THE COMPLETE ILLUSTRATED SHAKESPEARE.

OPHELIA

THE COMPLETE ILLUSTRATED SHAKESPEARE.

EDITED BY HOWARD STAUNTON.

THE ILLUSTRATIONS BY JOHN GILBERT
AND RAY ABEL.
ENGRAVINGS BY THE BROTHERS DALZIEL.

WITH A FOREWORD BY
SOLOMON J. SCHEPPS.

PARK LANE
NEW YORK

This book was originally published in three volumes as
The Plays of Shakespeare.

This edition is published by Park Lane,
a division of Crown Publishers, Inc.
a b c d e f g h
PARK LANE 1979 EDITION
Manufactured in the United States of America

Library of Congress Cataloging in Publication Data
Shakespeare, William, 1564-1616.
The complete illustrated Shakespeare.
Reprint of the 1858-61 ed. published by
G. Routledge, London, New York under title: The
plays of Shakespeare.
Includes index.
1. Staunton, Howard, 1810-1874. II. Title.
PR2753.S8 1979 822.3'3 78-27133
ISBN 0-517-27890-1

Contents.

VOLUME ONE.

VOLUME TWO.

VOLUME THREE.

FOREWORD TO THE 1979 EDITION.

In his early prose work *Spring and All,* William Carlos Williams said that Shakespeare is the greatest university of all. If a university is a place where we can learn about our world, this is surely the highest compliment one can pay to any man. Universities, of course, have often been criticized as repositories of barren learning, lacking the soul and pulse of life. But Shakespeare's medium was the stage. Although Jaques's bitterness leads him to remark that "All the world's a stage,/And all the men and women merely players" (*As You Like It*), we can fairly invert that to say that, properly used, the stage is a world, and the players real men and women.

In a recent American film the following bit of conversation stands out: "Who is your favorite writer?" "Shakespeare, I suppose." "Nobody's favorite writer is Shakespeare." The idea is that Shakespeare is too huge, too perfect to be anybody's favorite. In his plays and poems he covers the entire spectrum of human events and emotions more fully than any other writer. His achievement is all the more astounding when we consider the few things we know about his life. He was something of a social climber, a popular entertainer, and a shrewd businessman whose main aim in life was to make himself a gentleman landowner, which he did successfully.

Shakespeare was, in many ways, ahead of his time. He had psychological depth that is only in this century beginning to be fully understood. He is considered by many the only male writer of his day who could give accurate portrayals of women, even though he wrote at a time when only a queen could be accorded equality with men (all the parts in his plays were originally performed by men and boys). Yet he was very much a man of his age, an age that was still governed by the medieval world view of the Great Chain of Being, in which everything in creation was seen as a link in a chain with an absolute place. If any link were moved (or tried to move itself) it would upset the balance of the entire world. It is very likely that Shakespeare would have been more comfortable talking to Dante, who wrote 300 years earlier, than to Newton, who was born only twenty-six years after his death.

These contradictions, however, do nothing to diminish the breadth and depth of Shakespeare's imagination and the judiciousness with which he formed his works. His characters display a myriad of profound emotions, both alone and in interpersonal relationships. He gives us life at court and among peasants, in the city and the country, in England and Europe, on land and at sea. Most of the plays have subplots that mirror the main plot on a different level. And his language is universal. In his own day his plays were enjoyed by peasants and nobles alike. Today they are performed in repertory companies, in schools, and on Broadway, while scholars write doctoral and postdoctoral theses on them. Their art and appeal are limitless in a way that is rivaled only by the Bible.

The single most recurrent subject in Shakespeare's work is love, the most powerful and far-reaching of all emotions. Many of the plays, like *Romeo and Juliet, Antony and Cleopatra,* and *As You Like It,* are love stories. And the variety is immense.

Romeo and Juliet and *Antony and Cleopatra* are similar in that they are about love that is too great to bear: both plays end in double suicide. Also, both pairs of lovers belong to opposite sides of a battle. But the similarity ends there. Romeo and Juliet are the adolescent offspring of two feuding families and must keep their love secret. Their youth and inexperience make them impetuous, and in their clandestine romance they become so histrionic that some have, with reason, called the play a comedy. But their plan of escape is too complex and ill conceived: communications break down, and they kill themselves, each thinking the other dead. Their families are brought together by their deaths, but at too great a price.

Antony and Cleopatra, on the other hand, are both mature adults. Indeed, they are both painfully aware of the fact that they are no longer young. And they, lovers for years, are heads of state. Their love leads to their downfall too, but it also leads to the downfall of Egypt and the Roman triumvirate, ushering in an even more ruthless Rome under Augustus. The tragedy of their love causes far more than family bereavement: it causes the face of the world to be permanently changed.

As You Like It takes place in the Forest of Arden, and most of the characters are former city and court dwellers who became disenchanted with the complexity of urban life. Touchstone, a former court jester (court jesters had very quick and caustic wits), marries a simple country girl because she has no conventional graces. Rosalind orchestrates an enormously complex deception in the disguise of an adolescent boy and eloquently discourses on love throughout the play, finally revealing herself to Orlando, her beloved, only when she is certain of his love. And, although the play ends with a quadruple marriage, it is somewhat darkened by the wholly disenchanted Jaques, the ultimate misanthrope, whose cynicism is a sober reminder of how the paranoia and greed of city life can irreparably destroy the most beautiful things.

Shakespeare, then, examines love in its many ramifications, from personal to political. And love is present in all his works. But it is not only romantic love that he portrays. In *Julius Caesar,* for instance, the love between Brutus and Cassius is crucial. After the assassination of Caesar, chaos erupts in the senate, and the ensuing political struggle is encapsulated in an argument between Brutus and Cassius in Act IV that is couched in the language of a lovers' quarrel. In it, we see clearly that the end is near for both, for Brutus through his pride, and for Cassius through his remorse.

The power of love to build or destroy is also displayed in parent-child relationships. With regard to destruction, the great examples are, of course, *Hamlet* and *King Lear.*

In modern psychology, Hamlet's case is placed alongside that of Oedipus as a mythical symbol of some of our most secret longings and fears. While Oedipus' desire is for his mother and his rage is against his father, Hamlet's case is more complex. And in his obsession with avenging his father's murder, he also destroys Ophelia and Laertes, the two people closest to him. Is Hamlet's madness feigned or real? We can never be certain, anymore than we can be certain that the ghost's story is true. As Hamlet's famous soliloquies show, he was seriously contemplating suicide, and feigning madness can cover up a death wish. At any rate, *Hamlet* portrays a mysterious and essential question about fathers and sons, that is, can father and son maintain wholly separate identities? Although Shakespeare's statement in *Hamlet* is conjectural, he suggests that they cannot.

Lear's madness is clearer. He mistakes words of love from Goneril and Regan for true love, and entirely misses the honest love expressed by Cordelia. This causes him to lose his kingdom, his mind, and his only faithful daughter, Cordelia. *King Lear* is, in fact, a play in which love is only revealed in the midst of madness, violence, and death. Gloucester and Edgar undergo the same hardships as Lear and Cordelia. Lear and Gloucester mistake the public language of the court for the private language of the family. The play shows how the greed, plotting, and deceptions of life can turn love into evil, so that the world is irreparably changed.

Quite the opposite is true of the last plays, or the romances. Like *King Lear,* these plays are primarily concerned with father-daughter relationships, but here it is their power to heal. In *Pericles,* the Prince of Tyre, Pericles, suffers every imaginable offense and ignominy, including the loss of his daughter and wife. But, like Job, his spirit is strong, and all is finally made right, culminating with his being reunited with his daughter Marina (the sea). For twenty years he searches at sea, while also being chased by numerous enemies and vandals. When finally he is reunited with Marina, the sea is transformed from an enemy, in constant flux, to a friend, the cleansing water of life.

Similarly, Leontes is reunited with his daughter Perdita (the lost one) in *The Winter's Tale.* This case is even more wonderful, as a statue of the dead girl comes to life. And in *The Tempest,* Prospero's daugther Miranda (miracle) is a key figure in the resolution of a highly complex plot.

In each of these plays, the old order of the world falls apart and a new order begins. And in each it is a miracle between father and daughter that symbolizes the new order. The last plays express a Christian love (Paul's *caritas,* or charity), and the love between father and daughter, two generations, represents the progress of man towards a universal *caritas.*

Another predominant theme in Shakespeare's plays is the struggle for political power and all that such power entails. Shakespeare's greatest achievement in this vein is his imaginative reconstruction of English history. This is not to downplay the magnificence of the great political tragedies such as *Julius Caesar, Antony and Cleopatra, Macbeth,* and *Coriolanus.* But in the English history plays he presents a chronicle of the constant shifting of power over a great many years.

The English history plays are not a continuous historical sequence, although four kings who ruled in succession are covered: Richard II, a Plantagenet who held the throne by right, and three Lancastrian usurpers, Henrys IV, V, and VI. The most all-encompassing of these plays are *Henry IV, Parts I* and *II,* and *Richard III.*

In the two Henry IV plays we see Prince Hal, a young rake, become King Henry V. Hal, the black sheep who keeps unsavory companions, most notably the lusty and meddlesome Falstaff, reveals in a soliloquy that he is conducting his life so as to strengthen his position once he is king. If he leads a profligate life as Prince of Wales, he reasons, and, upon accession to the throne, suddenly straightens out, his subjects will marvel at how quickly he has matured and assumed responsibility. And he indeed fulfills his promise by banishing Falstaff immediately upon becoming King Henry V. For Hal was of a usurping line, and he knew that he had to rule by his wits.

Richard III, a Yorkist, has been unfairly treated by history, and this is mainly due to Shakespeare's portrayal. In the play, Richard speaks of himself as having a hunchback and a withered arm, and he too is a usurper. But there is no historical evidence for any of this. What we have, then, in his physical condition, is a symbol for his awareness that he did not hold the throne by legal succession. Richard is paranoid, and with good reason. His reign, which lasted only two years, was one of tremendous turmoil and insecurity. He could trust nobody, and the battle scene at the end of the play (perhaps the most brilliant battle scene in all dramatic literature) reaches its apex with Richard's famous cry, "A horse! a horse! my kingdom for a horse!" This, a moment before his death, is his final statement on the precariousness of his rule: surely no English king who held the throne legally could ever trade his kingdom to save his life. Although Richard was killed by his enemies, he was just as much hounded to death by his own conscience. Shakespeare concentrates on the psychological burden of the usurper in these plays, and the line of dissolution traced between Henry IV and Richard III is one of the great triumphs of his art.

What is not in Shakespeare's work? There are revenge tragedies, plays of madness, racism, demonic evil, jealousy, great heroism, and many light comedies that show man in all his social strengths and weaknesses. And, although each play makes a distinct statement, the more Shakespeare we read, the more we see themes from each play in all the plays, until the entire canon of his work becomes a series of interwoven dramatic essays on the subject of man and his world.

Because of this unparalleled scope and detail, Shakespeare has inspired more great art than any other writer. And any literary critic with aspirations to greatness must show his mind by writing on Shakespeare. This edition includes both of these important extensions of the Shakespearean universe.

Editor Howard Staunton was one of the great Shakespearean scholars of his age. His knowledge of the texts themselves and of Elizabethan language and customs was enormous. And, equally to his credit, he understood the importance of including extra material in this edition. The illustrations by Sir John Gilbert are most expressive: the costumes are accurate and the facial characterizations always complement the text well. And the criticism in the book is a good sampling of what was available at that date. Aside from Johnson and Coleridge, two of the most important English critics in history, and Schlegel, who translated the plays into German, there are remarks by Drake, Steevens, Hallam, Hunter, and Malone, giving the reader an excellent overview of how Shakespeare was viewed at the time this edition was first published. And all of these critics, especially Johnson and Coleridge, express ideas which will be forever fresh and important.

SOLOMON J. SCHEPPS

PUBLISHER'S NOTE TO THE 1979 EDITION.

ABOUT THE EDITOR

HOWARD STAUNTON (1810–1874), writer and journalist, devoted the last twenty years of his life to the study of Shakespeare. His edition of Shakespeare (November 1857–May 1860) is based on the first folio, early quartos, and texts of his contemporaries. His textual emendations display great familiarity with Elizabethan literature and language, and his notes are discerning and scholarly. During his last two years, he wrote nineteen articles on "Unsuspected Corruptions of Shakespeare's Text" for *Athenaeum*. Staunton was also perhaps the greatest English chess player up to that time and wrote many articles on chess.

ABOUT THE ILLUSTRATOR

SIR JOHN GILBERT (1817–1897), English historical painter and wood engraver, was considered one of the best illustrators of his time. Most noted as a designer of woodcut illustrations for editions of Shakespeare, Scott, Milton, and Cervantes, he was probably the most prolific illustrator of his day.

The following Shakespearean critics and scholars are mentioned in the Preface or are listed as authors of the Critical Opinions:

SAMUEL TAYLOR COLERIDGE (1772–1834), renowned poet and literary critic, wrote (with Wordsworth) *Lyrical Ballads* (1798), the most important single collection of English Romantic poetry.

NATHAN DRAKE (1776–1836), medical and literary scholar, wrote a two-volume work entitled *Shakespeare and His Times* and many essays on Shakespeare.

ALEXANDER DYCE (1798–1869), Scottish editor of dramas, was known chiefly for his editions of Shakespeare (1857, 1866).

HENRY HALLAM (1777–1859), historian, wrote several histories of England and Europe.

JAMES ORCHARD HALLIWELL (1820–1889), librarian and scholar, collected Shakespearean works and manuscripts and published in 1843 a description of the only extant manuscript of the plays.

JOSEPH HUNTER (1783–1861) was an illustrator and annotator of Shakespeare's works.

SAMUEL JOHNSON (1709–1784), poet, critic, essayist, and lexicographer, is acknowledged as an outstanding writer and thinker. The preeminent Shakespearean scholar of his time, he edited an eight-volume edition of his works in 1765.

CHARLES KNIGHT (1791–1873) wrote a biography of Shakespeare and published two editions of his works.

EDMUND MALONE (1741–1812), scholar and critic of the Elizabethan theater, edited a ten-volume edition of Shakespeare's works in 1790.

GEORGE STEEVENS (1736–1800) edited a 1773 ten-volume edition of Shakespeare's works with Samuel Johnson.

AUGUST WILHELM VON SCHLEGEL (1767–1845), German scholar, poet, and professor of art and literary history, is most noted for his translation of Shakespeare (1797–1810), later completed by Ludwig Tieck and others, which established Shakespeare's literary reputation in Germany.

PREFACE.

Of the personal history of Shakespeare, and of the usages of theatres formerly in relation to dramatic productions,[1] so little is now known, that it is impossible to say why he made no provision for the publication of his transcendent works. Whether, having written them for the stage, he was satisfied with their success in that arena, or had forfeited the power of giving them a wider circulation, or was confident enough in their merits to believe they must survive all accidents, no one probably will ever determine. All we know upon the subject is, that, unlike his learned contemporary, Jonson, he published no collection of his "Plays" as "Works," and that although some of them were printed during his life, and possibly with his sanction, there is no evidence to show that any one of them was ever corrected by his own hand. What is strange, too, of a writer so remarkable and of compositions so admired, not a poem, a play, or fragment of either, in his manuscript, has come down to us. What is still more surprising, with the exception of five or six signatures, not a word in his handwriting is known to exist!

The first collective edition of his dramas did not appear till seven years after his death. This was the famous folio of 1623, in which his "fellows" Heminge and Condell brought together rather than edited the whole of the plays, *Pericles* excepted, which are by common consent ascribed to him.

In the singular prefatory address "To the Great Variety of Readers," written, as Steevens supposed, mainly by Ben Jonson, the editors, so to call them, confess it had been a thing "worthie to have bene wished, that the Author himselfe had liv'd to have set forth, and overseen his owne writings;" though they claim credit for the care and pain they have bestowed in collecting and publishing them, so that—"where (before) *you were abus'd with*

---

[1] It is well ascertained that the printing of a play was considered injurious to its stage success; and although in the sale of a piece to the theatre there may have been no express contract to that effect between the vendor and vendee, the purchase apparently was understood to include, with the special right of performing such piece, the literary interest in it also. Authors, however, were not always faithful to this understanding. Thomas Heywood, in the address to the reader, prefixed to his *Rape of Lucrece*, 1608, observes, "Though some have used a double sale of their labours, first to the stage, and after to the press, for my own part, I here proclaim myself ever faithful in the first, and never guilty in the last."

Sometimes plays were printed surreptitiously without the cognizance of either the authors or the company to which they belonged, and there is an admonition directed to the Stationers' Company, in the office of the Lord Chamberlain, dated June 10, 1637, against the printing of plays, to the prejudice of the companies who had bought them:—"After my hearty commendations, Whereas complaint was heretofore presented to my dear brother and predecessor by his Majesty's servants the players, that some of the Company of Printers and Stationers had procured and printed divers of their books of Comedies, Tragedies, Interludes, Histories and the like, which they had for the special service of his Majesty, and their own use, bought and provided at very dear and high rates," &c.

Occasionally too, an author, from apprehension or in consequence of a corrupt version of his piece getting abroad, was induced to have it printed himself:—"One only thing affects me; to think, that scenes, invented merely to be spoken, should be enforcively published to be read, and that the least hurt I can receive is to do myself the wrong. But since others otherwise would do me more, the least inconvenience is to be accepted; I have therefore myself set forth this comedie," &c.—Marston's *Preface to the Malecontent*, 1604.

diverse stolne and surreptitious copies, maimed, and deformed by the frauds and stealthes of injurious impostors, that expos'd them: even those, are now offer'd to your view cur'd, and perfect of their limbes; and all the rest, absolute in their numbers, as he conceived them," and profess further to have printed at least a portion of the volume from "papers" in which they "scarse received from him a blot." By the "diverse stolne and surreptitious copies" they point evidently at the quartos; but the depreciation of those editions is merely a clap-trap to enhance the value of their own folio.[2] The facts, which are indisputable, that in many of the plays the folio text is a literal reprint of that in the quartos, even to the errors of the press, and that some of the publishers of the latter were bought off and included among the proprietors of the folio, prove that, if not absolutely authentic, the earlier copies had strong claims to accuracy and completeness.[3] The seventeen of Shakespeare's plays which appeared in the quarto form prior to the publication of the folio 1623, are: *King Richard II., King Richard III., Romeo and Juliet, Love's Labour's Lost, Henry IV.* P. I., *Henry IV.* P. II., *Henry V., The Merchant of Venice, A Midsummer Night's Dream, Much Ado about Nothing, Titus Andronicus, The Merry Wives of Windsor, Hamlet, King Lear, Troilus and Cressida, Pericles,* and *Othello.* The folio contains the whole of the above pieces (excepting *Pericles*), which had previously appeared in print, and twenty plays besides, which, so far as we know, till that time were only in manuscript.

---

[2] Malone observes that what Heminge and Condell state regarding the imperfection and mutilation of the quartos "is not strictly true of any but two of the whole number," and that *in general* the other quartos "are preferable to the exhibition of the same plays in the folio; for this plain reason, because, instead of printing these plays from a manuscript, the editors of the folio, to save labour, or from some other motive, printed the greater part of them from the very copies which they represented as maimed and imperfect, and frequently from a late, instead of the earliest edition."

[3] "It is demonstrable that Heminge and Condell printed *Much Ado About Nothing* from the quarto of 1600, omitting some short portions and words here and there, and making some trivial changes, mostly for the worse:—that they printed *Love's Labour's Lost* from the quarto of 1598, occasionally copying the old errors of the press; and though in a few instances they corrected the text, they more frequently corrupted it; spoilt the continuity of the dialogue in Act III. Sc. 1, by omitting several lines, and allowed the preposterous repetitions in Act IV. Sc. 3, and Act V. Sc. 2, to stand as in the quarto:—that their text of *A Midsummer Night's Dream* was mainly taken from Roberts's quarto,—by much the inferior of the two quartos of 1600,—its blunders being sometimes followed; and though they amended a few passages, they introduced not a few bad variations, to say nothing of their being chargeable with some small omissions:—that for *The Merchant of Venice* they used Heyes's quarto, 1600, retaining a good many of its misprints; and though in some places they improved the text, their deviations from the quarto are generally either objectionable readings, or positive errors:—that in *King Richard II.* they chiefly adhere to the quarto of 1615, copying some of its mistakes; and though they made one or two short additions, and some slight emendations, they occasionally corrupted the text, and greatly injured the tragedy by omitting sundry passages, one of which, in Act I. Sc. 3, extends to twenty-six lines:—that their text of *The First Part of King Henry IV.* is, on the whole, more faulty than that of the incorrect quarto of 1613, from which they printed the play:—that their text of *King Richard III.*, which materially differs from that of all the quartos,—now and then for the better, but oftener perhaps for the worse,—was in some parts printed from the quarto of 1602, as several corresponding errors prove, and though it has many lines not contained in any of the quartos, it leaves out a very striking and characteristic portion of the 2d scene of Act IV., and presents passages here and there which cannot be restored to sense without the assistance of the quartos:—that they formed their text of *Troilus and Cressida* on that of the quarto of 1609, from which some of their many blunders were derived; and though they made important additions in several passages, they omitted other passages, sometimes to the destruction of the sense:—that in *Hamlet*, while they added considerably to the prose-dialogue in Act II. Sc. 2, inserted elsewhere lines and words which are wanting in the quartos of 1604, &c., and rectified various mistakes of those quartos; they,—not to mention minor mutilations of the text, some of them accidental,—omitted in the course of the play about a hundred and sixty verses (including nearly the whole of the 4th scene of Act IV.), and left out a portion of the prose-dialogue in Act V. Sc. 2, besides allowing a multitude of errors to creep in *passim*:—that their text of *King Lear*, though frequently correct where the quartos are incorrect, and containing various lines and words omitted in the quartos, is, on the other hand, not only often incorrect where the quartos are correct, but is mutilated to a surprising extent, —the omissions, if we take prose and verse together, amounting to about two hundred and seventy lines, among which is an admirable portion of the 6th scene of Act III. * * * In short, Heminge and Condell made up the folio of 1623 partly from those very quartos which they denounced as worthless, and partly from manuscript stage-copies, some of which had been depraved, in not a few places, by the alterations and 'botchery of the players,' and awkwardly mutilated for the purpose of curtailing the pieces in representation."—DYCE.

This folio of 1623, then, forms the only authority we possess for above one half of Shakespeare's plays, and a very important one for the remainder which had been published before its appearance. Unhappily it is a very ill printed book; so badly edited, and so negligently "read," that it abounds not only with the most transparent typographical inaccuracies, but with readings disputable and nonsensical beyond belief. Such, indeed, are its errors and deficiencies that Mr. Knight, who professes more deference to the authority of its text than any other editor, and has gone the length of saying that "perhaps, all things considered, there never was a book so correctly printed,"[4] was constrained to abandon it in thousands of instances. The truth is, that no edition of Shakespeare founded literally on the folio would be endured by the general reader in the present day. Opinions may differ as to the extent to which the quartos are required in correcting and supplementing the players' copy; that they are invaluable for these purposes it would be the height of prejudice to deny. Some portion of the corruptions in the folio may be due to obscure or imperfect manuscript, papers originally received from the author's hands with scarce a blot, were probably much worn and soiled by years of use in the theatre, but the clusters of misprints, the ruthless disregard of metrical propriety, the absolute absurdities of punctuation, which deform this volume, too plainly indicate that it received little or no literary supervision, beyond that of the master printer who prepared it for the press.

The second folio, published in 1632, is no improvement on its predecessor in point of accuracy. It corrects a few of the most palpable typographical mistakes of the former folio; but the editor, as Malone has shown, was entirely ignorant of Shakespeare's phraseology and versification, and has left few pages undisfigured by some capricious innovations.

The third folio, bearing the date 1664, is very scarce, a large number of copies having been destroyed in the Great Fire of London, in 1666. Like the second folio, it is, as regards the acknowledged plays, merely a reprint, perpetuating the errors of the first, and adding new ones of its own. This edition, however, possesses a special interest, as it contains seven additional plays, "never before printed in folio:" viz. *Pericles Prince of Tyre; The London Prodigal; The History of Lord Cromwell; Sir John Oldcastle, Lord Cobham; The Puritan Widow; A Yorkshire Tragedy;* and *The Tragedy of Locrine.* No one of these plays, with the exception of *Pericles,* is ever now included in the editions of Shakespeare's works, nor has any other of them a claim to such distinction.

The fourth folio of 1685 is nothing more than a reproduction of the third copy, and, like its immediate precursor, not only presents blunders of its own, but repeats the most obvious errors found in the second folio. Such were the earliest collected editions of this poet's dramas, and such the only volumes in which these dramas were accessible for nearly a hundred years after his decease. At the beginning of the eighteenth century, a

---

[4] The Rev. Joseph Hunter gives a different and much truer character of the folio:—"Perhaps in the whole annals of English typography there is no record of any book of any extent, and any reputation, having been dismissed from the press with less care and attention than the first folio." --Preface to *New Illustrations of Shakespeare.*

new impulse to the study of his works was given by the editions of Rowe, in 1709 and 1714, and the reviving appreciation of his genius was strikingly shown by the long succession of distinguished editors that century produced:—Pope, 1725 and 1728; Theobald, 1733 and 1740; Hanmer, 1744; Warburton, 1747; Johnson, 1765; Capell, 1768; Johnson and Steevens, 1773, and 1779; Reed, 1785; Malone, 1790; and Rann, 1786—1794.

In addition to the early printed authorities for the formation of a text, there are two manuscript claimants, whose merits and pretensions demand some notice. The first of these, a version of the First and Second Parts of *Henry IV.* which by certain omissions and modifications is compressed into a single play, formerly belonged to Sir Edward Dering, of Surrenden, Kent, and is probably the oldest manuscript copy of any play by Shakespeare known. It is annotated in the hand-writing of Sir Edward Dering, and Mr. Halliwell inclines to think it was written after 1619, when, according to the family papers, Sir Edward purchased "twenty-seven play-books for nine shillings." This manuscript is certainly curious, and it has two or three conjectural emendations which are ingenious, but it is entitled to no consideration on the score of authority, being evidently formed upon the text of the quarto, 1613.

The other, and far more pretentious claimant to a voice in the regulation of Shakespeare's text, is the now notorious Collier folio, a copy of the 1632 edition, formerly belonging to Mr. John Payne Collier, and which was sold or presented by that gentleman to the late Duke of Devonshire. Mr. Collier's account of the way this volume came into his hands, and of the circumstances under which he first became aware of its MS. treasures, is as follows:—

"In the spring of 1849 I happened to be in the shop of the late Mr. Rodd, of Great Newport Street, at the time when a package of books arrived from the country; my impression is that it came from Bedfordshire, but I am not at all certain upon a point which I looked upon as a matter of no importance. He opened the parcel in my presence, as he had often done before in the course of my thirty or forty years' acquaintance with him, and looking at the backs and title-pages of several volumes, I saw that they were chiefly works of little interest to me. Two folios, however, attracted my attention, one of them gilt on the sides, and the other in rough calf: the first was an excellent copy of Florio's 'New World of Words,' 1611, with the name of Henry Osborn (whom I mistook at the moment for his celebrated namesake, Francis) upon the first leaf; and the other a copy of the second folio of Shakespeare's Plays, much cropped, the covers old and greasy, and, as I saw at a glance on opening them, imperfect at the beginning and end. Concluding hastily that the latter would complete another poor copy of the second folio, which I had bought of the same bookseller, and which I had had for some years in my possession, and wanting the former for my use, I bought them both,—the Florio for twelve, and the Shakespeare for thirty shillings.

"As it turned out, I at first repented my bargain as regarded the Shakespeare, because, when I took it home, it appeared that two leaves which I wanted were unfit for my purpose, not merely by being too short, but damaged and defaced: thus disappointed,

I threw it by, and did not see it again, until I made a selection of books I would take with me on quitting London. In the mean time, finding that I could not readily remedy the deficiencies in my other copy of the folio, 1632, I had parted with it; and when I removed into the country with my family, in the spring of 1850, in order that I might not be without some copy of the second folio for the purpose of reference, I took with me that which is the foundation of the present work.

"It was while putting my books together for removal, that I first observed some marks in the margin of this folio; but it was subsequently placed upon an upper shelf, and I did not take it down until I had occasion to consult it. It then struck me that Thomas Perkins, whose name, with the addition of 'his Booke,' was upon the cover, might be the old actor who had performed in Marlowe's 'Jew of Malta,' on its revival shortly before 1633. At this time I fancied that the binding was of about that date, and that the volume might have been his; but in the first place, I found that his name was Richard Perkins, and in the next, I became satisfied that the rough calf was not the original binding. Still, Thomas Perkins might have been a descendant of Richard; and this circumstance and others induced me to examine the volume more particularly. I then discovered, to my surprise, that there was hardly a page which did not present, in a handwriting of the time, some emendations in the pointing or in the text, while on most of them they were frequent, and on many numerous." Preface to *Notes and Emendations, &c.*

After due announcement of the extraordinary discovery, with samples of the emendations, in the chief literary newspapers, Mr. Collier, in 1852, published his volume entitled *Notes and Emendations to the Text of Shakespeare's Plays, from early Manuscript Corrections in a copy of the Folio,* 1632, &c. &c. The annotations excited great interest, and, among those not conversant with the language of our early literature and the labours of the poet's commentators, unbounded admiration. Shakespearian scholars, however, were by no means satisfied with the history of the "corrections," or disposed to concede the authority assumed for them. The late Mr. Singer, in particular, distinguished himself by a vigorous opposition to *Notes and Emendations,* and in an able though somewhat too trenchant work, *The Text of Shakespeare Vindicated from the Interpolations and Corruptions advocated by John Payne Collier, Esq.* &c. &c. very clearly proved that many of the best of the emendations were not new, and that most of the new were uncalled for or absurd. In this estimate of the readings he was followed and supported by Mr. Knight, Mr. Halliwell, and Mr. Dyce.

In spite of this antagonism, a second edition of *Notes and Emendations* was soon published. Nearly at the same time, too, Mr. Collier brought out a Monovolume of Shakespeare's Plays, in which all the "emendations," good, bad, and indifferent, were adopted without note or comment to distinguish them from the customary text. This was followed by a volume entitled by Mr. Collier, *Seven Lectures on Shakespeare and Milton, by the late S. T. Coleridge;* containing what professed to be a list of every manuscript note and emendation in Mr. Collier's folio. And finally appeared an edition of Shakespeare's Works edited by that gentleman, in which he adopted the greater part of the anonymous substitutions, and strenuously advocated the remainder. In the meantime, however, such sweeping changes in the text, and upon authority so questionable, became the subject of discussion and energetic protest in various quarters. Having myself, I may be permitted to say, from the first publication of *Notes and Emendations,* felt assured, by the internal evidence, that they were for the most part plagiarized from the chief Shakesperian editors and critics, and the rest of quite modern fabrication—I earnestly longed to have the writing tested. That which was a desire before, when the present book was undertaken became a necessity, and during the year 1858 I more than once communicated to Sir Frederic Madden, as the most eminent paleographer of the age, my motives for wishing that the volume should undergo inspection by persons skilled in ancient writing. Sir Frederic's official engagements at that time prevented his giving the subject the attention it perhaps merited. With the courtesy and consideration which have marked his conduct throughout this painful business, he did, however, I subsequently found, in consequence of my solicitations, apply to Mr. Collier to obtain him access to the volume. His letter, it appears, was not answered. In the spring of last year I again called upon him, and reiterated my reasons for desiring the volume should be examined, and if possible by him. This time I was more successful. Sir Frederic immediately wrote to the Duke of Devonshire, requesting permission to see the much talked of folio, and it was liberally forwarded to the British Museum for inspection by himself and friends.[5] While there, the writing was carefully examined by Sir Frederic Madden, Mr. Panizzi, Mr. Bond, Mr. T. Duffus Hardy, Professor Brewer, the Rev. Joseph Hunter, Mr. Hamilton, and other paleographers, and these gentlemen were unanimously of opinion that the MS. annotations on the margins and in the body of the book, though in an apparently antique character, were really of quite modern origin. The technical evidences upon

---

[5] In reply to the discreditable insinuations of Mr. Collier and his partisans, that Sir Frederic Madden was influenced by personal animosity to Mr. Collier, in the measures he has taken, and the opinion he has expressed respecting the disputed folio—Sir Frederic has published the following narrative of the circumstances which led to the book being placed in his hands:—

"During the summer and autumn of 1858 Dr. Mansfield Ingleby and Mr. Staunton had called more than once on me, to ask my opinion of the genuineness of the notes of the 'Old Corrector,' as printed by Mr. Collier, and also at the same time to express their opinion, from internal evidence, that the notes were of recent origin. So far from my having at that time 'aided the case' against Mr. Collier, as falsely asserted by him (p. 70 of his Reply), I call upon the two gentlemen above named to bear witness whether I did not express my great surprise at their statement, and manifest the utmost unwillingness to believe that so large a body of notes could have been fabricated, or, if fabricated, could escape detection. These interviews, however, led me to address a request to Mr. Collier, on Sept. 6, 1858, that he would procure me a sight of the Folio, which of itself ought to prove that I could at that time have entertained no doubt of his integrity in the matter. To this request I never received any answer, nor indeed, to the best of my belief, did Mr. Collier write to me at all subsequently; and, although I thought it strange, yet I certainly never took offence at it. I resolved, however, in my own mind, to prefer my request to the Duke of Devonshire himself; but official and other business constantly interfered to prevent my carrying out my intention until May 1859, when Professor Bodenstedt was introduced to me by Mr. Watts of the Museum, and having expressed his great desire to see the Collier Folio, I promised them to gratify, if possible, their and my own wishes on the subject, as well as to give several of my Shakesperian friends an opportunity of examining the volume. Accordingly, on the 13th of May, I wrote to the Duke, requesting the loan of the volume for a short time, and by his grace's liberality it was sent to me on the 26th of the same month, late in the day. In the evening of the same day I wrote letters to Professor Bodenstedt, the Rev. A. Dyce. Mr. W. J. Thoms (a friend of Mr. Collier), and I believe Mr. Staunton, inviting them to see the volume.

"Having thus succeeded in obtaining the volume, my next step was to examine it critically on palæographic grounds, and this I did on the following morning very carefully, together with Mr. Bond, the Assistant-Keeper of my Department, and we were both struck with the very suspicious character of the writing—certainly the work of one hand, but presenting varieties of forms assignable to different periods—the evident *painting* over of many of the letters, and the artificial look of the ink. The day had not passed before I had quite made up my mind that the 'Old Corrector' never lived in the seventeenth century, but that the notes were fabricated at a recent period."

which this decision was founded were immediately made public in a letter from Mr. Hamilton to the *Times* newspaper. The most striking of these were "an infinite number of faint pencil-marks and corrections on the margins, in obedience to which the supposed old corrector had made his emendations," which pencil-marks, without even a pretence to antiquity in character or spelling, but written in a bold hand of the present century, can sometimes be distinctly seen underneath the quasi-antique notes themselves. To the very grave and inevitable inferences supplied by this remarkable discovery, Mr. Collier replied in a letter to the same Journal, that he "never made a single pencil-mark on the pages of the book, excepting crosses, ticks, or lines, to direct [his] attention to particular emendations." That he had shown and sworn that the volume in its present annotated state, was formerly in the possession of a gentleman named Parry. That soon after the discovery of the folio, he had produced it before the Council of the Shakespeare Society, and at two or three assemblies of the Society of Antiquaries. That he had given, not sold the volume, as had been stated in some newspapers, to the late Duke of Devonshire, and unless before a proper legal tribunal he would not submit to say another word in print upon the subject.

A letter followed in the *Times* from Mr. Maskelyne, *Keeper of the Mineral Department*, in the British Museum, which stated that on examination of the writing by means of a microscope, the existence of the pencil-marks mentioned by Mr. Hamilton "is indisputable; that in some cases these pencillings underlie the ink, and that the ink, though apparently at times it has become mixed with ordinary ink, in its prevailing character is nothing more than a paint formed perhaps of sepia, or of sepia mixed with a little Indian ink. The publicity given to the investigation induced Mr. Parry, the gentleman cited by Mr. Collier as the former owner of the folio, to call at the British Museum to recognise his old possession. On seeing the volume, he at once denied not only that it was the book formerly his, but that it had ever been shown to him by Mr. Collier.[6] Some further controversy ensued which need not be detailed, and the question of the genuineness of the writing was warmly discussed both in the leading English and American papers. Shortly after the appearance of Mr. Hamilton's letter to the *Times*, a clever little work upon the subject by Dr. Ingleby, called *The Shakespeare Fabrications, or the Manuscript Notes of the Perkins Folio shown to be of recent Origin*, &c. was published. In this *opusculum* Mr. Collier's conduct in relation to the discovered volume was so severely handled, and the charge of complicity in the fabrications so plainly brought home to him, that his friends deemed it proper to announce that the volume was undergoing a careful examination by "four eminent antiquaries." As the result of this perquisition has not been made known, we may infer that these four gentlemen found nothing to invalidate the verdict passed upon the writing by the authorities who had preceded them in the task. A few months later Mr. Hamilton published his long promised

---

[6] Curiously enough, Mr. Parry, in searching through his library subsequently, has discovered a fly-leaf belonging to his lost folio, and on comparing it with the Collier volume, it is found to be a quarter of an inch too short, and a quarter of an inch too broad to match the latter. This substantiates the declaration of Mr. Parry when he first saw the Collier folio at the British Museum, that his book was wider than the one stated to have been his, and proves beyond future cavil that the Collier and the Parry folio were not the same.

pamphlet, *An Inquiry into the Genuineness of the Manuscript Corrections in Mr. J. Payne Collier's Annotated Shakespeare, folio,* 1632, &c. In this work he not only recapitulates all the former evidence against the Collier folio annotations, but publishes the result of an examination of certain other documents connected with Shakespeare, which Mr. Collier professed to have discovered in Devonshire House; among the archives of Lord Ellesmere, at Bridgewater House; in Dulwich College; and in the State Paper Office, proving, what had long been suspected, that a systematic series of Shakespearian forgeries has been perpetrated of late years, and apparently by one hand.

To the additional charges of uninquisitive credulity, not to say positive imposition, suggested in this "Inquiry," Mr. Collier has published a formal "Reply." In this reply he fails entirely to grapple with the main question at issue; he brings no evidence to rebut the technical and professional testimony against the impeached documents. He does not even propose the obvious course to any one circumstanced as he is, who believed the papers genuine—that of submitting them to the scrutiny of an authoritative tribunal of literary men and paleographers. Beyond the indulgence of much ill-judged personality against those gentlemen, who from a sense of duty have brought the subject before the public, he contents himself with a simple denial of culpability, an ignoring of the most palpable facts, and an appeal *ad misericordiam.*

But enough of this disreputable topic. Without taking into account these "New Particulars," the value of which will be more fittingly considered in the Memoir that follows, we may rest satisfied that the authority of the Collier folio is at an end. Such of its readings as are of value will be restored to their rightful owners, for the paternity of nearly all such is known; and the rest will speedily find the oblivion they so well deserve.

A few words may be desirable to explain the principle which has been followed in the present attempt to supply the best text of Shakespeare which the means at command allow. It has before been stated that we possess no play or poem, or even fragment of one, in the poet's writing. The early printed copies of his works are therefore the sole authority for what he wrote, and an accurate collation of them becomes the first and indispensable business of a modern editor. This portion of my duty has been performed at least with care, I hope with fidelity. Not only have I collated the quarto editions with the folio; but the former, where more than one of the same play existed, with themselves; and then, both quarto and folio with the best editions of modern times.[7]

Having mastered and noted the *variæ lectiones* in the old copies, the task of selection in a play found only in the folios was not difficult, the first copy, 1623, being in almost all cases preferable to the subsequent impressions. Where, however, a play exists both in quarto and folio form, and there are more than one edition of it in quarto, and, as is always the case, each copy abounds in corruptions, the choice is embarrassing. In these instances, taking the first folio as the basis of the text throughout, and when substituting a letter,

[7] The modern editions consulted are Rowe's, Pope's, Theobald's, Hanmer's, Warburton's, Johnson's and Steevens's. Those collated, Capell's, Malone's, Knight's, Collier's, and Dyce's; the two last-named, however, having appeared after great part of the present work was published, were available only for a portion of the plays.

word, or passage from any other source, always showing the folio reading in a note, I have trusted sometimes to the judgment of my predecessors, and occasionally to the dictates of my own. As a general rule it may be affirmed, that as in the folios, the first is freer from errors than the second, the second than the third, &c., so the earlier quartos exhibit a better text than the later ones, and, since the folio often prints from these later ones, of course in such cases a better one than the folio. When everything has been done in the shape of comparison which time, unwearied industry, and commodious access to old editions will allow, and when the labour of selecting from so many authorities in so many thousand instances has been fully accomplished, it is surprising how much remains to do. Dr. Johnson, after enumerating the various circumstances which tended to the corruption of Shakespeare's text, observes, "It is not easy for invention to bring together so many causes concurring to vitiate a text. No other author ever gave up his works to fortune and time with so little care; no books could be left in hands so likely to injure them, as plays frequently acted, yet continued in manuscript; no other transcribers were likely to be so little qualified for their task, as those who copied for the stage, at a time when the lower ranks of the people were universally illiterate; no other editions were made from fragments so minutely broken, and so fortuitously re-united; and in no other age was the art of printing in such unskilful hands." With a text thus pitiably depraved, it is not surprising that when collation is exhausted there should hardly be a page which does not present passages either dubious or positively corrupt. In those of the former category my rule has been to give the original lection in the text, but, as old Fuller well says, that "conjectures, if mannerly observing their distance, and not imprudently intruding themselves for certainties, deserve, if not to be received, to be considered,"— I have subjoined the emendations proposed by other commentators with my own, in the margin. The remedy for those of the latter class, I sought firstly in the modern editions, and did not often seek in vain. When they failed to rectify the error, recourse was had to my own sagacity. In no instance, however, has any deviation from the authentic copies been adopted without the change being notified. Mindful, too, of the Roman sentiment quoted by Johnson, "that it is more honourable to save a citizen than to destroy an enemy," I have in most cases, unless the emendation is indisputable on the ground of internal evidence, retained the ancient reading, and placed the proposed correction in a note. On the same principle, I have in some important instances, by citing examples of the disputed expression from Shakespeare himself, or from the authors he read, succeeded in restoring words found in the original, but which have been banished from all subsequent editions.

After exhibiting what Shakespeare wrote, according to the ancient copies, and the best modern glosses thereon, I have endeavoured, with the aid of those who have preceded me in the same task, and to the extent of a long familiarity with the literature and customs of his day, to explain his obscurities, to disentangle his intricacies, and to illustrate his allusions. In this attempt, the amount of reference and quotation will be seen to have been very great. It has, however, been much greater than it appears, since, with a few exceptions where the books or MSS. were unattainable, every extract throughout the work has been made at first hand. This is a circumstance I should have thought undeserving notice, but that in a standard edition of Shakespeare, like the *Variorum* of 1821, I have not found one quotation in ten without an error.

For the rest, it may suffice in this brief sketch of my plan to add, that by a careful regulation of the pointing, in some passages the lost sense has been retrieved, and in others the meaning has been rendered more conspicuous.

H. STAUNTON.

April, 1860.[8]

---

[8] *Suum cuique.* As some few of my readings have received the honour of adoption by more than one editor of Shakespeare, lately, the date above without explanation might expose me to the censure of plagiarism. I shall be forgiven therefore for stating that the present work was begun in Nov. 1857, and has been published month by month in parts up to the first of May, 1860.

THE COMPLETE ILLUSTRATED SHAKESPEARE.

VOLUME ONE.

Contents.

Page 33.

THE

TWO GENTLEMEN OF VERONA.

This play, indisputably one of the earliest complete productions of Shakespeare's mind, was first printed in the folio of 1623, where, owing to the arbitrary manner in which the dramas are disposed, it is preceded by The Tempest, assuredly one of the poet's latest creations. Some of the incidents in The Two Gentlemen of Verona, Steevens conjectures, were taken from Sidney's Arcadia (Book I. Chapter vi.), where Pyrocles consents to lead the Helots; but the amount of Shakespeare's obligations to this source does not appear to be considerable. For a portion of the plot he was unquestionably indebted to the episode of Felismena, in the Diana of George of Montemayor, a work very popular in Spain towards the end of the seventeenth century, and which exhibits several incidents, and even some expressions, in common with that part of the present play, which treats of the loves of Proteus and Julia. Of this work there were two translations, one by Bartholomew Yong, the other by Thomas Wilson.* There is a strong probability, however, that Shakespeare derived his knowledge of Felismena's story from another source, namely: "The History of Felix and Philiomena," which was played before the Queen at Greenwich in 1584.† Be this as it may, the story of Proteus and Julia so closely corresponds with that of Felix and Felismena, that no one who has read the two can doubt his familiarity with that portion of the Spanish romance.

Mr. Malone, in his "Attempt to ascertain the Order in which The Plays of Shakespeare were Written," originally assigned The Two Gentlemen of Verona to the year 1595; but he subsequently fixed the date of its production as 1591; a change which he has thus explained: "The following lines in Act I. Scene 3, had formerly induced me to ascribe this play to the year 1595:

'———— He wonder'd that your lordship
Would suffer him to spend his youth at home;
While other men, of slender reputation,
Put forth their sons to seek preferment out:
Some, to the wars, to try their fortune there;
Some, to discover islands far away.'

"Shakespeare, as has been often observed, gives to almost every country the manners of his own; and though the speaker is here a Veronese, the poet, when he wrote the last two lines,

* The translation by Yong was not *published* until 1598; but from his "Preface to divers learned gentlemen," we learn that it was written many years before. "It hath lyen by me finished," he remarks, "Horace's *ten, and six yeeres* more." He further observes:—"Well might I have excused these paines, if onely *Edward Paston*, Esquier, who heere and there for his own pleasure, as I understood, hath aptly turned out of Spanish into English some leaves that liked him best, had also made an absolute and complete translation of all the parts of Diana; the which, for his travell in that countrey, and great knowledge in that language, accompanied with other learned and good parts in him, had of all others that ever I heard translate these Bookes, prooved the rarest and worthiest to be embraced." Thomas Wilson's version, Dr. Farmer informs us, was published two or three years before that of Yong. "But," he adds, "this work, I am persuaded, was never published *entirely*."

† See Cunningham's "Revels at Court," p. 189.

was thinking of England, where voyages, for the purpose of *discovering islands far away*, were at this time much prosecuted. In 1595, Sir Walter Raleigh undertook a voyage to the island of Trinidado, from which he made an expedition up the river Oronoque to discover Guiana. Sir Humphry Gilbert had gone on a similar voyage of discovery the preceding year.

"The particular situation of England in 1595, I had supposed, might have suggested the line above quoted—'Some, to the wars,' &c. In that year it was generally believed that the Spaniards meditated a second invasion of England with a much more powerful and better-appointed Armada than that which had been defeated in 1588. Soldiers were levied with great diligence and placed on the seacoasts, and two great fleets were equipped—one to encounter the enemy in the British seas; the other to sail to the West Indies, under the command of Hawkins and Drake, to attack the Spaniards in their own territories. About the same time, also, Elizabeth sent a considerable body of troops to the assistance of King Henry IV. of France, who had entered into an offensive and defensive alliance with the English queen, and had newly declared war against Spain. Our author, therefore, we see, had abundant reason for both the lines before us:—

'Some, to the wars, to try their fortune there;
Some, to discover islands far away.'

"Among the marks of love, Speed in this play (Act II. Scene 1) enumerates the walking alone, 'like one that had the pestilence.' In the year 1593, there had been a great plague, which carried off near eleven thousand persons in London. Shakespeare was undoubtedly there at that time, and his own recollection might, I thought, have furnished him with this image. But since my former edition, I have been convinced that these circumstances by no means establish the date I had assigned to this play. When Lord Essex went in 1591, with 4,000 men, to assist Henry IV. of France, we learn from Sir Robert Carey's Memoirs, p. 59, that he was attended by many volunteers; and several voyages of discovery were undertaken about that very time by Raleigh, Cavendish, and others. There was a considerable plague in London in 1583."

Mr. Knight surmises that this play, Love's Labour's Lost, The Comedy of Errors, Midsummer-Night's Dream, Pericles, and Titus Andronicus, were written between 1585 and 1591; and we agree with him that this is a more probable division of the poet's labours, than ascribing to him the power of producing seventeen plays,—and such plays!—in seven years.

Persons Represented.

DUKE OF MILAN, *father of* SILVIA.
VALENTINE, } *Gentlemen of* VERONA.
PROTEUS, }
ANTONIO, *father of* PROTEUS.
THURIO, *a foolish rival to* VALENTINE.
EGLAMOUR, *agent for* SILVIA *in her escape.*
SPEED, *a clownish servant to* VALENTINE.
LAUNCE, *servant to* PROTEUS.

PANTHINO, *servant to* ANTONIO.
HOST, *with whom* JULIA *lodges in* MILAN.
Outlaws.

JULIA, *a lady of* VERONA, *beloved by* PROTEUS.
SILVIA, *beloved by* VALENTINE.
LUCETTA, *waiting-woman to* JULIA.

Servants, Musicians.

SCENE.—*Sometimes in* VERONA; *sometimes in* MILAN; *and on the frontiers of* MANTUA.

ACT I.

SCENE I.—*An open Place in* Verona.

Enter VALENTINE *and* PROTEUS.

VAL. Cease to persuade, my loving Proteus;[a]
Home-keeping youth have ever homely wits;[b]
Wer 't not affection chains thy tender days
To the sweet glances of thy honour'd love,
I rather would entreat thy company,
To see the wonders of the world abroad,
Than, living dully sluggardiz'd at home,
Wear out thy youth with shapeless idleness.
But, since thou lov'st, love still, and thrive therein,
Even as I would, when I to love begin.

PRO. Wilt thou be gone? Sweet Valentine, adieu!
Think on thy Proteus, when thou, haply, seest
Some rare note-worthy object in thy travel:
Wish me partaker in thy happiness,
When thou dost meet good hap: and in thy danger,
If ever danger do environ thee,
Commend thy grievance to my holy prayers,
For I will be thy bead's-man,[c] Valentine.

VAL. And on a love-book pray for my success?

---

[a] Proteus;] Throughout the old copy (folio 1623), the ancient spelling of Proteus, which was *Protheus*, is invariably adopted. "Our ancestors," Malone observes, "were fond of introducing the letter *h* into proper names to which it does not belong: and hence even to this day, our common Christian name, *Antony*, is written improperly *Anthony*."

[b] Homely *wits;*] Steevens has noted the same play of words in Milton's Comus:—

"*It is for* homely *features to* keep home,
They had their name thence."

[c] Bead's-man,—] A beadsman is one who offers up *prayers* for another. *Bead*, in Anglo-Saxon, meaning a prayer. "*To count one's beads,*" means, to say the Rosary, a favourite devotion in the Roman Catholic Church, composed for meditating on the principal events in the life of our Saviour. The better to fix the attention during this exercise, recourse is had to a chaplet con-

PRO. Upon some book I love, I'll pray for thee.
VAL. That's on some shallow story of deep love,
How young Leander cross'd the Hellespont.[a]
PRO. That's a deep story of a deeper love;
For he was more than over shoes in love.
VAL. 'T is true; for[b] you are over boots in love,
And yet you never swom the Hellespont.
PRO. Over the boots? nay, give me not the boots.(1)
VAL. No, I will not, for it boots thee not.
PRO. What?
VAL. To be in love, where scorn is bought with groans;
Coy looks with heart-sore sighs; one fading moment's mirth,
With twenty watchful, weary, tedious nights:
If haply won, perhaps a hapless gain;
If lost, why then a grievous labour won;
However,[c] but a folly bought with wit,
Or else a wit by folly vanquished.
PRO. So, by your circumstance, you call me fool.
VAL. So, by your circumstance,[d] I fear, you 'll prove.
PRO. 'T is love you cavil at; I am not love.
VAL. Love is your master, for he masters you:
And he that is so yoked by a fool,
Methinks should not be chronicled for wise.
PRO. Yet writers say, as in the sweetest bud
The eating canker[e] dwells, so eating love
Inhabits in the finest wits of all.
VAL. And writers say, as the most forward bud
Is eaten by the canker ere it blow,
Even so by love the young and tender wit
Is turn'd to folly; blasting in the bud,
Losing his verdure even in the prime,
And all the fair effects of future hopes.
But wherefore waste I time to counsel thee,
That art a votary to fond desire?
Once more adieu: my father at the road
Expects my coming, there to see me shipp'd.
PRO. And thither will I bring thee, Valentine.
VAL. Sweet Proteus, no; now let us take our leave.
To Milan let me hear from thee by letters,
Of thy success in love, and what news else
Betideth here in absence of thy friend;
And I likewise will visit thee with mine.
PRO. All happiness bechance to thee in Milan!
VAL. As much to you at home! and so, farewell. [*Exit* VALENTINE.
PRO. He after honour hunts, I after love:
He leaves his friends to dignify them more;
I leave[f] myself, my friends, and all for love.
Thou, Julia, thou hast metamorphos'd me;
Made me neglect my studies, lose my time,
War with good counsel, set the world at nought;
Made wit with musing weak, heart sick with thought.

Enter SPEED.

SPEED. Sir Proteus, save you: Saw you my master?

PRO. But now he parted hence, to embark for Milan.

SPEED. Twenty to one then he is shipp'd already;
And I have play'd the sheep[g] in losing him.

PRO. Indeed a sheep doth very often stray,
An* if the shepherd be awhile away.

SPEED. You conclude that my master is a shepherd then, and I a sheep?[h]

PRO. I do.

SPEED. Why, then my horns are his horns, whether I wake or sleep.

PRO. A silly answer, and fitting well a sheep.

SPEED. This proves me still a sheep.

PRO. True; and thy master a shepherd.

SPEED. Nay, that I can deny by a circumstance.

PRO. It shall go hard but I'll prove it by another.

SPEED. The shepherd seeks the sheep, and not the sheep the shepherd; but I seek my master, and my master seeks not me: therefore, I am no sheep.

PRO. The sheep for fodder follow the shepherd, the shepherd for food follows not the sheep; thou for wages followest thy master, thy master for wages follows not thee: therefore, thou art a sheep.

SPEED. Such another proof will make me cry baa.

PRO. But dost thou hear? gav'st thou my letter to Julia?

SPEED. Ay, sir; I, a lost mutton, gave your

---

sisting of either fifty or a hundred and fifty beads, on each of which is repeated a short prayer.

a *How young* Leander *cross'd the* Hellespont.] This is believed to have reference to the poem of Musæus, entitled, "Hero and Leander;" but as Marlowe's translation of this piece, though entered on the Stationers' books in 1593, was not published till 1598, a probability is raised that Shakespeare took his allusion from a classical source. The commentators, however, prefer the supposition that he saw Marlowe's version in MS.

b For *you are over boots in love,*—] *for* appears to be a misprint, perhaps instead of *and* or *but*.

c *However,*—] That is, *any way*.

d *So, by your* circumstance,—] Malone says, "circumstance is used equivocally. It here means conduct; in the preceding line, circumstantial deduction."

(*) First folio, *and*.

e *The* eating canker—] Allusions to the canker are common in the old writers. It is mentioned both in Shakespeare's plays, in his "Sonnets," and in the "Rape of Lucrece." Topsell in his "Serpents," 1608, gives a dissertation which he heads, "Of Caterpillars or Palmer-worms, called of some Cankers," and he tells us, "They gnaw off and consume by eating both leaves, boughs, and flowers, yea, and some fruits also, as I have often seen in peaches."

f *I* leave *myself,*—] The original reads, "I love myself," which Pope corrected.

g *And I have play'd the* sheep—] In many English counties, a sheep is commonly pronounced a *ship*, even to this day.

h *And I a sheep?*] So the second folio, 1632. The first omits the article.

letter to her, a laced mutton; (2) and she, a laced mutton, gave me, a lost mutton, nothing for my labour!

PRO. Here 's too small a pasture for such store of muttons.

SPEED. If the ground be overcharged, you were best stick her.

PRO. Nay, in that you are astray;[a] 't were best pound you.

SPEED. Nay, sir, less than a pound shall serve me for carrying your letter.

PRO. You mistake; I mean the pound, a pinfold.

SPEED. From a pound to a pin? fold it over and over,
'T is threefold too little for carrying a letter to your lover.

PRO. But what said she? [SPEED *nods.*] Did she nod?[b]

SPEED. I.[c]

PRO. Nod, I; why, that 's noddy.[d]

SPEED. You mistook, sir; I say she did nod: and you ask me if she did nod; and I say, I.

PRO. And that set together is—noddy.

SPEED. Now you have taken the pains to set it together, take it for your pains.

PRO. No, no, you shall have it for bearing the letter.

SPEED. Well, I perceive I must be fain to bear with you.

PRO. Why, sir, how do you bear with me?

SPEED. Marry, sir, the letter very orderly;[e] having nothing but the word, noddy, for my pains.

PRO. Beshrew me, but you have a quick wit.

SPEED. And yet it cannot overtake your slow purse.

PRO. Come, come, open the matter in brief: what said she?

SPEED. Open your purse, that the money, and the matter, may be both at once delivered.

PRO. Well, sir, here is for your pains: what said she?

SPEED. Truly, sir, I think you 'll hardly win her.

PRO. Why? Couldst thou perceive so much from her?

SPEED. Sir, I could perceive nothing at all from her; no, not so much as a ducat for delivering your letter: and being so hard to me that brought your mind, I fear she 'll prove as hard to you in telling your mind. Give her no token but stones; for she 's as hard as steel.

PRO. What, said she nothing?

SPEED. No, not so much as—*Take this for thy pains.* To testify your bounty, I thank you, you have testern'd me; (3) in requital whereof, henceforth carry your letters yourself: and so, sir, I 'll commend you to my master.

PRO. Go, go, be gone, to save your ship from wrack;
Which cannot perish, having thee aboard,
Being destin'd to a drier death on shore:—
I must go send some better messenger;
I fear my Julia would not deign my lines,
Receiving them from such a worthless post.
[*Exeunt.*

SCENE II.—*The same. Garden of* Julia's *House.*

Enter JULIA *and* LUCETTA.

JUL. But say, Lucetta, now we are alone,
Would'st thou then counsel me to fall in love?

LUC. Ay, madam; so you stumble not unheedfully.

JUL. Of all the fair resort of gentlemen,
That every day with parle encounter me,
In thy opinion, which is worthiest love?

LUC. Please you, repeat their names, I 'll show my mind
According to my shallow simple skill.

JUL. What think'st thou of the fair sir Eglamour?

LUC. As of a knight well-spoken, neat and fine;
But, were I you, he never should be mine.

JUL. What think'st thou of the rich Mercatio?

LUC. Well of his wealth; but of himself, so so.

JUL. What think'st thou of the gentle Proteus?

LUC. Lord, Lord! to see what folly reigns in us!

JUL. How now! what means this passion at his name?

LUC. Pardon, dear madam; 't is a passing shame,
That I, unworthy body as I am,

---

a *In that you are* astray;] It has been proposed, to keep up this bout of petty quibbles, that we should read *a stray, i. e.* a stray sheep.

b *Did she nod?*] This query, and the stage-direction, *Speed nods,* were added by Theobald. The latter seems essential to what follows; but I have ventured to insert it at a different place to that in which it has hitherto been given.

c *I.*] The old spelling of the affirmative particle *Ay,* without which the conceit of Proteus would be unintelligible.

d *Why, that's* noddy.] There is a game at cards called Noddy, but the allusion is rather to the common acceptation of Noddy, which is, a noodle, a simpleton. In "Wit's Private Wealth," 1612, we find, "If you see a trull, scarce give her a *nod*, but do not follow her, lest you prove a *noddy*."

e *The letter very* orderly;] For *orderly*, I have sometimes thought we should read, *motherly*, or, according to the ancient spelling, *moderly*. From the words *bearing, bear with you,* my *pains, a quick* wit, and *delivered*, the humour appears to consist of allusions to *child-bearing*. None of the editors have noticed this; and yet, unless such conceit be understood, there seems no significance whatever in the last few passages.

Should censure[a] thus on lovely gentlemen.

JUL. Why not on Proteus, as of all the rest?

LUC. Then thus: of many good I think him best.

JUL. Your reason?

LUC. I have no other but a woman's reason;
I think him so,—because I think him so.

JUL. And wouldst thou have me cast my love on him?

LUC. Ay, if you thought your love not cast away.

JUL. Why, he of all the rest hath never mov'd me.

LUC. Yet he of all the rest, I think, best loves ye.

JUL. His little speaking shows his love but small.

LUC. Fire,[b] that's closest kept, burns most of all.

JUL. They do not love, that do not show their love.

LUC. O, they love least, that let men know their love.

JUL. I would I knew his mind.

LUC. Peruse this paper, madam.

JUL. *To Julia*,—Say, from whom?

LUC. That the contents will show.

JUL. Say, say; who gave it thee?

LUC. Sir Valentine's page; and sent, I think, from Proteus:
He would have given it you, but I, being in the way,
Did in your name receive it; pardon the fault, I pray.

JUL. Now, by my modesty, a goodly broker![c]
Dare you presume to harbour wanton lines?
To whisper and conspire against my youth?
Now, trust me, 't is an office of great worth,
And you an officer fit for the place.
There, take the paper, see it be return'd;
Or else return no more into my sight.

LUC. To plead for love deserves more fee than hate.

JUL. Will you be gone?

LUC. That you may ruminate. [*Exit.*

JUL. And yet, I would I had o'erlook'd the letter.
It were a shame to call her back again,

---

[a] *Should* censure *thus* on *lovely gentlemen.*] The corrector of Mr. Collier's folio reads, for the sake of rhyme—

"That I, unworthy body as I can,
Should censure thus *a* lovely gentleman."

The alteration is specious, but uncalled for. To *censure*, in Shakespeare's time, usually meant to pass judgment or opinion, and Julia's "Why not *on* Proteus?" &c. proves, I think, that *on* occurred in the preceding line.

[b] Fire, *that 's closest kept,*—] *Fire* in old times was often spelt *fyer*, and appears here, as in other portions of these plays, to be used as a dissyllable.

[c] *A goodly* broker!] *A pander, a go-between, a procuress.*

And pray her to a fault for which I chid her.
What fool is she, that knows I am a maid,
And would not force the letter to my view!
Since maids, in modesty, say *No* to that
Which they would have the profferer construe *Ay*.
Fie, fie! how wayward is this foolish love,
That, like a testy babe, will scratch the nurse,
And presently, all humbled, kiss the rod!
How churlishly I chid Lucetta hence,
When willingly I would have had her here!
How angerly I taught my brow to frown,
When inward joy enforc'd my heart to smile!
My penance is, to call Lucetta back,
And ask remission for my folly past:—
What ho! Lucetta! (4)

Re-enter LUCETTA.

LUC. What would your ladyship?
JUL. Is 't near dinner-time?
LUC. I would it were;
That you might kill your stomach on your meat,
And not upon your maid.
JUL. What is 't that you
Took up so gingerly?
LUC. Nothing.
JUL. Why didst thou stoop then?
LUC. To take a paper up that I let fall.
JUL. And is that paper nothing?
LUC. Nothing concerning me.
JUL. Then let it lie for those that it concerns.
LUC. Madam, it will not lie where it concerns,
Unless it have a false interpreter.
JUL. Some love of yours hath writ to you in rhyme.
LUC. That I might sing it, madam, to a tune:
Give me a note: your ladyship can set.[a]
JUL. As little by such toys as may be possible:
Best sing it to the tune of *Light o' love*. (5)
LUC. It is too heavy for so light a tune.
JUL. Heavy? belike it hath some burthen then. (6)
LUC. Ay; and melodious were it, would you sing it.
JUL. And why not you?
LUC. I cannot reach so high.
JUL. Let 's see your song;—How now, minion?
LUC. Keep tune there still, so you will sing it out:
And yet, methinks, I do not like this tune.
JUL. You do not?
LUC. No, madam; 't is too sharp.
JUL. You, minion, are too saucy.
LUC. Nay, now you are too flat,
And mar the concord with too harsh a descant:[b]
There wanteth but a mean to fill your song.
JUL. The mean[c] is drown'd with your unruly base.[d]
LUC. Indeed, I bid the base for Proteus. (7)
JUL. This babble shall not henceforth trouble me.
Here is a coil with protestation!— [*Tears the letter.*
Go, get you gone; and let the papers lie:
You would be fingering them, to anger me.
LUC. She makes it strange; but she would be best pleas'd
To be so anger'd with another letter. [*Exit.*
JUL. Nay, would I were so anger'd with the same![e]
O hateful hands, to tear such loving words!
Injurious wasps! to feed on such sweet honey,
And kill the bees, that yield it, with your stings!
I 'll kiss each several paper for amends.
Look, here is writ—*kind Julia*:—unkind Julia!
As in revenge of thy ingratitude,
I throw thy name against the bruising stones,
Trampling contemptuously on thy disdain.
And, here is writ—*love wounded Proteus*:—
Poor wounded name! my bosom, as a bed,
Shall lodge thee, till thy wound be throughly heal'd;
And thus I search it with a sovereign kiss.
But twice, or thrice, was—*Proteus*—written down:
Be calm, good wind, blow not a word away,
Till I have found each letter in the letter,
Except mine own name: that some whirlwind bear
Unto a ragged, fearful, hanging rock,
And throw it thence into the raging sea!
Lo, here in one line is his name twice writ,—
Poor forlorn Proteus, passionate Proteus,
To the sweet Julia; that I'll tear away;
And yet I will not, sith so prettily
He couples it to his complaining names;
Thus will I fold them one upon another:
Now kiss, embrace, contend, do what you will.

[a] *Your ladyship can* set.] "When Lucetta says 'Give me a note [to sing to]: your ladyship can set [a song to music],' it adds one more to the many proofs of the superior cultivation of the science in those days. We should not now readily attribute to ladies, even to those who are generally considered to be well educated and accomplished, enough knowledge of harmony to enable them to set a song correctly to music, however agile their fingers may be."—CHAPPELL'S *Popular Music of the Olden Time*, p. 221.

[b] *Too harsh a* descant:] "The name of *Descant* is usurped of the musicians in divers significations; sometime they take it for the whole harmony of many voices; others sometime, for one of the voices or parts. Last of all, they take it for singing a part extempore upon a plain song, in which sense we commonly use it."—MORLEY'S *Plain and Easy Introduction to Practical Music*, 1597.

[c] *The* mean—] That is, the intermediate part between the tenor and the treble.

[d] *Your unruly* base.] The original has, "*you* unruly base." The alteration was made in the second folio.

[e] *Nay, would I were so anger'd with the same!*] It is surprising that no one has hitherto pointed out the inconsistency of Julia's replying to an observation evidently intended to be spoken by her attendant *aside*, or remarked the utter absence of all meaning in such reply. I have little doubt that the line above is part of Lucetta's side speech. The expression of the wish "would *I* were so anger'd with the same!" from her is natural and consistent. In the mouth of her mistress it seems senseless and absurd.

Re-enter LUCETTA.

LUC. Madam, dinner is ready, and your father stays.
JUL. Well, let us go.
LUC. What, shall these papers lie like tell-tales here?
JUL. If you respect them, best to take them up.
LUC. Nay, I was taken up for laying them down:
Yet here they shall not lie, for catching cold.[a]
JUL. I see you have a month's mind (8) to them.
LUC. Ay, madam, you may say what sights you see;
I see things too, although you judge I wink.
JUL. Come, come, will 't please you go?
[*Exeunt.*

SCENE III.—*The same. A Room in* Antonio's *House.*

Enter ANTONIO *and* PANTHINO.

ANT. Tell me, Panthino,[b] what sad[c] talk was that,
Wherewith my brother held you in the cloister?
PAN. 'T was of his nephew Proteus, your son.
ANT. Why, what of him?
PAN. He wonder'd that your lordship
Would suffer him to spend his youth at home;
While other men, of slender reputation,
Put forth their sons to seek preferment out:
Some, to the wars, to try their fortune there;
Some, to discover islands far away;
Some, to the studious universities.
For any, or for all these exercises,
He said that Proteus, your son, was meet:
And did request me to impórtune you,
To let him spend his time no more at home,
Which would be great impeachment to his age,
In having known no travel in his youth.
ANT. Nor need'st thou much impórtune me to that
Whereon this month I have been hammering.
I have consider'd well his loss of time;
And how he cannot be a perfect man,
Not being try'd and tutor'd in the world:
Experience is by industry achiev'd,
And perfected by the swift course of time:
Then, tell me, whither were I best to send him?
PAN. I think your lordship is not ignorant,
How his companion, youthful Valentine,
Attends the emperor in his royal court.
ANT. I know it well.
PAN. 'T were good, I think, your lordship sent him thither:
There shall he practise tilts and tournaments,
Hear sweet discourse, converse with noblemen;
And be in eye of every exercise,
Worthy his youth and nobleness of birth.
ANT. I like thy counsel; well hast thou advis'd:
And, that thou mayst perceive how well I like it,
The execution of it shall make known:
Even with the speediest expedition,
I will despatch him to the emperor's court.
PAN. To-morrow, may it please you, Don Alphonso,
With other gentlemen of good esteem,
Are journeying to salute the emperor,
And to commend their service to his will.
ANT. Good company; with them shall Proteus go:
And,—in good time.[d]—Now will we break[e] with him.

Enter PROTEUS.

PRO. Sweet love! sweet lines! sweet life!
Here is her hand, the agent of her heart;
Here is her oath for love, her honour's pawn:
O, that our fathers would applaud our loves,
To seal our happiness with their consents!
O, heavenly Julia!
ANT. How now? what letter are you reading there?
PRO. May 't please your lordship, 't is a word or two
Of commendation sent from Valentine,
Deliver'd by a friend that came from him.
ANT. Lend me the letter; let me see what news.
PRO. There is no news, my lord; but that he writes
How happily he lives, how well-belov'd,
And daily graced by the emperor;
Wishing me with him, partner of his fortune.
ANT. And how stand you affected to his wish?
PRO. As one relying on your lordship's will,
And not depending on his friendly wish.
ANT. My will is something sorted with his wish:
Muse not that I thus suddenly proceed;
For what I will, I will, and there an end.
I am resolv'd that thou shalt spend some time

---

a For *catching cold.*] *i. e.* for *fear* of catching cold. A mode of expression very common in our author's day.

b *Panthino,*—] In the list of persons represented in the old copy this name is spelt *Panthion.* In the play, Act I. Sc. 3, he is designated *Panthino;* and in Act II. Sc. 3, *Panthion.*

c Sad *talk*—] *Grave, serious* talk.

d *And,*—in good time.] That is, *he comes in good time, apropos.* We have a saying now, *in the nick of time.*

e *Now will we* break *with him.*] Break the matter to him. Open the subject.

With Valentinus in the emperor's court;
What maintenance he from his friends receives,
Like exhibition[a] thou shalt have from me.
To-morrow be in readiness to go:
Excuse it not, for I am peremptory.

PRO. My lord, I cannot be so soon provided;
Please you, deliberate a day or two.

ANT. Look, what thou want'st shall be sent after thee:
No more of stay; to-morrow thou must go.—
Come on, Panthino; you shall be employ'd
To hasten on his expedition.

[*Exeunt* ANT. *and* PAN.

PRO. Thus have I shunn'd the fire, for fear of burning;
And drench'd me in the sea, where I am drown'd:
I fear'd to show my father Julia's letter,
Lest he should take exceptions to my love;
And with the vantage of mine own excuse
Hath he excepted most against my love.
O, how this spring of love resembleth[b]
The uncertain glory of an April day;
Which now shows all the beauty of the sun,
And by and by a cloud takes all away!

Re-enter PANTHINO.

PAN. Sir Proteus, your father calls for you;
He is in haste; therefore, I pray you, go.

PRO. Why, this it is! my heart accords thereto;
And yet a thousand times it answers, No.

[*Exeunt.*

---

a *Like* exhibition—] *Pension, allowance.*

b *O, how this spring of love* resembleth—] *Resembleth* Mr. Tyrwhitt remarks, is here used as a quadrisyllable, and must be pronounced *resembeleth.*

ACT II.

SCENE I.—Milan. *A Room in the* Duke's *Palace.*

Enter Valentine *and* Speed.

Speed. Sir, your glove.

Val. Not mine; my gloves are on.

Speed. Why, then this may be yours, for this is but one.[a]

Val. Ha! let me see: ay, give it me, it's mine:—
Sweet ornament, that decks a thing divine!
Ah Silvia! Silvia!

Speed. Madam Silvia! madam Silvia!

Val. How now, sirrah?

Speed. She is not within hearing, sir.

Val. Why, sir, who bade you call her?

Speed. Your worship, sir; or else I mistook.

Val. Well, you'll still be too forward.

Speed. And yet I was last chidden for being too slow.

Val. Go to, sir; tell me, do you know madam Silvia?

Speed. She that your worship loves?

Val. Why, how know you that I am in love?

Speed. Marry, by these special marks: First, you have learned, like sir Proteus, to wreath your arms like a malcontent; to relish a love-song, like a robin-redbreast; to walk alone, like one that had the pestilence; to sigh, like a schoolboy that had lost his A B C; to weep, like a young wench that had buried her grandam; to fast, like one that takes diet;[b] to watch, like one that fears robbing; to speak puling, like a beggar at Hallowmas.(1) You were wont, when you laughed, to crow like a cock; when you walked, to walk like one of the lions; when you fasted, it was presently after dinner; when you looked sadly, it was for want of money: and now you are metamorphosed with a mistress, that, when I look on you, I can hardly think you my master.

Val. Are all these things perceived in me?

Speed. They are all perceived without ye.

---

[a] *For this is but* one.] *On* and *one* were formerly pronounced alike, not I believe as *on*, but as *own*. Hence Speed's quibble. See note in "King John," Act III. Sc. 3,—

"*Sound* one *into the drowsy race of night.*"

[b] *Like one that takes* diet;] One under regimen for the restoration of health.

VAL. Without me?[a] they cannot.

SPEED. Without you? nay, that's certain, for without you were so simple, none else would;[b] but you are so without these follies, that these follies are within you, and shine through you like the water in an urinal; that not an eye that sees you, but is a physician to comment on your malady.

VAL. But tell me, dost thou know my lady Silvia?

SPEED. She that you gaze on so, as she sits at supper?

VAL. Hast thou observed that? even she I mean.

SPEED. Why, sir, I know her not.

VAL. Dost thou know her by my gazing on her, and yet know'st her not?

SPEED. Is she not hard favoured, sir?

VAL. Not so fair, boy, as well favoured.

SPEED. Sir, I know that well enough.

VAL. What dost thou know?

SPEED. That she is not so fair as (of you) well favoured.

VAL. I mean, that her beauty is exquisite, but her favour infinite.

SPEED. That's because the one is painted, and the other out of all count.

VAL. How painted? and how out of count?

SPEED. Marry, sir, so painted, to make her fair, that no man counts of her beauty.

VAL. How esteemest thou me? I account of her beauty.[c]

SPEED. You never saw her since she was deformed.

VAL. How long hath she been deformed?

SPEED. Ever since you loved her.

VAL. I have loved her ever since I saw her; and still I see her beautiful.

SPEED. If you love her, you cannot see her.

VAL. Why?

SPEED. Because love is blind. O, that you had mine eyes; or your own eyes had the lights they were wont to have when you chid at sir Proteus for going ungartered![d]

VAL. What should I see then?

SPEED. Your own present folly, and her passing deformity: for he, being in love, could not see to garter his hose; and you, being in love, cannot see to put on your hose.[e]

VAL. Belike, boy, then you are in love; for last morning you could not see to wipe my shoes.

SPEED. True, sir; I was in love with my bed: I thank you, you swinged me for my love, which makes me the bolder to chide you for yours.

VAL. In conclusion, I stand affected to her.

SPEED. I would you were set; so your affection would cease.

VAL. Last night she enjoined me to write some lines to one she loves.

SPEED. And have you?

VAL. I have.

SPEED. Are they not lamely writ?

VAL. No, boy, but as well as I can do them;—Peace! here she comes.

Enter SILVIA.

SPEED. O excellent motion! O exceeding puppet![f]
Now will he interpret to her.[g]

VAL. Madam and mistress, a thousand good-morrows.

SPEED. O, give ye good ev'n! here's a million of manners. [*Aside.*

SIL. Sir Valentine and servant,(2) to you two thousand.

SPEED. He should give her interest, and she gives it him.

VAL. As you enjoin'd me, I have writ your letter
Unto the secret nameless friend of yours;
Which I was much unwilling to proceed in,
But for my duty to your ladyship.

SIL. I thank you, gentle servant: 't is very clerkly done.

VAL. Now trust me, madam, it came hardly off;
For, being ignorant to whom it goes,
I writ at random, very doubtfully.

SIL. Perchance you think too much of so much pains?

---

[a] Without *me?*] The *equivoque* consists in Speed's using the word *without* to signify his master's exterior, personal demeanour, &c., and Valentine taking it in the sense of non-existence, absence, &c., as, how could these peculiarities be seen in me unless I myself am present? In the next passage, Speed uses the word in its meaning of *unless.*

[b] None else would;] "None else would *be so simple,*" says Johnson; and this appears to be what is implied.

[c] *I* account of *her beauty.*] *i. e.* I *value, estimate, appreciate.* "There dwelled sometime in the citie of Rome a baker named Astatio, who for his honest behaviour was well *accounted of* amongst his neighbours."—TARLTON'S *Newes out of Purgatorie.*

[d] *For going* ungartered!] Negligence of dress, time out of mind, has been considered symptomatical of love, and going *ungartered,* an infallible and characteristic mark of Cupid's sworn liegemen.

[e] *Cannot see to* put on your hose.] The allusion, whatever it was, which gave point here, has evaporated, or a word on which to hang a quibble been misprinted.

[f] *O excellent* motion! *O exceeding* puppet!] *Motion,* the commentators say, meant a *puppet-show,* which is true; but assuredly it was also often used to signify one of the figures in it. Thus in "Measure for Measure," Act III. Sc. 2, Lucio, speaking of Angelo, calls him "a motion generative." So, too, in "Pericles," Act. V. Sc. 1:—

> "Have you a working pulse? and are no fairy?
> No *motion?*"

In the present case, Speed terms Silvia a *motion* and a *puppet,* because of her diminutive appearance. In "A Midsummer-Night's Dream," Act III. Sc. 2, Helena terms Hermia a *puppet,* whereupon the latter exclaims—

> "Puppet! why so? Ay, that way goes the game,
> Now I perceive that she hath made compare
> Between our statures."

So too in Massinger's play, "The Duke of Milan," Act II. Sc. 1, the tall Marcelia taunts the dwarfish Mariana—"For you, *puppet*—" which the latter retorts with—"What of me, pine-tree?"

[g] Interpret *to her.*] A motion or puppet-show was not complete without the interpreter, who probably sat behind the scenes and furnished the dialogue.

VAL. No, madam; so it stead you, I will write,
Please you command, a thousand times as much:
And yet,—

SIL. A pretty period! Well, I guess the sequel;
And yet—I will not name it;—and yet—I care not;—
And yet—take this again;—and yet—I thank you;
Meaning henceforth to trouble you no more.

SPEED. And yet—you will; and yet—another yet. [*Aside.*

VAL. What means your ladyship? do you not like it?

SIL. Yes, yes; the lines are very quaintly writ:[a]
But since unwillingly, take them again;
Nay, take them.

VAL. Madam, they are for you.

SIL. Ay, ay, you writ them, sir, at my request;
But I will none of them; they are for you:
I would have had them writ more movingly.

VAL. Please you, I'll write your ladyship another.

SIL. And when it's writ, for my sake read it over:
And if it please you, so; if not, why, so.

VAL. If it please me, madam! what then?

SIL. Why, if it please you, take it for your labour.
And so good morrow, servant. [*Exit* SILVIA.

SPEED. O jest unseen, inscrutable, invisible,
As a nose on a man's face, or a weathercock on a steeple!
My master sues to her; and she hath taught her suitor,
He being her pupil, to become her tutor.
O excellent device! was there ever heard a better,
That my master, being scribe, to himself should write the letter?

VAL. How now, sir? what are you reasoning with yourself?

SPEED. Nay, I was rhyming; 't is you that have the reason.

VAL. To do what?

SPEED. To be a spokesman from madam Silvia.

VAL. To whom?

SPEED. To yourself: why, she wooes you by a figure.

VAL. What figure?

SPEED. By a letter, I should say.

VAL. Why, she hath not writ to me?

SPEED. What needs she, when she hath made you write to yourself? Why, do you not perceive the jest?

VAL. No, believe me.

SPEED. No believing you, indeed, sir: but did you perceive her earnest?

VAL. She gave me none, except an angry word.

SPEED. Why, she hath given you a letter.

VAL. That's the letter I writ to her friend.

SPEED. And that letter hath she delivered, and there an end.

VAL. I would it were no worse.

SPEED. I'll warrant you 't is as well.

For often have you writ to her, and she, in modesty,
Or else for want of idle time, could not again reply;
Or fearing else some messenger, that might her mind discover,
Herself hath taught her love himself, to write unto her lover.—

All this I speak in print,[b] for in print I found it.—
Why muse you, sir? 't is dinner-time.

VAL. I have dined.

SPEED. Ay, but hearken, sir; though the cameleon Love can feed on the air,[c] I am one that am nourished by my victuals, and would fain have meat. O, be not like your mistress; be moved, be moved. [*Exeunt.*

SCENE II.—Verona. *A Room in* Julia's *House.*

Enter PROTEUS *and* JULIA.

PRO. Have patience, gentle Julia.

JUL. I must, where is no remedy.

PRO. When possibly I can, I will return.

JUL. If you turn not,[d] you will return the sooner:
Keep this remembrance for thy Julia's sake. [*Giving a ring.*

PRO. Why, then we'll make exchange; here, take you this.

JUL. And seal the bargain with a holy kiss.(3)

PRO. Here is my hand for my true constancy;
And when that hour o'erslips me in the day,
Wherein I sigh not, Julia, for thy sake,
The next ensuing hour some foul mischance
Torment me for my love's forgetfulness!
My father stays my coming; answer not;
The tide is now: nay, not thy tide of tears;
That tide will stay me longer than I should: [*Exit* JULIA.
Julia, farewell.—What! gone without a word?

---

a *Very* quaintly *writ:*] *Quaint* formerly meant *clever, adroit, skilful,* not as now, *pleasant, odd, fanciful.*

b *All this I speak* in print.] *In print,* meant *precisely, exactly, to the letter.* Old Burton, in his "Anatomy of Melancholy," says—"He must speak *in print,* walke *in print,* eat and drink *in print,* and that which is all in all, he must be mad *in print.*"

c *The* cameleon *Love can feed on the air.*] "Oh Palmerin, Palmerin, how cheaply dost thou furnish out thy table of love! Canst feed upon a thought! live upon hopes! feast upon a look! fatten upon a smile! and surfeit and die upon a kiss! What a Cameleon lover is a Platonick!"—*The World in the Moon,* 1697.

d If you turn not,—] If you remain constant to your love.

Ay, so true love should do: it cannot speak;
For truth hath better deeds than words to grace it.

Enter PANTHINO.

PAN. Sir Proteus, you are stay'd for.

PRO. Go; I come, I come:—
Alas! this parting strikes poor lovers dumb.
[*Exeunt.*

SCENE III.—*The same. A Street.*

Enter LAUNCE, *leading a Dog.*

LAUN. Nay, 't will be this hour ere I have done weeping; all the kind of the Launces have this very fault: I have received my proportion, like the prodigious son, and am going with sir Proteus to the imperial's court. I think Crab my dog be the sourest-natured dog that lives: my mother weeping, my father wailing, my sister crying, our maid howling, our cat wringing her hands, and all our house in a great perplexity, yet did not this cruel-hearted cur shed one tear: he is a stone, a very pebble-stone, and has no more pity in him than a dog: a Jew would have wept to have seen our parting; why, my grandam, having no eyes, look you, wept herself blind at my parting. Nay, I 'll show you the manner of it: This shoe is my father;—no, this left shoe is my father; no, no, this left shoe is my mother;—nay, that cannot be so neither:—yes, it is so, it is so; it hath the worser sole. This shoe, with the hole in it, is my mother, and this my father. A vengeance on 't! there 't is: now, sir, this staff is my sister; for, look you, she is as white as a lily, and as small as a wand: this hat is Nan, our maid; I am the dog:—no, the dog is himself, and I am the dog,—O, the dog is me, and I am myself; ay, so, so. Now come I to my father; *Father, your blessing;* now should not the shoe speak a word for weeping; now should I kiss my father; well, he weeps on:—now come I to my mother, (O, that shoe could speak now, like a wood woman;[a])—well, I kiss her;—why, there 't is; here 's my mother's breath up and down;[b] now come I to my sister; mark the moan she makes: now the dog all this while sheds not a tear, nor speaks a word; but see how I lay the dust with my tears.

Enter PANTHINO.

PAN. Launce, away, away, aboard; thy master is shipped, and thou art to post after with oars. What 's the matter? why weep'st thou, man? Away, ass; you 'll lose the tide if you tarry any longer.

LAUN. It is no matter if the tied were lost;[c] for it is the unkindest tied that ever man tied.

PAN. What 's the unkindest tide?

LAUN. Why, he that 's tied here; Crab, my dog.

PAN. Tut, man, I mean thou 'lt lose the flood; and, in losing the flood, lose thy voyage; and, in losing thy voyage, lose thy master; and, in losing thy master, lose thy service; and, in losing thy service,—Why dost thou stop my mouth?

LAUN. For fear thou shouldst lose thy tongue.

PAN. Where should I lose my tongue?

LAUN. In thy tale.

PAN. In thy tail?

LAUN. Lose the tide, and the voyage, and the master, and the service, and the tied! Why, man, if the river were dry, I am able to fill it with my tears; if the wind were down, I could drive the boat with my sighs.

PAN. Come, come away, man; I was sent to call thee.

LAUN. Sir, call me what thou darest.

PAN. Wilt thou go?

LAUN. Well, I will go. [*Exeunt.*

SCENE IV.—Milan. *A Room in the* Duke's *Palace.*

Enter VALENTINE, SILVIA, THURIO, *and* SPEED.

SIL. Servant!

VAL. Mistress.

SPEED. Master, sir Thurio frowns on you.

VAL. Ay, boy, it 's for love.

SPEED. Not of you.

VAL. Of my mistress then.

SPEED. 'T were good you knocked him.

SIL. Servant, you are sad.

VAL. Indeed, madam, I seem so.

THU. Seem you that you are not?

VAL. Haply I do.

THU. So do counterfeits.

VAL. So do you.

THU. What seem I that I am not?

VAL. Wise.

---

[a] *Like a* wood *woman;*] The folio, 1623, reads—"like a would woman." Theobald suggested the reading in the text. *Wood* means *mad, crazed, wild.*

The alteration of *she* to *shoe* in the same line was proposed by Blackstone, and after "now should not the shoe speak a word for weeping," seems a legitimate correction.

[b] Up and down;] An expression of the time, implying *exactly,* as we say "for all the world," or "all the world over." It occurs again in "Much Ado about Nothing," Act II. Sc. 1:—

"Here 's his dry hand *up and down.*"

[c] *If the* tied *were lost;*] A similar quibble is quoted by Steevens from Chapman's "Andromeda." It is found also as early as Heywood's "Epigrams."

"The *tyde taryeth* no man, but here to scan
Thou art *tyed* so that thou taryest every man."

THU. What instance of the contrary?

VAL. Your folly.

THU. And how quote you my folly?

VAL. I quote[a] it in your jerkin.

THU. My jerkin is a doublet.

VAL. Well, then, I 'll double your folly.

THU. How?

SIL. What, angry, sir Thurio? do you change colour?

VAL. Give him leave, madam; he is a kind of cameleon.

THU. That hath more mind to feed on your blood, than live in your air.

VAL. You have said, sir.

THU. Ay, sir, and done too, for this time.

VAL. I know it well, sir; you always end ere you begin.

SIL. A fine volley of words, gentlemen, and quickly shot off.

VAL. 'T is indeed, madam; we thank the giver.

SIL. Who is that, servant?

VAL. Yourself, sweet lady; for you gave the fire: Sir Thurio borrows his wit from your ladyship's looks, and spends what he borrows, kindly, in your company.

THU. Sir, if you spend word for word with me, I shall make your wit bankrupt.

VAL. I know it well, sir; you have an exchequer of words, and, I think, no other treasure to give your followers; for it appears, by their bare liveries, that they live by your bare words.

SIL. No more, gentlemen, no more; here comes my father.

Enter DUKE.

DUKE. Now, daughter Silvia, you are hard beset.
Sir Valentine, your father 's in good health:
What say you to a letter from your friends,
Of much good news?

VAL. My lord, I will be thankful
To any happy messenger from thence.

DUKE. Know you don Antonio, your countryman?

VAL. Ay, my good lord, I know the gentleman
To be of worth, and worthy estimation,
And not without desert so well reputed.

DUKE. Hath he not a son?

VAL. Ay, my good lord; a son that well deserves
The honour and regard of such a father.

DUKE. You know him well?

VAL. I know* him, as myself; for from our infancy
We have convers'd and spent our hours together:
And though myself have been an idle truant,
Omitting the sweet benefit of time
To clothe mine age with angel-like perfection,
Yet hath sir Proteus, for that 's his name,
Made use and fair advantage of his days;
His years but young, but his experience old;
His head unmellow'd, but his judgment ripe;
And, in a word, (for far behind his worth
Come all the praises that I now bestow,)
He is complete in feature[b] and in mind,
With all good grace, to grace a gentleman.

DUKE. Beshrew me, sir, but if he make this good,
He is as worthy for an empress' love,
As meet to be an emperor's counsellor.
Well, sir; this gentleman is come to me,
With commendation from great potentates;
And here he means to spend his time awhile:
I think 't is no unwelcome news to you.

VAL. Should I have wish'd a thing, it had been he.

DUKE. Welcome him then according to his worth;
Silvia, I speak to you: and you, sir Thurio:—
For Valentine, I need not 'cite him to it:
I will send him hither to you presently.
[*Exit* DUKE.

VAL. This is the gentleman I told your ladyship,
Had come along with me, but that his mistress
Did hold his eyes lock'd in her crystal looks.

SIL. Belike, that now she hath enfranchis'd them,
Upon some other pawn for fealty.

VAL. Nay, sure I think she holds them prisoners still.

SIL. Nay, then he should be blind; and, being blind,
How could he see his way to seek out you?

VAL. Why, lady, love hath twenty pair of eyes.

THU. They say that love hath not an eye at all—

VAL. To see such lovers, Thurio, as yourself;
Upon a homely object love can wink.

Enter PROTEUS.

SIL. Have done, have done; here comes the gentleman.

VAL. Welcome, dear Proteus!—Mistress, I beseech you,
Confirm his welcome with some special favour.

---

[a] *I* quote *it in your jerkin.*] A quibble springing from *quote* and *coat;* the former being pronounced and often spelt *cote*, in the time of our author.

[b] *He is complete in* feature *and in mind,*
With all good grace, to grace a gentleman.] *Feature* of old expressed both beauty of countenance and comeliness of person. Thus Spenser:—
"Which the fair *feature* of her limbs did hide."

(*) First folio, *knew*.

The punctuation I have adopted in this passage, though at variance with that of all the Editors, is fully authorized by the following one in "Henry VIII.," Act III. Sc. 2:—
"She is a gallant creature, and *complete*
In *mind and feature.*"

SIL. His worth is warrant for his welcome hither,
If this be he you oft have wish'd to hear from.
VAL. Mistress, it is: sweet lady, entertain him
To be my fellow servant to your ladyship.
SIL. Too low a mistress for so high a servant.
PRO. Not so, sweet lady; but too mean a servant
To have a look of such a worthy mistress.
VAL. Leave off discourse of disability:—
Sweet lady, entertain him for your servant.
PRO. My duty will I boast of, nothing else.
SIL. And duty never yet did want his meed;
Servant, you are welcome to a worthless mistress.
PRO. I'll die on him that says so, but yourself.
SIL. That you are welcome?
PRO. That you are worthless.

Enter SERVANT.

SER. Madam, my lord your father would speak with you.[a]
SIL. I wait upon his pleasure. [*Exit* SERVANT.
Come, sir Thurio,
Go with me:—once more, new servant, welcome:
I'll leave you to confer of home affairs;
When you have done, we look to hear from you.
PRO. We'll both attend upon your ladyship.
[*Exeunt* SILVIA, THURIO, *and* SPEED.
VAL. Now, tell me, how do all from whence you came?
PRO. Your friends are well, and have them much commended.
VAL. And how do yours?
PRO. I left them all in health.
VAL. How does your lady? and how thrives your love?
PRO. My tales of love were wont to weary you;
I know you joy not in a love-discourse.
VAL. Ay, Proteus, but that life is alter'd now:
I have done penance for contemning love;
Whose high imperious[b] thoughts have punish'd me
With bitter fasts, with penitential groans,
With nightly tears, and daily heart-sore sighs;
For, in revenge of my contempt of love,
Love hath chas'd sleep from my enthrall'd eyes,
And made them watchers of mine own heart's sorrow.
O, gentle Proteus, Love 's a mighty lord;
And hath so humbled me, as, I confess,
There is no woe to his correction,[c]
Nor to his service no such joy on earth!
Now, no discourse, except it be of love;
Now can I break my fast, dine, sup, and sleep,
Upon the very naked name of love.
PRO. Enough; I read your fortune in your eye;
Was this the idol that you worship so?
VAL. Even she; and is she not a heavenly saint?
PRO. No; but she is an earthly paragon.
VAL. Call her divine.
PRO. I will not flatter her.
VAL. O, flatter me, for love delights in praises.
PRO. When I was sick, you gave me bitter pills;
And I must minister the like to you.
VAL. Then speak the truth by her; if not divine,
Yet let her be a principality,[d]
Sovereign to all the creatures on the earth.
PRO. Except my mistress.
VAL. Sweet, except not any;
Except thou wilt except against my love.
PRO. Have I not reason to prefer mine own?
VAL. And I will help thee to prefer her too:
She shall be dignified with this high honour:
To bear my lady's train; lest the base earth
Should from her vesture chance to steal a kiss,
And, of so great a favour growing proud,
Disdain to root the summer-swelling flower,[e]
And make rough winter everlastingly.
PRO. Why, Valentine, what braggardism is this?
VAL. Pardon me, Proteus: all I can is nothing
To her, whose worth makes other worthies nothing;
She is alone.
PRO. Then let her alone.
VAL. Not for the world: why, man, she is mine own;
And I as rich in having such a jewel
As twenty seas, if all their sand were pearl,
The water nectar, and the rocks pure gold.
Forgive me, that I do not dream on thee,
Because thou seest me dote upon my love.
My foolish rival, that her father likes,
Only for his possessions are so huge,
Is gone with her along; and I must after,
For love, thou know'st, is full of jealousy.
PRO. But she loves you?
VAL. Ay, and we are betroth'd: Nay, more, our marriage hour,

---

[a] The first folio assigns this to Thurio.

[b] *Whose high* imperious *thoughts*—] Dr. Johnson proposed to read "Those high imperious thoughts;" conceiving the sense to be, "I have contemned love, and am punished." The misprint, if there is any, I rather take to be in the word *thoughts*, which our author has never elsewhere adopted to express *behests, dictates, commands*, &c.

[c] There is no woe to his correction,—] No sorrow *equal to* the punishment he inflicts. A very common idiom of the time.

"There is no comfort in the world,
To women that are kind."—*Cupid's Whirligig.*

An analogous ellipsis occurs in the very next line—

"Nor to his service no such joy on earth,"

i. e. "Nor, *compared* to his service," &c.

[d] *Yet let her be a* principality,—] If not a divinity, admit she is celestial. "The first he calleth Seraphim, the second, Cherubim, the third, thrones, the fourth, denominations, the fifth, virtues, the sixth, powers, the seventh, principalities, the eighth, archangels, the ninth and inferior sort, he calleth angels."—SCOT'S *Discoverie of Witchcraft*, 1584, p. 500.

[e] *The* summer-swelling *flower*,—] Mr. Collier's old corrector changes this fine epithet to *summer-smelling*. Steevens also says, "I once thought that our poet had written *summer-smelling;* but the epithet which stands in the text, I have since met with in the translation of Lucan by Sir Arthur Gorges, 1614, b. viii. p. 354."

With all the cunning manner of our flight,
Determin'd of: how I must climb her window;
The ladder made of cords; and all the means
Plotted and 'greed on, for my happiness.
Good Proteus, go with me to my chamber,
In these affairs to aid me with thy counsel.

PRO. Go on before; I shall inquire you forth:
I must unto the[a] road, to disembark
Some necessaries that I needs must use;
And then I 'll presently attend you.

VAL. Will you make haste?

PRO. I will.— [*Exit* VAL.
Even as one heat another heat expels,
Or as one nail by strength drives out another,
So the remembrance of my former love
Is by a newer object quite forgotten.
Is it her mien,[b] or Valentinus' praise,
Her true perfection, or my false transgression,
That makes me, reasonless, to reason thus?
She is fair; and so is Julia, that I love;—
That I did love, for now my love is thaw'd;
Which, like a waxen image 'gainst a fire,(4)
Bears no impression of the thing it was.
Methinks, my zeal to Valentine is cold;
And that I love him not, as I was wont:
O! but I love his lady too-too[c] much;
And that 's the reason I love him so little.
How shall I dote on her with more advice,
That thus without advice begin to love her!
'T is but her picture[d] I have yet beheld,
And that hath dazzled[e] my reason's light;
But when I look on her perfections,
There is no reason but I shall be blind.
If I can check my erring love, I will;
If not, to compass her I 'll use my skill. [*Exit.*

SCENE V.—*The same. A Street.*

Enter SPEED *and* LAUNCE.

SPEED. Launce! by mine honesty, welcome to Milan.*

LAUN. Forswear not thyself, sweet youth; for I am not welcome. I reckon this always—that a man is never undone till he be hanged; nor never welcome to a place till some certain shot be paid, and the hostess say, Welcome.

SPEED. Come on, you madcap, I 'll to the alehouse with you presently; where, for one shot of fivepence, thou shalt have five thousand welcomes. But, sirrah, how did thy master part with madam Julia?

LAUN. Marry, after they closed in earnest, they parted very fairly in jest.

SPEED. But shall she marry him?

LAUN. No.

SPEED. How then? shall he marry her?

LAUN. No, neither.

SPEED. What, are they broken?

LAUN. No, they are both as whole as a fish.

SPEED. Why then, how stands the matter with them?

LAUN. Marry, thus; when it stands well with him, it stands well with her.

SPEED. What an ass art thou! I understand thee not.

LAUN. What a block art thou, that thou canst not! My staff understands me.

SPEED. What thou say'st?

LAUN. Ay, and what I do, too: look thee, I'll but lean, and my staff understands me.

SPEED. It stands under thee, indeed.

LAUN. Why, stand under and understand is all one.

SPEED. But tell me true, will 't be a match?

LAUN. Ask my dog: if he say ay, it will; if he say no, it will; if he shake his tail, and say nothing, it will.

SPEED. The conclusion is then, that it will.

LAUN. Thou shalt never get such a secret from me but by a parable.

SPEED. 'T is well that I get it so. But, Launce, how say'st thou, that my master has become a notable lover?

LAUN. I never knew him otherwise.

SPEED. Than how?

LAUN. A notable lubber, as thou reportest him to be.

SPEED. Why, thou whoreson ass, thou mistakest me.

LAUN. Why, fool, I meant not thee, I meant thy master.

SPEED. I tell thee, my master is become a hot lover.

LAUN. Why, I tell thee, I care not though he burn himself in love. If thou wilt, go with me to

---

(*) First folio, *Padua.*

[a] *Unto the* road,—] *Roadstead, haven.* Place where vessels ride at anchor.

[b] Is it her mien,—] The original has—

"*It is mine* or Valentine's praise."

Steevens proposed—

"It is mine eye, or Valentine's praise."

The reading of the text was suggested to Malone by the Rev. Mr. Blakeway, and has since been generally adopted. It is certainly ingenious; but I believe we have not yet got what the poet wrote.

[c] *I love his lady* too-too *much;*] In this case I adopt the reading introduced by Halliwell, who has shown that *too-too* is "a genuine compound Archaism, used both as an adjective and an adverb, meaning *excessive* or *excessively.*"

[d] *'Tis but her* picture *I have yet beheld,*—] He has seen but her exterior yet, and that has *dazzled* his "reason's light;" when he looks upon her intellectual endowments, they will blind him quite. So in "Cymbeline," Act I. Sc. 7:—

"All of her that is *out of door*, most rich!
If she be furnish'd with a mind so rare,
She is alone the Arabian bird:—&c."

[e] *Dazzled*—] This word must be read here as a trisyllable *dazzeled;* so in the quotation Malone adduces from Drayton:—

"A diadem once *dazzling* the eye,
The day too darke to see affinitie."

the alehouse; if not, thou art an Hebrew, a Jew, and not worth the name of a Christian.

SPEED. Why?

LAUN. Because thou hast not so much charity in thee as to go to the ale(5) with a Christian: Wilt thou go?

SPEED. At thy service. [*Exeunt.*

SCENE VI.—*The same. A Room in the Palace.*

Enter PROTEUS.

PRO. To leave my Julia, shall I be forsworn;
To love fair Silvia, shall I be forsworn;
To wrong my friend, I shall be much forsworn;
And even that power, which gave me first my oath,
Provokes me to this threefold perjury.
Love bade me swear, and love bids me forswear:
O sweet-suggesting love,[a] if thou hast sinn'd,
Teach me, thy tempted subject, to excuse it.
At first I did adore a twinkling star,
But now I worship a celestial sun.
Unheedful vows may heedfully be broken;
And he wants wit that wants resolved will
To learn his wit to exchange the bad for better.—
Fie, fie, unreverend tongue! to call her bad,
Whose sovereignty so oft thou hast preferr'd
With twenty thousand soul-confirming oaths.
I cannot leave[b] to love, and yet I do;
But there I leave to love, where I should love.
Julia I lose, and Valentine I lose:
If I keep them, I needs must lose myself;
If I lose them, thus find I, by their loss,
For Valentine, myself; for Julia, Silvia.
I to myself am dearer than a friend,
For love is still most precious in itself:
And Silvia, witness Heaven, that made her fair!
Shows Julia but a swarthy Ethiope.
I will forget that Julia is alive,
Rememb'ring that my love to her is dead;
And Valentine I 'll hold an enemy,
Aiming at Silvia as a sweeter friend.
I cannot now prove constant to myself,
Without some treachery us'd to Valentine:—
This night, he meaneth with a corded ladder
To climb celestial Silvia's chamber-window;
Myself in counsel, his competitor:[c]
Now presently I 'll give her father notice
Of their disguising, and pretended flight;[d]
Who, all enrag'd, will banish Valentine;
For Thurio, he intends, shall wed his daughter:
But, Valentine being gone, I 'll quickly cross,
By some sly trick, blunt Thurio's dull proceeding.
Love, lend me wings to make my purpose swift,
As thou hast lent me wit to plot this drift! [*Exit.*

---

[a] *O sweet* suggesting *love,*—] *To suggest* is *to entice, to tempt, to seduce.* Thus, in "The Tempest," Act II. Sc. 1:—

"———— For all the rest
They'll take *suggestion* as a cat laps milk."

And in the present play, Act III. Sc. 1:—

"Knowing that tender youth is soon *suggested.*"

[b] *I cannot* leave *to love,*—] *i. e.* I cannot *cease* to love. This use of *leave* is very frequent in the old writers.

[c] *Myself in counsel, his* competitor:] *In counsel* is *in secret;* and *competitor* here, as in other places, means *coadjutor, auxiliary, confederate.* In "Richard III." Act IV. Sc. 4, we have,—

"——The Guildfords are in arms,
And every hour more *competitors*
Flock to the rebels;"

and in "Love's Labour 's Lost,"—

"The king and his *competitors* in oath."

[d] Pretended *flight;*] *i. e. intended, purposed* flight.

SCENE VII.—Verona. *A Room in* Julia's *House.*

Enter JULIA *and* LUCETTA.

JUL. Counsel, Lucetta! gentle girl, assist me!
And, even in kind love, I do conjure thee,—
Who art the table[a] wherein all my thoughts
Are visibly character'd and engrav'd,—
To lesson me; and tell me some good mean,
How, with my honour, I may undertake
A journey to my loving Proteus.

LUC. Alas! the way is wearisome and long.

JUL. A true devoted pilgrim is not weary
To measure kingdoms with his feeble steps;
Much less shall she that hath love's wings to fly!
And when the flight is made to one so dear,
Of such divine perfection, as sir Proteus.

LUC. Better forbear, till Proteus make return.

JUL. O, know'st thou not, his looks are my soul's food?
Pity the dearth that I have pined in,
By longing for that food so long a time.
Didst thou but know the inly touch of love,[b]
Thou wouldst as soon go kindle fire with snow,
As seek to quench the fire of love with words.

LUC. I do not seek to quench your love's hot fire;
But qualify the fire's extreme rage,
Lest it should burn above the bounds of reason.

JUL. The more thou damm'st it up, the more it burns;
The current that with gentle murmur glides,
Thou know'st, being stopp'd, impatiently doth rage;
But, when his fair course is not hindered,
He makes sweet music with the enamell'd stones,
Giving a gentle kiss to every sedge
He overtaketh in his pilgrimage;
And so by many winding nooks he strays,
With willing sport, to the wild ocean.
Then let me go, and hinder not my course:
I'll be as patient as a gentle stream,
And make a pastime of each weary step,
Till the last step have brought me to my love;
And there I'll rest, as, after much turmoil,
A blessed soul doth in Elysium.

---

a *Who art the* table—] Alluding to the table-book, or tables made of slate and ivory, and used as a note or memorandum-book. Thus Hamlet,—

"My *tables*—meet it is I set it down."

b *The* inly *touch of love*,—] *Inly*, Halliwell says, is used as an adjective:—

"Trust me, Lorrique, besides the *inlie* grief,
That swallowes my content."—*The Tragedy of Hoffman*, 4to. 1631.

LUC. But in what habit will you go along?
JUL. Not like a woman; for I would prevent
The loose encounters of lascivious men:
Gentle Lucetta, fit me with such weeds
As may beseem some well-reputed page.
LUC. Why, then, your ladyship must cut your hair.
JUL. No, girl; I'll knit it up in silken strings,
With twenty odd-conceited true-love knots:
To be fantastic, may become a youth
Of greater time than I shall show to be.
LUC. What fashion, madam, shall I make your breeches?
JUL. That fits as well as—"Tell me, good my lord,
What compass will you wear your farthingale?"
Why, ev'n what fashion thou best lik'st, Lucetta.
LUC. You must needs have them with a cod-piece, madam.
JUL. Out, out, Lucetta! that will be ill favour'd.
LUC. A round hose, madam, now 's not worth a pin,
Unless you have a cod-piece to stick pins on.
JUL. Lucetta, as thou lov'st me, let me have
What thou think'st meet, and is most mannerly.
But tell me, wench, how will the world repute me,
For undertaking so unstaid a journey?
I fear me, it will make me scandalis'd.
LUC. If you think so, then stay at home, and go not.
JUL. Nay, that I will not.
LUC. Then never dream on infamy, but go.
If Proteus like your journey, when you come,
No matter who 's displeas'd, when you are gone:
I fear me, he will scarce be pleas'd withal.
JUL. That is the least, Lucetta, of my fear:
A thousand oaths, an ocean of his tears,
And instances of infinite of love,[a]
Warrant me welcome to my Proteus.
LUC. All these are servants to deceitful men.
JUL. Base men, that use them to so base effect!
But truer stars did govern Proteus' birth:
His words are bonds, his oaths are oracles;
His love sincere, his thoughts immaculate;
His tears, pure messengers sent from his heart;
His heart as far from fraud as heaven from earth.
LUC. Pray Heaven he prove so, when you come to him!
JUL. Now, as thou lov'st me, do him not that wrong,
To bear a hard opinion of his truth:
Only deserve my love, by loving him;
And presently go with me to my chamber,
To take a note of what I stand in need of,
To furnish me upon my longing journey.
All that is mine I leave at thy dispose,
My goods, my lands, my reputation;
Only, in lieu thereof, despatch me hence;
Come, answer not, but to it presently:
I am impatient of my tarriance. [*Exeunt.*

[a] *And instances* of infinite of love,—] So in Fenton's "Tragicall Discourses," 4to. 1567, fol. 45:—"Wherewyth hee using the benefit of hys fortune, forgat not to embrace hys Lady with an *infinite* of kysses." The construction in the text seems harsh; but we are not for that reason to conclude the passage is corrupt. The second folio reads:—

"And instances *as* infinite of love."

ACT III.

SCENE I.—Milan. *An Ante-room in the* Duke's *Palace.*

Enter Duke, Thurio, *and* Proteus.

Duke. Sir Thurio, give us leave, I pray, awhile;
We have some secrets to confer about. [*Exit* Thurio.
Now, tell me, Proteus, what 's your will with me?
Pro. My gracious lord, that which I would discover,
The law of friendship bids me to conceal:
But, when I call to mind your gracious favours
Done to me, undeserving as I am,
My duty pricks me on to utter that
Which else no worldly good should draw from me.
Know, worthy prince, sir Valentine, my friend,
This night intends to steal away your daughter;
Myself am one made privy to the plot.
I know you have determin'd to bestow her
On Thurio, whom your gentle daughter hates;
And should she thus be stolen away from you,
It would be much vexation to your age.
Thus, for my duty's sake, I rather chose
To cross my friend in his intended drift,
Than, by concealing it, heap on your head
A pack of sorrows, which would press you down,
Being unprevented, to your timeless grave.
Duke. Proteus, I thank thee for thine honest care;
Which to requite, command me while I live.
This love of theirs myself have often seen,
Haply, when they have judg'd me fast asleep;
And oftentimes have purpos'd to forbid
Sir Valentine her company, and my court:
But, fearing lest my jealous aim [a] might err,
And so, unworthily, disgrace the man,
(A rashness that I ever yet have shunn'd,)
I gave him gentle looks; thereby to find
That which thyself hast now disclos'd to me.
And, that thou mayst perceive my fear of this,
Knowing that tender youth is soon suggested,[b]
I nightly lodge her in an upper tower,
The key whereof myself have ever kept;
And thence she cannot be convey'd away.
Pro. Know, noble lord, they have devis'd a mean
How he her chamber-window will ascend,

[a] *My jealous* aim *might err,*—] *Aim,* as Malone and Steevens remark, in this instance, implies *guess, surmise,* as in "Romeo and Juliet:"—

"I aim'd so near, when I supposed you lov'd."

[b] *Soon* suggested,—] See Note (a) at p. 17.

And with a corded ladder fetch her down;
For which the youthful lover now is gone,
And this way comes he with it presently;
Where, if it please you, you may intercept him.
But, good my lord, do it so cunningly,
That my discovery be not aimed at;[a]
For love of you, not hate unto my friend,
Hath made me publisher of this pretence.[b]
DUKE. Upon mine honour, he shall never know
That I had any light from thee of this.
PRO. Adieu, my lord; sir Valentine is coming. [*Exit.*

Enter VALENTINE.

DUKE. Sir Valentine, whither away so fast?
VAL. Please it your grace, there is a messenger
That stays to bear my letters to my friends,
And I am going to deliver them.
DUKE. Be they of much import?
VAL. The tenor of them doth but signify
My health, and happy being at your court.
DUKE. Nay then, no matter; stay with me a while;
I am to break with thee of some affairs,
That touch me near, wherein thou must be secret.
'T is not unknown to thee, that I have sought
To match my friend, sir Thurio, to my daughter.
VAL. I know it well, my lord; and, sure, the match
Were rich and honourable; besides, the gentleman
Is full of virtue, bounty, worth, and qualities
Beseeming such a wife as your fair daughter:
Cannot your grace win her to fancy him?
DUKE. No, trust me; she is peevish, sullen, froward,
Proud, disobedient, stubborn, lacking duty;
Neither regarding that she is my child,
Nor fearing me as if I were her father:
And, may I say to thee, this pride of hers,
Upon advice, hath drawn my love from her;
And, where[c] I thought the remnant of mine age
Should have been cherish'd by her childlike duty,
I now am full resolv'd to take a wife,
And turn her out to who will take her in:
Then let her beauty be her wedding-dower;
For me and my possessions she esteems not.
VAL. What would your grace have me to do in this?
DUKE. There is a lady, sir, in Milan[d] here,
Whom I affect; but she is nice, and coy,
And nought esteems my aged eloquence:
Now, therefore, would I have thee to my tutor,
(For long agone I have forgot to court;
Besides, the fashion of the time is chang'd:)
How, and which way, I may bestow myself,
To be regarded in her sun-bright eye.
VAL. Win her with gifts, if she respect not words;
Dumb jewels often, in their silent kind,
More than quick words, do move a woman's mind.
DUKE. But she did scorn a present that I sent her.
VAL. A woman sometimes scorns what best contents her:
Send her another; never give her o'er;
For scorn at first makes after-love the more.
If she do frown, 't is not in hate of you,
But rather to beget more love in you:
If she do chide, 't is not to have you gone;
For why, the fools are mad, if left alone.
Take no repulse, whatever she doth say:
For *get you gone*, she doth not mean *away*:
Flatter, and praise, commend, extol their graces;
Though ne'er so black, say they have angels' faces.
That man that hath a tongue, I say, is no man,
If with his tongue he cannot win a woman.
DUKE. But she I mean is promis'd by her friends
Unto a youthful gentleman of worth;
And kept severely from resort of men,
That no man hath access by day to her.
VAL. Why then I would resort to her by night.
DUKE. Ay, but the doors be lock'd, and keys kept safe,
That no man hath recourse to her by night.
VAL. What lets,[e] but one may enter at her window?
DUKE. Her chamber is aloft, far from the ground;
And built so shelving, that one cannot climb it
Without apparent hazard of his life.
VAL. Why, then, a ladder, quaintly[f] made of cords,
To cast up with a pair of anchoring hooks,
Would serve to scale another Hero's tower,
So bold Leander would adventure it.
DUKE. Now, as thou art a gentleman of blood,
Advise me where I may have such a ladder.
VAL. When would you use it? pray, sir, tell me that.
DUKE. This very night; for love is like a child,
That longs for everything that he can come by.
VAL. By seven o'clock I 'll get you such a ladder.
DUKE. But, hark thee; I will go to her alone;

---

[a] *Be not* aimed *at*;] *Guessed at*. The word has the same meaning as in the passage referred to in Note (a), p. 20.

[b] *This* pretence.] *Design, device*.

[c] *And*, where *I thought*—] *Where* for *whereas*. It may be observed of these words, as also of *when* and *whenas*, that, with the writers of Shakespeare's era, they were "convertible terms."

[d] *In* Milan *here*,—] The original reads,—

"There is a lady in *Verona* here."

An error of the same kind occurs in Act II. Sc. 5, where Speed says,—"Welcome to *Padua*," instead of *Milan*. The corrections were made by Pope.

[e] *What* lets,—] What *stops*, what *debars*. So "Hamlet," Act I. Sc. 4,—

"By Heaven, I 'll make a ghost of him that *lets* me."

[f] Quaintly *made of cords*,—] *Cleverly, skilfully* made of cords.

How shall I best convey the ladder thither?

VAL. It will be light, my lord, that you may bear it
Under a cloak, that is of any length.

DUKE. A cloak as long as thine will serve the turn?

VAL. Ay, my good lord.

DUKE. Then let me see thy cloak:
I 'll get me one of such another length.

VAL. Why, any cloak will serve the turn, my lord.

DUKE. How shall I fashion me to wear a cloak?—
I pray thee, let me feel thy cloak upon me.—
What letter is this same? What 's here?—*To Silvia?*
And here an engine fit for my proceeding!
I 'll be so bold to break the seal for once. [*Reads.*

My thoughts do harbour with my Silvia nightly;
And slaves they are to me, that send them flying:
O, could their master come and go as lightly,
Himself would lodge, where senseless they are lying.
My herald thoughts in thy pure bosom rest them;
While I, their king, that thither them importune,
Do curse the grace that with such grace hath bless'd them,
Because myself do want my servants' fortune:
I curse myself, for they are sent by me,
That they should harbour where their lord should be.

What 's here?

Silvia, this night I will enfranchise thee.

'T is so; and here 's the ladder for the purpose.
Why, Phaëton, (for thou art Merops' son,)[a]
Wilt thou aspire to guide the heavenly car,
And with thy daring folly burn the world?
Wilt thou reach stars, because they shine on thee?
Go, base intruder! overweening slave!
Bestow thy fawning smiles on equal mates;
And think, my patience, more than thy desert,
Is privilege for thy departure hence:
Thank me for this, more than for all the favours,
Which, all too much, I have bestow'd on thee.
But if thou linger in my territories,
Longer than swiftest expedition
Will give thee time to leave our royal court,
By Heaven, my wrath shall far exceed the love
I ever bore my daughter, or thyself.
Be gone; I will not hear thy vain excuse,
But, as thou lov'st thy life, make speed from hence.
[*Exit* DUKE.

VAL. And why not death, rather than living torment?
To die, is to be banish'd from myself;
And Silvia is myself: banish'd from her,
Is self from self: a deadly banishment!
What light is light, if Silvia be not seen?
What joy is joy, if Silvia be not by?
Unless it be to think that she is by,
And feed upon the shadow of perfection.
Except I be by Silvia in the night,
There is no music in the nightingale;
Unless I look on Silvia in the day,
There is no day for me to look upon:
She is my essence; and I leave to be,
If I be not by her fair influence
Foster'd, illumin'd, cherish'd, kept alive.
I fly not death, to fly his deadly doom:[b]
Tarry I here, I but attend on death;
But, fly I hence, I fly away from life.

Enter PROTEUS *and* LAUNCE.

PRO. Run, boy, run, run, and seek him out.

LAUN. So-ho! so-ho!

PRO. What seest thou?

LAUN. Him we go to find:
There 's not a hair[c] on 's head, but 't is a Valentine.

PRO. Valentine?

VAL. No.

PRO. Who then? his spirit?

VAL. Neither.

PRO. What then?

VAL. Nothing.

LAUN. Can nothing speak? Master, shall I strike?

PRO. Who wouldst thou strike?

LAUN. Nothing.

PRO. Villain, forbear.

LAUN. Why, sir, I 'll strike nothing: I pray you,—

PRO. Sirrah, I say, forbear: Friend Valentine, a word.

VAL. My ears are stopp'd, and cannot hear good news,
So much of bad already hath possess'd them.

PRO. Then in dumb silence will I bury mine,
For they are harsh, untuneable, and bad.

VAL. Is Silvia dead?

PRO. No, Valentine.

---

[a] Merops' son,—] "Thou art Phaëton in thy rashness, but without his pretensions: thou art not the son of a divinity, but a *terræ filius*, a low-born wretch; Merops is thy true father, with whom Phaëton was falsely reproached."—JOHNSON.

[b] I fly not death, to fly his deadly doom:] This is somewhat obscure. Mr. Singer reads:—

"————; to fly *is* deadly doom:"

but the original may mean,—

"I escape not death in flying his (the Duke's) deadly doom."

[c] *There's not* a hair—] "Launce is still quibbling. He is now running down the *hare* that he started when he entered."—MALONE.

VAL. No Valentine, indeed, for sacred Silvia!—
Hath she forsworn me?

PRO. No, Valentine.

VAL. No Valentine, if Silvia have forsworn me!—
What is your news?

LAUN. Sir, there is a proclamation that you are vanished.

PRO. That thou art banished. O, that 's the news;
From hence, from Silvia, and from me, thy friend.

VAL. O, I have fed upon this woe already,
And now excess of it will make me surfeit.
Doth Silvia know that I am banished?

PRO. Ay, ay; and she hath offer'd to the doom
(Which, unrevers'd, stands in effectual force)
A sea of melting pearl, which some call tears:
Those at her father's churlish feet she tender'd;
With them, upon her knees, her humble self;
Wringing her hands, whose whiteness so became them,
As if but now they waxed pale for woe:
But neither bended knees, pure hands held up,
Sad sighs, deep groans, nor silver-shedding tears,
Could penetrate her uncompassionate sire;
But Valentine, if he be ta'en, must die.
Besides, her intercession chaf'd him so,
When she for thy repeal was suppliant,
That to close prison he commanded her,
With many bitter threats of 'biding there.

VAL. No more; unless the next word that thou speak'st
Have some malignant power upon my life;
If so, I pray thee, breathe it in mine ear,
As ending anthem of my endless dolour.

PRO. Cease to lament for that thou canst not help,
And study help for that which thou lament'st.
Time is the nurse and breeder of all good.
Here if thou stay, thou canst not see thy love;
Besides, thy staying will abridge thy life.
Hope is a lover's staff; walk hence with that,
And manage it against despairing thoughts.
Thy letters may be here, though thou art hence:
Which, being writ to me, shall be deliver'd
Even in the milk-white bosom of thy love.
The time now serves not to expostulate:
Come, I 'll convey thee through the city gate;
And, ere I part with thee, confer at large
Of all that may concern thy love-affairs:
As thou lov'st Silvia, though not for thyself,
Regard thy danger, and along with me.

VAL. I pray thee, Launce, an if thou seest my boy,
Bid him make haste, and meet me at the north gate.

PRO. Go, sirrah, find him out. Come, Valentine.

VAL. O my dear Silvia! hapless Valentine!

[*Exeunt* VALENTINE *and* PROTEUS.

LAUN. I am but a fool, look you; and yet I have the wit to think my master is a kind of a knave: but that 's all one, if he be but one knave.[a] He lives not now that knows me to be in love: yet I am in love; but a team of horse shall not pluck that from me; nor who 't is I love, and yet 't is a woman: but what woman, I will not tell myself; and yet 't is a milkmaid; yet 't is not a maid, for she hath had gossips: yet 't is a maid, for she is her master's maid, and serves for wages. She hath more qualities than a water-spaniel,—which is much in a bare Christian. Here is the cate-log [*pulling out a paper*] of her conditions. Imprimis, *She can fetch and carry.* Why, a horse can do no more: nay, a horse cannot fetch, but only carry; therefore is she better than a jade. Item, *She can milk;* look you, a sweet virtue in a maid with clean hands.

Enter SPEED.

SPEED. How now, signior Launce? what news with your mastership?

LAUN. With my master's ship? why, it is at sea.

SPEED. Well, your old vice still; mistake the word: What news then in your paper?

LAUN. The blackest news that ever thou heard'st.

SPEED. Why, man, how black?

LAUN. Why, as black as ink.

SPEED. Let me read them.

LAUN. Fie on thee, jolt-head! thou canst not read.

SPEED. Thou liest, I can.

LAUN. I will try thee: tell me this: Who begot thee?

SPEED. Marry, the son of my grandfather.

LAUN. O illiterate loiterer! it was the son of thy grandmother: this proves that thou canst not read.

SPEED. Come, fool, come: try me in thy paper.

LAUN. There; and St. Nicholas be thy speed! (1)

SPEED. Imprimis, *She can milk.*

LAUN. Ay, that she can.

SPEED. Item, *She brews good ale.*

---

[a] *If he be but* one knave.] Warburton very plausibly proposed to read—"if he be but one *kind.*" Something, however, leading to Launce's love confession, appears to have been omitted. Possibly the poet wrote, "But that's all one, if he be but one *in love.*" The second *knave* may have been repeated, repetition being a very common compositor's error, instead of the words *in love*, which seem naturally enough to precede, "He lives not now that knows me to be in love."

LAUN. And thereof comes the proverb,—Blessing of your heart, you brew good ale.[a]

SPEED. Item, *She can sew.*

LAUN. That 's as much as to say, can she so?

SPEED. Item, *She can knit.*

LAUN. What need a man care for a stock with a wench, when she can knit him a stock?

SPEED. Item, *She can wash and scour.*

LAUN. A special virtue; for then she need not be washed and scoured.

SPEED. Item, *She can spin.*

LAUN. Then may I set the world on wheels, when she can spin for her living.

SPEED. Item, *She hath many nameless virtues.*

LAUN. That 's as much as to say, bastard virtues; that, indeed, know not their fathers, and therefore have no names.

SPEED. *Here follow her vices.*

LAUN. Close at the heels of her virtues.

SPEED. Item, *She is not to be fasting,*[b] *in respect of her breath.*

LAUN. Well, that fault may be mended with a breakfast: Read on.

SPEED. Item, *She hath a sweet mouth.*[c]

LAUN. That makes amends for her sour breath.

SPEED. Item, *She doth talk in her sleep.*

LAUN. It 's no matter for that, so she sleep not in her talk.

SPEED. Item, *She is slow in words.*

LAUN. O villain, that set this down among her vices! To be slow in words is a woman's only virtue: I pray thee, out with 't; and place it for her chief virtue.

SPEED. Item, *She is proud.*

LAUN. Out with that too; it was Eve's legacy, and cannot be ta'en from her.

SPEED. Item, *She hath no teeth.*

LAUN. I care not for that neither, because I love crusts.

SPEED. Item, *She is curst.*

LAUN. Well; the best is, she hath no teeth to bite.

SPEED. *She will often praise her liquor.*

LAUN. If her liquor be good, she shall: if she will not, I will; for good things should be praised.

SPEED. Item, *She is too liberal.*

LAUN. Of her tongue she cannot; for that 's writ down she is slow of: of her purse she shall not; for that I 'll keep shut: now of another thing she may; and that cannot I help. Well, proceed.

SPEED. Item, *She hath more hair than wit,*[d] *and more faults than hairs, and more wealth than faults.*

---

[a] *You* brew good ale.]

> "Our ale 's o' the best,
> And each good guest
> *Prays for their souls* that brew it."
> *Masque of Augurs*, BEN JONSON.

[b] *She is not to be fasting,*—] So the folio. The word *kissed*, which is found in the modern editions, was added by Rowe.

[c] *She hath a* sweet mouth.] As we now say, *a liquorish tooth.*

[d] More hair than wit,—] A well-known old English proverb. Steevens has given many instances of its occurrence in the old writers.

LAUN. Stop there; I 'll have her: she was mine, and not mine, twice or thrice in that last article: rehearse that once more.

SPEED. Item, *She hath more hair than wit*,—

LAUN. More hair than wit,—it may be; I 'll prove it: the cover of the salt hides the salt, and therefore it is more than the salt; the hair that covers the wit is more than the wit; for the greater hides the less. What 's next?

SPEED. *And more faults than hairs*,—

LAUN. That 's monstrous: O, that that were out!

SPEED. *And more wealth than faults.*

LAUN. Why, that word makes the faults gracious: well, I 'll have her: and if it be a match, as nothing is impossible,—

SPEED. What then?

LAUN. Why, then will I tell thee,—that thy master stays for thee at the north gate.

SPEED. For me?

LAUN. For thee? ay: who art thou? he hath stayed for a better man than thee.

SPEED. And must I go to him?

LAUN. Thou must run to him, for thou hast stayed so long, that going will scarce serve the turn.

SPEED. Why didst not tell me sooner? 'pox of your love-letters! [*Exit.*

LAUN. Now will he be swinged for reading my letter: an unmannerly slave, that will thrust himself into secrets!—I 'll after, to rejoice in the boy's correction. [*Exit.*

SCENE II.—*The same. A Room in the* Duke's *Palace.*

Enter DUKE *and* THURIO; PROTEUS *behind.*

DUKE. Sir Thurio, fear not but that she will love you,
Now Valentine is banish'd from her sight.
THU. Since his exile she hath despis'd me most,
Forsworn my company, and rail'd at me,
That I am desperate of obtaining her.
DUKE. This weak impress of love is as a figure
Trenched in ice; which with an hour's heat
Dissolves to water, and doth lose his form.
A little time will melt her frozen thoughts,
And worthless Valentine shall be forgot.—
How now, sir Proteus! Is your countryman,
According to our proclamation, gone?
PRO. Gone, my good lord.
DUKE. My daughter takes his going grievously.
PRO. A little time, my lord, will kill that grief.
DUKE. So I believe; but Thurio thinks not so.—
Proteus, the good conceit I hold of thee,
(For thou hast shown some sign of good desert,)
Makes me the better to confer with thee.
PRO. Longer than I prove loyal to your grace,
Let me not live to look upon your grace.
DUKE. Thou know'st how willingly I would effect
The match between sir Thurio and my daughter.
PRO. I do, my lord.
DUKE. And also, I think, thou art not ignorant
How she opposes her against my will.
PRO. She did, my lord, when Valentine was here.
DUKE. Ay, and perversely she persévers so.
What might we do, to make the girl forget
The love of Valentine, and love sir Thurio?
PRO. The best way is, to slander Valentine
With falsehood, cowardice, and poor descent;
Three things that women highly hold in hate.
DUKE. Ay, but she 'll think that it is spoke in hate.
PRO. Ay, if his enemy deliver it:
Therefore it must, with circumstance, be spoken
By one whom she esteemeth as his friend.
DUKE. Then you must undertake to slander him.
PRO. And that, my lord, I shall be loth to do:
'T is an ill office for a gentleman;
Especially, against his very friend.[a]
DUKE. Where your good word cannot advantage him,
Your slander never can endamage him;
Therefore the office is indifferent,
Being entreated to it by your friend.
PRO. You have prevail'd, my lord: if I can do it,
By aught that I can speak in his dispraise,
She shall not long continue love to him.
But, say this weed[b] her love from Valentine,
It follows not that she will love sir Thurio.
THU. Therefore, as you unwind her love from him,
Lest it should ravel, and be good to none,
You must provide to bottom it on me;[c]
Which must be done by praising me as much
As you in worth dispraise sir Valentine.
DUKE. And, Proteus, we dare trust you in this kind;
Because we know, on Valentine's report,

[a] *His* very *friend.*] *True friend.* In modern phraseology, *particular friend.*

[b] *Say this* weed—] Mr. Collier's corrector reads *wean;* and the same substitution was made by B. Victor in his alteration of this play, 1763.

[c] *To* bottom *it on me;*] A *bottom* of thread every housewife is familiar with:—

"A *bottome* for your silke it seems
My letters are become,
Which oft with winding off and on
Are wasted whole and some."
GRANGE'S *Garden*, 1557.

You are already love's firm votary,
And cannot soon revolt and change your mind.
Upon this warrant shall you have access
Where you with Silvia may confer at large;
For she is lumpish, heavy, melancholy,
And, for your friend's sake, will be glad of you;
Where you may temper her, by your persuasion,
To hate young Valentine, and love my friend.

PRO. As much as I can do, I will effect:—
But you, sir Thurio, are not sharp enough;
You must lay lime, to tangle her desires,
By wailful sonnets, whose composed rhymes
Should be full fraught with serviceable vows.

DUKE. Ay, much is the force of heaven-bred poesy.

PRO. Say that upon the altar of her beauty
You sacrifice your tears, your sighs, your heart.
Write till your ink be dry; and with your tears
Moist it again; and frame some feeling line,
That may discover such integrity:[a]
For Orpheus' lute was strung with poets' sinews;
Whose golden touch could soften steel and stones,
Make tigers tame, and huge leviathans
Forsake unsounded deeps to dance on sands.
After your dire lamenting elegies,
Visit by night your lady's chamber-window,
With some sweet consort:[b] to their instruments
Tune a deploring dump: the night's dead silence
Will well become such sweet complaining grievance:
This, or else nothing, will inherit her.[c]

DUKE. This discipline shows thou hast been in love.

THU. And thy advice this night I'll put in practice.
Therefore, sweet Proteus, my direction-giver,
Let us into the city presently
To sort some gentlemen well skill'd in music:
I have a sonnet that will serve the turn,
To give the onset to thy good advice.

DUKE. About it, gentlemen.

PRO. We'll wait upon your grace till after supper;
And afterward determine our proceedings.

DUKE. Even now about it: I will pardon you.

[*Exeunt.*

---

a *Discover* such integrity:] Malone supposed that a line following this had been lost. I rather suspect some corruption in the words *such integrity*.

b *With some sweet* consort:] *Consort* is the reading of the old copy, and is certainly correct. The modern editors, for the most part, read *concert*. *Consort*, in Shakespeare's time, appears to have been used as we use the word *band*, a *set* or *company of musicians*.

c *Will* inherit *her*.] That is, "*obtain possession* of her," Steevens says.

ACT IV.

SCENE I.—*A Forest, near* Mantua.

Enter certain Outlaws.

1 OUT. Fellows, stand fast; I see a passenger.

2 OUT. If there be ten, shrink not, but down with 'em.

Enter VALENTINE *and* SPEED.

3 OUT. Stand, sir, and throw us that you have about you;
If not, we 'll make you sit, and rifle you.

SPEED. Sir, we are undone! these are the villains
That all the travellers do fear so much.

VAL. My friends,—

1 OUT. That 's not so, sir; we are your enemies.

2 OUT. Peace! we 'll hear him.

3 OUT. Ay, by my beard, will we; for he is a proper man![a]

VAL. Then know, that I have little wealth to lose;
A man I am cross'd with adversity:
My riches are these poor habiliments,
Of which if you should here disfurnish me,
You take the sum and substance that I have.

2 OUT. Whither travel you?

VAL. To Verona.

1 OUT. Whence came you?

[a] *A* proper *man!*] *Well-proportioned, comely* man.

VAL. From Milan.
3 OUT. Have you long sojourn'd there?
VAL. Some sixteen months; and longer might have stay'd,
If crooked fortune had not thwarted me.
1 OUT. What, were you banish'd thence?
VAL. I was.
2 OUT. For what offence?
VAL. For that which now torments me to rehearse:
I kill'd a man, whose death I much repent;
But yet I slew him manfully in fight,
Without false vantage, or base treachery.
1 OUT. Why, ne'er repent it, if it were done so:
But were you banish'd for so small a fault?
VAL. I was, and held me glad of such a doom.
1 OUT. Have you the tongues?
VAL. My youthful travel therein made me happy;
Or else I often had been miserable.
3 OUT. By the bare scalp of Robin Hood's fat friar,[a]
This fellow were a king for our wild faction!
1 OUT. We 'll have him; sirs, a word.
SPEED. Master, be one of them;
It is an honourable kind of thievery.
VAL. Peace, villain!
2 OUT. Tell us this: have you anything to take to?
VAL. Nothing but my fortune.
3 OUT. Know then, that some of us are gentlemen,
Such as the fury of ungovern'd youth
Thrust from the company of awful men:[b]
Myself was from Verona banished,
For practising to steal away a lady,
An heir, and near allied unto the duke.[c]
2 OUT. And I from Mantua, for a gentleman,
Whom, in my mood, I stabb'd unto the heart.
1 OUT. And I, for such like petty crimes as these.
But to the purpose,—for we cite our faults,
That they may hold excus'd our lawless lives,
And, partly, seeing you are beautified
With goodly shape; and by your own report
A linguist; and a man of such perfection,

a *Of Robin Hood's* fat friar,—] Friar Tuck, the well-known associate and *quasi* confessor of Robin Hood, whom Scott has immortalized in his "Ivanhoe," and of whom Drayton sings in his "Polyolbion,"—

"Of *Tuck the merry friar*, which many a sermon made
In praise of Robin Hoode, his outlawes and his trade."

b *Of awful men*:] *Men of worth and station*. "An awful man is to this day used in the North to denote a man of dignity."—THOMAS WHITE, 1793.

c An *heir, and* near *allied unto the duke*.] The folio, 1623, reads,—

"And heire and Neece, alide vnto the Duke."

The folio, 1664, corrected the first word; Theobald substituted *near* for *neece*.

As we do in our quality[a] much want;—

2 OUT. Indeed, because you are a banish'd man,
Therefore, above the rest, we parley to you:
Are you content to be our general?
To make a virtue of necessity,
And live, as we do, in this wilderness?

3 OUT. What say'st thou? wilt thou be of our consort?[b]
Say, ay, and be the captain of us all:
We'll do thee homage, and be rul'd by thee,
Love thee as our commander, and our king.

1 OUT. But if thou scorn our courtesy, thou diest.

2 OUT. Thou shalt not live to brag what we have offer'd.

VAL. I take your offer, and will live with you;
Provided that you do no outrages
On silly women, or poor passengers.

3 OUT. No, we detest such vile base practices.
Come, go with us, we'll bring thee to our crews,[c]
And show thee all the treasure we have got;
Which, with ourselves, all rest at thy dispose.
[*Exeunt.*

SCENE II.—Milan. *Court of the Palace.*

Enter PROTEUS.

PRO. Already have I been false to Valentine,
And now I must be as unjust to Thurio.
Under the colour of commending him,
I have access my own love to prefer;
But Silvia is too fair, too true, too holy,
To be corrupted with my worthless gifts.
When I protest true loyalty to her,
She twits me with my falsehood to my friend:
When to her beauty I commend my vows,
She bids me think how I have been forsworn
In breaking faith with Julia whom I lov'd:
And, notwithstanding all her sudden quips,[d]
The least whereof would quell a lover's hope,
Yet, spaniel-like, the more she spurns my love,
The more it grows, and fawneth on her still.
But here comes Thurio: now must we to her window,
And give some evening music to her ear.

Enter THURIO *and* Musicians.

THU. How now, sir Proteus; are you crept before us?

PRO. Ay, gentle Thurio; for you know that love
Will creep in service where it cannot go.

THU. Ay, but I hope, sir, that you love not here.

PRO. Sir, but I do; or else I would be hence.

THU. Who?[e] Silvia?

PRO. Ay, Silvia,—for your sake.

THU. I thank you for your own. Now, gentlemen,
Let's tune, and to it lustily awhile.

Enter Host, *at a distance; and* JULIA, *in boy's clothes.*

HOST. Now, my young guest! methinks you're allycholly; I pray you, why is it?

JUL. Marry, mine host, because I cannot be merry.

HOST. Come, we'll have you merry: I'll bring you where you shall hear music, and see the gentleman that you asked for.

JUL. But shall I hear him speak?

HOST. Ay, that you shall.

JUL. That will be music. [*Music plays.*

HOST. Hark! hark!

JUL. Is he among these?

HOST. Ay: but peace, let's hear 'em.

SONG.

Who is Silvia? what is she,
That all our swains commend her?
Holy, fair, and wise[f] is she,
The heaven such grace did lend her,
That she might admired be.

Is she kind as she is fair?
For beauty lives with kindness:
Love doth to her eyes repair,
To help him of his blindness;
And, being help'd, inhabits there.

Then to Silvia let us sing,
That Silvia is excelling;
She excels each mortal thing,
Upon the dull earth dwelling:
To her let us garlands bring.

---

[a] *In our* quality—] *Our profession* or *calling.* Thus in "Hamlet," Act II. Sc. 2:—

"Will they pursue the *quality* no longer than they can sing?"

and subsequently:—

"Come, give us a taste of your *quality.*"

[b] *Of our* consort?] *Of our fellowship, confederacy, fraternity.*

[c] *We'll bring thee to our* crews,—] Mr. Collier's corrector reads, *cave;* Mr. Singer, *caves* I have not ventured to alter the original text; but can hardly believe *crews* to be what the poet wrote.

[d] *Her* sudden quips,—] *Her angry gibes, scoffs, taunts.*

[e] Who?] "Our author, throughout his plays, has confounded the personal pronouns, &c. and uses one for the other (*who* for *whom*, *she* for *her*, *him* for *he*); nor was this inaccuracy peculiar to him, being very common when he wrote, even among persons of good education."—MALONE.

[f] *Holy, fair, and* wise is *she,*—] Mr. Collier's corrector reads, wise as *free;* free is certainly a most inappropriate epithet applied to Silvia. Proteus had just before described her as

"too *fair*, too *true*, too *holy;*"

and *true*, no doubt, was the becoming term; but as the object of the serenade was to make her break faith, it would have been somewhat out of place in the song; and hence *wise* was substituted in its stead.

HOST. How now? are you sadder than you were before? How do you, man? the music likes you not.[a]

JUL. You mistake; the musician likes me not.

HOST. Why, my pretty youth?

JUL. He plays false, father.

HOST. How? out of tune on the strings?

JUL. Not so; but yet so false that he grieves my very heart-strings.

HOST. You have a quick ear.

JUL. Ay, I would I were deaf! it makes me have a slow heart.

HOST. I perceive you delight not in music.

JUL. Not a whit, when it jars so.

HOST. Hark, what fine change is in the music!

JUL. Ay, that change is the spite.

HOST. You would have them always play but one thing.

JUL. I would always have one play but one thing.
But, host, doth this sir Proteus, that we talk on,
Often resort unto this gentlewoman?

HOST. I tell you what Launce, his man, told me; he loved her out of all nick.[b]

JUL. Where is Launce?

HOST. Gone to seek his dog; which, to-morrow, by his master's command, he must carry for a present to his lady.

JUL. Peace! stand aside! the company parts.

PRO. Sir Thurio, fear not you! I will so plead,
That you shall say, my cunning drift excels.

THU. Where meet we?

PRO. At Saint Gregory's well.

THU. Farewell.

[*Exeunt* THURIO *and* Musicians.

SILVIA *appears above, at her window.*

PRO. Madam, good even to your ladyship.

SIL. I thank you for your music, gentlemen:
Who is that, that spake?

PRO. One, lady, if you knew his pure heart's truth,
You 'd quickly learn to know him by his voice.

SIL. Sir Proteus, as I take it.

PRO. Sir Proteus, gentle lady, and your servant.

SIL. What 's your will?

PRO. That I may compass yours.

---

a *The music* likes *you not.*] That is, *pleases you not.*

b *Out of all* nick.] *Beyond all reckoning.* It was the custom formerly to reckon by the *nicks* or *notches* cut upon the tally-stick. Steevens, in a note to this passage, quotes a very apposite passage from Rowley's play of "A Woman never Vexed," where the innkeeper says,—

"I have carried
The tallies at my girdle seven years together,
For I did ever love to deal honestly in the *nick*."

SIL. You have your wish; my will is even this,—
That presently you hie you home to bed.
Thou subtle, perjur'd, false, disloyal man!
Think'st thou, I am so shallow, so conceitless,
To be seduced by thy flattery,
That hast deceiv'd so many with thy vows?
Return, return, and make thy love amends.
For me,—by this pale queen of night I swear,
I am so far from granting thy request,
That I despise thee for thy wrongful suit;
And by and by intend to chide myself,
Even for this time I spend in talking to thee.

PRO. I grant, sweet love, that I did love a lady;
But she is dead.

JUL. 'T were false, if I should speak it;
For I am sure she is not buried. [*Aside.*

SIL. Say that she be; yet Valentine, thy friend,
Survives; to whom, thyself art witness,
I am betroth'd: And art thou not asham'd
To wrong him with thy importunacy?

PRO. I likewise hear that Valentine is dead.

SIL. And so suppose am I; for in his grave
Assure thyself my love is buried.

PRO. Sweet lady, let me rake it from the earth.

SIL. Go to thy lady's grave, and call hers thence;
Or, at the least, in hers sepulchre thine.

JUL. He heard not that. [*Aside.*

PRO. Madam, if your heart be so obdurate,
Vouchsafe me yet your picture for my love,
The picture that is hanging in your chamber;
To that I'll speak, to that I'll sigh and weep:
For, since the substance of your perfect self
Is else devoted, I am but a shadow;
And to your shadow will I make true love.

JUL. If 't were a substance, you would, sure, deceive it,
And make it but a shadow, as I am. [*Aside.*

SIL. I am very loth to be your idol, sir;
But, since your falsehood shall become you[a] well
To worship shadows, and adore false shapes,
Send to me in the morning, and I'll send it:
And so, good rest.

PRO. As wretches have o'er-night,
That wait for execution in the morn.

[*Exeunt* PROTEUS; *and* SILVIA, *from above.*

JUL. Host, will you go?

HOST. By my halidom,[b] I was fast asleep.

JUL. Pray you, where lies sir Proteus?

HOST. Marry, at my house: trust me, I think 't is almost day.

JUL. Not so; but it hath been the longest night
That e'er I watch'd, and the most heaviest.[c]

[*Exeunt.*

SCENE III.—*The same.*

Enter EGLAMOUR.

EGL. This is the hour that madam Silvia
Entreated me to call, and know her mind;
There's some great matter she'd employ me in.—
Madam, madam!

SILVIA *appears above, at her window.*

SIL. Who calls?

EGL. Your servant, and your friend;
One that attends your ladyship's command.

SIL. Sir Eglamour, a thousand times good-morrow.

EGL. As many, worthy lady, to yourself.
According to your ladyship's impose,[d]
I am thus early come, to know what service
It is your pleasure to command me in.

SIL. O Eglamour, thou art a gentleman,
(Think not I flatter, for I swear I do not,)
Valiant, wise, remorseful,[e] well accomplish'd.
Thou art not ignorant what dear good will
I bear unto the banish'd Valentine;
Nor how my father would enforce me marry
Vain Thurio, whom my very soul abhorr'd.
Thyself hast lov'd; and I have heard thee say,
No grief did ever come so near thy heart
As when thy lady and thy true love died,
Upon whose grave thou vow'dst pure chastity.(1)
Sir Eglamour, I would to Valentine,
To Mantua, where, I hear, he makes abode;
And, for the ways are dangerous to pass,
I do desire thy worthy company,
Upon whose faith and honour I repose.
Urge not my father's anger, Eglamour,
But think upon my grief, a lady's grief;
And on the justice of my flying hence,
To keep me from a most unholy match,
Which Heaven and fortune still reward with plagues.
I do desire thee, even from a heart
As full of sorrows as the sea of sands,
To bear me company, and go with me:
If not, to hide what I have said to thee,
That I may venture to depart alone.

---

[a] *Shall* become *you well*—] *i.e.* "'since your falsehood shall *adapt*, or *render you fit*, to worship shadows.' *Become* here answers to the Latin *convenire*, and is used according to its genuine Saxon meaning."—DOUCE.

[b] *By my* halidom,—] "*Halidome*, or *holidome*, an old word used by old countrywomen by manner of swearing; by my *halidome*, of the Saxon word, *haligdome*, ex. *halig*, i.e. *sanctum*, and *dome*, *dominium aut judicium*."—MINSHEU'S *Dict.*, folio, 1617.

[c] Most heaviest.] The use of the double superlative is not peculiar to Shakespeare; it is found in all the authors of his time.

[d] *Your ladyship's* impose,—] *Impose* is *bidding, injunction, requirement.*

[e] *Remorseful*,—] *Compassionate, full of pity.*

"——— he was none of those *remorseful* men,
Gentle and affable; but fierce at all times, and mad then."
G. CHAPMAN'S *Iliad*, 1598.

EGL. Madam, I pity much your grievances;[a]
Which since I know they virtuously are plac'd,
I give consent to go along with you;
Recking as little what betideth me
As much I wish all good befortune you.
When will you go?
SIL. This evening coming.
EGL. Where shall I meet you?
SIL. At friar Patrick's cell,
Where I intend holy confession.
EGL. I will not fail your ladyship:
Good morrow, gentle lady.
SIL. Good morrow, kind sir Eglamour. [*Exeunt.*

SCENE IV.—*The same.*

Enter LAUNCE, *with his dog.*

When a man's servant shall play the cur with him, look you, it goes hard: one that I brought up of a puppy; one that I saved from drowning, when three or four of his blind brothers and sisters went to it! I have taught him—even as one would say precisely, Thus I would teach a dog. I was sent to deliver him, as a present to mistress Silvia, from my master; and I came no sooner into the dining-chamber, but he steps me to her trencher, and steals her capon's leg. O, 't is a foul thing

---

a —— *I pity much your* grievances;
Which since I know they virtuously are plac'd, &c.]
Mr. Collier's old annotator, seeing the difficulty here, intercalates a line:—

"Madam, I pity much your grievances,
And the most true affections that you bear,
Which since I know," &c.

But this, as it has been remarked, would make Sir Eglamour bestow his pity on the *most true affections* as well as on the *grievances*. Unless, as I have sometimes thought, *grievances* in Shakespeare's age occasionally bore the meaning of *sorrowful* or *crossed affections*, the corruption would seem to lie in the word *plac'd*, which may have been a misprint for *caused*, or some word to the same effect.

when a cur cannot keep himself in all companies! I would have, as one should say, one that takes upon him to be a dog indeed, to be, as it were, a dog at all things. If I had not had more wit than he, to take a fault upon me that he did, I think verily he had been hanged for 't; sure as I live he had suffer'd for 't: you shall judge. He thrusts me himself into the company of three or four gentlemanlike dogs, under the duke's table: he had not been there (bless the mark!) a pissing while, but all the chamber smelt him. *Out with the dog*, says one; *What cur is that?* says another; *Whip him out*, says a third; *Hang him up*, says the duke. I, having been acquainted with the smell before, knew it was Crab; and goes me to the fellow that whips the dogs: *Friend*, quoth I, *you mean to whip the dog? Ay, marry, do I*, quoth he. *You do him the more wrong*, quoth I; *'t was I did the thing you wot of.* He makes me no more ado, but whips me out of the chamber. How many masters would do this for their * servant? Nay, I'll be sworn, I have sat in the stocks for puddings he hath stolen, otherwise he had been executed: I have stood on the pillory for geese he hath killed, otherwise he had suffered for 't: thou think'st not of this now!—Nay, I remember the trick you served me when I took my leave of madam Silvia; did not I bid thee still mark me, and do as I do? When didst thou see me heave up my leg, and make water against a gentlewoman's farthingale? didst thou ever see me do such a trick?

Enter PROTEUS *and* JULIA.

PRO. Sebastian is thy name? I like thee well,
And will employ thee in some service presently.

JUL. In what you please.—I'll do what I can.

PRO. I hope thou wilt.—How now, you whoreson peasant; [*To* LAUNCE.
Where have you been these two days loitering?

LAUN. Marry, sir, I carried mistress Silvia the dog you bade me.

PRO. And what says she to my little jewel?

LAUN. Marry, she says, your dog was a cur; and tells you, currish thanks is good enough for such a present.

PRO. But she received my dog?

LAUN. No, indeed, did she not: here have I brought him back again.

PRO. What, didst thou offer her this from me?

LAUN. Ay, sir; the other squirrel was stolen from me by the hangman's boys in the market-place: and then I offered her mine own; who is a dog as big as ten of yours, and therefore the gift the greater.

PRO. Go, get thee hence, and find my dog again,
Or ne'er return again into my sight.
Away, I say: Stay'st thou to vex me here?
[*Exit* LAUNCE.
A slave, that still an end[a] turns me to shame.
Sebastian, I have entertained thee,
Partly, that I have need of such a youth,
That can with some discretion do my business,
For 't is no trusting to yon foolish lout;
But, chiefly, for thy face and thy behaviour;
Which (if my augury deceive me not)
Witness good bringing up, fortune, and truth:
Therefore know thee, for this I entertain thee.
Go presently, and take this ring with thee,
Deliver it to madam Silvia:
She lov'd me well, deliver'd it to me.

JUL. It seems you lov'd not her to leave[b] her token:
She is dead, belike?

PRO. Not so; I think she lives.

JUL. Alas!

PRO. Why dost thou cry, alas!

JUL. I cannot choose but pity her.

PRO. Wherefore shouldst thou pity her?

JUL. Because, methinks, that she lov'd you as well
As you do love your lady Silvia:
She dreams on him that has forgot her love;
You dote on her that cares not for your love.
'T is pity, love should be so contrary;
And thinking on it makes me cry, alas!

PRO. Well, give her that ring, and therewithal
This letter;—that 's her chamber.—Tell my lady,
I claim the promise for her heavenly picture.
Your message done, hie home unto my chamber,
Where thou shalt find me, sad and solitary.
[*Exit* PROTEUS.

JUL. How many women would do such a message?
Alas, poor Proteus! thou hast entertain'd
A fox, to be the shepherd of thy lambs:
Alas, poor fool! why do I pity him
That with his very heart despiseth me?
Because he loves her, he despiseth me;
Because I love him, I must pity him.
This ring I gave him, when he parted from me,

(*) First folio, *his*.

a *That* still an end—] *Still an end* and *most an end* were common forms of speech, and signified *constantly, perpetually*.

"Now help, good heaven, 'tis such an uncouth thing
To be a widow out of term time! I
Do feel such aguish qualms, and dumps, and fits,
And shakings *still an end*."—*The Ordinary*.

b To leave *her token*:] The old copy has—

"It seems you lov'd not her, not leave her token."

The second *not*, there can be little doubt, was a misprint for *to*. *To leave* means *to part with, to give away*.

To bind him to remember my good will:
And now am I (unhappy messenger)
To plead for that, which I would not obtain;
To carry that, which I would have refus'd;
To praise his faith, which I would have disprais'd.
I am my master's true confirmed love;
But cannot be true servant to my master,
Unless I prove false traitor to myself.
Yet will I woo for him; but yet so coldly,
As, Heaven it knows, I would not have him speed.

Enter SILVIA, *attended.*

Gentlewoman, good day! I pray you, be my mean
To bring me where to speak with madam Silvia.
SIL. What would you with her, if that I be she?
JUL. If you be she, I do entreat your patience
To hear me speak the message I am sent on.
SIL. From whom?
JUL. From my master, sir Proteus, madam.
SIL. O!—he sends you for a picture?
JUL. Ay, madam.
SIL. Ursula, bring my picture there.
[*Picture brought.*
Go, give your master this: tell him, from me,
One Julia, that his changing thoughts forget,
Would better fit his chamber, than this shadow.
JUL. Madam, please you peruse this letter.——
Pardon me, madam; I have, unadvis'd
Deliver'd you a paper that I should not:
This is the letter to your ladyship.
SIL. I pray thee, let me look on that again.
JUL. It may not be; good madam, pardon me.
SIL. There, hold.
I will not look upon your master's lines:
I know they are stuff'd with protestations,
And full of new-found oaths; which he will break,
As easily as I do tear his paper.
JUL. Madam, he sends your ladyship this ring.
SIL. The more shame for him that he sends it me;
For, I have heard him say a thousand times,

His Julia gave it him at his departure:
Though his false finger have profan'd the ring,
Mine shall not do his Julia so much wrong.
Jul. She thanks you.
Sil. What say'st thou?
Jul. I thank you, madam, that you tender her:
Poor gentlewoman! my master wrongs her much.
Sil. Dost thou know her?
Jul. Almost as well as I do know myself:
To think upon her woes I do protest
That I have wept a hundred several times.
Sil. Belike, she thinks that Proteus hath forsook her.
Jul. I think she doth, and that's her cause of sorrow.
Sil. Is she not passing fair?
Jul. She hath been fairer, madam, than she is:
When she did think my master lov'd her well,
She, in my judgment, was as fair as you;
But since she did neglect her looking-glass,
And threw her sun-expelling mask away, (2)
The air hath starv'd the roses in her cheeks,
And pinch'd the lily-tincture of her face,
That now she is become as black as I.
Sil. How tall was she?
Jul. About my stature: for, at Pentecost,
When all our pageants of delight were play'd,
Our youth got me to play the woman's part,
And I was trimm'd in madam Julia's gown;
Which served me as fit, by all men's judgments,
As if the garment had been made for me:
Therefore, I know she is about my height.
And, at that time, I made her weep a-good,[a]
For I did play a lamentable part;
Madam, 't was Ariadne, passioning[b]
For Theseus' perjury and unjust flight;
Which I so lively acted with my tears,
That my poor mistress, moved therewithal,
Wept bitterly; and, would I might be dead,
If I in thought felt not her very sorrow!
Sil. She is beholden to thee, gentle youth!—
Alas, poor lady! desolate and left!—
I weep myself to think upon thy words.
Here, youth, there is my purse; I give thee this
For thy sweet mistress' sake, because thou lov'st her.
Farewell. [*Exit* Silvia.
Jul. And she shall thank you for 't, if e'er you know her.
A virtuous gentlewoman, mild, and beautiful.
I hope my master's suit will be but cold,
Since she respects my mistress' love so much.
Alas, how love can trifle with itself!
Here is her picture: let me see; I think,
If I had such a tire, this face of mine
Were full as lovely as is this of hers:
And yet the painter flatter'd her a little,
Unless I flatter with myself too much.
Her hair is auburn, mine is perfect yellow:
If that be all the difference in his love,
I 'll get me such a colour'd periwig.(3)
Her eyes are gray as glass;[c] and so are mine:
Ay, but her forehead 's low, and mine 's as high.
What should it be, that he respects in her,
But I can make respective[d] in myself,
If this fond love were not a blinded god?
Come, shadow, come, and take this shadow up,
For 't is thy rival. O thou senseless form,
Thou shalt be worshipp'd, kiss'd, lov'd, and ador'd;
And, were there sense in his idolatry,
My substance should be statue[e] in thy stead.
I 'll use thee kindly for thy mistress' sake,
That used me so; or else, by Jove I vow,
I should have scratch'd out your unseeing eyes,
To make my master out of love with thee! [*Exit.*

---

[a] *I made her* weep a-good,—] That is, *weep in good earnest.*
"And therewithall their knees have rankled so,
That I have laughed *a-good.*"—Marlowe's *Jew of Malta.*

[b] *'Twas Ariadne,* passioning—] *To passion* as, a verb, is not at all unfrequent in writers contemporary with our author, and meant, I believe, not merely to feel emotion, but to display it by voice or gesture, or both. So in "Venus and Adonis"—
"Dumbly she *passions,* franticly she doteth."

[c] *Her eyes are* gray as glass;] "By a *gray* eye was meant what we now call a blue eye: gray, when applied to the eye, is rendered by Coles in his Dict., 1679, *ceruleus, glaucus.*"—Malone. Old glass is said to have a bluish tinge.

[d] *I can make* respective—] That is, *regardful, considerative, observable.*

[e] *My substance should be* statue—] It is true enough, as the commentators have shown, that the words *statue* and *picture* were of old used indiscriminately; but is not *image* here meant? and had not the poet in his mind the story of Pygmalion? That he was conversant with it we know:—
"What, is there none of *Pygmalion's images,* newly made woman to be had—"—*Measure for Measure.*

ACT V.

SCENE I.—*The same. An Abbey.*

Enter EGLAMOUR.

EGL. The sun begins to gild the western sky;
And now it is about the very hour
That Silvia, at friar Patrick's cell, should meet me.
She will not fail; for lovers break not hours,
Unless it be to come before their time;
So much they spur their expedition.

Enter SILVIA.

See where she comes: Lady, a happy evening!
SIL. Amen, amen! go on, good Eglamour,
Out at the postern by the abbey-wall;
I fear I am attended by some spies.
EGL. Fear not; the forest is not three leagues off:
If we recover that, we are sure enough. [*Exeunt.*

SCENE II.—*The same. A Room in the* Duke's *Palace.*

Enter THURIO, PROTEUS, *and* JULIA.

THU. Sir Proteus, what says Silvia to my suit?
PRO. O, sir, I find her milder than she was;
And yet she takes exceptions at your person.
THU. What, that my leg is too long?
PRO. No, that it is too little.
THU. I'll wear a boot, to make it somewhat rounder.
PRO. But love will not be spurr'd to what it loathes.[a]
THU. What says she to my face?
PRO. She says it is a fair one.
THU. Nay then, the wanton lies; my face is black.
PRO. But pearls are fair; and the old saying is,

---

[a] But love will not be spurred, *&c.*] This line, as well as one a little lower, Mr. Boswell justly thought belonged to Julia. They are of a character with her other remarks, and intended to be spoken aside.

Black men are pearls in beauteous ladies' eyes.
JUL. 'T is true,[a] such pearls as put out ladies' eyes;
For I had rather wink than look on them. [*Aside.*
THU. How likes she my discourse?
PRO. Ill, when you talk of war.
THU. But well, when I discourse of love and peace?
JUL. But better, indeed, when you hold your peace. [*Aside.*
THU. What says she to my valour?
PRO. O, sir, she makes no doubt of that.
JUL. She needs not, when she knows it cowardice. [*Aside.*
THU. What says she to my birth?
PRO. That you are well deriv'd.
JUL. True; from a gentleman to a fool. [*Aside.*
THU. Considers she my possessions?
PRO. O, ay; and pities them.
THU. Wherefore?
JUL. That such an ass should owe them. [*Aside.*
PRO. That they are out by lease.[b]
JUL. Here comes the duke.

Enter DUKE.

DUKE. How now, sir Proteus? how now, Thurio?
Which of you saw sir Eglamour of late?
THU. Not I.
PRO. Nor I.
DUKE. Saw you my daughter?
PRO. Neither.
DUKE. Why, then, she 's fled unto that peasant Valentine;
And Eglamour is in her company.
'T is true; for friar Lawrence met them both,
As he in penance wander'd through the forest:
Him he knew well, and guess'd that it was she;
But, being mask'd, he was not sure of it:
Besides, she did intend confession
At Patrick's cell this even; and there she was not:
These likelihoods confirm her flight from hence.
Therefore, I pray you, stand not to discourse,
But mount you presently, and meet with me
Upon the rising of the mountain-foot
That leads toward Mantua, whither they are fled.
Despatch, sweet gentlemen, and follow me. [*Exit.*
THU. Why, this it is to be a peevish girl,
That flies her fortune when it follows her:
I 'll after; more to be reveng'd on Eglamour,
Than for the love of reckless Silvia. [*Exit.*
PRO. And I will follow, more for Silvia's love,
Than hate of Eglamour that goes with her. [*Exit.*
JUL. And I will follow, more to cross that love,
Than hate for Silvia, that is gone for love. [*Exit.*

SCENE III.—*Frontiers of* Mantua. *The Forest.*

Enter SILVIA *and* Outlaws.

1 OUT. Come, come;
Be patient, we must bring you to our captain.
SIL. A thousand more mischances than this one
Have learn'd me how to brook this patiently.
2 OUT. Come, bring her away.
1 OUT. Where is the gentleman that was with her?
3 OUT. Being nimble-footed, he hath outrun us,
But Moyses and Valerius follow him.
Go thou with her to the west end of the wood,
There is our captain: we 'll follow him that 's fled,
The thicket is beset, he cannot 'scape.
1 OUT. Come, I must bring you to our captain's cave;
Fear not; he bears an honourable mind,
And will not use a woman lawlessly.
SIL. O Valentine, this I endure for thee. [*Exeunt.*

SCENE IV.—*Another part of the Forest.*

Enter VALENTINE.

VAL. How use doth breed a habit in a man!
This shadowy desert, unfrequented woods,
I better brook than flourishing peopled towns:
Here can I sit alone, unseen of any,
And to the nightingale's complaining notes
Tune my distresses, and record[c] my woes.
O thou that dost inhabit in my breast,
Leave not the mansion so long tenantless;
Lest, growing ruinous, the building fall,
And leave no memory of what it was!
Repair me with thy presence, Silvia;
Thou gentle nymph, cherish thy forlorn swain!
What hallooing, and what stir, is this to-day?
These are my mates, that make their wills their law,
Have some unhappy passenger in chase:
They love me well; yet I have much to do,
To keep them from uncivil outrages.
Withdraw thee, Valentine; who 's this comes here?
[*Steps aside.*

---

[a] 'Tis true, *&c.*] In the folio, 1623, this line is given to Thurio. There can be no doubt that it belongs to Julia.

[b] *That they are* out by lease.] The meaning has been controverted. Lord Hailes explains it thus:—"By Thurio's *possessions* he himself understands his *lands*. But Proteus chooses to take the word likewise in a figurative sense, as signifying his *mental endowments;* and when he says they *are out by lease,* he means that they are no longer enjoyed by their master, (who is a fool,) but are *leased out* to another."

[c] *And* record *my woes.*] *To record* refers to the *singing of birds,* and is derived, Douce says, from the *recorder,*—a sort of flute *by* which they were taught to sing.

Enter PROTEUS, SILVIA, *and* JULIA.

PRO. Madam, this service I have done for you,
(Though you respect not aught your servant doth,)
To hazard life, and rescue you from him
That would have forc'd your honour and your love.
Vouchsafe me, for my meed, but one fair look;
A smaller boon than this I cannot beg,
And less than this, I am sure, you cannot give.

VAL. How like a dream is this I see and hear!
Love, lend me patience to forbear a while. [*Aside.*

SIL. O miserable, unhappy that I am!

PRO. Unhappy were you, madam, ere I came;
But, by my coming, I have made you happy.

SIL. By thy approach thou mak'st me most unhappy.

JUL. And me, when he approacheth to your presence. [*Aside.*

SIL. Had I been seized by a hungry lion,
I would have been a breakfast to the beast,
Rather than have false Proteus rescue me.
O, Heaven be judge how I love Valentine,
Whose life 's as tender to me as my soul;
And full as much (for more there cannot be)
I do detest false perjur'd Proteus:
Therefore be gone, solicit me no more.

PRO. What dangerous action, stood it next to death,
Would I not undergo for one calm look?
O, 't is the curse in love, and still approv'd,[a]
When women cannot love where they 're belov'd.

SIL. When Proteus cannot love where he 's belov'd.
Read over Julia's heart, thy first best love,
For whose dear sake thou didst then rend thy faith
Into a thousand oaths; and all those oaths
Descended into perjury, to love me.
Thou hast no faith left now, unless thou'dst two,
And that 's far worse than none; better have none
Than plural faith, which is too much by one:
Thou counterfeit to thy true friend!

PRO. In love,
Who respects friend?

SIL. All men but Proteus.

PRO. Nay, if the gentle spirit of moving words
Can no way change you to a milder form,
I 'll woo you like a soldier, at arms' end;
And love you 'gainst the nature of love, force you.

SIL. O Heaven!

PRO. I 'll force thee yield to my desire.

VAL. Ruffian, let go that rude uncivil touch;
Thou friend of an ill fashion!

PRO. Valentine!

VAL. Thou common friend, that 's without faith or love;
(For such is a friend now;) treacherous man!
Thou hast beguil'd my hopes; nought but mine eye
Could have persuaded me: now I dare not say
I have one friend alive; thou wouldst disprove me.
Who should be trusted when one's own* right hand
Is perjur'd to the bosom? Proteus,
I am sorry I must never trust thee more,
But count the world a stranger for thy sake.
The private wound is deepest: O time most accurs'd!
'Mongst all foes, that a friend should be the worst.

PRO. My shame, and guilt, confounds me.—
Forgive me, Valentine: if hearty sorrow
Be a sufficient ransom for offence,
I tender it here; I do as truly suffer
As e'er I did commit.

VAL. Then I am paid;
And once again I do receive thee honest:—
Who by repentance is not satisfied
Is nor of heaven, nor earth; for these are pleas'd;
By penitence the Eternal's wrath 's appeas'd,—
And, that my love may appear plain and free,
All that was mine, in Silvia, I give thee.[b]

JUL. O me, unhappy! [*Faints.*

PRO. Look to the boy.

VAL. Why, boy!
Why, wag! how now? what 's the matter? Look up; speak.

JUL. O good sir, my master charged me to deliver a ring to madam Silvia; which, out of my neglect, was never done.

PRO. Where is that ring, boy?

JUL. Here 't is: this is it. [*Gives a ring.*

PRO. How! let me see:
Why, this is the ring I gave to Julia.

JUL. O, cry you mercy, sir, I have mistook;

---

[a] *And* still approv'd,—] That is, *always proved.* So in "Othello," Act I. Sc. 3,—

"My very noble and *approv'd* good masters."

[b] All that was mine, in Silvia, I give thee.] No passage in the play has caused so much perplexity to the commentators as this. "It is, I think, very odd," remarks Pope, "to give up his mistress thus at once, without any reason alleged;"—and every reader thinks so too; and innumerable have been the expedients suggested to remove the anomaly. It has been proposed to transfer the lines to Thurio in another scene; and Mr. Knight intimates that, with a slight alteration, they might be given to Silvia. Mr. Baron Field suggested we should read,—

"All that was *thine*, in Silvia I give thee."

i.e. "I will make up my love for you as large as the love you once had for Silvia." The most plausible correction is, I think, the transferring the disputed lines to Proteus, but reading *Julia* for *Silvia*, thus:—

"And, that my love may appear plain and free,
All that was mine, in *Julia*, I give thee."

All the love I once felt for Julia, I will henceforth dedicate to my friendship for you.

Whatever may be thought of this conjecture, no one can believe the lines were spoken by Valentine, after seeing the vehemence with which he repels the advances of Thurio to his mistress subsequently, even in the presence of her father, the Duke:—

"Do not name Silvia thine; if once again,
Verona shall not hold thee. Here she stands;
Take but possession of her with a touch;—
I dare thee but to breathe upon my love."

(*) *Own* is not in First folio.

This is the ring you sent to Silvia.
[*Shows another ring.*
PRO. But how camest thou by this ring?
At my depart, I gave this unto Julia.
JUL. And Julia herself did give it me;
And Julia herself hath brought it hither.
PRO. How! Julia!
JUL. Behold her that gave aim[a] to all thy oaths,
And entertain'd them deeply in her heart:
How oft hast thou with perjury cleft the root?[b]
O Proteus, let this habit make thee blush!
Be thou asham'd, that I have took upon me
Such an immodest raiment; if shame live
In a disguise of love:
It is the lesser blot, modesty finds,
Women to change their shapes, than men their minds.
PRO. Than men their minds! 't is true; O Heaven! were man
But constant, he were perfect: that one error
Fills him with faults; makes him run through all th' sins:
Inconstancy falls off ere it begins:
What is in Silvia's face, but I may spy
More fresh in Julia's with a constant eye?
VAL. Come, come, a hand from either:
Let me be bless'd to make this happy close;
'T were pity two such friends should be long foes.
PRO. Bear witness, Heaven, I have my wish for ever.
JUL. And I mine.

Enter Outlaws, *with* DUKE *and* THURIO.

OUT. A prize, a prize, a prize!
VAL. Forbear, forbear, I say; it is my lord the duke.
Your grace is welcome to a man disgrac'd,
Banished Valentine.

---

[a] *That* gave aim—] *To give aim,* and *to cry aim,* have been so admirably explained and discriminated by Mr. Gifford, that we cannot do better than append his note upon the expressions:—"*Aim!* for so it should be printed, and not *cry aim,* was always addressed to the person about to shoot; it was an hortatory exclamation of the bystanders, or, as Massinger has it, of the *idle lookers-on,* intended for his encouragement. To cry *aim!* was *to encourage; to give aim* was *to direct;* and in these distinct and appropriate senses the words perpetually occur. Those who cried *aim!* stood by the archers; he who *gave it,* was stationed near the butts, and pointed out, after every discharge, how wide, or how short, the arrow fell of the mark."

[b] *Cleft* the root?] That is, of her heart. She is carrying on the allusion to archery. *To cleave the pin* was to split the wooden peg which attached the target to the butt.

DUKE. Sir Valentine!
THU. Yonder is Silvia; and Silvia's mine.
VAL. Thurio, give back, or else embrace thy death;
Come not within the measure of my wrath:
Do not name Silvia thine; if once again,
Verona shall not hold thee.[a] Here she stands;
Take but possession of her with a touch;—
I dare thee but to breathe upon my love.—
THU. Sir Valentine, I care not for her, I;
I hold him but a fool, that will endanger
His body for a girl that loves him not:
I claim her not, and therefore she is thine.
DUKE. The more degenerate and base art thou,
To make such means for her as thou hast done,
And leave her on such slight conditions.—
Now, by the honour of my ancestry,
I do applaud thy spirit, Valentine,
And think thee worthy of an empress' love!
Know then, I here forget all former griefs,
Cancel all grudge, repeal thee home again.—
Plead a new state in thy unrivall'd merit,[b]
To which I thus subscribe,—Sir Valentine,
Thou art a gentleman, and well deriv'd;
Take thou thy Silvia, for thou hast deserv'd her.
VAL. I thank your grace; the gift hath made me happy.
I now beseech you, for your daughter's sake,
To grant one boon that I shall ask of you.
DUKE. I grant it, for thine own, whate'er it be.
VAL. These banish'd men, that I have kept withal,
Are men endued with worthy qualities;
Forgive them what they have committed here,
And let them be recall'd from their exile:
They are reformed, civil, full of good,
And fit for great employment, worthy lord.
DUKE. Thou hast prevail'd; I pardon them, and thee;
Dispose of them, as thou know'st their deserts.
Come, let us go; we will include all jars
With triumphs, mirth, and rare solemnity.(1)
VAL. And, as we walk along, I dare be bold
With our discourse to make your grace to smile:
What think you of this page, my lord?
DUKE. I think the boy hath grace in him; he blushes.
VAL. I warrant you, my lord; more grace than boy.
DUKE. What mean you by that saying?
VAL. Please you, I'll tell you as we pass along,
That you will wonder what hath fortuned.—
Come, Proteus; 't is your penance, but to hear
The story of your loves discovered:
That done, our day of marriage shall be yours;
One feast, one house, one mutual happiness.
[*Exeunt.*

[a] Verona *shall not hold thee.*] This is the reading of the only authentic edition of the present play we possess. Theobald, upon the ground that Thurio was a Milanese, and that the scene is between the confines of Milan and Mantua, changed the reading to—

"*Milan* shall not *behold thee*;"

and he has been followed by nearly every editor but Malone.

[b] Plead a new state in thy unrivall'd merit,—] There is some obscurity here. Mr. Singer says,—"Do thou put in a plea for reinstatement in forfeited honours, or claim an enhancement of dignity, and I set my hand to it in these terms:—'Sir Valentine, thou art a gentleman!'"

ILLUSTRATIVE COMMENTS.

ACT I.

(1) SCENE I.—*Nay, give me not the boots.*] To give one the boots, like the French equivalent, *donner le change à quelqu'un,* means, to sell him a bargain.

> "*Acc.* What, doo you *give me the boots?*
> *Half.* Whether will they, here be right
> Cobler's cuts."
> LILLY'S *Mother Bombie,* 1594.

So also in "The Weakest go to the Wall," 1618 :—

> "'Tis not your big belly nor your fat bacon can carry it away, if you *offer us the boots.*"

Steevens thinks the expression arose from a sport the country people in Warwickshire use at their harvest-home, where one sits as judge to try misdemeanours committed in harvest; and the punishment for the men is to be laid on a bench and slapped on the breech with a *pair of boots.*

But he remarks, the allusion may be to the dreadful punishment known as the *boots.* In Harl. MSS., 6999—48, Mr. T. Randolph writes to Lord Hunsdon, and mentions in the P.S. to his letter, that George Fluke *had* yesterday night *the boots,* and is said to have confessed that the Earl of Morton was privy to the poisoning the Earl of Athol, 16th March, 1580; and in another letter, March 18th, 1580, "that the Laird of Wittingham *had the boots,* but without torment, confess'd," &c. The punishment consisted in putting on the victim a pair of iron boots, fitting close to the leg, and then driving wedges with a mallet between those and the limb. Not a great while before this play was written, Douce tells us it was inflicted on a poor wretch, one Fian, in Scotland, in the presence of King James (afterwards our James the First). Fian was supposed to be a wizard, and to have been concerned in raising the storms which the King encountered on his matrimonial expedition to Denmark. The account of the transaction, which is contained in a very curious old pamphlet, states that Fian "was with all convenient speed, by commandement, convaied againe to the *torment of the boots,* wherein he continued a long time, and did abide so many blows in them, that his legges were crushte and beaten togeather as small as might bee, and the bones and flesh so brused that the bloud and marrowe spouted forth in great abundance, whereby they were made unserviceable for ever." The miserable man was afterwards burned.

(2) SCENE I.—*I, a lost mutton, gave your letter to her, a laced mutton.*] *Laced mutton* was, from a very early period of our history, a cant phrase to express a courtesan. In our author's time, according to Malone, it was so established a term for one of these unfortunates, that a street in Clerkenwell, much frequented by them, was then called *Mutton* Lane. Mr. Dyce suggests that, in the present instance, the expression might not be regarded as synonymous with courtesan; and that Speed applied the term to Julia in the much less offensive sense of—*a richly-attired piece of woman's flesh.* We believe there was but one meaning attached to the term; and the only palliation for Speed's application of it in this case is, that in reality it was not the lady, but her waiting-maid, to whom he gave the letter.

(3) SCENE I.—*You have testern'd me.*] The old copy reads *cestern'd*—a palpable corruption. The *tester, testern, teston,* derives its name, some suppose, from the French *teston,* so called on account of the King's head first appearing on this coin,—Louis XII. 1513; or from an Italian coin of the same denomination. In England the name is said to have been first applied to the shilling (originally coined by Henry VII.), at the beginning of the reign of Henry VIII., and was at first of the value of twelve silver pennies; it subsequently became much reduced; and its debasement by an admixture of copper, temp. 1551, and again, 1560, is satirized in Heywood's "Epigrams :"—

> "These testons, look, read; how like you the same?
> 'Tis a token of grace—they blush for shame."

At the latter period named, it was so far reduced as to be worth but fourpence halfpenny; but it afterwards rose in value again to the value of sixpence.

> "*Sir Toby.* Come on; there is *sixpence* for you, let's have a song.
> *Sir Andrew.* There 's a *testril* of me too; if one knight give a—
> *Clown.* Would you have a love song," &c.
> *Twelfth Night,* Act II. Sc. 3.

And it appears to have ever since continued as a popular name for that coin.

(4) SCENE II.—*What ho! Lucetta!*] It may be interesting to compare this scene with the corresponding portion of Felismena's story in Book II. of Bartholomew Yong's translation of the "Diana" of Montemayor, 1598 :—

"But to see the meanes that Rosina made unto me (for so was she called), the dutifull services and unwoonted circumstances, before she did deliver it, the othes that she sware unto me, and the subtle words and serious protestations she used, it was a pleasant thing, and woorthie the noting. To whom (neverthelesse) with an angrie countenance I turned againe, saying, If I had not regard of mine owne estate, and what hereafter might be said, I would make this shamelesse face of thine be knowne ever after for a marke of an impudent and bolde minion: but bicause it is the first time, let this suffice that I have saide, and give thee warning to take heed of the second.

"Me thinkes I see now the craftie wench, how she helde her peace, dissembling very cunningly the sorrow that she conceived by my angrie answer; for she fained a counterfaite smiling, saying, Jesus, mistresse! I gave it you, bicause you might laugh at it, and not to moove your patience with it in this sort; for if I had any thought that it would have provoked you to anger, I praie God he may shew his wrath as great towards me as ever he did to the daughter of any mother. And with this she added many wordes more (as she could do well enough) to pacifie the fained anger and ill opinion that I had conceived of her, and taking her letter with her, she departed from me. This having passed thus, I began to imagine what might ensue thereof, and love (me thought) did put a certaine desire into my minde to see the letter, though modestie and shame forbad me to ask it of my maide, especially for the wordes that had passed betweene us, as you have heard. And so I continued all that day untill night, in varietie of many thoughts; but when *Rosina* came to helpe me to bedde, God knowes how desirous I was to have her entreat me againe to take the letter, but she woulde never speake unto me about it, nor (as it seemed) did so much as once thinke thereof. Yet to trie, if by giving her some occasion I might prevaile, I saide unto her: And is it so, *Rosina*, that *Don Felix*, without any regard to mine honour, dares write unto me? These are things, mistresse (saide she demurely to me againe), that are commonly incident to love, wherefore I beseech you pardon me, for if I had thought to have angred you with it, I would have first pulled out the bals of mine eies. How cold my hart was at that blow, God knowes, yet did I dissemble the matter, and suffer myselfe to remaine that night onely with my desire, and with occasion of little sleepe. And so it was, indeede, for that (me thought) was the longest and most painfull night that ever I passed. But when, with a slower pace (then I desired) the wished day was come, the discreet and subtle *Rosina* came into my chamber to helpe me to make me readie, in dooing whereof, of purpose she let the letter closely fall, which, when I perceived, What is that that fell downe? (said I) let me see it. It is nothing, mistresse, saide she. Come, come, let me see it (saide I): what! moove me not, or else tell me what it is. Good Lord, mistresse (said she) why will you see it: it is the letter I would have given you yesterday. Nay, that it is not (saide I) wherefore shewe it me, that I may see if you lie or no. I had no sooner said so, but she put it into my handes, saying, God never give me good if it be anie other thing; and although I knewe it well indeede, yet I saide, what, this is not the same, for I know that well enough, but it is one of thy lovers letters: I will read it, to see in what neede he standeth of thy favour."

(5) SCENE II.—*The tune of "Light o' love."*] "*Light of Love*" is so frequently mentioned by writers of the sixteenth century, that it is much to be regretted that the words of the original song are still undiscovered. When played slowly, and with expression, the air is beautiful. In the Collection of Mr. George Daniel, of Canonbury, is "A *very proper* dittie, to the tune of *Lightie Love*," which was printed in 1570. The original may not have been quite so "proper," if "Light o' Love" was used in the sense in which it was occasionally employed, instead of its more poetical meaning:—

> "One of your *London Light o' Loves*, a right one,
> Come over in thin pumps and half a petticoat."
> FLETCHER'S *Wild Goose Chase*, Act IV. Sc. 1.

CHAPPELL'S *Popular Music of the Olden Time*, p. 221.

Shakespeare refers to this tune in "Much Ado about Nothing," Act III. Sc. 4.

> "*Marg.* Clap us into—*Light o' love*, that goes without a burden; do you sing it, and I'll dance it."

(6) SCENE II.—*Belike it hath some burthen then.*] The burden of a song, in the old acceptation of the word, was the base, foot, or under-song. It was sung throughout, and not merely at the end of the verse. Burden is derived from *bourdoun*, a drone base (French, *bourdon*).

> "This Sompnour bear to him a stiff burdoun,
> Was never trompe of half so gret a'soun."
> CHAUCER.

We find, as early as 1250, that *Somer is icumen in*, was sung with a foot or burden in two parts throughout ("Sing, Cuckoo, Sing Cuckoo"); and in the preceding century Giraldus had noticed the peculiarity of the English in singing under-parts to their songs.—CHAPPELL'S *Popular Music, &c.*

(7) SCENE II.—*I bid the base for Proteus.*] Lucetta, playing on the word *base*, turns the allusion to an ancient and still practised sport, known as *the base*, or *prison base*, or *prison bars*. This game is frequently mentioned by the old writers. It consisted in a number of men or boys congregating within certain spaces, from whence one of them issued some hundred or more yards, and challenged any other to come out and catch him before the challenger could make his way to a privileged spot equi-distant from where the two parties were placed. The party who went out and challenged the other was said to *bid the base*.

> "—— lads more like to run
> The country *base*, than to commit such slaughter."
> *Cymbeline*, Act IV. Sc. 2.

> "To drinke half pots, or deale at the whole Canne:—
> To play at *Base* or Ben, and Inck-horn, Sir Ihan."
> *The Letting of Humours Blood in the Head Vaine*,
> S. ROWLAND, 1600

> "Yet was no better than our *prison base*."
> *Annalia Dubrensia*, 4to. 1636.

(8) SCENE II.—*I see you have a month's mind to them.*] The *month's mind*, i. e. the religious observances for the dead performed daily for one month after the death of the person on whose behalf they were offered, was generally prompted by regard for the deceased. To perform a *month's mind* might be taken, therefore, as a proof of *strong affection* for some one; and when these religious ceremonies ceased with the Reformation, the expression came by degrees to have only the meaning we find attached to it in Shakespeare and his contemporaries, implying a hankering after, or as we now express it, a *great mind* for, anything.

> "*Diss.* ———— I had of late
> A *moneth's mind*, sir, to you, y'ave the right make
> To please a lady."
> RANDOLPH'S *Jealous Lovers*, 1646.

"These verses Euphues sent also under his glasse, which having finished, he gave himself to his booke, determining to end his life in Athens, although he had a *moneth's minde* to England."—*Euphues and his England*, 1623.

ACT II.

(1) SCENE I.—*To speak puling, like a beggar at Hallowmas.*] "It is worth remarking," observes Tollet, "that on All-Saints'-Day the poor people in Staffordshire, and, perhaps, in other country places, go from parish to parish *a-souling*, as they call it; *i. e.* begging and *puling* (or singing small, as Bailey's Dictionary explains *puling*) for *soul-cakes*, or any good thing to make them merry. This custom is mentioned by Peck, and seems a remnant of Popish superstition to pray for departed souls, particularly those of friends." In Lancashire and Herefordshire it was usual at this period for the wealthy to dispense oaken cakes, called *soul-mass-cakes*, to the poor, who, upon receiving them, repeated the following couplet in acknowledgment:—

> God have poor soul,
> Bones and all.

(2) SCENE I.—*Sir Valentine and servant.*] By *servant*, in this and numerous instances of a similar kind, where the word occurs in the old writers, we are to understand, not an *accepted lover*, as some commentators suppose, but a *follower*, an *admirer*.

"Sweet sister, let's sit in judgement a little; faith upon my *servant*, Monsieur Laverdure.
Mel. Troth, well for a *servant*, but for a husband!"
What You Will, 1607.

(3) SCENE II.—*And seal the bargain with a holy kiss.*] "This," Douce remarks, "was the mode of plighting troth between lovers in private. It was sometimes done in the church with great solemnity; and the service on this occasion is preserved in some of the old rituals." The latter ceremony is described by the priest in "Twelfth Night," Act V. Sc. 1,

"A contract of eternal bond of love,
Confirm'd by mutual joinder of your hands,
Attested by the holy close of lips,
Strengthen'd by interchangement of your rings."

And will be further alluded to in the Notes to that Comedy.

(4) SCENE IV.—*Which, like a waxen image 'gainst a fire.*] Among the practices imputed to the hapless wretches who in former times had the misfortune to incur the charge of witchcraft, was that of making clay or waxen images of the individuals they were supposed to be hostile to, and roasting them before a fire. By doing which it was supposed they melted and wasted away the body of the person represented. Thus Holinshed, speaking of the witchcraft employed to destroy King Duffe,—"whereupon learning by her confessor in what house in the town (Fores) they wrought their mischiefous mysteries, he sent forth soldiers about the middest of the night, who, breaking into the house, found one of the witches rosting upon a wooden broch an image of wax at the fier, resembling in each feature the king's person, made and devised (as is to be thought) by craft and art of the devil; another of them sat reciting certein words of inchantment, and still basted the image with a certein liquor verie busilie . . . . . They confessed they went about such manner of inchantment to the end to make awaie with the king; for as the image did waste afore the fire, so did the bodie of the king break forth in sweat. And as for the words of the inchantment, they served to keepe him still waking from sleepe, so that as the wax ever melted so did the king's flesh; by the which means it should have come to passe, that when the wax was once cleane consumed, the death of the king should immediately follow."

So Webster also, in his *Dutchess of* MALFY, 1623:—

"—— it *wastes* me more
Than wert my picture fashion'd out of wax,
Stuck with a magick needle, and then buried
In some foul dunghill."

(5) SCENE V. — *To go to the ale with a Christian.*] Launce is here supposed, though I think erroneously, to refer *not* to the ale-house he had before mentioned, but to one of those periodical festivities which our rustic ancestors delighted in observing about the sixteenth century, called *Ales*. Such as the Leet-ale, Lamb-ale, Bride-ale, Clerk-ale, Church-ale, and Whitsun-ale.

The Church-ale, we learn from Drake, was instituted generally for the purpose of contributing towards the repair or decoration of the church. On this occasion, it was the business of the churchwardens to brew a considerable quantity of strong ale, which was sold to the populace in the churchyard, and to the better sort in the church itself—a practice which, independent of the profit arising from the sale of the liquor, led to great pecuniary advantages; for the rich thought it a meritorious duty, besides paying for their ale, to offer largely to the holy fund. Other *Ales*, however, were held by agreement, annually or oftener, by the inhabitants of one or more parishes, each individual contributing a certain sum towards the expenses. An interesting proof of this is found in a MS. from the "Dodsworth Collection" in the Bodleian Library: "The parishioners of Elveston and Okebrook, in Derbyshire, agree jointly to brew four *Ales*, and every *Ale* of one quarter of malt, betwixt this (the time of contract) and the feast of St. John Baptist, next coming; and that every inhabitant of the said town of Okebrook shall be at the several *Ales*; and every husband and his wife shall pay twopence, and every cottager one penny; and all the inhabitants of Elveston shall have and receive all the profits and advantages coming of the said *Ales*, to the use and behoof of the said church of Elveston. And the inhabitants of Elveston shall brew *eight Ales* betwixt this and the feast of Saint John Baptist, at the which *Ales* the inhabitants of Okebrook shall come and pay, as before rehearsed; and if he be away at one *Ale*, to pay at the toder *Ale* for both," &c.

ACT III.

(1) SCENE I.—*St. Nicholas be thy speed!*] Launce invokes St. Nicholas to be *Speed's speed*, because this saint was the patron of scholars. The reason of his being so chosen may be gathered, Douce tells us, from the following story in his life, translated from the French verse of *Maître Wace*, chaplain to Henry the Second:—"Three scholars were on their way to school, (I shall not make a long story of it,) their host murdered them in the night, and hid their bodies; their ——* he reserved. St. Nicholas was informed of it by God Almighty, and according to his pleasure, went to the place. He demanded the scholars of the host, who was not able to conceal them, and therefore showed them to him. St. Nicholas, by his prayers, restored the souls to their bodies. Because he conferred such honour on scholars, they at this day celebrate a festival."

Whether the election of St. Nicholas as the tutelary saint of scholars, had really its origin in the belief of this legend, is perhaps too much to say. He appears to have been very early and very generally so acknowledged in this country. The parish clerks of London were incorporated as a guild, with this saint for their patron, in 1233; and we find that the first statutes of St. Paul's School required the children to attend divine service in the cathedral on his anniversary.

* *A word defaced in the manuscript.*

ACT IV.

(1) Scene III.—*Upon whose grave thou vow'dst pure chastity.*] "It was common," Steevens observes, "in former ages for widowers and widows to make vows of chastity in honour of their deceased wives or husbands. In 'Dugdale's Antiquities of Warwickshire,' p. 10—13, there is the form of a commission by the bishop of the diocese for taking a vow of chastity made by a widow. It seems that, besides observing the vow, the widow was for life to wear a veil and a mourning habit. The same distinction we may suppose to have been made in respect of male votaries; and, therefore, this circumstance might inform the players how Sir Eglamour should be drest, and will account for Silvia's having chosen him as a person in whom she could confide without injury to her own character."

(2) Scene IV.—*And threw her sun-expelling mask away.*] "When they use to ride abroad they have *masks and vizors made of velvet*, wherewith they cover all their faces, having holes made in them against their eyes, whereout they looke. So that if a man that knew not their guise before, should chaunce to meet one of them, he would think he met a monster or a Devil, for face he can shew none, but two broad holes against their eyes, with glasses in them."—Stubb's *Anatomie of Abuses*, 4to. p. 59, 1595.

So Randle Holme, "Academy of Armory," book iii. c. 5, speaks of *vizard masks* that covered all the face, having holes only for the eyes, a case for the nose, and a slit for the mouth. They were easily disengaged, being held in the teeth by means of a round bead fastened in the inside. These masks were usually made of leather, covered with black velvet.

(3) Scene IV.—*I 'll get me such a colour'd periwig.*] *Periwigs* are said to have been first introduced into England about 1572, and were worn of different colours by ladies long before the use of false hair was adopted by men. Heywood has a passage in which he makes Sardanapalus exclaim :—

> "Curl'd periwigs upon my head I wore,
> And, being man, the shape of woman bore."

And *perwickes* are mentioned in one of Churchyard's earliest poems. So also in Barnabe Rich's "Honestie of the Age," 1615 :—"The attire-makers within this forty years were not known by that name, and but now very lately they kept their lowzie commodity of *periwigs*, and their monstrous attires closed in boxes; and those women that used to weare them would not buy them but in secret. But now they are not ashamed to set them forthe upon their stalls—such monstrous mop-powles of haire, so proportioned and deformed, that but within this twenty or thirty years would have drawne the passers-by to stand and gaze, and to wonder at them."

ACT V.

(1) Scene IV.—*With triumphs, mirth, and rare solemnity.*] We shall have occasion hereafter to speak at large on the subject of those magnificent and costly spectacles, the delight alike of the monarch and the people, called Triumphs, Masques and Pageants, of the grandeur and stateliness of which in Shakespeare's time, some conception may be formed from a description of an entertainment of the kind Ben Jonson has left us in his *Hymenæi*, or *the Solemnities of Masque and Barriers at a Marriage*. "Hitherto extended the first night's solemnity, whose grace in the execution left not where to add to it, with wishing; I mean (nor do I court them) in those, that sustained the nobler parts. Such was the *exquisite performance*, as (beside the *pomp, splendor*, or what we may call *apparelling* of such *presentments*), that alone (had all else been absent) was of power *to surprise with delight, and steal away the spectators from themselves.* Nor was there wanting whatsoever might give [add] to the furniture or complement; either in *riches*, or *strangeness of the habits, delicacy of dances, magnificence of the scene, or divine rapture of musick.* Only the envy was, that it lasted not still! or (now it is past) *cannot* by *imagination, much less description, be recovered to a part of that spirit it had in the gliding by.*" Speaking of the attire of those who on this occasion assumed the part of actors, he tells us, "that of the Lords had part of it taken from the *antique Greek* statues; mixed with some *moderne* additions; which made it both gracefull and strange. On their heads they wore Persick crowns that were with scroles of *gold-plate* turned outward and wreathed about with a *carnation* and *silver* net-lawne; the one end of which hung carelessly on the left shoulder; the other was tricked up before, in severall degrees of folds between the plaits, and set with *rich jewels* and *great pearles*. Their bodies were of *carnation* cloth of *silver*, richly wrought, and cut to express the *naked*, [the flesh] in manner of the *Greek Thorax;* girt under the brests with a *broad belt of cloth of gold imbroydered, and fastened before with jewels:* Their Labels were of *white cloth of silver, laced and wrought curiously between*, sutable to the upper halfe of their sleeves; whose nether parts with their bases, were of *watchet cloth of silver, chev'rond all over with lace.* Their Mantils were of *severall coloured silkes*, distinguishing their qualities, as they were coupled in paires; the first, *skie colour;* the second, *pearle colour;* the third, *flame colour;* the fourth, *tawny;* and these cut in leaves, which were subtilly tacked up and imbroydered with Oo's, and between every ranck of leaves, a *broad silver lace.* They were fastened on the right shoulder, and fell compasse down the back in gracious [graceful] folds, and were again tyed with a round knot, to the fastening of their swords. Upon their legs they wore *silver greaves.*" —*The Workes of* Benjamin Jonson, folio, 1640. Masques, p. 143.

CRITICAL OPINIONS

ON

THE TWO GENTLEMEN OF VERONA.

"In this play there is a strange mixture of knowledge and ignorance, of care and negligence. The versification is often excellent, the allusions are learned and just, but the author conveys his heroes by sea from one inland town to another in the same country. He places the Emperor at *Milan*, and sends his young men to attend him, but never mentions him more. He makes *Protheus*, after an interview with *Silvia*, say he has only seen her picture; and, if we may credit the old copies, he has, by mistaking places, left his scenery inextricable. The reason of all this confusion seems to be that he took his story from a novel, which he sometimes followed and sometimes forsook, sometimes remembered and sometimes forgot.

"That this play is rightly attributed to *Shakespeare*, I have little doubt. If it be taken from him, to whom shall it be given? This question may be asked of all the disputed plays, except *Titus Andronicus;* and it will be found more credible that *Shakespeare* might sometimes sink below his highest flights, than that any other should rise up to his lowest."—Johnson.

"Mr. Pope has expressed his surprise that 'the style of this comedy is less figurative, and more natural and unaffected, than the greater part of this author's, THOUGH supposed to be one of the first he wrote.' But I conceive it is natural and unaffected, and less figurative, than some of his subsequent productions, in consequence of the very circumstance which has been mentioned—because it was a youthful performance. Though many young poets of ordinary talents are led by false taste to adopt inflated and figurative language, why should we suppose that such should have been the course pursued by this master genius? The figurative style of 'Othello,' 'Lear,' and 'Macbeth,' written when he was an established and long-practised dramatist, may be ascribed to the additional knowledge of men and things which he had acquired during a period of fifteen years; in consequence of which his mind teemed with images and illustrations, and thoughts crowded so fast upon him, that the construction in these, and some other of his plays of a still later period, is much more difficult and involved than in the productions of his youth, which in general are distinguished by their ease and perspicuity; and this simplicity and unaffected elegance, and not its want of success, were, I conceive, the cause of its being less corrupted than some others. Its perspicuity rendered any attempt at alteration unnecessary. Who knows that it was not successful? For my own part, I have no doubt that it met with the highest applause. Nor is this mere conjecture; for we know from the testimony of a contemporary well acquainted with the stage, whose eulogy on our author I have already produced, that he was very early distinguished for his comic talents, and that before the end of the year 1592, he had excited the jealousy of one of the most celebrated dramatick poets of the time.

"In a note on the first scene of this comedy, Mr. Pope has particularly objected to the low and trifling conceits which, he says, are found there and in various other parts of the play before us; but this censure is pronounced without sufficient discrimination, or a due attention to the period when it was produced. Every composition must be examined with a constant reference to the opinions that prevailed when the piece under consideration was written ; and, if the present comedy be viewed in that light, it will be found that the conceits here objected to were not denominated by any person of Shakespeare's age low and trifling, but were very generally admired, and were considered pure and genuine wit. Nothing can prove the truth of this statement more decisively than a circumstance which I have had occasion to mention elsewhere,—that Sir John Harrington was commonly called by Queen Elizabeth her WITTY godson, and was very generally admired in his own time for the liveliness of his talents and the playfulness of his humour; yet, when we examine his writings,* we find no other proof of his wit than those very conceits which have been censured in some of our author's comedies as mean, low, and trifling. It is clear, therefore, that the notions of our ancestors on this subject were very different from ours. What we condemn, they highly admired; and what we denominate true wit, they certainly would not have relished, and perhaps would scarcely have understood.

"Mr. Pope should also have recollected that, in Shakespeare's time, and long before, it was customary in almost every play to introduce a jester, who, with no great propriety, was denominated a CLOWN, whose merriment made a principal part of the entertainment of the lower ranks, and, I believe, of a large portion of the higher orders also. When no clown or jester was introduced in a comedy, the servants of the principal personages sustained his part, and the dialogue attributed to them was written with a particular view to supply that deficiency, and to amuse the audience by the promptness of their pleasantry, and the liveliness of their conceits. Such is the province assigned to those characters in Lilly's comedies, which were performed with great success and admiration for several years before Shakespeare's time ; and such are some of the lower characters in this drama, 'The Comedy of Errors,' 'Love's Labour's Lost,' and some others. On what ground, therefore, is our poet to be condemned for adopting a mode of writing universally admired by his contemporaries, and for not foreseeing that, in a century after his death, these dialogues which set the audience in a roar would, by more fastidious criticks, be denominated low quibbles and trifling comments ? †

"With respect to his neglect of geography in this and some other plays, it cannot be defended by attributing his errour in this instance to his youth, for one of his latest productions is liable to the same objection. The truth, I believe, is, that as he neglected to observe the rules of the drama with respect to the unities, though before he began to write they had been enforced by Sidney in a treatise, which doubtless he had read, so he seems to have thought that the whole terraqueous globe was at his command; and as he brought in a child in the beginning of a play, who, in the fourth act, appears as a woman, so he seems to have wholly set geography at defiance, and to have considered countries as inland or maritime, just as it suited his fancy or convenience.

"With the qualifications and allowances which these considerations demand, the present comedy, viewed as a first production, may surely be pronounced a very elegant and extraordinary performance.

"Having already given the reasons why I suppose this to have been our author's first play, it is only necessary to say here, that I believe it to have been written in 1591. See the Essay on the Chronological Order of Shakespeare's Plays."—MALONE.

"The 'Two Gentlemen of Verona' paints the irresolution of love, and its infidelity to friendship, pleasantly enough, but in some degree superficially—we might almost say, with the levity of mind which a passion suddenly entertained, and as suddenly given up, presupposes. The faithless lover is at last, on account of a very ambiguous repentance, forgiven without much difficulty by his first mistress. For the more serious part, the premeditated flight of the daughter of a prince, the capture of her father along with herself by a band of robbers, of which one of the Two Gentlemen, the betrayed and banished friend, has been against his will elected captain: for all this a peaceful solution is soon found. It is as if the course of the world was obliged to accommodate itself to a transient youthful caprice, called love. Julia, who accompanies her faithless lover in the disguise of a page, is, as it were, a light sketch of the tender female figures of a Viola and an Imogen, who, in the latter pieces of Shakespeare, leave their home in similar disguises on love adventures, and to whom a peculiar charm is communicated by the display of the most virginly modesty in their hazardous and problematical situation."—SCHLEGEL.

* See particularly his "Supplie" (or Supplement) to Godwin's Account of the English Bishops, which abounds in almost every page with such conceits as we are now speaking of. The titles of some of our poet's comedies, which appear to have been written by the booksellers for whom they were printed, may also be cited for the same purpose; thus we have, "A pleasant *conceited* comedy called Love's Labour's Lost," &c. 1598; that is, a comedy full of pleasant *conceits*. The bookseller, doubtless, well knew the publick taste, and added this title as more likely to attract purchasers than any other he could devise. See also "A most pleasant and excellent *conceited* comedy of Syr John Falstaffe," &c., 1602, *i.e.* a comedy full of excellent *conceits*.

† See this topick further discussed in the preliminary observations to the "Comedy of Errors."

LOVE'S
LABOUR'S LOST.
DALZIEL

LOVE'S LABOUR 'S LOST.

"A Pleasant Conceited Comedie called Loves labor 's lost. As it was presented before her Highnes this last Christmas. Newly corrected and augmented. By W. Shakespeare. Imprinted at London by W. W., for Cuthbert Burby. 1598. 4to." Such is the title of the first edition we possess of the present comedy. Whether any impression was published prior to the corrections and augmentations mentioned, or between the date of this quarto and the folio, 1623, has yet to be discovered. Like The Two Gentlemen of Verona, Love's Labour 's Lost bears unmistakeable traces of Shakespeare's earliest style. We find in both, though in different degree, the same fluency and sweetness of measure, the same frequency of rhymes, the same laborious addiction to quibbling, repartees, and doggerel verse, and in both it is observable that depth of characterization is altogether subordinate to elegance and sprightliness of dialogue. In the former, however, the wit and fancy of the poet are infinitely more subdued; the events are within the range of probability; and the humour, for the most part, is confined to the inferior personages of the story. But Love's Labour 's Lost is an extravaganza for *Le bon Roi*, René, and the Court of Provence; "a humoursome display of frolic," as Schlegel calls it, "in which every one is a jester; and the sparkles of wit fly about in such profusion that they resemble a blaze of fireworks; while the dialogue is in the same hurried style in which the masks at a carnival attempt to banter each other."

From the circumstance that Armado is sometimes styled "the Braggart," and Holofernes "the Pedant," it has been conjectured that Shakespeare borrowed his plot from the Italian stage, where these buffoons once formed a staple source of entertainment.* But, judging from the names of the characters, and an evident Gallicism in the Fourth Act,† Douce attributes its origin to a French novel, and his opinion is in some degree countenanced by the following passage in the Chronicles of Monstrelet (Lond. 1810, i. 108, ed. Johnes), first pointed out by Mr. Hunter:—"Charles king of Navarre came to Paris to wait on the King. He negotiated so successfully with the King and Privy Council, that he obtained a gift of the castle of Nemours with some of its dependant castlewicks, which territory was made a duchy. He instantly did homage for it, and at the same time surrendered to the King the castle of Cherbourg, the county of Evreux, and all the other lordships he possessed within the kingdom of France, renouncing all claims or profits in them to the King and to his successors, on condition that with the duchy of Nemours the king of France *engaged to pay him two hundred thousand gold crowns of the coin of the King our lord.*" ‡

This passage is interesting because it shows that the original story, whether French or Italian, whence Shakespeare drew the outline of his plot, was founded in part at least upon an historical event, and because it enables us to fix the time of the play to about 1425, in which year

* "I was often," says Montaigne, "when a boy, wonderfully concerned to see in the Italian farce, a *pedant* always brought in as the *fool of the play*."—Vol. i. p. 190.

† Where the Princess speaking of the love-letter says,—

Boyet, you can carve:
Break up this *capon*.

using the same metaphor of a *poulet* for a love epistle, that the French adopt.

‡ King. Madam, your father here doth intimate
The payment of a hundred thousand crowns;
Being but the one-half of an entire sum,
Disbursed by my father in his wars. Act II. Sc. 1.

the king of Navarre died. To the date of its production we have no such clue; it is one of the plays enumerated by Meres in the oft-quoted passage from his *Palladis Tamia*, 1598, "As Plautus and Seneca are accounted the best for comedy and tragedy among the Latins, so Shakespeare among ye English is the most excellent in both kinds for the stage; for comedy, witness his Gētlemē of Verona, his Errors, his Love Labor 's Lost, his Love Labour 's Wonne, his Midsummer's Night Dreame, and his Merchant of Venice; for tragedy, his Richard the II., Richard the III., Henry the IV., King John, Titus Andronicus, and his Romeo and Juliet."

It is noticed also, and in a manner which seems to imply that the writer had seen it some time before, in the rare poem by R[obert T[ofte, intituled "Alba; or, The Month's Minde of a Melancholy Lover, 8vo, 1598."

"Love's Labour Lost! I *once* did see a play
Ycleped so, so called to my paine,
Which I to heare to my small joy did stay,
Giving attendance on my froward dame:
My misgiving minde presaging to me ill,
Yet was I drawne to see it 'gainst my will.

The play, no play, but plague was unto me,
For there I lost the love I liked most,
And what to others seemde a jest to be,
I that in earnest found unto my cost,
To every one save me, 'twas comicall;
While trajick-like to me it did befall.

Each actor plaid in cunning wise his part,
But chiefly those entrapt in Cupid's snare;
Yet all was fained, 'twas not from the hart,
They seeme to grieve, but yet they felt no care;
'Twas I that griefe indeed did beare in brest,
The others did but make a shew in jest."

Beyond these two allusions we have no external evidence positive or negative to aid us in ascertaining the precise date when this comedy was written. We do not despair, however, of the first draft, like the Hamlet of 1603, turning up some day, and in the meantime shall not be far wrong if we assign its production to a period somewhere between 1587 and 1591.

Persons Represented.*

FERDINAND, *king of* NAVARRE.
BIRON, LONGAVILLE, DUMAINE, } *Lords attending on the King.*
BOYET, MERCADE, } *Lords attending on the Princess of* FRANCE.
DON ADRIANO DE ARMADO, *a Spaniard.*
SIR NATHANIEL, *a Curate.*
HOLOFERNES, *a schoolmaster.*
DULL, *a constable.*
COSTARD, *a clown.*
MOTH, *page to* ARMADO.
A Forester.

Princess of FRANCE.
ROSALINE, MARIA, KATHERINE, } *Ladies attending on the Princess.*
JAQUENETTA, *a country wench.*

Officers and others, attendant on the King and Princess.

SCENE.—NAVARRE.

* This list of characters was first printed by Rowe.

ACT I.

SCENE I.—Navarre. *A Park, with a Palace in it.*

Enter the KING, BIRON,[a] LONGAVILLE, *and* DUMAIN.

KING. Let fame, that all hunt after in their lives,
Live register'd upon our brazen[b] tombs,
And then grace us in the disgrace of death;
When, spite of cormorant devouring time,
Th' endeavour of this present breath may buy
That honour, which shall bate his scythe's keen edge,
And make us heirs of all eternity.
Therefore, brave conquerors!—for so you are,
That war against your own affections,
And the huge army of the world's desires,—(1)
Our late edict shall strongly stand in force:
Navarre shall be the wonder of the world;
Our court shall be a little Academe,
Still and contemplative in living art.
You three, Biron, Dumain, and Longaville,
Have sworn for three years' term to live with me,
My fellow-scholars, and to keep those statutes
That are recorded in this schedule here:

[a] Biron,—] In the old copies the name is spelt *Berowne*, probably in accordance with the ancient pronunciation of Biron, which appears to have been *Beroon*, with the accent on the last syllable. Thus in Act IV. Sc. 3, we find it rhyming to *moon*—

"My love, her mistress, is a gracious moon;—
My eyes are then no eyes, nor I *Biron*."

[b] *Live register'd upon our* brazen *tombs*,—] The allusion here is to the figures and inscriptions on *plates of brass*, with which it was the fashion to ornament the tombs of distinguished persons, from the thirteenth to the seventeenth century. Numerous examples still remain in the churches throughout England, and in those of Belgium and Germany.

Your oaths are pass'd, and now subscribe your names;
That his own hand may strike his honour down,
That violates the smallest branch herein:
If you are arm'd to do, as sworn to do,
Subscribe to your deep oaths, and keep them* too.
LONG. I am resolv'd: 'tis but a three years' fast;
The mind shall banquet, though the body pine:
Fat paunches have lean pates,[a] and dainty bits
Make rich the ribs, but bankrupt† quite the wits.
DUM. My loving lord, Dumain is mortified.
The grosser manner of these world's delights
He throws upon the gross world's baser slaves:
To love, to wealth, to pomp, I pine and die;
With all these living in philosophy.
BIRON. I can but say their protestation over;
So much, dear liege, I have already sworn,
That is, to live and study here three years.
But there are other strict observances:
As, not to see a woman in that term;
Which, I hope well, is not enrolled there:
And, one day in a week to touch no food,
And but one meal on every day beside;
The which, I hope, is not enrolled there:
And then to sleep but three hours in the night,
And not be seen to wink of all the day;
(When I was wont to think no harm all night,
And make a dark night too of half the day;)
Which, I hope well, is not enrolled there:
O, these are barren tasks, too hard to keep;
Not to see ladies,—study,—fast,—not sleep.
KING. Your oath is pass'd to pass away from these.
BIRON. Let me say no, my liege, an if you please;
I only swore, to study with your grace,
And stay here in your court for three years' space.
LONG. You swore to that, Biron, and to the rest.
BIRON. By yea and nay, sir, then I swore in jest.
What is the end of study? let me know.
KING. Why, that to know, which else we should not know.
BIRON. Things hid and barr'd, you mean, from common sense?
KING. Ay, that is study's god-like recompense.
BIRON. Come on then, I will swear to study so,
To know the thing I am forbid to know:
As thus,—To study where I well may dine,
When I to feast‡ expressly am forbid;
Or, study where to meet some mistress fine,
When mistresses from common sense are hid:
Or, having sworn too hard-a-keeping oath,
Study to break it, and not break my troth.
If study's gain be thus, and this be so,
Study knows that, which yet it doth not know:
Swear me to this, and I will ne'er say, no.
KING. These be the stops that hinder study quite,
And train our intellects to vain delight.
BIRON. Why, all delights are vain; but* that most vain,
Which, with pain purchas'd, doth inherit pain:
As, painfully to pore upon a book,
To seek the light of truth; while truth the while
Doth falsely blind the eye-sight of his look:
Light, seeking light, doth light of light beguile:
So, ere you find where light in darkness lies,
Your light grows dark by losing of your eyes.
Study me how to please the eye indeed,
By fixing it upon a fairer eye;
Who dazzling so, that eye shall be his heed,
And give him light that it was blinded by.
Study is like the heaven's glorious sun,
That will not be deep-search'd with saucy looks;
Small have continual plodders ever won,
Save base authority from others' books.
These earthly godfathers of heaven's lights,
That give a name to every fixed star,
Have no more profit of their shining nights,
Than those that walk, and wot not what they are.
Too much to know, is, to know nought but fame;
And every godfather can give a name.
KING. How well he's read, to reason against reading!
DUM. Proceeded well, to stop all good proceeding!
LONG. He weeds the corn, and still lets grow the weeding.
BIRON. The spring is near, when green geese are a-breeding.
DUM. How follows that?
BIRON. Fit in his place and time.
DUM. In reason nothing.
BIRON. Something then in rhyme.
KING. Biron is like an envious sneaping frost,
That bites the first-born infants of the spring.
BIRON. Well, say I am; why should proud summer boast,
Before the birds have any cause to sing?
Why should I joy in any abortive birth?
At Christmas I no more desire a rose,
Than wish a snow in May's new-fangled shows;
But like of each thing that in season grows.
So you, to study now it is too late,
Climb o'er the house to unlock the little gate.[b]

(*) Old copies, *it*.
(†) The folio, 1623, *bankerout*, omitting *quite*.
(‡) Old copies, *fast*.
[a] Fat paunches have lean pates, &c.]

"*Pinguis venter non gignit sensum tenuem.*"

There is a more elegant Greek proverb, mentioned by Hierom, to the same effect; and the whole couplet is given in Clark's "Parœmiologia Anglo-Latina; or, Proverbs English and Latine," &c., 8vo. 1630—

"Fat paunches make lean pates; and grosser bits
Enrich the ribs, but bankrupt quite the wits."

(*) First folio, *and*.

[b] Climb o'er the house to unlock the little gate.] This is the reading of the quarto. The folio has—

"That were to climb o'er the house to unlock the gate."

KING. Well, sit you out;[a] go home, Biron; adieu!
BIRON. No, my good lord; I have sworn to stay with you:
And, though I have for barbarism spoke more,
Than for that angel knowledge you can say;
Yet, confident I'll keep what I have swore,(*)
And bide the penance of each three years' day.
Give me the paper,—let me read the same;
And to the strict'st decrees I'll write my name.
KING. How well this yielding rescues thee from shame!
BIRON. [*Reads.*]

Item, That no woman shall come within a mile of my court—

Hath this been proclaim'd?
LONG. Four days ago.
BIRON. Let 's see the penalty. [*Reads.*]

—*on pain of losing her tongue.*—

Who devis'd this penalty?
LONG. Marry, that did I.
BIRON. Sweet lord, and why?
LONG. To fright them hence with that dread penalty,
A dangerous law against gentility.[b]
BIRON. [*Reads.*]

Item, If any man be seen to talk with a woman within the term of three years, he shall endure such public shame as the rest of the court can(†) *possibly devise.*—

This article, my liege, yourself must break;
For, well you know, here comes in embassy
The French king's daughter, with yourself to speak,—
A maid of grace, and cómplete majesty,—
About surrender-up of Aquitain
To her decrepit, sick, and bed-rid father:
Therefore this article is made in vain,
Or vainly comes th' admired princess hither.
KING. What say you, lords? why, this was quite forgot.
BIRON. So study evermore is over-shot;
While it doth study to have what it would,
It doth forget to do the thing it should:
And when it hath the thing it hunteth most,
'T is won, as towns, with fire; so won, so lost.
KING. We must, of force, dispense with this decree;
She must lie[c] here on mere necessity.
BIRON. Necessity will make us all forsworn
Three thousand times within this three years' space;
For every man with his affects is born,
Not by might master'd, but by special grace.
If I break faith, this word shall speak(*) for me,
I am forsworn on mere necessity.—
So to the laws at large I write my name:
[*Subscribes.*
And he that breaks them in the least degree,
Stands in attainder of eternal shame:
Suggestions[d] are to others, as to me;
But, I believe, although I seem so loth,
I am the last that will last keep his oath.
But is there no quick[e] recreation granted?
KING. Ay, that there is: our court, you know, is haunted
With a refined traveller of Spain;
A man in all the world's new fashion planted,
That hath a mint of phrases in his brain:
One who the music of his own vain tongue
Doth ravish, like enchanting harmony;
A man of complements,[f] whom right and wrong
Have chose as umpire of their mutiny:
This child of fancy, that Armado hight,
For interim to our studies, shall relate,
In high-born words, the worth of many a knight
From tawny Spain, lost in the world's debate.
How you delight, my lords, I know not, I;
But, I protest, I love to hear him lie,
And I will use him for my minstrelsy.
BIRON. Armado is a most illustrious wight,
A man of fire-new words,[g] fashion's own knight.

(*) Old copies, *sworne.* (†) First folio, *shall.* (*) First folio, *break.*

a *Well,* sit *you out;*] The folio reads, *fit you out*, which is a palpable misprint. To *sit out*, a phrase borrowed from the card table, was a common expression in Shakespeare's age. Steevens quotes the following illustration from Bishop Sanderson:—

"They are glad, rather than *sit out*, to play very small game."

To this may be added another given by Mr. Dyce, from *The Tryall of Cheualry*, 1605, sig. G. 3:—

"*Lewis*. . . . .
King of Nauar, will onely *you sit out?*
"*Nau.* No, king of Fraunce, my bloud's as hot as thine:
And this my weapon shall confirme my words."

b LONG. *To fright them hence with that dread penalty,*
A dangerous law against gentility.]

So the old copies, but Theobald first, and all the modern editors since, have deprived Longaville of the second line, and given it to Biron. I have no hesitation in restoring it to the proper speaker. The only difficulty in the passage is the word *gentility*, (in the quarto, *gentletie*,) which could never have been the expression of the poet. Mr. Collier's old annotator proposes *garrulity*; that, or *scurrility*, certainly comes nearer to the sense, but neither is satisfactory. By a *dangerous* law, we are to understand a *biting* law. In Act I. Sc. 2, there is a similar use of the word:—

"A *dangerous* rhyme, master, against the reason of white and red."

c *She must* lie *here*—] *i. e.* reside here.

d Suggestions—] Temptations, seducements.

e *No* quick *recreation*—] i.e. *lively* pastime, *brisk* diversion.

"—— the *quick* comedians
Extemporally will stage us."
Antony and Cleopatra, Act V. Sc. 2.

f A *man of* complements,—] One versed in punctilios, of *point-de-vice* manners,—a formalist.

"He walks most commonly with a clove or pick-tooth in his mouth; he is the very mint of compliment; all his behaviours are printed; his face is another volume of essays; and his beard is an Aristarchus."—BEN JONSON'S *Cynthia's Revels*, (Gifford's Ed.) vol. ii. p. 264.

g Fire-new words,—] Words freshly coined; *brand-new*.

"Your *fire-new* stamp of honour scarce is current."
Richard the Third, Act I. Sc. 3.

Again, in "Twelfth Night," Act III. Sc. 2:—

"And with some excellent jest, *fire-new* from the mint," &c.

LONG. Costard the swain, and he, shall be our sport;
And, so to study, three years is but short.

Enter DULL,* *with a letter, and* COSTARD.

DULL. Which is the duke's own person?

BIRON. This, fellow; what wouldst?

DULL. I myself reprehend his own person, for I am his grace's tharborough;[a] but I would see his own person in flesh and blood.

BIRON. This is he.

DULL. Signior Arme—Arme—commends you. There's villainy abroad; this letter will tell you more.

COST. Sir, the contempts thereof are as touching me.

KING. A letter from the magnificent Armado.

BIRON. How low soever the matter, I hope in God for high words.

LONG. A high hope for a low heaven:[b] (2) God grant us patience!

BIRON. To hear? or forbear laughing?[c]

LONG. To hear meekly, sir, and to laugh moderately; or to forbear both.

BIRON. Well, sir, be it as the style shall give us cause to climb in the merriness.

COST. The matter is to me, sir, as concerning Jaquenetta. The manner of it is, I was taken with the manner.[d]

BIRON. In what manner?

COST. In manner and form following, sir; all

(*) Old copies, *constable*.

[a] Tharborough;] A corruption of *thirdborough;* a constable.

[b] A *high hope for a low* heaven:] This passage has occasioned a great deal of controversy. Theobald proposed to read *a low having;* Mr. Collier's manuscript-corrector reads, *a low hearing;* and some critics will have, *a low haven*. The allusion may be to the representations of *Heaven*, and the attendant personifications of Faith, *Hope*, &c. in the ancient Pageants.

[c] Or *forbear* laughing?] The old copies have, "forbear *hearing*." The emendation is due to Capell.

[d] I *was taken with the* manner.] Costard quibbles on *manner*, written *mainour* in the old law-books; *i.e.* the thing stolen, and *manor* house, where he was arrested. *With the manner*, meant *in the fact*.

"—— and being taken *with the manner*, had nothing to say for himself."—HEYWOOD'S *Rape of Lucrece*, 1630.

those three: I was seen with her in the manor house, sitting with her upon the form, and taken following her into the park; which, put together, is in manner and form following. Now, sir, for the manner,—it is the manner of a man to speak to a woman: for the form,—in some form.

BIRON. For the following, sir?

COST. As it shall follow in my correction: and God defend the right!

KING. Will you hear this letter with attention?

BIRON. As we would hear an oracle.

COST. Such is the simplicity of man to hearken after the flesh.

KING. [*Reads.*]

Great deputy, the welkin's vicegerent, and sole dominator of Navarre, my soul's earth's God, and body's fostering patron,—

COST. Not a word of Costard yet.

KING.

So it is,—

COST. It may be so: but if he say it is so, he is, in telling true, but so.

KING. Peace!

COST. —be to me, and every man that dares not fight!

KING. No words!

COST. —of other men's secrets, I beseech you.

KING.

So it is, besieged with sable-coloured melancholy, I did commend the black-oppressing humour to the most wholesome physic of thy health-giving air; and, as I am a gentleman, betook myself to walk. The time when? About the sixth hour; when beasts most graze, birds best peck, and men sit down to that nourishment which is called supper. So much for the time when: Now for the ground which; which, I mean, I walked upon: it is ycleped, thy park. Then for the place where; where, I mean, I did encounter that obscene and most preposterous event, that draweth from my snow-white pen the ebon-coloured ink, which here thou viewest, beholdest, surveyest, or seest: But to the place where,—it standeth north-north-east and by east from the west corner of thy curious-knotted[a] garden: there did I see that low-spirited swain, that base minnow of thy mirth,

COST. Me.

KING.

—that unletter'd small-knowing soul,

COST. Me.

KING.

—that shallow vassal,

COST. Still me.

KING.

—which, as I remember, hight Costard,

COST. O me!

KING.

—sorted, and consorted, contrary to thy established proclaimed edict and continent canon, with—with,—O with—but with this I passion to say wherewith,*

COST. With a wench.

KING.

—with a child of our grandmother Eve, a female; or, for thy more sweet understanding, a woman. Him I (as my ever-esteemed duty pricks me on) have sent to thee, to receive the meed of punishment, by thy sweet grace's officer, Antony Dull; a man of good repute, carriage, bearing, and estimation.

DULL. Me, an 't shall please you; I am Antony Dull.

KING.

For Jaquenetta, (so is the weaker vessel called, which I apprehended with the aforesaid swain,) I keep her as a vessel of thy law's fury; and shall, at the least of thy sweet notice, bring her to trial. Thine in all complements of devoted and heart-burning heat of duty,

DON ADRIANO DE ARMADO.

BIRON. This is not so well as I looked for, but the best that ever I heard.

KING. Ay, the best for the worst. But, sirrah, what say you to this?

COST. Sir, I confess the wench.

KING. Did you hear the proclamation?

COST. I do confess much of the hearing it, but little of the marking of it.

KING. It was proclaimed a year's imprisonment, to be taken with a wench.

COST. I was taken with none, sir; I was taken with a damosel.

KING. Well, it was proclaimed damosel.

COST. This was no damosel, neither, sir; she was a virgin.

KING. It is so varied too; for it was proclaimed virgin.

COST. If it were, I deny her virginity; I was taken with a maid.

KING. This maid will not serve your turn, sir.

COST. This maid will serve my turn, sir.

KING. Sir, I will pronounce your sentence: you shall fast a week with bran and water.

a *Thy* curious-knotted *garden*:] Ancient gardens, Steevens observes, abounded with figures, of which the lines intersected each other in many directions. Thus in "Richard II." Act III. Sc. 4:—

"Her fruit-trees all unprun'd, her hedges ruin'd,
Her *knots* disorder'd," &c.

(*) Old copies, *which* with.

COST. I had rather pray a month with mutton and porridge.

KING. And don Armado shall be your keeper.—
My lord Biron, see him deliver'd o'er.—
And go we, lords, to put in practice that
Which each to other hath so strongly sworn.—
[*Exeunt* KING, LONGAVILLE, *and* DUMAIN.

BIRON. I'll lay my head to any good man's hat,
These oaths and laws will prove an idle scorn.—
Sirrah, come on.

COST. I suffer for the truth, sir: for true it is, I was taken with Jaquenetta, and Jaquenetta is a true girl; and therefore, Welcome the sour cup of prosperity! Affliction may one day smile again, and till then, Sit thee down, sorrow!*
[*Exeunt.*

SCENE II.—*Another part of the same.* Armado's *House.*

Enter ARMADO *and* MOTH.

ARM. Boy, what sign is it, when a man of great spirit grows melancholy?

MOTH. A great sign, sir, that he will look sad.

ARM.[a] Why, sadness is one and the self-same thing, dear imp.

MOTH. No, no; O lord, sir, no.

ARM. How canst thou part sadness and melancholy, my tender juvenal?

MOTH. By a familiar demonstration of the working, my tough senior.†

ARM. Why tough senior?† why tough senior?†

MOTH. Why tender juvenal? why tender juvenal?

ARM. I spoke it, tender juvenal, as a congruent epitheton, appertaining to thy young days, which we may nominate, tender.

MOTH. And I, tough senior,† as an appertinent title to your old time, which we may name, tough.

ARM. Pretty, and apt.

MOTH. How mean you, sir; I pretty, and my saying apt? or I apt, and my saying pretty?

ARM. Thou pretty, because little.[b]

MOTH. Little pretty, because little: Wherefore apt?

ARM. And therefore apt, because quick.

MOTH. Speak you this in my praise, master?

ARM. In thy condign praise.

MOTH. I will praise an eel with the same praise.

ARM. What? that an eel is ingenious?*

MOTH. That an eel is quick.

ARM. I do say, thou art quick in answers: Thou heat'st my blood.

MOTH. I am answered, sir.

ARM. I love not to be crossed.

MOTH. He speaks the mere contrary, crosses[c] love not him. [*Aside.*

ARM. I have promised to study three years with the duke.

MOTH. You may do it in an hour, sir.

ARM. Impossible.

MOTH. How many is one thrice told?

ARM. I am ill at reckoning; it fitteth† the spirit of a tapster.

MOTH. You are a gentleman, and a gamester, sir.(3)

ARM. I confess both; they are both the varnish of a complete man.

MOTH. Then, I am sure, you know how much the gross sum of deuce-ace amounts to.

ARM. It doth amount to one more than two.

MOTH. Which the base vulgar do‡ call, three.

ARM. True.

MOTH. Why, sir, is this such a piece of study? Now here's three studied, ere you'll thrice wink: and how easy it is to put years to the word three, and study three years in two words, the dancing horse (4) will tell you.

ARM. A most fine figure!

MOTH. To prove you a cipher. [*Aside.*

ARM. I will hereupon confess, I am in love: and, as it is base for a soldier to love, so am I in love with a base wench. If drawing my sword against the humour of affection would deliver me from the reprobate thought of it, I would take Desire prisoner, and ransom him to any French courtier for a new devised courtesy. I think scorn to sigh; methinks, I should outswear Cupid. Comfort me, boy: What great men have been in love?

MOTH. Hercules, master.

ARM. Most sweet Hercules!—More authority, dear boy, name more; and, sweet my child, let them be men of good repute and carriage.

MOTH. Sampson, master; he was a man of

(*) First folio, *until then sit down*, &c.
(†) First folio, *signeur*.

(*) First folio, *ingenuous*. (†) First folio, *fits*.
(‡) First folio, *vulgar call*.

a Armado.] Here and throughout the scene in the old copies we have *Braggart*, instead of Armado.

b *Thou* pretty, because little:] So in Ben Jonson's play of "The Fox," (Gifford's edition,) vol. iii. p. 236:—

"First for your dwarf, he's little and witty,
And every thing, *as it is little is pretty.*"

c Crosses *love not him.*] A punning allusion, very frequent in Shakespeare's day, probably to the ancient penny, which Stowe describes as having a double cross, with a crest stamped on it, so that it might easily be broken in half or into quarters. In "Henry IV. Part II." Act I. Sc. 2, we meet with the same quibble:—

"Not a penny, not a penny; you are too impatient to *bear crosses.*" And again, in "As You Like It," Act II. Sc. 4:—

"For my part, I had rather bear with you than bear you; yet I should bear no *cross* if I did bear you."

good carriage, great carriage; for he carried the town-gates on his back, like a porter: and he was in love.

Arm. O well-knit Sampson! strong-jointed Sampson! I do excel thee in my rapier, as much as thou didst me in carrying gates. I am in love, too—Who was Sampson's love, my dear Moth?

Moth. A woman, master.

Arm. Of what complexion?

Moth. Of all the four, or the three, or the two; or one of the four.

Arm. Tell me precisely of what complexion?

Moth. Of the sea-water green, sir.

Arm. Is that one of the four complexions?

Moth. As I have read, sir: and the best of them too.

Arm. Green, indeed, is the colour of lovers; but to have a love of that colour, methinks, Sampson had small reason for it. He, surely, affected her for her wit.

Moth. It was so, sir; for she had a green wit.

Arm. My love is most immaculate white and red.

Moth. Most maculate * thoughts, master, are masked under such colours.

Arm. Define, define, well-educated infant.

Moth. My father's wit, and my mother's tongue, assist me.

Arm. Sweet invocation of a child; most pretty, and pathetical!

Moth. If she be made of white and red,
Her faults will ne'er be known;
For blushing † cheeks by faults are bred,
And fears by pale-white shown:

(*) First folio, *immaculate*. (†) Old copies, *blush-in*.

Then, if she fear, or be to blame,
By this you shall not know;
For still her cheeks possess the same,
Which native she doth owe.

A dangerous rhyme, master, against the reason of white and red.

ARM. Is there not a ballad, boy, of the King and the Beggar? (5)

MOTH. The world was very guilty of such a ballad some three ages since: but, I think, now 't is not to be found; or, if it were, it would neither serve for the writing, nor the tune.

ARM. I will have that subject newly writ o'er, that I may example my digression by some mighty precedent. Boy, I do love that country girl that I took in the park with the rational hind Costard; she deserves well.

MOTH. To be whipped; and yet a better love than my master. [*Aside.*

ARM. Sing, boy; my spirit grows heavy in love.

MOTH. And that 's great marvel, loving a light wench.

ARM. I say, sing.

MOTH. Forbear till this company be past.

**Enter* DULL, COSTARD, *and* JAQUENETTA.

DULL. Sir, the duke's pleasure is that you keep Costard safe: and you must let him take no delight, nor no penance; but a' † must fast three days a week. For this damsel, I must keep her at the park; she is allowed for the day-woman.[a] Fare you well.

ARM. I do betray myself with blushing.—Maid.

JAQ. Man.

ARM. I will visit thee at the lodge.

JAQ. That 's hereby.[b]

ARM. I know where it is situate.

JAQ. Lord, how wise you are!

ARM. I will tell thee wonders.

JAQ. With that face? [c]

ARM. I love thee.

JAQ. So I heard you say.

ARM. And so farewell.

JAQ. Fair weather after you!

DULL. Come, Jaquenetta, away.

[*Exeunt* DULL *and* JAQUENETTA.

ARM. Villain, thou shalt fast for thy offences ere thou be pardoned.

COST. Well, sir, I hope, when I do it, I shall do it on a full stomach.

ARM. Thou shalt be heavily punished.

COST. I am more bound to you than your fellows, for they are but lightly rewarded.

ARM. Take away this villain; shut him up.

MOTH. Come, you transgressing slave; away.

COST. Let me not be pent up, sir; I will fast, being loose.

MOTH. No, sir; that were fast and loose:[d] thou shalt to prison.

COST. Well, if ever I do see the merry days of desolation that I have seen, some shall see—

MOTH. What shall some see?

COST. Nay, nothing, master Moth, but what they look upon. It is not for prisoners to be too* silent in their words; and, therefore, I will say nothing: I thank God, I have as little patience as another man; and, therefore, I can be quiet.

[*Exeunt* MOTH *and* COSTARD.

ARM. I do affect[e] the very ground, which is base, where her shoe, which is baser, guided by her foot, which is basest, doth tread. I shall be forsworn (which is a great argument of falsehood) if I love: and how can that be true love, which is falsely attempted? Love is a familiar; love is a devil: there is no evil angel but love. Yet Sampson was so tempted; and he had an excellent strength: yet was Solomon so seduced; and he had a very good wit. Cupid's butt-shaft is too hard for Hercules' club, and therefore too much odds for a Spaniard's rapier. The first and second cause[f] will not serve my turn; the passado he respects not, the duello he regards not: his disgrace is to be called boy; but his glory is to subdue men. Adieu, valour! rust, rapier! be still, drum! for your manager[g] is in love; yea, he loveth. Assist me, some extemporal god of rhyme, for, I am sure, I shall turn sonnets. Devise, wit; write, pen; for, I am for whole volumes in folio.

[*Exit.*

(*) Old copies, *Enter Clowne, Constable, and Wench.*
(†) First folio, *he.*

(*) First folio omits *too.*

[a] —*for the* day-woman.] *A day-woman* is a *dairy*-woman, a *milk*-woman. Johnson, in his Dictionary, derives *dairy* from *day*, which, he says, though without adducing any authority, was an old word for *milk*.

[b] That 's hereby.] She means, scoffingly, *that's as it may happen; that's to be seen.* Armado understands her in the literal sense, *close by*.

[c] With that face?] An old bantering phrase, hardly obsolete now. The folio mars it by reading, "With *what* face?"

[d] *That were* fast and loose:] An allusion to a well-known game of the time, now called "pricking i' the garter."

[e] I *do* affect—] *i.e.* I do love, &c. *Affect*, in this sense, is so common an expression with the old writers, as scarcely to require explanation.

[f] The first and second cause *will not serve my turn;* the passado *he respects not,*—] These are terms borrowed from the school of fence, and the fantastical treatises on the Duello by Saviolo and Caranza. See the Illustrative Comments on Act II. of "Romeo and Juliet."

[g] —*for your* manager *is in love;*] The corrector of Mr. Collier's copy of the folio 1632, with much plausibility, suggests for *manager* that we should read *armiger;* and two lines lower, instead of *sonnet*, as in the old editions, *sonnet-maker*. In the latter case, I prefer *sonnets*, the happy emendation of an American critic, Dr. Verplanck.

ACT II.

SCENE I.—*Another part of the Park. A Pavilion and Tents at a distance.*

Enter the Princess of France, Rosaline, Maria, Katharine, Boyet, Lords, *and other* Attendants.

Boyet. Now, madam, summon up your dearest[a] spirits;
Consider who the king your father sends;
To whom he sends; and what's his embassy:
Yourself, held precious in the world's esteem,
To parley with the sole inheritor
Of all perfections that a man may owe,
Matchless Navarre: the plea, of no less weight
Than Aquitain, a dowry for a queen.
Be now as prodigal of all dear grace,
As Nature was in making graces dear,
When she did starve the general world beside,
And prodigally gave them all to you.

Prin. Good lord Boyet, my beauty, though but mean,
Needs not the painted flourish of your praise;
Beauty is bought by judgment of the eye,
Not utter'd by base sale of chapmen's tongues:
I am less proud to hear you tell my worth,
Than you much willing to be counted wise
In spending your wit in the praise of mine.
But now to task the tasker,—Good Boyet,
You are not ignorant, all-telling fame
Doth noise abroad, Navarre hath made a vow,
Till painful study shall out-wear three years,

a *Your* dearest *spirits;*] That is, your *choicest, rarest* spirits.

No woman may approach his silent court:
Therefore to us seemeth it a needful course,
Before we enter his forbidden gates,
To know his pleasure; and in that behalf,
Bold of your worthiness, we single you
As our best-moving fair solicitor:
Tell him, the daughter of the king of France,
On serious business, craving quick despatch,
Importunes personal conference with his grace.
Haste, signify so much; while we attend,
Like humble-visag'd suitors, his high will.

BOYET. Proud of employment, willingly I go. [*Exit.*

PRIN. All pride is willing pride, and yours is so.—
Who are the votaries, my loving lords,
That are vow-fellows with this virtuous duke? [a]

1 LORD. Longaville is one.

PRIN. Know you the man?

MAR. I know him, madam; at a marriage feast,
Between lord Perigort and the beauteous heir
Of Jaques Falconbridge, solemnized
In Normandy, saw I this Longaville:
A man of sovereign parts he is esteem'd;
Well fitted in the [b] arts, glorious in arms;
Nothing becomes him ill, that he would well.
The only soil of his fair virtue's gloss
(If virtue's gloss will stain with any soil),
Is a sharp wit match'd with too blunt a will;
Whose edge hath power to cut, whose will still wills
It should none spare that come within his power.

PRIN. Some merry mocking lord, belike: is't so?

MAR. They say so most, that most his humours know.

PRIN. Such short-liv'd wits do wither as they grow.
Who are the rest?

KATH. The young Dumain, a well-accomplish'd youth,
Of all that virtue love, for virtue lov'd:
Most power to do most harm, least knowing ill;
For he hath wit to make an ill shape good,
And shape to win grace though he* had no wit.
I saw him at the duke Alençon's once;
And much too little of that good I saw,
Is my report, to his great worthiness.

ROS. Another of these students at that time
Was there with him: if† I have heard a truth,
Biron they call him, but a merrier man,
Within the limit of becoming mirth,
I never spent an hour's talk withal:
His eye begets occasion for his wit;
For every object that the one doth catch,
The other turns to a mirth-moving jest;
Which his fair tongue (conceit's expositor)
Delivers in such apt and gracious words,
That aged ears play truant at his tales,
And younger hearings are quite ravished;
So sweet and voluble is his discourse.

PRIN. God bless my ladies! are they all in love
That every one her own hath garnished
With such bedecking ornaments of praise?

MAR. Here comes Boyet.

Re-enter BOYET.

PRIN. Now, what admittance, lord?

BOYET. Navarre had notice of your fair approach;
And he and his competitors in oath
Were all address'd to meet you, gentle lady,
Before I came. Marry, thus much I have learnt,
He rather means to lodge you in the field,
(Like one that comes here to besiege his court,)
Than seek a dispensation for his oath,
To let you enter his unpeopled house.
Here comes Navarre. [*The Ladies mask.*

Enter KING, LONGAVILLE, DUMAIN, BIRON, *and* Attendants.

KING. Fair princess, welcome to the court of Navarre.

PRIN. Fair, I give you back again; and welcome I have not yet: the roof of this court is too high to be yours; and welcome to the wide fields too base to be mine.

KING. You shall be welcome, madam, to my court.

PRIN. I will be welcome then; conduct me thither.

KING. Hear me, dear lady,—I have sworn an oath.

PRIN. Our Lady help my lord! he'll be forsworn.

KING. Not for the world, fair madam, by my will.

PRIN. Why, will shall break it; will, and nothing else.

KING. Your ladyship is ignorant what it is.

PRIN. Were my lord so, his ignorance were wise,
Where now his knowledge must prove ignorance.
I hear, your grace hath sworn-out house-keeping:
'T is deadly sin to keep that oath, my lord,
And sin to break it:
But pardon me, I am too sudden-bold;
To teach a teacher ill beseemeth me.
Vouchsafe to read the purpose of my coming,
And suddenly resolve me in my suit. [*Gives a paper.*

KING. Madam, I will, if suddenly I may.

PRIN. You will the sooner, that I were away;

(*) Folio, 1623, *she*. (†) Folio, 1623, *as*.

a — *this virtuous* duke?] The titles of *king* and *duke* were used indifferently both by Shakespeare and his contemporaries.

b *Well fitted in* the *arts*,—] The older copies omit the article, which was supplied in the second folio.

For you'll prove perjur'd, if you make me stay.

BIRON. Did not I dance with you in Brabant once?

ROS. Did not I dance with you in Brabant once?

BIRON. I know you did.

ROS. How needless was it then to ask the question!

BIRON. You must not be so quick.

ROS. 'T is long of you that spur me with such questions!

BIRON. Your wit's too hot, it speeds too fast, 't will tire.

ROS. Not till it leave the rider in the mire.

BIRON. What time o' day?

ROS. The hour that fools should ask.

BIRON. Now fair befall your mask!

ROS. Fair fall the face it covers!

BIRON. And send you many lovers!

ROS. Amen, so you be none.

BIRON. Nay, then will I be gone.

KING. Madam, your father here doth intimate
The payment of a hundred thousand crowns;
Being but the one-half of an entire sum,
Disbursed by my father in his wars.
But say, that he, or we, (as neither have,)
Receiv'd that sum; yet there remains unpaid
A hundred thousand more; in surety of the which,
One part of Aquitain is bound to us,
Although not valued to the money's worth.
If then the king your father will restore
But that one-half which is unsatisfied,

We will give up our right in Aquitain,
And hold fair friendship with his majesty.
But that, it seems, he little purposeth,
For here he doth demand to have repaid
An hundred thousand crowns; and not demands,
On payment of a hundred thousand crowns,
To have his title live in Aquitain;
Which we much rather had depart[a] withal,
And have the money by our father lent,
Than Aquitain so gelded as it is.
Dear princess, were not his requests so far
From reason's yielding, your fair self should make
A yielding, 'gainst some reason, in my breast,
And go well satisfied to France again.

PRIN. You do the king my father too much wrong,
And wrong the reputation of your name,
In so unseeming to confess receipt
Of that which hath so faithfully been paid.

KING. I do protest, I never heard of it;
And, if you prove it, I'll repay it back,
Or yield up Aquitain.

PRIN. We arrest your word:—
Boyet, you can produce acquittances,
For such a sum, from special officers
Of Charles his father.

KING. Satisfy me so.

BOYET. So please your grace, the packet is not come,
Where that and other specialties are bound;
To-morrow you shall have a sight of them.

KING. It shall suffice me: at which interview,
All liberal reason I will* yield unto.
Meantime, receive such welcome at my hand
As honour, without breach of honour, may
Make tender of to thy true worthiness:
You may not come, fair princess, in my gates;
But here without you shall be so receiv'd,
As you shall deem yourself lodg'd in my heart,
Though so denied fair† harbour in my house.
Your own good thoughts excuse me, and farewell:
To-morrow we shall visit you again.

PRIN. Sweet health and fair desires consort your grace!

KING. Thy own wish wish I thee in every place! [*Exeunt* KING *and his train.*

BIRON. Lady, I will commend you to my own heart.[b]

ROS. 'Pray you, do my commendations; I would be glad to see it.

BIRON. I would you heard it groan.

ROS. Is the fool sick?

BIRON. Sick at the heart.

ROS. Alack, let it blood.

BIRON. Would that do it good?

ROS. My physic says, ay.

BIRON. Will you prick't with your eye?

ROS. No *poynt*,[c] with my knife.

BIRON. Now, God save thy life!

ROS. And yours from long living!

BIRON. I cannot stay thanksgiving. [*Retiring.*

DUM. Sir, I pray you a word: What lady is that same?

BOYET. The heir of Alençon, Rosaline her name.

DUM. A gallant lady! Monsieur, fare you well. [*Exit.*

LONG. I beseech you a word: What is she in the white?

BOYET. A woman sometimes, an* you saw her in the light.

LONG. Perchance, light in the light: I desire her name.

BOYET. She hath but one for herself; to desire that were a shame.

LONG. Pray you, sir, whose daughter?

BOYET. Her mother's, I have heard.

LONG. God's blessing on your beard!

BOYET. Good sir, be not offended:
She is an heir of Falconbridge.

LONG. Nay, my choler is ended.
She is a most sweet lady.

BOYET. Not unlike, sir; that may be. [*Exit* LONG.

BIRON. What's her name, in the cap?

BOYET. Katharine, by good hap.

BIRON. Is she wedded, or no?

BOYET. To her will, sir, or so.

BIRON. You are welcome, sir; adieu!

BOYET. Farewell to me, sir, and welcome to you. [*Exit* BIRON.—*Ladies unmask.*

MAR. That last is Biron, the merry madcap lord;
Not a word with him but a jest.

BOYET. And every jest but a word.

PRIN. It was well done of you to take him at his word.

BOYET. I was as willing to grapple, as he was to board.

MAR. Two hot sheeps, marry!

BOYET. And wherefore not ships?
No sheep, sweet lamb, unless we feed on your lips.

MAR. You sheep, and I pasture: Shall that finish the jest?

BOYET. So you grant pasture for me. [*Offering to kiss her.*

MAR. Not so, gentle beast;

(*) First folio, *would I.* (†) First folio, *farther.*

a Depart *withal,*—] *Depart,* for *part.* " *Which we would much rather part with.*"

b Lady, I will commend you to my own heart.] In the folio, 1623, this speech, and the speeches of Biron immediately following, are given to Boyet.

(*) First folio, *if.*

c *No poynt,*—] The same diminutive pun on the French negation, *Non point,* is repeated in Act V. Sc. 2:—

" Dumain was at my service, and his sword;
No point, quoth I."

My lips are no common, though several [a] they be.
BOYET. Belonging to whom?
MAR. To my fortunes and me.
PRIN. Good wits will be jangling; but, gentles, agree:
This civil war of wits were much better us'd
On Navarre and his book-men; for here 't is abus'd.
BOYET. If my observation, (which very seldom lies,)
By the heart's still rhetoric, disclosed with eyes,
Deceive me not now, Navarre is infected.
PRIN. With what?
BOYET. With that which we lovers entitle, affected.
PRIN. Your reason?
BOYET. Why, all his behaviours did* make their retire
To the court of his eye, peeping thorough desire:
His heart, like an agate, with your print impressed,
Proud with his form, in his eye pride expressed:
His tongue, all impatient to speak and not see,
Did stumble with haste in his eye-sight to be;
All senses to that sense did make their repair,
To feel only looking on fairest of fair:
Methought all his senses were lock'd in his eye,
As jewels in crystal for some prince to buy;
Who, tend'ring their own worth, from where* they were glass'd,
Did point you† to buy them, along as you pass'd.
His face's own margent (1) did quote‡ such amazes,
That all eyes saw his eyes enchanted with gazes:
I'll give you Aquitain, and all that is his,
An you give him for my sake but one loving kiss.
PRIN. Come, to our pavilion: Boyet is dispos'd—
BOYET. But to speak that in words, which his eye hath disclos'd:
I only have made a mouth of his eye,
By adding a tongue which I know will not lie.
ROS. Thou art an old love-monger, and speak'st skilfully.
MAR. He is Cupid's grandfather, and learns news of him.
ROS. Then was Venus like her mother; for her father is but grim.
BOYET. Do you hear, my mad wenches?
MAR. No.
BOYET. What, then, do you see?
ROS. Ay, our way to be gone.
BOYET. You are too hard for me.
[*Exeunt.*

(*) First folio, *do*.

a *My lips are no* common, *though* several they be.] The difficulty in this passage has arisen from the particle *though*, which appears to destroy the antithesis between *common*, i.e. public land, and *several*, which, in the ordinary acceptation, implies enclosed or private property. If, however, we take both as places devoted to pasture,—the one for general, the other for particular use,—the meaning is easy enough. Boyet asks permission to graze on her lips. "Not so," she answers; "my lips, though intended for the purpose, are not for general use."

(*) First folio, *whence*. (†) First folio, *out*. (‡) Old editions, *coate*.

ACT III.

SCENE I.—*Another part of the Park.*

Enter Armado *and* Moth.

Arm. Warble, child; make passionate my sense of hearing.

Moth. *Concolinel,*(1)—— [*Singing.*

Arm. Sweet air!—Go, tenderness of years! take this key, give enlargement to the swain, bring him festinately hither; I must employ him in a letter to my love.

Moth. Master,* will you win your love with a French brawl? (2)

Arm. How meanest thou? brawling in French?

Moth. No, my complete master: but to jig off a tune at the tongue's end, canary[a] to it with your† feet, humour it with turning up your eyelids;‡ sigh a note, and sing a note; sometime through the throat, as if you swallowed love with singing love; sometime through the nose, as if you snuffed up love by smelling love; with your hat, penthouse-like, o'er the shop of your eyes; with your arms crossed on your thin-belly doublet,[b] like a rabbit on a spit; or your hands in your pocket, like a man after the old painting; and keep not too long in one tune, but a snip and away: These are complements, these are humours; these betray nice wenches, that would be betrayed without these; and make them men of note, (do you note, men?) that most are affected to these.

Arm. How hast thou purchased this experience?

Moth. By my penny[c] of observation.(3)

Arm. But O,—but O—

Moth. —the hobby-horse is forgot.(4)

(*) First folio omits *Master*. (†) First folio, *the*. (‡) First folio, *eye*.

[a] Canary *to it with your feet,*—] The *canary* was a favourite dance, probably of Spanish origin, and supposed to derive its name from the Canary Islands, where it was much in vogue. The folio, 1623, reads, "With *the* feet."

[b] *Your* thin-belly doublet,—] Modern editors, except Capell, have *thin belly-doublet;* but surely *thin-belly,* "like a rabbit on a spit," is more humorous.

[c] *By* my penny *of observation.*] The early copies read *penne,* which, with *peny, penni, pennie,* was an old form of spelling the word. "My penny," "his penny," "her penny," was a popular phrase formerly. See Note (3), Illustrative Comments on Act III.

ARM. Callest thou my love, hobby-horse?

MOTH. No, master; the hobby-horse is but a colt, and your love, perhaps, a hackney. But have you forgot your love?

ARM. Almost I had.

MOTH. Negligent student! learn her by heart.

ARM. By heart, and in heart, boy.

MOTH. And out of heart, master: all those three I will prove.

ARM. What wilt thou prove?

MOTH. A man, if I live; and this, by, in, and without, upon the instant: by heart you love her, because your heart cannot come by her: in heart you love her, because your heart is in love with her: and out of heart you love her, being out of heart that you cannot enjoy her.

ARM. I am all these three.

MOTH. And three times as much more, and yet nothing at all.

ARM. Fetch hither the swain; he must carry me a letter.

MOTH. A message well sympathised; a horse to be ambassador for an ass!

ARM. Ha, ha! what sayest thou?

MOTH. Marry, sir, you must send the ass upon the horse, for he is very slow-gaited: but I go.

ARM. The way is but short; away.

MOTH. As swift as lead, sir.

ARM. Thy meaning, pretty ingenious?
Is not lead a metal heavy, dull, and slow?

MOTH. *Minimè*, honest master; or, rather[a] master, no.

ARM. I say, lead is slow.

MOTH. You are too swift, sir, to say so:[b]
Is that lead slow which is fired from a gun?

ARM. Sweet smoke of rhetoric!
He reputes me a cannon; and the bullet, that's he:—
I shoot thee at the swain.

MOTH. Thump, then, and I flee. [*Exit.*

ARM. A most acute juvenal; voluble and free of grace!
By thy favour, sweet welkin, I must sigh in thy face:
Most rude melancholy, valour gives thee place.
My herald is return'd.

Re-enter MOTH *with* COSTARD.

MOTH. A wonder, master; here's a Costard[c] broken in a shin.

ARM. Some enigma, some riddle: come,—thy *l'envoy*;—begin.

COST. No egma, no riddle, no *l'envoy*; no salve in the male, sir:[d] O sir, plantain, a plain plantain; no *l'envoy*, no *l'envoy*, no salve, sir, but a plantain![e]

ARM. By virtue, thou enforcest laughter; thy silly thought, my spleen; the heaving of my lungs provokes me to ridiculous smiling: O, pardon me, my stars! Doth the inconsiderate take salve for *l'envoy*, and the word *l'envoy* for a salve?

MOTH. Do the wise think them other? is not *l'envoy* a salve?

ARM. No, page: it is an epilogue or discourse, to make plain
Some obscure precedence that hath tofore been sain.*
I will example it:
The fox, the ape, and the humble bee,
Were still at odds, being but three.
There's the moral: now the *l'envoy*.

MOTH. I will add the *l'envoy*; say the moral again.

ARM. The fox, the ape, and the humble bee,
Were still at odds, being but three.

MOTH. Until the goose came out of door,
And stay'd the odds by adding four.
Now will I begin your moral, and do you follow with my *l'envoy*.
The fox, the ape, and the humble bee,
Were still at odds, being but three:

ARM. Until the goose came out of door,
Staying the odds by adding four.

MOTH. A good *l'envoy*, ending in the goose; would you desire more?

COST. The boy hath sold him a bargain, a goose, that's flat:—
Sir, your pennyworth is good, an your goose be fat.—
To sell a bargain well is as cunning as fast and loose:
Let me see a fat *l'envoy*; ay, that's a fat goose.

a *Honest master*, or, rather *master*,—] This is always punctuated "or, rather, master." But, from the context, which is a play on *swift* and *slow*, I apprehend Moth to mean by *rather* master, *hasty* master; *rather*, of old, meaning *quick*, *eager*, *hasty*, &c.

b To say so:] Should we not read *slow* for *so*?

c *Here's* a Costard *broken in a shin.*] *Costard* means *head.* Thus:—

"I wyll rappe you on the *costard* with my horne."
HYCKE SCORNER.

And in "King Lear," Act IV. Sc. 6:—

"Keepe out, che vor'ye, or ice try whether your *costard* or my bat be the harder."

(*) First folio, *faine.*

d *No salve in* the male, *sir*:] The old copies have—"No salve in thee male, sir," which Johnson, Malone, and Steevens interpret, "in the bag or wallet." Tyrwhitt proposed to remove the ambiguity by reading: "No salve in them all, sir;" which, if not decisive, is certainly a very ingenious conjecture.

e —plantain!] "All the *plantanes* are singular good wound herbes, to heale fresh or old wounds and sores, either inward or outward."—PARKINSON'S *Theater of Plantes*, 1640, p. 498.

f I will example it:] This, and the eight lines following it, are omitted in the folio 1623.

ARM. Come hither, come hither; how did this argument begin?
MOTH. By saying that a Costard was broken in a shin.
Then called you for the *l'envoy*.
COST. True, and I for a plantain: thus came your argument in;
Then the boy's fat *l'envoy*, the goose that you bought.
And he ended the market.
ARM. But tell me; how was there a Costard broken in a shin?
MOTH. I will tell you sensibly.
COST. Thou hast no feeling of it, Moth; I will speak that *l'envoy*.
I, Costard, running out, that was safely within,
Fell over the threshold, and broke my shin.
ARM. We will talk no more of this matter.
COST. Till there be more matter in the shin.
ARM. Marry,* Costard, I will enfranchise thee.
COST. O, marry me to one Frances;—I smell some *l'envoy*, some goose, in this.
ARM. By my sweet soul, I mean, setting thee at liberty, enfreedoming thy person; thou wert immured, restrained, captivated, bound.
COST. True, true; and now you will be my purgation, and let me loose.
ARM. I give thee thy liberty, set thee from durance; and, in lieu thereof, impose on thee nothing but this: bear this significant to the country maid

(*) Old editions, *Sirrah Costard*. "*Marry*, Costard," was, I believe, first suggested in Mr. Knight's "Stratford Shakspere."

Jaquenetta: there is remuneration [*giving him money*]; for the best ward of mine honour* is rewarding my dependents. Moth, follow. [*Exit.*

MOTH. Like the sequel, I.—Signor Costard, adieu.

COST. My sweet ounce of man's flesh! my incony Jew![a] [*Exit* MOTH.

Now will I look to his remuneration. Remuneration! O, that's the Latin word for three farthings: three farthings—remuneration.—*What's the price of this inkle? a penny:—No, I'll give you a remuneration:* why, it carries it.—Remuneration!—why, it is a fairer name than French crown. I will never buy and sell out of this word.

Enter BIRON.

BIRON. O, my good knave Costard! exceedingly well met.

COST. Pray you, sir, how much carnation ribbon may a man buy for a remuneration?

BIRON. What is a remuneration?

COST. Marry, sir, half-penny farthing.

BIRON. O, why then, three-farthings-worth of silk.

COST. I thank your worship: God be wi' you!

BIRON. O, stay, slave; I must employ thee:
As thou wilt win my favour, good my knave,
Do one thing for me that I shall entreat.

COST. When would you have it done, sir?

BIRON. O, this afternoon.

COST. Well, I will do it, sir: fare you well.

BIRON. O, thou knowest not what it is.

COST. I shall know, sir, when I have done it.

BIRON. Why, villain, thou must know first.

COST. I will come to your worship to-morrow morning.

BIRON. It must be done this afternoon. Hark, slave, it is but this:—
The princess comes to hunt here in the park,
And in her train there is a gentle lady;
When tongues speak sweetly, then they name her name,
And Rosaline they call her; ask for her,
And to her white hand see thou do commend
This seal'd-up counsel. There's thy guerdon; go.
[*Gives him money.*

COST. Guerdon,—O sweet guerdon! better than remuneration,[b] eleven-pence farthing better: most sweet guerdon!—I will do it, sir, in print.—Guerdon—remuneration. [*Exit.*

BIRON. O!—And I, forsooth, in love! I that have been love's whip;
A very beadle to a humorous sigh;
A critic; nay, a night-watch constable;
A domineering pedant o'er the boy;
Than whom no mortal so magnificent!
This wimpled,[c] whining, purblind, wayward boy;
This senior-junior,(4) giant-dwarf, Dan Cupid:
Regent of love-rhymes, lord of folded arms,
The anointed sovereign of sighs and groans,
Liege of all loiterers and malcontents,
Dread prince of plackets, king of cod-pieces,
Sole imperator, and great general
Of trotting paritors.[d] O my little heart!—
And I to be a corporal of his field,[e]
And wear his colours like a tumbler's hoop!
What! I love! I sue! I seek a wife!
A woman, that is like a German clock,* (5)
Still a-repairing; ever out of frame;
And never going aright, being a watch,
But being watch'd that it may still go right!
Nay, to be perjur'd, which is worst of all;
And, among three, to love the worst of all;
A whitely[f] wanton with a velvet brow,
With two pitch-balls stuck in her face for eyes;

(*) First folio, *honours.*

a *My* incony Jew!] *Incony* is defined to mean *fine, delicate, pretty.* It occurs occasionally in our old plays, and is repeated in the present one, Act IV. Sc. I. Of *Jew*, as a term of endearment, I remember no other example, except that in "Midsummer Night's Dream," Act III. Sc. I, where Thisbe calls Pyramus "Most lovely Jew." (See note (b), p. 71.)

b Guerdon,—O *sweet* guerdon! better than remuneration,—] In reference to this passage, Farmer has pointed attention to a parallel one, which is given in a tract called "A Health to the Gentlemanly Profession of Serving-men," by J. M., 1598. "There was, sayth he, a man, (but of what estate, degree, or calling, I will not name, least thereby I might incurre displeasure of any,) that comming to his friend's house, who was a gentleman of good reckoning, and being there kindly entertayned and well used as well of his friende the gentleman, as of his servantes; one of the sayd servantes doing him some extraordinarie pleasure during his abode there, at his departure he comes unto the sayd servant and saith unto him, Holde thee, here is a remuneration for thy paynes; which the servant receyving, gave him utterly for it (besides his paynes) thankes, for it was but a three-farthing piece! and I holde thankes for the same a small price as the market goes. Now another comming to the sayd gentleman's house, it was the foresayd servant's good hap to be neare him at his going away, who, calling the servant unto him, sayd, Holde thee, heere is a guerdon for thy desartes. Now the servant payde no deerer for the guerdon than he did for the remuneration, though the guerdon was xj *d.* farthing better, for it was a shilling, and the other but a three-farthinges." The joke was probably older than either the play or the tract quoted.

(*) Old editions, *cloake.*

c *This* wimpled,—] *Hooded, veiled, blindfolded.*

"Justice herself there sitteth *wimpled* about the eyes," &c.
Comedy of Midas, 1592.

d *Of trotting* paritors.] An apparitor is an officer of the spiritual court. As his duty, in former times, often consisted in summoning offenders against chastity, he is very properly described as under Cupid's command.

e A corporal of his field,—] *A corporal of the field*, according to some authorities, was an officer like an *aide-de-camp*, whose employment was to convey instructions from head-quarters, or from the higher officers of the field.

f A whitely *wanton*—] The old editions have "*A whitly* wanton," which is, perhaps, a misprint for *witty* wanton. *Whitely* is not a suitable epithet to apply to a dark beauty. In Vicar's "Virgil," 1632, it is applied befittingly enough to the moon,—

"Night-gadding Cynthia with her *whitely* face."

Ay, and, by heaven, one that will do the deed,
Though Argus were her eunuch and her guard!
And I to sigh for her! to watch for her!
To pray for her! go to; it is a plague
That Cupid will impose for my neglect
Of his almighty dreadful little might.
Well, I will love, write, sigh, pray, sue, groan;
Some men must love my lady, and some Joan.
[*Exit.*

ACT IV.

SCENE I.—*Another part of the Park.*

Enter the PRINCESS, ROSALINE, MARIA, KATHARINE, BOYET, Lords, Attendants, *and a* Forester.

PRIN. Was that the King, that spurr'd his horse so hard
Against the steep uprising of the hill?
BOYET. I know not; but, I think, it was not he.
PRIN. Whoe'er he was, he show'd a mounting mind.
Well, lords, to-day we shall have our despatch;
On Saturday we will return to France.—
Then, forester, my friend, where is the bush
That we must stand and play the murtherer in?
FOR. Hereby, upon the edge of yonder coppice;
A stand where you may make the fairest shoot.
PRIN. I thank my beauty, I am fair that shoot
And thereupon thou speak'st, the fairest shoot.
FOR. Pardon me, madam, for I meant not so.
PRIN. What, what! first praise me, and (*) again say, no?
O short-liv'd pride! Not fair? alack for woe!
FOR. Yes, madam, fair.
PRIN. Nay, never paint me now;
Where fair is not, praise cannot mend the brow.
Here, good my glass, take this for telling true;
[*Giving him money.*
Fair payment for foul words is more than due.
FOR. Nothing but fair is that which you inherit.
PRIN. See, see, my beauty will be sav'd by merit.
O heresy in fair,[a] fit for these days!
A giving hand, though foul, shall have fair praise.—
But come, the bow:—now Mercy goes to kill,
And shooting well is then accounted ill.
Thus will I save my credit in the shoot:
Not wounding, pity would not let me do 't;
If wounding, then it was to show my skill,
That more for praise, than purpose, meant to kill.
And, out of question, so it is sometimes,
Glory grows guilty of detested crimes;
When, for fame's sake, for praise, an outward part,
We bend to that the working of the heart:
As I, for praise alone, now seek to spill
The poor deer's blood that my heart means no ill.
BOYET. Do not curst[b] wives hold that self-sovereignty
Only for praise' sake, when they strive to be
Lords o'er their lords?
PRIN. Only for praise: and praise we may afford
To any lady that subdues a lord.

Enter COSTARD.

BOYET. Here comes a member of the commonwealth.
COST. God dig-you-den all![c] Pray you, which is the head lady?
PRIN. Thou shalt know her, fellow, by the rest that have no heads.
COST. Which is the greatest lady, the highest?
PRIN. The thickest, and the tallest.
COST. The thickest, and the tallest! it is so; truth is truth.
An your waist, mistress, were as slender as my wit,
One o' these maids' girdles for your waist should be fit.
Are not you the chief woman? you are the thickest here.
PRIN. What's your will, sir? what's your will?
COST. I have a letter from monsieur Biron, to one lady Rosaline.
PRIN. O, thy letter, thy letter; he's a good friend of mine:
Stand aside, good bearer.—Boyet, you can carve;
Break up this capon.[d]

(*) First folio, and *then* again.

a O heresy in fair,—] Mr. Collier's old annotator suggests, "O heresy in *faith*," &c.; but this alteration would destroy the point of the allusion. *Fair* is used here, as in many other instances, for *beauty*; and the *heresy* is, that merit should be esteemed equivalent to beauty.

b *Do not* curst *wives*—] That is, *sour, cross-grained, intractable* wives. A very ancient sense of the word, and one in which it is repeatedly used by Shakespeare. Thus, in "Taming of the Shrew," Act I. Sc. 1:—

"Her elder sister is so *curst* and shrewd."

Again, in Act I. Sc. 2, of the same Play,—

"——— and as *curst* and shrewd
As Socrates' Xantippe."

c God dig-you-den *all!*—] A vulgar corruption of *God give you good even*. It is sometimes contracted to *God ye good den*; as in "Romeo and Juliet," Act II. Sc. 4.

d Break up this capon.] A Gallicism. *Poulet*, with the French, meaning both a young fowl and a *billet-doux*. The Italians use

BOYET. I am bound to serve,—
This letter is mistook, it importeth none here;
It is writ to Jaquenetta.

PRIN. We will read it, I swear:
Break the neck of the wax, and every one give ear.

BOYET. [*Reads.*]

By heaven, that thou art fair is most infallible; true, that thou art beauteous; truth itself, that thou art lovely: More fairer than fair, beautiful than beauteous, truer than truth itself, have commiseration on thy heroical vassal! The magnanimous and most illustrate king Cophetua *set eye upon the pernicious and indubitate beggar* Zenelophon;[a] *and he it was that might rightly say* veni, vidi, vici; *which to annothanize, in the vulgar, (O base and obscure vulgar!)* videlicet, *he came, saw, and overcame: he came, one; saw, two; overcame, three. Who came? the king; why did he come? to see; why did he see? to overcome: to whom came he? to the beggar; what saw he? the beggar; who overcame he? the beggar: the conclusion is victory; on whose side? the king's: the captive is enrich'd; On whose side? the beggar's: the catastrophe is a nuptial; on whose side? the king's?—no, on both in one, or one in both. I am the king; for so stands the comparison: thou the beggar; for so witnesseth thy lowliness. Shall I command thy love? I may: shall I enforce thy love? I could: shall I entreat thy love? I will: what shalt thou exchange for rags? robes: for tittles, titles: for thyself, me. Thus, expecting thy reply, I profane my lips on thy foot, my eyes on thy picture, and my heart on thy every part.*

Thine, in the dearest design of industry,
DON ADRIANO DE ARMADO.

Thus dost thou hear the Nemean lion roar
'Gainst thee, thou lamb, that standest as his prey;
Submissive fall his princely feet before,
And he from forage will incline to play:
But if thou strive, poor soul, what art thou then?
Food for his rage, repasture for his den.

PRIN. What plume of feathers is he that indited this letter?
What vane?* what weathercock? did you ever hear better?

BOYET. I am much deceived, but I remember the style.

PRIN. Else your memory is bad, going o'er it erewhile.

BOYET. This Armado is a Spaniard, that keeps here in court;
A phantasm, a Monarcho,(1) and one that makes sport
To the prince, and his book-mates.

PRIN. Thou, fellow, a word:
Who gave thee this letter?

COST. I told you; my lord.

PRIN. To whom shouldst thou give it?

COST. From my lord to my lady.

PRIN. From which lord, to which lady?

COST. From my lord Biron, a good master of mine,
To a lady of France, that he call'd Rosaline.

PRIN. Thou hast mistaken his letter. Come, lords, away,
Here, sweet, put up this; 't will be thine another day. [*Exeunt* PRINCESS *and train.*

BOYET. Who is the suitor? who is the suitor?[b]

ROS. Shall I teach you to know?

BOYET. Ay, my continent of beauty.

ROS. Why, she that bears the bow.
Finely put off!

BOYET. My lady goes to kill horns; but, if thou marry,
Hang me by the neck, if horns that year miscarry.
Finely put on!

ROS. Well, then, I am the shooter.

BOYET. And who is your deer?

ROS. If we choose by the horns, yourself: come not near.
Finely put on, indeed!—

MAR. You still wrangle with her, Boyet, and she strikes at the brow.

BOYET. But she herself is hit lower: have I hit her now?

ROS. Shall I come upon thee with an old saying, that was a man when king Pepin of France was a little boy, as touching the hit it?

BOYET. So I may answer thee with one as old, that was a woman when queen Guinever of Britain was a little wench, as touching the hit it.

ROS. [*Singing.*]

Thou canst not hit it,[c] *hit it, hit it,*
Thou canst not hit it, my good man.

(*) First folio, *veine.*

the same metaphor, calling a love-letter, *una pollicetta amorosa.* *To break up*, Percy says, was a peculiar phrase in carving. Undoubtedly,

"We carve a hare, or else *breake up* a hen."
FLORIO'S *Montaigne*, p. 166, 1603.

But Shakespeare is not singular in applying it to the opening of a letter. In Ben Jonson's "Every Man Out of His Humour," Act I. Sc. 1, Carlo Buffone recommends Sogliardo to have letters brought to him when dining or supping out,—"And there, while you intend circumstances of news, or inquiry of their health, or so, one of your familiars, whom you must carry about you still, *breaks it up*, as 't were in a jest, and reads it publicly at the table."

a Zenelophon;] In the old ballad of "A Song of a Beggar and a King," 1612, the name is *Penelophon*, but the misspelling may have been intentional.

b *Who is the* suitor?] The jest lies in pronouncing *suitor*, as it is spelt in the old copies, *shooter;* which, indeed, appears to have been the ancient pronunciation.

c Thou canst not hit it,—] Alluding to a song, or dance, mentioned in S. Gosson's "Pleasant Quippes for Upstart Newfangled Gentlewomen," 1596:—

"*Can you hit it?* is oft their daunce,
Deuce-ace fals stil to be their chance."

And in "Wily Beguiled," 1606:—

"And then dance, *Canst thou not hit it?*"

BOYET.

An I cannot, cannot, cannot,
An I cannot, another can.
[*Exeunt* ROS. *and* KATH.

COST. By my troth, most pleasant! how both did fit it!

MAR. A mark marvellous well shot: for they both did hit it.

BOYET. A mark! O, mark but that mark! A mark, says my lady!
Let the mark have a prick in 't to mete at, if it may be.

MAR. Wide o' the bow hand! I' faith your hand is out.

COST. Indeed, a' must shoot nearer, or he 'll ne'er hit the clout.

BOYET. An if my hand be out, then, belike your hand is in.

COST. Then will she get the upshot by cleaving the pin.[a]

MAR. Come, come, you talk greasily, your lips grow foul.

COST. She 's too hard for you at pricks, sir; challenge her to bowl.

BOYET. I fear too much rubbing. Good night, my good owl.
[*Exeunt* BOYET *and* MARIA.

COST. By my soul, a swain! a most simple clown!
Lord, lord! how the ladies and I have put him down!
O' my troth, most sweet jests! most incony vulgar wit!
When it comes so smoothly off, so obscenely, as it were, so fit.
Armado o' the one side,[b]—O, a most dainty man!
To see him walk before a lady, and to bear her fan!
To see him kiss his hand! and how most sweetly a' will swear!—
And his page o' t'other side, that handful of wit!
Ah, heavens, it is a most pathetical nit!
Sola, sola!
*Shouting within.** *Exit* COSTARD, *running.*

SCENE II.—*The same.*

Enter HOLOFERNES, *Sir* NATHANIEL, *and* DULL.

NATH. Very reverend sport, truly; and done in the testimony of a good conscience.

HOL. The deer was, as you know, *sanguis*,—in blood;[c] ripe as a pomewater, who now hangeth like a jewel in the ear of *cœlo*,—the sky, the welkin, the heaven; and anon falleth like a crab, on the face of *terra*,—the soil, the land, the earth.

NATH. Truly, master Holofernes, the epithets are sweetly varied, like a scholar at the least; but, sir, I assure ye, it was a buck of the first head.

HOL. Sir Nathaniel, *haud credo.*

DULL. 'T was not a *haud credo;* 't was a pricket.(2)

HOL. Most barbarous intimation! yet a kind of insinuation, as it were *in viâ*, in way, of explication; *facere*, as it were, replication, or, rather, *ostentare*, to show, as it were, his inclination,—after his undressed, unpolished, uneducated, unpruned, untrained, or rather unlettered, or, ratherest, unconfirmed fashion,—to insert again my *haud credo* for a deer.

DULL. I said the deer was not a *haud credo;* 't was a pricket.

HOL. Twice sod simplicity, *bis coctus!*—
O, thou monster, Ignorance, how deformed dost thou look!

NATH. Sir, he hath never fed of the dainties that are bred in a book.
He hath not eat paper, as it were; he hath not drunk ink: his intellect is not replenished; he is only an animal, only sensible in the duller parts;
And such barren plants are set before us, that we thankful should be
(Which we of[d] taste and feeling are) for those parts that do fructify in us more than he.
For as it would ill become me to be vain, indiscreet, or a fool,
So, were there a patch set on learning, to see him in a school:
But, *omne bene*, say I; being of an old father's mind,
Many can brook the weather, that love not the wind.

(*) Old copies, *shoote within.*

[a] By cleaving the pin.] The quarto, 1598, and the folio, 1623, read, by mistake, *is in*. *To cleave the pin* is explained in Act V. Sc. 4, of "The Two Gentlemen of Verona," p. 39.

[b] *Armado* o' the one side,—] *O' the one side*, is a modern correction: the quarto, 1598, reads, *ath toothen side;* and the folio, 1623, *ath to the side*. Nor are these, I believe, the only misdeeds in connexion with this particular passage for which the old copies are amenable. The reference to Armado and the Page is so utterly irrelevant to anything in the scene, that every one must be struck with its incongruity. I have more than a suspicion that the whole passage, from

"O' my troth, most sweet jests! most incony vulgar wit!"

or, at least, from

"Armado o' the one side," &c.

down to,

"Ah, heavens, it is a most pathetical nit!"

belongs to the previous Act, and in the original MS. followed Costard's panegyric on the Page,—

"My sweet ounce of man's flesh! my incony Jew!"

It is evidently out of place in the present scene, and quite appropriate in the one indicated.

[c] In blood;] To be *in blood*, a phrase of the chase, has been explained, *to be fit for killing;* but it appears also to have meant an animal with its *blood up*—ready to turn and attack its pursuers; like a stag at bay. See the passage in "Henry VI. Part I." Act IV. Sc. 2, beginning—

"If we be English deer, be then *in blood;*
Not rascal like," &c.

[d] *Which we* of *taste*—] The preposition *of* is not found in the old copies. It was inserted by Tyrwhitt.

DULL. You two are book-men: can you tell by your wit,
What was a month old at Cain's birth, that's not five weeks old as yet?

HOL. Dictynna,[a] goodman Dull; Dictynna, goodman Dull.

DULL. What is Dictynna?

NATH. A title to Phœbe, to Luna, to the moon.

HOL. The moon was a month old, when Adam was no more;
And raught not to five weeks, when he came to five-score.
The allusion holds in the exchange.

DULL. 'T is true indeed; the collusion holds in the exchange.

HOL. God comfort thy capacity! I say, the allusion holds in the exchange.

DULL. And I say the pollusion holds in the exchange; for the moon is never but a month old: and I say, beside, that 't was a pricket that the princess killed.

HOL. Sir Nathaniel, will you hear an extemporal epitaph on the death of the deer? and, to humour the ignorant, I have[b] called the deer the princess killed, a pricket.

NATH. *Perge*, good master Holofernes, *perge;* so it shall please you to abrogate scurrility.

HOL. I will something affect the letter; for it argues facility.

The preyful princess pierc'd and prick'd a pretty pleasing pricket;
Some say a sore; but not a sore, till now made sore with shooting.
The dogs did yell; put l to sore, then sorel jumps from thicket;
Or pricket, sore, or else sorel; the people fall a hooting.

[a] Dictynna, *goodman Dull;* Dictynna,—] The old copies have *Dictissima* and *Dictima.* Rowe made the corrections.

[b] I have *called the deer*—] *I have,* not in the ancient copies, was inserted by Rowe.

If sore be sore, then L to sore makes fifty sores;
O sore L!
Of one sore l an hundred make, by adding but one more L.

NATH. A rare talent!

DULL. If a talent be a claw, look how he claws him with a talent.[a]

HOL. This is a gift that I have, simple, simple; a foolish extravagant spirit, full of forms, figures, shapes, objects, ideas, apprehensions, motions, revolutions: these are begot in the ventricle of memory, nourished in the womb of *pia mater*,* and delivered upon the mellowing of occasion: but the gift is good in those in whom it is acute, and I am thankful for it.

NATH. Sir, I praise the Lord for you; and so may my parishioners; for their sons are well tutor'd by you, and their daughters profit very greatly under you: you are a good member of the commonwealth.

HOL. *Mehercle!* if their sons be ingenious, they shall want no instruction: if their daughters be capable, I will put it to them: but, *vir sapit qui pauca loquitur*. A soul feminine saluteth us.

Enter JAQUENETTA *and* COSTARD.

JAQ. God give you good morrow, master person.[b]

HOL. Master person,—*quasi* pers-on. And if one should be pierced, which is the one?

COST. Marry, master schoolmaster, he that is likest to a hogshead.

HOL. Of piercing a hogshead! a good lustre of conceit in a turf of earth; fire enough for a flint, pearl enough for a swine: 'tis pretty; it is well.

JAQ. Good master parson, be so good as read me this letter; it was given me by Costard, and sent me from don Armatho; I beseech you, read it.

HOL. *Fauste, precor gelidâ quando pecus omne sub umbrâ Ruminat*,[c]—and so forth. Ah, good old Mantuan! I may speak of thee as the traveller doth of Venice:

——Vinegia, Vinegia,
Chi non te vede, ei non te pregia.(3)

Old Mantuan! old Mantuan! who understandeth thee not, loves thee not.*—*Ut, re, sol, la, mi, fa.*—Under pardon, sir, what are the contents? Or, rather, as Horace says in his—What, my soul, verses?

NATH. Ay, sir, and very learned.

HOL. Let me hear a staff, a stanza, a verse; *Lege, domine.*

NATH.

If love make me forsworn, how shall I swear to love?
Ah, never faith could hold, if not to beauty vow'd!
Though to myself forsworn, to thee I'll faithful prove;
Those thoughts to me were oaks, to thee like osiers bow'd.
Study his bias leaves, and makes his book thine eyes,
Where all those pleasures live that art would comprehend:
If knowledge be the mark, to know thee shall suffice;
Well learned is that tongue that well can thee commend:
All ignorant that soul that sees thee without wonder;
(Which is to me some praise, that I thy parts admire;)
Thy eye Jove's lightning bears, thy voice his dreadful thunder,
Which, not to anger bent, is music, and sweet fire.
Celestial as thou art, oh, pardon, love, this wrong,
That sings heaven's praise with such an earthly tongue!

HOL. You find not the apostrophes, and so miss the accent: let me supervise the canzonet. Here are only numbers ratified;[d] but, for the elegancy, facility, and golden cadence of poesy, *caret*. Ovidius Naso was the man: and why, indeed, Naso; but for smelling out the odoriferous flowers of fancy, the jerks of invention? *Imitari*[e] is nothing: so doth the hound his master, the ape his keeper, the tired[f] horse his rider. But, damosella virgin, was this directed to you?

(*) Old copies, *primater*.

a *If a* talent *be a claw*, &c.—] Goodman Dull's small pun is founded on *talon* of a bird or beast being often of old spelt *talent*, and on *claw*, in one sense, meaning *to flatter, to fawn upon*.

b *Master* person.] *Parson* was formerly very often pronounced and spelt *person*; which, indeed, is more correct than *parson*, as the word comes from *persona ecclesiæ*. "Though we write *Parson* differently, yet 'tis but *Person*; that is, the individual Person set apart for the service of the Church, and 'tis in Latin *Persona*, and *Personatus* is a *Personage*."—SELDEN's *Table Talk*, Art. "Parson."

c *Fauste, precor gelidâ*—] In the old copies this passage is assigned to Nathaniel. There can be no doubt of its belonging to Holofernes, who probably reads it, or recites it from memory, while the curate is intent upon the letter. Like all quotations from a foreign language, the Latin here, and the Italian proverb which follows, are printed most vilely in both quarto and folio. The "good old Mantuan" was Baptista Spagnolus, a writer of poems, who flourished late in the fifteenth century, and was called Mantuanus, from the place of his birth.

(*) First folio omits *loves thee not*.

d Here are only numbers ratified;] In the old copies Sir Nathaniel is now made to proceed with this speech; so to other passages in the present scene, which clearly belong to Holofernes, *Nath.* has been mistakenly prefixed.

e Imitari *is nothing*:] The quarto and folio, 1623, read *invention imitarie*. Theobald made the obvious correction.

f *The* tired *horse*—] Banks' horse is thought to be here again alluded to; but perhaps by *tired horse* (in the original *tyred*) any horse adorned with ribbons or trappings may be meant.

JAQ. Ay, sir, from one monsieur Biron, one of the strange queen's lords.[a]

HOL. I will overglance the superscript. *To the snow-white hand of the most beauteous lady Rosaline.* I will look again on the intellect of the letter, for the nomination of the party writing* to the person written unto:

Your ladyship's in all desired employment,
BIRON.

Sir Nathaniel, this Biron is one of the votaries with the king; and here he hath framed a letter to a sequent of the stranger queen's, which, accidentally, or by way of progression, hath miscarried.—Trip and go, my sweet; deliver this paper into the royal† hand of the king; it may concern much: stay not thy compliment; I forgive thy duty; adieu!

JAQ. Good Costard, go with me.—Sir, God save your life!

COST. Have with thee, my girl.

[*Exeunt* COST. *and* JAQ.

NATH. Sir, you have done this in the fear of God, very religiously; and, as a certain father saith——

HOL. Sir, tell not me of the father, I do fear colourable colours. But, to return to the verses: did they please you, sir Nathaniel?

NATH. Marvellous well for the pen.

HOL. I do dine to-day at the father's of a certain pupil of mine; where if, before* repast, it shall please you to gratify the table with a grace,

(*) Old copies, *written*. (†) First folio omits *royal*.

(*) First folio, *being*.

[a] Monsieur Biron, one of the strange queen's lords.] Unless Jaquenetta is intended to blunder or prevaricate, the poet has committed an oversight here. As Mason remarks, "Jaquenetta knew nothing of Biron, and had said just before that the letter had been sent to her from *Don Armatho*, and given to her by Costard."

I will, on my privilege I have with the parents of the foresaid child or pupil, undertake your *ben venuto;* where I will prove those verses to be very unlearned, neither savouring of poetry, wit, nor invention: I beseech your society.

NATH. I thank you too: for society (saith the text) is the happiness of life.

HOL. And, certes, the text most infallibly concludes it.—Sir, [*to* DULL] I do invite you too; you shall not say me nay: *pauca verba.* Away; the gentles are at their game, and we will to our recreation. [*Exeunt.*

SCENE III.—*Another part of the same.*

Enter BIRON *with a paper.*

BIRON. The king he is hunting the deer; I am coursing myself: they have pitched a toil; I am toiling in a pitch; pitch, that defiles; defile! a foul word. Well, Set thee down, sorrow! for so they say the fool said, and so say I, and I the fool. Well proved, wit! By the Lord, this love is as mad as Ajax: it kills sheep; it kills me, I a sheep: well proved again o' my side! I will not love: if I do, hang me; i' faith, I will not. O, but her eye,—by this light, but for her eye, I would not love her; yes, for her two eyes. Well, I do nothing in the world but lie, and lie in my throat. By heaven, I do love; and it hath taught me to rhyme, and to be melancholy; and here is part of my rhyme, and here my melancholy. Well, she hath one o' my sonnets already: the clown bore it, the fool sent it, and the lady hath it: sweet clown, sweeter fool, sweetest lady! By the world, I would not care a pin if the other three were in. Here comes one with a paper; God give him grace to groan. [*Gets up into a tree.*[a]

Enter the KING, *with a paper.*

KING. Ay me!

BIRON. [*Aside.*] Shot by heaven!—Proceed, sweet Cupid; thou hast thump'd him with thy bird-bolt under the left pap.—I' faith, secrets.—

KING. [*Reads.*]

So sweet a kiss the golden sun gives not
To those fresh morning drops upon the rose,
As thy eye-beams, when their fresh rays have smot
The dew of night that on my cheeks down flows:*
Nor shines the silver moon one-half so bright
Through the transparent bosom of the deep,
As doth thy face through tears of mine give light:
Thou shin'st in every tear that I do weep;
No drop but as a coach doth carry thee,
So ridest thou triumphing in my woe:
Do but behold the tears that swell in me,
And they thy glory through my grief will show:
But do not love thyself; then thou wilt keep
My tears for glasses, and still make me weep.
O queen of queens, how far dost thou excel!
No thought can think, nor tongue of mortal tell.—

How shall she know my griefs? I'll drop the paper;
Sweet leaves, shade folly. Who is he comes here? [*Steps aside.*

Enter LONGAVILLE *with a paper.*

What, Longaville! and reading! listen, ear.

BIRON. Now, in thy likeness, one more fool appear! [*Aside.*

LONG. Ay me! I am forsworn.

BIRON. Why, he comes in like a perjure,[b] wearing papers. [*Aside.*

KING. In love, I hope:[c] sweet fellowship in shame! [*Aside.*

BIRON. One drunkard loves another of the name. [*Aside.*

LONG. Am I the first that have been perjur'd so?

BIRON. [*Aside.*] I could put thee in comfort; not by two, that I know:
Thou mak'st the triumviry, the corner cap of society,
The shape of Love's Tyburn that hangs up simplicity.[d]

LONG. I fear these stubborn lines lack power to move:
O sweet Maria, empress of my love!
These numbers will I tear, and write in prose.

BIRON. [*Aside.*] O, rhymes are guards on wanton Cupid's hose:
Disfigure not his shape.[e]

LONG. This same shall go.— [*He reads the sonnet.*

Did not the heavenly rhetoric of thine eye
('Gainst whom the world cannot hold argument)
Persuade my heart to this false perjury?
Vows for thee broke deserve not punishment.

(*) Old copies, *night of dew.*

[a] Gets up into a tree.] A modern stage direction. The old one is, "He stands aside."

[b] *He comes in like* a perjure, wearing papers.] For *perjure,* some modern editors, Mr. Collier among them, read *perjurer;* but in the old play of "King John," Act II., Constance says,—

"But now black-spotted *perjure* as he is,
He takes a truce with Elnor's damned brat."

Wearing papers is an allusion to the custom of making persons convicted of perjury wear papers, while undergoing punishment, descriptive of their offence. Thus Hollinshed, p. 383, says of Wolsey,—"he so punished a perjurie with open punishment, and *open paper wearing,* that in his time it was less used."

[c] In love, I hope:] The early copies give this line to Longaville.

[d] *Thou mak'st the triumviry, the corner cap of society,*
The shape of Love's Tyburn, &c.]

The old gallows at Tyburn was of a triangular form.

[e] *Disfigure not his* shape.] The quarto and folio, 1623, read *shop,* which has been altered by some editors to *slop.* If any change is necessary, of which I am not sure—for *shop* may have been an old word for *garb*—I prefer that in the text, which is a MS. correction in the margin of Lord Ellesmere's copy of the first folio.

A woman I forswore; but, I will prove,
Thou being a goddess, I forswore not thee:
My vow was earthly, thou a heavenly love;
Thy grace being gain'd, cures all disgrace in me.
Vows are but breath, and breath a vapour is:
Then thou, fair sun, which on my earth dost shine,
Exhal'st this vapour vow; in thee it is:
If broken then, it is no fault of mine,
If by me broke, what fool is not so wise,
To lose an oath to win a paradise?

BIRON. [*Aside.*] This is the liver vein, which makes flesh a deity;
A green goose, a goddess: pure, pure idolatry.
God amend us, God amend! we are much out o' the way.

Enter DUMAIN, *with a paper.*

LONG. By whom shall I send this?—Company! stay. [*Stepping aside.*

BIRON. [*Aside.*] All hid, all hid, an old infant play:
Like a demi-god here sit I in the sky,
And wretched fools' secrets heedfully o'er-eye.

More sacks to the mill! O heavens, I have my wish;
Dumain transform'd: four woodcocks in a dish!

DUM. O most divine Kate!

BIRON. O most profane coxcomb! [*Aside.*

DUM. By heaven, the wonder of a mortal eye!

BIRON. By earth, she is not; corporal, there you lie.[a] [*Aside.*

DUM. Her amber hairs for foul hath amber quoted.

BIRON. An amber-colour'd raven was well noted. [*Aside.*

DUM. As upright as the cedar.

BIRON. Stoop, I say;
Her shoulder is with child. [*Aside.*

DUM. As fair as day.

BIRON. Ay, as some days: but then no sun must shine. [*Aside.*

DUM. O that I had my wish!

LONG. And I had mine! [*Aside.*

KING. And I * mine too, good lord! [*Aside.*

BIRON. Amen, so I had mine! Is not that a good word? [*Aside.*

DUM. I would forget her; but a fever she
Reigns in my blood, and will remember'd be.

BIRON. A fever in your blood! why, then incision
Would let her out in saucers: sweet misprision! [*Aside.*

DUM. Once more I'll read the ode that I have writ.

BIRON. Once more I'll mark how love can vary wit. [*Aside.*

DUM.
On a day, (alack the day!)
Love, whose month is ever † May
Spied a blossom, passing fair,
Playing in the wanton air:
Through the velvet leaves the wind,
All unseen, 'gan ‡ passage find;
That the lover, sick to death,
Wish'd[b] *himself the heaven's breath.*
Air, quoth he, thy cheeks may blow;
Air, would I might triumph so!
But alack, my hand is sworn,
Ne'er to pluck thee from thy thorn!
Vow, alack, for youth unmeet;
Youth so apt to pluck a sweet.
Do not call it sin in me,
That I am forsworn for thee:
Thou for whom Jove would swear
Juno but an Ethiop were;
And deny himself for Jove,
Turning mortal for thy love.

This will I send; and something else more plain,
That shall express my true love's fasting pain.
O, would the King, Biron, and Longaville,
Were lovers too! Ill, to example ill,
Would from my forehead wipe a perjur'd note;
For none offend, where all alike do dote.

LONG. Dumain [*advancing*], thy love is far from charity,
That in love's grief desir'st society:
You may look pale, but I should blush, I know,
To be o'erheard, and taken napping so.

KING. Come, sir [*advancing*], you blush; as his, your case is such;
You chide at him, offending twice as much:
You do not love Maria; Longaville
Did never sonnet for her sake compile;
Nor never lay his wreathed arms athwart
His loving bosom, to keep down his heart.
I have been closely shrouded in this bush,
And mark'd you both, and for you both did blush.
I heard your guilty rhymes, observ'd your fashion;
Saw sighs reek from you, noted well your passion:
Ay me! says one; O Jove! the other cries;
One,* her hairs were gold, crystal the other's eyes
You would for paradise break faith and troth; [*To* LONG
And Jove, for your love, would infringe an oath. [*To* DUMAIN.
What will Biron say, when that he shall hear
Faith infringed, which such zeal did swear?
How will he scorn! how will he spend his wit!
How will he triumph, leap, and laugh at it!
For all the wealth that ever I did see,
I would not have him know so much by me.

BIRON. Now step I forth to whip hypocrisy.—
Ah, good my liege, I pray thee, pardon me: [*Descends from the tree.*
Good heart, what grace hast thou, thus to reprove
These worms for loving, that art most in love?
Your eyes do make no coaches;[c] in your tears
There is no certain princess that appears:
You'll not be perjur'd, 'tis a hateful thing;
Tush, none but minstrels like of sonneting.
But are you not asham'd? nay, are you not,
All three of you, to be thus much o'ershot?

(*) First folio and quarto omit *I*. (†) First folio, *every*. (‡) First folio and quarto, *can*.

(*) First folio, *On*.

[a] By earth, she is not; corporal, there you lie.] This is usually read—

"By earth she is *but* corporal," &c.

but the old lection is to me more intelligible than the new. Biron has previously called himself a *corporal* of Cupid's field; he now terms Dumain *corporal* in the same sense, but uses the word for *corporeal* also, in allusion to the *mortal* eye of the preceding line.

[b] Wish'd *himself*—] The old editions have *wish* here for *wish'd*; and, a little lower, *throne* instead of *thorn*. The corrections were made in "England's Helicon," 1600, where this poem appeared.

[c] *No* coaches;] An allusion to the line in the King's sonnet:—

"No drop but as a *coach* doth carry thee."

The old copies have *couches*.

You found his mote *; the king your mote * did see;
But I a beam do find in each of three.
O, what a scene of foolery have I seen,
Of sighs, of groans, of sorrow, and of teen!
O me, with what strict patience have I sat,
To see a king transformed to a gnat![a]
To see great Hercules whipping a gig,
And profound Solomon tuning a jig,
And Nestor play at push-pin with the boys,
And critic Timon laugh at idle toys!
Where lies thy grief, O tell me, good Dumain?
And, gentle Longaville, where lies thy pain?
And where my liege's? all about the breast:—
A caudle,† ho!

KING. Too bitter is thy jest.
Are we betray'd thus to thy over-view?

BIRON. Not you by me, but I betray'd to you:
I, that am honest; I that hold it sin
To break the vow I am engaged in;
I am betray'd, by keeping company
With men-like men, of strange inconstancy.[b]
When shall you see me write a thing in rhyme?
Or groan for Joan?[c] or spend a minute's time
In pruning me? When shall you hear that I
Will praise a hand, a foot, a face, an eye,
A gait, a state, a brow, a breast, a waist,
A leg, a limb?—

KING. Soft; whither away so fast?
A true man, or a thief, that gallops so?

BIRON. I post from love; good lover, let me go.

Enter JAQUENETTA *and* COSTARD.

JAQ. God bless the king!

KING. What present hast thou there?

COST. Some certain treason.

KING. What makes treason here?

COST. Nay, it makes nothing, sir.

KING. If it mar nothing neither,
The treason, and you, go in peace away together.

JAQ. I beseech your grace, let this letter be read;
Our person misdoubts it; it was treason, he said.

KING. Biron, read it over. [*Giving him the letter.*
Where hadst thou it?

JAQ. Of Costard.

KING. Where hadst thou it?

COST. Of Dun Adramadio, Dun Adramadio.
[*Biron tears the paper.*

KING. How now! what is in you? why dost thou tear it?

BIRON. A toy, my liege, a toy; your grace needs not fear it.

LONG. It did move him to passion, and therefore let's hear it.

DUM. It is Biron's writing, and here is his name. [*Picks up the pieces.*

BIRON. Ah, you whoreson loggerhead [*to* COSTARD], you were born to do me shame.—
Guilty, my lord, guilty; I confess, I confess.

KING. What?

BIRON. That you three fools lack'd me fool to make up the mess;
He, he, and you; and you, my liege, and I,
Are pick-purses in love, and we deserve to die.
O, dismiss this audience, and I shall tell you more.

DUM. Now the number is even.

BIRON. True, true; we are four:—
Will these turtles be gone?

KING. Hence, sirs; away.

COST. Walk aside the true folk, and let the traitors stay. [*Exeunt* COST. *and* JAQ.

BIRON. Sweet lords, sweet lovers, O let us embrace!
As true we are, as flesh and blood can be:
The sea will ebb and flow, heaven show his face;
Young blood doth not obey an old decree:
We cannot cross the cause why we were* born;
Therefore, of all hands must we be forsworn.

KING. What, did these rent lines show some love of thine?

BIRON. Did they, quoth you? Who sees the heavenly Rosaline,
That, like a rude and savage man of Inde,
At the first opening of the gorgeous east,
Bows not his vassal head; and, strucken blind,
Kisses the base ground with obedient breast?
What peremptory eagle-sighted eye
Dares look upon the heaven of her brow,
That is not blinded by her majesty?

KING. What zeal, what fury hath inspir'd thee now?
My love, her mistress, is a gracious moon;

(*) Old editions, *moth*. (†) First folio, *A candle*.

[a] *A king transformed* to a gnat!] Instead of *gnat*, which seems to be without meaning in this place, it has been proposed to read *knot* or *sot;* but both are rhythmically inadmissible. I have some notion that the true word is *quat*, which appears to have been a cant term applied to a simpleton, or green-horn. Thus Iago, "Othello," Act V. Sc. 1, speaking of his silly tool Roderigo, says:—"I have rubb'd this young *quat* almost to the sense," &c. So also, in Decker's "Gul's Hornbook," 1609: "—whether he be a *yong quat* of the first yeere's revennew, or some austere and sullen-fac'd steward." It is worth remarking, too, that in the passage from "Othello," quoted above, the early quarto prints *gnat* for *quat*.

* First folio, *are*.

[b] *With men-like men*, of strange *inconstancy*.] So the old copies, except that they omit *strange*, which was added by the editor of the folio, 1632. As the expression *men-like men* is obscure, Hanmer reads "*vane*-like men;" Mason proposes "*moon*-like men;" and Mr. Collier suggests that we should read—

"With men-like *women* of inconstancy."

Which, but that *men-like* might have been a term of reproach as *man-kind* was, I should have preferred to either of the other emendations.

[c] *Or groan for* Joan?] The quarto in the possession of the Duke of Devonshire reads, "Or grone for *Love*."

She, an attending star,[a] scarce seen a light.
BIRON. My eyes are then no eyes, nor I Biron:
O, but for my love, day would turn to night!
Of all complexions, the cull'd sovereignty
Do meet, as at a fair, in her fair cheek,
Where several worthies make one dignity;
Where nothing wants, that want itself doth seek.
Lend me the flourish of all gentle tongues,—
Fie, painted rhetoric! O, she needs it not:
To things of sale a seller's praise belongs;
She passes praise: then praise too short doth blot.
A wither'd hermit, five-score winters worn,
Might shake off fifty, looking in her eye:
Beauty doth varnish age, as if new-born,
And gives the crutch the cradle's infancy.
O, 't is the sun that maketh all things shine!
KING. By heaven, thy love is black as ebony.
BIRON. Is ebony like her? O wood* divine!
A wife of such wood were felicity.
O, who can give an oath? where is a book?
That I may swear, beauty doth beauty lack,
If that she learn not of her eye to look:
No face is fair, that is not full so black.
KING. O paradox! Black is the badge of hell,
The hue of dungeons, and the stole† of night;
And beauty's crest becomes the heavens well.
BIRON. Devils soonest tempt, resembling spirits of light.
O, if in black my lady's brows be deck'd,
It mourns, that painting, and[b] usurping hair,

[a] *She, an attending star,*—] It was a prevailing notion formerly that the moon had an attending star. Lilly calls it *Lunisequa*, and Sir Richard Hawkins, in his "Observations on a Voyage to the South Seas, in 1593," published in 1622, remarks:—"Some I have heard say, and others write, that there is a starre which never separateth itself from the moon, but a small distance," &c.

[b] And *usurping hair*,—] *And* is not in the early editions. The folio of 1632, *an*.

(*) Old editions, *word*. (†) Old editions, *school*.

Should ravish doters with a false aspect;
And therefore is she born to make black fair.
Her favour turns the fashion of the days,
For native blood is counted painting now;
And therefore red, that would avoid dispraise,
Paints itself black to imitate her brow.

DUM. To look like her, are chimney-sweepers black.

LONG. And, since her time, are colliers counted bright.

KING. And Ethiops of their sweet complexion crack.

DUM. Dark needs no candles now, for dark is light.

BIRON. Your mistresses dare never come in rain,
For fear their colours should be wash'd away.

KING. 'T were good, yours did; for, sir, to tell you plain,
I'll find a fairer face not wash'd to-day.

BIRON. I'll prove her fair, or talk till doomsday here.

KING. No devil will fright thee then so much as she.

DUM. I never knew man hold vile stuff so dear.

LONG. Look, here's thy love: my foot and her face see. [*Showing his shoe.*

BIRON. O, if the streets were paved with thine eyes,
Her feet were much too dainty for such tread!

DUM. O vile! then as she goes, what upward lies
The street should see as she walk'd over head.

KING. But what of this? Are we not all in love?

BIRON. O, nothing so sure; and thereby all forsworn.

KING. Then leave this chat; and, good Biron, now prove
Our loving lawful, and our faith not torn.

DUM. Ay, marry, there;—some flattery for this evil.

LONG. O, some authority how to proceed;
Some tricks, some quillets, how to cheat the devil.

DUM. Some salve for perjury.

BIRON. O, 't is more than need!—
Have at you then, affection's men at arms:[a]
Consider, what you first did swear unto;—
To fast,—to study,—and to see no woman:—
Flat treason 'gainst the kingly state of youth.
Say, can you fast? your stomachs are too young;
And abstinence engenders maladies.
And where that you have vow'd to study, lords,
In that each of you hath forsworn his book:
Can you still dream, and pore, and thereon look?
For when would you, my lord, or you, or you,
Have found the ground of study's excellence,
Without the beauty of a woman's face?
From women's eyes this doctrine I derive: (4)
They are the ground, the books, the academes,
From whence doth spring the true Promethean fire.
Why, universal plodding prisons up
The nimble spirits in the arteries;
As motion, and long-during action, tires
The sinewy vigour of the traveller.
Now, for not looking on a woman's face,
You have in that forsworn the use of eyes;
And study too, the causer of your vow:
For where is any author in the world,
Teaches such beauty[b] as a woman's eye?
Learning is but an adjunct to ourself,
And where we are, our learning likewise is.
Then, when ourselves we see in ladies' eyes,[c] (4)
Do we not likewise see our learning there?
O, we have made a vow to study, lords,
And in that vow we have forsworn our books;
For when would you, my liege, or you, or you,
In leaden contemplation, have found out
Such fiery numbers, as the prompting eyes
Of beauty's tutors have enrich'd you with?
Other slow arts entirely keep the brain;
And therefore finding barren practisers,
Scarce show a harvest of their heavy toil:
But love, first learned in a lady's eyes,
Lives not alone immured in the brain;
But with the motion of all elements,
Courses as swift as thought in every power;
And gives to every power a double power,
Above their functions and their offices.
It adds a precious seeing to the eye;
A lover's eyes will gaze an eagle blind:
A lover's ear will hear the lowest sound,
When the suspicious head of theft is stopp'd:
Love's feeling is more soft, and sensible,
Than are the tender horns of cockled snails:
Love's tongue proves dainty Bacchus gross in taste:
For valour, is not Love a Hercules,
Still climbing trees in the Hesperides?
Subtle as sphynx; as sweet, and musical,
As bright Apollo's lute, strung with his hair;
And when Love speaks, the voice of all the gods
Makes* heaven drowsy with the harmony.
Never durst poet touch a pen to write,
Until his ink were temper'd with Love's sighs;
O, then his lines would ravish savage ears,
And plant in tyrants mild humility.

---

[a] Affection's men at arms:] That is to say, *Love's soldiers.*

[b] *Such* beauty *as a woman's eye?*] Mr. Collier's annotator suggests, "Such *learning*," &c. If any change is necessary, I should prefer reading, "Such *study*," &c.

(*) Old editions, *Make.*

[c] We see in ladies' eyes,—] After this line, the words, "*With ourselves*," have, apparently by inadvertence, been inserted in the early copies. See Note (4), Illustrative Comments on Act IV.

From women's eyes this doctrine I derive:
They sparkle still the right Promethean fire;
They are the books, the arts, the academes,
That show, contain, and nourish all the world;
Else, none at all in aught proves excellent:
Then fools you were, these women to forswear;
Or, keeping what is sworn, you will prove fools.
For wisdom's sake, a word that all men love;
Or for love's sake, a word that loves all men;
Or for men's sake, the authors * of these women;
Or women's sake, by whom we men are men;
Let us once lose our oaths to find ourselves,
Or else we lose ourselves to keep our oaths:
It is religion to be thus forsworn:
For charity itself fulfils the law;
And who can sever love from charity?

KING. Saint Cupid, then! and, soldiers, to the field!

BIRON. Advance your standards, and upon them, lords;
Pell-mell, down with them! but be first advis'd,
In conflict that you get the sun of them.

LONG. Now to plain-dealing; lay these glozes by;
Shall we resolve to woo these girls of France?

KING. And win them too: therefore let us devise
Some entertainment for them in their tents.

BIRON. First, from the park let us conduct them thither;
Then, homeward, every man attach the hand
Of his fair mistress: in the afternoon
We will with some strange pastime solace them,
Such as the shortness of the time can shape;
For revels, dances, masks, and merry hours,
Forerun fair Love, strewing her way with flowers.

KING. Away, away! no time shall be omitted,
That will betime,[a] and may by us be fitted.

BIRON. *Allons! Allons!* [b] — Sow'd cockle reap'd no corn;
And justice always whirls in equal measure:
Light wenches may prove plagues to men forsworn;
If so, our copper buys no better treasure.

[*Exeunt.*

(*) Old editions, *author*.

[a] *That will* betime, &c.] This is invariably printed, "That will *be time*," &c.; with what meaning, I am at a loss to know. If *betime* is right, it appears to be used like *beteem*, from the Anglo-Saxon, *Tym-an*, to bear, to yield, &c.; but I suspect Shakespeare wrote, "That will *betide*," &c., i. e. *will fall out, will come to pass*, &c.

[b] *Allons! Allons!*—] The old copies, read, "Alone, alone;" which may be right, and mean *along*. The word occurs again at the end of the first scene of Act V. of this Play, in "The Tempest," Act IV. Sc. 1,—*Let's alone*, where it has been the source of interminable controversy; and in other places in these dramas,—in the sense of *along;* and, in every instance, it is spelt *alone*. I find it with the same meaning in Beaumont and Fletcher's Play of "The Loyal Subject," Act III. Sc. 5, where it rhymes to *gone;* and could hardly, therefore, in that case, be a misprint.

ACT V.

SCENE I.—*Another part of the same.*

Enter HOLOFERNES, *Sir* NATHANIEL, *and* DULL.[a]

HOL. *Satis quod*[b] *sufficit.*

NATH. I praise God for you, sir: your reasons at dinner have been sharp and sententious; pleasant without scurrility, witty without affection,[c] audacious without impudency, learned without opinion, and strange without heresy. I did converse this *quondam* day with a companion of the king's, who is intituled, nominated, or called, Don Adriano de Armado.

HOL. *Novi hominem tanquam te:* His humour is lofty, his discourse peremptory, his tongue filed, his eye ambitious, his gait majestical, and his general behaviour vain, ridiculous, and thrasonical. He is too picked,[d] too spruce, too affected, too odd, as it were, too peregrinate, as I may call it.

NATH. A most singular and choice epithet.

[*Takes out his table-book.*

HOL. He draweth out the thread of his verbosity finer than the staple of his argument. I abhor such fanatical phantasms, such insociable and point-devise companions; such rackers of

a Enter Holofernes, Sir Nathaniel, and Dull.] In the quarto and the folio. 1623, the direction here is, "Enter the Pedant, Curate, and Dull." And Holofernes is styled the "Pedant," to the end of the Scene.

b *Satis* quod sufficit.] The ancient copies have *quid;* and in them the errors in the Latinity are so frequent and so barbarous that, in mercy to the reader, I have refrained from noting them severally, and have silently adopted the obvious corrections of my predecessors.

c *Without* affection,—] That is, without *affectation.* Thus, in "Hamlet," Act II. Sc. 2,—

"No matter that might indite the author of *affection.*"

d *He is too* picked,—] *Picked* was applied both to manners and to dress. It seems to have meant, *scrupulously nice;* or, as we should now term it, *priggish, foppish.* "Hamlet," Act. V. Sc. 1, says,

"—— the age is grown so *picked.*"

So Chaucer, "Prologue to the Canterbury Tales," speaking of the dresses of the haberdasher, dyer, &c. tells us, l. 367,—

"Ful freshe and newe ther geare *ypicked* was."

Again, in Chapman's Play of "All Fools," Act. V. Sc. 1,—

"I think he was some barber's son, by the mass,
'Tis such a *picked* fellow, not a hair
About his whole bulk, but it stands in print."

orthography, as to speak, dout, fine, when he should say, doubt: det, when he should pronounce debt;—d, e, b, t; not d, e, t:—he clepeth a calf, cauf; half, hauf; neighbour, *vocatur*, nebour; neigh, abbreviated, ne: This is abhominable,[a] (which he would call abominable*) it insinuateth me of insanie:[b] *Ne intelligis, domine?* to make frantic, lunatic.

NATH. *Laus Deo, bone intelligo.*

HOL. *Bone?*——*bone*, for *benè*: Priscian a little scratch'd; 't will serve.

Enter ARMADO, MOTH, *and* COSTARD.

NATH. *Videsne quis venit?*

HOL. *Video et gaudeo.*

ARM. Chirra! [*To* MOTH.

HOL. *Quare* Chirra, not sirrah?

ARM. Men of peace, well encountered.

HOL. Most military sir, salutation.

MOTH. They have been at a great feast of languages, and stolen the scraps. [*To* COSTARD *aside.*

COST. O, they have lived long on the alms-basket of words! I marvel, thy master hath not eaten thee for a word; for thou art not so long by the head as *honorificabilitudinitatibus*: thou art easier swallowed than a flap-dragon.

MOTH. Peace! the peal begins.

ARM. Monsieur [*to* HOL.], are you not lettered?

MOTH. Yes, yes; he teaches boys the horn-book;—
What is a, b, spelt backward, with the horn on his head?

HOL. Ba, *pueritia*, with a horn added.

MOTH. Ba, most silly sheep, with a horn.—You hear his learning.

HOL. *Quis, quis*, thou consonant?

MOTH. The third † of the five vowels, if you repeat them; or the fifth, if I.

HOL. I will repeat them, a, e, i.—

MOTH. The sheep: the other two concludes it; o, u.

ARM. Now, by the salt wave of the Mediterraneum, a sweet touch, a quick venew (1) of wit: snip, snap, quick, and home; it rejoiceth my intellect: true wit.

MOTH. Offer'd by a child to an old man; which is wit-old.

HOL. What is the figure? what is the figure?

MOTH. Horns.

HOL. Thou disputest like an infant: go, whip thy gig.

MOTH. Lend me your horn to make one, and I will whip about your infamy *circùm circà*: A gig of a cuckold's horn!

COST. An I had but one penny in the world, thou shouldst have it to buy gingerbread: hold, there is the very remuneration I had of thy master, thou halfpenny purse of wit, thou pigeon-egg of discretion. O, an the heavens were so pleased that thou wert but my bastard! what a joyful father wouldst thou make me! Go to; thou hast it *ad dunghill*, at the fingers' ends, as they say.

HOL. O, I smell false Latin; dunghill for *unguem*.

ARM. Arts-man, *prœambula*; we will be singled from the barbarous. Do you not educate youth at the charge-house on the top of the mountain?

HOL. Or, *mons*, the hill.

ARM. At your sweet pleasure, for the mountain.

HOL. I do, sans question.

ARM. Sir, it is the king's most sweet pleasure and affection, to congratulate the princess at her pavilion, in the posteriors of this day; which the rude multitude call the afternoon.

HOL. The posterior of the day, most generous sir, is liable, congruent, and measurable for the afternoon: the word is well culled; choice,* sweet, and apt, I do assure you, sir, I do assure.

ARM. Sir, the king is a noble gentleman; and my familiar, I do assure you, very good friend:—For what is inward between us, let it pass:—I do beseech thee, remember thy courtesy:[c]—I beseech thee, apparel thy head:—And among other importunate and most serious designs,—and of great import indeed, too;—but let that pass:—for I must tell thee, it will please his grace (by the world) sometime to lean upon my poor shoulder; and with his royal finger, thus, dally with my excrement, with my mustachio: but, sweet heart, let that pass. By the world, I recount no fable; some certain special honours it

(*) Old copies, *abhominable*. (†) Old editions, The *last*.

[a] Abhominable,—] The antiquated mode of spelling the word, which appears to have been in a transition state at the period when the present Play was written.

[b] *It insinuateth me of* insanie:] The old editions have *infamie*. For this and other corrections in the speech we are indebted to Theobald.

[c] *I do beseech thee*, remember thy courtesy:] The words *remember thy courtesy* have been a stumbling-block to all the commentators. Mr. Malone wrote a very long note to prove that we should read, "remember *not* thy courtesy;" and Mr. Dyce says, nothing can be more evident than that Shakespeare so wrote. Whatever may have been the meaning of the words, or whether they were a mere complimentary periphrasis, without any precise signification, the following quotations prove, I think beyond question, that the old text is right; and that the expression refers—not, as Mr. Knight supposes, to any obligation of secrecy, but simply to the Pedant's standing bare-headed,—

"I pray you *be remembred*, and cover your head."
Lusty Juventus. Hawkins' Edition, p. 142.

"Then I pray *remember your courtesy*."
MARLOWE's *Faustus*, Act IV Sc. 3.

"Pray you *remember your courts'y* * *
* * * * * Nay, pray you be cover'd."
BEN JONSON's *Every Man in His Humour*, Act. I. Sc. 1. Gifford's Edition.

(*) First folio, *culd, chose*, &c.

pleaseth his greatness to impart to Armado, a soldier, a man of travel, that hath seen the world: but let that pass.—The very all of all is,—but, sweet heart, I do implore secrecy,—that the king would have me present the princess, sweet chuck, with some delightful ostentation, or show, or pageant, or antic, or fire-work. Now, understanding that the curate and your sweet self are good at such eruptions, and sudden breaking out of mirth, as it were, I have acquainted you withal, to the end to crave your assistance.

HOL. Sir, you shall present before her the nine Worthies.—Sir Nathaniel,* as concerning some entertainment of time, some show in the posterior of this day, to be rendered by our assistance,—the king's command, and this most gallant, illustrate, and learned gentleman,—before the princess; I say, none so fit as to present the nine Worthies.

NATH. Where will you find men worthy enough to present them?

HOL. Joshua, yourself; myself, or† this gallant gentleman, Judas Maccabæus; this swain, because of his great limb or joint, shall pass Pompey the great; the page, Hercules.

ARM. Pardon, sir, error: he is not quantity enough for that worthy's thumb: he is not so big as the end of his club.

HOL. Shall I have audience? he shall present Hercules in minority: his *enter* and *exit* shall be strangling a snake; and I will have an apology for that purpose.

MOTH. An excellent device! so, if any of the audience hiss, you may cry, *Well done, Hercules! now thou crushest the snake!* that is the way to make an offence gracious; though few have the grace to do it.

ARM. For the rest of the Worthies?—

HOL. I will play three myself.

MOTH. Thrice-worthy gentleman!

ARM. Shall I tell you a thing?

HOL. We attend.

ARM. We will have, if this fadge [a] not, an antic. I beseech you, follow.

HOL. *Via*, goodman Dull! thou hast spoken no word all this while.

DULL. Nor understood none neither, sir.

HOL. *Allons!* [b] we will employ thee.

DULL. I'll make one in a dance, or so; or I will play on the tabor to the Worthies, and let them dance the hay.[c]

HOL. Most dull, honest Dull, to our sport, away. [*Exeunt.*

SCENE II.—*Another part of the same. Before the* Princess's *Pavilion.*

Enter the PRINCESS, KATHARINE, ROSALINE, *and* MARIA.

PRIN. Sweet hearts, we shall be rich ere we depart,
If fairings come thus plentifully in:
A lady wall'd about with diamonds!
Look you, what I have from the loving king.

ROS. Madam, came nothing else along with that?

PRIN. Nothing but this? yes, as much love in rhyme,
As would be cramm'd up in a sheet of paper,
Writ on both sides of the leaf, margent and all;
That he was fain to seal on Cupid's name.

ROS. That was the way to make his godhead wax; [d]
For he hath been five thousand years a boy.

KATH. Ay, and a shrewd unhappy gallows too.

ROS. You'll ne'er be friends with him; 'a kill'd your sister.

KATH. He made her melancholy, sad, and heavy;
And so she died: had she been light, like you,
Of such a merry, nimble, stirring spirit,
She might have been a grandam ere she died:
And so may you; for a light heart lives long.

ROS. What's your dark meaning, mouse, of this light word?

KATH. A light condition in a beauty dark.

ROS. We need more light to find your meaning out.

KATH. You'll mar the light, by taking it in snuff; [e]
Therefore, I'll darkly end the argument.

(*) Old editions, Sir *Holofernes*. (†) Old editions, *and*.

[a] *If this* fadge *not*,—] *To fadge* is *to fit, to suit, to agree with.*

[b] Allons!] See note (b) at page 81.

[c] *And let them dance the* hay.] This dance, Douce informs us, was borrowed from the French, and is classed among the *brawls* in Thoinot Arbeau's "Orchesographie," 4to. 1588.

[d] *To make his godhead* wax;] *To wax*, is *to grow*. We say, he *waxes* in years. The moon *waxes* and *wanes*.

"So ripe is vice, so green is virtue's bud,
The world doth *wax* in ill, but wane in good."
SOUTHWELL, *Rursus ad Eundem.*

[e] *Taking it* in snuff;] This was a favourite conceit with Shakespeare and the writers of his time. To take anything *in snuff*, was *to take it in dudgeon, to be in ill temper*. Hence the equivoque, which was sometimes in allusion to snuff for the nose, and sometimes to the snuff of a candle. Everybody is familiar with Hotspur's fop and his pouncet-box,—

"—— which ever and anon
He gave his nose, and took 't away again;—
Who, therewith angry, when it next came there,
Took it in snuff."

So in "Midsummer-Night's Dream," Act. V. Sc. 1,—

"He dares not come there, for the candle; for you see, it is already *in snuff*."

So, too, in Decker's "Satiro-mastix," where the characters are speaking of tobacco,—

"—— 'tis enough,
Having so much fool, to *take him in snuff*."

Ros. Look, what you do; you do it still i' the dark.
Kath. So do not you; for you are a light wench.
Ros. Indeed, I weigh not you; and therefore light.
Kath. You weigh me not,—O, that's you care not for me.
Ros. Great reason; for, Past cure is still past care.[a]
Prin. Well bandied both; a set of wit well play'd.
But, Rosaline, you have a favour too:
Who sent it? and what is it?
Ros. I would, you knew:
An if my face were but as fair as yours,
My favour were as great; be witness this.
Nay, I have verses too, I thank Biron:
The numbers true; and, were the numb'ring too,
I were the fairest goddess on the ground:
I am compar'd to twenty thousand fairs.
O, he hath drawn my picture in his letter!
Prin. Anything like?
Ros. Much, in the letters; nothing in the praise.
Prin. Beauteous as ink; a good conclusion.
Kath. Fair as a text B in a copy-book.
Ros. 'Ware pencils,[b] Ho! let me not die your debtor,
My red dominical, my golden letter:[c]
O that your face were not so* full of O's!
Prin. A pox of that jest! and I[d] beshrew all shrows!
But, Katharine, what was sent to you from fair Dumain?
Kath. Madam, this glove.
Prin. Did he not send you twain?
Kath. Yes, madam; and moreover,
Some thousand verses of a faithful lover;
A huge translation of hypocrisy,
Vilely compil'd, profound simplicity.
Mar. This, and these pearls, to me sent Longaville;
The letter is too long by half a mile.
Prin. I think no less: Dost thou not † wish in heart,
The chain were longer, and the letter short?
Mar. Ay, or I would these hands might never part.
Prin. We are wise girls to mock our lovers so.
Ros. They are worse fools to purchase mocking so.
That same Biron I'll torture ere I go.
O, that I knew he were but in by the week![e]
How I would make him fawn, and beg, and seek;
And wait the season, and observe the times,
And spend his prodigal wits in bootless rhymes;
And shape his service wholly to my behests;*
And make him proud to make me proud that jests!
So portent-like[f] would I o'ersway his state,
That he should be my fool, and I his fate.
Prin. None are so surely caught, when they are catch'd,
As wit turn'd fool: folly, in wisdom hatch'd,
Hath wisdom's warrant, and the help of school;
And wit's own grace to grace a learned fool.
Ros. The blood of youth burns not with such excess,
As gravity's revolt to wantonness.†
Mar. Folly in fools bears not so strong a note,
As foolery in the wise, when wit doth dote;
Since all the power thereof it doth apply,
To prove, by wit, worth in simplicity.

Enter Boyet.

Prin. Here comes Boyet, and mirth is‡ in his face.
Boyet. O, I am stabb'd with laughter! Where's her grace?
Prin. Thy news, Boyet?
Boyet. Prepare, madam, prepare!—
Arm, wenches, arm! encounters mounted are
Against your peace: Love doth approach disguis'd,
Arm'd in arguments; you'll be surpris'd:
Muster your wits; stand in your own defence;
Or hide your heads like cowards, and fly hence.
Prin. Saint Dennis to Saint Cupid! What are they,
That charge their breath against us? say, scout, say.
Boyet. Under the cool shade of a sycamore,
I thought to close mine eyes some half an hour;
When, lo! to interrupt my purpos'd rest,

(*) First folio omits *not so*. (†) First folio omits *not*.

a Past cure is still past care.] The old editions transpose the words *cure* and *care*; but Rosaline is quoting a familiar adage,—"Things past *cure*, past *care*."

b 'Ware pencils, Ho!] The elder copies read, *Ware pensals. How?* Mr. Dyce has shown that, in books of the period, *Ho!* is frequently printed *How?* but he is wrong in saying that all editions have hitherto retained the old reading. Sir Thomas Hanmer, in his edition, 1744, gives the lection in the text.

c *My* golden *letter*:] Rosaline was a "darke ladye;" Katharine fair and golden haired; and, as in the early alphabets for children, A was printed in red, and B in black, ink, the taunting allusions are sufficiently expressive.

(*) The quarto and first folio have *device*.
(†) The quarto and first folio read *wantons be*.
(‡) First folio omits *is*.

d *And* I beshrew *all shrows!*] *To beshrew*, is *to imprecate sorrow*, or *evil*, on any person or thing, *to curse*, &c.

e *He were but* in by the week!] To be *in by the week*, i.e. for a fixed period, was a frequent saying in former times; and is supposed to be taken from the custom of hiring servants, or operatives, generally.

f *So* portent-like—] The old copies have *pertaunt-like*. Hanmer first suggested *portent-like*; and he has been followed by most of the subsequent editors.

Toward that shade I might behold address'd
The king and his companions: warily
I stole into a neighbour thicket by,
And overheard what you shall overhear;
That, by and by, disguis'd they will be here.
Their herald is a pretty knavish page,
That well by heart hath conn'd his embassage:
Action, and accent, did they teach him there;
Thus must thou speak, and thus thy body bear:
And ever and anon they made a doubt,
Presence majestical would put him out;
For, quoth the king, *an angel shalt thou see;*
Yet fear not thou, but speak audaciously.
The boy replied, *An angel is not evil;*
I should have fear'd her had she been a devil.
With that all laugh'd, and clapp'd him on the shoulder;
Making the bold wag by their praises bolder.
One rubb'd his elbow, thus; and fleer'd, and swore,
A better speech was never spoke before:
Another with his finger and his thumb,
Cried, *Via! we will do't, come what will come:*
The third he caper'd, and cried, *All goes well;*
The fourth turn'd on the toe, and down he fell.
With that, they all did tumble on the ground,
With such a zealous laughter, so profound,
That, in this spleen ridiculous, appears,
To check their folly, passion's solemn tears.[a]

PRIN. But what, but what, come they to visit us?

BOYET. They do, they do; and are apparell'd thus,—
Like Muscovites, or Russians, as I guess.
Their purpose is, to parle, to court, and dance:
And every one his love-feat will advance
Unto his several mistress; which they'll know
By favours several, which they did bestow.

PRIN. And will they so? the gallants shall be task'd:—
For, ladies, we will every one be mask'd;
And not a man of them shall have the grace,
Despite of suit, to see a lady's face.
Hold, Rosaline, this favour thou shalt wear,
And then the king will court thee for his dear;

[a] To check their folly, *passion's* solemn *tears.*] Mr. Collier's annotator, for "*solemn* tears," reads "*sudden* tears," which is, at least, a very plausible suggestion. But whether we have *sudden*, or *solemn* tears, I cannot help believing the line should run,—

To check their *folly's passion*, &c.

Hold, take thou this, my sweet, and give me thine;
So shall Biron take me for Rosaline.—
And change your favours too; so shall your loves
Woo contrary, deceiv'd by these removes.

ROS. Come on then; wear the favours most in sight.

KATH. But, in this changing, what is your intent?

PRIN. The effect of my intent is, to cross theirs:
They do it but in mocking merriment;
And mock for mock is only my intent.
Their several counsels they unbosom shall
To loves mistook; and so be mock'd withal,
Upon the next occasion that we meet,
With visages display'd, to talk and greet.

ROS. But shall we dance, if they desire us to't?

PRIN. No; to the death we will not move a foot,
Nor to their penn'd speech render we no grace:
But, while 't is spoke, each turn away her* face.

BOYET. Why, that contempt will kill the speaker's † heart,
And quite divorce his memory from his part.

PRIN. Therefore I do it; and, I make no doubt,
The rest will ne'er come in, if he be out.
There's no such sport as sport by sport o'erthrown;
To make theirs ours, and ours none but our own:
So shall we stay, mocking intended game;
And they, well mock'd, depart away with shame. [*Trumpets sound within.*

BOYET. The trumpet sounds; be mask'd, the maskers come. [*The ladies mask.*

Enter the KING, BIRON, LONGAVILLE, *and* DUMAIN, *in Russian habits, and masked;* MOTH, Musicians, *and* Attendants.

MOTH. *All hail the richest beauties on the earth!*

BIRON. Beauties no richer than rich taffata. [*Aside.*

MOTH. *A holy parcel of the fairest dames,* [The ladies turn their backs to him.
That ever turn'd their—backs—to mortal views!

BIRON. *Their eyes,* villain, *their eyes!*

MOTH. *That ever turn'd their eyes to mortal views!*
Out—

BOYET. True; *out,* indeed.

MOTH. *Out of your favours, heavenly spirits, vouchsafe*
Not to behold—

BIRON. *Once to behold,* rogue.

MOTH. *Once to behold with your sun-beamed eyes,—*
With your sun-beamed eyes—

BOYET. They will not answer to that epithet,
You were best call it, daughter-beamed eyes.

MOTH. They do not mark me, and that brings me out.

BIRON. Is this your perfectness? begone, you rogue!

ROS. What would these strangers? know their minds, Boyet:
If they do speak our language, 't is our will
That some plain man recount their purposes:
Know what they would.

BOYET. What would you with the princess?

BIRON. Nothing but peace, and gentle visitation.

ROS. What would they, say they?

BOYET. Nothing but peace, and gentle visitation.

ROS. Why, that they have; and bid them so be gone.

BOYET. She says, you have it, and you may be gone.

KING. Say to her, we have measur'd many miles,
To tread a measure(2) with her * on the grass.

BOYET. They say that they have measur'd many a mile,
To tread a measure with you on this grass.

ROS. It is not so; ask them how many inches
Is in one mile: if they have measur'd many,
The measure then of one is easily told.

BOYET. If, to come hither, you have measur'd miles,
And many miles, the princess bids you tell,
How many inches do † fill up one mile.

BIRON. Tell her, we measure them by weary steps.

BOYET. She hears herself.

ROS. How many weary steps,
Of many weary miles you have o'ergone,
Are number'd in the travel of one mile?

BIRON. We number nothing that we spend for you;
Our duty is so rich, so infinite,
That we may do it still without accompt.
Vouchsafe to show the sunshine of your face,
That we, like savages, may worship it.

ROS. My face is but a moon, and clouded too.

KING. Blessed are clouds, to do as such clouds do!
Vouchsafe, bright moon, and these thy stars, to shine
(Those clouds remov'd) upon our watery eyne.

ROS. O vain petitioner! beg a greater matter;
Thou now request'st but moonshine in the water.

KING. Then, in our measure, do but vouchsafe one change:
Thou bidd'st me beg; this begging is not strange.

ROS. Play, music, then: nay, you must do it soon. [*Music plays.*

(*) Old copies, *his.* (†) First folio, *keeper's.*

(*) First folio, *you.* (†) Old editions *doth.*

Not yet;—no dance:—thus change I like the moon.

KING. Will you not dance? How come you thus estrang'd?

ROS. You took the moon at full; but now she's chang'd.

KING. Yet still she is the moon, and I the man.[a]
The music plays; vouchsafe some motion to it.[b]

ROS. Our ears vouchsafe it.

KING. But your legs should do it.

ROS. Since you are strangers, and come here by chance,
We'll not be nice: take hands;—we will not dance.

KING. Why take we (*) hands, then?

ROS. Only to part friends:—
Court'sy, sweet hearts, and so the measure ends.

KING. More measure of this measure; be not nice.

ROS. We can afford no more at such a price.

KING. Prize you (†) yourselves: What buys your company?

---

[a] — *she is the* moon, *and I the* man.] An allusion to a stage character, with whom the audience of Shakespeare's day was perfectly familiar—*the Man in the Moon*.

(*) First folio, *you*. (†) First folio omits *you*.

[b] Vouchsafe some motion to it.] The early copies assign this line to Rosaline.

Ros. Your absence only.
King. That can never be.
Ros. Then cannot we be bought: and so adieu;
Twice to your visor, and half once to you!
King. If you deny to dance, let's hold more chat.
Ros. In private then.
King. I am best pleas'd with that.
[*They converse apart.*
Biron. White-handed mistress, one sweet word with thee.
Prin. Honey, and milk, and sugar; there is three.
Biron. Nay, then, two treys (an if you grow so nice),
Metheglin, wort, and malmsey.—Well run, dice!
There's half a dozen sweets.
Prin. Seventh sweet, adieu!
Since you can cog,[a] I'll play no more with you.
Biron. One word in secret.
Prin. Let it not be sweet.
Biron. Thou griev'st my gall.
Prin. Gall? bitter.
Biron. Therefore meet.
[*They converse apart.*
Dum. Will you vouchsafe with me to change a word?
Mar. Name it.
Dum. Fair lady,—
Mar. Say you so? Fair lord,—
Take* that for your fair lady.
Dum. Please it you,
As much in private, and I'll bid adieu.
[*They converse apart.*
Kath. What, was your visor made without a tongue?
Long. I know the reason, lady, why you ask.
Kath. O, for your reason! quickly, sir; I long.
Long. You have a double tongue within your mask,
And would afford my speechless visor half.
Kath. Veal, quoth the Dutchman:—Is not veal a calf?
Long. A calf, fair lady?
Kath. No, a fair lord calf.
Long. Let's part the word.
Kath. No, I'll not be your half:
Take all, and wean it; it may prove an ox.
Long. Look, how you butt yourself in these sharp mocks!
Will you give horns, chaste lady? do not so.
Kath. Then die a calf, before your horns do grow.
Long. One word in private with you, ere I die.
Kath. Bleat softly then, the butcher hears you cry. [*They converse apart.*
Boyet. The tongues of mocking wenches are as keen
As is the razor's edge invisible,
Cutting a smaller hair than may be seen;
Above the sense of sense: so sensible
Seemeth their conference; their conceits have wings,
Fleeter than arrows, bullets, wind, thought, swifter things.
Ros. Not one word more, my maids; break off, break off.
Biron. By heaven, all dry-beaten with pure scoff!
King. Farewell, mad wenches; you have simple wits.
[*Exeunt* King, Lords, Moth, *Music, and* Attendants.
Prin. Twenty adieus, my frozen Muscovits.—
Are these the breed of wits so wonder'd at?
Boyet. Tapers they are, with your sweet breaths puff'd out.
Ros. Well-liking wits they have; gross, gross; fat, fat.
Prin. O poverty in wit, kingly-poor flout![b]
Will they not, think you, hang themselves to-night?
Or ever, but in visors, show their faces?
This pert Biron was out of countenance quite.
Ros. O! they were all in lamentable cases!
The king was weeping-ripe for a good word.
Prin. Biron did swear himself out of all suit.
Mar. Dumain was at my service, and his sword:
No *point*,[c] quoth I; my servant straight was mute.
Kath. Lord Longaville said, I came o'er his heart;
And trow you what he call'd me?
Prin. Qualm, perhaps.
Kath. Yes, in good faith.
Prin. Go, sickness as thou art!
Ros. Well, better wits have worn plain statute-caps,(3)
But will you hear? the king is my love sworn.
Prin. And quick Biron hath plighted faith to me.
Kath. And Longaville was for my service born.
Mar. Dumain is mine, as sure as bark on tree.
Boyet. Madam, and pretty mistresses, give ear:

(*) First folio, "Take *you* that."
a *Since you can* cog,—] *To cog* the dice is to load them for cheating; and hence, when any one deceives or defrauds another, he is said *to cog*.
b *O poverty in wit*, kingly-poor flout!] No ingenuity has yet succeeded in extracting sense from this passage. It appears to me manifestly corrupt, and the misprint to have been occasioned by a transposition. *Kingly-poor*, I suspect, is no other than a printer's error for *poor-lyking*. Rosaline, in irony, speaks of their visitors having rich, *well-liking*, i.e. good-conditioned, wits; to which the Princess replies:—

"O poverty in wit, *poor-liking* flout!"

Liking, of old, was spelt, indifferently, *liking*, or *lyking*.
c *No* point,—] See note (c), p. 62.

Immediately they will again be here
In their own shapes; for it can never be,
They will digest this harsh indignity.

PRIN. Will they return?

BOYET. They will, they will, God knows,
And leap for joy, though they are lame with blows:
Therefore, change favours; and, when they repair,
Blow like sweet roses in this summer air.

PRIN. How blow? how blow? speak to be understood.

BOYET. Fair ladies, mask'd, are roses in their bud:
Dismask'd, their damask sweet commixture shown,
Are angels vailing clouds, or roses blown.

PRIN. Avaunt, perplexity! What shall we do,
If they return in their own shapes to woo?

ROS. Good madam, if by me you'll be advis'd,
Let's mock them still, as well known, as disguis'd:
Let us complain to them what fools were here,
Disguis'd like Muscovites, in shapeless gear;
And wonder what they were; and to what end
Their shallow shows, and prologue vilely penn'd,
And their rough carriage so ridiculous,
Should be presented at our tent to us.

BOYET. Ladies, withdraw: the gallants are at hand.

PRIN. Whip to our tents, as roes run over land.*

[*Exeunt* PRINCESS, ROS., KATH., *and* MARIA.

Enter the KING, BIRON, LONGAVILLE, *and* DUMAIN, *in their proper habits.*

KING. Fair sir, God save you! Where is† the princess?

BOYET. Gone to her tent: Please it your majesty,
Command me any service to her thither?‡

KING. That she vouchsafe me audience for one word.

BOYET. I will; and so will she, I know, my lord. [*Exit.*

BIRON. This fellow pecks § up wit, as pigeons peas,
And utters it again when God|| doth please:
He is wit's pedler; and retails his wares
At wakes, and wassails, meetings, markets, fairs;
And we that sell by gross, the Lord doth know,
Have not the grace to grace it with such show.
This gallant pins the wenches on his sleeve;
Had he been Adam, he had tempted Eve:
He can carve (4) too, and lisp: Why, this is he,
That kiss'd away his hand in courtesy;
This is the ape of form, monsieur the nice,
That, when he plays at tables, chides the dice
In honourable terms; nay, he can sing
A mean most meanly; and, in ushering,
Mend him who can: the ladies call him, sweet;
The stairs, as he treads on them, kiss his feet:
This is the flower that smiles on every one,
To show his teeth as white as whales' bone:
And consciences, that will not die in debt,
Pay him the due* of *honey-tongued* Boyet.

KING. A blister on his sweet tongue, with my heart,
That put Armado's page out of his part!

Enter the PRINCESS, *ushered by* BOYET; ROSALINE, MARIA, KATHARINE, *and* Attendants.

BIRON. See where it comes!—Behaviour, what wert thou,
Till this† man show'd thee? and what art thou now?

KING. All hail, sweet madam, and fair time of day!

PRIN. Fair, in all hail, is foul, as I conceive.

KING. Construe my speeches better, if you may.

PRIN. Then wish me better, I will give you leave.

KING. We came to visit you; and purpose now
To lead you to our court; vouchsafe it then.

PRIN. This field shall hold me; and so hold your vow:
Nor God, nor I, delights in perjur'd men.

KING. Rebuke me not for that which you provoke;
The virtue of your eye must break my oath.

PRIN. You nick-name virtue: vice you should have spoke;
For virtue's office never breaks men's troth.
Now, by my maiden honour, yet as pure
As the unsullied‡ lily, I protest,
A world of torments though I should endure,
I would not yield to be your house's guest:
So much I hate a breaking-cause to be
Of heavenly oaths, vow'd with integrity.

KING. O, you have liv'd in desolation here,
Unseen, unvisited, much to our shame.

PRIN. Not so, my lord, it is not so, I swear;
We have had pastimes here, and pleasant game;
A mess of Russians left us but of late.

KING. How, madam? Russians?

PRIN. Ay, in truth, my lord;
Trim gallants, full of courtship, and of state.

ROS. Madam, speak true:—It is not so, my lord;
My lady (to the manner of the days),
In courtesy, gives undeserving praise.
We four, indeed, confronted were with four

(*) Old copies, *runnes ore land.* (†) Old copies, *where's.* (‡) First folio omits *thither.* (§) First folio, *picks.* || First folio, *Jove.*

(*) First folio, *duty.* (†) Old editions, *madman.* (‡) Old editions, *unsallied.*

In Russian habit; here they stay'd an hour,
And talk'd apace; and in that hour, my lord,
They did not bless us with one happy word.
I dare not call them fools; but this I think,
When they are thirsty, fools would fain have drink.

BIRON. This jest is dry to me. Fair gentle-sweet,[a]
Your wit makes wise things foolish; when we greet
With eyes best seeing heaven's fiery eye,
By light we lose light: Your capacity
Is of that nature, that to your huge store
Wise things seem foolish, and rich things but poor.

ROS. This proves you wise and rich, for in my eye,—

BIRON. I am a fool, and full of poverty.

ROS. But that you take what doth to you belong,
It were a fault to snatch words from my tongue.

BIRON. O, I am yours, and all that I possess.

ROS. All the fool mine?

BIRON. I cannot give you less.

ROS. Which of the visors was it that you wore?

BIRON. Where? when? what visor? why demand you this?

ROS. There, then, that visor; that superfluous case,
That hid the worse, and show'd the better face.

KING. We are descried: they'll mock us now downright.

DUM. Let us confess, and turn it to a jest.

PRIN. Amaz'd, my lord? Why looks your highness sad?

ROS. Help, hold his brows! he'll swoon! Why look you pale?—
Sea-sick, I think, coming from Muscovy.

BIRON. Thus pour the stars down plagues for perjury.
Can any face of brass hold longer out?—
Here stand I, lady; dart thy skill at me;
Bruise me with scorn, confound me with a flout;
Thrust thy sharp wit quite through my ignorance;
Cut me to pieces with thy keen conceit;
And I will wish thee never more to dance
Nor never more in Russian habit wait.
O! never will I trust to speeches penn'd,
Nor to the motion of a schoolboy's tongue;
Nor never come in visor to my friend;
Nor woo in rhyme, like a blind harper's song:
Taffata phrases, silken terms precise,
Three-pil'd hyperboles, spruce affectation,*
Figures pedantical; these summer-flies
Have blown me full of maggot ostentation:
I do forswear them: and I here protest,
By this white glove, (how white the hand, God knows!)
Henceforth my wooing mind shall be express'd
In russet yeas, and honest kersey noes:
And, to begin, wench,—so God help me, la!—
My love to thee is sound, sans crack or flaw.

ROS. *Sans* SANS, I pray you.

BIRON. Yet I have a trick
Of the old rage:—bear with me, I am sick;
I'll leave it by degrees. Soft, let us see;—
Write *Lord have mercy on us*,(5) on those three;
They are infected, in their hearts it lies;
They have the plague, and caught it of your eyes:
These lords are visited; you are not free,
For the Lord's tokens on you do I see.

PRIN. No, they are free that gave these tokens to us.

BIRON. Our states are forfeit, seek not to undo us.

ROS. It is not so. For how can this be true,
That you stand forfeit, being those that sue?

BIRON. Peace; for I will not have to do with you.

ROS. Nor shall not, if I do as I intend.

BIRON. Speak for yourselves, my wit is at an end.

KING. Teach us, sweet madam, for our rude transgression
Some fair excuse.

PRIN. The fairest is confession.
Were you not here, but even now, disguis'd?

KING. Madam, I was.

PRIN. And were you well advis'd?

KING. I was, fair madam.

PRIN. When you then were here,
What did you whisper in your lady's ear?

KING. That more than all the world I did respect her.

PRIN. When she shall challenge this, you will reject her.

KING. Upon mine honour, no.

PRIN. Peace, peace, forbear;
Your oath once broke, you force[b] not to forswear.

KING. Despise me, when I break this oath of mine.

PRIN. I will: and therefore keep it:—Rosaline,
What did the Russian whisper in your ear?

ROS. Madam, he swore that he did hold me dear
As precious eye-sight: and did value me
Above this world: adding thereto, morever,
That he would wed me, or else die my lover.

PRIN. God give thee joy of him! the noble lord
Most honourably doth uphold his word.

(*) Old copies, *affection*.

a Fair *gentle-sweet*,—] *Fair* was supplied by the second folio, 1632. Mr. Malone reads "*My*."

b *You* force *not to forswear*.] To *force not* is *to care not*. Mr. Collier gives a very apposite illustration of this old use of the word,—

"O Lorde! some good body for God's sake, gyve me meate,
I *force* not what it were, so that I had to eate."
Int. of Jacob and Esau, 1568, Act II. Sc. 2.

KING. What mean you, madam? by my life, my troth,
I never swore this lady such an oath.

ROS. By heaven you did; and to confirm it plain,
You gave me this; but take it, sir, again.

KING. My faith, and this, the princess I did give;
I knew her by this jewel on her sleeve.

PRIN. Pardon me, sir, this jewel did she wear;
And lord Biron, I thank him, is my dear:—
What; will you have me, or your pearl again?

BIRON. Neither of either; I remit both twain.
I see the trick on 't:—Here was a consent,
(Knowing aforehand of our merriment,)
To dash it like a Christmas comedy:
Some carry-tale, some please-man, some slight zany,
Some mumble-news, some trencher-knight, some Dick,—
That smiles his cheek in years;[a] and knows the trick
To make my lady laugh, when she 's dispos'd,—
Told our intents before: which once disclos'd,
The ladies did change favours; and then we,
Following the signs, woo'd but the sign of she.
Now to our perjury to add more terror,
We are again forsworn: in will, and error.
Much upon this it is:*—And might not you, [*To* BOYET.
Forestal our sport, to make us thus untrue?
Do not you know my lady's foot by the squire,[b]
And laugh upon the apple of her eye?
And stand between her back, sir, and the fire,
Holding a trencher, jesting merrily?
You put our page out: Go, you are allow'd;[c]
Die when you will, a smock shall be your shroud.
You leer upon me, do you? there 's an eye,
Wounds like a leaden sword.

BOYET. Full merrily
Hath this brave manage,[d] this career, been run.

BIRON. Lo, he is tilting straight! Peace; I have done.

Enter COSTARD.

Welcome, pure wit! thou partest a fair fray.

COST. O Lord, sir, they would know,
Whether the three Worthies shall come in, or no.

BIRON. What, are there but three?

COST. No, sir; but it is vara fine,
For every one pursents three.

BIRON. And three times thrice is nine.

COST. Not so, sir: under correction, sir; I hope, it is not so:
You cannot beg us,(6) sir, I can assure you, sir; we know what we know;
I hope, sir, three times thrice, sir,—

BIRON. Is not nine.

COST. Under correction, sir, we know whereuntil it doth amount.

BIRON. By Jove, I always took three threes for nine.

COST. O Lord, sir, it were pity you should get your living by reckoning, sir.

BIRON. How much is it?

COST. O Lord, sir, the parties themselves, the actors, sir, will show whereuntil it doth amount: for mine own part, I am, as they say, but to parfect one man, in one poor man; Pompion the great, sir.

BIRON. Art thou one of the Worthies?

COST. It pleased them to think me worthy of Pompey the great;[e] for mine own part, I know not the degree of the Worthy; but I am to stand for him.

BIRON. Go, bid them prepare.

COST. We will turn it finely off, sir; we will take some care. [*Exit* COSTARD.

KING. Biron, they will shame us, let them not approach.

BIRON. We are shame-proof, my lord: and 't is some policy
To have one show worse than the king's and his company.

KING. I say, they shall not come.

PRIN. Nay, my good lord, let me o'er-rule you now:
That sport best pleases that doth least know how:
Where zeal strives to content, and the contents
Dies in the zeal of that which it presents,[f]
Their form confounded makes most form in mirth;
When great things labouring perish in their birth.

BIRON. A right description of our sport, my lord.

(*) Old copies, *'tis.*

[a] *That smiles his cheek* in years;] One that by incessant grinning wears his face into wrinkles. Thus, in the "Merchant of Venice," Act I. Sc. 1,—

"With mirth and *laughter* let old *wrinkles* come."

[b] *By the* squire,—] From the French *esquiere, a square,* or *rule.*

[c] Go, you are allow'd;] That is, you are *hired, licensed* as a fool or jester,—

"There is no slander in an *allow'd* fool."
Twelfth Night, Act I. Sc. 5.

[d] *Hath this brave* manage,—] The quarto has *nuage,* and the folio, 1623, *manager.*

[e] Pompey *the great;*] Some surprise has been expressed at Costard's first pronouncing the name *Pompion,* and then giving it, immediately after, correctly; but his former speeches show either that his rusticity is merely assumed, and put on and off at pleasure, or that Shakespeare had never finally settled whether to make him a fool natural or artificial, and so left him neither one nor the other.

[f] Where zeal strives to content, and the contents
Dies in the zeal of that which it presents,—]

This passage, as it stands, looks like a printer's jumble. Some editors have attempted to render it intelligible by substituting *die* for *dies,* and *them* for *that;* and others, *lies,* in place of *dies.* Perhaps we should read:—

Where zeal strives to content, and *discontent*
Dies in the zeal of them which it present.

Shakespeare has before indulged in the same antithesis,—

"Sister, *content* you in my *discontent.*"
Taming of the Shrew, Act I. Sc. 1.

Enter ARMADO.

ARM. Anointed, I implore so much expense of thy royal sweet breath, as will utter a brace of words. [ARMADO *converses with the* KING, *and delivers him a paper.*

PRIN. Doth this man serve God?

BIRON. Why ask you?

PRIN. He speaks not like a man of God's making.

ARM. That 's all one, my fair, sweet, honey monarch: for, I protest, the schoolmaster is exceedingly fantastical; too-too vain; too-too vain: But we will put it, as they say, to *fortuna della guerra.** I wish you the peace of mind, most royal couplement! [*Exit* ARMADO.

KING. Here is like to be a good presence of Worthies: He presents Hector of Troy; the swain, Pompey the great; the parish curate, Alexander; Armado's page, Hercules; the pedant, Judas Machabæus.
And if these four Worthies in their first show thrive,
These four will change habits, and present the other five.

BIRON. There is five in the first show.

KING. You are deceiv'd, 't is not so.

BIRON. The pedant, the braggart, the hedge-priest, the fool, and the boy:—
Abate[a] throw at novum; and the whole world again
Cannot prick out five such, take each one in his vein.

KING. The ship is under sail, and here she comes amain.

[*Seats brought for the* KING, PRINCESS, *&c.*

Pageant of the Nine Worthies.(7)

Enter COSTARD, *armed, for* Pompey.

COST. *I Pompey am,*—

BOYET. You lie,[b] you are not he.

COST. *I Pompey am,*—

BOYET. With libbard's head on knee.

BIRON. Well said, old mocker; I must needs be friends with thee.

COST. *I Pompey am, Pompey surnam'd the big,*—

DUM. *The great.*

COST. It is *great*, sir;—*Pompey surnam'd the great;*
That oft in field, with targe and shield, did make my foe to sweat:
And travelling along this coast, I here am come by chance;
And lay my arms before the legs of this sweet lass of France.
If your ladyship would say, *Thanks, Pompey,* I had done.

PRIN. Great thanks, great Pompey.

COST. 'T is not so much worth; but, I hope, I was perfect: I made a little fault in *great.*

BIRON. My hat to a halfpenny, Pompey proves the best Worthy.

Enter NATHANIEL, *armed, for* Alexander.

NATH. *When in the world I liv'd, I was the world's commander;*
By east, west, north, and south, I spread my conquering might:
My 'scutcheon plain declares that I am Alisander.

BOYET. Your nose says, no, you are not; for it stands too right.

BIRON. Your nose smells, no, in this, most tender-smelling knight.

PRIN. The conqueror is dismay'd: Proceed, good Alexander.

NATH. *When in the world I liv'd, I was the world's commander.*

BOYET. Most true, 't is right; you were so, Alisander.

BIRON. Pompey the great,—

COST. Your servant, and Costard.

BIRON. Take away the conqueror, take away Alisander.

COST. O, sir [*to* NATH.], you have overthrown Alisander the conqueror! You will be scraped out of the painted cloth for this: your lion, that holds his poll-ax sitting on a close stool, will be given to A-jax: he will be the ninth Worthy. A conqueror, and afeard* to speak! run away for shame, Alisander. [NATH. *retires.*] There, an 't shall please you; a foolish mild man; an honest man, look you, and soon dash'd! He is a marvellous good neighbour, in sooth; and a very good bowler: but, for Alisander, alas, you see how 't is;—a little o'erparted:—But there are Worthies a coming will speak their mind in some other sort.

PRIN. Stand aside, good Pompey.

(*) Old editions, *fortuna delaguar.*

a Abate throw at novum;] *Novum,* or *novem,* was a game played with dice, at which five and nine appear to have been the best throws; but what *abate* means here, has yet to be shown. The usual reading is,—

"Abate *a* throw," &c.

(*) First folio, *afraid.*

b *You* lie,—] We must suppose that, on his entrance, Costard prostrates himself before the court; hence Boyet's joke.

Enter HOLOFERNES *for* Judas, *and* MOTH *for* Hercules.

HOL. *Great Hercules is presented by this imp,*
Whose club kill'd Cerberus, that three-headed canus ;
And when he was a babe, a child, a shrimp,
Thus did he strangle serpents in his manus :
Quoniam, *he seemeth in minority ;*
Ergo, *I come with this apology.*—
Keep some state in thy *exit,* and vanish.
[*Exit* MOTH.
Judas, I am,—

DUM. A Judas!

HOL. Not Iscariot, sir,—
Judas, I am, ycleped Machabæus.

DUM. Judas Machabæus clipt, is plain Judas.

BIRON. A kissing traitor:—How art thou prov'd Judas?

HOL. *Judas, I am,*—

DUM. The more shame for you, Judas.

HOL. What mean you, sir?

BOYET. To make Judas hang himself.

HOL. Begin, sir; you are my elder.

BIRON. Well followed: Judas was hang'd on an elder.

HOL. I will not be put out of countenance.

BIRON. Because thou hast no face.

HOL. What is this?

BOYET. A cittern-head.

DUM. The head of a bodkin.

BIRON. A death's face in a ring.

LONG. The face of an old Roman coin, scarce seen.

BOYET. The pummel of Cæsar's faulchion.

DUM. The carved bone face[a] on a flask.

BIRON. St. George's half-cheek in a brooch.

DUM. Ay, and in a brooch of lead.

BIRON. Ay, and worn in the cap of a tooth-drawer. And now, forward; for we have put thee in countenance.

HOL. You have put me out of countenance.

BIRON. False: we have given thee faces.

HOL. But you have out-fac'd them all.

BIRON. An thou wert a lion, we would do so.

BOYET. Therefore, as he is an ass, let him go. And so adieu, sweet Jude! nay, why dost thou stay?

DUM. For the latter end of his name.

BIRON. For the ass to the Jude; give it him:—Jud-as,(8) away!

HOL. This is not generous; not gentle; not humble.

BOYET. A light for monsieur Judas: it grows dark, he may stumble.

PRIN. Alas, poor Machabæus, how hath he been baited!

Enter ARMADO, *armed, for* Hector.

BIRON. Hide thy head, Achilles; here comes Hector in arms.

DUM. Though my mocks come home by me, I will now be merry.

KING. Hector was but a Trojan in respect of this.

BOYET. But is this Hector?

DUM. I think Hector was not so clean-timbered.

LONG. His leg is too big for Hector.

DUM. More calf, certain.

BOYET. No; he is best indued in the small.

BIRON. This cannot be Hector.

DUM. He's a god or a painter; for he makes faces.

ARM. *The armipotent Mars, of lances the almighty,*
Gave Hector a gift,—

DUM. A gilt nutmeg.

BIRON. A lemon.

LONG. Stuck with cloves.

DUM. No, cloven.

ARM. Peace! *
The armipotent Mars, of lances the almighty,
Gave Hector a gift, the heir of Ilion:
A man so breath'd that certain he would fight ye
From morn till night, out of his pavilion.
I am that flower,—

DUM. That mint.

LONG. That columbine.

ARM. Sweet lord Longaville, rein thy tongue.

LONG. I must rather give it the rein, for it runs against Hector.

DUM. Ay, and Hector's a greyhound.

ARM. The sweet war-man is dead and rotten; sweet chucks, beat not the bones of the buried: when he breathed, he was a man[b]—But I will forward with my device: Sweet royalty [*to the* PRINCESS], bestow on me the sense of hearing.
[BIRON *whispers* COSTARD.

PRIN. Speak, brave Hector: we are much delighted.

ARM. I do adore thy sweet grace's slipper.

BOYET. Loves her by the foot.

DUM. He may not by the yard.

ARM. *This Hector far surmounted Hannibal,*—

COST. The party is gone, fellow Hector, she is gone; she is two months on her way.

[a] — bone face *on a flask.*] *Query, Boni-face,* or *Bon-face?*
[b] When he breathed, he was a man—] These words are from the quarto. The folio, 1623, omits them.

(*) First folio omits *Peace.* (†) Old copies, *yea.*

ARM. What meanest thou?

COST. Faith, unless you play the honest Trojan, the poor wench is cast away: she 's quick; the child brags in her belly already; 't is yours.

ARM. Dost thou infamonize me among potentates? thou shalt die.

COST. Then shall Hector be whipped for Jaquenetta that is quick by him; and hanged for Pompey that is dead by him.

DUM. Most rare Pompey!

BOYET. Renowned Pompey!

BIRON. Greater than great, great, great, great Pompey! Pompey the huge!

DUM. Hector trembles.

BIRON. Pompey is moved:—More Ates, more Ates; stir them on! stir them on!

DUM. Hector will challenge him.

BIRON. Ay, if he have no more man's blood in 's belly than will sup a flea.

ARM. By the north pole, I do challenge thee.

COST. I will not fight with a pole, like a northern man; I 'll slash; I 'll do it by the sword:—I pray you, let me borrow my arms again.

DUM. Room for the incensed Worthies.

COST. I 'll do it in my shirt.

DUM. Most resolute Pompey!

MOTH. Master, let me take you a button-hole lower. Do you not see, Pompey is uncasing for the combat? What mean you? you will lose your reputation.

ARM. Gentlemen, and soldiers, pardon me; I will not combat in my shirt.

DUM. You may not deny it; Pompey hath made the challenge.

ARM. Sweet bloods, I both may and will.

BIRON. What reason have you for 't?

ARM. The naked truth of it is, I have no shirt; I go woolward for penance.[a]

BOYET. True, and it was enjoin'd him in Rome for want of linen: since when, I 'll be sworn, he wore none but a dishclout of Jaquenetta's; and that 'a * wears next his heart, for a favour.

Enter MERCADE.

MER. God save you, madam!

PRIN. Welcome, Mercade;
But that thou interrupt'st our merriment.

MER. I am sorry, madam; for the news I bring
Is heavy in my tongue. The king, your father—

PRIN. Dead, for my life.

MER. Even so; my tale is told.

BIRON. Worthies, away; the scene begins to cloud.

ARM. For mine own part, I breathe free breath: I have seen the day of wrong through the little hole of discretion, and I will right myself like a soldier. [*Exeunt* Worthies.

KING. How fares your majesty?

PRIN. Boyet, prepare; I will away to-night.

KING. Madam, not so; I do beseech you, stay.

PRIN. Prepare, I say.—I thank you, gracious lords,
For all your fair endeavours; and entreat,
Out of a new-sad soul, that you vouchsafe
In your rich wisdom, to excuse, or hide,
The liberal opposition of our spirits:
If over-boldly we have borne ourselves
In the converse of breath, your gentleness
Was guilty of it.—Farewell, worthy lord!
A heavy heart bears not a humble tongue:[b]
Excuse me so, coming too * short of thanks
For my great suit so easily obtain'd.

KING. The extreme parts[c] of time extremely forms
All causes to the purpose of his speed;
And often, at his very loose, decides
That which long process could not arbitrate:
And though the mourning brow of progeny
Forbid the smiling courtesy of love,
The holy suit which fain it would convince;[d]
Yet, since love's argument was first on foot,
Let not the cloud of sorrow justle it
From what it purpos'd; since, to wail friends lost,
Is not by much so wholesome-profitable,
As to rejoice at friends but newly found.

PRIN. I understand you not; my griefs are double.[e]

(*) Folio, 1623, *he*.

a *I go* woolward *for penance*.] To go *woolward*, i. e. to go with a woollen garment next the skin, was a penance appointed for pilgrims and penitents; and from this arose the saying, when any one was shirtless, that he went *woolward*. Thus, in Lodge's "Incarnate Devils," 1596,—"His common course is to go always untrust; except when his *shirt is a washing*, and then he goes *woolward*."

And in Samuel Rowland's collection of Epigrams and Satyres, which he quaintly intitules, "The Letting of Humour's blood in the Head-Vaine," &c., Satyre 4:—

"He takes a common course to goe untrust,
Except his shirt 's a washing; then he must
Goe *wool-ward* for the time."

b A *heavy heart bears not* a humble *tongue*:] I am very doubtful of the genuineness of this line; the true lection is probably,—

"A heavy heart bears *but* a humble tongue."

Or, as Theobald suggested,—

"A heavy heart bears not a *nimble* tongue."

c *The extreme* parts *of time*—] The word *parts* here is an admitted misprint. Mr. Singer proposes to substitute *haste*. Mr. Collier's corrector rewrites the line,—

"The extreme *parting* time *expressly* forms," &c.

A much slighter change will render the sense clear. I would read,—

"The extreme *dart* of time extremely forms
All causes to the purpose of his speed," &c.

And I am strengthened in my belief that *parts* is a corruption for *dart* or *shaft* by the next line,—

"And often, at his very *loose*, decides," &c.

To *loose* an arrow is to discharge it from the bow:—"th' Archers terme, who is not said to finish the feate of his shot before he give the *loose*, and deliuer his arrow from his bow."—PUTTENHAM'S *Arte of English Poesie*, 1589, p. 145.

Thus, in "Midsummer-Night's Dream," Act II. Sc. 1,—

"And *loos'd* his love-shaft smartly from his bow,
As it should pierce a hundred thousand hearts."

So also in Ben Jonson's "Every Man out of His Humour," Act III. Sc. 3 (Gifford's Edition): "—— her brain 's a very quiver of jests! and she does dart them abroad with that sweet *loose*, and judicial aim, that you would —" &c. Where, from not knowing, strangely enough, the technical meaning of this term, the accomplished editor has punctuated the passage thus,—"She does dart them abroad with that sweet, loose, and judicial aim," &c.

By the *extreme dart* of time, the King means as he directly after explains it,—"The latest minute of the hour."

(*) First folio, *so*.

d *Which fain it would* convince;] *To convince* is *to conquer, to overcome*. So in "Macbeth," Act I. Sc. 7,

"—— his two chamberlains
Will I with wine and wassel so *convince*," &c.

e *I understand you not; my griefs are* double.] For *double*, which seems a very inapposite expression, Mr. Collier's corrector suggests *dull*,—a good conjecture; but, as coming nearer to the letters in the text, I think it more likely the poet wrote,

"—— my griefs *hear dully*."

Which, besides, appears to lead more naturally to Biron's rejoinder:—

"Honest plain words best pierce the ear of grief."

BIRON. Honest plain words best pierce the ear* of grief;—
And by these badges understand the king.
For your fair sakes have we neglected time;
Play'd foul play with our oaths: your beauty, ladies,
Hath much deform'd us, fashioning our humours
Even to the opposed end of our intents;
And what in us hath seem'd ridiculous,—
As love is full of unbefitting strains,
All wanton as a child, skipping, and vain;
Form'd by the eye, and, therefore, like the eye,
Full of strange† shapes, of habits, and of forms,
Varying in subjects as the eye doth roll
To every varied object in his glance:
Which party-coated presence of loose love
Put on by us, if, in your heavenly eyes,
Have misbecom'd our oaths and gravities,
Those heavenly eyes, that look into these faults,
Suggested us to make: Therefore, ladies,
Our love being yours, the error that love makes
Is likewise yours: we to ourselves prove false,
By being once false, for ever to be true
To those that make us both,—fair ladies, you:
And even that falsehood, in itself a sin,
Thus purifies itself, and turns to grace.

PRIN. We have receiv'd your letters, full of love;
Your favours, the ambassadors of love;
And, in our maiden council, rated them
At courtship, pleasant jest, and courtesy,
As bombast, and as lining to the time;[a]
But more devout than this, in ‡ our respects,
Have we not been; and therefore met your loves
In their own fashion, like a merriment.

DUM. Our letters, madam, show'd much more than jest.

LONG. So did our looks.

ROS. We did not quote § them so.

KING. Now, at the latest minute of the hour,
Grant us your loves.

PRIN. A time, methinks, too short
To make a world-without-end bargain in:
No, no, my lord, your grace is perjur'd much,
Full of dear guiltiness; and, therefore this,—
If for my love (as there is no such cause)
You will do aught, this shall you do for me:
Your oath I will not trust; but go with speed
To some forlorn and naked hermitage,
Remote from all the pleasures of the world;
There stay, until the twelve celestial signs
Have brought about their annual reckoning:
If this austere insociable life
Change not your offer made in heat of blood;
If frosts, and fasts, hard lodging, and thin weeds,
Nip not the gaudy blossoms of your love,
But that it bear this trial, and last love;[b]
Then, at the expiration of the year,
Come challenge me, challenge me by these deserts,
And, by this virgin palm, now kissing thine,
I will be thine; and, till that instant, shut
My woeful self up in a mourning house,
Raining the tears of lamentation
For the remembrance of my father's death.
If this thou do deny, let our hands part,
Neither intitled in the other's heart.

KING. If this, or more than this, I would deny,
To flatter up these powers of mine with rest,
The sudden hand of death close up mine eye!
Hence ever, then, my heart is in thy breast.[c]

DUM. But what to me, my love? but what to me?

KATH. A wife!—A beard, fair health, and honesty;
With three-fold love I wish you all these three.

DUM. O, shall I say, I thank you, gentle wife?

KATH. Not so, my lord;—a twelvemonth and a day,
I'll mark no words that smooth-fac'd wooers say:
Come when the king doth to my lady come,
Then, if I have much love, I'll give you some.

DUM. I'll serve thee true and faithfully till then.

KATH. Yet swear not, lest you be forsworn agen.[d]

LONG. What says Maria?

MAR. At the twelvemonth's end,
I'll change my black gown for a faithful friend.

LONG. I'll stay with patience; but the time is long.

MAR. The liker you; few taller are so young.

BIRON. Studies my lady? mistress, look on me,
Behold the window of my heart, mine eye,
What humble suit attends thy answer there;
Impose some service on me for thy* love.

(*) First folio, *ears*. † Old copies, *straying*.
(‡) The quarto omits *in*. First folio reads *these are*.
(§) First folio, *coat*.

(*) First folio, *my*.

a *As* bombast, *and as lining to the time*;] *Bombast* was a sort of wadding used to fill out the dresses formerly.

b — and last love;] The old copies concur in this reading, but *love* is not improbably a misprint for *proof*,—

"But that it bear this trial and last proof."

c In the old copies, and in most of the modern editions also, the following lines now occur:—

"BIRON. And what to me, my love? and what to me?
ROS. You must be purged too, your sins are rank;
You are attaint with faults and perjury;
Therefore if you my favour mean to get,
A twelvemonth shall you spend, and never rest,
But seek the weary beds of people sick."

On comparing these five lines of Rosaline with her subsequent speech, of which they are a comparatively tame and feeble abridgement, it is evident that Biron's question and the lady's reply in this place are only part of the poet's first draft, and were intended by him to be struck out when the Play was augmented and corrected. Their retention in the text answers no purpose but to detract from the force and elegance of Rosaline's expanded answer immediately afterwards, and to weaken the dramatic interest of the two leading characters. See Note (4) of the Illustrative Comments on Act IV.

d —*forsworn* agen.] So the old copies, and rightly. Modern editors, regardless of the rhyme, have substituted, *again*.

Ros. Oft have I heard of you, my lord Biron,
Before I saw you; and the world's large tongue
Proclaims you for a man replete with mocks;
Full of comparisons and wounding flouts,
Which you on all estates will execute,
That lie within the mercy of your wit:
To weed this wormwood from your fruitful brain,
And, therewithal, to win me, if you please,
(Without the which I am not to be won,)
You shall this twelvemonth term, from day to day,
Visit the speechless sick, and still converse
With groaning wretches; and your task shall be,
With all the fierce endeavour of your wit,
To enforce the pained impotent to smile.

Biron. To move wild laughter in the throat of death?
It cannot be; it is impossible:
Mirth cannot move a soul in agony.

Ros. Why, that 's the way to choke a gibing spirit,
Whose influence is begot of that loose grace
Which shallow laughing hearers give to fools:
A jest's prosperity lies in the ear
Of him that hears it, never in the tongue
Of him that makes it: then, if sickly ears,
Deaf'd with the clamours of their own dear groans,
Will hear your idle scorns, continue then,
And I will have you, and that fault withal;
But, if they will not, throw away that spirit,
And I shall find you, empty of that fault,
Right joyful of your reformation.

Biron. A twelvemonth? well, befal what will befal,
I 'll jest a twelvemonth in an hospital.

Prin. Ay, sweet my lord; and so I take my leave. [*To the* King.

King. No, madam, we will bring you on your way.

Biron. Our wooing doth not end like an old play;
Jack hath not Jill: these ladies' courtesy
Might well have made our sport a comedy.

King. Come, sir, it wants a twelvemonth and a day,
And then 't will end.

Biron. That 's too long for a play.

Enter Armado.

Arm. Sweet majesty vouchsafe me,—

Prin. Was not that Hector?

Dum. The worthy knight of Troy.

Arm. I will kiss thy royal finger, and take leave: I am a votary; I have vowed to Jaquenetta to hold the plough for her sweet love three years. But, most esteemed greatness, will you hear the dialogue that the two learned men have compiled, in praise of the owl and the cuckoo? it should have followed in the end of our show.

King. Call them forth quickly, we will do so.

Arm. Holla! approach.

Enter Holofernes, Nathaniel, Moth, Costard, *and others.**

This side is Hiems, winter: this Ver, the spring: the one maintained by the owl, the other by the cuckoo. Ver, begin.

The Song.

I.

Spring. *When daisies pied,*[a] *and violets blue,*
And lady-smocks all silver white,
And cuckoo-buds of yellow hue,[b]
Do paint the meadows with delight,
The cuckoo then, on every tree,
Mocks married men, for thus sings he,
Cuckoo;
Cuckoo, cuckoo,—O word of fear,
Unpleasing to a married ear!

II.

When shepherds pipe on oaten straws,
And merry larks are ploughmen's clocks,
When turtles tread, and rooks, and daws,
And maidens bleach their summer-smocks,
The cuckoo then, on every tree,
Mocks married men, for thus sings he,
Cuckoo;
Cuckoo, cuckoo,—O word of fear,
Unpleasing to a married ear!

III.

Winter. *When icicles hang by the wall,*
And Dick *the shepherd blows his nail,*
And Tom *bears logs into the hall,*
And milk comes frozen home in pail,
When blood is nipp'd, and ways be foul,
Then nightly sings the staring owl,
To-who;[c]
Tu-whit, to-who, a merry note,
While greasy Joan *doth keel the pot.*

[a] *When daisies pied,—*] *Pied* means *party-coloured*, of *different hues*. Thus, in the "Merchant of Venice," Act I. Sc. 3:—

"That all the eanlings which were streaked and *pied*."

[b] And cuckoo buds of yellow hue,] In the old copies the four first lines of the stanza are arranged in couplets, and run thus:—

"When daisies pied, and violets blue,
And cuckoo-buds of yellow hue,
And lady-smocks all silver white,
Do paint the meadows with delight."

But, as in all the other stanzas the rhymes are alternate, this was most probably an error of the compositor; and I have adopted the transposition, which Theobald was the first to make.

[c] To-who;] A modern addition, to correspond with "cuckoo" in the previous verses, and without which the two last verses could hardly be sung to the same tune.

* First folio, *Enter all.*

IV.

When all aloud the wind doth blow,
And coughing drowns the parson's saw,
And birds sit brooding in the snow,
And Marian's *nose looks red and raw;*
When roasted crabs hiss in the bowl,
Then nightly sings the staring owl,
To-who;
Tu-whit, to-who, a merry note,
While greasy Joan *doth keel the pot.*

ARM. The words of Mercury are harsh after the songs of Apollo. You, that way; we, this way. [*Exeunt.*

ILLUSTRATIVE COMMENTS.

ACT I.

(1) Scene I.—

> — *brave conquerors! —for so you are,*
> *That war against your own affections,*
> *And the huge army of the world's desires.*]

There is a passage in "The Hystorie of Hamblet, Prince of Denmarke," (London, 1608,) which strikingly resembles the above both in thought and expression. It is there said that Hamlet "in all his honorable actions made himselfe worthy of perpetuall memorie, if one onely spotte had not blemished and darkened a good part of his prayses. For that *the greatest victorie that a man can obtaine is to make himselfe victorious and lord over his owne affections, and that restraineth the unbridled desires of his concupiscence;*" see Mr. Collier's reprint in "Shakespeare's Library," vol. i. p. 180.

(2) Scene I.—*A high hope for a low heaven.*] Upon maturer consideration, I am disposed to believe the *low heaven*, and the *god* from whom Biron expected *high words*, refer to the *Stage* Heaven, and its hectoring Jupiter, whose lofty, huff-cap style was a favourite topic for ridicule.

> "If Jove speak English in a thundering cloud,
> 'Thwick, thwack,' and 'riff-raff,' roars he out aloud."
> Hall's *Satires, Book I. Sat. VI.*

See an interesting and suggestive article on the *Heaven* of the old theatres in "A Specimen of a Commentary on Shakspeare," by W. Whiter, 1794, pp. 153—166.

(3) Scene II.—*You are a gentleman, and a gamester.*] Of the extent to which the practice of gambling was carried in Shakespeare's time, we have abundant testimony in the literature of that period. There are few plays or books of any description, illustrative of the social habits of the people, which have not some allusion to this prevalent vice. According to Drake, it "had become almost universal in the days of Elizabeth; and," he remarks, "if we may credit George Whetstone,* had reached a prodigious degree of excess. Speaking of the licentiousness of the stage previous to the appearance of Shakspeare, he adds:—'But, there are in the bowels of this famous citie, farre more daungerous playes, & little reprehended: that wicked playes of the dice, first invented by the devyll, (as Cornelius Agrippa wryteth) & frequented by unhappy men: the detestable roote, upon which a thousand villanies growe.

"'The nurses of thease (worse than heathnysh) hellish exercises are places called *ordinary tables:* of which there are in London more in nomber, to honor the devyll, then churches to serve the living God.—P. 24.

"'I cōstantly determine to crosse the streets where these vile houses (ordinaries) are planted, to blesse me from thē enticements of thē, which in very deed are many, and the more dangerous, in that they please with a vain hope of gain. Insomuch on a time, I heard a distemperate dicer solemnly sweare that he faithfully beleeved, *that dice were first made of the bones of a witch, & cards of her skin,* in which there hath ever sithence remained an inchantment, y[t] whosoever once taketh delight in either, he shall never have power utterly to leave them; for quoth he, I a hundred times vowed to leave both, yet have not the grace to forsake either.'—P. 32.

"No opportunity for the practice of this ruinous habit seems to have been omitted, and we find the modern mode of gambling, by taking the odds, to have been fully established towards the latter end of the sixteenth century; for Gilbert Talbot, writing to his father, the Earl of Shrewsbury, on May the 15th, 1579, after informing His Lordship that the matter of the Queen's marriage with Monsieur 'is growne very colde,' subjoins, 'and yet I know a man may take a thousande pounds, in this towne, to be bounde to pay doble so muche when Mons[r] cūmethe into Inglande, and treble so muche when he marryethe the Q. Ma[tie], and if he nether doe the one nor the other, to gayne the thousande poundes cleare.'"

(4) Scene II.—*The dancing horse will tell you.*] This famous quadruped and his exploits are often referred to by the old writers. He was called *Marocco*, but is usually mentioned as "Bankes's horse," from the name of his owner, and appears to have been an animal of wonderful aptitude and docility. His first exhibition is said to have been in 1589; and Sir Kenelm Digby observes, that he "would restore a glove to the due owner, after the master had whispered the man's name in his ear; would tell the just number of pence in any piece of silver coin, newly showed him by his master," &c.—*A Treatise on Bodies*, c. xxxviii. p. 393.

His most celebrated performance was the ascent to the top of St. Paul's, in 1600, an exploit referred to in Decker's "Gull's Horn-Booke," 1609:—"from hence you may descend to talk about the horse that went up; and strive if you can to know his keeper;" &c. And also in the Blacke Booke, by Middleton, 1604:—"May not the devil, I pray you, walk in Paul's, as well as the horse go a' top of Paul's, for I am sure I was not far from his keeper."

In a rare quarto, called "Tarlton's Jests," &c. published in 1611, we are told,—"There was one Banks (in the time of Tarlton), who served the Earle of Essex, and had a horse of strange qualities; and being at the Crosse-keyes in Gracious street, getting money with him, as he was mightily resorted to; Tarlton, then (with his fellowes) playing at the Bell by, came into the Crosse-keyes (amongst many people) to see fashions; which Banks perceiving, (to make the people laugh,) saies, 'Signor,' (to his horse,) 'go fetch me the veryest foole in the company.' The jade comes immediately, and with his mouth drawes Tarlton forth. Tarlton (with merry words) said nothing but '*God a mercy, horse!*' In the end, Tarlton, seeing the people laugh so, was angry inwardly, and said, 'Sir, had I power of your horse, as you have, I would do more than that.' 'Whate'er it be,' said Banks (to please

* See the *second* part of his work, "The Enemie to Unthryftinesse" (1586), entitled, "An Addition or Touchstone for the times; exposing the dangerous Mischiefes, that the dycing Howses (commonly called) Ordinarie Tables, and other (like) Sanctuaries of Iniquitie do dayly breede within the Bowelles of the famous Citie of London, by George Whetstone, *Gent.*"

him), 'I will charge him to do it.' 'Then,' saies Tarlton, 'charge him to bring me the veriest —— master in the company.' 'He shall,' (saies Banks.) 'Signor,' (saies he,) 'bring master Tarlton here, the veriest —— master in the company.' The horse leades his master to him. '*Then, God a mercy, horse, indeed!*' saies Tarlton. The people had much ado to keep peace; but Banks and Tarlton had like to have squared, and the horse by to give aim. But ever after it was a by-word thorow London, '*God a mercy, horse!*' and is to this day."

In 1601 he was exhibited at the Golden Lion, Rue Saint Jaques, in Paris; and in the notes to a French translation of the "Golden Ass" of Apuleius, by Jean de Montlyard, Sieur de Melleray, first pointed out by Douce, he is described as *a middle-sized bay English gelding, about fourteen years old.* This work furnishes a very good account of his tricks, which seem to have been much of the same description as those practised by the learned pigs, dogs, and horses of our own time. While in France, poor Bankes and his curtail ran a narrow escape of being sacrificed as magicians,—a fate it has been feared, from a passage in Ben Jonson's 134th Epigram, and a note in the mock-romance of "Don Zara del Fogo," 1660, which really did befal them not long afterwards in Rome.

(5) SCENE II.—*Is there not a ballad, boy, of the King and the beggar?*] Two versions of this once popular ditty have come down to us. The elder is probably that printed in "Percy's Reliques," vol. i. p. 183, ed. 1767, from Richard Johnson's "Crown garland of Goulden Roses," 1612, and intituled, "A Song of a Beggar and a King." Whether this was the original of which Moth declares "The world was very guilty some three ages since," it is not easy to determine. It begins:—

"I read that once in Affrica,
A princely wight did raine,
Who had to name Cophetua,
As poets they did faine.
From nature's laws he did decline,
For sure he was not of my mind,
He cared not for women-kinde,
But did them all disdaine.
But marke what hapned on a day,
As he out of his window lay
He saw a beggar all in gray,
The which did cause his paine."

The second stanza is memorable, from Mercutio's quoting the opening line:—

"Young Abraham Cupid, he that *shot so trim*,
When King Cophetua lov'd the beggar-maid."
Romeo and Juliet, Act II. Sc. 1.

"The blinded boy that shootes so trim
From heaven downe did hie;
He drew a dart and shot at him
In place where he did lye;
Which soone did pierse him to the quicke,
And when he felt the arrow pricke,
Which in his tender heart did sticke,
He looketh as he would dye.
What sudden chance is this, quoth he,
That I to love must subject be,
Which never thereto would agree,
But still did it defie?"

There are in all ten stanzas, of which that descriptive of the wedding of the king with "Penelophon" is, perhaps, the best:—

"And when the wedding day was come
The king commanded strait
The noblemen, both all and some,
Upon the queene to wait.
And she behav'd herself that day
As if she had never walk't the way;
She had forgot her gowne of gray,
Which she did weare of late.
The proverbe old is come to passe,
The priest when he begins his masse,
Forgets that ever clerke l e was;
He knowth not his estate."

ACT II.

(1) SCENE I.—
His face's own margent did quote such amazes,
That all eyes saw his eyes enchanted with gazes.]

In the "Rape of Lucrece" we have the same metaphor:—

"But she, that never cop'd with stranger eyes,
Could pick no meaning from their parling looks,
Nor read the subtle shining secrecies
Writ in the glassy *margent* of such books."

Shakespeare was evidently fond of resembling the face to a book, and having once arrived at this similitude, the comparison, however odd, of the eyes to the margin, wherein of old the commentary on the text was printed, is not altogether unnatural. The following passage, which presents both the primary and subordinate metaphor, is the best example he has given us of this peculiar association of ideas:—

"What say you? can you love the gentleman?
This night you shall behold him at our feast;
Read o'er the *volume* of young Paris' *face*,
And find delight writ there with beauty's pen;
Examine every married lineament,
And see how one another lends content;
And what obscur'd in this fair *volume* lies,
Find written in the *margent* of his eyes."
Romeo and Juliet, Act I. Sc. 3.

ACT III.

(1) SCENE I.—*Concolinel,——* [*Singing.*]

This might have been the beginning, or the title of some *pastorale*, usually sung here by the actor who represented Moth.

Steevens has cited several passages to show that the songs introduced in the old Plays were frequently left to the taste of the singer. From among the instances he has produced, the following are sufficiently decisive:—

"In Marston's "Dutch Courtesan," 1605:—"*Cantat Gallice.*" But no song is set down. In the same Play, Act V.:—

"*Cantat sallatque cum Cithara.*"

"Not one out of the many songs supposed to be sung in Marston's 'Antonio's Revenge,' 1602, are inserted; but instead of them, *cantant.*"—STEEVENS.

He has shown, too, that occasionally a still greater latitude was allowed to the players. In Greene's "Tu Quoque," 1614, the stage direction says:—

"Here they two talk and rail *what they list.*"

And in "King Edward IV. Part II." 1619:—

"Jockey is led whipping over the stage, speaking some words, but of no importance."

(2) SCENE I.—*Master, will you win your love with a French brawl?*] Marston, in his "Malcontent," describes this dance, but in a way that is quite unintelligible. It appears to have been performed by several persons joined hand to hand in a circle, and to have been the opening dance of a ball. Douce quotes the following account of "*Le branle du bouquet*," from "*Deux dialogues du nouveau langage François, Italianizé*," &c. Anvers, 1579, 24mo:—"Un des gentil-hommes et une des dames, estans les premiers en la danse, laissent les autres (qui cependant continuent la danse) et se mettans dedans la dicte compagnie, *vont baisans par ordre toutes les personnes qui y sont:* à sçavoir le gentil-homme les dames, et la dame les gentilshommes. Puis ayans achevé leurs baisemens, au lieu qu'ils estoyent les premiers en la danse, se mettent les derniers. Et ceste façon de faire se continue par le gentilhomme et la dame qui sont les plus prochains, jusques à ce qu'on vienne aux derniers."—P. 385.

In Thoinot Arbeau's curious treatise on dancing, intituled "Orchesographie," Lengres, 1588, 4to, there is a *Scottish brawl,* the music of which is given in Douce's "Illustrations of Shakspeare," Vol. I. p. 219.

(3) SCENE I.—*By my penny of observation, &c.*] *Penny,* in days of yore, was used metaphorically to signify money, or means generally. In vol. i. p. 400, of the celebrated "Roxburgh Collection of Ballads," in the British Museum, is an old ballad,—"There's nothing to be had without Money;" the burden of which is, "But God a mercy penny." It is much too long to quote in full; but a few of the stanzas may be amusing to those who are not familiar with the quaint old lays which solaced and delighted our forefathers:—

"1. You gallants, and you swaggering blades,
Give ear unto my ditty;
I am a boon companion known
In country, town, or city;
I always lov'd to wear good clothes,
And ever scorned to take blows;
I am belov'd of all me know,
But God a mercy penny.

2. My father was a man well known,
That us'd to hoard up money;
His bags of gold, he said, to him
More sweeter were than honey.
But I, his son, will let it fly
In tavern, or in ordinary;
I am beloved in company,
But God a mercy penny.

8. Bear garden, when I do frequent,
Or the Globe on the Bankside,
They afford to me most rare content
As I full oft have tried.
The best pastime that they can make
They instantly will undertake,
For my delight and pleasure sake,
But God a mercy penny.

9. In every place whereas I came,
Both I and my sweet penny,
Got entertainment in the same,
And got the love of many;
Both tapsters, cooks, and vintners fine,
With other jovial friends of mine,
Will pledge my health in beer or wine,
But God a mercy penny."

If further proof of this figurative use of *penny* is required, it may readily be found in our old comedies; but perhaps the following will be sufficient:—

"—— a man may buy it with *his penny.*"
All Fools, Act IV. Sc. 1.

"She had purchased with *her penny.*"
BEAUMONT AND FLETCHER'S *Wit without Money.*
Act IV. Sc. 3.

(4) SCENE I.—*The hobby-horse is forgot.*] "The Morris and the May-game of Robin Hood attained their most perfect form," Drake remarks, "when united with the *Hobby-horse* and the *Dragon.* Of these, the former was the resemblance of the head and tail of a horse, manufactured in pasteboard, and attached to a person, whose business it was, whilst he seemed to ride gracefully on its back, to imitate the prancings and curvetings of that noble animal, whose supposed feet were concealed by a footcloth reaching to the ground." Considerable practice, and some little skill, must have been required for the most perfect specimens of this burlesque *manege.* In "The Vow Breaker" of Sampson, one of these centaurs, enraged with the mayor of the town for being his rival, exclaims,—"Let the mayor play the hobby-horse among his brethren, an he will, I hope our towne-lads cannot want a hobby-horse. Have I practic'd my reines, my careeres, my pranckers, my ambles, my false trotts, my smooth ambles and Canterbury paces, and shall master mayor put me besides the hobby-horse?"

One of the first steps taken by the puritanical zealots of those days, for the suppression of the ancient May-day sports, was to prohibit this popular favourite; and the playwrights and ballad-mongers seem never weary of satirizing his banishment by their ludicrous repining. Shakespeare again refers to it in "Hamlet," Act III. Sc. 2:—

"For O, for O, the *hobby-horse* is forgot."

And Ben Jonson, in his "Entertainment for the Queen and Prince at Althorpe:—

"But see *the hobby-horse is forgot.*
Fool, it must be your lot,
To supply his want with faces
And some other buffoon graces."

So, too, Beaumont and Fletcher, in their "Women Pleased," Act IV. Sc. 1:—

"Shall *the hobby-horse be forgot, then,*
The hopeful *hobby-horse,* shall he lie founder'd?"

And in Greene's "Tu Quoque," 1614:

"The other *hobby-horse,* I perceive, is not forgotten."

(5) SCENE I.—*Like a German clock.*] The earliest clocks used in this country came from Germany, and from their cumbrous, inartificial construction were likely to be often out of gear. Weston tells us he heard a French proverb that compared anything intricate and out of order to the coq de Strasburg, that belonged to the machinery of the town clock. The first clock of English manufacture is said to be the one at Hampton Court; which, according to the inscription once attached to it, was set up in 1540. Shakespeare is not singular in comparing a woman, from the elaboration of her toilet, to the complicated mechanism of a German clock. Ben Jonson, in his "Silent Woman," Act IV. Sc. 1. (Gifford's Ed.), has the same simile:—

"She takes herself asunder still when she goes to bed, into some twenty boxes; and about next day noon is put together again, like a great *German clock.*"

So, also, Middleton, in "A Mad World, My Masters," 1608:—

"What, is she took asunder from her clothes?
Being ready she consists of hundred pieces,
Much like a *German clock,* and near ally'd."

Thus, too, Decker and Webster in "Westward Hoe!" 1607:—

"No *German clock,* no mathematical engine
Whatsoever, requires such reparation."

ACT IV.

(1) SCENE I.—*A Monarcho.*] This *Monarcho* was a crazy Italian, to whom allusion is made by many writers of the age. His mania consisted in believing himself king of the world!—

"Sole Monarch of the universal earth."

In "A Brief Discourse of the Spanish State," &c. 4to 1590, p. 39, the following incident connected with his delusion is recorded:—"The actors were, that Bergamasco (for his phantastick humors) named *Monarcho*, and two of the Spanish embassadors retinue, who being about foure and twenty years past, in Paules Church in London, contended who was soveraigne of the world; the *Monarcho* maintained himself to be he, and named their King to be but his viceroy for Spain; the other two with great fury denying it." &c.

Churchyard wrote an epitaph, published in 1580, on this poor crack-brained being; an extract from which, as it contains the best account of him yet discovered, may not be unacceptable:—

"THE PHANTASTICALL *Monarckes* EPITAPHE.

"Though Dant be dedde, and Marrot lies in graue,
And Petrark's sprite bee mounted past our vewe,
Yet some doe liue (that poets humours haue)
To keepe old course with vains of verses newe:
Whose penns are prest to paint out people plaine,
That els a sleepe in silence should remaine:
Come poore old man that boare the *Monarks* name,
Thyne Epitaphe shall here set forthe thy fame.

Thy climyng mynde aspierd beyonde the starrs,
Thy loftie stile no yearthly titell bore:
Thy witts would seem to see through peace and warrs,
Thy tauntyng tong was pleasant sharpe and sore.
And though thy pride and pompe was somewhat vaine,
The *Monarcke* had a deepe discoursyng braine:
Alone with freend he could of wonders treate,
In publike place pronounce a sentence greate.

* * * * * *

When straungers came in presence any wheare,
Straunge was the talke the *Monarke* uttred than:
He had a voice could thonder through the eare,
And speake mutche like a merry Christmas man:
But sure small mirthe his matter harped on.
His forme of life who lists to look upon,
Did shewe some witte, though follie fedde his will:
The man is dedde, yet *Monarks* liueth still."

(2) SCENE II.—'*Twas a pricket.*] In the Play called "The Return from Parnassus," 1606, we have the several appellations of the deer at his different stages of growth:—"Now, sir, a Bucke the first yeare is a Fawne; the second yeare a *pricket;* the third yeare a Sorell; the fourth yeare a Soare; the fift, a Buck of the first head; the sixt yeare a compleat Buck."

(3) SCENE II.—

——*Vinegia, Vinegia,*
Chi non te vede, ei non te pregia.]

A well-known proverbial sentence. In Howell's "Letters," b. I. sect. i. l. 36, it is quoted thus:—

"*Venetia, Venetia, chi non te vede, non te pregia,*
Ma chi t'ha troppo veduto le dispregia."

"Venice, Venice, none thee unseen can prize,
Who thee hath seen too much, will thee despise."

(4) SCENE III. *For when would you, my lord, or you, or you.*] In the present speech, as in that of Rosaline (p. 97), we appear to have got both the first sketch and the completed form of the poet's intention, which makes it extremely probable that the 4to. 1598, was composed from his own MS. There can be little doubt that the passage beginning as above, and the one lower down, both enclosed in brackets, commencing—

"For where is any author in the world,"

are a portion of the original draft of Biron's address, and were meant by the author to be erased after he corrected and enlarged the play. In a subsequent part of the speech we have the same ideas, and even the same expressions. It has been contended, indeed, that these repetitions were intentional, and the iteration an artifice of rhetoric; but Shakespeare never repeats himself unnecessarily, and it is too much to believe that he would lengthen out an address, already long enough, by conveying the same thoughts in the same language. The words, too, "With ourselves," which in the old copies occur under a line that bears a similar expression, point irresistibly to the conclusion, that the passages indicated were inadvertently left uncancelled, and so got into print with the amended version.

ACT V.

(1) SCENE I. *A quick venew of wit.*] The meaning of *venew*, or *venue*, a term used of old by fencers, was made the subject of a very animated war of words between Steevens and Malone, the former defining it to be a *bout*, or *set-to*, and the latter, a *hit*. Mr. Douce has shown clearly that *venue, stoccato,* and *imbrocato* denoted the same thing—a *hit, thrust, foin,* or *touch.* See Saviolo's treatise, called "Use of the rapier and dagger," 4to. 1595; Florio's Italian dictionary, 1598; and Howel's "Lexicon tetraglotton," 1660.

(2) SCENE II. *To tread a measure with her on the grass.*] A *measure* seems originally to have meant any dance the motions of which kept due touch to music:—

"And dancing is a moving all in *measure.*"
Orchestra, by SIR JOHN DAVIES, 1622.

In time, however, it obtained a more precise signification, and was used to denote a movement slow, stately, and sweeping, like the modern minuet, which appears to be of the same character, and its legitimate successor:—

"But after these, as men more civil grew,
He did more *grave and solemn measures frame*
With such fair order and proportion true,
And correspondence ev'ry way the same,
That no fault-finding eye did ever blame."—*Orchestra.*

The *measures,* Reed tells us, "were performed at court, and at public entertainments of the societies of law and equity, at their halls, on particular occasions. It was formerly not deemed inconsistent with propriety even for the gravest persons to join in them; and accordingly at the revels which were celebrated at the inns of court, it has not been unusual for the first characters in the law to become performers in *treading the measures.*"

In "Riche his Farewell to Militarie Profession," Lond. 1581, there is a description of the *Measure* and other popular dances of the period too amusing to be omitted:—"Firste for dauncyng, although I like the *measures* verie well, yet I could never treade them aright, nor to use measure in any thyng that I went aboute, although I desired to performe all thynges by line and by leavell, what so ever I tooke in hande. Our *galliardes* are so curious, that thei are not for my daunsyng, for thei are so full of trickes and tournes, that he whiche hath no more but the plaine *sinquepace* is no better accoumpted of then a verie bongler; and for my part thei might assone teache me to make a capricornus, as a capre in the right kinde that it should bee.

"For a *jeigge* my heeles are too heavie: and these *braules* are so busie, that I love not to beate my braines about them.

"A *rounde* is too giddie a daunce for my diet; for let the dauncers runne about with as much speede as thei maie, yet are thei never a whit the nier to the ende of their course, unlesse with often tourning thei hap to catch a fall; and so thei ende the daunce with shame, that was begonne but in sporte.

"These *hornepipes* I have hated from my verie youth; and I knowe there are many other that love them as well as I.

"Thus you may perceive that there is no daunce but either I like not of theim, or thei like not of me, so that I can daunce neither."

(3) SCENE II. *Well, better wits have worn plain statute-caps.*] Johnson opined that the *statute-caps* alluded to were those worn by members of the Universities. "Lady Rosaline declares that her expectations were disappointed by these courtly students, and that *better wits* might be found in the common places of education." But in 1571, it was ordered by *Statute,* that citizens should wear woollen caps on Sundays and holidays, to encourage the trade of cappers; the more probable meaning, therefore, as Steevens suggested, is—*better wits* may *be found among the citizens,* an interpretation which is well supported by the following quotations: "— though my husband be a citizen, and his *cap's made of wool,* yet I have wit."—Marston's "Dutch Courtezan," 1605. "'Tis a law enacted by the common council of *statute-caps.*"—"The Family of Love," 1608. "— in a bowling alley in a *flat cap* like a shop-keeper."—"Newes from Hell," &c. 1606.

(4) SCENE II.—*He can carve too and lisp.*] Mr. Hunter ("New Illustrations of Shakespeare," vol. i. p. 215) was the first to point out that the commentators were all wrong in supposing that the word *carve* here, and the same expression in "The Merry Wives of Windsor," Act I. Sc. 3:—

"she discourses, she *carves,* she gives the leer of invitation;"

denoted the particular action of carving food at table. "*Carving,*" he remarks, "would seem to mean some form of action which indicated the desire that the person to whom it was addressed should be attentive and propitious." It was reserved for an American critic, Mr. R. G. White, to show by a happy illustration from Sir Thomas Overbury's "Characters," "her wrie little finger bewraies *carving,*" that the "form of action," acutely surmised by Mr. Hunter, was a sign of recognition made with the little finger, probably when the glass was raised to the mouth. (See "Shakespeare's Scholar," 8vo. New York, 1854, p. xxxiii.)

The following are instances, adduced by Mr. Hunter and Mr. Dyce, in which the word is used with this meaning:—

"Then did this Queen her wandering coach ascend,
Whose wheels were more inconstant than the wind:
A mighty troop this empress did attend;
There might you Caius Marius *carving* find
And martial Sylla courting Venus kind."
A description of Fortune from "A Prophecie of Cadwallader, last King of the Brittaines," by WILLIAM HERBERT, *4to.,* 1604.

"her amorous glances are her accusers, her very looks write Sonnets in thy commendations; she *carves* thee at boord, and cannot sleepe for dreaming on thee in bedde."—DAY'S *Ile of Guls,* 1606, Sig. D.

"And if thy rival be in presence too,
Seem not to mark, but do as others do;
Salute him friendly, give him gentle words,
Return all courtesies that he affords;
Drink to him, *carve* him, give him compliment;
This shall thy mistress more than thee torment."
BEAUMONT'S *Remedy of Love.*

(5) SCENE II. *Write* Lord have mercy on us, *on those three.*] During the plague, every infected or *visited* house was strictly guarded night and day that no person should leave it, and large red crosses were painted upon the doors and windows, over which was inscribed, LORD HAVE MERCY UPON US.

"But by the way he saw and much respected
A doore belonging to a house infected,
Whereon was plac'd (as 'tis the custom still)
The Lord have mercy on us; this sad bill
The sot perus'd ——."
Epigrams, by R. S., entitled "More Fools yet," 1610.

We have the same allusion in Sir Thomas Overbury's "Characters," art. "A Prison." Ed. 1616:—"*Lord have mercy upon us,* may well stand over these doores, for debt is a most dangerous and catching city pestilence."

The expression, the *Lord's tokens,* four lines lower, is a continuation of the metaphor; the discolourations, or *plague-spots* on the skin of an infected person, were commonly called "*The Lord's tokens.*"

(6) SCENE II.—*You cannot beg us.*] Allusive to a practice formerly prevalent of *begging the wardship* of *idiots and lunatics* from the sovereign, who was the legal guardian, in order to gain possession of their property. This odious custom is a source of constant satire to the old dramatists. In illustration of it, there is an amusing story extracted by Douce from the Harleian MSS. in the British Museum, No. 6395.

"The Lord North begg'd old Bladwell for a foole (though he could never prove him so), and having him in custodie as a lunaticke, he carried him to a gentleman's house, one day, that was his neighbour. The L. North and the gentleman retir'd awhile to private discourse, and left Bladwell in the dining roome, which was hung with a faire hanging; Bladwell walking up and downe, and viewing the imagerie, spyed a foole at last in the hanging, and without delay drawes his knife, flyes at the foole, cutts him cleane out, and layes him on the floore; my L., and the gentl. coming in againe, and finding the tapestrie thus defac'd, he ask'd Bladwell what he meant by such a rude uncivill act; he answered, Sr. be content, I have rather done you a courtesie than a wrong, for if ever my L. N. had seene the foole there, he would have begg'd him, and so you might have lost your whole suite."

(7) SCENE II.—*Pageant of the Nine Worthies.*] The Nine Worthies, originally comprising Joshua, David,

Judas Maccabæus, Hector, Alexander, Julius Cæsar, Arthur, Charlemagne, and Godfrey of Bulloigne, appear from a very early period to have been introduced occasionally in the shows and pageants of our ancestors. Ritson has extracted a curious specimen of the rude poetry spoken by the characters in a performance of this nature, from the original Manuscript, *temp.* Edward IV. (MSS. Tanner, 407).

IX. Wurthy.

ECTOR DE TROYE.	Thow Achylles in bataly me slow Of my wurthynes men speken i-now.
ALISANDER.	And in romaunce often am I leyt As conqueror gret thow I seyt.
JULIUS CESAR.	Thow my cenatoures me slow in Conllory, Fele londes byfore by conquest wan I.
JOSUE.	In holy Chyrche ye mowen here and rede Of my wurthynes and of my dede.
DAVIT.	Aftyr that slayn was Golyas By me the Sawter than made was.
JUDAS MACABEUS.	Of my wurthynesse, zyf ze wyll wete Seche the Byble, for ther it is wrete.
ARTHOUR.	The Round Tabyll I sette with knyghtes strong, Zyt shall I come agen, thow it be long.
CHARLES.	With me dwellyd Rouland Olyvere In all my conquest fer and nere.
GODEFREY DE BOLEYN.	And I was kyng of Iherusalem The crowne of thorn I wan fro hem.

In the Harl. MSS. 2057, f. 36, there is the draft of a show "Intended to be made upon the petition to Mr. Recorder, Aug. 1, 1621," of which the Nine Worthies form a part; and from the description it gives of these personages and their esquires, they must have presented a very imposing spectacle.

"The 9 wortheys in compleat armor with Crownes of gould on there heads, every on having his esq[s] to beare before him his sheild and penon of armes, dressed according as there lords where accostumed to be: 3 Issaralits, 3 Infidels, 3 Christians, &c."

As Shakespeare introduces Hercules and Pompey among his presence of Worthies, we may infer that the characters were sometimes varied to suit the circumstances of the period, or the taste of the auditory. A MS. preserved in the library of Trinity College, Dublin, mentions the *Six Worthies* having been played before the Lord Deputy Sussex in 1557.

(8) SCENE II.—
For the ass to the Jude; give it him:—Jud-as, away!]

Biron's quibble has not even the merit of novelty, but with the unfastidious audience of Shakespeare's age, that was far from indispensable to a joke's prosperity. It occurs as early as 1566, in Heywood's Poems, and if worth the search might probably be traced still further back,—

"ON AN YLL GOVERNOUR CALLED JUDE.

"A ruler there was in a countrey a fer,
And of people a greate extorcioner:
Who by name (as I understand) was caled Jude,
One gave him an asse, which gyft when he had veude,
He asked the gever, for what intent
He brought him that asse. For a present
I bryng maister Jude (quoth he) this as hyther,
To joygne maister Jude and this asse together.
Whiche two joygned in one, this is brought to pas,
I maie byd you good even maister Judas.
Macabe or Iscariot thou knave (quoth he?)
Whom it please your mastership, him let it be."

CRITICAL OPINIONS

ON

LOVE'S LABOUR'S LOST.

"Of 'Love's Labour's Lost,' as it was performed in the year 1591, we possess no exact transcript; for, in the oldest edition which has hitherto been found of this Play, namely that of 1598, it is said in the title-page to be *newly corrected and augmented*, with the further information, that it had been *presented before Her Highness the last Christmas;* facts which show that we are in possession not of the first draft or edition of this comedy, but only of that copy which represents it as it was *revived* and *improved* for the entertainment of the Queen, in 1597.

"The *original sketch*, whether printed or merely performed, we conceive to have been one of the pieces alluded to by Greene, in 1592, when he accuses Shakespeare of being *an absolute Johannes fac-totum* of the stage, *primarily* and *principally* from the mode of its execution, which, as we have already observed, betrays the earliness of its source in the strongest manner; *secondarily*, that, like *Pericles*, it occasionally copies the language of the *Arcadia*, then with all the attractive *novelty* of its reputation in full bloom;* and, *thirdly*, that, in the fifth Act, various allusions to the Muscovites or Russians seem evidently to point to a period when Russia and its inhabitants attracted the public consideration, a period which we find, from Hackluyt,† to have occupied the years 1590 and 1591, when, as Warburton and Chalmers have observed, the arrangement of Russian commerce engaged very particularly the attention, and formed the conversation of the court, the city, and the country.‡

"It may be also remarked, that while no Play among our author's works exhibits more decisive marks of juvenility than *Love's Labour's Lost*, none, at the same time, is more strongly imbued with the peculiar cast of his youthful genius; for in style and manner it bears a closer resemblance to the *Venus and Adonis*, the *Rape of Lucrece*, and the *earlier Sonnets*, than any other of his genuine dramas. It presents us, in short, with a continued contest of wit and repartee; the persons represented, whether high or low, vying with each other throughout the piece, in the production of the greatest number of jokes, sallies, and verbal equivoques. The profusion with which these are every-where scattered, has, unfortunately, had the effect of throwing an air of uniformity over all the characters, who seem solely intent on keeping up the ball of raillery; yet is *Biron* now and then discriminated by a few strong touches, and *Holofernes* is probably the portrait of an individual, some of his quotations having justly induced the commentators to infer, that *Florio*, the author of *First* and *Second Fruits*, dialogues in Italian and English, and of a *Dictionary* entitled *A World of Words*, was the object of the poet's satire.

"If in dramatic strength of painting this comedy be deficient, and it appears to us, in this quality, inferior to *Pericles*, we must, independent of the vivacity of its dialogue already noticed, acknowledge, that it displays several poetical gems, that it contains many just moral apophthegms, and that it affords, even in the closet, no small fund of amusement; and here it is worthy of being remarked, and may, indeed, without prejudice or prepossession, be asserted, that, even to the earliest and most unfinished

---

* Vide Chalmers's Supplemental Apology, pp, 281, 282; and Douce's Illustrations, vol. i. p. 238.

† Vol. i. p. 498-9, edit. 1598.

‡ Reed's Shakespeare, vol. vii. p. 151, note; and Chalmers's Supplemental Apology, p. 283.

dramas of our poet, a peculiar interest is felt to be attached, not arising from the fascination of a name, but from an intrinsic and almost inexplicable power of pleasing, which we in vain look for in the juvenile plays of other bards, and which serves, perhaps better than any other criterion, to ascertain the genuine property of Shakspeare ; it is, in fact, a touchstone, which, when applied to *Titus Andronicus*, and what has been termed the *First Part* of Henry the Sixth, must, if every other evidence were wanting, flash conviction on our senses."—DRAKE.

"I can never sufficiently admire the wonderful activity of thought throughout the whole of the first scene of this play, rendered natural, as it is, by the choice of the characters, and the whimsical determination on which the drama is founded. A whimsical determination certainly ;—yet not altogether so very improbable to those who are conversant in the history of the middle ages, with their Courts of Love, and all that lighter drapery of chivalry which engaged even mighty kings with a sort of serio-comic interest, and may well be supposed to have occupied more completely the smaller princes, at a time when the noble's or prince's court contained the only theatre of the domain or principality. This sort of story, too, was admirably suited to Shakspeare's times, when the English court was still the foster-mother of the state and the muses ; and when, in consequence, the courtiers, and men of rank and fashion, affected a display of wit, point, and sententious observation, that would be deemed intolerable at present,—but in which a hundred years of controversy, involving every great political, and every dear domestic, interest, had trained all but the lowest classes to participate. Add to this, the very style of the sermons of the time, and the eagerness of the Protestants to distinguish themselves by long and frequent preaching, and it will be found that, from the reign of Henry the Eighth to the abdication of James the Second, no country ever received such a national education as England.

"Hence the comic matter chosen in the first instance is a ridiculous imitation or apery of this constant striving after logical precision, and subtle opposition of thoughts, together with a making the most of every conception or image, by expressing it under the least expected property belonging to it, and this, again, rendered specially absurd by being applied to the most current subjects and occurrences. The phrases and modes of combination in argument were caught by the most ignorant from the custom of the age, and their ridiculous misapplication of them is most amusingly exhibited in Costard ; whilst examples suited only to the gravest propositions and impersonations, or apostrophes to abstract thoughts impersonated, which are in fact the natural language only of the most vehement agitations of the mind, are adopted by the coxcombry of Armado as mere artifices of ornament.

"The same kind of intellectual action is exhibited in a more serious and elevated strain in many other parts of this play. Biron's speech at the end of the fourth act is an excellent specimen of it. It is logic clothed in rhetoric ;—but observe how Shakspeare, in his two-fold being of poet and philosopher, avails himself of it to convey profound truths in the most lively images,—the whole remaining faithful to the character supposed to utter the lines, and the expressions themselves constituting a further development of that character. This speech is quite a study ;—sometimes you see this youthful god of poetry connecting disparate thoughts purely by means of resemblances in the words expressing them,—a thing in character in lighter comedy, especially of that kind in which Shakspeare delights, namely, the purposed display of wit, though sometimes, too, disfiguring his graver scenes ;—but more often you may see him doubling the natural connection or order of logical consequence in the thoughts, by the introduction of an artificial and sought-for resemblance in the words, as, for instance, in the third line of the play :—

'And then grace us in the disgrace of death ;'—

this being a figure often having its force and propriety, as justified by the law of passion, which, inducing in the mind an unusual activity, seeks for means to waste its superfluity,—when in the highest degree—in lyric repetitions and sublime tautology—(*at her feet he bowed, he fell, he lay down ; at her feet he bowed, he fell; where he bowed, there he fell down dead,*)—and, in lower degrees, in making the words themselves the subjects and materials of that surplus action, and for the same cause that agitates our limbs, and forces our very gestures into a tempest in states of high excitement.

"The mere style of narration in 'Love's Labour 's Lost,' like that of Ægeon in the first scene of the Comedy of Errors, and of the Captain in the second scene of Macbeth, seems imitated with its defects and its beauties from Sir Philip Sidney; whose Arcadia, though not then published, was already well known in manuscript copies, and could hardly have escaped the notice and admiration of Shakspeare as the friend and client of the Earl of Southampton. The chief defect consists in the parentheses and parenthetic thoughts and descriptions, suited neither to the passion of the speaker, nor the purpose of the person to whom the information is to be given, but manifestly betraying the author himself,—not by way of continuous under-song, but—palpably, and so as to show themselves addressed to the general reader. However, it is not unimportant to notice how strong a presumption the diction and allusions of this play afford, that, though Shakspeare's acquirements in the dead languages might not be such as we suppose in a learned education, his habits had, nevertheless, been scholastic, and those of a student. For a young author's first work almost always bespeaks his recent pursuits, and his first observations of life are either drawn from the immediate employments of his youth, and from the characters and images most deeply impressed on his mind in the situations in which those employments had placed him;—or else they are fixed on such objects and occurrences in the world, as are easily connected with, and seem to bear upon, his studies and the hitherto exclusive subjects of his meditation. Just as Ben Jonson, who applied himself to the drama after having served in Flanders, fills his earliest plays with true or pretended soldiers, the wrongs and neglects of the former, and the absurd boasts and knavery of their counterfeits. So Lessing's first comedies are placed in the universities, and consist of events and characters conceivable in an academic life."—COLERIDGE.

"LOVE'S LABOUR'S LOST is numbered among the pieces of Shakspeare's youth. It is a humorsome display of frolic; a whole cornucopia of the most vivacious jokes is emptied into it. Youth is certainly perceivable in the lavish superfluity of labour in the execution; the unbroken succession of plays on words, and sallies of every description, hardly leave the spectator time to breathe; the sparkles of wit fly about in such profusion, that they resemble a blaze of fireworks; while the dialogue, for the most part, is in the same hurried style in which the passing masks at a carnival attempt to banter each other. The young king of Navarre, with three of his courtiers, has made a vow to pass three years in rigid retirement, and devote them to the study of wisdom; for that purpose he has banished all female society from his court, and imposed a penalty on the intercourse with women. But scarcely has he, in a pompous harangue, worthy of the most heroic achievements, announced this determination, when the daughter of the king of France appears at his court, in the name of her old and bed-ridden father, to demand the restitution of a province which he held in pledge. Compelled to give her audience, he falls immediately in love with her. Matters fare no better with his companions, who on their parts renew an old acquaintance with the princess's attendants. Each, in heart, is already false to his vow, without knowing that the wish is shared by his associates; they overhear one another, as they in turn confide their sorrows in a love-ditty to the solitary forest; every one jeers and confounds the one who follows him. Biron, who from the beginning was the most satirical among them, at last steps forth, and rallies the king and the two others, till the discovery of a love-letter forces him also to hang down his head. He extricates himself and his companions from their dilemma by ridiculing the folly of the broken vow, and after a noble eulogy on women, invites them to swear new allegiance to the colours of love. This scene is inimitable, and the crowning beauty of the whole. The manner in which they afterwards prosecute their love-suits in masks and disguise, and in which they are tricked and laughed at by the ladies, who are also masked and disguised, is, perhaps, spun out too long. It may be thought, too, that the poet, when he suddenly announces the death of the king of France, and makes the princess postpone her answer to the young prince's serious advances till the expiration of the period of her mourning, and impose, besides, a heavy penance on him for his levity, drops the proper comic tone. But the tone of raillery which prevails throughout the piece, made it hardly possible to bring about a more satisfactory conclusion: after such extravagance, the characters could not return to sobriety, except under the presence of some foreign influence. The grotesque figures of Don Armado, a pompous fantastic Spaniard, a couple of pedants, and a clown, who between whiles contribute to the entertainment, are the creation of a whimsical imagination, and well adapted as foils for the wit of so vivacious a society."—SCHLEGEL.

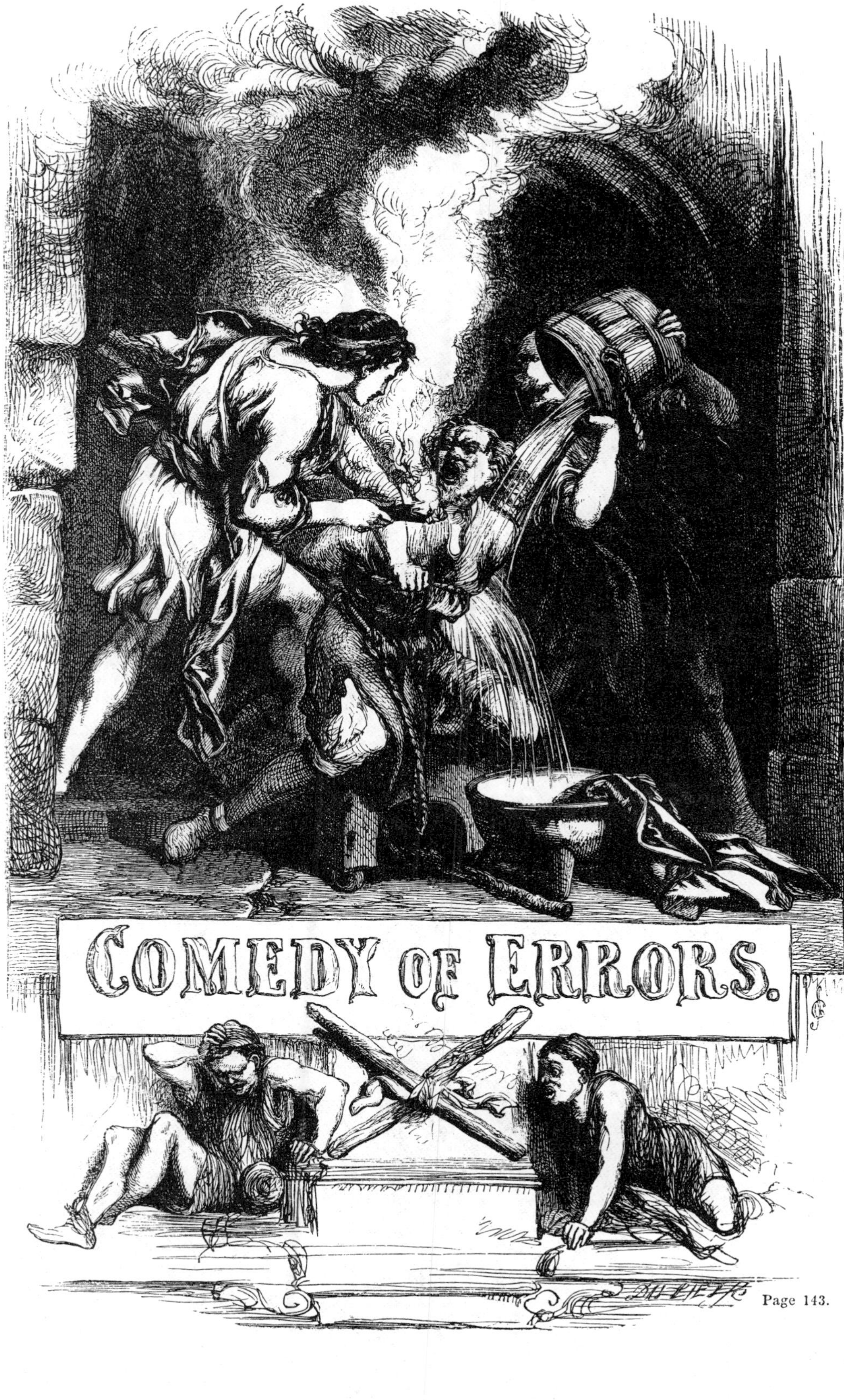

Page 143.

THE

COMEDY OF ERRORS.

"The Comedie of Errors" is one of those plays no copy of which has been discovered prior to that in the folio of 1623. It is noticed by Meres, (Palladis Tamia, 1598,) and, in all probability, was written, and acted first, in the very dawn of Shakespeare's genius. The main incident appears to have been taken from the *Menœchmi* of Plautus, but whether directly, or through the medium of some early translation of the Roman comedy, will most likely remain a subject of interesting speculation to editors and commentators for ages yet unborn.

Steevens conceived that our author was indebted to an English version by W. W[arner], printed in 1595, but there are circumstances which militate strongly against this presumption. In the first place, we have almost decisive proof that the present play was publicly performed a year before Warner's *Menœchmi* appeared, since in the Gesta Grayorum of 1594 (published in 4to, 1688) is the following entry:—"After such sports, a Comedy of Errors (like to Plautus his Menechmus) was played by the players; so that night was begun and continued to the end, in nothing but confusion and errors; whereupon it was ever afterwards called the Night of Errors." (P. 22.) Again, it is reasonable to expect, if Shakespeare had adopted Warner's version for the groundwork of his play, that some coincidence in the names of the characters, or at least some parallelism in the ideas and turns of expression, would be evident in the two works; but none has been detected. Another circumstance adverse to Steevens' conjecture, is the fact that the brothers Antipholus in Shakespeare's comedy are respectively distinguished, in the opening scenes, as Antipholus *Erotes*, or *Errotis*, and Antipholus *Sereptus* (corruptions, perhaps, of *erraticus* and *surreptus*), appellatives which are not found in Warner.* Taken singly, these facts are not of much weight, but together, they certainly tend to prove that the youthful dramatist either went at once to Plautus for so much of his fable and characters as are borrowed, or took them from some other source than the *Menœchmi* of Warner. The latter is the more probable and popular hypothesis. Without assenting to the opinion of those Commentators who deny to Shakespeare any acquaintance with Greek and Latin (languages, it should be remembered, which were better and more extensively cultivated in his day than in ours), we may safely suppose that,—engrossed as his time and mind must have been as an actor, a shareholder in the theatre, and a dramatic writer, whenever he had more than one source at command for the derivation of his story, he preferred that which gave him the least trouble to apprehend. That it was his practice, where the subject of his plot is taken from the ancients, to resort to existing translations, rather than apply to the originals themselves, we know, indeed, by comparing Coriolanus, Julius Cæsar, Antony and Cleopatra, &c. &c., with the translation of Plutarch extant in his time. The question then arises, did any English version of the *Menœchmi*, besides that by Warner, exist before the "Comedy of Errors" was written. We believe there did. The indefatigable Malone was the first to discover evidence of an old play called "The Historie of Error," which, according to the Accounts of the Revels in Queen Elizabeth's Court preserved in the Audit Office, was acted at Hampton Court on New Year's Night, 1576-77, "by the children of Powles."†

The same accounts contain an entry, under the date of 1582-3, which may be assumed to refer to this play, although the title, through the ignorance or carelessness of the scribe, is misprinted, "A Historie of *Ferrar* shewed before her Majestie at Wyndesor on Twelfdaie at night, enacted by the Lord Chamberlayne's servauntes," &c.

* In Plautus, these personages are designated,
Menæchmus Surreptus.
Menæchmus Sosicles.

† See Cunningham's Extracts from the Accounts of the Revels, p. 102.

In "The Historic of Error," then, we have possibly the foundation of Shakespeare's "Comedy of Errors," and the source whence he adopted the designations *erraticus* and *surreptus*, which the players or printers corrupted into *Erotes* and *Sereptus*.

Mr. Halliwell has observed that the title of this comedy was either a common proverb, or furnished the subject of one; and in his magnificent edition of the great dramatist he adduces the following instances where it is mentioned by contemporary writers:—"Anton, in his Philosophical Satires, 1616, p. 51, exclaims—'What Comedies of Errors swell the stage!' So also Decker, in his Knights Conjuring, 1607—'His ignorance, arising from his blindeness, is the onely cause of this Comedie of Errors;' and previously, in his Satiro-mastix, 1602, he seems to allude to the play itself—'Instead of the trumpets sounding thrice before the play begin, it shall not be amisse, for him that will read, first to behold this short Comedy of Errors, and where the greatest enter, to give them instead of a hisse, a gentle correction.' Again also, in the Meeting of Gallants at an Ordinarie, 1604,—'This was a prettie Comedie of Errors, my round host.'"

How long before the notice of it by Meres in 1598 the Comedy of Errors was acted, we can only conjecture from internal indications. The "long hobbling verses," as Blackstone termed them, that are found in it, and which were a marked peculiarity in the old plays anterior to Shakespeare's day, would alone determine it to have been one of his youthful efforts. Theobald was of opinion, too, that Dromio's reply (Act III. Sc. 2), to the question where he found France in the "globe"-like kitchen wench,—

> "In her forehead; arm'd and reverted, making war against her *heir*,"

was an allusion to the civil wars in France upon the succession of Henry IV. of Navarre; whose claim as *heir* was resisted by the States of France on account of his being a Protestant. If any such *equivoque* between hair and *heir* were really intended, which is fairly presumable, this passage would serve to fix the date of the play somewhere between 1589, when the war began, and 1593, the period of its termination.

Persons Represented.

SOLINUS, *duke of* EPHESUS.
ÆGEON, *a merchant of* SYRACUSE.
ANTIPHOLUS *of* EPHESUS, ANTIPHOLUS *of* SYRACUSE, } *Twin brothers, sons to* ÆGEON *and* ÆMILIA, *but unknown to each other.*
DROMIO *of* EPHESUS, DROMIO *of* SYRACUSE, } *Twin brothers, and attendants on the two Antipholuses.*
BALTHAZAR, *a merchant.*
ANGELO, *a goldsmith.*
A Merchant, friend to ANTIPHOLUS *of* SYRACUSE.
A Merchant, trading with ANGELO.*
PINCH, *a schoolmaster, and a conjurer.*

ÆMILIA, *wife to* ÆGEON, *an Abbess at* EPHESUS.
ADRIANA, *wife to* ANTIPHOLUS *of* EPHESUS.
LUCIANA, *her sister.*
LUCE, *her servant.*
A Courtezan.
Gaoler, Officers, and other Attendants.

SCENE.—EPHESUS.

* This personage, who plays no unimportant part in the drama, appears to have been altogether forgotten, or confounded with another character, in every list of the *Dramatis Personæ* of the play that has heretofore been published.

ACT I

SCENE I.—*A Hall in the* Duke's *Palace.*

Enter Duke, Ægeon, Gaoler, Officer, *and other* Attendants.

Æge. Proceed, Solinus, to procure my fall,
And, by the doom of death, end woes and all.
Duke. Merchant of Syracusa, plead no more;
I am not partial to infringe our laws.
The enmity and discord which of late
Sprung from the rancorous outrage of your duke,
To merchants, our well-dealing countrymen,—
Who, wanting guilders to redeem their lives,
Have seal'd his rigorous statutes with their bloods,—
Excludes all pity from our threat'ning looks.
For, since the mortal and intestine jars
'Twixt thy seditious countrymen and us,
It hath in solemn synods been decreed,
Both by the Syracusians and ourselves,
To admit no traffic to our adverse towns.

Nay, more: if any born at Ephesus be seen
At any Syracusian marts and fairs,—
Again, if any Syracusian born
Come to the bay of Ephesus, he dies,
His goods confiscate to the duke's dispose;
Unless a thousand marks be levied
To quit the penalty, and to ransom him.
Thy substance, valued at the highest rate,
Cannot amount unto a hundred marks;
Therefore, by law thou art condemn'd to die.
Æge. Yet this my comfort; when your words are done,
My woes end likewise with the evening sun.
Duke. Well, Syracusian, say in brief the cause
Why thou departedst from thy native home,
And for what cause thou cam'st to Ephesus.
Æge. A heavier task could not have been impos'd,
Than I to speak my griefs unspeakable.
Yet, that the world may witness that my end

Was wrought by nature,[a] not by vile offence,
I'll utter what my sorrow gives me leave.
In Syracusa was I born; and wed
Unto a woman, happy but for me,
And by me too,[b] had not our hap been bad.
With her I liv'd in joy; our wealth increas'd,
By prosperous voyages I often made
To Epidamnum, till my factor's death,
And the great care of goods at random left,[c]
Drew me from kind embracements of my spouse:
From whom my absence was not six months old,
Before herself (almost at fainting under
The pleasing punishment that women bear)
Had made provision for her following me;
And soon and safe arrived where I was.
There had she not been long, but she became
A joyful mother of two goodly sons;
And, which was strange, the one so like the other,
As could not be distinguish'd but by names.
That very hour, and in the self same inn,
A poor[d] mean woman was delivered
Of such a burden—male twins, both alike.
Those,—for their parents were exceeding poor,—
I bought, and brought up to attend my sons.
My wife, not meanly proud of two such boys,
Made daily motions for our home return.

---

[a] *Was wrought by* nature,—] Mr. Collier's corrector substitutes *fortune* for *nature*, a change which is unnecessary. The sense of the original is clear enough:—"My death was not a punishment for criminality, but brought about by the impulses of nature, which led me to Ephesus in search of my son."

[b] *And by me* too,—] The word *too* was added by the editor of the second folio. It was, no doubt, omitted by error in the first.

[c] *And the great care of goods at random left,*—] In the original we have, "And *he*," &c. The emendation, which is easy and happy, we owe to Malone.

[d] *A* poor *mean woman*—] *Poor* is an addition from the folio, 1632. It is questionable, however, whether this is the right word; for, as Malone observes, immediately below we have:—

"— for their parents were exceeding *poor*."

Perhaps, instead of *A mean woman*, the line should read, "A *moaning* woman," *i. e.* a woman in labour.

Unwilling I agreed—alas! too soon we came aboard:
A league from Epidamnum had we sail'd,
Before the always-wind-obeying deep
Gave any tragic instance of our harm;
But longer did we not retain much hope;
For what obscured light the heavens did grant
Did but convey unto our fearful minds
A doubtful warrant of immediate death;
Which, though myself would gladly have embrac'd,
Yet the incessant weepings of my wife,
Weeping before for what she saw must come,
And piteous plainings of the pretty babes,
That mourn'd for fashion, ignorant what to fear,
Forc'd me to seek delays for them and me.
And this it was—for other means was none:
The sailors sought for safety by our boat,
And left the ship, then sinking-ripe, to us.
My wife, more careful for the latter-born,
Had fasten'd him unto a small spare mast,
Such as seafaring men provide for storms:
To him one of the other twins was bound,
Whilst I had been like heedful of the other.
The children thus dispos'd, my wife and I,
Fixing our eyes on whom our care was fix'd,
Fasten'd ourselves at either end the mast;
And, floating straight, obedient to the stream,
Were carried towards Corinth, as we thought.
At length the sun, gazing upon the earth,
Dispers'd those vapours that offended us;
And, by the benefit of his wished light,
The seas wax'd calm, and we discovered
Two ships from far, making amain to us,—
Of Corinth that, of Epidaurus this:
But ere they came——O, let me say no more!
Gather the sequel by that went before.

DUKE. Nay, forward, old man, do not break off so;
For we may pity, though not pardon thee.

ÆGE. O, had the gods done so, I had not now
Worthily term'd them merciless to us!
For, ere the ships could meet by twice five leagues,
We were encounter'd by a mighty rock;
Which, being violently borne upon,*
Our helpful ship was splitted in the midst;
So that, in this unjust divorce of us,
Fortune had left to both of us alike,
What to delight in, what to sorrow for.
Her part, poor soul! seeming as burdened
With lesser weight, but not with lesser woe,
Was carried with more speed before the wind;
And, in our sight, they three were taken up
By fishermen of Corinth, as we thought.
At length another ship had seiz'd on us;
And, knowing whom it was their hap to save,
Gave healthful welcome to their shipwreck'd guests;
And would have reft the fishers of their prey,
Had not their bark been very slow of sail;
And therefore homeward did they bend their course.
Thus have you heard me sever'd from my bliss;
That by misfortunes was my life prolong'd,
To tell sad stories of my own mishaps.

DUKE. And, for the sake of them thou sorrowest for,
Do me the favour to dilate at full,
What hath befall'n of them and thee* till now.

ÆGE. My youngest boy, and yet my eldest care,
At eighteen years became inquisitive
After his brother; and importun'd me
That his attendant (so[a] his case was like,
Reft of his brother, but retain'd his name)
Might bear him company in the quest of him;
Whom, whilst I labour'd of a love to see,
I hazarded the loss of whom I lov'd.
Five summers have I spent in farthest Greece,
Roaming clean through the bounds of Asia,
And, coasting homeward, came to Ephesus;
Hopeless to find, yet loath to leave unsought
Or that or any place that harbours men.
But here must end the story of my life;
And happy were I in my timely death,
Could all my travels warrant me they live.

DUKE. Hapless Ægeon, whom the fates have mark'd
To bear the extremity of dire mishap!
Now, trust me, were it not against our laws,
Against my crown, my oath, my dignity,
Which princes, would they, may not disannul,
My soul should sue as advocate for thee.
But, though thou art adjudged to the death,
And passed sentence may not be recall'd
But to our honour's great disparagement;
Yet will I favour thee in what I can:
Therefore, merchant, I'll limit thee this day,
To seek thy hope by beneficial help:[b]
Try all the friends thou hast in Ephesus;
Beg thou, or borrow, to make up the sum,
And live; if no, then thou art doom'd to die:—
Gaoler, take him to thy custody.

GAOL. I will, my lord.

ÆGE. Hopeless and helpless doth Ægeon wend,
But to procrastinate his liveless end. [*Exeunt.*

(*) First folio, borne *up*.

* First folio, *they*.

[a] So *his case was like*,—] The second folio substituted *for* in place of *so*, and has been followed by most of the subsequent editors. Those who adopt the original reading, "*so his* case was like," interpret it to mean, *his case was so like*. But does it not rather mean, "*as* his case was like,"? This use of *so* we meet again shortly after,—"Am I *so* round with you, *as* you with me?" &c.

[b] *To seek thy* hope *by beneficial help*:] The folio, 1623, has *help*. Pope, and many of the modern editors, read, "To seek thy *life*," &c. Steevens proposed reading:—

"To seek thy help by beneficial *means*."

"To seek thy *fine*" has also been suggested; and is a plausible conjecture: but as Ægeon is made to repeat the Duke's words in *hope*-less, *help*-less, and *live*-less, I have no doubt *hope*, or *holp*, was what the poet wrote.

SCENE II.—*A Public Place.*

Enter ANTIPHOLUS[a] *and* DROMIO *of* Syracuse, *and a* Merchant.

MER. Therefore, give out you are of Epidamnum,
Lest that your goods too soon be confiscate.
This very day a Syracusian merchant
Is apprehended for arrival here;
And, not being able to buy out his life,
According to the statute of the town,
Dies ere the weary sun set in the west.
There is your money that I had to keep.

ANT. S. Go bear it to the Centaur, where we host,
And stay there, Dromio, till I come to thee.
Within this hour it will be dinner-time;
Till that, I'll view the manners of the town,
Peruse the traders, gaze upon the buildings,
And then return, and sleep within mine inn;
For with long travel I am stiff and weary.
Get thee away.

DRO. S. Many a man would take you at your word,
And go indeed, having so good a mean.
[*Exit* DRO. S.

ANT. S. A trusty villain,[b] sir; that very oft,
When I am dull with care and melancholy,
Lightens my humour with his merry jests.
What, will you walk with me about the town,
And then go to my inn, and dine with me?

MER. I am invited, sir, to certain merchants,
Of whom I hope to make much benefit;
I crave your pardon. Soon, at five o'clock,[c]
Please you, I'll meet with you upon the mart,
And afterward consort[d] you till bed-time:
My present business calls me from you now.

ANT. S. Farewell till then; I will go lose myself,
And wander up and down to view the city.

MER. Sir, I commend you to your own content.
[*Exit* Merchant.

ANT. S. He that commends me to mine own content,
Commends me to the thing I cannot get.
I to the world am like a drop of water,
That in the ocean seeks another drop;
Who, falling there to find his fellow forth,
Unseen inquisitive![e] confounds himself:
So I, to find a mother and a brother,
In quest of them, unhappy, lose myself.

---

[a] ANTIPHOLUS—] The folio, 1623, has, "Enter Antipholis Erotes, a Marchant, and Dromio."

[b] A *trusty* villain,—] *A faithful bondman, or slave.* By these appellations each Antipholus, throughout this Comedy, denominates the Dromio attached to him. So in our author's "Rape of Lucrece," where a Roman *slave* is mentioned:—

"The homely *villain* curt'sies to her low."—MALONE.

[c] *Soon, at five o'clock,*—] That is, *about five o'clock.*

[d] *And afterward* consort *you*—] Malone proposed to read, "consort *with* you;" but the original is probably right—*consort you* meaning *companion you, accompany you.*

[e] Unseen inquisitive!] This is invariably printed, "Unseen, inquisitive," &c.; but *inquisitive,* I believe, is used here for *inquisitor.*

Enter Dromio *of* Ephesus.

Here comes the almanack of my true date.[a]—
What now? how chance thou art return'd so soon?
Dro. E. Return'd so soon! rather approach'd too late.
The capon burns, the pig falls from the spit;
The clock hath strucken twelve upon the bell;
My mistress made it one upon my cheek:
She is so hot, because the meat is cold;
The meat is cold, because you come not home;
You come not home, because you have no stomach;
You have no stomach, having broke your fast;
But we, that know what 'tis to fast and pray,
Are penitent[b] for your default to-day.
Ant. S. Stop in your wind, sir: tell me this, I pray,—
Where have you left the money that I gave you?
Dro. E. O! sixpence, that I had o' Wednesday last,
To pay the saddler for my mistress' crupper,—
The saddler had it, sir; I kept it not.
Ant. S. I am not in a sportive humour now:
Tell me, and dally not, where is the money?
We being strangers here, how dar'st thou trust
So great a charge from thine own custody?
Dro. E. I pray you, jest, sir, as you sit at dinner:
I from my mistress come to you in post;
If I return, I shall be post[c] indeed,
For she will score* your fault upon my pate.
Methinks your maw, like mine, should be your clock,†
And strike you home without a messenger.
Ant. S. Come, Dromio, come, these jests are out of season;
Reserve them till a merrier hour than this.
Where is the gold I gave in charge to thee?
Dro. E. To me, sir? Why, you gave no gold to me.
Ant. S. Come on, sir knave; have done your foolishness,

---

a *The* almanack *of my true date.*] He thus denominates Dromio, because they were both born in the same hour, and therefore the date of Dromio's birth ascertains that of his master.—Malone.

b *Are* penitent —] That is, *performing penance.*

c — I *shall be* post *indeed,*
For she will score your fault upon my pate]

(*) First folio, *scoure.* (†) First folio, *cooke.*

In former times shopkeepers kept a reckoning of their petty dealings by chalk-marks, or notches, on a post of their shop, after the manner of our modern Bonifaces. We have the same quibbling allusion in "Henry IVth," Part I. Act V. Sc. 3:—"Though I could 'scape shot-free at London, I fear the shot here; here's no *scoring but upon the pate.*"

And tell me how thou hast dispos'd thy charge.
DRO. E. My charge was but to fetch you from the mart,
Home to your house, the Phœnix, sir, to dinner;
My mistress and her sister stay for you.
ANT. S. Now, as I am a Christian, answer me,
In what safe place you have bestow'd [a] my money;
Or I shall break that merry sconce of yours,
That stands on tricks when I am undispos'd:
Where is the thousand marks thou hadst of me?
DRO. E. I have some marks of yours upon my pate;
Some of my mistress' marks upon my shoulders;
But not a thousand marks between you both.
If I should pay your worship those again,
Perchance you will not bear them patiently.
ANT. S. Thy mistress' marks? What mistress, slave, hast thou?
DRO. E. Your worship's wife, my mistress, at the Phœnix;
She that doth fast till you come home to dinner,[b]
And prays that you will hie you home to dinner.
ANT. S. What! wilt thou flout me thus unto my face,
Being forbid? There, take you that, sir knave.
DRO. E. What mean you, sir? for God's sake, hold your hands;
Nay, an you will not, sir, I'll take my heels.
[*Exit* DRO. E.
ANT. S. Upon my life, by some device or other,
The villain is o'erraught of all my money.
They say this town is full of cozenage; (1)
As nimble jugglers, that deceive the eye,
Dark-working sorcerers, that change the mind,
Soul-killing witches, that deform the body,
Disguised cheaters, prating mountebanks,
And many such like liberties [c] of sin:
If it prove so, I will be gone the sooner.
I'll to the Centaur, to go seek this slave;
I greatly fear my money is not safe.

[a] Bestow'd *my money;*] That is, *stowed, secreted.*
[b] *She that doth* fast, &c.
And prays *that you will,* &c.]
The quibble here, on *fast* and *pray,* must be understood, or the only point in the passage is lost.
[c] Liberties *of sin:*] Hanmer recommended *libertines of sin;* and this is the reading countenanced by Mr. Collier's old corrector of the Perkins' folio.

ACT II.

SCENE I.—*A Public Place.*

Enter Adriana *and* Luciana.[a]

Adr. Neither my husband nor the slave return'd,
That in such haste I sent to seek his master!
Sure, Luciana, it is two o'clock.

Luc. Perhaps some merchant hath invited him,
And from the mart he's somewhere gone to dinner.
Good sister, let us dine, and never fret:
A man is master of his liberty;
Time is their master; and, when they see time,
They'll go or come: If so, be patient, sister.

Adr. Why should their liberty than ours be more?

Luc. Because their business still lies out o' door.

Adr. Look, when I serve him so, he takes it ill.[b]

Luc. O, know, he is the bridle of your will.

Adr. There's none but asses will be bridled so.

Luc. Why, headstrong liberty is lash'd[c] with woe.
There's nothing situate under heaven's eye
But hath his bound, in earth, in sea, in sky:
The beasts, the fishes, and the winged fowls,
Are their males' subjects, and at their controls.
Men,[d] more divine, the masters of all these,
Lords of the wide world and wild wat'ry seas,
Indued with intellectual sense and souls,
Of more pre-eminence than fish and fowls,

---

[a] Adriana *and* Luciana.] The folio, 1623, has "Enter Adriana, wife to Antipholis Sereptus, with Luciana her Sister."

[b] *He takes it* ill.] The first folio has *thus*, instead of *ill*. The latter word, which seems called for by the rhyme, was supplied in the folio of 1632.

[c] *Is* lash'd *with woe.*] It was suggested to Steevens by a lady, that we should read *leash'd*, i. e. coupled like a headstrong hound; but, as he remarks, "when the mariner *lashes* his guns, the sportsman *leashes* his dogs, the female *laces* her clothes, they all perform one act of fastening with a *lace* or *cord*." No alteration, therefore, is required.

[d] The first folio reads *Man*, and *master*, in this line, and *Lord*, in the next. Hanmer made the necessary corrections.

Are masters to their females, and their lords;
Then let your will attend on their accords.

ADR. This servitude makes you to keep unwed.

LUC. Not this, but troubles of the marriage-bed.

ADR. But, were you wedded, you would bear some sway.

LUC. Ere I learn love, I'll practise to obey.

ADR. How if your husband start some otherwhere?[a]

LUC. Till he come home again, I would forbear.

ADR. Patience unmov'd! no marvel though she pause;
They can be meek that have no other cause.
A wretched soul, bruis'd with adversity,
We bid be quiet, when we hear it cry;
But, were we burden'd with like weight of pain,
As much or more we should ourselves complain:
So thou, that hast no unkind mate to grieve thee,
With urging helpless[b] patience would relieve me;
But, if thou live to see like right bereft,
This fool-begg'd[c] patience in thee will be left.

LUC. Well, I will marry one day, but to try.
Here comes your man—now is your husband nigh.

Enter DROMIO *of* Ephesus.

ADR. Say, is your tardy master now at hand?

DRO. E. Nay, he's at two hands with me, and that my two ears can witness.

ADR. Say, didst thou speak with him? Know'st thou his mind?

DRO. E. Ay, ay; he told his mind upon mine ear.
Beshrew his hand, I scarce could understand it.

LUC. Spake he so doubtfully, thou couldst not feel his meaning?

DRO. E. Nay, he struck so plainly, I could too well feel his blows; and withal so doubtfully that I could scarce understand them.

ADR. But say, I pr'ythee, is he coming home?
It seems he hath great care to please his wife.

DRO. E. Why, mistress, sure my master is horn-mad.

ADR. Horn-mad, thou villain?

DRO. E. I mean not, cuckold-mad;
But sure he is stark mad.
When I desir'd him to come home to dinner,
He ask'd me for a thousand* marks in gold:
'Tis dinner time, quoth I.—*My gold*, quoth he:
Your meat doth burn, quoth I.—*My gold*, quoth he:
Will you come home?[d] quoth I.—*My gold*, quoth he:
Where is the thousand marks I gave thee, villain?
The pig, quoth I, *is burn'd.—My gold*, quoth he:
My mistress, sir, quoth I.—*Hang up thy mistress;*
I know not thy mistress: out on thy mistress!

LUC. Quoth who?

DRO. E. Quoth my master:
I know, quoth he, *no house, no wife, no mistress.*
So that my errand, due unto my tongue,
I thank him, I bare home upon my shoulders;
For, in conclusion, he did beat me there.

ADR. Go back again, thou slave, and fetch him home.

DRO. E. Go back again, and be new beaten home?
For God's sake, send some other messenger.

ADR. Back, slave, or I will break thy pate across.

DRO. E. And he will bless that cross with other beating.
Between you, I shall have a holy head.

ADR. Hence, prating peasant; fetch thy master home.

DRO. E. Am I so round[e] with you, as you with me,
That, like a football, you do spurn me thus?
You spurn me hence, and he will spurn me hither:
If I last in this service, you must case me in leather.[f] [*Exit.*

LUC. Fie!—how impatience low'reth in your face!

ADR. His company must do his minions grace,
Whilst I at home starve for a merry look.
Hath homely age the alluring beauty took

---

[a] *Start some* otherwhere?—] Johnson thought Shakespeare wrote:—

"— start some other *hare?*"

But *otherwhere* occurs three or four times in these Plays; and Adriana uses it again in the present Scene:—

"— his eye doth homage *otherwhere.*"

It signifies *other place*. The sense of the passage is, *How, if your husband goes roaming after some other woman?* as is shown by the rejoinder of Luciana:—

"*Till he come home again*, I would forbear."

The word is now quite obsolete; but our *elsewhere* has much the same meaning.

[b] Helpless *patience*—] *Helpless patience* is patience which imparts no help. Thus, in the poem of "Venus and Adonis:"—

"As those poor birds that *helpless* berries saw."

[c] *This* fool-begg'd *patience*—] Johnson suggested that the allusion was to the custom of begging an idiot to get the charge of his fortune. May not *begg'd* be a misprint for *bagg'd*, in reference to the *bag* which the fool usually carried? Or for *badg'd?* "*This patience with the fool's badge*," &c. (See Douce's Dissertation on the Clowns and Fools of Shakespeare.)

[d] *Will you come* home?] The word *home*, not in the original, was supplied by Capell.

[e] *Am I so* round *with you*,—] Dromio plays on the word *round*, applying it in the ordinary sense of spherical, *like a football*, to himself, and in the meaning of *plain spoken* to his mistress' language. Thus in "Twelfth Night," Act II. Sc. 3:—

"Sir Toby, I must be *round* with you."

So also, in "Henry V." Act IV. Sc. 1:—

"Your reproof is something too *round*."

[f] *You must case me in* leather.] Footballs, generally bladders, are covered with leather.

(*) First folio, a *hundred*.

From my poor cheek? then he hath wasted it.
Are my discourses dull?—barren my wit?
If voluble and sharp discourse be marr'd,
Unkindness blunts it more than marble hard.
Do their gay vestments his affections bait?
That's not my fault—he's master of my state.
What ruins are in me that can be found,
By him not ruin'd? Then is he the ground
Of my defeatures.[a] My decayed fair[b]
A sunny look of his would soon repair;
But, too unruly deer, he breaks the pale,
And feeds from home; poor I am but his stale.[c]

LUC. Self-harming jealousy!—Fie, beat it hence!

ADR. Unfeeling fools can with such wrongs dispense.
I know his eye doth homage otherwhere;
Or else, what lets it but he would be here?
Sister, you know he promis'd me a chain;
Would that alone, alone he would detain,[d]
So he would keep fair quarter with his bed!
I see the jewel best enamelled
Will lose his beauty; and, though gold 'bides still
That others touch, yet often-touching will
Wear gold;[e] and no man that hath a name,
But falsehood and corruption doth it shame.
Since that my beauty cannot please his eye,
I'll weep what's left away, and weeping die.

LUC. How many fond fools serve mad jealousy!
[*Exeunt.*

SCENE II.—*The same.*

Enter ANTIPHOLUS *of* Syracuse.*

ANT. S. The gold I gave to Dromio is laid up
Safe at the Centaur, and the heedful slave
Is wander'd forth in care to seek me out.
By computation, and mine host's report,
I could not speak with Dromio since at first
I sent him from the mart. See, here he comes.

Enter DROMIO *of* Syracuse.

How now, sir? Is your merry humour alter'd?
As you love strokes, so jest with me again.
You know no Centaur?—You receiv'd no gold?—
Your mistress sent to have me home to dinner?—
My house was at the Phœnix? Wast thou mad,
That thus so madly thou didst answer me?

DRO. S. What answer, sir? When spake I such a word?

ANT. S. Even now, even here,—not half an hour since.

DRO. S. I did not see you since you sent me hence,
Home to the Centaur, with the gold you gave me.

ANT. S. Villain, thou didst deny the gold's receipt,
And told'st me of a mistress and a dinner;
For which, I hope, thou felt'st I was displeas'd.

DRO. S. I am glad to see you in this merry vein:
What means this jest? I pray you, master, tell me.

ANT. S. Yea, dost thou jeer and flout me in the teeth?
Think'st thou I jest? Hold, take thou that, and that! [*Beats Dromio.*

DRO. S. Hold, sir, for God's sake! now your jest is earnest.
Upon what bargain do you give it me?

ANT. S. Because that I familiarly sometimes
Do use you for my fool, and chat with you,
Your sauciness will jest upon my love,
And make a common[f] of my serious hours.
When the sun shines, let foolish gnats make sport,
But creep in crannies when he hides his beams.
If you will jest with me, know my aspect,
And fashion your demeanour to my looks,
Or I will beat this method in your sconce.

---

* First folio, *Antipholis Errotis.*

[a] *Of my* defeatures.] That is, my *ill-looks, defacement.* We meet with the same expression in Act V. Sc. 1 of this Play:—

"And careful hours, with Time's deformed hand,
Have written strange *defeatures* in my face."

[b] *My decayed* fair—] *Fair,* for *fairness,* or *beauty.* Our author has several times used *fair* as a substantive:—

"Demetrius loves your *fair.*"
A Midsummer Night's Dream.

Again, in "Love's Labour's Lost," Act IV. Sc. 1:—

"Oh, heresy in *fair,*" &c.

[c] *Poor I am but his* stale.] That is, say the commentators, his *stalking-horse, a pretence, the mask,* under which he covers his amours. It may, however, imply, I am *out of date, insipid.* As in "Cymbeline," Act III. Sc. 4:—

"Poor I am *stale,* a garment out of fashion.

[d] *Would that alone,* alone he *would detain,*—] The original has:—

"Would that alone a *loue,*" &c.

The received reading is from the second folio. Both appear to be corrupt. Perhaps the poet wrote:—

"Would that alone, alone *she* would detain."

She being the *otherwhere.*

[e] *Wear gold;*] In the old copy this passage runs thus:—

"—— *Yet* the gold bides still
That others touch, *and* often touching will,
Where gold and no man that hath a name,
By falshood and corruption doth it shame."

The amended reading was formed by Pope, Warburton, and Steevens; but I am not at all satisfied that it expresses the meaning of the speaker.

[f] *And make a* common *of my serious hours.*] Steevens says, "That is, intrude on them when you please. The allusion is to those tracts of ground destined to *common* use, which are thence called *commons.*"

DRO. S. Sconce, call you it? So you would leave battering, I had rather have it a head: an you use these blows long, I must get a sconce for my head, and insconce it too; or else I shall seek my wit in my shoulders. But, I pray, sir, why am I beaten?

ANT. S. Dost thou not know?

DRO. S. Nothing, sir, but that I am beaten.

ANT. S. Shall I tell you why?

DRO. S. Ay, sir, and wherefore; for, they say, every why hath a wherefore.

ANT. S. Why, first,—for flouting me; and then,
—wherefore,
For urging it the second time to me.

DRO. S. Was there ever any man thus beaten
out of season?
When, in the why and the wherefore, is neither
rhyme nor reason?
Well, sir, I thank you.

ANT. S. Thank me, sir! for what?

DRO. S. Marry, sir, for this something, that you gave me for nothing.

ANT. S. I'll make you amends next, to give you nothing for something. But say, sir, is it dinner-time?

DRO. S. No, sir; I think the meat wants that I have.

ANT. S. In good time, sir, what's that?

DRO. S. Basting.

ANT. S. Well, sir, then 'twill be dry.

DRO. S. If it be, sir, I pray you eat none of it.

ANT. S. Your reason?

DRO. S. Lest it make you choleric, and purchase me another dry basting.

ANT. S. Well, sir, learn to jest in good time: there's a time for all things.

DRO. S. I durst have denied that, before you were so choleric.

ANT. S. By what rule, sir?

DRO. S. Marry, sir, by a rule as plain as the plain bald pate of father Time himself.

ANT. S. Let's hear it.

DRO. S. There's no time for a man to recover his hair that grows bald by nature.

ANT. S. May he not do it by fine and recovery?

DRO. S. Yes, to pay a fine for a periwig, and recover the lost hair of another man.

ANT. S. Why is Time such a niggard of hair, being, as it is, so plentiful an excrement?

DRO. S. Because it is a blessing that he bestows on beasts; and what he hath scanted men * in hair he hath given them in wit.

ANT. S. Why, but there's many a man hath more hair than wit.

DRO. S. Not a man of those but he hath the wit to lose his hair.

ANT. S. Why, thou didst conclude hairy men plain dealers without wit.

DRO. S. The plainer dealer, the sooner lost: yet he loseth it in a kind of jollity.[a]

ANT. S. For what reason?

DRO. S. For two; and sound ones too.

ANT. S. Nay, not sound, I pray you.

DRO. S. Sure ones, then.

ANT. S. Nay, not sure in a thing falsing.

DRO. S. Certain ones, then.

ANT. S. Name them.

DRO. S. The one, to save the money that he spends in tyring;[b] the other, that, at dinner, they should not drop in his porridge.

ANT. S. You would all this time have proved, there is no time for all things.

DRO. S. Marry, and did, sir; namely,[c] no time to recover hair lost by nature.

ANT. S. But your reason was not substantial, why there is no time to recover.

DRO. S. Thus I mend it:—Time himself is bald, and, therefore, to the world's end, will have bald followers.

ANT. S. I knew 'twould be a bald conclusion: but, soft! who wafts us yonder?

Enter ADRIANA *and* LUCIANA.

ADR. Ay, ay, Antipholus, look strange and
frown;
Some other mistress hath thy sweet aspects:
I am not Adriana, nor thy wife.
The time was once, when thou, unurg'd, wouldst
vow
That never words were music to thine ear,
That never object pleasing in thine eye,
That never touch well-welcome to thy hand,
That never meat sweet-savour'd in thy taste,
Unless I spake, or look'd, or touch'd, or carv'd to
thee.
How comes it now, my husband, oh, how
comes it,
That thou art then estranged from thyself?
Thyself I call it, being strange to me,
That, undividable, incorporate,
Am better than thy dear self's better part.
Ah! do not tear away thyself from me;
For know, my love, as easy mayst thou fall
A drop of water in the breaking gulf,
And take unmingled thence that drop again,

(*) First folio, *them*.

[a] *In a kind of* jollity.] This has been passed by all the editors without comment; but is not *jollity*, of old, spelt *jollitie*, a misprint for *pollicie?* There is a kind of *policy* in a man's losing his hair to save his money, and to prevent an uncleanly addition to his porridge; but where is the *jollity?*

[b] *In* tyring;] A correction of Pope's. The old copy reads *in trying*.

[c] *Namely*, no time—] The folio, 1623, has "namely, *in* no time."

Without addition or diminishing,
As take from me thyself, and not me too.
How dearly would it touch thee to the quick,
Shouldst thou but hear I were licentious!
And that this body, consecrate to thee,
By ruffian lust should be contaminate!
Wouldst thou not spit at me, and spurn at me,
And hurl the name of husband in my face,
And tear the stain'd skin off my harlot-brow,[a]
And from my false hand cut the wedding-ring,
And break it with a deep-divorcing vow?
I know thou canst, and therefore see thou do it.
I am possess'd with an adulterate blot;
My blood is mingled with the grime[b] of lust:
For, if we two be one, and thou play false,
I do digest the poison of thy flesh,
Being strumpeted by thy contagion.
Keep, then, fair league and truce with thy true bed;
I live dis-stain'd,[c] thou undishonoured.

ANT. S. Plead you to me, fair dame? I know you not:
In Ephesus I am but two hours old,
As strange unto your town as to your talk;
Who, every word by all my wit being scann'd,
Want * wit in all, one word to understand.

LUC. Fie, brother! how the world is chang'd with you:
When were you wont to use my sister thus?
She sent for you, by Dromio, home to dinner.

ANT. S. By Dromio?

DRO. S. By me?

---

[a] *And tear* the stain'd skin off my harlot brow,—] It would appear from this and other passages in our author that the practice of branding criminals on the forehead was extended, in the case of women, to notorious offenders against chastity. Thus in "Hamlet," Act IV. Sc. 5:—

"——; *brands the harlot*
Even here, *between the chaste, unsmirched brow*
Of my true mother."

Again, in the same Play, Act III. Sc. 4:—

"——; takes off the rose
From the fair forehead of an innocent love,
And *sets a blister there.*"

(*) First folio, *wants*.

[b] *My blood is mingled with the* grime *of lust:*] The folio, 1623, has "*crime* of lust." As Warburton, to whom we owe the emendation, remarks:—"Both the integrity of the metaphor and the word *blot* show that we should read '*grime* of lust.'" This reading is supported by a line in Hall's "Satires," Book IV. S. 1:—

"Besmeared all with loathsome *smoake of lust.*"

[c] Dis-stain'd,—] Probably a misprint for *unstain'd.*

ADR. By thee; and this thou didst return from him,—
That he did buffet thee, and, in his blows,
Denied my house for his,—me for his wife.
ANT. S. Did you converse, sir, with this gentlewoman?
What is the course and drift of your compact?
DRO. S. I, sir? I never saw her till this time.
ANT. S. Villain, thou liest! for even her very words
Didst thou deliver to me on the mart.
DRO. S. I never spake with her in all my life.
ANT. S. How can she thus, then, call us by our names,
Unless it be by inspiration?
ADR. How ill agrees it with your gravity,
To counterfeit thus grossly with your slave,
Abetting him to thwart me in my mood!
Be it my wrong,—you are from me exempt,[a]
But wrong not that wrong with a more contempt.
Come, I will fasten on this sleeve of thine;
Thou art an elm, my husband!—I, a vine![b]—
Whose weakness, married to thy stronger* state,
Makes me with thy strength to communicate.
If aught possess thee from me, it is dross,—
Usurping ivy, brier, or idle moss;
Who, all for want of pruning, with intrusion
Infect thy sap, and live on thy confusion.
ANT. S. To me she speaks, she moves me for her theme!
What, was I married to her in my dream?
Or, sleep I now, and think I hear all this?
What error drives our eyes and ears amiss?
Until I know this sure uncertainty,
I'll entertain the offer'd† fallacy.
LUC. Dromio, go bid the servants spread for dinner.
DRO. S. Oh, for my beads![c] I cross me for a sinner.
This is the fairy land!—O, spite of spites!—
We talk with goblins, owls, and elvish[d] sprites!
If we obey them not, this will ensue,—

(*) First folio, *stranger*. (†) First folio, *free'd*.

[a] *You are from me* exempt,—] Johnson interprets *exempt, separated, parted*. The sense appears to be, "*I am wronged* sufficiently in your separation from me; do not add to that another wrong, contempt."

[b] *Thou art an* elm, *my husband!—I, a* vine!—] So in Catullus:—

"Lenta, qui, velut assitas
Vitis implicat arbores,
Implicabitur in tuum
Complexum."

And in Milton, "Paradise Lost," Book V. l. 215:—

"——— they led the vine
To wed her elm; she, spous'd, about him twines
Her marriageable arms."

[c] *Oh, for my* beads!] See "Two Gentlemen of Verona," p. 3, note (c).

[d] *And* elvish *sprites!*] The old copy omits *elvish;* but the folio 1632, has *elves*, which Rowe changed to *elvish*.

They 'll suck our breath, or pinch us black and blue.
LUC. Why prat'st thou to thyself, and answer'st not?
Dromio, thou drone,*—thou snail,—thou slug,—thou sot!
DRO. S. I am transformed, master, am not I?†
ANT. S. I think thou art in mind; and so am I.
DRO. S. Nay, master, both in mind and in my shape.
ANT. S. Thou hast thine own form.
DRO. S. No, I am an ape.
LUC. If thou art chang'd to aught, 'tis to an ass.
DRO. S. 'Tis true; she rides me, and I long for grass.
'Tis so;—I am an ass; else it could never be,
But I should know her as well as she knows me.
ADR. Come, come, no longer will I be a fool,
To put the finger in the eye and weep,
Whilst man and master laugh my woes to scorn.—
Come, sir, to dinner.—Dromio, keep the gate.—
Husband, I 'll dine above with you to-day,
And shrive[a] you of a thousand idle pranks.—
Sirrah, if any ask you for your master,
Say he dines forth, and let no creature enter.—
Come, sister;—Dromio, play the porter well.
ANT. S. Am I in earth, in heaven, or in hell,—
Sleeping or waking,—mad or well advis'd?
Known unto these, and to myself disguis'd?
I 'll say as they say, and perséver so,
And in this mist at all adventures go.
DRO. S. Master, shall I be porter at the gate?
ADR. Ay; and let none enter, lest I break your pate.
LUC. Come, come, Antipholus, we dine too late.
[*Exeunt.*

(*) First folio, *thou Dromio.* (†) First folio, *am I not.*

[a] *And* shrive *you*—] That is, *bring you to confession, and absolve you.*

ACT III.

SCENE I.—*The same.*

Enter ANTIPHOLUS *of* Ephesus, DROMIO *of* Ephesus, ANGELO, *a Goldsmith, and* BALTHAZAR, *a Merchant.*

ANT. E. Good Signior Angelo, you must excuse us all;—
My wife is shrewish when I keep not hours:—
Say that I linger'd with you at your shop
To see the making of her carkanet,[a]
And that to-morrow you will bring it home.
But here's a villain that would face me down,
He met me on the mart; and that I beat him,
And charg'd him with a thousand marks in gold,
And that I did deny my wife and house!
Thou drunkard thou, what didst thou mean by this?

DRO. E. Say what you will, sir, but I know what I know:
That you beat me at the mart, I have your hand to show:

[a] Carkanet,—] A carcanet, from *carcan*, a chain or collar, is a necklace.
"Nay, I'll be matchless for a *carkanet*,
Whose pearls and diamonds plac'd with ruby rocks
Shall circle this fair neck to set it forth."
Histrio-mastix, 1610.

If the skin were parchment, and the blows you gave were ink,
Your own handwriting would tell you what I think.

ANT. E. I think thou art an ass.

DRO. E. Marry, so it doth appear,
By the wrongs I suffer and the blows I bear.
I should kick, being kick'd; and, being at that pass,
You would keep from my heels and beware of an ass.

ANT. E. You are sad, Signior Balthazar; pray God our cheer
May answer my good will, and your good welcome here.

BAL. I hold your dainties cheap, sir, and your welcome dear.

ANT. E. O, Signior Balthazar, either at flesh or fish,
A table full of welcome makes scarce one dainty dish.

BAL. Good meat, sir, is common; that every churl affords.

ANT. E. And welcome more common; for that's nothing but words.

BAL. Small cheer and great welcome makes a merry feast.

ANT E. Ay, to a niggardly host, and more sparing guest.
But, though my cates be mean, take them in good part;
Better cheer may you have, but not with better heart.
But, soft; my door is lock'd: go bid them let us in.

DRO. E. Maud, Bridget, Marian, Cicely, Gillian, Gin'!

DRO. S. [*Within.*] Mome,[a] malt-horse, capon, coxcomb, idiot, patch![b]
Either get thee from the door, or sit down at the hatch.
Dost thou conjure for wenches, that thou call'st for such store,
When one is one too many? go get thee from the door.

DRO. E. What patch is made our porter? my master stays in the street.

DRO. S. Let him walk from whence he came, lest he catch cold on 's feet.

ANT. E. Who talks within there? Ho!—open the door.

DRO. S. Right, sir; I'll tell you when, an you'll tell me wherefore.

ANT. E. Wherefore?—for my dinner; I have not din'd to-day.

DRO. S. Nor, to-day, here you must not; come again when you may.

ANT. E. What art thou, that keep'st me out from the house I owe?[c]

DRO. S. The porter for this time, sir, and my name is Dromio.

DRO. E. O villain! thou hast stolen both mine office and my name;—
The one ne'er got me credit, the other mickle blame.
If thou hadst been Dromio to-day in my place,
Thou wouldst have chang'd thy face for a name, or thy name for an ass.

LUCE. [*Within.*] What a coil is there! Dromio, who are those at the gate?

DRO. E. Let my master in, Luce.

LUCE. Faith, no; he comes too late;
And so tell your master.

DRO. E. O Lord! I must laugh—
Have at you with a proverb:—*Shall I set in my staff?*

LUCE. Have at you with another: that's—*When? Can you tell?*[d]

DRO. S. If thy name be called Luce,—Luce, thou hast answer'd him well.

ANT. E. Do you hear, you minion? you'll let us in, I hope?[e]

LUCE. I thought to have ask'd you.

DRO. S. And you said, no.

DRO. E. So come help,—Well struck!—there was blow for blow.

ANT. E. Thou baggage, let me in.

LUCE. Can you tell for whose sake?

---

[a] Mome,—] Sir J. Hawkins derives this word from the French *momon*, which signifies the gaming at dice in masquerade, the custom and rule of which is, that a strict silence is to be observed: whatever sum one stakes, another covers, but not a word is to be spoken; from hence also, he says, comes our word *Mum!* for silence. Douce thinks we have *mome* from one of those similar words found in many languages to imply something foolish. In this place it clearly means *blockhead, dolt, fool.*

[b] Patch!] This in Shakespeare's time, and long before, appears to have been the generic term for a fool or jester, derived, it is thought by some, from his *pied* or *patch'd* vestments. Mr. Tyrwhitt supposed *patch*, however, to be nothing more than a corruption of the Italian *pazzo*, which signifies, properly, *a fool.* Shakespeare uses it again in the present Scene, and elsewhere:—

"——— what soldiers *patch?*"
Macbeth, Act V. Sc. 3.

"What a pied ninny's this? Thou scurvy *patch!*"
Tempest, Act III. Sc. 2.

"The *patch* is kind enough."
Merchant of Venice, Act II. Sc. 5.

[c] I owe?] I *own.*

"Who *owes* that shield?
I — and who *owes* that?"
The Four Prentices of London, 1615.

[d] When? Can you tell?] This proverbial query, often met with in the old playwrights, occurs again in "Henry IV." Part I. Act II. Sc. 1:—

"Ay, when? canst tell?"

And is perhaps alluded to just before in this Scene, when Dromio S. says:—

"Right, sir; I'll *tell you when*, an you'll tell me wherefore."

[e] I hope?] Malone thought that a line following this, in which the speaker threatened Luce with the correction of a rope, has been lost. "In a subsequent Scene he puts the threat into execution, by ordering Dromio to go and buy a rope's-end." As all the rest of the dialogue is in rhyme, and *hope* here has no corresponding word, perhaps Malone was right.

DRO. E. Master, knock the door hard.
LUCE. Let him knock till it ache.
ANT. E. You'll cry for this, minion, if I beat the door down.
LUCE. What needs all that, and a pair of stocks in the town?
ADR. [*Within.*] Who is that at the door that keeps all this noise?
DRO. S. By my troth, your town is troubled with unruly boys.
ANT. E. Are you there, wife?—You might have come before.
ADR. Your wife, sir knave!—Go; get you from the door.
DRO. E. If you went in pain, master, this knave would go sore.
ANG. Here is neither cheer, sir, nor welcome; —we would fain have either.
BAL. In debating which was best, we shall part with neither.
DRO. E. They stand at the door, master;—bid them welcome hither.
ANT. E. There is something in the wind, that we cannot get in.
DRO. E. You would say so, master, if your garments were thin.
Your cake, here, is warm within;—you stand here in the cold;—
It would make a man mad as a buck, to be so bought and sold.
ANT. E. Go, fetch me something, I'll break ope the gate.
DRO. S. Break any breaking here, and I'll break your knave's pate.
DRO. E. A man may break a word with you, sir, and words are but wind;
Ay, and break it in your face, so he break it not behind.
DRO. S. It seems, thou want'st breaking, out upon thee, hind!
DRO. E. Here's too much, *out upon thee!* I pray thee let me in.
DRO. S. Ay, when fowls have no feathers, and fish have no fin.
ANT. E. Well, I'll break in; go, borrow me a crow.
DRO. E. A crow without feather?—Master, mean you so?
For a fish without a fin, there's a fowl without a feather:
If a crow help us in, sirrah, we'll pluck a crow together.
ANT. E. Go, get thee gone; fetch me an iron crow.
BAL. Have patience, sir, Oh, let it not be so:
Herein you war against your reputation,
And draw within the compass of suspect
The unviolated honour of your wife.
Once (1) this,[a]—your long experience of her * wisdom,
Her sober virtue, years, and modesty,
Plead, on her* part, some cause to you unknown;
And doubt not, sir, but she will well excuse
Why, at this time, the doors are made[b] against you.
Be rul'd by me, depart in patience,
And let us to the Tiger all to dinner,
And, about evening, come yourself, alone,
To know the reason of this strange restraint.
If by strong hand you offer to break in,
Now, in the stirring passage of the day,
A vulgar comment will be made of it;
And that supposed by the common rout
Against your yet ungalled estimation,
That may with foul intrusion enter in,
And dwell upon your grave when you are dead:
For slander lives upon succession;
For ever housed, where it gets possession.
ANT. E. You have prevail'd; I will depart in quiet,
And, in despite of mirth, mean to be merry.
I know a wench of excellent discourse,—
Pretty and witty—wild, and, yet too, gentle,—
There will we dine: this woman that I mean,
My wife (but, I protest, without desert)
Hath oftentimes upbraided me withal;

---

a Once *this*,—] "This expression," observes Malone, "appears to me so singular, that I cannot help suspecting the passage to be corrupt." Steevens thinks it may mean, *Once for all, at once*, and more recent editors accept this interpretation. The truth is, *once*, or *ones*, was very commonly used by the old writers in place of *nonce*, or *nones*, implying the *occasion*, the *purpose in hand*, the *time being*, &c., as in the following examples:—

"If any evyll come thereof, ye can consider to whome it must be imputed, *ones* the example is very straunge and perillous."—ELLIS's *Original Letters*, &c. 1st Series, vol. ii. p. 170.

Here the meaning I take to be, "meantime the example is very strange," &c. In a passage of the Ancient Morality, "Hycke Scorner," (Hawkins' Edition,) p. 85, we meet with a notable instance, where the word *ones* seems to be used both in the sense it bears in the present day and in that of *for the nonce*:—

"For as soone as they have sayd, *In manus tua, ones*
By God, theyr truthe is stopped *at ones*."

Again, in "Wily Beguiled," (Hawkins' Edition,) p. 344:—

"Thus craft by cunning *once* shall be beguiled."

Again, in Peele's "David and Bethsabe," (Dyce's Edition,) p. 44:—

"Live, Absalom, my son, *once* in peace."

In Ben Jonson's "Cynthia's Revels," Act IV. Sc. 1:—

"I would this water would arrive *once*."

Again, in Beaumont and Fletcher's Play of "The Nice Valour," Act II. Sc. 1:—

"I'll have all woman-kind struck in time for me,
After thirteen *once*."

So, also, in our author, "Timon of Athens," Act I. Sc. 2:—

"Nay, an you begin to rail on society, *once*, —"

And "Coriolanus," Act II. Sc. 3:—

"*Once*, if he do require our voices, we ought not to deny him."

"*Once* this," then, in the passage above, may mean, *for the nonce, this*, &c.; which is perfectly consistent with what precedes and what follows.

b *The doors are* made *against you*.] To *make* the door, *i. e.* to *bar* the door, is an expression still used in parts of England.

(*) First folio, *your*.

To her will we to dinner.—Get you home
And fetch the chain; by this I know 'tis made:
Bring it, I pray you, to the Porcupine;[a]
For there 's the house; that chain will I bestow
(Be it for nothing but to spite my wife)
Upon mine hostess there: good sir, make haste;
Since mine own doors refuse to entertain me,
I'll knock elsewhere, to see if they'll disdain me.

ANG. I'll meet you at that place some hour hence.

ANT. E. Do so; this iest shall cost me some expense. [*Exeunt.*

SCENE II.—*The same.*

Enter LUCIANA* *and* ANTIPHOLUS *of* Syracuse.

LUC. And may it be, that you have quite forgot
A husband's office? Shall Antipholus,
Even in the spring of love—thy love-springs rot?
Shall love, in building,† grow so ruinous?[b]
If you did wed my sister for her wealth,
Then, for her wealth's sake, use her with more kindness;
Or, if you like elsewhere,[c] do it by stealth;
Muffle your false love with some show of blindness:
Let not my sister read it in your eye;
Be not thy tongue thy own shame's orator;
Look sweet,—speak fair,—become disloyalty;[d]
Apparel Vice like Virtue's harbinger;
Bear a fair presence, though your heart be tainted;
Teach sin the carriage of a holy saint;
Be secret-false: what need she be acquainted?
What simple thief brags of his own attaint?‡
'Tis double wrong to truant with your bed,
And let her read it in thy looks at board.
Shame hath a bastard fame, well managed;
Ill deeds are doubled with an evil word.
Alas, poor women! make us but believe,*
Being compact of credit,[e] that you love us;
Though others have the arm, show us the sleeve:
We in your motion turn, and you may move us.
Then, gentle brother, get you in again;
Comfort my sister,—cheer her,—call her wife:
'Tis holy sport to be a little vain,
When the sweet breath of flattery conquers strife.

ANT. S. Sweet mistress (what your name is else I know not,
Nor by what wonder you do hit of mine),
Less, in your knowledge and your grace, you show not,
Than our earth's wonder; more than earth, divine!
Teach me, dear creature! how to think and speak;
Lay open to my earthy gross conceit,
Smother'd in errors,—feeble,—shallow,—weak,—
The folded meaning of your words' deceit.
Against my soul's pure truth, why labour you
To make it wander in an unknown field?
Are you a god? Would you create me new?
Transform me, then, and to your power I'll yield.
But if that I am I, then well I know,
Your weeping sister is no wife of mine,
Nor to her bed no homage do I owe;
Far more, far more to you do I decline.
Oh, train me not, sweet mermaid, with thy note,
To drown me in thy sister flood of tears;
Sing, syren, for thyself, and I will dote:
Spread o'er the silver waves thy golden hairs,
And as a bride[f] I'll take thee, and there lie;
And, in that glorious supposition, think
He gains by death, that hath such means to die:(2)
Let love, being light, be drowned if she sink!

LUC. What, are you mad, that you do reason so?

ANT. S. Not mad, but mated;[g] how, I do not know.

LUC. It is a fault that springeth from your eye.

ANT. S. For gazing on your beams, fair sun, being by.

(*) First folio, *Juliana*. (†) First folio, *buildings*. (‡) First folio, *attain*.

(*) First folio, *not* believe.

[a] Porcupine;] In the old editions, for *Porcupine*, we have always *Porpentine*.

[b] *Shall love*, in building, *grow so* ruinous?] The first folio reads,—

"Shall love, in *buildings*, grow so *ruinate*."

As a rhyme is evidently required to Antipholus, Mr. Steevens recommended *ruinous*, in place of *ruinate*; and this lection is almost invariably adopted. It is in some measure justified too, by a passage in "The Two Gentlemen of Verona," Act V. Sc. 4,—

"Leave not the mansion so long tenantless;
Lest, growing *ruinous*, the *building* fall."

"With respect to *love-springs*," or "the buds of love," Malone remarks,—"it may be observed that the word *springs*, in its primary signification, means the young shoots or buds of plants."

"This canker that eats up *love's* tender *spring*."
Venus and Adonis.

[c] *Or, if you like* elsewhere,—] See note, p. 120, on *otherwhere*.

[d] Become *disloyalty*;] That is, render it *becoming, set it off*.

[e] *Being* compact *of* credit,—] That is to say, *made up of credulity*.

"If he, *compact* of jars, grows musical."
As You Like It, Act II. Sc. 7.

"The lunatic, the lover, and the poet,
Are of imagination all *compact*."
A Midsummer Night's Dream, Act V. Sc. 1.

So, in Nash's "Pierce Pennilesse,"—"The Frenchman (not altered from his own nature) is whollie *compact* of deceivable courtship."

[f] *And as a* bride *I'll take thee*,—] For *bride*, I am responsible. The authentic copy reads *bud*, which was transformed to *bed* in the second folio, and this has been followed in every edition since!

[g] *Not mad, but* mated;] *Mated*, that is, *bewildered, fascinated*.

LUC. Gaze where* you should, and that will clear your sight.

ANT. S. As good to wink, sweet love! as look on night.

LUC. Why call you me love?—call my sister so.

ANT. S. Thy sister's sister.

LUC. That's my sister.

ANT. S. No;
It is thyself,—mine own self's better part,—
Mine eye's clear eye, my dear heart's dearer heart;
My food, my fortune, and my sweet hope's aim,
My sole earth's heaven, and my heaven's claim!

LUC. All this my sister is, or else should be.

ANT. S. Call thyself sister, sweet! for I aim[a] thee.
Thee will I love, and with thee lead my life!
Thou hast no husband yet, nor I no wife:—
Give me thy hand.

LUC. Oh, soft, sir!—hold you still!
I'll fetch my sister, to get her good will.
[*Exit* LUCIANA.

Enter, from the house of ANTIPHOLUS *of* Ephesus, DROMIO *of* Syracuse.

ANT. S. Why, how now, Dromio?—where run'st thou so fast?

DRO. S. Do you know me, sir?—am I Dromio?—am I your man?—am I myself?

ANT. S. Thou art Dromio;—thou art my man;—thou art thyself.

DRO. S. I am an ass;—I am a woman's man;—and besides myself.

ANT. S. What woman's man? and how besides thyself?

DRO. S. Marry, sir, besides myself, I am due to a woman;—one that claims me;—one that haunts me;—one that will have me!

ANT. S. What claim lays she to thee?

DRO. S. Marry, sir, such claim as you would lay to your horse; and she would have me as a beast: not that, I being a beast, she would have me; but that she, being a very beastly creature, lays claim to me.

ANT. S. What is she?

DRO. S. A very reverent body; ay, such a one as a man may not speak of, without he say, *sir-reverence:*[b] I have but lean luck in the match, and yet is she a wondrous fat marriage.

ANT. S. How dost thou mean, a fat marriage?

DRO. S. Marry, sir, she's the kitchen-wench, and all grease: and I know not what use to put her to, but to make a lamp of her, and run from her by her own light. I warrant, her rags, and the tallow in them, will burn a Poland winter: if she lives till doomsday, she'll burn a week longer than the whole world.

ANT. S. What complexion is she of?

DRO. S. Swart, like my shoe, but her face nothing like so clean kept. For why[c] she sweats,—a man may go over shoes in the grime of it.

ANT. S. That's a fault that water will mend.

DRO. S. No, sir, 'tis in grain; Noah's flood could not do it.

ANT. S. What's her name?

DRO. S. Nell, sir; but her name and* three quarters, that's an ell and three quarters, will not measure her from hip to hip.

ANT. S. Then she bears some breadth?

DRO. S. No longer from head to foot than from hip to hip; she is spherical like a globe,—I could find out countries in her.

ANT. S. In what part of her body stands Ireland?

DRO. S. Marry, sir, in her buttocks; I found it out by the bogs.

ANT. S. Where Scotland?

DRO. S. I found it by the barrenness; hard, in the palm of the hand.

ANT. S. Where France?

DRO. S. In her forehead; arm'd and reverted, making war against her heir.(3)

ANT. S. Where England?

DRO. S. I looked for the chalky cliffs, but I could find no whiteness in them; but I guess, it stood in her chin, by the salt rheum that ran between France and it.

ANT. S. Where Spain?

DRO. S. Faith, I saw it not; but I felt it hot in her breath.

ANT. S. Where America, the Indies?

DRO. S. O sir, upon her nose,—all o'er embellished with rubies, carbuncles, sapphires, declining their rich aspect to the hot breath of

(*) First folio, *when*.

(*) First folio, *is*.

[a] *For I* aim *thee.*] The folio, 1623, has, "I *am* thee." Steevens suggested, "I *aim* thee."

[b] *Without he say,* sir reverence:] A very common and a very old corruption of *salvâ reverentiâ, save reverence,* used as an apology before saying anything not very cleanly. "The time hath been, when, if we did speak of this loathsome stuff, tobacco, we used to put a '*Sir reverence*' before, but we forget our good manners."—Old tract on the origin of tobacco, quoted by Gifford, in his Edition of "Ben Jonson," vol. vi. p. 149. This interjection, and another, "saving your presence," are still adopted among the lower classes.

[c] For why *she sweats,*—] *For why,* Mr. Dyce tells us, is equivalent to *because, for this reason that,* and ought not, therefore, to have an interrogation point put after it; and he cites, among other examples, the following,—

> "But let me see; what time a day is't now?
> It cannot be imagined by the sunne,
> *For why* I have not seene it shine to-daie."
> *A Warning for Faire Women,* 1599, Sig. E. 4.

He might have added this, from our author's "Richard II." Act V. Sc. 1,—

> "*For why* the senseless brands will sympathise."

Spain, who sent whole armadoes of carracks to be ballast at her nose.[a]

Ant. S. Where stood Belgia, the Netherlands?

Dro. S. O sir, I did not look so low. To conclude, this drudge, or diviner, laid claim to me; call'd me Dromio; swore I was assured[b] to her; told me what privy marks I had about me,—as the mark of my shoulder, the mole in my neck, the great wart on my left arm,—that I, amazed, ran from her as a witch;
And I think, if my breast had not been made of faith, and my heart of steel,
She had transform'd me to a curtail-dog, and made me turn i' the wheel.

Ant. S. Go, hie thee presently, post to the road;
And, if the wind blow any way from shore,
I will not harbour in this town to-night.
If any bark put forth, come to the mart,
Where I will walk till thou return to me.
If every one knows us, and we know none,
'Tis time, I think, to trudge, pack, and be gone.

Dro. S. As from a bear a man would run for life,
So fly I from her that would be my wife. [*Exit.*

Ant. S. There's none but witches do inhabit here,
And, therefore, 'tis high time that I were hence.
She that doth call me husband, even my soul
Doth for a wife abhor: but her fair sister,
Possess'd with such a gentle sovereign grace,
Of such enchanting presence and discourse,
Hath almost made me traitor to myself:
But, lest myself be guilty to self-wrong,
I'll stop mine ears against the mermaid's song.

Enter Angelo, *with the chain.*

Ang. Master Antipholus.

Ant. S. Ay, that's my name.

Ang. I know it well, sir. Lo, here is the chain;
I thought to have ta'en you at the Porcupine;
The chain unfinish'd made me stay thus long.

Ant. S. What is your will that I shall do with this?

Ang. What please yourself, sir; I have made it for you.

Ant. S. Made it for me, sir! I bespoke it not.

---

[a] *To be* ballast *at her nose.*] *Ballast*, Mr. Malone remarks, was a contraction not of *ballasted*, but of *balased*, or *balaced*. Spain sent whole fleets of vessels to be freighted with the treasures of her nose.

[b] Assured *to her*;] *Affianced* to her.

ANG. Not once, nor twice, but twenty times you have.
Go home with it, and please your wife withal;
And soon at supper-time I'll visit you,
And then receive my money for the chain.

ANT. S. I pray you, sir, receive the money now,
For fear you ne'er see chain nor money more.

ANG. You are a merry man, sir; fare you well! [*Exit.*

ANT. S. What I should think of this, I cannot tell;
But this I think, there's no man is so vain,
That would refuse so fair an offer'd chain.
I see, a man here needs not live by shifts,
When in the streets he meets such golden gifts.
I'll to the mart, and there for Dromio stay;
If any ship put out, then straight away. [*Exit.*

ACT IV.

SCENE I.—*The same.*

Enter a Merchant,[a] ANGELO, *and an* Officer.

MER. You know since Pentecost the sum is due,
And since, I have not much impórtun'd you;
Nor now I had not, but that I am bound
To Persia, and want guilders for my voyage:
Therefore make present satisfaction,
Or I'll attach you by this officer.

ANG. Even just the sum that I do owe to you,
Is growing[b] to me by Antipholus;
And, in the instant that I met with you,
He had of me a chain; at five o'clock
I shall receive the money for the same.
Pleaseth you walk with me down to his house,
I will discharge my bond, and thank you too.

[a] A Merchant,] The folio, 1623, contains no list of the persons represented in this play; but in the list invariably adopted by modern editors, this character, strange to say, has been omitted altogether.

[b] *Is growing to me*—] *Accruing* to me. Thus, in Act IV. Sc. 4:—

"And, knowing how the debt *grows*, I will pay it."

Again, same Act and Scene:—

"Say, how *grows* it due?"

Enter ANTIPHOLUS *of Ephesus, and* DROMIO *of Ephesus, from the* Courtezan's.

OFF. That labour may you save; see where he comes.

ANT. E. While I go to the goldsmith's house, go thou
And buy a rope's end; that will I bestow
Among my wife and her * confederates,
For locking me out of my doors by day.
But, soft, I see the goldsmith; get thee gone;
Buy thou a rope, and bring it home to me.

DRO. E. I buy a thousand pound a year!—I buy a rope! [a] [*Exit* DROMIO.

ANT. E. A man is well holp up that trusts to you:
I promised your presence and the chain,
But neither chain nor goldsmith came to me:
Belike, you thought our love would last too long
If it were chain'd together, and therefore came not.

ANG. Saving your merry humour; here 's the note,
How much your chain weighs to the utmost carat,
The fineness of the gold, and chargeful fashion,
Which doth amount to three odd ducats more
Than I stand debted to this gentleman.
I pray you see him presently discharg'd,
For he is bound to sea, and stays but for it.

ANT. E. I am not furnish'd with the present money;
Besides, I have some business in the town:
Good signior, take the stranger to my house,
And with you take the chain, and bid my wife
Disburse the sum on the receipt thereof;
Perchance I will be there as soon as you.

ANG. Then you will bring the chain to her yourself?

ANT. E. No; bear it with you, lest I come not time enough.

ANG. Well, sir, I will. Have you the chain about you?

ANT. E. An if I have not, sir, I hope you have;
Or else you may return without your money.

ANG. Nay, come, I pray you, sir, give me the chain:
Both wind and tide stays for this gentleman,
And I, to blame, have held him here too long.

ANT. E. Good lord! you use this dalliance to excuse
Your breach of promise to the Porcupine.
I should have chid you for not bringing it,
But, like a shrew, you first begin to brawl.

MER. The hour steals on; I pray you, sir, despatch.

ANG. You hear how he impórtunes me; the chain—

ANT. E. Why, give it to my wife, and fetch your money.

ANG. Come, come; you know I gave it you even now:
Either send the chain, or send me by some token.[b]

ANT. E. Fie! now you run this humour out of breath.
Come, where 's the chain?—I pray you let me see it.

MER. My business cannot brook this dalliance.
Good sir, say whe'r you 'll answer me or no;
If not, I 'll leave him to the officer.

ANT. E. I answer you! What should I answer you?

ANG. The money that you owe me for the chain.

ANT. E. I owe you none till I receive the chain.

ANG. You know I gave it you half an hour since.

ANT. E. You gave me none; you wrong me much to say so.

ANG. You wrong me more, sir, in denying it.
Consider, how it stands upon my credit.

MER. Well, officer, arrest him at my suit.

OFF. I do; and charge you, in the duke's name, to obey me.

ANG. This touches me in reputation.
Either consent to pay this sum for me,
Or I attach you by this officer.

ANT. E. Consent to pay thee that I never had!
Arrest me, foolish fellow, if thou dar'st.

ANG. Here is thy fee; arrest him, officer.
I would not spare my brother in this case,
If he should scorn me so apparently.

OFF. I do arrest you, sir; you hear the suit.

ANT. E. I do obey thee, till I give thee bail;—
But, sirrah, you shall buy this sport as dear
As all the metal in your shop will answer.

ANG. Sir, sir, I shall have law in Ephesus,
To your notorious shame, I doubt it not.

Enter DROMIO *of* Syracuse *from the Bay.*

DRO. S. Master, there is a bark of Epidamnum,
That stays but till her owner comes aboard,
And then, sir, she bears away. Our fraughtage, sir,

(*) First folio, *their*.

[a] *I buy a thousand pound a year!—I buy a rope!*] What connexion is there between the purchase of a thousand pound a year and a rope? Here, as in many other instances of obscurity in Shakespeare, there may have been an allusion well understood at the time; but which, referring merely to some transitory event, or to some popular bye-word of the moment, has passed into oblivion, and will never be recovered.

[b] *Or send* me by *some token.*] It has been proposed to read,—*or send by me*, &c.; but the inversion was, doubtless, a peculiarity of the period.

I have convey'd aboard; and I have bought
The oil, the balsamum, and aqua vitæ.
The ship is in her trim; the merry wind
Blows fair from land: they stay for nought at all,
But for their owner, master, and yourself.

ANT. E. How now?—a madman?—Why, thou peevish sheep,[a]
What ship of Epidamnum stays for me?

DRO. S. A ship you sent me to, to hire waftage.

ANT. E. Thou drunken slave! I sent thee for a rope;
And told thee to what purpose and what end.

DRO. S. You sent me for a rope's end as soon.
You sent me to the bay, sir, for a bark.

ANT. E. I will debate this matter at more leisure,
And teach your ears to list me with more heed.
To Adriana, villain, hie thee straight;
Give her this key, and tell her, in the desk,
That 's cover'd o'er with Turkish tapestry,
There is a purse of ducats; let her send it:
Tell her, I am arrested in the street,
And that shall bail me:—hie thee, slave; begone.
On, officer, to prison, till it come.
[*Exeunt* Merchant, ANGELO, Officer, *and* ANT. E.

DRO. S. To Adriana!—that is where we din'd,
Where Dowsabel did claim me for her husband:
She is too big, I hope, for me to compass;
Thither I must, although against my will,
For servants must their masters' minds fulfil.
[*Exit.*

SCENE II.—*The same.*

Enter ADRIANA *and* LUCIANA.

ADR. Ah, Luciana, did he tempt thee so?
Might'st thou perceive austerely in his eye,
That he did plead in earnest, yea or no?
Look'd he or red or pale, or sad or merrily?
What observation mad'st thou in this case,
Of * his heart's meteors tilting in his face?[b]

LUC. First, he denied you had in him no right.[c]

ADR. He meant he did me none; the more my spite.

LUC. Then swore he, that he was a stranger here.

ADR. And true he swore, though yet forsworn he were.

LUC. Then pleaded I for you.

ADR. And what said he?

LUC. That love I begg'd for you, he begg'd of me.

ADR. With what persuasion did he tempt thy love?

LUC. With words that in an honest suit might move.
First, he did praise my beauty; then my speech.

ADR. Didst speak him fair?

LUC. Have patience, I beseech.

ADR. I cannot, nor I will not, hold me still;
My tongue, though not my heart, shall have his will.
He is deformed, crooked, old, and sere,
Ill-fac'd, worse-bodied, shapeless every where;
Vicious, ungentle, foolish, blunt, unkind,
Stigmatical in making,[d] worse in mind.

LUC. Who would be jealous, then, of such a one?
No evil lost is wail'd when it is gone.

ADR. Ah! but I think him better than I say,
And yet would herein others' eyes were worse:
Far from her nest the lapwing cries away;[e]
My heart prays for him, though my tongue do curse.

Enter DROMIO *of* Syracuse.

DRO. S. Here, go; the desk—the purse; sweet now, make haste.

LUC. How hast thou lost thy breath?

DRO. S. By running fast.

ADR. Where is thy master, Dromio? Is he well?

DRO. S. No; he 's in Tartar limbo, worse than hell.
A devil in an everlasting garment (1) hath him;
One, whose hard heart is button'd up with steel;
A fiend, a fairy, pitiless and rough;
A wolf,—nay, worse—a fellow all in buff;
A back-friend, a shoulder-clapper,—one that countermands
The passages of alleys, creeks, and narrow lands;
A hound that runs counter, and yet draws dry foot well; (2)

(*) First folio, *Oh*.

a *Why, thou peevish* sheep,
What ship—]
The same quibble on *sheep* and *ship* occurs, it will be remembered, in "The Two Gentlemen of Verona," Act I. Sc. 1.

b *Of his* heart's meteors *tilting in his face?*] A strange conceit. She means, What opinion did you form as to the reality of his solicitation from the varying emotions expressed by his visage? I suspect, however, that *case* is a misprint for *race*. The rapid changes of expression in the countenance may be not inaptly termed a *race*.

c *First, he* denied *you had in him* no right.] This was an idiom in the phraseology of Shakespeare's day. Thus, in "Richard III." Act I. Sc. 3:—
"You may *deny* that you were *not* the cause," &c.

d Stigmatical *in making*,—] That is, *branded by nature with deformity*.

e *Far from her nest the lapwing cries away;*] This allusion to the habits of the lapwing is not unfrequent in our old poets.

"You resemble the lapwing, who crieth most
Where her nest is not."—LILY'S *Campaspe*, 1584.

So, also, Greene, in his Second Part of "Coney Catching," 1592:—"But again to our priggers, who, as before I said,—*cry with the lapwing farthest from her nest*," &c.

And in Ben Jonson's "Underwoods:"—

"Where he that knowes, will *like a lapwing flie*,
Farre from the nest, and so himself belie."

One that, before the judgment, carries poor souls to hell.(3)

ADR. Why, man, what is the matter?

DRO. S. I do not know the matter; he is 'rested on the case.

ADR. What!—is he arrested?—tell me at whose suit.

DRO. S. I know not at whose suit he is arrested well;
But is in a suit of buff which 'rested him, that can I tell.
Will you send him, mistress, redemption, the money in his desk?

ADR. Go fetch it, sister. This I wonder at, [*Exit* LUCIANA.
That he,* unknown to me, should be in debt.
Tell me, was he arrested on a band?

DRO. S. Not on a band,[a] but on a stronger thing:
A chain—a chain; do you not hear it ring?

ADR. What, the chain?

DRO. S. No, no, the bell; 'tis time that I were gone:
It was two ere I left him, and now the clock strikes one.

ADR. The hours come back!—that did I never hear.

DRO. S. O, yes: if any hour meet a sergeant, a' turns back for very fear.

ADR. As if time were in debt!—how fondly dost thou reason!

DRO. S. Time is a very bankrupt, and owes more than he's worth to season.
Nay, he's a thief, too: have you not heard men say,
That Time comes stealing on by night and day?
If a'† be in debt, and theft, and a sergeant in the way,
Hath he not reason to turn back an hour in a day?

Enter LUCIANA.

ADR. Go, Dromio; there's the money—bear it straight;
And bring thy master home immediately.
Come, sister; I am press'd down with conceit,—
Conceit, my comfort and my injury. [*Exeunt.*

SCENE III.—*The same.*

Enter ANTIPHOLUS *of* Syracuse.

ANT. S. There's not a man I meet but doth salute me,
As if I were their well-acquainted friend;
And every one doth call me by my name.
Some tender money to me; some invite me;
Some other give me thanks for kindnesses;
Some offer me commodities to buy:
Even now, a tailor call'd me in his shop,
And show'd me silks that he had bought for me,
And therewithal took measure of my body.
Sure, these are but imaginary wiles,
And Lapland sorcerers inhabit here.

Enter DROMIO *of* Syracuse.

DRO. S. Master, here's the gold you sent me for.
What, have you got the picture of old Adam new apparell'd?[b]

ANT. S. What gold is this? What Adam dost thou mean?

DRO. S. Not that Adam that kept the paradise, but that Adam that keeps the prison: he that goes in the calf's-skin that was killed for the prodigal; he that came behind you, sir, like an evil angel, and bid you forsake your liberty.

ANT. S. I understand thee not.

DRO. S. No?—why, 'tis a plain case: he that went like a base-viol in a case of leather; the man, sir, that, when gentlemen are tired, gives them a fob,[c] and 'rests them; he, sir, that takes pity on decayed men, and gives them suits of durance; he that sets up his rest to do more exploits with his mace than a morris-pike.(4)

ANT. S. What!—thou mean'st an officer?

DRO. S. Ay, sir, the sergeant of the band; he that brings any man to answer it that breaks his band; one that thinks a man always going to bed, and says, *God give you good rest!*

ANT. S. Well, sir, there rest in your foolery. Is there any ship puts forth to-night? may we be gone?

DRO. S. Why, sir, I brought you word an hour since, that the bark Expedition put forth to-night; and then were you hindered by the sergeant, to tarry for the hoy, Delay. Here are the angels that you sent for to deliver you.

(*) First folio, *Thus.* (†) First folio, If *I.*

a *On a* band,—] Dromio equivocates between *band*, i.e. a legal bond, and a *band*, or tie for the neck.

b *What, have you got the picture of old Adam new apparell'd?*] Theobald conjectured that a word or two had slipped out in copying, or at press; and proposed to rectify the omission by reading, "What, have you got *rid of* the picture?" &c. The addition seems uncalled for. Dromio on his return, surprised to find his master unattended by the officer, asks, "Have you got the picture of old Adam new apparell'd?" that is, Have you *put him on a new suit,—changed his suit?* quibbling on *suit*, the action, and *suit*, the apparel. He terms the sergeant "old Adam," because both went in *buff-leather*. A very ancient jest on our first parents' costume. The sergeant's dress, however, was not always the "suit of durance." He at times wore a black cloak, or gown:—

> "Had we blacke gownes, upon my life I sweare
> Many would say that we foure Serjeants were."
> *The Knave of Hearts*, &c., S. ROWLAND, 1612.

c *When gentlemen are tired, gives them a* fob, *and 'rests them;*] The folio, 1623, has a *sob*, which is clearly wrong, but what is gained by substituting *fob?* Would not *sop* be more to the purpose?

ANT. S. The fellow is distract, and so am I,
And here we wander in illusions;
Some blessed power deliver us from hence!

Enter a Courtezan.

COUR. Well met, well met, master Antipholus.
I see, sir, you have found the goldsmith now:
Is that the chain you promis'd me to-day?

ANT. S. Satan, avoid! I charge thee tempt me not!

DRO. S. Master, is this Mistress Satan?

ANT. S. It is the devil!

DRO. S. Nay, she is worse—she is the devil's dam; and here she comes in the habit of a light wench: and thereof comes, that the wenches say, *God dam me;* that's as much as to say, *God make me a light wench.* It is written, they appear to men like angels of light: light is an effect of fire, and fire will burn; *ergo,* light wenches will burn. Come not near her.

COUR. Your man and you are marvellous merry, sir.
Will you go with me? we'll mend our dinner here.

DRO. S. Master, if you* do, expect spoon-meat, or bespeak a long spoon.

ANT. S. Why, Dromio?

DRO. S. Marry, he must have a long spoon that must eat with the devil.

ANT. S. Avoid, then, fiend! Why tell'st thou me of supping?
Thou art, as you are all, a sorceress.
I conjure thee to leave me, and be gone.

COUR. Give me the ring of mine you had at dinner,
Or, for my diamond, the chain you promis'd;
And I'll be gone, sir, and not trouble you.

DRO. S. Some devils ask but the paring of one's nail,
A rush, a hair, a drop of blood, a pin,
A nut, a cherry-stone; but she, more covetous,
Would have a chain.
Master, be wise; an' if you give it her,
The devil will shake her chain, and fright us with it.

COUR. I pray you, sir, my ring, or else the chain;
I hope you do not mean to cheat me so.

ANT. S. Avaunt, thou witch! Come, Dromio, let us go.

DRO. S. *Fly pride,* says the peacock: mistress, that you know.

[*Exeunt* ANT. S. *and* DRO. S.

COUR. Now, out of doubt, Antipholus is mad,
Else would he never so demean himself.
A ring he hath of mine worth forty ducats,(5)
And for the same he promis'd me a chain;—
Both one and other he denies me now.
The reason that I gather he is mad,
(Besides this present instance of his rage,)
Is a mad tale he told to-day at dinner,
Of his own doors being shut against his entrance.
Belike his wife, acquainted with his fits,
On purpose shut the doors against his way.
My way is now to hie home to his house,
And tell his wife, that, being lunatic,
He rush'd into my house, and took perforce
My ring away. This course I fittest choose;
For forty ducats is too much to lose. [*Exit,*

(*) The first folio omits *you.*

SCENE IV.—*The same.*

Enter ANTIPHOLUS *of* Ephesus, *and an* Officer.

ANT. E. Fear me not, man; I will not break away:
I'll give thee, ere I leave thee, so much money,
To warrant thee, as I am 'rested for.
My wife is in a wayward mood to-day,
And will not lightly trust the messenger:
That I should be attach'd in Ephesus,
I tell you, 'twill sound harshly in her ears.

Enter DROMIO *of* Ephesus, *with a rope's end.*

Here comes my man; I think he brings the money.
How now, sir? have you that I sent you for?

DRO. E. Here's that, I warrant you, will pay them all.

ANT. E. But where's the money?

DRO. E. Why, sir, I gave the money for the rope.

ANT. E. Five hundred ducats, villain, for a rope?

DRO. E. I'll serve you, sir, five hundred at the rate.

ANT. E. To what end did I bid thee hie thee home?

DRO. E. To a rope's end, sir, and to that end am I return'd.

ANT. E. And to that end, sir, I will welcome you. [*Beating him.*

OFF. Good sir, be patient.

DRO. E. Nay, 'tis for me to be patient; I am in adversity.

OFF. Good now, hold thy tongue.

DRO. E. Nay, rather persuade him to hold his hands.

ANT. E. Thou whoreson, senseless villain!

DRO. E. I would I were senseless, sir, that I might not feel your blows.

ANT. E. Thou art sensible in nothing but blows, and so is an ass.

DRO. E. I am an ass, indeed; you may prove it by my long ears. I have served him from the hour of my nativity to this instant, and have nothing at his hands for my service but blows. When I am cold, he heats me with beating; when I am warm, he cools me with beating: I am waked with it when I sleep; raised with it when I sit; driven out of doors with it when I go from home; welcomed home with it when I return; nay, I bear it on my shoulders as a beggar wont her brat; and, I think, when he hath lamed me, I shall beg with it from door to door.

Enter ADRIANA, LUCIANA, *the* Courtezan, *and a* Schoolmaster *called* PINCH.

ANT. E. Come, go along; my wife is coming yonder.

DRO. E. Mistress, *respice finem*, respect your end; or rather the prophecy, like the parrot,[a] *Beware the rope's end.*

ANT. E. Wilt thou still talk? [*Beats him.*

COUR. How say you now? Is not your husband mad?

ADR. His incivility confirms no less.
Good Doctor Pinch, you are a conjurer;
Establish him in his true sense again,
And I will please you what you will demand.

LUC. Alas, how fiery and how sharp he looks!

COUR. Mark how he trembles in his ecstasy![b]

PINCH. Give me your hand, and let me feel your pulse.

ANT. E. There is my hand, and let it feel your ear.

PINCH. I charge thee, Satan, hous'd within this man,
To yield possession to my holy prayers,
And to thy state of darkness hie thee straight:
I cónjure thee by all the saints in heaven.

ANT. E. Peace, doting wizard, peace; I am not mad.

ADR. O, that thou wert not, poor distressed soul!

ANT. E. You minion, you, are these your customers?
Did this companion[c] with the saffron face
Revel and feast it at my house to-day,
Whilst upon me the guilty doors were shut,
And I denied to enter in my house?

ADR. O, husband, God doth know you dined at home;
Where, would you had remain'd until this time,
Free from these slanders, and this open shame!

ANT. E. Din'd at home! Thou villain, what say'st thou?

DRO. E. Sir, sooth to say, you did not dine at home.

ANT. E. Were not my doors lock'd up, and I shut out?

DRO. E. Perdy,[d] your doors were lock'd, and you shut out.

ANT. E. And did not she herself revile me there?

DRO. E. *Sans* fable, she herself revil'd you there.

ANT. E. Did not her kitchen-maid rail, taunt, and scorn me?

DRO. E. Certes, she did; the kitchen-vestal scorn'd you.

ANT. E. And did not I in rage depart from thence?

DRO. E. In verity you did; my bones bear witness,
That since have felt the vigour of his rage.

ADR. Is 't good to soothe him in these contraries?

PINCH. It is no shame: the fellow finds his vein,
And, yielding to him, humours well his frenzy.

ANT. E. Thou hast suborn'd the goldsmith to arrest me.

ADR. Alas! I sent you money to redeem you,
By Dromio here, who came in haste for it.

DRO. E. Money by me!—Heart and good-will you might,
But surely, master, not a rag of money.

ANT. E. Went'st not thou to her for a purse of ducats?

ADR. He came to me, and I deliver'd it.

LUC. And I am witness with her that she did.

DRO. E. God and the rope-maker bear me witness,
That I was sent for nothing but a rope!

PINCH. Mistress, both man and master is possess'd,
I know it by their pale and deadly looks;
They must be bound, and laid in some dark room.

ANT. E. Say, wherefore didst thou lock me forth to-day?
And why dost thou deny the bag of gold?

ADR. I did not, gentle husband, lock thee forth.

---

[a] *Like the* parrot,—] Warburton says this alludes to people's teaching that bird unlucky words; with which, when any passenger was offended, it was the standing joke of the wise owner to say, "Take heed, sir, my parrot prophesies!" To this Butler hints when, speaking of Ralpho's skill in augury, he says:—

"Could tell what subtlest parrots mean
That speak, and think contrary clean;
What member 'tis of whom they talk,
When they cry *rope*, and *walk, knave, walk*."

[b] *How he trembles in his* ecstasy!] Thus, in our Author's "Venus and Adonis," 1593:—

"Thus stands she in a *trembling ecstasy*."

Ecstasy meant aberration of mind. "Extasie, or trance. G. extasé; Lat. ecstasis, abstractio mentis. Est propriè mentis emotio, et quasi de statione suâ deturbatio, seu furore, seu admiratione, seu timore, aliove casu decidat."—*Minsheu. Dict.* 1617.

[c] *This* companion—] *Companion* was formerly applied contemptuously, as we now use *fellow*.

"I scorn you, scurvy *companion*."
Henry IV. 2d Part, Act II. Sc. 4.

[d] Perdy,—] Corrupted from the French, *Pardieu*. It occurs frequently in old authors, and three or four times again in these Plays. Thus, in "Twelfth Night," Act IV. Sc. 2:—

"My lady is unkind, *perdy*."

and in "Hamlet," Act III. Sc. 2:—

"Belike he likes it not, *perdy*."

DRO. E. And, gentle master, I receiv'd no gold;
But I confess, sir, that we were lock'd out.
ADR. Dissembling villain, thou speak'st false in both!
ANT. E. Dissembling harlot, thou art false in all;
And art confederate with a damned pack,
To make a loathsome abject scorn of me:
But with these nails I'll pluck out these false eyes,
That would behold in me this shameful sport.
[*Enter three or four, and offer to bind him. He strives.**
ADR. O, bind him, bind him! let him not come near me.
PINCH. More company—the fiend is strong within him.
LUC. Ay me, poor man!—how pale and wan he looks!
ANT. E. What, will you murder me? Thou gaoler, thou,
I am thy prisoner: wilt thou suffer them
To make a rescue?
OFF. Masters, let him go;
He is my prisoner, and you shall not have him.
PINCH. Go, bind this man, for he is frantic too.
ADR. What wilt thou do, thou peevish officer?
Hast thou delight to see a wretched man
Do outrage and displeasure to himself?
OFF. He is my prisoner; if I let him go,
The debt he owes will be requir'd of me.
ADR. I will discharge thee ere I go from thee.
Bear me forthwith unto his creditor,
And, knowing how the debt grows, I will pay it.
Good Master Doctor, see him safe convey'd
Home to my house. O, most unhappy day!
ANT. E. O, most unhappy strumpet!
DRO. E. Master, I am here enter'd in bond for you.
ANT. E. Out on thee, villain! wherefore dost thou mad me?

* This is the stage direction in the authentic copy.

DRO. E. Will you be bound for nothing? Be mad, good master; Cry, the devil!—

LUC. God help poor souls, how idly do they talk!

ADR. Go bear him hence. Sister, go you with me.

[*Exeunt* PINCH *and* Assistants, *with* ANT. E. *and* DRO. E.

Say, now, whose suit is he arrested at?

OFF. One Angelo, a goldsmith; do you know him?

ADR. I know the man. What is the sum he owes?

OFF. Two hundred ducats.

ADR. Say, how grows it due?

OFF. Due for a chain your husband had of him.

ADR. He did bespeak a chain for me, but had it not.

COUR. Whenas[a] your husband, all in rage, to-day
Came to my house, and took away my ring,
(The ring I saw upon his finger now,)
Straight after did I meet him with a chain.

ADR. It may be so, but I did never see it.
Come, gaoler, bring me where the goldsmith is;
I long to know the truth hereof at large.

Enter ANTIPHOLUS *of* Syracuse, *with his rapier drawn, and* DROMIO *of* Syracuse.

LUC. God, for thy mercy! they are loose again!

ADR. And come with naked swords: let's call more help,
To have them bound again.

OFF. Away; they'll kill us.

[*Exeunt* Officer, ADR. *and* LUC.[b]

ANT. S. I see these witches are afraid of swords.

DRO. S. She that would be your wife now ran from you.

ANT. S. Come to the Centaur; fetch our stuff from thence:
I long that we were safe and sound aboard.

DRO. S. Faith, stay here this night; they will surely do us no harm.—You saw, they speak us fair, give us gold: methinks they are such a gentle nation, that, but for the mountain of mad flesh that claims marriage of me, I could find in my heart to stay here still, and turn witch.

ANT. S. I will not stay to-night for all the town;
Therefore away, to get our stuff[c] aboard.

[*Exeunt.*

---

a Whenas *your husband,*—] This is commonly printed *when as,* &c.; in some editions *when, as,* &c. As we remarked in note (c) p. 21, *when* as and *when, where*as and *where,* were of old used interchangeably.

b *Exeunt,* &c.] The old copy has two stage directions here. One, "*Runne all out,*" and immediately after, "*Exeunt omnes, as fast as may be, frighted.*"

c *To get our* stuff *aboard.*] One of the meanings attached to this commonly-used word, *stuff,* in early times, was *luggage.* In the orders issued for the royal progresses, Malone says, the king's baggage was always thus denominated.

ACT V.

SCENE I.—*The same. Before an Abbey.*

Enter Merchant *and* Angelo.

Ang. I am sorry, sir, that I have hinder'd you;
But, I protest, he had the chain of me,
Though most dishonestly he doth deny it.

Mer. How is the man esteem'd here in the city?

Ang. Of very reverent reputation, sir,—
Of credit infinite,—highly belov'd,—
Second to none that lives here in the city;
His word might bear my wealth at any time.

Mer. Speak softly; yonder, as I think, he walks.

Enter Antipholus *and* Dromio *of* Syracuse.

Ang. 'T is so; and that self chain about his neck,
Which he forswore most monstrously to have.
Good sir, draw near to me, I'll speak to him.
Signior Antipholus, I wonder much
That you would put me to this shame and trouble,
And not without some scandal to yourself,
With circumstance and oaths, so to deny
This chain, which now you wear so openly:
Beside the charge, the shame, imprisonment,
You have done wrong to this my honest friend;
Who, but for staying on our controversy,
Had hoisted sail and put to sea to-day:—
This chain you had of me,—can you deny it?

Ant. S. I think I had; I never did deny it.

Mer. Yes, that you did, sir; and forswore it too.

Ant. S. Who heard me to deny it, or forswear it?

Mer. These ears of mine, thou knowest, did hear thee:
Fie on thee, wretch! 'tis pity that thou liv'st
To walk where any honest men resort.

Ant. S. Thou art a villain to impeach me thus!

I'll prove mine honour and mine honesty
Against thee presently, if thou dar'st stand.
MER. I dare, and do defy thee for a villain.
[*They draw.*

Enter ADRIANA, LUCIANA, Courtezan, *and others.*

ADR. Hold!—hurt him not, for God's sake!—he is mad;
Some get within him;[a] take his sword away;—
Bind Dromio too, and bear them to my house.
DRO. S. Run, master, run; for God's sake, take a house;—
This is some priory;—in, or we are spoil'd.
[*Exeunt* ANT. S. *and* DRO. S. *to the Priory.*

Enter the Lady Abbess.

ABB. Be quiet, people! wherefore throng you hither?
ADR. To fetch my poor distracted husband hence:
Let us come in that we may bind him fast,
And bear him home for his recovery.
ANG. I knew he was not in his perfect wits.
MER. I am sorry now that I did draw on him.
ABB. How long hath this possession held the man?
ADR. This week he hath been heavy, sour, sad,
And much different from the man he was;
But, till this afternoon, his passion
Ne'er brake into extremity of rage.
ABB. Hath he not lost much wealth by wreck of sea?
Buried some dear friend? Hath not, else, his eye
Stray'd his affection in unlawful love?
A sin prevailing much in youthful men,
Who give their eyes the liberty of gazing.
Which of these sorrows is he subject to?
ADR. To none of these, except it be the last:
Namely, some love that drew him oft from home.
ABB. You should, for that, have reprehended him.
ADR. Why, so I did.
ABB. Ay, but not rough enough.
ADR. As roughly as my modesty would let me.
ABB. Haply in private.
ADR. And in assemblies too.
ABB. Ay, but not enough.
ADR. It was the copy of our conference.
In bed, he slept not for my urging it;
At board, he fed not for my urging it:
Alone, it was the subject of my theme;
In company, I often glanced it;
Still did I tell him it was vile and bad.

ABB. And thereof came it that the man was mad.
The venom clamour of a jealous woman
Poisons more deadly than a mad dog's tooth.
It seems, his sleeps were hinder'd by thy railing;
And thereof comes it, that his head is light.
Thou say'st, his meat was sauc'd with thy upbraidings:
Unquiet meals make ill digestions,—
Thereof the raging fire of fever bred;
And what's a fever but a fit of madness?
Thou say'st, his sports were hinder'd by thy brawls:
Sweet recreation barr'd, what doth ensue,
But moody and dull melancholy,
Kinsman to grim and comfortless Despair,
And, at her heels, a huge infectious troop
Of pale distemperatures and foes to life?
In food, in sport, and life-preserving rest,
To be disturb'd, would mad or man, or beast:
The consequence is, then, thy jealous fits
Have scar'd thy husband from the use of wits.
LUC. She never reprehended him but mildly,
When he demean'd himself rough, rude, and wildly.
Why bear you these rebukes and answer not?
ADR. She did betray me to my own reproof.
Good people, enter and lay hold on him!
ABB. No, not a creature enters in my house.
ADR. Then let your servants bring my husband forth.
ABB. Neither; he took this place for sanctuary,
And it shall privilege him from your hands,
Till I have brought him to his wits again,
Or lose my labour in assaying it.
ADR. I will attend my husband, be his nurse,
Diet his sickness, for it is my office,
And will have no attorney but myself;
And therefore let me have him home with me.
ABB. Be patient; for I will not let him stir,
Till I have us'd the approved means I have,
With wholesome syrups, drugs, and holy prayers,
To make of him a formal[b] man again:
It is a branch and parcel of mine oath,—
A charitable duty of my order;
Therefore depart, and leave him here with me.
ADR. I will not hence and leave my husband here;
And ill it doth beseem your holiness
To separate the husband and the wife.
ABB. Be quiet and depart, thou shalt not have him. [*Exit* Abbess.
LUC. Complain unto the duke of this indignity.
ADR. Come, go; I will fall prostrate at his feet,
And never rise until my tears and prayers
Have won his grace to come in person hither,
And take perforce my husband from the abbess.

[a] *Some get* within *him;*] *Get within his guard; close with him.*

[b] *A* formal *man*—] This seems to mean, A *reasonable* man. A well *regulated* man.

MER. By this, I think, the dial points at five:
Anon, I'm sure, the duke himself in person
Comes this way to the melancholy vale,
The place of death[a] and sorry[b] execution,
Behind the ditches of the abbey here.

ANG. Upon what cause?

MER. To see a reverend Syracusian merchant,
Who put unluckily into this bay
Against the laws and statutes of this town,
Beheaded publicly for his offence.

ANG. See where they come; we will behold his death.

LUC. Kneel to the duke before he pass the abbey.

Enter DUKE, *attended;* ÆGEON, *bare-headed; with the* Headsman *and other* Officers.

DUKE. Yet once again proclaim it publicly,
If any friend will pay the sum for him,
He shall not die,—so much we tender him.

ADR. Justice, most sacred duke, against the abbess!

DUKE. She is a virtuous and a reverend lady;
It cannot be that she hath done thee wrong.

ADR. May it please your grace, Antipholus, my husband,
Whom I made lord of me and all I had,
At your important[c] letters,(1) this ill day
A most outrageous fit of madness took him;
That desp'rately he hurried through the street,
(With him his bondman, all as mad as he,)
Doing displeasure to the citizens,
By rushing in their houses, bearing thence,
Rings, jewels,—any thing his rage did like.
Once did I get him bound, and sent him home,
Whilst to take order for the wrongs I went,
That here and there his fury had committed.
Anon, I wot not by what strong escape,
He broke from those that had the guard of him,
And, with his mad attendant and himself,
Each one, with ireful passion,—with drawn swords,
Met us again, and, madly bent on us,
Chas'd us away; till, raising of more aid,
We came again to bind them: then they fled
Into this abbey, whither we pursued them;
And here the abbess shuts the gates on us,
And will not suffer us to fetch him out,
Nor send him forth, that we may bear him hence.
Therefore, most gracious duke, with thy command,
Let him be brought forth, and borne hence for help.

DUKE. Long since, thy husband serv'd me in my wars;
And I to thee engag'd a prince's word,
When thou didst make him master of thy bed,
To do him all the grace and good I could.
Go, some of you, knock at the abbey-gate,
And bid the lady abbess come to me;
I will determine this before I stir.

Enter a Servant.

SERV. O mistress, mistress! shift and save yourself!
My master and his man are both broke loose,
Beaten the maids a-row,[d] and bound the doctor,
Whose beard they have singed off with brands of fire;
And, ever as it blazed, they threw on him
Great pails of puddled mire to quench the hair:
My master preaches patience to him, and the while,
His man, with scissors, nicks him[e] like a fool;
And, sure, unless you send some present help,
Between them they will kill the conjurer.

ADR. Peace, fool! thy master and his man are here,
And that is false thou dost report to us.

SERV. Mistress, upon my life I tell you true!
I have not breath'd, almost, since I did see it.
He cries for you, and vows, if he can take you,
To scorch[f] your face, and to disfigure you: [*Cry within.*
Hark, hark! I hear him, mistress!—fly!—be gone!

DUKE. Come, stand by me; fear nothing. Guard with halberts.

---

[a] *The place* of death—] The original has *depth* instead of *death;* and, as the Rev. Mr. Hunter thinks, rightly. According to his view, "New Illustrations of Shakespeare," vol. i. p. 225, "'The place of *depth*,' in the Greek story, the *Barathrum*, means the deep pit, into which offenders were cast."

[b] *And* sorry *execution*,—] Meaning *dismal, sorrowful* execution.

[c] *At your* important *letters*,—] That is, in the language of our old writers, your *importunate* letters. Thus, in "Much Ado about Nothing," Act II. Sc. 1:—"—if the Prince be too *important*, tell him there is measure in everything," &c.

So in "King Lear," Act IV. Sc. 4:—

"Therefore great France
My mourning and *important* tears hath pitied."

[d] *Beaten the maids* a-row,—] *A-row* is explained by the commentators, *one after another, successively*.

"A thousand time *a-row* he gan hire kisse."
CHAUCER, *Wife of Bathes Tale*, v. 6386, Tyrwhitt's Ed.

"The curtal Friar in Fountain Abbey
Well can a strong bow draw;
He will beat you and your yeomen
Set them all on *a-row*."
Old Ballads, Evans, vol. ii. p. 152.

[e] Nicks *him like a fool;*] The custom of *shaving* and *nicking* the head of a fool is very old. Tollet says there is a penalty of ten shillings, in one of Alfred's ecclesiastical laws, if one opprobriously *shave* a common man like a *fool;* and Malone cites a passage from "The Choice of Change," &c., by S. R. Gent, 4to. 1598,—"Three things used by monks, which provoke other men to laugh at their follies: 1. They are *shaven* and *notched* on the head like *fooles*."

[f] *To* scorch *your face*,—] So the old copy. The same spelling occurs in the folio, 1623, Act III. Sc. 2, of "Macbeth:"—

"We have *scorch'd* the snake, not killed it;"

where, however, the word meant is probably *scotch'd*.

Adr. Ah me, it is my husband! Witness you,
That he is borne about invisible:
Even now we hous'd him in the abbey here,
And now he's there, past thought of human reason!

Enter Antipholus *and* Dromio *of* Ephesus.

Ant. E. Justice, most gracious duke! Oh, grant me justice!
Even for the service that long since I did thee,
When I bestrid thee in the wars, and took
Deep scars to save thy life; even for the blood
That then I lost for thee, now grant me justice.

Æge. Unless the fear of death doth make me dote,
I see my son Antipholus, and Dromio.

Ant. E. Justice, sweet prince! against that woman there.
She whom thou gav'st to me to be my wife;—
That hath abused and dishonour'd me,
Even in the strength and height of injury!
Beyond imagination is the wrong,
That she this day hath shameless thrown on me.

Duke. Discover how, and thou shalt find me just.

Ant. E. This day, great duke, she shut the doors upon me,
While she with harlots[a] feasted in my house.

Duke. A grievous fault. Say, woman, didst thou so?

Adr. No, my good lord; myself, he, and my sister,
To-day did dine together: so befal my soul
As this is false, he burdens me withal!

[a] *While she with* harlots—] Antipholus does not mean *courtezans*, but *base companions, villains*. So in the "Winter's Tale," Act II. Sc. 3:—

"—— for the *harlot* king
Is quite beyond mine arm."

LUC. Ne'er may I look on day, nor sleep on night,
But she tells to your highness simple truth!

ANG. O perjur'd woman! they are both forsworn.
In this the madman justly chargeth them.

ANT. E. My liege, I am advised what I say;
Neither disturbed with the effect of wine,
Nor, heady-rash, provok'd with raging ire,
Albeit my wrongs might make one wiser mad.
This woman lock'd me out this day from dinner:—
That goldsmith there, were he not pack'd with her,
Could witness it, for he was with me then;
Who parted with me to go fetch a chain,
Promising to bring it to the Porcupine,
Where Balthazar and I did dine together.
Our dinner done, and he not coming thither,
I went to seek him: in the street I met him,
And, in his company, that gentleman.
There did this perjur'd goldsmith swear me down,
That I this day of him receiv'd the chain,
Which, God he knows, I saw not; for the which,
He did arrest me with an officer.
I did obey, and sent my peasant home
For certain ducats: he with none return'd.
Then fairly I bespoke the officer
To go in person with me to my house.
By the way we met
My wife, her sister, and a rabble more
Of vile confederates; along with them,
They brought one Pinch, a hungry lean-fac'd villain,
A mere anatomy, a mountebank,
A thread-bare juggler, and a fortune-teller;
A needy, hollow-ey'd, sharp-looking wretch,—
A living dead man: this pernicious slave,
Forsooth, took on him as a conjurer,
And, gazing in mine eyes, feeling my pulse,
And with no face, as 'twere, out-facing me,
Cries out I was possess'd: then, all together,
They fell upon me, bound me, bore me thence,
And, in a dark and dankish vault at home,
There left me and my man both bound together;
Till, gnawing with my teeth my bonds in sunder,
I gain'd my freedom, and immediately
Ran hither to your grace, whom I beseech
To give me ample satisfaction
For these deep shames and great indignities.

ANG. My lord, in truth, thus far I witness with him,
That he dined not at home, but was lock'd out.

DUKE. But had he such a chain of thee or no?

ANG. He had, my lord; and when he ran in here
These people saw the chain about his neck.

MER. Besides, I will be sworn these ears of mine
Heard you confess you had the chain of him,
After you first forswore it on the mart:
And thereupon I drew my sword on you;
And then you fled into this abbey here,
From whence, I think, you are come by miracle.

ANT. E. I never came within these abbey walls,
Nor ever didst thou draw thy sword on me;
I never saw the chain, so help me Heaven!
And this is false you burden me withal.

DUKE. Why, what an intricate impeach is this!
I think you all have drunk of Circe's cup.
If here you hous'd him, here he would have been.
If he were mad, he would not plead so coldly.
You say he dined at home; the goldsmith here
Denies that saying. Sirrah, what say you?

DRO. E. Sir, he dined with her there, at the Porcupine.

COUR. He did; and from my finger snatch'd that ring.

ANT. E. 'Tis true, my liege, this ring I had of her.

DUKE. Saw'st thou him enter at the abbey here?

COUR. As sure, my liege, as I do see your grace.

DUKE. Why, this is strange. Go, call the abbess hither.
I think you are all mated or stark mad.
[*Exit an* Attendant.

ÆGE. Most mighty duke, vouchsafe me speak a word:
Haply I see a friend will save my life,
And pay the sum that may deliver me.

DUKE. Speak freely, Syracusian, what thou wilt.

ÆGE. Is not your name, sir, call'd Antipholus?
And is not that your bondman, Dromio?

DRO. E. Within this hour I was his bondman, sir,
But he, I thank him, gnaw'd in two my cords.
Now am I Dromio, and his man, unbound.

ÆGE. I am sure you both of you remember me.

DRO. E. Ourselves we do remember, sir, by you;
For lately we were bound as you are now.
You are not Pinch's patient,—are you, sir?

ÆGE. Why look you strange on me? You know me well.

ANT. E. I never saw you in my life, till now.

ÆGE. Oh! grief hath chang'd me since you saw me last;
And careful hours,[a] with Time's deformed hand,
Have written strange defeatures in my face.[b]
But tell me yet, dost thou not know my voice?

ANT. E. Neither.

ÆGE. Dromio, nor thou?

DRO. E. No, trust me, sir, nor I.

ÆGE. I am sure thou dost.

---

[a] *And* careful *hours,*—] *Painful, anxious* hours.

[b] *Strange* defeatures *in my face.*] See Note ([a]), p. 121.

DRO. E. Ay, sir, but I am sure I do not; and whatsoever a man denies, you are now bound[a] to believe him.

ÆGE. Not know my voice? Oh, Time's extremity!
Hast thou so crack'd and splitted my poor tongue,
In seven short years, that here my only son
Knows not my feeble key of untun'd cares?
Though now this grained face of mine be hid
In sap-consuming winter's drizzled snow,
And all the conduits of my blood froze up;
Yet hath my night of life some memory—
My wasting lamps some fading glimmer left—
My dull deaf ears a little use to hear:
All these old witnesses (I cannot err)
Tell me, thou art my son, Antipholus.

ANT. E. I never saw my father in my life.

ÆGE. But seven years since, in Syracusa, boy,
Thou know'st we parted; but, perhaps, my son,
Thou sham'st to acknowledge me in misery.

ANT. E. The duke, and all that know me in the city,
Can witness with me that it is not so;
I ne'er saw Syracusa in my life.

DUKE. I tell thee, Syracusian, twenty years
Have I been patron to Antipholus,
During which time he ne'er saw Syracusa.
I see, thy age and dangers make thee dote.

Enter the Abbess, *with* ANTIPHOLUS *of* Syracuse, *and* DROMIO *of* Syracuse.

ABB. Most mighty duke, behold a man much wrong'd. [*All gather to see them.*

ADR. I see two husbands, or mine eyes deceive me.

DUKE. One of these men is Genius to the other;
And so of these, which is the natural man,
And which the spirit? Who deciphers them?

DRO. S. I, sir, am Dromio; command him away.

DRO. E. I, sir, am Dromio, pray let me stay.

ANT. S. Ægeon, art thou not? or else his ghost!

DRO. S. Oh, my old master! who hath bound him here?

ABB. Whoever bound him, I will loose his bonds,
And gain a husband by his liberty!
Speak, old Ægeon, if thou be'st the man
That hadst a wife once call'd Æmilia,
That bore thee at a burden two fair sons!
Oh, if thou be'st the same Ægeon, speak!

[a] *You are now* bound, &c.] Of course, a quibble on poor Ægeon's bonds.

And speak unto the same Æmilia!
ÆGE. If I dream not,[a] thou art Æmilia!
If thou art she, tell me, where is that son
That floated with thee on the fatal raft?
ABB. By men of Epidamnum he and I,
And the twin Dromio, all were taken up.
But, by and by, rude fishermen of Corinth,
By force, took Dromio and my son from them,
And me they left with those of Epidamnum.
What then became of them I cannot tell;
I, to this fortune that you see me in.
DUKE. Why, here begins his morning story right;
These two Antipholus',—these two so like,
And these two Dromios, one in semblance;
Besides her urging of her wreck at sea:
These are the parents to these children,[b]
Which accidentally are met together.
Antipholus, thou cam'st from Corinth first.
ANT. S. No, sir, not I; I came from Syracuse.
DUKE. Stay, stand apart; I know not which is which.
ANT. E. I came from Corinth, my most gracious lord.
DRO. E. And I with him.
ANT. E. Brought to this town by that most famous warrior,
Duke Menaphon, your most renowned uncle.
ADR. Which of you two did dine with me to-day?
ANT. S. I, gentle mistress.
ADR. And are not you my husband?
ANT. E. No; I say nay to that.
ANT. S. And so do I; yet did she call me so:
And this fair gentlewoman, her sister here,
Did call me brother. What I told you then,[c]
I hope I shall have leisure to make good;
If this be not a dream I see and hear.
ANG. That is the chain, sir, which you had of me.
ANT. S. I think it be, sir; I deny it not.
ANT. E. And you, sir, for this chain arrested me.
ANG. I think I did, sir; I deny it not.
ADR. I sent you money, sir, to be your bail,
By Dromio; but I think he brought it not.
DRO. E. No; none by me.
ANT. S. This purse of ducats I receiv'd from you,
And Dromio, my man, did bring them me:
I see, we still did meet each other's man,
And I was ta'en for him and he for me,
And thereupon these Errors [d] rare arose.
ANT. E. These ducats pawn I for my father here.
DUKE. It shall not need,—thy father hath his life.
COUR. Sir, I must have that diamond from you.
ANT. E. There, take it, and much thanks for my good cheer.
ABB. Renowned duke, vouchsafe to take the pains
To go with us into the abbey here,
And hear at large discoursed all our fortunes;
And all that are assembled in this place,
That, by this sympathized one day's error,
Have suffer'd wrong, go, keep us company,
And we shall make full satisfaction.
Twenty-five years have I but gone in travail
Of you, my sons; and, till this present hour,[e]
My heavy burden ne'er delivered.
The duke, my husband, and my children both,
And you the calendars of their nativity,
Go to a gossip's feast, and go with me;[f]
After so long grief, such festivity!
DUKE. With all my heart, I'll gossip at this feast.
[*Exeunt* DUKE, Abbess, ÆGEON, Courtezan, Merchant, ANGELO, *and* Attendants.
DRO. S. Master, shall I fetch your stuff from ship-board?
ANT. E. Dromio, what stuff of mine hast thou embark'd?
DRO. S. Your goods, that lay at host, sir, in the Centaur.
ANT. S. He speaks to me; I am your master, Dromio:

---

[a] *If I dream not,*—] In the folio, 1623, this speech of Ægeon, and the subsequent one of the Abbess, are misplaced, and come after the Duke's speech, commencing,—" Why, here begins," &c. Malone made the necessary transposition.

[b] *To these* children,—] *Children* must be pronounced as a trisyllable.

[c] What I told you then, &c.] This, and the two lines following, are addressed to Luciana, and should perhaps be spoken aside to her.

[d] *These* Errors rare *arose.*] The ancient copy has *errors are,* and this incontestable misprint is faithfully followed by modern editors. Mr. Collier's old corrector endeavours, not very successfully, to rectify it by reading *all* for *are.* I venture to substitute *rare,* which, besides being closer to the original, appears to give a better meaning.

[e] Twenty-five *years have I but gone in travail*
Of you, my sons; and, till this present hour,
My heavy burden ne'er *delivered.*]

The original copy has "thirtie three yeares." The rectification of time was made by Theobald, who pointed out that as Ægeon had related how at eighteen years his youngest boy "became inquisitive after his brother;" and, in the present Scene, says it is but seven years since they parted, the date of their birth is settled indisputably. For the emendation, *ne'er* for *are*, we are indebted to Mr. Dyce.

[f] *Go to a gossip's feast, and go with me;*
After so long grief, such festivity!]

The old copy gives us:—

" After so long grief, such *nativity*,"

which can hardly be right, "such nativity," that is, *equal*, or *proportionate nativity*, being without sense here. Johnson proposed *festivity*, which is most likely what the poet wrote. The compositor seems to have caught *nativity* from the line just above. I believe, however, this word is not the only corruption in the passage.

Come, go with us; we'll look to that anon;
Embrace thy brother there; rejoice with him.
[*Exeunt* ANTIPHOLUS S. *and* E., ADR. *and* LUC.

DRO. S. There is a fat friend at your master's house,
That kitchen'd me for you to-day at dinner;
She now shall be my sister,—not my wife.

DRO. E. Methinks you are my glass, and not my brother:
I see by you, I am a sweet-fac'd youth.
Will you walk in to see their gossiping?

DRO. S. Not I, sir; you are my elder.

DRO. E. That's a question: how shall we try it?

DRO. S. We'll draw cuts for the senior; till then, lead thou first.

DRO. E. Nay, then, thus;
We came into the world like brother and brother;
And now let's go hand in hand, not one before another. [*Exeunt.*

ILLUSTRATIVE COMMENTS.

ACT I.

(1) SCENE II.—*They say this town is full of cozenage, &c.*] This was the character attributed to Ephesus in remote ages. Steevens suggests that Shakespeare might have got the hint for this description from Warner's translation of the "Menæchmi," 1595. "For this assure yourselfe, this Towne *Epidamnum* is a place of outragious expences, exceeding in all ryot and lasciviousnesse: and (I heare) as full of Ribaulds, Parasites, Drunkards, Catchpoles, Cony-catchers, and Sycophants, as it can hold," &c. But it is observable that Shakespeare, with great propriety, makes Antipholus attach to the Ephesians higher and more poetical qualities of cozenage than those enumerated by the old translator. It is not merely as "catchpoles," "cony-catchers," and the like, but as "dark-working sorcerers," and "soul-killing witches," that he speaks of them. And hence we are prepared to find him attribute the cross-purposes of the scene to supernatura agency, and see no inconsistency in his wooing Luciana as an enchantress:—

"Teach me, dear creature! how to think and speak;
Lay open to my earthy gross conceit,
Smother'd in errors—feeble—shallow—weak—
The folded meaning of your words' deceit.
Against my soul's pure truth, why labour you
To make it wander in an unknown field?"

Or in his imagining that, to win the sibyl, he must lose himself:—

"Sing, syren, for thyself, and I will dote:
Spread o'er the silver waves thy golden hairs,
And as a bride I'll take thee, and there lie;
And, in that glorious supposition, think
He gains by death, that hath such means to die!"

ACT III.

(1) SCENE I.—*Once this.*] The following note in Gifford's "Ben Jonson" (vol. iii. p. 218) helps to confirm our opinion that *once* in this place, and in many other instances, is only another form of *nonce*, and means for the *occasion*, for the *time being*, &c. "For the *nonce*, is simply for the *once*, for the *one thing* in question, whatever it may be. This is invariably its meaning. The aptitude of many of our monosyllables beginning with a vowel to assume the *n* is well known; but the progress of this expression is distinctly marked in our early writers, 'a ones,' 'an anes,' 'for the anes,' 'for the nanes,' 'for the nones,' 'for the nonce.'"

(2) SCENE II.—*He gains by death, that hath such means to die.*] The allusion is obviously to the long current opinion that the syren, or mermaid, decoyed mortals to destruction by the witchery of her songs. This superstition has been charmingly illustrated by Leyden, in his poem, "The Mermaid," (*vide* Scott's "Minstrelsy of the Scottish Border," vol. iv. p. 294.)

"Thus, all to soothe the Chieftain's woe,
Far from the maid he loved so dear,
The song arose, so soft and slow,
He seem'd her parting sigh to hear.

* * * *

That sea-maid's form, of pearly light,
Was whiter than the downy spray,
And round her bosom, heaving bright,
Her glossy, yellow ringlets play.

Borne on a foamy-crested wave,
She reach'd amain the bounding prow,
Then clasping fast the Chieftain brave,
She, plunging, sought the deep below."

The reader desirous of particular information concerning the supposed existence and habits of these seductive beings, may consult Maillet's "Telliamed," Pontopiddan's "Natural History of Norway," and Waldron's "Account of the Isle of Man."

(3) SCENE II.—
ANT. S. *Where* France?
DRO. S. *In her forehead; arm'd and reverted, making war against her* heir.]
As Theobald first observed, an equivoque was, no doubt, intended between the words *hair* and *heir;* and by the latter, was meant Henry IV. the *heir* of France, concerning whose succession to the throne there was a civil war in the country from 1589 for several years. Henry, after struggling long against the League, extricated himself from all his difficulties by embracing the Roman Catholic religion at St. Denis, on Sunday, the 25th of July, 1593, and was crowned King of France in February, 1594. In 1591, Lord Essex was dispatched with 4,000 troops to the French king's assistance, and his brother Walter was killed before Rouen, in Normandy. From that time till Henry was peaceably settled on the throne, many bodies of troops were sent by Queen Elizabeth to his aid: so that his situation must at that period have been a matter of notoriety, and a subject of conversation in England. From the reference to this circumstance, Malone imagines the "Comedy of Errors" to have been written before 1594.

ACT IV.

(1) SCENE II.—*A devil in an everlasting garment hath him.*] A sergeant's buff leather garment was called *durance;* partly, it would appear, on account of its *everlasting* qualities, and partly from a quibble on the occupation of the wearer, which was that of arresting and clapping men in *durance.* In Greene's "Quip for an Upstart Courtier," sig. D, 3d edit. 1620, there is a graphic description of a sergeant, or sheriff's officer. "One of them had on a buffe-leather jerkin, all greasie before with the droppings of beere, that fell from his beard, and by his side, a skeine like a brewer's bung knife; and muffled he was in a cloke, turn'd over his nose, as though hee had beene ashamed to showe his face."

This peculiar garb is again referred to by our author in a passage of "Henry IV." Part I. Act I. Sc. 2,—

"And is not a *buff* jerkin a most sweet robe of *durance?*"

the point of which seems not to have been fully understood by the commentators. A *robe of durance* was a cant term, implying imprisonment; and the Prince, after dilating on purse-stealing, humorously calls attention to its probable consequences, by his query about the *buff jerkin.* See MIDDLETON'S "Blurt, Master Constable," Act III. Sc. 2:—

"Tell my lady, that I *go in a suit of durance.*"

(2) SCENE II.—*A hound that runs* counter, *and yet draws* dry foot *well.*] To run *counter* is to follow on a false scent; to *draw dry foot* means to track by the mere scent of the foot. A hound that does one is not likely to do the other; but the ambiguity is explained by the double meaning attached to the words *counter* and *dry foot.* The former implying both *false,* and a *prison,* and the latter, privation of *scent,* and *lack of means.* The sheriff's-officer, as he tracks for a prison, may be said to *run counter,* and, as he follows those who have expended their substance, he *draws dry foot.*

(3) SCENE II.—*One that, before* the judgment, *carries poor souls to* hell.] By *before the judgment,* in its secondary sense, Dromio is supposed to allude to arrest on *mesne-process. Hell* was a cant term for the worst dungeon in the wretched prisons of the time. There was the *Master's Side,* the *Knight's Ward,* the *Hole,* and last and most deplorable, the department called *Hell,* which was the receptacle for those who had no means to pay the extortionate fines exacted for better accommodation.

(4) SCENE III.—*He that* sets up his rest *to do more exploits with his mace* than a morris-pike.] Dromio plays on the word *rest, arrest,* and a metaphor, very common in our old writers, *setting up his rest,* which is taken from gaming, and means *staking his all* upon an event. Hence it was frequently applied to express fixed determination, steadfast purpose. Thus, in "All's Well that Ends Well," Act II. Sc. 1:—

"What I can do, can do no hurt to try,
Since you *set up your rest* 'gainst remedy."

The *Morris-pike* is often mentioned by old writers. It was the Moorish pike, and was constantly used both in land and sea warfare, during the sixteenth century.

(5) SCENE III.—*A ring he hath of mine worth forty ducats.*] The number *forty* was very anciently adopted to express a *great many,* in the same way that we now use *fifty,* or *a score.* In the Scriptures it is recorded that the flood was *forty* days on the earth; the Israelites were *forty* years, and our Saviour *forty* days in the wilderness; and Job mourned *forty* days. In Hindustani, the word chalis, *forty,* has the same indefinite acceptation; *chalis-sutun,* denoting literally *forty columns,* being applied to a palace with a number of pillars. So also in Persia, *chihal* signifies *forty,* and Persepolis, because it is a city of many towers, is called *chihal-minar,* "the forty towers." In like manner, too, the insect which we name *centipede,* is there known as *chihal-pâ,* "forty feet." The word in this sense is not at all uncommon among old English writers;—

"Quoth Niceness to Newfangle, thou art such a Jacke,
That thou devisest *fortie* fashions for my ladie's backe."
The Cobler's Prophecy, 1594.

And it is so used repeatedly by Shakespeare; for example,—

"I have learned these *forty* years."
Richard II. Act I. Sc. 3.

"I will have *forty* moys."
Henry V. Act IV. Sc. 4.

"I myself fight not once in *forty* years."
Henry VI. Part I. Act I. Sc. 3.

"Some *forty* truncheoneers draw."
Henry VIII. Act V. Sc. 3.

"I could beat *forty* of them."
Coriolanus, Act III. Sc. 1.

"I saw her once hop *forty* paces."
Antony and Cleopatra, Act II. Sc. 2.

"I had rather than *forty* pound."
Twelfth Night, Act V. Sc. 1.

ACT V.

(1) SCENE I.—*At your important letters, &c.*]
"Shakspeare, who gives to all nations the customs of his own, seems from this passage to allude to a *court* of *wards* in Ephesus. The *court* of *wards* was always considered as a grievous oppression. It is glanced at as early as in the old morality of Hycke Scorner:—

'—— these ryche men ben unkinde:
Wydowes do curse lordes and gentyllmen,
For they contrayne them to marry with their men;
Ye, wheder they wyll or no.'"—STEEVENS.

"In the passage before us, Shakspeare was thinking particularly on the interest which the king had in England in the marriage of his wards, who were the heirs of his tenants holding by knight's service, or in *capité,* and were under age; an interest which Queen Elizabeth in Shakspeare's time exerted on all occasions, as did her successors, till the abolition of the Court of Wards and Liveries; the poet attributes to the duke the same right to choose a wife or a husband for his wards at Ephesus."—MALONE.

CRITICAL OPINIONS

ON

THE COMEDY OF ERRORS.

"The alternate rhymes that are found in this play, as well as in 'A Midsummer Night's Dream,' 'Love's Labour 's Lost,' 'The Two Gentlemen of Verona,' and 'Romeo and Juliet,' are a further proof that these pieces were among our author's earliest productions. We are told by himself that 'Venus and Adonis' was 'the first heir of his invention.' The 'Rape of Lucrece' probably followed soon afterwards. When he turned his thoughts to the stage, the measure which he had used in those poems naturally presented itself to him in his first dramatick essays: I mean in those plays which were written *originally* by himself. In those which were grounded, like the Henries, on the preceding productions of other men, he naturally followed the example before him, and consequently in those pieces no alternate rhymes are found. The doggrel measure, which, if I recollect right, is employed in none of our author's plays except 'The Comedy of Errors,' 'The Taming of the Shrew,' and 'Love's Labour 's Lost,' also adds support to the dates assigned to these plays; for these long doggrel verses are written in that kind of metre which was usually attributed by the dramatic poets before his time to some of their inferior characters.* He was imperceptibly infected with the prevailing mode in these his early compositions; but soon learned to 'deviate boldly from the common track' left by preceding writers."—Malone.

"This drama of Shakspeare's is much more varied, rich, and interesting in its incidents than the Menæchmi of Plautus; and while, in rigid adherence to the unities of action, time, and place, our poet rivals the Roman play, he has contrived to insinuate the necessary previous information for the spectator, in a manner infinitely more pleasing and artful than that adopted by the Latin bard; for whilst Plautus has chosen to convey it through the medium of a prologue, Shakspeare has rendered it at once natural and pathetic, by placing it in the mouth of Ægeon, the father of the twin brothers.

"In a play, of which the plot is so intricate, occupied, in a great measure, by mere personal mistakes and their whimsical results, no elaborate development of character can be expected; yet is the portrait

---

LIKE WILL TO LIKE.
1568.

"Royst. If your name to me you will declare and showe,
You may in this matter my minde the sooner knowe.
Tos. Few wordes are best among freends, this is true,
Wherefore I shall briefly show my name unto you.
Tom Tospot it is, it need not to be painted,
Wherefore I with Raife Roister must needs be acquainted," &c.

COMMONS CONDITIONS.
(About 1570.)

"Shift. By gogs bloud, my maisters, we were not best longer here to staie,
I thinke was never such a craftie knave before this daie.
[*Ex.* Ambo.
Cond. Are thei all gone? Ha, ha, well fare old Shift at a neede:
By his woundes had I not devised this, I had hanged indeed.
Tinkers, (q[d] you) tinke me no tinkes; I'll meddle with them no more;
I thinke was never knave so used by a companie of tinkers before.
By your leave I'll be so bolde as to looke about me and spie,
Lest any knaves for my coming down in ambush do lie.
By your license I minde not to preache longer in this tree,
My tinkerly slaves are packed hence, as farre as I maie see;" &c.

PROMOS AND CASSANDRA.
1578.

"The wind is yl blows no man's gaine: for cold I neede not care:
Here is nine and twentie sutes of apparel for my share:
And some, berlady, very good, for so standeth the case,
As neither gentlemen nor other Lord Promos sheweth any grace;
But I marvel much, poore slaves, that they are hanged so soone,
They were wont to staye a day or two, now scarce an after-noone;" &c.

THE THREE LADIES OF LONDON.
1584.

"You think I am going to market to buy rost meate, do ye not?
I thought so, but you are deceived, for I wot what I wot:
I am neither going to the butchers, to buy veale, mutton, or beefe,
But I am going to a bloodsucker, and who is it? faith Usurie, that theefe."

THE COBLER'S PROPHECY.
1594.

"Quoth Niceness to Newfangle, thou art such a Jacke,
That thou devisest fortie fashions for my ladie's backe.
And thou, quoth he, art so possest with everie frantick toy,
That following of my ladie's humour thou dost make her coy,
For once a day for fashion-sake my lady must be sicke,
No meat but mutton, or at most the pinion of a chicke;
To-day her owne haire best becomes, which yellow is as gold
A periwig is better for to-morrow, blacke to behold:
To-day in pumps and cheveril gloves to walk she will be bold,
To-morrow cuffes and countenance, for feare of catching cold,
Now is she barefast to be seene, straight on her mufler goes;
Now is she hufft up to the crowne, straight nusled to the nose."

of Ægeon touched with a discriminative hand, and the pressure of age and misfortune is so painted, as to throw a solemn, dignified, and impressive tone of colouring over this part of the fable, contrasting well with the lighter scenes which immediately follow,—a mode of relief which is again resorted to at the close of the drama, where the re-union of Ægeon and Æmilia, and the recognition of their children, produce an interest in the denouëment of a nature more affecting than the tone of the preceding scenes had taught us to expect.

"As to the comic action which constitutes the chief bulk of this piece, if it be true, that, to excite laughter, awaken attention, and fix curiosity, be essential to its dramatic excellence, the *Comedy of Errors* cannot be pronounced an unsuccessful effort; both reader and spectator are hurried on to the close, through a series of thick-coming incidents, and under the pleasurable influence of novelty, expectation, and surprise; and the dialogue is uniformly vivacious, pointed, and even effervescing. Shakspeare is visible, in fact, throughout the entire play, as well in the broad exuberance of its mirth, as in the cast of its more chastised parts,—a combination of which may be found in the punishment and character of Pinch, the pedagogue and conjuror, who is sketched in the strongest and most marked style of our author.

"If we consider, therefore, the construction of the fable, the narrowness of its basis, and that its powers of entertainment are almost exclusively confined to a continued deception of the external senses, we must confess that Shakspeare has not only improved on the Plautian model, but, making allowance for a somewhat too coarse vein of humour, has given to his production all the interest and variety that the nature and the limits of his subject would permit."—DRAKE.

"Shakespeare has in this piece presented us with a legitimate farce in exactest consonance with the philosophical principles and character of farce, as distinguished from comedy and from entertainments. A proper farce is mainly distinguished from comedy by the license allowed, and even required, in the fable, in order to produce strange and laughable situations. The story need not be probable, it is enough that it is possible. A comedy would scarcely allow even the two Antipholuses, because although there have been instances of almost undistinguishable likeness in two persons, yet these are mere individual antecedents, *casus ludentis naturæ*, and the *verum* will not excuse the *inverisimile*. But farce dares add the two Dromios, and is justified in so doing by the laws of its end and constitution. In a word, farces commence in a postulate which must be granted."—COLERIDGE.

"'The Comedy of Errors' is the subject of the Menæchmi of Plautus, entirely recast and enriched with new developments. Of all works of Shakspeare this is the only example of imitation of, *or borrowing* from, the ancients. To the two twin brothers of the same name are added two slaves, also twins, impossible to be distinguished from each other, and of the same name. The improbability becomes by this means doubled; but when once we have lent ourselves to the first, which certainly borders on the incredible, we shall not perhaps be disposed to cavil at the second; and if the spectator is to be entertained by mere perplexities, they cannot be too much varied. * * * * In short, this is perhaps the best of all written or possible Menæchmi; and if the piece be inferior in worth to other pieces of Shakspeare, it is merely because nothing more could be made of the materials."—SCHLEGEL.

Act III. Sc. 5.

ROMEO AND JULIET.

The pathetic legend on which Shakespeare founded the plot of this beautiful tragedy has been cherished from time immemorial among the traditions of Italian history, although no such story has ever been discovered in the authentic records of any particular state. The Veronese, Lord Byron tells us, are tenacious to a degree of the truth of it, insisting on the fact, giving a date (1303), and showing the tomb. But this is only an instance of pardonable local vanity; no account exists of any actual Romeo and Juliet, but a tale more or less resembling that immortalized by our great dramatist may be found in several ancient writers. Mr. Douce has attempted to trace it to a Middle Greek author, one Xenophon Ephesius. The earliest writer, however, who set forth the romance in a connected narration is believed to be Masuccio di Salerno, in whose "Novellino," a collection of tales first printed at Naples in 1476, a similar event is recorded to have occurred, not at Verona, but in Sienna. He relates that in Sienna there lived a young man of good family, named Mariotto Mignanelli, who was enamoured of a lady, Gianozza, and succeeded in engaging her affections; some impediment standing in the way of a public marriage, they are secretly united by an Augustine monk. Shortly after the ceremony, Mariotto has the misfortune to slay a fellow-citizen of rank in a street brawl, for which he is condemned by the Podesta to perpetual banishment. He obtains a farewell interview with his wife, and departs to Alexandria, where resides a rich uncle of his, Sir Nicolo Mignanelli. After the flight of Mariotto, Gianozza is pressed by her father to accept a husband whom he has found for her. Having no reason which she dare allege to oppose her parent's wishes, she pretends to consent, and then determines to escape the hated nuptials by an act as daring as it was extraordinary. She discloses her miserable situation to the monk who had married her to Mariotto, and bribes him to prepare a soporific powder, which, drunk in water, will throw her into a death-like trance for three days; she drinks the narcotic, is supposed to be dead, and in due time is interred by her friends in the church of St. Augustine. Before this, she had despatched a special messenger to Alexandria, apprising her husband of her determination; but the messenger is unhappily seized by pirates, and her missive never reaches him; instead of it, he receives another letter written by his brother, informing him of her death and that of her father also, who had died of grief for the loss of his daughter. The wretched Mariotto resolves to return forthwith to Sienna, and die upon her tomb, or perish by the hand of justice. He is taken in an attempt to break open the vault, and is condemned to death. Gianozza, in the meanwhile, recovers from her lethargy, disguises herself in man's apparel, and sets out for Alexandria in search of her banished husband; here she learns, to her dismay, that Mariotto, believing her dead, had departed for Sienna. She returns to that place, and, arriving just three days after his execution, dies of anguish and a broken heart.*

A story closely corresponding with this in the preliminary incidents, though varying in the catastrophe, is told by Luigi da Porto in his Novella, "La Giulietta," first published in 1535. "Hystoria Novella mente Ritrovata di dui nobili Amanti: Con la loro Pietosa Morte: Intervenuta gia nella Citta di Verona Nel tempio del Signor Bartholomeo Scala." Luigi, in his dedication to Madonna Lucina Savorgnana, pretends to have derived the legend from an archer of Verona, one Peregrino, who quotes as his authority for it a relation of his father's. In the

* "La donna no'l trova in Alesandria, ritorna a Siena, e trova l'amunto decollato, e ella sopra il suo corpo per dolore si muore," are the words of the "Argument;" but in the novel itself she is said to retire to a monastery,—"Con intenso dolore e sanguinose lagrime con poco cibo e niente dormire, il suo' Mariotto di continovo chiamando, in brevissimo tempo finì li suvi miserimi giorni."

narrative of Peregrino, we first meet with the families of Montague and Capulet in connexion with the story, which he relates to have occurred in Verona. The real or supposititious archer expresses doubts of the historical truth of the event, since he had read in some ancient chronicles that the Capelletti and Montecchi had always been of the same party.*

In 1554, Bandello published at Lucca a novel on the same subject, which, like Da Porto, he says was related to him by one Peregrino. This was followed at a brief interval by another, in French, by Pierre Boisteau, founded on the narratives of Luigi da Porto and Bandello, but differing from them in many particulars. From the translation of Boisteau, the English versions of the tale—namely, the poem called "The Tragical Historye of Romeus and Juliet," (1562,) by Arthur Brooke, and the novel found in Paynter's "Palace of Pleasure," under the title of "The goodly hystory of the true and constant love betweene Rhomeo and Julietta"—were both derived; † and to these, more especially the poem, Shakespeare was certainly indebted, not for the story,—which seems to have been popular long before he adapted it for representation,—but for the names of his chief characters, and many of the incidents, and even expressions of his tragedy.

The first edition of "Romeo and Juliet" was printed by *John Danter*, in the year 1597, with the title of "An excellent conceited tragedie of Romeo and Juliet. As it hath been often (with great applause) plaid publiquely, by the right honourable the L. of Hunsdon his Seruants."

The second edition was printed by *Thomas Creede*, for *Cuthbert Burby*, in 1599, and is entitled "The most excellent and lamentable Tragedie of Romeo and Juliet; Newly corrected, augmented, and amended: As it hath been sundry times publiquely acted, by the right Honourable the Lord Chamberlaine his Seruants."

The two remaining editions, published before the folio collection of 1623, are a quarto printed in 1609, and another without date, both by the same publisher, *John Smethwicke*.

The first two of these editions are extremely rare and valuable; and there is every reason to conclude that the numerous corrections and amplifications in that of 1599 are exclusively Shakespeare's own, since the former evince the judgment and tact of the master, and the latter comprise some of the finest passages in the play. But a correct copy of the text can only be obtained by a collation of both these editions, as the first is free from certain typographical errors which disfigure and obscure the second, and *vice versâ*. The subsequent copies are all founded on the quarto, 1599, and contain but few deviations from its text.

As Shakespeare was only thirty-three years of age when this play was first published, it must obviously rank among his early productions. But the date of publication is no criterion to determine the period when it was written, or when it was first performed. The words on the titlepage of the first edition, "As it hath been often (with great applause) plaid publiquely, by the right honourable the L. of Hunsdon his Seruants," Malone considers proof that the play was first acted in 1596, because Henry, Lord Hunsdon, who held the office of Lord Chamberlain, died in that year, and his son George, Lord Hunsdon, only succeeded to the office in April, 1597. He is of opinion that the actors would only have designated themselves "Lord Hunsdon's servants" during the interval of these dates, because they would have been called "The Lord Chamberlain's servants" at a time when the office was really held by their noble patron. This argument, Mr. Knight remarks, is no doubt decisive as to the play being performed before George, Lord Hunsdon; but it is not in any degree decisive as to the play not having been performed without the advantage of this nobleman's patronage. Chalmers assigns its composition to the spring of 1592; and Drake places it a year later. The belief in its production at an earlier period than that ascribed by Malone, is strengthened by the indications

---

* This accords with a passage in Dante (Purgatorio, c. vi.), where the poet, reproaching "Alberto Tedesco," the German emperor Albert, for his treatment of Italy, exclaims:—

"Vieni a veder Montecchi e Capelletti,
Monaldi e Fillippeschi, uom senza cura!
Color già tristi e costor con sospetti."

Which Cary renders:—

"Come, see the Capulets and Montagues,
The Fillippeschi and Monaldi, man
Who car'st for nought! Those sunk in grief, and these
With dire suspicion rack'd."

† The story must have been eminently popular all over Europe from an early period. It forms the subject of a Spanish play by Lopez de Vega, entitled "Los Castelvies y Monteses," and another by Don Francisco de Roxas, under the name of "Los Vandos de Verona." In Italy, so early as 1578, it had been adapted to the stage by Luigi Groto, under the title of "Hadriana;" and Arthur Brooke, in the preface to the poem above mentioned, speaks of having seen "the same argument lately set forth on stage with more commendation than I can looke for (being there much better set forth then I have or can dooe):" an allusion most probably to some representation of it abroad, for the rude condition of our drama at the time, renders it unlikely that he should refer to any play of the kind performed in this country.

of matured reading and reflection which are displayed in the augmented edition of 1599, as compared with that of 1597. There is also a scrap of internal evidence which, as proof of an earlier authorship than 1596, is well entitled to consideration. The Nurse, describing Juliet's being weaned, says,—" On Lammas-eve at night shall she be fourteen; that shall she; marry, I remember it well. 'Tis since the earthquake now eleven years." Tyrwhitt was the first to suggest the probable reference of this passage to an earthquake which occurred in 1580, and of which Holinshed has given a striking and minute account:—" On the sixt of Aprill (1580), being wednesdaie in Easter weeke about six of the clocke toward euening, a sudden earthquake happening in London, and almost generallie throughout all England, caused such an amazednesse among the people as was wonderfull for the time, and caused them to make their earnest praiers to almightie God. The great clocke bell in the palace at Westminster strake of it selfe against the hammer with the shaking of the earth, as diverse other clocks and bels in the steeples of the citie of London and elswhere did the like. The gentlemen of the Temple being then at supper, ran from the tables, and out of their hall with their kniues in their hands. The people assembled at the plaie houses in the fields, * * * * were so amazed that doubting the ruine of the galleries, they made hast to be gone. A peece of the temple church fell down, some stones fell from saint Paules church in London: and at Christs church neere to Newgate market, in the sermon while, a stone fell from the top of the same church." Such an event would form a memorable epoch to the class which constituted the staple of a playhouse auditory in the sixteenth century; and if an allusion to it was calculated to awaken interest and fix attention, the anachronism, or the impropriety of its association with an historical incident of some centuries preceding, would hardly have deterred any playwright of that age from turning it to account. On the theory that the Nurse's observation really applied to the earthquake of 1580, we may ascribe the date of this play's composition to the year 1591; and, unfortunately, in the absence of everything in the shape of a history of our poet's writings, we can trust only to inferences and conjectures of this description to make even an approximate guess as to the period of its production.

Persons Represented.

ESCALUS, *Prince of* VERONA.

PARIS, *a young Nobleman, kinsman to the Prince.*

MONTAGUE, } *heads of two Houses, at variance with*
CAPULET, } *each other.*

An old Man, uncle to CAPULET.

ROMEO, *son to* MONTAGUE.

MERCUTIO, *kinsman to the Prince, and friend to* ROMEO.

BENVOLIO, *nephew to* MONTAGUE, *and friend to* ROMEO.

TYBALT, *nephew to* LADY CAPULET.

FRIAR LAURENCE, *a Franciscan.*

FRIAR JOHN, *of the same order.*

BALTHASAR, *servant to* ROMEO.

SAMPSON, } *servants to* CAPULET.
GREGORY, }

ABRAM, *servant to* MONTAGUE.

An Apothecary.

Three Musicians.

Chorus. Boy; Page to PARIS; PETER; *and an Officer.*

LADY MONTAGUE, *wife to* MONTAGUE.

LADY CAPULET, *wife to* CAPULET.

JULIET, *daughter to* CAPULET.

Nurse to JULIET.

Citizens of VERONA; *several men and women, Relations to both Houses; Maskers, Guards, Watchmen, and Attendants.*

SCENE, *during the greater part of the Play, in* VERONA; *once, in the fifth Act, at* MANTUA.

THE

PROLOGUE.[a]

CHORUS.

Two households, both alike in dignity,
(In fair Verona, where we lay our scene,)
From ancient grudge break to new mutiny,
Where civil blood makes civil hands unclean.
From forth the fatal loins of these two foes
A pair of star-cross'd lovers take their life;
Whose misadventur'd piteous overthrows
Doth, with their death, bury their parents' strife.
The fearful passage of their death-mark'd love,
And the continuance of their parents' rage,
Which, but their children's end, nought could remove,
Is now the two hours' traffick of our stage;
The which if you with patient ears attend,
What here shall miss, our toil shall strive to mend.

---

[a] This prologue appeared in its present form, in the first complete edition of "Romeo and Juliet," the quarto of 1599: it is omitted in the folio. In the incomplete sketch of the play, published in 1597, it stands as under;—

"Two houshold frends alike in dignitie,
(In faire *Verona*, where we lay our Scene)
From ciuill broyles broke into enmitie,
Whose ciuill warre makes ciuill hands vncleane.
From forth the fatall loynes of these two foes,
A paire of starre-crost louers tooke their life:
Whose misaduentures, piteous ouerthrowes,
(Through the continuing of their fathers strife,
And death-markt passage of their parents rage)
Is now the two howres traffique of our stage.
The which if you with patient eares attend,
What here we want wee'l studie to amend."

ACT I.

SCENE I.—*A Public Place.*

Enter SAMPSON *and* GREGORY, *armed with swords and bucklers.*

SAM. Gregory, o' my word, we'll not carry coals.[a]

GRE. No, for then we should be colliers.

SAM. I mean, an* we be in choler, we'll draw.

GRE. Ay, while you live, draw your neck out o' the collar.

SAM. I strike quickly, being moved.

GRE. But thou art not quickly moved to strike.

SAM. A dog of the house of Montague moves me.

GRE. To move, is—to stir; and to be valiant, is—to stand: therefore, if thou art moved, thou run'st away.

SAM. A dog of that house shall move me to stand: I will take the wall of any man or maid of Montague's.

GRE. That shows thee a weak slave; for the weakest goes to the wall.

SAM. True; and therefore women, being the weaker vessels, are ever thrust to the wall:—therefore I will push Montague's men from the wall, and thrust his maids to the wall.

GRE. The quarrel is between our masters, and us their men.

SAM. 'Tis all one, I will show myself a tyrant:

(*) First folio, *if*.

[a] We'll not carry coals.] *We will not submit to indignities.* A favourite expression with the authors of Shakespeare's era, and which probably originated, as Gifford suggests, in the fact that the meanest and most forlorn dependents of a great household were those employed in the servile drudgery of *carrying coals*.

when I have fought with the men, I will be cruel[a] with the maids; I will* cut off their heads.

GRE. The heads of the maids?

SAM. Ay, the heads of the maids, or their maiden-heads; take it in what sense thou wilt.

GRE. They must take it in† sense, that feel it.

SAM. Me they shall feel, while I am able to stand: and, 'tis known, I am a pretty piece of flesh.

GRE. 'Tis well, thou art not fish; if thou hadst, thou hadst been poor John.[b] Draw thy tool; here comes of the house of the Montagues.(1)

Enter ABRAM *and another* Servant *of* MONTAGUE.

SAM. My naked weapon is out; quarrel, I will back thee.

GRE. How? turn thy back, and run?

SAM. Fear me not.

GRE. No, marry; I fear thee!

SAM. Let us take the law of our sides; let them begin.

GRE. I will frown, as I pass by; and let them take it as they list.

SAM. Nay, as they dare. I will bite my thumb at them;[c] which is a disgrace to them, if they bear it.

ABR. Do you bite your thumb at us, sir?

SAM. I do bite my thumb, sir.

ABR. Do you bite your thumb at us, sir?

SAM. Is the law of our side, if I say—ay? [*Aside to* GREGORY.

GRE. No.

SAM. No, sir, I do not bite my thumb at you, sir; but I bite my thumb, sir.

GRE. Do you quarrel, sir?

ABR. Quarrel, sir? no, sir.

SAM. But if you do, sir, I am for you; I serve as good a man as you.

ABR. No better.

SAM. Well, sir.

(*) First folio, and *cut off*. (†) First folio omits *in*.

[a] I *will be* cruel *with the maids*;] The quarto of 1599, that of 1609, and the folio, 1623, which was printed from it, concur in reading *civill*. The correction appears in a quarto edition without date, published by John Smethwicke; "at his shop in Sainte Dunstanes Church, in Fleete Street, under the Dyall." Smethwicke also published the quarto, 1609; and the undated edition, which contains several important corrections of previous typographical errors, was probably issued soon after.

[b] Poor John.] The fish called *hake*, an inferior sort of cod, when dried and salted, was probably the staple fare of servants and the indigent during Lent; and this sorry dish is perpetually ridiculed by the old writers as "poor John."

[c] *I will* bite my thumb *at them*;] This contemptuous action, though obsolete in this country, is still in use both in France and Italy; but Mr. Knight is mistaken in supposing it identical with what is called *giving the fico*. *Biting the thumb* is performed by biting the thumb nail; or, as Cotgrave describes it, "by putting the thumbe naile into the mouth, and with a jerke (from the

Enter BENVOLIO, *at a distance.*

GRE. Say—better; here comes one of my master's kinsmen. [*Aside to* SAMPSON.

SAM. Yes, better, sir.*

ABR. You lie.

SAM. Draw, if you be men.—Gregory, remember thy swashing† blow.[d] [*They fight.*

BEN. Part, fools; put up your swords; you know not what you do. [*Beats down their swords.*

Enter TYBALT.

TYB. What, art thou drawn among these heartless hinds?
Turn thee, Benvolio, look upon thy death.

BEN. I do but keep the peace; put up thy sword,
Or manage it to part these men with me.

TYB. What, drawn,‡ and talk of peace? I hate the word,
As I hate hell, all Montagues, and thee:
Have at thee, coward! [*They fight.*

Enter several Followers *of both Houses*,[e] *who join the fray; then enter* Citizens, *with clubs.*

1 CIT. Clubs, bills, and partizans![f] strike! beat them down!
Down with the Capulets! down with the Montagues!

Enter CAPULET, *in his gown; and* LADY CAPULET.

CAP. What noise is this?—Give me my long sword, ho!

LA. CAP. A crutch, a crutch!—why call you for a sword?

CAP. My sword, I say!—Old Montague is come,
And flourishes his blade in spite of me.

(*) First folio omits *sir*.
(†) Old copies, except the undated quarto, *washing*.
(‡) First folio, *draw*.

upper teeth) make it to knacke." The more offensive gesticulation of *giving the fico* was by thrusting out the thumb between the fore-fingers, or putting it in the mouth so as to swell out the cheek.

[d] *Remember thy* swashing *blow*.] To *swash* perhaps originally meant, as Barret in his "Alvearie," 1580, describes it, "to make a noise with swords against tergats;" but *swashing blow* here, as in Jonson's "Staple of News," Act V. Sc. 2, "I do confess a *swashing blow*," means evidently a *smashing, crushing* blow.

[e] *Enter several* Followers, &c.] A modern direction. The old copies have merely—"*Enter three or four citizens with clubs or partysons.*"

[f] Clubs, *bills*, and *partizans!*—] Shakespeare, whose wont it is to assimilate the customs of all countries to those of his own, puts the ancient call to arms of the London 'prentices in the mouth of the Veronese citizen.

Enter MONTAGUE *and* LADY MONTAGUE.

MON. Thou villain, Capulet,—Hold me not, let me go.

LA. MON. Thou shalt not stir one* foot to seek a foe.(2)

Enter PRINCE, *with* Attendants.

PRIN. Rebellious subjects, enemies to peace,
Profaners of this neighbour-stained steel,—
Will they not hear?—what ho! you men, you beasts,—
That quench the fire of your pernicious rage
With purple fountains issuing from your veins,—
On pain of torture, from those bloody hands
Throw your mis-temper'd weapons to the ground,
And hear the sentence of your moved prince.—
Three civil brawls,† bred of an airy word,
By thee, old Capulet, and Montague,
Have thrice disturb'd the quiet of our streets;
And made Verona's ancient citizens
Cast by their grave beseeming ornaments,
To wield old partizans, in hands as old,
Canker'd with peace, to part your canker'd hate.
If ever you disturb our streets again,
Your lives shall pay the forfeit of the peace.
For this time, all the rest depart away:
You, Capulet, shall go along with me,
And, Montague, come you this afternoon,
To know our farther‡ pleasure in this case,
To old Free-town, our common judgment-place.
Once more, on pain of death, all men depart.

[*Exeunt* PRINCE *and* Attendants; CAPULET, LADY CAPULET, TYBALT, Citizens, *and* Servants.

MON. Who set this ancient quarrel new abroach?—
Speak, nephew, were you by, when it began?

BEN. Here were the servants of your adversary,
And yours, close fighting ere I did approach:
I drew to part them; in the instant came
The fiery Tybalt, with his sword prepar'd;
Which, as he breath'd defiance to my ears,
He swung about his head, and cut the winds,
Who, nothing hurt withal, hiss'd him in scorn:
While we were interchanging thrusts and blows,
Came more and more, and fought on part and part,
Till the prince came, who parted either part.

LA. MON. O, where is Romeo!—saw you him to-day?
Right glad am I, he was not at this fray.

BEN. Madam, an hour before the worshipp'd sun
Peer'd forth the golden window of the east,
A troubled mind drave me to walk abroad;
Where,—underneath the grove of sycamore,
That westward rooteth from this city's side,—
So early walking did I see your son:
Towards him I made; but he was 'ware of me,
And stole into the covert of the wood:
I, measuring his affections by my own,—
That most are busied when they are most alone,[a]—
Pursued my humour,* not pursuing his,
And gladly shunn'd who gladly fled from me.

MON. Many a morning hath he there been seen,[b]
With tears augmenting the fresh morning's dew,
Adding to clouds more clouds with his deep sighs:
But all so soon as the all-cheering sun
Should in the farthest east begin to draw
The shady curtains from Aurora's bed,
Away from light steals home my heavy son,
And private in his chamber pens himself,
Shuts up his windows, locks fair daylight out,
And makes himself an artificial night:
Black and portentous must this humour prove,
Unless good counsel may the cause remove.

BEN. My noble uncle, do you know the cause?

MON. I neither know it, nor can learn of him.

BEN. Have you impórtun'd him by any means?

MON. Both by myself, and many other† friends:
But he, his own affections' counsellor,
Is to himself—I will not say, how true—
But to himself so secret and so close,
So far from sounding and discovery,
As is the bud bit with an envious worm,
Ere he can spread his sweet leaves to the air,
Or dedicate his beauty to the sun.[c]
Could we but learn from whence his sorrows grow,
We would as willingly give cure, as know.

Enter ROMEO, *at a distance.*

BEN. See, where he comes: so please you, step aside;
I'll know his grievance, or be much denied.

MON. I would, thou wert so happy by thy stay,
To hear true shrift.—Come, madam, let's away.
[*Exeunt* MONTAGUE *and* Lady.

BEN. Good morrow, cousin.

ROM. Is the day so young?

(*) First folio, a *foot*. (†) First folio, *broils*. (‡) First folio, *father's*.

(*) First folio, *honour*. (†) First folio, *others*.

[a] That most are busied when they are most alone,—] This is the reading of the quarto, 1597. Subsequent editions, including the folio, 1623, read thus:—

"Which then most sought, where most might not be found;
Being one too many by my weary self,
Pursued my humour," &c.

[b] Many a morning hath he there been seen,—] This, and the lines following down to—

"And makes himself an artificial night,"

are first found in the quarto of 1599. Benvolio's inquiry,

"Have you impórtun'd him by any means?"

and the reply, are likewise wanting in the first quarto.

[c] *His beauty to the sun.*] The old editions have *same*. The emendation was made by Theobald.

BEN. But new struck nine.
ROM. Ay me! sad hours seem long.
Was that my father that went hence so fast?
BEN. It was.—What sadness lengthens Romeo's hours?
ROM. Not having that, which, having, makes them short.
BEN. In love?
ROM. Out—
BEN. Of love?
ROM. Out of her favour, where I am in love.(3)
BEN. Alas, that love, so gentle in his view,
Should be so tyrannous and rough in proof!
ROM. Alas, that love, whose view is muffled still,
Should, without eyes, see pathways to his will![a]
Where shall we dine?—O me!—What fray was here?
Yet tell me not, for I have heard it all.
Here's much to-do with hate, but more with love:—
Why then, O brawling love! O loving hate!
O any thing, of nothing first created;
O heavy lightness! serious vanity!
Mis-shapen chaos of well-seeming * forms!
Feather of lead, bright smoke, cold fire, sick health!
Still-waking sleep, that is not what it is!—
This love feel I, that feel no love in this.
Dost thou not laugh?
BEN. No, coz, I rather weep.
ROM. Good heart, at what?
BEN. At thy good heart's oppression.
ROM. Why, such is love's transgression.—
Griefs of mine own lie heavy in my breast,
Which thou wilt propagate, to have it prest
With more of thine: this love, that thou hast shown,
Doth add more grief to too much of mine own.
Love is a smoke made with the fume of sighs;
Being purg'd,[b] a fire sparkling in lovers' eyes;
Being vex'd, a sea nourish'd with loving tears;
What is it else? a madness most discreet,
A choking gall, and a preserving sweet.
Farewell, my coz. [*Going.*
BEN. Soft, I will go along;
An if you leave me so, you do me wrong.
ROM. Tut, I have lost myself; I am not here;
This is not Romeo, he's some otherwhere.

BEN. Tell me in sadness, who is that you love?
ROM. What, shall I groan, and tell thee?
BEN. Groan? why, no;
But sadly tell me, who.
ROM. Bid* a sick man in sadness make† his will:—
A word ill urg'd to one that is so ill!—
In sadness, cousin, I do love a woman.
BEN. I aim'd so near, when I suppos'd you lov'd.
ROM. A right good mark-man!—And she's fair I love.
BEN. A right fair mark, fair coz, is soonest hit.
ROM. Well, in that hit, you miss: she'll not be hit
With Cupid's arrow, she hath Dian's wit;
And, in strong proof of chastity well arm'd,
From love's weak childish bow she lives unharm'd.[c]
She will not stay the siege of loving terms,
Nor bide‡ the encounter of assailing eyes,
Nor ope her lap to saint-seducing gold:
O, she is rich in beauty; only poor,
That, when she dies, with beauty[d] dies her store.(4)
BEN. Then she hath sworn, that she will still live chaste?
ROM. She hath, and in that sparing makes huge waste;
For beauty, starv'd with her severity,
Cuts beauty off from all posterity.
She is too fair, too wise; wisely too fair,
To merit bliss by making me despair:
She hath forsworn to love; and, in that vow,
Do I live dead, that live to tell it now.
BEN. Be rul'd by me, forget to think of her.
ROM. O, teach me how I should forget to think.
BEN. By giving liberty unto thine eyes;
Examine other beauties.(5)
ROM. 'Tis the way
To call hers, exquisite, in question more:[e]
These happy masks, that kiss fair ladies' brows,
Being black, put us in mind they hide the fair;
He, that is strucken blind, cannot forget
The precious treasure of his eyesight lost:
Show me a mistress that is passing fair,
What doth her beauty serve, but as a note,
Where I may read, who pass'd that passing fair?
Farewell, thou canst not teach me to forget.
BEN. I'll pay that doctrine, or else die in debt.
[*Exeunt.*

(*) First folio, *well* seeing.

[a] See pathways to his will!] This is obscure. The earliest quarto, that of 1597, has,—

"Should without lawes give path-waies to our will."

And this may help us to the true reading, which very probably was:—

"Should without eyes *set* pathways to *our* will;"

in other words, "Make us walk in any direction he chooses to appoint."

[b] Being purg'd,—] Johnson suggested, and not without reason, that *purg'd* might be a misprint for *urg'd*. "To *urge* the fire," he observes, "is the technical term." Mr. Collier's corrector, with equal plausibility, changes *purg'd* to *puff'd*.

(*) First folio omits *bid*. (†) First folio, *makes*. (‡) First folio, *bid*.

[c] She lives unharm'd.] So the quarto of 1597. The subsequent quartos and the folio, 1623, read "*uncharm'd*."

[d] With beauty dies her store.] The reading of all the ancient copies, which Theobald altered to "—— with her dies beauty's store."

[e] *To call hers*, exquisite, *in question more*:] This is generally conceived to refer to the beauty of Rosaline. It may mean, however, "that is only the way to throw doubt upon any other beauty I may see;" an interpretation countenanced by the after lines:—

"Show me a mistress that is passing fair,
What doth her beauty serve, but as a note,
Where I may read, who pass'd that passing fair?"

SCENE II.—*A Street.*

Enter CAPULET, PARIS, *and* Servant.[a]

CAP. But* Montague is bound as well as I,
In penalty alike; and 'tis not hard, I think,
For men so old as we to keep the peace.
PAR. Of honourable reckoning are you both,
And pity 'tis, you liv'd at odds so long.
But now, my lord, what say you to my suit?
CAP. But saying o'er what I have said before:
My child is yet a stranger in the world,
She hath not seen the change of fourteen years;
Let two more summers wither in their pride,
Ere we may think her ripe to be a bride.
PAR. Younger than she are happy mothers made.
CAP. And too soon marr'd are those so early made.*
The† earth hath swallow'd all my hopes but she,
She is the hopeful lady of my earth:[b]
But woo her, gentle Paris, get her heart,
My will to her consent is but a part;
An she agree, within her scope of choice
Lies my consent and fair according voice.
This night I hold an old accustom'd feast, (6)
Whereto I have invited many a guest,
Such as I love; and you, among the store,
One more, most welcome, makes my number more.
At my poor house, look to behold this night

(*) First folio omits *But*.

(*) The first quarto, 1597, reads *married*.

(†) First folio omits *The*.

[a] And Servant.] The old editions have,—"*Enter Capulet, Countie Paris, and the Clowne.*" By Clown was meant the *merry-man;* and a character of this description was so general in the plays of Shakespeare's early period, that his title here ought perhaps to be retained.

[b] She is the hopeful lady of my earth:] A gallicism. Steevens says, *Fille de terre* being the French phrase for an heiress. But Shakespeare may have meant by, "my earth," *my corporal part,* as in his 146th Sonnet,—

"Poor soul, the centre of my sinful *earth*."

Earth-treading stars, that make dark heaven light:[a]
Such comfort, as do lusty young men feel,
When well-apparell'd April on the heel
Of limping winter treads, even such delight
Among fresh female* buds shall you this night
Inherit at my house; hear all, all see,
And like her most, whose merit most shall be:
Such, amongst view of many,[b] mine, being one,
May stand in number, though in reckoning none.
Come, go with me.—Go, sirrah, [*to* Serv.] trudge about
Through fair Verona; find those persons out,
Whose names are written there, [*gives a paper.*] and to them say,
My house and welcome on their pleasure stay.
[*Exeunt* CAPULET *and* PARIS.

SERV. Find them out, whose names are written here? It is written—that the shoemaker should meddle with his yard, and the tailor with his last, the fisher with his pencil, and the painter with his nets; but I am sent to find those persons, whose names are here† writ, and can never find what names the writing person hath here writ. I must to the learned:—In good time—

Enter BENVOLIO *and* ROMEO.

BEN. Tut, man! one fire burns out another's burning,
One pain is lessen'd by another's anguish;
Turn giddy, and be holp by backward turning;
One desperate grief cures with another's languish:
Take thou some new infection to thy‡ eye,
And the rank poison of the old will die.
ROM. Your plantain leaf is excellent for that.
BEN. For what, I pray thee?
ROM. For your broken shin.
BEN. Why, Romeo, art thou mad?
ROM. Not mad, but bound more than a madman is:
Shut up in prison, kept without my food,
Whipp'd, and tormented, and—God den, good fellow.

SERV. God ye good den.—I pray, sir, can you read?

ROM. Ay, mine own fortune in my misery.

SERV. Perhaps you have learn'd it without book:
But I pray, can you read any thing you see?
ROM. Ay, if I know the letters, and the language.
SERV. Ye say honestly; rest you merry!
ROM. Stay, fellow; I can read. [*Reads.*

SIGNIOR MARTINO, *and his wife, and daughter;* COUNTY ANSELME, *and his beauteous sisters; the lady widow of* VITRUVIO; SIGNIOR PLACENTIO, *and his lovely nieces;* MERCUTIO, *and his brother* VALENTINE; *mine uncle* CAPULET, *his wife, and daughters; my fair niece* ROSALINE; LIVIA; SIGNIOR VALENTIO, *and his cousin* TYBALT; LUCIO, *and the lively* HELENA.

A fair assembly; [*Gives back the note.*] Whither should they come?
SERV. Up.[c]
ROM. Whither to supper?
SERV. To our house.
ROM. Whose house?
SERV. My master's.
ROM. Indeed, I should have asked you that before.

SERV. Now I'll tell you without asking. My master is the great rich Capulet; and if you be not of the house of Montagues, I pray, come and crush[d] a cup of wine: rest you merry. [*Exit.*

BEN. At this same ancient feast of Capulet's
Sups the fair Rosaline, whom thou so lov'st;
With all the admired beauties of Verona:
Go thither; and, with unattainted eye,
Compare her face with some that I shall show,
And I will make thee think thy swan a crow.
ROM. When the devout religion of mine eye
Maintains such falsehood, then turn tears to fires!*
And these,—who, often drown'd, could never die,—
Transparent heretics, be burnt for liars!
One fairer than my love! the all-seeing sun
Ne'er saw her match, since first the world begun.
BEN. Tut! you saw her fair, none else being by,
Herself pois'd with herself in either eye:
But in that crystal scales, let there be weigh'd
Your lady's love[e] against some other maid
That I will show you, shining at this feast,
And she shall scant show well,† that now shows best.
ROM. I'll go along, no such sight to be shown,
But to rejoice in splendour of mine own. [*Exeunt.*

(*) First folio, *fennell.*
(†) First folio omits *here.* (‡) First folio, *the* eye.

[a] That make dark heaven light:] Warburton pronounces this nonsense, and Mason thinks it absurd. The former would read,—
"——that make dark *even* light;"
and the latter,—
"——that make dark heaven's light."
Mr. Knight adheres to the old reading, "as passages in the masquerade scene would seem to indicate that the banqueting room opened into a garden." A better reason for abiding by the original text is to consider that the "dark heaven," in Shakespeare's mind, was most probably the *Heaven* of the stage, hung, as was the custom during the performance of tragedy, with black.

[b] Such, amongst *view of many,*—] The reading of the quarto, 1597. The quarto, 1599, that of 1609, and the folio, 1623, have, "Which one more view," &c. Neither reading affords a clear sense.

(*) Old editions, *fire.*
(†) First folio, *she shew scant shell, well,* &c.

[c] Up.] Is this a misprint for "to sup?"

[d] *Come and* crush *a cup of wine:*] This, like the *crack a bottle* of later times, was a common invitation of old to a carouse. The following instances of its use, which might be easily multiplied, were collected by Steevens:—
"Fill the pot, hostess, &c., and we'll *crush* it."
The Two Angry Women of Abingdon, 1599.
"——we'll *crush a cup* of thine own country wine."
HOFFMAN'S *Tragedy,* 1631.
"Come, George, we'll *crush a pot* before we part."
The Pinder of Wakefield, 1599.

[e] Your lady's love—] A corruption, I suspect, for "lady-love." It was not Romeo's love for Rosaline, or hers for him, which was to be poised, but the lady herself "against some other maid."

SCENE III.—*A Room in* Capulet's *House.*

Enter LADY CAPULET *and* NURSE.

LA. CAP. Nurse, where's my daughter? call her forth to me.

NURSE. Now, by my maiden-head,—at twelve year old,—
I bad her come.—What, lamb! what, lady-bird!—
God forbid![a]—where's this girl?—what, Juliet!

Enter JULIET.

JUL. How now, who calls?

NURSE. Your mother.

JUL. Madam, I am here.
What is your will?

LA. CAP. This is the matter:—Nurse, give leave awhile,
We must talk in secret.—Nurse, come back again;
I have remember'd me, thou shalt* hear our counsel.
Thou knowest, my daughter's of a pretty age.

NURSE. 'Faith, I can tell her age unto an hour.

LA. CAP. She's not fourteen.

NURSE. I'll lay fourteen of my teeth,—
And yet, to my teen[b] be it spoken, I have but four,—
She's not fourteen: how long is it now
To Lammas-tide?

LA. CAP. A fortnight, and odd days.

NURSE. Even or odd, of all days in the year, come Lammas-eve at night, shall she be fourteen. Susan and she,—God rest all Christian souls!—were of an age:—Well, Susan is with God; she

* Old copies, *thou'se.*

[a] *What*, lady-bird!—*God forbid!*—] An exquisite touch of nature. The old nurse in her fond garrulity uses "lady-bird" as a term of endearment; but recollecting its application to a female of loose manners, checks herself;—"God forbid!" her darling should prove such a one!

[b] *And yet to my* teen—] That is, to my *sorrow.*

was too good for me: but, as I said, on Lammas-eve at night shall she be fourteen; that shall she; marry, I remember it well. 'Tis since the earthquake now eleven years; (7) and she was wean'd, —I never shall forget it,—of all the days of the year, upon that day: for I had then laid wormwood to my dug, sitting in the sun under the dove-house wall. My lord and you were then at Mantua:—nay, I do bear a brain:[a]—but, as I said, when it did taste the wormwood on the nipple of my dug, and felt it bitter, pretty fool! to see it tetchy, and fall out with the dug. Shake, quoth the dove-house: 'twas no need, I trow, to bid me trudge. And since that time it is eleven years, for then she could stand alone; nay, by the rood, she could have run and waddled all about. For even the day before, she broke her brow: and then my husband—God be with his soul! 'a was a merry man;—took up the child; *Yea*, quoth he, *dost thou fall upon thy face? thou wilt fall backward, when thou hast more wit; wilt thou not, Jule?* and, by my holy-dam, the pretty wretch left crying, and said—*Ay:* to see now, how a jest shall come about! I warrant, an I should* live a thousand years, I never should forget it; *wilt thou not, Jule?* quoth he: and, pretty fool, it stinted,[b] and said—*Ay.*

LA. CAP. Enough of this; I pray thee, hold thy peace.

NURSE. Yes, madam; yet I cannot choose but laugh, to think it should leave crying, and say—Ay: and yet, I warrant, it had upon its brow a bump as big as a young cockrel's stone; a par'lous knock; and it cried bitterly. *Yea*, quoth my husband, *fall'st upon thy face? thou wilt fall backward when thou com'st to age; wilt thou not, Jule?* it stinted, and said—*Ay.*

JUL. And stint thou too, I pray thee, nurse, say I.

NURSE. Peace, I have done. God mark thee to his grace!
Thou wast the prettiest babe that e'er I nurs'd:
An I might live to see thee married once,
I have my wish.

LA. CAP. Marry, that marry is the very theme
I came to talk of: tell me, daughter Juliet,
How stands your disposition to be married?

JUL. It is an honour[c] that I dream not of.

NURSE. An honour! were not I thine only nurse,
I'd say, thou hadst suck'd wisdom from thy teat.

LA. CAP. Well, think of marriage now; younger than you,
Here in Verona, ladies of esteem,
Are made already mothers: by my count,
I was your mother much upon these years (8)
That you are now a maid. Thus then, in brief;—
The valiant Paris seeks you for his love.

NURSE. A man, young lady! lady, such a man,
As all the world—why, he's a man of wax.

LA. CAP. Verona's summer hath not such a flower.

NURSE. Nay, he's a flower; in faith, a very flower.

LA. CAP. What say you? can you love the gentleman?[d]
This night you shall behold him at our feast:
Read o'er the volume of young Paris' face,
And find delight writ there with beauty's pen;
Examine every married* lineament,
And see how one another lends content;
And what obscur'd in this fair volume lies,
Find written in the margent of his eyes.[e]
This precious book of love, this unbound lover,
To beautify him, only lacks a cover:
The fish lives in the sea;[f] and 'tis much pride,
For fair without, the fair within to hide:
That book in many's eyes doth share the glory,
That in gold clasps locks in the golden story;
So shall you share all that he doth possess,
By having him, making yourself no less.

NURSE. No less? nay, bigger; women grow by men.

LA. CAP. Speak briefly, can you like of Paris' love?

JUL. I'll look to like, if looking liking move:
But no more deep will I endart mine eye,
Than your consent gives strength to make it† fly.

Enter a Servant.

SERV. Madam, the guests are come, supper served up, you call'd, my young lady ask'd for, the nurse curs'd in the pantry, and everything in extremity. I must hence to wait; I beseech you, follow straight.

LA. CAP. We follow thee.—Juliet, the county stays.

NURSE. Go, girl, seek happy nights to happy days. [*Exeunt.*

(*) First folio, *shall.*

[a] *Nay, I do* bear a brain:] I *can remember well.*
[b] It stinted,—] To *stint* is to stop.

"*Stint* thy babbling tongue."
Cynthia's Revels, Act I. Sc. 1.

"Pish! for shame. *stint* thy idle chat."
MARSTON'S *What You Will*, 1607, Induction.

(*) First folio, *several.* (†) First folio omits *it.*

[c] *It is an* honour—] In this and in the next line, for *honour*, the quarto, 1599, and the folio, 1623, have *houre.*
[d] Can you love the gentleman?] The whole of this speech was added after the publication of the first quarto.
[e] *In the* margent *of his eyes.*] See note, p. 101, in the Illustrative Comments on "Love's Labour's Lost."
[f] *The fish lives in the* sea;] Mason very properly observes that "the *sea* cannot be said to be a beautiful cover to a fish," and suggests that *sea* was a misprint for "shell."

SCENE IV.—*A Street.*

Enter ROMEO, MERCUTIO,(9) BENVOLIO, *with five or six other* Maskers, *and* Torch-bearers.

ROM. What, shall this speech be spoke for our excuse?
Or shall we on without apology?

BEN. The date is out of such prolixity:[a]
We'll have no Cupid hood-wink'd with a scarf,
Bearing a Tartar's painted bow of lath,
Scaring the ladies like a crow-keeper;
Nor no without-book prologue, faintly spoke
After the prompter, for our entrance:[b]
But, let them measure us by what they will,
We'll measure them a measure,[c] and be gone.

ROM. Give me a torch,(10)—I am not for this ambling;
Being but heavy, I will bear the light.

MER. Nay, gentle Romeo, we must have you dance.

ROM. Not I, believe me; you have dancing shoes,
With nimble soles: I have a soul of lead,
So stakes me to the ground, I cannot move.

MER. You are a lover;[d] borrow Cupid's wings,

---

[a] The date is out of such prolixity:] It appears to have been the custom formerly for guests who were desirous, for the purposes of intrigue or from other motives, of being incognito, to go in visors, when they visited an entertainment of the description given by Capulet, and to send a masked messenger before them with an apologetic and propitiatory address to the host or hostess.

[b] After the prompter, &c.] This and the preceding line are found only in the quarto of 1597. The word *entrance* here requires to be pronounced as a trisyllable, *enterance.*

[c] *We'll measure them* a measure, &c.] For an account of this dance, see the Illustrative Comments to Act V. of "Love's Labour's Lost."

[d] You are a lover;] The twelve lines which follow are not found in the first quarto.

And soar with them above a common bound.
ROM. I am too sore enpierced with his shaft,
To soar with his light feathers; and so* bound,
I cannot bound a pitch above dull woe;
Under love's heavy burden do I sink.
MER.†And, to sink in it, should you burden love;
Too great oppression for a tender thing.
ROM. Is love a tender thing? it is too rough,
Too rude, too boist'rous; and it pricks like thorn.
MER. If love be rough with you, be rough with love;
Prick love for pricking, and you beat love down,—
Give me a case to put my visage in:
[*Putting on a mask.*
A visor for a visor! what care I,
What curious eye doth quote deformities?
Here are the beetle-brows shall blush for me.
BEN. Come, knock, and enter; and no sooner in,
But every man betake him to his legs.
ROM. A torch for me: let wantons, light of heart,
Tickle the senseless rushes[a] with their heels;
For I am proverb'd with a grandsire phrase,—
I'll be a candle-holder, and look on,—
The game was ne'er so fair, and I am done.[b]
MER. Tut! dun's the mouse,(11) the constable's own word:
If thou art dun, we'll draw thee from the mire,
Or (save your reverence) love, wherein thou stick'st
Up to the ears: come, we burn day-light, ho.
ROM. Nay, that's not so.
MER. I mean, sir, in‡ delay
We waste our lights in vain, like lamps by day.§
Take our good meaning; for our judgment sits
Five times in that, ere once in our five[c] wits.
ROM. And we mean well in going to this mask;
But 'tis no wit to go.
MER. Why, may one ask?
ROM. I dreamt a dream to-night.
MER. And so did I.
ROM. Well, what was yours?
MER. That dreamers often lie.
ROM. In bed, asleep, while they do dream things true.
MER. O then, I see queen Mab hath been with you.
She is the fairies' midwife; and she comes
In shape no bigger than an|| agate-stone
On the fore-finger of an alderman,
Drawn with a team of little atomies
Athwart* men's noses as they lie asleep:
Her waggon-spokes made of long spinners' legs;
The cover, of the wings of grasshoppers;
Her traces, of the smallest spider's web;
Her collars, of the moonshine's wat'ry beams:
Her whip, of cricket's bone; the lash, of film:
Her waggoner, a small grey-coated gnat,
Not half so big as a round little worm
Prick'd from the lazy finger of a maid:†
Her chariot is an empty hazel-nut,
Made by the joiner squirrel, or old grub,
Time out o' mind the fairies' coach-makers.
And in this state she gallops night by night
Through lovers' brains, and then they dream of love:
On courtiers' knees, that dream on court'sies straight:
O'er lawyers' fingers, who straight dream on fees:
O'er ladies' lips, who straight on kisses dream;
Which oft the angry Mab with blisters plagues,
Because their breaths‡ with sweet-meats tainted are.
Sometime she gallops o'er a courtier's nose,
And then dreams he of smelling out a suit:[d]
And sometime comes she with a § tithe-pig's tail,
Tickling a parson's nose as 'a lies asleep,
Then dreams he|| of another benefice:
Sometime she driveth o'er a soldier's neck,
And then dreams he of cutting foreign throats,
Of breaches, ambuscadoes, Spanish blades,
Of healths five fathom deep; and then anon
Drums in his ear;¶ at which he starts, and wakes;
And, being thus frighted, swears a prayer or two,
And sleeps again. This is that very Mab,
That plats the manes of horses in the night;
And bakes the elf-locks** in foul sluttish hairs,
Which, once untangled, much misfortune bodes.
This is the hag, when maids lie on their backs,
That presses them, and learns them first to bear,
Making them women of good carriage.
This is she—(12)
ROM. Peace, peace, Mercutio, peace;
Thou talk'st of nothing.
MER. True, I talk of dreams;
Which are the children of an idle brain,
Begot of nothing but vain fantasy;
Which is as thin of substance as the air,

(*) First folio, *to bound.* (†) Old copies, HORATIO.
(‡) First folio, I *delay*
(§) First folio, *in vain,* lights lights *by day.*
(||) First folio omits *an.*

(*) First folio, *over.* (†) First folio, *man.*
(‡) First folio, *breath.* (§) First folio omits *a.*
(||) First folio, *he dreams.* (¶) First folio, *ears.*
(**) First folio, *elk-locks.*

a Tickle the senseless rushes—] Before the introduction of carpets it was customary, as everybody knows, to strew rooms with *rushes;* it is not so generally known, however, that the stage was strewn in the same manner.

"—— on the very *rushes,* when the comedy is to daunce."
DECKER'S *Gull's Hornbooke,* 1609.

b The game was ne'er so fair, and I am done.] An allusion, Ritson says, to an old proverbial saying, which advises to give over when the game was at the fairest; but we doubt if this is the true meaning of Romeo's "grandsire phrase."

c In *our* five wits.] Old copies *fine;* the correction was made by Malone.

d Of *smelling out* a suit:] By *suit* in this place is not meant, a *process* or *law-suit,* but an appointment in the gift of the crown.

"If you be a *courtier,* discourse of the obtaining of *suits.*"
DECKER'S *Gull's Hornbooke,* 1609.

And more inconstant than the wind, who wooes
Even now the frozen bosom of the north,
And, being anger'd, puffs away from thence,
Turning his face* to the dew-dropping south.

BEN. This wind, you talk of, blows us from ourselves;
Supper is done, and we shall come too late.

ROM. I fear, too early: for my mind misgives,
Some consequence, yet hanging in the stars,
Shall bitterly begin his fearful date
With this night's revels; and expire the term
Of a despised life, clos'd in my breast,
By some vile forfeit of untimely death:
But He, that hath the steerage of my course,
Direct my sail!†—On, lusty gentlemen.

BEN. Strike, drum. [*Exeunt.*[a]

SCENE V.—*A Hall in* Capulet's *House.*

Musicians *waiting.* *Enter* Servants.

1 SERV. Where's Potpan, that he helps not to take away? he shift a trencher! he scrape a trencher!

2 SERV. When good manners shall lie all‡ in one or two men's hands, and they unwash'd too, 'tis a foul thing.

1 SERV. Away with the joint-stools, remove the court-cupboard,[b] look to the plate:—good thou, save me a piece of marchpane;[c] and, as thou lovest me, let the porter let in Susan Grindstone, and Nell.—Antony! and Potpan!

2 SERV. Ay, boy; ready.

1 SERV. You are look'd for, and call'd for, ask'd for, and sought for, in the great chamber.

2 SERV. We cannot be here and there too.—Cheerly, boys; be brisk awhile, and the longer liver take all.[d] [*They retire behind.*

Enter CAPULET, &c. *with the* Guests, *and the* Maskers.

1 CAP. Welcome, gentlemen! ladies, that have their toes
Unplagu'd with corns, will have a bout[e] with you:—
Ah ha,* my mistresses! which of you all
Will now deny to dance? she that makes dainty,
She, I'll swear, hath corns; am I come near ye now?
Welcome, gentlemen![f] I have seen the day,
That I have worn a visor, and could tell
A whispering tale in a fair lady's ear,
Such as would please;—'tis gone, 'tis gone, 'tis gone:
You are welcome, gentlemen!—Come, musicians, play.
A hall! a hall! give room, and foot it, girls.
[*Music plays, and they dance.*
More light, you knaves; and turn the tables up,
And quench the fire, the room is grown too hot.—
Ah, sirrah, this unlook'd-for sport comes well.
Nay, sit, nay, sit, good cousin[g] Capulet,
For you and I are past our dancing days:
How long is 't now, since last yourself and I
Were in a mask?

2 CAP. By'r lady, thirty years.

1 CAP. What, man? 'tis not so much; 'tis not so much:
'Tis since the nuptial of Lucentio,
Come pentecost as quickly as it will,
Some five and twenty years; and then we mask'd.

2 CAP. 'Tis more, 'tis more, his son is elder, sir;
His son is thirty.

1 CAP. Will you tell me that?
His son was but a ward two years ago.

ROM. What lady's that, which doth enrich the hand
Of yonder knight? (13)

SERV. I know not, sir.

ROM. O, she doth teach the torches to burn bright!
It seems[h] she hangs upon the cheek of night
As a rich jewel in an Ethiop's ear:
Beauty too rich for use, for earth too dear!
So shows a snowy dove trooping with crows,
As yonder lady o'er her fellows shows.
The measure done, I'll watch her place of stand,
And, touching hers, make blessed my rude hand.

(*) First folio, *side*. (†) First folio, *suit*. (‡) First folio omits *all*.

[a] *Exeunt.*] The folio, 1623, has the following stage direction:—"*They march about the stage, and Serving-men come forth with their napkins.*"

[b] *Remove the* court-cupboard —] A *court-cupboard* appears to have been what we now call a cabinet, and was used to display the silver flagons, cups, beakers, ewers, &c., constituting the plate of the establishment.

[c] *Save me a piece of* marchpane;] A favourite confection with our ancestors; something like almond cakes, but richer, being composed of pistachio nuts, almonds, pine kernels, sugar of roses, and flour.

[d] This scene first appeared in the edition of 1599.

[e] Will have a bout—] So the quarto, 1597: the subsequent copies, and the folio, *walk about*.

[f] Welcome, gentlemen!—] The remainder of this speech, down to "More light, you knaves;" &c. was added after the printing of the 1597 quarto.

(*) Quartos, 1599, &c., and folio, Ah, *my mistresses!*

[g] *Good* cousin *Capulet,*—] Unless within the degree of parent and child, or brother and sister, one kinsman usually addressed another as cousin in Shakespeare's time. Thus the King in "Hamlet" calls his nephew and step-son

"—my *cousin* Hamlet,"

and Lady Capulet, in Act III. of the present play, speaks of her nephew as

"Tybalt, my *cousin!*"

[h] It seems she *hangs upon the cheek of night*—] This is the lection of the early quartos, and of the folio, 1623. The folio, 1632, substituted

"*Her beauty* hangs," &c.

which has been thought so great an improvement that it is almost invariably adopted.

Did my heart love till now? forswear it, sight!
For I ne'er saw true beauty till this night.
TYB. This, by his voice, should be a Montague:—
Fetch me my rapier, boy:—what! dares the slave
Come hither, cover'd with an antick face,
To fleer and scorn at our solemnity?
Now, by the stock and honour of my kin,
To strike him dead I hold it not a sin.
1 CAP. Why, how now, kinsman? wherefore storm you so?
TYB. Uncle, this is a Montague, our foe;
A villain, that is hither come in spite,
To scorn at our solemnity this night.
1 CAP. Young Romeo is't?
TYB. 'Tis he, that villain Romeo.
1 CAP. Content thee, gentle coz, let him alone,
He bears him like a portly gentleman;
And, to say truth, Verona brags of him,
To be a virtuous and well-govern'd youth:
I would not for the wealth of all this* town,
Here in my house, do him disparagement:
Therefore be patient, take no note of him,
It is my will; the which if thou respect,
Show a fair presence, and put off these frowns,
An ill-beseeming semblance for a feast.
TYB. It fits, when such a villain is a guest;
I'll not endure him.
1 CAP. He shall be endur'd;
What, goodman boy!—I say, he shall;—go to;
Am I the master here, or you? go to.
You'll not endure him!—God shall mend my soul—
You'll make a mutiny among my† guests!
You will set cock-a-hoop![a] you'll be the man!
TYB. Why, uncle, 'tis a shame.
1 CAP. Go to, go to,
You are a saucy boy:—is't so, indeed?
This trick may chance to scathe you;[b]—I know what.
You must contrary me! marry, 'tis time—
Well said, my hearts:—you are a princox;[c] go:
Be quiet, or—more light, more light: for shame!
I'll make you quiet; what!—cheerly, my hearts.
TYB. Patience perforce,[d] with wilful choler meeting,
Makes my flesh tremble in their different greeting.
I will withdraw: but this intrusion shall,
Now seeming sweet, convert to bitter gall. [*Exit.*

ROM. If I profane with my unworthiest hand
[*To* JULIET.
This holy shrine, the gentle sin is this,—
My lips, two blushing pilgrims, ready stand*
To smooth that rough touch with a tender kiss.
JUL. Good pilgrim, you do wrong your hand too much,
Which mannerly devotion shows in this;
For saints have hands that pilgrims' hands do touch,
And palm to palm is holy palmers' kiss.
ROM. Have not saints lips, and holy palmers too?
JUL. Ay, pilgrim, lips that they must use in prayer.
ROM. O then, dear saint, let lips do what hands do;
They pray, grant thou, lest faith turn to despair.
JUL. Saints do not move, though grant for prayers' sake.
ROM. Then move not, while my prayer's effect I take.
Thus from my lips, by thine, my sin is purg'd.
[*Kissing her.*
JUL. Then have my lips the sin that they have took.
ROM. Sin from my lips? O trespass sweetly urg'd!
Give me my sin again.
JUL. You kiss by the book.
NURSE. Madam, your mother craves a word with you.
ROM. What is her mother?
NURSE. Marry, bachelor,
Her mother is the lady of the house,
And a good lady, and a wise, and virtuous:
I nurs'd her daughter, that you talk'd withal;
I tell you,—he, that can lay hold of her,
Shall have the chinks.
ROM. Is she a Capulet?
O dear account! my life is my foe's debt.[e]
BEN. Away, begone; the sport is at the best.[f]
ROM. Ay, so I fear; the more is my unrest.
1 CAP. Nay, gentlemen, prepare not to be gone;
We have a trifling foolish banquet towards.—[g]
Is it e'en so? why, then I thank you all;
I thank you, honest gentlemen; good night:—
More torches here!—come on, then let's to bed.

(*) First folio, *the*. (†) First folio, *the*.

(*) First folio, did *ready stand*.

[a] *You will set* cock-a-hoop!—] A phrase of very doubtful origin. Some writers think it an allusion to a custom they say existed of taking the *cock* or spigot out of the barrel and laying it *on the hoop*. I rather suppose it to refer in some way to the boastful, provocative crowing of the cock, but can find nothing explanatory of its meaning in any author.

[b] *To* scathe *you;*] That is, to *damage* you.

[c] *You are a* princox;—] A *coxcomb*.

[d] Patience perforce,—] From the old adage,—"*Patience upon force* is a medicine for a mad dog."

[e] My life is my foe's debt.] He means that, as bereft of Juliet he should die, his existence is at the mercy of his enemy, Capulet. Thus in the old poem:—

"So hath he learnd her name and knowth she is no geast,
Her father was a Capilet, and master of the feast.
Thus hath his foe in choyse to geve him life or death,
That scarcely can his wofull brest keepe in the lively breath."

[f] The sport is at the best.] This seems to mean, "We have seen the best of the sport."

[g] Towards.—] *Approaching, near at hand.*

Ah, sirrah, [*to* 2 CAP.] by my fay, it waxes late;
I'll to my rest.

[*Exeunt all but* JULIET *and* Nurse.

JUL. Come hither, nurse: what is yon gentleman? (14)

NURSE. The son and heir of old Tiberio.

JUL. What's he, that now is going out of door?

NURSE. Marry, that, I think, be young Petruchio.

JUL. What's he, that follows there,* that would not dance?

(*) First folio, *here.*

NURSE. I know not.

JUL. Go, ask his name:—if he be married,
My grave is like to be my wedding* bed.

NURSE. His name is Romeo, and a Montague;
The only son of your great enemy.

JUL. My only love sprung from my only hate!
Too early seen unknown, and known too late!
Prodigious birth of love it is to me,
That I must love a loathed enemy.

NURSE. What's this? what's this?

JUL. A rhyme I learn'd† even now

(*) First folio, *wedded.* (†) First folio, *learne.*

Of one I danc'd withal.
[*One calls within*, JULIET.

NURSE. Anon, anon:—
Come, let 's away; the strangers all are gone.
[*Exeunt.*

Enter Chorus.[a]

Now old desire doth in his death-bed lie,
And young affection gapes to be his heir;
That fair, for which love groan'd for, and would die,
With tender Juliet match'd, is now not fair.
Now Romeo is belov'd, and loves again,
Alike bewitched by the charm of looks;
But to his foe suppos'd he must complain,
And she steal love's sweet bait from fearful hooks:
Being held a foe, he may not have access
To breathe such vows as lovers use to swear;
And she as much in love, her means much less,
To meet her new-beloved any where:
But passion lends them power, time means to meet,
Temp'ring extremities with extreme sweet. [*Exit.*

[a] Chorus.] First printed in the edition of 1599.

ACT II.

SCENE I.—*An open place adjoining* Capulet's *Garden.*

Enter ROMEO.

ROM. Can I go forward, when my heart is here?
Turn back, dull earth, and find thy centre out.
[*He climbs the wall, and leaps down within it.*

Enter BENVOLIO *and* MERCUTIO.

BEN. Romeo! my cousin Romeo! Romeo!
MER. He is wise;
And, on my life, hath stol'n him home to bed.
BEN. He ran this way, and leap'd this orchard wall:
Call, good Mercutio.
MER. Nay, I'll conjure too.—[a]
Romeo! humours! madman! passion! lover!
Appear thou in the likeness of a sigh,
Speak but one rhyme, and I am satisfied;
Cry but—*Ah me!* pronounce[b] but— *love* and *dove;*
Speak to my gossip Venus one fair word,
One nick-name for her purblind son and heir,*
Young Abraham Cupid, he that shot so trim,[c]
When king Cophetua lov'd the beggar-maid.—
He heareth not, he stirreth not, he moveth not;
The ape is dead, and† I must conjure him.—
I conjure thee by Rosaline's bright eyes,
By her high forehead, and her scarlet lip,
By her fine foot, straight leg, and quivering thigh,
And the demesnes that there adjacent lie,
That in thy likeness thou appear to us!
BEN. An if he hear thee, thou wilt anger him.
MER. This cannot anger him: 'twould anger him
To raise a spirit in his mistress' circle
Of some strange nature, letting it there stand

[a] Nay, I'll conjure too.—] The folio, 1623, assigns these words to Benvolio.

[b] We print this line according to the text of the earliest edition, 1597, all the others being singularly corrupt; for example, the first folio reads:—
Cry me *but ay me*, Provant, *but Love and* day.

(*) First folio, *her*.

(†) First folio omits *and*.

[c] So the quarto, 1597; later editions, *true*.

Till she had laid it, and conjur'd it down;
That were some spite: my invocation
Is fair and honest, and, in his mistress' name,
I conjure only but to raise up him.

BEN. Come, he hath hid himself among those* trees,
To be consorted with the humorous night:
Blind is his love, and best befits the dark.

MER. If love be blind, love cannot hit the mark.
Now will he sit under a medlar tree,
And wish his mistress were that kind of fruit,
As maids call medlars, when they laugh alone.—
Oh Romeo that she were, oh that she were,
An open *et cœtera*, thou, a poprin pear!
Romeo, good night;—I 'll to my truckle-bed;
This field-bed is too cold for me to sleep:
Come, shall we go?

BEN. Go, then; for 'tis in vain
To seek him here, that means not to be found.
[*Exeunt.*

SCENE II.—Capulet's *Garden.*

Enter ROMEO.

ROM. He jests at scars, that never felt a wound.—[a]
[JULIET *appears above, at a window.*
But, soft! what light through yonder window breaks!
It is the east, and Juliet is the sun!—
Arise, fair sun, and kill the envious moon,
Who is already sick and pale with grief,
That thou her maid art far more fair than she:
Be not her maid, since she is envious;
Her vestal livery is but sick and green,
And none but fools do wear it; cast it off.—
It is my lady; O, it is my love:
O, that she knew she were!—
She speaks, yet she says nothing; what of that?
Her eye discourses, I will answer it.
I am too bold, 'tis not to me she speaks:
Two of the fairest stars in all the heaven,
Having some business, do intreat her eyes
To twinkle in their spheres till they return.
What if her eyes were there, they in her head?
The brightness of her cheek would shame those stars,
As daylight doth a lamp; her eye in heaven
Would through the airy region stream so bright,
That birds would sing, and think it were not night.
See, how she leans her cheek upon her hand!
O, that I were a glove upon that hand,
That I might touch that cheek!

JUL. Ay me!

ROM. She speaks:—
O, speak again, bright angel! for thou art
As glorious to this night, being o'er my head,
As is a winged messenger of heaven
Unto the white-upturned wond'ring eyes
Of mortals, that fall back to gaze on him,
When he bestrides the lazy-pacing clouds,[b]
And sails upon the bosom of the air.

JUL. O Romeo, Romeo! wherefore art thou Romeo?
Deny thy father, and refuse thy name:
Or, if thou wilt not, be but sworn my love,
And I 'll no longer be a Capulet.

ROM. Shall I hear more, or shall I speak at this? [*Aside.*

JUL. 'Tis but thy name, that is my enemy;—
Thou art thyself though, not a Montague.(1)
What 's Montague? it is nor hand, nor foot,
Nor arm, nor face, nor any other part[c]
Belonging to a man. O, be some other name!
What 's in a name?* that which we call a rose,
By any other word would smell as sweet;
So Romeo would, were he not Romeo call'd,
Retain that dear perfection which he owes,
Without that title:—Romeo, doff thy name;
And for that name, which is no part of thee,
Take all myself.

ROM. I take thee at thy word:
Call me but love, and I'll be new baptiz'd;
Henceforth I never will be Romeo.

JUL. What man art thou, that, thus bescreen'd in night,
So stumblest on my counsel?

ROM. By a name
I know not how to tell thee who I am:
My name, dear saint, is hateful to myself,
Because it is an enemy to thee;
Had I it written, I would tear the word.

JUL. My ears have not yet drunk a hundred words
Of that tongue's utterance,† yet I know the sound;
Art thou not Romeo, and a Montague?

ROM. Neither, fair maid, if either thee dislike.

JUL. How cam'st thou hither, tell me? and wherefóre?
The orchard walls are high, and hard to climb;
And the place death, considering who thou art,

(*) First folio, *these.*

[a] He jests at scars, &c.] It has been disputed whether Romeo, overhearing Mercutio's banter, refers to that, or to his having believed himself, before he saw Juliet, so invincible in his love for Rosaline, that no other beauty could move him. We feel no doubt that the allusion is to Mercutio; indeed, the rhyme in *found* and *wound* seems purposely intended to carry on the connexion of the speeches; and at this moment Rosaline is wholly forgotten.

(*) First folio, *What? in a names.*
(†) First folio, *of thy tongues uttering.*

[b] The lazy-pacing clouds,—] So, the earliest edition, 1597; all the others have *lazy*-puffing, which Mr. Collier's MS. corrector alters to *lazy*-passing.

[c] Nor any other part—] These words are found only in the quarto of 1597.

It any of my kinsmen find thee here.
ROM. With love's light wings did I o'er-perch these walls,
For stony limits cannot hold love out:
And what love can do, that dares love attempt;
Therefore thy kinsmen are no stop to me.
JUL. If they do see thee, they will murder thee.
ROM. Alack! there lies more peril in thine eye,
Than twenty of their swords; look thou but sweet,
And I am proof against their enmity.
JUL. I would not for the world they saw thee here.
ROM. I have night's cloak to hide me from their eyes,
And, but [a] thou love me, let them find me here:
My life were better ended by their hate,
Than death prorogued, wanting of thy love.
JUL. By whose direction found'st thou out this place?
ROM. By love, that first did prompt me to inquire;
He lent me counsel, and I lent him eyes.
I am no pilot, yet, wert thou as far
As that vast shore wash'd with the farthest sea,
I would* adventure for such merchandise.
JUL. Thou know'st the mask of night is on my face,
Else would a maiden blush bepaint my cheek,
For that which thou hast heard me speak to-night.
Fain would I dwell on form, fain, fain deny
What I have spoke; but farewell complement! [b]
Dost thou love me?† I know, thou wilt say—Ay;
And I will take thy word: yet, if thou swear'st,
Thou may'st prove false; at lovers' perjuries,
They say, Jove laughs.‡ O, gentle Romeo,
If thou dost love, pronounce it faithfully:
Or if thou think'st I am too quickly won,
I'll frown, and be perverse, and say thee nay,
So thou wilt woo; but, else, not for the world.
In truth, fair Montague, I am too fond,
And therefore thou may'st think my 'haviour§ light:
But trust me, gentleman, I'll prove more true
Than those that have more cunning [c] to be strange. [d]
I should have been more strange, I must confess,
But that thou over-heard'st, ere I was 'ware,
My true love's passion: therefore pardon me,
And not impute this yielding to light love,
Which the dark night hath so discovered.
ROM. Lady, by yonder blessed|| moon I vow,
That tips with silver all these fruit-tree tops,—
JUL. O, swear not by the moon, the inconstant moon,
That monthly changes in her circled orb,
Lest that thy love prove likewise variable.
ROM. What shall I swear by?
JUL. Do not swear at all;
Or, if thou wilt, swear by thy gracious self,
Which is the god of my idolatry,
And I'll believe thee.
ROM. If my heart's dear love—
JUL. Well, do not swear. Although I joy in thee,
I have no joy of this contract to-night:
It is too rash, too unadvis'd, too sudden,
Too like the lightning, which doth cease to be,
Ere one can say—*it lightens*. Sweet, good night! [e]
This bud of love, by summer's ripening breath,
May prove a beauteous flower when next we meet.
Good night, good night! as sweet repose and rest
Come to thy heart, as that within my breast!
ROM. O, wilt thou leave me so unsatisfied?
JUL. What satisfaction canst thou have to-night?
ROM. The exchange of thy love's faithful vow for mine.
JUL. I gave thee mine before thou didst request it:
And yet I would it were to give again.
ROM. Would'st thou withdraw it? for what purpose, love?
JUL. But to be frank, and give it thee again.
And yet I wish but for the thing I have:
My bounty is as boundless as the sea,
My love as deep; the more I give to thee,
The more I have, for both are infinite.
[Nurse *calls within.*
I hear some noise within; dear love, adieu!
Anon, good nurse.—Sweet Montague, be true.
Stay but a little, I will come again. [*Exit.*
ROM. O blessed, blessed night! I am afeard,
Being in night, all this is but a dream,
Too flattering-sweet to be substantial.

Re-enter JULIET, *above.*

JUL. Three words, dear Romeo, and good night, indeed.
If that thy bent of love be honourable, (2)
Thy purpose marriage, send me word to-morrow,
By one that I'll procure to come to thee,

(*) First folio, *should*. (†) First folio omits *me*.
(‡) First folio, *laught*. (§) First folio, *behaviour*.
(||) First folio omits *blessed*.

a *And*, but *thou love me,*—] That is, *unless* thou love me.

b *But* farewell complement!] Away with formality and punctilio!

c Cunning—] So the quarto, 1597; later editions, including the first folio, *coying*.

d *To be* strange.] *To be strange* is to be *coy, reserved*. Thus in Act III. Sc. 2, of the present Play:—

"—— 'till *strange* love, grown bold,
Think true love acted, simple modesty."

So, too, in Greene's "Mamilia," 1593:—

"Is it the fashion in Padua to be so *strange* with your friends?"

e Sweet, good night!] This, and the intermediate lines down to "Stay but a little," &c., were added after the printing of the 1597 quarto.

Where, and what time, thou wilt perform the rite;
And all my fortunes at thy foot I'll lay,
And follow thee my lord throughout the world;—
[NURSE. [*Within.*] Madam!
JUL. I come, anon:—but, if thou mean'st not well,
I do beseech thee,—
[NURSE. [*Within.*] Madam!
JUL. By and by, I come:—
To cease thy suit,[a] and leave me to my grief:
To-morrow will I send.
ROM. So thrive my soul,—
JUL. A thousand times good night! [*Exit.*
ROM. A thousand times the worse, to want thy light.—
Love goes toward love, as school-boys from their books;
But love from love, toward school, with heavy looks.
[*Retiring slowly.*

Re-enter JULIET, *above.*

JUL. Hist! Romeo, hist!—O, for a falconer's voice,
To lure this tassel-gentle (3) back again!
Bondage is hoarse, and may not speak aloud;
Else would I tear the cave where echo lies,
And make her airy tongue more hoarse than mine,*
With repetition of my Romeo's name.[b]
ROM. It is my soul, that calls upon my name:
How silver-sweet sound lovers' tongues by night,
Like softest music to attending ears!
JUL. Romeo!
ROM. My dear![c]
JUL. What o'clock to-morrow
Shall I send to thee?
ROM. By the hour of nine.
JUL. I will not fail; 'tis twenty years till then.
I have forgot why I did call thee back.
ROM. Let me stand here till thou remember it.
JUL. I shall forget, to have thee still stand there,
Remembering how I love thy company.
ROM. And I'll still stay, to have thee still forget,
Forgetting any other home but this.
JUL. 'Tis almost morning; I would have thee gone:
And yet, no farther than a wanton's bird;
That lets it hop a little from her* hand,
Like a poor prisoner in his twisted gyves,
And with a silk† thread plucks it back again,
So loving-jealous of his liberty.
ROM. I would, I were thy bird.
JUL. Sweet, so would I:
Yet I should kill thee with much cherishing.
Good night, good night! parting is such sweet sorrow,[d]
That I shall say—good night, till it be morrow.
[*Exit.*
ROM. Sleep dwell upon thine eyes, peace in thy breast!—
Would I were sleep and peace, so sweet to rest!
Hence will I to my ghostly father's[e] cell;‡
His help to crave, and my dear hap to tell. [*Exit.*

SCENE III.—*Friar* Laurence's *Cell.*

Enter Friar LAURENCE, *with a basket.*

FRI. The grey-ey'd morn smiles on the frowning night,
Checkering the eastern clouds with streaks of light;
And flecked[f] darkness like a drunkard reels
From forth day's path, and Titan's fiery§ wheels:[g]
Now ere the sun advance his burning eye,
The day to cheer, and night's dank dew to dry,
I must up-fill this osier cage of ours,
With baleful weeds, and precious-juiced flowers.(4)
The earth, that's nature's mother, is her tomb;[h]
What is her burying grave, that is her womb:
And from her womb children of divers kind,
We sucking on her natural bosom find;
Many for many virtues excellent,
None but for some, and yet all different.
O, mickle is the powerful grace, that lies
In plants, herbs, stones, and their true qualities:

(*) First folio omits *mine*.

(*) Quarto, 1599, and first folio, *his*.
(†) Quarto, 1599, and first folio, *silken*.
(‡) First folio, *friar's close* cell.
(§) First folio, *burning*.

a So the undated quarto; the first folio reads *strife*.

b *My Romeo's* name.] So the quarto, 1597; that of 1599, and first folio, read only, "*of my Romeo.*"

c My dear!] The quarto, 1597, has *madam;* that of 1599, and folio, 1623, have *My neece*, which, in the second folio, was altered to *My sweet*. Our reading is that of the undated quarto.

d Parting is such sweet sorrow,—] In the folio, 1623, and some of the quartos, this speech is allotted to Romeo, and the first line of the next to Juliet.

e *My* ghostly father's *cell;*] My *ghostly* father is, my *spiritual* father.

f *And* flecked *darkness*—] *Flecked*, or, as the folio, 1623, spells it, *fleckled*, means *spotted, dappled, flaked.* We meet with the same image in "Much Ado About Nothing," Act V. Sc. 3:—

"—— and look, the gentle day,
Before the wheels of Phœbus, round about,
Dapples the drowsy east with spots of grey."

g From forth day's path, and Titan's fiery wheels:] This is the reading of the first quarto, 1597: in the other editions, these four lines, slightly varied in the concluding couplet, which runs thus,—

And darknesse fleckeld *like a drunkard reeles*
*From forth dayes path*way, made by *Titans wheeles,*—

are also printed in the middle of Romeo's speech above. The editor, or printer, of the folio, 1632, thought he was correcting the blunder by crossing the lines out of the friar's speech, and assigning them to Romeo.

h The earth, that's nature's mother, is her tomb;] So Lucretius:—

"Omniparens, eadem rerum commune sepulchrum."

And our author, in "Pericles," has a parallel idea:—

"—— Time 's the king of men,
For he's their parent, and he is their grave."

For nought so vile that on the earth doth live,
But to the earth some special good doth give;
Nor aught so good, but, strain'd from that fair use,
Revolts from true birth, stumbling on abuse:
Virtue itself turns vice, being misapplied;
And vice sometime 's by action dignified.[a]
Within the infant rind of this weak flower
Poison hath residence, and medicine power:
For this, being smelt, with that part cheers each part;
Being tasted, slays all senses with the heart.
Two such opposed kings encamp them still
In man as well as herbs,—grace, and rude will;
And, where the worser is predominant,
Full soon the canker death eats up that plant.

Enter ROMEO.

ROM. Good morrow, father!

FRI. *Benedicite!*
What early tongue so sweet saluteth me?—
Young son, it argues a distemper'd head,
So soon to bid good morrow to thy bed:
Care keeps his watch in every old man's eye,
And where care lodges, sleep will never lie:
But where unbruised youth with unstuff'd brain
Doth couch his limbs, there golden sleep doth reign:
Therefore thy earliness doth me assure,
Thou art up-rous'd with some distemperature;
Or if not so, then here I hit it right—

[a] By action dignified.] After these words the ancient copies, except the first quarto, which has no direction, have,—"*Enter Romeo;*" but it very frequently happens in old plays that the entrance of a character is marked some time before he really takes part in the scene. Such direction probably meaning that the actor is to be at hand, ready to enter when the cue is given.

Our Romeo hath not been in bed to-night.
ROM. That last is true, the sweeter rest was mine.
FRI. God pardon sin! wast thou with Rosaline?
ROM. With Rosaline, my ghostly father? no;
I have forgot that name, and that name's woe.
FRI. That's my good son: but where hast thou been then?
ROM. I'll tell thee, ere thou ask it me agen.
I have been feasting with mine enemy;
Where, on a sudden, one hath wounded me,
That's by me wounded; both our remedies
Within thy help and holy physic lies:
I bear no hatred, blessed man; for, lo,
My intercession likewise steads my foe.
FRI. Be plain, good son, and *homely in thy drift;
Riddling confession finds but riddling shrift.
ROM. Then plainly know, my heart's dear love is set
On the fair daughter of rich Capulet:
As mine on hers, so hers is set on mine;
And all combin'd, save what thou must combine
By holy marriage. When, and where, and how,
We met, we woo'd, and made exchange of vow,
I'll tell thee as we pass; but this I pray,
That thou consent to marry us to-day.
FRI. Holy saint Francis! what a change is here!
Is Rosaline, that thou didst love so dear,
So soon forsaken? young men's love then lies,
Not truly in their hearts, but in their eyes.
Jesu Maria! what a deal of brine
Hath wash'd thy sallow cheeks for Rosaline!
How much salt water thrown away in waste,
To season love, that of it doth not taste!
The sun not yet thy sighs from heaven clears,
Thy old groans ring† yet in my ancient ears;
Lo, here upon thy cheek the stain doth sit
Of an old tear that is not wash'd off yet:
If e'er thou wast thyself, and these woes thine,
Thou and these woes were all for Rosaline;
And art thou chang'd? pronounce this sentence then—
Women may fall, when there's no strength in men.
ROM. Thou chidd'st me oft for loving Rosaline.
FRI. For doting, not for loving, pupil mine.
ROM. And bad'st me bury love.
FRI. Not in a grave,
To lay one in, another out to have.
ROM. I pray thee, chide not: she whom I love now,[a]
Doth grace for grace, and love for love allow;
The other did not so.
FRI. O, she knew well,
Thy love did read by rote, and* could not spell.
But come, young waverer, come go with me,
In one respect I'll thy assistant be;
For this alliance may so happy prove,
To turn your households'† rancour to pure love.
ROM. O, let us hence; I stand on sudden haste.[b]
FRI. Wisely, and slow; they stumble, that run fast. [*Exeunt.*

SCENE IV.—*A Street.*

Enter BENVOLIO *and* MERCUTIO.

MER. Where the devil should this Romeo be?—
Came he not home to night?
BEN. Not to his father's; I spoke with his man.
MER. Why, that same pale hard-hearted wench, that Rosaline,
Torments him so, that he will sure run mad.
BEN. Tybalt, the kinsman to old Capulet,
Hath sent a letter to his father's house.
MER. A challenge, on my life.
BEN. Romeo will answer it.
MER. Any man, that can write, may answer a letter.

BEN. Nay, he will answer the letter's master, how he dares, being dared.

MER. Alas, poor Romeo, he is already dead! stabb'd with a white wench's black eye; shot‡ through the ear with a love-song; the very pin[c] of his heart cleft with the blind bow-boy's butt-shaft; and is he a man to encounter Tybalt?

BEN. Why, what is Tybalt?

MER. More than prince of cats,(5) I can tell you.[d] O, he's the courageous captain of complements:[e] he fights as you sing prick-song, keeps time, distance, and proportion; rests me his minim rest,§ one,—two,—and the third in your bosom: the very butcher of a silk button, a duellist, a duellist; a gentleman of the very first house,—of the first and second cause: Ah, the immortal passado! the punto reverso! the hay!—(6)

BEN. The what?

(*) First folio, rest *homely*. (†) First folio, *yet ringing*.

[a] She whom I love now,—] So the earliest quarto, 1597. The other old copies, including the folio, 1623, read—

"I pray thee, chide *me* not, *her* I love now."

[b] I stand on sudden haste.] It imports me much to be speedy. So in "Richard II." Act II. Sc. 3:—

"It *stands* your grace *upon*, to do him right."

Again, in "Richard III." Act IV. Sc. 2:—

"—— It *stands* me much *upon*,
To stop all hopes whose growth may danger me."

(*) First folio, *that*. (†) First folio, *household*.
(‡) First folio, *runne*. (§) First folio, he *rests his minum*.

[c] *The very* pin *of his heart* cleft—] See "The Two Gentlemen of Verona," Act V. Sc. 4, note (b), p. 39 of the present Vol.

[d] I can tell you.] These words are found only in the quarto, 1597.

[e] *Captain of* complements:] See Act I. Sc. 1, note (f), p. 53 of the present Vol.

MER. The pox of such antick, lisping, affecting fantasticoes; * these new tuners of accent!—*By* † *Jesu, a very good blade!—a very tall man!—a very good whore!*—Why, is not this a lamentable thing, grand sire, that we should be thus afflicted with these strange flies, these fashion-mongers, these *pardonnez-moys*, who stand so much on the new form, that they cannot sit at ease on the old bench? O, their *bons*, their *bons!*

Enter ROMEO.

BEN. Here comes Romeo, here comes Romeo.

MER. Without his roe, like a dried herring:—O flesh, flesh, how art thou fishified!—now is he for the numbers that Petrarch flowed in: Laura, to his lady, was a kitchen-wench;—marry, she had a better love to be-rhyme her: Dido, a dowdy; Cleopatra, a gipsy; Helen and Hero, hildings and harlots; Thisbé, a grey eye or so, but not to the purpose.—Signior Romeo, *bon jour!* there's a French salutation to your French slop; [a] you gave us the counterfeit fairly last night.

ROM. Good morrow to you both; what counterfeit did I give you?

MER. The slip, sir, the slip; [b] can you not conceive?

(*) All but the first copy read *phantacies.*
(†) First folio omits *By.*

[a] *Your French* slop;] The *slop* is said to have been a sort of loose kneed *breeches* or *trousers.*

[b] *The* slip, *sir, the* slip;] The equivoque here is well explained in the following passage from Greene's "Thieves falling out, True Men come by their Goods:"—"And therefore he went and got him certain *slips,* which are *counterfeit* pieces of money, being brasse, and covered over with silver, which the common people call *slips.*" Again, in Ben Jonson's "Magnetick Lady," Act III. Sc. 6:—

"I had like t' have been
Abus'd i' the business, had the *slip* slur'd on me,
A *counterfeit.*"

ROM. Pardon, good* Mercutio, my business was great; and, in such a case as mine, a man may strain courtesy.

MER. That's as much as to say—such a case as yours constrains a man to bow in the hams.

ROM. Meaning—to court'sy.

MER. Thou hast most kindly[a] hit it.

ROM. A most courteous exposition.

MER. Nay, I am the very pink of courtesy.

ROM. Pink, for flower?

MER. Right.

ROM. Why, then is my pump well flower'd.[b]

MER. Sure wit:[c] follow me this jest now, till thou hast worn out thy pump; that, when the single sole of it is worn, the jest may remain, after the wearing, solely-singular.

ROM. O single-soled jest, solely singular for the singleness!

MER. Come between us, good* Benvolio; my wit† faints.

ROM. Switch and spurs, switch and spurs; or I'll cry a match.

MER. Nay, if our wits run the wild-goose chase, (7) I am done; for thou hast more of the wild-goose in one of thy wits, than, I am sure, I have in my whole five. Was I with you there for the goose?

ROM. Thou wast never with me for any thing, when thou wast not there for the goose.

MER. I will bite thee by the ear for that jest.

ROM. Nay, good goose, bite not.[d]

MER. Thy wit is a very bitter-sweeting; it is a most sharp sauce.

ROM. And is it not well served in to a sweet goose?

MER. O, here's a wit of cheverel,[e] that stretches from an inch narrow to an ell broad!

ROM. I stretch it out for that word—broad: which added to the goose, proves thee far and wide a broad goose.[f]

MER. Why, is not this better now, than groaning for love? now art thou sociable, now art thou Romeo; now art thou what thou art, by art as well as by nature: for this drivelling love is like a great natural, that runs lolling up and down to hide his bauble in a hole.

BEN. Stop there, stop there.

MER. Thou desirest me to stop in my tale against the hair.

BEN. Thou would'st else have made thy tale large.

MER. O, thou art deceived, I would have made it short: for* I was come to the whole depth of my tale, and meant, indeed, to occupy the argument no longer.

ROM. Here's goodly geer!

Enter NURSE *and* PETER.

MER. A sail, a sail! a sail![g]

BEN. Two, two; a shirt, and a smock.

NURSE. Peter!

PETER. Anon?

NURSE. My fan, Peter.

MER. Good Peter, to hide her face; for her fan's the fairer face.

NURSE. God ye good morrow, gentlemen.

MER. God ye good den, fair gentlewoman.

NURSE. Is it good den?

MER. 'Tis no less, I tell you; for the bawdy hand of the dial is now upon the prick of noon.

NURSE. Out upon you! what a man are you?

ROM. One, gentlewoman, that God hath made, for† himself to mar.

NURSE. By my troth, it is well‡ said;—*for himself to mar,* quoth'a!—Gentlemen, can any of you tell me where I may find the young Romeo?

ROM. I can tell you; but young Romeo will be older when you have found him, than he was when you sought him: I am the youngest of that name, for 'fault of a worse.

NURSE. You say well.

(*) First folio omits *good*. (†) First folio, *wits*.

(*) First folio, *or*. (†) First folio omits *for*. (‡) First folio omits *well*.

[a] *Thou hast most* kindly *hit it.*] That is, most *pertinently* hit it. So in "Henry VI." Part I. Act III. Sc. 1, when Warwick says,—

"Sweet king! the bishop hath a *kindly gird,*"

he does not mean, as it has been interpreted, "a reproof meant in kindness," but an *apposite* reproof; a reproof *in kind*. This sense of the word is very clearly shown in a passage of Middleton's play, "The Mayor of Queenborough," Act III. Sc. 3, where Vortigern, having discovered the trick of Hengist in cutting the hide into *thongs*, tells him his castle shall be called *Thong* Castle; to which the latter replies:—

"—— there your grace quites me *kindly*."

[b] *Then is* my pump *well* flower'd.] The idea seems to be,—my shoe or *pump* being *pinked* or punched with holes is well *flower'd*; there may also be a latent allusion to the custom of wearing ribbons in the shape of flowers on the shoes.

[c] Sure *wit*:] The earliest quarto, 1597, has "Well said;" the subsequent quartos, and the folio, 1623, read, "Sure wit," which Malone conjectured to be a mistake for "*Sheer* wit."

[d] Good goose, bite not.] An old proverbial saying, "Good goose, do not bite."

[e] *A wit* of cheverel,—] *Cheverel*, or *cheveril*, is a soft leather used for gloves. Its capacity of extension is frequently referred to by our old poets. Thus, in "Henry VIII." Act II. Sc. 3,—

"—— your soft *cheveril* conscience."

So, too, in "Histriomastix," 1610:—

"The *cheveril* conscience of corrupted law."

And Drayton, in "The Owl:"—

"A *cheverel* conscience, and a searching wit."

[f] A broad *goose*.] The quibble here not being understood, it has been proposed that we should read:—

"—— proves thee far and wide abroad, goose."

But Romeo plays on the words *a broad*, and *a brode*. "The Turnament of Tottenham," Harl. MSS. No. 5396:—

"Forther would not Tyb then,
Tyl scho had hur *brode-hen*
Set in hur lap."

[g] A sail, a sail, a sail!] So the quarto, 1597. The other old copies give these words to Romeo.

MER. Yea, is the worst well? very well took, i' faith; wisely, wisely.

NURSE. If you be he, sir, I desire some confidence with you.

BEN. She will indite him to some supper.

MER. A bawd, a bawd, a bawd! So ho![a]

ROM. What hast thou found?

MER. No hare, sir; unless a hare, sir, in a lenten pie, that is something stale and hoar ere it be spent.

An old hare hoar,[b]
And an old hare hoar,
Is very good meat in Lent:
But a hare that is hoar,
Is too much for a score,
When it hoars ere it be spent.—

Romeo, will you come to your father's? we'll to dinner thither.

ROM. I will follow you.

MER. Farewell, ancient lady; farewell, *lady, lady, lady.*(8)

[*Exeunt* MERCUTIO *and* BENVOLIO.

NURSE. I pray you, sir, what saucy merchant[c] was this, that was so full of his ropery?[d]

ROM. A gentleman, nurse, that loves to hear himself talk; and will speak more in a minute, than he will stand to in a month.

NURSE. An 'a speak any thing against me, I'll take him down an 'a were lustier than he is, and twenty such Jacks; and if I cannot, I'll find those that shall. Scurvy knave! I am none of his flirt-gills; I am none of his skains-mates:[e]—And thou must stand by too, and suffer every knave to use me at his pleasure.

PET. I saw no man use you at his pleasure; if I had, my weapon should quickly have been out, I warrant you: I dare draw as soon as another man, if I see occasion in a good quarrel, and the law on my side.

NURSE. Now, afore God, I am so vexed, that every part about me quivers. Scurvy knave!—pray you, sir, a word: and as I told you, my young lady bid me inquire you out; what she bid me say, I will keep to myself: but first let me tell ye, if ye should lead her into* a fool's paradise, as they say, it were a very gross kind of behaviour, as they say: for the gentlewoman is young; and, therefore, if you should deal double with her, truly, it were an ill thing to be offered to any gentlewoman, and very weak dealing.

ROM. Nurse, commend me to thy lady and mistress. I protest unto thee,—

NURSE. Good heart! and, i' faith, I will tell her as much: Lord, lord, she will be a joyful woman.

ROM. What wilt thou tell her, nurse? thou dost not mark me.

NURSE. I will tell her, sir,—that you do protest; which, as I take it, is a gentlemanlike offer.

ROM. Bid her devise some means to come to shrift
This afternoon;
And there she shall at friar Laurence' cell
Be shriv'd, and married. Here is for thy pains.

NURSE. No, truly, sir; not a penny.

ROM. Go to; I say, you shall.

NURSE. This afternoon, sir? well, she shall be there.

ROM. And stay,[f] good † nurse, behind the abbey-wall:
Within this hour my man shall be with thee,
And bring thee cords made like a tackled stair,
Which to the high top-gallant of my joy
Must be my convoy in the secret night.
Farewell!—be trusty, and I'll quit thy pains:
Farewell!—commend me to thy mistress.

NURSE. Now God in heaven bless thee!—hark you, sir.

ROM. What say'st thou, my dear nurse?

NURSE. Is your man secret? Did you ne'er hear say—
Two may keep counsel, putting one away?

ROM. I warrant thee;[g] my man's as true as steel.

NURSE. Well, sir; my mistress is the sweetest lady—Lord, lord! when 'twas a little prating thing,—O,—there's a nobleman in town, one Paris, that

---

(*) First folio, *in*.

(†) First folio, thou *good*.

---

[a] So ho!] The huntsman's cry when the hare is found in her seat.

[b] An old hare hoar,—] This may be a snatch of some quaint old ballad, but is more probably an extempore rhyme sung by Mercutio for the nonce. In the quarto, 1597, it is headed by a stage direction,—"*He walkes by them, and sings.*"

[c] *What saucy* merchant—] *Merchant*, as Steevens has shown, was formerly often applied in the derogatory sense of pedlar or low dealer; thus our author, "Henry VI." Part I. Act II. Sc. 3,—

"This is a riddling *merchant* for the nonce."

So, too, in Churchyard's "Chance," 1580:—

"What *saucie marchaunt* speaketh now, said Venus in her rage."

[d] *So full of his* ropery?] That is, *ribaldry*.

[e] *I am none of his* flirt-gills; *I am none of his* skains-mates:—] The meaning of *flirt-gills* is not far to seek. It implied, like *fiz-gig*, another term of the same age, a *wild, flirting, romping wench;* but *skains-mates* has been a sore puzzle to all the commentators. Some have derived it from *skein*, a knife or dagger; others suppose it a mispronunciation of *kins-mates;* and Mr. Douce ventures a random conjecture that the *skains* in question might be *skeins of thread*, and that the Nurse meant nothing more than *sempstresses!* The difficulty, after all, proves of easy solution. The word *skain*, I am told by a Kentish man, was formerly a familiar term in parts of Kent to express what we now call a *scape-grace* or *ne'er-do-well;* just the sort of person the worthy old Nurse would entertain a horror of being considered a companion to. Even at this day, my informant says, *skain* is often heard in the Isle of Thanet, and about the adjacent coast, in the sense of a *reckless, dare-devil* sort of fellow.

[f] And stay,—] The remainder of this scene is not in the first edition, 1597.

[g] I *warrant thee;*] *I* was added by the editor of the second folio.

would fain lay knife aboard; but she, good soul, had as lieve see a toad, a very toad, as see him. I anger her sometimes, and tell her that Paris is the properer man; but, I'll warrant you, when I say so, she looks as pale as any clout in the varsal world. Doth not rosemary and Romeo begin both with a letter?

ROM. Ay, nurse; What of that? both with an R.

NURSE. Ah, mocker! that's the dog's name. R (9) is for the dog.* No; I know it begins with some other letter: and she hath the prettiest sententious of it, of you and rosemary, that it would do you good to hear it.

ROM. Commend me to thy lady. [*Exit.*

NURSE. Ay, a thousand times.—Peter!

PETER. Anon.

NURSE. Before, and apace. [*Exeunt.*

SCENE V.—Capulet's *Garden.*

Enter JULIET.

JUL. The clock struck nine, when I did send the nurse:
In half an hour she promis'd to return.
Perchance, she cannot meet him:—that's not so.—
O, she is lame! love's heralds † should be thoughts,[a]
Which ten times faster glide than the sun's beams,
Driving back shadows over lowring hills:
Therefore do nimble-pinion'd doves draw Love,
And therefore hath the wind-swift Cupid wings.
Now is the sun upon the highmost hill
Of this day's journey; and from nine till twelve
Is three long hours,—yet she is not come.
Had she affections, and warm youthful blood,
She'd be as swift in motion as a ball;
My words would bandy her to my sweet love,
And his to me:
But old folks, many feign as they were dead;
Unwieldly, slow, heavy and pale as lead.

Enter Nurse *and* PETER.

O God, she comes!—O honey nurse, what news?
Hast thou met with him? send thy man away.

NURSE. Peter, stay at the gate. [*Exit* PETER.

JUL. Now, good sweet nurse,—O lord! why look'st thou sad?
Though news be sad, yet tell them merrily;
If good, thou sham'st the music of sweet news
By playing it to me with so sour a face.

NURSE. I am aweary, give me leave awhile;
Fie, how my bones ache! what a jaunt have I had!

JUL. I would, thou hadst my bones, and I thy news:
Nay, come, I pray thee, speak;—good, good nurse, speak.

NURSE. Jesu, what haste? can you not stay awhile?
Do you not see that I am out of breath?

JUL. How art thou out of breath, when thou hast breath
To say to me—that thou art out of breath?
The excuse, that thou dost make in this delay,
Is longer than the tale thou dost excuse.
Is thy news good, or bad? answer to that;
Say either, and I'll stay the circumstance:
Let me be satisfied, is 't good or bad?

NURSE. Well, you have made a simple choice; you know not how to choose a man: Romeo! no, not he; though his face be better than any man's, yet his leg excels all men's; and for a hand, and a foot, and a body,—though they be not to be talk'd on, yet they are past compare: he is not the flower of courtesy,—but, I'll warrant him, as gentle as a lamb.—Go thy ways, wench; serve God:—what, have you dined at home?

JUL. No, no: but all this did I know before;
What says he of our marriage? what of that?

NURSE. Lord, how my head aches! what a head have I?
It beats as it would fall in twenty pieces.
My back o' t' other side,—O, my back, my back!—
Beshrew your heart, for sending me about,
To catch my death with jaunting up and down!

JUL. I' faith, I am sorry that thou art not well:*
Sweet, sweet, sweet nurse, tell me, what says my love?

NURSE. Your love says like an honest gentleman,
And a courteous, and a kind, and a handsome,
And, I warrant, a virtuous:—where is your mother?

JUL. Where is my mother?—why, she is within;
Where should she be? how oddly thou reply'st:
Your love says like an honest gentleman,—
Where is your mother?

NURSE. O, God's lady dear!
Are you so hot? marry come up, I trow;
Is this the poultice for my aching bones?
Henceforward do your messages yourself.

JUL. Here's such a coil;—come, what says Romeo?

NURSE. Have you got leave to go to shrift today?

(*) First folio omits *dog*. (†) First folio, *herald*.

[a] Should be thoughts,—] This scene was greatly augmented and improved after the first quarto. In that edition, Juliet's speech is continued from the above words, as follows:—

"And runne more swift, than hastie powder fierd,
Doth hurrie from the fearfull cannons mouth;
Oh now she comes. Tell me gentle nurse,
What sayes my loue?"

(*) First folio, so *well*.

JUL. I have.

NURSE. Then hie you hence to friar Laurence' cell,
There stays a husband to make you a wife:
Now comes the wanton blood up in your cheeks,
They'll be in scarlet straight at any news.
Hie you to church; I must another way,
To fetch a ladder, by the which your love
Must climb a bird's nest soon, when it is dark:
I am the drudge, and toil in your delight;
But you shall bear the burden soon at night.
Go, I'll to dinner; hie you to the cell.

JUL. Hie to high fortune!—honest nurse, farewell. [*Exeunt.*

SCENE VI.—*Friar* Laurence's *Cell.*(10)

Enter Friar LAURENCE *and* ROMEO.

FRI. So smile the heavens upon this holy act,
That after-hours with sorrow chide us not!

ROM. Amen, amen! but come what sorrow can,
It cannot countervail the exchange of joy
That one short minute gives me in her sight:
Do thou but close our hands with holy words,
Then love-devouring death do what he dare;
It is enough I may but call her mine.

FRI. These violent delights have violent ends,
And in their triumph die; like fire and powder,
Which, as they kiss, consume. The sweetest honey
Is loathsome in his own deliciousness,
And in the taste confounds the appetite:
Therefore, love moderately; long love doth so;
Too swift arrives as tardy as too slow.

Enter JULIET.

Here comes the lady:—O, so light a foot
Will ne'er wear out the everlasting flint:
A lover may bestride the gossamer
That idles in the wanton summer air,
And yet not fall, so light is vanity.

JUL. Good even to my ghostly confessor.
FRI. Romeo shall thank thee, daughter, for us both.
JUL. As much to him, else is* his thanks too much.
ROM. Ah, Juliet, if the measure of thy joy
Be heap'd like mine, and that thy skill be more
To blazon it, then sweeten with thy breath
This neighbour air, and let rich music's tongue,
Unfold the imagin'd happiness that both
Receive in either, by this dear encounter.
JUL. Conceit,[a] more rich in matter than in words,
Brags of his substance, not of ornament:
They are but beggars that can count their worth;
But my true love is grown to such excess,
I cannot sum up sum of half my wealth.[b]
FRI. Come, come with me, and we will make short work;
For, by your leaves, you shall not stay alone,
Till holy church incorporate two in one. [*Exeunt.*

(*) First folio, *in*.

a Conceit,—] *Conceit* here means *imagination*. So, in "The Rape of Lucrece,"—

"—— which the *conceited* painter drew so proud."—MALONE.

b I *cannot sum up* sum of half my wealth.] So the second quarto, 1599; and so, also, the undated quarto, and the folio, 1623, except that they misspell the second "sum," "*some*." The meaning seems plain enough, "I cannot sum up the sum or total of half my wealth;" but the passage has been modernized into,—

"I cannot sum up half my sum of wealth."

ACT III.

SCENE I.—*A Public Place.*

Enter MERCUTIO, BENVOLIO, Page, *and* Servants.

BEN. I pray thee, good Mercutio, let's retire;
The day is hot, the Capulets abroad,
And, if we meet, we shall not 'scape a brawl;
For now, these hot days, is the mad blood stirring.

MER. Thou art like one of these fellows, that, when he enters the confines of a tavern, claps me his sword upon the table, and says, *God send me no need of thee!* and, by the operation of the second cup, draws him on the drawer, when, indeed, there is no need.

BEN. Am I like such a fellow?

MER. Come, come, thou art as hot a Jack in thy mood as any in Italy; and as soon moved to be moody, and as soon moody to be moved.

BEN. And what too[a]?

MER. Nay, an there were two such, we should have none shortly, for one would kill the other. Thou! why thou wilt quarrel with a man that hath a hair more, or a hair less, in his beard, than thou hast. Thou wilt quarrel with a man for cracking nuts, having no other reason but because thou hast hazel eyes; what eye, but such an eye, would spy

---

[a] *And what* too?] So the old copies, meaning, "And what *else?*" or, "What *more?*" The modern editions read, "And what to?"

out such a quarrel? Thy head is as full of quarrels, as an egg is full of meat; and yet thy head hath been beaten as addle as an egg, for quarrelling. Thou hast quarrelled with a man for coughing in the street, because he hath wakened thy dog that hath lain asleep in the sun. Didst thou not fall out with a tailor for wearing his new doublet before Easter? with another, for tying his new shoes with old riband? and yet thou wilt tutor me from quarrelling!

BEN. An I were so apt to quarrel as thou art, any man should buy the fee-simple of my life for an hour and a quarter.

MER. The fee-simple? O simple!

BEN. By my head, here come the Capulets.

MER. By my heel, I care not.

Enter TYBALT *and others.*

TYB. Follow me close, for I will speak to them.—
Gentlemen, good den; a word with one of you.

MER. And but one word with one of us? couple it with something; make it a word and a blow.

TYB. You shall find me apt enough to that, sir, an you will give me occasion.

MER. Could you not take some occasion without giving?

TYB. Mercutio, thou consort'st with Romeo,—

MER. Consort![a] what, dost thou make us minstrels? an thou make minstrels of us, look to hear nothing but discords: here's my fiddlestick; here's that shall make you dance. 'Zounds,* consort!

BEN. We talk here in the public haunt of men:
Either withdraw into some private place,
Or reason coldly of your grievances,
Or else depart;[b] here all eyes gaze on us.

MER. Men's eyes were made to look, and let them gaze;
I will not budge for no man's pleasure, I.[c]

TYB. Well, peace be with you, sir! here comes my man.

MER. But I'll be hang'd, sir, if he wear your livery:
Marry, go before to field, he 'll be your follower;
Your worship, in that sense, may call him—man.

Enter ROMEO.

TYB. Romeo, the love[d] I bear thee, can afford
No better term than this—Thou art a villain.

ROM. Tybalt, the reason that I have to love thee,
Doth much excuse the appertaining rage
To such a greeting:—Villain am I none;
Therefore farewell; I see, thou know'st me not.

TYB. Boy, this shall not excuse the injuries
That thou hast done me; therefore turn, and draw.

ROM. I do protest, I never injured thee;
But love* thee better than thou canst devise,
Till thou shalt know the reason of my love:
And so, good Capulet,—which name I tender
As dearly as mine† own,—be satisfied.

MER. O calm, dishonourable, vile submission!
A la stoccata[e] carries it away.— [*Draws.*
Tybalt, you rat-catcher, will you walk?

TYB. What would'st thou have with me?

MER. Good king of cats, nothing but one of your nine lives; that I mean to make bold withal, and, as you shall use me hereafter, dry-beat the rest of the eight. Will you pluck your sword out of his pilcher[f] by the ears? make haste, lest mine be about your ears ere it be out.

TYB. I am for you. [*Drawing.*

ROM. Gentle Mercutio, put thy rapier up.

MER. Come, sir, your *passado.* [*They fight.*

ROM. Draw, Benvolio; beat down their weapons.
Gentlemen, for shame, forbear this outrage;—
Tybalt,—Mercutio,—the prince expressly hath
Forbidden bandying in Verona streets:—
Hold, Tybalt;—good Mercutio.

[*Exeunt* TYBALT *and his partizans.*[g]

MER. I am hurt.—
A plague o' both the houses!—I am sped:—
Is he gone, and hath nothing?

BEN. What, art thou hurt?

MER. Ay, ay, a scratch, a scratch; marry, 'tis enough;—
Where is my page?—go, villain, fetch a surgeon.
[*Exit* Page.

ROM. Courage, man; the hurt cannot be much.

MER. No, 'tis not so deep as a well, nor so wide as a church-door; but 'tis enough, 'twill

(*) First folio, *Come.*

a Consort!] See "Two Gentlemen of Verona," Act III. Sc. 2, note (b), p. 26 of the present Vol.

b Or else depart;] Or else *part.* See "Love's Labour 's Lost," Act. II. Sc. 1, note (a), p. 62 of the present Vol.

c *I will not budge for no man's pleasure,* I.] The duplication of the pronoun is a construction of frequent use in the language of Shakespeare's time. So in the "Tempest," Act III. Sc. 3:—

> '*You* are three men of sin, whom destiny
> (That hath to instrument this lower world
> And what is in 't) the never surfeited sea
> Hath caus'd to belch up *you.*"

d *The* love *I bear thee,*—] This is the reading of all the ancient copies, except the quarto, 1597, which has—"the *hate* I bear thee," &c.

(*) First folio, *lov'd.* (†) First folio, *my.*

e *A la* stoccata—] *Stoccato* or *stoccado* is an Italian term for a *thrust,* or stab, in fencing. The folio, 1623, spells it *stucatho.*

f *Out of his* pilcher—] A *pilch* was the name for some outer garment made of leather. Nash, in his "Pierce Penniless's Supplication to the Devil," 1592, speaks of "a carreman in a lether *pilche:*" and the word might be applied suitably enough for the leathern sheath of a rapier. Perhaps we should read, "out of his pilch, sir," &c. The quarto, 1597, has "come drawe your rapier out of your scabard," &c.

g Exeunt, &c.] The first quarto has here a stage direction, running thus:—
"Tibalt under Romeo's arme thrusts Mercutio, in and flyes."

serve: ask for me to-morrow, and you shall find me a grave man.(1) I am peppered, I warrant, for this world:—A plague o' both your houses!—'zounds,* a dog, a rat, a mouse, a cat, to scratch a man to death! a braggart, a rogue, a villain, that fights by the book of arithmetic!—Why the devil came you between us? I was hurt under your arm.

ROM. I thought all for the best.

MER. Help me into some house, Benvolio,
Or I shall faint: a plague o' both your houses!
They have made worm's meat of me;
I have it, and soundly too:—your houses!
[*Exeunt* MERCUTIO *and* BENVOLIO.

ROM. This gentleman, the prince's near ally,
My very friend, hath got his mortal hurt
In my behalf; my reputation stain'd
With Tybalt's slander, Tybalt, that an hour
Hath been my cousin:—O sweet Juliet,
Thy beauty hath made me effeminate,
And in my temper soften'd valour's steel.

Re-enter BENVOLIO.

BEN. O Romeo, Romeo! brave Mercutio's dead;
That gallant spirit hath aspir'd[a] the clouds,
Which too untimely here did scorn the earth.

ROM. This day's black fate on more days doth depend;
This but begins the woe, others must end.

Re-enter TYBALT.

BEN. Here comes the furious Tybalt back again.

ROM. Alive[b] in triumph! and Mercutio slain!
Away to heaven, respective lenity,[c]
And fire-ey'd fury† be my conduct[d] now!—
Now, Tybalt, take the *villain* back again,
That late thou gav'st me; for Mercutio's soul
Is but a little way above our heads,
Staying for thine to keep him company;
Either thou, or I, or both, must go with him.

TYB. Thou, wretched boy, that didst consort him here,
Shalt with him hence.

ROM. This shall determine that.
[*They fight;* TYBALT *falls.*

BEN. Romeo, away, be gone!
The citizens are up, and Tybalt slain:—
Stand not amaz'd:—the prince will doom thee death,
If thou art taken:—hence!—be gone!—away!

ROM. O! I am fortune's fool![e]

BEN. Why dost thou stay?
[*Exit* ROMEO.

Enter Citizens, *&c.*

1 CIT. Which way ran he, that kill'd Mercutio?
Tybalt, that murderer, which way ran he?

BEN. There lies that Tybalt.

1 CIT. Up, sir, go with me;
I charge thee in the prince's name, obey.

Enter PRINCE, *attended;* MONTAGUE, CAPULET, *their* Wives *and others.*

PRIN. Where are the vile beginners of this fray?

BEN. O noble prince, I can discover all
The unlucky manage of this fatal brawl:
There lies the man, slain by young Romeo,
That slew thy kinsman, brave Mercutio.

LA. CAP. Tybalt, my cousin!—O my brother's child!
O prince! O cousin! husband! O the blood is spill'd[f]
Of my dear kinsman!—Prince, as thou art true,
For blood of ours, shed blood of Montague.—
O cousin, cousin!

PRIN. Benvolio, who began this bloody* fray?

BEN. Tybalt, here slain, whom Romeo's hand did slay;
Romeo that spoke him fair, bid him bethink
How nice[g] the quarrel was,(2) and urg'd withal
Your high displeasure: all this—uttered
With gentle breath, calm look, knees humbly bow'd,—
Could not take truce with the unruly spleen,
Of Tybalt deaf to peace, but that he tilts
With piercing steel at bold Mercutio's breast;
Who, all as hot, turns deadly point to point,
And, with a martial scorn, with one hand beats
Cold death aside, and with the other sends
It back to Tybalt, whose dexterity
Retorts it: Romeo he cries aloud,

(*) First folio, *What.* (†) First folio, *fire and fury.*

a *Hath* aspir'd *the clouds,*—] In the use of *aspire*, some particle, as *to* or *after*, is now considered indispensable. So to the word *arrive* we always add *at, unto*, or *in;* but the old writers frequently adopted the construction in the text. Thus Marlowe, in "Tamburlaine," 1590,—

"And both our souls *aspire* celestial thrones."

And our author, "Henry VI." Part III. Act V. Sc. 3:—

"—— those powers that the Queen
Hath raised in Gallia, have *arriv'd* the coast."

b Alive in triumph!] So the quarto, 1597; that of 1599 has *he gan*, and the folio, 1623, reads *he gon* in triumph. Modern editors have, "Alive! in triumph!"

(*) First folio omits *bloody*.

c Respective lenity,—] Considerate mildness.

d *My* conduct *now!*] My guide, my conductor.

e O! I am fortune's fool!] I am the sport of fortune. The first quarto reads, "Ah, I am fortune's slave."

f The quarto, 1597, reads,

Unhappy sight! ah, the blood is spilt.

g *How* nice—] *Nice* here signifies, not *delicate, squeamish*, &c., as in some other instances in these Plays, but *trivial, unimportant*, as in Act V. Sc. 2,—

"The letter was not *nice*, but full of charge,
Of dear import."

Hold, friends! friends, part! and, swifter than his tongue,
His[a] agile arm beats down their fatal points,
And 'twixt them rushes; underneath whose arm
An envious thrust from Tybalt hit the life
Of stout Mercutio, and then Tybalt fled;
But by and by comes back to Romeo,
Who had but newly entertain'd revenge,
And to't they go like lightning; for, ere I
Could draw to part them, was stout Tybalt slain;
And, as he fell, did Romeo turn and fly:
This is the truth, or let Benvolio die.

LA. CAP. He is a kinsman to the Montague,
Affection makes him false, he speaks not true:
Some twenty of them fought in this black strife,
And all those twenty could but kill one life:
I beg for justice, which thou, prince, must give;
Romeo slew Tybalt, Romeo must not live.

PRIN. Romeo slew him, he slew Mercutio;
Who now the price of his dear blood doth owe?

MON.* Not Romeo, prince, he was Mercutio's friend;
His fault concludes but, what the law should end,
The life of Tybalt.

PRIN. And, for that offence,
Immediately we do exíle him hence:
I have an interest in your hates'[b] proceeding,
My blood for your rude brawls doth lie a bleeding;
But I'll amerce you with so strong a fine,
That you shall all repent the loss of mine:
I† will be deaf to pleading and excuses;
Nor tears, nor prayers, shall purchase out‡ abuses,
Therefore use none: let Romeo hence in haste,
Else, when he's found, that hour is his last.
Bear hence this body, and attend our will:
Mercy but§ murders, pardoning those that kill.
[*Exeunt.*

SCENE II.—*A Room in* Capulet's *House.*

Enter JULIET.

JUL. Gallop apace, you fiery-footed steeds,
Towards Phœbus' lodging;[c] such a waggoner
As Phaeton would whip you to the west,
And bring in cloudy night immediately.[d]—
Spread thy close curtain, love-performing night!
That run-aways' (3) eyes may wink, and Romeo
Leap to these arms, untalk'd of, and unseen!—
Lovers can see to do their amorous rites
By* their own beauties:[e] or, if love be blind,
It best agrees with night.—Come, civil night,
Thou sober-suited matron, all in black,
And learn me how to lose a winning match,
Play'd for a pair of stainless maidenhoods:
Hood my unmann'd blood bating in my cheeks,(4)
With thy black mantle; till strange love, grown[f] bold,
Think true love acted, simple modesty.
Come, night! come, Romeo! come, thou day in night!
For thou wilt lie upon the wings of night
Whiter than snow upon a raven's back.[g]—
Come, gentle night; come, loving, black-brow'd night,
Give me my Romeo: and, when he[h] shall die,
Take him and cut him out in little stars,
And he will make the face of heaven so fine,
That all the world will be in love with night,
And pay no worship to the garish[i] sun.—
O, I have bought the mansion of a love,
But not possess'd it; and, though I am sold,
Not yet enjoy'd: so tedious is this day,
As is the night before some festival
To an impatient child, that hath new robes,
And may not wear them. O, here comes my nurse,
And she brings news; and every tongue, that speaks
But Romeo's name, speaks heavenly eloquence.—

Enter Nurse, *with cords.*(5)

Now, nurse, what news? What hast thou there? the cords,
That Romeo bid thee fetch?

NURSE. Ay, ay, the cords.
[*Throws them down.*

JUL. Ah me! what news! why dost thou wring thy hands?

(*) First folio, *Cap.* (†) First folio, *It.* (‡) First folio, *our.* (§) First folio, *not.*

a *His* agile *arm*—] So the quarto, 1597; that of 1599, and folio, 1623, read *aged,* which the editor of the second folio altered to *able.*

b *Your* hates'—] The quarto, 1599, and folio, read *hearts.*

c Towards Phœbus' lodging;] The first quarto reads, To *Phœbus'* mansion.

d Immediately.—] Here Juliet's speech terminates in the first quarto, 1597; the whole scene is very much amplified in the edition of 1599.

e By their own beauties:] Steevens observed that Milton, in his "Comus," might have been indebted to this passage:—

> "Virtue could see to do what virtue would,
> By her own radiant light, though sun and moon
> Were in the flat sea sunk."

f Grown *bold,*—] An emendation of Rowe's; the old copies have, "*grow* bold."

(*) First folio, And *by.*

g Whiter than snow—] So the undated quarto; the other editions read,

> *Whiter than* new *snow upon a raven's back.*

h *And, when* he *shall die,*—] This is another valuable emendation of the undated quarto; all the other early editions read, "when *I* shall die."

i Garish sun.—] That is, *gaudy, blazing,* sun. Milton was not unmindful of this beautiful speech when he composed "*Il Penseroso;*" compare—

> "—— Come, *civil* night,
> Thou sober-suited matron,—"

and—

> "Pay no worship to the *garish* sun,"

with his—

> "Till *civil-suited* morn appear."

and—

> "Hide me from day's *garish* eye.'

NURSE. Ah, well-a-day! he's dead, he's dead, he 's dead!
We are undone, lady, we are undone!—
Alack the day!—he's gone, he's kill'd, he's dead!
JUL. Can heaven be so envious?
NURSE. Romeo can,
Though heaven cannot:—O Romeo! Romeo!—
Who ever would have thought it?—Romeo!
JUL. What devil art thou, that dost torment me thus?
This torture should be roar'd in dismal hell.
Hath Romeo slain himself? say thou but *I*,[a]
And that bare vowel *I* shall poison more
Than the death-darting eye of cockatrice:[b]
I am not I, if there be such an *I*;
Or those eyes shut,* that make thee answer, *I*.
If he be slain, say—*I*; or if not—*no*:
Brief sounds determine of my weal, or woe.
NURSE. I saw the wound, I saw it with mine eyes,—
God save the mark![c]—here on his manly breast:
A piteous corse, a bloody piteous corse;
Pale, pale as ashes, all bedaub'd in blood,
All in gore blood;—I swounded at the sight.
JUL. O break, my heart!—poor bankrupt, break at once!
To prison, eyes! ne'er look on liberty!
Vile earth, to earth resign; end motion here;
And thou, and Romeo, press one heavy bier!
NURSE. O Tybalt, Tybalt, the best friend I had!
O courteous Tybalt! honest gentleman!
That ever I should live to see thee dead!
JUL. What storm is this, that blows so contrary?
Is Romeo slaughter'd? and is Tybalt dead?
My dear-lov'd† cousin, and my dearer lord?—
Then, dreadful trumpet, sound the general doom!
For who is living, if those two are gone?
NURSE. Tybalt is gone, and Romeo banished;
Romeo, that kill'd him, he is banished.
JUL. O God!—did Romeo's hand shed Tybalt's blood?
NURSE. It did, it did; alas the day! it did.[d]
JUL. O serpent heart, hid with a flow'ring face!
Did ever dragon keep so fair a cave?
Beautiful tyrant! fiend angelical!
Dove-feather'd raven![e] wolvish-ravening lamb!
Despised substance of divinest show!
Just opposite to what thou justly seem'st,
A damned saint,[f] an honourable villain!
O, nature! what hadst thou to do in hell,
When thou didst bower the spirit of a fiend
In mortal paradise of such sweet flesh?—
Was ever book, containing such vile matter,
So fairly bound? O, that deceit should dwell
In such a gorgeous palace!
NURSE. There's no trust,
No faith, no honesty in men; all perjur'd,
All forsworn, all naught, all dissemblers.—
Ah, where's my man? give me some *aqua vitæ*:—
These griefs, these woes, these sorrows make me old.
Shame come to Romeo!
JUL. Blister'd be thy tongue,
For such a wish! he was not born to shame:
Upon his brow shame is ashamed to sit;
For 'tis a throne where honour may be crown'd
Sole monarch of the universal earth.
O, what a beast was I to chide at* him!
NURSE. Will you speak well of him that kill'd your cousin?
JUL. Shall I speak ill of him that is my husband?
Ah, poor my lord, what tongue shall smooth thy name,
When I, thy three-hours' wife, have mangled it?—
But, wherefore, villain, didst thou kill my cousin?
That villain cousin would have kill'd my husband:
Back, foolish tears, back to your native spring;
Your tributary drops belong to woe,
Which you, mistaking, offer up to joy.
My husband lives, that Tybalt would have slain;
And Tybalt's dead, that would have slain my husband:
All this is comfort; wherefore weep I then?
Some word there was, worser than Tybalt's death,
That murder'd me: I would forget it fain;
But, O! it presses to my memory,
Like damned guilty deeds to sinners' minds:
Tybalt is dead, and Romeo—banished;
That—*banished*, that one word—*banished*,
Hath slain ten thousand Tybalts. Tybalt's death
Was woe enough, if it had ended there:

(*) Old copies, *shot*. (†) First folio, *dearest*.

(*) First folio omits *at*.

[a] *Say thou but* I,—] The old spelling of the affirmative, *Ay*, is of necessity retained in this passage.

[b] *Death-darting eye of* cockatrice:] Shakespeare has several allusions to the supposed destructive power of this fabled monster's eye. Thus, in "Henry VI." Part II. Act III. Sc. 2:—

"——— Come, *basilisk*,
And *kill* the innocent gazer *with thy sight*."

So, also, in Part III. of the same Play, Act III. Sc. 2:—

"I'll *slay* more gazers than the *basilisk*."

And again, in "Twelfth Night," Act III. Sc. 4:—

"—— they will *kill* one another *by the* look, like *cockatrices*."

[c] God save the mark!—] This exclamation appears to have been proverbial, but its meaning has hitherto baffled the research and sagacity of every commentator. It occurs again in "Henry IV." Part I. Act I. Sc. 3, and in "The Merchant of Venice," Act II. Sc. 2; and in "Othello," Act I. Sc. 1, we have *God bless the mark*. In the quarto, 1597, instead of "God save the mark!" in the present passage, we have, "God save the *sample*," an expression equally obscure.

[d] Alas the day! it did.] The speeches here are misappropriated in the quarto, 1599, and the folio, 1623, but are correctly given in the undated quarto.

[e] Dove-feather'd raven!] The quarto, 1599, and folio read—

"*Ravenous* dove-feather'd raven, wolvish-ravening lamb."

[f] *A* damned *saint*,—] So the undated quarto. That of 1599 has *dimme*, the folio, 1623, *dimne*.

Or,—if sour woe delights in fellowship,[a]
And needly will be rank'd with other griefs,
Why follow'd not, when she said—*Tybalt's dead,*
Thy father, or *thy mother*, nay, or both,
Which modern [b] lamentation might have mov'd?
But, with* a rear-ward following Tybalt's death,
Romeo is banished,—to speak that word,
Is father, mother, Tybalt, Romeo, Juliet,
All slain, all dead:—*Romeo is banished!*—
There is no end, no limit, measure, bound,
In that word's death; no words can that woe sound.—
Where is my father, and my mother, nurse?

NURSE. Weeping and wailing over Tybalt's corse:
Will you go to them? I will bring you thither.

JUL. Wash they his wounds with tears; [c] mine shall be spent,
When theirs are dry, for Romeo's banishment.
Take up those cords: poor ropes, you are beguil'd,
Both you and I; for Romeo is exil'd:
He made you for a highway to my bed;
But I, a maid, die maiden-widowed.
Come, cords; come, nurse; I'll to my wedding bed;
And death, not Romeo, take my maidenhead!

NURSE. Hie to your chamber: I'll find Romeo
To comfort you:—I wot well where he is.
Hark ye, your Romeo will be here at night;
I'll to him; he is hid at Laurence' cell.

JUL. O find him! give this ring to my true knight,
And bid him come to take his last farewell.
[*Exeunt.*

SCENE III.—*Friar* Laurence's *Cell.*

Enter FRIAR LAURENCE *and* ROMEO.

FRI. Romeo, come forth; come forth, thou fearful man;
Affliction is enamour'd of thy parts,
And thou art wedded to calamity.

ROM. Father, what news? what is the prince's doom?
What sorrow craves acquaintance at my hand,
That I yet know not?

FRI. Too familiar
Is my dear son with such sour company:
I bring thee tidings of the prince's doom.

ROM. What less than dooms-day is the prince's doom?

FRI. A gentler judgment vanish'd from his lips,
Not body's death, but body's banishment.

ROM. Ha! banishment? be merciful, say—death:
For exile hath more terror in his look,
Much more than death: do not say—banishment.

FRI. Here from Verona art thou banished:
Be patient, for the world is broad and wide.

ROM. There is no world without Verona walls,
But purgatory, torture, hell itself.
Hence banished is banish'd from the world,
And world's exile is death:—then banished
Is death mis-term'd: calling death, banishment,*
Thou cutt'st my head off with a golden axe,
And smil'st upon the stroke that murders me.

FRI. O deadly sin! O rude unthankfulness!
Thy fault our law calls death; but the kind prince,
Taking thy part, hath rush'd aside the law,
And turn'd that black word, death, to banishment:
This is dear mercy, and thou seest it not.

ROM. 'Tis torture, and not mercy: heaven is here,
Where Juliet lives; and every cat, and dog,
And little mouse, every unworthy thing,
Live here in heaven, and may look on her,
But Romeo may not.—More validity,
More honourable state, more courtship lives
In carrion flies, than Romeo; they may seize
On the white wonder of dear Juliet's hand,
And steal immortal blessing from her lips;
Who, even in pure and vestal modesty,
Still blush, as thinking their own kisses sin;
This may flies do, when I from this must fly;
But Romeo may not; he is banished.[d]
And say'st thou yet, that exile is not death?—[e]
Hadst thou no poison mix'd, no sharp-ground knife,
No sudden mean of death, though ne'er so mean,
But—banished—to kill me; banished?
O friar, the damned use that word in hell;
Howlings attend it: how hast thou the heart,
Being a divine, a ghostly confessor,
A sin-absolver, and my friend profess'd,

(*) First folio, *which.*

(*) First folio, *banished.*

a Sour woe delights in fellowship,—] Compare—

"Solamen miseris socios habuisse doloris."

b Modern *lamentation*—] That is, *ordinary, well-known* lamentation. So, in "All's Well That Ends Well," Act II. Sc. 3:—

"—— Make *modern* and familiar things,
Supernatural and causeless."

And in "As You Like It," Act II. Sc. 9:—

"Full of wise saws, and *modern* instances."

c Wash they his wounds with tears;] All the modern editions place a note of interrogation after these words, but perhaps in error. The Nurse tells Juliet her father and mother are weeping over Tybalt's corse, and asks if she will go to them; to which Juliet replies,—"No, let them wash his wounds with tears; mine shall be spent in wailing Romeo's banishment."

d He is banished.] Here, in the quarto, 1599, occur the following two lines; they are omitted in the folio:—

"Flies may do this, but I from this must fly,
They are free men, but I am banished."

Capell rightly conjectures that the author's first draft of this passage was left standing in the MS., and so got printed with the after version.

e That exile is not death?—] This line and the preceding one are transposed in the old copies.

To mangle me with that word—banished?
FRI. Thou fond mad man, hear me a little speak.[a]
ROM. O, thou wilt speak again of banishment.
FRI. I'll give thee armour to keep off that word;
Adversity's sweet milk, philosophy,
To comfort thee, though thou art banished.
ROM. Yet *banished?*—hang up philosophy!
Unless philosophy can make a Juliet,
Displant a town, reverse a prince's doom;
It helps not, it prevails not; talk no more.
FRI. O, then I see that madmen have no ears.
ROM. How should they, when that* wise men have no eyes?
FRI. Let me dispute† with thee of thy estate.[b]
ROM. Thou canst not speak of that thou dost not feel:
Wert thou as young as I,* Juliet thy love,
An hour but married, Tybalt murdered,
Doting like me, and like me—banished,
Then might'st thou speak, then might'st thou tear thy hair,
And fall upon the ground, as I do now,
Taking the measure of an unmade grave.
[*Knocking within.*[c]
FRI. Arise, one knocks; good Romeo, hide thyself.
ROM. Not I; unless the breath of heart-sick groans,

(*) First folio omits, *that*. (†) First folio, *dispaire*.

(*) First folio, *as* Juliet my love.

a Thou fond mad man,—] So the undated quarto: the other quartos read *then* for *thou;* the folio, 1623,

"Then fond mad man, hear me speak."

b Dispute with thee of thy estate.] Let me *reason* with you upon your *affairs*.

c Knocking within.] The stage direction in the old copies is, "*Enter Nurse, and knockes.*"

Mist-like, infold me from the search of eyes.
[*Knocking.*

FRI. Hark, how they knock!—who's there?—Romeo, arise;
Thou wilt be taken:—Stay a while:—stand up;
[*Knocking.*
Run to my study:—By and by:—God's will!
What wilfulness[a] is this!—I come, I come.
[*Knocking.*
Who knocks so hard? whence come you? what's your will?

NURSE. [*within.*] Let me come in, and you shall know my errand;
I come from lady Juliet.

FRI. Welcome then.

Enter Nurse.

NURSE. O holy friar, O, tell me, holy friar,
Where is my lady's lord, where's Romeo?

FRI. There on the ground, with his own tears made drunk.

NURSE. O, he is even in my mistress' case,
Just in her case!

FRI. O woeful sympathy!
Piteous predicament![b]

NURSE. Even so lies she,
Blubbering and weeping, weeping and blubbering:—
Stand up, stand up; stand, an you be a man:
For Juliet's sake, for her sake, rise and stand;
Why should you fall into so deep an O?

ROM. Nurse!

NURSE. Ah sir! ah sir!—Well,* death's the end of all.

ROM. Spak'st† thou of Juliet? how is it with her?
Doth she not think me an old murderer,
Now I have stained the childhood of our joy
With blood remov'd but little from her own?
Where is she? and how doth she? and what says
My conceal'd lady to our cancell'd‡ love?

NURSE. O, she says nothing, sir, but weeps and weeps;
And now falls on her bed; and then starts up,
And Tybalt calls; and then on Romeo cries,
And then down falls again.

ROM. As if that name,
Shot from the deadly* level of a gun,
Did murder her; as that name's cursed hand
Murder'd her kinsman.—O tell me, friar, tell me,
In what vile part of this anatomy
Doth my name lodge? tell me, that I may sack
The hateful mansion. [*Drawing his sword.*[c]

FRI. Hold thy desperate hand:
Art thou a man? thy form cries out, thou art;(6)
Thy tears are womanish; thy wild acts denote
The unreasonable fury of a beast:
Unseemly woman, in a seeming man!
Or† ill-beseeming beast, in seeming both!
Thou hast amaz'd me: by my holy order,
I thought thy disposition better temper'd.
Hast thou slain Tybalt? wilt thou slay thyself?
And slay thy lady that in thy life lives,[d]
By doing damned hate upon thyself?
Why rail'st thou on thy birth,[e] the heaven, and earth?
Since birth, and heaven, and earth, all three do meet
In thee at once; which thou at once would'st lose.
Fie, fie! thou sham'st thy shape, thy love, thy wit;
Which, like an usurer, abound'st in all,
And usest none in that true use indeed,
Which should bedeck thy shape, thy love, thy wit.
Thy noble shape is but a form of wax,
Digressing from the valour of a man:
Thy dear love, sworn, but hollow perjury,
Killing that love which thou hast vow'd to cherish:
Thy wit, that ornament to shape and love,
Mis-shapen in the conduct of them both,
Like powder in a skill-less soldier's flask,
Is set o' fire by thine own ignorance,
And thou dismemoer'd with thine own defence.
What, rouse thee, man! thy Juliet is alive,
For whose dear sake thou wast but lately dead;
There art thou happy: Tybalt would kill thee,
But thou slew'st Tybalt; there art thou happy too:[f]
The law, that threaten'd death, became thy friend,
And turn'd it to exile; there art thou happy:
A pack of blessings‡ light upon thy back;
Happiness courts thee in her best array;
But, like a misbehav'd§ and sullen wench,
Thou pout'st upon thy fortune[g] and thy love:

(*) First folio omits, *Well.* (†) First folio, *speak'st.* (‡) First folio, *conceal'd.*

(*) First folio, *dead.* (†) First folio, *And.* (‡) First folio, *or blessing.* (§) First folio, *mishaped.*

[a] *What* wilfulness *is this!*—] So the first quarto, 1597: all the subsequent editions, quarto and folio, read *simpleness.*

[b] Piteous predicament!] These words form part of the Nurse's speech in the old copies. Farmer first suggested they must be the Friar's.

[c] Drawing his sword.] In the first quarto, 1597, is the following stage direction:—*He offers to stab himselfe, and nurse snatches the dagger away.*

[d] That in thy life lives,—] The quarto, 1597, has,—

"And slay thy lady too, that lives in thee."

The quarto, 1599, and folio, 1623, read,—

"And slay thy lady, that in thy life *lies.*"

[e] Why rail'st thou on thy birth,—] Malone justly remarked, that Romeo does not here rail on his birth, though in the old poem he is made to do so:—

"Fyrst *Nature* did he blame, the author of his lyfe,
In which his joyes had been so scant, and sorowes aye so ryfe;
The time and place of byrth he fiersly did reprove,
He cryed out (with open mouth) against the starres above."

"Shakspeare copied the remonstrance of the friar, without reviewing the former part of his scene."

[f] *There art thou happy* too:] Thus the quarto, 1597; in the subsequent quartos, and the folio, 1623, the word *too* is omitted.

[g] *Thou* pout'st upon *thy fortune*—] The quarto, 1599, reads, *puts up;* the folio, 1623, *puttest up;* and in the quarto, 1597, the line stands—

"Thou *frown'st upon* thy fate, that smiles on thee."

The true reading is got at through the undated quarto, which has *powts.*

Take heed, take heed, for such die miserable.
Go, get thee to thy love, as was decreed,
Ascend her chamber, hence and comfort her;
But look thou stay not till the watch be set,
For then thou canst not pass to Mantua;
Where thou shalt live, till we can find a time
To blaze your marriage, reconcile your friends,
Beg pardon of the* prince, and call thee back
With twenty hundred thousand times more joy
Than thou went'st forth in lamentation.—
Go before, nurse: commend me to thy lady;
And bid her hasten all the house to bed,
Which heavy sorrow makes them apt unto:
Romeo is coming.

NURSE. O Lord, I could have staid here all the† night,
To hear good counsel: O, what learning is!—
My lord, I 'll tell my lady you will come.

ROM. Do so, and bid my sweet prepare to chide.

NURSE. Here, sir, a ring she bid me give you, sir:
Hie you, make haste, for it grows very late.
[*Exit* Nurse.

ROM. How well my comfort is reviv'd by this!

FRI. Go hence: good night; and here stands all your state;—[a]
Either be gone before the watch be set,
Or by the break of day disguis'd from hence:
Sojourn in Mantua; I'll find out your man,
And he shall signify from time to time
Every good hap to you, that chances here:
Give me thy hand; 'tis late: farewell; good night.

ROM. But that a joy past joy calls out on me,
It were a grief, so brief to part with thee:
Farewell. [*Exeunt.*

SCENE IV.—*A Room in* Capulet'*s house.*

Enter CAPULET, LADY CAPULET, *and* PARIS.

CAP. Things have fallen out, sir, so unluckily,
That we have had no time to move our daughter:
Look you, she lov'd her kinsman Tybalt dearly,
And so did I;—well, we were born to die.—
'Tis very late, she'll not come down to-night:

(*) First folio, *thy*.

(†) First folio omits, *the*.

[a] And here stands all your state;—] "The whole of your fortune depends on this." JOHNSON.

I promise you, but for your company,
I would have been a-bed an hour ago.

PAR. These times of woe afford no time* to woo:
Madam, good night; commend me to your daughter.

LA. CAP. I will, and know her mind early to-morrow;
To-night she 's mew'd [a] up to her heaviness.

CAP. Sir Paris, I will make a desperate tender[b]
Of my child's love: I think, she will be rul'd
In all respects by me; nay more, I doubt it not.
Wife, go you to her ere you go to bed;
Acquaint her here of my son Paris' love;
And bid her, mark you me, on Wednesday next—
But, soft; what day is this?

PAR. Monday, my lord.

CAP. Monday? ha! ha! well, Wednesday is too soon,
O' Thursday let it be;—o' Thursday, tell her,
She shall be married to this noble earl:—
Will you be ready? do you like this haste?
We 'll keep no great ado;—a friend, or two:—
For hark you, Tybalt being slain so late,
It may be thought we held him carelessly,
Being our kinsman, if we revel much:
Therefore we 'll have some half a dozen friends,
And there an end. But what say you to Thursday?

PAR. My lord, I would that Thursday were to-morrow.

CAP. Well, get you gone:—o' Thursday be it then:
Go you to Juliet ere you go to bed,
Prepare her, wife, against this wedding-day.
Farewell, my lord. Light to my chamber, ho!
Afore me, it is so very† late, that we
May call it early by and by:—good night.
[*Exeunt.*

SCENE V.—Juliet's *chamber.*

Enter ROMEO *and* JULIET.

JUL. Wilt thou be gone? it is not yet near day:
It was the nightingale, and not the lark,
That pierc'd the fearful hollow of thine ear;
Nightly she sings on yon pomegranate tree: [c]
Believe me, love, it was the nightingale.

ROM. It was the lark, the herald of the morn,
No nightingale: look, love, what envious streaks
Do lace the severing clouds in yonder east:
Night's candles are burnt out,(7) and jocund day
Stands tiptoe on the misty mountain tops;
I must be gone and live, or stay and die.

JUL. Yon light is not day-light, I know it, I:
It is some meteor that the sun exhales.
To be to thee this night a torch-bearer,
And light thee on thy way to Mantua:
Therefore stay yet, thou need'st not to be gone.

ROM. Let me be ta'en, let me be put to death;
I am content, so thou wilt have it so.
I 'll say, yon grey is not the morning's eye,
'Tis but the pale reflex of Cynthia's brow; [d]
Nor that is not the lark, whose notes do beat
The vaulty heaven so high above our heads:
I have more care to stay, than will to go;—
Come, death, and welcome! Juliet wills it so.—
How is't, my soul? let's talk, it is not day.

JUL. It is, it is, hie hence, be gone, away;
It is the lark that sings so out of tune,
Straining harsh discords, and unpleasing sharps.
Some say, the lark makes sweet division; [e]
This doth not so, for she divideth us:
Some say, the lark and loathed toad change eyes; [f]
O, now I would they had changed voices too!
Since arm from arm that voice doth us affray,
Hunting thee hence with hunts-up(8) to the day.
O, now be gone; more light and light it grows.

ROM. More light and light!—more dark and dark our woes!

Enter Nurse.

NURSE. Madam!

JUL. Nurse!

NURSE. Your lady mother 's coming to your chamber:
The day is broke; be wary, look about.
[*Exit* Nurse.

JUL. Then, window, let day in, and let life out.

ROM. Farewell, farewell! one kiss, and I'll descend.
[ROMEO *descends.*

(*) First folio, *times*. (†) First folio omits, *very*.

a *To-night she's* mew'd *up*—] A phrase taken from falconry: the *mew* was the inclosure where the hawks were confined.

b ———*I will make a* desperate *tender*
Of my child's love:]
I will make a *confident offer*, or *promise*, of my daughter's love.

c Nightly she sings on yon pomegranate tree:] According to Steevens, this is not merely a poetical supposition. "It is observed," he says, "of the nightingale that, if undisturbed, she sits and sings upon the same tree for many weeks together." And Russell, in his account of Aleppo, tells us, "The nightingale sings from the pomegranate groves in the daytime."

d *The pale reflex of Cynthia's* brow;] The annotator of Mr. Collier's second folio substitutes *bow* for "brow;" a very happy conjecture, and one which certainly affords a better reading than the old text. It must be remembered, however, that *brow* is the word in all the ancient copies, and that Shakespeare has allowed himself great latitude in the use of it in other places. In "Othello" we meet with the "brow of the sea;" and in "King John" with the "brow of night."

e *Makes sweet* division;] *Division* in music, meant what we now term *variation;* where, instead of one note, two, three or more notes are sung to one syllable, or to one chord.

f The lark and loathed toad change eyes;] The lark has ugly eyes and the toad very fine ones; hence arose a common saying that *the toad and lark had changed eyes.* Poor Juliet wishes they had changed voices, too, because, as Heath suggested, the croak of the toad would have been no indication of the day's approach, and consequently no signal for Romeo's departure.

JUL. Art thou gone so? love! lord! ay, husband! friend!
I must hear from thee every day in the hour,
For in a minute there are many days:
O! by this count I shall be much in years,
Ere I again behold my Romeo.

ROM. Farewell! I will omit no opportunity,
That may convey my greetings, love, to thee.

JUL. O, think'st thou, we shall ever meet again?

ROM. I doubt it not; and all these woes shall serve
For sweet discourses in our time to come.

JUL. O God! I have an ill-divining soul;[a]
Methinks I see thee, now thou art so low,
As one dead in the bottom of a tomb:
Either my eyesight fails, or thou look'st pale.
ROM. And trust me, love, in my eye so do you:
Dry sorrow drinks our blood. Adieu! adieu!
[*Exit* ROMEO.
JUL. O fortune, fortune![b] all men call thee fickle:
If thou art fickle, what dost thou with him,
That is renown'd for faith? Be fickle, fortune;
For then, I hope, thou wilt not keep him long,
But send him back.
LA. CAP. [*within.*] Ho, daughter! are you up?
JUL. Who is't that calls? is it my lady mother?
Is she not down so late, or up so early?
What unaccustom'd cause procures her hither?

Enter LADY CAPULET.

LA. CAP. Why, how now, Juliet?
JUL. Madam, I am not well.
LA. CAP. Evermore weeping for your cousin's death?
What, wilt thou wash him from his grave with tears?
An if thou could'st, thou could'st not make him live;
Therefore, have done: some grief shows much of love;
But much of grief shows still some want of wit.
JUL. Yet let me weep for such a feeling loss.
LA. CAP. So shall you feel the loss, but not the friend,
Which you weep for.
JUL. Feeling so the loss,
I cannot choose but ever weep the friend.
LA. CAP. Well, girl, thou weep'st not so much for his death,
As that the villain lives which slaughter'd him.
JUL. What villain, madam?
LA. CAP. That same villain, Romeo.
JUL. Villain and he be many miles asunder.
God pardon him![c] I do, with all my heart;
And yet no man, like he, doth grieve my heart.
LA. CAP. That is, because the traitor murderer* lives.
JUL. Ay, madam, from the reach of these my hands.
Would none but I might venge my cousin's death!
LA. CAP. We will have vengeance for it, fear thou not:
Then weep no more. I'll send to one in Mantua,—
Where that same banish'd runagate doth live,—
Shall give him such an unaccustom'd dram,[d]
That he shall soon keep Tybalt company;
And then, I hope, thou wilt be satisfied.
JUL. Indeed, I never shall be satisfied
With Romeo, till I behold him—dead—
Is my poor heart so for a kinsman vex'd:—
Madam, if you could find out but a man
To bear a poison, I would temper it;
That Romeo should, upon receipt thereof,
Soon sleep in quiet. O, how my heart abhors
To hear him nam'd,—and cannot come to him,—
To wreak the love I bore my cousin Tybalt,[e]
Upon his body that hath slaughter'd him!
LA. CAP. Find thou the means, and I'll find such a man.
But now I'll tell thee joyful tidings, girl.
JUL. And joy comes well in such a needy time:
What are they, I † beseech your ladyship?
LA. CAP. Well, well, thou hast a careful father, child;
One, who, to put thee from thy heaviness,
Hath sorted out a sudden day of joy,
That thou expect'st not, nor I look'd not for.
JUL. Madam, in happy time, what day is that? ‡
LA. CAP. Marry, my child, early next Thursday morn,
The gallant, young, and noble gentleman,
The county Paris,[f] at saint Peter's church,
Shall happily make thee there § a joyful bride.
JUL. Now, by saint Peter's church, and Peter too,
He shall not make me there a joyful bride. (9)
I wonder at this haste; that I must wed
Ere he, that should be husband, comes to woo.
I pray you, tell my lord and father, madam,
I will not marry yet; and, when I do, I swear,
It shall be Romeo, whom you know I hate,

(*) First folio omits, *murderer*. (†) First folio omits, *I*.
(‡) First folio, *this*. (§) First folio omits, *there*.

a I have an ill-divining soul;] "This miserable prescience of futurity," Steevens observes, "I have always regarded as a circumstance particularly beautiful. The same kind of warning from the mind, Romeo seems to have been conscious of, on his going to the entertainment at the house of Capulet:—

'—— my mind misgives
Some consequence, yet hanging in the stars,
Shall bitterly begin his fearful date
With this night's revels.'"

b O fortune, fortune!] This and the intervening lines to the entrance of Lady Capulet are not found in the quarto, 1597. Indeed, the whole scene was considerably amplified and altered after the publication of that edition.

c *God pardon* him!] *Him* was first inserted in the folio, 1632.

d Shall give him such an unaccustom'd dram,—] The quarto, 1597, reads:—

"That should bestow on him so sure a draught."

e *My cousin* Tybalt,—] This line terminates at *cousin* in the older copies. *Tybalt* was added in the folio, 1632, yet we doubt if this were the omitted word, and think, with Malone, it was more probably some epithet to cousin.

f *The* county *Paris*,—] An earl in Shakespeare's time was commonly styled *county* or *countie*.

Rather than Paris:—These are news indeed!
LA. CAP. Here comes your father; tell him so yourself,
And see how he will take it at your hands.

Enter CAPULET *and* Nurse.

CAP. When the sun sets, the earth[a] doth drizzle dew;
But for the sunset of my brother's son,
It rains downright.—
How now! a conduit, girl? what, still in tears?
Evermore showering? In one little body
Thou counterfeit'st a bark, a sea, a wind:
For still thy eyes, which I may call the sea,
Do ebb and flow with tears; the bark thy body is,
Sailing in this salt flood; the winds, thy sighs;
Who,—raging with thy* tears, and they with them,—
Without a sudden calm, will overset
Thy tempest-tossed body: how now, wife?
Have you deliver'd to her our decree?
LA. CAP. Ay, sir; but she will none, she gives you thanks.
I would the fool were married to her grave!
CAP. Soft, take me with you, take me with you,[b] wife.
How! will she none? doth she not give us thanks?
Is she not proud? doth she not count her bless'd,
Unworthy as she is, that we have wrought
So worthy a gentleman to be her bridegroom?
JUL. Not proud, you have; but thankful, that you have:
Proud can I never be of what I hate; †
But thankful even for hate, that is meant love.
CAP. How now! how now, chop-logic![c] what is this?
Proud,—and, I thank you,—and, I thank you not;—
And yet not proud;—mistress minion, you![d]
Thank me no thankings, nor proud me no prouds,
But fettle[e] your fine joints 'gainst Thursday next,
To go with Paris to saint Peter's church,
Or I will drag thee on a hurdle thither.
Out, you green-sickness carrion! out, you baggage!
You tallow-face!
LA. CAP. Fie, fie! what, are you mad?
JUL. Good father, I beseech you on my knees,
Hear me with patience but to speak a word.
CAP. Hang thee, young baggage! disobedient wretch!
I tell thee what,—get thee to church o'Thursday,
Or never after look me in the face:
Speak not, reply not, do not answer me;
My fingers itch: wife, we scarce thought us bless'd,
That God had lent us but this only child;
But now I see this one is one too much,
And that we have a curse in having her:
Out on her, hilding!
NURSE. God in heaven bless her!—
You are to blame, my lord, to rate her so.
CAP. And why, my lady wisdom? hold your tongue,
Good prudence; smatter with your gossips,* go.
NURSE. I speak no treason.
CAP. O, God ye good den![f]
NURSE. May not one speak?
CAP. Peace, you mumbling fool!
Utter your gravity o'er a gossip's bowl,†
For here we need it not.
LA. CAP. You are too hot.
CAP. God's bread![g] it makes me mad:
Day, night, hour, tide, time, work, play,
Alone, in company, still my care hath been
To have her match'd: and having now provided
A gentleman of noble[h] parentage,
Of fair demesnes, youthful, and nobly train'd,[i]
Stuff'd (as they say,) with honourable parts,
Proportion'd as one's heart could wish a man,[k]—

(*) First folio, *the*. (†) First folio, *have*.

(*) First folio, *gossip*. (†) First folio, *bowls*.

a *The* earth *doth drizzle dew;*] So the quarto, 1599, and folio, 1623; the undated quarto reads, *air*. The reading of *earth*, besides being philosophically true, is strongly supported by a line in our author's Rape of Lucrece,—

"But as the *earth* doth *weep*, the *sun being* set."

b Take me with you,—] Let me understand you.

c *How now*, chop-logic!] So the earliest quarto. The other old copies, including the folio, 1623, read *chopt logicke*. Steevens remarks that Capulet uses *chop-logic* for a nickname, as it occurs in The XXIIII Orders of Knaves, bl. l. "*Choplogyk* is he that whan his mayster rebuketh his servaunt for his defawtes, he will gyve hym XX wordes for one, or elles he wyll bydde the devylles paternoster in scylence."

d And yet not proud;—mistress minion, you!] This line appears to have been accidentally omitted in the first folio, since it is found in the quarto, 1609, from which this play in the folio was printed, and occurs also in the quarto, 1599.

e *But* fettle *your fine joints*—] This is the reading of the folio, 1623, and the other old editions. To *fettle* means to *prepare*, to *make ready*:—

"When the sheriffe saw Little John bend his bow,
He *fettled* him to be gone."
PERCY'S *Reliques* I. 92, ed. 1767.

"Nor list he now go whistling to the carre,
But sells his teme and *fettleth* to the warre."
HALL'S *Satires*, B. IV. Sat. 6.

The word does not occur again in our author, and, curiously enough, it has been overlooked in this passage by every editor, from Rowe downwards; modern editions all reading *settle*.

f O, God ye good den!] *God give you good even*. In all the old copies but the quarto, 1597, this exclamation is given as part of the nurse's speech. There can be no question as to whom it belongs.

g God's bread!] The quarto of 1597, reads:—

"Gods blessed mother, wife, it mads me,
Day, night, early, late, at home, abroad,
Alone, in company, waking or sleeping,
Still my care hath beene to see her matcht."

h Of noble *parentage*,—] Quarto, 1597, has *princely*,

i *Nobly* train'd,—] So the quarto, 1597; the next edition reads *liand*, which is doubtless a typographical error for *train'd;* in the succeeding impressions it was altered to *allied*.

k *As one's* heart could *wish a man*,—] The reading of the quarto, 1597; the other old editions, folio 1623 included, have "as one's *thought would* wish a man."

And then to have a wretched puling fool,
A whining mammet,[a] in her fortunes' tender,
To answer—*I'll not wed,—I cannot love,*
I am too young,—I pray you, pardon me;—
But, an you will not wed, I'll pardon you!
Graze where you will, you shall not house with me;
Look to't, think on't, I do not use to jest.
Thursday is near; lay hand on heart, advise:
An you be mine, I'll give you to my friend;
An you be not, hang, beg, starve, die in the streets,
For, by my soul, I'll ne'er acknowledge thee,
Nor what is mine shall never do thee good:
Trust to't, bethink you, I'll not be forsworn. [*Exit.*

JUL. Is there no pity sitting in the clouds,
That sees into the bottom of my grief?
O, sweet my mother, cast me not away!
Delay this marriage for a month, a week;
Or, if you do not, make the bridal bed,
In that dim monument where Tybalt lies.

LA. CAP. Talk not to me, for I'll not speak a word;
Do as thou wilt, for I have done with thee. [*Exit.*

JUL. O God!—O nurse! how shall this be prevented?
My husband is on earth, my faith in heaven;
How shall that faith return again to earth,
Unless that husband send it me from heaven,
By leaving earth?—comfort me, counsel me.—
Alack, alack, that heaven should practise stratagems
Upon so soft a subject as myself!—
What say'st thou? hast thou not a word of joy?
Some comfort, nurse.

NURSE. 'Faith, here it is: Romeo
Is banished; and, all the world to nothing,
That he dares ne'er come back to challenge you;
Or, if he do, it needs must be by stealth.
Then, since the case so stands as now it doth,
I think it best you married with the county.
O, he's a lovely gentleman!
Romeo's a dishclout to him; an eagle, madam,
Hath not so green, so quick, so fair an eye,
As Paris hath; beshrew my very heart,
I think you are happy in this second match,
For it excels your first: or if it did not,
Your first is dead; or 'twere as good he were,
As living here, and you no use of him.

JUL. Speakest thou from thy heart?

NURSE. And from my soul too;
Or else beshrew them both.

JUL. Amen!

NURSE. What?

JUL. Well, thou hast comforted me marvellous much.
Go in; and tell my lady I am gone,
Having displeas'd my father, to Laurence' cell,
To make confession, and to be absolv'd.

NURSE. Marry, I will; and this is wisely done. [*Exit.*

JUL. Ancient damnation![b] O most wicked fiend!
Is it * more sin to wish me thus forsworn,
Or to dispraise my lord with that same tongue,
Which she hath prais'd him with above compare,
So many thousand times?—Go, counsellor;
Thou and my bosom henceforth shall be twain.—
I'll to the friar, to know his remedy;
If all else fail, myself have power to die. [*Exit.*

[a] A *whining* mammet,—] A *puppet*, a *doll;* supposed to be a corruption of *Mahomet*.

[b] Ancient damnation!] In the quarto, 1597, before this speech is a stage direction "*She looks after Nurse*," which, like similar prescripts in that early edition, is extremely interesting, as affording us a glimpse of the "stage business" of this play in Shakespeare's time.

(*) First folio, *It is*.

ACT IV.

SCENE I.—*Friar* Laurence's *Cell.*

Enter Friar LAURENCE *and* PARIS.

FRI. On Thursday, sir? the time is very short.
PAR. My father Capulet will have it so;
And I am nothing slow, to slack his haste.[a]
FRI. You say you do not know the lady's mind;
Uneven is the course, I like it not.
PAR. Immoderately she weeps for Tybalt's death,
And therefore have I little talk'd of love,
For Venus smiles not in a house of tears.
Now, sir, her father counts it dangerous,
That she doth give her sorrow so much sway;
And, in his wisdom, hastes our marriage,
To stop the inundation of her tears;
Which, too much minded by herself alone,
May be put from her by society:
Now do you know the reason of this haste.
FRI. I would I knew not why it should be slow'd. [*Aside.*
Look, sir, here comes the lady towards my cell.

Enter JULIET.

PAR. Happily met, my lady, and my wife!
JUL. That may be, sir, when I may be a wife.
PAR. That may be, must be, love, on Thursday next.
JUL. What must be, shall be.
FRI. That's a certain text.
PAR. Come you to make confession to this father?
JUL. To answer that, I should confess to you.
PAR. Do not deny to him, that you love me.
JUL. I will confess to you, that I love him.
PAR. So will you, I am sure, that you love me.
JUL. If I do so, it will be of more price,
Being spoke behind your back, than to your face.
PAR. Poor soul, thy face is much abus'd with tears.
JUL. The tears have got small victory by that;
For it was bad enough, before their spite.

---

[a] *And I am* nothing *slow, to slack his haste.*] Shakespeare's marvellous power of condensation sometimes renders his meaning obscure. In this instance, the sense appears to be, "and I am not slow *in my own preparations for the wedding, to give him any reason* to slacken his hasty proceedings."

PAR. Thou wrong'st it, more than tears, with that report.

JUL. That is no slander, sir, which is a truth;
And what I spake, I spake it to my* face.

PAR. Thy face is mine, and thou hast slander'd it.

JUL. It may be so, for it is not mine own.—
Are you at leisure, holy father, now,
Or shall I come to you at evening mass?[a]

FRI. My leisure serves me, pensive daughter, now:—
My lord, we† must entreat the time alone.

PAR. God shield, I should disturb devotion!—
Juliet, on Thursday early will I rouse you:
Till then, adieu! and keep this holy kiss.
[*Exit* PARIS.

JUL. O, shut the door! and when thou hast done so,
Come weep with me; Past hope, past cure,[b] past help!

FRI. Ah, Juliet, I already know thy grief;
It strains‡ me past the compass of my wits:
I hear thou must, and nothing may prorogue it,
On Thursday next be married to this county.

JUL. Tell me not, friar, that thou hear'st of this,
Unless thou tell me how I may prevent it:
If, in thy wisdom, thou canst give no help,
Do thou but call my resolution wise,
And with this knife I'll help it presently.
God join'd my heart and Romeo's, thou our hands;
And ere this hand, by thee to Romeo seal'd,
Shall be the label to another deed,[c]
Or my true heart with treacherous revolt
Turn to another, this shall slay them both:
Therefore, out of thy long-experienc'd time,[d]
Give me some present counsel; or, behold,
'Twixt my extremes and me, this bloody knife
Shall play the umpire, arbitrating that
Which the commission of thy years and art
Could to no issue of true honour bring.
Be not so long to speak; I long to die,
If what thou speak'st speak not of remedy.

FRI. Hold, daughter; I do spy a kind of hope,
Which craves as desperate an execution
As that is desperate which we would prevent.
If, rather than to marry county Paris,
Thou hast the strength of will to slay* thyself;
Then is it likely thou wilt undertake
A thing like death to chide away this shame,
That cop'st with death himself to scape from it;
And, if thou dar'st, I'll give thee remedy.

JUL. O, bid me leap, rather than marry Paris,
From off the battlements of yonder tower;[e]
Or walk in thievish ways; or bid me lurk
Where serpents are; chain me with roaring bears;
Or shut† me nightly in a charnel-house,
O'er-cover'd quite with dead men's rattling bones,
With reeky shanks, and yellow chapless sculls;
Or bid me go into a new-made grave,
And hide me with a dead man in his shroud;[f]
Things that, to hear them told, have made me tremble;
And I will do it without fear or doubt,
To live an unstain'd wife to my sweet love.

FRI. Hold, then; go home, be merry, give consent
To marry Paris: Wednesday is to-morrow;
To-morrow night look that thou lie alone,
Let not thy nurse lie with thee in thy chamber:
Take thou this phial, being then in bed,
And this distilled‡ liquor drink thou off: (1)
When, presently, through all thy veins shall run
A cold and drowsy humour, for no pulse
Shall keep his native progress, but surcease,
No warmth, no breath, shall testify thou liv'st;[g]
The roses in thy lips and cheeks shall fade
To paly ashes;[h] thy§ eyes' windows fall,
Like death, when he shuts‖ up the day of life;
Each part, depriv'd of supple government,
Shall, stiff, and stark, and cold, appear like death:
And in this borrow'd likeness of shrunk death
Thou shalt continue two and forty hours,
And then awake as from a pleasant sleep.
Now, when the bridegroom in the morning comes
To rouse thee from thy bed, there art thou dead:
Then (as the manner of our country is,) (2)
In thy best robes uncover'd on the bier,[i]

(*) First folio, *thy*. (†) First folio, *you*. (‡) First folio, *streames*.

[a] *At* evening *mass?*] It is strange that Shakespeare, who on other occasions has shown a competent knowledge of the doctrines and usages of the Roman Catholic Church, should have fallen into this error. The celebration of mass, it is well known, can only take place in the forenoon of the day.

[b] *Past* cure,—] So the edition of 1597, the other copies read *care*.

[c] *The* label *to another deed*,—] "The seals of deeds in our author's time were not impressed on the parchment itself on which the deed was written, but were appended on distinct slips or labels affixed to the deed."—MALONE.

[d] Thy long-experienc'd time,—] This scene was expanded considerably after the publication of the quarto, 1597. In that, the nine lines of this speech from the first couplet are all wanting.

[e] *Of* yonder *tower;*] This is the reading of the quarto, 1597. The subsequent old copies have "*any* tower."

[f] *A dead man in his* shroud;] *Shroud* is supplied from the undated quarto, the word having dropped out in the editions of 1599 and 1609. The folio, 1623, inserts *grave*.

(*) First folio, *stay*. (†) First folio, *hide*. (‡) First folio, *distilling*. (§) First folio, *the*. (‖) First folio, *shut*.

[g] Shall testify thou liv'st;] In the first quarto this passage stands thus:—

"A dull and heavy slumber, which shall seaze
Each vitall spirit; for no pulse shall keepe
His natural progresse, but surcease to beate:
No signe of breath shall testifie thou liust."

[h] To paly *ashes;*] So the undated quarto. That of 1599, and the folio, 1623, read, To *many* ashes.

[i] In thy best robes uncover'd on the bier,—] After this line, the early editions, quarto and folio, introduce the following,—

"Be borne to burial in thy kindred's grave."

Which, Steevens remarks, the poet very probably had struck out on his revisal, because the sense of it is repeated in the next line.

Thou shalt be borne to that same ancient vault,
Where all the kindred of the Capulets lie.
In the mean time, against thou shalt awake,
Shall Romeo by my letters know our drift;
And hither shall he come; and he and I
Will watch thy waking,[a] and that very night,
Shall Romeo bear thee hence to Mantua.
And this shall free thee from this present shame,
If no inconstant toy, nor womanish fear,
Abate thy valour in the acting it.

JUL. Give me, give me! O tell me not of fear.*

FRI. Hold; get you gone, be strong and prosperous
In this resolve: I'll send a friar with speed
To Mantua, with my letters to thy lord.

JUL. Love, give me strength! and strength shall help afford.
Farewell, dear father! [*Exeunt.*

SCENE II.—*A Room in* Capulet's *House.*

Enter CAPULET, LADY CAPULET, Nurse, *and* Servants.

CAP. So many guests invite as here are writ.— [*Exit* Servant.
Sirrah, go hire me twenty cunning cooks.

2 SERV. You shall have none ill, sir; for I'll try if they can lick their fingers.

CAP. How canst thou try them so?

2 SERV. Marry, sir, 'tis an ill cook that cannot lick his own fingers:[b] therefore he that cannot lick his fingers, goes not with me.

CAP. Go, begone.— [*Exit* Servant.
We shall be much unfurnish'd for this time.—
What, is my daughter gone to friar Laurence?

NURSE. Ay, forsooth.

CAP. Well, he may chance to do some good on her:
A peevish self-will'd harlotry it is.

Enter JULIET.

NUR. See, where she comes from shrift with merry look.

CAP. How now, my headstrong? where have you been gadding?

JUL. Where I have learn'd me to repent the sin
Of disobedient opposition
To you, and your behests; and am enjoin'd
By holy Laurence to fall prostrate here, (3)
To beg your pardon:—pardon, I beseech you!
Henceforward I am ever rul'd by you.

CAP. Send for the county; go tell him of this;
I'll have this knot knit up to-morrow morning.

JUL. I met the youthful lord at Laurence' cell;
And gave him what becomed love I might,
Not stepping o'er the bounds of modesty.

CAP. Why, I am glad on't; this is well,—stand up:
This is as 't should be: let me see the county;
Ay, marry, go, I say, and fetch him hither.
Now, afore God, this reverend holy friar,—
All our whole city is much bound to him.

JUL. Nurse, will you go with me into my closet,
To help me sort such needful ornaments
As you think fit to furnish me to-morrow?

LA. CAP. No, not till Thursday; there is time enough.

CAP. Go, nurse, go with her:—we'll to church to-morrow. [*Exeunt* JULIET *and* Nurse.

LA. CAP. We shall be short in our provision;
'Tis now near night.

CAP. Tush! I will stir about,
And all things shall be well, I warrant thee, wife:
Go thou to Juliet, help to deck up her;
I'll not to bed to-night;—let me alone;
I'll play the housewife for this once.—What, ho!—
They are all forth: well, I will walk myself
To county Paris, to prepare up him*
Against to-morrow: my heart is wondrous light,
Since this same wayward girl is so reclaim'd.
[*Exeunt.*

SCENE III.—Juliet's *Chamber.*

Enter JULIET *and* Nurse.

JUL. Ay, those attires are best:—but, gentle nurse,
I pray thee, leave me to myself to-night;
For I have need of many orisons
To move the heavens to smile upon my state,
Which, well thou know'st, is cross and full of sin.

Enter LADY CAPULET.

LA. CAP. What, are you busy, ho? need you my help?

JUL. No, madam; we have cull'd such necessaries,

(*) First folio, *care.*

a ——and he and I
Will watch thy waking,—]
These words are omitted in the folio, 1623, although they are found in the quarto, 1609, which the folio copied.

(*) First folio, *him up.*

b Lick his own fingers:] An old saw quoted by Puttenham in his "Arte of English Poesie, 1589," p. 157,—
"As the olde cocke crowes so doeth the chick:
A bad cooke that cannot his owne fingers lick."

As are behoveful for our state to-morrow:
So please you, let me now be left alone,
And let the nurse this night sit up with you;
For, I am sure, you have your hands full all,
In this so sudden business.

LA. CAP. Good night!
Get thee to bed, and rest; for thou hast need.

JUL. Farewell!—

[*Exeunt* LADY CAPULET *and* Nurse.

God knows, when we shall meet again.
I have a faint cold fear thrills through my veins,(4)
That almost freezes up the heat of life: *
I'll call them back again to comfort me;—
Nurse!—what should she do here?
My dismal scene I needs must act alone.—
Come, phial.—
What if this mixture do not work at all?
Shall I be married then to-morrow morning?
No, no;—this shall forbid it:—lie thou there.

[*Laying down a dagger.*

What if it be a poison, which the friar
Subtly hath minister'd to have me dead;
Lest in this marriage he should be dishonour'd,
Because he married me before to Romeo?
I fear, it is: and yet, methinks, it should not,
For he hath still been tried a holy man.
I will not entertain so bad a thought.[a]—
How if, when I am laid into the tomb,
I wake before the time that Romeo
Come to redeem me? there's a fearful point!
Shall I not then be stifled in the vault,
To whose foul mouth no healthsome air breathes in,
And there die strangled ere my Romeo comes?
Or, if I live, is it not very like,
The horrible conceit of death and night,
Together with the terror of the place,—
As in a vault, an ancient receptacle,
Where, for these many hundred years, the bones
Of all my buried ancestors are pack'd;
Where bloody Tybalt, yet but green in earth,
Lies fest'ring in his shroud; where, as they say,
At some hours in the night, spirits resort;—
Alack, alack! is it not like, that I,
So early waking,—what with loathsome smells,
And shrieks like mandrakes'(5) torn out of the earth,
That living mortals, hearing them, run mad;—
O! if I wake,† shall I not be distraught,
Environed with all these hideous fears?
And madly play with my forefathers' joints?
And pluck the mangled Tybalt from his shroud?
And, in this rage, with some great kinsman's bone,
As with a club, dash out my desperate brains?
O, look! methinks, I see my cousin's ghost
Seeking out Romeo, that did spit his body
Upon a * rapier's point:—stay, Tybalt, stay!—
Romeo, I come! this do I drink to thee.(6)

[*She throws herself on the bed.*

SCENE IV.—Capulet's *Hall.*

Enter LADY CAPULET *and* Nurse.

LA. CAP. Hold, take these keys, and fetch more spices, nurse.

NURSE. They call for dates and quinces in the pastry.[b]

Enter CAPULET.

CAP. Come, stir, stir, stir! the second cock hath crow'd,
The curfew bell hath rung, 'tis three o'clock:—
Look to the bak'd meats, good Angelica:
Spare not for cost.

NURSE. Go, you cot-quean,[c] go,
Get you to bed; 'faith, you'll be sick to-morrow
For this night's watching.

CAP. No, not a whit; what! I have watch'd ere now
All night for lesser † cause, and ne'er been sick.

LA. CAP. Ay, you have been a mouse-hunt[d] in your time;
But I will watch you from such watching now.

[*Exeunt* LADY CAPULET *and* Nurse.

CAP. A jealous-hood, a jealous-hood!—now, fellow,
What's there?

Enter Servants, *with spits, logs, and baskets.*

1 SERV. Things for the cook, sir; but I know not what.

CAP. Make haste, make haste. [*Exit* 1 Serv.]—Sirrah, fetch drier logs;
Call Peter, he will show thee where they are.

2 SERV. I have a head, sir, that will find out logs,
And never trouble Peter for the matter. [*Exit.*

CAP. 'Mass, and well said; a merry whoreson! ha,

(*) First folio, *fire.* (†) First folio, *walk.*

a I will not entertain so bad a thought.—] This line is found only in the quarto, 1597.

b *In the* pastry.] "That is, in the room where paste was made. So *laundry, spicery,* &c." says Malone; but as he gives no example of this use of the word, we subjoin one:—

"Now having seene all this, then shall you see, hard by,
The *pastrie,* mealehouse, and the roome wheras the coales do ly."
A Floorish upon Fancie, by N[ICHOLAS] B[RETON], *Gent.* 1582.

(*) First folio, *my.* (†) First folio, *less.*

c *You* cot-quean,—] *Cot-quean* was nothing more than another name for what housewives now term a *molly-coddle;* a man who busies himself in affairs which properly belong to the softer sex.

d A mouse-hunt—] The *marten,* an animal of the weazel tribe, is called *mouse-hunt;* and from Lady Capulet's use of it, the name appears to have been familiarly applied to any one of rakish propensities. Heywood has a proverb, "Cat after kinde, good *mouse-hunt.*"—JOHN HEYWOOD'S *Workes,* 4to. 1598.

Thou shalt be logger-head.—Good faith,* 'tis day:
The county will be here with music straight,
[*Music within.*
For so he said he would. I hear him near:—
Nurse!—Wife!—what, ho!—what, nurse, I say!

Enter Nurse.

Go, waken Juliet, go, and trim her up;
I'll go and chat with Paris:—hie, make haste,
Make haste! the bridegroom he is come already:
Make haste, I say! [a] [*Exeunt.*

SCENE V.—Juliet's *Chamber;* Juliet *on the Bed.*

Enter Nurse.

NURSE. Mistress!—what, mistress!—Juliet!—fast, I warrant her, she—
Why, lamb!—why, lady!—fie, you slug-a-bed!—
Why, love, I say!—madam! sweet-heart!—why, bride!—
What, not a word?—you take your pennyworths now;
Sleep for a week; for the next night, I warrant,
The county Paris hath set up his rest,[b]
That you shall rest but little.—God forgive me,
(Marry, and amen!) how sound is she asleep!
I needs must wake her:—madam, madam, madam!
Ay, let the county take you in your bed;
He'll fright you up, i'faith:—will it not be?
What, drest! and in your clothes! and down again!
I must needs wake you: lady! lady! lady!
Alas! alas!—help! help! my lady's dead!—
O, well-a-day, that ever I was born!—
Some aqua-vitæ, ho!—my lord! my lady!

Enter LADY CAPULET.

LA. CAP. What noise is here?
NURSE. O lamentable day!
LA. CAP. What is the matter?
NURSE. Look, look! O heavy day!
LA. CAP. O me, O me!—my child, my only life,
Revive, look up, or I will die with thee!
Help, help!—call help.

Enter CAPULET.

CAP. For shame, bring Juliet forth; her lord is come.
NURSE. She's dead, deceas'd, she's dead; alack the day!
LA. CAP. Alack the day! she's dead, she's dead, she's dead.
CAP. Ha! let me see her:—out, alas! she's cold;
Her blood is settled, and her joints are stiff;
Life and these lips have long been separated:
Death lies on her, like an untimely frost
Upon the sweetest flower of all the field.
NURSE. O lamentable day!
LA. CAP. O woful time!
CAP. Death, that hath ta'en her hence to make me wail,
Ties up my tongue, and will not let me speak.

Enter Friar LAURENCE *and* PARIS, *with* Musicians.

PAR.[c] Come, is the bride ready to go to church?
CAP. Ready to go, but never to return:
O son, the night before thy wedding day
Hath death lain with thy bride:*—see,† there she lies,
Flower as she was, deflowered by him.
Death is my son-in-law, death is my heir;
My daughter he hath wedded! I will die,
And leave him all; life, living,[d] all is death's.
PAR. Have I thought long to see this morning's face,
And doth it give me such a sight as this?
LA. CAP. Accurs'd, unhappy, wretched, hateful day!
Most miserable hour, that e'er time saw
In lasting labour of his pilgrimage!
But one, poor one, one poor and loving child,
But one thing to rejoice and solace in,
And cruel death hath catch'd it from my sight. (7)

(*) First folio, *Father*.

[a] Make haste, I say!] In the quarto, 1597, this speech consists only of four lines:—

"Well goe thy way, thou shalt be logger head.
Come, come, make hast, call up your daughter,
The countie will be heere with musicke straight,
Gods me hees come, nurse call vp my daughter."

[b] *Hath* set up his rest,—] A phrase borrowed from the gaming table. See note (4), p. 150 of the present Vol.

[c] Every edition, except the quarto, 1597, assigns this speech to the Friar; but at the present juncture he is too critically placed to be anxious to lead the conversation. Moreover, the answer of Capulet tends to show that Paris had asked the question.

(*) First folio, *wife*. (†) First folio omits, *see*.

[d] *Life*, living, *all is death's*.] So the old copies. Most of the modern editors follow Capell, and read,—

"——life leaving, all is death's."

The change is uncalled for; "*living*" here implies *possessions, fortunes*, not *existence*. We meet with the same distinction between *life* and *living* in the "Merchant of Venice," Act V. Sc. 1, where Antonio, whose life had been saved by Portia, says,—

"Sweet lady, you have given me *life* and *living;*
For here I read for certain, that my ships
Are safely come to road."

NURSE. O woe! O woful, woful, woful day!
Most lamentable day! most woful day,
That ever, ever, I did yet behold!
O day! O day! O day! O hateful day!
Never was seen so black a day as this:
O woful day, O woful day!

PAR. Beguil'd, divorced, wronged, spited, slain!
Most détestable death, by thee beguil'd
By cruel, cruel thee, quite overthrown!—
O love! O life!—not life, but love in death!

CAP. Despis'd, distressed, hated, martyr'd, kill'd!—
Uncomfortable time! why cam'st thou now
To murder, murder our solemnity?—
O child! O child!—my soul, and not my child!—
Dead art thou!—alack! my child is dead;
And, with my child, my joys are buried!

FRI. Peace, ho, for shame! confusion's cure[a] lives not
In these confusions. Heaven and yourself
Had part in this fair maid; now heaven hath all,
And all the better is it for the maid:
Your part in her you could not keep from death;
But heaven keeps his part in eternal life.
The most you sought was—her promotion;
For 'twas your heaven, she should be advanc'd:
And weep ye now, seeing she is advanc'd,
Above the clouds, as high as heaven itself?
O, in this love, you love your child so ill,
That you run mad, seeing that she is well:
She's not well married, that lives married long;
But she's best married, that dies married young.
Dry up your tears, and stick your rosemary
On this fair corse; and, as the custom is,
In all* her best array bear her to church:
For though fond[b] nature bids us all lament,
Yet nature's tears are reason's merriment.

CAP. All things, that we ordained festival,
Turn from their office to black funeral:
Our instruments, to melancholy bells;
Our wedding cheer, to a sad burial feast;
Our solemn hymns to sullen dirges change;
Our bridal flowers serve for a buried corse,
And all things change them to the contrary.

FRI. Sir, go you in,—and, madam, go with him;—
And go, sir Paris;—every one prepare
To follow this fair corse unto her grave:
The heavens do lour upon you, for some ill;
Move them no more, by crossing their high will.

[*Exeunt* CAPULET, LADY CAPULET, PARIS, *and* Friar.

1 MUS. 'Faith, we may put up our pipes, and be gone.

NURSE. Honest good fellows, ah, put up, put up;
For, well you know, this is a pitiful case.

[*Exit* Nurse.

1 MUS. Ay, by my troth, the case may be amended.

Enter PETER. (8)

PET. Musicians, O, musicians, *Heart's ease, heart's ease;* O, an you will have me live, play—*heart's ease.*

1 MUS. Why *heart's ease?*

PET. O, musicians, because my heart itself plays—*My heart is full of woe:*[c] O, play me some merry dump, to comfort me.[d]

2 MUS. Not a dump we; 'tis no time to play now.

PET. You will not then?

MUS. No.

PET. I will then give it you soundly.

1 MUS. What will you give us?

PET. No money, on my faith; but the gleek:[e] I will give you the minstrel.

1 MUS. Then will I give you the serving-creature.

PET. Then will I lay the serving-creature's dagger on your pate. I will carry no crotchets: I'll *re* you, I'll *fa* you; do you note me?[f]

1 MUS. An you *re* us, and *fa* us, you note us.

2 MUS. Pray you, put up your dagger, and put out your wit.

(*) First folio, *And in*, &c.

[a] *Confusion's* cure—] The old copies read *care;* corrected by Theobald.

[b] *For though* fond *nature*—] So the second folio; the previous editions read *some* nature.

[c] My heart is full of woe:] The words "of woe" are found only in the dateless quarto; all the other old editions reading, "My heart is full." "*My heart is full of woe,*" and "*Heart's ease,*" were popular tunes of the period. In the Pepys' collection is "A pleasant Ballad of two Lovers," beginning thus:—

"Complaine, my lute, complaine on him,
That stayes so long away;
He promis'd to be here ere this,
But still unkind doth stay;
But now the proverbe true I finde,
Once out of sight, then out of mind.
Hey ho! *my heart is full of woe.*"

[d] *O, play me some* merry dump, *to comfort me.*] This line is not found in the folio, 1623. In the "Two Gentlemen of Verona," we hear of "a deploring dump;" and in "The Arraignment of Paris," 1584, when the shepherds have sung an elegiac hymn over the hearse of Colin, Venus says to Paris,—

"——How cheers my lovely boy after this *dump* of woe?"

and Paris replies,—

"Such *dumps*, sweet lady, as bin these, are deadly *dumps* to prove."

Dumps appear to have been heavy, mournful tunes, and Master Peter's "*merry* dump" was a purposed contradiction in terms.

[e] The gleek:] *To give the gleek*, a phrase borrowed from the old game of cards called *gleek*, signified to *flout* or *scorn* any one; and as a *gleekman*, or *gligman*, was a name for minstrel, we get a notion of the quibble meant. A similar *equivoque* is, no doubt, intended in "the serving-creature," but the allusion is yet to be discovered.

[f] I'll *re* you, I'll *fa* you; do you note me?] This is in the same strain as the rest of the dialogue. *Re* and *Fa* are the syllables used in sol-faing the notes D and F in the scale of music. The pun on *note* is self evident, and the word appears to have been a favourite one to play upon, for Shakespeare has used it with a double meaning at least a score of times.

PET. Then have at you with my wit;[a] I will dry-beat you with an iron wit, and put up my iron dagger:—answer me like men:

When griping grief[b] the heart doth wound,
And doleful dumps the mind oppress,[c]
Then music, with her silver sound;

Why, *silver sound?* why, *music with her silver sound?* what say you, Simon Catling?

1 MUS. Marry, sir, because silver hath a sweet sound.

PET. Pretty!* what say you, Hugh Rebeck?[d]

2 MUS. I say—*silver sound*, because musicians sound for silver.

PET. Pretty too!—what say you, James Soundpost?

3 MUS. 'Faith, I know not what to say.

PET. O, I cry you mercy; you are the singer: I will say for you. It is—*music with her silver sound*, because such fellows[e] as you have seldom gold for sounding:—

Then music with her silver sound,
With speedy help doth lend redress.
[*Exit, singing.*

1 MUS. What a pestilent knave is this same!

2 MUS. Hang him, Jack! come, we'll in here; tarry for the mourners, and stay dinner.
[*Exeunt.*

(*) First folio, *pratest*.

a Then have at you with my wit;] The first folio has these words annexed to the second minstrel's speech.

b When griping grief the heart doth wound,—] These are the opening lines of a song, "In commendation of Musick," by Richard Edwards, printed in "The Paradise of Dayntie Devises," 1576.

"Where gripyng grief the hart would wound, and dolfull domps the mind oppresse,
There Musick with her silver soũd is wont with spede to give redresse."

c And doleful dumps the mind oppress,—] This line is omitted in all the old editions, except the quarto, 1597.

d *Hugh* Rebeck?] The *rebeck* was a sort of fiddle with three strings, played on with a bow. It is frequently noticed by the old writers,—

"He turned his *rebeck* to a mournful note,
And thereto sung this doleful elegy."
DRAYTON, *Ed.* 11.

"When the merry bells ring round,
And the jocund *rebecks* sound."
MILTON, *L'Allegro*, v. 91.

e *Such* fellows *as you* have seldom gold—] Thus the quarto, 1597. All the other old copies read, "because *musicians* have *no* gold," &c.

ACT V.

SCENE I.—Mantua. *A Street.*

Enter Romeo.

Rom. If I may trust the flattering eye[a] of sleep,
My dreams presage some joyful news at hand:
My bosom's lord sits lightly in his throne;
And, all this day, an unaccustom'd spirit
Lifts me above the ground with cheerful thoughts.
I dreamt, my lady came and found me dead;
(Strange dream! that gives a dead man leave to think,)
And breath'd such life with kisses in my lips,
That I reviv'd, and was an emperor.
Ah me! how sweet is love itself possess'd,
When but love's shadows are so rich in joy.

---

a *Flattering eye of sleep*,—] This is according to the earliest copy. The subsequent editions have "*truth* of sleep," which is still less intelligible. By "*eye* of sleep," Shakespeare perhaps meant *vision, view, prospect*. Thus, in "King John," Act II. Sc. 1.:—

"These flags of France, that are advanced here
Before the eye and prospect of your town."

And in "Much Ado about Nothing," Act IV. Sc. 1.:—

"And every lovely organ of her life
Shall come apparell'd in more precious habit,
More moving—delicate and full of life,
Into the eye and prospect of his soul."

Enter BALTHASAR.

News from Verona!—how now, Balthasar?
Dost thou not bring me letters from the friar?
How doth my lady? is my father well?
How doth my lady Juliet? that I ask again;
For nothing can be ill, if she be well.
BAL. Then she is well, and nothing can be ill;
Her body sleeps in Capels' monument,
And her immortal part with angels lives; *
I saw her laid low in her kindred's vault,
And presently took post to tell it you:
O pardon me for bringing these ill news,
Since you did leave it for my office, sir.
ROM. Is it even so? then I defy* you, stars!—
Thou knowest my lodging: get me ink and paper,
And hire post-horses; I will hence to-night.
BAL. I do beseech you, sir, have patience: [a]
Your looks are pale and wild, and do import
Some misadventure.

(*) First folio, *live*.

(*) First folio, *deny*.

[a] I do beseech you, sir, have patience:] The quarto, 1597, reads,—
"Pardon me, sir, I will not leave you thus."

ROM. Tush, thou art deceiv'd;
Leave me, and do the thing I bid thee do:
Hast thou no letters to me from the friar?
BAL. No, my good lord.
ROM. No matter: get thee gone,
And hire those horses; I'll be with thee straight.
[*Exit* BALTHASAR.
Well, Juliet, I will lie with thee to-night.
Let's see for means:—O, mischief! thou art swift
To enter in the thoughts of desperate men!
I do remember an apothecary,—(1)
And hereabouts he* dwells,—which late I noted
In tatter'd weeds, with overwhelming brows,
Culling of simples: meagre were his looks,
Sharp misery had worn him to the bones;
And in his needy shop a tortoise hung,
An alligator stuff'd,[a] and other skins
Of ill-shap'd fishes; and, about his shelves,
A beggarly account of empty boxes,
Green earthen pots, bladders, and musty seeds,
Remnants of packthread, and old cakes of roses,
Were thinly scatter'd, to make up a show.
Noting this penury, to myself I said—
An if a man did need a poison now,
Whose sale is present death in Mantua,
Here lives a caitiff wretch would sell it him.
O, this same thought did but fore-run my need;
And this same needy man must sell it me.
As I remember, this should be the house:
Being holiday, the beggar's shop is shut.—
What, ho! apothecary!

Enter Apothecary.

APOTH. Who calls so loud?
ROM. Come hither, man.—I see, that thou art poor;
Hold, there is forty ducats: let me have
A dram of poison; such soon-speeding gear
As will disperse itself through all the veins,
That the life-weary taker may fall dead;
And that the trunk may be discharg'd of breath
As violently, as hasty powder fir'd
Doth hurry from the fatal cannon's womb.
APOTH. Such mortal drugs I have; but Mantua's law
Is death, to any he that utters them.
ROM. Art thou so bare, and full of wretchedness,
And fear'st to die? famine is in thy cheeks,
Need and oppression starveth[b] in thy eyes,
Contempt and beggary hangs upon thy back,[c]
The world is not thy friend, nor the world's law:
The world affords no law to make thee rich;
Then be not poor, but break it, and take this.
APOTH. My poverty, but not my will, consents.
ROM. I pay* thy poverty, and not thy will.
APOTH. Put this in any liquid thing you will,
And drink it off; and, if you had the strength
Of twenty men, it would despatch you straight.
ROM. There is thy gold; worse poison to men's souls,
Doing more murder in this loathsome world,
Than these poor compounds that thou may'st not sell:
I sell thee poison, thou hast sold me none.
Farewell; buy food, and get thyself in flesh.—
Come, cordial, and not poison; go with me
To Juliet's grave, for there must I use thee.
[*Exeunt.*

SCENE II.—*Friar* Laurence's *Cell.*

Enter Friar JOHN.

JOHN. Holy Franciscan friar! brother, ho!

Enter Friar LAURENCE.

LAU. This same should be the voice of friar John.—
Welcome from Mantua: what says Romeo?
Or, if his mind be writ, give me his letter.
JOHN. Going to find a bare-foot brother out,
One of our order, to associate me,[d]
Here in this city visiting the sick,
And finding him, the searchers of the town,[e]
Suspecting that we both were in a house
Where the infectious pestilence did reign,

(*) First folio omits, *he*.

[a] An alligator stuff'd,—] "He made an anatomie of a rat, and after hanged her over his head, instead of an *apothecary's crocodile* or dried *alligator*." Nashe's "Have with You to Saffron Walden, 1596."

[b] *Need and oppression* starveth *in thy eyes*,—] Otway, in his Caius Marius, much of which is stolen from this play, exhibits the line thus:—

"Need and oppression *stareth* in thy eyes;"

but although this reading has been adopted by several of the modern editors, and is perhaps preferable to the other, I have not felt justified in departing from the old text. The quarto, 1597, has,—

"And starved famine dwelleth in thy cheeks."

(*) First folio, *pray*.

[c] Hangs upon thy back,—] The quarto, 1597, reads, with at least equal force of expression,—

"Upon thy back hangs ragged misery."

[d] To associate me,—] It was the custom for each friar who had leave of absence to have a companion appointed him by the superior. In the Visitatio Notabilis de Seleburne, printed in White's "Natural History, &c. of Selborne," Wykeham enjoins the canons not to go abroad without leave from the prior, who is ordered on such occasions to assign the brother a companion, "*ne suspicio sinistra vel scandalum oriatur*."

[e] Here in this city visiting the sick,
And finding him, the searchers of the town,—]
It has been suggested, and seems very probable, that these lines have got transposed.

Seal'd up the doors, and would not let us forth;
So that my speed to Mantua there was stay'd.

LAU. Who bare my letter then to Romeo?

JOHN. I could not send it,—here it is again,—
Nor get a messenger to bring it thee,
So fearful were they of infection.

LAU. Unhappy fortune! by my brotherhood,
The letter was not nice,[a] but full of charge,
Of dear import; and the neglecting it
May do much danger: Friar John, go hence;
Get me an iron crow, and bring it straight
Unto my cell.

JOHN. Brother, I'll go and bring it thee. [*Exit.*

LAU. Now must I to the monument alone;
Within this three hours will fair Juliet wake;
She will beshrew me much, that Romeo
Hath had no notice of these accidents:
But I will write again to Mantua,
And keep her at my cell till Romeo come;
Poor living corse, clos'd in a dead man's tomb!
[*Exit.*

SCENE III.—*A Church-yard; in it, a monument belonging to the* Capulets.

Enter PARIS, *and his* Page, *bearing flowers and a torch.*

PAR. Give me thy torch, boy: hence, and stand aloof;—*
Yet put it out, for I would not be seen.
Under yon yew-trees† lay thee all along,
Holding thine ear close to the hollow ground;
So shall no foot upon the churchyard tread,
(Being loose, unfirm with digging up of graves,)
But thou shalt hear it: whistle then to me,
As signal that thou hearest something approach.
Give me those flowers: do as I bid thee, go.

PAGE. I am almost afraid to stand alone,
Here in the churchyard; yet I will adventure.
[*Retires.*

PAR. Sweet flower, with flowers thy bridal bed I strew,[b]—
(O woe! thy canopy is dust and stones!)
Which with sweet water nightly I will dew,
Or wanting that, with tears distill'd by moans;
The obsequies that I for thee will keep,
Nightly shall be, to strew thy grave and weep.[c]
[*The boy whistles.*
The boy gives warning, something doth approach.
What cursed foot wanders this way* to-night,
To cross my obsequies, and true love's rite?
What, with a torch!—muffle me, night, a while.
[*Retires.*

Enter ROMEO *and* BALTHASAR *with a torch, mattock, &c.*

ROM. Give me that mattock, and the wrenching iron.
Hold, take this letter; early in the morning
See thou deliver it to my lord and father.
Give me the light: upon thy life I charge thee
Whate'er thou hear'st or see'st, stand all aloof,
And do not interrupt me in my course.
Why I descend into this bed of death,
Is, partly, to behold my lady's face:
But, chiefly, to take thence from her dead finger
A precious ring; a ring, that I must use
In dear employment: therefore hence, be gone:—
But if thou, jealous,[d] dost return to pry
In what I further shall intend to do,
By heaven, I will tear thee joint by joint,
And strew this hungry churchyard with thy limbs:
The time and my intents are savage-wild;
More fierce, and more inexorable far,
Than empty tigers, or the roaring sea.

BAL. I will be gone, sir, and not trouble you.

ROM. So shalt thou show me friendship: take thou that:
Live, and be prosperous; and farewell, good fellow.

BAL. For all this same, I'll hide me hereabout;
His looks I fear, and his intents I doubt. [*Retires.*

ROM. Thou détestable maw, thou womb of death,
Gorg'd with the dearest morsel of the earth,
Thus I enforce thy rotten jaws to ope,
[*Breaking open the door of the monument.*
And, in despite, I'll cram thee with more food!

PAR. This is that banish'd haughty Montague,
That murder'd my love's cousin;—with which grief,
It is supposed, the fair creature died,—
And here is come to do some villainous shame
To the dead bodies: I will apprehend him:
[*Advances.*
Stop thy unhallow'd toil, vile Montague;
Can vengeance be pursued further than death?
Condemned villain, I do apprehend thee:
Obey, and go with me, for thou must die.

ROM. I must, indeed; and therefore came I hither.—

(*) First folio, *aloft.* (†) First folio, *young trees.*

(*) First folio, *wayes.*

[a] *The letter was not* nice,—] Not trivial. See note g, Act III. Sc. 1. p. 187.

[b] With flowers thy bridal bed I strew,—] By the modern punctuation of this passage, Paris is made to promise that he will nightly water, not the flowers, but the *canopy* of Juliet's "bridal bed"!

[c] To strew thy grave and weep.] We subjoin this speech, as it stands in the original quarto edition, 1597:—

"Sweet flower, with flowers I strew thy bridal bed:
Sweete tombe, that in thy circuite dost containe
The perfect modell of eternitie;
Fair *Juliet*, that with angells dost remaine,
Accept this latest fauour at my hands;
That liuing honourd thee, and being dead,
With funerall praises doe adorne thy tombe."

[d] *But if thou,* jealous,—] *Suspicious.*

Good gentle youth, tempt not a desperate man;
Fly hence and leave me;—think upon these* gone;
Let them affright thee.—I beseech thee, youth,
Heap[a] not another sin upon my head,
By urging me to fury:—O, be gone!
By heaven, I love thee better than myself;
For I come hither arm'd against myself:
Stay not,—be gone;—live, and hereafter say—
A madman's mercy bade thee run away.

PAR. I do defy thy conjurations,[b]
And apprehend thee for a felon here.

ROM. Wilt thou provoke me? then have at thee, boy. [*They fight.*

PAGE. O lord! they fight: I will go call the watch. [*Exit* Page.

PAR. O, I am slain! [*falls.*]—If thou be merciful,
Open the tomb, lay me with Juliet. [*Dies.*

ROM. In faith, I will:—let me peruse this face;—
Mercutio's kinsman, noble county Paris:—
What said my man, when my betossed soul
Did not attend him as we rode? I think
He told me, Paris should have married Juliet:
Said he not so? or did I dream it so?
Or am I mad, hearing him talk of Juliet,
To think it was so?—O, give me thy hand!
One writ with me in sour misfortune's book!
I 'll bury thee in a triumphant grave,—
A grave? O, no! a lantern,[c] slaughter'd youth,
For here lies Juliet, and her beauty makes
This vault a feasting presence[d] full of light.
Death, lie thou there, by a dead man interr'd.
[*Laying* PARIS *in the monument.*
How oft when men are at the point of death,
Have they been merry! which their keepers call
A lightning before death; O, how may I
Call this a lightning?—O, my love! my wife!
Death, that hath suck'd the honey of thy breath,
Hath had no power yet upon thy beauty:
Thou art not conquer'd; beauty's ensign yet
Is crimson in thy lips, and in thy cheeks,
And death's pale flag is not advanced there.—
Tybalt, liest thou there in thy bloody sheet? (2)
O, what more favour can I do to thee,
Than with that hand that cut thy youth in twain,
To sunder his that was thine enemy?
Forgive me, cousin!—Ah, dear Juliet,
Why art thou yet so fair? Shall I believe[e]
That unsubstantial death is amorous;
And that the lean abhorred monster keeps
Thee here in dark to be his paramour?
For fear of that, I still will stay with thee;
And never from this palace of dim night
Depart again;[f] here, here will I remain
With worms that are thy chamber-maids; O, here
Will I set up my everlasting rest;
And shake the yoke of inauspicious stars
From this world-wearied flesh.—Eyes, look your last!
Arms, take your last embrace! and lips, O you
The doors of breath, seal with a righteous kiss
A dateless bargain to engrossing death!—
Come, bitter conduct,[g] come, unsavoury guide!
Thou desperate pilot, now at once run on
The dashing rocks thy sea-sick weary bark!
Here's to my love!—[*drinks.*] O, true apothecary!
Thy drugs are quick.—Thus with a kiss I die.
[*Dies.*

Enter, at the other end of the churchyard, Friar LAURENCE, *with a lantern, crow, and spade.*

FRI. Saint Francis be my speed! how oft to-night
Have my old feet stumbled at graves?—Who's there?

BAL. Here's one, a friend, and one that knows you well.

FRI. Bliss be upon you! tell me, good my friend,
What torch is yond', that vainly lends his light
To grubs and eyeless sculls? as I discern,
It burneth in the Capels' monument.

BAL. It doth so, holy sir; and there's my master,
One that you love.

FRI. Who is it?

BAL. Romeo.

FRI. How long hath he been there?

BAL. Full half an hour.

(*) First folio, *those.*

[a] Heap not—] Thus the quarto, 1597. The quartos of 1599 and 1609, and the folio, 1623, have "*Put* not," for which Mr. Rowe substituted *pull*

[b] Conjurations,—] This is the reading of the quarto, 1597. That of 1599 has "*commiration,*" which led to the "*commiseration*" of the quarto, 1609, and the first folio. The meaning in "I defy thy conjurations" may be simply "I contemn your entreaties;" or, as he suspected Romeo had come to do *some shame to the dead bodies*, he might use *conjurations* in its ordinary sense of supernatural arts, and mean that he defied his necromantic charms and influence.

[c] A lantern,—] The *lantern* signified here was a *louvre*, or, as it was styled in ancient records, *lanternium; i. e.* a spacious round or octagonal turret, full of windows, by means of which halls, and sometimes cathedrals, as in the noble example at Ely, are illuminated.

[d] A feasting presence—] *Presence* means *presence-chamber;* the state apartment of a palace.

[e] Shall I believe—] The old copies read,—

"—————*I will believe,*
Shall I believe," &c.

giving us a glimpse, as it were, of the author's own manuscript.

[f] Depart again;—] In the quartos, 1599 and 1609, and also in the folio, 1623, which was printed from the latter edition, the following lines occur here; they are omitted, however, in the undated quarto:—

"Come lie thou in my arms,
Here's to thy health, where'er thou tumblest in,
O true apothecary,
Thy drugs are quick; thus with a kiss I die.
Depart again;"

This, there can be no doubt, as Malone suggested, was a different version by the author, imperfectly cancelled in the manuscript.

[g] *Bitter* conduct—] *Guide, conductor.* So in Act III. Sc. I.:—

"And fire-eyed fury be my *conduct* now."

FRI. Go with me to the vault.
BAL. I dare not, sir:
My master knows not but I am gone hence;
And fearfully did menace me with death,
If I did stay to look on his intents.
FRI. Stay then, I'll go alone:—fear comes upon me;
O, much I fear some ill unlucky thing.
BAL. As I did sleep under this yew-tree* here,[a]
I dreamt my master and another fought,
And that my master slew him.
FRI. Romeo!—[*Advances.*
Alack, alack! what blood is this, which stains
The stony entrance of this sepulchre?
What mean these masterless and gory swords
To lie discolour'd by this place of peace?
[*Enters the monument.*
Romeo! O, pale!—who else? what, Paris too?
And steep'd in blood?—Ah, what an unkind hour
Is guilty of this lamentable chance!—
The lady stirs. [JULIET *wakes.*
JUL. O, comfortable friar! where is my lord?
I do remember well where I should be,
And there I am:—Where is my Romeo?
[*Noise within.*
FRI. I hear some noise.—Lady, come from that nest
Of death, contagion, and unnatural sleep;
A greater Power than we can contradict
Hath thwarted our intents; come, come away:
Thy husband in thy bosom there lies dead;
And Paris too; come, I'll dispose of thee
Among a sisterhood of holy nuns:
Stay not to question, for the watch is coming;
Come, go, good Juliet,—[*Noise again.*] I dare no longer stay. [*Exit.*
JUL. Go, get thee hence, for I will not away.—
What's here? a cup, clos'd in my true love's hand?
Poison, I see, hath been his timeless end:—
Ah churl! drink all; and leave no friendly drop,[b]
To help me after?—I will kiss thy lips;
Haply, some poison yet doth hang on them,
To make me die with a restorative. [*Kisses him.*
Thy lips are warm!
1 WATCH. [*within.*] Lead, boy; which way?
JUL. Yea, noise?—then I'll be brief.—O happy dagger! [*Snatching* ROMEO'*s dagger.*
This is thy sheath;† [*stabs herself.*] there rust, and let me die.
[*Falls on* ROMEO'*s body, and dies.*

Enter Watch, *with the* Page *of* PARIS.

PAGE. This is the place; there, where the torch doth burn.
1 WATCH. The ground is bloody; search about the churchyard:
Go, some of you, who e'er you find, attach.
[*Exeunt some.*
Pitiful sight! here lies the county slain;
And Juliet bleeding; warm, and newly dead,
Who here hath lain this two days buried.
Go, tell the prince,—run to the Capulets,—
Raise up the Montagues,—some others search;—
[*Exeunt other* Watchmen.
We see the ground whereon these woes do lie;
But the true ground of all these piteous woes,
We cannot without circumstance descry.

Re-enter some of the Watch, *with* BALTHASAR.

2 WATCH. Here's Romeo's man, we found him in the churchyard.
1 WATCH. Hold him in safety, till the prince come hither.

Re-enter another Watchman, *with Friar* LAURENCE.

3 WATCH. Here is a friar, that trembles, sighs, and weeps:
We took this mattock and this spade from him,
As he was coming from this churchyard side.
1 WATCH. A great suspicion; stay the friar too.

Enter the PRINCE *and* Attendants.

PRINCE. What misadventure is so early up,
That calls our person from our morning's rest?

Enter CAPULET, LADY CAPULET, *and others.*

CAP. What should it be, that they so shriek abroad?
LA. CAP. The people* in the street cry—Romeo,
Some—Juliet, and some—Paris; and all run,
With open outcry, toward our monument.
PRINCE. What fear is this, which startles in our ears?[c]

(*) First folio, *young tree.* (†) First folio, *'Tis in.*

a As I did sleep under this yew-tree here,—] "This is one of those touches of nature that would have escaped the hand of any painter less attentive to it than Shakespeare. What happens to a person while he is under the manifest influence of fear will seem to him, when he is recovered from it, like a dream."—STEEVENS.

(*) First folio, *O the people.*

b Ah churl! drink all; and leave no friendly drop,—] Thus the earliest quarto, 1597. The folio, 1623, has:—

"O churl! drink all and *left* no friendly drop."

c *In* our *ears?*] The old copies have "*your ears,*" which Johnson corrected.

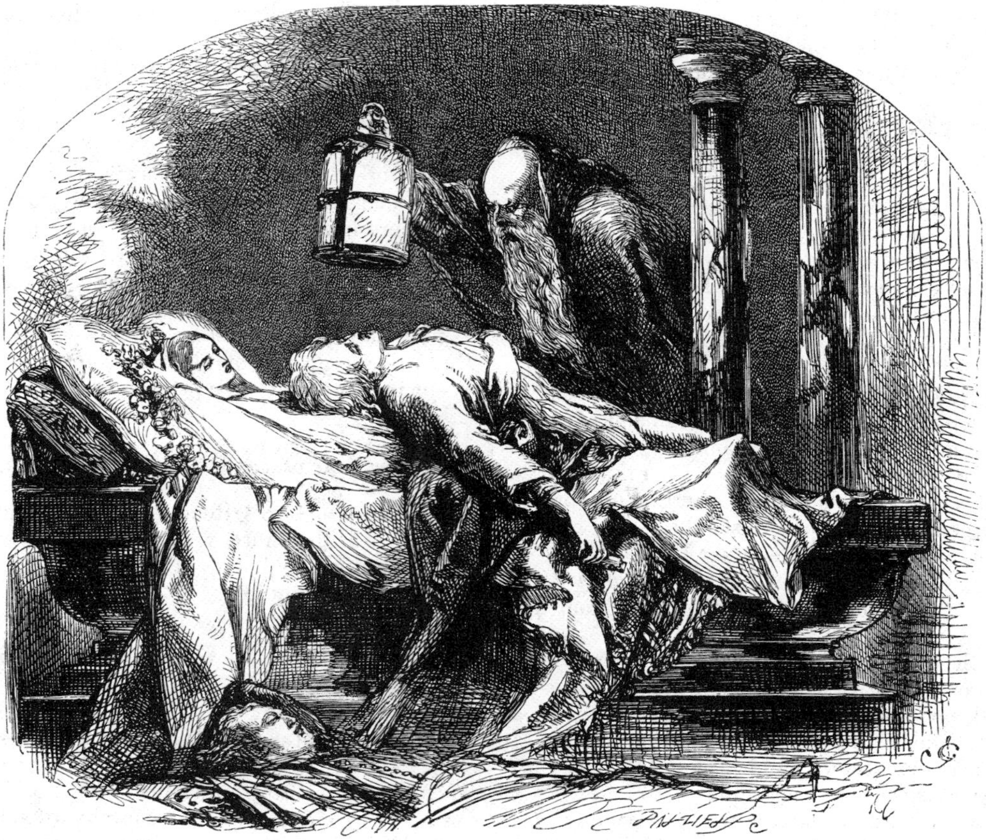

1 Watch. Sovereign, here lies the county Paris slain;
And Romeo dead; and Juliet, dead before,
Warm and new kill'd.

Prince. Search, seek, and know how this foul murder comes.

1 Watch. Here is a friar, and slaughter'd Romeo's man;
With instruments upon them, fit to open
These dead men's tombs.

Cap. O, heaven!—O, wife! look how our daughter bleeds!
This dagger hath mista'en,—for, lo! his house
Is empty on the back of Montague,—[a]
And is mis-sheathed in my daughter's bosom.

La. Cap. O me! this sight of death is as a bell,
That warns my old age to a sepulchre.

Enter Montague *and others.*

Prince. Come, Montague; for thou art early up,
To see thy son and heir more * early down.

Mon. Alas, my liege, my wife is dead to-night;
Grief of my son's exile hath stopp'd her breath:
What further woe conspires against mine age?

Prince. Look, and thou shalt see.

Mon. O thou untaught! what manners is in this,

---

a ——— for, lo! his house
Is empty on the back of Montague,—]
The dagger was anciently worn at the back. Thus, in "The Longer Thou Livest the More Fool Thou Art," 1570:—

"Thou must wear thy sword by thy side,
And thy *dagger* handsomely *at thy back.*"

(*) First folio, *now*.

To press before thy father to a grave?

PRINCE. Seal up the mouth of outrage[a] for a while,
'Till we can clear these ambiguities,
And know their spring, their head, their true descent;
And then will I be general of your woes,
And lead you even to death: mean time forbear,
And let mischance be slave to patience.—
Bring forth the parties of suspicion.

FRI. I am the greatest, able to do least,
Yet most suspected, as the time and place
Doth make against me, of this direful murder;
And here I stand, both to impeach and purge
Myself condemned and myself excus'd.

PRINCE. Then say at once what thou dost know in this.

FRI. I will be brief, for my short date of breath
Is not so long as is a tedious tale.
Romeo, there dead, was husband to that Juliet;
And she, there dead, that Romeo's faithful wife:
I married them; and their stolen marriage-day
Was Tybalt's dooms-day, whose untimely death
Banish'd the new-made bridegroom from this city;
For whom, and not for Tybalt, Juliet pin'd.
You—to remove that siege of grief from her,—
Betroth'd, and would have married her perforce,
To county Paris:—then comes she to me;
And, with wild looks, bid me devise some means
To rid her from this second marriage,
Or, in my cell there would she kill herself.
Then gave I her, so tutor'd by my art,
A sleeping potion; which so took effect
As I intended, for it wrought on her
The form of death: meantime I writ to Romeo,
That he should hither come as this dire night,
To help to take her from her borrow'd grave,
Being the time the potion's force should cease.
But he which bore my letter, friar John,
Was staid by accident: and yesternight
Return'd my letter back: then all alone,
At the prefixed hour of her waking,
Came I to take her from her kindred's vault;
Meaning to keep her closely at my cell,
Till I conveniently could send to Romeo:
But, when I came, (some minute ere the time
Of her awaking,) here untimely lay
The noble Paris, and true Romeo, dead.
She wakes; and I entreated her come forth,
And bear this work of heaven with patience:
But then a noise did scare me from the tomb;
And she, too desperate, would not go with me,
But (as it seems) did violence on herself.
All this I know; and to the marriage
Her nurse is privy: and, if aught in this
Miscarried by my fault, let my old life
Be sacrific'd, some hour before his * time,
Unto the rigour of severest law.

PRINCE. We still have known thee for a holy man.—
Where's Romeo's man? what can he say to this?

BAL. I brought my master news of Juliet's death;
And then in post he came from Mantua,
To this same place, to this same monument.
This letter he early bid me give his father;
And threaten'd me with death, going in the vault.
If I departed not, and left him there.

PRINCE. Give me the letter, I will look on it.—
Where is the county's page, that raised the watch?—
Sirrah, what made your master in this place?

PAGE. He came with flowers to strew his lady's grave;
And bid me stand aloof, and so I did:
Anon, comes one with light to ope the tomb;
And, by and by, my master drew on him;
And then I ran away to call the watch.

PRINCE. This letter doth make good the friar's words,
Their course of love, the tidings of her death:
And here he writes—that he did buy a poison
Of a poor 'pothecary, and therewithal
Came to this vault to die, and lie with Juliet.—
Where be these enemies? Capulet! Montague!—
See, what a scourge is laid upon your hate,
That heaven finds means to kill your joys with love!
And I, for winking at your discords too,
Have lost a brace of kinsmen: all are punish'd.

CAP. O, brother Montague! give me thy hand:
This is my daughter's jointure, for no more
Can I demand.

MON. But I can give thee more:
For I will raise her statue in pure gold;
That, whiles Verona by that name is known,
There shall no figure at such rate be set,
As that of true and faithful Juliet.

CAP. As rich shall Romeo by his lady lie;
Poor sacrifices of our enmity!

PRINCE. A glooming peace this morning with it brings;
The sun, for sorrow, will not show his head:
Go hence, to have more talk of these sad things;
Some shall be pardon'd, and some punished; (3)
For never was a story of more woe,
Than this of Juliet and her Romeo. [*Exeunt.*

---

[a] *The mouth of* outrage—] Mr. Collier's MS. annotator substitutes *outcry*, but no change is needed. In "Henry VI." Pt. I. Act IV. Sc. 1, we find the word with precisely the same signification as in the present passage:—

"——— Are you not asham'd,
With this immodest clamorous *outrage*
To trouble and disturb the king and us?"

(*) First folio, *the*.

ILLUSTRATIVE COMMENTS.

ACT I.

(1) SCENE I.—*Here comes of the house of the Montagues.*] Shakespeare was evidently acquainted with the tradition of the Montagues adopting a cognisance in their hats, that they might be distinguished from the Capulets, since in the play he has made them known at a distance. The circumstance, as Malone pointed out, is mentioned in a Devise of a Masque, written for the Right Honourable Viscount Mountacute, 1575:—

" And for a further proofe. he shewed in hys hat
Thys token which the *Mountacutes* did beare alwaies, for that
They covet to be known from Capels, where they pass,
For ancient grutch whych long ago, 'tweene these two houses was."

(2) SCENE I.—*Thou shalt not stir one foot to seek a foe.*] The earliest copy of Romeo and Juliet, the quarto of 1597,—which is peculiarly interesting from its presenting us with the poet's first projection of a play he subsequently expanded and elaborated with much care and skill, and is valuable too, in helping us to correct many typographical errors, and to supply some lines omitted, perhaps by negligence, in the later editions,—makes short work of this scene. In place of the dialogue, from the entrance of Benvolio to the arrival of the Prince, it has merely the following stage direction ;—" They draw, to them enters Tybalt, they fight, to them the Prince, old Mountague, and his wife, old Capulet and his wife, and other citizens, and part them."

(3) SCENE I.—*Out of her favour, where I am in love.*] In the old poem of "Romeus and Juliet," which Shakespeare adopted as the ground-work of his tragedy, the hero is first introduced to us as in the play, the victim to an unrequited passion.

Romeus, we are told,—

" Hath founde a mayde so fayre (he found so foule his happe),
Whose beauty, shape, and comely grace, did so his heart entrappe,
That from his owne affayres, his thought she did remove;
Onely he sought to honor her, to serve her and to love.
To her he writeth oft, oft messengers are sent,
At length (in hope of better spede) himselfe the lover went;
Present to pleade for grace, which absent was not founde:
And to discover to her eye his new receaved wounde.
But she that from her youth was fostred evermore
With vertues foode, and taught in schole of wisdomes skilfull lore:
By aunswere did cutte of thaffections of his love,
That he no more occasion had so vayne a sute to move.
So sterne she was of chere, (for all the payne he tooke)
That, in reward of toyle, she would not geve a frendly looke."

(4) SCENE I.—*That, when she dies, with beauty dies her store.*] The meaning of this somewhat complex passage seems to be ;—she is rich in the possession of unequalled beauty, but poor, because, having devoted herself to chastity, when she dies, her wealth, that is, beauty, dies with her. The same conceit occurs repeatedly in Shakespeare's poems :—

SONNET 1.

" From fairest creatures we desire increase,
That thereby *beauty's rose might never die*,
But as the riper should by time decease,
His tender heir might bear his memory :"

SONNET 4.

" Then how, when nature calls thee to be gone
What acceptable audit canst thou leave?
Thy unus'd beauty must be tomb'd with thee,
Which, used, lives thy executor to be."

See, also, Sonnets 2, 3, 5, 6, 10, 11, 12, 13, and 14.

(5) SCENE I.—*Examine other beauties.*] So "the trustiest of his feeres" counsels Romeus in the old poem :—

" Choose out some worthy dame, her honor thou and serve,
Who will geve eare to thy complaint, and pitty ere thou sterve.
But sow no more thy paynes in such a barrayne soyle:
As yeldes in harvest time no crop, in recompence of toyle.
Ere long the townishe dames together will resort:
Some one of bewty, favour, shape, and of so lovely porte,
With so fast fixed eye, perhaps thou mayst beholde:
That thou shalt quite forget thy love, and passions past of olde."

(6) SCENE II.—*This night I hold an old accustom'd feast.*] From the old poem :—

" The wery winter nightes restore the Christmas games,
And now the season doth invite to banquet townish dames.
And fyrst in Capels house, the chiefe of all the kyn
Sparth for no cost, the wonted use of banquets to begyn.
No Lady fayre or fowle was in Verona towne,
No knight or gentleman of high or lowe renowne;
But Capilet himselfe hath byd unto his feast,
Or by his name in paper sent, appoynted as a geast.

(7) SCENE III.—*'Tis since the earthquake now eleven years.*] We have already, in the Preliminary Observations, alluded to Tyrwhitt's conjecture that the earthquake spoken of by the Nurse was the one chronicled by Holinshed, as being felt in London and other parts of the kingdom in 1580. The Rev. Joseph Hunter ("New Illustrations, &c. &c., of Shakespeare," Vol. II. p. 120) contends, however, that it is much more probable the earthquake the Poet had in his mind was that which occurred ten years before, in the neighbourhood of Verona, and was so severe that it destroyed Ferrara. "When the church of St. Stephen at Ferrara was rebuilt," Mr. Hunter informs us, "an inscription was placed against it, from which we may collect the terrible nature of the visitation :—

—'Cum anno M. D. LXX die XVII Novembris tertia noctis hora, quam maximus terræ motus hanc præclarissimam urbem ita conquassasset, ut ejus fortissima mœnia, munitissimas arces, alta palatia, religiosa templa, sacratas turres, omnesque fere ædes omnino evertisset et prostrasset, una cum maximo civium damno, atque acerbâ clade.'"

There is a small tract, still extant, entitled "A coppie of the letter sent from Ferrara the xxii of November, 1570. Imprinted at London in Paules Churchyarde, at the signe of the Lucrece, by Thomas Purfoote;" in which the writer describes "the great and horrible earthquakes, the excessiue and vnrecouerable losses, with the greate mortalitie and death of people, the ruine and ouerthrowe of an infinite number of monasteries, pallaces and other howses, and the destruction of his graces excellencies castle." The first earthquake was on Thursday, the 11th, at ten at night, "whiche endured the space of an Aue

Marie;" on the 17th, "the earth quaked all the whole day." In all, "the earthquakes are numbered to haue been a hundred and foure in xl houres."

(8) SCENE III.—
I was your mother much upon these years
That you are now a maid.]
In the old poem Juliet's age is set down at sixteen; in Paynter's novel it is said to be eighteen. As Shakespeare makes his heroine only fourteen, if the words "*your* mother," which is the reading of the old editions, be correct, Lady Capulet would be eight and twenty, while her husband, having done masking some thirty years, must be at least three-score. Mr. Knight veils the disparity, and perhaps improves the passage, by printing, "I was *a* mother;" but we believe without authority.

(9) SCENE IV.—*Mercutio.*] The Mercutio of the play is Shakespeare's own, the only hint for all the wit, the gaiety, and the chivalry, with which he has indued this favourite character, being the following brief description of his prototype in the poem:—

"A courtier that eche where was highly had in pryce,
For he was coorteous of his speche, and pleasant of devise.
Even as a lyon would emong the lambes be bolde,
Such was emong the bashfull maydes, Mercutio to beholde."

(10) SCENE IV.—*Give me a torch.*] "The character which Romeo declares his resolution to assume, will be best explained by a passage in 'Westward Hoe,' by Decker and Webster, 1607; 'He is just like a *torch-bearer* to maskers; he wears good cloaths and is ranked in good company, but he doth nothing.' A *torch-bearer* seems to have been a constant appendage on every troop of masks. To *hold a torch* was anciently no degrading office. Queen Elizabeth's Gentlemen-Pensioners attended her to Cambridge, and *held torches* while a play was acted before her in the Chapel of King's College, on a Sunday evening."—STEEVENS.

(11) SCENE IV.—
Tut! dun's the mouse, the constable's own word:
If thou art dun, we'll draw thee from the mire.]
Dun's the mouse was a proverbial saying, the precise meaning of which has not come down to us. In the comedy of "Patient Grissil," 1603, Babulo says, "The sun hath play'd bo-peep in the element any time these two hours, as I do some mornings when you call. 'What, Babulo!' say you. 'Here, master,' say I; and then this eye opens, yet *don is the mouse*—lie still. 'What, Babulo!' says Grissil. 'Anon,' say I; and then this eye looks up, yet down I snug again. 'What, Babulo!' say you again; and then I start up, and see the sun," &c. The expression is found also in Decker and Webster's "Westward Hoe," 1607, and among Ray's proverbial similes. The allusion in the following line is to an ancient country sport, called *Dun is in the mire*, which Gifford thus describes:—"A log of wood is brought into the midst of the room; this is *Dun*, (the cart-horse,) and a cry is raised, that he is *stuck in the mire*. Two of the company advance, either with or without ropes, to draw him out. After repeated attempts, they find themselves unable to do it, and call for more assistance.—The game continues till all the company take part in it, when Dun is extricated of course; and the merriment arises from the awkward and affected efforts of the rustics to lift the log, and from sundry arch contrivances to let the ends of it fall on one another's toes."—*Works of Ben Jonson*, Vol. VII. p. 282.

(12) SCENE IV.—*This is she*—] It is instructive to compare the original draft of this famous speech as it appears in the quarto of 1597 with the finished version of the later editions, and observe the ease and mastery of touch by which the alterations are effected.

In the quarto, 1597, after the line—

"Ah, then I see Queen Mab hath been with you,"

Benvolio exclaims:—

"Queene Mab! whats she?"

The description then proceeds:—

"She is the Fairies Midwife and doth come
In shape no bigger than an Aggat stone
On the forefinger of a Burgomaster,
Drawne with a teeme of little Atomi,
A thwart mens noses when they lie a sleepe.
Her waggon spokes are made of spinners webs,
The couer, of the winges of Grashoppers,
The traces are the Moone-shine watrie beames,
The collers crickets bones, the lash of filmes,
Her waggoner is a small gray coated flie,
Not halfe so big as is a little worme,
Pickt from the lasie finger of a maide,
And in this sort she gallops vp and downe
Through Louers braines, and then they dream of loue.
O're Courtiers knees: who strait on cursies dreame,
O're Ladies lips, who dreame on kisses strait:
Which oft the angrie Mab with blisters plagues,
Because their breathes with sweet meats tainted are
Sometimes she gallops ore a Lawers lap,
And then dreames he of smelling out a sute,
And sometime comes she with a tithe pigs taile,
Tickling a Parson's nose that lies asleepe,
And then dreames he of another benefice:
Sometime she gallops ore a souldiers nose,
And then dreames he of cutting forraine throats,
Of breaches ambuscados, countermines,
Of healthes fiue fadome deepe, and then anon
Drums in his eare: at which he startes and wakes,
And sweares a Praier or two and sleepes againe.
This is that Mab that makes maids lie on their backes,
And proues them women of good cariage.
This is the verie Mab that plats the manes of Horses in the night,
And plats the Elfelocks in foule sluttish haire,
Which once vntangled much misfortune breedes.
ROM. Peace, peace,—" &c.

(13) SCENE V.—
What lady's that, which doth enrich the hand
Of yonder knight?]
Romeo's first sight of Juliet at the feast is thus quaintly described in the old poem:—

"At length he saw a mayd, right fayre of perfect shape,
Which Theseus or Paris would have chosen to their rape.
Whom erst he never sawe, of all she pleasde him most;
Within himselfe he sayd to her, thou justly mayst thee boste
Of perfit shapes renoune, and beauties sounding prayse,
Whose like ne hath, ne shalbe seene, ne liveth in our dayes.
And whilst he fixd on her his partiall perced eye,
His former love, for which of late he ready was to die,
Is nowe as quite forgotte, as it had never been."

(14) SCENE V.—*Come hither, nurse: what is yon gentleman?*] Compare the poem.—

"What twayne are those (quoth she) which prease unto the door,
Whose pages in their hand doe beare, two torches light before?
And then as eche of them had of his houshold name,
So she him named yet once agayne the yong and wily dame.
And tell me who is he with vysor in his hand,
That yender doth in masking weede besyde the window stand.
His name is Romeus (said shee) a Montagewe,
Whose Fathers pryde first styrd the strife which both your housholdes rewe.
The woord of Montagew her joyes did overthrow
And straight in steade of happy hope, despayre began to grow.
What hap have I quoth she, to love my father's foe?
What, am I wery of my wele? what, do I wishe my woe?
But though her grievouse paynes distraind her tender hart,
Yet with an outward shewe of joye she cloked inward smart;
And of the courtlyke dames her leave so courtly tooke,
That none dyd gesse the sodain change by changing of her looke."

ACT II.

(1) SCENE II.—*Thou art thyself, though not a Montague.*] So the old copies, and rightly. Malone appears to have been the first who adopted the punctuation, since invariably followed, of placing the comma after "*though*,"—

"Thou art thyself though, not a Montague."

"Juliet," he remarks, "is simply endeavouring to account for Romeo's being amiable and excellent, though he *is* a Montague; and, to prove this, she asserts that he merely bears that name, but has none of the qualities of that house." Nothing can be more foreign to her meaning. Her imagination is powerfully excited by the intelligence she has just received,—

"His name is Romeo, and a *Montague!*"

In that name she sees an insurmountable impediment to her new-formed wishes, and in the fancied apostrophe to her lover, she eloquently implores him to abandon it,—

"Deny thy father, and *refuse thy name.*

* * * * * * *

'Tis but thy *name*, that is my enemy;—
Thou art *thyself*, though not a *Montague*."

That is, as she afterwards expresses it, you would still retain all the perfections which adorn you, were you not *called Montague.*

"What's *Montague?* it is nor hand, nor foot," &c.

"———O be some other *name.*"

One is puzzled to conceive a difficulty in appreciating the meaning, especially as the thought is repeated immediately after,—

"What's in a *name?* that which we call a rose,
By *any other word* would smell as sweet."

The same idea occurs in Sir Thomas Overbury's poem of "A Wife,"—

"Things were first made, then words; she were the same
With, or *without*, that *title* or that *name.*"

(2) SCENE II.—
If that thy bent of love be honourable,
Thy purpose marriage.]
Thus the old poem:—

"But if your thought be chaste, and have on vertue ground,
If wedlocke be the ende and marke which your desire hath found,
Obedience set aside, unto my parents dewe,
The quarell eke that long agoe betwene our housholdes grewe,
Both me and myne I will all whole to you betake,
And following you where so you goe, my fathers house forsake."

(3) SCENE II.—
O, for a falconer's voice,
To lure this tassel-gentle back again!]
The tassel, or, more correctly, the *tiercel*, is the male of the gosshawk, and had the epithet *gentle* annexed to it from its docility and attachment to man. According to some authorities, the *tiercel* derives its name from being a *tierce*, or third, less than the female; but Tardif, in his "Treatise of Falconry," says it is so called from being one of three birds generally found in the aerie of a falcon, two of which are females, and the third a male: hence called *tiercelet*, or the *third*. This species of hawk was in high esteem; for the old books on the sport, which show that certain hawks were appropriated to certain ranks of society, tell us the falcon *gentle* and tiercel *gentle* "are for a prince."

(4) SCENE III.—*With baleful weeds, and precious-juiced flowers.*] Farmer has remarked, that Shakespeare, on his introduction of Friar Laurence, prepares us for the part he is afterwards to sustain; for, having thus early discovered him to be a chemist, we are not surprised when we find him furnishing the draught which produces the catastrophe of the piece.

(5) SCENE IV.—*More than prince of cats, I can tell you.*] *Tibert, Tybert*, or *Tybalt*, are forms of the ancient name *Thibault.* When or why the cat was first so called it is, perhaps, hopeless now to inquire. The earliest instance cited by the commentators, is in the old story-book of "Reynard the Fox,"—"Then the King called for *Sir Tibert*, the cat, and said to him, *Sir Tibert*, you shall go to Reynard, and summon him the second time."—Ch. vi.: and the association was evidently not uncommon; for Ben Jonson speaks of *cats* as *tiberts.* Decker, too, in his "Satiromastix," 1602, says:—

"— tho' you were *Tybert, the long-tail'd prince of cats.*"

And Nash, in "Have with You to Saffron Walden," 1598:—

"Not *Tibalt*, prince of *cats.*"

(6) SCENE IV.—*A duellist, a duellist; a gentleman of the very first house,—of the first and second cause: Ah, the immortal passado! the punto reverso! the hay!*] Mercutio's mockery is not directed against the practice of duelling in the abstract, for he appears to be almost as pugnacious as the fiery Tybalt himself. He is ridiculing the professors and *alumni* of those academies established in London during the latter part of the 16th century, for the study of "The Noble Science of Defence," as it was called. A class who appear to have prided themselves on the punctilious observance of certain absurd forms and an affected diction, which had been rendered fashionable by the treatises of Saviolo* and Caranza. The plainest and most obvious meaning of the words "A gentleman of the very first house" appears to be that Tybalt was a gentleman-scholar "of the very first house" or school of fencing, of the greatest teacher existing at the period. In George Silver's *Paradoxes of Defence*, London, 1599, quarto, it is stated that there were three "Italian Teachers of Offence;" the first of whom was Signior Rocco, who had come into England about thirty years before. "He disbursed a great summe of mony for the lease of a house in Warwicke-lane, which he called his colledge, for he thought it a great disgrace for him to keepe a fence-schoole, he being then thought to be the only famous maister of the arte of armes in the whole world." "He taught none commonly under twentie, forty, fifty, or an hundred pounds." To be, therefore, a gentleman of such a house as this, was really "a very ribband in the cap of youth." In the same tract occurs a curious illustration of another expression in the same speech of *Mercutio*:—"the very butcher of a silk button."—"One Austen Bagger, a verie tall gentleman of his handes," resolved to encounter Signior Rocco, and went to another house which he had in the Blackfriars, "and called to him in this manner: 'Signior Rocco, thou that art thought to be the only cunning man in the world with thy weapons; *thou that takest upon thee to hit anie Englishman with a thrust upon anie button;* thou that takest upon thee to come over the seas to teach the valiant noblemen and gentlemen of England to fight,—thou cowardly fellow, come out of thy house, if thou dare for thy life: I am come to fight with thee.'"

(*) *Practise of the Duello, in 2 books*, Vinc. Saviolo, 1595, 4to.

The expression, "a gentleman of the very first house," has been, however, usually understood in a genealogical sense; in which form it occurs also in Beaumont and Fletcher's "Women Pleased," Act I. Sc. 3:—

———"A gentleman's gone then:
A gentleman o' the first house!—there's the end on't!"

Warburton supposed the allusion was to Tybalt's pretending to be at the head of his family; to which Steevens objects that Capulet and Romeo were both before him; but the truth is, that neither of them at all interfered with such claim. Romeo was of the house of Capulet only by marriage with Juliet, and in the list of persons represented in the tragedy, Tybalt is called *Nephew to Lady Capulet.* The real heraldical reference, if that be the genuine sense of the passage, appears to have been quite overlooked. When the bearing of armorial-ensigns became reduced to a science, a series of differences was instituted, the more readily to distinguish between the arms borne by the several sons and descendants of the same family, and to show their order and consanguinity. They consisted of six small figures, called a label, crescent, mullet, martlet, annulet, and fleur-de-lis, which were always to be placed in the most prominent part of the coat-armour. These signs, borne singly, were for the sons of the original ancestors, who constituted that which heralds denominated "*the First House;*" the issue of those sons formed "the Second House," and carried their differences doubled, beginning with the crescent surmounted of a label, a crescent of a crescent, and so of the rest. It was ordained by Otho, Emperor of Germany, that the eldest son of the first member of the first house should be preferred in dignity before his uncle; and the same regulation was also established in France, and made to include females. Tybalt was, therefore, the eldest son of Lady Capulet's elder brother, and, without pretending to be at the head of his family, was still a gentleman descended of "the very first house."

The *passado,* more properly *passata,* meant a step forward or aside in fencing.

"If your enemy be first to strike at you, and if, at that instant, you would make him a *passata* or remove, it behoveth you to be very ready with your feet and hand, and, being to *passe* or enter, you must take heede," &c.—SAVIOLO, H. 3.

The *punto reverso* and the *hay* were also Italian terms, the former meaning a back-handed stroke:—

"——or, in both these false thrusts, when he beateth them by with his rapier, you may, with much sodainnesse make a passata with your lefte foote, and your Dagger commanding his Rapier, you maie give him a *punta,* either dritta, or *riversa.*"—SAVIOLO, K. 2.

And the latter being the exclamation *hai, thou hast* it, used when a thrust or blow tells; from whence Johnson supposes modern fencers, on the same occasion, cry out *ha!*

(7) SCENE IV.—*Nay, if our wits run the wild-goose chase, I am done.*] The *wild-goose chase* was a barbarous sort of horse-race, in which two horses were started together; and the rider who first got the lead compelled the other to follow him over whatever ground the foremost jockey chose to go. See Chambers' Dictionary, last edition, under the article CHASE; and Holt White's note to this passage in the *Variorum* Shakespeare.

(8) SCENE IV.—*Lady, lady, lady.*] This is the burden of an old ballad, of which a stanza is given in Percy's "Reliques of Ancient Poetry," vol. i. p. 204:—

"There dwelt a man in Babylon
Of reputation great by fame;
He took to wife a faire womán,
Susanna she was callde by name:
A woman fair and vertuous;
Lady, lady:
Why should we not of her learn thus
To live godly?"

(9) SCENE IV.—*Ah, mocker! that's the dog's name. R is for the dog.*] *R,* from its resemblance in sound to the growl of a dog, has, time out of mind, been known as the *dog's letter;* and was, therefore, a very unbefitting initial in the ear of the old woman for anything so sweet as rosemary and Romeo. The dog's letter is amusingly illustrated in a quotation Steevens has adduced from Barclay's "Ship of Fooles," 1578:—

"This man malicious which troubled is with wrath,
Nought els soundeth but the hoorse letter R.
Though all be well, yet he none aunswere hath
Save the *doggees letter* glowming with *nar, nar.*"

And Ben Jonson, in his "English Grammar," says "*R* is the *dog's* letter, and hurreth in the sound:"—

"—Sonat hic de nare caninâ
Litera."—*Pers. Sat.* 1.

Erasmus, as Douce has shown, in explaining the adage, "canina facundia," says, "R, litera quæ in rixando prima est, canina vocatur."

(10) SCENE VI.—*Friar* Laurence's *Cell.*] How much the dialogue in this scene was amplified and improved after the publication of the earliest quarto, let the reader judge from a comparison of it with the corresponding scene in that edition:—

Enter Romeo, Frier.

Rom. Now Father *Laurence,* in thy holy grant
Consists the good of me and *Iuliet.*
Fr. Without more words I will doo all I may,
To make you happie if in me it lye.
Rom. This morning here she pointed we should meet,
And consumate those neuer parting bands,
Witnes of our harts loue by ioyning hands,
And come she will.
Fr. I gesse she will indeed,
Youths loue is quicke, swifter than swiftest speed.

Enter Iuliet, somewhat fast, and embraceth Romeo.

See where she comes.
So light of foote nere hurts the troden flower:
Of loue and joy, see see the soueraigne power.
Iul. Romeo.
Rom. My *Iuliet* welcome. As doo waking eyes
(Cloasd in Nights mysts) attend the frolicke Day,
So *Romeo* hath expected *Iuliet,*
And thou art come.
Jul. I am (if I be Day)
Come to my Sunne: shine foorth, and make me faire.
Rom. All beauteous fairnes dwelleth in thine eyes.
Iul. Romeo from thine all brightnes doth arise.
Fr. Come wantons, come, the stealing houres do passe,
Defer imbracements till some fitter time,
Part for a while, you shall not be alone,
Till holy Church haue ioynd ye both in one.
Rom. Lead holy Father, all delay seemes long.
Iul. Make hast, make hast, this lingring doth vs wrong.
Fr. O, soft and faire makes sweetest worke they say.
Hast is a common hindrer in crosse way. *Exeunt omnes.*

ACT III.

(1) SCENE I.—*Ask for me to-morrow, and you shall find me a grave man.*] In Italy the funeral follows close upon death, and it was so formerly in England too; hence poor Mercutio's quibble, and the fact of the narcotic administered to Juliet being tempered to operate only "two-and-forty hours," are strictly in keeping with the usages of the period. The same play on the word *grave* Steevens has found in "The Revenger's Tragedy," 1608, where Vindici dresses up his Lady's skull:—

"She has a somewhat *grave* look with her."

It is met with also in Overbury's "Characters," ed. 1616, where, speaking of a sexton, the author says, "He could willingly all his life time be confinde to the church-yard; at least within five foot on 't: for at every church stile, commonly ther's an ale-house: where let him be found never so idle pated, hee is still a *grave drunkard*."

Mercutio's last words were improved after the 1597 quarto. There they stand thus:—

"I am pepperd for this world, I am sped yfaith, he hath made wormes meate of me, and ye aske for me to morrow you shall find me a graue-man. A poxe of your houses, I shall be fairely mounted vpon foure-mens shoulders: For your house of the *Mountegues* and the *Capolets:* and then some peasantly rogue, some Sexton, some base slaue shall write my Epitapth, that *Tybalt* came and broke the Princes Lawes, and *Mercutio* was slaine for the first and second cause. Wher's the Surgeon?"

Boy. Hee's come, sir.

Mer. Now heele keepe a mumbling in my guts on the other side, come *Benuolio*, lend me thy hand: a poxe of your houses.

Exeunt."

(2) SCENE I.—

——— *bid him bethink,*
How nice the quarrel was.]

In the quarto, 1597, the speech is continued as follows:—

"But *Tibalt* still persisting in his wrong,
The stout *Mercutio* drewe to calme the storme,
Which *Romeo* seeing cal'd stay Gentlemen,
And on me cry'd, who drew to part their strife,
And with his agill arme yong *Romeo*,
As fast as tung cryde peace, sought peace to make.
While they were enterchanging thrusts and blows,
Vnder yong *Romeos* laboring arme to part,
The furious *Tybalt* cast an enuious thrust,
That rid the life of stout *Mercutio*.
With that he fled, but presently return'd,
And with his rapier braued *Romeo:*
That had but newly entertain'd reuenge.
And ere I could draw forth my rapyer
To part their furie, downe did *Tybalt* fall,
And this way *Romeo* fled."

(3) SCENE II.—

Spread thy close curtain, love-performing night!
That run-aways' eyes may wink, and Romeo
Leap to these arms, untalk'd of, and unseen!]

The expression "run-aways' eyes," usually printed "run-away's eyes," in modern editions, has long been a subject of contention with the critics, and abundant are the emendations which have been suggested to make the meaning clear; for example:—

Rumour's eyes	by Heath.
Renomy's (Renomée, *Fr.*) eyes	— Monck Mason.
Unawares eyes	— Z. Jackson.
Rude day's eyes Soon day's eyes Roving eyes	— Dyce.
Luna's eyes	— Gent. Mag. June 1845.
Enemies' eyes	— Perkins' Folio.
Rumourer's eyes	— Singer.
Wary ones' eyes	—Anon.

Those who are in favour of retaining "run-aways interpret it diversely. Steevens says, Night is the run-away; Warburton thinks, Day is the run-away; Douce, that it is Juliet; and some one else, that it is Romeo; while Mr. Halpin, in an elegant contribution to the Shakespeare Society's Papers, called "The Bridal Run-away," (vol. ii. p. 24,) endeavours to prove the fugitive none other than Cupid himself. Of the proposed emendations, that of Zachary Jackson has found most favour, having been adopted by two very opposite authorities, Mr. Collier and Mr. Knight; but we must decline the invidious task of pronouncing an opinion upon the relative merits of these suggestions, believing that all are equally inadmissible. Whether Shakespeare's "run-away" applied to Romeo, or to Juliet, or to Day, or to Night, or to the Sun, for whom a good case might be made out,—

"You, grandsire Phœbus, with your lovely eye,
The firmament's eternal vagabond,
The Heav'n's promoter that doth peep and pry."
Return from Parnassus.

or to the moon, who has some claim to the distinction,—

"Blest night, wrap Cynthia in a sable sheet
That fearful lovers may securely sleep."
Blurt, Master Constable, Act III. Sc. I.

or to the stars, for whom much might be said; or whether "run-away" sometimes bore a wider signification, and implied a spy as well as a fugitive,—in which case the poet may have meant, any wandering, prying eyes,—we are convinced that the old word is the true word, and that "run-aways" (runnawayes) ought to retain its place in the text.

(4) SCENE II.—*Hood my unmann'd blood bating in my cheeks.*] The terms *hood, unmann'd*, and *bating*, are derived from falconry. The *hood* was a cap with which the hawk was usually hood-winked. An *unmann'd* hawk was one not sufficiently trained to be familiar with her keeper, and such birds commonly fluttered and beat their wings violently in efforts to escape. Thus Petruchio, speaking of Katharine, says:—

"Another way I have to *man* my haggard,
To make her come and know her keeper's call;
That is, to watch her, as we watch those kites,
That *bate*, and beat and will not be obedient."
Taming of the Shrew, Act IV. Sc. I.

(5) SCENE II.—*Enter* Nurse, *with cords.*] In the quarto, 1597, the stage direction is:—

"*Enter* Nurse *wringing her hands, with the ladder of cords in her lap;*"

and the dialogue, which is much abridged, begins,—

"*Iul.* But how now Nurse: O Lord, why lookst thou sad?
What hast thou there, the cordes?
Nur. I, I, the cordes: alacke we are vndone,
We are vndone, Ladie we are vndone.
Iul. What diuell art thou that torments me thus?
Nurs. Alack the day, hees dead, hees dead, hees dead.
Jul. This torture should be roard in dismall hell.
Can heauens be so enuious?
Nur. Romeo can if heauens cannot.
I saw the wound, I saw it with mine eyes,
God saue the sample, on his manly breast:
A bloodie coarse, a piteous bloodie coarse,
All pale as ashes, I swounded at the sight." &c. &c.

(6) SCENE III.—

Art thou a man? thy form cries out, thou art;
Thy tears are womanish.]

Here, Shakespeare has closely followed the old poem,—

"Art thou quoth he a man? thy shape saith, so thou art;
Thy crying, and thy weping eyes denote a woman's hart,
For manly reason is quite from of thy mynd outchased,
And in her stead affections lewd and fancies highly placed,
So that I stoode in doute, this howre (at the least)
If thou a man or woman wert, or els a brutish beast."

(7) SCENE V.—*Night's candles are burnt out.*] It has been noticed that this runs parallel with a passage in the Ajax of Sophocles,—

κεῖνος γὰρ ἄκρας νυκτὸς, ἡνίχ' ἕσπεροι
λαμπτῆρες οὐκέτ' ᾖθον. [v. 285.]

———"At dead of night,
What time the evening tapers were expired."

But Shakespeare certainly meant the stars, while Sophocles seems only to have thought of the less poetical lamps of earth.

(8) SCENE V.—*Hunting thee hence with hunts-up to the day.*] "Any song intended to arouse in the morning,—even a love-song,—was formerly called a *hunt's-up;* and the name was, of course, derived from a tune or song employed by early hunters. Butler in his *Principles of Musik*, 1636, defines a *hunt's-up* as 'morning music;' and Cotgrave defines 'Resveil' as a hunt's-up, or *Morning Song*, for a new married wife." See W. CHAPPELL'S *Popular Music of the Olden Time; &c.*

The following song, which is taken from a manuscript in Mr. Collier's possession, is of the character of a love-song:—

THE NEW HUNT'S-UP.

"THE hunt is up, the hunt is up,
Awake, my lady free,
The sun hath risen, from out his prison,
Beneath the glistering sea.

"The hunt is up, the hunt is up,
Awake, my lady bright,
The morning lark is high, to mark
The coming of day-light.

"The hunt is up, the hunt is up,
Awake, my lady fair,
The kine and sheep, but now asleep,
Browse in the morning air.

"The hunt is up, the hunt is up,
Awake, my lady gay,
The stars are fled to the ocean bed,
And it is now broad day.

"The hunt is up, the hunt is up,
Awake, my lady sheen,
The hills look out, and the woods about
Are drest in lovely green.

"The hunt is up, the hunt is up,
Awake, my lady dear,
A morn in spring is the sweetest thing
Cometh in all the year.

"The hunt is up, the hunt is up,
Awake, my lady sweet,
I come to thy bower, at this lov'd hour,
My own true love to greet."

(9) SCENE V.—*A joyful bride.*] In the later copies this dialogue between Lady Capulet and Juliet varies in some respects from the earliest quarto. The reader desirous of seeing it in its original form is referred to the *Variorum* Edition, where it is given at length.

ACT IV.

(1) SCENE I.—
Take thou this phial, being then in bed,
And this distilled liquor drink thou off.]

Compare the corresponding passage in the old poem:—

" Receive this vyoll small, and keepe it as thine eye;
And on the mariage day, before the sunne doe cleare the skye,
Fill it with water full up to the very brim,
Then drinke it of, and thou shalt feele throughout eche veyne and lim
A pleasant slumber slide, and quite dispred at length
On all thy partes, from every part reve all thy kindly strength;
Withouten moving thus thy ydle parts shall rest,
No pulse shall goe, ne hart once beate within thy hollow brest,
But thou shalt lye as she that dyeth in a traunce;
Thy kinsmen and thy trusty friendes shall wayle the sodain chaunce,
The corps then will they bring to grave in this churchyarde,
Where thy forefathers long agoe a costly tombe preparde,
Both for himselfe and eke for those that should come after,
Both deepe it is, and long and large, where thou shalt rest my daughter,
Till I to Mantua sende for Romeus, thy knight;
Out of the tombe both he and I will take thee forth that night."

(2) SCENE I.—
Then (as the manner of our country is,)
In thy best robes uncover'd on the bier,
Thou shalt be borne.]

The custom of bearing the dead body to burial clad in its ordinary habiliments, and with the face uncovered, appears to have been peculiar to Italy; it is mentioned in the old poem:—

" An other use there is, that whosoever dyes,
Borne to their church with *open face* upon the beere he lyes,
In wonted weede attyrde, not wrapt in winding sheete."

and in a passage quoted by Mr. Hunter, ("New Illustrations of Shakespeare," Vol. II. p. 139,) from "Coryat's *Crudities*:"—"The burials are so strange, both in Venice, and all other cities, towns, and parishes of Italy, that they differ not only from England, but from all other nations whatever in Christendom. For they carry the corse to church with the face, hands, and feet all naked, and wearing the same apparel that the person wore lately before it died, or that which it craved to be buried in; which apparel is interred together with their bodies."—Vol. II. p. 27.

(3) SCENE II.—
And am enjoin'd
By holy Laurence to fall prostrate here.]

From this point the scene is thus exhibited in the first quarto:—

" And craue remission of so foule a fact.

She kneeles downe.

Moth. Why thats well said.
Capo. Now before God this holy reuerent Frier
All our whole Citie is much bound vnto.
Goe tell the Countie presently of this,
For I will haue this knot knit vp to morrow.
Jul. Nurse, will you go with me to my Closet,
To sort such things as shall be requisite
Against to morrow.
Moth. I pree thee do, good Nurse goe in with her,
Helpe her to sort Tyres, Rebatoes, Chaines,
And I will come vnto you presently.
Nur. Come sweet hart, shall we goe;
Jul. I pree thee let vs. *Exeunt.*"

(4) SCENE III.—*I have a faint cold fear thrills through my veins.*] So the old poem :—

" Her dainty tender parts gan shever all for dred,
Her golden heares did stand upright upon her chillish hed.
Then pressed with the feare that she there lived in,
A sweat as colde as mountaine yse pearst through her slender skin."

(5) SCENE III.—
And shrieks like mandrakes' torn out of the earth,
That living mortals, hearing them, run mad.]

The plant called *mandrake* was fabulously endowed with a degree of animal life and feeling, and, when drawn from the earth, was said to utter cries so terrible as to kill the gatherer, and madden all who heard them : " Therefore, they did tye some dogge or other lyving beast unto the roote thereof wyth a corde, and digged the earth in compasse round about, and in the meane tyme stopped their own eares for feare of the terreble shriek and cry of this *Mandrack.* In whych cry it doth not only dye itselfe, but the feare thereof kylleth the dogge or beast which pulleth it out of the earth."—Bulleine's "Bulwarke of Defence Against Sickness," &c. 1575.

(6) SCENE III.—*Romeo, I come! this do I drink to thee.*] The reading of the quarto, 1597, which has been deservedly preferred to the redundant and seemingly corrupt line of the subsequent old copies,—

"Romeo, Romeo, Romeo, here's drink, I drink to thee."

In other respects the soliloquy is much superior in the latter editions, as will be seen by comparing their version with the following of the first quarto :—

"Ah, I doo take a fearfull thing in hand.
What if this Potion should not worke at all,
Must I of force be married to the Countie?
This shall forbid it. Knife, lye thou there.
What if the Frier should giue me this drinke
To poyson mee, for feare I should disclose
Our former marriage? Ah, I wrong him much,
He is a holy and religious Man :
I will not entertaine so bad a thought.
What if I should be stifled in the Toomb?
Awake an houre before the appointed time :
Ah then I feare I shall be lunaticke,
And playing with my dead forefathers bones,
Dash out my franticke brains. Me thinkes I see
My Cosin *Tybalt* weltring in his bloud,
Seeking for *Romeo:* stay *Tybalt* stay.
Romeo I come, this doe I drinke to thee."
[*She fals vpon her bed within the Curtaines.*

(7) SCENE V.—
But one thing to rejoice and solace in,
And cruel death hath catch'd it from my sight.]

In this part of the scene the quarto, 1597, has the following stage direction :—"*All at once cry out and wring their hands;*" and to the next couplet—

"And all our joy, and all our hope is dead,
Dead, lost, undone, absented, wholly fled"—

is prefixed, *All cry.* From which we must infer that all the characters present here spoke together. At the close of the scene the direction is :—"*They all but the Nurse goe foorth, casting Rosemary on her and shutting the Curtens.*"

(8) SCENE V.—*Enter Peter.*] The first quarto has "*Enter Seruingman;*" and the scene begins :—

"*Ser.* Alack alack what shal I doe, come Fidlers play me some mery dumpe.
1 *Mus.* A sir, this is no time to play.
Ser. You will not then?
1 —. No marry will wee.
Ser. Then will I giue it you, and soundly to.
1 —. What will you giue vs?
Ser. The fidler, Ile re you, Ile fa you, Ile sol you.
1 —. If you re vs and fa vs, we will note you, &c. &c. &c."

In the after quartos, 1599 and 1609, the direction is, "*Enter Will Kemp;*" from which it appears that Peter was one of the characters played by this popular actor.

ACT V.

(1) SCENE I.—*I do remember an apothecary.*] This well-known description was carefully elaborated after it appeared in the first quarto, where it reads :—

" ——— As I doo remember
Here dwells a Pothecarie whom oft I noted
As I past by, whose needie shop is stufft
With beggerly accounts of emptie boxes :
And in the same an *Aligarta* hangs,
Old ends of packthred, and cakes of Roses,
Are thinly strewed to make vp a show.
Him as I noted, thus with my selfe I thought:
And if a man should need a poyson now,
(Whose present sale is death in *Mantua*)
Here he might buy it. This thought of mine
Did but forerunne my need : and here about he dwels."

(2) SCENE III.—*Tybalt, liest thou there in thy bloody sheet?*] Compare the old poem :—

" Ah cosin dere, Tybalt, where so thy restles sprite now be,
With stretched handes to thee for mercy now I crye,
For that before thy kindly howre I forced thee to dye.
But if with quenched lyfe, not quenched be thine yre,
But with revengeing lust as yet thy hart be set on fyre,
What more amendes or cruel wreke desyrest thou
To see on me, then this which here is shewd forth to thee now?
Who reft by force of armes from thee thy living breath,
The same with his owne hand (thou seest,) doth poyson himselfe to death."

(3) SCENE III.—*Some shall be pardon'd, and some punished.*] "This line has reference to the novel from which the fable is taken. Here we read that Juliet's female attendant was banished for concealing the marriage : Romeo's servant set at liberty, because he had only acted in obedience to his master's orders : the apothecary taken, tortured, condemned and hanged : while Friar Laurence was permitted to retire to a hermitage in the neighbourhood of Verona, where he ended his life in penitence and tranquillity."—STEEVENS.

CRITICAL OPINIONS

ON

ROMEO AND JULIET.

"ROMEO AND JULIET is a picture of love and its pitiable fate, in a world whose atmosphere is too rough for this tenderest blossom of human life. Two beings created for each other feel mutual love at a first glance; every consideration disappears before the irresistible influence of living in one another; they join themselves secretly under circumstances hostile in the highest degree to their union, relying merely on the protection of an invisible power. By unfriendly events, following blow upon blow, their heroic constancy is exposed to all manner of trials, till, forcibly separated from each other, by a voluntary death they are united in the grave to meet again in another world. All this is to be found in the beautiful story which Shakspeare has not invented, and which, however simply told, will always excite a tender sympathy: but it was reserved for Shakspeare to unite purity of heart and the glow of imagination, sweetness and dignity of manners and passionate violence, in one ideal picture. By the manner in which he has handled it, it has become a glorious song of praise on that inexpressible feeling which ennobles the soul and gives to it its highest sublimity, and which elevates even the senses themselves into soul, and, at the same time, is a melancholy elegy on its frailty from its own nature and external circumstances: at once the deification and the burial of love. It appears here like a heavenly spark that, descending to the earth, is converted into a flash of lightning, by which mortal creatures are almost in the same moment set on fire and consumed. Whatever is most intoxicating in the odour of a southern spring, languishing in the song of the nightingale, or voluptuous on the first opening of the rose, is breathed into this poem. But even more rapidly than the earliest blossoms of youth and beauty decay, it hurries on from the first timidly-bold declaration of love and modest return, to the most unlimited passion, to an irrevocable union: then, amidst alternating storms of rapture and despair, to the death of the two lovers, who still appear enviable as their love survives them, and as by their death they have obtained a triumph over every separating power. The sweetest and the bitterest, love and hatred, festivity and dark forebodings, tender embraces and sepulchres, the fulness of life and self-annihilation, are all here brought close to each other: and all these contrasts are so blended, in the harmonious and wonderful work, into a unity of impression, that the echo which the whole leaves behind in the mind, resembles a single but endless sigh."—SCHLEGEL.

"Whence arises the harmony that strikes us in the wildest natural landscapes,—in the relative shapes of rocks, the harmony of colours in the heaths, ferns, and lichens, the leaves of the beech and the oak, the stems and rich brown branches of the birch and other mountain trees, varying from verging autumn to returning spring,—compared with the visual effect from the greater number of artificial plantations?—From this, that the natural landscape is affected, as it were, by a single energy, modified *ab intra* in each component part. And as this is the particular excellence of the Shakspearian drama generally, so is it especially characteristic of the Romeo and Juliet.

"The groundwork of the tale is altogether in family life, and the events of the play have their first origin in family feuds. Filmy as are the eyes of party-spirit, at once dim and truculent, still there is commonly some real or supposed object in view, or principle to be maintained; and though but the twisted wires on the plate of rosin in the preparation for electrical pictures, it is still a guide in some degree, an assimilation to an outline. But in family quarrels, which have proved scarcely less injurious to states, wilfulness and precipitancy, and passion from mere habit and custom, can alone be expected. With his accustomed judgment, Shakspeare has begun by placing before us a lively picture of all the impulses of the play; and, as nature ever presents two sides, one for Heraclitus, and one for Democritus, he has, by way of prelude, shown the laughable absurdity of the evil by the contagion of it reaching the servants, who have so little to do with it, but who are under the necessity of letting the superfluity of sensoreal power fly off through the escape-valve of wit-combats, and of quarrelling with weapons of sharper edge, all in humble imitation of their masters. Yet there is a sort of unhired fidelity, an *ourishness*, about all this that makes it rest pleasant on one's feelings. All the first scene, down to the conclusion of the Prince's speech, is a motley dance of all ranks and ages to one tune, as if the horn of Huon had been playing behind the scenes.

"Benvolio's speech—

> "'Madam, an hour before the worshipp'd sun
> Peer'd forth the golden window of the east'—

and, far more strikingly, the following speech of old Montague—

> "'Many a morning hath he there been seen
> With tears augmenting the fresh morning dew'—

prove that Shakspeare meant the Romeo and Juliet to approach to a poem, which, and indeed its early date, may be also inferred from the multitude of rhyming couplets throughout. And if we are right, from the internal evidence, in pronouncing this one of Shakspeare's early dramas, it affords a strong instance of the fineness of his insight into the nature of the passions, that Romeo is introduced already love-bewildered. The necessity of loving creates an object for itself in man and woman; and yet there is a difference in this respect between the sexes, though only to be known by a perception of it. It would have displeased us if Juliet had been represented as already in love, or as fancying herself so;—but no one, I believe, ever experiences any shock at Romeo's forgetting his Rosaline, who had been a mere name for the yearning of his youthful imagination, and rushing into his passion for Juliet. Rosaline was a mere creation of his fancy; and we should remark the boastful positiveness of Romeo in a love of his own making, which is never shown where love is really near the heart.

> "'When the devout religion of mine eye
> Maintains such falsehood, then turn tears to fires!
> * * * * *
> One fairer than my love! the all-seeing sun
> Ne'er saw her match, since first the world begun.'

"The character of the Nurse is the nearest of anything in Shakspeare to a direct borrowing from mere observation; and the reason is, that as in infancy and childhood the individual in nature is a representative of a class,—just as in describing one larch tree, you generalize a grove of them,—so it is nearly as much so in old age. The generalization is done to the poet's hand. Here you have the garrulity of age strengthened by the feelings of a long-trusted servant, whose sympathy with the mother's affections gives her privileges and rank in the household; and observe the mode of connection by accidents of time and place, and the child-like fondness of repetition in a second childhood, and also that happy, humble, ducking under, yet constant resurgence against, the check of her superiors!—

> "'Yes, madam!—Yet I cannot choose but laugh,' &c.

"In the fourth scene we have Mercutio introduced to us. O! how shall I describe that exquisite ebullience and overflow of youthful life, wafted on over the laughing waves of pleasure and prosperity, as a wanton beauty that distorts the face on which she knows her lover is gazing enraptured, and wrinkles her forehead in the triumph of its smoothness! Wit ever wakeful, fancy busy and procreative as an insect, courage, an easy mind that, without cares of its own, is at once disposed to laugh away those of others, and yet to be interested in them,—these and all congenial qualities, melting into the common *copula* of them all, the man of rank and the gentleman, with all its excellencies and all its weaknesses, constitute the character of Mercutio!"—COLERIDGE.

TAMING OF THE SHREW. Act III. Sc. 2.

THE

TAMING OF THE SHREW.

The earliest copy of this diverting comedy in its present form, yet known, is that of the folio 1623; but in the year 1594 was printed an anonymous play entitled "A Pleasant Conceited Historie, called The taming of a Shrew. As it was sundry times acted by the *Right Honorable the Earle of* Pembrook his seruants. Printed at London by Peter Short and *are to be sold by Cutbert Burbie, at his* shop at the Royall Exchange, 1594," * quarto, which from its remarkable resemblance to the drama acknowledged to be Shakespeare's, may be looked upon almost as a previous edition of the same play. The "Pleasant Conceited Historie," of 1594, has an Induction, the characters of which are, a Noble man, Slie, a Tapster, Page, Players, and Huntsmen. The incidents of this Prelude, and the story, the characters, and the events of the play that follows—with the exception of an underplot taken from George Gascoigne's translation of Ariosto's "*Il Suppositi,*"—all so closely resemble those in Shakespeare's drama, that one was evidently framed upon the other. This remarkable similarity, both in the titles and the contents of these two productions, has been the occasion of much interesting perquisition. The first impression would naturally be that they were by the same hand, and that the latter, wonderfully improved in the spirit of the dialogue and the ease and flow of the verse, was only a revised edition of the other. This was Pope's conjecture, and he acted upon it by boldly transferring passages from the anonymous play into his edition of Shakespeare. In favour of this supposition are the facts, that the authorship of the early play is still unknown,—the almost identity of the titles,—and that Shakespeare's comedy, though undoubtedly written and acted before the beginning of the seventeenth century, was not published, so far as we yet know, before 1623. Another theory, which has been maintained with much ingenuity by Mr. Hickson (see "Notes and Queries," Vol. I, pp. 194, 227, 345), is, that the anonymous comedy was produced after and in direct imitation of Shakespeare's. A third hypothesis gives priority to the "Taming of *a* Shrew," and supposes that our author adopted it as a popular subject, re-casting and re-writing the whole with as much originality as was compatible with a close adherence to the fundamental incidents of his predecessor. This last assumption is perfectly consonant to the customs of the theatre in those days. Nothing was more common than the reproduction of dramas once in vogue, with alterations and additions; and as a close examination and comparison of the two works prove to us convincingly, that the disputed play was neither written by nor borrowed from Shakespeare, we consider this the most satisfactory explanation of their affinity.

History furnishes us with two or three instances of such a trick as that put upon Christopher Sly in the prelude to this comedy, having been perpetrated for the amusement of some distinguished personage. The story of "The Sleeper Awakened" is one of the kind, and Mr. Lane is of opinion that it is founded on a real historical anecdote. In that story the *ruse* practised by the Caliph upon his humble victim is only the introduction to an acquaintance, which leads to a series of entertaining adventures, but it is precisely of the same character as that with which the present play is prefaced. Speaking of "The Sleeper Awakened," Mr. Lane says,— "The author by whom I have found the chief portion of this tale related as an historical

* This, the earliest edition known, is now in the library of the Duke of Devonshire. It was reprinted in 1596, and a copy of that edition is in the possession of Lord Ellesmere. The third impression, that of 1607, is with the first, in the collection of the Duke of Devonshire.

anecdote is El-Is-hakee, who finished his history shortly before the close of the reign of the 'Osmānlee Sultān Mustafa, apparently in the year of the Flight 1032 (A. D. 1623). He does not mention his authority; and whether it is related by an older historian I do not know, but perhaps it is founded upon fact." This is not a very decided expression of opinion on Mr. Lane's part, as to the historical character of the incident; but we find its counterpart in chronicles of the Middle Ages much more specifically related. (See Heuterus, *De Rebus Burgundicis.* Goulart, *Thrésor d'histoires admirables et merveilleuses de notre temps.*)

There is a kindred story, too, recorded by Sir Richard Barkley in "A Discource on the Felicitie of Man," (1598, p. 24,) who relates it as if he had been an eye-witness, and terms it "a pretie experiment practised by the Emperor Charles the Fifth upon a drunkard." His tale is that the Emperor encountered an unconscious drunkard in the streets of Ghent, had him carried home to his palace, dressed in princely habiliments, served by royal attendants, supplied with the most costly dainties, and surrounded by everything calculated to give him the impression that he was a prince of unlimited wealth and authority. As he thus sat "in his Majestie," eating and drinking, "he tooke to his cups so freelie," that he fell fast asleep again as he sat in his chair. His attendants then stripped him of his fresh apparel, clothed him with his own rags again, and carried him to the place where he was first found. When he awoke and joined his companions, he narrated the particulars of his adventure in the palace as the subject of a pleasant dream.

The more immediate source, however, whence the incident of the Induction was taken, is probably an anecdote in an old collection of many tales compiled by Richard Edwards, printed as early as 1570,* which will be found in the Illustrative Comments at the end of the play.

---

* No copy of this edition is now known; but what is believed to be a fragment of a subsequent edition has lately been discovered: and, curiously enough, it contains this particular story, and scarcely anything else.

Persons Represented.

A LORD.
CHRISTOPHER SLY, *a Tinker.*
Hostess, Page, Players, Huntsmen, and other Servants.
} *Characters in the Induction.*

BAPTISTA, *a rich gentleman of* PADUA.
VINCENTIO, *an old gentleman of* PISA.
LUCENTIO, *son to* VINCENTIO, *in love with* BIANCA.
PETRUCHIO, *a gentleman of* VERONA, *suitor to* KATHARINA.
GREMIO, *an old gentleman,* / HORTENSIO, } *suitors to* BIANCA.
TRANIO, / BIONDELLO, } *servants to* LUCENTIO.

GRUMIO, / CURTIS, } *servants to* PETRUCHIO.
The Pedant.

KATHARINA, / BIANCA, } *daughters to* BAPTISTA.
Widow.

Tailor, Haberdasher, and Servants attending on BAPTISTA *and* PETRUCHIO.

SCENE,—*sometimes in* PADUA; *and sometimes in* PETRUCHIO'S *House in the Country.*

INDUCTION.

SCENE I.—*Before an Alehouse on a Heath.*

Enter Hostess *and* Sly.[a]

Sly. I'll pheeze[b] you, in faith.

Host. A pair of stocks, you rogue!

Sly. Y' are a baggage; the Slys are no rogues: look in the chronicles, we came in with Richard Conqueror: therefore, *paucas pallabris;*[c] let the world slide:[d] *Sessa!*

Host. You will not pay for the glasses you have burst?

Sly. No, not a denier: go by, S. Jeronimy[e]—go to thy cold bed, and warm thee.[f]

---

a *Enter* Hostess *and* Sly.] In the old play of "The Taming of a Shrew," we have "*Enter a Tapster, beating out of his doores Slie droonken.*"

b *I'll* pheeze *you,*—] This phrase has been much discussed, but never satisfactorily explained. It was equivalent exactly to our figurative saying, *I'll tickle you*, and had a meaning, amorous or villainous, according to the circumstances under which it was uttered; thus Ricardo, in Beaumont and Fletcher's play of "The Coxcomb," Act I. Sc. 6,—

"Marry, sweet love, e'en here: lie down; [*Seizes her.*
I'll *feese* you."

And Ajax, in "Troilus and Cressida," Act II. Sc. 3,—

"An a be proud with me, I'll *pheeze* his pride."

c Paucas pallabris;] *Pocas palabras—few words*, a phrase of Spain, much in vogue here in the time of Shakespeare. *Sessa* or *cessa, be quiet*, was probably another scrap from Sly's Spanish vocabulary.

d Let the world slide:] An old proverbial saying:—

"———will you go drink,
And *let the world slide*, Uncle?"
Beaumont and Fletcher's *Wit Without Money*, Act V. Sc. 2.

e Go by, S. Jeronimy—] Mason suggested that the troublesome *S* was only the beginning of *says*, which the printers omitted to complete. This is not unlikely; or it may have been repeated inadvertently from the initial of Sly's name. The *Go by, Jeronimy*, is plainly an allusion to the old play called "The Spanish Tragedy," and the line,—

"Not I:—*Hieronimo*, beware! *go by, go by*."

f Go to thy cold bed, and warm thee.] Edgar, in "King Lear," uses the same expression,—

"Humph: go to thy cold bed and warm thee."
Act III. Sc. 4.

HOST. I know my remedy, I must go fetch the thirdborough.* [*Exit.*

SLY. Third, or fourth, or fifth borough, I'll answer him by law: I'll not budge an inch, boy; let him come, and kindly.

[*Lies down on the ground, and falls asleep.*

Wind horns. Enter a Lord *from hunting, with his Train.*

LORD. Huntsman, I charge thee, tender well my hounds:
Brach Merriman,—the poor cur is emboss'd;[a]
And couple Clowder with the deep-mouth'd brach.
Saw'st thou not, boy, how Silver made it good
At the hedge corner, in the coldest fault?
I would not lose the dog for twenty pound.

1 HUN. Why, Belman is as good as he, my lord;
He cried upon it at the merest loss,
And twice to-day pick'd out the dullest scent:
Trust me, I take him for the better dog.

LORD. Thou art a fool; if Echo were as fleet,
I would esteem him worth a dozen such.
But sup them well, and look unto them all;
To-morrow I intend to hunt again.

1 HUN. I will, my lord.

LORD. What's here? one dead, or drunk? see, doth he breathe?

2 HUN. He breathes, my lord: were he not warm'd with ale,
This were a bed but cold to sleep so soundly.

LORD. O monstrous beast! how like a swine he lies!
Grim death, how foul and loathsome is thine image!
Sirs, I will practise on this drunken man.
What think you, if he were convey'd to bed,
Wrapp'd in sweet clothes, rings put upon his fingers,
A most delicious banquet by his bed,
And brave attendants near him when he wakes,
Would not the beggar then forget himself?

1 HUN. Believe me, lord, I think he cannot choose.

2 HUN. It would seem strange unto him when he wak'd.

LORD. Even as a flattering dream, or worthless fancy.
Then take him up, and manage well the jest:—
Carry him gently to my fairest chamber,
And hang it round with all my wanton pictures:
Balm his foul head in warm distilled waters,
And burn sweet wood to make the lodging sweet:
Procure me music ready when he wakes,
To make a dulcet and a heavenly sound;
And if he chance to speak, be ready straight,
And, with a low submissive reverence,
Say,—What is it your honour will command?
Let one attend him with a silver bason,
Full of rose-water, and bestrew'd with flowers;
Another bear the ewer, the third a diaper,
And say,—Will 't please your lordship cool your hands?
Some one be ready with a costly suit,
And ask him what apparel he will wear;
Another tell him of his hounds and horse,
And that his lady mourns at his disease:
Persuade him that he hath been lunatic;
And, when he says he is—,[b] say, that he dreams,
For he is nothing but a mighty lord.
This do, and do it kindly,[c] gentle sirs;
It will be pastime passing excellent,
If it be husbanded with modesty.[d]

1 HUN. My lord, I warrant you, we'll play our part,
As he shall think, by our true diligence,
He is no less than what we say he is.

LORD. Take him up gently and to bed with him;
And each one to his office, when he wakes.

[*Some bear out* SLY. *A trumpet sounds.*

Sirrah, go see what trumpet 't is that sounds:

[*Exit* Servant.

Belike, some noble gentleman, that means,
Travelling some journey, to repose him here.

Re-enter a Servant.

How now? who is it?

SERV. An 't please your honour, players,
That offer service to your lordship.

LORD. Bid them come near.

Enter Players.(1)

Now, fellows, you are welcome.

PLAYERS. We thank your honour.

LORD. Do you intend to stay with me to-night?

2 PLAY. So please your lordship to accept our duty.

LORD. With all my heart. This fellow I remember,
Since once he play'd a farmer's eldest son;—
'T was where you woo'd the gentlewoman so well:

(*) Old copy, *headborough.*

[a] Brach Merriman,—the poor cur is emboss'd;] There is a difficulty here. "A *brach* is a *mannerly-name* for all hound-bitches," says an old book on sports; and *Merriman* could hardly be the name given to the female animal. Hanmer, therefore, proposed to read Leech Merriman; and Johnson, *Bathe* Merriman. *Emboss'd* is a term in hunting, applied to a deer or dog who foams at the mouth.

[b] And, when he says he is——,] The dash here is a modern interpolation, but Shakespeare evidently intended a break, leaving Sly's name to be understood; the Lord not being supposed to know what that was. Hanmer proposed to insert *poor*, and Johnson, *Sly*.

[c] *And do it* kindly,—] *Appropriately, naturally.*

[d] If it be husbanded *with* modesty.] That is, if it be kept within due bounds. If it be managed discreetly.

I have forgot your name; but, sure, that part
Was aptly fitted, and naturally perform'd.

1 PLAY. I think, 't was Soto that your honour means.[a]

LORD. 'T is very true;—thou didst it excellent.—
Well, you are come to me in happy time;
The rather for I have some sport in hand,
Wherein your cunning can assist me much.
There is a lord will hear you play to-night:
But I am doubtful of your modesties;
Lest, over-eyeing of his odd behaviour,
(For yet his honour never heard a play,)
You break into some merry passion,
And so offend him; for I tell you, sirs,
If you should smile, he grows impatient.

1 PLAY. Fear not, my lord; we can contain ourselves,
Were he the veriest antic in the world.

LORD. Go, sirrah, take them to the buttery,
And give them friendly welcome every one:
Let them want nothing that my house affords.—
[*Exeunt* Servant *and* Players.
Sirrah, go you to Bartholomew, my page,
[*To a* Servant.
And see him dress'd in all suits like a lady:
That done, conduct him to the drunkard's chamber,
And call him—madam, do him obeisance.
Tell him from me, as he will win my love,
He bear himself with honourable action,
Such as he hath observ'd in noble ladies
Unto their lords, by them accomplished:
Such duty to the drunkard let him do,
With soft low tongue, and lowly courtesy;
And say,—What is 't your honour will command,
Wherein your lady, and your humble wife,
May show her duty, and make known her love?
And then,—with kind embracements, tempting kisses,
And with declining head into his bosom,—
Bid him shed tears, as being overjoy'd
To see her noble lord restor'd to health,
Who, for this seven years, hath esteemed him[b]
No better than a poor and loathsome beggar:
And if the boy have not a woman's gift,
To rain a shower of commanded tears,
An onion will do well for such a shift;
Which in a napkin being close conveyed,[c]
Shall in despite enforce a watery eye.
See this despatch'd with all the haste thou canst;
Anon I'll give thee more instructions.
[*Exit* Servant.
I know the boy will well usurp the grace,
Voice, gait, and action of a gentlewoman:
I long to hear him call the drunkard, husband;
And how my men will stay themselves from laughter,
When they do homage to this simple peasant.
I'll in to counsel them: haply, my presence
May well abate the over-merry spleen,
Which otherwise would grow into extremes.
[*Exeunt.*

SCENE II.—*A Bedchamber in the* Lord's *house.*

SLY *is discovered*[d] *in a rich night-gown, with* Attendants; *some with apparel, some with bason, ewer, and other appurtenances. Enter* Lord, *dressed like a servant.*(2)

SLY. For God's sake, a pot of small ale.

1 SERV. Will 't please your lordship drink a cup of sack?

2 SERV. Will 't please your honour taste of these conserves?

3 SERV. What raiment will your honour wear to-day?

SLY. I am Christophero Sly; call not me *honour*, nor *lordship:* I ne'er drank sack in my life; and if you give me any conserves, give me conserves of beef: ne'er ask me what raiment I'll wear; for I have no more doublets than backs, no more stockings than legs, nor no more shoes than feet; nay, sometime, more feet than shoes, or such shoes as my toes look through the over-leather.

LORD. Heaven cease this idle humour in your honour!
O, that a mighty man of such descent,
Of such possessions, and so high esteem,
Should be infused with so foul a spirit!

SLY. What! would you make me mad? Am not I Christopher Sly, old Sly's son, of Burton-heath; by birth a pedlar, by education a card-maker, by transmutation a bear-herd, and now by present profession a tinker? Ask Marian Hacket, the fat ale-wife of Wincot,[e] if she know me not: if she say I am not fourteen pence on the score for sheer ale,[f] score me up for the lyingest knave

---

[a] *I think, 't was* Soto that your honour means.] The folio, 1623, prefixes the name of *Sinclo* to this line. Sinclo was an actor of minor parts in Shakespeare's fellowship of players; and this allusion to his excellence in *Soto* must have been flattering to him, and was no doubt pleasant to the audience. He is introduced by name again, in the "Second Part of Henry IV," and "Part Three of Henry VI."

[b] *Hath esteemed* him—] *Him*, here, is used for *himself.*

[c] Close *conveyed,*—] By *stealth* conveyed.

[d] Sly is discovered—] The stage direction in the folio is, "*Enter aloft the drunkard with attendants, some with apparel, bason and ewer, and other appurtenances, and Lord;*" by which it is to be understood that Sly, and those concerned in the induction, were placed in a balcony, at the back of the stage, the play being represented on the stage before them. This practice is reversed in the present day; the play within a play, as in Hamlet, being always exhibited on a temporary stage, behind the permanent one, on which the performers enact the main drama.

[e] Of Wincot,—] By *Wincot* the poet no doubt meant *Wilnecote*, commonly called *Wincot*, a village near Stratford; and the fat hostess was probably a real personage equally well-known to him. It is supposed, too, that the *Burton-heath* Sly speaks of just before, was *Barton-on-the-Heath*, in Warwickshire.

[f] Sheer *ale,*—] That is, *pure, unmixed* ale; as our brewers say, "*Entire* beer." In Beaumont and Fletcher's play of "The Double Marriage," Act V. Sc. 1, Castruccio is permitted to drink but wine and water; and he asks indignantly,—

"Shall I have no *sheer* wine then?"

in Christendom. What! I am not bestraught:[a]
here 's——

3 SERV. O, this it is that makes your lady mourn.

2 SERV. O, this it is that makes your servants droop.

LORD. Hence comes it that your kindred shuns your house,
As beaten hence by your strange lunacy.
O, noble lord, bethink thee of thy birth,
Call home thy ancient thoughts from banishment,
And banish hence these abject lowly dreams.
Look how thy servants do attend on thee,
Each in his office ready at thy beck.
Wilt thou have music? hark! Apollo plays, [*Music.*
And twenty caged nightingales do sing:
Or wilt thou sleep? we 'll have thee to a couch,
Softer and sweeter than the lustful bed
On purpose trimm'd up for Semiramis.
Say, thou wilt walk: we will bestrew the ground:
Or wilt thou ride? thy horses shall be trapp'd,
Their harness studded all with gold and pearl.
Dost thou love hawking? thou hast hawks will soar
Above the morning lark: or wilt thou hunt?
Thy hounds shall make the welkin answer them,
And fetch shrill echoes from the hollow earth.

1 SERV. Say, thou wilt course; thy greyhounds are as swift
As breathed stags, ay, fleeter than the roe.

2 SERV. Dost thou love pictures? we will fetch thee straight,
Adonis, painted by a running brook;
And Cytherea all in sedges hid,
Which seem to move and wanton with her breath,
Even as the waving sedges play with wind.

LORD. We 'll show thee Io, as she was a maid;
And how she was beguiled and surpris'd,
As lively painted as the deed was done.

3 SERV. Or Daphne, roaming through a thorny wood;
Scratching her legs that one shall swear she bleeds:
And at that sight shall sad Apollo weep,
So workmanly the blood and tears are drawn.

LORD. Thou art a lord, and nothing but a lord:
Thou hast a lady far more beautiful
Than any woman in this waning age.

1 SERV. And, till the tears that she hath shed for thee,
Like envious floods o'er-run her lovely face,
She was the fairest creature in the world;
And yet she is inferior to none.

SLY. Am I a lord? and have I such a lady?
Or do I dream, or have I dream'd till now?
I do not sleep: I see, I hear, I speak;
I smell sweet savours, and I feel soft things:—
Upon my life, I am a lord, indeed;
And not a tinker, nor Christopher Sly.—
Well, bring our lady hither to our sight;
And, once again, a pot o' the smallest ale.

2 SERV. Will 't please your mightiness to wash your hands?

[Servants *present an ewer, bason, and napkin.*

O, how we joy to see your wit restor'd!
O, that once more you knew but what you are!
These fifteen years you have been in a dream;
Or, when you wak'd, so wak'd as if you slept.

SLY. These fifteen years? by my fay, a goodly nap.
But did I never speak of all that time?

1 SERV. O yes, my lord; but very idle words:—
For though you lay here in this goodly chamber,
Yet would you say ye were beaten out of door,
And rail upon the hostess of the house;
And say, you would present her at the leet,[b]
Because she brought stone jugs and no seal'd quarts:
Sometimes you would call out for Cicely Hacket.

SLY. Ay, the woman's maid of the house.

3 SERV. Why, sir, you know no house, nor no such maid;
Nor no such men, as you have reckon'd up,—
As Stephen Sly, and old John Naps of Greece,[c]
And Peter Turf, and Henry Pimpernell;
And twenty more such names and men as these,
Which never were, nor no man ever saw.

SLY. Now, Lord be thanked for my good amends!

ALL. Amen.

SLY. I thank thee; thou shalt not lose by it.

Enter the Page, *as a lady, with* Attendants.(3)

PAGE. How fares my noble lord?

SLY. Marry, I fare well: for here is cheer enough.
Where is my wife?

PAGE Here, noble lord, what is thy will with her?

SLY. Are you my wife, and will not call me husband?
My men should call me lord; I am your goodman.

PAGE. My husband and my lord, my lord and husband;
I am your wife in all obedience.

SLY. I know it well. What must I call her?

LORD. Madam.

SLY. Al'ce madam, or Joan madam?

---

[a] Bestraught:] *Distraught, distracted:—*

"Now teares had drowned further speech, till she as one *bestrought*
Did crie," &c.—WARNER'S *Albion's England*, 1602.

[b] *You would present her at the* leet,—] That is, the *Court-leet*, where parties in the practice of using false weights and measures were presentable and punishable. The *seal'd quarts* were the licensed quart measures, certified by stamp to be capable of holding that quantity of liquid.

[c] *Old John Naps of* Greece,—] Probably *o' th' Green*, as Blackstone suggested.

LORD. Madam, and nothing else; so lords call ladies.

SLY. Madam wife, they say that I have dream'd,
And slept above some fifteen year or more.

PAGE. Ay, and the time seems thirty unto me;
Being all this time abandon'd from your bed.

SLY. 'Tis much: servants, leave me and her alone.
Madam, undress you, and come now to bed.

PAGE. Thrice noble lord, let me entreat of you
To pardon me yet for a night or two;
Or, if not so, until the sun be set:
For your physicians have expressly charg'd,
In peril to incur your former malady,
That I should yet absent me from your bed:
I hope, this reason stands for my excuse.

SLY. Ay, it stands so, that I may hardly tarry so long, but I would be loth to fall into my dreams again; I will therefore tarry, in despite of the flesh and the blood.

Enter a Servant.

SERV. Your honour's players, hearing your amendment,
Are come to play a pleasant comedy,
For so your doctors hold it very meet.
Seeing too much sadness hath congeal'd your blood,
And melancholy is the nurse of frenzy;
Therefore, they thought it good you hear a play,
And frame your mind to mirth and merriment,
Which bars a thousand harms, and lengthens life.

SLY. Marry, I will let them play. Is it not a commonty, a Christmas gambol, or a tumbling-trick?

PAGE. No, my good lord: it is more pleasing stuff.

SLY. What, household stuff?

PAGE. It is a kind of history.

SLY. Well, we'll see 't:
Come, madam wife, sit by my side,
And let the world slip; we shall ne'er be younger.
[*They sit down.*

ACT I.

SCENE I.—Padua. *A Public Place.*

Enter LUCENTIO *and* TRANIO.

LUC. Tranio,—since for the great desire I had
To see fair Padua, nursery of arts,—
I am arriv'd for fruitful Lombardy,
The pleasant garden of great Italy;
And, by my father's love and leave, am arm'd
With his good will, and thy good company,
My trusty servant, well approv'd in all;
Here let us breathe, and haply institute
A course of learning, and ingenious studies.
Pisa, renowned for grave citizens,
Gave me my being, and my father first,
A merchant of great traffic through the world:
Vincentio 's come of the Bentivolii;[a]
Vincentio's son, brought up in Florence,
It shall become, to serve all hopes conceiv'd,
To deck his fortune with his virtuous deeds:
And therefore, Tranio, for the time I study,
Virtue, and that part of philosophy
Will I apply,[b] that treats of happiness
By virtue specially to be achiev'd.

---

[a] Vincentio's come of the Bentivolii;] Thus the old copy; most modern editions read,—

" Vincentio, come of the Bentivolii."

But Tranio, it should be remembered, is the servant of Vincentio, has been brought up by him from childhood; and although for dramatic exigencies it might be allowable to inform him that his master was descended from the Bentivolii, nothing could excuse the absurdity of telling him this master's name.

[b] Will I apply,—] *Apply* is here used, as it is frequently found in old writers, in the sense of *ply*. So in Gascoigne's "Supposes," 1566, from which Shakespeare borrowed the underplot of this comedy,—" I feare he *applyes* his study so, that he will not leave the minute of an houre from his booke."

Tell me thy mind, for I have Pisa left,
And am to Padua come, as he that leaves
A shallow plash, to plunge him in the deep,
And with satiety seeks to quench his thirst.

TRA. *Mi perdonate,** gentle master mine,
I am in all affected as yourself;
Glad that you thus continue your resolve,
To suck the sweets of sweet philosophy.
Only, good master, while we do admire
This virtue, and this moral discipline,
Let 's be no stoics, nor no stocks, I pray;
Or so devote to Aristotle's checks,[a]
As Ovid be an outcast quite abjur'd:
Balk logic[b] with acquaintance that you have,
And practise rhetoric in your common talk:
Music and poesy use to quicken you;
The mathematics, and the metaphysics,
Fall to them, as you find your stomach serves you:
No profit grows where is no pleasure ta'en;—
In brief, sir, study what you most affect.

LUC. Gramercies, Tranio, well dost thou advise.
If, Biondello, thou wert come ashore,
We could at once put us in readiness;
And take a lodging, fit to entertain
Such friends as time in Padua shall beget.
But stay awhile; what company is this?

TRA. Master, some show, to welcome us to town.

Enter BAPTISTA, KATHARINA, BIANCA, GREMIO,(1) *and* HORTENSIO. LUCENTIO *and* TRANIO *stand aside.*

BAP. Gentlemen, impórtune me no farther,
For how I firmly am resolv'd you know:
That is, not to bestow my youngest daughter,
Before I have a husband for the elder:
If either of you both love Katharina,
Because I know you well, and love you well,
Leave shall you have to court her at your pleasure.

GRE. To cart her rather: she 's too rough for me:
There, there, Hortensio, will you any wife?

KATH. I pray you, sir, [*to* BAP.] is it your will
To make a stale of me amongst these mates?[c]

HOR. Mates, maid! how mean you that? no mates for you,
Unless you were of gentler, milder mould.

KATH. I' faith, sir, you shall never need to fear;
I—wis,(2) it is not half way to her heart:
But, if it were, doubt not her care should be
To comb your noddle with a three-legg'd stool,
And paint your face, and use you like a fool.

HOR. From all such devils, good Lord, deliver us!

GRE. And me too, good Lord!

TRA. Hush, master! here is some good pastime toward;
That wench is stark mad, or wonderful froward.

LUC. But in the other's silence do I see
Maids' mild behaviour and sobriety.
Peace, Tranio.

TRA. Well said, master; mum! and gaze your fill.

BAP. Gentlemen, that I may soon make good
What I have said, Bianca, get you in:
And let it not displease thee, good Bianca;
For I will love thee ne'er the less, my girl.

KATH. A pretty peat;[d] 't is best
Put finger in the eye—an she knew why.

BIAN. Sister, content you in my discontent.
Sir, to your pleasure humbly I subscribe:
My books and instruments shall be my company,
On them to look, and practise by myself.

LUC. Hark, Tranio! thou mayst hear Minerva speak. [*Aside.*

HOR. Signior Baptista, will you be so strange?
Sorry am I that our good will effects
Bianca's grief.

GRE. Why, will you mew her,
Signior Baptista, for this fiend of hell,
And make her bear the penance of her tongue?

BAP. Gentlemen, content ye; I am resolv'd:
Go in, Bianca. [*Exit* BIANCA.
And, for I know she taketh most delight
In music, instruments, and poetry,
Schoolmasters will I keep within my house,
Fit to instruct her youth.—If you, Hortensio,
Or signior Gremio, you,—know any such,
Prefer them[e] hither; for to cunning men[f]
I will be very kind, and liberal
To mine own children in good bringing-up;
And so farewell. Katharina, you may stay;
For I have more to commune with Bianca. [*Exit.*

KATH. Why, and I trust I may go, too, may I not?
What, shall I be appointed hours; as though, belike,
I knew not what to take, and what to leave, ha! [*Exit.*

GRE. You may go to the devil's dam; your gifts are so good here 's none will hold you.

(*) First folio, *Me Pardonato.*

[a] Aristotle's checks,] Blackstone proposed to read *ethics*, and *ethics* is the word substituted in the margin of his folio by Mr. Collier's annotator.

[b] Balk *logic*—] To *balk logic* meant to *chop logic*, to *dispute*, to *wrangle* logically, for the sake of exercise in reasoning. This sense of *balk* is now quite lost.

[c] To *make* a stale of *me amongst these* mates?] The primary meaning is, "Will you make a common harlot of me with these fellows?" but Douce is probably right in suspecting a quibbling allusion to the term *stale-mate* in chess.

[d] *A pretty* peat;] A *pet*, from the French *petite*, or Italian *petto*.

[e] Prefer *them*—] *Prefer* is defined to mean *recommend;* it seems to have implied something more, as to *advance*, or *promote*.

[f] Cunning *men*—] Knowing, skilful men.

Their love is not so great,[a] Hortensio, but we may blow our nails together, and fast it fairly out; our cake 's dough[b] on both sides. Farewell:—yet, for the love I bear my sweet Bianca, if I can by any means light on a fit man to teach her that wherein she delights, I will wish him to her father.[c]

HOR. So will I, signior Gremio: but a word, I pray. Though the nature of our quarrel yet never brooked parle, know now, upon advice, it toucheth us both,—that we may yet again have access to our fair mistress, and be happy rivals in Bianca's love,—to labour and effect one thing specially.

GRE. What 's that, I pray?

HOR. Marry, sir, to get a husband for her sister.

GRE. A husband! a devil.

HOR. I say, a husband.

GRE. I say, a devil: think'st thou, Hortensio, though her father be very rich, any man is so very a fool to be married to hell?

HOR. Tush! Gremio; though it pass your patience and mine to endure her loud alarums, why, man, there be good fellows in the world, an a man could light on them, would take her with all faults, and money enough.

GRE. I cannot tell; but I had as lief take her dowry with this condition,—to be whipped at the high-cross every morning.

HOR. 'Faith, as you say, there 's small choice in rotten apples; but, come, since this bar in law makes us friends, it shall be so far forth friendly maintained, till by helping Baptista's eldest daughter to a husband, we set his youngest free for a husband, and then have to 't afresh.—Sweet Bianca!—happy man be his dole![d] He that runs fastest gets the ring:[e] how say you, signior Gremio?

GRE. I am agreed: and would I had given him the best horse in Padua to begin his wooing, that would thoroughly woo her, wed her, and bed her, and rid the house of her. Come on.

[*Exeunt* GREMIO *and* HORTENSIO.

TRA. [*Advancing.*] I pray, sir, tell me,—is it possible
That love should of a sudden take such hold?

LUC. O Tranio, till I found it to be true,
I never thought it possible, or likely;
But see! while idly I stood looking on,
I found the effect of love in idleness:[f]
And now in plainness do confess to thee,
That art to me as secret, and as dear,
As Anna to the queen of Carthage was,—
Tranio, I burn, I pine, I perish, Tranio,
If I achieve not this young modest girl:
Counsel me, Tranio, for I know thou canst;
Assist me, Tranio, for I know thou wilt.

TRA. Master, it is no time to chide you now;
Affection is not rated from the heart:
If love have touch'd you, nought remains but so,—
Redime te captum quam queas minimo.

LUC. Gramercies, lad; go forward, this contents;
The rest will comfort, for thy counsel 's sound.

TRA. Master, you look'd so longly on the maid,
Perhaps you mark'd not what 's the pith of all.

LUC. O yes, I saw sweet beauty in her face,
Such as the daughter of Agenor[g] had,
That made great Jove to humble him to her hand,
When with his knees he kiss'd the Cretan strand.

TRA. Saw you no more? mark'd you not, how her sister
Began to scold; and raise up such a storm,
That mortal ears might hardly endure the din?

LUC. Tranio, I saw her coral lips to move,
And with her breath she did perfume the air;
Sacred, and sweet, was all I saw in her.

TRA. Nay, then, 't is time to stir him from his trance.
I pray, awake, sir: if you love the maid,
Bend thoughts and wits to achieve her. Thus it stands:—
Her elder sister is so curst and shrew'd,
That, till the father rids his hands of her,
Master, your love must live a maid at home;
And therefore has he closely mew'd her up,
Because she will[h] not be annoy'd with suitors.

LUC. Ah, Tranio, what a cruel father 's he!
But art thou not advis'd he took some care,
To get her cunning schoolmasters to instruct her?

TRA. Ay, marry, am I, sir; and now, 'tis plotted.

---

[a] Their *love is not so great*,—] Whose love? Perhaps, as Malone suggested, we ought to read *your* love; or with the third folio, *our* love.

[b] Our *cake's* dough—] Our hopes are frustrated; a proverbial saying. It occurs again, Act V. Sc. 1.:—

"My cake is dough."

And in "The Case is Altered," 1609,—

"Steward, your cake is dough, as well as mine."

[c] I *will* wish *him to her father*.] I will *commend* him. So in Act I. Sc. 2, Hortensio says, "And *wish* thee to a shrew'd, ill-favour'd wife."

[d] Happy man be his dole!] This trite phrase means literally, Let the share or lot dealt to him be happiness; but it was generally used in the sense of encouragement, as wishing good success to any one about to undertake a contest, or business of doubtful issue:—

"Now, my masters, *happy man be his dole*, say I
Every man to his business."—*Henry* IV. Pt. I. Act II. Sc. 2.

[e] *He that runs fastest gets the* ring:] An allusion, Douce remarks, "to the sport of running at the ring." Rather to the sport of running *for* the ring. A *ring* was one of the prizes formerly given in wrestling and running matches.

[f] *The effect of* love in idleness:] *Love in idleness* was a favourite flower, often mentioned by old authors.

[g] The daughter of Agenor—] *Europa*.

[h] *Because she* will *not*—] So the old copy. Several of the modern editors needlessly substitute *shall* for *will*.

LUC. I have it, Tranio.

TRA. Master, for my hand,
Both our inventions meet and jump in one.

LUC. Tell me thine first.

TRA. You will be schoolmaster,
And undertake the teaching of the maid:
That 's your device.

LUC. It is: may it be done?

TRA. Not possible: for who shall bear your part,
And be in Padua here Vincentio's son?
Keep house, and ply his book; welcome his friends;
Visit his countrymen, and banquet them?

LUC. Basta;[a] content thee; for I have it full.
We have not yet been seen in any house;
Nor can we be distinguish'd by our faces,
For man or master: then it follows thus;—
Thou shalt be master, Tranio, in my stead,
Keep house, and port,[b] and servants, as I should:
I will some other be; some Florentine,
Some Neapolitan, or meaner man of Pisa.
'T is hatch'd, and shall be so:—Tranio, at once
Uncase thee; take my colour'd hat and cloak:
When Biondello comes, he waits on thee;
But I will charm him first to keep his tongue.

TRA. So had you need. [*They exchange habits.*
In brief, sir, sith it your pleasure is,
And I am tied to be obedient,
(For so your father charg'd me at our parting;
Be serviceable to my son, quoth he,
Although, I think, 't was in another sense,)
I am content to be Lucentio,
Because so well I love Lucentio.

LUC. Tranio, be so, because Lucentio loves:
And let me be a slave, t' achieve that maid
Whose sudden sight hath thrall'd my wounded eye.

Enter BIONDELLO.

Here comes the rogue.—Sirrah, where have you been?

BION. Where have I been? nay, how now, where are you?
Master, has my fellow Tranio stol'n your clothes?
Or you stol'n his? or both? Pray, what's the news?

LUC. Sirrah, come hither; 't is no time to jest,
And therefore frame your manners to the time.
Your fellow Tranio here, to save my life,
Puts my apparel and my countenance on,
And I for my escape have put on his;
For in a quarrel, since I came ashore,
I kill'd a man, and fear I was descried.
Wait you on him, I charge you, as becomes,
While I make way from hence to save my life;
You understand me?

BION. I, sir? ne'er a whit.

LUC. And not a jot of Tranio in your mouth;
Tranio is chang'd into Lucentio.

BION. The better for him; would I were so too!

TRA. So would I,* faith, boy, to have the next wish after,—
That Lucentio indeed had Baptista's youngest daughter.
But, sirrah, not for my sake, but your master's, I advise
You use your manners discreetly in all kind of companies:
When I am alone, why, then I am Tranio;
But in all places else, your master Lucentio.

LUC. Tranio, let 's go:—
One thing more rests, that thyself execute;
To make one among these wooers: if thou ask me why,—
Sufficeth, my reasons are both good and weighty.
[*Exeunt.*

(*The Presenters above speak.*)[c]

1 SERV. *My lord, you nod; you do not mind the play.*

SLY. *Yes, by saint Anne, do I, a good matter, surely; comes there any more of it?*

PAGE. *My lord, 't is but begun.*

SLY. *'T is a very excellent piece of work, madam lady. 'Would 't were done!*
[*They sit and mark.*

SCENE II.—*The same. Before* Hortensio's *House.*

Enter PETRUCHIO *and* GRUMIO.

PET. Verona, for a while I take my leave,
To see my friends in Padua; but, of all,
My best beloved and approved friend,
Hortensio; and, I trow, this is his house:
Here, sirrah Grumio; knock, I say.

GRU. Knock, sir! whom should I knock? is there any man has rebused your worship?

---

[a] Basta;] *Enough*, Italian and Spanish.
[b] Port,—] That is, *show, state appearance*. Thus Bassanio, "Merchant of Venice," Act I. Sc. 1, attributes his diminished fortunes
"To something showing a more swelling *port*"
than his means warranted.

(*) First folio, *could*.

[c] *The Presenters above speak.*] This is the original stage direction; the *presenters* meaning Sly, &c., who are seated in the balcony behind.

PET. Villain, I say, knock me here[a] soundly.
GRU. Knock you here, sir? why, sir, what am I, sir, that I should knock you here, sir?
PET. Villain, I say, knock me at this gate,
And rap me well, or I'll knock your knave's pate.
GRU. My master is grown quarrelsome: I should knock you first,
And then I know after who comes by the worst.
PET. Will it not be?
'Faith, sirrah, an you'll not knock, I'll wring it;
I'll try how you can *sol, fa*, and sing it.
[*He wrings* GRUMIO *by the ears.*
GRU. Help, masters,[b] help! my master is mad.
PET. Now, knock when I bid you, sirrah villain!

[a] *Knock* me *here*—] An idiom, not unfrequent in old English writers, and which is familiar, Mr. Singer observes, in the French language:—

"——— Ah! mon Dieu! je vous prie,
Avant que de parler, prenez-*moi* ce mouchoir."
MOLIÈRE'S *Tartuffe*, Act III. Sc. 2.

And M. Dumarsais, in his "Principes de Grammaire," p. 388, thinks the same expletive form of speech is to be found in "The Heautontimorumenos" of Terence, Act I. Sc. 4.:—

"Fac *me* ut sciam."

[b] *Help*, masters,—] The old copy has, *mistris*. If this was not intentional, the mistake arose from the words *Master* and *Mistress* in ancient manuscripts being both denoted by the letter *M*.

Enter HORTENSIO.

HOR. How now? what 's the matter?—my old friend Grumio! and my good friend Petruchio![a]—how do you all at Verona?

PET. Signior Hortensio, come you to part the fray?
Con tutto il core bene trovato, may I say.

HOR. *Alla nostra casa bene venuto,*
Molto honorato signor mio Petrucio.
Rise, Grumio, rise; we will compound this quarrel.

GRU. Nay, 't is no matter, sir, what he 'leges in Latin.[b]—If this be not a lawful cause for me to leave his service,—look you, sir,—he bid me knock him, and rap him soundly, sir. Well, was it fit for a servant to use his master so; being, perhaps, (for aught I see,) two-and-thirty,—a pip out?[c]
Whom, would to God, I had well knock'd at first,
Then had not Grumio come by the worst.

PET. A senseless villain!—good Hortensio,
I bade the rascal knock upon your gate,
And could not get him for my heart to do it.

GRU. Knock at the gate?—O heavens!
Spake you not these words plain,—*Sirrah, knock me here,*
Rap me here, knock me well, and knock me soundly?
And come you now with—knocking at the gate?

PET. Sirrah, be gone, or talk not, I advise you.

HOR. Petruchio, patience; I am Grumio's pledge:
Why, this a heavy chance 'twixt him and you;
Your ancient, trusty, pleasant servant, Grumio!
And tell me now, sweet friend,—what happy gale
Blows you to Padua here, from old Verona?

PET. Such wind as scatters young men through the world,
To seek their fortunes farther than at home,
Where small experience grows. But, in a few,[d]
Signior Hortensio, thus it stands with me:
Antonio, my father, is deceas'd;
And I have thrust myself into this maze,
Haply to wive, and thrive, as best I may:
Crowns in my purse I have, and goods at home,
And so am come abroad to see the world.

HOR. Petruchio, shall I then come roundly to thee,
And wish thee to a shrew'd ill-favour'd wife?
Thou 'dst thank me but a little for my counsel,
And yet I'll promise thee she shall be rich,
And very rich:—but thou 'rt too much my friend,
And I'll not wish thee to her.

PET. Signior Hortensio, 'twixt such friends as we
Few words suffice; and, therefore, if thou know
One rich enough to be Petruchio's wife,
(As wealth is burthen of my wooing dance,)
Be she as foul as was Florentius' love,[e]
As old as Sibyl, and as curst and shrew'd
As Socrates' Xantippe, or a worse,
She moves me not; or not removes, at least,
Affection's edge in me, were she as rough[f]
As are the swelling Adriatic seas.
I come to wive it wealthily in Padua;
If wealthily, then happily in Padua.

GRU. Nay, look you, sir, he tells you flatly what his mind is: why, give him gold enough and marry him to a puppet, or an aglet-baby;[g] or an old trot with ne'er a tooth in her head, though she have as many diseases as two-and-fifty horses. Why, nothing comes amiss, so money comes withal.

HOR. Petruchio, since we are stepp'd thus far in,
I will continue that I broach'd in jest.
I can, Petruchio, help thee to a wife
With wealth enough, and young, and beauteous;
Brought up as best becomes a gentlewoman:
Her only fault (and that is faults enough)
Is,—that she is intolerable curst;
And shrew'd, and froward, so beyond all measure,
That, were my state far worser than it is,
I would not wed her for a mine of gold.

PET. Hortensio, peace; thou know'st not gold's effect:
Tell me her father's name, and 'tis enough;
For I will board her, though she chide as loud

---

a Petruchio!] In "The Supposes" this name is spelt correctly, *Petrucio*; and Malone suggests that Shakespeare wrote it *Petruchio* for the purpose of teaching the actors the right pronunciation.

b *Nay, 'tis no matter, what* he 'leges *in Latin.*—] Grumio, a native of Italy, is here made to mistake his own language for Latin! It is true that he speaks English all through the play, and Shakespeare might have thought of him only as a type of this country; but I am strongly in favour of Tyrwhitt's proposal to read, "Nay, 'tis no matter, sir, what *be leges*, in Latin, if this be not a lawful cause for me to leave his service," &c. The amendment is effected by the change of a single letter, and we obtain from it a very natural and humorous rejoinder, "'Tis no matter what is *law*, if this be not a lawful cause," &c. By the way, upon what plea do the majority of modern editors omit the *sir* in this passage?

c Two-and-thirty,—a pip out?] A *pip* is a spot upon a card, and the allusion is to the now obsolete diversion of *Bone-ace, or one-and-thirty*. So in Massinger's play of "The Fatal Dowry," Act II. Sc. 2,—

"You think, because you served my lady's mother, are *thirty-two years* old, which is *a pip out*, you know ——"

d *But, in* a few,—] *In a few* means, *in short, to be brief, in a few words.*

e Florentius' love,—] This refers to a story in Gower's "Confessio Amantis," b. I., where the hero, a knight named *Florent*, bound himself to marry a deformed hag on the condition that she taught him the solution of an enigma on which his life depended. The legend is very ancient and has been often repeated.

f *Were* she as *rough*—] The first folio reads, "Were she *is* as rough," which was corrected in the second folio.

g An aglet-baby;] 'Aglets (*aiguilettes*) were the tags to the strings used to fasten dresses, and these *aglets* sometimes represented small images. Mr. Singer has shown that *aglet* also signified a *brooch* or *jewel* in *one's cap*; *aglet-baby* might therefore mean a diminutive figure on the tags just mentioned, or one carved on a jewel.

As thunder, when the clouds in autumn crack.

HOR. Her father is Baptista Minola,
An affable and courteous gentleman:
Her name is Katharina Minola,
Renown'd in Padua for her scolding tongue.

PET. I know her father, though I know not her,
And he knew my deceased father well:
I will not sleep, Hortensio, till I see her;
And therefore let me be thus bold with you,
To give you over at this first encounter,
Unless you will accompany me thither.

GRU. I pray you, sir, let him go while the humour lasts. O' my word, an she knew him as well as I do, she would think scolding would do little good upon him. She may, perhaps, call him half a score knaves, or so: why, that 's nothing; an he begin once, he 'll rail in his rope-tricks.[a] I 'll tell you what, sir,—an she stand him but a little, he will throw a figure in her face, and so disfigure her with it, that she shall have no more eyes to see withal than a cat: you know him not, sir.

HOR. Tarry, Petruchio, I must go with thee;
For in Baptista's keep my treasure is:
He hath the jewel of my life in hold,
His youngest daughter, beautiful Bianca;
And her withholds from me, and other more[b]
Suitors to her, and rivals in my love:
Supposing it a thing impossible,
(For those defects I have before rehears'd,)
That ever Katharina will be woo'd;
Therefore this order hath Baptista ta'en,[c]
That none shall have access unto Bianca,
Till Katharine the curst have got a husband.

GRU. Katharine the curst!
A title for a maid, of all titles the worst.

HOR. Now shall my friend Petruchio do me grace;
And offer me, disguis'd in sober robes,
To old Baptista as a schoolmaster
Well seen[d] in music, to instruct Bianca:
That so I may by this device, at least,
Have leave and leisure to make love to her,
And, unsuspected, court her by herself.

Enter GREMIO; *with him* LUCENTIO *disguised, with books under his arm.*

GRU. Here's no knavery! see; to beguile the old folks, how the young folks lay their heads together! Master, master, look about you: who goes there? ha!

HOR. Peace, Grumio; it is the rival of my love:—
Petruchio, stand by a while.

GRU. A proper stripling, and an amorous!
[*They retire.*

GRE. O, very well: I have perus'd the note.
Hark you, sir; I'll have them very fairly bound:
All books of love, see that at any hand;
And see you read no other lectures to her:
You understand me:—over and beside
Signior Baptista's liberality,
I 'll mend it with a largess:—take your papers* too,
And let me have them very well perfum'd;
For she is sweeter than perfume itself,
To whom they go to; what will you read to her?

LUC. Whate'er I read to her, I'll plead for you,
As for my patron, (stand you so assur'd,)
As firmly as yourself were still in place:
Yea, and perhaps with more successful words
Than you, unless you were a scholar, sir.

GRE. O this learning! what a thing it is!

GRU. O this woodcock! what an ass it is!

PET. Peace, sirrah.

HOR. Grumio, mum!—God save you, signior Gremio!

GRE. And you 're well met, signior Hortensio: trow you,
Whither I am going?—to Baptista Minola.
I promis'd to inquire carefully
About a schoolmaster for the fair Bianca;
And, by good fortune, I have lighted well
On this young man; for learning, and behaviour,
Fit for her turn; well read in poetry
And other books,—good ones, I warrant ye.

HOR. 'T is well: and I have met a gentleman,
Hath promis'd me to help me† to another,
A fine musician to instruct our mistress;
So shall I no whit be behind in duty
To fair Bianca, so belov'd of me.

GRE. Belov'd of me,—and that my deeds shall prove.

GRU. And that his bags shall prove. [*Aside.*

HOR. Gremio, 't is now no time to vent our love:
Listen to me, and if you speak me fair,
I'll tell you news indifferent good for either.
Here is a gentleman, whom by chance I met;
Upon agreement from us to his liking,

---

[a] *He'll rail in his* rope-tricks.] *Ropery*, or *rope-tricks*, Malone says, originally signified abusive language, without any determinate idea. In this instance, Grumio, perhaps, plays upon the resemblance of *rhetoric* and *rope-tricks*, as he does upon the word *figure*, and *cat* for *Kate*, in the next sentence.

[b] *From me, and other more*—] The folio, 1623, reads, *from me. Other more.* Theobald, at the suggestion of Dr. Thirlby, added the conjunction, and his reading has been adopted by every editor since.

[c] This order hath Baptista ta'en,—] To *take order* meant to *adopt measures*: The expression in this sense is a common one not only with our author, but with his contemporaries. Thus in "Othello," Act V. Sc. 1,—

"Honest Iago *hath ta'en order* for 't."

Again in "Henry IV.," Part II. Act III. Sc. 2,—

"I will *take such order*, that thy friends shall ring for thee."

And in "Richard III." Act IV. Sc. 2,—

"I will *take order* for her keeping close."

[d] *Well* seen—] Well *versed*, well *skilled*. Thus Spenser,—

"Well *scene* in every science that *mote* bee."
Faërie Queen, b. iv. c. 2.

(*) First folio, *paper*. (†) First folio, *one*.

Will undertake to woo curst Katharine;
Yea, and to marry her, if her dowry please.
GRE. So said, so done, is well:—
Hortensio, have you told him all her faults?
PET. I know she is an irksome, brawling scold;
If that be all, masters, I hear no harm.
GRE. No, say'st me so, friend? what countryman?
PET. Born in Verona, old Antonio's* son:
My father dead, my fortune lives for me;
And I do hope good days, and long, to see.
GRE. O sir, such a life, with such a wife, were strange:
But if you have a stomach, to't o' God's name;
You shall have me assisting you in all.
But, will you woo this wild cat?
PET. Will I live?
GRU. Will he woo her? ay, or I'll hang her. [*Aside.*
PET. Why came I hither, but to that intent?
Think you, a little din can daunt mine ears?
Have I not in my time heard lions roar?
Have I not heard the sea, puff'd up with winds,
Rage like an angry boar, chafed with sweat?
Have I not heard great ordnance in the field,
And heaven's artillery thunder in the skies?
Have I not in a pitched battle heard
Loud 'larums, neighing steeds, and trumpets' clang,
And do you tell me of a woman's tongue
That gives not half so great a blow to hear,[a]
As will a chestnut in a farmer's fire?
Tush! tush! fear boys with bugs.[b]
GRU. For he fears none. [*Aside.*
GRE. Hortensio, hark!
This gentleman is happily arriv'd,
My mind presumes, for his own good, and yours.
HOR. I promis'd, we would be contributors,
And bear his charge of wooing, whatsoe'er.
GRE. And so we will, provided that he win her.
GRU. I would I were as sure of a good dinner. [*Aside.*

Enter TRANIO, *bravely apparelled; and* BIONDELLO.

TRA. Gentlemen, God save you! if I may be bold,
Tell me, I beseech you, which is the readiest way
To the house of signior Baptista Minola?
BION. He that has the two fair daughters; is't he you mean?
TRA. Even he, Biondello.
GRE. Hark you, sir; you mean not her to——
TRA. Perhaps, him and her, sir; what have you to do?
PET. Not her that chides, sir, at any hand, I pray.
TRA. I love no chiders, sir; Biondello, let's away.
LUC. Well begun, Tranio. [*Aside.*
HOR. Sir, a word ere you go;
Are you a suitor to the maid you talk of, yea or no?
TRA. An if I be, sir, is it any offence?
GRE. No; if, without more words, you will get you hence.
TRA. Why, sir, I pray, are not the streets as free
For me, as for you?
GRE. But so is not she.
TRA. For what reason, I beseech you?
GRE. For this reason if you'll know,
That she's the choice love of signior Gremio.
HOR. That she's the chosen of signior Hortensio.
TRA. Softly, my masters! if you be gentlemen,
Do me this right,—hear me with patience.
Baptista is a noble gentleman,
To whom my father is not all unknown;
And, were his daughter fairer than she is,
She may more suitors have, and me for one.
Fair Leda's daughter had a thousand wooers;
Then well one more may fair Bianca have,
And so she shall; Lucentio shall make one,
Though Paris came, in hope to speed alone.
GRE. What! this gentleman will out-talk us all.
LUC. Sir, give him head; I know, he'll prove a jade.
PET. Hortensio, to what end are all these words?
HOR. Sir, let me be so bold as ask you,
Did you yet ever see Baptista's daughter?
TRA. No, sir; but hear I do, that he hath two;
The one as famous for a scolding tongue,
As is the other for beauteous modesty.
PET. Sir, sir, the first's for me; let her go by.
GRE. Yea, leave that labour to great Hercules;
And let it be more than Alcides' twelve.
PET. Sir, understand you this of me, in sooth;—
The youngest daughter, whom you hearken for,
Her father keeps from all access of suitors,
And will not promise her to any man,
Until the elder sister first be wed:
The younger then is free, and not before.
TRA. If it be so, sir, that you are the man
Must stead us all, and me amongst the rest;
An if you break the ice, and do this feat,[c]—
Achieve the elder, set the younger free

(*) First folio, *Butonios*.

[a] A *blow* to hear,—] Thus the folio, 1623. The ordinary and perhaps preferable reading is, to *the ear*.

[b] Fear boys with bugs.] Fright children with *bugbears*. A *bug* meant an object of terror, a *goblin*.
"This hand shall hale them down to deepest hell,
Where none but furies, *bugs*, and tortures dwell."
The Spanish Tragedy, Act V.

[c] *And do this* feat,—] The old copies read "and do this *seek*;" *feat* was substituted by Rowe

For our access,—whose hap shall be to have her,
Will not so graceless be, to be ingrate.

HOR. Sir, you say well, and well you do conceive;
And since you do profess to be a suitor,
You must, as we do, gratify this gentleman,
To whom we all rest generally beholden.[a]

TRA. Sir, I shall not be slack: in sign whereof,
Please ye we may contrive this afternoon,[b]
And quaff carouses to our mistress' health;
And do as adversaries do in law,—
Strive mightily, but eat and drink as friends.

GRU. BION. O excellent motion! fellows, let's begone.

HOR. The motion's good indeed, and be it so;—
Petruchio, I shall be your *ben venuto*. [*Exeunt.*

[a] Beholden.] Here and elsewhere, the old editions have *beholding;* the active and past participle, in Shakespeare and his contemporaries, being used indiscriminately.

[b] *We may* contrive *this afternoon,*—] We may *pass away*, or *wear out*, this afternoon; from *contrivi*, the preterite of *contero*.

"Ambulando totum hunc *contrivi* diem."
TERENCE's *Hecyra*, Act V. Sc. 3.

ACT II.

SCENE I.—*The same. A Room in* Baptista's *House.*

Enter KATHARINA *and* BIANCA.

BIAN. Good sister, wrong me not, nor wrong yourself,
To make a bondmaid and a slave of me;
That I disdain: but for these other gawds,[a]
Unbind my hands, I'll pull them off myself,
Yea, all my raiment, to my petticoat;
Or, what you will command me, will I do,
So well I know my duty to my elders.

KATH. Of all thy suitors, here I charge thee,* tell
Whom thou lov'st best: see thou dissemble not.

BIAN. Believe me, sister, of all the men alive,
I never yet beheld that special face
Which I could fancy more than any other.

KATH. Minion, thou liest: is't not Hortensio?

BIAN. If you affect him, sister, here I swear,
I'll plead for you myself, but you shall have him.

KATH. O then, belike, you fancy riches more;
You will have Gremio to keep you fair.

BIAN. Is it for him you do envy me so?
Nay, then you jest; and now I well perceive,
You have but jested with me all this while:

(*) First folio omits, *thee*.

[a] Gawds,—] The folio, 1623, has *goods*, for which Theobald substituted *gawds*. Mr. Collier's MS. annotator reads *guards*, in the old sense of ornaments.

I prithee, sister Kate, untie my hands.

KATH. If that be jest, then all the rest was so. [*Strikes her.*

Enter BAPTISTA.

BAP. Why, how now, dame! whence grows this insolence?
Bianca, stand aside;—poor girl! she weeps:—
Go ply thy needle; meddle not with her.
For shame, thou hilding, of a devilish spirit,
Why dost thou wrong her that did ne'er wrong thee?
When did she cross thee with a bitter word?

KATH. Her silence flouts me, and I'll be reveng'd. [*Flies after* BIANCA.

BAP. What, in my sight?—Bianca, get thee in. [*Exit* BIANCA.

KATH. What, will you not suffer me? nay, now I see
She is your treasure, she must have a husband;
I must dance barefoot on her wedding-day,
And, for your love to her, lead apes in hell.[a]
Talk not to me. I will go sit and weep,
Till I can find occasion of revenge. [*Exit* KATHARINA.

BAP. Was ever gentleman thus griev'd as I?
But who comes here?

Enter GREMIO, *with* LUCENTIO *meanly habited;* PETRUCHIO, *with* HORTENSIO *as a musician;*[b] *and* TRANIO, *with* BIONDELLO *bearing a lute and books.*

GRE. Good morrow, neighbour Baptista.

BAP. Good morrow, neighbour Gremio; God save you, gentlemen.

PET. And you, good sir; pray, have you not a daughter
Call'd Katharina, fair and virtuous?

BAP. I have a daughter, sir, call'd Katharina.

GRE. You are too blunt, go to it orderly.

PET. You wrong me, signior Gremio; give me leave.
I am a gentleman of Verona, sir,
That, hearing of her beauty and her wit,
Her affability, and bashful modesty,
Her wondrous qualities, and mild behaviour,
Am bold to show myself a forward guest
Within your house, to make mine eye the witness
Of that report which I so oft have heard:
And, for an entrance to my entertainment,
I do present you with a man of mine, [*Presenting* HORTENSIO.
Cunning in music, and the mathematics,
To instruct her fully in those sciences,
Whereof, I know, she is not ignorant:
Accept of him, or else you do me wrong;
His name is Licio, born in Mantua.

BAP. You're welcome, sir; and he for your good sake:
But for my daughter Katharine, this I know,
She is not for your turn, the more my grief.

PET. I see you do not mean to part with her;
Or else you like not of my company.

BAP. Mistake me not, I speak but as I find.
Whence are you, sir? what may I call your name?

PET. Petruchio is my name; Antonio's son,
A man well known throughout all Italy.

BAP. I know him well: you are welcome for his sake.

GRE. Saving your tale, Petruchio, I pray,
Let us, that are poor petitioners, speak too:
Baccare![c] you are marvellous forward.

PET. O, pardon me, signior Gremio; I would fain be doing.

GRE. I doubt it not, sir; but you will curse your wooing.

Neighbour,* this is a gift very grateful, I am sure of it. To express the like kindness myself, that have been more kindly beholden to you than any, I freely give unto you[d] this young scholar, [*presenting* LUCENTIO] that hath been long studying at Rheims; as cunning in Greek, Latin, and other languages, as the other in music and mathematics: his name is Cambio; pray accept his service.

BAP. A thousand thanks, signior Gremio: welcome, good Cambio.—But, gentle sir, [*to* TRANIO] methinks, you walk like a stranger: may I be so bold to know the cause of your coming?

TRA. Pardon me, sir, the boldness is mine own
That, being a stranger in this city here,
Do make myself a suitor to your daughter,
Unto Bianca, fair, and virtuous.
Nor is your firm resolve unknown to me,
In the preferment of the eldest sister:
This liberty is all that I request,—
That, upon knowledge of my parentage,
I may have welcome 'mongst the rest that woo,
And free access and favour as the rest.

---

a Lead apes in hell.] "To lead apes," as Malone remarks, was one of the employments of a bear-ward, but why or when old maids were condemned to the care of them in hell, we are ignorant. Beatrice, in "Much Ado About Nothing," Act II. Sc. 1, has the same phrase,—

"I will even take sixpence in earnest of the *bear-herd*, and lead his *apes into hell.*"

b *As a musician;*] In the old copies Hortensio's entrance is not mentioned.

(*) First folio, *neighbours.*

c Baccare!] An old proverbial saying of doubtful derivation, but meaning *stand back.*

"*Backare*, quoth Mortimer to his sow,
Went that sow *backe* at that bidding, trow you?"
JOHN HEYWOOD'S *Book of Proverbs.*

d I *freely give unto* you—] The folio, 1623, omits *I* and *you*, which appear to have been first introduced by Capell.

And, toward the education of your daughters,
I here bestow a simple instrument,
And this small packet of Greek and Latin books:
If you accept them, then their worth is great.
BAP. Lucentio is your name? of whence, I pray?
TRA. Of Pisa, sir; son to Vincentio.
BAP. A mighty man of Pisa; by report
I know him well: you are very welcome, sir.
Take you [*to* HOR.] the lute, and you [*to* LUC.] the set of books,
You shall go see your pupils presently.
Holla, within!

Enter a Servant.

Sirrah, lead
These gentlemen to my daughters; and tell them both,
These are their tutors; bid them use them well.
[*Exit* Servant, *with* HORTENSIO, LUCENTIO, *and* BIONDELLO.
We will go walk a little in the orchard,
And then to dinner: you are passing welcome,
And so I pray you all to think yourselves.
PET. Signior Baptista, my business asketh haste,
And every day I cannot come to woo.
You knew my father well; and in him, me,
Left solely heir to all his lands and goods,
Which I have better'd rather than decreas'd:
Then tell me,—if I get your daughter's love,
What dowry shall I have with her to wife?
BAP. After my death, the one half of my lands;
And, in possession, twenty thousand crowns.
PET. And, for that dowry, I'll assure her of
Her widowhood,[a]—be it that she survive me,—
In all my lands and leases whatsoever:
Let specialties be therefore drawn between us,
That covenants may be kept on either hand.
BAP. Ay, when the special thing is well obtain'd,
That is,—her love; for that is all in all.
PET. Why, that is nothing; for I tell you, father,
I am as peremptory as she proud-minded;
And where two raging fires meet together,
They do consume the thing that feeds their fury:
Though little fire grows great with little wind,
Yet extreme gusts will blow out fire and all:
So I to her, and so she yields to me;
For I am rough, and woo not like a babe.
BAP. Well mayst thou woo, and happy be thy speed!
But be thou arm'd for some unhappy words.
PET. Ay, to the proof; as mountains are for winds,
That shake not, though they blow perpetually.

Re-enter HORTENSIO, *with his head broken.*

BAP. How now, my friend? why dost thou look so pale?
HOR. For fear, I promise you, if I look pale.
BAP. What, will my daughter prove a good musician?
HOR. I think, she'll sooner prove a soldier;
Iron may hold with her, but never lutes.
BAP. Why, then thou canst not break her to the lute?
HOR. Why, no; for she hath broke the lute to me.
I did but tell her she mistook her frets,[b]
And bow'd her hand to teach her fingering;
When, with a most impatient devilish spirit,
Frets, call you these? quoth she: *I'll fume with them:*
And, with that word, she struck me on the head,
And through the instrument my pate made way;
And there I stood amazed for a while,
As on a pillory, looking through the lute;
While she did call me,—rascal fiddler,
And twangling Jack; with twenty such vile terms,
As she had* studied to misuse me so.
PET. Now, by the world, it is a lusty wench;
I love her ten times more than e'er I did:
O, how I long to have some chat with her!
BAP. Well, go with me, and be not so discomfited:
Proceed in practice with my younger daughter;
She's apt to learn, and thankful for good turns.
Signior Petruchio, will you go with us:
Or shall I send my daughter Kate to you?
PET. I pray you do; I will attend her here,—
[*Exeunt* BAPTISTA, GREMIO, TRANIO, *and* HORTENSIO.
And woo her with some spirit when she comes.
Say, that she rail; why, then I'll tell her plain
She sings as sweetly as a nightingale:
Say, that she frown; I'll say, she looks as clear
As morning roses newly wash'd with dew:
Say, she be mute, and will not speak a word;
Then I'll commend her volubility,
And say she uttereth piercing eloquence:
If she do bid me pack, I'll give her thanks
As though she bid me stay by her a week;
If she deny to wed, I'll crave the day

---

[a] ——*I'll assure her of*
Her widowhood,—]

Her *widowhood*, that is, her *dower*.

(*) First folio, *had she*.

[b] *Mistook her* frets,—] A *fret* is the point at which a string on the lute or guitar is to be *stopped*.

When I shall ask the banns, and when be married:—
But here she comes; and now, Petruchio, speak.

Enter KATHARINA.

Good morrow, Kate; for that's your name, I hear.
KATH. Well have you heard, but something hard of hearing;
They call me—Katharine, that do talk of me.
PET. You lie, in faith; for you are call'd plain Kate,
And bonny Kate, and sometimes Kate the curst;
But Kate, the prettiest Kate in Christendom,
Kate of Kate-Hall, my super-dainty Kate,
For dainties are all cates; and therefore, Kate,
Take this of me, Kate of my consolation;—
Hearing thy mildness prais'd in every town,
Thy virtues spoke of, and thy beauty sounded,
(Yet not so deeply as to thee belongs,)
Myself am mov'd to woo thee for my wife.
KATH. Mov'd! in good time: let him that mov'd you hither
Remove you hence: I knew you at the first,
You were a moveable.
PET. Why, what's a moveable?
KATH. A joint-stool.[a]
PET. Thou hast hit it: come, sit on me.
KATH. Asses are made to bear, and so are you.
PET. Women are made to bear, and so are you.
KATH. No such jade as you, if me you mean.[b]
PET. Alas, good Kate! I will not burthen thee:
For, knowing thee to be but young and light,—
KATH. Too light for such a swain as you to catch;
And yet as heavy as my weight should be.
PET. Should be, should buz![c]
KATH. Well ta'en, and like a buzzard.
PET. O, slow-wing'd turtle! shall a buzzard take thee?
KATH. Ay, for a turtle, as he takes a buzzard.[d]
PET. Come, come, you wasp, i' faith, you are too angry.
KATH. If I be waspish, best beware my sting.
PET. My remedy is then, to pluck it out.
KATH. Ay, if the fool could find it where it lies.
PET. Who knows not where a wasp does wear his sting?
In his tail.
KATH. In his tongue.
PET. Whose tongue?
KATH. Yours, if you talk of tales; and so farewell.
PET. What, with my tongue in your tail? nay, come again.
Good Kate; I am a gentleman.
KATH. That I'll try.
[*She strikes him.*
PET. I swear I'll cuff you, if you strike again.
KATH. So may you lose your arms:
If you strike me, you are no gentleman,
And if no gentleman, why, then no arms.
PET. A herald, Kate? O, put me in thy books.
KATH. What is your crest? a coxcomb?
PET. A combless cock, so Kate will be my hen.
KATH. No cock of mine, you crow too like a craven.
PET. Nay, come, Kate, come, you must not look so sour.
KATH. It is my fashion, when I see a crab.
PET. Why, here's no crab, and therefore look not sour.
KATH. There is, there is.
PET. Then show it me.
KATH. Had I a glass, I would.
PET. What, you mean my face?
KATH. Well aim'd of such a young one.
PET. Now, by Saint George, I am too young for you.
KATH. Yet you are withered.
PET. 'Tis with cares.
KATH. I care not.
PET. Nay, hear you, Kate: in sooth, you 'scape not so.
KATH. I chafe you, if I tarry; let me go.
PET. No, not a whit; I find you passing gentle:
'Twas told me, you were rough, and coy, and sullen,
And now I find report a very liar;
For thou art pleasant, gamesome, passing courteous,
But slow in speech, yet sweet as spring-time flowers.
Thou canst not frown, thou canst not look askance,
Nor bite the lip, as angry wenches will;
Nor hast thou pleasure to be cross in talk;
But thou with mildness entertain'st thy wooers,
With gentle conference, soft and affable.
Why does the world report that Kate doth limp?
O slanderous world! Kate, like the hazel-twig,
Is straight, and slender; and as brown in hue,
As hazel-nuts, and sweeter than the kernels.
O, let me see thee walk: thou dost not halt.
KATH. Go, fool, and, whom thou keep'st, command.

---

[a] A joint-stool.] "Cry you mercy, I took you for a *join'd-stool*," is an old proverbial saying. It occurs as a proverb in Lyly's "Mother Bombie," 1594. and also in "King Lear," Act III. Sc. 6.

[b] *No such jade as you, if me* you mean.] Petruchio's reply shows clearly there is some omission or misprint in this line.

[c] Should be, should buz!] A quibble is intended on the *buzz* of the *bee*, and *buz*, applied to a din of words:—

"But you wyl choplogick
And be *Bee-to-busse*."
The Contention betwyxte Churchyeard and Camell, &c. 1560.

[d] A buzzard.] A beetle: so called on account of its *humming, buzzing* noise.

PET. Did ever Dian so become a grove,
As Kate this chamber with her princely gait?
O, be thou Dian, and let her be Kate;
And then let Kate be chaste, and Dian sportful.

KATH. Where did you study all this goodly speech?

PET. It is *extempore*, from my mother-wit.

KATH. A witty mother! witless else her son.

PET. Am I not wise?

KATH. Yes; keep you warm.[a]

PET. Marry, so I mean, sweet Katharine, in thy bed:
And, therefore, setting all this chat aside,
Thus in plain terms:—your father hath consented
That you shall be my wife; your dowry 'greed on;
And, will you, nill you, I will marry you.
Now, Kate, I am a husband for your turn;
For, by this light, whereby I see thy beauty,
(Thy beauty that doth make me like thee well,)
Thou must be married to no man but me;
For I am he am born to tame you, Kate;
And bring you from a wild Kate[b] to a Kate
Conformable, as other household Kates.
Here comes your father; never make denial,
I must and will have Katharine to my wife.

Re-enter BAPTISTA, GREMIO, *and* TRANIO.

BAP. Now, Signior Petruchio, how speed you with my daughter?

PET. How but well, sir? how but well?
It were impossible I should speed amiss.

BAP. Why, how now, daughter Katharine? in your dumps?

---

[a] *Yes; keep you warm.*] An allusion to a proverbial phrase, of which the sense is not apparent. It is found again in "Much Ado about Nothing," Act I. Sc. 1,—

"——— that if he have *wit* enough to keep himself *warm*—."

[b] *From a wild* Kate—] Modern editors usually read "a wild *cat*," but the intended play on the words Kate *cat*, and *Kates cats*, is sufficiently obvious without altering the text.

KATH. Call you me daughter? now I promise you,
You have show'd a tender fatherly regard,
To wish me wed to one half lunatic;
A mad-cap ruffian, and a swearing Jack,
That thinks with oaths to face the matter out.

PET. Father, 't is thus,—yourself and all the world,
That talk'd of her, have talk'd amiss of her;
If she be curst, it is for policy:
For she's not froward, but modest as the dove;
She is not hot, but temperate as the morn;
For patience, she will prove a second Grissel;
And Roman Lucrece for her chastity:
And to conclude,—we have 'greed so well together,
That upon Sunday is the wedding-day.

KATH. I'll see thee hanged on Sunday first.

GRE. Hark, Petruchio! she says she'll see thee hanged first.

TRA. Is this your speeding? nay, then, good night our part!

PET. Be patient, gentlemen; I choose her for myself;
If she and I be pleas'd, what's that to you?
'Tis bargain'd 'twixt us twain, being alone,
That she shall still be curst in company.
I tell you, 'tis incredible to believe
How much she loves me: O, the kindest Kate!
She hung about my neck; and kiss on kiss
She vied so fast, protesting oath on oath,
That in a twink she won me to her love.
O, you are novices! 'tis a world to see,[a]
How tame, when men and women are alone,
A meacock[b] wretch can make the curstest shrew.
Give me thy hand, Kate: I will unto Venice,
To buy apparel 'gainst the wedding-day:
Provide the feast, father, and bid the guests;
I will be sure my Katharine shall be fine.

BAP. I know not what to say: but give me your hands;
God send you joy, Petruchio! 'tis a match.

GRE. TRA. Amen, say we; we will be witnesses.

PET. Father, and wife, and gentlemen, adieu;
I will to Venice; Sunday comes apace:
We will have rings, and things, and fine array;
And, kiss me, Kate; we will be married o' Sunday.
[*Exeunt* PETRUCHIO *and* KATHARINA *severally*.(1)

GRE. Was ever match clapp'd up so suddenly?

BAP. Faith, gentlemen, now I play a merchant's part,
And venture madly on a desperate mart.

TRA. 'Twas a commodity lay fretting by you;
'Twill bring you gain, or perish on the seas.

BAP. The gain I seek is—quiet in* the match.

GRE. No doubt, but he hath got a quiet catch.
But now, Baptista, to your younger daughter;
Now is the day we long have looked for;
I am your neighbour, and was suitor first.

TRA. And I am one that love Bianca more
Than words can witness, or your thoughts can guess.

GRE. Youngling! thou canst not love so dear as I.

TRA. Greybeard! thy love doth freeze.

GRE. But thine doth fry.
Skipper, stand back; 'tis age that nourisheth.

TRA. But youth, in ladies' eyes that flourisheth.

BAP. Content you, gentlemen; I will compound this strife:
'Tis deeds must win the prize; and he, of both,
That can assure my daughter greatest dower,
Shall have† Bianca's love.
Say, signior Gremio, what can you assure her?

GRE. First, as you know, my house within the city
Is richly furnished with plate and gold;
Basins, and ewers, to lave her dainty hands;
My hangings all of Tyrian tapestry:
In ivory coffers I have stuff'd my crowns;
In cypress chests my arras, counterpoints,[c]
Costly apparel, tents,[d] and canopies,
Fine linen, Turkey cushions boss'd with pearl,
Valance of Venice gold in needlework,
Pewter[e] and brass, and all things that belong
To house, or housekeeping: then, at my farm,
I have a hundred milch-kine to the pail,
Six score fat oxen standing in my stalls,
And all things answerable to this portion.
Myself am struck in years, I must confess;
And, if I die to-morrow, this is hers,
If, whilst I live, she will be only mine.

TRA. That *only* came well in. Sir, list to me
I am my father's heir, and only son;
If I may have your daughter to my wife,
I'll leave her houses three or four as good,
Within rich Pisa walls, as any one
Old signior Gremio has in Padua;
Besides two thousand ducats by the year,
Of fruitful land, all which shall be her jointure.
What! have I pinch'd you, signior Gremio?

GRE. Two thousand ducats by the year of land!
My land amounts not to so much in all:[f]

---

[a] 'T is a world to see,—] An expression frequently found in the old writers, meaning, *it is wonderful to see*.

[b] A *meacock*—] A *milk-livered, chicken-hearted fellow*. The word, Nares thinks, was originally applied to denote a *hen-pecked* husband.

[c] Counterpoints,—] Coverings for beds, now called *counterpanes*. "*Counterpoints* were, in ancient times, extremely costly. In Wat Tyler's rebellion, Stowe informs us, when the insurgents broke into the wardrobe in the Savoy, 'they destroyed a coverlet, worth a thousand marks.'"—MALONE.

(*) First folio, *me*. (†) First folio, *my Bianca's*.

[d] Tents,—] *Hangings*; so called, it has been suggested, from the *tenters* upon which they were hung.

[e] Pewter—] This composite metal, common as it is now, was so expensive formerly, that vessels made of it were hired by some of the nobility by the year. See Holinshed's "Description of England," pp. 188, 189.

[f] *My land amounts* not *to so much in all*:] Warburton proposed to substitute *but* for *not*; and I believe either *but* or *yet* was Shakespeare's word.

That she shall have; besides an argosy[a]
That now is lying in Marseilles' road.[b]
What! have I chok'd you with an argosy?

TRA. Gremio, 'tis known my father hath no less
Than three great argosies; besides two galliasses,[c]
And twelve tight galleys: these I will assure her,
And twice as much, whate'er thou offer'st next.

GRE. Nay, I have offer'd all; I have no more;
And she can have no more than all I have.
If you like me, she shall have me and mine.

TRA. Why, then the maid is mine from all the world,
By your firm promise; Gremio is outvied.

BAP. I must confess your offer is the best;
And, let your father make her the assurance,
She is your own; else, you must pardon me:
If you should die before him, where's her dower?

TRA. That's but a cavil; he is old, I young.

GRE. And may not young men die, as well as old?

BAP. Well, gentlemen, I am thus resolv'd:—
On Sunday next you know
My daughter Katharine is to be married:
Now, on the Sunday following, shall Bianca
Be bride to you, if you make this assurance;
If not, to signior Gremio:
And so I take my leave, and thank you both. [*Exit.*

GRE. Adieu, good neighbour:—now I fear thee not;
Sirrah, young gamester, your father were a fool
To give thee all, and, in his waning age,
Set foot under thy table: tut! a toy!
An old Italian fox is not so kind, my boy. [*Exit.*

TRA. A vengeance on your crafty wither'd hide!
Yet I have fac'd it with a card of ten.(2)
'Tis in my head to do my master good:—
I see no reason, but suppos'd Lucentio
Must get a father call'd—suppos'd Vincentio;
And that's a wonder: fathers, commonly,
Do get their children; but, in this case of wooing,
A child shall get a sire, if I fail not of my cunning.(3) [*Exit.*

---

a An argosy—] An *argosy*, or *argosie*, was a large vessel employed for war, or in the conveyance of merchandise, more frequently the latter.

b Marseilles' *road.*] The folio, 1623, reads, "*Marcellus* road." It should be pronounced as a trisyllable.

c *Besides two* galliasses,—] *Galeazza*, Ital. A huge *galley*, having three masts and accommodation for thirty-two rowers, so that it could be propelled either by sails or oars, or by both.

ACT III.

SCENE I.—*A Room in* Baptista's *House.*

Enter Lucentio, Hortensio, *and* Bianca.

Luc. Fiddler, forbear; you grow too forward, sir:
Have you so soon forgot the entertainment
Her sister Katharine welcom'd you withal?
Hor. But, wrangling pedant, this is
The patroness of heavenly harmony:
Then give me leave to have prerogative,
And when in music we have spent an hour,
Your lecture shall have leisure for as much.
Luc. Preposterous ass![a] that never read so far
To know the cause why music was ordain'd!
Was it not, to refresh the mind of man,

---

[a] Preposterous *ass!*] Shakespeare uses *preposterous* closer to its primitive and literal sense of *inverted order*, *ὕστερον πρότερον*, than is customary now. With us it implies *monstrous, absurd, ridiculous*, and the like; with him it meant *misplaced, out of the natural or reasonable course.*

After his studies, or his usual pain?
Then give me leave to read philosophy,
And, while I pause, serve in your harmony.

HOR. Sirrah, I will not bear these braves of thine.

BIAN. Why, gentlemen, you do me double wrong,
To strive for that which resteth in my choice:
I am no breeching scholar in the schools;
I'll not be tied to hours, nor 'pointed times,
But learn my lessons as I please myself.
And, to cut off all strife, here sit we down:
Take you your instrument, play you the whiles;
His lecture will be done ere you have tun'd.

HOR. [*To* BIANCA.] You'll leave his lecture when I am in tune? [*Retires.*

LUC. That will be never;—tune your instrument.

BIAN. Where left we last?

LUC. Here, madam:—
Hac ibat Simois; hic est Sigeia tellus;
Hic steterat Priami regia celsa senis.[a]

BIAN. Construe them.

LUC. *Hac ibat*, as I told you before,[b]—*Simois*, I am Lucentio,—*hic est*, son unto Vincentio of Pisa,—*Sigeia tellus*, disguised thus to get your love;—*Hic steterat*, and that Lucentio that comes a wooing,—*Priami*, is my man Tranio,—*regia*, bearing my port,—*celsa senis*, that we might beguile the old pantaloon.

HOR. Madam, my instrument 's in tune. [*Returning.*

BIAN. Let 's hear;— [HORTENSIO *plays.*
O fie! the treble jars.

LUC. Spit in the hole, man, and tune again.

BIAN. Now let me see if I can construe it: *Hac ibat Simois*, I know you not; *hic est Sigeia tellus*, I trust you not;—*Hic steterat Priami*, take heed he hear us not;—*regia*, presume not;—*celsa senis*, despair not.

HOR. Madam, 'tis now in tune.

LUC. All but the base.

HOR. The base is right; 'tis the base knave that jars.
How fiery and forward our pedant is!
Now, for my life the knave doth court my love:
Pedascule, I'll watch you better yet.

BIAN. In time I may believe, yet I mistrust.

LUC. Mistrust it not; for, sure, Æacides
Was Ajax,—call'd so from his grandfather.

BIAN. I must believe my master; else, I promise you,
I should be arguing still upon that doubt:
But let it rest: now, Licio, to you:—
Good masters,* take it not unkindly, pray,
That I have been thus pleasant with you both.

HOR. You may go walk, [*to* LUCENTIO] and give me leave awhile;
My lessons make no music in three parts.

LUC. Are you so formal, sir? well, I must wait,
And watch withal; for, but I be deceiv'd,
Our fine musician groweth amorous. [*Aside.*

HOR. Madam, before you touch the instrument,
To learn the order of my fingering,
I must begin with rudiments of art;
To teach you gamut in a briefer sort,
More pleasant, pithy, and effectual,
Than hath been taught by any of my trade;
And there it is in writing, fairly drawn.

BIAN. Why, I am past my gamut long ago.

HOR. Yet read the gamut of Hortensio.

BIAN. [*Reads.*] Gamut *I am, the ground of all accord,*
A re, *to plead Hortensio's passion;*
B mi, *Bianca, take him for thy lord,*
C fa ut, *that loves with all affection:*
D sol re, *one cliff, two notes have I;*
E la mi, *show pity, or I die.*[1]
Call you this gamut? tut! I like it not:
Old fashions please me best; I am not so nice,
To change true rules for odd inventions.[c]

Enter a Servant.

SERV. Mistress, your father prays you leave your books,
And help to dress your sister's chamber up;
You know, to-morrow is the wedding-day.

BIAN. Farewell, sweet masters, both; I must be gone. [*Exeunt* BIANCA *and* Serv.

LUC. 'Faith, mistress, then I have no cause to stay. [*Exit.*

HOR. But I have cause to pry into this pedant;
Methinks, he looks as though he were in love:
Yet if thy thoughts, Bianca, be so humble,
To cast thy wand'ring eyes on every stale,
Seize thee that list: if once I find thee ranging,
Hortensio will be quit with thee by changing. [*Exit.*

SCENE II.—*The same. Before* Baptista's *House.*

Enter BAPTISTA, TRANIO, KATHARINA, BIANCA, LUCENTIO, *and* Attendants.

BAP. Signior Lucentio, [*to* TRANIO] this is the 'pointed day
That Katharine and Petruchio should be married,

(*) First folio, *master*.

[a] —celsa senis.] Ovid. Epist. Penelope Ulyssi, v. 33.

[b] *Hac ibat*, as I told you before,—] The humour of translating Latin into English of a different sense, as Malone remarks, was not at all uncommon among our old writers.

[c] To change *true rules for* odd *inventions.*] The first folio has "*charge*," the second "*change.*" The alteration of *odd* for *old*, the reading of the early copies, was made by Theobald, to whom we are indebted also for the correct distribution of the speeches, which in the folios are perversely confused in this part of the scene.

And yet we hear not of our son-in-law:
What will be said? what mockery will it be,
To want the bridegroom, when the priest attends
To speak the ceremonial rites of marriage?
What says Lucentio to this shame of ours?

KATH. No shame but mine: I must, forsooth, be forc'd
To give my hand, oppos'd against my heart,
Unto a mad-brain rudesby,[a] full of spleen;
Who woo'd in haste, and means to wed at leisure.
I told you, I, he was a frantic fool,
Hiding his bitter jests in blunt behaviour:
And, to be noted for a merry man,
He'll woo a thousand, 'point the day of marriage,
Make friends, invite, yes,[b] and proclaim the banns;
Yet never means to wed where he hath woo'd.
Now must the world point at poor Katharine,
And say,—*Lo, there is mad Petruchio's wife,*
If it would please him come and marry her.

TRA. Patience, good Katharine, and Baptista too;
Upon my life, Petruchio means but well,
Whatever fortune stays him from his word:
Though he be blunt, I know him passing wise;
Though he be merry, yet withal he's honest.

KATH. 'Would Katharine had never seen him, though!

[*Exit, weeping, followed by* BIANCA, *and others.*

BAP. Go, girl; I cannot blame thee now to weep;
For such an injury would vex a saint,
Much more a shrew of thy impatient humour.[c]

Enter BIONDELLO.

BION. Master, master! old news,[d] and such news as you never heard of!

BAP. Is it new and old too? how may that be?

BION. Why, is it not news, to hear* of Petruchio's coming?

BAP. Is he come?

BION. Why, no, sir.

BAP. What then?

BION. He is coming.

BAP. When will he be here?

BION. When he stands where I am, and sees you there.

TRA. But, say, what:—to thine old news.

BION. Why, Petruchio is coming, in a new hat and an old jerkin; a pair of old breeches, thrice turned; a pair of boots that have been candle-cases, one buckled, another laced; an old rusty sword ta'en out of the town armoury, with a broken hilt, and chapeless; with two broken points:[e] his horse hipped with an old mothy saddle, and stirrups of no kindred: besides, possessed with the glanders, and like to mose in the chine; troubled with the lampass, infected with the fashions,[f] full of wind-galls, sped with spavins, raied with the yellows, past cure of the fives,[g] stark spoiled with the staggers, begnawn with the bots; swayed* in the back, and shoulder-shotten; ne'er legged before; and with a half-checked bit, and a head-stall of sheep's leather, which, being restrained to keep him from stumbling, hath been often burst, and now repaired with knots; one girth six times pieced, and a woman's crupper of velure,[h] which hath two letters for her name, fairly set down in studs, and here and there pieced with packthread.

BAP. Who comes with him?

BION. O, sir, his lackey, for all the world caparisoned like the horse; with a linen stock on one leg, and a kersey boot-hose on the other, gartered with a red and blue list; an old hat, and *The humour of forty fancies*[i] pricked in't for a feather; a monster, a very monster in apparel; and not like a Christian footboy, or a gentleman's lackey.

TRA. 'Tis some odd humour pricks him to this fashion;
Yet oftentimes he goes but mean apparell'd.

BAP. I am glad he is come, howsoe'er he comes.

BION. Why, sir, he comes not.

BAP. Didst thou not say, he comes?

BION. Who? that Petruchio came?

(*) First folio, *heard*.

(†) First folio, *waid*.

[a] *Unto a mad-brain* rudesby,—] *Blusterer, swaggerer.* The same expression occurs in "Twelfth Night," Act IV. Sc. 1,—

"*Rudesby*, begone!"

[b] *Make friends, invite,* yes,—] The word *yes* was inserted by the editor of the second folio.

[c] *Of* thy *impatient humour.*] *Thy* was also added in the second folio.

[d] Old *news*,—] The folio, 1623, omits *old*, apparently by inadvertence, as the reply of Biondello shows it to be necessary. By "old news" the speaker obviously intends a reference to the "*old* jerkin," "*old* breeches," "*old* rusty sword," &c. &c., which form part of Petruchio's grotesque equipment.

[e] *Two broken* points:] *Points* were the long-tagged laces by which part of the outer dress was fastened. Among other services, they supplied the place of our present braces, and the result of their breaking must, therefore, have been sometimes peculiarly inconvenient and unseemly:—

"CL. I am resolved on two *points*.
MARIA. That, if one break, the other will hold; or, if both break, your gaskins fall."—*Twelfth Night*, Act I. Sc. 5.

Thus, too, in "Henry IV." Part I. Act II. Sc. 4,—

"FALS. Their *points* being *broken*,—
PRINCE. Down fell their hose."

[f] The fashions,—] The disease in horses called *farcin* or *farcy*. So Decker, "Gull's Hornbook," 1609. "*Fashions* was then counted a disease, and horses died of it." And S. Rowland, in his "Looke To it; for, Ile Stabbe Ye," 1604,—

"You gentle-puppets of the proudest size,
That are like Horses troubled with the Fashions." Sig. 6. 2.

[g] *The* fives,—] In farriery, the distemper known as *vives*, affecting the glands under the ear.

[h] *Velure*,—] *Velvet.*

[i] *The humour of forty fancies* pricked in't for a feather;] *The humour of forty fancies*, Warburton conjectured, was some popular ballad, or collection of ballads, of the time, which Petruchio had stuck in the lackey's hat as a ridiculous ornament.

BAP. Ay, that Petruchio came.

BION. No, sir; I say, his horse comes with him on his back.

BAP. Why, that 's all one.

BION. Nay, by Saint Jamy, I hold you a penny,
A horse and a man is more than one, and yet not many.

Enter PETRUCHIO *and* GRUMIO.(1)

PET. Come, where be these gallants? who 's at home?

BAP. You are welcome, sir.

PET. And yet I come not well.

BAP. And yet you halt not.

TRA. Not so well apparell'd
As I wish you were.

PET. Were it better, I should rush in thus.
But where is Kate? where is my lovely bride?
How does my father?—Gentles, methinks you frown:
And wherefore gaze this goodly company;
As if they saw some wondrous monument,
Some comet, or unusual prodigy?

BAP. Why, sir, you know, this is your wedding-day:
First were we sad, fearing you would not come;
Now sadder, that you come so unprovided.
Fie! doff this habit, shame to your estate,
An eyesore to our solemn festival.[a]

TRA. And tell us, what occasion of import
Hath all so long detain'd you from your wife,
And sent you hither so unlike yourself?

PET. Tedious it were to tell, and harsh to hear:
Sufficeth, I am come to keep my word,
Though in some part enforced to digress;
Which, at more leisure, I will so excuse
As you shall well be satisfied withal.
But, where is Kate? I stay too long from her;
The morning wears, 'tis time we were at church.

TRA. See not your bride in these unreverent robes;
Go to my chamber, put on clothes of mine.

PET. Not I, believe me; thus I'll visit her.

BAP. But thus, I trust, you will not marry her.

PET. Good sooth, even thus; therefore ha' done with words;
To me she's married, not unto my clothes:
Could I repair what she will wear in me,
As I can change these poor accoutrements,
'Twere well for Kate, and better for myself.
But what a fool am I, to chat with you,
When I should bid good-morrow to my bride,
And seal the title with a lovely kiss!

[*Exeunt* PETRUCHIO, GRUMIO *and* BIONDELLO.

TRA. He hath some meaning in his mad attire;
We will persuade him, be it possible,
To put on better ere he go to church.

BAP. I'll after him, and see the event of this. [*Exit.*

TRA. But, sir, to love[b] concerneth us to add
Her father's liking: which to bring to pass,
As I* before imparted to your worship,
I am to get a man,—whate'er he be,
It skills not much; we'll fit him to our turn,—
And he shall be Vincentio of Pisa;
And make assurance, here in Padua,
Of greater sums than I have promised.
So shall you quietly enjoy your hope,
And marry sweet Bianca with consent.

LUC. Were it not that my fellow schoolmaster
Doth watch Bianca's steps so narrowly,
'Twere good, methinks, to steal our marriage;
Which once perform'd, let all the world say—no,
I'll keep mine own, despite of all the world.

TRA. That by degrees we mean to look into,
And watch our vantage in this business:
We'll over-reach the greybeard, Gremio,
The narrow-prying father, Minola,
The quaint musician, amorous Licio;
All for my master's sake, Lucentio.

Enter GREMIO.

Signior Gremio! came you from the church?

GRE. As willingly as e'er I came from school.

TRA. And is the bride and bridegroom coming home?

GRE. A bridegroom, say you? 'tis a groom indeed,
A grumbling groom, and that the girl shall find.

TRA. Curster than she? why, 'tis impossible.

GRE. Why he's a devil, a devil, a very fiend.

TRA. Why, she's a devil, a devil, the devil's dam.

GRE. Tut! she's a lamb, a dove, a fool to him.
I'll tell you, sir Lucentio; when the priest
Should ask—if Katharine should be his wife,
Ay, by gogs-wouns, quoth he; and swore so loud
That, all amaz'd, the priest let fall the book:
And, as he stoop'd again to take it up,
This mad-brain'd bridegroom took him such a cuff,

(*) First folio omits *I*.

[a] *An eyesore to our* solemn *festival.*] It may be mentioned once for all, that *solemn*, beside its ordinary sense of *grave, serious, ceremonial*, bore, in our author's time, the meaning of *public, accustomed*, and the like. Thus, in the present instance, Baptista does not mean a grave religious festival, but the customary public entertainment provided at weddings.

[b] *But, sir, to love—*] The old copy omits the preposition, we presume by accident, since both sense and prosody require it.

That down fell priest and book, and book and priest;
Now take them up, quoth he, *if any list*.

TRA. What said the wench, when he rose up again? [a]

GRE. Trembled and shook; for why[b] he stamp'd, and swore,
As if the vicar meant to cozen him.
But after many ceremonies done,
He calls for wine:—*A health*, quoth he, as if
He had been aboard, carousing to his mates
After a storm:—quaff'd off the muscadel,(2)
And threw the sops all in the sexton's face;
Having no other reason,—
But that his beard grew thin and hungerly,
And seem'd to ask him sops as he was drinking.
This done, he took the bride about the neck,
And kiss'd her lips with such a clamorous smack,[c]
That, at the parting, all the church did echo.
And I, seeing this, came thence for very shame;
And after me, I know, the rout is coming:
Such a mad marriage never was before.
Hark, hark! I hear the minstrels play. [*Music.*

Enter PETRUCHIO, KATHARINA, BIANCA, BAPTISTA, HORTENSIO, GRUMIO, *and Train.*

PET. Gentlemen and friends, I thank you for your pains:
I know, you think to dine with me to-day,
And have prepar'd great store of wedding cheer;
But so it is, my haste doth call me hence,
And therefore here I mean to take my leave.

BAP. Is't possible you will away to-night?

PET. I must away to-day, before night come:
Make it no wonder; if you knew my business
You would entreat me rather go than stay.
And, honest company, I thank you all,
That have beheld me give away myself
To this most patient, sweet, and virtuous wife:
Dine with my father, drink a health to me;
For I must hence, and farewell to you all.

TRA. Let us entreat you stay till after dinner.

PET. It may not be.

GRE. Let me entreat you.

PET. It cannot be.

KATH. Let me entreat you.

PET. I am content.

KATH. Are you content to stay?

PET. I am content you shall entreat me stay;
But yet not stay, entreat me how you can.

KATH. Now, if you love me, stay.

PET. Grumio, my horse.[d]

GRU. Ay, sir, they be ready; the oats have eaten the horses.

KATH. Nay, then,
Do what thou canst, I will not go to-day;
No, nor to-morrow, not till I please myself.
The door is open, sir, there lies your way,
You may be jogging whiles your boots are green;
For me, I'll not be gone, till I please myself:
'T is like, you'll prove a jolly surly groom,
That take it on you at the first so roundly.

PET. O Kate, content thee; prithee be not angry.

KATH. I will be angry: what hast thou to do?
Father, be quiet; he shall stay my leisure.

GRE. Ay, marry, sir; now it begins to work.

KATH. Gentlemen, forward to the bridal dinner:
I see, a woman may be made a fool,
If she had not a spirit to resist.

PET. They shall go forward, Kate, at thy command:
Obey the bride, you that attend on her:
Go to the feast, revel and domineer,
Carouse full measure to her maidenhead,
Be mad and merry,—or go hang yourselves.
But for my bonny Kate, she must with me.
Nay, look not big, nor stamp, nor stare, nor fret;
I will be master of what is mine own:
She is my goods, my chattels; she is my house,
My household stuff, my field, my barn,
My horse, my ox, my ass, my anything;
And here she stands, touch her whoever dare,
I'll bring mine action on the proudest he
That stops my way in Padua. Grumio,
Draw forth thy weapon, we are beset with thieves;
Rescue thy mistress, if thou be a man:—
Fear not, sweet wench, they shall not touch thee, Kate;
I'll buckler thee against a million.
[*Exeunt* PETRUCHIO, KATHARINA, *and* GRUMIO.(3)

BAP. Nay, let them go, a couple of quiet ones.

GRE. Went they not quickly, I should die with laughing.

---

a *When he rose* up *again?*] So the second folio; the first omits *up*.

b For why—] That is, *because*. See Note (c), p. 130, of the present volume.

c And kiss'd her lips *with such a clamorous smack*,—] The salutation of the bride was part of the ancient marriage-ceremony:—"Surgant ambo, sponsus et sponsa, et accipiat sponsus pacem a sacerdote, et ferat sponsæ, *osculans eam*, et neminem alium, nec ipse, nec ipsa." *Manuale Sarum.* Paris, 1533. Quarto. So in Marston's *Insatiate Countess*;—

"The *kisse thou gav'st me in the church*, here take."

d *Grumio, my* horse.] From Grumio's reply, we must take *horse* to be used as a plural here. The after observation, that "the oats have eaten the horses," is, perhaps, allied to a saying common in the stable now:—"the horses have eaten their heads off," implying, that the money due for their provender is more than they are worth. In the corresponding passage of the old play, the meaning is expressed more openly:—

"SAN. The ostler will not let me have him: you owe tenpence
For his meat and 6 pence for stuffing my Mistris saddle."

TRA. Of all mad matches, never was the like!
LUC. Mistress, what's your opinion of your sister?
BIAN. That, being mad herself, she's madly mated.
GRE. I warrant him, Petruchio is Kated.
BAP. Neighbours and friends, though bride and bridegroom wants,
For to supply the places at the table,
You know there wants no junkets at the feast;
Lucentio, you shall supply the bridegroom's place;
And let Bianca take her sister's room.
TRA. Shall sweet Bianca practise how to bride it?
BAP. She shall, Lucentio.—Come, gentlemen, let's go. [*Exeunt.*

ACT IV.

SCENE I.—*A Hall in* Petruchio's *Country House.*

Enter GRUMIO.

GRU. Fie, fie, on all tired jades! on all mad masters! and all foul ways! Was ever man so beaten? was ever man so rayed?[a] was ever man so weary? I am sent before to make a fire, and they are coming after to warm them: now, were not I a little pot, and soon hot, my very lips might freeze to my teeth, my tongue to the roof of my mouth, my heart in my belly, ere I should come by a fire to thaw me; but, I, with blowing the fire, shall warm myself; for, considering the weather, a taller man than I will take cold. Holla, hoa! Curtis!

Enter CURTIS.

CURT. Who is that calls so coldly?

GRU. A piece of ice; if thou doubt it, thou mayst slide from my shoulder to my heel, with no

[a] *Was ever man so* rayed?] *Rayed*, say the commentators, is *befouled, bemired:* perhaps here it rather means, *chafed, excoriated, frayed*, from the French *rayer*.

greater a run but my head and my neck. A fire, good Curtis.

CURT. Is my master and his wife coming, Grumio?

GRU. O, ay, Curtis, ay: and therefore fire, fire; cast on no water.

CURT. Is she so hot a shrew as she 's reported?

GRU. She was, good Curtis, before this frost: but, thou know'st, winter tames man, woman, and beast; for it hath tamed my old master and my new mistress, and myself,[a] fellow Curtis.

CURT. Away, you three-inch fool! I am no beast.

GRU. Am I but three inches? why, thy horn is a foot; and so long am I, at the least: but wilt thou make a fire, or shall I complain on thee to our mistress, whose hand (she being now at hand) thou shalt soon feel, to thy cold comfort, for being slow in thy hot office?

CURT. I prithee, good Grumio, tell me, how goes the world?

GRU. A cold world, Curtis, in every office but thine; and, therefore, fire: do thy duty, and have thy duty; for my master and mistress are almost frozen to death.

CURT. There's fire ready; and, therefore, good Grumio, the news?

GRU. Why, *Jack, boy! ho, boy!*[b] and as much news as thou wilt.*

CURT. Come, you are so full of coneycatching.

GRU. Why, therefore, fire; for I have caught extreme cold. Where's the cook? is supper ready, the house trimmed, rushes strewed, cobwebs swept; the serving-men in their new fustian, the white stockings, and every officer his wedding garment on? Be the jacks fair within, the jills fair without,[c] the carpets laid,[d] and everything in order?

CURT. All ready: and, therefore, I pray thee, news?

GRU. First, know, my horse is tired; my master and mistress fallen out.

CURT. How?

GRU. Out of their saddles into the dirt: and thereby hangs a tale.

CURT. Let's ha't, good Grumio.

GRU. Lend thine ear.

CURT. Here.

GRU. There. [*Striking him.*

CURT. This 'tis to feel a tale, not to hear a tale.

GRU. And therefore 'tis called, a sensible tale; and this cuff was but to knock at your ear, and beseech listening. Now I begin: *Imprimis*, we came down a foul hill, my master riding behind my mistress:—

CURT. Both of one horse?

GRU. What's that to thee?

CURT. Why, a horse.

GRU. Tell thou the tale:—but hadst thou not crossed me, thou shouldst have heard how her horse fell, and she under her horse; thou shouldst have heard, in how miry a place: how she was bemoiled; how he left her with the horse upon her; how he beat me because her horse stumbled; how she waded through the dirt to pluck him off me; how he swore; how she prayed, that never prayed before; how I cried; how the horses ran away; how her bridle was burst;[e] how I lost my crupper; with many things of worthy memory, which now shall die in oblivion, and thou return unexperienced to thy grave.

CURT. By this reckoning, he is more shrew than she.

GRU. Ay; and that thou and the proudest of you all shall find when he comes home. But what talk I of this?—call forth Nathaniel, Joseph, Nicholas, Philip, Walter, Sugarsop, and the rest. Let their heads be slickly combed, their blue coats brushed, and their garters of an indifferent[f] knit: let them curtsey with their left legs; and not presume to touch a hair of my master's horse-tail, till they kiss their hands. Are they all ready?

CURT. They are.

GRU. Call them forth.

CURT. Do you hear, ho! you must meet my master, to countenance[g] my mistress.

GRU. Why, she hath a face of her own.

CURT. Who knows not that?

GRU. Thou, it seems, that calls for company to countenance her.

(*) Folio, 1623, *wilt thou.*

[a] *And* myself, *fellow Curtis.*] For *myself*, Warburton substituted *thyself*, and, notwithstanding the ingenious defence of *myself* by other critics, was perhaps right.

[b] Jack, boy! ho, boy!] This is the commencement of an old round in three parts, of which Hawkins has given the notes in the *Variorum* Shakespeare.

[c] Be the jacks fair within, the jills fair without,—] A quibble. Certain drinking vessels were called *Jacks and Jills*, which terms, too, were commonly applied to the male and female servants. The same pun is found in the "Puritan," 1607. "I owe money to several hostesses, and you know such *jills* will quickly be upon a man's *jack*."

[d] *The* carpets *laid*,—] The *carpets* here meant were coverings for the tables. The floors were strewed with rushes.

[e] Burst;] That is, *broken*. So in the opening scene of the Induction; the Hostess asks, "You will not pay for the glasses you have *burst?*"

[f] *Of an* indifferent *knit:*] Shakespeare sometimes uses indifferent in the sense of *impartial, free from bias*,—

"——— I beseech your grace,
Look on my wrongs with an *indifferent eye*."
Richard II. Act II. Sc. 3.

But by "*an indifferent knit*" is simply meant a *passable*, or *tolerable* knit. So in "Twelfth Night," Act I. Sc. 5,—

"—— as, item, two lips *indifferent* red."

[g] *To* countenance *my mistress.*] That is, to *receive* or *entertain* her. "The old Law was, that when a Man was Fin'd, he was to be Fin'd *Salvo Contenemento*, so as his Countenance might be safe, taking *Countenance* in the same sense as your Country man does, when he says, *if you will come unto my House, I will shew you the best Countenance I can*, that is not the best Face, but the best Entertainment."—SELDEN'S *Table-Talk*, Art. *Fines.*

CURT. I call them forth to credit her.

GRU. Why, she comes to borrow nothing of them.

Enter four or five Serving-men.

NATH. Welcome home, Grumio.

PHIL. How now, Grumio?

JOS. What, Grumio!

NICH. Fellow Grumio!

NATH. How now, old lad?

GRU. Welcome, you;—how now, you;—what, you;—fellow, you;—and thus much for greeting. Now, my spruce companions, is all ready, and all things neat?

NATH. All things is ready: how near is our master?

GRU. E'en at hand, alighted by this: and therefore be not—Cock's passion, silence!—I hear my master.

Enter PETRUCHIO *and* KATHARINA.

PET. Where be these knaves? what, no man at door,
To hold my stirrup, nor to take my horse?
Where is Nathaniel, Gregory, Philip?

ALL SERV. Here, here, sir; here, sir.

PET. *Here, sir! here, sir! here, sir! here, sir!*
You loggerheaded and unpolish'd grooms!
What? no attendance? no regard? no duty?
Where is the foolish knave I sent before?

GRU. Here, sir; as foolish as I was before.

PET. You peasant swain! you whoreson malt-horse drudge!
Did I not bid thee meet me in the park,

And bring along these rascal knaves with thee?

GRU. Nathaniel's coat, sir, was not fully made,
And Gabriel's pumps were all unpink'd i' the heel;
There was no link to colour Peter's hat,[a]
And Walter's dagger was not come from sheathing:
There were none fine but Adam, Ralph, and Gregory;
The rest were ragged, old, and beggarly;
Yet, as they are, here are they come to meet you.

PET. Go, rascals, go, and fetch my supper in.—
[*Exeunt some of the* Servants.
Where is the life that late I led— [*Sings.*
Where are those——sit down, Kate, and welcome.
Soud, soud, soud, soud![b]

Re-enter Servants, *with Supper.*

Why, when, I say?—nay, good sweet Kate, be merry.
Off with my boots, you rogues, you villains; when?
It was the friar of orders grey, [*Sings.*
As he forth walked on his way:
Out, you rogue! you pluck my foot awry:
Take that, and mend the plucking of the other.—
[*Strikes him.*
Be merry, Kate:—some water here; what, ho!
Where's my spaniel Troilus? Sirrah, get you hence,
And bid my cousin Ferdinand come hither:
[*Exit* Servant.
One, Kate, that you must kiss, and be acquainted with.
Where are my slippers?—shall I have some water?
[*A bason is presented to him.*
Come, Kate, and wash, and welcome heartily:—
[Servant *lets the ewer fall.*
You whoreson villain! will you let it fall?
[*Strikes him.*

KATH. Patience, I pray you; 't was a fault unwilling.

PET. A whoreson, beetle-headed, flap-ear'd knave!
Come, Kate, sit down; I know you have a stomach.
Will you give thanks, sweet Kate, or else shall I?
What's this? mutton?

1 SERV. Ay.

---

[a] No link to colour Peter's hat,—] "This cozenage is used likewise in selling old hats found upon dung-hills instead of newe, blackt over with *the smoake of an olde linke*."—GREENE'S *Mihil Mumchance*. In this ludicrous enumeration of his fellows' deficiencies, Grumio is evidently playing into his master's hands. It is all, as Lucio says, "according to the trick."

[b] Soud, soud, soud, soud!] Malone thought this *soud* a word coined by Shakespeare to express the noise made by a person heated and fatigued.

PET. Who brought it?
1 SERV. I.
PET. 'T is burnt; and so is all the meat:
What dogs are these!—where is the rascal cook?
How durst you, villains, bring it from the dresser,
And serve it thus to me that love it not?
There, take it to you, trenchers, cups, and all:
[*Throws the meat, &c., about the stage.*
You heedless joltheads, and unmanner'd slaves!
What, do you grumble? I'll be with you straight.
KATH. I pray you, husband, be not so disquiet;
The meat was well, if you were so contented.
PET. I tell thee, Kate, 'twas burnt and dried away;
And I expressly am forbid to touch it,
For it engenders choler, planteth anger;
And better 't were that both of us did fast,
Since, of ourselves, ourselves are choleric,
Than feed it with such over-roasted flesh.
Be patient; to-morrow it shall be mended,
And, for this night, we'll fast for company:
Come, I will bring thee to thy bridal chamber.
[*Exeunt* PETRUCHIO, KATHARINA, *and* CURTIS.
NATH. [*Advancing.*] Peter, didst ever see the like?
PETER. He kills her in her own humour.

Re-enter CURTIS.

GRU. Where is he?
CURT. In her chamber,
Making a sermon of continency to her:
And rails, and swears, and rates; that she, poor soul,
Knows not which way to stand, to look, to speak;
And sits as one new-risen from a dream.
Away, away! for he is coming hither. [*Exeunt.*

Re-enter PETRUCHIO.

PET. Thus have I politicly begun my reign,
And 'tis my hope to end successfully;
My falcon now is sharp, and passing empty,
And, till she stoop, she must not be full-gorg'd,
For then she never looks upon her lure.
Another way I have to man my haggard,
To make her come, and know her keeper's call;
That is, to watch her, as we watch these kites,
That bate, and beat, and will not be obedient.
She eat no meat to-day, nor none shall eat;
Last night she slept not, nor to-night she shall not;
As with the meat, some undeserved fault
I'll find about the making of the bed;
And here I'll fling the pillow, there the bolster,
This way the coverlet, another way the sheets:—
Ay, and amid this hurly, I intend,[a]
That all is done in reverend care of her;
And, in conclusion, she shall watch all night:
And, if she chance to nod, I'll rail and brawl,
And with the clamour keep her still awake.
This is a way to kill a wife with kindness;[b]
And thus I'll curb her mad and headstrong humour;
He that knows better how to tame a shrew,
Now let him speak; 'tis charity to shew. [*Exit.*(1)

SCENE II.—Padua. *Before* Baptista's *House.*

Enter TRANIO *and* HORTENSIO.

TRA. Is't possible, friend Licio, that mistress Bianca
Doth fancy any other but Lucentio?
I tell you, sir, she bears me fair in hand.[c]
HOR. Sir, to satisfy you in what I have said,
Stand by, and mark the manner of his teaching.
[*They stand aside.*

Enter BIANCA *and* LUCENTIO.

LUC. Now, mistress, profit you in what you read?
BIAN. What, master, read you? first resolve me that.
LUC. I read that I profess, the art to love.
BIAN. And may you prove, sir, master of your art!
LUC. While you, sweet dear, prove mistress of my heart. [*They retire.*
HOR. Quick proceeders, marry! now, tell me, I pray,
You that durst swear that your mistress Bianca
Lov'd none* in the world so well as Lucentio.
TRA. O despiteful love! unconstant woman-kind!
I tell thee, Licio, this is wonderful.
HOR. Mistake no more: I am not Licio,
Nor a musician, as I seem to be;
But one that scorn to live in this disguise,
For such a one as leaves a gentleman,
And makes a god of such a cullion:

---

[a] *Amid this hurly,* I intend,—] *Intend* for *pretend.* So in "Richard III." Act III. Sc. 7,—

"The mayor is here at hand; *intend* some fear."

[b] To kill a wife with kindness;] This has been thought an allusion to Thomas Heywood's play, "A Woman Killed with Kindness," which is mentioned in Henslowe's Diary, under the date of February, 1602-3. We believe the saying was much older than the play.

[c] She bears me fair in hand.] *To bear in hand* was to *encourage,* to *buoy up.* Thus in "Much Ado About Nothing," Act. IV. Sc. 1,—"What! *bear her in hand* until they come to take hands; and then."—

(*) First folio, *me.*

Know, sir, that I am call'd Hortensio.
TRA. Signior Hortensio, I have often heard
Of your entire affection to Bianca;
And since mine eyes are witness of her lightness,
I will with you,—if you be so contented,—
Forswear Bianca, and her love for ever.
HOR. See, how they kiss and court! Signior Lucentio,
Here is my hand, and here I firmly vow
Never to woo her more; but do forswear her,
As one unworthy all the former favours
That I have fondly flatter'd her* withal.
TRA. And here I take the like unfeigned oath,
Never to marry with her, though she would entreat:
Fie on her! see, how beastly she doth court him.
HOR. Would all the world, but he, had quite forsworn!
For me, that I may surely keep mine oath,
I will be married to a wealthy widow,
Ere three days pass, which hath as long lov'd me,

(*) First folio, *them.*

As I have lov'd this proud disdainful haggard:
And so farewell, signior Lucentio.
Kindness in women, not their beauteous looks,
Shall win my love: and so I take my leave,
In resolution as I swore before.
[*Exit* HORTENSIO.—LUCENTIO *and* BIANCA *advance.*
TRA. Mistress Bianca, bless you with such grace
As 'longeth to a lover's blessed case!
Nay, I have ta'en you napping, gentle love;
And have forsworn you with Hortensio.
BIAN. Tranio, you jest: but have you both forsworn me?
TRA. Mistress, we have.
LUC. Then we are rid of Licio.
TRA. I' faith, he'll have a lusty widow now,
That shall be woo'd and wedded in a day.
BIAN. God give him joy!
TRA. Ay, and he'll tame her.
BIAN. He says so, Tranio.
TRA. 'Faith, he 's gone unto the taming-school.

BIAN. The taming-school! what, is there such a place?

TRA. Ay, mistress, and Petruchio is the master;
That teacheth tricks eleven and twenty long,
To tame a shrew, and charm her chattering tongue.

Enter BIONDELLO, *running.*

BION. O master, master, I have watch'd so long
That I'm dog-weary; but at last I spied
An ancient angel(2) coming down the hill,
Will serve the turn.

TRA. What is he, Biondello?

BION. Master, a mercatante, or a pedant,[a]
I know not what; but formal in apparel,
In gait and countenance surely like a father.[b]

LUC. And what of him, Tranio?

TRA. If he be credulous, and trust my tale,
I'll make him glad to seem Vincentio;
And give assurance to Baptista Minola,
As if he were the right Vincentio.
Take in[c] your love, and then let me alone.
[*Exeunt* LUCENTIO *and* BIANCA.

Enter a Pedant.

PED. God save you, sir!

TRA. And you, sir! you are welcome.
Travel you far on, or are you at the farthest?

PED. Sir, at the farthest for a week or two;
But then up farther; and as far as Rome;
And so to Tripoli, if God lend me life.

TRA. What countryman, I pray?

PED. Of Mantua.

TRA. Of Mantua, sir?—marry, God forbid!
And come to Padua, careless of your life?

PED. My life, sir! how, I pray? for that goes hard.

TRA. 'T is death for any one in Mantua
To come to Padua. Know you not the cause?
Your ships are stay'd at Venice; and the duke
(For private quarrel 'twixt your duke and him)
Hath publish'd and proclaim'd it openly:
'T is marvel; but that you are but newly come,
You might have heard it else proclaim'd about.

PED. Alas, sir, it is worse for me than so;
For I have bills for money by exchange
From Florence, and must here deliver them.

TRA. Well, sir, to do you courtesy,
This will I do, and this I will advise you:
First, tell me, have you ever been at Pisa?

PED. Ay, sir, in Pisa have I often been;
Pisa, renowned for grave citizens.

TRA. Among them, know you one Vincentio?

PED. I know him not, but I have heard of him;
A merchant of incomparable wealth.

TRA. He is my father, sir; and, sooth to say,
In countenance somewhat doth resemble you.

BION. As much as an apple doth an oyster, and all one. [*Aside.*

TRA. To save your life in this extremity,
This favour will I do you for his sake;
And think it not the worst of all your fortunes
That you are like to sir Vincentio.[d]
His name and credit shall you undertake,
And in my house you shall be friendly lodg'd.
Look, that you take upon you as you should;
You understand me, sir;—so shall you stay
Till you have done your business in the city:
If this be court'sy, sir, accept of it.

PED. O, sir, I do; and will repute you ever
The patron of my life and liberty.

TRA. Then go with me, to make the matter good.
This, by the way, I let you understand;
My father is here look'd for every day,
To pass assurance of a dower in marriage
'Twixt me and one Baptista's daughter here:
In all these circumstances I'll instruct you:
Go with me, sir,[e] to clothe you as becomes you.
[*Exeunt.*

SCENE III.—*A Room in* Petruchio'*s House.*

Enter KATHARINA *and* GRUMIO.

GRU. No, no; forsooth, I dare not, for my life.

KATH. The more my wrong, the more his spite appears:
What, did he marry me to famish me?
Beggars that come unto my father's door,
Upon entreaty, have a present alms;
If not, elsewhere they meet with charity:
But I, who never knew how to entreat,
Nor never needed that I should entreat,
Am starv'd for meat, giddy for lack of sleep;
With oaths kept waking, and with brawling fed:
And that which spites me more than all these wants,
He does it under name of perfect love;

---

[a] A mercatante, or a pedant,—] *A merchant*, or a *schoolmaster*. In the old copy *Marcantant*.

[b] Surely *like a father*.] The second folio reads "*Surly* like a father," which is preferable; *surly* meaning *proud*, *lofty*, &c.

[c] *Take* in—] The first folio has "Take *me*," which Theobald corrected.

[d] Like to sir Vincentio.] We should probably read :—

"That you are like, sir, to Vincentio."

[e] *Go with me*, sir,—] The *sir* was added in the second folio.

As who should say, if I should sleep, or eat,
'Twere deadly sickness, or else present death.
I prithee go, and get me some repast;
I care not what, so it be wholesome food.

Gru. What say you to a neat's foot?

Kath. 'T is passing good; I prithee let me have it.

Gru. I fear, it is too choleric a meat:
How say you to a fat tripe, finely broil'd?

Kath. I like it well; good Grumio, fetch it me.

Gru. I cannot tell; I fear, 't is choleric.
What say you to a piece of beef, and mustard?

Kath. A dish that I do love to feed upon.

Gru. Ay, but the mustard is too hot a little.

Kath. Why, then the beef, and let the mustard rest.

Gru. Nay, then I will not; you shall have the mustard,
Or else you get no beef of Grumio.

Kath. Then both, or one, or anything thou wilt.

Gru. Why, then the mustard without the beef.

Kath. Go, get thee gone, thou false deluding slave, [*Beats him.*(3
That feed'st me with the very name of meat:
Sorrow on thee, and all the pack of you,
That triumph thus upon my misery!
Go, get thee gone, I say.

Enter PETRUCHIO, *with a dish of meat; and* HORTENSIO.

PET. How fares my Kate? what, sweeting, all amort?[a]
HOR. Mistress, what cheer?
KATH. 'Faith, as cold as can be.
PET. Pluck up thy spirits, look cheerfully upon me.
Here, love; thou seest how diligent I am,
To dress thy meat myself, and bring it thee:
[*Sets the dish on a table.*
I am sure, sweet Kate, this kindness merits thanks.
What, not a word? Nay, then thou lov'st it not;
And all my pains is sorted to no proof:
Here, take away this dish.
KATH. I pray you, let it stand.
PET. The poorest service is repaid with thanks;
And so shall mine, before you touch the meat.
KATH. I thank you, sir.
HOR. Signior Petruchio, fie! you are to blame:
Come, mistress Kate, I'll bear you company.
PET. Eat it up all, Hortensio, if thou lov'st me.
[*Aside.*
Much good do it unto thy gentle heart!
Kate, eat apace;—and now, my honey love,
Will we return unto thy father's house;
And revel it as bravely as the best,
With silken coats, and caps, and golden rings,
With ruffs, and cuffs, and farthingales, and things;
With scarfs, and fans, and double change of bravery,

---

[a] *All* amort?] A gallicism often met with in our old dramatists, meaning *dejected, dispirited, out of heart;* in which sense it is still used in the Eastern Counties. It occurs again in "Henry VI." Pt. I. Act III. Sc. 2,—

"What, *all amort?* Rouen hangs her head for grief."

With amber bracelets, beads, and all this knavery.
What, hast thou dined? The tailor stays thy leisure,
To deck thy body with his ruffling treasure.

Enter Tailor.

Come, tailor, let us see these ornaments;

Enter Haberdasher.

Lay forth the gown:—what news with you, sir?

HAB. Here is the cap your worship did bespeak.

PET. Why, this was moulded on a porringer;
A velvet dish;—fie, fie! 't is lewd and filthy;
Why, 't is a cockle, or a walnut-shell,
A knack, a toy, a trick, a baby's cap;
Away with it, come, let me have a bigger.

KATH. I'll have no bigger; this doth fit the time,
And gentlewomen wear such caps as these.

PET. When you are gentle, you shall have one too,
And not till then.

HOR. That will not be in haste. [*Aside.*

KATH. Why, sir, I trust, I may have leave to speak;

And speak I will. I am no child, no babe:
Your betters have endur'd me say my mind;
And, if you cannot, best you stop your ears.
My tongue will tell the anger of my heart;
Or else my heart, concealing it, will break;
And rather than it shall, I will be free
Even to the uttermost, as I please, in words.

PET. Why, thou say'st true; it is a* paltry cap,
A custard-coffin,[a] a bauble, a silken pie:
I love thee well, in that thou lik'st it not.

KATH. Love me, or love me not, I like the cap;
And it I will have, or I will have none.

PET. Thy gown? why, ay:—come, tailor, let us see 't.
O mercy, God! what masking stuff is here!
What 's this? a sleeve? 't is like a* demi-cannon:
What! up and down, carv'd like an apple tart?
Here 's snip, and nip, and cut, and slish, and slash,
Like to a censer[b] in a barber's shop:
Why, what, o' devil's name, tailor, call'st thou this?

HOR. I see, she 's like to have neither cap nor gown. [*Aside.*

TAI. You bid me make it orderly and well,
According to the fashion and the time.

PET. Marry, and did; but if you be remember'd,
I did not bid you mar it to the time.
Go, hop me over every kennel home,
For you shall hop without my custom, sir:
I'll none of it; hence, make your best of it.

KATH. I never saw a better fashion'd gown,
More quaint,[c] more pleasing, nor more commendable:
Belike, you mean to make a puppet of me.

PET. Why, true; he means to make a puppet of thee.

TAI. She says, your worship means to make a puppet of her.

PET. O monstrous arrogance! Thou liest, thou thread, thou thimble,
Thou yard, three-quarters, half-yard, quarter, nail,
Thou flea, thou nit, thou winter cricket thou:
Brav'd in mine own house with a skein of thread!
Away, thou rag, thou quantity, thou remnant;
Or I shall so be-mete thee with thy yard,
As thou shalt think on prating whilst thou liv'st!
I tell thee, I, that thou hast marr'd her gown.

TAI. Your worship is deceiv'd; the gown is made
Just as my master had direction:
Grumio gave order how it should be done.

GRU. I gave him no order; I gave him the stuff.

TAI. But how did you desire it should be made?

GRU. Marry, sir, with needle and thread.

TAI. But did you not request to have it cut?

GRU. Thou hast faced[d] many things.

TAI. I have.

GRU. Face not me: thou hast braved[e] many men; brave not me. I will neither be faced nor braved. I say unto thee—I bid thy master cut out the gown; but I did not bid him cut it to pieces: *ergo*, thou liest.

TAI. Why, here is the note of the fashion to testify.

PET. Read it.

GRU. The note lies in 's throat, if he say I said so.

TAI. *Imprimis, a loose-bodied gown:*

GRU. Master, if ever I said loose-bodied gown, sew me in the skirts of it, and beat me to death with a bottom of brown thread: I said, a gown.

PET. Proceed.

TAI. *With a small compassed cape;*

GRU. I confess the cape.

TAI. *With a trunk sleeve;*

GRU. I confess two sleeves.

TAI. *The sleeves curiously cut.*

PET. Ay, there's the villainy.

GRU. Error i' the bill, sir; error i' the bill. I commanded the sleeves should be cut out, and sewed up again: and that I'll prove upon thee, though thy little finger be armed in a thimble.

TAI. This is true, that I say; an I had thee in place where thou shouldst know it!

GRU. I am for thee straight; take thou the bill, give me thy mete-yard, and spare not me.

HOR. God-a-mercy, Grumio! then he shall have no odds.

PET. Well, sir, in brief, the gown is not for me.

GRU. You are i' the right, sir; 't is for my mistress.

PET. Go, take it up unto thy master's use.

GRU. Villain, not for thy life: take up my mistress' gown for thy master's use!

PET. Why, sir, what 's your conceit in that?

GRU. O, sir, the conceit is deeper than you think for:

(*) First folio omits, *a*.

[a] Custard-coffin,—] A *coffin*, Steevens tells us, was the old culinary term for the raised crust of a pie or custard.

[b] *Like to* a censer *in a barber's shop*:] A *censer* was a fire-pan with a pierced cover, in which perfumes were burnt to sweeten the place.

[c] *More* quaint,—] *Quaint* here means *dainty, neat;* but it sometimes implies, *nimbleness*, or *cleverness*, as in the "Tempest," Act I. Sc. 2,—

"——— My *quaint* Ariel."

[d] *Thou hast* faced *many things.*] *Turned over* many garments with *facings*. Thus in "Henry IV." Pt. I., Act V. Sc. 1,—

"To *face* the garment of rebellion
With some fine colour."

[e] *Thou hast* braved *many men*;] That is, *bedizened, ornamented*, many men. *Bravery* was an ancient term for sumptuous apparel; Petruchio uses it in this sense just before,—

"With scarfs, and fans, and *double change of bravery*."

And in Act I. Sc. 2, the old stage direction is,—

"Enter Tranio, *brave*."

Take up my mistress' gown to his master's use!
O, fie, fie, fie!

PET. Hortensio, say thou wilt see the tailor paid:— [*Aside.*
Go, take it hence; begone, and say no more.

HOR. Tailor, I'll pay thee for thy gown to-morrow.
Take no unkindness of his hasty words:
Away, I say; commend me to thy master. [*Exit* Tailor.

PET. Well, come, my Kate; we will unto your father's,
Even in these honest mean habiliments;
Our purses shall be proud, our garments poor:
For 't is the mind that makes the body rich;
And as the sun breaks through the darkest clouds,
So honour peereth in the meanest habit.
What, is the jay more precious than the lark,
Because his feathers are more beautiful?
Or is the adder better than the eel,
Because his painted skin contents the eye?
O, no, good Kate; neither art thou the worse
For this poor furniture and mean array.
If thou account'st it shame, lay it on me:
And therefore frolic; we will hence forthwith,
To feast and sport us at thy father's house.
Go, call my men, and let us straight to him;
And bring our horses unto Long-lane end,
There will we mount, and thither walk on foot.
Let's see; I think 't is now some seven o'clock,
And well we may come there by dinner-time.

KATH. I dare assure you, sir, 'tis almost two;
And 't will be supper-time ere you come there.

PET. It shall be seven, ere I go to horse:
Look, what I speak, or do, or think to do,
You are still crossing it.—Sirs, let 't alone:
I will not go to-day; and ere I do,
It shall be what o'clock I say it is.

HOR. Why, so! this gallant will command the sun. [*Exeunt.*(4)

SCENE IV.—Padua. *Before* Baptista's *House.*

Enter TRANIO, *and the* Pedant *dressed like* VINCENTIO.

TRA. Sir,* this is the house: please it you that I call?

PED. Ay, what else? and, but I be deceiv'd,
Signior Baptista may remember me,
Near twenty years ago, in Genoa,
Where we were lodgers at the Pegasus.[a]

TRA. 'T is well; and hold your own, in any case,
With such austerity as 'longeth to a father.

Enter BIONDELLO.

PED. I warrant you: but, sir, here comes your boy;
'T were good he were school'd.

TRA. Fear you not him. Sirrah Biondello,
Now do your duty thoroughly, I advise you;
Imagine 't were the right Vincentio.

BION. Tut! fear not me.

TRA. But hast thou done thy errand to Baptista?

BION. I told him, that your father was at Venice,
And that you look'd for him this day in Padua.

TRA. Thou 'rt a tall fellow; hold thee; that to drink.
Here comes Baptista:—set your countenance, sir.

Enter BAPTISTA *and* LUCENTIO.[b]

Signior Baptista, you are happily met:—
Sir, [*To the* Pedant] this is the gentleman I told you of:
I pray you, stand good father to me now,
Give me Bianca for my patrimony.

PED. Soft, son!
Sir, by your leave, having come to Padua
To gather in some debts, my son Lucentio
Made me acquainted with a weighty cause
Of love between your daughter and himself:
And,—for the good report I hear of you;
And for the love he beareth to your daughter,
And she to him,—to stay him not too long,
I am content, in a good father's care,
To have him match'd; and,—if you please to like
No worse than I,—upon some agreement,
Me shall you find ready and willing
With one consent to have her so bestow'd;
For curious[c] I cannot be with you,
Signior Baptista, of whom I hear so well.

BAP. Sir, pardon me in what I have to say;—
Your plainness and your shortness please me well.
Right true it is, your son Lucentio here
Doth love my daughter, and she loveth him,
Or both dissemble deeply their affections:
And, therefore, if you say no more than this,
That like a father you will deal with him,
And pass my daughter a sufficient dower,
The match is made, and all is done:
Your son shall have my daughter with consent.

(*) Old copy, *Sirs.*

[a] At the Pegasus.] In the old copy, 1623, this line is given to Tranio.

[b] *Enter* BAPTISTA *and* LUCENTIO.] The folio, 1623, adds, "Pedant booted and bare headed."

[c] Curious—] That is, *scrupulous.*

TRA. I thank you, sir: where then do you know best,
We be affied; and such assurance ta'en,
As shall with either part's agreement stand?

BAP. Not in my house, Lucentio; for, you know,
Pitchers have ears, and I have many servants:
Besides, old Gremio is heark'ning still;
And, happily, we might be interrupted.

TRA. Then at my lodging, an it like you, sir:[a]
There doth my father lie; and there, this night,
We 'll pass the business privately and well:
Send for your daughter by your servant here,
My boy shall fetch the scrivener presently.
The worst is this, that, at so slender warning,
You are like to have a thin and slender pittance.

BAP. It likes me well: Cambio, hie you home,
And bid Bianca make her ready straight;
And, if you will, tell what hath happened:
Lucentio's father is arriv'd in Padua,
And how she 's like to be Lucentio's wife!

LUC. I pray the gods she may, with all my heart![b]

TRA. Dally not with the gods, but get thee gone.
Signior Baptista, shall I lead the way?
Welcome! one mess is like to be your cheer;
Come, sir; we will better it in Pisa.

BAP. I follow you.

[*Exeunt* TRANIO, Pedant, *and* BAPTISTA.

BION. Cambio.

LUC. What say'st thou, Biondello?

BION. You saw my master wink and laugh upon you?

LUC. Biondello, what of that?

BION. 'Faith, nothing; but has left me here behind, to expound the meaning or moral of his signs and tokens.

LUC. I pray thee, moralize them.

BION. Then thus:—Baptista is safe talking with the deceiving father of a deceitful son.

LUC. And what of him?

BION. His daughter is to be brought by you to the supper.

LUC. And then?

BION. The old priest at Saint Luke's church is at your command at all hours.

LUC. And what of all this?

BION. I cannot tell: expect,[c] they are busied about a counterfeit assurance, take you assurance of her, *cum privilegio ad imprimendum solùm*, to the church;—take the priest, clerk, and some sufficient honest witnesses:

[a] *An it like you*, sir:] The word *sir* was added in the second folio.

[b] With all my heart!] In the old copy this line is assigned to Biondello, and the speaker is made to go out. The "business," no doubt, was, that Lucentio retired until Baptista, Tranio, and the Pedant, had left, and then came forward to confer privately with Biondello.

If this be not that you look for, I have no more to say,
But bid Bianca farewell for ever and a day.

[*Going.*

LUC. Hear'st thou, Biondello?

BION. I cannot tarry: I knew a wench married in an afternoon as she went to the garden for parsley to stuff a rabbit; and so may you, sir; and so adieu, sir. My master hath appointed me to go to Saint Luke's, to bid the priest be ready to come against you come with your appendix.

[*Exit.*

LUC. I may, and will, if she be so contented:
She will be pleas'd, then wherefore should I doubt?
Hap what hap may, I'll roundly go about her;
It shall go hard, if Cambio go without her. [*Exit.*

SCENE V.—*A Public Road.*

Enter PETRUCHIO, KATHARINA, *and* HORTENSIO.

PET. Come on, o' God's name; once more toward our father's.
Good Lord, how bright and goodly shines the moon!

KATH. The moon! the sun; it is not moonlight now.

PET. I say, it is the moon that shines so bright.

KATH. I know, it is the sun that shines so bright.

PET. Now, by my mother's son, and that's myself,
It shall be moon, or star, or what I list,
Or ere I journey to your father's house:—
Go on, and fetch our horses back again.—
Evermore cross'd and cross'd: nothing but cross'd!

HOR. Say as he says, or we shall never go.

KATH. Forward, I pray, since we have come so far,
And be it moon, or sun, or what you please:
An if you please to call it a rush candle,
Henceforth I vow it shall be so for me.

PET. I say, it is the moon.

KATH. I know it is the moon.

PET. Nay, then you lie; it is the blessed sun:

KATH. Then, God be bless'd, it is* the blessed sun:
But sun it is not, when you say it is not;
And the moon changes, even as your mind.
What you will have it nam'd, even that it is;
And so it shall be so, for Katharine.

(*) First folio, *in*.

[c] Expect,—] So the first folio. The second reads *except*. If *expect* is the poet's word, the meaning seems to be, *anticipate*. They are busied about a counterfeit assurance: Go you, anticipate their movements by obtaining a real one.

HOR. Petruchio, go thy ways; the field is won.
PET. Well, forward, forward: thus the bowl should run,
And not unluckily against the bias.
But soft! Company is coming here!

Enter VINCENTIO, *in a travelling dress.*

Good morrow, gentle mistress: where away?
[*To* VINCENTIO.
Tell me, sweet Kate, and tell me truly too,
Hast thou beheld a fresher gentlewoman?
Such war of white and red within her cheeks?
What stars do spangle heaven with such beauty,
As those two eyes become that heavenly face?
Fair lovely maid, once more good day to thee:
Sweet Kate, embrace her for her beauty's sake.
HOR. 'A will make the man mad, to make a[a] woman of him.
KATH. Young budding virgin, fair, and fresh, and sweet,
Whither away; or where[b] is thy abode?
Happy the parents of so fair a child;
Happier the man, whom favourable stars
Allots thee for his lovely bedfellow! (5)
PET. Why, how now, Kate? I hope thou art not mad:
This is a man, old, wrinkled, faded, wither'd;
And not a maiden, as thou say'st he is.
KATH. Pardon, old father, my mistaking eyes,
That have been so bedazzled with the sun,
That everything I look on seemeth green:
Now I perceive thou art a reverend father;
Pardon, I pray thee, for my mad mistaking.
PET. Do, good old grandsire; and, withal, make known
Which way thou travellest; if along with us,
We shall be joyful of thy company.
VIN. Fair sir, and you my merry mistress,
That with your strange encounter much amaz'd me,
My name is call'd Vincentio, my dwelling Pisa;
And bound I am to Padua; there to visit
A son of mine, which long I have not seen.
PET. What is his name?
VIN. Lucentio, gentle sir.
PET. Happily met; the happier for thy son.
And now by law, as well as reverent age,
I may entitle thee my loving father;
The sister to my wife, this gentlewoman,
Thy son by this hath married: wonder not,
Nor be not griev'd; she is of good esteem,
Her dowry wealthy, and of worthy birth;
Beside, so qualified as may beseem
The spouse of any noble gentleman.
Let me embrace with old Vincentio:
And wander we to see thy honest son,
Who will of thy arrival be full joyous.
VIN. But is this true? or is it else your pleasure,
Like pleasant travellers, to break a jest
Upon the company you overtake?
HOR. I do assure thee, father, so it is.
PET. Come, go along, and see the truth hereof;
For our first merriment hath made thee jealous.
[*Exeunt* PETRUCHIO, KATHARINA, *and* VINCENTIO.
HOR. Well, Petruchio, this has put me in heart.
Have to my widow; and if she be froward,[c]
Then hast thou taught Hortensio to be untoward.
[*Exit.*

[a] *To make a woman of him.*] Thus the second folio; the first has "*the* woman," &c.
[b] *Or* where—] The reading of the second folio; the first having "*whether*," &c.
[c] *And if she* be *froward,*—] The first folio omits *be*, which was supplied by the second.

ACT V.

SCENE I.—Padua. *Before* Lucentio's *House.*

Enter on one side BIONDELLO, LUCENTIO, *and* BIANCA; GREMIO *walking on the other side.*[a]

BION. Softly and swiftly, sir; for the priest is ready.

LUC. I fly, Biondello; but they may chance to need thee at home, therefore leave us.

BION. Nay, faith, I'll see the church o' your back; and then come back to my master* as soon as I can.

[*Exeunt* LUCENTIO, BIANCA, *and* BIONDELLO.

GRE. I marvel Cambio comes not all this while.

Enter PETRUCHIO, KATHARINA, VINCENTIO, *and* Attendants.

PET. Sir, here's the door, this is Lucentio's house,
My father's bears more toward the market-place;
Thither must I, and here I leave you, sir.

VIN. You shall not choose but drink before you go;
I think I shall command your welcome here,
And by all likelihood, some cheer is toward.
[*Knocks.*

GRE. They're busy within, you were best knock louder.

Enter Pedant *above at a window.*

PED. What's he that knocks as he would beat down the gate?

VIN. Is signior Lucentio within, sir?

PED. He's within, sir, but not to be spoken withal.

VIN. What if a man bring him a hundred pound or two to make merry withal?

PED. Keep your hundred pounds to yourself; he shall need none, as long as I live.

(*) Old copies, *Mistris.*

[a] GREMIO *walking on the other side.*] The original stage-direction is, *Enter Biondello, Lucentio and Bianca, Gremio is out before.*

PET. Nay, I told you your son was well beloved in Padua.—Do you hear, sir?—to leave frivolous circumstances,—I pray you, tell signior Lucentio, that his father is come from Pisa, and is here at the door to speak with him.

PED. Thou liest; his father is come from Pisa,* and here looking out at the window.

VIN. Art thou his father?

PED. Ay, sir; so his mother says, if I may believe her.

PET. Why, how now, gentleman! [*To* VINCEN.] why, this is flat knavery, to take upon you another man's name.

PED. Lay hands on the villain. I believe 'a means to cozen somebody in this city under my countenance.

Re-enter BIONDELLO.

BION. I have seen them in the church together; God send 'em good shipping!—but who is here? mine old master, Vincentio? now we are undone, and brought to nothing.

VIN. Come hither, crack-hemp.

[*Seeing* BIONDELLO.

BION. I hope I may choose, sir.

VIN. Come hither, you rogue; what, have you forgot me?

BION. Forgot you? no, sir: I could not forget you, for I never saw you before in all my life.

VIN. What, you notorious villain, didst thou never see thy master's father,[a] Vincentio?

BION. What, my old, worshipful old master? yes, marry, sir; see where he looks out of the window.

VIN. Is't so, indeed? [*Beats* BIONDELLO.

BION. Help, help, help! here's a madman will murder me. [*Exit.*

PED. Help, son! help, signior Baptista!

[*Exit from the window.*

PET. Prithee, Kate, let's stand aside, and see the end of this controversy. [*They retire.*

Re-enter Pedant *below;* BAPTISTA, TRANIO, *and* Servants.

TRA. Sir, what are you that offer to beat my servant?

VIN. What am I, sir? nay, what are you, sir? —O immortal gods! O fine villain! A silken doublet! a velvet hose! a scarlet cloak! and a copatain hat![b]—O, I am undone, I am undone! while I play the good husband at home, my son and my servant spend all at the university.

TRA. How now? what's the matter?

BAP. What, is the man lunatic?

TRA. Sir, you seem a sober ancient gentleman by your habit, but your words show you a madman. Why, sir, what concerns[c] it you if I wear pearl and gold? I thank my good father, I am able to maintain it.

VIN. Thy father? O villain! he is a sail-maker in Bergamo.

BAP. You mistake, sir; you mistake, sir; pray, what do you think is his name?

VIN. His name? as if I knew not his name: I have brought him up ever since he was three years old, and his name is Tranio.

PED. Away, away, mad ass! his name is Lucentio; and he is mine only son, and heir to the lands of me, signior Vincentio.

VIN. Lucentio! O, he hath murdered his master! lay hold on him, I charge you, in the duke's name: O, my son, my son!—tell me, thou villain, where is my son, Lucentio.

TRA. Call forth an officer:(1) carry this mad knave to the gaol:—Father Baptista, I charge you see that he be forthcoming.

VIN. Carry me to the gaol!

[*Enter one with an* Officer.

GRE. Stay, officer; he shall not go to prison.

BAP. Talk not, signior Gremio; I say he shall go to prison.

GRE. Take heed, signior Baptista, lest you be coney-catched[d] in this business; I dare swear this is the right Vincentio.

PED. Swear, if thou darest.

GRE. Nay, I dare not swear it.

TRA. Then thou wert best say that I am not Lucentio.

GRE. Yes, I know thee to be signior Lucentio.

BAP. Away with the dotard; to the gaol with him.

VIN. Thus strangers may be haled and abus'd. O monstrous villain!

Re-enter BIONDELLO, *with* LUCENTIO *and* BIANCA.

BION. O, we are spoiled, and—yonder he is; deny him, forswear him, or else we are all undone.

LUC. Pardon, sweet father. [*Kneeling.*

VIN. Lives my sweet son?

[BIONDELLO, TRANIO, *and* Pedant *run out.*[e]

BIAN. Pardon, dear father. [*Kneeling.*

(*) Old copies, *Padua.*

[a] *Thy master's father,*—] The first folio reads *mistris,* which was corrected in the second folio.

[b] A copatain hat!—] This was a high-crowned hat shaped like a sugar-loaf. "Upon their heads they ware felt-hats *copple-tanked,* a quarter of an ell high or more."—*Comines, trans. by Danet.*

[c] Concerns—] In the first folio, "*cerns.*" We read after the second edition.

[d] Coney-catched—] That is, *cheated, imposed upon.* We gather from Decker's "English Villanies," that formerly the sharpers termed their gang *a warren,* and their simpleton-victims *rabbit-suckers* (young rabbits), or *conies.* At other times their confederates were called *bird-catchers,* and their prey *gulls* (raw, unfledged greenhorns): and hence it was common to say of any person who had been swindled, or hoaxed, he was *coney-catched,* or *gulled.*

[e] *Run out.*] The old copy adds, "*as fast as may be.*"

BAP. How hast thou offended?
Where is Lucentio?
LUC. Here's Lucentio,
Right son unto* the right Vincentio;
That have by marriage made thy daughter mine,
While counterfeit supposes[a] blear'd thine eyne.
GRE. Here's packing[b] with a witness, to deceive us all!
VIN. Where is that damned villain, Tranio,
That fac'd and brav'd me in this matter so?
BAP. Why, tell me, is not this my Cambio?
BIAN. Cambio is chang'd into Lucentio.
LUC. Love wrought these miracles. Bianca's love
Made me exchange my state with Tranio,
While he did bear my countenance in the town;
And happily I have arrived at the last,
Unto the wished haven of my bliss:
What Tranio did, myself enforc'd him to;
Then pardon him, sweet father, for my sake.
VIN. I'll slit the villain's nose, that would have sent me to the gaol.
BAP. But do you hear, sir? [*To* LUCENTIO.] Have you married my daughter without asking my good-will?
VIN. Fear not, Baptista; we will content you: go to: but I will in, to be revenged for this villainy. [*Exit.*
BAP. And I, to sound the depth of this knavery. [*Exit.*
LUC. Look not pale, Bianca; thy father will not frown. [*Exeunt* LUC. *and* BIAN.
GRE. My cake is dough:[c] but I'll in among the rest;
Out of hope of all,—but my share of the feast. [*Exit.*

PETRUCHIO *and* KATHARINA *advance.*

KATH. Husband, let's follow, to see the end of this ado.
PET. First kiss me, Kate, and we will.
KATH. What, in the midst of the street?
PET. What, art thou ashamed of me?
KATH. No, sir; God forbid:—but ashamed to kiss.
PET. Why, then, let's home again:—come, sirrah, let's away.
KATH. Nay, I will give thee a kiss: now pray thee, love, stay.
PET. Is not this well?—come, my sweet Kate;
Better once than never, for never too late. [*Exeunt.*[d]

SCENE II.—*A Room in* Lucentio's *House.*

A banquet set out. Enter BAPTISTA, VINCENTIO, GREMIO, *the* Pedant, LUCENTIO, BIANCA, PETRUCHIO, KATHARINA, HORTENSIO, *and* Widow. TRANIO, BIONDELLO, GRUMIO, *and others, attending.*

LUC. At last, though long, our jarring notes agree;
And time it is, when raging war is done,[e]
To smile at 'scapes and perils overblown.
My fair Bianca, bid my father welcome,
While I with self-same kindness welcome thine:
Brother Petruchio,—sister Katharina,—
And thou, Hortensio, with thy loving widow,—
Feast with the best, and welcome to my house.
My banquet[f] is to close our stomachs up,
After our great good cheer: pray you, sit down;
For now we sit to chat, as well as eat. [*They sit at table.*
PET. Nothing but sit and sit, and eat and eat.
BAP. Padua affords this kindness, son Petruchio.
PET. Padua affords nothing but what is kind.
HOR. For both our sakes, I would that word were true.
PET. Now, for my life, Hortensio fears[g] his widow.
WID. Then never trust me if I be afeard.
PET. You are very sensible, and yet you miss my sense;
I mean, Hortensio is afeard of you.
WID. He that is giddy thinks the world turns round.

(*) Old copies, *to.*

[a] *While counterfeit* supposes—] *Supposes* is here used in the same sense as in Gascoigne's Comedy of that name, for *impostors, changelings,* &c.

[b] *Here's* packing—] *Iniquitous collusion, chicanery, plotting.* The word is used metaphorically from *packing* cards with the view to defraud.

[c] My cake is dough:] See Note (b), p. 234.

[d] *Exeunt.*] In the original, the following stage direction and dialogue occur, after the parallel scene to this,—

"*Slie* sleepes.
Lord. Whose within there? come hither sirs my Lords
Asleepe againe: go take him easily vp,
And put him in his one apparel againe,
And lay him in the place where we did find him,
Iust vnderneath the alehouse side below,
But see you wake him not in any case.
Boy. It shall be don my Lord come helpe to beare him hence,
Exit."

[e] *When raging war is* done,—] The old copies have, "When raging war is *come,*" which is obviously a misprint. Rowe substituted *done.*

[f] *My* banquet—] *A banquet,* with our old writers, sometimes meant what we call *a dessert*—a slight refection, consisting of fruit, sweetmeats, &c.; and was occasionally set out in a room separated from the dining apartment. Thus, in Massinger's "Unnatural Combat," Act III. Sc. 1,—

"We'll *dine* in the great room, but let the music
And *banquet* be prepared here."

See also *The City Madam,* Act II. Sc. 2. GIFFORD'S *Massinger.* More often, in Shakespeare, however, *a banquet* signifies a feast, as at the present day.

[g] *Hortensio* fears *his widow.*] To understand the equivoque, it must be remembered that *to fear* anciently had an active as well as a passive sense, and meant not only to feel alarm, but to frighten. So in Act I. Sc. 2,—

"——— *fear* boys with bugs,
For he *fears* none."

PET. Roundly replied.
KATH. Mistress, how mean you that?
WID. Thus I conceive by him.
PET. Conceives by me!—how likes Hortensio that?
HOR. My widow says, thus she conceives her tale.
PET. Very well mended: kiss him for that, good widow.
KATH. He that is giddy thinks the world turns round:—
I pray you, tell me what you meant by that.
WID. Your husband, being troubled with a shrew,[a]
Measures my husband's sorrow by his woe:
And now you know my meaning.
KATH. A very mean meaning.
WID. Right, I mean you.
KATH. And I am mean, indeed, respecting you.
PET. To her, Kate!
HOR. To her, widow!
PET. A hundred marks, my Kate does put her down.
HOR. That's my office.
PET. Spoke like an officer:—ha' to thee, lad.
[*Drinks to* HORTENSIO.
BAP. How likes Gremio these quick-witted folks?
GRE. Believe me, sir, they butt together well.
BIAN. Head, and butt? an hasty-witted body
Would say your head and butt were head and horn.
VIN. Ay, mistress bride, hath that awaken'd you?
BIAN. Ay, but not frighted me; therefore I'll sleep again.
PET. Nay, that you shall not; since you have begun,
Have at you for a bitter jest or two.[b]
BIAN. Am I your bird? I mean to shift my bush,
And then pursue me as you draw your bow:—
You are welcome all.
[*Exeunt* BIANCA, KATHARINA, *and* Widow.
PET. She hath prevented me: here, signior Tranio,
This bird you aim'd at, though you hit her not;
Therefore, a health to all that shot and miss'd.
TRA. O, sir, Lucentio slipp'd me like his greyhound,
Which runs himself, and catches for his master.
PET. A good swift simile, but something currish.
TRA. 'Tis well, sir, that you hunted for yourself;
'Tis thought, your deer does hold you at a bay.
BAP. O ho, Petruchio, Tranio hits you now.
LUC. I thank thee for that gird,[c] good Tranio.
HOR. Confess, confess, hath he not hit you here?

---

a Shrew,—woe:] *Shrew* was frequently pronounced, as well as spelt, *shrow*. Here it is evidently intended to rhyme with *woe*; and at the end of the play it couples with *so*.

b *A* bitter *jest or two*.] The old copies read, "a *better* jest." Capell suggested *bitter*, which was, no doubt, the poet's word. So in Act III. Sc. 2,—

"Hiding his *bitter* jests in blunt behaviour."

c I *thank thee for that* gird,—] *A sarcasm, a taunt, a bitter jest*. "His life is a perpetual satyr, and he is still *girding* the age's vanity, when this very anger shows he too much esteems it."—EARLE'S *Microcosmographie. Char.* 6.

PET. 'A has a little gall'd me, I confess;
And, as the jest did glance away from me,
'T is ten to one it maim'd you two* outright.

BAP. Now, in good sadness, son Petruchio,
I think thou hast the veriest shrew of all.

PET. Well, I say—no: and, therefore, for assurance,[a]
Let's each one send unto his wife;
And he, whose wife is most obedient
To come at first when he doth send for her,
Shall win the wager which we will propose.

HOR. Content: what is the wager?

LUC. Twenty crowns.

PET. Twenty crowns!
I'll venture so much of my hawk, or hound,
But twenty times so much upon my wife.

LUC. A hundred, then.

HOR. Content.

PET. A match; 'tis done.

HOR. Who shall begin?

LUC. That will I.
Go, Biondello, bid your mistress come to me.

BION. I go. [*Exit.*

BAP. Son, I will be your half, Bianca comes.

LUC. I'll have no halves; I'll bear it all myself.

Re-enter BIONDELLO.

How now! what news?

BION. Sir, my mistress sends you word
That she is busy, and she cannot come.

PET. How! she is busy, and she cannot come!
Is that an answer?

GRE. Ay, and a kind one too:
Pray God, sir, your wife send you not a worse.

PET. I hope, better.

HOR. Sirrah Biondello, go, and entreat my wife,
To come to me forthwith. [*Exit* BIONDELLO.

PET. O, ho! entreat her!
Nay, then she must needs come.

HOR. I am afraid, sir,
Do what you can, yours will not be entreated.

Re-enter BIONDELLO.

Now where 's my wife?

BION. She says, you have some goodly jest in hand;
She will not come; she bids you come to her.

PET. Worse and worse; she will not come! O vile,
Intolerable, not to be endur'd!
Sirrah Grumio, go to your mistress;
Say, I command her come to me. [*Exit* GRUMIO.

HOR. I know her answer.

PET. What?

HOR. She will not.

PET. The fouler fortune mine, and there an end.

Enter KATHARINA.

BAP. Now, by my holidam, here comes Katharina!

KATH. What is your will, sir, that you send for me?

PET. Where is your sister, and Hortensio's wife?

KATH. They sit conferring by the parlour fire.

PET. Go, fetch them hither; if they deny to come,
Swinge me them soundly forth unto their husbands:
Away, I say, and bring them hither straight. [*Exit* KATHARINA.

LUC. Here is a wonder, if you talk of a wonder.

HOR. And so it is; I wonder what it bodes.

PET. Marry, peace it bodes, and love, and quiet life,
An awful rule, and right supremacy;
And, to be short, what not, that's sweet and happy.

BAP. Now fair befall thee, good Petruchio!
The wager thou hast won; and I will add
Unto their losses twenty thousand crowns,
Another dowry to another daughter,
For she is chang'd, as she had never been.

PET. Nay, I will win my wager better yet;
And show more sign of her obedience,
Her new-built virtue and obedience.

Re-enter KATHARINA, *with* BIANCA *and* Widow.

See, where she comes; and brings your froward wives,
As prisoners to her womanly persuasion.
Katharine, that cap of yours becomes you not;
Off with that bauble, throw it under foot.
[KATHARINA *pulls off her cap, and throws it down.*

WID. Lord, let me never have a cause to sigh,
Till I be brought to such a silly pass!

BIAN. Fie! what a foolish duty call you this?

LUC. I would, your duty were as foolish too:
The wisdom of your duty, fair Bianca,
Hath cost me an hundred crowns[b] since supper-time.

BIAN. The more fool you, for laying on my duty.

PET. Katharine, I charge thee, tell these headstrong women,
What duty they do owe their lords and husbands.

WID. Come, come, you're mocking; we will have no telling.

PET. Come on, I say; and first begin with her.

WID. She shall not.

PET. I say, she shall;—and first begin with her.

KATH. Fie, fie! unknit that threat'ning unkind brow;

(*) First folio, *too*.

[a] For *assurance*,—] *For* is the correction of the second folio; the first has *sir*.

[b] An hundred *crowns*—] The old reading is, "Hath cost me *five hundred* crowns." Pope made the correction.

And dart not scornful glances from those eyes,
To wound thy lord, thy king, thy governor:
It blots thy beauty, as frosts do bite the meads,
Confounds thy fame, as whirlwinds shake fair buds,
And in no sense is meet or amiable.
A woman mov'd is like a fountain troubled,
Muddy, ill-seeming, thick, bereft of beauty;
And, while it is so, none so dry or thirsty
Will deign to sip, or touch one drop of it.
Thy husband is thy lord, thy life, thy keeper,
Thy head, thy sovereign; one that cares for thee,
And for thy maintenance: commits his body
To painful labour, both by sea and land;
To watch the night in storms, the day in cold,
Whilst thou liest warm at home, secure and safe;
And craves no other tribute at thy hands,
But love, fair looks, and true obedience,—
Too little payment for so great a debt.
Such duty as the subject owes the prince,
Even such, a woman oweth to her husband:
And, when she's froward, peevish, sullen, sour,
And not obedient to his honest will,
What is she, but a foul contending rebel,
And graceless traitor to her loving lord?
I am asham'd, that women are so simple
To offer war, where they should kneel for peace;
Or seek for rule, supremacy, and sway,
When they are bound to serve, love, and obey.
Why are our bodies soft, and weak, and smooth,
Unapt to toil, and trouble in the world,
But that our soft conditions, and our hearts,
Should well agree with our external parts?
Come, come, you froward and unable worms,
My mind hath been as big as one of yours,
My heart as great; my reason, haply, more,
To bandy word for word, and frown for frown;
But now, I see our lances are but straws,
Our strength as weak, our weakness past compare,
That seeming to be most, which we indeed least are.
Then vail your stomachs,[a] for it is no boot,
And place your hands below your husbands' foot:
In token of which duty, if he please,
My hand is ready, may it do him ease!

PET. Why, there's a wench!—come on, and kiss me, Kate.

LUC. Well, go thy ways, old lad; for thou shalt ha't.

VIN. 'Tis a good hearing, when children are toward.

LUC. But a harsh hearing when women are froward.

PET. Come, Kate, we'll to bed:—
We three are married, but you two are sped.
'Twas I won the wager, though you hit the white; [*To* LUCENTIO.
And being a winner, God give you good night!
[*Exeunt* PETRUCHIO *and* KATH.

HOR. Now go thy ways, thou hast tam'd a curst shrew.[b]

LUC. 'Tis a wonder, by your leave, she will be tam'd so. [*Exeunt.*(2)

---

[a] *Then* vail *your stomachs,*—] Abase your *pride*, your *spirit*. Thus, in "Henry IV." Part II. Act I. Sc. 1, we are told the bloody Douglas

"'Gan *vail his stomach*, and did grace the shame
Of those that turn'd their backs."

[b] *Thou hast tam'd a curst* shrew.] *Shrew* here was doubtless intended to be pronounced *shrow*. See Note (a), p. 271.

ILLUSTRATIVE COMMENTS.

INDUCTION.

(1) Scene I.—The following is the story mentioned in the Preliminary Notice as the most probable source whence the author of the "Taming of *a* Shrew" derived the notion of his Prelude :—

THE WAKING MAN'S DREAME.

In the time that *Phillip*, Duke of *Burgundy* (who by the gentlenesse and curteousnesse of his carriage purchaste the name of Good,) guided the reines of the country of *Flanders*, this prince, who was of an humour pleasing, and full of judicious goodnesse, rather then silly simplicitie, used pastimes which for their singularity are commonly called the pleasures of Princes: after this manner he no lesse shewed the quaintnesse of his wit then his prudence.

Being in *Bruxelles* with all his Court, and having at his table discoursed amply enough of the vanities and greatnesse of this world, he let each one say his pleasure on this subject, whereon was alleadged grave sentences and rare examples: walking towards the evening in the towne, his head full of divers thoughts, he found a Tradesman lying in a corner sleeping very soundly, the fumes of Bacchus having surcharged his braine. * * * * * He caused his men to carry away this sleeper, with whom, as with a blocke, they mighte doe what they would, without awaking him; he caused them to carry him into one of the sumptuousest parts of his Pallace, into a chamber most state-like furnished, and makes them lay him on a rich bed. They presently strip him of his bad cloathes, and put him on a very fine and cleane shirt, in stead of his own, which was foule and filthy. They let him sleepe in that place at his ease, and whilest hee settles his drinke the Duke prepares the pleasantest pastime that can be imagined.

In the morning, this drunkard being awake drawes the curtaines of this brave rich bed, sees himselfe in a chamber adorned like a Paradice, he considers the rich furniture with an amazement such as you may imagine: he beleeves not his eyes, but layes his finger on them, and feeling them open, yet perswades himselfe they are shut by sleep, and that all he sees is but a pure dreame.

Assoone as he was knowne to be awake, in comes the officers of the Dukes house, who were instructed by the Duke what they should do. There were pages bravely apparelled, Gentlemen of the chamber, Gentleman waiters, and the High Chamberlaine, who, all in faire order and without laughing, bring cloathing for this new guest: they honour him with the same great reverences as if hee were a Soveraigne Prince; they serve him bare headed, and aske him what suite hee will please to weare that day.

This fellow, affrighted at the first, beleeving these things to be inchantment or dreames, reclaimed by these submissions, tooke heart, and grew bold, and setting a good face on the matter, chused amongst all the apparell that they presented unto him that which he liked best, and which hee thought to be fittest for him: he is accommodated like a King, and served with such ceremonies, as he had never seene before, and yet beheld them without saying any thing, and with an assured countenance. This done, the greatest Nobleman in the Dukes Court enters the chamber with the same reverence and honour to him as if he had been their Soveraigne Prince. * * *

Being risen late, and dinner time approaching, they asked if he were pleased to have his tables covered. He likes that very well: * * * he eates with the same ceremony which was observed at the Dukes meales, he made good cheere, and chawed with all his teeth, but only drank with more moderation than he could have wisht, but the Majesty which he represented made him refraine. All taken away, he was entertained with new and pleasant things: * * * they made him passe the afternoone in all kinds of sports: musicke, dancing, and a Comedy, spent some part of the time. * * *

Super time approaching, * * * he was led with sound of Trumpets and Hoboyes into a faire hall, where long Tables were set, which were presently covered with divers sorts of dainty meates, the Torches shined in every corner, and made a day in the midst of a night. * * * Never was the imaginary Duke at such a feast: carousses begin after the manner of the Country; * * * They serve him with very strong wine, good *Hipocras*, which hee swallowed downe in great draughts, and frequently redoubled; so that, charged with so many extraordinaryes, he yeelded to death's cousin german, sleep. * * *

Then the right Duke, who had put himselfe among the throng of his Officers to have the pleasure of this mummery, commanded that this sleeping man should be stript out of his brave cloathes, and cloathed againe in his old ragges, and so sleeping carried and layd in the same place where he was taken up the night before. This was presently done, and there did he snort all the night long, not taking any hurt either from the hardnesse of the stones or the night ayre, so well was his stomacke filled with good preservatives. Being awakened in the morning by some passenger, or it may bee by some that the good Duke *Philip* had thereto appointed, ha! said he, my friends, what have you done? you have rob'd mee of a Kingdome, and have taken mee out of the sweetest, and happiest dreame that ever man could have fallen into. * * * Being returned home to his house, hee entertaines his wife, neighbours, and friends, with this his dreame, as hee thought. * * *

In his adaptation of the foregoing incident to the purposes of the stage, the writer of the old play has displayed a knowledge of character and an appreciation of humour and effect which entitle him, perhaps, to higher commendation than he has yet received. His Induction opens thus :—

"Enter a Tapster, beating out of his doores *Slie Droonken.**

Tapster. You whorson droonken slaue, you had best be gone,
And empty your droonken panch some where else
For in this house thou shalt not rest to night. *Exit* Tapster.
Slie. Tilly, vally, by crisee Tapster Ile fese you anon.
Fils the tother pot and alls paid for, looke you
I doo drinke it of mine owne Instegation, *Omne bene*
Heere Ile lie awhile, why Tapster I say,
Fils a fresh cushen heere.
Heigh ho, heers good warme lying.
He fals asleepe.

Enter a Noble man and his men from hunting.

Lord. Now that the gloomie shaddow of the night,
Longing to view Orions drisling lookes,
Leapes from th' antarticke world vnto the skie,
And dims the Welkin with her pitchie breath,
And darkesome night oreshades the christall heauens,
Here breake we off our hunting for to night;
Cupple vppe the hounds and let vs hie vs home,
And bid the huntsman see them meated well,
For they haue all deseru'd it well to daie,
But soft, what sleepie fellow is this lies heere?
Or is he dead, see one what he dooth lacke?
Seruingman. My lord, tis nothing but a drunken sleepe,
His head is too heauie for his bodie,
And he hath drunke so much that he can go no furder.
Lord. Fie, how the slauish villaine stinkes of drinke.
Ho, sirha arise. What so sounde asleepe?
Go take him vppe and beare him to my house,
And beare him easilie for feare he wake," &c. &c.

(2) Scene II.—*Enter* Lord, *dressed like a servant.*] Compare Shakespeare's admirable picture of the tinker's transmutation with the corresponding scene in the original :—

* Our extracts are quoted *literatim* from the edition of 1594.

" Enter two with a table and a banquet on it, and two otherwith *Slie* asleepe in a chaire, richlie apparelled, and the musicke plaieng.

One. So: sirha now go call my Lord,
And tel him that all things is ready as he wild it.
Another. Set thou some wine vpon the boord
And then Ile go fetch my Lord presentlie. *Exit.*

Enter the Lord and his men.

Lord. How now, what is all thinges readie?
One. I my Lord.
Lord. Then sound the musick, and Ile wake him straight,
And see you doo as earst I gaue in charge.
My lord, My lord, he sleepes soundlie: My Lord.
Slie. Tapster, gis a little small ale. Heigh ho.
Lord. Heers wine my lord, the purest of the grape.
Slie. For which Lord?
Lord. For your honour my Lord.
Slie. Who I, am I a Lord? Jesus what fine apparell haue I got.
Lord. More richer farre your honour hath to weare,
And if it please you I will fetch them straight.
Wil. And if your honour please to ride abroad,
Ile fetch you lustie steedes more swift of pace
Then winged *Pegasus* in all his pride,
That ran so swiftlie ouer the Persian plaines.
Tom. And if your honour please to hunt the deere,
Your hounds stand readie cuppeld at the doore.
Who in running will oretake the Row,
And make the long breathde Tygre broken winded.
Slie. By the masse I think I am a Lord indeed,
Whats thy name?
Lord. *Simon* and it please your honour.
Slie. *Simon*, thats as much as to say *Simion* or *Simon*
Put foorth thy hand and fill the pot.
Give me thy hand, *Sim* am I a lord indeed?" &c. &c.

(3) SCENE II.—*Enter the* Page, *&c.*] In the old play the scene proceeds as follows:—

" Enter the boy in Womans attire.

Slie. *Sim,* Is this she?
Lord. I my Lord.
Slie. Masse tis a prettie wench, what's her name?
Boy. Oh that my louelie Lord would once vouchsafe
To looke on me and leaue these frantike fits,
Or were I now but halfe so eloquent,
To paint in words what ile performe in deedes,
I know your honour then would pittie me.
Slie. Harke you mistrese, will you eat a peece of bread,
Come sit downe on my knee, *Sim* drinke to hir *Sim,*
For she and I will go to bed anon.
Lord. May it please you, your honors plaiers be come;
To offer your honour a plaie.
Slie. A plaie *Sim,* O braue, be they my plaiers?
Lord. I my Lord.
Slie. Is there not a foole in the plaie?
Lord. Yes my lord.
Slie. When wil they plaie *Sim?*
Lord. Euen when it please your honor, they be readie.
Boy. My lord Ile go bid them begin their plaie.
Slie. Doo, but looke that you come againe.
Boy. I warrant you, my lord, I will not leave you thus.
Exit boy.
Slie. Come *Sim,* where be the plaiers? *Sim* stand by me and weele flout the plaiers out of their cotes.
Lord. Ile cal them my lord. Hoe where are you there?"

ACT I.

(1) SCENE I.—*Gremio.*] In the first folio, Gremio is called "*a Pantelowne.*" *Il Pantalone* was the old baffled amoroso of the early Italian Comedy, and, like the Pedant and the Braggart, formed a never-failing source of ridicule upon the Italian stage.

(2) SCENE I.—*I wis, it is not half way to her heart.*] The word *I wis, in its origin,* is the Anglo-Saxon adjective *gewis, certain, sure,* which is still preserved in the modern German *gewiss,* and Dutch *gewis.* It is always used adverbially in the English writers of the thirteenth, fourteenth, and fifteenth centuries, and it invariably means *certainly, truly.* The change of the Anglo-Saxon *ge* to *y* or *i,* appears to have been made in the thirteenth century, and the letters *y* or *i* are used indifferently, one being as right as the other. But although the word is really an adverb, Sir Frederic Madden thinks it questionable whether, in the latter part of the fifteenth century, it was not regarded as a *pronoun and a verb,* equivalent to the German *ich weiss.** That it was so considered in the sixteenth and seventeenth centuries seems pretty generally admitted. In Shakespeare it is always printed with a capital letter, *I wis;* and we have no doubt he used it as a *pronoun and a verb,* not knowing its original sense *as an adverb.*

* See the Glossary to Sir Frederic Madden's "Syr Gawayne. *Printed for the Bannatyne Club,* 1839."

ACT II.

(1) SCENE I.—*Exeunt* PETRUCHIO *and* KATHARINA *severally.*] Compare the interview of the hero and heroine in the old comedy:—

" Enter *Kate.*

Alfon. Ha *Kate,* Come hither wench & list to me,
Vse this gentleman friendlie as thou canst.
Feran. Twentie good morrowes to my louely *Kate*
Kate. You iest I am sure, is she yours alreadie?
Feran. I tell thee *Kate* I know thou lou'st me well
Kate. The deuill you doo, who told you so?
Feran. My mind sweet *Kate* doth say I am the man,
Must wed, and bed, and marrie bonnie *Kate.*
Kate. Was euer seene so grose an asse as this?
Feran. I, to stand so long and neuer get a kisse.
Kate. Hands off I say, and get you from this place;
Or I wil set my ten commandments in your face.
Feran. I prethe doo *Kate;* they say thou art a shrew,
And I like thee the better for I would haue thee so.
Kate. Let go my hand for feare it reech your eare.
Feran. No *Kate,* this hand is mine and I thy loue.

Kate. In faith sir no, the woodcock wants his taile.
Feran. But yet his bil wil serue, if the other faile.
Alfon. How now, *Ferando*, what saies my daughter?
Feran. Shees willing sir and loues me as hir life.
Kate. Tis for your skin then, but not to be your wife.
Alfon. Come hither *Kate* and let me giue thy hand
To him that I haue chosen for thy loue,
And thou tomorrow shalt be wed to him.
Kate. Why father what do you meane to doo with me,
To giue me thus vnto this brainsick man,
That in his mood cares not to murder me?
She turnes aside and speakes.
But yet I will consent and marrie him,
For I methinkes haue liued too long a maid,
And match him to, or else his manhoods good.
Alfon. Giue me thy hand *Ferando* loues thee wel
And will with wealth and ease maintaine thy state,
Here *Ferando* take her for thy wife,
And Sunday next shall be your wedding day.
Feran. Why so, did I not tell thee I should be the man
Father, I leaue my louile *Kate* with you,
Prouide your selues against our mariage daie;
For I must hie me to my countrie house
In hast to see prouision may be made,
To entertaine my *Kate* when she dooth come.
Alfon. Doo so, come *Kate* why doost thou looke
So sad, be merrie wench thy wedding daies at hand.
Sonne fare you well, and see you keepe your promise.
Exit Alfonso and Kate."

(2) Scene I.—*Yet I have fac'd it with a card of ten.*] "A common phrase," says Nares, "which we may suppose to have been derived from some game (possibly *primero*), wherein the standing boldly upon a *ten* was often successful. *A card of ten* meant a tenth card, a ten, &c. I conceive the force of the phrase to have expressed, originally, the confidence or impudence of one who, with a ten, as at brag, *faced*, or *out-faced* one who had really a faced card against him. To face, meant, as it still does, to bully, to attack by impudence of face."

(3) Scene I.—*If I fail not of my cunning.*] At the termination of this scene in the original, the following bit of by-play is introduced:—

"*Slie. Sim*, when will the foole come againe?
Lord. Heele come againe my Lord anon.
Slie. Gis some more drinke here, souns wheres
The Tapster, here *Sim* eate some of these things.
Lord. So I doo my Lord.
Slie. Here *Sim*, I drinke to thee.
Lord. My Lord heere comes the plaiers againe,
Slie. O braue, heers two fine gentlewomen."

ACT III.

(1) Scene II.—*Enter* Petruchio *and* Grumio.] The answerable scene to this in the old piece, though not without humour, is much inferior:—

"Enter *Ferando* baselie attired, and a red cap on his head.

Feran. Godmorow father, *Polidor* well met,
You wonder I know that I haue staid so long.
Alfon. I marrie son, we were almost perswaded,
That we should scarse haue had our bridegroome heere,
But say, why art thou thus basely attired?
Feran. Thus richlie father you should haue said,
For when my wife and I am married once,
Shees such a shrew, if we should once fal out
Sheele pul my costlie sutes ouer mine eares,
And therefore am I thus attired awhile,
For manie thinges I tell you's in my head,
And none must know thereof but *Kate* and I,
For we shall liue like lammes and Lions sure,
Nor Lammes to Lions neuer was so tame,
If once they lie within the Lions pawes
As *Kate* to me if we were married once,
And therefore come let vs to church presently.
Pol. Fie *Ferando* not thus atired for shame
Come to my Chamber and there sute thy selfe,
Of twentie sutes that I did neuer were.
Feran. Tush *Polidor* I haue as many sutes
Fantasticke made to fit my humor so
As any in Athens and as richlie wrought
As was the Massie Robe that late adornd,
The stately legate of the Persian King,
And this from them haue I made choise to weare.
Alfon. I prethie *Ferando* let me intreat
Before thou goste vnto the church with vs
To put some other sute vpon thy backe.
Feran. Not for the world if I might gaine it so,
And therefore take me thus or not at all."

(2) Scene II.—
"*He calls for wine—*
——— *quaff'd off the muscadel,*" &c.]
The custom of taking wine and sops in the church upon the conclusion of the marriage ceremonies is very ancient, and in this country, in our author's time, it was almost universal. The beverage usually chosen was *Muscadel*, or *Muscadine*, or a medicated drink called *Hippocras*. Thus, in Robert Armin's Comedy of "The History of the Two Maids of Moreclacke," 1609, the play begins with:—

"*Enter a Maid strewing flowers, and a serving-man perfuming the door.*

Maid. Strew, strew.
Man. The *muscadine* stays for the bride at church:
The priest and Hymen's ceremonies tend
To make them man and wife."

So at the marriage of Mary and Philip in Winchester Cathedral, 1554, we read:—"The trumpets sounded, and they returned to their traverses in the quire, and there remayned untill masse was done; at which tyme, *wyne* and *sopes* were hallowed and delyvered to them both."—*Appendix to* Leland's *Collectanea.*

(3) Scene II.—*Exeunt* Petruchio, Katharina, *and* Grumio.] Perhaps in no part of the play is the immeasurable superiority of Shakespeare to his predecessor more evident than in the boisterous vigour and excitation of this scene. Compared with it, the corresponding situation in the original is torpidity itself:—

"Enter *Ferando and Kate and Alfonso and Polidor and Amelia and Aurelius and Philema.*

Feran. Father farwell, my *Kate* and I must home,
Sirra go make ready my horse presentlie.
Alfon. Your horse? What son I hope you doo but iest
I am sure you will not go so suddainly.
Kate. Let him go or tarry I am resolu'de to stay,
And not to trauell on my wedding day.
Feran. Tut *Kate* I tell thee we must needes go home,
Villaine hast thou saddled my horse?
San. Which horse, your curtall?
Feran. Sounes you slaue stand you prating here?
Saddell the bay gelding for your Mistris.
Kate. Not for me: for Ile not go.
San. The ostler will not let me haue him you owe tenpence
For his meate and 6 pence for stuffing my Mistris saddle.
Feran. Here villaine go pay him straight.
San. Shall I giue them another pecke of lauender.
Feran. Out slaue and bring them presently to the dore.
Alfon. Why son I hope at least youle dine with vs.
San. I pray you maister lets stay till dinner be don.
Feran. Sounes villaine art thou here yet? *Ex. Sander.*
Come *Kate* our dinner is prouided at home.

Kate. But not for me, for here I meane to dine
Ile haue my will in this as well as you,
Though you in madding mood would leaue your frends
Despite of you Ile tarry with them still.
Feran. I *Kate* so thou shalt but at some other time,
When as thy sisters here shall be espousd,
Then thou and I will keepe our wedding day
In better sort then now we can prouide,
For here I promise thee before them all,
We will ere long returne to them againe,
Come *Kate* stand not on termes we will awaie,
This is my day, tomorrow thou shalt rule,
And I will doo what euer thou commandes.
Gentlemen farwell, wele take our leues,
It will be late before that we come home.
Exit Ferando and Kate."

ACT IV.

(1) SCENE I.—
He that knows better how to tame a shrew,
Now let him speak; 'tis charity to shew. [*Exit.*]
Subjoined is the parallel scene of the older play:—

"*Enter Ferando and Kate.*

Feran. Now welcome *Kate:* where's these villains
Here, what? not supper yet vppon the borde:
Nor table spred nor nothing don at all,
Wheres that villaine that I sent before.
San. Now, *ad sum,* sir.
Feran. Come hether you villaine Ile cut your nose,
You Rogue: helpe me of with my bootes: wilt please
You to lay the cloth? sounes the villaine
Hurts my foote? pull easely I say; yet againe.
He beates them all.
They couer the bord and fetch in the meate.
Sounes? burnt and skorcht who drest this meate?
Will. Forsouth Iohn cooke.
He throwes downe the table and meate and all, and beates them.

Feran. Go you villaines bringe you me such meate,
Out of my sight I say and beare it hence,
Come *Kate* wele haue other meate prouided,
Is there a fire in my chamber sir?
San. I forsooth. *Exit Ferando and Kate.*

Manent seruing men and eate vp all the meate.

Tom. Sounes? I thinke of my conscience my Masters
Mad since he was maried.
Will. I laft what a boxe he gaue *Sander*
For pulling of his bootes.

Enter *Ferando* againe.

San. I hurt his foote for the nonce man.
Feran. Did you so you damned villaine.
He beates them all out againe.
This humor must I holde me to awhile,
To bridle and holde backe my headstrong wife,
With curbes of hunger: ease: and want of sleepe,
Nor sleepe nor meate shall she inioie to night,
Ile mew her vp as men do mew their hawkes,
And make her gentlie come vnto the lure,
Were she as stuborne or as full of strength
As were the *Thracian* horse *Alcides* tamde,
That King *Egeus* fed with flesh of men,
Yet would I pull her downe and make her come
As hungry hawkes do flie vnto there lure. *Exit.*"

(2) SCENE II.—
"——— *but at last I spied*
An ancient angel coming down the hill."]
For upwards of a century, the expression, "An ancient *angel,*" has been a puzzle to commentators. Theobald, Hanmer, and Warburton concurred in substituting *engle,* or *enghle* (the most innocent meaning of which is *gull,* or *dupe*) for "angel;" and this word has been supported strenuously by Gifford. In a note to Jonson's Poetaster, Act II. Sc. 1, he quotes a passage from Gascoigne's Supposes, the play Shakespeare is thought to have been under obligations to for this part of the plot, which he considers decisive:—"There Erostrato, the Biondello of Shakespeare, looks out for a person to gull by an idle story, judges *from appearances* that he has found him, and is not deceived:—'At the foot of the hill I met a gentleman, and *as methought by his habits and his looks he should be none of the wisest.*' Again, 'this gentleman being, as I guessed at the first, *a man of small sapientia.*' And Dulippo (the Lucentio of Shakespeare) as soon as he spies him coming, exclaims, 'Is this he? go meet him: by my truth, HE LOOKS LIKE A GOOD SOUL, he that fisheth for him might *be sure to catch a codshead.*'" But, after all, as Mr. Singer observes, it is not necessary to depart from the reading of the old copy. Cotgrave explains *Angelot à la grosse escaille,* "An old angell; and by metaphor a fellow of th' old, sound, honest, and worthie stamp." So *an ancient angel* may here have meant only *a good old simple soul.* It is singular that, while so much consideration has been bestowed on this expression, one very similar in "The Tempest," Act II. Sc. 1, "This *ancient morsel,*" should scarcely have been noticed.

(3) SCENE III.—*Go, get thee gone, thou false deluding slave.*] We subjoin the analogous scene from the original play:—

"Enter *Sander and his Mistres.*

San. Come Mistris.
Kate. Sander I prethe helpe me to some meate,
I am so faint that I can scarsely stande.
San. I marry mistris but you know my maister
Has giuen me a charge that you must eate nothing,
But that which he himselfe giueth you.
Kate. Why man thy Maister needs neuer know it.
San. You say true indede: why looke you Mistris,
What say you to a peese of beeffe and mustard now?
Kate. Why I say tis excellent meate, canst thou helpe me to some?
San. I, I could helpe you to some but that
I doubt the mustard is too colerick for you,
But what say you to a sheepes head and garlick?
Kate. Why any thing, I care not what it be.
San. I but the garlike I doubt will make your breath stincke,
and then my maister will course me for letting
You eate it: But what say you to a fat Capon?
Kate. Thats meate for a King sweet *Sander* helpe
Me to some of it.
San. Nay ber lady then tis too deere for vs, we must
Not meddle with the Kings meate.
Kate. Out villaine dost thou mocke me,
Take that for thy sawsinesse.
She beates him.

(4) SCENE III.—*Exeunt.*] The incidents in the foregoing scene closely resemble those in the following one from the old piece; it is in their treatment that the pre-eminence of Shakespeare is recognised:—

"Enter *Ferando and Kate and Sander.*

San. Master the haberdasher has brought my
Mistresse home hir cappe here.
Feran. Come hither sirra: what haue you there?
Habar. A veluet cappe sir and it please you.
Feran. Who spoake for it? didst thou *Kate?*
Kate. What if I did, come hither sirra, giue me
The cap, Ile see if it will fit me. She sets it one hir head.
Feran. O monstrous, why it becomes thee not,
Let me see it *Kate:* here sirra take it hence,
This cappe is out of fashion quite.
Kate. The fashion is good inough: belike you
meane to make a foole of me.
Feran. Why true he meanes to make a foole of thee
To haue thee put on such a curtald cappe,
Sirra begon with it.

Enter the *Taylor* with a gowne.

San. Here is the *Taylor* too with my Mistris gowne.
Feran. Let me see it *Taylor:* what with cuts and iagges.
Sounes you villaine, thou hast spoiled the gowne.
Taylor. Why sir I made it as your man gaue me direction.
You may reade the note here.
Feran. Come hither sirra *Taylor* reade the note.
Taylor. Item. a faire round compast cape.
San. I thats true.
Taylor. And a large truncke sleeue.
San. Thats a lie maister. I sayd two truncke sleeues.
Feran. Well sir goe forward.
Taylor. Item a loose bodied gowne.
San. Maister if euer I sayd loose bodies gowne,
Sew me in a seame and beate me to death,
With bottome of browne thred.
Taylor. I made it as the note bad me.
San. I say the note lies in his throute and thou too
And thou sayst it.
Taylor. Nay nay nere be so hot sirra, for I feare you not.
San. Doost thou heare *Taylor*, thou hast braued
Many men: braue not me.
Thou'st faste many men.
Taylor. Well sir.
San. Face not me Ile neither be faste nor braued.
At thy handes I can tell thee.
Kate. Come come I like the fashion of it well enough,
Heres more a do then needs Ile haue it, I
And if you do not like it hide your eies,
I thinke I shall haue nothing by your will.
Feran. Go I say and take it vp for your maisters vse.
San. Souns villaine not for thy life touch it not,
Souns take vp my mistris gowne to his
Maisters vse?
Feran. Well sir whats your conceit of it.
San. I haue a deeper conceite in it then you thinke for, take vp my mistris gowne
To his maisters vse?
Feran. *Taylor* come hether; for this time take it
Hence againe, and Ile content thee for thy paines.
Taylor. I thanke you sir. *Exit Taylor.*
Feran. Come *Kate* we now will go see thy fathers house
Euen in these honest meane abilliments,
Our purses shall be rich our garments plaine,
To shrowd our bodies from the winter rage,
And that's inough, what should we care for more
Thy sisters *Kate* to morrow must be wed,
And I haue promised them thou shouldst be there
The morning is well vp lets hast away,
It will be nine a clocke ere we come there.
Kate. Nine a clock, why tis allreadie past two
In the after noone by all the clocks in the towne.
Feran. I say tis but nine a clock in the morning.
Kate. I say tis two a clock in the after noone.
Feran. It shall be nine then ere we go to your fathers,
Come backe againe we will not go to day.
Nothing but crossing of me still,
Ile haue you say as I doo ere you go. *Exeunt Omnes.*"

(5) SCENE V.—*Allots thee for his lovely bed-fellow!*] Compare the opening of the original scene:—

" *Feran.* Come *Kate* the Moone shines cleare to night
Methinkes.
Kate. The moone? why husband you are deceiued
It is the sun.
Feran. Yet againe come backe againe it shall be
The moone ere we come at your fathers.
Kate. Why Ile say as you say it is the moone.
Feran. Iesus saue the glorious moone.
Kate. Iesus saue the glorious moone.
Feran. I am glad *Kate* your stomack is come downe,
I know it well thou knowest it is the sun,
But I did trie to see if thou wouldst speake,
And crosse me now as thou hast donne before,
And trust me *Kate* hadst thou not named the moone,
We had gon back againe as sure as death,
But soft whose this thats comming here."

ACT V.

(1) SCENE I.—*Call forth an officer.*] In the original the performance is interrupted at this point by the Tinker:—

" *Slie.* I say wele haue no sending to prison.
Lord. My Lord this is but the play, theyre but in iest.
Slie. I tell thee *Sim* wele haue no sending,
To prison thats flat: why *Sim* am not I *Don Christo Vary?* *
Therefore I say they shall not go to prison.
Lord. No more they shall not my Lord,
They be run away.
Slie. Are they run away *Sim?* thats well,
Then gis some more drinke, and let them play againe.
Lord. Here my Lord.
Slie drinkes and then falls asleepe."

(2) SCENE II.—*Exeunt.*] Shakespeare's piece terminates here, and no more is heard of the inimitable Christopher. Whether this is owing to the latter portion of the Induction having been lost, or whether the poet purposely dismissed the Tinker and the characters of the apologue, before whom we were to suppose the comedy was played, in the first act, we shall probably never know. In the old drama, at the end, the scene is supposed to change, from the nobleman's palace to the outside of the alehouse-door, and Sly is properly re-introduced in the same state in which he first appeared:—

" Then enter two bearing of *Slie* in his
Owne apparrell againe and leaues him
Where they found, him, and then goes out.
Then enter the *Tapster*.

Tapster. Now that the darkesome night is ouerpast,
And dawning day appeares in chrystall sky,
Now must I hast abroad: but soft whose this?
What *Slie* oh wondrous hath he laine here allnight,
Ile wake him, I thinke he's starued by this,
But that his belly was so stuft with ale,
What how *Slie*, Awake for shame.
Slie. *Sim* gis some more wine, whats all the
Plaiers gon: am not I a Lord?
Tapster. A lord with a murrin: come art thou dronken still?
Slie. Whose this? *Tapster*, oh Lord sirra, I haue had
The brauest dreame to night, that euer thou
Hardest in all thy life.
Tapster. I marry but you had best get you home,
For your wife will course you for dreaming here tonight.
Slie. Will she? I know now how to tame a shrew,
I dreamt vpon it all this night till now,
And thou hast wakt me out of the best dreame
That euer I had in my life, but Ile to my
Wife presently and tame her too.
And if she anger me.
Tapster. Nay tarry *Slie* for Ile go home with thee,
And heare the rest that thou hast dreamt to night.
Exeunt Omnes.'

* *Christo Vary?*] A humorous variation of Christopher; whence, probably, Shakespeare's *Christophero* Sly.

CRITICAL OPINIONS

ON

THE TAMING OF THE SHREW.

"FROM whatever source the Apologue to this drama may have been directly taken, we cannot but feel highly indebted to Shakspeare for its conversion into a lesson of exquisite moral irony, while, at the same time, it unfolds his wonted richness of humour, and minute delineation of character. The whole, indeed, is conducted with such lightness and frolic spirit, with so many happy touches of risible simplicity, yet chastised by so constant an adherence to nature and verisimilitude, as to form one of the most delightful and instructive sketches.

"So admirably drawn is the character of Sly, that we regret to find the interlocution of the group before whom the piece is supposed to be performed, has been dropped by our author after the close of the first scene of the play. Here we behold the jolly tinker nodding, and, at length, honestly exclaiming, '*Would 'twere done!*' and though the integrity of the representation requires that he should finally return to his former state, the transformation, as before, being effected during his sleep, yet we hear no more of this truly comic personage; whereas in the spurious play, he is frequently introduced commenting on the scene, is carried off the stage fast asleep, and on the termination of the drama, undergoes the necessary metamorphosis. It would appear, therefore, either that our bard's continuation of the Induction has been unaccountably lost, or that he trusted the remainder of Sly's part to the improvisatory ingenuity of the performers; or, what is more likely, that they were instructed to copy a certain portion of what had been written, for this subordinate division of the tinker's character, by the author of the elder play. Some of the observations, indeed, of Sly, as given by the writer of this previous comedy, are incompatible with the fable and *Dramatis Personæ* of Shakspeare's production; and have, consequently, been very injudiciously introduced by Mr. Pope; but there are two passages which, with the exception of but two names, are not only accordant with our poet's prelude, but absolutely necessary to its completion. Shakspeare, as we have seen, represents Sly as nodding at the end of the first scene, and the parts of the anonymous play to which we allude are those where the nobleman orders the sleeping tinker to be put into his own apparel again, and where he awakens in this garb, and believes the whole to have been a dream; the only alterations required in this *finale* being the omission of the Christian appellative *Sim*, and the conversion of *Tapster* into *Hostess*. These few lines were, most probably, those which Shakspeare selected as a necessary accompaniment to his piece, from the old drama supposed to have been written in 1590;* and these lines should be withdrawn from the notes in all the modern editions, and though distinguished as borrowed property, should be immediately connected with the text.

"As to the play itself, the rapidity and variety of its action, the skilful connexion of its double plot, and the strength and vivacity of its principal characters, must for ever ensure its popularity. There is, indeed, a depth and breadth of colouring in its execution, a boldness and prominency of relief, which may be thought to border upon coarseness; but the result has been an effect equally powerful and interesting, though occasionally, as the subject demanded, somewhat glaring and grotesque. *Petruchio*, *Katharina*, and *Grumio*, the most important personages of the play, are consistently supported throughout, and their peculiar features touched, and brought forward with singular sharpness and

* "I suspect," says Mr. Malone, "that the anonymous 'Taming of a Shrew' was written about the year 1590, either by George Peele or Robert Greene."

spirit; the wild fantastic humour of the first, the wayward and insolent demeanour of the second, contrasted with the meek, modest, and retired disposition of her sister, together with the inextinguishable wit and drollery of the third, form a picture, at once rich, varied, and pre-eminently diverting." —DRAKE.

"'The Taming of the Shrew' has the air of an Italian comedy: and indeed, the love of intrigue, which constitutes the main part of it, is derived, mediately or immediately, from a piece of Ariosto. The characters and passions are lightly sketched; the intrigue is introduced without much preparation, and in its rapid progress impeded by no sort of difficulties; however, in the manner in which Petruchio, though previously cautioned respecting Katharine, still runs the risk of marrying her, and contrives to tame her, the character and peculiar humour of the English are visible. The colours are laid somewhat coarsely on, but the ground is good. That the obstinacy of a young and untamed girl, possessed of none of the attractions of her sex, and neither supported by bodily nor mental strength, must soon yield to the still rougher and more capricious but assumed self-will of a man: such a lesson can only be taught on the stage, with all the perspicuity of a proverb.

"The prelude is still more remarkable than the play itself: the drunken tinker removed in his sleep to a palace, where he is deceived into the belief of being a nobleman. The invention, however, is not Shakspeare's; Holberg has handled the same subject in a masterly manner, and with inimitable truth; but he has spun it out to five acts, for which the matter is hardly sufficient. He probably did not borrow from the English dramatist, but like him took the hint from a popular story. There are several comic motives of this description, which go back to a very remote age, without ever becoming antiquated.—Shakspeare proves himself here, as well as everywhere else, a great poet: the whole is merely a light sketch, but in elegance and nice propriety it will hardly ever be excelled. Neither has he overlooked the irony which the subject naturally suggested to him, that the great lord who is driven by idleness and *ennui* to deceive a poor drunkard, can make no better use of his situation than the latter who every moment relapses into his vulgar habits. The last half of this prelude, that in which the tinker in his new state again drinks himself out of his senses, and is transformed in his sleep into his former condition, from some accident or other is lost. It ought to have followed at the end of the larger piece. The occasional observations of the tinker, during the course of the representation of the comedy, might have been improvisatory; but it is hardly credible that Shakspeare should have trusted to the momentary suggestions of the players, which he did not hold in high estimation, the conclusion of a work, however short, which he had so carefully commenced. Moreover, the only circumstance which connects the prelude with the play, is that it belongs to the new life of the supposed nobleman, to have plays acted in his castle by strolling actors. This invention of introducing spectators on the stage, who contribute to the entertainment, has been very wittily used by later English poets."—SCHLEGEL.

Act IV. Sc. 1.

KING JOHN.

"King John," which is the only uncontested play of Shakespeare's not entered on the books of the Stationers' Company, was first printed in the folio collection of 1623. Though enumerated in the list of our author's works by Meres, 1598, commentators have not succeeded in determining the time when it was written. Malone seems to have been of opinion that the maternal lamentations of Lady Constance, for the loss of Arthur, are an expression of the poet's own grief at the death of his son Hammet in 1596; and if this theory were admissible, we should, of course, be bound to conclude that "King John" was not written until after that date. But conjectures of this nature are very fanciful. There are undoubtedly high authorities in literature to justify a poet in availing himself of such an occasion to celebrate an event not strictly connected with his theme; but in those cases the writers worked on great historical subjects. It can scarcely be believed that a man of Shakespeare's incomparable sagacity would have interwoven a merely personal sentiment into a drama intended to interest the public at large. It savours of a reproach to the poet's memory to represent him giving utterance to his own sorrow for the loss of an obscure lad, twelve years old, when depicting the anguish of such a character as Constance for the loss of her princely Arthur. The language and ideas which would be appropriate in the one case would be out of keeping in the other; and those who are best acquainted with Shakespeare's habitual self-negation, will not suspect him of perpetrating this act of bathos.

Johnson has observed, that the description of the English army which Chatillon, the French Ambassador, gives to King Philip, in the first scene of the second act, beginning,—

"And all the unsettled humours of the land,"—

may have been suggested by the dramatist's acquaintance with the details of the grand fleet despatched against Spain in 1596. But here again we must be cautious in attaching particular meaning to descriptions which would apply with equal truth to almost any expedition. The fleet which the Earls of Nottingham and Essex led against Cadiz was not the only one which had been partly manned by gentlemen. History furnishes too many instances where men

"Have sold their fortunes at their native homes,
Bearing their birthrights proudly on their backs,"

that they might participate in adventures of a similar kind; and Shakespeare may have derived the materials of Chatillon's description from the chronicles of different periods and various countries. As if to show, indeed, how fallacious such guess-work often is, Johnson has attempted to make a similar deduction from another passage in this play. He conceived that Pandulph's denunciation of King John,—

"And meritorious shall that hand be call'd,
Canonized, and worshipp'd as a saint,
That takes away by any secret course
Thy hateful life,"—

might either refer to the bull published against Queen Elizabeth, or to the canonization of Garnet, Fawkes, and their accomplices, who, in a Spanish book which he had seen, are registered as saints. The latter theory would fix the writing of the play after 1605, and is at once demolished by a reference to the corresponding scene of the old piece of "King John," printed in 1591, upon which this is based, where the Legate denounces John:—

PRELIMINARY NOTICE.

"Then I Pandulph of Padua, legate from the apostolike sea doe in the name of Saint Peter and his successor our holy father Pope *Innocent*, pronounce thee accursed, discharging every of thy subjects of all dutie and fealtie that they doe owe te thee, and pardon and forgiveness of sinne to those or them whatsoever, which shall carrie armes against thee, or murder thee: this I pronounce, and charge all good men to abhorre thee as an excommunicate person."

Such hypotheses as these, however, if they do little towards establishing the chronology of Shakespeare's writings, are forcible confirmations of the fact that he wrote "not for an age, but for all time." His representations are so truthful and life-like that it is the easiest of all undertakings to find a model whence he may be presumed to have drawn them. He describes the ruinous extravagance into which noblemen and gentlemen are seduced in equipping themselves for a foreign enterprise, and the arrogant pretensions of the Catholic Church in dealing with a rebellious monarch, with such fidelity, that we seem to be reading a particular relation of whichever individual occurrence of the kind our memory first brings to notice.

The play of "King John" stands precisely in the same relation to the old drama called "The Troublesome Raigne of John King of England," &c., that "The Taming of the Shrew" does to its predecessor, "The Taming of *a* Shrew." In both cases the elder productions were probably current favourites on the stage when Shakespeare first joined it; and in obedience to the customs of the time, and perhaps to the dictates of his employers, he took them up as good dramatic subjects, and availing himself of the general plot and leading incidents of each, transfused a new vitality into the crude materials furnished by some other workman.

At the present day it can hardly be necessary to vindicate Shakespeare from the charge of having falsified history in those of his performances which are founded on historical subjects. The marvel, indeed, is, how he has contrived to combine the highest dramatic effect with so close an adherence to historic truth. It must be remembered that he wrote without any of the advantages we derive from the researches which modern investigation has brought to bear upon the characters of particular personages and the secrets of peculiar transactions. He has left us, notwithstanding, so many masterly and instructive pictures of historic characters and events, that it may be safely said, the youth of England would be far less acquainted with and interested in the veritable annals of their country, if Shakespeare had never written his series of Historical Plays.

Persons Represented.

JOHN, *King of* ENGLAND.

PRINCE HENRY, *his son; afterwards* HENRY III.

ARTHUR, *Duke of* BRETAGNE, *son of* GEFFREY, *late Duke of* BRETAGNE, *the elder brother of* KING JOHN.

WILLIAM MARESHALL, *Earl of* PEMBROKE.

GEFFREY FITZ-PETER, *Earl of* ESSEX.

WILLIAM LONGSWORD, *Earl of* SALISBURY.

ROBERT BIGOT, *Earl of* NORFOLK.

HUBERT DE BURGH, *Chamberlain to the* KING.

ROBERT FAULCONBRIDGE, *son of* SIR ROBERT FAULCONBRIDGE.

PHILIP FAULCONBRIDGE, *his half-brother, bastard son of* KING RICHARD THE FIRST.

JAMES GURNEY, *servant to* LADY FAULCONBRIDGE.

PETER *of* POMFRET, *a supposed prophet.*

PHILIP, *King of* FRANCE.

LEWIS, *the Dauphin; afterwards* LEWIS VIII.

ARCHDUKE *of* AUSTRIA.

PANDULPH, *the Pope's Legate.*

MELUN, *a French nobleman.*

CHATILLON, *ambassador from* FRANCE *to* KING JOHN.

ELINOR, *the widow of* HENRY II., *and mother of* KING JOHN.

CONSTANCE, *mother of* ARTHUR.

BLANCH, *daughter to* ALPHONSO, *King of* CASTILE, *and niece to* KING JOHN.

LADY FAULCONBRIDGE, *mother to* PHILIP *and* ROBERT FAULCONBRIDGE.

Lords, Ladies, and divers other attendants, Sheriff, Heralds, Citizens, Officers, Soldiers, and Messengers.

ACT I.

SCENE I.—Northampton. *A Room of State in the Palace.*

Enter KING JOHN, ELINOR, *the* Queen-Mother, PEMBROKE, ESSEX, SALISBURY, *and others, with* CHATILLON.[a]

K. JOHN. Now say, Chatillon, what would France with us?

CHAT. Thus, after greeting, speaks the king of France,
In my behaviour, to the majesty,
The borrow'd majesty, of England here.

ELI. A strange beginning;—borrow'd majesty!

K. JOHN. Silence, good mother; hear the embassy.

CHAT. Philip of France, in right and true behalf

[a] Chatillon.] In the old copy this name is spelt *Chattylion*, or *Chatillion*.

Of thy deceasèd brother Geffrey's son,
Arthur Plantagenet, lays most lawful claim
To this fair island, and the territories;
To Ireland, Poictiers, Anjou, Touraine, Maine:
Desiring thee to lay aside the sword
Which sways usurpingly these several titles,
And put the same into young Arthur's hand,
Thy nephew and right royal sovereign.

K. JOHN. What follows, if we disallow of this?

CHAT. The proud control of fierce and bloody war,
To enforce these rights so forcibly withheld.

K. JOHN. Here have we war for war, and blood for blood,
Controlment for controlment: so answer France.

CHAT. Then take my king's defiance from my mouth,
The farthest limit of my embassy.

K. JOHN. Bear mine to him, and so depart in peace.
Be thou as lightning in the eyes of France;
For ere thou canst report I will be there,
The thunder of my cannon shall be heard.
So hence! be thou the trumpet of our wrath,
And sullen[a] presage of your own decay.—
An honourable conduct let him have:
Pembroke, look to't.—Farewell, Chatillon.
[*Exeunt* CHATILLON *and* PEMBROKE.

ELI. What now, my son? have I not ever said,
How that ambitious Constance would not cease,
Till she had kindled France, and all the world,
Upon the right and party of her son?
This might have been prevented, and made whole,
With very easy arguments of love;
Which now the manage[b] of two kingdoms must
With fearful bloody issue arbitrate.

K. JOHN. Our strong possession, and our right, for us.

ELI. Your strong possession, much more than your right;
Or else it must go wrong with you and me:
So much my conscience whispers in your ear,
Which none but Heaven, and you, and I, shall hear.

Enter the Sheriff *of* Northamptonshire, *who whispers* ESSEX.

ESSEX. My liege, here is the strangest controversy,
Come from the country to be judged by you,
That e'er I heard: shall I produce the men?

K. JOHN. Let them approach.— [*Exit* Sheriff.
Our abbeys and our priories shall pay
This expedition's charge.

Re-enter Sheriff, *with* ROBERT FAULCONBRIDGE, *and* PHILIP, *his bastard Brother*.

What men are you?

BAST. Your faithful subject, I; a gentleman,
Born in Northamptonshire; and eldest son,
As I suppose, to Robert Faulconbridge,
A soldier, by the honour-giving hand
Of Cœur-de-lion, knighted in the field.

K. JOHN. What art thou?

ROB. The son and heir to that same Faulconbridge.

K. JOHN. Is that the elder, and art thou the heir?
You came not of one mother, then, it seems.

BAST. Most certain of one mother, mighty king,
That is well known; and, as I think, one father:
But, for the certain knowledge of that truth,
I put you o'er to Heaven, and to my mother;
Of that I doubt, as all men's children may.

ELI. Out on thee, rude man! thou dost shame thy mother,
And wound her honour, with this diffidence.

BAST. I, madam? no, I have no reason for it;
That is my brother's plea, and none of mine;
The which if he can prove, 'a pops me out
At least from fair five hundred pound a-year:
Heaven guard my mother's honour, and my land!

K. JOHN. A good blunt fellow —Why, being younger born,
Doth he lay claim to thine inheritance?

BAST. I know not why, except to get the land.
But once he slander'd me with bastardy:
But whe'r[c] I be as true begot, or no,
That still I lay upon my mother's head;
But, that I am as well begot, my liege,
(Fair fall the bones that took the pains for me!)
Compare our faces, and be judge yourself.
If old sir Robert did beget us both,
And were our father, and this son like him,
O, old sir Robert father, on my knee
I give Heaven thanks I was not like to thee!

K. JOHN. Why, what a madcap hath Heaven lent us here!

ELI. He hath a trick of Cœur-de-lion's face;
The accent of his tongue affecteth him:

---

[a] *And* sullen *presage*—] That is, *doleful, melancholy* presage. Thus, in "Henry IV." Part II. Act I. Sc. 1,—

"——— and his tongue
Sounds ever after as a *sullen* bell,
Remember'd knolling a departing friend."

[b] *The* manage—] *Manage* of old meant *government, control, administration*:—

"——— and to him put
The *manage* of my state."
The Tempest, Act I. Sc. 2.

[c] *But* whe'r *I be as true begot*,—] This contraction of *whether* is frequent both in Shakespeare and his contemporaries; but they seem usually to have written it *where*.

Do you not read some tokens of my son
In the large composition of this man?
K. JOHN. Mine eye hath well examinèd his parts,
And finds them perfect Richard.—Sirrah, speak,
What doth move you to claim your brother's land?
BAST. Because he hath a half-face, like my father;
With that half-face[a] would he have all my land:
A half-fac'd groat, five hundred pound a-year! (1)
ROB. My gracious liege, when that my father liv'd,
Your brother did employ my father much,—
BAST. Well, sir, by this you cannot get my land;
Your tale must be, how he employ'd my mother.
ROB. And once dispatch'd him in an embassy
To Germany, there, with the emperor,
To treat of high affairs touching that time.
The advantage of his absence took the king,
And in the mean time sojourn'd at my father's;
Where how he did prevail, I shame to speak;
But truth is truth: large lengths of seas and shores
Between my father and my mother lay,—
As I have heard my father speak himself,—
When this same lusty gentleman was got.
Upon his death-bed he by will bequeath'd
His lands to me; and took it, on his death,[b]
That this, my mother's son, was none of his;
And, if he were, he came into the world
Full fourteen weeks before the course of time.
Then, good my liege, let me have what is mine,
My father's land, as was my father's will.
K. JOHN. Sirrah, your brother is legitimate;
Your father's wife did after wedlock bear him:
And, if she did play false, the fault was hers;
Which fault lies on the hazards of all husbands
That marry wives. Tell me, how if my brother,
Who, as you say, took pains to get this son,
Had of your father claim'd this son for his?

---

[a] *With* that half-face—] This is a correction of Theobald's; the folio, 1623, reading, "with *half that face*."

[b] *And* took it, on his death,—] Steevens is the only one of the commentators who notices this expression; and he interprets it to mean, "entertained it as his fixed opinion, when he was dying." We believe it was a common form of speech, and signified that he swore, or *took oath, upon his death*, of the truth of his belief. Thus Falstaff, "Merry Wives of Windsor," Act II. Sc. 2, says, "——— and when mistress Bridget lost the handle of her fan, I *took 't upon my honour* thou hadst it not." And Prince Henry, in the First Part of "Henry IV." Act II. Sc. 4,—"They *take it already upon their salvation*." So, also, in Beaumont and Fletcher's play of "The Lover's Progress," Act V. Sc. 3,—

"——— *Upon my death*
I take it uncompelled, that they were guilty."

We still say, *upon my life, upon my honour*, meaning, *I swear or declare upon my life*, &c.

In sooth, good friend, your father might have kept
This calf, bred from his cow, from all the world;
In sooth, he might: then, if he were my brother's,
My brother might not claim him; nor your father,
Being none of his, refuse him. This concludes,[a]—
My mother's son did get your father's heir;
Your father's heir must have your father's land.
ROB. Shall, then, my father's will be of no force,
To dispossess that child which is not his?
BAST. Of no more force to dispossess me, sir,
Than was his will to get me, as I think.
ELI. Whether[b] hadst thou rather be a Faulconbridge,
And like thy brother, to enjoy thy land;
Or the reputed son of Cœur-de-lion,
Lord of thy presence,[c] and no land beside?
BAST. Madam, an if my brother had my shape,
And I had his, sir Robert* his, like him;
And if my legs were two such riding-rods,
My arms such eel-skins stuff'd, my face so thin,
That in mine ear I durst not stick a rose, [goes; (2)
Lest men should say, *Look, where three farthings*
And, to his shape, were heir to all this land,
Would I might never stir from off this place,
I'd † give it every foot to have this face;
I would not be sir Nob[d] in any case. [fortune,
ELI. I like thee well. Wilt thou forsake thy
Bequeath thy land to him, and follow me?
I am a soldier, and now bound to France.
BAST. Brother, take you my land, I'll take my chance:
Your face hath got five hundred pound a year;
Yet sell your face for five pence, and 'tis dear.—
Madam, I'll follow you unto the death.
ELI. Nay, I would have you go before me thither.
BAST. Our country manners give our betters way.
K. JOHN. What is thy name?
BAST. Philip, my liege; so is my name begun;
Philip, good old sir Robert's wife's eldest son.
K. JOHN. From henceforth bear his name whose form thou bearest:
Kneel thou down Philip, but arise ‡ more great;
Arise sir Richard, and Plantagenet.
BAST. Brother—by the mother's side, give me your hand;
My father gave me honour, yours gave land:—
Now blessed be the hour, by night or day,
When I was got, sir Robert was away.
ELI. The very spirit of Plantagenet!—
I am thy grandame, Richard; call me so.
BAST. Madam, by chance, but not by truth. What though?
Something about, a little from the right,
In at the window, or else o'er the hatch:[e]
Who dares not stir by day must walk by night,
And have is have, however men do catch:
Near or far off, well won is still well shot,
And I am I, howe'er I was begot.
K. JOHN. Go, Faulconbridge: now hast thou thy desire;
A landless knight makes thee a landed squire.—
Come, madam,—and come, Richard: we must speed,
For France, for France! for it is more than need.
BAST. Brother, adieu: good fortune come to thee!
For thou wast got i' the way of honesty.
[*Exeunt all except the* Bastard.
A foot of honour better than I was;
But many a many foot of land the worse.
Well, now can I make any Joan a lady:—
Good den, sir Richard.—God-a-mercy, fellow;
And if his name be George, I'll call him Peter,
For new-made honour doth forget men's names:
'Tis too respective,[f] and too sociable,
For your conversion. Now, your traveller,—
He and his toothpick at my worship's mess; (3)
And when my knightly stomach is suffic'd,
Why then I suck my teeth, and catechise
My pickéd man[g] of countries: *My dear sir,*
Thus, leaning on mine elbow, I begin,
I shall beseech you—that is Question now;
And then comes Answer like an A B C[h] book:
O, sir, says Answer, *at your best command;*
At your employment; at your service, sir:—
No, sir, says Question, *I, sweet sir, at yours:*
And so, ere Answer knows what Question would,
(Saving in dialogue of compliment,
And talking of the Alps and Apennines,
The Pyrenean, and the river Po,)

(*) First folio, *Roberts*. (†) First folio, *I would*. (‡) First folio, *rise*.

[a] This concludes,—] "This is a *decisive argument*. As your father, if he liked him, could not have been forced to resign him; so, not liking him, he is not at liberty to reject him."—JOHNSON.

[b] Whether—] According to strict prosody this word should have been contracted, as in an instance just noted, to *whe'r;* but the old writers, or their printers, exhibited great laxity in such cases.

[c] *Lord of* thy presence,—] Queen Elinor, prepossessed by Philip's gallant bearing and likeness to her son, frames her question so as to discover whether he prefers to rest his claim to future distinction as the heir of Faulconbridge, or as the supposed son of Cœur-de-lion:—"Would you rather be a Faulconbridge, *resembling your brother*, but possessed of five hundred pounds a-year in land; or the reputed son of King Richard, *with similar personal endowments to his*, and no land at all?"

[d] I *would not be sir Nob*—] So the second folio, 1632; the first has, "*It* would."

[e] In at the window, or else o'er the hatch:] Proverbial sayings applied to illegitimate children;—"Woe worth the time that ever I gave suck to a child that *came in at the window!*"—*The Family of Love*, 1608. So, also, in "The Witches of Lancashire," by Heywood and Broome, 1634:—"——— It appears you *came in at the window*."—"I would not have you think I scorn my grannam's cat to leap *over the hatch*."

[f] *Too* respective,—] Too *mindful, considerate, retrospective;* and not, I believe, as Steevens interprets it, "*respectful*," "*formal*."

[g] *My* pickéd *man*—] See Note (d), p. 82, of the present volume.

[h] *Like an* A B C *book:*] These letters are printed as they were pronounced, *Absey*, in the old copies. An *Absey*, or *A B C* book, was a book to teach the young their letters, *catechism*, &c.:—

"In the *A B C* of bokes the least,
Yt is written, *Deus charitas est*."

It draws toward supper in conclusion so.
But this is worshipful society,
And fits the mounting spirit like myself:
For he is but a bastard to the time,
That doth not smack* of observation;
(And so am I, whether I smack, or no;)
And not alone in habit and device,
Exterior form, outward accoutrement,
But from the inward motion, to deliver
Sweet, sweet, sweet poison for the age's tooth:
Which, though I will not practise to deceive,
Yet, to avoid deceit, I mean to learn;
For it shall strew the footsteps of my rising.—
But who comes in such haste, in riding robes?
What woman-post is this? hath she no husband,
That will take pains to blow a horn before her?
O me! it is my mother.

Enter LADY FAULCONBRIDGE *and* JAMES GURNEY.

How now, good lady?
What brings you here to court so hastily?

LA. FAULC. Where is that slave, thy brother? where is he?
That holds in chase mine honour up and down?

BAST. My brother Robert? old sir Robert's son?
Colbrand the giant,[a] that same mighty man?
Is it sir Robert's son that you seek so?

LA. FAULC. Sir Robert's son! ay, thou unreverend boy,
Sir Robert's son: why scorn'st thou at sir Robert?
He is sir Robert's son, and so art thou.

BAST. James Gurney, wilt thou give us leave a while?

GUR. Good leave,[b] good Philip.

BAST. *Philip!*—sparrow![c]—James,
There's toys abroad;[d] anon I'll tell thee more.
[*Exit* GURN.
Madam, I was not old sir Robert's son;
Sir Robert might have eat his part in me
Upon Good-Friday, and ne'er broke his fast:
Sir Robert could do well; Marry—to confess—
Could he† get me? Sir Robert could not do it;
We know his handiwork.—Therefore, good mother,
To whom am I beholden for these limbs?
Sir Robert never holp to make this leg.

LA. FAULC. Hast thou conspired with thy brother too,
That for thine own gain shouldst defend mine honour?
What means this scorn, thou most untoward knave?

BAST. Knight, knight, good mother,—Basilisco-like;(4)
What! I am dubb'd; I have it on my shoulder.
But, mother, I am not sir Robert's son;
I have disclaim'd sir Robert, and my land;
Legitimation, name, and all, is gone:
Then, good my mother, let me know my father;
Some proper man, I hope; who was it, mother?

LA. FAULC. Hast thou denied thyself a Faulconbridge?

BAST. As faithfully as I deny the devil.

LA. FAULC. King Richard Cœur-de-lion was thy father:
By long and vehement suit I was seduc'd
To make room for him in my husband's bed:—
Heaven lay not my transgression to my charge!—
Thou[e] art the issue of my dear offence,
Which was so strongly urg'd, past my defence.

BAST. Now, by this light, were I to get again,
Madam, I would not wish a better father.
Some sins do bear their privilege on earth,
And so doth yours; your fault was not your folly;
Needs must you lay your heart at his dispose,—
Subjected tribute to commanding love,—
Against whose fury and unmatchèd force
The awless lion could not wage the fight,
Nor keep his princely heart from Richard's hand.
He, that perforce robs lions of their hearts,
May easily win a woman's. Ay, my mother,
With all my heart I thank thee for my father!
Who lives and dares but say, thou didst not well
When I was got, I'll send his soul to hell.
Come, lady, I will show thee to my kin;
And they shall say, when Richard me begot,
If thou hadst said him nay, it had been sin:
Who says it was, he lies; I say, 'twas not.
[*Exeunt.*(5)

* Old copies, *smoake.* (†) Old copies omit, *he.*

a Colbrand the giant,—] This was the Danish giant whom the renowned Guy of Warwick overcame in the presence of Athelstan. A description of the combat will be found in Drayton's "Polyolbion," Twelfth Song.

b Good leave,—] "*Good leave,*" Steevens says, "means a *ready assent.*"

c Philip!—sparrow!—] The sparrow was very early known by the name Sir *Richard* disdains, perhaps from its note, to which Catullus alludes:—

"Sed circumsiliens modo huc, modo illuc,
Ad solam dominam usque *pipilabat.*"

Thus, in Lyly's "Mother Bombie:"—

"——— cry
Phip phip the *sparrowes* as they fly."

Skelton, too, has a long poem, the title of which is "*Phyllyp Sparowe.*"

d *There's* toys *abroad;*] *Toys* may mean here *rumours, idle reports,* and the like; or *tricks, devices,* &c.; for Shakespeare uses the word with great latitude.

e Thou *art the issue*—] The old copy has, "*That* art," &c.; for which Rowe substituted *Thou,* &c. Some alteration was certainly required; but this is not satisfactory. I am half persuaded the misprint to be corrected is in the preceding line, and that we ought to read,—

"Heaven lay not my transgression to *thy* charge
That art the issue of my dear offence!"

She had a moment before confessed that Richard Cœur-de-lion was his father; and "*Thou* art the issue" is a needless repetition of the avowal.

ACT II.

SCENE I.—France. *Before the Walls of* Angiers.

Enter on one side, the Archduke of Austria, *and Forces; on the other,* Philip, *King of* France, *and Forces;* Lewis, Constance, Arthur, *and* Attendants.

Lew. Before Angiers well met, brave Austria.—
Arthur, that great fore-runner of thy blood,
Richard, that robb'd the lion of his heart,(1)
And fought the holy wars in Palestine,
By this brave duke came early to his grave:
And, for amends to his posterity,
At our importance[a] hither is he come
To spread his colours, boy, in thy behalf;
And to rebuke the usurpation
Of thy unnatural uncle, English John:
Embrace him, love him, give him welcome hither.

Arth. God shall forgive you Cœur-de-lion's death,
The rather, that you give his offspring life,
Shadowing their right under your wings of war.
I give you welcome with a powerless hand,
But with a heart full of unstainèd love:
Welcome before the gates of Angiers, duke.

Lew. A noble boy! who would not do thee right?

Aust. Upon thy cheek lay I this zealous kiss,
As seal to this indenture of my love;

[a] *At our* importance—] At our *importunity.* See Note (c), p. 143, of the present volume.

That to my home I will no more return,
Till Angiers, and the right thou hast in France,
Together with that pale, that white-fac'd shore,
Whose foot spurns back the ocean's roaring tides,
And coops from other lands her islanders,
Even till that England, hedg'd in with the main,
That water-wallèd bulwark, still secure
And confident from foreign purposes,
Even till that utmost corner of the west
Salute thee for her king: till then, fair boy,
Will I not think of home, but follow arms.

CONST. O, take his mother's thanks, a widow's thanks,
Till your strong hand shall help to give him strength,
To make a more[a] requital to your love.

AUST. The peace of heaven is theirs, that lift their swords
In such a just and charitable war.

K. PHI. Well, then, to work; our cannon shall be bent
Against the brows of this resisting town.—
Call for our chiefest men of discipline,
To cull the plots of best advantages:—
We'll lay before this town our royal bones,
Wade to the market-place in Frenchmen's blood,
But we will make it subject to this boy.

CONST. Stay for an answer to your embassy,
Lest unadvis'd you stain your swords with blood:
My lord Chatillon may from England bring
That right in peace, which here we urge in war;
And then we shall repent each drop of blood
That hot-rash haste so indirectly shed.[b]

Enter CHATILLON.

K. PHI. A wonder, lady!—lo, upon thy wish,
Our messenger Chatillon is arriv'd.—
What England says, say briefly, gentle lord,
We coldly pause for thee; Chatillon, speak.

CHAT. Then turn your forces from this paltry siege,
And stir them up against a mightier task.
England, impatient of your just demands,
Hath put himself in arms; the adverse winds,
Whose leisure I have stay'd, have given him time
To land his legions all as soon as I:
His marches are expedient[c] to this town,
His forces strong, his soldiers confident.
With him along is come the mother-queen,
An Até,* stirring him to blood and strife:
With her her niece, the lady Blanch of Spain;
With them a bastard of the king's deceas'd:
And all the unsettled humours of the land,—
Rash, inconsiderate, fiery voluntaries,
With ladies' faces, and fierce dragons' spleens,—
Have sold their fortunes at their native homes,
Bearing their birthrights proudly on their backs,
To make a hazard of new fortunes here.
In brief, a braver choice of dauntless spirits,
Than now the English bottoms have waft o'er,
Did never float upon the swelling tide,
To do offence and scath in Christendom.
[*Drums beat.*
The interruption of their churlish drums
Cuts off more circumstance: they are at hand
To parley, or to fight; therefore, prepare.

K. PHI. How much unlook'd-for is this expedition!

AUST. By how much unexpected, by so much
We must awake endeavour for defence,
For courage mounteth with occasion:
Let them be welcome then, we are prepar'd.

Enter KING JOHN, ELINOR, BLANCH, *the* Bastard, PEMBROKE, *and Forces.*

K. JOHN. Peace be to France; if France in peace permit
Our just and lineal entrance to our own!
If not, bleed France, and peace ascend to heaven!
Whiles we, God's wrathful agent, do correct
Their proud contempt that beats his peace to heaven.

K. PHI. Peace be to England; if that war return
From France to England, there to live in peace!
England we love; and, for that England's sake,
With burden of our armour here we sweat:
This toil of ours should be a work of thine,
But thou from loving England art so far,
That thou hast under-wrought his lawful king,
Cut off the sequence of posterity,
Out-facèd infant state, and done a rape
Upon the maiden virtue of the crown.
Look here upon thy brother Geffrey's face;—
These eyes, these brows, were moulded out of his:
This little abstract doth contain that large,
Which died in Geffrey; and the hand of time
Shall draw this brief into as huge a volume.
That Geffrey was thy elder brother born,
And this his son; England was Geffrey's right,

---

a *A* more *requital*—] That is, a *greater* requital. Thus, in "Henry IV." Pt. I. Act IV. Sc. 3,—

"The *more* and less came in with cap and knee."

b *So* indirectly *shed.*] So *wrongfully* shed. The word occurs again with the same meaning in "Henry V." Act II. Sc. 4,—

"——— he bids you then resign
Your crown and kingdom *indirectly* held
From him, the native and true challenger."

c *Are* expedient—] *Expeditious, immediate.*

(*) First folio, *Ace.*

And this is Geffrey's. In the name of God
How comes it, then, that thou art call'd a king,
When living blood doth in these temples beat,
Which owe the crown that thou o'ermasterest?
K. JOHN. From whom hast thou this great commission, France,
To draw my answer from thy articles?
K. PHI. From that supernal Judge that stirs good thoughts
In any breast[a] of strong authority,
To look into the blots and stains of right.
That Judge hath made me guardian to this boy:
Under whose warrant, I impeach thy wrong,
And by whose help, I mean to chastise it.
K. JOHN. Alack, thou dost usurp authority.
K. PHI. Excuse—it is to beat usurping down.
ELI. Who is it, thou dost call usurper, France?
CONST. Let me make answer;—thy usurping son.
ELI. Out, insolent! thy bastard shall be king,
That thou mayst be a queen, and check the world![b]
CONST. My bed was ever to thy son as true,
As thine was to thy husband; and this boy
Liker in feature to his father Geffrey,
Than thou and John, in manners being as like
As rain to water, or devil to his dam.
My boy a bastard! By my soul, I think,
His father never was so true begot;
It cannot be, an if thou wert his mother.
ELI. There's a good mother, boy, that blots thy father.
CONST. There's a good grandame, boy, that would blot thee.
AUST. Peace!
BAST. Hear the crier.
AUST. What the devil art thou?
BAST. One that will play the devil, sir, with you,
An 'a may catch your hide and you alone.[c]
You are the hare of whom the proverb goes,[d]
Whose valour plucks dead lions by the beard.
I'll smoke your skin-coat, an I catch you right:
Sirrah, look to't; i' faith, I will, i' faith.
BLANCH. O, well did he become that lion's robe,
That did disrobe the lion of that robe!
BAST. It lies as sightly on the back of him,
As great Alcides' shows upon an ass:—(2)
But, ass, I'll take that burden from your back;
Or lay on that shall make your shoulders crack.
AUST. What cracker is this same, that deafs our ears
With this abundance of superfluous breath?
King Philip, determine what we shall do straight.[e]
K. PHI. Women and fools, break off your conference.
King John, this is the very sum of all,—
England and Ireland, Anjou,[f] Touraine, Maine,
In right of Arthur do I claim of thee:
Wilt thou resign them, and lay down thy arms?
K. JOHN. My life as soon!—I do defy thee, France.
Arthur of Bretagne, yield thee to my hand,
And, out of my dear love, I'll give thee more
Than e'er the coward hand of France can win:
Submit thee, boy.
ELI. Come to thy grandame, child.
CONST. Do, child, go to it(3) grandame, child;
Give grandame kingdom, and it grandame will
Give it a plum, a cherry, and a fig:
There's a good grandame.
ARTH. Good my mother, peace!
I would that I were low laid in my grave;
I am not worth this coil that's made for me.
ELI. His mother shames him so, poor boy, he weeps.
CONST. Now shame upon you, whe'r she does, or no!
His grandame's wrongs, and not his mother's shames,
Draw those heaven-moving pearls from his poor eyes,
Which Heaven shall take in nature of a fee;
Ay, with these crystal beads Heaven shall be brib'd,
To do him justice, and revenge on you.
ELI. Thou monstrous slanderer of heaven and earth!
CONST. Thou monstrous injurer of heaven and earth!
Call not me slanderer; thou, and thine, usurp
The dominations, royalties, and rights
Of this oppressed boy. This is thy eldest son's son,

---

a *In any* breast—] The first folio has *beast;* corrected in the edition of 1632.

b *That thou mayst be* a queen, *and* check *the world!*] It has been doubted whether Shakespeare, who appears to have had cognizance of nearly every sport and pastime of his age, was acquainted with the ancient game of chess; we believe the present passage may be taken to settle the question decisively. The allusion is obviously to the *Queen* of the chess-board, which, in this country, was invested with those remarkable powers that render her by far the most powerful piece in the game, somewhere about the second decade of the 16th century.

c *One that will play the devil, sir, with you,*
An 'a may catch your hide *and you alone.*]

The circumstance which more particularly awakens the wrath of Faulconbridge against Austria, namely, that after having caused the death of King Richard Cœur-de-lion, he now wore the lion's *hide* which had belonged to that prince, Shakespeare has omitted to mention. In the old play this incident is properly specified,—

Bastard. "——— how do my sinews shake?
My father's foe clad in my father's spoyle!
* * * * *
Base heardgroom, coward, peasant, worse than a threshing slave,
What mak'st thou with the trophie of a king?"

d *The* hare *of whom the proverb goes,*—] "Mortuo leoni et lepores insultant."—*Erasmi Adagia.*

e King Philip, *determine*—] The old copies have "King *Lewis*," &c., and prefix *Lewis* to the next speech, which evidently belongs to the King.

f Anjou,—] The old editions read *Angiers.* Theobald made the necessary alteration.

Infortunate in nothing but in thee;
Thy sins are visited in this poor child;
The canon of the law is laid on him,
Being but the second generation
Removed from thy sin-conceiving womb.

K. JOHN. Bedlam, have done.

CONST. I have but this to say,—
That he 's not only plagued for her sin,[a]
But God hath made her sin and her the plague
On this removed issue;—plagued for her,
And with her plagued; her sin, his injury
Her injury, the beadle to her sin;
All punish'd in the person of this child,
And all for her. A plague upon her!

ELI. Thou unadvisèd scold, I can produce
A will, that bars the title of thy son.

CONST. Ay, who doubts that? a will! a wicked will,
A woman's will, a canker'd grandame's will!

K. PHI. Peace, lady; pause, or be more temperate:
It ill beseems this presence, to cry *aim!*[b]
To these ill-tuned repetitions.
Some trumpet summon hither to the walls
These men of Angiers; let us hear them speak,
Whose title they admit, Arthur's or John's.

Trumpet sounds. Enter Citizens *upon the Walls.*

CIT. Who is it, that hath warn'd us to the walls?

K. PHI. 'T is France, for England.

K. JOHN. England, for itself:
You men of Angiers, and my loving subjects—

K. PHI. You loving men of Angiers, Arthur's subjects,
Our trumpet call'd you to this gentle parle—

K. JOHN. For our advantage,—therefore, hear us first.
These flags of France, that are advanced here
Before the eye and prospect of your town,
Have hither march'd to your endamagement.

---

[a] That he 's not only plagued for her sin, &c.] The only departure from the old text in this obscure passage is in the punctuation, and in the addition of a *d* in the sentence of the second clause—

"And with her plague*d* ——"

which was first suggested by Mr. Roderick.

In the original, where it runs as follows, the whole passage is pointed with a ruthless disregard of meaning:—

"—— I have but this to say,
That he is not only plagued for her sin,
But God hath made her sin and her, the plague
On this removed issue, plagued for her,
And with her plague her sin: his injury
Her injury the Beadle to her sin,
All punish'd in the person of this child,
And all for her, a plague upon her."

[b] To cry *aim!*] See note ([a]), page 39, of the present volume.

The cannons have their bowels full of wrath,
And ready mounted are they, to spit forth
Their iron indignation 'gainst your walls:
All preparation for a bloody siege,
And merciless proceeding, by these French,
Confronts[a] your city's eyes, your winking gates;
And but for our approach, those sleeping stones,
That as a waist do girdle you about,
By the compulsion of their ordinance,[b]
By this time from their fixed beds of lime
Had been dishabited, and wide havoc made
For bloody power to rush upon your peace.
But, on the sight of us, your lawful king,
Who painfully, with much expedient march,
Have brought a countercheck before your gates,
To save unscratch'd your city's threaten'd cheeks,—
Behold, the French, amaz'd, vouchsafe a parle;
And now, instead of bullets wrapp'd in fire,
To make a shaking fever in your walls,
They shoot but calm words, folded up in smoke,
To make a faithless error in your ears:
Which trust accordingly, kind citizens,
And let us in. Your king, whose labour'd spirits,
Forwearied in this action of swift speed,
Craves harbourage within your city walls.

K. PHI. When I have said, make answer to us both.
Lo, in this right hand, whose protection
Is most divinely vow'd upon the right
Of him it holds, stands young Plantagenet,
Son to the elder brother of this man,
And king o'er him, and all that he enjoys:
For this down-trodden equity, we tread
In warlike march these greens before your town;
Being no further enemy to you,
Than the constraint of hospitable zeal,
In the relief of this oppressed child,
Religiously provokes. Be pleased then
To pay that duty, which you truly owe,
To him that owes(4) it,—namely, this young prince:
And then our arms, like to a muzzled bear,
Save in aspéct, have all offence seal'd up;
Our cannons' malice vainly shall be spent
Against the invulnerable clouds of heaven;
And, with a blessed and unvex'd retire,
With unhack'd swords, and helmets all unbruis'd,
We will bear home that lusty blood again,
Which here we came to spout against your town,
And leave your children, wives, and you, in peace.
But if you fondly pass our proffer'd offer,
'Tis not the roundure[c] of your old-fac'd walls
Can hide you from our messengers of war,
Though all these English, and their discipline,
Were harbour'd in their rude circumference.
Then, tell us, shall your city call us lord,
In that behalf which we have challeng'd it?
Or shall we give the signal to our rage,
And stalk in blood to our possession?

CIT. In brief, we are the king of England's subjects;
For him, and in his right, we hold this town.

K. JOHN. Acknowledge then the king, and let me in.

CIT. That can we not: but he that proves the king,
To him will we prove loyal; till that time,
Have we ramm'd up our gates against the world.

K. JOHN. Doth not the crown of England prove the king?
And if not that, I bring you witnesses,
Twice fifteen thousand hearts of England's breed,—

BAST. Bastards, and else. [*Aside.*

K. JOHN. To verify our title with their lives.

K. PHI. As many, and as well-born bloods as those,—

BAST. Some bastards, too. [*Aside.*

K. PHI. Stand in his face, to contradict his claim.

CIT. Till you compound whose right is worthiest,
We, for the worthiest, hold the right from both.

K. JOHN. Then God forgive the sin of all those souls,
That to their everlasting residence,
Before the dew of evening fall, shall fleet,
In dreadful trial of our kingdom's king!

K. PHI. Amen, Amen!—Mount, chevaliers! to arms!

BAST. St. George, that swindg'd the dragon, and e'er since
Sits on his horseback at mine hostess' door,[d]
Teach us some fence!—Sirrah, were I at home,
At your den, sirrah [*to* AUSTRIA], with your lioness,
I'd set an ox-head to your lion's hide,
And make a monster of you.

AUST. Peace; no more.

BAST. O, tremble, for you hear the lion roar!

K. JOHN. Up higher to the plain; where we'll set forth,
In best appointment, all our regiments.

---

[a] Confronts *your city's eyes*,—] The original has *comfort*, which was altered by Rowe to *confront*. Mr. Collier's MS. annotator reads, *Come 'fore* your city's eyes.

[b] Ordinance,—] The old spelling of this word should be retained here for the measure's sake.

[c] *The* roundure—] *Roundure*, or, as the old copies spell it, *rounder*, means *circle*, from the French, *rondeur*.

[d] St. George, &c.] In the old text this passage runs thus,—
"St. George that swindg'd the dragon,
And ere since sits on 's horseback at mine hostess door," &c.

BAST. Speed then, to take advantage of the field.

K. PHI. It shall be so;—[*to* LEWIS] and at the other hill
Command the rest to stand.—God, and our right!
[*Exeunt.*

SCENE II.—*The same.*

Alarums and Excursions; then a Retreat. Enter a French Herald, *with Trumpets, to the gates.*

FR. HER. You men of Angiers, open wide your gates,
And let young Arthur, duke of Bretagne, in;
Who, by the hand of France, this day hath made
Much work for tears in many an English mother,
Whose sons lie scatter'd on the bleeding ground;
Many a widow's husband grovelling lies,
Coldly embracing the discolour'd earth;
And victory, with little loss, doth play
Upon the dancing banners of the French,
Who are at hand, triumphantly display'd,
To enter conquerors, and to proclaim
Arthur of Bretagne, England's king, and yours!

Enter an English Herald, *with Trumpets.*

ENG. HER. Rejoice, you men of Angiers, ring your bells;
King John, your king and England's, doth approach,
Commander of this hot malicious day!
Their armours, that march'd hence so silver-bright,
Hither return all gilt with Frenchmen's blood;
There stuck no plume in any English crest,
That is removed by a staff of France;
Our colours do return in those same hands
That did display them when we first march'd forth;
And, like a jolly troop of huntsmen,[a] come
Our lusty English, all with purpled hands,
Dyed in the dying slaughter of their foes:
Open your gates, and give the victors way.

HUBERT.[b] Heralds, from off our towers we might behold,
From first to last, the onset and retire
Of both your armies; whose equality
By our best eyes cannot be censured.
Blood hath bought blood, and blows have answer'd blows;
Strength match'd with strength, and power confronted power:
Both are alike, and both alike we like.
One must prove greatest: while they weigh so even,
We hold our town for neither; yet for both.

Re-enter, at one side, KING JOHN, *with his Power,* ELINOR, BLANCH, *and the* Bastard; *at the other,* KING PHILIP, LEWIS, AUSTRIA, *and Forces.*

K. JOHN. France, hast thou yet more blood to cast away?
Say, shall the current of our right run[c] on,
Whose passage, vex'd with thy impediment,
Shall leave his native channel, and o'erswell
With course disturb'd even thy confining shores,
Unless thou let his silver water keep
A peaceful progress to the ocean?

K. PHI. England, thou hast not sav'd one drop of blood
In this hot trial, more than we of France;
Rather, lost more. And by this hand I swear,
That sways the earth this climate overlooks,
Before we will lay down our just-borne arms,
We'll put thee down, 'gainst whom these arms we bear,
Or add a royal number to the dead;
Gracing the scroll, that tells of this war's loss,
With slaughter coupled to the name of kings.

BAST. Ha, majesty! how high thy glory towers,
When the rich blood of kings is set on fire!
O, now doth death line his dead chaps with steel,
The swords of soldiers are his teeth, his fangs;
And now he feasts, mousing[d] the flesh of men,
In undetermin'd differences of kings.
Why stand these royal fronts amazed thus?
Cry, havoc, kings! back to the stained field,
You equal-potents, fiery-kindled spirits!
Then let confusion of one part confirm
The other's peace; till then, blows, blood, and death!

K. JOHN. Whose party do the townsmen yet admit?

---

[a] And, like a jolly troop of huntsmen,—] It appears to have been a practice of the chase formerly for the huntsmen to steep their hands in the blood of the deer as a trophy. Thus in "Julius Cæsar," Act III. Sc. 1,—

"—— here thy hunters stand,
Sign'd in thy spoil and *crimson'd in thy lethe.*"

[b] *Hubert.*] In the early copies several speeches of the present scene have this prefix, and Shakespeare may have intended to represent Hubert as a citizen of Angiers; but the more probable explanation is, that the name was prefixed merely because it was the custom of the actor who personated the character of Hubert to "double" with it that of the Angiers' spokesman.

[c] *Say, shall the current of our right* run *on,*—] So the second folio; the first has *rome,* a likely misprint of *ronne.*

[d] Mousing *the flesh of men,*—] For *mousing* Pope substituted a less expressive term, *mouthing,* which Malone very properly rejected, and restored the old word. *Mousing* meant *gorging, devouring.* Thus, in Decker's "Wonderful Year," 1603,—

"Whilst Troy was swilling sack and sugar, and *mousing* fat venison," &c.

K. PHI. Speak, citizens, for England; who 's your king?

HUBERT. The king of England, when we know the king.

K. PHI. Know him in us, that here hold up his right.

K. JOHN. In us, that are our own great deputy,
And bear possession of our person here;
Lord of our presence, Angiers, and of you.

HUBERT. A greater power than we denies all this;
And, till it be undoubted, we do lock
Our former scruple in our strong-barr'd gates,
Kings, of our fear;[a] until our fears, resolv'd,
Be by some certain king purg'd and depos'd.

BAST. By heaven, these scroyles[b] of Angiers flout you, kings,
And stand securely on their battlements,
As in a theatre, whence they gape and point
At your industrious scenes and acts of death.
Your royal presences be rul'd by me;
Do like the mutines of Jerusalem,(5)
Be friends a while, and both conjointly bend
Your sharpest deeds of malice on this town:
By east and west let France and England mount
Their battering cannon chargèd to the mouths,
Till their soul-fearing clamours have brawl'd down
The flinty ribs of this contemptuous city:—
I 'd play incessantly upon these jades,
Even till unfenced desolation
Leave them as naked as the vulgar air.—
That done, dissever your united strengths,
And part your mingled colours once again,
Turn face to face, and bloody point to point:
Then, in a moment, fortune shall cull forth
Out of one side her happy minion;
To whom in favour she shall give the day,
And kiss him with a glorious victory.
How like you this wild counsel, mighty states?
Smacks it not something of the policy?

K. JOHN. Now, by the sky that hangs above our heads,
I like it well;—France, shall we knit our powers,
And lay this Angiers even with the ground;
Then, after, fight who shall be king of it?

BAST. An if thou hast the mettle of a king,
Being wrong'd, as we are, by this peevish town,
Turn thou the mouth of thy artillery,
As we will ours, against these saucy walls:
And when that we have dash'd them to the ground,
Why, then defy each other; and, pell-mell,
Make work upon ourselves, for heaven, or hell.

K. PHI. Let it be so.—Say, where will you assault?

K. JOHN. We from the west will send destruction
Into this city's bosom.

AUST. I, from the north.

K. PHI. Our thunder from the south,
Shall rain their drift of bullets on this town.

BAST. O prudent discipline! From north to south,
Austria and France shoot in each other's mouth: [*Aside.*
I'll stir them to it:—Come, away, away!

HUBERT. Hear us, great kings: vouchsafe a while to stay,
And I shall show you peace, and fair-fac'd league;
Win you this city without stroke or wound,
Rescue those breathing lives to die in beds,
That here come sacrifices for the field:
Persèver not, but hear me, mighty kings.

K. JOHN. Speak on, with favour; we are bent to hear.

HUBERT. That daughter there of Spain, the lady Blanch,[c]
Is near to England: look upon the years
Of Lewis the Dauphin, and that lovely maid:
If lusty love should go in quest of beauty,
Where should he find it fairer than in Blanch?
If zealous love should go in search of virtue,
Where should he find it purer than in Blanch?
If love ambitious sought a match of birth,
Whose veins bound richer blood than lady Blanch?
Such as she is, in beauty, virtue, birth,
Is the young Dauphin every way complete;
If not complete, O say,[d] he is not she:
And she again wants nothing, to name want,
If want it be not, that she is not he:
He is the half part of a blessed man,
Left to be finished by such a * she;
And she a fair divided excellence,
Whose fulness of perfection lies in him.
O, two such silver currents, when they join,
Do glorify the banks that bound them in;
And two such shores to two such streams made one,

---

[a] Kings, of our fear;] This passage has been a good deal discussed. Warburton and Johnson read,—

"Kings *are* our fears;"—

Tyrwhitt,—

"*King'd* of our fears;"—

which latter is the reading usually adopted. Mr. Knight adheres to the original text; but his interpretation of it is to us unfathomable. The meaning of the speaker, however quaintly expressed, we imagine to be simply this,—Each of you lays claim to our allegiance, but neither has produced satisfactory proof of his right to it; and until all doubts upon that point are resolved, we shall trust to *our strong-barred gates* as the protectors, or *Kings*, of our fear.

[b] *These* scroyles—] From the French *escrouelles, scabby* rogues.

[c] *The lady* Blanch,—] This lady was daughter to Alphonso the Ninth, King of Castile, and was niece to King John, by his sister Eleanor.

[d] *If not complete,* O *say,*—] The old copy reads:—

"If not complete *of*, say,—"

Hanmer first suggested the alteration.

(*) Old copies, *as*.

Two such controlling bounds shall you be, kings,
To these two princes, if you marry them.
This union shall do more than battery can,
To our fast-closed gates; for, at this match,
With swifter spleen than powder can enforce,
The mouth of passage shall we fling wide ope,
And give you entrance; but, without this match,
The sea enraged is not half so deaf,
Lions more confident, mountains and rocks
More free from motion, no, not death himself
In mortal fury half so peremptory,
As we to keep this city.

BAST. Here 's a stay,[a]
That shakes the rotten carcase of old death
Out of his rags! Here 's a large mouth, indeed,
That spits forth death, and mountains, rocks, and seas,
Talks as familiarly of roaring lions,
As maids of thirteen do of puppy-dogs!
What cannoneer begot this lusty blood?
He speaks plain cannon-fire, and smoke, and bounce;
He gives the bastinado with his tongue;
Our ears are cudgell'd; not a word of his,
But buffets better than a fist of France:
Zounds! I was never so bethump'd with words,
Since I first called my brother's father, dad.

ELI. Son, list to this conjunction, make this match;
Give with our niece a dowry large enough:
For by this knot thou shalt so surely tie
Thy now unsur'd assurance to the crown,
That yon green boy shall have no sun to ripe
The bloom that promiseth a mighty fruit.
I see a yielding in the looks of France;
Mark, how they whisper: urge them, while their souls
Are capable[b] of this ambition;
Lest zeal, now melted, by the windy breath
Of soft petitions, pity, and remorse,
Cool and congeal again to what it was.

HUBERT. Why answer not the double majesties,
This friendly treaty of our threaten'd town?

K. PHI. Speak England first, that hath been forward first
To speak unto this city. What say you?

K. JOHN. If that the Dauphin there, thy princely son,
Can in this book of beauty read—*I love*,
Her dowry shall weigh equal with a queen:
For Anjou,* and fair Touraine, Maine, Poictiers,
And all that we upon this side the sea
(Except this city now by us besieg'd)
Find liable to our crown and dignity,
Shall gild her bridal bed; and make her rich
In titles, honours, and promotions,
As she in beauty, education, blood,
Holds hand with any princess of the world.

K. PHI. What sayst thou, boy? look in the lady's face.

LEW. I do, my lord, and in her eye I find
A wonder, or a wondrous miracle,
The shadow of myself form'd in her eye;
Which being but the shadow of your son,
Becomes a sun, and makes your son a shadow:
I do protest, I never lov'd myself,
Till now infixed I beheld myself,
Drawn in the flattering table[c] of her eye.
[*Whispers with* BLANCH.

BAST. Drawn in the flattering table of her eye!—
Hang'd in the frowning wrinkle of her brow!—
And quarter'd in her heart!—he doth espy
Himself love's traitor: this is pity now,
That hang'd, and drawn, and quarter'd, there should be,
In such a love, so vile a lout as he. [*Aside.*

BLANCH. My uncle's will, in this respect, is mine.
If he see aught in you, that makes him like,
That anything he sees, which moves his liking,
I can with ease translate it to my will;
Or, if you will, to speak more properly,
I will enforce it easily to my love.
Further I will not flatter you, my lord,
That all I see in you is worthy love,
Than this,—that nothing do I see in you,
Though churlish thoughts themselves should be your judge,
That I can find should merit any hate.

K. JOHN. What say these young ones? What say you, my niece?

BLANCH. That she is bound in honour still to do
What you in wisdom still vouchsafe to say.

K. JOHN. Speak then, prince Dauphin; can you love this lady?

LEW. Nay, ask me if I can refrain from love;
For I do love her most unfeignedly.

---

[a] *Here's* a stay,—] *Stay*, if that be the poet's word, is used, we suppose, in the sense of a *sudden* check or obstacle. It may not be the most suitable expression to introduce the following line; but it appears at least as good as *flaw* or *say*, which have been proposed to supersede it.

[b] *Are* capable *of this ambition;*] *Capable* is *impressible, susceptible*. So, in the next Act, Constance says,—

"—— I am sick and *capable* of fears."

and "Hamlet," Act III. Sc. 4,—

"His form and cause conjoin'd, preaching to stones,
Would make them *capable*."

(*) Old copies, *Angiers*.

[c] *The flattering* table—] *Table* the expositors define to mean *picture*, or the board or canvas on which any object is painted.

K. JOHN. Then do I give Volquessen,[a] Touraine, Maine,
Poictiers, and Anjou, these five provinces,
With her to thee; and this addition more,
Full thirty thousand marks of English coin.
Philip of France, if thou be pleas'd withal,
Command thy son and daughter to join hands.

K. PHI. It likes us well. Young princes, close your hands.

AUST. And your lips too; for I am well assur'd
That I did so, when I was first assur'd.[b]

K. PHI. Now, citizens of Angiers, ope your gates;
Let in that amity which you have made,
For at saint Mary's chapel, presently,
The rites of marriage shall be solemniz'd.
Is not the lady Constance in this troop?
I know she is not; for this match, made up,
Her presence would have interrupted much:
Where is she and her son? tell me, who knows.

LEW. She is sad and passionate[c] at your highness' tent.

K. PHI. And, by my faith, this league that we have made,
Will give her sadness very little cure.
Brother of England, how may we content
This widow lady? In her right we came;
Which we, God knows, have turn'd another way,
To our own vantage.

K. JOHN. We will heal up all,
For we'll create young Arthur duke of Bretagne,
And earl of Richmond; and this rich fair town
We make him lord of.—Call the lady Constance;
Some speedy messenger bid her repair
To our solemnity:—I trust we shall,
If not fill up the measure of her will,
Yet in some measure satisfy her so,
That we shall stop her exclamation.
Go we, as well as haste will suffer us,
To this unlook'd-for, unprepared pomp.

[*Exeunt all but the* Bastard.—*The* Citizens *retire from the walls.*

BAST. Mad world! mad kings! mad composition!
John, to stop Arthur's title in the whole,
Hath willingly departed[d] with a part:
And France, whose armour conscience buckled on,
Whom zeal and charity brought to the field
As God's own soldier, rounded[e] in the ear
With that same purpose-changer, that sly devil,
That broker,[f] that still breaks the pate of faith;
That daily break-vow; he that wins of all,
Of kings, of beggars, old men, young men, maids,—
Who having no external thing to lose
But the word maid, cheats the poor maid of that;
That smooth-fac'd gentleman, tickling commodity,[g]
Commodity, the bias of the world;
The world, who of itself is peised[h] well,
Made to run even, upon even ground;
Till this advantage, this vile drawing bias,
This sway of motion, this commodity,
Makes it take head from all indifferency,
From all direction, purpose, course, intent:
And this same bias, this commodity,
This bawd, this broker, this all-changing word,
Clapp'd on the outward eye[i] of fickle France,
Hath drawn him from his own determin'd aid,[k]
From a resolv'd and honourable war,
To a most base and vile-concluded peace.—
And why rail I on this commodity?
But for because he hath not woo'd me yet:
Not that I have the power to clutch my hand,
When his fair angels would salute my palm;
But for my hand, as unattempted yet,
Like a poor beggar, raileth on the rich.
Well, whiles I am a beggar, I will rail,
And say,—there is no sin but to be rich;
And being rich, my virtue then shall be,
To say,—there is no vice but beggary:
Since kings break faith upon commodity,
Gain, be my lord! for I will worship thee!

[*Exit.*

---

a Volquessen,—] The ancient name of that part of France now called *Le Vexin;* in Latin, *Pagus Velocassinus.* Thus, in the old play,—

"And here in marriage I do give with her,
From me and my successors, English kings,
Volquesson, Poiters, Anjou, Torain, Main,
And thirtie thousand markes of stipened coyne."

b *When I was first* assur'd.] In the previous line *assured* is used in its ordinary sense; here it means *affianced* or *contracted.* The kiss was a part of the ceremony of betrothing. So, in "Twelfth Night," Act V. Sc. 1,—

"A contract of eternal bond of love
Attested by the *holy close of lips.*"

c *Sad and* passionate—] *Passionate* in this place signifies *perturbed, agitated,* not *irascible.*

d *Willingly* departed with—] That is, *parted* with. *Depart* and *part* were used of old synonymously. See note (a), page 62, of the present volume.

e Rounded *in the ear*—] *Insinuated, whispered* in the ear. Thus, in the "Spanish Tragedy," Act I.—

"Forthwith Revenge she *rounded* thee in *th' ear.*"

f *That* broker,—] Broker in old language usually meant *a pander,* or *procuress;* but sometimes also, as in this passage, *a dissembler, or cheat.*

g *Tickling* commodity,—] *Commodity* is *advantage, self-interest.* So, in "Barnaby Riche's Farewell to Militarie Profession:"—"In the whiche Fineo, to his greate contentment, had the *comoditie* daiely to see his Fiamma," &c.

h *Peised*—] That is, *balanced, poised.*

i *On the outward* eye—] A continuation of the well-sustained metaphor derived from the game of bowls. The aperture on one side which contains the *bias* or weight that inclines the bowl, in running, from a direct course, was sometimes called the eye.

k *His own determin'd aid,*—] Mason suggested, and perhaps rightly, that we should read *aim,* instead of *aid.*

ACT III.[a]

SCENE I.—*The same. The* French King's *Tent.*

Enter Constance, Arthur, *and* Salisbury.

Const. Gone to be married! gone to swear a peace!
False blood to false blood join'd! Gone to be friends!
Shall Lewis have Blanch? and Blanch those provinces?
It is not so; thou hast mis-spoke, misheard;
Be well advis'd,[b] tell o'er thy tale again:

[a] *Act III.*] In the old copy the Second Act extended to the conclusion of the speech of Lady Constance, when she throws herself upon the ground. The division now always adopted was made by Theobald.

[b] *Be well* advis'd.—] *Be thoroughly assured. Advised,* in this sense, is common both in Shakespeare and the books of his time.

It cannot be; thou dost but say 'tis so:
I trust I may not trust thee; for thy word
Is but the vain breath of a common man:
Believe me, I do not believe thee, man;
I have a king's oath to the contrary.
Thou shalt be punish'd for thus frighting me,
For I am sick, and capable[a] of fears,
Oppress'd with wrongs, and therefore full of fears;
A widow, husbandless, subject to fears;
A woman, naturally born to fears;
And though thou now confess thou didst but jest,
With my vex'd spirits I cannot take a truce,[b]
But they will quake and tremble all this day.
What dost thou mean by shaking of thy head?
Why dost thou look so sadly on my son?
What means that hand upon that breast of thine?
Why holds thine eye that lamentable rheum,
Like a proud river peering o'er his bounds?
Be these sad signs confirmers of thy words?
Then speak again; not all thy former tale,
But this one word,—whether thy tale be true.

SAL. As true as, I believe, you think them false,
That give you cause to prove my saying true.

CONST. O, if thou teach me to believe this sorrow,
Teach thou this sorrow how to make me die;
And let belief and life encounter so,
As doth the fury of two desperate men,
Which, in the very meeting, fall, and die.—
Lewis marry Blanch! O, boy, then where art thou?
France friend with England! what becomes of me?—
Fellow, be gone: I cannot brook thy sight;
This news hath made thee a most ugly man.

SAL. What other harm have I, good lady, done,
But spoke the harm that is by others done?

CONST. Which harm within itself so heinous is,
As it makes harmful all that speak of it.

ARTH. I do beseech you, madam, be content.

CONST. If thou that bid'st me be content, wert grim,
Ugly, and slanderous to thy mother's womb,
Full of unpleasing blots and sightless[c] stains,
Lame, foolish, crooked, swart, prodigious,[d]
Patch'd with foul moles and eye-offending marks,
I would not care, I then would be content,
For then I should not love thee; no, nor thou
Become thy great birth, nor deserve a crown.
But thou art fair; and at thy birth, dear boy,
Nature and Fortune join'd to make thee great;
Of Nature's gifts thou mayst with lilies boast,
And with the half-blown rose: but Fortune, O!
She is corrupted, chang'd, and won from thee;
She adulterates hourly with thine uncle John;
And with her golden hand hath pluck'd on France
To tread down fair respect of sovereignty,
And made his majesty the bawd to theirs.
France is a bawd to Fortune, and king John;
That strumpet Fortune, that usurping John:—
Tell me, thou fellow, is not France forsworn?
Envenom him with words; or get thee gone,
And leave those woes alone, which I alone
Am bound to under-bear.

SAL. Pardon me, madam,
I may not go without you to the kings.

CONST. Thou mayst, thou shalt, I will not go with thee;
I will instruct my sorrows to be proud,
For grief is proud, and makes his owner stout.(1)
To me, and to the state of my great grief,
Let kings assemble; for my grief's so great
That no supporter but the huge firm earth
Can hold it up: here I and sorrows sit;
Here is my throne, bid kings come bow to it.
[*She throws herself on the ground.*

Enter KING JOHN, KING PHILIP, LEWIS, BLANCH, ELINOR, Bastard, AUSTRIA, *and* Attendants.

K. PHI. 'Tis true, fair daughter; and this blessed day
Ever in France shall be kept festival:
To solemnize this day, the glorious sun
Stays in his course, and plays the alchymist;
Turning, with splendour of his precious eye,
The meagre cloddy earth to glittering gold:
The yearly course that brings this day about
Shall never see it but a holiday.

CONST. A wicked day, and not a holy day!— [*Rising.*
What hath this day deserv'd? what hath it done,
That it in golden letters should be set,
Among the high tides, in the kalendar?
Nay, rather, turn this day out of the week,
This day of shame, oppression, perjury:
Or, if it must stand still, let wives with child
Pray that their burthens may not fall this day,
Lest that their hopes prodigiously be cross'd:[e]
But on this day[f] let seamen fear no wrack;
No bargains break, that are not this day made:

a Capable *of fears*,—] See note (b), page 297.

b I *cannot* take a truce,—] To *take truce*, in the language of our author, meant to *make peace*. Thus, in "Romeo and Juliet," Act III. Sc. 1,—

"Romeo ——
Could not *take truce* with the unruly spleen
Of Tybalt deaf to peace ——."

c Sightless—] *Unsightly*.

d Prodigious,—] *Monstrous*.

e Prodigiously *be cross'd*:] That is, *be frustrated by their burdens proving monsters*, or prodigies.

f But on *this day*—] *Except*, or *unless*, on this day.

This day, all things begun come to ill end,
Yea, faith itself to hollow falsehood change!

K. PHI. By heaven, lady, you shall have no cause
To curse the fair proceedings of this day.
Have I not pawn'd to you my majesty?

CONST. You have beguil'd me with a counterfeit,
Resembling majesty; which, being touch'd, and tried,
Proves valueless. You are forsworn, forsworn;
You came in arms to spill mine enemies' blood,
But now in arms you strengthen it with yours.
The grappling vigour, and rough frown of war,
Is cold in amity and painted peace,[a]
And our oppression hath made up this league:—
Arm, arm, you heavens, against these perjur'd kings!
A widow cries; be husband to me, heavens!
Let not the hours of this ungodly day
Wear out the day* in peace; but, ere sunset,
Set armed discord 'twixt these perjur'd kings!
Hear me, O, hear me!

AUST. Lady Constance, peace.

CONST. War! war! no peace! peace is to me a war.
O Lymoges! O Austria!(2) thou dost shame
That bloody spoil: thou slave, thou wretch, thou coward,
Thou little valiant, great in villainy!
Thou ever strong upon the stronger side!
Thou Fortune's champion, that dost never fight
But when her humorous ladyship is by
To teach thee safety! thou art perjur'd too,
And sooth'st up greatness. What a fool art thou,
A ramping fool; to brag, and stamp, and swear,
Upon my party! Thou cold-blooded slave,
Hast thou not spoke like thunder on my side?
Been sworn my soldier? Bidding me depend
Upon thy stars, thy fortune, and thy strength?
And dost thou now fall over to my foes?
Thou wear a lion's hide! doff it for shame,
And hang a calf's-skin on those recreant limbs.

AUST. O, that a man should speak those words to me!

BAST. And hang a calf's-skin on those recreant limbs.

AUST. Thou dar'st not say so, villain, for thy life.

BAST. And hang a calf's-skin on those recreant limbs.

K. JOHN. We like not this; thou dost forget thyself.

Enter PANDULPH.

K. PHI. Here comes the holy legate of the pope.

PAND. Hail, you anointed deputies of heaven!—
To thee, king John, my holy errand is.
I, Pandulph, of fair Milan cardinal,
And from pope Innocent the legate here,
Do, in his name, religiously demand,
Why thou, against the church, our holy mother,
So wilfully dost spurn; and, force perforce,
Keep Stephen Langton, chosen archbishop
Of Canterbury, from that holy see?
This, in our 'foresaid holy father's name,
Pope Innocent, I do demand of thee.

K. JOHN. What earthly* name to interrogatories[b]
Can task† the free breath of a sacred king?
Thou canst not, cardinal, devise a name
So slight, unworthy, and ridiculous,
To charge me to an answer, as the pope.
Tell him this tale; and from the mouth of England
Add thus much more,—That no Italian priest
Shall tithe or toll in our dominions;
But as we under heaven are supreme head,
So, under Him, that great supremacy,
Where we do reign, we will alone uphold,
Without the assistance of a mortal hand:
So tell the pope; all reverence set apart,
To him, and his usurp'd authority.

K. PHI. Brother of England, you blaspheme in this.

K. JOHN. Though you, and all the kings of Christendom,
Are led so grossly by this meddling priest,
Dreading the curse that money may buy out;
And by the merit of vile gold, dross, dust,
Purchase corrupted pardon of a man,
Who, in that sale, sells pardon from himself;
Though you, and all the rest, so grossly led,
This juggling witchcraft with revènue cherish:
Yet I alone, alone do me oppose
Against the pope, and count his friends my foes.

PAND. Then, by the lawful power that I have,
Thou shalt stand curs'd, and excommunicate:
And blessed shall he be that doth revolt
From his allegiance to an heretic;
And meritorious shall that hand be call'd,
Canonized, and worshipp'd as a saint,
That takes away by any secret course
Thy hateful life.(3)

CONST. O, lawful let it be,
That I have room with Rome to curse a while!

(*) Old copies, *days*.

(*) Old copies, *earthie*. (†) Old copies, *tast*.

[a] The grappling vigour, and rough frown of war,
Is cold in amity, and painted peace,—]
The ingenious annotator of Mr. Collier's folio would read "*faint in* peace;" but if any alteration be required, of which I am by no means certain, it should be simply to read *coil'd* for cold. The meaning seems to be,—The vigorous arms are coiled in amity, and grim-visaged war become a smooth-faced peace.

[b] To interrogatories—] That is, *subjoined* to interrogatories.

Good father cardinal, cry thou, Amen,
To my keen curses: for, without my wrong,
There is no tongue hath power to curse him right.

PAND. There 's law and warrant, lady, for my curse.

CONST. And for mine too. When law can do no right,
Let it be lawful that law bar no wrong;
Law cannot give my child his kingdom here,
For he, that holds his kingdom, holds the law:
Therefore, since law itself is perfect wrong,
How can the law forbid my tongue to curse?

PAND. Philip of France, on peril of a curse,
Let go the hand of that arch-heretic,
And raise the power of France upon his head,
Unless he do submit himself to Rome.

ELI. Look'st thou pale, France? do not let go thy hand.

CONST. Look to that, devil! lest that France repent,
And, by disjoining hands, hell lose a soul.

AUST. King Philip, listen to the cardinal.

BAST. And hang a calf's-skin on his recreant limbs.

AUST. Well, ruffian, I must pocket up these wrongs,
Because——

BAST. Your breeches best may carry them.

K. JOHN. Philip, what say'st thou to the cardinal?

CONST. What should he say, but as the cardinal?

LEW. Bethink you, father; for the difference
Is, purchase of a heavy curse from Rome,
Or the light loss of England for a friend:
Forego the easier.

BLANCH. That 's the curse of Rome.

CONST. O Lewis, stand fast; the devil tempts thee here,
In likeness of a new uptrimmed[a] bride.

BLANCH. The lady Constance speaks not from her faith,
But from her need.

CONST. O, if thou grant my need,
Which only lives but by the death of faith,
That need must needs infer this principle,—
That faith would live again by death of need:
O, then, tread down my need, and faith mounts up,
Keep my need up, and faith is trodden down.

K. JOHN. The king is mov'd, and answers not to this.

CONST. O, be remov'd from him, and answer well.

AUST. Do so, king Philip, hang no more in doubt.

BAST. Hang nothing but a calf's-skin, most sweet lout.

K. PHI. I am perplex'd, and know not what to say.

PAND. What canst thou say, but will perplex thee more,
If thou stand excommunicate, and curs'd?

K. PHI. Good reverend father, make my person yours,
And tell me how you would bestow yourself.
This royal hand and mine are newly knit,
And the conjunction of our inward souls
Married in league, coupled and link'd together
With all religious strength of sacred vows.
The latest breath that gave the sound of words
Was deep-sworn faith, peace, amity, true love,
Between our kingdoms, and our royal selves:
And even before this truce, but new before,—
No longer than we well could wash our hands,
To clap this royal bargain up of peace,—
Heaven knows, they were besmear'd and overstain'd
With slaughter's pencil; where revenge did paint
The fearful difference of incensed kings:
And shall these hands, so lately purg'd of blood,
So newly join'd in love, so strong in both,
Unyoke this seizure, and this kind regreet?
Play fast and loose with faith? so jest with heaven,
Make such unconstant children of ourselves,
As now again to snatch our palm from palm?
Unswear faith sworn? and on the marriage bed
Of smiling peace to march a bloody host,
And make a riot on the gentle brow
Of true sincerity? O, holy sir,
My reverend father, let it not be so:
Out of your grace, devise, ordain, impose
Some gentle order; and then we shall be bless'd
To do your pleasure, and continue friends.

PAND. All form is formless, order orderless,
Save what is opposite to England's love.
Therefore, to arms! be champion of our church!
Or let the church, our mother, breathe her curse,
A mother's curse, on her revolting son.
France, thou mayst hold a serpent by the tongue,
A chafed[b] lion by the mortal paw,
A fasting tiger safer by the tooth,
Than keep in peace that hand which thou dost hold.

K. PHI. I may disjoin my hand, but not my faith.

PAND. So mak'st thou faith an enemy to faith;
And, like a civil war, sett'st oath to oath,

---

[a] *In likeness of a new* uptrimmed *bride.*] As *untrimmed,* the reading of the old copies, is usually conceived to mean *unadorned,* and the sense appears to require a word implying the reverse, we have adopted the happy and unforced emendation of Mr. Dyce. Theobald reads, "*and* trimmed bride."

[b] *A* chafed *lion*—] The old text has "A *cased* lion." *Chafed* was first suggested by Mr. Dyce, and receives support from a well-known passage in "Henry VIII." Act III. Sc. 2,—

"——— So looks the *chafed* lion
Upon the daring huntsman that has gall'd him."

Thy tongue against thy tongue. O, let thy vow
First made to heaven, first be to heaven perform'd;
That is, to be the champion of our church!
What since thou swor'st, is sworn against thyself,
And may not be performed by thyself:
For that which thou hast sworn to do amiss,
Is not[a] amiss when it is truly done;
And being not done, where doing tends to ill,
The truth is then most done not doing it:
The better act of purposes mistook
Is, to mistake again; though indirect,
Yet indirection thereby grows direct,
And falsehood falsehood cures, as fire cools fire
Within the scorched veins of one new burn'd.
It is religion that doth make vows kept;[b]
But thou hast sworn against religion,
By what thou swear'st against the thing thou swear'st;
And mak'st an oath the surety for thy truth
Against an oath: the truth thou art unsure
To swear, swears only not to be forsworn;
Else, what a mockery should it be to swear!
But thou dost swear only to be forsworn,
And most forsworn, to keep what thou dost swear.
Therefore, thy later vows, against thy first,
Is in thyself rebellion to thyself;
And better conquest never canst thou make,
Than arm thy constant and thy nobler parts
Against these giddy loose suggestions:
Upon which better part our prayers come in,
If thou vouchsafe them; but, if not, then know,
The peril of our curses light on thee
So heavy, as thou shalt not shake them off,
But, in despair, die under their black weight.

AUST. Rebellion, flat rebellion!

BAST. Will 't not be?
Will not a calf's-skin stop that mouth of thine?

LEW. Father, to arms!

BLANCH. Upon thy wedding-day?
Against the blood that thou hast married?
What, shall our feast be kept with slaughter'd men?
Shall braying trumpets, and loud churlish drums,
Clamours of hell, be measures to our pomp?
O husband, hear me!—aye, alack, how new
Is husband in my mouth!—even for that name,
Which till this time my tongue did ne'er pronounce,
Upon my knee I beg, go not to arms
Against mine uncle.

CONST. O, upon my knee,
Made hard with kneeling, I do pray to thee,
Thou virtuous Dauphin, alter not the doom
Fore-thought by heaven.

BLANCH. Now shall I see thy love. What motive may
Be stronger with thee than the name of wife?

CONST. That which upholdeth him that thee upholds,
His honour: O, thine honour, Lewis, thine honour!

LEW. I muse your majesty doth seem so cold,
When such profound respects do pull you on.

PAND. I will denounce a curse upon his head.

K. PHI. Thou shalt not need:—England, I will fall from thee.

CONST. O fair return of banish'd majesty!

ELI. O foul revolt of French inconstancy!

K. JOHN. France, thou shalt rue this hour within this hour.

BAST. Old Time the clock-setter, that bald sexton, Time,
Is it as he will? well then, France shall rue.

BLANCH. The sun's o'ercast with blood: fair day adieu!
Which is the side that I must go withal?
I am with both: each army hath a hand,
And, in their rage, I having hold of both,
They whirl asunder, and dismember me.
Husband, I cannot pray that thou mayst win;
Uncle I needs must pray that thou mayst lose;
Father, I may not wish the fortune thine;
Grandame, I will not wish thy wishes thrive:
Whoever wins, on that side shall I lose;
Assured loss, before the match be play'd.

LEW. Lady, with me; with me thy fortune lies.

BLANCH. There where my fortune lives, there my life dies.

K. JOHN. Cousin, go draw our puissance together.— [*Exit* Bastard.
France, I am burn'd up with inflaming wrath,
A rage whose heat hath this condition,
That nothing can allay, nothing but blood,
The blood, and dearest-valued blood, of France.

K. PHI. Thy rage shall burn thee up, and thou shalt turn

---

[a] *Is* not *amiss when it is truly done;*] Surely the argument proves beyond question that *not* is a misprint for *but*, and that we should read:—

"For that which thou hast sworn to do amiss,
Is *but* amiss, when it is truly done;
And being not done, where doing tends to ill,
The truth is then most done, not doing it."

[b] It is religion that doth make vows kept, &c. &c.] In the folios this passage is exhibited as follows:—

"It is religion that doth make vows kept,
But thou hast sworn against religion:
By what thou swear'st against the thing thou swear'st,
And mak'st an oath the surety for thy truth,
Against an oath the truth, thou art unsure
To swear, swears only not to be forsworn,
Else what a mockery should it be to swear!" &c.

There are critics who profess to understand this and similar textual imbroglios of the 1623 edition, which is more than the author himself would do. I venture to suggest the following as a probable reading of the passage in its original form:—

"It is religion that doth make vows kept,
But thou hast sworn against religion:
By *that*, thou swear'st against the thing thou swear'st,
And mak'st an oath, the surety for thy truth,
Against an oath, the proof thou art unsure.
Who swears swears only not to be forsworn,
Else what a mockery should it be to swear!" &c.

To ashes, ere our blood shall quench that fire:
Look to thyself, thou art in jeopardy.

K. JOHN. No more than he that threats.—To arms! let 's hie. [*Exeunt.*

SCENE II.—*The same. Plains near* Angiers.

Alarums; Excursions. Enter the Bastard *with* AUSTRIA'*s Head.*

BAST. Now, by my life, this day grows wondrous hot;
Some airy(4) devil hovers in the sky,
And pours down mischief. Austria's head, lie there;
While Philip breathes.(5)

Enter KING JOHN, ARTHUR, *and* HUBERT.

K. JOHN. Hubert, keep this boy:—Philip, make up:
My mother is assailed in our tent,
And ta'en, I fear.

BAST. My lord, I rescued her;
Her highness is in safety, fear you not:
But on, my liege; for very little pains
Will bring this labour to an happy end. [*Exeunt.*

SCENE III.—*The same.*

Alarums; Excursions; Retreat. Enter King John, Elinor, Arthur, *the* Bastard, Hubert, *and* Lords.

K. John. So shall it be; your grace shall stay behind, [*To* Elinor.
So strongly guarded.—Cousin, look not sad, [*To* Arthur.
Thy grandame loves thee, and thy uncle will
As dear be to thee as thy father was.

Arth. O, this will make my mother die with grief.

K. John. Cousin, [*to the* Bastard] away for England; haste before:
And, ere our coming, see thou shake the bags
Of hoarding abbots; imprisoned angels
Set at liberty; the fat ribs of peace
Must by the hungry now[a] be fed upon:
Use our commission in his utmost force.

Bast. Bell, book, and candle shall not drive me back,
When gold and silver becks me to come on.
I leave your highness.—Grandame, I will pray
(If ever I remember to be holy)
For your fair safety; so I kiss your hand.

Eli. Farewell, gentle cousin.

K. John. Coz, farewell. [*Exit* Bastard.

Eli. Come hither, little kinsman; hark, a word. [*She takes* Arthur *aside.*

K. John. Come hither, Hubert. O my gentle Hubert,
We owe thee much; within this wall of flesh
There is a soul counts thee her creditor,
And with advantage means to pay thy love:
And, my good friend, thy voluntary oath
Lives in this bosom, dearly cherished.
Give me thy hand. I had a thing to say,—
But I will fit it with some better tune.[b]
By heaven, Hubert, I am almost asham'd
To say what good respect I have of thee.

Hub. I am much bounden to your majesty.

K. John. Good friend, thou hast no cause to say so yet:
But thou shalt have: and, creep time ne'er so slow,
Yet it shall come, for me to do thee good.
I had a thing to say,—but let it go:
The sun is in the heaven, and the proud day,
Attended with the pleasures of the world,
Is all too wanton, and too full of gauds,
To give me audience.—If the midnight bell
Did, with his iron tongue and brazen mouth,
Sound one into the drowsy ear of night; (6)
If this same were a churchyard where we stand,
And thou possessed with a thousand wrongs;
Or if that surly spirit, melancholy,
Had bak'd thy blood, and made it heavy-thick,
(Which, else, runs tickling up and down the veins,
Making that idiot, laughter, keep[c] men's eyes,
And strain their cheeks to idle merriment,
A passion hateful to my purposes;)
Or if that thou couldst see me without eyes,
Hear me without thine ears, and make reply
Without a tongue, using conceit alone,
Without eyes, ears, and harmful sound of words;
Then, in despite of brooded[d] watchful day,
I would into thy bosom pour my thoughts:
But ah, I will not:—yet I love thee well;
And, by my troth, I think thou lov'st me well.

Hub. So well, that what you bid me undertake,
Though that my death were adjunct to my act,
By heaven, I would do it!

K. John. Do not I know thou wouldst?
Good Hubert, Hubert, Hubert, throw thine eye
On yon young boy: I'll tell thee what, my friend,
He is a very serpent in my way;
And wheresoe'er this foot of mine doth tread
He lies before me: dost thou understand me?
Thou art his keeper.

Hub. And I'll keep him so,
That he shall not offend your majesty.

K. John. Death.

Hub. My lord!

K. John. A grave.

Hub. He shall not live.

K. John. Enough.
I could be merry now: Hubert, I love thee.
Well, I'll not say what I intend for thee:
Remember.——Madam, fare you well:
I'll send those powers o'er to your majesty.

Eli. My blessing go with thee!

---

[a] *Must by the hungry* now *be fed upon:*] For *now*, Warburton proposed to read *war*; a substitution supported by the corresponding passage in the old play:—

> "Philip, I make thee chiefe in this affaire,
> Ransacke the abbeis, cloysters, priories,
> Convert their coyne unto my *souldiers* use."

[b] *Some better* tune.] So the old copies. Pope altered *tune* to *time*; perhaps without necessity, for these words were often used, of old, as synonymes.

[c] *Making that idiot, laughter,* keep *men's eyes,*—] From a passage in the "Merchant of Venice," Act I. Sc. 1:—

> "Some that will evermore *peep* through their eyes,
> And laugh—."

I, at one time, thought *keep* a misprint of *peep*, that is, *half close*, which agrees, too, with the context:—

> "And *strain their cheeks* to idle merriment."

Keep, however, in the sense of occupy, may be right; for Biron, "Love's Labour 's Lost," Act IV. Sc. 3, says:—

> "Other slow arts entirely *keep* the brain."

[d] *Then, in despite* of brooded *watchful day,*—] Pope reads *broad-eyed*, an unobjectionable emendation, if any change were required, for *broad-eyed* and *narrow-eyed* are expressions repeatedly to be found in the old writers; but *brooded* for *brooding*, in allusion to the vigilance of birds *on brood*, conveys the very sense intended. So, in Massinger's play of "The City Madam," Act III. Sc. 3:—

> "——— I did not slumber,
> And could wake ever with a *brooding* eye
> To gaze upon 't——."

So Milton also, in "L'Allegro:"—

> "——— Find out some uncouth cell,
> Where *brooding* darkness spreads his *jealous* wings."

K. JOHN. For England, cousin, go:
Hubert shall be your man, attend on you
With all true duty.—On toward Calais, ho!
[*Exeunt.*

SCENE IV.—*The same. The* French King's *Tent.*

Enter KING PHILIP, LEWIS, PANDULPH, *and* Attendants.

K. PHI. So, by a roaring tempest on the flood,
A whole armado of convicted[a] sail
Is scatter'd and disjoin'd from fellowship. [well.
PAND. Courage and comfort! all shall yet go
K. PHI. What can go well, when we have run so ill?
Are we not beaten? Is not Angiers lost?
Arthur ta'en prisoner? divers dear friends slain?
And bloody England into England gone,
O'erbearing interruption, spite of France?
LEW. What he hath won, that hath he fortified:
So hot a speed with such advice dispos'd,
Such temperate order in so fierce a course,[b]
Doth want example. Who hath read, or heard,
Of any kindred action like to this? [this praise,
K. PHI. Well could I bear that England had
So we could find some pattern of our shame.
Look, who comes here! a grave unto a soul;
Holding the eternal spirit, against her will,

Enter CONSTANCE.

In the vile prison of afflicted breath:—
I prithee, lady, go away with me. [peace!
CONST. Lo, now! now see the issue of your
K. PHI. Patience, good lady! comfort, gentle Constance!
CONST. No, I defy all counsel, all redress,
But that which ends all counsel, true redress.
Death, death, O amiable lovely death!
Thou odoriferous stench! sound rottenness!
Arise forth from the couch of lasting night,
Thou hate and terror to prosperity,
And I will kiss thy detestable bones,
And put my eyeballs in thy vaulty brows,
And ring these fingers with thy household worms,
And stop this gap of breath with fulsome dust,
And be a carrion monster like thyself.
Come, grin on me; and I will think thou smil'st,
And buss thee as thy wife! Misery's love,
O, come to me!
K. PHI. O fair affliction, peace! [cry:—
CONST. No, no, I will not, having breath to
O, that my tongue were in the thunder's mouth!
Then with a passion would I shake the world,
And rouse from sleep that fell anatomy,
Which cannot hear a lady's feeble voice,
Which scorns a modern[c] invocation.
PAND. Lady, you utter madness, and not sorrow.
CONST. Thou art unholy* to belie me so.
I am not mad: this hair I tear is mine;
My name is Constance, I was Geffrey's wife;
Young Arthur is my son, and he is lost.
I am not mad;—I would to heaven I were!
For then, 'tis like I should forget myself:
O, if I could, what grief should I forget!—
Preach some philosophy to make me mad,
And thou shalt be canoniz'd, cardinal.
For, being not mad, but sensible of grief,
My reasonable part produces reason
How I may be deliver'd of these woes,
And teaches me to kill or hang myself:
If I were mad, I should forget my son,
Or madly think a babe of clouts were he.
I am not mad; too well, too well I feel
The different plague of each calamity. [note
K. PHI. Bind up those tresses: O, what love I
In the fair multitude of those her hairs!
Where but by chance a silver drop hath fall'n,
Even to that drop ten thousand wiry friends †
Do glue themselves in sociable grief;
Like true, inseparable, faithful loves,
Sticking together in calamity.
CONST. To England, if you will![d]
K. PHI. Bind up your hairs.
CONST. Yes, that I will. And wherefore will I do it?
I tore them from their bonds, and cried aloud,
O that these hands could so redeem my son,
As they have given these hairs their liberty!
But now I envy at their liberty,
And will again commit them to their bonds,
Because my poor child is a prisoner.
And, father cardinal, I have heard you say,
That we shall see and know our friends in heaven;
If that be true, I shall see my boy again:
For, since the birth of Cain, the first male child,

(*) The old text has *holy*.
(†) Old text, *fiends*.

[a] *A whole armado of* convicted *sail*—] *Convicted* is the word in the old copies; and, as it may have been used in the sense of *vanquished*, or *overpowered*, we have not displaced it from the text, although every one admits a preference for *convented*, the reading adopted by Mr. Singer, and which is found in the margin of Mr. Collier's folio, 1632. Mr. Dyce suggests that the true word may have been *convected*, from the Latin *convectus*, but gives no example of its use.

[b] *In so fierce* a course,—] The old text has *cause*. Warburton proposed the change, but oddly enough interpreted *course* as a *march!* By *course* is no doubt meant the *carrière* of a horse, or a *charge*, in a passage of arms.

[c] *Which scorns* a modern *invocation.*] A *common*, an *ordinary* invocation. See note ([b]), page 190, of the present volume.

[d] To England, if you will!] It has been conjectured that the unhappy Constance, in her despair, addresses the absent King John:—"*Take my son to England*, if you will." Does she not rather apostrophize her hair, as she madly tears it from its bonds?

To him that did but yesterday suspire,
There was not such a gracious[a] creature born.
But now will canker sorrow eat my bud,
And chase the native beauty from his cheek,
And he will look as hollow as a ghost,
As dim and meagre as an ague's fit,
And so he'll die: and, rising so again,
When I shall meet him in the court of heaven
I shall not know him: therefore never, never
Must I behold my pretty Arthur more.

PAND. You hold too heinous a respect of grief.

CONST. He talks to me that never had a son.

K. PHI. You are as fond of grief as of your child.

CONST. Grief fills the room up of my absent child,
Lies in his bed, walks up and down with me,
Puts on his pretty looks, repeats his words,

[a] *A gracious creature born.*] Malone was correct in surmising that *gracious*, in Shakespeare's time, included the idea of beauty. Florio explains *Gratioso, gracious, favourable, loving, milde, gentle, comely, well-favoured*.

Remembers me of all his gracious parts,
Stuffs out his vacant garments with his form;
Then, have I reason to be fond of grief.
Fare you well: had you such a loss as I,
I could give better comfort[a] than you do.—
I will not keep this form upon my head,
[*Tearing off her head-dress.*
When there is such disorder in my wit.
O Lord! my boy, my Arthur, my fair son!
My life, my joy, my food, my all the world!
My widow-comfort, and my sorrows' cure! [*Exit.*

K. PHI. I fear some outrage, and I'll follow her. [*Exit.*

LEW. There's nothing in this world can make me joy:
Life is as tedious as a twice-told tale,
Vexing the dull ear of a drowsy man;
And bitter shame hath spoil'd the sweet world's[b] taste,
That it yields nought but shame and bitterness.

PAND. Before the curing of a strong disease,
Even in the instant of repair and health,
The fit is strongest; evils, that take leave,
On their departure most of all shew evil:
What have you lost by losing of this day?

LEW. All days of glory, joy, and happiness.

PAND. If you had won it, certainly, you had.
No, no: when fortune means to men most good,
She looks upon them with a threatening eye.
'Tis strange to think how much king John hath lost
In this, which he accounts so clearly won:
Are not you griev'd that Arthur is his prisoner?

LEW. As heartily, as he is glad he hath him.

PAND. Your mind is all as youthful as your blood.
Now hear me speak with a prophetic spirit;
For even the breath of what I mean to speak
Shall blow each dust, each straw, each little rub,
Out of the path which shall directly lead
Thy foot to England's throne. And, therefore, mark:—
John hath seiz'd Arthur, and it cannot be,
That, whiles warm life plays in that infant's veins,
The misplac'd John should entertain an hour,
One minute, nay, one quiet breath of rest.
A sceptre, snatch'd with an unruly hand,
Must be as boisterously maintain'd as gain'd:
And he that stands upon a slippery place
Makes nice of no vile hold to stay him up:
That John may stand then, Arthur needs must fall;
So be it, for it cannot be but so.

LEW. But what shall I gain by young Arthur's fall?

PAND. You, in the right of lady Blanch your wife,
May then make all the claim that Arthur did.

LEW. And lose it, life and all, as Arthur did.

PAND. How green you are, and fresh in this old world!
John lays you plots; the times conspire with you—
For he that steeps his safety in true blood
Shall find but bloody safety, and untrue.—
This act, so evilly borne, shall cool the hearts
Of all his people, and freeze up their zeal,
That none so small advantage shall step forth
To check his reign, but they will cherish it.
No natural exhalation in the sky,
No scope of nature, no distemper'd day,
No common wind, no customed event,
But they will pluck away his natural cause,
And call them meteors, prodigies, and signs,
Abortives, presages, and tongues of heaven,
Plainly denouncing vengeance upon John.

LEW. May be, he will not touch young Arthur's life,
But hold himself safe in his prisonment.

PAND. O, sir, when he shall hear of your approach,
If that young Arthur be not gone already,
Even at that news he dies: and then the hearts
Of all his people shall revolt from him,
And kiss the lips of unacquainted change,
And pick strong matter of revolt and wrath,
Out of the bloody fingers' ends of John.
Methinks, I see this hurly all on foot;
And, O, what better matter breeds for you,
Than I have nam'd!—The bastard Faulconbridge
Is now in England, ransacking the church,
Offending charity. If but a dozen French
Were there in arms, they would be as a call[c]
To train ten thousand English to their side;
Or, as a little snow, tumbled about,
Anon becomes a mountain. O noble Dauphin,
Go with me to the king; 't is wonderful
What may be wrought out of their discontent,
Now that their souls are topfull of offence.
For England go; I will whet on the king.

LEW. Strong reasons make strange actions. Let us go;
If you say ay, the king will not say no.
[*Exeunt.*

---

[a] I could give better comfort—] "This is a sentiment which great sorrow always dictates. Whoever cannot help himself casts his eyes on others for assistance, and often mistakes their inability for coldness."—JOHNSON.

[b] *The sweet* world's *taste*,—] For *world's* the old copies have *words*. The correction is Pope's.

[c] *They would be as* a call—] An allusion to the reed, or pipe, termed a *bird-call*; or to the practice of bird-catchers, who, in laying their nets, place a caged bird over them, which they term the *call*-bird or bird-*call*, to lure the wild birds to the snare. Thus, in Beaumont and Fletcher's play of "The Bloody Brother," Act IV. Sc. 2, Pippeau, the scout or decoy of the Astrologers, tells them:—

> "———— but it is I
> That bring you in your rents for 'em, 'tis Pippeau
> That is your *bird-call*."

ACT IV.

SCENE I.—*A Room in a Castle.*

Enter Hubert *and Two* Attendants.

Hub. Heat me these irons hot, and look thou stand
Within the arras: when I strike my foot
Upon the bosom of the ground, rush forth,
And bind the boy, which you shall find with me,
Fast to the chair: be heedful: hence, and watch.

1 Attend. I hope your warrant will bear out the deed.

Hub. Uncleanly scruples! Fear not you: look to 't.— [*Exeunt* Attendants.
Young lad, come forth; I have to say with you.

Enter Arthur.

Arth. Good morrow, Hubert.

Hub. Good morrow, little prince.

Arth. As little prince (having so great a title
To be more[a] prince) as may be.—You are sad.

Hub. Indeed, I have been merrier.

Arth. Mercy on me!
Methinks, nobody should be sad but I:
Yet, I remember, when I was in France,
Young gentlemen would be as sad as night,
Only for wantonness. By my christendom,
So I were out of prison, and kept sheep,
I should be as merry as the day is long;
And so I would be here, but that I doubt
My uncle practises more harm to me:

[a] *To be more prince*—] That is, *greater* prince. See note (a), page 291.

He is afraid of me, and I of him:
Is it my fault that I was Geffrey's son?
No, indeed is 't not; and I would to heaven
I were your son, so you would love me, Hubert.

HUB. If I talk to him, with his innocent prate
He will awake my mercy, which lies dead:
Therefore I will be sudden, and despatch. [*Aside.*

ARTH. Are you sick, Hubert? you look pale to-day:
In sooth, I would you were a little sick,
That I might sit all night, and watch with you:
I warrant I love you more than you do me.

HUB. His words do take possession of my bosom.—
Read here, young Arthur. [*Showing a paper.*
How now, foolish rheum! [*Aside.*
Turning dispiteous torture out of door?
I must be brief, lest resolution drop
Out at mine eyes, in tender womanish tears.
Can you not read it? is it not fair writ?

ARTH. Too fairly, Hubert, for so foul effect:
Must you with hot irons burn out both mine eyes?

HUB. Young boy, I must.

ARTH. And will you?

HUB. And I will.

ARTH. Have you the heart? When your head did but ache,
I knit my handkerchief about your brows,
(The best I had, a princess wrought it me,)
And I did never ask it you again.
And with my hand, at midnight held your head;
And, like the watchful minutes to the hour,
Still and anon cheer'd up the heavy time,
Saying, *What lack you?* and, *Where lies your grief?*
Or, *What good love may I perform for you?*
Many a poor man's son would have lain still,
And ne'er have spoke a loving word to you;
But you at your sick service had a prince.
Nay, you may think my love was crafty love,
And call it cunning; do, an if you will:
If heaven be pleas'd that you must use me ill,
Why, then you must.—Will you put out mine eyes?
These eyes, that never did, nor never shall,
So much as frown on you?

HUB. I have sworn to do it;
And with hot irons must I burn them out.

ARTH. Ah, none, but in this iron age, would do it!
The iron of itself, though heat red-hot,
Approaching near these eyes, would drink my tears,
And quench his* fiery indignation,
Even in the matter of mine innocence:
Nay, after that, consume away in rust,
But for containing fire to harm mine eye.

(*) Old copies, *this.*

Are you more stubborn-hard than hammer'd iron?
An if an angel should have come to me,
And told me, Hubert should put out mine eyes,
I would not have believ'd him: no tongue but Hubert's—

HUB. Come forth! [*Stamps.*

Re-enter Attendants, *with Cords, Irons, &c.*

Do as I bid you do.

ARTH. O, save me, Hubert, save me! my eyes are out,
Even with the fierce looks of these bloody men.

HUB. Give me the iron, I say, and bind him here.

ARTH. Alas, what need you be so boist'rous-rough?
I will not struggle, I will stand stone-still.
For heaven sake, Hubert, let me not be bound!
Nay, hear me, Hubert! drive these men away,
And I will sit as quiet as a lamb;
I will not stir, nor wince, nor speak a word,
Nor look upon the iron angerly:
Thrust but these men away, and I'll forgive you,
Whatever torment you do put me to.

HUB. Go, stand within; let me alone with him.

1 ATTEND. I am best pleas'd to be from such a deed. [*Exeunt* Attendants.

ARTH. Alas! I then have chid away my friend;
He hath a stern look, but a gentle heart:—
Let him come back, that his compassion may
Give life to yours.

HUB. Come, boy, prepare yourself.

ARTH. Is there no remedy?

HUB. None, but to lose your eyes.

ARTH. O heaven!—that there were but a mote in yours,
A grain, a dust, a gnat, a wandering hair,
Any annoyance in that precious sense!
Then, feeling what small things are boist'rous there,
Your vile intent must needs seem horrible.

HUB. Is this your promise? go to, hold your tongue.

ARTH. Hubert, the utterance of a brace of tongues
Must needs want pleading for a pair of eyes:
Let me not hold my tongue; let me not, Hubert!
Or, Hubert, if you will, cut out my tongue,
So I may keep mine eyes. O, spare mine eyes;
Though to no use, but still to look on you!
Lo, by my troth, the instrument is cold,
And would not harm me.

HUB. I can heat it, boy.

ARTH. No, in good sooth; the fire is dead with grief,
Being create for comfort, to be us'd

In undeserv'd extremes: see else yourself;
There is no malice in this burning coal;
The breath of heaven hath blown his spirit out,
And strew'd repentant ashes on his head.

HUB. But with my breath I can revive it, boy.

ARTH. An if you do, you will but make it blush
And glow with shame of your proceedings, Hubert:
Nay, it, perchance, will sparkle in your eyes,
And, like a dog that is compell'd to fight,
Snatch at his master that doth tarre[a] him on.
All things that you should use to do me wrong,
Deny their office: only you do lack
That mercy which fierce fire and iron extends,
Creatures of note for mercy-lacking uses.

HUB. Well, see to live. I will not touch thine eyes
For all the treasure that thine uncle owes:
Yet am I sworn, and I did purpose, boy,
With this same very iron to burn them out.

ARTH. O, now you look like Hubert! all this while
You were disguised.

HUB. Peace, no more: Adieu.
Your uncle must not know but you are dead:
I'll fill these dogged spies with false reports;
And, pretty child, sleep doubtless, and secure,
That Hubert, for the wealth of all the world,
Will not offend thee.

ARTH. O heaven!—I thank you, Hubert.

HUB. Silence! no more. Go closely in with me;[b]
Much danger do I undergo for thee.(1) [*Exeunt.*

SCENE II.—*A Room of State in the Palace.*

Enter KING JOHN, *crowned;* PEMBROKE, SALISBURY, *and other* Lords. *The* KING *takes his State.*

K. JOHN. Here once again we sit, once again* crown'd,
And look'd upon, I hope, with cheerful eyes.

PEM. This once again, but that your highness pleas'd,
Was once superfluous; you were crown'd before,
And that high royalty was ne'er pluck'd off,
The faiths of men ne'er stained with revolt,
Fresh expectation troubled not the land,
With any long'd-for change, or better state.

SAL. Therefore, to be possess'd with double pomp,
To guard[c] a title that was rich before,
To gild refined gold, to paint the lily,
To throw a perfume on the violet,
To smooth the ice, or add another hue
Unto the rainbow, or with taper-light
To seek the beauteous eye of heaven to garnish,
Is wasteful, and ridiculous excess.

PEM. But that your royal pleasure must be done,
This act is as an ancient tale new told,
And, in the last repeating, troublesome,
Being urged at a time unseasonable.

SAL. In this, the antique and well-noted face
Of plain old form is much disfigured;
And, like a shifted wind unto a sail,
It makes the course of thoughts to fetch about,
Startles and frights consideration;
Makes sound opinion sick, and truth suspected,
For putting on so new a fashion'd robe.

PEM. When workmen strive to do better than well,[d]
They do confound their skill in covetousness;
And oftentimes excusing of a fault
Doth make the fault the worse by the excuse;
As patches, set upon a little breach,
Discredit more in hiding of the fault,
Than did the fault before it was so patch'd.

SAL. To this effect, before you were new crown'd,
We breath'd our counsel; but it pleas'd your highness
To overbear it, and we are all well pleas'd,
Since all and every part of what we would,
Doth make a stand at what your highness will.

K. JOHN. Some reasons of this double coronation
I have possess'd you with, and think them strong;
And more, more strong, when[e] lesser is my fear,
I shall indue you with: meantime, but ask
What you would have reform'd that is not well,
And well shall you perceive how willingly
I will both hear and grant you your requests.

PEM. Then I, as one that am the tongue of these,
To sound the purposes of all their hearts,
Both for myself and them, (but, chief of all,
Your safety, for the which myself and them
Bend their best studies,) heartily request
The enfranchisement of Arthur; whose restraint
Doth move the murmuring lips of discontent
To break into this dangerous argument,—

(*) Old copies, *against*.

[a] Tarre *him on.*] *Tarre*, Horne Tooke derives from Tyrian, A. S. *exacerbare, irritare.* It was more probably coined from the sound, *arre*, usually made to incite a dog to attack anything. We meet with it again in "Hamlet," Act II. Sc. 2:—"And the nation holds it no sin to *tarre* them on to controversy;" and in "Troilus and Cressida," Act I. Sc. 3:—

"——— Pride alone
Must *tarre* the mastiffs on,——"

[b] *Go* closely *in with me;*] That is, *secretly, privately.* So in "Hamlet," Act III. Sc. 1:—

"For we have *closely* sent for Hamlet hither."

[c] *To* guard *a title*—] To *guard* meant *to ornament with a border.*

[d] *When workmen strive to* do better *than well,*—] This is painfully dissonant, perhaps we should read,—

"——— to *better do* than well."

[e] When *lesser is my fear,*—] The original has, "*Then* lesser," &c. Tyrwhitt made the alteration.

If what in rest[a] you have, in right you hold,
Why, then, your fears, which (as they say) attend
The steps of wrong, should move you to mew up
Your tender kinsman, and to choke his days

[a] *If what* in rest *you have, in right you hold,*
Why, then, your fears, which (as they say) attend
The steps of wrong, should move you to mew up
Your tender kinsman, &c.]

Steevens proposed to read, " If what in *wrest*," &c.; i.e., *if what you possess by an act of seizure or violence*, &c.; but even then, to restore the generally-understood sense of the passage, Henley's suggestion to make *then* and *should* change places, and insert a note of interrogation after *exercise*, would be necessary. After all, is the ordinary interpretation the true one? The alteration of a single word gives a meaning which squares better with the reasoning of the speaker, and does away with the necessity of transposing the words, or even altering the punctuation of the old text. Suppose we were to read,—

" If what in rest you have, *not* right you hold,
Why, then, your fears," &c.—

and the sense of the "dangerous argument" is at once clear and consistent. This reading is forcibly corroborated, too, by the parallel passage in the older play:—

" We crave my lord Essex, to please the commons with
The libertie of lady Constance soone:
Whose durance darkeneth your highnesse right,
As if you kept him prisoner, to the end
Your selfe were doubtfull of the thing you have."

With barbarous ignorance, and deny his youth
The rich advantage of good exercise.
That the time's enemies may not have this
To grace occasions, let it be our suit,
That you have bid us ask his liberty;
Which for our goods, we do no further ask,
Than whereupon our weal, on you depending,
Counts it your weal he have his liberty.

K. JOHN. Let it be so; I do commit his youth
To your direction:—

Enter HUBERT.

Hubert, what news with you? [*Taking him apart.*

PEM. This is the man should do the bloody deed;
He shew'd his warrant to a friend of mine:
The image of a wicked heinous fault
Lives in his eye; that close aspèct of his
Doth shew the mood of a much-troubled breast,
And I do fearfully believe 't is done,
What we so fear'd he had a charge to do.

SAL. The colour of the king doth come and go
Between his purpose and his conscience,
Like heralds 'twixt two dreadful battles set:
His passion is so ripe, it needs must break.

PEM. And, when it breaks, I fear will issue thence
The foul corruption of a sweet child's death.

K. JOHN. We cannot hold mortality's strong hand:— [*Coming forward.*
Good lords, although my will to give is living,
The suit which you demand is gone and dead:
He tells us, Arthur is deceas'd to-night.

SAL. Indeed we fear'd his sickness was past cure.

PEM. Indeed we heard how near his death he was,
Before the child himself felt he was sick:
This must be answer'd, either here, or hence.

K. JOHN. Why do you bend such solemn brows on me?
Think you I bear the shears of destiny?
Have I commandment on the pulse of life?

SAL. It is apparent[a] foul play; and 't is shame
That greatness should so grossly offer it:—
So thrive it in your game! and so farewell.

PEM. Stay yet, lord Salisbury: I'll go with thee,
And find the inheritance of this poor child,
His little kingdom of a forced grave.
That blood, which ow'd the breadth of all this isle,
Three foot of it doth hold. Bad world the while!
This must not be thus borne; this will break out
To all our sorrows, and ere long, I doubt.
[*Exeunt* Lords.

K. JOHN. They burn in indignation. I repent.
There is no sure foundation set on blood;
No certain life achiev'd by others' death.—

Enter a Messenger.

A fearful eye thou hast. Where is that blood,
That I have seen inhabit in those cheeks?
So foul a sky clears not without a storm:
Pour down thy weather.—How goes all in France?

MESS. From France to England.[b]—Never such a power,
For any foreign preparation,
Was levied in the body of a land!
The copy of your speed is learn'd by them;
For, when you should be told they do prepare,
The tidings come that they are all arriv'd.

K. JOHN. O, where hath our intelligence been drunk?
Where hath it slept? Where is my mother's care,[c]
That such an army could be drawn in France,
And she not hear of it?

MESS. My liege, her ear
Is stopp'd with dust; the first of April, died
Your noble mother. And, as I hear, my lord,
The lady Constance in a frenzy died
Three days before: but this from rumour's tongue
I idly heard; if true, or false, I know not.

K. JOHN. Withhold thy speed, dreadful occasion!
O, make a league with me, till I have pleas'd
My discontented peers!—What! mother dead!
How wildly then walks my estate in France.—
Under whose conduct came those powers of France,
That thou for truth giv'st out are landed here?

MESS. Under the dauphin.

Enter the Bastard *and* PETER *of* Pomfret.

K. JOHN. Thou hast made me giddy
With these ill tidings.—Now, what says the world
To your proceedings? do not seek to stuff
My head with more ill news, for it is full.

BAST. But, if you be afeard to hear the worst,
Then let the worst, unheard, fall on your head.

K. JOHN. Bear with me, cousin; for I was amaz'd
Under the tide; but now I breathe again
Aloft the flood, and can give audience
To any tongue, speak it of what it will.

BAST. How I have sped among the clergymen,
The sums I have collected shall express.
But, as I travell'd hither through the land,
I find the people strangely fantasied,
Possess'd with rumours, full of idle dreams;
Not knowing what they fear, but full of fear:
And here 's a prophet,(2) that I brought with me
From forth the streets of Pomfret, whom I found
With many hundreds treading on his heels;
To whom he sung, in rude harsh-sounding rhymes,
That, ere the next Ascension-day at noon,

---

[a] *It is* apparent *foul play;*] It is *obvious, evident* foul play.

[b] From France to England.—] All in France *goes* now *to* England.

[c] *My mother's* care,—] *Care* may be suspected, from the context, a misprint for *ears*.

Your highness should deliver up your crown.

K. JOHN. Thou idle dreamer, wherefore didst thou so?

PETER. Foreknowing that the truth will fall out so.

K. JOHN. Hubert, away with him; imprison him;
And on that day at noon, whereon, he says,
I shall yield up my crown, let him be hang'd:
Deliver him to safety, and return,
For I must use thee.—

[*Exit* HUBERT, *with* PETER.

O my gentle cousin,
Hear'st thou the news abroad, who are arriv'd?

BAST. The French, my lord; men's mouths are full of it:
Besides, I met lord Bigot, and lord Salisbury,
(With eyes as red as new-enkindled fire,)
And others more, going to seek the grave
Of Arthur, who, they say, is kill'd to-night
On your suggestion.

K. JOHN. Gentle kinsman, go,
And thrust thyself into their companies;
I have a way to win their loves again:
Bring them before me.

BAST. I will seek them out.

K. JOHN. Nay, but make haste, the better foot before.
O, let me have no subject-enemies,
When adverse foreigners affright my towns
With dreadful pomp of stout[a] invasion!
Be Mercury, set feathers to thy heels,
And fly, like thought, from them to me again.

BAST. The spirit of the time shall teach me speed. [*Exit.*

K. JOHN. Spoke like a spriteful noble gentleman.—
Go after him; for he, perhaps, shall need
Some messenger betwixt me and the peers,
And be thou he.

MESS. With all my heart, my liege. [*Exit.*

K. JOHN. My mother dead!

Re-enter HUBERT.

HUB. My lord, they say five moons were seen to-night:
Four fixed, and the fifth did whirl about
The other four, in wondrous motion.

K. JOHN. Five moons?

HUB. Old men, and beldams, in the streets
Do prophesy upon it dangerously:
Young Arthur's death is common in their mouths,
And when they talk of him, they shake their heads,

[a] Stout *invasion!*] That is, *bold, proud,* invasion.

And whisper one another in the ear;
And he that speaks doth gripe the hearer's wrist,
Whilst he that hears makes fearful action,
With wrinkled brows, with nods, with rolling eyes.
I saw a smith stand with his hammer, thus,
The whilst his iron did on the anvil cool,
With open mouth swallowing a tailor's news;
Who, with his shears and measure in his hand,
Standing on slippers, (which his nimble haste
Had falsely thrust upon contrary feet,)
Told of a many thousand warlike French,
That were embattailed and rank'd in Kent:
Another lean unwash'd artificer
Cuts off his tale, and talks of Arthur's death.

K. JOHN. Why seek'st thou to possess me with these fears?
Why urgest thou so oft young Arthur's death?
Thy hand hath murder'd him: I had a mighty cause
To wish him dead, but thou hadst none to kill him.

HUB. No had,[a] my lord! why, did you not provoke me?

K. JOHN. It is the curse of kings to be attended,
By slaves that take their humours for a warrant
To break within the bloody house of life;
And, on the winking of authority,
To understand a law; to know the meaning
Of dangerous majesty, when, perchance, it frowns
More upon humour than advis'd respect.

HUB. Here is your hand and seal for what I did.

K. JOHN. O, when the last account 'twixt heaven and earth
Is to be made, then shall this hand and seal
Witness against us to damnation!
How oft the sight of means to do ill deeds

---

[a] No had, *my lord!*] From ignorance of this archaism most editors alter it to "None had," or "Had none." *No had, no did, no will*, &c., were ordinary forms of expression with the old English writers:—"'Nay, veryly sir,' quoth I, 'my Lord hath yit no word,'" &c. "'*No had*,' quoth he, 'I mych mervaile therof,'" &c.—*Letter of Sir Thomas More to Wolsey.* (Ellis's "Original Letters," &c., vol. i. p. 253.)

"Chedsey. Christ said, 'Take, eat, this is my body;' and not, 'Take ye, eat ye.'

Philpot. *No did*, master doctor? &c."—FOXE'S *Acts and Monuments*, vol. vii. p. 637, (Cattley's edition.)

"Philpot. And as I remember it is even the saying of St. Bernard, * * * * as my Lord of Durham and my Lord of Chichester by their learning can discern, and will not reckon it evil said.

London. *No will?*"—*Ibid.* p. 658.

For further examples of this idiom see "Notes and Queries," vol. vii. p. 520.

Makes ill deeds done![a] Hadst thou not been by,
A fellow by the hand of nature mark'd,
Quoted, and sign'd, to do a deed of shame,
This murder had not come into my mind:
But, taking note of thy abhorr'd aspect,
Finding thee fit for bloody villainy,
Apt, liable, to be employ'd in danger,
I faintly broke with thee of Arthur's death;
And thou, to be endeared to a king,
Made it no conscience to destroy a prince.
HUB. My lord,—
K. JOHN. Hadst thou but shook thy head, or made a pause,
When I spake darkly what I purposed,
Or turn'd an eye of doubt upon my face,
As bid me tell my tale in express words,
Deep shame had struck me dumb, made me break off,
And those thy fears might have wrought fears in me:
But thou didst understand me by my signs,
And didst in signs again parley with sin;[b]
Yea, without stop, didst let thy heart consent,
And, consequently, thy rude hand to act
The deed, which both our tongues held vile to name.
Out of my sight, and never see me more!
My nobles leave me, and my state is brav'd,
Even at my gates, with ranks of foreign powers;
Nay, in the body of this fleshly land,
This kingdom, this confine of blood and breath,
Hostility and civil tumult reigns
Between my conscience and my cousin's death.
HUB. Arm you against your other enemies,
I'll make a peace between your soul and you;
Young Arthur is alive. This hand of mine
Is yet a maiden and an innocent hand,
Not painted with the crimson spots of blood.
Within this bosom never enter'd yet
The dreadful motion of a murderous thought;
And you have slander'd nature in my form,
Which, howsoever rude exteriorly,

---

a Makes ill deeds *done!*] The original has, *Make deeds ill* done.
b And didst in signs again parley with sin;] Mr. Collier's MS. annotator very plausibly suggests the reading of *sign* for *sin* in this line.

Is yet the cover of a fairer mind
Than to be butcher of an innocent child. [peers,
K. JOHN. Doth Arthur live? O, haste thee to the
Throw this report on their incensed rage,
And make them tame to their obedience!
Forgive the comment that my passion made
Upon thy feature; for my rage was blind,
And foul imaginary eyes of blood
Presented thee more hideous than thou art.
O, answer not; but to my closet bring
The angry lords, with all expedient haste;
I conjure thee but slowly, run more fast.
[*Exeunt.*

SCENE III.—*Before the Castle.*

Enter ARTHUR *on the Walls.*

ARTH. The wall is high, and yet will I leap down.—
Good ground, be pitiful, and hurt me not!—
There 's few, or none, do know me; if they did,
This ship-boy's semblance hath disguis'd me quite.
I am afraid; and yet I'll venture it.
If I get down, and do not break my limbs,
I'll find a thousand shifts to get away:
As good to die and go, as die and stay.
[*Leaps down.*
O me! my uncle's spirit is in these stones:—
Heaven take my soul, and England keep my bones! [*Dies.*(3)

Enter PEMBROKE, SALISBURY, *and* BIGOT.

SAL. Lords, I will meet him at St. Edmund's-Bury;
It is our safety, and we must embrace
This gentle offer of the perilous time.
PEM. Who brought that letter from the cardinal?
SAL. The count Melun, a noble lord of France,

Whose private[a] with me, of the dauphin's love,
Is much more general than these lines import.

BIG. To-morrow morning let us meet him then.

SAL. Or rather, then set forward: for 't will be
Two long days' journey, lords, or e'er we meet.

Enter the Bastard.

BAST. Once more to-day well met, distemper'd lords!
The king, by me, requests your presence straight.

SAL. The king hath dispossess'd himself of us.
We will not line his thin, bestained cloak
With our pure honours, nor attend the foot
That leaves the print of blood where'er it walks:
Return, and tell him so; we know the worst.

BAST. Whate'er you think, good words, I think, were best.

SAL. Our griefs, and not our manners, reason now.

BAST. But there is little reason in your grief;
Therefore, 't were reason you had manners now.

PEM. Sir, sir, impatience hath his privilege.

BAST. 'T is true; to hurt his master, no man* else.

SAL. This is the prison. What is he lies here? [*Seeing* ARTHUR.

PEM. O death, made proud with pure and princely beauty!
The earth had not a hole to hide this deed.

SAL. Murder, as hating what himself hath done,
Doth lay it open, to urge on revenge.

BIG. Or, when he doom'd this beauty to a grave,
Found it too precious-princely for a grave.

SAL. Sir Richard, what think you? Have you beheld,[b]
Or have you read, or heard? or could you think?
Or do you almost think, although you see,
That you do see? could thought, without this object,
Form such another? This is the very top,
The height, the crest, or crest unto the crest,
Of murder's arms: this is the bloodiest shame,
The wildest savagery, the vilest stroke,
That ever wall-ey'd wrath, or staring rage,
Presented to the tears of soft remorse.

PEM. All murders past do stand excus'd in this:
And this so sole, and so unmatchable,
Shall give a holiness, a purity,
To the yet-unbegotten sin of times;
And prove a deadly bloodshed but a jest,
Exampled by this heinous spectacle.

BAST. It is a damned and a bloody work;
The graceless action of a heavy hand,
If that it be the work of any hand.

SAL. If that it be the work of any hand?—
We had a kind of light what would ensue.
It is the shameful work of Hubert's hand;
The practice, and the purpose, of the king:—
From whose obedience I forbid my soul,
Kneeling before this ruin of sweet life,
And breathing to his breathless excellence
The incense of a vow, a holy vow,
Never to taste the pleasures of the world,
Never to be infected with delight,
Nor conversant with ease and idleness,
Till I have set a glory to this hand,[c]
By giving it the worship of revenge.

PEM., BIG. Our souls religiously confirm thy words.

Enter HUBERT.

HUB. Lords, I am hot with haste in seeking you:
Arthur doth live; the king hath sent for you.

SAL. O, he is bold, and blushes not at death:—
Avaunt, thou hateful villain, get thee gone!

HUB. I am no villain.

SAL. Must I rob the law? [*Drawing his sword.*

BAST. Your sword is bright, sir; put it up again.

SAL. Not till I sheathe it in a murderer's skin.

HUB. Stand back, lord Salisbury, stand back, I say;
By heaven, I think, my sword's as sharp as yours:
I would not have you, lord, forget yourself,
Nor tempt the danger of my true defence;
Lest I, by marking of your rage, forget
Your worth, your greatness, and nobility.

BIG. Out, dunghill! dar'st thou brave a nobleman?

HUB. Not for my life: but yet I dare defend
My innocent life against an emperor.

(*) First folio, *mans*.

a *Whose private with me*,—] Whose *confidential parley*. Mr. Collier's MS. annotator reads, "Whose private *missive*," &c.; and a little lower, for—

"——— thin, bestained cloak—"

has—

"——— *sin* bestained cloak."

b Have you *beheld*,—] This is the corrected lection in the third folio, 1664. In the two previous editions the passage stands—"*You have* beheld."

c *A glory to this* hand,—] Pope reads *head* for hand, which, perhaps, gives a more elegant sense; but Malone quotes a passage from "Troilus and Cressida," Act IV. Sc. 1. confirmatory of the old reading:—

"——— Jove, let Æneas live,
If *to my sword* his fate be not the *glory*,
A thousand complete courses of the sun!"

SAL. Thou art a murderer.
HUB. Do not prove me so;
Yet, I am none.[a] Whose tongue soe'er speaks false,
Not truly speaks; who speaks not truly, lies.
PEM. Cut him to pieces.
BAST. Keep the peace, I say.
SAL. Stand by, or I shall gall you, Faulconbridge.
BAST. Thou wert better gall the devil, Salisbury:
If thou but frown on me, or stir thy foot,
Or teach thy hasty spleen to do me shame,
I'll strike thee dead. Put up thy sword betime,
Or I'll so maul you and your toasting-iron,
That you shall think the devil is come from hell.
BIG. What wilt thou do, renowned Faulconbridge?
Second a villain and a murderer?
HUB. Lord Bigot, I am none.
BIG. Who kill'd this prince?
HUB. 'Tis not an hour since I left him well:
I honour'd him, I lov'd him; and will weep
My date of life out, for his sweet life's loss.
SAL. Trust not those cunning waters of his eyes,
For villainy is not without such rheum;
And he, long traded in it, makes it seem
Like rivers of remorse[b] and innocency.
Away, with me, all you whose souls abhor
The uncleanly savours of a slaughter-house;
For I am stifled with this smell of sin.
BIG. Away, toward Bury, to the Dauphin there!
PEM. There, tell the king, he may inquire us out. [*Exeunt* Lords.
BAST. Here's a good world!—Knew you of this fair work?
Beyond the infinite and boundless reach of mercy,
If thou didst this deed of death, art thou damn'd, Hubert.
HUB. Do but hear me, sir,—
BAST. Ha! I'll tell thee what;
Thou 'rt damn'd as black—nay, nothing is so black;
Thou art more deep damn'd than prince Lucifer:
There is not yet so ugly a fiend of hell
As thou shalt be, if thou didst kill this child.
HUB. Upon my soul,—
BAST. If thou didst but consent
To this most cruel act, do but despair,
And, if thou want'st a cord, the smallest thread
That ever spider twisted from her womb
Will serve to strangle thee; a rush will be a beam
To hang thee on; or, wouldst thou drown thyself,
Put but a little water in a spoon,
And it shall be, as all the ocean,
Enough to stifle such a villain up.—
I do suspect thee very grievously.
HUB. If I in act, consent, or sin of thought,
Be guilty of the stealing that sweet breath
Which was embounded in this beauteous clay,
Let hell want pains enough to torture me!
I left him well.
BAST. Go, bear him in thine arms.—
I am amaz'd, methinks, and lose my way
Among the thorns and dangers of this world.—
How easy dost thou take all England up!
From forth this morsel of dead royalty,
The life, the right, and truth of all this realm
Is fled to heaven; and England now is left
To tug and scamble,[c] and to part by the teeth
The unow'd interest of proud-swelling state.
Now, for the bare-pick'd bone of majesty
Doth dogged war bristle his angry crest,
And snarleth in the gentle eyes of peace:
Now powers from home, and discontents at home,
Meet in one line; and vast confusion waits,
As doth a raven on a sick-fallen beast,
The imminent decay of wrested pomp.
Now happy he, whose cloak and cincture[d] can
Hold out this tempest. Bear away that child,
And follow me with speed; I'll to the king:
A thousand businesses are brief in hand,
And heaven itself doth frown upon the land.
[*Exeunt.*

---

[a] Do not prove me so;
Yet, I am none.]
Do not compel me to become one. *Now, at present,* I am no murderer.

[b] *Like rivers of* remorse—] *Remorse,* in Shakespeare and his contemporaries, almost invariably signifies *pity.* See Note (e), p. 31, of the present volume.

[c] *To tug and* scamble,—] *To scamble* is *to seize, to scramble,*—

"*Fortune.* Right now thou madste confessyon of thy boldnesse, what sodaine bashfulnes possessed thee, that thou fearedst to snatch out of my hands, as wel as others?

"*Author.* Truelye Madame I was never instructed in the scoole of *scambling* and now I am too old to learne."
FULWEL's *Art of Flattery,* 1576.

[d] *Whose cloak and* cincture—] The old text has *center.* The emendation *cincture,* a belt or girdle, is Pope's.

ACT V.

SCENE I.—*A Room in the Palace.*

Enter King John, Pandulph *with the Crown, and* Attendants.

K. John. Thus have I yielded up into your hand
The circle of my glory.

Pand. Take again
From this my hand, as holding of the pope,
Your sovereign greatness and authority.
[*Giving* John *the crown.*

K. John. Now keep your holy word: go meet the French;

And from his holiness use all your power
To stop their marches, 'fore we are inflam'd.
Our discontented counties [a] do revolt,
Our people quarrel with obedience,
Swearing allegiance, and the love of soul,
To stranger blood, to foreign royalty.
This inundation of mistemper'd humour
Rests by you only to be qualified.
Then pause not; for the present time's so sick,
That present medicine must be minister'd,
Or overthrow incurable ensues.

PAND. It was my breath that blew this tempest up,
Upon your stubborn usage of the pope;
But, since you are a gentle convertite,
My tongue shall hush again this storm of war,
And make fair weather in your blustering land.
On this Ascension-day, remember well,
Upon your oath of service to the pope,
Go I to make the French lay down their arms. [*Exit.*

K. JOHN. Is this Ascension-day? Did not the prophet
Say, that before Ascension-day at noon,
My crown I should give off? Even so I have:
I did suppose it should be on constraint,
But, heaven be thank'd, it is but voluntary.

Enter the Bastard.

BAST. All Kent hath yielded; nothing there holds out
But Dover castle: London hath receiv'd,
Like a kind host, the Dauphin and his powers:
Your nobles will not hear you, but are gone
To offer service to your enemy;
And wild amazement hurries [b] up and down
The little number of your doubtful friends.

K. JOHN. Would not my lords return to me again,
After they heard young Arthur was alive?

BAST. They found him dead, and cast into the streets;
An empty casket, where the jewel of life
By some damn'd hand was robb'd and ta'en away.

K. JOHN. That villain Hubert told me he did live.

BAST. So, on my soul, he did, for aught he knew.
But wherefore do you droop? why look you sad?
Be great in act, as you have been in thought;
Let not the world see fear and sad distrust,
Govern the motion of a kingly eye.
Be stirring as the time; be fire with fire;
Threaten the threat'ner, and outface the brow
Of bragging horror: so shall inferior eyes,
That borrow their behaviours from the great,
Grow great by your example, and put on
The dauntless spirit of resolution.
Away; and glister like the god of war,
When he intendeth to become the field:
Shew boldness and aspiring confidence.
What, shall they seek the lion in his den,
And fright him there? and make him tremble there?
O, let it not be said!—Forage, and run [c]
To meet displeasure farther from the doors;
And grapple with him, ere he come so nigh.

K. JOHN. The legate of the pope hath been with me,
And I have made a happy peace with him;
And he hath promis'd to dismiss the powers
Led by the Dauphin.

BAST. O inglorious league!
Shall we upon the footing of our land,
Send fair-play orders, and make compromise,
Insinuation, parley, and base truce,
To arms invasive? shall a beardless boy,
A cocker'd silken wanton, brave our fields,
And flesh his spirit in a warlike soil,
Mocking the air with colours idly spread,
And find no check? Let us, my liege, to arms:
Perchance, the cardinal cannot make your peace,
Or if he do, let it at least be said,
They saw we had a purpose of defence.

K. JOHN. Have thou the ordering of this present time.

BAST. Away then, with good courage; yet I know,
Our party may well meet a prouder foe. [*Exeunt.*

SCENE II.—*A Plain, near* St. Edmund's-Bury.

Enter in arms, LEWIS, SALISBURY, MELUN, PEMBROKE, BIGOT, *and* Soldiers.

LEW. My lord Melun, let this be copied out,
And keep it safe for our remembrance:
Return the precedent [d] to these lords again,
That, having our fair order written down,
Both they, and we, perusing o'er these notes,
May know wherefore we took the sacrament,
And keep our faiths firm and inviolable.

SAL. Upon our sides it never shall be broken.

---

[a] *Our discontented* counties *do revolt,—*] *Counties* here mean *nobility,* the *peers,* &c.

[b] Hurries *up and down—*] Perhaps a misprint for *harries. To harry* is *to hunt, to harass.*

[c] Forage, *and run—*] The original sense of *to forage,* Johnson says is, *to range abroad.* If so, the meaning may be, "*To the field!*" &c.; but I suspect the word has no business here. Mr. Collier's annotator reads, "*Courage;* and run—."

[d] *The* precedent—] The original draft of the treaty between Lewis and the English barons.

And, noble Dauphin, albeit we swear
A voluntary zeal, and an unurg'd faith,
To your proceedings; yet, believe me, prince,
I am not glad that such a sore of time
Should seek a plaster by contemn'd revolt,
And heal the inveterate canker of one wound
By making many. O, it grieves my soul,
That I must draw this metal from my side
To be a widow-maker; O, and there,
Where honourable rescue, and defence,
Cries out upon the name of Salisbury:
But such is the infection of the time,
That, for the health and physic of our right,
We cannot deal but with the very hand
Of stern injustice and confused wrong.—
And is 't not pity, O my grieved friends,
That we, the sons and children of this isle,
Were born to see so sad an hour as this;
Wherein we step after a stranger, march
Upon her gentle bosom, and fill up
Her enemies' ranks, (I must withdraw and weep
Upon the spot[a] of this enforced cause,)
To grace the gentry of a land remote,
And follow unacquainted colours here?
What, here?—O nation, that thou couldst remove!
That Neptune's arms, who clippeth thee about,
Would bear thee from the knowledge of thyself,
And grapple* thee unto a pagan shore;
Where these two Christian armies might combine
The blood of malice in a vein of league,
And not to-spend it so unneighbourly!

LEW. A noble temper dost thou shew in this;
And great affections, wrestling in thy bosom,
Do make an earthquake of nobility.
O, what a noble combat hast thou[b] fought
Between compulsion and a brave respect!
Let me wipe off this honourable dew,
That silverly doth progress on thy cheeks:
My heart hath melted at a lady's tears,
Being an ordinary inundation;
But this effusion of such manly drops,
This shower, blown up by tempest of the soul,
Startles mine eyes, and makes me more amaz'd
Than had I seen the vaulty top of heaven
Figur'd quite o'er with burning meteors.
Lift up thy brow, renowned Salisbury,
And with a great heart heave away this storm;
Commend these waters to those baby eyes,
That never saw the giant world enrag'd;
Nor met with fortune other than at feasts,
Full warm of blood, of mirth, of gossiping.
Come, come; for thou shalt thrust thy hand as deep
Into the purse of rich prosperity,
As Lewis himself:—so, nobles, shall you all,
That knit your sinews to the strength of mine.
And even there, methinks, an angel spake:
Look, where the holy legate comes apace,
To give us warrant from the hand of heaven;
And on our actions set the name of right,
With holy breath.

Enter PANDULPH, *attended.*

PAND. Hail, noble prince of France!
The next is this,—King John hath reconcil'd
Himself to Rome; his spirit is come in,
That so stood out against the holy church,
The great metropolis and see of Rome:
Therefore thy threat'ning colours now wind up,
And tame the savage spirit of wild war;
That, like a lion foster'd up at hand,
It may lie gently at the foot of peace,
And be no further harmful than in show.

LEW. Your grace shall pardon me, I will not back;
I am too high-born to be propertied,
To be a secondary at control,
Or useful serving-man, and instrument,
To any sovereign state throughout the world.
Your breath first kindled the dead coal of wars
Between this chastis'd kingdom and myself,
And brought in matter that should feed this fire;
And now 'tis far too huge to be blown out
With that same weak wind which enkindled it.
You taught me how to know the face of right,
Acquainted me with interest to[c] this land,
Yea, thrust this enterprise into my heart;
And come you now to tell me, John hath made
His peace with Rome? What is that peace to me?
I, by the honour of my marriage-bed,
After young Arthur, claim this land for mine;
And now it is half-conquer'd, must I back
Because that John hath made his peace with Rome?
Am I Rome's slave? What penny hath Rome borne,
What men provided, what munition sent,
To underprop this action? Is 't not I
That undergo this charge? Who else but I,
And such as to my claim are liable,
Sweat in this business, and maintain this war?
Have I not heard these islanders shout out,
Vive le roy! as I have bank'd their towns?[d]
Have I not here the best cards for the game,
To win this easy match play'd for a crown?

(*) Old text, *cripple.*

[a] *Upon the* spot—] The *stain* or *disgrace.*

[b] *O, what a noble combat hast* thou *fought*—] In the early folios *thou* is omitted, but was restored in the edition of 1685.

[c] *With interest* to *this land,*—] A familiar construction at the time. Thus, in "Henry IV." Part II. Act III. Sc. 2:—

"He hath more worthy interest *to* the state
Than thou—."

[d] *As I have* bank'd their towns?] This is supposed to mean, *sail'd along beside their towns upon the rivers' banks;* but from the context it seems more probably an allusion to card-playing; and by "bank'd their towns" is meant, *won their towns, put them in bank or rest.*

And shall I now give o'er the yielded set?
No, no, on my soul, it never shall be said.
PAND. You look but on the outside of this work.
LEW. Outside or inside, I will not return
Till my attempt so much be glorified,
As to my ample hope was promised
Before I drew this gallant head of war,
And cull'd these fiery spirits from the world,
To outlook conquest, and to win renown
Even in the jaws of danger and of death.—
[*Trumpet sounds.*
What lusty trumpet thus doth summon us?

Enter the Bastard, *attended.*

BAST. According to the fair play of the world,
Let me have audience: I am sent to speak.
My holy lord of Milan, from the king,
I come to learn how you have dealt for him;
And, as you answer, I do know the scope
And warrant limited unto my tongue.
PAND. The Dauphin is too wilful-opposite,
And will not temporize with my entreaties;
He flatly says, he'll not lay down his arms.
BAST. By all the blood that ever fury breath'd,
The youth says well.—Now hear our English king;
For thus his royalty doth speak in me.
He is prepar'd, and reason too, he should:
This apish and unmannerly approach,
This harness'd masque, and unadvised revel,
This unhair'd [a] sauciness, and boyish troops,
The king doth smile at; and is well prepar'd
To whip this dwarfish war, these* pigmy arms,
From out the circle of his territories.
That hand, which had the strength, even at your [door,
To cudgel you, and make you take the hatch; [b]
To dive, like buckets, in concealed wells;
To crouch in litter of your stable planks;

[a] *This* unhair'd *sauciness,*—] *Unhair'd,* meaning *unbearded,* is the suggestion of Theobald, the old text having "*unheard.*"

(*) Old copies, *this.*

[b] *And make you* take *the hatch;*] *To take,* i.e. *to leap.*

To lie, like pawns, lock'd up in chests and trunks;
To hug with swine; to seek sweet safety out
In vaults and prisons; and to thrill, and shake,
Even at the crying of your nation's crow,[a]
Thinking this voice an armed Englishman:—
Shall that victorious hand be feebled here,
That in your chambers gave you chastisement?
No! Know, the gallant monarch is in arms,
And, like an eagle o'er his aiery, towers,
To souse annoyance that comes near his nest. (1)
And you degenerate, you ingrate revolts,
You bloody Neros, ripping up the womb
Of your dear mother England, blush for shame:
For your own ladies, and pale-visag'd maids,
Like Amazons, come tripping after drums;
Their thimbles into armed gauntlets change,
Their neelds to lances, and their gentle hearts
To fierce and bloody inclination. [in peace;

LEW. There end thy brave, and turn thy face
We grant thou canst outscold us, fare thee well;
We hold our time too precious to be spent
With such a brabbler.

PAND. Give me leave to speak.

BAST. No, I will speak.

LEW. We will attend to neither:—
Strike up the drums; and let the tongue of war
Plead for our interest, and our being here. [out;

BAST. Indeed, your drums, being beaten, will cry
And so shall you, being beaten. Do but start
An echo with the clamour of thy drum,
And even at hand a drum is ready brac'd
That shall reverberate all as loud as thine;
Sound but another, and another shall,
As loud as thine, rattle the welkin's ear,
And mock the deep-mouth'd thunder: for at hand
(Not trusting to this halting legate here,
Whom he hath us'd rather for sport than need),
Is warlike John; and in his forehead sits
A bare-ribb'd death, whose office is this day
To feast upon whole thousands of the French.

LEW. Strike up our drums, to find this danger out.

BAST. And thou shalt find it, Dauphin, do not doubt. [*Exeunt.*

SCENE III.—*The same. A Field of Battle.*

Alarums. Enter KING JOHN *and* HUBERT.

K. JOHN. How goes the day with us? O, tell me, Hubert.

HUB. Badly, I fear: how fares your majesty?

K. JOHN. This fever, that hath troubled me so long,
Lies heavy on me; O, my heart is sick!

Enter a Messenger.

MESS. My lord, your valiant kinsman, Faulconbridge,
Desires your majesty to leave the field,
And send him word by me which way you go.

K. JOHN. Tell him, toward Swinstead, to the abbey there.

MESS. Be of good comfort; for the great supply,
That was expected by the Dauphin here,
Are wrack'd three nights ago on Goodwin sands.
This news was brought to Richard but even now;
The French fight coldly, and retire themselves.

K. JOHN. Aye me! this tyrant fever burns me up,
And will not let me welcome this good news.
Set on toward Swinstead; to my litter straight:
Weakness possesseth me, and I am faint. [*Exeunt.*

SCENE IV.—*The same. Another part of the same.*

Enter SALISBURY, PEMBROKE, BIGOT, *and others.*

SAL. I did not think the king so stor'd with friends.

PEM. Up once again; put spirit in the French:
If they miscarry, we miscarry too.

SAL. That misbegotten devil, Faulconbridge,
In spite of spite, alone upholds the day.

PEM. They say, King John, sore sick, hath left the field.

Enter MELUN, *wounded, and led by* Soldiers.

MEL. Lead me to the revolts of England here.

SAL. When we were happy we had other names.

PEM. It is the count Melun.

SAL. Wounded to death.

MEL. Fly, noble English, you are bought and sold;
Unthread the rude eye of rebellion,[b]
And welcome home again discarded faith.
Seek out King John, and fall before his feet;
For, if the French be lords of this loud day,

---

[a] *Of your* nation's crow,—] "That is, at the crowing of a cock; *gallus* meaning both a cock and a Frenchman."—DOUCE.

[b] Unthread the rude eye of rebellion,—] Retrace the difficult path upon which you have entered. Theobald proposed to read, *untread* the rude *way*, &c., but to *thread one's way* through any intricacy is still an habitual figure, and to pass through the eye of a needle is an oriental metaphor for any troublesome undertaking, familiar to us all by the passage in St. Matthew, chap. xix., which Shakespeare has himself paraphrased in Richard II. Act V. Sc. 5:—

"It is as hard to come, as for a camel
To *thread* the *postern* of a *needle's eye*."

So in Coriolanus, Act III. Sc. 1, we have:—

"Even when the navel of the state was touch'd,
They would not *thread* the gates."

Moreover, the original spelling is *unthred*, and it is remarkable that in the folio, 1623, *thread*, which occurs many times, is invariably spelt *thred*, whilst *tread* is always exhibited in its present form.

He[a] means to recompense the pains you take
By cutting off your heads: thus hath he sworn,
And I with him, and many more with me,
Upon the altar at St. Edmund's-Bury,
Even on that altar where we swore to you
Dear amity and everlasting love.

SAL. May this be possible? may this be true?

MEL. Have I not hideous death within my view,
Retaining but a quantity of life
Which bleeds away, even as a form of wax
Resolveth from his figure 'gainst the fire?
What in the world should make me now deceive,
Since I must lose the use of all deceit?
Why should I then be false, since it is true
That I must die here, and live hence by truth?
I say again, if Lewis do win the day,
He is forsworn if e'er those eyes of yours
Behold another day break in the east.
But even this night,—whose black contagious breath
Already smokes about the burning crest
Of the old, feeble, and day-wearied sun,—
Even this ill night your breathing shall expire,
Paying the fine of rated treachery,
Even with a treacherous fine of all your lives,
If Lewis by your assistance win the day.
Commend me to one Hubert, with your king;
The love of him,—and this respect besides,
For that my grandsire was an Englishman,—
Awakes my conscience to confess all this.
In lieu whereof, I pray you, bear me hence
From forth the noise and rumour of the field;
Where I may think the remnant of my thoughts
In peace, and part this body and my soul
With contemplation and devout desires.(2)

SAL. We do believe thee.—And beshrew my soul,
But I do love the favour and the form
Of this most fair occasion, by the which
We will untread the steps of damned flight;
And, like a bated and retired flood,
Leaving our rankness[b] and irregular course,
Stoop low within those bounds we have o'erlook'd,[c]
And calmly run on in obedience,
Even to our ocean, to our great King John.—
My arm shall give thee help to bear thee hence;
For I do see the cruel pangs of death
Right[d] in thine eye.—Away, my friends! New flight,
And happy newness, that intends old right.
[*Exeunt, leading off* MELUN.

a He means—] *Lewis*, the *Frenchman*, means, &c.

b *Leaving our* rankness—] Rank is here used in a sense it has ceased to retain, that of *riotous*, *impetuous*, &c.

c *Those bounds we have* o'erlook'd,—] That is, *o'erborne*, *overcome*.

d Right *in thine eye.*—] Mr. Collier's annotator would read *bright*; but the old word, meaning *direct*, *immediate*, is preferable.

e *When* the *English* measur'd *backward their own ground*,—] The original has, "When English measure," &c.

SCENE V.—*The same. The* French *Camp.*

Enter LEWIS *and his Train.*

LEW. The sun of heaven, methought, was loth to set,
But stay'd, and made the western welkin blush,
When the English measur'd[e] backward their own ground,
In faint retire: O bravely came we off
When with a volley of our needless shot,
After such bloody toil, we bid good night;
And wound our tottering colours clearly up,[f]
Last in the field, and almost lords of it!

Enter a Messenger.

MESS. Where is my prince, the Dauphin?

LEW. Here:—What news?

MESS. The count Melun is slain; the English lords,
By his persuasion, are again fallen off:
And your supply, which you have wish'd so long,
Are cast away, and sunk, on Goodwin sands.

LEW. Ah, foul shrewd news!—Beshrew thy very heart!
I did not think to be so sad to-night
As this hath made me.—Who was he that said,
King John did fly, an hour or two before
The stumbling night did part our weary powers?

MESS. Whoever spoke it, it is true, my lord.

LEW. Well; keep good quarter and good care to-night;
The day shall not be up so soon as I,
To try the fair adventure of to-morrow. [*Exeunt.*

SCENE VI.—*An open Place in the Neighbourhood of* Swinstead Abbey.

Enter the Bastard *and* HUBERT, *meeting.*

HUB. Who's there? speak, ho! speak quickly, or I shoot.

BAST. A friend.—What art thou?

HUB. Of the part of England.

BAST. Whither dost thou go?

HUB. What's that to thee?
Why may not I demand of thine affairs,

f *And wound our* tottering *colours* clearly *up*,—] Mr. Collier's old corrector suggests—

"And wound our *tott'red* colours *closely* up."

Tottering, or *tottered*, is explained to mean *tattered*; but *to totter* signified also *to hang* or *droop*; and the *tottering*, or *drooping* colours, after a hard fight, contrast becomingly with the *spreading*, *waving* colours of an army advancing to battle. The main difficulty is the word *clearly*; for which we are more disposed to substitute Capell's "*chearly*" than the "*closely*" of the ancient annotator.

As well as thou of mine?
 BAST. Hubert, I think.
 HUB. Thou hast a perfect thought;
I will, upon all hazards, well believe
Thou art my friend, that know'st my tongue so well.
Who art thou?
 BAST. Who thou wilt: an if thou please,
Thou mayst befriend me so much, as to think
I come one way of the Plantagenets.
 HUB. Unkind remembrance! thou, and eyeless night,[a]
Have done me shame:—brave soldier, pardon me,
That any accent, breaking from thy tongue,
Should 'scape the true acquaintance of mine ear.
 BAST. Come, come; sans compliment, what news abroad?
 HUB. Why, here walk I, in the black brow of night,
To find you out.
 BAST. Brief, then; and what 's the news?
 HUB. O, my sweet sir, news fitting to the night,
Black, fearful, comfortless, and horrible.
 BAST. Show me the very wound of this ill news;
I am no woman, I'll not swoon at it.
 HUB. The king, I fear, is poison'd by a monk:
I left him almost speechless, and broke out
To acquaint you with this evil, that you might
The better arm you to the sudden time,
Than if you had at leisure known of this.
 BAST. How did he take it? who did taste to him?
 HUB. A monk, I tell you; a resolved villain,
Whose bowels suddenly burst out: the king
Yet speaks, and, peradventure, may recover.
 BAST. Who didst thou leave to tend his majesty?
 HUB. Why, know you not the lords are all come back,
And brought prince Henry in their company?
At whose request the king hath pardon'd them,
And they are all about his majesty.
 BAST. Withhold thine indignation, mighty heaven,
And tempt us not to bear above our power!
I'll tell thee, Hubert, half my power this night,
Passing these flats, are taken by the tide,
These Lincoln washes have devoured them;
Myself, well mounted, hardly have escap'd.
Away, before! conduct me to the king.
I doubt he will be dead, or e'er I come. [*Exeunt.*

SCENE VII.—*The Orchard of* Swinstead Abbey.

Enter PRINCE HENRY, SALISBURY, *and* BIGOT.

 P. HEN. It is too late; the life of all his blood
Is touch'd corruptibly; and his pure brain
(Which some suppose the soul's frail dwelling-house)
Doth, by the idle comments that it makes,
Foretell the ending of mortality.

Enter PEMBROKE.

 PEM. His highness yet doth speak; and holds belief,
That being brought into the open air
It would allay the burning quality
Of that fell poison which assaileth him.
 P. HEN. Let him be brought into the orchard here.—
Doth he still rage? [*Exit* BIGOT.
 PEM. He is more patient
Than when you left him; even now he sung.
 P. HEN. O vanity of sickness! fierce extremes,
In their continuance, will not feel themselves.
Death, having prey'd upon the outward parts,
Leaves them insensible;[b] and his siege is now
Against the mind,* the which he pricks and wounds
With many legions of strange fantasies;
Which, in their throng and press to that last hold,
Confound themselves. 'Tis strange that death should sing!
I am the cygnet † to this pale faint swan,
Who chants a doleful hymn to his own death;
And, from the organ-pipe of frailty, sings
His soul and body to their lasting rest.
 SAL. Be of good comfort, prince; for you are born
To set a form upon that indigest,
Which he hath left so shapeless and so rude.

Re-enter BIGOT *and* Attendants, *who bring in* KING JOHN *in a Chair.*[c]

 K. JOHN. Ay, marry, now my soul hath elbow room;
It would not out at windows, nor at doors.
There is so hot a summer in my bosom,
That all my bowels crumble up to dust:
I am a scribbled form, drawn with a pen
Upon a parchment; and against this fire
Do I shrink up.
 P. HEN. How fares your majesty?
 K. JOHN. Poison'd,—ill fare;—dead, forsook, cast off:
And none of you will bid the winter come,
To thrust his icy fingers in my maw;
Nor let my kingdom's rivers take their course

---

[a] *Thou, and* eyeless night,—] The old text has "*endless* night." *Eyeless*, which is peculiarly applicable, we owe to Theobald.

[b] *Leaves them* insensible;] The original lection is *invisible;* a word, notwithstanding Malone's defence of it, that appears to be without sense in this passage. Hanmer first suggested the reading in the text, and his emendation is in some degree verified by the corresponding passage in the earlier play,—

"Power after power forsake their proper power,
Onely the heart impugnes with faint resist."

(*) Old text, *winde*. (†) Old text, *Symet*.

[c] The stage direction in the old copies is simply, "*John brought in.*"

Through my burn'd bosom; nor entreat the north
To make his bleak winds kiss my parched lips,
And comfort me with cold:—I do not ask you much,
I beg cold comfort; and you are so strait,
And so ingrateful, you deny me that.

P. Hen. O, that there were some virtue in my tears,
That might relieve you!

K. John. The salt in them is hot.
Within me is a hell; and there the poison
Is, as a fiend, confin'd to tyrannize
On unreprievable condemned blood.

Enter the Bastard.

Bast. O, I am scalded with my violent motion,
And spleen of speed to see your majesty.

K. John. O cousin, thou art come to set mine eye:
The tackle of my heart is crack'd and burnt,
And all the shrouds, wherewith my life should sail,
Are turned to one thread, one little hair:
My heart hath one poor string to stay it by,
Which holds but till thy news be uttered;
And then all this thou seest is but a clod,
And module of confounded royalty.

Bast. The Dauphin is preparing hitherward,
Where, heaven he knows, how we shall answer him:
For, in a night, the best part of my power,
As I upon advantage did remove,
Were in the washes, all unwarily,
Devoured by the unexpected flood.

[*The* King *dies.* (3)

Sal. You breathe these dead news in as dead an ear.—
My liege! my lord!—But now a king,—now thus!

P. Hen. Even so must I run on, and even so stop.
What surety of the world, what hope, what stay,
When this was now a king, and now is clay!

BAST. Art thou gone so? I do but stay behind
To do the office for thee of revenge;
And then my soul shall wait on thee to heaven,
As it on earth hath been thy servant still.
Now, now, you stars, that move in your right spheres,
Where be your powers? Shew now your mended faiths;
And instantly return with me again,
To push destruction, and perpetual shame,
Out of the weak door of our fainting land:
Straight let us seek, or straight we shall be sought;
The Dauphin rages at our very heels.

SAL. It seems, you know not then so much as we:
The cardinal Pandulph is within at rest,
Who half an hour since came from the Dauphin;
And brings from him such offers of our peace
As we with honour and respect may take,
With purpose presently to leave this war.

BAST. He will the rather do it, when he sees
Ourselves well sinewed to our defence.

SAL. Nay, 'tis in a manner done already;
For many carriages he hath dispatch'd
To the sea-side, and put his cause and quarrel
To the disposing of the cardinal;
With whom yourself, myself, and other lords,
If you think meet, this afternoon will post
To consummate this business happily.

BAST. Let it be so.—And you, my noble prince,
With other princes that may best be spar'd,
Shall wait upon your father's funeral.

P. HEN. At Worcester must his body be interr'd; (4)
For so he will'd it.

BAST. Thither shall it then.
And happily may your sweet self put on
The lineal state and glory of the land!
To whom, with all submission, on my knee,
I do bequeath my faithful services
And true subjection everlastingly.

SAL. And the like tender of our love we make,
To rest without a spot for evermore.

P. HEN. I have a kind soul, that would give you[a] thanks,
And knows not how to do it, but with tears.

BAST. O, let us pay the time but needful woe,
Since it hath been beforehand with our griefs.—
This England never did, nor never shall,
Lie at the proud foot of a conqueror,
But when it first did help to wound itself.
Now these her princes are come home again,
Come the three corners of the world in arms,
And we shall shock them. Nought shall make us rue,
If England to itself do rest but true. (5) [*Exeunt.*

[a] *That would give you thanks,*—] The word *you*, which is wanting in the original, was supplied by Rowe.

ILLUSTRATIVE COMMENTS.

ACT I.

(1) SCENE I.—
With that half-face would he have all my land:
A half-fac'd groat, five hundred pound a-year!]
The old text, which has "with *half that* face," was corrected by Theobald. *Half-faced groat* appears to have been a popular epithet for a meagre visage; and was derived from the issue of *groats* by Henry VII., which, in opposition to the general coinage, bore a *half-face*, or profile, instead of a full-face. Steevens quotes a passage from "The Downfall of Robert Earl of Huntingdon," 1601, where we meet the same allusion:—

"You *half-fac'd groat*, you thick-cheek'd chitty face."

(2) SCENE I.—
That in mine ear I durst not stick a rose,
Lest men should say, Look, where three farthings goes.]
In his chapter "On the Coines of England," Holinshed tells us that, after the death of Mary, "The ladie Elizabeth her sister, and now our most gratious queene, sovereigne and princesse, did finish the matter wholie, utterly abolishing the use of copper and brasen coine, and converting the same into guns and great ordinance, she restored sundrie coines of fine silver, as peeces of *halfepenie farding*, of a penie, of three halfe pence, peeces of two pence, of three pence, of foure pence (called the groat), of six pence, usuallie named the testone, and shilling of twelve pence, whereon she hath imprinted her owne image, and emphatical superscription."

The silver three-farthings was, of course, very thin; and as with the profile of the sovereign it bore the emblem of *a rose*, its similitude to a weazen-faced beau with that flower stuck in his ear, according to a courtly fashion of Shakespeare's day, is sufficiently intelligible and humorous.

(3) SCENE I.—
——— *Now, your traveller,—*
He and his tooth-pick at my worship's mess.]
We may readily believe that in an "age of newly-excited curiosity," as Dr. Johnson describes it, when intelligence was transmitted with incredible slowness and uncertainty, the company of a travelled man, conversant with the manners and languages of foreign countries, must have been eagerly sought after. The craving, indeed, for such society appears to have been carried at one time to so extravagant a pitch that there are good grounds for believing a professed traveller, engaged to relate his adventures, formed a not unfrequent source of entertainment at the dinner-table of the opulent. The writers of the period abound in allusions, invariably sarcastic, to this Tom Odcomb tribe. According to them, your professed traveller was the synonyme for a formal, mendacious coxcomb. Thus, in Marlowe's "Edward II." Act I. Sc. 1, Gaveston asks one of the "three poor men:"—

"What art thou?
Man. A traveller.
Gav. Let me see—thou wouldst do well
To wait at my trencher, and tell me lies at dinner time."

So, too, in Jonson's "Cynthia's Revels," Act II. Sc. 1, Gifford's Edition:)—

"He that is with him is Amorphus, a traveller, one so made out of the mixture of shreds of forms that himself is truly deform'd. He walks most commonly with a clove or pick-tooth in his mouth. * * * He will lie cheaper than any beggar, and louder than most clocks."

Overbury, in his "Characters," has hit off the ridiculous peculiarities of "An Affectate Traveller" with his accustomed penetration: not omitting, any more than Shakespeare or Jonson, who, in such portraiture, omit nothing, the indispensable *tooth-pick:*—

"His attire speakes *French* or *Italian*, and his *gate* cries, *Behold me.* He censures all things by countenances, and shrugs and speakes his own language with shame and lisping: he will choake, rather than confess *beere* good drinke; and his pick-tooth is a maine part of his behaviour."

(4) SCENE I.—*Knight, knight, good mother,—Basilisco-like.*] A satirical reference to the old play of "Soliman and Perseda," in one scene of which the clownish servant, Piston, springs on the back of a certain swaggering, cowardly knight, called Basilisco, and compels him to swear as he dictates:—

"*Bas.* O, I swear, I swear.
Pist. By the contents of this blade,—
Bas. By the contents of this blade,—
Pist. I, the aforesaid Basilisco,—
Bas. I, the aforesaid Basilisco,—*knight*, good fellow, *knight*, *knight*,—
Pist. *Knave*, good fellow, *knave*, *knave*."

For the episode of the brothers Faulconbridge, appealing to the king to decide upon their respective right to old Sir Robert's estate, as, indeed, for nearly every other incident in the play, Shakespeare is indebted to "The Troublesome Raigne of King John." Malone had the temerity to assert, and his dictum has been taken for granted by the critics since, that, "In expanding the character of the Bastard, Shakspeare seems to have proceeded on the following slight hint in the original play:—

'Near them, a bastard of the king's deceas'd,
A hardie wild-head, rough and venturous.'"

How far this statement is justifiable, let the reader determine after perusing only a few extracts from the earlier work. In the parallel scene, King John decrees that the paternity of Philip shall be determined by his mother and himself; the mother, on being questioned, declares his father was Sir Robert Faulconbridge; whereupon the king says:—

"Aske Philip whose sonne he is.
Essex. Philip, who was thy father?
Philip. Mas my lord and that's a question: and you had not
Taken some paines with her before, I should have desired
You to aske my mother.
John. Say, who was thy father?
Philip. Faith (my lord) to answere you, sure hee is my
Father that was neerest my mother when I was begotten,
And him I think to be Sir Robert Fauconbridge.
John. Essex, for fashions sake demand agen,
And so an end to this contention.
Robert. Was ever man thus wrongd as Robert is?
Essex. Philip speake I say, who was thy father?
John. Young man how now, what art thou in a trance
Elinor. Philip awake, the man is in a dreame.
Philip. *Philippus atavis ædite Regibus.*
What saist thou Philip, sprung of auncient kings?

Quo me rapit tempestas?
What winde of honour blowes this furie forth?
Or whence proceede these fumes of majestie?
Me thinkes I heare a hollow eccho sound,
That Philip is the sonne unto a king:
The whistling leaves upon the trembling trees,
Whistle in consort I am Richard's sonne:
The bubling murmur of the waters fall,
Records *Philippus Regius filius:*
Birds in their flight make musicke with their wings,
Filling the aire with glorie of my birth:
Birds, bubbles, leaves and mountaines, eccho, all
Ring in mine eares, that I am Richard's sonne.
Fond man! ah whither art thou carried?
How are thy thoughts ywrapt in honors heaven?
Forgetfull what thou art, and whence thou camst.
Thy fathers land cannot maintaine these thoughts;
These thoughts are farre unfitting Fauconbridge:
And well they may; for why this mounting minde
Doth soare too high to stoupe to Fauconbridge.
Why how now? knowest thou where thou art?
And knowest thou who expects thine answer here?
Wilt thou upon a franticke madding vaine
Goe loose thy land, and say thyselfe base borne?
No, keepe thy land, though Richard were thy sire,
What ere thou thinkst, say thou art Fauconbridge.
John. Speake man, be sodaine, who thy father was.
Philip. Please it your majestie, Sir Robert—
Philip, that Fauconbridge cleaves to thy jawes:
It will not out, I cannot for my life
Say I am sonne unto a Fauconbridge.
Let land and living goe, tis honors fire
That makes me sweare King Richard was my sire.
Base to a king addes title of more state,
Than knights begotten though legitimate.
Please it your grace, I am King Richards sonne."

We miss in the original the keen but sportive wit, the exuberant vivacity, the shrewd worldliness and the military genius of Shakespeare's Bastard; but his archetype in the old piece was the work of no mean hand.

(5) Scene I.—Compare the corresponding passage in the old play, beginning,—

"Then *Robin Fauconbridge* I wish thee joy,
My sire a king, and I a landlesse boy," &c.

ACT II.

(1) Scene I.—*Richard, that robb'd the lion of his heart.*] The exploit by which this pattern of chivalry was supposed to have acquired his distinguishing appellation, *Cœur-de-lion*, is related in the ancient metrical romance which bears his name: * and from thence was probably transferred into our old chronicles:—"It is sayd that a *lyon* was put to Kynge *Richarde* beynge in prison to have devoured him, and when the *lyon* was gapynge he put his arme in his mouth and pulled the *lyon* by the harte so harde, that he slew the lyon, and therefore some say he is called *Rycharde Cure de Lyon:* but some say he is called *Cure de Lyon*, because of his boldenesse and hardy stomake."—Rastall's *Chronicle.*

(2) Scene I.—
It lies as sightly on the back of him,
As great Alcides' shows upon an ass.]
The old text has *shoes*, instead of *shows;* and the commentators have produced a formidable array of instances in our old comedies where the *shoes* of Hercules are mentioned. Notwithstanding these, I feel persuaded that the allusion, as Theobald pointed out, is to the fable of the ass in the lion's skin. *Shoe* and *show* were often spelt alike:—

"Yet, what is Love? I pray thee, *shoe.*
A thing that creepes, it cannot *goe.*"
The Phœnix nest, set foorth by R. S. Lond. 1593.

(3) Scene I.—
Do, child, go to it grandame, child;
Give grandame kingdom, and it grandame will
Give it a plum.]
"Mr. Guest ('Phil. Pro.' I. 280) has observed that, in the dialects of the North-Western Counties, formerly *it* was sometimes used for *its;* and that, accordingly, we have not only in Shakespeare's 'King John,' 'Goe to yt grandame, childe * * * * and it grandame will giue yt a plum,' but, in Ben Jonson's 'Silent Woman,' II. 3, 'It knighthood and it friends.' So in 'Lear,' I. 4, we have, in a speech of the Fool, 'For you know, Nunckle, the Hedge-Sparrow fed the Cuckoo so long, that it's had it head bit off by it young,' (that is, that it has had its head,—not that it had its head,) as the modern editors give the passage, after the Second Folio, in which it stands, 'that it had its head bit off by it young.' So likewise, long before *its* was generally received, we have *it self* commonly printed in two words, evidently under the impression that *it* was a possessive, of the same syntactical force with the pronouns in *my self, your self, her self.*"—*The English of Shakespeare*, &c., by George L. Craik, &c. &c.

(4) Scene I.—
——— *Be pleased then*
To pay that duty, which you truly owe,
To him that owes it.]
In this passage the verb *to owe* is used both in its current acceptation, *to be indebted*, and in the sense which it repeatedly bears in Shakespeare and his contemporaries of *own:*—

"To him that *owes* it"—

means—

"To him that it *belongs to.*"

Owe, when used for *own*, generally implies absolute possession. Thus, in "Othello," Act III. Sc. 3:—

"——— Not poppy, nor mandragora,
Nor all the drowsy syrups of the world,
Shall ever medicine thee to that sweet sleep
Which thou *owed'st* yesterday."

That is, which thou *possessed*, or which was thy property yesterday. So, also, in "The Two Gentlemen of Verona," Act V. Sc. 2:—

"*Thu.* Considers she my possessions?
Pro. O, ay; and pities them.
Thu. Wherefore?
Jul. That such an ass should *owe* them."

(5) Scene II.—*Do like the mutines of Jerusalem.*] *Mutines* for *mutineers*. An allusion to the combination of the civil factions in Jerusalem when the city was threatened by Titus. Malone thinks it probable that Shakespeare derived the reference from Joseph Ben Gorion's "History of the Latter Times of the Jewes Common-Weale," translated from Hebrew into English by Peter Morwyn, 1575.

* *See* Weber's *Metrical Romances*, ii. 44.

ACT III.

(1) SCENE I.—

I will instruct my sorrows to be proud,
For grief is proud, and makes his owner stout.]

This passage has long been, and will long continue to be, a torment to critics. The old text reads, "——— and makes his owner stoope." Hanmer first proposed the substitution of *stout* for *stoope;* and he has been generally, but not invariably, followed by the other editors. I must confess, despite the elaborate defence of the ancient reading by Malone, and its adoption by Messrs. Collier and Knight, that *stoop* appears to me entirely inconsistent both with the context and with the subsequent language and demeanour of Lady Constance before the Kings of France and England. Shakespeare, I conceive, intended to express the very natural sentiment, that grief is proud, and renders its possessor proud also; but wishing to avoid the repetition of *proud,* which had been introduced twice immediately before, he adopted a word, *stout,* which was commonly used in the same sense.

The argument that in other passages of these plays the effect of grief is to deject and dishearten has been so admirably answered by Dr. Johnson, that it would be presumptuous to add anything to a criticism so discriminative and profound. "In 'Much Ado About Nothing,' the father of Hero, depressed by her disgrace, declares himself so subdued by grief that a *thread may lead him.* How is it that grief, in Leonato and Lady Constance, produces effects directly opposite, and yet both agreeable to nature? Sorrow softens the mind while yet it is warmed by hope; but hardens it when it is congealed by despair. Distress, while there remains any prospect of relief, is weak and flexible; but when no succour remains, is fearless and stubborn: angry alike at those that injure, and at those that do not help; careless to please where nothing can be gained, and fearless to offend when there is nothing further to be dreaded. Such was this writer's knowledge of the passions!"

(2) SCENE I.—*O Lymoges! O Austria!*] Historically, these titles indicate two distinct personages. The one, Leopold Duke of Austria, by whom Richard Cœur-de-Lion was imprisoned in the year 1193; and the other, Vidomar, Viscount of Limoges, before whose Castle of Chaluz, in 1199, the King was wounded by an archer, one Bertrand de Gourdon, of which wound he died. The author of the old play ascribes the death of Richard to the Duke of Austria, uniting in his person both the well-known enemies of the lion-hearted Monarch, and Shakespeare has followed him.

(3) SCENE I.—

And meritorious shall that hand be call'd,
Canonized, and worshipp'd as a saint,
That takes away by any secret course
Thy hateful life.]

The similar denunciation from "The Troublesome Raigne," &c., which was the model of this play, is given in the Preliminary Notice; but there is a still older dramatic piece entitled "Kynge Johan," written by Bishop Bale, wherein the sentence of excommunication pronounced by the Pope upon the contumacious monarch is far more curious and circumstantial;—

"For as moch as Kyng Johan doth Holy Church so handle,
Here I do curse hym wyth crosse, boke, bell and candle.
Lyke as this same roode turneth now from my face,
So God I requyre to sequester hym of his grace.
As this boke doth speare by my worke mannuall,
I wyll God to close uppe from hym his benefyttes all.
As this burnyng flame goth from this candle in syght,
I wyll God to put hym from his eternal lyght.
I take hym from Crist, and after the sownd of this bell,
Both body and sowle I geve hym to the devyll of hell," &c.—P. 40.

Kynge Johan, a Play in two Parts, &c. &c., by John Bale. Printed for the Camden Society, from the MS. of the author in the library of the Duke of Devonshire.

(4) SCENE II.—*Some airy devil hovers in the sky.*] The demonologists distributed their good and evil spirits into many divisions and subordinations, each class having its peculiar attributes and functions. Of the *Sublunary devils,* Burton tells us,—

"*Psellus makes six kinds:·fiery, aeriall, terrestiall, watery, and subterranean devils, besides those faieries, satyres, nymphs,*" &c.—

"Fiery spirits or devills, are such as commonly worke by blazing starres, fire-drakes, or *ignes fatui;* * * * * likewise they counterfeit sunnes and moones, stars oftentimes, and sit on ship masts," &c. &c.

"Aeriall spirits or devils, such as keep quarter most part in the aire, cause many tempests, thunder and lightnings, teare oakes, fire steeples, houses, strike men and beasts, make it raine stones, as in Livy's time, woole, frogs, &c. * * * * These can corrupt the aire, and cause plagues, sicknesse, storms, shipwrecks, fires, inundations," &c. &c.

BURTON'S *Anatomie of Melancholy,* P. I. Sc. II.

(5) SCENE II.—

——— *Austria's head, lie there;*
While Philip breathes.]

Shakespeare follows the old play in making the Bastard kill Austria to revenge the death of Cœur-de-Lion:—

"Thus hath K. *Richards* son performed his vowes,
And offred Austria's blood for his sacrifice
Unto his father's everliving soule."

According to history, it was the Viscount of Lymoges who was slain by Philip:—"The same yere, Philip bastard sonne to King Richard, to whome his father had given the castell and honor of Coinacke, killed the Vicount of Limoges, in revenge of his father's death, who was slaine (as yee have heard) in besieging the castell of Chalus Cheverell."—HOLINSHED, *under the year* 1199.

(6) SCENE III.—

——— *If the midnight bell*
Did, with his iron tongue and brazen mouth,
Sound one into the drowsy ear of night.]

In the original the last line reads thus,—

"Sound *on* into the drowsy *race* of night."

The main pose in this troublesome passage is the word *race: on* was so frequently printed for *one,* both in these plays and in other books of the period, that there is great probability of its being so here; and *into* was often used formerly where we now employ *unto:* but *race* must be a corruption. What is meant by "the *drowsy race?*" I, at one time, conjectured that *race* was a misprint, by transposition of the letters, for *carr,* or *carre,* and that the "Sound on" might be applicable to "Night's black chariot:"—

"All *drowsy* night who in a *car* of jet
By steeds of iron grey * * *
* * * * * drawn through the sky."

BROWNE'S *Britannia's Pastorals.* B. II. Song 1.

I am now, however, firmly assured that it is a corruption of *eare,* a word which occurred to me many years ago, as it did to Mr. Dyce, Mr. Collier, and no doubt to a hundred people besides. It has been suggested that the "midnight bell" might mean the bell which summoned the monks to prayer at that time, and that the "Sound on" referred to repeated strokes rather than to the hour of *one* proclaimed by the clock; but is there not something infinitely more awful and impressive in the idea of the solemn, single, boom of a church clock, knelling the death of time, and startling the hushed and drowsy ear of Night, than in the clangour of a whole peal of bells? Steevens thought so:—"The repeated strokes have less of solemnity than the single notice, as they take from the horror and awful silence here described as so propitious to the dreadful purposes of the King. Though the hour of *one* be not the natural midnight, it is yet the most solemn moment of the poetical one; and Shakespeare himself has chosen to introduce his Ghost in Hamlet,—

'The bell then beating *one*.'"

ACT IV.

(1) SCENE I.—

Silence! no more. Go closely in with me;
Much danger do I undergo for thee. [*Exeunt.*]

Let the reader who would appreciate in some degree the infusive, enriching faculty which Shakespeare possessed—marvellous almost as his wisdom, and creative power—compare the foregoing scene with its original in the old drama:—

" Enter Arthur to Hubert de Burgh.

Arthur.

Gramercie *Hubert* for thy care of me,
In or to whom restraint is newly knowne,
The joy of walking is small benefit,
Yet will I take thy offer with small thanks,
I would not loose the pleasure of the eie.
But tell me curteous keeper if thou can,
How long the king will have me tarrie heere.

Hubert.

I know not prince, but as I gesse, not long.
God send you freedome, and God save the king.
[*They issue forth.*

Arthur.

Why how now sirs, what may this outrage meane?
O helpe me *Hubert*, gentle keeper help:
God send this sodaine mutinous approach
Tend not to reave a wretched guiltles life.

Hubert.

So sirs, depart, and leave the rest for me.

Arthur.

Then *Arthur* yeeld, death frowneth in thy face,
What meaneth this? good *Hubert* pleade the case.

Hubert.

Patience yong lord, and listen words of woe,
Harmefull and harsh, hells horror to be heard:
A dismall tale fit for a furies tongue.
I faint to tell, deepe sorrow is the sound.

Arthur.

What, must I die?

Hubert.

No newes of death, but tidings of more hate,
A wrathfull doome, and most unluckie fate:
Deaths dish were daintie at so fell a feast,
Be deafe, heare not, its hell to tell the rest.

Arthur.

Alas, thou wrongst my youth with words of feare,
Tis hell, tis horror, not for one to heare:
What is it man if it must needes be done,
Act it, and end it, that the paine were gone.

Hubert.

I will not chaunt such dolour with my tongue,
Yet must I act the outrage with my hand.
My heart, my head, and all my powers beside,
To aide the office have at once denide.
Peruse this letter, lines of trebble woe,
Reade ore my charge, and pardon when you know.

'*Hubert*, these are to commaund thee, as thou tendrest our quiet in minde, and the estate of our person, that presently upon the receipt of our commaund, thou put out the eies of *Arthur Plantaginet!*'

Arthur.

Ah monstrous damned man! his very breath infects the elements.
Contagious venome dwelleth in his heart,
Effecting meanes to poyson all the world.
Unreverent may I be to blame the heavens
Of great injustice, that the miscreant
Lives to oppresse the innocents with wrong.
Ah *Hubert!* makes he thee his instrument,
To sound the trump that causeth hell triumph?
Heaven weepes, the saints do shed celestiall teares,
They fear thy fall, and cite thee with remorse,
They knocke thy conscience, moving pitie there,
Willing to fence thee from the rage of hell;
Hell, *Hubert*, trust me all the plagues of hell
Hangs on performance of this damned deed.
This seale, the warrant of the bodies blisse,
Ensureth satan chieftaine of thy soule:
Subscribe not *Hubert*, give not Gods part away.
I speake not only for eies priviledge,
The chiefe exterior that I would enjoy:
But for thy perill, far beyond my paine,
Thy sweete soules losse, more than my eies vaine lacke:
A cause internall, and eternall too.
Advise thee *Hubert*, for the case is hard,
To loose salvation for a kings reward.

Hubert.

My lord, a subject dwelling in the land
Is tied to execute the kings commaund.

Arthur.

Yet God's commaunds whose power reacheth further,
That no commaund should stand in force to murther.

Hubert.

But that same essence hath ordained a law,
A death for guilt, to keepe the world in awe.

Arthur.

I pleade, not guilty, treasonlesse and free.

Hubert.

But that appeale, my lord, concernes not me.

Arthur.

Why thou art he that maist omit the perill.

Hubert.

I, if my soveraigne would omit his quarrell.

Arthur.

His quarrell is unhallowed false and wrong.

Hubert.

Then be the blame to whom it doth belong.

Arthur.

Why thats to thee if thou as they proceede,
Conclude their judgement with so vile a deede.

Hubert.

Why then no execution can be lawfull,
If judges doomes must be reputed doubtfull.

Arthur.

Yes where in forme of law in place and time,
The offender is convicted of the crime.

Hubert.

My lord, my lord, this long expostulation,
Heapes up more griefe, than promise of redresse;
For this I know, and so resolvde I end,
That subjects lives on kings commands depend.
I must not reason why he is your foe,
But do his charge since he commaunds it so.

Arthur.

Then do thy charge, and charged be thy soule
With wrongfull persecution done this day.
You rowling eyes, whose superficies yet
I do behold with eies that nature lent:
Send foorth the terror of your moovers frowne,
To wreake my wrong upon the murtherers
That rob me of your faire reflecting view:
Let hell to them (as earth they wish to me)
Be darke and direfull guerdon for their guilt,
And let the black tormenters of deepe *Tartary*
Upbraide them with this damned enterprise,
Inflicting change of tortures on their soules.
Delay not *Hubert*, my orisons are ended,
Begin I pray thee, reave me of my sight:
But to performe a tragedie indeede,
Conclude the period with a mortall stab.
Constance farewell, tormenter come away,
Make my dispatch the tyrants feasting day.

Hubert.

I faint, I feare, my conscience bids desist:
Faint did I say? feare was it that I named:
My king commaunds, that warrant sets me free:
But God forbids, and he commaundeth kings,
That great commaunder counterchecks my charge,
He stayes my hand, he maketh soft my heart.
Goe cursed tooles, your office is exempt,
Cheere thee yong lord, thou shalt not loose an eie,
Though I should purchase it with losse of life.
Ile to the king, and say his will is done,
And of the lauyor tell him thou art dead,
Goe in with me, for *Hubert* was not borne
To blinde those lampes that nature pollisht so.

Arthur.

Hubert, if ever *Arthur* be in state,
Looke for amends of this received gift,
I took my eiesight by thy curtesie,
Thou lentst them me, I will not be ingrate.
But now procrastination may offend
The issue that thy kindnesse undertakes:
Depart we, *Hubert*, to prevent the worst. [*Exeunt.*"

(2) SCENE II.—
And here's a prophet, that I brought with me
From forth the streets of Pomfret.]
"There was in this season an heremit, whose name was Peter, dwelling about Yorke, a man in great reputation with the common people, bicause that either inspired with some spirit of prophesie as the people beleeved, or else having some notable skill in art magike, he was accustomed to tell what should follow after. And for so much as oftentimes his saiengs prooved true, great credit was given to him as a verie prophet," &c. "This Peter about the firste of January last past, had tolde the king, that at the feast of the Ascension it should come to passe, that he should be cast out of his kingdome; and (whether, to the intent that his words should be better beleeved, or whether upon too much trust of his owne cunning) he offered himselfe to suffer death for it, if his prophesie prooved not true. Hereupon being committed to prison within the castell of Corf, when the day by him prefixed came without any other notable damage unto King John, he was by the kings commandement drawne from the said castell into the towne of Warham, and there hanged, togither with his sonne.

"The people much blamed King John for this extreame dealing, bicause that the heremit was supposed to be a man of great vertue, and his sonne nothing guiltie of the offence committed by his father (if any were) against the king. Moreover some thought that he had much wrong to die, bicause the matter fell out even as he had prophesied; for the day before the Ascension day, King John had resigned the superioritie of his kingdome (as they tooke the matter) unto the pope."—HOLINSHED, *under the year* 1213.

(3) SCENE III.—*Heaven take my soul, and England keep my bones!*] Shakespeare, in his incidents, adheres closely to the old play:—

"*Enter young* Arthur *on the walls.*

Now help good hap to farther mine entent,
Crosse not my youth with any more extremes:
I venter life to gaine my libertie,
And if I die, world's troubles have an end.
Feare gins disswade the strength of my resolve,
My holde will faile, and then alas I fall,
And if I fall, no question death is next:
Better desist, and live in prison still.
Prison said I? Nay, rather death than so:
Comfort and courage come again to me,
Ile venter sure: tis but a leape for life."

How the ill-fated Arthur really lost his life we have no authentic evidence. Holinshed only says,—"Touching the maner in verie deed of the end of this Arthur, writers make sundrie reports. Neverthelesse certeine it is, that in the yeare next insuing, he was remooved from Falais unto the castell or tower of Rouen, out of the which there was not any that would confesse that ever he saw him go alive. Some have written that as he assaied to have escaped out of prison, and prooving to clime over the wals of the castell, he fell into the river of Saine, and so was drowned. Other write, that through verie greefe and languor he pined awaie and died of natural sicknesse. But some affirme, that King John secretelie caused him to be murthered and made awaie, so as it is not throughly agreed upon, in what sort he finished his daies: but verelie King John was had in great suspicion, whether worthilie or not, the Lord knoweth."—*Chronicles, under the year* 1202.

ACT V.

(1) SCENE II.—
——— *the gallant monarch is in arms,*
And, like an eagle o'er his aiery, towers
To souse annoyance that comes near his nest.]
The only explanation of this passage usually given is that "aiery signifies a nest;" but, regarded as the purely technical phraseology of Falconry, the lines will be found susceptible of much more meaning than this interpretation attributes to them. By the ordinary punctuation of the second line,—

"And like an eagle o'er his aiery towers,"—

it would seem, too, as if the words were supposed to refer to the elevation of the nest, and were equivalent only to "airy towers;" while it is clear that Shakespeare uses *tower* here as he does in another part of the present play,—

"Ha, majesty! how high thy glory towers,"
Act II. Sc. 2,—

in the sense of a hawking-technical, descriptive of the soaring of a falcon or an eagle, towering spirally in the manner natural to birds of prey. In this ascent, when his flight has brought him directly over the object of his aim, the falcon makes a rapid and destructive plunge, or, technically speaking, *souce*, upon it. There is in Drayton's *Polyolbion*, Song XX., a description of a falcon flight at a brook for water fowl, which illustrates this passage vividly, both as to the circular flight, and the sanguinary pouncing of the hawk:—

"When making for the brook the Falconer doth spy
One river, plash, or mere, where store of fowl doth lie,—
Whence forced over-land, by skilful Falconer's trade,
A fair convenient flight may easily be made;
He whistleth off his hawks, whose nimble pinions straight
Do work themselves by turns into a stately height.
* * * * * *
Still as the fearful fowl attempt to 'scape away,
With many a *stooping* brave, them in again they lay:

But when the Falconers take their hawking-poles in hand,
And crossing of the brook, do put it over land:
The Hawk gives it a Souce, that makes it to rebound
Well near the height of man, sometimes, above the ground
Oft takes a leg or wing, oft takes away the head,
And oft from neck to tail the back in two doth shred."

With respect to the verb *towers*, as expressive of the flight of an eagle, a falcon, &c., it would appear then to have formerly denoted, not merely a soaring to a great height, but to fly spirally. When the latter only is implied, it should be spelt *tour*, which Cotgrave, 1660, explains as "a turn, round, circle, compasse, wheeling, revolution."

After the preceding extract from Drayton, a short note only will be required to illustrate the original sense of the word *Souce*. Beaumont and Fletcher employ it as a hawking-phrase in "The Chances," Act IV. Sc. 1,—

"Her conscience and her fears creeping upon her,
Dead as a fowle *at souce* she'll sink."

Spenser uses it to describe the heavy and irresistible blows of the hammer in the House of Care:—

"In which his worke he had six servants prest,
About the andvile standing evermore
With huge great hammers, that did never rest
From heaping *stroukes that thereon sousèd sore.*"
Faëry Queene, B. IV. Ch. V. St. XXX.

To souce is also still well known in the domestic meaning of plunging, and throwing provisions into salt and water, from the Latin *Salsum;* which sense agrees with the precipitate plunge of a bird of prey on a water-fowl. The German *Sausen*, however, may rather be considered as the real etymon of the word. It signifies to rush with whistling sound like the blustering of the wind: which is remarkably expressive of the *whirr* made by the wings of a falcon when swooping on his quarry.

(2) SCENE IV.—*With contemplation and devout desires.*] This circumstance is historical:—"About the same time, or rather in the yeare last past as some hold, it fortuned that the vicount of Melune, a French man, fell sicke at London, and perceiving that death was at hand, he called unto him certeine of the English Barons, which remained in the citie, upon safegard thereof, and to them made this protestation: I lament (saith he) your destruction and desolation at hand, bicause ye are ignorant of the perils hanging over your heads. For this understand, that Lewes, and with him 16 earles and barons of France, have secretlie sworne (if it shall fortune him to conquere this realme of England and to be crowned king) that he will kill, banish and confine all those of the English nobilitie (which now doe serve under him, and persecute their owne king) as traitours and rebels, and furthermore will dispossesse all their linage of such inheritances as they now hold in England. And bicause (saith he) you shall not have doubt hereof, I which lie here at the point of death, doo now affirm unto you, and take it on the perill of my soule that I am one of those sixteen that have sworne to performe this thing: wherefore I advise you to provide for your owne safeties, and your realmes which you now destroie, and keepe this thing secret which I have uttered unto you. After this speech was uttered he streightwaies died."—HOLINSHED, *under the year* 1216.

In the old play, the dying nobleman declares his motives for this confession to be,—

"The greatest for the freedome of my soule,
That longs to leave this mansion free from guilt:
The other on a naturall instinct,
For that my grandsire was an Englishman."

In Shakespeare he is impelled by another circumstance:—

"Commend me to one Hubert, with your king:
The love of him,—and this respect besides,
For that my grandsire was an Englishman,—
Awakes my conscience to confess all this."

(3) SCENE VII.—*The King dies.*] The chroniclers, who wrote within sixty years after his death, make no mention of John having died by poison. Shakespeare found the incident in "The Troublesome Raigne," &c., and it is interesting to contrast his treatment of the king's dying scene with that of the older workman:—

John.

Philip, some drinke, oh for the frozen Alpes,
To tumble on and coole this inward heate,
That rageth as the fornace seven-fold hote.
To burne the holy tree in *Babylon*,
Power after power forsake their proper power,
Onely the heart impugnes with faint resist
The fierce invade of him that conquers kings,
Helpe God, O paine! die *John*, O plague
Inflicted on thee for thy grievous sinnes.
Philip, a chaire, and by and by a grave,
My legges disdaine the carriage of a king.

Bastard.

A good my liege, with patience conquer griefe,
And beare this paine with kingly fortitude.

John.

Methinkes I see a catalogue of sinne,
Wrote by a fiend in marble characters,
The least enough to loose my part in heaven.
Methinkes the divell whispers in mine eares,
And tells me, tis in vaine to hope for grace,
I must be damn'd for *Arthur's* sodaine death,
I see I see a thousand thousand men
Come to accuse me for my wrong on earth,
And there is none so mercifull a God
That will forgive the number of my sinnes.
How have I liv'd, but by another's losse?
What have I lov'd, but wracke of others weale?
Where have I done a deede deserving well?
How, what, when, and where, have I bestow'd a day,
That tended not to some notorious ill?
My life repleate with rage and tyrannie,
Craues little pittie for so strange a death.
Or, who will say that *John* deceasde too soone?
Who will not say, he rather liv'd too long?
Dishonour did attaint me in my life,
And shame attendeth *John* unto his death.
Why did I scape the fury of the French,
And dide not by the temper of their swords?
Shamelesse my life, and shamefully it ends,
Scorned by my foes, disdained of my friends.

Bastard.

Forgive the world and all your earthly foes,
And call on Christ, who is your latest friend.

John.

My tongue doth falter; *Philip*, I tell thee man,
Since *John* did yeeld unto the priest of *Rome*,
Nor he nor his have prospered on the earth:
Curst are his blessings, and his curse is blisse.
But in the spirit I crie unto my God,
As did the kingly prophet *David* cry,
(Whose hands, as mine, with murder were attaint)
I am not he shall build the Lord a house,
Or roote these locusts from the face of earth:
But if my dying heart deceive me not,
From out these loynes shall spring a kingly branch
Whose armes shall reach unto the gates of *Rome*,
And with his feete treades downe the strumpets pride,
That sits upon the chaire of *Babylon*.
Philip, my heart strings breake, the poysons flame
Hath overcome in me weake natures power,
And in the faith of *Jesu John* doth die."

(4) SCENE VII.—
At Worcester must his body be interred;
For so he will'd it.]

According to Holinshed, King John was buried at Croxton Abbey, in Staffordshire; but a stone coffin, containing his body, was discovered in the Cathedral Church of Worcester, July 17, 1797.

(5) SCENE VII.—
Nought shall make us rue,
If England to itself do rest but true.]

This conclusion is borrowed from the old play:—

"Let *England* live but true within it selfe,
And all the world can never wrong her state.
Lewes, thou shalt be bravely shipt to Fraunce,
For never *Frenchman* got of *English* ground
The twentith part that thou hast conquered.
Dolphin, thy hand: to Worster we will march:
Lords all, lay hands to beare your soveraigne
With obsequies of honour to his grave:
If *England* peeres and people joyne in one,
Nor pope, nor France, nor Spaine can do them wrong."

CRITICAL OPINIONS ON KING JOHN.

"If 'King John,' as a whole, be not entitled to class among the very first-rate compositions of our author, it can yet exhibit some scenes of superlative beauty and effect, and two characters supported with unfailing energy and consistency.

"The bastard Faulconbridge, though not, perhaps, a very amiable personage, being somewhat too interested and worldly-minded in his conduct to excite much of our esteem, has, notwithstanding, so large a portion of *the very spirit of Plantagenet* in him; so much heroism, gaiety, and fire, in his constitution; and, in spite of his avowed accommodation to the times,—

> 'For he is but a bastard to the time,
> That doth not smack of observation,' &c.

such an open and undaunted turn of mind, that we cannot refuse him our admiration; nor, on account of his fidelity to John, however ill-deserved, our occasional sympathy and attachment. The alacrity and intrepidity of his daring spirit are nobly supported to the very last; where we find him exerting every nerve to rouse and animate the conscience-stricken soul of the tyrant.

"In the person of Lady Constance *Maternal Grief*, the most interesting passion of the play, is developed in all its strength; the picture penetrates to the inmost heart; and seared must those feelings be, which can withstand so powerful an appeal; for all the emotions of the fondest affection and the wildest despair, all the rapid transitions of anguish, and approximating frenzy, are wrought up into the scene with a truth of conception which rivals that of nature herself.

"The innocent and beauteous Arthur, rendered doubly attractive by the sweetness of his disposition and the severity of his fate, is thus described by his doting mother:—

> 'But thou art fair, and at thy birth, dear boy!
> Nature and Fortune join'd to make thee great;
> Of Nature's gifts thou may'st with lilies boast,
> And with the half-blown rose.'

When he is captured, therefore, and imprisoned by John, and consequently sealed for destruction, who but Shakspeare could have done justice to the agonizing sorrows of the parent? Her invocation to Death, and her address to Pandulph, paint maternal despair with a force which no imagination can augment, and of which the tenderness and pathos have never been exceeded.

"Independent of the scenes which unfold the striking characters of Constance and Faulconbridge, there are two others in the play which may vie with anything that Shakspeare has produced; namely, the scene between John and Hubert, and that between Hubert and Arthur. The former, where the usurper obscurely intimates to Hubert his bloody wishes, is conducted in a manner so masterly that we behold the dark and turbulent soul of John lying naked before us in all its deformity, and shrinking with fear even from the enunciation of its own vile purposes. 'It is one of the scenes,' as Mr. Steevens has well observed, 'to which may be promised a lasting commendation. Art could add little to its perfection; and time itself can take nothing from its beauties.'

"The scene with Hubert and the executioners, where the hapless Arthur supplicates for mercy, almost lacerates the heart itself; and is only rendered supportable by the tender and alleviating impression which the sweet innocence and artless eloquence of the poor child fix with indelible influence on the mind. Well may it be said, in the language of our poet, that he who can behold this scene without the gushing tribute of a tear,—

> 'Is fit for treasons, stratagems, and spoils;—
> Let no such man be trusted.'

CRITICAL OPINIONS.

"As for the character of John, which, from its meanness and imbecility, seems not well calculated for dramatic representation, Shakspeare has contrived, towards the close of the drama, to excite in his behalf some degree of interest and commiseration; especially in the dying scene, where the fallen monarch, in answer to the inquiry of his son as to the state of his feelings, mournfully exclaims,—

'Poison'd,—ill fare;—dead, forsook, cast off.'"

DRAKE.

"The dramas derived from the English history, ten in number, form one of the most valuable of Shakspeare's works, and partly the fruit of his maturest age. I say advisedly *one* of his works, for the poet evidently intended them to form one great whole. It is, as it were, an historical heroic poem in the dramatic form, of which the separate plays constitute the rhapsodies. The principal features of the events are exhibited with such fidelity; their causes, and even their secret springs, are placed in such a clear light, that we may attain from them a knowledge of history in all its truth, while the living picture makes an impression on the imagination which can never be effaced.

"In King John the political and warlike events are dressed out with solemn pomp, for the very reason that they possess but little of true grandeur. The falsehood and selfishness of the monarch speak in the style of a manifesto. Conventional dignity is most indispensable where personal dignity is wanting. The bastard Faulconbridge is the witty interpreter of this language; he ridicules the secret springs of politics without disapproving of them; for he owns that he is endeavouring to make his fortune by similar means, and wishes rather to belong to the deceivers than the deceived, for in his view of the world there is no other choice. His litigation with his brother respecting the succession of his pretended father, by which he effects his acknowledgment at court as natural son of the most chivalrous king of England, Richard Cœur-de-Lion, forms a very entertaining and original prelude in the play itself. When, amidst so many disguises of real sentiments, and so much insincerity of expression, the poet shows us human nature without a veil, and allows us to take deep views of the inmost recesses of the mind, the impression produced is only the more deep and powerful. The short scene in which John urges Hubert to put out of the way Arthur, his young rival for the possession of the throne, is superlatively masterly; the cautious criminal hardly ventures to say to himself what he wishes the other to do. The young and amiable prince becomes a sacrifice of unprincipled ambition; his fate excites the warmest sympathy. When Hubert, about to put out his eyes with the hot iron, is softened by his prayers, our compassion would be almost overwhelming, were it not sweetened by the winning innocence of Arthur's childish speeches. Constance's maternal despair on her son's imprisonment is also of the highest beauty; and even the last moments of John,—an unjust and feeble prince, whom we can neither respect nor admire,—are yet so portrayed as to extinguish our displeasure with him, and fill us with serious considerations on the arbitrary deeds and the inevitable fate of mortals."—SCHLEGEL.

A MIDSUMMER NIGHT'S
DREAM

A MIDSUMMER NIGHT'S DREAM.

THE earliest editions of this drama are two quartos, both published in 1600, one by Thomas Fisher, the other by James Roberts, entitled, "A Midsommer Nights dreame. As it hath beene sundry times publickely acted, by the Right honourable, the Lord Chamberlaine his seruants. Written by William Shakespeare." Fisher's impression was duly registered at Stationers' Hall; but no memorandum of Roberts's has ever been found: and from this circumstance, and the greater accuracy of its text, the former has usually been considered the authorized version. Yet, strange to say, the player editors of the first folio, when they reprinted the work twenty-three years afterwards, adopted the text of Roberts, and appear to have been unacquainted altogether with the more correct quarto of Fisher.

Malone, in his attempt to determine the chronological order in which these plays were written, assigns the composition of "A Midsummer Night's Dream" to 1594; and Titania's fine description of the unnatural succession of the seasons and the "progeny of evils," which fairy discords had brought upon the "human mortals," is singularly applicable to a state of things prevalent in England during the years 1593 and 1594. Strype (*Annals, b.* IV. *p.* 211) has printed an extract from one of Dr. J. King's "Lectures upon Jonas," preached at York in 1594, in which that divine reminds his hearers of the various signs of God's wrath with which England was visited in 1593 and 1594; as storms, pestilence, dearth, and unseasonable weather. Of the last he says, "Remember that the spring" (that year that the plague broke out) "was very unkind, by means of the abundance of rains that fell; our July hath been like to a February; our June even as an April; so that the air must needs be corrupted." Then, having spoken of the three successive years of scarcity, he adds—"and see whether the Lord doth not threaten us much more, by sending such unseasonable weather and storms of rain among us; which, if we will observe, and compare it with that which is past, we may say, that the course of nature is very much inverted; our years are turned upside down; our summers are no summers: our harvests are no harvests: our seeds-times are no seeds-times." The passage is quoted by Blakeway; and it certainly bears a striking resemblance to the picture drawn by the Fairy Queen, beginning,—

> "Therefore the winds piping to us in vain," &c.

But we are not disposed to attach much importance to these coincidences as settling the date of the play, and still less to the interpretation of the well-known lines,—

> "The thrice three Muses mourning for the death
> Of learning, late deceas'd in beggary,"—

which Warton and Malone conceive to be an allusion either to Spenser's poem, "The Tears of the Muses on the Neglect and Contempt of Learning," or to the death of Spenser. The poem in question was first published in 1591, three years before the period fixed for the production of this piece, and the death of Spenser did not take place till 1599, five years after it. Mr. Knight conjectures, with more plausibility, that the allusion was to the erring but unfortunate Robert Greene, who died in 1592. Whatever uncertainty may attend these speculations, the internal evidence of the play proves at least that it was written in the full vigour of Shakespeare's youthful genius, and subsequent, there is every probability, to "The Two Gentlemen of Verona," "Love's Labour 's Lost," "The Comedy of Errors," "The Taming of the Shrew," and "Romeo and Juliet."

The commentators have been even less successful in their attempts to discover the origin of "A Midsummer Night's Dream," than in fixing the period of its production. Their persistence in assigning the ground-work of the fable to Chaucer's "Knight's Tale," is a remarkable instance of the docility with which succeeding writers will adopt, one after the other, an assertion that has really little or no foundation in fact. There is scarcely any resemblance whatever between Chaucer's tale and Shakespeare's play, beyond that of the scene in both being laid at the Court of Theseus. The Palamon, Arcite, and Emilie of the former are very different persons indeed from the Demetrius, Lysander, Helena, and Hermia, of the latter. Chaucer has made Duke

Theseus a leading character in his story, and has ascribed the unearthly incidents to mythological personages, conformable to a legend which professes to narrate events that actually happened in Greece. Shakespeare, on the other hand, has merely adopted Theseus, whose exploits he was acquainted with through the pages of North's Plutarch, as a well-known character of romance, in subordination to whom the rest of the *dramatis personæ* might fret their hour; and has employed for supernatural machinery those "airy nothings" familiar to the literature and traditions of various people and nearly all ages. There is little at all in common between the two stories except the name Theseus, the representative of which appears in Shakespeare simply as a prince who lived in times when the introduction of ethereal beings, such as Oberon, Titania, and Puck, was in accordance with tradition and romance.

Beyond one or two passing allusions, there is no attempt to individualize either the man or the country, and, but for these, Theseus might have been called by any other name, and have been lord of any other territory. There is another enunciation of the critics, which requires to be taken with considerable modification: we are told that the characters of the play are classical, while the accessories are Gothic; but the distinction implied is not perhaps so great as we have been led to believe. Godwin has called Theseus the "knight-errant" of antiquity, from which it might be inferred that the knight-errant of the middle ages was a very different person to the romantic hero of ancient times: but, in truth, the two characters were almost identical, as the history of Theseus proves. What material difference, for example, is there between his victory over the Minotaur, and that of Guy, the renowned Earl of Warwick, over the Dun cow? The combats with dragons and other ferocious monsters, the protection of the virtuous and the weak against the wicked and the strong, fluctuation of good and evil fortune, adventures with the fair sex, and engagements with supernatural enemies, these were the incidents of every story in which a warrior was made to figure as the hero of romance. Nor is there anything peculiarly Gothic in the imaginary population of the fairy-world. It is not improbable that many of our legends connected with this fabulous race were derived indirectly from Greece itself. It is impossible to read the Golden Ass of Apuleius, one of the few prose works of imagination which have been transmitted to us from ancient times, without being struck by the similarity of classic and Gothic literature in this department of romance. The Fawns, Satyrs, and Dryads of the Greeks were undoubtedly of a kindred origin with the woodland fairies of more recent times, and the intervention of an agency known as witchcraft is alike traceable in both ages.

There can be little doubt that Golding's translation of the story of Pyramus and Thisbe suggested the interlude by the hard-handed men of Athens, as North's Plutarch certainly furnished the characters of Theseus and his "bouncing Amazon;" but that which constitutes the charm and essence of the play, the union of those gross materials with the delicate, benign, and sportive beings of fairy-land, "lighter than the gossamer, and smaller than a cowslip's bell," was the pure creation of Shakespeare's own illimitable and delightful fancy.

Persons Represented.

Theseus, *Duke of Athens.*
Egeus, *father to* Hermia.
Lysander, *in love with* Hermia.
Demetrius, *beloved of* Helena.
Philostrate, *master of the sports to* Theseus.

Quince, *the carpenter.*	*Clowns, representing in the* Interlude,—	*The Prologue.*
Snug, *the joiner.*		Pyramus.
Bottom, *the weaver.*		Thisbe.
Flute, *the bellows-mender.*		Wall.
Snout, *the tinker.*		Lion.
Starveling, *the tailor.*		Moonshine.

Hippolyta, *Queen of the* Amazons, *betrothed to* Theseus.

Hermia.
Helena.

Oberon, *king of the fairies.*
Titania, *queen of the fairies.*
Puck, *or* Robin Goodfellow, *a fairy.*

Peas-blossom.	*fairies.*
Cobweb.	
Moth.	
Mustard-seed.	

Other fairies attending the King and Queen.
Attendants upon Theseus *and* Hippolyta.

SCENE.—Athens, *and an adjacent Wood.*

ACT I.

SCENE I.—Athens. *A Room in the Palace of* Theseus.

Enter Theseus, Hippolyta, Philostrate, *and* Attendants.

The. Now, fair Hippolyta, our nuptial hour
Draws on apace; four happy days bring in
Another moon: but, oh, methinks, how slow
This old moon wanes! she lingers my desires,
Like to a step-dame, or a dowager,
Long withering out a young man's revenue.

Hip. Four days will quickly steep themselves in nights;
Four nights will quickly dream away the time;

And then the moon, like to a silver bow
New[a] bent in heaven, shall behold the night
Of our solemnities.

THE. Go, Philostrate,
Stir up the Athenian youth to merriments;
Awake the pert(1) and nimble spirit of mirth;
Turn melancholy forth to funerals,
The pale companion is not for our pomp.
[*Exit* PHILOSTRATE.
Hippolyta, I woo'd thee with my sword,
And won thy love, doing thee injuries;
But I will wed thee in another key,
With pomp, with triumph, and with revelling.

Enter EGEUS, HERMIA, LYSANDER, *and* DEMETRIUS.

EGE. Happy be Theseus, our renowned duke!

THE. Thanks, good Egeus. What 's the news with thee?

EGE. Full of vexation come I, with complaint
Against my child, my daughter Hermia:
Stand forth, Demetrius. My noble lord,
This man hath my consent to marry her.—
Stand forth, Lysander:—and, my gracious duke,
This man hath bewitch'd the bosom of my child:
Thou, thou, Lysander, thou hast given her rhymes,
And interchang'd love-tokens with my child:
Thou hast by moonlight at her window sung,
With feigning voice, verses of feigning love;
And stol'n the impression of her fantasy
With bracelets of thy hair, rings, gawds, conceits,
Knacks, trifles, nosegays, sweet-meats; messengers
Of strong prevailment in unharden'd youth:
With cunning hast thou filch'd my daughter's heart;
Turn'd her obedience, which is due to me,
To stubborn harshness.—And, my gracious duke,
Be it so, she will not here before your grace
Consent to marry with Demetrius,
I beg the ancient privilege of Athens,
As she is mine, I may dispose of her:
Which shall be either to this gentleman,
Or to her death; according to our law,
Immediately provided in that case.

THE. What say you, Hermia? be advis'd, fair maid:
To you your father should be as a god;
One that compos'd your beauties; yea, and one
To whom you are but as a form in wax,
By him imprinted, and within his power
To leave the figure, or disfigure it.
Demetrius is a worthy gentleman.

HER. So is Lysander.

THE. In himself he is:
But, in this kind, wanting your father's voice,
The other must be held the worthier.

HER. I would my father look'd but with my eyes!

THE. Rather, your eyes must with his judgment look.

HER. I do entreat your grace to pardon me.
I know not by what power I am made bold,
Nor how it may concern my modesty,
In such a presence here, to plead my thoughts:
But I beseech your grace that I may know
The worst that may befal me in this case,
If I refuse to wed Demetrius.

THE. Either to die the death, or to abjure
For ever the society of men.
Therefore, fair Hermia, question your desires,
Know of your youth,[b] examine well your blood,
Whether, if you yield not to your father's choice,
You can endure the livery of a nun;
For aye to be in shady cloister mew'd,
To live a barren sister all your life,
Chanting faint hymns to the cold fruitless moon.
Thrice blessed they that master so their blood,
To undergo such maiden pilgrimage:
But earthly happier* is the rose distill'd,
Than that, which, withering on the virgin thorn,
Grows, lives, and dies, in single blessedness.

HER. So will I grow, so live, so die, my lord,
Ere I will yield my virgin patent up
Unto his lordship,[c] whose unwished yoke
My soul consents not to give sovereignty.[d]

THE. Take time to pause; and, by the next new moon,
(The sealing-day betwixt my love and me,
For everlasting bond of fellowship,)
Upon that day either prepare to die,
For disobedience to your father's will;
Or else, to wed Demetrius, as he would;
Or on Diana's altar to protest,
For aye, austerity and single life.

---

[a] New *bent in heaven,*—] The early editions read *now*, which was corrected by Rowe.

[b] Know of your youth,—] *Know*, here, as in the Second Part of "Henry IV." Act I. Sc. 3,—

"—— Know our own estate,"

seems to be used in the sense of *ascertain*.

[c] *Unto his* lordship,—] That is, *dominion, authority.*

[d] "—— whose unwished yoke
My soul consents not to give sovereignty."]

That is, give sovereignty *to*. An elliptical mode of expression not unfrequent in Shakespeare. Thus, in the "Winter's Tale," Act II. Sc. 1:—

"—— even as bad as those,
That vulgars give bold'st titles" [*to*.]

Again, in "Othello," Act I. Sc. 3:—

"What conjuration and what mighty magic—
I won his daughter" [*with*.]

Again, in "Henry VII." Act II. Sc. 1:—

"—— whoever the king removes,
The cardinal instantly will find employment" [*for*.]

(*) Old editions, *earthlier happy*.

DEM. Relent, sweet Hermia;—and, Lysander, yield
Thy crazed title to my certain right.
LYS. You have her father's love, Demetrius;
Let me have Hermia's: do you marry him.
EGE. Scornful Lysander! true, he hath my love;
And what is mine my love shall render him;
And she is mine; and all my right of her
I do estate unto Demetrius.
LYS. I am, my lord, as well deriv'd as he,
As well possess'd; my love is more than his;
My fortunes every way as fairly rank'd,
If not with vantage, as Demetrius';
And, which is more than all these boasts can be,
I am belov'd of beauteous Hermia:
Why should not I then prosecute my right?
Demetrius, I'll avouch it to his head,
Made love to Nedar's daughter, Helena,
And won her soul; and she, sweet lady, dotes,
Devoutly dotes, dotes in idolatry,
Upon this spotted and inconstant man.
THE. I must confess that I have heard so much,
And with Demetrius thought to have spoke thereof,
But, being over-full of self-affairs,
My mind did lose it.—But, Demetrius, come;
And come, Egeus; you shall go with me,
I have some private schooling for you both.
For you, fair Hermia, look you arm yourself
To fit your fancies to your father's will;
Or else the law of Athens yields you up
(Which by no means we may extenuate)
To death, or to a vow of single life.
Come, my Hippolyta; what cheer, my love?
Demetrius, and Egeus, go along:
I must employ you in some business
Against our nuptial; and confer with you
Of something nearly that concerns yourselves.
EGE. With duty and desire, we follow you.
[*Exeunt* THES., HIP., EGE., DEM., *and Train.*
LYS. How now, my love? Why is your cheek so pale?
How chance the roses there do fade so fast?
HER. Belike for want of rain, which I could well
Beteem[a] them from the tempest of mine eyes.
LYS. Ay me! * for aught that I could ever† read,
Could ever hear by tale or history,
The course of true love never did run smooth:[b]
But, either it was different in blood;—
HER. O cross! too high to be enthrall'd to low!‡
LYS. Or else misgraffed, in respect of years;
HER. O spite! too old to be engag'd to young!
LYS. Or else it stood upon the choice of friends;§
HER. O hell! to choose love by another's eye!
LYS. Or, if there were a sympathy in choice,
War, death, or sickness did lay siege to it;
Making it momentany[c] as a sound,
Swift as a shadow, short as any dream,
Brief as the lightning in the collied[d] night,
That, in a spleen,(2) unfolds both heaven and earth,
And ere a man hath power to say,—Behold!
The jaws of darkness do devour it up:
So quick bright things come to confusion.
HER. If then true lovers have been ever cross'd,
It stands as an edict in destiny:
Then let us teach our trial patience,
Because it is a customary cross;
As due to love, as thoughts, and dreams, and sighs,
Wishes, and tears, poor fancy's[e] followers.
LYS. A good persuasion; therefore, hear me, Hermia.
I have a widow aunt, a dowager
Of great revénue, and she hath no child;
From Athens is her house remote || seven leagues;
And she respects me as her only son.
There, gentle Hermia, may I marry thee,
And to that place the sharp Athenian law
Cannot pursue us. If thou lov'st me then,
Steal forth thy father's house to-morrow night;
And in the wood, a league without the town,
Where I did meet thee once with Helena,
To do observance to ¶ a morn of May,(3)
There will I stay for thee.

(*) First folio omits, *Ay me.* (†) First folio, *ever I could.* (‡) Old copies, *love.* (§) First folio, *merit.* (||) First folio, *remov'd.* (¶) First folio, *for.*

a —— *which I could well*
Beteem *them*—]
Allow them. In this sense the word occurs in "Hamlet," Act I. Sc. 2:—

"—— so loving to my mother
That he might not *beteem* the winds of heaven
Visit her face too roughly."

And in Spenser's "Faërie Queen," II. viii. 19:—

"So would I, said the enchanter, glad and faine
Beteeme to you this sword you to defend."

b The course of true love never did run smooth:] This sentiment is not uncommon, but it has never been so beautifully expressed. It occurs in Milton's "Paradise Lost," Book x. 896, et seqq., and we meet with it in Middleton's "Blurt, Master Constable," Act III. Sc. 1:—

"—— I never heard
Of any true affection, but 't was nipt
With care."

c *Making it* momentany—] So the two quartos; the folio, 1623, reads *momentary*. We have improvidently permitted too many of our old expressions to become obsolete.

d *In the* collied *night*,—] In the *black* or *dark* night. *Collied*, literally, is *smutted with coal*. So, in "The Marriage of Witt and Wisdome," 1579:—"Then let her set a fooles bable on his head, and *colling* his face."

"And now of a scollar
I will make him a collier."
Ibid.

So, too, in Ben Jonson's "Poetaster:"—

"——Thou hast not *collied* thy face enough."

e Fancy's *followers*.] *Fancy* is used here in the same sense as in Act II. Sc. 2:—

"In maiden meditation, *fancy* free;—"

And in Act IV. Sc. 1:—

"Fair Helena in *fancy* following me."

HER. My good Lysander!
I swear to thee by Cupid's strongest bow;
By his best arrow with the golden head;
By the simplicity of Venus' doves;
By that which knitteth souls, and prospers loves;[a]
And by that fire which burn'd the Carthage queen,
When the false Trojan under sail was seen;
By all the vows that ever men have broke,
In number more than ever women spoke;—
In that same place thou hast appointed me,
To-morrow truly will I meet with thee.
LYS. Keep promise, love. Look, here comes Helena.

Enter HELENA.

HER. God speed fair Helena! Whither away?
HEL. Call you me fair? that fair again unsay.
Demetrius loves your fair:[b] O happy fair!
Your eyes are lode-stars;(4) and your tongue's sweet air
More tuneable than lark to shepherd's ear,
When wheat is green, when hawthorn buds appear.
Sickness is catching; O, were favour[c] so,
Your words I'd catch, fair Hermia, ere I go,[d]
My ear should catch your voice, my eye your eye,
My tongue should catch your tongue's sweet melody.
Were the world mine, Demetrius being bated,
The rest I'll give to be to you translated.
O, teach me how you look, and with what art
You sway the motion of Demetrius' heart.
HER. I frown upon him, yet he loves me still.
HEL. O that your frowns would teach my smiles such skill!
HER. I give him curses, yet he gives me love.
HEL. O that my prayers could such affection move!
HER. The more I hate, the more he follows me.
HEL. The more I love, the more he hateth me.
HER. His folly, Helena, is no fault of mine.[e]
HEL. None, but your beauty; would that fault were mine!
HER. Take comfort, he no more shall see my [face;
Lysander and myself will fly this place.
Before the time I did Lysander see,
Seem'd Athens like a paradise to me:
O then, what graces in my love do dwell,
That he hath turn'd a heaven unto a* hell!
LYS. Helen, to you our minds we will unfold:
To-morrow night, when Phœbe doth behold
Her silver visage in the wat'ry glass,
Decking with liquid pearl the bladed grass,
(A time that lovers' flights doth still conceal,)
Through Athens' gates have we devis'd to steal.
HER. And in the wood, where often you and I
Upon faint primrose beds were wont to lie,
Emptying our bosoms of their counsel sweet,
There my Lysander and myself shall meet:
And thence, from Athens, turn away our eyes,
To seek new friends and stranger companies.[f]
Farewell, sweet playfellow, pray thou for us,
And good luck grant thee thy Demetrius!—
Keep word, Lysander: we must starve our sight
From lovers' food, till morrow deep midnight.
[*Exit* HERMIA.
LYS. I will, my Hermia.—Helena, adieu:
As you on him, Demetrius dote† on you!
[*Exit* LYSANDER.
HEL. How happy some o'er other-some can be!
Through Athens I am thought as fair as she.
But what of that? Demetrius thinks not so;
He will not know what all but he do know.
And as he errs, doting on Hermia's eyes,
So I, admiring of his qualities.
Things base and vile, holding no quantity,
Love can transpose to form and dignity:
Love looks not with the eyes, but with the mind,
And therefore is wing'd Cupid painted blind.
Nor hath love's mind of any judgment taste,
Wings, and no eyes, figure unheedy haste;
And therefore is love said to be a child,
Because in choice he is so oft‡ beguil'd.
As waggish boys in game themselves forswear,
So the boy love is perjur'd everywhere:
For ere Demetrius look'd on Hermia's eyne,
He hail'd down oaths, that he was only mine;
And when this hail some heat from Hermia felt,
So he dissolv'd, and showers of oaths did melt.
I will go tell him of fair Hermia's flight:

(*) First folio, *into*. (†) First folio, *dotes*. (‡) First folio, *is often*.

[a] *And prospers* loves;] This is the reading of the quarto published by Fisher; that by Roberts, and the folio, have *love*.

[b] *Your* fair:] That is, your *beauty*. See "Love's Labour's Lost," note (a), p. 69, and the "Comedy of Errors," note (b), p. 121. The folio reads, *you* fair.

[c] *O, were* favour *so,*—] *Favour*, in Shakespeare sometimes means *countenance, features*, and occasionally, as here, *good graces* generally.

[d] *Your words* I'd catch, *fair Hermia, ere I* go,—] The old copies read, "Your words *I* catch, fair Hermia, ere I go." The very slight alteration, which gives intelligibility to the line, was first made in the folio, 1632. Helena would catch not only the beauty of her rival's aspect, and the melody of her tones, but her language also. If the lection here proposed is inadmissible, we must adopt that of Hanmer,—"Yours would I catch," for the old text will never be accepted as the author's.

[e] *His folly, Helena, is* no fault *of mine.*] Thus, Fisher's quarto; that by Roberts, and the folio, have, "*none* of mine."

[f] *And* stranger companies.] In the old text the passage runs as follows:—

"And in the wood, where often you and I
Upon faint primrose beds were wont to lie,
Emptying our bosoms of their counsel *swell'd*,
There my Lysander and myself shall meet,
And thence from Athens turn away our eyes
To seek new friends and *strange companions*."

The restoration of "counsel *sweet*," and "*stranger companies*," is due to Theobald, and as the rest of the scene from the entrance of Helena is in rhyme, there can be no reasonable doubt that these four lines were originally in rhyme also.

Then to the wood will he to-morrow night,
Pursue her; and for this* intelligence
If I have thanks, it is a dear expense:[a]
But herein mean I to enrich my pain,
To have his sight thither and back again. [*Exit.*

(*) First folio, *his*.

[a] *It is a* dear expense:] Steevens supposes this to mean "it will *cost him much* (be a severe constraint on his feelings), to make even so slight a return for my communication." Is not the meaning rather, that, as to gratify her lover with this intelligence she makes the most painful sacrifice of her feelings, his thanks, even if obtained, are dearly bought? Mr. Collier's MS. annotator reads,—

"If I have thanks, it is *dear recompense;*"

which cannot be right, since Helena expressly tells us her recompense will be,—

"To have his sight thither and back again."

SCENE II.—*The same. A Room in* Quince's *house.*

Enter Snug, Bottom, Flute, Snout, Quince, *and* Starveling.[b](5)

Quin. Is all our company here?

[b] *Enter* Quince, *&c.*] In the old stage direction, "Enter Quince the Carpenter, Snug the Joyner, Bottom the Weaver, Flute the Bellows-mender, Snout the Tinker, and Starveling the Taylor."

BOT. You were best to call them generally, man by man, according to the scrip.

QUIN. Here is the scroll of every man's name, which is thought fit, through all Athens, to play in our interlude before the duke and the duchess, on his wedding-day at night.

BOT. First, good Peter Quince, say what the play treats on; then read the names of the actors; and so grow* to a point.[a]

QUIN. Marry, our play is—The most lamentable comedy, and most cruel death of Pyramus and Thisbe.(6)

BOT. A very good piece of work, I assure you, and a merry. Now, good Peter Quince, call forth your actors by the scroll: Masters, spread yourselves.

QUIN. Answer, as I call you.—Nick Bottom, the weaver.

BOT. Ready. Name what part I am for, and proceed.

QUIN. You, Nick Bottom, are set down for Pyramus.

BOT. What is Pyramus? a lover, or a tyrant?

QUIN. A lover that kills himself most gallant† for love.

BOT. That will ask some tears in the true performing of it. If I do it, let the audience look to their eyes; I will move storms; I will condole in some measure. To the rest yet,[b] my chief humour is for a tyrant: I could play Ercles rarely, or a part to tear a cat in, to make all split[c] the raging rocks; and shivering shocks shall break the locks of prison-gates, and Phibbus' car shall shine from far, and make and mar the foolish fates.[d] This was lofty!—Now name the rest of the players.—This is Ercles' vein, a tyrant's vein; a lover is more condoling.

QUIN. Francis Flute, the bellows-mender.

FLU. Here, Peter Quince.

QUIN. Flute,‡ you must take Thisbe on you.

FLU. What is Thisbe? a wandering knight?

QUIN. It is the lady that Pyramus must love.

FLU. Nay, faith, let not me play a woman; I have a beard coming.

QUIN. That's all one; you shall play it in a mask, and you may speak as small as you will.

BOT. An I may hide my face, let me play Thisbe too: I'll speak in a monstrous little voice;—*Thisne, Thisne,*—*Ah, Pyramus, my lover dear;—thy Thisbe dear!* and—*lady dear!*

QUIN. No, no, you must play Pyramus; and, Flute, you Thisbe.

BOT. Well, proceed.

QUIN. Robin Starveling, the tailor.

STAR. Here, Peter Quince.

QUIN. Robin Starveling, you must play Thisbe's mother.—Tom Snout, the tinker.

SNOUT. Here, Peter Quince.

QUIN. You, Pyramus' father; myself, Thisbe's father;—Snug, the joiner, you, the lion's part:—and, I hope, here* is a play fitted.

SNUG. Have you the lion's part written? pray you, if it be, give it me, for I am slow of study.

QUIN. You may do it extempore, for it is nothing but roaring.

BOT. Let me play the lion too: I will roar, that I will do any man's heart good to hear me; I will roar, that I will make the duke say, *Let him roar again, let him roar again.*

QUIN. An† you should do it too terribly, you would fright the duchess and the ladies, that they would shriek; and that were enough to hang us all.

ALL. That would hang us, every mother's son.

BOT. I grant you, friends, if that you should fright the ladies out of their wits, they would have no more discretion but to hang us; but I will aggravate my voice so, that I will roar you as gently as any sucking dove; I will roar you‡ an't were any nightingale.

QUIN. You can play no part but Pyramus: for Pyramus is a sweet-faced man; a proper man as one shall see in a summer's day; a most lovely,

---

(*) First folio, *grow on*. (†) First folio, *gallantly*. (‡) First folio omits *Flute*.

(*) First folio, *there*. (†) First folio, *If*. (‡) First folio omits, *you*.

[a] *And so* grow to a point.] *And so to business.* A common colloquial phrase formerly:—

"Our reasons will be infinite I trow,
Unless *unto some other point we grow*."
The Arraignment of Paris, 1584.

[b] To the rest yet,—] So the old copies. The modern editors place a colon after *rest*, "To the rest: yet my chief humour," &c.; a deviation which originated perhaps in unconsciousness of one of the senses Shakespeare attributes to the word *yet*. "To the rest yet," is simply "To the rest now," or, as he shortly after repeats it, "*Now*, name the rest of the players."

[c] *I could play* Ercles *rarely, or a part to* tear a cat *in*,—] Hercules and his labours formed a popular subject of entertainment on the early English stage. The player in Greene's "Groat's-worth of Wit," 1592, recounts to Roberto how he had "terribly thundered" the Twelve Labours of Hercules. He could probably, too, have enumerated among his performances *a part to tear a cat in*, for this allusion was evidently to an incident familiar to the auditory. In "Histriomastix, or the Player Whipt," an anonymous production published in 1610, some soldiers drag in a company of players; and the captain addresses one of them with, "Sirrah, this is you that would rend and *tear a cat* upon the stage," &c. And in "The Roaring Girl," 1611, one of the characters is called *Tear-cat*.

The expression, *to make all split*, is thought to be of nautical extraction; it is met with in many of the old dramas:—"Two roaring boys of Rome, that *made all split*."—Beaumont and Fletcher's "Scornful Lady," Act II. Sc. 3. Again in Chapman's play of "The Widow's Tears:"—"Her wit I must employ upon this business to prepare my next encounter, but in such a fashion as shall *make all split*."

[d] The foolish fates.] The chief humour of Bottom's "lofty" rant consists in the speaker's barbarous disregard of sense and rhythm; yet, notwithstanding this, and that the whole is printed as prose, carefully punctuated to be unintelligible in all the old copies, modern editors will persist in presenting it in good set doggrel rhyme.

gentleman-like man; therefore you must needs play Pyramus.

BOT. Well, I will undertake it. What beard were I best to play it in?

QUIN. Why, what you will.

BOT. I will discharge it in either your straw-colour beard, your orange-tawny beard, your purple-in-grain beard, or your French-crown-colour* beard, your perfect yellow.

QUIN. Some of your French crowns have no hair at all, and then you will play bare-faced.—But, masters, here are your parts: and I am to intreat you, request you, and desire you, to con them by to-morrow night, and meet me in the palace wood, a mile without the town, by moonlight; there will we* rehearse: for if we meet in the city we shall be dogg'd with company, and our devices known. In the mean time I will draw a bill of properties such as our play wants. I pray you, fail me not.

BOT. We will meet; and there we may rehearse most† obscenely and courageously. Take pains; be perfect; adieu.

QUIN. At the duke's oak we meet.

BOT. Enough. Hold, or cut bow-strings.(7)

[*Exeunt.*

(*) First folio, *coloured*.

(*) First folio, *we will*. (†) First folio, *more*.

ACT II.

SCENE I.—*A Wood near* Athens.

Enter, from opposite sides, a Fairy, *and* Puck.[a]

Puck. How now, spirit! whither wander you?
Fai. Over hill, over dale,
Thorough* bush, thorough brier,
Over park, over pale,
Thorough* flood, thorough fire,
I do wander everywhere,
Swifter than the moon's sphere;
And I serve the fairy queen,
To dew her orbs[b] upon the green:
The cowslips tall her pensioners be;
In their gold coats spots you see;
Those be rubies, fairy favours,
In those freckles live their savours:

(*) First folio, *through*.

[a] *Enter*, &c.] The original stage direction is "*Enter a Fairy at one doore, and* Robin Good-fellow *at another;*" and in the prefixes to his speeches, until the entrance of Oberon and Titania, Puck is thus designated.

[b] To dew her orbs—] The *orbs* are those circles in fields known as fairy rings, and popularly supposed to be produced by these "demi-puppets" in their moonlight revelry:—

"And in their courses make that *round*,
In meadows and in marshes found,
Of them so called the fairy ground."
Drayton's *Nymphidia*.

There is a peculiar propriety in the office assigned to the fairy of refreshing these ringlets, since we learn from Olaus Magnus, that the night-tripping spirits always parched up the grass on which they danced.

I must go seek some dew-drops here,
And hang a pearl in every cowslip's ear.
Farewell, thou lob[a] of spirits, I'll be gone;
Our queen and all her elves come here anon.

PUCK. The king doth keep his revels here to-night;
Take heed, the queen come not within his sight,
For Oberon is passing fell and wrath,
Because that she, as her attendant, hath
A lovely boy stol'n from an Indian king;
She never had so sweet a changeling:
And jealous Oberon would have the child
Knight of his train, to trace the forests wild:
But she, perforce, withholds the loved boy,
Crowns him with flowers, and makes him all her joy:
And now they never meet in grove, or green,
By fountain clear, or spangled star-light sheen,
But they do square;[b] that all their elves, for fear,
Creep into acorn-cups, and hide them there.

FAI. Either I mistake your shape and making quite,
Or else you are that shrewd and knavish sprite,
Call'd Robin Goodfellow;(1) are not you* he,
That frights the maidens of the villagery;
Skim milk; and sometimes labour in the quern,[c]
And bootless make the breathless housewife churn;
And sometime make the drink to bear no barm;
Mislead night wanderers, laughing at their harm?
Those that Hobgoblin call you, and sweet Puck,
You do their work, and they shall have good luck:
Are not you he?

PUCK. Thou speak'st aright;
I am that merry wanderer of the night.
I jest to Oberon, and make him smile,
When I a fat and bean-fed horse beguile,
Neighing in likeness of a filly† foal:
And sometime lurk I in a gossip's bowl,
In very likeness of a roasted crab;[d]
And, when she drinks, against her lips I bob,

---

[a] *Thou* lob *of spirits,*—] *Lob* here, I believe, is no more than another name for *clown*, or *fool;* and does not necessarily denote inactivity either of mind or body.

[b] *But they do* square;] To *square* in this place means to *quarrel*, and was commonly used in that sense by the old writers. Some have thought it derived from the French *quarrer*, which Cotgrave interprets, "*To strut*, or *square it, looke big out*," &c.

(*) First folio, *you not*. (†) First folio, *silly*.

[c] The quern,—] The handmill.

[d] *A roasted* crab;] That is, the *crab*, or *wild apple:*—

"Yet we will have in store a *crab* in the fire,
With Nut-browne ale."
Anonymous play, called The Famous Victories of Henry V

And on her wither'd dewlap pour the ale.
The wisest aunt, telling the saddest tale,
Sometime for three-foot stool mistaketh me;
Then slip I from her bum, down topples she,
And *tailor* cries,[a] and falls into a cough;
And then the whole quire hold their hips, and loffe,
And waxen[b] in their mirth, and neeze, and swear
A merrier hour was never wasted there.—
But room, Faëry, here comes Oberon.
FAI. And here my mistress:—Would that he were gone!

[a] And *tailor* cries,—] "The custom of crying *tailor*, at a sudden fall backwards, I think I remember to have observed. He that slips beside his chair falls as a tailor squats upon his board."—JOHNSON.

[b] *And* waxen—] *Waxen*, as Farmer surmised, is most probably a corruption of the old Saxon word *yexen, to hiccup*.

Enter OBERON, *on one side, with his Train, and* TITANIA, *on the other, with hers.*[a]

OBE. Ill met by moonlight, proud Titania.(2)
TITA. What, jealous Oberon? Fairies,* skip hence;
I have forsworn his bed and company.
OBE. Tarry, rash wanton. Am not I thy lord?
TITA. Then I must be thy lady. But I know
When thou hast† stolen away from fairy land,
And in the shape of Corin sat all day,
Playing on pipes of corn, and versing love
To amorous Phillida. Why art thou here,
Come from the farthest steep of India?
But that, forsooth, the bouncing Amazon,
Your buskin'd mistress, and your warrior love,
To Theseus must be wedded; and you come
To give their bed joy and prosperity.
OBE. How canst thou thus, for shame, Titania,
Glance at my credit with Hippolyta,
Knowing I know thy love to Theseus?
Didst thou not lead him through the glimmering night
From Perigenia, whom he ravished?
And make him with fair Æglé‡ break his faith,
With Ariadne, and Antiopa?(3)
TITA. These are the forgeries of jealousy:
And never, since the middle summer's spring,
Met we on hill, in dale, forest, or mead,
By paved fountain, or by rushy brook,
Or in the beached margent of the sea,
To dance our ringlets to the whistling wind,
But with thy brawls thou hast disturb'd our sport.
Therefore, the winds, piping to us in vain,
As in revenge, have suck'd up from the sea
Contagious fogs; which, falling in the land,
Have every pelting[b] river made so proud,
That they have overborne their continents:
The ox hath therefore stretch'd his yoke in vain,
The ploughman lost his sweat; and the green corn
Hath rotted, ere his youth attain'd a beard:
The fold stands empty in the drowned field,
And crows are fatted with the murrain flock;
The nine men's morris is filled up with mud; (4)
And the quaint mazes in the wanton green,
For lack of tread, are undistinguishable;
The human mortals want their winter here,[c]
No night is now with hymn or carol bless'd:—
Therefore, the moon, the governess of floods,
Pale in her anger, washes all the air,
That rheumatic diseases do abound:
And thorough* this distemperature, we see
The seasons alter: hoary-headed† frosts
Fall in the fresh lap of the crimson rose;
And on old Hyems' thin[d] and icy crown,
An odorous chaplet of sweet summer buds
Is, as in mockery, set. The spring, the summer,
The childing[e] autumn, angry winter, change
Their wonted liveries; and the 'mazed world,
By their increase, now knows not which is which;
And this same progeny of evils comes
From our debate, from our dissension;
We are their parents and original.
OBE. Do you amend it then; it lies in you:
Why should Titania cross her Oberon?
I do but beg a little changeling boy,
To be my henchman.[f]
TITA. Set your heart at rest,
The fairy land buys not the child of me.
His mother was a votaress of my order:
And, in the spiced Indian air, by night,
Full often hath she gossip'd by my side,
And sat with me on Neptune's yellow sands,
Marking the embarked traders on the flood;
When we have laugh'd to see the sails conceive,
And grow big-bellied, with the wanton wind:
Which she, with pretty and with swimming gait,
Following, (her womb then rich with my young squire,)
Would imitate; and sail upon the land,
To fetch me trifles, and return again,
As from a voyage, rich with merchandise.
But she, being mortal, of that boy did die;
And, for her sake, do I‡ rear up her boy:
And, for her sake, I will not part with him.
OBE. How long within this wood intend you stay?

(*) Old copies, *Fairy*. (†) First folio, *wast*. (‡) Old copies, *Eagles*.

(*) First folio, *through*. (†) First folio, *hoared-headed*. (‡) First folio, *I do*.

[a] *Enter*, &c.] According to the old stage direction, "*Enter the* King of Fairies *at one doore with his traine, and the* Queene *at another with hers*." All the modern editors, except Mr. Collier, mark this entrance as a new scene; upon what principle it is not easy to divine.

[b] *Have every* pelting *river*—] The folio reads *petty*. *Pelting* is *paltry, peddling, despicable:*—

"——— Jove would ne'er be quiet,
For every *pelting*, petty officer," &c.
Measure for Measure, Act II. Sc. 2.

[c] *The human mortals* want *their winter here,*—] *Want*, in this passage, does not appear to mean *need, lack, wish for*, &c., but to be used in the sense of *be without*. The human mortals are *without* their winter here. Thus, in Harrison's "Description of Britaine," p. 42:—"In like sort they *want* venomous beasts, chiefelie such as doo delight in hotter soile." It occurs, with the same meaning, in a well-known passage of "Macbeth," Act III. Sc. 6:—

"——— Men must not walk too late
Who cannot *want* the thought, how monstrous
It was," &c.;—

and is repeatedly found in the old writers with this signification.

[d] *And on old Hyems'* thin *and icy crown,*—] The ancient copies concur in reading, "Hyems *chin* and icy crown." The change was proposed by Tyrwhitt.

[e] *The* childing *autumn,*—] That is, the *teeming* autumn, *frugifer autumnus*.

[f] Henchman.] Page. The derivation is uncertain.

TITA. Perchance, till after Theseus' wedding-day.
If you will patiently dance in our round,
And see our moonlight revels, go with us;
If not, shun me, and I will spare your haunts.
OBE. Give me that boy, and I will go with thee.
TITA. Not for thy fairy kingdom. Fairies, away:
We shall chide downright, if I longer stay.
[*Exeunt* TITANIA *and her Train.*
OBE. Well, go thy way: thou shalt not from this grove,
Till I torment thee for this injury:
My gentle Puck, come hither. Thou remember'st
Since once I sat upon a promontory,
And heard a mermaid, on a dolphin's back,
Uttering such dulcet and harmonious breath,
That the rude sea grew civil at her song;
And certain stars shot madly from their spheres,
To hear the sea-maid's music.
PUCK. I remember.
OBE. That very time I saw,[a] (but thou couldst not,)
Flying between the cold moon and the earth,
Cupid all arm'd: a certain aim he took
At a fair vestal, throned by the west;
And loos'd his love-shaft smartly from his bow,
As it should pierce a hundred thousand hearts:
But I might see young Cupid's fiery shaft
Quench'd in the chaste beams of the watery moon;
And the imperial votaress passed on,
In maiden meditation, fancy-free.
Yet mark'd I where the bolt of Cupid fell:
It fell upon a little western flower,—
Before, milk-white, now purple with love's wound,—
And maidens call it love-in-idleness.
Fetch me that flower: the herb I shew'd thee once;
The juice of it on sleeping eyelids laid,

[a] *That very time* I saw,—] The quarto, published by Roberts, and the folio, read, "I *say*."

Will make or man or woman madly dote
Upon the next live creature that it sees.
Fetch me this herb, and be thou here again,
Ere the leviathan can swim a league.
PUCK. I'll put a girdle round about the earth
In forty minutes.[a] [*Exit* PUCK.
OBE. Having once this juice,
I'll watch Titania when she is asleep,
And drop the liquor of it in her eyes:
The next thing then* she waking looks upon,
(Be it on lion, bear, or wolf, or bull,
On meddling monkey, or on busy ape,)
She shall pursue it with the soul of love:
And ere I take this charm from off† her sight,
(As I can take it, with another herb,)
I'll make her render up her page to me.
But who comes here? I am invisible; (5)
And I will overhear their conference.

Enter DEMETRIUS, HELENA *following him.*

DEM. I love thee not, therefore pursue me not.
Where is Lysander, and fair Hermia?
The one I'll slay, the other slayeth me.[b]
Thou told'st me, they were stol'n unto‡ this wood.
And here am I, and wood[c] within this wood,
Because I cannot meet my Hermia.
Hence, get thee gone, and follow me no more.
HEL. You draw me, you hard-hearted adamant;
But yet you draw not iron, for my heart
Is true as steel. Leave you your power to draw,
And I shall have no power to follow you.
DEM. Do I entice you? Do I speak you fair?
Or, rather, do I not in plainest truth
Tell you—I do not, nor I cannot, love you?
HEL. And even for that do I love you§ the more.
I am your spaniel; and, Demetrius,
The more you beat me, I will fawn on you:
Use me but as your spaniel, spurn me, strike me,
Neglect me, lose me; only give me leave,
Unworthy as I am, to follow you.
What worser place can I beg in your love,
(And yet a place of high respect with me,)
Than to be used as you use¶ your dog?
DEM. Tempt not too much the hatred of my [spirit,
For I am sick when I do look on thee.
HEL. And I am sick when I look not on you.
DEM. You do impeach your modesty too much,
To leave the city, and commit yourself
Into the hands of one that loves you not;
To trust the opportunity of night,
And the ill counsel of a desert place,
With the rich worth of your virginity.
HEL. Your virtue is my privilege; for that
It is not night, when I do see your face,
Therefore I think I am not in the night:
Nor doth this wood lack worlds of company,
For you, in my respect, are all the world:
Then how can it be said, I am alone,
When all the world is here to look on me?
DEM. I'll run from thee, and hide me in the brakes,
And leave thee to the mercy of wild beasts.
HEL. The wildest hath not such a heart as you.[d]
Run when you will; the story shall be chang'd;
Apollo flies, and Daphne holds the chase;
The dove pursues the griffin; the mild hind
Makes speed to catch the tiger: bootless speed!
When cowardice pursues, and valour flies.
DEM. I will not stay thy questions; let me go:
Or, if thou follow me, do not believe
But I shall do thee mischief in the wood.
HEL. Ay, in the temple, in the town, and field,
You do me mischief. Fie, Demetrius!
Your wrongs do set a scandal on my sex:
We cannot fight for love, as men may do;
We should be woo'd, and were not made to woo.
[*Exit* DEM.
I'll* follow thee, and make a heaven of hell,
To die upon the hand I love so well.
[*Exit* HEL.
OBE. Fare thee well, nymph: ere he do leave this grove,
Thou shalt fly him, and he shall seek thy love.

Re-enter PUCK.

Hast thou the flower there? Welcome, wanderer.
PUCK. Ay, there it is.
OBE. I pray thee, give it me.

(*) First folio, *when*. (†) First folio, *off from*. (‡) First folio, *into*. (§) First folio, *thee*. (¶) First folio, *do*.

a *I'll put a girdle* round *about the earth*
In forty minutes.]

Roberts's quarto and the folio omit *round*. *To put a girdle round about the earth* seems to have been a proverbial mode of expressing a voyage round the world. It occurs in Chapman's "Bussy d'Ambois," Act I. Sc. 1. 1613:—

"And as great seamen, using all their wealth
And skills in Neptune's deep invisible paths,
In tall ships richly built, and ribb'd with brass,
To put a girdle round about the world."

(*) First folio, *I*.

And in Shirley's "Humorous Courtier," Act I. Sc. 1:—

"Thou hast been a traveller, and convers'd
With the Antipodes, almost *put a girdle*
About the world."

b *The one I'll* slay, *the other* slayeth *me.*] The old copies read, "The one I'll *stay*, the other *stayeth* me." Dr. Thirlby first suggested the probability of a misprint.
c *And* wood—] That is, *raging, mad.*
d The wildest hath not such a heart as you.] So Ovid:—

"Mitius inveni quam te genus omne ferarum."

I know a bank where the wild thyme blows,
Where ox-lips and the nodding violet grows;
Quite over-canopied with luscious woodbine,
With sweet musk-roses, and with eglantine:
There sleeps Titania, sometime of the night,
Lull'd in these flowers with dances and delight;
And there the snake throws her enamell'd skin,
Weed wide enough to wrap a fairy in:
And with the juice of this I'll streak her eyes,
And make her full of hateful fantasies.
Take thou some of it, and seek through this grove,
A sweet Athenian lady is in love
With a disdainful youth: anoint his eyes;
But do it when the next thing he espies
May be the lady. Thou shalt know the man
By the Athenian garments he hath on.
Effect it with some care; that he may prove
More fond on her, than she upon her love:
And look thou meet me ere the first cock crow.

PUCK. Fear not, my lord, your servant shall do so. [*Exeunt.*

SCENE II.—*Another part of the Wood.*

Enter TITANIA, *with her Train.*

TITA. Come, now a roundel,[a] and a fairy song;
Then, for the third part of a minute, hence;
Some, to kill cankers in the musk-rose buds;
Some, war with rear-mice for their leathern wings,
To make my small elves coats; and some, keep back
The clamorous owl, that nightly hoots and wonders
At our quaint spirits: sing me now asleep,
Then to your offices, and let me rest.

SONG.

I.

1 FAI. *You spotted snakes, with double tongue,*
Thorny hedgehogs, be not seen;
Newts, and blind-worms, do no wrong;
Come not near our fairy queen:

CHORUS.

Philomel, with melody
Sing in our sweet lullaby;*
Lulla, lulla, lullaby; lulla, lulla, lullaby;
Never harm, nor spell nor charm,
Come our lovely lady nigh;
So, good night, with lullaby.

II.

2 FAI. *Weaving spiders, come not here:*
Hence, you long-legg'd spinners, hence:
Beetles black, approach not near;
Worm, nor snail, do no offence.

CHORUS.

Philomel, with melody, &c.

2 FAI. Hence, away; now all is well:
One, aloof, stand sentinel.
[*Exeunt* Fairies. TITANIA *sleeps.*

Enter OBERON.

OBE. What thou seest, when thou dost wake,
[*Squeezes the flower on* TITANIA'*s eyelids.*
Do it for thy true-love take;
Love and languish for his sake;
Be it ounce, or cat, or bear,
Pard, or boar with bristled hair,
In thy eye that shall appear
When thou wak'st, it is thy dear;
Wake, when some vile thing is near.
[*Exit.*

Enter LYSANDER *and* HERMIA.

LYS. Fair love, you faint with wandering in the woods,
And, to speak troth, I have forgot our way;
We'll rest us, Hermia, if you think it good,
And tarry for the comfort of the day.

HER. Be it so, Lysander, find you out a bed,
For I upon this bank will rest my head.

LYS. One turf shall serve as pillow for us both;
One heart, one bed, two bosoms and one troth.

HER. Nay, good Lysander; for my sake, my dear,
Lie further off yet, do not lie so near.

LYS. O, take the sense, sweet, of my innocence;
Love takes the meaning, in love's conference.
I mean, that my heart unto yours is knit,
So that but one heart can we* make of it:
Two bosoms interchained† with an oath;
So then, two bosoms, and a single troth.
Then, by your side no bed-room me deny,
For, lying so, Hermia, I do not lie.

HER. Lysander riddles very prettily:—
Now much beshrew my manners and my pride,
If Hermia meant to say, Lysander lied.

(*) First folio, *your.*

(*) First folio, *you.* (†) First folio, *interchanged.*

[a] *Come, now a* roundel,—] A *roundel,* a *dance,* where the parties joined hands and formed a ring. This kind of dance was sometimes called a *round,* and a *roundelay* also, according to Minshew, who explains, "Roundelay, *Shepheards daunce.*"

But, gentle friend, for love and courtesy
Lie further off; in human modesty,
Such separation, as, may well be said,
Becomes a virtuous bachelor and a maid:
So far be distant, and good night, sweet friend;
Thy love ne'er alter, till thy sweet life end!
LYS. Amen, Amen, to that fair prayer say I,
And then end life, when I end loyalty!
Here is my bed: Sleep give thee all his rest!
HER. With half that wish the wisher's eyes be press'd! [*They sleep.*

Enter PUCK.

PUCK. Through the forest have I gone,
But Athenian found* I none,
On whose eyes I might approve
This flower's force in stirring love.
Night and silence! who is here?
Weeds of Athens he doth wear:
This is he my master said
Despised the Athenian maid;
And here the maiden, sleeping sound,
On the dank and dirty ground.
Pretty soul, she durst not lie
Near this lack-love, this kill-court'sy.
Churl, upon thy eyes I throw
All the power this charm doth owe:[a]
When thou wak'st, let love forbid
Sleep his seat on thy eyelid.
So awake, when I am gone;
For I must now to Oberon. [*Exit.*

Enter DEMETRIUS *and* HELENA, *running.*

HEL. Stay, though thou kill me, sweet Demetrius.
DEM. I charge thee, hence, and do not haunt me thus.
HEL. O, wilt thou darkling[b] leave me? do not so.
DEM. Stay, on thy peril; I alone will go. [*Exit* DEMETRIUS.

(*) First folio, *find.*

[a] *Doth* owe:] That is, doth *own, possess.*
[b] O, *wilt thou* darkling *leave me?*] *Darkling* is, in the dark. Shakespeare uses this word again in "King Lear," Act I. Sc. 4:—
"So out went the candle, and we were left darkling."
And in "Antony and Cleopatra," Act IV. Sc. 13. It occurs, too, in the old play called "The Two Angry Women of Abingdon:"—
"We'll run away with the torch and leave them to fight darkling."

HEL. O, I am out of breath in this fond chase!
The more my prayer, the lesser is my grace.
Happy is Hermia, wheresoe'er she lies,
For she hath blessed and attractive eyes:
How came her eyes so bright? Not with salt tears;
If so, my eyes are oftener wash'd than hers.
No, no, I am as ugly as a bear,
For beasts that meet me run away for fear;
Therefore, no marvel, though Demetrius
Do, as a monster, fly my presence thus.
What wicked and dissembling glass of mine
Made me compare with Hermia's sphery eyne?
But who is here?—Lysander! on the ground!
Dead? or asleep? I see no blood, no wound!—
Lysander, if you live, good sir, awake.

LYS. [*Waking.*] And run through fire I will, for thy sweet sake:
Transparent Helena! Nature shows her art,[a]
That through thy bosom makes me see thy heart.
Where is Demetrius? O, how fit a word
Is that vile name to perish on my sword!

HEL. Do not say so, Lysander; say not so:
What though he love your Hermia? Lord, what though?
Yet Hermia still loves you; then be content.

LYS. Content with Hermia? No: I do repent
The tedious minutes I with her have spent.
Not Hermia, but Helena* I love:
Who will not change a raven for a dove?
The will of man is by his reason sway'd,
And reason says you are the worthier maid.
Things growing are not ripe until their season,
So I, being young, till now ripe not to reason;
And touching now the point of human skill,
Reason becomes the marshal to my will,
And leads me to your eyes; where I o'erlook
Love's stories, written in love's richest book.

HEL. Wherefore was I to this keen mockery born?
When, at your hands, did I deserve this scorn?
Is 't not enough, is 't not enough, young man,
That I did never, no, nor never can,
Deserve a sweet look from Demetrius' eye,
But you must flout my insufficiency?
Good troth, you do me wrong, good sooth, you do,
In such disdainful manner me to woo.
But fare you well: perforce I must confess,
I thought you lord of more true gentleness.
O, that a lady, of one man refus'd,
Should of another therefore be abus'd! [*Exit.*

LYS. She sees not Hermia:—Hermia, sleep thou there;
And never mayst thou come Lysander near!
For, as a surfeit of the sweetest things
The deepest loathing to the stomach brings;
Or, as the heresies that men do leave,
Are hated most of those they* did deceive;
So thou, my surfeit, and my heresy,
Of all be hated, but the most, of me!
And all my powers address your love and might,
To honour Helen, and to be her knight. [*Exit.*

HER. [*starting.*] Help me, Lysander, help me! do thy best,
To pluck this crawling serpent from my breast!
Ah me, for pity!—what a dream was here!
Lysander, look how I do quake with fear!
Methought a serpent ate my heart away,
And you† sat smiling at his cruel prey:
Lysander! what, remov'd? Lysander! lord!
What, out of hearing? gone? no sound, no word?
Alack, where are you? speak, an if you hear;
Speak, of all loves;[b] I swoon almost with fear.
No?—then I well perceive you are not nigh:
Either death, or you, I'll find immediately.
[*Exit.*

(*) First folio, *now I*.

(*) First folio, *that*. (†) First folio, *yet*.

[a] *Nature shows her art,*—] The quartos have,—"Nature shows art;" the folio, "Nature *her* shows art."

[b] *Speak, of all loves*;] This pretty imploration, with the sense of, *for love's sake*, is found again in "The Merry Wives of Windsor," Act II. Sc. 2:—"But Mistress Page would desire you to send her your little page, *of all loves*." And in "Othello," Act III. Sc. 1:—"But, Masters, here's money for you: and the general so likes your music, that he desires you, *of all loves*, to make no more noise with it."

ACT III.

SCENE I.—*The Wood. The Queen of Fairies lying asleep.*

Enter QUINCE, SNUG, BOTTOM, FLUTE, SNOUT, *and* STARVELING.[a]

BOT. Are we all met?

QUIN. Pat, pat; and here 's a marvellous convenient place for our rehearsal. This green plot shall be our stage, this hawthorn brake our tyring-house; and we will do it in action, as we will do it before the duke.

BOT. Peter Quince,—

QUIN. What say'st thou, bully Bottom?

BOT. There are things in this comedy of *Pyramus and Thisbe* that will never please. First, Pyramus must draw a sword to kill himself; which the ladies cannot abide. How answer you that?

SNOUT. By 'rlakin, a parlous fear.[b]

STAR. I believe we must leave the killing out, when all is done.

BOT. Not a whit; I have a device to make all well. Write me a prologue: and let the prologue seem to say, we will do no harm with our swords; and that Pyramus is not killed indeed: and, for the more better assurance, tell them, that I Pyramus am not Pyramus, but Bottom the weaver: this will put them out of fear.

QUIN. Well, we will have such a prologue: and it shall be written in eight and six.[c]

BOT. No, make it two more; let it be written in eight and eight.

SNOUT. Will not the ladies be afeard of the lion?

STAR. I fear it, I promise you.

BOT. Masters, you ought to consider with yourselves: to bring in, God shield us! a lion among ladies, is a most dreadful thing; for there is not a more fearful wild-fowl than your lion, living; and we ought to look to 't.

SNOUT. Therefore, another prologue must tell he is not a lion.

---

[a] *Enter* QUINCE, &c.] The old stage direction is simply, "Enter the Clownes."

[b] By 'rlakin, *a* parlous *fear.*] By our *lady kin*, or *little lady. Par'lous*, a popular corruption of *perilous*, occurs again in "Richard III," Act II. Sc. 4; in "Romeo and Juliet," Act I. Sc. 3; and in "As You Like It," Act III. Sc. 2.

[c] *And it shall be written in* eight *and* six.] In fourteen-syllable measure, which was frequently divided into two lines of *eight and six* syllables.

BOT. Nay, you must name his name, and half his face must be seen through the lion's neck; and he himself must speak through, saying thus, or to the same defect,—*Ladies, fair ladies, I would wish you, I would request you, I would entreat you, not to fear, not to tremble: my life for yours. If you think I come hither as a lion, it were pity of my life: no, I am no such thing; I am a man as other men are:* and there, indeed, let him name his name; and tell them* plainly he is Snug the joiner.

QUIN. Well, it shall be so. But there is two hard things; that is, to bring the moonlight into a chamber: for, you know, Pyramus and Thisbe meet by moonlight.

SNUG. Doth the moon shine that night we play our play?

BOT. A calendar, a calendar! look in the almanac; find out moonshine, find out moonshine.

QUIN. Yes, it doth shine that night.

BOT. Why, then may you leave a casement of the great chamber-window, where we play, open; and the moon may shine in at the casement.

QUIN. Ay; or else one must come in with a bush of thorns and a lantern, and say, he comes to disfigure, or to present, the person of Moonshine. Then there is another thing: we must have a wall in the great chamber; for Pyramus and Thisbe, says the story, did talk through the chink of a wall.

SNUG. You can never bring in a wall.—What say you, Bottom?

BOT. Some man or other must present wall: and let him have some plaster, or some loam, or some rough-cast, about him, to signify wall; or let him hold his fingers thus, and through that cranny shall Pyramus and Thisbe whisper.

QUIN. If that may be, then all is well. Come, sit down, every mother's son, and rehearse your parts. Pyramus, you begin: when you have spoken your speech, enter into that brake; and so every one according to his cue.

Enter PUCK *behind.*

PUCK. What hempen homespuns have we swaggering here,
So near the cradle of the fairy queen?
What, a play toward? I'll be an auditor;
An actor too, perhaps, if I see cause.

QUIN. Speak, Pyramus:—Thisbe, stand forth.

PYR. *Thisbe, the flowers of odious savours sweet.*

QUIN. Odours, odours.

PYR. ——*odours savours sweet:*
So hath thy breath, my dearest Thisbe, dear.
But, hark, a voice! stay thou but here a while,
And by and by I will to thee appear. [*Exit.*

PUCK. A stranger Pyramus than e'er play'd here! [*Aside.—Exit.*

THIS. Must I speak now?

QUIN. Ay, marry, must you: for you must understand he goes but to see a noise that he heard, and is to come again.

THIS. *Most radiant Pyramus, most lily white of hue,*
Of colour like the red rose on triumphant brier,
Most brisky juvenal, and eke most lovely Jew,
As true as truest horse, that yet would never tire,
I'll meet thee, Pyramus, at Ninny's tomb.

QUIN. Ninus' tomb, man: why you must not speak that yet; that you answer to Pyramus: you speak all your part at once, cues[a] and all.—Pyramus, enter; your cue is past; it is, *never tire.*

Re-enter PUCK, *and* BOTTOM *with an ass's head.*

THIS. O,—*As true as truest horse, that yet would never tire.*

PYR. *If I were fair, Thisbe*[b] *I were only thine:—*

QUIN. O monstrous! O strange! we are haunted. Pray, masters! fly, masters! help! [*Exeunt* Clowns.

PUCK. I'll follow you, I'll lead you about a round,
Through bog, through bush, through brake, through brier;
Sometime a horse I'll be, sometime a hound,
A hog, a headless bear, sometime a fire;
And neigh, and bark, and grunt, and roar, and burn,
Like horse, hound, hog, bear, fire, at every turn. [*Exit.*

BOT. Why do they run away? this is a knavery of them to make me afeard.

* First folio, *him.*

[a] *You speak all your part at once,* cues *and all.—*] A *cue* is the stage technical for the last words of a speech, which serve as an indication to an actor of when he is to enter, and when to speak. To appreciate the importance of *cues,* it must be borne in mind that when the "parts," or written language of a new play, are distributed, each performer receives only what he has himself to recite; consequently, if this were unaccompanied by *cues,* or catchwords, from the other parts, he would be utterly at a loss to know either when to make his entrance on the scene, or to join in the dialogue.

[b] If I were fair, Thisbe—] "Perhaps," Malone remarks, "we ought to point thus: If I were, [*i.e.* as true, &c.] fair Thisbe, I were only thine." There cannot be a doubt of it, if we absolutely insist upon making bully Bottom speak sensibly, which Shakespeare has taken some pains to show he was never designed to do.

Re-enter SNOUT.

SNOUT. O Bottom, thou art changed! what do I see on thee?

BOT. What do you see? you see an ass-head of your own; do you?

Re-enter QUINCE.

QUIN. Bless thee, Bottom! bless thee! thou art translated. [*Exit.*

BOT. I see their knavery: this is to make an ass of me; to fright me, if they could. But I will not stir from this place, do what they can: I will walk up and down here, and I will sing, that they shall hear I am not afraid. [*Sings.*

The oosel-cock, so black of hue,[a]
With orange-tawny bill,
The throstle with his note so true,
The wren with * *little quill;*

TITA. [*Waking.*] What angel wakes me from my flowery bed?

BOT. *The finch, the sparrow, and the lark,*
The plain-song cuckoo gray,
Whose note full many a man doth mark,
And dares not answer, nay—

for, indeed, who would set his wit to so foolish a bird? who would give a bird the lie, though he cry *cuckoo* never so?

TITA. I pray thee, gentle mortal, sing again:
Mine ear is much enamour'd of thy note,
So is mine eye enthralled to thy shape;
And thy fair virtue's force perforce doth move me,
On the first view, to say, to swear, I love thee.

BOT. Methinks, mistress, you should have little reason for that: and yet, to say the truth, reason and love keep little company together now-a-days. The more the pity, that some honest neighbours will not make them friends. Nay, I can gleek upon occasion.[b]

(*) First folio, *and.*

a *The* oosel-cock,—] That is, the blackbird. Florio explains *merlo* to be "the birde called an *owsell,* a *mearle, or a blacke-birde;*" and Minshew has, "blackbird, or *blacke-ousell.*"

b *Nay, I can* gleek *upon occasion*] The ordinary sense of *gleek* is, *to jest,* or *joke,* and it is with this meaning the word is used here. The all-accomplished Bottom is boasting of his versatility. He has shown, by his last profound observation on the disunion of love and reason, that he possesses a pretty turn for the didactic and sententious; but he wishes Titania to understand that, upon fitting occasion, he can be as waggish as he has just been grave.

TITA. Thou art as wise as thou art beautiful.

BOT. Not so, neither: but if I had wit enough to get out of this wood, I have enough to serve mine own turn.

TITA. Out of this wood do not desire to go;
Thou shalt remain here, whether thou wilt or no.
I am a spirit, of no common rate;
The summer still doth tend upon my state,
And I do love thee: therefore, go with me;
I'll give thee fairies to attend on thee;
And they shall fetch thee jewels from the deep,
And sing, while thou on pressed flowers dost sleep:
And I will purge thy mortal grossness so,
That thou shalt like an airy spirit go.—
Peas-blossom! Cobweb! Moth! and Mustard-seed!

Enter PEAS-BLOSSOM, COBWEB, MOTH, *and* MUSTARD-SEED, Fairies.

1 FAI. Ready.
2 FAI. And I.

3 FAI. And I.
4 FAI. And I.
ALL. Where shall we go?

TIT. Be kind and courteous to this gentleman;
Hop in his walks, and gambol in his eyes;
Feed him with apricocks, and dewberries,
With purple grapes, green figs, and mulberries;
The honey-bags steal from the humble-bees,
And, for night-tapers, crop their waxen thighs,
And light them at the fiery glow-worm's eyes,
To have my love to bed, and to arise;
And pluck the wings from painted butterflies,
To fan the moonbeams from his sleeping eyes:
Nod to him, elves, and do him courtesies.

1 FAI. Hail, mortal!
2 FAI. Hail!
3 FAI. Hail!
4 FAI. Hail!

BOT. I cry your worships mercy, heartily.—I beseech your worship's name.

COB. Cobweb.

BOT. I shall desire you of more acquaintance,[a] good master Cobweb. If I cut my finger, I shall make bold with you.—Your name, honest gentleman?

PEAS. Peas-blossom.

BOT. I pray you, commend me to mistress Squash,[b] your mother, and to master Peas-cod, your father. Good master Peas-blossom, I shall desire you of* more acquaintance too.—Your name, I beseech you, sir?

MUS. Mustard-seed.

BOT. Good master Mustard-seed, I know your patience well: that same cowardly, giant-like ox-beef hath devoured many a gentleman of your house: I promise you, your kindred hath made my eyes water ere now. I desire you more acquaintance, good master Mustard-seed.

TITA. Come, wait upon him; lead him to my bower.
The moon, methinks, looks with a watery eye;
And when she weeps, weeps every little flower,
Lamenting some enforced chastity.
Tie up my love's† tongue, bring him silently.
[*Exeunt.*

SCENE II.—*Another part of the Wood.*

Enter OBERON.

OBE. I wonder, if Titania be awak'd;
Then, what it was that next came in her eye,
Which she must dote on in extremity.

Enter PUCK.

Here comes my messenger.— How now, mad spirit?
What night-rule[c] now about this haunted grove?

PUCK. My mistress with a monster is in love.
Near to her close and consecrated bower,
While she was in her dull and sleeping hour,
A crew of patches, rude mechanicals,
That work for bread upon Athenian stalls,
Were met together to rehearse a play,
Intended for great Theseus' nuptial day.
The shallowest thick-skin of that barren sort,
Who Pyramus presented in their sport,
Forsook his scene, and enter'd in a brake:
When I did him at this advantage take,

(*) First folio, *of you*. (†) Old text, *lovers*.

[a] *I shall desire* you of *more acquaintance*,—] This construction is by no means unusual with our old writers. Thus, in "The Marriage of Witt and Wisdome," 1579:—

"Gentlewoman, this shalbe to *desier you of more* acquaintance."

Again, in the "Morality of Lusty Juventus:"—

"I shall desire you of better acquaintance."

So, also, in Greene's "Groat's-worth of Wit:"—

"—— craving *you of more* acquaintance."

[b] Squash,—] A *squash*, Steevens tells us, is an immature peascod.

[c] *What night*-rule now—] *Rule*, in this word, has the same meaning as in the "Christmas lord of Mis-*rule*," and is a corruption of *revel*, formerly written *reuel*.

An ass's nowl I fixed on his head ;(1)
Anon, his Thisbe must be answered,
And forth my mimic comes : when they him spy,
As wild geese that the creeping fowler eye,
Or russet-pated choughs, many in sort,
Rising and cawing at the gun's report,
Sever themselves, and madly sweep the sky ;
So, at his sight, away his fellows fly :
And, at our stamp, here o'er and o'er one falls,
He murder cries, and help from Athens calls.
Their sense thus weak, lost with their fears thus strong,
Made senseless things begin to do them wrong ;
For briers and thorns at their apparel snatch,
Some, sleeves ; some, hats ; from yielders all things catch.
I led them on in this distracted fear,
And left sweet Pyramus translated there :
When in that moment (so it came to pass)
Titania wak'd, and straightway lov'd an ass.

OBE. This falls out better than I could devise.
But hast thou yet latch'd[a] the Athenian's eyes
With the love-juice, as I did bid thee do?

PUCK. I took him sleeping,—that is finish'd too,—
And the Athenian woman by his side ;
That when he wak'd of force she must be ey'd.

Enter DEMETRIUS *and* HERMIA.

OBE. Stand close ; this is the same Athenian.

PUCK. This is the woman, but not this the man.

DEM. O, why rebuke you him that loves you so?
Lay breath so bitter on your bitter foe.

HER. Now I but chide, but I should use thee worse ;
For thou, I fear, hast given me cause to curse.
If thou hast slain Lysander in his sleep,
Being o'er shoes in blood, plunge in the deep,
And kill me too.
The sun was not so true unto the day,
As he to me : would he have stolen away
From sleeping Hermia? I 'll believe as soon,
This whole earth may be bor'd; and that the moon
May through the centre creep, and so displease
Her brother's noontide with the Antipodes.
It cannot be, but thou hast murder'd him ;
So should a murderer look ; so dead, so grim.

DEM. So should the murder'd* look ; and so should I,
Pierc'd through the heart with your stern cruelty :
Yet you, the murderer, look as bright, as clear,
As yonder Venus in her glimmering sphere.

HER. What's this to my Lysander? where is he?
Ah, good Demetrius, wilt thou give him me?

---

[a] Latch'd—] According to Hanmer, *letch'd, lick'd over;* but I have found no example of the word so used.

(*) First folio, *murderer.*

DEM. I'd rather give his carcase to my hounds.
HER. Out, dog! out, cur! thou driv'st me past the bounds
Of maiden's patience. Hast thou slain him then?
Henceforth be never number'd among men!
Oh, once tell true, tell true,* even for my sake;
Durst thou have look'd upon him, being awake,
And hast thou kill'd him sleeping? O, brave touch!
Could not a worm, an adder, do so much?
An adder did it: for with doubler tongue
Than thine, thou serpent, never adder stung.
DEM. You spend your passion on a mispris'd mood:[a]
I am not guilty of Lysander's blood;
Nor is he dead, for aught that I can tell.
HER. I pray thee, tell me then that he is well.
DEM. An if I could, what should I get therefore?
HER. A privilege, never to see me more.—
And from thy hated presence part I so:[b]
See me no more, whether he be dead or no. [*Exit.*
DEM. There is no following her in this fierce vein:
Here, therefore, for a while I will remain.
So sorrow's heaviness doth heavier grow
For debt that bankrupt sleep doth sorrow owe;
Which now, in some slight measure, it will pay,
If for his tender here I make some stay.
[*Lies down.*
OBE. What hast thou done? thou hast mistaken quite,
And laid the love-juice on some true-love's sight:
Of thy misprision must perforce ensue
Some true-love turn'd, and not a false turn'd true.
PUCK. Then fate o'er-rules; that, one man holding troth,
A million fail, confounding oath on oath.
OBE. About the wood go swifter than the wind,
And Helena of Athens look thou find:
All fancy-sick she is, and pale of cheer[c]
With sighs of love, that cost the fresh blood dear.[d]
By some illusion see thou bring her here;
I'll charm his eyes against she doth appear.
PUCK. I go, I go; look, how I go;
Swifter than arrow from the Tartar's bow. [*Exit.*
OBE. Flower of this purple dye,
Hit with Cupid's archery,
Sink in apple of his eye!
When his love he doth espy,
Let her shine as gloriously
As the Venus of the sky.
When thou wak'st, if she be by,
Beg of her for remedy.

Re-enter PUCK.

PUCK. Captain of our fairy band,
Helena is here at hand;
And the youth, mistook by me,
Pleading for a lover's fee;
Shall we their fond pageant see?
Lord, what fools these mortals be!
OBE. Stand aside: the noise they make,
Will cause Demetrius to awake.
PUCK. Then will two at once woo one—
That must needs be sport alone;
And those things do best please me,
That befal preposterously.[e]

Enter LYSANDER *and* HELENA.

LYS. Why should you think that I should woo in scorn?
Scorn and derision never come in tears.
Look, when I vow, I weep; and vows so born,
In their nativity all truth appears.
How can these things in me seem scorn to you,
Bearing the badge of faith, to prove them true?
HEL. You do advance your cunning more and more.
When truth kills truth, O devilish-holy fray!
These vows are Hermia's; will you give her o'er?
Weigh oath with oath, and you will nothing weigh:
Your vows to her and me, put in two scales,
Will even weigh; and both as light as tales.
LYS. I had no judgment, when to her I swore.
HEL. Nor none, in my mind, now you give her o'er.
LYS. Demetrius loves her, and he loves not you.
DEM. [*awaking.*] O Helen, goddess, nymph, perfect, divine!

(*) First folio omits the repetition of *tell true*.

[a] *You spend your passion on a* mispris'd mood:] This is not very intelligible, and we prefer the critical remedy applied, afforded by Mr. Collier's annotator, who reads,—

"You spend your passion *in* a mispris'd *flood*,"—

to any explication of the old text that has yet been given.

[b] *Part I* so:] *So*, omitted in the quartos and folio, was inserted by Pope.

[c] *And pale of* cheer—] Cheer, visage, from the French *chère*. The word occurs again in this sense in "Henry VI." Pt. I. Act I. Sc. 2:—

"Methinks, your looks are sad, your *cheer* appall'd."

[d] *With* sighs *of love, that* cost the fresh blood dear.] It was formerly supposed that the indulgence of every sigh cost a drop of blood, and the notion that sighing tends to impair the animal powers is still prevalent. Shakespeare has many allusions to this popular belief:—

"And then this *should* is like *a spendthrift sigh*,
That hurts by easing."—*Hamlet*, Act IV. Sc. 7.

Again:—

"I would be blind with weeping, sick with groans,
Look pale as primrose, with *blood-drinking sighs*."
Henry VI. Pt. II. Act III. Sc. 2.

Again:—

"Ay, ay, for this I draw in many a tear,
And stop the rising of *blood-sucking sighs*."
Henry VI. Pt. III. Act IV. Sc. 4.

[e] Preposterously.] *i.e. Inversely*. See note [a], p. 248.

To what, my love, shall I compare thine eyne?
Crystal is muddy. O, how ripe in show
Thy lips, those kissing cherries, tempting grow!
That pure congealed white, high Taurus' snow,
Fann'd with the eastern wind, turns to a crow,
When thou hold'st up thy hand: O, let me kiss
This impress of pure white, this seal of bliss![a]

HEL. O, spite! O, hell! I see you all* are bent
To set against me, for your merriment.
If you were civil and knew courtesy,
You would not do me thus much injury.
Can you not hate me, as I know you do,
But you must join, in souls, to mock me too?
If you were† men, as men you are in show,
You would not use a gentle lady so;
To vow, and swear, and superpraise my parts,
When, I am sure, you hate me with your hearts.
You both are rivals, and love Hermia,
And now both rivals, to mock Helena:
A trim exploit, a manly enterprise,
To conjure tears up in a poor maid's eyes
With your derision! None of noble sort
Would so offend a virgin; and extort
A poor soul's patience, all to make you sport.

LYS. You are unkind, Demetrius; be not so;
For you love Hermia: this, you know, I know;
And here, with all good will, with all my heart,
In Hermia's love I yield you up my part;
And yours of Helena to me bequeath,
Whom I do love, and will do to my death.

HEL. Never did mockers waste more idle breath.

DEM. Lysander, keep thy Hermia; I will none:
If e'er I lov'd her, all that love is gone.
My heart to her but as guest-wise sojourn'd;
And now to Helen is it‡ home return'd,
There to remain.

LYS. Helen,§ it is not so.

DEM. Disparage not the faith thou dost not know,
Lest, to thy peril, thou aby[b] it dear.—
Look, where thy love comes; yonder is thy dear.

Enter HERMIA.

HER. Dark night, that from the eye his function takes,
The ear more quick of apprehension makes;
Wherein it doth impair the seeing sense,
It pays the hearing double recompense:
Thou art not by mine eye, Lysander, found;
Mine ear, I thank it, brought me to thy* sound.
But why unkindly didst thou leave me so?

LYS. Why should he stay whom love doth press to go?

HER. What love could press Lysander from my side?

LYS. Lysander's love, that would not let him bide;
Fair Helena; who more engilds the night
Than all yon fiery oes[c] and eyes of light.
Why seek'st thou me? could not this make thee know,
The hate I bear thee made me leave thee so?

HER. You speak not as you think, it cannot be.

HEL. Lo, she is one of this confederacy!
Now I perceive they have conjoin'd, all three,
To fashion this false sport in spite of me.
Injurious Hermia! most ungrateful maid!
Have you conspir'd, have you with these contriv'd
To bait me with this foul derision?
Is all the counsel that we two have shar'd,
The sisters' vows, the hours that we have spent,
When we have chid the hasty-footed time
For parting us,—O, and† is all forgot?
All school-days' friendship, childhood innocence?
We, Hermia, like two artificial gods,
Have with our neelds created both one flower,
Both on one sampler, sitting on one cushion,
Both warbling of one song, both in one key;
As if our hands, our sides, voices, and minds,
Had been incorporate. So we grew together,
Like to a double cherry, seeming parted;
But yet a union in partition,
Two lovely berries moulded on one stem:
So, with two seeming bodies, but one heart,
Two of the first, like‡ coats in heraldry,(2)
Due but to one, and crowned with one crest.
And will you rent our ancient love asunder,
To join with men in scorning your poor friend?
It is not friendly, 't is not maidenly:
Our sex, as well as I, may chide you for it,
Though I alone do feel the injury.

HER. I am amazed at your passionate§ words:
I scorn you not; it seems that you scorn me.

HEL. Have you not set Lysander, as in scorn,

(*) First folio, *are all.* (†) First folio, *are.*
(‡) First folio, *it is.* (§) First folio omits *Helen.*

(*) First folio, *that.* (†) First folio omits *and.*
(‡) Old copies, *life.* (§) The quartos omit *passionate.*

a *This* impress *of pure white, this seal of bliss!*] The old copies have, "This *princess* of pure white," &c. Mr. Collier suggested the reading in the text; it has been subsequently found in the marginal notes of his old corrector, and is supported by a passage I have met with in Beaumont and Fletcher's "Double Marriage," Act IV. Sc. 3, where Virolet, apostrophizing Juliana's hand, calls it—

"—— *White seal of virtue.*"

b *Lest, to thy peril, thou* aby *it dear.*—] *Aby it dear* is, *pay dearly for it.* This form of *abide* is not at all unfrequent, it is found in the old version of the Psalms iii. v. 26, "Thou shalt dear *aby* this blow." And in "Gorboduc," Act IV. Sc. 2:—

"Thou Porrex, thou shalt dearely *abye* the same."

It occurs, too, in Beaumont and Fletcher's "Knight of the Burning Pestle," Act III. Sc. 4:—

"Fool-hardy knight, full soon thou shalt *aby*
This fond reproach: Thy body will I bang."

c *Than all yon fiery* oes—] *Oes* were small circular bosses of shining metal.

To follow me, and praise my eyes and face?
And made your other love, Demetrius,
(Who even but now did spurn me with his foot,)
To call me goddess, nymph, divine, and rare,
Precious, celestial? Wherefore speaks he this
To her he hates? and wherefore doth Lysander
Deny your love, so rich within his soul,
And tender me, forsooth, affection;
But by your setting on, by your consent?
What though I be not so in grace as you,
So hung upon with love, so fortunate;
But miserable most, to love unlov'd!
This you should pity, rather than despise.

HER. I understand not what you mean by this!

HEL. Ay, do, persèver, counterfeit sad looks,
Make mouths upon me when I turn my back,
Wink each at other, hold the sweet jest up:
This sport, well carried, shall be chronicled.
If you have any pity, grace, or manners,
You would not make me such an argument.
But, fare ye well: 'tis partly mine own fault,
Which death, or absence, soon shall remedy.

LYS. Stay, gentle Helena, hear my excuse;
My love, my life, my soul, fair Helena!

HEL. O, excellent!

HER. Sweet, do not scorn her so.

DEM. If she cannot entreat, I can compel.

LYS. Thou canst compel no more than she entreat;
Thy threats have no more strength, than her weak prayers.(*)—
Helen, I love thee; by my life I do;
I swear by that which I will lose for thee,
To prove him false that says I love thee not.

DEM. I say, I love thee more than he can do.

LYS. If thou say so, withdraw, and prove it too.

DEM. Quick, come,—

HER. Lysander, whereto tends all this?

LYS. Away, you Ethiope!

DEM. No, no, he'll—[a]
Seem to break loose; take on, as you would follow;
But yet come not. You are a tame man, go!

LYS. Hang off, thou cat, thou burr: vile thing, let loose;
Or I will shake thee from me, like a serpent.

HER. Why are you grown so rude? what change is this,
Sweet love?

LYS. Thy love? out, tawny Tartar, out!
Out, loathed medicine! O, hated potion,(†) hence!

HER. Do you not jest?

HEL. Yes, 'sooth; and so do you.

LYS. Demetrius, I will keep my word with thee.

DEM. I would I had your bond, for I perceive
A weak bond holds you; I'll not trust your word.

LYS. What, should I hurt her, strike her, kill her dead?
Although I hate her, I'll not harm her so.

HER. What, can you do me greater harm than hate?
Hate me! wherefore? O me! what means[b] my [love?
Am not I Hermia? Are not you Lysander?
I am as fair now as I was erewhile.
Since night, you lov'd me; yet, since night, you left me:
Why then you left me,—O, the gods forbid!—
In earnest, shall I say?

LYS. Ay, by my life;
And never did desire to see thee more.
Therefore, be out of hope, of question, doubt,*
Be certain, nothing truer, 'tis no jest,
That I do hate thee, and love Helena.

HER. O me! you juggler! you canker-blossom!
You thief of love! what, have you come by night,
And stol'n my love's heart from him?

HEL. Fine, i' faith
Have you no modesty, no maiden shame,
No touch of bashfulness? What, will you tear
Impatient answers from my gentle tongue?
Fie, fie! you counterfeit, you puppet, you!

HER. Puppet! why so? Ay, that way goes the game.
Now I perceive that she hath made compare
Between our statures, she hath urg'd her height;
And with her personage, her tall personage,
Her height, forsooth, she hath prevail'd with him.—
And are you grown so high in his esteem
Because I am so dwarfish, and so low?
How low am I, thou painted maypole? speak;
How low am I? I am not yet so low,
But that my nails can reach unto thine eyes.

HEL. I pray you, though you mock me, gentlemen,
Let her not hurt me; I was never curst;[c]
I have no gift at all in shrewishness;
I am a right maid for my cowardice;
Let her not strike me. You, perhaps, may think,
Because she's something lower than myself,
That I can match her.

HER. Lower! hark, again.

HEL. Good Hermia, do not be so bitter with me.
I evermore did love you, Hermia,
Did ever keep your counsels, never wrong'd you;
Save that, in love unto Demetrius,

(*) Old copies, *praise*. (†) First folio, *poison*.

[a] No, no, he'll—] This is the reading of Fisher's quarto; the folio has:—

"No, no, sir: seem to break loose:
Take on as you would follow."

* Old copies, *of doubt*.

[b] *O me! what* means *my love?*] The old copies have *newes*, a very probable misprint of *meanes*, the word substituted by Mr. Collier's annotator.

[c] *I was never* curst;] That is, *froward, irascible, shrewish.*

I told him of your stealth unto this wood:
He follow'd you; for love I follow'd him.
But he hath chid me hence; and threaten'd me
To strike me, spurn me, nay, to kill me too:
And now, so you will let me quiet go,
To Athens will I bear my folly back,
And follow you no further. Let me go;
You see how simple and how fond[a] I am.

HER. Why, get you gone: who is't that hinders you?

HEL. A foolish heart that I leave here behind.

HER. What, with Lysander?

HEL. With Demetrius.

LYS. Be not afraid: she shall not harm thee, Helena.

DEM. No, sir, she shall not, though you take her part.

HEL. O when she's angry, she is keen and shrewd;
She was a vixen, when she went to school,
And, though she be but little, she is fierce.

HER. Little again? nothing but low and little?
Why will you suffer her to flout me thus?
Let me come to her.

LYS. Get you gone, you dwarf;
You minimus, of hind'ring knot-grass made;[b]
You bead, you acorn.

DEM. You are too officious
In her behalf that scorns your services.
Let her alone; speak not of Helena;
Take not her part: for if thou dost intend
Never so little show of love to her,
Thou shalt aby it.

LYS. Now she holds me not;
Now follow, if thou dar'st, to try whose right,
Or* thine or mine, is most in Helena.

DEM. Follow? nay, I'll go with thee, cheek by jole. [*Exeunt* LYS. *and* DEM.

HER. You, mistress, all this coil is 'long of you:
Nay, go not back.

HEL. I will not trust you, I;
Nor longer stay in your curst company.
Your hands than mine are quicker for a fray,
My legs are longer though, to run away. [*Exit.*

HER. I am amaz'd, and know not what to say.[c] [*Exit, pursuing* HELENA.

OBE. This is thy negligence: still thou mistak'st,
Or else committ'st thy knaveries wilfully.†

PUCK. Believe me, king of shadows, I mistook.
Did not you tell me, I should know the man
By the Athenian garments he had* on?
And so far blameless proves my enterprise,
That I have 'nointed an Athenian's eyes:
And so far am I glad it so did sort,
As this their jangling I esteem a sport.

OBE. Thou seest, these lovers seek a place to fight:
Hie therefore, Robin, overcast the night;
The starry welkin cover thou anon
With drooping fog as black as Acheron;
And lead these testy rivals so astray,
As one come not within another's way.
Like to Lysander sometime frame thy tongue,
Then stir Demetrius up with bitter wrong;
And sometime rail thou like Demetrius;
And from each other look thou lead them thus,
Till o'er their brows death-counterfeiting sleep
With leaden legs and batty wings doth creep:
Then crush this herb into Lysander's eye,
Whose liquor hath this virtuous property,
To take from thence all error, with his might,
And make his eyeballs roll with wonted sight.
When they next wake, all this derision
Shall seem a dream, and fruitless vision;
And back to Athens shall the lovers wend,
With league, whose date till death shall never end.
Whiles I in this affair do thee employ,†
I'll to my queen, and beg her Indian boy;
And then I will her charmed eye release
From monster's view, and all things shall be peace.

PUCK. My fairy lord, this must be done with haste;
For night's swift‡ dragons cut the clouds full fast,
And yonder shines Aurora's harbinger;
At whose approach, ghosts, wandering here and there,
Troop home to churchyards: damned spirits all,
That in cross-ways and floods have burial,
Already to their wormy beds are gone;
For fear lest day should look their shames upon,
They wilfully themselves exile from light,
And must for aye consort with black-brow'd night.

OBE. But we are spirits of another sort:
I with the morning's love have oft made sport;[d]
And, like a forester, the groves may tread,
Even till the eastern gate, all fiery-red,
Opening on Neptune with fair blessed beams,
Turns into yellow gold his salt-green streams.

(*) Old copies, *Of.* (†) First folio, *willingly.*

[a] *And how* fond *I am.*] *How foolish I am.* This sense of *fond* is so trite in old books, that it scarcely requires explanation.

[b] You minimus, of hind'ring knot-grass made;] Knot-grass was formerly believed to possess the property of stunting animal growth. Thus, Beaumont and Fletcher, in "The Coxcomb," Act II. Sc. 2:—

"We want a boy extremely for this function,
Kept under for a year, *with milk and knot-grass.*"

[c] HER. *I am amaz'd,* &c.] This line is omitted in the folio.

(*) First folio, *hath.* (†) First folio, *imply.* (‡) First folio, *night-swift.*

[d] *I with the* morning's love *have oft made sport;*] Johnson would read, "the morning's *light,*" which is plausible; but I prefer to believe, with Holt White, that by the *morning's love* the poet intended Cephalus, the mighty hunter, and paramour of Aurora:—

"*Aurora* now began to rise againe
From watrie couch and from old *Tithon*'s side,
In hope to kisse upon Acteian plaine
Yong *Cephalus,*" &c.—*The Phœnix Nest,* 4to. 1593, p. 95.

But, notwithstanding, haste; make no delay:
We may effect this business yet ere day.
[*Exit* OBERON.

PUCK. Up and down, up and down,
I will lead them up and down;
I am fear'd in field and town;
Goblin, lead them up and down.
Here comes one.

Enter LYSANDER.

LYS. Where art thou, proud Demetrius? speak thou now.

PUCK. Here, villain; drawn and ready. Where art thou?

LYS. I will be with thee straight.

PUCK. Follow me then,
To plainer ground.
[*Exit* LYS. *as following the voice.*

Enter DEMETRIUS.

DEM. Lysander! speak again.
Thou runaway, thou coward, art thou fled—
Speak—in some bush? Where dost thou hide thy head?

PUCK. Thou coward, art thou bragging to the stars,
Telling the bushes that thou look'st for wars,
And wilt not come? Come, recreant; come, thou child;
I 'll whip thee with a rod: he is defil'd
That draws a sword on thee.

DEM. Yea; art thou there?

PUCK. Follow my voice: we 'll try no manhood here. [*Exeunt.*

Re-enter LYSANDER.

LYS. He goes before me, and still dares me on;
When I come where he calls, then he is gone.

The villain is much lighter heel'd than I,
I follow'd fast, but faster he did fly;
That fallen am I in dark uneven way,
And here will rest me. Come, thou gentle day!
[*Lies down.*
For if but once thou show me thy grey light,
I'll find Demetrius, and revenge this spite.
[*Sleeps.*

Re-enter PUCK *and* DEMETRIUS.

PUCK. Ho, ho, ho! (3) Coward, why com'st thou not?
DEM. Abide me, if thou dar'st; for well I wot,
Thou runn'st before me, shifting every place;
And dar'st not stand, nor look me in the face.
Where art thou now?*
PUCK. Come hither; I am here.
DEM. Nay, then, thou mock'st me. Thou shalt 'by this dear,[a]
If ever I thy face by daylight see:
Now, go thy way. Faintness constraineth me
To measure out my length on this cold bed.
By day's approach look to be visited.
[*Lies down and sleeps.*

Enter HELENA.

HEL. O, weary night, O, long and tedious night,
Abate thy hours: shine, comforts, from the east,
That I may back to Athens by daylight,
From these that my poor company detest:—
And sleep, that sometimes shuts up sorrow's eye,
Steal me awhile from mine own company. [*Sleeps.*

PUCK. Yet but three? Come one more;
Two of both kinds makes up four.
Here she comes, curst and sad:
Cupid is a knavish lad,
Thus to make poor females mad.

Enter HERMIA.

HER. Never so weary, never so in woe,
Bedabbled with the dew, and torn with briers;
I can no further crawl, no further go,
My legs can keep no pace with my desires.
Here will I rest me, till the break of day.
Heavens shield Lysander, if they mean a fray!
[*Lies down.*
PUCK. On the ground
Sleep sound:
I'll apply
To* your eye,
Gentle lover, remedy
[*Squeezing the juice on* LYSANDER'S *eye.*
When thou wak'st,
Thou tak'st
True delight
In the sight
Of thy former lady's eye:
And the country proverb known,
That every man should take his own,
In your waking shall be shown:
Jack shall have Jill;[b]
Nought shall go ill;
The man shall have his mare again, and all shall be well.
[*Exit* PUCK.—DEM., HEL., *&c., sleep.*[c]

(*) First folio omits, *now*.

[a] Thou shalt 'by this dear,—] The old text has "*buy* this dear," but there can be little doubt the true word was *'by*. See note [b], p. 364.

[b] Jack shall have Jill, &c.] A popular proverb of olden times, signifying, as Puck expresses it, "that every man should take his own," or, as we should say, "all ended happily." It occurs in Skelton's poem, "Magnyfycence," Dyce's Ed. Vol. I. p. 234:—

"—— Jack shall have Gyl?"

(*) Old copies omit, *To*.

And in Heywood, "Dialogue," Sig. F. 3, 1598:—

"Come chat at home, *all is well, Jack shall have Gill.*"

So, too, Biron, in "Love's Labour's Lost," Act V. Sc. 2:—

"Our wooing doth not end like an old play;
Jack hath not Jill ——."

[c] DEM., HEL., &c., *sleep.*] In the folio, the old stage direction is, "*They sleepe all the Acte.*"

ACT IV.

SCENE I.—*The Wood.*

Enter TITANIA *and* BOTTOM,[a] Fairies *attending;* OBERON *behind unseen.*

TITA. Come, sit thee down upon this flowery bed,
While I thy amiable cheeks do coy,
And stick musk-roses in thy sleek smooth head,
And kiss thy fair large ears, my gentle joy.

BOT. Where 's Peas-blossom?

PEAS. Ready.

BOT. Scratch my head, Peas-blossom.—Where 's monsieur Cobweb?

COB. Ready.

BOT. Monsieur Cobweb; good monsieur, get

[a] *And* BOTTOM,—] Bottom's was the *Clown's* part, and in the old copies he is sometimes designated *Clown*, and sometimes *Bottom*.

you* your weapons in your hand, and kill me a red-hipped humble-bee on the top of a thistle; and, good monsieur, bring me the honey-bag. Do not fret yourself too much in the action, monsieur; and, good monsieur, have a care the honey-bag break not; I would be loth to have you overflown with a honey-bag, signior. Where's monsieur Mustard-seed?

MUST. Ready.

BOT. Give me your neif,[a] monsieur Mustard-seed. Pray you, leave your courtesy, good monsieur.

MUST. What's your will?

BOT. Nothing, good monsieur, but to help cavalero Cobweb to scratch. I must to the barber's, monsieur; for, methinks, I am marvellous hairy about the face; and I am such a tender ass, if my hair do but tickle me, I must scratch.

TITA. What, wilt thou hear some music, my sweet love?

BOT. I have a reasonable good ear in music; let us have the tongs(1) and the bones.[b]

TITA. Or say, sweet love, what thou desir'st to eat.

BOT. Truly, a peck of provender: I could munch your good dry oats. Methinks I have a great desire to a bottle of hay: good hay, sweet hay, hath no fellow.

TITA. I have a venturous fairy that shall seek
The squirrel's hoard, and fetch thee new nuts.

BOT. I had rather have a handful, or two, of dried peas. But, I pray you, let none of your people stir me; I have an exposition of sleep come upon me.

TITA. Sleep thou, and I will wind thee in my [arms.
Fairies, be gone, and be all ways away.[c]
So doth the woodbine the sweet honeysuckle
Gently entwist; the female ivy so
Enrings the barky fingers of the elm.
O, how I love thee! how I dote on thee!
[*They sleep.*

OBERON *advances.* *Enter* PUCK.

OBE. Welcome, good Robin. See'st thou this sweet sight?
Her dotage now I do begin to pity:
For meeting her of late, behind the wood,
Seeking sweet favours[d] for this hateful fool,
I did upbraid her and fall out with her:
For she his hairy temples then had rounded
With coronet of fresh and fragrant flowers;
And that same dew, which sometime on the buds
Was wont to swell, like round and orient pearls,
Stood now within the pretty flow'rets' eyes,
Like tears, that did their own disgrace bewail.
When I had, at my pleasure, taunted her,
And she, in mild terms, begg'd my patience,
I then did ask of her her changeling child;
Which straight she gave me, and her fairy sent
To bear him to my bower in fairy land.
And now I have the boy, I will undo
This hateful imperfection of her eyes.
And, gentle Puck, take this transformed scalp
From off the head of this Athenian swain;
That he awaking when the other do,
May all to Athens back again repair,
And think no more of this night's accidents,
But as the fierce vexation of a dream.
But first I will release the fairy queen.
Be, as thou wast wont to be,
[*Touching her eyes with an herb.*
See, as thou wast wont to see:
Dian's bud o'er* Cupid's flower
Hath such force and blessed power.
Now, my Titania, wake you, my sweet queen.

TITA. My Oberon! what visions have I seen!
Methought I was enamour'd of an ass.

OBE. There lies your love.

TITA. How came these things to pass?
O, how mine eyes do loath his† visage now!

OBE. Silence a while.—Robin, take off this‡ head.—
Titania, music call; and strike more dead
Than common sleep, of all these five§ the sense.

TITA. Music, ho! music; such as charmeth sleep.
[*Still music.*[e]

PUCK. Now,‖ when thou wak'st, with thine own fool's eyes peep.

OBE. Sound, music. Come, my queen, take hands with me,
And rock the ground whereon these sleepers be.

(*) First folio omits, *you.*

[a] Neif,—] A north country word, meaning *fist.* Shakespeare uses it again in "Henry IV." Pt. II. Act II. Sc. 4:—

"Sweet knight, I kiss thy *neif.*"

[b] *Let us have* the tongs and the bones.] It appears to have been the custom of the old theatres to gratify Bottom's "reasonable good ear," for the folio has a stage direction in this part of the scene, "*Musicke Tongs, Rurall Musicke.*

[c] *And be* all ways *away.*] *Disperse yourselves in every direction.* Mr. Collier's annotator reads *a while* for *all ways.*

[d] *Seeking sweet* favours—] This is the reading of Fisher's quarto; that published by Roberts, and the folio, 1623, have *savours.*

[e] [*Still music.*] In the folio, the stage direction here, not as all modern editions place it, in Oberon's speech, is, "*Music still;*" "which means, probably," Mr. Collier observes, "that the music was to cease before Puck spoke, as Oberon afterwards exclaims 'Sound music' when it is to be renewed." We apprehend, rather, by "*Music still,*" or "*still music,*" was meant *soft, subdued music,* such music as Titania could command,—" as charmeth sleep;" the object of it being to—

"—— Strike more dead
Than common sleep ——."

This being effected, Oberon himself calls for more stirring strains while he and the Queen take hands—

"And rock the ground whereon these sleepers be."

(*) Old copies, *or.* (†) First folio, *this.* (‡) First folio, *his.* (§) Old copies, *fine.* (‖) First folio omits, *Now.*

Now thou and I are new in amity;
And will, to-morrow midnight, solemnly,
Dance in Duke Theseus' house triumphantly,
And bless it to all fair posterity:
There shall the pairs of faithful lovers be
Wedded, with Theseus, all in jollity.

PUCK. Fairy king, attend, and mark,
I do hear the morning lark.

OBE. Then, my queen, in silence sad,
Trip we after the night's shade:
We the globe can compass soon,
Swifter than the wand'ring moon.

TITA. Come, my lord; and in our flight,
Tell me how it came this night,
That I sleeping here was found,
With these mortals on the ground.
[*Exeunt.*
[*Horns sound within.*

Enter THESEUS, HIPPOLYTA, EGEUS, *and Train.*

THE. Go one of you, find out the forester,
For now our observation[a] is perform'd;
And since we have the vaward of the day,
My love shall hear the music of my hounds.
Uncouple in the western valley; let them go:
Despatch, I say, and find the forester.
We will, fair queen, up to the mountain's top,
And mark the musical confusion
Of hounds and echo in conjunction.

HIP. I was with Hercules and Cadmus once,
When in a wood of Crete they bay'd the bear
With hounds of Sparta: never did I hear
Such gallant chiding; for, besides the groves,
The skies, the fountains, every region near
Seem'd* all one mutual cry: I never heard
So musical a discord, such sweet thunder.

THE. My hounds are bred out of the Spartan kind,
So flew'd, so sanded; and their heads are hung
With ears that sweep away the morning dew;
Crook-knee'd and dew-lapp'd like Thessalian bulls;
Slow in pursuit, but match'd in mouth like bells,
Each under each.(2) A cry more tuneable
Was never holla'd to, nor cheer'd with horn,
In Crete, in Sparta, nor in Thessaly:
Judge, when you hear.—But, soft; what nymphs are these?

EGE. My lord, this is my daughter here asleep;
And this Lysander; this Demetrius is;
This Helena, old Nedar's Helena:
I wonder of their* being here together.

THE. No doubt they rose up early, to observe
The rite of May; and, hearing our intent,
Came here in grace of our solemnity.
But, speak, Egeus; is not this the day
That Hermia should give answer of her choice?

EGE. It is, my lord.

THE. Go, bid the huntsmen wake them with their horns.

Horns, and shout within. DEMETRIUS, LYSANDER, HERMIA, *and* HELENA, *wake and start up.*

THE. Good morrow, friends. Saint Valentine is past;
Begin these wood-birds but to couple now?

LYS. Pardon, my lord.
[*He and the rest kneel to* THESEUS.

THE. I pray you, all stand up.
I know, you two are rival enemies;
How comes this gentle concord in the world,
That hatred is so far from jealousy,
To sleep by hate, and fear no enmity?

LYS. My lord, I shall reply amazedly,
Half 'sleep, half waking: but as yet, I swear
I cannot truly say how I came here:
But, as I think, (for truly would I speak,—
And now I do bethink me, so it is;)
I came with Hermia hither: our intent
Was, to be gone from Athens, where we might be
Without[b] the peril of the Athenian law.

EGE. Enough, enough, my lord; you have enough:
I beg the law, the law, upon his head.
They would have stol'n away, they would, Demetrius,
Thereby to have defeated you and me:
You of your wife, and me of my consent,—
Of my consent that she should be your wife.

DEM. My lord, fair Helen told me of their stealth,
Of this their purpose hither, to this wood;
And I in fury hither follow'd them,
Fair Helena in fancy[c] following† me.
But, my good lord, I wot not by what power,
(But, by some power it is,) my love to Hermia,

(*) Old copies, *seem.*

(*) First folio, *this.*

(†) First folio, *followed.*

a *Our* observation—] The rites or *observance* due to the morn of May.

b Without *the peril of the Athenian law.*] That is, *beyond* the peril, &c. *Without*, in this sense, occurs repeatedly in Shakespeare and the books of his age. There is a memorable instance of it in a passage of "The Tempest," Act V. Sc. 1, where, from not being understood, it has been the occasion of perpetual discussion:—

"His mother was a witch, and one so strong
That could control the moon, make flows and ebbs,
And deal in her command *without* her power."

Here, "*without* her power" means, *beyond* her power, or *sphere*, as I am strongly inclined to think the poet wrote. Thus, too, in Ben Jonson's "Cynthia's Revels," Act I. Sc. IV. Gifford's Ed.—

"Oh, now I apprehend you: your phrase was
Without me before."

c *In fancy*—] That is, *love*, or *affection.*

Melted as the snow, seems to me now[a]
As the remembrance of an idle gaud,
Which in my childhood I did dote upon:
And all the faith, the virtue of my heart,
The object, and the pleasure of mine eye,
Is only Helena. To her, my lord,
Was I betroth'd ere I saw* Hermia:
But, like a sickness, did I loath this food:
But, as in health, come to my natural taste,
Now do I wish it, love it, long for it,
And will for evermore be true to it.

THE. Fair lovers, you are fortunately met:
Of this discourse we more will hear† anon.
Egeus, I will overbear your will,
For in the temple, by and by with us,
These couples shall eternally be knit.
And, for the morning now is something worn,
Our purpos'd hunting shall be set aside.
Away, with us, to Athens; three and three,
We'll hold a feast in great solemnity.
Come, Hippolyta.

[*Exeunt* THESEUS, HIPPOLYTA, EGEUS, *and Train.*

DEM. These things seem small and undistinguishable,
Like far-off mountains turned into clouds.

HER. Methinks I see these things with parted eye,
When everything seems double.

HEL. So methinks:
And I have found Demetrius like a jewel,[b]
Mine own, and not mine own.

DEM. Are you sure
That we are awake?[c] It seems to me,
That yet we sleep, we dream.—Do not you think,
The duke was here, and bid us follow him?

HER. Yea, and my father.

HEL. And Hippolyta.

LYS. And he did‡ bid us follow to the temple.

DEM. Why then, we are awake: let's follow him,
And, by the way, let us recount our dreams.

[*Exeunt.*

As they go out, BOTTOM *awakes.*

BOT. When my cue comes, call me, and I will answer:—my next is, *Most fair Pyramus.*—Hey, ho!—Peter Quince! Flute, the bellows-mender! Snout, the tinker! Starveling! God's my life! stolen hence, and left me asleep! I have had a most rare vision. I have* had a dream,—past the wit of man to say what dream it was.—Man is but an ass if he go about to expound this dream. Methought I was—there is no man can tell what. Methought I was—and methought I had.—But man is but a patched fool[d] if he will offer to say what methought I had. The eye of man hath not heard, the ear of man hath not seen, man's hand is not able to taste, his tongue to conceive, nor his heart to report, what my dream was. I will get Peter Quince to write a ballad of this dream: it shall be called Bottom's Dream, because it hath no bottom; and I will sing it in the latter end of a play, before the duke: peradventure, to make it the more gracious, I shall sing it after death.[e]

[*Exit.*

SCENE II.—Athens. *A Room in* Quince's *House.*

Enter QUINCE, FLUTE, SNOUT, *and* STARVELING.

QUIN. Have you sent to Bottom's house? is he come home yet?

STAR. He cannot be heard of. Out of doubt, he is transported.[f]

FLU. If he come not, then the play is marred. It goes not forward, doth it?

QUIN. It is not possible: you have not a man in all Athens able to discharge Pyramus, but he.

FLU. No; he hath simply the best wit of any handicraft man in Athens.

QUIN. Yea, and the best person too: and he is a very paramour for a sweet voice.

FLU. You must say, paragon: a paramour is, God bless us, a thing of naught.

Enter SNUG.

SNUG. Masters, the duke is coming from the temple, and there is two or three lords and ladies

(*) Old copies, *see.* (†) First folio, *shall hear more.* (‡) First folio omits, *did.*

(*) First folio omits, *have.*

[a] *Melted as* the snow, *seems to me now*—] To remedy the prosodical imperfection in this line, the modern editors adopt Capell's ungrammatical lection,—

"Melted as *doth* the snow," &c.

I should prefer,—

"*All* melted as the snow," &c.

[b] *And I have found Demetrius like* a jewel,
Mine own, and not mine own.]

For *jewel,* Warburton proposed to read *gemell,* from *gemellus,* a twin; a substitution preferable to any explanation yet given of the text as it stands.

[c] Are you sure
That we are awake?]

The folio omits these words.

[d] *But man is but* a patched fool—] See Note (b), p. 127. Since writing that note I have met with remarkable proof of the supposed connexion between the term *patch,* applied to a fool, and the garb such a character sometimes wore, in a Flemish picture of the sixteenth century. In this picture, which represents a grand *al fresco* entertainment of the description given to Queen Elizabeth during her "Progresses," there is a procession of masquers and mummers, led by a fool or jester, whose dress is covered with many-coloured coarse patches from head to heel.

[e] *I shall sing it* after *death.*] This is the extremely plausible emendation of Theobald. The old copy has, "—— *at her* death;" from which no ingenuity has ever succeeded in extracting a shred of humour or even meaning.

[f] *Out of doubt, he is* transported.] Or, as Snout expressed it when he first saw Bottom adorned with an ass's head, *translated,* that is, *transformed.*

more, married: if our sport had gone forward we had all been made men.

FLU. O sweet bully Bottom! Thus hath he lost sixpence a-day during his life; he could not have 'scaped sixpence a-day: an the duke had not given him sixpence a-day for playing Pyramus, I'll be hanged; he would have deserved it: sixpence a-day, in Pyramus, or nothing.

Enter BOTTOM.

BOT. Where are these lads? where are these hearts?

QUIN. Bottom!—O most courageous day! O most happy hour!

BOT. Masters, I am to discourse wonders: but ask me not what; for if I tell you I am no true Athenian. I will tell you everything, right* as it fell out.

QUIN. Let us hear, sweet Bottom.

BOT. Not a word of me. All that I will tell you is, that the duke hath dined. Get your apparel together; good strings to your beards, new ribbons to your pumps; meet presently at the palace; every man look o'er his part; for, the short and the long is, our play is preferred. In any case, let Thisbe have clean linen: and let not him that plays the lion pare his nails, for they shall hang out for the lion's claws. And, most dear actors, eat no onions, nor garlic, for we are to utter sweet breath; and I do not doubt but to hear them say, it is a sweet comedy. No more words; away; go, away. [*Exeunt.*

(*) First folio omits, *right*.

ACT V.

SCENE I.—Athens. *An Apartment in the Palace of* Theseus.

Enter Theseus, Hippolyta, Philostrate, Lords, *and* Attendants.

Hip. 'T is strange, my Theseus, that these lovers speak of.

The. More strange than true. I never may believe
These antique fables, nor these fairy toys.
Lovers and madmen have such seething brains,
Such shaping fantasies, that apprehend
More than cool reason ever comprehends.
The lunatic, the lover, and the poet,
Are of imagination all compact:
One sees more devils than vast hell can hold—

That is the madman: the lover, all as frantic,
Sees Helen's beauty in a brow of Egypt.
The poet's eye, in a fine frenzy rolling,
Doth glance from heaven to earth, from earth to heaven;
And, as imagination bodies forth
The forms of things unknown, the poet's pen
Turns them to shapes, and gives to airy nothing
A local habitation and a name.
Such tricks hath strong imagination,
That, if it would but apprehend some joy,
It comprehends some bringer of that joy;
Or, in the night, imagining some fear,
How easy is a bush suppos'd a bear.

HIP. But all the story of the night told over,
And all their minds transfigur'd so together,
More witnesseth than fancy's images,
And grows to something of great constancy;[a]
But, howsoever, strange, and admirable.

Enter LYSANDER, DEMETRIUS, HERMIA, *and* HELENA.

THE. Here come the lovers, full of joy and mirth.—
Joy, gentle friends! joy, and fresh days of love,
Accompany your hearts!

LYS. More than to us,
Wait in your royal walks, your board, your bed!

THE. Come now; what masks, what dances shall we have,
To wear away this long age of three hours,
Between our after-supper(1) and bed-time?
Where is our usual manager of mirth?
What revels are in hand? Is there no play,
To ease the anguish of a torturing hour?
Call Philostrate.[b]

PHILOST. Here, mighty Theseus.

THE. Say, what abridgment[c] have you for this evening?
What mask, what music? How shall we beguile
The lazy time, if not with some delight?

PHILOST. There is a brief, how many sports are ripe;*
Make choice of which your highness will see first.
[*Giving a paper.*

LYS. [*Reads.*] *The battle with the Centaurs, to be sung,*
By an Athenian eunuch to the harp.

THE. We'll none of that: that have I told my love,
In glory of my kinsman Hercules.

LYS. *The riot of the tipsy Bacchanals,*
Tearing the Thracian singer in their rage.

THE. That is an old device, and it was play'd
When I from Thebes came last a conqueror.

LYS. *The thrice three Muses mourning for the death*
Of learning, late deceased in beggary.

THE. That is some satire, keen, and critical,
Not sorting with a nuptial ceremony.

LYS. *A tedious brief scene of young Pyramus,*
And his love Thisbe; very tragical mirth.

THE. Merry and tragical? Tedious and brief?
That is, hot ice, and wondrous strange snow.[d]
How shall we find the concord of this discord?

PHILOST. A play there is, my lord, some ten words long;
Which is as brief as I have known a play;
But by ten words, my lord, it is too long;
Which makes it tedious: for in all the play,
There is not one word apt, one player fitted.
And tragical, my noble lord, it is;
For Pyramus therein doth kill himself.
Which, when I saw rehears'd, I must confess,
Made mine eyes water; but more merry tears
The passion of loud laughter never shed.

THE. What are they that do play it?

PHILOST. Hard-handed men, that work in Athens here,
Which never labour'd in their minds till now;
And now have toil'd their unbreath'd memories
With this same play, against your nuptial.

THE. And we will hear it.

PHILOST. No, my noble lord,
It is not for you: I have heard it over,
And it is nothing, nothing in the world,
(Unless you can find sport in their intents,)
Extremely stretch'd, and conn'd with cruel pain,
To do you service.

THE. I will hear that play;
For never anything can be amiss,
When simpleness and duty tender it.
Go, bring them in: and take your places, ladies.
[*Exit* PHILOSTRATE.

HIP. I love not to see wretchedness o'ercharg'd,
And duty in his service perishing.

THE. Why, gentle sweet, you shall see no such thing.

HIP. He says, they can do nothing in this kind.

THE. The kinder we, to give them thanks for nothing.

(*) First folio, *rife*.

a Constancy;] *Consistency, congruity.*

b *Call* Philostrate.] The folio has, "Call *Egeus*;" and, in that edition, nearly every speech spoken by Philostrate in this scene assigned to *Egeus*. We follow the two quartos.

c *What* abridgment—] That is, what *pastime*.

d *That is, hot ice, and wondrous* strange *snow.*] *Strange* is undoubtedly a corruption. It forms no antithesis where one certainly was intended. Upton's *black* snow comes nearest to the sense demanded; but *strange* could hardly have been a misprint for *black*. Perhaps we should read, *swarthy* snow. *Swarte*, as formerly spelt, is not so far removed from the word in the text as Upton's *black*, or Hanmer's *scorching*, or the old annotator's *seething*.

Our sport shall be, to take what they mistake:
And what poor duty cannot do, noble respect
Takes it in might,[a] not merit.
Where I have come, great clerks have purposed
To greet me with premeditated welcomes;
Where I have seen them shiver and look pale,
Make periods in the midst of sentences,
Throttle their practis'd accent in their fears,
And, in conclusion, dumbly have broke off,
Not paying me a welcome. Trust me, sweet,
Out of this silence yet I pick'd a welcome;
And in the modesty of fearful duty,
I read as much, as from the rattling tongue
Of saucy and audacious eloquence.
Love, therefore, and tongue-tied simplicity,
In least, speak most, to my capacity.

Enter PHILOSTRATE.

PHILOST. So please your grace, the prologue is address'd.[b]

THE. Let him approach. [*Flourish of trumpets.*

Enter Prologue.[c]

PROL. *If we offend, it is with our good will.*
That you should think, we come not to offend,
But with good will. To show our simple skill,
That is the true beginning of our end.
Consider then, we come but in despite.
We do not come, as minding to content you,
Our true intent is. All for your delight,
We are not here. That you should here repent you,
The actors are at hand; and by their show,
You shall know all, that you are like to know.(2)

THE. This fellow doth not stand upon points.

LYS. He hath rid his prologue like a rough colt; he knows not the stop. A good moral, my lord: it is not enough to speak, but to speak true.

HIP. Indeed he hath played on his prologue like a child on a recorder: a sound, but not in government.

THE. His speech was like a tangled chain; nothing impaired, but all disordered. Who is next?

Enter PYRAMUS *and* THISBE, WALL, MOONSHINE, *and* LION, *as in dumb show.*[d]

PROL. Gentles, perchance you wonder at this show;
But wonder on, till truth make all things plain.
This man is Pyramus, if you would know;
This beauteous lady Thisbe is, certain.
This man, with lime and rough-cast, doth present
Wall, that vile Wall which did these lovers sunder:
And through Wall's chink, poor souls, they are content
To whisper; at the which let no man wonder.
This man, with lantern, dog, and bush of thorn,
Presenteth Moonshine: for, if you will know,
By moonshine did these lovers think no scorn
To meet at Ninus' tomb, there, there to woo.
This grisly beast, which by name Lion hight,[e]
The trusty Thisbe, coming first by night,
Did scare away, or rather did affright:
And, as she fled, her mantle she did fall;
Which Lion vile with bloody mouth did stain.
Anon comes Pyramus, sweet youth and tall,
And finds his trusty * Thisbe's mantle slain:
Whereat with blade, with bloody blameful blade,
He bravely broach'd his boiling bloody breast; (3)
And, Thisbe tarrying in mulberry shade,
His dagger drew, and died. For all the rest,
Let Lion, Moonshine, Wall, and lovers twain,
At large discourse, while here they do remain.
[*Exeunt* PROLOGUE, THISBE, LION, *and* MOONSHINE.

THE. I wonder, if the lion be to speak.

DEM. No wonder, my lord: one lion may, when many asses do.

WALL. In this same interlude, it doth befall,
That I, one Snout by name, present a wall:
And such a wall as I would have you think,
That had in it a cranny'd hole, or chink,
Through which the lovers, Pyramus and Thisbe,
Did whisper often very secretly.
This loam, this rough-cast, and this stone doth show
That I am that same wall; the truth is so:
And this the cranny is, right and sinister,
Through which the fearful lovers are to whisper.

THE. Would you desire lime and hair to speak better?

DEM. It is the wittiest partition that ever I heard discourse, my lord.

THE. Pyramus draws near the wall: silence.

PYR. O grim-look'd night! O night with hue so black!
O night, which ever art when day is not!
O night, O night, alack, alack, alack,
I fear my Thisbe's promise is forgot!—
And thou, O wall, O sweet, O† lovely wall,
That stand'st between her father's ground and mine,
Thou wall, O wall, O sweet and lovely wall,
Show me thy chink, to blink through with mine eyne.
[WALL *holds up his fingers.*
Thanks, courteous wall: Jove shield thee well for this!
But what see I? No Thisbe do I see.
O wicked wall, through whom I see no bliss;
Curs'd be thy stones for thus deceiving me!

THE. The wall, methinks, being sensible, should curse again.

BOT. No, in truth, sir, he should not. *Deceiving me* is Thisbe's cue: she is to enter now,‡ and I am to spy her through the wall. You shall see, it will fall pat as I told you:—yonder she comes.

---

[a] *Takes it in* might, *not merit.*] This is very oddly expressed; but the sense appears to be, "Takes it in *will, intention,*" &c., as in Act II. Sc. 3:—

"Love takes the *meaning* in love's conference."

[b] Address'd.] That is, *prepared.*

[c] *Enter* Prologue.] The prologue was evidently spoken by Peter Quince, as in the folio, after the direction, "*Enter the Prologue,*" is "*Quince.*"

(*) First folio omits, *trusty.*
(†) First folio, *thou sweet and.*
(‡) First folio omits, *now.*

[d] *Enter* Pyramus, &c.] In the folio this stage direction is preceded by a direction, "*Tawyer with a trumpet before them.*"

[e] *Which* by name Lion hight,—] The old text reads, "Lion hight by name." Theobald suggested the transposition, to make this line and the two next lines form a triplet.

Enter THISBE.

THIS. O wall, full often hast thou heard my moans,
For parting my fair Pyramus and me:
My cherry lips have often kiss'd thy stones;
Thy stones with lime and hair knit up in thee.
PYR. I see a voice: now will I to the chink,
To spy an I can hear my Thisbe's face.
Thisbe!
THIS. My love! thou art my love, I think.
PYR. Think what thou wilt, I am thy lover's grace;
And like Limander[a] am I trusty still.
THIS. And I like Helen, till the fates me kill.
PYR. Not Shafalus to Procrus was so true.
THIS. As Shafalus to Procrus, I to you.
PYR. O, kiss me through the hole of this vile wall.
THIS. I kiss the wall's hole, not your lips at all.
PYR. Wilt thou at Ninny's tomb meet me straightway?
THIS. 'Tide life, 'tide death, I come without delay.
WALL. Thus have I, Wall, my part discharged so;
And, being done, thus Wall away doth go.
[*Exeunt* WALL, PYRAMUS, *and* THISBE.

THE. Now is the mural* down between the two neighbours.

DEM. No remedy, my lord, when walls are so wilful to hear without warning.

HIP. This is the silliest stuff that ever I heard.

THE. The best in this kind are but shadows; and the worst are no worse, if imagination amend them.

HIP. It must be your imagination, then, and not theirs.

THE. If we imagine no worse of them, than they of themselves, they may pass for excellent men. Here come two noble beasts in, a man and a lion.[b]

Enter LION *and* MOONSHINE.

LION. You, ladies, you, whose gentle hearts do fear
The smallest monstrous mouse that creeps on floor,
May now, perchance, both quake and tremble here,
When lion rough in wildest rage doth roar.
Then know that I, one Snug the joiner, am
A lion fell,[c] nor else no lion's dam:
For if I should as lion come in strife
Into this place, 't were pity on† my life.

THE. A very gentle beast, and of a good conscience.

DEM. The very best at a beast, my lord, that e'er I saw.

LYS. This lion is a very fox for his valour.

THE. True; and a goose for his discretion.

DEM. Not so, my lord; for his valour cannot carry his discretion; and the fox carries the goose.

THE. His discretion, I am sure, cannot carry his valour; for the goose carries not the fox. It is well: leave it to his discretion, and let us hearken to the moon.

MOON. This lantern doth the horned moon present—

DEM. He should have worn the horns on his head.

THE. He is no crescent, and his horns are invisible within the circumference.

MOON. This lantern doth the horned moon present;
Myself the man i' th' moon doth seem to be.(4)

THE. This is the greatest error of all the rest: the man should be put into the lantern: how is it else the man i' the moon?

DEM. He dares not come there for the candle; for, you see, it is already in snuff.[d]

HIP. I am aweary of this moon; would he would change.

THE. It appears, by his small light of discretion,[e] that he is in the wane: but yet, in courtesy, in all reason, we must stay the time.

LYS. Proceed, Moon.

MOON. All that I have to say, is to tell you, that the lantern is the moon; I, the man in the moon; this thorn-bush, my thorn-bush; and this dog, my dog.

DEM. Why, all these should be in the lantern; for they are in the moon. But, silence; here comes Thisbe.

Enter THISBE.

THIS. This is old Ninny's tomb. Where is my love?
LION. Oh—. [*The* LION *roars.*—THISBE *runs off.*

DEM. Well roared, lion.

THE. Well run, Thisbe.

HIP. Well shone, moon. Truly, the moon shines with a good grace.

THE. Well moused, lion.

[LION *tears* THISBE'*s mantle, and exit.*

DEM. And then came Pyramus.

LYS. And so the lion vanished.

Enter PYRAMUS.

PYR. Sweet moon, I thank thee for thy sunny beams.
I thank thee, moon, for shining now so bright;
For, by thy gracious, golden, glittering gleams,[f]
I trust to taste of truest Thisbe's sight.
But stay;—O spite!
But mark;—poor knight,
What dreadful dole is here?
Eyes, do you see?
How can it be?
O dainty duck! O dear!

(*) Old copies, *moral*. (†) First folio, *of*.

[a] *And like* Limander—] Bottom's *Limander* and *Helen* are intended for Leander and Hero; as his *Shafalus* and *Procrus* for Cephalus and Procris.

[b] *Here come two noble beasts* in, a *man and a lion.*] The conceit is not apparent; and Theobald plausibly suggested that we should read,—

"——— in a moon and a lion."

[c] A lion fell, *nor else no lion's dam*:] So the old copies. Mr. Barron Field proposed for *A lion fell*, to read, *A lion's fell*, which is extremely ingenious; but in the rehearsal of this scene Snug is expressly enjoined to show his face through the lion's neck, tell his name and trade, and say, "If you think I come hither as a lion, it were pity of my life: *No*, I am no such thing," &c. I am disposed, therefore, if *nor* is not to be taken as relating to both members of the sentence, to read,—

"*No* lion fell, nor else no lion's dam;"—

i. e. neither lion nor lioness.

[d] *Already* in snuff.] That is, *in anger*. See Note (e), p. 84.

[e] *By his* small light of discretion,—] So, in "Love's Labour's Lost," Act V. Sc. 2:—"I have seen the day of wrong *through the little hole of discretion.*" The expression was evidently familiar, though we have never met with any explanation of it.

[f] *Thy gracious, golden, glittering* gleams,—] The old copies read, *beams*. We adopt the emendation suggested by Mr. Knight.

Thy mantle good,
What, stain'd with blood?
Approach, ye furies fell!
O fates! come, come;
Cut thread and thrum;
Quail, crush, conclude, and quell!

THE. This passion, and the death of a dear friend, would go near to make a man look sad.(5)

HIP. Beshrew my heart, but I pity the man.

PYR. O, wherefore, nature, didst thou lions frame?
Since lion vile hath here deflower'd my dear:
Which is—no, no—which was the fairest dame,
That liv'd, that lov'd, that lik'd, that look'd with cheer.
Come, tears, confound;
Out, sword, and wound
The pap of Pyramus:
Ay, that left pap
Where heart doth hop:—
Thus die I, thus, thus, thus.
Now am I dead,
Now am I fled,
My soul is in the sky:
Tongue, lose thy light!
Moon, take thy flight!
Now, die, die, die, die, die.
[*Dies.—Exit* MOONSHINE.

DEM. No die, but an ace, for him; for he is but one.

LYS. Less than an ace, man, for he is dead; he is nothing.

THE. With the help of a surgeon, he might yet recover, and prove an ass.

HIP. How chance Moonshine is gone, before Thisbe comes back and finds her lover?

THE. She will find him by starlight.—Here she comes; and her passion ends the play.

Enter THISBE.

HIP. Methinks, she should not use a long one for such a Pyramus: I hope she will be brief.

DEM. A mote will turn the balance, which Pyramus, which Thisbe, is the better. He for a man, God warn'd us; she for a woman, God bless us.[a]

LYS. She hath spied him already with those sweet eyes.

DEM. And thus she moans,[b] *videlicet.*

THIS. Asleep, my love?
What, dead, my dove?
O Pyramus, arise,
Speak, speak. Quite dumb?
Dead, dead? A tomb
Must cover thy sweet eyes.
These lily lips,
This cherry nose,
These yellow cowslip cheeks,
Are gone, are gone:
Lovers, make moan!
His eyes were green as leeks.
O sisters three,
Come, come to me,
With hands as pale as milk;
Lay them in gore,
Since you have shore
With shears his thread of silk.
Tongue, not a word:
Come, trusty sword;
Come, blade, my breast imbrue;
And farewell, friends;
Thus Thisbe ends:
Adieu, adieu, adieu. [*Dies.*

THE. Moonshine and Lion are left to bury the dead.

DEM. Ay, and Wall too.

BOT. No, I assure you; the wall is down that parted their fathers. Will it please you to see the epilogue, or to hear a Bergomask[c] dance, between two of our company?

THE. No epilogue, I pray you; for your play needs no excuse. Never excuse; for when the players are all dead, there need none to be blamed. Marry, if he that writ it had played Pyramus, and hanged himself in Thisbe's garter, it would have been a fine tragedy: and so it is, truly; and very notably discharged. But come, your Bergomask: let your epilogue alone.
[*Here a dance of* Clowns.[d]
The iron tongue of midnight hath told twelve:—
Lovers to bed: 't is almost fairy time.
I fear we shall outsleep the coming morn,
As much as we this night have overwatch'd.
This palpable-gross play hath well beguil'd
The heavy gait of night.—Sweet friends, to bed.—
A fortnight hold we this solemnity,
In nightly revels, and new jollity. [*Exeunt.*

SCENE II.

Enter PUCK.

PUCK. Now the hungry lion roars,
And the wolf behowls* the moon;

---

[a] *He for a man, God* warn'd *us; she for a woman, God bless us.*] We should probably read, "God *ward* us." The meaning appears to be, "From such a man God defend us; from such a woman God save us." The passage is altogether omitted in the folio, on account of the statute, 3 Jac. ch. 21, against the profane using of the sacred name.

[b] *And thus she* moans,—] The old copies have *means.* The change was made by Theobald; but, perhaps, without necessity, as *means* appears formerly to have sometimes borne the same signification. Thus, in "The Two Gentlemen of Verona," Act V. Sc. 4:—

"The more degenerate and base art thou,
To make such *means* for her as thou hast done."

(*) Old copies, *beholds.*

[c] *A* Bergomask *dance,*—] This is supposed to have been a dance in the manner of the rustics of Bergomasco, a province of Italy.

[d] *Here a dance of Clowns.*] This stage direction was introduced by Malone.

Whilst the heavy ploughman snores,
All with weary task fordone.
Now the wasted brands do glow,
Whilst the scritch-owl, scritching loud,
Puts the wretch, that lies in woe,
In remembrance of a shroud.
Now it is the time of night,
That the graves, all gaping wide,
Every one lets forth his sprite,
In the church-way paths to glide.
And we fairies, that do run
By the triple Hecate's team,
From the presence of the sun,
Following darkness like a dream,
Now are frolic; not a mouse
Shall disturb this hallow'd house:
I am sent, with broom, before,
To sweep the dust behind the door.

Enter OBERON *and* TITANIA, *with their Train.*

OBE. Through the house give glimmering light,
By the dead and drowsy fire,
Every elf, and fairy sprite,
Hop as light as bird from brier;
And this ditty, after me,
Sing, and dance it trippingly.

TITA. First, rehearse your * song by rote:
To each word a warbling note,
Hand in hand, with fairy grace,
Will we sing, and bless this place.

SONG, AND DANCE.

OBE. Now, until the break of day,
Through this house each fairy stray.
To the best bride-bed will we,
Which by us shall blessed be:(6)
And the issue there create,
Ever shall be fortunate.
So shall all the couples three
Ever true in loving be;
And the blots of Nature's hand
Shall not in their issue stand;
Never mole, hare-lip, nor scar,
Nor mark prodigious, such as are
Despised in nativity,
Shall upon their children be.
With this field-dew consecrate,
Every fairy take his gait;
And each several chamber bless,
Through this palace with sweet peace,
And the owner of it blest,
Ever shall in safety rest.[a]
Trip away;
Make no stay:
Meet me all by break of day.
[*Exeunt* OBERON, TITANIA, *and Train.*

PUCK. If we shadows have offended,
Think but this, (and all is mended,)
That you have but slumber'd here,
While these visions did appear.
And this weak and idle theme,
No more yielding but a dream,
Gentles, do not reprehend;
If you pardon, we will mend.
And, as I am an honest Puck,
If we have unearned luck,
Now to 'scape the serpent's tongue,
We will make amends, ere long:
Else the Puck a liar call.
So, good night unto you all.
Give me your hands, if we be friends,
And Robin shall restore amends. [*Exit.*

(*) First folio, *this.*

a And the owner of it blest,
Ever shall in safety rest.]
In the old editions these lines run thus:—
"Ever shall in safety rest,
And the owner of it blest."
I, at one time, thought "*Ever shall*" a misprint for "*Every hall;*" and proposed to read,—
"Every hall in safety rest,
And the owner of it blest;"—
but it has since been suggested to me by Mr. Singer, and by an anonymous correspondent, that the difficulty in the passage arose from the printer's having transposed the two last lines.

ILLUSTRATIVE COMMENTS.

ACT I.

(1) SCENE I.—*Awake the pert and nimble spirit of mirth.*] The very peculiar use of the adjective *pert* in this line, shows that in the sixteenth century it was not always understood with the ordinary meaning of saucy or talkative, but that it was also employed to express, *quick, lively, subtle.* Hence Skinner, in 1671, derived it through the French *appert,* from the Latin *ad peritus,* skilful, *expert, prompt,* &c. He also cites Dr. Davies as stating that in the Cambro-British the word signified elegant, or beautiful, as it occurs in the English poetical version of the Romance of Sir Launfal, in the description of Dame Tryainous :—

"Sche was as whyt as lylye in May,
Or snow that sneweth yn wynterys day;
He seigh never none so *pert.*"
KEIGHTLEY'S *Fairy Mythology,* Ed. 1850, p. 36.

(2) SCENE I.—
Brief as the lightning in the collied night,
That, in a spleen, unfolds both heaven and earth,
And ere a man hath power to say,—Behold!
The jaws of darkness do devour it up.]

"The word *spleen* is laid under suspicion by Warburton, and is not justified by the later commentators. Nares says, 'We do not find it so used by other writers.' This is a mistake: and it will be seen that a happier choice could not have been made than the poet has made of this word :—

'Like winter fires that with disdainful heat
The opposition of the cold defeat;
And in an *angry spleen* do burn more fair
The more encountered by the frosty air.'
Verses by POOLE, *before his England's Parnassus,* 8vo. 1657.

So, in Lithgow's 'Nineteen Years' Travels,' quarto, 1632, p. 61 :—'All things below and above being cunningly perfected, and every one ranked in order with his harquebuse and pike, to stand in the centinel of his own defence, we recommend ourselves in the hands of the Almighty, and, in the meanwhile, attended their fiery salutations. In a *furious spleen,* the first holla of their courtesies was the progress of a martial conflict, thundering forth a terrible noise of gally-roaring pieces,' " &c.
HUNTER'S *New Illustrations of Shakespeare,* I. 289.

(3) SCENE I.—
——— *In the wood a league without the town,*
Where I did meet thee once with Helena,
To do observance to a morn of May.]

The principal ceremonies with which young persons of both sexes were formerly accustomed to honour the mornings of May, were the Maying, which belonged especially to the first day; and the collecting of May-dew, which appears to have been practised at any part of the month. "On the *Calends,* or the first day of May," says Bourne, "commonly called May-day, the juvenile part of both sexes were wont to rise a little after midnight, and walk to some neighbouring wood, accompany'd with music, and the blowing of horns, where they break down branches from the trees, and adorn them with *nosegays* and *crowns of flowers.* When this is done they return with their booty homewards about the rising of the sun, and make their doors and windows to triumph in the flowery spoil. The after part of the day is chiefly spent in dancing round a tall pole, which is called a *May Pole;* which being placed in a convenient part of the village, stands there, as it were, consecrated to the *Goddess of Flowers,* without the least violence offered it, in the whole circle of the year."

The general popularity of this custom of early rising "to go a Maying," may be inferred from a passage in "Henry VIII." Act V. Sc. 3, where the Porter's man exclaims of the crowd :—

"——— 'T is as much impossible
To scatter them, as 't is to make them sleep
On May-day morning, which will never be."

Herrick—for in his time, though half a century later than Shakespeare, bigotry had not succeeded in frowning down all the simple, healthful pleasures of the people—has a poem, *Corinna's going a Maying,* in which the May worship is delightfully pictured :—

"Get up———and see
The dew-bespangling herbe and tree :
Each flower has wept, and bow'd toward the east,
Above an houre since ;—it is sin,
Nay, profanation to keep in;
Whenas a thousand virgins on this day,
Spring sooner than the lark, to fetch in May!
Come, my Corinna, come; and coming marke
How each field turns a street, each street a parke,
Made green, and trimm'd with trees, see how
Devotion gives each house a bough,
Or branch: each porch, each doore, ere this,
An arke, a tabernacle is
Made up of white-thorn neatly interwove.—

There's not a budding boy, or girle, this day,
But is got up, and gone to bring in May:
A deale of youth ere this is come
Back, and with white-thorn laden home.
Some have dispatcht their cakes and creame,
Before that we have left to dreame:
And some have wept, and woo'd and plighted troth,
And chose their priest, ere we can cast off sloth."

The most direct and charming illustration of the homage paid to the month of love and flowers is, however, contained in two exquisite pictures from the Knightes Tale of Chaucer :—

This passeth yere by yere, and day by day,
Tille it felle ones in a morwè of May,
That Emelie that fayrer was to seene
Than is the lilie on hire stalkes grene,
And fresher than the May with flowrès newe,
(For with the rose colour strof hire hewe;
I n'ot which was the finer of hem two,)
Ere it was day, as sche was wont to do,
Sche was arisen and al redy dight;
For May wol have no slogardiè a-night.
The seson priketh every gentil herte,
And maketh him out of his sleepe sterte,
And seith, '*Aryse, and do thin observance.*'
This maketh Emilie han remembrance
To do honour to May, and for to ryse."—

And,—

"The busy larke, messager of day,
Saleweth in hir song the morwe gray;
And fiery Phœbus ryseth up so bright,
That all the orient laugheth of the light:
And with his strêmes drieth in the greves
The silver droppès hongyng on the leaves;
And Arcite, that is in the court ryal
With Theseus, his squier principal,
Is risen, and looketh on the mery day;
And for to do on his *observance to May*,
Remembring of the point of his desire,
He on his courser, sterting as the fire,
Is riden into fieldès him to pleye,
Out of the court, were it a mile or tway:
And to the grove, of which that I you told,
By aventure his way he 'gan to hold,
To maken him a garland of the greves,
Were it of woodewynde or hawthorn leaves,
And loud he song against the sonny scheen;
'May, with all thyn floures and thy greene,
Welcome be thou, wel faire freissche May.'"

All the ceremonial observed by Emelie is to walk in her garden at the sun-rising; and this primitively was perhaps the simple method of collecting the May-dew—receiving it on the face and hands before it had evaporated. In the seventeenth century, however, the dew, held sovereign as a cosmetic by the damsels of old, was evidently gathered in phials; for, in 1667, Mrs. Turner had taught Mrs. Pepys to collect the May-dew, as being "the only thing in the world to wash her face with."

(4) SCENE I.—*Your eyes are lode-stàrs.*] The *lode-star* is the *leading* or *guiding star*, the *pole-star*, by which navigators directed their course. Davies, in his "Dedication to Queen Elizabeth," calls her,—

"*Lode-stone* to hearts, and *lode-star* to all eyes."

And in another place speaks of her as,—

"Eagle-ey'd Wisdome, life's *lode-star*."
* * * * *
"If we this star once cease to see
No doubt our state will shipwreck'd be."

Milton adopts the same metaphor in his "L'Allegro:"—

"Towers and battlements it sees
Bosom'd high in tufted trees,
Where perhaps some beauty lies,
The *cynosure* of neighboring eyes."

(5) SCENE II.—*Enter Quince, Bottom, Flute, Snug, Snout, and Starveling.*] The old editions add the several occupations of these individuals after their names, when they make their first appearance. It is possible that in the rude dramatic performance of these handicraftsmen of Athens, Shakespeare was referring to the plays and pageants exhibited by the trading companies of Coventry, which were celebrated down to his own time, and which he might very probably have witnessed. The last of those performances recorded in the list which the late Mr. Thomas Sharpe published from the City Leet-books, took place in 1591; when it was agreed by the whole consent of the council, "that the Destrucyon of Jerusalem, the Conquest of the Danes, or the Historie of King Edward (the Confessor), should be plaied on the pagens on Midsomer daye and St. Peter's daye next, in this cittie, and none other playes." In 1656, Dugdale states that he had been told "by some old people, who, in their younger years were eye-witnesses of these pageants, that the yearly confluence of people to see that shew, was extraordinary great, and yielded no small advantage to this city." For the support therefor of the expenses of these profitable entertainments, the several municipal trading companies of Coventry were charged either to contribute in association to the exhibition of a joint performance; or else to furnish a pageant of their own. These theatrical unions were ordered by the Leet or Common Council; and the combination of trades which played together was often remarkably like that of the operatives of Athens in this drama:—

"A crew of patches, rude mechanicals,
That work for bread upon Athenian stalls,
(Who) met together to rehearse a play."—Act III. Sc. 2.

In 1434 it was ordered "that the Sadelers and the Peyntours, be fro this tyme contrebetory unto the pajont of the Cardemakers." In 1435 the council "will that the Carpenters be associate unto the Tilers and Pinners, to maynten ther pagent." In 1492 "it is ordeyned that the Chaundelers and Cookes of this Cite shall be contributory to the Smythes of this Cite;" and in subsequent years Bakers were added to the Smiths, the Barbers to the Girdlers, and the Shoemakers to the Tanners. So late as 1533 it was "enacted that such persons as are not associate or assistant to any craft which is charged with a pageant, such as Fishmongers, Bowyers, Fletchers, and others, shall now be associate or assistant to such crafts as the Mayor shall assign." As most of the performances of these companies were Religious Mysteries taken from the Scriptures, there appears to have been a priest attached to each society, who directed the exhibition probably and played the most important part, as well as taught the other actors.

(6) SCENE II.—QUIN. *Marry, our play is—The most lamentable comedy and most cruel death of Pyramus and Thisbe.*] In the title of this interlude Shakespeare doubtless intended a burlesque on the old play by Thomas Preston, entitled, "A lamentable tragedie *mixed full of pleasant mirth* containing the life of Cambises king of Persia." The sad tale of Pyramus and Thisbe is told in the fourth book of Ovid's Metamorphoses; and if we may judge by the number of versions put forth in the sixteenth century, the story must have been very popular with our forefathers. The book of "Perymus and Thesbye" was entered on the Stationers' registers in 1562–3. Arthur Golding's translation of Ovid was first published in 1567; and went through several editions. Another translation of the tale of the lovers appeared in the "Gorgious Gallery of Gallant Inventions," 1578; and a "new sonet of Pyramus and Thisbie" in "The Handefull of Pleasant Delites," 1584. Of course, the incidents are the same in all; but Shakespeare appears to have had recourse to Golding's version, some extracts from which are here given:—

"Within the towne (of whose huge walles so monstrous high and thicke
The fame is giuen Semyramis for making them of bricke)
Dwelt hard toogither twoo yoong folke in houses ioynde so nere
That vnder all one roofe well nie both twaine conueyed were.
The name of him was Pyramus and Thisbe cald was shee.
* * * * * *
And if that right had taken place, they had bin man and wife.
But still their Parents went about to let which (for their life)
They could not let. * * * *
The wall that parted house from house had riuen therein a cranie
Which shroonke at making of the wall, this fault not markt of anie
Of many hundred yeeres before (what doth not loue espie?)
These louers first of all found out, and made a way whereby
To talke togither secretly, and through the same did go
Their louing whisprings very light and safely to and fro.
Now as at one side Pyramus, and Thisbe on the tother
Stood often drawing one of them the pleasant breath from other,
O thou envious wall (they sayd) why letst thou louers thus
What matter were it if that thou permitted both of vs
In armes ech other to embrace? Or if thou thinke that this
Were ouer-much, yet mightest thou at least make roome to kisse.
* * * * * *
Thus hauing where they stoode in vaine complayned of their wo,
When night drew neere, they bade adew and eche gaue kisses sweete
Vnto the parget on their side, the whiche did neuer meete.
* * * * * *
And to thentent that in the feeldes they strayde not up and downe,
They did agree at Ninus Tumb to meet without the towne,
And tarie vnderneath a tree that by the same did grow
Which was a faire high Mulberie with fruite as white as snow.
* * * * * *
As soone as darkenesse once was come, straight Thisbe did deuyse
A shift to wind her out of doores, that none that were within
Perceiued her: and muffling her with clothes about her chin,
That no man might discerne her face, to Ninus Tombe she came
Vnto the tree; and set her downe there vnderneath the same.

Loue made her bold, but see the chance, there comes besmerde with blood
About the chappes a Lyonnesse all foming from the wood
From slaughter lately made of kine, to stanch her bloody thirst
With water of the foresaid spring. Whom Thisbe spying first
Afarre by moonelight, thereupon with fearefull steps gan flie
And in a dark and yrkesome caue did hide her selfe thereby
And as she fled away for haste she let her mantle fall
The which for feare she left behinde not looking backe at all.

* * * * * * *

The night was somewhat further spent ere Pyramus came there
Who seeing in the suttle sand the print of Lyons paw,
Waxt pale for feare. But when also the bloodie cloke he saw
All rent and torne: one night (he sayd) shall louers two confound
My soule deserves of this mischaunce the perill for to beare.

* * * * * * *

And when he had bewept and kist the garment which he knew,
Receiue thou my blood too, (quoth he) and therewithall he drew
His sword the which among his guts he thrust, and by and bie
Did draw it from the bleeding wound beginning for to die,
And cast himselfe vpon his backe, the blood did spinne on hie.

* * * * * * *

For doubt of disapoynting him comes Thisbe forth in hast,
And for her louer lookes about, reioycing for to tell
How hardly she had scapt that night the danger that befell.
* * * she cast her eye aside
And there beweltred in his bloud hir louer she espide.

* * * * * * *

She beate hir brest, she shricked out, she tare hir golden heares,
And taking him betweene hir armes did wash his wounds with teares,
She meynt hir weepying with his bloud, and kissing all his face
(Which now became as cold as yse) she cride in wofull case
Alas what chaunce my Pyramus hath parted thee and mee?
Make aunswere O my Pyramus: It is thy Thisb euen shee
Whome thou doste loue most heartely that speaketh unto thee.
Giue eare and raise thy heauie head. He hearing Thisbe's name
Lift vp his dying eyes and hauing seene hir closde the same.
But when she knew hir mantle there, and saw his scabberd lie
Without the sworde: Unhappy man thy loue hath made thee die:
Thy loue (she said) hath made thee slea thy selfe. This hand of mine
Is strong enough to doe the like. My loue no lesse than thine
Shall giue me force to work my wound. I will pursue the dead.

* * * * * * *

This said she tooke the sword yet warme with slaughter of hir loue
And setting it beneath hir brest, did to her heart it shoue."

(7) SCENE II.—*Hold, or cut bow-strings.*] Capell's explication of this disputed saying is no doubt the true one. "When a party was made at butts, assurance of meeting was given in the words of that phrase: the sense of the person using them being, that he would '*hold,*' or keep promise, or they might '*cut* his *bowstrings,*' demolish him for an archer." There is another proverbial expression of the same character, which none of the commentators, that I am aware of, has mentioned:—"Hold, or cut cod-piece point."

ACT II.

(1) SCENE I.—
Or else you are that shrewd and knavish sprite,
Called Robin Goodfellow.]

The frolics Shakespeare attributes to Puck, or, as he was usually called, Robin Goodfellow, correspond in every particular with the popular characteristics of this "shrewd and meddling elf." According to the rare tract entitled "The Mad Pranks and Merry Jests of Robin Goodfellow," reprinted by Mr. Collier from the original in Lord Francis Egerton's library, Robin Goodfellow was the son of Oberon, or Obreon, his mother being "a proper young wench" whom the fayry king was in the habit of visiting. Robin's knavish propensities as he grew up became so troublesome, that to avoid the punishment they entailed, he ran away from his mother and was engaged to a tailor. After a short time he leaves his master, and the tract relates—

"WHAT HAPNED TO ROBIN GOODFELLOW AFTER HE WENT FROM THE TAYLOR.

After Robin had travailed a good dayes journy from his masters house hee sate downe, and beeing weary hee fell a sleepe. No sooner had slumber tooken full possession of him, and closed his long opened eye-lids, but hee thought he saw many goodly proper personages in anticke measures tripping about him, and withall hee heard such musicke, as he thought that Orpheus, that famous Greeke fidler (had hee beene alive), compared to one of these had beene as infamous as a Welch-harper that playes for cheese and onions. As delights commonly last not long, so did those end sooner than hee would willingly they should have done; and for very griefe he awaked, and found by him lying a scroule, wherein was written these lines following in golden letters.

Robin, my only sonne and heire,
How to live take thou no care:
By nature thou hast cunning shifts,
Which Ile increase with other gifts.
Wish what thou wilt, thou shalt it have;
And for to vex both foole and knave,
Thou hast the power to change thy shape,
To horse, to hog, to dog, to ape.
Transformed thus, by any meanes
See none thou harm'st but knaves and queanes;
But love thou those that honest be,
And help them in necessity.
Do thus, and all the world shall know
The prankes of Robin Good-fellow;
For by that name thou cald shall be
To ages last posterity.
If thou observe my just command,
One day thou shalt see Fayry Land.
This more I give: who tels thy prankes
From those that heare them shall have thankes.

Robin having read this was very joyfull, yet longed he to know whether he had this power or not, and to try it hee wished for some meate: presently it was before him. Then wished hee for beere and wine: he straightway had it. This liked him well, and because he was weary, he wished himselfe a horse: no sooner was his wish ended, but he was transformed, and seemed a horse of twenty pound price, and leaped and curveted as nimble as if he had beene in stable at racke and manger a full moneth. Then wished he himselfe a dog, and was so: then a tree, and was so: so from one thing to another, till he was certaine and well assured that hee could change himselfe to any thing whatsoever."

Though the edition from which Mr. Collier made his reprint is dated 1628, there is little doubt that the tract, as he remarks, was published at least forty years earlier, and was evidently known to Shakespeare. The following account, "HOW ROBIN GOOD-FELLOW LED A COMPANY OF FELLOWES OUT OF THEIR WAY," is a good illustration of the passage,—

"Mislead night-wanderers, laughing at their harm."

"A company of young men having beene making merry with their sweet hearts, were at their comming home to come over a heath. Robin Good-fellow, knowing of it, met them, and to make some pastime, hee led them up and downe the heath a whole night, so that they could not get out of it: for hee went before them in the shape of a walking fire, which they all saw and followed till the day did appeare: then Robin left them, and at his departure spake these words:—

Get you home, you merry lads:
Tell your mammies and your dads,
And all those that newes desire,
How you saw a walking fire.
Wenches, that doe smile and lispe,
Use to call me Willy Wispe.
If that you but weary be,
It is sport alone for me.
Away: unto your houses goe
And I'll goe laughing *ho, ho, hoh!*

The fellowes were glad that he was gone, for they were all in a great feare that hee would have done them some mischiefe."

The line which we have italicized will recal the same expression used by Puck in the play:—

"Then will two at once woo one;
That must needs be *sport alone.*"—Act III. Sc. 2.

(2) SCENE I.—OBERON. *Ill met by moonlight, proud Titania.*] The names of Oberon and Titania were, no doubt, familiar in connexion with the race of *Faëry* before the time of Shakespeare. Oberon, the "dwarfe king of fayryes," is introduced into the popular romance of Huon de Bordeaux, translated by Lord Berners, probably earlier than 1558. The older part of Huon de Bordeaux, Mr. Keightley has shown to have been taken from the story of Otnit in the Heldenbuch, where the dwarf king Elberich performs nearly the same services to Otnit that Oberon does to Huon. The name of Oberon, in fact, according to Grimm, is only Elberich slightly altered. From the usual change of *l* into *u* (as *al, au, col, cou,* &c.), in the French language, Elberich or Albrich (derived from *Alp, Alf*) becomes Auberich; and *ich* not being a French termination, the dominative *on* was substituted, and thus the name became Auberon, or Oberon. The elf queen's name, Titania, was an appellation of Diana. "It was the belief, in those days, that the fairies were the same as the classic nymphs, the attendants of Diana. 'That fourth kind of sprites,' says King James, 'guhilk be the gentiles was called Diana, and her wandering court, and amongst us called the *Phairëe.*' The Fairy-queen was therefore the same as Diana, whom Ovid styles Titania."—KEIGHTLEY.

(3) SCENE I.—

Didst thou not lead him through the glimmering night
From Perigenia, whom he ravished?
And make him with fair Æglê break his faith,
With Ariadne, and Antiopa?]

Shakespeare's authority for all this was his diligently-read Plutarch:—

Perigenia.] "This Sinnis had a goodly faire daughter called Perigouna, which fled away when she saw her father slaine * * * but Theseus finding her, called her, and sware by his faith he would use her gently, and do her no hurt, nor displeasure her at all."

Ariadne. Æglê.] "They report many other things also touching this matter, and specially of Ariadne: but there is no troth nor certaintie in it. For some say that Ariadne hung herselfe for sorow, when she saw that Theseus had cast her off. Other write, that she was transported by mariners into the Ile of Naxos, where she was married unto Œnarus, the priest of Bacchus: and they think that Theseus left her, because he was in love with another, as by these verses should appeare:—

'Ægles the nymph was loved of Theseus,
Who was the daughter of Panopeus.'"

From this passage Shakespeare evidently got his "faire *Eagles,*" as the lady's name is spelt in all the old editions.

Antiopa.] "Touching the voyage he made by the sea Maior, Philochurus, and some other hold opinion, that he went thither with Hercules against the Amazons: and that to honour his valiantness, Hercules gave him Antiopa the Amazone. But the more part of the other Historiographers do write that Theseus went thither alone, after Hercules' voyage, and that he tooke this Amazone prisoner, which is likeliest to be true * * * Bion also the Historiographer saith that he brought her away by deceit and stealth * * * and that Theseus enticed her to come into his shippe, who brought him a present; and so soone as she was aboord, he hoysed his saile, and so carried her away."—NORTH'S *Plutarch* (*Life of Theseus*).

(4) SCENE I.—*The nine men's morris is filled up with mud.*] *Nine men's morris,* or *nine men's merrils,* as it was sometimes called, from *merelles,* an old French word for the counters with which it was originally conducted, is a rustic sport, played on a diagram cut out of the turf of which the figure consists of three squares, one within another. Sometimes the largest square is not more than a foot in diameter, at others it is four or five yards. These squares are united by cross lines, which extend from the middle of each line of the innermost square to the middle of the outermost line. The stations or houses for the men (usually represented by stones or pieces of tile) are at the corners of the squares, and at the junctures of the intersecting lines, and number in all twenty-four. The game is played by two persons, each of whom has *nine men,* or counters, which they begin by playing alternately, one at a time, to any of the stations they may select. When the men are all deposited in the places chosen, each party, moving alternately, as in chess or draughts, aims to place three of them *on a line;* and every time he achieves this object he is entitled to remove one of the adversary's men from the field. Of course his opponent, if he foresee the scheme, endeavours to frustrate it by playing a man of his own on to the line. When one player succeeds in removing all his antagonist's men from the board, he wins the game. The original game, called *Jeu de Merelles,* was probably played on a board or table like chess, with men made for the purpose. It is supposed to have come from France, and is undoubtedly very ancient. Douce speaks of a representation of two monkeys engaged at it in a German edition of Petrarch "de remedio utriusque fortunæ," b. 1, ch. 26, the cuts of which were executed in 1520; but in the Bibliothèque of Paris there is a beautiful manuscript on parchment (7391) by Nicholas de St. Nicolai, of the 12th century, containing some hundred of illuminated diagrams of remarkable positions in Chess and *in Merelles.* Whether the game is now obsolete in France, I am unable to say; but it is still practised, though rarely, in this country, both on the turf and on the table, its old title having undergone another mutation, and become "*Mill.*"

In Cotgrave's Dictionary, 1611, under the article Merelles, the following explanation is given: "Le Ieu des merelles. *The boyish game called Merills, or five-pennie Morris; played here most commonly with stones, but in France with pawnes, or men made of purpose, and tearmed Merelles.*"

(5) SCENE I.—*I am invisible.*] Theobald remarks that as Oberon and Puck may be frequently observed to speak, when there is no mention of their entering, they are designed by the poet to be supposed on the stage during the greatest part of the remainder of the play; and so mix, as they please, as spirits, with the other actors, and embroil the plot without being seen or heard but when they choose. Among the stage properties mentioned in Henslowe's Diary is "a robe for to go invisible." It is not improbable that a similar robe was worn by supernatural beings, such as Oberon, Ariel, &c.; who, when so habited, were understood by the audience to be invisible to the other characters.

ACT III.

(1) SCENE II.—*An ass's nowl I fixed on his head.*] Bottom's transformation might have been suggested, as Steevens observes, by a passage in the "History of the Damnable Life and Deserved Death of Dr. John Faustus," chap. xliii. :—"The guests having sat, and well eat and drank, Dr. Faustus made that every one had an ass's head on, with great and long ears, so they fell to dancing, and to drive away the time until it was midnight, and then every one departed home, and as soon as they were out of the house, each one was in his natural shape, and so they ended and went to sleep."

A receipt for this metamorphosis is given in Albertus Magnus de Secretis :—"Si vis quod caput hominis assimiletur *capiti asini,* sume de segimine aselli, et unge hominem in capite, et sic apparebit." And another, in Scott's "Discoverie of Witchcraft," b. 13, chap. xix. :—"Cutt off the head of a horsse or an asse (before they be dead), otherwise the vertue or strength thereof will be lesse effectuall, and make an earthern vessell of fit capacitie to containe the same, and let it be filled with the oile and fat thereof: cover it close, and daube it over with lome : let it boile over a soft fier three daies continuallie, that the flesh boiled may run into oile, so as the bare bones may be seene : beate the haire into powder, and mingle the same with the oile ; and annoint the *heads of the standers by,* and they shall seem to have horsses or *asses* heads."

In all likelihood, however, the trick was familiar to play-goers long before Shakespeare's time ; and Mr. Halliwell quotes a stage direction in the "Chester Mysteries," as proof of this :—"*Tunc percutiet Balaham asinam suam, et nota quod hic oportet aliquis transformari in speciem asine, et quando Balaham percutiet dicat asina—;*" which we take the liberty of rendering into befitting English :—*Then Balaham shall smyte his asse, and note that here it is fittyng that one shoulde bee dysguysed into the lykenesse of an asse, and when Balaham smyteth the asse shall saye—.* But it is not easy to see in what way this direction illustrates the passage of the text.

(2) SCENE II.—

So we grew together,
Like to a double cherry, seeming parted ;
But yet a union in partition,
Two lovely berries moulded on one stem :
So, with two seeming bodies, but one heart ;
Two of the first, like coats in heraldry,
Due but to one, and crowned with one crest.]

An important step towards the comprehension of this difficult passage was made by Martin Folkes, when he pointed out to Theobald that "*life coats,*" the reading of the old copies, was a misprint for "*like* coats." After the aid of this emendation, however, the commentators appear to have shown more ingenuity than sagacity in their endeavours to elucidate the sense. The plain heraldical allusion is to the simple impalements of two armorial ensigns, as they are marshalled side by side to represent a marriage ; and the expression "Two of the First," is to *that particular form of dividing the shield, being the first in order of the nine ordinary partitions of the Escutcheon.* These principles were familiarly understood in the time of Shakespeare by all the readers of the many very popular heraldical works of the period, and an extract from one of these will probably render the meaning of the passage clear. In "*The Accedence of Armorie,*" published by Gerard Leigh, in 1597, he says, "Now will I declare to you of IX sundrie Partitions :—the *First whereof is a partition from the highest part of the Escocheon to the lowest. And though it must be blazed so, yet is it a joining together.* It is also as a mariage, that is to say, *two cotes ;* the man's on the right side, and the woman's on the left : as it might be said that Argent had maried with Gules." In different words, this is nothing else than an amplification of Helena's own expression,—

"—— seeming parted ;
But yet a union in partition."

The shield bearing the arms of two married persons would of course be surmounted by one crest only, as the text properly remarks, that of the husband. In Shakespeare's day, the only pleas for bearing two crests were ancient usage, or a special grant. The modern practice of introducing a second crest by an heiress has been most improperly adopted from the German heraldical system ; for it should be remembered, that as a female cannot wear a helmet, so neither can she bear a crest.

(3) SCENE II.—*Ho, ho, ho !*] There is an ancient Norfolk proverb, "To laugh like Robin Goodfellow," which means, we presume, to laugh in mockery or scorn. This derision was always expressed by the exclamation in the text, which is as old as the Devil of the early mysteries, whose "ho, ho, ho !" was habitual upon the stage long before the introduction of Robin Goodfellow. In "Histriomastix" (quoted by Steevens) a *roaring devil* enters, with the *Vice* on his back, *Iniquity* in one hand, and *Juventus* in the other, crying ;—

"Ho, ho, ho! these babes mine are all."

In "Gammer Gurton's Needle," the same form of cachinnation is attributed to the Evil One :—

"But Diccon, Diccon, did not the devil cry, *ho, ho, ho?*"

It seems with our ancestors always to have conveyed the idea of something fiendish or supernatural, and is the established burden to the songs which describe the frolics of Robin Goodfellow. See the curious tract before mentioned, called "The Mad Pranks and Merry Jests of Robin Goodfellow."

ACT IV.

(1) Scene I.—*I have a reasonable good ear in music; let us have the tongs and the bones.*] If the employment of unusual instruments to produce a barbarous kind of music were ingeniously traced backward to extreme antiquity, the origin of it might perhaps be found when "Pyctagoras passed som tyme by a symythes' hous, and herde a swete sowne, accordynge to the mystynge of foure hamers upon an anvelt;" as Higden relates the story. The practice of performing rustic or burlesque music is, however, really ancient; and Strutt attributes the invention of it to the minstrels and joculators, who appear to have converted every species of amusement into a vehicle for mirth. He has engraved some parts of two illuminations of the fourteenth century, in one of which a youth is playing to a tumbler, by beating on a metal basin held on a staff; and in the other, an individual is depicted "holding a pair of bellows by way of fiddle, and using the tongs as the substitute for the bow." Mr. Halliwell has illustrated the passage which forms the subject of this note, by a reference to two figures in the original sketches of actors in the court masques, executed by Inigo Jones: one of which represents a performer with tongs and key; and the other a player on knackers of bone or wood, clacked together between the fingers. These instruments must be regarded as the immediate precursors of the more musical marrow-bones and cleavers, the introduction of which may, with great probability, be referred to the establishment of Clare Market, in the middle of the seventeenth century; since the butchers of that place were particularly celebrated for their performances. In Addison's description of John Dentry's remarkable "kitchen music" (Spectator, No. 570, 1714), the marrow-bones and cleavers form no part of the Captain's harmonious apparatus, but the tongs and key are represented to have become a little unfashionable some years before. By the year 1749, however, the former had obtained a considerable degree of vulgar popularity, and were introduced in Bonnell Thornton's burlesque "Ode on St. Cecilia's Day, adapted to the Ancient British Musick." Ten years afterwards, this poem was recomposed by Dr. Burney, and performed at Ranelagh, on which occasion cleavers were cast in bell-metal to accompany the verses wherein they are mentioned.

(2) Scene I.—
My hounds are bred out of the Spartan kind,
So flew'd, so sanded; and their heads are hung
With ears that sweep away the morning dew;
Crook-knee'd and dew-lapp'd like Thessalian bulls;
Slow in pursuit, but match'd in mouth like bells,
Each under each.]

The hounds of Sparta and Crete are classically celebrated:—"Tenet ora levis clamosa Molossi, *Spartanos*, Cretasque, ligat."—*Lucani Phars*, IV. 440: and the peculiarities of form and colour indicated, are those which were considered to mark the highest quality of the bloodhound breed. The flews are the large hanging chaps, which, with long thin pendant ears, were a peculiar recommendation in these animals. Thus, Golding, 1567:—

"——— with other twaine that had a syre of Crete,
And dam of Sparta: tone of them called Jollyboy a greate,
And *large-flew'd* hound."

And Heywood:—

"——— the fierce Thessalian hounds,
With their flag ears, ready to *sweep the dew*
From their moist breasts."
Brazen Age, 1613.

For "so sanded" some commentator proposed to read, "so sounded;" but Steevens correctly explains *sanded* to mean of *a sandy colour*, "one of the true denotements of a blood-hound."—See *The Gentleman's Recreation.*

ACT V.

(1) Scene I.—
What masks, what dances shall we have,
To wear away this long age of three hours,
Between our after-supper and bed-time?]

The accepted explanation of an *after-supper* conveys but an imperfect idea of what this refection really was. "*A rere-supper*," Nares says, "seems to have been a late or second supper." Not exactly. The *rere-supper* was to the supper itself what the *rere-banquet* was to the dinner—*a dessert.* On ordinary occasions, the gentlemen of Shakespeare's age appear to have dined about eleven o'clock, and then to have retired either to a garden-house, or other suitable apartment, and enjoyed their *rere-banquet* or dessert. Supper was usually served between five and six; and this, like the dinner, was frequently followed by a collation consisting of fruits and sweetmeats, called, in this country, the *rere-supper;* in Italy, Pocenio, from the Latin *Pocœnium.*

(2) Scene I.—*You shall know all, &c.*] The humour of distorting the meaning of a passage by mispunctuation was a favourite one formerly. There is a good example in Roister Doister's letter to Dame Custance, beginning,—

"Sweete mistresse, where as I love you nothing at all,
Regarding your substance and richesse chiefe of all," &c.
See *Ralph Roister Doister*, Act III. Sc. 4.

I find another specimen in a MS. collection of short poems, epigrams, &c., written evidently in the early part of the seventeenth century, which belonged to Dr. Percy.

JANUS BIFRONS.

"The Feminine kinde is counted-ill,
And is I sweare: the Contrary,
No man can find: that hurt they will,
But every where: doe shewe pitty,
To no kinde heart: they will be curst,
To all true Friends: they will beare trust,
In no parte: they will worke the worst,
With tongue and minde: but Honestye,
They do detest: Inconstancye,
They do embrace: honest intent,
They like least: lewd Fantasye
In evry case: are Patient,
At no season: doing amisse,
To it: truly Contrarye,
To all Reason: subject and meeke,
To no Bodye: malitiouse,
To Frende and Foe: of gentle sort
They be never: doing amisse,
In Weale and Woe: of Like report,
They be ever: be sure of this,
The feminine kinde shall have no hart
Nothing at all: false they will be,
In Worde and Minde: to suffer smart,
And ever shall: Believe thou me?"

Read thus, the lines are anything but complimentary; but, by transposing the colons and commas, they become highly eulogistic. Taylor, the water poet, in his "Address to Nobody," prefixed to Sir Gregory Nonsense, alludes to the Prologue in the text:—"So ending at the beginning, I say as it is applawsefully written and commended to posterity in the Midsummer Night's Dream, If we offend, it is with our good will, we came with no intent, but to offend and shew our simple skill."

(3) SCENE I.—
Whereat with blade, with bloody blameful blade,
He bravely broach'd his boiling bloody breast.]

The classical reader will remember the examples of alliterative trifling in Ennius, and his well-known—

"O Tite, tute, Tati, tibi tanta, Tyranne, tulisti,
At, Tuba terribili tonitru taratantara trusit."

Perhaps the most famous of these puerilities, in later times, is the "Pugna Porcorum" of Leo Placentius, wherein every word begins with P. There is also the poem written by Hugald, in honour of Charles the Bold, in which the initial of each word is C; and a long poem, written in 1576, called "Christus Crucifixus," every word beginning with C also. Langland, the author of "The Vision of Piers Ploughman," and Norton, who wrote "Gorboduc," both "affected the letter;" and Tusser's "Husbandry" contains a poem in which all the words begin with T. In this country, the foppery appears to have reached its culminating point in the reign of Henry VIII., if we may judge from the following exquisite specimen in a production by Wilfride Holme, on "The Fall and evil Success of Rebellion:"—

"Loe, leprous lurdeins, lubricke in loquacitie,
Vah, vaporous villeins, with venim vulnerate,
Proh, prating parenticides, plexious to pennositie,
Fie, frantike fabulators, furibund and fatuate,
Out, oblatrant, oblict, obstacle, and obsecate,
Ah addict algoes, in acerbitie acclamant,
Magnall in mischief, malicious to mugilate,
Repriving your Roy so renowned and radiant."

(4) SCENE I.—*Myself the man i' th' moon doth seem to be.*] "Although the legend of the man in the moon is perhaps one of the most singular and popular superstitions known, yet it is almost impossible to discover early materials for a connected account of its progress; nor have the researches of former writers been extended to this curious subject. It is very probable that the natural appearance of the moon, and those delineations on its disc, which modern philosophers have considered to belong to the geographical divisions of that body, may originally have suggested the similarity vulgarly supposed to exist between these outlines and a man 'pycchynde stake.' In fact, it is hardly possible to account for the universality of the legend by any other conjecture. * * * *

"A manuscript of about the fourteenth century, preserved in the British Museum (*Harl.* MS. 2253), contains an exceedingly curious early English poem on the Man in the Moon, beginning,—

'Mon in the mone stond and strit,
On his bot forke is burthen he bereth
Hit is muche wonder that he na doun slyt,
For doute leste he valle he shoddreth aut shereth.'

"Grimm, Deutsche Mythologie, p. 412, asserts that there are three legends connected with the Man in the Moon. The first, that this personage was Isaac, carrying a bundle of sticks for his own sacrifice; the second, that he was Cain; and the other, which is taken from the history of the Sabbath-breaker, as related in the Book of Numbers. Chaucer, in 'Troilus and Creseide,' I. 147, refers to 'the chorle' in the moon; and in the poem entitled the 'Testament of Creseide,' printed in Chaucer's works, there is an allusion to the same legend:—

'Next after him came lady Cynthia,
The laste of al, and swiftest in her sphere,
Of colour blake buskid with hornis twa
And in the night she listith best t'appere,
Hawe as the leed, of colour nothing clere,
For al the light she borowed at her brother
Titan, for of herselfe she hath non other.
Her gite was gray and ful of spottis blake,
And on her brest a chorle painted ful even,
Bering a bush of thornis on his bake,
Whiche for his theft might clime no ner the heven.'

"From Manningham's diary (*Harl.* MS. 5353) we learn that, among the devises at Whitehall, in 1601, was 'the man in the moone with thornes on his backe looking downeward.' Ben Jonson, in one of his Masques, fol. ed., p. 41, expressly alludes to the man in the moon having been introduced upon the English stage:—'*Fac.* Where? which is he? I must see his dog at his girdle, and the bushe of thornes at his backe, ere I beleeve it. 1 *Her.* Doe not trouble your faith then, for if that bush of thornes should prove a goodly grove of okes, in what case were you and your expectation? 2 *Her.* Those are stale ensignes o' the stages, man i' th moone, delivered doune to you by musty antiquitie, and are of as doubtfull credit as the makers.'"—HALLIWELL.

(5) SCENE I.—*This passion, and the death of a dear friend, would go near to make a man look sad.*] Mr. Collier's annotator reads, "This passion *on* the death of a dear friend," &c.;—one proof among many of his inability to appreciate anything like subtle humour. Had he never heard the old proverbial saying, "He that loseth his wife and sixpence, *hath lost a tester?*"

(6) SCENE II.—
To the best bride-bed will we,
Which by us shall blessed be.]

The ceremony of blessing the bridal-bed was observed, Douce says, at all marriages; and we are indebted to him for the formula, copied from the "Manual," of the use of Salisbury:—"Nocte vero sequente cum sponsus et sponsa *ad lectum pervenerint,* accedat sacerdos et benedicat thalamum, dicens: Benedic, Domine, thalamum istum et omnes habitantes in eo; ut in tua pace consistant, et in tua voluntate permaneant: et in amore tuo vivant et senescant et multiplicentur in longitudine dierum. Per Dominum.—Item *benedictio super lectum.* Benedic, Domine, hoc *cubiculum,* respice, qui non dormis neque dormitas. Qui custodis Israel, custodi famulos tuos in hoc lecto quiescentes *ab omnibus fantasmaticis demonum illusionibus:* custodi eos vigilantes ut in preceptis tuis meditentur dormientes, et te per soporem sentiant: ut hic et ubique defensionis tuæ muniantur auxilio. Per Dominum. —Deinde fiat benedictio *super eos in lecto* tantum cum Oremus. Benedicat Deus corpora vestra et animas vestras; et det super vos benedictionem sicut benedixit Abraham, Isaac et Jacob, Amen.—His peractis *aspergat aqua eos benedicta,* et sic discedat et dimittat eos in pace."

CRITICAL OPINIONS

ON

MIDSUMMER NIGHT'S DREAM.

"In 'The Midsummer Night's Dream,' there flows a luxuriant vein of the boldest and most fantastical invention; the most extraordinary combination of the most dissimilar ingredients seems to have been brought about without effort, by some ingenious and lucky accident, and the colours are of such clear transparency, that we think the whole of the variegated fabric may be blown away with a breath. The fairy world here described, resembles those elegant pieces of arabesque, where little genii with butterfly wings rise, half-embodied, above the flower-cups. Twilight, moonshine, dew, and spring perfumes, are the elements of these tender spirits ; they assist Nature in embroidering her carpet with green leaves, many-coloured flowers, and glittering insects; in the human world they do but make sport childishly and waywardly with their beneficent or noxious influences. Their most violent rage dissolves in good-natured raillery ; their passions, stripped of all earthly matter, are merely an ideal dream. To correspond with this, the loves of mortals are painted as a poetical enchantment, which, by a contrary enchantment, may be immediately suspended, and then renewed again. The different parts of the plot; the wedding of Theseus and Hippolyta, Oberon and Titania's quarrel, the flight of the two pair of lovers, and the theatrical manœuvres of the mechanics, are so lightly and happily interwoven, that they seem necessary to each other for the formation of a whole. Oberon is desirous of relieving the lovers from their perplexities, but greatly adds to them through the mistakes of his minister, till he at last comes really to the aid of their fruitless amorous pain, their inconstancy and jealousy, and restores fidelity to its old rights. The extremes of fanciful and vulgar are united, when the enchanted Titania awakes and falls in love with a coarse mechanic with an ass's head, who represents, or rather disfigures, the part of a tragical lover. The droll wonder of Bottom's transformation is merely the translation of a metaphor in its literal sense; but in his behaviour during the tender homage of the Fairy Queen, we have an amusing proof how much the consciousness of such a head-dress heightens the effect of his usual folly. Theseus and Hippolyta are, as it were, a splendid frame for the picture; they take no part in the action, but surround it with a stately pomp. The discourse of the hero and his Amazon, as they course through the forest with their noisy hunting-train, works upon the imagination like the fresh breath of morning, before which the shades of night disappear. Pyramus and Thisbe is not unmeaningly chosen as the grotesque play within the play: it is exactly like the pathetic part of the piece, a secret meeting of two lovers in the forest, and their separation by an unfortunate accident, and closes the whole with the most amusing parody."—Schlegel.

"The 'Midsummer Night's Dream' is the first play which exhibits the imagination of Shakspeare in all its fervid and creative power ; for though, as mentioned in Meres's Catalogue, as having numerous scenes of continued rhyme, as being barren in fable, and defective in strength of character—it may be pronounced the offspring of youth and inexperience—it will ever, in point of fancy, be considered as equal to any subsequent drama of the poet.

"In a piece where the imagery of the most wild and fantastic dream is actually embodied before our eyes—where the principal agency is carried on by beings lighter than the gossamer, and smaller than the cowslip's bell, whose elements are the moonbeams and the odoriferous atmosphere of flowers, and whose sport it is

'To dance in ringlets to the whistling winds,'

it was necessary, in order to give a filmy and assistant legerity to every part of the play, that the human agents should partake of the same evanescent and visionary character; accordingly both the higher and lower personages of this drama are the subjects of illusion and enchantment, and love and amusement their sole occupation; the transient perplexities of thwarted passion, and the grotesque adventures of humorous folly, touched as they are with the tenderest or most frolic pencil, blending admirably with the wild, sportive, and romantic tone of the scene, where

'Trip the light fairies and the dapper elves,'

and forming together a whole so variously yet so happily interwoven, so racy and effervescent in its composition, of such exquisite levity and transparency, and glowing with such luxurious and phosphorescent splendour, as to be perfectly without a rival in dramatic literature."—Drake.

"'A Midsummer Night's Dream!' At the sight of such a title we naturally ask—Who is the dreamer? The poet, any of the characters of the drama, or the spectators? The answer seems to be that there is much in this beautiful sport of imagination which was fit only to be regarded as a dream by the persons whom the fairies illuded: and that, as a whole, it comes before the spectators under the notion of a dream.

"'If we shadows have offended,
Think but this, (and all is mended,)
That you have but slumber'd here,
While these visions did appear.
And this weak and idle theme,
No more yielding but a dream,
Gentles, do not reprehend.'—

"Shakespeare was then but a young poet, rising into notice,—and it was a bold and hazardous undertaking to bring together classical story and the fairy mythology, made still more hazardous by the introduction of the rude attempts in the dramatic art of the hard-handed men of Athens. By calling it a dream he obviated the objection to its incongruities, since it is of the nature of a dream that things heterogeneous are brought together in fantastical confusion. Yet, to a person who by repeated perusals has become familiar with this play, it will not appear so incongruous a composition that it requires such an apology as we find in the Epilogue and title. It cannot, however, have been popular, any more than *Comus* is popular when brought upon the stage. Its great and surpassing beauties would be in themselves a hindrance to its obtaining a vulgar popularity.

"There is no apparent reason why it should be called a dream of Midsummer Night in particular. Midsummer night was of old in England a time of bonfires and rejoicings, and, in London, of processions and pageantries. But there is no allusion to anything of this kind in the play. Midsummer night cannot be the time of the action, which is very distinctly fixed to May morning and a few days before. May morning, even more than Midsummer night, was a time of delight in those times which, when looked back upon from these days of incessant toil, seem to have been gay, innocent, and paradisaical. See in what sweet language and in what a religious spirit the old topographer of London, Stowe, speaks of the universal custom of the people of the city on May-day morning, 'to walk into the sweet meadows and green woods, there to rejoice their spirits with the beauty and savour of sweet flowers, and with the harmony of birds praising God in their kinds.' We have abundant materials for a distinct and complete account of the May-day sports in the happy times of old England; but they would be misplaced in illustration of this play: for, though Shakespeare has made the time of his story the time when people went forth—

'To do observance to the morn of May,'

and has laid the scene of the principal event in one of those half-sylvan, half-pastoral spots which we may conceive to have been the most favourite haunts of the Mayers, he does not introduce any of the May-day sports, or show us anything of the May-day customs of the time. Yet he might have done so. His subject seemed even to invite him to it, since a party of Mayers with their garlands of sweet flowers would have harmonized well with the lovers and the fairies, and might have made sport for Robin Goodfellow. Shakespeare loved to think of flowers and to write of them, and it may seem that it was a part of his original conception to have made more use than he has done of May-day and Flora's followers."—Hunter.

Act IV. Sc. 1.

THE MERCHANT OF VENICE.

Of this popular drama two editions were published prior to its appearance in the 1623 folio. One, entitled, "The most excellent Historie of the Merchant of Venice. With the extreame crueltie of Shylocke the Iewe towards the sayd Merchant, in cutting a iust pound of his flesh: and the obtayning of Portia by the choyce of three chests. As it hath beene diuers times acted by the Lord Chamberlaine his Seruants. Written by William Shakespeare. At London, Printed by I. R., for Thomas Heyes, and are to be sold in Paules Church-yard, at the signe of the Greene Dragon. 1600," 4to. The other, "The excellent History of the Merchant of Venice. With the extreme cruelty of Shylocke the Iew towards the saide Merchant, in cutting a iust pound of his flesh. And the obtaining of Portia, by the choyse of three caskets. Written by W. Shakespeare. Printed by J. Roberts. 1600," 4to.

"The Merchant of Venice" is the last play of Shakespeare's mentioned in the list of Francis Meres, 1598; and we find, in the same year, it was entered on the register of the Stationers' Company:—"22. July, 1598, James Robertes] A booke of the Marchaunt of Venyce, or otherwise called the Jewe of Venyse," &c. &c. But that it was written and acted some years before there appears to be now very little doubt. Henslowe's "Diary" contains an entry, 25th of August, 1594, recording the performance of "The Venesyon Commodey." This Malone conjectured to refer to "The Merchant of Venice," which is the more probable as it has since been found that, in 1594, the fellowship of players to which Shakespeare belonged was performing at the theatre in Newington Butts, conjointly, it is believed, with the company managed by Henslowe.

The plot is composed of two distinct stories;—the incidents connected with the bond, and those of the caskets, which are interwoven with wonderful felicity. Both these fables are found separately related in the Latin "*Gesta Romanorum.*" The bond, in Chap. XLVIII. *of MS. Harl.* 2270; and the caskets, in Chap. XCIX. of the same collection. Some of the circumstances, however, connected with the bond in "The Merchant of Venice," resemble more closely the tale of the fourth day in the "*Pecorone*" of Ser Giovanni Fiorentino, in which it is noticeable too, that the scene of a portion of the hero's adventures is laid at *Belmont.* The "*Pecorone,*" though first printed in 1550, was written nearly two hundred years before. A translation of it in English was extant in our author's time, of which an abridgment will be found in the "Illustrative Comments" at the end of the play. Upon this translation the old ballad of "Gernutus," which is found in Percy's "Reliques," entitled,—"A New Song, Shewing the crueltie of Gernutus, a Jew, who lending to a Merchant a hundred Crownes, would have a pound of his fleshe, because he could not pay him at the day apointed.—To the Tune of *Black and Yellow,*"—was most likely founded. Whether the fusion of the two legends was the work of Shakespeare or of an earlier writer, we have not sufficient evidence to determine. Tyrwhitt was of opinion that he followed some hitherto unknown novelist, who had saved him the trouble of combining the two stories, and Steevens cites a passage from Gosson's "School of Abuse," 1579, which certainly tends to prove that a play comprising the double plot of "The Merchant of Venice" had been exhibited before Shakespeare began to write for the stage. The passage is as follows—Gosson is excepting some particular players and plays from the sweeping condemnation of his "pleasaunt inuective against Poets, Pipers, Plaiers, Iesters, and such like Caterpillers of a Commonwelth:"—"And as some of the players are farre from abuse, so some of their playes are without rebuke, which are easily remembered, as quickly rekoned. The two prose bookes played at the Belsavage, where you shall finde never a worde withoute witte, never a line without pith, never a letter placed in vaine. *The Jew,* and Ptolome, showne at the Bull; *the one representing the greedinesse of worldly chusers, and bloody mindes of usurers;*" &c.

The expression *worldly chusers* is so appropriate to the choosers of the caskets, and the *bloody mindes of usurers,* so applicable to the vindictive cruelty of Shylock, that it is very probable Shakespeare in this play, as in other plays, worked upon some rough model already prepared for him. The question is not of great importance. Be the merit of the fable whose it may, the characters, the language, the poetry, and the sentiment, are his and his alone. To no other writer of the period could we be indebted for the charming combination of womanly grace, and dignity, and playfulness, which is found in Portia; for the exquisite picture of friendship between Bassanio and Antonio; for the profusion of poetic beauties scattered over the play; and for the masterly delineation of that perfect type of Judaism in olden times, the character of Shylock himself.

In his treatment of the Jew, without doing such violence to the antipathies of his age as would have been fatal to the popularity of the play, Shakespeare has generously vindicated the claims of this despised race to the rights and privileges of the community in which they lived. If, in obedience to the story he followed, and to hereditary prejudice too deep-rooted and long cherished for his control, he has portrayed the Jew father as malignant and revengeful, he has represented the daughter as affectionate and loveable; and if the former is rendered an object of odium and contumely, the latter becomes the wife of a Venetian gentleman, and the companion of the nobles and merchant princes of the land. This was much. At the time when "The Merchant of Venice" was produced, as for ages before, the Jews were an abomination to the people. With the exception of such truly great men as Pope Gregory, Saint Bernard, Charlemagne, and a few others, no one had hardihood enough to venture a word in their defence. They were accounted Pariahs, born only to be reviled, and persecuted, and plundered. As a proof of the abhorrence with which they were regarded in Shakespeare's day, we need but refer to Marlowe's "Rich Jew of Malta." "Shylock," says Charles Lamb, "in the midst of his savage purpose, is a man. His motives, feelings, resentments, have something human in them. 'If you wrong us, shall we not revenge?' *Barabas* is a mere monster brought in with a large painted nose to please the rabble. He kills in sport—poisons whole nunneries—invents infernal machines. He is just such an exhibition as a century or two earlier might have been played before the Londoners, *by the Royal Command*, when a general pillage and massacre of the Hebrews had been previously resolved on in the cabinet."

Few plays have been more successful on the stage than "The Merchant of Venice," few are better adapted for popular reading. Dramas of a loftier kind, moving deeper feeling and dealing with nobler passions, have proceeded from the same exhaustless source; but we question if any one more diversified and picturesque than this exists. It is full of incident, character, poetry, and humour. The friendship of Antonio and Bassanio, "strong even unto death"—the love episode of Lorenzo and the fair Jewess—the quaint drolleries of Launcelot—the buoyant spirits and *brusque* wit of Gratiano—the beauty of the Casket scenes—the grandeur of the trial—and the tragic interest attached to the circumstances of the contract between the Merchant and his unrelenting creditor—combine to form a whole unapproached and unapproachable by any other dramatist.

Persons Represented.

DUKE OF VENICE.
PRINCE OF ARRAGON, PRINCE OF MOROCCO, } *suitors to* PORTIA.
ANTONIO, *the Merchant of* Venice.
BASSANIO, *friend to* ANTONIO.
SOLANIO, SALARINO, GRATIANO, } *friends to* ANTONIO *and* BASSANIO.
LORENZO, *in love with* JESSICA.
SHYLOCK, *a Jew.*
TUBAL, *a Jew, friend to* SHYLOCK.
LAUNCELOT GOBBO, *a Clown, servant to* SHYLOCK.

Old GOBBO, *father to* LAUNCELOT.
LEONARDO, *servant to* BASSANIO.
BALTHAZAR, STEPHANO, } *servants to* PORTIA.

PORTIA, *a rich heiress.*
NERISSA, *waiting-maid to* PORTIA.
JESSICA, *daughter to* SHYLOCK.

Magnificoes of Venice, *Officers of the Court of Justice, Gaoler, Servants, and other Attendants.*

SCENE,—*Partly at* VENICE; *and partly at* BELMONT, *the Seat of* PORTIA, *on the Continent.*

ACT I.

SCENE I.—Venice. *A Street.*

Enter ANTONIO, SALARINO, *and* SOLANIO.[a]

ANT. In sooth, I know not why I am so sad;
It wearies me; you say it wearies you;
But how I caught it, found it, or came by it,
What stuff 'tis made of, whereof it is born,
I am to learn;
And such a want-wit sadness makes of me,

[a] SALARINO *and* SOLANIO.] The uncertain orthography of these names in the first folio, where we have at one time *Salarino*, at another *Slarino*, *Solania*, *Salanio*, *Salino*, and *Salerio*, has led to such perplexity in their abbreviations prefixed to the speeches, that we are glad to avoid confusion by adopting the distinction proposed by Capell, of *Salar.* and *Solan.* as prefixes.

That I have much ado to know myself.
SALAR. Your mind is tossing on the ocean;
There where your argosies,[a] with portly sail,—
Like signiors and rich burghers on the flood,
Or, as it were, the pageants of the sea,—
Do overpeer the petty traffickers,
That curt'sy to them, do them reverence,
As they fly by them with their woven wings.
SOLAN. Believe me, sir, had I such venture forth,
The better part of my affections would
Be with my hopes abroad. I should be still
Plucking the grass,[b] to know where sits the wind;
Peering in maps, for ports, and piers, and roads:
And every object that might make me fear
Misfortune to my ventures, out of doubt
Would make me sad.
SALAR. My wind, cooling my broth,
Would blow me to an ague, when I thought
What harm a wind too great might do at sea.
I should not see the sandy hour-glass run,
But I should think of shallows and of flats;
And see my wealthy Andrew[c] dock'd* in sand,
Vailing her high-top lower than her ribs,
To kiss her burial. Should I go to church,
And see the holy edifice of stone,
And not bethink me straight of dangerous rocks,
Which, touching but my gentle vessel's side,
Would scatter all her spices on the stream,
Enrobe the roaring waters with my silks,
And, in a word, but even now worth this,
And now worth nothing? Shall I have the thought
To think on this; and shall I lack the thought
That such a thing, bechanc'd, would make me sad?
But tell not me; I know, Antonio
Is sad to think upon his merchandise.
ANT. Believe me, no; I thank my fortune for it,
My ventures are not in one bottom trusted,
Nor to one place; nor is my whole estate
Upon the fortune of this present year:
Therefore my merchandise makes me not sad.
SALAR. Why, then you are in love.
ANT. Fie, fie!
SALAR. Not in love neither? Then let us say, you are sad
Because you are not merry: and 'twere as easy
For you to laugh, and leap, and say you are merry,
Because you are not sad. Now, by two-headed Janus,
Nature hath fram'd strange fellows in her time:
Some that will evermore peep through their eyes,
And laugh, like parrots, at a bagpiper;
And other of such vinegar aspéct,
That they'll not show their teeth in way of smile,
Though Nestor swear the jest be laughable.
SOLAN. Here comes Bassanio, your most noble kinsman,
Gratiano, and Lorenzo: Fare you well;
We leave you now with better company.
SALAR. I would have stay'd till I had made you merry,
If worthier friends had not prevented me.
ANT. Your worth is very dear in my regard.
I take it, your own business calls on you,
And you embrace the occasion to depart.

Enter BASSANIO, LORENZO, *and* GRATIANO.

SALAR. Good morrow, my good lords.
BASS. Good signiors both, when shall we laugh? say, when?
You grow exceeding strange: must it be so?
SALAR. We'll make our leisures to attend on yours. [*Exeunt* SALARINO *and* SOLANIO.
LOR. My lord Bassanio, since you have found Antonio,
We two will leave you; but at dinner-time,
I pray you have in mind where we must meet.
BASS. I will not fail you.
GRA. You look not well, signior Antonio;
You have too much respect upon the world:
They lose it that do buy it with much care;
Believe me, you are marvellously chang'd.
ANT. I hold the world but as the world, Gratiano;
A stage, where every man must play a part,
And mine a sad one.
GRA. Let me play the Fool:
With mirth and laughter let old wrinkles come;
And let my liver rather heat with wine,
Than my heart cool with mortifying groans.
Why should a man whose blood is warm within
Sit like his grandsire cut in alabaster?
Sleep when he wakes? and creep into the jaundice
By being peevish? I tell thee what, Antonio,—
I love thee, and it is my love that speaks;—
There are a sort of men, whose visages
Do cream and mantle like a standing pond;
And do a wilful stillness entertain,
With purpose to be dress'd in an opinion
Of wisdom, gravity, profound conceit;

(*) Old text, *docks.*

[a] *There where your* argosies,—] Argosies were ships of huge bulk and burden, adapted either for commerce or war, and supposed to have been named from the classic ship *Argo*.

[b] Plucking the grass, to know where sits the wind;] A blade of grass held up to indicate, by the way it bends, the direction of the wind, is a very primitive kind of weather vane. Sailors, with whom grass is usually harder to come by than even to Venetians, adopt one equally simple and always at hand: they moisten a finger in the mouth, and holding it up, judge by a sensible coldness on one side the digit, whence the wind blows.

[c] *My wealthy* Andrew—] This name for a ship, it is not unlikely, was derived from the famous naval hero, Andrew Doria.

As who should say, *I am sir Oracle,**
And, when I ope my lips, let no dog bark!
O, my Antonio, I do know of these,
That therefore only are reputed wise,
For saying nothing; who,† I am very sure,
If they should speak, would almost damn those ears
Which, hearing them, would call their brothers, fools.[a]
I'll tell thee more of this another time:
But fish not with this melancholy bait,
For this fool-gudgeon, this opinion.
Come, good Lorenzo:—Fare ye well, a while;
I'll end my exhortation after dinner.

LOR. Well, we will leave you then till dinner-time:
I must be one of these same dumb wise men,
For Gratiano never lets me speak.

GRA. Well, keep me company but two years more,
Thou shalt not know the sound of thine own tongue.

ANT. Farewell:‡ I'll grow a talker for this gear.

GRA. Thanks, i' faith; for silence is only commendable
In a neat's tongue dried, and a maid not vendible.
[*Exeunt* GRATIANO *and* LORENZO.

ANT. Is§ that anything now?

BASS. Gratiano speaks an infinite deal of nothing, more than any man in all Venice: his reasons are as‖ two grains of wheat hid in two bushels of chaff; you shall seek all day ere you find them; and when you have them they are not worth the search.

ANT. Well; tell me now, what lady is the same
To whom you swore a secret pilgrimage,
That you to-day promis'd to tell me of?

BASS. 'Tis not unknown to you, Antonio,
How much I have disabled mine estate,
By something showing a more swelling port[b]
Than my faint means would grant continuance:
Nor do I now make moan to be abridg'd
From such a noble rate; but my chief care
Is to come fairly off from the great debts
Wherein my time, something too prodigal,
Hath left me gag'd. To you, Antonio,
I owe the most in money and in love;
And from your love I have a warranty
To unburthen all my plots and purposes,
How to get clear of all the debts I owe.

ANT. I pray you, good Bassanio, let me know [it;
And, if it stand, as you yourself still[c] do,
Within the eye of honour, be assur'd,
My purse, my person, my extremest means,
Lie all unlock'd to your occasions.

BASS. In my school-days, when I had lost one shaft,
I shot his fellow of the self-same flight
The self-same way, with more advised watch,
To find the other forth;[d] and by adventuring both
I oft found both:(1) I urge this childhood proof,
Because what follows is pure innocence.
I owe you much; and, like a wilful youth,
That which I owe is lost: but if you please
To shoot another arrow that self way
Which you did shoot the first, I do not doubt,
As I will watch the aim, or to find both,
Or bring your latter hazard back again,
And thankfully rest debtor for the first.

ANT. You know me well, and herein spend but time,
To wind about my love with circumstance;[e]
And, out of doubt, you do me now* more wrong
In making question of my uttermost,
Than if you had made waste of all I have.
Then do but say to me what I should do,
That in your knowledge may by me be done,
And I am prest[f] unto it: therefore speak.

(*) First folio, *sir, an oracle.* (†) Old copies, *when.*
(‡) First folio, *far you well.* (§) Old copies, *it is.*
(‖) First folio omits, *as.*

a If they should speak, would almost damn those ears
Which, hearing them, would call their brothers, fools.]
The meaning seems to be: There are people whose reputation for wisdom depends upon their purposed silence, who, if they could be brought to speak, would so expose their emptiness, that the hearers could hardly escape the penalty denounced on those who call their brethren fools; but the idea is not clearly expressed.

b A more swelling port—] A more ostentatious state. See note (b), p. 235.

c *As you yourself* still *do*,—] That is, *always, ever* do. This signification of the word is frequent in Shakespeare, although no commentator that I remember has noticed it.

d —— with more advised watch,
To find the other forth;]
"*To find forth,*" says an accomplished critic on the language of Shakespeare, "may, I apprehend, be safely pronounced to be neither English nor sense." It may not be English of the present day, but it was thought good sense and good English in the time of our author. *Forth* here means *out*,—"To find the other *out*," and with this import the word is used in the following, and in a hundred other, instances.

"Who, falling there *to find his fellow forth.*"
Comedy of Errors, Act I. Sc. 2.

(*) First folio omits, *me now.*

Where we have again the identical expression, "*find forth.*"

"Go on before; *I shall inquire you forth.*"
Two Gentlemen of Verona, Act II. Sc. 4.

"——for at this time the jealous rascally knave, her husband, *will be forth.*"—*Merry Wives of Windsor*, Act II. Sc. 2.

And already in this very play,—

"Believe me, sir, had I such venture *forth.*"

e *To wind about my love with* circumstance;] *Circumstance*, for *circumlocution*, or "*going about the bush*," as the old lexicographers define it, though in common use formerly, has now become quite obsolete:—

"Therefore it must, with *circumstance*, be spoken—"
Two Gentlemen of Verona, Act III. Sc. 2.

"And not without some scandal to yourself,
With *circumstance* and oaths, so to deny
This chain."—*The Comedy of Errors*, Act V. Sc. 1.

"And so, without more *circumstance* at all,
I hold it fit that we shake hands and part."
Hamlet, Act I. Sc. 5.

f *And I am* prest *unto it*:] *Prest*, signifying *ready*, is, as Steevens remarks, of common occurrence in the old writers; but it may be doubted whether in this instance the word is not used in the current sense of *bound* or *urged*.

BASS. In Belmont is a lady richly left,
And she is fair, and, fairer than that word,
Of wondrous virtues. Sometimes[a] from her eyes
I did receive fair speechless messages:
Her name is Portia; nothing undervalued
To Cato's daughter, Brutus' Portia.
Nor is the wide world ignorant of her worth;
For the four winds blow in from every coast
Renowned suitors: and her sunny locks
Hang on her temples like a golden fleece;
Which makes her seat of Belmont, Colchos' strand,
And many Jasons come in quest of her.
O, my Antonio! had I but the means
To hold a rival place with one of them,
I have a mind presages me such thrift,
That I should questionless be fortunate.

ANT. Thou know'st that all my fortunes are at sea;
Neither have I money, nor commodity
To raise a present sum: therefore go forth,
Try what my credit can in Venice do;
That shall be rack'd, even to the uttermost,
To furnish thee to Belmont, to fair Portia.
Go, presently inquire, and so will I,
Where money is; and I no question make,
To have it of my trust, or for my sake. [*Exeunt.*

SCENE II.—Belmont. *A Room in* Portia's *House.*

Enter PORTIA *and* NERISSA.

POR. By my troth, Nerissa, my little body is a-weary of this great world.

NER. You would be, sweet madam, if your miseries were in the same abundance as your good fortunes are; and yet, for aught I see, they are as sick that surfeit with too much, as they that starve with nothing. It is no mean* happiness, therefore, to be seated in the mean; superfluity comes sooner by white hairs, but competency lives longer.

POR. Good sentences, and well pronounced.

NER. They would be better, if well followed.

POR. If to do were as easy as to know what were good to do, chapels had been churches, and poor men's cottages princes' palaces. It is a good divine that follows his own instructions: I can easier teach twenty what were good to be done, than be one of the twenty to follow mine own teaching. The brain may devise laws for the blood; but a hot temper leaps o'er a cold decree: such a hare is madness the youth, to skip o'er the meshes of good counsel the cripple. But this reasoning* is not in the† fashion to choose me a husband:—O me, the word choose! I may neither choose whom I would, nor refuse whom I dislike; so is the will of a living daughter curbed by the will of a dead father:—Is it‡ not hard, Nerissa, that I cannot choose one, nor refuse none?

NER. Your father was ever virtuous; and holy men at their death have good inspirations; therefore, the lottery that he hath devised in these three chests, of gold, silver, and lead, (whereof who chooses his meaning chooses you,) will, no doubt, never be chosen by any rightly, but one who you shall rightly love. But what warmth is there in your affection towards any of these princely suitors that are already come?

POR. I pray thee, overname them; and as thou namest them I will describe them; and according to my description level at my affection.

NER. First, there is the Neapolitan prince.

POR. Ay, that's a colt, indeed, for he doth nothing but talk of his horse; and he makes it a great appropriation to his own good parts that he can shoe him himself: I am much afraid my lady his mother played false with a smith.

NER. Then, is there the county Palatine.(2)

POR. He doth nothing but frown; as who should say, *An you will not have me, choose;* he hears merry tales, and smiles not: I fear he will prove the weeping philosopher when he grows old, being so full of unmannerly sadness in his youth. I had rather be § married to a death's head with a bone in his mouth, than to either of these. God defend me from these two!

NER. How say you by the French lord, monsieur le Bon?

POR. God made him, and therefore let him pass for a man. In truth, I know it is a sin to be a mocker; but he! why, he hath a horse better than the Neapolitan's; a better bad habit of frowning than the count Palatine: he is every man in no man: if a throstle ‖ sing he falls straight a capering; he will fence with his own shadow: if I should marry him I should marry twenty husbands: if he would despise me I would forgive him; for if he love me to madness I shall ¶ never requite him.

NER. What say you then to Fauconbridge, the young baron of England?

POR. You know I say nothing to him; for he understands not me, nor I him: he hath neither Latin, French, nor Italian;[b] and you will come into the court, and swear that I have a poor

(*) First folio, *small.*

a Sometimes.] *Sometimes* here means, *formerly*, in *other times.*

b He hath neither Latin, French, nor Italian;] This satirical allusion to our ignorance in "the tongues" has not yet lost all its point.

(*) First folio, *reason.* (†) First folio omits, *the.* (‡) First folio, *it is.* (§) First folio, *to be.* (‖) Old copies, *trassell.* (¶) First folio, *should.*

pennyworth in the English. He is a proper man's picture;[a] but, alas! who can converse with a dumb show? How oddly he is suited! I think he bought his doublet in Italy, his round hose in France, his bonnet in Germany, and his behaviour everywhere.

NER. What think you of the Scottish lord,[b] his neighbour?

POR. That he hath a neighbourly charity in him; for he borrowed a box of the ear of the Englishman, and swore he would pay him again when he was able: I think the Frenchman became his surety, and sealed under for another.

NER. How like you the young German, the duke of Saxony's nephew?

POR. Very vilely in the morning, when he is sober; and most vilely in the afternoon, when he is drunk: when he is best, he is a little worse than a man; and when he is worst, he is little better than a beast: an the worst fall that ever fell, I hope I shall make shift to go without him.

NER. If he should offer to choose, and choose the right casket, you should refuse to perform your father's will, if you should refuse to accept him.

POR. Therefore, for fear of the worst, I pray thee set a deep glass of Rhenish wine on the contrary casket; for, if the devil be within, and that temptation without, I know he will choose it. I will do anything, Nerissa, ere I will be married to a sponge.

NER. You need not fear, lady, the having any of these lords: they have acquainted me with their determinations: which is, indeed, to return to their home, and to trouble you with no more suit; unless you may be won by some other sort than your father's imposition, depending on the caskets.

POR. If I live to be as old as Sibylla I will die as chaste as Diana, unless I be obtained by the manner of my father's will. I am glad this parcel of wooers are so reasonable; for there is not one among them but I dote on his very absence, and I pray God grant[c] them a fair departure.

NER. Do you not remember, lady, in your father's time, a Venetian, a scholar and a soldier, that came hither in company of the marquis of Montferrat?

POR. Yes, yes, it was Bassanio; as I think, so was he called.

NER. True, madam; he, of all the men that ever my foolish eyes looked upon, was the best deserving a fair lady.

POR. I remember him well; and I remember him worthy of thy praise.

Enter a Servant.

How now! what news?*

SERV. The four strangers seek for† you, madam, to take their leave: and there is a forerunner come from a fifth, the prince of Morocco; who brings word, the prince, his master, will be here to-night.

POR. If I could bid the fifth welcome with so good heart as I can bid the other four farewell, I should be glad of his approach: if he have the condition[d] of a saint, and the complexion of a devil, I had rather he should shrive me than wive me.
Come, Nerissa. Sirrah, go before;
Whiles we shut the gate upon one wooer, another
knocks at the door. [*Exeunt.*

SCENE III.—Venice. *A Public Place.*

Enter BASSANIO *and* SHYLOCK.(3)

SHY. *Three thousand ducats,*—well.

BASS. Ay, sir, for three months.

SHY. *For three months,*—well.

BASS. For the which, as I told you, Antonio shall be bound.

SHY. *Antonio shall become bound,*—well.

BASS. May you stead me? Will you pleasure me? Shall I know your answer?

SHY. *Three thousand ducats, for three months, and Antonio bound.*

BASS. Your answer to that.

SHY. Antonio is a good man.[e]

BASS. Have you heard any imputation to the contrary?

SHY. Ho! no, no, no, no;—my meaning in saying he is a good man, is, to have you understand me that he is sufficient: yet his means are in supposition: he hath an argosy bound to Tripolis, another to the Indies; I understand moreover upon the Rialto, he hath a third at

---

a A proper *man's picture;*] *Proper* meant *handsome, comely.* The word with this import is so common, that it is needless to give examples; they may be found in every play of the time.

b *The* Scottish *lord,*—] So the quartos, which were printed before the accession of James I. The folio, 1623, reads, "the *other* lord," to avoid giving offence to the king and his countrymen.

c I pray God grant them—] The first folio, in obedience to the Act passed in the reign of James I. prohibiting the profane use of holy names, has, "*I wish* them a fair departure."

d *The* condition of *a saint,*—] *Condition* for, *nature, disposition,* as in "Richard III." Act IV. Sc. 4:—

(*) First folio omits, *How now!* &c.
(†) First folio omits, *for.*

"Madam, I have a touch of your *condition,*
That cannot brook the accent of reproof."

And in "Othello," Act II. Sc. 1:—

"—— she is full of most bless'd *condition.*"

e *Antonio is* a good man.] That is, a man of substance and responsibility:—

——"*A good man,*
I have enquired him, eighteen hundred a year."
The Devil is An Ass, Act III. Sc. 1.

Mexico, a fourth for England; and other ventures he hath, squander'd[a] abroad. But ships are but boards, sailors but men: there be land-rats and water-rats, land-thieves and water-thieves;[b] I mean, pirates; and then, there is the peril of waters, winds, and rocks. The man is, notwithstanding, sufficient;—three thousand ducats;—I think I may take his bond.

BASS. Be assured you may.

SHY. I will be assured I may; and that I may be assured, I will bethink me. May I speak with Antonio?

BASS. If it please you to dine with us.

SHY. Yes, to smell pork; to eat of the habitation which your prophet, the Nazarite, conjured the devil into! I will buy with you, sell with you, talk with you, walk with you, and so following; but I will not eat with you, drink with you, nor pray with you.—What news on the Rialto?—Who is he comes here?

Enter ANTONIO.

BASS. This is signior Antonio.

SHY. [*Aside.*] How like a fawning publican he looks!
I hate him for he is a Christian:
But more, for that, in low simplicity,
He lends out money gratis, and brings down
The rate of usance here with us in Venice.
If I can catch him once upon the hip,(4)
I will feed fat the ancient grudge I bear him.
He hates our sacred nation; and he rails,
Even there where merchants most do congregate,
On me, my bargains, and my well-won * thrift,
Which he calls interest. Cursed be my tribe
If I forgive him!

BASS. Shylock, do you hear?

SHY. I am debating of my present store:
And, by the near guess of my memory,
I cannot instantly raise up the gross
Of full three thousand ducats. What of that?
Tubal, a wealthy Hebrew of my tribe,
Will furnish me. But soft: how many months
Do you desire?—Rest you fair, good signior: [*To* ANTONIO.
Your worship was the last man in our mouths.

ANT. Shylock, albeit I neither lend nor borrow,
By taking, nor by giving of excess,
Yet, to supply the ripe wants of my friend,
I'll break a custom:—Is he yet possess'd,[c]
How much you * would? [*To* BASSANIO.

SHY. Ay, ay, three thousand ducats.

ANT. And for three months.

SHY. I had forgot;—three months, you told me so.
Well then, your bond; and, let me see. But hear you:
Methought you said, you neither lend nor borrow,
Upon advantage.

ANT. I do never use it.

SHY. When Jacob graz'd his uncle Laban's sheep,
This Jacob from our holy Abraham was
(As his wise mother wrought in his behalf)
The third possessor; ay, he was the third.

ANT. And what of him? did he take interest?

SHY. No, not take interest; not, as you would say,
Directly interest: mark what Jacob did.
When Laban and himself were compromis'd,
That all the eanlings which were streak'd and pied
Should fall, as Jacob's hire; the ewes, being rank,
In end of autumn turned to the rams:
And when the work of generation was,
Between these woolly breeders, in the act,
The skilful shepherd pill'd me certain wands,
And, in the doing of the deed of kind,
He stuck them up before the fulsome ewes;
Who, then conceiving, did in eaning-time
Fall party-colour'd lambs, and those were Jacob's.
This was a way to thrive, and he was blest;
And thrift is blessing, if men steal it not.

ANT. This was a venture, sir, that Jacob serv'd for;
A thing not in his power to bring to pass,
But sway'd and fashion'd by the hand of Heaven.
Was this inserted to make interest good?
Or is your gold and silver ewes and rams?

SHY. I cannot tell; I make it breed as fast:
But note me, signior.

ANT. Mark you this, Bassanio,
The devil can cite scripture for his purpose.
An evil soul producing holy witness,
Is like a villain with a smiling cheek;
A goodly apple rotten at the heart;
O, what a goodly outside falsehood hath!

SHY. Three thousand ducats,—'tis a good round sum.
Three months from twelve, then let me see the rate.

ANT. Well, Shylock, shall we be beholden to you?

(*) First folio, *well-worn*.

a Squander'd *abroad*.] *Squandered*, of old, meant only *dispersed* or *scattered*, not as now, *wasted*, *dissipated*.

b Land-thieves and water-thieves;] The ancient copies read "water-thieves and land-thieves," which, there can be little doubt, was a printer's or transcriber's error.

(*) First folio, *he*.

c *Is he yet* possess'd,—] Is he yet *informed*. Thus in Act IV. Sc. 1:—

"I have *possess'd* your grace of what I purpose."

SHY. Signior Antonio, many a time and oft,[a]
In the Rialto (5) you have rated me
About my monies, and my usances:
Still have I borne it with a patient shrug,
For sufferance is the badge of all our tribe:
You call me,—misbeliever, cut-throat dog,
And spet upon my Jewish gaberdine,(6)
And all for use of that which is mine own.
Well then, it now appears you need my help:
Go to then: you come to me, and you say,
Shylock, we would have monies; You say so;
You, that did void your rheum upon my beard,
And foot me, as you spurn a stranger cur
Over your threshold; monies is your suit.
What should I say to you? Should I not say,
Hath a dog money? is it possible
A cur can lend three thousand ducats?* or
Shall I bend low, and in a bondman's key,
With 'bated breath, and whispering humbleness,
Say this,—
Fair sir, you spet on me on Wednesday last;
You spurn'd me such a day; another time
You call'd me—dog; and for these courtesies
I'll lend you thus much monies?

ANT. I am as like to call thee so again,
To spet on thee again, to spurn thee too.
If thou wilt lend this money, lend it not
As to thy friends; (for when did friendship take
A breed for† barren metal of his friend?)[b]
But lend it rather to thine enemy;
Who, if he break, thou mayst with better face
Exact the penalty.‡

SHY. Why, look you, how you storm!
I would be friends with you, and have your love,
Forget the shames that you have stain'd me with,
Supply your present wants, and take no doit
Of usance for my monies, and you'll not hear me:
This is kind I offer.

ANT. This were kindness.

SHY. This kindness will I show:
Go with me to a notary, seal me there
Your single bond; and, in a merry sport,[c]
If you repay me not on such a day,
In such a place, such sum, or sums, as are
Express'd in the condition, let the forfeit
Be nominated for an equal pound
Of your fair flesh, to be cut off and taken
In what part of your body pleaseth * me.

ANT. Content, in faith; I'll seal to such a bond,
And say there is much kindness in the Jew.

BASS. You shall not seal to such a bond for me;
I'll rather dwell[d] in my necessity.

ANT. Why, fear not, man, I will not forfeit it;
Within these two months,—that's a month before
This bond expires,—I do expect return
Of thrice three times the value of this bond.

SHY. O father Abraham, what these Christians are,
Whose own hard dealings teaches them suspect
The thoughts of others! Pray you, tell me this;
If he should break his day,(7) what should I gain
By the exaction of the forfeiture?
A pound of man's flesh, taken from a man,
Is not so estimable, profitable neither,
As flesh of muttons, beefs, or goats. I say,
To buy his favour, I extend this friendship;
If he will take it, so; if not, adieu;
And, for my love, I pray you wrong me not.

ANT. Yes, Shylock, I will seal unto this bond.

SHY. Then meet me forthwith at the notary's;
Give him direction for this merry bond,
And I will go and purse the ducats straight;
See to my house, left in the fearful[e] guard
Of an unthrifty knave; and presently
I will be with you. [*Exit.*

ANT. Hie thee, gentle Jew.
This Hebrew will turn Christian; he grows kind.

BASS. I like not fair terms and a villain's mind.

ANT. Come on; in this there can be no dismay,
My ships come home a month before the day.
[*Exeunt.*

(*) First folio, *should*. (†) First folio, *of*. (‡) First folio, *penalties*.

(*) First folio, *it pleaseth*.

[a] Many a time and oft,—] This old saying, equivalent to our "Many and many a time," occurs again in "Julius Cæsar," Act I. Sc. 1:—

"——— *Many a time and oft*
Have you climbed up to walls and battlements."

[b] A breed for barren metal of his friend?] By *breed* is apparently meant *fruit* or *interest*. Meres says, "Usurie and encrease by gold and silver is unlawful, because against nature; nature hath made them *sterile* and *barren*, usurie makes them procreative."

[c] ——— seal me there
Your single bond; and, in a merry sport,
If you repay me not, &c.]

So in the old ballad of "Gernutus."

"But we will have *a merry jeast*
For to be talked long;
You shall make me *a bond*, quoth he,
That shall be large and strong."

[d] *I'll rather* dwell, &c.] That is, *abide, continue*, &c.

[e] *Left in the* fearful *guard*—] This may denote either in the guard of one who makes you fearful to trust him; or a timorous, *faint-hearted guard*: the former is the usual interpretation.

ACT II.

SCENE I.—Belmont. *A Room in* Portia's *House.*

Flourish of Cornets. Enter the PRINCE OF MOROCCO, *and his Train;* PORTIA, NERISSA, *and other of her* Attendants.[a]

MOR. Mislike me not for my complexion,
The shadowed livery of the burnish'd sun,
To whom I am a neighbour, and near bred.
Bring me the fairest creature northward born,
Where Phœbus' fire scarce thaws the icicles,
And let us make incision for your love,
To prove whose blood is reddest,[b] his, or mine.
I tell thee, lady, this aspéct of mine
Hath fear'd the valiant; by my love, I swear,
The best-regarded virgins of our clime
Have lov'd it too: I would not change this hue,
Except to steal your thoughts, my gentle queen.
POR. In terms of choice I am not solely led
By nice[c] direction of a maiden's eyes:
Besides, the lottery of my destiny
Bars me the right of voluntary choosing:
But, if my father had not scanted me,
And hedg'd me by his wit,[d] to yield myself
His wife, who wins me by that means I told you,
Yourself, renowned prince, then stood as fair
As any comer I have look'd on yet,
For my affection.
MOR. Even for that I thank you;
Therefore, I pray you, lead me to the caskets,(1)
To try my fortune. By this scimitar,—
That slew the Sophy, and a Persian prince,

---

a *Enter*, &c.] The old stage direction is, "*Enter Morochus a tawnie Moore all in white, and three or foure followers accordingly, with Portia, Nerrissa, and their traine;*" which, as Mr. Collier remarks, is curious, as showing the manner in which Moors were usually dressed on the stage in Shakespeare's time.

b *To prove whose* blood is reddest,—] "It must be remembered," Johnson says, "that *red* blood is a traditionary sign of courage. Thus Macbeth calls one of his frighted soldiers, a *lily-liver'd boy;* again, in this play, cowards are said to *have livers as white as milk;* and an effeminate and timorous man is termed a *milksop.*"

Among the Saxons it was the custom to cover their distinguished dead with a *red* pall instead of a black one, "In remembrance," according to Glanville, "of theyr *hardynes* and *boldnes*, whyle they were in theyr bloude."

c *By* nice *direction of a maiden's eyes:*] *Nice*, from the Anglo-Saxon *nesc*, or *hnesc*, tender, gentle, here means *dainty*, *squeamish*, as in "The Two Gentlemen of Verona," Act III. Sc. 1, and in other places:—

"————but she is *nice* and coy,
And naught esteems my aged eloquence."

d *And hedg'd me by his* wit,—] *Wit* in this case is used with its old signification, of *knowledge, foresight, wisdom.*

That won three fields of sultan Solyman,—
I would o'erstare the sternest eyes that look,
Outbrave the heart most daring on the earth,
Pluck the young sucking cubs from the she-bear,
Yea, mock the lion when he roars for prey,
To win thee, lady. But, alas the while![a]
If Hercules and Lichas play at dice
Which is the better man, the greater throw
May turn by fortune from the weaker hand:
So is Alcides beaten by his page;*
And so may I, blind fortune leading me,
Miss that which one unworthier may attain,
And die with grieving.

POR. You must take your chance;
And either not attempt to choose at all,
Or swear, before you choose,—if you choose wrong,
Never to speak to lady afterward
In way of marriage; therefore be advis'd.

MOR. Nor will not; come, bring me unto my chance.

POR. First, forward to the temple; after dinner
Your hazard shall be made. [*Cornets.*

MOR. Good fortune, then!
To make me bless'd, or cursed'st among men.
[*Exeunt.*

SCENE II.—Venice. *A Street.*

Enter LAUNCELOT GOBBO.[b]

LAUN. Certainly, my conscience will serve me to run from this Jew, my master. The fiend is at mine elbow, and tempts me; saying to me,—*Gobbo, Launcelot Gobbo, good Launcelot,* or *good Gobbo,* or *good Launcelot Gobbo, use your legs, take the start, run away.*—My conscience says,—*no; take heed, honest Launcelot; take heed, honest Gobbo;* or (as aforesaid) *honest Launcelot Gobbo; do not run: scorn running with thy heels:*[c] well, the most courageous fiend bids me pack; *Via!* says the fiend; *away!* says the fiend, *for the heavens*[d] *rouse up a brave mind,* says the fiend, *and run.* Well, my conscience, hanging about the neck of my heart, says very wisely to me,—*my honest friend Launcelot, being an honest man's son:* or rather an honest woman's son;—for, indeed, my father did something smack, something grow to, he had a kind of taste;—well, my conscience says, *Launcelot, budge not: budge,* says the fiend; *budge not,* says my conscience: Conscience, say I, you counsel well; fiend, say I, you counsel well: to be ruled by my conscience, I should stay with the Jew my master, who (God bless the mark!) is a kind of devil; and to run away from the Jew, I should be ruled by the fiend, who, saving your reverence, is the devil himself. Certainly, the Jew is the very devil incarnation: and, in my conscience, my conscience is but* a kind of hard conscience, to offer to counsel me to stay with the Jew: the fiend gives the more friendly counsel: I will run, fiend; my heels are at your commandment, I will run.

Enter Old GOBBO,[e] *with a basket.*

GOB. Master, young man, you; I pray you, which is the way to master Jew's?

LAUN. [*Aside.*] O heavens, this is my true-begotten father! who, being more than sand-blind, high-gravel blind, knows me not: I will try confusions[f] with him.

GOB. Master, young gentleman, I pray you which is the way to master Jew's?

LAUN. Turn upon your right hand at the next turning, but, at the next turning of all, on your left; marry, at the very next turning, turn of no hand, but turn down indirectly to the Jew's house.

GOB. By God's sonties,[g] 'twill be a hard way to hit. Can you tell me whether one Launcelot, that dwells with him, dwell with him, or no?

LAUN. Talk you of young master Launcelot?—

(*) Old text, *rage.*

a *But,* alas the while!] The vernacular phrase, *alas,* or *woe the while,* appears to have been a parenthetical ejaculation of sorrow, with no more determinate meaning than Pistol's "lament therefore," or our "it's sad to think." It occurs again in "Henry V." Act IV. Sc. 7:—

"For many of our princes (*woe the while!*)
Lie drown'd and soak'd in mercenary blood."

And in "Julius Cæsar," Act I. Sc. 3:—

"——— for Romans now
Have thews and limbs like to their ancestors,
But, *woe the while!* our fathers' minds are dead."

b *Enter* LAUNCELOT GOBBO.] In the old copies, *Enter the* Clowne *alone;* throughout the play, too, this character is generally designated as "Clowne" on his *entrance and exit.*

c Scorn running with thy heels:] This figurative manner of expressing a scornful rejection of anything, is not so uncommon that it need have puzzled the critics as it has done. It occurs in "Much Ado about Nothing," Act III. Sc. 4:—"O illegitimate construction! *I scorn that with my heels.*" So also in Rowland's Collection of Epigrams and Satires, called "The Letting of Humours Blood in the Head Vaine," 1611,—

"Bidde me goe sleepe? *I scorne it with my heeles.*"

And again, in "A Crew of Kind Gossips," 1609:—

"And *with my heeles, I scorne it,* by the Lord."

(*) First folio omits, *but.*

d For the heavens—] Gifford, by a note on "Every Man Out of His Humour," Act II. Sc. 1, has saved this "pretty oath" from the prohibition with which it was threatened by the Shakespeare commentators. The meaning, as he has shown by a string of instances, is simply, *by heaven!*

e GOBBO,—] Steevens surmised that, as *Gobbo* is Italian for *crook-back,* Shakespeare designed the old man to be represented with that deformity.

f Confusions—] So the quarto by Heyes, and the folio; Roberts' quarto has, *conclusions.*

g *By God's* sonties,—] *Sonties* is a corruption of *sanctities.*

Mark me now—[*aside*]—now will I raise the waters.—Talk you of young master Launcelot?

GOB. No *master*, sir, but a poor man's son: his father, though I say it, is an honest exceeding poor man, and, God be thanked, well to live.

LAUN. Well, let his father be what a will, we talk of young master Launcelot.

GOB. Your worship's friend, and Launcelot, sir.*

LAUN. But I pray you *ergo*, old man, *ergo*, I beseech you, talk you of young master Launcelot.

GOB. Of Launcelot, an't please your mastership.

LAUN. *Ergo*, master Launcelot;[a] talk not of master Launcelot, father; for the young gentleman (according to fates and destinies, and such odd sayings, the sisters three, and such branches of learning) is, indeed, deceased; or, as you would say in plain terms, gone to heaven.

GOB. Marry, God forbid! the boy was the very staff of my age, my very prop.

LAUN. Do I look like a cudgel, or a hovel-post, a staff, or a prop? [*aside*]—Do you know me, father?

GOB. Alack the day, I know you not, young gentleman: but, I pray you tell me, is my boy (God rest his soul!) alive or dead?

LAUN. Do you not know me, father?

GOB. Alack, sir, I am sand-blind, I know you not.

LAUN. Nay, indeed, if you had your eyes you might fail of the knowing me: it is a wise father that knows his own child. Well, old man, I will tell you news of your son: give me your blessing: truth will come to light; murder cannot be hid long; a man's son may; but, in the end, truth will out. [*Kneels.*

GOB. Pray you, sir, stand up; I am sure you are not Launcelot, my boy.

LAUN. Pray you, let's have no more fooling about it, but give me your blessing; I am Launcelot, your boy that was, your son that is, your child that shall be.

GOB. I cannot think you are my son.

LAUN. I know not what I shall think of that: but I am Launcelot, the Jew's man; and I am sure Margery, your wife, is my mother.

GOB. Her name is Margery, indeed: I'll be sworn, if thou be Launcelot, thou art mine own flesh and blood. Lord worshipped might he be! what a beard hast thou got! thou hast got more hair on thy chin than Dobbin my phill-horse has on his tail.[b]

(*) First folio omits, *sir*.

[a] *Ergo*, master Launcelot;] The humour here, which consists in Launcelot's determination to be dignified by the title of *master*, and the old man's unwillingness so to honour him, is less apparent in writing than in acting, where the *master* Launcelot can be rendered sufficiently emphatic.

[b] Than Dobbin my phill-horse has on his tail.] Stage tradition, not improbably from the time of Shakespeare himself, makes Launcelot, at this point, kneel with his back to the sand-blind old father, who, of course, mistakes his long back hair for a beard, of which his face is perfectly innocent.

LAUN. It should seem then, that Dobbin's tail grows backward; I am sure he had more hair of his tail, than I have of my face, when I last saw him.

GOB. Lord, how art thou changed! How dost thou and thy master agree? I have brought him a present. How 'gree you now?

LAUN. Well, well; but for mine own part, as I have set up my rest to run away, so I will not rest till I have run some ground. My master 's a very Jew. Give him a present! give him a halter: I am famished in his service; you may tell every finger I have with my ribs. Father, I am glad you are come: give me[a] your present to one master Bassanio, who, indeed, gives rare new liveries; if I serve not him, I will run as far as God has any ground.—O rare fortune! here comes the man;—to him, father; for I am a Jew if I serve the Jew any longer.

Enter BASSANIO, *with* LEONARDO, *and other* Followers.

BASS. You may do so:—but let it be so hasted, that supper be ready at the farthest by five of the clock. See these letters delivered; put the liveries to making; and desire Gratiano to come anon to my lodging. [*Exit a* Servant.

LAUN. To him, father.

GOB. God bless your worship!

BASS. Gramercy! Wouldst thou aught with me?

GOB. Here's my son, sir, a poor boy,—

LAUN. Not a poor boy, sir, but the rich Jew's man; that would, sir, as my father shall specify,—

GOB. He hath a great infection, sir, as one would say, to serve,—

LAUN. Indeed, the short and the long is, I serve the Jew, and have a desire, as my father shall specify,—

GOB. His master and he (saving your worship's reverence) are scarce cater-cousins:—

LAUN. To be brief, the very truth is, that the Jew having done me wrong, doth cause me, as my father, being I hope an old man, shall frutify unto you,—

GOB. I have here a dish of doves, that I would bestow upon your worship; and my suit is,—

LAUN. In very brief, the suit is impertinent to myself, as your worship shall know by this honest old man; and, though I say it, though old man, yet, poor man, my father.

---

[a] *Give* me *your present to one master Bassanio,*—] "The *me,* in such a phrase as the present," Mr. Craik remarks, on a passage of the same construction, in "Julius Cæsar," "may be considered as being in the same predicament with the *my* in *my lord,* or the *mon* in the French *monsieur.* The best commentary on the use of the pronoun that we have here is in the dialogue between Petrucio and his servant Grumio in 'Taming of the Shrew,' Act I. Sc. 2:—'PET. Villain, I say, knock *me* here soundly,' &c."

BASS. One speak for both:—what would you?

LAUN. Serve you, sir.

GOB. That is the very defect of the matter, sir.

BASS. I know thee well, thou hast obtain'd thy suit:
Shylock, thy master, spoke with me this day,
And hath preferr'd thee, if it be preferment,
To leave a rich Jew's service, to become
The follower of so poor a gentleman.

LAUN. The old proverb is very well parted between my master Shylock and you, sir; you have the grace of God, sir, and he hath enough.[a]

BASS. Thou speak'st it well. Go, father, with thy son:—
Take leave of thy old master, and inquire
My lodging out:—give him a livery [*To his* Followers.
More guarded[b] than his fellows: see it done.

LAUN. Father, in:—I cannot get a service, no!—I have ne'er a tongue in my head!—Well [*looking on his palm*]; if any man in Italy have a fairer table,[c] which doth offer to swear upon a book, I shall have good fortune! Go to, here's a simple line of life! (2) here's a small trifle of wives: alas, fifteen wives is nothing; aleven[d] widows and nine maids, is a simple coming in for one man: and then, to 'scape drowning thrice; and to be in peril of my life with the edge of a feather bed; here are simple 'scapes! Well, if fortune be a woman, she's a good wench for this gear.—Father, come. I'll take my leave of the Jew in the twinkling of an eye.*

[*Exeunt* LAUNCELOT *and Old* GOBBO.

BASS. I pray thee, good Leonardo, think on this;
These things being bought, and orderly bestow'd,
Return in haste, for I do feast to-night
My best esteem'd acquaintance: hie thee, go.

LEON. My best endeavours shall be done herein.

Enter GRATIANO.

GRA. Where's your master?

LEON. Yonder, sir, he walks. [*Exit* LEON.

GRA. Signior Bassanio,—

BASS. Gratiano!

GRA. I have a suit to you.

BASS. You have obtain'd it.

GRA. You must not deny me: I must go with you to Belmont.

BASS. Why, then you must.—But hear thee, Gratiano;
Thou art too wild, too rude and bold of voice;
Parts, that become thee happily enough,
And in such eyes as ours appear not faults; [show
But where thou art* not known, why, there they
Something too liberal:[e]—pray thee, take pain
To allay with some cold drops of modesty, [viour,
Thy skipping spirit; lest, through thy wild beha-
I be misconster'd in the place I go to,
And lose my hopes.

GRA. Signior Bassanio, hear me:
If I do not put on a sober habit,
Talk with respect, and swear but now and then,
Wear prayer-books in my pocket, look demurely;
Nay more, while grace is saying, hood mine eyes
Thus with my hat, and sigh, and say *Amen*; (3)
Use all the observance of civility,
Like one well studied in a sad ostent[f]
To please his grandam,—never trust me more.

BASS. Well, we shall see your bearing.

GRA. Nay, but I bar to-night; you shall not gage me
By what we do to-night.

BASS. No, that were pity;
I would entreat you rather to put on
Your boldest suit of mirth, for we have friends
That purpose merriment. But fare you well,
I have some business.

GRA. And I must to Lorenzo and the rest;
But we will visit you at supper-time. [*Exeunt.*

SCENE III.—Venice. *A Room in* Shylock's *House.*

Enter JESSICA *and* LAUNCELOT.

JES. I am sorry thou wilt leave my father so;
Our house is hell, and thou, a merry devil,

(*) First folio omits, *of an eye*.

(*) First folio, *they are*.

a You have the grace of God, sir, and he hath enough.] The proverb referred to is, "The grace of God is better than riches;" or, in the Scots' form of it, "God's grace is gear enough."

b *More* guarded—] That is, more *ornamented*. A *guard* was, properly, the welt or border of a garment; and so called, from its guarding the stuff from being torn.

c *A fairer* table,—] *Table*, in palmistry, is the palm of the hand.—"*Beau.* Fairest one, I have skill in palmistry. *Wife.* Good my Lord, what do you find there? *Beau.* In good earnest, I do find written here all my good fortune lies in your hand. *Wife.* You'll keep a very bad house then; you may see by the smallness of the *table*."—MIDDLETON'S *Any Thing for a Quiet Life*, Act II. Sc. 1.

d Aleven.] So the old text, and rightly; *aleven* being a common vulgarism, which was, probably, pronounced "a'leven."

e *Something too* liberal:—] *Liberal* is used here in its ancient sense of *licentious;* as in "Much Ado about Nothing," Act. IV. Sc. 1:—

"Who hath, indeed, most like a *liberal* villain," &c.

And in "Hamlet," Act IV. Sc. 7:—

"——— and long purples,
That *liberal* shepherds give a grosser name."

f *Sad* ostent—] *Ostent* is meant perhaps for more than mere *appearance*, and implies *parade* or *display*. The word occurs again in the eighth scene of this act, with the same purport:—

"Be merry and employ your chiefest thoughts,
To courtships and such fair *ostents* of love."

And in "Henry V." (Chorus) Act V.:—

"Giving full trophy, signal, and *ostent*
Quite from himself, to God."

Didst rob it of some taste of tediousness:
But fare thee well: there is a ducat for thee.
And, Launcelot, soon at supper shalt thou see
Lorenzo, who is thy new master's guest:
Give him this letter; do it secretly,
And so farewell; I would not have my father
See me in * talk with thee.

LAUN. Adieu!—tears exhibit my tongue. Most beautiful pagan,—most sweet Jew! If a Christian did[a] not play the knave and get thee, I am much deceived. But, adieu! these foolish drops do something † drown my manly spirit: adieu! [*Exit.*

JES. Farewell, good Launcelot.
Alack, what heinous sin is it in me,
To be asham'd to be my father's child!
But though I am a daughter to his blood,
I am not to his manners: O Lorenzo!
If thou keep promise, I shall end this strife;
Become a Christian, and thy loving wife. [*Exit.*

SCENE IV.—Venice. *A Street.*

Enter GRATIANO, LORENZO, SALARINO, *and* SOLANIO.

LOR. Nay, we will slink away in supper-time,
Disguise us at my lodging, and return
All in an hour.

GRA. We have not made good preparation.

SALAR. We have not spoke us yet of torch-bearers.[b]

(*) First folio omits, *in*. (†) First folio, *somewhat*.

[a] If *a Christian* did *not play the knave*—] This, the true reading, is first found in the folio, 1632. All the earlier editions have, "*doe* not get thee," &c.

[b] Torchbearers.] See Note (10), p. 215.

SOLAN. 'T is vile, unless it may be quaintly ordered,
And better, in my mind, not undertook. [hours,
LOR. 'T is now but four o'clock; we have two
To furnish us.—

Enter LAUNCELOT *with a letter.*

Friend Launcelot, what's the news?
LAUN. An it shall please you to break up this,[a] it shall * seem to signify. [hand;
LOR. I know the hand: in faith, 't is a fair
And whiter than the paper it writ on,
Is † the fair hand that writ.
GRA. Love-news, in faith.
LAUN. By your leave, sir.
LOR. Whither goest thou?
LAUN. Marry, sir, to bid my old master the Jew to sup to-night with my new master the Christian.
LOR. Hold here, take this:—tell gentle Jessica,
I will not fail her;—speak it privately:
Go. Gentlemen, will you prepare you for this masque to-night?
[*Exit* LAUNCELOT.
I am provided of a torchbearer. [straight.
SALAR. Ay, marry, I'll be gone about it
SOLAN. And so will I.
LOR. Meet me and Gratiano,
At Gratiano's lodging some hour hence.
SALAR. 'T is good we do so.
[*Exeunt* SALAR. *and* SOLAN.
GRA. Was not that letter from fair Jessica?
LOR. I must needs tell thee all. She hath directed
How I shall take her from her father's house;
What gold and jewels she is furnish'd with;
What page's suit she hath in readiness.
If e'er the Jew her father come to heaven,
It will be for his gentle daughter's sake:
And never dare misfortune cross her foot,
Unless she do it under this excuse,—
That she is issue to a faithless Jew.
Come, go with me; peruse this as thou goest:
Fair Jessica shall be my torchbearer. [*Exeunt.*

SCENE V.—Venice. *Before* Shylock's *House.*

Enter SHYLOCK *and* LAUNCELOT.[b]

SHY. Well, thou shalt see, thy eyes shall be thy judge,
The difference of old Shylock and Bassanio:—
What, Jessica!—thou shalt not gormandise,
As thou hast done with me;—What, Jessica!—
And sleep, and snore, and rend apparel out;—
Why, Jessica, I say!
LAUN. Why, Jessica! [call.
SHY. Who bids thee call? I do not bid thee
LAUN. Your worship was wont to tell me, I could do nothing without bidding.

Enter JESSICA.

JES. Call you? What is your will?
SHY. I am bid forth[c] to supper, Jessica;
There are my keys.—But wherefore should I go?
I am not bid for love; they flatter me:
But yet I'll go in hate, to feed upon
The prodigal Christian.—Jessica, my girl,
Look to my house.—I am right loth to go;
There is some ill a-brewing towards my rest,
For I did dream of money-bags to-night.
LAUN. I beseech you, sir, go; my young master doth expect your reproach.
SHY. So do I, his.
LAUN. And they have conspired together,—I will not say, you shall see a masque; but if you do, then it was not for nothing that my nose fell a-bleeding on Black-Monday last, at six o'clock i' the morning, falling out that year on Ash-Wednesday was four year in the afternoon.
SHY. What! are there masques? Hear you me, Jessica:
Lock up my doors; and when you hear the drum,
And the vile squealing of the wry-neck'd fife,[d]
Clamber not you * up to the casements then,
Nor thrust your head into the public street,
To gaze on Christian fools with varnish'd faces:
But stop my house's ears, I mean my casements;
Let not the sound of shallow foppery enter
My sober house.—By Jacob's staff I swear,
I have no mind of feasting forth to-night:
But I will go.—Go you before me, sirrah;
Say, I will come.
LAUN. I will go before, sir.—
Mistress, look out at window for all this;
There will come a Christian by,
Will be worth a Jewess' eye. [*Exit* LAUN.
SHY. What says that fool of Hagar's offspring; ha?
JES. His words were, *Farewell, mistress;* nothing else.

(*) First folio, *shall it.* (†) First folio, *I.*

[a] To break up this,—] See Note (d), p. 69.
[b] *Enter* SHYLOCK and LAUNCELOT.] The original stage direction in Heyes' quarto and the folio is too curious to be omitted, "*Enter Jew, and his man that was the Clowne.*"

(*) First folio, *you not.*

[c] *I am* bid forth—] I am *invited out.* *Bid* in old language was frequently used for *invitation.*
[d] *The* wry-neck'd fife,—] The performer, not the instrument, is meant. "A *fife* is a *wry-neckt musician,* for he always looks away from his instrument."—BARNABY RICHE'S *Aphorismes,* 1618.

Shy. The patch[a] is kind enough; but a huge feeder,
Snail-slow in profit, and * he sleeps by day
More than the wild cat: drones hive not with me,
Therefore I part with him; and part with him
To one, that I would have him help to waste
His borrow'd purse.—Well, Jessica, go in;
Perhaps, I will return immediately;
Do as I bid you, shut doors after you:
Fast bind, fast find;
A proverb never stale in thrifty mind. [*Exit.*

Jes. Farewell; and if my fortune be not cross'd,
I have a father, you a daughter, lost. [*Exit.*

SCENE VI.—*The same.*

Enter Gratiano *and* Salarino, *masqued.*

Gra. This is the pent-house, under which Lorenzo
Desir'd us to make stand.*

Salar. His hour is almost past.

Gra. And it is marvel he out-dwells his hour,
For lovers ever run before the clock.

Salar. O, ten times faster Venus' pigeons fly
To seal † love's bonds new made, than they are wont
To keep obliged faith unforfeited!

Gra. That ever holds: who riseth from a feast
With that keen appetite that he sits down?
Where is the horse that doth untread again,
His tedious measures with the unbated fire,
That he did pace them first? All things that are,
Are with more spirit chased than enjoy'd.
How like a younker,[b] or a prodigal,
The scarfed bark [c] puts from her native bay,
Hugg'd and embraced by the strumpet wind!
How like a prodigal doth she return;
With over-weather'd ‡ ribs, and ragged sails,
Lean, rent, and beggar'd by the strumpet wind!

(*) First folio, *but*.

[a] *The* patch—] See note (d), p. 372.

[b] *How like* a younker, *or a prodigal,*—] The old copies read, *a younger;* the emendation, which was made by Rowe, is fully justified by the following passage in "Henry VI." Part III. Act II. Sc. 1:—

"See how the morning opes her golden gates,
And takes her farewell of the glorious sun!
How well resembles it the prime of youth,
Trimm'd like *a younker* prancing to his love!"

A younker meant a young gallant, from *Juncker* or *Jung Herr*, as Minshew defines him, "*Nobilis vel equestris ordinis vir.*"

[c] *The* scarfed *bark*—] The vessel decorated with flags and streamers.

(*) First folio, *a stand*. † First folio, *steale*. (‡) First folio, *wither'd*.

SALAR. Here comes Lorenzo;—more of this hereafter.

Enter LORENZO.

LOR. Sweet friends, your patience for my long abode:
Not I, but my affairs, have made you wait:
When you shall please to play the thieves for wives,
I'll watch as long for you then.—Approach;
Here dwells my father Jew—Ho! who's within?

Enter JESSICA, *above, in boy's clothes.*

JES. Who are you? Tell me, for more certainty,
Albeit I'll swear that I do know your tongue.

LOR. Lorenzo, and thy love.

JES. Lorenzo, certain; and my love, indeed;
For who love I so much? and now, who knows
But you, Lorenzo, whether I am yours?

LOR. Heaven, and thy thoughts, are witness that thou art.

JES. Here, catch this casket; it is worth the pains.
I am glad 't is night, you do not look on me,
For I am much asham'd of my exchange:
But love is blind, and lovers cannot see
The pretty follies that themselves commit;
For if they could, Cupid himself would blush,
To see me thus transformed to a boy.

LOR. Descend, for you must be my torchbearer.

JES. What, must I hold a candle to my shames?
They in themselves, good sooth, are too-too light.
Why, 't is an office of discovery, love;
And I should be obscur'd.

LOR. So are you,* sweet,
Even in the lovely garnish of a boy.
But come at once;
For the close night doth play the run-away,
And we are stay'd for at Bassanio's feast.

JES. I will make fast the doors, and gild myself
With some more ducats, and be with you straight.
[*Exit, from above.*

GRA. Now, by my hood, a Gentile† and no Jew.

LOR. Beshrew[a] me, but I love her heartily:
For she is wise, if I can judge of her;
And fair she is, if that mine eyes be true;
And true she is, as she hath prov'd herself;
And therefore, like herself, wise, fair, and true,
Shall she be placed in my constant soul.

Enter JESSICA, *below.*

What, art thou come?—On, gentlemen, away;
Our masking mates by this time for us stay.
[*Exit, with* JESSICA *and* SALARINO.

Enter ANTONIO.

ANT. Who's there?

GRA. Signior Antonio?

ANT. Fie, fie, Gratiano! where are all the rest?
'Tis nine o'clock, our friends all stay for you:
No masque to-night, the wind is come about;
Bassanio presently will go aboard:
I have sent twenty out to seek for you.

GRA. I am glad on't; I desire no more delight,
Than to be under sail and gone to-night.
[*Exeunt.*

SCENE VII.—Belmont. *A Room in* Portia's *House.*

Flourish of Cornets. Enter PORTIA, *with the* PRINCE OF MOROCCO, *and both their Trains.*

POR. Go, draw aside the curtains, and discover
The several caskets to this noble prince:—

(*) First folio, *you are.* (†) First folio, *gentle.*

[a] Beshrew me,—] See note (d), p. 85; to which may be added the following explanation by Florio: "*Museragno*, a kinde of mouse called a *shrew*, deadlie to other beasts if he bite them, and laming any bodie if he but touch them, *of which that curse came, I beshrew you.*"—*A Worlde of Wordes*, 1598.

Now make your choice.
MOR. The first, of gold, who this inscription bears:
Who chooseth me, shall gain what many men desire.*
The second, silver, which this promise carries:
Who chooseth me, shall get as much as he deserves.
This third, dull lead, with warning all as blunt:
Who chooseth me, must give and hazard all he hath.
How shall I know if I do choose the right?
POR. The one of them contains my picture, prince;
If you choose that, then I am yours withal.
MOR. Some god direct my judgment! Let me see.
I will survey the inscriptions back again:
What says this leaden casket:
Who chooseth me, must give and hazard all he hath.
Must give—For what? for lead? hazard for lead?
This casket threatens: men that hazard all
Do it in hope of fair advantages:
A golden mind stoops not to shows of dross;
I'll then nor give, nor hazard, aught for lead.
What says the silver, with her virgin hue?
Who chooseth me, shall get as much as he deserves.
As much as he deserves?—Pause there, Morocco,
And weigh thy value with an even hand:
If thou be'st rated by thy estimation,
Thou dost deserve enough; and yet enough
May not extend so far as to the lady:
And yet to be afeard of my deserving,
Were but a weak disabling of myself.
As much as I deserve!—Why, that's the lady:
I do in birth deserve her, and in fortunes,
In graces, and in qualities of breeding;
But more than these, in love I do deserve.
What if I strayed no farther, but chose here?—
Let's see once more this saying grav'd in gold:
Who chooseth me, shall gain what many men desire.
Why, that's the lady: all the world desires her:
From the four corners of the earth they come,
To kiss this shrine, this mortal, breathing, saint.
The Hyrcanian deserts, and the vasty wilds
Of wide Arabia, are as through-fares now,
For princes to come view fair Portia:
The watery kingdom, whose ambitious head
Spets in the face of heaven, is no bar
To stop the foreign spirits; but they come,
As o'er a brook, to see fair Portia.
One of these three contains her heavenly picture.
Is't like that lead contains her? 'Twere damnation
To think so base a thought: it were too gross
To rib her cerecloth in the obscure grave.
Or shall I think in silver she's immur'd,
Being ten times undervalued to tried gold?
O sinful thought! Never so rich a gem
Was set in worse than gold. They have in England,
A coin that bears the figure of an angel,
Stamped in gold; but that's insculp'd upon;
But here an angel in a golden bed
Lies all within.—Deliver me the key;
Here do I choose, and thrive I as I may!
POR. There, take it, prince, and if my form lie there,
Then I am yours. [*He unlocks the golden casket.*
MOR. O hell! what have we here?
A carrion death, within whose empty eye
There is a written scroll? I'll read the writing.

All that glisters is not gold,
Often have you heard that told:
Many a man his life hath sold,
But my outside to behold:
Gilded tombs[a] *do worms infold.*
Had you been as wise as bold,
Young in limbs, in judgment old,
Your answer had not been inscroll'd:
Fare you well; your suit is cold.

Cold, indeed; and labour lost:
Then, farewell heat; and welcome frost.—
Portia, adieu! I have too griev'd a heart
To take a tedious leave: thus losers part. [*Exit.*
POR. A gentle riddance:—Draw the curtains, go;—
Let all of his complexion choose me so. [*Exeunt.*

SCENE VIII.—Venice. *A Street.*

Enter SALARINO *and* SOLANIO.

SALAR. Why, man, I saw Bassanio under sail;
With him is Gratiano gone along;
And in their ship, I am sure, Lorenzo is not.
SOLAN. The villain Jew with outcries rais'd the duke;
Who went with him to search Bassanio's ship.
SALAR. He came* too late, the ship was under sail:

(*) First folio omits, *many*.

a *Gilded* tombs *do worms infold.*] The old copies have,—

"Gilded *timber* do worms infold."

Johnson proposed the reading, *tombs*, which is now universally accepted. If "timber" is right, then the redundant *do* is an interloper, and we should read,—

"Gilded timber worms infold."

(*) First folio, *comes*.

But there the duke was given to understand,
That in a gondola (4) were seen together
Lorenzo and his amorous Jessica;
Besides, Antonio certified the duke,
They were not with Bassanio in his ship.
SOLAN. I never heard a passion so confus'd,
So strange, outrageous, and so variable,
As the dog Jew did utter in the streets:
My daughter!—O my ducats!—O my daughter!
Fled with a Christian?—O my Christian ducats!—
Justice! the law! my ducats, and my daughter!
A sealed bag, two sealed bags of ducats,
Of double ducats, stol'n from me by my daughter!
And jewels; two stones, two rich and precious stones,
Stol'n by my daughter!—Justice! find the girl!
She hath the stones upon her, and the ducats!
SALAR. Why, all the boys in Venice follow him
Crying,—*his stones, his daughter*, and *his ducats.*
SOLAN. Let good Antonio look he keep his day,
Or he shall pay for this.
SALAR. Marry, well remember'd:
I reason'd [a] with a Frenchman yesterday,
Who told me,—in the narrow seas that part
The French and English, there miscarried
A vessel of our country, richly fraught:
I thought upon Antonio when he told me,
And wish'd in silence that it were not his.
SOLAN. You were best to tell Antonio what you hear;
Yet do not suddenly, for it may grieve him.
SALAR. A kinder gentleman treads not the earth.
I saw Bassanio and Antonio part:
Bassanio told him, he would make some speed
Of his return; he answer'd—*Do not so,*
Slubber not business for my sake, Bassanio,
But stay the very riping of the time;
And for the Jew's bond, which he hath of me,
Let it not enter in your mind of [b] *love:*
Be merry; and employ your chiefest thoughts
To courtship, and such fair ostents of love,
As shall conveniently become you there:
And even there, his eye being big with tears,

---

[a] I reason'd *with a Frenchman yesterday,*—] That is, I *discoursed*. This sense of *reason*, though unusual, is not singular, thus in Chapman's Translation of the "Odyssey," Book IV.:—

"The morning shall yield time to you and me,
To do what fits, and *reason* mutually."

[b] *And for the Jew's bond, which he hath of me,*
Let it not enter in your mind of love:]
Mind of love may be correct, but *bond of love* would be more in Shakespeare's manner, and is countenanced by a passage in "Twelfth Night," Act V. Sc. 1:—

"A contract of eternal *bond of love.*"

And by another in "The Winter's Tale," Act IV. Sc. 3:—

"—— besides you know
Prosperity 's the very *bond of love.*"

Turning his face, he put his hand behind him,
And, with affection wondrous sensible,
He wrung Bassanio's hand, and so they parted.
SOLAN. I think he only loves the world for him.
I pray thee, let us go and find him out,
And quicken his embraced heaviness,
With some delight or other.
SALAR. Do we so. [*Exeunt.*

SCENE IX.—Belmont. *A Room in* Portia's *House.*

Enter NERISSA, *with a* Servant.

NER. Quick, quick, I pray thee, draw the curtain straight;
The prince of Arragon hath ta'en his oath,
And comes to his election presently.

Flourish of Cornets. Enter the PRINCE OF ARRAGON, PORTIA, *and their Trains.*

POR. Behold, there stand the caskets, noble prince;
If you choose that wherein I am contain'd,
Straight shall our nuptial rites be solemnis'd;
But if you* fail, without more speech, my lord,
You must be gone from hence immediately.
ARR. I am enjoin'd by oath to observe three things:
First, never to unfold to any one,
Which casket 'twas I chose; next, if I fail
Of the right casket, never in my life
To woo a maid in way of marriage;
Lastly, if I do fail in fortune of my choice,
Immediately to leave you, and be gone.
POR. To these injunctions every one doth swear,
That comes to hazard for my worthless self.
ARR. And so have I address'd me:[a] Fortune now
To my heart's hope!—Gold, silver, and base lead.
Who chooseth me, must give and hazard all he hath.
You shall look fairer, ere I give, or hazard.
What says the golden chest? ha! let me see:
Who chooseth me, shall gain what many men desire.
What many men desire.—That *many* may be meant
By the fool multitude, that choose by show,
Not learning more than the fond eye doth teach;
Which pries not to th' interior, but, like the martlet,
Builds in the weather on the outward wall,
Even in the force and road of casualty.
I will not choose what many men desire,
Because I will not jump[b] with common spirits,
And rank me with the barbarous multitudes.
Why, then to thee, thou silver treasure-house;
Tell me once more what title thou dost bear:
Who chooseth me, shall get as much as he deserves.
And well said too. For who shall go about
To cozen fortune, and be honourable
Without the stamp of merit! Let none presume
To wear an undeserved dignity:
O, that estates, degrees, and offices,
Were not deriv'd corruptly! and that clear honour
Were purchas'd by the merit of the wearer!
How many then should cover that stand bare!
How many be commanded that command!
How much low peasantry * would then be glean'd
From the true seed of honour! and how much honour
Pick'd from the chaff and ruin[c] of the times,
To be new varnish'd! Well, but to my choice:
Who chooseth me, shall get as much as he deserves.
I will assume desert:—give me a key for this,
And instantly unlock my fortunes here.
POR. Too long a pause for that which you find there.
ARR. What's here? the portrait of a blinking idiot,
Presenting me a schedule! I will read it.
How much unlike art thou to Portia!
How much unlike my hopes and my deservings!
Who chooseth me, shall have as much as he deserves.
Did I deserve no more than a fool's head?
Is that my prize? are my deserts no better?
POR. To offend, and judge, are distinct offices,
And of opposed natures.
ARR. What is here?
The fire seven times tried this;
Seven times tried that judgment is,

(*) First folio, *thou.*

a *And so have* I address'd *me:*] *Prepared* me, *directed* me. Thus, in "A Midsummer Night's Dream," Act V. Sc. 1:—
"—— the prologue is *address'd.*"
And in "Macbeth," Act II. Sc. 2:—
"——But they did say their prayers,
And *address'd them* again to sleep."
To *dress*, is derived immediately from the French word *dresser*, and remotely from the Latin *rectus, directus;* and implies, to *direct, instruct, prepare.*

(*) First folio, *pleasantry.*

b *I will not* jump *with common spirits,*—] That is, *agree.* So, in "Twelfth Night," Act V. Sc. 1:—
"—— till each circumstance
Of place, time, fortune, do cohere and *jump.*"
Again, in "Henry IV." Part I. Act I. Sc. 2:—
"—— and in some sort it *jumps* with my humour."

c *Pick'd from the chaff and* ruin *of the times,*—] *Ruin* meant *refuse, rubbish. Chaff and ruin* is the same as *chaff and bran.*

That did never choose amiss :
Some there be that shadows kiss,
Such have but a shadow's bliss :
There be fools alive, I wis,[a]
Silver'd o'er ; and so was this.
Take what wife you will to bed,
I will ever be your head :
So begone : you are sped.

Still more fool I shall appear,
By the time I linger here :
With one fool's head I came to woo,
But I go away with two.
Sweet, adieu ! I'll keep my oath,
Patiently to bear my wroth.[b]
[*Exeunt* ARRAGON *and Train.*

POR. Thus hath the candle sing'd the moth.
O these deliberate fools ! when they do choose,
They have the wisdom by their wit to lose.

NER. The ancient saying is no heresy ;—
Hanging and wiving goes by destiny.

POR. Come, draw the curtain, Nerissa.

Enter a Messenger.

MESS. Where is my lady ?

POR. Here ; what would my lord ?[c]

MESS. Madam, there is alighted at your gate
A young Venetian, one that comes before
To signify the approaching of his lord ;
From whom he bringeth sensible regreets ;
To wit, besides commends and courteous breath,
Gifts of rich value ; yet I have not seen
So likely an ambassador of love :
A day in April never came so sweet,
To show how costly summer was at hand,
As this fore-spurrer comes before his lord.

POR. No more, I pray thee ; I am half afeard,
Thou wilt say anon he is some kin to thee,
Thou spend'st such high-day[d] wit in praising him.
Come, come, Nerissa ; for I long to see
Quick Cupid's post that comes so mannerly.

NER. Bassanio, lord Love, if thy will it be !
[*Exeunt.*

---

a I wis,—] See Note (2), p. 275.

b *Patiently to bear my* wroth.] The old editions have *wroath. Wroth* or *wroath*, in the sense of *calamity* or *misfortune*, is not unfrequent in early English books.

c MESS. *Where is* my lady?
POR. *Here; what would* my lord?]
Portia's playful rejoinder to the sudden inquiry of the attendant, which Mr. Collier seriously considers a proof that he was no mere servant, but "a person of rank," and which Tyrwhitt thinks "more proper in the mouth of Nerissa," was not thought unbecoming a lady in our author's time, whatever it might be deemed now. A dozen instances may be cited from kindred works, where a similar expression is used by an individual of station to one of very inferior rank. In "Richard II." Act V. Sc. 5, a groom enters the presence of the king, and exclaims,—

"Hail ! *royal prince !*"

to which Richard replies,—

"—— Thanks, *noble peer.*"

Again, in "Henry IV." Part I. Act II. Sc. 4 :—

"*Enter* Hostess.
HOST. *My lord the prince.*
PRINCE HEN. How now, *my lady the hostess ?*"

d *Thou spend'st such* high-day *wit*—] The expression recals Hotspur's—

"—— many *holiday* and lady terms."

ACT III.

SCENE I.—Venice. *A Street.*

Enter Solanio *and* Salarino.

Solan. Now, what news on the Rialto?

Salar. Why, yet it lives there unchecked, that Antonio hath a ship of rich lading wrack'd on the narrow seas,—the Goodwins, I think they call the place; a very dangerous flat, and fatal, where the carcases of many a tall ship lie buried, as they say, if my gossip * report, be an honest woman of her word.

Solan. I would she were as lying a gossip in that, as ever knapped ginger,[a] or made her neigh-

(*) First folio, *gossips*.

a *As ever* knapped *ginger*,—] To *knap*, is the same as to *snap*, *i.e.* to *break*, or *crack*.

bours believe she wept for the death of a third husband. But it is true,—without any slips of prolixity, or crossing the plain highway of talk,—that the good Antonio, the honest Antonio,—O that I had a title good enough to keep his name company!—

SALAR. Come, the full stop.

SOLAN. Ha,—what sayest thou?—Why the end is, he hath lost a ship.

SALAR. I would it might prove the end of his losses!

SOLAN. Let me say, *Amen*, betimes, lest the devil cross my prayer: for here he comes in the likeness of a Jew.—

Enter SHYLOCK.

How now, Shylock? what news among the merchants?

SHY. You knew, none so well, none so well as you, of my daughter's flight.

SALAR. That's certain. I, for my part, knew the tailor that made the wings she flew withal.

SOLAN. And Shylock, for his own part, knew the bird was fledged; and then it is the complexion of them all to leave the dam.

SHY. She is damn'd for it.

SALAR. That's certain, if the devil may be her judge.

SHY. My own flesh and blood to rebel!

SOLAN. Out upon it, old carrion! rebels it at these years?

SHY. I say, my daughter is my flesh and blood.

SALAR. There is more difference between thy flesh and hers, than between jet and ivory; more between your bloods, than there is between red wine and rhenish:—but tell us, do you hear whether Antonio have had any loss at sea or no?

SHY. There I have another bad match: a bankrupt, a prodigal, who dare scarce show his head on the Rialto; a beggar, that was used to come so smug upon the mart. Let him look to his bond: he was wont to call me usurer;—let him look to his bond: he was wont to lend money for a Christian courtesy;—let him look to his bond.

SALAR. Why, I am sure, if he forfeit, thou wilt not take his flesh? What's that good for?

SHY. To bait fish withal: if it will feed nothing else, it will feed my revenge. He hath disgraced me, and hindered me half a million; laughed at my losses, mocked at my gains, scorned my nation, thwarted my bargains, cooled my friends, heated mine enemies; and what's his* reason? I am a Jew: hath not a Jew eyes? hath not a Jew hands, organs, dimensions, senses, affections, passions? fed with the same food, hurt with the same weapons, subject to the same diseases, healed by the same means, warmed and cooled by the same winter and summer, as a Christian is? If you prick us, do we not bleed? if you tickle us, do we not laugh? if you poison us, do we not die? and if you wrong us, shall we not revenge? If we are like you in the rest, we will resemble you in that. If a Jew wrong a Christian, what is his humility? revenge. If a Christian wrong a Jew, what should his sufferance be by Christian example? why, revenge. The villainy you teach me I will execute; and it shall go hard but I will better the instruction.

(*) First folio, *the*.

Enter a Servant.

SERV. Gentlemen, my master Antonio is at his house, and desires to speak with you both.

SALAR. We have been up and down to seek him.

SOLAN. Here comes another of the tribe; a third cannot be matched, unless the devil himself turn Jew.

[*Exeunt* SOLANIO, SALARINO, *and* Servant.

Enter TUBAL.

SHY. How now, Tubal, what news from Genoa? hast thou found my daughter?

TUB. I often came where I did hear of her, but cannot find her.

SHY. Why, there, there, there, there! a diamond gone, cost me two thousand ducats in Frankfort! The curse never fell upon our nation till now; I never felt it till now:—two thousand ducats in that; and other precious, precious jewels.—I would my daughter were dead at my foot, and the jewels in her ear! 'would she were hearsed at my foot, and the ducats in her coffin! No news of them?—Why, so:—and I know not what's* spent in the search. Why, thou loss upon loss! the thief gone with so much, and so much to find the thief; and no satisfaction, no revenge: nor no ill luck stirring but what lights o' my shoulders; no sighs but o' my breathing: no tears but o' my shedding.

TUB. Yes, other men have ill luck too. Antonio, as I heard in Genoa,—

SHY. What, what, what? ill luck, ill luck?

TUB. —hath an argosy cast away, coming from Tripolis.

SHY. I thank God, I thank God:—Is it true? is it true?

TUB. I spoke with some of the sailors that escaped the wrack.

SHY. I thank thee, good Tubal;—Good news, good news: ha! ha!—Where?† in Genoa?

(*) First folio, *how much is*. (†) Old copies, *Here*.

TUB. Your daughter spent in Genoa, as I heard, one night, fourscore ducats!

SHY. Thou stick'st a dagger in me:—I shall never see my gold again. Fourscore ducats at a sitting! fourscore ducats!

TUB. There came divers of Antonio's creditors in my company to Venice, that swear he cannot choose but break.

SHY. I am very glad of it: I'll plague him; I'll torture him; I am glad of it.

TUB. One of them showed me a ring, that he had of your daughter for a monkey.

SHY. Out upon her! Thou torturest me, Tubal: it was my turquoise:(1) I had it of Leah, when I was a bachelor: I would not have given it for a wilderness of monkeys.

TUB. But Antonio is certainly undone.

SHY. Nay, that's true, that's very true. Go, Tubal, fee me an officer, bespeak him a fortnight before: I will have the heart of him, if he forfeit; for were he out of Venice, I can make what merchandise I will. Go, Tubal, and meet me at our synagogue; go, good Tubal; at our synagogue, Tubal. [*Exeunt.*

SCENE II.—Belmont. *A Room in* Portia's *House.*

Enter BASSANIO, PORTIA, GRATIANO, NERISSA, *and* Attendants. *The caskets are set out.*

POR. I pray you, tarry; pause a day or two,
Before you hazard; for, in choosing wrong,
I lose your company; therefore, forbear a while:
There's something tells me, (but it is not love,)
I would not lose you; and you know yourself,
Hate counsels not in such a quality:
But lest you should not understand me well,
(And yet a maiden hath no tongue but thought,)
I would detain you here some month or two,
Before you venture for me. I could teach you
How to choose right, but then I am forsworn;
So will I never be: so may you miss me;
But if you do, you'll make me wish a sin,
That I had been forsworn. Beshrew your eyes,
They have o'erlook'd[a] me, and divided me;
One half of me is yours, the other half yours,—
Mine own, I would say; but if* mine, then yours,
And so, all yours: O! these naughty times
Put bars between the owners and their rights;

---

[a] *They have* o'erlook'd *me*,—] An allusion to witchery. To *o'erlook*, or *forelook*, or *eye-bite*, was to *bewitch with the eyes*. In this sense, o'erlooked is used by Glanvil. *Sadducismus Triumphatus*, p. 95: and in "The Merry Wives of Windsor," Act V. Sc. 5:—

"Vile worm, thou wast *o'erlook'd* even in thy birth."

(*) First folio, *of*.

And so, though yours, not yours.—Prove it so,
Let fortune go to hell for it,—not I.
I speak too long; but 't is to peize[a] the time;
To eke* it, and to draw it out in length,
To stay you from election.

BASS. Let me choose;
For, as I am, I live upon the rack.

POR. Upon the rack, Bassanio? then confess
What treason there is mingled with your love.

BASS. None, but that ugly treason of mistrust,
Which makes me fear the enjoying of my love:
There may as well be amity and life
'Tween snow and fire, as treason and my love.

POR. Ay, but I fear you speak upon the rack,
Where men enforced do speak anything.

BASS. Promise me life, and I'll confess the truth.

POR. Well, then, confess, and live.

BASS. Confess, and love,
Had been the very sum of my confession:
O happy torment, when my torturer
Doth teach me answers for deliverance!
But let me to my fortune and the caskets.

POR. Away then: I am lock'd in one of them;
If you do love me, you will find me out.
Nerissa, and the rest, stand all aloof.
Let music sound, while he doth make his choice;
Then, if he lose, he makes a swan-like end,
Fading in music: that the comparison
May stand more proper, my eye shall be the stream,
And watery death-bed for him. He may win;
And what is music then? then music is
Even as the flourish, when true subjects bow
To a new-crowned monarch: such it is,
As are those dulcet sounds in break of day,
That creep into the dreaming bridegroom's ear,
And summon him to marriage. Now he goes,
With no less presence,[b] but with much more love,
Than young Alcides, when he did redeem
The virgin tribute paid by howling Troy
To the sea-monster: I stand for sacrifice,
The rest aloof are the Dardanian wives,
With bleared visages, come forth to view
The issue of the exploit. Go, Hercules!
Live thou, I live:—With much-much† more dismay
I view the fight, than thou that mak'st the fray.
[*Here Music.*

(*) First folio, *ich*. (†) First folio omits the second *much*.

[a] *To* peize *the time;*] To *peize* the time, means to put a clog or weight on the time that it may not run so fast.

[b] With no less presence,—] "With the same dignity of mien."—JOHNSON.

[c] *With a* gracious *voice,*—] A *pleasing, winning, plausible* voice.

[d] *And* approve *it*—] That is, *justify* it. Thus, in "King Lear," Act II. Sc. 2:—

"Good king, that must *approve* the common saw."

[e] *Valour's* excrement,—] A brave man's beard. The meaning is,—cowards, who, inwardly, are false and craven, by the assumption of what is merely the excrescence of true valour, think to be considered indomitable.

A song, whilst BASSANIO *comments on the caskets to himself.*

1. *Tell me where is fancy bred,*
Or in the heart, or in the head?
How begot, how nourished?
Reply, reply.

2. *It is engender'd in the eyes,*
With gazing fed; and fancy dies
In the cradle where it lies;
Let us all ring fancy's knell;
I'll begin it,—Ding, dong, bell.

ALL. *Ding, dong, bell.*

BASS. So may the outward shows be least themselves;
The world is still deceiv'd with ornament.
In law, what plea so tainted and corrupt,
But, being season'd with a gracious[c] voice,
Obscures the show of evil? In religion,
What damned error, but some sober brow
Will bless it, and approve[d] it with a text,
Hiding the grossness with fair ornament?
There is no vice* so simple, but assumes
Some mark of virtue on his outward parts.
How many cowards, whose hearts are all as false
As stairs of sand, wear yet upon their chins
The beards of Hercules and frowning Mars,
Who, inward search'd, have livers white as milk;
And these assume but valour's excrement,[e]
To render them redoubted! Look on beauty,
And you shall see 'tis purchas'd by the weight;
Which therein works a miracle in nature,
Making them lightest that wear most of it:
So are those crisped snaky golden locks,
Which make such wanton gambols with the wind,
Upon supposed fairness, often known
To be the dowry of a second head,
The scull, that bred them, in the sepulchre.(2)
Thus ornament is but the guiled shore
To a most dangerous sea; the beauteous scarf
Veiling an Indian beauty;[f] in a word,
The seeming truth which cunning times put on
To entrap the wisest. Therefore, thou† gaudy gold,
Hard food for Midas, I will none of thee;
Nor none of thee, thou pale and common drudge

(*) Old copies, *voice*. (†) First folio, *then thou*.

[f] —— the beauteous scarf
Veiling an Indian beauty; in a word,
The seeming truth, &c.]

I have always suspected an error of the press in this passage. The printer appears to have caught the word *beauty*, of all others most inappropriate here, from the *beauteous* of the preceding line, and permitted it to usurp the place of the original expression; but what that was must be left to the reader's sagacity to determine. Mr. Collier's MS. corrector reads,—

"—— the beauteous scarf
Veiling an Indian; beauty in a word," &c.

'Tween man and man. But thou, thou meagre lead,
Which rather threat'nest than dost promise aught,
Thy plainness moves me more than eloquence,[a]
And here choose I. Joy be the consequence!

POR. How all the other passions fleet to air,
As, doubtful thoughts, and rash-embrac'd despair,
And shudd'ring fear, and green-eyed jealousy.
O Love, be moderate, allay thy ecstasy,
In measure rain thy joy, scant this excess;
I feel too much thy blessing, make it less,
For fear I surfeit!

BASS. What find I here?
[*Opening the leaden casket.*
Fair Portia's counterfeit?[b] What demi-god
Hath come so near creation? Move these eyes?
Or whether, riding on the balls of mine,
Seem they in motion? Here are sever'd lips,
Parted with sugar breath; so sweet a bar
Should sunder such sweet friends. Here in her hairs,
The painter plays the spider; and hath woven
A golden mesh to entrap the hearts of men,
Faster than gnats in cobwebs: but her eyes,—
How could he see to do them? having made one,
Methinks it should have power to steal both his,
And leave itself unfurnish'd. Yet look, how far,
The substance of my praise doth wrong this shadow
In underprizing it, so far this shadow
Doth limp behind the substance.—Here's the scroll,
The continent and summary of my fortune.

You that choose not by the view,
Chance as fair, and choose as true!
Since this fortune falls to you,
Be content, and seek no new.
If you be well pleas'd with this,
And hold your fortune for your bliss,
Turn you where your lady is,
And claim her with a loving kiss.

A gentle scroll.—Fair lady, by your leave:
[*Kissing her.*
I come by note, to give and to receive.
Like one of two contending in a prize,
That thinks he hath done well in people's eyes,
Hearing applause and universal shout,
Giddy in spirit, still gazing in a doubt
Whether those peals of praise be his or no;
So, thrice fair lady, stand I, even so;
As doubtful whether what I see be true,
Until confirm'd, sign'd, ratified by you.

POR. You see me,* lord Bassanio, where I stand,
Such as I am: though, for myself alone,
I would not be ambitious in my wish,
To wish myself much better; yet, for you,
I would be trebled twenty times myself:
A thousand times more fair, ten thousand times more rich;
That only to stand high in your account,
I might in virtues, beauties, livings, friends,
Exceed account: but the full sum of me
Is sum of nothing;† which, to term in gross,
Is, an unlesson'd girl, unschool'd, unpractis'd:
Happy in this, she is not yet so old
But she may learn; happier than this,
She is not bred so dull but she can learn;
Happiest of all, is, that her gentle spirit
Commits itself to yours to be directed,
As from her lord, her governor, her king.
Myself, and what is mine, to you and yours
Is now converted: but now, I was the lord
Of this fair mansion, master of my servants,
Queen o'er myself; and even now, but now,
This house, these servants, and this same myself,
Are yours, my lord,—I give them with this ring;
Which when you part from, lose, or give away,
Let it presage the ruin of your love,
And be my vantage to exclaim on you.

BASS. Madam, you have bereft me of all words;
Only my blood speaks to you in my veins,
And there is such confusion in my powers,
As, after some oration fairly spoke
By a beloved prince, there doth appear
Among the buzzing pleased multitude;
Where every something, being blent together,
Turns to a wild of nothing, save of joy,
Express'd, and not express'd. But when this ring
Parts from this finger, then parts life from hence;
O, then be bold to say, Bassanio's dead.

NER. My lord and lady, it is now our time,
That have stood by, and seen our wishes prosper,
To cry, good joy; Good joy, my lord and lady!

GRA. My lord Bassanio, and my gentle lady,
I wish you all the joy that you can wish;
For I am sure you can wish none from me:[c]
And, when your honours mean to solemnise
The bargain of your faith, I do beseech you,
Even at that time I may be married too.

BASS. With all my heart, so thou canst get a wife.

GRA. I thank your lordship; you have got me one.

(*) First folio, *my*. (†) Quartos, *something*.

a *Thy* plainness *moves me more than eloquence,*—] The old copies read, *paleness*, for which Warburton substituted the word in the text. We admit his emendation, but demur to the reasoning by which he sought to establish it. The *plainness* which moves Bassanio *more than eloquence* is clearly not alone the unpretending appearance of the leaden coffer, as Warburton seems to have thought, but the plain speaking of the inscription on it,—

"Which rather threat'nest than dost promise aught,"—

contrasted with the tempting labels of its neighbours.

b *Fair Portia's* counterfeit?] *Counterfeit* formerly signified *a portrait, a picture*, or *an image*. Thus, in "The Wit of a Woman," 1604:—"I will see if I can agree with this stranger, for the drawing of my daughter's *counterfeit*."

c For I am sure you can wish none from me:] "That is, none *away from me*; none that I shall lose, if you gain it."—JOHNSON. Rather, none *beyond what I wish you*.

My eyes, my lord, can look as swift as yours:
You saw the mistress, I beheld the maid;
You lov'd, I lov'd for intermission;[a]
No more pertains to me, my lord, than you.[b]
Your fortune stood upon the caskets there,
And so did mine too, as the matter falls:
For wooing here, until I sweat again,
And swearing, till my very roof* was dry
With oaths of love, at last,—if promise last,—
I got a promise of this fair one here,
To have her love, provided that your fortune
Achiev'd her mistress.

POR. Is this true, Nerissa?

NER. Madam, it is,† so you stand pleas'd withal.

BASS. And do you, Gratiano, mean good faith?

GRA. Yes faith, my lord.

BASS. Our feast shall be much honour'd in your marriage.

GRA. We'll play with them, the first boy, for a thousand ducats.

NER. What, and stake down?

GRA. No; we shall ne'er win at that sport, and stake down.
But who comes here? Lorenzo, and his infidel?
What, and my old Venetian friend, Solanio?

Enter LORENZO, JESSICA, *and* SOLANIO.

BASS. Lorenzo, and Solanio, welcome hither;
If that the youth of my new interest here
Have power to bid you welcome:—By your leave,
I bid my very friends and countrymen,
Sweet Portia, welcome.

POR. So do I, my lord;
They are entirely welcome.

LOR. I thank your honour.—For my part, my lord,
My purpose was not to have seen you here;
But meeting with Solanio by the way,
He did entreat me, past all saying nay,
To come with him along.

SOLAN. I did, my lord,
And I have reason for it. Signior Antonio
Commends him to you. [*Gives* BASSANIO *a letter.*

BASS. Ere I ope his letter,
I pray you tell me how my good friend doth.

SOLAN. Not sick, my lord, unless it be in mind;
Nor well, unless in mind: his letter there
Will show you his estate.

GRA. Nerissa, cheer yon stranger; bid her welcome.
Your hand, Solanio. What's the news from Venice?
How doth that royal merchant, good Antonio?
I know he will be glad of our success;
We are the Jasons, we have won the fleece.

SOLAN. I would you had won the fleece that he hath lost!

POR. There are some shrewd contents in yon same paper,
That steals the colour from Bassanio's cheek;
Some dear friend dead; else nothing in the world
Could turn so much the constitution
Of any constant man. What, worse and worse?—
With leave, Bassanio; I am half yourself,
And I must freely have the half of anything
That this same paper brings you.

BASS. O sweet Portia,
Here are a few of the unpleasant'st words
That ever blotted paper! Gentle lady,
When I did first impart my love to you,
I freely told you, all the wealth I had
Ran in my veins,—I was a gentleman;
And then I told you true: and yet, dear lady,
Rating myself at nothing, you shall see,
How much I was a braggart. When I told you
My state was nothing, I should then have told you,
That I was worse than nothing; for, indeed,
I have engag'd myself to a dear friend,
Engag'd my friend to his mere enemy,
To feed my means. Here is a letter, lady;
The paper as the body of my friend,
And every word in it a gaping wound,
Issuing life-blood. But is it true, Solanio?
Have all his ventures fail'd? What, not one hit?
From Tripolis, from Mexico, and England,
From Lisbon, Barbary, and India?
And not one vessel 'scape the dreadful touch
Of merchant-marring rocks?

SOLAN. Not one, my lord.
Besides, it should appear, that if he had
The present money to discharge the Jew,
He would not take it. Never did I know
A creature that did bear the shape of man,
So keen and greedy to confound a man:
He plies the duke at morning, and at night,
And doth impeach the freedom of the state
If they deny him justice: twenty merchants,
The duke himself, and the magnificoes
Of greatest port, have all persuaded with him;
But none can drive him from the envious plea
Of forfeiture, of justice, and his bond.

JES. When I was with him, I have heard him swear
To Tubal, and to Chus, his countrymen,
That he would rather have Antonio's flesh,

(*) First folio, *rough*. (†) First folio, *it is so, so* &c.

[a] *You lov'd*, I lov'd for intermission;] So all the old copies. Modern editors read,

"You lov'd, I lov'd; for intermission
No more pertains," &c.

If *intermission* is not used, as I think it probably is, for *pass-time*, Gratiano may mean "for *fear of* intermission," *i.e.* to avoid delay or loss of time.

[b] No more pertains to me, my lord, than you.] I owe my wife as much to you, as to my own efforts.

Than twenty times the value of the sum
That he did owe him; and I know, my lord,
If law, authority, and power deny not,
It will go hard with poor Antonio.

POR. Is it your dear friend that is thus in trouble?

BASS. The dearest friend to me, the kindest man,
The best condition'd and unwearied spirit
In doing courtesies; and one in whom
The ancient Roman honour more appears,
Than any that draws breath in Italy.

POR. What sum owes he the Jew?

BASS. For me, three thousand ducats.(3)

POR. What, no more?
Pay him six thousand, and deface the bond;
Double six thousand, and then treble that,
Before a friend of this description
Shall lose a hair thorough Bassanio's fault.
First, go with me to church, and call me wife,
And then away to Venice to your friend;
For never shall you lie by Portia's side
With an unquiet soul. You shall have gold
To pay the petty debt twenty times over;
When it is paid, bring your true friend along:
My maid Nerissa, and myself, meantime,
Will live as maids and widows. Come, away,
For you shall hence upon your wedding-day:
Bid your friends welcome, show a merry cheer:[a]
Since you are dear bought, I will love you dear.
But let me hear the letter of your friend.

BASS. [*Reads.*]

Sweet Bassanio, my ships have all miscarried, my creditors grow cruel, my estate is very low, my bond to the Jew is forfeit; and since, in paying it, it is impossible I should live, all debts are cleared between you and I, if I might but see you at my death; notwithstanding, use your pleasure: if your love do not persuade you to come, let not my letter.*

POR. O love, despatch all business, and be gone.

BASS. Since I have your good leave to go away,
I will make haste: but, till I come again,
No bed shall e'er be guilty of my stay,
Nor rest be interposer 'twixt us twain.
[*Exeunt.*

SCENE III.—Venice. *A Street.*

Enter SHYLOCK, SALARINO, ANTONIO, *and* Gaoler.

SHY. Gaoler, look to him. Tell not me of mercy;—
This is the fool that lent† out money gratis;—

---

[a] Cheer:] *Aspect, countenance.* See Note (c), p. 363. To the example there given of this use of the word, the following, from Puttenham's "Arte of English Poesy," may be added:—
"—— as ourselves wrote, in a *Partheniade* praising her Majesties countenance thus,—
'A *cheare* where love and Majestie do raigne.'"
Edition 1591.

*) First folio omits, *but.* (†) First folio, *lends.*

Gaoler, look to him.
ANT. Hear me yet, good Shylock.
SHY. I'll have my bond; speak not against my bond;
I have sworn an oath that I will have my bond;
Thou call'dst me dog, before thou hadst a cause;
But, since I am a dog, beware my fangs:
The duke shall grant me justice.—I do wonder,
Thou naughty gaoler,[a] that thou art so fond[b]
To come abroad with him at his request.
ANT. I pray thee, hear me speak.
SHY. I'll have my bond; I will not hear thee speak;
I'll have my bond; and therefore speak no more.
I'll not be made a soft and dull-ey'd fool,
To shake the head, relent, and sigh, and yield
To Christian intercessors. Follow not;
I'll have no speaking; I will have my bond.
[*Exit* SHYLOCK.
SALAR. It is the most impenetrable cur
That ever kept[c] with men.
ANT. Let him alone;
I'll follow him no more with bootless prayers.
He seeks my life; his reason well I know:
I oft deliver'd from his forfeitures,
Many that have at times made moan to me;
Therefore he hates me.
SALAR. I am sure, the duke
Will never grant this forfeiture to hold.
ANT. The duke cannot deny the course of law,
For the commodity that strangers have
With us in Venice; if it be denied,
'Twill much impeach the justice of the state;[d]
Since that the trade and profit of the city
Consisteth of all nations. Therefore, go
These griefs and losses have so 'bated me,
That I shall hardly spare a pound of flesh
To-morrow, to my bloody creditor.
Well, gaoler, on:—Pray God, Bassanio come
To see me pay his debt, and then I care not!
[*Exeunt.*

SCENE IV.—Belmont. *A Room in* Portia's *House.*

Enter PORTIA, NERISSA, LORENZO, JESSICA, *and* BALTHAZAR.

LOR. Madam, although I speak it in your presence,
You have a noble and a true conceit
Of god-like amity; which appears most strongly
In bearing thus the absence of your lord.
But, if you knew to whom you show this honour,
How true a gentleman you send relief,
How dear a lover of my lord your husband,
I know you would be prouder of the work,
Than customary bounty can enforce you.
POR. I never did repent for doing good,
Nor shall not now; for in companions
That do converse and waste the time together,
Whose souls do bear an equal yoke of love,
There must be needs a like proportion
Of lineaments, of manners, and of spirit;
Which makes me think, that this Antonio,
Being the bosom lover of my lord,
Must needs be like my lord. If it be so,
How little is the cost I have bestow'd,
In purchasing the semblance of my soul
From out the state of hellish cruelty!
This comes too near the praising of myself,
Therefore, no more of it: hear other things.
Lorenzo, I commit into your hands
The husbandry and manage of my house,
Until my lord's return; for mine own part,
I have toward heaven breath'd a secret vow,
To live in prayer and contemplation,
Only attended by Nerissa here,
Until her husband and my lord's return:
There is a monastery two miles off,
And there we will abide. I do desire you
Not to deny this imposition,
The which my love, and some necessity,
Now lays upon you.
LOR. Madam, with all my heart,
I shall obey you in all fair commands.
POR. My people do already know my mind,

---

[a] *Thou* naughty *gaoler,*—] *Naughty*, in the present day, is commonly employed to express some venial or childish trespass. In old language it bore a stronger meaning, and was used indifferently with *wicked, bad, base*, &c. Thus, Leonato says of the villain Borachio,—

"—— this *naughty* man
Shall face to face be brought to Margaret."
Much Ado about Nothing, Act V. Sc. 2.

And Gloster, in "King Lear," addresses the savage and relentless Regan, when she plucks his beard, as,—

"—— *Naughty* lady."

[b] *Thou art so* fond—] That is, *foolish*.

[c] *That ever* kept *with men.*] To *keep*, in the sense of *to live* or *dwell*, is still preserved at the University; "Where do you *keep?*" being frequently heard with the meaning of "Where do you *reside?*"

[d] 'T will *much impeach the justice of the state;*] The old copies read, "*Will* much," &c. We adopt the slight alteration proposed by Capell; for the construction of the original is so perplexed that it seems impossible to extract from that any clear sense. Possibly,—

"For the commodity that strangers have"—

is in the same predicament with other lines in these plays; and being intended by the author to be cancelled, was carelessly inserted by the old printers, together with the better expression of the same idea which follows it:—

"Since that the trade and profit of the city
Consisteth of all nations."

Without this unaccommodating line, the passage is perfectly logical and easy:—

"The duke cannot deny the course of law
With us in Venice; if it be denied,
'T will much impeach the justice of the state;
Since," &c.

And will acknowledge you and Jessica,
In place of lord Bassanio and myself.
So fare you well, till we shall meet again.

LOR. Fair thoughts and happy hours attend on you!

JES. I wish your ladyship all heart's content.

POR. I thank you for your wish, and am well pleas'd
To wish it back on you: fare you well, Jessica.
[*Exeunt* JESSICA *and* LORENZO.
Now, Balthazar,
As I have ever found thee honest, true,
So let me find thee still: take this same letter,
And use thou all the endeavour of a man
In speed to Padua;* see thou render this
Into my cousin's hand, doctor Bellario;
And, look, what notes and garments he doth give thee,
Bring them, I pray thee, with imagin'd speed
Unto the tranect,[a] to the common ferry
Which trades to Venice:—waste no time in words,
But get thee gone; I shall be there before thee.

BALTH. Madam, I go with all convenient speed. [*Exit.*

POR. Come on, Nerissa; I have work in hand,
That you yet know not of; we'll see our husbands
Before they think of us.

NER. Shall they see us?

POR. They shall, Nerissa; but in such a habit,
That they shall think we are accomplished
With that we lack. I'll hold thee any wager,
When we are both accoutred like young men,
I'll prove the prettier fellow of the two,
And wear my dagger with the braver grace;
And speak, between the change of man and boy,
With a reed voice; and turn two mincing steps
Into a manly stride; and speak of frays,
Like a fine bragging youth: and tell quaint lies,
How honourable ladies sought my love,
Which I denying, they fell sick and died;
I could not do withal;[b] then I'll repent,
And wish, for all that, that I had not kill'd them:
And twenty of these puny lies I'll tell,
That men shall swear I have discontinued school
Above a twelvemonth:—I have within my mind
A thousand raw tricks of these bragging Jacks,
Which I will practise.

NER. Why, shall we turn to men?

POR. Fie! what a question's that,
If thou wert near a lewd interpreter!
But come, I'll tell thee all my whole device
When I am in my coach, which stays for us
At the park gate; and therefore haste away,
For we must measure twenty miles to-day.
[*Exeunt.*

SCENE V.—*The same. A Garden.*

Enter LAUNCELOT *and* JESSICA.

LAUN. Yes, truly;—for, look you, the sins of the father are to be laid upon the children; therefore, I promise you I fear you.[c] I was always plain with you, and so now I speak my agitation of the matter: therefore, be of good cheer; for, truly, I think you are damned. There is but one hope in it that can do you any good; and that is but a kind of bastard hope neither.

JES. And what hope is that, I pray thee?

LAUN. Marry, you may partly hope that your father got you not, that you are not the Jew's daughter.

JES. That were a kind of bastard hope, indeed; so,[d] the sins of my mother should be visited upon me.

LAUN. Truly then I fear you are damned both by father and mother: thus when I shun Scylla, your father, I fall into Charybdis,(4) your mother: well, you are gone both ways.

JES. I shall be saved by my husband; he hath made me a Christian.

LAUN. Truly, the more to blame he: we were Christians enow before; e'en as many as could well live, one by another: this making of Christians will raise the price of hogs; if we grow all to be pork-eaters we shall not shortly have a rasher on the coals for money.

JES. I'll tell my husband, Launcelot, what you say; here he comes.

Enter LORENZO.

LOR. I shall grow jealous of you shortly, Launcelot, if you thus get my wife into corners.

JES. Nay, you need not fear us, Lorenzo. Launcelot and I are out: he tells me flatly, there is no mercy for me in heaven, because I am a Jew's daughter: and he says, you are no good member of the commonwealth; for, in converting Jews to Christians, you raise the price of pork.

(*) Old copies, *Mantua.*

a *Unto the* tranect,—] *Traneet* is probably a misprint for *traject*, from the Italian *traghetto*, a ferry, or ford, from shore to shore.

b I could not do withal;] That is, *I could not help it.* See Gifford's edition of "Ben Jonson," vol. III. p. 470, where the meaning of the phrase is fully illustrated.

c *Therefore, I promise you* I fear you.] That is, "I fear *for* you." So in "Richard III." Act I. Sc. 1.:—

"The king is sickly, weak, and melancholy,
And his physicians *fear him* mightily."

d So, *the sins of my mother*—] *So* means, *in that case.* This passage may help to countenance my opinion that the line in "King John," Act I. Sc. 1,—

"Heaven lay not my transgression to my charge,"—

should read,—

"Heaven lay not my transgression to *thy* charge."

LOR. I shall answer that better to the commonwealth, than you can the getting up of the negro's belly; the Moor is with child by you, Launcelot.

LAUN. It is much, that the Moor should be more than reason: but if she be less than an honest woman, she is, indeed, more than I took her for.[a]

LOR. How every fool can play upon the word! I think, the best grace of wit will shortly turn into silence; and discourse grow commendable in none only but parrots.—Go in, sirrah; bid them prepare for dinner.

LAUN. That is done, sir; they have all stomachs.

LOR. Goodly lord, what a wit-snapper are you! then bid them prepare dinner.

LAUN. That is done too, sir: only, cover is the word.

LOR. Will you cover, then, sir?

LAUN. Not so, sir, neither; I know my duty.

LOR. Yet more quarrelling with occasion! Wilt thou show the whole wealth of thy wit in an instant? I pray thee, understand a plain man in his plain meaning; go to thy fellows; bid them cover the table, serve in the meat, and we will come in to dinner.

LAUN. For the table, sir, it shall be served in; for the meat, sir, it shall be covered; for your coming into dinner, sir, why let it be as humours and conceits shall govern. [*Exit* LAUNCELOT.

LOR. O dear discretion, how his words are suited!
The fool hath planted in his memory
An army of good words; and I do know
A many fools, that stand in better place,
Garnish'd like him, that for a tricksy word
Defy the matter. How cheer'st thou, Jessica?
And now, good sweet, say thy opinion;—
How dost thou like the lord Bassanio's wife?

JES. Past all expressing. It is very meet,
The lord Bassanio live an upright life;
For, having such a blessing in his lady,
He finds the joys of heaven here on earth;
And, if on earth he do not mean it, then
In reason he should never come to heaven.[b]
Why, if two gods should play some heavenly match,
And on the wager lay two earthly women,
And Portia one, there must be something else
Pawn'd with the other; for the poor rude world
Hath not her fellow.

LOR. Even such a husband
Hast thou of me, as she is for a wife.

JES. Nay, but ask my opinion too of that.

LOR. I will anon; first, let us go to dinner.

JES. Nay, let me praise you, while I have a stomach.

LOR. No, pray thee, let it serve for table-talk;
Then, howsoe'er thou speak'st, 'mong other things
I shall digest it.

JES. Well, I'll set you forth. [*Exeunt.*

---

[a] LAUN. It is much, that the Moor should be more than reason: but if she be less, &c.] The commentators have illustrated Launcelot's gingle on *Moor* and *more*, but have overlooked the quibble here on *More* and *less*, which, petty as it is, has been repeated in "Titus Andronicus:"—

"NURSE. O, tell me, did you see Aaron the Moor?
AARON. Well, *more* or *less*, or ne'er a whit at all,
Here Aaron is," &c.

[b] And, if on earth he do not mean it, then
In reason he should never come to heaven.]

So the quarto by Roberts; the folio reads,—

"——— he do not mean it, *it*
Is reason he should never come to heaven."

Both are equally unintelligible. What can be made of,—

"——— he do not mean it, it
Is reason he should never come to heaven?"

Mean what? The commentators afford us no assistance here, although the sense is more ambiguous than in many passages on which they have expended whole pages of comment. The allusion applies to the belief that suffering in this life is a necessary preparation for happiness hereafter. Haply we should read:—

"And if on earth, he do not *moan*, it *is*
In reason he should never come to heaven."

The meaning of Jessica appears to be this:—It is meet Bassanio live virtuously; for, possessing, with such a wife, the joys of paradise, he could not plead suffering here as an atonement for his errors, and, in reason, therefore, would be excluded from heaven.

ACT IV.

SCENE I.—Venice. *A Court of Justice.*

Enter the DUKE, *the* Magnificoes, ANTONIO, BASSANIO, GRATIANO, SALARINO, SOLANIO, *and others.*

DUKE. What, is Antonio here?
ANT. Ready, so please your grace.
DUKE. I am sorry for thee; thou art come to answer
A stony adversary, an inhuman wretch
Uncapable of pity, void and empty
From any dram of mercy.
ANT. I have heard,
Your grace hath ta'en great pains to qualify
His rigorous course; but since he stands obdurate,
And that no lawful means can carry me
Out of his envy's[a] reach, I do oppose
My patience to his fury; and am arm'd
To suffer, with a quietness of spirit,
The very tyranny and rage of his.
DUKE. Go one, and call the Jew into the court.
SOLAN. He's ready at the door: he comes, my lord.

Enter SHYLOCK.

DUKE. Make room, and let him stand before our face.
Shylock, the world thinks, and I think so too,
That thou but lead'st this fashion of thy malice
To the last hour of act; and then, 't is thought
Thou 'lt show thy mercy and remorse, more strange
Than is thy strange apparent cruelty:
And where[b] thou now exact'st the penalty,
(Which is a pound of this poor merchant's flesh,)
Thou wilt not only lose the forfeiture,
But, touch'd with human gentleness and love,
Forgive a moiety of the principal;
Glancing an eye of pity on his losses,
That have of late so huddled on his back,
Enough to press a royal merchant(1) down,
And pluck commiseration of his state
From brassy bosoms, and rough hearts of flint,*
From stubborn Turks and Tartars, never train'd
To offices of tender courtesy.
We all expect a gentle answer, Jew.

[a] *Out of his* envy's *reach,—*] *Envy* is so commonly found in old writers in the sense of *hatred* or *malice*, that it would be supererogation to adduce examples.

(*) First folio, *flints*.

[b] *And* where—] *Where* for *whereas*.

SHY. I have possess'd your grace of what I purpose;
And by our holy Sabbath have I sworn,
To have the due and forfeit of my bond:
If you deny it, let the danger light
Upon your charter, and your city's freedom.
You'll ask me, why I rather choose to have
A weight of carrion flesh, than to receive
Three thousand ducats: I'll not answer that:
But, say, it is my humour. Is it answer'd?
What, if my house be troubled with a rat,
And I be pleas'd to give ten thousand ducats
To have it ban'd? What, are you answer'd yet?
Some men there are love not a gaping pig; (2)
Some, that are mad if they behold a cat;
And others, when the bagpipe sings i' the nose,
Cannot contain their urine: for affection,
Master of passion, sways it* to the mood
Of what it likes, or loathes.[a] Now, for your answer.
As there is no firm reason to be render'd,
Why he, cannot abide a gaping pig;
Why he, a harmless necessary cat;
Why he, a woollen bagpipe,—but of force
Must yield to such inevitable shame,
As to offend himself,[b] being offended;
So can I give no reason, nor I will not,
More than a lodg'd hate, and a certain loathing,
I bear Antonio, that I follow thus
A losing suit against him. Are you answer'd?

BASS. This is no answer, thou unfeeling man,
To excuse the current of thy cruelty.

SHY. I am not bound to please thee with my answer.

BASS. Do all men kill the things they do not love?

SHY. Hates any man the thing he would not kill?

BASS. Every offence is not a hate at first.

SHY. What, wouldst thou have a serpent sting thee twice?

ANT. I pray you, think you question with the Jew,
You may as well go stand upon the beach,
And bid the main flood bate his usual height;
You may* as well use question with the wolf,
Why he hath made† the ewe bleat for the lamb;
You may as well forbid the mountain pines
To wag their high tops, and to make no noise
When they are fretted with the gusts of heaven;
You may as well do anything most hard,
As seek to soften that (than which what's‡ harder?)
His Jewish heart.—Therefore, I do beseech you,
Make no more offers, use no farther means,
But, with all brief and plain conveniency,
Let me have judgment, and the Jew his will.

BASS. For thy three thousand ducats here is six.

SHY. If every ducat in six thousand ducats
Were in six parts, and every part a ducat,
I would not draw them,—I would have my bond.

DUKE. How shalt thou hope for mercy, rendering none?

SHY. What judgment shall I dread, doing no wrong?
You have among you many a purchas'd slave,
Which, like your asses, and your dogs, and mules,
You use in abject and in slavish parts,
Because you bought them.—Shall I say to you,
Let them be free, marry them to your heirs?
Why sweat they under burthens? let their beds
Be made as soft as yours, and let their palates
Be season'd with such viands? You will answer,
The slaves are ours:—so do I answer you.
The pound of flesh, which I demand of him,
Is dearly bought; 'tis mine, and I will have it:
If you deny me, fie upon your law!
There is no force in the decrees of Venice:
I stand for judgment: answer, shall I have it?

DUKE. Upon my power, I may dismiss this court,
Unless Bellario, a learned doctor,
Whom I have sent for to determine this,
Come here to-day.

SOLAN. My lord, here stays without,
A messenger with letters from the doctor,
New come from Padua.

DUKE. Bring us the letters. Call the messenger.§

(*) First folio omits, *it*.

(*) First folio, *or even*. (†) First folio omits, *Why he hath made*. (‡) First folio, *what*. (§) First folio, *messengers*.

a —— for affection,
Master of passion, sways it to the mood
Of what it likes, or loathes.]

In the old copies this troublesome passage is exhibited thus:—

"And others, when the bag-pipe sings i' the nose,
Cannot contain their urine for affection.
Masters of passion swayes it to the moode
Of what it likes or loathes."

The reading we select, which affords a good meaning with less violence to the original text than any other proposed, was first suggested by Dr. Thirlby, and has been adopted by Mr. Singer and Mr. Knight. Rowe and Pope read,—

"*Masterless passion* sways it to the mood," &c.

Hawkins,—

"—— for *affections*,
Masters of passion sway it," &c.

Warburton, Malone, Ritson, and Heath, abide by the ancient text, and Steevens advocates an amendment of Waldron's,—

"—— for affection,
Mistress of passion, sways it to the mood," &c.

The true source of the difficulty, however, may lie neither in *masters* nor *affection*, but in the comparatively insignificant preposition, *of*. If *of* is a misprint for *our*, the passage would run,—

"—— for affection
Masters *our* passion, sways it to the mood
Of what it likes or loathes."

b As to offend himself, being offended;] Modern editors point this line,—

"As to offend, himself being offended,"—

which renders it near akin to nonsense.

BASS. Good cheer, Antonio! What, man! courage yet!
The Jew shall have my flesh, blood, bones, and all,
Ere thou shalt lose for me one drop of blood.

ANT. I am a tainted wether of the flock,
Meetest for death; the weakest kind of fruit
Drops earliest to the ground, and so let me:
You cannot better be employ'd, Bassanio,
Than to live still, and write mine epitaph.

Enter NERISSA, *habited like a Clerk.*

DUKE. Came you, from Padua, from Bellario?

NER. From both, my lord: Bellario greets your grace. [*Presents a letter.*

BASS. Why dost thou whet thy knife so earnestly?

SHY. To cut the forfeiture from that bankrupt there.

GRA. Not on thy sole, but on thy soul, harsh Jew,
Thou mak'st thy knife keen; but no metal can,
No, not the hangman's axe, bear half the keenness
Of thy sharp envy. Can no prayers pierce thee?

SHY. No, none that thou hast wit enough to make.

GRA. O, be thou damn'd, inexorable* dog!
And for thy life let justice be accus'd.
Thou almost mak'st me waver in my faith,
To hold opinion with Pythagoras,
That souls of animals infuse themselves
Into the trunks of men: thy currish spirit
Govern'd a wolf, who, hang'd for human slaughter,
Even from the gallows did his fell soul fleet,
And, whilst thou lay'st in thy unhallow'd dam,
Infus'd itself in thee; for thy desires
Are wolfish, bloody, sterv'd, and ravenous.

SHY. Till thou canst rail the seal from off my bond,
Thou but offend'st thy lungs to speak so loud:
Repair thy wit, good youth; or it will fall
To cureless† ruin.—I stand here for law.

DUKE. This letter from Bellario doth commend
A young and learned doctor to‡ our court:—
Where is he?

NER. He attendeth here hard by,
To know your answer, whether you'll admit him.

DUKE. With all my heart:—some three or four of you
Go give him courteous conduct to this place.—
Meantime, the court shall hear Bellario's letter.
[*Clerk reads.*

Your grace shall understand, that at the receipt of your letter, I am very sick: but in the instant that your messenger came, in loving visitation was with me a young doctor of Rome; his name is Balthazar: I acquainted him with the cause in controversy between the Jew and Antonio the merchant: we turned o'er many books together: he is furnished with my opinion; which, bettered with his own learning (the greatness whereof I cannot enough commend), comes with him, at my importunity, to fill up your grace's request in my stead. I beseech you, let his lack of years be no impediment to let him lack a reverend estimation; for I never knew so young a body with so old a head. I leave him to your gracious acceptance, whose trial shall better publish his commendation.

DUKE. You hear the learn'd Bellario, what he writes:
And here, I take it, is the doctor come.—

Enter PORTIA, *for* BALTHAZAR.

Give me your hand. Came you from old Bellario?

POR. I did, my lord.

DUKE. You are welcome: take your place.[a]
Are you acquainted with the difference
That holds this present question in the court?

POR. I am informed throughly of the cause.
Which is the merchant here, and which the Jew?

DUKE. Antonio and old Shylock, both stand forth.

POR. Is your name Shylock?

SHY. Shylock is my name.

POR. Of a strange nature is the suit you follow;
Yet in such rule, that the Venetian law
Cannot impugn you, as you do proceed.—
You stand within his danger,[b] do you not?
[*To* ANTONIO.

ANT. Ay, so he says.

POR. Do you confess the bond?

ANT. I do.

POR. Then must the Jew be merciful.

SHY. On what compulsion must I? tell me that.

POR. The quality of mercy is not strain'd,
It droppeth, as the gentle rain from heaven
Upon the place beneath: it is twice bless'd;
It blesseth him that gives, and him that takes:
'Tis mightiest in the mightiest; it becomes
The throned monarch better than his crown;
His sceptre shows the force of temporal power,

(*) Old copies, *inexecrable.* (†) First folio, *endless.* (‡) First folio, *in.*

[a] Take your place.] In the representation of this scene, pictorially, or on the stage, it seems never to be remembered that Portia throughout the trial appears as a judge, not an advocate, and that her proper place, therefore, is on the judgment-seat, below the Duke's throne, rather than on the supposed floor of the court in front of the stage.

[b] *You stand* within his danger,—] That is, within his power. To be in *debt* was of old synonymous with being in *danger*. Ducange explains the term as follows: "*Danger,* quidquid juri stricto, atque adeo confiscationi obnoxium est."

The attribute to awe and majesty,
Wherein doth sit the dread and fear of kings;
But mercy is above this sceptred sway,
It is enthroned in the hearts of kings,
It is an attribute to God himself;
And earthly power doth then show likest God's,
When mercy seasons justice. Therefore, Jew,
Though justice be thy plea, consider this—
That in the course of justice, none of us
Should see salvation: we do pray for mercy;
And that same prayer, doth teach us all to render
The deeds of mercy. I have spoke thus much,
To mitigate the justice of thy plea,
Which if thou follow, this strict court* of Venice
Must needs give sentence 'gainst the merchant there.

SHY. My deeds upon my head! I crave the law,
The penalty and forfeit of my bond.

POR. Is he not able to discharge the money?

BASS. Yes, here I tender it for him in the court;
Yea, twice the sum: if that will not suffice,
I will be bound to pay it ten times o'er,
On forfeit of my hands, my head, my heart:
If this will not suffice, it must appear
That malice bears down truth. And I beseech you,
Wrest once the law to your authority:
To do a great right do a little wrong;
And curb this cruel devil of his will.

POR. It must not be; there is no power in Venice
Can alter a decree established:
'T will be recorded for a precedent;
And many an error, by the same example,
Will rush into the state: it cannot be.

SHY. A Daniel come to judgment! yea, a Daniel!
O wise young judge, how do I honour thee!

POR. I pray you, let me look upon the bond.

SHY. Here 'tis, most reverend doctor, here it is.

POR. Shylock, there's thrice thy money offer'd thee.

SHY. An oath, an oath, I have an oath in heaven:
Shall I lay perjury upon my soul?
No, not for Venice.

(*) First folio, *course*.

POR. Why, this bond is forfeit;
And lawfully by this the Jew may claim
A pound of flesh, to be by him cut off
Nearest the merchant's heart.—Be merciful;
Take thrice thy money; bid me tear the bond.
SHY. When it is paid according to the tenor.
It doth appear you are a worthy judge;
You know the law, your exposition
Hath been most sound; I charge you by the law,
Whereof you are a well-deserving pillar,
Proceed to judgment: by my soul I swear,
There is no power in the tongue of man
To alter me: I stay here on my bond.
ANT. Most heartily I do beseech the court
To give the judgment.
POR. Why then, thus it is:
You must prepare your bosom for his knife.
SHY. O noble judge! O excellent young man!
POR. For the intent and purpose of the law,
Hath full relation to the penalty
Which here appeareth due upon the bond;—
SHY. 'Tis very true: O wise and upright judge!
How much more elder art thou than thy looks!
POR. Therefore, lay bare your bosom.
SHY. Ay, his breast:
So says the bond;—doth it not, noble judge?—
Nearest his heart, those are the very words.
POR. It is so. Are there balance here to weigh the flesh?
SHY. I have them ready.
POR. Have by some surgeon, Shylock, on your charge,
To stop his wounds, lest he do* bleed to death.
SHY. Is it so† nominated in the bond?
POR. It is not so express'd, but what of that?
'Twere good you do so much for charity.
SHY. I cannot find it; 'tis not in the bond.
POR. Come,‡ merchant, have you anything to say?
ANT. But little; I am arm'd, and well prepar'd.—
Give me your hand, Bassanio: fare you well!
Grieve not that I am fallen to this for you;
For herein fortune shows herself more kind
Than is her custom: it is still her use,
To let the wretched man out-live his wealth,
To view with hollow eye, and wrinkled brow,
An age of poverty; from which lingering penance
Of such misery doth she cut me off.
Commend me to your honourable wife:
Tell her the process of Antonio's end,
Say, how I lov'd you, speak me fair in death;
And, when the tale is told, bid her be judge
Whether Bassanio had not once a love.
Repent not you that you shall lose your friend,
And he repents not that he pays your debt;

(*) First folio, *should*. (†) First folio, *It is not*. (‡) Quartos, *You*.

For, if the Jew do cut but deep enough,
I'll pay it instantly with all my heart.
BASS. Antonio, I am married to a wife,
Which is as dear to me as life itself;
But life itself, my wife, and all the world
Are not with me esteem'd above thy life;
I would lose all, ay, sacrifice them all
Here to this devil, to deliver you.
POR. Your wife would give you little thanks for that,
If she were by, to hear you make the offer.
GRA. I have a wife, whom I protest I love;
I would she were in heaven, so she could
Entreat some power to change this currish Jew.
NER. 'Tis well you offer it behind her back;
The wish would make else an unquiet house.
SHY. These be the Christian husbands: I have a daughter;
Would any of the stock of Barrabas
Had been her husband, rather than a Christian!
[*Aside.*
We trifle time; I pray thee pursue sentence.
POR. A pound of that same merchant's flesh is thine;
The court awards it, and the law doth give it.
SHY. Most rightful judge!
POR. And you must cut this flesh from off his breast;
The law allows it, and the court awards it.
SHY. Most learned judge!—A sentence! come, prepare.
POR. Tarry a little;—there is something else.—
This bond doth give thee here no jot of blood;
The words expressly are, *a pound of flesh:*
Take then* thy bond, take thou thy pound of flesh;
But, in the cutting it, if thou dost shed
One drop of Christian blood, thy lands and goods
Are, by the laws of Venice, confiscate
Unto the state of Venice.
GRA. O upright judge!—Mark, Jew;—O learned judge!
SHY. Is that the law?
POR. Thyself shall see the act:
For, as thou urgest justice, be assur'd
Thou shalt have justice, more than thou desirest.
GRA. O learned judge!—Mark, Jew;—a learned judge!
SHY. I take this offer then,—pay the bond thrice,
And let the Christian go.
BASS. Here is the money.
POR. Soft;—
The Jew shall have all justice;—soft;—no haste;—
He shall have nothing but the penalty.
GRA. O Jew! an upright judge, a learned judge!
POR. Therefore, prepare thee to cut off the flesh.
Shed thou no blood; nor cut thou less, nor more,

(*) First folio, *Then take*.

But just a pound of flesh: if thou tak'st more,
Or less, than a just pound,—be it but so* much
As makes it light, or heavy, in the substance,
Or the division of the twentieth part
Of one poor scruple,—nay, if the scale do turn
But in the estimation of a hair,—
Thou diest, and all thy goods are confiscate.(3)

GRA. A second Daniel, a Daniel, Jew!
Now, infidel, I have thee on the hip.

POR. Why doth the Jew pause? take thy forfeiture.

SHY. Give me my principal, and let me go.

BASS. I have it ready for thee; here it is.

POR. He hath refus'd it in the open court;
He shall have merely justice, and his bond.

GRA. A Daniel, still say I; a second Daniel!—
I thank thee, Jew, for teaching me that word.

SHY. Shall I not have barely my principal?

POR. Thou shalt have nothing but the forfeiture,
To be so taken† at thy peril, Jew.

SHY. Why, then the devil give him good of it!
I'll stay no longer question.

POR. Tarry, Jew;
The law hath yet another hold on you.
It is enacted in the laws of Venice,—
If it be proved against an alien,
That by direct or indirect attempts
He seek the life of any citizen,
The party 'gainst the which he doth contrive,[a]
Shall seize one half his goods; the other half
Comes to the privy coffer of the state;
And the offender's life lies in the mercy
Of the duke only, 'gainst all other voice.
In which predicament, I say, thou stand'st:
For it appears by manifest proceeding,
That, indirectly, and directly too,
Thou hast contriv'd against the very life
Of the defendant; and thou hast incurr'd
The danger formerly by me rehears'd.
Down, therefore, and beg mercy of the duke.

GRA. Beg that thou mayst have leave to hang thyself:
And yet, thy wealth being forfeit to the state,
Thou hast not left the value of a cord;
Therefore, thou must be hang'd at the state's charge.

DUKE. That thou shalt see the difference of our spirit,
I pardon thee thy life before thou ask it:

(*) First folio omits, *but*. (†) First folio, *taken so*.

[a] Contrive,—] In "The Taming of the Shrew," Act I. Sc. 2, Shakespeare for once uses *contrive* in its scholastic sense, to *consume, spend*, and the like, from the Latin *contero, contrivi*. Here and elsewhere it means to *scheme*, to *devise*, to *plot*, and comes from the old French compound, *controuver*. As an example, take the passage, in "Julius Cæsar," Act II. Sc. 3:—

"If not, the fates with traitors do *contrive*."

And that in "Hamlet," Act I. Sc. 5:—

"Taint not thy mind, nor let thy soul *contrive*
Against thy mother aught."

For half thy wealth, it is Antonio's;
The other half comes to the general state,
Which humbleness may drive unto a fine.
POR. Ay, for the state;[a] not for Antonio.
SHY. Nay, take my life and all; pardon not that:
You take my house, when you do take the prop
That doth sustain my house; you take my life,
When you do take the means whereby I live.
POR. What mercy can you render him, Antonio?
GRA. A halter gratis; nothing else, for God's sake!
ANT. So please my lord the duke, and all the court,
To quit the fine for one half of his goods;
I am content, so he will let me have
The other half in use,(4) to render it,
Upon his death, unto the gentleman
That lately stole his daughter;
Two things provided more,—that for this favour,
He presently become a Christian;
The other, that he do record a gift,
Here in the court, of all he dies possess'd,
Unto his son Lorenzo and his daughter.
DUKE. He shall do this; or else I do recant
The pardon that I late pronounced here.
POR. Art thou contented, Jew? what dost thou say?
SHY. I am content.
POR. Clerk, draw a deed of gift.
SHY. I pray you give me leave to go from hence:
I am not well; send the deed after me,
And I will sign it.
DUKE. Get thee gone, but do it.
GRA. In christening, shalt thou* have two godfathers;
Had I been judge, thou shouldst have had ten more,[b]
To bring thee to the gallows, not the† font.
[*Exit* SHYLOCK.
DUKE. Sir, I entreat you home with me‡ to dinner.
POR. I humbly do desire your grace of pardon.[c]
I must away this night toward Padua,
And it is meet I presently set forth.
DUKE. I am sorry that your leisure serves you not.
Antonio, gratify this gentleman,
For, in my mind, you are much bound to him.
[*Exeunt* DUKE, Magnificoes, *and Train.*

BASS. Most worthy gentleman, I, and my friend,
Have by your wisdom been this day acquitted
Of grievous penalties; in lieu whereof,
Three thousand ducats, due unto the Jew,
We freely cope[d] your courteous pains withal.
ANT. And stand indebted, over and above,
In love and service to you evermore.
POR. He is well paid that is well satisfied:
And I, delivering you, am satisfied,
And therein do account myself well paid;
My mind was never yet more mercenary.
I pray you, know me, when we meet again;
I wish you well, and so I take my leave.
BASS. Dear sir, of force I must attempt you further;
Take some remembrance of us, as a tribute,
Not as fee: grant me two things, I pray you,
Not to deny me, and to pardon me.
POR. You press me far, and therefore I will yield.
Give me your gloves, I'll wear them for your sake;
And, for your love, I'll take this ring from you:—
Do not draw back your hand; I'll take no more;
And you in love shall not deny me this.
BASS. This ring, good sir?—alas it is a trifle;
I will not shame myself to give you this.
POR. I will have nothing else but only this;
And now, methinks, I have a mind to it.
BASS. There's more depends on this than on the value.
The dearest ring in Venice will I give you,
And find it out by proclamation;
Only for this I pray you pardon me.
POR. I see, sir, you are liberal in offers:
You taught me first to beg; and now, methinks,
You teach me how a beggar should be answer'd.
BASS. Good sir, this ring was given me by my wife;
And, when she put it on, she made me vow
That I should neither sell, nor give, nor lose it.
POR. That 'scuse serves many men to save their gifts.
An if your wife be not a mad woman,
And know how well I have deserv'd this ring,
She would not hold out enemy for ever,
For giving it to me. Well, peace be with you!
[*Exeunt* PORTIA *and* NERISSA.
ANT. My lord Bassanio, let him have the ring;
Let his deservings, and my love withal,

(*) First folio, *thou shalt.* (†) First folio, *not to the.* (‡) First folio, *with me home.*

a Ay, for the state;] "That is, the state's moiety may be commuted for a fine, but not Antonio's."—MALONE.

b *Had I been judge, thou shouldst have had* ten more,—] Meaning a jury of *twelve* men, to condemn him. This, as Malone remarks, was an old joke. In "A Dialogue both pleasant and pietifull," &c., by Dr. William Bulleyne, 1564, one of the speakers says:—"I did see him aske blessinge to XII. godfathers at ones."

c *Your grace* of pardon.] See note (a), p. 361.

d *We freely* cope *your courteous pains withal.*] *To cope* seems to be used here in the sense of *encounter* or *meet*, and not in that of *exchange.*

Be valued 'gainst your wife's commandment.
BASS. Go, Gratiano, run and overtake him;
Give him the ring; and bring him, if thou can'st,
Unto Antonio's house:—away! make haste.
[*Exit* GRATIANO.
Come, you and I will thither presently;
And in the morning early will we both
Fly toward Belmont. Come, Antonio. [*Exeunt.*

SCENE II.—Venice. *A Street.*

Enter PORTIA *and* NERISSA.

POR. Inquire the Jew's house out, give him this deed,
And let him sign it; we'll away to-night,
And be a day before our husbands home.
This deed will be well welcome to Lorenzo.

Enter GRATIANO.

GRA. Fair sir, you are well o'erta'en:
My lord Bassanio, upon more advice,[a]
Hath sent you here this ring; and doth entreat
Your company at dinner.
POR. That cannot be:
His ring I do accept most thankfully,
And so, I pray you, tell him: furthermore,
I pray you, show my youth old Shylock's house.
GRA. That will I do.
NER. Sir, I would speak with you:—
I'll see if I can get my husband's ring,
[*Aside to* PORTIA.
Which I did make him swear to keep for ever.
POR. Thou may'st, I warrant. We shall have old[b] swearing,
That they did give the rings away to men;
But we'll outface them, and outswear them too.
Away! make haste; thou know'st where I will tarry.
NER. Come, good sir, will you show me to this house? [*Exeunt.*

---

[a] Upon more advice,—] After more *consideration.*
[b] *We shall have* old *swearing,*—] "Of this common augmentative in colloquial language there are various instances in our author. Thus, in 'The Merry Wives of Windsor:'—'Here will be an *old* abusing of God's patience and the King's English.' Again, in 'King Henry IV.' (Part II. Act II. Sc. 4): '—— here will be *old* utis.' The same phrase also occurs in 'Macbeth.'"—STEEVENS.

ACT V.

SCENE I.—Belmont. *A Grove before* Portia's *House.*(1)

Enter LORENZO *and* JESSICA.

LOR. The moon shines bright :—in such a night as this,
When the sweet wind did gently kiss the trees,
And they did make no noise,—in such a night,
Troilus, methinks, mounted the Trojan walls,
And sigh'd his soul toward the Grecian tents,
Where Cressid lay that night.
JES. In such a night,
Did Thisbe fearfully o'ertrip the dew,
And saw the lion's shadow ere himself,
And ran dismay'd away.
LOR. In such a night,
Stood Dido, with a willow in her hand,
Upon the wild sea-banks, and waft her love
To come again to Carthage.
JES. In such a night,
Medea gather'd the enchanted herbs
That did renew old Æson.
LOR. In such a night,
Did Jessica steal from the wealthy Jew,
And with an unthrift love did run from Venice,
As far as Belmont.
JES. In such a night,
Did young Lorenzo swear he lov'd her well ;
Stealing her soul with many vows of faith,
And ne'er a true one.
LOR. In such a night,
Did pretty Jessica, like a little shrew,
Slander her love, and he forgave it her.
JES. I would out-night you, did no body come ;
But, hark, I hear the footing of a man.

Enter STEPHANO.

LOR. Who comes so fast in silence of the night?
STEPH. A friend.
LOR. A friend? what friend? your name, I pray you, friend?
STEPH. Stephāno is my name; and I bring word,
My mistress will before the break of day
Be here at Belmont ; she doth stray about
By holy crosses, where she kneels and prays
For happy wedlock hours.
LOR. Who comes with her?
STEPH. None, but a holy hermit, and her maid.
I pray you, is my master yet return'd?

LOR. He is not, nor we have not heard from him.—
But go we in, I pray thee, Jessica,
And ceremoniously let us prepare
Some welcome for the mistress of the house.

Enter LAUNCELOT.

LAUN. Sola, sola! wo ha, ho! sola, sola![a]
LOR. Who calls?
LAUN. Sola! Did you see master Lorenzo, and mistress Lorenzo? sola, sola!
LOR. Leave hollaing, man; here.
LAUN. Sola! Where? where?
LOR. Here.
LAUN. Tell him there's a post come from my master, with his horn full of good news; my master will be here ere morning. [*Exit.*
LOR. Sweet soul, let's in, and there expect their coming;
And yet no matter:—Why should we go in?
My friend Stepháno, signify, I* pray you,
Within the house, your mistress is at hand:
And bring your music forth into the air.
[*Exit* STEPHANO.
How sweet the moonlight sleeps upon this bank!
Here will we sit, and let the sounds of music
Creep in our ears; soft stillness, and the night,
Become the touches of sweet harmony.
Sit, Jessica. Look how the floor of heaven
Is thick inlaid with patines† of bright gold.
There's not the smallest orb which thou behold'st,
But in his motion like an angel sings,
Still quiring to the young-eyed cherubins:[b]
Such harmony is in immortal souls;(2)
But, whilst this muddy vesture of decay
Doth grossly close it in,‡ we cannot hear it.—

Enter Musicians.

Come, ho! and wake Diana with a hymn;
With sweetest touches pierce your mistress' ear,
And draw her home with music. [*Music.*
JES. I am never merry when I hear sweet music.
LOR. The reason is, your spirits are attentive:
For do but note a wild and wanton herd,
Or race of youthful and unhandled colts,
Fetching mad bounds, bellowing, and neighing loud,
Which is the hot condition of their blood,
If they but hear, perchance, a trumpet sound,
Or any air of music touch their ears,
You shall perceive them make a mutual stand,
Their savage eyes turn'd to a modest gaze,
By the sweet power of music. Therefore, the poet
Did feign that Orpheus drew trees, stones, and floods;
Since nought so stockish, hard, and full of rage,
But music for the* time doth change his nature.
The man that hath no music in himself,
Nor is not mov'd with concord of sweet sounds,
Is fit for treasons, stratagems, and spoils;
The motions of his spirit are dull as night,
And his affections dark as Erebus:
Let no such man be trusted.—Mark the music.

Enter PORTIA *and* NERISSA *at a distance.*

POR. That light we see is burning in my hall:
How far that little candle throws his beams!
So shines a good deed in a naughty world.
NER. When the moon shone, we did not see the candle.
POR. So doth the greater glory dim the less:
A substitute shines brightly as a king,
Until a king be by; and then his state
Empties itself, as doth an inland brook
Into the main of waters. Music! hark!
NER. It is your music, madam, of the house.
POR. Nothing is good, I see, without respect;[c]
Methinks it sounds much sweeter than by day.
NER. Silence bestows that virtue on it, madam.
POR. The crow doth sing as sweetly as the lark,
When neither is attended; and, I think,
The nightingale, if she should sing by day,
When every goose is cackling, would be thought
No better a musician than the wren.
How many things by season season'd are
To their right praise, and true perfection!—
Peace, ho! the moon sleeps with Endymion,[d]
And would not be awak'd! [*Music ceases.*

(*) First folio omits, *I*, and for *Stephano*, reads, *Stephen*.
(†) First folio, *pattens*. (‡) First folio, *in it*.

[a] Sola, sola! wo ha, ho! sola, sola!] Launcelot is imitating the horn of the courier, or "post," as he was called, who always wore that appendage suspended from his neck. Thus, in "The Untrussing of The Humourous Poet:"—

"The King will *hang a horn about thy neck*,
And make a *Post* of thee."

So, also, in Ben Jonson's "Silent Woman," Act II. Sc. 2:—

"*Enter* Truewit *with his horn*.
I had no other way to get in but by feigning to be a *post*."

[b] Cherubins:] This, and not *cherubims*, (or, properly, *cherubim*,) was the frequent orthography in Shakespeare's time.

(*) First folio omits, *the*.

[c] *Nothing is good, I see, without* respect;] By *respect*, in this place, is meant, *regard, attention, consideration*. When the mind is pre-engaged, it is influenced but little by the beautiful in nature or in art:—

"The crow doth sing as sweetly as the lark,
When neither is attended."

[d] Peace, ho! the moon sleeps with Endymion,—] All the old copies read,—

"Peace! *how* the moon sleeps," &c.

The emendation is Malone's; and, after the examples of this exclamation which he has cited from other plays, can hardly be disputed.

LOR. That is the voice,
Or I am much deceiv'd, of Portia.
POR. He knows me, as the blind man knows the cuckoo,
By the bad voice.
LOR. Dear lady, welcome home.
POR. We have been praying for our husbands' welfare,
Which speed, we hope, the better for our words.
Are they return'd?
LOR. Madam, they are not yet;
But there is come a messenger before,
To signify their coming.
POR. Go in, Nerissa;
Give order to my servants, that they take
No note at all of our being absent hence;
Nor you, Lorenzo:—Jessica, nor you.
[*A tucket*[a] *sounds.*
LOR. Your husband is at hand; I hear his trumpet:[b]
We are no tell-tales, madam; fear you not.
POR. This night, methinks, is but the daylight sick.
It looks a little paler; 't is a day,
Such as the day is, when the sun is hid.

Enter BASSANIO, ANTONIO, GRATIANO, *and their Followers.*

BASS. We should hold day with the Antipodes,
If you would walk in absence of the sun.
POR. Let me give light, but let me not be light;
For a light wife doth make a heavy husband,
And never be Bassanio so for me:
But God sort all!—You are welcome home, my lord.
BASS. I thank you, madam: give welcome to my friend.—
This is the man, this is Antonio,
To whom I am so infinitely bound.
POR. You should in all sense be much bound to him,
For, as I hear, he was much bound for you.
ANT. No more than I am well acquitted of.
POR. Sir, you are very welcome to our house:
It must appear in other ways than words,
Therefore, I scant this breathing courtesy.
GRA. [*To* NERISSA.] By yonder moon, I swear you do me wrong;
In faith, I gave it to the judge's clerk:
Would he were gelt that had it, for my part,
Since you do take it, love, so much at heart.
POR. A quarrel, ho, already! what 's the matter?
GRA. About a hoop of gold, a paltry ring
That she did give me; whose poesy was
For all the world, like cutlers' poetry
Upon a knife, *Love me, and leave me not!*[c]
NER. What talk you of the poesy, or the value?
You swore to me, when I did give it you,
That you would wear it till your* hour of death;
And that it should lie with you in your grave:
Though not for me, yet for your vehement oaths,
You should have been respective, and have kept it.
Gave it a judge's clerk!—no, God's my judge![d]
The clerk will ne'er wear hair on's face that had it.
GRA. He will, an if he live to be a man.
NER. Ay, if a woman live to be a man.
GRA. Now, by this hand, I gave it to a youth,—
A kind of boy; a little scrubbed[e] boy,
No higher than thyself, the judge's clerk;
A prating boy, that begg'd it as a fee;
I could not for my heart deny it him.
POR. You were to blame, I must be plain with you,
To part so slightly with your wife's first gift;
A thing stuck on with oaths upon your finger,
And riveted so† with faith unto your flesh.
I gave my love a ring, and made him swear
Never to part with it; and here he stands,—
I dare be sworn for him, he would not leave it,
Nor pluck it from his finger, for the wealth
That the world masters. Now, in faith, Gratiano,
You give your wife too unkind a cause of grief;
An 't were to me, I should be mad at it.
BASS. Why, I were best to cut my left hand off,
And swear, I lost the ring defending it. [*Aside.*
GRA. My lord Bassanio gave his ring away
Unto the judge that begg'd it, and, indeed,
Deserv'd it too; and then the boy, his clerk,
That took some pains in writing, he begg'd mine:
And neither man, nor master, would take aught
But the two rings.
POR. What ring gave you, my lord?
Not that, I hope, which you receiv'd of me.
BASS. If I could add a lie unto a fault,
I would deny it; but you see, my finger
Hath not the ring upon it, it is gone.
POR. Even so void is your false heart of truth.

---

[a] *A tucket*—] *A tucket* meant a flourish on a trumpet, perhaps from the Italian *toccata,* or the Spanish *tocár; tocár trompeta,* to sound a trumpet.

[b] I hear his trumpet:] In the time of Shakespeare it was customary for persons of distinction, when visiting, to be accompanied by a trumpeter, who announced their approach by a flourish on his instrument. To this practice we often find allusions in contemporary writers.

(*) First folio, *the.* (†) Old text, *so riveted.*

[c] *And* leave *me not!*] And *give* me not. So in "The Two Gentlemen of Verona," Act IV. Sc. 4:—
"It seems you lov'd not her, to *leave* her token."

[d] No, God's my judge!] The folio, in compliance with Act, 3 *Jac.* 1, reads, *but well I know.*

[e] *A little* scrubbed *boy,*—] That is, *a stunted* or *shrubbed* boy.

By heaven, I will ne'er come in your bed
Until I see the ring.
NER. Nor I in yours,
Till I again see mine.
BASS. Sweet Portia,
If you did know to whom I gave the ring,
If you did know for whom I gave the ring,
And would conceive for what I gave the ring,
And how unwillingly I left the ring,
When nought would be accepted but the ring,
You would abate the strength of your displeasure.
POR. If you had known the virtue of the ring,
Or half her worthiness that gave the ring,
Or your own honour to contain[a] the ring,
You would not then have parted with the ring.
What man is there so much unreasonable,
If you had pleas'd to have defended it
With any terms of zeal, wanted the modesty
To urge the thing held as a ceremony?
Nerissa teaches me what to believe;
I'll die for 't, but some woman had the ring.
BASS. No, by mine honour, madam, by my soul,
No woman had it, but a civil doctor,(3)
Which did refuse three thousand ducats of me,
And begg'd the ring; the which I did deny him,
And suffer'd him to go displeas'd away;
Even he that had held up the very life
Of my dear friend. What should I say, sweet lady?
I was enforc'd to send it after him;
I was beset with shame and courtesy;
My honour would not let ingratitude
So much besmear it. Pardon me, good lady;
For,* by these blessed candles of the night,
Had you been there, I think, you would have begg'd
The ring of me to give the worthy doctor.
POR. Let not that doctor e'er come near my house:
Since he hath got the jewel that I lov'd,
And that which you did swear to keep for me,
I will become as liberal as you;
I'll not deny him anything I have,
No, not my body, nor my husband's bed:
Know him I shall, I am well sure of it:
Lie not a night from home; watch me, like Argus;
If you do not, if I be left alone,
Now, by mine honour, which is yet mine own,
I'll have that† doctor for my bedfellow.
NER. And I his clerk; therefore be well advis'd,
How you do leave me to mine own protection.
GRA. Well, do you so: let not me take him then,
For, if I do, I'll mar the young clerk's pen.
ANT. I am the unhappy subject of these quarrels.
POR. Sir, grieve not you; you are welcome notwithstanding.
BASS. Portia, forgive me this enforced wrong;
And, in the hearing of these many friends,
I swear to thee, even by thine own fair eyes,
Wherein I see myself,—
POR. Mark you but that!
In both my eyes he doubly sees himself:
In each eye, one:—swear by your double self,
And there's an oath of credit.
BASS. Nay, but hear me:
Pardon this fault, and by my soul I swear,
I never more will break an oath with thee.
ANT. I once did lend my body for his* wealth;[b]
Which, but for him that had your husband's ring,
Had quite miscarried: I dare be bound again,
My soul upon the forfeit, that your lord
Will never more break faith advisedly.
POR. Then you shall be his surety. Give him this;
And bid him keep it better than the other.
ANT. Here, lord Bassanio; swear to keep this ring.
BASS. By heaven, it is the same I gave the doctor!
POR. I had it of him: pardon me,† Bassanio;
For by this ring the doctor lay with me.
NER. And pardon me, my gentle Gratiano;
For that same scrubbed boy, the doctor's clerk,
In lieu of this, last night did lie with me.
GRA. Why, this is like the mending of highways
In summer, where the ways are fair enough:
What! are we cuckolds, ere we have deserv'd it?
POR. Speak not so grossly.—You are all amaz'd:
Here is a letter, read it at your leisure;
It comes from Padua, from Bellario:
There you shall find, that Portia was the doctor;
Nerissa there, her clerk: Lorenzo here
Shall witness, I set forth as soon as you,
And but e'en now return'd; I have not yet
Enter'd my house.—Antonio, you are welcome;
And I have better news in store for you,
Than you expect: unseal this letter soon;
There you shall find, three of your argosies
Are richly come to harbour suddenly:
You shall not know by what strange accident
I chanced on this letter.
ANT. I am dumb.

(*) First folio, *And*. (†) First folio, *the*.

(*) First folio, *thy*. (†) First folio omits, *me*.

[a] Contain *the ring,*—] *Hold* or *retain* the ring.

[b] *For his* wealth;] That is, for his *weal, advantage, prosperity*. "*Wealth*," Johnson says, "was, at that time, the term opposite to *adversity*, or *calamity*." Thus, in the "Litany:"—
"In all time of our tribulation; in all time of our *wealth*."

BASS. Were you the doctor, and I knew you not?
GRA. Were you the clerk, that is to make me cuckold?
NER. Ay, but the clerk that never means to do it,
Unless he live until he be a man.
BASS. Sweet doctor, you shall be my bedfellow;
When I am absent, then lie with my wife.
ANT. Sweet lady, you have given me life, and living;[a]
For here I read for certain, that my ships
Are safely come to road.
POR. How now, Lorenzo?
My clerk hath some good comforts too for you.
NER. Ay, and I'll give them him without a fee.—
There do I give to you and Jessica,
From the rich Jew, a special deed of gift,
After his death, of all he dies possess'd of.
LOR. Fair ladies, you drop manna in the way
Of starved people.
POR. It is almost morning,
And yet, I am sure, you are not satisfied
Of these events at full. Let us go in;
And charge us there upon inter'gatories,
And we will answer all things faithfully.
GRA. Let it be so. The first inter'gatory,
That my Nerissa shall be sworn on, is,
Whether till the next night she had rather stay,
Or go to bed now, being two hours to day:
But were the day come, I should wish it dark,
That* I were couching with the doctor's clerk.
Well, while I live, I'll fear no other thing
So sore, as keeping safe Nerissa's ring. [*Exeunt.*

[a] *Life, and* living;] *Living* signified *riches, resources,* &c. See Note (d), p. 203.

(*) First folio, *Till.*

ILLUSTRATIVE COMMENTS.

ACT I.

(1) Scene I.—
In my school-days, when I had lost one shaft,
I shot his fellow of the self-same flight
The self-same way, with more advised watch,
To find the other forth; and by adventuring both
I oft found both.]

This expedient for discovering a stray shaft is probably as old as archery. It was prescribed by P. Crescentius in his "Treatise de Agricultura," lib. x. cap. xxviii., and is mentioned frequently by the writers of our author's age. Thus in Decker's "Villanies discovered by Lanthorne and Candlelight:"—"And yet I have seene a Creditor in Prison weepe when he beheld the Debtor, and to lay out money of his owne purse to free him: *he shot a second arrow to find the first,*" 4to. 1616. Again, in Howel's Letters ("Epistolæ Ho-Elianæ"):—"I sent you one of the 3d current, but it was not answered: I sent another of the 13th, *like a second arrow to find out the first,* but I know not what's become of either: I send this to find out the other two; and if this fail, there shall go no more out of my Quiver." *Letter XV.*, 19 *July*, 1626. And in Taylor the Water Poet's "Kicksey Winsey, or, a Lerry Come Twang," folio 1630, p. 41:—

"I, like a boy that shooting with a bow
Hath lost his shaft where weedes and bushes growe:
Who having search'd, and rak'd, and scrap'd, and tost,
To find his arrow that he late hath lost;
At last a crotchet comes into his braine,
To stand at his first shooting place againe:
Then shoots and lets another arrow flye,
Neere as he thinkes his other shaft may lye:
Thus ventring, he perhaps findes both or one,
The worst is, if he lose both, he findes none."

(2) Scene II.—*The county Palatine.*] It is possible that Shakespeare, with his fondness of allusion to contemporaneous events and characters, referred here to an individual whose career would be familiar enough to the public of that period—the Polish Palatine of Siradz, Albert Laski, a nobleman of immense possessions, who visited England in 1583, and was received by Queen Elizabeth with unusual distinction. The prodigality of this Polonian is said to have been so extraordinary, that in a few years he dissipated the greater part of his enormous fortune, and was fain to become the disciple of the notorious alchymists, Dee and Kelly, in the hope of discovering the philosopher's stone. In company with these men and their families, he returned to his palace near Cracow, and there began operations for transmuting iron into gold. In these processes, the already deeply mortgaged estates of the infatuated Count were in a short time swallowed up; and it was not until ruin stared him in the face, that the credulous dupe awoke from his delusions, and dismissed the charlatans in time to save himself from utter beggary.

(3) Scene III.—*Shylock.*] This name, it has been thought, was derived from the Jewish appellation *Scialac*, borne in the poet's day by a Maronite of Mount Libanus. It may, however, have been an Italian name, *Scialocca*, the change of which into Shylock was natural. At all events, it was a name current among the Jews, for, at the end of an extremely rare tract, called "A Jewes Prophesy, or Newes from Rome of two mightie Armies as well footemen as horsmen," 1607, is a piece entitled, "Caleb Shilock his prophesie for the yeere 1607," which begins as follows:—"Be it knowne unto all men, that in the yeare 1607, when as the moone is in the watrye signe, the world is like to bee in great danger; for a learned Jew named Caleb Shilock doth write that, in the foresaid yeere, the sun shall be covered with the dragon in the morning, from five of the clocke untill nine, and will appeare like fire: therefore it is not good that any man do behold the same, for by beholding thereof, hee may lose his sight." Although pretending to be a prophecy for the year 1607, this edition was a reprint of a much older copy, the date of the predicted event being altered, to give interest to the publication.

(4) Scene III.—*If I can catch him once upon the hip.*] That is, *at advantage.* The phrase is taken from wrestling, and in its metaphorical sense is frequently found in the old authors. Thus Sir John Harington, in his Translation of Orlando Furioso, Booke XLVI., Stanza 117:—

"Full oft the valiant knight his hold doth shift,
And with much prettee sleight the same doth slippe;
In fine he doth applie one special drift,
Which was to *get the Pagan on the hippe;*
And having caught him right, he doth him lift,
By nimble sleight, and in such wise doth trippe;
That downe he threw him, and his fall was such,
His head-piece was the first that ground did tuch."

And in Bishop Andrewes' "Sermon preached before the King's Majesty at Whitehall, 1617:"—"If he have us *at the advantage, on the hip* as we say, it is no great matter then to get service at our hands." For additional examples of the use of this phrase, see "Notes and Queries," Vol. VII., p. 375, and Mr. Dyce's "Remarks on Knight's and Collier's Shakespeare."

(5) Scene III.—*In the Rialto.*] There were in ancient Venice three distinct places properly called *Rialto;* namely, the island on the farther side of the Grand Canal; the Exchange erected on that island; and the Ponte di Rialto, which connected the island with St. Mark's Quarter. The first of these places, according to Daru, received the name of *Rialto,* on account of its convenience to fishermen, its height, its contiguity to the sea, and its situation in the centre of a basin. If this conjecture be accurate, the original name was perhaps *Riva Alta,* a high bank-shore, or *Rilevato,* an elevated margin; since the island was the highest, and probably the oldest, of those in the lagune to which the Veneti fled. Early in the fifth century the church of San Jacopo was erected on this spot, near the fish-market; and adjoining to it were built the *Fabbricche,* a series of edifices connected by arcades, employed as warehouses and custom-houses; in the open space opposite to which was held the Exchange. Sabellicus, who wrote on Venetian history in the seventeenth century, states that this "most noble piazza" was crowded from morning to night. The part where the merchants transacted the most weighty and important affairs was near the double portico at the end of the piazza, opposite San Jacopo's church, where the *Banco Giro* was established.

The following is Coryat's description of the Rialto, or

Exchange, as it appeared when he visited Venice :—"The Rialto which is at the farthest side of the bridge as you come from St. Mark's, is a most stately building, being the Exchange of Venice, where the Venetian gentlemen and the merchants doe meete twice a day, betwixt eleven and twelve of the clocke in the morning, and betwixt five and sixe of the clocke in the afternoone. This Rialto is of a goodly height, built all with bricke as the palaces are, adorned with many faire walkes or open galleries that I have before mentioned, and hath a pretty quadrangular court adjoining to it. But it is inferior to our Exchange in London, though indeede there is a farre greater quantity of building in this than in ours."—*Coryat's Crudities* (1611), p. 169.

(6) *My Jewish gaberdine.*] A gaberdine was a large loose cloak, and it does not appear that this habiliment, as worn by the Jews, was in any respect different from that in ordinary use, though Mr. Halliwell observes, "According to a memorandum, the source of which is unknown to me, Shylock 'should assuredly wear a large red cross, embroidered upon his shoulder, the senate of Venice having passed an edict to mortify the Jews—many of whom quitted their territory to avoid its infliction—that no Israelite should appear upon the Rialto without the emblem or badge above specified.'" The distinguishing peculiarity in the costume of the Jews, as we learn from Coryat, was the colour of their head gear; those born in the western part of the world being compelled to wear red hats, and those in the east yellow turbans, or bonnets :—"I was at the place where the whole fraternity of the Jews dwelleth together, which is called the Ghetto, being an iland: for it is inclosed round about with water. It is thought there are of them in all five and sixe thousand. They are distinguished and discerned from the Christians by their habites on their heads: for some of them doe weare hats and those redde, only those Jewes that are borne in the Westerne parts of the world, as in Italy, &c., but the easterne Jewes, being otherwise called the Levantine Jewes which are borne in Hierusalem, Alexandria, Constantinople, &c., weare turbents upon their heads, as the Turkes do: but the difference is this; the Turkes weare white, the Jewes yellow. By that word turbent I understand a rowle of fine linnen wrapped together upon their heads, which serveth them instead of hats, whereof many have bin often worne by the Turkes in London."—CORYAT'S *Crudities* (ed. 1611, p. 130). As Shylock was a Levantine Jew, he should be represented with a yellow turban or bonnet.

(7) SCENE III.—*If he should break his day.*] To *break his day* was the current expression formerly to imply a breach of contract. "Every day he surveighs his grounds and the buttals therof, lest there be any incroaching or any thing remov'd. If any debtor *misse his day* but a minute, hee is sure to pay soundly for forbearance: besides usurie upon usury, if he continue it."—*Characters of Theophrastus*, translated by HEALEY. So, also, in "The Fayre Mayde of the Exchange," 1607, Act II. Sc. 2 :—

> "If you do *break your day*, assure yourself,
> That I will take the forfeit of your bond."

ACT II.

(1) SCENE I.—*Lead me to the caskets.*]—The incident of the caskets is generally believed to have been derived, directly or remotely, from a story in the Latin "Gesta Romanorum," which relates that a certain king of Apulia sent his daughter to be married to the only son of Anselmo the emperor, and that the ship in which she sailed was wrecked, and all on board lost except the princess. After undergoing some incredible adventures, the lady reaches the court of the emperor, her destined father-in-law :—

"Then was the emperour right glad of her safety and comming, and had great compassion on her, saying: Ah faire lady, for the love of my sonne thou hast suffered much woe, nevertheless if thou be worthie to be his wife, soone shall I prove.

"And when he had thus said, he commanded to bring forth three vessels, the first was made of pure gold, beset with precious stones without, and within full of dead mens bones, and thereupon was ingraven this posey: Who so chooseth me shall finde that he deserveth.

"The second vessel was made of fine silver, filled with earth and wormes, and the superscription was thus: Who so chooseth me shall find that his nature desireth.

"The third vessel was made of lead, full within of precious stones, and the superscription, Who so chooseth me shall finde that God hath disposed to him.

"These three vessels the emperour shewed to the maiden and said, Lo, here daughter, these be faire vessels, if thou choose one of these, wherein is profit to thee and to other, then shalt thou have my sonne: but if thou choose that wherein is no profit to thee nor to none other, soothly thou shalt not marrie him.

"When the mayden saw this, she lift up her hands to God and said: Thou Lord that knowest all things, grant me grace this houre so to choose, that I may receive the emperours sonne. And with that shee beheld the first vessell of gold, which was engraven, and read the superscription, Who so chooseth me, &c. saying thus: Though this vessel be full precious and made of pure gold, neverthelesse I know not what is within, and therefore my deare lord, this vessel will I not choose.

"And then shee beheld the second vessel that was of pure silver, and read the superscription, Who so chooseth mee shall finde that his nature desireth. Thinking thus within her selfe, If I choose this vessel, what is within it I know not, but well I wot there shall I finde that nature desireth, and my nature desireth the lust of the flesh, therefore this vessel will I not choose. When she had seene these two vessels, and given an answere as touching them, shee beheld the third vessell of lead, and read the superscription, Who so chooseth mee, shall finde that God hath disposed. Thincking within her selfe this vessel is not passing rich, nor throughly precious: nevertheless, the superscription saith: Who so chooseth mee, shall finde that God hath disposed: and without doubt God never disposeth any harme, therefore now I will choose this vessell, by the leave of God.

"When the emperour saw this, hee said, O faire mayden open thy vessell, and see if thou hast well chosen or no. And when this yong lady had opened it, she found it full of fine gold and precious stones, like as the emperour had told her before.

"And then said the emperour, O my deere daughter, because thou hast wisely chosen, therefore shalt thou marry my sonne. And when he had so said, he ordained a marriage, and married them together with great solempnitie and much honour, and they lived peaceably a long time together."—*Abridged from a translation by* ROBERT ROBINSON, *in Mr.* COLLIER'S *Shakespeare's Library*, vol. II. p. 102.

(2) SCENE II.—*Here's a simple line of life.*] Chiromantically, the *linea vitæ*, or *line of life*, is the indentation which runs round the root of the thumb, dividing it from the palm of the hand. In an ancient MS. possessed by

Mr. Halliwell, we are told, "Hit ys to know yf the lyne of the lyf strecche to the wryst, and that it be of good coloure sufficiently, it is a signe of long lyf. Yf it be short, it ys a signe of short lyf." If this authority be correct, we were not strictly so in stating that *the table* signified *the palm of the hand*. (See Note (c), p. 404.) "The lyne that begyniyth under the litille fynger and streccheth toward the rote of the fynger next the thombe, ys cleped *mensalis* that is, *the table*." But another writer on palmistry says, "The space between the natural line and the line of fortune is called *mensa*, the table."—SAMSON'S *Polygraphice*, 1675.

The *table line*, or *line of fortune*, then, is the line running from the fore-finger below the other three fingers to the side of the hand. *The natural line* is the line which curves in a different direction, through the middle of the palm; and the *line of life*, as before mentioned, is the circular line surrounding the ball of the thumb. The space between the two former lines being technically known as *the table*.

(3) SCENE II.—

Nay more, while grace is saying, hood mine eyes
Thus with my hat, and sigh, and say Amen.]

The practice of wearing the hat at meals, and especially at ceremonial feasts, was probably derived from the age of chivalry. In the present day, at the installation banquet of the Knights of the Garter, all the Knights Companions wear their hats and plumes. It appears to have been usual formerly for all persons above the rank of attendants to keep on their hats at the dinner-table. Lilly, in his Autobiography, gives an edifying account of his wooing his widowed mistress, who finally signified her acceptance of his suit by making him sit down with her to dinner with his hat on. And the custom may be inferred from the following:—"Roger the Canterburian, that cannot Say Grace for his meat with a low-crowned hat before his face: or the character of a prelatical man affecting great heighths. Newly written by G. T. Lond. sm. 4to." As also, from the Recipe for Dressing a Knuckle of Veal, sent by Dr. Delany to Swift:—

"Then skimming the fat off,
Say Grace with your hat off."

(4) SCENE VIII.—*That in a gondola.*] A good account of the gondola, as it was in Shakespeare's time, is found in Coryat's "Crudities," ed. 1611, pp. 170, 171. "The channels which are called in Latin *euripi*, or *æstuaria*, that is, pretty little armes of the sea, because they ebbe and flow every sixe houres, are very singular ornaments to the citie, through the which they runne even as the veynes doe through the body of a man, and doe disgorge into the *Canal il grande*, which is the common receptacle of them all. They impart two principall commodities to the citie, the one that it carryeth away all the garbage and filthinesse that falleth into them from the citie, which by meanes of the ebbing and flowing of the water, is the sooner conveighed out of the channels, though indeede not altogether so well, but that the people doe eftsoones adde their own industry to clense and purge them: the other that they serve the Venetians in stead of streetes to passe with farre more expedition on the same, then they can do on their land streetes, and that by certaine little boates, which they call gondolas, the fayrest that ever I saw in any place. For none of them are open above, but fairely covered, first with some fifteene or sixteene little round pieces of timber that reach from one end to the other, and make a pretty kinde of arch or vault in the gondola; then with faire black cloth which is turned up at both ends of the boate, to the end that if the passenger meaneth to be private, he may drawe downe the same, and after row so secretly that no man can see him: in the inside the benches are finely covered with blacke leather, and the bottomes of many of them, together with the sides under the benches, are very neatly garnished with fine linnen cloth, the edge whereof is laced with bonelace: the ends are beautified with two pretty and ingenuous devices. For each end hath a crooked thing made in the forme of a dolphin's tayle, with the fins very artificially represented, and it seemeth to be tinned over. The watermen that row these never sit as ours doe in London, but alwaies stand, and that at the farther end of the gondola, sometimes one, but most commonly two; and in my opinion they are altogether as swift as our rowers about London. Of these gondolaes they say there are ten thousand about the citie, whereof sixe thousand are private, serving for the gentlemen and others; and foure thousand for mercenary men, which get their living by the trade of rowing."

ACT III.

(1) SCENE I.—*It was my turquoise.*] The *turquoise* was esteemed precious of old, not alone from its rarity and beauty, but on account of the imaginary properties attributed to it. Among other virtues, it was supposed to have the power to quell enmity, and reconcile man and wife; and to possess the inestimable quality of forewarning its wearer, if any evil approached him:—"The turkesse doth move when there is any peril prepared to him that weareth it." FENTON'S *Certain Secrete Wonders of Nature*, 1569. "Turcois," says Swan, 1635, "is a compassionate stone: if the wearer of it be not well, it changeth colour, and looketh pale and dim; but increaseth to his perfectnesse, as the wearer recovereth to his health."

(2) SCENE II.—*The scull, that bred them, in the sepulchre.*] The fashion of wearing false hair seems to have been epidemical among the ladies of the *beau-monde* in the sixteenth century, and to have exposed them to unceasing raillery and sarcasm from contemporary pens. The crabbed Stubbes avers that it was the practice to decoy children who had beautiful hair to some secluded spot and there despoil them of their envied locks. Even the dead, as Shakespeare tells us here and elsewhere, were pillaged, to satisfy the demand occasioned by this morbid vanity:—

"—— The golden tresses of the dead,
The right of sepulchres, were shorn away,
To live a second life on second head!"
Sonnet 68.

"The hair thus obtained," says Drake, "was often dyed of a sandy colour, in complement to the Queen, whose locks were of that tint; and these false ornaments, or 'thatches,' as Timon terms them, were called 'periwigs.'" (See note (3), p. 44.)

(3) SCENE II.—*For me, three thousand ducats.*] In Venice there were two sorts of ducats: one, the *ducat de Banco*, worth 4*s.* 4*d.*; the other, of St. Mark, valued at about 2*s.* 10*d.* The ducat took its name, according to some, from the legend on it:—

"Sit tibi, Christi, datus, quem tu regis, iste Ducatus."

(4) SCENE V.—*Thus when I shun Scylla, your father, I fall into Charybdis, your mother.*] The famous old proverbial line,

"Incidis in Scyllam, cupiens vitare Charybdim,"

is said to have originally appeared in the Latin poem, "Alexandreis sive Gesta Alexandri Magni," by Philip Gualtier; there applied to Darius, who, escaping from Alexander, fell into the hands of Bessus. The proverb itself, however, has been pointed out in a much older writer, St. Augustine, in Joan. Evang., Tract. xxxvi. § 9: "Ne iterum quasi fugiens Charybdim, in Scyllam incurras." Again:—"A Charybdi quidem evasisti, sed in Scyllæis scopulis naufragasti. In medio naviga, utrumque periculosum latus evita." It was common in English books of the sixteenth and seventeenth century; and Mr. Halliwell quotes an old Somersetshire saying to a similar effect,—"He got out of the muxy and fell into the pucksy."

ACT IV.

(1) SCENE I.—*A royal merchant.*] This epithet is strictly appropriate, a *royal* merchant being one who transacted the commercial business of a sovereign. Thus King John calls Brand de Doway, "homo noster et dominicus mercator noster;" and on the same account, the famous Gresham was ordinarily dignified with the title of the *royal merchant.* About the period when Shakespeare wrote this play, there was at Palermo a celebrated merchant called Antonio, of whom it was said that he had at one time two kingdoms mortgaged to him by the King of Spain. (See Hunter's "New Illustrations of Shakespeare.")

(2) SCENE I.—*Some men there are love not a gaping pig.*] By a *gaping* pig Shakespeare may have meant a pig roasted for the table. Thus, in Nash's "Pierce Pennylesse his Supplication to the Devil:"—"The causes conducting unto wrath are as diverse as the actions of a man's life. Some will take on like a madman, if they see a *pig come to the table.*" So, in Fletcher's play of "The Elder Brother," Act II. Sc. 2:—"And they stand *gaping* like a *roasted pig.*" Again, in Webster's "Dutchess of Malfi," Act III. Sc. 2, 1623:—"He could not abide to see *a pig's head gaping;* I thought your grace would find him a Jew." In the "Newe Metamorphosis," a poem quoted by Mr. Halliwell, and written in the seventeenth century, there are some singular instances of antipathy:—

"I knewe the like by one that nould endure
To see a goose come to the table sure;
Some cannot brooke to se a custarde there,
Some of a cheese doe ever stand in feare;
And I knowe one, if she tobacco see,
Or smels the same, she swoones imediately:
The like of roses I have heard some tell,
Touch but the skyn and presently 'twill swell,
And growe to blisters: the reason it is this,
'Twixt them and these there's such antithisis."

(3) SCENE I.—*Thou diest, and all thy goods are confiscate.*] In the conduct of this part of Antonio's trial, we have a curious picture of Italian manners in the sixteenth century; one which shows that the most esteemed forensic talent of the period, consisted less in sound legal knowledge, than in the subtle acumen which could discover a flaw in an indictment, or detect an unsuspected omission in a bond. Portia here brings forth at last the most fatal charge against Shylock, that namely by which he had already forfeited both property and life, after the validity of the deed had been overthrown and the cause actually gained, by insisting on the fulfilment of overlooked impossibilities. Firstly, she urges,

"This bond doth give thee here no jot of blood."

And then,

"——In the cutting of it, if thou dost shed
One drop of Christian blood, thy lands and goods
Are by the laws of Venice confiscate."

Finally, she requires the plaintiff to cut off at once the precise weight, not the twentieth part of a scruple more or less than an exact pound. After all these objections had been urged and admitted, she adduces the Venetian law which made the whole transaction a criminal offence involving the penalty of forfeiture and death. In these two distinct parts of the pleading, we may fancy we can perceive the operations of two different minds; Doctor Bellario, of Padua, and Portia, of Belmont. To the former may be attributed the sound and irresistible legal attack upon the sanguinary bond; as appears to be expressed in his letter to the courts,—"We turned o'er many books together: he is furnish'd with *my opinion.*" But it seems also as if the female wit of Portia may be traced in the ingenious perception of the less criminal objections which first gained the cause; and that the old advocate covertly alludes to it in the words, "better'd with his own learning (the greatness whereof I cannot enough commend)."

There is, in Mr. Rogers' volume of Italy, a charming old Italian story, entitled "The Bag of Gold," which had been related to the author by a retired cardinal, and which, as he says, bears some resemblance to the tale of "The Merchant of Venice." It is altogether too long to be extracted entire, and the reader will probably thank us for sending him to the book; but as it especially illustrates the ancient Italian practice of gaining a cause by ingenious sophistry, we shall abstract the narrative and give the conclusion.

Three of the half-robber soldiers of the sixteenth or seventeenth century, desired to leave a stolen bag of gold with the hostess of a small inn called the White Cross, on the road to Bologna. They drew up an acknowledgment for it, which she signed, undertaking to deliver it when applied for; "but to be delivered, these were the words, not to one, nor to two, but to the three; words wisely introduced by those to whom it belonged, knowing what they knew of each other." After they had gone, one of them, who seemed to be a Venetian, returned, and requested to be allowed to set his seal on the bag as the others had done. She placed it before him for the purpose, but being at the same moment called away to receive a guest, when she came back the soldier and the money were gone. The other two robbers soon after claimed the gold; and as it was not forthcoming, they commenced a process against the hostess on her written acknowledgment. In great distress, she sent her daughter to several advocates to defend her; but some of them demanded too large a fee, others were already retained against her: all considered the case to be hopeless, and the trial was to come on the next day.

It happened that the hostess' daughter had a lover, Lorenzo Martelli, who was a law-student of great promise and already at the bar, though he had never spoken: and he volunteered his hearty support. The trial came on, the claim was proved,—there was no defence made by the defendant, and the judges were about to give sentence, when Lorenzo rose and addressed the court. "Much has been said," he pleaded, "on the sacred nature of the obligation, and we acknowledge it in its full force. Let it be fulfilled, and to the last letter. It is what we solicit, what we require. But to whom is the bag of gold to be delivered?

What says the bond? Not *to one,* not *to two,* but *to the three.* Let the three stand forth and claim it." From that day,—for who can doubt the issue?—none were sought, none employed, but the *subtle,* the eloquent Lorenzo.

(4) SCENE I.—

——— *So he will let me have*
The other half in use.]

"That is, in trust for Shylock during his life, for the purpose of securing it at his death to Lorenzo. Some critics explain *in use,* upon interest—a sense which the phrase certainly sometimes bore; but that interpretation is altogether inconsistent, in the present passage, with the generosity of Antonio's character. In conveyances of land, where it is intended to give the estate to any person after the death of another, it is necessary that a third person should be possessed of the estate, and the *use* be declared to the one after the death of the other, or the estate to the future possessor would be rendered insecure. This is called a conveyance to *uses,* and the party is said to be possessed, or rather *seised* to the *use* of such an one, or to the use that he render or convey the land to such an one, which is expressed in law French by the terms *seisie al use,* and in Latin, *seisitus in usum alicujus,* viz., A B, or C D. This latter phrase Shakespeare has rendered with all the strictness of a technical conveyancer, and has made Antonio desire to have one-half of Shylock's goods in *use,*—to render it upon his, Shylock's, death to Lorenzo."—ANON.

ACT V.

(1) SCENE I.—*A Grove before* Portia'*s house.*] "The 'poet's pen' has nowhere given more striking proof of its power than in the scene of the garden of Belmont. We find ourselves transported into the grounds of an Italian palazzo of the very first class, and we soon perceive them to be of surpassing beauty and almost boundless extent. It is not a garden of parterres and flowers, but more like Milton's 'Paradise,' full of tall shrubs and lofty trees—the tulip-tree, the poplar, and the cedar. But it is not, like Milton's, a garden in which the hand of Nature is alone visible. There are terraces and flights of steps, cascades and fountains, broad walks, avenues and risings, with alcoves and banquetting-houses in the rich architecture of Venice. It is evening: a fine evening of summer, which tempts the masters of the scene to walk abroad and enjoy the breezes which ruffle the gentle foliage. The moon is in the heavens, full orbed and shining with a steady lustre; no light clouds disturbing the deep serene. On the green sward fall the ever-changing shadows of the lofty trees, which may be mistaken for fairies sporting by the moonlight; where trees are not the moonbeams sleep upon the bank. The distant horn is heard; and even sweeter music floats upon the breeze."—HUNTER'S *New Illustrations, &c.*

(2) SCENE I.—*Such harmony is in immortal souls.*] "Touching musical harmony," observed Hooker, "whether by instrument or by voice, it being but of high or low sounds in a due proportionable disposition, such, notwithstanding, is the force thereof, and so pleasing effects it hath in every part of man which is most divine, that some have been thereby induced to think that the soul itself by nature is, or hath in it, harmony."

Ecclesiastical Polity, Book 5.

(3) SCENE I.—*No woman had it, but a civil doctor.*] In the Pecorone of Ser Giovanni, with which there can be little reason to doubt Shakespeare was in some way acquainted, this pleasant little incident about the ring forms a part of the story. The tale is much too long to be given in full, but the following analysis of it, extracted from Dunlop's "History of Fiction," preserves enough of the original to show that it was closely connected with the *bond* fable in "The Merchant of Venice." A young man, named Giannetto, is adopted by Ansaldo, a rich Venetian merchant. He obtains permission to go to Alexandria, and sets sail in a ship richly laden. On his voyage he enters the port of Belmont, where a lady of great wealth resided, and who announced herself as the prize of any person who could enjoy her. Giannetto is entertained in her palace, and having partaken of wine purposely mixed with soporific ingredients, he falls asleep on going to bed, and his vessel is confiscated next morning, according to the stipulated conditions. He returns to Venice, fits out a vessel richly loaded, for Belmont, and acts in a similar manner. The third time, Ansaldo is forced to borrow ten thousand ducats from a Jew, on condition of his creditor being allowed to take a pound of flesh from his body if he did not pay by a certain time. Giannetto's expedition is now more fortunate. He obtains the lady in marriage, by refraining from the wine, according to a hint he received from a waiting maid. Occupied with his bride, he forgets the bond of Ansaldo till the day it is due: he then hastens to Venice, but as the time had elapsed the Jew refuses to accept ten times the money. At this crisis the new-married lady arrives disguised as a lawyer, and announces, as was the custom in Italy, that she had come to decide difficult cases: for in that age, delicate points were not determined by the ordinary judges of the provinces, but by doctors of law who were called from Bologna, and other places at a distance. The pretended lawyer being consulted on the claim of the Jew, decides that he is entitled to insist on the pound of flesh, but that he should be beheaded if he draw one drop of blood from his debtor. The judge then takes from Giannetto his marriage-ring as a fee, and afterwards banters him in her own character for having parted with it.

CRITICAL OPINIONS ON THE MERCHANT OF VENICE.

"The 'Merchant of Venice' is one of Shakspeare's most perfect works: popular to an extraordinary degree, and calculated to produce the most powerful effect on the stage, and, at the same time, a wonder of ingenuity and art for the reflecting critic. Shylock, the Jew, is one of the inimitable master-pieces of characterization which are to be found only in Shakspeare. It is easy for both poet and player to exhibit a caricature of national sentiments, modes of speaking, and gestures. Shylock, however, is everything but a common Jew: he possesses a strongly-marked and original individuality, and yet we perceive a light touch of Judaism in everything he says or does. We almost fancy we can hear a light whisper of the Jewish accent even in the written words, such as we sometimes still find in the higher classes, notwithstanding their social refinement. In tranquil moments, all that is foreign to the European blood and Christian sentiments is less perceptible; but in passion the national stamp comes out more strongly marked. All these inimitable niceties the finished art of a great actor can alone properly express. Shylock is a man of information, in his own way, even a thinker, only he has not discovered the region where human feelings dwell; his morality is founded on the disbelief in goodness and magnanimity. The desire to avenge the wrongs and indignities heaped upon his nation is, after avarice, his strongest spring of action. His hate is naturally directed chiefly against those Christians who are actuated by truly Christian sentiments: a disinterested love of our neighbour seems to him the most unrelenting persecution of the Jews. The letter of the law is his idol; he refuses to lend an ear to the voice of mercy, which, from the mouth of Portia, speaks to him with heavenly eloquence: he insists on rigid and inflexible justice, and at last it recoils on his own head. Thus he becomes a symbol of the general history of his unfortunate nation. The melancholy and self-sacrificing magnanimity of Antonio is affectingly sublime. Like a princely merchant, he is surrounded with a whole train of noble friends. The contrast which this forms to the selfish cruelty of the usurer Shylock was necessary to redeem the honour of human nature. The danger which almost to the close of the fourth act hangs over Antonio, and which the imagination is almost afraid to approach, would fill the mind with too painful anxiety, if the poet did not also provide for its recreation and diversion. This is effected in an especial manner by the scenes at Portia's country-seat, which transport the spectator into quite another world. And yet they are closely connected with the main business by the chain of cause and effect: Bassanio's preparations for his courtship are the cause of Antonio's subscribing the dangerous bond; and Portia again, by the counsel and advice of her uncle, a famous lawyer, effects the safety of her lover's friend. But the relations of the dramatic composition are the while admirably observed in yet another respect. The trial between Shylock and Antonio is indeed recorded as being a real event; still, for all that, it must ever remain an unheard-of and singular case. Shakspeare has therefore associated it with a love intrigue not less extraordinary: the one consequently is rendered natural and probable by means of the other. A rich, beautiful, and clever heiress, who can only be won by the solving the riddle—the locked caskets—the foreign princes, who come to try the venture—all this powerfully excites the imagination with the splendour of an olden tale of marvels. The two scenes in which, first the Prince of Morocco, in the language of Eastern hyperbole, and then the self-conceited Prince of Arragon, make their choice among the caskets, serve merely to raise our curiosity, and give employment to our wits; but on the third, where the two lovers stand trembling before the inevitable choice, which in one moment must unite or separate them for ever, Shakspeare has lavished all the charms of feeling—all the magic of poesy. We share in the rapture of Portia and Bassanio at the fortunate choice: we easily conceive why they are so fond of each other, for they are both most deserving of love. The judgment scene, with which the fourth act is occupied, is in itself a perfect drama, concentrating in itself the interest of the whole. The knot is now untied, and, according to the common ideas of theatrical satisfaction, the curtain ought to drop. But the poet was unwilling to dismiss his audience with the gloomy impressions which Antonio's acquittal, effected with so much difficulty, and contrary to all expectation, and the condemnation of Shylock, were calculated to leave behind them; he has therefore added the fifth act by way of a musical afterlude in the piece itself. The episode of Jessica, the fugitive daughter of the Jew, in whom Shakspeare has contrived to throw a veil of sweetness over the national features, and the artifice by which Portia and her companion are enabled to rally their newly-married husbands, supply him with the necessary materials. The scene opens with the playful prattling of two lovers in a summer evening; it is followed by soft music, and a rapturous eulogy on this powerful disposer of the human mind and the world; the principal characters then make their appearance, and, after a simulated quarrel, which is gracefully maintained, the whole ends with the most exhilarating mirth."—Schlegel.

Act II. Sc. I.

THE LIFE AND DEATH OF

KING RICHARD THE SECOND.

SHAKESPEARE'S "King Richard II." was entered at Stationers' Hall, August 29, 1597, by Andrew Wise, who published the first edition that year under the title of "The tragedie of King Richard the Second. As it hath beene publikely acted by the Right Honourable the Lord Chamberlaine his Servants, London, *Printed by Valentine Simmes, for Androw Wise,* and are to be sold at his shop in Paules church yard at the signe of the Angel. 1597." 4to. This is much the most accurate copy of the play extant. Three other quarto editions were published before the first folio, one in 1598, another in 1608, "with new additions of the Parliament sceane, and the Deposing of King Richard," and the last in 1615; each of which bears the author's name, "William Shake-speare," on the title-page; that of 1615 being apparently the copy followed in the folio, 1623. There can now be scarcely a doubt that there was an older Richard II. than Shakespeare's, and one that kept its place as an acting drama, even at the Globe theatre, long after his had been played and printed. In a passage of Camden's Annals, it is related that Sir Gillie Merrick, who was concerned in the desperate insurrection of the Earl of Essex, was accused, among other charges, of having caused to be acted, by money in a public theatre, the obsolete tragedy (*exoletum tragediam*) of the abdication of Richard the Second. This transaction is related more circumstantially in the official declarations, where it is stated that, "The Afternoon before the Rebellion, Merrick with a great company of others, who were all afterwards in the action, had procured to be play'd before them the Play of deposing King Richard the Second; neither was it casual, but a play bespoke by Merrick; and when it was told him by one of the Players, that the Play was old, and they should have Loss in playing it, because few would come to it, there were forty Shillings extraordinary given for it, and so it was play'd." The deposition of Richard II. appears to have been a subject upon which Elizabeth was peculiarly sensitive. It was probably on this account, that the Parliament scene in Shakespeare's play, containing the actual deposition of the King, was not inserted in the quartos until after her death. In 1599, Sir John Haywarde was severely censured in the Star Chamber, and committed to prison, for his History of the First Part of the Life and Reign of King Henry IV., which contained the deposition of Richard II.

The revival of an old play on this prohibited topic must therefore have been highly offensive to the Queen: it certainly made a deep impression upon her; for, in a conversation with the accomplished William Lambarde, twelve months afterwards, on the occasion of his presenting her with his pandect of her Rolls in the Tower, when, looking through the records, she came to the reign of Richard II., she remarked:—"I am Richard II., know ye not that?" Lambarde replied, in allusion to the Essex attempt, "Such a wicked imagination was determined and attempted by a most unkind gent, the most adorned creature that ever your Majesty made:" to this her Majesty rejoined: "He that will forget God, will also forget his benefactors: this tragedy was played 40^{tie} times in open streets and houses."

That the drama in question was not Shakespeare's Richard II., is tolerably evident, from its being described as an obsolete play; but a discovery made by Mr. Collier places this fact beyond controversy. In a MS. diary kept by the notorious Dr. Simon Forman, and preserved in the Bodleian Library, Mr. Collier has found an entry under the date, Thursday, April 30, 1611, wherein Forman records his having been present at the Globe theatre, and witnessed the play of Richard II., some incidents in which he notes for his future guidance:—"Remember therein how Jack Straw, by his overmuch boldness, not being politic nor suspecting anything, was suddenly, at Smithfield Bars, stabbed by Walworth, the Mayor of London, and so he and his whole army was overthrown. Therefore, in such case, or the like, never admit any party without a bar between, for a man cannot be too wise, nor keep himself too safe. Also remember how the Duke of

Glocester, the Earl of Arundel, Oxford, and others, crossing the king in his humour about the Duke of Erland and Bushy, were glad to fly and raise a host of men; and being in his castle, how the Duke of Erland came by night to betray him, with three hundred men; but, having privy warning thereof, kept his gates fast, and would not suffer the enemy to enter, which went back again with a fly in his ear, and after, was slain by the Earl of Arundel in the battle. Remember also, when the Duke (*i. e.* of Gloucester,) and Arundel, came to London with their army, King Richard came forth to them and met them, and gave them fair words, and promised them pardon, and that all should be well if they would discharge their army, upon whose promises and fair speeches, they did it; and after, the king bid them all to a banquet, and so betrayed them, and cut off their heads, &c., because they had not his pardon under his hand and seal before, but his word.

"Remember therein, also, how the Duke of Lancaster privily contrived all villainy to set them all together by the ears, and to make the nobility to envy the King, and mislike him and his government: by which means he made his own son king, which was Henry Bolingbroke. Remember, also, how the Duke of Lancaster asked a wise man whether himself should ever be a king, and he told him No, but his son should be a king; and when he had told him, he hanged him up for his labour, because he should not bruit abroad, or speak thereof to others. This was a policy in the commonwealth's opinion, but I say it was a villain's part, and a Judas's kiss to hang the man for telling him the truth. Beware by this example of noblemen and their fair words, and say little to them, lest they do the like to thee for thy goodwill."

This play, then, it is clear, embraced the earlier portion of Richard's reign, and may have contained its close, and have been the one which the partizans of Essex contrived to get acted. Shakespeare's tragedy, on the contrary, comprises little more than the last two years of the reign of Richard II., and the facts appear to have been dramatized exclusively from Holinshed, some of the speeches being copied with scarcely any alteration from that old chronicler. Of the date of its composition we have no reliable evidence; Malone fixes it in 1593, Chalmers and Drake in 1596.

Persons Represented.

KING RICHARD THE SECOND.
EDMUND OF LANGLEY, *Duke of* YORK. } *Uncles to the* KING.
JOHN OF GAUNT, *Duke of* LANCASTER. }
HENRY, *surnamed* BOLINGBROKE, *Duke of* HEREFORD, *son to* JOHN OF GAUNT; *afterwards* KING HENRY THE FOURTH.
DUKE OF AUMERLE,* *son to the Duke of* YORK.
MOWBRAY, *Duke of* NORFOLK.
DUKE OF SURREY.
EARL OF SALISBURY.
EARL OF BERKLEY.
EARL OF NORTHUMBERLAND.
HENRY PERCY, *his Son.*
LORD ROSS.†
LORD WILLOUGHBY.
LORD FITZWATER.
LORD MARSHAL; *and other Lords.*
BISHOP OF CARLISLE.
ABBOT OF WESTMINSTER.
SIR PIERCE OF EXTON.
SIR STEPHEN SCROOP.
BUSHY, }
BAGOT, } *creatures to* KING RICHARD.
GREEN, }
Captain of a band of Welshmen.

QUEEN TO KING RICHARD.
DUCHESS OF GLOUCESTER.
DUCHESS OF YORK.
Lady attending on the QUEEN.

Lords, Heralds, Officers, Soldiers, Gardeners, Keeper, Messengers, Groom, and other attendants.

SCENE,—*Dispersedly in* ENGLAND *and* WALES.

* *Aumerle*, or *Aumale*, is the French for what we term *Albemarle*, a town in Normandy.
† Now spelt *Roos*.

ACT I.

SCENE I.—London. *A Room in the Palace.*

Enter KING RICHARD, *attended;* JOHN OF GAUNT, *and other* Nobles, *with him.*

K. RICH. Old John of Gaunt, time-honour'd Lancaster,(1)
Hast thou, according to thy oath and band,
Brought hither Henry Hereford,[a] thy bold son;
Here to make good the boisterous late appeal,
Which then our leisure would not let us hear,

[a] Hereford,—] This name is usually spelt *Herford* in the old copies, and must be pronounced as a dissyllable.

Against the duke of Norfolk, Thomas Mowbray?(2)
GAUNT. I have, my liege.
K. RICH. Tell me, moreover, hast thou sounded him,
If he appeal the duke on ancient malice;
Or worthily, as a good subject should,
On some known ground of treachery in him?
GAUNT. As near as I could sift him on that argument,
On some apparent danger seen in him,
Aim'd at your highness,—no inveterate malice.
K. RICH. Then call them to our presence; face to face,
And frowning brow to brow, ourselves will hear
The accuser, and the accused, freely speak:—
[*Exeunt some* Attendants.
High-stomach'd are they both, and full of ire,
In rage, deaf as the sea, hasty as fire.

Re-enter Attendants, *with* BOLINGBROKE [a] *and* NORFOLK.

BOLING. Many years of happy days befal
My gracious sovereign, my most loving liege!
NOR. Each day still better other's happiness;
Until the heavens, envying earth's good hap,
Add an immortal title to your crown!
K. RICH. We thank you both: yet one but flatters us,
As well appeareth by the cause you come; [b]
Namely, to appeal each other of high treason.—
Cousin of Hereford, what dost thou object
Against the duke of Norfolk, Thomas Mowbray?
BOLING. First, (heaven be the record to my speech!)
In the devotion of a subject's love,
Tendering the precious safety of my prince,
And free from other misbegotten hate,
Come I appellant to this princely presence.
Now, Thomas Mowbray, do I turn to thee,
And mark my greeting well; for what I speak
My body shall make good upon this earth,
Or my divine soul answer it in heaven.
Thou art a traitor, and a miscreant;
Too good to be so, and too bad to live;
Since the more fair and crystal is the sky,
The uglier seem the clouds that in it fly.
Once more, the more to aggravate the note,
With a foul traitor's name stuff I thy throat;
And wish (so please my sovereign), ere I move,
What my tongue speaks, my right-drawn sword may prove.
NOR. Let not my cold words here accuse my zeal:
'Tis not the trial of a woman's war,
The bitter clamour of two eager tongues,
Can arbitrate this cause betwixt us twain:
The blood is hot that must be cool'd for this.
Yet can I not of such tame patience boast,
As to be hush'd, and nought at all to say:
First, the fair reverence of your highness curbs me
From giving reins and spurs to my free speech;
Which else would post, until it had return'd
These terms of treason doubled * down his throat.
Setting aside his high blood's royalty,
And let him be no kinsman to my liege,
I do defy him, and I spit at him,
Call him a slanderous coward, and a villain:
Which to maintain, I would allow him odds,
And meet him, were I tied to run a-foot
Even to the frozen ridges of the Alps,
Or any other ground inhabitable [c]
Wherever Englishman durst set his foot.
Meantime, let this defend my loyalty,—
By all my hopes, most falsely doth he lie.
BOLING. Pale trembling coward, there I throw my gage,
Disclaiming here the kindred of the † king;
And lay aside my high blood's royalty,
Which fear, not reverence, makes thee to except: [d]
If guilty dread hath left thee so much strength,
As to take up mine honour's pawn, then stoop;
By that, and all the rites of knighthood else,
Will I make good against thee, arm to arm,
What I have spoke, ‡ or thou canst worse § devise.
NOR. I take it up; and, by that sword I swear,
Which gently laid my knighthood on my shoulder,
I'll answer thee in any fair degree,
Or chivalrous design of knightly trial:
And, when I mount, alive may I not light,
If I be traitor, or unjustly fight!
K. RICH. What doth our cousin lay to Mowbray's charge?
It must be great, that can inherit [e] us
So much as of a thought of ill in him.
BOLING. Look, what I speak ‖ my life shall prove it true;—
That Mowbray hath receiv'd eight thousand nobles,
In name of lendings, for your highness' soldiers;

[a] BOLINGBROKE—] Henry Plantagenet, Earl of Hereford, eldest son of John of Gaunt, the Duke of Lancaster, was surnamed Bolingbroke from the castle of that name in Lincolnshire, where he was born. According to Drayton, however, he was not distinguished by this name until after he assumed the crown.

[b] By the cause you come;] Meaning, by the cause *for which* you come.

[c] Inhabitable—] That is, *unhabitable, not habitable;* a primitive use of the word, common in old books. "Where all the country was scorched by the heat of the sun, and the place almost *inhabitable* for the multitude of serpents."—T. HEYWOOD'S *General History of Women*, 1624.

(*) First folio, *doubly*. (†) First folio, *a*.
(‡) First folio, *spoken*. (§) First folio omits, *worse*.
(‖) First folio, *said*.

[d] *Makes thee to* except:] *Except* is here employed in the old sense, to *put a bar to*, or *stay*, action.

[e] *That can* inherit *us*—] *Inherit* here means *possess;* but this use of the word is quite exceptional.

The which he hath detain'd for lewd[a] employments,
Like a false traitor and injurious villain.
Besides I say, and will in battle prove,—
Or here, or elsewhere, to the furthest verge
That ever was survey'd by English eye,—
That all the treasons, for these eighteen years
Complotted and contrived in this land,
Fetch* from false Mowbray their first head and spring.
Further I say,—and further will maintain
Upon his bad life, to make all this good,—
That he did plot the duke of Gloster's death;[b]
Suggest[c] his soon-believing adversaries;
And, consequently, like a traitor coward,
Sluic'd out his innocent soul through streams of blood:
Which blood, like sacrificing Abel's, cries,
Even from the tongueless caverns of the earth,
To me for justice and rough chastisement;
And, by the glorious worth of my descent,
This arm shall do it, or this life be spent.

K. RICH. How high a pitch his resolution soars!—
Thomas of Norfolk, what say'st thou to this?

NOR. O, let my sovereign turn away his face,
And bid his ears a little while be deaf,
Till I have told this slander of his blood,
How God, and good men, hate so foul a liar.

K. RICH. Mowbray, impartial are our eyes and ears:
Were he my brother, nay, my† kingdom's heir,
(As he is but my father's brother's son,)
Now by my‡ sceptre's awe I make a vow,
Such neighbour nearness to our sacred blood
Should nothing privilege him, nor partialize
The unstooping firmness of my upright soul:
He is our subject, Mowbray, so art thou;
Free speech, and fearless, I to thee allow.

NOR. Then, Bolingbroke, as low as to thy heart,
Through the false passage of thy throat, thou liest!
Three parts of that receipt I had for Calais
Disburs'd I duly§ to his highness' soldiers:
The other part reserv'd I by consent;
For that my sovereign liege was in my debt,
Upon remainder of a dear[d] account,
Since last I went to France to fetch his queen:(3)
Now swallow down that lie.—For Gloster's death,—
I slew him not; but, to mine own disgrace,
Neglected my sworn duty in that case.
For you, my noble lord of Lancaster,
The honourable father to my foe,
Once did I* lay an ambush for your life,
A trespass that doth vex my grieved soul:
But, ere I last receiv'd the sacrament,
I did confess it; and exactly[e] begg'd
Your grace's pardon, and, I hope, I had it.
This is my fault: as for the rest appeal'd,
It issues from the rancour of a villain,
A recreant and most degenerate traitor:
Which in myself I boldly will defend;
And interchangeably hurl down my gage
Upon this overweening traitor's foot,
To prove myself a loyal gentleman,
Even in the best blood chamber'd in his bosom:
In haste whereof, most heartily I pray
Your highness to assign our trial day.

K. RICH. Wrath-kindled gentlemen, be rul'd by me;
Let 's purge this choler without letting blood:
This we prescribe, though no physician;
Deep malice makes too deep incision:
Forget, forgive; conclude, and be agreed;
Our doctors say, this is no month† to bleed.
Good uncle, let this end where it begun;
We'll calm the duke of Norfolk, you, your son.

GAUNT. To be a make-peace shall become my age:—
Throw down, my son, the duke of Norfolk's gage.

K. RICH. And, Norfolk, throw down his.

GAUNT. When, Harry? when?
Obedience bids, I should not bid agen.[f]

K. RICH. Norfolk, throw down, we bid; there is no boot.[g]

NOR. Myself I throw, dread sovereign, at thy foot:
My life thou shalt command, but not my shame:
The one my duty owes; but my fair name,

(*) First folio, *fetch'd.* (†) First folio, *our.* (‡) Quartos omit, *my.* (§) First folio omits, *duly.*

(*) First folio, *I did.* (†) First folio, *time.*

a *For* lewd *employments,*—] *Lewd* here signifies *wicked, base, malicious.*

b The duke of Gloster's death;] Thomas of Woodstock, the youngest son of Edward III., who was murdered at Calais in 1397.

c Suggest—] *Incite, prompt.* See Note (a), p. 17.

d *Upon remainder of a* dear *account,*—] Mr. Collier's annotator has thrown suspicion on the word *dear* in the present passage, by proposing to read, "*clear* account;"—a poor and needless innovation. *Dear*, in this place, means, *precious, momentous, pressing, all-important;* and it assumes the same sense frequently in Shakespeare. Thus, in "King Lear," Act IV. Sc. 3:—

"——— Some *dear* cause,
Will in concealment wrap me up awhile."

Again, in "Romeo and Juliet," Act I. Sc. 5.:—

"O *dear* account! my life is my foe's debt."

In the same play, Act V. Sc. 2:—

"The letter was not nice, but full of charge
Of *dear* import."

And *ibid.*, Act V. Sc. 3:—

"A precious ring; a ring that I must use
In *dear* employment."

e *And* exactly *begg'd*—] That is, *duly* begged.

f When, Harry? when? &c.] In the old copies this speech is given thus:—

"When Harrie when? Obedience bids,
Obedience bids I should not bid agen."

When? was an exclamation of impatience, not unfrequent with the old writers. Shakespeare has it again in the "Taming of the Shrew," Act IV. Sc. 1:—

"Why, *when*, I say?—nay, good sweet Kate, be merry."

g *There is no* boot.] There is no *help, it is vain to resist.*

(Despite of death,) that lives upon my grave,
To dark dishonour's use thou shalt not have.
I am disgrac'd, impeach'd, and baffled[a] here;
Pierc'd to the soul with slander's venom'd spear;
The which no balm can cure, but his heart-blood
Which breath'd this poison.

K. RICH. Rage must be withstood:
Give me his gage:—lions make leopards tame.[b]

NOR. Yea, but not change his spots: take but my shame,
And I resign my gage. My dear-dear lord,
The purest treasure mortal times afford
Is—spotless reputation; that away,
Men are but gilded loam, or painted clay.
A jewel in a ten-times-barr'd-up chest,
Is—a bold spirit in a loyal breast.
Mine honour is my life; both grow in one;
Take honour from me, and my life is done:
Then, dear my liege, mine honour let me try;
In that I live, and for that will I die.

K. RICH. Cousin, throw up* your gage; do you begin.

BOLING. O God[c] defend my soul from such deep† sin!
Shall I seem crest-fallen in my father's sight?
Or with pale beggar-fear impeach my height
Before this outdared dastard? Ere my tongue
Shall wound mine honour with such feeble wrong,
Or sound so base a parle, my teeth shall tear
The slavish motive of recanting fear,
And spit it bleeding, in his high disgrace,
Where shame doth harbour, even in Mowbray's face. [*Exit* GAUNT.

K. RICH. We were not born to sue, but to command:
Which since we cannot do to make you friends,
Be ready, as your lives shall answer it,
At Coventry, upon Saint Lambert's day;
There shall your swords and lances arbitrate
The swelling difference of your settled hate;
Since we cannot atone[d] you, we‡ shall see
Justice design the victor's chivalry.
Lord marshal, command our officers at arms
Be ready to direct these home-alarms. [*Exeunt.*

(*) First folio, *down*. (†) First folio, *foul*. (‡) First folio, *you*.

[a] Baffled—] *Baffled* is here employed in the general sense of being treated with ignominy; but it particularly, and Nares says originally, meant, a degrading punishment inflicted on recreant knights; one part of which consisted in hanging them up by the heels. Thus, Spenser:—

"And after all for greater infamie
He *by the heels him hung upon a tree,*
And *bafful'd* so, that all which passed by
The picture of his punishment might see."
Faërie Queen, B. VI. vii. 27.

To this signification of the word Falstaff seems to allude when he says ("Henry IV." Part I. Act I. Sc. 2),—

"An I do not, call me villain, and *baffle* me."

And afterwards, *ibid.*, Act II. Sc. 4:—

"If thou do it half so gravely, so majestically both in word and matter, *hang me up by the heels* for a rabbit-sucker," &c.

SCENE II.—London. *A Room in the Duke of* Lancaster's *Palace.*

Enter GAUNT *and* DUCHESS OF GLOUCESTER.[e]

GAUNT. Alas! the part I had in Woodstock's* blood
Doth more solicit me than your exclaims,
To stir against the butchers of his life.
But since correction lieth in those hands
Which made the fault that we cannot correct,
Put we our quarrel to the will of heaven;
Who, when they see the hours ripe on earth,
Will rain hot vengeance on offenders' heads.

DUCH. Finds brotherhood in thee no sharper spur?
Hath love in thy old blood no living fire?
Edward's seven sons, whereof thyself art one,
Were as seven phials of his sacred blood,
Or seven fair branches springing from one root:
Some of those seven are dried by nature's course,
Some of those branches by the destinies cut:
But Thomas, my dear lord, my life, my Gloster,—
One phial full of Edward's sacred blood,
One flourishing branch of his most royal root,
Is crack'd, and all the precious liquor spilt;
Is hack'd down, and his summer leaves all faded,†
By envy's hand, and murder's bloody axe.
Ah, Gaunt! his blood was thine; that bed, that womb,
That metal, that self-mould, that fashion'd thee,
Made him a man; and though thou liv'st and breath'st,
Yet art thou slain in him: thou dost consent
In some large measure to thy father's death,
In that thou seest thy wretched brother die,
Who was the model of thy father's life.
Call it not patience, Gaunt, it is despair:
In suffering thus thy brother to be slaughter'd,
Thou show'st the naked pathway to thy life,
Teaching stern murder how to butcher thee:
That which in mean men we entitle patience,
Is pale cold cowardice in noble breasts.
What shall I say? to safeguard thine own life,
The best way is to 'venge my Gloster's death.

(*) First folio, *Gloster's*. (†) First folio, *vaded*.

[b] Lions make leopards tame.] Malone was the first to discover an allusion, in this passage, to the Norfolk crest, which was a golden *leopard*.

[c] O God defend my soul—] In obedience to the Act, 3 *Jac.* 1, the folio here and elsewhere throughout the play, substitutes *heaven* for God.

[d] Atone *you*,—] *Reconcile* you, make you *at one*. Thus, in "Cymbeline," Act I. Sc. 5:—

"I was glad I did *atone* my country man and you."

And in "Othello," Act IV. Sc. 1:—

"I would do much to *atone* them."

[e] DUCHESS OF GLOUCESTER.] This was Eleanor Bohun, widow of Duke Thomas, son of Edward III., whose tomb, richly inlaid with brass, still remains in Westminster Abbey.

GAUNT. God's* is the quarrel; for God's* substitute,
His deputy anointed, in His sight,
Hath caus'd his death: the which, if wrongfully,
Let heaven revenge; for I may never lift
An angry arm against His minister.

DUCH. Where then, alas! † may I complain[a] myself?

GAUNT. To God,‡ the widow's champion and§ defence.

DUCH. Why then, I will. Farewell, old Gaunt.
Thou go'st to Coventry, there to behold
Our cousin Hereford and fell Mowbray fight:
O, sit my husband's wrongs on Hereford's spear,
That it may enter butcher Mowbray's breast!
Or, if misfortune miss the first career,
Be Mowbray's sins so heavy in his bosom,
That they may break his foaming courser's back,
And throw the rider headlong in the lists,
A caitiff recreant to my cousin Hereford!
Farewell, old Gaunt; thy sometimes brother's wife,
With her companion, Grief, must end her life.

GAUNT. Sister, farewell; I must to Coventry:
As much good stay with thee, as go with me!

DUCH. Yet one word more;—Grief boundeth where it falls,
Not with the empty hollowness, but weight:
I take my leave before I have begun,
For sorrow ends not when it seemeth done.
Commend me to my brother, Edmund York.
Lo, this is all:—nay, yet depart not so,
Though this be all, do not so quickly go;
I shall remember more. Bid him—O, what?—
With all good speed at Plashy visit me.
Alack, and what shall good old York there see,
But empty lodgings and unfurnish'd walls,(4)
Unpeopled offices, untrodden stones?
And what hear there for welcome but my groans?
Therefore commend me; let him not come there,
To seek out sorrow;—that dwells everywhere:
Desolate, desolate, will I hence, and die:
The last leave of thee, takes my weeping eye.
[*Exeunt.*

SCENE III.—Coventry. *A Public Place.*

Lists set out, and a Throne. Heralds, *&c. attending.*

Enter the Lord Marshal *and* AUMERLE.

MAR. My lord Aumerle, is Harry Hereford arm'd?

(*) First folio, *heavens*. (†) First quarto omits, *alas!*
(‡) First folio, *heaven*. (§) First folio, *to*.

[a] Complain *myself?*] *Complain* is here a verb active, as in "The Queenes Majesties Entertainment in Suffolke and Norfolke," by Thomas Churchyard:—"Cupid encountring the Queene, beganne to *complayne* hys state and his mothers," &c.

AUM. Yea, at all points; and longs to enter in.

MAR. The duke of Norfolk, sprightfully and bold,
Stays but the summons of the appellant's trumpet.

AUM. Why, then the champions are prepar'd, and stay
For nothing but his majesty's approach.

Flourish of trumpets. Enter KING RICHARD, *to his throne;* GAUNT, *and several* Noblemen, *who take their places. A trumpet sounded, and answered by another trumpet within. Then enter* NORFOLK *in armour, preceded by a* Herald.

K. RICH. Marshal, demand of yonder champion
The cause of his arrival here in arms:
Ask him his name; and orderly proceed
To swear him in the justice of his cause.

MAR. In God's name and the king's, say who thou art,
And why thou com'st thus knightly clad in arms;
Against what man thou com'st, and what * thy quarrel:
Speak truly, on thy knighthood, and thine oath,
As so defend thee heaven, and thy valour!

NOR. My name is Thomas Mowbray, duke of Norfolk;
Who hither come † engaged by my oath,
(Which God ‡ defend a knight should violate!)
Both to defend my loyalty and truth
To God, my king, and his [a] succeeding issue,
Against the duke of Hereford that appeals me;
And, by the grace of God, and this mine arm,
To prove him, in defending of myself,
A traitor to my God, my king, and me:
And, as I truly fight, defend me, heaven!
[*He takes his seat.*

Trumpet sounds. Enter BOLINGBROKE, *in armour, preceded by a* Herald.

K. RICH. Marshal, ask yonder knight in arms,
Both who he is, and why he cometh hither,
Thus plated § in habiliments of war;
And formally || according to our law
Depose him in the justice of his cause.

MAR. What is thy name? and wherefore com'st thou hither,
Before King Richard, in his royal lists?

(*) First folio, *what's*. (†) First folio, *comes*. (‡) First folio, *heaven*. (§) First folio, *placed*. (||) First folio, *formerly*.

[a] *And his succeeding issue,—*] So the first folio; all the quartos read, "and *my* succeeding issue."

Against whom comest thou? and what's thy quarrel?
Speak like a true knight, so defend thee heaven!

BOLING. Harry of Hereford, Lancaster, and Derby,
Am I; who ready here do stand in arms,
To prove, by God's * grace, and my body's valour,
In lists, on Thomas Mowbray, duke of Norfolk,
That he's a traitor, foul and dangerous,
To God of heaven, King Richard, and to me;
And, as I truly fight, defend me heaven!

MAR. On pain of death, no person be so bold,
Or daring-hardy, as to touch the lists,(5)
Except the marshal, and such officers
Appointed to direct these fair designs.

BOLING. Lord marshal, let me kiss my sovereign's hand,
And bow my knee before his majesty:
For Mowbray and myself are like two men
That vow a long and weary pilgrimage;
Then let us take a ceremonious leave,
And loving farewell of our several friends.

MAR. The appellant in all duty greets your highness,
And craves to kiss your hand, and take his leave.

K. RICH. We will descend, and fold him in our arms.
Cousin of Hereford, as thy cause is right, †
So be thy fortune in this royal fight!
Farewell, my blood; which if to-day thou shed,
Lament we may, but not revenge thee dead.

BOLING. O, let no noble eye profane a tear
For me, if I be gor'd with Mowbray's spear;
As confident as is the falcon's flight
Against a bird, do I with Mowbray fight.—
My loving lord, [*to* Lord Marshal] I take my leave of you;
Of you, my noble cousin, lord Aumerle:—
Not sick, although I have to do with death,
But lusty, young, and cheerly drawing breath.
Lo, as at English feasts, so I regreet
The daintiest last, to make the end most sweet:
O thou, the earthly ‡ author of my blood,—
[*To* GAUNT.
Whose youthful spirit, in me regenerate,
Doth with a two-fold vigour § lift me up
To reach at victory above my head,—
Add proof unto mine armour with thy prayers,
And with thy blessings steel my lance's point,
That it may enter Mowbray's waxen [b] coat,
And furbish || new the name of John of Gaunt,
Even in the lusty 'haviour of his son.

(*) First folio, *heaven's*. (†) First folio, *just*. (‡) First folio, *earthy*. (§) First folio, *rigor*. (||) First folio, *furnish*.

[b] *Mowbray's* waxen *coat,—*] This is supposed to mean, *soft*, or *penetrable* coat: but we may reasonably suspect *waxen* to be a misprint for some more suitable epithet.

Cast off his chains of bondage, and embrace
His golden uncontroll'd enfranchisement,
More than my dancing soul doth celebrate
This feast of battle with mine adversary.
Most mighty liege, and my companion peers,
Take from my mouth the wish of happy years:
As gentle and as jocund, as to jest,[a]
Go I to fight; truth hath a quiet breast.

K. RICH. Farewell, my lord: securely I espy
Virtue with valour couched in thine eye.
Order the trial, marshal, and begin.

[*The* KING *and* Lords *return to their seats.*

MAR. Harry of Hereford, Lancaster, and Derby,
Receive thy lance; and God * defend the † right!

BOLING. [*Rising.*] Strong as a tower in hope, I cry—Amen.

MAR. [*To an* Officer.] Go bear this lance to Thomas, duke of Norfolk.

1 HER. Harry of Hereford, Lancaster, and Derby,
Stands here for God, his sovereign, and himself,
On pain to be found false and recreant,
To prove the duke of Norfolk, Thomas Mowbray,
A traitor to his God, his king, and him,
And dares him to set forward ‡ to the fight.

2 HER. Here standeth Thomas Mowbray, duke of Norfolk,
On pain to be found false and recreant,
Both to defend himself, and to approve
Henry of Hereford, Lancaster, and Derby,
To God, his sovereign, and to him, disloyal;
Courageously, and with a free desire,
Attending but the signal to begin.

MAR. Sound, trumpets; and set forward, combatants. [*A charge sounded.*
Stay, the king hath thrown his warder down.(6)

K. RICH. Let them lay by their helmets and their spears,
And both return back to their chairs again.—
Withdraw with us; and let the trumpets sound,
While we return these dukes what we decree.—

[*A long flourish.*

Draw near, [*To the Combatants.*
And list, what with our council we have done.
For that our kingdom's earth should not be soil'd
With that dear blood which it hath fostered;
And for our eyes do hate the dire aspect
Of civil § wounds plough'd up with neighbours' swords;
And for we think [b] the eagle-winged pride
Of sky-aspiring and ambitious thoughts,
With rival-hating envy, set on you
To wake our peace, which in our country's cradle
Draws the sweet infant-breath of gentle sleep;
Which so rous'd up with boisterous untun'd drums,
With harsh resounding trumpets' dreadful bray,
And grating shock of wrathful iron arms,
Might from our quiet confines fright fair peace,
And make us wade even in our kindred's blood;
Therefore, we banish you our territories:—
You, cousin Hereford, upon pain of life,*
Till twice five summers have enrich'd our fields,
Shall not regreet our fair dominions,
But tread the stranger paths of banishment.

BOLING. Your will be done. This must my comfort be,
That sun, that warms you here, shall shine on me;
And those his golden beams, to you here lent,
Shall point on me, and gild my banishment.

K. RICH. Norfolk, for thee remains a heavier doom,
Which I with some unwillingness pronounce:
The fly-slow hours [c] shall not determinate
The dateless limit of thy dear exile;—
The hopeless word of—Never to return,
Breathe I against thee, upon pain of life.

NOR. A heavy sentence, my most sovereign liege,
And all unlook'd for from your highness' mouth:
A dearer merit,[d] not so deep a maim
As to be cast forth in the common air,
Have I deserved at your highness' hands.
The language I have learn'd these forty years,
My native English, now I must forego:
And now my tongue's use is to me no more
Than an unstringed viol, or a harp;
Or like a cunning instrument cas'd up,
Or, being open, put into his hands
That knows no touch to tune the harmony.
Within my mouth you have engaol'd my tongue,
Doubly portcullis'd with my teeth and lips;
And dull, unfeeling, barren ignorance
Is made my gaoler to attend on me.
I am too old to fawn upon a nurse,
Too far in years to be a pupil now;
What is thy sentence, then, but speechless death,
Which robs my tongue from breathing native breath?

(*) First folio, *heaven*. (†) First folio, *thy*.
(‡) First folio, *forwards*. (§) First quarto, *cruel*.

(*) First folio, *death*.

a *As to jest,*—] To *jest* sometimes signified to take part in a masque or revel.

b *And for we think,* &c.] This and the four following lines are omitted in the folio.

c *The* fly-slow *hours*—] This is the reading of the second folio, and is eminently happy. The older copies have, "*sly slow;*" an epithet which conveys but a feeble meaning, if any.

d *A dearer* merit,—] *Merit* is here used for *guerdon, meed, reward;* in which peculiar sense it again occurs in "King John," Act III. Sc. 1:—

"And, by the *merit* of vile gold, dross, dust,
Purchase corrupted pardon of a man."

GAUNT. God * in thy good cause make thee
prosperous!
Be swift like lightning in the execution;
And let thy blows, doubly redoubled,
Fall like amazing[a] thunder on the casque
Of thy adverse † pernicious enemy:
Rouse up thy youthful blood, be valiant and live.

(*) First folio, *heaven*. (†) First folio, *amaz'd*.

[a] *Fall like* amazing *thunder*—] That is, *confounding, appalling* thunder.

BOLING. Mine innocency,* and Saint George
to thrive. [*He takes his seat.*
NOR. [*Rising.*] However God, † or fortune,
cast my lot, [throne,
There lives, or dies, true to King ‡ Richard's
A loyal, just, and upright gentleman:
Never did captive with a freer heart,

(*) Old copies, *innocence*. (†) First folio, *heaven*.
(‡) First folio, *kings*.

K. RICH. It boots thee not to be compassionate;[a]
After our sentence, plaining comes too late.

NOR. Then thus I turn me from my country's light,
To dwell in solemn shades of endless night. [*Retiring.*

K. RICH. Return again, and take an oath with thee:
Lay on our royal sword your banish'd hands;(7)
Swear by the duty that you owe to God,*
(Our part therein we banish with yourselves,)[b]
To keep the oath that we administer:—
You never shall (so help you truth and God!*)
Embrace each other's love in banishment;
Nor never † look upon each other's face;
Nor never † write, regreet, nor ‡ reconcile
This low'ring tempest of your home-bred hate;
Nor never † by advised purpose meet
To plot, contrive, or complot any ill
'Gainst us, our state, our subjects, or our land.

BOLING. I swear.

NOR. And I, to keep all this.

BOLING. Norfolk,—so far as to mine enemy;[c]—
By this time, had the king permitted us,
One of our souls had wandered in the air,
Banish'd this frail sepulchre of our flesh,
As now our flesh is banish'd from this land:
Confess thy treasons ere thou fly the § realm;
Since thou hast far to go, bear not along
The clogging burthen of a guilty soul.

NOR. No, Bolingbroke; if ever I were traitor
My name be blotted from the book of life,
And I from heaven banish'd, as from hence!
But what thou art, God,* thou, and I do know;
And all too soon, I fear, the king shall rue.
Farewell, my liege.—Now no way can I stray;
Save back to England, all the world's my way.[d] [*Exit.*

K. RICH. Uncle, even in the glasses of thine eyes
I see thy grieved heart; thy sad aspéct
Hath from the number of his banish'd years
Pluck'd four away.—[*To* BOLING.] Six frozen winters spent,
Return with welcome home from banishment.

BOLING. How long a time lies in one little word!
Four lagging winters, and four wanton springs,
End in a word. Such is the breath of kings.

GAUNT. I thank my liege, that, in regard of me
He shortens four years of my son's exile;
But little vantage shall I reap thereby;
For, ere the six years that he hath to spend
Can change their moons, and bring their times about,
My oil-dried lamp, and time-bewasted light,
Shall be extinct with age and endless night;
My inch of taper will be burnt and done,
And blindfold death not let me see my son.

K. RICH. Why, uncle, thou hast many years to live.

GAUNT. But not a minute, king, that thou canst give:
Shorten my days thou canst with sullen * sorrow,
And pluck nights from me, but not lend a morrow
Thou canst help time to furrow me with age,
But stop no wrinkle in his pilgrimage;
Thy word is current with him for my death,
But, dead, thy kingdom cannot buy my breath.

K. RICH. Thy son is banish'd upon good advice,
Whereto thy tongue a party-verdict gave;
Why at our justice seem'st thou then to lour?

GAUNT. Things sweet to taste prove in digestion sour.
You urg'd me as a judge; but I had rather
You would have bid me argue like a father:
O, had it been a stranger,[e] not my child,
To smooth his fault I should have been more mild:
A partial slander[f] sought I to avoid,
And in the sentence my own life destroy'd.
Alas, I look'd when some of you should say,
I was too strict, to make mine own away;
But you gave leave to my unwilling tongue,
Against my will, to do myself this wrong.

K. RICH. Cousin, farewell:—and, uncle, bid him so;
Six years we banish him, and he shall go.
[*Flourish. Exeunt* K. RICHARD *and Train.*

AUM. Cousin, farewell: what presence must not know,

(*) First folio, *heaven*. (†) First folio, *ever*.
(‡) First folio, *or*. (§) First folio, *this*.

(*) First folio, *sudden*.

a Compassionate;] As this is the only instance at present known of *compassionate* being employed to denote *lamenting*, it has been suspected to be a misprint for "*so passionate;*" but I apprehend the error, if there be one, consists in the latter part of *become* having got connexed by a very common typographical mishap, with the next word, and that we ought to read,—

"It boots thee not to *become* passionate."

Passionate is employed by the old writers with considerable freedom. Sometimes it is used to imply an *outward expression of emotion*, what Richard subsequently calls the "external manners of lament;" as in "Titus Andronicus," Act III. Sc. 2:—

"Thy niece and I, poor creatures, want our hands,
And cannot *passionate* our tenfold grief."

And occasionally it is adopted to signify *a passive endurance of affliction*, as in "King John," Act II. Sc. 2:—

"She is sad and *passionate* at your highness' tent."

See Note (c), p. 298.

b (Our part therein we banish with yourselves,)—] Writers on the law of nations are divided in opinion whether an exile is still bound by his allegiance to the State that banished him. Shakespeare here is of the side of those who hold the negative.

c Norfolk,—so far as to mine enemy;—] This seems to mean, *So far as I am now permitted to address my enemy*. The first folio, reads,—"so *fare*," &c.

d All the world's my way.] Upon his banishment, the Duke of Norfolk went to Venice; where, according to Holinshed, "for thought and melancholy he deceased."

e O, had it been a stranger, &c.] Four lines, commencing here, are omitted in the folio.

f A partial slander—] *The reproach of partiality*.

From where you do remain, let paper show.

MAR. My lord, no leave take I; for I will ride,
As far as land will let me, by your side.

GAUNT. O, to what purpose dost thou hoard thy words,
That thou return'st no greeting to thy friends?

BOLING. I have too few to take my leave of you,
When the tongue's office should be prodigal
To breathe the abundant dolour of the heart.

GAUNT. Thy grief is but thy absence for a time. [time.

BOLING. Joy absent, grief is present for that

GAUNT. What is six winters? they are quickly gone. [hour ten.

BOLING. To men in joy; but grief makes one

GAUNT. Call it a travel that thou tak'st for pleasure.

BOLING. My heart will sigh when I miscall it so,
Which finds it an enforced pilgrimage.

GAUNT. The sullen passage of thy weary steps
Esteem a foil,* wherein thou art to set
The precious jewel of thy home-return. [make

BOLING. Nay, rather, every tedious stride I
Will but remember me, what a deal of world
I wander from the jewels that I love.
Must I not serve a long apprenticehood
To foreign passages; and in the end,
Having my freedom, boast of nothing else
But that I was a journeyman to grief?

GAUNT. All places that the eye of heaven visits,
Are to a wise man ports and happy havens:
Teach thy necessity to reason thus;
There is no virtue like necessity.
Think not, the king did banish thee,
But thou the king: woe doth the heavier sit,
Where it perceives it is but faintly borne.
Go, say—I sent thee forth to purchase honour,
And not,—the king exil'd thee: or suppose,
Devouring pestilence hangs in our air,
And thou art flying to a fresher clime.
Look, what thy soul holds dear, imagine it
To lie that way thou go'st, not whence thou com'st.
Suppose the singing birds, musicians; [strew'd;
The grass whereon thou tread'st, the presence
The flowers, fair ladies; and thy steps, no more
Than a delightful measure, or a dance:
For gnarling sorrow hath less power to bite
The man that mocks at it, and sets it light.[a]

BOLING. O, who can hold a fire in his hand,
By thinking on the frosty Caucasus?
Or cloy the hungry edge of appetite,
By bare imagination of a feast?
Or wallow naked in December snow,
By thinking on fantastic summer's heat?
O, no! the apprehension of the good
Gives but the greater feeling to the worse:
Fell sorrow's tooth doth never * rankle more,
Than when it bites but lanceth not the sore.

GAUNT. Come, come, my son, I'll bring thee on thy way:
Had I thy youth and cause, I would not stay.

BOLING. Then, England's ground, farewell; sweet soil, adieu,
My mother, and my nurse, that † bears me yet!
Where'er I wander, boast of this I can,
Though banish'd, yet a true-born Englishman.
[*Exeunt.*

SCENE IV.—*A Room in the* King's *Palace.*

Enter KING RICHARD, BAGOT, *and* GREEN; AUMERLE *meeting them.*

K. RICH. We did observe.—Cousin Aumerle,
How far brought you high Hereford on his way?

AUM. I brought *high Hereford,* if you call him so,
But to the next highway, and there I left him.

K. RICH. And, say, what store of parting tears were shed? [wind,

AUM. 'Faith, none for me,[b] except the north-east
Which then blew ‡ bitterly against our faces,§
Awak'd the sleeping|| rheum; and so, by chance,
Did grace our hollow parting with a tear.

K. RICH. What said our cousin when you parted with him?

AUM. *Farewell:*
And for my heart disdained that my tongue
Should so profane the word, that, taught me craft
To counterfeit oppression of such grief,
That words ¶ seem'd buried in my sorrow's grave.
Marry, would the word *farewell* have lengthen'd hours,
And added years to his short banishment,
He should have had a volume of farewells;
But, since it would not, he had none of me.

K. RICH. He is our cousin, cousin; but 'tis doubt,
When time shall call him home from banishment,
Whether our kinsman come to see his friends.
Ourself and Bushy, Bagot here, and Green,[c]
Observ'd his courtship to the common people:—
How he did seem to dive into their hearts,

(*) First folio, *soyle.*

[a] The man that mocks at it, and sets it light.] The whole of this speech and the preceding one are omitted in the folio.

[b] 'Faith, none for me,—] *None on my part.*

(*) First folio, *ever.* (†) First folio, *which.* (‡) First folio, *grew.* (§) First folio, *face.* (||) First folio, *sleepie.* (¶) First folio, *word.*

[c] Bagot here, and Green,—] This half-line is omitted in the quartos. The folio reads, *here Bagot,* &c.

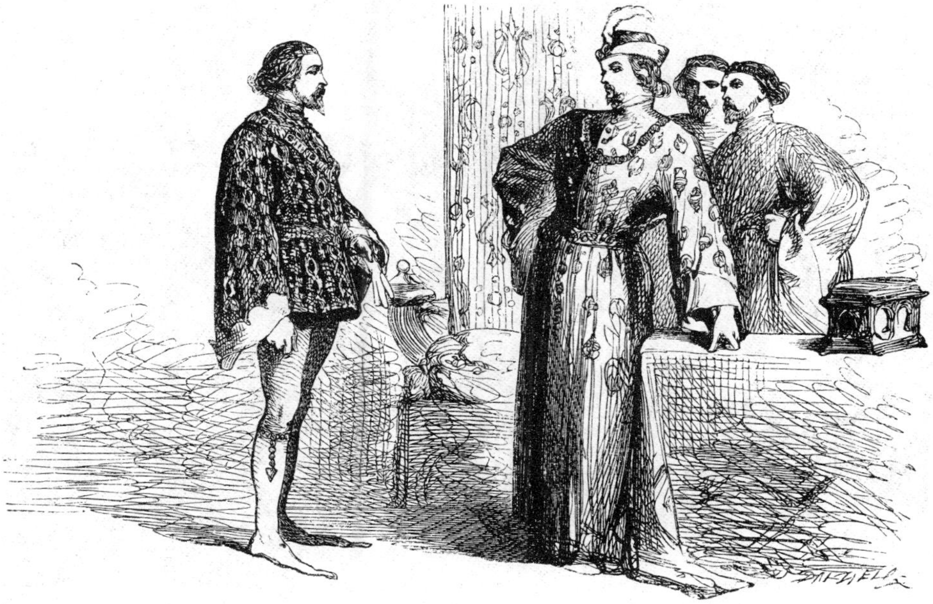

With humble and familiar courtesy;
What* reverence he did throw away on slaves,
Wooing poor craftsmen with the craft of smiles,†
And patient underbearing of his fortune.
As 't were to banish their affects with him,
Off goes his bonnet to an oyster-wench;
A brace of draymen bid—God speed him well,
And had the tribute of his supple knee, [*friends;*
With—*Thanks, my countrymen, my loving*
As were our England in reversion his,
And he our subjects' next degree in hope.
GREEN. Well, he is gone: and with him go these thoughts.
Now for the rebels, which stand out in Ireland;
Expedient[a] manage must be made, my liege,
Ere further leisure yield them further means,
For their advantage, and your highness' loss.
K. RICH. We will ourself in person to this war.
And for our coffers, with too great a court,
And liberal largess, are grown somewhat light,
We are enforc'd to farm our royal realm;
The revenue whereof shall furnish us
For our affairs in hand. If that come short,
Our substitutes at home shall have blank charters;(8)
Whereto, when they shall know what men are rich,
They shall subscribe them for large sums of gold,
And send them after to supply our wants;
For we will make for Ireland presently.

Enter BUSHY.

Bushy, what news?[b] [my lord;
BUSHY. Old John of Gaunt is grievous* sick,
Suddenly taken; and hath sent post haste,
To entreat your majesty to visit him.
K. RICH. Where lies he?
BUSHY. At Ely-house. [mind,
K. RICH. Now put it, God,† in his physician's
To help him to his grave immediately!
The lining of his coffers shall make coats
To deck our soldiers for these Irish wars.
Come, gentlemen, let's all go visit him: [late!
Pray God† we may make haste, and come too
ALL. Amen.[c] [*Exeunt.*

(*) Quarto, *with*. (†) First folio, *soules*.

[a] Expedient—] That is, *expeditious*.

[b] Bushy, what news?] The quartos omit this line, but have a stage direction:—"*Enter Bushie with newes.*"

(*) First folio, *very*. (†) First folio, *heaven*.

[c] Amen.] This is omitted in the folio, but appears in all the quarto copies, without, however, any prefix. It was doubtless intended to be uttered by all present.

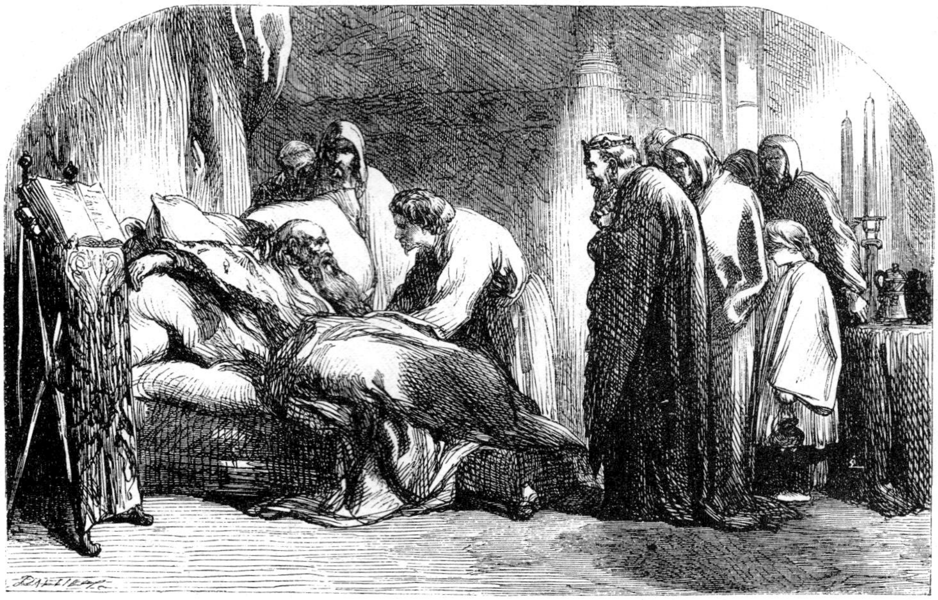

ACT II.

SCENE I.—London. *A Room in* Ely House.

GAUNT *on a couch; the* DUKE OF YORK (1) *and others, standing by him.*

GAUNT. Will the king come, that I may breathe my last
In wholesome counsel to his unstaid youth?
YORK. Vex not yourself, nor strive not with your breath;
For all in vain comes counsel to his ear.
GAUNT. O, but they say, the tongues of dying men,
Enforce attention, like deep harmony;
Where words are scarce, they are seldom spent in vain,
For they breathe truth, that breathe their words in pain.
He, that no more must say, is listen'd more
Than they whom youth and ease have taught to glose;
More are men's ends mark'd, than their lives before;
The setting sun, and music at* the close,
As the last taste of sweets is sweetest, last
Writ in remembrance, more than things long past;
Though Richard my life's counsel would not hear,
My death's sad tale may yet undeaf his ear.
YORK. No; it is stopp'd with other, flattering, sounds,
As praises of his state: then, there are found[a]
Lascivious metres; to whose venom sound
The open ear of youth doth always listen:
Report of fashions in proud Italy;
Whose manners still, our tardy apish nation
Limps after, in base imitation.
Where doth the world thrust forth a vanity,
(So it be new, there's no respect how vile,)
That is not quickly buzz'd into his ears?
Then† all too late comes counsel to be heard,
Where will doth mutiny with wit's regard.[b]

[a] As praises of his state: then, there are found—] So the folio. The first quarto reads, "*of whose taste the wise* are found;" in the second edition, 1598, *taste* was altered to *state*, but no further correction of the passage was attempted.

(*) First folio, *is*. (†) First folio, *That*.

[b] Where will doth mutiny with wit's regard.] "Where the will rebels against the notices of the understanding."—JOHNSON.

Direct not him, whose way himself will choose,
'Tis breath thou lack'st, and that breath wilt thou lose.

GAUNT. Methinks I am a prophet new inspir'd,
And thus, expiring, do foretell of him:
His rash fierce blaze of riot cannot last,
For violent fires soon burn out themselves;
Small showers last long, but sudden storms are short;
He tires betimes, that spurs too fast betimes;
With eager feeding, food doth choke the feeder:
Light vanity, insatiate cormorant,
Consuming means, soon preys upon itself.
This royal throne of kings, this sceptred isle,
This earth of Majesty, this seat of Mars,
This other Eden, demi-paradise;
This fortress, built by nature for herself,
Against infection[a] and the hand of war;
This happy breed of men, this little world,
This precious stone set in the silver sea,
Which serves it in the office of a wall,
Or as a moat defensive to a house,
Against the envy of less happier lands;
This blessed plot, this earth, this realm, this England,
This nurse, this teeming womb of royal kings,
Fear'd by their breed, and famous by* their birth,
Renowned for their deeds as far from home,
(For Christian service, and true chivalry,)
As is the sepulchre in stubborn Jewry
Of the world's ransom, blessed Mary's son.
This land of such dear souls, this dear-dear land,
Dear for her reputation through the world,
Is now leas'd out, (I die pronouncing it,)
Like to a tenement, or pelting[b] farm:
England, bound in with the triumphant sea,
Whose rocky shore beats back the envious siege
Of watery Neptune, is now bound in with shame,
With inky blots, and rotten parchment bonds;
That England, that was wont to conquer others,
Hath made a shameful conquest of itself:
O,† would the scandal vanish with my life,
How happy then were my ensuing death!

Enter KING RICHARD *and* QUEEN; AUMERLE, BUSHY, GREEN, BAGOT, ROSS, *and* WILLOUGHBY.

YORK. The king is come: deal mildly with his youth;
For young hot colts, being rag'd,[c] do rage the more.

QUEEN. How fares our noble uncle, Lancaster?

K. RICH. What! comfort, man. How is't with aged Gaunt?

GAUNT. O, how that name befits my composition!
Old Gaunt, indeed; and gaunt in being old:
Within me grief hath kept a tedious fast;
And who abstains from meat, that is not gaunt?
For sleeping England long time have I watch'd;
Watching breeds leanness, leanness is all gaunt:
The pleasure that some fathers feed upon
Is my strict fast,—I mean my children's looks,
And, therein fasting, hast thou made me gaunt;
Gaunt am I for the grave, gaunt as a grave,
Whose hollow womb inherits nought but bones.

K. RICH. Can sick men play so nicely with their names?

GAUNT. No, misery makes sport to mock itself:
Since thou dost seek to kill my name in me,
I mock my name, great king, to flatter thee.

K. RICH. Should dying men flatter with* those that live?

GAUNT. No, no; men living flatter those that die.

K. RICH. Thou, now a-dying, say'st thou flatterest me.

GAUNT. Oh! no; thou diest, though I the sicker be.

K. RICH. I am in health, I breathe, and† see thee ill.

GAUNT. Now, He that made me, knows I see thee ill;
Ill in myself to see, and in thee seeing ill.
Thy death-bed is no lesser than thy‡ land
Wherein thou liest in reputation sick:
And thou, too careless patient as thou art,
Committ'st thy anointed body to the cure
Of those physicians that first wounded thee.
A thousand flatterers sit within thy crown,
Whose compass is no bigger than thy head;
And yet, incaged § in so small a verge,
The waste is no whit lesser than thy land.
O, had thy grandsire, with a prophet's eye,
Seen how his son's son should destroy his sons,
From forth thy reach he would have laid thy shame,
Deposing thee before thou wert possess'd,
Which art possess'd now to depose thyself.
Why, cousin, wert thou regent of the world,
It were a shame to let this‖ land by lease;
But, for thy world, enjoying but this land,

(*) First folio, *for*. (†) First folio, *Ah*.

[a] *Against* infection—] So all the ancient copies; but as this country, up to 1665, had not for centuries been exempt from the ravages of the plague, which, in Shakespeare's time, destroyed hundreds of the inhabitants yearly in London alone, the poet could hardly boast that our insularity secured us from pestilential contagion. Farmer proposed *infestion*, in the sense of *infestation*, and his suggestion has been adopted by Malone and other editors.

[b] Pelting *farm*:] That is, *peddling, paltry* farm. See note ([b]), p. 351.

(*) First folio omits, *with*. (†) First folio, *I*.
(‡) First folio, *the*. (§) Quarto, *inraged*.
(‖) First folio, *his*.

[c] *For young hot colts, being* rag'd, *do* rage *the more*.] Ritson suggested, "being *rein'd*, do rage the more," and Mr. Collier's annotator reads, "being *urg'd*;" an alteration to which the following passage, from G. Withers' "Abuses Stript and Whipt," lends some support:—

"Do not incense my Satyr for thy life:
Hee's patient enough unlesse thou *urge*."

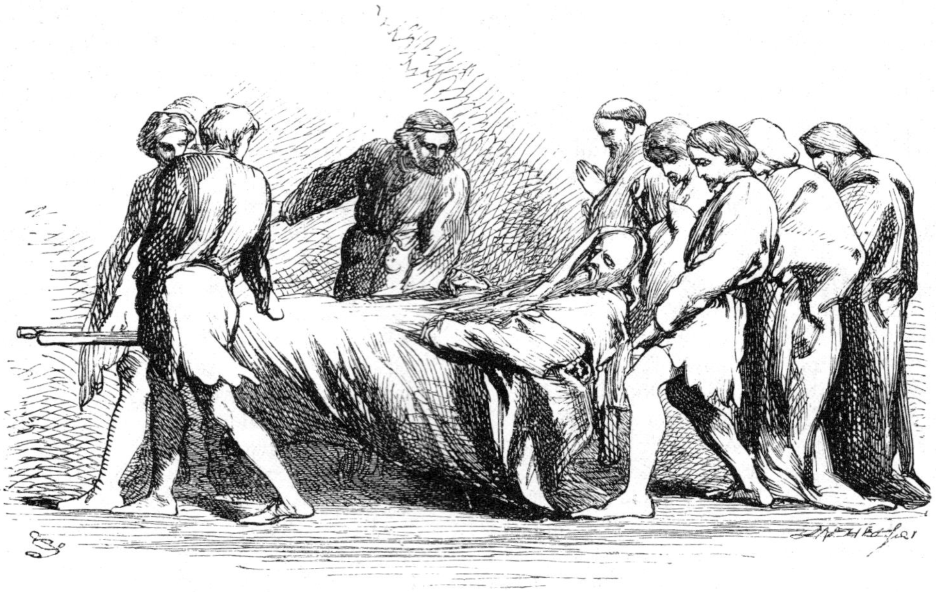

Is it not more than shame to shame it so?
Landlord of England art thou now,* not king:
Thy state of law is bondslave to the law;
And thou—

K. RICH. A lunatic lean-witted fool,[a]
Presuming on an ague's privilege,
Dar'st with thy frozen admonition
Make pale our cheek; chasing † the royal blood,
With fury, from his native residence.
Now by my seat's right royal majesty,
Wert thou not brother to great Edward's son,
This tongue, that runs so roundly in thy head,
Should run thy head from thy unreverent shoulders.

GAUNT. O, spare me not, my brother ‡ Edward's son,
For that I was his father Edward's son;
That blood already, like the pelican,
Hast thou § tapp'd out, and drunkenly carous'd:
My brother Gloster, plain well-meaning soul,
(Whom fair befal in heaven 'mongst happy souls!)
May be a precedent and witness good,
That thou respect'st not spilling Edward's blood:
Join with the present sickness that I have;
And thy unkindness be like crooked age,
To crop at once a too-long wither'd flower.
Live in thy shame, but die not shame with thee,—
These words hereafter thy tormentors be!—
Convey me to my bed, then to my grave;
Love they to live, that love and honour have.
[*Exit, borne out by his* Attendants.

K. RICH. And let them die, that age and sullens have;
For both hast thou, and both become the grave.

YORK. I do beseech your majesty, impute his words
To wayward sickliness and age in him:
He loves you, on my life, and holds you dear
As Harry duke of Hereford, were he here.

K. RICH. Right, you say true, as Hereford's love, so his;
As theirs, so mine, and all be as it is.

Enter NORTHUMBERLAND.

NORTH. My liege, old Gaunt commends him to your majesty.

K. RICH. What says he?

(*) First folio, *and*. (†) First folio, *chafing*.
(‡) First folio, *brothers*. (§) First folio, *Thou hast*.

a A lunatic lean-witted fool,—] The regulation in the folio is somewhat different; there, the lines run thus:—

"GAUNT. *And* ——————
K. RICH. *And thou*," &c.

NORTH. Nay, nothing; all is said:
His tongue is now a stringless instrument;
Words, life, and all, old Lancaster hath spent.

YORK. Be York the next that must be bankrupt so!
Though death be poor, it ends a mortal woe.

K. RICH. The ripest fruit first falls, and so doth he;
His time is spent, our pilgrimage must be;
So much for that.—Now for our Irish wars:
We must supplant those rough rug-headed kerns,[a]
Which live like venom, where no venom else,
But only they, have privilege to live.
And, for these great affairs do ask some charge,
Towards our assistance, we do seize to us
The plate, coin, revenues, and moveables,
Whereof our uncle Gaunt did stand possess'd.

YORK. How long shall I be patient? Ah,* how long
Shall tender duty make me suffer wrong?
Not Gloster's death, nor Hereford's banishment,
Nor Gaunt's rebukes, nor England's private wrongs,
Nor the prevention of poor Bolingbroke
About his marriage,[b] nor my own disgrace,
Have ever made me sour my patient cheek,
Or bend one wrinkle on my sovereign's face.
I am the last of noble Edward's sons,
Of whom thy father, prince of Wales, was first;
In war, was never lion rag'd more fierce,
In peace, was never gentle lamb more mild,
Than was that young and princely gentleman:
His face thou hast, for even so look'd he,
Accomplish'd with the † number of thy hours;
But when he frown'd, it was against the French,
And not against his friends; his noble hand
Did win what he did spend, and spent not that
Which his triumphant father's hand had won:
His hands were guilty of no kindred ‡ blood,
But bloody with the enemies of his kin.
O, Richard! York is too far gone with grief,
Or else he never would compare between.

K. RICH. Why, uncle, what's the matter?

YORK. O, my liege,
Pardon me, if you please; if not, I, pleas'd
Not to be pardon'd, am content withal.§
Seek you to seize, and gripe into your hands,
The royalties and rights of banish'd Hereford?
Is not Gaunt dead? and doth not Hereford live?
Was not Gaunt just? and is not Harry true?
Did not the one deserve to have an heir?
Is not his heir a well-deserving son?
Take Hereford's rights away, and take from time
His charters, and his customary rights;
Let not to-morrow then ensue to-day;
Be not thyself; for how art thou a king,
But by fair sequence and succession?
Now, afore God (God forbid, I say true!)
If you do wrongfully seize Hereford's right,
Call in the * letters-patents that he hath
By his attorneys-general to sue
His livery,(2) and deny his offer'd homage,—
You pluck a thousand dangers on your head,
You lose a thousand well-disposed hearts,
And prick my tender patience to those thoughts
Which honour and allegiance cannot think.

K. RICH. Think what you will; we seize into our hands
His plate, his goods, his money, and his lands.

YORK. I'll not be by the while. My liege, farewell,
What will ensue hereof, there's none can tell;
But by bad courses may be understood,
That their events can never fall out good. [*Exit.*

K. RICH. Go, Bushy, to the earl of Wiltshire straight;
Bid him repair to us to Ely-house,
To see this business. To-morrow next,
We will for Ireland; and 'tis time, I trow;
And we create, in absence of ourself,
Our uncle York, lord governor of England,
For he is just, and always loved us well.
Come on, our queen: to-morrow must we part;
Be merry, for our time of stay is short.
[*Flourish.*
[*Exeunt* KING, QUEEN, BUSHY, AUMERLE, GREEN, *and* BAGOT.

NORTH. Well, lords, the duke of Lancaster is dead.

ROSS. And living too, for now his son is duke.

WILLO. Barely in title, not in revenue.

NORTH. Richly in both, if justice had her right.

ROSS. My heart is great; but it must break with silence,
Ere't be disburthen'd with a liberal tongue.

NORTH. Nay, speak thy mind, and let him ne'er speak more,
That speaks thy words again to do thee harm

WILLO. Tends that thou'dst speak, to the duke of Hereford?
If it be so, out with it boldly, man;
Quick is mine ear to hear of good towards him.

ROSS. No good at all that I can do for him;
Unless you call it good to pity him,
Bereft and gelded of his patrimony.

(*) First folio, *Oh.* (†) Quarto, *a.* (‡) First folio, *kindred's.* (§) First folio, *with all.*

(*) First folio, *his.*

[a] *Those rough rug-headed* kerns,—] *Kernes* were the rude foot soldiery of Ireland.

[b] About his marriage,—] "When the duke of Hereford, after his banishment, went into France, he was honourably entertained at that court, and would have obtained in marriage the only daughter of the duke of Berry, uncle to the French king, had not Richard prevented the match."—STEEVENS.

NORTH. Now, afore God! * 'tis shame such wrongs are borne,
In him a royal prince, and many more
Of noble blood in this declining land.
The king is not himself, but basely led
By flatterers; and what they will inform,
Merely in hate, 'gainst any of us all,
That will the king severely prosecute
'Gainst us, our lives, our children, and our heirs.
ROSS. The commons hath he pill'd[a] with grievous taxes,
And quite lost their hearts: the nobles hath he fin'd
For ancient quarrels, and quite lost their hearts.
WILLO. And daily new exactions are devis'd—
As—blanks, benevolences, and I wot not what;
But what, o' God's name, doth become of this?
NORTH. Wars hath not wasted it, for warr'd he hath not,
But basely yielded upon compromise
That which his noble † ancestors achiev'd with blows:
More hath he spent in peace, than they in wars.
ROSS. The earl of Wiltshire hath the realm in farm.
WILLO. The king's grown bankrupt, like a broken man.
NORTH. Reproach and dissolution hangeth over him.
ROSS. He hath not money for these Irish wars,
(His burthenous taxations notwithstanding,)
But by the robbing of the banish'd duke—
NORTH. His noble kinsman; Most degenerate king!
But, lords, we hear this fearful tempest sing,
Yet seek no shelter to avoid the storm;
We see the wind sit sore upon our sails,
And yet we strike not, but securely[b] perish.
ROSS. We see the very wreck that we must suffer;
And unavoided is the danger now,
For suffering so the causes of our wreck.
NORTH. Not so: even through the hollow eyes of death,
I spy life peering; but I dare not say,
How near the tidings of our comfort is.
WILLO. Nay, let us share thy thoughts, as thou dost ours.
ROSS. Be confident to speak, Northumberland:
We three are but thyself, and, speaking so,
Thy words are but as thoughts;[c] therefore, be bold.
NORTH. Then thus:—I have from Port le Blanc,
A bay in Brittany, receiv'd intelligence
That Harry duke of Hereford, Reignold lord Cobham,
That late broke from the duke of Exeter,[d]
His brother, archbishop late of Canterbury,
Sir Thomas Erpingham, sir John Ramston; *
Sir John Norbery, sir Robert Waterton, and Francis Quoint,—
All these, well furnish'd by the duke of Bretagne,
With eight tall ships, three thousand men of war,
Are making hither with all due expedience,
And shortly mean to touch our northern shore: (3)
Perhaps, they had ere this, but that they stay
The first departing of the king for Ireland.
If then we shall shake off our slavish yoke,
Imp[e] out our drooping country's broken wing,
Redeem from broking pawn the blemish'd crown,
Wipe off the dust that hides our sceptre's gilt,
And make high majesty look like itself,—
Away with me in post to Ravenspurg:
But if you faint, as fearing to do so,
Stay and be secret, and myself will go.
ROSS. To horse, to horse! urge doubts to them that fear.
WILLO. Hold out my horse, and I will first be there. [*Exeunt.*

SCENE II.—*The same. A Room in the Palace.*

Enter QUEEN, BUSHY, *and* BAGOT.

BUSHY. Madam, your majesty is too much sad:
You promis'd, when you parted with the king,
To lay aside life-harming † heaviness,
And entertain a cheerful disposition.
QUEEN. To please the king, I did; to please myself,
I cannot do it; yet I know no cause,
Why I should welcome such a guest as grief,
Save bidding farewell to so sweet a guest

(*) First folio, *heaven*. (†) First folio omits, *noble*.

(*) First folio, *Rainston*. (†) First folio, *self-harming*.

a Hath he *pill'd*—] That is, *robbed, pillaged;* from the French, *piller*.

b *But* securely *perish.*] *Securely*, in this place, as in other instances, is used in the sense of *carelessly, over-confidently, foolhardily*. Thus, in the "Merry Wives of Windsor," Act II. Sc. 2:—"She dwells so *securely* on the excellency of her honour;" and in the same play, Act II. Sc. 2:—"Page is an ass, a *secure* ass."

c Thy words are but as thoughts;] Mr. Collier's annotator would read "*our* thoughts,"—an unhappy conjecture; for if they knew the intelligence Northumberland possessed, why need he impart it? The meaning is obviously, "We are all leagued together, and whatever you speak will be as safe in our keeping as if you only thought it."

d That late broke from the duke of Exeter,—] There is a *lacuna* here. It was Thomas, the earl of Arundel's son, who was in custody of the duke of Exeter. (See Holinshed, under the year 1399.) Malone therefore inserted the following line to perfect the sense:—

["*The son of Richard, earl of Arundel.*"]

e Imp *out our drooping country's broken wing,*—] To *imp* is an expression borrowed from falconry, and means, to supply or repair any wing-feathers of a hawk, which had fallen out or were broken. It is supposed to come from the Saxon *impan*, to *graft* or *inoculate*.

As my sweet Richard. Yet, again, methinks,
Some unborn sorrow, ripe in fortune's womb,
Is coming towards me; and my inward soul
With nothing trembles: at something it grieves,
More than with parting from my lord the king.
 BUSHY. Each substance of a grief hath twenty
 shadows,
Which shows like grief itself, but is not so:
For sorrow's eye, glazed with blinding tears,
Divides one thing entire, to many objects,
Like perspectives,(4) which, rightly gaz'd upon,
Show nothing but confusion,—ey'd awry,
Distinguish form: so your sweet majesty,
Looking awry upon your lord's departure,
Finds* shapes of griefs more than himself to wail;
Which, look'd on as it is, is nought but shadows
Of what it is not. Then, thrice-gracious queen,
More than your lord's departure, weep not;
 more 's not seen;
Or if it be, 'tis with false sorrow's eye,
Which, for things true, weeps* things imaginary.
 QUEEN. It may be so; but yet my inward soul
Persuades me it is otherwise: howe'er it be,
I cannot but be sad; so heavy-sad,
As—though, in[a] thinking, on no thought I think—
Makes me with heavy nothing faint and shrink.
 BUSHY. 'T is nothing but conceit,[b] my gracious
 lady.
 QUEEN. 'T is nothing less: conceit is still
 deriv'd
From some forefather grief, mine is not so;
For nothing hath begot my something grief,
Or something hath, the nothing that I grieve;
'Tis in reversion that I do possess;

(*) Old text, *Find*.

a *As—though*, in *thinking*,—] The old copies all read, "*on* thinking."

(*) First folio, *weep*.

b *'T is nothing but* conceit,—] *Imagination, fanciful conception*.

But what it is, that is not yet known, what,
I cannot name; 't is nameless woe, I wot.

Enter GREEN.

GREEN. God * save your majesty!—and—well met, gentlemen:—
I hope the king is not yet shipp'd for Ireland.
QUEEN. Why hop'st thou so? 't is better hope he is;
For his designs crave haste, his haste good hope;
Then wherefore dost thou hope he is not shipp'd?
GREEN. That he, our hope, might have retir'd his power,
And driven into despair an enemy's hope,
Who strongly hath set footing in this land:
The banish'd Bolingbroke repeals himself,
And with uplifted arms is safe arriv'd
At Ravenspurg.
QUEEN. Now God in heaven forbid!
GREEN. O, madam, 't is too true; and, that is worse,
The lord Northumberland, his son, young † Henry [Percy,
The lords of Ross, Beaumond, and Willoughby,
With all their powerful friends, are fled to him.
BUSHY. Why have you not proclaim'd Northumberland
And all ‡ the rest of the revolted faction, traitors?
GREEN. We have: whereupon the earl of Worcester
Hath broke his staff, resign'd his stewardship,
And all the household servants fled with him,
To Bolingbroke.
QUEEN. So, Green, thou art the midwife to § [my woe,
And Bolingbroke my sorrow's dismal heir:
Now hath my soul brought forth her prodigy;
And I, a gasping new-deliver'd mother,
Have woe to woe, sorrow to sorrow, join'd.
BUSHY. Despair not, madam.
QUEEN. Who shall hinder me?
I will despair, and be at enmity
With cozening hope; he is a flatterer,
A parasite, a keeper-back of death,
Who gently would dissolve the bands of life
Which false hope lingers ‖ in extremity.

Enter YORK.

GREEN. Here comes the duke of York.
QUEEN. With signs of war about his aged neck;
O, full of careful business are his looks!
Uncle, for God's* sake, speak comfortable words.
YORK. Should I do so, I should belie my thoughts:[a]
Comfort's in heaven; and we are on the earth,
Where nothing lives, but crosses, cares,† and grief.
Your husband he is gone to save far off,
Whilst others come to make him lose at home:
Here am I left to underprop his land,
Who, weak with age, cannot support myself:
Now comes the sick hour that his surfeit made,
Now shall he try his friends that flatter'd him.

Enter a Servant.

SERV. My lord, your son was gone before I came.
YORK. He was?—Why, so!—go all which way it will!
The nobles they are fled, the commons they are cold,
And will, I fear, revolt on Hereford's side.—
Sirrah, get thee to Plashy, to my sister Gloucester;—
Bid her send me presently a thousand pound:
Hold, take my ring.
SERV. My lord, I had forgot to tell your lordship:
To-day, as I came by, I called there;[b]—
But I shall grieve you to report the rest.
YORK. What is it, knave?
SERV. An hour before I came, the duchess died.
YORK. God ‡ for his mercy! what a tide of woes
Comes § rushing on this woeful land at once!
I know not what to do:—I would to God ‡
(So my untruth[c] had not provok'd him to it,)
The king had cut off my head with my brother's.—
What, are there no ‖ posts despatch'd for Ireland?—
How shall we do for money for these wars?—
Come, sister,—cousin, I would say: pray, pardon me.—
Go, fellow, [*to the* Servant] get thee home, provide some carts,
And bring away the armour that is there.—
[*Exit* Servant.
Gentlemen, will you go ¶ muster men?
If I know how, or which way,[d] to order these affairs,
Thus disorderly thrust into my hands,
Never believe me. Both are my kinsmen;—
The one is my sovereign, whom both my oath
And duty bids defend; the other again

(*) First folio, *heaven*. (†) First folio, *young son*.
(‡) First folio omits, *all*. (§) First folio, *of*.
(‖) First folio, *hopes linger*.

[a] Should I do so, I should belie my thoughts:] This line is wanting in the folio.
[b] *To-day*, as *I came by*, I *called there*;—] This is the reading of the first copy, 1597: subsequent editions, including the folio 1623, read lamely and prosaically:—
"To-day I came by *and* called there;"—

(*) First folio, *heaven's*. (†) First folio, *care*.
(‡) First folio, *Heaven*. (§) First folio, *Come*.
(‖) First folio omits, *no*. (¶) First folio omits, *go*.

[c] *So my* untruth—] That is, *faithlessness, disloyalty*.
[d] *If I know how*, or which way,—] The redundant, *or which way*, I have always suspected to be an interlineation of the poet's, who had not decided whether to read, "*how* to order these affairs," or, "*which way* to order."

Is my kinsman, whom the king hath wrong'd,
Whom conscience and my kindred bids to right.
Well, somewhat we must do.—Come, cousin,
I'll dispose of you:—Gentlemen, go muster up your men,
And meet me presently at Berkley Castle.
I should to Plashy too;—
But time will not permit:—All is uneven,
And everything is left at six and seven.
[*Exeunt* YORK *and* QUEEN.

BUSHY. The wind sits fair for news to go to Ireland,
But none returns. For us to levy power,
Proportionable to the enemy,
Is all unpossible.*

GREEN. Besides, our nearness to the king in love,
Is near the hate of those love not the king.

BAGOT. And that's the wavering commons; for their love
Lies in their purses, and whoso empties them,
By so much fills their hearts with deadly hate.

BUSHY. Wherein the king stands generally condemn'd.

BAGOT. If judgment lie in them, then so do we,
Because we ever have been† near the king.

GREEN. Well, I'll for refuge straight to Bristol castle;
The earl of Wiltshire is already there.

BUSHY. Thither will I with you: for little office
Will the hateful commons perform for us;
Except, like curs, to tear us all to‡ pieces.—
Will you go along with us?

BAGOT. No; I will to Ireland to his majesty.
Farewell: if heart's presages be not vain,
We three here part, that ne'er shall meet again.

BUSHY. That's as York thrives to beat back Bolingbroke.

GREEN. Alas, poor duke! the task he undertakes,
Is—numbering sands, and drinking oceans dry;
Where one on his side fights, thousands will fly.

BUSHY. Farewell at once; for once, for all, and ever.

GREEN. Well, we may meet again.

BAGOT. I fear me, never.
[*Exeunt.*

SCENE III.—*The Wilds in* Gloucestershire.

Enter BOLINGBROKE *and* NORTHUMBERLAND, *with Forces.*

BOLING. How far is it, my lord, to Berkley now?

NORTH. Believe me, noble lord,
I am a stranger here in Gloucestershire.
These high wild hills, and rough uneven ways,
Draw* out our miles, and make* them wearisome:
And yet your† fair discourse hath been as sugar,
Making the hard way sweet and délectable.
But, I bethink me, what a weary way
From Ravenspurg to Cotswold, will be found
In Ross, and Willoughby, wanting your company;
Which, I protest, hath very much beguil'd
The tediousness and process of my travel:
But theirs is sweetened with the hope to have
The present benefit which‡ I possess:
And hope to joy,[a] is little less in joy,
Than hope enjoy'd. By this, the weary lords
Shall make their way seem short, as mine hath done,
By sight of what I have, your noble company.

BOLING. Of much less value is my company,
Than your good words. But who comes here?

Enter HARRY PERCY.

NORTH. It is my son, young Harry Percy,
Sent from my brother Worcester, whencesoever.—
Harry, how fares your uncle?

PERCY. I had thought, my lord, to have learn'd his health of you.

NORTH. Why, is he not with the queen?

PERCY. No, my good lord; he hath forsook the court,
Broken his staff of office, and dispers'd
The household of the king.

NORTH. What was his reason?
He was not so resolv'd when last we§ spake together.

PERCY. Because your lordship was proclaimed traitor.
But he, my lord, is gone to Ravenspurg,
To offer service to the duke of Hereford;
And sent me over by Berkley, to discover
What power the duke of York had levied there;
Then with directions‖ to repair to Ravenspurg.

NORTH. Have you forgot the duke of Hereford, boy?

PERCY. No, my good lord; for that is not forgot
Which ne'er I did remember: to my knowledge,
I never in my life did look on him.

NORTH. Then learn to know him now; this is the duke.

PERCY. My gracious lord, I tender you my service,
Such as it is, being tender, raw, and young;

(*) First folio, *impossible*. (†) First folio, *have been ever*. (‡) First folio, *in*.

a *And hope to* joy,—] To *joy* is used here as to *enjoy*.

(*) Old copies, *draws—makes*. (†) First folio, *our*. (‡) First folio, *that*. (§) First folio, *we last*. (‖) First folio, *direction*.

Which elder days shall ripen, and confirm
To more approved service and desert.
BOLING. I thank thee, gentle Percy; and be sure,
I count myself in nothing else so happy,
As in a soul rememb'ring my good friends;
And as my fortune ripens with thy love,
It shall be still thy true love's recompense:
My heart this covenant makes, my hand thus seals it.
NORTH. How far is it to Berkley? and what stir,
Keeps good old York there, with his men of war?
PERCY. There stands the castle, by yon tuft of trees,
Mann'd with three hundred men, as I have heard:
And in it are the lords of York, Berkley, and Seymour,
None else of name and noble estimate.

Enter ROSS *and* WILLOUGHBY.

NORTH. Here come the lords of Ross and Willoughby,
Bloody with spurring, fiery-red with haste.
BOLING. Welcome, my lords: I wot your love pursues
A banish'd traitor; all my treasury
Is yet but unfelt thanks, which, more enrich'd,
Shall be your love and labour's recompense.
ROSS. Your presence makes us rich, most noble lord.
WILLO. And far surmounts our labour to attain it.
BOLING. Evermore thanks, the exchequer of the poor;
Which, till my infant fortune comes to years,
Stands for my bounty. But who comes here?

Enter BERKLEY.

NORTH. It is my lord of Berkley, as I guess.
BERK. My lord of Hereford, my message is to you.
BOLING. My lord, my answer is—to Lancaster:[a]
And I am come to seek that name in England:
And I must find that title in your tongue,
Before I make reply to aught you say.
BERK. Mistake me not, my lord, 't is not my meaning
To raze one title of your honour out:—
To you, my lord, I come, (what lord you will,)
From the most gracious regent[b] of this land,
The duke of York; to know what pricks you on
To take advantage of the absent time,
And fright our native peace with self-born arms.

Enter YORK, *attended.*

BOLING. I shall not need transport my words by you;
Here comes his grace in person.—My noble uncle! [*Kneels.*
YORK. Show me thy humble heart, and not thy knee,
Whose duty is deceivable and false.
BOLING. My gracious uncle!
YORK. Tut, tut!
Grace me no grace, nor uncle me no uncle.*
I am no traitor's uncle; and that word, grace,
In an ungracious mouth, is but profane.
Why have these banish'd and forbidden legs
Dar'd once to touch a dust of England's ground?
But then more† why;—why have they dar'd to march
So many miles upon her peaceful bosom,
Frighting her pale-fac'd villages with war,
And ostentation of despised[c] arms?
Com'st thou because the anointed king is hence?
Why, foolish boy, the king is left behind,
And in my loyal bosom lies his power.
Were I but now the lord of such hot youth
As when brave Gaunt, thy father, and myself,
Rescued the Black Prince, that young Mars of men,
From forth the ranks of many thousand French,
O, then, how quickly should this arm of mine,
Now prisoner to the palsy, chastise thee,
And minister correction to thy fault!
BOLING. My gracious uncle, let me know my fault;
On what condition stands it, and wherein?
YORK. Even in condition of the worst degree,—
In gross rebellion, and detested treason:
Thou art a banish'd man, and here art come,
Before the expiration of thy time,
In braving arms against thy sovereign.
BOLING. As I was banish'd, I was banish'd Hereford:
But as I come, I come for Lancaster.
And, noble uncle, I beseech your grace,
Look on my wrongs with an indifferent[d] eye:
You are my father, for methinks in you

---

[a] My lord, my answer is—to Lancaster:] My answer will be given only to the title of *Lancaster*.

[b] *From the most* gracious regent *of this land,*—] The folio reads, From the most *glorious* of this land.

[c] *And ostentation of* despised *arms?*] *Despised* is not a satisfactory epithet in this place, but we cannot consent to eject it for the sake of Warburton's "*disposed*," or Hanmer's "*despightful*," or even for the old annotator's "*despoiling*."

(*) First folio omits, *no uncle*. (†) First folio, *more then*.

[d] Indifferent—] That is, *impartial*. Thus, in "Henry VIII." Act II. Sc. 4, Queen Katherine says:—

"I am a most poor woman, and a stranger,
Born out of your dominions: having here
No judge *indifferent*."

I see old Gaunt alive. O, then, my father,
Will you permit that I shall stand condemn'd
A wandering vagabond; my rights and royalties
Pluck'd from my arms perforce, and given away
To upstart unthrifts? Wherefore was I born?
If that my cousin king, be king of England,
It must be granted I am duke of Lancaster.
You have a son, Aumerle, my noble kinsman;
Had you first died, and he been thus trod down,
He should have found his uncle Gaunt a father,
To rouse his wrongs, and chase them to the bay.
I am denied to sue my livery here,
And yet my letters-patents give me leave:
My father's goods are all distrain'd, and sold,
And these, and all, are all amiss employ'd.
What would you have me do? I am a subject,
And I* challenge law: attorneys are denied me;
And therefore personally I lay my claim
To my inheritance of free descent.

NORTH. The noble duke hath been too much abus'd.

ROSS. It stands your grace upon,[a] to do him right.

WILLO. Base men by his endowments are made great.

YORK. My lords of England, let me tell you this,—
I have had feeling of my cousin's wrongs,
And labour'd all I could to do him right:
But in this kind to come, in braving arms,
Be his own carver,[b] and cut out his way,
To find out right with wrong,† it may not be;
And you that do abet him in this kind,
Cherish rebellion, and are rebels all.

NORTH. The noble duke hath sworn, his coming is
But for his own: and, for the right of that,
We all have strongly sworn to give him aid;
And let him ne'er see joy that breaks that oath.

YORK. Well, well, I see the issue of these arms;
I cannot mend it, I must needs confess,
Because my power is weak, and all ill left:
But, if I could, by Him that gave me life,
I would attach you all, and make you stoop
Unto the sovereign mercy of the king;
But, since I cannot, be it known to you,
I do remain as neuter. So, fare you well;—
Unless you please to enter in the castle,
And there repose you for this night.

BOLING. An offer, uncle, that we will accept.
But we must win your grace to go with us
To Bristol castle; which, they say, is held
By Bushy, Bagot, and their complices,
The caterpillars of the commonwealth,
Which I have sworn to weed, and pluck away.

YORK. It may be I will go with you:—but yet I'll pause;
For I am loth to break our country's laws.
Nor friends, nor foes, to me welcome you are:
Things past redress are now with me past care.
[*Exeunt.*

SCENE IV.—*A Camp in* Wales.

Enter SALISBURY[c] *and a* Captain.

CAP. My lord of Salisbury, we have stay'd ten days,
And hardly kept our countrymen together,
And yet we hear no tidings from the king;
Therefore we will disperse ourselves: farewell.(5)

SAL. Stay yet another day, thou trusty Welshman;
The king reposeth all his confidence in thee.

CAP. 'T is thought the king is dead; we will not stay.
The bay-trees in our country are all withered,(6)
And meteors fright the fixed stars of heaven;
The pale-fac'd moon looks bloody on the earth,
And lean-look'd prophets whisper fearful change;
Rich men look sad, and ruffians dance and leap,
The one, in fear to lose what they enjoy,
The other, to enjoy by rage and war:
These signs forerun the death or fall[d] of kings.—
Farewell; our countrymen are gone and fled,
As well assur'd Richard their king is dead. [*Exit.*

SAL. Ah, Richard! with the* eyes of heavy mind,
I see thy glory, like a shooting star,
Fall to the base earth from the firmament.
Thy sun sets weeping in the lowly west,
Witnessing storms to come, woe, and unrest;
Thy friends are fled, to wait upon thy foes,
And crossly to thy good, all fortune goes. [*Exit.*

(*) First folio omits, *I*. (†) First folio, *wrongs*.

a It stands your grace upon,—] The meaning of this now obsolete form of expression is, *it is incumbent upon you, it is of import to you*. See note (b). p. 178.

b *Be his own* carver, *and* cut out *his way*,—] So in "Othello," Act II. Sc. 3:—

"He that stirs next to *carve forth* his own rage."

(*) First folio omits, *the*.

c SALISBURY.] John Montacute, earl of Salisbury.

d *The death* or fall *of kings*—] So the first quarto only: other editions, folio included, omit the words, *or fall*.

ACT III.

SCENE I.—Bolingbroke's *Camp at* Bristol.

Enter BOLINGBROKE, YORK, NORTHUMBERLAND, PERCY, WILLOUGHBY, ROSS: Officers *behind, with* BUSHY *and* GREEN, *prisoners.*

BOLING. Bring forth these men.—
Bushy, and Green, I will not vex your souls
(Since presently your souls must part your bodies,)
With too much urging your pernicious lives,
For 'twere no charity: yet, to wash your blood
From off my hands, here, in the view of men,
I will unfold some causes of your deaths.
You have misled a prince, a royal king,
A happy gentleman in blood and lineaments,
By you unhappied and disfigur'd clean.[a]
You have, in manner, with your sinful hours,
Made a divorce betwixt his queen and him;
Broke the possession of a royal bed,
And stain'd the beauty of a fair queen's cheeks
With tears drawn from her eyes by* your foul wrongs.
Myself—a prince, by fortune of my birth;
Near to the king in blood, and near in love,
Till you did make him misinterpret me,—
Have stoop'd my neck under your injuries,
And sigh'd my English breath in foreign clouds,
Eating the bitter bread of banishment:
While you have fed upon my seignories,
Dispark'd[b] my parks, and fell'd my forest woods;
From mine own windows torn my household coat,
Raz'd out my impress,[c] leaving me no sign—
Save men's opinions, and my living blood—
To show the world I am a gentleman.
This, and much more, much more than twice all this,
Condemns you to the death.—See them deliver'd over

(*) First folio, *with*.

[a] Clean.] That is, *utterly, completely.*

[b] Dispark'd *my parks.*—] "To *dispark*, is a legal term, and signifies, to divest a park, constituted by royal grant or prescription, of its name and character, by destroying the enclosures of such a park, and also the vert (or whatever bears green leaves, whether wood or underwood), and the beasts of chase therein; and laying it open."—MALONE.

[c] *Raz'd out my* impress,—] An *impress* signified a device or motto.

To execution and the hand of death.

BUSHY. More welcome is the stroke of death to me,
Than Bolingbroke to England. Lords, farewell.*

GREEN. My comfort is, that heaven will take our souls,
And plague injustice with the pains of hell.

BOLING. My lord Northumberland, see them despatch'd.

[*Exeunt* NORTHUMBERLAND *and others, with Prisoners.*

Uncle, you say, the queen is at your house;
For God's† sake, fairly let her be entreated:
Tell her, I send to her my kind commends;
Take special care my greetings be deliver'd.

YORK. A gentleman of mine I have dispatch'd
With letters of your love to her at large.

BOLING. Thanks, gentle uncle.—Come, lords, away;
To fight with Glendower and his complices;
Awhile to work, and, after, holiday. [*Exeunt.*

SCENE II.—*The Coast of* Wales. *A Castle in View.*

Flourish: Drums and Trumpets. Enter KING RICHARD, BISHOP OF CARLISLE, AUMERLE, *and* Soldiers.

K. RICH. Barkloughly castle call they‡ this at hand?

AUM. Yea, my lord. How brooks your grace the air,
After your late tossing on the breaking seas?

K. RICH. Needs must I like it well; I weep for joy,
To stand upon my kingdom once again.
Dear earth, I do salute thee with my hand,
Though rebels wound thee with their horses' hoofs:
As a long-parted mother with her child,
Plays fondly with her tears and smiles, in meeting;
So, weeping, smiling,[a] greet I thee, my earth,
And do thee favour with my royal hands.
Feed not thy sovereign's foe, my gentle earth,
Nor with thy sweets comfort his ravenous sense:
But let thy spiders, that suck up thy venom,
And heavy-gaited toads, lie in their way,
Doing annoyance to the treacherous feet,
Which with usurping steps do trample thee.
Yield stinging nettles to mine enemies;
And when they from thy bosom pluck a flower,
Guard it, I pray thee, with a lurking adder,
Whose double tongue may with a mortal touch
Throw death upon thy sovereign's enemies.
Mock not my senseless conjuration, lords;
This earth shall have a feeling, and these stones
Prove armed soldiers, ere her native king
Shall falter under foul rebellion's* arms.

CAR. Fear not, my lord; that Power that made you king,
Hath power to keep you king, in spite of all.[b]
The means that heaven yields† must be embrac'd,
And not neglected; else, if[c] heaven would,
And we will not, heaven's offer we refuse,
The proffer'd means of succour and redress.

AUM. He means, my lord, that we are too remiss;
Whilst Bolingbroke, through our security,[d]
Grows strong and great, in substance, and in power.‡

K. RICH. Discomfortable cousin! know'st thou not,
That, when the searching eye of heaven is hid
Behind the globe that lights the lower world,[e]
Then thieves and robbers range abroad unseen,
In murders, and in outrage bloody, here;
But when, from under this terrestrial ball,
He fires the proud tops of the eastern pines,[f]
And darts his light§ through every guilty hole,
Then murders, treasons, and detested sins,
The cloak of night being pluck'd from off their backs,
Stand bare and naked, trembling at themselves?
So when this thief, this traitor, Bolingbroke,—
Who all this while hath revell'd in the night,
Whilst we were wandering with the Antipodes,[g]—
Shall see us rising in our throne, the east,
His treasons will sit blushing in his face,
Not able to endure the sight of day,
But, self-affrighted, tremble at his sin.
Not all the water in the rough rude sea
Can wash the balm from an anointed king:
The breath of worldly men cannot depose
The deputy elected by the Lord:
For every man that Bolingbroke hath press'd,
To lift shrewd steel against our golden crown,
God|| for his Richard hath in heavenly pay

(*) First folio omits, *Lords, farewell.* (†) First folio, *Heavens.* (‡) First folio, *you.*

[a] *So,* weeping, smiling,—] These words were probably intended to form a compound, "*weeping-smiling.*"

[b] In spite of all.] The four lines that follow are omitted in the folio.

[c] If *heaven would,*—] Pope inserted *if.*

[d] *Through our* security,—] See note ([b]), p. 462.

[e] *Behind the globe* that *lights the lower world,*—] It is customary to read "*and* lights," but no alteration can reconcile the confused imagery of a passage which Shakespeare, intending to say poetically "after sunset," evidently wrote *currente calamo.*

[f] He fires the proud tops of the eastern pines,—] "It is not easy to point out an image more striking and beautiful than this in any poet, whether ancient or modern."—STEEVENS.

[g] Whilst we were wandering with the Antipodes,—] This line is not in the first folio.

(*) First folio, *rebellious.* (†) Old copies, *heavens yield.* (‡) First folio, *friends.* (§) First folio, *lightning.* (||) First folio, *Heaven.*

A glorious angel: then, if angels fight,
Weak men must fall, for heaven still guards the right.

Enter SALISBURY.

Welcome, my lord. How far off lies your power?
SAL. Nor near, nor farther off, my gracious lord,
Than this weak arm. Discomfort guides my tongue,
And bids me speak of nothing but despair.
One day too late, I fear, my noble lord,
Hath clouded all thy happy days on earth:
O, call back yesterday, bid time return,
And thou shalt have twelve thousand fighting men!
To-day, to-day, unhappy day, too late,
O'erthrows thy joys, friends, fortune, and thy state;
For all the Welshmen, hearing thou wert dead,
Are gone to Bolingbroke, dispers'd, and fled.
AUM. Comfort, my liege; why looks your grace so pale?
K. RICH. But now, the blood of twenty thousand men
Did triumph in my face, and they are fled;
And, till so much blood thither come again,
Have I not reason to look pale and dead?
All souls that will be safe fly from my side;
For time hath set a blot upon my pride.
AUM. Comfort, my liege; remember who you are.
K. RICH. I had forgot myself. Am I not king?
Awake thou sluggard* majesty! thou sleepest.
Is not the king's name twenty† thousand names?
Arm, arm, my name! a puny subject strikes
At thy great glory.—Look not to the ground,
Ye favourites of a king. Are we not high?
High be our thoughts: I know, my uncle York
Hath power enough to serve our turn. But who comes here?

Enter SCROOP.

SCROOP. More health and happiness betide my liege,
Than can my care-tun'd tongue deliver him.
K. RICH. Mine ear is open,(1) and my heart prepar'd;
The worst is worldly loss thou canst unfold.
Say, is my kingdom lost? why, 'twas my care;
And what loss is it to be rid of care?
Strives Bolingbroke to be as great as we?
Greater he shall not be; if he serve God,
We 'll serve him too, and be his fellow so.
Revolt our subjects? that we cannot mend;
They break their faith to God, as well as us:
Cry, woe, destruction, ruin, loss, decay;
The worst is—death, and death will have his day.
SCROOP. Glad am I that your highness is so arm'd
To bear the tidings of calamity.
Like an unseasonable stormy day,
Which makes the silver rivers drown their shores,
As if the world were all dissolv'd to tears;
So high above his limits swells the rage
Of Bolingbroke, covering your fearful land
With hard bright steel, and hearts harder than steel.
White-beards* have arm'd their thin and hairless scalps
Against thy majesty; and boys, with women's voices,
Strive to speak big, and clap their female joints
In stiff unwieldy arms; against thy crown
Thy very beadsmen learn to bend their bows
Of double-fatal yew;[a] against thy state,
Yea, distaff-women manage rusty bills;
Against thy seat both young and old rebel,[b]
And all goes worse than I have power to tell.
K. RICH. Too well, too well, thou tell'st a tale so ill.
Where is the earl of Wiltshire? where is Bagot?
What is become of Bushy? where is Green?
That they have let the dangerous enemy
Measure our confines with such peaceful steps?
If we prevail, their heads shall pay for it.
I warrant they have made peace with Bolingbroke.
SCROOP. Peace have they made with him, indeed, my lord.
K. RICH. O villains, vipers, damn'd without redemption!
Dogs, easily won to fawn on any man!
Snakes, in my heart-blood warm'd, that sting my heart!
Three Judases, each one thrice worse than Judas!
Would they make peace? terrible hell make war
Upon their spotted souls for this offence!†
SCROOP. Sweet love, I see, changing his property,
Turns to the sourest and most deadly hate:
Again uncurse their souls; their peace is made
With heads, and not with hands: those whom you curse,
Have felt the worst of death's destroying wound,‡
And lie full low, grav'd in the hollow ground.
AUM. Is Bushy, Green, and the earl of Wiltshire, dead?

(*) Quartos, *coward*. (†) First folio, *forty*.

(*) First folio, *White beares*. (†) First quarto omits, *offence*. (‡) First folio, *hand*.

a *Of double-fatal yew*—] Fatal alike from the poisonous nature of the leaves, and from the wood being formed into instruments of death.

b *Both young and old rebel*,—] The punctuation of this passage, beginning "and boys, with women's voices," is that of the folio, 1623, which certainly yields a finer and more impressive sense than the pointing adopted in all modern editions.

SCROOP. Yea, all of them at Bristol lost their heads.

AUM. Where is the duke my father with his power?

K. RICH. No matter where. Of comfort no man speak:
Let's talk of graves, of worms, and epitaphs;
Make dust our paper, and with rainy eyes
Write sorrow on the bosom of the earth.
Let's choose executors, and talk of wills:
And yet not so,—for what can we bequeath,
Save our deposed bodies to the ground?
Our lands, our lives, and all, are Bolingbroke's,
And nothing can we call our own but death;
And that small model[a] of the barren earth,
Which serves as paste and cover to our bones.
For God's* sake, let us sit upon the ground,
And tell sad stories of the death of kings:—
How some have been depos'd, some slain in war,
Some haunted by the ghosts they have depos'd;
Some poison'd by their wives, some sleeping kill'd;
All murder'd.—For within the hollow crown
That rounds the mortal temples of a king,
Keeps Death his court; and there the antic sits,
Scoffing his state, and grinning at his pomp;(2)
Allowing him a breath, a little scene
To monarchize, be fear'd, and kill with looks;
Infusing him with self and vain conceit,—
As if this flesh, which walls about our life,
Were brass impregnable,—and, humour'd thus,
Comes at the last, and with a little pin
Bores through his castle wall,† and—farewell king!
Cover your heads, and mock not flesh and blood
With solemn reverence; throw away respect,
Tradition, form, and ceremonious duty,
For you have but mistook me all this while:
I live with bread like you, feel want, taste grief,
Need friends:—subjécted thus,
How can you say to me—I am a king?

CAR. My lord, wise men ne'er sit and wail their woes,[b]
But presently prevent the ways to wail.
To fear the foe, since fear oppresseth strength,
Gives, in your weakness, strength unto your foe,
And so your follies fight against yourself.[c]
Fear, and be slain? no worse can come, to fight:
And fight and die, is death destroying death;
Where fearing-dying, pays death servile breath.

AUM. My father hath a power, inquire of him;
And learn to make a body of a limb.

K. RICH. Thou chid'st me well.—Proud Bolingbroke, I come,
To change blows with thee for our day of doom.
This ague-fit of fear is over-blown,
An easy task it is to win our own.——
Say, Scroop, where lies our uncle with his power?
Speak sweetly, man, although thy looks be sour.

SCROOP. Men judge by the complexion of the sky
The state and inclination of the day;
So may you by my dull and heavy eye,
My tongue hath but a heavier tale to say.
I play the torturer, by small and small,
To lengthen out the worst that must be spoken:—
Your uncle York is join'd with Bolingbroke,
And all your northern castles yielded up,
And all your southern gentlemen in arms,
Upon his party.*

K. RICH. Thou hast said enough.—
Beshrew thee, cousin, which didst lead me forth [*To* AUM.
Of that sweet way I was in, to despair!
What say you now? What comfort have we now?
By heaven, I'll hate him everlastingly,
That bids me be of comfort any more.
Go to Flint castle, there I'll pine away;
A king, woe's slave, shall kingly woe obey.
That power I have, discharge; and let them go
To ear[d] the land that hath some hope to grow,
For I have none. Let no man speak again
To alter this, for counsel is but vain.

AUM. My liege, one word—

K. RICH. He does me double wrong,
That wounds me with the flatteries of his tongue.
Discharge my followers, let them hence away,
From Richard's night to Bolingbroke's fair day. [*Exeunt.*

SCENE III.—Wales. *Before* Flint Castle.

Enter, with drum and colours, BOLINGBROKE *and Forces;* YORK, NORTHUMBERLAND, *and others.*

BOLING. So that by this intelligence we learn,
The Welshmen are dispers'd; and Salisbury
Is gone to meet the king, who lately landed,
With some few private friends, upon this coast.

NORTH. The news is very fair and good, my lord;

(*) First folio, *Heaven.* (†) First folio, *walls.*

a *And that small* model *of the barren earth,—*] Douce and other critics thought *model*, in the present passage, meant no more than a *measure, portion,* or *quantity;* but with Shakespeare's intense objectivity, it was more probably intended to signify the hillock of mould which, covering the dead body, assumes its shape.

b *Wise men ne'er sit* and *wail their woes,—*] So the quarto copies. The folio reading, usually adopted, is,—

"Wise men *ne'er wail* their *present* woes."

(*) First folio, *faction.*

c And so your follies, &c.] This line is not found in the first folio.

d *To* ear *the land—*] That is, to *plough*, to *till* it. So, in "All's Well that Ends Well," Act I. Sc. 3:—

"He that *ears* my land, spares my team."

And also in Shakespeare's Dedication of "Venus and Adonis" to Lord Southampton: "And never after *ear* so barren a land, for fear it yield me still so bad a harvest."

Richard, not far from hence, hath hid his head.
  YORK. It would beseem the lord Northumberland
To say, King Richard. Alack the heavy day,
When such a sacred king should hide his head!
  NORTH. Your grace mistakes; only to be brief,
Left I his title out.
  YORK. The time hath been,
Would you have been so brief with him, he would
Have been so brief with you,* to shorten you,
For taking so the head, your whole head's length.
  BOLING. Mistake not, uncle, further than you should.
  YORK. Take not, good cousin, further than you should,
Lest you mis-take. The heavens are o'er our heads.†
  BOLING. I know it, uncle; and oppose not myself
Against their will.—But who comes here?

Enter PERCY.

Welcome, Harry: what, will not this castle yield?
  PERCY. The castle royally is mann'd, my lord,
Against thy entrance.
  BOLING. Royally?
Why, it contains no king?
  PERCY. Yes, my good lord,
It doth contain a king; King Richard lies
Within the limits of yon lime and stone:
And with him are‡ the lord Aumerle, lord Salisbury,
Sir Stephen Scroop; besides a clergyman
Of holy reverence, who, I cannot learn.
  NORTH. Oh! belike it is the bishop of Carlisle.
  BOLING. Noble lord,[a] [*To* NORTH.
Go to the rude ribs of that ancient castle:
Through brazen trumpet send the breath of parle
Into his ruin'd ears, and thus deliver.
Henry Bolingbroke
On both[b] his knees doth kiss King Richard's hand;
And sends allegiance, and true faith of heart,
To his most § royal person: hither come
Even at his feet to lay my arms and power;
Provided that, my banishment repeal'd,
And lands restor'd again, be freely granted:
If not, I'll use the advantage of my power,
And lay the summer's dust with showers of blood,
Rain'd from the wounds of slaughter'd Englishmen:
The which, how far off from the mind of Bolingbroke
It is such crimson tempest should bedrench
The fresh green lap of fair King Richard's land,
My stooping duty tenderly shall show.
Go, signify as much; while here we march
Upon the grassy carpet of this plain.
  [NORTH. *advances to the castle with a trumpet.*
Let's march without the noise of threat'ning drum,
That from the * castle's totter'd[c] battlements
Our fair appointments may be well perus'd.
Methinks, King Richard and myself should meet
With no less terror than the elements
Of fire and water, when their thund'ring shock[d]
At meeting tears the cloudy cheeks of heaven.
Be he the fire, I'll be the yielding water:
The rage be his, while on the earth I rain
My waters; on the earth, and not on him.
March on, and mark King Richard how he looks.

A parle sounded; answered by another trumpet within. Flourish. Enter on the walls, KING RICHARD, *the* BISHOP OF CARLISLE, AUMERLE, SCROOP, *and* SALISBURY.

  BOLING. See, see, King Richard doth himself appear,
As doth the blushing discontented sun,
From out the fiery portal of the east,
When he perceives the envious clouds are bent
To dim his glory, and to stain the track †
Of his bright passage to the occident.
  YORK. Yet looks he like a king; behold, his eye,
As bright as is the eagle's, lightens forth
Controlling majesty; alack, alack, for woe,
That any harm should stain so fair a show!
  K. RICH. We are amaz'd; and thus long have we stood
To watch the fearful bending of thy knee,
[*To* NORTH.
Because we thought ourself thy lawful king:
And if we be, how dare thy joints forget
To pay their awful duty to our presence?
If we be not, show us the hand of God
That hath dismiss'd us from our stewardship;
For well we know, no hand of blood and bone
Can gripe the sacred handle of our sceptre,
Unless he do profane, steal, or usurp.
And though you think that all, as you have done,
Have torn their souls, by turning them from us,
And we are barren, and bereft of friends;
Yet know,—my master, God omnipotent,
Is mustering in his clouds, on our behalf,
Armies of pestilence; and they shall strike

(*) The quarto omits, *with you*. (†) First folio, *your head*.
(‡) First folio omits, *are*. (§) First folio omits, *most*.

a Noble lord,—] Malone has remarked, with judgment, that Shakespeare frequently in his addresses to persons, begins with an hemistich, and, in many instances, blends short prosaic sentences with his metrical dialogues.

b On both *his knees*—] So the quarto. The folio reads, *Upon* his knees.

(*) First folio, *this*. (†) First folio, *tract*.

c Totter'd *battlements*—] *Totter'd* is the reading of the two earliest quartos, and may be used for *tottering*, the passive for the active participle. The other ancient copies have *tattered* and *tatter'd*.

d *Their thund'ring* shock—] So the first quarto, 1597. The folio, and the other quarto copies, read, *smoake*.

Your children yet unborn, and unbegot,
That lift your vassal hands against my head,
And threat the glory of my precious crown.
Tell Bolingbroke, (for yond', methinks, he stands,*)
That every stride he makes upon my land
Is dangerous treason. He is come to ope
The purple testament[a] of bleeding war;
But ere the crown he looks for, live in peace,
Ten thousand bloody crowns of mothers' sons
Shall ill become the flower of England's face,
Change the complexion of her maid-pale peace
To scarlet indignation, and bedew
Her pastures' grass with faithful English blood.

NORTH. The king of heaven forbid, our lord the king
Should so with civil and uncivil arms
Be rush'd upon! Thy thrice-noble cousin,
Harry Bolingbroke, doth humbly kiss thy hand;
And by the honourable tomb he swears,
That stands upon your royal grandsire's bones;
And by the royalties of both your bloods,
Currents that spring from one most gracious head;
And by the buried hand of warlike Gaunt,
And by the worth and honour of himself,
Comprising all that may be sworn or said,—
His coming hither hath no further scope,
Than for his lineal royalties, and to beg
Enfranchisement immediate on his knees;
Which on thy royal party granted once,
His glittering arms he will commend to rust,
His barbed steeds to stables, and his heart,
To faithful service of your majesty.
This swears he, as he is a prince, is just;
And, as I am a gentleman, I credit him.

K. RICH. Northumberland, say thus,—the king returns,—
His noble cousin is right welcome hither;
And all the number of his fair demands
Shall be accomplish'd without contradiction:
With all the gracious utterance thou hast,
Speak to his gentle hearing kind commends.—
We do debase ourself, cousin, do we not, [*To* AUMERLE.
To look so poorly, and to speak so fair?
Shall we call back Northumberland, and send
Defiance to the traitor, and so die?

AUM. No, good my lord; let's fight with gentle words,
Till time lend friends, and friends their helpful swords.

K. RICH. O God! O God! that e'er this tongue of mine,
That laid the sentence of dread banishment
On yon proud man, should take it off again
With words of sooth![b] O, that I were as great
As is my grief, or lesser than my name!
Or that I could forget what I have been!
Or not remember what I must be now!
Swell'st thou, proud heart? I'll give thee scope to beat,
Since foes have scope to beat both thee and me.

AUM. Northumberland comes back from Bolingbroke.

K. RICH. What must the king do now? Must he submit?
The king shall do it. Must he be depos'd?
The king shall be contented. Must he lose
The name of king? o' God's name, let it go:
I'll give my jewels for a set of beads,
My gorgeous palace, for a hermitage,
My gay apparel, for an alms-man's gown,
My figur'd goblets, for a dish of wood,
My sceptre, for a palmer's walking-staff,
My subjects, for a pair of carved saints,
And my large kingdom, for a little grave,
A little, little, grave, an obscure grave:—
Or I'll be buried in the king's highway,
Some way of common trade,[c] where subjects' feet
May hourly trample on their sovereign's head:
For on my heart they tread, now whilst I live;
And, buried once, why not upon my head?
Aumerle, thou weep'st; my tender-hearted cousin!
We'll make foul weather with despised tears;
Our sighs, and they, shall lodge[d] the summer corn,
And make a dearth in this revolting land.
Or shall we play the wantons with our woes,
And make some pretty match with shedding tears?
As thus;—To drop them still upon one place,
Till they have fretted us a pair of graves
Within the earth; and, therein laid,—*There lies
Two kinsmen, digg'd their graves with weeping eyes?*

(*) First folio, *is*.

[a] The purple testament of bleeding war;] Steevens believed that *testament* is here used in its legal sense, but Mr. Whiter, in his ingenious "Specimen of a Commentary on Shakspeare," quotes a parallel passage from the first part of the old play "Jeronimo,"—

"Then I *unclasp* the *purple leaves of war;*"

and remarks, "Whatever be the *direct* meaning of the words in question, I am persuaded that the idea of a *book* with a *purple* covering suggested this combination to the mind of our poet."

[b] *With words of* sooth!] *Sooth*, from the Anglo Saxon *sóth*, primarily meant *truth*, as in *soothsayer*=truth-teller; in this place it signifies *sweetness*, or *softness*, as in the verb to *soothe*.

[c] *Some way of common* trade,—] That is, a place of *common resort*, as we now talk of,

"A road of frequent traffic."

Thus in Lord Surrey's Translation of the Second Book of the Æneid:

"A postern with a blind wicket there was,
A *common trade*, to pass through Priam's house."

[d] *Shall* lodge *the summer corn*,—] Corn beaten down by rain or wind in modern language is said to be *lay'd*. Formerly *lodg'd* had the same import. So, in "Macbeth," Act IV. Sc. 1:—

"Though bladed corn be *lodg'd*."

And again, in "Henry VI." Part II. Act III. Sc. 2:—

"Like to the summer corn by tempest *lodg'd*."

Would not this ill, do well?—Well, well, I see
I talk but idly, and you mock at me.—
Most mighty prince, my lord Northumberland,
What says king Bolingbroke? will his majesty
Give Richard leave to live till Richard die?
You make a leg, and Bolingbroke says—*ay*.

NORTH. My lord, in the base[a] court he doth attend
To speak with you; may it please you to come down?

K. RICH. *Down?* down, I come; like glistering Phaeton,
Wanting the manage[b] of unruly jades.
[NORTH. *retires to* BOLING.
In the base court? Base court, where kings grow base,
To come at traitors' calls, and do them grace.
In the base court? Come down? Down court! down king!
For night-owls shriek, where mounting larks should sing. [*Exeunt from above.*

BOLING. What says his majesty?

NORTH. Sorrow, and grief of heart,
Makes him speak fondly, like a frantic man:
Yet he is come.

Enter KING RICHARD, *and his* Attendants, *below.*

BOLING. Stand all apart,
And show fair duty to his majesty.——
My gracious lord,— [*Kneeling.*

K. RICH. Fair cousin, you debase your princely knee,
To make the base earth proud with kissing it:
Me rather had my heart might feel your love,
Than my unpleas'd eye see your courtesy.
Up, cousin, up; your heart is up, I know,
Thus high at least, [*touching his own head*] although your knee be low.

[a] *In the* base *court*—] *Base* court is simply *lower* court, from the French, *basse cour.*

[b] Wanting the manage—] *i.e.* Not possessing the control.

BOLING. My gracious lord, I come but for mine own.

K. RICH. Your own is yours, and I am yours, and all. [lord,

BOLING. So far be mine, my most redoubted
As my true service shall deserve your love.

K. RICH. Well you deserve:*—They well deserve to have,
That know the strong'st and surest way to get.
Uncle, give me your hand: nay, dry your eyes;
Tears show their love, but want their remedies.—
Cousin, I am too young to be your father,
Though you are old enough to be my heir.
What you will have, I'll give, and willing too;
For do we must, what force will have us do.—
Set on towards London:—Cousin, is it so?

BOLING. Yea, my good lord.

K. RICH. Then I must not say, no.(3)
[*Flourish. Exeunt.*

SCENE IV.—Langley. *The Duke of* York's *Garden.*

Enter the QUEEN *and two* Ladies.

QUEEN. What sport shall we devise here in this garden,
To drive away the heavy thought of care?

1 LADY. Madam, we'll play at bowls. [of rubs,

QUEEN. 'Twill make me think the world is full
And that my fortune runs against the bias.

1 LADY. Madam, we'll dance.

QUEEN. My legs can keep no measure in delight,
When my poor heart no measure keeps in grief:
Therefore, no dancing, girl; some other sport.

1 LADY. Madam, we'll tell tales.

QUEEN. Of joy or grief?[a]

1 LADY. Of either, madam.

QUEEN. Of neither, girl:
For if of joy, being altogether wanting,
It doth remember me the more of sorrow;
Or if of grief, being altogether had,
It adds more sorrow to my want of joy:
For what I have, I need not to repeat;
And what I want, it boots not to complain.

1 LADY. Madam, I'll sing.

QUEEN. 'Tis well that thou hast cause;
But thou shouldst please me better wouldst thou weep. [good.

1 LADY. I could weep, madam, would it do you

QUEEN. And I could sing, would weeping do me good,[b]
And never borrow any tear of thee.
But stay, here come the gardeners:
Let's step into the shadow of these trees.—

Enter a Gardener *and two* Servants.

My wretchedness unto a row of pins,
They'll talk of state: for every one doth so
Against a change: woe is forerun with woe.
[QUEEN *and* Ladies *retire.*

GARD. Go, bind thou up yon' dangling apricocks,
Which, like unruly children, make their sire
Stoop with oppression of their prodigal weight:
Give some supportance to the bending twigs.
Go thou, and, like an executioner,
Cut off the heads of too-fast-growing sprays,
That look too lofty in our commonwealth:
All must be even in our government.
You thus employ'd, I will go root away
The noisome weeds, that without profit suck
The soil's fertility from wholesome flowers.

1 SERV. Why should we, in the compass of a pale,
Keep law, and form, and due proportion,
Showing, as in a model, our firm estate?
When our sea-walled garden, the whole land,
Is full of weeds; her fairest flowers chok'd up,
Her fruit-trees all unprun'd, her hedges ruin'd,
Her knots[c] disorder'd, and her wholesome herbs
Swarming with caterpillars?

GARD. Hold thy peace:—
He that hath suffer'd this disorder'd spring
Hath now himself met with the fall of leaf:
The weeds, that his broad-spreading leaves did shelter,
That seem'd, in eating him, to hold him up,
Are pluck'd* up, root and all, by Bolingbroke;
I mean the earl of Wiltshire, Bushy, Green.

1 SERV. What, are they dead?

GARD. They are; and Bolingbroke
Hath† seiz'd the wasteful king.—Oh! what pity is it,
That he had not so trimm'd and dress'd his land,
As we this garden! We[d] at time of year
Do‡ wound the bark, the skin of our fruit-trees;
Lest, being over-proud in § sap and blood,
With too much riches it confound itself:
Had he done so to great and growing men,

(*) First folio, *deserv'd.*

a Of joy or grief?] All the old copies read, "Of *sorrow or of* grief." The text adopted here is the amendment of Capell.

b *And I could* sing, *would weeping do me good,*—] The reading of all the old copies; but which Pope, perhaps without necessity, altered to "I could *weep*," &c. The meaning appears to be this:—Were my griefs of so light a nature that weeping would remedy them, I could sing for joy, and would never ask any one to shed a tear for me. It may be worth considering, however, whether the poet did not write,—

"And I could sing, would *singing* do me good."

(*) First folio, *pull'd.* (†) First folio, *Hast.* (‡) First folio, *And.* (§) First folio, *with.*

c *Her knots disorder'd,*—] Knots, as we have before explained (see note (a) p. 55), were the intricate figures into which the beds of a garden were formed in old fashioned horticulture.

d We *at time of year*—] *We,* wanting in the old copies, was supplied by Capell.

They might have liv'd to bear, and he to taste,
The fruits of duty. Superfluous branches
We lop away, that bearing boughs may live:
Had he done so, himself had borne the crown,
Which waste of* idle hours hath quite thrown
down. [be depos'd?
1 SERV. What, think you then,† the king shall
GARD. Depress'd he is already; and depos'd,
'Tis doubt‡ he will be. Letters came last night
To a dear friend of the good§ duke of York's,
That tell black tidings.
QUEEN. O, I am press'd to death through want
of speaking!—
Thou, old Adam's likeness, [*Coming forward*] set
to dress this garden,
How dares thy harsh rude tongue sound this
unpleasing news?
What Eve, what serpent hath suggested thee
To make a second fall of cursed man?
Why dost thou say, King Richard is depos'd?
Dar'st thou, thou little better thing than earth,
Divine his downfall? Say where, when, and how
Cam'st thou by these‖ ill-tidings? speak, thou
wretch.
GARD. Pardon me, madam: little joy have I
To breathe this¶ news: yet what I say is true.
King Richard, he is in the mighty hold
Of Bolingbroke; their fortunes both are weigh'd:
In your lord's scale, is nothing but himself,
And some few vanities that make him light;
But in the balance of great Bolingbroke,
Besides himself, are all the English peers,
And with that odds he weighs King Richard down.
Post you to London, and you'll find it so:
I speak no more than every one doth know. [foot,
QUEEN. Nimble mischance, that art so light of
Doth not thy embassage belong to me,
And am I last that knows it? O, thou think'st
To serve me last, that I may longest keep
Thy sorrow in my breast. Come, ladies, go,
To meet, at London, London's king in woe.
What! was I born to this! that my sad look
Should grace the triumph of great Bolingbroke?
Gardener, for telling me this news[a] of woe,
Pray God* the plants thou graft'st, may never grow.
[*Exeunt* QUEEN *and* Ladies.
GARD. Poor queen! so that thy state might be
no worse,
I would my skill were subject to thy curse.—
Here did she fall† a tear; here, in this place,
I'll set a bank of rue, sour herb of grace:
Rue, even for ruth, here shortly shall be seen,
In the remembrance of a weeping queen.
[*Exeunt.*

(*) First folio, *and*. (†) First folio omits, *then*.
(‡) First folio, *doubted*. (§) First folio omits, *good*.
(‖) First folio, *this*. (¶) First folio, *these*.

(*) First folio, *I would*. (†) First folio, *drop*.

a This *news*—] Here, as in the instance above, the folio has "*these* news." News appears to have been used by our ancestors either as singular or plural, indifferently.

ACT IV.

SCENE I.—London. Westminster Hall.[a] *The Lords spiritual on the right side of the throne; the Lords temporal on the left: the Commons below.*

Enter BOLINGBROKE, AUMERLE, SURREY, NORTHUMBERLAND, PERCY, FITZWATER, *another* Lord, BISHOP OF CARLISLE, *the* ABBOT OF WESTMINSTER, *and* Attendants. Officers *behind, with* BAGOT.

BOLING. Call forth Bagot.——
Now, Bagot, freely speak thy mind;
What thou dost know of noble Gloster's death;
Who wrought it with the king, and who perform'd
The bloody office of his timeless end.

BAGOT. Then set before my face the lord Aumerle.

BOLING. Cousin, stand forth, and look upon that man.

BAGOT. My lord Aumerle, I know your daring tongue
Scorns to unsay what once it hath* deliver'd.
In that dead time when Gloster's death was plotted,
I heard you say,—*Is not my arm of length,*
That reacheth from the restful English court
As far as Calais, to mine uncle's head?*—
Amongst much other talk, that very time,
I heard you say, that you had rather refuse
The offer of an hundred thousand crowns,
Than Bolingbroke's return to England; adding withal,
How bless'd this land would be in this your cousin's death.

AUM. Princes, and noble lords,
What answer shall I make to this base man?
Shall I so much dishonour my fair stars,[b]
On equal terms to give him chastisement?
Either I must, or have mine honour soil'd

(*) First folio, *it hath once.*

(*) First folio, *my.*

a Westminster Hall.] The rebuilding of this magnificent Hall was begun by Richard II. in 1397; it was finished in 1399, and the first assemblage of Parliament in the new edifice was for the purpose of deposing him.

b *My fair stars,*—] As the birth of an individual was supposed to be influenced by the *stars,* the latter, not unnaturally, was a term sometimes used to express the former. Thus, in "Richard III." Sc. 7, Gloster, speaking of his nephew, the heir to the crown, says:—

"On him I lay what you would lay on me,
The right and fortune of his happy stars."

With the attainder of his slanderous lips.
There is my gage, the manual seal of death,
That marks thee out for hell: I say,[a] thou liest,
And will maintain what thou hast said, is false,
In thy heart-blood, though being all too base
To stain the temper of my knightly sword.

BOLING. Bagot, forbear, thou shalt not take it up.

AUM. Excepting one, I would he were the best
In all this presence, that hath mov'd me so.

FITZ. If that thy valour stand on sympathy,[b]
There is my gage, Aumerle, in gage to thine:
By that fair sun which* shows me where thou stand'st,
I heard thee say, and vauntingly thou spak'st it,
That thou wert cause of noble Gloster's death.
If thou deny'st it, twenty times thou liest;
And I will turn thy falsehood to thy heart,
Where it was forged, with my rapier's point.

AUM. Thou dar'st not, coward, live to see the day.

FITZ. Now, by my soul, I would it were this hour.

AUM. Fitzwater, thou art damn'd to hell for this.

PERCY. Aumerle, thou liest; his honour is as true,
In this appeal, as thou art all unjust:
And, that thou art so, there I throw my gage,
To prove it on thee to the extremest point
Of mortal breathing; seize it, if thou dar'st.

AUM. And if I do not, may my hands rot off,
And never brandish more revengeful steel
Over the glittering helmet of my foe!

LORD. I task the earth to the like, forsworn Aumerle;[c]
And spur thee on with full as many lies
As † may be holla'd in thy treacherous ear
From sun to sun: ‡ there is my honour's pawn;
Engage it to the trial, if thou dar'st.

AUM. Who sets me else? by heaven, I'll throw at all:
I have a thousand spirits in one breast,
To answer twenty thousand such as you.

SURREY. My lord Fitzwater, I do remember well
The very time Aumerle and you did talk.

FITZ. 'Tis very true:[d] you were in presence then;
And you can witness with me, this is true.

SURREY. As false, by heaven, as heaven itself is true.

FITZ. Surrey, thou liest.

SURREY. Dishonourable boy!
That lie shall lie so heavy on my sword,
That it shall render vengeance and revenge,
Till thou the lie-giver, and that lie, do lie
In earth, as quiet as thy father's skull.
In proof whereof, there is mine honour's pawn;
Engage it to the trial, if thou dar'st.

FITZ. How fondly dost thou spur a forward horse!
If I dare eat, or drink, or breathe, or live,—
I dare meet Surrey in a wilderness,[e]
And spit upon him, whilst I say, he lies,
And lies, and lies: there is my bond of faith,
To tie thee to my strong correction.
As I intend to thrive in this new world,
Aumerle is guilty of my true appeal:
Besides, I heard the banish'd Norfolk say
That thou, Aumerle, didst send two of thy men
To execute the noble duke at Calais.

AUM. Some honest Christian trust me with a gage,
That Norfolk lies: here do I throw down this,
If he may be repeal'd to try his honour.

BOLING. These differences shall all rest under gage,
Till Norfolk be repeal'd: repeal'd he shall be,
And, though mine enemy, restor'd again
To all his land and seignories; when he's return'd,
Against Aumerle we will enforce his trial.

CAR. That honourable day shall ne'er be seen.
Many a time hath banish'd Norfolk fought
For Jesu Christ, in glorious Christian field,
Streaming the ensign of the Christian cross,
Against black pagans, Turks, and Saracens:
And, toil'd with works of war, retired himself
To Italy; and there, at Venice, gave
His body to that pleasant country's earth,
And his pure soul unto his captain Christ,
Under whose colours he had fought so long.

BOLING. Why, Bishop, is Norfolk dead?

CAR. As surely* as I live, my lord.

BOLING. Sweet peace conduct his sweet soul to the bosom

(*) First folio, *that*. (†) Old copies, *As it may*. (‡) Old copies, *sinne to sinne*.

(*) First folio, *sure*.

a I say, *thou liest*,—] The folio, and other early editions, except the first quarto, omit the words, *I say*.

b If that thy valour stand on sympathy,—] The use of *sympathy*, in the sense of equality, is peculiar. Aumerle affects to think it a derogation from his high birth to accept the defiance of Bagot; whereupon Fitzwater, whose pretensions to blood equal Aumerle's, flings down his gauntlet, with the taunt,—

"If that thy valour stand on *sympathy*,
There is my gage."

The folio 1623 reads, *sympathize*.

c LORD. I task the earth, &c.] This speech, and Aumerle's answer, are omitted in the folio. And all the quartos, except the first, read, "I *take* the earth."—By "*task* the earth," we are apparently to understand, "challenge the whole world."

d 'Tis very true:] So the quarto. The folio reads, *My lord*, 'tis very true.

e *I dare meet Surrey in a* wilderness,—] So, in Beaumont and Fletcher's play of "The Lovers' Progress," Act V. Sc. 2:—

"Maintain thy treason with thy sword? With what
Contempt I hear it! in a *wilderness*
I durst encounter it."

Of good old Abraham!—Lords appellants,
Your differences shall all rest under gage,
Till we assign you to your days of trial.

Enter YORK, *attended.*

YORK. Great duke of Lancaster, come to thee
From plume-pluck'd Richard; who with willing soul
Adopts thee heir, and his high sceptre yields
To the possession of thy royal hand:
Ascend his throne, descending now from him,—
And long live Henry, of that name the fourth!

BOLING. In God's name, I'll ascend the regal throne.

CAR. Marry, God * forbid!—
Worst in this royal presence may I speak,
Yet best, beseeming me to speak the truth.
Would God, that any in this noble presence
Were enough noble to be upright judge
Of noble Richard; then true noblesse † would
Learn him forbearance from so foul a wrong.
What subject can give sentence on his king?
And who sits here that is not Richard's subject?
Thieves are not judg'd but they are by to hear,
Although apparent guilt be seen in them;
And shall the figure of God's majesty,
His captain, steward, deputy elect,
Anointed, crowned, planted many years,
Be judg'd by subject and inferior breath,
And he himself not present? O, forfend ‡ it, God,
That, in a Christian climate, souls refin'd
Should show so heinous, black, obscene a deed!
I speak to subjects, and a subject speaks,
Stirr'd up by God * thus boldly for his king.
My lord of Hereford here, whom you call king,
Is a foul traitor to proud Hereford's king:
And if you crown him, let me prophesy,—
The blood of English shall manure the ground,
And future ages groan for this § foul act;
Peace shall go sleep with Turks and infidels,
And, in this seat of peace, tumultuous wars
Shall kin with kin, and kind with kind confound;
Disorder, horror, fear, and mutiny,
Shall here inhabit, and this land be call'd
The field of Golgotha, and dead men's sculls.
O, if you raise || this house against this house,
It will the woefullest division prove
That ever fell upon this cursed earth:
Prevent it, resist it, let ¶ it not be so,
Lest child, child's children, cry against you—woe! (1)

NORTH. Well have you argued, sir; and, for your pains,
Of capital treason we arrest you here:
My lord of Westminster, be it your charge
To keep him safely till his day of trial.
May 't please you, lords, to grant the commons' suit? [a]

BOLING. Fetch hither Richard, that in common view
He may surrender; so we shall proceed
Without suspicion.

YORK. I will be his conduct. [*Exit.*

BOLING. Lords, you that here are under our arrest,
Procure your sureties for your days of answer:
Little are we beholden to your love, [*To* CARLISLE.
And little look'd for at your helping hands.

Re-enter YORK, *with* KING RICHARD, *and* Officers *bearing the crown, &c.*

K. RICH. Alack, why am I sent for to a king,
Before I have shook off the regal thoughts
Wherewith I reign'd? I hardly yet have learn'd
To insinuate, flatter, bow, and bend my limbs: *
Give sorrow leave awhile to tutor me
To this submission. Yet I well remember
The favours [b] of these men: were they not mine?
Did they not sometime cry, *all hail!* to me?
So Judas did to Christ: but he, in twelve,
Found truth in all but one; I, in twelve thousand, none.
God save the king!—Will no man say, *Amen?*
Am I both priest and clerk? well then, *Amen.*
God save the king! although I be not he;
And yet, *Amen,* if heaven do think him me.—
To do what service am I sent for hither?

YORK. To do that office, of thine own good will,
Which tired majesty did make thee offer,—
The resignation of thy state and crown
To Henry Bolingbroke.

K. RICH. Give me the crown.—Here, cousin, seize the crown; [c]
On this side my hand, and on that side yours.
Now is this golden crown like a deep well,
That owes [d] two buckets, filling one another;
The emptier ever dancing in the air,
The other down, unseen, and full of water:
That bucket down, and full of tears, am I,

(*) First folio, *Heaven.* (†) First folio, *nobleness.*
(‡) First folio, *forbid.* (§) First folio, *his.*
(||) First folio, *rear.* (¶) First folio, *and let.*

[a] May't please you, lords, &c.] The remainder of this Act, with the exception of a few lines at the end (see p. 482), forms the "new additions of the parliament scene and the deposing of King Richard," first published in the quarto of 1608.

(*) First folio, *knee.*

[b] *The* favours—] That is, the *countenances,* the *features.*
[c] Give me the crown.—Here, cousin, seize the crown;] This is the reading of the folio. The quarto has only, *Seize the crown.*
[d] *That* owes—] That *owns,* or *possesses.* See note (4), p. 330.

Drinking my griefs, whilst you mount up on high.

BOLING. I thought you had been willing to resign.

K. RICH. My crown I am, but still my griefs are mine:
You may my glories and my state depose,
But not my griefs; still am I king of those.

BOLING. Part of your cares you give me with your crown.

K. RICH. Your cares set up, do not pluck my cares down.
My care is—loss of care, by old care done;
Your care is—gain of care, by new care won:
The cares I give, I have, though given away;
They tend the crown, yet still with me they stay.

BOLING. Are you contented to resign the crown?

K. RICH. Ay, no;—no, ay; for I must nothing be;
Therefore no, no, for I resign to thee.
Now mark me how I will undo myself:—
I give this heavy weight from off my head,
And this unwieldy sceptre from my hand,
The pride of kingly sway from out my heart.
With mine own tears I wash away my balm,
With mine own hands I give away my crown,
With mine own tongue deny my sacred state,
With mine own breath release all duties, rites: *
All pomp and majesty I do forswear,
My manors, rents, revenues, I forego,
My acts, decrees, and statutes, I deny:
God pardon all oaths that are broke to me!
God keep all vows unbroke that swear † to thee!
Make me, that nothing have, with nothing griev'd;
And thou with all pleas'd, that hast all achiev'd!
Long may'st thou live in Richard's seat to sit,
And soon lie Richard in an earthy pit!
God save King Henry, unking'd Richard says,
And send him many years of sunshine days!
What more remains?

NORTH. No more, but that you read [*Offering a paper.*
These accusations, and these grievous crimes,
Committed by your person, and your followers,
Against the state and profit of this land;
That, by confessing them, the souls of men
May deem that you are worthily depos'd.

K. RICH. Must I do so? and must I ravel out
My weav'd-up follies! Gentle Northumberland,
If thy offences were upon record,
Would it not shame thee, in so fair a troop,
To read a lecture of them? If thou wouldst,
There shouldst thou find one heinous article,—
Containing the deposing of a king,
And cracking the strong warrant of an oath.—
Mark'd with a blot, damn'd in the book of heaven:—
Nay, all of you, that stand and look upon me,
Whilst that my wretchedness doth bait myself,
Though some of you, with Pilate, wash your hands,
Showing an outward pity; yet you Pilates
Have here deliver'd me to my sour cross,
And water cannot wash away your sin.

NORTH. My lord, despatch; read o'er these articles.

K. RICH. Mine eyes are full of tears, I cannot see:
And yet salt water blinds them not so much,
But they can see a sort [a] of traitors here.
Nay, if I turn mine eyes upon myself,
I find myself a traitor with the rest:
For I have given here my soul's consent
To undeck the pompous body of a king;
Made glory base, and* sovereignty a slave;
Proud majesty, a subject; state, a peasant.

NORTH. My lord,——

K. RICH. No lord of thine, thou haught, insulting man,
Nor† no man's lord; I have no name, no title,—
No, not that name was given me at the font,—
But 'tis usurp'd.—Alack the heavy day,[b]
That I have worn so many winters out,
And know not now what name to call myself!
O, that I were a mockery king of snow,
Standing before the sun of Bolingbroke,
To melt myself away in water-drops!—
Good king,—great king,—and yet not greatly good,
An if my name ‡ be sterling yet in England,
Let it command a mirror hither straight,
That it may show me what a face I have,
Since it is bankrupt of his [c] majesty.

BOLING. Go, some of you, and fetch a looking-glass. [*Exit an* Attendant.

NORTH. Read o'er this paper, while the glass doth come.

K. RICH. Fiend! thou torment'st me ere I come to hell.

BOLING. Urge it no more, my lord Northumberland.

NORTH. The commons will not then be satisfied.

K. RICH. They shall be satisfied: I'll read enough,
When I do see the very book indeed
Where all my sins are writ, and that's myself.

(*) First folio, *duteous oaths*. (†) First folio, *are made*.

(*) First folio, *a*. (†) First folio, *No, nor*. (‡) First folio, *word*.

[a] *A sort of traitors—*] That is, *a gang, a knot, a crew*. Thus, in "Richard III." Act V. Sc. 3:—

"A *sort* of vagabonds, rascals, and runaways."

[b] Alack the heavy day,—] This is equivalent with, and serves to interpret, the old phrase "*Woe the while*."

[c] *Of* his *majesty*.] With the old writers, *his* was neuter as well as personal; the genitive of *his* and *it* also. *Its* is found but rarely in Shakespeare, though in many more instances than Mr. Trench or Mr. Singer appear to suppose. In the authorized translation of the Bible the word is said never to occur, its place being always supplied by *his* or *thereof*:—"But if the salt have lost *his* savour" (Matt. chap. v. ver. 13). "But if the salt have lost *his* saltness" (Mark, chap. ix. ver. 50).

Re-enter Attendant, *with a glass.*

Give me that glass, and therein will I read.[a]
No deeper wrinkles yet? Hath sorrow struck
So many blows upon this face of mine,
And made no deeper wounds?—O, flattering glass,
Like to my followers in prosperity,
Thou dost beguile me! Was this face the face
That every day under his household roof
Did keep ten thousand men? Was this the face
That, like the sun, did make beholders wink?
Was * this the face that faced so many follies,
And † was at last outfaced by Bolingbroke?
A brittle glory shineth in this face,
As brittle as the glory, is the face;
[*Dashes the glass to the ground.*

For there it is, crack'd in an hundred shivers.
Mark, silent king, the moral of this sport,—
How soon my sorrow hath destroy'd my face.

BOLING. The shadow of your sorrow hath destroy'd
The shadow of your face.

K. RICH. Say that again.
The shadow of my sorrow? Ha! let's see:—
'Tis very true, my grief lies all within,
And these external manners * of laments
Are merely shadows to the unseen grief,
That swells with silence in the tortur'd soul;
There lies the substance: and I thank thee, king,
For thy great bounty, that not only giv'st
Me cause to wail, but teachest me the way
How to lament the cause. I'll beg one boon,

(*) First folio, *Is*. (†) First folio, *That*.

(*) First folio, *manner*.

a And therein will I read.] These words, and two or three other lines of this speech, are omitted in the quartos.

And then be gone, and trouble you no more.
Shall I obtain it?
BOLING. Name it, fair cousin.
K. RICH. *Fair cousin!* I am greater than a king:
For when I was a king, my flatterers
Were then but subjects; being now a subject,
I have a king here to my flatterer.
Being so great, I have no need to beg.
BOLING. Yet ask.
K. RICH. And shall I have?
BOLING. You shall.
K. RICH. Then give me leave to go.
BOLING. Whither?
K. RICH. Whither you will, so I were from [your sights.
BOLING. Go, some of you, convey him to the Tower.
K. RICH. O, good! *Convey!*[a]—Conveyers are [you all,
That rise thus nimbly by a true king's fall.
[*Exeunt* K. RICHARD, *some* Lords, *and a* Guard.

BOLING. On Wednesday next,[b] we solemnly set down
Our coronation: lords, prepare yourselves.(2)
[*Exeunt all but the* Abbot, BISHOP OF CARL. *and* AUM.
ABBOT. A woeful pageant have we here beheld.
CAR. The woe's to come; the children yet unborn
Shall feel this day as sharp to them as thorn.
AUM. You holy clergymen, is there no plot
To rid the realm of this pernicious blot?
ABBOT. My lord,* before I freely speak my mind herein,
You shall not only take the sacrament
To bury mine intents, but also to effect
Whatever I shall happen to devise.
I see your brows are full of discontent,
Your hearts † of sorrow, and your eyes of tears;
Come home with me to supper; I will lay
A plot shall show us all a merry day. [*Exeunt.*

a Convey!—Conveyers *are you all,*—] *Convey*, in Shakespeare's time, was frequently used in a bad sense, implying *fraud*, and *trickery*. Thus Pistol ("Merry Wives of Windsor," Act I. Sc. 3) adopts it as a genteel synonym for filching,—

"*Convey*, the wise it call;"

and Gloster, in "Henry VI." Part I. Act I. Sc. 3, suspecting collusion, remarks,—

"Since Henry's death, I fear there is *conveyance*."

(*) First folio omits, *My lord*. (†) First folio, *heart*.

b On Wednesday next,—] So the enlarged quarto, 1608. In the first edition, 1597, this speech, which there follows that of Northumberland when he arrests the Bishop of Carlisle (see p. 479), is rendered thus:—

"Let it be so, and lo! on Wednesday next,
We solemnly proclaim our coronation:
Lords, be ready, all."

ACT V.

SCENE I.—London. *A Street leading to the* Tower.

Enter Queen *and* Ladies.

Queen. This way the king will come; this is the way
To Julius Cæsar's ill-erected[a] tower,
To whose flint bosom, my condemned lord
Is doom'd a prisoner by proud Bolingbroke:
Here let us rest, if this rebellious earth
Have any resting for her true king's queen.

Enter King Richard *and* Guards.

But soft, but see, or rather do not see,
My fair rose wither: yet look up; behold,
That you in pity may dissolve to dew,
And wash him fresh again with true-love tears.
Ah, thou, the model where old Troy did stand;
Thou map of honour; thou King Richard's tomb,
And not King Richard; thou most beauteous inn,[b]

---

[a] Ill-erected *tower*,—] Steevens' conjecture, that by *ill-erected* was meant *erected for bad purposes*, is extremely plausible.

[b] *Thou most beauteous* inn,—] Steevens surmised that *inn* does not here signify a house of public entertainment, but a dignified mansion. We believe the term was applied without distinction to any building, whether public or private, which was appropriated to human habitation, and that the expression, *beauteous inn*, meant no more than *beauteous abode*. We meet with it in precisely the same sense in "The Lovers' Progress" of Beaumont and Fletcher, Act V. Sc. 3:—

> "She's a book
> To be with care perused; and 't is my wonder,
> If such misshapen guests as Lust and Murder,
> At any price should ever find a lodging
> In such a *beauteous inn!*"

Why should hard-favour'd grief be lodg'd in thee,
When triumph is become an alehouse guest?

K. RICH. Join not with grief, fair woman, do not so,
To make my end too sudden: learn, good soul,
To think our former state a happy dream;
From which awak'd, the truth of what we are
Shows us but this: I am sworn brother,[a] sweet,
To grim necessity; and he and I
Will keep a league till death. Hie thee to France,
And cloister thee in some religious house:
Our holy lives must win a new world's crown,
Which our profane hours here have stricken down.

QUEEN. What! is my Richard both in shape and mind
Transform'd and weakened? Hath Bolingbroke
Depos'd thine intellect? Hath he been in thy heart?
The lion, dying, thrusteth forth his paw,
And wounds the earth, if nothing else, with rage
To be o'erpower'd; and wilt thou, pupil-like,
Take thy correction mildly? kiss the rod;
And fawn on rage with base humility,
Which art a lion, and a king of beasts?

K. RICH. A king of beasts, indeed; if aught but beasts,
I had been still a happy king of men.
Good sometime queen, prepare thee hence for France:
Think I am dead; and that even here thou tak'st,
As from my death-bed, my last living leave.
In winter's tedious nights sit by the fire
With good old folks; and let them tell thee tales
Of woeful ages, long ago betid:
And, ere thou bid good night, to quit their grief,
Tell thou the lamentable tale* of me,
And send the hearers weeping to their beds.
For why, the senseless brands will sympathise
The heavy accent of thy moving tongue,
And, in compassion, weep the fire out:
And some will mourn in ashes, some coal-black,
For the deposing of a rightful king.

Enter NORTHUMBERLAND, *attended.*

NORTH. My lord, the mind of Bolingbroke is chang'd;
You must to Pomfret, not unto the Tower.(1)
And, madam, there is order ta'en for you;
With all swift speed you must away to France.(2)

K. RICH. Northumberland, thou ladder, wherewithal
The mounting Bolingbroke ascends my throne,
The time shall not be many hours of age
More than it is, ere foul sin, gathering head,
Shall break into corruption. Thou shalt think,
Though he divide the realm, and give thee half,
It is too little, helping him to all:
He shall think, that thou, which knowest the way
To plant unrightful kings, wilt know again,
Being ne'er so little urg'd, another way
To pluck him headlong from the usurped throne.
The love of wicked friends converts to fear;
That fear to hate; and hate turns one, or both,
To worthy danger, and deserved death.

NORTH. My guilt be on my head, and there an end.
Take leave, and part; for you must part forthwith.

K. RICH. Doubly divorc'd?—Bad men, ye violate
A twofold marriage; 'twixt my crown and me;
And then betwixt me and my married wife.
Let me unkiss the oath 'twixt thee and me;
And yet not so, for with a kiss 'twas made.
Part us, Northumberland; I, towards the north,
Where shivering cold and sickness pines the clime;
My wife* to France; from whence, set forth in pomp,
She came adorned hither like sweet May,
Sent back like Hallowmas, or short'st of day.

QUEEN. And must we be divided? must we part?

K. RICH. Ay, hand from hand, my love, and heart from heart.

QUEEN. Banish us both, and send the king with me.

NORTH. That were some love, but little policy.

QUEEN. Then whither he goes, thither let me go.

K. RICH. So two, together weeping, make one woe.
Weep thou for me in France, I for thee here;
Better far off, than—near be, ne'er the near.[b]
Go, count thy way with sighs; I mine with groans.

QUEEN. So longest way shall have the longest moans.

K. RICH. Twice for one step I'll groan, the way being short,
And piece the way out with a heavy heart.
Come, come, in wooing sorrow let's be brief,
Since, wedding it, there is such length in grief.
One kiss shall stop our mouths, and dumbly part;

(*) First folio, *fall.*

(*) First folio, *queen.*

[a] Sworn brother,—] *Sworn brother* came originally from the *fratres jurati,* military adventurers who bound themselves by mutual obligation to share each others' fortunes. When William the Conqueror invaded England, Robert de Oily and Roger de Ivery were *fratres jurati,* and the former gave one of the honours he received to his sworn brother, Roger.

[b] Near be, ne'er the near.] That is, *be near, but never the nigher.* A proverbial saying implying, to come near the object, yet never achieve it. Thus, in Ben Jonson's Epilogue to "The Tale of a Tub:"—

"Wherein the poet's fortune is, I fear,
Still to be early up but ne'er the near."

Thus give I mine, and thus take I thy heart.
[*They kiss.*

QUEEN. Give me mine own again; 't were no good part,
To take on me to keep, and kill thy heart.
[*Kiss again.*
So, now I have mine own again, begone,
That I may strive to kill it with a groan.

K. RICH. We make woe wanton with this fond delay;
Once more, adieu; the rest, let sorrow say.
[*Exeunt.*

SCENE II.—*The same. A Room in the Duke of* York's *Palace.*

Enter YORK *and his* DUCHESS.

DUCH. My lord, you told me you would tell the rest,
When weeping made you break the story off,
Of our two cousins coming into London.

YORK. Where did I leave?

DUCH. At that sad stop, my lord,
Where rude misgovern'd hands, from windows' tops,
Threw dust and rubbish on King Richard's head.

YORK. Then, as I said, the duke, great Bolingbroke,
Mounted upon a hot and fiery steed,
Which his aspiring rider seem'd to know,
With slow but stately pace, kept on his course,
While all tongues cried—*God save thee, Bolingbroke!*
You would have thought the very windows spake,
So many greedy looks of young and old,
Through casements darted their desiring eyes
Upon his visage; and that all the walls,
With painted imagery had said at once,—
Jesu preserve thee! welcome, Bolingbroke!
Whilst he, from one side to the other turning,
Bare-headed, lower than his proud steed's neck,
Bespake them thus,—*I thank you, countrymen:*
And thus still doing, thus he pass'd along.

DUCH. Alack,* poor Richard! where rode† he the whilst?

YORK. As in a theatre,[a] the eyes of men,
After a well-grac'd actor leaves the stage,
Are idly bent on him that enters next,
Thinking his prattle to be tedious:—
Even so, or with much more contempt, men's eyes
Did scowl on Richard; no man cried, God save him;
No joyful tongue gave him his welcome home,
But dust was thrown upon his sacred head;
Which with such gentle sorrow he shook off,
His face still combating with tears and smiles,
The badges of his grief and patience,
That had not God, for some strong purpose, steel'd
The hearts of men, they must perforce have melted,
And barbarism itself have pitied him.
But heaven hath a hand in these events;
To whose high will we bound our calm contents.(3)
To Bolingbroke are we sworn subjects now,
Whose state and honour I for aye allow.

DUCH. Here comes my son Aumerle.

YORK. Aumerle that was;[b]
But that is lost, for being Richard's friend,
And, madam, you must call him Rutland now:
I am in parliament pledge for his truth,
And lasting fealty to the new-made king.

Enter AUMERLE.

DUCH. Welcome, my son. Who are the violets now,
That strew the green lap of the new-come spring?

AUM. Madam, I know not, nor I greatly care not;
God knows, I had as lief be none, as one.

YORK. Well, bear you well in this new spring of time,
Lest you be cropt before you come to prime.
What news from Oxford? hold those justs and triumphs?

AUM. For aught I know, my lord, they do.

YORK. You will be there, I know.

AUM. If God prevent it not; I purpose so.

YORK. What seal is that, that hangs without thy bosom?[c]
Yea, look'st thou pale? let me see the writing.

AUM. My lord, 't is nothing.

YORK. No matter then who sees it:
I will be satisfied,—let me see the writing.

AUM. I do beseech your grace to pardon me;
It is a matter of small consequence,
Which for some reasons I would not have seen.

YORK. Which for some reasons, sir, I mean to see.
I fear, I fear,—

DUCH. What should you fear?
'T is nothing but some bond, that he is enter'd into

(*) First folio, *Alas.* (†) First folio, *rides.*

a As in a theatre,—] "The painting of this description is so lively, and the words so moving, that I have scarce read anything comparable to it in any other language."—DRYDEN.

b Aumerle that was;] We learn from Holinshed that the dukes of Aumerle, Surrey, and Exeter, were deprived of their dukedoms by an act of Henry's first parliament, but were allowed to retain the earldoms of *Rutland*, Kent, and Huntingdon.

c *What seal is that, that* hangs without thy bosom?] The seals on deeds were in old time not impressed on the documents themselves, but appended to them by labels or slips of parchment. See note (c), p. 200.

For gay apparel, 'gainst the triumph day.*

YORK. Bound to himself? what doth he with a bond
That he is bound to? Wife, thou art a fool.—
Boy, let me see the writing.

AUM. I do beseech you, pardon me; I may not show it.

YORK. I will be satisfied; let me see it, I say.
[*Snatches it, and reads.*
Treason! foul treason!—villain! traitor! slave!

DUCH. What is the matter, my lord?

YORK. Ho! who's within there?

Enter a Servant.

Saddle my horse.
God† for his mercy! what treachery is here!

DUCH. Why, what is't, my lord?

YORK. Give me my boots, I say; saddle my horse:—
Now by mine honour, by‡ my life, my troth,
I will appeach the villain. [*Exit* Servant.

DUCH. What's the matter?

YORK. Peace, foolish woman.

DUCH. I will not peace:—What is the matter, son?

AUM. Good mother, be content: it is no more
Than my poor life must answer.

DUCH. Thy life answer!

Re-enter Servant, *with boots.*

YORK. Bring me my boots, I will unto the king.

DUCH. Strike him, Aumerle.—Poor boy, thou art amaz'd:
Hence, villain! never more come in my sight.—
[*To the* Servant.

YORK. Give me my boots, I say.

DUCH. Why, York, what wilt thou do?
Wilt thou not hide the trespass of thine own?
Have we more sons? or are we like to have?
Is not my teeming date drunk up with time?
And wilt thou pluck my fair son from mine age,
And rob me of a happy mother's name?
Is he not like thee? is he not thine own?

YORK. Thou fond mad woman,
Wilt thou conceal this dark conspiracy?
A dozen of them here have ta'en the sacrament,
And interchangeably set down their hands,
To kill the king at Oxford.

DUCH. He shall be none;
We'll keep him here: then what is that to him?

YORK. Away, fond[a] woman! were he twenty times my son,
I would appeach him.

DUCH. Hadst thou groan'd for him,
As I have done, thou'dst be more pitiful.
But now I know thy mind; thou dost suspect
That I have been disloyal to thy bed,
And that he is a bastard, not thy son.
Sweet York, sweet husband, be not of that mind:
He is as like thee as a man may be,
Not like to me, nor any of my kin,
And yet I love him.

YORK. Make way, unruly woman! [*Exit.*

DUCH. After, Aumerle! mount thee upon his horse;
Spur, post, and get before him to the king,
And beg thy pardon ere he do accuse thee.
I'll not be long behind; though I be old,
I doubt not but to ride as fast as York:
And never will I rise up from the ground,
Till Bolingbroke have pardon'd thee: Away!
Begone. [*Exeunt.*

SCENE III.—Windsor. *A Room in the Castle.*

Enter BOLINGBROKE, *as* King; PERCY, *and other* Lords.

BOLING. Can no man tell of my unthrifty son?(4)
'T is full three months since I did see him last:
If any plague hang over us, 'tis he.
I would to God,* my lords, he might be found:
Inquire at London, 'mongst the taverns there,
For there, they say, he daily doth frequent,
With unrestrained loose companions—
Even such, they say, as stand in narrow lanes,
And beat† our watch, and rob‡ our passengers;
Which he, young, wanton, and effeminate boy,
Takes on the point of honour, to support
So dissolute a crew.[b]

PERCY. My lord, some two days since I saw the prince,
And told him of these triumphs held at Oxford.

BOLING. And what said the gallant?

PERCY. His answer was,—he would unto the stews,
And from the commonest creature pluck a glove,
And wear it as a favour; and with that
He would unhorse the lustiest challenger.

BOLING. As dissolute as desperate: yet through both,
I see some sparkles of a better hope,[c]

(*) First folio omits, *day*. (†) First folio, *Heaven*. (‡) First folio omits, *by*.

[a] Fond *woman!*] *Fond* is here used for *foolish*,—perhaps its original meaning. Chaucer has *fonne* for fool, and Skelton, both *fonne, fon*, and *fonde*, in the same sense.

[b] So dissolute a crew.] This seems to have been part of a line which was intended to be cancelled, or to supply the place of:

(*) First folio, *Heaven*. (†) First folio, *rob*. (‡) First folio, *beat*.

"*Even such they say.*"
The passage should obviously terminate at *support*.

[c] *I see some* sparkles *of* a *better hope,*—] *Sparkles* is found in three of the quartos, but the first quarto and folio read, *sparkes*; and all the old copies omit the article.

Which elder days may happily bring forth.
But who comes here?

Enter AUMERLE, *hastily.*[a]

AUM. Where is the king?
BOLING. What means
Our cousin, that he stares and looks so wildly?
AUM. God save your grace. I do beseech your majesty,
To have some conference with your grace alone.
BOLING. Withdraw yourselves, and leave us here alone. [*Exeunt* PERCY *and* Lords.
What is the matter with our cousin now?
AUM. For ever may my knees grow to the earth, [*Kneels.*
My tongue cleave to my roof within my mouth,
Unless a pardon, ere I rise, or speak.
BOLING. Intended, or committed, was this fault?
If on the first, how heinous ere it be,
To win thy after-love, I pardon thee.
AUM. Then give me leave that I may turn the key,
That no man enter till my tale be done.
BOLING. Have thy desire.
[AUMERLE *locks the door.*
YORK. [*Without.*][b] My liege, beware; look to thyself;
Thou hast a traitor in thy presence there.
BOLING. Villain, I'll make thee safe. [*Drawing.*
AUM. Stay thy revengeful hand;
Thou hast no cause to fear.
YORK. [*Without.*] Open the door, secure, foolhardy king;
Shall I, for love, speak treason to thy face?
Open the door, or I will break it open.
[BOLINGBROKE *opens the door.*

---

[a] *Hastily.*] The stage direction in some of the old editions is, *Enter* Aumerle *amazed.*

[b] YORK. [*Without.*] The old stage prescript is: "The Duke of York knocks at the door and crieth."

Enter YORK.

BOLING. What is the matter, uncle? speak;
Recover breath; tell us how near is danger,
That we may arm us to encounter it.
YORK. Peruse this writing here, and thou shalt know
The treason that my haste forbids me show.
AUM. Remember, as thou read'st, thy promise past:
I do repent me; read not my name there,
My heart is not confederate with my hand.
YORK. It was, villain, ere thy hand did set it down.—
I tore it from the traitor's bosom, king;
Fear, and not love, begets his penitence:
Forget to pity him, lest thy pity prove
A serpent that will sting thee to the heart.
BOLING. O heinous, strong, and bold conspiracy!
O loyal father of a treacherous son!
Thou sheer,[a] immaculate, and silver fountain,
From whence this stream through muddy passages
Hath held* his current, and defil'd himself!
Thy overflow of good converts to bad;
And thy abundant goodness shall excuse
This deadly blot in thy digressing son.
YORK. So shall my virtue be his vice's bawd;
And he shall spend mine honour with his shame,
As thriftless sons their scraping father's gold.
Mine honour lives when his dishonour dies,
Or my sham'd life in his dishonour lies;
Thou kill'st me in his life, giving him breath,
The traitor lives, the true man's put to death.
DUCH. [*Without.*] What ho, my liege! for God's† sake let me in.
BOLING. What shrill-voic'd suppliant makes this eager cry?
DUCH. A woman, and thine aunt, great king; ['tis I.
Speak with me, pity me, open the door;
A beggar begs that never begg'd before.
BOLING. Our scene is alter'd, from a serious thing,
And now chang'd to *The Beggar and the King.*[b]
My dangerous cousin, let your mother in;
I know she's come to pray for your foul sin.
YORK. If thou do pardon, whosoever pray,
More sins, for this forgiveness, prosper may.
This fester'd joint cut off, the rest rests sound;
This, let alone, will all the rest confound.

(*) First folio, *had*. (†) First folio, *Heaven's*.

[a] *Thou* sheer, *immaculate,—*] *Sheer* meant *pure, unmixed.* Thus in Spenser's "Faerie Queene," B. III. C. 2:—

"Who having viewed in a fountain *shere*
Her face," &c.

[b] The Beggar and the King.] An evident allusion to the ancient ballad called "A Song of a Beggar and a King." See note (5), p. 101.

[c] Ill mayst thou thrive, &c.] This line is not in the folio.

Enter DUCHESS.

DUCH. O king, believe not this hard-hearted man;
Love, loving not itself, none other can.
YORK. Thou frantic woman, what dost thou make here?
Shall thy old dugs once more a traitor rear?
DUCH. Sweet York, be patient. Hear me, gentle liege. [*Kneels.*
BOLING. Rise up, good aunt.
DUCH. Not yet, I thee beseech:
For ever will I kneel* upon my knees,
And never see day that the happy sees,
Till thou give joy; until thou bid me joy,
By pardoning Rutland, my transgressing boy.
AUM. Unto my mother's prayers I bend my knee. [*Kneels.*
YORK. Against them both my true joints bended be. [*Kneels.*
Ill mayst thou thrive, if thou grant any grace![c]
DUCH. Pleads he in earnest? look upon his face;
His eyes do drop no tears, his prayers are in jest;
His words come from his mouth, ours from our breast:
He prays but faintly, and would be denied;
We pray with heart, and soul, and all beside:
His weary joints would gladly rise, I know;
Our knees shall kneel till to the ground they grow:
His prayers are full of false hypocrisy;
Ours of true zeal and deep integrity.
Our prayers do out-pray his; then let them have
That mercy which true prayers ought to have.
BOLING. Good aunt, stand up.
DUCH. Nay, do not say—*stand up;*
Say,† pardon, first; and afterwards, *stand up.*
An if I were thy nurse, thy tongue to teach,
Pardon—should be the first word of thy speech.
I never long'd to hear a word till now;
Say—pardon, king; let pity teach thee how:
The word is short, but not so short as sweet;
No word like pardon, for kings' mouths so meet.
YORK. Speak it in French, king: say, *pardonnez moy.*[d]
DUCH. Dost thou teach pardon pardon to [destroy?
Ah, my sour husband, my hard-hearted lord,
That sett'st the word itself against the word!
Speak, pardon, as 'tis current in our land,

(*) Quarto, *walk*. (†) First folio, *But*.

[d] *Pardonnez* moy.] Moy rhymes here with *destroy*, and this was probably the usual pronunciation of the word formerly. Thus, in Skelton's "Elynour Rummyng," vol. I. p. 113, Dyce's Ed.:—

"She made it as koy
As a lege de *moy.*"

And again, in his "Colyn Cloute," vol. I. p. 348, *ibid.*:—

"And howe Parys of Troy
Daunced a lege de *moy.*"

The chopping [a] French we do not understand.
Thine eye begins to speak, set thy tongue there,
Or, in thy piteous heart plant thou thine ear,
That, hearing how our plaints and prayers do pierce,
Pity may move thee pardon to rehearse.

BOLING. Good aunt, stand up.

DUCH. I do not sue to stand,
Pardon is all the suit I have in hand.

BOLING. I pardon him, as God* shall pardon me.

DUCH. O happy vantage of a kneeling knee!
Yet am I sick for fear: speak it again;
Twice saying pardon doth not pardon twain,
But makes one pardon strong.

BOLING. With all my heart,
I pardon him.[b]

DUCH. A god on earth thou art.

BOLING. But for our trusty brother-in-law, and † the abbot,
With all the rest of that consorted crew,
Destruction straight shall dog them at the heels.
Good uncle, help to order several powers
To Oxford, or where'er these traitors are:
They shall not live within this world, I swear,
But I will have them, if I once know where.
Uncle, farewell,—and cousin mine,[c] adieu:
Your mother well hath pray'd, and prove you true.

DUCH. Come, my old son;—I pray God* make thee new. [*Exeunt.*

SCENE IV.—*The same.*

Enter EXTON *and a* Servant.

EXTON. Didst thou not mark the king, what words he spake?
Have I no friend will rid me of this living fear?
Was it not so?

SERV. These† were his very words.

EXTON. *Have I no friend?* quoth he: he spake it twice.

(*) First folio, *Heaven*. (†) First folio omits, *and*.

[a] The chopping French we do not understand.] This passage has occasioned discussion; *chopping* being supposed a contemptuous epithet applied to the French language. We apprehend the duchess means no more than "we are ignorant how to *chop* or *exchange* French." To *chop* logic, in the sense of interchanging logic, is an old Academic phrase.

(*) First folio, *Heaven*. (†) First folio, *Those*.

[b] With all my heart,
I pardon him.]
The old copies, regardless of the rhyming couplet, read, *I pardon him with all my heart*.

[c] *And cousin* mine, *adieu*:] The word *mine*, prosodially necessary, is the addition of Mr. Collier's MS. Annotator.

And urg'd it twice together; did he not?
SERV. He did.
EXTON. And, speaking it, he wistly look'd on me;
As who should say,[a]—I would thou wert the man
That would divorce this terror from my heart;
Meaning the king at Pomfret. Come, let's go,
I am the king's friend, and will rid[b] his foe.
[*Exeunt.*

SCENE V.—Pomfret. *The Dungeon of the Castle.*

Enter KING RICHARD.

K. RICH. I have been studying how I may[c] compare
This prison, where I live, unto the world:
And, for because[d] the world is populous,
And here is not a creature but myself,
I cannot do it;—yet I'll hammer it out.
My brain I'll prove the female to my soul;
My soul, the father; and these two beget
A generation of still-breeding thoughts,
And these same thoughts people this little world,
In humours like the people of this world,
For no thought is contented. The better sort,—
As thoughts of things divine,—are intermix'd
With scruples, and do set the word* itself
Against the word.*
As thus,—*Come, little ones;* and then again,—
It is as hard to come, as for a camel
To thread the postern of a needle's eye.
Thoughts tending to ambition, they do plot
Unlikely wonders; how these vain weak nails
May tear a passage through the flinty ribs
Of this hard world, my ragged prison walls;
And, for they cannot, die in their own pride.
Thoughts tending to content, flatter themselves
That they are not the first of fortune's slaves,
Nor shall not be the last; like silly beggars,
Who, sitting in the stocks, refuge their shame,—
That many have, and others must sit there:
And in this thought they find a kind of ease,
Bearing their own misfortunes† on the back
Of such as have before endur'd the like.
Thus play I, in one person,* many people,
And none contented. Sometimes am I king;
Then treasons make† me wish myself a beggar,
And so I am. Then, crushing penury
Persuades me I was better when a king;
Then, am I king'd again: and by-and-by,
Think that I am unking'd by Bolingbroke,
And straight am nothing. But, whate'er I be‡
Nor I, nor any man, that but man is, [*Music.*
With nothing shall be pleas'd, till he be eas'd
With being nothing. Music do I hear?
Ha, ha! keep time:—how sour sweet music is,
When time is broke, and no proportion kept!
So is it in the music of men's lives.
And here have I the daintiness of ear,
To check§ time, broke in a disordered string;
But, for the concord of my state and time,
Had not an ear to hear my true time broke.
I wasted time, and now doth time waste me;
For now hath Time made me his numbering clock:
My thoughts are minutes, and, with sighs they jar
Their watches on unto mine eyes, the outward watch,[e]
Whereto my finger, like a dial's point,
Is pointing still, in cleansing them from tears.
Now, sir, the sound that tells what hour it is
Are clamorous groans, which‖ strike upon my heart,
Which is the bell: so sighs, and tears, and groans,
Show minutes, times, and hours:¶—but my time
Runs posting on in Bolingbroke's proud joy,
While I stand fooling here, his jack o' the clock.
This music mads me, let it sound no more;
For, though it have holp madmen to their wits,
In me it seems it will make wise men mad.
Yet blessing on his heart that gives it me!
For 't is a sign of love; and love to Richard
Is a strange brooch in this all-hating world.

Enter Groom.

GROOM. Hail, royal prince!
K. RICH. Thanks, noble peer![f]
The cheapest of us is ten groats too dear.

(*) First folio, *Faith*. (†) First folio, *misfortune*.

(*) First folio, *prison*. (†) First folio, *treason makes*. (‡) First folio, *am*. (§) First folio, *hear*. (‖) First folio, *that*. (¶) First folio, *hours and times*.

[a] As who should say,—] Meaning, "As *one* who should say." This elliptical phrase, so frequent with the old writers, has gone quite out of use.

[b] *And will* rid *his foe.*] That is, *destroy*, or *get rid of*. In this sense we have the word in "Henry VI." Part II. Act V. Sc. 5:—

"As deathsmen you have *rid* this sweet young prince."

And again, in "The Tempest," Act I. Sc. 2.

"——the red plague *rid* you."

[c] *How* I may *compare*—] So the first quarto, 1597. The subsequent quartos and the folio, 1623, read, how *to* compare.

[d] And, for because—] A tautological form of expression no longer current, though very common when Shakespeare wrote.

[e] The outward watch,—] This passage is obscure, and no explication we have seen, nor any we are prepared to suggest, renders it as perspicuous as could be wished. The best is that by Henley:—"There are three ways in which a clock notices the progress of time; viz. by the vibration of the pendulum, the index on the dial, and the striking of the hour. To these, the king, in his comparison, severally alludes; his sighs corresponding to the *jarring* of the pendulum, which at the same time that it *watches*, or numbers, the seconds, marks also their progress in minutes on the dial or outward watch, to which the king compares his eyes; and their want of figures is supplied by a succession of tears, or (to use an expression of Milton) *minute drops:* his finger, by as regularly wiping these away, performs the office of the dial's point:—his clamorous groans are the sounds that tell the hour." In "Henry IV." Part II. *tears* are used in a similar manner:—

"But Harry lives, that shall convert those *tears*,
By number, into *hours* of happiness."

[f] Thanks, noble peer!] See note (c), p. 413.

What art thou? and how comest thou hither,
Where no man never* comes, but that sad dog
That brings me food, to make misfortune live?
GROOM. I was a poor groom of thy stable, king,
When thou wert king; who, travelling towards
York,
With much ado, at length have gotten leave
To look upon my sometimes[a] royal master's face.
O, how it yearn'd my heart, when I beheld,
In London streets, that coronation day,
When Bolingbroke rode on roan Barbary!
That horse that thou so often hast bestrid;
That horse that I so carefully have dress'd.
K. RICH. Rode he on Barbary? Tell me,
gentle friend,
How went he under him?
GROOM. So proudly as if he disdain'd† the ground.[b]
K. RICH. So proud that Bolingbroke was on his
back!
That jade hath eat bread from my royal hand;
This hand hath made him proud with clapping him.
Would he not stumble? Would he not fall down,
(Since pride must have a fall,) and break the neck
Of that proud man that did usurp his back?
Forgiveness, horse! why do I rail on thee,
Since thou, created to be aw'd by man,
Wast born to bear? I was not made a horse,
And yet I bear a burthen like an ass,
Spur-gall'd,* and tir'd, by jauncing[c] Bolingbroke.

Enter Keeper, *with a dish of meat.*

KEEP. Fellow, give place; here is no longer
stay. [*To the* Groom.

(*) First folio, *ever.* (†) First folio, *had disdained.*

[a] Sometimes—] See note (a), p. 396.
[b] So proudly as if he disdain'd the ground.] In the folio, 1623, —"As if he had disdain'd the ground." We should perhaps read,—
"*So proud, as if he had disdain'd the ground.*"

(*) First quarto, *spurn'd, gall'd.*

[c] Jauncing *Bolingbroke.*] Jauncing may mean *hard riding*, as Cotgrave explains *jancer*, "To stir a horse in the stable 'till he sweat withal;" or as our to *jaunt.*

K. Rich. If thou love me, 'tis time thou wert away.

Groom. What my tongue dares not, that my heart shall say. [*Exit.*

Keep. My lord, will 't please you to fall to?

K. Rich. Taste of it first, as thou art* wont to do. [who

Keep. My lord, I dare not; Sir Pierce of Exton,
Lately came from the king, commands the contrary.

K. Rich. The devil take Henry of Lancaster, and thee! [*Strikes the* Keeper.
Patience is stale, and I am weary of it.

Keep. Help, help, help!

Enter Exton, *and* Servants, *armed.*

K. Rich. How now? What means death in this rude assault? [a]
Villain, thine own hand yields thy death's instrument.
[*Snatching a weapon, and killing one of the* Servants.
Go thou, and fill another room in hell.
[*He kills another, then* Exton *strikes him down.*
That hand shall burn in never-quenching fire,
That staggers thus my person.—Exton, thy fierce hand
Hath with the king's blood stain'd the king's own land.
Mount, mount, my soul; thy seat is up on high;
Whilst my gross flesh sinks downward, here to die.(5) [*Dies.*

Exton. As full of valour as of royal blood:
Both have I spill'd; O, would the deed were good!
For now the devil, that told me I did well,
Says that this deed is chronicled in hell.
This dead king to the living king I'll bear;—
Take hence the rest, and give them burial here.
[*Exeunt.*

(*) First folio, *wert.*

[a] How now? &c.] There is some obscurity here. Perhaps we should read, How now? What? mean'st death in this rude assault?

SCENE VI.—Windsor. *A Room in the Castle.*

Flourish. Enter BOLINGBROKE *and* YORK, *with* Lords *and* Attendants.

BOLING. Kind uncle York, the latest news we hear
Is, that the rebels have consum'd with fire
Our town of Cicester [a] in Glostershire;
But whether they be ta'en, or slain, we hear not.

Enter NORTHUMBERLAND.

Welcome, my lord: what is the news?
NORTH. First, to thy sacred state wish I all happiness.
The next news is,—I have to London sent
The heads of Salisbury, Spencer, Blunt, and Kent:
The manner of their taking may appear
At large discoursed in this paper here.
[*Presenting a paper.*
BOLING. We thank thee, gentle Percy, for thy pains;
And to thy worth will add right worthy gains.

Enter FITZWATER.

FITZ. My lord, I have from Oxford sent to London
The heads of Brocas, and Sir Bennet Seely;
Two of the dangerous consorted traitors
That sought at Oxford thy dire overthrow.
BOLING. Thy pains, Fitzwater, shall not be forgot;
Right noble is thy merit, well I wot.

Enter PERCY, *with the* BISHOP OF CARLISLE.

PERCY. The grand conspirator, abbot of Westminster,
With clog of conscience and sour melancholy,
Hath yielded up his body to the grave;
But here is Carlisle living, to abide
Thy kingly doom, and sentence of his pride.
BOLING. Carlisle, this is your doom:—
Choose out some secret place, some reverend room,
More than thou hast, and with it joy thy life;
So, as thou liv'st in peace, die free from strife:
For though mine enemy thou hast ever been,
High sparks of honour in thee have I seen.

Enter EXTON, *with* Attendants *bearing a coffin.*

EXTON. Great king, within this coffin I present
Thy buried fear; herein all breathless lies
The mightiest of thy greatest enemies,
Richard of Bordeaux, by me hither brought.
BOLING. Exton, I thank thee not; for thou hast wrought
A deed of slander,* with thy fatal hand,
Upon my head, and all this famous land.
EXTON. From your own mouth, my lord, did I this deed.
BOLING. They love not poison that do poison need,
Nor do I thee; though I did wish him dead,
I hate the murderer, love him murdered.
The guilt of conscience take thou for thy labour,
But neither my good word, nor princely favour:
With Cain go wander through the shades † of night,
And never show thy head by day nor light.
Lords, I protest, my soul is full of woe
That blood should sprinkle me to make me grow:
Come, mourn with me for that I do lament,
And put on sullen black, incontinent;
I'll make a voyage to the Holy Land,
To wash this blood off from my guilty hand:—
March sadly after; grace my mournings here,
In weeping after this untimely bier. [*Exeunt.*

---

[a] Cicester—] Cirencester is still pronounced according to the spelling in the text. Two tracts published during the civil wars of the seventeenth century also exhibit the same colloquial title:—"A Relation of the Taking of the Town of Cicester, in the County of Gloucester, on Thursday, Feb. 2d, 1642 (1643)"—and "An exact Relation of the Proceedings of the Cavaleers at Cicester, Feb. 14th, 1643."

(*) First folio, *slaughter*. (†) First folio, *shade*.

ILLUSTRATIVE COMMENTS.

ACT I.

(1) SCENE I.—*Old John of Gaunt.*] "Our ancestors, in their estimate of old age, appear to have reckoned somewhat differently from us, and to have considered men as old, whom we should now esteem middle aged. With them, every man that had passed fifty seems to have been accounted an old man. John of Gaunt, who is here introduced in that character with the additional of '*time-honour'd* Lancaster,' was at this time only fifty-eight years old. He was born at Ghent in 1340, and our present play commences in 1398; he died in 1399, aged fifty-nine.

"King Henry is represented by Daniel, in his poem of Rosamond, as extremely old when he had a child by that lady. Henry was born at Mentz in 1133, and died on the 7th of July, 1189, at the age of fifty-six. Robert, Earl of Leicester, is called an old man by Spencer in a letter to Gabriel Harvey in 1582; and the French Admiral Coligny is represented by his biographer, Lord Huntington, as a very old man, though at the time of his death he was but fifty-three.

"These various instances fully ascertain what has been stated, and account for the appellation here given to John of Gaunt. I believe this is made in some measure to arise from its being customary to enter into life, in former times, at an earlier period than we do now. Those who were married at fifteen, had at fifty been masters of a house and family for thirty-five years."—MALONE.

(2.) SCENE I.—

Hast thou, according to thy oath and band,
Brought hither Henry Hereford, thy bold son;
Here to make good the boisterous late appeal,
Which then our leisure would not let us hear,
Against the duke of Norfolk, Thomas Mowbray?]

In a subsequent part of this note, is given Holinshed's account of the circumstances of the particular Appeal of Treason referred to in the preceding passage. But before proceeding to that narrative, it may be desirable to state some of the ancient ceremonies attending such an Appeal when it was made for a Trial by Battle, as it was in the present instance.

An Appeal of Battle, according to the French practice, was an accusation wherein, says Favine, "it is the purpose of one party to call another by the name of a villain before the bench of justice." The appealer, or appellant, thus derived his designation from being the *caller* of another person, whom he affirmed to be guilty of a certain crime; which the accused was then bound either immediately to disprove, or to deny, and to declare his readiness to answer body against body, without resorting to any other remedy;—or else to be regarded as guilty. This process of appeal could be brought for certain crimes only, the chief being treason and murder, and for acts of the commission of which full proof could not be made. If the accuser appealed without any witness to the charge which he brought forward, he was obliged to combat in his own person; but otherwise he might answer by deputy, on adducing one of the many excuses which were allowed to be valid. When the appeal was made, both parties appeared before the judge who heard it, and the accused person was not permitted to leave his presence until he had either satisfied the law that he ought not to have been so appealed, or had engaged to defend his denial by himself or by a substitute. In the fourteenth century, when the French ceremonial of appeals and trial by battle was in its greatest perfection, the Gage or glove was thrown down and taken up at this part of the process, and the accusation and denial pronounced according to established forms, which may be seen in Andrew Favine's "Theatre of Honour and Knighthood." In England these declarations were also reduced to written copies called "bills," which were again produced and sworn to shortly before the combat. The judge was then to receive the gages of the parties, and especially to take good security of the appellant for the pursuit of the appeal; after which the proceedings were laid before the King and Parliament, to order the combat if it were considered to be lawful.

It will be observed in the ensuing extract from Holinshed that pledges were delivered for the Duke of Hereford, the appellant, but that the Duke of Norfolk was not suffered to put in pledges; he being sent to Windsor Castle under arrest. The old French law of Appeals also was, that "he that *followeth the judgment needeth not to give any surety*, in regard that he is the man who, if he bring not the judgment to good effect, he shall lose the judgment, and pay threescore pounds to his lord. But for him that appealed," continues Messire Philip De Beaumanoir, "if the judgment fall foul on his side, he is to pay threescore pounds fine; and to him against whom he made the appeal, threescore pounds more; and if he appeal many men, he must make amends to every man by himself, and the amends to each man is threescore pounds: in which respect it is very requisite that he deliver good security for pursuing his appeal." Such were the general features of this species of process, and the circumstances of the appeal, referred to in this play, are thus related by Holinshed:—

"In the parliament holden at Shrewsburie, Henry duke of Hereford, accused Thomas Mowbraie duke of Norfolke, of certin words which he should utter in talke had betwixt them, as they rode togither latelie before betwixt London and Brainford, sounding highlie to the King's dishonor. And for further proofe thereof, he presented a supplication to the King, *wherein he appealed the duke of Norfolke in field of batell, for a traitor, false and disloiall to the King, and enimie unto the realme.* This supplication was red before both the dukes in presence of the King: which doone, the duke of Norfolke toke upon him to answer it, declaring that whatsoever the duke of Hereford had said against him other than well, he lied falselie like an untrue knight as he was. And when the King asked of the duke of Hereford what he said to it, he taking his hood off his head, said; My sovereigne lord, even as the supplication which I tooke you importeth, right so I saie for truth, that Thomas Mowbraie duke of Norfolke is a traitour, false and disloiall to your roiall maiestie, your crowne and to all the states of your realme.

"Then the duke of Norfolke being asked what he said to this, he answered: 'Right deere lord, with your fauour that I make answer unto your cousine here, I saie (your reverence saved) that Henrie of Lancaster duke of

Hereford, like a false and disloiall traitor as he is, dooth lie, in that he hath or shall say of me otherwise than well.' No more, said the King, we have heard enough; and herewith commanded the duke of Surrie for that turne Marshall of England, to arrest in his name the two dukes: the duke of Lancaster, father to the duke of Hereford, the duke of Yorke, the duke of Aumerle constable of England: and the duke of Surrie, Marshall of the realme, *undertooke as pledges bodie for bodie for the duke of Hereford;* but the duke of Northfolke was not suffered to put in pledges, and so under arrest was led into Windsor castell; and there garded with keepers that were appointed to see him safelie kept."—HOLINSHED, under the year 1398.

(3) SCENE I.—*Since last I went to France to fetch his queen.*] "The Duke of Norfolk was joined in commission with Edward, Earl of Rutland, (the Aumerle of this play,) to go to France in the year 1395, in the King's name, to demand in marriage (Isabel, the queen of our present drama) the eldest daughter of Charles the Sixth, then between seven and eight years of age. The contract of marriage was confirmed by the French King in March, 1396; and in November, 1396, Richard was married to his young consort in the chapel of St. Nicholas, in Calais, by Arundel, Archbishop of Canterbury. His first wife, Anne, daughter to the Emperor of Germany, Charles the Fourth, whom he had married in 1382, died at Shene, on Whitsunday, 1394. His marriage with Isabella, as is manifest from her age, was merely political; and, accordingly it was accompanied with an agreement for a truce between France and England, for thirty years."—MALONE.

(4) SCENE II.—*But empty lodgings and unfurnish'd walls.*] In old castles, the walls of the chambers were covered during the residence of the family with tapestry or arras hung upon tenter hooks, but these hangings were taken down at every removal, and the walls then left quite bare. One department of the king's wardrobe, indeed, was called the "Removing Wardrobe," which consisted principally of the arras that was to be hung up against the naked walls of the king's bedchamber, &c. See Dr. Percy's preface to the Household Book of the fifth Earl of Northumberland.

(5) SCENE III.—

On pain of death, no person be so bold,
Or daring-hardy, as to touch the lists.]

In the Chorus before the commencement of King Henry V., Shakespeare eloquently expresses the impossibility of representing the great events of the play within the narrow limits of his theatre:—

"————Can this cockpit hold
The vasty fields of France? or may we cram
Within this wooden O, the very casques
That did affright the air at Agincourt?"

The poet, however, did not regard himself as being in any such difficulty, when he directed the present scene to consist of "Lists set out, and a throne," for the Trial by Battle between the Dukes of Norfolk and Hereford, on a charge of treason against the former. "The place where the lists were appointed," says Sir William Segar, "was ever upon plaine and drie ground, without ridges, hilles, or other impediments;" and in the present instance they were made on Gosford-green, near Coventry. Such enclosures appear to have received their name originally from the list, or border of cloth covering the rails that staked out the ground. Their established dimensions were sixty paces in length by forty in breadth; and, as those proportions would very far exceed the extent of any stage in Shakespeare's time, we may conceive that whenever this play was performed, the lists, the king's throne, and the champions, very much resembled those in an illumination of the time of Richard II. engraved in Strutt's *Regal and Ecclesiastical Antiquities*, Plate lviii. It represents two figures in complete armour fighting, within a very small octagonal enclosure formed of high posts and rails, on one side of which the king sits on an elevated throne, in his robes, and with his crown and sceptre. Below the king, and close to the lists, are the constable and marshal leaning on the rails and watching the combat.

Shakespeare has twice introduced the ceremonies of the Trial by Battle in his dramas: in the present instance, as taking place between two noblemen of the highest rank, and in the Second Part of Henry VI. between two persons of the lowest degree. In both cases, however, the parties were equals to each other, and both the accusations were for treason, which was always one of the great causes for which combats might be allowed. As each of these trials had ceremonies proper to itself, those relating to the present play only will be considered in this place; and as the text exactly follows "the order of combats for life in England, as they are anciently recorded in the Office of Arms," the reader may probably be interested and amused by a short heraldical commentary on the opening of this scene.

The action commences with Thomas Holland, Duke of Surrey, who officiated on the occasion as Earl Marshal, and Edward Plantagenet, second Duke of Aumerle,—who performed the office of High Constable,—waiting for the arrival of the king. Richard then enters and takes his seat on the throne, for, "on the day of battell," says Segar, "the king used to sit on a high seat or scaffold purposely made, at the foote whereof was another seat for the Constable and Marshall." Richard then orders the Earl Marshal to make the usual enquiries of the Duke of Norfolk, who enters in armour, and some of these speeches are so exceedingly close to the words of the record in the College of Arms, as to make it quite possible that Shakespeare had seen a copy of it. "The challenger did commonly come to the east gate of the lists," continues this ancient document, "and brought with him such armours as were appointed by the Court, and wherewith he was determined to fight. Being at the gate, there he stayed until such time as the Constable and Marshall arose from their seate and went thither. They being come to the said gate of the lists, and beholding the Challenger there, the Constable said, "For what cause art thou come hither thus armed, and what is thy name?" Unto whom the Challenger answered thus: "My name is A. B., and I am hither come armed and mounted to perform my challenge against C. D. and acquit my pledges." It is to be remarked, however that Shakespeare has departed equally from history and the established practice of combats, in bringing in the Duke of Norfolk, who was the defendant, before the Duke of Hereford, the appellant. "The appellant," says Favine, "ought to present himself first in the field, and before mid-day." Mowbray then "takes his seat," which, as the respondent's, was placed on the king's left hand; and Holinshed says that it was of crimson velvet, curtained about with white and red damask, the livery-colours of his family. Bolingbroke enters next, and the same ceremony is repeated of enquiring his name, and the cause of his coming thither in arms. After his reply, the Marshal makes proclamation that none shall touch the lists: but Holinshed states that this was done by a king of arms, and Segar says that the herald pronounced the order by command of the Constable and Marshal at the four corners of the lists.

The next ceremony represented in the play and mentioned by Holinshed, is the delivery of their spears to the combatants, and the sounding of the charge for commencing the battle. But in the official order of such a proceeding, the contending parties had previously to take three oaths before the Constable and Marshal, the king or judge of the fight, and a priest who attended in the middle of the lists with an altar, having on it a crucifix and a copy of the Gospels. The first oath maintained the truth of the contents of the bills given in by the two parties, affirming and denying the charge in question. The second oath was that they had not brought into the lists any other armour or weapons than such as were allowed; nor any unlawful instrument, or charm, or enchantment, for their defence. The third oath was rather a promise in reply to a solemn admonition of the Marshal, that each of the combatants should exert his utmost endeavours to prove by strength and valour the truth of his own cause. Both in France and England about the year 1306 these oaths were appointed to be taken with many imposing ceremonies; after which the lists were cleared by the proclamation of the herald, who also cried out three several times, "Gentlemen, do your devoire." At this signal the combatants mounted, and the Marshal having viewed their spears, to see that they were of equal length, delivered one lance himself to the duke of Hereford, as in the play, and sent the other to the duke of Norfolk by a knight. The last proclamations given in the text, are those of two heralds describing the respective champions; which ended, the Marshal and Constable were to withdraw to their places by the throne, and the former cried out with a loud voice, "Let them go! let them go! let them go! and do their best."

"The duke of Hereford," says Holinshed, "was quicklie horsed and closed his beaver, and cast his speare into the rest; and when the trumpet sounded set forward courageouslie towards his enemie six or seven paces. The duke of Norfolke was not so fullie set forward, when the king cast downe his warder, and the heralds cried 'Ho! Ho!'" This peculiar manner of exercising the sovereign privilege of arresting a Trial by Battle, is illustrated in the ensuing note. The king had the power of taking the quarrel into his own hands, even after the combat had begun, and of making peace between the parties without longer fight. "Then," continues the old ceremonial, "did the Constable lead the one, and the Marshall the other out of the listes at severall gates, armed and mounted as they were, having speciall regard that neither of them should goe the one before the other. For the quarrell resting in the king's hands, might not be renued, nor any violence offered, without prejudice to the king's honour." If the sovereign commanded that the combatants should be parted immediately after he had cast down his warder, two knights and four esquires who were in the lists, in attendance on the Marshall and Constable, were to cross the headless lances which they carried between the contending parties. The cry of the heralds, "Ho! Ho!" for stopping the combat seems to have been very familiar in the time of Elizabeth, for in Robert Laneham's Letter describing the Queen's entertainment at Kenilworth in 1575, the expression is introduced in a manner that is scarcely intelligible.—"Here was no 'Ho,' Master Marten, in devout drinking alway, that brought a lack unlooked for."

The only other ceremony mentioned in this part of the drama requiring illustration, is the command of Richard—

> "Let them lay by their helmets and their spears,
> And both return back to their chairs again,—
> Withdraw with us; and let the trumpets sound,
> While we return these dukes what we decree."

The stage-direction is "a long flourish," by which Shakespeare ingeniously disposed of the two long hours noticed by Holinshed, that passed whilst the combatants remained in their chairs, and "the king and his council deliberately consulted what order was best to be had in so weighty a cause."

(6) SCENE III.—*Stay, the king hath thrown his warder down.*] The ceremony referred to in this passage, is noticed by Favine, in 1620, as being one of those "held and observed in these fields of battaile—forgotten or let sleepe in silence, but to be the better knowne in these times because then they were in full execution." He then proceeds to instance the giving to the King by "the constable or marshall that carrieth command in the field of battaile, a rod, or wand, or warder, *guilded:* which, like to the caduceus of Mercury, being cast in the midst betweene the combattants causeth them to sunder each from other."

In his description of the proceedings connected with the appointed combat between the dukes of Hereford and Mowbray, the poet has closely followed the chronicler.

"The duke of Aumerle, that daie being high constable of England, and the Duke of Surrie, marshall, placed themselves betwixt them, well armed and appointed; and when they saw their time, they first entered into the listes with a great companie of men apparelled in silke sendall, imbrodered with silver, both richlie and curiouslie, everie man having a tipped staffe to keepe the field in order. About the houre of prime came to the barriers of the listes the duke of Herford, mounted on a white courser, barded with greene and blue velvet, imbrodered sumptuouslie with swans and antelops of goldsmiths woorke armed at all points. The constable and marshall came to the barriers, demanding of him what he was,—he answered; I am Henrie of Lancaster duke of Hereford, which am come hither to do mine indevour against Thomas Mowbraie duke of Norfolke, as a traitor untrue to God, the king, his realme, and me. Then, incontinentlie, he sware upon the holie evangelists that his quarrell was true and iust, and upon that point he required to enter the lists. Then he put up his sword, which before he held naked in his hand, and putting downe his visor, made a crosse on his horsse, and with speare in hand, entered into the lists, and descended from his horsse, and set him downe in a chaire of greene velvet, at the one end of the lists, and there reposed himselfe, abiding the comming of his adversarie.

"Soone after him, entered into the field with great triumph king Richard accompanied with all the peeres of the realme, and in his companie was the earle of saint Paule, which was come out of France in post to see this challenge performed. The king had there above ten thousand men in armour, least some fraie or tumult might rise amongst his nobles by quarrelling or partaking. When the king was set in his seat, which was richlie hanged and adorned, a king at arms made open proclamation, prohibiting all men in the name of the king, and of the high constable and marshall, to enterprise or attempt to approch or touch any part of the lists upon paine of death, except such as were appointed to order or marshall the field. The proclamation ended, an other herald cried; Behold here Henrie of Lancaster duke of Hereford appellant, which is entred into the lists roiall to do his devoir against Thomas Mowbraie duke of Norfolke defendant, upon paine to be found false and recreant.

"The duke of Norfolke hovered on horssebacke at the entrie of the lists, his horsse being barded with crimosen velvet, imbrodered richlie with lions of silver and mulberie trees; and when he had made his oth before the constable and marshall that his quarrell was iust and true, he entred the field manfullie saieng alowd; God aid him that hath the right, and then he departed from his horsse, and sate him downe in his chaire, which was of crimosen velvet, courtined about with white and red damaske. The lord marshall viewed their speares to see that they were of equal length, and delivered the one speare himselfe to the duke of Hereford, and sent the other unto the duke of Norfolke by a knight. Then the herald proclamed that the traverses and chaires of the champions should be remooved, commanding them on the kings behalfe to mount on horssebacke, and addresse themselves to the battell and combat.

"The duke of Hereford was quicklie horssed, and closed his bavier, and cast his speare into the rest, and when the trumpet sounded set forward couragiouslie towards his enimie six or seven pases. The duke of Norfolke was not fullie set forward, when the king cast downe his warder, and the heralds cried, Ho, ho. Then the king caused their speares to be taken from them, and commanded them to repaire againe to their chaires, where they remained two long houres, while the king and his councell deliberatlie consulted what order was best to be had in so weightie a cause.

"Finallie, after they had devised, and fullie determined what should be done therein, the heralds cried silence; and sir John Bushie the kings secretarie read the sentence and determination of the king and his councell, in a long roll, the effect wherof was, that Henry duke of Hereford should within fifteene daies depart out of the realme, and not to returne before the terme of ten yeares were expired, except by the king he should be repealed againe, and this upon paine of death; and that Thomas Mowbraie duke of Norfolke, bicause he had sowen sedition in the relme by his words, should likewise avoid the realme, and never to return againe into England, nor approch the borders or confines thereof upon paine of death."—HOLINSHED, 1398.

(7) SCENE III.—*Lay on our royal sword your banish'd hands.*] That is, Place your hands on the cross-hilt of this sword, and swear by all your hopes in that sign of common salvation

"To keep the oath that we administer."

There are two instances in Shakespeare's plays of the very ancient ceremony of Swearing by or on the Sword: the present, which shows the Christian practice, and that in the first act of "Hamlet," which may be properly regarded as belonging to the old customs of Denmark and the northern nations, in their pagan state. The last example will be most appropriately considered in its own place; and therefore the following remarks refer solely to the passage cited above.

The rudiments, as it were, of the modern cross-guard to a sword-handle, were very commonly to be found both in the *Xiphos* of the Greeks, and the *Gladius* of the Romans; and it is probable that this improvement of the weapon was first introduced into Britain by the latter nation; for in the most ancient swords of the British and Irish, where they have been found with the remains of handles and scabbards, there was not space enough for any cross-guard. As this Christian characteristic, however, existed on the Anglo-Saxon weapons before the mission of Augustine, it is possible that he preserved this relique of paganism and converted it into a Christian symbol, in conformity with the prudent counsel of Gregory the Great. He would eagerly adopt the cruciform figure of the weapon, as being especially fitted to make a deep and constant impression on a soldier; and even the pagan practice of swearing "by the edge of a sword," he purified into a solemn oath, to be taken on the cross of the handle; which would thus become a military substitute for the same sign on the cover of a copy of the Gospels. If these conjectures be true, a careful distinction should be made by the actors of "Hamlet" and "Richard II." in the manner in which they present the swords to the parties who are to swear; to mark the difference between the pagan and the Christian ceremonies. In "Hamlet," the oath is by the "edge" of the weapon, according to the old northern form: and the Prince should therefore hold the sword, and Horatio and Marcellus should place their hands on the blade. Retzsch, in his outline of this scene, has represented the characters in these positions; though he has also compromised the act by making the soldiers who are swearing, touch a cross engraved on the blade of the sword close to the handle. In the present play, Richard should hold the sword itself sheathed, and the two dukes should lay their hands on the cross-handle.

In the swords of the Norman period, and the later middle age, the transverse-guard was gradually increased in size, and the centre cross made more important and ornamental; and the badge of the Order of St. James, instituted in A.D. 1158, exhibits a very remarkable example of the close identity between a cross and a sword. The emblem seems to have been universally adopted throughout civilized Europe; and to have been regarded as sacred, down, perhaps, to the commencement of the 17th century. In a note furnished by Steevens, in illustration of the passage in 'Hamlet,' there is a copy of 'the oath taken by a Master of Defence when his degree was conferred on him,' derived from a manuscript in the Sloanian collection, which gives the following old form of a protestation on the sword, but as it had been retained down to the year 1583: 'First you shall sweare—so help you God and Halidome, and by all the christendome which God gave you at the fount-stone, and *by the crosse of this sword, which doth represent unto you the Crosse which our Saviour suffered his most paynefull deathe upon,*—that you shall upholde, maynteyne, and kepe, to your power, all soch articles as shall be heare declared unto you, and receve in the presence of me, your maister, and these the rest of the maisters my brethren, heare with me at this tyme.'"

(8.) SCENE IV.—

——— *If that come short,*
Our substitutes at home shall have blank charters.]

Of the numerous schemes devised by Richard to replenish his exchequer and to oppress obnoxious subjects, none, except the abominable poll-tax, excited such general indignation as the compelling all classes to sign or seal *blank* bonds which the king's officers filled up according to his exigencies or pleasure. Stow records that some of the Commons were mulcted to the extent of a thousand marks, and some were even made to pay as much as a thousand pounds by these intolerable means. But a day of retribution came, and when Bolingbroke, surrounded by the magnates of the church, the greater part of the nobility, and multitudes of the people, appeared at Westminster a claimant for the throne, the "blank charters" were not forgotten:—

"An hundreth thousande cryed all at ones,
At Westmynster to croune hym for kyng,
So hated they king Richard for the nones,
For his mysrule and wrong gouernyng,
For taxes and for *blank charters* sealyng,
For murder of duke Thomas of Woodstoke,
That loved was well more than all the floke."—
HARDYNG'S *Chronicle, chap.* 197.

ACT II.

(1) SCENE I.—*The Duke of York.*] Edmund Duke of York, was the fifth of the seven sons of Edward the Third. He was born in 1441, at Langley, near St. Alban's, in Hertfordshire, and thence derived his surname. From the graphic description given of him by Hardyng the Chronicler, who was a contemporary, he appears to have been of an easy, amiable disposition, and too much devoted to sports and pleasure, to take a willing part in the turbulent transactions of the period in which he lived:—

"Whān all lordes went to counsels and parlement,
He wolde to huntes and also to haukynge,
All gentilnes disporte that myrth appent
He used aie and to the poore supportynge
Wher euer he wase in any place bidynge
Without supprise or any extorciōn
Of the poraile or any oppressiōn.
* * * * * *
The Kynge thān made the Duke of York be name,
Maister of the Mewehouse and of haukes feire
Of his venerie and maister of his game,
In whatt cuntraie that he dide repeire
Whiche wase to hym withoute any dispeire
Well more comforte and a gretter gladenes
Thān beeñ a lorde of worldely grete riches."—
HARL. MS. 661

(2.) SCENE I.—

If you do wrongfully seize Hereford's right,
Call in the letters-patents that he hath
By his attorneys-general to sue
His livery.]

"The duke of Lancaster departed out of this life at the bishop of Elies place in Holborne, and lieth buryed in the cathedral churche of saint Paule in London, on the northside of the high altar, by the die Blanch his first wife. The death of this duke gave occasion of encreasing more hatred in the people of this realme toward the king, for he seased into his handes all the goods that belonged to hym, and also receyved all the rents and revenues of his landes which ought to have descended unto the duke of Hereforde by lawfull inheritaunce, in revoking his letters patents, which he had graunted to him before, by vertue wherof, he might make his attorneis general to *sue livery for hym*, of any maner of inheritaunces or possessions that myghte from thenceforthe fall unto hym, and that hys homage myghte bee respited, wyth making reasonable fine: whereby it was evident, that the king ment his utter undooing.

"Thys harde dealing was much mysliked of all the nobilitie, and cried out against, of the meaner sorte: But namely the Duke of Yorke was therewyth sore amoved, who before this time, had borne things with so pacient a minde as he could, though the same touched him very near, as the death of his brother the duke of Gloucester, the banishment of hys nephewe the said duke of Hereford, and other mo iniuries in greate number, which for the slipperie youth of the king, he passed over for the time, and did forget as well as he might."—HOLINSHED, 1399.

(3) SCENE I.—

With eight tall ships, three thousand men of war,
Are making hither with all due expedience,
And shortly mean to touch our northern shore.]

"There were certeine ships rigged, and made readie for him [the duke of Lancaster] at a place in base Britaine, called Le portblanc, as we find in the chronicles of Britaine: and when all his provision was made readie, he took the sea, togither with the said archbishop of Canturburie and his nephue Thomas Arundell, sonne and heire to the late earle of Arundell, beheaded at the Tower-hill, as you have heard. There were also with him, Reginald, lord Cobham, sir Thomas Erpingham, and sir Thomas Ramston, knights, John Norburie, Robert Waterton, and Francis Coint, esquires; few else were there, for (as some write) he had not past fifteene lances, as they tearmed them in those daies, that is to saie, men of armes, furnished and appointed as the vse then was. Yet other write that the duke of Britaine delivered unto him three thousand men of warre, to attend him, and that he had eight ships well furnished for the warre where Froissard yet speaketh but of three. * * * The duke of Lancaster, after that he had coasted along the shore a certeine time, and had got some intelligence how the people's minds were affected towards him, landed about the beginning of Julie in Yorkshire, at a place sometime called Ravenspur, betwixt Hull and Bridlington, and with him not past threescore persons, as some write: but he was so ioifullie received of the lords, knights, and gentlemen of those parts, that he found means (by their helpe) forthwith to assemble a great number of people, that were willing to take his part. The first that came to him, were the lords of Lincolneshire, and other countries adioining, as the lords Willoughbie, Ros, Darcie, and Beaumont."—HOLINSHED, 1399.

(4) SCENE II.—

Like perspectives, which, rightly gaz'd upon,
Show nothing but confusion,—ey'd awry,
Distinguish form.]

Authorities are at variance as to what these "perspectives" were. Warburton describes them as an optical delusion, consisting of a figure drawn with all the rules of *perspective inverted:* so that, when held in the same position with those pictures which are drawn in accordance with the principles of perspective, it can present nothing but confusion: while to be seen in form, it must be looked upon from a contrary station; or, as Shakespeare says, *ey'd awry*.

Dr. Plot, on the other hand, in his "Natural History of Staffordshire," fol. Oxford, 1686, p. 391, gives the following account of some perspectives he had seen at Lord Gerard's house:—

"At the right Honorable the Lord *Gerards* at *Gerards Bromley*, there are the pictures of *Henry* the great of *France* and his *Queen*, both upon the same *indented board*, which if beheld *directly*, you only perceive a confused piece of work; but if *obliquely*, of one side you see the king's and on the other the queen's picture, which I am told (and not unlikely), were made thus. The *board* being *indented* according to the magnitude of the *Pictures*, the *prints* or *paintings* were cut into *parallel pieces*, equal to the depth and number of the indentures on the board; which being nicely done, the *parallel pieces* of the *king's* picture, were pasted on the *flatts* that strike the eye beholding it *obliquely*, on one side of the *board;* and those of the *queens* on the other; so that the edges of the *parallel pieces* of the prints or paintings exactly joyning on the edges of the *indentures*, the *work* was done."

(5) SCENE IV.—

——————*We have stay'd ten days,*
And hardly kept our countrymen together,
And yet we hear no tidings from the king;
Therefore we will disperse ourselves: farewell.]

"It fortuned at the same time, in which the Duke of Hereford or Lancaster, whether ye list to call him, arrived thus in England, the seas were so troubled by tempests, and the winds blew so contrarie for anie passage, to come over forth of England to the king, remaining still in Ireland, that for the space of six weeks, he received no advertisements from thence: yet at length, when the seas became calme, and the wind once turned aniething favourable, there came over a ship, whereby the king understood the manner of the duke's arrivall, and all his proceedings till that daie, in which the ship departed from the coast of England, whereupon he meant forthwith to have returned over into England, to make resistance against the duke; but through persuasion of the duke of Aumarle (as was thought) he staied till he might have all his ships and other provision, fullie readie for his passage.

"In the meane time he sent the earle of Salisburie over into England, to gather a power togither, by helpe of the king's freends in Wales and Cheshire, with all speed possible, that they might be readie to assist him against the duke upon his arrivall, for he meant himself to follow the earle, within six daies after. The earl passing over into Wales, landed at Conwaie, and sent foorth letters to the kings freends, both in Wales and Cheshire, to leauie their people, and to come with all speed to assist the king, whose request, with great desire, and very willing minds they fulfilled, hoping to have found the king himselfe at Conwaie, insomuch that within four daies space there were to the number of fortie thousand men assembled, readie to march with the king against his enimies, if he had beene there himselfe in person.

"But when they missed the king, there was a brute spred amongst them, that the king was suerlie dead, which wrought such an impression, and evill disposition in the minds of the Welshmen and others, that for anie persuasion which the earle of Salisburie might vse, they would not go foorth with him, till they saw the king; onelie they were contented to staie foureteene daies to see if he should come or not; but when he came not within that tearme, they would no longer abide, but scaled and departed awaie; wheras, if the king had come before their breaking up, no doubt but they would have put the duke of Hereford in adventure of a field: so that the king's lingering of time before his comming over, gave opportunitie to the duke to bring things to passe as he could haue wished, and tooke from the king all occasion to recover afterwards anie forces sufficient to resist him."

Holinshed, from whom the foregoing extract is taken, agrees here in the main with the other historians; but the most entertaining and circumstantial narrative of all the events connected with Richard's sojourn in Ireland, his skirmishes with the Irish chieftain, Macmore, his reception of the terrible news of Bolingbroke's landing, of the people's insurrection, of his tardy return to England, down to his deposition and death, is contained in a manuscript entitled "Histoire du Roy d'Angleterre Richard, Traictant particulierement la Rebellion de ses subiectz et prinse de sa personne. Composee par un gentlehom'e Francois de Marque, qui fut a la suite du dict Roy, avecq permission du Roy de France, 1399." This metrical history, of which a beautifully illuminated copy is preserved in the library of the British Museum, has been ably translated by the Rev. John Webb, and published in vol. xx. of the "Archæologia." From this invaluable contribution to English history, we are tempted to extract the author's account, as witnessed by himself, of the dispersion of the Welsh army:—

"He [the king] sent for the earl of Salisbury, saying, 'Cousin, you must go to England and resist this mad enterprise of the duke, and let his people be put to death, or taken prisoners; and learn too, how and by what means he hath thus troubled my land, and set it against me.' The earl said, 'Sir, upon mine honour I will perform it in such manner, that in a short time you shall hear of this disturbance, or I will suffer the penalty of death.' 'Fair cousin, I know it well,' said the king, 'and will myself set forward to pass over as speedily as I may, for never shall I have comfort or repose so long as the false traitor, who hath now played me such a trick, shall be alive. If I can but get him in my power, I will cause him to be put to death in such a manner that it shall be spoken of long enough, even in Turkey.' The earl caused his people and vessels to be made ready for immediate departure, gravely took leave of the king, and entreated him to proceed with all possible haste. The king, upon his advice, promised him, happen what might, that he would put to sea within six days. At that time the earl, who had great desire to set out in defence of the right of king Richard, had earnestly prayed me to go over with him, for the sake of merriment and song, and thereto I heartily agreed. My companion and myself went over the sea with him. Now it came to pass that the earl landed at Conway. I assure you, it was the strongest and fairest town in Wales.

"There we were told of the enterprise of the duke; a more cruel one shall, I think, never be spoken of in any land. For they told us, that he had already conquered the greater part of England, and taken towns and castles; that he had displaced officers, and everywhere set up a different establishment in his own name; that he had put to death, without mercy, as a sovereign lord, all those whom he held in displeasure.

"When the earl heard these doleful tidings, it was no wonder that he was alarmed, for the duke had gained over the greater part of the nobles of England, and we were assured that there were full sixty thousand men ready for war. The earl then quickly sent his summons, throughout Wales and Chester, that all gentlemen, archers, and other persons, should come to him without delay, upon pain of death, to take part with King Richard who loved them. This they were very desirous to do, thinking of a truth that the king had arrived at Conway: I am certain that forty thousand were trained and mustered in the field within four days, every one eager to fight with all who wished ill to the ever preux and valiant King Richard. Then the earl, who endured great pain and trouble, went to them all, and declared to them with a solemn oath, that before three days were ended, he would so straiten the duke and his people, that for this time they should advance no farther to waste the land. Soon after, he found the whole of his friends assembled together in the field; he spake to them well-advisedly, 'My good gentlemen, let us all make haste to avenge King Richard in his absence, that he may be satisfied with us for the time to come: for mine own part I purpose neither to stop nor to take rest, till such time as I shall have made my attempt upon those who are so traitorous and cruel towards him. Let us go hence, and march directly towards them. God will help us, if we are diligent in assaulting them; for, according to our law, it is the duty of every one in many cases to support the right until death.'

"When the Welshmen understood that the king was not there, they were all sorrowful, murmuring to one another in great companies, full of alarm, thinking that the king was dead of grief, and dreading the horrible and great severity of the Duke of Lancaster and his people. They were not well satisfied with the earl, saying, 'Sir, be assured that for the present we will advance no farther, since the king is not here; and do you know wherefore? Behold the duke is subduing everything to himself, which is a great terror and trouble to us; for indeed we think that the king is dead, since he is not arrived with you at the port; were he here, right or wrong, each of us would be eager to assail his enemies. But now we will not go with you.' The earl at this was so wroth at heart, that he had almost gone out of his senses with vexation; he shed tears. It was a great pity to see how he was treated. 'Alas!' said he, 'what shame befalleth me this day! O death, come unto me without delay; put an end to me; I loath my destiny. Alas! now will the king suppose that I have devised treason.'

"While thus he mourned, he said, 'My comrades, as you hope for mercy, come with me, I beseech you; so shall we be champions for King Richard, who within four days and a half will be here; for he told me when I quitted Ireland, that he would upon his life embark before the week was ended. Sirs, I pray you let us hasten to depart.' It availed nothing; they stood all mournfully, like men afraid; a great part of them were disposed to betake themselves to the duke, for fear of death. But the earl kept them in the field fourteen days, expecting the coming of King Richard. Many a time said the good earl apart, 'Small portion will you have of England, in my opinion, my rightful lord, since you delay so long. What can this mean? certes, I believe you are betrayed, since I hear no true tidings of you in word or deed. Alas! I see these people are troubled with fear, lest the duke should hem them in. They are but common ignorant people. They will desert me.' So said the good earl to himself in the field; while he was serving with those who in a little time all abandoned him; some went their way straight to the duke, and the rest returned into Wales; so they left the earl encamped with none but his own men, who did not, I think, amount to a hundred. He lamented it greatly, saying, in a sorrowful manner, 'Let us make our retreat, for our enterprise goeth on very badly.'"

(6) Scene IV.—

The bay-trees in our country are all withered.]

"In this year in a manner throughout all the realme of England, old baie trees withered, and afterwards, contrarie to all men's thinking, grew greene againe, a strange sight, and supposed to import some unknown event.—Holinshed, 1399.

This was usually held to be an evil prognostic, for the bay-tree, from very early ages, was believed to exercise a powerfully beneficial influence upon the place where it flourished:—"Neyther falling sycknes, neyther devyll, wyl infest or hurt one in that place whereas a *Bay-tree* is. The Romaynes calles it the plant of the good angell," &c. —Lupton's *Syxt Booke of Notable Thinges.*

ACT III.

(1) SCENE II.—*Mine ear is open, &c.*] "It seems to be the design of the poet to raise Richard to esteem in his fall, and consequently to interest the reader in his favour. He gives him only passive fortitude,—the virtue of a confessor, rather than of a king. In his prosperity we saw him imperious and oppressive; but in his distress he is wise, patient, and pious."—JOHNSON.

(2) SCENE II.—

——— For within the hollow crown
That rounds the mortal temples of a king,
Keeps Death his court; and there the antic sits,
Scoffing his state, and grinning at his pomp.]

"Some part of this fine description might have been suggested from the seventh print in the *Imagines Mortis*, a celebrated series of wooden cuts which have been improperly attributed to Holbein. It is probable that Shakespeare might have seen some spurious edition of this work; for the great scarcity of the original in this country in former times is apparent, when Hollar could not procure the use of it for his *copy* of the Dance of Death."—DOUCE. An admirable modern illustration of this noble passage, may be seen in J. H. Mortimer's etching of Richard II. in a series of twelve characteristic heads from Shakespeare.

(3) SCENE III.—*Then I must not say, no.*] The interview between King Richard and Bolingbroke, at Flint, is thus narrated by the author of the French Metrical History, who was an eye witness of all that passed.

"The Duke entered the castle armed at all points, except his basinet. Then they made the king, who had dined in the donjon, come down to meet Duke Henry, who, as soon as he perceived him at a distance, bowed very low to the ground; and as they approached each other, he bowed a second time, with his cap in his hand; and then the king took off his bonnet, and spake first in this manner: 'Fair cousin of Lancaster, you be right welcome.' Then Duke Henry replied, bowing very low to the ground, 'My Lord, I am come sooner than you sent for me: the reason wherefore I will tell you. The common report of your people is such, that you have, for the space of twenty or two and twenty years, governed them very badly and very rigorously, and in so much that they are not well contented therewith. But if it please our Lord, I will help you to govern them better than they have been governed in time past.' King Richard then answered him, 'Fair cousin, since it pleaseth you, it pleaseth us well.' And be assured that these are the very words that they two spake together, without taking away or adding anything: for I heard and understood them very well. And the earl of Salisbury also rehearsed them to me in French, and another aged knight who was one of the council of Duke Henry. He told me as we rode to Chester, that Merlin and Bede had, from the time in which they lived, prophesied of the taking and ruin of the king, and that if I were in his castle he would show it me in form and manner as I had seen it come to pass. * * * * * Thus, as you have heard, came Duke Henry to the castle and spake unto the king, to the Bishop of Carlisle, and the two knights, Sir Stephen Scroope and Ferriby; howbeit unto the earl of Salisbury he spake not at all, but sent word to him by a knight in this manner, 'Earl of Salisbury, be assured that no more than you deigned to speak to my lord the duke of Lancaster, when he and you were in Paris at Christmas last past, will he speak unto you.' Then was the earl much abashed, and had great fear and dread at heart, for he saw plainly that the duke mortally hated him: The said Duke Henry called aloud with a stern and savage voice, 'Bring out the king's horses;' and then they brought him two little horses that were not worth forty franks: the king mounted one, and the earl of Salisbury the other. Everyone got on horseback, and we set out from the said castle of Flint about two hours after mid-day."

ACT IV.

(1) SCENE I.—

Lest child, child's children, cry against you—woe!]

In the Bishop's bold and animated defence of the rights of kings, Shakespeare followed his favourite historical authority, Holinshed:—

"On Wednesdaie following, request was made by the commons, that sith King Richard had resigned, and was lawfullie deposed from his roiall dignitie, he might have judgement decreed against him, so as the realme were not troubled by him, and that the causes of his deposing might be published through the realme for satisfying of the people: which demand was granted. Whereupon the Bishop of Carleill, a man both learned, wise, and stout of stomach, boldlie shewed forth his opinion concerning that demand; affirming that there was none amongst them worthie or meet to give judgement upon so noble a prince as Richard was, whom they had taken for their sovereigne and liege lord, by the space of two and twentie yeares and more; And I assure you (said he) there is not so ranke a traitor, nor so errant a theef, nor yetso cruel a murthere apprehended or deteined in prison for his offense, but he shall be brought before the iustice to heare his iudgement; and will ye proceed to the iudgement of an anointed king, hearing neither his answer nor excuse? I say, that the duke of Lancaster whom ye call king, hath more trespassed to king Richard and his realme, than king Richard hath doone either to him or us: for it is manifest and well knowne, that the duke was banished the realme by king Richard and his councell, and by the iudgement of his own father, for the space of ten yeares, for what cause ye know, and yet without license of king Richard, he is returned againe into the realme, and (that is worse) hath taken upon him the name, title, and preheminence of king. And therfore I say, that you have doone manifest wrong, to proceed in anie thing against King Richard, without calling him openlie to his answer and defense. As soone as the bishop had ended this tale, he was attached by the Earle-Marshall, and committed to ward in the abbeie of saint Albons."—HOLINSHED, 1399.

(2) SCENE I.—

On Wednesday next, we solemnly set down
Our coronation: lords, prepare yourselves.]

The following is the description of the proceedings at Westminster on the occasion of Richard's deposition; from the "Metrical History:"—

"First sat Duke Henry, and next to him the Duke of York, his fair cousin, whose heart was not right faithful towards his nephew, King Richard. After him, on the same side, sat the Duke of Aumarle, the son of the Duke of York; and then the Duke of Surrey, who was ever loyal and true. After him sat the Duke of Exeter, who had no reason to rejoice, for he saw before him preparation made for the ruin of the king, his brother. Early and late this was the wish of them all. Then came another on that side, who was called the Marquess,* lord of a great country. And next the Earl of Arundel, who is right young and active. The Earl of Norvic † next, was not forgotten in the account, neither he of La Marche.‡ There was one who was Earl of Stamford,§ and never could agree with his lord, King Richard; on this side also sat one whom I heard called Earl of Pembroke,‖ and a baron. And close to him was seated the Earl of Salisbury, who so faithfully loved the king that he was loyal to the last. The Earl of Devonshire was there, as I heard. All other earls and lords, the greatest in the kingdom, were present at this assembly, their desire and intention being to choose another king. There, in fair fashion, stood the Earl of Northumberland and the Earl of Westmoreland, the whole of the day, and for the better discharge of their duty, they kneeled very often: wherefore, or how it was, I cannot tell.

"The archbishop of Canterbury next arose, and preached before all the people in Latin. The whole of his sermon was upon this, 'Habuit Jacob benedictionem a patre suo:'—'How Jacob had gotten the blessing instead of Esau, although he were the eldest son.' This he set forth as true. Alas, what a text for a sermon! He made it to prove, in conclusion, that King Richard ought to have no part in the Crown of England, and that the prince ought to have had the realm and territory. These were very ungrateful people; after they had all held him to be rightful king and lord for two-and-twenty years, by a great error they ruined him with one accord.

"When the archbishop had finished his sermon in the Latin language, a lawyer, who was a most sage doctor, and also a notary, arose and commanded silence. For he began to read aloud an instrument which contained how Richard, some time King of England, had avowed and confessed, of his own will, without compulsion, that he was neither capable nor worthy, wise nor prudent, nor gentle enough to bear the crown; and that it was his wish to resign it into the hand of another worthy man of noble birth and greater wisdom than himself. Thus right or wrong, they by agreement caused King Richard to make a declaration in the Tower of London, in a most wicked manner; and then in this parliament read the instrument before all. Its witnesses were bishops and abbots, who affirmed and testified that the instrument was entirely true. Now consider this testimony: never was such an outrage heard of.

"When the reading of the instrument was ended, all kept silence, and the archbishop then rose and took up anew his discourse, laying his foundation upon the instrument aforesaid, and speaking so loud, that he was plainly heard of the people. 'Forasmuch as it is thus, and that Richard, sometime King of England, hath by his words and of his own goodwill acknowledged and confessed that he is not sufficiently able, worthy, or well skilled to govern the kingdom, it were right good to advise and chuse another king.' Alas! fair sirs, what an evil deed! There were they, judge, and party accusing. It was not a thing justly divided nor of legal right; because there was no man in that place for the old king, save three or four who durst upon no account gainsay them. All that they said or did was the greatest mockery; for, great and small, they all agreed, without any dividing, that they would have a king who better knew how to discharge his duty than Richard had done. And when the archbishop had completely made an end in the English language of declaring his will and his evil intention, and the people had replied according to that which they had heard, he began to interrogate and question each man by himself. 'Will you that the duke of York be your king?' All in good order answered 'No.'—'Will you then have his eldest son, who is duke of Aumarle?' They answered aloud, 'Let no one speak to us of him.' Once more again he asked, 'Will you then have his youngest son?' They said, 'Nay, truly.' He asked them concerning many others, but the people stopped at none of those that he had named. And then the archbishop ceased to say much. He next inquired aloud, 'Will you have the duke of Lancaster?' They all at once replied with so loud a voice, that the account which I heard appears marvellous to me, 'Yea, we will have no other.' Then they praised Jesus Christ."

Immediately the ceremony of the deposition of Richard is concluded and the deprived King has departed, Bolingbroke announces the day of his own coronation, the ensuing Wednesday. The real day, however, was Monday, and is so set down in Holinshed; and it is therefore difficult to understand how Shakespeare was led into the mistake, unless it were derived from the old play on this part of English History which has never yet been found.

The Coronation of Henry IV. took place on the Translation of St. Edward the Confessor, Monday, Oct. 13th, 1399, on which occasion the Court of Claims for services was held with great ceremony. It is remarkable as being the first coronation in which the creation of Knights of the Bath is particularly noticed by historians; though there can be no doubt of the practice having prevailed in much earlier times. Forty-six gentlemen, four of whom were Henry's sons, received the Order at the Tower the day before the festival, and watched there the vigil of the Coronation. In this ceremony the new king's policy appears to have been to make the most imposing display of wealth and magnificence possible, as may be seen in the elaborate account of it given by Froissart. There were six thousand horses employed in the cavalcade which attended Henry to Westminster; and the coronation-feast lasted two days, during which nine conduits of wine were kept flowing in Cheapside.

* John Beaufort, eldest son of John of Gaunt, by Catherine Swinford, created, 20 Rich. II., Marquess of Dorset and Somerset.

† An error of the transcriber; it should, perhaps, be Warwick. There was no Earl of Norwich till the 2d Charles I.

‡ Edmund Mortimer, son of Roger, Earl of March, could not have been more than seven years of age.

§ Query, *Stafford*.

‖ This must be an error, as the last earl had been killed in a tournament at Windsor some years before.

ACT V.

(1) SCENE I.—*You must to Pomfret, not unto the Tower.*] This is not historically correct; in the prose MSS. concerning the deposition of Richard the Second, preserved in the national library of Paris, there is an extremely interesting and characteristic narrative of an interview which took place between the king and Henry of Lancaster while the former was confined in the Tower. These MSS. record that, when the Dukes of Lancaster and York went to the Tower to see the king, Lancaster desired the Earl of Arundel to send the king to them. When this message was delivered to Richard, he replied, "Tell Henry of Lancaster from me, that I will do no such thing, and that, if he wishes to speak with me, he must come to me." On entering none shewed any respect to the king, except Lancaster, who took off his hat and saluted him respectfully, and said to him; "Here is our cousin, the Duke of Aumarle, and our uncle, the Duke of York, who wish to speak with you;" to which Richard answered, "Cousin, they are not fit to speak to me." "But have the goodness to hear them," replied Lancaster; upon which Richard uttered an oath, and turning to York, "Thou villain, what wouldst thou say to me? and thou, traitor of Rutland, thou art neither good nor worthy enough to speak to me, nor to bear the name of duke, earl, or knight; thou, and the villain thy father have both of you foully betrayed me; in a cursed hour were ye born: by your false counsel was my uncle of Gloucester put to death." The Earl of Rutland replied to the king that, in what he said he lied; and threw down his bonnet at his feet: on which the king said, "I am king, and thy lord; and will still continue king; and will be a greater lord than I ever was, in spite of all my enemies." Upon this Lancaster imposed silence on Rutland. Richard, turning then with a fierce countenance to Lancaster, asked why he was in confinement, and why under a guard of armed men. "Am I your servant or your king? What mean you to do with me?" Lancaster replied, "You are my king and lord, but the council of the realm have ordered that you should be kept in confinement till full decision (*jugement*) in parliament." The king again swore; and desired he might see his wife. "Excuse me," replied the duke, "it is forbidden by the council." Then the king in great wrath walked about the room; and at length broke out into passionate exclamations, and appeals to heaven; called them "false traitors," and offered to fight any four of them; boasted of his father and grandfather, his reign of twenty-two years; and ended by throwing down his bonnet. Lancaster then fell on his knees, and besought him to be quiet till the meeting of parliament, and then every one would bring forward his reason.—*See Notes by the* Rev. JOHN WEBB, *to his Translation of the French Metrical History,* &c.; *Archæologia,* vol. xx.

(2) SCENE I.—*With all swift speed you must away to France.*] At this period, Isabel in reality was a mere child. Upon the deposition of Richard, the French made a formal demand for the restitution of the Queen and part of her dowry, which by the contract of marriage was to be returned in the event of her becoming a widow before she had completed her twelfth year. The negotiations were delayed from the end of November, 1399, to May 27th, 1401, when the treaty for her return was signed at Leulinghen. The account of her return to France is thus related in the Metrical History. "On Tuesday the twenty-fifth day of July, about (*the hour of*) prime, the queen of the English passed from Dover to Calais, in the year one thousand four hundred and one. I understand she was most grandly attended, for she had in her company some of the greatest ladies of England. When they had landed, Hugueville, who had come over with her, wrote presently of the matter to the ambassadors at Boulogne, how she had made the passage, and that they all purposed to restore her, as they had given him to understand.

"On the following Sunday, being the last day of July, the queen set out from Calais without farther delay, together with the English, who could find no right reason for detaining her longer, so often were they reminded by the French. But they brought her straight to Lolinghehen, whither those who had heard the news of it went to meet her; these were the upright Count of Saint Pol, as every one calls him, and with him the ambassadors of France, who had used great diligence that they might behold her again.

"The queen, indeed, alighted below Lolinghehen at a tent, that the English had handsomely pitched for her in the valley. She was met by the ladies of France, who most heartily desired to see her. Soon after, they set out, it seems, together, and took the queen to the chapel of Lolinghehen; what it is, every one knows who has seen it. And when she had alighted, they made her enter, attended by few persons, except the ambassadors of France and England, who had taken great pains to do this. When they were assembled in the chapel, a knight, who is highly esteemed of the English, Sir Thomas Percy, took up his discourse, saying thus, 'King Henry, King of England, my sovereign lord on earth, desiring the fulfilment of his promise, hath without reserve and of right pure will, caused us to bring hither my lady, the Queen of England, to render and restore her to her father, loosed, quit, and free of all bonds of marriage, and of every other service, debt, or obligation; and declareth, moreover, that he would most solemnly pledge himself as he took it (or so far as he understood it), that she was as pure and entire as on the day when she was brought in her litter to King Richard. And if there should be any where a king, duke, or earl, christian, or otherwise, great or little, who would deny this, he would, without farther say or any long consultation, find a man of equal rank in England, to maintain this quarrel, and expose his person before any competent judge, in support of all this.' And when he had most sagely declared his pleasure, the Count of St. Pol told him that Jesus Christ should be praised therefore, and that they firmly believed it, without any scruple. Then Sir Thomas Percy, with many tears, took the young queen by the arms, and delivered her with good grace to the messengers there present, and received certain letters of acquittance, which had been promised by the French. And know, that before the two parties separated, they wept most piteously; but when they came to quit the chapel, the queen, whose heart is enlightened by goodness, brought all the English ladies, who made sore lamentations, to the French tents, where they purposed to dine together. So it seems, they did. And after dinner the queen caused a great abundance of very fair jewels to be brought out, and presented them to the great ladies and lords of England, who wept mightily for sorrow; but the queen bade them be of good cheer; and when she was forced to part from them, they renewed their lamentation."

(3) SCENE II.—

But heaven hath a hand in these events;
To whose high will we bound our calm contents.]

On comparing this scene with a parallel passage in Drayton's "Civil Warres," published in 1595, no one can doubt that either Shakespeare had Drayton's version in his mind's eye, or that the latter was indebted to York's magnificent description of the entry of Richard and Bolingbroke into London. We incline to the opinion of Mr. Knight, that the "Civil Warres" was produced and published before Richard II. was written. In Drayton the incident is told as follows:—

"He that in glory of his fortune sate,
Admiring what he thought could never be,
Did feel his blood within salute his state,
And lift up his rejoicing soul, to see
So many hands and hearts congratulate
Th' advancement of his long-desir'd degree;
When, prodigal of thanks, in passing by,
He re-salutes them all with cheerful eye.

Behind him, all aloof, came pensive on
The unregarded king; that drooping went.
Alone, and (but for spite) scarce look'd upon:
Judge, if he did more envy, or lament.
See what a wondrous work this day is done;
Which th' image of both fortunes doth present:
In th' one, to shew the best of glories face;
In th' other, worse than worst of all disgrace."

(4) SCENE III.—*Can no man tell of my unthrifty son?*] This speech may be regarded as striking the key-note of the three plays which continue the history of England at this period; and is, as Johnson observes, "a very proper introduction to the future character of Henry the Fifth, to his debaucheries in his youth, and his greatness in his manhood." Shakespeare's authority for thus delineating the Prince, was in all probability either the old play of Richard II. or a passage in Holinshed, which may be better adduced as an illustration in another place. Holinshed has founded his statement "on the authority," as Mr. Hunter points out, "of the chroniclers immediately preceding himself, Fabyan, Polydore Vergil, and Caxton, who wrote while the memory of the Prince's extravagance may well be supposed to have been alive, as they were all writers of his own century. But as this testimony," he adds, "may be regarded as coming late, and it may be thought that they are so far removed from the actual time, that they are in some degree at least copyists from each other, and not wholly independent authorities;" he refers to Henry's own contemporaries, Hardyng, Walsingham, Otterburne, the historian who called himself Titus Livius, and Thomas of Elmham: all of whom notice the vicious life of his youth in connexion with the entire change which took place in him on his accession to the throne. How early Henry became thus dissolute, it is not possible even to conjecture, but Malone's note on this passage is quite worthy of attention. "The Prince," he observes, "was at this time but twelve years old; for he was born in 1388, and the conspiracy on which the present scene is formed, was discovered in the beginning of the year 1400. He scarcely frequented taverns or stews at so early an age:" and it may be noticed that his answer declaring his prowess as a tilter, is that of an inexperienced young champion in his full strength.

(5) SCENE V.—*Whilst my gross flesh sinks downward, here to die.*] The circumstantial detail of the murder of Richard II., as it is represented in the close of this play, was popularly considered, even long after the time of Shakespeare, to be in reality the true history of his death: and down to the present day, the manner in which he came to his end constitutes one of the most interesting Problems of English history. Holinshed is again the principal authority of the dramatist; and his statements are avowedly founded on the report of Abraham Fleming, who was one of the compilers of the series of chronicles collectively called by the name of Holinshed. Fleming derived his information from the "Short History by Thomas of Walsingham, from Edward I. to Henry V." Walsingham appears to record his narrative for the purpose of disproving "the common fame," that the king's death was to be attributed to *compulsory famine:* and, continues Fleming, "he referreth it altogether to *voluntarie pining of himselfe.* For, when he heard that the complots and attempts of such of his favourers as sought *his restitution, and their own advancement,* were annihilated, and the chiefe agents shamefullie executed; he tooke such a conceit at these misfortunes,—for *so* Thomas Walsingham termeth them—and was so beaten out of heart,—that *wilfullie he starved himselfe, and so died in Pomfret Castle.*" So far as this statement can be received, it is not at all inconsistent with the ordinary account of the murder of Richard, nor with his "desperate manhood," as Holinshed properly calls it, on that occasion; excited as he was by his injuries, and his own fierce self-will and impetuous disposition.

In the termination of the life of the dethroned king, by whatsoever means it was effected,—if the guilty wish for his death, were ever expressed by Bolingbroke as related by Walsingham, and transferred by Fleming into Holinshed; the passage seems not only to have furnished matter for the present play, but also to have suggested almost the very words which Shakespeare has employed in two very noble and well-known parallel passages.

The first of these is in "King John," Act III. Scene 1.

"Good Hubert, Hubert,—Hubert, throw thine eye
On yon young boy:—I'll tell thee what, my friend;—
He is a very serpent in my way;—
And wheresoe'er this foot of mine doth tread,
He lies before me. Dost thou understand me?
Thou art his keeper!"

The other passage is of course the celebrated temptation of Buckingham by the Duke of Gloucester to the murder of Edward V. and his brother, in "The Life and Death of Richard the Third," Act IV. Scene 2.

"Thus high, by thy advice and thy assistance,
Is Richard seated.
But, shall we wear these glories for a day,
Or shall they last, and we rejoice in them?
* * * * *
Now, Buckingham, now do I play the touch
To try if thou be current gold, indeed.———
Young Edward *lives*——Think *now* what I would speak!"

"One writer," says Holinshed, "which seemeth to have great knowledge of King Richard's doings, saith that King Henrie, sitting on a daie at his table, sore sighing, said, 'Have I *no* faithfull friend which will deliver me of *him,* whose life will be my death, and whose death will be the preservation of my life?' This saying was much noted of them that were present, and especiallie of one called Sir Piers of Exton." It is added that "this knight incontinentlie departed from the court, with eight strong persons in his companie, and came to Pomfret;" where the remaining act of the tragedy was suddenly performed. In the Chronicle of Gervase of Dover, relating to the reign of Henry II., 1171, there is a very remarkable historical parallel to this passage, in the passionate expression of that sovereign in reference to the Archbishop Thomas à Becket. The historian states that the king became so enraged beyond the majestic decency of his condition, that he aloud lamented that of all the numbers, both of nobles and others, whom he had maintained, there was not one of them who would undertake to redress his injuries. These and the like complaints of the king so much irritated four knights, that they bound themselves together by an oath, and withdrew from court to execute their design.

After the death of Richard, Shakespeare sagaciously shows that the first policy of Bolingbroke was to disclaim any participation in it, as he does even to Exton himself: and here again appears a remarkable similarity between this part of the present play and the speech of King John to Hubert after the supposed murder of Arthur, in the fine passage in Act IV. Scene 2, of that play. Bolingbroke's second and more imposing act of policy was to appear publicly to declare that he was altogether innocent of the death of the late king, by honourably exposing and interring a body affirmed to be that of Richard. Holinshed thus sets down the circumstances of this ceremony:—"After he was thus dead, his bodie was embalmed and cered, and covered with lead, all save the face, to the intent that all men might see him, and perceive that he *was* departed from life. For, as the corpse was conveied from Pomfret to London, in all the townes and places where those that had the conveiance of it did staie with it all night,—they caused '*Dirige*' to be sung in the evening, and masse of '*Requiem*' in the morning; and, as well after the one service as the other, his face, dis-covered, was shewed to all that coveted to behold it. Thus was the corpse first brought to the Tower, and after through the citie to the cathedrall church of saint Paule, bare-faced, where it laie three daies together, that all men might behold it. There was a solemne obsequie done for him, both at Paule's and after at Westminster; at which time both at *Dirige* over night, and in the morning at *Requiem*, the king and the citizens of London were present." Up to this point the remains were treated with great ceremony, but they were next removed to the church of the Friars Predicants at Abbot's Langley in Hertfordshire; where they were obscurely interred by the Bishop of Chester and the Abbots of St. Alban's and Waltham, "none of the nobles," adds Holinshed, "nor anie of the commons—to accompt of—being present; *neither was there anie to bid them to dinner after they had laid him in the ground, and finished the funerall service.*"

Throughout the whole of these proceedings, as well in the first ostentatious display of a corse, affirmed to have been that of the dethroned monarch, as afterwards,—it seems as if the policy of Bolingbroke might everywhere be traced. After having effected his first object, that of showing, in the most public places, the uninjured body of a person, which is declared by Froissart to have been seen by *twenty thousand witnesses*;—and after having performed all the principal rites, the rest of the funeral was passed over in silence. There is also the curious evidence of a contemporaneous poetical historian, relating first the exposure of a body said to have been King Richard's, and afterwards the obscure burial of it. In a manuscript copy of John Hardyng's Chronicle, preserved in the Lansdowne Collection, there are the following notices of this funeral:—

> "Sone after that kyng Richerde so was dede,
> And brought to Paule's with gret solempnite,—
> (Men sayd he was for-hungred)—and lapp'd in lede;
> But that his masse was done, and "*Dirige*,"
> *In Herse Rial his corse lay there, I se:*
> And after Masse to Westmynster was ladde,
> Where '*Placebo*' and '*Dyryge*' he hadde."

The printed editions of the Chronicle differ entirely in the text of this stanza; but the following verse, and the title of the chapter in which they occur, appear to indicate that the author probably thought it more prudent not to declare his having seen the body. He states, however, that when the funeral ceremonies were performed at St. Paul's:—

> "'The kynge and lordes clothes of golde there offered,
> Some viii, some ix, upon his herse were profferde.
>
> At Westmynster then did they so the same;
> When trustynge he should there have buryed bene,
> In at that Mynster lyke a Prince of name,
> In his owne tombe, together with the quene
> Anne, that afore his fyrst wyfe had bene.
> But then the kyng him fast to Langley sent,
> There in 'the Freers' to be buryed secretement."

Hardyng adds, in the title to this chapter, that the body was removed thither "for men should have no remembraunce of him."

No part of this narrative indicates any doubt that the remains which had been exhibited were really those of Richard; nor is there any notice of the other reports concerning the cause of his death. The author of the Metrical History of the Deposition, on the contrary, seems not only to have very much doubted the identity of the deceased individual, but also to have disbelieved that the dethroned king was really dead. His narrative of these particulars may be thus rendered in the familiar style and measure of the original:—

> "When the King was these tidings shew'd,
> The which were neither fair nor good;
> So sadly on his heart they sank
> That never more he ate or drank;
> But, vanquish'd from that hour, denied
> All food to take, and so he died.
> This some have said and have received,
> But shall not be by me believed;
> For certain others yet do tell
> That he is still alive and well,
> Though shut within their prison-fort;—
> And therefore some do mis-report.
> It matters not that they display'd
> A dead man's corse uncover'd laid,
> Through London with such honours borne
> As should a lifeless king adorn;
> Declaring that it was the corse
> Of Richard lying on that hearse.
> * * * * * *
> But I believe not certainly
> That it the former king *could* be:
> 'Twas but his chaplain, Maudelain,
> Was carried by that solemn train;
> Who in face, size, and height, and limb,
> So closely did resemble him,
> That each one firmly thought he knew
> 'T was good King Richard met his view.
> *If it were he*, both morn and eve
> My hearty prayers to God I give,
> Who merciful and piteous is,
> That he may take his soul to bliss."

The priest Maudelaine, who is mentioned in these verses, had already represented Richard in the conspiracy of the Earls of Rutland and Kent; and he was afterwards taken with many others at Cirencester, and was one of those hanged at London. Hence it was that his body could be so opportunely brought forward as that of the late king; and it is not impossible that Henry might even have indulged in a bitter jest, by so calling the lifeless remains of one who, whilst living, had been really put forward as the royal substitute. Throughout a great part of the reign of Henry IV. the very general belief that Richard was not dead, was a source of the most serious vexation to him; and it is especially remarkable that he should have experienced much of his anxiety from the appearance of other false Richards after Maudelaine, against whom he issued proclamations so late as 1402.

The illustration of the removal of the body obscurely interred at Abbot's Langley, with royal honours to Westminster, rightly belongs to the play of Henry V. to which we refer it. But there is one circumstance, arising out of that translation, which may be properly noticed in this place,—the opportunity which it afforded of examining some skulls in the royal tomb, by Sir Joseph Ayloffe, Edward King, Richard Gough, and others, in the latter part of the last century; when the skull which was believed to be that of the king did not exhibit any marks of violence. Mr. King states that "a small cleft that was visible on one side, appeared, on close inspection, to be merely the opening of a suture from length of time and decay: and it was beside in such a part of the head that it must have been visible when the visage was exposed, had it been the consequence of a wound given by a battle-axe, it being at the top of what the anatomists call the *os temporis*." In answer to these arguments it is to be observed, firstly, that the skulls examined were contained in the sub-basement of the tomb, and not in the monument itself, under the effigies, where the royal bodies might be supposed to be laid. Secondly, that only the lower part of the face was uncovered when the remains were carried through London, and the temporal bones were hidden. The rumour of starvation by his keepers, which Holinshed says was the most commonly believed, might have been the cause of the death of Richard; or he might even, as another account states, have remained by his own will too long without food, and then have been unable to receive it, and so have died. A heavy suspicion of the guilt of destroying him must always, however, rest upon the memory of Henry of Bolingbroke; though at the present time he is commonly believed to have been innocent, and Richard to have expired at Pomfret from purely natural causes.

Act II. Sc. 4.

THE FIRST PART OF

KING HENRY THE FOURTH.

"The History of Henrie the Fovrth; With the battell at Shrewsburie, betweene the King and Lord Henry Percy, surnamed Henrie Hotspur of the North. With the humorous conceits of Sir John Falstalffe. At London, Printed by P. S. for Andrew Wise, dwelling in Paules Church-yard, at the signe of the Angell. 1598." Such is the title of the first and best edition of this famous historic drama. A second edition was issued in 1599, which was followed by a third in 1604, a fourth in 1608, a fifth in 1613, and a sixth in 1622. That six distinct impressions of it should have been published before its incorporation in the folio of 1623, is proof of its enduring popularity.

The First Part of King Henry IV. was entered on the books of the Stationers' Company in 1597, to which year Malone ascribes its production. Chalmers and Drake assign it to 1596, but the evidence for either date is so extremely vague and unsubstantial that no dependance can be placed upon it. All we really know is, that the play was written before 1598, because Meres, in his list published that year, enumerates "Henry the IVth." as one of our poet's works. Shakespeare, it is thought, selected the stirring period of our history comprehended in the reigns of Henry IV. and V. for dramatic illustration, in consequence of the success achieved by an old and worthless piece which had long retained possession of the stage, called "The Famous Victories of Henry the Fifth;" though Dr. Johnson conceived that he had planned a regular connexion of these dramatic histories from Richard the Second to Henry the Fifth. From a similarity in some of the incidents and in the names of two or three of the characters, it is quite clear that he was acquainted with "The Famous Victories," and the circumstance of his having chosen the same events for representation, may have occasioned the revival of that old piece by Henslowe's company in 1595, and its re-publication in 1598. As Mr. Collier observes, "It is impossible to institute any parallel between 'The Famous Victories' and Shakespeare's dramas; for, besides that the former has reached us evidently in an imperfect shape, the immeasurable superiority of the latter is such, as to render any attempt to trace resemblance a matter of contrast rather than of comparison."

In the year 1844, a manuscript copy of the play of Henry the Fourth was found among the family papers of Sir Edward Dering, Bart., of Surrenden, Kent. Mr. Halliwell, who edited the MS. for the Shakespeare Society, observes, in his Introduction to the volume, that it "does not contain the whole of Shakespeare's Henry IV., but the two parts condensed into one, and, as we may presume, for the purpose of representation." And he goes on to say that "the variations are so numerous, that we can hardly believe the MS. was transcribed from any printed edition. At all events, we cannot discover any which contains them. If the adapter was a player, there seems to be no preponderating reason why the MS. should not originally have been the property of one of the metropolitan theatres, and have been prepared for the use of such an establishment."

The discovery of any of Shakespeare's plays in manuscript of a date even approaching his own time, is alone sufficiently interesting in a literary point of view; the editor's suggestion that the Dering MS. may have been derived from some independent source, cannot, however, be maintained. There is abundant internal evidence to show that it was copied, in the first instance, from the quarto edition of 1613; and as the transcript was apparently made during the reign of James I, with a view to private performance, by the friends of Sir Edward Deryng, the first baronet, the language was, as usual, altered to suit the taste of the day; the various readings, therefore, whatever their merit, cannot be accepted as of any authority in elucidating the text.

Persons Represented.

King Henry the Fourth.
Henry, *Prince of Wales*, } *Sons to the* King.
Prince John *of* Lancaster, } *Sons to the* King.
Earl of Westmoreland.
Sir Walter Blunt.
Thomas Percy, *Earl of* Worcester.
Henry Percy, *Earl of* Northumberland.
Henry Percy, *surnamed* Hotspur, *his son.*
Edward Mortimer, *Earl of* March.
Scroop, *Archbishop of* York.
Sir Michael, *a friend of the* Archbishop.
Archibald, *Earl of* Douglas.
Owen Glendower.

Sir Richard Vernon.
Sir John Falstaff.
Poins.
Gadshill.
Peto.
Bardolph.

Lady Percy, *wife to* Hotspur.
Lady Mortimer, *daughter to* Glendower.
Mrs. Quickly, *hostess of a tavern in* Eastcheap.

Lords, Officers, Sheriff, Vintner, Chamberlain, Drawers, Travellers, Carriers, and Attendants.

SCENE,—England.

ACT I.

SCENE I.—London. *A Room in the Palace.*

Enter KING HENRY, WESTMORELAND, SIR WALTER BLUNT, *and others.*

K. HEN. So shaken as we are, so wan with care,
Find we a time for frighted peace to pant,
And breathe short-winded accents of new broils
To be commenc'd in strands[a] afar remote.

[a] Strands—] The old text has *stronds*,

No more the thirsty entrance[a] of this soil
Shall daub her lips with her own children's blood;
No more shall trenching war channel her fields,
Nor bruise her flowrets with the armed hoofs
Of hostile paces: those opposed eyes,
Which,—like the meteors of a troubled heaven,
All of one nature, of one substance bred,——
Did lately meet in the intestine shock
And furious close of civil butchery,
Shall now, in mutual, well-beseeming ranks,
March all one way; and be no more oppos'd
Against acquaintance, kindred, and allies:
The edge of war, like an ill-sheathed knife,
No more shall cut his master. Therefore, friends,
As far as to the sepulchre of Christ,[b]
(Whose soldier now, under whose blessed cross
We are impressed and engaged to fight,)
Forthwith a power of English shall we levy;
Whose arms were moulded in their mothers' womb
To chase these pagans, in those holy fields,
Over whose acres walk'd those blessed feet,
Which, fourteen hundred years ago, were nail'd
For our advantage, on the bitter cross.
But this our purpose now[c] is twelve-months old,
And bootless 'tis to tell you—we will go;
Therefore we meet not now. Then let me hear
Of you, my gentle cousin Westmoreland,
What yesternight our council did decree,
In forwarding this dear expedience.

WEST. My liege, this haste was hot in question,
And many limits of the charge set down
But yesternight: when, all athwart, there came
A post from Wales, loaden with heavy news;
Whose worst was, that the noble Mortimer,
Leading the men of Herefordshire to fight
Against the irregular and wild Glendower,
Was by the rude hands of that Welchman taken,
And a thousand of his people butchered:
Upon whose dead corps[d] there was such misuse,
Such beastly, shameless transformation,
By those Welchwomen done, as may not be,
Without much shame, retold or spoken of.

K. HEN. It seems then, that the tidings of this broil
Brake off our business for the Holy Land.

WEST. This, match'd with other, did[e], my gracious lord;
For* more uneven and unwelcome news
Came from the north, and thus it did import.†
On Holy-rood day, the gallant Hotspur there,
Young Harry Percy, and brave Archibald,
That ever-valiant and approved Scot,
At Holmedon met,
Where they did spend a sad and bloody hour;
As by discharge of their artillery,
And shape of likelihood, the news was told;
For he that brought them, in the very heat
And pride of their contention, did take horse,
Uncertain of the issue any way.

K. HEN. Here is a dear and‡ true-industrious friend,
Sir Walter Blunt, new lighted from his horse,
Stain'd§ with the variation of each soil
Betwixt that Holmedon and this seat of ours;
And he hath brought us smooth and welcome|| news.
The earl of Douglas is discomfited;
Ten thousand bold Scots, two and twenty knights,
Balk'd[f] in their own blood, did sir Walter see
On Holmedon's plains: of prisoners, Hotspur took
Mordake the¶ earl of Fife, and eldest son
To beaten Douglas;[g] and the earl of Athol,
Of Murray, Angus, and Menteith.
And is not this an honourable spoil?
A gallant prize? ha, cousin, is it not?

WEST. In faith, it is;
A conquest for a prince to boast of.

K. HEN. Yea, there thou mak'st me sad, and mak'st me sin

(*) First folio, *Far*.
(†) First folio, *report*.
(‡) First quarto, *a*.
(§) First folio, *strain'd*.
(||) First folio, *welcomes*.
(¶) Old copies omit, *the*.

[a] *No more the thirsty* entrance *of this soil*—] Long and fruitless has been the controversy upon the word *entrance*, here. For a time, indeed, the ingenious and classical *Erinnys* of Monck Mason was permitted to supersede it in some editions; and a few critics advocated the substitution of *entrants* recommended by Steevens, or the less elegant *entrails* proposed by Douce; but these readings have had their day, and the general feeling is now in favour of retaining the old expression. *Thirsty entrance* is certainly obscure, but it might be used metaphorically for the parched crevices of the earth after long drought, without any serious impropriety. There is something similar in a passage of the "Troublesome Raigne of King John," with which Shakespeare was perfectly familiar:—

> "Is all the *blood* yspilt on either part,
> Closing the *cranies* of the *thirstie earth*
> Growne to a love-game and a bridall feast?"

[b] As far as to the sepulchre of Christ,
* * * * * *
Forthwith a power of English shall we levy.]

To *levy* a power as far as *to* the sepulchre of Christ, Steevens objected was an expression quite unexampled. Gifford has shown, however, [Ben Jonson, Vol. V. p. 138,] that the construction was not peculiar, by quoting an instance of it from *Gosson's School of Abuse*, 1587, "Scipio, before he *levied* his force *to* the walles of Carthage, gave his soldiers the print of the citie on a cake to be devoured."

[c] Now *is twelve* months *old*,—] So the first quarto; the folio reads, is *a* twelve*month* old.

[d] *Upon whose dead* corps—] The folio has *corpes*. We should, perhaps, read *corses*.

[e] *This, match'd with other*, did, *my gracious lord;*] The folio, following the quarto of 1613, from which it appears to have been printed, reads, This match'd with other *like*, &c.

[f] Balk'd *in their own blood*,—] For Balk'd, that is *ridged*, or *heaped* up, there is classic authority: "Ingentes Rutulæ spectabit cædis *Acervos*." Æn. X. 245, and "ingentes Rutulorum linquis *Acervos*:" X. 509; but many will prefer the conjectural reading *bak'd*, of Steevens: which he well supports by the following passages from Heywood's "Iron Age," 1632:—

> "—— Troilus lies *embak'd*
> In his cold blood"——

And,

> "—— *bak'd* in blood and dust."

[g] Mordake the earl of Fife, and eldest son
To beaten Douglas;—]
This is an error into which the poet was led by a mispointed passage in Holinshed. Mordake Earl of Fife was the son of the Duke of Albany, Regent of Scotland.

In envy that my lord Northumberland
Should be the father to* so blest a son:
A son, who is the theme of honour's tongue;
Amongst a grove, the very straightest plant;
Who is sweet fortune's minion, and her pride:
Whilst I, by looking on the praise of him,
See riot and dishonour stain the brow
Of my young Harry. O, that it could be prov'd,
That some night-tripping fairy had exchang'd
In cradle-clothes our children where they lay,
And call'd mine, Percy, his, Plantagenet!
Then would I have his Harry, and he mine.
But let him from my thoughts. What think you, coz',
Of this young Percy's pride? the prisoners,
Which he in this adventure hath surpris'd,
To his own use he keeps; and sends me word,
I shall have none but Mordake earl of Fife.[a]

WEST. This is his uncle's teaching, this is Worcester,
Malevolent to you in all aspécts,
Which makes him prune himself, and bristle up
The crest of youth against your dignity.

K. HEN. But I have sent for him to answer this;
And, for this cause, awhile we must neglect
Our holy purpose to Jerusalem.
Cousin, on Wednesday next our council we
Will hold at Windsor,† so inform the lords:
But come yourself with speed to us again;
For more is to be said, and to be done,
Than out of anger can be uttered.

WEST. I will, my liege. [*Exeunt.*

SCENE II.—*The same. An apartment in a Tavern.*(1)

Enter HENRY, *Prince of Wales, and* FALSTAFF.

FAL. Now, Hal, what time of day is it, lad?

P. HEN. Thou art so fat-witted, with drinking of old sack, and unbuttoning thee after supper, and sleeping upon benches ‡ after noon, that thou hast forgotten to demand that truly which thou would'st truly know.[b] What a devil hast thou to do with the time of the day? unless hours were cups of sack, and minutes capons, and clocks the tongues of bawds, and dials the signs of leaping-houses, and the blessed sun himself a fair hot wench in flame-coloured taffata, I see no reason why thou should'st be so superfluous to demand the time of the day.

FAL. Indeed, you come near me now, Hal: for we, that take purses, go by the moon and the* seven stars; and not by Phœbus,—he, *that wandering knight so fair*. And, I pr'ythee, sweet wag, when thou art king,—as, God save thy grace, (majesty, I should say; for grace thou wilt have none,)——

P. HEN. What! none?

FAL. No, by my troth;† not so much as will serve to be prologue to an egg and butter.

P. HEN. Well, how then? come, roundly, roundly.

FAL. Marry, then, sweet wag, when thou art king, let not us, that are squires of the night's body, be called thieves of the day's beauty;[c] let us be—*Diana's foresters, Gentlemen of the shade, Minions of the moon;* and let men say, we be men of good government; being governed as the sea is, by our noble and chaste mistress the moon, under whose countenance we—steal.

P. HEN. Thou say'st well; and it holds well too: for the fortune of us, that are the moon's men, doth ebb and flow like the sea; being governed as the sea is, by the moon. As, for proof, now: a purse of gold most resolutely snatched on Monday night, and most dissolutely spent on Tuesday morning; got with swearing—*lay by;* and spent with crying—*bring in:* now, in as low an ebb as the foot of the ladder; and, by and by, in as high a flow as the ridge of the gallows.

FAL. By the Lord,‡ thou say'st true, lad. And is not my hostess of the tavern a most sweet wench?[e]

P. HEN. As the honey of Hybla,[f] my old lad of the castle. And is not a buff jerkin[g] a most sweet robe of durance?

(*) First folio, *of*. (†) First folio inserts, *and*. (‡) First folio inserts, *in the*.

(*) First folio omits, *the*. (†) First folio omits, *by my troth* (‡) First folio omits, *By the Lord*.

[a] I shall have none but Mordake earl of Fife.] In this refusal Hotspur was justified by the law of arms; every prisoner whose redemption did not exceed ten thousand crowns being at the disposal of his captor, either for ransom or acquittal. Mordake, however, being a prince of the royal blood could be rightfully claimed by the king.

[b] To demand that truly which thou would'st truly know.] The prince appears to object that Falstaff asks the time of *day*, when all his pursuits have reference to *night*.

[c] *Thieves of the day's* beauty;] For *beauty*, Theobald reads *booty;* but Malone conjectures that a pun was intended on the word *beauty*, which was to be pronounced as it still is in some counties, *booty*.

[d] *Got with swearing*—lay by; *and spent with crying*—bring in;] *Lay by*, is a nautical phrase meaning *slacken sail*, and may have been a slang term for the highwayman's "*stand*." The *bring in*, was the tavern call for more wine.

[e] And is not my hostess of the tavern a most sweet wench?] The humour of asking a question or making an observation quite irrelevant to the conversation going on, is very ancient. It must have been common in Shakespeare's time, for it is frequently found in the old dramas, and he himself indulges in this vein again in the present play, where the prince mystifies poor Francis,—"Why then, your brown bastard is your only drink." It occurs also in Hamlet more than once. Ben Jonson calls it *a game of vapours*.

[f] As the honey of Hybla,—] The folio reads, As *is* the honey, omitting the words, *of Hybla*.

[g] And is not a buff jerkin a most sweet robe of durance?] See note (1), p. 150.

FAL. How now, how now, mad wag? what, in thy quips and thy quiddities? what a plague have I to do with a buff jerkin?

P. HEN. Why, what a pox have I to do with my hostess of the tavern?

FAL. Well, thou hast called her to a reckoning, many a time and oft.

P. HEN. Did I ever call for thee to pay thy part?

FAL. No; I'll give thee thy due, thou hast paid all there.

P. HEN. Yea, and elsewhere, so far as my coin would stretch; and, where it would not, I have used my credit.

FAL. Yea, and so used it, that were it not* here apparent that thou art heir apparent,—But, I pr'ythee, sweet wag, shall there be gallows standing in England when thou art king? and resolution thus fobbed as it is, with the rusty curb of old father antic the law? Do not thou, when thou art* king, hang a thief.

P. HEN. No; thou shalt.

FAL. Shall I? O rare! By the Lord,† I'll be a brave judge.[a]

P. HEN. Thou judgest false already; I mean, thou shalt have the hanging of the thieves, and so become a rare hangman.

FAL. Well, Hal, well; and in some sort it jumps with my humour, as well as waiting in the court, I can tell you.

P. HEN. For obtaining of suits?

FAL. Yea, for obtaining of suits: whereof the hangman hath no lean wardrobe. 'Sblood,‡ I am as melancholy as a gib cat,[b] or a lugged bear.

P. HEN. Or an old lion; or a lover's lute.

FAL. Yea, or the drone of a Lincolnshire bagpipe.(2)

P. HEN. What say'st thou to a hare,[c] or the melancholy of Moor-ditch? (3)

(*) First folio omits, *not*.

(*) First folio inserts, *a*. (†) First folio omits, *By the Lord*. (‡) First folio omits, *S'blood*.

[a] *I'll be* a brave judge.] Shakespeare had probably in his mind a passage from the old play of "The Famous Victories of Henry the Fifth,"—

"Henry V. But Ned, so soone as I am king, the first thing I will doo, shal be to put my Lord chiefe Justice out of office, and thou shalt be my Lord chiefe Justice of England."

"Ned. Shall I be Lorde chiefe Justice?
By gog's wounds ile be the *bravest* Lorde chiefe Justice
That ever was in England."

[b] *A* gib *cat*,—] *Gilbert* and *Tibert*, contracted into *Gib* and *Tib*, were the common names for cats in former times, *Gib* being usually applied to an *old cat*. Why this animal or "an old lion," or a "lugged bear," should be accounted melancholy, unless from the gravity of its carriage, has never been shown, but the simile "as melancholy as a cat," was in frequent use:—thus in Lilly's "Midas,"—

"Pet. How now, Motto, all amort?
Mot. I am *as melancholy as a cat*."

[c] A hare,—] The following extract, from Turberville's Book on Hunting and Falconry, is a better explanation of this passage than any given by the commentators:—"The Hare first taught us the use of the hearbe called wyld Succory, which is very excellent for those which are disposed to be melancholicke: *Shee herselfe is one of the most melancholicke beasts that is*, and to heale her own infirmitie she goeth commonly to sit under that hearbe."

FAL. Thou hast the most unsavoury similes;* and art, indeed, the most comparative,[a] rascalliest,†—sweet young prince,—But Hal, I pr'ythee, trouble me no more with vanity. I would to God,‡ thou and I knew where a commodity of good names were to be bought: an old lord of the council rated me the other day in the street about you, sir; but I marked him not: and yet he talked very wisely; but I regarded him not: and yet he talked wisely, and in the street too.

P. HEN. Thou did'st well; for wisdom cries out in the streets, and no man regards it.(4)

FAL. O, thou hast damnable iteration; and art, indeed, able to corrupt a saint. Thou hast done much harm upon§ me, Hal,—God forgive thee for it! Before I knew thee, Hal, I knew nothing; and now am I,|| if a man should speak truly, little better than one of the wicked. I must give over this life, and I will give it over; by the Lord,¶ an I do not, I am a villain; I'll be damn'd for never a king's son in Christendom.

P. HEN. Where shall we take a purse to-morrow, Jack?

FAL. Zounds!** where thou wilt, lad, I'll make one; an I do not, call me villain, and baffle me.

P. HEN. I see a good amendment of life in thee; from praying, to purse-taking.

Enter POINS *at a distance.*

FAL. Why, Hal, 'tis my vocation, Hal; 'tis no sin for a man to labour in his vocation. Poins!—Now shall we know if Gadshill have set a match.[b] O, if men were to be saved by merit, what hole in hell were hot enough for him? This is the most omnipotent villain, that ever cried, *Stand*, to a true man.

P. HEN. Good morrow, Ned.

POINS. Good morrow, sweet Hal.—What says monsieur Remorse? What says sir John Sack-and-Sugar? Jack, how agrees the devil and thee about thy soul, that thou soldest him on Good-Friday last, for a cup of Madeira, and a cold capon's leg?

P. HEN. Sir John stands to his word, the devil shall have his bargain; for he was never yet a breaker of proverbs, he will *give the devil his due.*

POINS. Then art thou damned for keeping thy word with the devil.

P. HEN. Else he had been* damned for cozening the devil.

POINS. But my lads, my lads, to-morrow morning, by four o'clock, early at Gadshill:(5) there are pilgrims going to Canterbury with rich offerings, and traders riding to London with fat purses: I have visors for you all, you have horses for yourselves; Gadshill lies to-night in Rochester; I have bespoke supper to-morrow night† in Eastcheap; we may do it as secure as sleep: if you will go, I will stuff your purses full of crowns: if you will not, tarry at home, and be hanged.

FAL. Hear ye, Yedward;[c] if I tarry at home, and go not, I'll hang you for going.

POINS. You will, chops?

FAL. Hal, wilt thou make one?

P. HEN. Who, I rob? I a thief? not I, by my faith.‡

FAL. There's neither honesty, manhood, nor good fellowship in thee, nor thou cam'st not of the blood royal, if thou dar'st not stand for ten shillings.[d]

P. HEN. Well, then, once in my days I'll be a mad-cap.

FAL. Why, that's well said.

P. HEN. Well, come what will, I'll tarry at home.

FAL. By the Lord,§ I'll be a traitor then, when thou art king.

P. HEN. I care not.

POINS. Sir John, I pr'ythee, leave the prince and me alone; I will lay him down such reasons for this adventure, that he shall go.

FAL. Well, God give thee[e] the spirit of persuasion, and him the ears of profiting, that what thou speakest may move, and what he hears may be believed, that the true prince may (for recreation sake,) prove a false thief; for the poor abuses of the time want countenance. Farewell: you shall find me in Eastcheap.

P. HEN. Farewell, thou || latter spring! Farewell, All-hallown summer![f] [*Exit* FALSTAFF.

(*) First folio, *smiles*. (†) First folio, *rascallest*.
(‡) First folio omits, *to God*. (§) First folio, *unto*.
(||) First folio, *I am*. (¶) First folio omits, *by the Lord*.
(**) First folio omits, *Zounds*.

[a] *Most* comparative,] This may mean, that is *readiest in comparisons or similes*.

[b] *Have* set a match.] The first folio has "set a *watch*." *Setting a match* was occasionally used for *making an appointment*; thus, in Ben Jonson's "Bartholomew Fair;"—"Peace, Sir, they'll be angry if they hear you eves-dropping, now they are *setting* their *match*." But it was also employed in rogues' language to mean *planning a robbery*; as in "Ratsey's Ghost," a black letter quarto, quoted by Farmer, supposed to be about 1606. "I have been many times beholding to Tapsters and Chamberlaines for directions and *setting of matches*."

[c] *Hear ye*, Yedward;] *Yedward* is a popular corruption of "Edward," still used in some parts of England.

(*) First folio omits, *been*. (†) First folio omits, *night*.
(‡) First folio omits, *by my faith*.
(§) First folio omits, *by the Lord*. (||) Old text, *the*.

[d] Thou cam'st not of the blood royal, if thou darest not stand for ten shillings.] We should perhaps read, as many of the modern editors do, "*cry*, stand," since a quibble is evidently intended on the word *royal*. The coin called *real* or *royal* was of *ten shillings* value.

[e] *Well*, God give thee *the spirit of persuasion, and* him *the ears of profiting*,—] The folio reads, Well, *may'st thou have* the spirit of persuasion, and *he* the ears, &c.

[f] All-hallown summer!] *All-hallown tide*, or *All Saints' day*, is the first of November. Nothing could be more happy than the likening Falstaff, with his old age and young passions, to this November summer.

POINS. Now, my good sweet honey lord, ride with us to-morrow; I have a jest to execute, that I cannot manage alone. Falstaff, Bardolph, Peto, and Gadshill,[a] shall rob those men that we have already way-laid; yourself, and I, will not be there: and when they have the booty, if you and I do not rob them, cut this head from my shoulders.

P. HEN. But how shall we part with them in setting forth?

POINS. Why, we will set forth before or after them, and appoint them a place of meeting, wherein it is at our pleasure to fail; and then will they adventure upon the exploit themselves: which they shall have no sooner achieved, but we'll set upon them.

P. HEN. Ay, but, 'tis like, that they will know us, by our horses, by our habits, and by every other appointment, to be ourselves.

POINS. Tut! our horses they shall not see, I'll tie them in the wood; our visors we will change after we leave them; and, sirrah, I have cases of buckram for the nonce,[b] to immask our noted outward garments.

P. HEN. But I doubt, they will be too hard for us.

POINS. Well, for two of them, I know them to be as true-bred cowards as ever turned back; and for the third, if he fight longer than he sees reason, I'll forswear arms. The virtue of this jest will be, the incomprehensible lies that this same* fat rogue will tell us, when we meet at supper: how thirty at least, he fought with; what wards, what blows, what extremities he endured; and, in the reproof of this, lies† the jest.

P. HEN. Well, I'll go with thee; provide us all things necessary, and meet me to-night[c] in Eastcheap, there I'll sup. Farewell.

POINS. Farewell, my lord. [*Exit* POINS.

P. HEN. I know you all, and will a while uphold
The unyok'd humour of your idleness:
Yet herein will I imitate the sun,
Who doth permit the base contagious clouds
To smother up his beauty from the world,
That, when he please again to be himself,
Being wanted, he may be more wonder'd at,
By breaking through the foul and ugly mists
Of vapours, that did seem to strangle him.
If all the year were playing holidays,
To sport would be as tedious as to work;
But when they seldom come, they wish'd-for come,
And nothing pleaseth but rare accidents.
So, when this loose behaviour I throw off,
And pay the debt I never promised,
By how much better than my word I am,
By so much shall I falsify men's hopes;[d]
And, like bright metal on a sullen ground,
My reformation, glittering o'er my fault,
Shall show more goodly, and attract more eyes,
Than that which hath no foil* to set it off.
I'll so offend, to make offence a skill;
Redeeming time, when men think least I will.(6)
[*Exit.*

SCENE III.—*The same. A Room in the Palace.*

Enter KING HENRY, NORTHUMBERLAND, WORCESTER, HOTSPUR, SIR WALTER BLUNT, *and others.*

K. HEN. My blood hath been too cold and temperate,
Unapt to stir at these indignities,
And you have found me; for, accordingly,
You tread upon my patience: but, be sure,
I will from henceforth rather be myself,
Mighty, and to be fear'd, than my condition;[e]
Which hath been smooth as oil, soft as young down,
And therefore lost that title of respect,
Which the proud soul ne'er pays, but to the proud.

WOR. Our house, my sovereign liege, little deserves
The scourge of greatness to be used on it;
And that same greatness too which our own hands
Have holp to make so portly.

NORTH. My lord,——

K. HEN. Worcester, get thee gone, for I do see
Danger and disobedience in thine eye:
O, sir, your presence is too bold and peremptory,
And majesty might never yet endure

(*) First folio omits, *same*. (†) First quarto, *lives*.

(*) First folio, *soil*.

a Falstaff, Bardolph, Peto, and Gadshill,—] The old copies read, Falstaff, *Harvey*, *Rossil*, and Gadshill. *Harvey* and *Rossil* being, no doubt, the names of the actors who personated Bardolph and Peto.

b *For the* nonce,] For the *occasion*. See note (a), p. 128.

c Meet me to-night—] The old copies have "to-morrow night," which is an obvious mistake.

d *Shall I falsify men's* hopes;] Hopes here means *expectations*, a use of the word not at all uncommon formerly, and hardly obsolete even now in some counties.

"This speech is very artfully introduced to keep the Prince from appearing vile in the opinion of the audience; it prepares them for his future reformation; and what is yet more valuable, exhibits a natural picture of a great mind offering excuses to itself, and palliating those follies which it can neither justify nor forsake."
JOHNSON

e Than my condition.] *Condition* in this place means, *natural disposition*. See note (d), p. 397.

The moody frontier of a servant brow.
You have good leave to leave us; when we need
Your use and counsel, we shall send for you.—
[*Exit* WORCESTER.
You were about to speak. [*To* NORTH.
NORTH. Yea, my good lord.
Those prisoners in your highness' name* demanded,
Which Harry Percy here at Holmedon took,
Were, as he says, not with such strength denied
As is† deliver'd to your majesty:
Either envy, therefore, or misprision
Is guilty of this fault, and not my son.[a]
HOT. My liege, I did deny no prisoners.
But, I remember, when the fight was done,
When I was dry with rage, and extreme toil,
Breathless and faint, leaning upon my sword,
Came there a certain lord, neat, and trimly dress'd,
Fresh as a bridegroom; and his chin, new reap'd,
Show'd like a stubble land at harvest-home:
He was perfumed like a milliner,
And 'twixt his finger and his thumb he held
A pouncet-box,[b] which ever and anon
He gave his nose, and took't away again;——
Who, therewith angry, when it next came there,
Took it in snuff:[c]—and still he smil'd, and talk'd;
And, as the soldiers bore* dead bodies by,
He call'd them—untaught knaves, unmannerly,
To bring a slovenly unhandsome corse
Betwixt the wind and his nobility.
With many holiday and lady terms†
He question'd me: among the rest, demanded
My prisoners, in your majesty's behalf.
I then, all smarting, with my wounds being cold,—
To be so pester'd with a popinjay,—
Out of my grief and my impatience,
Answer'd neglectingly, I know not what,—

(*) First folio omits, *name*. (†) First folio, *was*.

a Either envy, therefore, or *misprision*
Is *guilty of this fault, and not my son*.]
So the early quarto copies. The folio reads,—
"*Who either through envy*, or misprision,
Was guilty of this fault," &c.

(*) First folio, *bare*.
(†) First folio, *term*.

b *A pouncet box*.] A box with the lid pierced, containing scents.
c Took it in snuff.—] See note (e), p. 84.

He should, or he* should not;—for he made me mad,
To see him shine so brisk, and smell so sweet,
And talk so like a waiting-gentlewoman,
Of guns, and drums, and wounds, (God save the mark!)
And telling me, the sovereign'st thing on earth
Was parmaceti,[a] for an inward bruise;
And that it was great pity, so it was,
That villainous salt-petre should be digg'd
Out of the bowels of the harmless earth,
Which many a good tall fellow had destroy'd
So cowardly; and, but for these vile guns,
He would himself have been a soldier.
This bald unjointed chat of his, my lord,
I answer'd,† indirectly, as I said;
And, I beseech you, let not his‡ report
Come current for an accusation,
Betwixt my love and your high majesty.

BLUNT. The circumstance consider'd, good my lord,
Whatever Harry Percy then had said,
To such a person, and in such a place,
At such a time, with all the rest re-told,
May reasonably die, and never rise
To do him wrong, or any way impeach
What then he said, so he unsay it now.

K. HEN. Why, yet he* doth deny his prisoners;
But with proviso, and exception,—
That we, at our own charge, shall ransom straight
His brother-in-law, the foolish Mortimer; (7)
Who, on† my soul, hath wilfully betray'd
The lives of those, that he did lead to fight
Against the great magician, damn'd Glendower;
Whose daughter, as we hear, the earl of March
Hath lately married. Shall our coffers then
Be emptied, to redeem a traitor home?
Shall we buy treason? and indent with feers,[b]
When they have lost and forfeited themselves?
No, on the barren mountains‡ let him starve;
For I shall never hold that man my friend,
Whose tongue shall ask me for one penny cost
To ransom home revolted Mortimer.

HOT. Revolted Mortimer!
He never did fall off, my sovereign liege,
But by the chance of war. To prove that true,
Needs no more but one tongue for all those wounds,
Those mouthed wounds, which valiantly he took,

(*) First folio omits, *he*.
(†) First folio, *Made me to answer*. (‡) First folio, *this*.

a Parmaceti.] This was the ancient pronunciation of *spermaceti*. Sir Richard Hawkins, in his "Voyage into the South Sea," 1593, p. 46, says—"This we corruptly call *parmacettie*, of the Latin word *Sperma Ceti*."

b *And indent with* feers.] The old copies all read *fears*, which was only one of the many forms of spelling *feers*:—

"And Hero fayre vnto her *feare*,
Leander fyne did take."—

The Pleasant fable of Hermaphroditus and Salmacis, by T. Peend, Gent. &c. &c. 1565

(*) First folio omits, *he*. (†) First folio, *in*.
(‡) First folio, *mountain*.

When on the gentle Severn's sedgy bank,
In single opposition, hand to hand,
He did confound the best part of an hour
In changing hardiment with great Glendower:
Three times they breath'd, and three times did they drink,
Upon agreement, of swift Severn's flood:
Who then, affrighted [a] with their bloody looks,
Ran fearfully among the trembling reeds,
And hid his crisp head in the hollow bank
Blood-stained with these valiant combatants.
Never did base and rotten policy
Colour her working with such deadly wounds;
Nor never could the noble Mortimer
Receive so many, and all willingly:
Then let him not be slander'd with revolt.

K. HEN. Thou dost belie him, Percy, thou dost belie him;
He never did encounter with Glendower; [alone,
I tell thee, he durst as well have met the devil
As Owen Glendower for an enemy.
Art thou not asham'd? But, sirrah, henceforth,
Let me not hear you speak of Mortimer:
Send me your prisoners with the speediest means,
Or you shall hear in such a kind from me
As will displease you. My lord Northumberland,
We license your departure with your son:—
Send us your prisoners, or you'll hear of it.

[*Exeunt* KING HENRY, BLUNT, *and Train.*

HOT. And if the devil come and roar for them,
I will not send them: I will after straight,
And tell him so; for I will ease my heart,
Albeit I make a hazard of my head.[b]

NORTH. What, drunk with choler! stay, and pause awhile;
Here comes your uncle.

Re-enter WORCESTER.

HOT. Speak of Mortimer!
'Zounds,* I will speak of him; and let my soul
Want mercy, if I do not join with him:
Yea, on his part,† I'll empty all these veins,
And shed my dear blood drop by drop i' the dust,
But I will lift the down-trod‡ Mortimer
As high i' the air as this unthankful king,
As this ingrate and canker'd Bolingbroke.

NORTH. Brother, the king hath made your nephew mad. [*To* WORCESTER.

WOR. Who struck this heat up after I was gone?

HOT. He will, forsooth, have all my prisoners;
And when I urg'd the ransom once again
Of my wife's brother, then his cheek look'd pale;
And on my face he turn'd an eye of death,[c]
Trembling even at the name of Mortimer.

WOR. I cannot blame him: was he not proclaim'd,
By Richard that dead is, the next of blood?

NORTH. He was; I heard the proclamation;
And then it was, when the unhappy king
(Whose wrongs in us God pardon!) did set forth
Upon his Irish expedition;
From whence he, intercepted, did return
To be depos'd, and, shortly murdered.

WOR. And for whose death, we in the world's wide mouth
Live scandaliz'd, and foully spoken of. [then

HOT. But, soft, I pray you; did king Richard
Proclaim my brother Edmund* Mortimer
Heir to the crown?

NORTH. He did; myself did hear it.

HOT. Nay, then I cannot blame his cousin king,
That wish'd him on the barren mountains starv'd.
But shall it be, that you, that set the crown
Upon the head of this forgetful man;
And, for his sake, wear† the detested blot
Of murd'rous subornation,—shall it be,
That you a world of curses undergo;
Being the agents, or base second means,
The cords, the ladder, or the hangman rather?—
O, pardon me,‡ that I descend so low,
To show the line, and the predicament,
Wherein you range under this subtle king.
Shall it, for shame, be spoken in these days,
Or fill up chronicles in time to come,
That men of your nobility and power,
Did 'gage them both in an unjust behalf,—
As both of you, God pardon it! have done,—
To put down Richard, that sweet lovely rose,
And plant this thorn, this canker, Bolingbroke?
And shall it, in more shame, be further spoken,
That you are fool'd, discarded, and shook off
By him, for whom these shames ye underwent?
No; yet time serves, wherein you may redeem
Your banish'd honours,[d] and restore yourselves

(*) First folio, *yes.* (†) First folio, *In his behalf.* (‡) First folio, *downfall.*

[a] "Severn is here not the flood, but the tutelary power of the flood, who was affrighted, and hid his head in the hollow bank."—JOHNSON.

[b] Albeit I make a *hazard of my head.*] So all the quarto copies; the folio reads, *Although it be with* hazard, &c.

[c] An eye of death.] Not surely, as Johnson and Steevens interpret it, *an eye menacing death*, but, *an eye of deadly fear.*

——*You may redeem*
your banish'd honours,—]

(*) First folio omits, *Edmund.* (†) First folio, *were.* (‡) First folio omits, *me*, and inserts, *if.*

Mr. Collier's annotator, in the very wantonness of emendation, substitutes "*tarnish'd*" for "*banish'd.*" In Massinger's play of "The Maid of Honour," Act I. Sc. 1, we have

"——Rouse us, sir, from the sleep
Of idleness, and *redeem our mortgaged honours*"

And in "The Custom of the Country," (Beaumont and Fletcher,) Act II. Sc. 1:—

"—— Upon my life, this gallant
Is bribed to repeal *banish'd swords.*"

Into the good thoughts of the world again:
Revenge the jeering, and disdain'd contempt,
Of this proud king; who studies, day and night,
To answer all the debt he owes to* you,
Even with the bloody payment of your deaths.
Therefore I say,——
WOR. Peace, cousin, say no more:
And now I will unclasp a secret book,
And to your quick-conceiving discontents
I'll read you matter deep and dangerous;
As full of peril, and adventurous spirit,
As to o'er-walk a current, roaring loud,
On the unsteadfast footing of a spear.
HOT. If he fall in, good night:—or sink, or swim:—
Send danger from the east unto the west,
So honour cross it from the north to south,
And let them grapple;—O!† the blood more stirs,
To rouse a lion, than to start a hare.[a]
NORTH. Imagination of some great exploit
Drives him beyond the bounds of patience.
HOT. By heaven, methinks, it were an easy leap,
To pluck bright honour from the pale-fac'd moon;
Or dive into the bottom of the deep,
Where fathom-line could never touch the ground,
And pluck up drowned honour by the locks,
So he, that doth redeem her thence, might wear
Without corrival, all her dignities:
But out upon this half-fac'd fellowship!
WOR. He apprehends a world of figures here,
But not the form of what he should attend.
Good cousin, give me audience for a while.[b]
HOT. I cry you mercy.
WOR. Those same noble Scots,
That are your prisoners,——
HOT. I'll keep them all;
By God,‡ he shall not have a Scot of them;
No, if a Scot would save his soul, he shall not:
I'll keep them, by this hand.
WOR. You start away,
And lend no ear unto my purposes.—
Those prisoners you shall keep.
HOT. Nay, I will; that's flat:—
He said, he would not ransom Mortimer;
Forbad my tongue to speak of Mortimer;
But I will find him when he lies asleep,
And in his ear I'll holloa—*Mortimer!*
Nay, I'll have a starling shall be taught to speak
Nothing but, *Mortimer*, and give it him,
To keep his anger still in motion.
WOR. Hear you, cousin; a word.
HOT. All studies here I solemnly defy,[c]
Save how to gall and pinch this Bolingbroke:
And that same sword-and-buckler[d] prince of Wales,—
But that I think his father loves him not,
And would be glad he met with some mischance,
I'd have him poison'd* with a pot of ale.
WOR. Farewell, kinsman! I will talk to you,
When you are better temper'd to attend.
NORTH. Why, what a wasp-stung[e] and impatient fool
Art thou, to break into this woman's mood:
Tying thine ear to no tongue but thine own?
HOT. Why, look you, I am whipp'd and scourg'd with rods,
Nettled and stung with pismires, when I hear
Of this vile politician, Bolingbroke.
In Richard's time,—what do you call the place?—
A plague upon't!—it is in Glostershire;—
'Twas where the mad-cap duke his uncle kept;
His uncle York;—where I first bow'd my knee
Unto this king of smiles, this Bolingbroke,—'sblood!†
When you and he came back from Ravenspurg,—
NORTH. At Berkley castle.
HOT. You say true:——
Why, what a candy‡ deal of courtesy
This fawning greyhound then did proffer me!
Look,—*when his infant fortune came to age*,—
And,—*gentle Harry Percy*—and, *kind cousin*,—[f]
O, the devil take such cozeners!——God forgive me!——
Good uncle, tell your tale, for I have done.
WOR. Nay, if you have not, to't again;
We'll stay your leisure.
HOT. I have done, i'faith,§
WOR. Then once more to your Scottish prisoners.
Deliver them up without their ransom straight,
And make the Douglas' son your only mean

(*) First folio, *unto*. (†) First folio omits, *O*. (‡) First folio, *Heaven*.

(*) First folio, *poison'd him*. (†) First folio omits, *'sblood*. (‡) First folio, *caudie*. (§) First folio, *in sooth*.

a *To rouse a lion, than to start a hare.*] That Shakespeare was an accomplished "woodman," may be inferred from his perfect acquaintance with the technical phraseology of the craft. The appropriate expression for raising the nobler animals for the chase was to *rouse;* the boar was *reared;* the fox *unkennelled;* and the hare *started*.

b Good cousin, give me audience for a while.] The folio, weakening the force of the passage, adds, *And list to me*.

c I *solemnly* defy,] *Defy* was sometimes employed in old language in the sense of *renounce*.

d *And that same* sword-and-buckler *prince of Wales*,—] Upon the introduction of the rapier and dagger, the sword-and-buckler fell into desuetude among the higher classes, and were accounted fitting weapons for the vulgar only, such as Hotspur implies were the associates of the prince. Thus in "Florio's First Fruites," 1578:—"What weapons bear they?—Some sword and dagger, some *sword* and *buckler*.—What weapon is that *buckler?*—A clownish dastardly weapon, and not fit for a gentleman."

e *Why, what a* wasp stung *and impatient fool*—] So the first quarto, 1598; in the second edition, 1599, *wasp-stung* was altered to *wasp-tongue;* and in the folio, 1623, it is, *wasp-tongu'd*.

f *When his infant fortune came to age,—*
And,—*gentle Harry Percy*—and, *kind cousin*,—]

The empty compliments, recollection of which so galled the fiery Percy, occur in his interview with Bolingbroke, in "Richard II." Act II. Sc. 3.

For powers in Scotland; which,—for divers reasons,
Which I shall send you written,—be assur'd,
Will easily be granted.—You, my lord,—
[*To* NORTHUMBERLAND.
Your son in Scotland being thus employ'd,—
Shall secretly into the bosom creep
Of that same noble prelate, well belov'd,
The archbishop.

HOT. Of York, is't not?

WOR. True; who bears hard
His brother's death at Bristol, the lord Scroop.
I speak not this in estimation,[a]
As what I think might be, but what I know
Is ruminated, plotted, and set down;
And only stays but to behold the face
Of that occasion that shall bring it on.

HOT. I smell it; upon my life, it will do well.*

NORTH. Before the game's afoot, thou still let'st slip.[b]

HOT. Why, it cannot choose[c] but be a noble plot:—
And then the power of Scotland, and of York,
To join with Mortimer, ha?

WOR. And so they shall.

HOT. In faith, it is exceedingly well aim'd.

WOR. And 'tis no little reason bids us speed,
To save our heads by raising of a head:
For, bear ourselves as even as we can,
The king will always think him in our debt,
And think we think ourselves unsatisfied,
Till he hath found a time to pay us home.
And see already, how he doth begin
To make us strangers to his looks of love.

HOT. He does, he does; we'll be reveng'd on him.

WOR. Cousin, farewell.—No further go in this,
Than I by letters shall direct your course.
When time is ripe, (which will be suddenly,)
I'll steal to Glendower, and lord* Mortimer;
Where you and Douglas, and our powers at once,
(As I will fashion it,) shall happily meet,
To bear our fortunes in our own strong arms,
Which now we hold at much uncertainty.

NORTH. Farewell, good brother: we shall thrive, I trust.

HOT. Uncle, adieu:—O, let the hours be short,
Till fields, and blows, and groans applaud our sport! [*Exeunt.*

(*) First folio, *wondrous well.*

(*) First folio, *loe.*

[a] I *speak not this in* estimation,—] *Estimation* here means *supposition, conjecture.*

[b] *Thou* still *let'st slip*] Thou *always* let'st slip. To let slip is a hunting technical; the hounds are held by the *leash* until the game is roused, and then are loosened for the chace.

[c] *Why* it cannot choose—] A form of expression now changed into *it cannot help*, &c.

ACT II.

SCENE I.—Rochester. *An Inn Yard.*

Enter a Carrier, *with a lantern in his hand.*

1 Car. Heigh ho! An't be not four by the day, I'll be hanged: Charles' wain[a] is over the new chimney, and yet our horse not packed. What, ostler!

Ost. [*Within.*] Anon, anon.

1 Car. I pr'ythee, Tom, beat Cut's saddle, put a few flocks in the point; the poor jade is wrung in the withers out of all cess.[b]

Enter another Carrier.

2 Car. Peas and beans are as dank here as a dog, and that* is the next way to give poor jades the bots: this house is turned upside down, since Robin† ostler died.

1 Car. Poor fellow! never joyed since the price of oats rose; it was the death of him.

2 Car. I think, this be‡ the most villainous house in all London road for fleas: I am stung like a tench.

---

a Charles' wain,—] The vulgar appellation for the constellation called the Bear, and a corruption of the *Chorles* or *Churls* (*i. e.* rustic's) wain.

b Out of all cess—] Out of all *measure.* The phrase, according to Cotgrave, is the same as the French, *sans cesse.*

(*) First folio, *this.* (†) First folio inserts, *the.* (‡) First folio, *is.*

1 Car. Like a tench? by the mass,* there is ne'er a king in Christendom[a] could be better bit than I have been since the first cock.

2 Car. Why, they† will allow us ne'er a jordan, and then we leak in your chimney; and your chamber-lie breeds fleas like a loach.(1)

1 Car. What, ostler! come away, and be hanged! come away.

2 Car. I have a gammon of bacon, and two razes of ginger,[b] to be delivered as far as Charing-cross.

1 Car. Godsbody!‡ the turkies in my pannier are quite starved.—What, ostler!—A plague on thee! hast thou never an eye in thy head? can'st not hear? An 'twere not as good a deed as drink, to break the pate of thee, I am a very villain.—Come, and be hanged:—hast no faith in thee?

Enter Gadshill.

Gads. Good-morrow, carriers. What's o'clock?

1 Car. I think it be two o'clock.[c]

Gads. I pr'ythee, lend me thy lantern, to see my gelding in the stable.

1 Car. Nay, soft, I pray ye;[d] I know a trick worth two of that, i'faith.§

Gads. I pr'ythee, lend me thine.

2 Car. Ay, when, can'st tell?[e]—*Lend me thy lantern,* quoth a?—marry, I'll see thee hanged first.

Gads. Sirrah carrier, what time do you mean to come to London?

2 Car. Time enough to go to bed with a candle, I warrant thee.—Come, neighbour Mugs, we'll call up the gentlemen; they will along with company, for they have great charge.

[*Exeunt* Carriers.

Gads. What, ho! chamberlain!

Cham. [*Within.*] At hand, quoth pick-purse.[f]

Gads. That's even as fair as—*at hand, quoth the chamberlain:* for thou variest no more from picking of purses, than giving direction doth from labouring; thou lay'st the plot, how.(2)

Enter Chamberlain.

Cham. Good morrow, master Gadshill. It holds current, that I told you yesternight. There's a franklin in the wild of Kent, hath brought three hundred marks with him in gold: I heard him tell it to one of his company, last night at supper; a kind of auditor; one that hath abundance of charge too, God knows what. They are up already, and call for eggs and butter;[g] they will away presently.

Gads. Sirrah, if they meet not with saint Nicholas' clerks,[h] I'll give thee this neck.

Cham. No, I'll none of it; I pr'ythee, keep that for the hangman; for, I know, thou worship'st saint Nicholas as truly as a man of falsehood may.

Gads. What talk'st thou to me of the hangman? if I hang, I'll make a fat pair of gallows: for, if I hang, old sir John hangs with me; and, thou know'st, he's no starveling. Tut! there are other Trojans that thou dream'st not of, the which, for sport sake, are content to do the profession some grace; that would, if matters should be looked into, for their own credit sake, make all whole. I am joined with no foot land-rakers, no long-staff, sixpenny strikers; none of these mad, mustachio-purple-hued malt-worms: but with nobility, and tranquillity; burgomasters, and great oneyers;(3) such as can hold in; such as will strike sooner than speak, and speak sooner than drink, and drink sooner than pray:[i] and yet, zounds!* I lie; for they pray continually to† their saint, the commonwealth; or, rather, not‡ pray to her, but prey on her; for they ride up and down on her, and make her their boots.

Cham. What, the commonwealth their boots? will she hold out water in foul way?

Gads. She will, she will; justice hath liquored her. We steal as in a castle, cock-sure: we have the receipt of fern-seed, we walk invisible.(4)

Cham. Nay, by my faith,[k] I think you are more beholden to the night, than to§ fern-seed, for your walking invisible.

(*) First folio omits, *by the mass.* (†) First folio, *you.*
(‡) First folio omits, *God'sbody.* (§) First folio omits, *i'faith.*

[a] *There is ne'er a king* in Christendom—] So the folio: the quartos read, ne'er a king *christen.*

[b] And two razes of ginger.] Supposed to mean *roots* of ginger.

[c] *I think it be* two o'clock.] Steevens suggests that the Carrier, suspecting Gadshill, tries to deceive him as to the hour; because the first observation made in the scene is, that it is *four o'clock.*

[d] Nay, soft, I pray ye; I know a trick, &c.—] Here the quarto copies have, Nay, *by God,* soft, I know, &c. The reading in the text is that of the folio.

[e] Ay, when, can'st tell?—] A proverbial saying. See note (d) p. 127, of the present volume.

[f] At hand, quoth pick-purse.] A proverbial expression of common currency in Shakespeare's time.

[g] Eggs and butter.] Buttered eggs constituted the usual breakfast formerly, especially in Lent.

[h] Saint Nicholas' clerks.] Under what circumstances St. Nicholas became the patron of scholars, an account is given in note (1), p. 43; but why he was reckoned the tutelary guardian of cut-purses has not yet been satisfactorily explained, although the expression so applied is repeatedly met with in old books. Thus in *Glareanus Vadeanus's Panegyrick upon Tom Coryat:*—

> "A mandrake grown under some heavy tree,
> There where *Saint Nicholas knights* not long before,
> Had dropt their fat *axungia* to the lee."

And again, in Rowley's play of "A Match at Midnight:"—"I think yonder comes prancing down the hills from Kingston a couple of *St. Nicholas's clerks.*"

[i] *Such as can* hold in; such as will strike sooner than speak, and speak sooner than drink, &c.] By *such as can hold in,* Gadshill, in his professional jargon, may mean such as can *hold on,* or *stick to the purpose;* but the subsequent gradation is not very intelligible, unless by *speak* is to be understood, *cry,* "*stand.*"

[k] *Nay,* by my faith, *I think you are,* &c.—] The folio omits *by my faith,* and reads,—Nay, I think *rather,* you, &c.

(*) First folio omits, *zounds.* (†) First folio, *unto.*
(‡) First folio inserts, *to.* (§) First folio inserts, *the.*

GADS. Give me thy hand: thou shalt have a share in our purchase,[a] as I am a true man.

CHAM. Nay, rather let me have it, as you are a false thief.

GADS. Go to; *Homo* is a common name to all men. Bid the ostler bring my* gelding out of the stable. Farewell, you muddy knave. [*Exeunt.*

SCENE II.—*The Road near* Gads-hill.

Enter PRINCE HENRY, *and* POINS.

POINS. Come, shelter, shelter; I have removed Falstaff's horse, and he frets like a gummed velvet.[b]

P. HEN. Stand close.

Enter FALSTAFF.

FAL. Poins! Poins, and be hanged! Poins!

P. HEN. Peace, ye fat-kidney'd rascal; what a brawling dost thou keep!

FAL. Where's* Poins, Hal?

P. HEN. He is walked up to the top of the hill; I'll go seek him. [*Pretends to seek* POINS.

FAL. I am accurst to rob in that thief's company: the† rascal hath removed my horse, and tied him I know not where. If I travel but four foot by the squire[c] further afoot, I shall break my wind. Well, I doubt not but to die a fair death for all this, if I 'scape hanging for killing that rogue. I have forsworn his company hourly any time this two-and-twenty year, and yet I am bewitched with the rogue's company. If the rascal

(*) First folio, *the.*

(*) First folio, *What.* (†) First folio, *that.*

a *Our* purchase] In the rogue's language, *purchase* was anciently a slang synonym for *stolen goods*. Thus in Henry V. Act III. Sc. 2:—

"They will steal anything, and call it *purchase.*"

The first folio reads, *purpose.*

b *And he* frets like a gummed velvet,] So in Marston's play of "The Malcontent:"—"I'll come among you, like gum into taffata, to *fret, fret.*"

c *By the* squire—] That is, by the *rule*. The word is derived from the French *esquiere;* and occurs again in the "Winter's Tale," Act IV. Sc. 3:—"Not the worst of the three, but jumps twelve foot and a half *by the squire.*" See, also, Note (b), p. 92.

have not given me medicines, to make me love him, I'll be hanged; it could not be else; I have drunk medicines.—Poins!—Hal!—a plague upon you both!—Bardolph!—Peto!—I'll starve, ere I'll* rob a foot further. An 'twere not as good a deed as† drink, to turn true[a] man, and to leave these rogues, I am the veriest varlet that ever chewed with a tooth. Eight yards of uneven ground is threescore and ten miles afoot with me; and the stony-hearted villains know it well enough. A plague upon't, when thieves cannot be true to one another! [*They whistle.*] Whew!—A plague‡ upon you all! Give me§ my horse, you rogues; give me my horse, and be hanged.

P. Hen. Peace, ye fat-guts! lie down; lay thine ear close to the ground, and list if thou can'st‖ hear the tread of travellers.

Fal. Have you any levers to lift me up again, being down? 'Sblood,¶ I'll not bear mine own flesh so far afoot again, for all the coin in thy father's exchequer. What a plague mean ye, to colt[b] me thus?

P. Hen. Thou liest, thou art not colted, thou art uncolted.

(*) First folio, *I*.
(†) First folio inserts, *to*.
(‡) First folio inserts, *light*.
(§) First folio omits, *me*.
(‖) First folio, *can*.
(¶) First folio omits, *'Sblood*.

[a] True *man*,—] *Honest* man. In old language *thief* and *true* *man* are always placed in opposition.

[b] *To colt me thus?*] To *colt* meant to *gull*.

Fal. I pr'ythee, good prince Hal, help me to my horse; good king's son.

P. Hen. Out, you rogue! shall I be your ostler?

Fal. Go, hang thyself in thine own heir-apparent garters! If I be ta'en, I'll peach for this. An I have not ballads made on you* all, and sung to filthy tunes, let a cup of sack be my poison: when a jest is so forward, and afoot too,—I hate it.

Enter Gadshill; Bardolph *and* Peto *with him.*

Gads. Stand.

Fal. So I do, against my will.

Poins. O, 'tis our setter: I know his voice. Bardolph, what news?

Bar. Case ye, case ye; on with your visors; there's money of the king's coming down the hill; 'tis going to the king's exchequer.

Fal. You lie, you rogue; 'tis going to the king's tavern.

Gads. There's enough to make us all.

Fal. To be hanged.

(*) First folio omits, *you*.

P. Hen. Sirs,* you four shall front them in the narrow lane; Ned Poins† and I will walk lower: if they 'scape from your encounter, then they light on us.

Peto. How many be there of them?[a]

Gads. Some eight, or ten.

Fal. Zounds!‡ will they not rob us?

P. Hen. What, a coward, sir John Paunch?

Fal. Indeed, I am not John of Gaunt, your grandfather; but yet no coward, Hal.

P. Hen. Well,§ we || leave that to the proof.

Poins. Sirrah Jack, thy horse stands behind the hedge; when thou need'st him, there thou shalt find him. Farewell, and stand fast.

Fal. Now cannot I strike him, if I should be hanged.

P. Hen. Ned, where are our disguises?

Poins. Here, hard by; stand close.

[P. Henry *and* Poins *retire.*

(*) First folio omits, *Sirs.* (†) First folio omits, *Poins.* (‡) First folio omits, *Zounds.* (§) First folio omits, *Well.* (||) First folio, *wee'l.*

a How many be there of them?] So the first quarto. The folio reads,—*But* how many be of them?

Fal. Now, my masters, happy man be his dole,[b] say I; every man to his business.

Enter Travellers.

1 Trav. Come, neighbour; the boy shall lead our horses down the hill: we'll walk afoot a while, and ease our legs.

Thieves. Stand!*

Trav. Jesu bless us!

Fal. Strike! down with them! cut the villains' throats! Ah! whorson caterpillars! bacon-fed knaves! they hate us youth: down with them! fleece them!

1 Trav. O, we are undone, both we and ours, for ever.

Fal. Hang ye, gorbellied[c] knaves: are ye undone? No, ye fat chuffs; I would your store

(*) First folio, *Stay.*

b Happy man be his dole,—] See Note (d), p. 234.

c Gorbellied—] *Pot-bellied, swag-bellied.* Perhaps corrupted from *gorge-bellied.* That Falstaff, the "tun of man," should reproach his victims with corpulence is exquisitely humorous.

were here! On, bacons, on! What, ye knaves! young men must live: you are grand jurors are ye? we'll jure ye, i'faith.

[*Exeunt* FALSTAFF, &c. *driving them out.*[a]

P. HEN. The thieves have bound the true men: now could thou and I rob the thieves, and go merrily to London, it would be argument for a week, laughter for a month, and a good jest for ever.

POINS. Stand close, I hear them coming.

[*Retire again.*

Re-enter Thieves.

FAL. Come, my masters, let us share, and then to horse before day. An the Prince and Poins be not two arrant cowards, there's no equity stirring: there's no more valour in that Poins, than in a wild duck.

P. HEN. Your money!

[*Rushing out upon them.*

POINS. Villains!

[*As they are sharing,*[b] *the* Prince *and* POINS *set upon them. They all run away, and* FALSTAFF *after a blow or two runs away too, leaving the booty behind them.*

P. HEN. Got with much ease. Now merrily to horse:
The thieves are scatter'd, and possess'd with fear
So strongly, that they dare not meet each other:
Each takes his fellow for an officer.
Away, good Ned. Falstaff sweats to death,
And lards the lean earth as he walks along:
Wer't not for laughing, I should pity him.

POINS. How the rogue roar'd! [*Exeunt.*

SCENE III.

Warkworth. *A Room in the Castle.*

Enter HOTSPUR, *reading a letter.*[c]

——*But, for mine own part, my lord, I could be well contented to be there, in respect of the love I bear your house.*—He could be contented,—why is he not then? In respect of the love he bears our house:—he shows in this, he loves his own barn better than he loves our house. Let me see some more. *The purpose you undertake, is dangerous;*—Why, that's certain; 'tis dangerous to take a cold, to sleep, to drink: but I tell you, my lord fool, out of this nettle, danger, we pluck this flower, safety. *The purpose you undertake, is dangerous; the friends you have named, uncertain; the time itself unsorted; and your whole plot too light, for the counterpoise of so great an opposition.*—Say you so, say you so? I say unto you again, you are a shallow cowardly hind, and you lie. What a lack-brain is this! By the Lord,* our plot is a good† plot as ever was laid; our friends‡ true and constant: a good plot, good friends, and full of expectation: an excellent plot, very good friends. What a frosty-spirited rogue is this! Why, my lord of York commends the plot, and the general course of the action. Zounds, an§ I were now by this rascal, I could brain him with his lady's fan. Is there not my father, my uncle, and myself? lord Edmund Mortimer, my lord of York, and Owen Glendower? Is there not, besides, the Douglas? Have I not all their letters, to meet me in arms by the ninth of the next month? and are they not, some of them, set forward already? What a pagan rascal is this! an infidel! Ha! you shall see now, in very sincerity of fear and cold heart, will he to the king, and lay open all our proceedings. O, I could divide myself, and go to buffets, for moving such a dish of skimmed milk with so honourable an action! Hang him! let him tell the king. We are prepared; I will set forward‖ to-night.

Enter Lady PERCY.

How now, Kate? I must leave you within these two hours.

LADY. O my good lord, why are you thus alone?
For what offence have I, this fortnight, been
A banish'd woman from my Harry's bed?
Tell me, sweet lord, what is't that takes from thee
Thy stomach, pleasure, and thy golden sleep?
Why dost thou bend thine eyes upon the earth,
And start so often when thou sit'st alone?
Why hast thou lost the fresh blood in thy cheeks,
And given my treasures, and my rights of thee,
To thick-ey'd musing, and curs'd melancholy?
In thy¶ faint slumbers, I by thee have watch'd,
And heard thee murmur tales of iron wars:
Speak terms of manage to thy bounding steed;
Cry, *Courage!—to the field!* And thou hast talk'd
Of sallies, and retires; of** trenches, tents,
Of palisadoes, frontiers, parapets;
Of basilisks,[d] of cannon, culverin:
Or prisoners' ransom, and of soldiers slain,
And all the current of a heady fight.

---

[a] Exeunt Falstaff, &c.] The old stage direction is,—"Heere they rob them, and binde them. Enter the Prince and Poines."

[b] As they are sharing, &c.] This is the stage direction exactly as it stands in the quarto copies.

[c] Reading a letter.] This letter, Mr. Edwards says, in his MS. Notes, was from George Dunbar, Earl of March, in Scotland.

(*) First folio, *I protest.* (†) First folio, *as good a.*
(‡) First folio, *friend.* (§) First folio, *By this hand if.*
(‖) First folio, *forwards.* (¶) First folio, *my.*
(**) First folio omits *of.*

[d] Basilisks,—] Huge pieces of ordnance. So called from their supposed resemblance to the basilisk.

Thy spirit within thee hath been so at war,
And thus hath so bestir'd thee in thy sleep,
That beads* of sweat have† stood upon thy brow,
Like bubbles in a late disturbed stream:
And in thy face strange motions have appear'd,
Such as we see when men restrain their breath
On some great sudden haste. O, what portents are these?
Some heavy business hath my lord in hand,
And I must know it, else he loves me not.

HOT. What, ho! Is Gilliams with the packet gone?

Enter Servant.

SERV. He is, my lord, an hour ago.‡

HOT. Hath Butler brought those horses from the sheriff?

SERV. One horse, my lord, he brought even now.

HOT. What horse? a roan, a crop-ear, is it not?

SERV. It is, my lord.

HOT. That roan shall be my throne.
Well, I will back him straight: O *esperance!* [a]—
Bid Butler lead him forth into the park.
[*Exit* Servant.

LADY. But hear you, my lord.

HOT. What say'st thou, my lady? [b]

LADY. What is it carries you away?

HOT. Why, my horse,
My love, my horse.

LADY. Out, you mad-headed ape!

(*) First folio, *beds*. (†) First folio, *hath*. (‡) First folio, *agone*.

[a] O *esperance!*—] The "O" is omitted in the folio, though clearly required, since *Esperance* (the motto of the Percy family) is pronounced as a word of three syllables,

[b] *But hear you*, my lord.
What say'st thou, my lady?]

See note (c), p. 413.

A weasel hath not such a deal of spleen,
As you are tossed with. In faith,*
I 'll know your business, Harry, that I will.
I fear, my brother Mortimer doth stir
About his title; and hath sent for you
To line [a] his enterprise: but if you go——

HOT. So far afoot, I shall be weary, love.

LADY. Come, come, you paraquito, answer me
Directly unto this question that I† ask.
In faith,‡ I 'll break thy little finger, Harry,
An if thou wilt not tell me all things true.[b]

HOT. Away, away, you trifler!—Love?—I love thee not,
I care not for thee, Kate: this is no world
To play with mammets, and to tilt with lips:
We must have bloody noses, and crack'd crowns,
And pass them current too.—Gods me, my horse!—
What say'st thou, Kate? what would'st thou have with me?

LADY. Do you§ not love me? do you§ not, indeed?
Well, do not then; for, since you love me not,
I will not love myself. Do you not love me?
Nay, tell me, if you speak|| in jest, or no.

HOT. Come, wilt thou see me ride?
And when I am o' horseback, I will swear
I love thee infinitely. But hark you, Kate;
I must not have you henceforth question me
Whither I go, nor reason whereabout:
Whither I must, I must; and, to conclude,
This evening must I leave you,¶ gentle Kate.
I know you wise; but yet no further wise,
Than Harry Percy's wife: constant you are,
But yet a woman: and for secrecy,
No lady closer; for I well** believe,
Thou wilt not utter what thou dost not know;[c]
And so far will I trust thee, gentle Kate!

LADY. How! so far?

HOT. Not an inch further. But hark you, [Kate,
Whither I go, thither shall you go too;
To-day will I set forth, to-morrow you.—
Will this content you, Kate?

LADY. It must, of force. [*Exeunt.*

(*) First folio, *sooth.* (†) Old text inserts, *shall.*
(‡) First folio, *indeed.* (§) First folio, *ye.*
(||) First folio, *thou speak'st.* (¶) First folio, *thee.*
(**) First folio, *will.*

a *To line his enterprise:*] To *line* means here to *strengthen.* It occurs, with the same sense, in "Macbeth," Act I. Sc. 3:—

"—— did *line* the rebel
With hidden help and vantage."

And in "King John," Act IV. Sc. 3:—

"We will not *line* his thin, bestained cloak."

b An if thou wilt not tell me all things true.] So the quartos. The folio, which prints the speech as prose, reads,—*if thou wilt not tell me true.*

c Thou wilt not utter what thou dost not know;] This was proverbial,—(see Ray's "Proverbs,")—and as old at least as Chaucer:—"Ye sayn that the janglerie of wommen *can hyde things that they wot not of.*"—MELIBEUS' *Tale.*

d And tell *me flatly*—] The folio reads,—*Telling* me, &c.

e *And when you* breathe in your watering,—] That is, take breath while drinking. Thus, in Rowland's "Letting of Humours Blood in the Head Vaine," Satyre 6:—

"Fill him his Beaker, he will never flinch,
To give a full quart pot the emptie pinch.
Heele looke vnto your *water* well enough,
And hath an eye that no man leaues a snuffe,
A pox of peece-meale drinking (William sayes)
Play it away, weele have no stoppes and stayes."

SCENE IV.—Eastcheap. *A Room in the* Boar's Head Tavern.(5)

Enter PRINCE HENRY *and* POINS.

P. HEN. Ned, pr'ythee, come out of that fat room, and lend me thy hand to laugh a little.

POINS. Where hast been, Hal?

P. HEN. With three or four loggerheads, amongst three or fourscore hogsheads. I have sounded the very base string of humility. Sirrah, I am sworn brother to a leash of drawers; and can call them all by their Christian* names, as—Tom, Dick, and Francis. They take it already upon their salvation,† that, though I be but prince of Wales, yet I am the king of courtesy; and tell[d] me flatly I am no proud Jack, like Falstaff; but a Corinthian, a lad of mettle, a good boy,—by the Lord, so they call me;‡ and when I am king of England, I shall command all the good lads in Eastcheap. They call—drinking deep, *dyeing scarlet:* and when you breathe in your watering,[e] they cry§—*hem!* and bid you play it off.—To conclude, I am so good a proficient in one quarter of an hour, that I can drink with any tinker in his own language during my life. I tell thee, Ned, thou hast lost much honour, that thou wert not with me in this action. But, sweet Ned,—to sweeten which name of Ned, I give thee this pennyworth of sugar,[f] clapped even now into my hand by an under-skinker;[g] one that never spake other English in his life, than—*Eight shillings and sixpence,* and—*You are welcome;* with this shrill addition,—*Anon, anon, sir! Score a pint of bastard in the Half-moon,* or so. But, Ned, to drive away the|| time till Falstaff come, I pr'ythee, do thou stand in some by-room, while I question my puny drawer, to what end he gave me the sugar; and do thou¶ never leave calling—*Francis!* that his tale to me may be nothing but—*anon.* Step aside, and I'll show thee a precedent.

POINS. Francis!

P. HEN. Thou art perfect.

POINS. Francis! [*Exit* POINS.

(*) First folio omits, *all,* and *Christian.*
(†) First folio, *confidence.*
(‡) First folio omits, *by the Lord, so they call me.*
(§) First folio, *then they cry.* (||) First folio omits, *the.*
(¶) First folio omits, *thou.*

f I give thee this pennyworth of sugar,—] It was not unusual in Shakespeare's day, to put sugar in wine; and the drawers, therefore, kept small papers of it, ready folded up, for the supply of customers.

g Under-skinker;] An *under-drawer,* or *waiter,* from *Schencken,* Dutch, to pour out drink.

Enter FRANCIS.

FRAN. Anon, anon, sir.—Look down into the Pomegranate, Ralph.

P. HEN. Come hither, Francis.

FRAN. My lord.

P. HEN. How long hast thou to serve, Francis?

FRAN. Forsooth, five years, and as much as to—

POINS. [*Without.*] Francis!

FRAN. Anon, anon, sir.

P. HEN. Five years! by'r lady, a long lease for the clinking of pewter. But, Francis, darest thou be so valiant, as to play the coward with thy indenture, and show it a fair pair of heels, and run from it?

FRAN. O lord, sir! I'll be sworn upon all the books in England, I could find in my heart—

POINS. [*Without.*] Francis!

FRAN. Anon, anon, sir.

P. HEN. How old art thou, Francis?

FRAN. Let me see,—about Michaelmas next I shall be—

POINS. [*Without.*] Francis!

FRAN. Anon, sir.—Pray you, stay a little, my lord.

P. HEN. Nay, but hark you, Francis; for the sugar thou gavest me,—'twas a pennyworth, was't not?

FRAN. O lord, sir! I would it had been two.

P. HEN. I will give thee for it a thousand pound; ask me when thou wilt, and thou shalt have it.

POINS. [*Without.*] Francis!

FRAN. Anon, anon.

P. HEN. *Anon*, Francis? No, Francis: but to-morrow, Francis; or, Francis, on Thursday; or, indeed, Francis, when thou wilt. But, Francis,—

FRAN. My lord?

P. HEN. Wilt thou rob this leathern-jerkin, crystal-button, nott-pated,[a] agate-ring, puke-stocking,[b] caddis-garter,[c] smooth-tongue, Spanish-pouch,—

FRAN. O lord, sir, who do you mean?

---

[a] Nott-pated,—] *Round-headed*, from the hair being polled close. In Chaucer's "Canterbury Tales," it is told of the Yeman:—

"A *nott head* had he with a brown visage."

[b] Puke-stocking,—] That is, *puce-stocking*. Either from the colour, which was a kind of dark drab, or from the material, which was worsted or woollen.

[c] Caddis-garter,—] *Caddis*, Malone says, was *worsted galloon*.

P. HEN. Why then, your brown bastard[a] is your only drink: for, look you, Francis, your white canvas doublet will sully: in Barbary, sir, it cannot come to so much.

FRAN. What, sir?

POINS. [*Without.*] Francis!

P. HEN. Away, you rogue; dost thou not* hear them call?

[*Here they both call him; the drawer stands amazed, not knowing which way to go.*

Enter Vintner.

VINT. What! stand'st thou still, and hear'st such a calling? look to the guests within. [*Exit* FRAN.] My lord, old sir John, with half a dozen more, are at the door; shall I let them in?

P. HEN. Let them alone awhile, and then open the door. [*Exit* Vintner.] Poins!

Re-enter POINS.

POINS. *Anon, anon,* sir.

P. HEN. Sirrah, Falstaff and the rest of the thieves are at the door; shall we be merry?

POINS. As merry as crickets, my lad. But hark ye; what cunning match have you made with this jest of the drawer? come, what's the issue?

P. HEN. I am now of all humours, that have showed themselves humours, since the old days of goodman Adam, to the pupil age of this present twelve o'clock at midnight. [*Re-enter* FRANCIS *with wine.*] What's o'clock, Francis?

FRAN. Anon, anon, sir. [*Exit.*

P. HEN. That ever this fellow should have fewer words than a parrot, and yet the son of a woman!—His industry is—up-stairs, and down-stairs; his eloquence, the parcel of a reckoning. I am not yet of Percy's mind, the Hotspur of the north; he that kills me some six or seven dozen of Scots at a breakfast, washes his hands, and says to his wife,—*Fie upon this quiet life! I want work. O my sweet Harry,* says she, *how many hast thou killed to-day? Give my roan horse a drench,* says he; and answers, *Some fourteen,* an hour after, *a trifle, a trifle.* I pr'ythee, call in Falstaff; I'll play Percy, and that damned brawn shall play dame Mortimer his wife. *Rivo,* says the drunkard. Call in ribs, call in tallow.

Enter FALSTAFF, GADSHILL, BARDOLPH, *and* PETO.

POINS. Welcome, Jack; where hast thou been?

FAL. A plague of all cowards, I say, and a vengeance too! marry, and amen!—Give me a cup of sack, boy.—Ere I lead this life long, I'll sew nether-stocks,[b] and mend them, and foot them* too. A plague of all cowards!—Give me a cup of sack, rogue. [*Re-enter* FRANCIS *with wine.*] Is there no virtue extant? [*He drinks.*

P. HEN. Didst thou never see Titan kiss a dish of butter? pitiful-hearted Titan, that melted at the sweet tale of the sun![c] if thou didst, then behold that compound.

FAL. You rogue, here's lime in this sack too: there is nothing but roguery to be found in villainous man: yet a coward is worse than a cup of sack with lime in it;† a villainous coward.—Go thy ways, old Jack, die when thou wilt; if manhood, good manhood, be not forgot upon the face of the earth, then am I a shotten herring. There lives not three good men unhanged in England; and one of them is fat, and grows old: God help the while! A bad world, I say! I would I were a weaver; I could sing psalms or any thing[d]: A plague of all cowards, I say still!

P. HEN. How now, wool-sack? what mutter you?

FAL. A king's son! If I do not beat thee out of thy kingdom with a dagger of lath, and drive all thy subjects afore thee like a flock of wild geese, I'll never wear hair on my face more. You prince of Wales!

P. HEN. Why, you whoreson round man! what's the matter?

FAL. Are not‡ you a coward? answer me to that; and Poins there?

POINS. 'Zounds,§ ye fat paunch, an ye call me coward, by the Lord, || I'll stab thee.

FAL. I call thee coward! I'll see thee damned ere I call thee coward: but I would give a thousand pound, I could run as fast as thou canst. You are straight enough in the shoulders, you care not who sees your back: call you that, backing of your friends? A plague upon such backing! give me them that will face me.—Give me a cup of sack:—I am a rogue, if I drunk to-day.

(*) First folio omits, *not.*

(*) First folio omits, *and foot them.* (†) First folio omits, *in it.* (‡) First folio, *you not.* (§) First folio omits, *'Zounds.* (||) First folio omits, *by the Lord.*

a Brown bastard—] A kind of sweet wine.

b Nether-stocks,—] That is, low or short stockings; what the French called *bas de chausses.*

c Pitiful-hearted Titan, that melted at the sweet tale of the sun!] Thus the later quartos, and the folio, 1623. The first and second quartos read, *sonnes* for *sun.* In this much-disputed passage we prefer the punctuation recommended by Warburton, reading "*pitiful-hearted Titan*" parenthetically; but have some disposition to think, with Theobald, that the compositor, by inadvertence, repeated the word "Titan" instead of "butter," and that the true lection is, "pitiful-hearted *butter,* that melted at the sweet tale of the sun."

d I could sing psalms or any thing:] The weeding of expressions that were considered objectionable, has been carried to a greater extent in this play than in any other of our author's; probably from its being often performed. The above words are altered in the folio to, *I could sing all manner of songs.* The censor has, however, overlooked, "God help the while!" just before.

P. HEN. O villain! thy lips are scarce wiped since thou drunk'st last.

FAL. All's one for that. A plague of all cowards, still say I. [*He drinks.*

P. HEN. What's the matter?

FAL. What's the matter! there* be four of us here† have ta'en a thousand pound this day morning.[a]

P. HEN. Where is it, Jack? where is it?

FAL. Where is it? taken from us it is: a hundred upon poor four of us.

P. HEN. What, a hundred, man?

FAL. I am a rogue, if I were not at half-sword with a dozen of them two hours together. I have 'scaped by miracle. I am eight times thrust through the doublet; four, through the hose; my buckler[b] cut through and through; my sword hacked like a handsaw, *ecce signum*. I never dealt better since I was a man: all would not do. A plague of all cowards!—Let them speak: if they speak more or less than truth, they are villains, and the sons of darkness.

P. HEN. Speak, sirs; how was it?

GADS. We four set upon some dozen,——

FAL. Sixteen, at least, my lord.

GADS. And bound them;—

PETO. No, no, they were not bound.

FAL. You rogue, they were bound, every man of them; or I am a Jew else, an Ebrew Jew.

GADS. As we were sharing, some six or seven fresh men set upon us,——

FAL. And unbound the rest, and then come in the other.

P. HEN. What, fought ye with them all?

FAL. All? I know not what ye call, all; but if I fought not with fifty of them, I am a bunch of radish: if there were not two or three and fifty upon poor old Jack, then am I no two-legged creature.

P. HEN. Pray God,‡ you have not murdered some of them.

FAL. Nay, that's past praying for; I have peppered two of them: two, I am sure, I have paid; two rogues in buckram suits. I tell thee what, Hal,—if I tell thee a lie, spit in my face, call me horse—thou knowest my old ward: §—here I lay, and thus I bore my point. Four rogues in buckram let drive at me,——

P. HEN. What, four? thou said'st but two, even now.

FAL. Four, Hal; I told thee four.

POINS. Ay, ay, he said four.

FAL. These four came all a-front, and mainly thrust at me. I made me* no more ado, but took all their seven points in my target, thus.

P. HEN. Seven? why there were but four, even now.

FAL. In buckram?

POINS. Ay, four in buckram suits.

FAL. Seven, by these hilts, or I am a villain else.

P. HEN. Pr'ythee, let him alone; we shall have more anon.

FAL. Dost thou hear me, Hal?

P. HEN. Ay, and mark thee too, Jack.

FAL. Do so, for it is worth the listening to. These nine in buckram, that I told thee of,——

P. HEN. So, two more already.

FAL. Their points being broken,——

POINS. Down fell their† hose.[c]

FAL. Began to give me ground: but I followed me close, came in foot and hand; and, with a thought, seven of the eleven I paid.

P. HEN. O monstrous! eleven buckram men grown out of two!

FAL. But, as the devil would have it, three misbegotten knaves, in Kendal green,[d] came at my back, and let drive at me;—for it was so dark, Hal, that thou could'st not see thy hand.

P. HEN. These lies are like the father that begets them; gross as a mountain, open, palpable. Why, thou clay-brained guts; thou knotty-pated fool; thou whoreson, obscene, greasy tallow-keech,[e]——

FAL. What, art thou mad? art thou mad? is not the truth, the truth?

P. HEN. Why, how could'st thou know these men in Kendal green, when it was so dark thou could'st not see thy hand? come, tell us your reason; what say'st thou to this?

POINS. Come, your reason, Jack, your reason.

FAL. What, upon compulsion? No; were I at

(*) First folio, *here*. (†) First folio omits, *here*.
(‡) First folio, *Heaven*. (§) First folio, *word*.

a *This* day *morning*.] So the two earliest quartos. Subsequent editions omit *day*. "*Day-morning*" is, however, an expression not yet quite obsolete.

b My buckler—] The adherence to the old weapons of combat, which were rapidly giving place to the more fashionable rapier and dagger, was thought derogatory to a gentleman in Shakespeare's time. See Note (b), p. 518.—"I see by this dearth of good swords, that sword-and-buckler-fight begins to grow out. I am sorry for it: I shall never see good manhood again. If it be once gone, this poking fight of rapier and dagger will come up then."—*The Two Angry Women of Abingdon*, 1599.

c Down fell their hose.] Poins plays on the double meaning of *point*, as *the sharp end of a sword* and *the laces which fastened up the garments*. See Note (e), p. 250.

(*) First folio omits, *me*. (†) First folio, *his*.

d Kendal green,—] Kendal, in Westmoreland, was famous, time out of mind, for its manufacture and dyeing of cloths:—

"—— where *Kendal* town doth stand,
For making of our *cloth* scarce match'd in all the land."
DRAYTON'S *Polyolbion*, *Song* XX.

e *Tallow*-keech,——] The old copies have, "*tallow-catch*," which conveys no meaning at present discoverable. A *keech*, Dr. Percy says, is the fat of an ox or cow rolled up by the butcher into a round lump, to be carried to the chandler. In "Henry IV." Part II. Act II. Sc. 1, the butcher's wife is called "*dame Keech*."

the strappado,[a] or all the racks in the world, I would not tell you on compulsion. Give you a reason on compulsion! if reasons were as plenty as blackberries, I would give no man a reason upon compulsion, I.

P. HEN. I'll be no longer guilty of this sin; this sanguine coward, this bed-presser, this horse-back-breaker, this huge hill of flesh;——

FAL. Away! you starveling, you elf-skin,[b] you dried neat's-tongue, bull's pizzle, you stock-fish,—O, for breath to utter what is like thee!—you tailor's yard, you sheath, you bow-case, you vile standing tuck;——

P. HEN. Well, breathe a while, and then to it again: and when thou hast tired thyself in base comparisons, hear me speak but this.*

POINS. Mark, Jack.

P. HEN. We two saw you four set on four; you bound them,[c] and were masters of their wealth. Mark now, how a plain tale shall put you down. Then did we two set on you four: and, with a word, out-faced you from your prize, and have it; yea, and can show it you here* in the house:—and, Falstaff, you carried your guts away as nimbly, with as quick dexterity, and roared for mercy, and still ran and roared, as ever I heard bull-calf. What a slave art thou, to hack thy sword as thou hast done, and then say it was in fight! What trick, what device, what starting-hole, canst thou now find out, to hide thee from this open and apparent shame?

POINS. Come, let's hear, Jack; what trick hast thou now?

FAL. By the Lord,† I knew ye as well as he

(*) First folio, *thus*.

(*) First folio omits, *here*. (†) First folio omits, *By the Lord*.

[a] The strappado,—] This frightful punishment, so frequently mentioned in old books, is described in Randle Holme's "Academy of Arms and Blazon," B. III. Ch. VII. p. 310, as follows:—"The *strappado* is when the person is drawn up to his height, and then suddenly to let him fall half way with a jerk, which not only breaketh his arms to pieces, but also shaketh all his joints out of joint; which punishment is better to be hanged, than for a man to undergo."

[b] Elf-skin,—] Hanmer and Warburton read, "*eel-skin*."

[c] You *bound them*,—] The old editions read "*and* bound them." Pope made the necessary correction.

that made ye. Why, hear ye, my masters: was it for me to kill the heir apparent? should I turn upon the true prince? Why, thou knowest, I am as valiant as Hercules: but beware instinct; the lion will not touch the true prince.[a] Instinct is a great matter; I was a coward on instinct. I shall think the better of myself, and thee, during my life; I, for a valiant lion, and thou, for a true prince. But, by the Lord,* lads, I am glad you have the money. Hostess, clap to the doors; watch to-night, pray to-morrow. Gallants! lads! boys! hearts of gold! All the titles of good† fellowship come to you! What, shall we be merry? shall we have a play extempore?

P. HEN. Content;—and the argument shall be, thy running away.

FAL. Ah! no more of that, Hal, an thou lovest me.

Enter Hostess.

HOST. O Jesu!‡ my lord the prince,———

P. HEN. How now, my lady the hostess? what say'st thou to me?

HOST. Marry, my lord, there is a nobleman of the court at door, would speak with you: he says, he comes from your father.

P. HEN. Give him as much as will make him a royal man,[b] and send him back again to my mother.

FAL. What manner of man is he?

HOST. An old man.

FAL. What doth gravity out of his bed at midnight?—Shall I give him his answer?

P. HEN. Pr'ythee, do, Jack.

FAL. 'Faith, and I'll send him packing. [*Exit.*

P. HEN. Now, sirs; by'r lady,§ you fought fair;—so did you, Peto;—so did you, Bardolph: you are lions too, you ran away upon instinct, you will not touch the true prince; no,—fie!

BARD. 'Faith, I ran when I saw others run.

P. HEN. Tell me now in earnest, how came Falstaff's sword so hacked?

PETO. Why, he hacked it with his dagger; and said, he would swear truth out of England, but he would make you believe it was done in fight; and persuaded us to do the like.

BARD. Yea, and to tickle our noses with spear-grass to make them bleed; and then to beslubber our garments with it, and swear it was the blood of true men. I did that I did not this seven year* before: I blushed, to hear his monstrous devices.

P. HEN. O villain, thou stolest a cup of sack eighteen years ago, and wert taken with the manner, and ever since thou hast blushed extempore: thou hadst fire and sword on thy side, and yet thou ran'st away; what instinct hadst thou for it?

BARD. My lord, do you see these meteors? do you behold these exhalations?

P. HEN. I do.

BARD. What think you they portend?

P. HEN. Hot livers, and cold purses.

BARD. Choler, my lord, if rightly taken.

P. HEN. No, if rightly taken, halter.

Re-enter FALSTAFF.

Here comes lean Jack, here comes bare-bone. How now, my sweet creature of bombast? How long is't ago, Jack, since thou saw'st thine own knee?

FAL. My own knee? when I was about thy years, Hal, I was not an eagle's talon in the waist; I could have crept into any alderman's thumb-ring: a plague of sighing and grief! it blows a man up like a bladder. There's villainous news abroad: here was sir John Bracy from your father; you must† to the court in the morning. That‡ same mad fellow of the north, Percy; and he of Wales, that gave Amaimon the bastinado, and made Lucifer cuckold, and swore the devil his true liegeman upon the cross of a Welsh hook,—what, a plague, call you him?——

POINS. O! Glendower.

FAL. Owen, Owen; the same;—and his son-in-law, Mortimer; and old Northumberland; and that§ sprightly Scot of Scots, Douglas, that runs o'horseback up a hill perpendicular.

P. HEN. He that rides at high speed, and with his‖ pistol kills a sparrow flying.

FAL. You have hit it.

P. HEN. So did he never the sparrow.

FAL. Well, that rascal hath good mettle in him; he will not run.

(*) First folio omits, *by the Lord*. (†) First folio, *good titles of*.
(‡) First folio omits, *O Jesu*. (§) First folio omits, *by'r lady*.

(*) First folio, *years*. (†) First folio inserts, *go*.
(‡) First folio, *the*. (§) First folio, *the*.
(‖) First folio, *a*.

[a] The lion will not touch the true prince.] So in "Palmerin d'Oliva," Part II. c. 5, translated by Anthony Monday, 1588:—"Palmerin being in the Lyons denne, because none of the lyons should get forth to hurt any other however God disposed of him, made faste the doore after him and with his sword drawne and his mantle wraped about his arme went to see how the Beastes would deal with him. The Lyons coming about him smelling on his clothes would *not touch him; but* (*as it were knowing the blood royal*) lay downe at his feete and licked him, and afterwards went to their places againe."

[b] *There is a* nobleman———
Give him as much as will make him a royal man,—] The jest lies in the difference in the value of the two coins, a *royal* and a *noble*. The former was worth 10*s*.; the latter, only 6*s*. 8*d*. The prince bids the hostess give the *nobleman* 3*s*. 4*d*. and make him a *royal man*. The origin of this joke was probably an anecdote related of Queen Elizabeth. Mr. John Blower, in a sermon before her Majesty, first said, "my *royal* Queen," and shortly after, "my *noble* Queen." Upon which says the Queen: "What! am I *ten groats* worse than I was?"

P. HEN. Why, what a rascal art thou then, to praise him so for running?

FAL. O' horseback, ye cuckoo! but, afoot, he will not budge a foot.

P. HEN. Yes, Jack, upon instinct.

FAL. I grant ye, upon instinct. Well, he is there too, and one Mordake, and a thousand blue-caps more: Worcester is stolen away to-night:(*) thy father's beard is turned white with the news; you may buy land now as cheap as stinking mackerel.

P. HEN. Why(†) then, 't is like, if there come a hot June,(‡) and this civil buffeting hold, we shall buy maidenheads as they buy hob-nails, by the hundreds.

FAL. By the mass, lad, thou say'st true; it is like we shall have good trading that way.—But, tell me, Hal, art thou not(§) horribly afeard? thou being heir apparent, could the world pick thee out three such enemies again, as that fiend Douglas, that spirit Percy, and that devil Glendower? Art thou not horribly afraid? doth not thy blood thrill at it?

P. HEN. Not a whit, i' faith;(||) I lack some of thy instinct.

FAL. Well, thou wilt be horribly chid to-morrow, when thou comest to thy father; if thou(¶) love me, practise an answer.

P. HEN. Do thou stand for my father, and examine me upon the particulars of my life.

FAL. Shall I? content.—This chair shall be my state,[a] this dagger my sceptre, and this cushion my crown.

P. HEN. Thy state is taken for a joint-stool, thy golden sceptre for a leaden dagger, and thy precious rich crown, for a pitiful bald crown!

FAL. Well, an the fire of grace be not quite out of thee, now shalt thou be moved.—Give me a cup of sack, to make mine eyes look red, that it may be thought I have wept; for I must speak in passion, and I will do it in king Cambyses'[b] vein.

P. HEN. Well, here is my leg.[c]

FAL. And here is my speech.—Stand aside, nobility.

HOST. O Jesu!(**) this is excellent sport, i' faith.

FAL. Weep not, sweet queen, for trickling
tears are vain.

HOST. O the father, how he holds his countenance!

FAL. For God's sake, lords, convey my tristful(*)
queen,
For tears do stop the flood-gates of her eyes.

HOST. O Jesu!(†) he doth it as like one of these harlotry players, as ever I see.

FAL. Peace, good pint-pot; peace, good tickle-brain.—Harry, I do not only marvel where thou spendest thy time, but also how thou art accompanied: for though the camomile,[d] the more it is trodden on,(‡) the faster it grows, yet youth, the more it is wasted, the sooner it wears. That(§) thou art my son, I have partly thy mother's word, partly my own(||) opinion; but chiefly, a villainous trick of thine eye, and a foolish hanging of thy nether lip, that doth warrant me. If then thou be son to me, here lieth the point—why, being son to me, art thou so pointed at? Shall the blessed sun of heaven prove a micher,[e] and eat blackberries? a question not to be asked. Shall the son of England prove a thief, and take purses? a question to be asked. There is a thing, Harry, which thou hast often heard of, and it is known to many in our land by the name of pitch: this pitch, as ancient writers do report, doth defile; so doth the company thou keepest: for, Harry, now I do not speak to thee in drink, but in tears; not in pleasure, but in passion: not in words only, but in woes also:—and yet there is a virtuous man whom I have often noted in thy company, but I know not his name.

P. HEN. What manner of man, an it like your majesty?

FAL. A goodly portly man, i' faith, and a corpulent; of a cheerful look, a pleasing eye, and a most noble carriage; and, as I think, his age some fifty, or, by 'r lady, inclining to threescore; and now I remember me, his name is Falstaff; if that man should be lewdly given, he deceiveth me; for, Harry, I see virtue in his looks. If then the tree may be known by the fruit, as the fruit by the tree, then, peremptorily I speak it, there is virtue in that Falstaff: him keep with, the rest banish. And tell me now, thou naughty varlet, tell me, where hast thou been this month?

P. HEN. Dost thou speak like a king? Do thou stand for me, and I 'll play my father.

FAL. Depose me? if thou dost it half so gravely, so majestically, both in word and matter, hang me

(*) First folio, *by night*. (†) First folio omits, *Why*.
(‡) First folio, *Sun*. (§) First folio, *not thou*.
(||) First folio omits, *i'faith*. (¶) First folio inserts, *do*.
(**) First folio omits, *O Jesu*.

[a] *This chair shall be my* state,—] A *state* or *estate* meant originally perhaps only the canopy which surmounted the seat of princes; but it afterwards came to signify the throne or chair itself. Thus, "Macbeth," Act IV. Sc. 4,—

"Our hostess keeps her *state*."

[b] *In king* Cambyses' *vein*.] The reference is to a play by Thomas Preston, 1570, called "A Lamentable Tragedy, mixed ful of Pleasant Mirth, conteyning the Life of *Cambises*, King of Percia."

(*) Old copies, *trustful*. (†) First folio, *rare*.
(‡) First folio omits, *on*. (§) First folio omits, *That*.
(||) First folio omits, *own*.

[c] *Here is my* leg.] My obeisance to my father.

[d] Though the camomile,—] In ridicule, probably, of a passage in Lily's "Euphues":—"Though the *camomile* the more it is trodden and pressed downe, the more it spreadeth; yet the *violet* the oftener it is handled and touched, the sooner it withereth and decayeth," &c.

[e] *A* micher,—] A *vagabond*, a petty *rogue*.

up by the heels for a rabbit-sucker,[a] or a poulter's[b] hare.

P. HEN. Well, here I am set.

FAL. And here I stand:—judge, my masters.

P. HEN. Now, Harry? whence come you?

FAL. My noble lord, from Eastcheap.

P. HEN. The complaints I hear of thee are grievous.

FAL. 'Sblood,* my lord, they are false:—nay, I'll tickle ye for a young prince, i' faith.†

P. HEN. Swearest thou, ungracious boy? henceforth ne'er look on me. Thou art violently carried away from grace: there is a devil haunts thee, in the likeness of a fat old man: a tun of man is thy companion. Why dost thou converse with that trunk of humours, that bolting-hutch[c] of beastliness, that swoln parcel of dropsies, that huge bombard[d] of sack, that stuffed cloak-bag of guts, that roasted Manningtree ox[e] with the pudding in his belly, that reverend vice, that grey iniquity, that father ruffian, that vanity in years?[f] Wherein is he good, but to taste sack and drink it? wherein neat and cleanly, but to carve a capon and eat it? wherein cunning, but in craft? wherein crafty, but in villainy? wherein villainous, but in all things? wherein worthy, but in nothing?

FAL. I would your grace would take me with you;[g] whom means your grace?

P. HEN. That villainous abominable misleader of youth, Falstaff, that old white-bearded Satan.

FAL. My lord, the man I know.

P. HEN. I know, thou dost.

FAL. But to say, I know more harm in him than in myself, were to say more than I know. That he is old, (the more the pity,) his white hairs do witness it: but that he is (saving your reverence) a whoremaster, that I utterly deny. If sack and sugar be a fault, God‡ help the wicked! If to be old and merry be a sin, then many an old host that I know, is damned: if to be fat be to be hated, then Pharaoh's lean kine are to be loved. No, my good lord; banish Peto, banish Bardolph, banish Poins: but for sweet Jack Falstaff, kind Jack Falstaff, true Jack Falstaff, valiant Jack Falstaff, and therefore more valiant, being as he is, old Jack Falstaff, banish not him thy Harry's company, banish not him thy Harry's company; banish plump Jack, and banish all the world. [*A knocking heard.*

[*Exeunt* Hostess, FRANCIS, *and* BARDOLPH.

P. HEN. I do, I will.

Re-enter BARDOLPH, *running.*

BARD. O, my lord, my lord! the sheriff, with a most monstrous watch, is at the door.

FAL. Out, you rogue! play out the play: I have much to say in the behalf of that Falstaff.

Re-enter Hostess, *hastily.*

HOST. O Jesu,* my lord, my lord!——

FAL. Heigh, heigh![h] the devil rides upon a fiddle-stick. What's the matter?

HOST. The sheriff and all the watch are at the door: they are come to search the house; shall I let them in?

FAL. Dost thou hear, Hal? Never call a true piece of gold a counterfeit: thou art essentially mad,†[i] without seeming so.

P. HEN. And thou a natural coward, without instinct.

FAL. I deny your *major:* if you will deny the sheriff, so;[k] if not, let him enter: if I become not a cart as well as another man, a plague on my bringing up! I hope I shall as soon be strangled with a halter, as another.

P. HEN. Go, hide thee behind the arras;—the rest walk up above. Now, my masters, for a true face, and good conscience.

FAL. Both which I have had; but their date is out, and therefore I'll hide me.

[*Exeunt all but the* PRINCE *and* PETO.

P. HEN. Call in the sheriff.——

Enter Sheriff *and* Carrier.

Now, master sheriff; what's your will with me?

SHER. First, pardon me, my lord. A hue and cry
Hath follow'd certain men unto this house.

(*) First folio, *Yfaith.* (†) First folio omits, *i' faith.* (‡) First folio, *Heaven.*

[a] A rabbit-sucker,—] That is, a sucking rabbit.

[b] A poulter's—] The old spelling and pronunciation of *poulterer.*

[c] Bolting-hutch—] According to Steevens, the bin into which the meal is *bolted.*

[d] Bombard—] A *barrel.*

[e] Roasted Manningtree ox—] Alluding, it is thought, to the custom of roasting an ox at Manningtree fair. *Manningtree,* as we gather from Nash, Heywood, and Decker, enjoyed the privilege of fairs by exhibiting certain stage-performances called "Moralities" every year.

[f] *That reverend* vice, *that grey* iniquity, ... *that* vanity *in years?*] The *Vice, Iniquity,* and *Vanity,* were the characters of the ancient Moralities.

(*) First folio omits, *Jesu.* (†) Old copies, *made.*

[g] Would take me with you;] See note (b), p. 197.

[h] FAL. Heigh, heigh! &c.] The quarto gives this speech to the Prince, but the folio is undoubtedly right in assigning it to Falstaff.

[i] Thou art essentially mad,—] This speech has never been explained. The key to it, we believe, is, that when the Hostess asks, "Shall I let them in?" the Prince boldly replies by gesture, "Yes," which so alarms Falstaff that he breaks forth, first imploringly, "Dost thou hear, Hal?" and then with vehemence, "Never call," &c.

[k] *I deny your* major: *if you will deny the* sheriff, *so;*] A quibble is obviously meant between the chief corporate officer the *mayor,* and his subordinate the sheriff, and *major* the proposition of a syllogism.

P. HEN. What men?
SHER. One of them is well known, my gracious lord;
A gross fat man.
CAR. As fat as butter.
P. HEN. The man, I do assure you, is not here;
For I myself at this time have employ'd him.
And, sheriff, I will engage my word to thee,
That I will, by to-morrow dinner-time,
Send him to answer thee, or any man,
For any thing he shall be charg'd withal:
And so let me entreat you leave the house.
SHER. I will, my lord. There are two gentlemen
Have in this robbery lost three hundred marks.
P. HEN. It may be so; if he have robb'd these men,
He shall be answerable; and so, farewell.
SHER. Good night, my noble lord.
P. HEN. I think it is good morrow; is it not?
SHER. Indeed, my lord, I think it be two o'clock. [*Exeunt* Sheriff *and* Carrier.

P. HEN. This oily rascal is known as well as Paul's: go, call him forth.

PETO. Falstaff!—fast asleep behind the arras, and snorting like a horse.

P. HEN. Hark, how hard he fetches breath: search his pockets. [*He searcheth his pockets, and findeth certain papers.*][a] What hast thou found?

PETO. Nothing but papers, my lord.

P. HEN. Let's see what they be:* read them.

PETO. *Item, a capon* . . . . . 2*s.* 2*d.*
Item, Sauce . . . . 4*d.*
Item, Sack, two gallons . . . . . 5*s.* 8*d.*
Item, Anchovies, and sack after supper. 2*s.* 6*d.*
Item, Bread . . . . *ob.*[b]

P. HEN. O monstrous! but one half-pennyworth of bread to this intolerable deal of sack!—What there is else, keep close; we'll read it at more advantage: there let him sleep till day. I'll to the court in the morning: we must all to the wars, and thy place shall be honourable. I'll procure this fat rogue a charge of foot; and, I know, his death will be a march† of twelve-score.[c] The money shall be paid back again with advantage. Be with me betimes in the morning; and so good morrow, Peto.

PETO. Good morrow, good my lord. [*Exeunt.*

[a] He searcheth his pockets, &c.] The original stage direction.
[b] *Ob.*] For *obolum*, the usual way in old times of writing a halfpenny.

(*) First folio, *be they.* (†) First folio, *match.*

[c] Of twelve-score.] In archers' phraseology, twelve-score *yards.*

ACT III.

SCENE I.—Bangor. *A Room in the* Archdeacon's *House.*

Enter HOTSPUR, WORCESTER, MORTIMER, *and* GLENDOWER.

MOR. These promises are fair, the parties sure,
And our induction[a] full of prosperous hope.

HOT. Lord Mortimer,—and cousin Glendower,—
Will you sit down?——
And, uncle Worcester:—a plague upon it!
I have forgot the map.

GLEND. No, here it is. Sit, cousin Percy,
Sit, good cousin Hotspur: for by that name
As oft as Lancaster doth speak of you,
His cheek looks* pale; and, with a rising sigh,
He wisheth you in heaven.

HOT. And you in hell, as oft as he hears
Owen Glendower spoke of.

GLEND. I cannot blame him: at my nativity,
The front of heaven was full of fiery shapes,
Of burning cressets; and, at my birth,
The frame and huge† foundation of the earth
Shak'd like a coward.

HOT. Why, so it would have done at the same

[a] Induction—] That is, *Beginning, entrance.*

(*) First folio, *cheeks look.* (†) First folio omits, *huge.*

season, if your mother's cat had but kitten'd, though yourself had never been born.

GLEND. I say, the earth did shake when I was born.

HOT. And I say, the earth was not of my mind,
If you suppose, as fearing you, it shook.

GLEND. The heavens were all on fire, the earth did tremble.

HOT. O, then the earth shook to see the heavens on fire,
And not in fear of your nativity.
Diseased nature oftentimes breaks forth
In strange eruptions; oft* the teeming earth
Is with a kind of colic pinch'd and vex'd
By the imprisoning of unruly wind
Within her womb; which, for enlargement striving,
Shakes the old beldame earth, and topples† down
Steeples, and moss-grown towers. At your birth,
Our grandam earth, having this distemperature,
In passion shook.

GLEND. Cousin, of many men
I do not bear these crossings. Give me leave
To tell you once again,—that, at my birth,
The front of heaven was full of fiery shapes;
The goats ran from the mountains, and the herds
Were strangely clamorous to the frighted fields.
These signs have mark'd me extraordinary;
And all the courses of my life do show,
I am not in the roll of common men.
Where is the living,—clipp'd in with the sea
That chides the banks of England, Scotland,‡ Wales,——
Which calls me pupil, or hath read to me?
And bring him out, that is but woman's son,
Can trace me in the tedious ways of art,
And hold me pace in deep experiments.

HOT. I think there is no man speaks better Welsh:——I will to dinner.

MORT. Peace, cousin Percy, you will make him mad.

GLEND. I can call spirits from the vasty deep.

HOT. Why, so can I; or so can any man;
But will they come, when you do call for them?

GLEND. Why, I can teach thee, cousin, to command the devil.

HOT. And I can teach thee, coz, to shame the devil,
By telling truth. *Tell truth, and shame the devil.*—[a]
If thou have power to raise him, bring him hither,
And I'll be sworn, I have power to shame him hence.
O, while you live, *tell truth, and shame the devil.*

MORT. Come, come,
No more of this unprofitable chat.

GLEND. Three times hath Henry Bolingbroke made head
Against my power: thrice from the banks of Wye,
And sandy-bottom'd Severn, have I sent* him
Bootless home, and weather-beaten back.

HOT. Home without boots, and in foul weather too!
How 'scapes he agues, in the devil's name?

GLEND. Come, here's the map: shall we divide our right,
According to our threefold order ta'en?

MORT. The archdeacon hath divided it
Into three limits, very equally:
England, from Trent and Severn hitherto,
By south and east, is to my part assign'd:
All westward, Wales beyond the Severn shore,
And all the fertile land within that bound,
To Owen Glendower:—and, dear coz, to you
The remnant northward, lying off from Trent.
And our indentures tripartite are drawn;
Which being sealed interchangeably,
(A business that this night may execute,)
To-morrow, cousin Percy, you, and I,
And my good lord of Worcester, will set forth,
To meet your father, and the Scottish power,
As is appointed us, at Shrewsbury.
My father Glendower is not ready yet,
Nor shall we need his help these fourteen days:—
Within that space, [*To* GLEND.] you may have drawn together
Your tenants, friends, and neighbouring gentlemen.

GLEN. A shorter time shall send me to you, lords,
And in my conduct shall your ladies come:
From whom you now must steal, and take no leave;
For there will be a world of water shed,
Upon the parting of your wives and you.

HOT. Methinks, my moiety,[b] north from Burton here,
In quantity equals not one of yours;
See, how this river comes me cranking in,
And cuts me,[c] from the best of all my land,
A huge half-moon, a monstrous cantle[d] out.

(*) First folio, *and*. (†) First folio, *tombles*. (‡) First folio inserts, *and*.

(*) First folio, *hent*.

[a] Tell truth, and shame the devil.—] A well-known and very ancient proverb.

[b] *My* moiety,—] *Moiety* of old was sometimes used to signify any portion of a thing, and sometimes, as now, the half part.

[c] *Comes* me *cranking in*, &c.] *Me* in this passage does not apply to the speaker; it is merely an expletive common among the old writers, and found frequently in these plays. Thus, in the "Second Part of Henry the Fourth," Act IV. Sc. 3:—"A good sherris-sack hath a twofold operation in it: it ascends *me* into the brain; dries *me* there all the foolish, and dull, and cruddy vapours which environ it;" &c. Again in "Julius Cæsar," Act I. Sc. 2.—

"He pluck'd *me* ope his doublet."

And in the same play, Act III. Sc. 3:—

"You'll bear *me* a bang for this."

You and *your* were often employed in the same way:—"Here's Wart;—you see what a ragged appearance it is: he shall charge *you*, and discharge *you*, with the motion of a pewterer's hammer;" &c.—HENRY IV. Pt. II. Act III. Sc. 2.

"*Your* Dane, *your* German, and *your* swag-bellied Hollander,—Drink, hoa! are nothing to *your* English."—OTHELLO, Act II. Sc. 3.

[d] *A monstrous* cantle—] *Cantle* is a *slice* or corner.

"Not so much as a *cantell* of cheese or crust of bread."—*A New Trick to Cheat the Devil.* 1636. Quoted by Steevens.

I'll have the current in this place damm'd up,
And here the smug and silver Trent shall run,
In a new channel, fair and evenly;
It shall not wind with such a deep indent,
To rob me of so rich a bottom here.

GLEND. Not wind? it shall, it must; you see, it doth.

MORT. Yea, but mark how he bears his course, and runs me up
With like advantage on the other side;
Gelding the opposed continent as much,
As on the other side it takes from you.

WOR. Yea, but a little charge will trench him here,
And on this north side win this cape of land;
And then he runs straight and even.[a]

HOT. I'll have it so; a little charge will do it.

GLEND. I will not have it alter'd.

HOT. Will not you?

GLEND. No, nor you shall not.

HOT. Who shall say me nay?

GLEND. Why, that will I.

HOT. Let me not understand you then;
Speak it in Welsh.

GLEND. I can speak English, lord, as well as you:
For I was train'd up in the English court: (1)
Where, being but young, I framed to the harp
Many an English ditty, lovely well,
And gave the tongue a helpful ornament;
A virtue that was never seen in you.

HOT. Marry, and I am glad of it with all my heart;
I had rather be a kitten, and cry—*mew*,
Than one of these same metre ballad-mongers:
I had rather hear a brazen canstick* turn'd,
Or a dry wheel grate on the axle-tree;
And that would set my teeth nothing on edge,
Nothing so much as mincing poetry;
'T is like the forc'd gait of a shuffling nag.

GLEND. Come, you shall have Trent turn'd.

HOT. I do not care; I'll give thrice so much land
To any well-deserving friend.
But, in the way of bargain, mark ye me,
I'll cavil on the ninth part of a hair.
Are the indentures drawn? shall we be gone?

GLEND. The moon shines fair, you may away by night:
I'll haste the writer, and, withal,
Break with your wives of your departure hence:
I am afraid, my daughter will run mad,
So much she doteth on her Mortimer. [*Exit.*

MORT. Fie, cousin Percy! how you cross my father!

HOT. I cannot choose: sometimes he angers me,
With telling me of the moldwarp and the ant,[b]
Of the dreamer Merlin, and his prophecies;
And of a dragon, and a finless fish,
A clip-wing'd griffin, and a moulten raven,
A couching lion, and a ramping cat,
And such a deal of skimble-skamble stuff
As puts me from my faith. I tell you what,—
He held me, last night, at least nine hours,[c]
In reckoning up the several devils' names,
That were his lackeys: I cry'd, *hum*,—and, *well*, —*go to*,—
But mark'd him not a word. O, he is as tedious
As a tired horse,[d] a railing wife;
Worse than a smoky house:—I had rather live
With cheese and garlic, in a windmill, far,
Than feed on cates, and have him talk to me,
In any summer-house in Christendom.

MORT. In faith, he is* a worthy gentleman;
Exceedingly† well read, and profited
In strange concealments; valiant as a lion,
And wondrous affable; and as bountiful
As mines of India. Shall I tell you, cousin?
He holds your temper in a high respect,
And curbs himself even of his natural scope,
When you do cross his humour; 'faith, he does;
I warrant you, that man is not alive,
Might so have tempted him as you have done,
Without the taste of danger and reproof;
But do not use it oft, let me entreat you.

WOR. In faith, my lord, you are too wilful-blame;
And since your coming hither, have done enough
To put him quite beside his patience.
You must needs learn, lord, to amend this fault:
Though sometimes it show greatness, courage, blood,
(And that's the dearest grace it renders you,)
Yet oftentimes it doth present harsh rage,
Defect of manners, want of government,
Pride, haughtiness, opinion, and disdain:
The least of which, haunting a nobleman,
Loseth men's hearts; and leaves behind a stain
Upon the beauty of all parts besides,

(*) First folio, *candlestick*.

a And then he runs straight and even.] This line is so unmetrical that we may well suspect a syllable has been dropped. Might it not read,

"And then he runs *me* straight and even"?

b The moldwarp and the ant,—] The *moldwarp* is the mole. Hotspur alludes to an ancient prophecy mentioned in the "Chronicles":—"This [the dividing the realm between Mortimer, Glendower, and Percy] was done (as some have sayde) through a foolish credite given to a vaine prophecie, as though King Henry was the *molde-warpe*, cursed of God's owne mouth, and they three were the *dragon*, the *lion*, and the *wolfe* which should divide this realme between them."

(*) First folio, *was*. (†) First folio, *Exceeding*.

c At least nine hours,—] Capell reads, and perhaps correctly,

"He held me last night at *the* least nine hours."

d As a tired horse,—] Query,

"As *is* a tired horse,"

the reading of most of the modern editions?

Beguiling them of commendation.

HOT. Well, I am school'd; good manners be your speed!
Here come our* wives, and let us take our leave.

Re-enter GLENDOWER, *with the* Ladies.

MORT. This is the deadly spite that angers me,—
My wife can speak no English, I no Welsh.

GLEND. My daughter weeps; she will not part with you;
She'll be a soldier too, she'll to the wars.

MORT. Good father, tell her,—that she, and my aunt Percy,
Shall follow in your conduct speedily.

[GLENDOWER *speaks to his daughter in Welsh, and she answers him in the same.*

GLEND. She's desperate here; a peevish self-will'd harlotry,[a]
One that no persuasion can do good upon.

[Lady M. *speaks to* MORTIMER *in Welsh.*

MORT. I understand thy looks: that pretty Welsh
Which thou pour'st down from these swelling heavens,[b]
I am too perfect in; and, but for shame,
In such a parley should I answer thee.

[Lady M. *speaks.*

I understand thy kisses, and thou mine,
And that's a feeling disputation:
But I will never be a truant, love,
Till I have learn'd thy language; for thy tongue
Makes Welsh as sweet as ditties highly penn'd,
Sung by a fair queen in a summer's bower,
With ravishing division, to her lute.

GLEND. Nay, if you† melt, then will she run mad. [Lady M. *speaks again.*

MORT. O, I am ignorance itself in this.

GLEND. She bids you on the wanton rushes lay you down,
And rest your gentle head upon her lap,
And she will sing the song that pleaseth you,
And on your eyelids crown the god of sleep,
Charming your blood with pleasing heaviness;
Making such difference 'twixt wake and sleep,
As is the difference betwixt day and night,
The hour before the heavenly-harness'd team
Begins his golden progress in the east.

MORT. With all my heart I'll sit, and hear her sing;
By that time will our book,[c] I think, be drawn.

GLEND. Do so;
And those musicians that shall play to you,
Hang in the air a thousand leagues from hence;*
Yet straight they shall be here: sit, and attend.

HOT. Come, Kate, thou art perfect in lying down: come, quick, quick; that I may lay my head in thy lap.

LADY P. Go, ye giddy goose.

GLENDOWER *speaks some Welsh words; then the music plays.*

HOT. Now I perceive, the devil understands Welsh;
And 't is no marvel he's so humorous,
By'r lady, he's a good musician.

LADY P. Then should† you be nothing but musical; for you are altogether governed by humours. Lie still, ye thief, and hear the lady sing in Welsh.

HOT. I had rather hear *Lady*, my brach, howl in Irish.

LADY P. Would'st thou‡ have thy head broken?

HOT. No.

LADY P. Then be still.

HOT. Neither; 't is a woman's fault.

LADY P. Now God help thee!

HOT. To the Welsh lady's bed.

LADY P. What's that?

HOT. Peace! she sings.

A Welsh Song sung by LADY MORTIMER.

HOT. Come, Kate,§ I'll have your song too.

LADY P. Not mine, in good sooth.

HOT. Not yours, *in good sooth!* 'Heart,‖ you swear like a comfit-maker's wife! Not you, *in good sooth;* and, *As true as I live;* and, *As God shall mend me;* and, *As sure as day:*
And giv'st such sarcenet surety for thy oaths,
As if thou never walk'dst further than Finsbury.
Swear me, Kate, like a lady, as thou art,
A good mouth-filling oath; and leave *in sooth,*
And such protest of pepper-gingerbread,

(*) First folio, *your.* (†) First folio, *thou.*

[a] A peevish self-will'd harlotry,—] So in "Romeo and Juliet," Act IV. Sc. 2:—

"A peevish self-will'd harlotry it is."

[b] Which thou pour'st down from these swelling heavens,—] Steevens conceived by "swelling heavens" were meant her *prominent lips.* Douce thought they were her *eyes swollen with tears.* Mr. Collier's annotator interprets the passage as Douce does, but ingeniously reads "*welling* heavens." Perhaps, after all, Mortimer alludes neither to lips nor eyes, but to her swelling bosom. In "Love's Labour 's Lost," Act IV. Sc. 3, the King says,—

"Do but behold the tears that *swell my heart;*"

and in Webster's "Sir Thomas Wyatt," Dyce's edition, p. 267, we meet with a passage still more to the purpose:—

"*Pouring down* tears sent from my *swelling heart.*"

[c] *Our* book,—] The tripartite indentures between them. In Shakespeare's day it was common to call any draft or deed "*a book.*"

(*) First folio, *thence.* (†) First folio, *would.* (‡) First folio omits, *thou.* (§) First folio omits, *Kate.* (‖) First folio omits, *Heart.*

To velvet-guards,[a] and Sunday-citizens.
Come, sing.

LADY P. I will not sing.

HOT. 'T is the next[b] way to turn tailor, or be redbreast teacher. An the indentures be drawn, I'll away within these two hours; and so come in when ye will. [*Exit.*

GLEND. Come, come, lord Mortimer; you are as slow,
As hot lord Percy is on fire to go.
By this our book is drawn; we will but seal,
And then to horse immediately.

MORT. With all my heart. [*Exeunt.*

SCENE II.—London. *A Room in the Palace.*

Enter KING HENRY, PRINCE OF WALES, *and* Lords.

K. HEN. Lords, give us leave; the prince of Wales and I
Must have some private conference; but be near at hand,
For we shall presently have need of you.— [*Exeunt* Lords.
I know not whether God* will have it so,
For some displeasing service I have done,
That, in his secret doom, out of my blood
He'll breed revengement and a scourge for me;
But thou dost, in thy passages of life,
Make me believe,—that thou art only mark'd
For the hot vengeance and the rod of heaven,
To punish my mistreadings. Tell me else,
Could such inordinate and low desires,
Such poor, such bare, such lewd, such mean attempts,
Such barren pleasures, rude society,
As thou art match'd withal, and grafted to,
Accompany the greatness of thy blood,
And hold their level with thy princely heart?

P. HEN. So please your majesty, I would I could
Quit all offences with as clear excuse,
As well as, I am doubtless, I can purge
Myself of many I am charg'd withal:
Yet such extenuation let me beg,
As, in reproof[c] of many tales devis'd,—
Which oft the ear of greatness needs must hear,
By smiling pick-thanks and base newsmongers,—
I may, for some things true, wherein my youth
Hath faulty wander'd and irregular,
Find pardon on my true submission.

K. HEN. God* pardon thee!—Yet let me wonder, Harry,
At thy affections, which do hold a wing
Quite from the flight of all thy ancestors.
Thy place in council thou hast rudely lost,
Which by thy younger brother is supplied;
And art almost an alien to the hearts
Of all the court and princes of my blood:
The hope and expectation of thy time
Is ruin'd; and the soul of every man
Prophetically does forethink thy fall.
Had I so lavish of my presence been,
So common-hackney'd in the eyes of men,
So stale and cheap to vulgar company;
Opinion, that did help me to the crown,
Had still kept loyal to possession,
And left me in reputeless banishment,
A fellow of no mark, nor likelihood.
By being seldom seen, I could not stir,
But, like a comet, I was wonder'd at:
That men would tell their children, *This is he;*
Others would say,—*Where? which is Bolingbroke?*
And then I stole all courtesy from heaven,
And dress'd myself in such humility,
That I did pluck allegiance from men's hearts,
Loud shouts and salutations from their mouths,
Even in the presence of the crowned king.
Thus did I keep my person fresh, and new;
My presence, like a robe pontifical,
Ne'er seen, but wonder'd at: and so my state,
Seldom, but sumptuous, showed like a feast;
And won, by rareness, such solemnity.
The skipping king, he ambled up and down
With shallow jesters, and rash bavin[d] wits,
Soon kindled, and soon burn'd: carded[e] his state;
Mingled his royalty with carping[f] fools;
Had his great name profaned with their scorns,
And gave his countenance, against his name,
To laugh at gibing boys, and stand the push
Of every beardless vain comparative;[g]
Grew a companion to the common streets,
Enfeoff'd himself to popularity:
That, being daily swallow'd by men's eyes,

(*) First folio, *Heaven.*

(*) First folio, *Heaven.*

[a] Velvet-guards,—] Gowns *guarded*, or bordered, with velvet were a favourite dress of the City ladies:—"At public meetings the aldermen of London weere skarlet gownes, and their wives a close gown of skarlet, with *gardes* of black *velvet.*"—FYNES MORISON, *Itin.* 1617, Pt. III. p. 179.

[b] *The* next *way*—] That is, the *nearest* way.

[c] *As, in* reproof—] *Reproof* in this place means *refutation, disproof.*

[d] *And* rash bavin wits,—] *Fierce, flashing wits.* A *bavin* is a faggot made of brushwood, used for lighting fires. "*Bavins* will have their flashes, and youth their fancies, the one as soon quenched as the other burnt."—*Mother Bombie*, 1594.

[e] Carded *his state;*] According to Warburton, *discarded*, threw away his state. Ritson, however, believed it to mean played away his consequence at cards. And Steevens imagined the metaphor was taken from mingling *coarse* wool with *fine.*

[f] Carping fools;] *Taunting* fools.

[g] *Vain* comparative.] See note (a), p. 513.

They surfeited with honey; and began
To loathe the taste of sweetness, whereof a little
More than a little, is by much too much:
So, when he had occasion to be seen,
He was but as the cuckoo is in June,
Heard, not regarded; seen, but with such eyes,
As, sick and blunted with community,
Afford no extraordinary gaze,
Such as is bent on sun-like majesty
When it shines seldom in admiring eyes:
But rather drows'd, and hung their eyelids down,
Slept in his face, and render'd such aspéct
As cloudy men use to * their adversaries;
Being with his presence glutted, gorg'd, and full.
And in that very line, Harry, stand'st thou:
For thou hast lost thy princely privilege,
With vile participation; not an eye,
But is a-weary of thy common sight,
Save mine, which hath desir'd to see thee more;
Which now doth that I would not have it do,
Make blind itself with foolish tenderness.

P. HEN. I shall hereafter, my thrice gracious lord,
Be more myself.

K. HEN. For all the world,
As thou art to this hour, was Richard then
When I from France set foot at Ravenspurg;
And even as I was then, is Percy now.
Now by my sceptre, and my soul to boot,
He hath more worthy interest to[a] the state,
Than thou, the shadow of succession:
For, of no right, nor colour like to right,
He doth fill fields with harness in the realm;
Turns head against the lion's armed jaws;
And, being no more in debt to years than thou,
Leads ancient lords and reverend bishops on,
To bloody battles, and to bruising arms.
What never-dying honour hath he got
Against renowned Douglas! whose high deeds,
Whose hot incursions, and great name in arms,
Holds from all soldiers chief majority,
And military title capital,
Through all the kingdoms that acknowledge Christ.
Thrice hath this† Hotspur, Mars in swathing clothes,
This infant warrior, in his enterprises
Discomfited great Douglas: ta'en him once,
Enlarged him, and made a friend of him,
To fill the mouth of deep defiance up,
And shake the peace and safety of our throne.
And what say you to this? Percy, Northumberland,
The archbishop's grace of York, Douglas, Mortimer,
Capitulate against us, and are up.
But wherefore do I tell these news to thee?
Why, Harry, do I tell thee of my foes,
Which art my near'st and dearest enemy?
Thou that art like enough,—through vassal fear,
Base inclination, and the start of spleen,——
To fight against me under Percy's pay,
To dog his heels, and court'sy at his frowns,
To show how much thou art degenerate.

P. HEN. Do not think so, you shall not find it so:
And God * forgive them, that so much have sway'd
Your majesty's good thoughts away from me!
I will redeem all this on Percy's head,
And, in the closing of some glorious day,
Be bold to tell you, that I am your son;
When I will wear a garment all of blood,
And stain my favours[b] in a bloody mask,
Which, wash'd away, shall scour my shame with it.
And that shall be the day, whene'er it lights,
That this same child of honour and renown,
This gallant Hotspur, this all-praised knight,
And your unthought-of Harry, chance to meet:
For every honour sitting on his helm,
'Would they were multitudes; and on my head
My shames redoubled! for the time will come,
That I shall make this northern youth exchange
His glorious deeds for my indignities.
Percy is but my factor, good my lord,
To engross up glorious deeds on my behalf;
And I will call him to so strict account,
That he shall render every glory up,
Yea, even the slightest worship of his time,
Or I will tear the reckoning from his heart.
This, in the name of God,* I promise here:
The which if He be pleas'd I shall perform,[c]
I do beseech your majesty, may salve
The long-grown wounds of my intemperance;†
If not, the end of life cancels all bands;
And I will die a hundred thousand deaths,
Ere break the smallest parcel of this vow.

K. HEN. A hundred thousand rebels die in this:—(2)
Thou shalt have charge, and sovereign trust herein.

Enter BLUNT.

How now, good Blunt? thy looks are full of speed.

BLUNT. So hath the business that I come to speak of.
Lord Mortimer of Scotland hath sent word,

(*) First folio inserts, *do to*. (†) First folio, *the*.

(*) First folio, *Heaven*. (†) First folio, *intemperature*.

[a] *More worthy interest to the state*,—] This construction was not uncommon in old language, and is even now not altogether obsolete; witness the saying, "*To* the fore."

[b] *My* favours—] My *features*, but, as Warburton suggests, we should, perhaps, read *favour*, that is, countenance.

[c] If He be pleas'd I shall perform,—] So the quarto copies; the folio reads, if *I perform and do survive*.

That Douglas, and the English rebels, met,
The eleventh of this month, at Shrewsbury:
A mighty and a fearful head they are,
(If promises be kept on every hand,)
As ever offer'd foul play in a state.

K. HEN. The earl of Westmoreland set forth to-day;
With him my son, lord John of Lancaster;
For this advertisement is five days old:—
On Wednesday next, Harry, you shall* set forward;
On Thursday, we ourselves will march:
Our meeting is Bridgnorth: and, Harry, you
Shall march through Glostershire; by which account,
Our business valued, some twelve days hence
Our general forces at Bridgnorth shall meet.
Our hands are full of business: let's away;
Advantage feeds him fat, while men delay.
[*Exeunt.*

(*) First folio, *thou shalt.*

[a] *In some* liking;] In some *condition.* So, in "Love's Labour's Lost," Act V. Sc. 2:—

"*Well-liking* wits they have; gross, gross, fat, fat."

SCENE III.—Eastcheap. *A Room in the* Boar's Head Tavern.

Enter FALSTAFF *and* BARDOLPH.

FAL. Bardolph, am I not fallen away vilely since this last action? Do I not bate? do I not dwindle? Why, my skin hangs about me like an old lady's loose gown; I am withered like an old apple-John. Well, I'll repent, and that suddenly, while I am in some liking;[a] I shall be out of heart shortly, and then I shall have no strength to repent. An I have not forgotten what the inside of a church is made of, I am a peppercorn, a brewer's horse: the inside of a church! Company, villainous company, hath been the spoil of me.

BARD. Sir John, you are so fretful, you cannot live long.

FAL. Why, there is it:—come, sing me a bawdy song; make me merry. I was as virtuously given, as a gentleman need to be; virtuous enough: swore little; diced not above seven times—a week; went to a bawdy-house, not above once in a quarter—of an hour: paid money that I borrowed,—three or four times; lived well, and in good compass: and now I live out of all order, out of all* compass.

BARD. Why, you are so fat, sir John, that you must needs be out of all compass; out of all reasonable compass, sir John.

FAL. Do thou amend thy face, and I'll amend my† life. Thou art our admiral,[a] thou bearest the lantern in the poop,—but 't is in the nose of thee; thou art the knight of the burning lamp.

BARD. Why, sir John, my face does you no harm.

FAL. No, I'll be sworn; I make as good use of it as many a man doth of a death's head, or a *memento mori*: I never see thy face, but I think upon hell-fire, and Dives that lived in purple; for there he is in his robes, burning, burning. If thou wert any way given to virtue, I would swear by thy face; my oath should be, *By this fire, that's God's angel*:‡ but thou art altogether given over; and wert indeed, but for the light in thy face, the son of utter darkness. When thou ran'st up Gadshill in the night to catch my horse, if I did not think § thou hadst been an *ignis fatuus*, or a ball of wildfire, there's no purchase in money. O, thou art a perpetual triumph, an everlasting bonfire-light! Thou hast saved me a thousand marks in links and torches, walking with thee in the night betwixt tavern and tavern: but the sack that thou hast drunk me, would have bought me lights as good cheap,[b] at ‖ the dearest chandler's in Europe. I have maintained that salamander of yours with fire, any time this two and thirty years; God¶ reward me for it!

BARD. 'Sblood,** I would my face were in your belly!

FAL. God-a-mercy††! so should I be sure to be heart-burned.

Enter Hostess.

How now, dame Partlet[c] the hen? have you inquired yet, who picked my pocket?

HOST. Why, sir John! what do you think, sir John? Do you think I keep thieves in my house? I have searched, I have inquired, so has my husband, man by man, boy by boy, servant by servant: the tithe* of a hair was never lost in my house before.

FAL. You lie, hostess; Bardolph was shaved, and lost many a hair: and I'll be sworn, my pocket was picked: go to, you are a woman, go.

HOST. Who I? no,† I defy thee: God's light!‡ I was never called so in mine own house before.

FAL. Go to, I know you well enough.

HOST. No, sir John, you do not know me, sir John; I know you, sir John; you owe me money, sir John, and now you pick a quarrel to beguile me of it: I bought you a dozen of shirts to your back.

FAL. Dowlas, filthy dowlas: I have given them away to bakers' wives, and they have made bolters[d] of them.

HOST. Now, as I am a true woman, holland of eight shillings an ell.(3) You owe money here besides, sir John, for your diet, and by-drinkings; and money lent you, four and twenty pound.§

FAL. He had his part of it; let him pay.

HOST. He! alas, he is poor; he hath nothing.

FAL. How! poor? look upon his face; what call you rich? let them coin his nose, let them coin his cheeks: I'll not pay a denier. What, will you make a younker[e] of me? shall I not take mine ease in mine inn,[f] but I shall have my pocket picked? I have lost a seal-ring of my grandfather's, worth forty mark.

HOST. O Jesu! ‖ I have heard the prince tell him, I know not how oft, that that ring was copper

FAL. How! the prince is a Jack, a sneak-cup; 'sblood¶ an he were here, I would cudgel him like a dog if he would say so.

Enter PRINCE HENRY *and* POINS, *marching.* FALSTAFF *meets the* PRINCE, *playing on his truncheon, like a fife.*

FAL. How now, lad? is the wind in that door, i'faith?** must we all march?

BARD. Yea, two and two, Newgate-fashion.

(*) First folio omits, *all*. (†) First folio, *thy*.
(‡) First folio omits, *that's God's angel*.
(§) First folio inserts, *that*. (‖) First folio, *as*.
(¶) First folio, *Heaven*. (**) First folio omits, *'Sblood*.
(††) First folio omits, *God-a-mercy*.

a Thou art our admiral,—] Decker (says Steevens), in his "Wonderful Yeare," 1603, has the same thought; he is describing the host of a country inn:—"An antiquary might have pickt rare matter out of his *nose*.—The Hamburghers offered I know not how many dollars for his companie in an East-Indian voyage, to have stoode a nightes in the Poope of their Admirall, onely to save the charges of candles."

b As *good* cheap,—] *Cheap* is the old name for market; *good cheap* is, therefore, the same as the French *à bon marché*.

c Dame Partlet—] The name of the hen in the popular old story-book of "Reynard the Fox;" it occurs, also, in Chaucer's "*Nonnes Preestes Tale*," and in Skelton's "*Phyllyp Sparrowe*." Ruddiman conjectures that the name was applied to a hen because of the ruff (the *partlet*), or ring of feathers about her neck.

(*) Old copies, *tight*. (†) First folio omits, *no*.
(‡) First folio omits, *God's light!* (§) First folio, *pounds*.
(‖) First folio omits, *O Jesu!* (¶) First folio omits, *'Sblood*.
(**) First folio omits, *i'faith*.

d *Made* bolters *of them*.] *Bolters* are sieves: nothing could better express the coarseness of their texture.

e *Will you make a* younker *of me?*] *Younker* was not always used in the contemptuous sense it bears here, of a *greenhorn* or *noddy*. See note (b), p. 407.

f Shall I not take mine ease in mine inn,—] In early times an *inn* signified a dwelling, and "To take mine ease in mine inne" was a proverb, Percy remarks, not very different in its application from the maxim, "Every man's house is his castle." When the word *inne* had changed its import, and came to mean a house of public entertainment, the proverb continuing in force, was applied in the latter sense.

HOST. My lord, I pray you, hear me.

P. HEN. What say'st thou, mistress Quickly? How does thy husband? I love him well; he is an honest man.

HOST. Good my lord, hear me.

FAL. Pr'ythee, let her alone, and list to me.

P. HEN. What say'st thou, Jack?

FAL. The other night I fell asleep here behind the arras, and had my pocket picked: this house is turned bawdy-house, they pick pockets.

P. HEN. What didst thou lose, Jack?

FAL. Wilt thou believe me, Hal? three or four bonds of forty [a] pound a-piece, and a seal-ring of my grandfather's.

P. HEN. A trifle, some eight-penny matter.

HOST. So I told him, my lord; and I said, I heard your grace say so; and, my lord, he speaks most vilely of you, like a foul-mouthed man as he is; and said, he would cudgel you.

P. HEN. What! he did not?

HOST. There's neither faith, truth, nor womanhood in me else.

FAL. There's no more faith in thee than in* a stewed prune; [b] nor no more truth in thee than in a drawn fox; [c] and for womanhood, maid Marian may be the deputy's wife of the ward to thee.[d] Go, you thing,† go.

HOST. Say, what thing? what thing?

FAL. What thing? why, a thing to thank God ‡ on.

---

[a] *Of* forty *pound a-piece,*—] See note (5), p. 150.

[b] *There's no more faith in thee than in a* stewed prune;] The reader will find the subject of *stewed prunes* very amply discussed in Boswell's *Variorum* Edition, Vol. XVI. p. 345.

[c] A drawn fox;] The allusion is probably to the subtlety displayed by a fox in his efforts to escape after being drawn from his kennel. It was believed that sometimes he even counterfeited death.

[d] Maid Marian may be, &c.] Maid Marian was the traditional "ladie love" of the noted Robin Hood, and, in after times, an adopted character in the Morris-dances. It is not at all unlikely that she was often represented by a man, whence it might happen that any very masculine specimen of womankind was likened to Maid Marian.

(*) First folio omits, *in*. (†) First folio, *nothing*. (‡) First folio, *Heaven*.

HOST. I am no thing to thank God* on, I would thou should'st know it; I am an honest man's wife: and, setting thy knighthood aside, thou art a knave to call me so.

FAL. Setting thy womanhood aside, thou art a beast to say otherwise.

HOST. Say, what beast, thou knave, thou?

FAL. What beast? why, an otter?

P. HEN. An otter, sir John! why an otter?

FAL. Why, she's neither fish nor flesh; a man knows not where to have her.

HOST. Thou art an † unjust man in saying so; thou or any man knows where to have me, thou knave thou!

P. HEN. Thou say'st true, hostess; and he slanders thee most grossly.

HOST. So he doth you, my lord; and said this other day, you ought him a thousand pound.

P. HEN. Sirrah, do I owe you a thousand pound?

FAL. A thousand pound, Hal? a million: thy love is worth a million; thou owest me thy love.

HOST. Nay, my lord, he called you Jack, and said, he would cudgel you.

FAL. Did I, Bardolph?

BARD. Indeed, sir John, you said so.

FAL. Yea; if he said my ring was copper.

P. HEN. I say, 't is copper: darest thou be as good as thy word now?

FAL. Why, Hal, thou knowest, as thou art but ‡ man, I dare: but as thou art ‡ prince, I fear thee, as I fear the roaring of the lion's whelp.

P. HEN. And why not as the lion?

FAL. The king himself is to be feared as the lion: dost thou think, I'll fear thee as I fear thy father? nay, an I do, I pray God, my girdle break! [a]

P. HEN. O, if it should, how would thy guts fall about thy knees! But, sirrah, there's no room for faith, truth, nor honesty, in this bosom of thine; it is all filled up with guts, and midriff. Charge an honest woman with picking thy pocket! Why, thou whoreson, impudent, embossed rascal, if there were anything in thy pocket but tavern-reckonings, memorandums of bawdy-houses, and one poor pennyworth of sugar-candy to make thee long-winded; if thy pocket were enriched with any other injuries but these, I am a villain. And yet you will stand to it, you will not pocket up wrong:[b] art thou not ashamed?

FAL. Dost thou hear, Hal? thou knowest, in the state of innocency, Adam fell; and what should poor Jack Falstaff do, in the days of villainy? Thou seest, I have more flesh than another man; and therefore more frailty.——You confess then, you picked my pocket?

P. HEN. It appears so by the story.

FAL. Hostess, I forgive thee. Go, make ready breakfast; love thy husband, look to thy servants,* cherish thy guests: thou shalt find me tractable to any honest reason: thou seest, I am pacified still.[c] Nay, † pr'ythee, be gone. [*Exit* Hostess.] Now, Hal, to the news at court: for the robbery, lad,—How is that answered?

P. HEN. O, my sweet beef, I must still be good angel to thee:—the money is paid back again.

FAL. O, I do not like that paying back, 'tis a double labour.

P. HEN. I am good friends with my father and may do any thing.

FAL. Rob me the exchequer the first thing thou dost, and do it with unwashed hands too.[d]

BARD. Do, my lord.

P. HEN. I have procured thee, Jack, a charge of foot.

FAL. I would it had been of horse. Where shall I find one that can steal well? O for a fine thief, of two-and-twenty, or thereabout! I am heinously unprovided. Well, God be thanked for these rebels, they offend none but the virtuous; I laud them; I praise them.

P. HEN. Bardolph!——

BARD. My lord.

P. HEN. Go bear this letter to lord John of Lancaster,
To my brother John; this to my lord of Westmoreland.—
Go, Poins, to horse, to horse; ‡—for thou and I
Have thirty miles to ride yet[e] ere dinner time.——
Jack, meet me to-morrow in the Temple hall
At two o'clock i' the afternoon:
There shalt thou know thy charge, and there receive
Money, and order for their furniture.
The land is burning, Percy stands on high;
And either they, or we, must lower lie.

[*Exeunt* PRINCE, POINS, *and* BARDOLPH.

FAL. Rare words! brave world!——Hostess, my breakfast; come:—
O, I could wish, this tavern were my drum!

[*Exit.*

(*) First folio, *Heaven*. (†) First folio omits, *an*. (‡) First folio inserts, *a*.

[a] *Nay*, an *I do*, I pray God, *my girdle break!*] The folio reads, Nay *if* I do *let* my girdle break.

[b] And yet you will stand to it, you will not pocket up wrong:] Johnson's conjecture that some part of this "merry dialogue," wherein Falstaff had declared his resolution *not to pocket up wrongs or injuries*, has been lost, is extremely credible.

[c] I *am pacified* still.] I am *always* pacified.

(*) First folio inserts, *and*. (†) First folio inserts, *I*. (‡) First folio reads, *to horse*, once only, and *Peto* for *Poins*.

[d] Do it with unwashed hands too.] Not, I believe, do it at once, without even the ceremony of washing your hands, but—do it *without repentance*, without "*that paying back*."

[e] *Have thirty miles to ride* yet—] The *yet* here overloads the line, and, unless the whole passage, down to "at two o'clock i' the afternoon," was intended for prose, is better omitted.

ACT IV.

SCENE I.—*The Rebel Camp near* Shrewsbury.

Enter Hotspur, Worcester, *and* Douglas.

Hot. Well said, my noble Scot; if speaking truth,
In this fine age, were not thought flattery,
Such attribution should the Douglas have,
As not a soldier of this season's stamp
Should go so general current through the world.
By God,* I cannot flatter; I defy
The tongues of soothers; but a braver place
In my heart's love, hath no man than yourself:
Nay, task me to my word; approve me, lord.

(*) First folio, *Heaven*.

DOUG. Thou art the king of honour;
No man so potent breathes upon the ground,
But I will beard him.[a]
HOT. Do so, and 't is well:—

Enter a Messenger, *with Letters.*

What letters hast thou* there?—I can but thank you.
MESS. These letters come from your father,—
HOT. Letters from him! why comes he not himself?
MESS. He cannot come, my lord; he's grievous sick.
HOT. 'Zounds!† how has he the leisure to be sick,‡
In such a justling time? Who leads his power?
Under whose government come they along?
MESS. His letters bear his mind, not I, my lord.[b]
WOR. I pr'ythee, tell me, doth he keep his bed?
MESS. He did, my lord, four days ere I set forth;
And, at the time of my departure thence,
He was much fear'd by his physicians.§
WOR. I would the state of time had first been whole,
Ere he by sickness had been visited;
His health was never better worth than now.
HOT. Sick now! droop now! this sickness doth infect
The very life-blood of our enterprise;
'T is catching hither, even to our camp.——
He writes me here,—that inward sickness—
And that his friends by deputation
Could not so soon be drawn; nor did he think it meet,
To lay so dangerous and dear a trust
On any soul remov'd, but on his own.
Yet doth he give us bold advertisement,
That with our small conjunction, we should on,
To see how fortune is dispos'd to us:
For, as he writes, there is no quailing now;
Because the king is certainly possess'd
Of all our purposes. What say you to it?
WOR. Your father's sickness is a maim to us.
HOT. A perilous gash, a very limb lopp'd off;—
And yet, in faith, 't is not; his present want
Seems more than we shall find it;—were it good,
To set the exact wealth of all our states
All at one cast? to set so rich a main
On the nice hazard of one doubtful hour?
It were not good: for therein should we read
The very bottom and the soul of hope;[c]
The very list, the very utmost bound
Of all our fortunes.
DOUG. 'Faith, and so we should;
Where now remains a sweet reversion:
We may boldly spend upon the hope
Of what is to come in;
A comfort of retirement lives in this.
HOT. A rendezvous, a home to fly unto,
If that the devil and mischance look big
Upon the maidenhead of our affairs.
WOR. But yet, I would your father had been here.
The quality and hair[d] of our attempt
Brooks no division: it will be thought
By some that know not why he is away,
That wisdom, loyalty, and mere dislike
Of our proceedings, kept the earl from hence;
And think, how such an apprehension
May turn the tide of fearful faction,
And breed a kind of question in our cause:
For, well you know, we of the offering side
Must keep aloof from strict arbitrement;
And stop all sight-holes, every loop, from whence
The eye of reason may pry in upon us:
This absence of your father's* draws a curtain,
That shows the ignorant a kind of fear
Before not dreamt of.
HOT. You strain too far.
I, rather, of his absence make this use;—

(*) First folio omits, *thou*. (†) First folio omits, *'Zounds!*
(‡) First folio adds, *now*. (§) First folio, *physician*.

(*) First folio, *father*.

[a] But I will beard him.] This hemistich is always allied to the preceding line, but it may be intended to refer to something supposed to have been said by Douglas, before the opening of the scene. Some threat of confronting the King, which had called forth the "Well said, my noble Scot."

[b] *His letters bear his mind, not I*, my lord.] The first quarto has, "not I, my *mind*," clearly a printer's error. The folio, copying a later quarto, reads, "Not I, *his mind*." We adopt the reading of Capell.

[c] —— For therein should we read
The very bottom and the soul of hope;]

If *read* was not occasionally used for *tread*, and in Middleton's play of "Your Five Gallants," Act III. Sc. 4, it occurs in that sense:—

"Nay, *read* forward;"

then it may be suspected a misprint for *tread*, as *soul* certainly appears to be of *sound*. In the MS. *soūd* would easily be mistaken for *soul*, and the original perhaps ran:—

"—— For therein should we *tread*
The very bottom and the *sound* of hope."

[d] The quality and hair of our attempt
Brooks no division:]

Hair, for *complexion*, may be the poet's word, yet it is worth considering, perhaps, whether "and hair" was not mistaken for "*and dare:*"—

"The quality and *dare* of our attempt
Brooks no division."

The nature and boldness of our enterprise cannot afford the appearance of dissension. This reading, too, receives some support from Hotspur's reply:—

"I, rather, of his absence make this use;—
It lends a lustre, and more great opinion,
A larger *dare* to our great enterprise," &c.

It lends a lustre, and more great opinion,
A larger dare to our* great enterprise,
Than if the earl were here: for men must think,
If we, without his help, can make a head
To push against the kingdom; with his help,
We shall o'erturn it topsy-turvy down.—
Yet, all goes well; yet, all our joints are whole.

DOUG. As heart can think: there is not such a word
Spoke of in Scotland, as this dream of fear.[a]

Enter SIR RICHARD VERNON.

HOT. My cousin Vernon! welcome, by my soul.

VER. Pray God, my news be worth a welcome, lord.
The earl of Westmoreland, seven thousand strong,
Is marching hitherwards; with him,† prince John.

HOT. No harm: what more?

VER. And further, I have learn'd,—
The king himself in person is‡ set forth,
Or hitherwards intended speedily,
With strong and mighty preparation.

HOT. He shall be welcome too. Where is his son,
The nimble-footed[b] mad-cap prince of Wales,
And his comrádes, that daff'd the world aside,
And bid it pass?

VER. All furnish'd, all in arms,
All plum'd like estridges, that wing[c] the wind;
Bated like eagles having lately bath'd;
Glittering in golden coats, like images;
As full of spirit as the month of May,
And gorgeous as the sun at midsummer;
Wanton as youthful goats, wild as young bulls.
I saw young Harry,—with his beaver on,
His cuisses on his thighs, gallantly arm'd,—
Rise from the ground like feather'd Mercury,
And vaulted with such ease into his seat,
As if an angel dropp'd down from the clouds,
To turn and wind a fiery Pegasus,
And witch the world with noble horsemanship.

HOT. No more, no more; worse than the sun in March,
This praise doth nourish agues. Let them come;
They come like sacrifices in their trim,
And to the fire-eyed maid of smoky war,
All hot and bleeding will we offer them:
The mailed Mars shall on his altar sit,
Up to the ears in blood. I am on fire,
To hear this rich reprisal is so nigh,
And yet not ours.—Come, let me take my horse,
Who is to bear me like a thunderbolt,
Against the bosom of the prince of Wales:
Harry to Harry shall, hot* horse to horse,
Meet, and ne'er part, till one drop down a corse.—
O, that Glendower were come!

VER. There is more news:
I learn'd in Worcester, as I rode along,
He cannot draw his power this† fourteen days.

DOUG. That's the worst tidings that I hear of yet.

WOR. Ay, by my faith, that bears a frosty sound.

HOT. What may the king's whole battle reach unto?

VER. To thirty thousand.

HOT. Forty let it be!
My father and Glendower being both away,
The powers of us may serve so great a day.
Come, let us take a muster speedily:
Doomsday is near; die all, die merrily.

DOUG. Talk not of dying; I am out of fear
Of death, or death's hand, for this one half year.
[*Exeunt.*

SCENE II.—*A public Road near* Coventry.

Enter FALSTAFF *and* BARDOLPH.

FAL. Bardolph, get thee before to Coventry; fill me a bottle of sack: our soldiers shall march through; we'll to Sutton-Cop-hill to-night.

BARD. Will you give me money, captain?

FAL. Lay out, lay out.

BARD. This bottle makes an angel.

FAL. An if it do, take it for thy labour; and if it make twenty, take them all, I'll answer the coinage. Bid my lieutenant Peto meet me at the town's end.

BARD. I will, captain: farewell. [*Exit.*

FAL. If I be not ashamed of my soldiers, I am a soused gurnet. I have misused the king's press damnably. I have got, in exchange of a hundred and fifty soldiers, three hundred and odd pounds.

(*) First folio, *your.* (†) First folio omits, *him.* (‡) First folio, *hath.*

[a] As this dream of fear.] The quartos before 1613 read "*term* of fear," and they are followed by all the modern editors. We prefer "*dream* of fear," because Douglas appears to be scornfully alluding to an expression in the previous speech of Worcester:—

"This absence of your father's draws a curtain,
That shows the ignorant a *kind of fear*
Before *not dreamt of.*"

[b] Nimble-footed—] Stowe relates that the prince was so surpassingly swift as a runner, that with two of his lords, "without hounds, bow, or engine," he would capture a wild buck or doe in a large park.

[c] *All plum'd like estridges, that* wing *the wind;*] The old text has, *with* the wind; Johnson substituted *wing* for *with*, in the opinion of some without necessity; the passage only requiring to be pointed thus:—

"All plum'd like estridges, that with the wind
Bated,—like eagles having lately bath'd;
Glittering in golden coats, like images."

(*) First folio, *not.* (†) First folio, *these.*

I press me none but good householders, yeomen's sons: inquire me out contracted bachelors, such as had been asked twice on the bans; such a commodity of warm slaves, as had as lief hear the devil as a drum; such as fear the report of a caliver, worse than a struck fowl, or a hurt wild-duck. I pressed me none but such toasts and butter,[a] with hearts in their bellies no bigger than pins' heads, and they have bought out their services; and now my whole charge consists of ancients, corporals, lieutenants, gentlemen of companies, slaves as ragged as Lazarus in the painted cloth, where the glutton's dogs licked his sores: and such as, indeed, were never soldiers; but discarded unjust[b] serving-men, younger sons to younger brothers, revolted tapsters, and ostlers trade-fallen; the cankers of a calm world, and a* long peace; ten times more dishonourable ragged than an old faced ancient:[c] and such have I, to fill up the rooms of them that have bought out their services; that you would think, that I had a hundred and fifty tattered prodigals, lately come from swine-keeping, from eating draff and husks. A mad fellow met me on the way, and told me I had unloaded all the gibbets, and pressed the dead bodies. No eye hath seen such scare-crows. I'll not march through Coventry with them, that's flat:—nay, and the villains march wide betwixt the legs, as if they had gyves on; for, indeed, I had the most of them out of prison. There's but* a shirt and a half in all my company: and the half-shirt is two napkins, tacked together, and thrown over the shoulders like a herald's coat without sleeves: and the shirt, to say the truth, stolen from my host at† saint

(*) First folio omits, *a*.

a Toasts and butter,—] An old term of contempt for persons cockered up and peaceably nurtured:—

"They love young *toasts and butter*, (Bow-bell suckers.)"
Beaumont and Fletcher's "Wit without Money," Act V. Sc. 2.

(*) Old copies, *not*. (†) First folio, *of*.

b Unjust *serving-men*,—] That is, *dishonest* serving-men.
c An old faced ancient:] According to Steevens, an old standard *faced* or mended with a different colour.

Alban's, or the red-nose innkeeper of Daventry. But that's all one; they'll find linen enough on every hedge.

Enter PRINCE HENRY *and* WESTMORELAND.

P. HEN. How now, blown Jack? how now, quilt?[a]

FAL. What, Hal? How now, mad wag? what a devil dost thou in Warwickshire?—My good lord of Westmoreland, I cry you mercy; I thought your honour had already been at Shrewsbury.

WEST. 'Faith, sir John, 't is more than time that I were there, and you too; but my powers are there already: the king, I can tell you, looks for us all; we must away all* night.

FAL. Tut! never fear me; I am as vigilant as a cat to steal cream.

P. HEN. I think, to steal cream indeed: for thy theft hath already made thee butter. But tell me, Jack; whose fellows are these that come after?

FAL. Mine, Hal, mine.

P. HEN. I did never see such pitiful rascals.

FAL. Tut, tut; good enough to toss;[b] food for powder, food for powder; they'll fill a pit, as well as better: tush, man, mortal men, mortal men.

WEST. Ay, but, sir John, methinks, they are exceeding poor and bare; too beggarly.

FAL. 'Faith, for their poverty,—I know not where they had that: and for their bareness,—I am sure, they never learned that of me.

P. HEN. No, I'll be sworn; unless you call three fingers on the ribs, bare. But, sirrah, make haste: Percy is already in the field.

FAL. What, is the king encamped?

WEST. He is, sir John; I fear, we shall stay too long.

FAL. Well,
To the latter end of a fray, and the beginning of a feast,
Fits a dull fighter, and a keen guest. [*Exeunt.*

SCENE III.—*The Rebel Camp near* Shrewsbury.

Enter HOTSPUR, WORCESTER, DOUGLAS, *and* VERNON.

HOT. We'll fight with him to-night.
WOR. It may not be.
DOUG. You give him then advantage.
VER. Not a whit.
HOT. Why say you so? looks he not for supply?
VER. So do we.
HOT. His is certain, ours is doubtful.
WOR. Good cousin, be advis'd; stir not to-night.
VER. Do not, my lord.
DOUG. You do not counsel well;
You speak it out of fear, and cold heart.
VER. Do me no slander, Douglas: by my life,
(And I dare well maintain it with my life,)
If well-respected honour bid me on,
I hold as little counsel with weak fear,
As you, my lord, or any Scot that this day lives:[c]
Let it be seen to-morrow in the battle,
Which of us fears.
DOUG. Yea, or to-night.
VER. Content.
HOT. To-night, say I.
VER. Come, come, it may not be: I wonder much,
Being men of such great leading as you are,
That you foresee not what impediments
Drag back our expedition: certain horse
Of my cousin Vernon's are not yet come up:
Your uncle Worcester's horse came but to-day;
And now their pride and mettle is asleep,
Their courage with hard labour tame and dull,
That not a horse is half the half of himself.
HOT. So are the horses of the enemy
In general, journey-bated, and brought low;
The better part of ours are full of rest.
WOR. The number of the king exceedeth ours:
For God's sake, cousin, stay till all come in..
[*The Trumpet sounds a parley.*

Enter SIR WALTER BLUNT.

BLUNT. I come with gracious offers from the king,
If you vouchsafe me hearing, and respect.
HOT. Welcome, sir Walter Blunt, and would to God
You were of our determination!
Some of us love you well; and even those some
Envy your great deservings, and good name,
Because you are not of our quality,
But stand against us like an enemy.
BLUNT. And God* defend, but still I should stand so,
So long as, out of limit, and true rule,
You stand against anointed majesty!

(*) First folio inserts, *to*.

(*) First folio, *Heaven*.

[a] Quilt?] Mr. Hunter is the only commentator, we believe, who has noticed this word, and he quite misapprehends its meaning; a *quilt* was a *flock-bed*.

[b] Good enough to toss;] To toss upon a pike. Thus in "Henry VI." Part III. Act I. Sc. 1:—

"The soldiers should have *toss'd me on their pikes*,
Before," &c.

[c] As you, my lord, or any Scot that this day lives:] Mason would omit the words, *this day*, as they "weaken the sense and destroy the measure." It is not improbable that the line originally stood:—

"As you, or any Scot that this day lives,"

and was subsequently altered by the poet to,—

"As you, my lord, or any Scot that lives;"

but the compositor, while adding the words "my lord," neglected to omit "this day."

But, to my charge.—The king hath sent to know
The nature of your griefs; and whereupon
You conjure from the breast of civil peace
Such bold hostility, teaching his duteous land
Audacious cruelty. If that the king
Have any way your good deserts forgot,—
Which he confesseth to be manifold,—
He bids you name your griefs;[a] and, with all speed,
You shall have your desires, with interest;
And pardon absolute for yourself, and these
Herein misled by your suggestion.

HOT. The king is kind; and, well we know, the king
Knows at what time to promise, when to pay.
My father, and* my uncle, and myself,
Did give him that same royalty he wears:
And,—when he was not six and twenty strong,
Sick in the world's regard, wretched and low,
A poor unminded outlaw sneaking home,—
My father gave him welcome to the shore;
And,—when he heard him swear, and vow to God,
He came but to be duke of Lancaster,
To sue his livery, and beg his peace;—
With tears of innocency, and terms of zeal,
My father, in kind heart and pity mov'd,
Swore him assistance, and perform'd it too.
Now, when the lords and barons of the realm
Perceiv'd Northumberland did lean to him,
The more and less came in with cap and knee;
Met him in boroughs, cities, villages:
Attended him on bridges, stood in lanes,
Laid gifts before him, proffer'd him their oaths,
Gave him their heirs as pages; follow'd him,
Even at the heels, in golden multitudes.
He presently,—as greatness knows itself,—
Steps me a little higher than his vow
Made to my father, while his blood was poor,
Upon the naked shore at Ravenspurg;
And now, forsooth, takes on him to reform
Some certain edicts, and some strait decrees,
That lie too heavy on the commonwealth;
Cries out upon abuses, seems to weep
Over his country's wrongs; and, by this face,
This seeming brow of justice, did he win
The hearts of all that he did angle for.
Proceeded further; cut me off the heads
Of all the favourites, that the absent king
In deputation left behind him here,
When he was personal in the Irish war.

BLUNT. Tut, I came not to hear this.

HOT. Then, to the point.——
In short time after, he depos'd the king;
Soon after that, depriv'd him of his life;
And, in the neck of that, task'd[b] the whole state:
To make that worse, suffer'd his kinsman March
(Who is, if every owner were well * plac'd,
Indeed his king,) to be engag'd[c] in Wales,
There without ransom to lie forfeited:
Disgrac'd me in my happy victories,
Sought to entrap me by intelligence,
Rated my uncle from the council-board,
In rage dismiss'd my father from the court,
Broke oath on oath, committed wrong on wrong,
And, in conclusion, drove us to seek out
This head of safety; and, withal, to pry
Into his title, the which we find
Too indirect for long continuance.

BLUNT. Shall I return this answer to the king?

HOT. Not so, sir Walter; we 'll withdraw a while.
Go to the king: and let there be impawn'd
Some surety for a safe return again,
And in the morning early shall mine † uncle
Bring him our purposes: ‡ and so farewell.

BLUNT. I would you would accept of grace and love.

HOT. And,§ may be, so we shall.

BLUNT. 'Pray God,|| you do!

[*Exeunt.*

SCENE IV.—York. *A Room in the* Archbishop's *House.*

Enter the ARCHBISHOP OF YORK, *and a* Gentleman.

ARCH. Hie, good sir Michael; bear this sealed brief,
With winged haste, to the lord mareshal;
This, to my cousin Scroop; and all the rest,
To whom they are directed; if you knew
How much they do import, you would make haste.

GENT. My good lord,
I guess their tenor.

ARCH. Like enough, you do.
To-morrow, good sir Michael, is a day,
Wherein the fortune of ten thousand men
Must bide the touch: for, sir, at Shrewsbury,
As I am truly given to understand,
The king, with mighty and quick-raised power,
Meets with lord Harry: and I fear, sir Michael,—

(*) First folio omits, *and*.

a Griefs;] That is, *grievances*.

b Task'd *the whole state*:] *Task'd* and *tax'd* were often used indifferently:—"Duke Philip, by the space of many years, levied neither subsidies nor *tasks*."—*Memoirs of P. de Comines*, by Danert, folio 1674, p. 136. Quoted by Steevens.

(*) First folio omits, *well*. (†) First folio, *my*. (‡) First folio, *purpose*. (§) First folio, *And't*. (||) First folio, *Heaven*.

c Engag'd in Wales,—] This is the reading of all the ancient copies, which Theobald altered to "*incag'd*." Engag'd means *detained as a pledge* or *hostage*. So in Act V. Sc. 2, of this play:—
"And Westmoreland that was *engag'd*, did bear it."

What with the sickness of Northumberland,
(Whose power was in the first proportion,)
And what with Owen Glendower's absence thence,
(Who with them was a rated sinew [a] too,
And comes not in, o'er-rul'd by prophecies,)—
I fear, the power of Percy is too weak
To wage an instant trial with the king.

GENT. Why, my good lord, you need not fear; there 's Douglas,
And lord Mortimer.

ARCH. No, Mortimer's not there.

GENT. But there is Mordake, Vernon, lord Harry Percy,
And there 's my lord of Worcester; and a head
Of gallant warriors, noble gentlemen.

ARCH. And so there is: but yet the king hath drawn
The special head of all the land together;—
The prince of Wales, lord John of Lancaster,
The noble Westmoreland, and warlike Blunt;
And many more corrivals, and dear men
Of estimation and command in arms.

GENT. Doubt not, my lord, they * shall be well oppos'd.

ARCH. I hope no less, yet needful 'tis to fear;
And, to prevent the worst, sir Michael, speed;
For, if lord Percy thrive not, ere the king
Dismiss his power, he means to visit us,—
For he hath heard of our confederacy,—
And 't is but wisdom to make strong against him;
Therefore, make haste; I must go write again
To other friends; and so farewell, sir Michael.

[*Exeunt severally.*

---

[a] *Who with them was a rated* sinew *too,*—] *A valued strength.* The folio reads—
"Was rated *firmly* too."

(*) First folio, *he*.

ACT V.

SCENE I.—*The* King's *Camp near* Shrewsbury.

Enter King Henry, Prince Henry, Prince John of Lancaster, Sir Walter Blunt, *and* Sir John Falstaff.

K. Hen. How bloodily the sun begins to peer
Above yon busky[a] hill! the day looks pale
At his distemperature.

P. Hen. The southern wind
Doth play the trumpet to his purposes;
And, by his hollow whistling in the leaves,
Foretells a tempest, and a blustering day.

K. Hen. Then with the losers let it sympathise;
For nothing can seem foul to those that win.—

Trumpet sounds. Enter Worcester *and* Vernon.

How now, my lord of Worcester? 't is not well,
That you and I should meet upon such terms
As now we meet. You have deceiv'd our trust;
And made us doff our easy robes of peace,
To crush our old limbs in ungentle steel:
This is not well, my lord, this is not well.
What say you to it? will you again unknit
This churlish knot of all-abhorred war?
And move in that obedient orb again,
Where you did give a fair and natural light;

[a] *Above yon* busky *hill!*] *Busky* is woody, and should, perhaps, be spelt *bosky*, from the Latin *boscus*, or the French *bosque;* as in the "Tempest," Act IV. Sc. 1:—
"My *bosky* acres, and my unshrubb'd down."

And be no more an exhal'd meteor,
A prodigy of fear, and a portent
Of broached mischief to the unborn times?

WOR. Hear me, my liege:
For mine own part, I could be well content
To entertain the lag-end of my life
With quiet hours; for, I do protest,
I have not sought the day of this dislike.

K. HEN. You have not sought it! how comes it then?

FAL. Rebellion lay in his way, and he found it.

P. HEN. Peace, chewet,[a] peace.

WOR. It pleas'd your majesty to turn your looks
Of favour, from myself, and all our house;
And yet I must remember you, my lord,
We were the first and dearest of your friends.
For you, my staff of office did I break
In Richard's time; and posted day and night
To meet you on the way, and kiss your hand,
When yet you were in place and in account
Nothing so strong and fortunate as I.
It was myself, my brother, and his son,
That brought you home, and boldly did outdare
The dangers (*) of the time. You swore to us,—
And you did swear that oath at Doncaster,—
That you did nothing (†) purpose 'gainst the state;
Nor claim no further than your new-fall'n right,
The seat of Gaunt, dukedom of Lancaster:
To this we swore (‡) our aid. But, in short space,
It rain'd down fortune showering on your head;
And such a flood of greatness fell on you,—
What with our help, what with the absent king;
What with the injuries of a (§) wanton time;
The seeming sufferances that you had borne;
And the contrarious winds, that held the king
So long in his (||) unlucky Irish wars,
That all in England did repute him dead,—
And, from this swarm of fair advantages,
You took occasion to be quickly woo'd
To gripe the general sway into your hand:
Forgot your oath to us at Doncaster;
And, being fed by us, you us'd us so
As that ungentle gull, the cuckoo's bird,[b]
Useth the sparrow; did oppress our nest,
Grew by our feeding to so great a bulk,
That even our love durst not come near your sight,
For fear of swallowing; but with nimble wing
We were enforc'd, for safety sake, to fly
Out of your sight, and raise this present head;
Whereby we stand opposed by such means
As you yourself have forg'd against yourself,
By unkind usage, dangerous countenance,
And violation of all faith and troth
Sworn to us in your (*) younger enterprise.

K. HEN. These things, indeed, you have articulated,
Proclaim'd at market-crosses, read in churches,
To face the garment of rebellion
With some fine colour, that may please the eye
Of fickle changelings, and poor discontents,
Which gape, and rub the elbow, at the news
Of hurly-burly innovation:
And never yet did insurrection want
Such water-colours, to impaint his cause;
Nor moody beggars, starving for a time
Of pell-mell havoc and confusion.

P. HEN. In both our armies, there is many a soul
Shall pay full dearly for this encounter,
If once they join in trial. Tell your nephew,
The prince of Wales doth join with all the world
In praise of Henry Percy. By my hopes,—
This present enterprise set off his head,—
I do not think a braver gentleman,
More active-valiant, or more valiant-young,
More daring, or more bold, is now alive,
To grace this latter age with noble deeds.
For my part, I may speak it to my shame,
I have a truant been to chivalry;
And so, I hear, he doth account me too:
Yet this,—before my father's majesty,—
I am content, that he shall take the odds
Of his great name and estimation,
And will, to save the blood on either side,
Try fortune with him in a single fight.

K. HEN. And, prince of Wales, so dare we venture thee,
Albeit, considerations infinite
Do make against it.—No, good Worcester, no,
We love our people well; even those we love,
That are misled upon your cousin's part;
And, will they take the offer of our grace,
Both he, and they, and you, yea, every man
Shall be my friend again, and I'll be his:
So tell your cousin, and bring me word
What he will do:—but if he will not yield,
Rebuke and dread correction wait on us,
And they shall do their office. So, be gone;
We will not now be troubled with reply;
We offer fair, take it advisedly.

[*Exeunt* WORCESTER *and* VERNON.

(*) First folio, *danger*. (†) First folio inserts, *of*.
(‡) First folio, *sware*. (§) First folio omits, *a*.
(||) First folio, *the*.

(*) First folio omits, *your*.

a *Peace*, chewet,—] *Chewit*, from the French *choüette*, meant "a noisy, chattering bird," a *chough* or *jackdaw*.

b *As that ungentle* gull, the cuckoo's bird,
Useth the sparrow;] By *gull* was meant a young unfeathered bird. The cuckoo often lays its eggs in the sparrow's nest, and when the chicken or *cuckoo's bird*, hatched and reared by the sparrow, grows of bulk and strength enough, it frequently expels its nurse.

P. HEN. It will not be accepted, on my life:
The Douglas and the Hotspur both together
Are confident against the world in arms.

K. HEN. Hence, therefore, every leader to his charge;
For, on their answer, will we set on them:
And God befriend us, as our cause is just!

[*Exeunt* KING, BLUNT, *and* PRINCE JOHN.

FAL. Hal, if thou see me down in the battle, and bestride me, so; 't is a point of friendship.

P. HEN. Nothing but a colossus can do thee that friendship. Say thy prayers, and farewell.

FAL. I would it were bed-time, Hal, and all well.

P. HEN. Why, thou owest God* a death. [*Exit.*

FAL. 'T is not due yet; I would be loth to pay him before his day. What need I be so forward with him that calls not on me? Well, 't is no matter; Honour pricks me on. Yea,† but how if Honour prick me off when I come on? how then? Can Honour set to a leg? No. Or an arm? No. Or take away the grief of a wound? No. Honour hath no skill in surgery then? No. What is Honour? A word. What is that word, Honour? Air.[a] A trim reckoning!—Who hath it? He that died o' Wednesday. Doth he feel it? No. Doth he hear it? No. Is it insensible then? Yea, to the dead. But will it not live with the living? No. Why? Detraction will not suffer it:—therefore I'll none of it: Honour is a mere 'scutcheon, and so ends my catechism.

[*Exit.*

SCENE II.—*The Rebel Camp.*

Enter WORCESTER *and* VERNON.

WOR. O, no, my nephew must not know, sir Richard,(1)
The liberal and ‡ kind offer of the king.

VER. 'T were best, he did.

WOR. Then are we § all undone.
It is not possible, it cannot be,
The king should || keep his word in loving us;
He will suspect us still, and find a time
To punish this offence in other ¶ faults:
Suspicion,** all our lives, shall be stuck full of eyes:
For treason is but trusted like the fox;
Who, ne'er so tame, so cherish'd, and lock'd up,
Will have a wild trick of his ancestors.
Look how we* can, or sad, or merrily,
Interpretation will misquote our looks,
And we shall feed like oxen at a stall,
The better cherish'd, still the nearer death.
My nephew's trespass may be well forgot,
It hath the excuse of youth, and heat of blood,
And an adopted name of privilege,—
A hair-brain'd Hotspur, govern'd by a spleen:
All his offences live upon my head,
And on his father's;—we did train him on;
And, his corruption being ta'en from us,
We, as the spring of all, shall pay for all.
Therefore, good cousin, let not Harry know,
In any case, the offer of the king.

VER. Deliver what you will, I'll say, 'tis so.
Here comes your cousin.

Enter HOTSPUR *and* DOUGLAS; Officers *and* Soldiers, *behind.*

HOT. My uncle is return'd:—deliver up
My lord of Westmoreland.—Uncle, what news?

WOR. The king will bid you battle presently.

DOUG. Defy him by the lord of Westmoreland.[b]

HOT. Lord Douglas, go you and tell him so.

DOUG. Marry, and shall, and very willingly.

[*Exit.*

WOR. There is no seeming mercy in the king.

HOT. Did you beg any? God forbid!

WOR. I told him gently of our grievances,
Of his oath-breaking, which he mended thus,—
By now forswearing that he is forsworn:
He calls us, rebels, traitors; and will scourge
With haughty arms this hateful name in us.

Re-enter DOUGLAS.

DOUG. Arm, gentlemen! to arms! for I have thrown
A brave defiance in King Henry's teeth,
And Westmoreland, that was engag'd, did bear it;
Which cannot choose but bring him quickly on.

WOR. The prince of Wales stepp'd forth before the king,
And, nephew, challeng'd you to single fight.

HOT. O, would the quarrel lay upon our heads;
And that no man might draw short breath to-day,
But I, and Harry Monmouth! Tell me, tell me,
How show'd his tasking?[c] seem'd it in contempt?

(*) First folio, *Heaven.* (†) First folio omits, *yea.*
(‡) First folio omits, *and.* (§) First folio, *we are.*
(||) First folio, *would.* (¶) First folio, *others.*
(**) Old copies, *supposition.*

[a] *What is that word, Honour? Air.*] This is the reading of the fifth quarto and the folio 1623, and it is decidedly preferable to the redundant lection of the other copies.

[b] Defy him by the lord of Westmoreland.] This line is given in all the old copies to Douglas. Capell, perhaps rightly, assigned it to Hotspur, observing that his station and his temper would have rendered him the first to take fire at his uncle's intelligence.

[c] *How show'd his tasking?*] Tasking here means *challenging.* So in "Richard II." Act IV. Sc. 1.:—

"I *task* the earth to the like."

All the old editions after the first quarto read, *talking.*

(*) First folio, *he.*

VER. No, by my soul; I never in my life
Did hear a challenge urg'd more modestly,
Unless a brother should a brother dare
To gentle exercise and proof of arms.
He gave you all the duties of a man,
Trimm'd up your praises with a princely tongue,
Spoke your deservings like a chronicle;
Making you ever better than his praise,
By still dispraising praise, valued with you:
And, which became him like a prince indeed,
He made a blushing cital of himself,
And chid his truant youth with such a grace,
As if he master'd there a double spirit,
Of teaching and of learning, instantly.
There did he pause. But let me tell the world,—
If he outlive the envy of this day,
England did never owe so sweet a hope,
So much misconstrued in his wantonness.

HOT. Cousin, I think, thou art enamoured
On his follies; never did I hear
Of any prince, so wild a libertine:[a]
But, be he as he will, yet once ere night
I will embrace him with a soldier's arm,
That he shall shrink under my courtesy.——
Arm, arm, with speed!——And, fellows, soldiers, friends,
Better consider what you have to do,
Than I, that have not well the gift of tongue,
Can lift your blood up with persuasion.

Enter a Messenger.

MESS. My lord, here are letters for you.

HOT. I cannot read them now.—
O gentlemen, the time of life is short;
To spend that shortness basely, were too long,
If life did ride upon a dial's point,

[a] *So wild* a libertine:] The first three quartos read, so wild *a libertie;* the folio 1623, so wild *at liberty.* The emendation in the text was made by Capell.

Still ending at the arrival of an hour.
An if we live, we live to tread on kings;
If die, brave death, when princes die with us!
Now for our consciences,—the arms are* fair,
When the intent of† bearing them is just.

Enter another Messenger.

MESS. My lord, prepare; the king comes on apace.
HOT. I thank him, that he cuts me from my tale,
For I profess not talking. Only this—
Let each man do his best; and here draw I‡
A sword, whose § temper I intend to stain
With the best blood that I can meet withal
In the adventure of this perilous day.
Now,—Esperance!—Percy!—and set on.—
Sound all the lofty instruments of war,
And by that music let us all embrace:
For, heaven to earth,[a] some of us never shall
A second time do such a courtesy.
[*Flourish of trumpets. They embrace, and exeunt.*

SCENE III.—*Plain near* Shrewsbury.

Alarum to the battle. Excursions, and Parties fighting. Then enter DOUGLAS *and* BLUNT, *meeting.*

BLUNT. What is thy name, that in the || battle thus
Thou crossest me? what honour dost thou seek
Upon my head?
DOUG. Know then, my name is Douglas;
And I do haunt thee in the battle thus,
Because some tell me that thou art a king.
BLUNT. They tell thee true.
DOUG. The lord of Stafford dear to-day hath bought
Thy likeness; for, instead of thee, king Harry,
This sword hath ended him: so shall it thee,
Unless thou yield thee as my¶ prisoner.
BLUNT. I was not born a yielder, thou proud Scot;[b]

(*) First folio, *is*.
(†) First folio, *for*.
(‡) First folio, *I draw*.
(§) First folio inserts, *worthy*.
(||) Old text omits, *the*.
(¶) First folio, *a*.

[a] For, heaven to earth,—] *It is the odds of heaven to earth.* Why doubt should have been thrown upon a passage so clear and satisfactory, not only by Mr. Collier's annotator, but even by his trenchant opponent, Mr. Singer, is quite inexplicable; the former proposes the poor substitution of,

"*Fore* heaven *and*," &c.

and the latter suggests that we should read,

"For *here on earth*," &c.

Let the reader compare with the old text, the following, from "Romeo and Juliet," Act III. Sc. 5:—

And thou shalt find a king that will revenge
Lord* Stafford's death.
[*They fight, and* BLUNT *is slain.*

Enter HOTSPUR.

HOT. O Douglas, hadst thou fought at Holmedon thus,
I never had triumphéd o'er a Scot.
DOUG. All's done, all's won; here breathless lies the king.
HOT. Where?
DOUG. Here.
HOT. This, Douglas? no, I know this face full well:
A gallant knight he was, his name was Blunt,
Semblably furnish'd like the king himself.
DOUG. A† fool go with thy soul, whither it goes:
A borrow'd title hast thou bought too dear.
Why didst thou tell me that thou wert a king?
HOT. The king hath many marching[c] in his coats.
DOUG. Now, by my sword, I will kill all his coats;
I'll murder all his wardrobe, piece by piece,
Until I meet the king.
HOT. Up and away;
Our soldiers stand full fairly for the day.
[*Exeunt.*

Other Alarums. Enter FALSTAFF.

FAL. Though I could 'scape shot-free at London, I fear the shot here; here's no scoring, but upon the pate.—Soft! who art thou? Sir Walter Blunt!—there's Honour for you! Here's no vanity!—I am as hot as molten lead, and as heavy too: God‡ keep lead out of me! I need no more weight than mine own bowels.—I have led my ragamuffins § where they are peppered: there's but || three of my hundred and fifty left alive, and they are¶ for the town's end, to beg during life. But who comes here?

Enter PRINCE HENRY.

P. HEN. What, stand'st thou idle here? lend me thy sword:

(*) First folio, *Lords*.
(†) Old copies, *Ah*.
(‡) First folio, *Heaven*.
(§) Old text, *rag of muffins*.
(||) Old text, *not*.
(¶) First folio omits, *are*.

"——— And *all the world to nothing*
That he dares ne'er come back."—

And,

"Should I miscarry in the present journey,
From whence it is *all number to a cipher*
I ne'er return with honour."
MASSINGER'S *Duke of Milan*, Act I. Sc. 3.

[b] *I was not born* a yielder, *thou* proud *Scot;*] So the first quarto; the folio reads, I was not born *to yield*, thou *haughty* Scot.
[c] *The king hath many* marching *in his coats.*] For *marching* Mr. Collier's annotator reads, *masking*.

Many a nobleman lies stark and stiff
Under the hoofs of vaunting enemies,
Whose deaths are unreveng'd. Pr'ythee, lend me thy sword.

FAL. O Hal, I pr'ythee, give me leave to breathe a while.—Turk Gregory[a] never did such deeds in arms, as I have done this day. I have paid Percy, I have made him sure.

P. HEN. He is, indeed; and living to kill thee. I pr'ythee, lend me thy sword.

FAL. Nay, before God,* Hal, if Percy be alive, thou get'st not my sword; but take my pistol, if thou wilt.

P. HEN. Give it me: what, is it in the case?

FAL. Ay, Hal; 'tis hot, 'tis hot;† there's that will sack a city.

[*The* PRINCE *draws out a bottle of sack.*

P. HEN. What, is it a time to jest and dally now? [*Throws it at him and exit.*

FAL. Well,‡ if Percy be alive, I'll pierce him. If he do come in my way, so; if he do not, if I come in his willingly, let him make a carbonado[b] of me. I like not such grinning honour as sir Walter hath. Give me life; which if I can save, so; if not, honour comes unlooked for, and there's an end. [*Exit.*

SCENE IV.—*Another Part of the Field.*

Alarums. Excursions. Enter the KING, PRINCE HENRY, PRINCE JOHN, *and* WESTMORELAND.

K. HEN. I pr'ythee,
Harry, withdraw thyself; thou bleed'st too much:—
Lord John of Lancaster, go you with him.

P. JOHN. Not I, my lord, unless I did bleed too.

P. HEN. I beseech your majesty, make up,
Lest your§ retirement do amaze your friends.

K. HEN. I will do so:—
My lord of Westmoreland, lead him to his tent.

WEST. Come, my lord, I'll lead you to your tent.

P. HEN. Lead me, my lord? I do not need your help:
And God‖ forbid, a shallow scratch should drive
The prince of Wales from such a field as this,
Where stain'd nobility lies trodden on,
And rebels' arms triumph in massacres!

P. JOHN. We breathe too long:—come, cousin Westmoreland,
Our duty this way lies; for God's* sake, come.

[*Exeunt* PRINCE JOHN *and* WESTMORELAND.

P. HEN. By heaven, thou hast deceiv'd me, Lancaster;
I did not think thee lord of such a spirit:
Before, I lov'd thee as a brother, John;
But now, I do respect thee as my soul.

K. HEN. I saw him hold lord Percy at the point,
With lustier maintenance than I did look for
Of such an ungrown warrior.

P. HEN. O, this boy
Lends mettle to us all! [*Exit.*

Alarums. Enter DOUGLAS.

DOUG. Another king! they grow like Hydra's heads:
I am the Douglas, fatal to all those
That wear those colours on them.—What art thou,
That counterfeit'st the person of a king?

K. HEN. The king himself; who, Douglas, grieves at heart,
So many of his shadows thou hast met,
And not the very king. I have two boys
Seek Percy, and thyself, about the field:
But seeing thou fall'st on me so luckily,
I will assay thee; so defend thyself.

DOUG. I fear, thou art another counterfeit;
And yet, in faith, thou bear'st thee like a king:
But mine, I am sure, thou art, whoe'er thou be,
And thus I win thee.

[*They fight; the* KING *being in danger, enter* PRINCE HENRY.

P. HEN. Hold up thy head, vile Scot, or thou art like
Never to hold it up again! the spirits
Of valiant Shirley, Stafford, Blunt, are in my arms:
It is the Prince of Wales, that threatens thee;
Who never promiseth, but he means to pay.—

[*They fight;* DOUGLAS *flies.*

Cheerly, my lord; how fares your grace?—
Sir Nicholas Gawsey hath for succour sent,
And so hath Clifton; I'll to Clifton straight.

K. HEN. Stay, and breathe a while:—(2)
Thou hast redeem'd thy lost opinion;[c]

(*) First folio omits, *before God.*
(†) First folio omits the repetition. (‡) First folio omits, *Well.*
(§) First folio, *you.* (‖) First folio, *Heaven.*

(*) First folio, *Heavens.*

[a] Turk Gregory—] Gregory the Seventh, called Hildebrand. "Fox, in his History hath made Gregory so odious, that I don't doubt but the good Protestants of that time were well pleased to hear him thus characterised, as uniting the attributes of their two great enemies, the Turk and Pope, in one."—WARBURTON.

[b] Carbonado—] A collop cooked on the coals.

[c] *Thou hast redeem'd thy lost* opinion;] That is, *reputation, estimation.* So in "The Gamester," by Shirley, "Patience! I mean you have the *opinion* of a valiant gentleman; one that dares fight and maintain your honour against odds."

And show'd, thou mak'st some tender of my life,
In this fair rescue thou hast brought to me.

P. Hen. O God,* they did me too much injury,
That ever said, I hearken'd for † your death.
If it were so, I might have let alone
The insulting hand of Douglas over you;
Which would have been as speedy in your end,
As all the poisonous potions in the world,
And sav'd the treacherous labour of your son.

K. Hen. Make up to Clifton, I'll to Sir Nicholas Gawsey. [*Exit* King Henry.

Enter Hotspur.

Hot. If I mistake not, thou art Harry Monmouth.

P. Hen. Thou speak'st as if I would deny my name.

Hot. My name is Harry Percy.

P. Hen. Why, then I see
A very valiant rebel of that name.
I am the Prince of Wales; and think not, Percy,
To share with me in glory any more:
Two stars keep not their motion in one sphere;
Nor can one England brook a double reign,
Of Harry Percy, and the Prince of Wales.

Hot. Nor shall it, Harry, for the hour is come
To end the one of us; and would to God,*
Thy name in arms were now as great as mine!

P. Hen. I'll make it greater, ere I part from thee;
And all the budding honours on thy crest
I'll crop, to make a garland for my head.

Hot. I can no longer brook thy vanities.
[*They fight.*

Enter Falstaff.

Fal. Well said, Hal! to it, Hal!—Nay, you shall find no boy's play here, I can tell you.

Enter Douglas; *he fights with* Falstaff, *who falls down as if he were dead, and exit* Douglas. Hotspur *is wounded, and falls.*

Hot. O, Harry, thou hast robb'd me of my youth!
I better brook the loss of brittle life,
Than those proud titles thou hast won of me;
They wound my thoughts, worse than thy † sword my flesh:——
But thought's the slave of life, and life, Time's fool,
And Time, that takes survey of all the world,
Must have a stop.[a] O, I could prophesy,[b]

(*) First folio, *Heaven*. (†) First folio, *to*.

(*) First folio, *Heaven*. (†) First folio, *the*.

a *But thought's the slave of life, and* life, Time's fool,
And Time, that takes survey of all the world,
Must have a stop.]

The fine gradation in this noble passage is quite ruined in all modern editions by the mistaken punctuation of the first line,—

"But thought's the slave of life, and *life time's fool.*"

b O, I could prophesy,—] The belief that the dying are endowed with a faculty of prevision, is of high antiquity. Allusions to it are met with in the Scriptures, and in many of the early Greek writers. Shakespeare has before illustrated the superstition in "Richard II." Act II. Sc. 1, when John of Gaunt, upon his death-bed, predicts the downfal of the reckless King:—

"Methinks, I am a prophet new inspir'd,
And thus, expiring, do foretell of him."

But that the earthy and cold hand of death[a]
Lies on my tongue:—No, Percy, thou art dust,
And food for—— [*Dies.*

P. HEN. For worms, brave Percy. Fare thee* well, great heart!—
Ill-weav'd ambition, how much art thou shrunk!
When that this body did contain a spirit,
A kingdom for it was too small a bound;
But now, two paces of the vilest earth
Is room enough. This earth, that bears thee dead,
Bears not alive so stout a gentleman.
If thou wert sensible of courtesy,
I should not make so dear† a show of zeal:
But let my favours hide thy mangled face,
And, even in thy behalf, I'll thank myself
For doing these fair rites of tenderness.
Adieu, and take thy praise with thee to heaven!
Thy ignomy[b] sleep with thee in the grave,
But not remember'd in thy epitaph!
[*He sees* FALSTAFF *on the ground.*
What! old acquaintance! could not all this flesh
Keep in a little life? Poor Jack, farewell!
I could have better spar'd a better man.
O, I should have a heavy miss of thee,
If I were much in love with vanity.
Death hath not struck so fat a deer to-day,
Though many dearer, in this bloody fray:
Embowell'd will I see thee by and by;
Till then, in blood by noble Percy lie. [*Exit.*

FAL. [*Rising slowly.*] Embowelled! if thou embowel me to-day, I'll give you leave to powder[c] me, and eat me too, to-morrow. 'Sblood,‡ 'twas time to counterfeit, or that hot termagant Scot had paid me scot and lot too. Counterfeit? I lie,§ I am no counterfeit: to die, is to be a counterfeit; for he is but the counterfeit of a man, who hath not the life of a man: but to counterfeit dying, when a man thereby liveth, is to be no counterfeit, but the true and perfect image of life indeed. The better part of valour is, discretion; in the which better part, I have saved my life. 'Zounds,|| I am afraid of this gunpowder Percy, though he be dead. How if he should counterfeit too, and rise? By my faith,¶ I am afraid, he would prove the better counterfeit. Therefore I'll make him sure: yea, and I'll swear I killed him. Why may not he rise, as well as I? Nothing confutes me but eyes, and nobody sees me: therefore, sirrah, [*Stabbing him.*] with a new wound in your thigh, come you along with** me. [*Takes* HOTSPUR *on his back.*

Re-enter PRINCE HENRY *and* PRINCE JOHN.

P. HEN. Come, brother John; full bravely hast thou flesh'd
Thy maiden sword.

P. JOHN. But, soft! whom * have we here?
Did you not tell me this fat man was dead?

P. HEN. I did; I saw him dead,
Breathless and bleeding on the ground.——
Art thou alive? or is it fantasy
That plays upon our eyesight? I pr'ythee, speak;
We will not trust our eyes, without our ears:—
Thou art not what thou seem'st.

FAL. No, that's certain; I am not a double man: but if I be not Jack Falstaff, then am I a Jack. There is Percy: [*Throwing the body down.*] if your father will do me any honour, so; if not, let him kill the next Percy himself. I look to be either earl or duke, I can assure you.

P. HEN. Why, Percy I killed myself, and saw thee dead.

FAL. Didst thou?—Lord, Lord, how this † world is given to lying!—I grant you, I was down, and out of breath; and so was he: but we rose both at an instant, and fought a long hour by Shrewsbury clock. If I may be believed, so; if not, let them, that should reward valour, bear the sin upon their own heads. I'll take it upon‡ my death, I gave him this wound in the thigh: if the man were alive, and would deny it, 'zounds!§ I would make him eat a piece of my sword.

P. JOHN. This is the strangest tale that e'er I heard.

P. HEN. This is the strangest fellow, brother John.——
Come, bring your luggage nobly on your back:
For my part, if a lie may do thee grace,
I'll gild it with the happiest terms I have.
[*A retreat is sounded.*
The trumpet sounds || retreat, the day is ours.
Come, brother, let's to the highest of the field,
To see what friends are living, who are dead.
[*Exeunt* PRINCE HENRY *and* PRINCE JOHN.

FAL. I'll follow, as they say, for reward. He that rewards me, God¶ reward him!! If I do grow great,** I'll grow less; for I'll purge, and leave sack, and live cleanly, as a nobleman should do.
[*Exit, bearing off the body.*

(*) First folio omits, *thee.* (†) First folio, *great.*
(‡) First folio omits, *'Sblood.* (§) First folio omits, *I lie.*
(||) First folio omits, *'Zounds.* (¶) First folio omits, *By my faith.*
(**) First folio omits, *with.*

(*) First folio, *who.* (†) First folio, *the.*
(‡) First folio, *on.* (§) First folio omits, *'zounds.*
(||) First folio, *trumpets sound.* (¶) First folio, *Heaven.*
(**) First folio adds, *again.*

[a] *But that the* earthy *and cold hand of death*—] The folio reads, the *earth* and *the* cold hand, &c.

[b] *Thy* ignomy—] This abridgement of *ignominy* is not unfrequent with our early writers.

[c] To powder me,—] To *powder*, was to *salt*, and we still retain the word in *powdered* beef.

SCENE V.—*Another part of the Field.*

The trumpets sound. Enter KING HENRY, PRINCE HENRY, PRINCE JOHN, WESTMORELAND, *and others, with* WORCESTER *and* VERNON, *prisoners.*

K. HEN. Thus ever did rebellion find rebuke.—
Ill-spirited Worcester! did not we * send grace,
Pardon, and terms of love to all of you?
And would'st thou turn our offers contrary?
Misuse the tenor of thy kinsman's trust?
Three knights upon our party slain to-day,
A noble earl, and many a creature else,
Had been alive this hour,
If, like a Christian, thou hadst truly borne,
Betwixt our armies, true intelligence.

WOR. What I have done, my safety urg'd me to;
And I embrace this fortune patiently,
Since not to be avoided it falls on me.

K. HEN. Bear Worcester to the† death, and Vernon too:
Other offenders we will pause upon.—
[*Exeunt* WORCESTER *and* VERNON *guarded:*
How goes the field?

P. HEN. The noble Scot, lord Douglas, when he saw
The fortune of the day quite turn'd from him,
The noble Percy slain, and all his men
Upon the foot of fear,—fled with the rest;
And falling from a hill, he was so bruis'd,
That the pursuers took him. At my tent
The Douglas is; and I beseech your grace,
I may dispose of him.

K. HEN. With all my heart.

P. HEN. Then, brother John of Lancaster, to you
This honourable bounty shall belong:
Go to the Douglas, and deliver him
Up to his pleasure, ransomless, and free:
His valour, shown upon our crests to-day,
Hath taught us how to cherish such high deeds,
Even in the bosom of our adversaries.[a]

K. HEN. Then this remains,—that we divide our power.—
You, son John, and my cousin Westmoreland,
Towards York shall bend you, with your dearest speed,
To meet Northumberland, and the prelate Scroop,
Who, as we hear, are busily in arms:
Myself,—and you, son Harry,—will towards Wales,
To fight with Glendower, and the earl of March.
Rebellion in this land shall lose his sway,*
Meeting the check of such another day:
And since this business so fair is done,
Let us not leave till all our own be won.
[*Exeunt.*

(*) First folio, *we not.* (†) First folio omits, *the.*

[a] Even in the bosom of our adversaries.] After this speech, in the first four quartos, Prince John replies to his brother thus:—

"I thank your grace for this high courtesy,
Which I shall give away immediately."

(*) First folio, *way.*

ILLUSTRATIVE COMMENTS.

ACT I.

(1) Scene II.—*An apartment in a Tavern.*] According to the modern editions, the action of this scene takes place in a room of the king's palace. Now, not to dwell upon the improbability of the prince of Wales surrounding himself with licentious companions, and planning a vulgar robbery in such a place, we are compelled to infer that he was not in the practice of making the court his home. In the last Act of "Richard II." King Henry asks:—

"Can no man tell of my unthrifty son?
'Tis full three months since I did see him last."

And in a subsequent scene in the present play, when Falstaff personates the monarch, one of his inquiries, founded upon his knowledge of the prince's habits, is—

———"*Where hast thou been this month?*"

(2) Scene II.—*Or the drone of a Lincolnshire bagpipe.*] Steevens acutely conceived that the "drone of a Lincolnshire bagpipe," meant the *dull croak of a frog,* one of the native minstrels of that fenny county; but it is more credible that Lincolnshire was celebrated for the making or playing on this instrument. In "A Nest of Ninnies," by Robert Armin, 1608, a *Lincolnshire bagpipe* is mentioned in a way to show it was familiarly known:—"At a Christmas time, when great logs furnish the hall-fire—when brawne is in season, and, indeede, all reveling is regarded, this gallant knight kept open house for all commers, where beefe, beere, and bread was no niggard. Amongst all the pleasures prouided, a noyse of minstrells and a *Lincolnshire bagpipe* was prepared—the minstrels for the great chamber, the bagpipe for the hall—the minstrells to serue vp the knight's meat, and the bagpipe for the common dauncing."

(3) Scene II.—*The melancholy of Moor-ditch.*] Moor-ditch was a part of the great ditch or moat, which, with the well-known wall, surrounded and formed the defence of London. This ditch was begun in 1211, and finished in 1213. That portion of it known as Moor-ditch, extending from the Postern called Moorgate, to Bishopsgate, was cleansed and widened in 1595; but Stowe relates that it soon filled again, and, flanked as it was on the one side with miserable dwellings, and on the other by an unwholesome and sometimes impassable morass, it is easy to understand how the sombre, melancholy aspect of this filthy stream should have become proverbial. Taylor in his "Pennylesse Pilgrimage," 1618, says—"Walking thus downe the street, (my body being tyred with trauell, and my mind attyred with moody, muddy, *Moore-ditch melancholly,*") &c.

(4) Scene II.—*Wisdom cries out in the streets.*] In the first folio, this scriptural expression is omitted, in compliance, it has been thought, with the Act 3 Jac. I.; but that Act, which we append, was restricted to preventing the profane use of the sacred names. The numberless omissions of phrases like the above, as well as "by my faith," "by my troth," "by the mass," &c. &c. in the folio, must therefore be attributed not to the Act of Parliament in question, but to the increasing influence of the Puritans.

3 Jac. I. c. 21. An Acte to restrain the Abuses of Players, (1605-6.)

For the preventing and avoyding of the greate Abuse of the Holy Name of God in Stageplayes, Interludes Maygames Shewes and such like;—Be it enacted by our Soveraigne Lorde the Kings Majesty, and by the Lordes Spirituall and Temporall, and Commons in this present Parliament assembled, and by the authoritie of the same, That if at any tyme or tymes, after the end of this present Session of Parliament any person or persons doe or shall in any Stage play Interlude Shewe Maygame or Pageant jestingly or prophanely speake or use the holy Name of God or of Christ Jesus, or of the Holy Ghoste or of the Trinitie, which are not to be spoken but with feare and reverence, shall forfeite for everie such Offence by hym or them comitted Tenne Pounde, the one Moytie thereof to the Kings Majestie his Heires and Successors, the other Moytie thereof to hym or them that will sue for the same in any Courte of Recorde at Westminster, wherein no Essoigne Proteccion or Wager of Lawe shalbe allowed.

(5) Scene II.—*Gadshill.*] This place, which is on the Kentish road near Rochester, appears at one time to have enjoyed the same kind of unenviable notoriety which rendered Shooters Hill and Hounslow Heath the terror of travellers in later days. So early as 1558, a ballad was entered on the books of the Stationers' Company, entitled *The Robbery at Gadshill,* and there is still extant among the Lansdowne Manuscripts in the British Museum a circumstantial narrative in the handwriting of Sir Roger Manwood, Chief Baron of the Exchequer, dated July 3d, 1590, of the exploits of a daring gang of robbers, who at that period infested Gadshill and its vicinity. We extract a portion of this curious account; the whole of which may be seen in Boswell's edition of Malone's Shakespeare, vol. xvi. p. 432.

"In October, at begynninge of last Mychaelmas Terme, iij or iiij robberyes done at Gadeshill by certen foote theves, vppon hughe and crye, one of the Theves named Hachfeild flying and squatted in a bushe, was broughte to me, and vppon examynacion findinge a purse and things about him suspiciouse, and his cause of being there and his flyinge and other circumstances very suspiciouse, I commytted him to the Jayle, and he ys of that robberye indyted.

"In the course of that Michaelmas Terme, I being at London, many robberyes weare done in the hye wayes at Gadeshill on the west parte of Rochester, and at Chatham downe on the east parte of Rochester, by horse theves, with suche fatt and lustye horses, as weare not lyke hackney horsses, nor farr jorneying horsses, and one of them sometyme wearing a vizarde greye bearde (by reason that to the persons robbed, the Theves did use to mynister an othe that there should bee no hue and crye made after, and also did gyve a watche woorde for the parties robbed, the better to escape other of their theves companye devyded vppon the hyghe-waye,) he was by common report in the country called Justice Greye Bearde; and no man durst travell that waye without great companye.

"After the end of that Mychaelmas Terme, iij or iiij gentn. from London rydinge home towardes Canterburye, at the west end of Gadeshill, weare overtaken by v or vj horsemen all in clokes vpp about their faces, and fellowe lyke all, and none lyke servants or waytinge on the other, and swiftly ridinge by them gatt to the east end of Gadeshill, and there turned about all their horsses on the faces of the trewe men, wherby they became in feare; but by chanse one of the trewe men did knowe this Curtall to bee one of the v or vj swift ryders, and after some speache betwene them of the manyfold robberyes there done and that by company of this Curtall, that gentleman hoped to have the more saffetye from robbing. This Curtall with the other v or vj swifte ryders, rode awaye to Rochester before, and the trewe men coming afterwards neere Rochester they did mete this Curtall retorning on horsebacke, rydinge towards Gadeshill againe; and after they had passed Rochester, in Chatham streete, at a Smyths fordge they did see the reste of the swyft ryders tarying about shoing of their horsses, and then the trewe men doubted to be set vppon at Chatham downe, but their company being the greater, they passed without troble to Sittingborne that nyghte where they harde of robberyes daylye done at Chatham downe and Gadeshill, and that this Curtall with v or vj other as lustye companyons, and well horssed, much havnted the innes and typlinge howses at Raynham, Sittingborne, and Rochester, with liberall expences."

In another memorandum belonging to the same collection, which relates to similar depredations in other parts of the country, we find the word *match*, used precisely as in "Ratsey's Ghost," (see note [b], p. 513) to signify the plot, or scheme of a robbery, showing that the "*set a match*" of the quartos is the true reading, and the "set a *watch*" of the folio, a misprint:—

"There maner of robbinge is to robbe in suche companies as afore saide if *the matche* soe require, and sometimes doe devide themselves and robbe three or fower together onelie, in a companie."

* * * * *

This, indeed, is put beyond all question by Minsheu's explanation of "*Outeparters.*" "Some are of opinion, that those which are tearmed *outparters*, are at this day called *out-putters*, and are such as *set matches* for the robbing any man or house; as by discovering which way he rideth or goeth, or where the house is weakest and fittest to be entred."

(6) Scene II.—*Redeeming time, when men think least I will.*] We had purposed in this scene, to say a few words on the contrast presented by the traditional character of the prince, familiarized as it is to us by the delightful fancies of the poet, and that ascribed to him by Mr. Luders and Mr. Tyler, the historians, who have laboured so zealously to exculpate him from the imputation of youthful riot and dishonour; but, upon reflection, prefer reserving our observations until Henry appears as King of England.

(7) Scene III.—*His brother-in-law, the foolish Mortimer.* Every historian, from Walsingham to Sharon Turner, has fallen into the error of confounding Sir Edmund Mortimer with his nephew, Edmund Earl of March, who at this period was a boy not more than ten years of age, and in custody of the king at Windsor.

Sir Edmund Mortimer was taken prisoner by Owen Glendower, at the battle fought June 12, 1402, near Melienydd in Radnorshire; became devotedly attached to the Welsh chieftain, and married his daughter. By this connexion, Owen shortly after obtained another accession to his power and influence in the person of Hotspur, who, incensed, it was thought, at the king's refusal to ransom his brother-in-law (for Hotspur had married Mortimer's sister), suddenly revolted from his side, and allied himself to the cause of his old opponent, Glendower.

ACT II.

(1) Scene I. —— *breeds fleas like a loach.*] The efforts of critics who gravely labour to establish the pertinence and integrity of such comparisons as these, are as profitable, to adopt a characteristic simile of Gifford's, as the milking he-goats in a sieve. When the obtuse carrier tells us that his horse provender is as *dank as a dog*—that chamber-lie *breeds fleas like a loach*, and that he himself is *stung like a tench* and as *well bitten as a king*, he means no more, than that the peas and beans are very damp, that chamberlie breeds many fleas, and that he is severely stung. So, when the immortal Mrs. Quickly declares Sir John and his Dulcinea to be "as rheumatic as two dried toasts," she intends only to convey, what she wants language to describe in words, or imagination to portray properly by figure, that they are inordinately quarrelsome. An appropriate and congruous resemblance would be as inappropriate and incongruous in such mouths, as forcible and well chosen phraseology. The Water Poet, John Taylor, has very happily derided such inapposite similitudes:—"But many pretty ridiculous aspersions are cast upon Dogges, so that it would make a Dogge laugh to heare and understand them. As I have heard a Man say, I am as hot as a Dogge, or as cold as a Dogge, I sweate like a Dogge, (when a Dogge never sweates) as drunke as a Dogge, hee swore like a Dogge, and one told a man once That his Wife was not to be believ'd for she would lye like a Dogge," &c. —*A Dogge of Warre*, 1630.

(2) Scene I.—*Thou lay'st the plot, how.*] The collusion between the Chamberlains and Ostlers, and the "Gentlemen of the Road," in old times, is often referred to in works of the period. In Harrison's "Description of England," (Holinshed, Vol. I. p. 246,) there is an interesting account of old English Inns, wherein the villainy of tapsters, drawers, chamberlains, and ostlers, forms a prominent topic:—"Those townes that we call thorowfaires have great and sumptuous innes builded in them, for the receiving of such travellers and strangers as pass to and fro. The manner of harbouring wherein, is not like to that of some other countries, in which the host or good man of the house doth chalenge a lordlie authoritie over his ghests, but cleane otherwise, sith everie man may use his inne as his owne house in England, and have for his monie how great or little varietee of vittels, and what other service himselfe shall thinke expedient to call for. Our innes are also verie well furnished with naperie, bedding and tapisterie, especiallie with naperie; for beside the linnen used at the tables which is commonlie washed dailie, is such and so much as belongeth unto the estate and calling of the ghest. Ech commer is sure to lie in cleane sheets, wherein no man hath been lodged since they came from the landresse, or out of the water wherein they were last washed. If the traveller have an horsse, his bed doth cost him nothing, but if he go on foot he is sure to paie a penie for the same; but whether he be horsseman or footman, if his chamber be once appointed he may carie the kaie with him, as of his own house so long as he lodgeth there. If he loose oughte whilest he abideth in the inne, the host is bound by a generall custome to restore the damage, so that there is no greater securitie anie,

where for travellers than in the gretest ins of England. There horsses in like sort are walked, dressed, and looked unto by certain hostelers or hired servants, appointed at the charges of the goodman of the house, who in hope of extraordinarie reward will deale verie deligentlie after outward appeerance in this their function and calling. Herein neverthelesse are manie of them blameworthie, in that they doo not onelie deceive the beast oftentimes of his allowance by sundrie meanes, except their owners looke well to them, but also make such packs with slipper merchants which hunt after preie (for what place is sure from evill and wicked persons) that manie an honest man is spoiled of his goods as he travelleth to and fro, in which feat also the counsells of the tapsters or drawers of drink, and chamberleins is not seldome behind or wanting. Certes I beleeve not that chapman or traveller in England is robbed by the waie without the knowledge of some of them, for when he commeth into the inne and alighteth from his horsse, the hostler forthwith is verie busie to take downe his budget or capcase in the yard from his sadle bow, which he poiseth slilie in his hand to feele the weight thereof: or if he misse of this pitch, when the ghest hath taken up his chamber, the chamberleine that looketh to the making of the beds, will be sure to remove it from the place where the owner hath set it as if it were to set it more convenientlie some where else, whereby he getteth an inkling whether it be monie or other short wares and thereof giveth warning to such od ghests as hant the house and are of his confederacie, to the utter undoing of manie an honest yeoman as he journieth by the waie. The tapster in like sort for his part doth marke his behaviour, and what plentie of monie he draweth when he paieth the shot, to the like end: so that it shall be an hard matter to escape all their subtile practises. Some thinke it a gay matter to commit their budgets at their comming to the goodman of the house: but thereby they oft bewraie themselves. For albeit their monie be safe for the time that it is in his hands (for you shall not heare that a man is robbed in his inne) yet after their departure the host can make no warrantize of the same, sith his protection extendeth no further than the gate of his owne house: and there cannot be a surer token unto such as prie and watch for those booties, than to see anie ghest deliver his capcase in such manner."

(3) SCENE I.—*Great oneyers.*] For *oneyers* of the ancient text, Pope proposed *oneraires*,—trustees or commissioners; Theobald, *Moneyers;* Capell, *Mynheers;* Malone, *onyers*, that is, public accountants; and Hanmer, *owners*. Of all these conjectures we prefer the last, not merely because it better suits the context than any of the others, but because *one* having, as we believe, of old, the pronunciation of *own*, a sound it still retains in *only*, (or *onelie*, as it was once written,) *oneyers* might easily have been misprinted for *owners*.

(4) SCENE I.—*We have the receipt of fern-seed, we walk invisible.*] This superstition appears to have originated partly in an imperfect knowledge of the natural history of the fern, and partly in obscure traditions, which represented the seed of that plant as possessed of many occult virtues. The first cause of error is attributable to Pliny, who says, that "there are two kinds of fern, which bear neither flower nor seed;" and hence it was supposed that, as it was produced by invisible seed, such persons as could by any means possess themselves of it would partake of its qualities, and also become invisible. Gerard, in his "Great Herbal," published in 1597, explained this phenomenon by stating fern to be "one of those plants which have their seede on the back of the leafe, so small as to escape the sighte. Those who perceived that ferne was propagated by semination, and yet could never see the seede, were much at a losse for a solution of the difficultie; and, as wonder always endeavours to augment itself, they ascribed to ferne-seede many strange properties, some of which the rusticke vergins have not yet forgotten or exploded." To make these marvellous powers available, the seed was to be gathered at noon, or at midnight, on Midsummer Eve—June 23d—fasting, and in silence; but the attempt to secure it is reported to have been very frequently unsuccessful, for the minute seed fell spontaneously without being caught, and often disappeared altogether, when apparently in safe keeping. Ben Jonson makes Ferret refer to the latent virtue of this seed in "The New Inn," Act I. Sc. 6:—

> "I had
> No medicine, sir, to go invisible,
> No *fern-seed* in my pocket."

Beside the bestowing invisibility, there seem to have been other qualities attributed to this seed, even by scientific persons, in the 17th century, of which John Parkinson, in his "Theater of Plants," 1640, speaks as follows:—"The seede which this and the female Ferne doe beare, and to be gathered onely on Midsommer eve at night, with I know not what conjuring words,—is superstitiously held by divers, not onely Mountebankes and Quacksalvers, but by other learned men, (yet it cannot be said but by those that are too superstitiously addicted,) to be of some secret hidden vertue, but I cannot finde it exprest what it should be: for *Bauhinus*, in his *Synonimies* upon *Matthiolus*, saith these tales are neither fabulous nor superstitious." It must be observed that the "*conjuring words*" mentioned in this extract constitute Shakespeare's "*receipt of fern-seed*" as being the formula and directions with which it was to be effectually gathered.

(5) SCENE IV.—*The Boar's Head Tavern.*] Were it practicable to obtain original and pertinent illustrations of the famous Boar's Head Tavern of Shakespeare, there would be little difficulty in composing an interesting article on the subject. But all that is really known, or that is likely to be known relating to the edifice, has been repeatedly told; and its story belongs rather to poetical and speculative history, than to antiquarian or topographical research. Yet the name and the locality were familiar in connexion, so early as the end of the fourteenth century, when William Warden gave "all that his tenement called 'the Boar's Head,' in East Cheap," towards the support of certain priests serving a chapel founded by Sir William Walworth, in the adjoining church of St. Michael, Crooked Lane.

There is no existing evidence to prove, whether any part of those premises were at that time a tavern; though there is a strong probability, even arising out of their peculiar designation, that they might have been one of many places established in the vicinity for the sale of provisions ready dressed. The practice of appropriating such dealers to this particular part of London dates from a very early period, for Fitz-Stephen tells us that "the followers of the several trades, the vendors of various commodities, and the labourers of every kind, are daily to be found in their proper and distinct places, according to their employments." This statement refers to the close of the twelfth century, at which time there stood on the river-bank at Billingsgate a very extensive tavern or provision store, that being then the common landing-place for all passengers who came to London by water. Fitz-Stephen says of it, that no number so great of soldiers or travellers could enter the city, or leave it, at any hour of the day or night, but that all might be supplied with food. The restaurants of ancient London afterwards spread themselves to the north and west of their original locality, until they formed part of the East-Cheap, or market; so called in contradistinction to the Stocks Market and West-Cheap. In this place, the shops of cooks were interspersed with those of the butchers; the contiguous "Poultry" supplied the capons for which Falstaff ran into debt with Mrs. Quickly; and fish and wine were easily procurable from Billingsgate, and the ships lying near.

So early as the reign of Henry V. Lydgate celebrated the fame of East-Cheap, as being pre-eminent for good cheer, a reputation it seems to have maintained throughout the sixteenth century. It is remarked by Stow, in one of those many incidental passages in which he has preserved traces of ancient manners, not to be found elsewhere, that—"When friends did meete, and were disposed to be merrie, they wente not to dine or sup in tavernes, but to the cooke's, where they called for what they liked: which they always found readie dressed, and at a reasonable rate." There is on contemporaneous record a curious anecdote of an affray on this spot, at one of these houses of public entertainment, in which two of the sons of Henry IV. were actually concerned; and it might very well suggest to a sagacious dramatist, the idea of transferring their revelries to Prince Henry, Falstaff, Mrs. Quickly, and the Boar's Head. The disturbance in question took place June 23d, 1410, the Eve of St. John the Baptist, when, says Stow, "Thomas and John, the king's sonnes, being at London in East Cheape, at supper, after midnight, a great debate happened between their men and men of the court, till the Maior and Sheriffes with other citizens ceased the same."

In the sixteenth century these premises had become established as a tavern, and in the tract entitled "Newes from Bartholomew Fair" the house is mentioned as "the Bore's Head neere London-stone." It continued in the same occupation during the next century and a half. In Mr. J. H. Burn's Descriptive Catalogue of the collection of Tradesmen's Tokens at Guildhall, there are notices of two which were issued from the Boar's Head Tavern, in Great East Cheap, and the same work contains also several interesting memorials relating to the house. One of these tokens is anterior to the Great Fire of 1666, which completely destroyed the whole premises. They were re-erected two years afterwards, and a carving of the sign in stone, bearing the date with the initials J. T., was inserted between the windows of the first and second floor. The building was subsequently divided into two houses, at which time it probably ceased to be a tavern, and the sign remained in its original situation between them. In 1831, however, the premises were taken down for the London Bridge improvements, and the carved Boar's Head was removed to the Corporation Museum at Guildhall.

ACT III.

(1) Scene I.—

I can speak English, lord, as well as you:
For I was train'd up in the English court.]

The brave but ill-fated Owen Glendower, who contrived for twelve years to sustain a desultory warfare against the English, often so successfully that his enemies were fain to attribute their defeats to supernatural agency, was descended from Llewellin ap Jorwarth Droyndon, Prince of Wales, and was called Owen-ap-Gryffyth Vaughan. He is said to have inherited a large estate, and to have taken his surname from a lordship of his property, called Glyndourdwy. When a youth, he was sent to London for his education, where he entered himself of the Temple, and subsequently became an esquire of the body to Richard the Second, and was one of the very few who faithfully adhered to the fallen monarch up to the moment when he was captured at Flint Castle.

Mr. Tyler, who, in his History of Henry of Monmouth, has paid a just tribute to the unconquerable courage and untiring perseverance of this remarkable man, thus touchingly alludes to the termination of his chequered career. "Owyn Glyndowr failed, and he was denounced as a rebel and a traitor. But had the issue of the 'sorry fight' of Shrewsbury been otherwise than it was; had Hotspur so devised and digested, and matured his plan of operations, as to have enabled Owyn with his forces to join heart and hand in that hard-fought field; had Bolingbroke and his son fallen on that fatal day;—instead of lingering among his native mountains, as a fugitive and a branded felon, bereft of his lands, his friends, his children, and his wife, waiting only for the blow of death to terminate his earthly sufferings, and, when the blow fell, leaving no memorial behind him to mark either the time or place of his release,—Owyn Glendowr might have been recognised even by England, as he actually had been by France, in the character of an independent sovereign; and his people might have celebrated his name as the avenger of his country's wrongs, the scourge of her oppressors, and the restorer of her independence.

"The anticipations of his own bard, Gryffydd Llydd, might have been amply realized:—

"'Strike then your harps, ye Cambrian bards!
The song of triumph best rewards
An hero's toils. Let Henry weep
His warriors wrapt in everlasting sleep:
Success and victory are thine,
Owain Glyndurdwy divine!
Dominion, honour, pleasure, praise,
Attend upon thy vigorous days.
And, when thy evening's sun is set,
May grateful Cambria ne'er forget
Thy noontide blaze; but on thy tomb
Never-fading laurels bloom.'"

(2) Scene II.—

A hundred thousand rebels die in this.]

The interview between the King and Prince Henry, upon which the present Scene is founded, was brought about by the anxiety of the latter to disabuse his father of a suspicion which he had been led to entertain, that the prince aspired to the throne, and is thus related by Holinshed; after narrating that the prince came to the court accompanied by many noblemen and others his friends, whom he had commanded to attend him no farther than to the fire in Westminster Hall, and that he himself was then admitted to the presence of his father, the chronicle proceeds:—

"The prince, kneeling downe before his father, said: Most redoubted and sovereigne lord and father, I am at this time come to your presence as your liege man, and as your naturall sonne, in all things to be at your commandement. And where I understand you have in suspicion my demeanour against your grace, you know verie well, that if I knew any man within this realme of whom you should stand in feare, my dutie were to punish that person, thereby to remove that griefe from your heart. Then how much more ought I to suffer death, to ease your grace of that greefe which you have of me, being your natural sonne and liege man: and to that end I have this daie made myselfe readie by confession and receiving of the sacrament. And therefore I beseech you, most redoubted lord and deare father, for the honour of God, to ease your heart of all such suspicion as you have of me, and to dispatch me heere before your knees with this same dagger [and withall delivered unto the king his dagger in all humble reverence, adding further, that his life was not so deare to him that he wished to live one daie with his displeasure], and therefore, in thus ridding me out of life, and yourselfe from all suspicion, here, in presence of these lords, and before God at the daie of the generall judgement, I faithfullie protest clearlie to forgive you.

"The king moved herewith, cast from him the dagger, and imbracing the prince, kissed him, and with shedding teares confessed, that in deed he had him partlie in suspicion, though now (as he perceived) not with just cause, and therefore from thenceforth no mis-report should cause him to have him in mistrust, and this he promised of his honour. So by his great wisedome was the wrongfull suspicion which his father had conceived against him removed, and he restored to his favour. And further, where he could not but grievously complaine of them that had slandered him so greatlie, to the defacing not onelie of his honor, but also putting him in danger of his life, he humblie besought the king that they might answer their unjust accusation; and in case they were found to have forged such matters upon a malicious purpose, that then they might suffer some punishment for their faults, though not to the full of that they had deserved."—HOLINSHED, (1402).

(3) SCENE III.—*Now, as I am a true woman, holland of eight shillings an ell.*] Dame Quickly has been suspected of exaggerating the price of her holland, since, according to this estimate, and making due allowance for the difference in the value of money between her time and ours, each shirt of Falstaff's must have cost as much as would now suffice to clothe a man handsomely from head to foot. But Shakespeare was thinking only of the price of linen in his day; and, at eight shillings an ell, the expense of each shirt would have been about five pounds,—a sum not considered particularly extravagant for this article of apparel in the 16th century; for what says Stubbes upon the subject in his "Anatomie of Abuses"?—"In so much as I have heard of shirtes that have cost some ten shillinges, some twentie, some fortie, some five pound, some twentie nobles, and (which is horrible to heare,) some ten pound apeece, yea, the meanest shirte that commonly is worne of any, doest cost a crowne or a noble at the least; and yet that is scarcely thought fine enough for the simplest person."

ACT V.

(1) SCENE II.—

O, no, my nephew must not know, sir Richard,
The liberal and kind offer of the king.]

There is unquestioned evidence to show that the king made advances for the purpose of averting this conflict. He sent both the Abbot of Shrewsbury and the Clerk of the Privy Seal to Hotspur's camp with offers of pardon if his opponents would return to their allegiance. Hotspur is represented as being much moved by this unexpected act of grace, and to have dispatched his uncle, the Earl of Worcester, to negotiate. This nobleman, however, is reported to have addressed the king with such bitterness, and so to have misinterpreted the conversation between them, that both sides resolved to put their cause to the issue of a battle.

(2) SCENE IV.—*Stay, and breathe awhile.*] "The prince that daie holpe his father like a lustie yong gentleman: for although he was hurt in the face with an arrow, so that diverse noble men that were about him, would have conveied him foorth of the field, yet he would not suffer them so to do, least his departure from amongst his men might happilie have striken some feare into their harts; and so without regard of his hurt, he continued with his men, and never ceassed either to fight where the battell was most hot, or to incourage his men where it seemed most need. This battell lasted three long houres, with indifferent fortune on both parts, till at length, the king crieng saint George victorie, brake the arraie of his enemies and adventured so farre that (as some write) the earl Douglas strake him downe, and at that instant, slue Sir Walter Blunt and three other, apparelled in the king's sute and clothing, saieng: I marvell to see so many kings thus suddenlie arise one in the necke of an other. The king in deed was raised, and did that daie manie a noble feat of armes, for as it is written, he slue that daie with his owne hands six and thirtie persons of his enimies."

Act IV. Sc. 4.

THE SECOND PART OF

KING HENRY THE FOURTH.

THE Registers of the Stationers' Company contain the following memorandum relative to this drama :—

"*23rd August*, 1600.

And. Wise Wm. Apsley.]—Two books the one called Much Adoe about Nothinge, and the other The Seconde Parte of the History of King Henry the iiii, with the Humors of Sir John Fallstaff : wrytten by Mr. Shakespeare." In the same year Wise and Apsley published the only quarto edition of it known, under the title of "The Second Part of Henrie the fourth, continuing to his death and coronation of Henrie the Fift. With the humours of Sir Iohn Falstaffe, and swaggering Pistoll. As it hath been sundrie times publikely acted by the right honourable, the Lord Chamberlaine his seruants. Written by William Shakespeare."

This edition appears to have been printed without proper supervision, for, independently of minor omissions, at the beginning of Act III. a whole scene was left out. Nor does the mistake seem to have been discovered until the greater part of the impression had been worked off: sheet E was then reprinted and the missing scene incorporated. The folio text of the play was printed from an independent and more complete copy than that of the quarto, depraved, however, as usual by playhouse alterations and the negligence of successive transcribers.

Malone assigns the composition of the Second Part of King Henry IV. to 1598 ; but from the circumstance of one speech of Falstaff's in Act I. Sc. 2, bearing the prefix of *Old, i.e. Oldcastle,* it is evident that the great humourist retained the name of Oldcastle when this play was written, and as it is known that the name was changed anterior to the entry of Part I. in the Stationers' books, on the 25th of February, 1597-8, we are warranted in assuming that the Second Part was produced before that date.

The historical transactions comprehended in this piece, extend over a period of about nine years ; beginning with the account of Hotspur's defeat and death in 1403, and terminating with the decease of Henry IV. and the accession and coronation of Henry V. in 1412-13.

Persons Represented.

KING HENRY THE FOURTH.

HENRY, *Prince of* WALES; *afterwards* KING HENRY V. THOMAS, *Duke of* CLARENCE, *Prince* JOHN *of* LANCASTER, *Prince* HUMPHREY *of* GLOUCESTER.	*His Sons.*
Earl of WARWICK, *Earl of* WESTMORELAND, *Lord Chief Justice of the King's Bench,* GOWER; HARCOURT, *A gentleman attending on the Chief Justice.*	*Of the King's party.*
Earl of NORTHUMBERLAND, SCROOP, *Archbishop of York,* *Lord* MOWBRAY, *Lord* HASTINGS, *Lord* BARDOLPH, *Sir* JOHN COLEVILE, TRAVERS *and* MORTON.	*Opposites to the King.*

Sir JOHN FALSTAFF.
POINS *and* PETO.
SHALLOW *and* SILENCE, *Country Justice*
BARDOLPH, PISTOL, *and Page.*
DAVY, SHALLOW'S *Servant.*
MOULDY, SHADOW, BULL-CALF, WART, *and* FEEBLE, *Recruits.*
FANG *and* SNARE, *Sergeants.*
RUMOUR.
A PORTER.
A DANCER, *Speaker of the Epilogue.*

Lady NORTHUMBERLAND.
Lady PERCY.
Hostess QUICKLY, *and* DOLL TEAR-SHEET.

Lords and Attendants, Officers, Soldiers, Messengers, Drawers, Grooms, &c. &c.

SCENE,—ENGLAND.

INDUCTION.

Warkworth. *Before* Northumberland's *Castle.*

Enter Rumour, *painted full of Tongues.*[a]

Rum. Open your ears; for which of you will stop
The vent of hearing, when loud Rumour speaks?
I, from the orient to the drooping west,
Making the wind my posthorse, still unfold
The acts commenced on this ball of earth:
Upon my tongues* continual slanders ride,
The which in every language I pronounce,
Stuffing the ears of men† with false reports.
I speak of peace, while covert enmity,
Under the smile of safety, wounds the world:
And who but Rumour, who but only I,
Make fearful musters, and prepar'd defence;
Whilst the big year, swol'n with some other grief,‡
Is thought with child by the stern tyrant war?
And no such matter. Rumour is a pipe
Blown by surmises, jealousies, conjectures;
And of so easy and so plain a stop,
That the blunt monster with uncounted heads,
The still discordant wavering multitude,
Can play upon it. But what need I thus
My well-known body to anatomize
Among my household? Why is Rumour here?
I run before king Harry's victory;
Who, in a bloody field by Shrewsbury,
Hath beaten down young Hotspur, and his troops,
Quenching the flame of bold rebellion
Even with the rebels' blood. But what mean I
To speak so true at first? my office is
To noise abroad,—that Harry Monmouth fell
Under the wrath of noble Hotspur's sword;
And that the king before the Douglas' rage
Stoop'd his anointed head as low as death.
This have I rumour'd through the peasant towns[b]
Between that§ royal field of Shrewsbury
And this worm-eaten hole of ragged stone,
Where Hotspur's father, old Northumberland,
Lies crafty-sick: the posts come tiring on,
And not a man of them brings other news
Than they have learn'd of me. From Rumour's tongues
They bring smooth comforts false, worse than true wrongs. [*Exit.*

(*) First folio, *tongue.*
(†) First folio, *them.*
(‡) First folio, *griefs.*
(§) First folio, *the.*

[a] Painted full of Tongues.] This description is omitted in the folio.

[b] *Through the* peasant *towns*—] Mr. Collier's MS. annotator reads *pleasant* towns.

ACT I.

SCENE I.—*The same.* *The* Porter *before the Gate.*

Enter Lord Bardolph.

Bard. Who keeps the gate here, ho?—Where is the earl?
Port. What shall I say you are?
Bard. Tell thou the earl,
That the lord Bardolph doth attend him here.
Port. His lordship is walk'd forth into the orchard;
Please it your honour, knock but at the gate,
And he himself will answer.
Bard. Here comes the earl.

Enter Northumberland.

North. What news, lord Bardolph? every minute now
Should be the father of some stratagem:
The times are wild; contention, like a horse
Full of high feeding, madly hath broke loose
And bears down all before him.
Bard. Noble earl,
I bring you certain news from Shrewsbury.
North. Good, an God* will!
Bard. As good as heart can wish:—
The king is almost wounded to the death;
And, in the fortune of my lord your son,
Prince Harry slain outright; and both the Blunts
Kill'd by the hand of Douglas: young prince John,
And Westmoreland, and Stafford, fled the field;
And Harry Monmouth's brawn, the hulk sir John,

(*) First folio, *heaven*.

Is prisoner to your son: O, such a day,
So fought, so follow'd, and so fairly won,
Came not, till now, to dignify the times,
Since Cæsar's fortunes!
NORTH. How is this deriv'd?
Saw you the field? came you from Shrewsbury?
BARD. I spake with one, my lord, that came from thence;
A gentleman well bred, and of good name,
That freely render'd me these news for true.
NORTH. Here comes my servant Travers, whom I sent
On Tuesday last to listen after news.
BARD. My lord, I over-rode him on the way;
And he is furnish'd with no certainties,
More than he haply may retail from me.

Enter TRAVERS.

NORTH. Now, Travers, what good tidings comes with* you?
TRA. My lord, sir John Umfrevile turn'd me [back
With joyful tidings; and, being better hors'd,
Out-rode me. After him, came, spurring hard,†
A gentleman almost forespent with speed,
That stopp'd by me to breathe his bloodied horse:
He ask'd the way to Chester; and of him
I did demand, what news from Shrewsbury.
He told me, that rebellion had bad‡ luck,
And that young Harry Percy's spur was cold:
With that he gave his able horse the head,
And, bending forward, struck his armed§ heels
Against the panting sides of his poor jade
Up to the rowel-head; and, starting so,
He seem'd in running to devour the way,
Staying no longer question.
NORTH. Ha!——Again.
Said he, young Harry Percy's spur was cold?
Of Hotspur, coldspur? that rebellion
Had met ill luck?
BARD. My lord, I'll tell you what;—
If my young lord your son have not the day,
Upon mine honour, for a silken point
I'll give my barony: never talk of it.
NORTH. Why should that|| gentleman, that rode by Travers,
Give, then, such instances of loss?
BARD. Who, he?
He was some hilding[a] fellow, that had stol'n
The horse he rode on; and, upon my life,
Spoke at a venture.¶ Look, here comes more news.

(*) First folio, *from*. (†) First folio, *head*.
(‡) First folio, *ill*. (§) First folio, *able*.
(||) First folio, *the*. (¶) First folio, *adventure*.

[a] *Some* hilding *fellow*,—] Some *degenerate* fellow. The epithet *hilding* was applied indiscriminately to either sex. Thus Capulet says of his daughter, "Romeo and Juliet," Act III. Sc. 5:—

"Out on her, hilding."

NORTH. Yea, this man's brow, like to a title-leaf,[b]
Foretells the nature of a tragic volume:
So looks the strand, whereon* the imperious flood
Hath left a witness'd usurpation.——

Enter MORTON.

Say, Morton, did'st thou come from Shrewsbury?
MOR. I ran from Shrewsbury, my noble lord;
Where hateful death put on his ugliest mask,
To fright our party.
NORTH. How doth my son, and brother?
Thou tremblest; and the whiteness in thy cheek
Is apter than thy tongue to tell thy errand.
Even such a man, so faint, so spiritless,
So dull, so dead in look, so woe-begone,
Drew Priam's curtain in the dead of night,
And would have told him, half his Troy was burn'd;
But Priam found the fire, ere he his tongue,
And I my Percy's death, ere thou report'st it.
This thou would'st say,—Your son did thus, and thus;
Your brother, thus; so fought the noble Douglas;
Stopping my greedy ear with their bold deeds,
But in the end, to stop mine ear indeed,
Thou hast a sigh to blow away this praise,
Ending with—brother, son, and all are dead.
MOR. Douglas is living, and your brother, yet;
But, for my lord your son,——
NORTH. Why, he is dead.
See, what a ready tongue suspicion hath!
He, that but fears the thing he would not know,
Hath, by instinct, knowledge from others' eyes,
That what he fear'd is chanced. Yet speak, Morton;
Tell thou thy earl, his divination lies;
And I will take it as a sweet disgrace,
And make thee rich for doing me such wrong.
MOR. You are too great to be by me gainsaid:
Your spirit is too true, your fears too certain.
NORTH. Yet, for all this, say not that Percy's dead.
I see a strange confession in thine eye:
Thou shak'st thy head, and hold'st it fear, or sin,
To speak a truth. If he be slain, say so:
The tongue offends not, that reports his death;
And he doth sin, that doth belie the dead,
Not he, which says the dead is not alive.
Yet the first bringer of unwelcome news
Hath but a losing office; and his tongue
Sounds ever after as a sullen bell,

(*) First folio, *when*.

[b] *Like to a* title-leaf,—] Elegiac poems in former times were usually printed with a black border round the title-page, and sometimes with that leaf totally black.

Remember'd knolling (*) a departing friend.

BARD. I cannot think, my lord, your son is dead.

MOR. I am sorry, I should force you to believe
That, which I would to God (†) I had not seen:
But these mine eyes saw him in bloody state,
Rend'ring faint quittance,[a] wearied and out-breath'd
To Harry (‡) Monmouth; whose swift wrath beat down
The never-daunted Percy to the earth,
From whence with life he never more sprung up.
In few,[b] his death, (whose spirit lent a fire
Even to the dullest peasant in his camp,)
Being bruited once, took fire and heat away
From the best temper'd courage in his troops:
For from his metal was his party steel'd;
Which once in him abated, all the rest
Turn'd on themselves, like dull and heavy lead.
And as the thing that's heavy in itself,
Upon enforcement, flies with greatest speed,
So did our men, heavy in Hotspur's loss,
Lend to this weight such lightness with their fear,
That arrows fled not swifter toward their aim,
Than did our soldiers, aiming at their safety,
Fly from the field. Then was that noble Worcester
Too soon ta'en prisoner; and that furious Scot,
The bloody Douglas, whose well-labouring sword
Had three times slain the appearance of the king,
'Gan vail his stomach,[c] and did grace the shame
Of those that turn'd their backs; and, in his flight,
Stumbling in fear, was took. The sum of all
Is,—that the king hath won; and hath sent out
A speedy power, to encounter you, my lord,
Under the conduct of young Lancaster,
And Westmoreland: this is the news at full.

NORTH. For this I shall have time enough to mourn.
In poison there is physic; and these (§) news,
Having been well, that would have made me sick;
Being sick, have in some measure made me well:
And as the wretch, whose fever-weaken'd joints,
Like strengthless hinges, buckle[d] under life,
Impatient of his fit, breaks like a fire
Out of his keeper's arms; even so my limbs,
Weaken'd with grief, being now enrag'd with grief,
Are thrice themselves: hence therefore, thou nice[e] crutch;
A scaly gauntlet now, with joints of steel,
Must glove this hand: and hence, thou sickly coif;
Thou art a guard too wanton for the head,
Which princes, flesh'd with conquest, aim to hit.
Now bind my brows with iron; and approach
The ragged'st[f] hour that time and spite dare bring,
To frown upon the enrag'd Northumberland!
Let heaven kiss earth! Now let not nature's hand
Keep the wild flood confin'd! let order die!
And let this (*) world no longer be a stage,
To feed contention in a lingering act,
But let one spirit of the first-born Cain
Reign in all bosoms, that, each heart being set
On bloody courses, the rude scene may end,
And darkness be the burier of the dead!

TRA. This strained passion doth you wrong, my lord.[g]

BARD. Sweet earl, divorce not wisdom from your honour.

MOR. The lives of all your loving complices
Lean on your health; the which, if you give o'er
To stormy passion, must perforce decay.[h]
You cast the event of war, my noble lord,
And summ'd the account of chance, before you said,—
Let us make head. It was your presurmise,
That, in the dole[i] of blows, your son might drop:
You knew, he walk'd o'er perils, on an edge,
More likely to fall in, than to get o'er;
You were advis'd,[k] his flesh was capable[l]
Of wounds, and scars; and that his forward spirit
Would lift him where most trade[m] of danger rang'd;
Yet did you say,—*Go forth;* and none of this,
Though strongly apprehended, could restrain
The stiff-borne action. What hath then befallen,
Or what hath this bold enterprise brought forth,
More than that being which was like to be?

BARD. We all that are engaged to this loss,
Knew that we ventur'd on such dangerous seas,
That, if we wrought out life, 't was (†) ten to one;
And yet we ventur'd, for the gain propos'd
Chok'd the respect of likely peril fear'd;
And, since we are o'erset, venture again.
Come, we will all put forth; body and goods.

(*) Quarto, *tolling*. (†) First folio, *heaven*.
(‡) First folio, *Henry*. (§) First folio, *this*.

(*) First folio, *the*. (†) First folio, *was*.

[a] *Rend'ring faint* quittance,—] *Quittance* here means *requital*, as in "Henry V." Act II. Sc. 2:—

"And shall forget the office of our hand,
Sooner than *quittance* of desert and merit."

[b] In few,—] That is, *in short*, in a *few* words. So in "The Tempest," Act I. Sc. 2:—

"*In few*, they hurried us aboard a bark;"

and in "Measure for Measure," Act III. Sc. 1:—

"*In few*, bestowed her on her own lamentation."

See note (d) p. 237.

[c] 'Gan vail his stomach,—] Lower his *pride* or *courage*. See note (a), p. 273.

[d] Buckle *under*—] *Bend* under.

[e] *Thou* nice *crutch;*] *Nice* means here *effeminate*.

[f] *The* ragged'st *hour*—] The *roughest* hour.

[g] TRA. This strained passion doth you wrong, my lord.] This line is omitted in the folio.

[h] Must perforce decay.] The remainder of Morton's speech, after this line, is omitted in the quarto.

[i] *The* dole *of blows*,—] The *dealing*, the *distribution* of blows.

[k] *You were* advis'd,—] You were *aware*.

[l] Capable—] That is, *susceptible, sensible*. "Alongst the galupin or silver paved way of heaven, conducted into the great hall of the gods, Mercury sprinkled me with water, which made me *capable* of their divine presence."—GREENE'S *Orpharion*, 4to, 1599, p. 7. See note (b), p. 297.

[m] *Where most* trade—] Most *traffic*. See note (c), p. 473.

MOR. 'Tis more than time: and, my most noble lord,
I hear for certain, and do* speak the truth,[a]——
The gentle archbishop of York is up,
With well-appointed powers; he is a man,
Who with a double surety binds his followers.
My lord your son had only but the corps,
But shadows, and the shows of men, to fight:
For that same word, *rebellion*, did divide
The action of their bodies from their souls;
And they did fight with queasiness, constrain'd,
As men drink potions; that their weapons only
Seem'd on our side, but, for their spirits and souls,
This word, *rebellion*, it had froze them up,
As fish are in a pond: but now the bishop
Turns insurrection to religion:
Suppos'd sincere and holy in his thoughts,
He's follow'd both with body and with mind;
And doth enlarge his rising with the blood
Of fair king Richard, scrap'd from Pomfret stones;
Derives from heaven his quarrel, and his cause;
Tells them, he doth bestride a bleeding land,
Gasping for life under great Bolingbroke;
And more and less,[b] do flock to follow him.

NORTH. I knew of this before; but, to speak truth,
This present grief had wip'd it from my mind.
Go in with me; and counsel every man
The aptest way for safety, and revenge:
Get posts, and letters, and make friends with speed;
Never so few, and† never yet more need.
[*Exeunt.*

SCENE II.—London. *A Street.*

Enter SIR JOHN FALSTAFF, *with his* PAGE *bearing his sword and buckler.*

FAL. Sirrah, you giant, what says the doctor to my water?

PAGE. He said, sir, the water itself was a good healthy water: but, for the party that owed it, he might have more diseases than he knew for.

FAL. Men of all sorts take a pride to gird at me. The brain of this foolish-compounded clay, man, is not able to invent any thing that tends to laughter, more than I invent, or is invented on me: I am not only witty in myself, but the cause that wit is in other men. I do here walk before thee, like a sow, that hath overwhelmed all her litter but one. If the prince put thee into my service for any other reason than to set me off, why then I have no judgment. Thou whoreson mandrake, thou art fitter to be worn in my cap, than to wait at my heels. I was never manned with an agate[c] till now: but I will in-set* you neither in gold nor silver, but in vile apparel, and send you back again to your master, for a jewel; the juvenal, the prince your master, whose chin is not yet fledged. I will sooner have a beard grow in the palm of my hand, than he shall get one on his cheek; and yet he will not stick to say, his face is a face-royal: God† may finish it when he will, it is not a hair amiss yet: he may keep it still as‡ a face-royal, for a barber shall never earn sixpence out of it; and yet he will be crowing, as if he had writ man ever since his father was a bachelor. He may keep his own grace, but he is almost out of mine, I can assure him.——What said master Dombledon about the satin for my short cloak, and my § slops?

PAGE. He said, sir, you should procure him better assurance than Bardolph: he would not take his bond and yours; he liked not the security.

FAL. Let him be damned like the glutton! pray God‖ his tongue be hotter!—A whoreson Achitophel! a rascally yea-forsooth knave! to bear a gentleman in hand,[d] and then stand upon security!—The whoreson smooth-pates do now wear nothing but high shoes, and bunches of keys at their girdles; and if a man is thorough with them in honest taking up,[e] then they must stand upon—*security*. I had as lief they would put ratsbane in my mouth, as offer to stop it with—*security*. I looked he should have sent me two and twenty yards of satin, as I am a true knight, and he sends me—*security*. Well, he may sleep in security; for he hath the horn of abundance, and the lightness of his wife shines through it; and yet cannot he see, though he have his own lantern to light him.—Where's Bardolph?

PAGE. He's gone into Smithfield to buy your worship a horse.

FAL. I bought him in Paul's, and he'll buy me a horse in Smithfield: an¶ I could get me but** a wife in the stews, I were manned, horsed, and wived.[f]

(*) Quarto, *dare*. (†) First folio, *nor*.

a And do speak the truth,——] Here, again, the quarto omits what follows of Morton's speech.

b More and less,—] That is, *great and small*. So in "Henry IV." Part I. Act IV. Sc. 3:—

"The *more and less* came in with cap and knee."

c I was never manned with an agate—] An agate stone was frequently cut to represent the human form, and was occasionally worn in the hat by gallants.

d To bear a gentleman in hand,—] To *bear in hand*, was to *buoy up*. See note (c), p. 258.

(*) First folio, *set*. (†) First folio, *Heaven*.
(‡) Old text, *at*. (§) First folio omits, *my*.
(‖) First folio, *may*. (¶) First folio, *if*.
(**) First folio omits, *but*.

e *If a man is* thorough *with them in honest* taking up,—] Falstaff appears to mean if a man is *resolute* with them to have honest goods dealt to him.

f I were manned, horsed, and wived.] Alluding to a proverb often quoted by the old writers: "Who goes to Westminster for a wife, to St. Paul's for a man, and to Smithfield for a horse, may meet with a queane, a knave, and a jade."

Enter the Lord Chief Justice,(1) *and an* Attendant.

PAGE. Sir, here comes the nobleman that committed the prince for striking him about Bardolph.

FAL. Wait close, I will not see him.

CH. JUST. What's he that goes there?

ATTEN. Falstaff, an't please your lordship.

CH. JUST. He that was in question for the robbery?

ATTEN. He, my lord: but he hath since done good service at Shrewsbury: and, as I hear, is now going with some charge to the lord John of Lancaster.

CH. JUST. What, to York? Call him back again.

ATTEN. Sir John Falstaff!

FAL. Boy, tell him, I am deaf.

PAGE. You must speak louder, my master is deaf.

CH. JUST. I am sure he is, to the hearing of any thing good.—Go, pluck him by the elbow; I must speak with him.

ATTEN. Sir John,——

FAL. What! a young knave, and beg! Is there not wars? Is there not employment? Doth not the king lack subjects? do not the rebels need * soldiers? Though it be a shame to be on any side but one, it is worse shame to beg than to be on the worst side, were it worse than the name of rebellion can tell how to make it.

ATTEN. You mistake me, sir.

FAL. Why, sir, did I say you were an honest man? setting my knighthood and my soldiership aside, I had lied in my throat (2) if I had said so.

ATTEN. I pray you, sir, then set your knighthood and your soldiership aside; and give me leave to tell you, you lie in your throat, if you say I am any other than an honest man.

FAL. I give thee leave to tell me so! I lay aside that which grows to me! If thou get'st any leave of me, hang me; if thou takest leave, thou wert better be hanged: you hunt-counter,[a] hence! avaunt!

ATTEN. Sir, my lord would speak with you.

CH. JUST. Sir John Falstaff, a word with you.

(*) First folio, *want.*

a *You* hunt-counter,—] A quibble may have been intended on the cant term *hunt-counter* for a sheriff's officer, and the fault of a hound in turning and following the scent the way the chase has come.

FAL. My good lord!—God* give your lordship good time of day. I am glad to see your lordship abroad: I heard say, your lordship was sick: I hope, your lordship goes abroad by advice. Your lordship, though not clean past your youth, hath yet some smack of age in you, some relish of the saltness of time; and I most humbly beseech your lordship, to have a reverend care of your health.

CH. JUST. Sir John, I sent for† you before your expedition to Shrewsbury.

FAL. An't‡ please your lordship, I hear, his majesty is returned with some discomfort from Wales.

CH. JUST. I talk not of his majesty:—you would not come when I sent for you.

FAL. And I hear moreover, his highness is fallen into this same whoreson apoplexy.

CH. JUST. Well, heaven mend him! I pray, let me speak with you.

FAL. This apoplexy is, as I take it, a kind of lethargy, an't please your lordship; a kind of sleeping in the blood,[a] a whoreson tingling.

CH. JUST. What tell you me of it? be it as it is.

FAL. It hath it original from much grief; from study, and perturbation of the brain: I have read the cause of his effects in Galen; it is a kind of deafness.

CH. JUST. I think, you are fallen into the disease; for you hear not what I say to you.

FAL. Very well, my lord, very well: rather, an't please you, it is the disease of not listening, the malady of not marking, that I am troubled withal.

CH. JUST. To punish you by the heels, would amend the attention of your ears; and I care not, if I do become§ your physician.

FAL. I am as poor as Job, my lord, but not so patient: your lordship may minister the potion of imprisonment to me, in respect of poverty; but how I should be your patient to follow your prescriptions, the wise may make some dram of a scruple, or, indeed, a scruple itself.

CH. JUST. I sent for you, when there were matters against you for your life, to come speak with me.

FAL. As I was then advised by my learned counsel in the laws of this land-service, I did not come.

CH. JUST. Well, the truth is, sir John, you live in great infamy.

FAL. He that buckles him in my belt, cannot live in less.

CH. JUST. Your means are very slender, and your waste is* great.

FAL. I would it were otherwise; I would my means were greater, and my waist slenderer.

CH. JUST. You have misled the youthful prince.

FAL. The young prince hath misled me: I am the fellow with the great belly, and he my dog.[b]

CH. JUST. Well, I am loth to gall a new-healed wound; your day's service at Shrewsbury hath a little gilded over your night's exploit on Gads-hill: you may thank the unquiet time for your quiet o'er-posting that action.

FAL. My lord?

CH. JUST. But since all is well, keep it so: wake not a sleeping wolf.

FAL. To wake a wolf, is as bad as to smell a fox.

CH. JUST. What! you are as a candle, the better part burnt out.

FAL. A wassel candle, my lord; all tallow: if I did say of wax, my growth would approve the truth.

CH. JUST. There is not a white hair on your face, but should have his effect of gravity.

FAL. His effect of gravy, gravy, gravy.

CH. JUST. You follow the young prince up and down, like his ill† angel.

FAL. Not so, my lord; your ill angel is light;[c] but, I hope, he that looks upon me, will take me without weighing; and yet, in some respects, I grant, I cannot go, I cannot tell:[d] Virtue is of so little regard in these costar-mongers' times‡, that true valour is turned bear-herd: pregnancy[e] is made a tapster, and hath his quick wit wasted in giving reckonings: all the other gifts appertinent to man, as the malice of this age shapes them, are not worth a gooseberry. You, that are old, consider not the capacities of us that are young; you measure the heat of our livers with the bitterness of your galls: and we that are in the vaward of our youth, I must confess, are wags too.

CH. JUST. Do you set down your name in the scroll of youth, that are written down old with all the characters of age? Have you not a moist eye? a dry hand? a yellow cheek? a white beard? a decreasing leg? an increasing belly? Is not your

(*) First folio omits, *God*. (†) First folio omits, *for*.
(‡) First folio, *If it*. (§) First folio, *if I be*.

(*) First folio omits, *is*. (†) First folio, *evil*.
(‡) First folio omits, *times*.

a An't please your lordship: *a* kind of *sleeping* in *the blood*,—] So the quarto, for which the folio reads only, "a sleeping *of* the blood."

b The fellow with the great belly, and he my dog.] A supposed allusion to a fat blind beggar, well known at the time, who was led by his dog.

c *Your* ill angel *is light*;] The Chief Justice means *evil genius*; Falstaff evades the application by alluding to the coin called an *angel*, which was frequently made light enough by the process of clipping.

d I cannot tell:] This phrase usually signifies, as Gifford has shown, no more than, *I cannot tell what to think of it*, or *I cannot account for it*: but, in the present instance, the interpretation assigned to it by Johnson, "I cannot be taken; I cannot pass current," seems preferable.

e Pregnancy—] That is, Ready wit.

voice broken? your wind short? your chin double?* your wit single?[a] and every part about you blasted with antiquity; and will you yet† call yourself young? Fie, fie, fie, sir John!

FAL. My lord, I was born about three of the clock in the afternoon,‡ with a white head, and something a round belly. For my voice,—I have lost it with hollaing, and singing of anthems. To approve my youth further, I will not: the truth is, I am only old in judgment and understanding; and he that will caper with me for a thousand marks, let him lend me the money, and have at him. For the box of the ear that the prince gave you,—he gave it like a rude prince, and you took it like a sensible lord. I have checked him for it; and the young lion repents; marry, not in ashes, and sackcloth; but in new silk, and old sack.

CH. JUST. Well, God§ send the prince a better companion!

FAL. God§ send the companion a better prince! I cannot rid my hands of him.

CH. JUST. Well, the king hath severed you and prince Harry: I hear, you are going with lord John of Lancaster, against the archbishop, and the earl of Northumberland.

FAL. Yea; || I thank your pretty sweet wit for it. But look you pray, all you that kiss my lady peace at home, that our armies join not in a hot day; for, by the Lord,¶ I take but two shirts out with me, and I mean not to sweat extraordinarily: if it be a hot day, an** I brandish anything but my bottle, would I might never spit white again.[b] There is not a dangerous action can peep out his head, but I am thrust upon it. Well, I cannot last ever;[c] but it was always yet the trick of our English nation, if they have a good thing, to make it too common. If ye will needs say, I am an old man, you should give me rest. I would to God, my name were not so terrible to the enemy as it is. I were better to be eaten to death with rust, than to be scoured to nothing with perpetual motion.

CH. JUST. Well, be honest, be honest; and God†† bless your expedition!

FAL. Will your lordship lend me a thousand pound, to furnish me forth?

CH. JUST. Not a penny, not a penny; you are too impatient to bear crosses.[d] Fare you well. Commend me to my cousin Westmoreland.

[*Exeunt* Chief Justice *and* Attendant.

FAL. If I do, fillip me with a three-man beetle.[e] —A man can no more separate age and covetousness, than he can part young limbs and lechery: but the gout galls the one, and the pox pinches the other; and so both the degrees prevent[f] my curses.—Boy!——

PAGE. Sir?

FAL. What money is in my purse?

PAGE. Seven groats and two-pence.

FAL. I can get no remedy against this consumption of the purse: borrowing only lingers and lingers it out, but the disease is incurable.—Go bear this letter to my lord of Lancaster; this to the prince; this to the earl of Westmoreland; and this to old mistress Ursula, whom I have weekly sworn to marry since I perceived the first white hair on my chin: about it; you know where to find me. [*Exit* Page.] A pox of this gout! or, a gout of this pox! for the one or the other plays the rogue with my great toe. 'Tis no matter, if I do halt; I have the wars for my colour, and my pension shall seem the more reasonable. A good wit will make use of anything; I will turn diseases to commodity. [*Exit.*

SCENE III.—York. *A Room in the Archbishop's Palace.*

Enter the ARCHBISHOP OF YORK, *the Lords* HASTINGS, MOWBRAY, *and* BARDOLPH.

ARCH. Thus have you heard our cause,* and know our means;
And, my most noble friends, I pray you all,
Speak plainly your opinions of our hopes:—
And first, lord marshal, what say you to it?

MOWB. I well allow the occasion of our arms;
But gladly would be better satisfied,
How, in our means, we should advance ourselves,
To look with forehead bold and big enough
Upon the power and puissance of the king.

HAST. Our present musters grow upon the file
To five and twenty thousand men of choice;
And our supplies live largely in the hope
Of great Northumberland, whose bosom burns
With an incensed fire of injuries.

BARD. The question then, lord Hastings, standeth thus;—

(*) First folio omits, *your chin double.* (†) First folio omits, *yet.*
(‡) First folio omits, *about three of the clock in the afternoon.*
(§) First folio, *Heaven.* (||) First folio, *Yes.*
(¶) First folio omits, *by the Lord,* and inserts, *if.*
(**) First folio, *if.* (††) First folio, *Heaven.*

(*) First folio, *causes.*

[a] *Your wit* single?] *Single* meant *simple, silly, weak.*

[b] Never spit white again.] Steevens interprets this "never have my stomach inflamed again with liquor." Mr. Collier thinks the expression "may have reference to his exertions and wounds in the expected conflicts, which might compel him to spit blood." The meaning is simply, *may I never be thirsty again,* want of drink being supposed to have the effect of making people *spit white.* Thus Spungius in Massinger's "Virgin Martyr," Act III. Sc. 3:—"Had I been a pagan still, I should not have *spit white* for want of drink."

[c] Well, I cannot last ever;] Falstaff's speech ends here in the folio, 1623.

[d] *You are too impatient* to bear crosses.] The same pun is met with in "Love's Labour's Lost." See note (c), p. 56.

[e] A three-man beetle.] An implement made of wood, and having two long handles and a short one, which was used for driving piles.

[f] Prevent—] i. e. *Anticipate, come before.*

Whether our present five and twenty thousand
May hold up head without Northumberland?
HAST. With him we may.
BARD. Ay, marry there's the point;
But if without him we be thought too feeble,
My judgment is, we should not step too far,[a]
Till we had his assistance by the hand:
For, in a theme so bloody-fac'd as this,
Conjecture, expectation, and surmise
Of aids incertain, should not be admitted.
ARCH. 'Tis very true, lord Bardolph; for, indeed,
It was young Hotspur's case * at Shrewsbury.
BARD. It was, my lord; who lin'd himself with hope,
Eating the air on promise of supply,
Flattering himself in † project of a power
Much smaller than the smallest of his thoughts:
And so, with great imagination,
Proper to madmen, led his powers to death,
And, winking, leap'd into destruction.
HAST. But, by your leave, it never yet did hurt,
To lay down likelihoods, and forms of hope.
BARD. Yes, if this present quality of war,
Indeed the instant action: a cause on foot,
Lives so in hope, as in an early spring
We see the appearing buds; which, to prove fruit,
Hope gives not so much warrant, as despair,
That frosts will bite them.[b] When we mean to build,
We first survey the plot, then draw the model;
And when we see the figure of the house,
Then must we rate the cost of the erection;
Which if we find outweighs ability,
What do we then, but draw anew the model
In fewer offices; or, at least,[c] desist
To build at all? Much more, in this great work,
(Which is, almost, to pluck a kingdom down,
And set another up,) should we survey
The plot of situation, and the model;
Consent upon a sure foundation;
Question surveyors; know our own estate,
How able such a work to undergo,
To weigh against his opposite;[d] or else,

(*) Quarto, *cause*. (†) First folio, *with*.

[a] We should not step too far,—] The remainder of this speech is omitted in the quarto.

[b] Yes, if this present quality of war;—
* * * * *
That frosts will bite them.] In this opening clause of Lord Bardolph's speech, something has apparently been lost or misprinted; and as the passage only occurs in the folio, the omission or error, it is to be feared, is irremediable.

[c] *At* least,—] Capell proposed, and we think judiciously, to read, at *last*.

[d] ——— know our own estate,
How able such a work to undergo,
To weigh against his opposite;]
Mr. Collier's Annotator, from not reflecting that *his* was in Shakespeare's time *neuter* as well as masculine, and that in this passage it does duty as *its*, has gone to the extreme length of interpolating a new line; reading:—

"——— Know our own estate,
How able such a work to undergo.
A careful leader sums what force he brings
To weigh against his opposite."

The only alteration required is to read "*And* weigh," instead of "*To* weigh," in the last line.

We fortify in paper,[a] and in figures,
Using the names of men instead of men :
Like one, that draws the model of a house
Beyond his power to build it ; who, half through,
Gives o'er, and leaves his part-created cost
A naked subject to the weeping clouds,
And waste for churlish winter's tyranny.

HAST. Grant, that our hopes (yet likely of fair birth)
Should be still-born, and that we now possess'd
The utmost man of expectation ;
I think we are a body strong enough,
Even as we are, to equal with the king.

BARD. What! is the king but five and twenty thousand?

HAST. To us, no more ; nay, not so much, lord Bardolph.
For his divisions, as the times do brawl,
Are in three heads ; one power against the French,
And one against Glendower ; perforce, a third
Must take up us : so is the unfirm king
In three divided ; and his coffers sound
With hollow poverty and emptiness.

ARCH. That he should draw his several strengths together,
And come against us in full puissance,
Need not be dreaded.

HAST. If he should do so,
He leaves his back unarm'd, the French and Welsh
Baying him at the heels : never fear that.

BARD. Who, is it like, should lead his forces hither?

HAST. The duke of Lancaster, and Westmoreland :
Against the Welsh, himself, and Harry Monmouth :
But who is substituted 'gainst the French,
I have no certain notice.

ARCH. Let us on ;[b]
And publish the occasion of our arms.
The commonwealth is sick of their own choice,
Their over-greedy love hath surfeited :—
An habitation giddy and unsure
Hath he, that buildeth on the vulgar heart.
O thou fond many ! with what loud applause
Didst thou beat heaven with blessing Bolingbroke,
Before he was what thou would'st have him be?
And being now trimm'd in thine own desires,
Thou, beastly feeder, art so full of him,
That thou provok'st thyself to cast him up.
So, so, thou common dog, didst thou disgorge
Thy glutton bosom of the royal Richard ;
And now thou would'st eat thy dead vomit up,
And howl'st to find it. What trust is in these times?
They that, when Richard liv'd, would have him die,
Are now become enamour'd on his grave :
Thou, that threw'st dust upon his goodly head,
When through proud London he came sighing on
After the admired heels of Bolingbroke,
Cry'st now, *O earth, yield us that king again,*
And take thou this ! O thoughts of men accurst !
Past, and to come, seem best ; things present, worst.

MOWB. Shall we go draw our numbers, and set on?

HAST. We are time's subjects, and time bids, be gone. [*Exeunt.*

[a] We fortify in paper,—] In the quarto, the speech of Bardolph begins here, the previous lines being omitted.

[b] ARCH. Let us on ;] This speech is omitted in the quarto.

ACT II.

SCENE I.—London. *A Street.*

Enter Hostess; Fang, *and his* Boy, *with her; and* Snare *following.*

Host. Master Fang, have you entered the action?

Fang. It is entered.

Host. Where's your yeoman?[a] Is it a lusty yeoman? will a'* stand to't?

Fang. Sirrah, where's Snare?

Host. O Lord, † ay; good master Snare.

Snare. Here, here.

Fang. Snare, we must arrest sir John Falstaff.

Host. Yea, ‡ good master Snare; I have entered him and all.

Snare. It may chance cost some of us our lives, for § he will stab.

Host. Alas the day! take heed of him: he stabbed me in mine own house, and that most beastly: in good faith,* he cares not what mischief he doth, if his weapon be out: he will foin like any devil; he will spare neither man, woman, nor child.

Fang. If I can close with him, I care not for his thrust.

Host. No, nor I neither; I'll be at your elbow.

Fang. An † I but fist him once; an † a' come but within my vice;——

Host. I am undone by ‡ his going; I warrant you, § he's an infinitive thing upon my score.—Good master Fang, hold him sure:—good master Snare, let him not 'scape. A' comes continuantly to Pye-corner, (saving your manhoods,) to buy a saddle; and he is indited to dinner to the lubbar's head in Lumbert || street, to master Smooth's the silkman: I pray ye, since my exion is entered, and my case so openly known to the world, let him be

(*) First folio, *he*.
(†) First folio omits, *O Lord*.
(‡) First folio, *Ay*.
(§) First folio omits, *for*.

(*) First folio omits, *in good faith*.
(†) First folio, *If*.
(‡) First folio, *with*.
(§) First folio omits, *you*.
(||) First folio, *Lombard*.

a *Where's your yeoman?*] The follower of a serjeant of the mace, or as we now term him, sheriff's officer, was called a serjeant's *yeoman*.

brought in to his answer. A hundred mark is a long one for a poor lone woman to bear: and I have borne, and borne, and borne; and have been fubbed off, and fubbed off, and fubbed off, from this day to that day, that it is a shame to be thought on. There is no honesty in such dealing; unless a woman should be made an ass, and a beast, to bear every knave's wrong. Yonder he comes; and that arrant malmsey-nose knave,* Bardolph, with him. Do your offices, do your offices, master Fang, and master Snare; do me, do me, do me your offices.

Enter SIR JOHN FALSTAFF, Page, *and* BARDOLPH.

FAL. How now? whose mare's dead? what's the matter?

FANG. Sir John, I arrest you at the suit of mistress Quickly.

FAL. Away, varlets!—Draw, Bardolph; cut me off the villain's head; throw the quean in the channel.

HOST. Throw me in the channel? I'll throw thee in the channel.[a] Wilt thou? wilt thou? thou bastardly rogue!—Murder, murder! O thou honey-suckle villain! wilt thou kill God's officers, and the king's! O thou honey-seed rogue![b] thou art a honey-seed; a man-queller,[c] and a woman-queller.

FAL. Keep them off, Bardolph.

FANG. A rescue! a rescue!

HOST. Good people, bring a rescue or two.[d]—Thou wo't, wo't thou? thou wo't, wo't thou? do, do, thou rogue! do, thou hemp-seed!

FAL. Away, you scullion! you rampallian; you fustilarian! I'll tickle your catastrophe.

Enter the Lord Chief Justice, *attended.*

CH. JUST. What is the matter? keep the peace here, ho!

HOST. Good my lord, be good to me! I beseech you stand to me!

CH. JUST. How now, sir John? what, are you brawling here?
Doth this become your place, your time, and [business?
You should have been well on your way to York.—
Stand from him, fellow; wherefore hang'st upon him?

HOST. O my most worshipful lord, an't please your grace, I am a poor widow of Eastcheap, and he is arrested at my suit.

CH. JUST. For what sum?

HOST. It is more than for some, my lord; it is for all, all I have: he hath eaten me out of house and home; he hath put all my substance into that fat belly of his:—but I will have some of it out again, or I'll ride thee o' nights, like the mare.

FAL. I think, I am as like to ride the mare, if I have any vantage of ground to get up.

CH. JUST. How comes this, sir John? Fie! what * man of good temper would endure this tempest of exclamation? Are you not ashamed to enforce a poor widow to so rough a course to come by her own?

FAL. What is the gross sum that I owe thee?

HOST. Marry if thou wert an honest man, thyself, and the money too. Thou didst swear to me upon a parcel-gilt goblet,[e] sitting in my Dolphin chamber, at the round table, by a sea-coal fire, upon † Wednesday in Whitsun-week, when the prince broke thy head for liking ‡ his father to a singing-man of Windsor; thou didst swear to me then, as I was washing thy wound, to marry me, and make me my lady thy wife. Canst thou deny it? Did not goodwife Keech, the butcher's wife, come in then, and call me gossip Quickly? coming in to borrow a mess of vinegar; telling us, she had a good dish of prawns; whereby thou didst desire to eat some; whereby I told thee, they were ill for a green wound? And didst thou not, when she was gone down stairs, desire me to be no more so familiarity § with such poor people; saying, that ere long they should call me madam? And didst thou not kiss me, and bid me fetch thee thirty shillings? I put thee now to thy book-oath; deny it, if thou canst.

FAL. My lord, this is a poor mad soul; and she says, up and down the town, that her eldest son is like you: she hath been in good case, and, the truth is, poverty hath distracted her. But for these foolish officers, I beseech you, I may have redress against them.

CH. JUST. Sir John, sir John, I am well acquainted with your manner of wrenching the true cause the false way. It is not a confident brow, nor the throng of words that come with such more than impudent sauciness from you, can thrust me from a level consideration; you have, as it appears

(*) First folio omits, *knave*.

(*) First folio inserts, *a*. (†) First folio, *on*. (‡) First folio, *lik'ning*. (§) First folio, *no more familiar*.

[a] *I'll throw thee* in the channel.] The folio reads, I'll throw thee *there*.

[b] Honey-suckle villain! .... honey-seed rogue!] Our hostess means, *homicidal*, and *homicide*.

[c] Man-queller,—] An old word for manslayer or murderer.

[d] *Bring a rescue* or two.—Thou wo't, &c.] The folio reading is, "Bring a rescue. *Thou wilt not? Thou wilt not?* do, do," &c.

[e] Parcel-gilt *goblet*,—] "*Parcel-gilt* means what is now called by artists *party-gilt*, that is, where part of the work is gilt, and part left plain, or ungilded."—MALONE.

to me,[a] practised upon the easy-yielding spirit of this woman, and made her serve your uses both in purse and person.

HOST. Yes, in troth, my lord.

CH. JUST. Pr'ythee, peace :—Pay her the debt you owe her, and unpay the villainy you have done with * her ; the one you may do with sterling money, and the other with current repentance.

FAL. My lord, I will not undergo this sneap[b] without reply. You call honourable boldness, impudent sauciness: if a man will make † court'sy, and say nothing, he is virtuous. No, my lord, my ‡ humble duty remembered, I will not be your suitor ; I say to you, I do § desire deliverance from these officers, being upon hasty employment in the king's affairs.

CH. JUST. You speak as having power to do wrong : but answer in the effect of your reputation,[c] and satisfy the poor woman.

FAL. Come hither, hostess. [*Taking her aside.*

Enter GOWER.

CH. JUST. Now, master Gower ; what news ?

GOW. The king, my lord, and Henry, prince of Wales,
Are near at hand : the rest the paper tells.

FAL. As I am a gentleman ;——

HOST. Nay, you said so before.

FAL. As I am a gentleman ;——come, no more words of it.

HOST. By this heavenly ground I tread on, I must be fain to pawn both my plate and the tapestry of my dining-chambers.

(*) First folio omits, *with*. (†) First folio omits, *make*.
(‡) First folio, *your*. (§) First folio omits, *do*.

[a] You have, as it appears to me, &c.] So the quarto. In the folio, we read only, "I know you have practised upon the easy-yielding spirit of this woman."

[b] *This* sneap—] *Sneap*, Icelandic, *sneipa*—contumelia, convitium, *a check*, *sarcasm*, *set-down*.

[c] In the effect of your reputation,—] "That is," Johnson says, "in a manner suitable to your reputation ;" rather, perhaps, in the peril of your reputation.

FAL. Glasses, glasses, is the only drinking: and for thy walls, a pretty slight drollery, or the story of the prodigal, or the German hunting in water-work,(1) is worth a thousand of these bed-hangings, and these fly-bitten tapestries. Let it be ten pound, if thou canst. Come, an * it were not for thy humours, there is not a better wench in England. Go, wash thy face, and 'draw thy action. Come, thou must not be in this humour with me; dost not know me? † Come, come, ‡ I know thou wast set on to this.

HOST. Pray thee, sir John, let it be but twenty nobles; i' faith I am § loth to pawn my plate, in good earnest, la.

FAL. Let it alone; I'll make other shift: you'll be a fool still.

HOST. Well, you shall have it, though I pawn my gown. I hope, you'll come to supper: you'll pay me all together?

(*) First folio, *if*. (†) First folio omits, *dost not know me?*
(‡) First folio, *come;* once only.
(§) First folio omits, *i' faith*, and, *am*.

FAL. Will I live?—Go, with her, with her; [*To* BARDOLPH.] hook on, hook on.

HOST. Will you have Doll Tear-sheet meet you at supper?

FAL. No more words; let's have her.

[*Exeunt* Hostess, BARDOLPH, Officers, *and* Boy.

CH. JUST. I have heard better * news.

FAL. What's the news, my good lord?

CH. JUST. Where lay the king last night?

GOW. At Basingstoke,[a] my lord.

FAL. I hope, my lord, all's well: what is the news, my lord?

CH. JUST. Come all his forces back?

GOW. No: fifteen hundred foot, five hundred horse,
Are march'd up to my lord of Lancaster,
Against Northumberland, and the archbishop.

FAL. Comes the king back from Wales, my noble lord?

(*) First folio, *bitter*.

a *At* Basingstoke, *my lord.*] The quarto makes a ludicrous mistake here, by reading *Billingsgate* instead of Basingstoke.

CH. JUST. You shall have letters of me presently: Come, go along with me, good master Gower.

FAL. My lord!

CH. JUST. What's the matter?

FAL. Master Gower, shall I entreat you with me to dinner?

GOW. I must wait upon my good lord here: I thank you, good sir John.

CH. JUST. Sir John, you loiter here too long, being you are to take soldiers up in counties * as you go.

FAL. Will you sup with me, master Gower?

CH. JUST. What foolish master taught you these manners, sir John?

FAL. Master Gower, if they become me not, he was a fool that taught them me.—This is the right fencing grace, my lord; tap for tap, and so part fair.

CH. JUST. Now the Lord lighten thee! thou art a great fool. [*Exeunt.*

SCENE II.—The same. *Another Street.*

Enter PRINCE HENRY *and* POINS.[a]

P. HEN. Trust me, I am exceeding weary.

POINS. Is it come to that? I had thought, weariness durst not have attached one of so high blood.

P. HEN. 'Faith,† it does me; though it discolours the complexion of my greatness to acknowledge it. Doth it not show vilely in me, to desire small beer?

POINS. Why, a prince should not be so loosely studied, as to remember so weak a composition.

P. HEN. Belike then, my appetite was not princely got: for, by my‡ troth, I do now remember the poor creature, small beer. But, indeed, these humble considerations make me out of love with my greatness. What a disgrace is it to me, to remember thy name? or to know thy face to-morrow? or to take note how many pair of silk stockings thou hast; *viz.* these, and those that were thy peach-coloured ones? or to bear the inventory of thy shirts; as, one for superfluity, and one other for use?—but that, the tennis-court keeper knows better than I; for it is a low ebb of linen with thee, when thou keepest § not racket there; as thou hast not done a great while, because the rest of thy low-countries have made a shift to eat up thy holland: and God knows,[b] whether those that bawl out the ruins of thy linen, shall inherit his kingdom: but the midwives say, the children are not in the fault; whereupon the world increases, and kindreds are mightily strengthened.

POINS. How ill it follows, after you have laboured so hard, you should talk so idly? Tell me, how many good young princes would do so, their fathers being so sick as yours at this time is?[c]

P. HEN. Shall I tell thee one thing, Poins?

POINS. Yes; and let it be an excellent good thing.

P. HEN. It shall serve among wits of no higher breeding than thine.

POINS. Go to; I stand the push of your one thing that you will tell.

P. HEN. Marry,* I tell thee,—it is not meet that I should be sad, now my father is sick: albeit I could tell to thee, (as to one it pleases me, for fault of a better, to call my friend,) I could be sad, and sad indeed too.

POINS. Very hardly, upon such a subject.

P. HEN. By this hand,† thou thinkest me as far in the devil's book, as thou and Falstaff, for obduracy and persistency: let the end try the man. But I tell thee,—my heart bleeds inwardly, that my father is so sick: and keeping such vile company as thou art, hath in reason taken from me all ostentation of sorrow.

POINS. The reason?

P. HEN. What wouldst thou think of me, if I should weep?

POINS. I would think thee a most princely hypocrite.

P. HEN. It would be every man's thought: and thou art a blessed fellow to think as every man thinks; never a man's thought in the world keeps the roadway better than thine: every man would think me an hypocrite indeed. And what accites your most worshipful thought, to think so?

POINS. Why, because you have been so lewd, and so much engraffed to Falstaff.

P. HEN. And to thee.

POINS. By this light, I am well spoke on,‡ I can hear it with mine own ears: the worst that they can say of me is, that I am a second brother, and that I am a proper fellow of my hands; and those two things I confess I cannot help. Look, look, here comes Bardolph.

P. HEN. And the boy that I gave Falstaff: he

(*) First folio, *countries*. (†) First folio omits, *'Faith* (‡) First folio, *in*. (§) First folio, *kept'st*.

[a] *And* Poins.] The stage direction in the quarto is, "*Enter the prince*, Poynes, sir John Russel, *with other*."

[b] *And God knows*, &c.] The remainder of the speech is omitted in the folio, having been struck out, most probably by the Master of the Revels.

(*) First folio, *Why*. (†) First folio omits, *By this hand*. (‡) First folio, *Nay, I am well spoken of*.

[c] *Their fathers* being *so sick as yours* at this time *is?*] So the quarto. The folio reads, "their fathers *lying* so sick, as yours is."

had him from me Christian; and look * if the fat villain have not transformed him ape.

Enter BARDOLPH *and* Page.

BARD. God † save your grace!

P. HEN. And yours, most noble Bardolph!

BARD. Come, you virtuous ‡ ass, [*To the* Page.] you bashful fool, must you be blushing? wherefore blush you now? What a maidenly man-at-arms are you become? Is it such a matter to get a pottle-pot's maidenhead? [a]

PAGE. He called me even now, my lord, through a red lattice,(2) and I could discern no part of his face from the window: at last, I spied his eyes; and methought he had made two holes in the ale-wife's new petticoat, and peeped through.

P. HEN. Hath not the boy profited?

BARD. Away, you whoreson upright rabbit, away!

PAGE. Away, you rascally Althea's dream, away!

P. HEN. Instruct us, boy: what dream, boy?

PAGE. Marry, my lord, Althea dreamed [b] she was delivered of a fire-brand; and therefore I call him her dream.

P. HEN. A crown's worth of good interpretation.—There it is, boy. [*Gives him money.*

POINS. O, that this good blossom could be kept from cankers!—Well, there is sixpence to preserve thee.

BARD. An § you do not make him be hanged among you, the gallows shall have wrong. ||

P. HEN. And how doth thy master, Bardolph?

BARD. Well, my good lord. He heard of your grace's coming to town; there's a letter for you.

POINS. Delivered with good respect.—And how doth the martlemas, [c] your master?

BARD. In bodily health, sir.

POINS. Marry, the immortal part needs a physician: but that moves not him; though that be sick, it dies not.

P. HEN. I do allow this wen to be as familiar with me as my dog: and he holds his place, for look you how ¶ he writes.

POINS. [*Reads.*] *John Falstaff, knight,*—— Every man must know that, as oft as he hath occasion to name himself. Even like those that are kin to the king; for they never prick their finger, but they say, *There is some of the king's blood spilt. How comes that?* says he, that takes upon him not to conceive: the answer is as ready as a borrowed cap; *I am the king's poor cousin, sir.*

P. HEN. Nay, they will be kin to us, but they will fetch it from Japhet. But to the letter:—

POINS.[d] *Sir John Falstaff, knight, to the son of the king, nearest his father, Harry prince of Wales, greeting.*—Why, this is a certificate.

P. HEN. Peace!

POINS. *I will imitate the honourable Romans in brevity:*—sure he means brevity in breath; short-winded.—*I commend me to thee, I commend thee, and I leave thee. Be not too familiar with* Poins; *for he misuses thy favours so much, that he swears, thou art to marry his sister* Nell. *Repent at idle times as thou may'st, and so farewell.*

Thine, by yea and no, (which is as much as to say, as thou usest him,) Jack Falstaff, with my familiars; John, with my brothers and sisters; * *and Sir John, with all Europe.*

My lord, I will steep this letter in sack, and make him eat it.

P. HEN. That's to make him eat twenty of his words. But do you use me thus, Ned? must I marry your sister?

POINS. God send the wench no worse fortune! [e] but I never said so.

P. HEN. Well, thus we play the fools with the time; and the spirits of the wise sit in the clouds, and mock us.—Is your master here in London?

BARD. Yes, my lord.

P. HEN. Where sups he? doth the old boar feed in the old frank? [f]

BARD. At the old place, my lord; in Eastcheap.

P. HEN. What company?

PAGE. Ephesians, my lord; of the old church.

P. HEN. Sup any women with him?

PAGE. None, my lord, but old mistress Quickly, and mistress Doll Tear-sheet.

P. HEN. What pagan may that be?

PAGE. A proper gentlewoman, sir, and a kinswoman of my master's.

(*) First folio, *see*. (†) First folio omits, *God*.
(‡) First folio, *pernicious*. (§) First folio, *If*.
(||) First folio, *be wrong'd*. (¶) First folio omits, *how*.

a Pottle-pot's maidenhead?] In the old editions, this speech is given to Poins. Theobald, with more propriety, assigned it to Bardolph.

b Althea dreamed—] The page confounds the fire-brand upon which depended the life of Althea's son, Meleager, with the imaginary torch which Hecuba, when pregnant of Paris, dreamed she brought into the world.

c The martlemas, *your master?*] Martlemas, correctly Martinmass, fell about the twelfth of November, and was the period when beef was hung up for smoking; whether Falstaff is so designated from his resemblance to Martlemas beef, or from his being like "the latter spring," is not clear.

(*) First folio, *sister*.

d POINS.] In the old copies this forms part of the Prince's speech.

e God send *the wench no worse fortune!*] The folio reads, "*May* the wench *have* no worse fortune."

f *The old* frank?] The old *sty*.

P. Hen. Even such kin, as the parish heifers are to the town bull.—Shall we steal upon them, Ned, at supper?

Poins. I am your shadow, my lord; I'll follow you.

P. Hen. Sirrah, you boy,—and Bardolph;—no word to your master, that I am yet come to[a] town: there's for your silence.

Bard. I have no tongue, sir.

Page. And for mine, sir,—I will govern it.

P. Hen. Fare ye well; go. [*Exeunt* Bardolph *and* Page.]—This Doll Tear-sheet should be some road.

Poins. I warrant you, as common as the way between saint Alban's and London.

P. Hen. How might we see Falstaff bestow himself to-night in his true colours, and not ourselves be seen?

Poins. Put on two leathern jerkins, and aprons, and wait upon him at his table as* drawers.

(*) First folio, *like*.

[a] *Yet* come to *town*:] The folio has, "yet *in* town."

P. Hen. From a god to a bull? a heavy declension! it was Jove's case. From a prince to a prentice? a low transformation! that shall be mine: for, in every thing, the purpose must weigh with the folly. Follow me, Ned. [*Exeunt.*

SCENE III.—Warkworth. *Before the Castle.*

Enter Northumberland, Lady Northumberland, *and* Lady Percy.

North. I pray thee, loving wife, and gentle daughter,
Give* even way unto my rough affairs:
Put not you on the visage of the times,
And be, like them, to Percy troublesome.

Lady N. I have given over, I will speak no more:
Do what you will; your wisdom be your guide.

(*) First folio inserts, *an*.

NORTH. Alas, sweet wife, my honour is at pawn;
And, but my going, nothing can redeem it.

LADY P. O, yet for God's* sake, go not to these wars!
The time was, father, that† you broke your word,
When you were more endear'd to it than now;
When your own Percy, when my heart-dear Harry,
Threw many a northward look, to see his father
Bring up his powers; but he did long in vain.
Who then persuaded you to stay at home?
There were two honours lost; yours, and your son's.
For yours,—the God of heaven[a] brighten it!
For his,—it stuck upon him, as the sun
In the grey vault of heaven: and, by his light,
Did all the chivalry of England move
To do brave acts; he was, indeed, the glass
Wherein the noble youth did dress themselves.[b]
He had no legs, that practis'd not his gait:
And speaking thick,[c] which nature made his blemish,
Became the accents of the valiant;
For those that could speak low, and tardily,
Would turn their own perfection to abuse,
To seem like him. So that, in speech, in gait,
In diet, in affections of delight,
In military rules, humours of blood,
He was the mark and glass, copy and book,
That fashion'd others. And him,—O wondrous him!
O miracle of men!—him did you leave,
(Second to none, unseconded by you,)
To look upon the hideous god of war
In disadvantage; to abide a field,
Where nothing but the sound of Hotspur's name
Did seem defensible:—so you left him:
Never, O never, do his ghost the wrong,
To hold your honour more precise and nice
With others, than with him; let them alone;
The marshal, and the archbishop, are strong:
Had my sweet Harry had but half their numbers,
To-day might I, hanging on Hotspur's neck,
Have talk'd of Monmouth's grave.

NORTH. Beshrew your heart,
Fair daughter! you do draw my spirits from me,
With new lamenting ancient oversights.
But I must go, and meet with danger there;
Or it will seek me in another place,
And find me worse provided.

LADY N. O, fly to Scotland,
Till that the nobles, and the armed commons,
Have of their puissance made a little taste.

LADY P. If they get ground and vantage of the king,
Then join you with them, like a rib of steel,
To make strength stronger; but, for all our loves,
First let them try themselves: so did your son;
He was so suffer'd; so came I a widow;
And never shall have length of life enough,
To rain upon remembrance with mine eyes,
That it may grow and sprout as high as heaven,
For recordation to my noble husband.

NORTH. Come, come, go in with me: 'tis with my mind,
As with the tide swell'd up unto his height,
That makes a still-stand, running neither way.
Fain would I go to meet the archbishop,
But many thousand reasons hold me back:——
I will resolve for Scotland; there am I,
Till time and vantage crave my company.
[*Exeunt.*

SCENE IV.—London. *A Room in the* Boar's Head Tavern, *in* Eastcheap.

Enter two Drawers.

1 DRAW. What the devil* hast thou brought there? apple-Johns? thou knowest sir John cannot endure an apple-John.[d]

2 DRAW. Mass,† thou say'st true. The prince once set a dish of apple-Johns before him, and told him, there were five more sir Johns: and, putting off his hat, said, I *will now take my leave of these six dry, round, old, withered knights.* It angered him to the heart; but he hath forgot that.

1 DRAW. Why then, cover, and set them down: and see if thou canst find out Sneak's noise;[e] mistress Tear-sheet would fain hear some music. Dispatch. The room where they supped, is too hot; they'll come in straight.[f]

2 DRAW. Sirrah, here will be the prince, and master Poins anon: and they will put on two of our jerkins, and aprons; and sir John must not know of it: Bardolph hath brought word.

(*) First folio, *Heaven's.* (†) First folio, *when.*

[a] The God of heaven *bright'n it!*] So the quarto. The folio reading is, *may heavenly glory* brighten it.

[b] Wherein the noble youth did dress themselves.] This concludes the speech in the quarto.

[c] *And speaking* thick,—] That is, speaking *rapidly.* Thus, in "Cymbeline," Act III. Sc. 2:—

"—— say, and *speak thick,*
Love's counsellor should fill the bores of hearing."

(*) First folio omits, *the devil.* (†) First folio omits, *Mass.*

[d] An apple-John.] An apple which may be kept without much injury for a couple of years, but, after some time, appears to be shrunk and dried up. The French call it *deux-ans,* whence, in this country formerly, it was corruptly known as *deusants.*

[e] *Sneak's* noise:] "A *noise* of musicians" signified a band or company of them. *Sneak* was probably a jocular name applied to the leader of an itinerant "noise."

[f] Dispatch. The room where they supped, is too hot; they'll come in straight.] The folio omits this passage.

1 Draw. By the mass,* here will be old utis :[a] it will be an excellent stratagem.

2 Draw. I'll see if I can find out Sneak. [*Exit.*

Enter Hostess *and* Doll Tear-sheet.

Host. I'faith,† sweet heart, methinks now you are in an excellent good temperality: your pulsidge beats as extraordinarily as heart would desire; and your colour, I warrant you, is as red as any rose in good truth, la! ‡ But, i'faith,† you have drunk too much canaries; and that's a marvellous searching wine, and it perfumes the blood ere one § can say,—what's this? How do you now?

Doll. Better than I was. Hem!

Host. Why, that's ‖ well said; a good heart's worth gold. Look, here comes sir John.

Enter Falstaff, *singing.*

Fal. *When Arthur first in court*—Empty the jordan.—*And was a worthy king:* (3) [*Exit* Drawer.] How now, Mistress Doll?

Host. Sick of a calm:[b] yea, and good faith.*

Fal. So is all her sect; an † they be once in a calm, they are sick.

Doll. You muddy rascal, is that all the comfort you give me?

Fal. You make fat rascals, mistress Doll.

Doll. I make them! gluttony and diseases make them; I make them not.

Fal. If the cook help to‡ make the gluttony, you help to make the diseases, Doll: we catch of you, Doll, we catch of you; grant that, my poor virtue, grant that.

Doll. Ay, marry; our chains, and our jewels.

Fal. *Your brooches, pearls, and owches:*[c]—for

(*) First folio omits, *By the mass.* (†) First folio omits, *I'faith.*
(‡) First folio omits, *in good truth, la!*
(§) First folio, *we.* (‖) First folio, *was well.*

[a] *Here will be old* utis:] *Old utis* is, rare fun. *Old* here is nothing more than an augmentative. *Utis*, according to Skinner, from the French, *huit*, mean , a merry festival; properly, the *octave, huit, octo*, of a saint's day.

[b] A calm:] A *qualm.*

Your brooches, pearls, and owches:—] A fragment of an old ballad, "The Boy and the Mantle," which is reprinted in Percy's "Reliques," vol. III. p. 401, Edit. 1812:—

"A kirtle and a mantle,
This boy had him upon,
With brooches, rings, and owches
Full daintily bedone."

(*) First folio, *yea good sooth.* (†) First folio, *if.*
(‡) First folio omits, *help to.*

to serve bravely, is to come halting off, you know: to come off the breach with his pike bent bravely, and to surgery bravely; to venture upon the charged chambers bravely:——

DOLL. Hang yourself, you muddy conger, hang yourself![a]

HOST. Why, this is the old fashion; you two never meet, but you fall to some discord: you are both, in good troth, as rheumatic as two dry toasts; you cannot one bear with another's confirmities. What the good-year! one must bear, and that must be you: [*To* DOLL.] you are the weaker vessel, as they say, the emptier vessel.

DOLL. Can a weak empty vessel bear such a huge full hogshead? there's a whole merchant's venture of Bordeaux stuff in him; you have not seen a hulk better stuffed in the hold.—Come, I'll be friends with thee, Jack: thou art going to the wars; and whether I shall ever see thee again, or no, there is nobody cares.

Re-enter Drawer.

DRAW. Sir, ancient Pistol's[b] below, and would speak with you.

DOLL. Hang him, swaggering rascal! let him not come hither: it is the foul-mouth'dst rogue in England.

HOST. If he swagger, let him not come here: no, by my faith;* I must live amongst my neighbours; I'll no swaggerers: I am in good name and fame with the very best.—Shut the door; there comes no swaggerers here! I have not lived all this while, to have swaggering now: shut the door, I pray you.

FAL. Dost thou hear, hostess?—

HOST. Pray you, pacify yourself, sir John; there comes no swaggerers here.

FAL. Dost thou hear? it is mine ancient.

HOST. Tilly-fally, sir John, never tell me; your ancient swaggerer comes not in my doors. I was before master Tisick, the deputy, the other day; and, as he said to me,—'twas no longer ago than Wednesday last,—*Neighbour Quickly*, says he;—master Dumb, our minister, was by then:—*Neighbour Quickly*, says he, *receive those that are civil; for*, saith he, *you are in an ill name;*—now he said so, I can tell whereupon; *for*, says he, *you are an honest woman, and well thought on; therefore take heed what guests you receive: receive*, says he, *no swaggering companions.*——There comes none here;—you would bless you to hear what he said:—no, I'll no swaggerers.

FAL. He's no swaggerer, hostess; a tame cheater,[c] he; you may stroke him as gently as a puppy greyhound: he will not swagger with a Barbary hen, if her feathers turn back in any show of resistance.—Call him up, drawer.

[*Exit* Drawer.

HOST. *Cheater*, call you him? I will bar no honest man my house, nor no cheater: but I do not love swaggering; by my troth,* I am the worse, when one says—*swagger:* feel, masters, how I shake; look you, I warrant you.

DOLL. So you do, hostess.

HOST. Do I? yea, in very truth, do I, an† 'twere an aspen leaf: I cannot abide swaggerers.

Enter PISTOL, BARDOLPH, *and* Page.

PIST. God‡ save you, sir John!

FAL. Welcome, ancient Pistol. Here, Pistol, I charge you with a cup of sack: do you discharge upon mine hostess.

PIST. I will discharge upon her, sir John, with two bullets.

FAL. She is pistol-proof, sir; you shall hardly offend her.

HOST. Come, I'll drink no proofs, nor no bullets; I'll drink no more than will do me good, for no man's pleasure, I.

PIST. Then to you, mistress Dorothy; I will charge you.

DOLL. Charge me? I scorn you, scurvy companion. What! you poor, base, rascally, cheating, lack-linen mate! Away, you mouldy rogue, away! I am meat for your master.

PIST. I know you, mistress Dorothy.

DOLL. Away, you cut-purse rascal! you filthy bung, away! by this wine, I'll thrust my knife in your mouldy chaps, an § you play the saucy cuttle with me. Away, you bottle-ale rascal! you basket-hilt stale juggler, you!—Since when, I pray you, sir?—What! with two points on your shoulder? much![d]

PIST. I will murder your ruff for this.

FAL. No more, Pistol; || I would not have you

(*) First folio omits, *no, by my faith.*

[a] DOLL. Hang yourself, &c.] This speech is omitted in the folio.

[b] Ancient *Pistol*—] In modern phrase, *ensign* Pistol. The banner and banner-bearer of old were called *ancient*, as they are both now termed *ensign*.

[c] A tame cheater,—] *Cheater*, in old language, usually means *gamester*, or *cozener*:—"They call their art by a new-found name, as *cheating*, themselves *cheators*, and the dice *cheters*, borrowing the term from among our lawyers, with whom all such casuals as fall to the lord at the holding of his leets as waifes and straies, and such like, be called *chetes*, and are accustomably said to be escheted to the lord's use."—MIHIL MUMCHAUNCE, *his Discovery of the art of Cheating in False Dyce Play.* *Tame cheater*, however, in the sense of a craven bird of some kind, was undoubtedly a cant phrase applied to a petty rogue. Thus, in Beaumont and Fletcher's "Fair Maid of the Inn," Act IV, Sc. 2:—"You are worse than simple widgeons, and will be drawn into the net by this decoy-duck, this *tame cheater*."

[d] Much!] An expression of supreme contempt.

(*) First folio omits, *by my troth.* (†) First folio, *if it.*
(‡) First folio omits, *God.* (§) First folio, *if.*
(||) First folio omits this speech.

go off here: discharge yourself of our company, Pistol.

HOST. No, good captain Pistol; not here, sweet captain.

DOLL. Captain! thou abominable damned cheater, art thou not ashamed to be called—captain? An* captains were of my mind, they would truncheon you out, for taking their names upon you before you have earned them. You a captain, you slave! for what? for tearing a poor whore's ruff in a bawdy-house?—He a captain? hang him, rogue! he lives upon mouldy stewed prunes, and dried cakes. A captain! God's light! these villains will make the word captain as odious as the word *occupy*;[a] which was an excellent good word before it was ill sorted: therefore captains had need look to it.

BARD. Pray thee, go down, good ancient.

FAL. Hark thee hither, mistress Doll.

PIST. Not I: I tell thee what, corporal Bardolph;—
I could tear her:—I'll be reveng'd on her.

PAGE. Pray thee, go down.

PIST. I'll see her damned first to Pluto's damned lake; by this hand! † to the infernal deep, with ‡ Erebus and tortures vile also. Hold hook and line, say I. Down! down, dogs! down, faitors! § Have we not Hiren here? [b]

HOST. Good captain Peesel, be quiet; it is very late, i'faith: ‖ I beseek you now, aggravate your choler.

PIST. These be good humours, indeed! Shall pack-horses,
And hollow pamper'd jades of Asia,
Which cannot go but thirty miles a day,
Compare with Cæsars, ¶ and with Cannibals,[c]
And Trojan Greeks? nay, rather damn them with
King Cerberus; and let the welkin roar.
Shall we fall foul for toys?

HOST. By my troth, captain, these are very bitter words.

BARD. Be gone, good ancient: this will grow to a brawl anon.

PIST. Die men, like dogs; give crowns like pins; have we not Hiren here?

HOST. O' my word, captain, there's none such here. What the good-year! do you think, I would deny her? for God's sake, ** be quiet.

PIST. Then, feed, and be fat, my fair Calipolis.[d]
Come, give's * some sack.

Sè fortuna me tormenta, la sperânza me contenta,[e]

Fear we broadsides? no, let the fiend give fire:
Give me some sack;—and, sweetheart, lie thou there. [*Laying down his sword.*
Come we to full points here; and are *et cetera*'s nothing?

FAL. Pistol, I would be quiet.

PIST. Sweet knight, I kiss thy neif:[f] what! we have seen the seven stars.

DOLL. For God's sake,† thrust him down stairs; I cannot endure such a fustian rascal.

PIST. Thrust him down stairs! know we not Galloway nags?

FAL. Quoit him down, Bardolph, like a shove-groat shilling:(4) nay, an ‡ he do nothing but speak nothing, he shall be nothing here.

BARD. Come, get you down stairs.

PIST. What! shall we have incision? shall we imbrue?—— [*Snatching up his sword.*
Then death rock me asleep, abridge my doleful days! (5)
Why then, let grievous, ghastly, gaping wounds
Untwine the sisters three! Come, Atropos, I say!

HOST. Here's goodly stuff toward!

FAL. Give me my rapier, boy.

DOLL. I pr'ythee, Jack, I pr'ythee, do not draw.

FAL. Get you down stairs. [*Drawing.*

HOST. Here's a goodly tumult! I'll forswear keeping house, afore § I'll be in these tirrits and frights. So; murder, I warrant now.——Alas, alas! put up your naked weapons, put up your naked weapons.

[*Exeunt* PISTOL *and* BARDOLPH.

DOLL. I pr'ythee, Jack, be quiet; the rascal is gone. Ah, you whoreson little valiant villain, you.

HOST. Are you not hurt i' the groin? methought, a' made a shrewd thrust at your belly.

Re-enter BARDOLPH.

FAL. Have you turned him out of doors?

BARD. Yea, sir. The rascal's drunk: you have hurt him, sir, in the shoulder.

FAL. A rascal! to brave me!

(*) First folio, *if*. (†) First folio omits, *by this hand*.
(‡) First folio, *where*. (§) First folio, *Fates*.
(‖) First folio omits, *i'faith*. (¶) First folio, *Cæsar*.
(**) First folio, *I pray*.

[a] As odious as the word *occupy*;] The perversion of this word to the offensive sense, which a reference to dictionaries of the period will explain, would appear to have been recent when our author wrote. It has now resumed its place as "an excellent good word." The folio omits the passage altogether; reading thus:—"A captaine? These Villaines will make the word Captaine odious: Therefore Captaines had neede looke to it."

[b] Have we not Hiren here?] Pistol's rant is chiefly made up of bombastic quotations stolen from the playhouse. Thus, the line above was no doubt taken from an old play now lost, by George Peele, called "The Turkish Mahomet and Hyren the Fair Greek;" as the "hollow pamper'd jades of Asia" was borrowed from Marlowe's robustious drama of "Tamburlaine the Great," 1590:—

"Holla, ye pamper'd jades of Asia,
What! can you draw but twenty miles a day?"

[c] Cannibals,—] He means *Hannibals*.

[d] My fair Calipolis.] From a line in "The Battle of Alcazar," 1594, a play Mr. Dyce attributes to Peele:—

"Feed then, and faint not, my fair Calipolis."

[e] *Sè fortuna, &c.*] In the original this motto is corruptly printed *si fortune me tormente, sperato me contento*, perhaps intentionally.

[f] Neif:] *Neif* is *fist*.

(*) First folio, *give me*. (†) First folio omits, *For God's sake*.
(‡) First folio, *if*. (§) First folio, *before*.

DOLL. Ah, you sweet little rogue, you! Alas poor ape, how thou sweat'st? Come, let me wipe thy face;—come on, you whoreson chops:—Ah, rogue! i'faith,* I love thee. Thou art as valorous as Hector of Troy, worth five of Agamemnon, and ten times better than the nine worthies: ah, villain!

FAL. A rascally slave! I will toss the rogue in a blanket.

DOLL. Do, an † thou darest, for thy heart: if thou dost, I'll canvas thee between a pair of sheets.

PAGE. The music is come, sir.

Enter Music.

FAL. Let them play.—Play, sirs.—Sit on my knee, Doll. A rascal bragging slave! the rogue fled from me like quicksilver.

DOLL. I'faith,* and thou follow'dst him like a church. Thou whoreson little tidy[a] Bartholomew boar-pig,(6) when wilt thou leave fighting o' days, and foining o' nights, and begin to patch up thine old body for heaven?

Enter behind, PRINCE HENRY *and* POINS, *disguised like* Drawers.

FAL. Peace, good Doll! do not speak like a death's head; do not bid me remember mine end.

DOLL. Sirrah, what humour is the prince of?

FAL. A good shallow young fellow: he would have made a good pantler, he would have chipped bread well.

DOLL. They say, Poins hath a good wit.

FAL. He a good wit? hang him, baboon! his wit is as thick as Tewksbury mustard; there is no more conceit in him, than is in a mallet.

DOLL. Why doth the prince love him so then?

(*) First folio omits, *I'faith.*

(†) First folio, *if.*

[a] Tidy—] *Tidy* meant *plump:* from the Teutonic, *tydigh, ripe, mature,* in *good condition.*

FAL. Because their legs are both of a bigness; and he plays at quoits well; and eats conger and fennel; and drinks off candles' ends for flap-dragons;(7) and rides the wild mare[a] with the boys; and jumps upon joint-stools; and swears with a good grace; and wears his boot very smooth, like unto the sign of the leg; and breeds no bate with telling of discreet stories: and such other gambol faculties he hath, that show a weak mind and an able body, for the which the prince admits him: for the prince himself is such another; the weight of a hair will turn the scales between their avoirdupois.

P. HEN. Would not this nave of a wheel have his ears cut off?

POINS. Let's beat him before his whore.

P. HEN. Look, if the withered elder hath not his poll clawed like a parrot.

POINS. Is it not strange that desire should so many years outlive performance?

FAL. Kiss me, Doll.

P. HEN. Saturn and Venus this year in conjunction! what says the almanac to that?

POINS. And, look, whether the fiery Trigon,[b] his man, be not lisping to his master's old tables; his note-book, his counsel-keeper.

FAL. Thou dost give me flattering busses.

DOLL. Nay, truly, I kiss thee with a most constant heart.

FAL. I am old, I am old.

DOLL. I love thee better than I love e'er a scurvy young boy of them all.

FAL. What stuff wilt* have a kirtle of? I shall receive money on Thursday: thou shalt have a cap to-morrow. A merry song, come: it grows late, we'll to bed. Thou'lt forget me, when I am gone.

DOLL. By my troth † thou'lt set me a weeping, an ‡ thou say'st so: prove that ever I § dress myself handsome till thy return.——Well, hearken the end.

FAL. Some sack, Francis.

P. HEN. POINS. Anon, anon, sir. [*Advancing.*

FAL. Ha! a bastard son of the king's?—And art not thou Poins his brother?[c]

P. HEN. Why, thou globe of sinful continents, what a life dost thou lead?

FAL. A better than thou; I am a gentleman, thou art a drawer.

P. HEN. Very true, sir; and I come to draw you out by the ears.

HOST. O, the Lord preserve thy good grace! welcome to London.—Now, heaven bless that sweet face of thine! What! are you come from Wales?

FAL. Thou whoreson mad compound of majesty,—by this light flesh and corrupt blood, thou art welcome. [*Leaning his hand upon* DOLL.

DOLL. How! you fat fool, I scorn you.

POINS. My lord, he will drive you out of your revenge, and turn all to a merriment, if you take not the heat.

P. HEN. You whoreson candle-mine, you, how vilely did you speak of me even now, before this honest, virtuous, civil gentlewoman?

HOST. God's* blessing of † your good heart! and so she is, by my troth.

FAL. Didst thou hear me?

P. HEN. Yes; and you knew me, as you did when you run away by Gads-hill: you knew, I was at your back, and spoke it on purpose, to try my patience.

FAL. No, no, no; not so; I did not think thou wast within hearing.

P. HEN. I shall drive you, then, to confess the wilful abuse; and then I know how to handle you.

FAL. No abuse, Hal, on mine honour; no abuse.

P. HEN. Not! to dispraise me; and call me—pantler, and bread-chipper,‡ and I know not what?

FAL. No abuse, Hal.

POINS. No abuse!

FAL. No abuse, Ned, in the world; honest Ned, none. I dispraised him before the wicked, that the wicked might not fall in love with him:—in which doing, I have done the part of a careful friend, and a true subject, and thy father is to give me thanks for it. No abuse, Hal;—none, Ned, none;—no, boys, none.

P. HEN. See now, whether pure fear, and entire cowardice, doth not make thee wrong this virtuous gentlewoman, to close with us? Is she of the wicked? Is thine hostess here of the wicked? Or is thy§ boy of the wicked? Or honest Bardolph, whose zeal burns in his nose, of the wicked?

POINS. Answer, thou dead elm, answer.

FAL. The fiend hath pricked down Bardolph irrecoverable; and his face is Lucifer's privy-kitchen, where he doth nothing but roast malt-worms. For the boy,—there is a good angel about him; but the devil outbids him too.

P. HEN. For the women?

FAL. For one of them,—she is in hell already,

(*) First folio inserts, *thou*. (†) First folio omits, *By my troth*. (‡) First folio, *if*. (§) First folio, *I ever*.

(*) First folio omits, *God's*. (†) First folio, *on*. (‡) First folio, *chopper*. (§) First folio, *the*.

[a] The wild mare—] The name given to the sport of *see-saw*, or what the French call *bascule* and *balançoire*.

[b] *The* fiery Trigon,—] Among astrologers, *Trigon* or *Triplicity* imports the meeting of three signs of the same nature and quality; and *Aries*, *Leo*, and *Sagittarius* are *the Fiery Trigon*, but this does not much assist us in understanding the allusion intended.

[c] Poins his brother?] *Poins's brother*.

and burns, poor soul!* For the other,—I owe her money; and whether she be damned for that, I know not.

HOST. No, I warrant you.

FAL. No, I think thou art not; I think, thou art quit for that: marry, there is another indictment upon thee, for suffering flesh to be eaten in thy house, contrary to the law: for the which, I think, thou wilt howl.

HOST. All victuallers do so; what's a joint of mutton or two, in a whole Lent?

P. HEN. You, gentlewoman,—

DOLL. What says your grace?

FAL. His grace says that which his flesh rebels against. [*Knocking without.*

HOST. Who knocks so loud at door? look to the door there, Francis.

Enter PETO.

P. HEN. Peto! how now? what news?

PETO. The king your father is at Westminster;
And there are twenty weak and wearied posts,
Come from the north: and, as I came along,
I met and overtook a dozen captains,
Bare-headed, sweating, knocking at the taverns,
And asking everyone for sir John Falstaff.

P. HEN. By heaven, Poins, I feel me much to blame,
So idly to profane the precious time,
When tempest of commotion, like the south
Borne with black vapour, doth begin to melt,
And drop upon our bare unarmed heads.

(*) Old text, *souls.*

Give me my sword and cloak:—Falstaff, good night.

[*Exeunt* P. HENRY, POINS, PETO, *and* BARDOLPH.

FAL. Now comes in the sweetest morsel of the night, and we must hence, and leave it unpicked. [*Knocking heard.*] More knocking at the door!

Re-enter BARDOLPH.

How now? what's the matter?

BARD. You must away to court, sir, presently; a dozen captains stay at door for you.

FAL. Pay the musicians, sirrah. [*To the* Page.] —Farewell, hostess;—farewell, Doll.—You see, my good wenches, how men of merit are sought after: the undeserver may sleep, when the man of action is called on. Farewell, good wenches:—if I be not sent away post, I will see you again ere I go.

DOLL. I cannot speak.—If my heart be not ready to burst:—well, sweet Jack, have a care of thyself.

FAL. Farewell, farewell.

[*Exeunt* FALSTAFF *and* BARDOLPH.

HOST. Well, fare thee well: I have known thee these twenty-nine years, come peascod-time; but an honester and truer-hearted man,—Well, fare thee well.

BARD. [*Without.*] Mistress Tear-sheet,——

HOST. What's the matter?

BARD. Bid mistress Tear-sheet come to my master.

HOST. O run, Doll, run; run, good Doll.[a] [*Exeunt.*

[a] Run, good Doll.] The quarto adds, "Come, shee comes blubberd, yea? wil you come, Doll?"

ACT III.

SCENE I.[a]—*A Room in the Palace.*

Enter King Henry *in his nightgown, with a* Page.

K. Hen. Go, call the earls of Surrey and of Warwick;
But, ere they come, bid them o'er-read these letters,
And well consider of them: make good speed.—
[*Exit* Page.
How many thousand of my poorest subjects
Are at this hour asleep!—O sleep! O gentle sleep!
Nature's soft nurse, how have I frighted thee,
That thou no more wilt weigh my eyelids down,

[a] SCENE I.—] This scene does not appear in the first quarto, published in 1600; but another edition was issued in the same year to supply the omission.

And steep my senses in forgetfulness?
Why rather, sleep, liest thou in smoky cribs,
Upon uneasy pallets stretching thee,
And hush'd with buzzing night-flies to thy slumber;
Than in the perfum'd chambers of the great,
Under the canopies of costly state,
And lull'd with sounds of sweetest melody?
O thou dull god! why liest thou with the vile,
In loathsome beds, and leav'st the kingly couch,
A watch-case, or a common 'larum bell?
Wilt thou upon the high and giddy mast
Seal up the ship-boy's eyes, and rock his brains
In cradle of the rude imperious surge,
And in the visitation of the winds,
Who take the ruffian billows by the top,
Curling their monstrous heads, and hanging them
With deaf'ning clamours in the slippery clouds,
That, with the hurly, death itself awakes?
Can'st thou, O partial sleep! give thy repose
To the wet sea-boy in an hour so rude;
And, in the calmest and most stillest night,
With all appliances and means to boot,
Deny it to a king? Then, happy low, lie down!
Uneasy lies the head that wears a crown.

Enter WARWICK *and* SURREY, *and* SIR JOHN BLUNT.

WAR. Many good morrows to your majesty!
K. HEN. Is it good morrow, lords?
WAR. 'Tis one o'clock, and past.
K. HEN. Why then, good morrow to you all, my lords.
Have you read o'er the letters that I sent you?
WAR. We have, my liege.
K. HEN. Then you perceive, the body of our kingdom,
How foul it is: what rank diseases grow,
And with what danger, near the heart of it.
WAR. It is but as a body, yet distemper'd;[a]
Which to his former strength may be restor'd,
With good advice, and little medicine:——
My lord Northumberland will soon be cool'd.
K. HEN. O God!* that one might read the book of fate,
And see the revolution of the times
Make mountains level, and the continent
(Weary of solid firmness) melt itself
Into the sea! and, other times, to see
The beachy girdle of the ocean
Too wide for Neptune's hips; how chances mock,
And changes fill the cup of alteration
With divers liquors! O, if this were seen,[b]
The happiest youth,—viewing his progress through,
What perils past, what crosses to ensue,—
Would shut the book, and sit him down and die.
'Tis not ten years gone,
Since Richard, and Northumberland, great friends,
Did feast together, and, in two years after,
Were they at wars: it is but eight years, since
This Percy was the man nearest my soul;
Who, like a brother, toil'd in my affairs,
And laid his love and life under my foot;
Yea, for my sake, even to the eyes of Richard,
Gave him defiance. But which of you was by,
(You, cousin Nevil, as I may remember,)
[*To* WARWICK.
When Richard,—with his eye brim-full of tears,
Then check'd and rated by Northumberland,—
Did speak these words, now prov'd a prophecy?
Northumberland, thou ladder, by the which
My cousin Bolingbroke ascends my throne;—
Though then, God* knows, I had no such intent;
But that necessity so bow'd the state,
That I and greatness were compell'd to kiss:——
The time shall come, thus did he follow it,
The time will come, that foul sin, gathering head,
Shall break into corruption:—so went on,
Foretelling this same time's condition,
And the division of our amity.
WAR. There is a history in all men's lives,
Figuring the nature of the times deceas'd:
The which observ'd, a man may prophesy,
With a near aim, of the main chance of things
As yet not come to life; which in their seeds,
And weak beginnings, lie intreasured.
Such things become the hatch and brood of time;
And, by the necessary form of this,
King Richard might create a perfect guess,
That great Northumberland, then false to him,
Would, of that seed, grow to a greater falseness;
Which should not find a ground to root upon,
Unless on you.
K. HEN. Are these things, then, necessities?
Then let us meet them like necessities:—
And that same word even now cries out on us.
They say, the bishop and Northumberland
Are fifty thousand strong.
WAR. It cannot be, my lord;
Rumour doth double, like the voice and echo,
The numbers of the fear'd.—Please it your grace,
To go to bed; upon my soul,† my lord,
The powers that you already have sent forth,
Shall bring this prize in very easily.
To comfort you the more, I have receiv'd
A certain instance, that Glendower is dead.
Your majesty hath been this fortnight ill;

(*) First folio, *Heaven*.

[a] Yet *distemper'd*;] That is, *now* distemper'd. See note (b), p. 346.

(*) First folio, *Heaven*. (†) First folio, *life*.

[b] O, if this were seen,—] This half-line, and the three lines that follow, are not in the folio.

And these unseason'd hours, perforce, must add
Unto your sickness.

K. HEN. I will take your counsel:
And, were these inward wars once out of hand,
We would, dear lords, unto the Holy Land.
[*Exeunt.*

SCENE II.—*Court before* JUSTICE SHALLOW'*s House in* Gloucestershire.

Enter SHALLOW *and* SILENCE, *meeting;* MOULDY, SHADOW, WART, FEEBLE, BULL-CALF, *and* Servants, *behind.*

SHAL. Come on, come on, come on: give me your hand, sir; give me your hand, sir; an early stirrer, by the rood.[a] And how doth my good cousin Silence?

SIL. Good morrow, good cousin Shallow.

SHAL. And how doth my cousin, your bed-fellow? and your fairest daughter and mine, my god-daughter Ellen?

SIL. Alas, a black ouzel, cousin Shallow.

SHAL. By yea and nay, sir, I dare say, my cousin William is become a good scholar: he is at Oxford, still, is he not?

SIL. Indeed, sir; to my cost.

SHAL. He must then to the inns of court shortly: I was once of Clement's-inn;(1) where, I think, they will talk of mad Shallow yet.

SIL. You were called lusty Shallow, then, cousin.

SHAL. By the mass,* I was called any thing; and I would have done any thing, indeed, and roundly too. There was I, and little John Doit of Staffordshire, and black George Bare, and Francis Pickbone, and Will Squele, a Cotsole man,[b]—you had not four such swinge-bucklers in all the inns of court again: and, I may say to you, we knew where the *bona-robas* were, and had the best of them all at commandment. Then was Jack Falstaff, now sir John, a boy; and page to Thomas Mowbray, duke of Norfolk.

SIL. This sir John, cousin, that comes hither anon about soldiers?

SHAL. The same sir John, the very same. I saw him break Skogan's(2) head at the court gate, when he was a crack, not thus high: and the very

---

[a] *By the* rood.] The *cross* and the *rood* are usually taken to be the same, but there is some reason to believe that in early times the *rood* properly signified the image of Christ upon the cross, and not a representation of the cross alone.

[b] A Cotsole *man*,—] Cotswold was celebrated for athletic sports in the time of our author, and, as Steevens observes, "Shallow, by distinguishing Will Squele as a Cotswold man, meant to have him understood as one who was well versed in manly exercises."

(*) First folio omits, *By the mass.*

same day did I fight with one Sampson Stockfish, a fruiterer, behind Gray's-inn. O, the mad days that I have spent! and to see how many of mine old acquaintance are dead!

SIL. We shall all follow, cousin.

SHAL. Certain, 'tis certain; very sure, very sure: death, as the Psalmist saith,* is certain to all; all shall die. How a good yoke of bullocks at Stamford fair?

SIL. Truly, cousin, I was not there.

SHAL. Death is certain.—Is old Double of your town living yet?

SIL. Dead, sir.

SHAL. Jesu, Jesu![a] dead!—he drew a good bow;—and dead!—he shot a fine shoot:—John of Gaunt loved him well, and betted much money on his head. Dead!—he would have clapped i'the clout[b] at twelve score, and carried you a forehand shaft a† fourteen and fourteen and a half, that it would have done a man's heart good to see.——How a score of ewes now?

SIL. Thereafter as they be:[c] a score of good ewes may be worth ten pounds.

SHAL. And is old Double dead?

SIL. Here come two of sir John Falstaff's men, as I think.

Enter BARDOLPH, *and one with him.*

BARD. Good morrow, honest gentlemen: I beseech you, which is justice Shallow?

SHAL. I am Robert Shallow, sir; a poor esquire of this county, and one of the king's justices of the peace: what is your good pleasure with me?

BARD. My captain, sir, commends him to you; my captain, sir John Falstaff: a tall gentleman, by heaven,‡ and a most gallant leader.

SHAL. He greets me well, sir; I knew him a good backsword man: how doth the good knight? may I ask, how my lady his wife doth?

BARD. Sir, pardon; a soldier is better accommodated, than with a wife.

SHAL. It is well said, in faith,§ sir; and it is well said indeed too. Better accommodated!—it is good; yea, indeed, is it: good phrases are surely, and ever ‖ were, very commendable. Accommodated!—it comes of *accommodo:* very good; a good phrase.

BARD. Pardon, sir; I have heard the word. *Phrase,* call you it? By this day, I know not the *phrase:* but I will maintain the word with my sword, to be a soldier-like word, and a word of exceeding good command. Accommodated; that is, when a man is, as they say, accommodated: or, when a man is,—being,—whereby,—he may be* thought to be accommodated; which is an excellent thing.

Enter FALSTAFF.

SHAL. It is very just.—Look, here comes good sir John.—Give me your hand, give me your worship's good hand: by my troth,† you look well, and bear your years very well: welcome, good sir John.

FAL. I am glad to see you well, good master Robert Shallow:—Master Sure-card, as I think.

SHAL. No, sir John; it is my cousin Silence, in commission with me.

FAL. Good master Silence, it well befits you should be of the peace.

SIL. Your good worship is welcome.

FAL. Fie! this is hot weather.—Gentlemen, have you provided me here half a dozen sufficient men?

SHAL. Marry, have we, sir. Will you sit?

FAL. Let me see them, I beseech you.

SHAL. Where's the roll? where's the roll? where's the roll?—Let me see, let me see. So, so, so, so: yea, marry, sir:—Ralph Mouldy:—let them appear as I call; let them do so, let them do so——Let me see; where is Mouldy?

MOUL. Here, an't ‡ please you.

SHAL. What think you, sir John? a good limbed fellow: young, strong, and of good friends.

FAL. Is thy name Mouldy?

MOUL. Yea, an't ‡ please you.

FAL. 'Tis the more time thou wert used.

SHAL. Ha, ha, ha! most excellent, i'faith! § things, that are mouldy, lack use: very singular good!—Well said, sir John; very well said.

FAL. Prick him. [*To* SHALLOW.

MOUL. I was pricked well enough before, an ‖ you could have let me alone: my old dame will be undone now, for one to do her husbandry, and her drudgery: you need not to have pricked me; there are other men fitter to go out than I.

FAL. Go to; peace, Mouldy, you shall go. Mouldy, it is time you were spent.

MOUL. Spent!

SHAL. Peace, fellow, peace; stand aside; know

(*) First folio omits, *as the Psalmist saith.*
(†) First folio, *at.* (‡) First folio omits, *by heaven.*
(§) First folio omits, *in faith.* (‖) First folio, *every.*

[a] Jesu, Jesu! *dead!—he drew a good bow;—*] So the quarto. The folio reads, Dead! *see, see!* he drew, &c.

[b] He would have clapped i' the clout—] Hit the nail or pin which sustained the target.

[c] Thereafter as they be:] That depends upon their quality.

(*) First folio omits, *may be.* (†) First folio, *trust me.*
(‡) First folio, *if it.* (§) First folio omits, *i'faith.*
(‖) First folio, *if.*

you where you are?—For the other, sir John:—let me see;—Simon Shadow!

Fal. Ay marry, let me have him to sit under: he's like to be a cold soldier.

Shal. Where's Shadow?

Shad. Here, sir.

Fal. Shadow, whose son art thou?

Shad. My mother's son, sir.

Fal. Thy mother's son![a] like enough; and thy father's shadow: so the son of the female is the shadow of the male: it is often so, indeed; but not much[b] of the father's substance.

Shal. Do you like him, Sir John?

Fal. Shadow will serve for summer,—prick him;—for we have a number of shadows to fill up the muster-book.

Shal. Thomas Wart!

Fal. Where's he?

Wart. Here, sir.

Fal. Is thy name Wart?

Wart. Yea, sir.

Fal. Thou art a very ragged wart.

Shal. Shall I prick him,* sir John?

Fal. It were superfluous; for his apparel is built upon his back, and the whole frame stands upon pins: prick him no more.

Shal. Ha, ha, ha!—you can do it, sir; you can do it: I commend you well.—Francis Feeble!

Fee. Here, sir.

Fal. What trade art thou, Feeble?

Fee. A woman's tailor, sir.

Shal. Shall I prick him, sir?

Fal. You may: but if he had been a man's tailor, he would have pricked you.—Wilt thou make as many holes in an enemy's battle, as thou hast done in a woman's petticoat?

Fee. I will do my good will, sir; you can have no more.

Fal. Well said, good woman's tailor! well said, courageous Feeble! Thou wilt be as valiant as the wrathful dove, or most magnanimous mouse.—Prick the woman's tailor well, master Shallow; deep, master Shallow.

Fee. I would, Wart might have gone, sir.

Fal. I would, thou wert a man's tailor; that thou might'st mend him, and make him fit to go. I cannot put him to a private soldier, that is the

---

(*) First folio adds, *down*.

a *Thy mother's son!*] Falstaff has indulged in the same quibble on *son* and *sun* in the First Part of "Henry IV." Act II. Sc. 1:—"Shall the *son* of England prove a thief," &c.

b But not much *of the father's substance.*] The quarto omits, *not*, reading,—

"But much of the father's substance."

And the folio omits *much*, both it would seem by mistake; unless *but* is to be understood in the sense of *without*, in which case the text of the quarto affords a pointed meaning.

leader of so many thousands: let that suffice, most forcible Feeble.

FEE. It shall suffice, sir.*

FAL. I am bound to thee, reverend Feeble.—Who is† next?

SHAL. Peter Bull-calf of the green!

FAL. Yea, marry, let us see Bull-calf.

BULL. Here, sir.

FAL. 'Fore God,‡ a likely fellow!—Come, prick me Bull-calf, till he roar again.

BULL. O lord!§ good my lord captain,—

FAL. What! dost thou roar before thou art pricked?

BULL. O lord,§ sir! I am a diseased man.

FAL. What disease hast thou?

BULL. A whoreson cold, sir; a cough, sir; which I caught with ringing in the king's affairs, upon his coronation day, sir.

FAL. Come, thou shalt go to the wars in a gown; we will have away thy cold; and I will take such order, that thy friends shall ring for thee.—Is here all?

SHAL. Here is two more called than your number; you must have but four here, sir;—and so, I pray you, go in with me to dinner.

FAL. Come, I will go drink with you, but I cannot tarry dinner. I am glad to see you, in good troth, master Shallow.

SHAL. O, sir John, do you remember since we lay all night in the windmill in Saint George's fields.

FAL. No more of that, good master Shallow, no more of that.

SHAL. Ha, it was a merry night. And is Jane Night-work alive?

FAL. She lives, master Shallow.

SHAL. She never could away with me.

FAL. Never, never: she would always say, she could not abide master Shallow.

SHAL. By the mass,|| I could anger her to the heart. She was then a *bona-roba*. Doth she hold her own well?

FAL. Old, old, master Shallow.

SHAL. Nay, she must be old; she cannot choose but be old; certain, she's old; and had Robin Night-work by old Night-work, before I came to Clement's-inn.

SIL. That's fifty-five year¶ ago.

SHAL. Ha, cousin Silence, that thou hadst seen that that this knight and I have seen!—Ha, sir John, said I well?

FAL. We have heard the chimes at midnight, master Shallow.

SHAL. That we have, that we have, that we have; in faith, sir John, we have; our watch-word was, *Hem, boys!* (3)—Come, let's to dinner; come, let's to dinner:—O the days that we have seen!—Come, come.

[*Exeunt* FALSTAFF, SHALLOW, *and* SILENCE.

BULL. Good master corporate Bardolph, stand my friend, and here is four Harry ten shillings in French crowns for you. In very truth, sir, I had as lief be hanged, sir, as go: and yet, for mine own part, sir, I do not care; but, rather, because I am unwilling, and for mine own part, have a desire to stay with my friends; else, sir, I did not care, for mine own part, so much.

BARD. Go to; stand aside.

MOUL. And, good master corporal captain, for my old dame's sake, stand my friend: she has nobody to do anything about her, when I am gone; and she is old, and cannot help herself: you shall have forty, sir.

BARD. Go to; stand aside.

FEE. By my troth* I care not;—a man can die but once;—we owe God† a death!—I'll ne'er bear a base mind:—an't‡ be my destiny, so; an't‡ be not, so. No man's too good to serve his prince; and, let it go which way it will, he that dies this year, is quit for the next.

BARD. Well said; thou 'rt a good fellow.

FEE. 'Faith,§ I'll bear no base mind.

Re-enter FALSTAFF, *and* Justices.

FAL. Come, sir, which men shall I have?

SHAL. Four, of which you please.

BARD. Sir, a word with you:—I have three pound[a] to free Mouldy and Bull-calf.

FAL. Go to; well.

SHAL. Come, sir John, which four will you have?

FAL. Do you choose for me.

SHAL. Marry then,—Mouldy, Bull-calf, Feeble, and Shadow.

FAL. Mouldy, and Bull-calf:—for you, Mouldy, stay at home till you are past service:—and, for your part, Bull-calf,—grow till you come unto it; I will none of you.

SHAL. Sir John, sir John, do not yourself wrong; they are your likeliest men, and I would have you served with the best.

FAL. Will you tell me, master Shallow, how to choose a man? Care I for the limb, the thews,[b] the stature, bulk, and big assemblance of a man?

(*) First folio omits, *sir*. (†) First folio inserts, *the*. (‡) First folio, *Trust me*. (§) First folio omits, *lord*. (||) First folio omits, *By the mass*. (¶) First folio, *years*.

[a] I have three pound—] Johnson pointed out the wrong computation, and suggested, what no doubt was true, that Bardolph meant to pocket a portion of the profit.

(*) First folio omits, *By my troth*. (†) First folio omits, *God*. (‡) First folio, *if it*. (§) First folio, *Nay*.

[b] *The* thews,—] Shakespeare is almost the first writer who used this word in the sense of bodily vigour; its common application of old being to manners, or qualities of the mind.

Give me the spirit, master Shallow.—Here's* Wart;—you see what a ragged appearance it is: he shall charge you, and discharge you, with the motion of a pewterer's hammer; come off, and on, swifter than he that gibbets on the brewer's bucket. And this same half-faced fellow, Shadow,—give me this man; he presents no mark to the enemy; the foeman may with as great aim level at the edge of a penknife: and, for a retreat, how swiftly will this Feeble, the woman's tailor, run off? O, give me the spare men, and spare me the great ones.—Put me a caliver[a] into Wart's hand, Bardolph.

BARD. Hold, Wart, traverse; thus, thus, thus.

FAL. Come, manage me your caliver. So:—very well:—go to:—very good:—exceeding good.—O, give me always a little, lean, old, chapped, bald shot.—Well said,[b] Wart; thou 'rt a good scab: hold, there 's a tester for thee.

SHAL. He is not his craft's master, he doth not do it right. I remember at Mile-end green, (when I lay at Clement's inn,)—I was then sir Dagonet in Arthur's show, (4) there was a little quiver[c] fellow, and 'a would manage you his piece thus: and 'a would about, and about, and come you in, and come you in: *rah, tah, tah*, would 'a say; *bounce*, would 'a say; and away again would 'a go, and again would 'a come:—I shall never see such a fellow.

FAL. These fellows will do well, Master Shallow.—God keep you,† master Silence; I will not use many words with you:—fare you well, gentlemen both: I thank you: I must a dozen mile to-night.—Bardolph, give the soldiers coats.

SHAL. Sir John, the Lord ‡ bless you, and prosper your affairs; God § send us peace! At your || return, visit my house; let our old acquaintance be renewed: peradventure, I will with you to the court.

FAL. I would you would, master Shallow.

(*) First folio, *Where's*. (†) First folio, *Farewell*.
(‡) First folio, *heaven*. (§) First folio, *and*.
(||) First folio, *As you*.

[a] A caliver—] Was a hand gun; smaller and lighter than the ordinary musket.

[b] Well said,—] This hortatory phrase, meaning "*Well done*," was very common. It occurs in Henry IV. Part I. Act IV. Sc. 4, where Falstaff exclaims to the Prince, who is engaged in combat with Hotspur:—"*Well said*, Hal! to it, Hal!" And again, in the present play, Act V. Sc. 3, where Justice Shallow encourages his man of all work, with,—"Spread, Davy; spread, Davy; *Well said*, Davy."

SHAL. Go to; I have spoke at a word. Fare you well. [*Exeunt* SHALLOW *and* SILENCE.

FAL. Fare you well, gentle gentlemen. On, Bardolph; lead the men away. [*Exeunt* BARDOLPH, Recruits, *&c.*] As I return, I will fetch off these justices: I do see the bottom of justice Shallow. Lord, lord,* how subject we old men are to this vice of lying! This same starved justice hath done nothing but prate to me of the wildness of his youth, and the feats he hath done about Turnbull street; and every third word a lie, duer paid to the hearer than the Turk's tribute. I do remember him at Clement's-inn, like a man made after supper of a cheese-paring: when he was naked, he was, for all the world, like a forked radish, with a head fantastically carved upon it with a knife: he was so forlorn, that his dimensions to any thick sight were invisible: † he was the very genius of famine;[d] yet lecherous as a monkey, and the whores call'd him—mandrake: he came ever in the rearward of the fashion; and sung those tunes to the over-scutched huswifes that he heard the carmen whistle, and sware—they were his *fancies*, or his *good-nights*.[e] And now is this Vice's dagger (5) become a squire; and talks as familiarly of John of Gaunt, as if he had been sworn brother to him: and I 'll be sworn he never saw him, but once in the Tilt-yard; and then he burst[f] his head, for crowding among the marshal's men. I saw it; and told John of Gaunt, he beat his own name: for you might have trussed him, and all his apparel, into an eel-skin; the case of a treble hautboy was a mansion for him, a court; and now hath he land and beeves. Well; I will be acquainted with him, if I return: and it shall go hard, but I will make him a philosopher's two stones to me. If the young dace be a bait for the old pike, I see no reason, in the law of nature, but I may snap at him. Let time shape, and there an end. [*Exit.*

(*) First folio omits, *Lord, lord*. (†) Old text, *invincible*.

[c] *A little* quiver *fellow*,—] *Quiver* meant *smart, nimble*.

[d] The very genius of famine;] The folio omitting the intermediate lines, reads,—"he was the very Genius of famine: he came ever in the rearward of the fashion: And now is this Vice's dagger," &c.

[e] *His* fancies, *or his* good-nights.] Slight lyrical pieces were by the old poets sometimes called their "*Fancies*," or "*Good-nights*."

[f] Burst *his head*,—] To *burst* was to *break*. Thus in "The Taming of the Shrew," Induction, Sc. 1,—"You will not pay for the glasses you have *burst*?"

ACT IV.

SCENE I.—*A Forest in* Yorkshire.

Enter the ARCHBISHOP OF YORK, MOWBRAY, HASTINGS, *and others.*

ARCH. What is this forest call'd?

HAST. 'Tis Gaultree forest, an't shall please your grace.

ARCH. Here stand, my lords; and send discoverers forth,
To know the numbers of our enemies.

HAST. We have sent forth already.

ARCH. 'Tis well done.
My friends and brethren in these great affairs,
I must acquaint you that I have receiv'd
New-dated letters from Northumberland;
Their cold intent, tenor and substance, thus:—
Here doth he wish his person, with such powers
As might hold sortance with his quality,
The which he could not levy; whereupon

He is retir'd, to ripe his growing fortunes,
To Scotland; and concludes in hearty prayers,
That your attempts may overlive the hazard,
And fearful meeting of their opposite.[a]

MOWB. Thus do the hopes we have in him touch ground,
And dash themselves to pieces.

Enter a Messenger.

HAST. Now, what news?

MESS. West of this forest, scarcely off a mile,
In goodly form comes on the enemy: [number
And, by the ground they hide, I judge their
Upon, or near, the rate of thirty thousand. [out.

MOWB. The just proportion that we gave them
Let us sway on, and face them in the field.

ARCH. What well-appointed leader fronts us here?

MOWB. I think, it is my lord of Westmoreland.

Enter WESTMORELAND.

WEST. Health and fair greeting from our general,
The prince, lord John and duke of Lancaster.

ARCH. Say on, my lord of Westmoreland, in peace;
What doth concern your coming?

WEST. Then, my lord,
Unto your grace do I in chief address
The substance of my speech. If that rebellion
Came like itself, in base and abject routs,
Led on by bloody youth, guarded with rags,[b]
And countenanc'd by boys, and beggary;
I say, if damn'd commotion so appear'd,*
In his true, native, and most proper shape,
You, reverend father, and these noble lords,
Had not been here, to dress the ugly form
Of base and bloody insurrection
With your fair honours. You, lord archbishop,—
Whose see is by a civil peace maintain'd;
Whose beard the silver hand of peace hath touch'd;
Whose learning and good letters peace hath tutor'd;
Whose white investments figure innocence,
The dove and very blessed spirit of peace,—
Wherefore do you so ill translate yourself,
Out of the speech of peace, that bears such grace,
Into the harsh and boist'rous tongue of war?
Turning your books to greaves,[c] your ink to blood,
Your pens to lances; and your tongue divine
To a loud trumpet, and a point of war?[d] [stands.

ARCH. Wherefore do I this?—so the question
Briefly, to this end:—We are all diseas'd;[e]
And, with our surfeiting, and wanton hours,
Have brought ourselves into a burning fever,
And we must bleed for it: of which disease
Our late king, Richard, being infected, died.
But, my most noble lord of Westmoreland,
I take not on me here as a physician;
Nor do I, as an enemy to peace,
Troop in the throngs of military men:
But, rather, show awhile like fearful war,
To diet rank minds, sick of happiness;
And purge the obstructions, which begin to stop
Our very veins of life. Hear me more plainly;
I have in equal balance justly weigh'd [suffer,
What wrongs our arms may do, what wrongs we
And find our griefs heavier than our offences.
We see which way the stream of time doth run,
And are enforc'd from our most quiet there[f]
By the rough torrent of occasion:
And have the summary of all our griefs,
When time shall serve, to show in articles;
Which, long ere this, we offer'd to the king,
And might by no suit gain our audience:
When we are wrong'd, and would unfold our griefs,
We are denied access unto his person,
Even by those men that most have done us wrong.
The dangers of the days but newly gone,
(Whose memory is written on the earth
With yet-appearing blood,) and the examples
Of every minute's instance, (present now,)
Hath put us in these ill-beseeming arms:
Not to break peace, or any branch of it,
But to establish here a peace, indeed,
Concurring both in name and quality.

WEST. When ever yet was your appeal denied?
Wherein have you been galled by the king?
What peer hath been suborn'd to grate on you?
That you should seal this lawless bloody book
Of forg'd rebellion with a seal divine,
And consecrate commotion's bitter edge?[g]

ARCH. My brother general, the commonwealth,
To brother born an household cruelty,[h]
I make my quarrel in particular.

(*) Old text, *appear*.

[a] Opposite.] That is, *adversary, opponent*.

[b] *Guarded with* rags,—] The old text has "guarded with *rage*;" the emendation is due to Mr. Collier's MS. annotator.

[c] Turning your books to greaves,—] *Greaves* are leather, or other armour for the legs. The old copies have *graves*, which was only a more ancient mode of spelling the word.

[d] A point of war?] Mr. Collier's annotator, in strange ignorance of a most familiar expression, reads:—

"A loud trumpet and *report of war*;"

with what necessity and propriety may be judged from the following, out of a hundred instances which might be adduced, of the use of the phrase in our old writers:—

"To play him hunt's up, with a *point of war*."—
GREENE'S *Orlando Furioso*, Dyce's Ed. p. 19.

"Sound proudly here a perfect *point of war*."—
PEELE'S *Edward 1st*, 1593, Act I. Sc. 1.

"Sa, sa, sa! Now sound *a point of war*."—
The Duke's Mistress, by Shirley, Act IV. Sc. 1.

[e] We are all diseas'd;] The remainder of this speech, excepting the last eight lines, is omitted in the quarto.

[f] *Quiet* there—] The old text. Warburton suggested we should read, *sphere*.

[g] And consecrate commotion's bitter edge?] This line is omitted in the folio.

[h] To brother born an household cruelty,—] Another line, omitted in the folio.

WEST. There is no need of any such redress ;
Or, if there were, it not belongs to you.
MOWB. Why not to him, in part, and to us all,
That feel the bruises of the days before,
And suffer the condition of these times
To lay a heavy and unequal hand
Upon our honours ?[a]
WEST. O my good lord Mowbray,
Construe the times to their necessities,
And you shall say indeed,—it is the time,
And not the king, that doth you injuries.
Yet, for your part, it not appears to me,
Either from the king, or in the present time,
That you should have an inch of any ground
To build a grief on. Were you not restor'd
To all the duke of Norfolk's seigniories,
Your noble and right-well-remember'd father's ?
MOWB. What thing, in honour, had my father lost,
That need to be reviv'd, and breath'd in me ?
The king, that lov'd him, as the state stood then,
Was, force* perforce, compell'd to banish him :
And then, that Harry Bolingbroke, and he,—
Being mounted, and both roused in their seats,
Their neighing coursers daring of the spur,
Their armed staves in charge, their beavers down,
Their eyes of fire sparkling through sights[b] of steel,
And the loud trumpet blowing them together,
Then, then—when there was nothing could have stay'd
My father from the breast of Bolingbroke,—
O, when[c] the king did throw his warder down,
(His own life hung upon the staff he threw)
Then threw he down himself, and all their lives,
That, by indictment, and by dint of sword,
Have since miscarried under Bolingbroke.
WEST. You speak, lord Mowbray, now, you know not what :
The earl of Hereford was reputed then
In England the most valiant gentleman ;
Who knows, on whom fortune would then have smil'd?
But, if your father had been victor there,
He ne'er had borne it out of Coventry :
For all the country, in a general voice,
Cried hate upon him ; and all their prayers, and [love,
Were set on Hereford, whom they doted on,
And bless'd, and grac'd indeed,[d] more than the king.
But this is mere digression from my purpose.—
Here come I from our princely general,
To know your griefs ; to tell you from his grace,
That he will give you audience : and wherein
It shall appear that your demands are just,
You shall enjoy them ; every thing set off,
That might so much as think you enemies.
MOWB. But he hath forc'd us to compel this offer ;
And it proceeds from policy, not love.
WEST. Mowbray, you overween, to take it so ;
This offer comes from mercy, not from fear :
For, lo ! within a ken, our army lies ;
Upon mine honour, all too confident
To give admittance to a thought of fear.
Our battle is more full of names than yours,
Our men more perfect in the use of arms,
Our armour all as strong, our cause the best ;
Then reason wills,* our hearts should be as good :—
Say you not then our offer is compell'd.
MOWB. Well, by my will, we shall admit no parley.
WEST. That argues but the shame of your [offence :
A rotten case abides no handling.
HAST. Hath the prince John a full commission,
In very ample virtue of his father,
To hear, and absolutely to determine
Of what conditions we shall stand upon ?
WEST. That is intended[e] in the general's name :
I muse you make so slight a question.
ARCH. Then take, my lord of Westmoreland, this schedule,
For this contains our general grievances :—
Each several article herein redress'd ;
All members of our cause, both here and hence,
That are insinew'd to this action,
Acquitted by a true substantial form ;
And present execution of our wills
To us, and to our purposes, confirm'd ; †—
We come within our awful banks again,
And knit our powers to the arm of peace.
WEST. This will I show the general. Please you, lords,
In sight of both our battles we may meet :
And ‡ either end in peace, which God § so frame !
Or to the place of difference call the swords
Which must decide it.
ARCH. My lord, we will do so.
[*Exit* WEST.
MOWB. There is a thing within my bosom tells me,
That no conditions of our peace can stand.
HAST. Fear you not that : if we can make our [peace

(*) Old text, *forc'd*.

(*) Old text, *will*. (†) Old text, *confin'd*.
(‡) Old text, *At*. (§) First folio, *Heaven*.

[a] Upon our honours ?] The next two speeches, and the first ten lines of the third speech, are omitted in the quarto.

[b] Sights of steel,—] The apertures for seeing through in a helmet.

[c] When—] By reading here, "O *then* the king," &c.—and a few lines above—"And *when*, that Harry Bolingbroke," &c., the whole speech is so infinitely improved, that it is difficult to believe the words *when* and *then* were not mistakenly transposed by the compositor.

[d] Indeed,—] In the old text "*and did*." The emendation, which is easy and probable, was suggested by Thirlby.

[e] Intended—] That is, *implied*, or *understood*.

Upon such large terms, and so absolute,
As our conditions shall consist upon,
Our peace shall stand as firm as rocky mountains.

MOWB. Ay, but our valuation shall be such,
That every slight and false-derived cause,
Yea, every idle, nice, and wanton reason,
Shall, to the king, taste of this action:
That, were our royal faiths martyrs in love,
We shall be winnow'd with so rough a wind,
That even our corn shall seem as light as chaff,
And good from bad find no partition.

ARCH. No, no, my lord; note this,—the king is weary
Of dainty and such picking grievances:
For he hath found,—to end one doubt by death,
Revives two greater in the heirs of life.
And therefore will he wipe his tables clean,
And keep no tell-tale to his memory,
That may repeat and history his loss
To new remembrance: for full well he knows,
He cannot so precisely weed this land,
As his misdoubts present occasion:
His foes are so enrooted with his friends,
That, plucking to unfix an enemy,
He doth unfasten so, and shake a friend.
So that this land, like an offensive wife,
That hath enrag'd him on to offer strokes,
As he is striking, holds his infant up,
And hangs resolv'd correction in the arm
That was uprear'd to execution.

HAST. Besides, the king hath wasted all his rods
On late offenders, that he now doth lack
The very instruments of chastisement:
So that his power, like to a fangless lion,
May offer, but not hold.

ARCH. 'Tis very true;—
And therefore be assur'd, my good lord marshal,
If we do now make our atonement well,
Our peace will, like a broken limb united,
Grow stronger for the breaking.

MOWB. Be it so.
Here is return'd my lord of Westmoreland.

Re-enter WESTMORELAND.

WEST. The prince is here at hand: pleaseth your lordship,
To meet his grace just distance 'tween our armies?

MOWB. Your grace of York, in God's* name then set† forward.

ARCH. Before, and greet his grace:—my lord, we come. [*Exeunt.*

SCENE II.—*Another Part of the Forest.*

Enter from one side MOWBRAY, *the* ARCHBISHOP, HASTINGS, *and others; from the other side,* PRINCE JOHN *of* LANCASTER, WESTMORELAND, Officers, *and* Attendants.

P. JOHN. You are well encounter'd here, my cousin Mowbray:—
Good day to you, gentle lord archbishop;—
And so to you, lord Hastings,—and to all.—
My lord of York, it better show'd with you,
When that your flock, assembled by the bell,
Encircled you, to hear with reverence
Your exposition on the holy text;
Than now to see you here an iron man,
Cheering a rout of rebels with your drum,
Turning the word to sword, and life to death.
That man, that sits within a monarch's heart,
And ripens in the sunshine of his favour,
Would he abuse the countenance of the king,
Alack, what mischiefs might he set abroach,
In shadow of such greatness! with you, lord bishop,
It is even so.—Who hath not heard it spoken,
How deep you were within the books of God?*
To us, the speaker in His parliament;
To us, the imagin'd† voice of heaven itself.
The very opener, and intelligencer,
Between the grace, the sanctities of heaven,
And our dull workings: O, who shall believe,
But you misuse the reverence of your place;
Employ the countenance and grace of heaven,
As a false favourite doth his prince's name,
In deeds dishonourable? You have taken up,
Under the counterfeited seal[a] of God,*
The subjects of His* substitute, my father;
And, both against the peace of heaven and him,
Have here up-swarm'd them.

ARCH. Good my lord of Lancaster,
I am not here against your father's peace:
But, as I told my lord of Westmoreland,
The time misorder'd doth, in common sense,
Crowd us, and crush us, to this monstrous form,
To hold our safety up. I sent your grace
The parcels and particulars of our grief,
The which hath been with scorn shov'd from the court:
Whereon this Hydra-son of war is born,
Whose dangerous eyes may well be charm'd asleep,
With grant of our most just and right desires;
And true obedience, of this madness cur'd,
Stoop tamely to the foot of majesty.

MOWB. If not, we ready are to try our fortunes
To the last man.

(*) First folio, *Heaven's*. (†) First folio omits, *set*.

(*) First folio, *heaven*. (†) Old text, *imagine*.

[a] Seal of God,—] The old text has *zeal*, a misprint, first corrected, we believe, by Mr. Collier's annotator.

HAST. And though we here fall down,
We have supplies to second our attempt;
If they miscarry, theirs shall second them,
And so, success of mischief shall be born,
And heir from heir shall hold this quarrel up,
Whiles England shall have generation.
P. JOHN. You are too shallow, Hastings, much too shallow,
To sound the bottom of the after-times.

WEST. Pleaseth your grace, to answer them directly,
How far-forth you do like their articles?
P. JOHN. I like them all, and do allow them well:
And swear here by the honour of my blood,
My father's purposes have been mistook;
And some about him have too lavishly
Wrested his meaning, and authority.—
My lord, these griefs shall be with speed redress'd;

Upon my soul,* they shall. If this may please you,
Discharge your powers unto their several counties,
As we will ours; and here, between the armies,
Let's drink together friendly, and embrace;
That all their eyes may bear those tokens home,
Of our restored love and amity.

ARCH. I take your princely word for these redresses.

P. JOHN. I give it you, and will maintain my word;
And thereupon I drink unto your grace.

HAST. Go, captain, [*To an* Officer.] and deliver to the army
This news of peace; let them have pay, and part:
I know, it will well please them; hie thee, captain.
[*Exit* Officer.

ARCH. To you, my noble lord of Westmoreland.

WEST. I pledge your grace: and, if you knew what pains
I have bestow'd, to breed this present peace,
You would drink freely: but my love to ye
Shall show itself more openly hereafter.

ARCH. I do not doubt you.

WEST. I am glad of it.—
Health to my lord, and gentle cousin, Mowbray.

MOWB. You wish me health in very happy season;
For I am, on the sudden, something ill.

ARCH. Against ill chances, men are ever merry;
But heaviness fore-runs the good event.

WEST. Therefore be merry, coz; since sudden sorrow
Serves to say thus,—Some good thing comes to-morrow.

ARCH. Believe me, I am passing light in spirit.

MOWB. So much the worse, if your own rule be true. [*Shouts without.*

P. JOHN. The word of peace is render'd; hark, how they shout!

MOWB. This had been cheerful, after victory.

ARCH. A peace is of the nature of a conquest;
For then both parties nobly are subdued,
And neither party loser.

P. JOHN. Go, my lord,
And let our army be discharged too.
[*Exit* WESTMORELAND.
And, good my lord, so please you, let our trains
March by us; that we may peruse the men
We should have cop'd withal.

ARCH. Go, good lord Hastings,
And ere they be dismiss'd, let them march by.
[*Exit* HASTINGS.

P. JOHN. I trust, lords, we shall lie to-night together.—

Re-enter WESTMORELAND.

Now, cousin, wherefore stands our army still?

WEST. The leaders, having charge from you to stand,
Will not go off until they hear you speak.

P. JOHN. They know their duties.

Re-enter HASTINGS.

HAST. My lord,* our army is dispers'd already:
Like youthful steers unyok'd, they take their courses†
East, west, north, south; or, like a school broke up,
Each hurries toward his home, and sporting-place.

WEST. Good tidings, my lord Hastings; for the which
I do arrest thee, traitor, of high treason:— (1)
And you, lord archbishop,—and you, lord Mowbray,—
Of capital treason I attach you both.

MOWB. Is this proceeding just and honourable?

WEST. Is your assembly so?

ARCH. Will you thus break your faith?

P. JOHN. I pawn'd thee none:
I promis'd you redress of these same grievances,
Whereof you did complain; which, by mine honour,
I will perform with a most Christian care.
But, for you, rebels,—look to taste the due
Meet for rebellion, and such acts as yours.
Most shallowly did you these arms commence,
Fondly brought here, and foolishly sent hence.—
Strike up our drums, pursue the scatter'd stray;
God,‡ and not we, hath§ safely fought to-day.—
Some guard these traitors to the block of death;
Treason's true bed, and yielder up of breath.
[*Exeunt.*

SCENE III.—*Another Part of the Forest.*

Alarums. Excursions. Enter FALSTAFF *and* COLEVILE, *meeting.*

FAL. What's your name, sir? of what condition are you; and of what place, I pray?

COLE. I am a knight, sir; and my name is Colevile of the dale.

FAL. Well then, Colevile is your name; a knight is your degree; and your place, the dale, Colevile shall still be your name; a traitor your degree; and the dungeon your place,—a place[a] deep enough; so shall you be still Colevile of the dale.

COLE. Are not you sir John Falstaff?

(*) First folio, *life.*

[a] A place *deep enough;*] We should perhaps read, as Tyrwhitt suggested, "a *dale* deep enough."

(*) First folio omits, *my lord,* and *already.*
(†) First folio, *took their course.*
(‡) First folio, *Heaven.* (§) First folio, *have.*

FAL. As good a man as he, sir, whoe'er I am. Do ye yield, sir? or shall I sweat for you? If I do sweat, they are the drops of thy lovers, and they weep for thy death: therefore rouse up fear and trembling, and do observance to my mercy.

COLE. I think you are sir John Falstaff; and, in that thought, yield me.

FAL. I have a whole school of tongues in this belly of mine; and not a tongue of them all speaks any other word but my name. An I had but a belly of any indifferency, I were simply the most active fellow in Europe: my womb, my womb, my womb undoes me.—Here comes our general. [*A Retreat sounded.*

Enter PRINCE JOHN *of* LANCASTER, WESTMORELAND, *and others.*

P. JOHN. The heat is past, follow no further now;—
Call in the powers, good cousin Westmoreland.— [*Exit* WEST.
Now, Falstaff, where have you been all this while?
When every thing is ended, then you come:—
These tardy tricks of yours will, on my life,
One time or other break some gallows' back.

FAL. I would be sorry, my lord, but it should be thus: I never knew yet, but rebuke and check was the reward of valour. Do you think me a swallow, an arrow, or a bullet? have I, in my poor and old motion, the expedition of thought? I have speeded hither with the very extremest inch of possibility; I have foundered nine-score and odd posts: and here, travel-tainted as I am, have, in my pure and immaculate valour, taken sir John Colevile of the dale, a most furious knight, and valorous enemy: but what of that? he saw me, and yielded; that I may justly say with the hook-nosed fellow of Rome,——I came, saw, and overcame.

P. JOHN. It was more of his courtesy than your deserving.

FAL. I know not; here he is, and here I yield him; and I beseech your grace, let it be booked with the rest of this day's deeds; or, by the lord,* I will have it in a particular ballad else,† with mine own picture on the top of it, Colevile kissing my foot: to the which course if I be enforced, if you do not all show like gilt two-pences to me; and I, in the clear sky of fame, o'ershine you as much as the full moon doth the cinders of the element, which show like pins' heads to her, believe not the word of the noble: therefore let me have right, and let desert mount.

P. JOHN. Thine's too heavy to mount.

FAL. Let it shine then.

P. JOHN. Thine's too thick to shine.

FAL. Let it do something, my good lord, that may do me good, and call it what you will.

P. JOHN. Is thy name Colevile?

COLE. It is, my lord.

P. JOHN. A famous rebel art thou, Colevile.

FAL. And a famous true subject took him.

COLE. I am, my lord, but as my betters are,
That led me hither: had they been rul'd by me,
You should have won them dearer than you have.

FAL. I know not how they sold themselves, but thou, like a kind fellow, gavest thyself away gratis;* and I thank thee for thee.

Re-enter WESTMORELAND.

P. JOHN. Now,† have you left pursuit?

WEST. Retreat is made, and execution stay'd.

P. JOHN. Send Colevile, with his confederates,
To York, to present execution:—
Blunt, lead him hence; and see you guard him sure. [*Exeunt some with* COLEVILE.
And now despatch we toward the court, my lords;
I hear, the king my father is sore sick:
Our news shall go before us to his majesty,—
Which, cousin, you shall bear,—to comfort him;
And we with sober speed will follow you.

FAL. My lord, I beseech you, give me leave to go through Gloucestershire; and, when you come to court, stand my good lord,[a] pray, in your good report.

P. JOHN. Fare you well, Falstaff: I, in my condition,[b]
Shall better speak of you than you deserve. [*Exit.*

FAL. I would you had but the wit; 'twere better than your dukedom.—Good faith, this same young sober-blooded boy doth not love me; nor a man cannot make him laugh;—but that's no marvel, he drinks no wine. There's never any of these demure boys come to any proof; for thin drink doth so over-cool their blood, and making many fish-meals, that they fall into a kind of male green sickness; and then, when they marry, they get wenches: they are generally fools and cowards;—which some of us should be too, but for inflammation. A good sherris-sack (2) hath a two-fold operation in it. It ascends me into the brain; dries me there all the foolish, and dull, and crudy vapours which environ it: makes it apprehensive, quick, forgetive,[c] full of nimble, fiery, and delectable shapes; which delivered o'er to the

(*) First folio, *I swear*. (†) First folio omits, *else*.

(*) First folio omits, *gratis*. (†) First folio omits, *Now*.

a Stand my good lord,—] Be my *good friend* or *advocate*.

b *I, in my* condition,—] *Condition* seems used here in the sense of *official statement*, "In my report I shall speak better of you than you deserve," although we remember no other instance of its being so employed.

c Forgetive,—] *Inventive, imaginative.*

voice, (the tongue,)[a] which is the birth, becomes excellent wit. The second property of your excellent sherris is,—the warming of the blood; which, before cold and settled, left the liver white and pale, which is the badge of pusillanimity and cowardice: but the sherris warms it, and makes it course from the inwards to the parts extreme.* It illumineth† the face; which, as a beacon, gives warning to all the rest of this little kingdom, man, to arm; and then the vital commoners, and inland petty spirits, muster me all to their captain, the heart, who, great, and puffed up with his retinue, doth any deed of courage; and this valour comes of sherris. So that skill in the weapon is nothing without sack, for that sets it a-work; and learning, a mere hoard of gold kept by a devil,[b] till sack commences it, and sets it in act and use. Hereof comes it, that prince Harry is valiant; for the cold blood he did naturally inherit of his father, he hath, like lean, steril, and bare land, manured, husbanded, and tilled, with excellent endeavour of drinking good, and good store of fertile sherris; that he is become very hot, and valiant. If I had a thousand sons, the first human‡ principle I would teach them, should be,—to forswear thin potations, and to addict themselves to sack.

Enter BARDOLPH.

How now, Bardolph?

BARD. The army is discharged all, and gone.

FAL. Let them go. I'll through Gloucestershire; and there will I visit master Robert Shallow, esquire: I have him already tempering between my finger and my thumb, and shortly will I seal with him. Come away. [*Exeunt.*

SCENE IV.—Westminster. *A Room in the Palace.*

Enter KING HENRY, CLARENCE, PRINCE HUMPHREY, WARWICK, *and others.*

K. HEN. Now, lords, if God§ doth give successful end
To this debate that bleedeth at our doors,
We will our youth lead on to higher fields,
And draw no swords but what are sanctified.
Our navy is address'd,[c] our power collected,
Our substitutes in absence well invested,
And every thing lies level to our wish:
Only, we want a little personal strength;
And pause us, till these rebels, now a-foot,
Come underneath the yoke of government.

WAR. Both which, we doubt not but your majesty
Shall soon enjoy.

K. HEN. Humphrey, my son of Gloster,
Where is the prince your brother?

P. HUMPH. I think, he's gone to hunt, my lord, at Windsor.

K. HEN. And how accompanied?

P. HUMPH. I do not know, my lord.

K. HEN. Is not his brother, Thomas of Clarence, with him?

P. HUMPH. No, my good lord; he is in presence here.

CLA. What would my lord and father?

K. HEN. Nothing but well to thee, Thomas of Clarence.
How chance, thou art not with the prince thy brother?
He loves thee, and thou dost neglect him, Thomas;
Thou hast a better place in his affection,
Than all thy brothers: cherish it, my boy;
And noble offices thou may'st effect,
Of mediation, after I am dead,
Between his greatness and thy other brethren:
Therefore, omit him not; blunt not his love:
Nor lose the good advantage of his grace,
By seeming cold, or careless of his will,
For he is gracious, if he be observ'd;[d]
He hath a tear for pity, and a hand
Open as day, for melting charity:
Yet notwithstanding, being incens'd, he's flint;
As humorous as winter, and as sudden
As flaws congealed in the spring of day.
His temper, therefore, must be well observ'd:
Chide him for faults, and do it reverently,
When you perceive his blood inclin'd to mirth.
But, being moody, give him line and scope,
Till that his passions, like a whale on ground,
Confound themselves with working. Learn this, Thomas,
And thou shalt prove a shelter to thy friends;
A hoop of gold, to bind thy brothers in,
That the united vessel of their blood,
Mingled with venom of suggestion,
(As, force perforce, the age will pour it in,)
Shall never leak, though it do work as strong
As aconitum, or rash gunpowder.

CLA. I shall observe him with all care and love.

K. HEN. Why art thou not at Windsor with him, Thomas?

CLA. He is not there to-day; he dines in London.

K. HEN. And how accompanied? can'st thou tell that?

(*) Old text, *extremes.* (†) First folio, *illuminateth.*
(‡) First folio omits, *human.* (§) First folio, *heaven.*

[a] The voice, (the tongue,)—] *Tongue* was, possibly, only an interlineation, the poet not having determined whether to adopt "*voice*" or "*tongue.*"

[b] Kept by a devil,—] It was superstitiously believed formerly that mines of gold were guarded by evil spirits.

[c] Address'd,—] *Prepared.* See note (a), p. 412.

[d] *If he be* observ'd;] That is, respectfully treated.

CLA. With Poins, and other his continual followers.

K. HEN. Most subject is the fattest soil to weeds,
And he, the noble image of my youth,
Is over-spread with them: therefore my grief
Stretches itself beyond the hour of death.
The blood weeps from my heart, when I do shape,
In forms imaginary, the unguided days,
And rotten times, that you shall look upon
When I am sleeping with my ancestors.
For when his headstrong riot hath no curb,
When rage and hot blood are his counsellors,
When means and lavish manners meet together,
O, with what wings shall his affections fly
Towards fronting peril and oppos'd decay!

WAR. My gracious lord, you look beyond him quite:
The prince but studies his companions,
Like a strange tongue; wherein, to gain the language,
'T is needful, that the most immodest word
Be look'd upon, and learn'd; which once attain'd,
Your highness knows, comes to no further use,
But to be known, and hated.[a] So, like gross terms,
The prince will, in the perfectness of time,
Cast off his followers; and their memory
Shall as a pattern or a measure live,
By which his grace must mete the lives of others,
Turning past evils to advantages.

K. HEN. 'T is seldom-when[b] the bee doth leave her comb
In the dead carrion.—Who's here? Westmoreland?

[a] But to be known, and hated.—] This is very like a passage in Terence:—

"——— quo modo adolescentulus
Meretricum ingenia et mores posset noscere,
Mature ut cum cognovit, perpetuo oderit."

[b] Seldom-when:—] This is usually printed "seldom, when." Mr. Singer first suggested that it was a compound word, signifying *rarely, not often*.

Enter WESTMORELAND.

WEST. Health to my sovereign! and new happiness
Added to that that I am to deliver!
Prince John, your son, doth kiss your grace's hand:
Mowbray, the bishop Scroop, Hastings, and all,
Are brought to the correction of your law;
There is not now a rebel's sword unsheath'd,
But peace puts forth her olive everywhere.
The manner how this action hath been borne,
Here, at more leisure, may your highness read,
With every course, in his particular.

K. HEN. O Westmoreland, thou art a summer bird,
Which ever in the haunch of winter sings
The lifting up of day. Look! here's more news.

Enter HARCOURT.

HAR. From enemies heaven keep your majesty;
And, when they stand against you, may they fall
As those that I am come to tell you of!
The earl Northumberland, and the lord Bardolph,
With a great power of English, and of Scots,
Are by the shrieve* of Yorkshire overthrown:
The manner and true order of the fight,
This packet, please it you, contains at large.

K. HEN. And wherefore should these good news make me sick?
Will fortune never come with both hands full,
But write her fair words still in foulest letters?[a]
She either gives a stomach, and no food,—
Such are the poor, in health: or else a feast,
And takes away the stomach,—such are the rich,
That have abundance, and enjoy it not.
I should rejoice now at this happy news,
And now my sight fails, and my brain is giddy:—
O me! come near me, now I am much ill.
[*Swoons*

(*) First folio, *sheriff*.

a But write her fair words still in foulest letters?] The quarto reads:—
"But *wet* her faire words still in foulest *termes*."

P. HUMPH. Comfort, your majesty!
CLA. O my royal father!
WEST. My sovereign lord, cheer up yourself, look up! [fits
WAR. Be patient, princes; you do know, these
Are with his highness very ordinary.
Stand from him, give him air; he'll straight be well. [pangs:
CLA. No, no; he cannot long hold out these
The incessant care and labour of his mind
Hath wrought the mure,[a] that should confine it in,
So thin, that life looks through, and will break out.
P. HUMPH. The people fear me;[b] for they do observe[c]
Unfather'd heirs,(3) and loathly births of nature:
The seasons change their manners, as the year[d]
Had found some months asleep, and leap'd them over. [between;
CLA. The river hath thrice flow'd, no ebb
And the old folk, time's doting chronicles,
Say, it did so, a little time before
That our great grandsire, Edward, sick'd and died.
WAR. Speak lower, princes, for the king recovers. [end.
P. HUMPH. This apoplexy will, certain, be his
K. HEN. I pray you, take me up, and bear me hence
Into some other chamber; softly, pray.
[*They convey the* KING *to an inner part of the room, and place him on a bed.*
Let there be no noise made, my gentle friends;
Unless some dull[e] and favourable hand
Will whisper music to my weary spirit.
WAR. Call for the music in the other room.
K. HEN. Set me the crown upon my pillow here.
CLA. His eye is hollow, and he changes much.
WAR. Less noise, less noise.

Enter PRINCE HENRY.

P. HEN. Who saw the duke of Clarence?
CLA. I am here, brother, full of heaviness.
P. HEN. How now! rain within doors, and none abroad!
How doth the king?
P. HUMPH. Exceeding ill.
P. HEN. Heard he the good news yet?
Tell it him. [it.
P. HUMPH. He alter'd much upon the hearing
P. HEN. If he be sick with joy,
He will recover without physic.
WAR. Not so much noise, my lords:—sweet prince, speak low;
The king your father is dispos'd to sleep.
CLA. Let us withdraw into the other room.
WAR. Will't please your grace to go along with us?
P. HEN. No; I will sit and watch here by the king. [*Exeunt all but* PRINCE HENRY.
Why doth the crown lie there upon his pillow,
Being so troublesome a bedfellow?
O polish'd perturbation! golden care!
That keep'st the ports of slumber open wide
To many a watchful night!—sleep with it now!
Yet not so sound, and half so deeply sweet,
As he, whose brow, with homely biggin[f] bound,
Snores out the watch of night. O majesty!
When thou dost pinch thy bearer, thou dost sit
Like a rich armour worn in heat of day,
That scalds with safety. By his gates of breath
There lies a downy feather, which stirs not:
Did he suspire, that light and weightless down
Perforce must move.—My gracious lord! my father!—
This sleep is sound indeed; this is a sleep,
That from this golden rigol[g] hath divorc'd
So many English kings. Thy due, from me,
Is tears, and heavy sorrows of the blood;
Which nature, love, and filial tenderness,
Shall, O dear father, pay thee plenteously:
My due, from thee, is this imperial crown,
Which, as immediate from thy place and blood,
Derives itself to me. Lo, here it sits,—
[*Putting it on his head.*
Which God* shall guard; and put the world's whole strength
Into one giant arm, it shall not force
This lineal honour from me. This from thee
Will I to mine leave, as 'tis left to me. [*Exit.*
K. HEN. Warwick! Gloster! Clarence!

Re-enter WARWICK, *and the rest.*

CLA. Doth the king call?
WAR. What would your majesty? How fares your grace?
K. HEN. Why did you leave me here alone, my lords?
CLA. We left the prince my brother here, my liege,
Who undertook to sit and watch by you.

---

a *Hath* wrought *the* mure,—] Hath worn the wall, &c. Daniel, in his "Civil Wars," 1595, Book III. st. 116, referring to the sickness of Henry the Fourth, has a parallel thought:—

"Wearing the wall so thin, that now the mind
Might well look thorough, and his frailtie find."

b *The people* fear *me;*] The people alarm me, make me afraid.

(*) First folio, *heaven.*

c Observe—] That is, *reverence.*
d As the year—] As *if* the year.
e *Some* dull—] *Dull* here appears to signify, *quiet, soft.*
f *Homely* biggin—] *Biggin* was a coif, so named, according to Steevens, from the cap worn by an order of nuns, called *Beguines.*
g Rigol—] A word thought peculiar to Shakespeare, signifying a *round* or *circle.*

K. Hen. The prince of Wales? where is he? let me see him:
He is not here.*

War. This door is open; he is gone this way.

P. Humph. He came not through the chamber where we stay'd.

K. Hen. Where is the crown? who took it from my pillow?

(*) First folio omits, *he is not here.*

War. When we withdrew, my liege, we left it here.

K. Hen. The prince hath ta'en it hence:—go, [seek him out.
Is he so hasty, that he doth suppose
My sleep my death?——
Find him, my lord of Warwick; chide him hither.
[*Exit* Warwick.
This part of his conjoins with my disease,
And helps to end me.—See, sons, what things you are!

How quickly nature falls into revolt,
When gold becomes her object!
For this, the foolish over-careful fathers
Have broke their sleep* with thought, their brains with care,
Their bones with industry;
For this, they have engrossed and pil'd up
The canker'd heaps of strange-achieved gold;
For this they have been thoughtful to invest
Their sons with arts, and martial exercises:
When, like the bee, culling from every flower
The virtuous sweets;
Our thighs packed with wax, our mouths with honey,
We bring it to the hive; and, like the bees,
Are murder'd for our pains. This bitter taste
Yields his engrossments to the ending father.—

Re-enter WARWICK.

Now, where is he that will not stay so long
Till his friend sickness hath determin'd me?[a]

WAR. My lord, I found the prince in the next room,
Washing with kindly tears his gentle cheeks;
With such a deep demeanour in great sorrow,
That tyranny, which never quaff'd but blood,
Would, by beholding him, have wash'd his knife
With gentle eye-drops. He is coming hither.

K. HEN. But wherefore did he take away the crown?

Re-enter PRINCE HENRY.

Lo, where he comes.—Come hither to me, Harry:—
Depart the chamber, leave us here alone.
[*Exeunt* CLARENCE, PRINCE HUMPHREY, Lords, &c.

P. HEN. I never thought to hear you speak again.

K. HEN. Thy wish was father, Harry, to that thought:
I stay too long by thee, I weary thee.
Dost thou so hunger for my empty chair,
That thou wilt needs invest thee with mine honours
Before thy hour be ripe? O foolish youth!
Thou seek'st the greatness that will overwhelm thee.
Stay but a little; for my cloud of dignity
Is held from falling with so weak a wind,
That it will quickly drop: my day is dim.
Thou hast stol'n that, which, after some few hours,
Were thine without offence; and, at my death,
Thou hast seal'd up my expectation:
Thy life did manifest, thou lov'dst me not,
And thou wilt have me die assur'd of it.
Thou hid'st a thousand daggers in thy thoughts;
Which thou hast whetted on thy stony heart,
To stab at half an hour of my life.
What! can'st thou not forbear me half an hour?
Then get thee gone, and dig my grave thyself,
And bid the merry bells ring to thine* ear,
That thou art crowned, not that I am dead.
Let all the tears that should bedew my hearse,
Be drops of balm to sanctify thy head:
Only compound me with forgotten dust;
Give that, which gave thee life, unto the worms.
Pluck down my officers, break my decrees;
For now a time is come to mock at form,
Harry† the fifth is crown'd!—Up, vanity!
Down, royal state! all you sage counsellors, hence!
And to the English court assemble now,
From every region, apes of idleness!
Now, neighbour confines, purge you of your scum:
Have you a ruffian, that will swear, drink, dance,
Revel the night; rob, murder, and commit
The oldest sins the newest kind of ways?
Be happy, he will trouble you no more:
England shall double gild his treble guilt;
England shall give him office, honour, might:
For the fifth Harry, from curb'd licence plucks
The muzzle of restraint, and the wild dog
Shall flesh his tooth in every innocent.
O my poor kingdom, sick with civil blows!
When that my care could not withhold thy riots,
What wilt thou do, when riot is thy care?
O, thou wilt be a wilderness again,
Peopled with wolves, thy old inhabitants!

P. HEN. O, pardon me, my liege! but for my tears, [*Kneeling.*
The moist‡ impediments unto my speech,
I had forestall'd this dear and deep rebuke,
Ere you with grief had spoke, and I had heard
The course of it so far. There is your crown;
And He that wears the crown immortally,
Long guard it yours! If I affect it more,
Than as your honour, and as your renown,
Let me no more from this obedience rise,
Which my most true and inward-duteous spirit
Teacheth this prostrate and exterior bending.
God§ witness with me, when I here came in,
And found no course of breath within your majesty,
How cold it struck my heart! if I do feign,
O, let me in my present wildness die;
And never live to show the incredulous world
The noble change that I have purposed!
Coming to look on you, thinking you dead,
(And dead almost, my liege, to think you were,)
I spake unto the crown, as having sense,
And thus upbraided it. *The care on thee depending,*

(*) First folio, *sleepes*.

(*) First folio, *thy*. (†) First folio, *Henry*. (‡) First folio, *most*. (§) First folio, *Heaven*.

[a] *Till his friend sickness hath* determin'd me?—] Hath *ended* me. The quarto reads:—
"Till his friend sickness' *hands*," &c.

Hath fed upon the body of my father;
Therefore, thou, best of gold, art worst of gold.
Other, less fine in carat, is more precious,
Preserving life in med'cine potable:[a]
But thou, most fine, most honour'd, most renown'd,
Hast eat thy bearer up.* Thus, my most† royal liege,
Accusing it, I put it on my head;
To try with it,—as with an enemy,
That had before my face murder'd my father,—
The quarrel of a true inheritor.
But if it did infect my blood with joy,
Or swell my thoughts to any strain of pride;
If any rebel, or vain spirit of mine
Did, with the least affection of a welcome,
Give entertainment to the might of it,
Let God‡ for ever keep it from my head!
And make me as the poorest vassal is,
That doth with awe and terror kneel to it!
K. HEN. O my son!
Heaven put it in thy mind, to take it hence,
That thou might'st win§ the more thy father's love,
Pleading so wisely in excuse of it.
Come hither, Harry, sit thou by my bed,
And hear, I think, the very latest counsel
That ever I shall breathe. Heaven knows, my son,
By what by-paths, and indirect crook'd ways,
I met this crown; and I myself know well,
How troublesome it sat upon my head:
To thee, it shall descend with better quiet,
Better opinion, better confirmation;
For all the soil of the achievement goes
With me into the earth. It seem'd in me,
But as an honour snatch'd with boisterous hand;
And I had many living, to upbraid
My gain of it by their assistances;
Which daily grew to quarrel, and to bloodshed,
Wounding supposed peace: all these bold fears,[b]
Thou see'st, with peril I have answered:
For all my reign hath been but as a scene
Acting that argument; and now my death
Changes the mode: for what in me was purchas'd,[c]
Falls upon thee in a more fairer sort;
So thou the garland wear'st successively.
Yet, though thou stand'st more sure than I could do,
Thou art not firm enough, since griefs are green;
And all thy[d] friends, which thou must make thy friends,
Have but their stings and teeth newly ta'en out;
By whose fell working I was first advanc'd,
And by whose power I well might lodge a fear
To be again displac'd: which to avoid,
I cut them off; and had a purpose now
To lead out many to the Holy Land;
Lest rest, and lying still, might make them look
Too near unto my state. Therefore, my Harry,
Be it thy course to busy giddy minds
With foreign quarrels; that action, hence borne out,
May waste the memory of the former days.
More would I, but my lungs are wasted so,
That strength of speech is utterly denied me.
How I came by the crown, O God,* forgive!
And grant it may with thee in true peace live!
P. HEN. My gracious liege,
You won it, wore it, kept it, gave it me:
Then plain and right must my possession be;
Which I, with more than with a common pain,
'Gainst all the world will rightfully maintain.

Enter PRINCE JOHN *of* LANCASTER, WARWICK, Lords, *and others.*

K. HEN. Look, look, here comes my John of Lancaster.
P. JOHN. Health, peace, and happiness, to my royal father!
K. HEN. Thou bring'st me happiness, and peace, son John;
But health, alack, with youthful wings is flown
From this bare, wither'd trunk: upon thy sight,
My worldly business makes a period.——
Where is my lord of Warwick?
P. HEN. My lord of Warwick!
K. HEN. Doth any name particular belong
Unto the lodging where I first did swoon?
WAR. 'Tis call'd Jerusalem, my noble lord.
K. HEN. Laud be to God!*—even there my life must end.(4)
It hath been prophesied to me many years,
I should not die but in Jerusalem;
Which vainly I suppos'd, the Holy Land:—
But, bear me to that chamber; there I'll lie;
In that Jerusalem shall Harry die. [*Exeunt.*

(*) First folio, *the*. (†) First folio omits, *most*.
(‡) First folio, *heaven*. (§) First folio, *joyne*.

(*) First folio, *heaven*.

a Med'cine potable:] In allusion to the once prevalent notion that a solution of gold was the "sovereign'st thing on earth" for bodily ailments, and that "the incorruptibility of the metal might be communicated to the body impregnated with it."

b *All these* bold fears,—] "Fear," Johnson says, "is here used in the active sense, for that which causes *fear*." Fears are objects of fear; but, by these "*bold fears*," may be meant, "bold *feers*," that is, *allies* or *companions*, in the same sense that we apprehend the king uses the word in Act I. Sc. 3, of the first portion of this play:—

"Shall we buy treason? and indent with *feers*."

c *Was* purchas'd,—] Gained by force. *Purchase*, with our old writers, was obliquely used in the sense of goods obtained by dishonest means, or at least by might rather than right.

d *And all* thy *friends*,—] Tyrwhitt conjectured we should read "*my* friends," but there is still a difficulty, as the king is recommending the prince to ingratiate himself with persons whom he tells us immediately afterwards, he has cut off. Monck Mason, for "I cut *them* off," would therefore print "I cut *some* off."

ACT V.

SCENE I.—Gloucestershire. *A Hall in* Shallow's *House.*

Enter SHALLOW, FALSTAFF, BARDOLPH, *and* Page.

SHAL. By cock and pye,(1) sir,* you shall not away to-night.——What, Davy, I say!

FAL. You must excuse me, master Robert Shallow.

SHAL. I will not excuse you; you shall not be excused; excuses shall not be admitted; there is no excuse shall serve; you shall not be excused.—Why, Davy!

Enter DAVY.

DAVY. Here, sir.

SHAL. Davy, Davy, Davy, Davy,—let me see, Davy;—let me see, Davy:—let me see;—yea, marry,* William cook,[a] bid him come hither.—Sir John, you shall not be excused.

DAVY. Marry, sir, thus;—those precepts[b] cannot be served: and, again, sir,—shall we sow the head-land with wheat?

SHAL. With red wheat, Davy. But for William cook;——are there no young pigeons?

DAVY. Yes, sir.—Here is now the smith's note, for shoeing, and plough-irons.

SHAL. Let it be cast, and paid: sir John, you shall not be excused.

DAVY. Now,† sir, a new link to the bucket must needs be had:—And, sir, do you mean to stop any of William's wages, about the sack he lost the other day at Hinckley fair?

(*) First folio omits, *sir.*

(*) First folio omits, *yea, marry.* (†) First folio omits, *now.*

[a] William cook,—] Servants, and the lower orders of people generally, were commonly distinguished of old by surnames derived from their respective callings.

[b] Precepts—] *Warrants.*

SHAL. He shall answer it.——Some pigeons, Davy; a couple of short-legged hens; a joint of mutton, and any pretty little tiny kickshaws, tell William cook.

DAVY. Doth the man of war stay all night, sir?

SHAL. Yes, Davy. I will use him well; A friend i' the court is better than a penny in purse. Use his men well, Davy; for they are arrant knaves, and will backbite.

DAVY. No worse than they are back*-bitten, sir; for they have marvellous foul linen.

SHAL. Well conceited, Davy. About thy business, Davy.

DAVY. I beseech you, sir, to countenance William Visor of Wincot† against Clement Perkes of the hill.

SHAL. There are many complaints, Davy, against that Visor; that Visor is an arrant knave, on my knowledge.

DAVY. I grant your worship, that he is a knave, sir: but yet, God‡ forbid, sir, but a knave should have some countenance at his friend's request. An honest man, sir, is able to speak for himself, when a knave is not. I have served your worship truly, sir, this§ eight years; and if I cannot once or twice in a quarter bear out a knave against an honest man, I have but a very little credit with your worship. The knave is mine honest friend, sir; therefore, I beseech your worship, let him be countenanced.

SHAL. Go to; I say, he shall have no wrong. Look about, Davy. [*Exit* DAVY.] Where are you, sir John? Come, come, come, off with your boots.—Give me your hand, master Bardolph.

BARD. I am glad to see your worship.

SHAL. I thank thee with all my heart, kind master Bardolph:—and welcome, my tall fellow. [*To the* Page.] Come, sir John. [*Exit* SHALLOW.

FAL. I'll follow you, good master Robert Shallow. Bardolph, look to our horses. [*Exeunt* BARDOLPH *and* Page.] If I were sawed into quantities, I should make four dozen of such bearded hermits'-staves as master Shallow. It is a wonderful thing, to see the semblable coherence of his men's spirits and his: they, by observing him, do bear themselves like foolish justices; he, by conversing with them, is turned into a justice-like serving-man: their spirits are so married in conjunction with the participation of society, that they flock together in consent,[a] like so many wild geese. If I had a suit to master Shallow, I would humour his men, with the imputation of being near their master;[b] if to his men, I would curry with master Shallow, that no man could better command his servants. It is certain, that either wise bearing, or ignorant carriage, is caught, as men take diseases, one of another: and therefore, let men take heed of their company. I will devise matter enough out of this Shallow, to keep prince Harry in continual laughter, the wearing-out of six fashions, (which is four terms, or two actions,) and he shall laugh without* *intervallums*. O, it is much, that a lie, with a slight oath, and a jest with a sad brow, will do with a fellow that never had the ache in his shoulders! O, you shall see him laugh, till his face be like a wet cloak ill laid up.

SHAL. [*Within.*] Sir John!

FAL. I come, master Shallow; I come, master Shallow. [*Exit* FALSTAFF.

(*) First folio omits, *back*. (†) Old text, *Woncot*.
(‡) First folio, *heaven*. (§) First folio, *these*.

a *They flock together in* consent,—] In *agreement*, in *union*.

SCENE II.—Westminster. *A Room in the Palace.*

Enter WARWICK, *and the* Lord Chief Justice.

WAR. How now, my lord chief justice? whither away?

CH. JUST. How doth the king?

WAR. Exceeding well; his cares are now all ended.

CH. JUST. I hope, not dead.

WAR. He's walk'd the way of nature;
And, to our purposes, he lives no more.

CH. JUST. I would his majesty had call'd me with him:
The service that I truly did his life,
Hath left me open to all injuries.

WAR. Indeed, I think, the young king loves you not.

CH. JUST. I know he doth not, and do arm myself,
To welcome the condition of the time;
Which cannot look more hideously upon me,
Than I have drawn it in my fantasy.

Enter PRINCE JOHN, PRINCE HUMPHREY, CLARENCE, WESTMORELAND, *and others*.

WAR. Here come the heavy issue of dead Harry:
O, that the living Harry had the temper
Of him, the worst of these three gentlemen!
How many nobles then should hold their places,
That must strike sail to spirits of vile sort!

CH. JUST. Alas! I fear, all will be overturn'd.

P. JOHN. Good morrow, cousin Warwick, good morrow.

P. HUMPH. *and* CLA. Good morrow, cousin.

P. JOHN. We meet like men that had forgot to speak.

(*) First folio, *with*.

b Being near their master;] This may mean either *resembling their master*, or *being able to influence him*.

WAR. We do remember; but our argument
Is all too heavy to admit much talk.

P. JOHN. Well, peace be with him that hath made us heavy!

CH. JUST. Peace be with us, lest we be heavier!

P. HUMPH. O, good my lord, you have lost a friend, indeed:
And I dare swear, you borrow not that face
Of seeming sorrow; it is sure, your own.

P. JOHN. Though no man be assur'd what grace to find,
You stand in coldest expectation:
I am the sorrier; would 'twere otherwise.

CLA. Well, you must now speak sir John Falstaff fair,
Which swims against your stream of quality.

CH. JUST. Sweet princes, what I did, I did in honour,
Led by the impartial* conduct of my soul;
And never shall you see, that I will beg
A ragged and forestall'd remission.—[a]
If truth and upright innocency fail me,
I'll to the king my master that is dead,
And tell him who hath sent me after him.

WAR. Here comes the prince.

Enter KING HENRY V.

CH. JUST. Good morrow; and God* save your majesty!

KING. This new and gorgeous garment, majesty,
Sits not so easy on me as you think.—
Brothers, you mix your sadness with some fear;
This is the English, not the Turkish court;
Not Amurath an Amurath(2) succeeds,
But Harry, Harry. Yet be sad, good brothers,
For, to speak truth, it very well becomes you;
Sorrow so royally in you appears,
That I will deeply put the fashion on,
And wear it in my heart. Why then, be sad:
But entertain no more of it, good brothers,
Than a joint burthen laid upon us all.
For me, by heaven, I bid you be assur'd,
I'll be your father and your brother too;
Let me but bear your love, I'll bear your cares.
Yet† weep, that Harry's dead; and so will I:
But Harry lives, that shall convert those tears,
By number, into hours of happiness.

(*) First folio, *imperial*.

[a] A ragged and forestall'd remission.—] *Ragged* in this place means *base*, *ignominious*, as in Shakespeare's eighth sonnet:—

" Thy secret pleasure turns to open shame,
Thy smoothing titles to a ragged name;"

but of "*forestall'd remission*," we believe the import is yet to be sought. That it was a familiar expression is evident, for it occurs twice in Massinger, (in "The Duke of Milan," Act III. Sc. 1; and in "The Bondman," Act III. Sc. 3;) though in neither case does the context assist us to its meaning.

(*) First folio, *heaven*. (†) First folio, *But*.

PRINCES.[a] We hope no other from your majesty. [you most;
KING. You all look strangely on me:—and
You are, I think, assur'd I love you not.
[*To the* Lord Chief Justice.
CH. JUST. I am assur'd, if I be measur'd rightly,
Your majesty hath no just cause to hate me.
KING. No!
How might a prince of my great hopes forget
So great indignities you laid upon me?
What! rate, rebuke, and roughly send to prison
The immediate heir of England! Was this easy?
May this be wash'd in Lethe, and forgotten?
CH. JUST. I then did use the person of your father;
The image of his power lay then in me:
And, in the administration of his law,
Whiles I was busy for the commonwealth,
Your highness pleased to forget my place,
The majesty and power of law and justice,
The image of the king whom I presented,
And struck me in my very seat of judgment;
Whereon, as an offender to your father,
I gave bold way to my authority,
And did commit you. If the deed were ill,
Be you contented, wearing now the garland,
To have a son set your decrees at nought;
To pluck down justice from your awful bench;
To trip the course of law, and blunt the sword
That guards the peace and safety of your person:
Nay, more; to spurn at your most royal image,
And mock your workings in a second body.
Question your royal thoughts, make the case yours;
Be now the father, and propose a son:
Hear your own dignity so much profan'd,
See your most dreadful laws so loosely slighted,
Behold yourself so by a son disdain'd;
And then imagine me taking your part,
And, in your power, soft silencing your son:
After this cold considerance, sentence me;
And, as you are a king, speak in your state,
What I have done, that misbecame my place,
My person, or my liege's sovereignty.
KING. You are right, justice, and you weigh this well;
Therefore still bear the balance, and the sword:
And I do wish your honours may increase,
Till you do live to see a son of mine
Offend you, and obey you, as I did.
So shall I live to speak my father's words;
Happy am I, that have a man so bold,
That dares do justice on my proper son:
And not * *less happy, having such a son,*
That would deliver up his greatness so
Into the hands of justice.—You did commit me:
For which, I do commit into your hand
The unstain'd sword that you have us'd to bear;
With this remembrance,—That you use the same
With the like bold, just, and impartial spirit,
As you have done 'gainst me. There is my hand;
You shall be as a father to my youth;
My voice shall sound as you do prompt mine ear;
And I will stoop and humble my intents
To your well-practis'd, wise directions.——
And, princes all, believe me, I beseech you;—
My father is gone wild into his grave,[b]
For in his tomb lie my affections;
And with his spirit sadly I survive,
To mock the expectation of the world;
To frustrate prophecies, and to raze out
Rotten opinion, who hath writ me down
After my seeming. The tide of blood in me
Hath proudly flow'd in vanity, till now;
Now doth it turn, and ebb back to the sea;
Where it shall mingle with the state of floods,
And flow henceforth in formal majesty.
Now call we our high court of parliament;
And let us choose such limbs of noble counsel,
That the great body of our state may go
In equal rank with the best-govern'd nation;
That war, or peace, or both at once, may be
As things acquainted and familiar to us;——
In which you, father, shall have foremost hand.—
[*To the* Lord Chief Justice.
Our coronation done, we will accite,
As I before remember'd, all our state:
And (God* consigning to my good intents,)
No prince, nor peer, shall have just cause to say,—
Heaven shorten Harry's happy life one day.
[*Exeunt.*

SCENE III.—Gloucestershire. *The Garden of* Shallow's *House.*

Enter FALSTAFF, SHALLOW, SILENCE, BARDOLPH, *the* Page, *and* DAVY.

SHAL. Nay, you shall see mine orchard; where, in an arbour, we will eat a last year's pippin of my own graffing, with a dish of carraways, and so forth;—come, cousin Silence;—and then to bed.

FAL. 'Fore God,† you have here a goodly dwelling, and a rich.

SHAL. Barren, barren, barren; beggars all, beggars all, sir John:—marry, good air.—Spread, Davy; spread, Davy: well said, Davy.

FAL. This Davy serves you for good uses; he is your serving-man, and your husband.

SHAL. A good varlet, a good varlet, a very good

(*) First folio, *no*.

a Princes.] The prefix to this speech in the quarto is *Bro.* for "*Brothers;*" and in the folio, "*John,* &c.:" it was intended to be spoken by all the Princes together.

(*) First folio, *heaven*. (†) First folio omits, *'Fore God.*

b My father is gone wild into his grave,—] He means, because he has exchanged his own wildness, burying it in that grave, for his father's serious spirit.

varlet, sir John.—By the mass,* I have drunk too much sack at supper:—a good varlet. Now sit down, now sit down:—come, cousin.

SIL. Ah, sirrah! quoth-a,—we shall

[Singing.

Do nothing but eat, and make good cheer,
And praise heaven for the merry year;
When flesh is cheap and females dear,
And lusty lads roam here and there,
So merrily,
And ever among so merrily.

FAL. There's a merry heart!—Good master Silence, I'll give you a health for that anon.

SHAL. Give† master Bardolph some wine, Davy.

DAVY. Sweet sir, sit; [*Seating* BARDOLPH *and the* Page *at another table.*] I'll be with you anon:—most sweet sir, sit.——Master page, good master page, sit: proface![a] What you want in meat we'll have in drink. But you must* bear; the heart's all. [*Exit.*

SHAL. Be merry, Master Bardolph;—and my little soldier there, be merry.

[Singing.

SIL. *Be merry, be merry, my wife has all;*[b]
For women are shrews, both short and tall:
'Tis merry in hall, when beards wag all,[c]
And welcome merry shrove-tide.
Be merry, be merry, &c.

FAL. I did not think, master Silence had been a man of this mettle.

SIL. Who I? I have been merry twice and once, ere now.

(*) First folio omits, *By the mass.* (†) First folio, *Good.*

a Proface!] An Italian phrase, signifying *much good may it do you*, and equivalent to our "*welcome.*" It is found in Florio's Dictionary, "Buon pro vi faccia, *much good may it do you*," and in many of the early writers.

b *My wife* has all;] So the old copy. Farmer suggested we should read, "My wife 's as all."

(*) First folio omits, *must.*

c 'T is merry in hall, &c.] This rhyme is of great antiquity. Warton found it in a poem by Adam Davie, called "The Life of Alexander:"—

"Merrie swithe it is in hall
When the berdes waveth all."

Re-enter DAVY.

DAVY. There is a dish of leather-coats for you.[a]
[*Setting them before* BARDOLPH.

SHAL. Davy,—

DAVY. Your worship?—I'll be with you straight.
[*To* BARD.]—A cup of wine, sir?
[Singing.

SIL. *A cup of wine, that's brisk and fine,*
And drink unto the leman mine;
And a merry heart lives long-a.

FAL. Well said, master Silence.

SIL. An* we shall be merry, now comes in the sweet of the night.

FAL. Health and long life to you, master Silence!

SIL. *Fill the cup, and let it come;*
I'll pledge you a mile to the bottom.

SHAL. Honest Bardolph, welcome: if thou want'st any thing, and wilt not call, beshrew thy heart.—Welcome, my little tiny thief? [*To the* Page.] and welcome, indeed, too.—I'll drink to master Bardolph, and to all the cavaleroes about London.

DAVY. I hope to see London once ere I die.

BARD. An* I might see you there, Davy,—

SHAL. By the mass,† you'll crack a quart together. Ha! will you not, master Bardolph?

BARD. Yes, sir, in a pottle pot.

SHAL. I thank thee:—the knave will stick by thee, I can assure thee that: he will not out;[b] he is true bred.

BARD. And I'll stick by him, sir.

SHAL. Why, there spoke a king. Lack nothing: be merry. [*Knocking heard.*] Look, who 's at door there, ho! who knocks! [*Exit* DAVY.

FAL. Why, now you have done me right.
[*To* SILENCE, *who drinks a bumper.*

SIL. *Do me right,* [Singing.
And dub me knight.
Samingo.[c]
Is 't not so?

FAL. 'T is so.

SIL. Is 't so? Why then, say an old man can do somewhat.

(*) First folio, *If*. (†) First folio omits, *By the mass.*

[a] Leather-coats.] Apples usually known as *russetines*.

[b] He will not out; he is true bred.] A sportsman's saying applied to hounds, and which serves to expound Gadshill's expression:—

"Such as can *hold in*."—*Henry IV*. Part I. Act II. Sc. 1.

"If they run it endways orderly and make it good, then when they *hold in* together merrily, we say, *They are in crie.*" —TURBERVILE's "*Booke of Hunting.*"

[c] *Samingo.*] Silence is in his cups, or he would probably have sung *San Domingo. Domingo*, for some unexplained reason, was an old burden to topers' songs and catches. Thus in "Summer's Last Will and Testament," 1600:—

"Monsieur *Mingo* for quaffing doth surpass
In cup, in can, or glass;
God Bacchus, do me right,
And dub me knight,
Domingo."

Re-enter DAVY.

DAVY. An* it please your worship, there 's one Pistol come from the court with news.

FAL. From the court? let him come in.—

Enter PISTOL.

How now, Pistol?

PIST. Sir John, God save you! †

FAL. What wind blew you hither, Pistol?

PIST. Not the ill wind which blows no man‡ to good.—Sweet knight, thou art now one of the greatest men in the realm.

SIL. By'r lady,§ I think 'a be; but[d] goodman Puff of Barson.

PIST. Puff?
Puff in thy teeth, most recreant coward base!—
Sir John, I am thy Pistol, and thy friend,
And || helter-skelter have I rode to thee;
And tidings do I bring, and lucky joys,
And golden times, and happy news of price.

FAL. I pr'ythee now, deliver them like a man of this world.

PIST. A foutra for the world, and worldlings base!
I speak of Africa, and golden joys.

FAL. O base Assyrian knight, what is thy news?
Let king Cophetua know the truth thereof.

SIL. *And Robin Hood, Scarlet, and John.*
[Sings.

PIST. Shall dunghill curs confront the Helicons?
And shall good news be baffled?
Then, Pistol, lay thy head in Furies' lap.

SHAL. Honest gentleman, I know not your breeding.

PIST. Why then, lament therefore.

SHAL. Give me pardon, sir;—if, sir, you come with news from the court, I take it, there is but two ways; either to utter them, or to conceal them. I am, sir, under the king, in some authority.

PIST. Under which king, Bezonian?[e] speak, or die.

SHAL. Under king Harry.

PIST. Harry the fourth? or fifth?

SHAL. Harry the fourth.

PIST. A foutra for thine office!—
Sir John, thy tender lambkin now is king;

(*) First folio, *If*. (†) First folio, *Save you, sir.*
(‡) First folio, *none*. (§) *Indeed.*
(||) First folio omits, *And.*

[d] But *goodman Puff*—] That is, *except* goodman, &c.

[e] Bezonian?] A term of contempt derived, it is thought, from the Italian *bisogno*, which Cotgrave explains, "a filthie knave, or clowne, a raskall, a *bisonian*, base humoured scoundrel."

Harry the fifth 's the man. I speak the truth.
When Pistol lies, do this ; and fig me,[a] like
The bragging Spaniard.

FAL. What ! is the old king dead ?

PIST. As nail in door: the things I speak are just.

FAL. Away, Bardolph ; saddle my horse.—Master Robert Shallow, choose what office thou wilt in the land, 't is thine.—Pistol, I will double charge thee with dignities.

BARD. O joyful day !—I would not take a knighthood for my fortune.

PIST. What ! I do bring good news ?

FAL. Carry master Silence to bed.—Master Shallow, my lord Shallow, be what thou wilt, I am fortune's steward. Get on thy boots ; we 'll ride all night :—O, sweet Pistol :—Away, Bardolph. [*Exit* BARD.]—Come, Pistol, utter more to me ; and, withal, devise something to do thyself good. —Boot, boot, master Shallow; I know the young king is sick for me. Let us take any man's horses ; the laws of England are at my commandment. Happy are they which have been my friends ; and woe unto my lord chief justice !

PIST. Let vultures vile seize on his lungs also !
Where is the life that late I led,[b] say they :
Why, here it is ; welcome these* pleasant days.
[*Exeunt.*

SCENE IV.—London. *A Street.*

Enter Beadles, *dragging along* HOSTESS QUICKLY, *and* DOLL TEAR-SHEET.[c]

HOST. No, thou arrant knave; I would I might die, that I might have thee hanged: thou hast drawn my shoulder out of joint.

1 BEAD. The constables have delivered her over to me; and she shall have whipping-cheer enough, I warrant her: there hath been a man or two lately killed about her.

DOLL. Nut-hook, nut-hook,[d] you lie. Come on ; I'll tell thee what, thou damned tripe-visaged rascal ; an† the child I now go with, do miscarry, thou hadst better thou hadst struck thy mother, thou paper-faced villain!

HOST. O the lord,‡ that sir John were come ! he would make this a bloody day to somebody. But I pray God,§ the fruit of her womb|| miscarry !

1 BEAD. If it do, you shall have a dozen of cushions again ; you have but eleven now. Come, I charge you both go with me ; for the man is dead, that you and Pistol beat among you.

DOLL. I'll tell thee what, thou thin man in a censer ! I will have you as soundly swinged for this, you blue-bottled rogue ; you filthy famished correctioner ! if you be not swinged, I'll forswear half-kirtles.

1 BEAD. Come, come, you she knight-errant, come.

HOST. O, that right should thus overcome might! Well ; of sufferance comes ease.

DOLL. Come, you rogue, come ; bring me to a justice.

HOST. Yes ; come, you starved blood-hound !

DOLL. Goodman death ! goodman bones !

HOST. Thou atomy* thou !

DOLL. Come, you thin thing ; come, you rascal !

1 BEAD. Very well. [*Exeunt.*

SCENE V.—*A public Place near* Westminster Abbey.

Enter two Grooms, *strewing rushes.*

1 GROOM. More rushes, more rushes.

2 GROOM. The trumpets have sounded twice.

1 GROOM. It will be two o'clock ere they come from the coronation: despatch, despatch.†
[*Exeunt* Grooms.

Enter FALSTAFF, SHALLOW, PISTOL, BARDOLPH, *and the* Page.

FAL. Stand here by me, master Robert Shallow ; I will make the king do you grace : I will leer upon him, as he comes by ; and do but mark the countenance that he will give me.

PIST. God‡ bless thy lungs, good knight !

FAL. Come here, Pistol; stand behind me,—O, if I had had time to have made new liveries, I would have bestowed the thousand pound I borrowed of you. [*To* SHALLOW.] But 't is no matter ; this poor show doth better ; this doth infer the zeal I had to see him.

SHAL. It doth so.

FAL. It shows my earnestness in affection.

SHAL. It doth so.

(*) First folio, *those*. (†) First folio, *if*. (‡) First folio omits, *the lord*. (§) First folio, *I would*. (||) First folio inserts, *might*.

[a] And fig me,—] This odious gesture, the Spanish *higas dar*, was performed by thrusting out the thumb between the fore and middle finger. See note (c), p. 160.

[b] Where is the life that late I led,—] This scrap from some old ballad is sung also by Petruchio in "The Taming of the Shrew," Act IV. Sc. 1.

(*) First folio, *anatomy*. (†) First folio omits these two words. (‡) First folio omits, *God*.

[c] Enter Beadles, &c.] The stage direction in the quarto, is "Enter Sincklo and three or foure officers;" and the name of *Sincklo* is prefixed to the speeches of the Beadle, or as the folio calls him, *officer*. Sincklo was an actor of Shakespeare's company.

[d] Nut-hook,—] This appears to have been a cant title formerly for a beadle or catchpoll.

FAL. My devotion.

SHAL. It doth, it doth, it doth.

FAL. As it were, to ride day and night; and not to deliberate, not to remember, not to have patience to shift me.

SHAL. It is most certain.

FAL. But to stand stained with travel, and sweating with desire to see him: thinking of nothing else; putting all affairs else in oblivion; as if there were nothing else* to be done, but to see him.

PIST. 'T is *semper idem*, for *absque hoc nihil est:* 'T is all in every part.

SHAL. 'T is so, indeed.

PIST. My knight, I will inflame thy noble liver,
And make thee rage.
Thy Doll, and Helen of thy noble thoughts,
Is in base durance, and contagious prison;
Hal'd thither by most mechanical and dirty hand:—
Rouse up revenge from ebon den with fell Alecto's snake,
For Doll is in; Pistol speaks nought but truth.

FAL. I will deliver her.

[*Shouts without, and the trumpets sound.*

PIST. There roar'd the sea, and trumpet-clangor sounds.

(*) First folio omits, *else*.

Enter the KING, *and his train, the* Chief Justice *among them.*

FAL. God save thy grace, king Hal! my royal Hal.

PIST. The heavens thee guard and keep, most royal imp of fame!

FAL. God save thee, my sweet boy!

KING. My lord chief justice, speak to that vain [man.

CH. JUST. Have you your wits? know you what 't is you speak?

FAL. My king! my Jove! I speak to thee, my heart!

KING. I know thee not, old man: fall to thy [prayers;
How ill white hairs become a fool, and jester!
I have long dream'd of such a kind of man,
So surfeit-swell'd, so old, and so profane;
But, being awake, I do despise my dream.
Make less thy body hence,[a] and more thy grace;
Leave gormandizing; know, the grave doth gape
For thee thrice wider than for other men:—
Reply not to me with a fool-born jest;
Presume not, that I am the thing I was:
For God* doth know, so shall the world perceive,
That I have turn'd away my former self;
So will I those that kept me company.

(*) First folio, *heaven*.

[a] Hence,—] That is, *henceforward*.

When thou dost hear I am as I have been,
Approach me; and thou shalt be as thou wast,
The tutor and the feeder of my riots:
Till then, I banish thee, on pain of death,—
As I have done the rest of my misleaders,—
Not to come near our person by ten mile.
For competence of life, I will allow you,
That lack of means enforce you not to evil:
And, as we hear you do reform yourselves,
We will,—according to your strength, and qualities,—
Give you advancement.(3)—Be it your charge, my lord, [*To the* Chief Justice.
To see perform'd the tenor of our word.—
Set on. [*Exeunt* KING, *and his train.*

FAL. Master Shallow, I owe you a thousand pound.

SHAL. Ay, marry, sir John; which I beseech you to let me have home with me.

FAL. That can hardly be, master Shallow. Do not you grieve at this; I shall be sent for in private to him: look you, he must seem thus to the world. Fear not your advancement; I will be the man yet, that shall make you great.

SHAL. I cannot perceive how; unless you should give me your doublet, and stuff me out with straw. I beseech you, good sir John, let me have five hundred of my thousand.

FAL. Sir, I will be as good as my word: this that you heard, was but a colour.

SHAL. A colour, I fear, that you will die in, sir John.

FAL. Fear no colours; go with me to dinner. Come, lieutenant Pistol;—come, Bardolph:—I shall be sent for soon at night.

Re-enter PRINCE JOHN, *the* Chief Justice, Officers, &c.

CH. JUST. Go, carry sir John Falstaff to the Fleet;(4)
Take all his company along with him.

FAL. My lord, my lord,——

CH. JUST. I cannot now speak: I will hear you soon.
Take them away.

PIST. *Se fortuna me tormenta, la speranza me contenta.*

[*Exeunt* FAL. SHAL. PIST. BARD. Page, *and* Officers.

P. JOHN. I like this fair proceeding of the king's:
He hath intent, his wonted followers
Shall all be very well provided for;
But all are banish'd, till their conversations
Appear more wise and modest to the world.

CH. JUST. And so they are.

P. JOHN. The king hath call'd his parliament, my lord.

CH. JUST. He hath.

P. JOHN. I will lay odds,—that, ere this year expire,
We bear our civil swords, and native fire,
As far as France: I heard a bird so sing,
Whose music, to my thinking, pleas'd the king.
Come, will you hence? [*Exeunt.*

EPILOGUE.

Spoken by a Dancer.

FIRST, my fear; then, my court'sy: last, my speech. My fear is your displeasure; my court'sy, my duty; and my speech, to beg your pardons. If you look for a good speech now, you undo me: for what I have to say, is of mine own making; and what, indeed, I should say, will, I doubt, prove mine own marring. But to the purpose, and so to the venture.—Be it known to you, (as it is very well,) I was lately here in the end of a displeasing play, to pray your patience for it, and to promise you a better. I did mean, indeed, to pay you with this; which, if, like an ill venture, it come unluckily home, I break, and you, my gentle creditors, lose. Here, I promised you, I would be, and here I commit my body to your mercies: bate me some, and I will pay you some, and, as most debtors do, promise you infinitely.

If my tongue cannot entreat you to acquit me, will you command me to use my legs? and yet that were but light payment,—to dance out of your debt. But a good conscience will make any possible satisfaction, and so will I. All the gentlewomen here have forgiven me; if the gentlemen will not, then the gentlemen do not agree with the gentlewomen, which was never seen before in such an assembly.

One word more, I beseech you. If you be not too much cloyed with fat meat, our humble author will continue the story, with Sir John in it, and make you merry with fair Katharine of France: where, for any thing I know, Falstaff shall die of a sweat, unless already he be killed with your hard opinions; for Oldcastle died a martyr, and this is not the man. My tongue is weary; when my legs are too, I will bid you good night: and so kneel down before you;—but, indeed, to pray for the queen.(1)

ILLUSTRATIVE COMMENTS.

ACT I.

(1) SCENE II.—*The Lord Chief Justice.*] This was Sir William Gascoigne, Chief Justice of the King's Bench, to whom tradition ascribes the honour of having vindicated the authority of the law, by committing Prince Henry to prison for insulting him in the execution of his office. According to Holinshed, whom Shakespeare copied, the prince on this occasion so far forgot himself and the dignity of the judge, as actually to strike him on the seat of judgment. "Where on a time *hee stroke the chiefe justice on the face with his fiste,* for emprisoning one of his mates, he was not only committed to straighte prison himselfe by the sayde chief Justice, but also of his father putte out of the privie counsell and banished the courte." The blow was probably an exaggeration, as it is not mentioned in the earliest and most interesting account of the incident which we possess, that by Sir Thomas Elyot, in his collection of moral discourses, entitled "The Governor," which is as follows:—

"*A good Judge, a good Prince, a good King.*—The most renouned Prince, King Henry the Fift, late King of Englande, duringe the lyfe of his father was noted to be fierce, and of wanton courage. It happened, that one of his servants, whom he favoured well, was for felony by him committed arreyned at the King's Bench; whereof the prince being advertized, and incensed by light persons about him, in furious rage came hastily to the barre, where his servaunt stood as a prisoner, and commaunded him to be ungived and sette at libertie. Whereat all men were abashed, reserved the chiefe Justice, who humbly exhorted the Prince to be contented that his servaunt might be ordered, according to the aunciente lawes of this realme: or if he would have him saved from the rigour of the lawes, that he should obtayne, if he might, of the king his father his gracious pardon, whereby no Law or Justice should be derogate.

"With which aunswere the Prince nothing appeased, but rather more inflamed, endeavoured himselfe to take away his servaunt. The Judge, considering the perilous example and inconvenience that might thereby ensue, with a valyant spirite and courage, commaunded the Prince uppon his alleagaunce, to leave the prisoner and depart his way; at which commaundemet the Prince beinge set all in a furye, all chaufed, and in a terrible maner, came up to the place of Judgement, men thinking he would have slain the Judge, or have done to him some domage: But the Judge sitting still without moving, declaring the majestie of the King's place of Judgement, and with an assured and bold countenaunce, had to the Prince these words following: 'Sir, remember your selfe. I keepe heere the place of the king your sovereigne lord and father, to whom ye owe double obedience: wherefore eftsoones in his name, I charge you to desist of your wilfulnesse and unlawfull enterprise, and from hencefoorth give good example to those which hereafter shall be your proper subjects. And now, for your contempte and disobedience, goe you to the prison of the Kinge's Bench, where unto I commit you, and remaine ye there prisoner until pleasure of the kinge your father be further knowen.' With which words being abashed, and also wondering at the marvailous gravitie of that worshipful Justice, the noble Prince laying his weapone aparte, doing reverence departed and went to the Kinge's Bench as he was commaunded. Whereat his servaunts disdayned, came and shewed to the King al the whole affayre, whereat he a whiles studying, after as a man all ravished with gladnesse, holding his eyes and handes up towards heaven, abrayded with a loud voice: 'O mercifull God, how much am I bound to your infinite goodness, specially for that you have given me a judge who feareth not to minister Justice, and also a son who can suffer semblably and obey Justice.'"

For this occurrence, which Shakespeare repeatedly adverts to in the play, he had, then, historical authority—but in making Henry, upon his accession to the throne, magnanimously forgive and re-appoint the lord chief justice:—

> —— "You did commit me:
> For which, I do commit into your hand
> The unstain'd sword—"

he has rendered himself amenable to the charge of departing from history for the sake of elevating his hero. It is true, indeed, that Sir William Gascoigne survived King Henry, notwithstanding his biographers have fixed his death to have happened the 17th of December, 1412; for Mr. Foss, in his "Judges of England," has shown, first, that he is judge in a case reported in Hilary term, 1413; secondly, that he was summoned to the first parliament of Henry V., in Easter, 1413; and, lastly, that his will has been found in the ecclesiastical court at York, bearing date, December 15th, 1419: but it is equally indisputable that he was not present at the parliament in question, and that the appointment of his successor, Sir William Hankford, took place March 29th, 1413, only eight days after Henry's accession, and ten days before his coronation.

"The peculiar period chosen for this act," Mr. Foss observes, "and its precipitancy in contrast with the delay in issuing the new patents to the other judges, tend strongly to show that it resulted from the king's peremptory mandate, rather than Gascoigne's personal choice; and, consequently, to raise a suspicion that the indignity he had laid upon the prince was not 'washed in Lethe and forgotten' by the king."

It is just to add that Sir William Gascoigne's claim to the distinction of having punished the wild young prince is not undisputed. In the memorandum book of Sir Robert Markham, preserved in the British Museum, "Add. MSS. 18,721," the first few leaves contain numerous extracts from early historians respecting Sir John Markham, a judge of the Common Pleas, in the time of Henry IV. and Henry V., at the end of which the writer remarks:—"Now, the reason I have thus diligently inquired into the authorities among the historians, concerning the name of the judge that committed Henry V., then Prince of Wales, is, because my own father alwais persisted in it as a tradition in our family, that it was Sir John Markham whom the prince struck, for which he was committed."

(2) SCENE II.—*Setting my knighthood and my soldiership aside, I had lied in my throat if I had said so.*]—*To lie in the throat*, an expression which is frequently met with in Shakespeare, and other of our early writers, appears to have borne a deeper meaning than is usually supposed. In a curious old treatise on War and the Duello, which has escaped the researches of all the commentators, entitled "VALLO LIBRO CON*tinente appertenentie ad Capitanii, retenere & fortificare una Citta cō bastioni con noui artificii de fuoco aggioti, come nella tabola appare, & de diuerse sorte poluere, et de expugnare una Citta co poti, scale, argani, trobe, trenciere, artegliare, caue, dare auisa menti senza messo allo amico, fare ordinanze, battaglioni, Et ponti de disfida con lo pingere, opera molto utile con la experientia de l'arte militare*," 1524, there is a chapter in the part devoted to the duello, which is headed "DELA DIVISIONE DEL MENTIRE," and which contains the following remarks on giving the lie:—

"Eda notare che uno honesto mentire se suole dire tu non dice il uero, anchora ue e laltro mentire dicendo tu ne menti *per la gola*, & laltro mentire se dice tu ne menti *per la gola* como ad un tristo, laltro anchora se dice tu ne menti *p* la *gola* como ad un tristo che tu sei, siche luno procede dallaltro, & luno e differente dallaltro, prendendo el caso che un dicessi tu, ne menti *per la gola* como un tristo, nō se intēde chel sia tristo, ma che lhabia mentito come fa un tristo in q̄lla uolta, & lui non deue combattere per querela chel sia ditto tristo, ma dicendo tu ne menti *per la gola*, come un tristo che tu sei la querela e de cobattere che li e ditto tristo per causa che dice tu sei."

ACT II.

(1) SCENE I.—*For thy walls, a pretty slight drollery, or the story of the prodigal, or the German hunting in water-work, is worth a thousand of these bed-hangings, and these fly-bitten tapestries.*]—In this, and in another passage where he declares his recruits to be "slaves *as ragged as Lazarus in the painted cloth*," Falstaff intimates the subjects usually found in the decoration of houses formerly. The mural-painting referred to, appears to have both preceded and followed the use of tapestry-hangings; and it also became a substitute for them, when it was executed on loose cloths to be suspended against the walls. In palaces and mansions, both the art and the subject were of a much superior kind. Martial scenes, classical and romantic histories, armorial ensigns or heraldical devices, adorned the apartments of the great; and, not unfrequently, moral sentences in Latin, French, or English, were inscribed in golden letters on richly-coloured panels. All of which would have been out of place in any such houses as that referred to by Falstaff: where the popular taste was shown in familiar Scripture narratives, forest-sports, or scenes of broad humour. There is a curious indication of this difference of decoration in the two poems called "Chaucer's Dream;" in one of which, the author, imagining an apartment embellished in the highest style of art, says that it was—

> "Full well depainted—— ——
> And all the walls with colours fine,
> Were painted to the text and glose,
> And all the Romaunt of the Rose."

In the second poem, on his waking, he sees nothing better in his own chamber—

> "Save on the walls old portraiture
> Of horsemen, hawkis, and houndis,
> And hurt dere, all full of woundis."

It is thus evident that hunting-subjects had been commonly employed, in the fourteenth century, for the adornment of interiors; and "The German Hunting" appears to have been one of the most popular of the class at the period. There is more than one explanation to be offered of this expression. The first is, that it implied no more than the representation of a chase after the manner of the Germans, as if the passage had been written, "your German hunting:" and the picture might then have consisted of a wild-boar hunt, in a German forest, taken from some old foreign print. But the words may possibly have reference to the famous German legend of "the Wild Huntsman," which had, perhaps, found its way to England during the reign of Elizabeth.

There can be no doubt, from the very name, that the "drolleries" proposed by Falstaff for the garniture of "The Boar's Head," were some of those scenes of coarse humour which the painters of the Dutch school introduced, between the end of the sixteenth, and the middle of the seventeenth century. They comprised representations of low tavern-parties, soldiers' quarters, country-fairs and mountebanks; and in some of them apes and cats were represented as drinking, playing on musical instruments, or acting as constables and watchmen. There were several very common specimens of this kind of tavern-painting formerly existing in an apartment of "The Elephant" in Fenchurch Street.

(2) SCENE II.—*A red lattice.*]—The *lattice*, or crossed laths, the ordinary denotement of an ale-house, was probably derived from the ancient sign of the *chequers*, common among the Romans. The designation, Douce remarks, "is not altogether lost, though the original meaning of the word is, the sign being converted into a *green lettuce;* of which an instance occurs in Brownlow Street, Holborn. In The Last Will and Testament of Lawrence Lucifer, the old Batchiler of Limbo, at the end of the 'Blacke Booke,' 1604, 4to, is the following passage: '—watched sometimes ten houres together in an ale-house, ever and anon peeping forth, and *sampling thy nose with the red Lattis.*'"

(3) SCENE IV.—

> *When Arthur first in court—*
> *And was a worthy king.*]

The old ballad of which Sir John hums a snatch, was one in honour of Sir Launcelot du Lake, and is given at length in Percy's Reliques, vol. i. p. 198, ed. 1767, and with the tune to which it was sung, in W. Chappell's Popular Music, &c., I. 271. The opening stanza runs:—

> "When Arthur first in court began,
> And was approved king,
> By force of armes great victoryes wanne,
> And conquest home did bring."

(4) SCENE IV.—*Quoit him down, Bardolph, like a shove-groat shilling.*]—The following is Strutt's account of *Shove-groat*, which appears to have been originally played with the silver groat, and afterwards with the broad shilling of Edward VI. "Shove-groat, named also Slyp-groat, and Slide-thrift, are sports occasionally mentioned by writers of the sixteenth and seventeenth centuries, and probably were analogous to the modern pastime called Justice Jervis, or Jarvis, which is confined to common pot-houses, and only practised by such as frequent the tap-rooms. It requires a parallelogram to be made with chalk, or by lines cut upon the middle of a table, about twelve or fourteen inches in breadth, and three or four feet in length; which is divided, latitudinally, into nine equal partitions, in every

one of which is placed a figure, in regular succession, from one to nine. Each of the players provides himself with a smooth halfpenny, which he places upon the edge of the table, and striking it with the palm of his hand, drives it towards the marks; and according to the value of the figure affixed to the partition wherein the halfpenny rests, his game is reckoned; which generally is stated at thirty-one, and must be made precisely: if it be exceeded, the player goes again for nine, which must also be brought exactly, or the turn is forfeited; and if the halfpenny rests upon any of the marks that separate the partitions, or overpasses the external boundaries, the go is void."

(5) SCENE IV.—

Then death rock me asleep, abridge my doleful days!]

This is the beginning of a mournful ballad, of which we append the first and last stanzas, said to have been composed by Anne Boleyne, but which Ritson thought was more likely to have been written by her brother, George, Viscount Rochford, who was reputed to be the author of several poems, songs, and sonnets. Mr. W. Chappell (Popular Music, &c., vol. i. p. 238) has published the first stanza, with the tune, from a manuscript of the latter part of the reign of Henry VIII.

"O Death, rocke me on slepe,
Bring me on quiet reste,
Let passe my verye giltless goste,
Out of my carefull brest;
Toll on the passinge bell,
Ringe out the dolefull knell,
Let the sound my dethe tell,
For I must dye,
There is no remedye,
For now I dye."

"Farewell my pleasures past,
Welcum my present payne,
I fele my torments so inerese,
That lyfe cannot remayne.
Cease now the passing-bell,
Rong is my doleful knell,
For the sound my deth doth tell.
Deth doth draw nye,
Sound my end dolefully,
For now I dye."

(6) SCENE IV.—*Bartholomew boar-pig.*]—*Roast pig*, even down to the middle of the last century, appears to have constituted one of the staple attractions of Bartholomew fair. See Ben Jonson's play of "Bartholomew Fair," and D'Avenant's burlesque poem on a long vacation:—

"Now London's chief, on sadle new,
Rides to the Fare of *Bartholemew;*
He twirles his chain, and looketh big,
As if to fright the Head of Pig,
That gaping lies on greasy stall."—Folio 1673.

(7) SCENE IV.—*Flap-dragons.*]—The sport of placing a plum or raisin in a shallow dish of spirit, and then setting light to it, and while the whole was in a flame, snatching out the *flap-dragon*, as it was called, with the mouth, was borrowed from the Dutch. Our gallants, who vied with each other in disgusting extravagances while toasting their mistresses, improved upon the Dutch practice, by making even a candle's end into a flap-dragon, and swallowing that off. An allusion to this, and another frantic absurdity of the fast youths of former times—that of puncturing their arms, and drinking the health of their charmers in blood, occurs in an old ballad, called "The Man in the Moon drinks Claret:"—

"Bacchus the father of drunken nowles,
Full mazers, beakers, glasses, bowls,
Greasie flap-dragons, flamish upsefriese,
With healths stab'd in arms upon naked knees."

ACT III.

(1) SCENE II.—*I was once of Clement's-inn.*]—This Inn was so called, says Stow, "because it standeth near to St. Clement's Church, but nearer to the fair fountain called Clement's Well." How long before 1479, nineteenth of Edward IV., it was occupied by students of the law is not known, but that it had been so inhabited for some time previously is quite certain; and we have the testimony of Strype to show that in after-times the roisterers of the Inns of Court fully maintained the reputation which Shallow took so much pride in claiming for himself and his fellow swinge-bucklers: "Here about this Church," he is speaking of St. Clement's, "and in the parts adjacent, were frequent disturbances by reason of the unthrifts of the Inns of Chancery, who were so unruly on nights, walking about to the disturbance and danger of such as passed along the streets, that the inhabitants were fain to keep watches. In the year 1582, the Recorder himself, with six more of the honest inhabitants, stood by St. Clement s Church, to see the lanthorn hung out, and to observe if he could meet with any of these outrageous dealers."—Strype's Stow, vol. ii. p. 108, ed. 1755.

(2) SCENE II.—*I saw him break Skogan's head.*]—Some of the commentators contend there were two Skogans, one—

"—— A fine gentleman, and a master of arts,
Of Henry the Fourth's time, that made disguises
For the king's sons, and writ in ballad royal
Daintily well," &c.

as described by Ben Jonson in his Masque of "The Fortunate Isles." This was *Henry* Scogan. The other, *John* Scogan, whom Holinshed mentions as "a learned gentleman of Edward the Fourth's reign, student for a time in Oxford, of a pleasaunte witte, and bent to mery devises, in respect whereof he was called into the courte, where guiding himselfe to his naturall inclination of mirthe and pleasaunt pastime, he plaied many sporting parts," &c.

Others believe there was but one poet of the name, and that the compositions attributed to the supposed Scogan of Edward the Fourth's time were written by him of Henry IV. It is needless to prolong the controversy. There was certainly a book published in the reign of Henry VIII. by Andrew Borde, called "Scoggin's Jests," which was reprinted in 1565; and the father of these jokes was no doubt considered by Shakespeare and his auditory as a court-jester of a former period, whether in the reign of Henry IV. or Edward IV. was not material.

(3) SCENE II.—*Our watch-word was, Hem, boys!*]—There was an old rollicking song, whose burden, *hem, boys, hem!* still lingered in Justice Shallow's memory, and of which the only verse now extant is quoted by Brome in his comedy of *A Jovial Crew, or the Merry Beggars*, first acted in 1641:—

"There was an old fellow at Waltham Cross,
Who merrily sung when he liv'd by the loss,
He never was heard to sigh with hey-ho,
But sent it out with a hey trolly-lo!
He cheer'd up his heart, when his goods went to wrack,
With a *hem, boys, hem!* and a cup of old sack."
Act II. Sc. 1.

Mr. Chappell ("Popular Music of the Olden Time," i. 262), acquaints us with the interesting fact, that the original air to which the above burden was sung, is the same still heard in the well-known chorus,—

"A very good song, and very well sung;
Jolly companions every one."

(4) SCENE II.—*I was then Sir Dagonet in Arthur's show.*]—*Arthur's show* appears to have been an exhibition performed by a band of Toxopholites, calling themselves "The Auncient Order, Society, and Unitie laudablè of Prince Arthure and his Knightly Armory of the Round Table," the associates of which took the names of the knights who figure in the famous romance, and were fifty-eight in number. Their ordinary place of rendezvous was *Mile End Green,* for ages the spot chosen by the Londoners for their martial sports and exercises, but they occasionally presented their spectacle in Smithfield and in other parts of the city. Of the origin of this Society nothing is known; but from a passage in the dedication of a rare tract by Richard Robinson, its historian and poet, we learn that it was confirmed by charter under Henry VIII.; who, "when he sawe a good archer indeede, he chose him, and ordained such a one for a knight of this order." That it flourished in Shakespeare's time is proved by the following extract from a treatise on the training of children, by Richard Mulcaster (1581), Master of St. Paul's School, where the writer, expatiating on the utility of *Archerie* as a preservative of health, says:—"how can I but prayse them, who professe it throughly, and maintaine it nobly, the friendly and frank *fellowship* of Prince Arthur's Knights, in and about the citie of London? which, if I had sacred to silence, would not my good friend in the citie, Maister Hewgh Offly, and the same my noble fellow in that order, Syr Launcelot, at our next meeting have given me a soure nodde, being the chief furtherer of the fact which I commend, and the famousest *knight* of the *fellowship* which I am of. Nay, would not even Prince Arthur himselfe, Maister Thomas Smith, and the whole *table* of those well-known knights, and most active archers, have laid in their challenge against their *fellow-knight,* if speaking of their pastime, I should have spared their names?"

The complacency with which Justice Shallow refers to his personification of poor Sir Dagonet, who in the romance is the fool of King Arthur, is charmingly characteristic, and must have been highly relished by an auditory familiar with all the personages of *La Morte d'Arthure.*

(5) SCENE II.—*And now is this Vice's dagger become a squire.*]—The following particulars concerning the old stage favourite, called the VICE, are mainly taken from an instructive article on the subject, in Mr. Collier's "History of English Dramatic Poetry." Mr. Douce is of opinion that the name was derived from the nature of the character; and certain it is that he is represented most wicked by design, and never good but by accident. As the Devil now and then appeared without the Vice, so the Vice sometimes appeared without the Devil. Malone tells us that "the principal employment of the Vice was to belabour the Devil;" but although he was frequently so engaged, he had also higher duties. He figured now and then in the religious plays of a later date; and in *The Life and Repentance of Mary Magdalen,* 1567, he performed the part of her lover, before her conversion, under the name of Infidelity: in *King Darius,* 1565, he also acted a prominent part, by his own impulses to mischief, under the name of Iniquity, without any prompting from the representative of the principle of evil. Such was the general style of the Vice, and as Iniquity he is spoken of by Shakespeare ("Richard III." III. 1,) and Ben Jonson, ("Staple of News," second Intermean.) The Vice and Iniquity seem, however, sometimes to have been distinct persons,* and he was not unfrequently called by the name of particular vices: thus, in *Lusty Juventus,* the Vice performs the part of Hypocrisy; in *Common Conditions,* he is called Conditions; in *Like Will to Like,* he is named Nichol Newfangle; in *The Trial of Treasure,* his part is that of Inclination; in *All for Money,* he is called Sin; in *Tom Tyler and his Wife,* Desire; and in *Appius and Virginia,* Hap-hazard.

Gifford designates the Vice "the Buffoon of the Old Mysteries and Moralities," as if he had figured in the Miracle-plays represented at Chester, Coventry, York, and elsewhere. Malone, also, speaks of him as the "constant attendant" of the Devil in "the ancient religious plays;" but the fact is, that the Vice was wholly unknown in our religious plays, which have hitherto gone by the name of Mysteries. *The Life and Repentance of Mary Magdalen,* and *King Darius,* already mentioned as containing the character of the Vice, were not written until after the reign of Mary. The same remark will apply to the *Interlude of Queen Hester,* 1561, which differs from other religious plays, inasmuch as the Vice there is a court-jester and servant, and is named Hardydardy.

On the external appearance of the Vice, Mr. Douce has observed, that, "being generally dressed in a fool's habit," he was gradually and undistinguishably blended with the domestic fool. Ben Jonson, in his *Devil is an Ass,* alludes to this very circumstance, when he is speaking of the fools of old kept in the houses of the nobility and gentry:—

——————"fifty years agone and six,
When every great man had his Vice stand by him
In his long coat, shaking his wooden dagger!"

The Vice here spoken of was the domestic fool of the nobility about the year 1560, to whom also Puttenham, in his *Arte of English Poesie,* alludes under the terms "buffoon or vice in plays."

In the first Intermean of Ben Jonson's *Staple of News,* Mirth leads us to suppose that it was a very common termination of the adventures of the Vice, for him to be carried off to hell on the back of the devil: "he would carry away the Vice on his back, quick to hell, in every play where he came." In *The longer thou livest the more Fool thou art,* and in *Like Will to Like,* the Vice is disposed of nearly in this summary manner. In *King Darius,* the Vice runs to hell of his own accord, to escape from Constancy, Equity, and Charity. According to Bishop Harsnet, in a passage cited by Malone, the Vice was in the habit of riding and beating the Devil, at other times than when he was thus carried against his will to punishment.

* In the play of "Histriomastix," 1610, we read:—"Enter a roaring Devil with the *Vice* on his back, *Iniquity* on one hand, and *Juventus* on the other."

ACT IV.

(1) SCENE II.]—*I do arrest thee, traitor, of high treason.*]—Holinshed's account of the insurrection does not, perhaps, directly implicate Prince John in this unparalleled breach of faith and honour; but it cannot be forgotten that the earl was acting under the orders of his general.

"The archbishop, accompanied with the Erle Marshall, devised certaine articles of such matters as it was supposed, that not onely the commonaltie of the Realme, but also the Nobilitie, found themselves agrieved with: which articles they shewed first unto such of their adherents as were neare aboute them, and after sent them abrode to theyr friendes further of, assuring them that for redresse of such oppressions, they woulde shedde the last droppe of bloud in theyr bodyes, if neede were. The Archbishop not meaning to stay after he saw hymselfe accompanied with a greate number of men, that came flocking to Yorke to take his parte in this quarrell, forthwith discovered his enterprice, causing the articles aforesayde to be set up in the publicke streetes of the Citie of Yorke and upon the gates of the monasteries, that eche man might understande the cause that moved him to rise in armes against the King, the reforming whereof did not yet apperteyne unto him. Hereupon knights, esquiers, gentlemen, yeomen, and other of the commons, * * * * assembled togither in great numbers, and the Archbishop comming forth amongst them clad in armor, encouraged, exhorted, and, by all means he coulde, pricked them forth to take the enterprise in hand, * * * * and thus not only all the citizens of York, but all other in the countries about, that were able to bear weapon, came to the Archbishop, and to the Erle Marshal. Indeed, the respect that men had to the Archbishop, caused them to like the better of the cause, since the gravitie of his age, his integrity of life, and incomparable learning, with the reverend aspect of his amiable personage, moved all menne to have him in no small estimation. The King advertised of these matters, meaning to prevent them, left his journey into Wales, and marched with al speed towards the north partes. Also Raufe Nevill, Erle of Westmerlande, that was not farre off, togither with the lorde John of Lancaster the king's sonne, being enformed of this rebellious attempt, assembled togither such power as they might make, * * * * and comming into a plaine within the forest of Galtree, caused theyr standarts to be pight downe in like sort as the Archbishop had pight his, over agaynst them, being farre stronger in number of people than the other, for (as some write) there were of the rebels at the least 20 thousand men. When the Erle of Westmerlande perceyved the force of adversaries, and that they lay still and attempted not to come forwarde upon him, he subtilly devised how to quail their purpose, and foorthwith dispatched Messengeres unto the Archbyshoppe to understande the cause as it were of that greate assemble, and for what cause contrarye to the kings peace they came so in armor. The Archbishop answered, that he tooke nothing in hande agaynste the king's peace, but that whatsover he did, tended rather to advaunce the peace and quiet of the common wealth, than otherwise, and where he and his companie were in armes, it was for feare of the king, to whom hee could have no free accesse by reason of such a multitude of flatterers as were about him, and therefore he mainteyned that his purpose was good and profitable, as well for the king himselfe, as for the realme, if men were willing to understand a truth: and herewith hee shewed forthe a skroll in which the articles were written, wherof before ye have heard. The Messengers returning unto the Earle of Westmerlande shewed him what they had heard and brought from the Archbishop. When he had read the articles, hee shewed in word and countenance outwardly that he lyked of the Archbyshoppes holy and vertuous intent and purpose, promising that he and his woulde prosecute the same in assysting the Archebishop, who rejoycing hereat, gave credite to the Earle, and perswaded the Earle Marshall agaynst hys will as it were to go with him to a place appoynted for them to common togyther. Here when they were mette with like number on eyther part, the articles were reade over, and without any more adoe, the earle of Westmerlande and those that were with him, agreed to doe theyr best to see that a reformation might bee had, according to the same. The Earle of Westmerlande using more policie than the rest: well (sayde he) then our travaile is come to the wished ende: and where our people have beene long in armour, let them depart home to their wonted trades and occupations: in the meane time let us drinke togyther, in signe of agreement, that the people on both sydes may see it, and know that it is true, that we be light at a poynt. They had no sooner shaked handes togither, but that a knight was sent streightwayes from the Archbishop to bring worde to the people that there was peace concluded, commanding eche man to lay aside his armes, and to resort home to their houses. The people beholding such tokens of peace, as shaking of handes, and drinking togither of the Lordes in loving manner, they being alreadie wearied with the unaccustomed travell of warre; brake up their fielde and returned homewardes; but in the meane time whilest the people of the Archbishoppes side withdrew away, the number of the contrarie part increased, according to order given by the earle of Westmerland, and yet the Archbishop perceyved not that he was deceyved, untill the Earl of Westmerland arrested both him and the earle Marshall with diverse other. * * * The Archbishop and the Earle Marshall were brought to Pomfret to the king, who in this meane while was advanced thither with his power, and from thence he went to Yorke, whither the prisoners were also brought, and there beheaded the morrow after Whitsundaie in a place without the citie, that is to understand, the Archbishop himselfe, the Earle marshall, Sir John Lampleie, and Sir Robert Plumpton. Unto all which persons though indemnitie were promised, yet was the same to none of them at anie hand performed. By the issue hereof, I meane the death of the foresaid, but speciallie of the archbishop, the prophesie of a sickelie canon of Bridlington in Yorkeshire fell out to be true, who darklie inough foretold this matter, and the infortunate event thereof in these words hereafter following, saieng:—

Pacem tractabunt, sed fraudem subter arabunt,
Pro nulla marca, salvabitur ille hierarcha.

(2.) SCENE III.—*A good sherris-sack hath a two-fold operation in it.*]—When we consider how familiar nearly everybody in this country must have been with the wine called *Sack*, from the sixteenth to the eighteenth century, it seems remarkable that any doubt should exist as to what that liquor really was; yet, after all the labour and research expended by the commentators on the older dramatists, the question is still not positively determined. The reason of this uncertainty appears to be, that when Sack was the universal wine sold in London and other great cities, the simple name was enough to distinguish it; one kind only was expressed, because one kind only was intended. But as commercial enterprise and maritime discovery became extended, other wines were introduced, very different from the genuine Sack, but which were assumed to have the same characteristics and qualities, and which therefore received the generical name, though occasionally with a local distinction prefixed to it, until at length its original meaning became indefinite, if not altogether unknown. In the slight notices of Sack contained in his "Illustrations of Shakespeare," Mr. Douce observes that there are two principal questions on the subject: first, whether Sack was known in the time of Henry IV.; second, whether it was a dry or a sweet wine, when this play was written? The first of these inquiries is altogether valueless, inasmuch as Shakespeare certainly never contemplated the historical age of Henry IV., but exhibited only the manners of his own time. The second question is relevant, and deserves attention.

It would weary the reader, however, and occupy far too much space, to insert a tithe of the passages collected from the old writers in illustration of the qualities of Sack. The most descriptive and important are before us, and the conclusions deducible from them appear to be, that Sack, properly so called, was a *Spanish wine*, and hence was named *Sherris*, or *Xeres Sack;* that it was a *hot, stimulating*, and especially *dry* wine, from which last quality its name of *Sack* (*sec*) was indubitably derived; that the name was also expressive of a class of wines comprehending several very different species of Sack, some of which were usually medicated or prepared according to the taste of the drinker; and that the *genuine* old Sack in reality closely resembled, if it were not indeed the very same liquor as the modern sherry, the simple name of which was not older than the end of the seventeenth century:—

"The next that stood up, with a countenance merry,
Was a pert sort of wine *that the moderns call Sherry*."
Bacchanalian Sessions, 1693.

That Sack, in the general meaning of the name, was a *Spanish wine*, is established, without going beyond the older dictionaries. Florio, in defining the liquor called "*Tibidrago*," says that it is "a kind of strong Spanish wine, or Sacke; we call it *Rubiedavy*." A name, by the way, which does not appear to have been noticed by any authors who have written on wines. Cotgrave translates sack into "*Vin d'Espagne:*" Coles renders the word "*Vinum Hispanicum;*" and Minsheu gives it the same signification in eleven languages, as if that were to be regarded as the best explanation in all.

Of its hot and stimulating qualities, we need no further evidence than the copious and eloquent eulogy of Falstaff in the present speech, and Herrick's "Welcome" and "Farewell to Sack," published in 1648; and its dryness, by which is to be understood the contrary of a sweet wine, is sufficiently indicated both by its name, and by the practice of sweetening and preparing it for different purposes, or according to the taste of the imbiber. *Sack and sugar, burnt Sack*, and *Sack-posset* are well-known names of these preparations, and even the "lime in the sack," which Sir John condemns as a vile adulteration, may be shown to belong to the same class of medicated liquors.

Dr. Venner, 1622, considered the sugar which was occasionally added to the Sack to be quite as much of a medicine as a luxury; but Fynes Moryson, in 1617, regarded it as simply indicative of the national liking for sweetness in general. "Clownes and vulgar men only," he remarks, "use large drinking of beere, or ale; but gentlemen *garrawse* only in wine; with which they mix sugar; which I never observed in any other place or kingdom to be used for that purpose. And, because the taste of the English is thus delighted with sweetness, the wines in taverns,—for I speak not of merchantes' or gentlemen's cellars—are mixed at the filling thereof, to make them pleasant."

The next artificial preparation of Sack, the "burning" it, seems to have been designed partly to warm the liquor, partly to enrich the flavour, and partly to abate the strength of the spirit; but it was probably a slight process, that simple preparation only, to which Falstaff refers, when he says, "Go, brew me a pottle of sack finely;" a brewage altogether different to the elaborate concoction called *Sack-posset*, the excellence of which, however,—the method of making it in Shakespeare's days, and the proper hour when it ought to be found in perfect projection—will be more fittingly set forth in the commentary on "The Merry Wives of Windsor," where the "posset" is twice mentioned.

(3) Scene IV.—
—— *they do observe*
Unfather'd heirs, and loathly births of nature.]

This passage has been strangely misunderstood. By *loathly births of nature*, are, of course, meant, *monstrous mis-shapen* productions of nature. Such prodigies, we know, from the many broadside descriptions of them which are registered in the books of the Stationers' Company, or are still extant, and from the good-humoured sarcasms of Shakespeare—"*A strange fish! Were I in England now, (as once I was,) and had but this fish painted, not a holiday fool there but would give a piece of silver: there would this monster make a man; any strange beast there makes a man*,"—possessed an extraordinary fascination for our credulous and sight-loving forefathers. But the *unfather'd heirs*, whom Prince Humphrey is alarmed to see the people reverence, were certain so-called *prophets*, who pretended to have been conceived by miracle, like Merlin—

"And, sooth, men say that he was not the sonne
Of mortall syre or other living wight,
But wondrously begotten, and begoune
By false illusion of a guilefull spright
On a faire lady Nonne, that whilome hight
Matilda, daughter to Pubidius
Who was the lord of Mathtraval by right,
And coosen unto king Ambrosius;
Whence he indued was with skill so merveilous."
Faerie Queene, III. 3, St. 13.

and assumed, on that account, to be endowed, like him, with the prophetic character. Walter Scott, it will be remembered, imputes a kindred origin to his wizard Hermit, Brian, in "The Lady of the Lake"—

"Of Brian's birth strange tales were told," &c.
Canto III. St. 5.

And Montaigne refers to such supposed miraculous conceptions in his Essay entitled the *Apology for Raymond Sebond*, "In *Mahomet's* religion, by the easie beleefe of that people, are many *Merlins* found; That is to say, *fatherles children;* Spiritual children, conceived and borne devinely in the wombs of virgins, and that in their language beare names, importing as much."—"Florio's Montaigne," folio 1603, p. 308.

If the meaning here attributed to the expression *unfather'd heirs*, be that intended by the poet, it may, perhaps, afford a key to another in "The Merry Wives of Windsor, Act V. Scene 5, which has been long discussed, but never yet explained,—

"*You orphan heirs of fixed destiny*."

(4) Scene IV.—

War. '*Tis call'd Jerusalem, my noble lord.*
K. Hen. *Laud be to God!—even there my life must end.*]

In looking at this representation of Henry's death, in connection with the beginning of his dramatic history, we are reminded of the words of the Duke of Ephesus, at the end of "The Comedy of Errors," "Why, here begins his morning story right." The king discovers in the present scene, that one reason at least for his pressing forward an expedition to the Holy Land, was the fulfilment of a prediction that he should die in Jerusalem. Such a prophecy, as to the death of an important personage, appears to have been not unusual in the middle ages; and a remarkable illustration of it is on record, concerning Pope Sylvester II. Cardinal Benno states, that when he inquired of spiritual agency as to the length of his life, he was assured that he should not die until he had said mass at Jerusalem; on which he promised himself a very long existence. In the fifth year of his pontificate, however, A.D. 1003, he happened to celebrate mass in the church called "The Holy Cross in Jerusalem;" and there he was suddenly taken ill, and soon after died. Holinshed seems to doubt the prediction respecting Henry IV. "Whether this was true, that so he spake as one that gave too much credit to foolish prophesies and vaine tales, or whether it was fained, as in such cases it commonlie happeneth, we leave to the admired reader to judge." There does not appear, however, to be any sufficient reason to doubt either that such a prediction was uttered, or that Henry declared it. His purpose of levying "a power of English" to recover the city of Jerusalem from the infidels, was universally known, and the prophecy, that he would die there, seemed to be a very natural conclusion, and a politic flattering of his design as well. Henry had brought forward this measure at a very early period of his reign, and it continued to be "the ruling passion strong in death." Shortly before he was attacked by apoplexy at Eltham, about Christmas, 1413, he held a council at Whitefriars, which ordered the fitting out of ships and galleys, and other preparations to be made for the voyage. And even after his partial recovery, when "hee was taken with his last sicknesse, he was making his prayers at Sainte Edwardes shrine, *there as it were to take his leave, and so to proceede forthe on hys iourney;* and was then "so suddaynely and greevouslie taken that suche as were about him, feared least he would have dyed presently, wherefore to relieve him if it were possible, they bare him into a chamber that was nexte at hand, belonging to the Abbot of Westminster, where they layd him on a pallet before the fier, and used all remedyes to revive him: at length, hee recovered hys speeche, and understanding and perceiving himselfe in a strange place which he knew not, hee willed to know if the chamber had any particular name, whereunto aunswere was made, that it was called '*Jerusalem.*' Then saide the king, laudes be gyven to the father of heaven, for now I knowe that I shall dye heere in thys chamber, according to the prophecie of me declared, that I shoulde depart this life in Jerusalem." * * *

It is quite possible that his early and active military employment in foreign countries might have given the first impetus to his design of an expedition to Palestine; but it is still more probable that he contemplated it as a meritorious atonement for the means by which he had obtained the crown.

The effigy of Henry IV. upon his tomb at Canterbury, is considered to be the most splendid of our regal series. No doubt was entertained that the King was really buried there, until the discovery by Wharton of a MS. in Corpus Christi College, Cambridge, written by Clement Maydestone, a contemporary and an ecclesiastic, entitled—"A History of the Martyrdom of Archbishop Scroop," in which the following passage occurs:—

"Within thirty days after the death of the said king Henry the Fourth, a certain man of his household came to the house of the Holy Trinity at Houndeslow to eat, and the standers-by discoursing of that king's probity of life, the aforesaid person made answer to an esquire, whose name was Thomas Maydestone, then sitting at the same table, *God knows whether he was a good man; but this I certainly know, that when his body was carried from Westminster towards Canterbury, in a small vessel to be buried, I was one of the three persons that threw his body into the sea between Berkyng and Gravesend.* And he added, confirming it with an oath,—*So great a storm of wind and waves came upon us, that many noblemen that followed us in eight small vessels, were dispersed, and narrowly escaped the danger of death. But we that were with the body despairing of our lives, by common consent threw it into the sea, and a great calm ensued; but the chest it was in, covered with cloth of gold, we carried in very honourable manner to Canterbury, and buried it.* The monks of Canterbury may therefore say, The tomb of King Henry the Fourth is with us, but not his body, as Peter said of holy David, Acts ii. Almighty God is witness and judge that I, Clement Maydestone, saw that man, and heard him swear to my father, Thomas Maydestone, that all abovesaid was true."

It had long been the wish of historians and antiquaries to test the value of this story, and at length on the 21st of August, 1832, the tomb was opened by the cathedral authorities, when the body was found cased in lead, within a rude elm coffin, so much larger than necessary, that the intervening spaces were filled with hay-bands. On removing the wrapper, "to the astonishment of all present, the face of the deceased king was seen in remarkable preservation. The nose elevated, the cartilage even remaining, though, on the admission of the air, it sunk rapidly away, and had entirely disappeared before the examination was finished. The skin of the chin was entire, of the consistence and thickness of the upper leather of a shoe, brown and moist; the beard thick and matted and of a deep russet color."

ACT V.

(1) SCENE I.—*By cock and pye.*]—This popular adjuration was once supposed to refer to the sacred name, and to the table of services in the Romish Church, called *The Pie:* but it is now thought to be what Hotspur termed a mere "protest of pepper-gingerbread," as innocent as Slender's, "By these gloves," or "By this hat." In "Soliman and Perseda," 1599, it occurs coupled with *mouse-foot;* "By *cock and pie* and mouse-foot;" and again, in "The Plaine Man's Pathway to Heaven," by Arthur Dent, 1607, where we have the following dialogue: Asunctus—"I know a man that will never swear but by *cock* or *py,* or *mouse-foot.* I hope you will not say these be oaths. For he is as honest a man as ever brake bread. You shall not hear an oath come out of his mouth." Theologus—"I do not think he is so honest a man as you make him. For it is no small sin to *swear by creatures.*" The *Cock* and *Pye, i. e.,* and *Magpie,* was an ordinary ale-house sign, and may thus have become a subject for the vulgar to swear by. Douce, however, ascribes to it a less ignoble origin, and his interpretation is much too ingenious to be passed in silence:—"It will, no doubt, be recollected, that in the days of ancient chivalry it was the practice to make solemn vows or engagements for the performance of some considerable enterprise. This ceremony was usually performed during some grand feast or entertainment, at which a roasted peacock or pheasant being served up by ladies in a dish of gold or silver, was thus presented to each knight, who then made the particular vow which he had chosen, with great solemnity. When this custom had fallen into disuse, the peacock nevertheless continued to be a favourite dish, and was introduced on the table in a *pie,* the head, with gilded beak, being proudly elevated above the crust, and the splendid tail expanded. Other birds of smaller value were introduced in the same manner, and the recollection of the old peacock vows might occasion the less serious, or even burlesque, imitation of swearing not only by the bird itself but also by the *pie;* and hence probably the oath *by cock and pie,* for the use of which no very old authority can be found. The vow to the peacock had even got into the mouths of such as had no pretensions to knighthood. Thus in *The merchant's second tale, or the history of Beryn,* the host is made to say,—

"*I make a vowe to the pecock* there shal wake a foul mist."

(2) SCENE II.—

This is the English, not the Turkish court;
Not Amurath an Amurath succeeds,
But Harry, Harry.]

Amurath the Third, who was the seventh Emperor of the Turks, died in 1595, and the people, being disaffected to his eldest son, Mahomet, and inclined to a younger one, the death of the emperor was kept secret for some days by the Janissaries, until Mahomet came from Amasia to Constantinople. On his arrival, he was saluted Emperor by the Bassas and others with whom he was a favourite; whereupon, without informing his brothers of their father's demise, he invited all of them to a solemn entertainment, and there had them strangled. Mr. Malone conceives it highly probable that Shakespeare alludes to this transaction in the present passage, and that the period when it happened may fix the date of the play to the beginning of the year 1596. There is no solid reason, however, for believing that the poet had this particular circumstance in his mind, or that it is in any way connected with the date of the piece. The barbarous and unnatural custom which prevailed among the Turkish kings and emperors, of slaughtering all their brethren and nearest kinsmen, on coming to the throne, that they might relieve themselves from the apprehension of competitors, originated many years before with Bajazet, son to Amurath the First (third emperor of the Turks), and it is much more likely that Shakespeare in this instance referred to a general practice, rather than to a special event.

(3) SCENE V.—

We will,—according to your strength, and qualities,—
Give you advancement.]

There is a speech somewhat similar to this in the corresponding scene of "The famous Victories of Henry the Fifth:"—

"Ah Tom, your former life grieves me,
And makes me to abandon and abolish your company for ever,
And therefore not upon pain of death to approch my presence,
By ten miles space, then if I heare well of you,
It may bee I will doe somewhat for you,
Otherwise looke for no more favour at my hands
Then at any other mans."

Both dramatists were indebted for the incident to Holinshed, who records it as follows:—"Immediately after that hee was invested Kyng, and had receyved the Crowne, he determined with himselfe to putte upon him the shape of a new man, turning insolencie and wildnesse into gravitie and sobernesse; And whereas hee hadde passed his youth in wanton pastime and riotous misorder, with a sort of misgoverned mates, and unthriftie playfeers, he nowe banished them from his presence (not unrewarded nor yet unpreferred), inhibiting them uppon a greate payne, not once to approche, lodge, or sojourn within tenne miles of his Courte or mansion; and in their places he elected and chose men of gravitie, witte, and high policie, by whose wise counsell, and prudent advertisement, he might at all times rule to his honoure, and governe to his profyte; whereas if he should have reteined the other lustie companions aboute him, he doubted least they might have allured him to such lewde and lighte partes, as with them beforetyme he had youthfully used."

(4) SCENE V.—*Go, carry sir John Falstaff to the Fleet.*]—"Everybody will agree with Dr. Johnson in the impropriety of Falstaff's cruel and unnecessary commitment to prison. The king had already given him a fit admonition as to his future conduct, and banished him to a proper distance from the court. We must suppose therefore that the chief justice had far exceeded his royal master's commands on this occasion, or that the king had repented of his lenity. The latter circumstance would indeed augur but unfavourably of the sovereign's future regard to justice; for had he not himself been a partaker, and consequently an encourager, of Falstaff's excesses?"—DOUCE.

EPILOGUE.

(1) *And so kneel down, &c.*]—At the termination of the performance, from a very early period, it was customary for the players to kneel down and pray for their patrons, the king or queen, or House of Commons, &c. Hence probably, as Steevens suggests, the *Vivant Rex et Regina*, still appended at the bottom of the play-bills. Thus, at the end of "Apius and Virginia," 1575:—

"Beseeching God, as duty is, our gracious queene to save,
The nobles and the commons eke, with prosperous life I crave."

Again in Middleton's "A Mad World, my Masters:"—

"This shows like kneeling after the play; I praying for my lord Owemuch, and his good countess, our honourable lady and mistress."

And also in "New Custom:"—

"Preserve our noble Queen Elizabeth, and her counsell all."

CRITICAL OPINIONS

ON THE

FIRST AND SECOND PARTS OF KING HENRY IV.

"None of *Shakespeare's* plays are more read than the *First and Second Parts of Henry the Fourth.* Perhaps no author has ever in two plays afforded so much delight. The great events are interesting, for the fate of kingdoms depends upon them; the slighter occurrences are diverting, and, except one or two, sufficiently probable: the incidents are multiplied with wonderful fertility of invention, and the characters diversified with the utmost nicety of discernment, and the profoundest skill in the nature of man.

"The prince, who is the hero both of the comick and tragick part, is a young man of great abilities and violent passions, whose sentiments are right, though his actions are wrong; whose virtues are obscured by negligence, and whose understanding is dissipated by levity. In his idle hours he is rather loose than wicked; and when the occasion forces out his latent qualities, he is great without effort, and brave without tumult. The trifler is roused into a hero, and the hero again reposes in the trifler. This character is great, original, and just.

"*Percy* is a rugged soldier, cholerick, and quarrelsome, and has only the soldier's virtues, generosity and courage.

"But *Falstaff,* unimitated, unimitable *Falstaff,* how shall I describe thee? Thou compound of sense and vice; of sense which may be admired, but not esteemed; of vice which may be despised, but hardly detested. *Falstaff* is a character loaded with faults, and with those faults which naturally produce contempt. He is a thief and a glutton, a coward and a boaster, always ready to cheat the weak, and prey upon the poor; to terrify the timorous, and insult the defenceless. At once obsequious and malignant, he satirizes in their absence those whom he lives by flattering. He is familiar with the prince only as an agent of vice, but of this familiarity he is so proud, as not only to be supercilious and haughty with common men, but to think his interest of importance to the duke of *Lancaster.* Yet the man thus corrupt, thus despicable, makes himself necessary to the prince that despises him, by the most pleasing of all qualities, perpetual gaiety; by an unfailing power of exciting laughter, which is the more freely indulged, as his wit is not of the splendid or ambitious kind, but consists in easy scapes and sallies of levity, which make sport, but raise no envy. It must be observed, that he is stained with no enormous or sanguinary crimes, so that his licentiousness is not so offensive but that it may be borne for his mirth.

"The moral to be drawn from this representation is, that no man is more dangerous than he that, with a will to corrupt, hath the power to please; and that neither wit nor honesty ought to think themselves safe with such a companion, when they see *Henry* seduced by *Falstaff.*"—Johnson.

"The first part of *Henry the Fourth* is particularly brilliant in the serious scenes, from the contrast between two young heroes, Prince Henry and Percy (with the characteristical name of Hotspur). All the amiability and attractiveness is certainly on the side of the prince: however familiar he makes himself with bad company, we can never mistake him for one of them: the ignoble does indeed touch, but it does not contaminate him; and his wildest freaks appear merely as witty tricks, by which his restless mind sought to burst through the inactivity to which he was constrained, for on the first occasion which wakes him out of his unruly levity he distinguishes himself without effort in the most chivalrous guise. Percy's boisterous valour is not without a mixture of rude manners, arrogance, and boyish obstinacy ; but these errors, which prepare for him an early death, cannot disfigure the majestic image of his noble youth ; we are carried away by his fiery spirit at the very moment we would most censure it. Shakspeare has admirably shown why so formidable a revolt against an unpopular and really an illegitimate prince was not attended with success : Glendower's superstitious fancies respecting himself, the effeminacy of the young Mortimer, the ungovernable disposition of Percy, who will listen to no prudent counsel, the irresolution of his older friends, the want of unity of plan and motive, are all characterized by delicate but unmistakable traits. After Percy has departed from the scene, the splendour of the enterprise is, it is true, at an end ; there remain none but the subordinate participators in the revolts, who are reduced by Henry IV., more by policy than by warlike achievements. To overcome this dearth of matter, Shakspeare was in the Second Part obliged to employ great art, as he never allowed himself to adorn history with more arbitrary embellishments than the dramatic form rendered indispensable. The piece is opened by confused rumours from the field of battle : the powerful impression produced by Percy's fall, whose name and reputation were peculiarly adapted to be the watchword of a bold enterprise, make him in some degree an acting personage after his death. The last acts are occupied with the dying king's remorse of conscience, his uneasiness at the behaviour of the prince, and lastly, the clearing up of the misunderstanding between father and son, which make up several most affecting scenes. All this, however, would still be inadequate to fill the stage, if the serious events were not interrupted by a comedy which runs through both parts of the play, which is enriched from time to time with new figures, and which first comes to its catastrophe at the conclusion of the whole, namely, when Henry V., immediately after ascending the throne, banishes to a proper distance the companions of his youthful excesses, who had promised to themselves a rich harvest from his kingly favour.

"Falstaff is the crown of Shakspeare's comic invention. He has, without exhausting himself, continued this character throughout three plays, and exhibited him in every variety of situation ; the figure is drawn so definitely and individually, that even to the mere reader it conveys the clear impression of personal acquaintance. Falstaff is the most agreeable and entertaining knave that ever was portrayed. His contemptible qualities are not disguised : old, lecherous, and dissolute ; corpulent beyond measure, and always intent upon cherishing his body with eating, drinking, and sleeping ; constantly in debt, and anything but conscientious in his choice of means by which money is to be raised ; a cowardly soldier, and a lying braggart ; a flatterer of his friends before their face, and a satirist behind their backs ; and yet we are never disgusted with him. We see that his tender care of himself is without any mixture of malice towards others ; he will only not be disturbed in the pleasant repose of his sensuality, and this he obtains through the activity of his understanding. Always on the alert, and good-humoured, ever ready to crack jokes on others, and to enter into those of which he is himself the subject, so that he justly boasts he is not only witty himself, but the cause of wit in others, he is an admirable companion for youthful idleness and levity. Under a helpless exterior, he conceals an extremely acute mind ; he has always at command some dexterous turn whenever any of his free jokes begin to give displeasure ; he is shrewd in his distinctions, between those whose favour he has to win and those over whom he may assume a familiar authority. He is so convinced that the part which he plays can only pass under the cloak of wit, that even when alone he is never altogether serious, but gives the drollest colouring to his love-intrigues, his intercourse with others, and to his own sensual philosophy. Witness his inimitable soliloquies on honour, on the influence of wine on bravery, his descriptions of the beggarly vagabonds whom he enlisted, of Justice Shallow, &c. Falstaff has about him a whole court of amusing caricatures, who by turns make their appearance, without ever throwing him into the shade. The adventure, in which the Prince, under the disguise of a robber, compels him to give up the spoil which he had just taken ; the scene where the two act the part of the King and the Prince ; Falstaff's behaviour in the field, his mode of raising recruits, his patronage of Justice Shallow, which afterwards takes such an unfortunate turn :—all this forms a series of characteristic scenes of the most original description, full of pleasantry, and replete with nice and ingenious observation, such as could only find a place in a historical play like the present."—SCHLEGEL.

Act I. Sc. 1.

THE

MERRY WIVES OF WINDSOR.

"A Most pleasaunt and excellent conceited Comedie, of Syr *Iohn Falstaffe,* and the merrie Wives of *Windsor.* Entermixed with sundrie variable and pleasing humors, of Syr *Hugh* the Welch Knight, Iustice *Shallow,* and his wise Cousin M. *Slender.* With the swaggering vaine of Auncient *Pistoll,* and Corporall *Nym.* By *William Shakespeare.* As it hath bene diuers times Acted by the right Honorable my Lord Chamberlaines seruants. Both before her Maiestie, and else-where. London: Printed by T. C. for Arthur Iohnson, and are to be sold at his shop in Powles Church-yard, at the signe of the Flower de Leuse and the Crowne, 1602." Such is the title of the earliest edition of this play, the entry of which on the Registers of the Stationers' Company is as follows:—

"18 Jan., 1601—2.

"John Busby.] An excellent and pleasant conceited Commedie of Sir John Faulstof, and the Merry Wyves of Windesor.

"Arth. Johnson.] By assignement from John Busbye a book, An excellent and pleasant conceited comedie of Sir John Faulstafe and the mery wyves of Windsor."

A second edition of this quarto was published by Arthur Johnson, in 1619:—"A most pleasant and excellent conceited Comedy, of Sir John Falstaffe and the Merry Wives of Windsor. With the swaggering vaine of Ancient Pistoll and Corporall Nym. Written by W. Shakespeare." Of the original version of the Merry Wives of Windsor, Mr. Collier says,—"It has been universally admitted that the 4to, 1602, was piratical, and our conviction is, that like the first edition of 'Henry IV.,' in 1600, it was made up, for the purpose of sale, partly from notes taken at the theatre, and partly from memory, without even the assistance of any of the parts as delivered by the copyist of the theatre to the actors."

Mr. Halliwell and Mr. Knight take a very different view of this edition, which, with the earlier editors, they conceive to have been a transcript of the play as first produced, and the basis of the complete and admirable Comedy as it stands in the folio of 1623. With this opinion most people who have well examined the quarto, 1602, will probably concur, though few we apprehend are likely to agree with these gentlemen in assigning it to a period as early as 1592, upon so slender a foundation as the supposed connexion between the visit of the Duke of Würtenburg to England in that year, and the imposition practised upon the Host of the Garter by some German travellers. If any allusion to a visitor received by the Court with so much distinction, were intended, an offensive one would hardly have been ventured during the life-time of the Queen. Another forbidding consideration to this theory is, its involving the conclusion that "The Merry Wives of Windsor" was written and acted before even the First

Part of "Henry IV.," and that the fat humorist, whose love adventures afford so much entertainment, was *Oldcastle,* and not *Falstaff.* But the most serious objection to it is, that it strikes at the root of the long-cherished tradition, of Elizabeth being so well pleased with the Falstaff of "Henry IV.," that she commanded a play to be written, in which the knight should be exhibited in love, and was so eager to see it acted, that she directed it should be finished in fourteen days. We can by no means afford to part with this tradition: it accounts for the many evidences of haste observable in the first draft of the piece, and reconciles all the difficulties which are experienced in attempting to determine whether the incidents are to be taken as occurring before the historical plays of "Henry IV.," Parts I. and II., and "Henry V.," or between any two of them, or after the whole. The title of the original sketch, "Syr John Falstaff," &c., the "Merry Wives" being at first considered subordinate attractions only, and the delineation of Falstaff and his satellites, both in that and in the finished version, are to us conclusive as to these characters being *old favourites* with the public; and if we accept the pleasant tradition of their revival at the bidding of the Queen, there need be no hesitation in receiving them "without regard to their situations and catastrophes in former plays."

An excellent reprint of the first edition of "The Merry Wives of Windsor," was made by Mr. Halliwell for the Shakespeare Society in 1842, in the appendix to which he has given the tales from which a few of the incidents in this comedy are thought to be derived. These consist, I. of a story from "Le tredici piacevoli notti del S. Gio. Francesco Straparola," 8vo. Vineg. 1569, vol. i. fol. 47. II. A tale from "Il Pecorone di Ser Giovanni Fiorentino," 4to. Trevig. 1640, fol. 7. III. A story from a scarce collection of early English tales, entitled "The Fortunate, the Deceived, and the Unfortunate Lovers," 4to. Lond. 1632. IV. Another story from "Le tredici piacevoli notti del S. Gio. Fr. Straparola," Vineg. 1569, vol. i. fol. 129. V. A tale from Tarlton's "Newes out of Purgatorie," 4to. London, 1590, taken from the preceding novel of "Straparola." Dr. Farmer was of opinion that Falstaff's mishaps with the Merry Wives were taken from this story. And, VI. a tale extracted from a rare work, called "Westward for Smelts," 4to. Lond. 1620, which Malone thought led Shakespeare to lay the scene of Falstaff's love adventures at Windsor.

Persons Represented.

Sir JOHN FALSTAFF.
FENTON, *a young Gentleman.*
SHALLOW, *a Country Justice.*
SLENDER, *Cousin to* Shallow.
FORD, PAGE, } *Two Gentlemen dwelling at Windsor.*
WILLIAM PAGE, *a boy, son to* Page.
SIR HUGH EVANS, *a Welsh Parson.*
Dr. CAIUS, *a French Physician.*
Host of the Garter Inn.
BARDOLPH, PISTOL, NYM, } *Followers of* Falstaff.

ROBIN, *page to* Falstaff.
SIMPLE, *servant to* Slender.
RUGBY, *servant to* Dr. Caius.

Mistress FORD.
Mistress PAGE.
Mistress ANNE PAGE, *her Daughter.*
Mistress QUICKLY, *servant to* Dr. Caius.

Servants to Page, Ford, &c. &c.

SCENE,—WINDSOR, *and the parts adjacent.*

ACT I.

SCENE I.—Windsor. *Before* Page's *House.*

Enter Justice Shallow, Slender, *and* Sir Hugh Evans.

Shal. Sir Hugh,(1) persuade me not; I will make a Star-chamber(2) matter of it: if he were twenty sir John Falstaffs, he shall not abuse Robert Shallow, esquire.

Slen. In the county of Gloster, justice of peace, and *coram.*

Shal. Ay, cousin Slender, and *Cust-alorum.*[a]

Slen. Ay, and *ratolorum* too; and a gentleman born, master parson; who writes himself *armigero* in any bill, warrant, quittance, or obligation; *armigero.*

[a] *Cust-alorum.*] The provincial abbreviation, probably, of *Custos Rotulorum.* Correctly, Shallow's designation was, "Justice of the Peace, and of the Quorum and Custos Rotulorum."

Shal. Ay, that I do; and have done any time these three hundred years.

Slen. All his successors, gone before him, hath done't; and all his ancestors, that come after him, may: they may give the dozen white luces in their coat.

Shal. It is an old coat.

Eva. The dozen white louses do pecome an old coat well; it agrees well, *passant:* it is a familiar peast to man, and signifies—love.

Shal. The luce is the fresh fish; the salt fish is an old coat.(3)

Slen. I may quarter, coz?

Shal. You may, by marrying.

Eva. It is marring, indeed, if he quarter it.

Shal. Not a whit.

Eva. Yes, per-lady; if he has a quarter of

your coat, there is put three skirts for yourself, in my simple conjectures: but that is all one: if sir John Falstaff have committed disparagements unto you, I am of the church, and will be glad to do my penevolence, to make atonements and compromises petween you.

SHAL. The Council shall hear it; it is a riot.

EVA. It is not meet the Council hear a riot; there is no fear of Got in a riot: the Council, look you, shall desire to hear the fear of Got, and not to hear a riot; take your vizaments in that.

SHAL. Ha! o' my life, if I were young again, the sword should end it.

EVA. It is petter that friends is the sword, and end it: and there is also another device in my prain, which, peradventure, prings goot discretions with it. There is Anne Page, which is daughter to master George * Page, which is pretty virginity.

SLEN. Mistress[a] Anne Page? she has brown hair, and speaks small like a woman.

EVA. It is that fery person for all the 'orld, as just as you will desire; and seven hundred pounds of monies, and gold, and silver, is her grandsire, upon his death's-ped, (Got deliver to a joyful resurrections!) give, when she is aple to overtake seventeen years old: it were a goot motion, if we leave our pribbles and prabbles, and desire a marriage petween master Abraham and mistress Anne Page.

SHAL. Did her grandsire leave her seven hundred pound?[b]

EVA. Ay, and her father is make her a petter penny.[c]

SHAL. I know the young gentlewoman; she has good gifts.

EVA. Seven hundred pounds, and possibilities, is goot gifts.

SHAL. Well, let us see honest master Page: is Falstaff there?

EVA. Shall I tell you a lie? I do despise a liar, as I do despise one that is false; or, as I despise one that is not true. The knight, sir John, is there; and, I peseech you, pe ruled by your well-willers. I will peat the door [*Knocks.*] for master Page. What, hoa! Got pless your house here!

Enter PAGE.

PAGE. Who's there?

EVA. Here is Got's plessing, and your friend, and justice Shallow: and here young master Slender; that, peradventures, shall tell you another tale, if matters grow to your likings.

PAGE. I am glad to see your worships well: I thank you for my venison, master Shallow.

SHAL. Master Page, I am glad to see you; much good do it your good heart! I wished your venison better; it was ill killed.—How doth good mistress Page?—and I thank you always with my heart, la; with my heart.

PAGE. Sir, I thank you.

SHAL. Sir, I thank you; by yea and no, I do.

PAGE. I am glad to see you, good master Slender.

SLEN. How does your fallow greyhound, sir? I heard say, he was out-run on Cotsale.(4)

PAGE. It could not be judged, sir.

SLEN. You'll not confess, you'll not confess.

SHAL. That he will not;—'t is your fault, 't is your fault:[d]—'t is a good dog.

PAGE. A cur, sir.

SHAL. Sir, he's a good dog, and a fair dog; can there be more said? he is good, and fair.—Is sir John Falstaff here?

PAGE. Sir, he is within; and I would I could do a good office between you.

EVA. It is spoke as a Christians ought to speak.

SHAL. He hath wronged me, master Page.

PAGE. Sir, he doth in some sort confess it.

SHAL. If it be confessed, it is not redressed: is not that so, master Page? He hath wronged me; indeed, he hath; at a word, he hath; believe me; Robert Shallow, esquire, saith, he is wronged.

PAGE. Here comes sir John.

Enter SIR JOHN FALSTAFF, BARDOLPH, NYM, *and* PISTOL.

FAL. Now, master Shallow; you'll complain of me to the king?

SHAL. Knight, you have beaten my men, killed my deer, and broke open my lodge.

FAL. But not kissed your keeper's daughter!

SHAL. Tut, a pin! this shall be answered.

FAL. I will answer it straight: I have done all this: that is now answered.

SHAL. The Council shall know this.

FAL. 'Twere better for you, if it were known in counsel:[e] you'll be laughed at.

(*) Old text, *Thomas*.

[a] Mistress *Anne Page?*] So late as to the beginning of the last century an unmarried lady was styled *Mistress*.

[b] Did her grandsire, &c.] The folio gives this and a succeeding speech, "I know the young gentlewoman," &c. to Slender. From the context it is evident they belong to Shallow.

[c] Petter penny.] *Better penny* was proverbial, but its precise meaning has not come down to us.

[d] *Your* fault:] That is, your *misfortune*. This meaning of the word is illustrated by a passage in "Pericles," Act IV. Sc. 3:—

"BAWD. You are lit into my hands, where you are like to live.
MARINA. The more my *fault*,
To 'scape his hands, where I was like to die."

It occurs again in the present play, Act III. Sc. 3, with the same sense:—

"PAGE. I would not have your distemper in this kind, for the wealth of Windsor Castle.
FORD. 'T is my *fault*, Master Page; I suffer for it."

[e] Counsel:] Falstaff quibbles on the words *council* and *counsel;* the latter signifying *secrecy*. "'Twere better for you it were known only to those who will not talk of it, or you will become ridiculous."

EVA. *Pauca verba*, sir John, good worts.

FAL. Good worts! good cabbage.[a]—Slender, I broke your head; what matter have you against me?

SLEN. Marry, sir, I have matter in my head against you; and against your coney-catching[b] rascals, Bardolph, Nym, and Pistol. They carried me to the tavern, and made me drunk, and afterwards picked my pocket.[c]

BARD. You Banbury cheese![d]

SLEN. Ay, it is no matter.

PIST. How now, Mephostophilus?[e]

SLEN. Ay, it is no matter.

NYM. Slice, I say! *pauca, pauca;* slice! that's my humour.

SLEN. Where's Simple, my man?—can you tell, cousin?

EVA. Peace, I pray you! Now let us understand: there is three umpires in this matter, as I understand: that is—master Page, *fidelicet*, master Page; and there is myself, *fidelicet*, myself; and the three party is, lastly and finally, mine Host of the Garter.

PAGE. We three, to hear it, and end it between them.

EVA. Fery goot: I will make a prief of it in my note-book; and we will afterwards 'ork upon the cause, with as great discreetly as we can.

FAL. Pistol,—

PIST. He hears with ears.

EVA. The tevil and his tam! what phrase is this, *He hears with ear?* Why, it is affectations.

FAL. Pistol, did you pick master Slender's purse?

---

a *Good* worts! *good* cabbage.] *Worts* meant *coleworts, cabbages*, and any kind of pot-herbs, formerly.

b *Your* coney-catching *rascals*,—] A *coney-catcher*, by metaphor from those that rob warrens or coney-grounds, was a *sharper*, a *trickster*.

c They carried me to the tavern, &c.] These words, which seem to introduce Falstaff's subsequent question, ("Pistol, did you pick Master Slender's purse?") are restored from the quarto, 1602.

d *You* Banbury cheese!] A soft, thin cream-cheese. "Put off your cloathes, and you are like a *Banbery cheese*, nothing but paring."—JACK DRUM'S ENTERTAINMENT, 1601.

e Mephostophilus?] The name of an evil spirit in the popular history of Dr. Faustus. It was also a cant word for a gaunt-faced, lanthorn-jawed fellow.

SLEN. Ay, by these gloves, did he, (or I would I might never come in mine own great chamber again else,) of seven groats in mill-sixpences,[a] and two Edward shovel-boards, that cost me two shilling and two pence a-piece of Yead Miller, by these gloves.

FAL. Is this true, Pistol?

EVA. No; it is false, if it is a pick-purse.

PIST. Ha, thou mountain-foreigner!—Sir John and master mine,
I combat challenge of this latten bilbo:[b]
Word of denial in thy *labras*[c] here;
Word of denial: froth and scum, thou liest.

SLEN. By these gloves, then 'twas he.

NYM. Be avised, sir, and pass good humours: I will say, *marry trap*, with you, if you run the nuthook's[d] humour on me; that is the very note of it.

SLEN. By this hat, then he in the red face had it; for though I cannot remember what I did when you made me drunk, yet I am not altogether an ass.

FAL. What say you, *Scarlet and John?*

BARD. Why, sir, for my part, I say, the gentleman had drunk himself out of his five sentences.

EVA. It is his five senses: fie, what the ignorance is!

BARD. And being fap, sir, was, as they say, cashiered;[e] and so conclusions passed the careires.

SLEN. Ay, you spake in Latin then too; but 'tis no matter: I'll ne'er be drunk whilst I live again, but in honest, civil, godly company, for this trick: if I be drunk, I'll be drunk with those that have the fear of God, and not with drunken knaves.

EVA. So Got 'udge me, that is a virtuous mind.

FAL. You hear all these matters denied, gentlemen; you hear it.

Enter ANNE PAGE *with wine;* MISTRESS FORD *and* MISTRESS PAGE *following.*

PAGE. Nay, daughter, carry the wine in; we'll drink within. [*Exit* ANNE PAGE.

SLEN. O heaven! this is mistress Anne Page.

PAGE. How now, mistress Ford?

FAL. Mistress Ford, by my troth, you are very well met: by your leave, good mistress. [*Kissing her.*

PAGE. Wife, bid these gentlemen welcome: come, we have a hot venison pasty to dinner; come, gentlemen, I hope we shall drink down all unkindness.

[*Exeunt all but* SHAL. SLENDER, *and* EVANS.

SLEN. I had rather than forty shillings, I had my book of Songs and Sonnets here:—

Enter SIMPLE.

how now, Simple! where have you been? I must wait on myself, must I? You have not *The Book of Riddles* about you, have you?

SIM. *Book of Riddles!* why, did you not lend it to Alice Shortcake upon Allhallowmas last, a fortnight afore Michaelmas?[f]

SHAL. Come, coz; come, coz; we stay for you. A word with you, coz: marry, this, coz; there is, as 'twere, a tender, a kind of tender, made afar off by sir Hugh here;—do you understand me?

SLEN. Ay, sir, you shall find me reasonable; if it be so, I shall do that that is reason.

SHAL. Nay, but understand me.

SLEN. So I do, sir.

EVA. Give ear to his motions, master Slender: I will description the matter to you, if you pe capacity of it.

SLEN. Nay, I will do as my cousin Shallow says: I pray you, pardon me; he's a justice of peace in his country, simple though I stand here.

EVA. But that is not the question; the question is concerning your marriage.

SHAL. Ay, there's the point, sir.

EVA. Marry, is it; the very point of it; to mistress Anne Page.

SLEN. Why, if it be so, I will marry her, upon any reasonable demands.

EVA. But can you affection the 'oman? Let us command to know that of your mouth, or of your lips; for divers philosophers hold, that the lips is parcel[g] of the mouth;—therefore, precisely, can you carry your good will to the maid?

SHAL. Cousin Abraham Slender, can you love her?

SLEN. I hope, sir,—I will do, as it shall become one that would do reason.

EVA. Nay, Got's lords and his ladies, you must speak possitable, if you can carry her your desires towards her.

---

[a] Mill-sixpences,—] The mill-sixpences used in 1561 and 1562, were the first milled money used in England.

[b] Latten bilbo:] *Bilboa*, in Spain, was once famous for its fine-tempered sword-blades, and hence a sword was often called a *Bilbo*. A *latten bilbo* (*Latten* being a mixed metal akin to brass) means a sword wanting both edge and temper.

[c] *In thy* labras *here;*] In thy *lips* The old quarto reads:—

——"I do retort the lie
Even in thy gorge, thy gorge, thy gorge."

[d] *The* nuthook's humour—] *Nuthook* was the slang title of a catchpole. Nym threatens poor Slender with the *marry trap* if he *comes the constable over him*, by charging him with theft.

[e] *And being fap, sir, was, as they say*, cashiered;] Equipollent to, *being drunk, was cleaned out.*

[f] *A fortnight afore* Michaelmas?] Theobald proposed to read *Martlemas*, but the blunder was perhaps designed.

[g] Parcel *of the mouth;*] *Parcel* is *part;* and is still so used in law language.

SHAL. That you must: will you, upon good dowry, marry her?

SLEN. I will do a greater thing than that, upon your request, cousin, in any reason.

SHAL. Nay, conceive me, conceive me, sweet coz: what I do, is to pleasure you, coz: can you love the maid?

SLEN. I will marry her, sir, at your request; but if there be no great love in the beginning, yet heaven may decrease it upon better acquaintance, when we are married, and have more occasion to know one another: I hope, upon familiarity will grow more contempt*: but if you say, *marry her*, I will marry her, that I am freely dissolved, and dissolutely.

EVA. It is a fery discretion answer; save, the faul' is in the 'ort *dissolutely:* the 'ort is, according to our meaning, resolutely;—his meaning is goot.

SHAL. Ay, I think my cousin meant well.

SLEN. Ay, or else I would I might be hanged, la.

SHAL. Here comes fair mistress Anne:

(*) Old copy, *content.*

Re-enter ANNE PAGE.

Would I were young, for your sake, Mistress Anne!

ANNE. The dinner is on the table; my father desires your worships' company.

SHAL. I will wait on him, fair mistress Anne.

EVA. Od's plessed will! I will not pe absence at the grace.

[*Exeunt* SHALLOW *and* SIR HUGH EVANS.

ANNE. Will't please your worship to come in, sir?

SLEN. No, I thank you, forsooth, heartily; I am very well.

ANNE. The dinner attends you, sir.

SLEN. I am not a-hungry, I thank you, forsooth: go, sirrah, for all you are my man, go, wait upon my cousin Shallow. [*Exit* SIMPLE.] A justice of peace sometime may be beholden to his friend for a man:—I keep but three men and a boy yet, till my mother be dead: but what though? yet I live like a poor gentleman born.

ANNE. I may not go in without your worship: they will not sit till you come.

SLEN. I'faith, I'll eat nothing; I thank you as much as though I did.

ANNE. I pray you, sir, walk in.

SLEN. I had rather walk here, I thank you: I bruised my shin the other day with playing at sword and dagger with a master of fence,[a] three veneys[b] for a dish of stewed prunes; and, by my troth, I cannot abide the smell of hot meat since. Why do your dogs bark so? be there bears i' th' town?

ANNE. I think there are, sir; I heard them talked of.

SLEN. I love the sport well; but I shall as soon quarrel at it, as any man in England. You are afraid, if you see the bear loose, are you not?

ANNE. Ay, indeed, sir.

SLEN. That's meat and drink to me now: I have seen Sackerson (5) loose, twenty times; and have taken him by the chain: but, I warrant you, the women have so cried and shrieked at it, that it passed:[c]—but women, indeed, cannot abide 'em: they are very ill-favoured rough things.

Re-enter PAGE.

PAGE. Come, gentle master Slender, come; we stay for you.

SLEN. I'll eat nothing, I thank you, sir.

PAGE. By cock and pye, you shall not choose, sir: come, come.

SLEN. Nay, pray you, lead the way.

PAGE. Come on, sir.

SLEN. Mistress Anne, yourself shall go first.

ANNE. Not I, sir; pray you, keep on.

SLEN. Truly, I will not go first; truly, la: I will not do you that wrong.

ANNE. I pray you, sir.

SLEN. I'll rather be unmannerly, than troublesome: you do yourself wrong, indeed, la.
[*Exeunt.*

SCENE II.—*The same.*

Enter SIR HUGH EVANS *and* SIMPLE.

EVA. Go your ways, and ask of Doctor Caius' house, which is the way: and there dwells one mistress Quickly, which is in the manner of his nurse, or his dry nurse, or his cook, or his laundry, his washer, and his wringer.

SIM. Well, sir?

EVA. Nay, it is petter yet:—give her this letter; for it is a 'oman that altogether's acquaintance with mistress Anne Page: and the letter is to desire and require her to solicit your master's desires to mistress Anne Page: I pray you, pe gone; I will make an end of my dinner; there's pippins and cheese to come. [*Exeunt.*

SCENE III.—*A Room in the* Garter Inn.

Enter FALSTAFF, Host, BARDOLPH, NYM, PISTOL, *and* ROBIN.

FAL. Mine Host of the Garter,—

HOST. What says my bully-rook?[d] speak scholarly, and wisely.

FAL. Truly, mine host, I must turn away some of my followers.

HOST. Discard, bully Hercules; cashier: let them wag; trot, trot.

FAL. I sit at ten pounds a week.

HOST. Thou'rt an emperor, Cæsar, Keisar, and Pheezar. I will entertain Bardolph; he shall draw, he shall tap: said I well, bully Hector?

FAL. Do so, good mine host.

HOST. I have spoke; let him follow. Let me see thee, froth and lime:[e] I am at a word; follow.
[*Exit* Host.

FAL. Bardolph, follow him; a tapster is a good trade: an old cloak makes a new jerkin; a withered serving-man, a fresh tapster: go; adieu.

BARD. It is a life that I have desired; I will thrive. [*Exit* BARD.

PIST. O base Gongarian* wight! wilt thou the spigot wield?

NYM. He was gotten in drink: is not the humour conceited? His mind is not heroic, and there's the humour of it.[f]

FAL. I am glad, I am so acquit of this tinder-box; his thefts were too open: his filching was like an unskilful singer, he kept not time.

(*) First folio, *Hungarian.*

a A master of fence,—] One who had taken his *master's* degree n the "Noble Science of Defence."

b *Three* veneys—] Three *hits;* from the French, *venue* or *veney,* a *touch* or *hit* in fencing.

c *That it* passed:] Meaning it *surpassed* belief or expression. So in "Troilus and Cressida," Act I. Sc. 2: "And all the rest so laughed, that it *passed;*" again, in the present play, Act IV. Sc. 2, Page, amazed at Ford's vehemence, exclaims, "*this passes!*" And in "The Two Gentlemen of Verona," Act II. Sc. 1: "Your own present folly and her *passing* deformity," i.e. *surpassing* deformity. So, too, in the Scriptures, "And the peace of God, which *passeth* all understanding, shall keep your hearts and minds through Christ Jesus."—Phil. iv. 7.

d Bully-rook?] In Shakespeare's day this epithet bore much the same meaning as "jolly dog" now; but it came subsequently to have a more offensive signification, and was applied to a cheat and sharper.

e Froth and lime:] The folio reads *live,* for lime. *Froth and lime* was an old cant term for a tapster, in allusion to the practice of frothing beer, and adulterating sack. The host means, let me see thee turn tapster. "*To keep a tapster from frothing his pots*—Provide in a readiness the skin of a red-herring, and when the tapster is absent, do but rub a little on the inside of the pots, and he will not be able to froth them, do what he can in a good while after."—COTGRAVE'S *Wit's Interpreter,* 1671, p. 92, *ap.* Halliwell.

f He was gotten in drink, &c.] This speech of Nym's is made up from the quarto of 1602, and the folio 1623, the latter part being only found in the early sketch.

NYM. The good humour is, to steal at a minute's rest.

PIST. Convey, the wise it call: steal! foh; a fico for the phrase!

FAL. Well, sirs, I am almost out at heels.

PIST. Why then, let kibes[a] ensue.

FAL. There is no remedy; I must coney-catch; I must shift.

PIST. Young ravens must have food.

FAL. Which of you know Ford of this town?

PIST. I ken the wight; he is of substance good.

FAL. My honest lads, I will tell you what I am about.

PIST. Two yards, and more.

FAL. No quips now, Pistol; indeed I am in the waist two yards about: but I am now about no waste; I am about thrift. Briefly, I do mean to make love to Ford's wife; I spy entertainment in her; she discourses, she carves,[b] she gives the leer of invitation: I can construe the action of her familiar style; and the hardest voice of her behaviour, to be englished rightly, is, *I am sir John Falstaff's.*

PIST. He hath studied her will, and translated her will; out of honesty into English.

NYM. The anchor is deep:[c] will that humour pass?

FAL. Now, the report goes, she has all the rule of her husband's purse; she hath legions of angels.[d]

PIST. As many devils entertain; and, *To her, boy*, say I.

NYM. The humour rises; it is good: humour me the angels.

---

[a] Kibes—] *Chilblains.*

[b] *She* carves—] See note (4), page 104.

[c] The anchor is deep:] Nym, in his fustian language, perhaps means, that he does not fathom the object of this love to Ford's wife; when he hears, however, that the ultimate end is to pocket her "legions of angels," "the humour rises; it is good."

[d] She *hath* legions *of angels.*] So the quarto; the folio reads, "*he* hath *a legend* of angels."

FAL. I have writ me here a letter to her: and here another to Page's wife; who even now gave me good eyes too, examined my parts with most judicious œiliads:[a] sometimes the beam of her view gilded my foot, sometimes my portly belly.

PIST. Then did the sun on dung-hill shine.

NYM. I thank thee for that humour.

FAL. O, she did so course o'er my exteriors with such a greedy intention, that the appetite of her eye did seem to scorch me up like a burning glass! Here's another letter to her: she bears the purse too; she is a region in Guiana, all gold and bounty. I will be cheaters[b] to them both, and they shall be exchequers to me; they shall be my East and West Indies, and I will trade to them both. Go, bear thou this letter to mistress Page; and thou this to mistress Ford: we will thrive, lads, we will thrive.

PIST. Shall I sir Pandarus of Troy become,
And by my side wear steel? then, Lucifer take all!

NYM. I will run no base humour: here, take the humour letter; I will keep the 'haviour of reputation.

FAL. Hold, sirrah, [*To* ROBIN.] bear you these letters tightly;[c]
Sail like my pinnace to these golden shores.
Rogues, hence, avaunt! vanish like hail-stones, go!
Trudge, plod, away, o' th'* hoof; seek shelter, pack!
Falstaff will learn the humour of this † age,
French thrift, you rogues; myself, and skirted page.[d] [*Exeunt* FALSTAFF *and* ROBIN.

PIST. Let vultures gripe thy guts! for gourd, and fullam holds,
And high and low beguiles the rich and poor:[e]
Tester I'll have in pouch, when thou shalt lack,
Base Phrygian Turk!

NYM. I have operations in my head, ‡ which be humours of revenge.

PIST. Wilt thou revenge?

NYM. By welkin, and her star![f]

PIST. With wit, or steel?

---

[a] Œiliads:] From the French *Oëillade*, an *ogle*, or amorous glance, to cast a sheep's eye. Sometimes written *eye-lids*.

[b] Cheaters—] The popular name for *escheators*, those officers employed to certify to the Exchequer what *escheats* fall to the Crown through forfeiture, the death of tenants without heirs, &c.

[c] Tightly;] *Briskly, promptly.*

[d] French thrift, *you rogues;* myself, and skirted page.] Alluding to the custom then prevalent in France of making a smart page serve the purpose of a tribe of retainers.

[e] *For* gourd, *and* fullam *holds,*
And high *and* low *beguiles the rich and poor:*]

(*) First folio, *i' th'*. (†) First folio, *honor of the.* (‡) First folio omits, *in my head.*

Gourd, *fullam*, *high*-men, and *low*-men, were the professional terms for false dice.

"What should I say more of false dice, of *fulloms*, *high*-men, *lowe*-men, *gourds* and brizled dice, graviers, demies, and contraries?"—GREEN's *Art of Juggling*, &c. 1612, quoted by Steevens.

[f] *By welkin, and her* star!] For *star*, the quarto reads *Fairies.*

NYM. With both the humours, I:
I will discuss the humour of this love to Page.*

PIST. And I to Ford † shall eke unfold,
How Falstaff, varlet vile,
His dove will prove, his gold will hold,
And his soft couch defile.

NYM. My humour shall not cool: I will incense Page * to deal with poison; I will possess him with yellowness, for the revolt of mine[a] is dangerous: that is my true humour.

PIST. Thou art the Mars of malcontents: I second thee; troop on. [*Exeunt.*

SCENE IV.—*A Room in* Dr. Caius's *House.*

Enter MISTRESS QUICKLY, SIMPLE, *and* RUGBY.

QUICK. What; John Rugby!—I pray thee, go to the casement, and see if you can see my master, master Doctor Caius, coming: if he do, i'faith, and find any body in the house, here will be an old[b] abusing of God's patience, and the king's English.

RUG. I'll go watch.

QUICK. Go; and we'll have a posset for't soon at night, in faith, at the latter end of a sea-coal fire. [*Exit* RUGBY.] An honest, willing, kind fellow, as ever servant shall come in house withal; and, I warrant you, no tell-tale, nor no breed-bate: his worst fault is, that he is given to prayer; he is something peevish that way: but nobody but has his fault;—but let that pass. Peter Simple, you say your name is?

SIM. Ay, for fault of a better.

QUICK. And master Slender's your master?

SIM. Ay, forsooth.

QUICK. Does he not wear a great round beard, like a glover's paring-knife?

SIM. No, forsooth: he hath but a little wee face, with a little yellow beard; a Cain-coloured beard.(6)

QUICK. A softly-sprighted man, is he not?

(*) First folio, *Ford*. (†) First folio, *Page*.

[a] *For the revolt* of mine—] The poet probably wrote "*this* revolt of mine." Steevens proposed to read "the revolt of *mien*," but the change is no improvement. In "Henry V." Act II. Sc. 2, we have:—

"*For this revolt of thine*, methinks, is like
Another fall of man."

[b] *An* old *abusing*—] *An old*, i.e. a *famous*, a *rare*, a *plentiful* abusing.

SIM. Ay, forsooth: but he is as tall a man of his hands,[a] as any is between this and his head; he hath fought with a warrener.

QUICK. How say you?—O, I should remember him; does he not hold up his head, as it were, and strut in his gait?

SIM. Yes, indeed, does he.

QUICK. Well, heaven send Anne Page no worse fortune! Tell master parson Evans, I will do what I can for your master: Anne is a good girl, and I wish—

Re-enter RUGBY.

RUG. Out, alas! here comes my master.

QUICK. We shall all be shent:[b] run in here, good young man; go into this closet. [*Shuts* SIMPLE *in the closet.*] He will not stay long.—What, John Rugby! John! what, John! I say!—Go, John, go inquire for my master; I doubt, he be not well, that he comes not home:—*and down, down, adown a,* &c. [*Sings.*

Enter DOCTOR CAIUS.

CAIUS. Vat is you sing? I do not like dese toys; pray you, go and vetch me in my closet *un boitier verd;* a box, a green-a box; do intend vat I speak? a green-a box.

QUICK. Ay, forsooth, I'll fetch it you. I am glad he went not in himself: if he had found the young man, he would have been horn-mad. [*Aside.*

CAIUS. *Fe, fe, fe, fe! ma foi, il fait fort chaud.*[c] *Je m'en vais à la Cour,—la grande affaire.*

QUICK. Is it this, sir?

CAIUS. *Ouy; mette le au mon* pocket; *depêche,* quickly: vere is dat knave Rugby?

QUICK. What, John Rugby! John!

RUG. Here, sir.

CAIUS. You are John Rugby, and you are Jack[d] Rugby: come, take-a your rapier, and come after my heel to de court.

RUG. 'Tis ready, sir, here in the porch.

CAIUS. By my trot, I tarry too long:—Od's me! *Qu'ay j'oublié?* dere is some simples in my closet, dat I vill not for the varld I shall leave behind.

QUICK. Ay me! he'll find the young man there, and be mad.

CAIUS. *O diable, diable!* vat is in my closet?—Villainy! *larron!* [*Pulling* SIMPLE *out.*] Rugby, my rapier.

QUICK. Good master, be content.

CAIUS. Verefore[e] shall I be content-a?

QUICK. The young man is an honest man.

CAIUS. Vat shall de honest man do in my closet? dere is no honest man dat shall come in my closet.

QUICK. I beseech you, be not so flegmatick; hear the truth of it: he came of an errand to me from parson Hugh.

CAIUS. Vell?

SIM. Ay, forsooth, to desire her to—

QUICK. Peace, I pray you.

CAIUS. Peace-a your tongue:—speak-a your tale.

SIM. To desire this honest gentlewoman, your maid, to speak a good word to mistress Anne Page for my master, in the way of marriage.

QUICK. This is all, indeed, la; but I'll ne'er put my finger in the fire, and need not.

CAIUS. Sir Hugh send-a you?—Rugby, *baillez* me some paper: tarry you a little-a while. [*Writes.*

QUICK. I am glad he is so quiet: if he had been throughly moved, you should have heard him so loud, and so melancholy;—but notwithstanding, man, I'll do you your master what good I can: and the very yea and the no is, the French doctor, my master,—I may call him my master, look you, for I keep his house; and I wash, wring, brew, bake, scour, dress meat and drink, make the beds, and do all myself;—

SIM. 'Tis a great charge, to come under one body's hand.

QUICK. Are you avised[f] o' that? you shall find it a great charge: and to be up early and down late;—but notwithstanding, (to tell you in your ear, I would have no words of it;) my master himself is in love with mistress Anne Page: but notwithstanding that,—I know Anne's mind,—that's neither here nor there.

CAIUS. You jack'nape; give-a dis letter to Sir Hugh; by gar, it is a shallenge: I vill cut his troat in de park; and I vill teach a scurvy jack-a-nape priest to meddle or make: you may be gone; it is not good you tarry here: by gar, I vill cut all his two stones; by gar, he shall not have a stone to trow at his dog. [*Exit* SIMPLE.

QUICK. Alas, he speaks but for his friend.

CAIUS. It is no matter-a vor dat:—do not you

---

[a] *As* tall *a man* of his hands,—] That is, as *able,* or bold a man of his hands. Florio translates *Manesco, readie* or *nimble-handed, a tall man of his hands.*

[b] Shent:] *Shent* here means *undone, ruined.*

[c] Il fait fort chaud, &c.] The printers of the folio make sorry work of both French and Latin; there the above reads, *il fait for ehando, Ie man voi a le Court,* &c.

[d] *And you are* Jack *Rugby:*] The Doctor had been long enough in England to learn that *Jack* was another name for *knave.*

[e] Verefore, &c.] The old text, which here reads *wherefore,* is not consistent in its mode of rendering the Doctor's broken English; but, in common with all modern editions, we render it uniform throughout.

[f] *Are you* avised o' that?] A household phrase at one time, equivalent to, Have you found out that? Has it occurred to you? O, you think so, do you? Thus, in "The Isle of Gulls," Act II. Sc. 1:—

"HIP. And in good earnest wee are not father'd much amisse.
VIST. Are you *avis'd of that?*"

tell-a me dat I shall have Anne Page for myself? by gar, I vill kill de Jack priest; and I have appointed mine Host of *de Jarterre* to measure our weapon: by gar, I vill myself have Anne Page.

QUICK. Sir, the maid loves you, and all shall be well: we must give folks leave to prate: what, the good-year!

CAIUS. Rugby, come to the court vit me;—by gar, if I have not Anne Page, I shall turn your head out of my door:—follow my heels, Rugby.

[*Exeunt* CAIUS *and* RUGBY.

QUICK. You shall have An fools-head of your own. No, I know Anne's mind for that: never a woman in Windsor knows more of Anne's mind than I do; nor can do more than I do with her, I thank heaven.

FENT. [*Without.*] Who's within there? ho!

QUICK. Who's there, I trow? Come near the house, I pray you.

Enter FENTON.

FENT. How now, good woman; how dost thou?

QUICK. The better, that it pleases your good worship to ask.

FENT. What news? how does pretty mistress Anne?

QUICK. In truth, sir, and she is pretty, and honest, and gentle; and one that is your friend, I can tell you that by the way; I praise heaven for it.

FENT. Shall I do any good, thinkest thou? Shall I not lose my suit?

QUICK. Troth, sir, all is in his hands above: but notwithstanding, master Fenton, I'll be sworn on a book, she loves you:—have not your worship a wart above your eye?

FENT. Yes, marry, have I; what of that?

QUICK. Well, thereby hangs a tale;—good faith, it is such another Nan;—but, I detest, an honest maid as ever broke bread:—we had an hour's talk of that wart;—I shall never laugh but in that maid's company!—But, indeed, she is given too much to allicholly and musing: but for you—well, go to.

FENT. Well, I shall see her to-day: hold, there's money for thee; let me have thy voice in my behalf: if thou seest her before me, commend me—

QUICK. Will I? i' faith, that we will: and I will tell your worship more of the wart, the next time we have confidence; and of other wooers.

FENT. Well, farewell; I am in great haste now.

QUICK. Farewell to your worship [*Exit* FENTON. Truly, an honest gentleman; but Anne loves him not; for I know Anne's mind as well as another does: out upon't! what have I forgot! [*Exit.*

ACT II.

SCENE I.—*Before* Page's *House.*

Enter Mistress Page, *with a letter.*

Mrs. Page. What! have I* 'scaped love-letters in the holy-day time of my beauty, and am I now a subject for them? Let me see: [*Reads.*

Ask me no reason why I love you; for though love use reason for his physician,[a] *he admits him not for his counsellor. You are not young, no more am I; go to then, there's sympathy; you are merry, so am I; ha! ha! then there's more sympathy: you love sack, and so do I; would you desire better sympathy? Let it suffice thee, mistress Page, (at the least, if the love of soldier can suffice,) that I love thee. I will not say, pity me, 'tis not a soldier-like phrase; but I say, love me. By me,*

Thine own true knight,
By day or night,
Or any kind of light,
With all his might,
For thee to fight. John Falstaff.

(*) First folio omits, *I*.

a *— though love use reason for his* physician,—] Old copies, *precisian.* The emendation is Johnson's, and, supported by the line,

"My *reason,* the *physician* to my *love,*"

in our author's 147th Sonnet, it should have found a place in every modern edition.

What a Herod of Jewry is this?—O wicked, wicked, world!—one that is well nigh worn to pieces with age, to show himself a young gallant! What an unweighed behaviour hath this Flemish drunkard picked (with the devil's name) out of my conversation, that he dares in this manner assay me? Why, he hath not been thrice in my company!—What should I say to him? I was then frugal of my mirth: heaven forgive me!—Why, I'll exhibit a bill in the parliament for the putting down of fat men.[a] How shall I be revenged on him? for revenged I will be, as sure as his guts are made of puddings.

Enter MISTRESS FORD.

MRS. FORD. Mistress Page! trust me, I was going to your house.

MRS. PAGE. And, trust me, I was coming to you: you look very ill.

MRS. FORD. Nay, I'll ne'er believe that; I have to show to the contrary.

MRS. PAGE. 'Faith, but you do, in my mind.

MRS. FORD. Well, I do then; yet, I say, I could show you to the contrary: O, mistress Page, give me some counsel!

MRS. PAGE. What's the matter, woman?

MRS. FORD. O woman, if it were not for one trifling respect, I could come to such honour!

MRS. PAGE. Hang the trifle, woman, take the honour: What is it? dispense with trifles; what is it?

MRS. FORD. If I would but go to hell for an eternal moment, or so, I could be knighted.

MRS. PAGE. What?—thou liest!—Sir Alice Ford! These knights will hack;[b] and so thou shouldst not alter the article of thy gentry.

MRS. FORD. We burn day-light: here, read, read; perceive how I might be knighted. I shall think the worse of fat men, as long as I have an eye to make difference of men's liking:[c] and yet he would not swear; praised* women's modesty: and gave such orderly and well-behaved reproof to all uncomeliness, that I would have sworn his disposition would have gone to the truth of his words: but they do no more adhere and keep place together, than the hundredth psalm† to the tune of *Green Sleeves*.(1) What tempest, I trow, threw this whale, with so many tuns of oil in his belly, ashore at Windsor? How shall I be revenged on him? I think, the best way were to entertain him with hope, till the wicked fire of lust have melted him in his own grease. Did you ever hear the like?

MRS. PAGE. Letter for letter; but that the name of Page and Ford differs! To thy great comfort in this mystery of ill opinions, here's the twin-brother of thy letter: but let thine inherit first; for, I protest, mine never shall. I warrant, he hath a thousand of these letters, writ with blank space for different names, (sure more,) and these are of the second edition: he will print them out of doubt; for he cares not what he puts into the press, when he would put us two. I had rather be a giantess, and lie under mount Pelion. Well, I will find you twenty lascivious turtles, ere one chaste man.

MRS. FORD. Why, this is the very same; the very hand, the very words: what doth he think of us?

MRS. PAGE. Nay, I know not: it makes me almost ready to wrangle with mine own honesty. I'll entertain myself like one that I am not acquainted withal; for, sure, unless he know some strain[d] in me, that I know not myself, he would never have boarded me in this fury.

MRS. FORD. Boarding, call you it? I'll be sure to keep him above deck.

MRS. PAGE. So will I; if he come under my hatches, I'll never to sea again. Let's be revenged on him; let's appoint him a meeting; give him a show of comfort in his suit; and lead him on with a fine-baited delay, till he hath pawned his horses to mine Host of the Garter.

MRS. FORD. Nay, I will consent to act any villainy against him, that may not sully the chariness of our honesty. O, that[e] my husband saw this letter! it would give eternal food to his jealousy.

MRS. PAGE. Why, look, where he comes; and my good man too: he's as far from jealousy, as I am from giving him cause; and that, I hope, is an unmeasurable distance.

MRS. FORD. You are the happier woman.

MRS. PAGE. Let's consult together against this greasy knight: come hither. [*They retire.*

(*) Old text, *praise*. (†) Old text, *hundred psalms*.

[a] *For the putting down of* fat *men*.] Theobald first inserted *fat*, and the correction seems warranted by the context, as well as by the parallel passage of the early quarto:—

"Well, I shall trust *fat* men the worse while I live, for his sake."

[b] These knights will hack;] Nothing like a satisfactory explanation of this passage has yet been given. It is generally understood to be an allusion to the extravagant creation of knights by James I. in the early part of his reign. "These knights will become *hackneyed*," &c.; but there must be in it a meaning more pertinent than this.

[c] *Of men's* liking:] Of men's condition of body. *Good*, or *well-liking*, meant *plump*, in *good plight; ill-liking*, the reverse.

[d] *Some* strain *in me*,—] Some *turn, tendency*.

[e] O, that *my husband*—] That is, O, *if that* my husband, &c. The early quarto reads,—

"O Lord, if my husband should see this letter!"

Enter FORD, PAGE, PISTOL, *and* NYM.

FORD. Well, I hope it be not so.

PIST. Hope is a curtail dog[a] in some affairs:
Sir John affects thy wife.

FORD. Why, sir, my wife is not young.

PIST. He woos both high and low, both rich and poor,
Both young and old, one with another, Ford;
He loves the gally-mawfry; Ford, perpend.

FORD. Love my wife?

PIST. With liver burning hot: prevent:
Or go thou, like sir Actæon he, with
Ring-wood at thy heels. O, odious is the name!

FORD. What name, sir?

PIST. The horn, I say: farewell.
Take heed; have open eye; for thieves do foot by night:
Take heed, ere summer comes, or cuckoo-birds do sing.—
Away, sir corporal Nym.——
Believe it, Page; he speaks sense. [*Exit* PISTOL.

FORD. I will be patient; I will find out this.

NYM. And this is true; [*To* PAGE.] I like not the humour of lying. He hath wronged me in some humours: I should have borne the humoured letter to her; but I have a sword, and it shall bite upon my necessity. He loves your wife; there's the short and the long. My name is corporal Nym; I speak, and I avouch. 'Tis true:—my name is Nym, and Falstaff loves your wife.—Adieu! I love not the humour of bread and cheese; and there's the humour of it.[b] Adieu. [*Exit* NYM.

PAGE. *The humour of it*, quoth 'a! here's a fellow frights humour [c] out of his wits.(2)

FORD. I will seek out Falstaff.

PAGE. I never heard such a drawling-affecting rogue.

FORD. If I do find it; well.

PAGE. I will not believe such a Cataian,[d] though the priest o' th' town (3) commended him for a true man.

FORD. 'Twas a good sensible fellow: well.[e]

PAGE. How now, Meg?

MRS. PAGE. Whither go you, George? hark you.

---

[a] A curtail dog—] It was supposed that the tail of a dog assisted him in running. A curtail dog may mean a *halting, lingering* dog, as it certainly implied a worthless one; "*A curtald dogg, chien courtaud, c'est à dire chien sans queuë ou esqueuè bon à tout service.*"—HOWELL's *Lexicon Tet.* 1660.

[b] And there's the humour of it.] These words, so necessary to the sense because echoed by Page, are omitted in the folio.

[c] *Frights* humour *out of his wits.*] So the quarto: the folio reads, Frights *English*, &c.

[d] Cataian,—] A term of reproach, of which the precise meaning is not known. Sir Toby, in "Twelfth Night," Act II. Sc. 3, applies it to Olivia:—

"My lady 's a *Cataian;*"

and it occurs in Sir William D'Avenant's play, called "Love and Honour," 1649, Act II. Sc. 1,—

"Hang him, bold *Cataian!*"

[e] 'Twas a good sensible fellow:] In this and the two preceding speeches, Ford must be supposed to be speaking to himself.

MRS. FORD. How now, sweet Frank? why art thou melancholy?

FORD. I melancholy! I am not melancholy. Get you home, go.

MRS. FORD. 'Faith, thou hast some crotchets in thy head now. Will you go, Mistress Page?

MRS. PAGE, Have with you. You'll come to dinner, George? Look, who comes yonder: she shall be our messenger to this paltry knight.

[*Aside to* MRS. FORD.

MRS. FORD. Trust me, I thought on her: she'll fit it.

Enter MISTRESS QUICKLY.

MRS. PAGE. You are come to see my daughter Anne?

QUICK. Ay, forsooth; and, I pray, how does good mistress Anne?

MRS. PAGE. Go in with us, and see; we have an hour's talk with you.

[*Exeunt* MISTRESS PAGE, MISTRESS FORD, *and* MISTRESS QUICKLY.

PAGE. How now, master Ford?

FORD. You heard what this knave told me, did you not?

PAGE. Yes; and you heard what the other told me?

FORD. Do you think there is truth in them?

PAGE. Hang 'em, slaves; I do not think the knight would offer it: but these that accuse him in his intent towards our wives, are a yoke of his discarded men; very rogues, now they be out of service.

FORD. Were they his men?

PAGE. Marry, were they.

FORD. I like it never the better for that: does he lie at the Garter?

PAGE. Ay, marry, does he. If he should intend this voyage toward my wife, I would turn her loose to him; and what he gets more of her than sharp words, let it lie on my head.

FORD. I do not misdoubt my wife; but I would be loath to turn them together: a man may be too confident: I would have nothing lie on my head: I cannot be thus satisfied.

PAGE. Look, where my ranting Host of the Garter comes: there is either liquor in his pate, or money in his purse, when he looks so merrily. How now, mine Host?

Enter Host, *and* SHALLOW, *behind.*

HOST. How now, bully-rook? thou'rt a gentleman: cavalero-justice, I say.

SHAL. I follow, mine Host, I follow.—Good even and twenty,[a] good master Page! Master Page, will you go with us? we have sport in hand.

HOST. Tell him, cavalero-justice; tell him, bully-rook.

SHAL. Sir, there is a fray to be fought, between sir Hugh the Welsh priest, and Caius the French doctor.

FORD. Good mine Host o' th' Garter, a word with you.

HOST. What say'st thou, my bully-rook?

[*They go aside.*

SHAL. Will you [*To* PAGE.] go with us to behold it? My merry Host hath had the measuring of their weapons; and, I think, hath appointed them contrary places: for, believe me, I hear the parson is no jester. Hark, I will tell you what our sport shall be.

HOST. Hast thou no suit against my knight, my guest-cavalier?

FORD. None, I protest: but I'll give you a pottle of burnt sack to give me recourse to him, and tell him, my name is Brook;[b] only for a jest.

HOST. My hand, bully: thou shalt have egress and regress; said I well? and thy name shall be Brook: It is a merry knight. Will you go, myn-heers?[c]

SHAL. Have with you, mine Host.

PAGE. I have heard the Frenchman hath good skill in his rapier.

SHAL. Tut, sir, I could have told you more. In these times you stand on distance, your passes, stoccadoes, and I know not what: 'tis the heart, master Page; 'tis here, 'tis here. I have seen the time, with my long sword, I would have made you four tall fellows skip like rats.

HOST. Here, boys, here, here! shall we wag?

PAGE. Have with you:—I had rather hear them scold than fight.

[*Exeunt* Host, SHALLOW, *and* PAGE.

FORD. Though Page be a secure[d] fool, and stands so firmly on his wife's fealty,[e] yet I cannot put off my opinion so easily: she was in his company at Page's house; and, what they made[f]

---

a Good even and twenty,—] An old popular salutation, meaning twenty good evenings. Similar to which is, "*God night and a thousand* to every body."—ELIOT'S *Fruits of the French*, 1593, quoted by Halliwell.

b *My name is* Brook;] The folio prints *Broome* throughout, as the assumed name of Ford, and assigns the present speech to Shallow.

c *Will you go*, myn-heers?] The folio reads, *An-heires*, an evident corruption, for which Theobald proposed the word we adopt. Warburton *Heris*, an old Scotch word for master; Malone, *and hear us;* Steevens, *on, heroes*, or *on, hearts;* Boaden, *Cavaliers;* and Mr. Collier's annotator, *on here*.

d *A* secure *fool*,—] An *over-confident*, or *careless* fool.

e And stands so firmly on his wife's fealty,—] That is, insists so stoutly upon his wife's fidelity. The old text has, "on his wife's frailty;" "*fealty*" is the correction of Theobald, and to us appears a very happy restoration.

f *And, what they* made *there*,—] A mode of speech now almost obsolete, implying, "What they *did* there." As in "Hamlet," Act I. Sc. 2,—

"And what *make* you from Wittenberg, Horatio?"

there, I know not. Well, I will look further into 't: and I have a disguise to sound Falstaff: if I find her honest, I lose not my labour; if she be otherwise, 't is labour well bestowed. [*Exit.*

SCENE II.—*A Room in the* Garter Inn.

Enter FALSTAFF *and* PISTOL.

FAL. I will not lend thee a penny.

PIST. Why, then the world's mine oyster,
Which I with sword will open.—
I will retort the sum in equipage.[a]

FAL. Not a penny. I have been content, sir, you should lay my countenance to pawn: I have grated upon my good friends for three reprieves for you and your coach-fellow Nym; or else you had looked through the grate, like a geminy of baboons. I am damned in hell, for swearing to gentlemen my friends, you were good soldiers, and tall fellows: and when mistress Bridget lost the handle of her fan, I took't upon mine honour, thou hadst it not.

PIST. Didst thou not share? hadst thou not fifteen pence?

FAL. Reason, you rogue, reason. Think'st thou, I'll endanger my soul *gratis?* At a word, hang no more about me, I am no gibbet for you: go. A short knife and a throng;[b] to your manor of Pickt-hatch,(4) go. You'll not bear a letter for me, you rogue! you stand upon your honour! Why, thou unconfinable baseness, it is as much as I can do, to keep the terms of my honour precise. I, I, I myself sometimes, leaving the fear of heaven on the left hand, and hiding mine honour in my necessity, am fain to shuffle, to hedge, and to lurch; and yet you, rogue, will ensconce your rags, your cat-a-mountain looks, your red-lattice[c] phrases, and your bold-beating oaths, under the shelter of your honour! You will not do it, you!

PIST. I do relent;[d] what would thou more of man?

Enter ROBIN.

ROB. Sir, here's a woman would speak with you.

FAL. Let her approach.

Enter MISTRESS QUICKLY.

QUICK. Give your worship good-morrow.

FAL. Good-morrow, good wife.

[a] I will retort the sum in equipage.] This line is not in the olio, and it forms the whole of Pistol's reply in the quarto.

[b] A short knife and a throng;] Falstaff bids him get a cut-purse's knife, and seek out a crowd. Purses, it must be remembered, were formerly hung at the girdle.

[c] Red-lattice *phrases*,—] *Ale-house expressions*. Ale-houses, in old times, were distinguished by *red-lattices*, as dairies have since been by *green* ones.

[d] *I do* relent;] *Relent* here must mean *repent*. The quarto has *recant*, which is the better word.

QUICK. Not so, an't please your worship.

FAL. Good maid, then.

QUICK. I'll be sworn; as my mother was, the first hour I was born.

FAL. I do believe the swearer: what with me?

QUICK. Shall I vouchsafe your worship a word or two?

FAL. Two thousand, fair woman; and I'll vouchsafe thee the hearing.

QUICK. There is one mistress Ford, sir; I pray, come a little nearer this ways: I myself dwell with master doctor Caius.

FAL. Well, on: mistress Ford, you say,——

QUICK. Your worship says very true: I pray your worship, come a little nearer this ways.

FAL. I warrant thee, nobody hears; mine own people, mine own people.

QUICK. Are they so? Heaven bless them, and make them his servants!

FAL. Well: mistress Ford;—what of her?

QUICK. Why, sir, she's a good creature. Lord, Lord! your worship's a wanton: well, heaven forgive you, and all of us, I pray!

FAL. Mistress Ford;—come, mistress Ford,—

QUICK. Marry, this is the short and the long of it; you have brought her into such a canaries,[a] as 'tis wonderful. The best courtier of them all, when the court lay at Windsor, could never have brought her to such a canary. Yet there has been knights, and lords, and gentlemen, with their coaches; I warrant you, coach after coach, letter after letter, gift after gift; smelling so sweetly, (all musk,) and so rushling, I warrant you, in silk and gold; and in such alligant terms; and in such wine and sugar of the best, and the fairest, that would have won any woman's heart; and I warrant you, they could never get an eye-wink of her.—I had myself twenty angels given me this morning: but I defy all angels, (in any such sort, as they say,) but in the way of honesty:

[a] Canaries,—] Mrs. Q. means, *quandaries*.

and, I warrant you, they could never get her so much as sip on a cup with the proudest of them all: and yet there has been earls, nay, which is more, pensioners;[a] but, I warrant you, all is one with her.

FAL. But what says she to me? be brief, my good she-Mercury.

QUICK. Marry, she hath received your letter for the which she thanks you a thousand times: and she gives you to notify, that her husband will be absence from his house between ten and eleven.

FAL. Ten and eleven.

QUICK. Ay, forsooth; and then you may come and see the picture, she says, that you wot of; master Ford, her husband, will be from home. Alas! the sweet woman leads an ill life with him; he's a very jealousy man; she leads a very frampold[b] life with him, good heart.

FAL. Ten and eleven; woman, commend me to her; I will not fail her.

QUICK. Why, you say well. But I have another messenger to your worship: mistress Page hath her hearty commendations to you too;—and let me tell you in your ear, she's as fartuous a civil modest wife, and one, I tell you, that will not miss you morning nor evening prayer, as any is in Windsor, whoe'er be the other: and she bade me tell your worship, that her husband is seldom from home; but she hopes there will come a time. I never knew a woman so dote upon a man; surely, I think you have charms, la; yes, in truth.

FAL. Not I, I assure thee; setting the attraction of my good parts aside, I have no other charms.

QUICK. Blessing on your heart for't!

FAL. But, I pray thee, tell me this: has Ford's wife, and Page's wife, acquainted each other how they love me?

QUICK. That were a jest, indeed!—they have not so little grace, I hope:—that were a trick, indeed! but mistress Page would desire you to send her your little page, of all loves;[c] her husband has a marvellous infection to the little page: and, truly, master Page is an honest man. Never a wife in Windsor leads a better life than she does; do what she will, say what she will, take all, pay all, go to bed when she list, rise when she list, all is as she will; and, truly, she deserves it: for if there be a kind woman in Windsor, she is one. You must send her your page; no remedy.

FAL. Why, I will.

QUICK. Nay, but do so then: and, look you, he may come and go between you both; and, in any case, have a nay-word, that you may know one another's mind, and the boy never need to understand anything; for 'tis not good that children should know any wickedness: old folks, you know, have discretion, as they say, and know the world.

FAL. Fare thee well: commend me to them both: there's my purse; I am yet thy debtor.—Boy, go along with this woman.—This news distracts me! [*Exeunt* QUICKLY *and* ROBIN.

PIST. This punk is one of Cupid's carriers:—
Clap on more sails; pursue! up with your fights;[d]
Give fire! she is my prize, or ocean whelm them all! [*Exit* PISTOL.

FAL. Say'st thou so, old Jack? go thy ways; I'll make more of thy old body than I have done. Will they yet look after thee? Wilt thou, after the expense of so much money, be now a gainer? Good body, I thank thee: let them say, 't is grossly done; so it be fairly done, no matter.

Enter BARDOLPH.

BARD. Sir John, there's one master Brook below would fain speak with you, and be acquainted with you; and hath sent your worship a morning's draught of sack.(5)

FAL. Brook, is his name?

BARD. Ay, sir.

FAL. Call him in. [*Exit* BARDOLPH.] Such Brooks are welcome to me, that o'erflow such liquor. Ah! ha! mistress Ford and mistress Page, have I encompassed you? go to; *via!*

Re-enter BARDOLPH, *with* FORD *disguised.*

FORD. 'Bless you, sir.

FAL. And you, sir: would you speak with me?

FORD. I make bold, to press with so little preparation upon you.

FAL. You're welcome; what's your will? Give us leave, drawer. [*Exit* BARDOLPH.

FORD. Sir, I am a gentleman that have spent much; my name is Brook.

FAL. Good master Brook, I desire more acquaintance of you.

FORD. Good sir John, I sue for yours: not to charge you; for I must let you understand, I think myself in better plight for a lender than you are: the which hath something emboldened me to this unseasoned intrusion; for they say, if money go before, all ways do lie open.

---

[a] Pensioners;] Gentlemen of the band of Pensioners, whose duty was to be in immediate attendance on the sovereign, and whose splendid uniform might well induce Mrs. Quickly to rank them above the magnates of the Court.

[b] Frampold *life*—] *Frampold*, equivalent to our *cantankerous*.

[c] Of all loves;] *For love's sake.* See note (b), page 356.

[d] Up with your fights;] "The Waste-cloaths that hang round about the Ship in a Fight, to hinder the Men from being seen by the Enemy: Also any Place wherein men may cover themselves, and yet use their Fire-arms."—PHILLIPS' *New World of Words*, 1706.

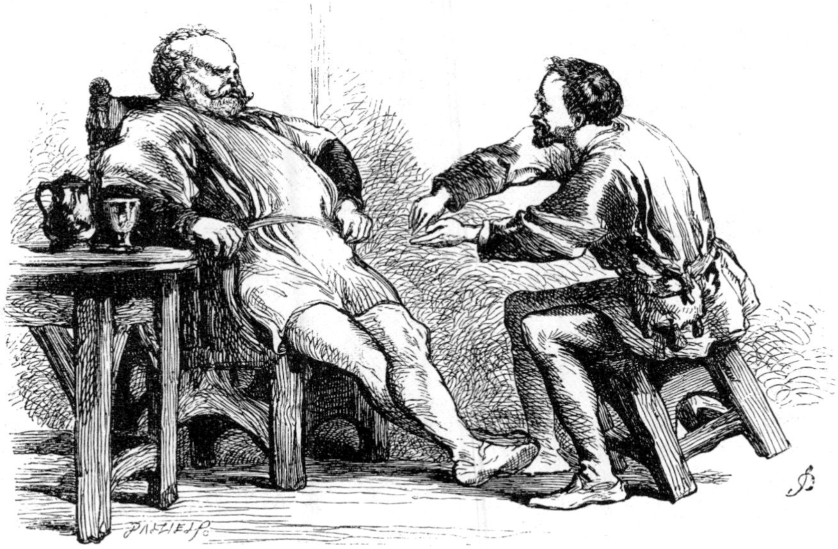

FAL. Money is a good soldier, sir, and will on.

FORD. Troth, and I have a bag of money here, troubles me: if you will help to bear it, sir John, take half, or all, for easing me of the carriage.

FAL. Sir, I know not how I may deserve to be your porter.

FORD. I will tell you, sir, if you will give me the hearing.

FAL. Speak, good master Brook; I shall be glad to be your servant.

FORD. Sir, I hear you are a scholar. I will be brief with you; and you have been a man long known to me, though I had never so good means, as desire, to make myself acquainted with you. I shall discover a thing to you, wherein I must very much lay open mine own imperfection: but, good sir John, as you have one eye upon my follies, as you hear them unfolded, turn another into the register of your own; that I may pass with a reproof the easier, sith you yourself know, how easy it is to be such an offender.

FAL. Very well, sir; proceed.

FORD. There is a gentlewoman in this town, her husband's name is Ford.

FAL. Well, sir.

FORD. I have long loved her, and, I protest to you, bestowed much on her; followed her with a doting observance; engrossed opportunities to meet her; fee'd every slight occasion, that could but niggardly give me sight of her; not only bought many presents to give her, but have given largely to many, to know what she would have given: briefly, I have pursued her, as love hath pursued me; which hath been, on the wing of all occasions. But whatsoever I have merited, either in my mind, or in my means, meed, I am sure, I have received none; unless experience be a jewel: that I have purchased at an infinite rate; and that hath taught me to say this:

Love like a shadow flies, when substance love pursues;
Pursuing that that flies, and flying what pursues.

FAL. Have you received no promise of satisfaction at her hands?

FORD. Never.

FAL. Have you importuned her to such a purpose?

FORD. Never.

FAL. Of what quality was your love then?

FORD. Like a fair house, built upon another man's ground; so that I have lost my edifice, by mistaking the place where I erected it.

FAL. To what purpose have you unfolded this to me?

FORD. When I have told you that, I have told you all. Some say, that, though she appear honest to me, yet, in other places, she enlargeth her mirth so far, that there is shrewd construction made of her. Now, sir John, here is the heart of my purpose: you are a gentleman of excellent breeding, admirable discourse, of great admittance,[a] authentic in your place and person, generally allowed for your many war-like, court-like, and learned preparations.

FAL. O, sir!

FORD. Believe it, for you know it: there is money; spend it, spend it; spend more; spend all I have; only give me so much of your time in exchange of it, as to lay an amiable siege to the honesty of this Ford's wife: use your art of wooing, win her to consent to you; if any man may, you may as soon as any.

FAL. Would it apply well to the vehemency of your affection, that I should win what you would enjoy? Methinks, you prescribe to yourself very preposterously.[b]

FORD. O, understand my drift! she dwells so securely on the excellency of her honour,[c] that the folly of my soul dares not present itself; she is too bright to be looked against. Now, could I come to her with any detection in my hand, my desires had instance and argument to commend themselves; I could drive her then from the ward[d] of her purity, her reputation, her marriage vow, and a thousand other her defences, which now are too strongly embattled against me. What say you to't, sir John?

FAL. Master Brook, I will first make bold with your money; next, give me your hand; and last, as I am a gentleman, you shall, if you will, enjoy Ford's wife.

FORD. O, good sir!

FAL. I say you shall.

FORD. Want no money, sir John, you shall want none.

FAL. Want no mistress Ford, master Brook, you shall want none. I shall be with her, (I may tell you,) by her own appointment—even as you came in to me, her assistant, or go-between, parted from me—I say, I shall be with her between ten and eleven; for at that time the jealous rascally knave, her husband, will be forth. Come you to me at night; you shall know how I speed.

FORD. I am blest in your acquaintance. Do you know Ford, sir?

FAL. Hang him, poor cuckoldly knave! I know him not: yet I wrong him, to call him poor; they say, the jealous wittolly knave hath masses of money; for the which his wife seems to me well-favoured. I will use her as the key of the cuckoldly rogue's coffer; and there's my harvest-home.

FORD. I would you knew Ford, sir; that you might avoid him, if you saw him.

FAL. Hang him, mechanical salt-butter rogue! I will stare him out of his wits; I will awe him with my cudgel: it shall hang like a meteor o'er the cuckold's horns: master Brook, thou shalt know, I will predominate over the peasant, and thou shalt lie with his wife. Come to me soon at night: Ford's a knave, and I will aggravate his stile; thou, master Brook, shalt know him for knave and cuckold: come to me soon at night. [*Exit.*

FORD. What a damned Epicurean rascal is this!—My heart is ready to crack with impatience. Who says, this is improvident jealousy? My wife hath sent to him, the hour is fixed, the match is made. Would any man have thought this? See the hell of having a false woman! my bed shall be abused, my coffers ransacked, my reputation gnawn at; and I shall not only receive this villainous wrong, but stand under the adoption of abominable terms, and by him that does me this wrong. Terms! names! Amaimon sounds well; Lucifer, well; Barbason, well; yet they are devils' additions, the names of fiends: but cuckold! wittol-cuckold! the devil himself hath not such a name. Page is an ass, a secure ass; he will trust his wife, he will not be jealous: I will rather trust a Fleming with my butter, parson Hugh the Welshman with my cheese, an Irishman with my aqua-vitæ bottle, or a thief to walk my ambling gelding, than my wife with herself: then she plots, then she ruminates, then she devises: and what they think in their hearts they may effect, they will break their hearts but they will effect. Heaven be praised for my jealousy! eleven o'clock the hour; I will prevent this, detect my wife, be revenged on Falstaff, and laugh at Page. I will about it; better three hours too soon, than a minute too late. Fie, fie, fie! cuckold! cuckold! cuckold! [*Exit.*

SCENE III.—Windsor Park.

Enter CAIUS *and* RUGBY.

CAIUS. Jack Rugby!

RUG. Sir.

CAIUS. Vat is de clock, Jack?

RUG. 'Tis past the hour, sir, that sir Hugh promised to meet.

CAIUS. By gar, he has save his soul, dat he is no come; he has pray his pible vell, dat he is no come: by gar, Jack Rugby, he is dead already, if he be come.

---

a Of great admittance,—] *i.e.* Of great *vogue, fashion,* &c.

b Preposterously.] See note (a), page 248.

c She dwells so securely on the excellency of her honour,—] This passage serves in some degree to support Theobald's reading of the very similar one in Scene 1:—"Though Page be a secure fool, and *stands* so firmly on his wife's *fealty.*" See note (c), page 653.

d Ward—] *Guard.*

RUG. He is wise, sir; he knew, your worship would kill him, if he came.

CAIUS. By gar, de herring is no dead, so as I vill kill him. Take your rapier, Jack; I vill tell you how I vill kill him.

RUG. Alas, sir, I cannot fence.

CAIUS. Villainy, take your rapier.

RUG. Forbear; here's company.

Enter Host, SHALLOW, SLENDER, *and* PAGE.

HOST. 'Bless thee, bully doctor.

SHAL. 'Save you, master doctor Caius.

PAGE. Now, good master doctor!

SLEN. 'Give you good-morrow, sir.

CAIUS. Vat be all you, one, two, tree, four, come for?

HOST. To see thee fight, to see thee foin,[a] to see thee traverse, to see thee here, to see thee there; to see thee pass thy punto, thy stock, thy reverse, thy distance, thy montánt.[b] Is he dead, my Ethiopian? is he dead, my Francisco? ha, bully! What says my Æsculapius? my Galen? my heart of elder? ha! is he dead, bully Stale? is he dead?

CAIUS. By gar, he is de coward Jack priest of de vorld; he is not show his face.

HOST. Thou art a Castilian, king Urinal! Hector of Greece, my boy!

CAIUS. I pray you, bear vitness that me have stay six or seven, two, tree hours for him, and he is no come.

SHAL. He is the wiser man, master doctor: he is a curer of souls, and you a curer of bodies; if you should fight, you go against the hair of your professions; is it not true, master Page?

PAGE. Master Shallow, you have yourself been a great fighter, though now a man of peace.

SHAL. Bodykins, master Page, though I now be old, and of the peace, if I see a sword out, my finger itches to make one: though we are justices, and doctors, and churchmen, master Page, we have some salt of our youth in us; we are the sons of women, master Page.

PAGE. 'Tis true, master Shallow.

SHAL. It will be found so, master Page. Master doctor Caius, I am come to fetch you home. I am sworn of the peace; you have showed yourself a wise physician, and sir Hugh hath shown himself a wise and patient churchman: you must go with me, master doctor.

HOST. Pardon, guest justice: a word,* monsieur Mock-water.

CAIUS. Mock-vater! vat is dat?

HOST. Mock-water, in our English tongue, is valour, bully.

CAIUS. By gar, then I have as much mock-vater as de Englishman.——Scurvy jack-dog priest! by gar, me vill cut his ears.

HOST. He will clapper-claw thee tightly, bully.

CAIUS. Clapper-de-claw! vat is dat?

HOST. That is, he will make thee amends.

CAIUS. By gar, me do look, he shall clapper-de-claw me; for, by gar, me vill have it.

HOST. And I will provoke him to't, or let him wag.

CAIUS. Me tank you vor dat.

HOST. And moreover, bully,—but first, master guest, and master Page, and eke cavalero Slender, go you through the town to Frogmore. [*Aside to them.*

PAGE. Sir Hugh is there, is he?

HOST. He is there: see what humour he is in; and I will bring the doctor about by the fields: will it do well?

SHAL. We will do it.

PAGE, SHAL. *and* SLEN. Adieu, good master doctor. [*Exeunt* PAGE, SHALLOW, *and* SLENDER.

CAIUS. By gar, me vill kill de priest; for he speak for a jack-an-ape to Anne Page.

HOST. Let him die: but first† sheath thy impatience; throw cold water on thy choler: go about the fields with me through Frogmore; I will bring thee where mistress Anne Page is, at a farm-house a-feasting; and thou shalt woo her; Cried game,[c] said I well?

CAIUS. By gar, me tank you vor dat: by gar, I love you; and I shall procure-a you de good guest, de earl, de knight, de lords, de gentlemen, my patients.

HOST. For the which, I will be thy adversary toward Anne Page; said I well?

CAIUS. By gar, 'tis good; vell said.

HOST. Let us wag then.

CAIUS. Come at my heels, Jack Rugby. [*Exeunt.*

---

a *To see thee* foin,—] To *foin* is to make a pass, or thrust, in fencing.

b *Pass thy* punto, &c.] The *punto*, the *stoccado*, the *reverso*, &c. are all technical terms, derived from the Italian masters of Fence See note (6), page 216.

c Cried game,—] The old text has, *Cride game*, which we mention in hope that some one more fortunate than previous guessers, may shape these apparently senseless words into the epithet, laughable and contemptuous, which the jolly Host intended to convey. Theobald proposed to substitute *Try'd game;* Warburton, *Cry aim;* and Douce, not infelicitously, *Cry'd I aim.* The conjecture of Mr. Collier's annotator, "curds and cream," is far removed from probability.

(*) First folio omits, *word.*
(†) First folio omits, *but first.*

ACT III.

SCENE I.—*A Field near* Frogmore.

Enter SIR HUGH EVANS *and* SIMPLE.

EVA. I pray you now, good master Slender's serving-man, and friend Simple py your name, which way have you looked for master Caius, that calls himself *Doctor of Physic?*

SIM. Marry, sir, the pittie-ward,[a] the park-ward, every way; old Windsor way, and every way but the town way.

EVA. I most fehemently desire you, you will also look that way.

SIM. I will, sir.

EVA. 'Pless my soul! how full of cholers I am, and trempling of mind!—I shall be glad, if he have deceived me:—how melancholies I am!—I will knog his urinals about his knave's costard, when I have good opportunities for the 'ork:—'pless my soul! [*Sings.*

To shallow rivers, to whose falls (1)
Melodious pirds sing madrigals;
There will we make our peds of roses,
And a thousand fragrant posies.
To shallow——

[a] Pittie-ward,—] Supposed to mean *petty-ward*.

'Mercy on me! I have a great dispositions to cry.

Melodious pirds sing madrigals;—
When as I sat in Pabylon,——
And a thousand vagram posies,
To shallow——

SIM. Yonder he is coming, this way, sir Hugh.

EVA. He's welcome:——

To shallow rivers, to whose falls——

Heaven prosper the right!—What weapons is he?

SIM. No weapons, sir: there comes my master, master Shallow, and another gentleman; from Frogmore, over the stile, this way.

EVA. Pray you, give me my gown; or else keep it in your arms.

Enter PAGE, SHALLOW, *and* SLENDER.

SHAL. How now, master parson? Good-morrow, good sir Hugh. Keep a gamester from the dice, and a good student from his book, and it is wonderful.

SLEN. Ah, sweet Anne Page!

PAGE. 'Save you, good sir Hugh!

EVA. 'Pless you from his mercy sake, all of you!

SHAL. What! the sword and the word! do you study them both, master parson?

PAGE. And youthful still, in your doublet and hose, this raw rheumatic day?

EVA. There is reasons and causes for it.

PAGE. We are come to you, to do a good office, master parson.

EVA. Fery well: what is it?

PAGE. Yonder is a most reverend gentleman, who belike, having received wrong by some person, is at most odds with his own gravity and patience, that ever you saw.

SHAL. I have lived fourscore years, and upward; I never heard a man of his place, gravity, and learning, so wide of his own respect.

EVA. What is he?

PAGE. I think you know him; master doctor Caius, the renowned French physician.

EVA. Got's will, and his—Passion of my heart! I had as lief you would tell me of a mess of porridge.

PAGE. Why?

EVA. He has no more knowledge in Hippocrates and Galen,—and he is a knave pesides; a cowardly knave, as you would desires to pe acquainted withal.

PAGE. I warrant you, he's the man should fight with him.

SLEN. O, sweet Anne Page!

SHAL. It appears so, by his weapons:—keep them asunder;—here comes doctor Caius.

Enter HOST, CAIUS, *and* RUGBY.

PAGE. Nay, good master parson, keep in your weapon.

SHAL. So do you, good master doctor.

HOST. Disarm them, and let them question; let them keep their limbs whole, and hack our English.

CAIUS. I pray you, let-a me speak a vord vit your ear: verefore vill you not meet a-me?

EVA. Pray you, use your patience: in good time.

CAIUS. By gar, you are de coward, de Jack dog, John ape.

EVA. [*Aside to* CAIUS.] Pray you, let us not be laughing-stogs to other men's humours; I desire you in friendship, and I will one way or other make you amends:—[*Aloud.*] I will knog your urinal about your knave's cogscomb, for missing your meetings and appointments.[a]

CAIUS. *Diable!*—Jack Rugby, mine *Host de Jarterre*, have I not stay for him, to kill him? have I not, at de place I did appoint?

EVA. As I am a Christians soul, now, look you, this is the place appointed; I'll be judgment py mine Host of the Garter.

HOST. Peace, I say, Guallia and Gaul, French and Welsh; soul-curer and body-curer.

CAIUS. Ay, dat is very good! excellent!

HOST. Peace, I say; hear mine Host of the Garter. Am I politic? am I subtle? am I a Machiavel? Shall I lose my doctor? no; he gives me the potions, and the motions. Shall I lose my parson? my priest? my sir Hugh? no; he gives me the proverbs and the no-verbs.—Give me thy hand, terrestrial; so[b]:—give me thy hand celestial; so.——Boys of art, I have deceived you both; I have directed you to wrong places: your hearts are mighty, your skins are whole, and let burnt sack be the issue.—Come, lay their swords to pawn:—follow me, lad of peace; follow, follow, follow.

SHAL. Trust me, a mad Host.—Follow, gentlemen, follow.

SLEN. O, sweet Anne Page!

[*Exeunt* SHALLOW, SLENDER, PAGE, *and* HOST.

CAIUS. Ha! do I perceive dat? have you make-a de sot of us? ha, ha!

EVA. This is well; he has made us his vlouting-stog.—I desire you, that we may pe friends; and let us knog our prains together, to pe revenge on this same scall, scurvy, cogging companion, the Host of the Garter.

CAIUS. By gar, vit all my heart; he promise to bring me vere is Anne Page: by gar, he deceive me too.

EVA. Well, I will smite his noddles:—pray you, follow. [*Exeunt.*

SCENE II.—*The Street in* Windsor.

Enter MISTRESS PAGE *and* ROBIN.

MRS. PAGE. Nay, keep your way, little gallant; you were wont to be a follower, but now you are a leader: whether had you rather, lead mine eyes, or eye your master's heels?

ROB. I had rather, forsooth, go before you like a man, than follow him like a dwarf.

MRS. PAGE. O you are a flattering boy; now, I see, you'll be a courtier.

---

[a] For missing your meetings and appointments.] These words, from the quarto, are omitted in the folio; another instance of strange neglect in the compilers of that volume, as without them the answer of Caius loses its point.

[b] Give me thy hand, terrestrial; so:] These words also are found only in the quarto.

Enter FORD.

FORD. Well met, mistress Page; whither go you?

MRS. PAGE. Truly, sir, to see your wife: is she at home?

FORD. Ay, and as idle as she may hang together, for want of company; I think, if your husbands were dead, you two would marry.

MRS. PAGE. Be sure of that,—two other husbands.

FORD. Where had you this pretty weather-cock?

MRS. PAGE. I cannot tell what the dickens his name is, my husband had him of: what do you call your knight's name, sirrah?

ROB. Sir John Falstaff.

FORD. Sir John Falstaff!

MRS. PAGE. He, he; I can never hit on's name.—There is such a league between my good man and he!—Is your wife at home, indeed?

FORD. Indeed, she is.

MRS. PAGE. By your leave, sir;—I am sick, till I see her. [*Exeunt* MRS. PAGE *and* ROBIN.

FORD. Has Page any brains? hath he any eyes? hath he any thinking? Sure, they sleep; he hath no use of them. Why, this boy will carry a letter twenty mile, as easy as a cannon will shoot point-blank twelve score. He pieces out his wife's inclination; he gives her folly motion and advantage: and now she's going to my wife, and Falstaff's boy with her. A man may hear this shower sing in the wind;—and Falstaff's boy with her!—Good plots!—they are laid: and our revolted wives share damnation together. Well; I will take him, then torture my wife, pluck the borrowed veil of modesty from the so-seeming mistress Page, divulge Page himself for a secure and wilful Actæon; and to these violent proceedings all my neighbours shall cry *aim*.[a] [*Clock strikes.*] The clock gives me my cue, and my assurance bids me search; there I shall find Falstaff: I shall be rather praised for this, than mocked; for it is as positive as the earth is firm, that Falstaff is there: I will go.

Enter PAGE, SHALLOW, SLENDER, Host, SIR HUGH EVANS, CAIUS, *and* RUGBY.

SHAL. PAGE, &c. Well met, master Ford.

FORD. Trust me, a good knot: I have good cheer at home; and, I pray you, all go with me.

SHAL. I must excuse myself, master Ford.

SLEN. And so must I, sir; we have appointed to dine with mistress Anne, and I would not break with her for more money than I'll speak of.

SHAL. We have lingered about a match between Anne Page and my cousin Slender, and this day we shall have our answer.

SLEN. I hope, I have your good will, father Page.

PAGE. You have, master Slender; I stand wholly for you:—but my wife, master doctor, is for you altogether.

CAIUS. Ay, by gar: and de maid is love-a me; my nursh-a Quickly tell me so mush.

HOST. What say you to young master Fenton? he capers, he dances, he has eyes of youth, he writes verses, he speaks holyday, he smells April and May: he will carry 't, he will carry 't; 'tis in his buttons;[b] he will carry 't.

PAGE. Not by my consent, I promise you. The gentleman is of no having:[c] he kept company with the wild Prince and Poins; he is of too high a region, he knows too much. No, he shall not knit a knot in his fortunes with the finger of my substance: if he take her, let him take her simply; the wealth I have waits on my consent, and my consent goes not that way.

FORD. I beseech you, heartily, some of you go home with me to dinner: besides your cheer, you shall have sport; I will show you a monster.——Master doctor, you shall go;—so shall you, master Page;—and you, sir Hugh.

SHAL. Well, fare you well:—we shall have the freer wooing at master Page's.

[*Exeunt* SHALLOW *and* SLENDER.

CAIUS. Go home, John Rugby; I come anon.

[*Exit* RUGBY.

HOST. Farewell, my hearts: I will to my honest knight Falstaff, and drink canary with him. [*Exit* Host.

FORD. [*Aside.*] I think, I shall drink in pipe-wine first with him; I'll make him dance. Will you go, gentles?

ALL. Have with you, to see this monster.

[*Exeunt.*

SCENE III.—*A Room in* Ford's *House.*

Enter MISTRESS FORD *and* MISTRESS PAGE.

MRS. FORD. What, John! what, Robert!

MRS. PAGE. Quickly, quickly: is the buck-basket——

MRS. FORD. I warrant:—what, Robin, I say!

Enter Servants *with a Basket.*

MRS. PAGE. Come, come, come.

MRS. FORD. Here, set it down.

---

[a] *Cry aim.*] See note (a), page 39.

[b] 'Tis in his buttons;] Mr. Knight suggests that this phrase may have the same meaning as the modern one, "It does not lie in your breeches," *i.e.* it is not within your compass.

[c] *Of no* having:] No *fortune,* no *revenue.*

MRS. PAGE. Give your men the charge; we must be brief.

MRS. FORD. Marry, as I told you before, John, and Robert, be ready here hard by in the brew-house; and when I suddenly call you, come forth, and without any pause, or staggering, take this basket on your shoulders: that done, trudge with it in all haste, and carry it among the whitsters[a] in Datchet mead, and there empty it in the muddy ditch, close by the Thames side.

MRS. PAGE. You will do it?

MRS. FORD. I have told them over and over; they lack no direction: be gone, and come when you are called. [*Exeunt* Servants.

MRS. PAGE. Here comes little Robin.

Enter ROBIN.

MRS. FORD. How now, my eyas-musket?[b] what news with you?

ROB. My master sir John is come in at your back-door, mistress Ford, and requests your company.

MRS. PAGE. You little Jack-a-lent,[c] have you been true to us?

ROB. Ay, I 'll be sworn: my master knows not of your being here; and hath threatened to put me into everlasting liberty, if I tell you of it; for, he swears, he 'll turn me away.

MRS. PAGE. Thou'rt a good boy; this secrecy

a The whitsters—] *Bleachers* of linen.
b Eyas-musket?] A young male sparrow-hawk.
c Jack-a-lent,—] A puppet stuck up to be thrown at in Lent, in imitation of the barbarous diversion of throwing at cocks about Shrovetide.

of thine shall be a tailor to thee, and shall make thee a new doublet and hose.—I'll go hide me.

MRS. FORD. Do so:—go tell thy master, I am alone. Mistress Page, remember you your cue. [*Exit* ROBIN.

MRS. PAGE. I warrant thee; if I do not act it, hiss me. [*Exit* MRS. PAGE.

MRS. FORD. Go to then; we'll use this unwholesome humidity, this gross watery pumpion;—we'll teach him to know turtles from jays.

Enter FALSTAFF.

FAL. *Have I caught* thee, *my heavenly jewel?* [a] Why, now let me die, for I have lived long enough; this is the period of my ambition: O this blessed hour!

MRS. FORD. O sweet sir John!

FAL. Mistress Ford, I cannot cog, I cannot prate, mistress Ford. Now shall I sin in my wish: I would thy husband were dead! I'll speak it before the best lord, I would make thee my lady.

MRS. FORD. I your lady, sir John! alas, I should be a pitiful lady.

FAL. Let the court of France show me such another; I see how thine eye would emulate the diamond: thou hast the right arched beauty of the brow, that becomes the ship-tire, the tire-valiant, or any tire of Venetian admittance.(2)

MRS. FORD. A plain kerchief, sir John: my brows become nothing else; nor that well neither.

FAL. Thou art a traitor * to say so; thou would'st make an absolute courtier; and the firm fixture of thy foot would give an excellent motion to thy gait, in a semi-circled farthingale. I see what thou wert, if Fortune thy foe,(3) were not

[a] *Have I caught* thee, *my heavenly jewel?*] The second song of Sidney's "Astrophel and Stella," begins:—

"*Have I caught my heav'nly jewell,*
Teaching sleepe most faire to be?"

And as Falstaff probably intended to sing the first line, the impertinent *thee*, which is not in the quarto, may have been an addition of the players.

(*) First folio, *tyrant*.

Nature, thy friend:[a] come, thou canst not hide it.

Mrs. Ford. Believe me, there's no such thing in me.

Fal. What made me love thee? let that persuade thee, there's something extraordinary in thee. Come, I cannot cog, and say thou art this and that, like a many of these lisping hawthorn buds, that come like women in men's apparel, and smell like Bucklersbury in simple-time;[b] I cannot: but I love thee, none but thee; and thou deservest it.

Mrs. Ford. Do not betray me, sir; I fear you love mistress Page.

Fal. Thou might'st as well say, I love to walk by the Counter-gate;[c] which is as hateful to me as the reek of a lime-kiln.

Mrs. Ford. Well, heaven knows how I love you; and you shall one day find it.

Fal. Keep in that mind; I'll deserve it.

Mrs. Ford. Nay, I must tell you, so you do; or else I could not be in that mind.

Rob. [*without.*] Mistress Ford, mistress Ford! here's mistress Page at the door, sweating, and blowing, and looking wildly, and would needs speak with you presently.

Fal. She shall not see me; I will ensconce me behind the arras.

Mrs. Ford. Pray you, do so; she's a very tattling woman.— [Falstaff *hides himself.*

Enter Mistress Page *and* Robin.

What's the matter? how now?

Mrs. Page. O mistress Ford, what have you done? You're shamed, you are overthrown, you are undone for ever.

Mrs. Ford. What's the matter, good mistress Page?

Mrs. Page. O well-a-day, mistress Ford! having an honest man to your husband, to give him such cause of suspicion!

Mrs. Ford. What cause of suspicion?

---

a I see what thou wert, if Fortune thy foe, were not Nature, thy friend:] It seems impossible to make good sense of this passage as it stands. We are disposed to believe the obscurity arises from the common error in these plays of misprinting *but* and *not*, and that the poet wrote, "I see what thou wert, if fortune thy foe, were *but* nature thy friend."

b Bucklersbury in simple-time;] In Shakespeare's days, Bucklersbury was the head-quarters of the druggists, who dealt in all kinds of medicinal herbs, (*simples* as they were then called,) whether dry or green.

c The Counter-gate;] The old dramatists and writers on manners, are unsparing in allusions to the Counter-prison, and constantly labour to extract some pleasantry from its name, which, to any who had tasted of the horrors of an English prison in former times, must have been odious enough even in jest:—Thus in Baret's "Alvearie," 1573:—"We saie merrily of him who hath been in the *Counter*, or such like places of prison; He can sing his *counter-tenor* very well. And in anger we say, I will make you sing a *counter-tenor* for this geare: meaning imprisonment."

Again Overbury, in his character of "A Sargeant," 1616:—

"His habit is a long gowne, made at first to cover his knavery, but that growing too monstrous, hee now goes in buffe: his conscience and that, being both cut out of one hide, and are of one toughnesse. *The countergate* is his kennell, the whole city his Paris garden, the misery of poore men (but especially of bad livers) are the offalles on which hee feeds."

MRS. PAGE. What cause of suspicion!—Out upon you! how am I mistook in you!

MRS. FORD. Why, alas! what's the matter?

MRS. PAGE. Your husband's coming hither, woman, with all the officers in Windsor, to search for a gentleman, that, he says, is here now in the house, by your consent, to take an ill advantage of his absence: you are undone.

MRS. FORD. 'T is not so, I hope.

MRS. PAGE. Pray heaven it be not so, that you have such a man here; but 't is most certain your husband's coming with half Windsor at his heels, to search for such a one. I come before to tell you: if you know yourself clear, why I am glad of it: but if you have a friend here, convey, convey him out. Be not amazed; call all your senses to you; defend your reputation, or bid farewell to your good life for ever.

MRS. FORD. What shall I do?—There is a gentleman, my dear friend; and I fear not mine own shame, so much as his peril: I had rather than a thousand pound, he were out of the house.

MRS. PAGE. For shame, never stand *you had rather*, and *you had rather;* your husband's here at hand, bethink you of some conveyance: in the house you cannot hide him.—O, how have you deceived me!—Look, here is a basket; if he be of any reasonable stature, he may creep in here; and throw foul linen upon him, as if it were going to bucking: or, it is whiting-time,[a] send him by your two men to Datchet mead.

MRS. FORD. He's too big to go in there: what shall I do?

Re-enter FALSTAFF.

FAL. Let me see't, let me see't! O let me see't! I'll in, I'll in;—follow your friend's counsel;—I'll in.

MRS. PAGE. What! sir John Falstaff! Are these your letters, knight?

FAL. I love thee, and none but thee;[b] help me away: let me creep in here; I'll never——

[*He goes into the basket; they cover him with foul linen.*

MRS. PAGE. Help to cover your master, boy: call your men, mistress Ford:—you dissembling knight!

MRS. FORD. What, John, Robert, John! [*Exit* ROBIN. *Re-enter* Servants.] Go take up these clothes here, quickly; where's the cowl-staff?[c] look, how you drumble: carry them to the laundress in Datchet mead; quickly, come.

Enter FORD, PAGE, CAIUS, *and* SIR HUGH EVANS.

FORD. 'Pray you, come near: if I suspect without cause, why then make sport at me, then let me be your jest; I deserve it.—How now? whither bear you this?

SERV. To the laundress, forsooth.

MRS. FORD. Why, what have you to do whither they bear it? You were best meddle with buck-washing.

FORD. Buck! I would I could wash myself of the buck! Buck, buck, buck! Ay, buck; I warrant you, buck; and of the season too, it shall appear. [*Exeunt* Servants *with the basket.*] Gentlemen, I have dreamed to-night; I'll tell you my dream. Here, here, here be my keys: ascend my chambers, search, seek, find out: I'll warrant, we'll unkennel the fox:—let me stop this way first:—so, now uncape.[d]

PAGE. Good master Ford, be contented: you wrong yourself too much.

FORD. True, master Page.—Up, gentlemen; you shall see sport anon: follow me, gentlemen. [*Exit.*

EVA. This is fery fantastical humours, and jealousies.

CAIUS. By gar, 't is no de fashion of France: it is not jealous in France.

PAGE. Nay, follow him, gentlemen; see the issue of his search.

[*Exeunt* EVANS, PAGE, *and* CAIUS.

MRS. PAGE. Is there not a double excellency in this?

MRS. FORD. I know not which pleases me better, that my husband is deceived, or sir John.

MRS. PAGE. What a taking was he in, when your husband asked what[e] was in the basket!

MRS. FORD. I am half afraid he will have need of washing; so, throwing him into the water will do him a benefit.

MRS. PAGE. Hang him, dishonest rascal! I would all of the same strain[f] were in the same distress.

MRS. FORD. I think, my husband hath some special suspicion of Falstaff's being here; for I never saw him so gross in his jealousy till now.

MRS. PAGE. I will lay a plot to try that: and

[a] Whiting-time,—] *Bleaching-time.*

[b] And none but thee;] These words are restored from the quarto, in most of the modern editions. Mr. Collier, and Mr. Knight, indeed, reject them, but somewhat inconsistently, since they admit other readings from the same source with no greater claims to insertion.

[c] Cowl-staff?] A staff or pole, for carrying a bucket at each end, or to sling a *cowl* or *tub*, with two handles on, to be borne by two men. "Bicollo, *a coule-staffe to carry behinde and before.*"—FLORIO'S *Dict.* 1611.

[d] *So, now* uncape] To *uncape* a fox, was the old technical term for *unearth* him.

[e] What was in the basket!] The folio has, "*who* was in the basket!" but Ford, in fact, asked neither *who*, nor *what*, was in the basket. The quarto, 1602, is more consistent: there, Ford directs the servants to set down the basket; and Mistress Ford afterwards asks, "I wonder what he thought when my husband bad them set down the basket?"

[f] Of *the same* strain.] See note (d), page 651.

we will yet have more tricks with Falstaff: his dissolute disease will scarce obey this medicine.

MRS. FORD. Shall we send that foolish carrion, mistress Quickly, to him, and excuse his throwing into the water; and give him another hope, to betray him to another punishment?

MRS. PAGE. We will do it; let him be sent for to-morrow, eight o'clock, to have amends.

Re-enter FORD, PAGE, CAIUS, *and* SIR HUGH EVANS.

FORD. I cannot find him: may be the knave bragged of that he could not compass.

MRS. PAGE. Heard you that?

MRS. FORD. Ay, ay, peace:*—you use me well, master Ford, do you?

FORD. Ay, I do so.

MRS. FORD. Heaven make you better than your thoughts!

FORD. Amen.

MRS. PAGE. You do yourself mighty wrong, master Ford.

FORD. Ay, ay; I must bear it.

EVA. If there pe any pody in the house, and in the chambers, and in the coffers, and in the presses, heaven forgive my sins at the day of judgment!

CAIUS. By gar, nor I too; dere is no bodies.

PAGE. Fie, fie, master Ford! are you not ashamed? What spirit, what devil suggests this imagination? I would not have your distemper in this kind, for the wealth of Windsor Castle.

FORD. 'Tis my fault,[a] master Page; I suffer for it.

EVA. You suffer for a pad conscience: your wife is as honest a 'omans, as I will desires among five thousand, and five hundred too.

CAIUS. By gar, I see 'tis an honest woman.

FORD. Well;—I promised you a dinner:—come, come, walk in the park: I pray you, pardon me, I will hereafter make known to you, why I have done this.—Come, wife;—come, mistress Page; I pray you pardon me; pray heartily, pardon me.

PAGE. Let's go in, gentlemen; but, trust me, we'll mock him. I do invite you to-morrow morning to my house to breakfast; after, we'll a birding together; I have a fine hawk for the bush: shall it be so?

FORD. Any thing.

EVA. If there is one, I shall make two in the company.

CAIUS. If there be one or two, I shall make-a de tird.

(*) First folio omits, *Ay, ay, peace.*

a *'Tis my* fault,—] That is, my *misfortune.* See note (d), p. 640.

FORD. Pray you go, master Page.

EVA. I pray you now, remembrance to-morrow on the lousy knave, mine Host.

CAIUS. Dat is good; by gar, vit all my heart.

EVA. A lousy knave; to have his gibes, and his mockeries. [*Exeunt.*

SCENE IV.—*A Room in* PAGE'S *House.*

Enter FENTON *and* ANNE PAGE.

FENT. I see, I cannot get thy father's love;
Therefore, no more turn me to him, sweet Nan.
ANNE. Alas! how then?
FENT. Why, thou must be thyself.
He doth object, I am too great of birth;
And that, my state being gall'd with my expense,
I seek to heal it only by his wealth:
Besides these, other bars he lays before me,
My riots past, my wild societies;
And tells me, 'tis a thing impossible
I should love thee, but as a property.
ANNE. May be, he tells you true.
FENT. No, heaven so speed me in my time to come!
Albeit, I will confess, thy father's wealth
Was the first motive that I woo'd thee, Anne:
Yet, wooing thee, I found thee of more value
Than stamps in gold, or sums in sealed bags:
And 'tis the very riches of thyself
That now I aim at.
ANNE. Gentle master Fenton,
Yet seek my father's love: still seek it, sir:
If opportunity and humblest suit
Cannot attain it, why then,—hark you hither.
[*They converse apart.*

Enter SHALLOW, SLENDER, *and* MISTRESS QUICKLY.

SHAL. Break their talk, mistress Quickly; my kinsman shall speak for himself.

SLEN. I'll make a shaft or a bolt on't:[b] 'slid, 'tis but venturing.

SHAL. Be not dismayed.

SLEN. No, she shall not dismay me: I care not for that,—but that I am afeard.

QUICK. Hark ye; master Slender would speak a word with you.

ANNE. I come to him. This is my father's choice.
O, what a world of vile ill-favour'd faults
Looks handsome in three hundred pounds a-year!
[*Aside.*

b I'll make a shaft or a bolt on't:] *To make a bolt or a shaft of a thing* is an old proverbial expression, equivalent to our saying, Here goes, *hit or miss.*

QUICK. And how does good master Fenton? Pray you, a word with you.

SHAL. She 's coming; to her, coz. O boy, thou hadst a father!

SLEN. I had a father, mistress Anne;—my uncle can tell you good jests of him:—pray you, uncle, tell mistress Anne the jest, how my father stole two geese out of a pen, good uncle.

SHAL. Mistress Anne, my cousin loves you.

SLEN. Ay, that I do; as well as I love any woman in Glostershire.

SHAL. He will maintain you like a gentlewoman.

SLEN. Ay, that I will, come cut and long-tail,[a] under the degree of a 'squire.

SHAL. He will make you a hundred and fifty pounds jointure.

ANNE. Good master Shallow, let him woo for himself.

SHAL. Marry, I thank you for it; I thank you for that good comfort. She calls you, coz: I'll leave you.

ANNE. Now, master Slender.

SLEN. Now, good mistress Anne.

ANNE. What is your will?

SLEN. My will? od's heartlings, that's a pretty jest, indeed! I ne'er made my will yet, I thank heaven; I am not such a sickly creature, I give heaven praise.

ANNE. I mean, master Slender, what would you with me?

SLEN. Truly, for mine own part, I would little or nothing with you: your father, and my uncle, hath made motions: if it be my luck, so: if not, happy man be his dole![b] They can tell you how things go, better than I can: you may ask your father; here he comes.

Enter PAGE, *and* MISTRESS PAGE.

PAGE. Now, master Slender:—love him, daughter Anne.—
Why, how now! what does master Fenton here?
You wrong me, sir, thus still to haunt my house:
I told you, sir, my daughter is disposed of.

FENT. Nay, master Page, be not impatient.

MRS. PAGE. Good master Fenton, come not to my child.

PAGE. She is no match for you.

FENT. Sir, will you hear me?

PAGE. No, good master Fenton.
Come, master Shallow; come, son Slender; in:—
Knowing my mind, you wrong me, master Fenton.

[*Exeunt* PAGE, SHALLOW, *and* SLENDER.

QUICK. Speak to mistress Page.

FENT. Good mistress Page, for that I love your daughter
In such a righteous fashion as I do,
Perforce, against all checks, rebukes, and manners,
I must advance the colours of my love,
And not retire: let me have your good will.

ANNE. Good mother, do not marry me to yond' fool.

MRS. PAGE. I mean it not; I seek you a better husband.

QUICK. That's my master, master doctor.

ANNE. Alas, I had rather be set quick i' th' earth,
And bowl'd to death with turnips.

MRS. PAGE. Come, trouble not yourself: good master Fenton,
I will not be your friend nor enemy:
My daughter will I question how she loves you,
And as I find her, so am I affected;
'Till then, farewell, sir:—she must needs go in;
Her father will be angry.

[*Exeunt* MISTRESS PAGE *and* ANNE.

FENT. Farewell, gentle mistress; farewell, Nan.

QUICK. This is my doing now;—*nay*, said I, *will you cast away your child on a fool, and a physician?* Look on master Fenton:—this is my doing.

FENT. I thank thee; and I pray thee, once[c] to-night,
Give my sweet Nan this ring: there's for thy pains.

[*Exit.*

QUICK. Now heaven send thee good fortune! A kind heart he hath: a woman would run through fire and water for such a kind heart. But yet, I would my master had mistress Anne; or I would master Slender had her; or, in sooth, I would master Fenton had her: I will do what I can for them all three; for so I have promised, and I'll be as good as my word; but speciously for master Fenton. Well, I must of another errand to sir John Falstaff from my two mistresses; what a beast am I to slack it! [*Exit.*

SCENE V.—*A Room in the* Garter Inn.

Enter FALSTAFF *and* BARDOLPH.

FAL. Bardolph, I say,—

BARD. Here, sir.

FAL. Go fetch me a quart of sack; put a toast in't. [*Exit* BARD.] Have I lived to be carried in a basket, like a barrow of butcher's offal; and to be thrown in the Thames? Well, if I be

---

[a] *Come cut and long-tail,—*] *Let any come that may; good and bad.* This phrase was, no doubt, originally applied to dogs, or horses.

[b] Happy man be his dole!] See note (d), page 234.

[c] Once *to-night,—*] *Some time* to-night.

served such another trick, I'll have my brains ta'en out, and buttered, and give them to a dog for a new year's gift. The rogues slighted me into the river with as little remorse as they would have drowned a blind bitch's puppies,[a] fifteen i' th' litter: and you may know by my size, that I have a kind of alacrity in sinking; if the bottom were as deep as hell, I should down. I had been drowned, but that the shore was shelvy and shallow; a death that I abhor; for the water swells a man; and what a thing should I have been, when I had been swelled! I should have been a mountain of mummy.

Re-enter BARDOLPH, *with the wine.*

BARD. Here's mistress Quickly, sir, to speak with you.

[a] A blind bitch's puppies,—] So the old text; a colloquial inversion of a *bitch's blind puppies*.

FAL. Come, let me pour in some sack to the Thames water; for my belly's as cold, as if I had swallowed snow-balls for pills to cool the reins. Call her in.

BARD. Come in, woman.

Enter MISTRESS QUICKLY.

QUICK. By your leave; I cry you mercy: give your worship good-morrow.

FAL. Take away these chalices: go brew me a pottle of sack finely.

BARD. With eggs, sir?

FAL. Simple of itself; I'll no pullet-sperm in my brewage.—[*Exit* BARDOLPH.]—How now?

QUICK. Marry, sir, I come to your worship from mistress Ford.

FAL. Mistress Ford! I have had ford enough: I was thrown into the ford: I have my belly full of ford.

QUICK. Alas the day! good heart, that was not

her fault: she does so take on with her men; they mistook their erection.

FAL. So did I mine, to build upon a foolish woman's promise.

QUICK. Well, she laments, sir, for it, that it would yearn your heart to see it. Her husband goes this morning a birding; she desires you once more to come to her between eight and nine: I must carry her word quickly; she'll make you amends, I warrant you.

FAL. Well, I will visit her: tell her so; and bid her think, what a man is: let her consider his frailty, and then judge of my merit.

QUICK. I will tell her.

FAL. Do so. Between nine and ten, say'st thou?

QUICK. Eight and nine, sir.

FAL. Well, be gone: I will not miss her.

QUICK. Peace be with you, sir! [*Exit.*

FAL. I marvel, I hear not of master Brook: he sent me word to stay within: I like his money well. O, here he comes.

Enter FORD.

FORD. 'Bless you, sir! [a]

FAL. Now, master Brook, you come to know what hath passed between me and Ford's wife?

FORD. That, indeed, sir John, is my business.

FAL. Master Brook, I will not lie to you; I was at her house the hour she appointed me.

FORD. And sped you, sir?

FAL. Very ill-favouredly, master Brook.

FORD. How so, sir? did she change her determination?

FAL. No, master Brook; but the peaking cornuto her husband, master Brook, dwelling in a continual larum of jealousy, comes me in the instant of our encounter, after we had embraced, kissed, protested, and, as it were, spoke the prologue of our comedy; and at his heels a rabble of his companions, thither provoked and instigated by his distemper, and, forsooth, to search his house for his wife's love.

FORD. What, while you were there?

FAL. While I was there.

FORD. And did he search for you, and could not find you?

FAL. You shall hear. As good luck would have it, comes in one mistress Page; gives intelligence of Ford's approach; and, by* her invention, and Ford's wife's distraction, they conveyed me into a buck-basket.

FORD. A buck-basket!

FAL. By the Lord,[b] a buck-basket: rammed me in with foul shirts and smocks, socks, foul stockings, greasy napkins; that, master Brook, there was the rankest compound of villainous smell, that ever offended nostril.

FORD. And how long lay you there?

FAL. Nay, you shall hear, master Brook, what I have suffered to bring this woman to evil for your good. Being thus crammed in the basket, a couple of Ford's knaves, his hinds, were called forth by their mistress, to carry me in the name of foul clothes to Datchet-lane: they took me on their shoulders; met the jealous knave their master in the door, who asked them once or twice what they had in their basket: I quaked for fear, lest the lunatic knave would have searched it; but fate, ordaining he should be a cuckold, held his hand. Well; on went he for a search, and away went I for foul clothes. But mark the sequel, master Brook: I suffered the pangs of three several deaths: first, an intolerable fright, to be detected with[c] a jealous rotten bell-wether: next, to be compassed, like a good bilbo, in the circumference of a peck, hilt to point, heel to head: and then, to be stopped in, like a strong distillation, with stinking clothes that fretted in their own grease: think of that,—a man of my kidney,—think of that; that am as subject to heat, as butter; a man of continual dissolution and thaw; it was a miracle, to 'scape suffocation. And in the height of this bath, when I was more than half stewed in grease, like a Dutch dish, to be thrown into the Thames, and cooled, glowing hot, in that surge, like a horse shoe; think of that,—hissing hot,—think of that, master Brook.

FORD. In good sadness, sir, I am sorry that for my sake you have suffered all this. My suit then is desperate; you'll undertake her no more?

FAL. Master Brook, I will be thrown into Ætna, as I have been into Thames, ere I will leave her thus. Her husband is this morning gone a birding: I have received from her another embassy of meeting; 'twixt eight and nine is the hour, master Brook.

FORD. 'T is past eight already, sir.

FAL. Is it? I will then address[d] me to my appointment. Come to me at your convenient leisure, and you shall know how I speed; and the conclusion shall be crowned with your enjoying her: adieu. You shall have her, master Brook; master Brook, you shall cuckold Ford. [*Exit.*

FORD. Hum! ha! is this a vision? is this a dream? do I sleep? Master Ford, awake; awake, master Ford; there's a hole made in your best coat, master Ford. This 'tis to be married! this 'tis to have linen, and buck-baskets!—Well, I will proclaim myself what I am: I will now take the lecher; he is at my house: he cannot 'scape me; 'tis impossible he should; he cannot creep into a halfpenny purse, nor into a pepper-box: but, lest the devil that guides him should aid him, I will search impossible places. Though what I am I cannot avoid, yet to be what I would not, shall not make me tame: if I have horns to make me[e] mad, let the proverb go with me, I'll be horn mad.

[*Exit.*

(*) First folio, *in*.

[a] 'Bless you, sir!] The greeting in the quarto, "God save you, sir!" is certainly preferable.

[b] By the Lord,—] This is the reading of the quarto. The folio has only, *Yes*.

[c] *An intolerable fright, to be detected* with,—] That is, an intolerable fear of being discovered *by*. *With*, *by*, *of*, *for*, &c. were used with indiscriminate licence formerly.

[d] Address me—] *Prepare* me; make myself ready.

[e] *Make* me *mad*,—] Old text, *one*. The correction was made by Mr. Dyce.

ACT IV.

SCENE I.—*The Street.*

Enter MISTRESS PAGE, MISTRESS QUICKLY, *and* WILLIAM PAGE.

MRS. PAGE. Is he at master Ford's already, think'st thou?

QUICK. Sure, he is by this; or will be presently: but truly, he is very courageous mad, about his throwing into the water. Mistress Ford desires you to come suddenly.

MRS. PAGE. I'll be with her by and by;[a] I'll but bring my young man here to school: look, where his master comes; 'tis a playing-day, I see.

Enter SIR HUGH EVANS.

How now, sir Hugh? no school to-day?

EVA. No: master Slender is let the boys leave to play.

[a] By and by;] *By and by*, in Shakespeare's day, signified *immediately;* not, as now, some time hence.

QUICK. 'Blessing of his heart!

MRS. PAGE. Sir Hugh, my husband says, my son profits nothing in the world at his book; I pray you, ask him some questions in his accidence.(1)

EVA. Come hither, William; hold up your head; come.

MRS. PAGE. Come on, sirrah; hold up your head; answer your master, be not afraid.

EVA. William, how many numbers is in nouns?

WILL. Two.

QUICK. Truly, I thought there had been one number more; because they say, od's nouns.

EVA. Peace your tattlings. What is *fair*, William?

WILL. *Pulcher*.

QUICK. *Poul-cats!* there are fairer things than poul-cats, sure.

EVA. You are a very simplicity 'oman; I pray you, peace. What is *lapis*, William?

WILL. A stone.

EVA. And what is a stone, William?

WILL. A pebble.

EVA. No, it is *lapis;* I pray you remember in your prain.

WILL. *Lapis.*

EVA. That is a good William. What is he, William, that does lend articles?

WILL. Articles are borrowed of the pronoun; and be thus declined, *Singulariter, nominativo, hic, hæc, hoc.*

EVA. *Nominativo, hig, hag, hog;*—pray you, mark: *genitivo, hujus:* well, what is your *accusative case?*

WILL. *Accusativo, hinc.*

EVA. I pray you, have your remembrance, child; *Accusativo, hing, hang, hog.*

QUICK. *Hang hog* is Latin for bacon, I warrant you.

EVA. Leave your prabbles, 'oman. What is the focative case, William?

WILL. O—*vocativo,* O.

EVA. Remember, William; *focative* is *caret.*

QUICK. And that's a good root.

EVA. 'Oman, forbear.

MRS. PAGE. Peace.

EVA. What is your *genitive case plural,* William?

WILL. *Genitive case?*

EVA. Ay.

WILL. *Genitive,—horum, harum, horum.*

QUICK. 'Vengeance of *Jenny's case!* fie on her!—never name her, child, if she be a whore.

EVA. For shame, 'oman.

QUICK. You do ill to teach the child such words; he teaches him to *hick* and to *hack,* which they'll do fast enough of themselves; and to call *horum:*—fie upon you!

EVA. 'Oman, art thou lunatics? hast thou no understandings for thy cases, and the numbers of the genders? Thou art as foolish Christian creatures as I would desires.

MRS. PAGE. Pr'ythee hold thy peace.

EVA. Show me now, William, some declensions of your pronouns.

WILL. Forsooth, I have forgot.

EVA. It is *ki, kæ, cod;* if you forget your *kies,* your *kæs,* and your *cods,* you must be preeches. Go your ways, and play; go.

MRS. PAGE. He is a better scholar than I thought he was.

EVA. He is a good sprag[a] memory. Farewell, mistress Page.

MRS. PAGE. Adieu, good sir Hugh.

[*Exit* SIR HUGH.

Get you home, boy.—Come, we stay too long.

[*Exeunt.*

SCENE II.—*A Room in* Ford's *House.*

Enter FALSTAFF *and* MISTRESS FORD.

FAL. Mistress Ford, your sorrow hath eaten up my sufferance: I see, you are obsequious in your love, and I profess requital to a hair's breadth; not only, mistress Ford, in the simple office of love, but in all the accoutrement, complement, and ceremony of it. But are you sure of your husband now?

MRS. FORD. He's a birding, sweet sir John.

MRS. PAGE. [*Without.*] What hoa, gossip Ford! what hoa!

MRS. FORD. Step into the chamber, sir John.

[*Exit* FALSTAFF.

Enter MISTRESS PAGE.

MRS. PAGE. How now, sweetheart? who's at home besides yourself?

MRS. FORD. Why, none but mine own people.

MRS. PAGE. Indeed?

MRS. FORD. No, certainly.—Speak louder.

[*Aside, to her.*

MRS. PAGE. Truly, I am so glad you have nobody here.

MRS. FORD. Why?

MRS. PAGE. Why, woman, your husband is in his old lunes[b] again; he so takes on yonder with my husband; so rails against all married mankind; so curses all Eve's daughters, of what complexion soever; and so buffets himself on the forehead, crying, *Peer-out, peer-out!* that any madness, I ever yet beheld, seemed but tameness, civility, and patience, to this his distemper he is in now: I am glad the fat knight is not here.

MRS. FORD. Why, does he talk of him?

MRS. PAGE. Of none but him; and swears, he was carried out, the last time he searched for him, in a basket: protests to my husband, he is now here; and hath drawn him and the rest of their company from their sport, to make another experiment of his suspicion: but I am glad the knight is not here; now he shall see his own foolery.

MRS. FORD. How near is he, mistress Page?

MRS. PAGE. Hard by, at street end; he will be here anon.

MRS. FORD. I am undone!—the knight is here.

MRS. PAGE. Why, then you are utterly shamed, and he's but a dead man. What a woman are you!—Away with him, away with him; better shame than murder.

MRS. FORD. Which way should he go? how

---

a Sprag—] *Sprack,* i.e. *quick, ready, sprightly.*

b *In his old* lunes *again;*] The folio reads, *lines;* the correction was made by Theobald. The quarto reads, in his old *vaine* again.

should I bestow him? shall I put him into the basket again?

Re-enter FALSTAFF.

FAL. No, I'll come no more i' th' basket; may I not go out, ere he come?

MRS. PAGE. Alas, three of master Ford's brothers watch the door with pistols, that none shall issue out; otherwise you might slip away ere he came. But what make you here?

FAL. What shall I do?—I'll creep up into the chimney.

MRS. FORD. There they always use to discharge their birding-pieces: creep into the kiln-hole.

FAL. Where is it?

MRS. FORD. He will seek there, on my word. Neither press, coffer, chest, trunk, well, vault, but he hath an abstract for the remembrance of such places, and goes to them by his note: there is no hiding you in the house.

FAL. I'll go out then.

MRS. PAGE. If you go out[a] in your own semblance, you die, sir John. Unless you go out disguised,—

MRS. FORD. How might we disguise him?

MRS. PAGE. Alas the day! I know not. There is no woman's gown big enough for him; otherwise, he might put on a hat, a muffler,(2) and a kerchief, and so escape.

FAL. Good hearts, devise something: any extremity, rather than a mischief.

MRS. FORD. My maid's aunt, the fat woman of Brentford, has a gown above.

MRS. PAGE. On my word, it will serve him; she's as big as he is: and there's her thrummed hat, and her muffler too: run up, sir John.

MRS. FORD. Go, go, sweet sir John: mistress Page and I will look some linen for your head.

MRS. PAGE. Quick, quick; we'll come dress you straight: put on the gown the while.

[*Exit* FALSTAFF.

MRS. FORD. I would my husband would meet him in this shape: he cannot abide the old woman of Brentford; he swears, she's a witch; forbade her my house, and hath threatened to beat her.

MRS. PAGE. Heaven guide him to thy husband's cudgel; and the devil guide his cudgel afterwards!

MRS. FORD. But is my husband coming?

MRS. PAGE. Ay, in good sadness, is he; and talks of the basket too, howsoever he hath had intelligence.

MRS. FORD. We'll try that; for I'll appoint my men to carry the basket again, to meet him at the door with it, as they did last time.

MRS. PAGE. Nay, but he'll be here presently: let's go dress him like the witch of Brentford.(3)

MRS. FORD. I'll first direct my men, what they shall do with the basket. Go up, I'll bring linen for him straight. [*Exit.*

MRS. PAGE. Hang him, dishonest varlet! we cannot misuse him enough.

We'll leave a proof, by that which we will do,
Wives may be merry, and yet honest too:
We do not act, that often jest and laugh;
'Tis old but true, *Still swine eat all the draff.*
[*Exit.*

Re-enter MISTRESS FORD, *with two* Servants.

MRS. FORD. Go, sirs, take the basket again on your shoulders; your master is hard at door; if he bid you set it down, obey him: quickly, despatch. [*Exit.*

1 SERV. Come, come, take it up.

2 SERV. Pray heaven, it be not full of knight again.

1 SERV. I hope not; I had as lief* bear so much lead.

Enter FORD, PAGE, SHALLOW, CAIUS, *and* SIR HUGH EVANS.

FORD. Ay, but if it prove true, master Page, have you any way then to unfool me again?—Set down the basket, villain:—somebody call my wife:——Youth in a basket!—O, you panderly rascals! there's a knot, a ging,[b] a pack, a conspiracy against me: now shall the devil be shamed. What! wife, I say! come, come forth; behold what honest clothes you send forth to bleaching!

PAGE. Why, this passes,[c] master Ford! you are not to go loose any longer; you must be pinioned.

EVA. Why, this is lunatics! this is mad as a mad dog!

SHAL. Indeed, master Ford, this is not well; indeed.

Enter MISTRESS FORD.

FORD. So say I too, sir.—Come hither, mistress Ford; mistress Ford, the honest woman, the modest wife, the virtuous creature, that hath the jealous fool to her husband!—I suspect without cause, mistress, do I?

---

[a] MRS. PAGE. If you go out, &c.] This, as well as the next speech, is given to Mrs. Ford in the folio, 1623.

[b] A ging,—] The old text reads *gin*. *Ging*, from the Anglo-Saxon, *genge*, a flock, is an old word used for *gang*. Thus, in Ben Jonson's "New Inn," Act I. Sc. 1:—

——"I would not willingly
See, or be seen, to any of this *ging*."

[c] This passes,—] *Surpasses* belief. See note (c), page 644.

(*) First folio, *liefe as*.

MRS. FORD. Heaven be my witness, you do, if you suspect me in any dishonesty.

FORD. Well said, brazen-face; hold it out.—— Come forth, sirrah!

[*Pulls the clothes out of the basket.*

PAGE. This passes!

MRS. FORD. Are you not ashamed? let the clothes alone.

FORD. I shall find you anon.

EVA. 'Tis unreasonable! Will you take up your wife's clothes? Come away.

FORD. Empty the basket, I say.

MRS. FORD. Why, man, why?

FORD. Master Page, as I am a man, there was one conveyed out of my house yesterday in this basket: why may not he be there again? In my house I am sure he is: my intelligence is true; my jealousy is reasonable: pluck me out all the linen.

MRS. FORD. If you find a man there, he shall die a flea's death.

PAGE. Here's no man.

SHAL. By my fidelity, this is not well, master Ford; this wrongs you.

EVA. Master Ford, you must pray, and not follow the imaginations of your own heart: this is jealousies.

FORD. Well, he's not here I seek for.

PAGE. No, nor nowhere else but in your brain.

FORD. Help to search my house this one time: if I find not what I seek, show no colour for my extremity, let me for ever be your table-sport; let them say of me, *As jealous as Ford, that searched a hollow walnut for his wife's leman.*[a] Satisfy me once more; once more search with me.

MRS. FORD, What hoa, mistress Page! come you, and the old woman, down; my husband will come into the chamber.

FORD. Old woman! what old woman's that?

MRS. FORD. Why, it is my maid's aunt of Brentford.

FORD. A witch, a quean, an old cozening quean! Have I not forbid her my house? She comes of errands, does she? We are simple men; we do not know what's brought to pass under the profession of fortune-telling. She works by charms, by spells, by the figure, and such daubery as this,[b] is beyond our element: we know nothing. Come down, you witch, you hag you; come down, I say!

MRS. FORD. Nay, good, sweet husband;—good gentlemen, let him not[c] strike the old woman.

---

a *His wife's* leman.] Leman, *lover, paramour.* It was applied to both sexes, though more frequently to females.

b Such daubery as this, &c.] Daubery means *gullery, juggling,* and the like; but from the invariable punctuation of the passage in modern editions, it appears to have been taken for some abusive epithet applied to the supposed witch.

c *Let him* not *strike the old woman.*] The folio, 1623, omits, *not,* which was supplied in that of 1632.

Enter FALSTAFF *disguised like an old woman, led by* MISTRESS PAGE.

MRS. PAGE. Come, mother Prat, come, give me your hand.

FORD. I'll *prat* her:——Out of my door, you witch! [*Beats him.*] you rag, you baggage, you polecat, you ronyon! out! out! I'll conjure you! I'll fortune-tell you! [*Exit* FALSTAFF.

MRS. PAGE. Are you not ashamed? I think, you have killed the poor woman.

MRS. FORD. Nay, he will do it:—'t is a goodly credit for you.

FORD. Hang her, witch!

EVA. By yea and no, I think, the 'oman is a witch indeed: I like not when a 'oman has a great peard; I spy a great peard under her* muffler.

FORD. Will you follow, gentlemen? I beseech you follow; see but the issue of my jealousy: if I cry out thus upon no trail, never trust me when I open again.

PAGE. Let's obey his humour a little further: come, gentlemen.

[*Exeunt* PAGE, FORD, SHALLOW, CAIUS, *and* EVANS.

MRS. PAGE. Trust me, he beat him most pitifully.

MRS. FORD. Nay, by the mass, that he did not; he beat him most unpitifully, methought.

MRS. PAGE. I'll have the cudgel hallowed, and hung o'er the altar; it hath done meritorious service.

MRS. FORD. What think you? May we, with the warrant of womanhood, and the witness of a good conscience, pursue him with any further revenge?

MRS. PAGE. The spirit of wantonness is, sure, scared out of him; if the devil have him not in fee-simple, with fine and recovery, he will never, I think, in the way of waste, attempt us again.

MRS. FORD. Shall we tell our husbands how we have served him?

MRS. PAGE. Yes, by all means; if it be but to scrape the figures out of your husband's brains. If they can find in their hearts, the poor unvirtuous fat knight shall be any further afflicted, we two will still be the ministers.

MRS. FORD. I'll warrant, they'll have him publicly shamed: and, methinks, there would be no period to the jest, should he not be publicly shamed.

MRS. PAGE. Come, to the forge with it then, shape it: I would not have things cool. [*Exeunt.*

(*) First folio, *his*.

[a] *They must* come off;] That is, pay. The expression in this sense is met with as early as Chaucer:—

"*Come off*, and let me riden hastily;
Give me twelve pence; I may no longer tarrie."
The Friar's Tale.

SCENE III.—*A Room in the* Garter Inn.

Enter Host *and* BARDOLPH.

BARD. Sir, the Germans* desire to have three of your horses: the duke himself will be to-morrow at court, and they are going to meet him.

HOST. What duke should that be, comes so secretly? I hear not of him in the court: let me speak with the gentlemen; they speak English?

BARD. Ay, sir; I'll call them† to you.

HOST. They shall have my horses; but I'll make them pay, I'll sauce them: they have had my house‡ a week at command; I have turned away my other guests: they must come off;[a] I'll sauce them. Come. [*Exeunt.*

SCENE IV.—*A Room in* Ford's *House.*

Enter PAGE, FORD, MISTRESS PAGE, MISTRESS FORD, *and* SIR HUGH EVANS.

EVA. 'T is one of the pest discretions of a 'oman as ever I did look upon.

PAGE. And did he send you both these letters at an instant?

MRS. PAGE. Within a quarter of an hour.

FORD. Pardon me, wife: henceforth do what thou wilt;
I rather will suspect the sun with cold,§
Than thee with wantonness; now doth thy honour stand,
In him that was of late an heretic,
As firm as faith.

PAGE. 'T is well, 't is well; no more.
Be not as éxtreme in submission, as in offence;
But let our plot go forward: let our wives
Yet once again, to make us public sport,
Appoint a meeting with this old fat fellow,
Where we may take him, and disgrace him for it.

FORD. There is no better way than that they spoke of.

PAGE. How! to send him word they'll meet him in the park at midnight! fie, fie; he'll never come.

EVA. You say, he has peen thrown in the rivers; and has peen grievously peaten, as an old 'oman: methinks, there should pe terrors in him, that he should not come; methinks, his flesh is punished, he shall have no desires.

PAGE. So think I too.

(*) First folio, *Germane desires*. (†) First folio, *him*. (‡) First folio, *houses*. (§) Old text, *gold*.

MRS. FORD. Devise but how you'll use him when he comes,
And let us two devise to bring him thither.
MRS. PAGE. There is an old tale goes, that Herne the hunter,
Sometime a keeper here in Windsor forest,
Doth all the winter time, at still midnight,
Walk round about an oak, with great ragg'd horns;
And there he blasts the tree, and takes[a] the cattle;
And makes* milch-kine yield blood, and shakes a chain
In a most hideous and dreadful manner:
You have heard of such a spirit; and well you know,
The superstitious idle-headed eld
Receiv'd and did deliver to our age,
This tale of Herne the hunter for a truth.
PAGE. Why, yet there want not many, that do fear
In deep of night to walk by this Herne's oak:
But what of this?
MRS. FORD. Marry, this is our device;
That Falstaff at that oak shall meet with us,
Disguis'd like Herne, with huge horns on his head.[b]
PAGE. Well, let it not be doubted but he'll come,
And in this shape; when you have brought him thither,
What shall be done with him? what is your plot?
MRS. PAGE. That likewise have we thought upon, and thus:
Nan Page my daughter, and my little son,
And three or four more of their growth, we'll dress
Like urchins, ouphes,[c] and fairies, green and white,
With rounds of waxen tapers on their heads,
And rattles in their hands; upon a sudden,
As Falstaff, she, and I, are newly met,
Let them from forth a saw-pit rush at once
With some diffused[d] song; upon their sight,
We two in great amazedness will fly:
Then let them all encircle him about,
And, fairy-like, to-pinch[e] the unclean knight;
And ask him, why, that hour of fairy revel,
In their so sacred paths, he dares to tread,
In shape profane.
MRS. FORD. And till he tell the truth,
Let the supposed fairies pinch him sound,
And burn him with their tapers.

MRS. PAGE. The truth being known,
We'll all present ourselves; dis-horn the spirit,
And mock him home to Windsor.
FORD. The children must
Be practis'd well to this, or they'll ne'er do't.
EVA. I will teach the children their pehaviours; and I will pe like a jack-an-apes also, to purn the knight with my taper.
FORD. That will be excellent. I'll go buy them vizards.
MRS. PAGE. My Nan shall be the queen of all the fairies,
Finely attired in a robe of white.
PAGE. That silk will I go buy;—and in that tire[f]
Shall master Slender steal my Nan away, [*Aside.*
And marry her at Eton.——Go, send to Falstaff straight.
FORD. Nay, I'll to him again in name of Brook:
He'll tell me all his purpose: sure, he'll come.
MRS. PAGE. Fear not you that: go, get us properties,
And tricking for our fairies.
EVA. Let us about it: it is admirable pleasures, and fery honest knaveries.
[*Exeunt* PAGE, FORD, *and* EVANS.
MRS. PAGE. Go, mistress Ford,
Send Quickly to sir John, to know his mind.
[*Exit* MISTRESS FORD.
I'll to the doctor; he hath my good will,
And none but he, to marry with Nan Page.
That Slender, though well landed, is an idiot;
And he my husband, best of all, affects:
The doctor is well money'd, and his friends
Potent at court; he, none but he, shall have her,
Though twenty thousand worthier come to crave her. [*Exit.*

SCENE V.—*A Room in the* Garter Inn.

Enter Host *and* SIMPLE.

HOST. What would'st thou have, boor? what, thick-skin?[g] speak, breathe, discuss; brief, short, quick, snap.
SIM. Marry, sir, I come to speak with sir John Falstaff from master Slender.
HOST. There's his chamber, his house, his

(*) First folio, *make.*

[a] *And* takes *the cattle;*] To *take*, meant to *bewitch*, to *blast with disease.* Thus in "Hamlet," Act I. Sc. 1:—

——"then no planets strike,
No fairy *takes*, nor witch hath power to charm."

[b] Disguis'd like Herne, with huge horns on his head.] This line, restored from the quarto, is shown by Page's next speech to be indispensable.

[c] Ouphes,—] *Elves, goblins.*

[d] Diffused song;] *Irregular, wild.*

[e] To-pinch—] *To* was very anciently used in connexion with verbs, as we conjoin *be.* Thus Gower, De Confessione Amantis, b. iv. fol. 7:—

"All *to-tore* is myn araie."

And Chaucer, Reeve's Tale, l. 4275:—

——"nose and mouth *to-broke.*"

And Spenser has all *to-rent*, all *to-torn*, where we should say all-*be*-torn, all-*be*-rent, &c.

[f] *In that* tire—] The first folio has, "in that *time*," which was corrected by Theobald.

[g] *What,* thick-skin?] This term of abuse, bearing the same meaning as our, *thick-head*, occurs again in "A Midsummer Night's Dream," Act III. Sc. 2, where Puck, speaking of Bottom, says:—

"The shallowest *thick-skin* of that barren sort,
Who Pyramus presented in their sport."

castle, his standing-bed, and truckle-bed;[a] 'tis painted about with the story of the prodigal, fresh and new: go, knock and call; he'll speak like an *Anthropophaginian* unto thee; knock, I say.

SIM. There's an old woman, a fat woman, gone up into his chamber; I'll be so bold as stay, sir, till she come down: I come to speak with her, indeed.

HOST. Ha! a fat woman! the knight may be robbed: I'll call.—Bully knight! Bully sir John! speak from thy lungs military: art thou there? it is thine host, thine Ephesian, calls.

FAL. [*above.*] How now, mine Host?

HOST. Here's a Bohemian-Tartar tarries the coming down of thy fat woman: let her descend, bully, let her descend; my chambers are honourable: fie! privacy? fie!

Enter FALSTAFF.

FAL. There was, mine Host, an old fat woman even now with me; but she's gone.

SIM. Pray you, sir, was't not the wise woman of Brentford?

FAL. Ay, marry, was it, muscle-shell;[b] what would you with her?

SIM. My master, sir, my master Slender, sent to her, seeing her go through the streets, to know, sir, whether one Nym, sir, that beguiled him of a chain, had the chain, or no.

FAL. I spake with the old woman about it.

SIM. And what says she, I pray, sir?

FAL. Marry, she says, that the very same man, that beguiled master Slender of his chain, cozened him of it.

SIM. I would, I could have spoken with the woman herself; I had other things to have spoken with her too, from him.

FAL. What are they? let us know.

HOST. Ay, come; quick!

SIM. I may not conceal them, sir.[c]

HOST. Conceal them, or thou diest!

SIM. Why, sir, they were nothing but about mistress Anne Page; to know, if it were my master's fortune to have her, or no.

FAL. 'Tis, 'tis his fortune.

SIM. What, sir?

FAL. To have her,—or no: go; say, the woman told me so.

SIM. May I be bold to say so, sir?

FAL. Ay, sir Tike; who more bold?[d]

SIM. I thank your worship: I shall make my master glad with these tidings. [*Exit* SIMPLE.

HOST. Thou art clerkly, thou art clerkly, sir John: was there a wise woman with thee?

FAL. Ay, that there was, mine Host; one, that hath taught me more wit than ever I learned before in my life: and I paid nothing for it neither, but was paid for my learning.[e]

Enter BARDOLPH.

BARD. Out, alas, sir! cozenage! mere cozenage!

HOST. Where be my horses? speak well of them, varletto.

BARD. Run away with the cozeners: for so soon as I came beyond Eton, they threw me off, from behind one of them, in a slough of mire; and set spurs, and away, like three German devils, three Doctor Faustuses.

HOST. They are gone but to meet the duke, villain: do not say, they be fled; Germans are honest men.

Enter SIR HUGH EVANS.

EVA. Where is mine Host?

HOST. What is the matter, sir?

EVA. Have a care of your entertainments: there is a friend of mine come to town, tells me, there is three couzin germans, that has cozened all the hosts of Readings, of Maidenhead, of Colebrook, of horses and money.(4) I tell you for good-will, look you: you are wise, and full of gipes and vlouting stogs; and 'tis not convenient you should pe cozened: fare you well. [*Exit.*

Enter DOCTOR CAIUS.

CAIUS. Vere is mine *Host de Jarterre?*

HOST. Here, master doctor, in perplexity, and doubtful dilemma.

CAIUS. I cannot tell vat is dat: but it is tell-a me, dat you make grand preparation for a duke *de Jarmany:* by my trot, dere is no duke, dat de court is know to come: I tell you for good vill: adieu. [*Exit.*

HOST. Hue and cry, villain, go!—assist me, knight; I am undone:—fly, run, hue and cry, villain! I am undone!

[*Exit* Host *and* BARDOLPH.

---

[a] His standing-bed, and truckle-bed;] In the poet's time, chambers were usually furnished with a standing bedstead, on which the superior reposed, and a truckle (from *trochlia*, a castor) or running one for the attendant. In the day-time, the latter, which was much lower than the standing bed, was wheeled under it, to afford more room in the apartment.

[b] Muscle-shell;] "He calls him Muscle-shell, because he stands with his mouth open."—JOHNSON.

[c] I may not conceal them, sir.] The old text gives this speech to Falstaff. For *conceal*, in both instances, Dr. Farmer proposes to read *reveal;* that is, to quench the little humour intended, which all depends on Slender's blunder, and the Host's jocular repetition of it.

[d] *Ay, sir* Tike; *who more bold?*] The folio reads, "Ay, sir. like who more bold." but the reading in the text is supported by the quarto, which has, Ay, *Tike*, &c. *Tike* meaning *clown*, or *clodpole*.

[e] *I* paid *nothing for it neither, but was* paid for my learning.] He quibbles on the meaning of *paid:* one sense of to *pay* formerly being to *beat*.

FAL. I would, all the world might be cozened; for I have been cozened, and beaten too. If it should come to the ear of the court, how I have been transformed, and how my transformation hath been washed and cudgeled, they would melt me out of my fat, drop by drop, and liquor fishermen's boots with me; I warrant, they would whip me with their fine wits, till I were as crestfallen as a dried pear. I never prospered since I foreswore myself at *primero*.[a] Well, if my wind were but long enough to say my prayers,[b] I would repent.—

Enter MISTRESS QUICKLY.

Now! whence come you?

QUICK. From the two parties, forsooth.

FAL. The devil take one party, and his dam the other, and so they shall be both bestowed! I have suffered more for their sakes, more, than the villainous inconstancy of man's disposition is able to bear.

QUICK. And have not they suffered? Yes, I warrant; speciously one of them; mistress Ford, good heart, is beaten black and blue, that you cannot see a white spot about her.

FAL. What tell'st thou me of black and blue? I was beaten myself into all the colours of the rainbow; and I was like to be apprehended for the witch of Brentford; but that my admirable dexterity of wit, my counterfeiting the action of an old woman, delivered me, the knave constable had set me i' th' stocks, i' th' common stocks, for a witch.

QUICK. Sir, let me speak with you in your chamber: you shall hear how things go, and, I warrant, to your content. Here is a letter will say somewhat. Good hearts, what ado here is to bring you together! Sure, one of you does not serve heaven well, that you are so crossed.

FAL. Come up into my chamber. [*Exeunt.*

SCENE VI.—*Another Room in the* Garter Inn.

Enter FENTON *and* Host.

HOST. Master Fenton, talk not to me; my mind is heavy, I will give over all.

FENT. Yet hear me speak: assist me in my purpose,
And, as I am a gentleman, I'll give thee
A hundred pound in gold, more than your loss.

HOST. I will hear you, master Fenton; and I will, at the least, keep your counsel.

FENT. From time to time I have acquainted you
With the dear love I bear to fair Anne Page;
Who, mutually, hath answer'd my affection
(So far forth as herself might be her chooser),
Even to my wish: I have a letter from her
Of such contents as you will wonder at;
The mirth whereof so larded with my matter,
That neither, singly, can be manifested,
Without the show of both;—wherein (*) fat Falstaff
Hath a great scene: the image of the jest [*Showing the letter.*
I'll show you here at large. Hark, good mine Host:
To-night at Herne's oak, just 'twixt twelve and one,
Must my sweet Nan present the fairy queen;
The purpose why, is here; in which disguise,
While other jests are something rank on foot,
Her father hath commanded her to slip
Away with Slender, and with him at Eton
Immediately to marry: she hath consented. Now, sir,
Her mother, even[c] strong against that match,
And firm for doctor Caius, hath appointed
That he shall likewise shuffle her away,
While other sports are tasking of their minds,
And at the deanery, where a priest attends,
Straight marry her: to this her mother's plot
She, seemingly obedient, likewise hath
Made promise to the doctor.—Now, thus it rests:
Her father means she shall be all in white;
And in that habit, when Slender sees his time
To take her by the hand, and bid her go,
She shall go with him:—her mother hath intended,
The better to denote(†) her to the doctor,
(For they must all be mask'd and vizarded,)
That, quaint in green, she shall be loose enrob'd,
With ribands pendant, flaring 'bout her head;
And when the doctor spies his vantage ripe,
To pinch her by the hand, and, on that token,
The maid hath given consent to go with him.

HOST. Which means she to deceive? father or mother?

FENT. Both, my good Host, to go along with me:
And here it rests,—that you'll procure the vicar
To stay for me at church, 'twixt twelve and one,
And, in the lawful name of marrying,
To give our hearts united ceremony.

HOST. Well, husband your device; I'll to the vicar:
Bring you the maid, you shall not lack a priest.

FENT. So shall I evermore be bound to thee;
Besides, I'll make a present recompense. [*Exeunt.*

---

a I never prospered since I foreswore myself at *primero.*] Shakespeare has nothing more profoundly characteristic of an old sinner, than this and the analogous reflection of Mistress Quickly upon the failure of their schemes:—"Sure, one of you does not serve heaven well, that you are so crossed."

(*) First folio omits, *wherein*. (†) Old text, *devote*.

b To say my prayers,—] These words are from the quarto.

c Even *strong*—] *Equally* strong. But as the quarto reads "*still* against," it may be doubted whether "even" is not a misprint for *ever*.

ACT V.

SCENE I.—*A Room in the* Garter Inn.

Enter FALSTAFF *and* MISTRESS QUICKLY.

FAL. Pr'ythee, no more prattling;—go.——I'll hold: this is the third time; I hope good luck lies in odd numbers. Away, go; they say, there is divinity in odd numbers,[a] either in nativity, chance, or death.—Away.

QUICK. I'll provide you a chain; and I'll do what I can to get you a pair of horns.

FAL. Away, I say; time wears: hold up your head, and mince.[b] [*Exit* MISTRESS QUICKLY.

Enter FORD.

How now, master Brook? Master Brook, the matter will be known to-night, or never. Be you in the Park about midnight, at Herne's oak,(1) and you shall see wonders.

FORD. Went you not to her yesterday, sir, as you told me you had appointed?

FAL. I went to her, master Brook, as you see, like a poor old man: but I came from her, master Brook, like a poor old woman. That same knave, Ford her husband, hath the finest mad devil of jealousy in him, master Brook, that ever governed frenzy. I will tell you. He beat me grievously, in the shape of a woman; for in the shape of man, master Brook, I fear not Goliath with a weaver's beam; because I know also, life is a shuttle. I am in haste; go along with me; I'll tell you all, master Brook. Since I plucked geese, played truant, and whipped top, I knew not what it was to be beaten, till lately. Follow me: I'll tell you strange things of this knave Ford: on whom to-night I will be revenged, and I will deliver his wife into your hand.—Follow: strange things in hand, master Brook! follow. [*Exeunt.*

SCENE II.—Windsor Park.

Enter PAGE, SHALLOW, *and* SLENDER.

PAGE. Come, come; we'll couch i' th' castle-ditch, till we see the light of our fairies. Remember, son Slender, my daughter.*

SLEN. Ay, forsooth; I have spoke with her, and we have a nay-word,[c] how to know one another.

---

[a] There is divinity in odd numbers,—]

——"numero deus impare gaudet."
VIRGIL, *Eclogue* viii.

(*) First folio omits, *daughter*.

[b] *And* mince.] To *mince* meant to walk with affected modesty.

[c] A nay-word,—] That is, a watch-word.

I come to her in white, and cry *mum;* she cries, *budget;* and by that we know one another.

SHAL. That's good too: but what needs either your *mum*, or her *budget?* the white will decipher her well enough.—It hath struck ten o'clock.

PAGE. The night is dark; light and spirits will become it well. Heaven prosper our sport! No man means evil but the devil, and we shall know him by his horns. Let's away; follow me. [*Exeunt.*

SCENE III.—*The Street in* Windsor.

Enter MISTRESS PAGE, MISTRESS FORD, *and* DR. CAIUS.

MRS. PAGE. Master doctor, my daughter is in green: when you see your time, take her by the hand, away with her to the deanery, and despatch it quickly: go before into the park; we two must go together.

CAIUS. I know vat I have to do; adieu.

MRS. PAGE. Fare you well, sir. [*Exit* CAIUS.] My husband will not rejoice so much at the abuse of Falstaff, as he will chafe at the doctor's marrying my daughter: but 'tis no matter; better a little chiding, than a great deal of heart-break.

MRS. FORD. Where is Nan now, and her troop of fairies? and the Welsh devil, Hugh?*

MRS. PAGE. They are all couched in a pit hard by Herne's oak, with obscured lights; which, at the very instant of Falstaff's and our meeting, they will at once display to the night.

MRS. FORD. That cannot choose but amaze him.

MRS. PAGE. If he be not amazed, he will be mocked; if he be amazed, he will every way be mocked.

MRS. FORD. We'll betray him finely.

MRS. PAGE. Against such lewdsters, and their lechery,
Those that betray them do no treachery.

MRS. FORD. The hour draws on; to the oak, to the oak! [*Exeunt.*

SCENE IV.—Windsor Park.

Enter SIR HUGH EVANS *and* Fairies.

EVA. Trib, trib, fairies; come; and remember your parts: be pold, I pray you; follow me into the pit; and when I give the watch-'ords, do as I pid you. Come, come; trib, trib. [*Exeunt.*

SCENE V.—*Another part of the* Park.

Enter FALSTAFF *disguised, with a buck's head on.*

FAL. The Windsor bell hath struck twelve; the minute draws on: now, the hot-blooded gods assist me. Remember, Jove, thou wast a bull for thy Europa; love set on thy horns. O powerful love! that, in some respects, makes a beast a man; in some other, a man a beast. You were also, Jupiter, a swan, for the love of Leda; O, omnipotent love! how near the god drew to the complexion of a goose! A fault done first in the form of a beast; O Jove, a beastly fault! and then another fault in the semblance of a fowl; think on't, Jove; a foul fault! When gods have hot backs, what shall poor men do? For me, I am here a Windsor stag; and the fattest, I think, i' th' forest: send me a cool rut-time, Jove, or who can blame me to piss my tallow? Who comes here? my doe?

Enter MISTRESS FORD *and* MISTRESS PAGE.

MRS. FORD. Sir John? art thou there, my deer? my male deer?

FAL. My doe with the black scut?—Let the sky rain potatoes; let it thunder to the tune of *Green Sleeves;* hail kissing-comfits, and snow eringoes; let there come a tempest of provocation, I will shelter me here. [*Embracing her.*

MRS. FORD. Mistress Page is come with me, sweetheart.

FAL. Divide me like a brib'd-buck, each a haunch: I will keep my sides to myself, my shoulders for the fellow of this walk,[a] and my horns I bequeath your husbands. Am I a woodman? ha! Speak I like Herne the hunter?—Why, now is Cupid a child of conscience; he makes restitution. As I am a true spirit, welcome! [*Noise without.*

MRS. PAGE. Alas! what noise?

MRS. FORD. Heaven forgive our sins!

FAL. What should this be?

MRS. FORD. MRS. PAGE. } Away! away! [*They run off.*

FAL. I think, the devil will not have me damned, lest the oil that is in me should set hell on fire; he would never else cross me thus.

(*) Old copy, *Herne.*

[a] My shoulders for the fellow of this walk,—] By *fellow of this walk* is meant the *forester*, to whom it was customary, on the "*breaking up*" of a deer, to present one or both of the shoulders. For the process, we must refer the reader to the "Booke of Hunting," by the venerable Dame Juliana Berners, who says:—

"And the right shoulder, where so ever he be,
Bere it to the *foster*, for that is his fee."

Or to Turberville's "Booke of Hunting," 1575, where the distribution is prescribed with all the exactness so important a ceremony deserved.

Enter Sir Hugh Evans, *like a satyr ;* Mistress Quickly, *and* Pistol ; Anne Page, *as the Fairy Queen, attended by her brother and others, dressed like fairies, with waxen tapers on their heads.*[a]

Queen.[b] Fairies, black, grey, green, and white,
You moon-shine revellers, and shades of night,
You orphan-heirs of fixed destiny,[c]
Attend your office, and your quality.——
Crier Hobgoblin, make the fairy o-yes. [toys.[d]
Pist. Elves, list your names ; silence, you airy
Cricket, to Windsor chimnies shalt thou leap :
Where fires thou find'st unrak'd, and hearths unswept,
There pinch the maids as blue as bilberry:
Our radiant queen hates sluts, and sluttery.
Fal. They are fairies ; he that speaks to them, shall die :
I'll wink and couch : no man their works must eye. [*Lies down upon his face.*
Eva. Where's Pede ?*—Go you, and where you find a maid,
That, ere she sleep, has thrice her prayers said,
Raise up the organs of her fantasy,
Sleep she as sound as careless infancy ;
Put those as sleep, and think not on their sins,
Pinch them, arms, legs, packs, shoulders, sides, and shins.
Queen. About, about ;
Search Windsor castle, elves, within and out ;
Strew good luck, ouphes, on every sacred room ;

---

a *Enter Sir Hugh Evans,* &c.] This stage-direction is chiefly made up from that in the early quarto. The folio has only, "*Enter fairies.*" The introduction of Pistol and Mistress Quickly in this scene, is to be accounted for on the supposition that the necessity of the theatre compelled the performers of these characters to take part among the fairies, and that the names thus got inserted in the printed copies.

b Queen.] There is nothing inconsistent in the prefix *Quic.* to these speeches in the quarto, because Mistress Quickly, or rather the actor who personated that character, was intended to "double" with it the Fairy Queen ; but in the enlarged play, as Anne Page enacts the latter part, the prefix should certainly be "Queen."

c You orphan-heirs of fixed destiny,—] Warburton proposed, with plausibility, to read, "*Ouphen* heirs," but see note (3), page 630.

d Queen. *Crier Hobgoblin, make the fairy* o-yes.
Pist *Elves, list your names; silence, you airy* toys.]

"These two lines were certainly intended to rhyme together, as the preceding and subsequent couplets do; and accordingly, in the old editions, the final words of each line are printed *oyes* and *toyes*. This therefore is a striking instance of the inconvenience which has arisen from modernizing the orthography of Shakespeare."—Tyrwhitt.

(*) First folio, *Bede*.

That it may stand till the perpetual doom,
In state as wholesome, as in state 't is fit;
Worthy the owner, and the owner it.
The several chairs of Order look you scour
With juice of balm,[a] and every precious flower:
Each fair installment, coat, and several crest,
With loyal blazon, evermore be blest!
And nightly, meadow-fairies, look, you sing,
Like to the Garter's compass, in a ring:
The expressure that it bears, green let it be,
More fertile-fresh than all the field to see;
And, *Hony soit qui mal y pense*, write,
In emerald tufts, flowers purple, blue, and white;
Like sapphire, pearl, and rich embroidery,
Buckled below fair knighthood's bending knee:
Fairies use flowers for their charactery.
Away; disperse: but, till 'tis one o'clock,
Our dance of custom, round about the oak
Of Herne the hunter, let us not forget.

EVA. Pray you, lock hand in hand; yourselves in order set:
And twenty glow-worms shall our lanterns be,
To guide our measure round about the tree.
But, stay; I smell a man of middle earth.

FAL. Heavens defend me from that Welsh fairy! lest he transform me to a piece of cheese!

PIST. Vile worm, thou wast o'er-look'd[b] even in thy birth.

QUEEN. With trial-fire touch me his finger-end:
If he be chaste, the flame will back descend,
And turn him to no pain; but if he start,
It is the flesh of a corrupted heart.

PIST. A trial, come!

EVA. Come, will this wood take fire?

[*They put the tapers to his fingers, and he starts.*

FAL. Oh, oh, oh!

QUEEN. Corrupt, corrupt, and tainted in desire!
About him, fairies; sing a scornful rhyme:
And, as you trip, still pinch him to your time.

SONG.

Fie on sinful fantasy!
Fie on lust and luxury!
Lust is but a bloody fire,
Kindled with unchaste desire,
Fed in heart, whose flames aspire,
As thoughts do blow them, higher and higher.
Pinch him, fairies, mutually;
Pinch him for his villainy;
Pinch him, and burn him, and turn him about,
Till candles, and star-light, and moonshine be out.

During this song,[c] *the fairies pinch* FALSTAFF. DOCTOR CAIUS *comes one way, and steals away a fairy in green;* SLENDER *another way, and takes off a fairy in white; and* FENTON *comes, and steals away* ANNE PAGE. *A noise of hunting is made without. All the fairies run away.* FALSTAFF *pulls off his buck's head, and rises.*

Enter PAGE, FORD, MISTRESS PAGE, *and* MISTRESS FORD. *They lay hold on him.*

PAGE. Nay, do not fly: I think, we have watch'd[d] you now;
Will none but Herne the hunter serve your turn?

MRS. PAGE. I pray you, come; hold up the jest no higher:—
Now, good sir John, how like you Windsor wives?
See you these, husband? do not these fair yokes
Become the forest better than the town?

FORD. Now, sir, who's a cuckold now?—*Master Brook*, Falstaff's a knave, a cuckoldly knave; here are his horns, *master Brook:* and, *master Brook*, he hath enjoyed nothing of Ford's but his buck-basket, his cudgel, and twenty pounds of money; which must be paid to *master Brook;* his horses are arrested for it, *master Brook.*

MRS. FORD. Sir John, we have had ill luck; we could never meet. I will never take you for my love again, but I will always count you my deer.

FAL. I do begin to perceive that I am made an ass.

FORD. Ay, and an ox too; both the proofs are extant.

FAL. And these are not fairies? I was three or four times in the thought, they were not fairies: and yet the guiltiness of my mind, the sudden surprise of my powers, drove the grossness of the foppery into a received belief, in despite of the teeth of all rhyme and reason, that they were fairies. See now, how wit may be made a Jack-a-lent, when 'tis upon ill employment!

---

[a] The several chairs of Order look you scour
With juice of balm,—]

As Steevens has observed, it was an article of ancient luxury to rub tables, &c. with aromatic herbs. Thus, in Ovid's "Baucis and Philemon," Metamorphoses viii.:—

——"Mensam—
æquatam *Mentha* abstersere virenti."

[b] O'er-look'd *even in thy birth.*] That is, bewitched. See note (a), page 416.

[c] *During this song,*—] Much of this direction is derived from the quarto. The folio has none whatever.

[d] *I think, we have* watch'd *you now;*] That is, *tamed* you. The allusion, which seems to have been overlooked by all the commentators, is to one of the methods employed to tame, or "reclaim," hawks. It was customary when a hawk was first taken, for the falconers to sit up by turns and "watch" it; in other words, prevent it from sleeping, sometimes for three successive nights. Shakespeare has referred to the practice in the "Taming of the Shrew," Act IV. Sc. 2:—

"Another way I have to man my haggard,
To make her come, and know her keeper's call,
That is, to *watch* her,"—

And again, in "Othello," Act III. Sc. 3:—

——"My lord shall never rest,
I 'll *watch* him tame."

EVA. Sir John Falstaff, serve Got, and leave your desires, and fairies will not pinse you.

FORD. Well said, fairy Hugh.

EVA. And leave you your jealousies too, I pray you.

FORD. I will never mistrust my wife again, till thou art able to woo her in good English.

FAL. Have I laid my brain in the sun, and dried it, that it wants matter to prevent so gross o'er-reaching as this? Am I ridden with a Welsh goat too? Shall I have a coxcomb of frieze? [a] 'tis time I were choked with a piece of toasted cheese.

EVA. Seese is not good to give putter; your pelly is all putter.

FAL. *Seese* and *putter!* have I lived to stand at the taunt of one that makes fritters of English? This is enough to be the decay of lust and late-walking, through the realm.

MRS. PAGE. Why, sir John, do you think, though we would have thrust virtue out of our hearts by the head and shoulders, and have given ourselves without scruple to hell, that ever the devil could have made you our delight?

FORD. What, a hodge-pudding? a bag of flax?

MRS. PAGE. A puffed man?

PAGE. Old, cold, withered, and of intolerable entrails?

FORD. And one that is as slanderous as Satan?

PAGE. And as poor as Job?

FORD. And as wicked as his wife?

EVA. And given to fornications, and to taverns, and sack, and wine, and metheglins, and to drinkings, and swearings, and starings, pribbles and prabbles?

[a] A coxcomb of frieze?] *A fool's cap* made of *frieze*. Wales was celebrated for this description of cloth.

FAL. Well, I am your theme: you have the start of me; I am dejected; I am not able to answer the Welsh flannel: ignorance itself is a plummet[a] o'er me: use me as you will.

FORD. Marry, sir, we'll bring you to Windsor, to one master Brook, that you have cozened of money, to whom you should have been a pander: over and above that you have suffered, I think, to repay that money will be a biting affliction.

PAGE. Yet be cheerful, knight: thou shalt eat a posset(2) to-night at my house; where I will desire thee to laugh at my wife, that now laughs at thee: tell her, master Slender hath married her daughter.

MRS. PAGE. Doctors doubt that: if Anne Page be my daughter, she is, by this, doctor Caius' wife. [*Aside.*

Enter SLENDER.

SLEN. Whoo, ho! ho! father Page!

PAGE. Son! how now? how now, son? have you despatched?

SLEN. Despatched!—I'll make the best in Gloucestershire know on't; would I were hanged, la, else.

PAGE. Of what, son?

SLEN. I came yonder at Eton to marry mistress Anne Page, and she's a great lubberly boy: if it had not been i' th' church, I would have swinged him, or he should have swinged me. If I did not think it had been Anne Page, would I might never stir, and 'tis a post-master's boy.

PAGE. Upon my life then you took the wrong.

SLEN. What need you tell me that? I think so, when I took a boy for a girl: if I had been married to him, for all he was in woman's apparel, I would not have had him.

PAGE. Why, this is your own folly. Did not I tell you, how you should know my daughter by her garments?

SLEN. I went to her in white,* and cried, *mum*, and she cried *budget*, as Anne and I had appointed; and yet it was not Anne, but a post-master's boy.

MRS. PAGE. Good George, be not angry: I knew of your purpose; turned my daughter into green;† and, indeed, she is now with the doctor at the deanery, and there married.

Enter CAIUS.

CAIUS. Vere is mistress Page? By gar, I am cozened; I ha' married *un garçon*, a boy; *un paisan*, by gar, a boy; it is not Anne Page: by gar, I am cozened.

MRS. PAGE. Why, did you take her in green?*

CAIUS. Ay, be gar, and 'tis a boy: be gar, I'll raise all Windsor. [*Exit* CAIUS.

FORD. This is strange: who hath got the right Anne?

PAGE. My heart misgives me: here comes master Fenton.

Enter FENTON *and* ANNE.

How now, master Fenton?

ANNE. Pardon, good father! good my mother, pardon!

PAGE. Now, mistress! how chance you went not with master Slender?

MRS. PAGE. Why went you not with master doctor, maid?

FENT. You do amaze[b] her: hear the truth of it.
You would have married her most shamefully,
Where there was no proportion held in love.
The truth is, she and I, long since contracted,
Are now so sure, that nothing can dissolve us.
The offence is holy, that she hath committed:
And this deceit loses the name of craft,
Of disobedience, or unduteous title;[c]
Since therein she doth evitate and shun
A thousand irreligious cursed hours,
Which forced marriage would have brought upon her.

FORD. Stand not amaz'd: here is no remedy:—
In love, the heavens themselves do guide the state;
Money buys lands, and wives are sold by fate.

FAL. I am glad, though you have ta'en a special stand(3) to strike at me, that your arrow hath glanced.

PAGE. Well, what remedy?(4) Fenton, heaven give thee joy!
What cannot be eschew'd, must be embrac'd.

FAL. When night-dogs run, all sorts of deer are chas'd.

MRS. PAGE. Well, I will muse no further:—master Fenton,
Heaven give you many, many merry days!—
Good husband, let us every one go home,
And laugh this sport o'er by a country fire;
Sir John and all.

FORD. Let it be so.—Sir John,
To master Brook you yet shall hold your word;
For he, to-night, shall lie with mistress Ford.
[*Exeunt.*

(*) Old text, *green*. (†) Old text, *white*.

a *Ignorance itself is a* plummet o'er me:] Farmer conjectured that *plummet* was a misprint for *planet*; but the following passage, in Shirley's "Love in a Maze," Act IV. Sc. 2, supports the old reading:—

"Yongrave, how is't, man? what! *art melancholy?*
What hath hung *plummets* on thy nimble soul,
What sleepy rod hath charm'd thy mounting spirit?"

(*) Old text, *white*.

b Amaze *her*:] *Confound* her by these questions.

c *Unduteous* title;] Mr. Collier's annotator reads, very speciously, "unduteous *guile*."

ILLUSTRATIVE COMMENTS.

ACT I.

(1) Scene I.—*Sir Hugh.*] The title of *Sir* was probably at one time applied to priests and curates without distinction, but subsequently became appropriated only to the inferior clergy, such as are called *Readers.* It was no more than the translation of *Dominus,* the academical distinction of a Bachelor of Arts. Fuller, in his Church History, says, there were formerly more *Sirs* than *Knights* in England, and adds, "Such priests as have the addition of *Sir* before their Christian name, were men not graduated in the university, being in orders, but not in degrees, whilst others entituled Masters had commenced in the arts."

(2) Scene I.—*I will make a Star-chamber matter of it.*] The Court of *Star Chamber,* as it was familiarly called from the sitting being held *en la chambre des estoyers,* was the King's Council, the nature and extent of whose jurisdiction, even so early as the reign of Henry VII. when it was remodelled, were sufficiently extraordinary. The preamble of the Act relating to this Court, which was passed in the third of his reign, sets forth, that "the King, remembering how by unlawful maintenances, giving of liveries, signs and tokens, and retaining by indentures, promises, oaths, writings or otherwise, embraceries of his subjects, untrue demeanings of Sheriffs, in making of pannels and other untrue returns, by taking of money by juries, by great riots and unlawful assemblies, the policy and good rule of this realm is almost subdued:" &c. &c. "whereby the laws of the land in execution may take little effect, to the increase of murders, robberies, perjuries and unsureties of all men living," &c. For the reformation of which, it was now ordained that the chancellor, treasurer, and privy seal, or two of them, calling to them a bishop and a temporal lord, being of the Council, and the two Chief Justices, or in their absence, two other justices upon bill of information put to the Chancellor for the King, or any other, against any person for any misbehaviour above mentioned, have authority to call before them by writ or privy-seal, the offenders and others as it shall seem fit, by whom the truth may be known, and to examine and punish, after the form and effect of statutes thereof made, in like manner, as they ought to be punished, if they were convict after the due order of the law.

A tribunal, paramount as this, whose proceedings were summary, and whose punishments, though professedly in accordance with the laws, were administered with much more promptitude than those of the ordinary courts, soon acquired under the Tudors a formidable and dangerous authority,—an authority, as we know from history, which at length became tremendous, and ultimately led to its final abolition in the reign of Charles I.

The ridicule in the play is the making the vain and imbecile old Justice suppose his petty squabble with Falstaff of sufficient importance to be adjudicated by such a Court.

(3) Scene I.—*The luce is the fresh fish; the salt fish is an old coat.*] Much has been written upon this perplexing passage to little purpose. It still remains, as Mr. Knight terms it, "an heraldic puzzle." There is, unquestionably, an allusion to the arms of Shakespeare's old foe, Sir Thomas Lucy, and it is conjecturable that the "dozen *white* luces," which were borne by one branch of the Lucy family, may have implied the *salt-water pike,* and have been an older scutcheon than the "three lucies hauriant" of the Warwickshire branch.

(4) Scene I.—*I heard say, he was out-run on Cotsale.*] The Cotswold hills in Gloucestershire, a large tract of fine turfed downs, were among the places famous in times of yore for rural games; but the sports here and elsewhere appear to have declined during the latter part of the sixteenth century, owing perhaps, to the rigorous puritanical crusade carried on against all popular diversions. About the end of Elizabeth's reign, or, as some say, at the beginning of her successor's, they were revived, however, with increased spirit, through the exertions of Mr. Robert Dover, an attorney of Barton-on-the-Heath in Warwickshire, who instituted an annual celebration of rustic amusements, which he conducted in person; consisting of wrestling, leaping, pitching the bar, managing the pike, dancing and coursing the hare with greyhounds.

(5) Scene I.—*I have seen Sackerson loose, twenty times.*] Sackerson, so named in all likelihood after his keeper, was a famous bear belonging to the Paris bear-baiting Garden on the Bankside; and the allusions to him and *Harry Hunks* and *George Stone,* two contemporary beasts of prowess, by the old writers, sufficiently attest the popularity of this savage sport in former time:—

> "Publius, a student of the common law,
> To *Paris-garden* doth himself withdraw;—
> Leaving old Ployden, Dyer and Broke alone,
> To see old *Harry Hunkes* and *Sacarson.*"
> *Epigrams* by Sir John Davies.

"Ile be sworne they tooke away a mastie dogge of mine by commission. Now I thinke on't, makes my teares stand in my eyes with grief. I had rather lost the dearest friend that ever I lay withal in my life. Be this light, never stir if hee fought not with great Sekerson foure hours to one, foremoste take up hindmoste, and tooke so many loaves from him, that hee sterv'd him presently. So, at last, the dogg cood doe no more then a beare cood, and the beare being heavie with hunger you know, fell uppon the dogge, broke his backe, and the dogge never stird more."—*Sir Gyles Goosecappe Knight,* a Comedie presented by the Chil. of the Chappell, 1606.

(6) Scene IV.—*A Cain-coloured beard.*] In the old tapestries and pictures, Cain and Judas were represented with yellowish-red beards. A conceit very frequently alluded to in early books:—

> "And let their beards be of *Judas* his own *colour.*"
> *The Spanish Tragedy.*

Again, in "The Insatiate Countess," by Marston:—

> "I ever thought by his *red beard* he would prove a *Judas.*"

ACT II.

(1) SCENE I.—*The tune of Green sleeves.*] "*Green Sleeves, or Which nobody can deny,*" we gather from Mr. Chappell's learned and entertaining account of our early National Music, "has been a favourite tune from the time of Elizabeth to the present day; and is still frequently to be heard in the streets of London to songs with the well-known burden, 'Which nobody can deny.'" Mr. Chappell, indeed, carries its antiquity still higher, and thinks it was sung in the reign of Henry VIII. The earliest words to the air known to us, however, do not date farther back than 1580; in which year "*A new northen dittye of the Lady greene sleeves*" was licensed to Richard Jones by the Stationers' Company. This song, which evidently attained an uncommon share of popular favour even in that age of universal ballatry, was reprinted, four years after, by the same printer in the poetical miscellany entitled,—"*A Handefull of Pleasant Delites: containing sundrie new Sonets and delectable Histories in divers kindes of meeter. Newly devised to the newest tunes, that are now in use to be sung: everie sonet orderlie pointed to his proper tune. With new additions of certain songs, to verie late devised notes, not commonly knowen, nor used heretofore. By Clement Robinson: and divers others. At London, printed by Richard Ihones: dwelling at the signe of the Rose and Crowne, near Holborne Bridge.* 1584."

(2) SCENE I.—*The humour of it, quoth 'a! here's a fellow frights humour out of his wits.*] Ben Jonson, the best delineator of that species of affectation, so fashionable in his time, called *humours*, has pointed out, with his usual force and discrimination, the difference between the real and pseudo-humourist. Between those who by a natural bias of mind were led into singularity of thought and action, and those who, with no pretensions to originality, endeavoured to establish a reputation for it by ridiculous eccentricities in manners or apparel:—

"As when some one peculiar quality
Doth so possess a man, that it doth draw
All his affects, his spirits, and his powers,
In their confluctions, all to run one way,
This may be truly said to be a HUMOUR.
But that a rook, by wearing a pyed feather,
The cable hat-band, or the three-piled ruff,
A yard of shoe-tye, or the Switzer's knot
On his French garters, should affect a HUMOUR!
O, it is more than most ridiculous!"
"*Every man out of his Humour.*"—

GIFFORD'S *Ben Jonson*, v. II. p. 16.

(3) SCENE I.—*The priest o' th' town.*] The following hexameters may be seen in black letter over an ancient doorway in Northgate-street, Gloucester:—

"En ruinosa domus quondam quam tunc renovavit,
Monachus urbanus Osborne John rite vocatus."

(4) SCENE II.—*To your manor of Pickt-hatch, go.*] This notorious haunt of profligacy, so called from the *spiked* half-door, or *hatch*, the usual denotement of houses of ill-fame formerly, was a collection of tenements situated near the end of Old Street and the garden of the Charterhouse in Goswell Street. The allusions to it and to similar colonies of depraved characters, in *Whitefriars, Lambeth Marsh,* and *Turnmill Street,* are innumerable in our old out-spoken writers; but two or three examples will be sufficient, for the subject and the references are alike unsavoury:—

ON LIEUTENANT SHIFT.

"Shift here, in towne, not meanest amongst squires,
That haunt *Pickt-hatch*, Mersh-Lambeth and White-fryer's
Keepes himselfe, with halfe a man, and defrayes
The charge of that state, with this charme, God payes."
BEN JONSON'S *Epigrams*, No. XII

"Sometimes shining in Lady-like resplendent brightnesse with admiration, and suddenly againe eclipsed with the pitchy and *tenebrous* clouds of contempt and deserved defamation. Sometimes at the *Full* at *Pickt-hatch*, and sometimes in the *Wane* at *Bridewell*."—TAYLOR, the Water Poet, fol., 1630, p. 95.

(5) SCENE II.—*One master Brook below would fain speak with you, and be acquainted with you; and hath sent your worship a morning's draught of sack.*] The custom of taking a "morning draught" of ale, beer, wine, or spirits, prevailed long before our author's time; and that of making acquaintance, in the manner indicated by the text, was nearly coeval. Speaking of the former habit, Dr. Venner, *Via Recta ad Vitam Longam*, 1637, says:—"The custome of drinking in the mornings fasting, a large draught of white wine, or of beere, hath almost with all men so farre prevailed, as that they judge it a principall means for the preservation of their health; where as in very deed, it is, being without respect had of the state or constitution of the body, inconsiderably used, the occasion of much hurt and discommoding." Of the latter practice there is a pleasant illustration in an anecdote told of Ben Jonson and Dr. Corbet:—"Ben Jonson was at a tavern, and in comes Bishop Corbet (but not so then) into the next room. Ben Jonson calls for a quart of *raw* wine and gives it to the tapster. 'Sirrah,' says he, 'carry this to the gentleman in the next chamber, and tell him, I sacrifice my service to him.' The fellow did, and in these words, 'Friend,' says Dr. Corbet, 'I thank him for his love: but pr'ythee tell him from me that he is mistaken; for sacrifices are always burnt.'"—*Merry Passages and Jeasts*, Harl. MSS. 6395.

ACT III.

(1) SCENE I.—
To shallow rivers, to whose falls
Melodious pirds sing madrigals.]

This couplet, slightly varied by Sir Hugh's trepidation, is from a charming little pastoral once thought to be Shakespeare's, and as such inserted in his "Passionate Pilgrim," but which, in "England's Helicon," and by Isaac Walton in his "Complete Angler," is attributed to Marlowe. In both these works, it is accompanied by "The Nymph's Reply," asserted to be by Sir Walter Raleigh. Though repeatedly quoted, and familiar to every one acquainted with our early poesy, we should be held inexcusable for omitting Kit Marlowe's "smooth song;" "old-fashioned poetry," indeed, as Walton calls it, "but choicely good:"—

"THE PASSIONATE SHEPHEARD TO HIS LOVE.

Come live with me, and be my love,
And we will all the pleasures prove,
That vallies, groves, hills, and fields,
Woods, or steepie mountaines yeelds.

And we will sit upon the rockes,
Seeing the Shepheards feede their flockes,
By shallow riuers, to whose falls
Melodious birds sing madrigalls.

And I will make thee beds of roses,
And a thousand fragrant poesies,
A cap of flowers and a kirtle
Imbroydered all with leaues of mirtle:

A gowne made of the finest wooll
Which from our pretty lambs we pull:
Faire lined slippers for the cold,
With buckles of the purest gold:

A belt of straw, and ivie buds,
With corall clasps and amber studs,
And if these pleasures may thee move,
Come live with me and be my love.

The Shepheard swaines shall dance and sing
For thy delights each May-morning;
If these delights thy mind may move,
Then live with me, and be my love."

(2) SCENE III.—*The ship-tire, the tire-valiant, or any tire of Venetian admittance.*] By the *ship-tire* was, perhaps, understood some fanciful head-dress, with ornaments of glass or jewellery fashioned to resemble a ship:—"The attyre of her head was in forme of two little ships, made of emeraulds, with all the shrouds and tackling of cleere sapphyres."—"*Diana*," *of George of Montemeyor*, 1598. Or it may have been an open kind of head-dress with ribbons streaming from it like the pennons of a ship. The *tire-valiant* was another of the innumerable "new-fangled tires," as Burton calls them, which an over-weening love of dress had imported from abroad, and of which the form is lost, and not worth seeking. Both were, no doubt, of "Venetian *admittance*," or fashion, as the coiffures of that nation were all the mode at the end of the sixteenth, and beginning of the seventeenth century:—"Let her have the Spanish gait, the *Venetian tire*, Italian complements and endowments."—BURTON'S *Anatomy of Melancholy*, 1624.

(3) SCENE III.—*Fortune thy foe.*] It is not, perhaps, quite certain that the ballad, of which the first and second stanzas are subjoined, is the original *Fortune my Foe* that Falstaff had in mind, though there is strong reason, from the fact of the opening verse being quoted in Lilly's "Maydes Metamorphosis," 1600, for believing it to be the authentic version. Of the tune, which will be found, with much interesting matter connected with it, in Mr. Chappell's "Popular Music of the Olden Time," vol. i. p. 162, there can be no doubt. It had the good or evil fortune to be selected as an appropriate chaunt for the dismal effusions attributed to condemned criminals, and for the relation of murders, fires, judgments, and calamities of all kinds; and hence, for more than two hundred years, it maintained a popularity almost unexampled. *Fortune my Foe* is alluded to again by Shakespeare, in "Henry V." Act III. Sc. 6, and is mentioned by Lodge, Chettle, Ben Jonson, Beaumont and Fletcher, Shirley, and a host of other writers.

"*A sweet Sonnet, wherein the Lover exclaimeth against Fortune for the loss of his Ladies Favour, almost past hope to get it again, &c. &c. The Tune is Fortune, my Foe.*

THE LOVER'S COMPLAINT FOR THE LOSS OF HIS LOVE.

Fortune my Foe why dost thou froun on me?
And will thy favours never better be?
Wilt thou I say for ever breed my pain,
And wilt thou not restore my joys again?

Fortune hath wrought my grief and great annoy,
Fortune hath falsly stoln my Love away,
My love my joy, whose sight did make me glad,
Such great misfortunes never young man had."

ACT IV.

(1) SCENE I.—*I pray you, ask him some questions in his accidence.*] The particular work here referred to is the old English introduction to Latin Grammar called "Lily's Accidence." One of the efforts of Henry VIII. and Edward VI. for the advancement of learning, was an endeavour to establish an uniformity of books for teaching Latin. In 1541, in the proheme to "The Castel of Helthe," Sir Thomas Elyot says that the king had "not himselfe disdained to be the chiefe authour and setter forthe of an Introduction into Grammar, for the childerne of his loving subjectes." This was the famous "Introduction of the Eyght Partes of Speche, and the Construction of the same," usually known as "Lily's Accidence," but really composed by Dean Colet for his school at St. Paul's, in the years 1510 and 1513. The whole collection of tracts forming this Grammar,—written by Colet, Erasmus, Lily, Robertson, and Ritwise,—had appeared either in London or abroad, before they received the Royal sanction; but in 1542 they were printed entire as having been "compiled and set forth by the commandement of our most gracious soverayne lorde the King." After the death of Henry VIII. his son continued the royal patronage to "Lily's Grammar," which then became known as "King Edward's Grammar;" "*Edvardus*" being inserted as the example of proper names in the English, as those of "*Henricus*" and "*Anglia*" were in the Latin Institution. This was the book taught by authority at the public schools down even to the first half of the seventeenth century, the Accidence mentioned in the text, and the identical source whence Shakespeare himself acquired the elements of Latin. In "Twelfth Night," Act II. Sc. 3, Sir Toby Belch refers familiarly, as having learned it in his own youth, to the example given in the First Concord, of the infinitive mood being the nominative case to a verb,—"*Diluculo surgere*— thou know'st,—" The clown in the same comedy, Act V. Sc. 1, misquotes, or perverts, the nouns of number requiring a genitive case, "*Primo, secundo, tertio*, is a good play:" and Benedick, in "Much Ado about Nothing," Act IV. Sc. 1, takes an illustration from another part of the Accidence, when he says, "How now! interjections? why, then, some be of laughing, as, ha! ha! he!" In the examination of William Page, Sir Hugh inquires, "What is he, William, that does lend Articles?" And to this the child replies in the very words of the Accidence, "Articles are borrowed of the pronoun; and be thus declined." Even in the difference between the teacher and the pupil, the rules of the Introduction are to be traced; for when young Page says, "O, vocativo O," he repeats the sense of the definition, "the vocative case is known by calling or speaking to, as *O magister;*" whilst Sir Hugh follows the declension of the article, and rightly says, "*vocativo caret.*"

(2) SCENE II.—*A muffler.*] The muffler, a contrivance adopted by women to conceal a portion of their face, consisted usually of a linen bandage which covered the mouth and chin. Douce states that "it was enacted by a Scottish statute in 1547, that 'na woman cum to kirk, nor mercat, with her face *mussaled* or covered that scho may not be kend.'"

(3) SCENE II.—*The witch of Brentford.*] The "wise-woman of Brentford" was an actual personage, the fame of whose vaticinations must have been traditionally well known to an audience of the time, although the records we possess of her are scant enough. The chief of them is a black letter tract, printed by William Copland in the middle of the sixteenth century, entitled, "Jyl of Braintford's Testament," from which it appears she was hostess of a tavern at Brentford. She is mentioned also in "Westward Hoe!"—"I doubt that old hag, Gillian of Brentford, has bewitched me."

(4) SCENE V.—*There is three couzin Germans, that has cozened all the hosts of Readings, of Maidenhead, of Cole-prook, of horses and money.*] In the preliminary notice of this play we mentioned an ingenious hypothesis of Mr. Knight in his "Pictorial Shakspere," that the deception practised upon mine *Host de Jarterre* pointed to some incidents connected with a visit made to Windsor, in 1592, by the Duke of Würtemberg. The Duke, it appears, was known here as "Count Mombeliard," (query, "Mumpelgard") of which title both Mr. Knight and Mr. Halliwell conceive the expression "cosen garmombles" in the quarto, to be a jocular corruption. "This nobleman visited Windsor, was shown 'the splendidly beautiful and royal Castle,' he 'hunted a stag for a long time over a broad and pleasant plain, with a pack of remarkably good hounds;' and, after staying some days, departed for Hampton Court.'" From these and other circumstances, not omitting that he was provided with a passport from Lord Howard, containing instructions to the authorities of towns through which he passed to furnish him with post horses, &c.; and at the sea-side with shipping, *for which he was to pay nothing*. Mr. Knight infers this to have been "one of those local and temporary allusions which Shakespeare seized upon to arrest the attention of his audience."

Our objections to this theory, inasmuch as the visit in 1592 is concerned, have already been mentioned in the Introduction; but it is far from improbable that an allusion was covertly intended to some other visit of the same nobleman. From the following interesting article by Sir Frederic Madden, we learn that the Duke of Würtemberg—Mümplegard was in England in 1610; and it is not unreasonable to suppose he might have visited us more than twice in the long interval of eighteen years.

"Among the Additional Manuscripts in the British Museum is a small thin quarto, containing the autograph diary, written in French, of Hans Jacob Wurmsser von Vendenheym, who accompanied Louis Frederic, Duke of Wurtemberg-Mumpelgard, in his diplomatic mission to England in 1610, on the part of the united Protestant German Princes. This diary extends from 16th March to 24th July of that year, and affords brief but interesting notices of the places visited by the Duke, both in coming and returning. He embarked from Flushing (where an English garrison was stationed) on Tuesday, 12th April, and arrived at Gravesend on the following day, where he was waited on by Sir Lewis Lewkenor, Master of the Ceremonies, and the next day conveyed in the Royal barges to London, 'au logis de l'Aigle noir.' On the 16th the Duke had his audience of the King, who received him sitting under a 'des' of cloth of gold, accompanied by the Queen, the Prince (Henry), the Duke of York (afterwards Charles I.), the Princess (Madame Arabella Stuart), and the young Prince of Brunswick, at that time also on a visit to James. Several days were afterwards spent in receiving and paying visits, and on the 23rd the Feast of St. George was kept with the usual ceremonies. On the 30th we have an entry of some interest to Shakspearean readers—'S. E. alla au Globe, lieu ordinaire ou l'on joue les Commedies; y fut representé l'histoire du More de Venise.'

We know from the evidence produced by Mr. Collier that 'Othello' appeared as early as 1602; and this entry proves that it retained its popularity in 1610. On the following day, 1st May, is another entry, of scientific interest:—

'S. E. alla au parc d'Elthon (Eltham) pour veoir *la perpetuum mobile*. L'inventeur s'appelle Cornelius Trebel, natif d'Alkmar, homme fort blond et beau, et d'une très douce façon, tout au contraire des espricts de la sorte. Nous y vismes aussy des Espinettes, qui jouent d'elle mesmes.'

I have not met with any mention of this philosopher in other papers of the period; but it is certain that in 1621 he published a work in Latin, entitled 'De quintessentia, et Epistola ad Jacobum Regem de perpetui mobili inventione.'

The King had previously left London (on the 24th) to go to his hunting-box in Northamptonshire; and on the 4th of May the Duke followed him and slept at Ware, at the inn called the Stag, where, says the author of the Diary, 'Je fus couché dans ung lict de plume de cigne, qui avoit huiet pieds de largeur.' This is, perhaps, the earliest precise notice yet found of this famous bed, and it serves to illustrate the passage in Shakspeare's 'Twelfth Night,' Act III. Sc. 2, in which he alludes to the 'Bed of Ware.' This bed still exists, and is engraved in Shaw's 'Ancient Furniture,' where it is stated to be 10 ft. 9 in. in length, by 10 ft. 9 in. in width, and to have been made in the reign of Elizabeth.

On leaving Ware the Duke proceeded to Royston, Cambridge, Newmarket, and Thetford, where he rejoined the King on the 7th; and the next morning the Duke went to church with his Majesty, as it was the day 'que sa Majesté observe infalliblement pour estre celuy de sa dellivrance de l'assasinat des Contes de Gaury (Gowry).' This is a remarkable passage, since other authorities give the 5th of August as the anniversary of this conspiracy. On the same day James took his guests with him to hunt the hare (his favourite amusement), and they saw a hawk seize some doterels, 'oiseau qui se laisse prendre par une estrange manière;' and also the trained cormorants, which, at the word of command, plunged into the water and brought up eels and other fish, which they, on a sign given, vomited up alive—'chose bien merveilleuse à voir!' On the same day, also, arrived the news of the assassination of Henry IV. of France, which took place on the 4th May. The news, however, did not prevent the King from hunting the hare the next day; and after dinner the whole party returned towards London, which they reached on the 10th. On the 25th the Duke of Wurtenberg left London and travelled by Rochester and Canterbury to Dover; whence, on the 29th, he embarked with his suite, and arrived safely at the port of Veer, in Zealand, on the following day."

ACT V.

(1) Scene I.—*Herne's oak.*] One of the many pleasing features in this sprightly comedy is the amount of local colouring with which it is imbued. Within the last few years the researches of various writers have shown, to use the words of Mr. Halliwell, "that 'The Merry Wives of Windsor' is to be regarded, in all essential particulars, as a purely English local drama, in which the actors and incidents, though spiritually belonging to all time, are really founded and engrafted upon living characters, amidst scenes existing, in a provincial town of England and its neighbourhood, in the lifetime of the poet." With regard to Herne's oak, the fact is now established, that a family of the name of Herne was living at Windsor in the sixteenth century, one Gylles Herne being married there in 1569. The old tradition was that Herne, one of the keepers in the park, having committed an offence for which he feared to be disgraced, hung himself upon an oak, which was ever after haunted by his ghost.

The earliest notice of this oak, since immortalized by Shakespeare, is in a "Plan of the Town and Castle of Windsor and little Park," published at Eton, in 1742. In the map, a tree, marked "Sir John Falstaff's oak," is represented as being on the edge of a pit, (Shakespeare's fairy pit!) just on the outside of an avenue which was formed in the seventeenth century, and known as Queen Elizabeth's Walk. The oak, a pollard, was described in 1780 as being twenty-seven feet in circumference, hollow, and the only tree in the neighbourhood into which boys could get. Although in a rapid state of decay, acorns were obtained from it as late as 1783, and it would in all probability have stood the scath of time and shocks of weather, but that unfortunately it was marked down inadvertently in a list of decayed and unsightly trees which had been ordered to be destroyed by George III., and fell a victim to the woodman's axe in 1796.

(2) Scene V.—*Yet be cheerful, knight: thou shalt eat a posset to-night at my house.*] To *posset*, whatever its derivation, meant to *coagulate*, or *curd*:—

> "And with a sudden vigour it doth *posset*,
> And curd, like aigre droppings into milk,
> The thin and wholesome blood":
>
> *Hamlet*, Act I. Sc. 8.

and the posset originally was, perhaps, no more than curdled milk, taken to promote perspiration. Hence, the hour of projection, the appropriate time for the administration of the posset proper, such as we are now considering, was *at night*, shortly before retiring to rest; Mrs. Quickly, in the present play, promises John Rugby "A posset soon at night,—at the end of a sea-coal fire:" Lady Macbeth, at night, speaks of having "drugged the possets" of Duncan's "grooms." Martha, in Beaumont and Fletcher's "Scornful Lady," Act II. Sc. 1, remarks to Welford, "Sir, 'tis so late, and our entertainment (meaning our posset) by this time is grown so cold, that 'twere an unmannerly part longer to hold you from your rest." And in Sir John Suckling's ballad on the wedding of Lord Broghill, the last ceremony described in the bridal chamber is:—

> "In come the bride's-maids with the posset,
> The bridegroom ate in spite:
> For, had he left the women to 't,
> It would have cost an hour to do 't,—
> Which were too much that night."

On the nature and qualities of Sack, "Simple of itself," the commentators are profuse in information. On this, its crowning luxury,—the famous and universally popular *sack-posset*,—they afford us none at all. Luckily, we are enabled to supply this grave omission, having at hand two recipes, infallibly authentic, for the precious brewage. The first of these is taken from a work published near the end of the seventeenth century, entitled "A True Gentlewoman's Delight:" the other is from the pen of Sir Fleetwood Shepherd.

"To Make a Sack-Posset.—Take Two Quarts of pure good Cream, and a Quarter of a Pound of the best Almonds. Stamp them in the Cream and boyl, with *Amber* and *Musk* therein. Then take a Pint of Sack in a basin, and set it on a Chafing-dish, till it be blood-warm; then take the Yolks of Twelve Eggs, with Four of their Whites, and beat them well together; and so put the Eggs into the Sack. Then stir all together over the coals, till it is all as thick as you would have it. If you now take some *Amber* and *Musk*, and grind the same quite small, with sugar, and strew this on the top of your Possit, I promise you that it shall have a most delicate and pleasant taste."

He must be the veriest Pythagorean who could doubt it; and the marvel is how such a "night-cap" ever went out of fashion. The Knight's preparation seems hardly so ambrosial, but that too must have been a palatable "comforter:"—

> "From fam'd *Barbadoes* in the *Western Main*,
> Fetch *Sugar*, ounces four; fetch *Sack* from *Spain*
> A Pint; and from the *Eastern Indian* coast,
> *Nutmeg*, the glory of our Northern toast:
> O'er flaming coals let them together heat,
> Till the all-conquering *Sack* dissolve the Sweet.
> O'er such another fire, put Eggs just Ten,
> New-born from tread of cock and rump of hen;
> Stir them, with steady hand, and conscience pricking,
> To see the untimely end of ten fine chicken.
> From shining shelf take down the brazen skillet,
> A quart of Milk from gentle cow will fill it.
> When boil'd and cold, put Milk and Sack to Egg,
> Unite them firmly, like the Triple League;
> And on the fire let them together dwell,
> Till Miss sing twice—'*You must not kiss and tell.*'
> Then lad and lass take up a Silver Spoon:
> And fall on 't fiercely, like a starved Dragoon."

(3) Scene V.—*I am glad, though you have ta'en a special stand to strike at me, that your arrow hath glanced.*] Deer shooting was a favourite sport of both sexes in the time of Shakespeare, and to enable ladies to enjoy it in safety and without fatigue, *stands*, or *standings*, with flat roofs, ornamented and concealed by boughs and bushes, were erected in many parks. Here, armed with the cross-bow or bow and arrow, the fair huntresses were wont to take aim at the animal which the keepers compelled to pass before them. To this practice the poet alludes again in "Love's Labour's Lost," Act IV. Sc. 1:—

> "Prin. ——— where is the bush
> That we must stand and play the murderer in?
> For. Hereby, upon the edge of yonder coppice;
> *A stand* where you may make the fairest shoot."

And in "Cymbeline," Act III. Sc. 4:—

> ———"When thou hast ta'en thy *stand*,
> The elected deer before thee!"

(4) Scene V.—*Well, what remedy?*] In the quarto, after Falstaff's speech, the dialogue proceeds as follows:—

> "Mrs. Ford. Come, mistris Page, Ile be bold with you,
> 'Tis pity to part love that is so true.
> Mrs. Page. Altho' that I have missed in my intent,
> Yet I am glad my husband's match was crossed;
> Here, M. Fenton, take her, and God give thee joy.
> Sir Hu. Come, Master Page, you must needs agree.
> Ford. I yfaith, sir, come, you see your wife is wel pleased.
> Page. I cannot tel, and yet my hart's well eased.
> And yet it doth me good the Doctor missed.
> Come hither, Fenton, and come hither, daughter;
> Go too. you might have stai'd for my good will,
> But since your choise is made of one you love,
> Here take her, Fenton, and both happie prove."

Act IV. Sc. I.

MUCH ADO ABOUT NOTHING.

The only edition of this comedy known before the folio 1623, is a quarto printed in 1600, entitled:—"Much adoe about Nothing, as it hath been sundrie times publikely acted by the right honourable the Lord Chamberlaine his seruants. *Written by William Shakespeare.* London Printed by V. S. for Andrew Wise and William Aspley, 1600." It is supposed originally to have been acted under the title of "Benedick and Beatrix," and, from being unnoticed by Meres, to have been written not earlier than 1598.

The serious incidents of his plot, some writers conjecture, Shakespeare derived from the story of Ariodante and Geneura, in Ariosto's Orlando Furioso, which, in 1582-3, was made the subject of dramatic representation, and played before Queen Elizabeth by "Mulcaster's children," that is, the children of St. Paul's school, and of which an English translation by Sir John Harrington, Elizabeth's "merry poet," and godson, was published in 1591. Others, with more probability, believe the source from whence he took them was some now extinct version of Bandello's twenty-second novel, "*Como il S. Timbreo di Cardona, essendo col Re Piero d'Aragona in Messina, s'innamora, di Fenicia Leonata: e i varii fortunevoli accidenti, che avvennero prima che per moglie la prendesse.*" In Bandello's story the scene, like that of the comedy, is laid at Messina; the name of the slandered lady's father is the same, Lionato, or Leonato; and the friend of her lover is Don Piero, or Pedro. These coincidences alone are sufficient to establish some near or remote connexion between the novel and the play, but a brief sketch of the romance will place their affinity almost beyond doubt. Don Piero of Arragon returns from a victorious campaign, and, with the gallant cavalier Timbreo di Cardona, is at Messina. Timbreo falls in love with Fenicia, the daughter of Lionato di Leonati, a gentleman of Messina, and, like Claudio in the play, courts her by proxy. He is successful in his suit, and the lovers are betrothed: but the course of true love is impeded by one Girondo, a disappointed admirer of the lady, who determines to prevent the marriage. In pursuance of this object, he insinuates to Timbreo that Fenicia is false, and offers to show him a stranger scaling her chamber window. The unhappy lover consents to watch; and at the appointed hour, Girondo and a servant in the plot, pass him disguised, and the latter is seen to ascend a ladder and enter the house of Lionato. In an agony of rage and jealousy, Timbreo in the morning accuses the lady of disloyalty, and rejects the alliance. Fenicia falls into a swoon; a dangerous illness supervenes; and the father, to stifle all rumours hurtful to her fame, removes her to a retired house of his brother, proclaims her death, and solemnly performs her funeral obsequies. Girondo is now struck with remorse at having "slandered to death" a creature so innocent and beautiful. He confesses his treachery to Timbreo, and both determine to restore the reputation of the lost one, and undergo any penance her family may impose. Lionato is merciful, and requires only from Timbreo, that he shall wed a lady whom he recommends, and whose face shall be concealed till the marriage ceremony is over. The *dénouement* is obvious. Timbreo espouses the mysterious fair one, and finds in her his injured, loving, and beloved Fenicia.

The comic portion of "Much Ado about Nothing," involving the pleasant stratagems by which the principal characters are decoyed into matrimony with each other, is Shakespeare's own design, and the amalgamation of the two plots is managed with so much felicity, that no one, perhaps, who read the comedy for entertainment only, ever thought them separable.

Persons Represented.

DON PEDRO, *Prince of* Arragon.

DON JOHN, *his bastard Brother.*

CLAUDIO, *a young nobleman of* Florence, } *Friends of* Don Pedro.
BENEDICK, *a young nobleman of* Padua, } *Friends of* Don Pedro.

LEONATO, *Governor of* Messina.

ANTONIO, *his Brother.*

BORACHIO, } *Followers of* Don John.
CONRADE, } *Followers of* Don John.

BALTHAZAR, *an Attendant on* Don Pedro.

SEXTON.

DOGBERRY, } *Two City Officers.*
VERGES, } *Two City Officers.*

A FRIAR.

A BOY, *attending on* Benedick.

HERO, *Daughter to* Leonato.

BEATRICE, *Niece to* Leonato.

MARGARET, } *Gentlewomen attending on* Hero *and* Beatrice.
URSULA, } *Gentlewomen attending on* Hero *and* Beatrice.

Messengers, Watchmen, and Attendants.

SCENE,—MESSINA.

ACT I.

SCENE I.—*Before* Leonato's *House.*

Enter LEONATO, HERO, BEATRICE, *and others, with a* Messenger.[a]

LEON. I learn in this letter, that don Pedro* of Arragon comes this night to Messina.

MESS. He is very near by this; he was not three leagues off when I left him.

LEON. How many gentlemen have you lost in this action?

(*) Old text, *Peter*.

[a] Enter Leonato, &c.] The stage-direction in the old copies is, "*Enter Leonato governour of Messina,* Innogen his wife, *Hero his daughter, and Beatrice his Neece, with a Messenger.*" As the wife of Leonato takes no part in the action, and neither speaks nor is spoken to throughout the play, she was probably no more than a character the poet had designed in his first sketch of the plot, and which he found reason to omit afterwards.

MESS. But few of any sort,[a] and none of name.

LEON. A victory is twice itself, when the achiever brings home full numbers. I find here, that don Pedro* hath bestowed much honour on a young Florentine, called Claudio.

MESS. Much deserved on his part, and equally remembered by don Pedro: he hath borne himself beyond the promise of his age, doing, in the figure of a lamb, the feats of a lion: he hath, indeed, better bettered expectation, than you must expect of me to tell you how.

LEON. He hath an uncle here in Messina will be very much glad of it.

MESS. I have already delivered him letters, and there appears much joy in him; even so much, that joy could not show itself modest enough, without a badge of bitterness.

LEON. Did he break out into tears?

MESS. In great measure.

LEON. A kind overflow of kindness: there are no faces truer than those that are so washed. How much better is it to weep at joy, than to joy at weeping!

BEAT. I pray you, is signior Montanto[b] returned from the wars, or no?

MESS. I know none of that name, lady; there was none such in the army of any sort.[c]

LEON. What is he that you ask for, niece?

HERO. My cousin means signior Benedick of Padua.

MESS. O, he is returned; and as pleasant as ever he was.

BEAT. He set up his bills(1) here in Messina, and challenged Cupid at the flight: and my uncle's fool, reading the challenge, subscribed for Cupid, and challenged him at the bird-bolt.(2)—I pray you, how many hath he killed and eaten in these wars? But how many hath he killed? for, indeed, I promised to eat all of his killing.

LEON. Faith, niece, you tax signior Benedick too much; but he'll be meet with you, I doubt it not.

MESS. He hath done good service, lady, in these wars.

BEAT. You had musty victual, and he hath holp to eat it: he is a very valiant trencher-man, he hath an excellent stomach.

MESS. And a good soldier too, lady.

BEAT. And a good soldier to a lady!—But what is he to a lord?

MESS. A lord to a lord, a man to a man; stuffed with all honourable virtues.

BEAT. It is so, indeed, he is no less than a stuffed man, but for the stuffing,—Well, *we are all mortal.*

LEON. You must not, sir, mistake my niece: there is a kind of merry war betwixt signior Benedick and her: they never meet, but there is a skirmish of wit between them.

BEAT. Alas! he gets nothing by that. In our last conflict, four of his five wits[d] went halting off, and now is the whole man governed with one: so that if he have wit enough to keep himself warm, let him bear it for a difference[e] between himself and his horse: for it is all the wealth that he hath left, to be known a reasonable creature.—Who is his companion now? he hath every month a new sworn brother.

MESS. Is it possible?

BEAT. Very easily possible: he wears his faith but as the fashion of his hat, it ever changes with the next block.[f]

MESS. I see, lady, the gentleman is not in your books.

BEAT. No: an he were, I would burn my study. But, I pray you, who is his companion? Is there no young squarer[g] now, that will make a voyage with him to the devil?

MESS. He is most in the company of the right noble Claudio.

BEAT. O Lord! he will hang upon him like a disease: he is sooner caught than the pestilence, and the taker runs presently mad. God help the noble Claudio! if he have caught the Benedick, it will cost him a thousand pound ere he be cured.

MESS. I will hold friends with you, lady.

BEAT. Do, good friend.

(*) Old text, *Peter.*

a *But few of any* sort, *and none of name.*] It may be questionable whether *any sort*, in this instance, is to be understood in the ordinary sense we attach to it, of any *kind*, or *description*, or whether it means any *of rank*, or *distinction;* but every one acquainted with our early literature is aware that *sort* was commonly used—as in a subsequent speech of the same character, "there was none such in the army of any *sort*" —to imply *stamp, degree, quality,* &c. Thus, in Ben Jonson's "Every Man out of his Humour," Act II. Sc. 6:—"Look you, sir, you presume to be a gentleman of *sort.*" Again, in the same author's "Every Man in his Humour," Act I. Sc. 2:—"A gentleman of your *sort*, parts," &c. And in "Ram Alley," Act IV. Sc. 1:—"Her husband is a gentleman of *sort.*" "A gentleman of *sort!* why, what care I?"

b Montanto—] A term borrowed from the Italian schools of fence:—" —— your punto, your reverso, your stoccata, your imbrocata, your passada, your *Montanto.*"—*Every Man in his Humour.*

c *Of any* sort.] See note (a).

d *His five* wits—] With our early writers the five senses were usually so called:—"Certes delites been after the appetites of the *five wittis;* as sight, hereing, smelling, savouring, and touching."—*The Persones Tale* of CHAUCER.

"I am callyd Sensuall Apetyte,
All craturs in me delyte;
I comforte the wyttys fyve,
The tastyng, smellyng, and herynge;
I refresh the syght and felynge
To all creaturs alyve."
Interlude of *The Four Elements.*

e *Bear it for a* difference—] That is, heraldically, *for a distinction.* So poor Ophelia, in "Hamlet," Act IV. Sc. 5:—

"You may wear your rue with *a difference.*"

f The next block.] The *block* was the mould on which the felt hats of our ancestors were shaped; and, as the mutability of fashion was shown in nothing so much as in the head-dresses of both sexes, these blocks must have been perpetually changing their form.

g Squarer—] *Squarer* may perhaps mean *quarreller*, as to *square* is to *dispute.*

Leon. You will never run mad, niece.
Beat. No, not till a hot January.
Mess. Don Pedro is approached.

Enter Don Pedro, *attended by* Balthazar, *and others*, Don John, Claudio, *and* Benedick.[a]

D. Pedro. Good signior Leonato, you are come

[a] *Enter*, &c.] In the old copies the direction is, "*Enter don Pedro, Claudio, Benedicke, Balthasar, and Iohn the bastard.*"

to meet your trouble: the fashion of the world is to avoid cost, and you encounter it.

Leon. Never came trouble to my house in the likeness of your grace: for trouble being gone, comfort should remain; but when you depart from me, sorrow abides, and happiness takes his leave.

D. Pedro. You embrace your charge too willingly. I think, this is your daughter.

Leon. Her mother hath many times told me so.

BENE. Were you in doubt, sir,* that you asked her?

LEON. Signior Benedick, no; for then were you a child.

D. PEDRO. You have it full, Benedick: we may guess by this what you are, being a man. Truly, the lady fathers herself.[a] Be happy, lady! for you are like an honourable father.

BENE. If signior Leonato be her father, she would not have his head on her shoulders, for all Messina, as like him as she is.

BEAT. I wonder that you will still[b] be talking, signior Benedick; nobody marks you.

BENE. What, my dear lady Disdain! are you yet living?

BEAT. Is it possible Disdain should die, while she hath such meet food to feed it, as signior Benedick? Courtesy itself must convert to disdain, if you come in her presence.

BENE. Then is courtesy a turn-coat. But it is certain, I am loved of all ladies, only you excepted: and I would I could find in my heart that I had not a hard heart, for truly I love none.

BEAT. A dear happiness to women; they would else have been troubled with a pernicious suitor. I thank God, and my cold blood, I am of your humour for that; I had rather hear my dog bark at a crow, than a man swear he loves me.

BENE. God keep your ladyship still in that mind! so some gentleman or other shall 'scape a predestinate scratched face.

BEAT. Scratching could not make it worse, an 'twere such a face as yours were.

BENE. Well, you are a rare parrot-teacher.

BEAT. A bird of my tongue, is better than a beast of yours.

BENE. I would my horse had the speed of your tongue, and so good a continuer: but keep your way o' God's name! I have done.

BEAT. You always end with a jade's trick; I know you of old.

D. PEDRO. This is the sum of all: Leonato,—signior Claudio, and signior Benedick,—my dear friend Leonato hath invited you all. I tell him, we shall stay here at the least a month; and he heartily prays, some occasion may detain us longer: I dare swear he is no hypocrite, but prays from his heart.

LEON. If you swear, my lord, you shall not be forsworn.—Let me bid you welcome, my lord; being reconciled to the prince your brother, I owe you all duty.

D. JOHN. I thank you: I am not of many words, but I thank you.

LEON. Please it your grace lead on?

D. PEDRO. Your hand, Leonato; we will go together.

[*Exeunt all but* BENEDICK *and* CLAUDIO.

CLAUD. Benedick, didst thou note the daughter of signior Leonato?

BENE. I noted her not, but I looked on her.

CLAUD. Is she not a modest young lady?

BENE. Do you question me, as an honest man should do, for my simple true judgment; or would you have me speak after my custom, as being a professed tyrant to their sex?

CLAUD. No, I pray thee, speak in sober judgment.

BENE. Why, i'faith, methinks she's too low for a high praise, too brown for a fair praise, and too little for a great praise: only this commendation I can afford her, that were she other than she is, she were unhandsome; and being no other but as she is, I do not like her.

CLAUD. Thou thinkest, I am in sport; I pray thee, tell me truly how thou likest her.

BENE. Would you buy her, that you inquire after her?

CLAUD. Can the world buy such a jewel?

BENE. Yea, and a case to put it into. But speak you this with a sad brow? or do you play the flouting Jack, to tell us Cupid is a good hare-finder, and Vulcan a rare carpenter?[c] Come, in what key shall a man take you, to go in the song?

CLAUD. In mine eye she is the sweetest lady that ever I looked on.

BENE. I can see yet without spectacles, and I see no such matter: there's her cousin, an she were not possessed with a fury, exceeds her as much in beauty, as the first of May doth the last of December. But I hope you have no intent to turn husband, have you?

CLAUD. I would scarce trust myself, though I had sworn the contrary, if Hero would be my wife.

BENE. Is't come to this? in faith, hath not the world one man, but he will wear his cap with suspicion? Shall I never see a bachelor of three-score again? Go to, i' faith; an thou wilt needs thrust thy neck into a yoke, wear the print of it, and sigh away Sundays. Look, don Pedro is returned to seek you.

(*) First folio omits, *sir*.

[a] The lady fathers herself.] This phrase, Steevens observes, is still common in Dorsetshire. "Jack fathers himself," is like his father. There was a French saying to the same effect, older than Shakespeare's time:—"*Il pourtrait fort bien à son père.*"

[b] Still *be talking*,—] *Always* be talking.

[c] To tell us Cupid is a good hare-finder, and Vulcan a rare carpenter?] This, which has so puzzled all the commentators, is nothing more than an example of what Puttenham terms "*Antiphrasis*, or the *Broad floute*." "Or when we deride by plaine and flat contradiction, as he that saw a dwarfe go in the streete said to his companion that walked with him; See yonder gyant; and to a Negro or woman blackemoore, In good sooth ye are a faire one."—*The Arte of English Poesie*, 1589.

Re-enter DON PEDRO.

D. PEDRO. What secret hath held you here, that you followed not to Leonato's?

BENE. I would your grace would constrain me to tell.

D. PEDRO. I charge thee on thy allegiance.

BENE. You hear, count Claudio: I can be secret as a dumb man, I would have you think so; but on my *allegiance*,—mark you this, on my *allegiance*:—he is in love. With who?—now that is your grace's part.—Mark, how short his answer is:—*With Hero, Leonato's short daughter.*

CLAUD. If this were so, so were it uttered.

BENE. Like the old tale, my lord: *it is not so, nor 't was not so;* but, indeed, *God forbid it should be so.*(3)

CLAUD. If my passion change not shortly, God forbid it should be otherwise.

D. PEDRO. Amen, if you love her; for the lady is very well worthy.

CLAUD. You speak this to fetch me in, my lord.

D. PEDRO. By my troth, I speak my thought.

CLAUD. And, in faith, my lord, I spoke mine.

BENE. And, by my two faiths and troths, my lord, I spoke* mine.

CLAUD. That I love her, I feel.

D. PEDRO. That she is worthy, I know.

BENE. That I neither feel how she should be loved, nor know how she should be worthy, is the opinion, that fire cannot melt out of me; I will die in it at the stake.

D. PEDRO Thou wast ever an obstinate heretic in the despite of beauty.

CLAUD. And never could maintain his part, but in the force of his will.

BENE. That a woman conceived me, I thank her; that she brought me up, I likewise give her most humble thanks: but that I will have a recheat winded in my forehead, or hang my bugle in an invisible baldrick,[a] all women shall pardon me. Because I will not do them the wrong to mistrust any, I will do myself the right to trust none; and the fine[b] is, (for the which I may go the finer,) I will live a bachelor.

D. PEDRO. I shall see thee, ere I die, look pale with love.

BENE. With anger, with sickness, or with hunger, my lord, not with love: prove that ever I lose more blood with love, than I will get again with drinking, pick out mine eyes with a ballad-maker's pen, and hang me up at the door of a brothel-house, for the sign of blind Cupid.

D. PEDRO. Well, if ever thou dost fall from this faith, thou wilt prove a notable argument.

BENE. If I do, hang me in a bottle like a cat,[c] and shoot at me; and he that hits me, let him be clapped on the shoulder, and called Adam.(4)

D. PEDRO. Well, as time shall try:
In time the savage bull doth bear the yoke.[d]

BENE. The savage bull may; but if ever the sensible Benedick bear it, pluck off the bull's horns, and set them in my forehead; and let me be vilely painted; and in such great letters as they write, *Here is good horse to hire*, let them signify under my sign,—*Here you may see Benedick the married man.*

CLAUD. If this should ever happen, thou would'st be horn-mad.

D. PEDRO. Nay, if Cupid have not spent all his quiver in Venice, thou wilt quake for this shortly.

BENE. I look for an earthquake too, then.

D. PEDRO. Well, you will temporize with the hours. In the mean time, good signior Benedick, repair to Leonato's; commend me to him, and tell him, I will not fail him at supper; for, indeed, he hath made great preparation.

BENE. I have almost matter enough in me for such an embassage; and so I commit you—

CLAUD. *To the tuition of God. From my house,* (if I had it,)—

D. PEDRO. *The sixth of July: Your loving friend, Benedick.*[e]

BENE. Nay, mock not, mock not: the body of your discourse is sometime guarded with fragments, and the guards are but slightly basted on neither: ere you flout old ends any further, examine your conscience; and so I leave you.

[*Exit* BENEDICK.

CLAUD. My liege, your highness now may do me good.

D. PEDRO. My love is thine to teach; teach it [but how,
And thou shalt see how apt it is to learn
Any hard lesson that may do thee good.

CLAUD. Hath Leonato any son, my lord?

D. PEDRO. No child but Hero, she's his only heir.
Dost thou affect her, Claudio?

(*) First folio, *speake*.

[a] *But that I will have a recheat winded in my forehead, or hang my bugle in an invisible baldrick,*—] A *recheat* was a note upon the horn, usually employed to recal the dogs from the wrong scent. Benedick's meaning appears to be, I will neither be a wittol, glorying in my shame, nor a poor cuckold who must endure and conceal it.

[b] The fine—] The *conclusion*.

[c] Hang me in a bottle like a cat, and shoot at me;] This was one of the barbarous sports of former times. The practice was to enclose a cat in a suspended coop of open bars, and shoot at it with arrows till the poor animal was killed:—"——— arrowes flew faster than they did at a *catte in a baskət*, when Prince Arthur, or the Duke of Shoreditch, strucke up drumme in field."—*Warres; or, The Peace is Broken*, a black-letter tract, quoted by Steevens.

[d] *In time*, &c.] A line from the old stage butt, "The Spanish Tragedy," by Thomas Kyd; but which originally occurs in Watson's "Passionate Centurie of Love," printed in 1582.

[e] Your loving friend, Benedick.] The "old ends," here ridiculed, were the formal conclusions of letters in the poet's time, which usually ran, "*And so*, wishing you health, *I commend you to the tuition of God*," &c. &c.

CLAUD. O my lord,
When you went onward on this ended action,
I look'd upon her with a soldier's eye,
That lik'd, but had a rougher task in hand
Than to drive liking to the name of love:
But now I am return'd, and that war-thoughts
Have left their places vacant, in their rooms
Come thronging soft and delicate desires,
All prompting me how fair young Hero is,
Saying, I lik'd her ere I went to wars—
D. PEDRO. Thou wilt be like a lover presently,
And tire the hearer with a book of words:
If thou dost love fair Hero, cherish it,
And I will break with her, and with her father,
And thou shalt have her:[a] was't not to this end,
That thou began'st to twist so fine a story?
CLAUD. How sweetly do you minister to love,
That know love's grief by his complexion!
But lest my liking might too sudden seem,
I would have salv'd it with a longer treatise.
D. PEDRO. What need the bridge much broader than the flood?
The fairest grant is the necessity:[b]
Look, what will serve, is fit: 'tis once,[c] thou lov'st;
And I will fit thee with the remedy.
I know, we shall have revelling to-night;
I will assume thy part in some disguise,
And tell fair Hero I am Claudio;
And in her bosom I'll unclasp my heart,
And take her hearing prisoner with the force
And strong encounter of my amorous tale:
Then, after, to her father will I break,
And, the conclusion is, she shall be thine:
In practice let us put it presently. [*Exeunt.*

a ———And with her father,
And thou shalt have her:]

These words are omitted in the folio, 1623.

b The fairest grant is the necessity:] Mr. Hayley proposed to read "The fairest grant is *to* necessity, that is, *necessitas quod cogit defendit*," but surely the sense is clear enough—the best boon is that which answers the necessities of the case: or, as Don Pedro pithily explains it, "what will serve, is fit."

c 'Tis once,—] See note (a), p. 128.

SCENE II.—*A Room in* Leonato's *House.*

Enter LEONATO *and* ANTONIO.[a]

LEON. How now, brother? where is my cousin, your son? hath he provided this music?

ANT. He is very busy about it. But, brother, I can tell you news that you yet dreamed not of.

LEON. Are they good?

ANT. As the event* stamps them; but they have a good cover, they show well outward. The prince and count Claudio, walking in a thick-pleached alley[b] in my orchard, were thus much† overheard by a man of mine. The prince discovered to Claudio, that he loved my niece your daughter, and meant to acknowledge it this night in a dance; and, if he found her accordant, he meant to take the present time by the top, and instantly break with you of it.

LEON. Hath the fellow any wit, that told you this?

ANT. A good sharp fellow: I will send for him, and question him yourself.

LEON. No, no; we will hold it as a dream, till it appear itself:—but I will acquaint my daughter withal, that she may be the better prepared for an answer, if peradventure this be true. Go you, and tell her of it. [*Several persons cross the stage.*] Cousins, you know what you have to do.—O, I cry you mercy, friend: go you with me, and I will use your skill.—Good cousins,‡ have a care this busy time. [*Exeunt.*

SCENE III.—*Another Room in* Leonato's *House.*

Enter DON JOHN *and* CONRADE.[c]

CON. What the good year, my lord! why are you thus out of measure sad?

D. JOHN. There is no measure in the occasion that breeds, therefore the sadness is without limit.

CON. You should hear reason.

D. JOHN. And when I have heard it, what blessing bringeth it?

CON. If not a present remedy, yet a patient sufferance.

D. JOHN. I wonder that thou, being (as thou say'st thou art) born under Saturn, goest about to apply a moral medicine to a mortifying mischief. I cannot hide what I am: I must be sad when I have cause, and smile at no man's jests; eat when I have stomach, and wait for no man's leisure; sleep when I am drowsy, and tend on no man's business; laugh when I am merry, and claw[d] no man in his humour.

CON. Yea, but you must not make the full show of this, till you may do it without controlment. You have of late stood out against your brother, and he hath ta'en you newly into his grace; where it is impossible you should take true* root, but by the fair weather that you make yourself: it is needful that you frame the season for your own harvest.

D. JOHN. I had rather be a canker in a hedge, than a rose in his grace; and it better fits my blood to be disdained of all, than to fashion a carriage to rob love from any: in this, though I cannot be said to be a flattering honest man, it must not be denied but I am a plain-dealing villain. I am trusted with a muzzle, and enfranchised with a clog; therefore I have decreed not to sing in my cage: if I had my mouth, I would bite; if I had my liberty, I would do my liking: in the meantime, let me be that I am, and seek not to alter me.

CON. Can you make no use of your discontent?

D. JOHN. I† make all use of it, for I use it only. Who comes here? what news, Borachio?

Enter BORACHIO.

BORA. I came yonder from a great supper; the prince, your brother, is royally entertained by Leonato; and I can give you intelligence of an intended marriage.

D. JOHN. Will it serve for any model to build mischief on? What is he for a fool[e] that betroths himself to unquietness?

BORA. Marry, it is your brother's right hand.

D. JOHN. Who? the most exquisite Claudio?

BORA. Even he.

D. JOHN. A proper squire! And who, and who? which way looks he?

BORA. Marry, on Hero, the daughter and heir of Leonato.

(*) Old text, *events.* (†) First folio omits, *much.* (‡) Old copies, *cousin.*

(*) First folio omits, *true.* (†) First folio, *will make.*

[a] Enter Leonato and Antonio.] In the old copies, "Enter Leonato *and an old man, brother to Leonato.*"

[b] Thick-pleached *alley*—] A thickly intertwined avenue.

[c] Enter Don John and Conrade.] The original stage-direction is, "Enter Sir John the Bastard, and Conrade, his companion."

[d] *And* claw *no man*—] To *claw* or *scratch*, is, metaphorically, to *flatter*.

[e] What is he for a fool—] This construction, though no longer permissible, was trite enough in the poet's time. The meaning is, *what kind of fool is he?* It is found in Peele's "Edward I." Sc. 2:—"What's he for a man?" in Ben Jonson's "Every Man out of his Humour," Act III. Sc. 6:—

"What is he for a creature?"

And in "Ram Alley," Act IV. Sc. 2:—

"What is he for a man?"
"Nothing for a man, but much for a beast."

D. JOHN. A very forward March chick! How came you to this?

BORA. Being entertained for a perfumer, as I was smoking a musty room,(5) comes me the prince and Claudio, hand in hand, in sad [a] conference: I whipt me * behind the arras, and there heard it agreed upon, that the prince should woo Hero for himself, and having obtained her, give her to count Claudio.

D. JOHN. Come, come, let us thither; this may prove food to my displeasure: that young start-up hath all the glory of my overthrow. If I can cross him any way, I bless myself every way: you are both sure, and will assist me?

CON. To the death, my lord.

D. JOHN. Let us to the great supper; their cheer is the greater that I am subdued: would the cook were of my mind!—Shall we go prove what's to be done?

BORA. We'll wait upon your lordship.

[*Exeunt.*

(*) First folio omits, *me*.

[a] Sad *conference:*] *Sad* here, and in most other instances where it occurs in these plays, signifies, *serious*.

ACT II.

SCENE I.—*A Hall in* Leonato's *House.*

Enter LEONATO, ANTONIO, HERO, BEATRICE, *and others.*[a]

LEON. Was not count John here at supper?

ANT. I saw him not.

BEAT. How tartly that gentleman looks! I never can see him, but I am heart-burned an hour after.

HERO. He is of a very melancholy disposition.

BEAT. He were an excellent man, that were made just in the mid-way between him and Benedick: the one is too like an image, and says nothing; and the other, too like my lady's eldest son, evermore tattling.

LEON. Then half signior Benedick's tongue in count John's mouth, and half count John's melancholy in signior Benedick's face,—

BEAT. With a good leg, and a good foot, uncle, and money enough in his purse, such a man could win any woman in the world,—if he could get her good will.

LEON. By my troth, niece, thou wilt never get thee a husband, if thou be so shrewd of thy tongue.

ANT. In faith, she 's too curst.

[a] Enter Leonato, &c.] The original copies again introduce Leonato's wife here.

BEAT. Too curst is more than curst: I shall lessen God's sending that way, for it is said, *God sends a curst cow short horns;* but to a cow too curst he sends none.

LEON. So, by being too curst, God will send you no horns.

BEAT. Just, if he send me no husband; for the which blessing, I am at him upon my knees every morning and evening: Lord! I could not endure a husband with a beard on his face; I had rather lie in the woollen.

LEON. You may light upon a husband that hath no beard.

BEAT. What should I do with him? dress him in my apparel, and make him my waiting-gentlewoman? He that hath a beard is more than a youth; and he that hath no beard is less than a man: and he that is more than a youth, is not for me; and he that is less than a man, I am not for him. Therefore I will even take sixpence in earnest of the bear-ward, and lead his apes into hell.

LEON. Well then, go you into hell?

BEAT. No; but to the gate; and there will the devil meet me, like an old cuckold, with horns on his head, and say, *Get you to heaven, Beatrice, get you to heaven; here's no place for you maids:* so deliver I up my apes, and away to Saint Peter; for the heavens![a] he shows me where the bachelors sit, and there live we as merry as the day is long.

ANT. Well, niece, [*To* HERO.] I trust you will be ruled by your father.

BEAT. Yes, faith; it is my cousin's duty to make courtesy, and say, *Father,(*) as it please you:*—but yet for all that, cousin, let him be a handsome fellow, or else make another courtesy, and say, *Father, as it please me.*

LEON. Well, niece, I hope to see you one day fitted with a husband.

BEAT. Not till God make men of some other metal than earth. Would it not grieve a woman to be over-mastered with a piece of valiant dust? to make account of her life to a clod of wayward marl? No, uncle, I'll none: Adam's sons are my brethren; and truly, I hold it a sin to match in my kindred.

LEON. Daughter, remember what I told you: if the prince do solicit you in that kind, you know your answer.

BEAT. The fault will be in the music, cousin, if you be not wooed in good time: if the prince be too important,[b] tell him there is measure[c] in every thing, and so dance out the answer. For hear me, Hero; wooing, wedding, and repenting, is as a Scotch jig, a measure,[d] and a cinque-pace: the first suit is hot and hasty, like a Scotch jig, and full as fantastical: the wedding, mannerly-modest, as a measure, full of state and ancientry; and then comes repentance, and, with his bad legs, falls into the cinque-pace faster and faster, till he sink(*) into his grave.

LEON. Cousin, you apprehend passing shrewdly.

BEAT. I have a good eye, uncle; I can see a church by day-light.

LEON. The revellers are entering, brother; make good room.

Enter DON PEDRO, DON JOHN, CLAUDIO, BENEDICK, BALTHAZAR; BORACHIO, MARGARET, URSULA, *and others, masked.*[e]

D. PEDRO. Lady, will you walk about with your friend?[f]

HERO. So you walk softly, and look sweetly, and say nothing, I am yours for the walk: and, especially, when I walk away.

D. PEDRO. With me in your company?

HERO. I may say so, when I please.

D. PEDRO. And when please you to say so?

HERO. When I like your favour; for God defend, the lute should be like the case!

D. PEDRO. My visor is Philemon's roof; within the house is Jove.[g]

HERO. Why then your visor should be thatch'd.

D. PEDRO. Speak low, if you speak love.

[*Takes her aside.*

BALTH. Well, I would you did like me.[h]

MARG. So would not I, for your own sake; for I have many ill qualities.

BALTH. Which is one?

(*) First folio omits, *Father.*

(*) First folio, *sinks.*

[a] For the heavens!] This adjuration, which Gifford says is no more than *by heaven!* has before occurred in "The Merchant of Venice." See note (d), p. 401.

[b] *Too* important,—] That is, *importunate.* See note (c), p. 143.

[c] *There is* measure *in every thing,*—] That is, *moderation* in every thing; but Beatrice plays on the word *measure,* which, in addition to its ordinary acceptation, once signified, any kind of *dance.* See (2), p. 103.

[d] A measure,—] *A measure* here means, a particular dance, slow and dignified, like the minuet. See note (2), p. 103.

[e] Enter Don Pedro, &c.] The stage-direction in the quarto is, "*Enter Prince, Pedro, Claudio, and Benedicke, and Balthaser, or dumb John.*" The folio adds, "*Maskers with a drum.*"

[f] *Your* friend?] *Friend,* in former times, was the ordinary term, applicable to both sexes, for *lover.*

[g] *Within the house is* Jove.] The folio has *love,* which is plainly wrong, as Shakespeare, in this reference to the story of Baucis and Philemon, obviously intended to form a couplet in the long fourteen-syllable verse of Golding's Ovid:—

"D. PEDRO. My visor is Philemon's roof; within the house is *Jove.*
"HERO. Why then your visor should be thatch'd.
"D. PEDRO. Speak low, if you speak *love.*"

[h] Well, I would you did like me.] It can hardly be doubted that this and the next two speeches, assigned to Benedick in the old editions, belong rightly to Balthazar. As Mr. Dyce remarks, "Benedick is now engaged with Beatrice, as is evident from what they presently say." The error probably arose like a similar one in "Love's Labour's Lost," Act II. Sc. 1. See note (b), p. 62,—from each of the two prefixes beginning with the same letter.

MARG. I say my prayers aloud.

BALTH. I love you the better; the hearers may cry, *Amen.*

MARG. God match me with a good dancer!

BALTH. *Amen.*

MARG. And God keep him out of my sight, when the dance is done!—Answer, clerk.

BALTH. No more words; the clerk is answered.

URS. I know you well enough; you are signior Antonio.

ANT. At a word, I am not.

URS. I know you by the waggling of your head.

ANT. To tell you true, I counterfeit him.

URS. You could never do him so ill well,[a] unless you were the very man: here's his dry hand up and down;[b] you are he, you are he.

ANT. At a word, I am not.

URS. Come, come; do you think I do not know you by your excellent wit? Can virtue hide itself? Go to, mum, you are he: graces will appear, and there's an end.

BEAT. Will you not tell me who told you so?

BENE. No, you shall pardon me.

BEAT. Nor will you not tell me who you are?

BENE. Not now.

BEAT. That I was disdainful,—and that I had my good wit out of the *Hundred merry tales*;—(1) Well, this was signior Benedick that said so.

BENE. What's he?

BEAT. I am sure you know him well enough.

BENE. Not I, believe me.

BEAT. Did he never make you laugh?

BENE. I pray you, what is he?

BEAT. Why, he is the prince's jester: a very dull fool; only his gift is in devising impossible[c] slanders: none but libertines delight in him; and the commendation is not in his wit, but in his villainy; for he both pleases* men, and angers them, and then they laugh at him, and beat him: I am sure, he is in the fleet; I would he had boarded me.

BENE. When I know the gentleman, I'll tell him what you say.

BEAT. Do, do: he'll but break a comparison or two on me; which, peradventure, not marked, or not laughed at, strikes him into melancholy; and then there's a partridge' wing saved, for the fool will eat no supper that night. [*Music within.*] We must follow the leaders.

BENE. In every good thing.

BEAT. Nay, if they lead to any ill, I will leave them at the next turning.

[*Dance. Then exeunt all but* DON JOHN, BORACHIO, *and* CLAUDIO.

D. JOHN. Sure, my brother is amorous on Hero, and hath withdrawn her father, to break with him about it: the ladies follow her, and but one visor remains.

BORA. And that is Claudio: I know him by his bearing.

D. JOHN. Are not you signior Benedick?

CLAUD. You know me well; I am he.

D. JOHN. Signior, you are very near[d] my brother in his love: he is enamoured on Hero; I pray you, dissuade him from her, she is no equal for his birth: you may do the part of an honest man in it.

CLAUD. How know you he loves her?

D. JOHN. I heard him swear his affection.

BORA. So did I too; and he swore he would marry her to-night.

D. JOHN. Come, let us to the banquet.

[*Exeunt* DON JOHN *and* BORACHIO.

CLAUD. Thus answer I, in name of Benedick,
But hear these ill news with the ears of Claudio.—
'Tis certain so;—the prince woos for himself.
Friendship is constant in all other things,
Save in the office and affairs of love:
Therefore, all hearts in love use their own tongues;
Let every eye negotiate for itself,
And trust no agent: for beauty is a witch,
Against whose charms faith melteth into blood:
This is an accident of hourly proof,
Which I mistrusted not. Farewell, therefore,
Hero!

Re-enter BENEDICK.

BENE. Count Claudio?

CLAUD. Yea, the same.

BENE. Come, will you go with me?

CLAUD. Whither?

BENE. Even to the next willow, about your own business, count. What fashion will you wear the garland of? about your neck, like an usurer's chain? or under your arm, like a lieutenant's scarf? You must wear it one way, for the prince hath got your Hero.

CLAUD. I wish him joy of her.

(*) First folio, *pleaseth.*

a You could never do him so ill well, &c.] You could never represent one, who is so ill-qualified, to the life, unless you were the very man.

b *Here's his dry hand up and down*;] See note (b), p. 13.

c Impossible slanders:] *Incredible, inconceivable* slanders. Thus, in "The Merry Wives of Windsor," Act III. Sc. 5:—"I will search *impossible* places." Again, in "Julius Cæsar," Act II. Sc. 1:—

"And I will strive with things *impossible*,
Yea, get the better of them."

And in "Twelfth Night," Act III. Sc. 2:—"—for there is no Christian can ever believe such *impossible* passages of grossness."

d *You are very near my brother*—] You are in *close confidence* with my brother. This explains a passage in "Henry IV." Part II. Act V. Sc. 2:—"If I had a suit to Master Shallow, I would humour his men, with the imputation of *being near their master.*"

BENE. Why, that's spoken like an honest drover; so they sell bullocks. But did you think, the prince would have served you thus?

CLAUD. I pray you, leave me.

BENE. Ho! now you strike like the blind man; 'twas the boy that stole your meat, and you'll beat the post.

CLAUD. If it will not be, I'll leave you. [*Exit.*

BENE. Alas, poor hurt fowl! Now will he creep into sedges.—But, that my lady Beatrice should know me, and not know me! *The prince's fool!* —Ha! it may be, I go under that title, because I am merry.—Yea: but so, I am apt to do myself wrong: I am not so reputed: it is the base, though bitter disposition[a] of Beatrice, that puts the world into her person, and so gives me out. Well, I'll be revenged as I may.

Re-enter DON PEDRO.

D. PEDRO. Now, signior, where's the count; did you see him?

BENE. Troth, my lord, I have played the part of lady Fame. I found him here as melancholy as a lodge in a warren;(2) I told him, and, I think, I* told him true, that your grace had got the good† will of this young lady; and I offered him my company to a willow tree, either to make him a garland, as being forsaken, or to bind him up‡ a rod, as being worthy to be whipped.

D. PEDRO. To be whipped! What's his fault?

BENE. The flat transgression of a school-boy; who, being overjoyed with finding a bird's nest, shows it his companion, and he steals it.

D. PEDRO. Wilt thou make a trust a transgression? the transgression is in the stealer.

BENE. Yet it had not been amiss, the rod had been made, and the garland too; for the garland he might have worn himself; and the rod he might have bestowed on you, who, as I take it, have stolen his bird's nest.

D. PEDRO. I will but teach them to sing, and restore them to the owner.

BENE. If their singing answer your saying, by my faith, you say honestly.

D. PEDRO. The lady Beatrice hath a quarrel to you; the gentleman that danced with her told her, that she is much wronged by you.

BENE. O, she misused me past the endurance of a block; an oak, but with one green leaf on it, would have answered her; my very visor began to assume life, and scold with her: she told me, not thinking I had been myself, that I was the prince's jester; that I was duller than a great thaw: huddling jest upon jest, with such impossible[b] conveyance upon me, that I stood like a man at a mark, with a whole army shooting at me. She speaks poniards, and every word stabs: if her breath were as terrible as her* terminations, there were no living near her, she would infect to the north star. I would not marry her, though she were endowed with all that Adam had left him before he transgressed: she would have made Hercules have turned spit; yea, and have cleft his club to make the fire too. Come, talk not of her; you shall find her the infernal Até in good apparel. I would to God, some scholar would conjure her; for, certainly, while she is here, a man may live as quiet in hell, as in a sanctuary,[c] (and people sin upon purpose, because they would go thither;) so, indeed, all disquiet, horror, and perturbation follow her.

Re-enter CLAUDIO, BEATRICE, HERO, *and* LEONATO.

D. PEDRO. Look, here she comes.

BENE. Will your grace command me any service to the world's end? I will go on the slightest errand now to the Antipodes, that you can devise to send me on; I will fetch you a tooth-picker now from the furthest inch of Asia; bring you the length of Prester John's foot; fetch you a hair off the great Cham's beard; do you any embassage to the Pigmies, rather than hold three words' conference with this harpy: You have no employment for me?

D. PEDRO. None, but to desire your good company.

BENE. O God, sir, here's a dish I love not; I cannot endure my† lady Tongue. [*Exit.*

D. PEDRO. Come, lady, come; you have lost the heart of signior Benedick.

BEAT. Indeed, my lord, he lent it me a while; and I gave him use[d] for it, a double heart for his‡ single one: marry, once before, he won it of me with false dice, therefore your grace may well say, I have lost it.

D. PEDRO. You have put him down, lady; you have put him down.

(*) First folio omits, *I*. (†) First folio omits, *good*. (‡) First folio omits, *up*.

[a] *It is the base*, though *bitter disposition*—] So both quarto and folio, but not very intelligibly. Some editors adopt the suggestion of Johnson, and read:—"the base, *the* bitter," &c.

[b] *Such* impossible conveyance—] Such *incredible dexterity*. *Conveyance* was a professional term for *legerdemain* in the poet's time. See also note (c), p. 705.

[c] *While she is here, a man may live* as quiet in hell, as in a sanctuary, &c.] This passage is very ambiguous. The obscurity may have arisen from the author having first written "*in hell,*" and afterwards substituted "*in a sanctuary,*" without cancelling the former, so that, as in many other cases, both got into the text. Or the compositor may have inserted the second *as*, instead of *or*, in which case we should read,—"While she is here, a man may live as quiet in hell, *or* in a sanctuary, (and people sin, &c.)"

[d] *Use*—] That is, *interest*.

(*) First folio omits, *her*. (†) First folio, *this*. (‡) First folio, *a*.

BEAT. So I would not he should do me, my lord, lest I should prove the mother of fools. I have brought count Claudio, whom you sent me to seek.

D. PEDRO. Why, how now, count? wherefore are you sad?

CLAUD. Not sad, my lord.

D. PEDRO. How then? sick?

CLAUD. Neither, my lord.

BEAT. The count is neither sad, nor sick, nor merry, nor well: but civil[a] count; civil as an orange, and something of that* jealous complexion.

D. PEDRO. I' faith, lady, I think your blazon to be true; though, I'll be sworn, if he be so, his conceit is false. Here, Claudio, I have wooed in thy name, and fair Hero is won; I have broke with her father, and his good will obtained: name the day of marriage, and God give thee joy!

LEON. Count, take of me my daughter, and with her my fortunes: his grace hath made the match, and all grace say *Amen* to it!

BEAT. Speak, count, 't is your cue.

CLAUD. Silence is the perfectest herald of joy: I were but little happy, if I could say how much.—Lady, as you are mine, I am yours: I give away myself for you, and dote upon the exchange.

BEAT. Speak, cousin: or, if you cannot, stop his mouth with a kiss, and let not him speak, neither.

D. PEDRO. In faith, lady, you have a merry heart.

BEAT. Yea, my lord; I thank it, poor fool, it keeps on the windy side of care.—My cousin tells him in his ear, that he is in her† heart.

CLAUD. And so she doth, cousin.

BEAT. Good Lord, for alliance![b]—Thus goes every one to the world[c] but I, and I am sun-burned;[d] I may sit in a corner, and cry, *heigh-ho for a husband!*

D. PEDRO. Lady Beatrice, I will get you one.

BEAT. I would rather have one of your father's getting: hath your grace ne'er a brother like you? Your father got excellent husbands, if a maid could come by them.

D. PEDRO. Will you have me, lady?

BEAT. No, my lord, unless I might have another for working-days; your grace is too costly to wear every day:—But, I beseech your grace, pardon me; I was born to speak all mirth, and no matter.

D. PEDRO. Your silence most offends me, and to be merry best becomes you; for, out of question, you were born in a merry hour.

BEAT. No, sure, my lord, my mother cried; but then there was a star danced, and under that was I born.—Cousins, God give you joy!

LEON. Niece, will you look to those things I told you of?

BEAT. I cry you mercy, 'uncle.—By your grace's pardon. [*Exit* BEATRICE.

D. PEDRO. By my troth, a pleasant-spirited lady.

LEON. There's little of the melancholy element in her, my lord: she is never sad, but when she sleeps; and not ever sad then; for I have heard my daughter say, she hath often dreamed of unhappiness, and waked herself with laughing.

D. PEDRO. She cannot endure to hear tell of a husband.

LEON. O, by no means; she mocks all her wooers out of suit.

D. PEDRO. She were an excellent wife for Benedick.

LEON. O Lord, my lord, if they were but a week married, they would talk themselves mad.

D. PEDRO. Count Claudio, when mean you to go to church?

CLAUD. To-morrow, my lord. Time goes on crutches, till love have all his rites.

LEON. Not till Monday, my dear son, which is hence a just seven-night; and a time too brief too, to have all things answer my* mind.

D. PEDRO. Come, you shake the head at so long a breathing; but, I warrant thee, Claudio, the time shall not go dully by us; I will, in the interim, undertake one of Hercules' labours; which is, to bring signior Benedick and the lady Beatrice into a mountain of affection, the one with the other. I would fain have it a match; and I doubt not but to fashion it, if you three will but minister such assistance as I shall give you direction.

(*) First folio, *a*. (†) First folio, *my*.

(*) First folio omits, *my*.

[a] *But* civil *count;* civil as an orange,—] That is, we believe, *sour, bitter* as an orange; and if this colloquial sense of the word *civil*, originating probably in a conceit upon *Seville*, really obtained, it is doubtful whether in instances where *civil* has been treated as a misprint of *cruel*, it was not the true word. For example, in the first edition of "Gorboduc," 1565; we have the line:—

"Brings them to *civill* and reproachful death:"

which was subsequently altered to,—

"*Cruel* and reproachful death."

And in "Romeo and Juliet," some of the early editions make Gregory say:—"—— when I have fought with the men, I will be *civill* with the maids, I will cut off their heads;" while others read, "*cruel* with the maids."

[b] Good Lord, for alliance!] This was an exclamation equivalent to "Heaven send me a husband!"

[c] *Thus* goes every one to the world *but I,*—] To *go to the world*, was a popular expression for *going to be married*. Thus in "All's Well that Ends Well," Act I. Sc. 3:—

——"if I may have your ladyship's good-will *to go to the world*, Isbel the woman and I will do as we may."

[d] *And I am* sun-burned.] That is, *homely, ill-favoured:* in this sense the word occurs in "Troilus and Cressida," Act I. Sc. 3:—

"The Grecian dames are *sun-burn'd*, and not worth
The splinter of a lance."

Leon. My lord, I am for you, though it cost me ten nights' watchings.

Claud. And I, my lord.

D. Pedro. And you too, gentle Hero?

Hero. I will do any modest office, my lord, to help my cousin to a good husband.

D. Pedro. And Benedick is not the unhopefullest husband that I know: thus far can I praise him; he is of a noble strain, of approved valour, and confirmed honesty. I will teach you how to humour your cousin, that she shall fall in love with Benedick:—and I, with your two helps, will so practise on Benedick, that, in despite of his quick wit and his queasy[a] stomach, he shall fall in love with Beatrice. If we can do this, Cupid is no longer an archer; his glory shall be ours, for we are the only love-gods. Go in with me, and I will tell you my drift. [*Exeunt.*

---

[a] Queasy *stomach*,—] That is, *fastidious, squeamish.*

SCENE II.—*Another Room in* Leonato's *House.*

Enter Don John *and* Borachio.

D. John. It is so; the count Claudio shall marry the daughter of Leonato.

Bora. Yea, my lord; but I can cross it.

D. John. Any bar, any cross, any impediment will be medicinable to me; I am sick in displeasure to him; and whatsoever comes athwart his affection, ranges evenly with mine. How canst thou cross this marriage?

Bora. Not honestly, my lord; but so covertly that no dishonesty shall appear in me.

D. John. Show me briefly how.

Bora. I think, I told your lordship, a year since, how much I am in the favour of Margaret, the waiting-gentlewoman to Hero.

D. John. I remember.

Bora. I can, at any unseasonable instant of

the night, appoint her to look out at her lady's chamber-window.

D. JOHN. What life is in that, to be the death of this marriage?

BORA. The poison of that lies in you to temper. Go you to the prince your brother; spare not to tell him, that he hath wronged his honour in marrying the renowned Claudio (whose estimation do you mightily hold up) to a contaminated stale, such a one as Hero.

D. JOHN. What proof shall I make of that?

BORA. Proof enough to misuse the prince, to vex Claudio, to undo Hero, and kill Leonato? Look you for any other issue?

D. JOHN. Only to despite them, I will endeavour anything.

BORA. Go then, find me a meet hour to draw don* Pedro and the count Claudio, alone: tell them that you know that Hero loves me; intend a kind of zeal both to the prince and Claudio, as —in† love of your brother's honour who hath made this match; and his friend's reputation, who is thus like to be cozened with the semblance of a maid,—that you have discovered thus. They will scarcely believe this without trial: offer them instances, which shall bear no less likelihood, than to see me at her chamber-window; hear me call Margaret, Hero; hear Margaret term me Claudio,[a] and bring them to see this, the very night before the intended wedding; for, in the mean time, I will so fashion the matter, that Hero shall be absent; and there shall appear such seeming truth‡ of Hero's disloyalty, that jealousy shall be called assurance, and all the preparation overthrown.

D. JOHN. Grow this to what adverse issue it can, I will put it in practice. Be cunning in the working this, and thy fee is a thousand ducats.

BORA. Be thou constant in the accusation, and my cunning shall not shame me.

D. JOHN. I will presently go learn their day of marriage. [*Exeunt.*

SCENE III.—Leonato's *Garden.*

Enter BENEDICK *and a* BOY *following.*

BENE. Boy!—

BOY. Signior.

BENE. In my chamber-window lies a book; bring it hither to me in the orchard.

BOY. I am here already, sir.

BENE. I know that;—but I would have thee hence, and here again. [*Exit* Boy.]—I do much wonder, that one man, seeing how much another man is a fool when he dedicates his behaviours to love, will, after he hath laughed at such shallow follies in others, become the argument of his own scorn, by falling in love: and such a man is Claudio. I have known, when there was no music with him but the drum and the fife; and now had he rather hear the tabor and the pipe: I have known, when he would have walked ten mile afoot, to see a good armour; and now will he lie ten nights awake, carving the fashion of a new doublet. He was wont to speak plain, and to the purpose, like an honest man, and a soldier; and now is he turned orthography;[b] his words are a very fantastical banquet, just so many strange dishes. May I be so converted, and see with these eyes? I cannot tell; I think not: I will not be sworn, but love may transform me to an oyster; but I'll take my oath on it, till he have made an oyster of me, he shall never make me such a fool. One woman is fair, yet I am well: another is wise, yet I am well: another virtuous, yet I am well: but till all graces be in one woman, one woman shall not come in my grace. Rich she shall be, that's certain; wise, or I'll none; virtuous, or I'll never cheapen her; fair, or I'll never look on her; mild, or come not near me; noble, or not I* for an angel; of good discourse, an excellent musician, and her hair shall be of what colour it please God.(3) Ha! the prince and monsieur Love! I will hide me in the arbour. [*Withdraws.*

Enter DON PEDRO, LEONATO, CLAUDIO, *and* BALTHAZAR.[c]

D. PEDRO. Come, shall we hear this music?

CLAUD. Yea, my good lord:—How still the evening is,
As hush'd on purpose to grace harmony!

D. PEDRO. See you where Benedick hath hid himself?

CLAUD. O, very well, my lord: the music ended,
We'll fit the kid-fox with a penny-worth.

D. PEDRO. Come, Balthazar, we'll hear that song again.

(*) First folio, *on*. (†) First folio inserts, *a*. (‡) First folio, *truths*.

[a] *Hear Margaret term me* Claudio,—] Theobald suggested that, as Claudio was to be a spectator of the scene, we ought to read *Borachio*.

[b] *And now is he turned* orthography;] So the old copies: and, if as we believe, correctly, the change of "*sonnet*," to "*sonnets*," or "*sonneteer*,"—in "Love's Labour's Lost," Act I. Sc. 2, "Assist me some extemporal god of rhyme, for I am sure I *shall turn sonnet*,"—was uncalled for and injurious. The modern editors read "orthographer."

(*) First folio omits, *I*.

[c] Enter Don Pedro, &c.] The stage-direction in the quarto is, "Enter Prince, Leonato, Claudio, musicke." Instead of "musicke," the folio has, "*and Jacke Wilson*." (4)

BALTH. O good my lord, tax not so bad a voice,
To slander music any more than once.[a]

D. PEDRO. It is the witness still of excellency,
To put a strange face on his own perfection :—
I pray thee, sing, and let me woo no more.

BALTH. Because you talk of wooing, I will sing ;
Since many a wooer doth commence his suit
To her he thinks not worthy ; yet he woos ;
Yet will he swear, he loves.

D. PEDRO. Nay, pray thee, come :
Or, if thou wilt hold longer argument,
Do it in notes.

BALTH. Note this before my notes,
There's not a note of mine that's worth the noting.

D. PEDRO. Why, these are very crotchets that he speaks,
Note, notes, forsooth, and *nothing !* [*Music.*

BENE. [*Aside.*] Now, *Divine air !* now is his soul ravished !—Is it not strange, that sheep's guts should hale souls out of men's bodies !—Well, a horn for my money, when all's done.

THE SONG.

I.

BALTH. *Sigh no more, ladies, sigh no more,*
Men were deceivers ever ;
One foot in sea, and one on shore,
To one thing constant never :
Then sigh not so,
But let them go,
And be you blithe and bonny ;
Converting all your sounds of woe
Into, Hey nonny, nonny.

II.

Sing no more ditties, sing no mo,
Of dumps so dull and heavy ;
*The fraud of men was * ever so,*
Since summer first was leafy.
Then sigh not so, &c.

D. PEDRO. By my troth, a good song !

BALTH. And an ill singer, my lord.

D. PEDRO. Ha ! no, no, 'faith ; thou singest well enough for a shift.

BENE. [*Aside.*] An he had been a dog that should have howled thus,[b] they would have hanged him : and, I pray God, his bad voice bode no mischief. I had as lief have heard the night-raven, come what plague could have come after it.

D. PEDRO. Yea, marry ; [*To* CLAUDIO.]—Dost thou hear, Balthazar ? I pray thee, get us some excellent music ; for to-morrow night we would have it at the lady Hero's chamber-window.

BALTH. The best I can, my lord.

D. PEDRO. Do so : farewell. [*Exit* BALTHAZAR.] Come hither, Leonato. What was it you told me of to-day ? that your niece Beatrice was in love with signior Benedick ?

CLAUD. [*Aside to* PEDRO.] O, ay :—Stalk on, stalk on ; the fowl sits.(5) [*Aloud.*] I did never think that lady would have loved any man.

LEON. No, nor I neither ; but most wonderful that she should so dote on signior Benedick, whom she hath in all outward behaviours seemed ever to abhor.

BENE. [*Aside.*] Is't possible ? Sits the wind in that corner ?

LEON. By my troth, my lord, I cannot tell what to think of it ; but that she loves him with an enraged affection,—it is past the infinite of thought.

D. PEDRO. May be, she doth but counterfeit.

CLAUD. 'Faith, like enough.

LEON. O God ! *counterfeit !* There was never counterfeit of passion came so near the life of passion, as she discovers it.

D. PEDRO. Why, what effects of passion shows she ?

CLAUD. [*Aside.*] Bait the hook well ; this fish will bite.

LEON. What effects, my lord ! She will sit you,—you heard my daughter tell you how.

CLAUD. She did, indeed.

D. PEDRO. How, how, I pray you ? you amaze me : I would have thought her spirit had been invincible against all assaults of affection.

LEON. I would have sworn it had, my lord ; especially against Benedick.

BENE. [*Aside.*] I should think this a gull, but that the white-bearded fellow speaks it : knavery cannot sure hide himself in such reverence.

CLAUD. [*Aside.*] He hath ta'en the infection ; hold it up.

D. PEDRO. Hath she made her affection known to Benedick ?

LEON. No ; and swears she never will : that's her torment.

CLAUD. 'T is true, indeed ; so your daughter says. *Shall I,* says she, *that have so oft encountered him with scorn, write to him that I love him ?*

LEON. This says she now, when she is beginning to write to him : for she'll be up twenty times a night, and there will she sit in her smock, till she have writ a sheet of paper :—my daughter tells us all.

CLAUD. Now you talk of a sheet of paper, I remember a pretty jest your daughter told us of.

LEON. O !—when she had writ it, and was

(*) First folio, *were.*

[a] To slander music any more than once.] This and the following line are printed twice in the folio, 1623.

[b] An he had been a dog that should have howled thus, &c.] The howling of a dog was supposed to be a sound of luckless omen.

reading it over, she found Benedick and Beatrice between the sheet?—

Claud. That.

Leon. O! she tore the letter into a thousand half-pence; railed at herself, that she should be so immodest to write to one that she knew would flout her: *I measure him*, says she, *by my own spirit; for I should flout him, if he writ to me; yea, though I love him, I should.*

Claud. Then down upon her knees she falls, weeps, sobs, beats her heart, tears her hair, prays, curses;—*O sweet Benedick! God give me patience!*

Leon. She doth indeed; my daughter says so: and the ecstacy hath so much overborne her, that my daughter is sometime afeard she will do a desperate outrage to herself; it is very true.

D. Pedro. It were good that Benedick knew of it by some other, if she will not discover it.

Claud. To what end? He would but make a sport of it, and torment the poor lady worse.

D. Pedro. An he should, it were an alms to hang him: she's an excellent sweet lady; and, out of all suspicion, she is virtuous.

Claud. And she is exceeding wise.

D. Pedro. In everything, but in loving Benedick.

Leon. O my lord, wisdom and blood combating in so tender a body, we have ten proofs to one, that blood hath the victory. I am sorry for her, as I have just cause, being her uncle and her guardian.

D. PEDRO. I would she had bestowed this dotage on me; I would have daffed all other respects, and made her half myself: I pray you, tell Benedick of it, and hear what he will say.

LEON. Were it good, think you?

CLAUD. Hero thinks surely, she will die: for she says, she will die if he love her not; and she will die ere she make her love known; and she will die if he woo her, rather than she will 'bate one breath of her accustomed crossness.

D. PEDRO. She doth well; if she should make tender of her love, 'tis very possible he'll scorn it; for the man, as you know all, hath a contemptible[a] spirit.

CLAUD. He is a very proper man.

D. PEDRO. He hath, indeed, a good outward happiness.

CLAUD. 'Fore God, and in my mind, very wise.

D. PEDRO. He doth, indeed, show some sparks that are like wit.[b]

LEON. And I take him to be valiant.

D. PEDRO. As Hector, I assure you; and in the managing of quarrels you may say* he is wise; for either he avoids them with great discretion, or undertakes them with a most† Christian-like fear.

LEON. If he do fear God, he must necessarily keep peace; if he break the peace, he ought to enter into a quarrel with fear and trembling.

D. PEDRO. And so will he do; for the man doth fear God, howsoever it seems not in him, by some large jests he will make. Well, I am sorry for your niece: shall we go seek* Benedick, and tell him of her love?

CLAUD. Never tell him, my lord; let her wear it out with good counsel.

LEON. Nay, that's impossible; she may wear her heart out first.

D. PEDRO. Well, we will hear further of it by your daughter: let it cool the while. I love Benedick well; and I could wish he would modestly examine himself, to see how much he is unworthy‡ so good a lady.

LEON. My lord, will you walk? dinner is ready.

CLAUD. [*Aside.*] If he do not dote on her upon this, I will never trust my expectation.

D. PEDRO. [*Aside.*] Let there be the same net spread for her; and that must your daughter and her gentlewoman carry. The sport will be, when they hold one an opinion of another's dotage, and no such matter; that's the scene that I would see, which will be merely[c] a dumb show. Let us send her to call him in to dinner.

[*Exeunt* DON PEDRO, CLAUDIO, *and* LEONATO.

BENE. [*Advancing.*] This can be no trick. The conference was sadly borne.[d]—They have the truth of this from Hero. They seem to pity the lady; it seems, her affections have their* full bent. Love me! why, it must be requited. I hear how I am censured: they say, I will bear myself proudly, if I perceive the love come from her; they say too, that she will rather die than give any sign of affection.—I did never think to marry:—I must not seem proud:—happy are they that hear their detractions, and can put them to mending. They say the lady is fair; 'tis a truth, I can bear them witness: and virtuous;—'tis so, I cannot reprove it; and wise,—but for loving me.—By my troth, it is no addition to her wit;—nor no great argument of her folly, for I will be horribly in love with her.—I may chance have some odd quirks and remnants of wit broken on me, because I have railed so long against marriage;—but doth not the appetite alter? A man loves the meat in his youth, that he cannot endure in his age: shall quips, and sentences, and these paper bullets of the brain, awe a man from the career of his humour? No; the world must be peopled. When I said, I would die a bachelor, I did not think I should live till I were married.—Here comes Beatrice. By this day, she's a fair lady: I do spy some marks of love in her.

Enter BEATRICE.

BEAT. Against my will, I am sent to bid you come in to dinner.

BENE. Fair Beatrice, I thank you for your pains.

BEAT. I took no more pains for those thanks, than you take pains to thank me; if it had been painful, I would not have come.

BENE. You take pleasure, then, in the message?

BEAT. Yea, just so much as you may take upon a knife's point, and choke a daw withal.—You have no stomach, signior; fare you well. [*Exit.*

BENE. Ha! *Against my will I am sent to bid you come in to dinner*—there's a double meaning in that. *I took no more pains for those thanks than you took pains to thank me*—that's as much as to say, Any pains that I take for you is as easy as thanks.—If I do not take pity of her, I am a villain; if I do not love her, I am a Jew: I will go get her picture. [*Exit.*

(*) First folio, *see*. (†) First folio omits, *most*. (‡) First folio inserts, *to have*.

(*) First folio, *the*.

a A contemptible *spirit.*] A *mocking, contemptuous* spirit.

b *That are like* wit.] *Wisdom* and *wit*, it must be remembered, were synonymous.

c Merely *a dumb show.*] *Entirely* a dumb show.

d Sadly borne.] Seriously carried on.

ACT III.

SCENE I.—Leonato's *Garden.*

Enter HERO, MARGARET, *and* URSULA.

HERO. Good Margaret, run thee to the parlour;
There shalt thou find my cousin Beatrice
Proposing[a] with the Prince and Claudio;
Whisper her ear, and tell her, I and Ursula
Walk in the orchard, and our whole discourse
Is all of her; say, that thou overheard'st us;
And bid her steal into the pleached bower,
Where honeysuckles, ripen'd by the sun,
Forbid the sun to enter;—like favourites,
Made proud by princes, that advance their pride
Against that power that bred it:—there will she hide her,
To listen our propose;* this is thy office,
Bear thee well in it, and leave us alone.

MARG. I'll make her come, I warrant you, presently. [*Exit.*

HERO. Now, Ursula, when Beatrice doth come,
As we do trace this alley up and down,
Our talk must only be of Benedick:
When I do name him, let it be thy part
To praise him more than ever man did merit.
My talk to thee must be, how Benedick

a Proposing *with the Prince and Claudio;*] That is, *discoursing*, from the French *propos.*

(*) First folio, *purpose.*

Is sick in love with Beatrice: of this matter
Is little Cupid's crafty arrow made,
That only wounds by hearsay. Now begin;

Enter BEATRICE, *behind.*

For look where Beatrice, like a lapwing, runs
Close by the ground, to hear our conference.
URS. The pleasant'st angling is to see the fish
Cut with her golden oars the silver stream,
And greedily devour the treacherous bait:
So angle we for Beatrice; who even now
Is couched in the woodbine coverture:
Fear you not my part of the dialogue.
HERO. Then go we near her, that her ear lose nothing
Of the false sweet bait that we lay for it.—
No, truly, Ursula, she is too disdainful;
I know, her spirits are as coy and wild
As haggards[a] of the rock.
URS. But are you sure,
That Benedick loves Beatrice so entirely?
HERO. So says the prince, and my new-trothed lord.
URS. And did they bid you tell her of it, madam?
HERO. They did entreat me to acquaint her of it;
But I persuaded them, if they lov'd Benedick,
To wish him wrestle with affection,
And never to let Beatrice know of it.
URS. Why did you so? doth not the gentleman
Deserve as full as fortunate a bed,[b]
As ever Beatrice shall couch upon?
HERO. O God of love! I know he doth deserve
As much as may be yielded to a man:
But nature never fram'd a woman's heart
Of prouder stuff than that of Beatrice;
Disdain and scorn ride sparkling in her eyes,
Misprising what they look on; and her wit
Values itself so highly, that to her
All matter else seems weak: she cannot love,
Nor take no shape nor project of affection,
She is so self-endeared.
URS. Sure, I think so;
And therefore, certainly, it were not good
She knew his love, lest she make sport at it.
HERO. Why, you speak truth: I never yet saw man,
How wise, how noble, young, how rarely featur'd,
But she would spell him backward:[c] if fair-faced,
She'd swear, the gentleman should be her sister;
If black, why, nature, drawing of an antic,
Made a foul blot; if tall, a lance ill-headed;
If low, an agate[d] very vilely cut;
If speaking, why, a vane blown with all winds;
If silent, why, a block moved with none.
So turns she every man the wrong side out,
And never gives to truth and virtue that,
Which simpleness and merit purchaseth.
URS. Sure, sure, such carping is not commendable.
HERO. No: not[e] to be so odd, and from all fashions,
As Beatrice is, cannot be commendable:
But who dare tell her so? If I should speak,
She would mock me into air; O, she would laugh me
Out of myself, press me to death with wit.
Therefore let Benedick, like cover'd fire,
Consume away in sighs, waste inwardly;
It were a better death than * die with mocks,
Which is as bad as die with tickling.
URS. Yet tell her of it; hear what she will say.
HERO. No; rather I will go to Benedick,
And counsel him to fight against his passion:
And, truly, I'll devise some honest slanders
To stain my cousin with: one doth not know
How much an ill word may empoison liking.
URS. O, do not do your cousin such a wrong.
She cannot be so much without true judgment,
(Having so swift[f] and excellent a wit,
As she is priz'd to have,) as to refuse
So rare a gentleman as signior Benedick.
HERO. He is the only man of Italy,
Always excepted my dear Claudio.
URS. I pray you, be not angry with me, madam,
Speaking my fancy; signior Benedick,
For shape, for bearing, argument, and valour,
Goes foremost in report through Italy.
HERO. Indeed, he hath an excellent good name.
URS. His excellence did earn it, ere he had it.—
When are you married, madam?
HERO. Why, every day[g] to-morrow: come, go in;
I'll show thee some attires, and have thy counsel,
Which is the best to furnish me to-morrow.

---

[a] As haggards of the rock.] The haggard-hawk was of a nature peculiarly unsocial, and difficult to tame; Latham, in his Falconry, 1663, says of her,—"Such is the greatnesse of her spirit, *she will* not *admit of any societie*, untill such time as nature worketh in her an inclination to put that in practice which all hawkes are subject unto at the spring time."

[b] As full as fortunate a bed,—] That is, as full fortunate a bed.

[c] Spell him backward:] Turn his good gifts to defects. So, in Lyly's "Anatomy of Wit," 1581, p. 44, (b),—"if he be cleanly, they term him proud: if meene [moderate] in apparel, a sloven; if tall, a lungis: if short, a dwarf: if bold, blunt: if shamefast, [modest] a coward," &c.

[d] *An* agate—] See note (c), p. 575.

(*) First folio, *to*.

[e] Not *to be so odd*,—] The word *not* here is redundant, and reverses the sense.

[f] *So* swift *and excellent a wit*,—] *Swift* means *ready, quick*. Thus in "As you Like It," Act V. Sc. 4, the Duke says of Touchstone—

"he is very *swift* and sententious."

[g] *Why*, every day to-morrow:] Hero plays on the form of Ursula's interrogatory, "*When are you married?*"

"I am a married woman every day, after to-morrow."

URS. [*Aside.*] She's lim'd,[*] I warrant you; we have caught her, madam.

HERO. [*Aside.*] If it prove so, then loving goes by haps:
Some, Cupid kills with arrows, some, with traps.
[*Exeunt* HERO *and* URSULA.

BEAT. [*advancing.*] What fire is in mine ears? can this be true?
Stand I condemn'd for pride and scorn so much?
Contempt, farewell! and maiden pride, adieu!
No glory lives behind the back of such.[a]
And, Benedick, love on, I will requite thee;
Taming my wild heart to thy loving hand;
If thou dost love, my kindness shall incite thee
To bind our loves up in a holy band:
For others say, thou dost deserve; and I
Believe it better than reportingly. [*Exit.*

SCENE II.—*A Room in* LEONATO'*s House.*

Enter DON PEDRO, CLAUDIO, BENEDICK, *and* LEONATO.

D. PEDRO. I do but stay till your marriage be consummate, and then go I toward Arragon.

CLAUD. I'll bring you thither, my lord, if you'll vouchsafe me.

D. PEDRO. Nay, that would be as great a soil in the new gloss of your marriage, as to show a child his new coat, and forbid him to wear it. I will only be bold with Benedick for his company; for, from the crown of his head to the sole of his foot, he is all mirth; he hath twice or thrice cut Cupid's bowstring, and the little hangman[b] dare not shoot at him: he hath a heart as sound as a

---

(*) First folio, *ta'en.*

a No glory lives behind the back of such.] The proud and contemptuous are never extolled in their absence,—a sense so obvious, and so pertinent, considering the part of listener Beatrice has just been playing, that it is with more than surprise we find Mr. Collier's MS. annotator substituting:—

"No glory lives *but in the lack* of such."

b Hangman—] That is, *rogue, rascal.*

bell, and his tongue is the clapper; for what his heart thinks, his tongue speaks.

BENE. Gallants, I am not as I have been.

LEON. So say I; methinks, you are sadder.

CLAUD. I hope, he be in love.

D. PEDRO. Hang him, truant; there's no true drop of blood in him, to be truly touched with love: if he be sad, he wants money.

BENE. I have the tooth-ache.

D. PEDRO. Draw it.

BENE. Hang it!

CLAUD. You must hang it first, and draw it afterwards.

D. PEDRO. What! sigh for the tooth-ache?

LEON. Where is but a humour or a worm?

BENE. Well, every one can * master a grief, but he that has it.

CLAUD. Yet say I, he is in love.

D. PEDRO. There is no appearance of fancy in him, unless it be a fancy that he hath to strange disguises; as, to be a Dutchman to-day; a Frenchman to-morrow; or in the shape of two countries at once, as, a German from the waist downward, all slops; and a Spaniard from the hip upward, no doublet.[a] Unless he have a fancy to this foolery, as it appears he hath, he is no fool for fancy, as you would have it † appear he is.

CLAUD. If he be not in love with some woman, there is no believing old signs: he brushes his hat o' mornings; what should that bode?

D. PEDRO. Hath any man seen him at the barber's?

CLAUD. No, but the barber's man hath been seen with him; and the old ornament of his cheek hath already stuffed tennis balls.

LEON. Indeed, he looks younger than he did, by the loss of a beard.

D. PEDRO. Nay, he rubs himself with civet: can you smell him out by that?

CLAUD. That's as much as to say, The sweet youth's in love.

D. PEDRO. The greatest note of it is his melancholy.

CLAUD. And when was he wont to wash his face?

D. PEDRO. Yea, or to paint himself? for the which, I hear what they say of him.

CLAUD. Nay, but his jesting spirit, which is now crept into a lute-string, and now governed by stops.

D. PEDRO. Indeed, that tells a heavy tale for him: conclude, conclude, ‡ he is in love.

CLAUD. Nay, but I know who loves him.

D. PEDRO. That would I know too; I warrant, one that knows him not.

CLAUD. Yes, and his ill conditions; and, in despite of all, dies for him.

D. PEDRO. She shall be buried with her face upwards.

BENE. Yet is this no charm for the tooth-ache.(1)—Old Signior, walk aside with me: I have studied eight or nine wise words to speak to you, which these hobby-horses must not hear.

[*Exeunt* BENEDICK *and* LEONATO.

D. PEDRO. For my life! to break with him about Beatrice.

CLAUD. 'Tis even so: Hero and Margaret have by this played their parts with Beatrice; and then the two bears will not bite one another, when they meet.

Enter DON JOHN.

D. JOHN. My lord and brother, God save you.

D. PEDRO. Good den, brother.

D. JOHN. If your leisure served, I would speak with you.

D. PEDRO. In private?

D. JOHN. If it please you;—yet count Claudio may hear; for what I would speak of, concerns him.

D. PEDRO. What's the matter?

D. JOHN. [*To* CLAUDIO.] Means your lordship to be married to-morrow?

D. PEDRO. You know, he does.

D. JOHN. I know not that, when he knows what I know.

CLAUD. If there be any impediment, I pray you discover it.

D. JOHN. You may think, I love you not; let that appear hereafter, and aim better at me by that I now will manifest: for my brother, I think, he holds you well; and in dearness of heart hath holp to effect your ensuing marriage: surely, suit ill spent, and labour ill bestowed!

D. PEDRO. Why, what's the matter?

D. JOHN. I came hither to tell you; and, circumstances shortened, (for she hath been too long a talking of,) the lady is disloyal.

CLAUD. Who? Hero?

D. JOHN. Even she; Leonato's Hero, your Hero, every man's Hero.

CLAUD. *Disloyal!*

D. JOHN. The word is too good to paint out her wickedness; I could say, she were worse; think you of a worse title, and I will fit her to it. Wonder not till further warrant: go but with me to-night, you shall see her chamber-window entered, even the night before her wedding-day: if you love her then, to-morrow wed her; but it would better fit your honour to change your mind.

(*) Old copies, *cannot*. (†) First folio inserts, *to*. (‡) First folio, *conclude*, once only.

a Or in the shape of two countries at once, &c.] This passage, down to *no doublet*, inclusively, is omitted in the folio.

CLAUD. May this be so?

D. PEDRO. I will not think it.

D. JOHN. If you dare not trust that you see, confess not that you know: if you will follow me, I will show you enough; and when you have seen more, and heard more, proceed accordingly.

CLAUD. If I see anything to-night why I should not marry her to-morrow; in the congregation, where I should wed, there will I shame her.

D. PEDRO. And, as I wooed for thee to obtain her, I will join with thee to disgrace her.

D. JOHN. I will disparage her no farther, till you are my witnesses: bear it coldly but till night, and let the issue show itself.

D. PEDRO. O day untowardly turned!

CLAUD. O mischief strangely thwarting!

D. JOHN. O plague right well prevented! So will you say, when you have seen the sequel.

[*Exeunt.*

SCENE III.—*A Street.*

Enter DOGBERRY *and* VERGES, *with the* Watch.[a]

DOGB. Are you good men and true?

VERG. Yea, or else it were pity but they should suffer salvation, body and soul.

DOGB. Nay, that were a punishment too good for them, if they should have any allegiance in them, being chosen for the prince's watch.

VERG. Well, give them their charge, neighbour Dogberry.

DOGB. First, who think you the most desartless man to be constable?

1 WATCH. Hugh Oatcake, sir, or George Seacoal; for they can write and read.

DOGB. Come hither, neighbour Seacoal. God hath blessed you with a good name: to be a well-favoured man is the gift of fortune, but to write and read comes by nature.

2 WATCH. Both which, master constable,—

DOGB. You have; I knew it would be your answer. Well, for your favour, sir, why, give God thanks, and make no boast of it; and for your writing and reading, let that appear when there is no need of such vanity. You are thought here to be the most senseless and fit man for the constable of the watch; therefore bear you the lantern. This is your charge; you shall comprehend all vagrom men: you are to bid any man stand, in the prince's name.

2 WATCH. How if 'a will not stand?

DOGB. Why then, take no note of him, but let him go; and presently call the rest of the watch together, and thank God you are rid of a knave.

VERG. If he will not stand when he is bidden, he is none of the prince's subjects.

DOGB. True, and they are to meddle with none but the prince's subjects. You shall also make no noise in the streets; for, for the watch to babble and talk, is most tolerable and not to be endured.

2 WATCH. We will rather sleep than talk; we know what belongs to a watch.

DOGB. Why, you speak like an ancient and most quiet watchman;(2) for I cannot see how sleeping should offend: only, have a care that your bills be not stolen. Well, you are to call at all the ale-houses, and bid those* that are drunk get them to bed.

2 WATCH. How if they will not?

DOGB. Why then, let them alone till they are sober: if they make you not then the better answer, you may say, they are not the men you took them for.

2 WATCH. Well, sir.

DOGB. If you meet a thief, you may suspect him, by virtue of your office, to be no true man; and, for such kind of men, the less you meddle or make with them, why, the more is for your honesty.

2 WATCH. If we know him to be a thief, shall we not lay hands on him?

DOGB. Truly, by your office you may; but, I think, they that touch pitch will be defiled: the most peaceable way for you, if you do take a thief, is, to let him show himself what he is, and steal out of your company.

VERG. You have been always called a merciful man, partner.

DOGB. Truly, I would not hang a dog by my will; much more a man who hath any honesty in him.

VERG. If you hear a child cry in the night, you must call to the nurse, and bid her still it.

2 WATCH. How if the nurse be asleep, and will not hear us?

DOGB. Why then, depart in peace, and let the child wake her with crying: for the ewe that will not hear her lamb when it baes, will never answer a calf when he bleats.

VERG. 'Tis very true.

DOGB. This is the end of the charge. You, constable, are to present the prince's own person; if you meet the prince in the night, you may stay him.

VERG. Nay, by'r lady, that, I think, 'a cannot.

---

a Enter Dogberry and Verges.] In the original, "Enter Dogbery *and his compartner.*"

(*) First folio, *them.*

DOGB. Five shillings to one on't, with any man that knows the statues, he may stay him: marry, not without the prince be willing; for, indeed, the watch ought to offend no man, and it is an offence to stay a man against his will.

VERG. By'r lady, I think, it be so.

DOGB. Ha, ha, ha! Well, masters, good night: an there be any matter of weight chances, call up me: keep your fellows' counsels and your own, and good night.—Come, neighbour.

2 WATCH. Well, masters, we hear our charge: let us go sit here upon the church-bench till two, and then all to bed.

DOGB. One word more, honest neighbours: I

pray you, watch about signior Leonato's door; for the wedding being there to-morrow, there is a great coil to-night. Adieu, be vigitant, I beseech you. [*Exeunt* DOGBERRY *and* VERGES.

Enter BORACHIO *and* CONRADE.

BORA. What, Conrade!

1 WATCH. [*Aside.*] Peace, stir not.

BORA. Conrade, I say!

CON. Here, man, I am at thy elbow.

BORA. Mass, and my elbow itched; I thought, there would a scab follow.

CON. I will owe thee an answer for that; and now forward with thy tale.

BORA. Stand thee close then under this pent-house, for it drizzles rain; and I will, like a true drunkard, utter all to thee.

1 WATCH. [*Aside.*] Some treason, masters; yet stand close.

BORA. Therefore know, I have earned of don John a thousand ducats.

CON. Is it possible that any villainy should be so dear?

BORA. Thou should'st rather ask, if it were possible any villainy should be so rich; for when rich villains have need of poor ones, poor ones may make what price they will.

CON. I wonder at it.

BORA. That shows, thou art unconfirmed: thou knowest, that the fashion of a doublet, or a hat, or a cloak, is nothing to a man.

CON. Yes, it is apparel.

BORA. I mean, the fashion.

CON. Yes, the fashion is the fashion.

BORA. Tush! I may as well say, the fool's the fool. But see'st thou not what a deformed thief this fashion is?

1 WATCH. [*Aside.*] I know that *Deformed;* 'a has been a vile thief this seven year:* 'a goes up and down like a gentleman: I remember his name.

BORA. Didst thou not hear somebody?

CON. No; 'twas the vane on the house.

BORA. See'st thou not, I say, what a deformed thief this fashion is? how giddily he turns about all the hot bloods, between fourteen and five-and-thirty? sometimes fashioning them like Pharaoh's soldiers in the reechy[a] painting; sometime, like god Bel's priests in the old church window; sometime, like the shaven Hercules in the smirched, worm-eaten tapestry, where his cod-piece seems as massy as his club?

CON. All this I see; and I† see that the fashion wears out more apparel than the man: but art not thou thyself giddy with the fashion too, that

(*) First folio, *years.* (†) First folio omits, *I.*

a Reechy *painting;*] Painting discoloured by smoke, Steevens says.

thou hast shifted out of thy tale into telling me of the fashion?

BORA. Not so neither: but know, that I have to-night wooed Margaret, the lady Hero's gentlewoman, by the name of Hero: she leans me out at her mistress' chamber window, bids me a thousand times good night,—I tell this tale vilely:—I should first tell thee, how the prince, Claudio, and my master, planted, and placed, and possessed by my master don John, saw afar off in the orchard this amiable encounter.

CON. And thought they,* Margaret was Hero?

BORA. Two of them did, the prince and Claudio; but the devil my master knew she was Margaret; and partly by his oaths, which first possessed them, partly by the dark night, which did deceive them, but chiefly by my villainy, which did confirm any slander that don John had made, away went Claudio enraged; swore he would meet her as he was appointed, next morning at the temple, and there, before the whole congregation, shame her with what he saw over-night, and send her home again without a husband.

1 WATCH. We charge you in the prince's name, Stand!

2 WATCH. Call up the right master constable: we have here recovered the most dangerous piece of lechery that ever was known in the commonwealth.

1 WATCH. And one Deformed is one of them; I know him, 'a wears a lock.(3)

CON. Masters! masters,—

2 WATCH. You'll be made bring Deformed forth, I warrant you.

CON. Masters,—

1 WATCH. Never speak;[a] we charge you, let us obey you to go with us.

BORA. We are like to prove a goodly commodity, being taken up of these men's bills.[b]

CON. A commodity in question, I warrant you. Come, we'll obey you. [*Exeunt.*

SCENE IV.—*A Room in* Leonato's *House.*

Enter HERO, MARGARET, *and* URSULA.

HERO. Good Ursula, wake my cousin Beatrice, and desire her to rise.

URS. I will, lady.

HERO. And bid her come hither.

URS. Well. [*Exit* URSULA.

MARG. Troth, I think, your other rebato[c] were better.

HERO. No, pray thee, good Meg, I'll wear this.

MARG. By my troth's[d] not so good; and I warrant, your cousin will say so.

HERO. My cousin's a fool, and thou art another; I'll wear none but this.

MARG. I like the new tire within excellently, if the hair were a thought browner: and your gown's a most rare fashion, i'faith. I saw the duchess of Milan's gown, that they praise so.

HERO. O, that exceeds, they say.

MARG. By my troth's but a night-gown in respect of yours: cloth o'gold, and cuts, and laced with silver; set with pearls, down-sleeves, side-sleeves,[e] and skirts round, underborne with a blueish tinsel: but for a fine, quaint, graceful, and excellent fashion, yours is worth ten on't.

HERO. God give me joy to wear it, for my heart is exceeding heavy!

MARG. 'T will be heavier soon, by the weight of a man.

HERO. Fie upon thee! art not ashamed?

MARG. Of what, lady? of speaking honourably? Is not marriage honourable in a beggar? Is not your lord honourable without marriage? I think, you would have me say, saving your reverence,—*a husband:* an bad thinking do not wrest true speaking, I'll offend nobody: Is there any harm in—*the heavier for a husband?* None, I think, an it be the right husband, and the right wife; otherwise 't is light, and not heavy: ask my lady Beatrice else, here she comes.

Enter BEATRICE.

HERO. Good morrow, coz.

BEAT. Good morrow, sweet Hero.

HERO. Why, how now! do you speak in the sick tune?

BEAT. I am out of all other tune, methinks.

MARG. Clap us into—*Light o' love;*[f] that goes without a burden; do you sing it, and I'll dance it.

BEAT. Yea,* *Light o' love,* with your heels!—then if your husband have stables enough, you'll see† he shall lack no barns.[g]

(*) First folio, *thy.*

(*) Old text, *Ye.* (†) First folio, *look.*

a Never speak, &c.] This speech, which clearly belongs to the Watchman, is given to Conrade in the old copies. Theobald transferred it to the proper speaker.

b *A goodly* commodity, *being* taken up *of these men's bills.*] "Here is a cluster of conceits. *Commodity* was formerly, as now, the usual term of an article of merchandise. To *take up,* besides its common meaning, (*to apprehend,*) was the phrase for obtaining goods on credit. 'If a man is thorough with them in honest *taking up,*' says Falstaff, 'then they must stand upon security.' *Bill* was the term both for a *single bond* and a *halberd.* We have the same conceit in 'King Henry VI.' Part II: 'My lord, when shall we go to Cheapside, and *take up commodities* upon our *bills?*'"—MALONE.

c Rebato—] A kind of ruff.

d *By my* troth's *not so good;*] In this passage, and in another of the same construction just after, "By my *troth's* but a night-gown," &c. where modern editors silently insert *it,* reading, "By my troth *it's,*" &c. we adhere to the idiomatic contraction of the old text.

e Side-*sleeves,*—] *Long* sleeves.

f *Light o' love,*—] See note (5), p. 42.

g *No* barns.] A quibble on *bairns,* and *barns,* both being formerly pronounced, and often spelt alike: so in "The Winter's Tale," Act III. Sc. 3:—"Mercy on's, a *barne!* a very pretty *barne!*"

MARG. O illegitimate construction! I scorn that with my heels.[a]

BEAT. 'Tis almost five o'clock, cousin; 'tis time you were ready. By my troth I am exceeding ill:—hey ho!

MARG. For a hawk, a horse, or a husband?

BEAT. For the letter that begins them all, H.[b]

MARG. Well, an you be not turned Turk,[c] there's no more sailing by the star.

BEAT. What means the fool, trow?[d]

MARG. Nothing I; but God send every one their heart's desire!

HERO. These gloves the count sent me, they are an excellent perfume.

BEAT. I am stuffed, cousin, I cannot smell.

MARG. A maid, and stuffed! there's goodly catching of cold.

BEAT. O, God help me! God help me! how long have you professed apprehension?

MARG. Ever since you left it: doth not my wit become me rarely?

BEAT. It is not seen enough; you should wear it in your cap.—By my troth, I am sick.

MARG. Get you some of this distilled Carduus Benedictus,(4) and lay it to your heart; it is the only thing for a qualm.

HERO. There thou prick'st her with a thistle.

BEAT. *Benedictus!* why *Benedictus?* you have some moral in this *Benedictus*.

MARG. Moral? no, by my troth, I have no moral meaning; I meant, plain holy-thistle. You may think, perchance, that I think you are in love: nay, by'r lady, I am not such a fool to think what I list; nor I list not to think what I can; nor, indeed, I cannot think, if I would think my heart out of thinking, that you are in love, or that you will be in love, or that you can be in love: yet Benedick was such another, and now is he become a man, he swore he would never marry; and yet now, in despite of his heart, he eats his meat without grudging: and how you may be converted, I know not, but methinks, you look with your eyes as other women do.

BEAT. What pace is this that thy tongue keeps?

MARG. Not a false gallop.

Re-enter URSULA.

URS. Madam, withdraw; the prince, the count, signior Benedick, don John, and all the gallants of the town, are come to fetch you to church.

HERO. Help to dress me, good coz, good Meg, good Ursula. [*Exeunt.*

SCENE V.—*Another Room in* Leonato's *House.*

Enter LEONATO, *with* DOGBERRY *and* VERGES.[e]

LEON. What would you with me, honest neighbour?

DOGB. Marry, sir, I would have some confidence with you, that decerns you nearly.

LEON. Brief, I pray you; for you see, it is a busy time with me.

DOGB. Marry, this it is, sir.

VERG. Yes, in truth it is, sir.

LEON. What is it, my good friends?

DOGB. Goodman Verges, sir, speaks a little off* the matter: an old man, sir, and his wits are not so blunt, as, God help, I would desire they were; but, in faith, honest as the skin between his brows.[f]

VERG. Yes, I thank God, I am as honest as any man living, that is an old man, and no honester than I.

DOGB. Comparisons are odorous: *palabras*,[g] neighbour Verges.

LEON. Neighbours, you are tedious.

DOGB. It pleases your worship to say so, but we are the poor[h] duke's officers: but, truly, for mine own part, if I were as tedious as a king, I could find in my heart to bestow it all of your worship.

LEON. All thy tediousness on me? ha!

DOGB. Yea, an 'twere a thousand pound† more than 'tis: for I hear as good exclamation on your worship, as of any man in the city; and though I be but a poor man, I am glad to hear it.

VERG. And so am I.

LEON. I would fain know what you have to say.

VERG. Marry, sir, our watch to-night, excepting your worship's presence, have ta'en a couple of as arrant knaves as any in Messina.

---

a I scorn that with my heels.] See note (c), p. 401.

b For the letter that begins them all, H.] The following epigrams supply a solution of this petty riddle, and show the usual pronunciation of *ache* formerly:—

"H is worst among letters in the crosse-row,
For if thou find him either in thine elbow,
In thy arm, or leg, in any degree;
In thine head, or teeth, or toe, or knee;
Into what place soever H may pike him,
Wherever thou find *ache*, thou shalt not like him."
HEYWOOD'S *Epigrams*, 1566.

"*Dolor intimus.*
Nor hawk, nor hound, nor horse, those *h h h*,
But *ach* itself, 'tis Brutus' bones att*aches*."
Wits' Recreation, 1640.

(*) Old text, *of*. (†) First folio, *times*.

c Turned Turk,—] Changed your faith, or condition. A proverbial saying.

d Trow?] A corruption, Mr. Singer says, of *think you? believe you?*

e Dogberry and Verges.] Here in the old copy these worthies are styled, "*the Constable, and the Headborough.*"

f Honest as the skin between his brows.] A proverbial expression. See note (a), p. 123.

g Palabras,—] Meaning *pocas palabrus*, few words. A scrap of Spanish we have had before from Christophero Sly, in "The Taming of the Shrew."

h *The* poor duke's *officers*:] In "Measure for Measure," Act II. Sc. 1, Elbow makes the same ludicrous transposition of the epithet *poor*:—"I am the *poor duke's* constable."

DOGB. A good old man, sir; he will be talking; as they say, When the age is in, the wit is out; God help us! it is a world to see![a]—Well said, i'faith, neighbour Verges:—well, God's a good man; an two men ride of a horse, one must ride behind.—An honest soul, i'faith, sir; by my troth he is, as ever broke bread: but, God is to be worshipped: all men are not alike; alas, good neighbour!

LEON. Indeed, neighbour, he comes too short of you.

DOGB. Gifts, that God gives.

LEON. I must leave you.

DOGB. One word, sir: our watch, sir, have, indeed, comprehended two aspicious persons, and we would have them this morning examined before your worship.

LEON. Take their examination yourself, and bring it me; I am now in great haste, as it* may appear unto you.

(*) First folio omits, *it*.

[a] It is a world to see!] It is *marvellous* to see. A very common apostrophe of old.

DOGB. It shall be suffigance.

LEON. Drink some wine ere you go: fare you well.

Enter a Messenger.

MESS. My lord, they stay for you to give your daughter to her husband.

LEON. I'll wait upon them; I am ready.

[*Exeunt* LEONATO *and* Messenger.

DOGB. Go, good partner, go, get you to Francis Seacoal, bid him bring his pen and inkhorn to the gaol: we are now to examination these* men.

VERG. And we must do it wisely.

DOGB. We will spare for no wit, I warrant you; here's that [*Touching his forehead.*] shall drive some of them to a *non com:* only get the learned writer to set down our excommunication, and meet me at the gaol. [*Exeunt.*

(*) First folio, *examine those.*

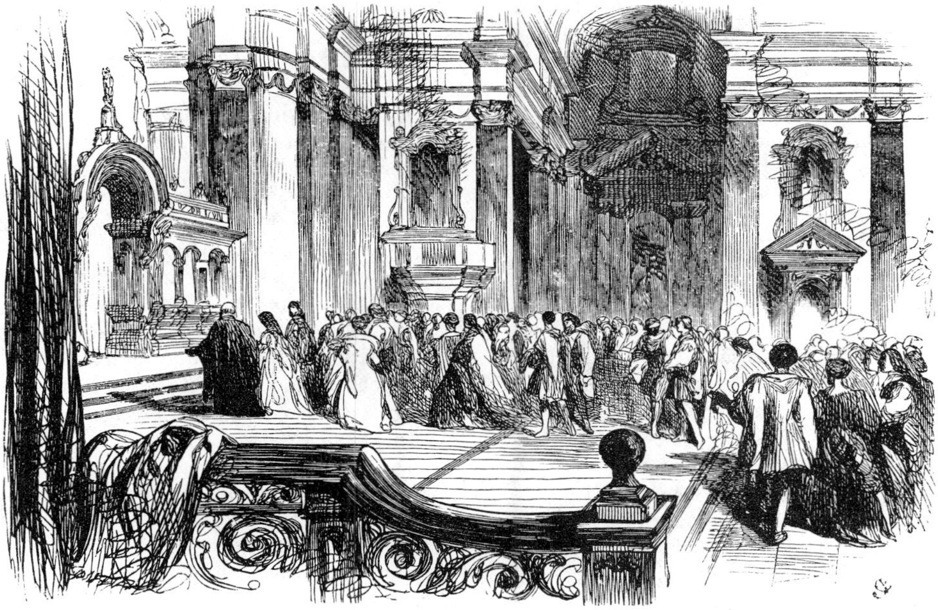

ACT IV.

SCENE I.—*A Church.*

Enter Don Pedro, Don John, Leonato, Friar, Claudio, Benedick, Hero, Beatrice, *and* Attendants.

Leon. Come, friar Francis, be brief; only to the plain form of marriage, and you shall recount their particular duties afterwards.

Friar. You come hither, my lord, to marry this lady?

Claud. No.

Leon. To be married to her, friar; you come to marry her.

Friar. Lady, you come hither to be married to this count?

Hero. I do.

Friar. If either of you know any inward impediment why you should not be conjoined, I charge you, on your souls, to utter it.

Claud. Know you any, Hero?

Hero. None, my lord.

Friar. Know you any, count?

Leon. I dare make his answer, none.

Claud. O, what men dare do! what men may do! what men daily do! not knowing what they do! [a]

Bene. How now! Interjections? Why, then some be of laughing, as, ha! ha! he!

Claud. Stand thee by, friar.—Father, by your leave,
Will you with free and unconstrained soul
Give me this maid, your daughter?

Leon. As freely, son, as God did give her me.

Claud. And what have I to give you back, whose worth
May counterpoise this rich and precious gift.

D. Pedro. Nothing, unless you render her again.

Claud. Sweet prince, you learn me noble thankfulness.—
There, Leonato, take her back again;
Give not this rotten orange to your friend;
She's but the sign and semblance of her honour:—
Behold, how like a maid she blushes here:

[a] Not knowing what they do!] The folio omits these words.

O, what authority and show of truth
Can cunning sin cover itself withal!
Comes not that blood, as modest evidence,
To witness simple virtue? Would you not swear,
All you that see her, that she were a maid,
By these exterior shows? But she is none:
She knows the heat of a luxurious bed;
Her blush is guiltiness, not modesty.

LEON. What do you mean, my lord?

CLAUD. Not to be married;
Not to knit my soul to an approved wanton.

LEON. Dear my lord, if you, in your own proof,
Have vanquish'd the resistance of her youth,
And made defeat of her virginity,——

CLAUD. I know what you would say; if I have known her,
You'll say, she did embrace me as a husband,
And so extenuate the 'forehand sin. No, Leonato,
I never tempted her with word too large;
But, as a brother to his sister, show'd
Bashful sincerity and comely love.

HERO. And seem'd I ever otherwise to you?

CLAUD. Out on thee! seeming![a] I will write against it:
You seem to me as Dian in her orb;
As chaste as is the bud ere it be blown;
But you are more intemperate in your blood
Than Venus, or those pamper'd animals
That rage in savage sensuality.

HERO. Is my lord well, that he doth speak so wide?

LEON. Sweet prince, why speak not you?

D. PEDRO. What should I speak?
I stand dishonour'd, that have gone about
To link my dear friend to a common stale.

LEON. Are these things spoken? or do I but dream?

D. JOHN. Sir, they are spoken, and these things are true.

BENE. This looks not like a nuptial.

HERO. *True?* O God![b]

CLAUD. Leonato, stand I here?
Is this the prince? Is this the prince's brother?
Is this face Hero's? Are our eyes our own?

LEON. All this is so: but what of this, my lord?

CLAUD. Let me but move one question to your daughter;
And, by that fatherly and kindly power
That you have in her, bid her answer truly.

LEON. I charge thee do so,* as thou art my child.

HERO. O God defend me! how am I beset!—
What kind of catechising call you this?

CLAUD. To make you answer truly to your name.

HERO. Is it not Hero? who can blot that name
With any just reproach?

CLAUD. Marry, that can Hero;
Hero itself can blot out Hero's virtue.
What man was he talk'd with you yesternight
Out at your window, betwixt twelve and one?
Now, if you are a maid, answer to this.

HERO. I talk'd with no man at that hour, my lord.

D. PEDRO. Why, then are you no maiden.—Leonato,
I am sorry you must hear. Upon mine honour,
Myself, my brother, and this grieved count,
Did see her, hear her, at that hour last night
Talk with a ruffian at her chamber-window;
Who hath, indeed, most like a liberal[c] villain,
Confess'd the vile encounters they have had
A thousand times in secret.

D. JOHN. Fie, fie!
They are not to be nam'd, my lord, not to be spoke* of;
There is not chastity enough in language,
Without offence, to utter them: thus, pretty lady,
I am sorry for thy much misgovernment.

CLAUD. O Hero! what a Hero hadst thou been,
If half thy outward graces had been plac'd
About thy thoughts, and counsels of thy heart!
But, fare thee well, most foul, most fair! farewell,
Thou pure impiety, and impious purity!
For thee, I'll lock up all the gates of love,
And on my eye-lids shall conjecture hang,
To turn all beauty into thoughts of harm,
And never shall it more be gracious.[d]

LEON. Hath no man's dagger here a point for me? [HERO *swoons.*

BEAT. Why, how now, cousin? wherefore sink you down?

D. JOHN. Come, let us go: these things, come thus to light,
Smother her spirits up.

[*Exeunt* DON PEDRO, DON JOHN, *and* CLAUDIO.

BENE. How doth the lady?

BEAT. Dead, I think;—help, uncle;—
Hero! why, Hero!—Uncle!—Signior Benedick!—friar!

LEON. O fate, take not away thy heavy hand!
Death is the fairest cover for her shame,
That may be wish'd for.

(*) First folio omits, *so*.

[a] Out on thee! seeming!] Pope altered the old text to—

"Out on *thy* seeming!"

and his lection is usually followed. Mr. Collier, however, adheres to the ancient copies; but, considering that Claudio addresses Hero as the personification of "seeming," he punctuates the passage thus:—

"Out on thee, seeming!"

(*) First folio, *spoken*.

[b] *True?* O God!] She is thinking of Don John's declaration:—

"—— these things are *true*."

[c] A liberal *villain*,—] A *licentious* villain.

[d] *And never shall it more be* gracious.] That is, *loveable, attractive*. See note (a), p. 307.

BEAT. How now, cousin Hero?
FRIAR. Have comfort, lady.
LEON. Dost thou look up?
FRIAR. Yea; wherefore should she not?
LEON. Wherefore? why, doth not every earthly thing
Cry shame upon her? Could she here deny
The story that is printed in her blood?—
Do not live, Hero; do not ope thine eyes:
For did I think thou wouldst not quickly die,
Thought I thy spirits were stronger than thy shames,
Myself would, on the rearward* of reproaches,
Strike at thy life. Griev'd I, I had but one?
Chid I for that at frugal nature's frame? [a]
O, one too much by thee! Why had I one?
Why ever wast thou lovely in my eyes?
Why had I not, with charitable hand,
Took up a beggar's issue at my gates?
Who, smirched† thus, and mired with infamy,
I might have said, *No part of it is mine,*
This shame derives itself from unknown loins;
But mine, and mine I lov'd, and mine I prais'd,
And mine that I was proud on; mine so much,
That I myself was to myself not mine,
Valuing of her; why, she—O, she is fallen
Into a pit of ink! that the wide sea
Hath drops too few to wash her clean again;
And salt too little, which may season give
To her foul tainted flesh! [b]
BENE. Sir, sir, be patient:
For my part, I am so attir'd in wonder,
I know not what to say.
BEAT. O, on my soul, my cousin is belied!
BENE. Lady, were you her bedfellow last night?
BEAT. No, truly, not; although, until last night,
I have this twelvemonth been her bedfellow.
LEON. Confirm'd, confirm'd! O, that is stronger made,
Which was before barr'd up with ribs of iron!
Would the two‡ princes lie? and Claudio lie?
Who lov'd her so, that, speaking of her foulness,
Wash'd it with tears? Hence from her; let her die.
FRIAR. Hear me a little;
For I have only been silent so long,
And given way unto this course of fortune,
By noting of the lady: I have mark'd
A thousand blushing apparitions
To start into her face; a thousand innocent shames
In angel whiteness beat* away those blushes;
And in her eye there hath appear'd a fire,
To burn the errors that these princes hold
Against her maiden truth.—Call me a fool;
Trust not my reading, nor my observations,
Which with experimental seal doth warrant
The tenour of my book; [c] trust not my age,
My reverence, calling, nor divinity,
If this sweet lady lie not guiltless here
Under some biting [d] error.
LEON. Friar, it cannot be:
Thou seest, that all the grace that she hath left
Is, that she will not add to her damnation
A sin of perjury; she not denies it:
Why seek'st thou then to cover with excuse,
That which appears in proper nakedness?
FRIAR. Lady, what man is he you are accused of?
HERO. They know, that do accuse me; I know none:
If I know more of any man alive,
Than that which maiden modesty doth warrant,
Let all my sins lack mercy!—O my father,
Prove you that any man with me convers'd
At hours unmeet, or that I yesternight
Maintain'd the change of words with any creature,
Refuse me, hate me, torture me to death.
FRIAR. There is some strange misprision in the princes.
BENE. Two of them have the very bent of honour;
And if their wisdoms be misled in this,
The practice of it lives in John the bastard,
Whose spirits toil in frame of villainies.
LEON. I know not; if they speak but truth of her,
These hands shall tear her; if they wrong her honour,
The proudest of them shall well hear of it.
Time hath not yet so dried this blood of mine,
Nor age so eat up my invention,
Nor fortune made such havoc of my means,
Nor my bad life reft me so much of friends,
But they shall find, awak'd in such a kind,
Both strength of limb, and policy of mind,
Ability in means, and choice of friends,
To quit me of them throughly.
FRIAR. Pause a while,
And let my counsel sway you in this case.
Your daughter here, the princes† left for dead;
Let her awhile be secretly kept in,
And publish it, that she is dead indeed:
Maintain a mourning ostentation,
And on your family's old monument

(*) First folio, *reward*. (†) First folio, *smeared*. (‡) First folio omits, *two*.

a At frugal nature's frame?] *Frame*, in this place, is interpreted *order, contrivance, disposition of things*. May it not mean *limit, restriction?* Mr. Collier's annotator reads,—

"———— nature's *frown?*"

(*) First folio, *bear*. (†) Old copies, *princess*.

b *To her* foul tainted flesh!] Mr. Collier's annotator substitutes

"———— *soul-tainted* flesh!"

c Of my book;] That is, my studies.

d Some biting error.] Mr. Collier's annotator suggests

"———— *blighting* error."

Hang mournful epitaphs, and do all rites
That appertain unto a burial.
LEON. What shall become of this? What will this do?
FRIAR. Marry, this, well carried, shall on her behalf
Change slander to remorse; that is some good:
But not for that dream I on this strange course,
But on this travail look for greater birth.
She dying, as it must be so maintain'd,
Upon the instant that she was accus'd,
Shall be lamented, pitied, and excus'd,
Of every hearer: for it so falls out,
That what we have we prize not to the worth,
Whiles we enjoy it; but being lack'd and lost,
Why, then we rack[a] the value; then we find
The virtue, that possession would not show us
Whiles it was ours.—So will it fare with Claudio:
When he shall hear she died upon[b] his words,
The idea of her life shall sweetly creep
Into his study of imagination;
And every lovely organ of her life
Shall come apparell'd in more precious habit,
More moving-delicate, and full of life,
Into the eye and prospect of his soul,
Than when she liv'd indeed:—then shall he mourn,
(If ever love had interest in his liver,)
And wish he had not so accused her;
No, though he thought his accusation true.
Let this be so, and doubt not but success
Will fashion the event in better shape,
Than I can lay it down in likelihood.
But if all aim but this be levell'd false,
The supposition of the lady's death
Will quench the wonder of her infamy:
And, if it sort not well, you may conceal her
(As best befits her wounded reputation,)

---

[a] *We* rack *the value;*] We *stretch, extend, exaggerate* the value.

[b] *She died* upon *his words,—*] That is, died *by* them. So in "A Midsummer Night's Dream," Act II. Sc. 1:—

"To die *upon* the hand I love so well."

In some reclusive and religious life,
Out of all eyes, tongues, minds, and injuries.

BENE. Signior Leonato, let the friar advise[a] you:
And though, you know, my inwardness[b] and love
Is very much unto the prince and Claudio,
Yet, by mine honour, I will deal in this
As secretly, and justly, as your soul
Should with your body.

LEON. Being that I flow in grief,
The smallest twine may lead me.

FRIAR. 'T is well consented; presently away;
For to strange sores strangely they strain the cure.—
Come, lady, die to live: this wedding day,
Perhaps, is but prolong'd; have patience, and endure.

[*Exeunt* Friar, HERO, *and* LEONATO.

BENE. Lady Beatrice, have you wept all this while?

BEAT. Yea, and I will weep a while longer.

BENE. I will not desire that.

BEAT. You have no reason, I do it freely.

BENE. Surely, I do believe your fair cousin is wronged.

BEAT. Ah, how much might the man deserve of me, that would right her!

BENE. Is there any way to show such friendship?

BEAT. A very even way, but no such friend.

BENE. May a man do it?

BEAT. It is a man's office, but not yours.

BENE. I do love nothing in the world so well as you; is not that strange?

BEAT. As strange as the thing I know not. It were as possible for me to say, I loved nothing so well as you: but believe me not; and yet I lie not; I confess nothing, nor I deny nothing:—I am sorry for my cousin.

BENE. By my sword, Beatrice, thou lovest me.

BEAT. Do not swear by it, and eat it.

BENE. I will swear by it, that you love me; and I will make him eat it, that says, I love not you.

BEAT. Will you not eat your word?

BENE. With no sauce that can be devised to it: I protest, I love thee.

BEAT. Why then, God forgive me!

BENE. What offence, sweet Beatrice?

BEAT. You have stayed me in a happy hour; I was about to protest—I loved you.

BENE. And do it with all thy heart.

BEAT. I love you with so much of my heart that none is left to protest.

BENE. Come, bid me do anything for thee.

BEAT. Kill Claudio.

BENE. Ha! not for the wide world.

BEAT. You kill me to deny it:* farewell.

BENE. Tarry, sweet Beatrice.

BEAT. I am gone, though I am here;—there is no love in you:—nay, I pray you, let me go.

BENE. Beatrice,—

BEAT. In faith, I will go.

BENE. We'll be friends first.

BEAT. You dare easier be friends with me, than fight with mine enemy.

BENE. Is Claudio thine enemy?

BEAT. Is he not approved in the height a villain, that hath slandered, scorned, dishonoured my kinswoman?—O, that I were a man!—What! bear her in hand[c] until they come to take hands; and then with public accusation, uncovered slander, unmitigated rancour,—O God, that I were a man! I would eat his heart in the market-place.

BENE. Hear me, Beatrice;—

BEAT. Talk with a man out at a window!—a proper saying!

BENE. Nay but, Beatrice;—

BEAT. Sweet Hero!—she is wronged, she is slandered, she is undone.

BENE. Beat—

BEAT. Princes, and counties! Surely, a princely testimony! a goodly count! Count Confect;[d] a sweet gallant surely! O that I were a man for his sake! or that I had any friend would be a man for my sake! But manhood is melted into courtesies, valour into complement, and men are only turned into tongue, and trim ones too: he is now as valiant as Hercules, that only tells a lie, and swears it:—I cannot be a man with wishing, therefore I will die a woman with grieving.

BENE. Tarry, good Beatrice: by this hand, I love thee.

BEAT. Use it for my love some other way than swearing by it.

BENE. Think you in your soul the count Claudio hath wronged Hero?

BEAT. Yea, as sure as I have a thought, or a soul.

BENE. Enough!—I am engaged.—I will challenge him; I will kiss your hand, and so leave you. By this hand, Claudio shall render me a dear account: as you hear of me, so think of me. Go, comfort your cousin: I must say, she is dead; and so, farewell. [*Exeunt.*

---

a *Let the friar* advise *you*:] *Advise* here, and in many other instances, implies *persuade*.
b *My* inwardness—] *Confidence, intimacy.*
c Bear her in hand—] See note (c), p. 258.

(*) First folio omits, *it*.

d Count Confect;] A title in derision, as my *Lord Lollipop* The folio reads, *a goodly Count Comfect*.

SCENE II.—*A Prison.*

Enter DOGBERRY,[a] VERGES, *and* Sexton, *in gowns; and the* Watch, *with* CONRADE *and* BORACHIO.

DOGB.[b] Is our whole dissembly appeared?

VERG. O, a stool and a cushion for the sexton!

SEXTON. Which be the malefactors?

DOGB.[c] Marry, that am I and my partner.

VERG. Nay, that's certain; we have the exhibition to examine.

SEXTON. But which are the offenders that are

---

[a] Enter Dogberry, &c.] The old stage-direction is, "*Enter the Constables, Borachio, and the Towne Clerke, in gownes.*" By the *town-clerk* is meant the *Sexton*, and not, as some of the commentators have supposed, another character. —"But this office [the sexton] is now swallowed up in the clerk."—Holme's *Academy of Armory*, 1688.

[b] DOGB.] The old text here has *Keeper*, but in much of this scene the prefixes to the speeches belonging to Dogberry and Verges are *Kemp* and *Cowley*, a proof that those actors originally performed the parts.

[c] DOGB.] In both quarto and folio the prefix here is "Andrew."

to be examined? let them come before master constable.

DOGB. Yea, marry, let them come before me.—What is your name, friend?

BORA. Borachio.

DOGB. Pray write down—Borachio—Yours, sirrah?

CON. I am a gentleman, sir, and my name is Conrade.

DOGB. Write down—master gentleman Conrade.—Masters, do you serve God?

CON. BORA. Yea, sir, we hope.[a]

DOGB. Write down—that they hope they serve God:—and write *God* first; for God defend but God should go before such villains! Masters, it is proved already that you are little better than false knaves, and it will go near to be thought so shortly. How answer you for yourselves?

CON. Marry, sir, we say we are none.

DOGB. A marvellous witty fellow, I assure you; but I will go about with him.—Come you hither, sirrah; a word in your ear, sir; I say to you, it is thought you are false knaves.

BORA. Sir, I say to you, we are none.

DOGB. Well, stand aside.—'Fore God, they are both in a tale. Have you writ down—that they are none?

SEXTON. Master constable, you go not the way to examine; you must call forth the watch that are their accusers.

DOGB. Yea, marry, that's the eftest[b] way:—Let the watch come forth.—Masters, I charge you, in the prince's name, accuse these men.

1 WATCH. This man said, sir, that don John, the prince's brother, was a villain.

DOGB. Write down—prince John a villain.—Why, this is flat perjury, to call a prince's brother—*villain.*

BORA. Master constable,—

DOGB. 'Pray thee, fellow, peace; I do not like thy look, I promise thee.

SEXTON. What heard you him say else?

2 WATCH. Marry, that he had received a thousand ducats of don John, for accusing the lady Hero wrongfully.

DOGB. Flat burglary, as ever was committed.

VERG. Yea, by the mass, that it is.

SEXTON. What else, fellow?

1 WATCH. And that count Claudio did mean, upon his words, to disgrace Hero before the whole assembly, and not marry her.

DOGB. O villain! thou wilt be condemned into everlasting redemption for this.

SEXTON. What else?

2 WATCH. This is all.

SEXTON. And this is more, masters, than you can deny. Prince John is this morning secretly stolen away; Hero was in this manner accused, in this very manner refused, and upon the grief of this, suddenly died.—Master constable, let these men be bound, and brought to Leonato; I will go before, and show him their examination. [*Exit.*

DOGB. Come, let them be opinioned.

VERG. Let them be in the hands of——

CON. Coxcomb![c]

DOGB. God's my life! where's the sexton? let him write down—the prince's officer, *coxcomb.*—Come, bind them:——thou naughty varlet!

CON. Away! you are an ass, you are an ass.[d]

DOGB. Dost thou not suspect my place? Dost thou not suspect my years?—O that he were here to write me down—*an ass!*—but, masters, remember, that I am *an ass;* though it be not written down, yet forget not that I am *an ass.*—No, thou villain, thou art full of piety, as shall be proved upon thee by good witness. I am a wise fellow; and, which is more, an officer; and, which is more, a householder; and, which is more, as pretty a piece of flesh as any in Messina; and one, that knows the law, go to; and a rich fellow enough, go to; and a fellow that hath had losses; and one that hath two gowns, and every thing handsome about him.—Bring him away. O, that I had been writ down—*an ass.* [*Exeunt.*

---

[a] Yea, sir, we hope.] This speech, and part of the next, down to "such villains," inclusive, is omitted in the folio.

[b] Eftest—] *Quickest, readiest.*

[c] Coxcomb!] The old copies have evidently jumbled two speeches into one reading,—

"Let them be in the hands of coxcomb."

[d] You are an ass.] This speech, both in quarto and folio, bears the prefix "*Couley,*" as if belonging to "Verges."

ACT V.

SCENE I.—*Before* Leonato's *House*.

Enter LEONATO *and* ANTONIO.

ANT. If you go on thus, you will kill yourself;
And 'tis not wisdom thus to second grief,
Against yourself.
LEON. I pray thee, cease thy counsel,
Which falls into mine ears as profitless
As water in a sieve: give not me counsel;
Nor let no comforter* delight mine ear,
But such a one whose wrongs do suit with mine.
Bring me a father, that so lov'd his child,
Whose joy of her is overwhelm'd like mine,
And bid him speak of patience;
Measure his woe the length and breadth of mine,
And let it answer every strain for strain;
As thus for thus, and such a grief for such,
In every lineament, branch, shape, and form:
If such a one will smile, and stroke his beard,
Bid sorrow wag,[a] cry *hem* when he should groan;
Patch grief with proverbs, make misfortune drunk
With candle-wasters;[b] bring him yet to me,
And I of him will gather patience.

(*) First folio, *comfort*.

[a] Bid sorrow wag,—] In the old copies,—
"And sorrow, wagge."
The suggestions to elucidate this hopeless crux are legion. We adopt one by Capell, which deviates little from the original, and affords a plausible meaning, but have not much confidence in its integrity.

[b] Candle-wasters;] *Bacchanals, revellers*.

But there is no such man: for, brother, men
Can counsel, and speak comfort to that grief
Which they themselves not feel; but, tasting it,
Their counsel turns to passion, which before
Would give preceptial medicine to rage,
Fetter strong madness in a silken thread,
Charm ache with air, and agony with words;
No, no; 'tis all men's office to speak patience
To those that wring under the load of sorrow;
But no man's virtue nor sufficiency,
To be so moral, when he shall endure
The like himself: therefore give me no counsel;
My griefs cry louder than advertisement.

ANT. Therein do men from children nothing differ.

LEON. I pray thee, peace: I will be flesh and blood;
For there was never yet philosopher,
That could endure the tooth-ache patiently;
However they have writ the style of gods,
And made a push[a] at chance and sufferance.

ANT. Yet bend not all the harm upon yourself;
Make those, that do offend you, suffer too.

LEON. There thou speak'st reason: nay, I will do so:
My soul doth tell me, Hero is belied,
And that shall Claudio know; so shall the prince,
And all of them, that thus dishonour her.

ANT. Here comes the prince, and Claudio, hastily.

Enter DON PEDRO *and* CLAUDIO.

D. PEDRO. Good den, good den.

CLAUD. Good day to both of you.

LEON. Hear you, my lords,—

D. PEDRO. We have some haste, Leonato.

LEON. Some haste, my lord!—well, fare you well, my lord:—
Are you so hasty now? well, all is one.

D. PEDRO. Nay, do not quarrel with us, good old man.

ANT. If he could right himself with quarrelling,
Some of us would lie low.

CLAUD. Who wrongs him?

LEON. Marry, thou dost wrong me; thou dissembler, thou:—
Nay, never lay thy hand upon thy sword,
I fear thee not.

CLAUD. Marry, beshrew my hand,
If it should give your age such cause of fear:
In faith, my hand meant nothing to my sword.

LEON. Tush, tush, man, never fleer and jest at me:
I speak not like a dotard, nor a fool,
As, under privilege of age, to brag
What I have done being young, or what would do,
Were I not old. Know, Claudio, to thy head,
Thou hast so wrong'd mine innocent child and me,
That I am forc'd to lay my reverence by,
And, with grey hairs, and bruise of many days,
Do challenge thee to trial of a man.
I say, thou hast belied mine innocent child;
Thy slander hath gone through and through her heart,
And she lies buried with her ancestors:
O! in a tomb where never scandal slept,
Save this of hers, fram'd by thy villainy.

CLAUD. My villainy!

LEON. Thine, Claudio; thine, I say.

D. PEDRO. You say not right, old man.

LEON. My lord, my lord,
I'll prove it on his body, if he dare;
Despite his nice fence, and his active practice,
His May of youth, and bloom of lustyhood.

CLAUD. Away! I will not have to do with you.

LEON. Canst thou so daff me? Thou hast kill'd my child;
If thou kill'st me, boy, thou shalt kill a man.

ANT. He shall kill two of us, and men indeed:
But that's no matter; let him kill one first;—
Win me and wear me,—let him answer me,—
Come, follow me, boy! come, sir boy, come, follow me:
Sir boy, I'll whip you from your foining fence;
Nay, as I am a gentleman, I will.

LEON. Brother,—

ANT. Content yourself; God knows, I lov'd my niece;
And she is dead, slander'd to death by villains,
That dare as well answer a man, indeed,
As I dare take a serpent by the tongue:
Boys, apes, braggarts, Jacks, milksops!—

LEON. Brother Antony,—

ANT. Hold you content; what, man! I know them, yea,
And what they weigh, even to the utmost scruple:
Scambling, out-facing, fashion-monging boys,
That lie, and cog, and flout, deprave, and slander,
Go anticly, and show outward hideousness,
And speak off half a dozen dangerous words,
How they might hurt their enemies, if they durst,
And this is all.

LEON. But, brother Antony,—

ANT. Come, 'tis no matter;
Do not you meddle, let me deal in this.

D. PEDRO. Gentlemen both, we will not wake your patience.

---

[a] *And made* a push *at chance and sufferance.*] *Push* was an interjection equivalent to *pish*, or *pshaw*. Thus, in "The Old Law," Act II. Sc. 1:—

"*Push!* I'm not for you yet."

And, as quoted by Mr. Dyce:—

"*Pem.* Deare friend—
Fer. Push! Meet me."
The Tryall of Cheualry, 1560, sig. C 4.

My heart is sorry for your daughter's death;
But, on my honour, she was charg'd with nothing
But what was true, and very full of proof.

LEON. My lord, my lord,—

D. PEDRO. I will not hear you.

LEON. No?
Come, brother, away:—I will be heard;—

ANT. And shall,
Or some of us will smart for it.

[*Exeunt* LEONATO *and* ANTONIO.

Enter BENEDICK.

D. PEDRO. See, see: here comes the man we went to seek.

CLAUD. Now, signior! what news?

BENE. Good day, my lord.

D. PEDRO. Welcome, signior: you are almost come to part almost a fray.

CLAUD. We had like to have had our two noses snapped off with two old men without teeth.

D. PEDRO. Leonato and his brother: what think'st thou? Had we fought, I doubt, we should have been too young for them.

BENE. In a false quarrel there is no true valour. I came to seek you both.

CLAUD. We have been up and down to seek thee; for we are high-proof melancholy, and would fain have it beaten away: wilt thou use thy wit?

BENE. It is in my scabbard; shall I draw it?

D. PEDRO. Dost thou wear thy wit by thy side?

CLAUD. Never any did so, though very many have been beside their wit.—I will bid thee draw, as we do the minstrels; draw, to pleasure us.

D. PEDRO. As I am an honest man, he looks pale:—art thou sick, or angry?

CLAUD. What! courage, man! What, though care killed a cat, thou hast mettle enough in thee to kill care.

BENE. Sir, I shall meet your wit in the career, an you charge it against me:—I pray you, choose another subject.

CLAUD. Nay, then give him another staff; this last was broke cross.[a]

D. PEDRO. By this light, he changes more and more; I think, he be angry indeed.

CLAUD. If he be, he knows how to turn his girdle.[b]

[a] *This last was* broke cross.] A metaphor taken, like Benedick's, from the Tilt-yard. In tilting, to break the weapon *across* an opponent's person, was accounted more disgraceful than even being unhorsed.

[b] He knows how to turn his girdle.] The sword was formerly worn much at the back, and, to bring it within reach, the buckle of the belt or girdles had to be turned behind. Mr. Holt White suggests another explanation:—"Large belts were worn with the buckle before, but for wrestling the buckle was turned behind, to give the adversary a fairer grasp at the girdle. To turn the buckle behind, therefore, was a challenge."

BENE. Shall I speak a word in your ear?

CLAUD. God bless me from a challenge!

BENE. You are a villain!—I jest not.—I will make it good how you dare, with what you dare, and when you dare.—Do me right,[a] or I will protest your cowardice: you have killed a sweet lady, and her death shall fall heavy on you. Let me hear from you.

CLAUD. Well, I will meet you, so I may have good cheer.

D. PEDRO. What, a feast? a feast?

CLAUD. I' faith, I thank him; he hath bid me to a calf's head and a capon; the which if I do not carve most curiously, say my knife's naught.—Shall I not find a woodcock[b] too?

BENE. Sir, your wit ambles well; it goes easily.

D. PEDRO. I'll tell thee how Beatrice praised thy wit the other day: I said, thou hadst a fine wit; *True*, said* she, *a fine little one*: *No*, said I, *a great wit*; *Right*, says she, *a great gross one*: *Nay*, said I, *a good wit*; *Just*, said she, *it hurts nobody*: *Nay*, said I, *the gentleman is wise*; *Certain*, said she, *a wise gentleman*:[c] *Nay*, said I, *he hath the tongues*; *That I believe*, said she, *for he swore a thing to me on Monday night, which he foreswore on Tuesday morning; there's a double tongue; there's two tongues.* Thus did she, an hour together, trans-shape thy particular virtues; yet, at last, she concluded with a sigh, thou wast the properest man in Italy.

CLAUD. For the which she wept heartily, and said, she cared not.

D. PEDRO. Yea, that she did; but yet, for all that, an if she did not hate him deadly, she would love him dearly: the old man's daughter told us all.

CLAUD. All, all; and moreover, *God saw him when he was hid in the garden.*

D. PEDRO. But when shall we set the savage bull's horns on the sensible Benedick's head?

CLAUD. Yea, and text underneath, *Here dwells Benedick the married man?*

BENE. Fare you well, boy; you know my mind; I will leave you now to your gossip-like humour: you break jests as braggarts do their blades, which, God be thanked, hurt not.—My lord, for your many courtesies I thank you: I must discontinue your company: your brother, the bastard, is fled from Messina: you have, among you, killed a sweet and innocent lady. For my lord Lack-beard, there, he and I shall meet; and till then, peace be with him. [*Exit* BENEDICK.

D. PEDRO. He is in earnest.

CLAUD. In most profound earnest; and, I'll warrant you, for the love of Beatrice.

D. PEDRO. And hath challenged thee?

CLAUD. Most sincerely.

D. PEDRO. What a pretty thing man is, when he goes in his doublet and hose, and leaves off his wit!

CLAUD. He is then a giant to an ape: but then is an ape a doctor to such a man.

D. PEDRO. But, soft you, let me be; pluck up my heart,[d] and be sad. Did he not say my brother was fled?

Enter DOGBERRY, VERGES, *and the* Watch, *with* CONRADE *and* BORACHIO.

DOGB. Come, you, sir; if justice cannot tame you, she shall ne'er weigh more reasons[e] in her balance: nay, an you be a cursing hypocrite once, you must be looked to.

D. PEDRO. How now, two of my brother's men bound! Borachio, one!

CLAUD. Hearken[f] after their offence, my lord!

D. PEDRO. Officers, what offence have these men done?

DOGB. Marry, sir, they have committed false report; moreover, they have spoken untruths; secondarily, they are slanders; sixth and lastly, they have belied a lady; thirdly, they have verified unjust things; and, to conclude, they are lying knaves.

D. PEDRO. First, I ask thee what they have done; thirdly, I ask thee what's their offence; sixth and lastly, why they are committed; and, to conclude, what you lay to their charge?

CLAUD. Rightly reasoned, and in his own division; and, by my troth, there's one meaning well suited.

D. PEDRO. Who have you offended, masters, that you are thus bound to your answer? this

---

(*) First folio, *says*.

a Do me right,—] Accept my challenge.

b *Shall I not find* a woodcock *too?*] A woodcock was supposed to have no brains, and hence became a synonym for a simpleton.

c A wise gentleman:] Another synonym for a witling.

d Let me be; pluck up my heart, and be sad.] So the original copies: but it may be suspected that the poet wrote, "let me pluck up my heart," &c.; the meaning being, rouse my spirits to serious business. It was a phrase in common use. Thus, in Gascoigne's play of "The Supposes," Act V. Sc. 7:—"pluck up your spirits and rejoice." So also, in "Gammer Gurton's Needle," Act III. Sc. 3:—"What devill woman *plucke up your hart*, and leve all this gloming."

e *More* reasons—] This ancient quibble between *reasons* and *raisins* was a favourite with Shakespeare. It is met with in "Troilus and Cressida," Act II. Sc. 2:—

"No marvel though, you bite so sharp at *reasons*,
You are so empty of them."

And in "As You Like It," Act II. Sc. 7:—

"ORL. He dies that touches any of this fruit.
JAQ. An you will not be answer'd with *reason*, I must die."

f Hearken *after their offence, my lord!*] *Hearken* appears to be used here in the peculiar sense which it bears in "Henry IV. Part I. Act V. Sc. 4:—

"——They did me too much injury,
That ever said, I *hearken'd* for your death."

learned constable is too cunning to be understood. What's your offence?

BORA. Sweet prince, let me go no farther to mine answer; do you hear me, and let this count kill me. I have deceived even your very eyes: what your wisdoms could not discover, these shallow fools have brought to light; who, in the night, overheard me confessing to this man, how don John your brother incensed me to slander the lady Hero: how you were brought into the orchard, and saw me court Margaret in Hero's garment; how you disgraced her, when you should marry her: my villainy they have upon record; which I had rather seal with my death, than repeat over to my shame: the lady is dead upon mine and my master's false accusation; and, briefly, I desire nothing but the reward of a villain.

D. PEDRO. Runs not this speech like iron through your blood?

CLAUD. I have drunk poison, whiles he utter'd it.

D. PEDRO. But did my brother set thee on to this?

BORA. Yea, and paid me richly for the practice of it.

D. PEDRO. He is compos'd and fram'd of treachery:—
And fled he is upon this villainy.

CLAUD. Sweet Hero! now thy image doth appear
In the rare semblance that I lov'd it first.

DOGB. Come, bring away the plaintiffs; by this time our sexton hath reformed signior Leonato of the matter; and, masters, do not forget to specify, when time and place shall serve, that I am *an ass.*

VERG. Here, here comes master signior Leonato and the sexton too.

Re-enter LEONATO *and* ANTONIO, *with the* Sexton.

LEON. Which is the villain? let me see his eyes,
That when I note another man like him,
I may avoid him: which of these is he?

BORA. If you would know your wronger, look on me.

LEON. Art thou the* slave, that with thy breath hast kill'd
Mine innocent child?

BORA. Yea, even I alone.

LEON. No, not so, villain; thou beliest thyself:
Here stand a pair of honourable men,
A third is fled, that had a hand in it:—
I thank you, princes, for my daughter's death;
Record it with your high and worthy deeds;
'Twas bravely done, if you bethink you of it.

CLAUD. I know not how to pray your patience,
Yet I must speak. Choose your revenge yourself;
Impose me to what penance your invention
Can lay upon my sin: yet sinn'd I not,
But in mistaking.

D. PEDRO. By my soul, nor I;
And yet, to satisfy this good old man,
I would bend under any heavy weight
That he'll enjoin me to.

LEON. I cannot bid you bid my daughter live,
That were impossible; but, I pray you both
Possess the people in Messina here
How innocent she died: and, if your love
Can labour aught in sad invention,
Hang her an epitaph upon her tomb,(1)
And sing it to her bones; sing it to-night:—
To-morrow morning come you to my house;
And since you could not be my son-in-law,
Be yet my nephew: my brother hath a daughter,
Almost the copy of my child that's dead,
And she alone is heir to both of us;
Give her the right you should have given her cousin,
And so dies my revenge.

CLAUD. O, noble sir,
Your over-kindness doth wring tears from me!
I do embrace your offer; and dispose
For henceforth of poor Claudio.

LEON. To-morrow then I will expect your coming;
To-night I take my leave.—This naughty man
Shall face to face be brought to Margaret,
Who, I believe, was pack'd[a] in all this wrong,
Hired to it by your brother.

BORA. No, by my soul, she was not;
Nor knew not what she did, when she spoke to me;
But always hath been just and virtuous,
In anything that I do know by her.

DOGB. Moreover, sir, (which, indeed, is not under white and black,) this plaintiff here, the offender, did call me *ass:* I beseech you, let it be remembered in his punishment. And also, the watch heard them talk of one *Deformed:* they say, he wears a key in his ear, and a lock hanging by it; and borrows money in God's name; the which he hath used so long, and never paid, that now men grow hard-hearted, and will lend nothing for God's sake: pray you examine him upon that point.

LEON. I thank thee for thy care and honest pains.

DOGB. Your worship speaks like a most thankful and reverend youth; and I praise God for you.

(*) First folio, *thou thou.*

[a] Pack'd *in all this wrong,*—] *Confederated, mixed up.*

LEON. There's for thy pains.

DOGB. God save the foundation!

LEON. Go, I discharge thee of thy prisoner, and I thank thee.

DOGB. I leave an arrant knave with your worship; which, I beseech your worship, to correct yourself, for the example of others. God keep your worship; I wish your worship well; God restore you to health: I humbly give you leave to depart; and if a merry meeting may be wished, God prohibit it.—Come, neighbour.

[*Exeunt* DOGBERRY, VERGES, *and* Watch.

LEON. Until to-morrow morning, lords, farewell.

ANT. Farewell, my lords: we look for you to-morrow.

D. PEDRO. We will not fail.

CLAUD. To-night I'll mourn with Hero.

[*Exeunt* DON PEDRO *and* CLAUDIO.

LEON. Bring you these fellows on; we'll talk with Margaret,
How her acquaintance grew with this lewd[a] fellow.

[*Exeunt.*

---

[a] *This* lewd *fellow.*] *Lewd,* of old, meant sometimes *lustful;* but more often *ignorant,* or *wicked.* The last is the sense it bears here.

SCENE II.—Leonato's *Garden.*

Enter BENEDICK *and* MARGARET, *meeting.*

BENE. 'Pray thee, sweet mistress Margaret, deserve well at my hands, by helping me to the speech of Beatrice.

MARG. Will you then write me a sonnet in praise of my beauty?

BENE. In so high a style, Margaret, that no man living shall come over it; for, in most comely truth, thou deservest it.

MARG. To have no man come over me? why, shall I always keep below stairs?

BENE. Thy wit is as quick as the greyhound's mouth, it catches.

MARG. And yours as blunt as the fencer's foils, which hit, but hurt not.

BENE. A most manly wit, Margaret, it will not hurt a woman; and so, I pray thee, call Beatrice: I give thee the bucklers.(2)

MARG. Give us the swords, we have bucklers of our own.

BENE. If you use them, Margaret, you must

put in the pikes with a vice; and they are dangerous weapons for maids.

MARG. Well, I will call Beatrice to you, who, I think, hath legs. [*Exit* MARGARET.

BENE. And therefore will come.

The god of love,[a] [Singing.
That sits above,
And knows me, and knows me,
How pitiful I deserve,—

I mean, in singing; but in loving—Leander the good swimmer, Troilus the first employer of panders, and a whole book-full of these quondam carpet-mongers, whose names yet run smoothly in the even road of a blank verse, why, they were never so truly turned over and over as my poor self, in love. Marry, I cannot show it in* rhyme; I have tried; I can find out no rhyme to *lady* but *baby*, an innocent rhyme; for *scorn, horn*, a hard rhyme; for *school, fool*, a babbling rhyme; very ominous endings: no, I was not born under a rhyming planet, nor † I cannot woo in festival terms.

Enter BEATRICE.

Sweet Beatrice, would'st thou come when I called thee?

BEAT. Yea, signior, and depart when you bid me.

BENE. O, stay but till then!

BEAT. *Then*, is spoken; fare you well now:—and yet, ere I go, let me go with that I came, which is, with knowing what hath passed between you and Claudio.

BENE. Only foul words; and thereupon I will kiss thee.

BEAT. Foul words is but foul wind, and foul wind is but foul breath, and foul breath is noisome; therefore I will depart unkissed.

BENE. Thou hast frighted the word out of his right sense, so forcible is thy wit: but, I must tell thee plainly, Claudio undergoes my challenge; and either I must shortly hear from him, or I will subscribe him a coward. And, I pray thee now, tell me, for which of my bad parts didst thou first fall in love with me?

BEAT. For them all together; which maintained so politic a state of evil, that they will not admit any good part to intermingle with them. But for which of my good parts did you first suffer love for me?

BENE. *Suffer* love; a good epithet! I do suffer love, indeed, for I love thee against my will.

BEAT. In spite of your heart, I think; alas! poor heart! if you spite it for my sake, I will spite it for yours; for I will never love that which my friend hates.

BENE. Thou and I are too wise to woo peaceably.

BEAT. It appears not in this confession: there's not one wise man among twenty that will praise himself.

BENE. An old, an old instance, Beatrice, that lived in the time of good neighbours: if a man do not erect in this age his own tomb ere he dies, he shall live no longer in monument* than the bell rings, and the widow weeps.

BEAT. And how long is that, think you?

BENE. Question!—Why, an hour in clamour, and a quarter in rheum: therefore is it most expedient for the wise, if don Worm his conscience, find no impediment to the contrary, to be the trumpet of his own virtues, as I am to myself: so much for praising myself, (who, I myself will bear witness, is praiseworthy,) and now tell me, how doth your cousin?

BEAT. Very ill.

BENE. And how do you?

BEAT. Very ill too.

BENE. Serve God, love me, and mend: there will I leave you too, for here comes one in haste.

Enter URSULA.

URS. Madam, you must come to your uncle; yonder's old coil[b] at home: it is proved my lady Hero hath been falsely accused, the prince and Claudio mightily abused; and don John is the author of all, who is fled and gone: will you come presently?

BEAT. Will you go hear this news, signior?

BENE. I will live in thy heart, die in thy lap, and be buried in thy eyes; and, moreover, I will go with thee to thy uncle's. [*Exeunt.*

SCENE III.—*The Inside of a Church.*

Enter DON PEDRO, CLAUDIO, *and* Attendants, *with Music and Tapers.*

CLAUD. Is this the monument of Leonato?

ATTEN. It is, my lord.

CLAUD. [*Reads from a Scroll.*]

(*) First folio omits, *in*. (†) First folio, *for*.

(*) First folio, *monuments*.

a The god of love,—] This, according to Ritson, was the beginning of a song by the famous ballad-monger, Elderton; of which a puritanical parody, by W. Birch, entitled "The Complaint of a Sinner," &c., is still extant, and commences,—

"*The God of love, that sits above,*
Doth know us, doth know us,
How sinful that we be."

b Old *coil*—] See note (a), p. 589.

EPITAPH.

Done to death by slanderous tongues
Was the Hero that here lies:
Death, in guerdon of her wrongs,
Gives her fame which never dies:
So the life, that died with shame,
Lives in death with glorious fame.

Hang thou there upon the tomb,
Praising her when I am dumb.
[*Affixing it.*

Now, music, sound, and sing your solemn hymn.

SONG.

Pardon, goddess of the night,
Those that slew thy virgin knight;
For the which, with songs of woe,
Round about her tomb they go.
Midnight, assist our moan,
Help us to sigh and groan,
Heavily, heavily:
Graves yawn and yield your dead,
Till death be uttered,
Heavenly, heavenly.[a]

CLAUD. Now unto thy bones good night!
Yearly will I do this rite.[b]

D. PEDRO. Good morrow, masters; put your torches out:
The wolves have prey'd; and look, the gentle day,
Before the wheels of Phœbus, round about
Dapples the drowsy east with spots of grey:
Thanks to you all, and leave us; fare you well.

CLAUD. Good morrow, masters; each his several way.

---

[a] Heavenly, heavenly.] The quarto reads, "*Heavily, heavily*."

[b] Yearly will I do this rite.] The old editions give this couplet to the Attendant, whom they style, "Lord:" it undoubtedly belongs to Claudio.

D. PEDRO. Come, let us hence, and put on other weeds,
And then to Leonato's we will go.
CLAUD. And, Hymen, now with luckier issue speeds,
Than this, for whom we render'd up this woe!
[*Exeunt.*

SCENE IV.—*A Room in* Leonato'*s House.*

Enter LEONATO, ANTONIO, BENEDICK, BEATRICE, URSULA, Friar, *and* HERO.

FRIAR. Did I not tell you she was innocent?
LEON. So are the prince and Claudio, who accus'd her,
Upon the error that you heard debated:
But Margaret was in some fault for this;
Although against her will, as it appears
In the true course of all the question.
ANT. Well, I am glad that all things sort so well.
BENE. And so am I, being else by faith enforc'd
To call young Claudio to a reckoning for it.
LEON. Well, daughter, and you gentlewomen all,
Withdraw into a chamber by yourselves,
And, when I send for you, come hither mask'd:
The prince and Claudio promis'd by this hour
To visit me:—you know your office, brother;
You must be father to your brother's daughter,
And give her to young Claudio. [*Exeunt* Ladies.
ANT. Which I will do with confirm'd countenance.
BENE. Friar, I must entreat your pains, I think.
FRIAR. To do what, signior?
BENE. To bind me, or undo me, one of them.—
Signior Leonato, truth it is, good signior,
Your niece regards me with an eye of favour.
LEON. That eye my daughter lent her; 'tis most true.
BENE. And I do with an eye of love requite her.
LEON. The sight whereof, I think, you had from me,
From Claudio, and the prince. But what's your will?
BENE. Your answer, sir, is enigmatical:
But, for my will, my will is, your good will
May stand with ours, this day to be conjoin'd
In the estate* of honourable marriage:—
In which, good friar, I shall desire your help.
LEON. My heart is with your liking.
FRIAR. And my help.
Here come the prince, and Claudio.[a]

Enter DON PEDRO, *and* CLAUDIO, *with* Attendants.

D. PEDRO. Good morrow to this fair assembly.
LEON. Good morrow, prince; good morrow, Claudio;
We here attend you; are you yet determined
To-day to marry with my brother's daughter?
CLAUD. I'll hold my mind, were she an Ethiope.
LEON. Call her forth, brother, here's the friar ready. [*Exit* ANTONIO.
D. PEDRO. Good morrow, Benedick: why, what's the matter,
That you have such a February face,
So full of frost, of storm, and cloudiness?
CLAUD. I think, he thinks upon the savage bull:—
Tush, fear not, man, we'll tip thy horns with gold,
And all Europa shall rejoice at thee,
As once Europa did at lusty Jove,
When he would play the noble beast in love.
BENE. Bull Jove, sir, had an amiable low,
And some such strange bull leap'd your father's cow,
And* got a calf in that same† noble feat,
Much like to you, for you have just his bleat.

Re-enter ANTONIO, *with the* Ladies *masked.*

CLAUD. For this I owe you: here come other reckonings.
Which is the lady I must seize upon?
ANT. This same is she, and I do give you her.[b]
CLAUD. Why, then she's mine. Sweet, let me see your face.
LEON. No, that you shall not, till you take her hand
Before this friar, and swear to marry her.
CLAUD. Give me your hand before this holy friar;
I am your husband, if you like of me.
HERO. And when I liv'd, I was your other wife: [*Unmasking.*
And when you lov'd, you were my other husband.
CLAUD. Another Hero?
HERO. Nothing certainer:
One Hero died defil'd;‡ but I do live,
And, surely as I live, I am a maid.
D. PEDRO. The former Hero! Hero that is dead!
LEON. She died, my lord, but whiles her slander liv'd.
FRIAR. All this amazement can I qualify,
When, after that the holy rites are ended,

(*) Old text, *state.*

[a] Here come the prince, and Claudio.] This line is not in the folio.

[b] And I do give you her.] In the old copies, this speech is assigned to Leonato, but erroneously, as Theobald first pointed out, since it had been agreed in an early part of the scene that Antonio should give the lady away.

(*) First folio, *A.* (†) First folio, *some.* (‡) First folio omits, *defil'd.*

I'll tell you largely of fair Hero's death:
Mean time, let wonder seem familiar,
And to the chapel let us presently.

BENE. Soft and fair, friar.—Which is Beatrice?

BEAT. I answer to that name; what is your will? [*Unmasking.*

BENE. Do not you love me?

BEAT. Why no, no more than reason.

BENE. Why, then your uncle, and the prince, and Claudio,
Have been deceived; they swore you did.

BEAT. Do not you love me?

BENE. Troth, no, no more than reason.

BEAT. Why, then, my cousin, Margaret, and Ursula,
Are much deceiv'd; for they did swear you did.

BENE. They swore that* you were almost sick for me.

BEAT. They swore that* you were well-nigh dead for me.

BENE. 'Tis no such† matter:—then you do not love me?

BEAT. No, truly, but in friendly recompense.

LEON. Come, cousin, I am sure you love the gentleman.

CLAUD. And I'll be sworn upon't, that he loves her;
For here's a paper, written in his hand,
A halting sonnet of his own pure brain,
Fashion'd to Beatrice.

HERO. And here's another,
Writ in my cousin's hand, stolen from her pocket,
Containing her affection unto Benedick.

BENE. A miracle! here's our own hands against our hearts!—Come, I will have thee; but, by this light, I take thee for pity.

BEAT. I would not deny you; but, by this good day, I yield upon great persuasion; and, partly, to save your life, for I was told you were in a consumption.

BENE. Peace, I will stop your mouth.[a] [*Kissing her.*

D. PEDRO. How dost thou, *Benedick the married man?*

BENE. I'll tell thee what, prince; a college of wit-crackers cannot flout me out of my humour. Dost thou think, I care for a satire, or an epigram? No: if a man will be beaten with brains, he shall wear nothing handsome about him; in brief, since I do purpose to marry, I will think nothing to any purpose that the world can say against it; and therefore never flout at me for what* I have

(*) First folio omits, *that*. (†) First folio omits, *such*.

(*) First folio omits, *what*.

a Peace, I will stop your mouth.] The old editions give this speech to Leonato.

said against it; for man is a giddy[a] thing, and this is my conclusion.—For thy part, Claudio, I did think to have beaten thee; but in that thou art like to be my kinsman, live unbruised, and love my cousin.

CLAUD. I had well hoped, thou wouldst have denied Beatrice, that I might have cudgelled thee out of thy single life, to make thee a double dealer;[b] which, out of question, thou wilt be, if my cousin do not look exceeding narrowly to thee.

BENE. Come, come, we are friends:—let's have a dance ere we are married, that we may lighten our own hearts, and our wives' heels.

LEON. We'll have dancing afterwards.

BENE. First, o' my word; therefore, play music.—Prince, thou art sad; get thee a wife, get thee a wife: there is no staff more reverend than one tipped with horn.

Enter a Messenger.

MESS. My lord, your brother John is ta'en in flight,
And brought with armed men back to Messina.

BENE. Think not on him till to-morrow, I'll devise thee brave punishments for him.—Strike up, pipers! [*Dance.—Exeunt.*

---

[a] Giddy—] That is, *inconstant*. So in "Henry V." Act I. Sc. 2:—

"—— the Scot,
Who hath been still a *giddy* neighbour to us."

[b] A double dealer;] To appreciate the equivoque, it must be understood that *double dealer* was a term jocosely applied to any one notoriously unfaithful in love or wedlock.

ILLUSTRATIVE COMMENTS.

ACT I.

(1) SCENE I.—*He set up his bills here in Messina.*] The only mode of advertising practised in Shakespeare's time appears to have been the very obvious one of attaching notices to posts and walls in places of great public resort: and these *affiches* were, of course, miscellaneous enough. Prominent among them were to be seen the *play-bills*, a step in advance of the ordinary placards, in being often *printed*; the "terrible billes" of "*quack-salving emperickes*;" the notification of servants who wanted employment, and masters who required servants; of landlords wanting to let, and tenants wishing to occupy; of those who had something to teach, and those who had much to learn; of the many who had lost, and the few who had found; and, which has more immediate reference to the passage in the text, the *challenges of scholars, fencers, archers, wrestlers, watermen,* &c. &c. with whom it was customary to "set up their bills," defying all comers, or sometimes only a particular rival, to a trial of skill.

(2) SCENE I.—*And challenged Cupid at the flight: and my uncle's fool, reading the challenge, subscribed for Cupid, and challenged him at the bird-bolt.*] The meaning of this, Douce says, is, "Benedick, from a vain conceit of his influence over women, challenged Cupid at *roving* (a particular kind of archery, in which *flight*-arrows are used). In other words, he challenged him to shoot *at hearts*. The fool, to ridicule this piece of vanity, in his turn challenged Benedick to shoot at crows with the cross-bow and bird-bolt; an inferior kind of archery used by fools, who, for obvious reasons, were not permitted to shoot with pointed arrows; whence the proverb, 'A fool's bolt is soon shot.'"

(3) SCENE I.—*Like the old tale, my lord: it is not so, nor 't was not so; but, indeed, God forbid it should be so.*] The old tale referred to—which has been preserved by Blakeway, a contributor of some intelligent notes to the Variorum edition, who took it down from the recitation of an aged female relative—is as follows:—

"Once upon a time, there was a young lady (called Lady Mary in the story), who had two brothers. One summer they all three went to a country seat of theirs, which they had not before visited. Among the other gentry in the neighbourhood who came to see them, was a Mr. Fox, a batchelor, with whom they, particularly the young lady, were much pleased. He used often to dine with them, and frequently invited Lady Mary to come and see his house. One day that her brothers were absent elsewhere, and she had nothing better to do, she determined to go thither; and accordingly set out unattended. When she arrived at the house, and knocked at the door, no one answered.* At length she opened it, and went in; over the portal of the hall was written, '*Be bold, be bold, but not too bold*:' she advanced: over the staircase the same inscription: she went up: over the entrance of a gallery, the same: she proceeded: over the door of a chamber,—'*Be bold, be bold, but not too bold, lest that your heart's blood should run cold.*' She opened it; it was full of skeletons, tubs full of blood, &c. She retreated in haste; coming down stairs, she saw out of a window Mr. Fox advancing towards the house, with a drawn sword in one hand, while with the other he dragged along a young lady by her hair. Lady Mary had just time to slip down, and hide herself under the stairs, before Mr. Fox and his victim arrived at the foot of them. As he pulled the young lady up stairs, she caught hold of one of the *bannisters* with her hand, on which was a rich bracelet. Mr. Fox cut it off with his sword: the hand and bracelet fell into Lady Mary's lap, who then contrived to escape unobserved, and got home safe to her brother's house.

"After a few days, Mr. Fox came to dine with them as usual (whether by invitation, or of his own accord, this deponent saith not). After dinner, when the guests began to amuse each other with extraordinary anecdotes, Lady Mary at length said, she would relate to them a remarkable dream she had lately had. I dreamt, said she, that as you, Mr. Fox, had often invited me to your house, I would go there one morning. When I came to the house, I knocked, &c., but no one answered. When I opened the door, over the hall was written, '*Be bold, be bold, but not too bold.*' But, said she, turning to Mr. Fox, and smiling, '*It is not so, nor it was not so*;' then she pursues the rest of the story, concluding at every turn with, '*It is not so, nor it was not so*,' till she comes to the room full of dead bodies, when Mr. Fox took up the burden of the tale, and said, '*It is not so, nor it was not so, and God forbid it should be so*;' which he continues to repeat at every subsequent turn of the dreadful story, till she came to the circumstance of his cutting off the young lady's hand, when upon his saying as usual, '*It is not so, nor it was not so, and God forbid it should be so*,' Lady Mary retorts, '*But it is so, and it was so, and here the hand I have to show*,' at the same time producing the hand and bracelet from her lap; whereupon the guests drew their swords, and instantly cut Mr. Fox into a thousand pieces."

(4) SCENE I.—*And he that hits me, let him be clapped on the shoulder, and called Adam.*] Adam Bel, Clym of the Clough, and William of Cloudesley, three famous archers of the "north countrey," are the heroes of an ancient, curious, and once popular ballad, of near 700 lines, "imprinted at London, in Lothburye, by Wyllyam Copland," (*b. l.* no date) beginning:—

---

* This circumstance in the story, Mr. Dyce supposes to have been borrowed from Spenser's *Faërie Queene*:—

"And, as she lookt about, she did behold
How over that same dore was likewise writ,
Be bolde, be bolde, and every where, *Be bold*;
That much she muz'd, yet could not construe it
By any ridling skill or commune wit.
At last she spyde at that rowmes upper end
Another yron dore: on which was writ,
Be not too bold; whereto though she did bend
Her earnest minde, yet wist not what it might intend."

The Faërie Queene, b. iii. c. xi. st. 54.

" Mery it was in grene forest,
Among the leues grene,
Wher that men walke east and west,
Wyth bowes and arrowes kene,
To ryse the dere out of theyr denne,
Such sightes hath ofte bene sene,
As by thre yemen of the north countrey,
By them it is I meane :
The one of them hight Adam Bel,
The other Clym of the Clough,
The thyrd was William of Cloudesly,
An archer good ynough."

The place of residence of these noted outlaws was the forest of Englewood, not far from Carlisle ; but the period when they flourished is unknown.

(5) Scene III.—*As I was smoking a musty room.*] The disregard of ventilation and cleanliness in early times was such as to render this precaution very necessary. Steevens has quoted from the Harleian MSS. No. 6850, a paper of directions drawn up by Sir John Puckering's steward, relative to Suffolk Place, before Queen Elizabeth's visit to it, in 1594. The 15th article is—" The swetynynge of the house in all places by any means." And old Burton, in his "Anatomy of Melancholy," ed. 1632, p. 261, tells us that "the smoake of juniper is in great request with us at Oxford, to *sweeten* our chambers."

ACT II.

(1) Scene I.—*The Hundred merry tales.*] Of this popular old jest book, printed by John Rastell, 1517—1533, a fragment, containing nearly all the tales, was fortunately discovered by the Rev. J. J. Conybeare some years ago, and has been carefully reprinted by Mr. Singer, under the title of " Shakspeare's Jest Book." The stories thus rescued from oblivion are so sadly deficient in point, and sometimes in decency also, that Beatrice might well resent the imputation of having derived her wit from such a source.

(2) Scene I.—*As melancholy as a lodge in a warren.*] " They used in the old time in their vineyards and cucumber gardens, to erect and builde little cotages and lodges for their watchfolkes and keepers that looked to the same, for feare of filchers and stealers ; which lodges and cotages, so soone as the grapes and cucumbers were gathered, were abandoned of the watchmen and keepers, and no more frequented. From this forsaking and leaving of these lodges and cotages, the prophet Isaiah taketh a similitude, and applieth the same against Jerusalem, the which hee pronounceth, should be so ruinated and laid waste, that no relick thereof should be left, and that it should become even as an empty and tenantlesse cotage or lodge in a forsaken vineyard and abandoned cucumber garden."—Newton's *Herbal for the Bible*, 1587.

" By the *solitarinesse* of the house I judged it *a lodge in a forest*, but there was no bawling of dogges thereabout." —*The Man in the Moone telling Strange Fortunes*, 1609. Quoted by Mr. Halliwell.

(3) Scene III.—*Her hair shall be of what colour it please God.*] A sarcasm upon the practice so prevalent in Elizabeth's reign of dyeing the hair :—

" If any have haire of her own naturall growing, which is not faire enough, then will they die it in divers colours, almost chaunging the substaunce into accidentes by their devilish and more than thrice cursed devises. So, whereas their haire was given them as a signe of subjection, and therefore they were commanded to cherish the same, now have they made it an ornament of pride and destruction to themselves for ever excepte they repent."—*The Anatomie of Abuses, by Phillip Stubs*, 1584.

Mr. Halliwell has discovered several ancient recipes for dyeing the hair : among them is one in " The Treasure of Evonymus," 1559, which is peculiar :—

" Sponsa solis beeten, otherwyse the siedes of solsosium beeten, put it in milke of a woman that nurseth a boy ten otherwise xi. daies, and then make an oyl ; this oyll, sod with leved gold, seething it gentely by the space of one day, is marvelous, for if a man washe his heares therewith they shall become lyke gold ; if the face be wet, and rubbed with the same, it shall be plaine and cleare, that it shall seeme angellike, continuing for the space of v. dayes."

(4) Scene III.—*Jacke Wilson.*] " John Wilson, the composer, was born in 1594. Anthony Wood tells us, that having an early taste for music, he became one of the most eminent masters of that science. In 1626 he was constituted ' a gentleman of the Royal Chapel,' and about the same time, according to Wood, ' musician in ordinary' to Charles I. He was created Doctor of Music in the University of Oxford, in 1644. At the Restoration, he was appointed chamber musician to Charles II. ; and on the death of Henry Lawes, in 1662, was again received into the Chapel Royal. He died in 1673, at nearly seventy-nine years of age."—Rimbault.

(5) Scene III. — *Stalk on, stalk on ; the fowl sits.*] Claudio alludes to the stalking-horse, behind which the fowlers of old were used to screen themselves from the sight of their game.

" But sometime it so happeneth, that the Fowl are so shie, there is no getting a shoot at them without a Stalking-horse, which must be some old Jade trained up for that purpose, who will gently, and as you will have him, walk up and down in the water which way you please, flodding and eating on the grass that grows therein.

" You must shelter yourself and Gun behind his fore-shoulder, bending your Body down low by his side, and keeping his Body still full between you and the Fowl : Being within shot, take your Level from before the fore-part of the Horse, shooting as it were between the Horse's Neck and the Water. * * * * Now to supply the want of a Stalking-horse, which will take up a great deal of Time to instruct and make fit for this Exercise ; you may make one of any Pieces of old Canvas, which you must shape into the Form of an Horse, with the Head bending downwards as if he grazed. You may stuff it with any light matter ; and do not forget to paint it of the Colour of an Horse, of which the Brown is the best. * * * * It must be made so portable, that you may bear it with ease in one Hand, moving it so as it may seem to Graze as you go.

" Sometimes the Stalking-horse was made in shape or an Ox ; sometimes in the form of a Stag—and sometimes to represent a tree, shrub, or bush. In every case the Stalking-horse had a spike at the bottom to stick into the ground while the fowler took his level."—*The Gentleman's Recreation*.

ACT III.

(1) SCENE II.—*Yet is this no charm for the tooth-ache.*] In Aubrey's Miscellanies, p. 141, is one of these charms:—"*To cure the tooth-ach:* Out of Mr. Ashmole's manuscript writ with his own hand:—'Mars, hur, abursa, aburse: Jesus Christ for Mary's sake,—Take away this Tooth-Ach.' Write the words three times; and as you say the words, let the party burn one paper, then another, and then the last. He says, he saw it experimented, and the party immediately cured."

(2) SCENE III.—*You speak like an ancient and most quiet watchman.*] Of the functionary whom Shakespeare had in view, the ancient watchman of London, there are two or three representations preserved. He was clad in a long loose cloak or coat, which reached to his heels, and was belted at the waist, and he usually carried the pike or halbert called "a bill," with a lantern and a great bell. The "charge," or duties of his office, are clearly laid down in the accompanying extract from Dalton's "Country Justice:"—

"This watch is to be kept yearly from the feast of the Ascention until Michaelmas, in every towne, and shall continue all the night, *sc.* from the sunne setting to the sunne rising. All such strangers, or persons suspected, as shall in the night time passe by the watchmen (appointed thereto by the towne constable, or other officer), may be examined by the said watchmen, whence they come, and what they be, and of their businesse, &c. And if they find cause of suspition, they shall stay them; and if such persons will not obey the arrest of the watchmen, the said watchmen shall levie hue and crie, that the offendors may be taken: or else they may justifie to beate them (for that they resist the peace and Justice of the Realme), and may also set them in the stockes (for the same) untill the morning; and then, if no suspition be found, the said persons shall be let go and quit: But if they find cause of suspition, they shall forthwith deliver the said persons to the sherife, who shall keepe them in prison untill they bee duely delivered; or else the watchmen may deliver such person to the constable, and so to convey them to the Justice of peace, by him to be examined, and to be bound over, or committed, untill the offenders be acquitted in due manner."

(3) SCENE III.—*And one Deformed is one of them; I know him, 'a wears a lock.*] The custom, imported from the Continent, of wearing a long lock of hair, sometimes ornamented with gaudy ribbons, came into fashion in the sixteenth century. In Greene's "Quip for an Upstart Courtier," 1592, quoted by Mr. Halliwell, a barber asks his customer, "Will you be Frenchified with a love-lock down to your shoulders, wherein you may hang your mistres' favor?" Against this practice Prynne wrote a treatise, entitled "The Unlovelinesse of Love-lockes, or a Discourse proving the wearing of a Locke to be unseemely," 1628 and from a passage in his Histriomastix, it appears that the fashion had become prevalent in a class not unlikely to be under the surveillance of worthy Dogberry's "compartners," Hugh Oatcake and George Seacole, "—— and more especially in long, unshorne, womanish, frizled, love-provoking haire, and *love-lockes* growne now too much in fashion with comly pages, youthes, and lewd, effeminate, ruffianly persons."

Manzoni informs us that in Lombardy during the same period, the custom was affected by a lawless class of the community as a cloak for their iniquity, and numerous edicts were promulgated, forbidding the use of locks either before or behind the ears, under a penalty of three hundred crowns, or three years' imprisonment in the galleys. "Bravoes by profession and villains of every kind, used to wear a long lock of hair, which they drew over the face like a vizor on meeting any one, so that the lock might almost be considered a part of the armour, and a distinctive mark of bravoes and vagabonds, whence those characters commonly bore the name of *Ciuffi, i. e. Locks.*"—*I Promessi Sposi, Cap.* 3.

(4) SCENE IV.—*Carduus Benedictus.*] "Blessed Thistle is called in Latine every where *Carduus Benedictus,* and in shops by a compound word, *Cardo-benedictus;* it is a kinde of wilde bastard Saffron.

"Blessed Thistle, taken in meate or drinke, is good for the swimming and giddinesse of the head, it strengthneth memorie, and is a singular remedie against deafnesse."—GERARD'S *Herbal.*

"Carduus Benedictus, or blessed Thistell, so worthily named for the singular vertues that it hath.* * * Howsoever it be used it strengtheneth all the principall partes of the bodie, it sharpeneth both the wit and memory, quickeneth all the senses, comforteth the stomacke, procureth appetite, and hath a special vertue against poison, and preserveth from the pestilence, and is excellent good against any kind of Fever being used in this manner: Take a dramme of the powder, put it into a good draught of ale or wine, warme it and drinke it a quarter of an hour before the fit doth come, then goe to bed, cover you well with clothes, and procure sweate, which by the force of the herbe will easily come foorth, and so continue until the fit be past: or else you may take the distilled water after the same maner. By this meanes you may recover in a short time, yea if it were a pestilentiall fever. So that this remedie be used before twelve houres be past after the disease felt. For which notable effects this herb may worthily be called *Benedictus* or *Omnimorbia,* that is a salve for everie sore, not known to Physitians of old time, but lately revealed by the speciall providence of Almightie God."—*The Haven of Health, by Thomas Cogan, Maister of Artes and Bacheler of Physicke. Lond. 4to. b. l.* 1596.

ACT V.

(1) Scene I.—
Hang her an epitaph upon her tomb.]

In some curious observations attached to Pietro Aretino's book of "The Three Impostors," M. De la Monnoie refers to the practice of suspending epitaphs on the hearses and monuments of important personages, as being common in the sixteenth century. "It is the custom with Catholics," he remarks, "to attach to some pillar or other place near to the tombs of deceased persons, and especially such as were of reputation, papers of funeral inscriptions. These inscriptions were, in fact, as they always ought to be, to the honour of the departed individual; but as Aretino had been a notorious libertine, it is quite possible that after *his* interment some satirist hung the condemnatory epitaph preserved by Moréri, on the door of St. Luke's church, where he was buried." The custom was still general in England when Shakespeare lived; many fine and interesting examples of it existing in the old cathedral of St. Paul's, and other churches of London, down to the time of the Great Fire, in the form of pensile-tables of wood and metal, painted or engraved with poetical memorials, suspended against the columns and walls.* Among these may be particularized the well-known verses on Queen Elizabeth, beginning:—

"Spaines Rod, Romes Ruine, Netherlands Reliefe;"

which appear to have been very generally displayed in the churches of the realm.

* See *Stow, Weever, and Dugdale.*

There is another allusion to this graceful custom in the present Comedy, Act IV. Sc. 1:—

"Maintain a mourning ostentation;
And, on your family's old monument,
Hang mournful epitaphs."

And Izaak Walton, in his "Life of Dr. Donne," supplies a curious illustration of it under the date of 1631. "The next day after his burial some one of the many lovers and admirers of his virtue and learning, writ this epitaph with a coal on the wall over his grave:—

'Reader! I am to let Thee know
Donne's Body only lies below;
For, *could the Earth his Soul comprise,*
Earth would be Richer than the Skies!'"

(2) Scene II.—*I give thee the bucklers.*] This is an expression borrowed from Sword and Buckler play, and often adopted by our old writers, meaning, I yield myself vanquished. Thus, in P. Holland's translation of "Pliny's Natural History," B. x. Ch. xxi.:—"It goeth against his stomach (the cock's) to yeeld the gantlet and *give the bucklers.*"

Again, in Greene's Second Part of "Coney-Catching," 1592:—"At this his master laught, and was glad for further advantage, to *yield the bucklers* to his prentice."

And in Chapman's "May-Day," 1611:—

"And now I lay *the bucklers* at your feet."

ANCIENT BALLAD OF "LIGHT O' LOVE," (see p. 720.)

From the original black-letter copy in the Library of GEORGE DANIEL, ESQ.

A very proper dittie to the tune of Lightie love.

Leave Lightie love Ladies for feare of yll name:
And True love embrace ye, to purchase your fame.

By force I am stred my fancie to write,
Ingratitude willeth mee not to refraine:
Then blame me not Ladies although I indite
What lighty love now amongst you doth raigne.
Your traces in places, in outward allurements
Doth moove my endevour to be the more playne;
Your nicyngs and ticings with sundrie procurementes
To publish your lightie love doth mee constrayne.

Deceite is not daintie, it coms at eche dish,
Fraude goes a fisshyng with frendly lookes,
Throughe frendship is spoyled the seely poore fish,
That hoover and shover upon your false hookes,
With baight, you lay waight, to catch here and there,
Whiche causeth poore fisshes their freedome to lose:
Then loute ye, and floute ye, wherby doth appere,
Your lightie love Ladies, styll cloaked with glose.

With DIAN so chaste, you seeme to compare,
When HELLENS you bee, and hang on her trayne:
Mee thinkes faithfull Thisbies bee now very rare,
Not one CLEOPATRA, I doubt doth remayne:
You wincke, and you twincke, tyll Cupid have caught,
And forceth through flames your Lovers to sue:
Your lyghtie love Ladies, too deere they have bought,
When nothyng wyll moove you, their causes to rue.

I speake not for spite, ne do I disdayne,
Your beautie fayre Ladies, in any respect:
But ones Ingratitude doth mee constrayne,
A childe hurt with fire, the same to neglect:
For proovyng in lovyng, I finde by good triall,
When Beautie had brought mee unto her becke:
She staying, not waying, but made a deniall,
And shewyng her lightie love, gave me the checke.

Thus fraude for frendship, did lodge in her brest,
Suche are most women, that when they espie,
Their lovers inflamed with sorowes opprest,
They stande then with Cupid against their replie
They taunte, and they vaunte, they smile when they vew,
How Cupid had caught them under his trayne,
But warned, discerned, the proofe is most true,
That lightie love Ladies, amongst you doth reigne.

It seemes by your doynges, that Cressed doth scoole ye,
Penelopes vertues are cleane out of thought:
Mee thinkes by your constantnesse, Heleyne doth rule ye,
Whiche, both Greece and Troy, to ruyne hath brought:
No doubt, to tell out, your manyfolde driftes,
Would shew you as constant, as is the Sea sande:
To truste so unjust, that all is but shieftes,
With lightie love bearyng your lovers in hande.

If ARGUS were lyvying whose eyes were in nomber,
The Peacockes plume painted, as Writers replie,
Yet Women by wiles, full sore would him cumber,
For all his quicke eyes, their driftes to espie:
Suche feates, with disceates, they dayly frequent,
To conquere Mennes mindes, their humours to feede,
That bouldly I may geve Arbittrement:
Of this your lightie love, Ladies in deede.

Ye men that are subject to Cupid his stroke,
And therein seemeth to have your delight:
Thinke when you see baight theres hidden a hooke,
Whiche sure wyll have you, if that you do bight:
Suche wiles, and suche guiles, by women are wrought,
That halfe their mischiefes, men cannot prevent,
When they are most pleasant unto your thought,
Then nothyng but lightie love, is their intent.

Consider that poyson doth lurke often tyme
In shape of sugre, to put some to payne:
And fayre wordes paynted, as Dames can desire,
The olde Proverbe saith doth make some fooles faine:
Be wise and precise, take warning by mee,
Trust not the Crocodile, least you do rue:
To womens faire wordes, do never agree:
For all is but lightie love, this is most true.

ANEXES so daintie, Example may bee,
Whose lightie love caused young IPHIS his woe,
His true love was tryed by death, as you see,
Her lightie love forced the knight therunto:
For shame then refrayne you Ladies therefore,
The Cloudes they doo vanish, and light doth appeare:
You can not dissemble, nor hide it no more,
Your love is but lightie love, this is most cleare.

For Troylus tried the same over well,
In lovyng his Ladie, as Fame doth reporte:
And likewise Menander, as Stories doth tell,
Who swam the salt Seas, to his love, to resorte:
So true, that I rue, such lovers should lose
Their labour in seekyng their Ladies unkinde:
Whose love, thei did proove, as the Proverbe nowe goes
Even very lightie love, lodgde in their minde.

I touche no suche Ladies, as true love imbrace,
But suche as to lightie love dayly applie:
And none wyll be grieved, in this kinde of case,
Save suche as are minded, true love to denie:
Yet frendly and kindly, I shew you my minde,
Fayre Ladies I wish you, to use it no more,
But say what you list, thus I have definde,
That lightie love Ladies, you ought to abhore.

To trust womens wordes, in any respect,
The danger by mee right well it is seene:
And Love and his Lawes, who would not neglect,
The tryall whereof, moste peryllous beene:
Pretendyng, the endyng, if I have offended,
I crave of you Ladies an Answere againe:
Amende, and whats said, shall soone be amended,
If case that your lightie love, no longer do rayne.

Finis. By Leonard Gybson. Imprinted at LONDON, in the upper end of Fleet lane, by Richard Ihones: and are to be solde at his shop joyning to the South-West Dore of Saint Paules Church.

CRITICAL OPINIONS

ON

MUCH ADO ABOUT NOTHING.

"THE main plot in *Much Ado about Nothing* is the same with the story of *Ariodante and Ginevra*, in Ariosto; the secondary circumstances and development are no doubt very different. The mode in which the innocent Hero before the altar at the moment of the wedding, and in the presence of her family and many witnesses, is put to shame by a most degrading charge, false indeed, yet clothed with every appearance of truth, is a grand piece of theatrical effect in the true and justifiable sense. The impression would have been too tragical had not Shakspeare carefully softened it, in order to prepare for a fortunate catastrophe. The discovery of the plot against Hero has been already partly made, though not by the persons interested; and the poet has contrived, by means of the blundering simplicity of a couple of constables and watchmen, to convert the arrest and the examination of the guilty individuals into scenes full of the most delightful amusement. There is also a second piece of theatrical effect not inferior to the first, where Claudio, now convinced of his error, and in obedience to the penance laid on his fault, thinking to give his hand to a relation of his injured bride, whom he supposes dead, discovers, on her unmasking, Hero herself. The extraordinary success of this play in Shakspeare's own day, and even since in England, is, however, to be ascribed more particularly to the parts of Benedick and Beatrice, two humorsome beings, who incessantly attack each other with all the resources of raillery. Avowedly rebels to love, they are both entangled in its net by a merry plot of their friends to make them believe that each is the object of the secret passion of the other. Some one or other, not over-stocked with penetration, has objected to the same artifice being twice used in entrapping them; the drollery, however, lies in the very symmetry of the deception. Their friends attribute the whole effect to their own device, but the exclusive direction of their raillery against each other is in itself a proof of a growing inclination. Their witty vivacity does not even abandon them in the avowal of love; and their behaviour only assumes a serious appearance for the purpose of defending the slandered Hero. This is exceedingly well imagined; the lovers of jesting must fix a point beyond which they are not to indulge in their humour, if they would not be mistaken for buffoons by trade."—SCHLEGEL.

VOLUME TWO.

Contents.

ALL'S WELL THAT ENDS WELL.

Vol. II. Act IV. Sc. 1.

ALL'S WELL THAT ENDS WELL.

THE earliest version of this comedy we possess is that of the folio, 1623. If a prior edition were ever printed, a copy of it would be inestimably valuable; for of all the plays of Shakespeare this appears to have suffered most from the negligence of transcribers and compositors. Malone, in his latest chronological arrangement, upon a supposed allusion to the fanaticism of the Puritans, dates its production in 1606; but there need be little hesitation in believing that it was one of the author's youthful productions, and most probably the piece indicated by Meres, in his "Palladis Tamia," 1598, as "Love Labors Wonne;" that it was intended as a counter-play to "Love's Labour's Lost," and was originally intituled "Love's Labour's Won; or, All's Well that Ends Well."

The fable is derived from the story of "Giletta of Narbona," forming the ninth novel of the third day in Boccaccio's "Decamerone," a translation of which is given in the first volume of Painter's "Palace of Pleasure," quarto, 1566; where the argument is thus set forth:—"Giletta, a phisician's daughter of Narbon, healed the Frenche Kyng of a fistula, for reward wherof she demaunded Beltramo counte of Rossigniole to husband. The counte beyng maried againste his will, for despite fled to Florence and loved an other. Giletta his wife, by pollicie founde meanes to lye with her husbande in place of his lover, and was begotten with child of two soonnes; whiche knowen to her husbande, he received her againe and afterwards she lived in greate honor and felicitie." In the leading incidents Shakespeare has closely adhered to the story; but the characters of the Countess, Parolles, the Clown, and Lafeu, as well as all the circumstances of the secondary plot, sprang from the inexhaustible resources of his own mind.

"All's well that ends well," is an English proverbial saying of great antiquity. It was used in a slightly varied form during the celebrated rebellion of Jack Straw, by one of the insurgents, in a speech recorded in the chronicle of Henry de Knyghton;—"Jak Carter prayeth you alle that ye make a gode end of that ye have begunne, and doth wele aye better and better, for atte the evyn men hereth the day, for if *the ende be wele, thanne is al wele.*" And, in Fulwell's "*Ars Adulandi,*" 1579, to this passage in the text:—"Wherefore, gentle Maister Philodoxus, I bid you adew with this motion or caveat; *Respice Finem:*" the marginal note says, "All is Well that Endes Well."

Persons Represented.

KING OF FRANCE.

DUKE OF FLORENCE.

BERTRAM, *Count of* Rousillon.

LAFEU,* *an old Lord.*

PAROLLES,* *a Follower of* Bertram.

Divers young French *Lords, who serve with* Bertram *in the* Florentine *war.*

Steward,
Clown,
A Page, } *Servants to the Countess of* Rousillon.

COUNTESS OF ROUSILLON, *Mother to* Bertram.

HELENA, *a gentlewoman protected by the* Countess.

An old Widow of Florence.

DIANA, *daughter to the Widow.*

VIOLENTA,
MARIANA, } *Neighbours and friends to the Widow.*

Lords, attending on the King; *Officers, Soldiers,* &c., French and Florenti

SCENE,—*Partly in* FRANCE *and partly in* TUSCANY.

* According to Steevens, we should write *Lefeu* and *Paroles.*

ACT I.

SCENE I.—Rousillon. *A Room in the* Countess's *Palace.*

Enter BERTRAM, *the* COUNTESS *of* ROUSILLON, HELENA, *and* LAFEU, *all in black.*

COUNT. In delivering my son from me, I bury a second husband.

BER. And I, in going, madam, weep o'er my father's death anew: but I must attend his majesty's command, to whom I am now in ward,(1) evermore in subjection.

LAF. You shall find of the king a husband, madam;—you, sir, a father. He that so generally is at all times good, must of necessity hold his virtue to you, whose worthiness would stir it up where it wanted, rather than lack it where there is such abundance.

COUNT. What hope is there of his majesty's amendment?

LAF. He hath abandoned his physicians, madam; under whose practices he hath persecuted time with hope; and finds no other advantage in the process, but only the losing of hope by time.

COUNT. This young gentlewoman had a father, (O, that *had!* how sad a passage 'tis!) whose skill was almost as great as his honesty; had it stretched so far, would have made nature immortal, and death should have play for lack of work.[a] Would, for the king's sake, he were living! I think it would be the death of the king's disease.

LAF. How called you the man you speak of, madam?

COUNT. He was famous, sir, in his profession, and it was his great right to be so; Gerard de Narbon.

LAF. He was excellent, indeed, madam; the king very lately spoke of him, admiringly, and mourningly: he was skilful enough to have lived still, if knowledge could be set up against mortality.

BER. What is it, my good lord, the king languishes of?

LAF. A fistula,[b] my lord.

BER. I heard not of it before.

LAF. I would it were not notorious.—Was this gentlewoman the daughter of Gerard de Narbon?

COUNT. His sole child, my lord, and bequeathed to my overlooking. I have those hopes of her good, that her education promises; her dispositions she inherits,[c] which makes fair gifts fairer; for where an unclean mind carries virtuous qualities, there commendations go with pity, they are virtues and traitors too; in her they are the better for their simpleness; she derives her honesty, and achieves her goodness.

LAF. Your commendations, madam, get from her, tears.

COUNT. 'Tis the best brine a maiden can season her praise in. The remembrance of her father never approaches her heart, but the tyranny of her sorrows takes all livelihood from her cheek. No more of this, Helena, go to,—no more; lest it be rather thought you affect a sorrow, than to have.[d]

HEL. I do affect a sorrow, indeed, but I have it too.

LAF. Moderate lamentation is the right of the dead; excessive grief the enemy to the living.

HEL. If the living be enemy to the grief, the excess makes it soon mortal.[e]

BER. Madam, I desire your holy wishes.

LAF. How understand we that?

COUNT. Be thou blest, Bertram! and succeed
thy father
In manners, as in shape; thy blood, and virtue,
Contend for empire in thee; and thy goodness,
Share with thy birth-right. Love all, trust a few,
Do wrong to none: be able for thine enemy
Rather in power, than use; and keep thy friend
Under thy own life's key: be check'd for silence,
But never tax'd for speech. What heaven more
will,
That thee may furnish, and my prayers pluck
down,
Fall on thy head! Farewell.—My lord,
'Tis an unseason'd courtier; good my lord,
Advise him.

LAF. He cannot want the best
That shall attend his love.

COUNT. Heaven bless him!—Farewell, Bertram.
[*Exit* COUNTESS.

BER. The best wishes, that can be forged in your thoughts, [*To* HELENA.] be servants to you! Be comfortable to my mother, your mistress, and make much of her.

LAF. Farewell, pretty lady: you must hold the credit of your father.
[*Exeunt* BERTRAM *and* LAFEU.

HEL. O, were that all!—I think not on my
father,
And these great tears grace his remembrance
more
Than those I shed for him.[f] What was he like?
I have forgot him: my imagination

---

[a] Whose skill was almost as great as his honesty; had it stretched so far, would have made nature immortal, &c.] Mr. Collier's annotator modernizes this passage, and reads, "*whose skill, almost as great as his honesty, had it stretched so far, would,*" &c.; but the original is quite as intelligible, and far more Shakespearian than the proposed reformation.

[b] *A* fistula, *my lord.*] In Painter's version of Boccaccio's story, the king's disorder is said to have been "a swellyng upon his breast, whiche, by reason of ill cure, was growen to a *fistula,*" &c.

[c] *Her dispositions she inherits,* &c.] There is scarcely a passage of importance in the earlier scenes of this comedy the meaning of which is not destroyed or impaired by some scandalous textual error. In the present instance some expression implying *chaste* or *pure*, before "*dispositions,*" appears to have been omitted. Perhaps we should read, "*The honesty of* her dispositions she inherits;"—*honesty* being understood in the sense of *chastity*, as in the last clause of the passage—"she derives her *honesty*, and achieves her goodness;" which we apprehend to signify, "she is chaste by temperament, and good by the practice of benevolence."

[d] *Lest it be rather thought,* &c.] The meaning here is sufficiently obvious; and, though the construction of the sentence appear to us somewhat strange and harsh, it was by no means peculiar to Shakespeare.

[e] *If the living be enemy to the grief, the excess makes it soon mortal.*] In the old copy this speech is assigned to the Countess. Tieck first suggested that it belongs to Helena; and that he is right is almost proved by Lafeu's rejoinder—"How understand we that?"

[f] *And these great tears grace his remembrance more*
Than those I shed for him.]
This is interpreted to mean, that her "great tears," being attributed to grief for the loss of her father, do his memory more grace than those she truly shed for him; but some defect in the text may be suspected; such a meaning is very tame and unsatisfying.

Carries no favour in 't, but Bertram's.
I am undone; there is no living, none,
If Bertram be away. 'T were all one,
That I should love a bright particular star,
And think to wed it, he is so above me:
In his bright radiance and collateral light
Must I be comforted, not in his sphere.
The ambition in my love thus plagues itself:
The hind, that would be mated by the lion,
Must die for love. 'T was pretty, though a plague,
To see him every hour; to sit and draw
His arched brows, his hawking eye, his curls,
In our heart's table;[a] heart, too capable
Of every line and trick of his sweet favour:
But now he's gone, and my idolatrous fancy
Must sanctify his relics. Who comes here?
One that goes with him: I love him for his sake;
And yet I know him a notorious liar,
Think him a great way fool, solely a coward;
Yet these fix'd evils sit so fit in him,
That they take place, when virtue's steely bones
Look bleak i' the cold wind: withal, full oft we see
Cold wisdom waiting on superfluous folly.

Enter PAROLLES.

PAR. Save you, fair queen.
HEL. And you, monárch.[b]
PAR. No.
HEL. And no.

---

[a] *In our heart's* table;] *Table* is used here in the sense of *panel*, or *surface*, on which a picture was painted. So, in "King John," Act II. Sc. 2:—

"Drawn in the flattering *table* of her eye!"

[b] And you, monárch.] This is conceived to be an allusion to the fantastic Italian, styled *Monarcho;* of whom an account will be found in note (1), p. 103, Vol. I. It is perhaps only anothe example of that species of repartée before noticed in "The Merchant of Venice," Act II. Sc. 9:—

"MESS. Where is *my lady?*
POR. Here; what would *my lord?*"

See note (c), p. 413, Vol. I.

PAR. Are you meditating on virginity?

HEL. Ay. You have some stain[a] of soldier in you; let me ask you a question: Man is enemy to virginity; how may we barricado it against him?

PAR. Keep him out.

HEL. But he assails; and our virginity, though valiant in the defence, yet is weak: unfold to us some warlike resistance.

PAR. There is none; man, sitting down before you, will undermine you, and blow you up.

HEL. Bless our poor virginity from underminers, and blowers up!—Is there no military policy, how virgins might blow up men?

PAR. Virginity, being blown down, man will quicklier be blown up: marry, in blowing him down again, with the breach yourselves made, you lose your city. It is not politic in the commonwealth of nature, to preserve virginity. Loss of virginity is rational increase; and there was never virgin got,* till virginity was first lost. That, you were made of, is metal to make virgins. Virginity, by being once lost, may be ten times found; by being ever kept, it is ever lost: 'tis too cold a companion: away with it.

HEL. I will stand for't a little, though therefore I die a virgin.

PAR. There's little can be said in't; 'tis against the rule of nature. To speak on the part of virginity, is to accuse your mothers; which is most infallible disobedience. He, that hangs himself, is a virgin: virginity murders itself; and should be buried in highways, out of all sanctified limit, as a desperate offendress against nature. Virginity breeds mites, much like a cheese; consumes itself to the very paring, and so dies with feeding his own stomach. Besides, virginity is peevish, proud, idle, made of self-love, which is the most inhibited[b] sin in the canon. Keep it not; you cannot choose but lose by't: out with't: within ten year it will make itself ten,[c] which is a goodly increase; and the principal itself not much the worse. Away with't.

HEL. How might one do, sir, to lose it to her own liking?

PAR. Let me see. Marry, ill, to like him that ne'er it likes. 'Tis a commodity will lose the gloss with lying; the longer kept, the less worth: off with't, while 't is vendible: answer the time of request. Virginity, like an old courtier, wears her cap out of fashion; richly suited, but unsuitable: just like the brooch and the toothpick, which wear not now. Your date is better in your pie and your porridge, than in your cheek: and your virginity, your old virginity, is like one of our French withered pears; it looks ill, it eats drily; marry, 'tis a withered pear; it was formerly better, marry, yet,[d] 'tis a withered pear: will you any thing with it?

HEL. Not my virginity yet.
There shall your master have a thousand loves,[e]
A mother, and a mistress, and a friend,
A phœnix, captain, and an enemy,
A guide, a goddess, and a sovereign,
A counsellor, a traitress, and a dear;
His humble ambition, proud humility,
His jarring concord, and his discord dulcet,
His faith, his sweet disaster; with a world
Of pretty, fond, adoptious christendoms,
That blinking Cupid gossips. Now shall he——
I know not what he shall:—God send him well!—
The court's a learning-place;—and he is one——

PAR. What one, i'faith?

HEL. That I wish well.—'Tis pity——

PAR. What's pity?

HEL. That wishing well had not a body in't,
Which might be felt: that we, the poorer born,
Whose baser stars do shut us up in wishes,
Might with effects of them follow our friends,
And show what we alone must think; which never
Returns us thanks.

Enter a Page.

PAGE. Monsieur Parolles, my lord calls for you. [*Exit* Page.

PAR. Little Helen, farewell: if I can remember thee, I will think of thee at court.

HEL. Monsieur Parolles, you were born under a charitable star.

PAR. Under Mars, I.

HEL. I especially think, *under* Mars.

PAR. Why *under* Mars?

HEL. The wars have so kept you under, that you must needs be born under Mars.

PAR. When he was predominant.

HEL. When he was retrograde, I think, rather.

PAR. Why think you so?

HEL. You go so much backward, when you fight.

(*) First folio, *goe*.

a *Some* stain—] Some *tinct*, some *mark*.

b Inhibited *sin*—] *Forbidden, prohibited.*

c *Within ten year it will make itself ten,*—] The folio reads, "—— make it selfe *two*," &c. The alteration of "two" to "ten," which was first made by Hanmer, is countenanced by a previous observation of the speaker—"Virginity, by being once lost, may be ten times found."

d *It was formerly better, marry, yet, 'tis a withered pear:*] This is a notable instance of "*yet*" being used in the sense of *now*. See note (b), p. 346, Vol. I.

e There shall your master have a thousand loves,—] Something is evidently wanting here; this rhapsody having no connexion with what precedes it. Hanmer remedies the defect by making Helena say, "*You're for the court;*" but the deficiency is more probably in Parolles' speech, where the words "*We are for the court*" may have been omitted by the compositor.

PAR. That's for advantage.

HEL. So is running away, when fear proposes the safety: but the composition, that your valour and fear makes in you, is a virtue of a good wing, and I like the wear well.

PAR. I am so full of businesses, I cannot answer thee acutely: I will return perfect courtier; in the which, my instruction shall serve to naturalize thee, so thou wilt be capable of a courtier's counsel, and understand what advice shall thrust upon thee; else thou diest in thine unthankfulness, and thine ignorance makes thee away: farewell. When thou hast leisure, say thy prayers; when thou hast none, remember thy friends: get thee a good husband, and use him as he uses thee: so farewell. [*Exit.*

HEL. Our remedies oft in ourselves do lie,
Which we ascribe to heaven: the fated sky
Gives us free scope; only, doth backward pull
Our slow designs, when we ourselves are dull.
What power is it, which mounts my love so high;
That makes me see, and cannot feed mine eye?
The mightiest space[a] in fortune, nature brings
To join like likes, and kiss like native things.
Impossible be strange attempts, to those
That weigh their pains in sense; and do suppose,
What hath been cannot be.[b] Who ever strove
To show her merit, that did miss her love?
The king's disease—my project may deceive me,
But my intents are fix'd, and will not leave me.
[*Exit.*

SCENE II.—Paris. *A Room in the* King's *Palace.*

Flourish of cornets. Enter the KING OF FRANCE, *with letters;* Lords *and others attending.*

KING. The Florentines and Senoys are by the ears;
Have fought with equal fortune, and continue
A braving war.

1 LORD.[c] So 'tis reported, sir,

KING. Nay, 'tis most credible; we here receive it

---

a *The* mightiest space *in fortune, nature brings*
To join like likes, and kiss like native things.]
It would improve both the sense and metre were we to read,—
"The *wid'st apart* in fortune," &c.
Mightiest space is clearly one of the swarm of typographical blemishes by which the old text of this comedy is disfigured.

b *What* hath *been cannot be.*] The very opposite of what the speaker intended to express! Mason, therefore, proposed—
"What ha'n't been, cannot be;"
and Hanmer substituted—
"What hath not been, can't be."
We suspect the error arose from the transcriber mistaking *n'ath*, the old contraction of *ne hath, hath not,* for *hath;* and that we should read,—
"What *n'ath* been cannot be."

c 1 *Lord.*] The folio distinguishes the two Lords who speak, as "1 Lord *G.*, and 2 Lord *E.*"

A certainty, vouch'd from our cousin Austria,
With caution, that the Florentine will move us
For speedy aid; wherein our dearest friend
Prejudicates the business, and would seem
To have us make denial.

1 LORD. His love and wisdom,
Approv'd so to your majesty, may plead
For amplest credence.

KING. He hath arm'd our answer,
And Florence is denied before he comes:
Yet, for our gentlemen that mean to see
The Tuscan service, freely have they leave
To stand on either part.

2 LORD. It may well serve
A nursery to our gentry, who are sick
For breathing and exploit.

KING. What's he comes here?

Enter BERTRAM, LAFEU, *and* PAROLLES.

1 LORD. It is the count Rousillon, my good lord,
Young Bertram.

KING. Youth, thou bear'st thy father's face;
Frank nature, rather curious than in haste,
Hath well compos'd thee. Thy father's moral parts
May'st thou inherit too! Welcome to Paris.

BER. My thanks and duty are your majesty's.

KING. I would I had that corporal soundness now,
As when thy father, and myself, in friendship
First tried our soldiership! He did look far
Into the service of the time, and was
Discipled of the bravest: he lasted long;
But on us both did haggish age steal on,
And wore us out of act. It much repairs me
To talk of your good father: in his youth
He had the wit, which I can well observe
To-day in our young lords; but they may jest,
Till their own scorn return to them unnoted,
Ere they can hide their levity in honour.
So like a courtier: contempt nor bitterness
Were in his pride, or sharpness;[a] if they were,
His equal had awak'd them; and his honour,
Clock to itself, knew the true minute when
Exception bid him speak, and, at this time,
His tongue obey'd his[b] hand. Who were below him
He us'd as creatures of another place;
And bow'd his eminent top to their low ranks,
Making them proud of his humility,
In their poor praise he humbled:[c] such a man
Might be a copy to these younger times;
Which, follow'd well, would démonstrate them now
But goers backward.

BER. His good remembrance, sir,
Lies richer in your thoughts, than on his tomb;
So in approof lives not his epitaph,
As in your royal speech.

KING. Would I were with him! He would always say,
(Methinks, I hear him now: his plausive words
He scatter'd not in ears, but grafted them,
To grow there, and to bear,)—*Let me not live,*——
This his good melancholy oft began,
On the catastrophe and heel of pastime,
When it was out,[d]—*let me not live,* quoth he,
After my flame lacks oil, to be the snuff
Of younger spirits, whose apprehensive senses
All but new things disdain; whose judgments are
Mere fathers of their garments; whose constancies
Expire before their fashions.——This he wish'd:
I, after him, do after him wish too,
Since I nor wax nor honey can bring home,
I quickly were dissolved from my hive,
To give some labourers room.

2 LORD. You are lov'd, sir:
They, that least lend it you, shall lack you first.

KING. I fill a place, I know't.—How long is't, count,
Since the physician at your father's died?
He was much fam'd.

BER. Some six months since, my lord.

KING. If he were living, I would try him yet;—
Lend me an arm;—the rest have worn me out
With several[e] applications:—nature and sickness
Debate it at their leisure. Welcome, count;
My son's no dearer.

BER. Thank your majesty.
[*Exeunt. Flourish.*

SCENE III.—Rousillon. *A Room in the Countess's Palace.*

Enter COUNTESS, Steward, *and* Clown.(2)

COUNT. I will now hear: what say you of this gentlewoman?

---

a ——— *contempt nor bitterness*
Were in his *pride, or sharpness;*]

Capell, with some plausibility, reads,—

"——— *no* contempt nor bitterness
Were in *him*, pride or sharpness."

b *His tongue obey'd* his *hand:*] His hand for *its* hand. The latter vocable had hardly come into use at the time when this play was written. See note (c), p. 480, Vol. I.

c *Making them proud of his humility,*
In their poor praise he humbled:]

A very slight alteration would lessen the ambiguity of this passage. We should, perhaps, read,—

"In their poor praise *be-humbled.*"

d *When* it *was* out,—] When what was out? The commentators are mute. Does not the whole tenor of the context tend to show that *it* is a misprint of *wit?* With this simple change, and supposing the ordinary distribution of the lines to be correct, the purport would be, "Often towards the end of some *spirituel* disport, *when wit was exhausted,* he would say," &c.

e *With* several *applications:*—] *Manifold* applications.

STEW. Madam, the care I have had to even[a] your content, I wish might be found in the calendar of my past endeavours: for then we wound our modesty, and make foul the clearness of our deservings, when of ourselves we publish them.

COUNT. What does this knave here? Get you gone, sirrah: the complaints, I have heard of you, I do not all believe; 'tis my slowness, that I do not: for I know you lack not folly to commit them, and have ability enough to make such knaveries yours.

CLO. 'Tis not unknown to you, madam, I am a poor fellow.

COUNT. Well, sir.

CLO. No, madam, 'tis not so well, that I am poor, though many of the rich are damned: but, if I may have your ladyship's good-will to go to the world,[b] Isbel the woman and I* will do as we may.

COUNT. Wilt thou needs be a beggar?

CLO. I do beg your good-will in this case.

COUNT. In what case?

CLO. In Isbel's case, and mine own. Service is no heritage: and, I think, I shall never have the blessing of God, till I have issue o' my body; for, they say, barns are blessings.

COUNT. Tell me thy reason why thou wilt marry.

CLO. My poor body, madam, requires it: I am driven on by the flesh; and he must needs go, that the devil drives.

COUNT. Is this all your worship's reason?

CLO. 'Faith, madam, I have other, holy reasons, such as they are.

COUNT. May the world know them?

---

[a] *To* even *your content,*—] *Even* is used here, seemingly, as in Act II. Sc. 1:—"But will you make it *even?*"—in the sense of *keep pace with, strike a balance with, equate,* &c.

(*) First folio, *w*.

[b] To go to the world,—] That is, *to be married*. See note (c), p. 707, Vol. I.

CLO. I have been, madam, a wicked creature, as you and all flesh and blood are; and, indeed, I do marry, that I may repent.

COUNT. Thy marriage, sooner than thy wickedness.

CLO. I am out o' friends, madam; and I hope to have friends for my wife's sake.

COUNT. Such friends are thine enemies, knave.

CLO. You are shallow, madam, in great friends;[a] for the knaves come to do that for me, which I am a-weary of. He, that ears my land, spares my team, and gives me leave to inn the crop: if I be his cuckold, he's my drudge. He, that comforts my wife, is the cherisher of my flesh and blood; he, that cherishes my flesh and blood, loves my flesh and blood; he, that loves my flesh and blood, is my friend; *ergo*, he that kisses my wife, is my friend. If men could be contented to be what they are, there were no fear in marriage: for young Charbon the puritan, and old Poysam[b] the papist, howsome'er their hearts are severed in religion, their heads are both one, they may jowl horns together, like any deer i' the herd.

COUNT. Wilt thou ever be a foul-mouthed and calumnious knave?

CLO. A prophet(3) I, madam; and I speak the truth the next way:[c]

For I the ballad will repeat,
Which men full true shall find;
Your marriage comes by destiny,
Your cuckoo sings by kind.[d]

COUNT. Get you gone, sir, I'll talk with you more anon.

STEW. May it please you, madam, that he bid Helen come to you; of her I am to speak.

COUNT. Sirrah, tell my gentlewoman, I would speak with her; Helen I mean.

CLO. [Singing.]
Was this fair face the cause, quoth she,
Why the Grecians sacked Troy?
Fond done, done fond,
Was this king Priam's joy.[e]
With that she sighed as she stood,
With that she sighed as she stood,
And gave this sentence then;
Among nine bad if one be good,
Among nine bad if one be good,
There's yet one good in ten.

COUNT. What, one good in ten? you corrupt the song, sirrah.

CLO. One good woman in ten, madam; which is a purifying o' the song.(4) Would God would serve the world so all the year! we'd find no fault with the tithe-woman, if I were the parson: one in ten, quoth a'! an we might have a good woman born but 'fore* every blazing star, or at an earthquake, 'twould mend the lottery well; a man may draw his heart out, ere 'a pluck one.

COUNT. You'll be gone, sir knave, and do as I command you.

CLO. That man should be at woman's command, and yet no hurt done!—Though honesty be no puritan, yet it will do no hurt; it will wear the surplice of humility over the black gown of a big heart.(5)—I am going, forsooth; the business is for Helen to come hither. [*Exit* Clown.

COUNT. Well, now.

STEW. I know, madam, you love your gentlewoman entirely.

COUNT. 'Faith, I do: her father bequeathed her to me; and she herself, without other advantage, may lawfully make title to as much love as she finds; there is more owing her than is paid; and more shall be paid her, than she'll demand.

STEW. Madam, I was very late more near her than, I think, she wished me: alone she was, and did communicate to herself, her own words to her own ears; she thought, I dare vow for her, they touched not any stranger sense. Her matter was, she loved your son: Fortune, she said, was no goddess, that had put such difference betwixt their two estates; Love, no god, that would not extend his might, only where qualities were level; Diana, no[f] queen of virgins, that would suffer her poor knight surprised,[g] without rescue, in the first assault, or ransome afterward. This she delivered in the most bitter touch of sorrow, that e'er I heard virgin exclaim in: which I held my duty, speedily to acquaint you withal; sithence, in the

---

[a] *You are shallow, madam*, in great friends;] This is usually read, "You are shallow, madam; *e'en* great friends;" and the instances, both in these plays and in contemporaneous books, of *in* being misprinted for *e'en*, suggests the probability of a like error here; but the meaning may be, "You are shallow in *the uses* of great friends."

[b] *Young Charbon the puritan, and old* Poysam *the papist,*—] Malone suggested that the original word was *Poisson*; an allusion to the practice of eating fish on fast-days, as Charbon might be to the fiery zeal of the puritans.

[c] The next way:] The *nearest* way.

[d] Your marriage comes by destiny,
Your cuckoo sings by kind.]
A new version of an old proverb. So, in "Grange's Garden," quarto, 1577:—

"Content yourselfe as well as I,
Let reason rule your minde;
As cuckoldes come by destinie,
So cuckowes sing by kinde."

[e] *Was this fair face the cause, quoth she,*—] This is, perhaps, a snatch of some antique ballad, which the fool craftily corrupts, to intimate, in the enigmatical manner of his calling, that he was not altogether ignorant of the subject which his mistress and her steward had met to speak about.

[f] Diana, no *queen of virgins*,—] The old text has only "Queene of Virgins;" the two words prefixed by Theobald, are probably as near to the original as can be supplied.

[g] *That would suffer her poor* knight surprised,—] This is the lection of the old text, and the phraseology of the poet's age. Theobald inserted the words *to be*, reading,—"that would suffer her poor knight *to be* surprised," and he has been followed by every subsequent editor.

(*) First folio, *ore*.

loss that may happen, it concerns you something to know it.

COUNT. You have discharged this honestly; keep it to yourself: many likelihoods informed me of this before, which hung so tottering in the balance, that I could neither believe nor misdoubt. 'Pray you, leave me: stall this in your bosom, and I thank you for your honest care: I will speak with you further anon. [*Exit* Steward.

COUNT. Even so it was with me, when I was young:
If we are nature's, these are ours; this thorn
Doth to our rose of youth rightly belong:
Our blood to us, this to our blood is born;
It is the show and seal of nature's truth,
Where love's strong passion is impress'd in youth:
By our remembrances of days foregone,
Such were our faults;—or them we thought then[a] none.

Enter HELENA.

Her eye is sick on't; I observe her now.

HEL. What is your pleasure, madam?

COUNT. You know, Helen,
I am a mother to you.

HEL. Mine honourable mistress.

COUNT. Nay, a mother;
Why not a mother? when I said, a mother,
Methought you saw a serpent: what's in *mother*,
That you start at it? I say, I am your mother;
And put you in the catalogue of those
That were enwombed mine. 'T is often seen,
Adoption strives with nature; and choice breeds
A native slip to us from foreign seeds:
You ne'er oppress'd me with a mother's groan,
Yet I express to you a mother's care:—
God's mercy, maiden! does it curd thy blood,
To say, I am thy mother? What's the matter,
That this distemper'd messenger of wet,
The many-colour'd Iris, rounds thine eye?
Why?——that you are my daughter?

HEL. That I am not.

COUNT. I say, I am your mother.

HEL. Pardon, madam;
The count Rousillon cannot be my brother:
I am from humble, he from honour'd name;
No note upon my parents, his, all noble:
My master, my dear lord he is: and I
His servant live, and will his vassal die:
He must not be my brother.

COUNT. Nor I your mother?

HEL. You are my mother, madam; would you were
(So that my lord, your son, were not my brother,)
Indeed my mother!—or were you both our mothers,
I care no more for,[b] than I do for heaven,
So I were not his sister: can't no other,
But, I your daughter, he must be my brother?

COUNT. Yes, Helen, you might be my daughter-in-law;
God shield, you mean it not! *daughter*, and *mother*,
So strive upon your pulse: what, pale again?
My fear hath catch'd your fondness: now I see
The mystery of your loneliness,* and find
Your salt tears' head. Now to all sense 't is gross,[c]
You love my son; invention is asham'd,
Against the proclamation of thy passion,
To say, thou dost not: therefore tell me true;
But tell me then, 't is so:—for, look, thy cheeks
Confess it, th' one to th' other:† and thine eyes
See it so grossly shown in thy behaviours,
That in their kind they speak it: only sin
And hellish obstinacy tie thy tongue,
That truth should be suspected. Speak, is't so?
If it be so, you have wound a goodly clue;
If it be not, forswear't: howe'er, I charge thee,
As heaven shall work in me for thine avail,
To tell me truly.

HEL. Good madam, pardon me!

COUNT. Do you love my son?

HEL. Your pardon, noble mistress!

COUNT. Love you my son?

HEL. Do not you love him, madam?

COUNT. Go not about; my love hath in 't a bond,
Whereof the world takes note: come, come, disclose
The state of your affection, for your passions
Have to the full appeach'd.

HEL. Then, I confess,
Here on my knee, before high heaven and you,
That before you, and next unto high heaven,
I love your son:—
My friends were poor, but honest; so's my love:
Be not offended, for it hurts not him,
That he is lov'd of me; I follow him not
By any token of presumptuous suit,
Nor would I have him, till I do deserve him;
Yet never know how that desert should be.
I know I love in vain, strive against hope;
Yet, in this captious[d] and intenible‡ sieve,

[a] *Or* them *we thought* then *none.*] The old copy reads,—
"—— Or then we thought them none."
For the transposition of *them* and *then*, I am responsible.

[b] I care no more for,—] "There is a designed ambiguity: 'I care no more for,' is 'I care *as much for.*'"—FARMER. It would somewhat lessen the perplexity of this difficult passage, if we suppose the present line to be spoken aside; but, in truth, the text throughout the speech is palpably corrupt.

[c] Gross,—] That is, *palpable.*

[d] *This* captious *and intenible sieve,*—] We incline to believe, with Farmer, that *captious* here is only a contraction of *capacious.*

(*) First folio, *louelinesse.* (†) First folio, *'ton tooth to th' other.* (‡) First folio, *intemible.*

I still pour in the waters of my love,
And lack not to lose still: thus, Indian-like,
Religious in mine error, I adore
The sun, that looks upon his worshipper,
But knows of him no more. My dearest madam,
Let not your hate encounter with my love,
For loving where you do: but, if yourself,
Whose aged honour cites a virtuous youth,
Did ever, in so true a flame of liking,
Wish chastely, and love dearly, that your Dian
Was both herself and Love; O then, give pity
To her, whose state is such that cannot choose,
But lend and give where she is sure to lose;
That seeks not to find that her search implies,
But, riddle-like, lives sweetly where she dies.
COUNT. Had you not lately an intent, speak truly,
To go to Paris?
HEL. Madam, I had.
COUNT. Wherefore? tell true.
HEL. I will tell truth; by grace itself, I swear.
You know, my father left me some prescriptions
Of rare and prov'd effects,(6) such as his reading,
And manifest experience, had collected
For general sovereignty; and that he will'd me
In heedfullest reservation to bestow them,
As notes, whose faculties inclusive were,
More than they were in note: amongst the rest,
There is a remedy, approv'd, set down,
To cure the desperate languishings, whereof
The king is render'd lost.
COUNT. This was your motive
For Paris, was it? speak.
HEL. My lord your son made me to think of this;
Else Paris, and the medicine, and the king,
Had, from the conversation of my thoughts,
Haply been absent then.
COUNT. But think you, Helen,
If you should tender your supposed aid,
He would receive it? He and his physicians
Are of a mind; he, that they cannot help him,

They, that they cannot help. How shall they
credit
A poor unlearned virgin, when the schools,
Embowell'd of their doctrine, have left off
The danger to itself?
HEL. There's something hints,[a]
More than my father's skill, which was the greatest
Of his profession, that his good receipt
Shall, for my legacy, be sanctified
By the luckiest stars in heaven: and, would your
honour
But give me leave to try success,[b] I'd venture
The well-lost life of mine on his grace's cure,
By such a day, and* hour.
COUNT. Dost thou believe't?
HEL. Ay, madam, knowingly.
COUNT. Why, Helen, thou shalt have my
leave, and love,
Means, and attendants, and my loving greetings
To those of mine in court; I'll stay at home,
And pray God's blessing into[c] thy attempt:
Be gone to-morrow; and be sure of this,
What I can help thee to, thou shalt not miss.
[*Exeunt.*

---

a *There's something* hints,—] The old copy has "*in't.*" Hanmer made the obvious correction.

b *To try* success,—] *Success* here means the *consequence*, the *issue*. So in "Much Ado About Nothing," Act IV. Sc. I:—

"—— And doubt not but *success*
Will fashion the event," &c.

(*) First folio, *an*.

"In this sense," as Johnson remarks, "*successo* is employed in Italian."

c Into—] *Into* or *unto* were often used indiscriminately by the old writers.

ACT II.

SCENE I.—Paris. *A Room in the* King's *Palace.*

Flourish. Enter King, *with divers young* Lords, *taking leave for the* Florentine *war;* Bertram, Parolles, *and* Attendants.

King. Farewell, young lords,[a] these warlike principles
Do not throw from you:—and you, my lords, farewell:—
Share the advice betwixt you; if both gain all,
The gift doth stretch itself as 't is receiv'd,
And is enough for both.

1 Lord. 'T is our hope, sir,
After well-entered soldiers, to return
And find your grace in health.

King. No, no, it cannot be, and yet my heart
Will not confess he owes the malady
That doth my life besiege. Farewell, young lords;
Whether I live or die, be you the sons

[a] *Farewell, young* lords,—] Thus the old copy. Many of the modern editors read, "Farewell, young *lord*," supposing there are only two French lords about to serve in Italy; but this is an error. There are "*divers*" young noblemen taking leave, and to these the King first addresses himself; he then turns to the two lords who are the spokesmen in the scene, and bids them share in the advice just given to their young companions.

Of worthy Frenchmen: let higher Italy(1)
(Those 'bated, that inherit but the fall
Of the last monarchy) see that you come
Not to woo honour, but to wed it; when
The bravest questant shrinks, find what you seek,
That fame may cry you loud: I say, farewell.

2 LORD. Health, at your bidding, serve your majesty!

KING. Those girls of Italy, take heed of them;
They say, our French lack language to deny,
If they demand; beware of being captives,
Before you serve.

BOTH. Our hearts receive your warnings.

KING. Farewell.—Come hither to me.

[*The* KING *retires to a couch.*

1 LORD. O my sweet lord, that you will stay behind us!

PAR. 'T is not his fault, the spark.

2 LORD. O, 't is brave wars!

PAR. Most admirable; I have seen those wars.

BER. I am commanded here, and kept a coil with,
Too young, and *the next year*, and *'t is too early.*

PAR. An thy mind stand to 't, boy, steal away bravely.

BER. I shall stay here the fore-horse to a smock,[a]
Creaking my shoes on the plain masonry,
Till honour be bought up, and no sword worn,
But one to dance with!(2) By heaven, I'll steal away.

1 LORD. There's honour in the theft.

PAR. Commit it, count.

2 LORD. I am your accessary; and so farewell.

BER. I grow to you, and our parting is a tortured body.[b]

1 LORD. Farewell, captain.

2 LORD. Sweet monsieur Parolles!

PAR. Noble heroes, my sword and yours are kin. Good sparks and lustrous, a word, good metals. You shall find in the regiment of the Spinii, one captain Spurio, with his cicatrice,* an emblem of war, here on his sinister cheek; it was this very sword entrenched it: say to him, I live; and observe his reports for me.

2 LORD. We shall, noble captain.

PAR. Mars dote on you for his novices! [*Exeunt* Lords.] What will you* do?

BER. Stay: the king——

PAR. Use a more spacious ceremony to the noble lords; you have restrained yourself within the list of too cold an adieu: be more expressive to them; for they wear themselves in the cap of the time; there, do muster true gait, eat, speak, and move under the influence of the most received star; and though the devil lead the measure, such are to be followed: after them, and take a more dilated farewell.

BER. And I will do so.

PAR. Worthy fellows; and like to prove most sinewy sword-men.

[*Exeunt* BERTRAM *and* PAROLLES.

Enter LAFEU.

LAF. Pardon, my lord, [*Kneeling.*] for me and for my tidings.

KING. I'll sue[c] thee to stand up.

LAF. Then here's a man stands, that has brought his pardon. [mercy;
I would you had kneel'd, my lord, to ask me
And that, at my bidding, you could so stand up.

KING. I would I had; so I had broke thy pate,
And ask'd thee mercy for't. ['t is thus;

LAF. Good faith, across:[d] but, my good lord,
Will you be cur'd of your infirmity?

KING. No.

LAF. O, will you eat no grapes, my royal fox?
Yes, but you will, my noble grapes,[e] an if
My royal fox could reach them: I have seen a medicine,
That's able to breathe life into a stone,
Quicken a rock, and make you dance canary,[f]
With sprightly fire and motion; whose simple touch
Is powerful to araise king Pepin, nay,

(*) First folio, *his cicatrice with.*

[a] *The* fore-horse *to a smock,*—] The *fore-horse* of a team was gaily ornamented with tufts, and ribbons, and bells. Bertram complains that, bedizened like one of these animals, he will have to squire ladies at the court, instead of achieving honour in the wars.

[b] Our parting is a tortured body.] *As* is understood:—

"—— Our parting is *as* a tortured body."

[c] *I'll* sue *thee to stand up.*] The old copy reads, "I'll *see* thee," &c. When any one kneels to a sovereign, it is to ask permission to stand in his presence. Thus, in "Richard II." Act V. Sc. 3, Bolingbroke says—

"Good aunt, stand up;"

to which she answers,—

"I do not *sue to stand.*"

Upon Lafeu prostrating himself, the afflicted king, mindful of his own debility, remarks,—"Instead of your begging permission of me to rise, I'll sue thee for the same grace;"—Lafeu immediately responds,—

"I would you *had* kneel'd, my lord," &c.

(*) Old text, *ye.*

[d] *Good faith,* across:] *Across,* in reference to the sports of chivalry, in which, to break a spear *across* the body of an opponent was disgraceful, came to be used in derision when any pass of wit miscarried. Here, however, we believe Lafeu alludes rather to some game, where certain successes entitle the achiever to mark *a cross.*

[e] *Yes, but you will,* my *noble grapes,*—] *My* in this passage has been changed in some modern editions to *ay,* but needlessly; we have only to read "*my*" emphatically, and the sense is obvious:—

"O, will you eat no grapes? &c.
Yes, but you will, *my* noble grapes."

[f] *And make you dance* canary,—] To what has already been said on the nature of this sprightly dance (see note ([a]), vol. I. p. 64), may be added, that the dancers accompanied their movements with castagnets: see Florio, who defines *Chioppare* "to clacke or snap, or phip, or click, or lirp with ones fingers, *as they that dance the Canaries,* or as some barbers."

To give great Charlemaine a pen in's hand,
And write to her a love-line.
KING. What *her* is this?
LAF. Why, doctor she; my lord, there's one arriv'd,
If you will see her,—now, by my faith and honour,
If seriously I may convey my thoughts
In this my light deliverance, I have spoke
With one, that, in her sex, her years, profession,
Wisdom, and constancy, hath amaz'd me more
Than I dare blame my weakness. Will you see her,
(For that is her demand,) and know her business?
That done, laugh well at me.
KING. Now, good Lafeu,
Bring in the admiration; that we with thee
May spend our wonder too, or take off thine,
By wond'ring how thou took'st it.
LAF. Nay, I'll fit you,
And not be all day neither. [*Exit* LAFEU.
KING. Thus he his special nothing ever prologues.

Re-enter LAFEU; HELENA *following.*

LAF. Nay, come your ways.
KING. This haste hath wings indeed.
LAF. Nay, come your ways;
This is his majesty, say your mind to him:
A traitor you do look like, but such traitors
His majesty seldom fears: I am Cressid's uncle,
That dare leave two together: fare you well. [*Exit.*
KING. Now, fair one, does your business follow us?
HEL. Ay, my good lord. Gerard de Narbon was my father;
In what he did profess, well found.
KING. I knew him.
HEL. The rather will I spare my praises towards him;
Knowing him, is enough. On's bed of death
Many receipts he gave me; chiefly one,
Which, as the dearest issue of his practice,
And of his old experience th' only darling,
He bade me store up, as a triple eye,
Safer than mine own two more dear: I have so;
And, hearing your high majesty is touch'd
With that malignant cause, wherein the honour
Of my dear father's gift stands chief in power,
I come to tender it, and my appliance,
With all bound humbleness.
KING. We thank you, maiden;
But may not be so credulous of cure,
When our most learned doctors leave us; and
The congregated college have concluded
That labouring art can never ransom nature
From her inaidable estate; I say we must not
So stain our judgment, or corrupt our hope,
To prostitute our past-cure malady
To émpirics; or to dissever so
Our great self and our credit, to esteem
A senseless help, when help past sense we deem.
HEL. My duty then shall pay me for my pains:
I will no more enforce mine office on you;
Humbly entreating from your royal thoughts
A modest one, to bear me back again.
KING. I cannot give thee less, to be call'd grateful:
Thou thought'st to help me, and such thanks I give,
As one near death to those that wish him live:
But, what at full I know, thou know'st no part;
I knowing all my peril, thou no art.
HEL. What I can do, can do no hurt to try,
Since you set up your rest 'gainst remedy:
He that of greatest works is finisher,
Oft does them by the weakest minister:
So holy writ in babes hath judgment shown,
When judges have been babes.(3) Great floods have flown
From simple sources; and great seas have dried,
When miracles have by the greatest been denied.
Oft expectation fails, and most oft there
Where most it promises; and oft it hits,
Where hope is coldest, and despair most fits.*
KING. I must not hear thee; fare thee well, kind maid;
Thy pains, not us'd, must by thyself be paid:
Proffers, not took, reap thanks for their reward.
HEL. Inspired merit so by breath is barr'd:
It is not so with him that all things knows,
As 't is with us that square our guess by shows:
But most it is presumption in us, when
The help of heaven we count the act of men.
Dear sir, to my endeavours give consent;
Of heaven, not me, make an experiment.
I am not an impostor, that proclaim
Myself against the level of mine aim,
But know I think, and think I know most sure,
My art is not past power, nor you past cure.
KING. Art thou so confident? within what space
Hop'st thou my cure?
HEL. The great'st grace lending grace,
Ere twice the horses of the sun shall bring
Their fiery torcher his diurnal ring;
Ere twice in murk and occidental damp
Moist Hesperus hath quench'd his† sleepy lamp;
Or four and twenty times the pilot's glass
Hath told the thievish minutes how they pass;
What is infirm, from your sound parts shall fly,
Health shall live free, and sickness freely die.
KING. Upon thy certainty and confidence,
What dar'st thou venture?
HEL. Tax of impudence,—
A strumpet's boldness, a divulged shame,—
Traduc'd by odious ballads; my maiden's name

(*) First folio, *shifts*. (†) First folio, *her*.

Sear'd otherwise; ne worse of worst extended,[a]
With vilest torture let my life be ended. [speak
KING. Methinks, in thee some blessed spirit doth
His powerful sound, within an organ weak:
And what impossibility[b] would slay
In common sense, sense saves another way.
Thy life is dear; for all that life can rate
Worth name of life, in thee hath estimate;
Youth, beauty, wisdom, courage, all
That happiness and prime can happy call:
Thou this to hazard, needs must intimate
Skill infinite, or monstrous desperate.
Sweet practiser, thy physic I will try;
That ministers thine own death, if I die.
HEL. If I break time, or flinch in property
Of what I spoke, unpitied let me die;
And well deserv'd. Not helping, death's my fee;
But, if I help, what do you promise me?
KING. Make thy demand.
HEL. But will you make it even?[c]
KING. Ay, by my sceptre, and my hopes of heaven.[d] [hand,
HEL. Then shalt thou give me, with thy kingly
What husband in thy power I will command:
Exempted be from me the arrogance
To choose from forth the royal blood of France;
My low and humble name to propagate
With any branch or image of thy state:
But such a one thy vassal, whom I know
Is free for me to ask, thee to bestow.
KING. Here is my hand; the premises observ'd,
Thy will by my performance shall be serv'd;
So make the choice of thy own time, for I,
Thy resolv'd patient, on thee still rely.
More should I question thee, and more I must,
Though, more to know, could not be more to trust;
From whence thou cam'st, how tended on,—but rest
Unquestion'd welcome, and undoubted blest.—
Give me some help here, ho!—If thou proceed
As high as word, my deed shall match thy deed.
[*Flourish. Exeunt.*

SCENE II.—Rousillon. *A Room in the Countess's Palace.*

Enter COUNTESS *and* Clown.

COUNT. Come on, sir; I shall now put you to the height of your breeding.

CLO. I will show myself highly fed, and lowly taught: I know my business is but to the court.

COUNT. To the court, why, what place make you special, when you put off that with such contempt? *But to the court!*

CLO. Truly, madam, if God have lent a man any manners, he may easily put it off at court: he that cannot make a leg, put off's cap, kiss his hand, and say nothing, has neither leg, hands, lip, nor cap; and indeed, such a fellow, to say precisely, were not for the court: but, for me, I have an answer will serve all men.

COUNT. Marry, that's a bountiful answer, that fits all questions.

CLO. It is like a barber's chair, that fits all buttocks; the pin-buttock, the quatch-buttock, the brawn-buttock, or any buttock.

COUNT. Will your answer serve fit to all questions?

CLO. As fit as ten groats is for the hand of an attorney, as your French crown for your taffata punk, as Tib's rush for Tom's fore-finger, as a pancake for Shrove-Tuesday, a morris for May-day,(4) as the nail to his hole, the cuckold to his horn, as a scolding quean to a wrangling knave, as the nun's lip to the friar's mouth; nay, as the pudding to his skin.

COUNT. Have you, I say, an answer of such fitness for all questions?

CLO. From below your duke, to beneath your constable, it will fit any question.

COUNT. It must be an answer of most monstrous size, that must fit all demands.

CLO. But a trifle neither, in good faith, if the learned should speak truth of it: here it is, and all that belongs to't: ask me, if I am a courtier; it shall do you no harm to learn.

COUNT. To be young again, if we could. I will be a fool in question, hoping to be the wiser by your answer. I pray you, sir, are you a courtier?

CLO. *O Lord, sir!*[e]—There's a simple putting off;—more, more, a hundred of them.

COUNT. Sir, I am a poor friend of yours, that loves you.

CLO. *O Lord, sir!*—Thick, thick, spare not me.

COUNT. I think, sir, you can eat none of this homely meat.

CLO. *O Lord, sir!*—Nay, put me to't, I warrant you.

COUNT. You were lately whipped, sir, as I think.

CLO. *O Lord, sir!*—Spare not me.

COUNT. Do you cry, *O Lord, sir,* at your whip-

---

[a] Ne *worse of worst* extended,—] This is the lection of the old copy, and, although unquestionably corrupt, it is not worse than the commentators' suggestions for its amendment. We should, perhaps, approach nearer to what the poet really wrote by treating *ne* and *extended* as palpable misprints, and reading:—

"—— *and*, worse of worst *expended*,
With vilest torture let my life be ended."

[b] Impossibility—] That is, *incredibility*.

[c] *But will you make it* even?] That is, Will you *equate* it? Will you *match it?* See note ([a]), p. 11, of the present volume.

[d] *And my hopes of* heaven.] The old copy has *help*. The correction, which is due to Dr. Thirlby, seems called for both by the context and the rhyme. It is observable that much of this scene is in smooth, rhyming verses; it was a portion probably of the poet's first youthful conception, for we cannot divest ourselves of the impression that at a subsequent period of his career he rewrote a considerable part of this play.

[e] O Lord, sir!] The use of this expletive, which appears to have been thought the mode both in court and city, has been finely ridiculed by Jonson also. See "Every Man out of his Humour," Act III. Sc. 1, and *passim*.

ping, and *spare not me?* Indeed, your *O Lord, sir,* is very sequent to your whipping; you would answer very well to a whipping, if you were but bound to't.

CLO. I ne'er had worse luck in my life, in my —*O Lord, sir:* I see things may serve long, but not serve ever.

COUNT. I play the noble housewife with the time, to entertain it so merrily with a fool.

CLO. *O Lord, sir!*—Why, there't serves well again.

COUNT. An* end, sir: to your business. Give Helen this,
And urge her to a present answer back:
Commend me to my kinsmen, and my son;
This is not much.

CLO. Not much commendation to them.

COUNT. Not much employment for you: you understand me?

CLO. Most fruitfully; I am there before my legs.

COUNT. Haste you again. [*Exeunt severally.*

SCENE III.—Paris. *A Room in the* King's *Palace.*

Enter BERTRAM, LAFEU, *and* PAROLLES.

LAF. They say, miracles are past; and we have our philosophical persons, to make modern and familiar, things supernatural and causeless. Hence is it, that we make trifles of terrors, ensconcing ourselves into seeming knowledge, when we should submit ourselves to an unknown fear.

PAR. Why, 't is the rarest argument of wonder, that hath shot out in our latter times.

BER. And so 't is.

LAF. To be relinquished of the artists,——

PAR. So I say; both of Galen and Paracelsus.

LAF. Of all the learned and authentic fellows,—

PAR. Right, so I say.

LAF. That gave him out incurable,—

PAR. Why, there 't is; so say I too.

LAF. Not to be helped,—

PAR. Right: as 't were, a man assured of a—

LAF. Uncertain life, and sure death.

PAR. Just, you say well; so would I have said.

LAF. I may truly say, it is a novelty to the world.

PAR. It is, indeed: if you will have it in showing, you shall read it in,——what do ye call there?—

LAF. A showing of a heavenly effect in an earthly actor.

PAR. That's it I would have said; the very same.

LAF. Why, your dolphin is not lustier: 'fore me I speak in respect——

PAR. Nay, 't is strange, 't is very strange, that is the brief and the tedious of it; and he is of a most facinorous* spirit, that will not acknowledge it to be the—

LAF. Very hand of heaven.

PAR. Ay, so I say.

LAF. In a most weak——

PAR. And debile minister, great power, great transcendence: which should, indeed, give us a further use to be made, than alone the recovery of the king, as to be——

LAF. Generally thankful.

PAR. I would have said it; you say well. Here comes the king.

LAF. *Lustique,*[a] as the Dutchman says: I'll like a maid the better, whilst I have a tooth in my head: why, he's able to lead her a coranto.[b]

PAR. *Mort du Vinaigre!* Is not this Helen?

LAF. 'Fore God, I think so.

Enter KING, HELENA, *and* Attendants.

KING. Go, call before me all the lords in court.
[*Exit an* Attendant.
Sit, my preserver, by thy patient's side;
And with this healthful hand, whose banish'd sense
Thou hast repeal'd, a second time receive
The confirmation of my promised gift,
Which but attends thy naming.

Enter several Lords.

Fair maid, send forth thine eye: this youthful parcel
Of noble bachelors stand at my bestowing,
O'er whom both sovereign power and father's voice
I have to use: thy frank election make,
Thou hast power to choose, and they none to forsake.

HEL. To each of you, one fair and virtuous mistress

(*) First folio, *And.*

a *Lustique,*—] "An old play, that has a great deal of merit, call'd '*The weakest goeth to the Wall,*' (printed in 1600, but how much earlier written, or by whom written, we are no where inform'd,) has in it a Dutchman, call'd—Jacob van Smelt, who speaks a jargon of Dutch and our language; and upon several occasions uses this very word, which in English is—lusty."—CAPELL.

(*) First folio, *facinerious.*

b A coranto.] The *coranto* was a dance distinguished for the liveliness and rapidity of its movements:—

"And teach lavoltas high, and *swift corantos.*"—
Henry V. Act III. Sc. 5.

Fall, when Love please!—marry, to each, but one!
LAF. I'd give bay Curtal, and his furniture,
My mouth no more were broken than these boys',
And writ as little beard.
KING. Peruse them well:
Not one of those, but had a noble father.
HEL. Gentlemen,
Heaven hath, through me, restored the king to health.

ALL. We understand it, and thank heaven for you.
HEL. I am a simple maid; and therein wealthiest,
That, I protest, I simply am a maid:——
Please it your majesty, I have done already:
The blushes in my cheeks thus whisper me,
We blush, that thou should'st choose; but, be refus'd,

Let the white death sit on thy cheek for ever;
We'll ne'er come there again.

KING. Make choice; and, see,
Who shuns thy love, shuns all his love in me.

HEL. Now, Dian, from thy altar do I fly,
And to imperial Love, that god most high,
Do my sighs stream.—Sir, will you hear my suit?

1 LORD. And grant it.

HEL. Thanks, sir; all the rest is mute.

LAF. I had rather be in this choice, than throw ames-ace for my life.

HEL. The honour, sir, that flames in your fair [eyes,
Before I speak, too threat'ningly replies:
Love make your fortunes twenty times above
Her that so wishes, and her humble love!

2 LORD. No better, if you please.

HEL. My wish receive,
Which great Love grant! and so I take my leave.

LAF. Do all they deny her? An they were sons of mine, I'd have them whipped; or I would send them to the Turk, to make eunuchs of.

HEL. Be not afraid [*To a* Lord.] that I your hand should take,
I'll never do you wrong for your own sake:
Blessing upon your vows! and in your bed
Find fairer fortune, if you ever wed!

LAF. These boys are boys of ice, they'll none have her: sure, they are bastards to the English; the French ne'er got them.

HEL. You are too young, too happy, and too [good,
To make yourself a son out of my blood.

4 LORD. Fair one, I think not so.

LAF. There's one grape yet,—I am sure thy father drank wine.[a] But if thou be'st not an ass, I am a youth of fourteen; I have known thee already.

HEL. I dare not say, I take you; [*To* BERTRAM.] but I give
Me and my service, ever whilst I live,
Into your guiding power.—This is the man.

KING. Why then, young Bertram, take her, she's thy wife.

BER. My wife, my liege? I shall beseech your highness,
In such a business give me leave to use
The help of mine own eyes.

KING. Know'st thou not, Bertram,
What she has done for me?

BER. Yes, my good lord;
But never hope to know why I should marry her.

KING. Thou know'st, she has rais'd me from my sickly bed.

BER. But follows it, my lord, to bring me down,
Must answer for your raising? I know her well;
She had her breeding at my father's charge:
A poor physician's daughter my wife!—Disdain
Rather corrupt me ever!

KING. 'Tis only title thou disdain'st in her, the which
I can build up. Strange is it, that our bloods,
Of colour, weight, and heat, pour'd all together,
Would quite confound distinction, yet stand off
In differences so mighty. If she be
All that is virtuous, (save what thou dislik'st,
A poor physician's daughter,) thou dislik'st
Of virtue for the name: but do not so:
From lowest place when* virtuous things proceed,
The place is dignified by the doer's deed:
Where great additions swell us, and virtue none,
It is a dropsied honour: good alone
Is good, without a name; vileness is so:
The property by what it† is should go,
Not by the title. She is young, wise, fair;
In these to nature she's immediate heir;
And these breed honour: that is honour's scorn,
Which challenges itself as honour's born,
And is not like the sire: honours thrive,
When rather from our acts we them derive
Than our fore-goers; the mere word's a slave,
Debosh'd on every tomb; on every grave,
A lying trophy, and as oft is dumb,
Where dust, and damn'd oblivion, is the tomb
Of honour'd bones indeed. What should be said?
If thou canst like this creature as a maid,
I can create the rest: virtue, and she,
Is her own dower; honour, and wealth, from me.

BER. I cannot love her, nor will strive to do't.

KING. Thou wrong'st thyself, if thou should'st strive to choose.

HEL. That you are well restor'd, my lord, I'm [glad;
Let the rest go.

KING. My honour's at the stake; which to defeat,
I must produce my power. Here, take her hand,
Proud scornful boy, unworthy this good gift,
That dost in vile misprision shackle up
My love, and her desert; that canst not dream,
We, poising us in her defective scale,
Shall weigh thee to the beam; that wilt not know,
It is in us to plant thine honour, where
We please to have it grow. Check thy contempt:
Obey our will, which travails in thy good:
Believe not thy disdain, but presently
Do thine own fortunes that obedient right,
Which both thy duty owes, and our power claims;
Or I will throw thee from my care for ever,

---

[a] There's one grape yet.—I am sure thy father drank wine.] We are to suppose that Lafeu, who has been in conversation with Parolles, had not heard the discourse between Helena and the young courtiers, but believed she had propose l to each, and been refused by all but the one now in question. The after-part of his speech, "But if thou be'st not an ass," &c. refers, (aside,) to Parolles.

(*) Old text, *whence*. (†) First folio, *is*.

Into the staggers,[a] and the careless lapse [hate,
Of youth and ignorance; both my revenge and
Loosing upon thee in the name of justice,
Without[b] all terms of pity. Speak; thine answer.

BER. Pardon, my gracious lord; for I submit,
My fancy to your eyes. When I consider,
What great creation, and what dole of honour,
Flies where you bid it, I find, that she, which late
Was in my nobler thoughts most base, is now
The praised of the king; who, so ennobled,
Is, as 'twere, born so.

KING. Take her by the hand,
And tell her, she is thine: to whom I promise
A counterpoise; if not to thy estate,
A balance more replete.

BER. I take her hand. [king,

KING. Good fortune, and the favour of the
Smile upon this contract; whose ceremony[c]
Shall seem expedient on the now-born brief,
And be perform'd to-night: the solemn feast
Shall more attend upon the coming space,
Expecting absent friends. As thou lov'st her,
Thy love's to me religious; else, does err.

[*Exeunt* KING, BERTRAM, HELENA, Lords, *and* Attendants.[d]

LAF. Do you hear, monsieur? a word with you.

PAR. Your pleasure, sir?

LAF. Your lord and master did well to make his recantation.

PAR. *Recantation?*—My *lord?*—my *master?*

LAF. Ay; is it not a language, I speak?

PAR. A most harsh one; and not to be understood without bloody succeeding. My *master?*

LAF. Are you companion to the count Rousillon?

PAR. To any count; to all counts; to what is man.

LAF. To what is count's man; count's master is of another style.

PAR. You are too old, sir; let it satisfy you, you are too old.

LAF. I must tell thee, sirrah, I write man; to which title age cannot bring thee.

PAR. What I dare too well do, I dare not do.

LAF. I did think thee, for two ordinaries, to be a pretty wise fellow; thou didst make tolerable vent of thy travel; it might pass: yet the scarfs and the bannerets about thee, did manifoldly dissuade me from believing thee a vessel of too great a burthen. I have now found thee; when I lose thee again, I care not: yet art thou good for nothing but taking up, and that thou art scarce worth.

PAR. Hadst thou not the privilege of antiquity upon thee,——

LAF. Do not plunge thyself too far in anger, lest thou hasten thy trial;—which if—Lord have mercy on thee for a hen! So, my good window of lattice,[e] fare thee well; thy casement I need not open, for I look through thee. Give me thy hand.

PAR. My lord, you give me most egregious indignity.

LAF. Ay, with all my heart; and thou art worthy of it.

PAR. I have not, my lord, deserved it.

LAF. Yes, good faith, every dram of it: and I will not bate thee a scruple.

PAR. Well, I shall be wiser.

LAF. E'en as soon as thou canst, for thou hast to pull at a smack o' the contrary. If ever thou be'st bound in thy scarf, and beaten, thou shalt find what it is to be proud of thy bondage. I have a desire to hold my acquaintance with thee, or rather my knowledge; that I may say, in the default, he is a man I know.

PAR. My lord, you do me most insupportable vexation.

LAF. I would it were hell-pains for thy sake, and my poor doing eternal: for doing I am past; as I will by thee, in what motion age will give me leave.[f] [*Exit.*

PAR. Well, thou hast a son shall take this disgrace off me; scurvy, old, filthy, scurvy lord!—Well, I must be patient; there is no fettering of authority. I'll beat him, by my life, if I can meet him with any convenience, an he were double and double a lord. I'll have no more pity of his age, than I would have of—I'll beat him, an if I could but meet him again.

Re-enter LAFEU.

LAF. Sirrah, your lord and master's married, there's news for you; you have a new mistress.

PAR. I most unfeignedly beseech your lordship

---

a The staggers,—] This expression occurs again in "Cymbeline," Act V. Sc. 2,—

"How came these *staggers* on me?"

Mr. Singer explains it as "*The reeling and unsteady course of a drunken or sick man;*" but we apprehend it has a meaning, in both instances, more relevant than this.

b Without—] That is, *beyond.*

c *Whose* ceremony—] It has never, that we are aware, been noticed that Shakespeare usually pronounces *cere* in *ceremony, ceremonies, ceremonials,* (but not in *ceremonious, ceremoniously,*) as a monosyllable, like *cere-cloth, cerement.* Thus, in "The Merry Wives of Windsor," Act IV. Sc. 6,—

"To give our hearts united ceremony."

Again, in "A Midsummer Night's Dream," Act V. Sc. 1,—

"Not sorting with a nuptial ceremony."

Again, in "Julius Cæsar," Act I. Sc. 1,—

"If you do find them deckt with ceremonies."

and, Act II. Sc. 2:—

"Cæsar, I never stood on ceremonies."

d *Exeunt* King, &c.] The stage-direction, in the original text, is, "*Exeunt. Parolles and Lafeu stay behind, commenting of this wedding.*"

e My good window of lattice—] See note (2). p. 626, Vol. i.

f *For doing I am past; as I will by thee, in what motion age will give me leave.*] If instead of *as*, we read, *so*, the conceit on the word *past* is then intelligible: "For doing I am past, so I will [*pass*] by thee," &c.

to make some reservation of your wrongs: he is my good lord: whom I serve above, is my *master*.

LAF. Who? God?

PAR. Ay, sir.

LAF. The devil it is, that's thy master. Why dost thou garter up thy arms o' this fashion? dost make hose of thy sleeves? do other servants so? Thou wert best set thy lower part where thy nose stands. By mine honour, if I were but two hours younger, I'd beat thee: methinks, thou art a general offence, and every man should beat thee. I think, thou wast created for men to breathe themselves upon thee.

PAR. This is hard and undeserved measure, my lord.

LAF. Go to, sir; you were beaten in Italy for picking a kernel out of a pomegranate; you are a vagabond, and no true traveller: you are more saucy with lords, and honourable personages, than the heraldry of your birth and virtue gives you commission.[a] You are not worth another word, else I'd call you knave. I leave you. [*Exit.*

Enter BERTRAM.

PAR. Good, very good; it is so then.—Good, very good; let it be concealed a while.

BER. Undone, and forfeited to cares for ever!

PAR. What is the matter, sweet-heart?

BER. Although before the solemn priest I have sworn, I will not bed her.

PAR. What? what, sweet-heart?

BER. O my Parolles, they have married me:—
I'll to the Tuscan wars, and never bed her.

PAR. France is a dog-hole, and it no more merits
The tread of a man's foot: to the wars!

BER. There's letters from my mother; what the import is,
I know not yet.

PAR. Ay, that would be known. To the wars, my boy, to the wars!
He wears his honour in a box unseen,
That hugs his kicky-wicky here at home;
Spending his manly marrow in her arms,
Which should sustain the bound and high curvet
Of Mars's fiery steed. To other regions!
France is a stable; we, that dwell in't, jades;
Therefore, to the war!

BER. It shall be so; I'll send her to my house,
Acquaint my mother with my hate to her,*
And wherefore I am fled; write to the king
That which I durst not speak: his present gift
Shall furnish me to those Italian fields,
Where noble fellows strike. War is no strife
To the dark house, and the detested* wife.

PAR. Will this capriccio hold in thee, art sure?

---

[a] *Than the* heraldry *of your birth and virtue gives you* commission.] This transposition of the words *heraldry* and *commission*, as they stand in the old text, was made by Hanmer.

(*) Old text, *detected*.

BER. Go with me to my chamber, and advise me.
I'll send her straight away. To-morrow
I'll to the wars, she to her single sorrow.

PAR. Why, these balls bound; there's noise
in it. 'T is hard;
A young man, married, is a man that's marr'd:
Therefore away, and leave her bravely; go:
The king has done you wrong: but, hush! 'tis so.
[*Exeunt.*

SCENE IV.—*The same. Another Room in the same.*

Enter HELENA *and* Clown.

HEL. My mother greets me kindly: is she well?

CLO. She is not well, but yet she has her health: she's very merry, but yet she is not well:

but thanks be given, she's very well, and wants nothing i'the world; but yet she is not well.

HEL. If she be very well, what does she ail, that she's not very well?

CLO. Truly, she's very well, indeed, but for two things.

HEL. What two things?

CLO. One, that she's not in heaven, whither God send her quickly! the other, that she's in earth, from whence God send her quickly!

Enter PAROLLES.

PAR. 'Bless you, my fortunate lady!

HEL. I hope, sir, I have your good will to have mine own good fortunes.*

PAR. You had my prayers to lead them on: and to keep them on, have them still.—O, my knave! how does my old lady?

CLO. So that you had her wrinkles, and I her money, I would she did as you say.

PAR. Why, I say nothing.

CLO. Marry, you are the wiser man; for many a man's tongue shakes out his master's undoing. To say nothing, to do nothing, to know nothing, and to have nothing, is to be a great part of your title; which is within a very little of nothing.

PAR. Away, thou'rt a knave.

CLO. You should have said, sir, before a knave thou'rt a knave; that is, before me thou art a knave: this had been truth, sir.

PAR. Go to, thou art a witty fool, I have found thee.

CLO. Did you find me in yourself, sir? or were you taught to find me? The search, sir, was profitable;[a] and much fool may you find in you, even to the world's pleasure, and the increase of laughter.

PAR. A good knave, i'faith, and well fed.—
Madam, my lord will go away to-night;
A very serious business calls on him.
The great prerogative and rite of love,
Which, as your due, time claims, he does acknowledge;
But puts it off to a compelled restraint;
Whose want, and whose delay, is strewed with sweets,
Which they distil now in the curbed time,
To make the coming hour o'erflow with joy,
And pleasure drown the brim.

HEL. What's his will else?

PAR. That you will take your instant leave o' the king,
And make this haste as your own good proceeding,
Strengthen'd with what apology you think
May make it probable need.

HEL. What more commands he?

PAR. That, having this obtain'd, you presently
Attend his further pleasure.

HEL. In every thing I wait upon his will.

PAR. I shall report it so.

HEL. I pray you.—Come, sirrah.
[*Exeunt.*

SCENE V.—*Another Room in the same.*

Enter LAFEU *and* BERTRAM.

LAF. But, I hope, your lordship thinks not him a soldier.

BER. Yes, my lord, and of very valiant approof.

LAF. You have it from his own deliverance?

BER. And by other warranted testimony.

LAF. Then my dial goes not true; I took this lark for a bunting.

BER. I do assure you, my lord, he is very great in knowledge, and accordingly[b] valiant.

LAF. I have then sinned against his experience, and transgressed against his valour; and my state that way is dangerous, since I cannot yet find in my heart to repent. Here he comes; I pray you, make us friends, I will pursue the amity.

Enter PAROLLES.

PAR. These things shall be done, sir.
[*To* BERTRAM.

LAF. Pray you, sir, who's his tailor?

PAR. Sir?

LAF. O, I know him well: ay, sir; he, sir, is a good workman, a very good tailor.

BER. Is she gone to the king?
[*Aside to* PAROLLES.

PAR. She is.

BER. Will she away to-night?

PAR. As you'll have her.

BER. I have writ my letters, casketed my treasure,
Given order for our horses; and to-night,
When I should take possession of the bride,

(*) Old text, *fortune.*

a The search, sir, was profitable;] This begins as a new speech in the folio, with a second prefix of *Clo.*; and it seems very likely, from the context, that Parolles had made some reply, which is lost.

b *And* accordingly *valiant.*] That is, *conformably, proportionally*, valiant. So in "The Lovers' Progress," of Beaumont and Fletcher, Act III. Sc. 6:—

"I fear ye are not used *accordingly*."

End[a] ere I do begin.

Laf. A good traveller is something at the latter end of a dinner; but one* that lies three-thirds, and uses a known truth to pass a thousand nothings with, should be once heard, and thrice beaten.—God save you, captain.

Ber. Is there any unkindness between my lord and you, monsieur?

Par. I know not how I have deserved to run into my lord's displeasure.

Laf. You have made shift to run into 't, boots and spurs and all, like him that leaped into the custard: (5) and out of it you'll run again, rather than suffer question for your residence.

Ber. It may be you have mistaken him, my lord.

Laf. And shall do so ever, though I took him at his prayers. Fare you well, my lord; and believe this of me, there can be no kernel in this light nut; the soul of this man is his clothes: trust him not in matter of heavy consequence; I have kept of them tame, and know their natures.—Farewell, monsieur: I have spoken better of you, than you have or will† deserve at my hand; but we must do good against evil. [*Exit.*

Par. An idle[b] lord, I swear.

Ber. I think[c] so.

Par. Why, do you not know him?

Ber. Yes, I do know him well; and common [speech

Gives him a worthy pass. Here comes my clog.

Enter Helena.

Hel. I have, sir, as I was commanded from you,
Spoke with the king, and have procur'd his leave
For present parting; only, he desires
Some private speech with you.

Ber. I shall obey his will.
You must not marvel, Helen, at my course,
Which holds not colour with the time, nor does
The ministration and required office
On my particular: prepar'd I was not
For such a business, therefore am I found
So much unsettled. This drives me to entreat you,
That presently you take your way for home,
And rather muse, than ask, why I entreat you;
For my respects are better than they seem,
And my appointments have in them a need,
Greater than shows itself at the first view,
To you that know them not. This to my mother:
[*Giving a letter.*
'T will be two days ere I shall see you; so
I leave you to your wisdom.

Hel. Sir, I can nothing say,
But that I am your most obedient servant.

Ber. Come, come, no more of that.

Hel. And ever shall
With true observance seek to eke out that,
Wherein toward me my homely stars have fail'd
To equal my great fortune.

Ber. Let that go:
My haste is very great: farewell; hie home.

Hel. Pray, sir, your pardon.

Ber. Well, what would you say?

Hel. I am not worthy of the wealth I owe,[d]
Nor dare I say, 't is mine; and yet it is;
But, like a timorous thief, most fain would steal
What law does vouch mine own.

Ber. What would you have?

Hel. Something; and scarce so much:—nothing, indeed.—
I would not tell you what I would: my lord—'faith, yes;—
Strangers, and foes, do sunder, and not kiss.

Ber. I pray you, stay not, but in haste to horse.

Hel. I shall not break your bidding, good my lord.

Ber. Where are my other men, monsieur?—Farewell.[e] [*Exit* Helena.
Go thou toward home; where I will never come,
Whilst I can shake my sword, or hear the drum.—
Away, and for our flight.

Par. Bravely, coragio! [*Exeunt.*

(*) First folio, *on*. (†) First folio inserts, *to*.

a End *ere I do begin*.] In the old copy,

"*And* ere I do begin."

The emendation was found in the margin of Lord Ellesmere's copy of the first folio, and is supported by a passage in "The Two Gentlemen of Verona," Act II. Sc. 4:—

"I know it well, sir; you always *end ere you begin*."

b *An* idle *lord*,—] *Idle*, here, as in many other passages, means, *crazy, wild, mad-brained*: thus, again in Act III. Sc. 7:—

"———yet, in his *idle* fire," &c.

and in "Hamlet," Act III. Sc. 6, Hamlet says—

"They are coming to the play; I must be *idle*."

c I think so.] The context testifies the poet wrote "I think *not* so."

d *The wealth* I owe.—] The wealth I *own, possess*.

e Where are my other men, &c.] This line, in the old copies, is given to Helena.

ACT III.

SCENE I.—Florence. *A Room in the* Duke's *Palace.*

Flourish. Enter the DUKE *of* FLORENCE, *attended; two* French Lords, *and others.*

DUKE. So that, from point to point, now have you heard
The fundamental reasons of this war;
Whose great decision hath much blood let forth,
And more thirsts after.
1 LORD. Holy seems the quarrel
Upon your grace's part; black and fearful
On the opposer. [France
DUKE. Therefore we marvel much, our cousin
Would, in so just a business, shut his bosom
Against our borrowing prayers.
2 LORD. Good my lord,
The reasons of our state I cannot yield,
But like a common and an outward man,
That the great figure of a council frames
By self-unable motion: therefore dare not
Say what I think of it, since I have found
Myself in my incertain grounds to fail
As often as I guess'd.
DUKE. Be it his pleasure.
2 LORD. But I am sure, the younger of our nature,
That surfeit on their ease, will, day by day,
Come here for physic.
DUKE. Welcome shall they be;
And all the honours, that can fly from us,
Shall on them settle. You know your places well;
When better fall, for your avails they fell.
To-morrow to the field. [*Flourish. Exeunt.*

SCENE II.—Rousillon. *A Room in the* Countess's *Palace.*

Enter Countess *and* Clown.

COUNT. It hath happened all as I would have had it, save, that he comes not along with her.

CLO. By my troth, I take my young lord to be a very melancholy man.

COUNT. By what observance, I pray you?

CLO. Why, he will look upon his boot, and

sing; mend the ruff,[a] and sing; ask questions, and sing; pick his teeth, and sing: I know a man that had this trick of melancholy, sold* a goodly manor for a song.

COUNT. Let me see what he writes, and when he means to come. [*Opening a letter.*

CLO. I have no mind to Isbel, since I was at court; our old ling† and our Isbels o' the country are nothing like your old ling and your Isbels o' the court: the brains of my Cupid 's knocked out; and I begin to love, as an old man loves money, with no stomach.

COUNT. What have we here?

CLO. E'en‡ that you have there. [*Exit.*

COUNT. [Reads.] *I have sent you a daughter-in-law: she hath recovered the king, and undone me. I have wedded her, not bedded her; and sworn to make the* not *eternal. You shall hear, I am run away; know it, before the report come. If there be breadth enough in the world, I will hold a long distance. My duty to you.*

Your unfortunate son,

BERTRAM.

This is not well, rash and unbridled boy,
To fly the favours of so good a king;
To pluck his indignation on thy head,
By the misprizing of a maid too virtuous
For the contempt of empire.

Re-enter Clown.

CLO. O madam, yonder is heavy news within, between two soldiers and my young lady.

COUNT. What is the matter?

CLO. Nay, there is some comfort in the news, some comfort; your son will not be killed so soon as I thought he would.

COUNT. Why should he be killed?

CLO. So say I, madam, if he run away, as I hear he does: the danger is in standing to 't; that 's the loss of men, though it be the getting of children. Here they come, will tell you more: for my part, I only hear your son was run away. [*Exit* Clown.

Enter HELENA *and two* Gentlemen.

1 GEN. 'Save you, good madam.

HEL. Madam, my lord is gone, for ever gone.

2 GEN. Do not say so.

COUNT. Think upon patience.—'Pray you, gentlemen,—
I have felt so many quirks of joy and grief,
That the first face of neither, on the start,
Can woman me unto 't.—Where is my son, I pray you?

2 GEN. Madam, he 's gone to serve the duke of Florence:
We met him thitherward: for thence we came,
And, after some despatch in hand at court,
Thither we bend again.

HEL. Look on his letter, madam; here 's my passport.
[Reads.] *When thou canst get the ring upon my finger which never shall come off, and show me a child begotten of thy body, that I am father to, then call me husband: but in such a* then *I write a* never.
This is a dreadful sentence.

COUNT. Brought you this letter, gentlemen?

1 GEN. Ay, madam;
And, for the contents' sake, are sorry for our pains.

COUNT. I pr'ythee, lady, have a better cheer;
If thou engrossest all the griefs are thine,
Thou robb'st me of a moiety: he was my son;
But I do wash his name out of my blood,
And thou art all my child.—Towards Florence is he?

2 GEN. Ay, madam.

COUNT. And to be a soldier?

2 GEN. Such is his noble purpose: and, believe 't,
The duke will lay upon him all the honour
That good convenience claims.

COUNT. Return you thither?

1 GEN. Ay, madam, with the swiftest wing of speed.

HEL. [Reads.] *Till I have no wife, I have nothing in France.*
'T is bitter.

COUNT. Find you that there?

HEL. Ay, madam.

1 GEN. 'T is but the boldness of his hand, haply, which his heart was not consenting to.

COUNT. Nothing in France, until he have no wife!
There's nothing here, that is too good for him,
But only she; and she deserves a lord,
That twenty such rude boys might tend upon,
And call her hourly, mistress. Who was with him?

1 GEN. A servant only, and a gentleman
Which I have sometime known.

COUNT. Parolles, was it not?

1 GEN. Ay, my good lady, he.

COUNT. A very tainted fellow, and full of wickedness.
My son corrupts a well-derived nature
With his inducement.

1 GEN. Indeed, good lady,
The fellow has a deal of that, too much,

(*) Old text, *hold*. (†) Old text, *Lings*. (‡) First folio, *In*.

[a] The ruff,—] The top of the boot which turned over, and was sometimes ornamented with lace, was called *the ruff*.

Which holds him much to have.[a]
COUNT. You are welcome, gentlemen.
I will entreat you, when you see my son,
To tell him, that his sword can never win
The honour that he loses: more I'll entreat you
Written to bear along.
2 GEN. We serve you, madam,
In that and all your worthiest affairs.
COUNT. Not so, but as we change our courtesies.
Will you draw near?
[*Exeunt* COUNTESS *and* Gentlemen.
HEL. *Till I have no wife, I have nothing in France.*
Nothing in France, until he has no wife!
Thou shalt have none, Rousillon, none in France,
Then hast thou all again. Poor lord! is't I
That chase thee from thy country, and expose
Those tender limbs of thine to the event
Of the none-sparing war? and is it I [thou
That drive thee from the sportive court, where
Wast shot at with fair eyes, to be the mark
Of smoky muskets? O you leaden messengers,
That ride upon the violent speed of fire,
Fly with false aim; move the still-piecing air,[b]
That sings with piercing, do not touch my lord!
Whoever shoots at him, I set him there;
Whoever charges on his forward breast,
I am the caitiff, that do hold him to it;
And, though I kill him not, I am the cause
His death was so effected. Better 't were
I met the ravin lion when he roar'd
With sharp constraint of hunger; better 't were
That all the miseries, which nature owes, [sillon,
Were mine at once. No, come thou home, Rou-
Whence honour but of danger wins a scar,
As oft it loses all; I will be gone:
My being here it is, that holds thee hence:
Shall I stay here to do't? no, no, although
The air of paradise did fan the house,
And angels offic'd all: I will be gone,
That pitiful rumour may report my flight,
To consolate thine ear. Come, night; end, day!
For, with the dark, poor thief, I'll steal away. [*Exit.*

SCENE III.—Florence. *Before the* Duke's *Palace.*

Flourish. Enter the DUKE *of* FLORENCE, BERTRAM, Lords, Officers, Soldiers, *and others.*

DUKE. The general of our horse thou art; and we,
Great in our hope, lay our best love and credence,
Upon thy promising fortune.
BER. Sir, it is
A charge too heavy for my strength; but yet
We'll strive to bear it for your worthy sake,
To the extreme edge of hazard.
DUKE. Then go thou forth;
And fortune play upon thy prosperous helm,
As thy auspicious mistress!
BER. This very day,
Great Mars, I put myself into thy file:
Make me but like my thoughts, and I shall prove
A lover of thy drum, hater of love. [*Exeunt.*

SCENE IV.—Rousillon. *A Room in the* Countess's *Palace.*

Enter COUNTESS *and* Steward.

COUNT. Alas! and would you take the letter of her?
Might you not know, she would do as she has done,
By sending me a letter? Read it again.
STEW. [Reads.]
I am St. Jaques' pilgrim, thither gone:
Ambitious love hath so in me offended,
That bare-foot plod I the cold ground upon,
With sainted vow my faults to have amended.
Write, write, that, from the bloody course of war,
My dearest master, your dear son, may hie;
Bless him at home in peace, whilst I from far,
His name with zealous fervour sanctify:
His taken labours bid him me forgive;
I, his despiteful Juno, sent him forth
From courtly friends, with camping foes to live,
Where death and danger dog the heels of worth:
He is too good and fair for death and me;
Whom I myself embrace, to set him free.
COUNT. Ah, what sharp stings are in her mildest words!——
Rinaldo, you did never lack advice so much,
As letting her pass so; had I spoke with her,
I could have well diverted her intents,
Which thus she hath prevented.
STEW. Pardon me, madam:
If I had given you this at over-night,
She might have been o'er-ta'en; and yet she writes,
Pursuit would be but vain.
COUNT. What angel shall

---

a The fellow has a deal of that, too much,
Which holds him much to have.]

Of this passage no one has yet succeeded in making sense. It is, we fear, irremediably corrupt.

b —*Move the still-piecing air,*—] The old text has "*still peering.*" *Still-piecing*, that is, *ever closing*, was proposed by Malone. Tyrwhitt thought a farther alteration necessary, and would have substituted *rove* for move:—

—"*rove* the still-piecing air;"

but there is authority for *move*, in the sense of *penetrate*, or *wound*.

"High preasse thy flames, *the chrystall aire to move.*"
A Sonnet by WILLIAM LITHGOW, 1615.

Bless this unworthy husband? he cannot thrive.
Unless her prayers, whom heaven delights to hear,
And loves to grant, reprieve him from the wrath
Of greatest justice.—Write, write, Rinaldo,
To this unworthy husband of his wife:
Let every word weigh heavy of her worth,
That he does weigh too light: my greatest grief,
Though little he do feel it, set down sharply.
Despatch the most convenient messenger:—
When, haply, he shall hear that she is gone,
He will return; and hope I may, that she,
Hearing so much, will speed her foot again,
Led hither by pure love: which of them both
Is dearest to me, I have no skill in sense
To make distinction:—Provide this messenger:—
My heart is heavy, and mine age is weak;
Grief would have tears, and sorrow bids me speak.
[*Exeunt.*

SCENE V.—*Without the Walls of* Florence.

A tucket afar off. Enter an old Widow *of* Florence, DIANA, VIOLENTA, MARIANA, *and other* Citizens.

WID. Nay, come; for if they do approach the city, we shall lose all the sight.

DIA. They say, the French count has done most honourable service.

WID. It is reported that he has taken their greatest commander; and that with his own hand he slew the duke's brother. We have lost our labour; they are gone a contrary way: hark! you may know by their trumpets.

MAR. Come, let's return again, and suffice ourselves with the report of it. Well, Diana, take heed of this French earl: the honour of a maid is her name; and no legacy is so rich as honesty.

WID. I have told my neighbour, how you have been solicited by a gentleman his companion.

MAR. I know that knave; hang him! one Parolles: a filthy officer he is in those suggestions for the young earl.—Beware of them, Diana; their promises, enticements, oaths, tokens, and all these engines of lust, are not the things they go under:[a] many a maid hath been seduced by them; and the misery is, example, that so terrible shows in the wreck of maidenhood, cannot for all that dissuade succession, but that they are limed with the twigs that threaten them. I hope I need not to advise you further; but I hope your own grace will keep you where you are, though there were

[a] Are not the things they go under:] "They are not the things for which their names would make them pass."—JOHNSON.

no further danger known, but the modesty which is so lost.

DIA. You shall not need to fear me.

WID. I hope so.——Look, here comes a pilgrim: I know she will lie at my house: thither they send one another; I'll question her.—

Enter HELENA, *in the dress of a Pilgrim.*

God save you, pilgrim! Whither are you bound?

HEL. To Saint Jaques le grand.
Where do the palmers(1) lodge, I do beseech you?

WID. At the Saint Francis here, beside the port.

HEL. Is this the way?

WID. Ay, marry, is it.—Hark you! They come this way: [*A march afar off.*
If you will tarry, holy pilgrim, but till the troops come by,
I will conduct you where you shall be lodg'd;
The rather, for, I think, I know your hostess
As ample as myself.

HEL. Is it yourself?

WID. If you shall please so, pilgrim.

HEL. I thank you, and will stay upon your leisure.

WID. You came, I think, from France?

HEL. I did so.

WID. Here you shall see a countryman of yours,
That has done worthy service.

HEL. His name, I pray you.

DIA. The count Rousillon; know you such a one?

HEL. But by the ear, that hears most nobly of him:
His face I know not.

DIA. Whatsoe'er he is,
He's bravely taken here. He stole from France,
As 'tis reported, for the king had married him
Against his liking. Think you it is so?

HEL. Ay, surely, mere[a] the truth; I know his lady.

DIA. There is a gentleman, that serves the count,
Reports but coarsely of her.

HEL. What's his name?

DIA. Monsieur Parolles.

HEL. O, I believe with him,
In argument of praise, or to the worth
Of the great count himself, she is too mean
To have her name repeated; all her deserving
Is a reserved honesty,[b] and that
I have not heard examin'd.

DIA. Alas, poor lady!
'T is a hard bondage, to become the wife
Of a detesting lord.

WID. I write good creature:[c] wheresoe'er she is,
Her heart weighs sadly: this young maid might do her
A shrewd turn, if she pleas'd.

HEL. How do you mean?
May be, the amorous count solicits her
In the unlawful purpose.

WID. He does, indeed;
And brokes[d] with all that can in such a suit
Corrupt the tender honour of a maid:
But she is arm'd for him, and keeps her guard
In honestest defence.

Enter, with drum and colours, a Party of the Florentine *army,* BERTRAM, *and* PAROLLES.

MAR. The gods forbid else!

WID. So, now they come:—
That is Antonio, the duke's eldest son;
That, Escalus.

HEL. Which is the Frenchman?

DIA. He;
That with the plume: 'tis a most gallant fellow;
I would, he lov'd his wife: if he were honester,
He were much goodlier.—Is't not a handsome gentleman?

HEL. I like him well.

DIA. 'T is pity he is not honest. Yond's that same knave,
That leads him to these places; were I his lady,
I'd poison that vile rascal.

HEL. Which is he?

DIA. That jack-an-apes with scarfs: why is he melancholy?

HEL. Perchance he's hurt i' the battle.

PAR. Lose our drum! well.

MAR. He's shrewdly vexed at something: look, he has spied us.

WID. Marry, hang you!

MAR. And your courtesy, for a ring-carrier!
[*Exeunt* BERTRAM, PAROLLES, Officers, *and* Soldiers.

WID. The troop is past. Come, pilgrim, I will bring you
Where you shall host: of enjoin'd penitents
There's four or five, to great Saint Jaques bound,

---

[a] Mere *the truth;*] *Quite* the truth.

[b] Honesty,—] That is, *chastity.*

[c] I write good creature;] So the first folio, but which the editor of the second, not perhaps understanding, altered to,—"I right, good creature." The phrase to *write*, in the sense of to *proclaim*, &c. was not at all uncommon formerly. It occurs, indeed, three or four times in Shakespeare: thus, in the present play, Act II. Sc. 3, Lafeu says,—

"Sirrah, I *write man*," &c.

And,—

"I'd give bay Curtal, and his furniture,
My mouth no more were broken than these boys',
And writ as little beard."

Again, in "King Lear," Act V. Sc. 3:—

"About it; and *write happy*, when thou hast done."

[d] *And* brokes—] That is, *panders.*

Already at my house.
Hel. I humbly thank you:
Please it this matron, and this gentle maid,
To eat with us to-night, the charge, and thanking,
Shall be for me; and, to requite you further,
I will bestow some precepts of[a] this virgin,
Worthy the note.
Both. We'll take your offer kindly.
[*Exeunt.*

SCENE VI.—*Camp before* Florence.

Enter Bertram, *and the two* French Lords.

1 Lord. Nay, good my lord, put him to't; let him have his way.

2 Lord. If your lordship find him not a hilding, hold me no more in your respect.

1 Lord. On my life, my lord, a bubble.

Ber. Do you think, I am so far deceived in him?

1 Lord. Believe it, my lord, in mine own direct knowledge, without any malice, but to speak of him as my kinsman, he's a most notable coward, an infinite and endless liar, an hourly promise-breaker, the owner of no one good quality worthy your lordship's entertainment.

2 Lord. It were fit you knew him, lest reposing too far in his virtue, which he hath not, he might, at some great and trusty business, in a main danger fail you.

Ber. I would I knew in what particular action to try him.

2 Lord. None better than to let him fetch off his drum, which you hear him so confidently undertake to do.

1 Lord. I, with a troop of Florentines, will

a Of *this virgin*,—] This is only one of the frequent instances in Shakespeare where *of* is employed for *on*.

suddenly surprise him; such I will have, whom, I am sure, he knows not from the enemy: we will bind and hoodwink him so, that he shall suppose no other but that he is carried into the leaguer[a] of the adversaries, when we bring him to our own tents: be but your lordship present at his examination; if he do not, for the promise of his life, and in the highest compulsion of base fear, offer to betray you, and deliver all the intelligence in his power against you, and that with the divine forfeit of his soul upon oath, never trust my judgment in any thing.

2 LORD. O, for the love of laughter, let him fetch his drum; he says, he has a stratagem for't: when your lordship sees the bottom of his* success in't, and to what metal this counterfeit lump of ore† will be melted, if you give him not John Drum's entertainment,(2) your inclining cannot be removed. Here he comes.

1 LORD. O, for the love of laughter, hinder not the honour of his design: let him fetch off his drum in any hand.

Enter PAROLLES.

BER. How now, monsieur? this drum sticks sorely in your disposition.

2 LORD. A pox on't, let it go; 'tis but a drum.

PAR. *But a drum!* Is't *but a drum?* A drum so lost!—There was an excellent command! to charge in with our horse upon our own wings, and to rend our own soldiers.

2 LORD. That was not to be blamed in the command of the service; it was a disaster of war that Cæsar himself could not have prevented, if he had been there to command.

BER. Well, we cannot greatly condemn our success; some dishonour we had in the loss of that drum; but it is not to be recovered.

PAR. It might have been recovered.

BER. It might, but it is not now.

PAR. It is to be recovered: but that the merit of service is seldom attributed to the true and exact performer, I would have that drum or another, or *hic jacet*.

BER. Why, if you have a stomach to't, monsieur, if you think your mystery in stratagem can bring this instrument of honour again into his native quarter, be magnanimous in the enterprise, and go on; I will grace the attempt for a worthy exploit; if you speed well in it, the duke shall both speak of it, and extend to you what further becomes his greatness, even to the utmost syllable of your worthiness.

PAR. By the hand of a soldier, I will undertake it.

BER. But you must not now slumber in it.

PAR. I'll about it this evening: and I will presently pen down my dilemmas, encourage myself in my certainty, put myself into my mortal preparation, and, by midnight, look to hear further from me.

BER. May I be bold to acquaint his grace, you are gone about it?

PAR. I know not what the success will be, my lord; but the attempt I vow.

BER. I know thou art valiant; and, to the possibility of thy soldiership, will subscribe for thee. Farewell.

PAR. I love not many words. [*Exit.*

1 LORD. No more than a fish loves water.—Is not this a strange fellow, my lord? that so confidently seems to undertake this business, which he knows is not to be done: damns himself to do, and dares better be damned than to do't.

2 LORD. You do not know him, my lord, as we do: certain it is, that he will steal himself into a man's favour, and, for a week, escape a great deal of discoveries; but when you find him out, you have him ever after.

BER. Why, do you think he will make no deed at all of this, that so seriously he does address himself unto?

1 LORD. None in the world; but return with an invention, and clap upon you two or three probable lies: but we have almost embossed[b] him; you shall see his fall to-night; for, indeed, he is not for your lordship's respect.

2 LORD. We'll make you some sport with the fox, ere we case him. He was first smoked by the old lord Lafeu: when his disguise and he is parted, tell me what a sprat you shall find him; which you shall see this very night.

1 LORD. I must go look my twigs; he shall be caught.

BER. Your brother, he shall go along with me.

1 LORD. As't please your lordship: I'll leave you. [*Exit.*

BER. Now will I lead you to the house, and show you the lass I spoke of.

2 LORD. But, you say, she's honest.

BER. That's all the fault: I spoke with her but once,
And found her wondrous cold; but I sent to her,
By this same coxcomb that we have i' the wind,

(*) First folio, *this*. (†) First folio, *ours*.

[a] The leaguer—] The *camp*.

[b] Embossed him,—] In the old language of the chase, the stag was said to be *embossed*, when, exhausted and outrun, he foamed and frothed at the mouth. The meaning is, we have hunted him almost to his fall.

Tokens and letters, which she did re-send,
And this is all I have done: she's a fair creature;
Will you go see her?
2 Lord. With all my heart, my lord.
[*Exeunt.*

SCENE VII.—Florence. *A Room in the* Widow's *House.*

Enter Helena *and* Widow.

Hel. If you misdoubt me that I am not she,
I know not how I shall assure you further,
But I shall lose the grounds I work upon.
Wid. Though my estate be fallen, I was well born,
Nothing acquainted with these businesses;
And would not put my reputation now
In any staining act.
Hel. Nor would I wish you.
First, give me trust, the count he is my husband;
And, what to your sworn counsel[a] I have spoken,
Is so, from word to word; and then you cannot,
By the good aid that I of you shall borrow,
Err in bestowing it.
Wid. I should believe you;
For you have show'd me that, which well approves
You are great in fortune.
Hel. Take this purse of gold,
And let me buy your friendly help thus far,
Which I will over-pay, and pay again,
When I have found it. The count he woos your daughter,
Lays down his wanton siege before her beauty,
Resolves to carry her; let her, in fine, consent,

[a] *Your* sworn counsel—] Your *pledged secrecy.*

As we 'll direct her how 't is best to bear it.
Now his important[a] blood will nought deny
That she 'll demand: a ring the county wears,
That downward hath succeeded in his house,
From son to son, some four or five descents
Since the first father wore it: this ring he holds
In most rich choice; yet, in his idle[b] fire,
To buy his will, it would not seem too dear,
Howe'er repented after.

WID. Now I see
The bottom of your purpose.

HEL. You see it lawful then: it is no more,
But that your daughter, ere she seems as won,
Desires this ring; appoints him an encounter;
In fine, delivers me to fill the time,
Herself most chastely absent; after this,*
To marry her, I'll add three thousand crowns
To what is pass'd already.

WID. I have yielded:
Instruct my daughter how she shall persévér,
That time and place, with this deceit so lawful,
May prove coherent. Every night he comes
With musics of all sorts, and songs compos'd
To her unworthiness: it nothing steads us,
To chide him from our eaves, for he persists,
As if his life lay on't.

HEL. Why then, to-night,
Let us assay our plot; which, if it speed,
Is wicked meaning in a lawful deed,
And lawful meaning in a lawful[c] act;
Where both not sin, and yet a sinful fact:
But let's about it. [*Exeunt.*

(*) First folio omits, *this*.

a *His* important *blood*—] Here and elsewhere, *important* means *importunate*.

b *His* idle *fire*,—] *Mad-brained* fire. See note (b), p. 27.
c *And lawful meaning in* a lawful *act*;] We should perhaps read:
"And lawful meaning in a *wicked* act."

ACT IV.

SCENE I.—*Without the* Florentine *Camp.*

Enter First Lord, *with five or six* Soldiers *in ambush.*

1 Lord. He can come no other way but by this hedge corner. When you sally upon him, speak what terrible language you will; though you understand it not yourselves, no matter; for we must not seem to understand him, unless some one among us, whom we must produce for an interpreter.

1 Sold. Good captain, let me be the interpreter.[a]

[a] *Let me be the* interpreter.] In conformity with this proposal, the first soldier is so styled in the old text, throughout the subsequent scenes with Parolles.

1 Lord. Art not acquainted with him? knows he not thy voice?

1 Sold. No, sir, I warrant you.

1 Lord. But what linsy-woolsy hast thou to speak to us again?

1 Sold. E'en such as you speak to me.

1 Lord. He must think us some band of strangers i' the adversary's entertainment. Now he hath a smack of all neighbouring languages; therefore we must every one be a man of his own fancy, not to know what we speak one to another; so we seem to know, is to know straight our purpose: chough's language, gabble enough, and good enough. As for you, interpreter, you must seem very politic. But couch, ho! here he comes, to

beguile two hours in a sleep, and then to return and swear the lies he forges.

Enter PAROLLES.

PAR. Ten o'clock; within these three hours 'twill be time enough to go home. What shall I say I have done? It must be a very plausive invention that carries it. They begin to smoke me: and disgraces have of late knocked too often at my door. I find, my tongue is too fool-hardy; but my heart hath the fear of Mars before it, and of his creatures, not daring the reports of my tongue.

1 LORD. [*Aside.*] This is the first truth that e'er thine own tongue was guilty of.

PAR. What the devil should move me to undertake the recovery of this drum, being not ignorant of the impossibility, and knowing I had no such purpose? I must give myself some hurts, and say, I got them in exploit; yet slight ones will not carry it: they will say, *Came you off with so little?* and great ones I dare not give. Wherefore? what's the instance?[a] Tongue, I must put you into a butter-woman's mouth, and buy myself another of Bajazet's mule, if you prattle me into these perils.

1 LORD. [*Aside.*] Is it possible, he should know what he is, and be that he is?

PAR. I would the cutting of my garments would serve the turn; or the breaking of my Spanish sword.

1 LORD. [*Aside.*] We cannot afford you so.

PAR. Or the baring of my beard; and to say, it was in stratagem.

1 LORD. [*Aside.*] 'Twould not do.

PAR. Or to drown my clothes, and say, I was stripped.

1 LORD. [*Aside.*] Hardly serve.

PAR. Though I swore I leaped from the window of the citadel—

1 LORD. [*Aside.*] How deep?

PAR. Thirty fathom.

1 LORD. [*Aside.*] Three great oaths would scarce make that be believed.

PAR. I would I had any drum of the enemy's; I would swear, I recovered it.

1 LORD. [*Aside.*] You shall hear one anon.
[*Alarum within.*

PAR. A drum now of the enemy's!

1 LORD. *Throca movousus, cargo! cargo! cargo!*

ALL. *Cargo! cargo! villianda par corbo, cargo!*

[a] Wherefore? what's the instance?] Wherefore did I volunteer this exploit? For what object?

PAR. O! ransom, ransom:—do not hide mine eyes. [*They seize and blindfold him.*

1 SOLD. *Boskos thromuldo boskos!*

PAR. I know you are the Muskos' regiment,
And I shall lose my life for want of language.
If there be here German, or Dane, low Dutch,
Italian, or French, let him speak to me:—
I will discover that which shall undo
The Florentine.

1 SOLD. *Boskos vauvado:*—
I understand thee, and can speak thy tongue.
Kerelybonto:——Sir,
Betake thee to thy faith, for seventeen poniards
Are at thy bosom.

PAR. Oh!

1 SOLD. O, pray, pray, pray. *Manka revania dulche.*

1 LORD. *Oscorbidulchos volivorco.*

1 SOLD. The general is content to spare thee yet,
And, hood-wink'd as thou art, will lead thee on
To gather from thee: haply, thou may'st inform
Something to save thy life.

PAR. O, let me live,
And all the secrets of our camp I'll show,
Their force, their purposes: nay, I'll speak that
Which you will wonder at.

1 SOLD. But wilt thou faithfully?

PAR. If I do not, damn me.

1 SOLD. *Acordo linta.*——
Come on, thou art granted space.
[*A short alarum without. Exit, with* PAROLLES *guarded.*

1 LORD. Go, tell the count Rousillon, and my brother,
We have caught the woodcock, and will keep him muffled,
Till we do hear from them.

2 SOLD. Captain, I will.

1 LORD. He will betray us all unto ourselves;—
Inform on that.

2 SOLD. So I will, sir.

1 LORD. Till then, I'll keep him dark, and safely lock'd. [*Exeunt.*

SCENE II.—Florence. *A Room in the* Widow's *House.*

Enter BERTRAM *and* DIANA.

BER. They told me, that your name was Fontibell.

DIA. No, my good lord, Diana.

BER. Titled goddess;
And worth it, with addition! But, fair soul,
In your fine frame hath love no quality?
If the quick fire of youth light not your mind,

You are no maiden, but a monument:
When you are dead, you should be such a one
As you are now, for you are cold and stern;[a]
And now you should be as your mother was,
When your sweet self was got.

DIA. She then was honest.

BER. So should you be.

DIA. No:
My mother did but duty; such, my lord,
As you owe to your wife.

BER. No more of that!
I pr'ythee, do not strive against my vows:
I was compell'd to her, but I love thee
By love's own sweet constraint, and will for ever
Do thee all rights of service.

DIA. Ay, so you serve us,
Till we serve you: but when you have our roses,
You barely leave our thorns to prick ourselves,
And mock us with our bareness.

BER. How have I sworn!

DIA. 'Tis not the many oaths, that makes the truth,
But the plain single vow, that is vow'd true.
What is not holy, that we swear not by,
But take the Highest to witness: then, pray you, tell me,
If I should swear by Jove's great attributes,
I lov'd you dearly, would you believe my oaths,
When I did love you ill? this has no holding,
To swear by him whom I protest to love,
That I will work against him.[b] Therefore, your oaths
Are words, and poor conditions, but unseal'd;
At least, in my opinion.

BER. Change it, change it;
Be not so holy-cruel: love[c] is holy,
And my integrity ne'er knew the crafts,
That you do charge men with: stand no more off,
But give thyself unto my sick desires,
Who then recovers; say, thou art mine, and ever
My love, as it begins, shall so persévor.

DIA. I see, that men make hopes, in such a snare,[d]
That we'll forsake ourselves. Give me that ring.

BER. I'll lend it thee, my dear, but have no power
To give it from me.

DIA. Will you not, my lord?

BER. It is an honour 'longing to our house,
Bequeathed down from many ancestors;
Which were the greatest obloquy i' the world,
In me to lose.

DIA. Mine honour's such a ring:
My chastity's the jewel of our house,
Bequeathed down from many ancestors;
Which were the greatest obloquy i' the world,
In me to lose. Thus your own proper wisdom
Brings in the champion *honour* on my part,
Against your vain assault.

BER. Here, take my ring:
My house, mine honour, yea, my life be thine,
And I'll be bid by thee.

DIA. When midnight comes, knock at my chamber window;
I'll order take, my mother shall not hear.
Now will I charge you in the band of truth,
When you have conquer'd my yet maiden bed,
Remain there but an hour, nor speak to me:
My reasons are most strong, and you shall know them,
When back again this ring shall be deliver'd:
And on your finger, in the night, I'll put
Another ring; that, what in time proceeds,
May token to the future our past deeds.
Adieu, till then: then, fail not: you have won
A wife of me, though there my hope be done.

BER. A heaven on earth I have won, by wooing thee. [*Exit.*

DIA. For which live long to thank both heaven and me!
You may so in the end.——
My mother told me just how he would woo,
As if she sat in his heart; she says, all men
Have the like oaths: he had sworn to marry me,
When his wife's dead; therefore I'll lie with him,
When I am buried. Since Frenchmen are so braid,[e]
Marry that will, I live and die a maid:
Only, in this disguise, I think't no sin
To cozen him, that would unjustly win. [*Exit.*

---

[a] *Cold and* stern;] *Stern* is *rigid, unyielding.*

"Can generous hearts in nature be so *stern?*"
GREENE's *James the Fourth.*

"In former times, some countries have been so chary in this behalf, so *stern*, that if a child were crooked or deformed in body or mind, they made him away."—BURTON's *Anatomy of Melancholy.*

[b] 'Tis not the many oaths, &c. &c.] All the best modern editors have laboured earnestly to render this passage intelligible. That they have failed is, we believe, owing to their not perceiving that the accomplished compositors or transcribers of the folio, 1623, have contrived, with their customary dexterity, to graft a speech of Bertram on to that of Diana. If we read the dialogue as follows, much in it that was nebulous becomes clear, and a way is seen to the comprehension of the rest:—

"BER. How have I sworn!
DIA. 'Tis not the many oaths, that makes the truth,
But the plain single vow, that is vow'd true.
What is not holy, that we swear not by,
But take the Highest to witness.
BER. Then, pray you, tell me,
If I should swear by Jove's great attributes,
I lov'd you dearly, would you believe my oaths,
When I did love you ill?
DIA. This has no holding,
To swear by him whom I protest to love,
That I will work against him."

[c] Love is holy,—] We should, perhaps, read, "*My* love is holy."

[d] *I see, that men make* hopes, *in such a* snare,—] The old copy has,—

"I see that men make *rope's* in such a *scarre;*"

which, though some critics have attempted to explain, none has yet succeeded in making intelligible. The alteration of *hopes* for *rope's* was proposed by Rowe, who reads,—

"I see that men make *hopes* in such *affairs.*"

[e] *Since Frenchmen are so* braid,—] *Braid,* in this place, means *false, tricking, deceitful.*

SCENE III.—*The* Florentine *Camp.*

Enter the two French Lords, *and two or three* Soldiers.

1 LORD. You have not given him his mother's letter?

2 LORD. I have delivered it an hour since: there is something in't that stings his nature, for, on the reading it, he changed almost into another man.

1 LORD. He has much worthy blame laid upon him, for shaking off so good a wife, and so sweet a lady.

2 LORD. Especially he hath incurred the everlasting displeasure of the king, who had even tuned his bounty to sing happiness to him. I will tell you a thing, but you shall let it dwell darkly with you.

1 LORD. When you have spoken it, 'tis dead, and I am the grave of it.

2 LORD. He hath perverted a young gentlewoman here in Florence, of a most chaste renown, and this night he fleshes his will in the spoil of her honour: he hath given her his monumental ring, and thinks himself made[a] in the unchaste composition.

1 LORD. Now, God delay our rebellion; as we are ourselves, what things are we!

2 LORD. Merely[b] our own traitors. And as in the common course of all treasons, we still see them reveal themselves, till they attain to their abhorred ends;[c] so he, that in this action contrives against his own nobility, in his proper stream o'erflows himself.

1 LORD. Is it not meant[d] damnable in us, to be trumpeters of our unlawful intents? We shall not then have his company to-night?

2 LORD. Not till after midnight, for he is dieted to his hour.

1 LORD. That approaches apace: I would gladly have him see his company[e] anatomized; that he might take a measure of his own judgments, wherein so curiously he had set this counterfeit.

2 LORD. We will not meddle with him till he come; for his presence must be the whip of the other.

1 LORD. In the mean time, what hear you of these wars?

2 LORD. I hear, there is an overture of peace.

1 LORD. Nay, I assure you, a peace concluded.

2 LORD. What will count Rousillon do then? will he travel higher, or return again into France?

1 LORD. I perceive, by this demand, you are not altogether of his council.

2 LORD. Let it be forbid, sir! so should I be a great deal of his act.

1 LORD. Sir, his wife, some two months since, fled from his house: her pretence is a pilgrimage to Saint Jaques le grand; which holy undertaking, with most austere sanctimony, she accomplished: and, there residing, the tenderness of her nature became as a prey to her grief; in fine, made a groan of her last breath, and now she sings in heaven.

2 LORD. How is this justified?

1 LORD. The stronger part of it by her own letters; which makes her story true, even to the point of her death: her death itself, which could not be her office to say, is come, was faithfully confirmed by the rector of the place.

2 LORD. Hath the count all this intelligence?

1 LORD. Ay, and the particular confirmations, point from point, to the full arming of the verity.

2 LORD. I am heartily sorry, that he'll be glad of this.

1 LORD. How mightily, sometimes, we make us comforts of our losses!

2 LORD. And how mightily, some other times, we drown our gain in tears! The great dignity, that his valour hath here acquired for him, shall at home be encountered with a shame as ample.

1 LORD. The web of our life is of a mingled yarn, good and ill together: our virtues would be proud, if our faults whipped them not, and our crimes would despair, if they were not cherished by our virtues.

Enter a Servant.

How now? where's your master?

SERV. He met the duke in the street, sir, of whom he hath taken a solemn leave; his lordship will next morning for France. The duke hath offered him letters of commendations to the king.

2 LORD. They shall be no more than needful there, if they were more than they can commend.

1 LORD. They cannot be too sweet for the king's tartness. Here's his lordship now.

Enter BERTRAM.

How now, my lord, is't not after midnight?

BER. I have to-night despatched sixteen busi-

---

[a] *And thinks himself* made—] *Made* seems strangely inapplicable. We should, perhaps, read, "*paid*."

[b] Merely—] That is, *absolutely*.

[c] *To their* abhorred ends;] Their *disgraceful punishments*; and not, as the words are usually explained, *the opportunity of effecting their treachery*;—an opportunity not very likely to occur, if they were always revealing the object they had in hand.

[d] *Is it not* meant *damnable*—] This is commonly altered to "*most* damnable;" but the context supports the ancient reading, the sense of which appears to be, "Are we not designedly, for our own condemnation, made trumpeters of our unlawful purposes."

[e] *His* company—] His *companion*.

nesses, a month's length a-piece, by an abstract of success; I have conge'd with the duke, done my adieu with his nearest, buried a wife, mourned for her, writ to my lady mother, I am returning; entertained my convoy; and, between these main parcels of despatch, effected many nicer needs; the last was the greatest, but that I have not ended yet.

2 LORD. If the business be of any difficulty, and this morning your departure hence, it requires haste of your lordship.

BER. I mean, the business is not ended, as fearing to hear of it hereafter. But shall we have this dialogue between the fool and the soldier? Come, bring forth this counterfeit module; he has deceived me, like a double-meaning prophesier.

2 LORD. Bring him forth: [*Exeunt* Soldiers.] he has sat i' the stocks all night, poor gallant knave.

BER. No matter; his heels have deserved it, in usurping his spurs so long. How does he carry himself?

1 LORD. I have told your lordship already, the stocks carry him. But to answer you as you would be understood, he weeps like a wench that had shed her milk: he hath confessed himself to Morgan, whom he supposes to be a friar, from the time of his remembrance, to this very instant disaster of his setting i' the stocks: and what think you he hath confessed?

BER. Nothing of me, has he?

2 LORD. His confession is taken, and it shall be read to his face: if your lordship be in't, as I believe you are, you must have the patience to hear it.

Re-enter Soldiers, *with* PAROLLES.

BER. A plague upon him! muffled! he can say nothing of me; hush! hush!

1 LORD. Hoodman(1) comes!—*Portotartarossa.*

1 SOLD. He calls for the tortures; what will you say without 'em?

PAR. I will confess what I know without constraint; if ye pinch me like a pasty, I can say no more.

1 SOLD. *Bosko chimurcho.*

2 LORD. *Boblibindo chicurmurco.*

1 SOLD. You are a merciful general.—Our general bids you answer to what I shall ask you out of a note.

PAR. And truly, as I hope to live.

1 SOLD. *First demand of him how many horse the duke is strong.* What say you to that?

PAR. Five or six thousand; but very weak and unserviceable: the troops are all scattered, and the commanders very poor rogues, upon my reputation and credit, and as I hope to live.

1 SOLD. Shall I set down your answer so?

PAR. Do; I'll take the sacrament on't, how and which way you will.

BER. All's one to him.[a] What a past-saving slave is this!

1 LORD. You are deceived, my lord; this is monsieur Parolles, the gallant militarist, (that was his own phrase,) that had the whole theorick of war in the knot of his scarf, and the practice in the chape of his dagger.

2 LORD. I will never trust a man again, for keeping his sword clean; nor believe he can have every thing in him, by wearing his apparel neatly.

1 SOLD. Well, that's set down.

PAR. Five or six thousand horse, I said,—I will say true,—or thereabouts, set down,—for I'll speak truth.

1 LORD. He's very near the truth in this.

BER. But I con him no thanks for't, in the nature he delivers it.[b]

PAR. Poor rogues, I pray you, say.

1 SOLD. Well, that's set down.

PAR. I humbly thank you, sir: a truth's a truth, the rogues are marvellous poor.

1 SOLD. *Demand of him of what strength they are afoot.* What say you to that?

PAR. By my troth, sir, if I were to live[c] this present hour, I will tell true. Let me see: Spurio a hundred and fifty, Sebastian so many, Corambus so many, Jaques so many,[d] Guiltian, Cosmo, Lodowick, and Gratii, two hundred fifty each: mine own company, Chitopher, Vaumond, Bentii, two hundred fifty each: so that the muster-file, rotten and sound, upon my life amounts not to fifteen thousand poll; half of the which dare not shake the snow from off their cassocks, lest they shake themselves to pieces.

BER. What shall be done to him?

1 LORD. Nothing, but let him have thanks. Demand of him my condition,[e] and what credit I have with the duke?

1 SOLD. Well, that's set down. *You shall demand of him, whether one captain Dumain be i' the camp, a Frenchman; what his reputation is with the duke, what his valour, honesty, and expertness in wars; or whether he thinks, it were not possible, with well-weighing sums of gold, to corrupt him to a revolt.* What say you to this? what do you know of it?

---

a All's one to him.] In the old text these words are given to Parolles.

b But I con him no thanks for't, in the nature he delivers it.] No thanks to him for truth, however, considering the purpose for which he tells it.

c *If I were to* live *this present hour,*—] "If I were to *die* this present hour" seems more germane to his position. *Live*, possibly, is a misprint of *leave*. He may have meant, "If I were free to *depart* this very hour."

d *Sebastian* so *many, Corambus* so *many, Jacques* so *many,*—] *So* many means, *as* many.

e *My* condition,—] That is, *disposition* and *character*.

PAR. I beseech you, let me answer to the particular of the intergatories. Demand them singly.

1 SOLD. Do you know this captain Dumain?

PAR. I know him: he was a botcher's 'prentice in Paris, from whence he was whipped for getting the shrieve's fool with child; a dumb innocent, that could not say him nay.

[DUMAIN *lifts up his hand in anger.*

BER. Nay, by your leave, hold your hands; though I know, his brains are forfeit to the next tile that falls.

1 SOLD. Well, is this captain in the duke of Florence's camp?

PAR. Upon my knowledge, he is, and lousy.

1 LORD. Nay, look not so upon me; we shall hear of your lordship* anon.

1 SOLD. What is his reputation with the duke?

PAR. The duke knows him for no other but a poor officer of mine; and writ to me this other day, to turn him out of the band: I think, I have his letter in my pocket.

1 SOLD. Marry, we'll search.

PAR. In good sadness, I do not know; either it is there, or it is upon a file, with the duke's other letters, in my tent.

1 SOLD. Here 't is; here's a paper. Shall I read it to you?

PAR. I do not know, if it be it, or no.

BER. Our interpreter does it well.

1 LORD. Excellently.

1 SOLD. *Dian, The count's a fool, and full of gold,—*

PAR. That is not the duke's letter, sir; that is an advertisement to a proper maid in Florence, one Diana, to take heed of the allurement of one count Rousillon, a foolish idle boy, but, for all that, very ruttish: I pray you, sir, put it up again.

1 SOLD. Nay, I'll read it first, by your favour.

PAR. My meaning in't, I protest, was very honest in the behalf of the maid: for I knew the young count to be a dangerous and lascivious boy, who is a whale to virginity, and devours up all the fry it finds.

BER. Damnable both-sides rogue!

1 SOLD. *When he swears oaths, bid him drop gold, and take it;*
After he scores, he never pays the score:
Half won, is match well made; match, and well make it;
He ne'er pays after debts, take it before;
And say, a soldier, Dian, told thee this,
Men are to mell with, boys are not to kiss:
For count of this, the count's a fool, I know it,
Who pays before, but not when he does owe it.

Thine, as he vowed to thee in thine ear,
PAROLLES.

BER. He shall be whipped through the army, with this rhyme in his forehead.

2 LORD. This is your devoted friend, sir, the manifold linguist, and the armipotent soldier.

BER. I could endure anything before but a cat, and now he's a cat to me.

1 SOLD. I perceive, sir, by our[a] general's looks, we shall be fain to hang you.

PAR. My life, sir, in any case! not that I am afraid to die, but that, my offences being many, I would repent out the remainder of nature: let me live, sir, in a dungeon, i' the stocks, or anywhere, so I may live.

1 SOLD. We'll see what may be done, so you confess freely; therefore, once more to this captain Dumain. You have answered to his reputation with the duke, and to his valour. What is his honesty?

PAR. He will steal, sir, an egg[b] out of a cloister; for rapes and ravishments he parallels Nessus. He professes not keeping of oaths; in breaking them he is stronger than Hercules. He will lie, sir, with such volubility, that you would think truth were a fool: drunkenness is his best virtue, for he will be swine-drunk, and in his sleep he does little harm, save to his bed-clothes about him; but they know his conditions, and lay him in straw. I have but little more to say, sir, of his honesty; he has everything that an honest man should not have; what an honest man should have, he has nothing.

1 LORD. I begin to love him for this.

BER. For this description of thine honesty? A pox upon him! for me, he is more and more a cat.

1 SOLD. What say you to his expertness in war?

PAR. 'Faith, sir, he has led the drum before the English tragedians,(2)—to belie him, I will not,—and more of his soldiership I know not; except, in that country, he had the honour to be the officer at a place there called Mile-end,[c] to instruct for the doubling of files: I would do the man what honour I can, but of this I am not certain.

1 LORD. He hath out-villained villainy so far, that the rarity redeems him.

BER. A pox on him! he's a cat still![d]

1 SOLD. His qualities being at this poor price, I

(*) Old copy, *Lord.*

[a] *I perceive, sir, by our general's looks,—*] The old text has "*your* general's looks;" altered by Capell.

[b] *He will steal, sir, an egg out of a cloister;*] If *an egg* is not a misprint, it may have been used metaphorically for a young girl; one of the murderers of Macduff's family ("Macbeth," Act IV. Sc. 2) calls the boy "*egg*," and "young fry." So also Costard, in "Love's Labour's Lost," Act V. Sc. 1, terms Moth "pigeon-egg of discretion."

[c] Mile-end,—] See note (4), p. 628, Vol. I.

[d] He's a cat still!] Bertram had before told us that a *cat* was his particular aversion, and that Parolles was now a *cat* to him. When the rogue becomes more scurrilous in his revelations, Bertram says, "He is more and more a *cat*;" and, finally, when he had "out-villained villany," the count impetuously exclaims, "—— he's a cat still!" that is, a cat *always*, a cat *evermore*.

need not to ask you, if gold will corrupt him to revolt.

PAR. Sir, for a *quart d'écu*(3) he will sell the fee-simple of his salvation, the inheritance of it; and cut the entail from all remainders, and a perpetual succession for it perpetually.

1 SOLD. What's his brother, the other captain Dumain?

2 LORD. Why does he ask him of me?

1 SOLD. What's he?

PAR. E'en a crow of the same nest; not altogether so great as the first in goodness, but greater a great deal in evil. He excels his brother for a coward, yet his brother is reputed one of the best that is. In a retreat he out-runs any lackey; marry, in coming on he has the cramp.

1 SOLD. If your life be saved, will you undertake to betray the Florentine?

PAR. Ay, and the captain of his horse, count Rousillon.

1 SOLD. I'll whisper with the general, and know his pleasure.

PAR. [*Aside.*] I'll no more drumming: a plague of all drums! Only to seem to deserve well, and to beguile the supposition of that lascivious young boy the count, have I run into this danger. Yet, who would have suspected an ambush where I was taken?

1 SOLD. There is no remedy, sir, but you must die: the general says, you, that have so traitorously discovered the secrets of your army, and made such pestiferous reports of men very nobly held, can serve the world for no honest use; therefore you must die. Come, headsman, off with his head.

PAR. O Lord, sir; let me live, or let me see my death!

1 SOLD. That shall you, and take your leave of all your friends. [*Unmuffling him.*
So, look about you; know you any here?

BER. Good morrow, noble captain.

2 LORD. God bless you, captain Parolles.

1 LORD. God save you, noble captain.

2 LORD. Captain, what greeting will you to my lord Lafeu? I am for France.

1 LORD. Good captain, will you give me a copy of the sonnet you writ to Diana in behalf of the count Rousillon? an I were not a very coward, I'd compel it of you; but fare you well.
[*Exeunt* BERTRAM, Lords, *&c.*

1 SOLD. You are undone, captain: all but your scarf, that has a knot on't yet.

PAR. Who cannot be crushed with a plot?

1 SOLD. If you could find out a country where but women were that had received so much shame, you might begin an impudent nation. Fare you well, sir; I am for France too; we shall speak of you there. [*Exit.*

PAR. Yet am I thankful: if my heart were great,
'T would burst at this. Captain, I'll be no more;
But I will eat and drink, and sleep as soft
As captain shall: simply the thing I am
Shall make me live. Who knows himself a braggart
Let him fear this; for it will come to pass,
That every braggart shall be found an ass.
Rust, sword! cool, blushes! and, Parolles, live
Safest in shame! being fool'd, by foolery thrive!
There's place, and means, for every man alive.
I'll after them. [*Exit.*

SCENE IV.—Florence. *A Room in the* Widow's *House.*

Enter HELENA, Widow, *and* DIANA.

HEL. That you may well perceive I have not wrong'd you,
One of the greatest in the Christian world
Shall be my surety; 'fore whose throne 't is needful,
Ere I can perfect mine intents, to kneel.
Time was, I did him a desired office,
Dear almost as his life; which gratitude
Through flinty Tartar's bosom would peep forth,
And answer, thanks: I duly am inform'd,
His grace is at Marseilles;[a] to which place
We have convenient convoy. You must know,
I am supposed dead: the army breaking,
My husband hies him home; where, heaven aiding,
And by the leave of my good lord the king,
We'll be, before our welcome.

WID. Gentle madam,
You never had a servant, to whose trust
Your business was more welcome.

HEL. Nor you,* mistress,
Ever a friend, whose thoughts more truly labour
To recompense your love; doubt not, but heaven
Hath brought me up to be your daughter's dower,
As it hath fated her to be my motive
And helper to a husband. But O strange men!
That can such sweet use make of what they hate,
When saucy trusting of the cozen'd thoughts
Defiles the pitchy night,[b] so lust doth play
With what it loaths, for that which is away:
But more of this hereafter. You, Diana,
Under my poor instructions yet must suffer
Something in my behalf.

DIA. Let death and honesty
Go with your impositions, I am yours
Upon your will to suffer.

HEL. Yet, I pray you [c]

---

[a] Marseilles;] *Marseilles*, in the old copy *Marcellæ*, must be pronounced as a word of three syllables—*Marsellis*. See note (b), p. 247, Vol. I.

[b] When saucy trusting of the cozen'd thoughts
Defiles the pitchy night,—]
Hanmer reads *fancy*; *saucy*, however, is sometimes employed by Shakespeare in the sense of *prurient*, and it may bear that meaning here. But how is the context to be understood?

[c] Yet, I pray you
But with the word;]
Blackstone proposed an ingenious emendation of this passage:—
"Yet, I *fray* you
But with the word."
"I only frighten you by mentioning the word *suffer*: for a short time will bring on the season of happiness and delight."
With much diffidence we venture to suggest that *Yet* apparently stands for *Now*; and that we should read,—
"Yet, I *pay* you
But with the word," &c.
Now I can only compensate your kindness by the word of promise; but the time approaches when all that you undergo for my sake shall be substantially requited.

(*) Old text, *your*.

But with the word; the time will bring on summer,
When briars shall have leaves as well as thorns,
And be as sweet as sharp. We must away;
Our waggon is prepar'd, and time revives[a] us:
All's well that ends well still: the fine's the crown;[b]
Whate'er the course, the end is the renown.
[*Exeunt.*

SCENE V.—Rousillon. *A Room in the Countess's Palace.*

Enter COUNTESS, LAFEU, *and* Clown.

LAF. No, no, no, your son was misled with a snipt-taffata fellow there, whose villainous saffron[c] would have made all the unbaked and doughy youth of a nation in his colour; your daughter-in-law had been alive at this hour, and your son here at home, more advanced by the king, than by that red-tailed humble-bee I speak of.

COUNT. I would I had not known him! it was the death of the most virtuous gentlewoman, that ever nature had praise for creating: if she had partaken of my flesh, and cost me the dearest groans of a mother, I could not have owed her a more rooted love.

LAF. 'Twas a good lady, 'twas a good lady: we may pick a thousand salads, ere we light on such another herb.

CLO. Indeed, sir, she was the sweet-marjoram of the salad, or, rather the herb of grace.

LAF. They are not salad-herbs,[d] you knave; they are nose-herbs.

CLO. I am no great Nebuchadnezzar, sir, I have not much skill in grass.*

LAF. Whether dost thou profess thyself, a knave or a fool?

CLO. A fool, sir, at a woman's service, and a knave at a man's.

LAF. Your distinction?

CLO. I would cozen the man of his wife, and do his service.

LAF. So you were a knave at his service, indeed.

CLO. And I would give his wife my bauble, sir, to do her service.

LAF. I will subscribe for thee; thou art both knave and fool.

CLO. At your service.

LAF. No, no, no.

CLO. Why, sir, if I cannot serve you, I can serve as great a prince as you are.

LAF. Who's that? a Frenchman?

CLO. Faith, sir, he has an English name,* but his phisnomy is more hotter in France, than there.

LAF. What prince is that?

CLO. The black prince, sir; *alias*, the prince of darkness; *alias*, the devil.

LAF. Hold thee, there's my purse; I give thee not this to suggest[e] thee from thy master thou talkest of; serve him still.

CLO. I am a woodland fellow, sir, that always loved a great fire; and the master I speak of, ever keeps a good fire. But, sure,[f] he is the prince of the world; let his nobility remain in his court. I am for the house with the narrow gate, which I take to be too little for pomp to enter: some, that humble themselves, may; but the many will be too chill and tender; and they'll be for the flowery way, that leads to the broad gate, and the great fire.

LAF. Go thy ways, I begin to be a-weary of thee; and I tell thee so before, because I would not fall out with thee. Go thy ways; let my horses be well looked to, without any tricks.

CLO. If I put any tricks upon 'em, sir, they shall be jades' tricks; which are their own right by the law of nature. [*Exit.*

LAF. A shrewd knave, and an unhappy.[g]

COUNT. So he is. My lord, that's gone, made himself much sport out of him; by his authority he remains here, which he thinks is a patent for his sauciness, and, indeed, he has no pace, but runs where he will.

LAF. I like him well; 'tis not amiss: and I was about to tell you. Since I heard of the good lady's death, and that my lord your son was upon his return home, I moved the king my master, to speak in the behalf of my daughter; which, in the minority of them both, his majesty, out of a self-gracious remembrance, did first propose: his highness hath promised me to do it; and, to stop up the displeasure he hath conceived against your son, there is no fitter matter. How does your ladyship like it?

(*) Old text, *grace*.

a *Time* revives *us*:] Johnson suggested *invites*; Warburton, *revies* us—an old word signifying challenges, borrowed from the card-table; and Mr. Collier's MS. annotator has *reviles*. Of these proposals, Warburton's is by far the most plausible. *Revives us*, however, in the sense of *reproaches us, mocks us*, may be right. See Middleton's "Michaelmas Term," Act II. Sc. 1:—

"Thou *revivest* us, rascal!"

b *The* fine's *the crown*;] The *end's* the crown:—Finis coronat opus.

c *Whose* villainous saffron—] This *villainous saffron*, the commentators suppose, must be a reference to the fantastic fashion of stiffening and colouring the ruffs and bands with *yellow starch*. The allusion, we imagine, is rather to that constant subject of obloquy among the old writers,—"the dissembling colour" of the arch-deceiver Judas' hair.

(*) First folio, *maine*.

d *They are not* salad-herbs,—] The old text has "herbs" only: Rowe inserted "salad," which the context appears to require.

e *To* suggest *thee*—] That is, to *seduce* thee, to *tempt* thee.

f *But*, sure,—] Some commentators would read, *since*.

g Unhappy.] *Waggish, mischievous.*

COUNT. With very much content, my lord, and I wish it happily effected.

LAF. His highness comes post from Marseilles, of as able body as when he numbered thirty: he will be here to-morrow, or I am deceived by him that in such intelligence hath seldom failed.

COUNT. It rejoices me, that I hope I shall see him ere I die. I have letters, that my son will be here to-night: I shall beseech your lordship, to remain with me till they meet together.

LAF. Madam, I was thinking, with what manners I might safely be admitted.

COUNT. You need but plead your honourable privilege.

LAF. Lady, of that I have made a bold charter, but, I thank my God, it holds yet.

Re-enter Clown.

CLO. O madam, yonder's my lord your son with a patch of velvet on's face; whether there be a scar under it, or no, the velvet knows, but 'tis a goodly patch of velvet; his left cheek is a cheek of two pile and a half, but his right cheek is worn bare.

LAF. A scar nobly got, or a noble scar, is a good livery of honour; so, belike, is that.

CLO. But it is your carbonadoed face.

LAF. Let us go see your son, I pray you; I long to talk with the young noble soldier.

CLO. 'Faith, there's a dozen of 'em, with delicate fine hats, and most courteous feathers, which bow the head, and nod at every man. [*Exeunt.*

ACT V.

SCENE I.—Marseilles. *A Street.*

Enter HELENA, WIDOW, *and* DIANA, *with two* Attendants.

HEL. But this exceeding posting, day and night,
Must wear your spirits low: we cannot help it;
But, since you have made the days and nights as one,
To wear your gentle limbs in my affairs,
Be bold, you do so grow in my requital,
As nothing can unroot you. In happy time;——

Enter a Gentleman.(1)

This man may help me to his majesty's ear,
If he would spend his power.—God save you, sir.

GENT. And you.

HEL. Sir, I have seen you in the court of France.

GENT. I have been sometimes there.

HEL. I do presume, sir, that you are not fallen
From the report that goes upon your goodness;
And therefore, goaded with most sharp occasions,
Which lay nice manners by, I put you to
The use of your own virtues, for the which
I shall continue thankful.

GENT. What's your will?

HEL. That it will please you
To give this poor petition to the king,
And aid me with that store of power you have,
To come into his presence.

GENT. The king's not here.

HEL. Not here, sir?
GENT. Not, indeed:
He hence remov'd last night, and with more haste
Than is his use.
WID. Lord, how we lose our pains!
HEL. *All's well that ends well*, yet;
Though time seem so advérse, and means unfit.—
I do beseech you, whither is he gone?
GENT. Marry, as I take it, to Rousillon;
Whither I am going.
HEL. I do beseech you, sir,
Since you are like to see the king before me,
Commend the paper to his gracious hand;
Which, I presume, shall render you no blame,
But rather make you thank your pains for it.
I will come after you, with what good speed
Our means will make us means.
GENT. This I'll do for you.
HEL. And you shall find yourself to be well thank'd,
Whate'er falls more. We must to horse again;—
Go, go, provide. [*Exeunt.*

SCENE II.—Rousillon. *The inner Court of the* Countess's *Palace.*

Enter Clown *and* PAROLLES.

PAR. Good monsieur Lavatch, give my lord Lafeu this letter: I have ere now, sir, been better known to you, when I have held familiarity with fresher clothes; but I am now, sir, muddied in fortune's mood,[a] and smell somewhat strong of her strong displeasure.

CLO. Truly, fortune's displeasure is but sluttish, if it smell so strong as thou speakest of: I will henceforth eat no fish of fortune's buttering. Pr'ythee, allow the wind.

PAR. Nay, you need not stop your nose, sir; I spake but by a metaphor.

CLO. Indeed, sir, if your metaphor stink, I will stop my nose; or against any man's metaphor. Pr'ythee, get thee further.

[a] *Muddied in fortune's* mood,—] Warburton reads, *moat*, and we have an impression that *moat* was the author's word.

PAR. 'Pray you, sir, deliver me this paper.

CLO. Foh! pr'ythee stand away; a paper from fortune's close-stool to give to a nobleman! Look, here he comes himself.

Enter LAFEU.

Here is a pur of fortune's, sir, or of fortune's cat, (but not a musk-cat,) that has fallen into the unclean fishpond of her displeasure, and, as he says, is muddied withal: pray you, sir, use the carp as you may, for he looks like a poor, decayed, ingenious, foolish, rascally knave. I do pity his distress in my smiles of comfort, and leave him to your lordship. [*Exit* Clown.

PAR. My lord, I am a man whom fortune hath cruelly scratched.

LAF. And what would you have me to do? 'tis too late to pare her nails now. Wherein have you played the knave with fortune, that she should scratch you, who of herself is a good lady, and would not have knaves thrive long under her?[a] There's a *quart d'écu* for you: let the justices make you and fortune friends; I am for other business.

PAR. I beseech your honour, to hear me one single word.

LAF. You beg a single penny more: come, you shall ha't; save your word.

PAR. My name, my good lord, is Parolles.

LAF. You beg more than word,[b] then.—Cox' my passion! give me your hand. How does your drum?

PAR. O my good lord, you were the first that found me.

LAF. Was I, in sooth? and I was the first that lost thee.

PAR. It lies in you, my lord, to bring me in some grace, for you did bring me out.

LAF. Out upon thee, knave! dost thou put upon me at once both the office of God and the devil? one brings thee in grace, and the other brings thee out. [*Trumpets sound.*] The king's coming, I know by his trumpets.—Sirrah, inquire further after me; I had talk of you last night; though you are a fool and a knave, you shall eat; go to, follow.

PAR. I praise God for you. [*Exeunt.*

SCENE III.—*The same. A Room in the Countess's Palace.*

Flourish. Enter KING, COUNTESS, LAFEU, Lords, Gentlemen, Guards, *&c.*

KING. We lost a jewel of her; and our esteem[c]
Was made much poorer by it: but your son,
As mad in folly, lack'd the sense to know
Her estimation home.

COUNT. 'T is past, my liege:
And I beseech your majesty to make it
Natural rebellion, done i' the blade[d] of youth;
When oil and fire, too strong for reason's force,
O'erbears it, and burns on.

KING. My honour'd lady,
I have forgiven and forgotten all;
Though my revenges were high bent upon him,
And watch'd the time to shoot.

LAF. This I must say,——
But first I beg my pardon,—the young lord
Did to his majesty, his mother, and his lady,
Offence of mighty note; but to himself
The greatest wrong of all: he lost a wife,
Whose beauty did astonish the survey
Of richest eyes, whose words all ears took captive;
Whose dear perfection, hearts that scorn'd to serve,
Humbly call'd mistress.

KING. Praising what is lost,
Makes the remembrance dear. Well, call him hither;
We are reconcil'd, and the first view shall kill
All repetition.[e]—Let him not ask our pardon;
The nature of his great offence is dead,
And deeper than oblivion we do bury
The incensing relics of it: let him approach,
A stranger, no offender; and inform him,
So 'tis our will he should.

GENT. I shall, my liege.
[*Exit* Gentleman.

KING. What says he to your daughter? have you spoke?

LAF. All that he is hath reference to your highness.

KING. Then shall we have a match. I have letters sent me,
That set him high in fame.

Enter BERTRAM.

LAF. He looks well on't.

KING. I am not a day of season,
For thou may'st see a sun-shine and a hail
In me at once: but to the brightest beams
Distracted clouds give way; so stand thou forth,
The time is fair again.

BER. My high-repented blames,
Dear sovereign, pardon to me.

KING. All is whole;
Not one word more of the consumed time.
Let's take the instant by the forward top,
For we are old, and on our quick'st decrees

---

[a] *Under* her?] The word *her*, omitted in the first, is supplied by the second folio, 1632.

[b] You beg more than word, then.—] Because *Parolles* is plural, and signifies *words*.

[c] *And our* esteem—] The sum of what we hold estimable.

[d] *Done i' the* blade *of youth*;] Theobald and Mr. Collier's annotator, read "*blaze* of youth."

[e] Repetition,—] That is, *recrimination*.

The inaudible and noiseless foot of time
Steals, ere we can effect them. You remember
The daughter of this lord?
BER. Admiringly, my liege: at first
I stuck my choice upon her, ere my heart
Durst make too bold a herald of my tongue:
Where the impression of mine eye infixing,
Contempt his scornful pérspective did lend me,
Which warp'd the line of every other favour;
Scorn'd a fair colour, or express'd it stol'n;
Extended or contracted all proportions,
To a most hideous object: thence it came, [self,
That she, whom all men prais'd, and whom my-
Since I have lost, have lov'd, was in mine eye
The dust that did offend it.
KING. Well excus'd;
That thou didst love her, strikes some scores away
From the great compt: but love that comes too late,
Like a remorseful pardon slowly carried,
To the great sender turns a sour offence,
Crying, That's good that's gone. Our rash faults
Make trivial price of serious things we have,
Not knowing them, until we know their grave:
Oft our displeasures, to ourselves unjust,
Destroy our friends, and after weep their dust:
Our own love waking cries to see what's done,
While shameful hate sleeps out the afternoon.
Be this sweet Helen's knell, and now forget her.
Send forth your amorous token for fair Maudlin:
The main consents are had, and here we'll stay
To see our widower's second marriage-day.
COUNT. Which better than the first, O dear heaven, bless!
Or, ere they meet, in me O nature cesse![a] [name
LAF. Come on, my son, in whom my house's
Must be digested, give a favour from you,
To sparkle in the spirits of my daughter,
That she may quickly come. By my old beard,
And every hair that's on't, Helen, that's dead,
Was a sweet creature; such a ring as this,
The last that e'er I took her leave at court,[b]
I saw upon her finger.
BER. Hers it was not.
KING. Now, pray you, let me see it; for mine eye,
While I was speaking, oft was fasten'd to 't.
This ring was mine; and, when I gave it Helen,
I bade her, if her fortunes ever stood
Necessitied to help, that by this token
I would relieve her. Had you that craft, to 'reave her
Of what should stead her most?
BER. My gracious sovereign,
Howe'er it pleases you to take it so,
The ring was never hers.
COUNT. Son, on my life,
I have seen her wear it; and she reckon'd it
At her life's rate.
LAF. I am sure, I saw her wear it.
BER. You are deceiv'd, my lord, she never saw it.
In Florence was it from a casement thrown me,
Wrapp'd in a paper, which contain'd the name
Of her that threw it: noble she was, and thought
I stood ingag'd:[c] but when I had subscrib'd
To mine own fortune, and inform'd her fully,
I could not answer in that course of honour
As she had made the overture, she ceas'd,
In heavy satisfaction, and would never
Receive the ring again.
KING. Plutus* himself,
That knows the tinct and multiplying medicine,
Hath not in nature's mystery more science,
Than I have in this ring: 'twas mine, 't was Helen's,
Whoever gave it you: then, if you know
That you are well acquainted with yourself,
Confess 'twas hers, and by what rough enforcement
You got it from her. She call'd the saints to surety,
That she would never put it from her finger,
Unless she gave it to yourself in bed,
(Where you have never come,) or sent it us
Upon her great disaster.
BER. She never saw it.
KING. Thou speak'st it falsely, as I love mine honour:
And mak'st conjectural† fears to come into me,
Which I would fain shut out. If it should prove
That thou art so inhuman,—'twill not prove so;—
And yet I know not:—thou didst hate her deadly,
And she is dead; which nothing, but to close
Her eyes myself, could win me to believe,
More than to see this ring.—Take him away.—
My fore-past proofs, howe'er the matter fall,
Shall tax‡ my fears of little vanity,[d]
Having vainly fear'd too little.—Away with him;—
We'll sift this matter further.
BER. If you shall prove
This ring was ever hers, you shall as easy
Prove that I husbanded her bed in Florence,
Where yet she never was.
[*Exit* BERTRAM, *guarded.*

---

a Which better than the first, &c.] These two lines form part of the King's speech in the original. Theobald made the present arrangement.

b The last that e'er I took her leave at court,—] Which means, The last *time* that ever I took leave of her at court.

c Ingag'd:] *Ingaged* is here used to imply *unengaged*, or *disengaged*, as the old writers employ *inhabited* to express *uninhabited*.

(*) Old text, *Platus*. (†) First folio, *connectural*. (‡) First folio, *taze*.

d Shall tax my fears of little vanity,—] "The *proofs which I have already had* are sufficient to show that my *fears* were not *vain* and irrational, I have rather been hitherto more easy than I ought, and have *unreasonably had too little fear*."—JOHNSON.

Enter a Gentleman.

KING. I am wrapp'd in dismal thinkings.
GENT. Gracious sovereign,
Whether I have been to [a] blame, or no, I know not;
Here's a petition from a Florentine,
Who hath, for four or five removes, come short
To tender it herself. I undertook it,
Vanquish'd thereto by the fair grace and speech
Of the poor suppliant, who by this, I know,
Is here attending: her business looks in her
With an importing visage, and she told me,
In a sweet verbal brief, it did concern
Your highness with herself.

KING. [Reads.] *Upon his many protestations to marry me, when his wife was dead, I blush to say it, he won me. Now is the count Rousillon a widower; his vows are forfeited to me, and my honour's paid to him. He stole from Florence, taking no leave, and I follow him to his country for justice. Grant it me, O king, in you it best lies; otherwise a seducer flourishes, and a poor maid is undone.* DIANA CAPULET.

LAF. I will buy me a son-in-law in a fair, and toll; for this, I'll none of him. [Lafeu,
KING. The heavens have thought well on thee,
To bring forth this discovery.—Seek these suitors:—
Go, speedily, and bring again the count.
[*Exeunt* Gentleman, *and some* Attendants.
I am afeard, the life of Helen, lady,
Was foully snatch'd.
COUNT. Now, justice on the doers!

Enter BERTRAM, *guarded.*

KING. I wonder, sir, since [b] wives are monsters to you,
And that you fly them as you swear them lordship,
Yet you desire to marry.—

Re-enter Gentleman, *with* Widow *and* DIANA.[c]

What woman's that?
DIA. I am, my lord, a wretched Florentine,
Derived from the ancient Capulet;
My suit, as I do understand, you know,
And therefore know how far I may be pitied.
WID. I am her mother, sir, whose age and honour
Both suffer under this complaint we bring,
And both shall cease, without your remedy.
KING. Come hither, count; do you know these women?

BER. My lord, I neither can, nor will deny
But that I know them. Do they charge me further?
DIA. Why do you look so strange upon your [wife?
BER. She's none of mine, my lord.
DIA. If you shall marry,
You give away this hand, and that is mine;
You give away heaven's vows, and those are mine;
You give away myself, which is known mine;
For I by vow am so embodied yours,
That she, which marries you, must marry me,
Either both or none.
LAF. Your reputation [*To* BERTRAM.] comes too short for my daughter, you are no husband for her.
BER. My lord, this is a fond and desperate creature,
Whom sometime I have laugh'd with: let your [highness
Lay a more noble thought upon mine honour,
Than for to think that I would sink it here.
KING. Sir, for my thoughts, you have them ill to friend,
Till your deeds gain them: fairer prove your [honour,
Than in my thought it lies!
DIA. Good my lord,
Ask him upon his oath, if he does think
He had not my virginity.
KING. What say'st thou to her?
BER. She's impudent, my lord,
And was a common gamester to the camp.
DIA. He does me wrong, my lord; if I were so,
He might have bought me at a common price:
Do not believe him: O, behold this ring,
Whose high respect, and rich validity,
Did lack a parallel; yet, for all that,
He gave it to a commoner o' the camp,
If I be one.
COUNT. He blushes, and 'tis it:
Of six preceding ancestors, that gem
Conferr'd by testament to the sequent issue,
Hath it been ow'd and worn. This is his wife;
That ring's a thousand proofs.
KING. Methought, you said,
You saw one here in court could witness it.
DIA. I did, my lord, but loath am to produce
So bad an instrument; his name's Parolles.
LAF. I saw the man to-day, if man he be.
KING. Find him, and bring him hither.
[*Exit* Attendants.
BER. What of him?
He's quoted for a most perfidious slave,
With all the spots o' the world tax'd and debosh'd;
Whose nature sickens, but to speak a truth.

a *Whether I have been to blame,*—] The original has "*too* blame," and the same reading occurs so frequently in the early editions of these plays, as to raise a doubt whether "*too* blame," was not an expression of the time. In "Henry IV." First Part, Act III. Scene 1, it will be remembered, we have:—"You are *too wilful blame.*"

b *I wonder, sir,* since *wives,* &c.] The old text is, "I wonder *sir, sir,* wives," &c. The correction is due to Tyrwhitt.
c Re-enter, &c.] In the ancient stage direction, "*Enter Widow, Diana, and Parolles.*"

Am I or that, or this, for what he'll utter,
That will speak any thing?
KING. She hath that ring of yours.
BER. I think, she has: certain it is, I lik'd her,
And boarded her i' the wanton way of youth:
She knew her distance, and did angle for me,
Madding my eagerness with her restraint,
As all impediments in fancy's course
Are motives of more fancy; and, in fine,
Her infinite cunning[a] with her modern grace,
Subdued me to her rate; she got the ring,
And I had that, which any inferior might
At market-price have bought.
DIA. I must be patient;
You, that turn'd off a first so noble wife,
May justly diet me. I pray you yet,
(Since you lack virtue, I will lose a husband,)
Send for your ring, I will return it home,
And give me mine again.
BER. I have it not.
KING. What ring was yours, I pray you?
DIA. Sir, much like
The same upon your finger. [of late.
KING. Know you this ring? this ring was his
DIA. And this was it I gave him, being a-bed.
KING. The story then goes false, you threw it him
Out of a casement.
DIA. I have spoke the truth.

Enter PAROLLES.

BER. My lord, I do confess the ring was hers.
KING. You boggle shrewdly, every feather starts you.——
Is this the man you speak of?
DIA. Ay, my lord.
KING. Tell me, sirrah, but, tell me true, I charge you,
Not fearing the displeasure of your master,
(Which, on your just proceeding, I'll keep off,)
By him, and by this woman here, what know you?
PAR. So please your majesty, my master hath been an honourable gentleman; tricks he hath had in him, which gentlemen have.
KING. Come, come, to the purpose: did he love this woman?
PAR. 'Faith, sir, he did love her; but how!
KING. How, I pray you? [a woman.
PAR. He did love her, sir, as a gentleman loves
KING. How is that?
PAR. He loved her, sir, and loved her not.
KING. As thou art a knave, and no knave:—what an equivocal companion is this?
PAR. I am a poor man, and at your majesty's command.
LAF. He's a good drum, my lord, but a naughty orator.
DIA. Do you know, he promised me marriage?
PAR. 'Faith, I know more than I'll speak.
KING. But wilt thou not speak all thou know'st?
PAR. Yes, so please your majesty; I did go between them, as I said; but more than that, he loved her—for, indeed, he was mad for her, and talked of Satan, and of limbo, and of furies, and I know not what: yet I was in that credit with them at that time, that I knew of their going to bed, and of other motions, as, promising her marriage, and things that would derive me ill-will to speak of, therefore I will not speak what I know.
KING. Thou hast spoken all already, unless thou canst say they are married. But thou art too fine[b] in thy evidence; therefore stand aside.—
This ring, you say, was yours?
DIA. Ay, my good lord.
KING. Where did you buy it? or who gave it you?
DIA. It was not given me, nor I did not buy it.
KING. Who lent it you?
DIA. It was not lent me neither.
KING. Where did you find it then?
DIA. I found it not.
KING. If it were yours by none of all these ways,
How could you give it him?
DIA. I never gave it him.
LAF. This woman's an easy glove, my lord; she goes off and on at pleasure.
KING. This ring was mine, I gave it his first wife.
DIA. It might be yours, or hers, for aught I [know.
KING. Take her away, I do not like her now;
To prison with her, and away with him.—
Unless thou tell'st me where thou hadst this ring,
Thou diest within this hour.
DIA. I'll never tell you.
KING. Take her away.
DIA. I'll put in bail, my liege.
KING. I think thee now some common customer.[c]
DIA. By Jove, if ever I knew man, 't was you.
KING. Wherefore hast thou accus'd him all this while?
DIA. Because he's guilty, and he is not guilty;
He knows I am no maid, and he'll swear to't:
I'll swear, I am a maid, and he knows not.
Great king, I am no strumpet, by my life;
I am either maid, or else this old man's wife.
[*Pointing to* LAFEU.

[a] *Her* infinite cunning *with her modern grace,*—] The old copy reads, "Her *insuite comming*," &c. The extremely happy emendation in the text was first suggested by the late Mr. Sidney Walker, and has since been found among the annotations of Mr. Collier's "Old Corrector."

[b] Too fine *in thy evidence;*] *Trop fine*, too full of *finesse*.

[c] Customer.] *Customer* was a term applied to a loose woman. Thus, in "Othello," Act IV. Sc. 1:—

"I marry her! what? a *customer*."

KING. She does abuse our ears; to prison with her.
DIA. Good mother, fetch my bail.—Stay, royal sir; [*Exit* Widow.
The jeweller, that owes the ring, is sent for,
And he shall surety me. But for this lord,
Who hath abus'd me, as he knows himself,
Though yet he never harm'd me, here I quit him:
He knows himself my bed he hath defil'd;
And at that time he got his wife with child:
Dead though she be, she feels her young one kick;
So there's my riddle, One that's dead is quick,
And now behold the meaning.

Re-enter Widow, *with* HELENA.

KING. Is there no exorcist
Beguiles the truer office of mine eyes?
Is't real, that I see?
HEL. No, my good lord;
'Tis but the shadow of a wife you see,
The name and not the thing.
BER. Both, both; O, pardon!
HEL. O, my good lord, when I was like this maid,
I found you wondrous kind. There is your ring,
And, look you, here's your letter; this it says,
When from my finger you can get this ring,
And are by me with child*, &c.—This is done:
Will you be mine, now you are doubly won?

BER. If she, my liege, can make me know this clearly,
I'll love her dearly, ever, ever dearly.
HEL. If it appear not plain, and prove untrue,
Deadly divorce step between me and you!—
O, my dear mother, do I see you living?
LAF. Mine eyes smell onions, I shall weep anon:—
Good Tom Drum, [*To* PAROLLES.] lend me a handkerchief: so, I thank thee; wait on me home, I'll make sport with thee. Let thy courtesies alone, they are scurvy ones.
KING. Let us from point to point this story [know,
To make the even truth in pleasure flow:—
If thou be'st yet a fresh uncropped flower,
[*To* DIANA.
Choose thou thy husband, and I'll pay thy dower;
For I can guess, that by thy honest aid,
Thou kept'st a wife herself, thyself a maid.—
Of that, and all the progress, more and less,
Resolvedly, more leisure shall express:
All yet seems well, and, if it end so meet,
The bitter past, more welcome is the sweet.
[*Flourish.*

(*Advancing.*)

The king's a beggar, now the play is done:
All is well ended, *if this suit be won,*
That you express content; which we will pay,
With strife to please you, day exceeding day:
Ours be your patience then, and yours our parts,
Your gentle hands lend us, and take our hearts.
[Exeunt.

(*) First folio, *is*.

ILLUSTRATIVE COMMENTS.

ACT I.

(1) Scene I.—*To whom I am now in ward.*] The heirs of great fortunes, from the feudal ages down to as late as the middle of the seventeenth century, were, both in this country and in parts of France, under the wardship of the sovereign.

(2) Scene III.—*Clown.*] "The practice of retaining fools," Douce observes, "can be traced in very remote times throughout almost all civilized and even among some barbarous nations. With respect to the antiquity of this custom in our own country, there is reason to suppose that it existed even during the period of our Saxon history; but we are quite certain of the fact in the reign of William the Conqueror. * * * The accounts of the household expenses of our sovereigns contain many payments and rewards to fools both foreign and domestic, the motives for which do not appear, but might perhaps have been some witty speech or comic action that had pleased the donors. Some of these payments are annual gifts at Christmas. Dr. Fuller, speaking of the court jester, whom, he says, some count a necessary evil, remarks, in his usual quaint manner, that it is an office which none but he that hath wit can perform, and none but he that wants it will perform. * * *

"The sort of entertainment that fools were expected to afford, may be collected, in great variety, from our old plays, and particularly from those of Shakspeare; but perhaps no better idea can be formed of their general mode of conduct than from the following passage in a singular tract by Lodge, entitled *Wit's Miserie*, 1599, 4to:—'Immoderate and disordinate joy became incorporate in the bodie of a jeaster; this fellow in person is comely, in apparell courtly, but in behaviour a very ape, and no man; his studie is to coine bitter jeasts, or to shew antique motions, or to sing baudie sonnets and ballads: give him a little wine in his head, he is continually flearing and making of mouthes: he laughs intemperately at every little occasion, and dances about the house, leaps over tables, out-skips mens heads, trips up his companions heeles, burns sack with a candle, and hath all the feats of a lord of misrule in the countrie: feed him in his humor, you shall have his heart, in meere kindness he will hug you in his armes, kisse you on the cheeke, and rapping out an horrible oth, crie Gods soule Tum, I love you, you know my poore heart, come to my chamber for a pipe of tabacco, there lives not a man in this world that I more honor. In these ceremonies you shall know his courting, and it is a speciall mark of him at the table, he sits and makes faces: keep not this fellow company, for in *jugling* with him, your wardropes shall be wasted, your credits crackt, your crownes consumed, and time (the most precious riches of the world) utterly lost.' This is the picture of a real hireling or artificial fool." The reader desirous of further information on the duties of the domestic jester will find them pleasantly illustrated in a curious and valuable tract, called Armin's "Nest of Ninnies," 1608; of which a reprint has been made, from the only known copy, for the Shakespeare Society.

(3) Scene III.—*A prophet I, madam.*] "It is a supposition, which has run through all ages and people, that *natural fools* have something in them of divinity; on which account they were esteemed sacred. Travellers tell us in what esteem the Turks now hold them; nor had they less honour paid them heretofore in France, as appears from the old word *bênet*, for a *natural fool*."—Warburton.

(4) Scene III.—*One good woman in ten, madam; which is a purifying o' the song.*] As Warburton suggested, it is probable the second stanza of the old ballad, which related to the ten remaining sons of Priam, ran:—

> "If one be bad amongst nine good,
> There's but one *bad* in ten."

The Countess objects, therefore, that in singing—"One *good* in ten," the Clown corrupts the song; whereupon he rejoins that inasmuch as the text says nothing whatever about *good women*, his emendation of "*One good woman in ten*" in reality renders it more complimentary.

(5) Scene III.—*Though honesty be no puritan,* &c. &c.] A correspondent in Knight's "Pictorial Shakspere" remarks: "This passage refers to the sour objection of the puritans to the use of the surplice in divine service, for which they wished to substitute the black Geneva gown. At this time the controversy with the puritans raged violently. Hooker's fifth book of 'Ecclesiastical Polity,' which, in the 29th Chapter, discusses this matter at length, was published in 1597. But the question itself is much older—as old as the Reformation, when it was agitated between the British and continental reformers. During the reign of Mary it troubled Frankfort, and on the accession of Elizabeth it was brought back to England, under the patronage of Archbishop Grindal, whose residence in Germany, during his exile in Mary's reign, had disposed him to Genevan theology. The dispute about ecclesiastical vestments may seem a trifle, but it was at this period made the ground upon which to try the first principles of Church authority: a point in itself unimportant becomes vital when so large a question is made to turn upon it. Hence its prominency in the controversial writings of Shakspere's time; and few among his audience would be likely to miss an allusion to a subject fiercely debated at Paul's Cross and elsewhere."

(6) Scene III.—

> ——*My father left me some prescriptions*
> *Of rare and prov'd effects.*]

The text exhibits a very early and curious instance of the use of the word "Prescription" as a medical formula, for which it was not generally current until the close of the seventeenth century. Previously to that time, the ordinary expression was "Recipe;" but in 1599 Bishop Hall employs both words in connexion, showing that they were to be regarded as synonymous:—

> "And give a dose for everie disease
> In Prescripts long, and endless Recipes."
> *Satires*, IV. B. 3.

Dryden does the same also, in his Thirteenth Epistle, in which he likewise alludes to the custom of preserving such papers,—

> "From files a random Recipe they take,
> And many deaths of one Prescription make."

In this manner the Hon. Robert Boyle appears to have made it his practice to preserve methodically all the recipes which had been written for himself in any sickness; one of his Occasional Reflections being on "his reviewing and tacking together the several bills filed in the apothecary's shop."

The practice was probably commenced at an early period of the history of medicine, and was continued in family recipe books, especially in country places, throughout the greater part of the last century, with "*Probatum est*" attached to the formulæ, where their virtues had been experienced. Dr. Cæsar Adelmare, who died in 1569, left among his papers a number of very extraordinary prescriptions, which Sir Hans Sloane copied neatly out, and preserved in his collection of manuscripts.

ACT II.

(1) Scene I.—

——Let higher Italy
(Those 'bated, that inherit but the fall
Of the last monarchy) see that you come
Not to woo honour, but to wed it; &c.]

In 1494, Charles VIII. of France invaded Italy, under pretence of being the legitimate heir to the kingdom of Naples, to which he marched almost without opposition, and, as Sismondi says, ravaged all the country with the violence and force of a hurricane.

Having subsequently entered into a convention with the Florentines, he proceeded to Sienna, which he attempted to secure by establishing in it a French garrison. This city had long been regarded as the most powerful in Tuscany, after Florence, to which it had formerly been subject, as well as to the crown of Naples; but at the period in question the citizens had set up in it an independent government, and had separated themselves from both, and also from their confederacy with the German Emperor. This disruption had produced the most inveterate hatred between the Florentines and the Siennois; and in 1495 began that "braving war," in which "the Florentines and Senoys were by the ears." Finding that the powers of the north of Italy were so much disgusted by the insolence of the French, as to enter into a league against them, because they appeared to consider themselves as masters of the whole peninsula, Charles resolved on returning to France. He accordingly re-crossed the Apennines, October 22, 1495, leaving half his army at Naples, under his relative, Gilbert De Montpensier, as Viceroy.

In this brief outline of the French invasion of Italy, will be found an explanation both of the policy of the king, and of a peculiar expression in the passage cited above. In virtue of the convention already mentioned, the Florentines were about to ask assistance from him, which the Emperor had written to desire they might not have; and Charles accordingly refused to furnish any troops, as king of France. He was willing, however, to permit those young French noblemen who desired to be known as having served in the wars, to enter themselves as gentlemen-volunteers in a neutral foreign service, with either the Florentine or Siennois, the Guelph or the Ghibelline party, in conformity with the practice of the period, which proved so favourable to many soldiers of fortune. But in his parting address to these noblemen, the king excepts those States which had been formed in the barbaric confusion that prevailed upon the dismemberment of the Roman empire, States which literally inherited the spoils only of the "last monarchy," or single government of Italy. In this exception it may be thought that Charles refers especially to the principalities of the north of Italy, which had entered into a coalition against him; but Shakespeare's history in this play, and in others, must not be examined too rigidly.

(2) Scene I.— *——And no sword worn,*
But one to dance with.]

As it was the fashion in Shakespeare's time for gentlemen to dance with swords on, and the ordinary weapon was liable to impede their motions, rapiers, light and short, were made for the purpose:—"I think wee were as much dread or more of our enemies, when our gentlemen went simply and our serving-men plainely, without cuts or gards, bearing their heavy swordes and buckelers on their thighes, instead of cuts and gardes and *light daunsing swordes;* and when they rode carrying good speares in theyr hands in stede of white rods, which they carry now more like ladies or gentlewomen than men; all which delicacyes maketh our men cleare effeminate and without strength."—Stafford's *Briefe Conceipt of English Pollicy,* 1581, 4to.

(3) Scene I.—

He that of greatest works is finisher,
Oft does them by the weakest minister:
So holy writ in babes hath judgment shown,
When judges have been babes.]

The ordinary explanation of these lines refers them either to those passages in Scripture which set forth the mischiefs incident to a kingdom that is governed by a child, as Ecclesiastes x. 16, and Isaiah iii. 4, 12; or to St. Matthew xi. 25,—"I thank thee, O Father, Lord of heaven and earth, because thou hast hid these things from the wise and prudent, and hast revealed them unto babes:" and 1 Corinthians i. 27, "But God hath chosen the foolish things of the world to confound the wise; and God hath chosen the weak things of the world to confound the things which are mighty." It seems probable, however, that the particular allusion is to the four children of the noble families of Israel who were appointed to be brought up for the king's service; Daniel, Hananiah, Mishael and Azariah,—"As for these four children, God gave them knowledge and skill in all learning and wisdom; therefore stood they before the king:" and Nebuchadnezzar set them "over the affairs of the province of Babylon," Daniel i. 3, 4, 17, 19; iii. 48, 49.

The Hebrew word signifies *youths,* but the usual translation is children. In Coverdale's version, 1535, they are called "young springalds."

(4) Scene II.—*A morris for May-day.*] The Morris, or *Morisco* dance, is generally supposed to have been derived originally from the Moors, and to have come to us through Spain; where, indeed, according to Douce, it still continues to delight both natives and strangers, under the name of the *Fandango.* On its first introduction, it was probably a sort of military dance, like that of the *Matachins* in France and Italy; but subsequently the May games, the games of Robin Hood, the Church and other "Ales," and the Morris dance got inextricably blended together. See Douce's "Illustrations of Shakspeare," under *Antient English Morris Dance.* Of the appearance and behaviour of the dancers, Stubbes, in his "Anatomie of Abuses," 1595, supplies a lively but no doubt exaggerated picture:—"They bedecke themselves with scarffes, ribbons and laces, hanged all over with golde ringes, precious stones, and other jewels: this done, they tie about either legge twentie or fortie belles with rich handkerchiefes in their handes, and sometimes laid acrosse over their shoulders and neckes, borrowed for the most part of their pretie Mopsies and loving Bessies, for bussing them in the darke. Thus all things set in order, then have they their hobby-horses, their dragons and other antiques, togither with their baudie pipers, and thundering drummers, to strike up the Devil's Daunce withall: then martch this heathen company towards the church and church-yarde, their pypers pyping, their drummers thundering, their stumpes dauncing, their belles jyngling, their handkerchеefes fluttering about their heades like madde men, their hobbie-horses, and other monsters skirmishing amongst the throng: and in this sorte they goe to the church, though the minister be at prayer or preaching, dauncing and swinging their handkerchiefes over their heades in the church like devils incarnate, with such a confused noise, that no man can heare his own voyce." * * *

One of the most curious notices of the morris, as practised in modern times, is given by Waldron, who says that, in the summer of 1783, he "saw at Richmond, in Surrey, a company of Morrice-Dancers from Abington, accompanied by a Fool in a motley-jacket, &c. who carried in his hand a staff or truncheon, about two feet long, having a blown-up bladder fastened to one end of it; with which he either buffeted the crowd, to keep them at a proper distance from the dancers, or played tricks for the spectators' diversion. The Dancers and the Fool were Berkshire husbandmen, taking an annual circuit, collecting money from whoever would give them any; and (I apprehend) had derived the appendage of the bladder from custom immemorial; not from old plays, or the commentaries thereon."

(5) SCENE V.—*You have made shift to run into't, boots and spurs and all, like him that leaped into the custard.*] One of the absurdities practised at the great civic festivals formerly, was for the Lord Mayor's or Sheriff's fool to spring on to the table, and, after uttering some doggerel balderdash, leap bodily into a huge custard; prepared, it may be supposed, for the purpose:—

" He may per hance, in tail of a sheriff's dinner,
Skip with a rhyme o' the table, from New-nothing,
And take his *Almain leap into a custard*,
Shall make my lady mayoress and her sisters
Laugh all their hoods over their shoulders."
BEN JONSON.—" *The Devil is an Ass*," Act I. Sc. 1.

ACT III.

(1) SCENE V.—
WID. *God save you, pilgrim! Whither are you bound?*
HEL. *To Saint Jaques le grand.*
Where do the palmers lodge, I do beseech you?]

By St. James the Great, Shakespeare no doubt signified the apostle so called, whose celebrated shrine was at Compostella, in Spain; and Dr. Johnson rightly observes that Florence was somewhat out of the road in going thither from Rousillon. There was, however, subsequently, another James, of La Marca of Ancona, a Franciscan confessor of the highest eminence for sanctity, who died at the convent of the Holy Trinity, near Naples, in A.D. 1476. He was not beatified until the seventeenth century, nor canonised until 1726; but it is quite possible that his reputation was very great in connexion with Italy, even at the period of this play; and that Shakespeare adopted the name without considering any other distinction. The same disregard of special peculiarities is evinced also in another part of the above passage, which makes palmers and pilgrims synonymous names, as they were generally supposed to be in England in the seventeenth century, when the original distinction was forgotten. There were differences between them; but it may be doubted whether those specified by Somner and Blount rest upon any sufficient authority. When pilgrims or crusaders returned from the Holy Land, it was customary for them to carry in their hands, or have bound to their staves, branches of the palm which grows in Syria, as signs of their having completely performed the journey. They were then called *Palmiferi*, or Palm-bearers; and on the day following their arrival, when they went to a church to give thanks to God for their safe return, these palms were offered on the altar. Thus it will be perceived that all palmers were pilgrims; but all pilgrims were not palmers, inasmuch as the "signs" of the performance of other pilgrimages were altogether different, and comprised a great variety of their own peculiar emblems.

(2) SCENE VI.—*John Drum's entertainment.*] To give any one *John*, or *Tom, Drum's entertainment*, meant to drive him *vi et armis* out of your company. It was a very old proverbial saying, the origin of which has never been satisfactorily explained. Holinshed, in speaking of the Mayor of Dublin, says, "His porter or anie other officer, durst not for both his eares give the simplest man that resorted to his house *Tom Drum his entertainment*, which is, to hale a man in by the head, and thrust him out by both the shoulders."

ACT IV.

(1) SCENE III.—*Hoodman comes!*] An allusion to the sport now known as "Blind Man's Buff," formerly called "Hoodman Blind," because the player, who was blinded, had his *hood* turned round to cover his eyes. Shakespeare refers to this pastime again, in "Hamlet," Act III. Sc. 4:—

——————" What devil was't
That thus hath cozen'd you at *hoodman blind?*"

(2) SCENE III.—*He has led the drum before the English tragedians.*] The practice of announcing their arrival by beat of drum is still observed by some itinerant performers, and appears to have been a very old one. In Kemp's "Nine Daies Wonder," 1600, there is a representation of Kemp, attired as a morris-dancer, preceded by a character whom he called Thomas Slye, his taberer; and Dr. Hunter has cited an instance from the annals of Doncaster, where, in 1684, the actors' drum going round the town, a part of the military then stationed there took offence at it, and a serious riot was the consequence.

(3) SCENE III.—*Quart d'écu.*] "The *quart d'écu*, or, as it was sometimes written, *cardecue*," Douce says, "was a French piece of money, first coined in the reign of Henry III. It was the fourth part of the *gold* crown, and worth fifteen sols. It is a fact not generally known, that many foreign coins were current at this time in England; some English coins were likewise circulated on the Continent. The French crown and its parts passed by weight only."

Mr. Halliwell gives an engraving of the quarter ecu, copied from the original of the time of Charles IX. "It is dated 1573, and was struck at the Paris mint, the large letter A beneath the shield being the distinguishing mark used there. The superior workmanship and the purity of metal used for these coins, originated the French proverb, applied to persons of honour and probity, 'Etre marqué a l'A.'" In old English books it is almost always called either *cardecue*, or *quardecue*. "I compounded with them for a *cardakew*, which is eighteen pence English."—CORYAT.

" The Spanish Royall, piece of foure and eight,
On me for my antiquity may waite,
The Floren, Guelder, and French *Cardecue*
To me are upstarts, if records be true."
TAYLOR'S *Workes*, 1630.

ACT V.

(1) SCENE I.—*Enter a Gentleman.*] The original has 'Enter a *Gentle Astringer*," which is said to mean a *gentleman falconer;* the term *Astringer*, derived from *osturcus*, or austurcus, having been formerly applied to one who kept goshawks. The introduction of such a retainer, however, appears so utterly uncalled for, and the title "*gentle* Astringer" is so peculiar, that we may reasonably suspect it to be an error of the press. The folio, 1632, reads, "a gentle Astranger;" that of 1685, "a gentleman, a stranger."

CRITICAL OPINIONS

ON

ALL'S WELL THAT ENDS WELL.

"*All's Well that Ends Well* is the old story of a young maiden whose love looked much higher than her station. She obtains her lover in marriage from the hand of the King, as a reward for curing him of a hopeless and lingering disease, by means of a hereditary arcanum of her father, who had been in his lifetime a celebrated physician. The young man despises her virtue and beauty; concludes the marriage only in appearance, and seeks in the dangers of war, deliverance from a domestic happiness which wounds his pride. By faithful endurance and an innocent fraud, she fulfils the apparently impossible conditions on which the Count had promised to acknowledge her as his wife. Love appears here in humble guise; the wooing is on the woman's side; it is striving, unaided by a reciprocal inclination, to overcome the prejudices of birth. But as soon as Helena is united to the Count by a sacred bond, though by him considered an oppressive chain, her error becomes her virtue. She affects us by her patient suffering: the moment in which she appears to most advantage is when she accuses herself as the persecutor of her inflexible husband, and, under the pretext of a pilgrimage to atone for her error, privately leaves the house of her mother-in-law. Johnson expresses a cordial aversion for Count Bertram, and regrets that he should be allowed to come off at last with no other punishment than a temporary shame, nay, even be rewarded with the unmerited possession of a virtuous wife. But has Shakspeare ever attempted to soften the impression made by his unfeeling pride and light-hearted perversity? He has but given him the good qualities of a soldier. And does not the poet paint the true way of the world, which never makes much of man's injustice to woman, if so-called family honour is preserved? Bertram's sole justification is, that by the exercise of arbitrary power, the King thought proper to constrain him, in a matter of such delicacy and private right as the choice of a wife. Besides, this story, as well as that of Grissel and many similar ones, is intended to prove that woman's truth and patience will at last triumph over man's abuse of his superior power, while other novels and *fabliaux* are, on the other hand, true satires on woman's inconsistency and cunning. In this piece old age is painted with rare favour; the plain honesty of the King, the good-natured impetuosity of old Lafeu, the maternal indulgence of the Countess to Helena's passion for her son, seem all, as it were, to vie with each other in endeavours to overcome the arrogance of the young Count. The style of the whole is more sententious than imaginative; the glowing colours of fancy could not with propriety have been employed on such a subject. In the passages where the humiliating rejection of the poor Helena is most painfully affecting, the cowardly Parolles steps in to the relief of the spectator. The mystification by which his pretended valour and his shameless slanders are unmasked, must be ranked among the most comic scenes that ever were invented: they contain matter enough for an excellent comedy, if Shakspeare were not always rich even to profusion. Falstaff has thrown Parolles into the shade, otherwise, among the poet's comic characters, he would have been still more famous."—SCHLEGEL.

Act IV. Sc. 7.

KING HENRY V.

The earliest edition of this play was published in 1600, under the title of—"The Chronicle History of Henry the fift, With his battell fought at Agin Court in France. Togither with Auntient Pistoll. As it hath bene sundry times playd by the Right honorable the Lord Chamberlaine his seruants. London,—*Printed by Thomas Creede*, for Tho. Millington and Iohn Busby." This was followed by another edition in 1602, and a third, in 1608.

The question whether the copy from which these quartos were printed was a maimed and surreptitious version of the perfect play, made up from what could be collected by short-hand, or remembered from the stage representation, as Mr. Collier believes, or whether it was an authentic transcript of the poet's first draft of the piece, but corrupted by the ordinary printing-house blunders, involves so much that is important in connexion with Shakespeare's method of production, that it will be best considered when we come to his Life.

Upon the evidence of a passage in the Chorus to the Fifth Act,—

> "Were now the general of our gracious empress
> (As, in good time, he may,) from Ireland coming,
> Bringing rebellion broached on his sword,
> How many would the peaceful city quit,
> To welcome him!"—

which bears an unmistakeable reference to the Irish expedition of the Earl of Essex, begun and terminated in 1599, this play is supposed to have been written in that year. Long before this date, however, Henry's exploits in France had been commemorated upon the stage. Nash, in his "Pierce Pennilesse," 1592, says,—"What a glorious thing it is to have Henry the Fifth represented on the stage, leading the French King prisoner, and forcing both him and the Dolphin sweare fealtie;" and "The famous Victories of Henry the Fift," already spoken of in "Henry IV.," was no doubt both acted and printed prior to Shakespeare's "Henry V."

Malone assumes the old historical drama alluded to by Nash, and "The famous Victories, &c." to be the same piece, which he says was exhibited before the year 1588, as Tarlton, who performed in it both the Chief Justice and the Clown, died in that year. Steevens speaks of them as distinct plays.

The events comprehended in "Henry V." begin in the first year of the king's reign, and terminate with his marriage of Katharine, the French princess, about eight years afterwards.

Persons Represented.

KING HENRY THE FIFTH.
DUKE OF GLOUCESTER, } *Brothers to the* KING.
DUKE OF BEDFORD, }
DUKE OF EXETER, *Uncle to the* KING.
DUKE OF YORK.
ARCHBISHOP OF CANTERBURY.
EARLS OF SALISBURY, WESTMORELAND, *and* WARWICK.
BISHOP OF ELY.
EARL OF CAMBRIDGE, }
LORD SCROOP, } *Conspirators against the* KING.
SIR THOMAS GREY, }
SIR THOMAS ERPINGHAM, GOWER, FLUELLEN, MACMORRIS, *and* JAMY, *Officers in* KING HENRY'*s Army.*
BATES, COURT, WILLIAMS, *Soldiers in the same.*
PISTOL, NYM, *and* BARDOLPH.

A Herald.
Boy.
Chorus.

CHARLES THE SIXTH, *King of* France.
LEWIS, *the* Dauphin.
DUKES OF BURGUNDY, ORLEANS, *and* BOURBON.
The CONSTABLE *of* France.
RAMBURES *and* GRANDPRÉ, French *Lords.*
MONTJOY, *a* French *Herald.*
Ambassadors to the King of England.
Governor of Harfleur.

ISABEL, *Queen of* France.
KATHARINE, *Daughter of* CHARLES *and* ISABEL.
ALICE, *a Lady attending on the Princess* KATHARINE.
QUICKLY, PISTOL'*s Wife, an Hostess.*

Lords, Ladies, Officers, English and French Soldiers, Messengers, and Attendants.

The Action at the beginning takes place in ENGLAND, *but afterwards, wholly in* FRANCE.

Enter Chorus.*

O, for a muse of fire, that would ascend
The brightest heaven of invention!
A kingdom for a stage, princes to act,
And monarchs to behold the swelling scene!
Then should the warlike Harry, like himself,
Assume the port of Mars; and, at his heels,
Leash'd in like hounds, should famine, sword, and
fire,
Crouch for employment. But pardon, gentles all,
The flat unraised spirits, that have† dar'd,
On this unworthy scaffold, to bring forth
So great an object. Can this cock-pit hold
The vasty fields of France? or may we cram,
Within this wooden O, the very casques,[a]
That did affright the air at Agincourt?
O, pardon! since a crooked figure may
Attest, in little place, a million;
And let us, cyphers to this great accompt,
On your imaginary forces work.
Suppose, within the girdle of these walls
Are now confin'd two mighty monarchies,
Whose high-upreared and abutting fronts
The perilous, narrow ocean parts asunder.
Piece out our imperfections with your thoughts;
Into a thousand parts divide one man,
And make imaginary puissance:
Think, when we talk of horses, that you see them
Printing their proud hoofs i' the receiving earth:
For 'tis your thoughts that now must deck our
kings;
Carry them here and there; jumping o'er times;
Turning the accomplishment of many years
Into an hour-glass; for the which supply,
Admit me Chorus to this history;
Who, prologue-like, your humble patience pray,
Gently to hear, kindly to judge, our play.

(*) First folio, *Enter Prologue*.

(†) First folio, *hath*.

a *The* very casques,—] The *mere helmets*.

ACT I.

SCENE I.—London. *An Antechamber in the* King's *Palace.*

Enter the ARCHBISHOP *of* CANTERBURY, *and the* BISHOP *of* ELY.

CANT. My lord, I'll tell you—that self bill is urg'd
Which in the eleventh year o' the last king's reign
Was like, and had indeed against us pass'd,
But that the scambling[a] and unquiet time
Did push it out of farther question.

---

[a] Scambling—] See note (c), p. 319. Vol. I.; to which may be added another example of the word, from Florio, who explains *Ruffare*, to *rifle*, to *scamble*.

ELY. But how, my lord, shall we resist it now?
CANT. It must be thought on. If it pass against us,
We lose the better half of our possession:
For all the temporal lands, which men devout
By testament have given to the church,
Would they strip from us; being valued thus,—
As much as would maintain, to the king's honour,
Full fifteen earls, and fifteen hundred knights;
Six thousand and two hundred good esquires;
And, to relief of lazars and weak age,
Of indigent faint souls past corporal toil,
A hundred alms-houses, right well supplied;
And to the coffers of the king beside,
A thousand pounds by the year. Thus runs the bill.
ELY. This would drink deep.
CANT. 'T would drink the cup and all.
ELY. But what prevention?
CANT. The king is full of grace and fair regard.
ELY. And a true lover of the holy church.
CANT. The courses of his youth promis'd it not.
The breath no sooner left his father's body,
But that his wildness, mortified in him,
Seem'd to die too: yea, at that very moment,
Consideration, like an angel, came,
And whipp'd the offending Adam out of him;
Leaving his body as a paradise,
To envelop and contain celestial spirits.
Never was such a sudden scholar made;
Never came reformation in a flood,
With such a heady currance, scouring faults;
Nor never Hydra-headed wilfulness
So soon did lose his seat, and all at once,[a]
As in this king.
ELY. We are blessed in the change.
CANT. Hear him but reason in divinity,
And, all-admiring, with an inward wish
You would desire, the king were made a prelate:
Hear him debate of commonwealth affairs,
You would say,—it hath been all-in-all his study:
List his discourse of war, and you shall hear
A fearful battle render'd you in music:
Turn him to any cause of policy,
The Gordian knot of it he will unloose,
Familiar as his garter; that, when he speaks,
The air, a charter'd libertine, is still,
And the mute wonder lurketh in men's ears,
To steal his sweet and honey'd sentences;
So that the art and practic part of life
Must be the mistress to this theoric:
Which is a wonder, how his grace should glean it,
Since his addiction was to courses vain;
His companies[b] unletter'd, rude, and shallow;
His hours fill'd up with riots, banquets, sports;
And never noted in him any study,
Any retirement, any sequestration
From open haunts and popularity.
ELY. The strawberry grows underneath the nettle,
And wholesome berries thrive and ripen best,
Neighbour'd by fruit of baser quality:
And so the prince obscur'd his contemplation
Under the veil of wildness; which, no doubt,
Grew like the summer grass, fastest by night,
Unseen, yet crescive in his faculty.
CANT. It must be so: for miracles are ceas'd;
And therefore we must needs admit the means,
How things are perfected.
ELY. But, my good lord,
How now for mitigation of this bill
Urg'd by the commons? Doth his majesty
Incline to it, or no?
CANT. He seems indifferent;
Or, rather, swaying more upon our part,
Than cherishing the exhibiters against us:
For I have made an offer to his majesty,—
Upon our spiritual convocation,
And in regard of causes now in hand,
Which I have open'd to his grace at large,
As touching France,—to give a greater sum
Than ever at one time the clergy yet
Did to his predecessors part withal.
ELY. How did this offer seem receiv'd, my lord?
CANT. With good acceptance of his majesty;
Save, that there was not time enough to hear
(As I perceiv'd his grace would fain have done,)
The severals, and unhidden passages,[c]
Of his true titles to some certain dukedoms,
And, generally, to the crown and seat of France,
Deriv'd from Edward, his great-grandfather.
ELY. What was the impediment that broke this off?
CANT. The French ambassador, upon that instant,
Crav'd audience:—and the hour, I think, is come,
To give him hearing. Is it four o'clock?
ELY. It is.

---

a And all at once,—] This was a trite phrase in Shakespeare's day, though not one of his editors has noticed it. In "As you Like It," Act III. Sc. 5, where it again occurs,—

"——— Who might be your mother?
That you insult, exult, *and all at once*
Over the wretched?"—

some of them have even suspected a misprint, and proposed to read,—

"——— and *rail* at once."

It is frequently met with in the old writers. Thus, in "The Fisherman's Tale," 1594, by F. Sabie:—

"She wept, she cride, she sob'd, *and all at once*."

And in Middleton's "Changeling," Act IV. Sc. 3:—

"Does love turn fool, run mad, *and all at once?*"

b Companies—] That is, *Companions*.

c The severals, and unhidden passages,—] "This line I suspect of corruption, though it may be fairly enough explained.—The *passages* of his *titles* are the *lines* of *succession* by which his claims descend. *Unhidden* is *open, clear*."—JOHNSON.

CANT. Then go we in, to know his embassy,
Which I could with a ready guess declare,
Before the Frenchman speak a word of it.
ELY. I'll wait upon you, and I long to hear it.
[*Exeunt.*

SCENE II.—*The same. A Room of State in the same.*

Enter KING HENRY, GLOUCESTER, BEDFORD, EXETER, WARWICK, WESTMORELAND, *and* Attendants.

K. HEN. Where is my gracious lord of Canterbury?
EXE. Not here in presence.
K. HEN. Send for him, good uncle.
WEST. Shall we call in the ambassador, my liege? [a]

[a] In the quartos the play begins with this speech.

K. HEN. Not yet, my cousin; we would be resolv'd,
Before we hear him, of some things of weight,
That task our thoughts, concerning us and France.

Enter the ARCHBISHOP *of* CANTERBURY, *and the* BISHOP *of* ELY.

CANT. God and his angels guard your sacred throne,
And make you long become it!
K. HEN. Sure, we thank you.
My learned lord, we pray you to proceed,
And justly and religiously unfold,
Why the law Salique, that they have in France,
Or should, or should not, bar us in our claim.
And God forbid, my dear and faithful lord,
That you should fashion, wrest, or bow your reading,
Or nicely charge your understanding soul
With opening titles miscreate, whose right
Suits not in native colours with the truth

For God doth know, how many, now in health,
Shall drop their blood in approbation
Of what your reverence shall incite us to:
Therefore take heed how you impawn our person,
How you awake our sleeping sword of war;
We charge you in the name of God, take heed:
For never two such kingdoms did contend,
Without much fall of blood, whose guiltless drops
Are every one a woe, a sore complaint
'Gainst him, whose wrongs give edge unto the swords
That make such waste in brief mortality.
Under this conjuration, speak, my lord:
For we will hear, note, and believe in heart,
That what you speak is in your conscience wash'd
As pure as sin with baptism.

CANT. Then hear me, gracious sovereign,—and you peers,(1)
That owe your lives, your faith, and services,[a]
To this imperial throne.—There is no bar
To make against your highness' claim to France,
But this, which they produce from Pharamond,—
In terram Salicam mulieres nè succedant,
No woman shall succeed in Salique land:
Which Salique land the French unjustly gloze[b]
To be the realm of France, and Pharamond
The founder of this law and female bar.
Yet their own authors faithfully affirm,
That the land Salique is in Germany,
Between the floods of Sala and of Elbe:
Where Charles the great, having subdued the Saxons,
There left behind and settled certain French;
Who, holding in disdain the German women,
For some dishonest manners of their life,
Establish'd then this law,—to wit, no female
Should be inheritrix in Salique land;
Which Salique, as I said, 'twixt Elbe and Sala,
Is at this day, in Germany call'd Meisen.
Then doth it well appear, the Salique law
Was not devised for the realm of France;
Nor did the French possess the Salique land
Until four hundred one and twenty years
After defunction of king Pharamond,
Idly suppos'd the founder of this law;
Who died within the year of our redemption
Four hundred twenty-six; and Charles the great
Subdued the Saxons, and did seat the French
Beyond the river Sala, in the year
Eight hundred five. Besides, their writers say,
King Pepin, which deposed Childeric,
Did, as heir general, being descended
Of Blithild, which was daughter to king Clothair,
Make claim and title to the crown of France.
Hugh Capet also,—who usurp'd the crown
Of Charles the duke of Lorraine, sole heir male
Of the true line and stock of Charles the great,—
To fine[c] his title with some show* of truth,
(Though, in pure truth, it was corrupt and naught,)
Convey'd[d] himself as heir to the lady Lingare,(2)
Daughter to Charlemain, who was the son
To Lewis the emperor, and Lewis the son
Of Charles the great. Also king Lewis the tenth,[e]
Who was sole heir to the usurper Capet,
Could not keep quiet in his conscience,
Wearing the crown of France, till satisfied
That fair queen Isabel, his grandmother,
Was lineal of the lady Ermengare,
Daughter to Charles, the foresaid duke of Lorraine:
By the which marriage, the line of Charles the great
Was re-united to the crown of France.
So that, as clear as is the summer's sun,
King Pepin's title, and Hugh Capet's claim,
King Lewis his satisfaction, all appear
To hold in right and title of the female:
So do the kings of France unto this day;
Howbeit they would hold up this Salique law,
To bar your highness claiming from the female,
And rather choose to hide them in a net,
Than amply to imbare[f] their crooked titles
Usurp'd from you and your progenitors.

K. HEN. May I with right and conscience make this claim?

CANT. The sin upon my head, dread sovereign!
For in the Book of Numbers is it writ,—
When the son† dies, let the inheritance
Descend unto the daughter. Gracious lord,
Stand for your own; unwind your bloody flag;
Look back into your mighty ancestors;[1]
Go, my dread lord, to your great-grandsire's tomb,
From whom you claim; invoke his warlike spirit,
And your great-uncle's, Edward the black prince;
Who on the French ground play'd a tragedy,

(*) First folio, *shewes*. (†) First folio, *man*.

[a] *That owe your* lives, *your* faith, *and services,*—] The folio reading is—"your *selves*, your *lives*," &c.

[b] Gloze—] That is, *misinterpret, put a false construction on;* and not, we believe, as the commentators say, *expound*, or *explain*.

[c] *To* fine *his title*—] The first folio reads, "To *find*," &c. To *fine his title* may mean, to *embellish*, or *prank up his title;* or to *point* his title, as Shakespeare makes use of *fine* in both these and in other senses. Mason conjectured that the metaphor was derived from the *fining* of liquors, which is also probable.

[d] Convey'd *himself as heir to the lady Lingare,*—] Thus the quartos. The folio, unmetrically, reads,—

"Convey'd himself as th' heir to th' lady Lingare."

The sense of *convey'd*, in this passage, is rendered plainly by Bishop Cooper:—"Conjicere se in familiam; *to convey himself* to be of some noble family."

[e] *King Lewis* the tenth,—] This should be "Lewis the *ninth*." Shakespeare adopted the error from Holinshed.

[f] *Than amply to* imbare—] The folio has, *imbarre;* the first two quartos, *imbace;* and the third, *embrace*. We adopt the accepted reading, which was first suggested by Warburton, and signifies, *to lay bare*.

Making defeat on the full power of France;
Whiles his most mighty father on a hill
Stood smiling to behold his lion's whelp
Forage in blood of French nobility.(3)
O noble English, that could entertain
With half their forces the full pride of France,
And let another half stand laughing by,
All out of work, and cold for action![a]
ELY. Awake remembrance of these valiant dead,
And with your puissant arm renew their feats:
You are their heir, you sit upon their throne;
The blood and courage, that renowned them,
Runs in your veins; and my thrice-puissant liege
Is in the very May-morn of his youth,
Ripe for exploits and mighty enterprizes.
EXE. Your brother kings and monarchs of the earth
Do all expect that you should rouse yourself,
As did the former lions of your blood.
WEST. They know your grace hath cause and means and might;
So hath your highness;[b] never king of England
Had nobles richer and more loyal subjects;
Whose hearts have left their bodies here in England,
And lie pavilion'd in the fields of France.
CANT. O, let their bodies follow, my dear liege,
With blood * and sword and fire to win your right:
In aid whereof, we of the spiritualty
Will raise your highness such a mighty sum,
As never did the clergy at one time,
Bring in to any of your ancestors.
K. HEN. We must not only arm to invade the French;
But lay down our proportions to defend
Against the Scot, who will make road upon us
With all advantages.
CANT. They of those marches, gracious sovereign,
Shall be a wall sufficient to defend
Our inland from the pilfering borderers.
K. HEN. We do not mean the coursing snatchers only,
But fear the main intendment of the Scot,
Who hath been still a giddy neighbour to us;
For you shall read, that my great-grandfather
Never went with his forces into France,
But that the Scot on his unfurnish'd kingdom
Came pouring, like the tide into a breach,
With ample and brim fulness of his force;
Galling the gleaned land with hot assays;
Girding with grievous siege castles and towns;
That England, being empty of defence,
Hath shook, and trembled at the ill neighbourhood.[c]
CANT. She hath been then more fear'd than harm'd, my liege:
For hear her but exampled by herself,—
When all her chivalry hath been in France,
And she a mourning widow of her nobles,
She hath herself not only well defended,
But taken, and impounded as a stray,
The king of Scots; whom she did send to France,
To fill king Edward's fame with prisoner kings;
And make your[d] chronicle as rich with praise,
As is the ooze and bottom of the sea
With sunken wreck and sumless treasuries.
WEST. But there's a saying, very old and true,—

If that you will France win,
Then with Scotland first begin:

For once the eagle England being in prey,
To her unguarded nest the weasel Scot
Comes sneaking, and so sucks her princely eggs;
Playing the mouse, in absence of the cat,
To spoil * and havoc more than she can eat.
EXE. It follows then, the cat must stay at home?
Yet that is but a crush'd[e] necessity,
Since we have locks to safeguard necessaries,
And pretty traps to catch the petty thieves.
While that the armed hand doth fight abroad,
The advised head defends itself at home;
For government, though high, and low, and lower,
Put into parts, doth keep in one concent,(4)
Congreeing in a full and natural close,
Like music.
CANT. Therefore doth heaven divide
The state of man in divers functions,
Setting endeavour in continual motion;
To which is fixed, as an aim or butt,

(*) Old copy, *bloods.*

a *And cold* for action!] That is, for *want of* action.
b *They know your* grace hath cause *and means and might;*
So hath your highness;]
So, tautologically, reads the passage in the folio, 1623, where alone it appears. We should, perhaps, transpose the words *grace* and *cause*, reading:—

"They know your *cause* hath *grace* and means and might;—
So hath your highness;"

or, retaining their original sequence, substitute *haste* for *hath* in the second line;—

"So *haste*, your highness."

c *At the* ill neighbourhood.] The quartos have,—

(*) First folio, *tame.*

"Hath shook and trembled at the *bruit hereof;*"—
which we much prefer.
d *And make* your chronicle—] The quartos read,—
"——— *your chronicles,*" &c.;—
the folio:—
"——— *their chronicle,*" &c.
As Johnson suggested, we ought, probably, to substitute,—
"——— *her chronicle.*"
e Yet that is but a crush'd necessity,—] Thus the folio. The quartos have, "a *curs'd* necessity;" neither affords a perspicuous meaning. Mason proposed to read,—
"Yet that is *not* a curs'd necessity."
Warburton, "a *'scus'd* necessity." Capell, "a *crude* necessity."

Obedience: for so work the honey bees,
Creatures that, by a rule in nature, teach
The act of order to a peopled kingdom.
They have a king, and officers of sorts:
Where some, like magistrates, correct at home;
Others, like merchants, venture trade abroad;
Others, like soldiers, armed in their stings,
Make boot upon the summer's velvet buds;
Which pillage they with merry march bring home
To the tent-royal of their emperor;
Who, busied in his majesty, surveys
The singing masons building roofs of gold,
The civil citizens kneading-up the honey;
The poor mechanic porters crowding in
Their heavy burdens at his narrow gate;
The sad-ey'd justice, with his surly hum,
Delivering o'er to éxecutors pale
The lazy yawning drone. I this infer,—
That many things, having full reference
To one concent, may work contrariously;
As many arrows, loosed several ways,
Fly* to one mark; as many ways meet in one town;
As many fresh streams run† in one salt sea;
As many lines close in the dial's centre;
So may a thousand actions, once afoot,
End‡ in one purpose, and be all well borne
Without defeat. Therefore to France, my liege.
Divide your happy England into four;
Whereof take you one quarter into France,
And you withal shall make all Gallia shake.
If we, with thrice such powers left at home,
Cannot defend our own doors from the dog,
Let us be worried, and our nation lose
The name of hardiness and policy.

K. HEN. Call in the messengers sent from the Dauphin. [*Exit an* Attendant.
Now are we well resolv'd: and, by God's help,
And yours, the noble sinews of our power,
France being ours, we'll bend it to our awe,
Or break it all to pieces. Or there we'll sit,
Ruling, in large and ample empery,
O'er France, and all her almost kingly dukedoms,
Or lay these bones in an unworthy urn,
Tombless, with no remembrance over them:
Either our history shall, with full mouth,
Speak freely of our acts; or else our grave,
Like Turkish mute, shall have a tongueless mouth,
Not worshipp'd with a waxen § epitaph.

(*) First folio, *Come.* (†) First folio, *meet.*
(‡) First folio, *And.* (§) Quarto, *paper.*

[a] A nimble galliard—] Sir John Davies in his "Orchestra," 1622, describes the *galliard* as:—

"A gallant daunce, that lively doth bewray
A spirit and a vertue Masculine.
Impatient that her house on earth should stay,
Since she her selfe is fiery and divine:
Oft doth she make her body upward fline;
With lofty turnes and capriols in the ayre,
Which with the lusty tunes accordeth faire."

[b] Chases.] *Hazard, courts,* and *chases,* are terms borrowed from the game of tennis.

Enter Ambassadors *of* France.

Now are we well prepar'd to know the pleasure
Of our fair cousin Dauphin; for, we hear,
Your greeting is from him, not from the king.

AMB. May't please your majesty to give us leave,
Freely to render what we have in charge;
Or shall we, sparingly, show you far off
The Dauphin's meaning and our embassy?

K. HEN. We are no tyrant, but a Christian king;
Unto whose grace our passion is as subject,
As are* our wretches fetter'd in our prisons:
Therefore, with frank and with uncurbed plainness,
Tell us the Dauphin's mind.

AMB. Thus then, in few.
Your highness, lately sending into France,
Did claim some certain dukedoms, in the right
Of your great predecessor, king Edward the third.
In answer of which claim, the prince our master
Says,—that you savour too much of your youth;
And bids you be advis'd, there's nought in France,
That can be with a nimble galliard[a] won;
You cannot revel into dukedoms there:
He therefore sends you, meeter for your spirit,
This tun of treasure; and, in lieu of this,
Desires you let the dukedoms that you claim
Hear no more of you. This the Dauphin speaks.

K. HEN. What treasure, uncle?

EXE. Tennis-balls, my liege.

K. HEN. We are glad the Dauphin is so pleasant with us;
His present and your pains, we thank you for.
When we have match'd our rackets to these balls,
We will, in France, by God's grace, play a set
Shall strike his father's crown into the hazard:
Tell him, he hath made a match with such a wrangler,
That all the courts of France will be disturb'd
With chases.[b] And we understand him well,
How he comes o'er us with our wilder days,
Not measuring what use we made of them.
We never valued this poor seat of England;
And therefore, living hence, did give ourself
To barbarous licence; as 'tis ever common,
That men are merriest when they are from home.
But tell the Dauphin,—I will keep my state,

(*) First folio, *is.*

Be like a king, and show my sail [a] of greatness,
When I do rouse me in my throne of France:

For that I have laid by my majesty,
And plodded like a man for working-days;

---

[a] *And show my* sail of *greatness*,—] Mr. Collier's annotator reads, speciously,—

"—— my *soul* of greatness;"—

but *sail* we believe to have been Shakespeare's expression. Thus in the Third Part of "Henry VI." Act III. Sc. 3:—

"—— now Margaret
Must *strike her sail*, and learn awhile to serve,
Where kings command."

Again, in Massinger's play of "The Picture," Act II. Sc. 2:—

"Such is my *full-sail'd* confidence."—

And in Beaumont and Fletcher's "Thierry and Theodoret," Act II. Sc. 1:—

"——— I do begin
To feel an alteration in my nature,
And, in his *full-sail'd* confidence, a shower
Of gentle rain," &c.

But I will rise there with so full a glory,
That I will dazzle all the eyes of France,
Yea, strike the Dauphin blind to look on us.
And tell the pleasant prince,—this mock of his
Hath turn'd his balls to gun-stones;(5) and his soul
Shall stand sore charged for the wasteful vengeance
That shall fly with them: for many a thousand widows
Shall this his mock mock out of their dear husbands,
Mock mothers from their sons, mock castles down,
And some are yet ungotten and unborn,
That shall have cause to curse the Dauphin's scorn.
But this lies all within the will of God,
To whom I do appeal; and in whose name,
Tell you the Dauphin, I am coming on,
To venge me as I may, and to put forth
My rightful hand in a well-hallow'd cause.
So, get you hence in peace; and tell the Dauphin,
His jest will savour but of shallow wit,
When thousands weep, more than did laugh at it.—
Convey them with safe conduct.—Fare you well.
[*Exeunt* Ambassadors.

EXE. This was a merry message.

K. HEN. We hope to make the sender blush at it.
Therefore, my lords, omit no happy hour
That may give furtherance to our expedition·
For we have now no thought in us but France,
Save those to God, that run before our business.
Therefore, let our proportions for these wars
Be soon collected, and all things thought upon,
That may with reasonable [a] swiftness add
More feathers to our wings: for, God before,[b]
We'll chide this Dauphin at his father's door.
Therefore, let every man now task his thought,
That this fair action may on foot be brought.
[*Exeunt.*

---

[a] *With* reasonable *swiftness*—] Mr. Collier's annotator has,—

"*Seasonable* swiftness,"—

which, however plausible, is tame and prosaic; by *reasonable* swiftness, is meant the *speed of thought;* as in "Hamlet," we have,—

"——— *wings as swift*
As *meditation,*"—

And in "Troilus and Cressida," Act II. Sc. 2:—

"The very *wings of reason.*"

[b] God before,—] That is, "I *swear before God,*" or "*God witness.*"

Enter CHORUS.

Now all the youth of England are on fire,
And silken dalliance in the wardrobe lies;
Now thrive the armourers, and honour's thought
Reigns solely in the breast of every man.
They sell the pasture now, to buy the horse;
Following the mirror of all Christian kings,
With winged heels, as English Mercuries.
For now sits Expectation in the air;
And hides a sword, from hilts unto the point,
With crowns imperial, crowns and coronets,
Promis'd to Harry, and his followers.
The French, advis'd by good intelligence
Of this most dreadful preparation,
Shake in their fear; and with pale policy
Seek to divert the English purposes.
O England!—model to thy inward greatness,
Like little body with a mighty heart,—
What mightst thou do, that honour would thee do,
Were all thy children kind and natural!
But see thy fault! France hath in thee found out
A nest of hollow bosoms, which he fills
With treacherous crowns: and three corrupted men,—
One, Richard earl of Cambridge; and the second,
Henry lord Scroop of Masham; and the third,
Sir Thomas Grey, knight, of Northumberland,—
Have for the gilt of France, (O guilt, indeed!)
Confirm'd conspiracy with fearful France;
And by their hands this grace of kings must die
(If hell and treason hold their promises,)
Ere he take ship for France, and in Southampton.
Linger your patience on; and we'll digest
The abuse of distance; force[a] a play.
The sum is paid: the traitors are agreed;
The king is set from London; and the scene
Is now transported, gentles, to Southampton.
There is the playhouse now, there must you sit,
And thence to France shall we convey you safe,
And bring you back, charming the narrow seas
To give you gentle pass; for, if we may,
We'll not offend one stomach with our play.
But, till the king come forth, and not till then,
Unto Southampton do we shift our scene. [*Exit.*

[a] Force *a play.*] So in the original. Possibly, however, an allusion is intended to the *dumb shows* which of old preceded each act, and we should read:—

"Linger your patience on; and we'll digest
The abuse of distance; *foresee* a play."

See the Chorus before Act III.

ACT II.

SCENE I.—London. Eastcheap.

Enter, severally, NYM *and* BARDOLPH.

BARD. Well met, corporal Nym.

NYM. Good morrow, lieutenant Bardolph.

BARD. What, are ancient Pistol and you friends yet?

NYM. For my part, I care not: I say little; but when time shall serve, there shall be smiles;—but that shall be as it may. I dare not fight, but I will wink, and hold out mine iron: it is a simple one, but what though? it will toast cheese, and it will endure cold as another man's sword will: and there's an end.[a]

BARD. I will bestow a breakfast, to make you friends, and we'll be all three sworn brothers[b] to France: let it be so, good corporal Nym.

NYM. 'Faith, I will live so long as I may, that's the certain of it; and when I cannot live any longer, I will do[c] as I may: that is my rest, that is the rendezvous of it.

BARD. It is certain, corporal, that he is married to Nell Quickly: and, certainly, she did you wrong; for you were troth-plight to her.

NYM. I cannot tell; things must be as they may: men may sleep, and they may have their throats about them at that time; and, some say, knives have edges. It must be as it may: though patience be a tired mare,* yet she will plod.

[a] *And there's* an end.] The quartos read, "And there's *the humour of it.*"

[b] *And we'll be all three* sworn brothers—] See note (a), p. 484, Vol. I.

(*) First folio, *name.*

[c] *I will* do *as I may*:] Monck Mason, with some reason, proposed to read:—

"—— *die* as I may."

There must be conclusions:—well, I cannot tell.

BARD. Here comes ancient Pistol, and his wife:—good corporal, be patient here.—

Enter PISTOL *and* Hostess.[a]

How now, mine host Pistol!

PIST. Base tike, call'st thou me—host?
Now, by this hand, I swear I scorn the term;
Nor shall my Nell keep lodgers.

HOST. No, by my troth, not long: for we cannot lodge and board a dozen or fourteen gentlewomen, that live honestly by the prick of their needles, but it will be thought we keep a bawdy-house straight. [NYM *draws his sword.*] O well-a-day, Lady, if he be not drawn![b] now we shall see wilful adultery and murder committed.

BARD. Good lieutenant,—good corporal,—offer nothing here.[c]

NYM. Pish![d]

PIST. Pish for thee, Iceland dog! (1) thou prick-ear'd cur of Iceland!

HOST. Good corporal Nym, show thy valour, and put up your sword.

NYM. Will you shog off? I would have you *solus.* [*Sheathing his sword.*

PIST. *Solus*, egregious dog! O viper vile!
The *solus* in thy most marvellous face;
The *solus* in thy teeth, and in thy throat,
And in thy hateful lungs, yea, in thy maw, perdy;
And, which is worse, within thy nasty mouth!
I do retort the *solus* in thy bowels:
For I can take, and Pistol's cock is up,
And flashing fire will follow.

NYM. I am not Barbason; you cannot conjure me. I have an humour to knock you indifferently well: if you grow foul with me, Pistol, I will scour you with my rapier, as I may, in fair terms: if you would walk off, I would prick your guts a little, in good terms, as I may; and that's the humour of it.

PIST. O braggart vile, and damned furious wight!
The grave doth gape, and doting death is near;
Therefore exhale.

[PISTOL *and* NYM *draw their swords.*

BARD. Hear me, hear me what I say:—he that strikes the first stroke, I'll run him up to the hilts, as I am a soldier. [*Draws his sword.*

PIST. An oath of mickle might; and fury shall abate.
Give me thy fist, thy fore-foot to me give;
Thy spirits are most tall.

NYM. I will cut thy throat, one time or other, in fair terms; that is the humour of it.

PIST. *Coupe le gorge!*
That is the word?—I thee defy* again.
O hound of Crete, think'st thou my spouse to get?
No; to the spital go,
And from the powdering-tub of infamy
Fetch forth the lazar kite of Cressid's kind,
Doll Tear-sheet she by name, and her espouse:
I have, and I will hold, the *quondam* Quickly
For the only she; and—*Pauca*, there's enough, to—
Go to.

Enter the Boy.

BOY. Mine host Pistol, you must come to my master,—and you,† hostess;—he is very sick, and would to bed.—Good Bardolph, put thy nose between his sheets, and do the office of a warming-pan: 'faith, he's very ill.

BARD. Away, you rogue!

HOST. By my troth, he'll yield the crow a pudding one of these days: the king has killed his heart. Good husband, come home presently.

[*Exeunt* Hostess *and* Boy.

BARD. Come, shall I make you two friends? We must to France together; why the devil should we keep knives to cut one another's throats?

PIST. Let floods o'erswell, and fiends for food howl on!

NYM. You'll pay me the eight shillings I won of you at betting?

PIST. Base is the slave that pays.

NYM. That now I will have; that's the humour of it.

PIST. As manhood shall compound; push home.

[PISTOL *and* NYM *draw their swords.*

BARD. By this sword, he that makes the first thrust, I'll kill him; by this sword, I will.

PIST. Sword is an oath; and oaths must have their course.

---

[a] Hostess.] The old copies have "Quickly," but evidently through inadvertence, as she is always afterwards called "Hostess," which, or "Mistress Pistol," is now her proper appellation.

[b] *O well-a-day, Lady, if he be not* drawn! *now we shall see,* &c.] In the folio, "if he be not *hewne now.*" The correction was made by Theobald.

[c] Good lieutenant,—good corporal,—offer nothing here.] To obviate the inconsistency of Bardolph, himself the lieutenant, designating Pistol by that title, Capell prints, "Good ancient," and Malone makes the sentence a part of the Hostess's speech. This, however, is not the only anomaly of the same kind. In the opening of the present scene, Nym addresses Bardolph as "lieutenant," while in Act III. Sc. 2, he calls him "corporal." Again, in the Second Part of "Henry IV." Act V. Sc. 5, Falstaff styles Pistol "lieutenant," though his military rank is only that of "ancient." Whether these incongruities are the effect of design or inattention on Shakespeare's part, (they could hardly arise from carelessness in the printing office,) it is now, perhaps, impossible to determine; we prefer therefore to adhere to the old text.

[d] Pish!] In the quartos "Push!" the older form of the same contemptuous exclamation. See note (a), p. 731, Vol. I.

(*) First folio, *defy thee.* (†) First folio, *your.*

BARD. Corporal Nym, an thou wilt be friends, be friends; an thou wilt not, why then be enemies with me too. Pr'ythee, put up.

NYM. I shall have my eight shillings, I won of you at betting?[a]

PIST. A noble shalt thou have, and present pay;
And liquor likewise will I give to thee,
And friendship shall combine, and brotherhood.
I'll live by Nym, and Nym shall live by me;—
Is not this just?—for I shall sutler be
Unto the camp, and profits will accrue.
Give me thy hand.

NYM. I shall have my noble?

PIST. In cash most justly paid.

NYM. Well then, that's* the humour of it.

Re-enter Hostess.

HOST. As ever you came† of women, come in quickly to sir John: ah, poor heart! he is so shaked of a burning quotidian tertian, that it is most lamentable to behold. Sweet men, come to him.

NYM. The king hath run bad humours on the knight, that's the even of it.

PIST. Nym, thou hast spoke the right;
His heart is fracted, and corroborate.

NYM. The king is a good king, but it must be as it may; he passes some humours and careers.

PIST. Let us condole the knight,
For, lambkins, we will live. [*Exeunt.*

SCENE II.—Southampton. *A Council Chamber.*

Enter EXETER, BEDFORD, *and* WESTMORELAND.

BED. 'Fore God, his grace is bold, to trust these traitors.

EXE. They shall be apprehended by and by.

(*) First folio, *that*.

(†) First folio, *come*.

[a] NYM. I shall have my eight shillings, &c.] This speech is omitted in the folio.

WEST. How smooth and even they do bear themselves!
As if allegiance in their bosoms sat,
Crowned with faith, and constant loyalty.
BED. The king hath note of all that they intend,
By interception which they dream not of.
EXE. Nay, but the man that was his bedfellow,
Whom he hath dull'd and cloy'd[a] with gracious favours,—
That he should, for a foreign purse, so sell
His sovereign's life to death and treachery!

Trumpets sound. Enter KING HENRY, SCROOP, CAMBRIDGE, GREY, Lords, *and* Attendants.

K. HEN. Now sits the wind fair, and we will aboard.
My lord of Cambridge,—and my kind lord of Masham,—
And you, my gentle knight, give me your thoughts:
Think you not, that the powers we bear with us,
Will cut their passage through the force of France,
Doing the execution, and the act,
For which we have in head assembled them?
SCROOP. No doubt, my liege, if each man do his best.
K. HEN. I doubt not that, since we are well persuaded,
We carry not a heart with us from hence,
That grows not in a fair concent with ours;
Nor leave not one behind, that doth not wish
Success and conquest to attend on us.
CAM. Never was monarch better fear'd and lov'd,
Than is your majesty; there's not, I think, a subject,
That sits in heart-grief and uneasiness
Under the sweet shade of your government.
GREY. True: those that were your father's enemies
Have steep'd their galls in honey, and do serve you
With hearts create of duty and of zeal.
K. HEN. We therefore have great cause of thankfulness,
And shall forget the office of our hand,
Sooner than quittance of desert and merit,
According to the weight and worthiness.
SCROOP. So service shall with steeled sinews toil,
And labour shall refresh itself with hope,
To do your grace incessant services.
K. HEN. We judge no less.—Uncle of Exeter,
Enlarge the man committed yesterday,
That rail'd against our person: we consider,
It was excess of wine that set him on;
And, on his more advice,[b] we pardon him.
SCROOP. That's mercy, but too much security;
Let him be punish'd, sovereign, lest example
Breed, by his sufferance, more of such a kind.
K. HEN. O, let us yet be merciful.
CAM. So may your highness, and yet punish too.
GREY. Sir, you show great mercy, if you give him life,
After the taste of much correction.
K. HEN. Alas, your too much love and care of me
Are heavy orisons 'gainst this poor wretch.
If little faults, proceeding on distemper,
Shall not be wink'd at, how shall we stretch our eye,
When capital crimes, chew'd, swallow'd, and digested,
Appear before us!—We'll yet enlarge that man,
Though Cambridge, Scroop, and Grey, in their dear care
And tender preservation of our person,
Would have him punish'd. And now to our French causes;
Who are the late commissioners?
CAM. I one, my lord;
Your highness bade me ask for it to-day.
SCROOP. So did you me, my liege.
GREY. And me,[c] my royal sovereign.
K. HEN. Then, Richard earl of Cambridge, there is yours;—
There yours, lord Scroop of Masham;—and, sir knight,
Grey of Northumberland, this same is yours:
Read them; and know, I know your worthiness.
My lord of Westmoreland,—and uncle Exeter,
We will aboard to-night. Why, how now, gentlemen!
What see you in those papers, that you lose
So much complexion?—look ye, how they change!
Their cheeks are paper.—Why, what read you there,
That hath* so cowarded and chas'd your blood
Out of appearance?
CAM. I do confess my fault;
And do submit me to your highness' mercy.
GREY. SCROOP. To which we all appeal.
K. HEN. The mercy, that was quick in us but late,
By your own counsel is suppress'd and kill'd:
You must not dare, for shame, to talk of mercy;
For your own reasons turn into your bosoms,
As dogs upon their masters, worrying you.
See you, my princes, and my noble peers,

[a] Dull'd and cloy'd—] So the folio; the quartos read, "*cloy'd and grac'd.*"

[b] *And, on his* more advice,—] This is variously interpreted. We believe it to mean, on his further representations.

(*) First folio, *have*.

[c] *And* me, *my royal sovereign.*] The folio has, "And *I*," &c. The quarto, "And *me*, my lord."

These English monsters! My lord of Cambridge here,—
You know how apt our love was to accord
To furnish him with all appertinents
Belonging to his honour; and this man
Hath, for a few light crowns, lightly conspir'd,
And sworn unto the practices of France,
To kill us here in Hampton: to the which,
This knight,—no less for bounty bound to us
Than Cambridge is,—hath likewise sworn.—But, O!
What shall I say to thee, lord Scroop? thou cruel,
Ingrateful, savage, and inhuman creature!
Thou, that didst bear the key of all my counsels,
That knew'st the very bottom of my soul,
That almost mightst have coined me into gold,
Wouldst thou have practis'd on me for thy use?
May it be possible, that foreign hire
Could out of thee extract one spark of evil,
That might annoy my finger? 'tis so strange,
That, though the truth of it stands off as gross
As black from white,[a] my eye will scarcely see it.
Treason and murder ever kept together,
As two yoke-devils sworn to either's purpose,
Working so grossly in a* natural cause,[b]
That admiration did not whoop † at them:
But thou, 'gainst all proportion, didst bring in
Wonder, to wait on treason and on murder:
And whatsoever cunning fiend it was,
That wrought upon thee so preposterously,
Hath got the voice in hell for excellence;
And other devils that suggest by treasons,
Do botch and bungle up damnation
With patches, colours, and with forms being fetch'd
From glistering semblances of piety;
But he that temper'd[c] thee, bade thee stand up,
Gave thee no instance why thou shouldst do treason,
Unless to dub thee with the name of traitor.
If that same dæmon, that hath gull'd thee thus,
Should with his lion-gait walk the whole world,
He might return to vasty Tartar[d] back,
And tell the legions—*I can never win*
A soul so easy as that Englishman's.
O, how hast thou with jealousy infected
The sweetness of affiance! Show men dutiful?
Why, so didst thou. Seem they grave and learned?
Why, so didst thou. Come they of noble family?
Why, so didst thou. Seem they religious?
Why, so didst thou. Or are they spare in diet,
Free from gross passion, or of mirth or anger,
Constant in spirit, not swerving with the blood,
Garnish'd and deck'd in modest complement;[e]
Not working with the eye, without the ear,
And, but in purged judgment, trusting neither?
Such and so finely boulted didst thou seem;
And thus thy fall hath left a kind of blot
To mark the* full-fraught man, and best indued,
With some suspicion. I will weep for thee;
For this revolt of thine, methinks, is like
Another fall of man.[f]—Their faults are open,
Arrest them to the answer of the law;—
And God acquit them of their practices!

EXE. I arrest thee of high treason, by the name of Richard earl of Cambridge.

I arrest thee of high treason, by the name of Henry† lord Scroop of Masham.

I arrest thee of high treason, by the name of Thomas Grey, knight, of Northumberland.

SCROOP. Our purposes God justly hath discovered,
And I repent my fault more than my death;
Which I beseech your highness to forgive,
Although my body pay the price of it.

CAM. For me,—the gold of France did not seduce,
Although I did admit it as a motive
The sooner to effect what I intended:
But God be thanked for prevention;
Which I‡ in sufferance heartily will rejoice,
Beseeching God and you to pardon me.

GREY. Never did faithful subject more rejoice
At the discovery of most dangerous treason,
Than I do at this hour joy o'er myself,
Prevented from a damned enterprize:
My fault, but not my body, pardon, sovereign.

K. HEN. God quit you in his mercy! Hear your sentence.
You have conspir'd against our royal person,
Join'd with an enemy proclaim'd, and from his coffers
Receiv'd the golden earnest of our death;
Wherein you would have sold your king to slaughter,
His princes and his peers to servitude,
His subjects to oppression and contempt,
And his whole kingdom into desolation.
Touching our person, seek we no revenge;
But we our kingdom's safety must so tender,

(*) First folio, *an*. (†) First folio, *hoope*.

[a] *Black from white,*—] So the quartos. The folio has "black *and* white."

[b] A *natural* cause,—] *Cause* was probably a misprint for *course*.

[c] Temper'd *thee,*—] *Moulded* thee. Johnson proposed to read "*tempted* thee."

[d] *Vasty* Tartar—] That is, *Tartarus*.

[e] *Garnish'd and deck'd in modest* complement;] Complement signified *accomplishments, perfection, completeness:* and was applied sometimes to mental, sometimes to physical attainments, and occasionally, as in the present instance, merely to the taste and elegance displayed in dress. Thus, in a note of Drayton's upon the Epistle from Geraldine to Lord Surrey; "but Apparell and the outward Appearance intituled *Complement.*"

[f] *Another fall of man.*—] The whole of this speech from the line,—

"Treason and murder ever kept together,"

inclusive, is omitted in the quartos.

(*) Old text, *make thee*. (†) First folio, *Thomas*. (‡) First folio omits, *I*.

Whose ruin you have* sought, that to her laws
We do deliver you. Get you therefore hence,
Poor miserable wretches, to your death:
The taste whereof, God, of his mercy, give
You patience to endure, and true repentance
Of all your dear offences!—Bear them hence.
[*Exeunt* Conspirators, *guarded.*
Now, lords, for France; the enterprize whereof
Shall be to you, as us, like glorious.
We doubt not of a fair and lucky war,
Since God so graciously hath brought to light
This dangerous treason, lurking in our way,
To hinder our beginnings. We doubt not now,
But every rub is smoothed on our way:
Then forth, dear countrymen; let us deliver
Our puissance into the hand of God,
Putting it straight in expedition.
Cheerly to sea; the signs of war advance:
No king of England, if not king of France.
[*Exeunt.*

SCENE III.—London. Pistol's *House in Eastcheap.*

Enter PISTOL, Hostess, BARDOLPH, NYM, *and* Boy.

HOST. Pr'ythee, honey-sweet husband, let me bring thee to Staines.

PIST. No; for my manly heart doth yearn.—
Bardolph, be blithe;—Nym, rouse thy vaunting veins;—
Boy, bristle thy courage up;—for Falstaff he is [dead,
And we must yearn therefore.

BARD. Would I were with him, wheresome'er he is, either in heaven or in hell!

HOST. Nay, sure, he's not in hell; he's in Arthur's bosom, if ever man went to Arthur's bosom. 'A made a finer end, and went away, an it had been any christom child;(2) 'a parted even just between twelve and one, even at the turning o' the tide:(3) for after I saw him fumble with the sheets, and play with flowers, and smile upon his fingers' ends,† I knew there was but one way; for his nose was as sharp as a pen, and 'a babbled of green fields.[a] *How now, sir John?* quoth I: *what, man! be o' good cheer.* So 'a cried out—*God, God, God!* three or four times: now I, to comfort him, bid him, 'a should not think of God; I hoped there was no need to trouble himself with any such thoughts yet: so, 'a bade me lay more clothes on his feet: I put my hand into the bed, and felt them, and they were as cold as any stone; then I felt to his knees, and so upward,* and upward, and all was as cold as any stone.

NYM. They say, he cried out of sack.

HOST. Ay, that 'a did.

BARD. And of women.

HOST. Nay, that 'a did not.

BOY. Yes, that 'a did; and said, they were devils incarnate.

HOST. 'A could never abide carnation: 'twas a colour he never liked.

BOY. 'A said once, the devil would have him about women.

HOST. 'A did in some sort, indeed, handle women: but then he was rheumatic;[b] and talked of the whore of Babylon.

BOY. Do you not remember, 'a saw a flea stick upon Bardolph's nose, and 'a said, it was a black soul burning in hell?

BARD. Well, the fuel is gone that maintained that fire: that's all the riches I got in his service.

NYM. Shall we shog? the king will be gone from Southampton.

PIST. Come, let's away.—My love, give me thy lips,
Look to my chattels, and my movables:
Let senses rule; the word† is, *Pitch and pay;*[c]
Trust none, for oaths are straws, men's faiths are wafer-cakes,
And hold-fast is the only dog, my duck;
Therefore, *caveto* be thy counsellor.
Go, clear thy crystals.—Yoke-fellows in arms,
Let us to France! like horse-leeches, my boys;
To suck, to suck, the very blood to suck!

BOY. And that is but unwholesome food, they say.

PIST. Touch her soft mouth, and march.

BARD. Farewell, hostess. [*Kissing her.*

NYM. I cannot kiss, that is the humour of it; but adieu.

PIST. Let housewifery appear; keep close, I thee command.

HOST. Farewell; adieu. [*Exeunt.*

(*) First folio omits, *have.* (†) First folio, *end.*

(*) First folio, *up-peer'd.* (†) First folio, *world.*

[a] *And 'a babbled of green fields.*] In the folio,—"his nose was as sharpe as a Pen, and a *Table* of greene fields." The quartos have simply, "His nose was as sharp as a pen." Theobald's famous emendation of "'a *babbled* of green fields," has now become so completely a part of the text, that no editor will ever have the temerity to displace it. The conjecture of Pope, therefore, that "a table of green fields," was a stage-direction for the property-man, (whom he supposed to be named *Greenfield,*) to have a table ready on the stage—"a table of Greenfield's;" and the equally atrocious sophistication of Mr. Collier's annotator—"his nose was as sharp as a pen *on* a table of green *frieze!*" need only be mentioned to be laughed at.

[b] *Was* rheumatic;] Was *lunatic,* the "*quondam* Quickly" means.

[c] *Pitch and pay;*] A proverbial saying, equivalent to our "*pay on delivery.*" One of the old laws of Blackwell-hall, Farmer says, "was that a *penny be paid* by the owner of every bale of cloth for *pitching.*" Tusser, in his description of Norwich, calls it,—

"A city trim;
Where strangers well may seem to dwell,
That *pitch and pay,* or keep their day."

SCENE IV.—France. *A Room in the* French King's *Palace.*

Flourish. Enter KING CHARLES, *attended; the* DAUPHIN, *the* DUKE *of* BURGUNDY, *the* Constable, *and others.*

K. CHA. Thus come the English with full power upon us,
And more than carefully it us concerns,
To answer royally in our defences.
Therefore the dukes of Berry, and of Bretagne,
Of Brabant, and of Orleans, shall make forth,—
And you, prince Dauphin,—with all swift despatch,
To line and new repair our towns of war,
With men of courage, and with means defendant:
For England his approaches makes as fierce,
As waters to the sucking of a gulf.
It fits us then to be as provident
As fear may teach us, out of late examples
Left by the fatal and neglected English,
Upon our fields.
DAU. My most redoubted father,
It is most meet we arm us 'gainst the foe;
For peace itself should not so dull a kingdom,
(Though war, nor no known quarrel, were in question,)
But that defences, musters, preparations,
Should be maintain'd, assembled, and collected,
As were a war in expectation.
Therefore, I say, 't is meet we all go forth,
To view the sick and feeble parts of France;
And let us do it with no show of fear,
No, with no more, than if we heard that England
Were busied with a Whitsun morris-dance:
For, my good liege, she is so idly king'd,
Her sceptre so fantastically borne
By a vain, giddy, shallow, humorous youth,
That fear attends her not.
CON. O peace, prince Dauphin!
You are too much mistaken in this king:
Question, your grace, the late ambassadors,—
With what great state he heard their embassy,
How well supplied with noble counsellors,
How modest in exception, and, withal,
How terrible in constant resolution,—
And you shall find, his vanities forespent
Were but the outside of the Roman Brutus,
Covering discretion with a coat of folly;
As gardeners do with ordure hide those roots
That shall first spring, and be most delicate.
DAU. Well, 't is not so, my lord high constable;
But though we think it so, it is no matter:
In cases of defence, 't is best to weigh
The enemy more mighty than he seems,
So the proportions of defence are fill'd;
Which, of[a] a weak and niggardly projection,
Doth, like a miser, spoil his coat, with scanting
A little cloth.
K. CHA. Think we king Harry strong;
And, princes, look you strongly arm to meet him.
The kindred of him hath been flesh'd upon us;
And he is bred out of that bloody strain,
That haunted us in our familiar paths:
Witness our too—much memorable shame,
When Cressy battle fatally was struck,
And all our princes captiv'd, by the hand
Of that black name, Edward, black prince of Wales;
Whiles that his mountain[b] sire,—on mountain standing,
Up in the air, crown'd with the golden sun,—
Saw his heroical seed, and smil'd to see him
Mangle the work of nature, and deface
The patterns that by God and by French fathers
Had twenty years been made. This is a stem
Of that victorious stock; and let us fear
The native mightiness and fate of him.

Enter a Messenger.

MESS. Ambassadors from Harry king of England
Do crave admittance to your majesty.
K. CHA. We'll give them present audience. Go, and bring them.
[*Exeunt* Messenger *and certain* Lords.
You see, this chase is hotly follow'd, friends.
DAU. Turn head, and stop pursuit: for coward dogs
Most spend their mouths, when what they seem to threaten,
Runs far before them. Good my sovereign,
Take up the English short, and let them know
Of what a monarchy you are the head;
Self-love, my liege, is not so vile a sin,
As self-neglecting.

Re-enter Lords, *with* EXETER *and train.*

K. CHA. From our brother of England?
EXE. From him; and thus he greets your majesty.
He wills you, in the name of God Almighty,
That you divest yourself, and lay apart
The borrow'd glories, that, by gift of heaven,
By law of nature and of nations, 'long
To him, and to his heirs; namely, the crown,
And all wide-stretched honours that pertain,

---

[a] Which, of a weak and niggardly projection,—] We should, perhaps, read, "Which *if*," or "Which *oft.*"

[b] Mountain *sire,*—] Theobald suggested, *Mounting* sire.

By custom and the ordinance of times,
Unto the crown of France. That you may know,
'T is no sinister, nor no awkward[a] claim,
Pick'd from the worm-holes of long-vanish'd days,
Nor from the dust of old oblivion rak'd,
He sends you this most memorable line,[b]
[*Gives a paper.*
In every branch truly demonstrative;
Willing you, overlook this pedigree,
And, when you find him evenly deriv'd
From his most fam'd of famous ancestors,
Edward the third, he bids you then resign
Your crown and kingdom, indirectly held
From him the native and true challenger.

K. CHA. Or else what follows? [crown

EXE. Bloody constraint; for if you hide the
Even in your hearts, there will he rake for it:
Therefore in fierce tempest is he coming,
In thunder, and in earthquake, like a Jove;
(That, if requiring fail, he will compel;)
And bids you, in the bowels of the Lord,
Deliver up the crown, and to take mercy
On the poor souls, for whom this hungry war
Opens his vasty jaws: and on your head
Turning the widows' tears, the orphans' cries,
The dead men's blood, the pining[c] maidens' groans,
For husbands, fathers, and betrothed lovers,
That shall be swallow'd in this controversy.
This is his claim, his threat'ning, and my message;
Unless the Dauphin be in presence here,
To whom expressly I bring greeting too.[d]

K. CHA. For us, we will consider of this further:
To-morrow shall you bear our full intent
Back to our brother of England.

DAU. For the Dauphin,
I stand here for him; what to him from England?

EXE. Scorn and defiance; slight regard, contempt,
And any thing that may not misbecome
The mighty sender, doth he prize you at.
Thus says my king: an if your father's highness
Do not, in grant of all demands at large,
Sweeten the bitter mock you sent his majesty,
He'll call you to so hot an answer of it,
That caves and womby vaultages of France
Shall chide[e] your trespass, and return your mock
In second accent of his ordinance.[f]

DAU. Say, if my father render fair return,
It is against my will: for I desire
Nothing but odds with England; to that end,
As matching to his youth and vanity,
I did present him with the Paris balls.

EXE. He'll make your Paris Louvre shake for it,
Were it the mistress-court of mighty Europe:
And, be assur'd, you'll find a difference,
(As we, his subjects, have in wonder found,)
Between the promise of his greener days,
And these he masters now; now he weighs time,
Even to the utmost grain; that you shall read
In your own losses, if he stay in France.

K. CHA. To-morrow shall you know our mind at full.

EXE. Despatch us with all speed, lest that our king
Come here himself to question our delay;
For he is footed in this land already.

K. CHA. You shall be soon despatch'd, with fair conditions:
A night is but small breath,[g] and little pause,
To answer matters of this consequence. [*Exeunt.*

---

a Awkward—] *Distorted.*
b *Memorable* line,—] *Line* is *lineage, genealogy.*
c Pining—] So the quartos; the folio has "*privy.*"
d *Greeting* too.] Thus the quartos; the folio reads, "greeting *to.*"
e Shall chide *your trespass,*—] Chide is here employed in its double sense of *rebuke* and *re-ound*, or *echo*.
f Ordinance.] This was anciently spelt indifferently, *ordnance*, or *ordinance*. Here the metre requires it to be pronounced as a trisyllable.
g Small breath,—] Short breathing time.

Enter Chorus.

Thus with imagin'd wing our swift scene flies,
In motion of no less celerity
Than that of thought. Suppose, that you have seen
The well-appointed king at Hampton* pier
Embark his royalty; and his brave fleet
With silken streamers the young Phœbus fanning.†
Play with your fancies; and in them behold
Upon the hempen tackle, ship-boys climbing:
Hear the shrill whistle, which doth order give
To sounds confus'd: behold the threaden sails,
Borne with the invisible and creeping wind,
Draw the huge bottoms through the furrow'd sea,
Breasting the lofty surge. O, do but think,
You stand upon the rivage,[a] and behold
A city on the inconstant billows dancing;
For so appears this fleet majestical,
Holding due course to Harfleur. Follow, follow!
Grapple your minds to sternage[b] of this navy;
And leave your England, as dead midnight, still,
Guarded with grandsires, babies, and old women,
Either past, or not arriv'd to, pith and puissance:
For who is he, whose chin is but enrich'd
With one appearing hair, that will not follow
These cull'd and choice-drawn cavaliers to France?
Work, work, your thoughts, and therein see a siege:
Behold the ordnance on their carriages,
With fatal mouths gaping on girded Harfleur.
Suppose the ambassador from the French comes back;
Tells Harry—that the king doth offer him
Katharine his daughter; and with her, to dowry,
Some petty and unprofitable dukedoms.
The offer likes not: and the nimble gunner
With linstock now the devilish cannon touches,
[*Alarum; and chambers go off.*
And down goes all before them. Still be kind,
And eke out our performance with your mind.
[*Exit.*

(*) Old copy, *Dover*. (†) Old copy, *fayning*.

a Rivage,—] The *shore* or *bank*. The word is not unfrequent with our old writers, although this is the only instance of its occurrence in Shakespeare.

b *To sternage of this navy*;] To the *steerage*, or *course*, of the fleet.

ACT III.

SCENE I.—France. *Before* Harfleur.

Alarums. Enter KING HENRY, EXETER, BEDFORD, GLOUCESTER, *and* Soldiers, *with scaling ladders.*

K. HEN. Once more unto the breach, dear friends, once more;
Or close the wall up with our English dead!
In peace, there's nothing so becomes a man,
As modest stillness and humility:
But when the blast of war blows in our ears,
Then imitate the action of the tiger;
Stiffen the sinews, summon* up the blood,
Disguise fair nature with hard-favour'd rage:
Then lend the eye a terrible aspéct;
Let it pry through the portage[a] of the head,
Like the brass cannon; let the brow o'erwhelm it,
As fearfully as doth a galled rock
O'erhang and jutty[b] his confounded[c] base,
Swill'd with the wild and wasteful ocean.
Now set the teeth, and stretch the nostril wide:
Hold hard the breath, and bend up every spirit
To his full height!—On, on, you noble* English,
Whose blood is fet[d] from fathers of war-proof!—
Fathers that, like so many Alexanders,
Have in these parts from morn till even fought,
And sheath'd their swords for lack of argument:—
Dishonour not your mothers; now attest,
That those, whom you call'd fathers, did beget you!
Be copy now to men† of grosser blood,
And teach them how to war!—And you, good yeomen,
Whose limbs were made in England, show us here
The mettle of your pasture; let us swear
That you are worth your breeding; which I doubt not;
For there is none of you so mean and base,
That hath not noble lustre in your eyes.
I see you stand like greyhounds in the slips,
Straining‡ upon the start. The game's afoot;
Follow your spirit: and, upon this charge,
Cry—God for Harry! England and saint George!

[*Exeunt. Alarum; and chambers go off.*

(*) Old copy, *commune*.

[a] Portage—] The *port-holes*.
[b] Jutty—] *Project, jut out*.
[c] Confounded *base*,—] *Demolished* base.

(*) Old copy, *Noblish*. (†) Old copy, *me*. (‡) Old copy, *Straying*.

[d] *Whose blood is* fet—] *Fet* is frequently found in our early poets; it is the participle of the Anglo-Saxon verb *fet ian*, to fetch.

SCENE II.—*The same.*

Forces pass over; then enter BARDOLPH, NYM, PISTOL, *and* BOY.

BARD. On, on, on, on, on! to the breach, to the breach!

NYM. Pray thee, corporal,[a] stay; the knocks are too hot; and, for mine own part, I have not a case[b] of lives: the humour of it is too hot, that is the very plain-song of it.

PIST. The plain-song is most just; for humours do abound;

Knocks go and come;
God's vassals drop and die;
And sword and shield,
In bloody field,
Doth win immortal fame.

BOY. Would I were in an alehouse in London! I would give all my fame for a pot of ale, and safety.

PIST. And I:

If wishes would prevail with me,
My purpose should not fail with me,
But thither would I hie.

BOY. *As duly, but not as truly,*
As bird doth sing on bough.

Enter FLUELLEN.[c]

FLU. Got's plood![d]—Up to the preach, you dogs! avaunt, you cullions! [*Driving them forward.*

PIST. Be merciful, great duke,[e] to men of mould!
Abate thy rage, abate thy manly rage!
Abate thy rage, great duke!
Good bawcock, bate thy rage! use lenity, sweet chuck!

NYM. These be good humours!—your honour wins bad humours.

[*Exeunt* NYM, PISTOL, *and* BARDOLPH, *followed by* FLUELLEN.

BOY. As young as I am, I have observed these three swashers:[f] I am boy to them all three: but all they three, though they would serve me, could not be man to me; for, indeed, three such antics do not amount to a man. For Bardolph,—he is white-livered, and red-faced; by the means whereof, 'a faces it out, but fights not. For Pistol,—he hath a killing tongue, and a quiet sword; by the means whereof 'a breaks words, and keeps whole weapons. For Nym,—he hath heard that men of few words are the best men; and therefore he scorns to say his prayers, lest 'a should be thought a coward: but his few bad words are matched with as few good deeds; for 'a never broke any man's

---

a *Pray thee*, corporal,—] See note (c), p. 74.
b *A* case of *lives*:] A *brace*, or *pair* of lives.
c Fluellen.] The Welsh pronunciation of Lluellyn.

d Got's plood!] Omitted in the folio, probably on account of the Act 3 Jac. I. c. 21. See note (4), p. 562, Vol. I.
e *Great* duke,—] Great *leader*.
f Swashers.] *Swaggerers, braggadochios.*

head but his own; and that was against a post, when he was drunk. They will steal any thing, and call it,—purchase. Bardolph stole a lute-case, bore it twelve leagues, and sold it for three halfpence. Nym and Bardolph are sworn brothers in filching; and in Calais they stole a fire shovel: I knew by that piece of service, the men would carry coals.[a] They would have me as familiar with men's pockets, as their gloves or their handkerchers; which makes much against my manhood, if I should take from another's pocket, to put into mine; for it is plain pocketing-up of wrongs. I must leave them, and seek some better service: their villainy goes against my weak stomach, and therefore I must cast it up. [*Exit* Boy.

Re-enter FLUELLEN, GOWER *following*.

GOW. Captain Fluellen, you must come presently to the mines; the duke of Gloucester would speak with you.

FLU. To the mines! tell you the duke, it is not so goot to come to the mines: for, look you, the mines is not according to the disciplines of the war; the concavities of it is not sufficient; for, look you, th' athversary (you may discuss unto the duke, look you,) is digt himself four yard under the countermines: py Cheshu, I think, 'a will plow up all, if there is not petter directions.

GOW. The duke of Gloucester, to whom the order of the siege is given, is altogether directed by an Irishman, a very valiant gentleman, i'faith.

FLU. It is captain Macmorris, is it not?

GOW. I think it be.

FLU. Py Cheshu, he is an ass, as in the 'orld: I will verify as much in his peard: he has no more directions in the true disciplines of the wars, look you, of the Roman disciplines, than is a puppy-dog.

GOW. Here 'a comes; and the Scots captain, captain Jamy, with him.

FLU. Captain Jamy is a marvellous falorous gentleman, that is certain; and of great expedition, and knowledge, in the auncient wars, upon my particular knowledge of his directions: py Cheshu, he will maintain his argument as well as any military man in the world, in the disciplines of the pristine wars of the Romans.

Enter MACMORRIS *and* JAMY.

JAMY. I say, gude-day, captain Fluellen.

FLU. God-den to your worship, goot captain James.

GOW. How now, captain Macmorris! have you quit the mines? have the pioneers given o'er?

MAC. By Chrish la, tish ill done; the work ish give over, the trompet sound the retreat. By my hand, I swear, and my father's soul, the work ish ill done; it ish give over: I would have blowed up the town, so Chrish save me, la, in an hour. O, tish ill done, tish ill done; by my hand, tish ill done!

FLU. Captain Macmorris, I peseech you now, will you voutsafe me, look you, a few disputations with you, as partly touching or concerning the disciplines of the war, the Roman wars, in the way of argument, look you, and friendly communication; partly, to satisfy my opinion, and partly, for the satisfaction, look you, of my mind, as touching the direction of the military discipline; that is the point.

JAMY. It sall be very gude, gude feith, gude captains baith: and I sall quit you with gude leve, as I may pick occasion; that sall I, mary.

MAC. It ish no time to discourse, so Chrish save me: the day ish hot, and the weather, and the wars, and the king, and the dukes; it ish no time to discourse. The town ish beseech'd, and the trompet call us to the breach; and we talk, and, by Chrish, do nothing; tish shame for us all: so God sa' me, tish shame to stand still; it ish shame, by my hand: and there ish throats to be cut, and works to be done; and there ish nothing done; so Chrish sa' me, la.

JAMY. By the mess, ere theise eyes of mine take themselves to slomber, aile do gude service, or aile ligge i'the grund for it; ay, or go to death; and aile pay't as valorously as I may, that sal I surely do, that is the breff and the long: mary, I wad full fain heard some question 'tween you tway.

FLU. Captain Macmorris, I think, look you, under your correction, there is not many of your nation——

MAC. Of my nation? What ish my nation? ish a villain, and a bastard, and a knave, and a rascal? What ish my nation? Who talks of my nation?[b]

FLU. Look you, if you take the matter otherwise than is meant, captain Macmorris, peradventure, I shall think you do not use me with that affability as in discretion you ought to use me, look you; peing as goot a man as yourself, both in the disciplines of wars, and in the derivation of my pirth, and in other particularities.

MAC. I do not know you so good a man as myself: so Chrish save me, I will cut off your head.

GOW. Gentlemen both, you will mistake each other.

JAMY. Au! that's a foul fault.

[*A parley sounded.*

---

[a] Carry coals.] See note (a), p. 159, Vol. I.

[b] *What ish my nation?* &c.] Mr. Knight suggests that by a common mistake in printing, the second and third lines were transposed, and that we should read,—"Who talks of my nation, ish a villain, and a bastard, and a knave, and a rascal." This is not unlikely; yet it is equally probable, that the incoherence of the original was designed to mark the impetuosity of the speaker.

GOW. The town sounds a parley.

FLU. Captain Macmorris, when there is more petter opportunity to be required, look you, I will pe so pold as to tell you, I know the disciplines of war; and there is an end.[a] [*Exeunt.*

SCENE III.—*The same. Before the Gates of* Harfleur.

The Governor *and some* Citizens *on the walls; the* English *Forces below. Enter* KING HENRY, *and his Train.*

K. HEN. How yet resolves the governor of the town?
This is the latest parle we will admit:
Therefore, to our best mercy give yourselves,
Or, like to men proud of destruction,
Defy us to our worst: for, as I am a soldier,
(A name, that, in my thoughts, becomes me best,)
If I begin the battery once again,
I will not leave the half-achieved Harfleur,
Till in her ashes she lie buried.
The gates of mercy shall be all shut up,
And the flesh'd soldier, rough and hard of heart,
In liberty of bloody hand, shall range
With conscience wide as hell; mowing like grass
Your fresh-fair virgins, and your flowering infants.
What is it then to me, if impious war,
Array'd in flames, like to the prince of fiends,
Do, with his smirch'd complexion, all fell feats
Enlink'd to waste and desolation?
What is't to me, when you yourselves are cause,
If your pure maidens fall into the hand
Of hot and forcing violation?
What rein can hold licentious wickedness,
When down the hill he holds his fierce career?
We may as bootless spend our vain command
Upon the enraged soldiers in their spoil,
As send precépts to the Leviathan
To come ashore. Therefore, you men of Harfleur,
Take pity of your town, and of your people,
Whiles yet my soldiers are in my command;
Whiles yet the cool and temperate wind of grace
O'erblows the filthy and contagious clouds
Of deadly * murder, spoil, and villainy.
If not, why, in a moment, look to see
The blind and bloody soldier, with foul hand,
Defile† the locks of your shrill-shrieking daughters;
Your fathers taken by the silver beards,
And their most reverend heads dash'd to the walls;
Your naked infants spitted upon pikes,
Whiles the mad mothers with their howls confus'd
Do break the clouds, as did the wives of Jewry,
At Herod's bloody-hunting slaughtermen.
What say you? will you yield, and this avoid?
Or, guilty in defence, be thus destroy'd?

GOV. Our expectation hath this day an end:
The Dauphin, whom of succours we entreated,
Returns us—that his powers are yet not ready
To raise so great a siege. Therefore, great king,
We yield our town and lives to thy soft mercy:
Enter our gates, dispose of us and ours,
For we no longer are defensible.

K. HEN. Open your gates.—Come, uncle Exeter,
Go you and enter Harfleur; there remain,
And fortify it strongly 'gainst the French:
Use mercy to them all. For us, dear uncle,—
The winter coming on, and sickness growing
Upon our soldiers,—we'll retire to Calais.
To-night in Harfleur will we be your guest,
To-morrow for the march are we address'd.
[*Flourish. The* KING, *&c. enter the Town.*

SCENE IV.—Rouen. *A Room in the Palace.*

Enter KATHARINE *and* ALICE.[b]

KATH. *Alice, tu as été en Angleterre, et tu parles bien le langage.*

ALICE. *Un peu, madame.*

KATH. *Je te prie, m'enseignez; il faut que j'apprenne à parler. Comment appelez-vous la main, en Anglais?*

ALICE. *La main? elle est appelée,* de hand.

KATH. De hand. *Et les doigts?*

ALICE. *Les doigts? ma foi, j'oublie les doigts; mais je me souviendrai. Les doigts? je pense, qu'ils sont appelés* de fingres; *oui,* de fingres.

KATH. *La main,* de hand! *les doigts,* de fingres. *Je pense, que je suis le bon écolier. J'ai gagné deux mots d'Anglais vîtement. Comment appelez-vous les ongles?*

ALICE. *Les ongles? les appelons,* de nails.

KATH. De nails. *Ecoutez; dites-moi, si je parle bien:* de hand, de fingres, *et* de nails.

ALICE. *C'est bien dit, madame; il est fort bon Anglais.*

KATH. *Dites-moi l'Anglais pour le bras.*

ALICE. De arm, *madame.*

KATH. *Et le coude.*

(*) Old text, *headly.* (†) Old text, *desire.*

[a] *And there is an end.*] This scene was well calculated to be effective in representation. The appearance at one time of an English, a Scotch, an Irish, and a Welsh man, could hardly fail to be an entertaining novelty on the early stage; but the profane gibberish put into the mouths of Irish characters in Shakespeare's day, would indicate but a very limited intercourse between this country and the sister Isle.

[b] Enter Katharine and Alice.] So the quarto: the folio, instead of Alice, has "*an old gentlewoman.*"

ALICE. De elbow.

KATH. De elbow. *Je m'en fais la répétition de tous les mots, que vous m'avez appris dès à présent.*

ALICE. *Il est trop difficile, madame, comme je pense.*

KATH. *Excusez-moi, Alice; écoutez:* de hand, de fingre, de nails, de arm, de bilbow.

ALICE. De elbow, *madame.*

KATH. *O Seigneur Dieu! je m'en oublie!* De elbow. *Comment appelez-vous le col?*

ALICE. De neck, *madame.*

KATH. De nick: *Et le menton?*

ALICE. De chin.

KATH. De sin. *Le col,* de nick: *le menton,* de sin.

ALICE. *Oui. Sauf votre honneur; en vérité, vous prononcez les mots aussi droit que les natifs d'Angleterre.*

KATH. *Je ne doute point d'apprendre par la grace de Dieu, et en peu de temps.*

ALICE. *N'avez-vous pas déjà oublié ce que je vous ai enseignée?*

KATH. *Non, je reciterai à vous promptement:* de hand, de fingre, de mails,—

ALICE. De nails, *madame.*

KATH. De nails, de arm, de ilbow.

ALICE. *Sauf votre honneur,* de elbow.

KATH. *Ainsi dis-je;* de elbow, de nick; *et* de sin: *Comment appelez-vous le pied et la robe?*

ALICE. De foot, *madame; et* de coun.

KATH. De foot, *et* de coun! *O Seigneur Dieu ces sont mots de son mauvais, corruptible, gros, et impudique, et non pour les dames d'honneur d'user: je ne voudrais prononcer ces mots devant les seigneurs de France, pour tout le monde. Il faut* de foot, *et* de coun, *néanmoins. Je reciterai une autre fois ma leçon ensemble:* de hand, de fingre, de nails, de arm, de elbow, de nick, de sin, de foot, de coun.

ALICE. *Excellent, madame!*

KATH. *C'est assez pour une fois; allons-nous à dîner.* [*Exeunt.*

SCENE V.—*The same. Another Room in the same.*

Enter KING CHARLES, *the* DAUPHIN, DUKE *of* BOURBON, *the* Constable *of* France, *and others.*

K. CHA. 'T is certain, he hath pass'd the river Somme.

CON. An if he be not fought withal, my lord,
Let us not live in France; let us quit all,
And give our vineyards to a barbarous people.

DAU. *O Dieu vivant!* shall a few sprays of us,—
The emptying of our fathers' luxury,
Our scions, put in wild and savage stock,
Spirt up so suddenly into the clouds,
And overlook their grafters?

BOUR. Normans, but bastard Normans, Norman bastards!
Mort de ma vie! if they march along
Unfought withal, but I will sell my dukedom,
To buy a slobbery and a dirty farm
In that nook-shotten[a] isle of Albion.

CON. *Dieu de battailes!* where have they this mettle?
Is not their climate foggy, raw, and dull?
On whom, as in despite, the sun looks pale,
Killing their fruit with frowns? Can sodden water,
A drench for sur-rein'd jades,[b] their barley broth,
Decoct their cold blood to such valiant heat?
And shall our quick blood, spirited with wine,
Seem frosty? O, for honour of our land,
Let us not hang like roping icicles
Upon our houses' thatch, whiles a more frosty people
Sweat drops of gallant youth in our rich fields;
Poor—we may* call them, in their native lords.

DAU. By faith and honour,
Our madams mock at us, and plainly say,
Our mettle is bred out; and they will give
Their bodies to the lust of English youth,
To new-store France with bastard-warriors.

BOUR. They bid us—to the English dancing-schools,
And teach lavoltas high, and swift corantos;(1)
Saying, our grace is only in our heels,
And that we are most lofty runaways.

K. CHA. Where is Montjoy the herald? speed him hence;
Let him greet England with our sharp defiance.—
Up, princes! and, with spirit of honour edg'd
More sharper than your swords, hie to the field:
Charles De-la-bret,[c] high-constable of France;
You dukes of Orleans, Bourbon, and of Berri,
Alençon, Brabant, Bar, and Burgundy;
Jaques Chatillon, Rambures, Vaudemont,
Beaumont, Grandpré, Roussi, and Fauconberg,
Foix,[d] Lestrale, Bouciqualt, and Charolois;
High dukes, great princes, barons, lords, and knights,[e]
For your great seats, now quit you of great shames.
Bar Harry England, that sweeps through our land
With pennons painted in the blood of Harfleur:
Rush on his host, as doth the melted snow
Upon the valleys, whose low vassal seat
The Alps doth spit and void his rheum upon:
Go down upon him,—you have power enough,—
And in a captive chariot, into Rouen
Bring him our prisoner.

CON. This becomes the great.
Sorry am I, his numbers are so few,
His soldiers sick, and famish'd in their march;
For, I am sure, when he shall see our army,
He'll drop his heart into the sink of fear,
And, for[f] achievement, offer us his ransom.

KING CHA. Therefore, lord constable, haste on Montjoy,
And let him say to England, that we send
To know what willing ransom he will give.—
Prince Dauphin, you shall stay with us in Rouen.

DAU. Not so, I do beseech your majesty.

K. CHA. Be patient, for you shall remain with us.—
Now, forth, lord constable, and princes all,
And quickly bring us word of England's fall.
[*Exeunt.*

SCENE VI.—*The* English *Camp in* Picardy.

Enter, severally, GOWER *and* FLUELLEN.

GOW. How now, captain Fluellen? come you from the bridge?

FLU. I assure you, there is very excellent services committed at the pridge.

GOW. Is the duke of Exeter safe?

(*) Old text omits, *may*.

[a] Nook-shotten—] "*Shotten,*" according to Warburton, "signifies any thing *projected;* so *nook-shotten isle,* is an isle that shoots out into capes, promontories, and necks of land, the very figure of Great Britain." "Nook-shotten isle," however, may mean only, *an isle, flung in a corner.*

[b] Sur-rein'd—] Perhaps, *over-ridden.*

[c] *Charles* De-la-bret,—] Correctly, "Charles D'Albret," but Shakespeare followed Holinshed, who calls the Constable *Delabreth.*

[d] Foix,—] The old text has Loys, which was not the name of any French house of distinction, in the books of that time.

[e] Knights,—] Old text, *kings;* altered by Theobald.

[f] *And,* for *achievement,*—] Should we not read, "And *'fore* achievement?" The import being, At sight of our army he will be so intimidated, as to offer us his ransom *before* we have captured him. In Act IV. Sc. 3, Henry says,—

"Bid them *achieve* me, and then sell my bones."

FLU. The duke of Exeter is as magnanimous as Agamemnon; and a man that I love and honour with my soul, and my heart, and my duty, and my life, and my living, and my uttermost power: he is not, (Got pe praised and plessed!) any hurt in the 'orld; but keeps the pridge most valiantly, with excellent discipline. There is an auncient lieutenant[a] there at the pridge,—I think, in my very conscience, he is as valiant a man as Mark Antony; and he is a man of no estimation in the 'orld; put I did see him do as gallant service.

GOW. What do you call him?

FLU. He is called—auncient Pistol.

GOW. I know him not.

Enter PISTOL.

FLU. Here is the man.

PIST. Captain, I thee beseech to do me favours:
The duke of Exeter doth love thee well.

FLU. Ay, I praise Got; and I have merited some love at his hands.

PIST. Bardolph, a soldier, firm and sound of heart,
*Of buxom[b] valour, hath,—by cruel fate,
And giddy Fortune's furious fickle wheel,—
That goddess blind,
That stands upon the rolling restless stone,—

FLU. Py your patience, auncient Pistol. Fortune is painted plind, with a muffler pefore her† eyes, to signify to you that fortune is plind, and she is painted also with a wheel, to signify to you, which is the moral of it, that she is turning, and inconstant, and mutability, and variation: and her foot, look you, is fixed upon a spherical stone, which rolls, and rolls, and rolls;—in good truth, the poet is make[c] a most excellent description of it: Fortune, look you,[d] is an excellent moral.

PIST. Fortune is Bardolph's foe, and frowns on him;
For he hath stol'n a *pax*,(2) and hanged must 'a be.
A damned death!
Let gallows gape for dog, let man go free,
And let not hemp his wind-pipe suffocate;
But Exeter hath given the doom of death,
For *pax* of little price.
Therefore, go speak, the duke will hear thy voice;
And let not Bardolph's vital thread be cut
With edge of penny cord, and vile reproach:
Speak, captain, for his life, and I will thee requite.

FLU. Auncient Pistol, I do partly understand your meaning.

PIST. Why then rejoice therefore.

FLU. Certainly, auncient, it is not a thing to rejoice at: for if, look you, he were my prother, I would desire the duke to use his goot pleasure, and put him to executions; for disciplines[e] ought to be used.

PIST. Die and be damn'd; and *figo*[f] for thy friendship!

FLU. It is well.

PIST. The fig of Spain![g] [*Exit* PISTOL.

FLU. Very goot.

GOW. Why, this is an arrant counterfeit rascal; I remember him now; a bawd, a cutpurse.

FLU. I'll assure you, 'a utter'd as prave 'ords at the pridge, as you shall see in a summer's day: but it is very well; what he has spoke to me, that is well, I warrant you, when time is serve.

GOW. Why, 'tis a gull, a fool, a rogue, that now and then goes to the wars, to grace himself, at his return into London, under the form of a soldier. And such fellows are perfect in the great commanders' names: and they will learn you by rote, where services were done;—at such and such a sconce, at such a breach, at such a convoy; who came off bravely, who was shot, who disgraced, what terms the enemy stood on; and this they con perfectly in the phrase of war, which they trick up with new-tuned oaths: and what a beard of the general's cut,(3) and a horrid suit of the camp, will do among foaming bottles, and ale-washed wits, is wonderful to be thought on! but you must learn to know such slanders of the age, or else you may be marvellously mistook.

FLU. I tell you what, captain Gower;—I do perceive, he is not the man that he would gladly

(*) Old text prefixes, *And*.
(†) First folio, *afore his*.

[a] *An* auncient lieutenant—] If Fluellen were not designed to blunder, we may suppose that *lieutenant* having been inadvertently inserted in the first instance, and *ancient* afterwards interlineated, both by accident got printed in the text. The quartos read,

"There is an *ensigne* there."

[b] Buxom *valour*,—] The earliest meaning of this word was, *pliant, yielding, obedient*; but in Shakespeare's time it was commonly used in the sense it appears to bear here, and in "Pericles," Act I. (Gower) that of *lusty, sprightly, buoyant*.

[c] The poet is make—] Thus the quartos; the folio has, "the poet makes," &c.

[d] Look you,—] These words are found only in the quartos.

[e] To executions; for disciplines, &c.] In the folio, to *execution*; for *discipline*, &c. As Mr. Knight both here and in other instances in the present scene has adopted, though silently, the reading of the quartos, it is not uncharitable to suppose that his objection to such a proceeding on the part of his brother-editors was a little more strongly expressed than felt.

[f] *An*! figo *for thy friendship*!] This is simply "a *fig* for thy friendship;" as in the "Merry Wives of Windsor," Act I. Sc. 3, he says, "A *fico* for the phrase;" there is no allusion apparently to the loathsome gesticulation mentioned in note (c), p. 160, Vol. I.

[g] The fig of Spain!] From the corresponding passage in the quartos,—"the fig of Spain *within thy jaw*," and "the fig within thy *bowels and thy dirty maw*,"—Pistol obviously refers here to the custom of administering poisoned figs, which appears to have been but too common both in Spain and Italy at one time:—

"It may fall out that thou shalt be entic'd
To sup sometimes with a magnifico,
And have a *fico* foisted in thy dish."
GASCOIGNE'S *Poems*.

Where a quibble was perhaps intended between magni*fico* and *fico*. So also in Vittoria Corombona:—

"I look now for a *Spanish fig*, or an Italian sallad daily."

make show to the 'orld he is; if I find a hole in his coat, I will tell him my mind. [*Drum heard.*] Hark you, the king is coming; and I must speak with him from the pridge.

Enter KING HENRY, GLOUCESTER, *and* Soldiers.[a]

FLU. Got pless your majesty!

K. HEN. How now, Fluellen? cam'st thou from the bridge?

FLU. Ay, so please your majesty. The duke of Exeter has very gallantly maintained the pridge: the French is gone off, look you, and there is gallant and most prave passages: marry, th' athversary was have possession of the pridge, but he is enforced to retire, and the duke of Exeter is master of the pridge: I can tell your majesty, the duke is a prave man.

K. HEN. What men have you lost, Fluellen?

FLU. The perdition of th' athversary hath been very great, reasonable great: marry, for my part, I think the duke hath lost never a man, but one that is like to be executed for robbing a church, one Bardolph, if your majesty know the man: his face is all bubukles, and whelks, and knobs, and flames of fire; and his lips plows at his nose, and it is like a coal of fire, sometimes plue, and sometimes red: but his nose is executed, and his fire's out.

K. HEN. We would have all such offenders so cut off:—and we give express charge, that, in our marches through the country, there be nothing compelled from the villages, nothing taken but paid for; none of the French upbraided, or abused in disdainful language; for when lenity and cruelty play for a kingdom, the gentler gamester is the soonest winner.

Tucket sounds. *Enter* MONTJOY.

MONT. You know me by my habit.

K. HEN. Well then, I know thee. What shall I know of thee?

MONT. My master's mind.

K. HEN. Unfold it.

MONT. Thus says my king:—Say thou to Harry of England: Though we seemed dead, we did but sleep; advantage is a better soldier than rashness. Tell him, we could have rebuked him at Harfleur, but that we thought not good to bruise an injury, till it were full ripe:—now we speak upon our cue, and our voice is imperial. England shall repent his folly, see his weakness, and admire our sufferance. Bid him, therefore, consider of his ransom; which must proportion the losses we have borne, the subjects we have lost, the disgrace we have digested; which, in weight to re-answer, his pettiness would bow under. For our losses, his exchequer is too poor; for the effusion of our blood, the muster of his kingdom too faint a number; and for our disgrace, his own person kneeling at our feet, but a weak and worthless satisfaction. To this add—defiance: and tell him, for conclusion, he hath betrayed his followers, whose condemnation is pronounced. So far my king and master; so much my office.

K. HEN. What is thy name? I know thy quality.

MONT. Montjoy.

K. HEN. Thou dost thy office fairly. Turn thee back,
And tell thy king,—I do not seek him now,
But could be willing to march on to Calais
Without impeachment:[b] for, to say the sooth,
(Though 'tis no wisdom to confess so much
Unto an enemy of craft and vantage,)
My people are with sickness much enfeebled;
My numbers lessen'd; and those few I have,
Almost no better than so many French;
Who when they were in health, I tell thee, herald,
I thought, upon one pair of English legs
Did march three Frenchmen,—Yet, forgive me, [God,
That I do brag thus!—this your air of France
Hath blown that vice in me; I must repent.
Go, therefore, tell thy master, here I am;
My ransom, is this frail and worthless trunk,
My army, but a weak and sickly guard;
Yet, God before,[c] tell him we will come on,
Though France himself, and such another neighbour,
Stand in our way. There's for thy labour, Montjoy.(4)
Go, bid thy master well advise himself:
If we may pass, we will; if we be hinder'd,
We shall your tawny ground with your red blood
Discolour: and so, Montjoy, fare you well.
The sum of all our answer is but this:
We would not seek a battle as we are,
Nor, as we are, we say, we will not shun it;
So tell your master.

MONT. I shall deliver so. Thanks to your highness. [*Exit* MONTJOY.

GLO. I hope, they will not come upon us now.

K. HEN. We are in God's hand, brother, not in theirs.
March to the bridge; it now draws toward night:—
Beyond the river we 'll encamp ourselves,
And on to-morrow bid them march away.
[*Exeunt.*

[a] *And Soldiers.*] The folio has, "*Enter the King and his poor souldiers.*"

[b] Impeachment:] *Hindrance.*

[c] Yet, God before,—] See note (b), page 71.

SCENE VII.—*The* French *Camp, near* Agincourt.

Enter the CONSTABLE *of* FRANCE, *the* DUKE *of* ORLEANS, *the* DAUPHIN, *the* LORD RAMBURES, *and others.*

CON. Tut! I have the best armour of the world.
Would it were day!

ORL. You have an excellent armour; but let my horse have his due.

CON. It is the best horse of Europe.

ORL. Will it never be morning?

DAU. My lord of Orleans, and my lord high-constable, you talk of horse and armour,—

ORL. You are as well provided of both, as any prince in the world.

DAU. What a long night is this!——I will not change my horse with any that treads but on four pasterns.[a] *Ça, ha!** He bounds from the earth, as if his entrails were hairs; *le cheval volant,* the Pegasus, *qui a les narines de feu!* When I bestride him, I soar, I am a hawk: he trots the air; the earth sings when he touches it; the basest horn of his hoof is more musical than the pipe of Hermes.

ORL. He's of the colour of the nutmeg.

DAU. And of the heat of the ginger. It is a a beast for Perseus: he is pure air and fire, and the dull elements of earth and water never appear in him, but only in patient stillness while his rider mounts him: he is, indeed, a horse, and all other jades[b] you may call—beasts.

CON. Indeed, my lord, it is a most absolute and excellent horse.

DAU. It is the prince of palfreys; his neigh is like the bidding of a monarch, and his countenance enforces homage.

ORL. No more, cousin.

DAU. Nay, the man hath no wit, that cannot, from the rising of the lark to the lodging of the lamb, vary deserved praise on my palfrey; it is a theme as fluent as the sea; turn the sands into eloquent tongues, and my horse is argument for them all: 'tis a subject for a sovereign to reason on, and for a sovereign's sovereign to ride on; and for the world (familiar to us, and unknown,) to lay apart their particular functions, and wonder at him. I once writ a sonnet in his praise, and began thus: *Wonder of nature,*—

ORL. I have heard a sonnet begin so to one's mistress.

DAU. Then did they imitate that which I composed to my courser; for my horse is my mistress.

ORL. Your mistress bears well.

DAU. Me well; which is the prescript praise and perfection of a good and particular mistress.

CON. Nay, for methought yesterday your mistress shrewdly shook your back.

DAU. So, perhaps, did yours.

CON. Mine was not bridled.

DAU. O! then, belike, she was old and gentle; and you rode, like a kerne of Ireland, your French hose off, and in your strait strossers.

CON. You have good judgment in horsemanship.

DAU. Be warned by me, then: they that ride so, and ride not warily, fall into foul bogs; I had rather have my horse to my mistress.

CON. I had as lief have my mistress a jade.

DAU. I tell thee, constable, my mistress wears his[c] own hair.

CON. I could make as true a boast as that, if I had a sow to my mistress.

DAU. *Le chien est retourné à son propre vomissement, et la truie lavée au bourbier:* thou makest use of any thing.

CON. Yet do I not use my horse for my mistress; or any such proverb, so little kin to the purpose.

RAM. My lord constable, the armour, that I saw in your tent to-night,—are those stars, or suns, upon it?

CON. Stars, my lord.

DAU. Some of them will fall to-morrow, I hope.

CON. And yet my sky shall not want.

DAU. That may be, for you bear a many superfluously, and 'twere more honour, some were away.

CON. Even as your horse bears your praises, who would trot as well, were some of your brags dismounted.

DAU. Would I were able to load him with his desert!—Will it never be day? I will trot to-morrow a mile, and my way shall be paved with English faces.

CON. I will not say so, for fear I should be faced out of my way: but I would it were morning, for I would fain be about the ears of the English.

RAM. Who will go to hazard with me for twenty prisoners?

CON. You must first go yourself to hazard, ere you have them.

(*) Old copy, *ch, ha'.*

[a] *On four* pasterns.] So the folio, 1632, correcting the error of its predecessor, which has, *postures.*

[b] *And all other* jades *you may call—beasts.*] *Jade,* it may be noticed, was not invariably applied to a horse in a depreciatory sense.

[c] His *own hair.*] So the folio. In the quartos we have, "*her* own hair." *His* may have been used f.r the impersonal pronoun, *its.*

DAU. 'T is midnight, I'll go arm myself. [*Exit.*

ORL. The Dauphin longs for morning.

RAM. He longs to eat the English.

CON. I think he will eat all he kills.

ORL. By the white hand of my lady, he's a gallant prince.

CON. Swear by her foot, that she may tread out the oath.

ORL. He is, simply, the most active gentleman of France.

CON. Doing is activity, and he will still be doing.[a]

ORL. He never did harm that I heard of.

CON. Nor will do none to-morrow; he will keep that good name still.

ORL. I know him to be valiant.

CON. I was told that, by one that knows him better than you.

ORL. What's he?

CON. Marry, he told me so himself; and he said, he cared not who knew it.

ORL. He needs not, it is no hidden virtue in him.

CON. By my faith, sir, but it is; never any body saw it, but his lackey: 'tis a hooded valour, and when it appears it will bate.[b]

ORL. *Ill-will never said well.*

CON. I will cap that proverb with—*There is flattery in friendship.*[c]

ORL. And I will take up that with—*Give the devil his due.*

CON. Well placed; there stands your friend for the devil; have at the very eye of that proverb, with—*A pox of the devil.*

ORL. You are the better at proverbs, by how much—*A fool's bolt is soon shot.*

CON. You have shot over.

ORL. 'Tis not the first time you were overshot.

Enter a Messenger.

MESS. My lord high-constable, the English lie within fifteen hundred paces of your tents.

CON. Who hath measured the ground?

MESS. The lord Grandpré.

CON. A valiant and most expert gentleman.—Would it were day!—Alas, poor Harry of England! he longs not for the dawning, as we do.

ORL. What a wretched and peevish fellow is this king of England, to mope with his fat-brained followers so far out of his knowledge!

CON. If the English had any apprehension, they would run away.

ORL. That they lack: for if their heads had any intellectual armour, they could never wear such heavy head-pieces.

RAM. That island of England breeds very valiant creatures; their mastiffs are of unmatchable courage.

ORL. Foolish curs, that run winking into the mouth of a Russian bear, and have their heads crushed like rotten apples! You may as well say,—that's a valiant flea, that dare eat his breakfast on the lip of a lion.

CON. Just, just; and the men do sympathize with the mastiffs, in robustious and rough coming on, leaving their wits with their wives: and then give them great meals of beef, and iron and steel, they will eat like wolves, and fight like devils.

ORL. Ay, but these English are shrewdly out of beef.

CON. Then shall we find to-morrow—they have only stomachs to eat, and none to fight. Now is it time to arm; come, shall we about it?

ORL. It is now two o'clock: but, let me see,—
by ten,
We shall have each a hundred Englishmen.
[*Exeunt.*

---

a *He will* still be doing.] He will *always* be doing. This was a familiar saying; *doing* being used equivocally.

b 'Tis a hooded valour, and when it appears it will bate.] The allusion is to the ordinary action of a hawk when unhooded, which is to beat and flutter with its wings; but a quibble may be intended between *bate*, the hawking technical, and *bate*, to *dwindle*, *abate*, &c.

c *There is* flattery *in friendship.*] The usual form of the proverb is, "There is *falsehood* in friendship."

Enter Chorus.

Now entertain conjecture of a time
When creeping murmur and the poring dark
Fills the wide vessel of the universe.
From camp to camp, through the foul womb of night,
The hum of either army stilly[a] sounds,
That the fix'd sentinels almost receive
The secret whispers of each other's watch.
Fire answers fire, and through their paly flames
Each battle sees the other's umber'd[b] face:
Steed threatens steed, in high and boastful neighs
Piercing the night's dull ear; and from the tents,
The armourers, accomplishing the knights,(1)
With busy hammers closing rivets up,
Give dreadful note of preparation.
The country cocks do crow, the clocks do toll,
And the third hour of drowsy morning name.*
Proud of their numbers, and secure in soul,
The confident and over-lusty French
Do the low-rated English play at dice;
And chide the cripple tardy-gaited night,
Who, like a foul and ugly witch, doth limp
So tediously away. The poor condemned English,
Like sacrifices, by their watchful fires
Sit patiently, and inly ruminate
The morning's danger; and their gesture sad,
Investing[c] lank-lean cheeks, and war-worn coats,
Presenteth† them unto the gazing moon
So many horrid ghosts. O, now, who will behold
The royal captain of this ruin'd band,
Walking from watch to watch, from tent to tent,
Let him cry,—Praise and glory on his head!

(*) Old copy, *nam'd*. (†) Old copy, *Presented*.

a Stilly *sounds*,—] That is, *gently*, *softly* sounds. The word recals an illustration of "*still* music," which properly belonged to note (e), p. 370, Vol. I. but was there accidentally omitted, taken from "A true reportarie of the most triumphant and royal accomplishment of the Baptisme of the most excellent, right high and mightie Prince, Frederik Henry," &c. &c. 1594:—"After which ensued a *still* noyse of recorders and flutes."

b Umber'd face:] That is, *shadowed* face.

c Investing—] This has no meaning; might we read *Infestive?*

For forth he goes, and visits all his host;
Bids them good morrow, with a modest smile;
And calls them—brothers, friends, and countrymen.
Upon his royal face there is no note,
How dread an army hath enrounded him;
Nor doth he dedicate one jot of colour
Unto the weary and all-watched night;
But freshly looks, and over-bears attaint,
With cheerful semblance, and sweet majesty;
That every wretch, pining and pale before,
Beholding him, plucks comfort from his looks:
A largess universal, like the sun,
His liberal eye doth give to every one,
Thawing cold fear. Then,[a] mean and gentle all
Behold, as may unworthiness define,
A little touch of Harry in the night;[b]
And so our scene must to the battle fly,
Where, (O for pity!) we shall much disgrace—
With four or five most vile and ragged foils,
Right ill dispos'd, in brawl ridiculous,—
The name of Agincourt. Yet, sit and see,
Minding true things, by what their mockeries be.
[*Exit.*

ACT IV.

SCENE I.—*The* English *Camp at* Agincourt.

Enter KING HENRY, BEDFORD, *and* GLOUCESTER.

K. HEN. Gloster, 'tis true, that we are in great danger,
The greater therefore should our courage be.—
Good morrow, brother Bedford. God Almighty!
There is some soul of goodness in things evil,
Would men observingly distil it out;
For our bad neighbour makes us early stirrers,
Which is both healthful, and good husbandry:
Besides, they are our outward consciences,
And preachers to us all; admonishing,
That we should dress[c] us fairly for our end:

---

a Then, *mean and gentle all,*—] This is the reading adopted by Theobald; the folio having,—"*that* mean and gentle all," which, as "*mean and gentle all*" clearly refers to the audience, and not to the soldiers, must be an error.

b *In the* night;] Is it not more than probable the poet wrote, "in the *fight?*" We have already seen "a touch of Harry in the *night*."

c Dress *us*—] That is, *prepare* us.

Thus may we gather honey from the weed,
And make a moral of the devil himself.

Enter ERPINGHAM.

Good morrow, old sir Thomas Erpingham:
A good soft pillow for that good white head
Were better than a churlish turf of France.

ERP. Not so, my liege; this lodging likes me better,
Since I may say—Now lie I like a king.

K. HEN. 'Tis good for men to love their present pains;
Upon example so, the spirit is eased:
And, when the mind is quicken'd, out of doubt,
The organs, though defunct and dead before,
Break up their drowsy grave, and newly move
With casted slough and fresh legerity.
Lend me thy cloak, sir Thomas.—Brothers both,
Commend me to the princes in our camp;
Do my good morrow to them, and, anon,
Desire them all to my pavilion.

GLO. We shall, my liege.
[*Exeunt* GLOUCESTER *and* BEDFORD.

ERP. Shall I attend your grace?

K. HEN. No, my good knight;
Go with my brothers to my lords of England:
I and my bosom must debate awhile,
And then I would no other company.

ERP. The Lord in heaven bless thee, noble Harry! [*Exit* ERPINGHAM.

K. HEN. God-a-mercy, old heart! thou speak'st cheerfully.

Enter PISTOL.

PIST. *Qui va là?*

K. HEN. A friend.

PIST. Discuss unto me; art thou officer?
Or art thou base, common, and popular?

K. HEN. I am a gentleman of a company.

PIST. Trail'st thou the puissant pike?

K. HEN. Even so. What are you?

PIST. As good a gentleman as the emperor.

K. HEN. Then you are a better than the king.

PIST. The king's a bawcock, and a heart of gold,
A lad of life, an imp of fame;[a]
Of parents good, of fist most valiant:
I kiss his dirty shoe, and from heart-strings
I love the lovely bully. What's thy name?

K. HEN. Harry *le Roy*.

PIST. *Le Roy!* a Cornish name: art thou of Cornish crew?

K. HEN. No, I am a Welshman.

PIST. Know'st thou Fluellen?

K. HEN. Yes.

PIST. Tell him, I'll knock his leek about his pate,
Upon saint David's day.

K. HEN. Do not you wear your dagger in your cap that day, lest he knock that about yours.

PIST. Art thou his friend?

K. HEN. And his kinsman too.

PIST. The *figo* for thee, then!

K. HEN. I thank you: God be with you!

PIST. My name is Pistol call'd. [*Exit.*

K. HEN. It sorts well with your fierceness. [*Retires.*

Enter FLUELLEN *and* GOWER, *severally.*

GOW. Captain Fluellen!

FLU. So! in the name of Cheshu Christ, speak lower.[b] It is the greatest admiration in the universal 'orld, when the true and auncient prerogatifes and laws of the wars is not kept: if you would take the pains but to examine the wars of Pompey the great, you shall find, I warrant you, that there is no tiddle-taddle, nor pibble-pabble, in Pompey's camp; I warrant you, you shall find the ceremonies of the wars, and the cares of it, and the forms of it, and the sobriety of it, and the modesty of it, to be otherwise.

GOW. Why, the enemy is loud; you hear him all night.

FLU. If the enemy is an ass and a fool, and a prating coxcomb, is it meet, think you, that we should also, look you, be an ass, and a fool, and a prating coxcomb; in your own conscience now?

GOW. I will speak lower.

FLU. I pray you, and peseech you, that you will. [*Exeunt* GOWER *and* FLUELLEN.

K. HEN. Though it appear a little out of fashion,
There is much care and valour in this Welshman.

Enter BATES, COURT, *and* WILLIAMS.[c]

COURT. Brother John Bates, is not that the morning which breaks yonder?

---

[a] *An imp of fame;*] Primitively, *imp* means shoot, and here a *son*. Pistol applies the same expression to the King in the Second Part of "Henry IV." Act V. Sc. 5:—

"The heavens thee guard and keep, most royal *imp* of *fame*."

[b] *Speak* lower.] So the quarto 1608. That of 1600 reads *lewer*; while the folio has *fewer*. It is evident from Gower's reply, that *lower* is correct.

[c] Bates, Court, and Williams.] The old stage-direction runs, "*Enter three souldiers, John Bates, Alexander Court, and Michael Williams.*"

BATES. I think it be, but we have no great cause to desire the approach of day.

WILL. We see yonder the beginning of the day, but, I think, we shall never see the end of it.—Who goes there?

K. HEN. A friend.

WILL. Under what captain serve you?

K. HEN. Under sir Thomas* Erpingham.

WILL. A good old commander, and a most kind gentleman: I pray you, what thinks he of our estate?

K. HEN. Even as men wrecked upon a sand, that look to be washed off the next tide.

BATES. He hath not told his thought to the king?

K. HEN. No; nor it is not meet he should. For, though I speak it to you, I think the king is but a man, as I am: the violet smells to him, as it doth to me; the element shows to him, as it doth to me; all his senses have but human conditions; his ceremonies laid by, in his nakedness he appears but a man; and though his affections are higher mounted than ours, yet, when they stoop, they stoop with the like wing; therefore when he sees reason of fears, as we do, his fears, out of doubt, be of the same relish as ours are: yet, in reason, no man should possess him with any appearance of fear, lest he, by showing it, should dishearten his army.

BATES. He may show what outward courage he will; but, I believe, as cold a night as 'tis, he could wish himself in Thames up to the neck; and so I would he were, and I by him, at all adventures, so we were quit here.

K. HEN. By my troth, I will speak my conscience of the king; I think he would not wish himself any where but where he is.

BATES. Then I would he were here alone; so should he be sure to be ransomed, and a many poor men's lives saved.

K. HEN. I dare say, you love him not so ill, to wish him here alone, howsoever you speak this, to feel other men's minds: methinks, I could not die any where so contented, as in the king's company; his cause being just, and his quarrel honourable.

WILL. That's more than we know.

BATES. Ay, or more than we should seek after; for we know enough, if we know we are the king's subjects: if his cause be wrong, our obedience to the king wipes the crime of it out of us.

WILL. But if the cause be not good, the king himself hath a heavy reckoning to make, when all those legs, and arms, and heads, chopped off in a battle, shall join together at the latter day, and cry all—We died at such a place; some swearing, some crying for a surgeon, some, upon their wives left poor behind them; some, upon the debts they owe; some, upon their children rawly left. I am afeard there are few die well, that die in a battle; for how can they charitably dispose of any thing, when blood is their argument? Now, if these men do not die well, it will be a black matter for the king that led them to it; who to disobey, were against all proportion of subjection.

K. HEN. So, if a son, that is by his father sent about merchandise, do sinfully miscarry upon the sea, the imputation of his wickedness, by your rule, should be imposed upon his father that sent him: or if a servant, under his master's command, transporting a sum of money, be assailed by robbers, and die in many irreconciled iniquities, you may call the business of the master the author of the servant's damnation. But this is not so: the king is not bound to answer the particular endings of his soldiers, the father of his son, nor the master of his servant; for they purpose not their death, when they purpose their services. Besides, there is no king, be his cause never so spotless, if it come to the arbitrement of swords, can try it out with all unspotted soldiers: some, peradventure, have on them the guilt of premeditated and contrived[a] murder; some, of beguiling virgins with the broken seals of perjury; some, making the wars their bulwark, that have before gored the gentle bosom of peace with pillage and robbery. Now, if these men have defeated the law, and outrun native punishment, though they can outstrip men, they have no wings to fly from God: war is his beadle; war is his vengeance; so that here men are punished, for before-breach of the king's laws, in now the king's quarrel: where they feared the death, they have borne life away, and where they would be safe, they perish: then if they die unprovided, no more is the king guilty of their damnation, than he was before guilty of those impieties for the which they are now visited. Every subject's duty is the king's, but every subject's soul is his own. Therefore should every soldier in the wars do as every sick man in his bed,—wash every mote out of his conscience; and dying so, death is to him advantage; or not dying, the time was blessedly lost, wherein such preparation was gained: and in him that escapes, it were not sin to think, that making God so free an offer, he let him outlive that day to see his greatness, and to teach others how they should prepare.

WILL. 'Tis certain, every man that dies ill, the ill upon his own head, the king is not to answer it.

BATES. I do not desire he should answer for me, and yet I determine to fight lustily for him.

(*) Old copy, *John*.

[a] Contrived *murder*;] *Plotted, preconcerted* murder. Thus, in "Othello," Act I. Sc. 2:—

"Yet do I hold it very stuff o' th' conscience,
To do no *contriv'd* murder."

K. HEN. I myself heard the king say, he would not be ransomed.

WILL. Ay, he said so, to make us fight cheerfully; but, when our throats are cut, he may be ransomed, and we ne'er the wiser.

K. HEN. If I live to see it, I will never trust his word after.

WILL. 'Mass,* you pay him then! That's a perilous shot out of an elder-gun, that a poor and private displeasure can do against a monarch! you may as well go about to turn the sun to ice with fanning in his face with a peacock's feather. You'll *never trust his word after!* come, 'tis a foolish saying.

K. HEN. Your reproof is something too round; I should be angry with you, if the time were convenient.

WILL. Let it be a quarrel between us, if you live.

K. HEN. I embrace it.

WILL. How shall I know thee again?

K. HEN. Give me any gage of thine, and I will wear it in my bonnet; then, if ever thou darest acknowledge it, I will make it my quarrel.

WILL. Here's my glove; give me another of thine.

K. HEN. There.

WILL. This will I also wear in my cap; if ever thou come to me and say, after to-morrow, *This is my glove,* by this hand, I will take thee a box on the ear.

K. HEN. If ever I live to see it, I will challenge it.

WILL. Thou darest as well be hanged.

K. HEN. Well, I will do it, though I take thee in the king's company.

WILL. Keep thy word: fare thee well.

BATES. Be friends, you English fools, be friends; we have French quarrels enow, if you could tell how to reckon.

K. HEN. Indeed, the French may lay twenty French crowns to one, they will beat us; for they bear them on their shoulders: but it is no English treason, to cut French crowns, and, to-morrow, the king himself will be a clipper.

[*Exeunt* Soldiers.

Upon the king! let us our lives, our souls,
Our debts, our careful wives,
Our children, and our sins, lay on the king;—
We must bear all.
O hard condition! twin-born with greatness,
Subject to the breath of every fool, whose sense
No more can feel, but his own wringing!
What infinite heart's-ease must kings neglect,
That private men enjoy?
And what have kings, that privates have not too,
Save ceremony, save general ceremony?
And what art thou, thou idol ceremony?[a]
What kind of god art thou, that suffer'st more
Of mortal griefs, than do thy worshippers?
What are thy rents? what are thy comings-in?
O ceremony, show me but thy worth!
What is thy soul, O adoration?[b]
Art thou aught else but place, degree, and form,
Creating awe and fear in other men?
Wherein thou art less happy being fear'd,
Than they in fearing.
What drink'st thou oft, instead of homage sweet,
But poison'd flattery? O, be sick, great greatness,
And bid thy ceremony give thee cure!
Think'st thou the fiery fever will go out
With titles blown from adulation?
Will it give place to flexure and low bending?
Can'st thou, when thou command'st the beggar's knee,
Command the health of it? No, thou proud dream,
That play'st so subtly with a king's repose;
I am a king, that find thee; and I know,
'Tis not the balm, the sceptre, and the ball,
The sword, the mace, the crown imperial,
The intertissu'd robe of gold and pearl,
The farced title running 'fore the king,
The throne he sits on, nor the tide of pomp
That beats upon the high shore of this world,—
No, not all these, thrice-gorgeous ceremony,
Not all these, laid in bed majestical,
Can sleep so soundly as the wretched slave,
Who, with a body fill'd, and vacant mind,
Gets him to rest, cramm'd with distressful[c] bread;
Never sees horrid night, the child of hell;
But, like a lackey, from the rise to set,
Sweats in the eye of Phœbus, and all night
Sleeps in Elysium; next day, after dawn,
Doth rise, and help Hyperion to his horse;
And follows so the ever-running year
With profitable labour, to his grave:
And, but for ceremony, such a wretch,
Winding up days with toil, and nights with sleep,
Had the fore-hand and vantage of a king.
The slave, a member of the country's peace,
Enjoys it; but in gross brain little wots,
What watch the king keeps to maintain the peace,
Whose hours the peasant best advantages.

(*) First folio omits, *'Mass.*

[a] Ceremony?] See note (c), p. 23.

[b] What is thy soul, O adoration?] The folio reads,—

"What? is thy Soule of Odoration?"

We adopt the easy emendation, proposed by Dr. Johnson, which gives a clear and forcible meaning to what, in the original, is inexplicable.

[c] *Gets him to rest, cramm'd with* distressful *bread;*] Mr. Collier's remorseless annotator substitutes, "*distasteful* bread." If any change were needed, "*disrestful* bread" would be more in Shakespeare's manner; but "*distressful* bread," *the hard fare of poverty,* is strikingly expressive, and better than anything suggested in its stead.

Enter Erpingham.

Erp. My lord, your nobles, jealous of your absence,
Seek through your camp to find you.
K. Hen. Good old knight,
Collect them all together at my tent:
I'll be before thee.
Erp. I shall do't, my lord. [*Exit.*
K. Hen. O God of battles! steel my soldiers' hearts;
Possess them not with fear; take from them now
The sense of reck'ning, if[a] the opposed numbers
Pluck their hearts from them!—Not to-day, O Lord,
O, not to-day, think not upon the fault
My father made in compassing the crown!
I Richard's body have interred new,
And on it have bestow'd more contrite tears,
Than from it issued forced drops of blood.
Five hundred poor I have in yearly pay,
Who twice a day their wither'd hands hold up

a ——— Take from them now
The sense of reck'ning, if the opposed numbers
Pluck their hearts from them!—Not to-day, O Lord,
O, not to-day, think not upon the fault, &c.]

In the second line, which the folio prints,—

"The sense of reck'ning *of* th' opposed numbers:"

Tyrwhitt first suggested *if* for *of*;—the reading we adopt. Mr. Singer and Mr. Knight exhibit the passage as follows:—

"——— Take from them now
The sense of reckoning of the opposed numbers!
Pluck their hearts from them not to-day, O Lord,
O not to-day! Think not upon the fault," &c.

Toward heaven, to pardon blood; and I have built
Two chantries, where the sad and solemn priests
Sing still[a] for Richard's soul. More will I do:
Though all that I can do, is nothing worth,
Since that my penitence comes after all,
Imploring pardon.

Enter GLOUCESTER.

GLO. My liege!
K. HEN. My brother Gloster's voice?—Ay;
I know thy errand, I will go with thee:—
The day, my friends,* and all things stay for me.
[*Exeunt.*

SCENE II.—*The* French *Camp.*

Enter the DAUPHIN, ORLEANS, RAMBURES, *and others.*

ORL. The sun doth gild our armour; up, my lords!
DAU. *Montez à cheval;*—My horse! *varlet! lacquay!* ha!
ORL. O brave spirit!
DAU. *Via!—les eaux et la terre,*——
ORL. *Rien puis? l'air et le feu,*——
DAU. *Ciel!* cousin Orleans.——

Enter Constable.

Now, my lord Constable!
CON. Hark, how our steeds for present service neigh!
DAU. Mount them, and make incision in their hides,
That their hot blood may spin in English eyes,
And dout[b] them with superfluous courage. Ha!
RAM. What, will you have them weep our horses' blood?
How shall we then behold their natural tears?

(*) First folio, *friend*.

[a] *Sing* still *for Richard's soul.*] That is, sing *ever*.

[b] *And* dout *them with superfluous courage.*] Meaning, *do out*, *extinguish* them. The folio has, "*doubt* them;" which Mr. Collier and Mr. Singer retain in the sense of *awe*, or *make them afraid*. Mr. Knight also reads *doubt*, although, in "Hamlet," Act IV Sc. 7,—

"I have a speech of fire that faine would blaze,
But that this folly *doubts* it;"—

he changes *doubts* to *douts*.

Enter a Messenger.

MESS. The English are embattled, you French peers.

CON. To horse, you gallant princes! straight to horse!
Do but behold yond poor and starved band,
And your fair show shall suck away their souls,
Leaving them but the shales and husks of men.
There is not work enough for all our hands;
Scarce blood enough in all their sickly veins,
To give each naked curtle-axe a stain,
That our French gallants shall to-day draw out,
And sheath for lack of sport. Let us but blow on them,
The vapour of our valour will o'erturn them.
'Tis positive 'gainst all exceptions, lords,
That our superfluous lackeys, and our peasants,—
Who, in unnecessary action, swarm
About our squares of battle,—were enow
To purge this field of such a hilding foe,
Though we, upon this mountain's basis by
Took stand for idle speculation:
But that our honours must not. What's to say?
A very little-little let us do,
And all is done. Then let the trumpets sound
The tucket-sonance, and the note to mount;
For our approach shall so much dare the field,
That England shall couch down in fear, and yield.

Enter GRANDPRE.

GRAND. Why do you stay so long, my lords of France?
Yond island carrions,(1) desperate of their bones,
Ill-favour'dly become the morning field:
Their ragged curtains poorly are let loose,
And our air shakes them passing scornfully.
Big Mars seems bankrupt in their beggar'd host,
And faintly through a rusty beaver peeps.
The horsemen sit like fixed candlesticks,
With torch-staves in their hand: and their poor jades
Lob down their heads, dropping the hides and hips,
The gum down-roping from their pale-dead eyes,
And, in their pale dull mouths, the gimmal-bit[a]
Lies foul with chaw'd grass, still and motionless;
And their executors, the knavish crows,
Fly o'er them, all impatient for their hour.
Description cannot suit itself in words,
To demonstrate the life of such a battle
In life so lifeless as it shows itself.

CON. They have said their prayers, and they stay for death.

DAU. Shall we go send them dinners and fresh suits,
And give their fasting horses provender,
And after fight with them?

CON. I stay but for my guard;[b] on, to the field:
I will the banner from a trumpet take,
And use it for my haste. Come, come away!
The sun is high, and we outwear the day.
[*Exeunt.*

SCENE III.—*The* English *Camp.*

Enter the English *Host;* GLOUCESTER, BEDFORD, EXETER, SALISBURY, *and* WESTMORELAND.

GLO. Where is the king?

BED. The king himself is rode to view their battle.

WEST. Of fighting men they have full three-score thousand.

EXE. There's five to one; besides, they all are fresh.

SAL. God's arm strike with us! 'tis a fearful odds.
God buy'[c] you, princes all; I'll to my charge:
If we no more meet, till we meet in heaven,
Then, joyfully,—my noble lord of Bedford,—
My dear lord Gloster,—and my good lord Exeter,—
And my kind kinsman,—warriors all, adieu!

BED. Farewell, good Salisbury, and good luck go with thee!

EXE. Farewell, kind lord; fight valiantly to-day:
And yet I do thee wrong to mind thee of it,[d]
For thou art fram'd of the firm truth of valour.
[*Exit* SALISBURY.

BED. He is as full of valour, as of kindness,
Princely in both.

WEST. O that we now had here

---

[a] *The* gimmal-*bit*—] Spelt *Iymold*, in the old text. A bit in two parts; and so called from the Latin *gemellus, double* or *twinned*.

[b] *I stay but for my* guard; on, *&c.*] A correspondent of Mr. Knight's ingeniously suggests, what certainly seems called for by the context, that we ought to read,—

"I stay but for my *guidon*.—To the field!"

The emendation is enforced, too, by a passage in Holinshed, where, speaking of the French, he says,—"They thought themselves so sure of victory, that diverse of the noblemen made such haste towards the battle, that they left many of their servants and *men of war* behind them, and some of them would not once *stay for their standards;* as amongst other the Duke of Brabant, when his standard was not come, caused a *banner* to be taken from a *trumpet*, and fastened to a speare, the which he commanded to be borne before him, instead of a standard."

[c] God buy' *you, princes all;*] *God buy'* is the same as our "Good-bye,"—a corruption of "*God be with you;*" and in this instance, for the sake of the metre, the old form of it should be retained.

[d] And yet I do thee wrong, &c.] The last two lines in this speech are annexed to the preceding one of Bedford in the folio: the present arrangement was suggested by Thirlby.

Enter KING HENRY.

But one ten thousand of those men in England,
That do no work to-day!
K. HEN. What's he, that wishes so?
My cousin Westmoreland?—No, my fair cousin:
If we are mark'd to die, we are enow
To do our country loss; and if to live,
The fewer men, the greater share of honour.
God's will! I pray thee, wish not one man more.
By Jove, I am not covetous for gold,
Nor care I, who doth feed upon my cost;
It yearns me not, if men my garments wear;
Such outward things dwell not in my desires:
But, if it be a sin to covet honour,
I am the most offending soul alive.
No, 'faith, my coz, wish not a man from England:
God's peace! I would not lose so great an honour,
As one man more, methinks, would share from me,
For the best hope I have. O, do not wish one more!
Rather proclaim it, Westmoreland, through my host,
That he which hath no stomach to this fight,
Let him depart; his passport shall be made,
And crowns for convoy put into his purse:
We would not die in that man's company,
That fears his fellowship to die with us.
This day is call'd—the feast of Crispian: (2)
He that outlives this day, and comes safe home,
Will stand a tip-toe when this day is nam'd,
And rouse him at the name of Crispian.
He that outlives this day, and sees old age,[a]
Will yearly on the vigil feast his friends,*
And say, To-morrow is saint Crispian:
Then will he strip his sleeve, and show his scars,
And say, These wounds I had on Crispin's day.[b]
Old men forget; yet all shall be forgot,
But he'll remember, with advantages,
What feats he did that day. Then shall our names,
Familiar in their mouths as household words,—[c]
Harry the king, Bedford and Exeter,
Warwick and Talbot, Salisbury and Gloster,—
Be in their flowing cups freshly remember'd.
This story shall the good man teach his son;
And Crispin Crispian shall ne'er go by
From this day to the ending of the world,
But we in it shall be remembered,—
We few, we happy few, we band of brothers;
For he to-day that sheds his blood with me,
Shall be my brother; be he ne'er so vile,
This day shall gentle his condition:[d]
And gentlemen in England, now a-bed,
Shall think themselves accurs'd, they were not here;
And hold their manhoods cheap, whiles any speaks,
That fought with us upon saint Crispin's day.

Re-enter SALISBURY.

SAL. My sovereign lord, bestow yourself with speed:
The French are bravely in their battles set,
And will with all expedience charge on us.
K. HEN. All things are ready, if our minds be so.
WEST. Perish the man, whose mind is backward now!
K. HEN. Thou dost not wish more help from England, coz?
WEST. God's will, my liege, would you and I alone!
Without more help, could fight this royal battle!
K. HEN. Why, now thou hast unwish'd five thousand men,
Which likes me better, than to wish us one.—
You know your places: God be with you all!

Tucket. Enter MONTJOY.

MONT. Once more I come to know of thee, king Harry,
If for thy ransom thou wilt now compound,
Before thy most assured overthrow:
For, certainly, thou art so near the gulf,
Thou needs must be englutted. Besides, in mercy,
The constable desires thee thou wilt mind
Thy followers, of repentance; that their souls
May make a peaceful and a sweet retire
From off these fields, where, wretches, their poor bodies
Must lie and fester.
K. HEN. Who hath sent thee now?
MONT. The constable of France.
K. HEN. I pray thee, bear my former answer back;
Bid them achieve me, and then sell my bones.

(*) First folio, *neighbours*.

[a] He that outlives this day, and sees old age,—] This is from the quartos, and is surely preferable to the lection of the folio:—

"He that shall see this day, and live old age."

[b] And say, These wounds I had on Crispin's day.] This line is found only in the quartos.

[c] *Familiar in* their mouths *as household words,*—] So the quartos. In the folio the line runs,—

"Familiar in *his mouth* as household words."

[d] Shall gentle his condition:] "King Henry V. inhibited any person but such as had a right by inheritance, or grant, to assume coats of arms, except those who fought with him at the battle of Agincourt; and, I think, these last were allowed the chief seats of honour at all feasts and publick meetings."—TOLLET.

Good God! why should they mock poor fellows thus?
The man that once did sell the lion's skin
While the beast liv'd, was kill'd with hunting him.
A many of our bodies shall no doubt
Find native graves; upon the which, I trust,
Shall witness live in brass[a] of this day's work:
And those that leave their valiant bones in France,
Dying like men, though buried in your dunghills,
They shall be fam'd; for there the sun shall greet them,
And draw their honours reeking up to heaven,
Leaving their earthly parts to choke your clime,
The smell whereof shall breed a plague in France.
Mark, then, abounding valour in our English;
That, being dead, like to the bullet's grazing,*
Break out into a second course of mischief,
Killing in relapse of mortality.
Let me speak proudly;—Tell the constable
We are but warriors for the working day:
Our gayness and our gilt are all besmirch'd
With rainy marching in the painful field;
There's not a piece of feather in our host,
(Good argument, I hope, we will not fly,)
And time hath worn us into slovenry:
But, by the mass, our hearts are in the trim:
And my poor soldiers tell me—yet ere night
They'll be in fresher robes, or they will pluck
The gay new coats o'er the French soldiers' heads,
And turn them out of service. If they do this,
(As, if God please, they shall,) my ransom then
Will soon be levied. Herald, save thou thy labour;
Come thou no more for ransom, gentle herald;
They shall have none, I swear, but these my joints,—
Which if they have as I will leave 'em them,
Shall yield them little, tell the constable.

MONT. I shall, king Harry. And so, fare thee well:
Thou never shalt hear herald any more. [*Exit.*

K. HEN. I fear thou wilt once more come again for ransom.[b]

Enter the DUKE *of* YORK.

YORK. My lord, most humbly on my knee I beg
The leading of the vaward.

K. HEN. Take it, brave York.—Now, soldiers, march away:—
And how thou pleasest, God, dispose the day! [*Exeunt.*

SCENE IV.—*The Field of Battle.*

Alarums; Excursions. Enter PISTOL, French Soldier, *and* Boy.

PIST. Yield, cur!

FR. SOL. *Je pense, que vous êtes le gentilhomme de bonne qualité.*

PIST. *Quality! cality!* construe me,[c] art thou a gentleman? What is thy name? discuss!

FR. SOL. *O seigneur Dieu!*

PIST. *O signieur Dew* should be a gentleman:—
Perpend my words, O signieur Dew, and mark;—
O signieur Dew, thou diest on point of fox,[d]
Except, O signieur, thou do give to me
Egregious ransom.

FR. SOL. *O, prennez miséricorde! ayez pitié de moi!*

PIST. Moy shall not serve, I will have forty [moys;
For I will fetch thy rim[e] out at thy throat,
In drops of crimson blood.

FR. SOL. *Est-il impossible d'échapper la force de ton bras?*

PIST. Brass, cur!
Thou damned and luxurious mountain goat,
Offer'st me brass?

FR. SOL. *O pardonnez-moi!*

PIST. Say'st thou me so? is that a ton of [moys?—
Come hither, boy; ask me this slave in French,
What is his name.

BOY. *Ecoutez; comment etes-vous appelé?*

FR. SOL. *Monsieur le Fer.*

(*) Old text, *crasing.*

[a] *Shall witness live in brass*—] The effigy, engraved on brass, of John Leventhorp, Esq. one of the heroes of Agincourt, who died in 1433, still remains in Sawbridgeworth church, Herts.

[b] I fear thou wilt once more come again for ransom.] This is not in the quartos; and the folio has,—

"I fear thou wilt once more come again for *a* ransom."

[c] *Quality! cality!* construe me, art thou a gentleman?] In the folio (the line is not found in the quartos) this is printed,—"*Qualitie calmie custure me.*" Malone, having met with "A Sonet of a Lover in the Praise of his Lady, to *Calen o custure me*, sung at every line's end," concluded that the incomprehensible jargon of the folio was nothing else than this very burden, and he accordingly gave the line,—

"Quality? Calen o custure me."

Subsequently, Boswell discovered that "Callino, castore me" is an old Irish song, still preserved in Playford's "Musical Companion." The line is now, therefore, usually printed,—

"*Quality? Callino, castore me!*"

This solution of the difficulty is certainly curious and very captivating; but to us the idea of Pistol holding a prisoner by the throat and quoting the fag end of a ballad at the same moment, is too preposterous, and in default of any better explanation of the mysterious syllables, we have adopted that of Warburton.

[d] *On point of* fox,—] The modern editors all agree in informing us that "*Fox* was an old cant word for a sword;" but why a sword was so called none of them appears to have been aware. The name was given from the circumstance that Andrea Ferrara, and, since his time, other foreign sword-cutlers, adopted a fox as the blade-mark of their weapons. Swords, with a running-fox rudely engraved on the blades, are still occasionally to be met with in the old curiosity-shops of London.

[e] *For I will fetch thy* rim *out at thy throat,*—] *Rim* was a term formerly used, not very definitively, for a part of the intestines; but Pistol's *rim* (the folio spells it *rymme*) was, perhaps, as Mr. Knight conjectured, no more than a word coined for the nonce, in mimickry of the Frenchman's guttural pronunciation.

Boy. He says, his name is—master Fer.

Pist. *Master Fer!* I'll fer him, and firk him, and ferret him:—discuss the same in French unto him.

Boy. I do not know the French for *fer*, and *ferret*, and *firk*.

Pist. Bid him prepare, for I will cut his throat.

Fr. Sol. *Que dit-il, monsieur?*

Boy. *Il me commande de vous dire que vous faites vous prêt; car ce soldat ici est disposé tout à cette heure de couper votre gorge.*

Pist. *Oui, coupe le gorge, par ma foi, pesant,*
Unless thou give me crowns, brave crowns;
Or mangled shalt thou be by this my sword.

Fr. Sol. *O, je vous supplie, pour l'amour de Dieu, me pardonner! Je suis gentilhomme de bonne maison: gardez ma vie, et je vous donnerai deux cents écus.*

Pist. What are his words?

Boy. He prays you to save his life: he is a gentleman of a good house, and for his ransom, he will give you two hundred crowns.

Pist. Tell him my fury shall abate,
And I the crowns will take.

Fr. Sol. *Petit monsieur, que dit-il?*

Boy. *Encore qu'il est contre son jurement de pardonner aucun prisonnier; néanmoins, pour les écus que vous l'avez promis, il est content de vous donner la liberté, le franchisement.*

Fr. Sol. *Sur mes genoux, je vous donne mille remercimens: et je m'estime heureux que je suis tombé entre les mains d'un chevalier, je pense, le plus brave, vaillant, et très distingué seigneur d'Angleterre.*

Pist. Expound unto me, boy.

Boy. He gives you, upon his knees, a thousand thanks: and he esteems himself happy that he hath fallen into the hands of one, (as he thinks,) the most brave, valorous, and thrice-worthy signieur of England.

Pist. As I suck blood, I will some mercy show.—
Follow me! [*Exit* Pistol.

Boy. *Suivez-vous le grand capitaine.*

[*Exit* French Soldier.

I did never know so full a voice issue from so empty a heart: but the saying is true,—The empty vessel makes the greatest sound. Bardolph and Nym had ten times more valour than this roaring devil i' the old play, that every one may pare his nails with a wooden dagger;(3) and they are both hanged; and so would this be, if he durst steal any thing adventurously. I must stay with the lackeys, with the luggage of our camp: the French might have a good prey of us, if he knew of it; for there is none to guard it, but boys.

[*Exit.*

SCENE V.—*Another Part of the Field.*

Alarums. Enter the DAUPHIN, ORLEANS, BOURBON, CONSTABLE, RAMBURES, *and others.*

CON. *O diable!*

ORL. *O seigneur!—le jour est perdu, tout est perdu!*

DAU. *Mort de ma vie!* all is confounded, all!
Reproach and everlasting shame
Sits mocking in our plumes.—*O méchante fortune!*
Do not run away. [*A short alarum.*

CON. Why, all our ranks are broke.

DAU. O perdurable shame!—let's stab ourselves.
Be these the wretches that we play'd at dice for?

ORL. Is this the king we sent to for his ransom?

BOUR. Shame, and eternal shame, nothing but shame!
Let's die in honour:[a] once more back again;
And he that will not follow Bourbon now,
Let him go hence, and, with his cap in hand,
Like a base pander hold the chamber-door,
Whilst by a slave,* no gentler than my dog,
His fairest daughter is contaminate.†

CON. Disorder, that hath spoil'd us, friend us now!
Let us, on heaps, go offer up our lives
Unto these English, or else die with fame.[b]

ORL. We are enow, yet living in the field,
To smother up the English in our throngs,
If any order might be thought upon.

BOUR. The devil take order now! I'll to the throng;
Let life be short: else, shame will be too long!
[*Exeunt.*

SCENE VI.—*Another Part of the Field.*

Alarums. Enter KING HENRY *and Forces;* EXETER, *and others.*

K. HEN. Well have we done, thrice-valiant countrymen;
But all's not done, yet keep the French the field.

EXE. The duke of York commends him to your majesty.

K. HEN. Lives he, good uncle? thrice, within this hour,
I saw him down; thrice up again, and fighting;
From helmet to the spur, all blood he was.

EXE. In which array, (brave soldier,) doth he lie,
Larding the plain: and by his bloody side,
(Yoke-fellow to his honour-owing wounds,)
The noble earl of Suffolk also lies.
Suffolk first died: and York, all haggled o'er,
Comes to him, where in gore he lay insteep'd,
And takes him by the beard; kisses the gashes,
That bloodily did yawn upon his face;
And* cries aloud,—*Tarry, dear† cousin Suffolk!*
My soul shall thine keep company to heaven:
Tarry, sweet soul, for mine, then fly a-breast,
As, in this glorious and well-foughten field,
We kept together in our chivalry!
Upon these words I came, and cheer'd him up:
He smil'd me in the face, raught me his hand,
And, with a feeble gripe, says,—*Dear my lord,*
Commend my service to my sovereign.
So did he turn, and over Suffolk's neck
He threw his wounded arm, and kiss'd his lips;
And so, espous'd to death, with blood he seal'd
A testament of noble-ending love.
The pretty and sweet manner of it forc'd
Those waters from me, which I would have stopp'd;
But I had not so much of man in me,
And all my mother came into mine eyes,
And gave me up to tears.

K. HEN. I blame you not;
For, hearing this, I must perforce compound
With mistful‡ eyes, or they will issue too.—
[*Alarum.*
But, hark! what new alarum is this same?—
The French have reinforc'd their scatter'd men:—
Then every soldier kill his prisoners; (4)
Give the word through. [*Exeunt.*

SCENE VII.—*Another Part of the Field.*

Alarums. Enter FLUELLEN *and* GOWER.

FLU. Kill the poys and the luggage! 'tis expressly against the law of arms: 'tis as arrant a piece of knavery, mark you now, as can pe offered; in your conscience now, is it not?

GOW. 'Tis certain, there's not a boy left alive; and the cowardly rascals, that ran from the battle, have done this slaughter: besides, they have burned and carried away all that was in the king's tent; wherefore the king, most worthily, hath caused every soldier to cut his prisoner's throat. O, 'tis a gallant king!

FLU. Ay, he was porn at Monmouth, captain Gower: what call you the town's name, where Alexander the pig was porn?

(*) First folio, *whilst a base slave.*
(†) First folio, *contaminated.*

(*) First folio, *He.* (†) First folio, *my.*
(‡) Old text, *mixtful.*

[a] Let's die in honour:] In the folio, the passage stands,—
"*Let us dye in once more backe againe.*"
The reading of the text, which was suggested by Mr. Knight, is supported by a line in the corresponding scene of the quartos:—
"*Let's dye with honor, our shame doth last too long.*"

[b] Unto these English, or else die with fame.] This line is not in the folio.

Gow. Alexander the great.

Flu. Why, I pray you, is not pig, great? The pig, or the great, or the mighty, or the huge, or the magnanimous, are all one reckonings, save the phrase is a little variations.

Gow. I think Alexander the great was born in Macedon; his father was called—Philip of Macedon, as I take it.

Flu. I think it is in Macedon, where Alexander is porn. I tell you, captain, if you look in the maps of the 'orld, I warrant, you sall find, in the comparisons petween Macedon and Monmouth, that the situations, look you, is poth alike. There is a river in Macedon; and there is also moreover a river at Monmouth: it is called Wye, at Monmouth; put it is out of my prains, what is the name of the other river: put 'tis all one, 'tis alike as my fingers is to my fingers, and there is salmons in poth. If you mark Alexander's life well, Harry of Monmouth's life is come after it indifferent well, for there is figures in all things. Alexander (Got knows, and you know,) in his rages, and his furies, and his wraths, and his cholers, and his moods, and his displeasures, and his indignations, and also peing a little intoxicates in his prains, did, in his ales and his angers, look you, kill his pest friend, Clytus.

Gow. Our king is not like him in that; he never killed any of his friends.

Flu. It is not well done, mark you now, to take the tales out of my mouth, ere it is made an end* and finished. I speak put in the figures and comparisons of it: as Alexander killed his friend Clytus, peing in his ales and his cups; so also Harry Monmouth, peing in his right wits and his goot judgments, turned away the fat knight with the great pelly doublet: he was full of jests, and gipes, and knaveries, and mocks; I have forgot his name.

Gow. Sir John Falstaff.

Flu. That is he: I'll tell you, there is goot men porn at Monmouth.

Gow. Here comes his majesty.

Alarum. Enter King Henry, *with a part of the* English *Forces;* Warwick, Gloucester, Exeter, *and others.*

K. Hen. I was not angry since I came to France,
Until this instant.—Take a trumpet, herald;
Ride thou unto the horsemen on yond hill;
If they will fight with us, bid them come down,
Or void the field: they do offend our sight:
If they 'll do neither, we will come to them,
And make them skir away, as swift as stones
Enforced from the old Assyrian slings:
Besides, we 'll cut the throats of those we have;
And not a man of them that we shall take,
Shall taste our mercy:—Go, and tell them so.

Exe. Here comes the Herald of the French, my liege.

Glo. His eyes are humbler than they us'd to be.

Enter Montjoy.

K. Hen. How now! what means this, herald? know'st thou not,
That I have fin'd these bones of mine for ransom?
Com'st thou again for ransom?

Mont. No, great king:
I come to thee for charitable licence,
That we may wander o'er this bloody field,
To book[a] our dead, and then to bury them;
To sort our nobles from our common men,—
For many of our princes (woe the while!)
Lie drown'd and soak'd in mercenary blood;
(So do our vulgar drench their peasant limbs
In blood of princes;) and their* wounded steeds
Fret fetlock deep in gore, and with wild rage
Yerk out their armed heels at their dead masters,
Killing them twice. O, give us leave, great king,
To view the field in safety, and dispose
Of their dead bodies.

K. Hen. I tell thee truly, herald,
I know not if the day be ours or no;
For yet a many of your horsemen peer
And gallop o'er the field.

Mont. The day is yours.

K. Hen. Praised be God, and not our strength, for it!—
What is this castle call'd, that stands hard by?

Mont. They call it—Agincourt.

K. Hen. Then call we this the field of Agincourt,
Fought on the day of Crispin Crispianus.

Flu. Your grandfather of famous memory, an 't please your majesty, and your great-uncle

(*) First folio omits, *an end.*

(*) Old text, *with.*

a *To book our dead,*—] Mr. Collier's annotator reads "to *look* our dead," which is at least a very plausible emendation. Thus, in "The Merry Wives of Windsor," Act IV. Sc. 2,—

"Mistress Page and I *will look some linen* for your head."

Again, in "As You Like It," Act II. Sc. 5,—

"He hath been all this day *to look you.*"

And again, in "All's Well That Ends Well," Act III. Sc. 6,—

"I must go *look my twigs.*"

To book our dead, was, however, we have no doubt, the poet's phrase.

Edward the plack prince of Wales, as I have read in the chronicles, fought a most prave pattle here in France.

K. HEN. They did, Fluellen.

FLU. Your majesty says very true. It your majesties is remembered of it, the Welshmen did goot service in a garden where leeks did grow, wearing leeks in their Monmouth caps, which, your majesty know, to this hour is an honourable padge of the service: and, I do pelieve, your majesty takes no scorn to wear the leek upon saint Tavy's day.

K. HEN. I wear it for a memorable honour:
For I am Welsh, you know, good countryman.

FLU. All the water in Wye cannot wash your majesty's Welsh plood out of your pody, I can tell you that: Got pless it and preserve it, as long as it pleases his grace, and his majesty too!

K. HEN. Thanks, good my countryman.*

FLU. By Cheshu, I am your majesty's countryman, I care not who know it; I will confess it to all the 'orld: I need not be ashamed of your majesty, praised pe God, so long as your majesty is an honest man.

K. HEN. God† keep me so!—Our heralds go with him;
Bring me just notice of the numbers dead
On both our parts. Call yonder fellow hither.
[*Points to* WILLIAMS. *Exeunt* MONTJOY, *and others.*

EXE. Soldier, you must come to the king.

K. HEN. Soldier, why wear'st thou that glove in thy cap?

WILL. An't please your majesty, 't is the gage of one that I should fight withal, if he be alive.

K. HEN. An Englishman?

WILL. An't please your majesty, a rascal, that swaggered with me last night: who, if 'a live, and ever dare to challenge this glove, I have sworn to take him a box o' the ear: or, if I can see my glove in his cap, (which he swore, as he was a soldier, he would wear, if alive,) I will strike it out soundly.

K. HEN. What think you, captain Fluellen? is it fit this soldier keep his oath?

FLU. He is a craven and a villain else, an't please your majesty, in my conscience.

K. HEN. It may be his enemy is a gentleman of great sort, quite from the answer of his degree.

FLU. Though he pe as goot a gentleman as the tevil is, as Lucifer and Pelzebub himself, it is necessary, look your grace, that he keep his vow and his oath: if he pe perjured, see you now, his reputation is as arrant a villain, and a Jack-sauce, as ever his plack shoe trod upon Got's ground and his earth, in my conscience, la.

(*) First folio, *countrymen.* (†) First folio, *Good.*

K. HEN. Then keep thy vow, sirrah, when thou meet'st the fellow.

WILL. So I will, my liege, as I live.

K. HEN. Who servest thou under?

WILL. Under captain Gower, my liege.

FLU. Gower is a goot captain, and is goot knowledge and literatured in the wars.

K. HEN. Call him hither to me, soldier.

WILL. I will, my liege. [*Exit.*

K. HEN. Here, Fluellen; wear thou this favour for me, and stick it in thy cap: when Alençon and myself were down together, I plucked this glove from his helm: if any man challenge this, he is a friend to Alençon, and an enemy to our person; if thou encounter any such, apprehend him, an thou dost me love.

FLU. Your grace does me as great honours, as can be desired in the hearts of his subjects: I would fain see the man, that has put two legs, that shall find himself aggriefed at this glove, that is all; put I would fain see it once; an please Got of his grace, that I might see.

K. HEN. Knowest thou Gower?

FLU. He is my dear friend, an please you.

K. HEN. Pray thee, go seek him, and bring him to my tent.

FLU. I will fetch him. [*Exit.*

K. HEN. My lord of Warwick,—and my brother Gloster,
Follow Fluellen closely at the heels:
The glove which I have given him for a favour,
May haply purchase him a box o' the ear;
It is the soldier's; I, by bargain, should
Wear it myself. Follow, good cousin Warwick:
If that the soldier strike him, (as, I judge
By his blunt bearing, he will keep his word,)
Some sudden mischief may arise of it;
For I do know Fluellen valiant,
And, touch'd with choler, hot as gunpowder,
And quickly will return an injury:
Follow, and see there be no harm between them.—
Go you with me, uncle of Exeter. [*Exeunt.*

SCENE VIII.—*Before* King Henry's *Pavilion.*

Enter GOWER *and* WILLIAMS.

WILL. I warrant it is to knight you, captain.

Enter FLUELLEN.

FLU. Got's will and his pleasure, captain, I peseech you now, come apace to the king: there is more goot toward you, peradventure, than is in your knowledge to dream of.

WILL. Sir, know you this glove?

FLU. Know the glove? I know the glove is a glove.

WILL. I know this, and thus I challenge it. [*Strikes him.*

FLU. 'Splud, an arrant traitor, as any's in the universal 'orld, or in France, or in England.

GOW. How now. sir? you villain!

WILL. Do you think I'll be forsworn?

FLU. Stand away, captain Gower; I will give treason his payment into plows, I warrant you.

WILL. I am no traitor.

FLU. That's a lie in thy throat.—I charge you in his majesty's name, apprehend him; he's a friend of the duke Alençon's.

Enter WARWICK *and* GLOUCESTER.

WAR. How now! how now! what's the matter?

FLU. My lord of Warwick, here is (praised be Got for it!) a most contagious treason come to light, look you, as you shall desire in a summer's day. Here is his majesty.

Enter KING HENRY *and* EXETER.

K. HEN. How now! what's the matter?

FLU. My liege, here is a villain and a traitor, that, look your grace, has struck the glove which your majesty is take out of the helmet of Alençon.

WILL. My liege, this was my glove; here is the fellow of it: and he, that I gave it to in change, promised to wear it in his cap; I promised to strike him, if he did: I met this man with my glove in his cap, and I have been as good as my word.

FLU. Your majesty hear now (saving your majesty's manhood,) what an arrant, rascally, peggarly, lousy knave it is: I hope your majesty is pear me testimony, and witness, and will avouchment that this is the glove of Alençon, that your majesty is give me, in your conscience, now.

K. HEN. Give me thy glove, soldier; look, here is the fellow of it.
'T was I, indeed, thou promised'st to strike;
And thou hast given me most bitter terms.

FLU. An please your majesty, let his neck answer for it, if there is any martial law in the 'orld.

K. HEN. How canst thou make me satisfaction?

WILL. All offences, my liege,* come from the heart: never came any from mine, that might offend your majesty.

K. HEN. It was ourself thou didst abuse.

WILL. Your majesty came not like yourself: you appeared to me but as a common man; witness the night, your garments, your lowliness; and what your highness suffered under that shape, I beseech you, take it for your own fault, and not mine: for had you been as I took you for, I made no offence; therefore, I beseech your highness, pardon me.

K. HEN. Here, uncle Exeter, fill this glove with crowns,
And give it to this fellow.—Keep it, fellow,
And wear it for an honour in thy cap,
Till I do challenge it.—Give him the crowns:—
And, captain, you must needs be friends with him.

FLU. Py this day and this light, the fellow has mettle enough in his pelly.—Hold, there is twelve-pence for you, and I pray you to serve Got, and keep you out of prawls, and prabbles, and quarrels, and dissensions, and I warrant you, it is the petter for you.

WILL. I will none of your money.

FLU. It is with a goot will; I can tell you, it will serve you to mend your shoes: come, wherefore should you be so pashful? your shoes is not so goot: 'tis a goot silling, I warrant you, or I will change it.

Enter an English Herald.

K. HEN. Now, herald; are the dead number'd?

HER. Here is the number of the slaughter'd French. [*Delivers a paper.*

K. HEN. What prisoners of good sort are taken, uncle?

EXE. Charles duke of Orleans, nephew to the king;
John duke of Bourbon, and lord Bouciqualt:
Of other lords and barons, knights and squires,
Full fifteen hundred, besides common men.

K. HEN. This note doth tell me of ten thousand French,
That in the field lie slain: of princes, in this number,
And nobles bearing banners, there lie dead
One hundred twenty-six: added to these,
Of knights, esquires, and gallant gentlemen,
Eight thousand and four hundred; of the which,
Five hundred were but yesterday dubb'd knights:
So that, in these ten thousand they have lost,
There are but sixteen hundred mercenaries;
The rest are princes, barons, lords, knights, squires,
And gentlemen of blood and quality.
The names of those their nobles that lie dead,—
Charles De-la-bret, high-constable of France;
Jaques of Chatillon, admiral of France;
The master of the cross-bows, lord Rambures;
Great-master of France, the brave sir Guischard Dauphin;
John duke of Alençon; Antony duke of Brabant,

(*) First folio, my *Lord.*

The brother to the duke of Burgundy;
And Edward duke of Bar: of lusty earls,
Grandpré, and Roussi, Fauconberg and Foix,
Beaumont, and Marle, Vaudemont, and Lestrale.
Here was a royal fellowship of death!——
Where is the number of our English dead?
[Herald *presents another paper.*
Edward the duke of York, the earl of Suffolk,
Sir Richard Ketly, Davy Gam, esquire:
None else of name; and, of all other men,
But five and twenty. O God, thy arm was here,
And not to us, but to thy arm alone,
Ascribe we all!—When, without stratagem,
But in plain shock and even play of battle,
Was ever known so great and little loss,
On one part and on th' other?—Take it, God,
For it is none but thine!

EXE. 'Tis wonderful!

K. HEN. Come, go we* in procession to the village:
And be it death proclaimed through our host,
To boast of this, or take that praise from God,
Which is his only.

FLU. Is it not lawful, an please your majesty, to tell how many is killed?

K. HEN. Yes, captain; but with this acknowledgment,
That God fought for us.

FLU. Yes, my conscience, he did us great goot.

K. HEN. Do we all holy rites;
Let there be sung *Non nobis*, and *Te Deum*.(5)
The dead with charity enclos'd in clay,
And then to Calais; and to England then,
Where ne'er from France arriv'd more happy men.
[*Exeunt.*

(*) First folio, *me*.

Enter CHORUS.

Vouchsafe to those that have not read the story,
That I may prompt them: and of such as have,
I humbly pray them to admit th' excuse
Of time, of numbers, and due course of things,
Which cannot in their huge and proper life
Be here presented. Now we bear the king
Toward Calais: grant him there; there seen,
Heave him away upon your winged thoughts,
Athwart the sea: behold, the English beach
Pales in the flood with men, and* wives, and boys,
Whose shouts and claps out-voice the deep-mouth'd sea,
Which, like a mighty whiffler(1) 'fore the king,
Seems to prepare his way: so let him land,
And solemnly see him set on to London.
So swift a pace hath thought, that even now
You may imagine him upon Blackheath:
Where that his lords desire him, to have borne
His bruised helmet and his bended sword,
Before him through the city, he forbids it;
Being free from vainness and self-glorious pride;
Giving full trophy, signal, and ostent,
Quite from himself to God. But now behold,
In the quick forge and working-house of thought,
How London doth pour out her citizens!
The mayor, and all his brethren, in best sort,—
Like to the senators of the antique Rome,
With the plebeians swarming at their heels,—
Go forth, and fetch their conqu'ring Cæsar in:
As, by a lower but by loving likelihood,
Were now the general of our gracious empress
(As in good time he may,) from Ireland coming,
Bringing rebellion broached on his sword,
How many would the peaceful city quit,
To welcome him?[a] much more, and much more cause,
Did they this Harry. Now in London place him;
(As yet the lamentation of the French
Invites the king of England's stay at home.
The emperor's coming in behalf of France,
To order peace between them;) and omit
All the occurrences, whatever chanc'd,
Till Harry's back-return again to France;
There must we bring him; and myself have play'd
The interim, by remembering you—'tis past.
Then brook abridgment, and your eyes advance
After your thoughts, straight back again to France.

(*) Old copy omits, *and*.

[a] To welcome him?] See the Preliminary Notice.

ACT V.

SCENE I.—France. *An* English *Court of Guard.*

Enter FLUELLEN *and* GOWER.

GOW. Nay, that's right; but why wear you your leek to-day? saint Davy's day is past.

FLU. There is occasions and causes why and wherefore in all things: I will tell you, as my friend, captain Gower;—the rascally, scald, peggarly, lousy, pragging knave, Pistol,—which you and yourself, and all the 'orld, know to pe no petter than a fellow, look you now, of no merits,—he is come to me, and prings me pread and salt yesterday, look you, and pid me eat my leek: it was in a place where I could not preed no contention with him; but I will pe so pold as to wear it in my cap till I see him once again, and then I will tell him a little piece of my desires.

GOW. Why, here he comes, swelling like a turkey-cock.

FLU. 'Tis no matter for his swellings, nor his turkey-cocks.

Enter PISTOL.

Got pless you, auncient Pistol! you scurvy, lousy knave, Got pless you!

PIST. Ha! art thou Bedlam? dost thou thirst, base Trojan,
To have me fold up Parca's fatal web?
Hence! I am qualmish at the smell of leek.

FLU. I peseech you heartily, scurvy, lousy knave, at my desires, and my requests, and my petitions, to eat, look you, this leek; pecause, look you, you do not love it, nor your affections, and your appetites, and your disgestions, does not agree with it, I would desire you to eat it.

PIST. Not for Cadwallader, and all his goats.

FLU. There is one goat for you. [*Strikes him.* Will you be so goot, scald knave, as eat it?

PIST. Base Trojan, thou shalt die.

FLU. You say very true, scald knave,—when Got's will is: I will desire you to live in the mean time, and eat your victuals; come, there is sauce for it. [*Striking him again.*] You called me yesterday, *mountain-squire;* put I will make you to-day a squire of low degree. I pray you, fall to; if you can mock a leek, you can eat a leek.

Gow. Enough, captain; you have astonished him.

Flu. I say, I will make him eat some part of my leek, or I will peat his pate four days.—Pite, I pray you; it is goot for your green wound, and your ploody coxcomb.

Pist. Must I bite?

Flu. Yes, certainly; and out of doubt, and out of question too, and ampiguities.

Pist. By this leek, I will most horribly revenge; I eat, and eat,—I swear—

Flu. Eat, I pray you: will you have some more sauce to your leek? there is not enough leek to swear py.

Pist. Quiet thy cudgel; thou dost see I eat.

Flu. Much goot do you, scald knave, heartily. Nay, pray you, throw none away; the skin is goot for your proken coxcomb. When you take occasions to see leeks hereafter, I pray you, mock at them; that is all.

Pist. Good.

Flu. Ay, leeks is goot:—hold you, there is a groat to heal your pate.

Pist. Me a groat!

Flu. Yes, verily and in truth, you shall take it; or I have another leek in my pocket, which you shall eat.

Pist. I take thy groat in earnest of revenge.

Flu. If I owe you any thing, I will pay you in cudgels; you shall pe a woodmonger, and puy nothing of me put cudgels. Got pe wi' you, and keep you, and heal your pate. [*Exit.*

Pist. All hell shall stir for this!

Gow. Go, go; you are a counterfeit cowardly knave. Will you mock at an ancient tradition,—begun upon an honourable respect, and worn as a memorable trophy of predeceased valour,—and dare not avouch in your deeds any of your words? I have seen you gleeking and galling at this gentleman twice or thrice. You thought, because he could not speak English in the native garb, he could not therefore handle an English cudgel: you find it otherwise; and, henceforth, let a Welsh correction teach you a good English condition. Fare ye well. [*Exit.*

Pist. Doth fortune play the huswife with me
now?
News have I, that my Nell* is dead i'the spittal
Of† malady of France;
And there my rendezvous is quite cut off.
Old I do wax; and from my weary limbs
Honour is cudgell'd. Well, bawd I'll turn,
And something lean to cutpurse of quick hand.
To England will I steal, and there I'll steal:
And patches will I get unto these scars,*
And swear,† I got them in the Gallia wars.
[*Exit.*

(*) Old copy, *Doll.* (†) Old copy inserts, *a.*

SCENE II.—Troyes *in* Champagne. *An Apartment in the* French King's *Palace.*

Enter, at one door, King Henry, Bedford, Gloucester, Exeter, Warwick, Westmoreland, *and other* Lords; *at another,* King Charles, Queen Isabel, *the* Princess Katharine, Lords, Ladies, *&c. the* Duke *of* Burgundy, *and his Train.*

K. Hen. Peace to this meeting, wherefore we are met!
Unto our brother France,—and to our sister,
Health and fair time of day:—joy and good wishes
To our most fair and princely cousin Katharine;
And (as a branch and member of this royalty,
By whom this great assembly is contriv'd,)
We do salute you, duke of Burgundy;—
And, princes French, and peers, health to you all!

K. Cha. Right joyous are we to behold your face,
Most worthy brother England; fairly met:—
So are you, princes English, every one.

Q. Isa. So happy be the issue, brother England,‡
Of this good day, and of this gracious meeting,
As we are now glad to behold your eyes;
Your eyes, which hitherto have borne in them
Against the French, that met them in their bent,
The fatal balls of murdering basilisks:
The venom of such looks, we fairly hope,
Have lost their quality; and that this day
Shall change all griefs and quarrels into love.

K. Hen. To cry Amen to that, thus we appear.

Q. Isa. You English princes all, I do salute you.

Bur. My duty to you both, on equal love,
Great kings of France and England! That I have labour'd
With all my wits, my pains, and strong endeavours,
To bring your most imperial majesties
Unto this bar and royal interview,
Your mightiness on both parts best can witness.
Since, then, my office hath so far prevail'd,

(*) First folio, *cudgeld scarres.* (†) Old copy, *swore.*
(‡) First folio, *Ireland.*

That, face to face, and royal eye to eye,
You have congreeted, let it not disgrace me,
If I demand, before this royal view,
What rub or what impediment there is,
Why that the naked, poor, and mangled Peace,
Dear nurse of arts, plenties, and joyful births,
Should not, in this best garden of the world,
Our fertile France, put up her lovely visage?
Alas! she hath from France too long been chas'd,
And all her husbandry doth lie on heaps,
Corrupting in it own fertility.
Her vine, the merry cheerer of the heart,
Unpruned dies: her hedges even-pleach'd,—
Like prisoners wildly overgrown with hair,

Put forth disorder'd twigs: her fallow leas,
The darnel, hemlock, and rank fumitory*
Doth root upon; while that the coulter rusts,
That should deracinate such savagery:
The even mead, that erst brought sweetly forth
The freckled cowslip, burnet, and green clover,
Wanting the scythe, all† uncorrected, rank,
Conceives by idleness; and nothing teems
But hateful docks, rough thistles, kecksies, burs,
Losing both beauty and utility.
And as our vineyards, fallows, meads, and hedges,
Defective in their natures, grow to wildness;
Even so our houses, and ourselves, and children,
Have lost, or do not learn, for want of time,
The sciences that should become our country;
But grow, like savages,—as soldiers will,
That nothing do but meditate on blood,—
To swearing, and stern looks, diffus'd attire,
And every thing that seems unnatural.
Which to reduce into our former favour,
You are assembled; and my speech entreats,
That I may know the let, why gentle Peace
Should not expel these inconveniencies,
And bless us with her former qualities.

K. HEN. If, duke of Burgundy, you would the peace,
Whose want gives growth to th' imperfections
Which you have cited, you must buy that peace
With full accord to all our just demands;
Whose tenours and particular effects
You have, enschedul'd briefly, in your hands.

BUR. The king hath heard them; to the which, as yet,
There is no answer made.

K. HEN. Well then, the peace, which you before so urg'd,
Lies in his answer.

K. CHA. I have but with a cursorary‡ eye
O'erglanc'd the articles: pleaseth your grace
To appoint some of your council presently
To sit with us once more, with better heed
To re-survey them, we will, suddenly,
Pass our accept, and peremptory answer.

K. HEN. Brother, we shall.—Go, uncle Exeter,—
And brother Clarence,—and you, brother Gloster,—
Warwick,—and Huntington,—go with the king;
And take with you free power to ratify,
Augment, or alter, as your wisdoms best
Shall see advantageable for our dignity,
Any thing in or out of our demands,
And we'll consign thereto.—Will you, fair sister,
Go with the princes, or stay here with us?

Q. ISA. Our gracious brother, I will go with them;
Haply a woman's voice may do some good,
When articles too nicely urg'd be stood on.

K. HEN. Yet leave our cousin Katharine here with us;
She is our capital demand, compris'd
Within the fore-rank of our articles.

Q. ISA. She hath good leave.

[*Exeunt all but* HENRY, KATHARINE, *and* ALICE.

K. HEN. Fair Katharine, and most fair!
Will you vouchsafe to teach a soldier terms,
Such as will enter at a lady's ear,
And plead his love-suit to her gentle heart?

KATH. Your majesty sall mock at me; I cannot speak your England.

K. HEN. O fair Katharine, if you will love me soundly with your French heart, I will be glad to hear you confess it brokenly with your English tongue. Do you like me, Kate?

KATH. *Pardonnez-moi*, I cannot tell vat is—*like me.*

K. HEN. An angel is like you, Kate; and you are like an angel.

KATH. *Que dit-il? que je suis semblable à les anges?*

ALICE. *Oui, vraiment, (sauf votre grace) ainsi dit-il.*

K. HEN. I said so, dear Katharine, and I must not blush to affirm it.

KATH. *O bon Dieu! les langues des hommes sont pleines de tromperies.*

K. HEN. What says she, fair one? that the tongues of men are full of deceits?

ALICE. *Oui;* dat de tongues of de mans is be full of deceits: dat is de princess.

K. HEN. The princess is the better Englishwoman. I'faith, Kate, my wooing is fit for thy understanding: I am glad, thou canst speak no better English, for, if thou couldst, thou wouldst find me such a plain king, that thou wouldst think, I had sold my farm to buy my crown. I know no ways to mince it in love, but directly to say—I love you: then, if you urge me farther than to say—Do you in faith? I wear out my suit. Give me your answer: i'faith, do; and so clap hands, and a bargain. How say you, lady?

KATH. *Sauf votre honneur*, me understand well.

K. HEN. Marry, if you would put me to verses, or to dance for your sake, Kate, why you undid me: for the one, I have neither words nor measure; and for the other, I have no strength in measure, yet a reasonable measure in strength. If I could win a lady at leap-frog, or by vaulting into my saddle with my armour on my back, under the correction of bragging be it spoken, I should quickly leap into a wife. Or, if I might buffet for my love, or bound my horse for her favours, I could lay on like a butcher, and sit like a jack-an-apes, never

(*) Old copy, *femetary*. (†) Old copy, *withal*. (‡) First folio, *curselarie*.

off: but, before God, Kate, I cannot look greenly, nor gasp out my eloquence, nor I have no cunning in protestation; only downright oaths, which I never use till urged, nor never break for urging. If thou canst love a fellow of this temper, Kate, whose face is not worth sun-burning, that never looks in his glass for love of any thing he sees there, let thine eye be thy cook. I speak to thee plain soldier: if thou canst love me for this, take me: if not, to say to thee that I shall die, is true,—but for thy love, by the Lord, no; yet I love thee too. And while thou livest, dear Kate, take a fellow of plain and uncoined constancy, for he perforce must do thee right, because he hath not the gift to woo in other places: for these fellows of infinite tongue, that can rhyme themselves into ladies' favours, they do always reason themselves out again. What! a speaker is but a prater; a rhyme is but a ballad. A good leg will fall; a straight back will stoop; a black beard will turn white; a curled pate will grow bald; a fair face will wither; a full eye will wax hollow: but a good heart, Kate, is the sun and the moon; or, rather, the sun, and not the moon; for it shines bright, and never changes, but keeps his course truly. If thou would have such a one, take me: and take me, take a soldier; take a soldier, take a king: and what sayest thou then to my love? speak, my fair, and fairly, I pray thee.

KATH. Is it possible dat I sould love de enemy of France?

K. HEN. No, it is not possible, you should love the enemy of France, Kate: but, in loving me, you should love the friend of France; for I love France so well, that I will not part with a village of it; I will have it all mine: and, Kate, when France is mine, and I am yours, then yours is France, and you are mine.

KATH. I cannot tell vat is dat.

K. HEN. No, Kate? I will tell thee in French; which, I am sure, will hang upon my tongue like a new-married wife about her husband's neck, hardly to be shook off. *Quand j'ai la possession de France, et quand vous avez la possession de moi,* (let me see, what then? Saint Denis be my speed!) *donc votre est France, et vous êtes mienne.* It is as easy for me, Kate, to conquer the kingdom, as to speak so much more French: I shall never move thee in French, unless it be to laugh at me.

KATH. *Sauf votre honneur, le Français que vous parlez, est meilleur que l'Anglais lequel je parle.*

K. HEN. No, 'faith, is't not, Kate: but thy speaking of my tongue, and I thine, most truly falsely, must needs be granted to be much at one. But, Kate, dost thou understand thus much English,—Canst thou love me?

KATH. I cannot tell.

K. HEN. Can any of your neighbours tell, Kate? I'll ask them. Come, I know, thou lovest me: and at night when you come into your closet, you'll question this gentlewoman about me; and I know, Kate, you will, to her, dispraise those parts in me that you love with your heart: but, good Kate, mock me mercifully; the rather, gentle princess, because I love thee cruelly. If ever thou beest mine, Kate, (as I have a saving faith within me, tells me, thou shalt,) I get thee with scambling, and thou must therefore needs prove a good soldier-breeder: shall not thou and I, between saint Denis and saint George, compound a boy, half French, half English, that shall go to Constantinople, and take the Turk by the beard? shall we not? what sayest thou, my fair flower-de-luce?

KATH. I do not know dat.

K. HEN. No; 'tis hereafter to know, but now to promise: do but now promise, Kate, you will endeavour for your French part of such a boy: and, for my English moiety, take the word of a king and a bachelor. How answer you, *la plus belle Katharine du monde, mon très chère et divine déesse?*

KATH. Your *majesté* ave *fausse* French enough to deceive de most *sage demoiselle* dat is *en France.*

K. HEN. Now, fie upon my false French! By mine honour, in true English, I love thee, Kate: by which honour I dare not swear thou lovest me, yet my blood begins to flatter me that thou dost, notwithstanding the poor and untempering effect of my visage. Now, beshrew my father's ambition! he was thinking of civil wars when he got me; therefore was I created with a stubborn outside, with an aspect of iron, that, when I come to woo ladies, I fright them. But, in faith, Kate, the elder I wax, the better I shall appear: my comfort is, that old age, that ill layer-up of beauty, can do no more spoil upon my face: thou hast me, if thou hast me, at the worst, and thou shalt wear me, if thou wear me, better and better;—and therefore tell me, most fair Katharine, will you have me? Put off your maiden blushes; avouch the thoughts of your heart with the looks of an empress; take me by the hand, and say—Harry of England, I am thine: which word thou shalt no sooner bless mine ear withal, but I will tell thee aloud,—England is thine, Ireland is thine, France is thine, and Henry Plantagenet is thine; who, though I speak it before his face, if he be not fellow with the best king, thou shalt find the best king of good fellows. Come, your answer in broken music;(1) for thy voice is music, and thy English broken; therefore, queen of all, Katharine, break thy mind to me in broken English,—wilt thou have me?

KATH. Dat is, as it sall please de *roi mon père.*

K. HEN. Nay, it will please him well, Kate; it shall please him, Kate.

KATH. Den it sall also content me.

K. HEN. Upon that, I kiss your hand, and I call you—my queen.

KATH. *Laissez, mon seigneur, laissez, laissez: ma foi, je ne veux point que vous abaissez votre grandeur, en baisant la main d'une votre indigne serviteur; excusez-moi, je vous supplie, mon très puissant seigneur.*

K. HEN. Then I will kiss your lips, Kate.

KATH. *Les dames, et demoiselles, pour être baiseés devant leur nôces, il n'est pas le coûtume de France.*

K. HEN. Madam my interpreter, what says she?

ALICE. Dat it is not be de fashion *pour les* ladies of France,—I cannot tell vat is *baiser en* English.

K. HEN. To kiss.

ALICE. Your majesty *entendre* bettre *que moi.*

K. HEN. It is not a fashion for the maids in France to kiss before they are married, would she say?

ALICE. *Oui, vraiment.*

K. HEN. O, Kate, nice customs court'sy to great kings. Dear Kate, you and I cannot be confined within the weak list of a country's fashion: we are the makers of manners, Kate; and the liberty that follows our places, stops the mouths of all find-faults,—as I will do yours, for upholding the nice fashion of your country, in denying me a kiss: therefore, patiently and yielding. [*Kissing her.*] You have witchcraft in your lips, Kate: there is more eloquence in a sugar touch of them, than in the tongues of the French council; and they should sooner persuade Harry of England, than a general petition of monarchs. Here comes your father.

Enter KING CHARLES *and* QUEEN ISABEL, BURGUNDY, BEDFORD, GLOUCESTER, EXETER, WARWICK, WESTMORELAND, *and other* French *and* English Lords.

BUR. God save your majesty! my royal cousin, teach you our princess English?

K. HEN. I would have her learn, my fair cousin, how perfectly I love her; and that is good English.

BUR. Is she not apt?

K. HEN. Our tongue is rough, coz, and my condition is not smooth; so that, having neither the voice nor the heart of flattery about me, I cannot so conjure up the spirit of love in her, that he will appear in his true likeness.

BUR. Pardon the frankness of my mirth, if I answer you for that. If you would conjure in her, you must make a circle: if conjure up love in her in his true likeness, he must appear naked and blind. Can you blame her then, being a maid yet rosed over with the virgin crimson of modesty, if she deny the appearance of a naked blind boy in her naked seeing self? It were, my lord, a hard condition for a maid to consign to.

K. HEN. Yet they do wink, and yield,—as love is blind and enforces.

BUR. They are then excused, my lord, when they see not what they do.

K. HEN. Then, good my lord, teach your cousin to consent winking.

BUR. I will wink on her to consent, my lord, if you will teach her to know my meaning: for maids, well summered and warm kept, are like flies at Bartholomew-tide, blind, though they have their eyes; and then they will endure handling, which before would not abide looking on.

K. HEN. This moral ties me over to time and a hot summer; and so I shall catch the fly, your cousin, in the latter end, and she must be blind too.

BUR. As love is, my lord, before it loves.

K. HEN. It is so: and you may, some of you, thank love for my blindness, who cannot see many a fair French city, for one fair French maid that stands in my way.

K. CHA. Yes, my lord, you see them perspectively, the cities turned into a maid; for they are all girdled with maiden walls, that war hath never* entered.

K. HEN. Shall Kate be my wife?

K. CHA. So please you.

K. HEN. I am content; so the maiden cities you talk of, may wait on her: so the maid that stood in the way for my wish, shall show me the way to my will.

K. CHA. We have consented to all terms of reason.

K. HEN. Is it so, my lords of England?

WEST. The king hath granted every article:
His daughter, first; and then,† in sequel, all,
According to their firm proposed natures.

EXE. Only, he hath not yet subscribed this:—
Where your majesty demands, that the king of France, having any occasion to write for matter of grant, shall name your highness in this form and with this addition, in French—*Notre très cher fils Henri roi d'Angleterre, héritier de France;* and thus in Latin,—*Præclarissimus*[a] *filius noster Henricus, rex Angliæ, et hæres Franciæ.*

K. CHA. Nor this I have not, brother, so
denied,

(*) Old copy omits, *never*. (†) Old copy omits, *then*.

[a] *Notre* très cher *fils*,——*and thus in Latin*,—Præclarissimus filius—] In the preamble of the original treaty of Troyes, Henry is correctly styled *Præcarissimus*; the mistake, however, did not originate with Shakespeare, it occurs in Holinshed as well as in previous historians.

But your request shall make me let it pass.
K. HEN. I pray you then, in love and dear alliance,
Let that one article rank with the rest,
And, thereupon, give me your daughter.
K. CHA. Take her, fair son; and from her blood raise up
Issue to me; that the contending kingdoms [pale
Of France and England, whose very shores look
With envy of each other's happiness,
May cease their hatred; and this dear conjunction
Plant neighbourhood and christian-like accord
In their sweet bosoms, that never war advance
His bleeding sword 'twixt England and fair France.
ALL. Amen! [witness, all,
K. HEN. Now, welcome, Kate:—and bear me
That here I kiss her as my sovereign queen.
[*Flourish.*
Q. ISA. God, the best maker of all marriages,
Combine your hearts in one, your realms in one!
As man and wife, being two, are one in love,
So be there 'twixt your kingdoms such a spousal,
That never may ill office, or fell jealousy,
Which troubles oft the bed of blessed marriage,
Thrust in between the paction[a] of these kingdoms,
To make divorce of their incorporate league;
That English may as French, French Englishmen,
Receive each other!—God speak this Amen!
ALL. Amen! [which day,
K. HEN. Prepare we for our marriage;—on
My lord of Burgundy, we'll take your oath,
And all the peers, for surety of our leagues.—
Then shall I swear to Kate, and you to me;
And may our oaths well kept and prosperous be!
[*Exeunt.*

Enter CHORUS.

Thus far, with rough and all-unable pen,
Our bending author hath pursu'd the story;
In little room confining mighty men,
Mangling by starts the full course of their glory.
Small time, but, in that small, most greatly liv'd
This star of England: Fortune made his sword;
By which the world's best garden he achiev'd,
And of it left his son imperial lord.
Henry the sixth, in infant bands crown'd king
Of France and England, did this king succeed;
Whose state so many had the managing,
That they lost France, and made his England bleed:
Which oft our stage hath shown: and, for their sake,
In your fair minds let this acceptance take.
[*Exeunt.*

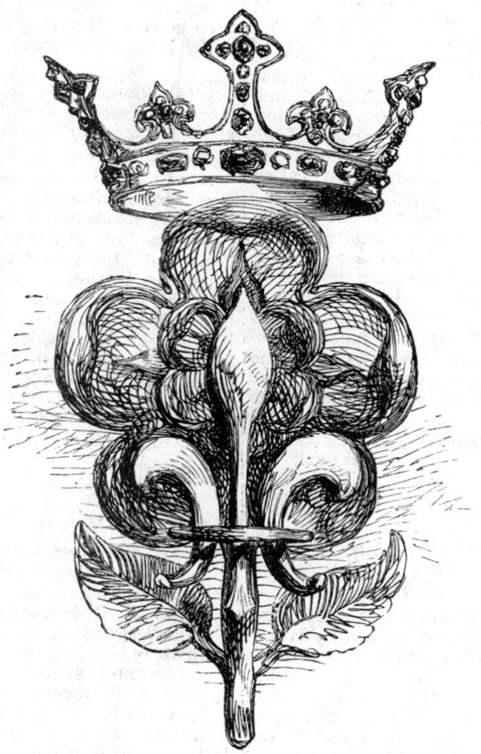

[a] *The* paction *of these kingdoms,*—] The old text has *Pation*, which was altered by Theobald.

ILLUSTRATIVE COMMENTS.

ACT I.

(1) SCENE II.—*Then hear me, gracious sovereign,—and you peers.*] This speech is taken almost verbatim from Holinshed; and as it may interest the reader to observe the facility with which Shakespeare converted prose into verse, we subjoin a few parallel lines.

HOLINSHED.	SHAKESPEARE.
In terram Salicam mulieres ne succedant, that is to saye, lette not women succeede in the land Salique, whiche the French glosers expound to bee the Realme of France, and that this law was made by King Pharamond, wheras yet their owne authors affirme, that the land Salique is in Germanie, between the rivers of Elbe and Sala, and that when Charles the great had overcome the Saxons, hee placed there certaine Frenchmen, which having in disdeine the dishonest maners of the Germain women, made a lawe, that the females should not succeede to anye inheritance within that lande.	*In terram Salicam mulieres nè succedant,* *No woman shall succeed in Salique land:* Which Salique land the French unjustly gloze To be the realm of France, and Pharamond The founder of this law and female bar. Yet their own authors faithfully affirm, That the land Salique is in Germany, Between the floods of Sala and of Elbe: Where Charles the great, having subdued the Saxons, There left behind and settled certain French; Who, holding in disdain the German women, For some dishonest manners of their life, Establish'd then this law,—to wit, no female Should be inheritrix in Salique land.

(2) SCENE II.—
—— the lady Lingare,
Daughter to Charlemain.]

"By Charles the Great is meant the Emperor Charlemagne, son of Pepin: Charlemain is Charlechauve, or Charles the Bald, who, as well as Charles le Gros, assumed the title of Magnus. See Goldasti Animadversiones in Einhardum. Edit. 1711, p. 157. But then Charlechauve had only one daughter, named Judith, married, or, as some say, only betrothed, to our king Ethelwulf, and carried off, after his death, by Baldwin the Forester, afterwards Earl of Flanders, whom it is very certain Hugh Capet was neither heir to, nor any way descended from. This Judith, indeed, had a great grand-daughter, called Luitgarde, married to a Count Wichman, of whom nothing further is known. It was likewise the name of Charlemagne's fifth wife; but no such female as Lingare is to be met with in any French historian. In fact, these fictitious personages and pedigrees seem to have been devised by the English heralds, to 'fine a title with some show of truth,' which 'in pure truth was corrupt and naught.' It was manifestly impossible that Henry, who had no hereditary title to his own dominions, could derive one by the same colour, to another person's. He merely proposes the invasion and conquest of France, in prosecution of the dying advice of his father:—

——— to busy giddy minds
With foreign quarrels; that action, thence borne out,
Might waste the memory of the former days."

RITSON.

(3) SCENE II.—
Whiles his most mighty father on a hill
Stood smiling to behold his lion's whelp
Forage in blood of French nobility.]

Alluding to the battle of Cressy, fought 26th August, 1346: the incident in the text is thus described by Holinshed:—"The earle of Northampton, and others sent to the king, *where he stood aloft on a windmill hill*, requiring him to advance forward, and come to their aid, they being as then sore laid to of their enimies. The king hereupon demanded if his sonne were slaine, hurt, or felled to the earth. No, (said the knight that brought the message,) but he is sore matched. Well, (said the king,) returne to him and them that sent you, and saie to them that they send no more to me for any adventure that falleth, as long as my son is alive, for I will that this iournie be his, with the honor thereof. With this answer the knight returned, which greatlie incouraged them to doo their best to win the spurs, being half abashed in that they had so sent to the king for aid. * * * The slaughter of the French was great and lamentable."

(4) SCENE II.—
For government, though high, and low, and lower,
Put into parts, doth keep in one concent.]

Concent, a term in music, signifies consonance of harmony; whence we use *consent* to express, by metaphor, *concord* or *agreement*. The foundation of the simile, Theobald conjectured, was borrowed from Cicero's "De Republica," lib. ii.; but, as a correspondent of Mr. Knight's suggests, the thought was more probably derived from a passage in the fourth book of Plato's "Republic:"—"It is not alone wisdom and strength which make a state simply wise and strong, but it (Order), like that harmony called the Diapason, is diffused throughout the whole state, making both the weakest and the strongest, and the middling people concent the same melody." Again: "The harmonic power of political justice is the same as that musical concent which connects the three chords, the octave, the bass, and the fifth."

(5) SCENE II.—
——— this mock of his
Hath turn'd his balls to gun-stones.]

One of the most familiar charges of armorial ensigns is the circular figure called a Roundle, the name of which, in English heraldry, varies according to the metal or colour of which it is composed. Black Roundles are called Pellets, Ogresses, or Gunstones, the first and last of which terms readily convey the idea of shot for ordnance; and the second is supposed to be derived from the mediæval Latin word *Agressus*, which was considered to be synonymous with the old French *Agresser*, to attack. The ancient use of stone-shot for cannon, before the introduction of iron balls, both explains the reason why these roundles were always black, and also discovers a stern concealed satire in this line of Henry's speech. Tennis balls were covered with white leather, but gun-stones became black from being discoloured by the powder and smoke of the cannon. And such a change Henry hints that he would certainly effect. In illustration of this passage Steevens quotes "The Brut of England," in which it is said that, when Henry the Fifth, before Hare-flewe, received a taunting message from the Dauphin of France, and a ton of tennis-balls by way of contempt, "he anone lette make tennis-balls for *The Dolfyn* (Henry's ship) in alle the haste that they might; and they were great *gunne-stones* for the Dolfyn to playe withall. But this game at tennis was too rough for the besieged, when Henry played at the tennis with his hard gunne-stones." The provision of this kind of ammunition, made by the king, is mentioned by Grose in his "History of the English Army," i. p. 400, as stated in a writ directed to the Clerk of the Ordnance and John Bonet, mason, of Maidstone, to cut 7,000 stone-shot in the quarries at that place. As Henry's gun-stones were all to be transported across the sea, they were probably not very large; but when Mahomet the Second besieged Constantinople in 1453, he battered the walls with stone-shot, and some of his pieces were of the calibre of 1,200 lbs.; but they could not be fired more than four times in the day. The well-known circumstance of the tennis-balls, which Shakespeare has introduced into this scene, is noticed by several contemporaneous historians; but the probability of it is questioned by Hume. For an examination into the truth of the story, see Sir N. H. Nicolas's "History of the Battle of Agincourt," pp. 8—13.

ACT II.

(1) SCENE I.—*Pish for thee, Iceland dog! thou prick-ear'd cur of Iceland!*] The *Iceland*, or *Island* dog, as the name is often spelt by our old authors, was a shag-haired animal, imported in great numbers from Iceland, which it was the fashion for ladies to carry about with them.—"Use and custome hath entertained other Dogs of an Out-landish kinde, but a few and the same being of a pretty bigness, I mean *Island Dogs*, curled and rough all over, which by reason of the length of their hair make shew neither of face nor of body: And yet these Curs, forsooth, because they be so strange, are greatly set by, esteemed, taken up, and many times in the room of the Spaniel gentle or comforter." *—TOPSEL'S *History of Four-footed Beasts*, 1658.

It is mentioned in the play of "Ram-Alley, or Merry Tricks," 1611:—

> " ——— you shall have jewels,
> A baboon, a parrot, and an *Izeland dog*."

And again in the Masque of "Britannia Triumphans," 1636:—

> " ——— she who hath been bred to stand
> Near chair of queen, with *Island shock* in hand."

(2) SCENE III.—*'A made a finer end, and went away, an it had been any christom child.*] The *chrisom*, so called from *chrism*, the holy oil which was anciently used in baptism, was a white cloth, placed on the child's head, and always worn by it for seven days afterwards. After the Reformation the sacred oil was no longer used, but the *chrisom* was retained, the child wearing it until the purification of the mother by the rite of churching. If an infant died before this latter ceremony, the *chrisom* formed its shroud, from which circumstance, probably, children, in the old bills of mortality, are denominated *chrisoms*.

(3) SCENE III.—*'A parted even just between twelve and one, even at the turning o' the tide.*] The opinion that animals, more particularly man, die only at the ebb of tide is of great antiquity, and was not peculiar to the profane vulgar. In the short chapter in which Pliny notices the marvels of the sea, he says that Aristotle affirms "that no living creature dieth but in the reflux and ebb of the sea. This is much observed in the Gallic Ocean, but is found true, in experience, only as to man."—*Hist. Nat.*, lib. ii. c. xcviii. Dr. Mead, in his Tract, *On the Influence of the Sun and Moon on Bodies*, originally published in 1704, chap. ii., enters into an elaborate examination of this question, in which, having shown the moon's power over the tides when new and full, he illustrates his inquiry by several cases, ancient and modern, of great and fatal changes having taken place at those periods. If, at the present day, any importance is to be attributed to those seasons as critical times, it is probably on the principle that a great external disturbance, whether meteorological or otherwise, unduly excites and quickens the nervous-action, to bring on a more rapid crisis; and, in the case of dying persons, unnaturally agitates and expends those vital powers which were already nearly exhausted.

ACT III.

(1) SCENE V.—*And teach lavoltas high, and swift corantos.*] *Lavolta*, a dance of Italian origin, appears by the description given of it in Thoinot Arbeau's "Orchesographie," and in Florio's "*World of Words*," to have somewhat resembled the modern "Polka." It is frequently mentioned by our earlier writers, and was evidently much in vogue about Shakespeare's time:—

> "So may you see by two *Lavalto* danced,
> Who face to face about the house do hop;
> And when one mounts, the other is advanced,
> At once they move, at once they both do stop."
> *An old-fashioned Love.* Poem by J. T. 1594.

> "Yet there is one the most delightfull kind,
> A loftie iumping or a leaping round,
> Where arme in arme, two dauncers are entwin'd,
> And whirle themselves with strict embracements bound,
> And still their feet an Anapest do sound:
> An Anapest is all their musick's song,
> Whose first two feet are short, and third is long."
> *Orchestra*, by SIR JOHN DAVIES, 1622. Stanza 70.

The *Coranto* has been already spoken of as a dance characterised by the spirit and rapidity of its movements. See note (b), p. 20. It is thus described in Davies' "Orchestra:"—

> "What shall I name those currant travases,
> That on a triple Dactile foot doe runne
> Close by the ground with sliding passages,
> Wherein that Dauncer greatest praise hath wonne:
> Which with best order can all orders shunne:
> For every where he wantonly must range,
> And turne and wind, with unexpected change."
> Stanza 69.

* This description we find Topsel has borrowed from Abraham Fleming's translation of "Caius de Canibus," 1576, "Of English Dogges."

(2) SCENE VI.—

Fortune is Bardolph's foe, and frowns on him;
For he hath stol'n a pax.]

It was customary, in the early Church, for Christians, in conformity with the words of St. Paul, "to salute one another with a holy kiss." This ceremony appears to have obtained until about the twelfth or thirteenth century, when, for some reason not clearly defined, the laity (for the clergy of the Roman Catholic Church still practise it at High Mass,) were required to kiss, instead, an instrument called indifferently a *pax*, a *tabula pacis*, or an *osculatorium*. This was a small plate of metal, precious or otherwise, according to circumstances, having a religious subject engraved upon its surface, generally a representation of the crucifixion; and the proper time for using it was at that part of the mass just before the communion, where the priest recites the prayer for peace.

The *pax* itself became disused in its turn, owing, it is said, to certain jealousies about precedence, an irregularity rebuked by Chaucer's "Persone:"—"And yit is ther a prive spice of pride, that wayteth first to be saluet er he saliewe, al be he lasse worth than that other is, paradventure; and eek wayteth or desireth to sitte above him, or to go above him in the way, or *kisse the pax*, or ben encensed, or gon to the offringe biforn his neighebore." Nevertheless, the use of the *pax* was not at first abrogated at the Reformation in England, but, on the contrary, enforced by the Royal Ecclesiastical Commissioners of Edward VI.

The act of sacrilege which Shakespeare has fathered upon Bardolph agrees in the main with Holinshed's statement:—"That a folish soldiour stale a pixe out of a churche, for which cause he was apprehended, and the king would not once remove till the box was restored, and the offender strangled."

The elder commentators thought it necessary to reconcile Shakespeare's text with Holinshed, by reading *pix* instead of *pax;* but without reason, as the alteration was most likely deliberate on the part of the poet. The *pix* was a sacred vessel, made sometimes of precious metal, but more usually of copper gilt, and intended to receive the consecrated host for conveyance to the sick. Shakespeare might well shrink from bringing anything of this nature in contact with Falstaff's worthless old retainer.

We may add that the first line of Pistol's speech—

"Fortune is Bardolph's foe, and frowns on him"—

conveys an allusion to the famous old ballad, "Fortune my Foe,"—

"*Fortune my Foe,* why dost thou *frown on me?*"

See note (3), p. 688, Vol. I.

(3) SCENE VI.—*A beard of the general's cut.*] Not the least odd among the fantastic fashions of our forefathers, was the custom of distinguishing certain professions and classes by the cut of the beard: thus we hear, *inter alia,* of the *bishop's-beard,* the *judge's-beard,* the *soldier's-beard,* the *citizen's-beard,* and even the *clown's-beard.* The peculiar shape appropriated to the Bench we have failed to discover: but Randle Holme tells us, "the *broad* or *cathedral* beard [is] so called because bishops and gownmen of the church anciently did wear such beards." By the military man, the cut adopted was known as the *stiletto* or the *spade:*—"he [the barber] descends as low as his beard, and asketh whether he please to be shaven or no? whether he will have his peak cut short and sharp, amiable, like an *inamorato,* or broade pendante, like a *spade,* to be terrible, *like a warrior and soldado?*"—GREENE'S *Quip for an Upstart Courtier,* 1592.

The beard of the citizen was usually worn *round,* as Mrs. Quickly describes it, "like a glover's paring-knife;" and that of the clown was left bushy or untrimmed:—

"Next the *clown* doth out-rush,
With the beard of *the bush.*"
Old Ballad, quoted by Malone from a Miscellany, entitled, "Le Prince d'Amour," 1660.

For additional particulars on the subject of beards, consult F. W. Fairholt's "Costume in England." Lond. 1846.

(4) SCENE VI.—

There's for thy labour, Montjoy.
Go, bid thy master well advise himself:
If we may pass, we will; if we be hinder'd,
We shall your tawny ground with your red blood
Discolour: and so, Montjoy, fare you well.]

The embassy here referred to, and even the words of Henry on that occasion, are taken from the following passage in Holinshed. Thirty of the French King's council "agreed that the Englishmen should not depart unfought withall, and five were of a contrary opinion; but the greater number ruled the matter: and so Montjoy, King at Armes, was sent to the King of England, to defie him as the enemie of France, and to tell him that he should shortlie have battell. King Henrie advisedlie answered, 'Mine intent is to doo as it pleaseth God. I will not seeke your maister at this time; but if he or his seeke me I will meete with them God willing. If anie of your nation attempt once to stop me in my journie now towards Callis, at their jeopardie be it: and yet wish I not anie of you so unadvised as to be the occasion that I dye your tawnie ground with your red blood.' When he had thus answered the herald, he gave him a princelie reward and monie to depart."

It has been supposed that many of the English nobility retained heralds in their households, who bore their names, and proclaimed their titles, even before the reign of Edward III. when Heraldry and officers of arms began to rise into the greatest eminence. Both the private heralds and the royal heralds received regular stipends, and wore surcoats or tabards embroidered with the armorial ensigns of their patrons; and considerable gratuities or largesses were at one period given to them at all ceremonials in which they performed any duty, either for the king or the nobility. These consisted of coronations, creations of peers and knights, embassies, displaying of banners in the field or at tournaments, processions and progresses, great banquets, baptisms, and funerals; the annual festivals of the Church, and the enthronisation of prelates. Some notion of the amount of these fees is supplied by a record of the reign of Richard II. of the dues and largesses anciently accustomed to be paid to the Kings of Arms and Heralds on such occasions, printed in the Rev. James Dallaway's *Inquiries into the Origin and Progress of Heraldry in England,* p. 142—148.

ACT IV.

CHORUS.

(1) *The armourers, accomplishing the knights,*
With busy hammers closing rivets up,
Give dreadful note of preparation.]

The din of preparation before battle has always been a favourite theme of poets. Chaucer has a passage much resembling the above, which Shakespeare probably remembered:—

"Ther fomen steedes, on the golden bridel
Gnawyng, *and faste armurers also*
With fyle and hamer prikyng to and fro."
The Knightes Tale, l. 2508.

To both descriptions some poetical licence must be accorded; and it is difficult to repress a smile at the gravity with which the commentators assume they are to be construed literally. Doubtless, in actual warfare, armour frequently wanted repair; but surely the poor knight had enough to endure in his cumbrous equipment without being made a blacksmith's anvil. No such necessity is recognised in any of the instructions "how to arme a man," still extant. From these we learn, that about Henry the Fifth's time, when plate armour had superseded chain mail, the "accomplishing" a knight consisted in first encasing him in garments of leather or fustian, fitting tight to the person and padded. The arming then began at the feet, and was continued gradually upward, each piece being fastened by "points," *i.e.* laces with tags at the end, or buckles and leather straps. The last thing fixed was the bascinet, or steel skull cap, which was "pynned upon two grete staples before the breste," and rendered firm by "a double bocle," or two buckles and straps "behynde upon the back."*

Thus it is apparent that arming a knight for battle or tourney, although a tedious business, was yet one simply and easily performed, and necessarily so, or the wounded man might die before he could be unharnessed. When Arcite is injured by a fall from his steed, Chaucer tells us that,—

> "——— he was y-born out of the place
> With herte sore, to Theseus paleys,
> Tho *was he corven out of his harneys.*"
>
> *The Knightes Tale*, l. 2696.

i. e. cut out of his armour, meaning that the laces which held it together were cut, for greater expedition.

(1) SCENE II.—

> *Why do you stay so long, my lords of France?*
> *Yond island carrions, desperate of their bones,*
> *Ill-favour'dly become the morning field.*]

The miserable condition of the English army previous to the battle is feelingly depicted by Holinshed:—

"The Englishemen were brought into great misery in this iorney, their victuall was in maner spent, and nowe coulde they get none; for their enimies had destroied all the corne before they came: Reste coulde they none take, for their enimies were ever at hande to give them alarmes: daily it rained, and nightly it freesed: of fewell there was great scarsitie, but of fluxes greate plenty: money they hadde ynoughe, but wares to bestowe it uppon, for their reliefe or comforte, hadde they little or none."

(2) SCENE III.—*The feast of Crispian.*] Of the martyrs Crispin and Crispinian, whose festival was formerly kept with especial honour in France on the 25th of October, the "Golden Legende" says,—

"In the tyme whan the furyous persecucyon of crysten men was vnder Dyoclesyan and Maxymyan toogydre regnynge, Cryspyn and Cryspynyan borne at Rome of noble lygnage came with the blessyd sayntes Quyntyn, Faustyan, and Victoryn vnto Parys in Fraunce; and they there chese dyverse places for to preche the fayth of Cryste. Cryspyn and Cryspynyan came to the cyte of Suessyon [Soissons] and chosen that cyte for the place of theyr pylgrymage where they folowed the steppes of saynt Poule the appostle, that is to saye, To laboure with theyr hondes for to provyde to them necessaryly to lyve, and exercysed the craft of makynge of shoes. In whiche craft they passed other and toke by constraynt no reward of no body, wherefore the gentyles and paynems overcome by love of them, not only for nede of the craft, but also for the love of God came oft to them and left the error of the ydollys and byleuyd in very God."

After a series of persecutions and torments, borne with great constancy, these saints "receyved the crowne of martyrdome on the x kalendes of Novembre," about the year 287.

* Archeologia, xx. 505.

(3) SCENE IV.—*This roaring devil i' the old play, that every one may pare his nails with a wooden dagger.*] In the ancient religious dramas, called "Mysteries," the Devil was usually a very prominent personage. He was hideously apparelled; wore a mask with goggle eyes, wide mouth, and huge nose; had a red beard, horned head, cloven feet, and hooked nails to his fingers. He was generally armed with a massive club, stuffed with wool, which he laid about him, during the performance, on all within his reach. To frighten others, he was wont to bellow out, "Ho, ho, ho!" and when himself alarmed, he roared, "Out haro, out!" As these popular representations assumed a more secular tone, an addition was made to the *dramatis personæ*, in the shape of a character called the "*Vice*," (see note 5, p. 628, Vol. I.) whose chief humour consisted in belabouring the evil-one with a wooden lath or dagger similar to that employed by the modern Harlequin, in skipping on to his back, and, as a crowning affront, in pretending to *pare his nails.* Shakespeare again alludes to this last exploit in "Twelfth Night," Act IV. Sc. 2:—

> "I'll be with you again
> In a trice,
> Like to the old *vice*,
> Your need to sustain.
>
> Who with dagger of lath,
> In his rage and his wrath,
> Cries, ah, ha! to the devil.
> Like a mad lad,
> *Pare thy nails, dad,*
> Adieu, goodman devil."

(4) SCENE VI.—*Then every soldier kill his prisoners.*] "In the meane season, while the battaile thus continued, and that the englishemen had taken a greate number of prisoners, certayne frenchemen on horse back, whereof were capteines Robinet of Bornevill, Rifflart of Clamas, Isambert of Agincourt, and other men of armes, to the number of six hundred horssemen, which were the first that fled,—hearing that the english tents and pavilions were a good way distant from the army, without any sufficient gard to defend the same, either upon a covetous meaning to gaine by the spoile, or upon a desire to be revenged, entred upon the kings camp, and there spoiled the bales, robbed the tents, brake up chests, and carried away caskets, and slew suche servants as they founde to make any resistance. For the which acte they were after committed to prison, and had loste their lives, if the Dolphin had longer lived: for when the outcrye of the lackies and boys which ran away for feare of the frenchmen thus spoiling the campe, came to the kings eares, he doubting least his enemies should gather togither againe and begin a newe fielde; and mistrusting further that the prisoners would either be an aide to his enimies, or verie enimies to their takers in deed if they were suffred to live, contrary to his accustomed gentlenes, commanded by sound of trumpet, that every man (upon paine of death) should incontinently slaie his prisoner."—HOLINSHED.

(5) SCENE VIII.—*Let there be sung* "Non nobis," *and* "Te Deum."] The incidents referred to in the preceding passage appear to be the last for which Shakespeare was indebted to Holinshed in this play; as well as the last of the more serious parts of the noble dramatic history of the French wars of Henry V. "Aboute foure of the clocke in the after noone," says the old chronicler, deriving his information from the contemporaneous historian known by the name of Titus Livius,—"the king, when he saw no appearance of enemies, caused the retreit to be blowen; and, gathering his armie together, gave thanks to Almightie God for so happie a victorie: causing his prelates and chapleins to sing this psalm, '*In Exitu Israel de Ægypto,*' and commanded everie man to kneele downe on the ground at this verse, '*Non nobis, Domine, non nobis, sed Nomini Tuo da gloriam:*' which done, he caused 'Te Deum,' with certaine anthems to be sung, giving laud and praise to God, without boasting of his owne force, or anie humane power." In the English version Psalm cxiii. commences, "When

Israel came out of Egypt," and the verse "*Non nobis*" forms the beginning of that following; answering to Psalms cxiv. cxv. of the ordinary Vulgate; though in the older psalters they are united into one. It will be remembered that Shakespeare has given to Henry a very fine paraphrase of the "*Non nobis*" in his speech on receiving the account of the loss sustained by both armies:—

"——— O God, thy arm was here,
And not to us, but to thy arm alone,
Ascribe we all!"

The command which the king issues in his next speech:—

"And be it death proclaimed through our host,
To boast of this, or take that praise from God,
Which is his only,"—

would appear to have been derived from the following very curious passage in Holinshed, though it really refers to Henry's entry into London. "The king, like a grave and sober personage, and as one remembering from whom all victories are sent, seemed little to regard such vaine pompe and shewes as were in triumphant sort devised for his welcoming home from so prosperous a journie; insomuch that he would not suffer his helmet to be carried before him, whereby might have appeared to the people the blowes and dints that were to be seene in the same: neither would he suffer any ditties to be made and sung by minstrels of his glorious victorie, for that he would have the praise and thanks altogether given to God."

In our Illustrative Comments on Act V. of "Richard II." we referred to this play our notice of the removal of the deposed king's body from Abbot's Langley to Westminster, in A.D. 1414. That ceremony appears to have been one of the earliest acts of Henry V. and he refers to it as an act of penitential restitution, in his speech immediately before the battle of Agincourt, Act IV. Sc. 1:—

"——— Not to-day, O Lord,
O! not to-day, think not upon the fault
My father made in compassing the crown!
I Richard's body have interred new,
And on it have bestow'd more contrite tears,
Than from it issued forcéd drops of blood.
Five hundred poor I have in yearly pay,
Who twice a day their wither'd hands hold up
Toward heaven, to pardon blood; and I have built
Two chantries, where the sad and solemn priests
Sing still for Richard's soul. More will I do:
Though all that I can do, is nothing worth,
Since that my penitence comes after all,
Imploring pardon."

Shakespeare derived the materials of this speech partly rom Holinshed, and partly from the contemporaneous chronicler Fabyan. The former historian says that "when the king had settled things much to his purpose, he caused the bodie of King Richard to be removed, with all funerall dignities convenient to his estate, from Langley to Westminster, where he was honourablie interred, with Queen Anne, his first wife, in a solemne toome, made and set up at the charges of this king. *Polychronicon* saith that after the bodie of the dead king was taken up out of the earth, this new king, happily tendering the magnificence of a prince, and abhorring obscure buriall, caused the same to be conveied to Westminster in a roiall seat or chaire of estate, covered all over with black velvet, and adorned with banners of divers armes round about." Fabyan adds that "after a solemne terrement there holden, he provided that fower tapers should bren day and night about his grave while the world endureth; and one day in the weeke a solempne *Dirige*, and upon the morowe a masse of *Requiem-song* by note: after which masse ended to be geven wekely unto the poore people an xis. and viii. pense, in pense. And upon the daye of his anniversary, after the saide masse of *Requiem-song*, to be yerely distributed for his soule, xx pounde in pense." But notwithstanding Holinshed's praise of the princely disposition which Henry V. exhibited towards the remains of Richard II. it seems to be almost certain that, so far as related to the translation of his body to Westminster, it was only restoring to him the occupation of his own sepulchre. His will proves that the tomb had been actually erected during his own life; and there are in Rymer's *Fœdera* two indentures made for its erection, between Richard and Henry Yevell and Stephen Lote, Citizens and Masons of London, and Nicholas Broker and Godfrey Prest, Citizens and Coppersmiths.

There is but one other point requiring illustration, which refers to the meaning of Henry in saying, "*More* will I do," in the way of satisfaction for the death of Richard II.: and a passage in the Chronicles of Monstrelet shews that, like his father, he designed another crusade. When Henry was informed that he could not live more than two hours, he "sent for his confessor, some of his household, and his chaplains, whom he ordered to chaunt the Seven Penitential Psalms. When they came to '*Benedic fac Domine*,' where mention is made of the '*Muri Hierusalem*,' (Psalm li. 18,) he stopped them, and said aloud that he had fully intended, after he had wholly subdued the realm of France to his obedience and restored it to peace, to have gone to conquer the kingdom of Jerusalem, if it had pleased his Creator to have granted him longer life." In the play also, in his courtship of the Princess Katharine, Act V. Sc. 2, Henry makes the following humorous reference to the same intention:—"Shall not thou and I, between St. Denis and St. George, compound a boy, half French, half English, that shall go to Constantinople and take the Turk by the beard? Shall we not? What sayest thou, my fair flower-de-luce?"

ACT V.

CHORUS.

(1) *A mighty whiffler.*] The term is supposed by some to be derived from *whiffle*, a name for a *fife* or flute; and *whifflers*, Douce surmises, were originally those who preceded armies or processions as fifers or pipers. Other authorities derive it from *whiffle*, to disperse as by a puff of wind, and affirm that a *whiffler*, in its original signification, meant a staff-bearer. In the old play of "Clyomen, Knight of the Golden Shield," &c. 1599, a *whiffler* presents himself at the tourney, clearing a passage for the king; and in Day's "Ile of Gulls," 1606, Miso says:—"And Manasses shall goe afore like a *whiffler*, and make way with his horns."

(1) SCENE II.—*Come, your answer in broken music.*] "Broken music," says Mr. Chappell, who was the first to explain the term, "means the music of stringed instruments, in contradistinction to those played by wind. The term originated probably from harps, lutes, and such other stringed instruments as were played without a bow, not having the capability to sustain a long note to its full duration of sound." See also *Popular Music of the Olden Time*, vol. i. p. 246.

Shakespeare quibbles on the expression in "Troilus and Cressida," Act III. Sc. 1:—

"Fair prince, here is good *broken* music;"

proving, as Mr. Chappell remarks, that the musicians on the stage were then performing on stringed instruments.

And again in "As You Like It," Act I. Sc. 2:—

"But is there any else longs to see this broken music in his sides?"

CRITICAL OPINIONS

ON

KING HENRY THE FIFTH.

"King Henry the Fifth is manifestly Shakspeare's favourite hero in English history: he paints him as endowed with every chivalrous and kingly virtue; open, sincere, affable, yet, as a sort of reminiscence of his youth, still disposed to innocent raillery, in the intervals between his perilous but glorious achievements. However, to represent on the stage his whole history subsequent to his accession to the throne, was attended with great difficulty. The conquests in France were the only distinguished event of his reign; and war is an epic rather than a dramatic object. For wherever men act in masses against each other, the appearance of chance can never wholly be avoided; whereas it is the business of the drama to exhibit to us those determinations which, with a certain necessity, issue from the reciprocal relations of different individuals, their characters and passions. In several of the Greek tragedies, it is true, combats and battles are exhibited, that is, the preparations for them and their results; and in historical plays war, as the *ultima ratio regum*, cannot altogether be excluded. Still, if we would have dramatic interest, war must only be the means by which something else is accomplished, and not the last aim and substance of the whole. For instance, in *Macbeth*, the battles which are announced at the very beginning merely serve to heighten the glory of Macbeth and to fire his ambition: and the combats which take place towards the conclusion, before the eyes of the spectator, bring on the destruction of the tyrant. It is the very same in the Roman pieces, in the most of those taken from English history, and, in short, wherever Shakspeare has introduced war in a dramatic combination. With great insight into the essence of his art, he never paints the fortune of war as a blind deity who sometimes favours one and sometimes another; without going into the details of the art of war, (though sometimes he even ventures on this,) he allows us to anticipate the result from the qualities of the general, and their influence on the minds of the soldiers; sometimes, without claiming our belief for miracles, he yet exhibits the issue in the light of a higher volition: the consciousness of a just cause and reliance on the protection of Heaven give courage to the one party, while the presage of a curse hanging over their undertaking weighs down the other. In *Henry the Fifth* no opportunity was afforded Shakspeare of adopting the last-mentioned course, namely, rendering the issue of the war dramatic; but he has skilfully availed himself of the first.—Before the battle of Agincourt he paints in the most lively colours the light-minded impatience of the French leaders for the moment of battle, which to them seemed infallibly the moment of victory; on the other hand, he paints the uneasiness of the English King and his army in their desperate situation, coupled with their firm determination, if they must fall, at least to fall with honour. He applies this as a general contrast between the French and English national characters; a contrast which betrays a partiality for his own nation, certainly excusable in a poet, especially when he is backed with such a glorious document as that of the memorable battle in question. He has surrounded the general events of the war with a fulness of individual, characteristic, and even sometimes comic features. A heavy Scotchman, a hot Irishman, a well-meaning, honourable, but pedantic Welshman, all speaking in their peculiar dialects, are intended to show us that the warlike genius of Henry did not merely carry the English with him, but also the other natives of the two islands, who were either not yet fully united or in no degree subject to him. Several good-for-nothing associates of Falstaff among the dregs of the army either afford an opportunity for proving Henry's strictness of discipline, or are sent home in disgrace. But all this variety still seemed to the poet insufficient to animate a play of which the subject was a conquest, and nothing but a conquest. He has, therefore, tacked a prologue (in the technical language of that day *a chorus*) to the beginning of each act. These prologues, which unite epic pomp and solemnity with lyrical sublimity, and among which the description of the two camps before the battle of Agincourt forms a most admirable night-piece, are intended to keep the spectators constantly in mind, that the peculiar grandeur of the actions described cannot be developed on a narrow stage, and that they must, therefore, supply, from their own imaginations, the deficiencies of the representation. As the matter was not properly dramatic, Shakspeare chose to wander in the form also beyond the bounds of the species, and to sing, as a poetical herald, what he could not represent to the eye, rather than to cripple the progress of the action by putting long descriptions in the mouths of the dramatic personages. The confession of the poet that "four or five most vile and ragged foils, right ill-disposed, can only disgrace the name of Agincourt," (a scruple which he has overlooked in the occasion of many other great battles, and among others of that of Philippi,) brings us here naturally to the question how far, generally speaking, it may be suitable and advisable to represent wars and battles on the stage. The Greeks have uniformly renounced them: as in the whole of their theatrical system they proceeded on ideas of grandeur and dignity, a feeble and petty imitation of the unattainable would have appeared insupportable in their eyes. With them, consequently, all fighting was merely recounted. The principle of the romantic dramatists was altogether different: their wonderful pictures were infinitely larger than their theatrical means of visible execution; they were everywhere obliged to count on the willing imagination of the spectators, and consequently they also relied on them in this point. It is certainly laughable enough that a handful of awkward warriors in mock armour, by means of two or three swords, with which we clearly see they take especial care not to do the slightest injury to one another, should decide the fate of mighty kingdoms. But the opposite extreme is still much worse. If we in reality succeed in exhibiting the tumult of a great battle, the storming of a fort, and the like, in a manner any way calculated to deceive the eye, the power of these sensible impressions is so great that they render the spectator incapable of bestowing that attention which a poetical work of art demands; and thus the essential is sacrificed to the accessory. We have learned from experience, that whenever cavalry combats are introduced, the men soon become secondary personages beside the four-footed players. Fortunately, in Shakspeare's time, the art of converting the yielding boards of the theatre into a riding course had not yet been invented. He tells the spectators in the first prologue in *Henry the Fifth*:—

> Think, when we talk of horses, that you see them
> Printing their proud hoofs in the receiving earth.

When Richard the Third utters the famous exclamation,—

> A horse! a horse! my kingdom for a horse!

it is no doubt inconsistent to see him both before and afterwards constantly fighting on foot. It is however better, perhaps, that the poet and player should by overpowering impressions dispose us to forget this, than by literal exactness to expose themselves to external interruptions. With all the disadvantages which I have mentioned, Shakspeare and several Spanish poets have contrived to derive such great beauties from the immediate representation of war, that I cannot bring myself to wish they had abstained from it. A theatrical manager of the present day will have a middle course to follow: his art must, in an especial manner, be directed to make what he shows us appear only as separate groups of an immense picture, which cannot be taken in at once by the eye; he must convince the spectators that the main action takes place behind the stage; and for this purpose he has easy means at his command in the nearer or more remote sound of warlike music and the din of arms.

"However much Shakspeare celebrates the French conquest of Henry, still he has not omitted to hint after his way, the secret springs of this undertaking. Henry was in want of foreign war to secure himself on the throne; the clergy also wished to keep him employed abroad, and made an offer of rich contributions to prevent the passing of a law which would have deprived them of the half of their revenues. His learned bishops consequently are as ready to prove to him his indisputable right to the crown of France, as he is to allow his conscience to be tranquillized by them. They prove that the Salic law is not, and never was, applicable to France; and the matter is treated in a more succinct and convincing manner than such subjects usually are in manifestoes. After his renowned battles, Henry wished to secure his conquests by marriage with a French princess; all that has reference to this is intended for irony in the play. The fruit of this union, from which two nations promised to themselves such happiness in future, was the weak and feeble Henry VI., under whom every thing was so miserably lost. It must not, therefore, be imagined that it was without the knowledge and will of the poet that a heroic drama turns out a comedy in his hands, and ends in the manner of Comedy with a marriage of convenience."—SCHLEGEL.

Act III. Sc. 5.

AS YOU LIKE IT.

THIS charming dramatic pastoral was first printed, it is believed, in the folio, 1623. On the Stationers' Registers, however, is an entry, conjectured, with good reason, to belong to the year 1600, which may induce a different conclusion. It runs thus:—

> "4 Augusti.
>
> "As you like yt, a book. Henry the ffift, a book. Every Man in his humor, a book. The Commedie of Much Adoo about Nothinge, a book. To be staied."

The object of the "stay," as Mr. Collier supposes, was no doubt to prevent the publication of these plays by any other booksellers than Wise and Apsley; and as the three other "books" were issued by them in a quarto form, probabilities are in favour of the fourth having been so published also. At all events, there are sufficient grounds for hope that a quarto edition may some day come to light. "As You Like It" is founded on Lodge's novel, entitled "Rosalynde, Euphues Golden Legacy," &c., 1590; which in turn was derived from the "Coke's Tale of Gamelyn," attributed to Chaucer, and sometimes printed in his works, though now very generally believed to be the work of another and much inferior hand.

The quotation, in Act. III. Sc. 5, from Marlowe's poem of "Hero and Leander,"—

> "*Who ever lov'd, that lov'd not at first sight?*"—

which appeared in 1598; the circumstance of its not being included in the list by Meres; and the memorandum above mentioned in the Stationers' Registers, have led Malone and others, we think rightly, to assign the composition of "As You Like It" to the year 1599.

In connexion with this comedy there is a tradition too pleasing to be forgotten. It is related, on the authority of the poet's brother Gilbert, who survived till after the Restoration of Charles II, that Shakespeare himself personated the faithful old Adam on the Stage. "One of Shakespeare's younger brothers," Oldys relates, "who lived to a good old age, even some years, as I compute, after the restoration of King Charles II, would in his younger days come to London to visit his brother Will, as he called him, and be a spectator of him as an actor in some of his own plays. This custom, as his brother's fame enlarged, and his dramatick entertainments grew the greatest support of our principal, if not of all our theatres, he continued, it seems, so long after his brother's death as even to the latter end of his own life. The curiosity at this time of the most noted actors to learn something from him of his brother, &c. they justly held him in the highest veneration. And it may be well believed, as there was besides a kinsman and descendant of the family, who was then a celebrated actor among them, this opportunity made them greedily inquisitive into every little circumstance, more especially in his dramatick character, which his brother could relate of him. But he, it seems, was so stricken in years, and possibly his memory so weakened with infirmities, which might make him the easier pass for a man of weak intellects, that he could give them but little light into their enquiries; and all that could be recollected from him of his brother Will in that station was the faint, general, and almost lost ideas he had of having once seen him 'act a part in one of his own comedies, wherein, being to personate a decrepit old man, he wore a long beard, and appeared so weak and drooping, and unable to walk, that he was forced to be supported and carried by another person to a table, at which he was seated among some company, who were eating, and one of them sung a song.'"

This description accords in all essential particulars with the introduction of Adam to the banished duke and his followers, at their sylvan banquet, in Act II. Sc. 7.

Persons Represented.

DUKE, *living in banishment.*	CHARLES, *a Wrestler.*
FREDERICK, *his Brother, and usurper of his Dominions.*	TOUCHSTONE, *a Clown, or Domestic Fool.*
AMIENS, JAQUES, } *Gentlemen attending on the Exiled* DUKE.	CORIN, SILVIUS, } *Shepherds.*
LE BEAU, *a Courtier attending upon* FREDERICK.	WILLIAM, *a Peasant, in love with* AUDREY.
OLIVER, JAQUES, ORLANDO, } *Sons of* SIR ROLAND DE BOIS.	*The Representative of Hymen.*
ADAM, DENIS, } *Servants to* OLIVER.	ROSALIND, *Daughter to the banished* DUKE.
SIR OLIVER MARTEXT, *a Vicar.*	CELIA, *Daughter to* FREDERICK.
	PHEBE, *a Shepherdess.*
	AUDREY, *a Country wench.*

Followers and Attendants on the two Dukes, Pages, Foresters, &c. &c.

SCENE,—*First, (and in Act II. Sc. 3,) near* OLIVER'S *House; intermediately and afterwards, partly in the* usurper's *Court, and partly in the Forest of* Arden.

ACT I.

SCENE I.—*An Orchard, adjoining* Oliver's *House.*

Enter ORLANDO *and* ADAM.

ORL. As I remember, Adam, it was upon this fashion,—bequeathed[a] me by will, but poor a[b] thousand crowns, and, as thou sayest, charged my brother, on his blessing, to breed me well: and there begins my sadness. My brother Jaques he keeps at school, and report speaks goldenly of his profit: for my part, he keeps me rustically at home, or, to speak more properly, stays me here at home unkept. For call you that keeping, for a gentleman of my birth, that differs not from the stalling of an ox? His horses are bred better: for, besides that they are fair with their feeding, they are taught their manage, and to that end riders dearly hired: but I, his brother, gain nothing under him but growth; for the which his animals on his dunghills are as much bound to him as I. Besides this nothing that he so plentifully gives me, the something that nature gave me, his countenance[c] seems to take from me: he lets me feed with his hinds, bars me the place of a brother, and, as much as in him lies, mines my gentility with my education. This is it, Adam, that grieves me; and the spirit of my father, which I think is within me, begins to mutiny against this servitude: I will no longer endure it, though yet I know no wise remedy how to avoid it.

---

[a] Bequeathed me—] Some of the modern editions read, "*he* bequeathed me:" and it is not improbable that the pronoun was omitted by the carelessness of the transcriber or compositor.

[b] *But* poor *a thousand crowns,*—] So the folio, 1623, but most editors have adopted the reading of the folio, 1632:—"*a poor* thousand crowns;" and those who adhere to the original have failed to produce a single instance of similar phraseology to support them. This is the more strange, since the idiom was at least as old as the time of Chaucer, and by no means uncommon:—

"And so I followed, till it me brought
To *right a* pleasaunt herber."
CHAUCER: *Flower and Leaf*, l. 49.

"At Leycester came to the Kynge *ryght a* fayre felawship of folks, to the nombar of three thousand men."—*Arrival of Edward IV.* p. 8.

"The Kynge * * * * travaylynge all his people, whereof were moo than three thousand foteman, that Fryday, which was *right-an-hot* day, thirty myle and more."—*Ibid.* p. 27.

[c] *His* countenance *seems to take from me*:] The commentators appear to have misunderstood this expression. It does not here import *aspect, carriage,* and the like, but *entertainment.* See note (g), p. 255, Vol. I.

ADAM. Yonder comes my master, your brother.

ORL. Go apart, Adam, and thou shalt hear how he will shake me up. [ADAM *retires.*

Enter OLIVER.

OLI. Now, sir! what make[a] you here?

ORL. Nothing: I am not taught to make any thing.

OLI. What mar you then, sir?

ORL. Marry, sir, I am helping you to mar that which God made, a poor unworthy brother of yours, with idleness.

OLI. Marry, sir, be better employed, and be naught awhile.[b]

ORL. Shall I keep your hogs, and eat husks with them? What prodigal portion have I spent, that I should come to such penury?

OLI. Know you where you are, sir?

ORL. O, sir, very well: here in your orchard.

OLI. Know you before whom, sir?

ORL. Ay, better than him I am before knows me. I know, you are my eldest brother; and, in the gentle condition of blood, you should so know me: the courtesy of nations allows you my better, in that you are the first-born; but the same tradition takes not away my blood, were there twenty brothers betwixt us: I have as much of my father in me, as you; albeit, I confess, your coming before me is nearer to his reverence.

OLI. What, boy!

ORL. Come, come, elder brother, you are too young in this.[c]

---

[a] *What* make *you here?*] What *do* you here?

[b] Be naught awhile.] A proverbial phrase, equivalent to *a mischief on you.*

[c] *Come, come,* elder *brother,* you *are too* young *in this.*] The obscurity in this speech is at once cleared up by a passage in the original story:—"Though I am *eldest* by birth, yet, never having attempted any deeds of arms, I am *youngest* to perform any martial exploits."—LODGE'S *Rosalynd*, p. 17 of reprint in *Shakespeare's Library*. Stung by the sarcastic allusion to his *reverence,* Oliver attempts to strike his brother, who seizes him, observing at the same time, "You are *too young* at this game of manly prowess; in this, I am the elder."

OLI. Wilt thou lay hands on me, villain?

ORL. I am no villain: I am the youngest son of sir Roland de Bois: he was my father; and he is thrice a villain that says such a father begot villains. Wert thou not my brother, I would not take this hand from thy throat, till this other had pulled out thy tongue for saying so; thou hast railed on thyself.

ADAM. [*Coming forward.*] Sweet masters, be patient; for your father's remembrance, be at accord.

OLI. Let me go, I say.

ORL. I will not, till I please; you shall hear me. My father charged you in his will to give me good education: you have trained me like a peasant, obscuring and hiding from me all gentleman-like qualities. The spirit of my father grows strong in me, and I will no longer endure it: therefore allow me such exercises as may become a gentleman, or give me the poor allottery my father left me by testament; with that I will go buy my fortunes.

OLI. And what wilt thou do? beg, when that is spent? Well, sir, get you in: I will not long be troubled with you: you shall have some part of your will: I pray you, leave me.

ORL. I will no further offend you than becomes me for my good.

OLI. Get you with him, you old dog.

ADAM. Is *old dog* my reward? Most true, I have lost my teeth in your service.—God be with my old master! he would not have spoke such a word. [*Exeunt* ORLANDO *and* ADAM.

OLI. Is it even so? begin you to grow upon me? I will physic your rankness, and yet give no thousand crowns neither. Holla, Denis!

Enter DENIS.

DEN. Calls your worship?

OLI. Was not Charles, the duke's wrestler, here to speak with me?

DEN. So please you, he is here at the door, and importunes access to you.

OLI. Call him in. [*Exit* DENIS.]—'Twill be a good way; and to-morrow the wrestling is.

Enter CHARLES.

CHA. Good morrow to your worship.

OLI. Good monsieur Charles!—what's the new news at the new court?

CHA. There's no news at the court, sir, but the old news: that is, the old duke is banished by his younger brother the new duke; and three or four loving lords have put themselves into voluntary exile with him, whose lands and revenues enrich the new duke; therefore he gives them good leave to wander.

OLI. Can you tell if Rosalind, the duke's daughter, be banished with her father?

CHA. O, no; for the duke's daughter, her cousin, so loves her,—being ever from their cradles bred together,—that she* would have followed her exile, or have died to stay behind her. She is at the court, and no less beloved of her uncle than his own daughter; and never two ladies loved as they do.

OLI. Where will the old duke live?

CHA. They say, he is already in the forest of Arden, and a many merry men with him; and there they live like the old Robin Hood of England: they say many young gentlemen flock to him every day, and fleet the time carelessly, as they did in the golden world.

OLI. What,—you wrestle to-morrow before the new duke?

CHA. Marry, do I, sir; and I came to acquaint you with a matter. I am given, sir, secretly to understand that your younger brother, Orlando, hath a disposition to come in disguised against me to try a fall. To-morrow, sir, I wrestle for my credit; and he that escapes me without some broken limb shall acquit him well. Your brother is but young and tender; and, for your love, I would be loth to foil him, as I must, for my own honour, if he come in: therefore, out of my love to you, I came hither to acquaint you withal; that either you might stay him from his intendment, or brook such disgrace well as he shall run into; in that it is a thing of his own search, and altogether against my will.

OLI. Charles, I thank thee for thy love to me, which thou shalt find I will most kindly requite. I had myself notice of my brother's purpose herein, and have by under-hand means laboured to dissuade him from it; but he is resolute. I'll tell thee, Charles,—it is the stubbornest young fellow of France; full of ambition, an envious emulator of every man's good parts, a secret and villainous contriver against me his natural brother; therefore use thy discretion; I had as lief thou didst break his neck as his finger: and thou wert best look to't; for if thou dost him any slight disgrace, or if he do not mightily grace himself on thee, he will practise against thee by poison, entrap thee by some treacherous device, and never leave thee till he hath ta'en thy life by some indirect means or other; for, I assure thee, and almost with tears I speak it, there is not one so young and so villainous this day living. I speak but brotherly of him; but should I anatomise him to thee as he is, I must blush and weep, and thou must look pale and wonder.

(*) First folio, *hee*.

CHA. I am heartily glad I came hither to you. If he come to-morrow, I'll give him his payment: if ever he go alone again, I'll never wrestle for prize more: and so, God keep your worship! (1)
[*Exit.*

OLI. Farewell, good Charles.—Now will I stir this gamester: I hope, I shall see an end of him; for my soul, yet I know not why, hates nothing more than he. Yet he's gentle: never schooled, and yet learned; full of noble device; of all sorts enchantingly beloved; and, indeed, so much in the heart of the world, and especially of my own people, who best know him, that I am altogether misprised: but it shall not be so long; this wrestler shall clear all: nothing remains, but that I kindle the boy thither, which now I'll go about.
[*Exit.*

SCENE II.—*A Lawn before the* Duke's *Palace.*

Enter ROSALIND *and* CELIA.

CEL. I pray thee, Rosalind, sweet my coz, be merry.

ROS. Dear Celia, I show more mirth than I am mistress of; and would you yet I* were merrier? Unless you could teach me to forget a banished father, you must not learn me how to remember any extraordinary pleasure.

CEL. Herein I see thou lovest me not with the full weight that I love thee: if my uncle, thy banished father, had banished thy uncle, the duke my father, so thou hadst been still with me, I could have taught my love to take thy father for mine; so wouldst thou, if the truth of thy love to me were so righteously tempered as mine is to thee.

ROS. Well, I will forget the condition of my estate, to rejoice in yours.

CEL. You know my father hath no child but I, nor none is like to have; and, truly, when he dies, thou shalt be his heir: for what he hath taken away from thy father perforce, I will render thee again in affection; by mine honour, I will; and when I break that oath, let me turn monster; therefore, my sweet Rose, my dear Rose, be merry.

ROS. From henceforth I will, coz, and devise sports: let me see;—what think you of falling in love?

(*) Old copy omits, *I*.

CEL. Marry, I pr'ythee, do, to make sport withal: but love no man in good earnest; nor no further in sport neither, than with safety of a pure blush thou mayst in honour come off again.

ROS. What shall be our sport then?

CEL. Let us sit and mock the good housewife Fortune from her wheel, that her gifts may henceforth be bestowed equally.

ROS. I would we could do so; for her benefits are mightily misplaced: and the bountiful blind woman doth most mistake in her gifts to women.

CEL. 'Tis true; for those that she makes fair, she scarce makes honest:[a] and those that she makes honest, she makes very ill-favouredly.

ROS. Nay, now thou goest from Fortune's office to Nature's: fortune reigns in gifts of the world, not in the lineaments of nature.

CEL. No? When Nature hath made a fair creature, may she not by Fortune fall into the fire?— Though Nature hath given us wit to flout at Fortune, hath not Fortune sent in this fool to cut off the argument?

Enter TOUCHSTONE.[b]

ROS. Indeed, there is fortune too hard for nature; when fortune makes nature's natural the cutter off of nature's wit.

CEL. Peradventure, this is not Fortune's work neither, but Nature's; who perceiving* our natural wits too dull to reason of such goddesses, hath sent this natural for our whetstone: for always the dulness of the fool is the whetstone of the wits.— How now, wit! whither wander you?[c]

TOUCH. Mistress, you must come away to your father.

[a] Honest:] That is, *chaste*.
[b] TOUCHSTONE.] In the old copy he is called "Clown."

(*) First folio, *perceiveth*.

[c] How now, wit! whither wander you?] The beginning, probably, of some ancient ballad.

CEL. Were you made the messenger?

TOUCH. No, by mine honour; but I was bid to come for you.

ROS. Where learned you that oath, fool?

TOUCH. Of a certain knight, that swore by his honour they were good pancakes, and swore by his honour the mustard was naught: now, I'll stand to it, the pancakes were naught, and the mustard was good; and yet was not the knight forsworn.

CEL. How prove you that, in the great heap of your knowledge?

ROS. Ay, marry; now unmuzzle your wisdom.

TOUCH. Stand you both forth now: stroke your chins and swear by your beards that I am a knave.

CEL. By our beards, if we had them, thou art.

TOUCH. By my knavery, if I had it, then I were: but if you swear by that that is not, you are not forsworn: no more was this knight, swearing by his honour, for he never had any;[a] or if he had, he had sworn it away before ever he saw those pancakes or that mustard.

CEL. Pr'ythee, who is't that thou meanest?

TOUCH. One that old Frederick, your father, loves.

CEL.[b] My father's love is enough to honour him. Enough! speak no more of him: you'll be whipped for taxation,[c] one of these days.

TOUCH. The more pity, that fools may not speak wisely, what wise men do foolishly.

CEL. By my troth, thou sayest true: for since the little wit that fools have was silenced, the little foolery that wise men have makes a great show.—Here comes monsieur Le Beau.*

ROS. With his mouth full of news.

CEL. Which he will put on us, as pigeons feed their young.

ROS. Then we shall be news-crammed.

CEL. All the better; we shall be the more marketable.

Enter LE BEAU.

Bon jour, monsieur Le Beau: what's the news?

LE BEAU. Fair princess, you have lost much good sport.

CEL. Sport? of what colour?

LE BEAU. What colour, madam! how shall I answer you?

ROS. As wit and fortune will.

TOUCH. Or as the Destinies decree.

CEL. Well said; that was laid on with a trowel.[d]

TOUCH. Nay, if I keep not my rank,——

ROS. Thou losest thy old smell.

LE BEAU. You amaze me, ladies: I would have told you of good wrestling, which you have lost the sight of.

ROS. Yet tell us the manner of the wrestling.

LE BEAU. I will tell you the beginning, and, if it please your ladyships, you may see the end; for the best is yet to do; and here, where you are, they are coming to perform it.

CEL. Well,—the beginning, that is dead and buried.

LE BEAU. There comes an old man, and his three sons,——

CEL. I could match this beginning with an old tale.

LE BEAU. Three proper young men, of excellent growth and presence;—

ROS. With bills on their necks,[e]—*Be it known unto all men by these presents*,[f]——

LE BEAU. The eldest of the three wrestled with Charles, the duke's wrestler; which Charles in a moment threw him, and broke three of his ribs, that there is little hope of life in him: so he served the second, and so the third; yonder they lie; the poor old man, their father, making such pitiful dole over them, that all the beholders take his part with weeping.

ROS. Alas!

TOUCH. But what is the sport, monsieur, that the ladies have lost?

LE BEAU. Why, this that I speak of.

TOUCH. Thus men may grow wiser every day! it is the first time that ever I heard breaking of ribs was sport for ladies.

CEL. Or I, I promise thee.

ROS. But is there any else longs to see this broken music[g] in his sides? is there yet another dotes upon rib-breaking?—Shall we see this wrestling, cousin?

LE BEAU. You must, if you stay here: for here is the place appointed for the wrestling, and they are ready to perform it.

CEL. Yonder, sure, they are coming: let us now stay and see it.

(*) First folio, *the Beu*.

[a] By his honour, for he never had any;] This was an ancient gibe. Boswell quotes a passage in which it occurs, from the play of "Damon and Pithias," 1573:—

"I have taken a wise othe on him; have I not, trow ye,
To trust such a false knave upon his honestie?
As he is *an honest man* (quoth you?) he may bewray all to the Kinge
And breke his oth for this never a whit."

[b] CELIA.] In the old copy, this speech is assigned to Rosalind, manifestly in error, since *Frederick* was the name of Celia's father. The correction is due to Theobald.

[c] Taxation,—] *Satire, invective, sarcasm.*

[d] *Laid on with* a trowel.] An old proverbial expression, which means, *laid on thickly*. We still say, when any one bespatters another with gross flattery, that he lays it on with a trowel.

[e] With bills on their necks,—] From a passage in Lodge's *Rosalynde*, the story whence Shakespeare derived the plot of this comedy:—"Rosader came pacing towardes them with his *forest bill on his neck*," Farmer conjectured, perhaps rightly, that these words originally formed part of Le Beau's speech.

[f] *Be it known*, &c.] Rosalind plays on the word *bills*, converting the forester's weapons into advertising bills, which, in Shakespeare's day, very commonly began with the phrase she quotes.

[g] Broken music—] See note (1), p. 120.

Flourish. Enter DUKE FREDERICK, Lords, ORLANDO, CHARLES, *and* Attendants.

DUKE F. Come on; since the youth will not be entreated, his own peril on his forwardness.

ROS. Is yonder the man?

LE BEAU. Even he, madam.

CEL. Alas, he is too young: yet he looks successfully.

DUKE F. How now, daughter and cousin! are you crept hither to see the wrestling?

ROS. Ay, my liege, so please you give us leave.

DUKE F. You will take little delight in it, I can tell you, there is such odds in the men.* In pity of the challenger's youth, I would fain dissuade him, but he will not be entreated. Speak to him, ladies; see if you can move him.

CEL. Call him hither, good monsieur Le Beau.

DUKE F. Do so; I'll not be by.

[DUKE *goes apart.*

LE BEAU. Monsieur the challenger, the princesses† call for you.

ORL. I attend them with all respect and duty.

ROS. Young man, have you challenged Charles the wrestler?

ORL. No, fair princess; he is the general challenger: I come but in, as others do, to try with him the strength of my youth.

CEL. Young gentleman, your spirits are too bold for your years: you have seen cruel proof of this man's strength: if you saw yourself with your eyes, or knew yourself with your judgment, the fear of your adventure would counsel you to a more equal enterprise. We pray you, for your own sake, to embrace your own safety, and give over this attempt.

ROS. Do, young sir; your reputation shall not therefore be misprised: we will make it our suit to the duke that the wrestling might not go forward.

ORL. I beseech you, punish me not with your hard thoughts; wherein I confess me much guilty,[a] to deny so fair and excellent ladies any thing. But let your fair eyes and gentle wishes go with me to my trial: wherein if I be foiled, there is but one shamed that was never gracious; if killed, but one dead that is willing to be so: I shall do my friends no wrong, for I have none to lament me; the world no injury, for in it I have nothing; only in the world I fill up a place, which may be better supplied when I have made it empty.

ROS. The little strength that I have, I would it were with you.

CEL. And mine, to eke out hers.

ROS. Fare you well. Pray heaven I be deceived in you!

CEL. Your heart's desires be with you!

CHA. Come, where is this young gallant that is so desirous to lie with his mother earth?

ORL. Ready, sir; but his will hath in it a more modest working.

DUKE F. You shall try but one fall.

CHA. No, I warrant your grace; you shall not entreat him to a second, that have so mightily persuaded him from a first.

ORL. You mean to mock me after; you should not have mocked me before; but come your ways.

ROS. Now Hercules be thy speed, young man!

CEL. I would I were invisible, to catch the strong fellow by the leg.

[ORLANDO *and* CHARLES *wrestle.*

ROS. O excellent young man!

CEL. If I had a thunderbolt in mine eye, I can tell who should down.

[CHARLES *is thrown.*(2) *Shout.*

DUKE F. No more, no more.

ORL. Yes, I beseech your grace; I am not yet well breathed.

DUKE F. How dost thou, Charles?

LE BEAU. He cannot speak, my lord.

DUKE F. Bear him away.

[CHARLES *is borne out.*

What is thy name, young man?

ORL. Orlando, my liege; the youngest son of sir Roland de Bois.

DUKE F. I would thou hadst been son to some man else.
The world esteem'd thy father honourable,
But I did find him still mine enemy:
Thou shouldst have better pleas'd me with this deed,
Hadst thou descended from another house.
But fare thee well; thou art a gallant youth;
I would thou hadst told me of another father.

[*Exeunt* DUKE FRED. Train, *and* LE BEAU.

CEL. Were I my father, coz, would I do this?

ORL. I am more proud to be sir Roland's son,
His youngest son;—and would not change that calling,
To be adopted heir to Frederick.

ROS. My father lov'd sir Roland as his soul,
And all the world was of my father's mind:
Had I before known this young man his son,
I should have given him tears unto entreaties,
Ere he should thus have ventur'd.

CEL. Gentle cousin,
Let us go thank him and encourage him:

(*) Old text, *man*. (†) Old text, *princesse*.

[a] Wherein I confess me much guilty,—] This is somewhat perplexed. Malone's gloss is:—"*Punish me not with your hard thoughts, which, however, I confess, I deserve to incur*, for denying such fair ladies any request."

My father's rough and envious disposition
Sticks me at heart.—Sir, you have well deserv'd:
If you do keep your promises in love,
But justly, as you have exceeded all promise,
Your mistress shall be happy.
Ros. Gentleman,
Wear this for me, one out of suits with fortune,
That could give more, but that her hand lacks means.—
[*Giving him a chain from her neck.*
Shall we go, coz?
Cel. Ay.—Fare you well, fair gentleman.
Orl. Can I not say, I thank you? My better parts
Are all thrown down; and that which here stands [up,
Is but a quintain,(3) a mere lifeless block.
Ros. He calls us back. My pride fell with my [fortunes;
I'll ask him what he would.—Did you call, sir?—
Sir, you have wrestled well, and overthrown
More than your enemies.

CEL. Will you go, coz?

ROS. Have with you.—Fare you well.

[*Exeunt* ROSALIND *and* CELIA.

ORL. What passion hangs these weights upon my tongue?
I cannot speak to her, yet she urg'd conference.
O poor Orlando, thou art overthrown!
Or Charles, or something weaker, masters thee.

Re-enter LE BEAU.

LE BEAU. Good sir, I do in friendship counsel you
To leave this place. Albeit you have deserv'd
High commendation, true applause, and love;
Yet such is now the duke's condition,[a]
That he misconstrues all that you have done.
The duke is humorous;[b] what he is, indeed,
More suits you to conceive than I to speak of.

ORL. I thank you, sir; and, pray you, tell me this,—
Which of the two was daughter of the duke
That here was at the wrestling?

LE BEAU. Neither his daughter, if we judge by manners;
But yet, indeed, the lower* is his daughter:
The other is daughter to the banish'd duke,
And here detain'd by her usurping uncle,
To keep his daughter company; whose loves
Are dearer than the natural bond of sisters.
But I can tell you, that of late this duke
Hath ta'en displeasure 'gainst his gentle niece;
Grounded upon no other argument,
But that the people praise her for her virtues,
And pity her for her good father's sake;
And, on my life, his malice 'gainst the lady
Will suddenly break forth.—Sir, fare you well;
Hereafter, in a better world than this,
I shall desire more love and knowledge of you.

ORL. I rest much bounden to you: fare you well. [*Exit* LE BEAU.
Thus must I from the smoke into the smother;
From tyrant duke, unto a tyrant brother:—
But heavenly Rosalind! [*Exit.*

SCENE III.—*A Room in the Palace.*

Enter CELIA *and* ROSALIND.

CEL. Why, cousin; why, Rosalind;—Cupid have mercy!—Not a word?

ROS. Not one to throw at a dog.

CEL. No, thy words are too precious to be cast away upon curs, throw some of them at me; come, lame me with reasons.

ROS. Then there were two cousins laid up; when the one should be lamed with reasons, and the other mad without any.

CEL. But is all this for your father?

ROS. No, some of it is for my child's father.[c] O, how full of briars is this working-day world!

CEL. They are but burs, cousin, thrown upon thee in holiday foolery; if we walk not in the trodden paths, our very petticoats will catch them.

ROS. I could shake them off my coat; these burs are in my heart.

CEL. Hem them away.

ROS. I would try, if I could cry *hem* and have him.

CEL. Come, come, wrestle with thy affections.

ROS. O, they take the part of a better wrestle than myself!

CEL. O, a good wish upon you! you will try in time, in despite of a fall. But, turning these jests out of service, let us talk in good earnest. Is it possible, on such a sudden, you should fall into so strong a liking with old sir Roland's youngest son?

ROS. The duke my father loved his father dearly.

CEL. Doth it therefore ensue, that you should love his son dearly? By this kind of chase, I should hate him, for my father hated his father dearly;[d] yet I hate not Orlando.

ROS. No, 'faith, hate him not, for my sake.

CEL. Why should I not? doth he not deserve well?

ROS. Let me love him for that; and do you love him, because I do. Look, here comes the duke.

CEL. With his eyes full of anger.

Enter DUKE FREDERICK, *with* Lords.

DUKE F. Mistress, despatch you with your safest haste,
And get you from our court.

ROS. Me, uncle?

DUKE F. You, cousin.
Within these ten days if that thou be'st found
So near our public court as twenty miles,
Thou diest for it.

(*) Old text, *taller*.

[a] Condition,—] *Temper, frame of mind.*

[b] *The duke is* humorous;] *Humorous* here means *contrarious, perverse, capricious.*

[c] For my child's father.] Thus the old text, which, as involving an "indelicate anticipation," is enervated in nearly all the modern editions into "for my father's child." The meaning is simply, as Theobald long ago explained it, "for him whom I hope to marry," and the idea and its expression are perfectly conformable to the freedom of thought and speech in Shakespeare's age. It is remarkable that Rowe, who first suggested, and all the editors who have since adopted, the prudish substitution of "my father's child," should have overlooked its obvious incompatibility with Rosalind's subsequent observation:—

"I would try, if I could cry *hem* and have *him*."

[d] For my father hated his father dearly;] See note on the word *dear*, in "Hamlet," Act I. Sc. 2:—

"Would I had met my *dearest* foe in heaven."

Ros. I do beseech your grace,
Let me the knowledge of my fault bear with me:
If with myself I hold intelligence,
Or have acquaintance with mine own desires;
If that I do not dream, or be not frantic,
(As I do trust I am not,) then, dear uncle,
Never so much as in a thought unborn,
Did I offend your highness.

Duke F. Thus do all traitors;
If their purgation did consist in words,
They are as innocent as grace itself:
Let it suffice thee, that I trust thee not. [traitor:

Ros. Yet your mistrust cannot make me a
Tell me, whereon the likelihood* depends.

Duke F. Thou art thy father's daughter, there's enough. [dukedom;

Ros. So was I when your highness took his
So was I when your highness banish'd him:
Treason is not inherited, my lord:
Or, if we did derive it from our friends,
What's that to me? my father was no traitor:
Then, good my liege, mistake me not so much,
To think my poverty is treacherous.

Cel. Dear sovereign, hear me speak. [sake,

Duke F. Ay, Celia; we stay'd her for your
Else had she with her father rang'd along.

Cel. I did not then entreat to have her stay;
It was your pleasure and your own remorse;
I was too young that time to value her,
But now I know her; if she be a traitor,
Why so am I: we still have slept together,
Rose at an instant, learn'd, play'd, eat together;
And wheresoe'er we went, like Juno's swans,
Still we went coupled and inseparable.(4)

Duke F. She is too subtle for thee; and her smoothness,
Her very silence, and her patience,
Speak to the people, and they pity her.
Thou art a fool: she robs thee of thy name,
And thou wilt show more bright and seem more virtuous,
When she is gone: then open not thy lips;
Firm and irrevocable is my doom
Which I have pass'd upon her;—she is banish'd.

Cel. Pronounce that sentence then on me, my liege;
I cannot live out of her company. [yourself;

Duke F. You are a fool.—You, niece, provide
If you outstay the time, upon mine honour,
And in the greatness of my word, you die.

[*Exeunt* Duke Frederick *and* Lords.

Cel. O my poor Rosalind! whither wilt thou go?
Wilt thou change fathers? I will give thee mine.
I charge thee, be not thou more griev'd than I am.

Ros. I have more cause.

Cel. Thou hast not, cousin;
Pr'ythee, be cheerful: know'st thou not, the duke
Hath banish'd me his daughter?

Ros. That he hath not.

Cel. No, hath not?[a] Rosalind lacks, then, the love
Which teacheth thee that thou and I am one:
Shall we be sunder'd? shall we part, sweet girl?
No; let my father seek another heir.
Therefore devise with me how we may fly,
Whither to go, and what to bear with us:
And do not seek to take your change upon you,[b]
To bear your griefs yourself, and leave me out;
For, by this heaven, now at our sorrows pale,
Say what thou canst, I'll go along with thee.(5)

Ros. Why, whither shall we go?

Cel. To seek my uncle in the forest of Arden.

Ros. Alas, what danger will it be to us,
Maids as we are, to travel forth so far!
Beauty provoketh thieves sooner than gold.

Cel. I'll put myself in poor and mean attire,
And with a kind of umber smirch my face;
The like do you; so shall we pass along,
And never stir assailants.

Ros. Were it not better,
Because that I am more than common tall,[c]
That I did suit me all points like a man?
A gallant curtle-ax upon my thigh,
A boar-spear in my hand; and (in my heart
Lie there what hidden woman's fear there will,)
We'll have a swashing and a martial outside;
As many other mannish cowards have,
That do outface it with their semblances.

Cel. What shall I call thee when thou art a man? [own page,

Ros. I'll have no worse a name than Jove's
And therefore look you call me, Ganymede.
But what will you be* call'd? [state;

Cel. Something that hath a reference to my
No longer Celia, but Aliena.

Ros. But, cousin, what if we assay'd to steal
The clownish fool out of your father's court?
Would he not be a comfort to our travel?

Cel. He'll go along o'er the wide world with me;
Leave me alone to woo him. Let's away,
And get our jewels and our wealth together;
Devise the fittest time, and safest way
To hide us from pursuit that will be made
After my flight. Now go we in† content
To liberty, and not to banishment. [*Exeunt.*

(*) First folio, *likelihoods*.

(*) First folio, *by*. (†) First folio, *in we*.

[a] No, hath not?] Mr. Singer looks upon this as an idiomatic phrase similar to the "No had, my lord?" in Act IV. Sc. 2, of "King John." See note (a), p. 315, Vol. I., but we believe he is mistaken.

[b] *And do not seek to take your* change *upon you*,—] That is, says Malone, *your reverse of fortune*. The second folio, 1632, reads *charge*, which is perhaps right.

[c] Because that I am more than common tall,—] So Lodge's *Rosalynde*—"Tush (quoth Rosalynde) art thou a woman, and hast not a sodeine shift to prevent a misfortune? I (thou seest) am of a tall stature, and would very well become the person and apparel of a page."—Reprint in *Shakespeare's Library*, p. 32.

ACT II.

SCENE I.—*The Forest of* Arden.

Enter DUKE *senior*, AMIENS, *and other* Lords, *like Foresters.*

DUKE S. Now, my co-mates and brothers in exíle,
Hath not old custom made this life more sweet
Than that of painted pomp? Are not these woods
More free from peril than the envious court?

Here feel we not[a] the penalty of Adam,
The seasons' difference: as the icy fang
And churlish chiding of the winter's wind,—
Which, when it bites and blows upon my body,
Even till I shrink with cold, I smile, and say,
This is no flattery:—these are counsellors,
That feelingly persuade me what I am.
Sweet are the uses of adversity,
Which, like the toad, ugly and venomous,
Wears yet a precious jewel in his head;
And this our life, exempt from public haunt,
Finds tongues in trees, books in the running brooks,
Sermons in stones, and good in every thing.

AMI. I would not change it.[b] Happy is your grace,
That can translate the stubbornness of fortune
Into so quiet and so sweet a style.

DUKE S. Come, shall we go and kill us venison?
And yet it irks me, the poor dappled fools,
Being native burghers of this desert city,
Should, in their own confines, with forked heads
Have their round haunches gor'd.

1 LORD. Indeed, my lord,
The melancholy Jaques grieves at that;
And, in that kind, swears you do more usurp
Than doth your brother that hath banish'd you.
To-day my lord of Amiens and myself,
Did steal behind him, as he lay along
Under an oak, whose antique root peeps out
Upon the brook that brawls along this wood:
To the which place a poor sequester'd stag,
That from the hunters' aim had ta'en a hurt,
Did come to languish; and, indeed, my lord,
The wretched animal heav'd forth such groans,
That their discharge did stretch his leathern coat
Almost to bursting; and the big round tears
Cours'd one another down his innocent nose
In piteous chase: and thus the hairy fool,
Much marked of the melancholy Jaques,
Stood on the extremest verge of the swift brook,
Augmenting it with tears.

DUKE S. But what said Jaques?
Did he not moralize this spectacle?

1 LORD. O, yes, into a thousand similes.
First, for his weeping in[c] the needless stream;
Poor deer, quoth he, *thou mak'st a testament*
As worldlings do, giving thy sum of more
*To that which had too much:** then, being there alone,
Left and abandon'd of his velvet friends; †
'Tis right, quoth he, *thus misery doth part*
The flux of company: anon, a careless herd,
Full of the pasture, jumps along by him,
And never stays to greet him; *Ay*, quoth Jaques,
Sweep on, you fat and greasy citizens;
'Tis just the fashion; wherefore do you look
Upon that poor and broken bankrupt there?
Thus most invectively he pierceth through
The body of the ‡ country, city, court,
Yea, and of this our life; swearing that we
Are mere usurpers, tyrants, and what's worse,
To fright the animals, and to kill them up,
In their assign'd and native dwelling place.

DUKE S. And did you leave him in this contemplation?

2 LORD. We did, my lord, weeping and commenting
Upon the sobbing deer.

DUKE S. Show me the place;
I love to cope him in these sullen fits,
For then he's full of matter.

2 LORD. I'll bring you to him straight.
[*Exeunt.*

SCENE II.—*A Room in the Palace.*

Enter DUKE FREDERICK, Lords, *and* Attendants.

DUKE F. Can it be possible that no man saw them?
It cannot be: some villains of my court
Are of consent and sufferance in this.

1 LORD. I cannot hear of any that did see her.
The ladies, her attendants of her chamber,
Saw her a-bed; and, in the morning early,
They found the bed untreasur'd of their mistress.

2 LORD. My lord, the roynish[d] clown at whom so oft

---

a *Here feel we* not *the penalty of Adam,*
The seasons' difference:]

The usual reading, suggested by Theobald, is "Here feel we *but*," &c. Neither is satisfactory, nor do we think *not* the only corruption in the speech,—the word *as* is equally open to suspicion. The passage, it is presumable, may have run thus in the original manuscript:—

"Here feel we *yet* the penalty of Adam,
The seasons' difference: *At* the icy fang,
And churlish chiding of the winter's wind,—
Which, when it bites and blows upon my body,
Even till I shrink with cold—I smile, and say,
This is no flattery."

The Duke is contrasting the dangers and sophistications of a court life with the safety and primitive simplicity of their sylvan state; and glories in the privilege of undergoing Adam's penalty—the seasons' difference.

b I would not change it.] Upton is perhaps right in suggesting that these words belong to the Duke, rather than to Amiens, who, as a courtier, would naturally agree with his master, and begin, "Happy is your grace," &c.

c In *the needless stream;*] The old copy has *into*. As Malone remarks, that word was probably caught by the compositor's eye from the line above.

d *The* roynish *clown*—] From the French *rogneux, scurvy, mangy*. It may, however, be no more than a misprint of *roguish*.

(*) First folio, *must*. (†) Old text, *friend*. (‡) First folio omits, *the*.

Your grace was wont to laugh, is also missing.
Hesperia, the princess' gentlewoman,
Confesses, that she secretly o'erheard
Your daughter and her cousin much commend
The parts and graces of the wrestler
That did but lately foil the sinewy Charles;
And she believes, wherever they are gone,
That youth is surely in their company.

DUKE F. Send to his brother; fetch that gallant hither:
If he be absent, bring his brother to me,
I'll make him find him: do this suddenly;
And let not search and inquisition quail
To bring again these foolish runaways. [*Exeunt.*

SCENE III.—*Before* Oliver's *House.*

Enter ORLANDO *and* ADAM, *meeting.*

ORL. Who's there?

ADAM. What! my young master?—O, my gentle master!
O, my sweet master! O you memory[a]
Of old sir Roland! why, what make you here?
Why are you virtuous? Why do people love you?
And wherefore are you gentle, strong, and valiant?
Why would you be so fond to overcome
The bony* priser of the humorous duke?
Your praise is come too swiftly home before you.
Know you not, master, to some† kind of men
Their graces serve them but as enemies?
No more do yours; your virtues, gentle master,
Are sanctified and holy traitors to you.
O, what a world is this, when what is comely
Envenoms him that bears it!

ORL. Why, what's the matter?[b]

ADAM. O unhappy youth,
Come not within these doors! within this roof
The enemy of all your graces lives:
Your brother—(no, no brother; yet the son—
Yet not the son;—I will not call him son—
Of him I was about to call his father,)—
Hath heard your praises; and this night he means
To burn the lodging where you use to lie,
And you within it: if he fail of that,
He will have other means to cut you off;
I overheard him and his practices.
This is no place; this house is but a butchery;
Abhor it, fear it, do not enter it.

ORL. Why, whither, Adam, wouldst thou have me go?

ADAM. No matter whither, so you come not here.

ORL. What, wouldst thou have me go and beg my food?
Or, with a base and boisterous sword, enforce
A thievish living on the common road?
This I must do, or know not what to do:
Yet this I will not do, do how I can;
I rather will subject me to the malice
Of a diverted blood and bloody brother.

ADAM. But do not so: I have five hundred crowns,
The thrifty hire I sav'd under your father,
Which I did store, to be my foster-nurse,
When service should in my old limbs lie lame,
And unregarded age in corners thrown;
Take that; and He that doth the ravens feed,
Yea, providently caters for the sparrow,
Be comfort to my age! Here is the gold;
All this I give you. Let me be your servant;
Though I look old, yet I am strong and lusty:
For in my youth I never did apply
Hot and rebellious liquors in my blood,
Nor did not with unbashful forehead woo
The means of weakness and debility;
Therefore my age is as a lusty winter,
Frosty, but kindly: let me go with you;
I'll do the service of a younger man
In all your business and necessities.

ORL. O good old man, how well in thee appears
The constant service of the antique world,
When service sweat for duty, not for meed!
Thou art not for the fashion of these times,
Where none will sweat but for promotion;
And having that, do choke their service up
Even with the having: it is not so with thee.
But, poor old man, thou prun'st a rotten tree,
That cannot so much as a blossom yield,
In lieu of all thy pains and husbandry:
But come thy ways, we'll go along together;
And ere we have thy youthful wages spent,
We'll light upon some settled low content.

ADAM. Master, go on; and I will follow thee,
To the last gasp, with truth and loyalty.—
From seventeen* years till now almost fourscore
Here lived I, but now live here no more.
At seventeen years many their fortunes seek,
But at fourscore, it is too late a week:
Yet fortune cannot recompense me better,
Than to die well, and not my master's debtor. [*Exeunt.*

(*) Old text, *bonnie*. (†) First folio, *seeme*.

(*) Old text, *seventy*.

a O *you* memory—] *Memory* was often used for *memorial*. Thus in "King Lear," Act IV. Sc. 1:—

"Those words are *memories* of those worser hours."

and in "Coriolanus," Act IV. Sc. 5:—

——— "a good *memory*
And witness."

b Why, what's the matter?] In the folio, 1623, this line is part of Adam's speech, but the error was set right in the edition of 1632, which, as regards this play, corrects many of the typographical blunders of its predecessor.

SCENE IV.—*The Forest of* Arden.

Enter ROSALIND *in boy's clothes*, CELIA *dressed like a shepherdess, and* TOUCHSTONE.

ROS. O Jupiter! how weary[a] are my spirits!

TOUCH. I care not for my spirits, if my legs were not weary.

ROS. I could find in my heart to disgrace my man's apparel, and to cry like a woman; but I must comfort the weaker vessel, as doublet and hose ought to show itself courageous to petticoat: therefore, courage, good Aliena.

CEL. I pray you, bear with me; I can go no further.[b]

---

a *O Jupiter! how* weary *are my spirits!*] In the original, "how *merry* are my spirits." The correction, which is favoured by the resemblance of the two words in their old spelling, was made by Theobald.

b I can *go no further*.] So the second folio; the first has, "I *cannot* go no further."

TOUCH. For my part, I had rather bear with you than bear you: yet I should bear no cross,[a] if I did bear you; for I think you have no money in your purse.

ROS. Well, this is the forest of Arden.

TOUCH. Ay, now am I in Arden; the more fool I; when I was at home, I was in a better place; but travellers must be content.

ROS. Ay, be so, good Touchstone.—Look you, who comes here; a young man and an old, in solemn talk.

Enter CORIN *and* SILVIUS.

COR. That is the way to make her scorn you still.

SIL. O Corin, that thou knew'st how I do love her!

COR. I partly guess, for I have lov'd ere now.

SIL. No, Corin, being old, thou canst not guess;
Though in thy youth thou wast as true a lover
As ever sigh'd upon a midnight pillow:
But if thy love were ever like to mine,
(As sure I think did never man love so,)
How many actions most ridiculous
Hast thou been drawn to by thy fantasy?

COR. Into a thousand that I have forgotten.

SIL. O, thou didst then ne'er love so heartily!
If thou remember'st not the slightest folly
That ever love did make thee run into,
Thou hast not lov'd:
Or if thou hast not sat as I do now,
Wearing thy hearer in thy mistress' praise,
Thou hast not lov'd:
Or if thou hast not broke from company,
Abruptly, as my passion now makes me,
Thou hast not lov'd. O Phebe, Phebe, Phebe!
[*Exit* SILVIUS.

ROS. Alas, poor shepherd! searching of thy wound,[b]
I have by hard adventure found mine own.

TOUCH. And I mine: I remember, when I was in love, I broke my sword upon a stone, and bid him take that for coming a-night to Jane Smile: and I remember the kissing of her batlet,[c] and the cow's dugs that her pretty chapped hands had milked: and I remember the wooing of a peascod instead of her; from whom[d] I took two cods, and, giving her them again, said with weeping tears, *Wear these for my sake.* We, that are true lovers, run into strange capers; but as all is mortal in nature, so is all nature in love mortal in folly.[e]

ROS. Thou speakest wiser than thou art 'ware of.

TOUCH. Nay, I shall ne'er be 'ware of mine own wit, till I break my shins against it.

ROS. Jove! Jove! this shepherd's passion
Is much upon my fashion.

TOUCH. And mine; but it grows something stale with me.

CEL. I pray you, one of you question yond man,
If he for gold will give us any food;
I faint almost to death.

TOUCH. Holla; you clown!

ROS. Peace, fool; he's not thy kinsman.

COR. Who calls?

TOUCH. Your betters, sir.

COR. Else are they very wretched.

ROS. Peace, I say:—
Good even to you,* friend.

COR. And to you, gentle sir, and to you all.

ROS. I pr'ythee, shepherd, if that love, or gold,
Can in this desert place buy entertainment,
Bring us where we may rest ourselves and feed:
Here's a young maid with travel much oppress'd,
And faints for succour.

COR. Fair sir, I pity her,
And wish, for her sake more than for mine own,
My fortunes were more able to relieve her;
But I am shepherd to another man,
And do not shear the fleeces that I graze;
My master is of churlish disposition,
And little recks to find the way to heaven
By doing deeds of hospitality:
Besides, his cote, his flocks, and bounds of feed,
Are now on sale, and at our sheepcote now,
By reason of his absence, there is nothing
That you will feed on; but what is, come see,
And in my voice most welcome shall you be.

ROS. What is he that shall buy his flock and pasture?

COR. That young swain that you saw here but erewhile,
That little cares for buying anything.

ROS. I pray thee, if it stand with honesty,
Buy thou the cottage, pasture, and the flock,
And thou shalt have to pay for it of us.

CEL. And we will mend thy wages: I like this place,

(*) First folio, *your*.

[a] I *should bear no* cross,—] This quibble on *cross* was a stereotype jest of which the writers, readers, and play-goers of Shakespeare's time seem never to have had enough. See note (c), p. 56, Vol. I.

[b] *Searching of* thy wound,—] The second folio, 1632, reads, "*their wound*," only partially correcting the error of the first edition, 1623, which has, "searching of *they would*"

[c] Batlet,—] The bat used to beat linen in washing. In the first folio, *batler*.

[d] From whom—] "From his mistress," Mr. Knight says, and other editors have fallen into the same error. Touchstone surely means that he both took the cods from and returned them to the *peascod*, the representative of his mistress. In like manner he tells us, just before, he broke his sword upon a stone, and bid *him*, his imagined rival, "take that."

[e] But as all is mortal in nature, so is all nature in love mortal in folly.] As the commentators appear not to suspect corruption here, the passage probably contains a meaning we have failed to discover.

And willingly could waste my time in it.
COR. Assuredly, the thing is to be sold:
Go with me; if you like, upon report,
The soil, the profit, and this kind of life,
I will your very faithful feeder be,
And buy it with your gold right suddenly. [*Exeunt.*

SCENE V.—*Another part of the Forest.*

Enter AMIENS, JAQUES, *and others.*

SONG.

AMI. *Under the greenwood tree,*
Who loves to lie with me,
And turn[a] *his merry note*
Unto the sweet bird's throat,
Come hither, come hither, come hither;
Here shall he see
No enemy,
But winter and rough weather.

JAQ. More, more, I pr'ythee, more.

AMI. It will make you melancholy, monsieur Jaques.

JAQ. I thank it. More, I pr'ythee, more. I can suck melancholy out of a song, as a weazel sucks eggs; more, I pr'ythee, more.

AMI. My voice is ragged;[b] I know I cannot please you.

JAQ. I do not desire you to please me, I do desire you to sing; come, more; another stanza; call you 'em stanzas?

AMI. What you will, monsieur Jaques.

JAQ. Nay, I care not for their names; they owe me nothing. Will you sing?

AMI. More at your request than to please myself.

JAQ. Well then, if ever I thank any man, I'll thank you: but that they call compliment, is like the encounter of two dog-apes;[c] and when a man thanks me heartily, methinks I have given him a penny, and he renders me the beggarly thanks. Come, sing; and you that will not, hold your tongues.

AMI. Well, I'll end the song. Sirs, cover[d] the while; the duke will drink under this tree: he hath been all this day to look you.

JAQ. And I have been all this day to avoid him. He is too disputable for my company: I think of as many matters as he, but I give heaven thanks, and make no boast of them. Come, warble, come.

SONG.

Who doth ambition shun, [All together here.
And loves to live i' the sun,
Seeking the food he eats,
And pleas'd with what he gets,
Come hither, come hither, come hither;
Here shall he see
No enemy,
But winter and rough weather.

JAQ. I'll give you a verse to this note, that I made yesterday in despite of my invention.

AMI. And I'll sing it.

JAQ. Thus it goes:

If it do come to pass,
That any man turn ass,
Leaving his wealth and ease,
A stubborn will to please,
Ducdame, ducdame, ducdame;[e]
Here shall he see
Gross fools as he,
An if he will come to me.

AMI. What's that *ducdame?*

JAQ. 'Tis a Greek invocation, to call fools into a circle. I'll go sleep if I can; if I cannot, I'll rail against all the first-born of Egypt.

AMI. And I'll go seek the duke; his banquet is prepared. [*Exeunt severally.*

SCENE VI.—*Another part of the Forest.*

Enter ORLANDO *and* ADAM.

ADAM. Dear master, I can go no further: O, I die for food! Here lie I down, and measure out my grave. Farewell, kind master.

ORL. Why, how now, Adam! no greater heart in thee? Live a little; comfort a little; cheer thyself a little: if this uncouth forest yield any thing savage, I will either be food for it, or bring it for food to thee. Thy conceit is nearer death than thy powers. For my sake, be comfortable; hold death awhile at the arm's end. I will here

---

[a] *And* turn *his merry note*—] In many modern editions we have "*tune* his merry note;" but *turn* was the poet's phrase:—

"Whiles threadbare Martiall *turns* his merry note."
HALL'S *Satires*, Bk. VI. Sat. 1, quoted by Mr. Singer.

[b] Ragged;] That is, *rough, rugged.*

[c] Dog-apes;] "Some be called *cenophe;* and be lyke to an *hounde* in the face, and in the body lyke to an *ape.*"—BARTHOLOMÆUS, *De propr. rerum*, xviii. 96, quoted by Douce.

[d] *Sirs,* cover *the while;*] That is, prepare the table; equivalent to our "lay the cloth;"—"bid them *cover the table,* serve in the meat, and we will come in to dinner."—*Merchant of Venice,* Act. III. Sc. 5.

[e] Ducdame;] After all that has been written in elucidation of "*ducdame,*" we are disposed to believe the "invocation," like the Clown's—

"Fond done, done fond;"

in "All's Well That Ends Well," is mere unmeaning babble coined for the occasion.

be with thee presently, and if I bring thee not something to eat, I'll give thee leave to die; but if thou diest before I come, thou art a mocker of my labour. Well said![a] thou lookest cheerly; and I'll be with thee quickly. Yet thou liest in the bleak air: come, I will bear thee to some shelter; and thou shalt not die for lack of a dinner, if there live any thing in this desert. Cheerly, good Adam! [*Exeunt.*

SCENE VII.—*Another part of the Forest.*

A table set out. Enter DUKE *senior,* AMIENS, *and others.*[b]

DUKE S. I think he be transform'd into a beast;
For I can no where find him like a man.
1 LORD. My lord, he is but even now gone hence;
Here was he merry, hearing of a song.
DUKE S. If he, compact of jars, grow musical,
We shall have shortly discord in the spheres.—
Go, seek him; tell him, I would speak with him.
1 LORD. He saves my labour by his own approach.

Enter JAQUES.

DUKE S. Why, how now, monsieur! what a life is this,
That your poor friends must woo your company?
What! you look merrily.
JAQ. A fool, a fool! I met a fool i'the forest,
A motley fool;—a miserable world!—
As I do live by food, I met a fool,
Who laid him down and bask'd him in the sun,
And rail'd on lady Fortune in good terms,
In good set terms,—and yet a motley fool.
Good-morrow, fool, quoth I: *No, sir,* quoth he,
Call me not fool, till heaven hath sent me fortune:
And then he drew a dial from his poke,
And looking on it with lack-lustre eye,
Says very wisely, *It is ten o'clock:*
Thus we may see, quoth he, *how the world wags:*
'Tis but an hour ago, since it was nine,
And after one hour more, 'twill be eleven;
And so, from hour to hour, we ripe and ripe,
And then, from hour to hour, we rot and rot;
And thereby hangs a tale. When I did hear
The motley fool thus moral on the time,
My lungs began to crow like chanticleer,
That fools should be so deep-contemplative;
And I did laugh, sans intermission,
An hour by his dial.—O noble fool!
A worthy fool! Motley's the only wear.
DUKE S. What fool is this?
JAQ. O worthy fool!—One that hath been a courtier,
And says, if ladies be but young and fair,
They have the gift to know it; and in his brain,—
Which is as dry as the remainder biscuit
After a voyage,—he hath strange places cramm'd
With observation, the which he vents
In mangled forms.—O, that I were a fool!
I am ambitious for a motley coat.
DUKE S. Thou shalt have one.
JAQ. It is my only suit;[c]
Provided, that you weed your better judgments
Of all opinion that grows rank in them,
That I am wise. I must have liberty
Withal, as large a charter as the wind,
To blow on whom I please; for so fools have:
And they that are most galled with my folly,
They most must laugh. And why, sir, must they so?
The *why* is plain as way to parish church:
He that a fool doth very wisely hit,
Doth very foolishly, although he smart,
Not to seem[d] senseless of the bob: if not,
The wise man's folly is anatomiz'd
Even by the squandering glances of the fool.
Invest me in my motley; give me leave
To speak my mind, and I will through and through
Cleanse the foul body of the infected world,
If they will patiently receive my medicine.
DUKE S. Fie on thee! I can tell what thou wouldst do.
JAQ. What, for a counter, would I do, but good?
DUKE S. Most mischievous foul sin, in chiding sin:*
For thou thyself hast been a libertine,
As sensual as the brutish sting itself;
And all the embossed sores, and headed evils,
That thou with licence of free foot hast caught,
Wouldst thou disgorge into the general world.
JAQ. Why, who cries out on pride,
That can therein tax any private party?
Doth it not flow as hugely as the sea,

a Well said!] Meaning, *well done.*
b Enter Duke, &c.] In the folio, 1623, "*Enter Duke Sen. and Lord, like Out-lawes.*"
c *My only* suit;] The old, old play on the double meaning of the word.
d Not to *seem*—] The original text reads only:—
"Seem senseless of the bob."
The words *not to*, were supplied by Theobald. If any addition is really called for, that proposed by Mr. Collier's annotator—"*But to* seem," &c.—is well entitled to consideration.

(*) First folio, *fin.*

Till that the weary very[a] means do ebb?
What woman in the city do I name,
When that I say, The city-woman bears
The cost of princes on unworthy shoulders?
Who can come in, and say that I mean her,
When such a one as she, such is her neighbour?
Or what is he of basest function,
That says his bravery[b] is not on my cost,
(Thinking that I mean him,) but therein suits
His folly to the mettle of my speech?
There then; how then? what then? Let me see wherein
My tongue hath wrong'd him: if it do him right,
Then he hath wrong'd himself: if he be free,
Why then my taxing like a wild-goose flies,
Unclaim'd of any man.—But who comes here?

Enter ORLANDO, *with his sword drawn.*

ORL. Forbear, and eat no more.
JAQ. Why, I have eat none yet.
ORL. Nor shalt not, till necessity be serv'd.
JAQ. Of what kind should this cock come of?
DUKE S. Art thou thus bolden'd, man, by thy distress,
Or else a rude despiser of good manners,
That in civility thou seem'st so empty?
ORL. You touch'd my vein at first; the thorny point
Of bare distress hath ta'en from me the show
Of smooth civility: yet am I inland[c] bred,
And know some nurture.[d] But forbear, I say;
He dies that touches any of this fruit,
Till I and my affairs are answered.
JAQ. An you will not be answered with reason,[e]
I must die.
DUKE S. What would you have? Your gentleness shall force,
More than your force move us to gentleness.
ORL. I almost die for food, and let me have it.
DUKE S. Sit down and feed, and welcome to our table.
ORL. Speak you so gently? Pardon me, I pray you:
I thought, that all things had been savage here,
And therefore put I on the countenance
Of stern commandment. But whate'er you are,
That in this desert inaccessible,
Under the shade of melancholy boughs,
Lose and neglect the creeping hours of time;
If ever you have look'd on better days,
If ever been where bells have knoll'd to church,
If ever sat at any good man's feast,
If ever from your eyelids wip'd a tear,
And know what 'tis to pity and be pitied,—
Let gentleness my strong enforcement be:
In the which hope I blush, and hide my sword.
DUKE S. True is it that we have seen better days,
And have with holy bell been knoll'd to church,
And sat at good men's feasts; and wip'd our eyes
Of drops that sacred pity hath engender'd:
And therefore sit you down in gentleness,
And take upon command what help we have,
That to your wanting may be minister'd.
ORL. Then, but forbear your food a little while,
Whiles, like a doe, I go to find my fawn,
And give it food. There is an old poor man,
Who after me hath many a weary step
Limp'd in pure love; till he be first suffic'd,—
Oppress'd with two weak evils, age and hunger,—
I will not touch a bit.
DUKE S. Go find him out,
And we will nothing waste till you return.
ORL. I thank ye; and be bless'd for your good comfort! [*Exit.*
DUKE S. Thou seest we are not all alone unhappy:
This wide and universal theatre
Presents more woeful pageants than the scene
Wherein we play in.
JAQ. All the world's a stage,(1)
And all the men and women merely players:
They have their exits and their entrances,
And one man in his time plays many parts,
His acts being seven ages. At first the infant,
Mewling and puking in the nurse's arms:
Then the whining school-boy, with his satchel

---

[a] *Till that the* weary very *means do ebb?*] This, the reading of the old text, is not very clear; neither are the emendations of it which have been adopted or proposed.

Pope changed it to,—

"Till that the *very very* means do ebb."

Mr. Singer gives, "Till that the *wearer's* very means do ebb;" and Mr. Collier's annotator suggests, "Till that the *very means of wear* do ebb."

The disputed words should, perhaps, be printed with a hyphen, "*weary-very*," or "*very-weary*." See a collection of old musical airs, entitled "Ayeres, or Phantastique Spirites for three voices, made and newly published by Thomas Weilkes," &c. 1608:—

"I will be blithe and briske,
Leap and skip, hop and trip,
Turne about, in the rout,
Until *very weary* ioyntes can scarce friske."

[b] Bravery—] Finery.

[c] Inland—] Opposed to *upland*. Orlando means that he is urbanely bred; brought up in civilized society; "—or, finally, in any *uplandish* village or corner of a Realme where is no resort but of poore rusticall or uncivill people."—PUTTENHAM'S *Arte of Poesie*, 1589.

[d] *And know some* nurture.] And possess some *courtesy, breeding, manners*:—"It is a point of *nurture*, or *good manners*, to salute them that you meete. Urbanitas est salutare obvios."—BARET'S *Alvearie*, 1580.

[e] *With* reason,—] We should, possibly, read *reasons*. Here, as in other places, Shakespeare evidently indulged in the perennial pun on *reasons* and *raisins*. A quibble, by the way, which Skelton long before found irresistible:—

"Grete *reysons* with *resons* be now reprobitante,
For *reysons* are no *resons*, but *resons current*."
Speke Parrot. Dyce's Ed. vol. ii. p. 22.

And shining morning-face, creeping like snail
Unwillingly to school. And then the lover,
Sighing like furnace, with a woeful ballad
Made to his mistress' eyebrow. Then a soldier,
Full of strange oaths, and bearded like the pard,
Jealous in honour, sudden,[a] and quick in quarrel,
Seeking the bubble reputation,
Even in the cannon's mouth. And then the justice,
In fair round belly with good capon lin'd,
With eyes severe and beard of formal cut,
Full of wise saws and modern instances;
And so he plays his part. The sixth age shifts
Into the lean and slipper'd pantaloon,
With spectacles on nose and pouch on side;
His youthful hose, well sav'd, a world too wide
For his shrunk shank; and his big manly voice,
Turning again toward childish treble, pipes
And whistles in his sound. Last scene of all,
That ends this strange eventful history,
Is second childishness, and mere oblivion,
Sans teeth, sans eyes, sans taste, sans everything.

Re-enter ORLANDO, *with* ADAM.(2)

DUKE S. Welcome. Set down your venerable burden,
And let him feed.

ORL. I thank you most for him.

ADAM. So had you need,
I scarce can speak to thank you for myself.

DUKE S. Welcome; fall too: I will not trouble you
As yet, to question you about your fortunes.—
Give us some music; and, good cousin, sing.

a Sudden,—] *Violent.*

b *Thy tooth is not so keen*
Because thou art not seen,—]

The second line has provoked some discussion. Johnson supposed the original was lost, and this line substituted merely to fill up the measure and the rhyme. Warburton proposed—

"Because thou art *not sheen*;"

and Farmer,—

"Because *the heart's not seen*;"

neither of which conjectures can be thought happy. If change is imperative, one less violent will afford a meaning quite in harmony with the sentiment of the song; we might read,—

"Thy tooth is not so keen,
Because thou art *foreseen*."

But the original text is, perhaps, susceptible of a different interpretation to that it has received. The poet certainly could not intend that the wintry blast was less cutting because invisible; he might mean, however, that the keenness of the wind's tooth was inherent, and not a quality developed (like the malice of a false friend), by the opportunity of inflicting a hurt unseen.

SONG.

I.

AMI. *Blow, blow, thou winter wind,*
Thou art not so unkind
As man's ingratitude;
Thy tooth is not so keen
Because thou art not seen,[b]
Although thy breath be rude.
Heigh-ho! sing, heigh-ho! unto the green holly;
Most friendship is feigning, most loving mere folly:
Then, heigh-ho, the holly!*
This life is most jolly.

II.

Freeze, freeze, thou bitter sky,
That dost not bite so nigh
As benefits forgot:
Though thou the waters warp,
Thy sting is not so sharp
As friend remember'd not.
Heigh-ho! sing, heigh-ho! &c.

DUKE S. If that you were the good sir Roland's son,—
As you have whisper'd faithfully you were,
And as mine eye doth his effigies witness
Most truly limn'd and living in your face,—
Be truly welcome hither: I am the duke,
That lov'd your father. The residue of your fortune,
Go to my cave and tell me.—Good old man,
Thou art right welcome as thy master† is:
Support him by the arm.—Give me your hand,
And let me all your fortunes understand. [*Exeunt.*

(*) Old text, *The*. (†) First folio, *masters*.

ACT III.

SCENE I.—*A Room in the Palace.*

Enter Duke Frederick, Oliver, Lords, *and* Attendants.

Duke F. Not see him since? Sir, sir, that cannot be:
But were I not the better part made mercy,
I should not seek an absent argument
Of my revenge, thou present: but look to it;
Find out thy brother, wheresoe'er he is:
Seek him with candle;(1) bring him dead or living,
Within this twelvemonth, or turn thou no more
To seek a living in our territory.
Thy lands, and all things that thou dost call thine,
Worth seizure, do we seize into our hands;
Till thou canst quit thee by thy brother's mouth,
Of what we think against thee.

Oli. O, that your highness knew my heart in this!
I never lov'd my brother in my life.

Duke F. More villain thou.—Well, push him out of doors;
And let my officers of such a nature
Make an extent upon his house and lands:
Do this expediently,[a] and turn him going. [*Exeunt.*

SCENE II.—*The Forest.*

Enter Orlando, *with a paper.*

Orl. Hang there, my verse, in witness of my love:
And, thou, thrice-crowned(2) queen of night, survey
With thy chaste eye, from thy pale sphere above,
Thy huntress' name, that my full life doth sway.
O Rosalind! these trees shall be my books,
And in their barks my thoughts I'll character,
That every eye, which in this forest looks,
Shall see thy virtue witness'd every where.
Run, run, Orlando; carve on every tree,
The fair, the chaste, and unexpressive[b] she. [*Exit.*

---

a Expediently,—] *Expeditiously.* So in "King John," Act II. Sc. 1, "His marches are *expedient* to this town;" and in the Second Part of "Henry VI." Act III. Sc. 1:—

"A breach that craves a quick *expedient* stop."

b Unexpressive—] *Inexpressible.* So Milton, in his "Lycidas," v. 176:—

"And hears the *unexpressive* nuptial song."

And again, in the "Hymn on the Nativity:"—

"Harping in loud and solemn quire,
With *unexpressive* notes to heaven's new-born heir."

Enter CORIN *and* TOUCHSTONE.

COR. And how like you this shepherd's life, master Touchstone?

TOUCH. Truly, shepherd, in respect of itself, it is a good life; but in respect that it is a shepherd's life, it is naught. In respect that it is solitary, I like it very well; but in respect that it is private, it is a very vile life. Now in respect it is in the fields, it pleaseth me well; but in respect it is not in the court, it is tedious. As it is a spare life, look you, it fits my humour well; but as there is no more plenty in it, it goes much against my stomach. Hast any philosophy in thee, shepherd?

COR. No more but that I know, the more one sickens, the worse at ease he is; and that he that wants money, means, and content, is without three good friends.—That the property of rain is to wet, and fire to burn; that good pasture makes fat sheep; and that a great cause of the night, is lack of the sun; that he that hath learned no wit by nature nor art, may complain of good breeding,[a] or comes of a very dull kindred.

TOUCH. Such a one is a natural philosopher. Wast ever in court, shepherd?

COR. No, truly.

TOUCH. Then thou art damned.

COR. Nay, I hope,——

TOUCH. Truly, thou art damned, like an ill-roasted egg, all on one side.

COR. For not being at court? your reason?

TOUCH. Why, if thou never wast at court, thou never sawest good manners; if thou never sawest good manners, then thy manners must be wicked; and wickedness is sin, and sin is damnation. Thou art in a parlous state, shepherd.

COR. Not a whit, Touchstone: those, that are

[a] *May complain* of good breeding,—] That is, of *a deficiency* of good breeding. An elliptical mode of speech, which, as Whiter remarked, is not peculiar to Shakespeare, or indeed to the English language.

good manners at the court, are as ridiculous in the country, as the behaviour of the country is most mockable at the court. You told me, you salute not at the court, but you kiss your hands; that courtesy would be uncleanly, if courtiers were shepherds.

Touch. Instance, briefly: come, instance.

Cor. Why, we are still handling our ewes, and their fells, you know, are greasy.

Touch. Why, do not your courtier's hands sweat? and is not the grease of a mutton as wholesome as the sweat of a man? Shallow, shallow: a better instance, I say; come.

Cor. Besides, our hands are hard.

Touch. Your lips will feel them the sooner. Shallow, again: a more sounder instance, come.

Cor. And they are often tarred over with the surgery of our sheep; and would you have us kiss tar? The courtier's hands are perfumed with civet.

TOUCH. Most shallow man! Thou worms-meat, in respect of a good piece of flesh, indeed!—Learn of the wise, and perpend: civet is of a baser birth than tar; the very uncleanly flux of a cat. Mend the instance, shepherd.

COR. You have too courtly a wit for me; I'll rest.

TOUCH. Wilt thou rest damned? God help thee, shallow man! God make incision in thee, thou art raw.[a]

COR. Sir, I am a true labourer; I earn that I eat, get that I wear; owe no man hate, envy no man's happiness; glad of other men's good, content with my harm: and the greatest of my pride is, to see my ewes graze, and my lambs suck.

TOUCH. That is another simple sin in you; to bring the ewes and the rams together, and to offer to get your living by the copulation of cattle; to be bawd to a bell-wether; and to betray a she-lamb of a twelvemonth, to a crooked-pated, old cuckoldly ram, out of all reasonable match. If thou beest not damned for this, the devil himself will have no shepherds; I cannot see else how thou shouldst 'scape.

COR. Here comes young master Ganymede, my new mistress's brother.

Enter ROSALIND, *reading a paper.*

ROS. *From the east to western Ind,*
No jewel is like Rosalind.
Her worth, being mounted on the wind,
Through all the world bears Rosalind.
All the pictures fairest lin'd
Are but black to Rosalind.
Let no face be kept in mind,
But the fair[b] *of Rosalind.*

TOUCH. I'll rhyme you so, eight years together, dinners, and suppers, and sleeping hours excepted; it is the right butter-women's rank[c] to market.

ROS. Out, fool!

TOUCH. For a taste:——

If a hart do lack a hind,
Let him seek out Rosalind.
If the cat will after kind,
So, be sure, will Rosalind.
Winter garments must be lin'd,*
So must slender Rosalind.
They that reap must sheaf and bind,
Then to cart with Rosalind.
Sweetest nut hath sourest rind,
Such a nut is Rosalind.
He that sweetest Rose will find,
Must find love's prick and Rosalind.

This is the very false gallop of verses; why do you infect yourself with them?

ROS. Peace, you dull fool! I found them on a tree.

TOUCH. Truly, the tree yields bad fruit.

ROS. I'll graff it with you, and then I shall graff it with a medlar: then it will be the earliest fruit in the country: for you'll be rotten ere you be half ripe, and that's the right virtue of the medlar.

TOUCH. You have said; but whether wisely or no, let the forest judge.

ROS. Peace!
Here comes my sister, reading; stand aside.

Enter CELIA, *reading a paper.*

CEL. *Why should this a† desert be?*
For it is unpeopled? No;
Tongues I'll hang on every tree,
That shall civil sayings show.
Some, how brief the life of man
Runs his erring pilgrimage;
That the stretching of a span
Buckles in his sum of age.
Some, of violated vows
'Twixt the souls of friend and friend:
But upon the fairest boughs,
Or at every sentence' end,
Will I Rosalinda write;
Teaching all that read, to know
The quintessence of every sprite
Heaven would in little[d] *show.*
Therefore heaven nature charg'd
That one body should be fill'd
With all graces wide enlarg'd:
Nature presently distill'd
Helen's cheek, but not her‡ heart;
Cleopatra's majesty,

(*) Old text, *Wintred.* (†) Old text omits, *a.* (‡) Old text, *his.*

[a] God make incision in thee, thou art raw.] Steevens suggests, very plausibly, that the allusion is to the common expression of *cutting for the simples.*

[b] Fair—] *Beauty.* See note (a), p. 69, Vol. I.

[c] *Right butter-women's* rank *to market.*] *Rank,* here, Whiter says, "means the *jog-trot rate* with which butter-women *uniformly* travel *one after another* in their road to market." But this is not satisfactory. From a passage in Drayton's poem, "The Shepherd's Sirena," it might be inferred that "*rank*" was a familiar term for *chorus,* or *rhyme*:—

"On thy bank,
In *a rank,*
Let thy swans sing her."

And *butter-women's rank* may have been only another term for verse which rhymed in couplets, called of old, "riding ryme."

[d] *In* little *show.*] In *miniature* show. So in "Hamlet," Act II. Sc. 2:—"Those that would make mowes at him while my father lived, give twenty, forty, fifty, an hundred ducats a-piece, *for his picture* in *little.*"

Atalanta's better part,
Sad Lucretia's modesty.
Thus Rosalind of many parts
By heavenly synod was devis'd,
Of many faces, eyes, and hearts,
To have the touches dearest priz'd.
Heaven would that she these gifts should have,
And I to live and die her slave.

Ros. O most gentle Jupiter!—what tedious homily of love have you wearied your parishioners withal, and never cried, *Have patience, good people!*

Cel. How now! back friends;—shepherd, go off a little: go with him, sirrah.

Touch. Come, shepherd, let us make an honourable retreat; though not with bag and baggage, yet with scrip and scrippage.

[*Exeunt* Corin *and* Touchstone.

Cel. Didst thou hear these verses?

Ros. O, yes, I heard them all, and more too; for some of them had in them more feet than the verses would bear.

Cel. That's no matter; the feet might bear the verses.

Ros. Ay, but the feet were lame, and could not bear themselves without the verse, and therefore stood lamely in the verse.

Cel. But didst thou hear without wondering how thy name should be hanged and carved upon these trees?

Ros. I was seven of the nine days out of the wonder before you came; for look here what I found on a palm-tree: I was never so be-rhymed since Pythagoras' time, that I was an Irish rat,(3) which I can hardly remember.

Cel. Trow you who hath done this?

Ros. Is it a man?

Cel. And a chain, that you once wore, about his neck: change you colour?

Ros. I pr'ythee, who?

Cel. O lord, lord! it is a hard matter for friends to meet; but mountains may be removed with earthquakes, and so encounter.

Ros. Nay, but who is it?

Cel. Is it possible?

Ros. Nay, I pray thee now, with most petitionary vehemence, tell me who it is.

Cel. O wonderful, wonderful, and most wonderful wonderful! and yet again wonderful, and after that, out of all whooping!

Ros. Good my complexion![a] dost thou think, though I am caparisoned like a man, I have a doublet and hose in my disposition? One inch of delay more is a South-sea of discovery.[b] I pr'ythee, tell me who is it, quickly, and speak apace: I would thou couldst stammer, that thou mightst pour this concealed man out of thy mouth, as wine comes out of a narrow-mouthed bottle,—either too much at once, or not at all. I pr'ythee take the cork out of thy mouth, that I may drink thy tidings.

Cel. So you may put a man in your belly.

Ros. Is he of God's making? What manner of man? Is his head worth a hat, or his chin worth a beard?

Cel. Nay, he hath but a little beard.

Ros. Why, God will send more, if the man will be thankful: let me stay the growth of his beard, if thou delay me not the knowledge of his chin.

Cel. It is young Orlando, that tripped up the wrestler's heels and your heart, both in an instant.

Ros. Nay, but the devil take mocking; speak sad brow and true maid.

Cel. I'faith, coz, 'tis he.

Ros. Orlando?

Cel. Orlando.

Ros. Alas the day! what shall I do with my doublet and hose?—What did he, when thou sawest him? What said he? How looked he? Wherein went he? What makes he here? Did he ask for me? Where remains he? How parted he with thee? and when shalt thou see him again? Answer me in one word.

Cel. You must borrow me Gargantua's(4) mouth first: 'tis a word too great for any mouth of this age's size. To say *ay* and *no*, to these particulars, is more than to answer in a catechism.

Ros. But doth he know that I am in this forest, and in man's apparel? Looks he as freshly as he did the day he wrestled?

Cel. It is as easy to count atomies as to resolve the propositions of a lover:—but take a taste of my finding him, and relish it with good observance. I found him under a tree, like a dropped acorn.

Ros. It may well be called Jove's tree, when it drops forth such[c] fruit.

Cel. Give me audience, good madam.

Ros. Proceed.

Cel. There lay he, stretched along, like a wounded knight.

[a] Good my complexion!] Celia is triumphing in Rosalind's heightened colour, and the latter's petulant exclamation may be equivalent to "plague on my complexion." Or "*Good*" may be a misprint for "*Hood*." Thus Juliet:—

"*Hood* my unmann'd blood bating in my cheeks."
Romeo and Juliet, Act III. Sc. 2.

[b] *One inch of delay more is* a South-sea of discovery.] This is painfully obscure, and the efforts of the commentators have by no means lessened its ambiguity. Does Rosalind mean that though "caparisoned like a man," she has so much of a woman's curiosity in her disposition, that "one inch of delay more" would cause her to betray her sex?

[c] *When it drops forth* such *fruit.*] The folio, 1623, reads, "when it drops *forth* fruit;" *such* was inserted by the editor of the second folio.

Ros. Though it be pity to see such a sight, it well becomes [a] the ground.

Cel. Cry, holla! [b] to thy* tongue, I pr'ythee; it curvets unseasonably. He was furnished like a hunter.

Ros. O ominous! he comes to kill my heart.

Cel. I would sing my song without a burden: thou bringest me out of tune.

Ros. Do you not know I am a woman? when I think, I must speak. Sweet, say on.

Cel. You bring me out.—Soft! comes he not here?

Ros. 'Tis he; slink by, and note him.

[Celia *and* Rosalind *retire.*

Enter Orlando *and* Jaques.

Jaq. I thank you for your company; but, good faith, I had as lief have been myself alone.

Orl. And so had I; but yet, for fashion sake, I thank you too for your society.

Jaq. God be wi' you; let's meet as little as we can.

Orl. I do desire we may be better strangers.

Jaq. I pray you, mar no more trees with writing love-songs in their barks.

Orl. I pray you, mar no more† of my verses with reading them ill-favouredly.

Jaq. Rosalind is your love's name?

Orl. Yes, just.

Jaq. I do not like her name.

Orl. There was no thought of pleasing you when she was christened.

Jaq. What stature is she of?

Orl. Just as high as my heart.

Jaq. You are full of pretty answers. Have you not been acquainted with goldsmiths' wives, and conned them out of rings?

Orl. Not so; but I answer you right painted cloth,[c] from whence you have studied your questions.

Jaq. You have a nimble wit; I think it was made of Atalanta's heels. Will you sit down with me? and we two will rail against our mistress the world, and all our misery.

Orl. I will chide no breather in the world but myself; against whom I know most faults.

Jaq. The worst fault you have is to be in love.

Orl. 'Tis a fault I will not change for your best virtue. I am weary of you.

Jaq. By my troth, I was seeking for a fool when I found you.

Orl. He is drowned in the brook; look but in and you shall see him.

Jaq. There I shall see mine own figure.

Orl. Which I take to be either a fool or a cypher.

Jaq. I'll tarry no longer with you; farewell, good signior Love. [*Exit* Jaques.

Orl. I am glad of your departure; adieu, good monsieur Melancholy.

[Celia *and* Rosalind *come forward.*

Ros. I will speak to him like a saucy lackey, and under that habit play the knave with him.—Do you hear, forester?

Orl. Very well; what would you?

Ros. I pray you, what is't o'clock?

Orl. You should ask me, what time o'day; there's no clock in the forest.

Ros. Then there is no true lover in the forest; else sighing every minute, and groaning every hour, would detect the lazy foot of time as well as a clock.

Orl. And why not the swift foot of time? had not that been as proper?

Ros. By no means, sir. Time travels in divers paces with divers persons: I'll tell you who Time ambles withal, who Time trots withal, who Time gallops withal, and who he stands still withal.

Orl. I pr'ythee who doth he trot withal?

Ros. Marry, he trots hard with a young maid, between the contract of her marriage, and the day it is solemnized; if the interim be but a se'nnight, Time's pace is so hard that it seems the length of seven year.

Orl. Who ambles Time withal?

Ros. With a priest that lacks Latin, and a rich man that hath not the gout: for the one sleeps easily, because he cannot study; and the other lives merrily, because he feels no pain: the one lacking the burden of lean and wasteful learning; the other knowing no burden of heavy tedious penury: these Time ambles withal.

Orl. Who doth he gallop withal?

Ros. With a thief to the gallows: for though he go as softly as foot can fall, he thinks himself too soon there.

Orl. Who stays it still withal?

Ros. With lawyers in the vacation: for they

(*) Old text, *the*. (†) First folio, *moe*.

[a] *It well becomes the ground.*] It well *adorns*, or *graces*, or *sets off* the ground. To *become*, in the present day, signifies usually *to befit, to be suitable;* formerly it meant more than this. Thus, in "The Comedy of Errors," Act III. Sc. 2, Luciana bids Antipholus,—

"—— *become* disloyalty;
Apparel Vice like Virtue's harbinger;"

And in "King John," Act V. Sc. 1, Falconbridge exhorts the King to,—

"—— glister like the god of war,
When he intendeth to *become* the field."

[b] Holla!] This was a term of the *manège*, by which a rider stopped his horse. Thus, in Shakespeare's "Venus and Adonis," Stanza 48:—

"What recketh he his rider's angry stir,
His flattering '*Holla*,' or his 'Stand, I say?'"

[c] I answer you right painted cloth,—] Alluding to the mottoes and "wise saws," inscribed on old mural hangings. See note (1), p. 626, Vol. I.

sleep between term and term, and then they perceive not how Time moves.

ORL. Where dwell you, pretty youth?

ROS. With this shepherdess, my sister, here in the skirts of the forest, like fringe upon a petticoat.

ORL. Are you native of this place?

ROS. As the coney, that you see dwell where she is kindled.

ORL. Your accent is something finer than you could purchase in so removed a dwelling.

ROS. I have been told so of many: but, indeed, an old religious uncle of mine taught me to speak, who was in his youth an inland[a] man; one that knew courtship too well, for there he fell in love. I have heard him read many lectures against it; and I thank God I am not a woman, to be touched with so many giddy offences as he hath generally taxed their whole sex withal.

ORL. Can you remember any of the principal evils, that he laid to the charge of women?

ROS. There were none principal; they were all like one another as half-pence are: every one fault seeming monstrous, till his fellow fault came to match it.

[a] An inland man;] See note (c), p. 144.
[b] *An* unquestionable spirit,—] One averse to question or discourse.

ORL. I pr'ythee, recount some of them.

ROS. No; I will not cast away my physic, but on those that are sick. There is a man haunts the forest, that abuses our young plants with carving *Rosalind* on their barks; hangs odes upon hawthorns, and elegies on brambles; all, forsooth, deifying* the name of Rosalind: if I could meet that fancy-monger, I would give him some good counsel, for he seems to have the quotidian of love upon him.

ORL. I am he that is so love-shaked; I pray you, tell me your remedy.

ROS. There is none of my uncle's marks upon you: he taught me how to know a man in love; in which cage of rushes I am sure you are† not a prisoner.

ORL. What were his marks?

ROS. A lean cheek,—which you have not; a blue eye and sunken,—which you have not; an unquestionable[b] spirit,—which you have not; a beard neglected,—which you have not; but I pardon you for that; for simply your having in beard is a younger brother's revenue.—Then your hose should be ungartered,[c] your bonnet unbanded,

(*) First folio, *defying*. (†) First folio, *art*.

[c] Your hose should be ungartered,—] See note (d), p. 11, Vol. I.

your sleeve unbuttoned, your shoe untied, and everything about you demonstrating a careless desolation;—but you are no such man;—you are rather point-device in your accoutrements; as loving yourself than seeming the lover of any other.

ORL. Fair youth, I would I could make thee believe I love.

ROS. Me believe it? you may as soon make her that you love believe it; which, I warrant, she is apter to do, than to confess she does; that is one of the points in the which women still give the lie to their consciences. But, in good sooth, are you he that hangs the verses on the trees, wherein Rosalind is so admired?

ORL. I swear to thee, youth, by the white hand of Rosalind, I am that he, that unfortunate he.

ROS. But are you so much in love as your rhymes speak?

ORL. Neither rhyme nor reason can express how much.

ROS. Love is merely[a] a madness; and, I tell you, deserves as well a dark house and a whip as madmen do: and the reason why they are not so punished and cured is, that the lunacy is so ordinary that the whippers are in love too: yet I profess curing it by counsel.

ORL. Did you ever cure any so?

ROS. Yes, one; and in this manner. He was to imagine me his love, his mistress; and I set him every day to woo me: at which time would I, being but a moonish[b] youth, grieve, be effeminate, changeable, longing, and liking; proud, fantastical, apish, shallow, inconstant, full of tears, full of smiles; for every passion something, and for no passion truly anything, as boys and women are for the most part cattle of this colour: would now like him, now loathe him; then entertain him, then forswear him; now weep for him, then spit at him; that I drave my suitor from his mad humour of love, to a loving* humour of madness; which was, to forswear the full stream of the world, and to live in a nook merely monastic: and thus I cured him; and this way will I take upon me to wash your liver as clean as a sound sheep's heart, that there shall not be one spot of love in't.

ORL. I would not be cured, youth.

ROS. I would cure you, if you would but call me Rosalind, and come every day to my cote, and woo me.

ORL. Now, by the faith of my love, I will; tell me where it is.

ROS. Go with me to it, and I'll show it you; and, by the way, you shall tell me where in the forest you live. Will you go?

ORL. With all my heart, good youth.

ROS. Nay, you must call me Rosalind.—Come, sister, will you go? [*Exeunt.*

SCENE III.—*Another part of the Forest.*

Enter TOUCHSTONE *and* AUDREY; JAQUES *behind, observing them.*

TOUCH. Come apace, good Audrey; I will fetch up your goats, Audrey: And how, Audrey? am I the man yet? doth my simple feature content you?

AUD. Your features! Lord warrant us! what features?

TOUCH. I am here with thee and thy goats, as the most capricious[c] poet, honest Ovid, was among the Goths.

JAQ. O knowledge ill-inhabited! worse than Jove in a thatched house![d] [*Aside.*

TOUCH. When a man's verses cannot be understood, nor a man's good wit seconded with the forward child, understanding, it strikes a man more dead than a great reckoning in a little room.—Truly, I would the gods had made thee poetical.

AUD. I do not know what *poetical* is: is it honest in deed and word? is it a true thing?

TOUCH. No, truly; for the truest poetry is the most feigning; and lovers are given to poetry; and what they swear in poetry, may be said, as lovers, they do feign.

AUD. Do you wish then, that the gods had made me poetical?

TOUCH. I do, truly, for thou swearest to me, thou art honest; now, if thou wert a poet, I might have some hope thou didst feign.

AUD. Would you not have me honest?

TOUCH. No, truly, unless thou wert hard-

(*) Old text, *living.*

a Merely—] It may not be impertinent to say, once for all, that *merely*, from the Latin *merus* and *mere*, in old language meant *absolutely, altogether, purely.* Thus in the present play:—

"And all the men and women *merely* players."

Again,—

"——*Merely*, thou art death's fool."
Measure for Measure, Act III. Sc. 1.

Again,—

"We are *merely* cheated of our lives."
The Tempest, Act I. Sc. 1.

Again,—

"Things rank and gross in nature possess it *merely*."
Hamlet, Act I. Sc. 2.

And in Lodge's *Rosalynde*, on which this comedy is based:—
"And forth they pulled such victuals as they had, and fed as *merely* as if they had been in Paris."

b Moonish—] Variable, inconstant, like the *moon*.

c Capricious—] "*Caper, capri, capritious*, capricious, fantastical, capering, goatish; and by a similar sort of process are we to smooth *Goths* into *goats*."—CALDECOTT.

d Jove in a thatched house!] "*Stipulis et cannâ tecta palustri.*" We have the same allusion in "Much Ado about Nothing," Act II. Sc. 1:—

"My visor is Philemon's roof; within the house is Jove."

favoured; for honesty coupled to beauty, is to have honey a sauce to sugar.

JAQ. A material fool![a] [*Aside.*

AUD. Well, I am not fair; and therefore I pray the gods make me honest!

TOUCH. Truly, and to cast away honesty upon a foul slut, were to put good meat into an unclean dish.

AUD. I am not a slut, though I thank the gods I am foul.[b]

---

a *A* material *fool!*] According to Johnson, a fool with matter him, one stocked with notions. In Act II. Sc. 1, the Duke, it will be remembered, remarks that Jaques, in his "sullen fits," is "full of matter."

b I *am* foul.] That is, *plain, homely.*

TOUCH. Well, praised be the gods for thy foulness! sluttishness may come hereafter. But be it as it may be, I will marry thee, and to that end, I have been with sir Oliver Martext, the vicar of the next village; who hath promised to meet me in this place of the forest, and to couple us.

JAQ. I would fain see this meeting. [*Aside.*

AUD. Well, the gods give us joy!

TOUCH. Amen. A man may, if he were of a fearful heart, stagger in this attempt; for here we have no temple but the wood, no assembly but horn-beasts. But what though?[a] Courage! As horns are odious, they are necessary. It is said,—Many a man knows no end of his goods: right,—many a man has good horns, and knows no end of them. Well, that is the dowry of his wife; 'tis none of his own getting. Horns? even so:——poor men alone?[b]——No, no; the noblest deer hath them as huge as the rascal.[c] Is the single man therefore blessed? No: as a walled town is more worthier than a village, so is the forehead of a married man more honourable than the bare brow of a bachelor: and by how much defence is better than no skill, by so much is a horn more precious than to want. Here comes sir Oliver.

Enter SIR OLIVER MARTEXT.

Sir Oliver Martext, you are well met: will you dispatch us here under this tree, or shall we go with you to your chapel?

SIR OLI. Is there none here to give the woman?

TOUCH. I will not take her on gift of any man.

SIR OLI. Truly, she must be given, or the marriage is not lawful.

JAQ. [*Coming forward.*] Proceed, proceed; I'll give her.

TOUCH. Good even, good master *What-ye-call't*: how do you, sir? You are very well met: God 'ild you for your last company: I am very glad to see you:—even a toy in hand here, sir.—Nay, pray be covered.

JAQ. Will you be married, motley?

TOUCH. As the ox hath his bow,[d] sir, the horse his curb, and the falcon her bells, so man hath his desires; and as pigeons bill, so wedlock would be nibbling.

JAQ. And will you, being a man of your breeding, be married under a bush, like a beggar? Get you to church, and have a good priest that can tell you what marriage is: this fellow will but join you together as they join wainscot; then one of you will prove a shrunk panel, and, like green timber, warp, warp.

TOUCH. [*Aside.*] I am not in the mind but I were better to be married of him than of another, for he is not like to marry me well; and not being well married, it will be a good excuse for me hereafter to leave my wife.

JAQ. Go thou with me, and let me counsel thee.

TOUCH. Come, sweet Audrey;
We must be married, or we must live in bawdry.—
Farewell, good master Oliver:—not,—

O sweet Oliver,
O brave Oliver,
Leave me not behind thee;

but,— *Wind away,*
Begone, I say,
I will not to wedding with thee. (5)

[*Exeunt* JAQUES, TOUCHSTONE, *and* AUDREY.

SIR OLI. 'Tis no matter; ne'er a fantastical knave of them all shall flout me out of my calling. [*Exit.*

SCENE IV.—*Another part of the Forest. Before a Cottage.*

Enter ROSALIND *and* CELIA.

ROS. Never talk to me; I will weep.

CEL. Do, I pr'ythee; but yet have the grace to consider, that tears do not become a man.

ROS. But have I not cause to weep?

CEL. As good cause as one would desire; therefore weep.

ROS. His very hair is of the dissembling colour.

CEL. Something browner than Judas's: marry, his kisses are Judas's own children.

ROS. I' faith, his hair is of a good colour.

CEL. An excellent colour: your chestnut was ever the only colour.

ROS. And his kissing is as full of sanctity as the touch of holy bread.

CEL. He hath bought a pair of cast[e] lips of Diana: a nun of winter's sisterhood kisses not more religiously; the very ice of chastity is in them.

ROS. But why did he swear he would come this morning, and comes not?

CEL. Nay, certainly, there is no truth in him.

ROS. Do you think so?

CEL. Yes; I think he is not a pick-purse nor a horse-stealer; but for his verity in love, I do think him as concave as a covered goblet,[f] or a worm-eaten nut.

---

[a] *What* though?] That is, what *then?*

[b] Horns, &c.] In the folio, 1623, this hopeless passage stands, "*Hornes, even so poore men alone.*" We adopt the ordinary punctuation, though with reluctance. Mr. Collier's annotator reads: "*Are* horns *given to* poor men alone?"

[c] Rascal.] *Rascal* was the huntsman's term for a deer lean and out of season.

[d] His bow,—] His *yoke.*

[e] *A pair of* cast *lips of Diana:*] So the folio, 1623; the second folio reads, "*chaste* lips."

[f] *As concave as a* covered goblet,—] A *covered* goblet, Warburton says, "because a goblet is never kept covered but when *empty.*"

Ros. Not true in love?

Cel. Yes, when he is in; but I think he is not in.

Ros. You have heard him swear downright, he was.

Cel. *Was* is not *is*: besides, the oath of a* lover is no stronger than the word of a tapster; they are both the confirmers† of false reckonings. He attends here in the forest on the duke your father.

Ros. I met the duke yesterday, and had much question with him: he asked me of what parentage I was; I told him, of as good as he; so he laughed, and let me go. But what talk we of fathers, when there is such a man as Orlando?

Cel. O, that's a brave man! he writes brave verses, speaks brave words, swears brave oaths, and breaks them bravely, quite traverse athwart the heart of his lover; as a puny tilter, that spurs his horse but on one side, breaks his staff like a noble goose: but all's brave, that youth mounts and folly guides.—Who comes here?

Enter Corin.

Cor. Mistress and master, you have oft inquir'd
After the shepherd that complain'd of love
Who you saw sitting by me on the turf,
Praising the proud disdainful shepherdess
That was his mistress.

Cel. Well, and what of him?

Cor. If you will see a pageant truly play'd,
Between the pale complexion of true love,
And the red glow of scorn and proud disdain,
Go hence a little, and I shall conduct you,
If you will mark it.

Ros. O, come, let us remove;
The sight of lovers feedeth those in love:—
Bring us to this sight, and you shall say
I'll prove a busy actor in their play. [*Exeunt.*

SCENE V.—*Another part of the Forest.*

Enter Silvius *and* Phebe.

Sil. Sweet Phebe, do not scorn me; do not, Phebe:
Say, that you love me not; but say not so
In bitterness. The common executioner,
Whose heart the accustom'd sight of death makes hard,
Falls not the axe upon the humbled neck,
But first begs pardon: will you sterner be
Than he that dies and lives by bloody drops?

Enter Rosalind, Celia, *and* Corin, *behind.*

Phe. I would not be thy executioner;
I fly thee, for I would not injure thee.
Thou tell'st me, there is murder in mine eye:
'Tis pretty, sure, and very probable,
That eyes,—that are the frail'st and softest things,
Who shut their coward gates on atomies,—
Should be call'd tyrants, butchers, murderers!
Now I do frown on thee with all my heart,
And, if mine eyes can wound, now let them kill thee;
Now counterfeit to swoon; why now fall down;
Or, if thou canst not, O, for shame, for shame,
Lie not, to say mine eyes are murderers!
Now show the wound mine eye hath made in thee;
Scratch thee but with a pin, and there remains
Some scar of it; lean upon a rush,
The cicatrice and capable[a] impressure
Thy palm some moment keeps: but now mine eyes,
Which I have darted at thee, hurt thee not;
Nor, I am sure, there is no force in eyes
That can do hurt.

Sil. O dear Phebe,
If ever (as that *ever* may be near)
You meet in some fresh cheek the power of fancy,
Then shall you know the wounds invisible
That love's keen arrows make.

Phe. But, till that time,
Come not thou near me: and, when that time comes,
Afflict me with thy mocks, pity me not,
As, till that time, I shall not pity thee.

Ros. [*Advancing.*] And why, I pray you? (6)
Who might be your mother,
That you insult, exult, and all at once,[b] [beauty,
Over the wretched? What though you have no
(As, by my faith, I see no more in you
Than without candle may go dark to bed,)
Must you be therefore proud and pitiless? [me?
Why, what means this? Why do you look on
I see no more in you, than in the ordinary
Of nature's sale-work:—Od's my little life,
I think she means to tangle my eyes too!—
No, 'faith, proud mistress, hope not after it;
'Tis not your inky brows, your black-silk hair,
Your bugle eyeballs, nor your cheek of cream,
That can entame my spirits to your worship.—
You foolish shepherd, wherefore do you follow her,
Like foggy south, puffing with wind and rain?
You are a thousand times a properer man

(*) First folio omits, *a*. (†) Old text, *confirmer*.

[a] *The* cicatrice *and* capable *impressure*—] Mr. Collier's annotator speciously, but without necessity, changes *capable* to *palpable*. *Capable* means *sensible*. The only difficulty in the line is the word *cicatrice*, which certainly appears here to be used in an exceptional sense.

[b] All at once,—] See note (a), p. 65.

Than she a woman. 'Tis such fools as you,
That make the world full of ill-favour'd children:
'Tis not her glass, but you, that flatters her;
And out of you she sees herself more proper,
Than any of her lineaments can show her.—
But, mistress, know yourself; down on your knees,
And thank heaven, fasting, for a good man's love:
For I must tell you friendly in your ear,—
Sell when you can; you are not for all markets:
Cry the man mercy; love him; take his offer:
Foul is most foul, being foul to be a scoffer.
So, take her to thee, shepherd;—fare you well.

PHE. Sweet youth, I pray you chide a year together;
I had rather hear you chide, than this man woo.

ROS. He's fallen in love with your[a] foulness, and she'll fall in love with my anger: If it be so, as fast as she answers thee with frowning looks, I'll sauce her with bitter words.—Why look you so upon me?

PHE. For no ill will I bear you.

ROS. I pray you, do not fall in love with me,
For I am falser than vows made in wine:
Besides, I like you not: if you will know my house,
'Tis at the tuft of olives here hard by:—
Will you go, sister?—Shepherd, ply her hard:—
Come, sister.—Shepherdess, look on him better,
And be not proud; though all the world could see,
None could be so abus'd in sight as he.
Come, to our flock.

[*Exeunt* ROSALIND, CELIA, *and* CORIN.

PHE. Dead shepherd! now I find thy saw of might;
Who ever lov'd, that lov'd not at first sight?(7)

SIL. Sweet Phebe,—

PHE. Ha! what say'st thou, Silvius?

SIL. Sweet Phebe, pity me.

PHE. Why, I am sorry for thee, gentle Silvius.

SIL. Wherever sorrow is, relief would be;
If you do sorrow at my grief in love,
By giving love, your sorrow and my grief
Were both extermin'd.

PHE. Thou hast my love; is not that neighbourly?

SIL. I would have you.

PHE. Why, that were covetousness.
Silvius, the time was, that I hated thee;
And yet it is not, that I bear thee love;
But since that thou canst talk of love so well,
Thy company, which erst was irksome to me,
I will endure; and I'll employ thee too:
But do not look for further recompense,
Than thine own gladness that thou art employ'd.

SIL. So holy and so perfect is my love,
And I in such a poverty of grace,
That I shall think it a most plenteous crop
To glean the broken ears after the man
That the main harvest reaps: loose now and then
A scatter'd smile, and that I'll live upon.

PHE. Know'st thou the youth that spoke to me ere while?

SIL. Not very well, but I have met him oft;
And he hath bought the cottage and the bounds,
That the old carlot[b] once was master of.

PHE. Think not I love him, though I ask for him;
'Tis but a peevish boy:—yet he talks well;—
But what care I for words? yet words do well,
When he that speaks them pleases those that hear.
It is a pretty youth:—not very pretty:—
But, sure, he's proud; and yet his pride becomes him:
He'll make a proper man: the best thing in him
Is his complexion; and faster than his tongue
Did make offence, his eye did heal it up.
He is not very tall; yet for his years he's tall:
His leg is but so so; and yet 'tis well:
There was a pretty redness in his lip,
A little riper and more lusty red
Than that mix'd in his cheek; 'twas just the difference
Betwixt the constant red and mingled damask.
There be some women, Silvius, had they mark'd him
In parcels as I did, would have gone near
To fall in love with him: but, for my part,
I love him not, nor hate him not; and yet
Have[c] more cause to hate him than to love him:
For what had he to do to chide at me?
He said mine eyes were black, and my hair black;
And, now I am remember'd, scorn'd at me;
I marvel, why I answer'd not again:
But that's all one, omittance is no quittance.
I'll write to him a very taunting letter,
And thou shalt bear it; wilt thou, Silvius?

SIL. Phebe, with all my heart.

PHE. I'll write it straight;
The matter's in my head and in my heart:
I will be bitter with him, and passing short:
Go with me, Silvius. [*Exeunt.*

a *With* your *foulness,—*] So the old copy. The usual lection is "*her* foulness." Caldecott observes,—"If Rosalind here turns to the parties before her," the original reading may stand.

b Carlot—] From *carl, churl.*

c Have more cause—] The second folio reads, "*I* have more cause," and has been followed by most of the modern editors, perhaps rightly, unless we should read:—"Have *much* more cause," &c.

ACT IV.

SCENE I.—*The Forest of* Arden.

Enter ROSALIND, CELIA, *and* JAQUES.

JAQ. I pr'ythee, pretty youth, let me be* better acquainted with thee.

ROS. They say you are a melancholy fellow.

JAQ. I am so; I do love it better than laughing.

ROS. Those that are in extremity of either, are abominable fellows, and betray themselves to every modern censure, worse than drunkards.

JAQ. Why, 'tis good to be sad and say nothing.

ROS. Why then, 'tis good to be a post.

JAQ. I have neither the scholar's melancholy, which is emulation; nor the musician's, which is fantastical; nor the courtier's, which is proud; nor the soldier's, which is ambitious; nor the lawyer's, which is politic; nor the lady's, which is nice; nor the lover's, which is all these: but it is a melancholy of mine own, compounded of many simples, extracted from many objects, and, indeed, the sundry contemplation of my travels, which,[a] by often rumination, wraps me in a most humorous sadness.

ROS. A traveller! By my faith, you have great reason to be sad: I fear, you have sold your

(*) First folio omits, *be*.

[a] Which, by *often rumination*,—] The first folio inserts *in* before *which*, the compositor's eye having probably caught the preposition from the line which followed in the MS. The second folio reads, "in which *my* often rumination."

own lands, to see other men's; then, to have seen much, and to have nothing, is to have rich eyes[a] and poor hands.

JAQ. Yes, I have gained my experience.

ROS. And your experience makes you sad: I had rather have a fool to make me merry than experience to make me sad; and to travel for it too!

Enter ORLANDO.

ORL. Good day, and happiness, dear Rosalind!

JAQ. Nay then, God be wi' you, an you talk in blank verse. [*Exit.*

ROS. Farewell, monsieur Traveller: look you lisp, and wear strange suits; disable all the benefits of your own country; be out of love with your nativity, and almost chide God for making you that countenance you are; or I will scarce think you have swam in a gondola.*—Why, how now, Orlando! where have you been all this while? you a lover? an you serve me such another trick, never come in my sight more.

ORL. My fair Rosalind, I come within an hour of my promise.

ROS. Break an hour's promise in love! He that will divide a minute into a thousand parts, and break but a part of the thousandth† part of a minute in the affairs of love, it may be said of him, that Cupid hath clapped him o' the shoulder, but I warrant him heart-whole.

ORL. Pardon me, dear Rosalind.

ROS. Nay, an you be so tardy, come no more in my sight; I had as lief be wooed of a snail.

ORL. Of a snail?

ROS. Ay, of a snail; for though he comes slowly, he carries his house on his head; a better jointure, I think, than you make a woman: besides, he brings his destiny with him.

ORL. What's that?

ROS. Why, horns; which such as you are fain to be beholden to your wives for: but he comes armed in his fortune, and prevents the slander of his wife.

ORL. Virtue is no horn-maker, and my Rosalind is virtuous.

ROS. And I am your Rosalind.

CEL. It pleases him to call you so; but he hath a Rosalind of a better leer[b] than you.

ROS. Come, woo me, woo me; for now I am in a holiday humour, and like enough to consent.—What would you say to me now, an I were your very very Rosalind?

ORL. I would kiss, before I spoke.

ROS. Nay, you were better speak first; and when you were gravelled for lack of matter, you might take occasion to kiss. Very good orators, when they are out, they will spit; and for lovers, lacking (God warn us!) matter, the cleanliest shift is to kiss.

ORL. How if the kiss be denied?

ROS. Then she puts you to entreaty, and there begins new matter.

ORL. Who could be out, being before his beloved mistress?

ROS. Marry, that should you, if I were your mistress: or I should think my honesty ranker than my wit.[c]

ORL. What, of my suit?

ROS. Not out of your apparel, and yet out of your suit. Am not I your Rosalind?

ORL. I take some joy to say you are, because I would be talking of her.

ROS. Well, in her person, I say, I will not have you.

ORL. Then, in mine own person, I die.

ROS. No, 'faith, die by attorney. The poor world is almost six thousand years old, and in all this time there was not any man died in his own person, *videlicet*, in a love-cause. Troilus had his brains dashed out with a Grecian club; yet he did what he could to die before, and he is one of the patterns of love. Leander, he would have lived many a fair year, though Hero had turned nun, if it had not been for a hot midsummer night; for good youth, he went but forth to wash him in the Hellespont, and being taken with the cramp, was drowned, and the foolish chroniclers[d] of that age found it was—Hero of Sestos. But these are all lies; men have died from time to time, and worms have eaten them, but not for love.

ORL. I would not have my right Rosalind of this mind, for, I protest, her frown might kill me.

ROS. By this hand, it will not kill a fly. But come, now I will be your Rosalind in a more coming-on disposition; and ask me what you will, I will grant it.

ORL. Then love me, Rosalind.

ROS. Yes, faith will I, Fridays, and Saturdays, and all.

ORL. And wilt thou have me?

ROS. Ay, and twenty such.

ORL. What sayest thou?

(*) Old text, *Gundello*. (†) Old text, *thousand*.

[a] Rich eyes—] So in "All's Well that Ends Well," Act V. Sc. 3:—

"Whose beauty did astonish the survey
Of *richest eyes*."

[b] Leer—] *Countenance, favour*

[c] Or *I should* think *my honesty* ranker *than my wit.*] Mr. Collier's annotator reads, "Or I should *thank* my honesty *rather* than my wit."

[d] *And the foolish* chroniclers *of that age found it was—Hero of Sestos.*] Hanmer substituted *coroners* for "chroniclers," and the same change was made by Mr. Collier's annotator.

ROS. Are you not good?

ORL. I hope so.

ROS. Why then, can one desire too much of a good thing?—Come, sister, you shall be the priest, and marry us.—Give me your hand, Orlando:—What do you say, sister?

ORL. Pray thee, marry us.

CEL. I cannot say the words.

ROS. You must begin,——*Will you, Orlando,*—

CEL. Go to.——Will you, Orlando, have to wife this Rosalind?

ORL. I will.

ROS. Ay, but when?

ORL. Why now; as fast as she can marry us.

ROS. Then you must say,—*I take thee, Rosalind, for wife.*

ORL. I take thee, Rosalind, for wife.

ROS. I might ask you for your commission; but,—*I do take thee, Orlando, for my husband*: there's a girl goes before the priest; and, certainly, a woman's thought runs before her actions.

ORL. So do all thoughts,—they are winged.

ROS. Now tell me, how long you would have her, after you have possessed her.

ORL. For ever and a day.

ROS. Say a day, without the ever. No, no, Orlando; men are April when they woo, December when they wed: maids are May when they are maids, but the sky changes when they are wives. I will be more jealous of thee than a Barbary cock-pigeon over his hen; more clamorous than a parrot against rain; more new-fangled than an ape; more giddy in my desires than a monkey: I will weep for nothing, like Diana in the fountain, and I will do that when you are disposed to be merry; I will laugh like a hyen, and that when thou art inclined to sleep.

ORL. But will my Rosalind do so?

ROS. By my life, she will do as I do.

ORL. O, but she is wise.

ROS. Or else she could not have the wit to do this: the wiser, the waywarder. Make[a] the doors upon a woman's wit, and it will out at the casement; shut that, and 'twill out at the key-hole; stop that, 'twill fly with the smoke out at the chimney.

ORL. A man that had a wife with such a wit, he might say,—*Wit, whither wilt?*[b]

ROS. Nay, you might keep that check for it, till you met your wife's wit going to your neighbour's bed.

ORL. And what wit could wit have to excuse that?

ROS. Marry, to say,—she came to seek you there. You shall never take her without her answer, unless you take her without her tongue. O, that woman that cannot make her fault her husband's occasion,[c] let her never nurse her child herself, for she will breed it like a fool.

ORL. For these two hours, Rosalind, I will leave thee.

ROS. Alas, dear love, I cannot lack thee two hours.

ORL. I must attend the duke at dinner; by two o'clock I will be with thee again.

ROS. Ay, go your ways, go your ways; I knew what you would prove; my friends told me as much, and I thought no less: that flattering tongue of yours won me:—'tis but one cast away, and so,—come death!—Two o'clock is your hour?

ORL. Ay, sweet Rosalind.

ROS. *By my troth*, and *in good earnest*, and *so God mend me*, and by all pretty oaths that are not dangerous, if you break one jot of your promise, or come one minute behind your hour, I will think you the most pathetical break-promise, and the most hollow lover, and the most unworthy of her you call Rosalind, that may be chosen out of the gross band of the unfaithful: therefore beware my censure, and keep your promise.

ORL. With no less religion, than if thou wert indeed my Rosalind: so, adieu.

ROS. Well, Time is the old justice that examines all such offenders, and let Time try: adieu!

[*Exit* ORLANDO.

CEL. You have simply misused our sex in your love-prate: we must have your doublet and hose plucked over your head, and show the world what the bird hath done to her own nest.

ROS. O coz, coz, coz, my pretty little coz, that thou didst know how many fathom deep I am in love! But it cannot be sounded; my affection hath an unknown bottom, like the bay of Portugal.

CEL. Or rather, bottomless; that as fast as you pour affection in, it(*) runs out.

ROS. No, that same wicked bastard of Venus, that was begot of thought, conceived of spleen, and born of madness; that blind rascally boy, that abuses every one's eyes, because his own are out, let him be judge, how deep I am in love:—I'll tell thee, Aliena, I cannot be out of the sight of Orlando: I'll go find a shadow, and sigh till he come.

CEL. And I'll sleep. [*Exeunt.*

---

[a] Make *the doors*—] That is, *bar the doors*. See note (b), p. 128, Vol. I.

[b] Wit, whither wilt?] A proverbial saying, repeatedly met with in our early writers.

[c] *Her husband's* occasion,—] Hanmer reads *accusation*; Mr. Collier's annotator, *accusing*. If any deviation is required, we might perhaps better, and without departing far from the text, read, "her husband's *confusion*."

(*) First folio, *in*.

SCENE II.—*Another part of the Forest.*

Enter JAQUES, *and* Lords *in the habit of Foresters.*

JAQ. Which is he that killed the deer?

1 LORD. Sir, it was I.

JAQ. Let's present him to the duke, like a Roman conqueror; and it would do well to set the deer's horns upon his head, for a branch of victory. Have you no song, forester, for this purpose?

1 LORD. Yes, sir.

JAQ. Sing it; 't is no matter how it be in tune, so it make noise enough.

SONG.

What shall he have that kill'd the deer?
His leather skin, and horns to wear.
Then sing him home.[a] [The rest shall bear this burden.]
Take thou no scorn to wear the horn,
It was a crest ere thou wast born.
Thy father's father wore it,
And thy father bore it:
The horn, the horn, the lusty horn,
Is not a thing to laugh to scorn. [Exeunt.

SCENE III.—*Another part of the Forest.*

Enter ROSALIND *and* CELIA.

ROS. How say you now? is it not past two o'clock? and here much[b] Orlando!

CEL. I warrant you, with pure love and troubled brain, he hath ta'en his bow and arrows, and is gone forth—to sleep.—Look, who comes here?

Enter SILVIUS.

SIL. My errand is to you, fair youth;—
My gentle Phebe did bid me give you this:
[*Giving a letter.*
I know not the contents, but, as I guess,
By the stern brow and waspish action
Which she did use as she was writing of it,
It bears an angry tenour: pardon me,
I am but as a guiltless messenger.

ROS. Patience herself would startle at this letter,
And play the swaggerer; bear this, bear all!
She says, I am not fair; that I lack manners;
She calls me proud; and, that she could not love me
Were man as rare as phœnix; Od's my will!
Her love is not the hare that I do hunt:
Why writes she so to me?—Well, shepherd, well,
This is a letter of your own device.

SIL. No, I protest, I know not the contents;
Phebe did write it.

ROS. Come, come, you are a fool,
And turn'd into the extremity of love.
I saw her hand: she has a leathern hand,
A freestone-colour'd hand; I verily did think
That her old gloves were on, but 'twas her hands;
She has a huswife's hand; but that's no matter:
I say, she never did invent this letter;
This is a man's invention, and his hand.

SIL. Sure, it is hers.

ROS. Why, 't is a boisterous and a cruel style,
A style for challengers; why, she defies me,
Like Turk to Christian: woman's* gentle brain
Could not drop forth such giant-rude invention,
Such Ethiop words, blacker in their effect
Than in their countenance.—Will you hear the letter?

SIL. So please you, for I never heard it yet;
Yet heard too much of Phebe's cruelty.

ROS. She Phebes me: mark how the tyrant writes.—[Reads.

Art thou god to shepherd turn'd,
That a maiden's heart hath burn'd?—

Can a woman rail thus?

SIL. Call you this railing?

ROS. [Reads.] *Why, thy godhead laid apart,*
Warr'st thou with a woman's heart?

Did you ever hear such railing?—[Reads.

Whiles the eye of man did woo me,
That could do no vengeance to me.—

Meaning me a beast.—[Reads.

If the scorn of your bright eyne
Have power to raise such love in mine,
Alack, in me what strange effect
Would they work in mild aspéct!
Whiles you chid me, I did love,
How then might your prayers move!
He that brings this love to thee,
Little knows this love in me:
And by him seal up thy mind,
Whether that thy youth and kind
Will the faithful offer take
Of me, and all that I can make;
Or else by him my love deny,
And then I'll study how to die.

---

[a] Then sing him home.] In the original these words, and "the rest shall bear this burden," are printed in one line as part of the song, and some editors suppose the whole to be only a stage-direction. We rather take "*Then sing him home,*" to form the burden; and conjecture it ought to be repeated after each couplet.

(*) Old text, *women's*.

[b] *And here* much *Orlando!*] This ironical mode of speech is not yet in desuetude. We still occasionally hear "*Much* you'll see of him!" "*Much* I get by this!" and the like.

SIL. Call you this chiding?

CEL. Alas, poor shepherd!

ROS. Do you pity him? no, he deserves no pity. Wilt thou love such a woman? What, to make thee an instrument, and play false strains upon thee! not to be endured!—Well, go your way to her, (for I see love hath made thee a tame snake,) and say this to her;—that if she love me, I charge her to love thee: if she will not, I will never have her, unless thou entreat for her. If you be a true lover, hence, and not a word; for here comes more company. [*Exit* SILVIUS.

Enter OLIVER.

OLI. Good morrow, fair ones. Pray you, if you know,
Where in the purlieus of this forest stands
A sheep-cote, fenc'd about with olive-trees?

CEL. West of this place, down in the neighbour bottom,
The rank of osiers, by the murmuring stream,
Left on your right hand, brings you to the place:
But at this hour the house doth keep itself.
There's none within.

OLI. If that an eye may profit by a tongue,
Then I should know you by description;
Such garments, and such years:—*The boy is fair,*
Of female favour, and bestows himself
Like a ripe sister:[a] *the woman low,*
And browner than her brother. Are not you
The owner of the house I did inquire for?

CEL. It is no boast, being ask'd, to say we are.

OLI. Orlando doth commend him to you both,
And to that youth he calls his Rosalind,
He sends this bloody napkin:—are you he?

ROS. I am: what must we understand by this?

OLI. Some of my shame; if you will know of me
What man I am, and how, and why, and where
This handkercher was stain'd.

CEL. I pray you, tell it.

OLI. When last the young Orlando parted from you,
He left a promise to return again
Within an hour; and, pacing through the forest,
Chewing the cud[b] of sweet and bitter fancy,
Lo, what befel! he threw his eye aside,
And, mark, what object did present itself!
Under an* oak, whose boughs were moss'd with age,
And high top bald with dry antiquity,
A wretched ragged man, o'ergrown with hair,
Lay sleeping on his back: about his neck
A green and gilded snake had wreath'd itself,
Who with her head, nimble in threats, approach'd
The opening of his mouth; but suddenly
Seeing Orlando, it unlink'd itself,
And with indented glides did slip away
Into a bush: under which bush's shade
A lioness, with udders all drawn dry,
Lay couching, head on ground, with cat-like watch,
When that the sleeping man should stir; for 't is
The royal disposition of that beast,
To prey on nothing that doth seem as dead:
This seen, Orlando did approach the man,
And found it was his brother, his elder brother.

CEL. O, I have heard him speak of that same brother;
And he did render him the most unnatural
That liv'd 'mongst men.

OLI. And well he might so do,
For well I know he was unnatural.

ROS. But, to Orlando: did he leave him there,
Food to the suck'd and hungry lioness?

OLI. Twice did he turn his back, and purpos'd so:
But kindness, nobler ever than revenge,
And nature, stronger than his just occasion,
Made him give battle to the lioness,
Who quickly fell before him; in which hurtling[c]
From miserable slumber I awak'd.(1)

CEL. Are you his brother?

ROS. Was 't you he rescu'd?

CEL. Was't you that did so oft contrive to kill him?

OLI. 'T was I, but 't is not I: I do not shame
To tell you what I was, since my conversion
So sweetly tastes, being the thing I am.

ROS. But, for the bloody napkin?

OLI. By and by.
When from the first to last, betwixt us two,
Tears our recountments had most kindly bath'd,
As, how I came into that desert place;——
In* brief, he led me to the gentle duke,
Who gave me fresh array and entertainment,
Committing me unto my brother's love;
Who led me instantly unto his cave,
There stripp'd himself, and here upon his arm
The lioness had torn some flesh away,
Which all this while had bled; and now he fainted,
And cried, in fainting, upon Rosalind.

(*) Old text inserts, *old*.

(*) First folio, *I*.

a ——— *And* bestows *himself*
Like a ripe sister:]
Bestow is here used in the same unusual sense which it bears in the Second Part of "Henry IV." Act II. Sc. 2:—"How might we see Falstaff *bestow* himself to-night in his true colours?" For, *Like a ripe sister*, Mr. W. N. Lettsom ingeniously proposes, "Like a *right forester*."

b *Chewing the* cud—] The old text has *food*, undoubtedly a misprint. "To chew the *cud*," metaphorically, to *ruminate*, to *revolve in the mind*, is an expression of frequent occurrence in our old authors.

c Hurtling—] *Justling.* So in "Julius Cæsar," Act II. Sc. 2:—
"The noise of battle *hurtled* in the air."

Brief, I recover'd him; bound up his wound;
And, after some small space, being strong at heart,
He sent me hither, stranger as I am,
To tell this story, that you might excuse
His broken promise, and to give this napkin,
Dy'd in his* blood, unto the shepherd youth
That he in sport doth call his Rosalind.

[ROSALIND *faints.*

CEL. Why, how now, Ganymede! sweet Ganymede! [blood.

OLI. Many will swoon when they do look on

CEL. There is more in it.—Cousin—Ganymede!

OLI. Look, he recovers.

ROS. I would I were at home.

CEL. We'll lead you thither:—
I pray you, will you take him by the arm?

OLI. Be of good cheer, youth: you a man?—you lack a man's heart.

(*) First folio, *this*.

ROS. I do so, I confess it. Ah, sirrah, a body would think this was well counterfeited: I pray you, tell your brother how well I counterfeited.—Heigh-ho!

OLI. This was not counterfeit; there is too great testimony in your complexion, that it was a passion of earnest.

ROS. Counterfeit, I assure you.

OLI. Well then, take a good heart, and counterfeit to be a man.

ROS. So I do: but, i' faith I should have been a woman by right.

CEL. Come, you look paler and paler; pray you, draw homewards.—Good sir, go with us.

OLI. That will I, for I must bear answer back, how you excuse my brother, Rosalind.

ROS. I shall devise something: but, I pray you commend my counterfeiting to him.—Will you go? [*Exeunt.*

ACT V.

SCENE I.—*The Forest of* Arden.

Enter Touchstone *and* Audrey.

Touch. We shall find a time, Audrey; patience, gentle Audrey.

Aud. Faith, the priest was good enough, for all the old gentleman's saying.

Touch. A most wicked Sir Oliver, Audrey, a most vile Martext. But, Audrey, there is a youth here in the forest lays claim to you.

Aud. Ay, I know who 'tis; he hath no interest in me in the world: here comes the man you mean.

Touch. It is meat and drink to me to see a clown: by my troth, we that have good wits have much to answer for; we shall be flouting; we cannot hold.

Enter William.

Will. Good even, Audrey.

Aud. God ye good even, William.

Will. And good even to you, sir.

Touch. Good even, gentle friend. Cover thy head, cover thy head; nay, pr'ythee, be covered. How old are you, friend?

Will. Five and twenty, sir.

Touch. A ripe age. Is thy name William?

Will. William, sir.

Touch. A fair name. Wast born i' the forest here?

Will. Ay, sir, I thank God.

Touch. *Thank God;*—a good answer. Art rich?

Will. 'Faith, sir, so-so.

Touch. *So-so* is good, very good, very excellent good:—and yet it is not; it is but so-so. Art thou wise?

Will. Ay, sir, I have a pretty wit.

Touch. Why, thou sayest well. I do now remember a saying: *The fool doth think he is wise, but the wise man knows himself to be a fool.*

The heathen philosopher, when he had a desire to eat a grape, would open his lips when he put it into his mouth, meaning thereby, that grapes were made to eat, and lips to open. You do love this maid?

WILL. I do, sir.

TOUCH. Give me your hand. Art thou learned?

WILL. No, sir.

TOUCH. Then learn this of me; To have, is to have: for it is a figure in rhetoric, that drink, being poured out of a cup into a glass, by filling the one doth empty the other: for all your writers do consent that *ipse* is he; now, you are not *ipse*, for I am he.

WILL. Which *he*, sir?

TOUCH. He, sir, that must marry this woman. Therefore, you clown, abandon,—which is in the vulgar, leave,—the society,—which in the boorish is, company,—of this female,—which in the common is, woman; which together is, abandon the society of this female, or, clown, thou perishest; or, to thy better understanding, diest; or, to wit, I kill thee, make thee away, translate thy life into death, thy liberty into bondage: I will deal in poison with thee, or in bastinado, or in steel; I will bandy with thee in faction; I will o'er-run thee with policy; I will kill thee a hundred and fifty ways; therefore tremble, and depart.

AUD. Do, good William.

WILL. God rest you merry, sir. [*Exit.*

Enter CORIN.

COR. Our master and mistress seeks you; come, away, away!

TOUCH. Trip, Audrey, trip, Audrey;—I attend, I attend. [*Exeunt.*

SCENE II.—*Another part of the Forest.*

Enter ORLANDO *and* OLIVER.

ORL. Is't possible that, on so little acquaintance, you should like her? that, but seeing, you should love her? and, loving, woo? and, wooing, she should grant? and will you persêver to enjoy her?

OLI. Neither call the giddiness of it in question, the poverty of her, the small acquaintance, my sudden wooing, nor her [a] sudden consenting; but say with me, I love Aliena; say with her, that she loves me; consent with both, that we may enjoy each other; it shall be to your good; for my father's house, and all the revenue that was old sir Roland's, will I estate upon you, and here live and die a shepherd.

ORL. You have my consent. Let your wedding be to-morrow: thither will I invite the duke, and all his contented followers. Go you, and prepare Aliena: for, look you, here comes my Rosalind.

Enter ROSALIND.

ROS. God save you, brother.

OLI. And you, fair sister.

ROS. O, my dear Orlando, how it grieves me to see thee wear thy heart in a scarf!

ORL. It is my arm.

ROS. I thought, thy heart had been wounded with the claws of a lion.

ORL. Wounded it is, but with the eyes of a lady.

ROS. Did your brother tell you how I counterfeited to swoon, when he showed me your handkercher?

ORL. Ay, and greater wonders than that.

ROS. O, I know where you are:—nay, 'tis true: there was never any thing so sudden, but the fight of two rams, and Cæsar's thrasonical brag of—*I came, saw,* and *overcame:** for your brother and my sister no sooner met, but they looked; no sooner looked, but they loved; no sooner loved, but they sighed; no sooner sighed, but they asked one another the reason; no sooner knew the reason, but they sought the remedy: and in these degrees have they made a pair of stairs to marriage, which they will climb incontinent, or else be incontinent before marriage: they are in the very wrath of love, and they will together; clubs cannot part them.[b]

ORL. They shall be married to-morrow, and I will bid[c] the duke to the nuptial. But, O, how bitter a thing it is to look into happiness through another man's eyes! By so much the more shall I to-morrow be at the height of heart-heaviness, by how much I shall think my brother happy in having what he wishes for.

ROS. Why, then, to-morrow I cannot serve your turn for Rosalind?

ORL. I can live no longer by thinking.

ROS. I will weary you no longer then with idle

---

[a] *Nor* her *sudden consenting;*] *Her*, wanting in the old copies, was inserted by Rowe.

[b] Clubs cannot part them.] The chief preservers, and sometimes disturbers, of the public peace in London during Shakespeare's time were the civic apprentices, who, upon the breaking out of a fray, were summoned to the scene of action by the well-known cry of "Clubs! Clubs!" From this circumstance it became a common custom, when a *fracas* occurred, to call out "Clubs!" to part the belligerents.

(*) First folio, *overcome.*

[c] Bid *the duke*—] *Invite* the duke. So in "The Merchant of Venice," Act II. Sc. 5:—

"I am *bid* forth to supper, Jessica."

talking. Know of me, then, (for now I speak to some purpose,) that I know you are a gentleman of good conceit: I speak not this, that you should bear a good opinion of my knowledge, insomuch, I say, I know you are; neither do I labour for a greater esteem than may in some little measure draw a belief from you, to do yourself good, and not to grace me. Believe, then, if you please, that I can do strange things: I have, since I was three year old, conversed with a magician, most profound in his art, and yet not damnable. If you do love Rosalind so near the heart as your gesture cries it out, when your brother marries Aliena, shall you marry her. I know into what straits of fortune she is driven, and it is not impossible to me, if it appear not inconvenient to you, to set her before your eyes to-morrow, human as she is, and without any danger.

ORL. Speakest thou in sober meanings?

ROS. By my life, I do; which I tender dearly, though I say I am a magician: therefore, put you in your best array, bid[a] your friends; for if you will be married to-morrow, you shall; and to Rosalind, if you will.—Look, here comes a lover of mine, and a lover of hers.

Enter SILVIUS *and* PHEBE.

PHE. Youth, you have done me much ungentleness,
To show the letter that I writ to you.

ROS. I care not, if I have: it is my study,
To seem despiteful and ungentle to you:
You are there follow'd by a faithful shepherd;
Look upon him, love him; he worships you.

PHE. Good shepherd, tell this youth what 'tis to love.

SIL. It is to be all made of sighs and tears;—
And so am I for Phebe.

PHE. And I for Ganymede.

ORL. And I for Rosalind.

ROS. And I for no woman.

SIL. It is to be all made of faith and service;—
And so am I for Phebe.

PHE. And I for Ganymede.

ORL. And I for Rosalind.

ROS. And I for no woman.

SIL. It is to be all made of fantasy,
All made of passion, and all made of wishes;
All adoration, duty, and observance;
All humbleness, all patience, and impatience,
All purity, all trial, all observance;[b]
And so am I for Phebe.

PHE. And so am I for Ganymede.

ORL. And so am I for Rosalind.

ROS. And so am I for no woman.

PHE. If this be so, why blame you me to love you? [*To* ROSALIND.

SIL. If this be so, why blame you me to love you? [*To* PHEBE.

ORL. If this be so, why blame you me to love you?

ROS. Who * do you speak to, *why blame you me to love you?*

ORL. To her, that is not here, nor doth not hear.

ROS. Pray you, no more of this; 'tis like the howling of Irish wolves against the moon.—I will help you, [*To* SILVIUS.] if I can:—I would love you [*To* PHEBE.] if I could.—To-morrow meet me all together. I will marry you, [*To* PHEBE.] if ever I marry woman, and I'll be married to-morrow. I will satisfy you, [*To* ORLANDO.] if ever I satisfied man, and you shall be married to-morrow.—I will content you, [*To* SILVIUS.] if what pleases you contents you, and you shall be married to-morrow. As you [*To* ORLANDO.] love Rosalind, meet; as you [*To* SILVIUS.] love Phebe, meet; and as I love no woman, I'll meet.—So, fare you well; I have left you commands.

SIL. I'll not fail, if I live.

PHE. Nor I.

ORL. Nor I. [*Exeunt.*

SCENE III.—*Another part of the Forest.*

Enter TOUCHSTONE *and* AUDREY.

TOUCH. To-morrow is the joyful day, Audrey; to-morrow will we be married.

AUD. I do desire it with all my heart: and I hope it is no dishonest desire, to desire to be a woman of the world.[c] Here come two of the banished duke's pages.

Enter two Pages.

1 PAGE. Well met, honest gentleman.

TOUCH. By my troth, well met: come, sit, sit, and a song.

2 PAGE. We are for you; sit i'the middle.

1 PAGE. Shall we clap into't roundly, without hauking, or spitting, or saying we are hoarse; which are the only prologues to a bad voice?

2 PAGE. I'faith, i'faith; and both in a tune, like two gypsies on a horse.

---

[a] Bid *your friends*;] See note (c), p. 165.

[b] *All purity, all trial, all* observance;] The same word having been employed just before, *observance* is here probably a misprint for *obedience*, or *obeisance*.

(*) Old text, *why;* altered by Rowe.

[c] A woman of the world.] That is, a *married woman*.

SONG.

I.

It was a lover and his lass,
With a hey, and a ho, and a hey nonino,
That o'er the green corn-field did pass
In the spring time, the only pretty ring[a] *time,*
When birds do sing, hey ding a ding, ding;
Sweet lovers love the spring.

II.

Between the acres of the rye,
With a hey, and a ho, and a hey nonino,
These pretty country-folks would lie
In spring time, &c.

III.

This carol they began that hour,
With a hey, and a ho, and a hey nonino,
How that a life was but a flower
In spring time, &c.

IV.

And therefore take the present time,[b]
With a hey, and a ho, and a hey nonino;
For love is crowned with the prime
In spring time, &c.

TOUCH. Truly, young gentlemen, though there was no great matter in the ditty, yet the note was very untuneable.[c]

1 PAGE. You are deceived, sir; we kept time, we lost not our time.

TOUCH. By my troth, yes; I count it but time lost to hear such a foolish song. God be wi' you; and God mend your voices! Come, Audrey. [*Exeunt.*

SCENE IV.—*Another part of the Forest.*

Enter DUKE *senior*, AMIENS, JAQUES, ORLANDO, OLIVER, *and* CELIA.

DUKE S. Dost thou believe, Orlando, that the boy
Can do all this that he hath promised?

ORL. I sometimes do believe, and sometimes do not;
As those that fear they hope, and know they fear.[d]

Enter ROSALIND, SILVIUS, *and* PHEBE.

ROS. Patience once more, whiles our compact is urg'd:[e]——
You say, if I bring in your Rosalind, [*To the* DUKE.
You will bestow her on Orlando here?

DUKE S. That would I, had I kingdoms to give with her.

ROS. And you say, you will have her, when I bring her? [*To* ORLANDO.

ORL. That would I, were I of all kingdoms king.

ROS. You say, you'll marry me, if I be willing?— [*To* PHEBE.

PHE. That will I, should I die the hour after.

ROS. But if you do refuse to marry me,
You'll give yourself to this most faithful shepherd?

PHE. So is the bargain.

ROS. You say, that you'll have Phebe, if she will? [*To* SILVIUS.

SIL. Though to have her and death were both one thing.

ROS. I have promis'd to make all this matter even.
Keep you your word, O duke, to give your daughter;—
You yours, Orlando, to receive his daughter:—
Keep you your word, Phebe, that you'll marry me;
Or else, refusing me, to wed this shepherd:—
Keep your word, Silvius, that you'll marry her,
If she refuse me:—and from hence I go,
To make these doubts all even.
[*Exeunt* ROSALIND *and* CELIA.

DUKE S. I do remember in this shepherd boy,
Some lively touches of my daughter's favour.

ORL. My lord, the first time that I ever saw him,
Methought he was a brother to your daughter;
But, my good lord, this boy is forest-born,
And hath been tutor'd in the rudiments
Of many desperate studies by his uncle,
Whom he reports to be a great magician,
Obscured in the circle of this forest.

---

[a] Ring *time*,—] The old edition has "*rang* time;" the reading in the text was proposed by Steevens, and has since been found in a MS. copy of the song of the seventeenth century, formerly belonging to Mr. Heber, and now in the Advocates' Library, Edinburgh.

[b] And therefore take the present time, &c.] This is printed as the second stanza in the old text.

[c] *The note was very* untuneable.] Theobald altered the last word to *untimeable;* and the same change is made by Mr. Collier's annotator; but *time* and *tune* were once synonymous.

[d] As those that fear they hope, and know they fear.] This line, not without reason, has been suspected of corruption, and innumerable emendations have been proposed; of these it may be sufficient to particularize the suggestion of Johnson:—

"As those that fear, *they* hope, and *now* they fear;"

that of Heath:—

"As those that fear *their* hope, and know their fear;"

and that of Mr. Collier's annotator:—

"As those that fear *to* hope, and know they fear."

A somewhat similar form of expression is found in "All's Well That Ends Well," Act II. Sc. 2:—

"But know I think, and think I know most sure."

[e] *Whiles our compact is* urg'd:] Mr. Collier's annotator needlessly changes *urg'd* to *heard.*

JAQ. There is, sure, another flood toward, and these couples are coming to the ark! Here comes a pair of very strange beasts, which in all tongues are called fools.

Enter TOUCHSTONE *and* AUDREY.

TOUCH. Salutation and greeting to you all!

JAQ. Good my lord, bid him welcome. This is the motley-minded gentleman, that I have so often met in the forest: he hath been a courtier, he swears.

TOUCH. If any man doubt that, let him put me to my purgation. I have trod a measure; I have flattered a lady; I have been politic with my friend, smooth with mine enemy; I have undone three tailors; I have had four quarrels, and like to have fought one.

JAQ. And how was that ta'en up?

TOUCH. Faith, we met, and found the quarrel was upon the seventh cause.

JAQ. How seventh cause?—Good, my lord, like this fellow.

DUKE S. I like him very well.

TOUCH. God 'ild you,[a] sir; I desire you[b] of the like. I press in here, sir, amongst the rest of the country copulatives, to swear and to forswear; according as marriage binds and blood breaks:—a poor virgin, sir, an ill-favoured thing, sir, but mine own; a poor humour of mine, sir, to take that that no man else will. Rich honesty dwells like a miser, sir, in a poor house, as your pearl in your foul oyster.

DUKE S. By my faith, he is very swift[c] and sententious.

TOUCH. According to the fool's bolt, sir, and such dulcet diseases.

JAQ. But, for the seventh cause; how did you find the quarrel on the seventh cause?

TOUCH. Upon a lie seven times removed:—bear your body more seeming, Audrey:—as thus, sir. I did dislike[d] the cut of a certain courtier's beard; he sent me word, if I said his beard was not cut well, he was in the mind it was: this is called the *Retort courteous*. If I sent him word again, it was not well cut, he would send me word, he cut it to please himself: this is called the *Quip modest*. If again, it was not well cut, he disabled[e] my judgment: this is called the *Reply churlish*. If again, it was not well cut, he would answer, I spake not true: this is called the *Reproof valiant*. If again, it was not well cut, he would say, I lie: this is called the *Countercheck quarrelsome:* and so to the* *Lie circumstantial*, and the *Lie direct*.

JAQ. And how oft did you say, his beard was not well cut?

TOUCH. I durst go no further than the *Lie circumstantial*, nor he durst not give me the *Lie direct;* and so we measured swords, and parted.

JAQ. Can you nominate in order now the degrees of the lie?

TOUCH. O, sir, we quarrel in print, by the book,(1) as you have books for good manners:(2) I will name you the degrees. The first, the Retort courteous; the second, the Quip modest; the third, the Reply churlish; the fourth, the Reproof valiant; the fifth, the Countercheck quarrelsome; the sixth, the Lie with circumstance; the seventh, the Lie direct. All these you may avoid, but the Lie direct; and you may avoid that too, with an *If*. I knew when seven justices could not take up a quarrel; but when the parties were met themselves, one of them thought but of an *If*, as, *If you said so, then I said so;* and they shook hands, and swore brothers. Your *If* is the only peace-maker; much virtue in *If*.

JAQ. Is not this a rare fellow, my lord? he's as good at any thing, and yet a fool.

DUKE S. He uses his folly like a stalking-horse, and under the presentation of that, he shoots his wit.

Still music.[f] *Enter* HYMEN,[g] *leading* ROSALIND *in woman's clothes; and* CELIA.

HYM. *Then is there mirth in heaven,*
When earthly things made even,
Atone together.
Good duke, receive thy daughter,
Hymen from heaven brought her,
Yea, brought her hither,
That thou might'st join her† hand with his,
Whose heart within her† bosom is.

ROS. To you I give myself, for I am yours. [*To* DUKE S.

---

a *God 'ild you,*—] God *yield* you, reward you.

b I *desire you of the like.*] For examples of this mode of construction, see note (a), p. 361, Vol. I.

c Swift—] See note (f), p. 714, Vol. I.

d I *did* dislike—] *Dislike* here imports not merely the entertaining an aversion, but the expressing it; so in "Measure for Measure," Act I. Sc. 2:—"I never *heard* any soldier *dislike* it." So, also, in Beaumont and Fletcher's "Queen of Corinth," Act IV. Sc. 1:—

——"Has he familiarly
Disliked your yellow starch, or said your doublet
Was not exactly frenchified?"

(*) First folio omits, *the*. (†) Old copy, *his*.

e *He* disabled *my judgment:*] He *disparaged, impugned* my judgment; so in Act IV. Sc. 1:—"*disable* all the benefits of your own country."

f Still music.] That is, *soft, low, gentle* music;—"then, calling softly to the Gentlemen who were witnesses about him, he bade them that they should command some *still* musicke to sound."—*A Patterne of the painefull Adventures of Pericles, prince of Tyre*, 1608. See note (a), p. 92.

g Hymen,—] "Rosalind is imagined by the rest of the company to be brought by enchantment, and is therefore introduced by a supposed aerial being in the character of Hymen."—JOHNSON.

To you I give myself, for I am yours.
[*To* ORLANDO.

DUKE S. If there be truth in sight, you are my daughter.

ORL. If there be truth in sight, you are my Rosalind.

PHE. If sight and shape be true,
Why then,—my love adieu!

ROS. I'll have no father, if you be not he:—
[*To* DUKE S.
I'll have no husband, if you be not he:—
[*To* ORLANDO.
Nor ne'er wed woman, if you be not she.
[*To* PHEBE.

HYM. Peace, ho! I bar confusion:
'T is I must make conclusion
Of these most strange events:
Here 's eight that must take hands,
To join in Hymen's bands,
If truth holds true contents.
You and you no cross shall part:
[*To* ORLANDO *and* ROSALIND.
You and you are heart in heart:
[*To* OLIVER *and* CELIA.
You [*To* PHEBE.] to his love must accord,
Or have a woman to your lord:—
You and you are sure together,
[*To* TOUCHSTONE *and* AUDREY.
As the winter to foul weather.
Whiles a wedlock-hymn we sing,
Feed yourselves with questioning;
That reason wonder may diminish,
How thus we met, and these things finish.

SONG.

Wedding is great Juno's crown;
O blessed bond of board and bed!
'T is Hymen peoples every town;
High wedlock, then, be honoured:
Honour, high honour and renown,
To Hymen, god of every town!

DUKE S. O my dear niece, welcome thou art to me!
Even daughter, welcome in no less degree.

PHE. I will not eat my word; now thou art mine;
Thy faith my fancy to thee doth combine.
[*To* SILVIUS.

Enter JAQUES DE BOIS.

JAQ. DE B. Let me have audience for a word, or two;
I am the second son of old sir Roland,
That bring these tidings to this fair assembly:—
Duke Frederick, hearing how that every day
Men of great worth resorted to this forest,
Address'd[a] a mighty power, which were on foot,
In his own conduct, purposely to take
His brother here, and put him to the sword:
And to the skirts of this wild wood he came,
Where meeting with an old religious man,
After some question with him, was converted
Both from his enterprize and from the world:
His crown bequeathing to his banish'd brother,
And all their lands restor'd to them* again
That were with him exíl'd. This to be true,
I do engage my life.

DUKE S. Welcome, young man;
Thou offer'st fairly to thy brothers' wedding:
To one, his lands withheld; and to the other,
A land itself at large, a potent dukedom.
First, in this forest, let us do those ends
That here were well begun and well begot:
And after, every of this happy number,
That have endur'd shrewd days and nights with us,
Shall share the good of our returned fortune,
According to the measure of their states.
Meantime, forget this new-fall'n dignity,
And fall into our rustic revelry:—
Play, music!—and you, brides and bridegrooms all,
With measure heap'd in joy, to the measures fall.

JAQ. Sir, by your patience.—If I heard you rightly,
The duke hath put on a religious life,
And thrown into neglect the pompous court?

JAQ. DE B. He hath.

JAQ. To him will I: out of these convertites
There is much matter to be heard and learn'd.—
You [*To* DUKE S.] to your former honour I bequeath;
Your patience and your virtue well deserves it:—
You [*To* ORLANDO.] to a love, that your true faith doth merit:—
You [*To* OLIVER.] to your land, and love, and great allies:—
You [*To* SILVIUS.] to a long and well deserved bed;—
And you [*To* TOUCHSTONE.] to wrangling; for thy loving voyage
Is but for two months victuall'd.—So to your pleasures;
I am for other than for dancing measures.

DUKE S. Stay, Jaques, stay.

JAQ. To see no pastime I:—what you would have
I'll stay to know at your abandon'd cave. [*Exit.*

DUKE S. Proceed, proceed: we will begin these rites,
As we do trust they'll end, in true delights.
[*A dance.*

[a] Address'd—] *Prepared.*

(*) Old text, *him.*

EPILOGUE.

Ros. It is not the fashion to see the lady the epilogue; but it is no more unhandsome, than to see the lord the prologue. If it be true, that *good wine needs no bush*,(1) 'tis true, that a good play needs no epilogue: yet to good wine they do use good bushes; and good plays prove the better by the help of good epilogues. What a case am I in, then, that am neither a good epilogue, nor cannot insinuate with you in the behalf of a good play! I am not furnished like a beggar, therefore to beg will not become me: my way is, to conjure you, and I'll begin with the women. I charge you, O women, for the love you bear to men, to like as much of this play as please you: and I charge you, O men, for the love you bear to women, (as I perceive by your simpering, none of you hates them,) that between you and the women the play may please. If I were a woman, I would kiss as many of you as had beards that pleased me, complexions that liked me, and breaths that I defied not: and, I am sure, as many as have good beards, or good faces, or sweet breaths, will, for my kind offer, when I make curtsy, bid me farewell.

[*Exeunt.*

ILLUSTRATIVE COMMENTS.

ACT I.

(1) Scene I.—*And so, God keep your worship!*] In Lodge's novel the complot between Saladyne (the Oliver of the play) and the wrestler is related as follows:—"A champion there was to stand against all commers, a Norman, a man of tall stature and of great strength; so valiant, that in many such conflicts he alwaies bare away the victorie, not onely overthrowing them which hee incountred, but often with the weight of his bodie killing them outright. Saladyne hearing of this, thinking now not to let the ball fal to the ground, but to take opportunitie by the forehead, first by secret meanes convented with the Norman, and procured him with rich rewards to sweare, that if Rosader came within his clawes hee would never more return to quarrel with Saladyne for his possessions. The Norman desirous of pelfe, as (*quis nisi mentis inops oblatum respuit aurum*) taking great gifts for litle gods, tooke the crownes of Saladyne to performe the stratagem."—Rosalynde. *Euphues' Golden Legacy*, &c. reprinted by Mr. Collier in his *Shakespeare's Library*.

(2) Scene II.—*Charles is thrown.*] In the novel, after an account of the Norman's victory over the poor Franklin's two sons, both of whom are killed, Rosader's (Orlando) encounter with the "bony prizer" is thus described:—"With that Rosader vailed bonnet to the king, and lightly leapt within the lists, where noting more the companie then the combatant, he cast his eye upon the troupe of ladies that glistered there lyke the starres of heaven; but at last Love willing to make him as amorous as hee was valiant, presented him with the sight of Rosalynd, whose admirable beautie so inveagled the eye of Rosader, that forgetting himselfe, he stood and fedde his lookes on the favour of Rosalyndes face; which shee perceiving, blusht, which was such a doubling of her beauteous excellence, that the bashful redde of Aurora at the sight of unacquainted Phaeton, was not halfe so glorious. The Normane, seeing this young gentleman fettered in the lookes of the ladyes drave him out of his memento with a shake by the shoulder. Rosader looking backe with an angrie frowne, as if hee had been wakened from some pleasaunt dreame, discovered to all by the furye of his countenance that hee was a man of some high thoughts; but when they all noted his youth, and the sweetnesse of his visage, with a general applause of favours, they grieved that so goodly a yoong man should venture in so base an action; but seeing it were to his dishonour to hinder him from his enterprize, they wisht him to bee graced with the palme of victorie. After Rosader was thus called out of his memento by the Norman, he roughly clapt to him with so fierce an incounter, that they both fel to the ground, and with the violence of the fal were forced to breathe: in which space the Norman called to minde by all tokens, that this was hee whom Saladyne had appoynted him to kil; which conjecture made him stretch every limbe, and try every sinew, that working his death hee might recover the golde which so bountifuly was promised him. On the contrary part, Rosader while he breathed was not idle, but stil cast his eye upon Rosalynde, who to incourage him with a favour, lent him such an amorous looke, as might have made the most coward desperate: which glance of Rosalynd so fiered the passionate desires of Rosader, that turning to the Norman hee ranne upon him and braved him with a strong encounter. The Norman received him as valiantly, that there was a sore combat, hard to judge on whose side fortune would be prodigal. At last Rosader, calling to minde the beautie of his new mistresse, the fame of his fathers honours, and the disgrace that should fal to his house by his misfortune, rowsed himselfe and threw the Norman against the ground, falling uppon his chest with so willing a weight, that the Norman yielded nature her due and Rosader the victorie."—*Ibid.* p. 20.

(3) Scene II.—

——— My better parts
Are all thrown down; and that which here stands up,
Is but a quintain, a mere lifeless block.]

Much has been written on the origin and use of the *quintain*. The following is the account of it by Strutt in his "Sports and Pastimes:" those who seek for further information on the subject may consult advantageously the notes appended to this play in the Variorum Edition:—"Tilting or combating at the quintain is certainly a military exercise of high antiquity, and antecedent, I doubt not, to the justs and tournaments. The quintain originally was nothing more than the trunk of a tree or post set up for the practice of the tyros in chivalry. Afterward a staff or spear was fixed in the earth, and a shield being hung upon it, was the mark to strike at: the dexterity of the performer consisted in smiting the shield in such a manner as to break the ligatures and bear it to the ground. In process of time this diversion was improved, and instead of the staff and shield the resemblance of a human figure carved in wood was introduced. To render the appearance of this figure more formidable, it was generally made in the likeness of a Turk or a Saracen, armed at all points, bearing a shield upon his left arm, and brandishing a club or a sabre with his right. Hence this exercise was called by the Italians, 'running at the armed man or at the Saracen.' The quintain thus fashioned was placed upon a pivot, and so contrived as to move round with facility. In running at this figure, it was necessary for the horseman to direct his lance with great adroitness, and make his stroke upon the forehead between the eyes or upon the nose; for if he struck wide of those parts, especially upon the shield, the quintain turned about with much velocity, and, in case he was not exceedingly careful, would give him a severe blow upon the back with the wooden sabre held in the right hand, which was considered as highly disgraceful to the performer, while it excited the laughter and ridicule of the spectators." To this description of quintain there can be little doubt Shakespeare refers in Orlando's speech.

(4) Scene III.—

And wheresoe'er we went, like Juno's swans,
Still we went coupled and inseparable.]

Compare this brief but affecting appeal with that of Celia's prototype, Alinda, in the novel:—

"Alinda's Oration to her Father in Defence of Rosalynde.

"If (mighty Torismond) I offend in pleading for my friend, let the law of amitie crave pardon for my boldnesse; for where there is depth of affection, there friendship alloweth a priviledge. Rosalynd and I have beene fostered up from our infancies, and noursed under the harbour of our conversing togeather with such private familiarities, that custome had wrought an unyon of our nature, and the sympathie of our affections such a secret love, that we have two bodies and one soule. Then marvel not (great Torismond) if, seeing my friend distrest, I finde myselfe perplexed with a thousand sorrowes; for her vertuous and honourable thoughts (which are the glories that maketh women excellent) they be such as may challenge love, and race out suspition. Her obedience to your majestie I referre to the censure of your own eye, that since her fathers exile hath smothered al griefs with patience, and in the absence of nature, hath honored you with all dutie, as her owne father by nouriture, not in word uttering any discontent, nor in thought (as far as my conjecture may reach) hammering on revenge; only in all her actions seeking to please you, and to win my favor. Her wisdome, silence, chastitie, and other such rich qualities, I need not decypher; onely it rests for me to conclude in one word, that she is innocent. If then, fortune who tryumphs in variety of miseries, hath presented some envious person (as minister of her intended stratagem) to tainte Rosalynde with any surmise of treason, let him be brought to her face, and confirme his accusation by witnesses; which proved, let her die, and Alinda wil execute the massacre. If none can avouch any confirmed relation of her intent, use justice, my lord, it is the glory of a king, and let her live in your wonted favour; for if you banish her, myselfe, as copartner of her harde fortunes, will participate in exile some part of her extremities."—ROSALYNDE, p. 28.

(5) SCENE III.—*Say what thou canst, I'll go along with thee.*] "Why then doth my Rosalynd grieve at the frowne of Torismond, who by offering her a prejudice proffers her a greater pleasure? and more (mad lasse) to be melancholy, when thou hast with thee Alinda, a friend who wil be a faithful copartner of al thy misfortunes; who hath left her father to follow thee, and chooseth rather to brooke al extremities then to forsake thy presence. What, Rosalynd,

Solamen miseris socios habuisse doloris.

Cheerly, woman; as wee have been bed-fellowes in royaltie, we wil be felow mates in povertie: I wil ever be thy Alinda, and thou shalt ever rest to me Rosalynd; so shall the world canonize our friendship, and speake of Rosalynd and Alinda, as they did of Pilades and Orestes. And if ever fortune smile, and we returne to our former honour, then folding our selves in the sweete of our friendship, we shal merily say (calling to mind our forepassed miseries),

Olim hæc meminisse juvabit."—

ROSALYNDE, p. 31.

ACT II.

(1) SCENE VII.—

———All the world's a stage,
And all the men and women merely players:
They have their exits and their entrances,
And one man in his time plays many parts,
His acts being seven ages.]

Totus mundus agit histrionem, an observation which occurs in one of the fragments of Petronius, and may even be traced still higher, is said to have been the motto over Shakespeare's theatre, the Globe, and was probably in his day a familiar apothegm. The division of human life into certain stages, or epochs, had also a classical origin. In some Greek verses attributed to Solon,—and whether written by him or not, certainly as old as the first half of the first century, being introduced by Philo Judæus into his *Liber de Mundi opificio*,—the life of man is separated into ten ages of seven years each. Other Greek authors, Hippocrates and Proclus, apportioned his existence into seven parts, and Varro the Roman into five. A Hebrew doctor of the ninth century, and a Hebrew poet of the twelfth, have made a similar distribution.

In that miscellaneous collection of the fifteenth century, denominated "Arnold's Chronicle," is a chapter entitled "THE VIJ AGES OF MAN LIVING IN THE WORLD."—"The first age is infancie, and lastyth from the byrth unto vij yere of age. The ij is childhood, and endurith unto xv yere age. The iij age is adholocencye, and endurith unto xxv yere of age. The iiij age is youthe, and endurith unto xxxv yere age. The v age is manhood, and endurith unto l yere age. The vi age is elde, and lasteth unto lxx yere age. The vij age of man is crepill, and endurith unto dethe." But the favourite mode of inculcating the moral of human life has been by pictorial illustration; in Shakespeare's time, as in France at the present day, the subject was a popular theme for prints, broadsides, and ballads. An Italian engraving of the sixteenth century, by Christopher Bertello, is still extant, valuable for its intrinsic merit, and interesting from its analogy to the exquisite moralization of Jaques. The school-boy is carrying his books; the lover, a youth of twenty, bears a branch of myrtle, and at his feet is a young Cupid bending his bow; the soldier, armed *cap-à-pie*, is "bearded like the pard;" the justice has an aspect of grave severity; the representative of our author's sixth age is a senile personage, bending with years, attired in a long furred robe, his feet in slippers, and "spectacles on nose." Last scene of all exhibits the man of eighty, blind and helpless, with one foot in the tomb already gaping to receive him.

For further information on this subject, the reader may consult two elaborate articles, one in Volume xxvii. of the "Archæologia," the other, in the Gentleman's Magazine, for May, 1853: to the mediæval representations of the ages of life there recorded, we will add one hitherto undescribed, being a series of fourteen subjects engraved on a Monumental Brass of the date of 1487, preserved in the Hôpital S. Marie, Ypres, in Belgium.

(2) SCENE VII.—*Re-enter Orlando, with Adam.*] The scene in which Orlando confronts the banished Duke and his companions in the forest, demanding food for his famished retainer, is closely copied from the novel:—

"It chaunced that day, that Gerismond, the lawfull King of France banished by Torismond, who with a lustie crue of outlawes lived in that forest, that day in honour of his birth made a feast to all his bolde yeomen, and frolickt it with store of wine and venison, sitting all at a long table under the shadow of lymon trees. To that place by chance fortune conducted Rosader, who seeing such a crue of brave men, having store of that for want of which hee and Adam perished, hee stept boldly to the boords end, and saluted the company thus:—

"Whatsoever thou be that art maister of these lustie squiers, I salute thee as graciously as a man in extreame distresse may: know, that I and a fellow friend of mine are here famished in the forrest for want of food: perish wee must, unlesse relieved by thy favours. Therefore, if thou be a gentleman, give meate to men, and to such as are everie way woorthie of life. Let the proudest squire that sits at thy table rise and incounter with mee in any honorable point of activitie whatsoever, and if hee and thou prove me not a man, send me away comfortlesse. If thou refuse this, as a niggard of thy cates, I will have amonst you with my sword; for rather wil I dye valiantly, then perish with so cowardly an extreame. Gerismond, looking him earnestly in the face, and seeing so proper a gentleman in so bitter a passion, was mooved with so great pitie, that rising from the table, he tooke him by the hand and badde him welcome, willing him to sit downe in his place, and in his roome not onely to eat his fill, but the lord of the feast. Gramercy, sir, (quoth Rosader,) but I have a feeble friend that lyes hereby famished almost for food, aged and therefore lesse able to abide the extremitie of hunger then my selfe, and dishonour it were for me to taste one crumme, before I made him partner of my fortunes: therefore I will runne and fetch him, and then I will gratefully accept of your proffer. Away hies Rosader to Adam Spencer, and tels him the newes, who was glad of so happie fortune, but so feeble he was that he could not go; wherupon Rosader got him up on his backe, and brought him to the place. Which when Gerismond and his men saw, they greatly applauded their league of friendship; and Rosader, having Gerismonds place assigned him, would not sit there himselfe, but set downe Adam Spencer."—ROSALYNDE, p. 53.

ACT III.

(1) SCENE I.—*Seek him with candle.*] Referring, it is supposed, to the passage in St. Luke, ch. xv. ver. 8:—"Either what woman having ten pieces of silver, if she lose one piece, doth not light a *candle*, and sweep the house, and *seek* diligently till she find it?"

(2) SCENE II.—*And thou, thrice-crowned queen of night.*] Johnson conjectured this was an allusion to the triple character of Proserpine, Cynthia, and Diana, given by some mythologists to the same goddess:—

> "*Terret, lustrat, agit, Proserpina, Luna, Diana,*
> *Ima, superna, feras, sceptro, fulgore, sagittis;*"

but Mr. Singer quotes a passage from one of Chapman's Hymns, which he thinks was probably in Shakespeare's mind:—

> "Nature's bright *eye-sight*, and the Night's fair soul,
> That with thy *triple forehead* dost control
> Earth, seas, and hell."
> *Hymnus in Cynthiam*, 1594.

(3) SCENE II.—*I was never so be-rhymed since Pythagoras' time, that I was an Irish rat.*] Rosalind is a very learned lady. She alludes to the Pythagorean doctrine, which teaches that souls transmigrate from one animal to another, and relates that in his time she was an *Irish rat*, and by some metrical charm was rhymed to death. The power of killing rats with rhymes Donne mentions in his Satires, and Temple in his Treatises. Dr. Grey has produced a similar passage from Randolph:—

> "——— My poets
> Shall with a satire, steep'd in gall and vinegar,
> Rhyme them to death, as they do rats in Ireland."

JOHNSON.

(4) SCENE II.—*Gargantua's mouth.*] "Although there had been no English translation of Rabelais in Shakespeare's time, yet it is evident, from several notices, that a chap-book history of the giant Garagantua, who swallowed five pilgrims, their staves and all, in a salad, was very popular in this country in the sixteenth century. The 'witless devices of Gargantua' are decried among 'the vain and lewd books of the age' by Edward Dering, in his epistle to the reader, prefixed to A Brief and Necessary Instruction, 1572. The history of Garagantua formed one of the pieces in the singular library of Captain Cox, so ludicrously described by Laneham, in the Letter from Kenilworth, 1575:—'King Arthurz book, Huon of Burdeaus, Friar Rous, Howleglass, and Gargantua.' The 'monstrous fables of Garagantua' are also enumerated among many other 'infortunate treatises' in Hanmer's Eusebius, 1577. In the books of the Stationers' Company for 1592, is found an entry of 'Gargantua his Prophecie;' and in those for 1594 of 'a booke entitled the History of Garagantua.'"—HALLIWELL.

(5) SCENE III.—*I will not to wedding with thee.*] These lines are probably quoted from the old ballads mentioned in the following entries on the Registers of the Stationers' Company, 1584-5:—

"6 AUGUSTI.

"Ric. Jones. Rd of him, for his licence to printe A Ballat of O swete Olyver, Leave me not behind thee . . . . iiij*d*."

"VICESSIMO DIE AUGUSTI.

"Henry Carre. Rd of him, for printinge of the answeare of O sweete Olyver . . . . . iiij*d*."

(6) SCENE V.—*And why, I pray you?*] Compare the parallel scene in "Rosalynde:"—

"Ganimede, overhearing all these passions of Montanus, could not brooke the crueltie of Phœbe, but starting from behind the bush said: And if, damzell, you fled from mee, I would transforme you as Daphne to a bay, and then in contempt trample your branches under my feet. Phœbe at this sodaine replye was amazed, especially when shee saw so faire a swaine as Ganimede; blushing therefore, she would have bene gone, but that he held her by the hand, and prosecuted his reply thus: What, shepheardesse, so faire and so cruell? Disdaine beseemes not cottages, nor coynesse maids; for either they be condemned to be too proud, or too froward. Take heed, faire nymph, that in despising love, you be not over-reacht with love, and in shaking off all, shape yourselfe to your owne shadow, and so with Narcissus prove passionat and yet unpitied. Oft have I heard, and sometime have I seene, high disdaine turned to hot desires. Because thou art beautifull be not so coy: as there is nothing more fair, so there is nothing more fading; as momentary as the shaddowes which growes from a clowdy sunne. Such (my faire shepheardesse) as disdaine in youth desire in age, and then are they hated in the winter, that might have been loved in the prime. A wringled mayd is like to a parched rose, that is cast up in coffers to please the smell, not worne in the hand to content the eye. There is no folly in love to had I wist, and therefore be rulde by mee. Love while thou art yoong, least thou be disdained when thou art olde. Beautie nor time cannot be recalde, and if thou love, like of Montanus; for if his desires are many, so his deserts are great."—ROSALYNDE, p. 97.

(7) SCENE V.—

> *Dead shepherd! now I find thy saw of might;*
> *Who ever lov'd, that lov'd not at first sight?*]

The "dead shepherd" here apostrophised was Marlowe, and the line Phebe quotes is from his once popular poem of "Hero and Leander," first published in 1598:—

> "It lies not in our power to love or hate,
> For will in us is over-rul'd by fate.
> When two are stripp'd, long ere the course begin,
> We wish that one should lose, the other win.
> And one especially do we affect
> Of two gold ingots, like in each respect:
> The reason no man knows; let it suffice,
> What we behold is censur'd by our eyes.
> Where both deliberate the love is slight:
> *Who ever lov'd, that lov'd not at first sight?*"
> P. 10, Edit. 1821.

Shakespeare has before referred to this favourite poem in "The Two Gentlemen of Verona," Act I. Sc. 1.

ACT IV.

(1) Scene III.—

———— *in which hurtling*
From miserable slumber I awak'd.]

The touching incident of the meeting of the two brothers is thus narrated in Lodge's story :—"Saladyne, wearie with wandring up and downe, and hungry with long fasting, finding a little cave by the side of a thicket, eating such fruite as the forest did affoord, and contenting himselfe with such drinke as nature had provided and thirst made delicate, after his repast he fell in a dead sleepe. As thus he lay, a hungry lyon came hunting downe the edge of the grove for pray, and espying Saladyne began to ceaze upon him : but seeing he lay still without any motion, he left to touch him, for that lyons hate to prey on dead carkasses ; and yet desirous to have some foode, the lyon lay downe and watcht to see if he would stirre. While thus Saladyne slept secure, fortune that was careful of her champion began to smile, and brought it so to passe, that Rosader (having stricken a deere that but slightly hurt fled through the thicket) came pacing downe by the grove with a boare-speare in his hande in great haste. He spyed where a man lay a sleepe, and a lyon fast by him : amazed at this sight, as he stoode gazing, his nose on the sodaine bledde, which made him conjecture it was some friend of his. Whereuppon drawing more nigh, he might easily discerne his visage, perceived by his phisnomie that it was his brother Saladyne, which drove Rosader into a deepe passion, as a man perplexed at the sight of so unexpected a chance, marvelling what should drive his brother to traverse those secrete desarts, without any companie, in such distresse and forlorne sorte. But the present time craved no such doubting ambages, for he must eyther resolve to hazard his life for his reliefe, or else steale away and leave him to the crueltie of the lyon. In which doubt hee thus briefly debated with himselfe. * * * * With that his brother began to stirre, and the lyon to rowse himselfe, whereupon Rosader sodainly charged him with the boare speare, and wounded the lion very sore at the first stroke. The beast feeling himselfe to have a mortall hurt, leapt at Rosader, and with his pawes gave him a sore pinch on the brest that he had almost faln ; yet as a man most valiant, in whom the sparks of Sir John Bourdeaux remained, he recovered himselfe, and in short combat slew the lion, who at his death roared so lowd that Saladyne awaked, and starting up, was amazed at the sudden sight of so monstrous a beast lying slaine by him, and so sweet a gentleman wounded."—Rosalynde, p. 79.

ACT V.

(1) Scene IV.—*O, sir, we quarrel in print, by the book.*] The particular book here ridiculed, is conjectured to be a treatise in 4to. published in 1595, entitled "Vincentio Saviolo his Practice. In two Bookes. The first intreating of the use of the Rapier and Dagger. The second of Honor and honorable Quarrels." "A Discourse," says the author, speaking of the second part, "most necessarie for all Gentlemen that have in regarde their honors, touching the giving and receiving of the Lie, whereupon the *Duello* and the *Combats* in divers sortes doth insue, and many other inconveniences, for lack only of the true knowledge of honor and the contrarie : and the right understanding of wordes." The contents of the several chapters are as follows :—"I. What the reason is, that the partie unto whom the lie is given ought to become Challenger : and of the nature of Lies. II. Of the manner and diversitie of Lies. III. Of Lies certaine. IV. Of conditionall Lyes. V. Of the Lye in generall. VI. Of the Lye in particular. VII. Of foolish Lyes. VIII. A conclusion touching the Challenger and the Defender, and of the wresting and returning back of the Lye, or Dementie." In the chapter of conditional lies, he says : "Conditionall lyes be such as are given conditionally : as if a man should saie or write these wordes :—*If* thou hast saide that I have offered my Lord abuse, thou lyest ; or *if* thou saiest so hereafter, thou shalt lye. * * * * Of these kind of lyes given in this manner, often arise much contention in words * * * * whereof no sure conclusion can arise." "By which," observes Warburton, "he means, they cannot proceed to cut one another's throat, while there is an *if* between." See note (6), p. 216, Vol. I.

(2) Scene IV.—*As you have books for good manners.*] Such works were not uncommon in the sixteenth and seventeenth centuries. Mr. Halliwell mentions a book of this description, published by Wynkyn de Worde in 1507, the colophon of which is as follows,—"Here endeth and fynysshed the boke named and Intytled Good Maners." There was also "The Boke of Nurture, or Schoole of Good Maners for Men, Servants, and Children," 8vo. 1577, written by Hugh Rhodes; another called "Galateo of Maister John Della Casa, Archebishop of Beneventa. Or rather, A treatise of the maners and behaviours, it behoveth a man to use and eschewe, in his familiar conversation. A worke very necessary and profitable for all Gentlemen or other. First written in the Italian tongue, and now done into English by Robert Peterson, of Lincoln's Inne Gentleman," 4to. 1576 : and in the Stationers' Registers, under the year 1576, is an entry—

> "Ric. Jones. Receyved of him, for his lycense to
> ymprinte a booke intituled how a yonge gentleman may behave him self in all cumpanies, &c.
> . . . . iiij*d*. and a copie."

EPILOGUE.

(1) *Good wine needs no bush.*] Mr. Halliwell remarks that the custom of hanging out a bush as a sign for a tavern, or a place where wine was to be sold, was of great antiquity in this country ; and he supplies an interesting example from an illuminated MS. of the fourteenth century, preserved in the Hunterian Museum at Glasgow, where a party of travellers are observed approaching a wayside inn, indicated by a huge bush depending from the sign. Chaucer alludes to the custom, and in an early poem in MS., Cotton. Tiber. A. vii. fol. 72, we read :—

> "Ryght as off a *tavernere*,
> The *greene busche* that hangeth out,
> Is a sygne, it is no dowte,
> Outward ffolkys ffor to telle
> That within is wyne to selle."

The bush is very frequently alluded to as having been formed of ivy, in which there appears a trace of classical allusion, as the ivy was always sacred to Bacchus ; perhaps continued from heathen times. So in "Gascoigne's Glass of Government," 1575 : "Now-a-days the good wyne needeth none *ivye garland.*" And in Florio's "Second Frutes," 1591 : "Like unto an *ivy bush*, that cals men to the tavern, but hangs itselfe without to winde and wether." Kennett, in his Glossary, says, that "the tavern-bush, or frame of wood, was drest round with ivy forty years since, though now left off for tuns or barrels hung in the middle of it. This custom gave birth to the present practice of putting out a green bush at the door of those private houses which sell drink during the fair, a practice stated to be still prevalent in many of the provinces." Notices of the tavern-bush abound in our early writers, and the name is traced in the sign of the "Bush," still retained by many inns in England. The petty taverns of Normandy are, indeed, to this day distinguished by bushes.

CRITICAL OPINIONS

ON

AS YOU LIKE IT.

"It would be difficult to bring the contents within the compass of an ordinary narrative; nothing takes place, or rather what is done is not so essential as what is said; even what may be called the *dénouement* is brought about pretty arbitrarily. Whoever can perceive nothing but what can, as it were, be counted on the fingers, will hardly be disposed to allow that it has any plan at all. Banishment and flight have assembled together, in the forest of Arden, a strange band: a Duke dethroned by his brother, who, with the faithful companions of his misfortune, lives in the wilds on the produce of the chase; two disguised Princesses, who love each other with a sisterly affection; a witty court fool; lastly, the native inhabitants of the forest, ideal and natural shepherds and shepherdesses. These lightly-sketched figures form a motley and diversified train; we see always the shady dark-green landscape in the background, and breathe in imagination the fresh air of the forest. The hours are here measured by no clocks, no regulated recurrence of duty or of toil: they flow on unnumbered by voluntary occupation or fanciful idleness, to which, according to his humour or disposition, every one yields himself, and this unrestrained freedom compensates them all for the lost conveniences of life. One throws himself down in solitary meditation under a tree, and indulges in melancholy reflections on the changes of fortune, the falsehood of the world, and the self-inflicted torments of social life; others make the woods resound with social and festive songs, to the accompaniment of their hunting-horns. Selfishness, envy, and ambition, have been left behind in the city; of all the human passions, love alone has found an entrance into this wilderness, where it dictates the same language alike to the simple shepherd and the chivalrous youth, who hangs his love-ditty to a tree. A prudish shepherdess falls at first sight in love with Rosalind, disguised in men's apparel; the latter sharply reproaches her with her severity to her poor lover, and the pain of refusal, which she feels from experience in her own case, disposes her at length to compassion and requital. The fool carries his philosophical contempt of external show, and his raillery of the illusion of love so far, that he purposely seeks out the ugliest and simplest country wench for a mistress. Throughout the whole picture, it seems to be the poet's design to show that to call forth the poetry which has its indwelling in nature and the human mind, nothing is wanted but to throw off all artificial constraint, and restore both to mind and nature their original liberty. In the very progress of the piece, the dreamy carelessness of such an existence is sensibly expressed: it is even alluded to by Shakspeare in the title. Whoever affects to be displeased, if in this romantic forest the ceremonial of dramatic art is not duly observed, ought in justice to be delivered over to the wise fool, to be led gently out of it to some prosaical region."—SCHLEGEL.

"Though this play, with the exception of the disguise and self-discovery of Rosalind, may be said to be destitute of plot, it is yet one of the most delightful of the dramas of Shakspeare. There is something inexpressibly wild and interesting both in the characters and in the scenery; the former disclosing the moral discipline and the sweets of adversity, the purest emotions of love and friendship, of gratitude and fidelity, the melancholy of genius, and the exhilaration of innocent mirth, as opposed to the desolating effects of malice, envy, and ambition; and the latter unfolding, with the richest glow of fancy, landscapes to which, as objects of imitation, the united talents of Ruysdale, Claude, and Salvator Rosa could alone do justice.

"From the forest of Arden, from that wild wood of oaks,

——"whose boughs were moss'd with age,
And high tops bald with dry antiquity,"—

from the bosom of sequestered glens and pathless solitudes, has the poet called forth lessons of the most touching and consolatory wisdom. Airs from paradise seem to fan with refreshing gales, with a soothing consonance of sound, the interminable depth of foliage, and to breathe into the hearts of those who have sought its shelter from the world, an oblivion of their sorrows and their cares. The banished Duke, the much-injured Orlando, and the melancholy Jaques, lose in meditation on the scenes which surround them, or in sportive freedom, or in grateful occupation, all corrosive sense of past affliction. Love seems the only passion which has penetrated this romantic seclusion, and the sigh of philosophic pity, or of wounded sensibility, (the legacy of a deserted world,) the only relique of the storm which is passed and gone.

"Nothing, in fact, can blend more harmoniously with the romantic glades and magic windings of Arden, than the society which Shakspeare has placed beneath its shades. The effect of such scenery, on the lover of nature, is to take full possession of the soul, to absorb its very faculties, and, through the charmed imagination, to convert the workings of the mind into the sweetest sensations of the heart, into the joy of grief, into a thankful endurance of adversity, into the interchange of the tenderest affections: and find we not here, in the person of the Duke, the noblest philosophy of resignation; in Jaques, the humorous sadness of an amiable misanthropy; in Orlando, the mild dejection of self-accusing humility; in Rosalind and Celia, the purity of sisterly affection; whilst love in all its innocence and gaiety binds in delicious fetters, not only the younger exiles, but the pastoral natives of the forest? A day thus spent, in all the careless freedom of unsophisticated nature, seems worth an eternity of common-place existence!"—DRAKE.

Act V. Sc. 3.

PERICLES, PRINCE OF TYRE.

This play is not found in the folio of 1623. The first edition of it known is the quarto, published in 1609, under the title of "The late and much admired Play, called Pericles, Prince of Tyre. With the true relation of the whole Historie, adventures, and fortunes of the said Prince: As also the no lesse strange and worthy accidents in the Birth and Life, of his Daughter Mariana. As it hath been divers and sundry times acted by his Maiesties Servants, at the Globe on the Banck-side. By William Shakespeare. Imprinted at London for *Henry Gosson,* and are to be sold at the signe of the Sunne, in Pater-noster row, &c. 1609." This was followed by other quarto editions, respectively dated 1611, 1619, 1630, 1635, 1639, and it was afterwards inserted in the folio of 1664, and in that of 1685. Although there is no evidence that Pericles was printed earlier than 1609, or, beyond the slight memorandum in an inventory of Alleyn's theatrical wardrobe, of "spangled hoes" for Pericles,* that it was acted before 1607 or 1608, we believe that, in an imperfect form, this piece was the work of an older play-wright than Shakespeare, and, being founded upon a story which for ages had retained extensive popularity, that it was placed in the latter's hands very early in his dramatic career for adaptation to the Blackfriars' stage. This impression is derived partly from the style, the general structure of the verse, and the want of individualization in the characters, and partly from the nature of the fable: the revolting story of Antiochus and his daughter being one which it is not easy to believe Shakespeare would ever have chosen as a subject for representation. Moreover, we conclude, from the conflicting testimony as to its success, that Pericles, on the first occasion of its re-production, was not prosperous; but that, having been re-modelled, and in part re-written by Shakespeare, especially in the fifth Act, it was again revived in 1607 or 1608, and then met with unusual favour. One proof of its popularity at this period was the publication of a prose-tract, written by George Wilkins, entitled "*The Painfull Adventures of Pericles Prince of Tyre. Being The true History of the Play of Pericles as it was lately presented by the worthy and ancient Poet John Gower.* 1608,"—a story (lately reprinted with most laudable accuracy

* See Collier's *Memoirs of Alleyn,* p. 21.

by Professor Mommsen) which was composed from notes taken during the performance of the play and extracts from the English version of "Apollonius Tyrius."

The original source of Pericles is the fabulous story of King Apollonius of Tyre, a romance of great antiquity and of such renown, that, of the Latin version alone,—Historia Apollonii Tyrii, first edited about 1470,—Professor Haupt, of Berlin University, declares he is acquainted with *one hundred* MSS. The author of the play, however, appears to have been immediately indebted for his fable and incidents to that portion of Gower's *Confessio Amantis,* which treats of King Appolin of Tyre, and to the English translation of the *Historia Apollonii* entitled *The Patterne of painefull Adventures: containing the most excellent, pleasant, and variable Historie of the strange accidents that befell unto Prince Apollonius, the Lady Lucina his wife, and Tharsia his daughter. Wherein the uncertainty of this world and the fickle state of man's life are lively described. Gathered into English by Lawrence Twine, Gentleman,*—first printed in 1576.

Persons Represented.

Antiochus, *King of* Antioch.
Pericles, *Prince of* Tyre.
Helicanus, } *two Lords of* Tyre.
Escanes, }
Simonides, *King of* Pentapolis.
Cleon, *Governor of* Tharsus.
Lysimachus, *Governor of* Mitylene.
Cerimon, *a Lord of* Ephesus.
Thaliard, *a Lord of* Antioch.
Philemon, *Servant to* Cerimon.
Leonine, *Servant to* Dionyza.
Marshal.

A Pander.
Boult, *his Servant.*

Gower, *as Chorus.*

The Daughter of Antiochus.
Thaisa, *Daughter to* Simonides.
Marina, *Daughter to* Pericles *and* Thaisa.
Dionyza, *Wife to* Cleon.
Lychorida, *Nurse to* Marina.
Diana.
A Bawd.

Lords, Knights, Gentlemen, Sailors, Pirates, Fishermen, and Messengers.

SCENE,—*Dispersedly in various Countries.*

PERICLES, PRINCE OF TYRE.

Enter GOWER.

Before the Palace of Antioch.

GOW. To sing a song that old was sung,
From ashes ancient Gower is come;
Assuming man's infirmities,
To glad your ear, and please your eyes.
It hath been sung, at festivals,
On ember-eves, and holy-ales;[a]
And lords and ladies, in their lives
Have read it for restoratives.
The purchase[b] is to make men glorious;
Et bonum quo antiquius, eo melius.
If you, born in these latter times,
When wit's more ripe, accept my rhymes,
And that to hear an old man sing,
May to your wishes pleasure bring,
I life would wish, and that I might
Waste it for you, like taper-light.—
This Antioch, then, Antiochus the Great
Built up, this city, for his chiefest seat;
The fairest in all Syria;—
I tell you what mine authors say:—
This king unto him took a pheere,[c]
Who died and left a female heir,
So buxom, blithe, and full of face,
As Heaven had lent her all his grace;
With whom the father liking took,
And her to incest did provoke;—
Bad child, worse father! to entice his own
To evil, should be done by none.
But custom what they did begin
Was with long use account no sin.
The beauty of this sinful dame
Made many princes thither frame,
To seek her as a bed-fellow,
In marriage-pleasures play-fellow:
Which to prevent, he made a law,
To keep her still, and men in awe,—
That whoso ask'd her for his wife,
His riddle told not, lost his life:
So for her many a wight did die,
As yon grim looks do testify.
What now ensues, to the judgment of your eye
I give, my cause who best can justify. [*Exit.*

---

[a] *Holy*-ales;] Old copies, holy-*days:* amended by Dr. Farmer.
[b] *The* purchase—] That is, the *profit*, the *advantage*. Modern editions, *purpose*.
[c] *Peer*, in the original copies; altered by Malone.

ACT I.

SCENE I.—Antioch. *A Room in the Palace.*

Enter ANTIOCHUS, PERICLES, *and* Attendants.

ANT. Young prince of Tyre, you have at large receiv'd,
The danger of the task you undertake.

PER. I have, Antiochus, and with a soul
Embolden'd with the glory of her praise,
Think death no hazard, in this enterprise.

ANT. Bring in our daughter, clothed like a bride,
For the* embracements even of Jove himself;
At whose conception (till Lucina reign'd)

(*) Old copies omit, *the*.

Nature this dowry gave, to glad her presence,
The senate-house of planets all did sit,
To knit in her their best perfections.

Music. *Enter the* Daughter *of* ANTIOCHUS.

PER. See where she comes, apparel'd like the spring,
Graces her subjects, and her thoughts the king
Of every virtue gives renown to men!
Her face the book of praiess, where is read
Nothing but curious pleasures, as from thence
Sorrow were ever ras'd, and testy wrath
Could never be her mild[a] companion.
You gods that made me man, and sway in love,
That have inflam'd desire in my breast
To taste the fruit of yon celestial tree,
Or die in the adventure, be my helps,
As I am son and servant to your will,
To compass such a boundless* happiness!
ANT. Prince Pericles—
PER. That would be son to great Antiochus.
ANT. Before thee stands this fair Hesperides,
With golden fruit, but dangerous to be touch'd,
For death-like dragons here affright thee hard:
Her face, like heav'n, enticeth thee to view
Her countless glory, which desert must gain:
And which, without desert, because thine eye
Presumes to reach, all thy† whole heap must die.
Yon sometime famous princes, like thyself,
Drawn by report, adventurous by desire,
Tell thee, with speechless tongues and semblance pale,
That, without covering, save yon field of stars,(1)
Here they stand martyrs, slain in Cupid's wars;
And with dead cheeks advise thee to desist
For going on death's net, whom none resist.
PER. Antiochus, I thank thee, who hath taught
My frail mortality to know itself,
And by those fearful objects to prepare
This body, like to them, to what I must:
For death remember'd should be like a mirror,
Who tells us, life 's but breath, to trust it, error.
I'll make my will then; and, as sick men do,
Who know the world, see heaven,[b] but feeling woe,
Gripe not at earthly joys, as erst they did;
So I bequeath a happy peace to you
And all good men, as every prince should do;
My riches to the earth from whence they came;—
But my unspotted fire of love to you.
[*To the* Daughter *of* ANTIOCHUS.
Thus ready for the way of life or death,
I wait the sharpest blow.
ANT. Scorning advice; read the conclusion then;[c]
Which read and not expounded, 't is decreed,
As these before thee, thou thyself shalt bleed.
DAUGH. Of all 'say'd[d] yet, mayst thou prove prosperous!
Of all 'say'd yet, I wish thee happiness!
PER. Like a bold champion I assume the lists,
Nor ask advice of any other thought,
But faithfulness and courage.

HE READS THE RIDDLE.

"*I am no viper, yet I feed*
On mother's flesh which did me breed:
I sought a husband, in which labour
I found that kindness in a father:
He's father, son, and husband mild,
I mother, wife, and yet his child.
How they[e] *may be, and yet in two,*
As you will live, resolve it you."

Sharp physic is the last: but O, you powers!
That give heaven countless eyes to view men's acts,
Why cloud they not their sights perpetually,
If this be true, which makes me pale to read it?
Fair glass of light, I lov'd you, and could still,
[*Takes the hand of the* Princess.
Were not this glorious casket stor'd with ill:
But I must tell you,—now, my thoughts revolt,
For he's no man on whom perfections wait,
That, knowing sin within, will touch the gate.
You're a fair viol, and your sense the strings;
Who, finger'd to make man his lawful music,
Would draw heav'n down, and all the gods to hearken;
But being play'd upon before your time,
Hell only danceth at so harsh a chime:
Good sooth, I care not for you.
ANT. Prince Pericles, touch not, upon thy life,
For that 's an article within our law,
As dangerous as the rest. Your time's expir'd;
Either expound now, or receive your sentence.
PER. Great king,
Few love to hear the sins they love to act;
'T would 'braid yourself too near for me to tell it.
Who has a book of all that monarchs do,
He 's more secure to keep it shut, than shown:
For vice repeated 's like the wandering wind,
Blows dust in others' eyes, to spread itself;

(*) Old copies, *bondlesse*. (†) Old copies, *the*.

[a] *Her* mild *companion*.] That is, companion of her mildness.—MASON.
[b] *Who know the world*, see heaven, but feeling woe,—] We should, perhaps, read:—

"Who know the *world's heaven*," &c.

[c] Read the conclusion then;] In the old copies these lines are thus arranged:—

"I wayt the sharpest blow (Antiochus),
Scorning advice: read the conclusion then:
Which read," &c.

[d] *Of all* 'say'd *yet*, &c.] That is, Of all who have yet *assay'd*.
[e] *How* they *may be*,—] In Wilkins' novel, "How *this* may be," which is probably the genuine reading.

And yet the end of all is bought thus dear,
The breath is gone, and the sore eyes see clear
To stop the air would hurt them. The blind mole casts
Copp'd hills towards heaven, to tell the earth is throng'd[a]
By man's oppression; and the poor worm doth die for't.
Kings are earth's gods; in vice their law's their will,
And if Jove stray, who dares say Jove doth ill?
It is enough you know; and it is fit,
What being more known grows worse, to smother it.—
All love the womb that their first being bred,
Then give my tongue like leave to love my head.

ANT. [*Aside.*] Heaven, that I had thy head! he has found the meaning!
But I will gloze with him. Young prince of Tyre,
Though by the tenour of our* strict edict,
Your exposition misinterpreting,
We might proceed to cancel† of your days;
Yet hope, succeeding from so fair a tree
As your fair self, doth tune us otherwise:
Forty days longer we do respite you,
If by which time our secret be undone,
This mercy shows we'll joy in such a son:
And until then your entertain shall be,
As doth befit our honour, and your worth.
[*Exeunt all but* PERICLES.

PER. How courtesy would seem to cover sin,
When what is done is like an hypocrite,
The which is good in nothing but in sight!
If it be true that I interpret false,
Then were it certain you were not so bad,

[a] *To tell the earth is* throng'd—] That is, *oppressed*, or *shrunk*. So in Act II. Sc. 1:—"A man *throng'd* up."

(*) Quartos, *your*. (†) Quartos, *counsel*.

As with foul incest to abuse your soul;
Where now you're both a father and a son,
By your untimely claspings with your child,
(Which pleasure fits an husband, not a father,)
And she an eater of her mother's flesh,
By the defiling of her parent's bed;
And both like serpents are, who though they feed
On sweetest flowers, yet they poison breed.
Antioch, farewell! for wisdom sees, those men
Blush not in actions blacker than the night,
Will shun* no course to keep them from the light.
One sin, I know, another doth provoke;
Murder's as near to lust, as flame to smoke.
Poison and treason are the hands of sin,
Ay, and the targets, to put off the shame:
Then, lest my life be cropp'd to keep you clear,
By flight I'll shun the danger which I fear. [*Exit.*

Re-enter ANTIOCHUS.

ANT. He hath found the meaning, for which we mean
To have his head.
He must not live to trumpet forth my infamy,
Nor tell the world, Antiochus doth sin
In such a loathed manner:
And therefore instantly this prince must die;
For by his fall my honour must keep high.
Who attends us there?

Enter THALIARD.[a]

THAL. Doth your highness call?
ANT. Thaliard, you are of our chamber, and our mind
Partakes[b] her private actions to your secrecy;
And for your faithfulness we will advance you.
Thaliard, behold here's poison, and here's gold;
We hate the prince of Tyre, and thou must kill him;
It fits thee not to ask the reason why,
Because we bid it.(2) Say, is it done?
THAL. My lord, 't is done.
ANT. Enough.

Enter a Messenger.

Let your breath cool yourself, telling your haste.
MES. My lord, prince Pericles is fled.
ANT. As thou
Wilt live, fly after; and like an arrow shot
From a well-experienc'd archer hits the mark
His eye doth level at, so thou; never return,
Unless thou say'st, *prince Pericles is dead!*
THAL. My lord, if I can get him within my pistol's length,
I'll make him sure enough: so farewell to your highness.
ANT. Thaliard, adieu! [*Exit* THAL.] Till Pericles be dead,
My heart can lend no succour to my head. [*Exit.*

SCENE II.—Tyre. *A Room in the Palace.*

Enter PERICLES.[c]

PER. [*To those without.*] Let none disturb us.
Why should this change of thoughts?[d]
The sad companion, dull-ey'd melancholy,
By me so[e] us'd a guest, as not an hour,
In the day's glorious walk, or peaceful night,
(The tomb where grief should sleep,) can breed me quiet.
Here pleasures court mine eyes, and mine eyes shun them,
And danger, which I feared, is at Antioch,
Whose arm seems far too short to hit me here;
Yet neither pleasure's art can joy my spirits,
Nor yet the other's distance comfort me.
Then it is thus; the passions of the mind,
That have their first conception by mis-dread,
Have after-nourishment and life by care;
And what was first but fear what might be done,
Grows elder now, and cares it be not done.
And so with me;—the great Antiochus,—
'Gainst whom I am too little to contend,
Since he's so great, can make his will his act,—
Will think me speaking, though I swear to silence;
Nor boots it me to say I honour him,*
If he suspect I may dishonour him:
And what may make him blush in being known,
He'll stop the course by which it might be known;
With hostile forces he'll o'erspread the land,
And with th' ostent[f] of war will look so huge,
Amazement shall drive courage from the state;
Our men be vanquish'd ere they do resist,
And subjects punish'd, that ne'er thought offence:

(*) Old copies, *shew;* corrected by Malone.

a Thaliard.] In Twine's translation this character is called *Thaliarch* and *Thaliarchus:* in Wilkins' novel, *Thalyart*, and *Thaliart*, and in Gower's poem, *Taliart*.

b Partakes—] *Imparts.*

c *Enter* Pericles.] The first quarto has here, "Enter Pericles and his Lords;" and after Pericles' speech, which certainly reads like a soliloquy, it has another stage-direction, "Enter all the Lords to Pericles." The other old copies have only the first direction; but we must not infer from that, the lords entered at the same time as the Prince. Nothing is more common in early plays than to have the entrance of all the characters who are to take part in a scene indicated at the beginning of it.

(*) *Him* was added by Rowe.

d *Why should this* change *of thoughts?*] So the old copies. The usual reading in modern editions is, "Why should this *charge* of thoughts?" Neither lection is very perspicuous. We might, with advantage to the sense, read:—

"——— why should this change *our* thoughts?"

or,

"——— why should this *charge our* thoughts?"

e *By* me *so us'd*—] Query, "By *me's* so used,"? &c.

f *And with* th' ostent *of war*—] The old editions have "the *stent* of warre." *Ostent* was suggested by Tyrwhitt.

Which care of them, not pity of myself,—
Who am* no more but as the tops of trees,
Which fence the roots they grow by, and defend them,—
Makes both my body pine, and soul to languish,
And punish that before that he would punish.

Enter HELICANUS, *and other* Lords.

1 LORD. Joy and all comfort in your sacred breast! [us,
2 LORD. And keep your mind till you return to
Peaceful and comfortable!
HEL. Peace, peace, and give experience tongue:
They do abuse the king that flatter him,
For flattery is the bellows blows up sin;
The thing the which is flatter'd, but a spark,
To which that blast[a] gives heat and stronger glowing;
Whereas reproof, obedient, and in order,
Fits kings as they are men, for they may err.
When signior Sooth here doth proclaim a† peace,
He flatters you, makes war upon your life.
Prince, pardon me, or strike me if you please;
I cannot be much lower than my knees.
PER. All leave us else; but let your cares o'erlook
What shipping and what lading's in our haven,
And then return to us. [*Exeunt* Lords.] Helicanus, thou
Hast moved us; what seest thou in our looks?
HEL. An angry brow, dread lord.
PER. If there be such a dart in princes' frowns,
How durst thy tongue move anger to our face?
HEL. How dare the plants look up to heaven, from whence
They have their nourishment?
PER. Thou know'st I have power
To take thy life from thee.
HEL. I have ground the axe myself;
Do you but strike the blow.
PER. Rise, pr'ythee, rise:
Sit down, thou art no flatterer;
I thank thee for it; and heaven forbid,
That kings should let their ears hear their faults hid![b]
Fit counsellor, and servant for a prince,
Who by thy wisdom mak'st a prince thy servant,
What wouldst thou have me do?
HEL. To bear with patience
Such griefs as you yourself do lay upon yourself.
PER. Thou speak'st like a physician, Helicanus;
That minister'st a potion unto me,
That thou wouldst tremble to receive thyself.
Attend me then; I went to Antioch,
Where, as thou know'st, against the face of death,
I sought the purchase of a glorious beauty,
From whence an issue I might propagate,
Are[c] arms to princes, and bring joys to subjects.
Her face was to mine eye beyond all wonder;
The rest (hark in thine ear) as black as incest;
Which by my knowledge found, the sinful father,
Seem'd not to strike, but smooth: but thou know'st this,
'Tis time to fear, when tyrants seem to kiss.
Which fear so grew in me, I hither fled,
Under the covering of a careful night,
Who seem'd my good protector: and, being here,
Bethought me* what was past, what might succeed;
I knew him tyrannous, and tyrants' fears
Decrease not, but grow faster than the years:
And should he doubt[d] it, (as no doubt he doth,)
That I should open to the listening air,
How many worthy princes' bloods were shed,
To keep his bed of blackness unlaid ope,—
To lop that doubt, he'll fill this land with arms,
And make pretence of wrong that I have done him;
When all, for mine, if I may call't,† offence,
Must feel war's blow, who spares not innocence:
Which love to all—of which thyself art one,
Who now reprov'st me for it——
HEL. Alas, sir!
PER. Drew sleep out of mine eyes, blood from my cheeks,
Musings into my mind, with thousand doubts
How I might stop this tempest ere it came;
And finding little comfort to relieve them,
I thought it princely charity to grieve them.
HEL. Well, my lord, since you have given me leave to speak,
Freely will I speak. Antiochus you fear,
And justly too, I think, you fear the tyrant,
Who either by public war, or private treason,
Will take away your life.
Therefore, my lord, go travel for a while,
Till that his rage and anger be forgot;

(*) Old copies, *once;* corrected by Farmer.
(†) Old editions omit, *a.*

(*) Old editions omit, *me.* (†) Old copies, *call.*

[a] To *which that* blast *gives heat,* &c.] The old copies have "that *sparke,*" a word caught by the compositor from the preceding line. *Blast,* a judicious emendation, was proposed by Mason.

[b] That kings should let their ears hear their faults hid!] Thus the old editions; the meaning appearing to be, as Holt White explained it, "Forbid it, heaven, that kings should *suffer* their ears to hear their failings palliated." Mr. Dyce, however, whose excellent edition of the poet's works has been published while the sheets of this play are preparing for press, conceives that *let* bears here its old signification *to hinder,* and reads,—

"—— and heaven forbid
That kings should let their ears hear their faults *chid.*"

[c] Are *arms to princes, and bring joys to subjects.*] Steevens reads:—

"Bring arms to princes, and to subjects joys."

That the text of the old editions is corrupted here, there can be no question; but whether by misprint or the omission of a line, who shall determine?

[d] *And should he* doubt it,—] Adapted by Malone upon the reading of the quarto 1609:—

"And shold he *doo't,*" &c.

Or till the Destinies do cut his thread of life:
Your rule direct to any; if to me,
Day serves not light more faithful than I'll be.
PER. I do not doubt thy faith;
But should he wrong my liberties in my absence—
HEL. We'll mingle our bloods together in the earth,
From whence we had our being and our birth.
PER. Tyre, I now look from thee, then, and to Tharsus
Intend my travel, where I'll hear from thee;
And by whose letters I'll dispose myself.
The care I had and have of subjects' good,
On thee I lay, whose wisdom's strength can bear it.
I'll take thy word for faith, not ask thine oath;
Who shuns not to break one, will sure crack both:
But in our orbs we'll* live so round and safe,
That time of both this truth shall ne'er convince,
Thou show'dst a subject's shine, I a true prince.
[*Exeunt.*

SCENE III.—*The same. An Ante-chamber in the Palace.*

Enter THALIARD.

THAL. So, this is Tyre, and this the court. Here must I kill king Pericles; and if I do it not, I am sure to be hanged at home: 't is dangerous. — Well, I perceive, he was a wise fellow, and had good discretion, that, being bid to ask what he would of the king, desired he might know none of his secrets.(3) Now do I see he had some reason for it: for if a king bid a man be a villain, he is bound by the indenture of his oath to be one. Hush! here come the lords of Tyre.

Enter HELICANUS, ESCANES, *and other* Lords.

HEL. You shall not need, my fellow-peers of Tyre,
Further to question me of your king's departure:
His seal'd commision, left in trust with me,
Doth speak sufficiently, he's gone to travel.
THAL. [*Aside.*] How! the king gone!
HEL. If further yet you will be satisfied,
Why, as it were unlicens'd of your loves,
He would depart, I'll give some light unto you.
Being at Antioch——
THAL. [*Aside.*] What from Antioch?
HEL. Royal Antiochus (on what cause I know not)
Took some displeasure at him; at least he judg'd so:
And doubting lest he had err'd or sinned,
To show his sorrow, he'd correct himself;
So puts himself unto the shipman's toil,
With whom each minute threatens life or death.
THAL. [*Aside.*] Well, I perceive
I shall not be hang'd now, although I would;
But since he's gone, the king it sure must please [a]
He 'scap'd the land, to perish at the sea.—
I'll present myself. Peace to the lords of Tyre!
HEL. Lord Thaliard from Antiochus is welcome.
THAL. From him I come
With message unto princely Pericles;
But since my landing I have understood,[b]
Your lord hath betook himself to unknown travels,
My message must return from whence it came.
HEL. We have no reason to desire it,
Commended to our master, not to us:
Yet ere you shall depart, this we desire,—
As friends to Antioch, we may feast in Tyre.
[*Exeunt.*

SCENE IV.—Tharsus. *A Room in the* Governor's *House.*

Enter CLEON, DIONYZA, *and* Attendants.

CLE. My Dionyza, shall we rest us here,
And by relating tales of others' griefs,
See if 't will teach us to forget our own?
DIO. That were to blow at fire in hope to quench it;
For who digs hills because they do aspire,
Throws down one mountain to cast up a higher.
O my distressed lord, even such our griefs are;
Here they're but felt, unseen* with mischief's eyes,
But like to groves, being topp'd, they higher rise.
CLE. O Dionyza,
Who wanteth food, and will not say he wants it,
Or can conceal his hunger till he famish?
Our tongues and sorrows do sound deep
Our woes into the air; our eyes do weep,
Till lungs† fetch breath that may proclaim them louder;
That if heaven slumber while their creatures want,
They may awake their helps‡ to comfort them.

(*) Quarto 1609, *will*; that of 1619, *we*.

a *But since he's gone*, the king it sure must please—] More corruption! Of the text of this play, Malone well observes: "There is, I believe, no play of our author's, perhaps I might say, in the English language, so incorrect as this. The most corrupt of Shakespeare's other dramas, compared with Pericles, is purity itself." In the old copies, the line above reads:

"But since he 's gone, the *king's seas must please*,"

which Malone interprets,—

"Must *do their pleasure!*"

We adopt, as a make-sense, the emendation of Percy, though with little confidence.

b But since my landing—] That is, "But *as* since my landing," &c.

(*) Old editions, *and seen*.
(†) Old copies, *tongues*; corrected by Steevens.
(‡) Old copies, *helpers*.

I'll then discourse our[a] woes felt several years,
And, wanting breath to speak, help me with tears.
 DIO. I'll do my best, sir. [government,
 CLE. This Tharsus, over which I have the
A city on whom plenty held full hand,
For riches strew'd herself even in the streets;
Whose towers bore heads so high they kiss'd the
 clouds,
And strangers ne'er beheld, but wonder'd at;
Whose men and dames so jetted and adorn'd,
Like one another's glass to trim them by:
Their tables were stor'd full, to glad the sight,
And not so much to feed on, as delight;
All poverty was scorn'd, and pride so great,
The name of help grew odious to repeat.
 DIO. Oh, 'tis too true. [change,
 CLE. But see what heaven can do! By this our
These mouths, whom but of late, earth, sea, and air
Were all too little to content and please,
Although they gave their creatures in abundance,
As houses are defil'd for want of use,
They are now starv'd for want of exercise;
Those palates who, not yet two summers younger,[b]
Must have inventions to delight the taste,

---

[a] *I'll then discourse* our *woes felt several years,*—] This speech is inveterately depraved; and in the present line, the word *our* is an obvious misprint. Cleon desires to banish the recollection of their *own* sorrows by relating "others' griefs;" we ought therefore to read:—

"I'll then discourse *of* woes," &c.

The necessity for this correction is enforced by the words "*several* years." Shakespeare uses *several* for *distinct, separate, particular, various,* but never in the sense it now commonly bears of *many;* a sense, indeed, clearly inapplicable in this instance, because, from the context,—

"These mouths, whom *but of late,* earth, sea, and air
Were all too little to content and please,"—

as well as from the novel, it is plain the famine at Tharsus was not *two summers* old.

[b] *Those palates who,* not yet two summers younger,—] In the old copy, "not yet *too savers* younger," which the modern editors have altered to

——"not *us'd to hunger's savour.*"

and

——"not *us'd to savour hunger.*"

The reading in the text was suggested by Mason long before the discovery of Wilkins' novel, which, in the corresponding scene, contains the very expression pre-supposed: "the ground of which forced lamentation was to see the power of change, that this their city, *who not two summers younger,* did so excell in pompe," &c.

Would now be glad of bread, and beg for it;
Those mothers who, to nouzle up their babes,
Thought nought too curious, are ready now,
To eat those little darlings whom they lov'd.
So sharp are hunger's teeth, that man and wife
Draw lots who first shall die to lengthen life:
Here stands a lord, and there a lady weeping;
Here many sink, yet those which see them fall
Have scarce strength left to give them burial.
Is not this true?
DIO. Our cheeks and hollow eyes do witness it.
CLE. O let those cities that of Plenty's cup
And her prosperities so largely taste,
With their superfluous riots, hear these tears!
The misery of Tharsus may be theirs.

Enter a Lord.

LORD. Where's the lord governor?
CLE. Here.
Speak out thy sorrows, which thou bring'st, in haste,
For comfort is too far for us to expect.
LORD. We have descried, upon our neighbouring shore,
A portly sail of ships make hitherward.
CLE. I thought as much.
One sorrow never comes but brings an heir,
That may succeed as his inheritor;
And so in ours: some neighbouring nation,
Taking advantage of our misery,
Hath* stuff'd these hollow vessels with their power,
To beat us down, the which are down already;
And make a conquest of unhappy me,
Whereas no glory's got to overcome.
LORD. That's the least fear; for, by the semblance
Of their white flags display'd, they bring us peace,
And come to us as favourers, not as foes.
CLE. Thou speak'st like him's untutor'd to repeat; [a]
Who makes the fairest show, means most deceit.
But bring they what they will, and what they can,
What need we fear?
The ground's the lowest, and we are half-way there:
Go tell their general we attend him here,
To know for what he comes, and whence he comes,
And what he craves.
LORD. I go, my lord.
CLE. Welcome is peace, if he on peace consist;
If wars, we are unable to resist.

Enter PERICLES, *with* Attendants.

PER. Lord governor, for so we hear you are,
Let not our ships, and number of our men,
Be, like a beacon fir'd, to amaze your eyes.
We have heard your miseries as far as Tyre,
And seen the desolation of your streets:
Nor come we to add sorrow to your tears,
But to relieve them of their heavy load;
And these our ships (you happily may think
Are, like the Trojan horse was, stuff'd within,
With bloody veins expecting overthrow) [b]
Are stor'd with corn to make your needy bread,
And give them life, whom hunger starv'd half dead.
ALL. The gods of Greece protect you!
And we will pray for you.
PER. Arise, I pray you, rise;
We do not look for reverence, but for love,
And harbourage for ourself, our ships, and men.
CLE. The which when any shall not gratify,
Or pay you with unthankfulness in thought,
Be it our wives, our children, or ourselves,
The curse of heaven and men succeed their evils!
Till when—the which, I hope, shall ne'er be seen—
Your grace is welcome to our town and us.
PER. Which welcome we'll accept; feast here a while,
Until our stars that frown lend us a smile.
[*Exeunt.*

(*) Old text, *That.*

[a] Thou speak'st like him's untutor'd to repeat;] This should possibly be read and pointed thus.—

"Thou speak'st like him's untutor'd: to defeat
Who makes the fairest show means most deceit."

When the object is to overthrow, the fairer the outward appearance, the more it is to be suspected.

[b] *Are, like the Trojan horse* was, stuff'd within,
With bloody veins,—]

For this, the somewhat confused but not unintelligible reading of the old text, Steevens ingeniously substituted,—

"—— *war*-stuff'd within
With bloody *views.*"

Enter GOWER.

GOW. Here have you seen a mighty king
His child, I wis, to incest bring:
A better prince and benign lord,
That will prove awful both in deed and word.
Be quiet, then, as men should be,
Till he hath pass'd necessity.
I'll show you those in trouble's reign,
Losing a mite, a mountain gain.
The good, in conversation,—
To whom I give my benizon,—
Is still at Tharsus, where each man
Thinks all is writ he spoken can:
And, to remember what he does,
Build his statue to make him glorious: (1)
But tidings to the contrary
Are brought your eyes; what need speak I?

Dumb show.

Enter at one door PERICLES *talking with* CLEON; *all the* Train *with them. Enter at another door a* Gentleman, *with a letter to* PERICLES; PERICLES *shows the letter to* CLEON; *then gives the* Messenger *a reward, and knights him. Exit* PERICLES *at one door, and* CLEON *at another.*

Good Helicane that[a] stay'd at home,
Not to eat honey, like a drone,
From others' labours; for though he strive
To killen bad, keeps good alive;
And, to fulfil his prince' desire,
Sends word* of all that haps in Tyre:
How Thaliard came full bent with sin,
And hid intent to murder him;
And that in Tharsus 't was not best
Longer for him to make his rest:
He, knowing so,† put forth to seas,
Where when men been, there 's seldom ease;
For now the wind begins to blow;
Thunder above, and deeps below,
Make such unquiet, that the ship
Should house him safe, is wreck'd and split;
And he, good prince, having all lost,
By waves from coast to coast is toss'd:
All perishen of man, of pelf,
Ne aught escapen but himself;
Till fortune, tir'd with doing bad,
Threw him ashore to give him glad:
And here he comes; what shall be next,
Pardon old Gower; this 'longs the text. [*Exit.*

a *Good Helicane* that *stay'd at home,*—] Steevens reads "*hath* stay'd," but this hardly restores the passage to sense. We should perhaps read,—

"Good Helicane that stay'd at home
* * * * *
But to fulfil his prince' desire," &c.

(*) Old copies, *sav'd one of all.*

(†) In the original, *doing so.*

ACT II.

SCENE I.—Pentapolis. *An open Place on the Sea-side.*

Enter PERICLES, *wet.*

PER. Yet cease your ire, you angry stars of heaven!
Wind, rain, and thunder, remember, earthly man
Is but a substance that must yield to you;
And I, as fits my nature, do obey you.
Alas, the sea hath cast me on the rocks,
Wash'd me from shore to shore, and left me* breath,
Nothing to think on, but ensuing death:
Let it suffice the greatness of your powers,
To have bereft a prince of all his fortunes;
And having thrown him from your wat'ry grave,
Here to have death in peace, is all he'll crave.

Enter three Fishermen.

1 FISH. What, ho, Pilche!†

2 FISH. Ho! come and bring away the nets.

1 FISH. What, Patch-breech, I say!

3 FISH. What say you, master?

1 FISH. Look how thou stirrest now! come away, or I'll fetch thee with a wannion.

(*) Old editions, *my*.
(†) Old editions, What *to pelch*.

3 FISH. Faith, master, I am thinking of the poor men that were cast away before us, even now.

1 FISH. Alas, poor souls! it grieved my heart to hear what pitiful cries they made to us, to help them, when, well-a-day, we could scarce help ourselves.

3 FISH. Nay, master, said not I as much when I saw the porpus how he bounced and tumbled? they say, they're half fish, half flesh; a plague on them! they ne'er come but I look to be washed. Master, I marvel how the fishes live in the sea.

1 FISH. Why, as men do a-land; the great ones eat up the little ones. I can compare our rich misers to nothing so fitly as to a whale; 'a plays and tumbles, driving the poor fry before him, and at last devours them all at a mouthful. Such whales have I heard on o' the land, who never leave gaping, till they've swallowed the whole parish, church, steeple, bells and all.

PER. [*Aside.*] A pretty moral.

3 FISH. But, master, if I had been the sexton, I would have been that day in the belfry.

2 FISH. Why, man?

3 FISH. Because he should have swallowed me too: and when I had been in his belly, I would

have kept such a jangling of the bells, that he should never have left, till he cast bells, steeple, church, and parish, up again. But if the good king Simonides were of my mind——

PER. [*Aside.*] Simonides?

3 FISH. We would purge the land of these drones, that rob the bee of her honey.

PER. How from the finny[a] subjects of the sea
These fishers tell the infirmities of men;
And from their watery empire recollect
All that may men approve, or men detect!
Peace be at your labour, honest fishermen.

2 FISH. Honest! good fellow, what's that? If it be a day fits you, scratch out of the calendar and nobody look after it.[b]

PER. You may see the sea hath cast me on your coast.[c]

2 FISH. What a drunken knave was the sea, to cast thee in our way!

PER. A man whom both the waters and the wind,
In that vast tennis-court, hath made the ball
For them to play upon, entreats you pity him;
He asks of you, that never us'd to beg.

1 FISH. No, friend, cannot you beg? here's them in our country of Greece gets more with begging than we can do with working.

2 FISH. Canst thou catch any fishes then?

PER. I never practised it.

2 FISH. Nay, then thou wilt starve sure; for here's nothing to be got now-a-days, unless thou canst fish for 't.

PER. What I have been, I have forgot to know;
But what I am, want teaches me to think on;
A man throng'd up[d] with cold; my veins are chill,
And have no more of life than may suffice
To give my tongue that heat to ask your help:
Which if you shall refuse, when I am dead,
For that I am a man, pray see me buried.(2)

1 FISH. Die, quoth-a? Now gods forbid! I have a gown here; come, put it on, keep thee warm. Now, afore me, a handsome fellow! Come, thou shalt go home, and we'll have flesh for holidays, fish for fasting-days, and moreo'er puddings and flap-jacks;[e] and thou shalt be welcome.

PER. I thank you, sir.

2 FISH. Hark you, my friend, you said you could not beg.

PER. I did but crave.

2 FISH. But crave! Then I'll turn craver too, and so I shall 'scape whipping.

PER. Why, are all your beggars whipped then?

2 FISH. O, not all, my friend, not all; for if all your beggars were whipped, I would wish no better office than to be a beadle. But, master, I'll go draw up the net.

[*Exeunt two of the* Fishermen.

PER. [*Aside.*] How well this honest mirth becomes their labour!

1 FISH. Hark you, sir, do you know where ye are?

PER. Not well.

1 FISH. Why, I'll tell you; this is called Pentapolis, and our king, the good Simonides.

PER. The good king Simonides, do you call him?

1 FISH. Ay, sir, and he deserves so to be called for his peaceable reign and good government.

PER. He is a happy king, since he gains from his subjects the name of good by his government. How far is his court distant from this shore?

1 FISH. Marry, sir, half a-day's journey; and I'll tell you, he hath a fair daughter, and to-morrow is her birthday; and there are princes and knights come from all parts of the world to joust and tourney for her love.

PER. Were my fortunes equal to my desires, I could wish to make one there.

1 FISH. O, sir, things must be as they may; and what a man cannot get, he may lawfully deal for—his wife's soul.[f]

Re-enter the two Fishermen, *drawing up a net.*

2 FISH. Help, master, help! here's a fish hangs in the net, like a poor man's right in the law; 'twill hardly come out. Ha! bots on 't, 't is come at last, and 't is turned to a rusty armour.

PER. An armour, friends! I pray you, let me see it.
Thanks, Fortune, yet, that after all my crosses,*
Thou giv'st me somewhat to repair myself;

---

[a] *The* finny *subjects*—] Old editions, "*fenny subject;*" but see Wilkins' novel,—"And prince Pericles wondring that from the *finny subjects* of the sea these poore country people learned the infirmities of men."—*Reprint*, p. 27.

[b] Scratch *out of the calendar and* nobody look after it.] The old text has "*search* out," &c. Steevens first suggested *scratch*—we believe, rightly; thus in Beaumont and Fletcher's play of "The Coxcomb," Act IV. Sc. 4:—

"That would quite *scratch me out of the Calendar.*"

But this emendation only partially restores the integrity of the dialogue; something in the preceding speech of Pericles is evidently missing, and his next is equally defective.

[c] You may see the sea hath cast me on your coast.] So the folio, 1664. The earlier editions in quarto read,—

(*) Old copies, *all crosses; my* was added by Malone.

"May see the sea hath cast upon your coast."

[d] Throng'd up—] See note [a], p. 184.

[e] Flap-jacks;] *Pancakes.* In the old editions the passage stands, "Flesh for *all day*, fish for fasting days, and *more, or* puddings and flap-jacks."

[f] And what a man cannot get, he may lawfully deal for—his wife's soul.] This passage has hitherto successfully resisted exposition. Its obscurity would perhaps be lessened by reading, "his wife's sole—." The meaning appears to be a gross one,—although a man cannot get a child, he may lawfully try for it; his wife is sole judge of its paternity.

And though it was my own, part of my heritage,
Which my dead father did bequeath to me,
With this strict charge (even as he left his life),
Keep it, my Pericles, it hath been a shield
'Twixt me and death—and pointed to this brace;—
For that it sav'd me, keep it; in like necessity,
The which the gods protect thee from! may't defend thee.[a]
It kept where I kept, I so dearly lov'd it;
Till the rough seas, that spare not any man,
Took it in rage, though calm'd, have given it again:
I thank thee for 't; my shipwreck now 's no ill,
Since I have here my father's gift in 's will.

1 Fish. What mean you, sir?

Per. To beg of you, kind friends, this coat of worth,
For it was sometime target to a king;
I know it by this mark. He lov'd me dearly,
And for his sake, I wish the having of it;
And that you'd guide me to your sovereign's court,
Where with it I may appear a gentleman;
And if that ever my low fortunes better,[b]
I'll pay your bounties; till then, rest your debtor.

1 Fish. Why, wilt thou tourney for the lady?

Per. I'll show the virtue I have borne in arms.

1 Fish. Why, do ye take it, and the gods give thee good on't!

2 Fish. Ay, but hark you, my friend; 'twas we that made up this garment through the rough seams of the water; there are certain condolements, certain vails. I hope, sir, if you thrive, you'll remember from whence you had it.*

Per. Believe it, I will;
By your furtherance I am cloth'd in steel;
And spite of all the rapture[c] of the sea,
This jewel holds his building on my arm;
Unto thy value I will mount myself
Upon a courser, whose delightful steps
Shall make the gazer joy to see him tread.—
Only, my friend, I yet am unprovided
Of a pair of bases.

2 Fish. We'll sure provide: thou shalt have my best gown to make thee a pair; and I'll bring thee to the court myself.

Per. Then honour be but a goal[d] to my will!
This day I'll rise, or else add ill to ill. [*Exeunt.*

---

a The old copies read:—

"The which the gods protect thee, *fame* may defend thee."

b *My low* fortunes *better*,—] In the old copies, *fortune's* better.

c *The* rapture *of the sea*,—] Old text, *rupture*; but see the paraphrase of this passage in Wilkins' novel:—"Which horse he provided with a jewel, whom all the *raptures* of the sea could not bereave from his arme."—*Reprint*, p. 29.

(*) Old editions, *them*.

d *Then honour be but a* goal *to my will!*] This is alike repugnant both to sense and harmony. Surely we should read,—

"Then honour be but *equal* to my will!"

as he had just before said,—

"Were *my fortunes equal to my desires*."

SCENE II.—*The same. A public Way or Platform, leading to the Lists. A Pavilion by the side of it for the reception of the* King, Princess, Lords, *&c.*

Enter SIMONIDES, THAISA, Lords, *and* Attendants.

SIM. Are the knights ready to begin the triumph?

1 LORD. They are, my liege;
And stay your coming to present themselves.

SIM. Return them, we are ready; and our daughter,*
In honour of whose birth these triumphs are,
Sits here, like beauty's child, whom nature gat
For men to see, and seeing wonder at.

[*Exit a* Lord.

THAI. It pleaseth you, my royal father, to express
My commendations great, whose merit's less.

SIM. 'Tis fit it should be so; for princes are
A model, which heaven makes like to itself:
As jewels lose their glory if neglected,
So princes their renown, if not respected.
'Tis now your honour, daughter, to explain*
The labour of each knight, in his device.

THAI. Which, to preserve mine honour, I'll perform.

[*Enter a* Knight; *he passes over the stage, and his* Squire *presents his shield to the* Princess.

SIM. Who is the first that doth prefer himself?

THAI. A knight of Sparta, my renowned father;
And the device he bears upon his shield
Is a black Æthiop reaching at the sun;
The word, *Lux tua vita mihi.*

SIM. He loves you well that holds his life of you.

[*The second* Knight *passes over.*

(*) Old editions insert, *heere.*

(*) Old copies, *entertaine;* altered by Steevens.

Who is the second that presents himself?
THAI. A prince of Macedon, my royal father;
And the device he bears upon his shield
Is an arm'd knight, that's conquer'd by a lady;
The motto thus, in Spanish, *Piu*[a] *por dulzura que por fuerza.*
[*The third* Knight *passes over.*
SIM. And what's the third?
THAI. The third of Antioch;
And his device a wreath of chivalry;
The word, *Me pompæ* provexit apex.*
[*The fourth* Knight *passes over.*
SIM. What is the fourth?
THAI. A burning torch, that's turned upside down;
The word, *Quod † me alit, me extinguit.*
SIM. Which shows that beauty hath his power and will,
Which can as well inflame, as it can kill.
[*The fifth* Knight *passes over.*
THAI. The fifth, an hand environed with clouds,
Holding out gold that's by the touchstone tried;
The motto thus, *Sic spectanda fides.*
[*The sixth* Knight *passes over.*
SIM. And what's the sixth and last, the which the knight himself
With such a graceful courtesy deliver'd?
THAI. He seems to be a stranger, but his present is
A wither'd branch, that's only green at top;
The motto, *In hac spe vivo.*
SIM. A pretty moral;
From the dejected state wherein he is,
He hopes by you his fortunes yet may flourish.
1 LORD. He had need mean better than his outward show
Can any way speak in his just commend;
For, by his rusty outside, he appears
To have practis'd more the whipstock than the lance.
2 LORD. He well may be a stranger, for he comes
To an honour'd triumph, strangely furnished.
3 LORD. And on set purpose let his armour rust
Until this day, to scour it in the dust.
SIM. Opinion's but a fool, that makes us scan
The outward habit by the inward man.
But stay, the knights are coming; we'll withdraw
Into the gallery. [*Exeunt.*
Great shouts without, and all cry, "The mean Knight!"

SCENE III.—*The same. A Hall of State. A Banquet prepared.*

Enter SIMONIDES, THAISA, Marshal, Lords, Attendants, *and the* Knights *from tilting.*

SIM. Knights,
To say you're welcome, were superfluous.
To* place upon the volume of your deeds,
As in a title-page, your worth in arms,
Were more than you expect, or more than's fit,
Since every worth in show commends itself.
Prepare for mirth, for mirth becomes a feast:
You are princes and my guests.
THAI. But you, my knight and guest;
To whom this wreath of victory I give,
And crown you king of this day's happiness.
PER. 'Tis more by fortune, lady, than by merit.
SIM. Call it by what you will, the day is yours;
And here, I hope, is none that envies it.
In framing an artist, art hath thus decreed,
To make some good, but others to exceed;
And you're her labour'd scholar. Come, queen o' the feast,
(For, daughter, so you are,) here take your place:
Marshal the rest, as they deserve their grace.
KNIGHTS. We are honour'd much by good Simonides.
SIM. Your presence glads our days; honour we love,
For who hates honour, hates the gods above.
MARSH. Sir, yonder is your place.
PER. Some other is more fit.
1 KNIGHT. Contend not, sir; for we are gentlemen,
That neither in our hearts nor outward eyes,
Envy the great nor do the low despise.[b]
PER. You are right courteous knights.
SIM. Sit, sir, sit.
By Jove, I wonder, that is king of thoughts,
These cates resist me, he not thought upon.[c]
THAI. By Juno, that is queen of marriage,
All viands that I eat do seem unsavoury,
Wishing him my meat: sure he's a gallant gentleman.
SIM. He's but a country gentleman;
Has done no more than other knights have done;
Has broken a staff, or so; so let it pass.
THAI. To me he seems like diamond to glass.
PER. Yon king's to me like to my father's picture,

(*) Old copies, *Pompey.* (†) Old copies, *Qui.*

(*) Old copies, until the fourth folio, 1685, I *place.*

a Piu—] This is an Italian, not a Spanish word.

b That neither in our hearts, &c.] So the quarto, 1619; the first, 1609, reads:—

"Have *neither in our hearts, nor outward eyes,*
Envies *the great, nor* shall *the low despise.*"

c *By Jove, I wonder, that is king of thoughts,*
These cates resist me, he not thought upon.]

In most of the modern editions these lines are assigned to Pericles, *she* being substituted for *he*; but compare the corresponding passage in Wilkins' novel,—"In the end, all being seated by the Marshall at a table, placed directly over-against where the king and his daughter sate, as it were by some divine operation, *both king and daughter, at one instant were so strucke in love with the noblenesse of his woorth, that they could not spare so much time to satisfie themselves with the delicacie of their viands, for talking of his prayses.*" We incline to think, with Steevens, that the second line should be read,—

"The cates resist me, *be* not thought upon."

Which tells me in that glory once he was;
Had princes sit, like stars, about his throne,
And he the sun, for them to reverence.
None that beheld him, but, like lesser lights,
Did vail their crowns to his supremacy; [night,
Where now his son's* like a glow-worm in the
The which hath fire in darkness, none in light;

(*) Old copies, *sonne*.

Whereby I see that Time's the king of men,
For he's their parent, and he is their grave,
And gives them what he will, not what they crave.
SIM. What, are you merry, knights?
1 KNIGHT. Who can be other in this royal presence? [brim,
SIM. Here, with a cup that's stor'd* unto the

(*) Old copies, *sturd*, *stirr'd*.

(As you do love, fill to your mistress' lips,)
We drink this health to you.
KNIGHTS. We thank your grace.
SIM. Yet pause a while;
Yon knight doth sit too melancholy,
As if the entertainment in our court
Had not a show might countervail his worth.
Note it not you, Thaisa?
THAI. What is it
To me, my father?
SIM. O attend, my daughter;
Princes, in this, should live like gods above,
Who freely give to every one that comes
To honour them:
And princes, not doing so, are like to gnats,
Which make a sound, but kill'd are wonder'd at.
Therefore to make his entrance[a] more sweet,
Here, say we drink this standing-bowl of wine to him.
THAI. Alas, my father, it befits not me
Unto a stranger knight to be so bold;
He may my proffer take for an offence,
Since men take women's gifts for impudence.
SIM. How! do as I bid you, or you'll move me else.
THAI. [*Aside.*] Now, by the gods, he could not please me better.
SIM. And further * tell him, we desire to know of him,
Of whence he is, his name and parentage.(3)
THAI. The king, my father, sir, has drunk to you.
PER. I thank him.
THAI. Wishing it so much blood unto your life.
PER. I thank both him and you, and pledge him freely.
THAI. And further he desires to know of you,
Of whence you are, your name and parentage.
PER. A gentleman of Tyre,—my name Pericles;
My education been, in arts and arms;[b]—
Who, looking for adventures in the world,
Was by the rough seas reft of ships and men,
And, after shipwreck, driven upon this shore.
THAI. He thanks your grace; names himself Pericles,
A gentleman of Tyre,
Who only by misfortune of the seas
Bereft of ships and men, cast on this shore.
SIM. Now, by the gods, I pity his misfortune,
And will awake him from his melancholy.—
Come, gentlemen, we sit too long on trifles,
And waste the time, which looks for other revels.
Even in your armours, as you are address'd,
Will very well become a soldier's dance:
I will not have excuse, with saying, this
Loud music is too harsh for ladies' heads;
Since they love men in arms, as well as beds.
[*The* Knights *dance.*
So[c] this was well ask'd; 'twas so well perform'd.
Come, sir; here is a lady that wants breathing too:
And I have heard, you knights of Tyre
Are excellent in making ladies trip;
And that their measures are as excellent.
PER. In those that practise them they are, my lord.
SIM. Oh, that's as much as, you would be denied
Of your fair courtesy.
[*The* Knights *and* Ladies *dance.*
Unclasp, unclasp;
Thanks, gentlemen, to all; all have done well,
But you the best. [*To* PERICLES.] Pages and lights, to conduct
These knights unto their several lodgings! Yours, sir,
We have given order to be next our own.
PER. I am at your grace's pleasure.
SIM. Princes, it is too late to talk of love,
And that's the mark I know you level at:
Therefore each one betake him to his rest;
To-morrow, all for speeding do their best.
[*Exeunt.*

SCENE IV.—Tyre. *A Room in the* Governor's *House.*

Enter HELICANUS *and* ESCANES.

HEL. No, Escanes, know this of me,
Antiochus from incest liv'd not free;
For which, the most high gods not minding longer
To withhold the vengeance that they had in store,
Due to this heinous capital offence;
Even in the height and pride of all his glory,
When he was seated[d] in a chariot
Of an inestimable value, and his daughter with him,
A fire from heaven came, and shrivell'd up
Their * bodies, even to loathing; for they so stunk,

(*) Old copies, *furthermore.*

[a] Entrance—] *Entrance* here means *reverie, trance,* &c., but the line has been mutilated.

[b] *My education* been, in *arts,* &c.] This is usually changed to,—

"My education *has* been," &c.

or,—

"My education *being,*" &c.

but the parallel passage in Wilkins' novel confirms the old reading:—"That he was a gentleman of Tyre, his name Pericles; his education beene in artes and armes," &c.

(*) Old editions, *Those.*

[c] So *this was well* ask'd, &c.] That is, *As* this was well ask'd.

[d] When he was seated, &c.] This passage, miserably corrupted in printing or transcription, is usually exhibited in modern editions thus:—

"When he was seated, and his daughter with him,
In a chariot of inestimable value,
A fire," &c.

That all those eyes ador'd them ere their fall,
Scorn now their hand should give them burial.

ESCA. 'Twas very strange.

HEL. And yet but justice; for though
This king were great, his greatness was no guard
To bar heav'n's shaft, but sin had his reward.

ESCA. 'Tis very true.

Enter three Lords.

1 LORD. See, not a man in private conference
Or council hath respect with him but he.

2 LORD. It shall no longer grieve without reproof.

3 LORD. And curs'd be he that will not second it.

1 LORD. Follow me, then: lord Helicane, a word.

HEL. With me? and welcome: happy day, my lords.

1 LORD. Know that our griefs are risen to the top,
And now at length they overflow their banks.

HEL. Your griefs! for what? wrong not your prince you love.

1 LORD. Wrong not yourself, then, noble Helicane;
But, if the prince do live, let us salute him,
Or know what ground's made happy by his breath.
If in the world he live, we'll seek him out;
If in his grave he rest, we'll find him there;
And be resolv'd, he lives to govern us,
Or dead, gives cause to mourn his funeral,
And leaves us to our free election.

2 LORD. Whose death's,* indeed, the strongest in our censure:
And knowing this kingdom is without a head,
(Like goodly buildings left without a roof
Soon fall to ruin,) your noble self,
That best know'st how to rule, and how to reign,
We thus submit unto,—our sovereign.

ALL. Live, noble Helicane.

HEL. For† honour's cause forbear your suffrages:
If that you love prince Pericles, forbear.
Take I your wish, I leap into the seas,
Where's hourly trouble for a minute's ease.
A twelvemonth longer, let me entreat you
To forbear the absence of your king;
If in which time expir'd, he not return,
I shall with aged patience bear your yoke.
But if I cannot win you to this love,
Go search like nobles, like noble subjects,
And in your search spend your adventurous worth;
Whom if you find, and win unto return,
You shall like diamonds sit about his crown.

(*) Old editions, *death*.
(†) Old copies, *Try*: amended by Mr. Dyce.

1 LORD. To wisdom he's a fool that will not yield;
And since lord Helicane enjoineth us,
We with our travels will endeavour it.*

HEL. Then you love us, we you, and we'll clasp hands;
When peers thus knit, a kingdom ever stands.
[*Exeunt.*

SCENE V.—Pentapolis. *A Room in the Palace.*

Enter SIMONIDES, *reading a Letter; the* Knights *meet him.*

1 KNIGHT. Good morrow to the good Simonides.

SIM. Knights, from my daughter this I let you know,
That for this twelvemonth she'll not undertake
A married life:
Her reason to herself is only known,
Which yet from her by no means can I get.

2 KNIGHT. May we not get access to her, my lord?

SIM. Faith, by no means: she hath so strictly tied her
To her chamber, that it is impossible.
One twelve moons more she'll wear Diana's livery;
This by the eye of Cynthia hath she vow'd,
And on her virgin honour will not break it.

3 KNIGHT. Loth to bid farewell, we take our leaves.
[*Exeunt.*

SIM. So, they're well despatch'd; now to my daughter's letter:
She tells me here, she'll wed the stranger knight,
Or never more to view nor day nor light.
'T is well, mistress, your choice agrees with mine;
I like that well;—nay, how absolute she's in't,
Not minding whether I dislike or no!
Well, I do commend her choice,
And will no longer have it be delay'd.—
Soft! here he comes;—I must dissemble it.

Enter PERICLES.

PER. All fortune to the good Simonides!

SIM. To you as much, sir! I am beholden to you,
For your sweet music this last night: I do
Protest my ears were never better fed
With such delightful pleasing harmony.

PER. It is your grace's pleasure to commend;
Not my desert.

SIM. Sir, you are music's master.

PER. The worst of all her scholars, my good lord.

(*) The *it* is not in the old copies.

SIM. Let me ask you one thing.
What do you think of my daughter, sir?
PER. A most virtuous princess.
SIM. And she is fair too, is she not?
PER. As a fair day in summer,—wondrous fair.
SIM. Sir, my daughter thinks very well of you;
Ay, so well, that you must be her master,
And she will be your scholar: therefore look to it.
PER. I am unworthy for her schoolmaster.
SIM. She thinks not so: peruse this writing else.
PER. [*Aside.*] What's here!
A letter, that she loves the knight of Tyre!
'T is the king's subtilty to have my life.—
O, seek not to entrap me, gracious lord,
A stranger and distressed gentleman,
That never aimed so high to love your daughter,
But bent all offices to honour her.
SIM. Thou hast bewitch'd my daughter, and thou art
A villain.
PER. By the gods I have not;
Never did thought of mine levy offence;
Nor never did my actions yet commence
A deed might gain her love, or your displeasure.
SIM. Traitor, thou liest.
PER. Traitor!
SIM. Ay, traitor.
PER. Even in his throat (unless it be a king),
That calls me traitor, I return the lie.

SIM. [*Aside.*] Now, by the gods, I do applaud
his courage.
PER. My actions are as noble as my thoughts,
That never relish'd of a base descent.
I came unto your court for honour's cause,
And not to be a rebel to her state;
And he that otherwise accounts of me,
This sword shall prove, he's honour's enemy.
SIM. No!—
Here comes my daughter, she can witness it.

Enter THAISA.

PER. Then, as you are as virtuous as fair,
Resolve your angry father, if my tongue
Did e'er solicit, or my hand subscribe
To any syllable that made love to you?
THAI. Why, sir, say if you had,
Who takes offence at that would make me glad?
SIM. Yea, mistress, are you so peremptory?
[*Aside.*] I'm glad of it with all my heart.
I'll tame you; I'll bring you in subjection.
Will you, not having my consent, bestow
Your love and your affections on* a stranger?—
Who, for aught I know, may be, nor can I think
The contrary,—[*Aside.*] as great in blood as I
myself.—
Therefore, hear you, mistress; either frame
Your will to mine—and you, sir, hear you,
Either be rul'd by me, or I will make you—
Man and wife:
Nay, come, your hands and lips must seal it too:
And being join'd I'll thus your hopes destroy;—
And for a† further grief,—God give you joy!—
What, are you both pleas'd?
THAI. Yes, if you love me, sir.
PER. Even as my life, or blood that fosters it.
SIM. What, are you both agreed?
BOTH. Yes, if it please your majesty.
SIM. It pleaseth me so well, that I will see you
wed;
Then, with what haste you can, get you to bed.
[*Exeunt.*(4)

(*) Old copies, *upon*. (†) Old copies omit, *a*.

Enter GOWER.

GOW. Now sleep yslaked hath the rout;
No din but snores, the house about,*
Made louder by the o'er-fed breast
Of this most pompous marriage-feast.
The cat, with eyne of burning coal,
Now couches from the mouse's hole;
And crickets sing at th' oven's mouth,
Aye † the blither for their drouth.
Hymen hath brought the bride to bed,
Where, by the loss of maidenhead,
A babe is moulded.—Be attent,
And time that is so briefly spent,
With your fine fancies quaintly eche;
What's dumb in show, I'll plain with speech.

Dumb show.

Enter PERICLES *and* SIMONIDES, *at one door, with* Attendants; *a* Messenger *meets them, kneels, and gives* PERICLES *a letter.* PERICLES *shows it to* SIMONIDES; *the* Lords *kneel to the former. Then enter* THAISA *with child, and* LYCHORIDA, *a nurse.* SIMONIDES *shows his daughter the letter: she r joices; she and* PERICLES *take leave of her father, and depart with* LYCHORIDA *and* Attendants. *Then exeunt* SIMONIDES *and the rest.*

By many a derne[a] and painful perch,
Of Pericles the careful search,
By the four opposing coigns,‡
Which the world together joins,
Is made; with all due diligence,
That horse and sail and high expense
Can stead the quest. At last from Tyre
(Fame answering the most strange inquire)
To the court of king Simonides
Are letters brought; the tenour these:—
Antiochus and his daughter dead;
The men of Tyrus on the head
Of Helicanus would set on
The crown of Tyre, but he will none;
The mutine there[b] he hastes t' oppress;
Says to them, if king Pericles
Come not home in twice six moons,
He, obedient to their dooms,
Will take the crown. The sum of this,
Brought hither to Pentapolis,
Y-ravished[c] the regions round,
And every one with claps can sound,
Our heir apparent is a king:
Who dream'd, who thought of such a thing?
Brief, he must hence depart to Tyre;
His queen with child, makes her desire
(Which who shall cross?) along to go:—
Omit we all their dole and woe:—
Lychorida her nurse she takes,
And so to sea. Their vessel shakes
On Neptune's billow; half the flood
Hath their keel cut; but fortune's mood[d]
Varies again: the grisly north
Disgorges such a tempest forth,
That, as a duck for life that dives,
So up and down the poor ship drives.
The lady shrieks, and well-a-near
Doth fall in travail with her fear:
And what ensues in this fell storm,
Shall for itself, itself perform;
I nill relate; action may
Conveniently the rest convey:
Which might not what by me is told.
In your imagination hold
This stage the ship, upon whose deck
The sea-tost* Pericles appears to speak. [*Exit.*

(*) Old copies, *about the house.*
(†) Old copies, *Are;* corrected by Mr. Dyce.
(‡) Old copies, *criges;* corrected by Tyrwhitt.

(*) Old editions, *seas-tost.*

a Derne—] *Derne* is usually explained to mean, *lonely;* it appears, however, in the instances of its use that we have met with, to signify *earnest, eager,* and the like. Thus:—

"Then if *derne* love of thy deare loving Lord,—"
BARNES' *Spirituall Sonnets,* 1595.

b The mutine there he—] In the old text, "*The mutiny he there.*"

c Y-ravished—] Old copies, *Iranished,* and *Irony shed;* Steevens made the emendation.

d *But* fortune's mood—] The old copies have, "But fortune *moou'd,*" and "fortune *mou'd.*"

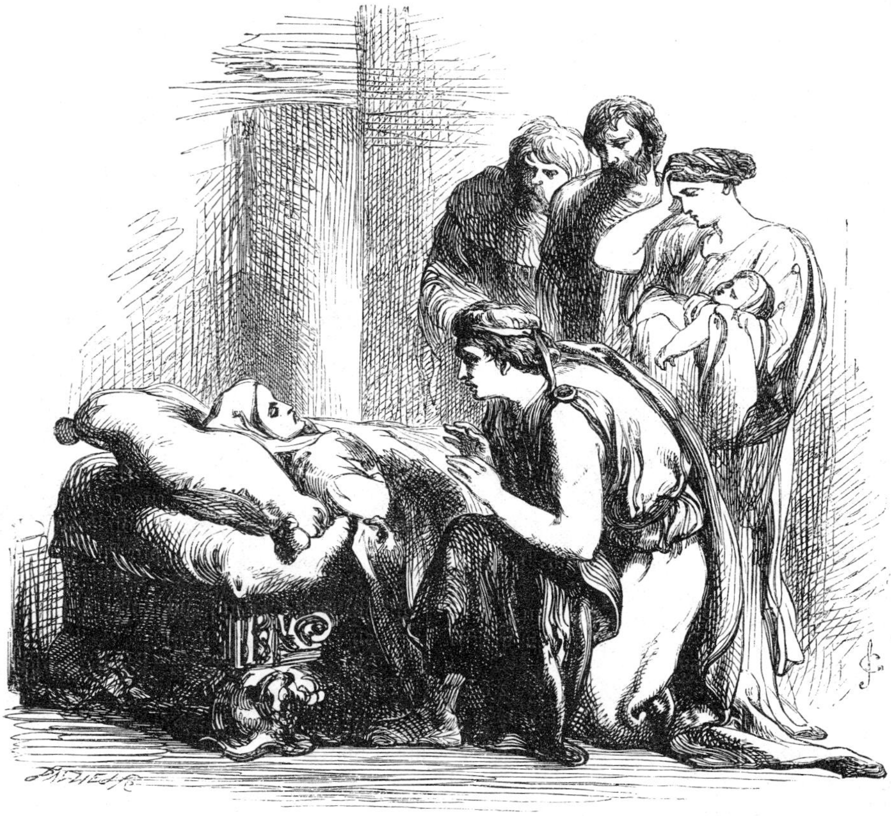

ACT III.

SCENE I.—*On a Ship at Sea.*

Enter PERICLES.

PER. The God of this great vast, rebuke these surges,
Which wash both heaven and hell; and thou, that hast
Upon the winds command, bind them in brass,
Having call'd them from the deep! O still
Thy deaf'ning, dreadful thunders; gently quench
Thy nimble, sulphurous flashes!—O how, Lychorida,
How does my queen?—thou* storm, venomously,
Wilt thou spit all thyself?—the seaman's whistle
Is, as a whisper in the ears of death,
Unheard.—Lychorida!—Lucina, O
Divinest patroness, and midwife† gentle
To those that cry by night, convey thy deity
Aboard our dancing boat; make swift the pangs
Of my queen's travails!

Enter LYCHORIDA, *with an Infant.*

Now, Lychorida—
LYC. Here is a thing too young for such a place,
Who, if it had conceit, would die, as I
Am like to do: take in your arms this piece
Of your dead queen.
PER. How! how, Lychorida!
LYC. Patience, good sir, do not assist the storm.
Here's all that is left living of your queen,—
A little daughter; for the sake of it,
Be manly, and take comfort.
PER. O, you gods!
Why do you make us love your goodly gifts,
And snatch them straight away? We, here below,
Recall not what we give, and therein may
Use[a] honour with you.

(*) Old copies, *then*.
(†) Old copies, *my* wife; corrected by Steevens.

[a] Use *honour*—] Steevens and Mason both conjectured *use* to be a misprint for *vie*, as it probably was.

LYC. Patience, good sir,
Even for this charge.
PER. Now, mild may be thy life!
For a more blust'rous birth had never babe:
Quiet and gentle thy conditions!
For thou art the rudeliest welcome[a] to this world,
That ere was prince's child. Happy what follows!
Thou hast as chiding a nativity,
As fire, air, water, earth, and heaven can make,
To herald thee from the womb: even at the first,
Thy loss is more than can thy portage quit,
With all thou canst find here.—Now the good gods
Throw their best eyes upon it! (1)

Enter two Sailors.

1 SAIL. What courage, sir? God save you!
PER. Courage enough: I do not fear the flaw;
It hath done to me the worst: yet, for the love
Of this poor infant, this fresh-new sea-farer,
I would it would be quiet.

1 SAIL. Slack the bolins there! Thou wilt not, wilt thou? Blow and split thyself.

2 SAIL. But sea-room, an the brine and cloudy billow kiss the moon, I care not.

1 SAIL. Sir, your queen must overboard; the sea works high, the wind is loud, and will not lie till the ship be cleared of the dead.

PER. That's your superstition.

1 SAIL. Pardon us, sir; with us at sea it hath been still observed, and we are strong in custom:[b] therefore briefly yield her, for she must overboard straight.

PER. As you think meet. — Most wretched queen!
LYC. Here she lies, sir.
PER. A terrible childbed hast thou had, my dear;
No light, no fire: the unfriendly elements
Forgot thee utterly; nor have I time
To give thee hallow'd to thy grave, but straight
Must cast thee, scarcely coffin'd, in the ooze;*
Where, for a monument upon thy bones,
And aye-remaining[c] lamps, the belching whale
And humming water must o'erwhelm thy corpse,
Lying with simple shells. O, Lychorida,
Bid Nestor bring me spices, ink and paper,
My casket and my jewels; and bid Nicander
Bring me the satin coffer:† lay the babe
Upon the pillow; hie thee, whiles I say
A priestly farewell to her; suddenly, woman.
[*Exit* LYCHORIDA.

2 SAIL. Sir, we have a chest beneath the hatches, caulked and bitumed ready.

PER. I thank thee.—Mariner, say, what coast is this?
2 SAIL. We are near Tharsus.
PER. Thither, gentle mariner!
Alter thy course for Tyre; when canst thou reach it?
2 SAIL. By break of day, if the wind cease.
PER. O make for Tharsus!—
There will I visit Cleon, for the babe
Cannot hold out to Tyrus; there I'll leave it
At careful nursing.—Go thy ways, good mariner;
I'll bring the body presently. [*Exeunt.*

SCENE II.—Ephesus. *A Room in* Cerimon's *House.*

Enter CERIMON, *a* Servant, *and some persons who have been shipwrecked.*

CER. Philemon, ho!

Enter PHILEMON.

PHIL. Doth my lord call?
CER. Get fire and meat for these poor men;
'T has been a turbulent and stormy night.
SER. I have been in many; but such a night as this,
Till now, I ne'er endur'd.
CER. Your master will be dead ere you return;
There's nothing can be minister'd to nature,
That can recover him. Give this to the 'pothecary,
And tell me how it works. [*To* PHILEMON.
[*Exeunt all but* CERIMON.

Enter two Gentlemen.

1 GENT. Good morrow.
2 GENT. Good morrow to your lordship.
CER. Gentlemen, why do you stir so early?
1 GENT. Sir,
Our lodgings, standing bleak upon the sea,
Shook as the earth did quake;
The very principals[d] did seem to rend,
And all to-topple: pure surprise and fear
Made me to quit the house.

(*) Old copies, *oare;* corrected by Steevens.
(†) Old copies, *coffin.*

[a] *For thou art the rudeliest* welcome—] Malone changed *welcome* to *welcom'd;* but the former is the word adopted in Wilkins' novel:—"Poor inch of nature (quoth he) thou arte *as rudely welcome* to the worlde, as ever Princesse Babe was, and hast as chiding a nativitie as fire, ayre, earth and water can affoord thee."

[b] *We are strong in* custom:] The old editions read *eastern;* we adopt the emendation proposed by Boswell, in preference to the *credence* of Steevens, the *earnest* of Mason, or the *astern* of Knight.

[c] And aye-*remaining lamps,*—] The original has "The ayre-*remaining.*"

[d] Principals—] The *principals* are the strongest rafters in the roof of a building.

2 GENT. That is the cause we trouble you so early;
'Tis not our husbandry.
CER. O, you say well.
1 GENT. But I much marvel that your lordship, having
Rich tire about you, should at these early hours
Shake off the golden slumber of repose:
It is most strange,
Nature should be so conversant with pain,
Being thereto not compell'd.
CER. I hold it ever,
Virtue and cunning[a] were endowments greater
Than nobleness and riches: careless heirs
May the two latter darken and expend;
But immortality attends the former,
Making a man a god. 'Tis known, I ever
Have studied physic, through which secret art,
By turning o'er authorities, I have
(Together with my practice) made familiar
To me and to my aid, the bless'd infusions
That dwell in vegetives, in metals, stones;
And I[b] can speak of the disturbances
That nature works, and of her cures; which doth give me
A more content in course of true delight
Than to be thirsty after tottering honour,
Or tie my treasure * up in silken bags,
To please the fool and death.
2 GENT. Your honour has through Ephesus pour'd forth
Your charity, and hundreds call themselves
Your creatures, who by you have been restor'd:
And not your knowledge, your personal pain, but even
Your purse, still open, hath built lord Cerimon
Such strong renown as time shall ne'er decay.

Enter two Servants *with a Chest.*

SER. So; lift there.
CER. What is that?
SER. Sir, even now
Did the sea toss † upon our shore this chest;
'Tis of some wreck.
CER. Set't down, let's look upon't.
2 GENT. 'Tis like a coffin, sir.
CER. Whate'er it be,
'Tis wondrous heavy; wrench it open straight;
If the sea's stomach be o'ercharg'd with gold,
'Tis a good constraint of Fortune it belches upon us.[c]
2 GENT. It is so, my lord.

---

a Cunning—] *Cunning* here signifies *knowledge, skill,* &c.
b *And I can speak*—] The old copies exhibit these lines thus:—

"And can speak of the disturbances that nature
Works, and of her cures; which doth give me
A more content," &c.

(*) Old text, *pleasure,* corrected by Steevens.
(†) Old editions, *up upon.*

c 'Tis a good constraint of Fortune it belches upon us.] Manifestly and incorrigibly corrupt.

CER. How close 't is caulk'd and bitum'd! *
Did the sea cast it up?
SER. I never saw so huge a billow, sir,
As toss'd it upon shore.
CER. Wrench it open;
Soft!—it smells most sweetly in my sense.
2 GENT. A delicate odour.

(*) Old editions, *bottomed*.

CER. As ever hit my nostril; so,—up with it.—
Oh you most potent gods! what 's here? a corse!
1 GENT. Most strange!
CER. Shrouded in cloth of state; balm'd and entreasur'd
With full bags of spices! A passport too!
Apollo, perfect me in the characters!
[*Reads from a scroll.*

" Here I give to understand,—
If e'er this coffin drive a-land,—
I, king Pericles, have lost
This queen, worth all our mundane cost.
Who finds her, give her burying;
She was the daughter of a king:
Besides this treasure for a fee,
The gods requite his charity!"

If thou liv'st, Pericles, thou hast a heart
That even cracks* for woe! This chanc'd to-night.
2 GENT. Most likely, sir.
CER. Nay, certainly to-night; [rough
For look how fresh she looks!—They were too
That threw her in the sea. Make a fire within;
Fetch hither all my boxes in my closet.
Death may usurp on nature many hours,
And yet the fire of life kindle again
The o'erpress'd spirits. I have heard†
Of an Egyptian that had nine hours lien dead,
Who was by good appliance recovered.[a]

Re-enter a Servant, *with boxes, napkins, and fire.*

Well said, well said; the fire and cloths.—
The rough and woeful music that we have,
Cause it to sound, 'beseech you.
The viol once more;—how thou stirr'st, thou block!—
The music there!—I pray you, give her air;—
Gentlemen,
This queen will live; nature awakes; a warmth
Breathes‡ out of her: she hath not been entranc'd
Above five hours. See how she 'gins to blow
Into life's flower again!
1 GENT. The heavens
Through you, increase our wonder, and set up
Your fame for ever.
CER. She is alive; behold
Her eyelids, cases to those heavenly jewels
Which Pericles hath lost,
Begin to part their fringes of bright gold;
The diamonds of a most praised water
Do appear, to make the world twice rich. Live,
And make us weep to hear your fate, fair creature,
Rare as you seem to be! [*She moves.*
THAI. O dear Diana,
Where am I? Where's my lord? What world is this?
2 GENT. Is not this strange?
1 GENT. Most rare.

(*) First edition, 1609, *ever* cracks.
(†) Old copies, *I heard; have* inserted by Malone.
(‡) Old copies, *warmth breath*, and *warm breath.*

[a] By good appliance recovered.] This passage, seems hopelessly depraved. In the novel founded on the play it runs as follows:—"I have read of some Egyptians, who after four houres death, (if man may call it so) have raised impoverished bodies, like to this, unto their former health."

[b] Wand'ringly—] Steevens's emendation; the old editions reading, *wond'ringly.*

CER. Hush, my gentle neighbours!
Lend me your hands; to the next chamber bear her.
Get linen; now this matter must be look'd to,
For her relapse is mortal. Come, come,
And Æsculapius guide us! (2)
[*Exeunt, carrying her away.*

SCENE III.—Tharsus. *A Room in* Cleon's *House.*

Enter PERICLES, CLEON, DIONYZA, *and* LYCHORIDA, *with* MARINA *in her arms.*

PER. Most honour'd Cleon, I must needs be gone;
My twelve months are expir'd, and Tyrus stands
In a litigious peace. You and your lady
Take from my heart all thankfulness! the gods
Make up the rest upon you!
CLE. Your shafts* of fortune, though they hurt† you mortally,
Yet glance full wand'ringly [b] on us.
DION. O your sweet queen!
That the strict fates had pleas'd you had brought her hither,
To have bless'd mine eyes with her!
PER. We cannot but obey
The powers above us. Could I rage and roar
As doth the sea she lies in, yet the end
Must be as 't is. My gentle babe, Marina,—whom,
For she was born at sea, I have nam'd so,—here
I charge your charity withal, leaving her
The infant of your care, beseeching you
To give her princely training, that she may be
Manner'd as she is born.
CLE. Fear not, my lord; but think,
Your grace, that fed my country with your corn,
(For which the people's prayers still fall upon you,)
Must in your child be thought on. If neglection
Should therein make me vile, the common body,
By you reliev'd, would force me to my duty:
But if to that my nature need a spur,
The gods revenge it upon me and mine,
To the end of generation!
PER. I believe you;
Your honour and your goodness teach me to 't,
Without your vows. Till she be married, madam,
By bright Diana, whom we honour, all
Unscissar'd[c] shall this hair of mine remain,
Though I show ill [d] in 't. So I take my leave:
Good madam, make me blessed in your care
In bringing up my child.

(*) Old copies, *shakes.*
(†) First quarto, *haunt;* folio, 1664, *hate.*

[c] Unscissar'd—] The old copies read, "unsister'd *shall this* heir." The correction, which was made by Steevens, is established by the corresponding passage in Wilkins' novel: "Vowing solemnely by othe to himselfe, his head should grow *uncisserd*, his beard untrimmed, himself in all uncomely," &c.

[d] *Though I show* ill *in 't.*] The old copies have *will.* We adopt Mr. Dyce's reading.

DION. I have one myself,
Who shall not be more dear to my respect,
Than yours, my lord.

PER. Madam, my thanks and prayers.

CLE. We'll bring your grace even to the edge o' the shore;
Then give you up to the mask'd Neptune, and
The gentlest winds of heaven.

PER. I will embrace your offer. Come, dearest madam.—
O, no tears, Lychorida, no tears:
Look to your little mistress, on whose grace
You may depend hereafter.—Come, my lord.(3)

[*Exeunt.*

SCENE IV.—Ephesus. *A Room in* Cerimon's *House.*

Enter CERIMON *and* THAISA.

CER. Madam, this letter, and some certain jewels,
Lay with you in your coffer; which are now*
At your command. Know you the character?

THAI. It is my lord's. That I was shipp'd at sea
I well remember, even on my yearning† time;
But whether there delivered or no,
By the holy gods, I cannot rightly say;
But since king Pericles, my wedded lord,
I ne'er shall see again, a vestal livery
Will I take me to, and never more have joy.

CER. Madam, if this you purpose as you speak,
Diana's temple is not distant far,
Where you may 'bide[a] until your date expire:
Moreover, if you please, a niece of mine
Shall there attend you.

THAI. My recompense is thanks, that's all;
Yet my good will is great, though the gift small.

[*Exeunt.*

(*) The word *now* was inserted by Malone.
(†) First quarto, *learning;* second quarto, *eaning.*

[a] *Where you may* 'bide until—] The old editions have, "Where you may *abide till.*"

Enter GOWER.

GOW. Imagine Pericles arriv'd at Tyre,
Welcom'd and settled to his own desire.
His woeful queen we leave at Ephesus,
Unto Diana there* a votaress.
Now to Marina bend your mind,
Whom our fast-growing scene must find
At Tharsus, and by Cleon train'd
In music,† letters; who hath gain'd
Of education all the grace,
Which makes her both the heart and place[a]
Of general wonder. But, alack!
That monster Envy, oft the wrack
Of earned praise, Marina's life
Seeks to take off by treason's knife.
And in this kind hath our Cleon
One daughter, and a wench full grown,[b]
Even ripe[c] for marriage fight; this maid
Hight Philoten: and it is said
For certain in our story, she
Would ever with Marina be.
Be't when she‡ weav'd the sleided silk
With fingers long, small, white as milk;
Or when she would with sharp neeld[d] wound
The cambric, which she made more sound
By hurting it; or when to the lute
She sung, and made the night-bird§ mute
That still records with moan; or when
She would with rich and constant pen
Vail to her mistress Dian; still
This Philoten contends in skill
With absolute Marina: so
With the dove of Paphos might the crow[e]
Vie feathers white. Marina gets
All praises, which are paid as debts,
And not as given. This so darks
In Philoten all graceful marks,
That Cleon's wife, with envy rare,
A present murderer does prepare
For good Marina, that her daughter
Might stand peerless by this slaughter.
The sooner her vile thoughts to stead,
Lychorida, our nurse, is dead.
And cursed Dionyza hath
The pregnant instrument of wrath
Prest for this blow. The unborn event
I do commend to your content;
Only I carry* winged time
Post on the lame feet of my rhyme;
Which never could I so convey,
Unless your thoughts went on my way.—
Dionyza doth appear,
With Leonine, a murderer. [*Exit.*

(*) Old copies, *there's;* altered by Malone.
(†) Old copies, *musick's;* also altered by Malone.
(‡) Old copies, *they.* (§) Old copies, *night bed.*

(*) Old text, *carried.*

[a] *Which makes her*, &c.] The old editions read—

"Which makes *high* both the art and place."

Steevens made the emendation.

[b] A wench full grown,—] In the original this couplet stands,—

"And in this kind our Cleon hath
One daughter, and a full-grown wench."

All Gower's speeches are in rhyme; and Steevens regulated these two lines as they now stand in the text.

[c] *Even* ripe—] So the first quarto, in the library of the Duke of Devonshire; other copies of that edition read, *right.*

[d] *With sharp* neeld—] The old copies read *needle.* In the old play of "Gammer Gurton's Needle," the word is used in both its forms of *neeld* and *needle*, according as it suits the metre.

[e] With the dove of Paphos might the crow, &c.] The old text reads, "The dove of Paphos might with the crow." Corrected by Mason.

ACT IV.

SCENE I.—Tharsus. *An open Place near the Sea-shore.*

Enter DIONYZA *and* LEONINE.

DION. Thy oath remember; thou hast sworn to do 't:
'T is but a blow, which never shall be known.
Thou canst not do a thing in the world so soon,
To yield thee so much profit. Let not conscience,
Which is but cold, inflaming love i' thy bosom,[a]
Inflame too nicely; nor let pity, which
Even women have cast off, melt thee, but be
A soldier to thy purpose.
LEON. I'll do't; but yet she is a goodly creature.
DION. The fitter then the gods should have her.
Here she comes weeping for her only mistress' death.[b]
Thou art resolv'd?
LEON. I am resolv'd.

Enter MARINA, *with a basket of flowers.*

MAR. No, I will rob Tellus of her weed,
To strew thy green with flowers: the yellows, blues,
The purple violets, and marigolds,
Shall, as a carpet, hang upon thy grave,
While summer days do last. Ay me! poor maid,
Born in a tempest when my mother died,
This world to me is like a lasting storm,
Whirring me from my friends.
DION. How now, Marina! why do you keep alone?
How chance my daughter is not with you? Do not
Consume your blood with sorrowing; you have
A nurse of me. Lord! how your favour 's chang'd
With this unprofitable woe! Come,
Give me your flowers: ere the sea mar it,
Walk with Leonine; the air is quick there,
And it pierces and sharpens the stomach.—Come,
Leonine, take her by the arm, walk with her.
MAR. No, I pray you;
I'll not bereave you of your servant.
DION. Come, come;
I love the king your father, and yourself,
With more than foreign heart. We every day

---

[a] Inflaming love i' thy bosom,—] The old copies read, *inflaming thy love bosome;* and, *in flaming, thy love bosome.*

[b] Here she comes weeping for her only mistress' death.] Assuredly corrupt. Malone reads,—

"Here she comes weeping for her only mistress.
Death—thou art resolv'd."

And Percy surmised, "Here *comes* she weeping for her *old nurse's* death."

Expect him here: when he shall come, and find
Our paragon to all reports thus blasted,
He will repent the breadth of his great voyage;
Blame both my lord and me, that we have ta'en
No care to your best courses. Go, I pray you,
Walk, and be cheerful once again; reserve
That excellent complexion which did steal
The eyes of young and old. Care not for me;
I can go home alone.

MAR. Well, I will go;
But yet I have no desire to it.

DION. Come, come, I know 't is good for you.—
Walk half an hour, Leonine, at the least;
Remember what I have said.

LEON. I warrant you, madam.

DION. I 'll leave you, my sweet lady, for a while;
Pray walk softly, do not heat your blood:
What! I must have a care of you.

MAR. My thanks, sweet madam.—
[*Exit* DIONYZA.
Is this wind westerly that blows?

LEON. South-west.

MAR. When I was born, the wind was north.

LEON. Was 't so?

MAR. My father, as nurse said, did never fear,
But cried, *Good seamen!* to the sailors, galling
His kingly hands with haling of the ropes;[a]
And, clasping to the mast, endur'd a sea
That almost burst the deck.

[a] With *haling of the ropes*;] Malone inserted the words, *with* and *of*; the old copies have only—
"His kingly hands haling ropes."

LEON. When was this?

MAR. When I was born.
Never was waves nor wind more violent;
And from the ladder-tackle washes off
A canvas-climber: *Ha!* says one, *wilt out?*
And with a dropping industry they skip
From stem to stern;* the boatswain whistles, and
The master calls, and trebles their confusion.

LEON. Come, say your prayers.

MAR. What mean you?

LEON. If you require a little space for prayer,
I grant it: pray; but be not tedious,
For the gods are quick of ear, and I am sworn
To do my work with haste.

MAR. Why will you kill me?

LEON. To satisfy my lady.

MAR. Why would she have me kill'd?
Now, as I can remember, by my troth,
I never did her hurt in all my life;
I never spake bad word, nor did ill turn,
To any living creature: believe me, la,
I never kill'd a mouse, nor hurt a fly:
I trod upon a worm against my will,
But I wept for it. How have I offended,
Wherein my death might yield her any profit,
Or my life imply her any danger?

LEON. My commission
Is not to reason of the deed, but do it.

MAR. You will not do 't for all the world, I hope.

(*) *Sterne* to sterne, in the original.

You are well-favour'd, and your looks foreshow
You have a gentle heart. I saw you lately,
When you caught hurt in parting two that fought:
Good sooth, it show'd well in you; do so now:
Your lady seeks my life;—come you between,
And save poor me, the weaker.

LEON. I am sworn,
And will despatch.

Whilst MARINA *is struggling, enter* Pirates.

1 PIRATE. Hold, villain!
[LEONINE *runs away.*

2 PIRATE. A prize! a prize!

3 PIRATE. Half-part! mates, half-part! Come, let's have her aboard suddenly.
[*Exeunt* Pirates *with* MARINA.

Re-enter LEONINE.

LEON. These roguing thieves serve the great pirate Valdes;
And they have seiz'd Marina. Let her go;
There's no hope she'll return. I'll swear she's dead,
And thrown into the sea.—(1) But I'll see further;
Perhaps they will but please themselves upon her,
Not carry her aboard. If she remain,
Whom they have ravish'd must by me be slain.
[*Exit.*

SCENE II.—Mitylene. *A Room in a Brothel.*

Enter Pander, Bawd, *and* BOULT.

PAND. Boult,—

BOULT. Sir.

PAND. Search the market narrowly; Mitylene is full of gallants. We lost too much money this mart by being too wenchless.

BAWD. We were never so much out of creatures. We have but poor three, and they can do no more than they can do; and* with continual action are even as good as rotten.

PAND. Therefore let's have fresh ones, whate'er we pay for them. If there be not a conscience to be used in every trade, we shall never prosper.

BAWD. Thou sayest true: 'tis not our bringing up of poor bastards,—as, I think, I have brought up some eleven——

BOULT. Ay, to eleven, and brought them down again.—But shall I search the market?

(*) Old editions insert, *they.*

BAWD. What else, man? The stuff we have, a strong wind will blow it to pieces, they are so pitifully sodden.

PAND. Thou sayest true; they're too* unwholesome o' conscience. The poor Transylvanian is dead, that lay with the little baggage.

BOULT. Ay, she quickly pooped him; she made him roast-meat for worms:—but I'll go search the market. [*Exit* BOULT.

PAND. Three or four thousand chequins were as pretty a proportion to live quietly, and so give over.

BAWD. Why to give over, I pray you? is it a shame to get when we are old?

PAND. O, our credit comes not in like the commodity; nor the commodity wages not with the danger: therefore, if in our youths we could pick up some pretty estate, 't were not amiss to keep our door hatched. Besides, the sore terms we stand upon with the gods, will be strong with us for giving over.

BAWD. Come, other sorts offend as well as we.

PAND. *As well as we!* ay, and better too; we offend worse. Neither is our profession any trade; it's no calling.—But here comes Boult.

Re-enter BOULT *with* MARINA, *and the* Pirates.

BOULT. [*To* MARINA.] Come your ways.—My masters, you say she's a virgin?

1 PIRATE. O sir, we doubt it not.

BOULT. Master, I have gone through for this piece, you see: if you like her, so; if not, I have lost my earnest.

BAWD. Boult, has she any qualities?

BOULT. She has a good face, speaks well, and has excellent good clothes; there's no further necessity of qualities can make her be refused.

BAWD. What's her price, Boult?

BOULT. I cannot be baited one doit of a thousand pieces.

PAND. Well, follow me, my masters; you shall have your money presently.—Wife, take her in; instruct her what she has to do, that she may not be raw in her entertainment.
[*Exeunt* Pander *and* Pirates.

BAWD. Boult, take you the marks of her;—the colour of her hair, complexion, height, age, with warrant of her virginity; and cry, *He that will give most shall have her first.* Such a maidenhead were no cheap thing, if men were as they have been. Get this done as I command you.

BOULT. Performance shall follow. [*Exit.*

(*) Old copies, *ther's* [and *there's*] *two.*

MAR. Alack, that Leonine was so slack, so slow!—
He should have struck, not spoke;—or that these pirates, [me,
Not enough barbarous, had not o'erboard thrown
For to seek my mother!

BAWD. Why lament you, pretty one?

MAR. That I am pretty.

BAWD. Come, the gods have done their part in you.

MAR. I accuse them not.

BAWD. You are lit into my hands, where you are like to live.

MAR. The more my fault,[a]
To 'scape his hands, where I was like to die.

BAWD. Ay, and you shall live in pleasure.

MAR. No.

BAWD. Yes, indeed shall you, and taste gentlemen of all fashions. You shall fare well; you shall have the difference of all complexions. What! do you stop your ears?

MAR. Are you a woman?

BAWD. What would you have me be, an I be not a woman?

MAR. An honest woman, or not a woman.

BAWD. Marry, whip thee, gosling: I think I shall have something to do with you. Come, you're a young foolish sapling, and must be bowed as I would have you.

MAR. The gods defend me!

BAWD. If it please the gods to defend you by men, then men must comfort you, men must feed you, men must stir you up.—Boult's returned.

Re-enter BOULT.

Now, sir, hast thou cried her through the market?

BOULT. I have cried her almost to the number of her hairs; I have drawn her picture with my voice.

BAWD. And I pr'ythee tell me, how dost thou find the inclination of the people, especially of the younger sort?

BOULT. Faith, they listened to me as they would have hearkened to their father's testament. There was a Spaniard's mouth so watered, that he went to bed to her very description.

BAWD. We shall have him here to-morrow, with his best ruff on.

BOULT. To-night, to-night. But, mistress, do you know the French knight that cowers i' the hams?

BAWD. Who? monsieur Veroles?

BOULT. Ay; he offered to cut a caper at the proclamation; but he made a groan at it, and swore he would see her to-morrow.

BAWD. Well, well; as for him, he brought his disease hither: here he doth but repair it. I know he will come in our shadow, to scatter his crowns in the sun.

BOULT. Well, if we had of every nation a traveller, we should lodge them with this sign.

BAWD. Pray you, come hither a while. You have fortunes coming upon you. Mark me; you must seem to do that fearfully which you commit willingly; to* despise profit where you have most gain. To weep that you live as you do makes pity in your lovers: seldom but that pity begets you a good opinion, and that opinion a mere profit.

MAR. I understand you not.

BOULT. O take her home, mistress, take her home: these blushes of hers must be quenched with some present practice.

BAWD. Thou sayest true, i' faith, so they must; for your bride goes to that with shame, which is her way to go with warrant.

BOULT. Faith, some do, and some do not. But, mistress, if I have bargained for the joint,—

BAWD. Thou mayst cut a morsel off the spit?

BOULT. I may so.

BAWD. Who should deny it? Come, young one, I like the manner of your garments well.

BOULT. Ay, by my faith, they shall not be changed yet.

BAWD. Boult, spend thou that in the town: report what a sojourner we have; you'll lose nothing by custom. When nature framed this piece, she meant thee a good turn; therefore say what a paragon she is, and thou hast the harvest out of thine own report.

BOULT. I warrant you, mistress, thunder shall not so awake the beds of eels, as my giving out her beauty stir up the lewdly-inclined. I'll bring home some to-night.

BAWD. Come your ways; follow me.

MAR. If fires be hot, knives sharp, or waters deep,
Untied I still my virgin knot will keep.
Diana, aid my purpose!

BAWD. What have we to do with Diana? pray you, will you go with us? [*Exeunt.*

SCENE III.—Tharsus. *A Room in* Cleon's *House.*

Enter CLEON *and* DIONYZA.

DION. Why, are you foolish? can it be undone?

CLE. O Dionyza, such a piece of slaughter
The sun and moon ne'er look'd upon!

---

[a] *The more my* fault,—] *Fault*, here, means misfortune. See note (d), p. 640, Vol. I.

(*) Old editions omit, *to*.

DION. I think you'll turn a child again. [world,
CLE. Were I chief lord of all this spacious
I'd give it to undo the deed. O lady,
Much less in blood than virtue, yet a princess
To equal any single crown o' the earth,
I' the justice of compare! O villain Leonine!
Whom thou hast poison'd too;
If thou hadst drunk to him, it had been a kindness
Becoming well thy fact:[a] what canst thou say,
When noble Pericles shall demand his child?
DION. That she is dead. Nurses are not the fates,
To foster it, nor ever to preserve.
She died at night; I'll say so. Who can cross it?
Unless you play the pious innocent,
And for an honest attribute, cry out,
She died by foul play.
CLE. O, go to. Well, well,
Of all the faults beneath the heavens, the gods
Do like this worst.
DION. Be one of those that think
The petty wrens of Tharsus will fly hence,
And open this to Pericles. I do shame
To think of what a noble strain you are,
And of how coward a spirit.

CLE. To such proceeding
Who ever but his approbation added,
Though not his pre-consent,[b] he did not flow
From honourable courses.[c]
DION. Be it so, then:
Yet none does know, but you, how she came dead,
Nor none can know, Leonine being gone.
She did distain[d] my child, and stood between
Her and her fortunes: none would look on her,
But cast their gazes on Marina's face;
Whilst ours was blurted at, and held a malkin
Not worth the time of day.[e] It pierc'd me thorough;
And though you call my course unnatural,
You not your child well loving, yet I find,
It greets me as an enterprise of kindness
Perform'd to your sole daughter.
CLE. Heavens forgive it!
DION. And as for Pericles,
What should he say? We wept after her hearse,
And yet we mourn: her monument
Is almost finish'd, and her epitaphs
In glittering golden characters express
A general praise to her, and care in us
At whose expense 'tis done.

---

a *Becoming well thy* fact:] In the old copies, *face*. The emendation is due to Mr. Dyce. Steevens suggested "*feat*."

b *Though not his* pre-*consent*,—] The quarto, 1609, has "*prince* consent," &c.; the other old editions have "*whole* consent." The reading in the text was proposed by Steevens.

c *From honourable* courses.] Mr. Dyce reads *sources*; perhaps rightly.

d *She did* distain *my child*,—] Old copies, *disdaine*. To *distain* meant *to cloud, to eclipse, cast into the shade*.

e ——A malkin
Not worth the time of day.]
A *homely wench*, not deserving the poor courtesy of "Good morning," or "Good even."

CLE. Thou art like the harpy,
Which, to betray, dost, with thine angel's face,
Seize with thine eagle's talons.*

DION. You are like one, that superstitiously
Doth swear to the gods that winter kills the flies:
But yet I know you'll do as I advise. [*Exeunt.*

SCENE IV.—*The same. Before the Monument of* MARINA.

Enter GOWER.

GOW. Thus time we waste, and longest leagues make short,
Sail seas in cockles, have an wish but for 't;
Making,—to take your† imagination,—
From bourn to bourn, region to region.
By you being pardon'd, we commit no crime
To use one language, in each several clime
Where our scenes seem to live. I do beseech you,
To learn of me, who stand i' the gaps to teach you
The stages of our story. Pericles
Is now again thwarting the wayward seas,
Attended on by many a lord and knight,
To see his daughter, all his life's delight.
Old Escanes, whom Helicanus late[a]
Advanc'd in time to great and high estate,
Is left to govern. Bear you it in mind;
Old Helicanus goes along behind.
Well-sailing ships and bounteous winds have [brought
This king to Tharsus,—think his pilot thought;
So with his steerage shall your thoughts grow on,—[b]
To fetch his daughter home, who first is gone.
Like motes and shadows see them move a while;
Your ears unto your eyes I'll reconcile.

Dumb show.

Enter PERICLES *at one door, with his* Train; CLEON *and* DIONYZA *at the other.* CLEON *shows* PERICLES *the tomb of* MARINA; *whereat* PERICLES *makes lamentation, puts on sackcloth, and in a mighty passion departs. Then exeunt* CLEON *and* DIONYZA.

See how belief may suffer by foul show!
This borrow'd passion stands for true old woe;
And Pericles, in sorrow all devour'd,
With sighs shot through, and biggest tears o'er- [show'r'd,
Leaves Tharsus, and again embarks. He swears
Never to wash his face, nor cut his hairs;
He puts on sackcloth, and to sea. He bears
A tempest, which his mortal vessel tears,
And yet he rides it out. Now please you wit
The epitaph is for Marina writ
By wicked Dionyza.
[*Reads the inscription on* MARINA'*s monument.*

The fairest, sweet'st, and best lies here,
Who wither'd in her spring of year:
She was of Tyrus the king's daughter,
On whom foul death hath made this slaughter;
Marina was she call'd; and at her birth,
Thetis, being proud, swallow'd some part o' the earth:
Therefore the earth, fearing to be o'erflow'd,
Hath Thetis' birth-child on the heavens bestow'd;
Wherefore she does, and swears she'll never stint,
Make raging battery upon shores of flint.

No vizor does become black villainy,
So well as soft and tender flattery.
Let Pericles believe his daughter's dead,
And bear his courses to be ordered
By lady Fortune; while our scene* must play
His daughter's woe and heavy well-a-day,
In her unholy service. Patience, then,
And think you now are all in Mitylen. [*Exit.*

SCENE V.—Mitylene. *A Street before the Brothel.*

Enter, from the Brothel, two Gentlemen.

1 GENT. Did you ever hear the like?

2 GENT. No, nor never shall do in such a place as this, she being once gone.

1 GENT. But to have divinity preached there! did you ever dream of such a thing?

2 GENT. No, no. Come, I am for no more bawdy-houses: shall 's go hear the vestals sing?

1 GENT. I'll do anything now that is virtuous, but I am out of the road of rutting for ever. [*Exeunt.*

SCENE VI.—*The same. A Room in the Brothel.*

Enter Pander, Bawd, *and* BOULT.

PAND. Well, I had rather than twice the worth of her she had ne'er come here.

(*) Old editions, *talents.* (†) Old editions, *our.*

[a] Old Escanes, whom Helicanus late, &c.] The present arrangement of these lines was made by Steevens: in the old copies they are thus misplaced:—

"Old Helicanus goes along behind
Is left to governe it, you beare in mind.
Old Escanes whom Helicanus late
Advancde in time to great and hie estate.
Well sailing ships," &c.

[b] —— *Think* his *pilot thought;* &c.] The old copies read:—
"Think *this* pilot thought,
So with his steerage shall your thoughts *groan,*"—
corrected by Malone.

(*) Old copies, *steare.*

BAWD. Fie, fie upon her! she is able to freeze the god Priapus, and undo a whole generation. We must either get her ravished, or be rid of her. When she should do for clients her fitment, and do me the kindness of our profession, she has me her quirks, her reasons, her master-reasons, her prayers, her knees; that she would make a puritan of the devil, if he should cheapen a kiss of her.

BOULT. Faith, I must ravish her, or she'll disfurnish us of all our cavaliers, and make all our swearers priests.

PAND. Now, the pox upon her green-sickness for me!

BAWD. Faith, there's no way to be rid on't, but by the way to the pox.—Here comes the lord Lysimachus, disguised.

BOULT. We should have both lord and lown, if the peevish baggage would but give way to customers.

Enter LYSIMACHUS.

LYS. How now! How a dozen of virginities?

BAWD. Now, the gods to-bless your honour!

BOULT. I am glad to see your honour in good health.

LYS. You may so; 't is the better for you that your resorters stand upon sound legs. How now, wholesome iniquity! Have you that a man may deal withal and defy the surgeon?

BAWD. We have here one, sir, if she would—but there never came her like in Mitylene.

LYS. If she'd do the deed of darkness, thou wouldst say.

BAWD. Your honour knows what 't is to say, well enough.

LYS. Well; call forth, call forth.

BOULT. For flesh and blood, sir, white and red, you shall see a rose; and she were a rose indeed, if she had but——

LYS. What, pr'ythee?

BOULT. O, sir, I can be modest. [*Exit* BOULT.

LYS. That dignifies the renown of a bawd, no less than it gives a good report to a number to be chaste.

BAWD. Here comes that which grows to the stalk;—never plucked yet, I can assure you. Is she not a fair creature?

Re-enter BOULT *with* MARINA.

LYS. Faith, she would serve after a long voyage at sea. Well, there's for you;—leave us.

BAWD. I beseech your honour, give me leave: a word, and I'll have done presently.

LYS. I beseech you, do.

BAWD. [*To* MARINA.] First, I would have you note, this is an honourable man.

MAR. I desire to find him so, that I may worthily note him.

BAWD. Next, he's the governor of this country, and a man whom I am bound to.

MAR. If he govern the country, you are bound to him indeed; but how honourable he is in that, I know not.

BAWD. Pray you, without any more virginal fencing, will you use him kindly? He will line your apron with gold.

MAR. What he will do graciously I will thankfully receive.

LYS. Have you done?

BAWD. My lord, she's not paced yet; you must take some pains to work her to your manage. Come, we will leave his honour and her together.

[*Exeunt* Bawd, Pander, *and* BOULT.

LYS. Go thy ways.[a]—Now, pretty one, how long have you been at this trade?

MAR. What trade, sir?

LYS. What * I cannot name but I shall offend.

MAR. I cannot be offended with my trade; please you to name it.

LYS. How long have you been of this profession?

MAR. Ever since I can remember.

LYS. Did you go to it so young? were you a gamester at five or at seven?

MAR. Earlier too, sir, if now I be one.

LYS. Why, the house you dwell in proclaims you to be a creature of sale.

MAR. Do you know this house to be a place of such resort, and will come into it? I hear say you are of honourable parts, and are the governor of this place.(2)

LYS. Why, hath your principal made known unto you who I am?

MAR. Who is my principal?

LYS. Why, your herb-woman; she that sets seeds and roots of shame and iniquity. O, you have heard something of my power, and so stand aloof † for more serious wooing. But I protest to thee, pretty one, my authority shall not see thee, or else look friendly upon thee. Come, bring me to some private place: come, come.

MAR. If you were born to honour, show it now;
If put upon you, make the judgment good
That thought you worthy of it.

LYS. How's this? how's this?—Some more;—be sage.

MAR. For me,
That am a maid, though most ungentle fortune
Hath plac'd me in this sty, where, since I came,
Diseases have been sold dearer than physic,—
O that the gods
Would set me free from this unhallow'd place,
Though they did change me to the meanest bird
That flies i' the purer air!

LYS. I did not think
Thou couldst have spoke so well; ne'er dream'd thou couldst.
Had I brought hither a corrupted mind,
Thy speech had alter'd it. Hold, here's gold for thee:
Perséver in that clear way thou goest,
And the gods strengthen thee!

MAR. The good gods preserve you!

LYS. For me, be you thoughten
That I came with no ill intent; for to me
The very doors and windows savour vilely.
Fare thee well. Thou art a piece of virtue, and
I doubt not but thy training hath been noble.—
Hold, here's more gold for thee.—
A curse upon him, die he like a thief,
That robs thee of thy goodness! If thou dost
Hear from me, it shall be for thy good.

Re-enter BOULT.

BOULT. I beseech your honour, one piece for me.

LYS. Avaunt, thou damned door-keeper!
Your house, but for this virgin that doth prop it,
Would sink and overwhelm you. Away! [*Exit.*

BOULT. How's this? We must take another course with you. If your peevish chastity, which is not worth a breakfast in the cheapest country under the cope, shall undo a whole household, let me be gelded like a spaniel. Come your ways.

MAR. Whither would you have me?

BOULT. I must have your maidenhead taken off, or the common hangman shall execute it. Come your ways. We'll have no more gentlemen driven away. Come your ways, I say.

Re-enter Bawd.

BAWD. How now! what's the matter?

BOULT. Worse and worse, mistress; she has here spoken holy words to the lord Lysimachus.

BAWD. O abominable!

BOULT. She * makes our profession as it were to stink afore the face of the gods.

BAWD. Marry, hang her up for ever!

BOULT. The nobleman would have dealt with her like a nobleman, and she sent him away as cold as a snowball; saying his prayers too.

(*) Old editions, *Why*. (†) Old copies, *aloft*.

(*) Old copies, *he*.

[a] Go thy ways.—] These words are found only in the quarto of 1609, and there are appended to the Bawd's speech; they seem more appropriate to Lysimachus.

BAWD. Boult, take her away; use her at thy pleasure: crack the glass of her virginity, and make the rest malleable.

BOULT. An if she were a thornier piece of ground than she is, she shall be ploughed.

MAR. Hark, hark, you gods!

BAWD. She conjures: away with her! Would she had never come within my doors! Marry hang you! She's born to undo us.—Will you not go the way of women-kind? Marry come up, my dish of chastity with rosemary and bays!

[*Exit* Bawd.

BOULT. Come, mistress; come your ways with me.

MAR. Whither wilt thou have me?

BOULT. To take from you the jewel you hold so dear.

MAR. Pr'ythee, tell me one thing first.

BOULT. Come now, your one thing.

MAR. What canst thou wish thine enemy to be?

BOULT. Why, I could wish him to be my master, or rather, my mistress.

MAR. Neither of these are so bad as thou art,
Since they do better thee in their command.
Thou hold'st a place, for which the pained'st fiend
Of hell would not in reputation change:
Thou art the damned door-keeper to every
Coistrel that comes inquiring for his Tib;
To the choleric fisting of every rogue
Thy ear is liable; thy food is such
As hath been belch'd on by infected lungs.

BOULT. What would you have me do? go to the wars, would you? where a man may serve seven years for the loss of a leg, and have not money enough in the end to buy him a wooden one?

MAR. Do anything but this thou doest. Empty
Old receptacles, or common sewers, of filth;
Serve by indenture to the common hangman;
Any of these ways are yet better than this:
For what thou professest, a baboon, could he speak,
Would own a name too dear. O, that the gods
Would safely deliver me from this place!
Here, here's gold for thee.
If that thy master would gain aught * by me,
Proclaim that I can sing, weave, sew, and dance,
With other virtues, which I'll keep from boast;
And I will undertake all these to teach.
I doubt not but this populous city will
Yield many scholars.

BOULT. But can you teach all this you speak of?

MAR. Prove that I cannot, take me home again,
And prostitute me to the basest groom
That doth frequent your house.

BOULT. Well, I will see what I can do for thee: if I can place thee, I will.

MAR. But amongst honest women? (3)

BOULT. Faith, my acquaintance lies little amongst them. But since my master and mistress have bought you, there's no going but by their consent: therefore I will make them acquainted with your purpose, and I doubt not but I shall find them tractable enough. Come, I'll do for thee what I can; come your ways. [*Exeunt.*

(*) Old copies omit, *aught*.

Enter GOWER.

GOW. Marina thus the brothel scapes, and chances
Into an honest house, our story says.
She sings like one immortal, and she dances
As goddess-like to her admired lays:
Deep clerks she dumbs; and with her neeld composes
Nature's own shape, of bud, bird, branch, or berry;
That even her art sisters the natural roses;
Her inkle, silk, twin * with the rubied cherry:
That pupils lacks she none of noble race,
Who pour their bounty on her; and her gain
She gives the cursed bawd. Here we her place;
And to her father turn our thoughts again,
Where we left him, on the sea. We there him lost:
Whence, driven before the winds, he is arriv'd [a]
Here where his daughter dwells; and on this coast
Suppose him now at anchor. The city striv'd
God Neptune's annual feast to keep: from whence
Lysimachus our Tyrian ship espies,
His banners sable, trimm'd with rich expense;
And to him in his barge with fervour hies.
In your supposing once more put your sight
Of heavy Pericles; think this his bark:
Where what is done in action, more, if might,
Shall be discover'd; please you, sit, and hark.
[*Exit.*

(*) Old copies, *twine*.

[a] Where we left him, on the sea. We there him lost:
Whence, driven before the winds, he is arriv'd, &c.]

This is the reading of Malone. In the quarto of 1609, the lines run,—

"Where wee left him on the sea, wee there him *left*,
Where driven before the windes, he is arriv'de," &c.

In the subsequent old copies,—

"Where we left him *at* sea, *tumbled and tost*,
And driven before the winde, he is arriv'de," &c.

ACT V.

SCENE I.—Mitylene. *On board* PERICLES' *ship. A close Pavilion on deck, with a curtain before it;* PERICLES *within, reclined on a couch. A barge lying beside the* Tyrian *vessel.*

Enter two Sailors, *one belonging to the* Tyrian *vessel, the other to the barge.*

TYR. SAIL. [*To the* Sailor *of* Mitylene.] Where is the lord Helicane?[a] he can resolve you.
O, here he is.—

Enter HELICANUS.

Sir, there 's a barge put off from Mitylene,
And in it is Lysimachus the governor,
Who craves to come aboard. What is your will?

HEL. That he have his. Call up some gentlemen.

TYR. SAIL. Ho, gentlemen! my lord calls.

Enter two Gentlemen.

1 GENT. Doth your lordship call?

HEL. Gentlemen,
There is some of worth[b] would come aboard; I pray,
Greet him fairly.

[*The* Gentlemen *and* Sailors *go on board the barge.*

Enter from thence LYSIMACHUS, *attended; the* Gentlemen, *and* Sailors.

TYR. SAIL. Sir,
This is the man that can, in aught you would,
Resolve you.

LYS. Hail, reverend sir! The gods preserve you!

HEL. And you, sir, to outlive the age I am,
And die as I would do.

LYS. You wish me well.
Being on shore, honouring of Neptune's triumphs,
Seeing this goodly vessel ride before us,
I made to it, to know of whence you are.

HEL. First, what is your place?

LYS. I am the governor of this place you lie before.

HEL. Sir,
Our vessel is of Tyre, in it the king;
A man, who for this three months hath not spoken
To any one, nor taken sustenance,
But to prorogue his grief.

LYS. Upon what ground is his distemperature?

---

[a] *Where is the lord* Helicane?] The old editions (except that of 1609, which omits *the*) read, "Where is the Lord *Helicanus?*" We believe, here and in some other instances, where the old text has *Helicanus*, the author wrote *Helicane*.

[b] Some *of worth*—] So the old copies; but the usual reading has been,—Some *one* of worth. The late Mr. Barron Field, however, produced a passage from Heywood to show that the expression *some* was formerly employed for *some person*,—

"Besides a sudden noise
Of *some* that swiftly ran towards your fields:
Make haste; 'twas now; *he* cannot be far off."—
Fortune by Land and Sea, Act II. Sc. 3.

HEL. 'T would be too tedious to repeat;
But the main grief[a] springs from the loss
Of a beloved daughter and a wife.
LYS. May we not see him?
HEL. You may, [to any.
But bootless is your sight;—he will not speak
LYS. Yet let me obtain my wish.
HEL. Behold him. [PERICLES *discovered.*] This was a goodly person,
Till the disaster that, one mortal night,*
Drove him to this.
LYS. Sir king, all hail! the gods preserve you!
Hail, royal sir!
HEL. It is in vain; he will not speak to you.
LORD. Sir,
We have a maid in Mitylen, I durst wager,
Would win some words of him.
LYS. 'T is well bethought.
She, questionless, with her sweet harmony,
And other chosen attractions, would allure,
And make a battery through his deafen'd parts,
Which now are midway stopp'd:
She is all happy as the fair'st of all,
And, with her fellow-maids, is[b] now upon
The leafy shelter that abuts against
The island's side.
[*Whispers a* Lord, *who goes off in the barge of* LYSIMACHUS.
HEL. Sure, all's† effectless; yet nothing we'll omit [kindness
That bears recovery's name. But since your
We have stretch'd thus far, let us beseech you,
That for our gold we may provision have,
Wherein we are not destitute for want,
But weary for the staleness.
LYS. O, sir, a courtesy
Which if we should deny, the most just gods
For every graff would send a caterpillar,
And so inflict our province.—Yet once more,
Let me entreat to know at large the cause
Of your king's sorrow.
HEL. Sit, sir, I will recount it to you:—
But see, I am prevented.

Re-enter from the barge, Lord, *with* MARINA, *and a* Lady.

LYS. O, here is
The lady that I sent for. Welcome, fair one!
Is't not a goodly presence?*
HEL. She's a gallant lady.
LYS. She's such a one, that were I well assur'd
Came of a gentle kind and noble stock, [wed.—
I'd wish no better choice, and think me rarely
Fair one, all goodness that consists in bounty†
Expect even here, where is a kingly patient:
If that thy prosperous and artificial feat[c]
Can draw him but to answer thee in aught,
Thy sacred physic shall receive such pay
As thy desires can wish.
MAR. Sir, I will use
My utmost skill in his recovery,
Provided none but I and my companion ‡
Be suffer'd to come near him.
LYS. Come, let us leave her,
And the gods make her prosperous!
[MARINA *sings.*(1)
LYS. Mark'd he your music?
MAR. No, nor look'd on us.
LYS. See, she will speak to him.
MAR. Hail, sir! my lord, lend ear.—
PER. Hum, ha!
MAR. I am a maid,
My lord, that ne'er before invited eyes,
But have been gaz'd on like a comet: she speaks,
My lord, that, may be, hath endur'd a grief
Might equal yours, if both were justly weigh'd.
Though wayward fortune did malign my state,
My derivation was from ancestors
Who stood equivalent with mighty kings:
But time hath rooted out my parentage,
And to the world and awkward casualties
Bound me in servitude.—[*Aside.*] I will desist;
But there is something glows upon my cheek,
And whispers in mine ear, *Go not till he speak.*
PER. My fortunes—parentage—good parentage—
To equal mine!—was it not thus? what say you?
MAR. I said, my lord, if you did know my parentage
You would not do me violence. [upon me.
PER. I do think so. Pray you, turn your eyes
You are like something, that—What countrywoman?
Here of these shores?[d]
MAR. No, nor of any shores:
Yet I was mortally brought forth, and am
No other than I appear.

(*) *Wight,* in all the old copies. (†) Old editions, *all.*

[a] But the main grief—] Something has evidently dropped out. The omission is ordinarily supplied by reading,—

"But the main grief *of all* springs from the loss," &c.

[b] *And,* with *her fellow-maids,* is *now upon*—] The words *with* and *is* are of modern interpolation.

[c] *Artificial* feat—] Dr. Percy suggested this reading, the old copies having *fate.*

[d] *Here of these* shores?] The emendation of *shores* for *shewes* was suggested to Malone by the Earl of Charlemont. The passage as it stands in the old editions, will afford the reader some notion of the state in which this most unfortunate of dramas has come down to us:—

"PER. I do thinke so, pray you turne your eyes upon me, your like something that, what countrey women heare of these shewes.
MAR. No, nor of any shewes, &c."

(*) Old editions, *present.*
(†) Old copies, *beauty;* corrected by Steevens.
(‡) Old editions add, *maid.*

PER. I am great with woe, and shall deliver weeping.
My dearest wife was like this maid, and such a one
My daughter might have been: my queen's square brows;
Her stature to an inch; as wand-like straight;
As silver-voic'd; her eyes as jewel-like,
And cas'd as richly: in pace another Juno;
Who starves the ears she feeds, and makes them hungry,
The more she gives them speech. Where do you live?

MAR. Where I am but a stranger: from the deck
You may discern the place.

PER. Where were you bred?
And how achiev'd you these endowments, which
You make more rich to owe?

MAR. If I should tell my history, it would seem
Like lies disdain'd in the reporting.

PER. Pr'ythee, speak;
Falseness cannot come from thee, for thou look'st
Modest as Justice, and thou seem'st a palace
For the crown'd Truth to dwell in: I will believe thee,
And make my senses credit thy relation
To points that seem impossible; for thou look'st
Like one I lov'd indeed. What were thy friends?
Didst thou not say,* when I did push thee back,
(Which was when I perceiv'd thee,) that thou cam'st
From good descending?

MAR. So indeed I did.

PER. Report thy parentage. I think thou said'st
Thou hadst been toss'd from wrong to injury,
And that thou thought'st thy griefs might equal mine,
If both were open'd.

MAR. Some such thing I said,
And said no more but what my thoughts
Did warrant me was likely.

PER. Tell thy story;
If thine consider'd prove the thousandth part
Of my endurance, thou art a man, and I
Have suffer'd like a girl: yet thou dost look
Like Patience gazing on kings' graves and smiling
Extremity out of act. What were thy friends?
How lost thou them?† Thy name, my most kind virgin?
Recount, I do beseech thee; come, sit by me.

MAR. My name is Marina.

(*) Old copies, *stay*
(†) Old copies, *How lost thou thy name?* corrected by Malone.

PER. O, I am mock'd,
And thou by some incensed god sent hither
To make the world to laugh at me.
MAR. Patience, good sir,
Or here I'll cease.
PER. Nay, I'll be patient;
Thou little know'st how thou dost startle me,
To call thyself Marina.
MAR. The name
Was given me by one that had some power;
My father and a king.
PER. How! a king's daughter?
And call'd Marina?
MAR. You said you would believe me;
But, not to be a troubler of your peace,
I will end here.
PER. But are you flesh and blood?
Have you a working pulse? and are no fairy?
Motion?—Well; speak on. Where were you born?
And wherefore called Marina?
MAR. Call'd Marina,
For I was born at sea.
PER. At sea! what mother?
MAR. My mother was the daughter of a king;
Who died the very * minute I was born,
As my good nurse Lychorida hath oft
Deliver'd weeping.
PER. O, stop there a little!
[*Aside.*] This is the rarest dream that e'er dull sleep
Did mock sad fools withal: this cannot be:
My daughter's† buried. Well;—where were you bred?
I'll hear you more, to the bottom of your story,
And never interrupt you.
MAR. You scorn to believe me;[a] 't were best I did give o'er.
PER. I will believe you by the syllable
Of what you shall deliver. Yet give me leave—
How came you in these parts? where were you bred?
MAR. The king my father did in Tharsus leave me;
Till cruel Cleon, with his wicked wife,
Did seek to murder me: and having woo'd
A villain to attempt it, who having drawn to do 't,
A crew of pirates came and rescued me;
Brought me to Mitylene. But, good sir, whither
Will you have me? Why do you weep? It may be
You think me an impostor; no, good faith;
I am the daughter to king Pericles,
If good king Pericles be.
PER. Ho, Helicanus!
HEL. Calls my lord?
PER. Thou art a grave and noble counsellor,
Most wise in general; tell me, if thou canst,
What this maid is, or what is like to be,
That thus hath made me weep?
HEL. I know not; but
Here is the regent, sir, of Mitylene
Speaks nobly of her.
LYS. She would never * tell
Her parentage; being demanded that,
She would sit still and weep.
PER. O, Helicanus, strike me, honour'd sir;
Give me a gash, put me to present pain;
Lest this great sea of joys rushing upon me
O'erbear the shores of my mortality,
And drown me with their sweetness. O, come hither,
Thou that begett'st him that did thee beget;
Thou that wast born at sea, buried at Tharsus,
And found at sea again!—O, Helicane,†
Down on thy knees, thank the holy gods as loud
As thunder threatens us: this is Marina.—
What was thy mother's name? tell me but that,
For truth can never be confirm'd enough,
Though doubts did ever sleep.
MAR. First, sir, I pray,
What is your title?
PER. I am Pericles of Tyre; but tell me now
My drown'd queen's name:—as in the rest you said,
Thou hast been god-like perfect,—the heir of kingdoms,
And another-life[b] to Pericles thy father.
MAR. Is it no more to be your daughter, than
To say my mother's name was Thaisa?
Thaisa was my mother, who did end
The minute I began.
PER. Now, blessing on thee! rise; thou art my child.—(2)
Give me fresh garments. Mine own Helicane,†
She is not dead at Tharsus, as she should have been,
By savage Cleon: she shall tell thee all;
When thou shalt kneel, and justify in knowledge,
She is thy very princess.—Who is this?
HEL. Sir, 'tis the governor of Mitylene,
Who, hearing of your melancholy state,
Did come to see you.
PER. I embrace you.—

(*) *Very* added by Malone. (†) Old editions, *daughter*.

(*) Old editions, *She never would.*
(†) Old editions, *Helicanus.*

[a] *You scorn to believe me;* &c.] The old editions have, "*You scorn believe me,*" &c., which Malone changed to, "You'll scarce believe me," &c.

[b] *And* another-life to *Pericles* thy father.] In the old text,—"And another like," &c. We adopt the easy alteration proposed by Mason, though we have doubts whether the author did not write,—"And *mother*-like to Pericles thy father," *i.e.* like one to whom he owed existence, by whom he was new-born.

Give me my robes.—I am wild in my beholding.—
O heavens bless my girl! — But hark, what music?—
Tell Helicanus, my Marina, tell him
O'er point by point, for yet he seems to doubt,*
How sure you are my daughter.—But what music?
HEL. My lord, I hear none.
PER. None!
The music of the spheres!—List, my Marina.
LYS. It is not good to cross him; give him way.
PER. Rarest sounds! do ye not hear?
LYS. My lord, I hear— [*Music.*
PER. Most heavenly music!
It nips me unto listening, and thick slumber
Hangs upon mine eyes; let me rest. [*He sleeps.*
LYS. A pillow for his head:—
So leave him all.—Well, my companion-friends,
If this but answer to my just belief,
I'll well remember you.
[*Exeunt all except* PERICLES.

DIANA *appears to* PERICLES *as in a vision.*

DIA. My temple stands in Ephesus; hie thee thither,
And do upon mine altar sacrifice.
There, when my maiden priests are met together,
Before the people all
Reveal how thou at sea didst lose thy wife:
To mourn thy crosses, with thy daughter's, call,
And give them repetition to the life.[a]
Or perform my bidding, or thou liv'st in woe:
Do it, and happy:[b] by my silver bow!
Awake and tell thy dream. [DIANA *disappears.*(3)
PER. Celestial Dian, goddess argentine,
I will obey thee!—Helicanus!

Enter LYSIMACHUS, HELICANUS, *and* MARINA.

HEL. Sir?
PER. My purpose was for Tharsus, there to strike
Th' inhospitable Cleon; but I am
For other service first: toward Ephesus
Turn our blown sails: eftsoons I'll tell thee why.—
Shall we refresh us, sir, upon your shore,
[*To* LYSIMACHUS.
And give you gold for such provision
As our intents will need?
LYS. Sir,
With all my heart; and when you come ashore,

(*) Old copies, *doat.*

[a] *Repetition to the* life.] The old copies read *like;* but, as Malone observes, this vision is founded upon a corresponding passage in Gower:—

"To Ephesim he bade hym drawe,
And as it was that tyme lawe
He shal do ther hys sacrafice:
And eke he bade in alle wise,
That in the temple amonges alle
His fortune, as it is byfalle
Towchyng his douhter, and his wiff,
He shalle be knowe uppon his liff."
Confessio Amantis.

[b] And happy:] That is, and *be* happy.

I have another suit.*

PER. You shall prevail,
Were it to woo my daughter; for it seems
You have been noble towards her.

LYS. Sir, lend me your arm.

PER. Come, my Marina. [*Exeunt.*

SCENE II.—Ephesus. *Before the Temple of* DIANA.

Enter GOWER.

GOW. Now our sands are almost run:
More a little, and then dumb.
This, as my last boon, give me,[a]
(For such kindness must relieve me,)
That you aptly will suppose
What pageantry, what feats, what shows,
What minstrelsy, and pretty din,
The regent made in Mitylin,
To greet the king. So he thriv'd,
That he is promis'd to be wiv'd
To fair Marina; but in no wise,
Till he had done his sacrifice,
As Dian bade: whereto being bound
The interim, pray you, all confound.
In feather'd briefness sails are fill'd,
And wishes fall out as they 're will'd.
At Ephesus, the temple see,
Our king, and all his company.
That he can hither come so soon,
Is by your fancy's thankful doom.

[*Exit.*

SCENE III.—*The same. The interior of the Temple;* THAISA *standing near the altar, as* High Priestess; *a number of* Virgins *on each side;* CERIMON *and other* Inhabitants *of* Ephesus *attending.*

Enter PERICLES *with his* Train; LYSIMACHUS, HELICANUS, MARINA, *and a* Lady.

PER. Hail, Dian! to perform thy just command,
I here confess myself the king of Tyre;
Who, frighted from my country, did wed
The fair Thaisa at Pentapolis.[b]
At sea, in childbed died she, but brought forth
A maid-child called Marina; who, O goddess,
Wears yet thy silver livery. She at Tharsus
Was nurs'd with Cleon; who at fourteen years
He sought to murder: but her better stars
Brought her to Mitylene; against whose shore
Riding, her fortunes brought the maid aboard us,
Where, by her own most clear remembrance, she
Made known herself my daughter.

THAI. Voice and favour!—
You are, you are—O royal Pericles!—

[*She faints.*

PER. What means the woman? she dies! help, gentlemen!

CER. Noble sir,
If you have told Diana's altar true,
This is your wife.

PER. Reverend appearer, no;
I threw her o'erboard with these very arms.

CER. Upon this coast, I warrant you.

PER. 'Tis most certain.

CER. Look to the lady;—O, she's but o'erjoyed.—
Early in blust'ring morn this lady was
Thrown upon this shore. I op'd the coffin,
Found there rich jewels; recover'd her, and plac'd her
Here in Diana's temple.

PER. May we see them?

CER. Great sir, they shall be brought you to my house,
Whither I invite you. Look, Thaisa is
Recovered.

THAI. O, let me look!
If he be none of mine, my sanctity
Will to my sense bend no licentious ear,
But curb it, spite of seeing. O, my lord,
Are you not Pericles? Like him you speak,
Like him you are: did you not name a tempest,
A birth, and death?

PER. The voice of dead Thaisa!

THAI. That Thaisa am I, supposed dead
And drowned.

PER. Immortal Dian!

THAI. Now I know you better.—
When we with tears parted Pentapolis,
The king, my father, gave you such a ring.

[*Shows a ring.*

PER. This, this; no more, you gods! your present kindness
Makes my past miseries sport: you shall do well,
That on the touching of her lips I may
Melt, and no more be seen. O, come, be buried
A second time within these arms.

MAR. My heart
Leaps to be gone into my mother's bosom.

[*Kneels to* THAISA.

PER. Look, who kneels here! Flesh of thy flesh, Thaisa;
Thy burthen at the sea, and call'd Marina

(*) Old copies, *sleight.*

[a] This, as my last boon, give me,—] We should perhaps read,—"This my last boon *freely* give me." Steevens partially remedied the defective measure by inserting "*as*."—"This *as* my last," and his lection has been usually followed.

[b] The fair Thaisa at Pentapolis.] The old editions have,—
"At Pentapolis the fair Thaisa."

For she was yielded there.
THAI. Bless'd, and mine own!
HEL. Hail, madam, and my queen!
THAI. I know you not.
PER. You have heard me say, when I did fly from Tyre,
I left behind an ancient substitute.
Can you remember what I call'd the man?
I have nam'd him oft.
THAI. 'T was Helicanus then.
PER. Still confirmation:
Embrace him, dear Thaisa; this is he.
Now do I long to hear how you were found;
How possibly preserv'd; and who to thank,
Besides the gods, for this great miracle.
THAI. Lord Cerimon, my lord; this man,
Through whom the gods have shown their power; that can
From first to last resolve you.
PER. Reverend sir,
The gods can have no mortal officer
More like a god than you. Will you deliver
How this dead queen re-lives?
CER. I will, my lord.
Beseech you, first go with me to my house,
Where shall be shown you all was found with her;
How she came placed here in the temple;
No needful thing omitted.
PER. Pure Dian! bless thee for thy vision!
I will offer night-oblations to thee.—Thaisa,
This prince, the fair-betrothed of your daughter,
Shall marry her at Pentapolis.—And now,
This ornament
Makes me look dismal, will I clip to form,
And what these fourteen years no razor touch'd,
To grace thy marriage-day, I'll beautify.
THAI. Lord Cerimon hath letters of good credit, sir;
My father's dead.
PER. Heavens make a star of him! Yet there, my queen,
We'll celebrate their nuptials, and ourselves
Will in that kingdom spend our following days;
Our son and daughter shall in Tyrus reign.—
Lord Cerimon, we do our longing stay,
To hear the rest untold.—Sir, lead 's (4) the way.
[*Exeunt omnes.*

Enter GOWER.

GOW. In Antiochus and his daughter, you have heard
Of monstrous lust the due and just reward:
In Pericles, his queen and daughter, seen
(Although assail'd with fortune fierce and keen)
Virtue preserv'd* from fell destruction's blast,
Led on by heaven, and crown'd with joy at last.
In Helicanus may you well descry
A figure of truth, of faith, of loyalty:
In reverend Cerimon there well appears
The worth that learned charity aye wears.
For wicked Cleon and his wife, when fame
Had spread their cursed deed, and† honour'd name
Of Pericles, to rage the city turn;
That him and his they in his palace burn.
The gods for murder seemed so content
To punish them;‡ although not done, but meant.
So, on your patience ever more attending,
New joy wait on you! Here our play hath ending.
[*Exit* GOWER.

(*) *Preferr'd*, in all the old copies; corrected by Malone.
(†) Quartos, *the*.
(‡) Old copies omit, *them*, which was added by Malone.

ILLUSTRATIVE COMMENTS.

ACT I.

(1) SCENE I.—

That, without covering, save yon field of stars,
Here they stand martyrs, slain in Cupid's wars.]

"The fader, whanne he understode
That thei his deuhter thus bysouhte,
With alle his wit he caste and souhte
Howe that he miht fynde a lette;
And thus a statute than he sette,
And in this wise his lawe he taxeth—
That what man that his douhter axeth,
But if he couth his questionn
Assoile, uponne suggestion
Of certen thinges that bifelle,
The wich he wolde unto hym telle,
He sholde in certeyn lese his hede.
And thus ther were many dede,
Here hedes stondyng on the gate
Tille atte laste, longe and late,
For lakke of answere in the wise,
The remenaunt, that weren wise,
Escheweden to make assaie."
GOWER: *Confessio Amantis.*

(2) SCENE I.—

It fits thee not to ask the reason why,
Because we bid it.]

In Twine's translation of Apollonius Tyrius, Antiochus confides to Thaliard the cause of his animosity to the Prince. The author follows Gower:—

"He hadde a felowe bacheler
Wich was the pryve conceiler,
And Taliart by name he hiht,
The kynge a stronge puysone diht
With inne a boxe, and golde therto,
In all hast and badde hym go
Strauht unto Tyr, and for no coste
Ne spare, til he hadde loste
The prynce, wich he wolde spille."

(3) SCENE III.—*Well, I perceive, he was a wise fellow, and had good discretion, that, being bid to ask what he would of the king, desired he might know none of his secrets.*] "Who this wise fellow was, may be known from the following passage in Barnabie Riche's 'Souldier's Wishe to Briton's Welfare, or Captaine Skill and Captaine Pill,' 1604, p. 27:—'I will therefore commende the poet Philipides, who, being demaunded by King Lisimachus, what favour he might doe unto him for that he loved him, made this answere to the king, That your majesty would never impart unto me *any of your secrets.*'"—STEEVENS.

ACT II.

(1) GOWER.—*And, to remember what he does,*
Build his statue to make him glorious.]

So in the *Confessio Amantis*:—

"That they for ever in remembraunce
Made a figure in resemblaunce
Of hym, and in comonne place
They sett it upp; so that his face
Miht every maner man by holde,
So that the cite was by holde.
It was of latonn over gilte;
Thus hath he not his yifte spilte."

(2) SCENE I.—

Which if you shall refuse, when I am dead,
For that I am a man, pray see me buried.]

This scene is apparently formed upon the corresponding description in Twine's version:—"And whilest he spake these wordes, hee sawe a man comming towardes him, and he was a rough fisherman, with an hoode upon his head, and a filthie leatherne pelt upon his backe, unseemely clad, and homely to beholde.

"When hee drewe neare, Apollonius, the present necessitie constraining him thereto, fell down prostrate at his feet, and powring forth a floud of teares he said unto him: Whosoever thou art, take pitie upon a poore sea-wracked man, cast up nowe naked, and in simple state, yet borne of no base degree, but sprung foorth of noble parentage. And that thou maiest in helping me knowe whome thou succourest, I am that Apollonius, Prince of Tyrus, whome most part of the worlde knoweth; and I beseech thee to preserve my life by shewing mee friendly reliefe. When the fisherman beheld the comlinesse and beautie of the yoong gentleman, hee was mooved with compassion towardes him, and lifted him up from the grounde and lead him into his house, and feasted him with such fare as he presently had; and the more amplie to expresse his great affection towardes him, he disrobed himselfe of his poore and simple cloke, and, dividing it into two parts, gave the one halfe thereof unto Apollonius, saying: Take here at my handes such poore entertainment and furniture as I have, and goe into the citie, where perhappes thou shalt finde some of better abilitie, that will rue thine estate: and if thou doe not, returne then againe hither unto mee, and thou shalt not want what may be performed by the povertie of a poore fisherman."

(3) SCENE III.—

And further tell him, we desire to know of him,
Of whence he is, his name and parentage.]

Thus in Gower:—

"The kynge behelde his hevynesse,
And of his grete gentilesse

His douhter, wich was faire and gode,
And att the borde by fore hym stode,
As it was thilke tyme usage,
He bade to go on his message,
And fonde for to make him gladde.
And she dede as her fader bade,
And goth to hym the softe pas,
And axeth whence and what he was."

(4) SCENE V.—*Exeunt.*] In the *Confessio Amantis*, as in the play, the princess reveals her love for the knight of Tyre in a letter to her father :—

"So write I to yowe, fader, thus .—
But if y have Appolinus,
Of alle this worlde what so bytide,
I wolle noon othir man abide;
And certes if I of hym faile,
I wote riht welle, with outen faile,
Ye shull for me be douhterles.
This lettir came, and ther was prees
To fore the kyng, there as he stode ;
And whan that he it understode,
He yaff hem answere by and by :
Bot that was do so pryvely,
That noon of othir counceile wiste.

* * * * * * *

And whan that he to chambre is come,
He hath in to his conceile nome
This man of Tyr, and let hym se
This lettir, and alle the pryvete
The wiche his douhter to hym sente."

ACT III.

(1) SCENE I.—

——— *Now the good gods*
Throw their best eyes upon it!]

It may be interesting to compare this scene with the one Wilkins worked up from it and the parallel description in the old novel :—"With which stirre (good Lady) her eies and eares, hauing not till then bin acquainted, she is strucke into such a hasty fright, that welladay she falles in travell, is delivered of a daughter, and in this childe-birth dies, while her princely husband being above the hatches, is one while praying to heaven for her safe deliverance, an other while suffering for the sorow wherwith he knew his Quéene was imburthened. he chid the contrary storme (as if it had béen sensible of hearing) to be so unmanerly, in this unfitting season, and when so good a Quéene was in labor, to kéep such a blustering : thus while the good Prince remayned reprooving the one, and pittying the other, up comes Lycorida the Nurse, sent along by good Symonides with his daughter, and into his armes delivers his Sea-borne Babe, which he taking to kisse, and pittying it with these words : Poore inch of Nature (quoth he) thou arte as rudely welcome to the worlde, as ever Princesse Babe was, and hast as chiding a nativitie, as fire, ayre, earth, and water can affoord thee, when, as if he had forgot himselfe, he abruptly breaks out : but say Licorida, how doth my Quéene ? O sir (quoth she) she hath now passed all daungers, and hath giuen uppe her griefes by ending her life. At which wordes, no tongue is able to expresse the tide of sorrowe that overbounded Pericles, first looking on his Babe, and then crying out for the mother, pittying the one that had lost her bringer ere shée had scarce saluted the worlde, lamenting for himselfe that had béene bereft of so inestimable a Iewell by the losse of his wife, in which sorrowe as he would haue procéeded, uppe came the Maister to him, who for that the storme continued still in his tempestuous height, brake off his sorrowe with these sillables. Sir, the necessitie of the time affoordes no delay, and we must intreate you to be contented, to have the dead body of your Quéene throwne over-boorde. How varlet ! quoth Pericles, interrupting him, wouldest thou have me cast that body into the sea for buriall, who being in misery received me into favour ? We must intreate you to temperance sir (quoth the Maister) as you respect your owne safety, or the prosperitie of that prety Babe in your armes. At the naming of which word Babe, Pericles, looking mournfully upon it, shooke his heade, and wept. But the Maister going on, tolde him, that by long experience they had tried, that a shippe may not abide to carry a dead carcasse, nor would the lingering tempest cease while the dead body remayned with them. But the Prince, séeking againe to perswade them, tolde them, that it was but the fondnes of their superstition to thinke so. Call it by what you shal please sir (quoth the Maister) but we that by long practise have tried the proofe of it, if not with your graunt, then without your consent (for your owne safety, which wée with all duety tender) must so dispose of it. So calling for his servants about him, he willed one of them, to bring him a chest, which he foorthwith caused to be well bitumed and well leaded for her coffin, then taking up the body of his (even in death) faire Thaysa, he arrayed her in princely apparrell, placing a Crowne of golde uppon her head, with his owne hands, (not without store of funerall teares) he layed her in that Toombe, then placed hée also store of golde at her head, and great treasure of silver at her féete, and having written this Letter, which he layd upon her breast, with fresh water flowing in his eyes, as loath to leave her sight, he nayled up the Chest, the Tenor of which writing was in forme as followeth :—

If ere it hap this Chest be driven
On any shoare, or coast or haven,
I Pericles the Prince of Tyre,
(That loosing her, lost all desire,)
Intreat you give her burying,
Since she was daughter to a king :
This golde I giue you as a fee,
The Gods requite your charitie."

(2) SCENE II.—*And Æsculapius guide us.*] Compare this incident with its prototype in Gower :—

"Riht as the corps was throwe on londe,
There came walkying uponn the stronde,
A worthy clerk, a surgyen,
And eke a grete phisicien,
Of all that londe the wisest oon,
Wich hiht maister Cerymon :
There were of his disciples somme,
This maister to the cofre is come,
And peyseth ther was sommewhat inne,
And bade hem bere it to his inne,
And goth hymself forth with alle,
All that shall falle, falle shalle.

Thei comen home, and tarye nouht :
This cofre in to chambre brouht,
Wich that thei fynde faste stoke,
Bot thei with crafte it have unloke.
Thei loken inne, where as thei founde
A body ded, wich was i wounde
In cloth of golde, as I seide er :
The tresour eke they founden ther

Forth with the letter, wich thei rede,
And tho thei token bettir hede.
Unsowed was the body sone:
As he that knewe what was to done,
This noble clerke, with alle haste
Be ganne the veynes for to taste,
And seih hire age was of youthe:
*   *   *   *   *
Thei leide hire on a couche softe,
And with a shete warmed ofte
Here colde breste be ganne to hete
Here herte also to flakke and bete.
This maister hath here every joynt
With certeyn oyle and bawme enoynt,
And put a liquour in here mouthe,
Wich is to fewe clerkes couthe,
So that she covereth att the laste.
And fyrst hir yhen uppe she caste,
And whan she more of strenth cauht,
Here armes both forth she strauht,
Helde up here honde, and petously
She spake, and seide, A! where am I?
Where is my lorde? What worlde is this?
As she that wote nouht how it is."

(3) Scene III.—*Come, my lord.*] So in Gower:—

"——— My frende Strangulio,
Lo thus, and thus it is by falle:
And thou thi self arte oon of alle,
Forth with thy wiff, that I most triste:
For thi if it yow both liste,
My douhter Thayse, by youre leve,
I thenke shalle with yow bileve
As for a tyme; and thus I pray
That she be kepte by alle weye:
And whan she hath of age more,
That she be sette to bokes lore.
And this avowe to God I make
That I shal never for hire sake
My berde for no lykyng shave,
Tille it befalle that I have,
In covenable tyme of age,
By sette hire unto mariage."

ACT IV.

(1) Scene I.—

Whom they have ravish'd must by me be slain.]

In the present scene the author appears to have followed Twine, rather than Gower, as the latter makes no mention of Marina's affectionate visits to her nurse's tomb. The name of Dionyza's confederate is, however, borrowed from Gower; Leonine, in the *Confessio Amantis,* being the name of the brothel-keeper at Mitylene:—

"When Dionisiades heard Tharsia commended, and her owne daughter Philomacia so dispraised, shee returned home wonderfull wroth, and, withdrawing herselfe into a solitary place, began thus secretly to discourse of the matter:—It is now fourteen yeares since Apollonius, this foolish girles father, departed from hence, and he never sendeth letters for her, nor any remembrance unto her, whereby I conjecture that he is dead. Ligozides, her nurce, is departed, and there is no bodie now of whom I should stand in feare, and therefore I will now slay her, and dresse up mine owne daughter in her apparell and jewels. When shee had thus resolved her selfe uppon this wicked purpose, in the meane while there came home one of their countrey villaines, called Theophilus, whom shee called, and said thus unto him:—Theophilus, my trustie friend, if ever thou looke for libertie, or that I shoulde doe thee pleasure, doe so much for me as to slay Tharsia. Then said Theophilus: Alas! mistresse, wherein hath that innocent maiden offended, that she should be slaine? Dionisiades answered, Shee innocent! nay she is a wicked wretch, and therefore, thou shalt not denie to fulfill my request, but doe as I commaund thee, or els I sweare by God thou shalt dearely repent it. But how shall I best doe it, mistres? said the villaine. She aunswered: Shee hath a custome, as soon as shee returneth home from schoole, not to eate meat before that she have gone into her nurces sepulchre, where I would have thee stand readie, with a dagger drawn in thine hand; and when she is come in, gripe her by the haire of the head, and so slay her: then take her bodie, and cast it into the sea, and when thou hast so done, I will make thee free, and besides reward thee liberally.

"Then tooke the villaine a dagger, and girded himselfe therewith, and with an heavy heart and weeping eies went forth towards the grave, saying within himselfe: Alas, poore wretch that I am! alas, poore Theophilus, that canst not deserve thy libertie but by shedding of innocent bloud! And with that hee went into the grave, and drue his dagger, and made him readie for the deede. Tharsia was nowe come from schoole, and made haste unto the grave with a flagon of wine, as shee was wont to doe, and entred within the vault. Then the villaine rushed violently upon her, and caught her by the haire of the head, and threw her to the ground. And while he was now readie to stab her with the dagger, poore silly Tharsia, all amazed, casting up her eies upon him, knew the villaine, and, holding up her handes, said thus unto him: O, Theophilus! against whom have I so greevously offended, that I must die therefore? The villaine answered, Thou hast not offended, but thy father hath, which left thee behind him in Stranguilios house, with so great a treasure in money and princely ornaments. O, said the mayden, would to God he had not done so! but I pray thee, Theophilus, since there is no hope for me to escape with life, give mee licence to say my praiers before I die. I give thee licence, saide the villaine; and I take God to record that I am constrained to murther thee against my will.

"As fortune, or rather the providence of God served, while Tharsia was devoutly making her praiers, certaine pyrats which were come aland, and stood under the side of an hill watching for some prey, beholding an armed man offering violence unto a mayden, cried unto him, and said," &c. &c.

(2) Scene VI.—*I hear say you are of honourable parts, and are the governor of this place.*] Speaking of the novel by Wilkins, Mr. Collier remarks,—"It is my firm conviction that it supplies many passages, written by Shakespeare and recited by the performers, which were garbled, mangled, or omitted in the printed play of 'Pericles,' as it has come down to us in the quartos of 1609, 1619, and 1630, and in the folios of 1664 and 1685."

The corresponding speech of Marina at this point, as given by Wilkins, is certainly confirmatory of Mr. Collier's opinion, for it exhibits a terseness of expression and a vigour of thought, which are quite Shakespearian:—"If as you say (my Lorde) you are the Governour, let not your authoritie, which should teach you to rule others, be the meanes to make you mis-governe your selfe: If the eminence of your place came unto you by discent, and the royalty of your blood, let not your life proove your birth a bastard: If it were throwne upon you by opinion, make good, that opinion was the cause to make you great. What reason is there in your Iustice, who hath power over all, to undoe any? If you take from mee mine honour, you are like him, that makes a gappe into forbidden ground, after whome too many enter, and you are guiltie of all their evilles: my life is yet unspotted, my chastitie unstained in thought. Then if your violence deface this building, the workemanship of heaven, made up for good, and not to be the exercise of sinnes intemperaunce, you do kill your owne honour, abuse your owne justice, and impoverish me."

(3) SCENE VI.—*But amongst honest women.*] From the words, *honest women,* which occur in the *Confessio Amantis,* it is evident the author here had Gower before him:—

"If so be, that thi maister wolde
That I his golde encrece sholde,
It may nott falle by this weye;
But soffre me to go my weye
Oute of this hous, where I am inne,
And I shall make hym for to wynne
In somme place elles of the towne,
Be so it be of religioun
Where that honest women dwelle."

ACT V.

(1) SCENE I.—*Marina sings.*] The song sung by Marina was very probably that given by Twine (an exact translation of the Latin original), and printed in Wilkins' novel, where it is introduced thus;—"Which when Marina heard, shee went boldely downe into the cabine to him, and with a milde voyce saluted him, saying; God save you sir, and be of good comfort, for an innocent Virgin, whose life hath bin distressed by shipwrack, and her chastity by dishonesty, and hath yet bin preserved from both, thus curteously saluteth thee: but perceiving him to yeeld her no answer, she began to record in verses, and therewithall to sing so sweetly, that Pericles, notwithstanding his great sorrow, woondered at her, at last, taking up another instrument unto his eares she preferred this:—

"Amongst the harlots foule I walke,
But harlot none am I;
The Rose amongst the Thornes doth grow,
And is not hurt thereby.
The Thiefe that stole me sure I thinke,
Is slaine before this time,
A Bawde me bought, yet am I not
Defilde by fleshly crime;
Nothing were pleasanter to me,
Then parents mine to know.
I am the issue of a King,
My blood from Kings dooth flow:
In time the heavens may mend my state
And send a better day,
For sorrow addes unto our griefes,
But helps not any way:
Shew gladnesse in your countenaunce,
Cast up your cheerefull eies,
That God remaines, that once of nought
Created Earth and Skies."

(2) SCENE I.—*Thou art my child.*] So Gower:—

"And he tho toke here in his arme;
Bot such a joye as he tho made
Was never seen; thus be thei glade
That sorry hadden be to forn.
Fro this day forth fortune hath swerne
To sett hym upwarde on the whiel:
So goth the worlde, now wo, now weel."

(3) SCENE I.—*Diana disappears.*] The vision is related as follows in Twine's translation:—"All things being in a readinesse, he tooke shipping with his sonne in lawe and his daughter and weyghed anchor, and committed the sailes unto the winde, and went their way, directing their course evermore towarde Tharsus, by which Apollonius purposed to passe unto his owne countrie Tyrus. And when they had sailed one whole day, and night was come, that Apollonius laide him downe to rest, there appeared an angell in his sleepe, commaunding him to leave his course toward Tharsus, and to saile unto Ephesus, and to go into the temple of Diana, accompanied with his sonne in lawe and his daughter, and there with a loude voyce to declare all his adventures, whatsoever had befallen him from his youth unto that present day."

(4) SCENE III.—*Sir, lead's the way.*] The leading incident in this scene, which so strikingly resembles the much grander one of the same nature in "The Winter's Tale," is related by the old poet with a simplicity and pathos which are irresistible:—

"With worthi knyhtes environed,
The kynge hym self hath abandoned
In to the temple in good entente,
The dore is uppe, and in he wente,
Where as with gret devocioun
Of holy contemplacioun
With inne his herte he made his shrifte,
And aftir that a rich yefte
He offreth with grete reverence;
And there in open audience
Of hem that stoden alle aboute
He tolde hem, and declareth owte
His happe, suche as hym is byfalle:
Ther was no thyng foryete of alle.
His wiff, as it was goddes grace,
Wich was professed in the place,
As she that was abbesse there,
Unto his tale hath leide hir ere.
She knew the voys, and the visage:
For pure joye, as inne a rage,
She strauht unto hym alle att ones,
And felle a swone upponn the stones
Wherof the temple flore was paved.
She was anon with water laved,
Til she came to here selfe ayeyn,
And thanne she began to seyn:
A bleased be the hihe soonde,
That I may se myn husbonde,
Wich whilom he and I were oone.

The kynge with that knewe here anoon,
And tooke her in his arme, and kyste,
And alle the towne the soone it wiste.
Tho was there joye many folde,
For every man this tale hath tolde
As for myracle, and weren glade."

CRITICAL OPINIONS ON PERICLES.

"PERICLES is generally reckoned to be in part, and only in part, the work of Shakespeare. From the poverty and bad management of the fable, the want of any effective or distinguishable character, for Marina is no more than the common form of female virtue, such as all the dramatists of that age could draw, and a general feebleness of the tragedy as a whole, I should not believe the structure to have been Shakespeare's. But many passages are far more in his manner than in that of any contemporary writer with whom I am acquainted; and the extrinsic testimony, though not conclusive, being of some value, I should not dissent from the judgment of Steevens and Malone, that it was, in no inconsiderable degree, repaired and improved by his touch. Drake has placed it under the year 1590, as the earliest of Shakespeare's plays, for no better reason, apparently, than that he thought it inferior to all the rest. But if, as most will agree, it were not quite his own, this reason will have less weight; and the language seems to me rather that of his second or third manner than of his first. Pericles is not known to have existed before 1609."—HALLAM.

"This piece was acknowledged by Dryden to be a work, but a youthful work of Shakespeare's. It is most undoubtedly his, and it has been admitted into several late editions of his works. The supposed imperfections originate in the circumstance, that Shakespeare here handled a childish and extravagant romance of the old poet Gower, and was unwilling to drag the subject out of its proper sphere. Hence he even introduces Gower himself, and makes him deliver a prologue in his own antiquated language and versification. This power of assuming so foreign a manner is at least no proof of helplessness." —SCHLEGEL.

Act III. Sc. 4.

TWELFTH NIGHT; OR, WHAT YOU WILL.

THIS enchanting comedy was first printed in the folio of 1623, and no quarto edition of it has ever been found. Though long supposed, upon the authority of Malone and Chalmers, to have been one of Shakespeare's very latest productions, we now know that it was acted in the Middle Temple, as early as the beginning of the seventeenth century. This fact was first made public by Mr. Collier and Mr. Hunter, who discovered, almost simultaneously, a small manuscript diary, among the Harleian Collection in the library of the British Museum, which appears to have been made by a student of the Temple, named Manningham, and contains the following interesting entry:—

"Feb. 2, 1601 [2].

At our feast, wee had a play called Twelve Night or what you will, much like the Comedy of errors, or Menechmi in Plautus, but most like and neere to that in Italian, called *Inganni*. A good practice in it to make the steward believe his lady widdowe was in love with him by counterfayting a letter, as from his lady in general termes telling him what shee liked best in him, and prescribing his gestures, inscribing his apparaile, &c.; and then when he came to practice, making beleeve they tooke him to be mad."

This is decisive, and, as there can be no doubt that, before being acted in the Temple, it had been represented in the public theatre, and, since it is not mentioned by Meres in his list of 1598, its production may be confidently ascribed to the period between that year and February, 1602.

The story whence the serious incidents of "Twelfth Night" are derived, is found in Bandello, Parte Seconda, Novella 36:—"*Nicuola innamorata di Lattantio và a servirlo vestita da paggio; edopo Molti casi seco si marita, e ciò che ad un suo fratello avvenne;*" but whether Shakespeare borrowed them from the fountain-head, or through the English translation of Barnabie Riche, called "*The Historie of Apollonius and Silla,*" or whether he found them in the Italian play referred to by Manningham, still remains a subject for investigation. The diarist notices only one comedy called *Inganni,* but there are two Italian plays bearing the title *Gl' Inganni,* both founded upon Bandello's novel; one (*commedia recitata in Milano l'anno* 1547, *dinanzi la Maestà del Re Filippo*) by Niccolò Secchi, 1562; the other, written by Curzio Gonzago, and printed in 1592. To neither of these plays does our poet appear to have been under much, if any, obligation. There is, however, a third Italian comedy of the *Accademici Intronati,* to which Mr. Hunter first called attention (*New Illustrations of Shakespeare,* vol. i. pp. 391—2), that presents much stronger claims to consideration as the immediate origin of the plot of "Twelfth Night." This drama is entitled *Gl' Ingannati* (*Commedia celebrata ni' Giuochi del Carnevale in Siena, l'anno* 1531, *sotto il Sodo dignissimo Archintronato*), first printed in 1537, and having for its general title *Il Sacrificio.* "That it was on the model of this play," Mr. Hunter remarks, "and not on any of the *Ingannis*, that Shakespeare formed the plan of the serious part of the *Twelfth Night*, will appear evidently by the following analysis of the main parts of the story. Fabritio and Lelia, a brother and sister, are separated at the sack of Rome, in 1527. Lelia is carried to Modena, where resides Flamineo, to whom she had formerly been attached. Lelia disguises herself as a boy, and enters his service: Flamineo had forgotten Lelia and was a suitor to Isabella, a Modenese lady. Lelia, in her male attire, is employed in love-embassies from Flamineo to Isabella. Isabella is insensible to the importunities of Flamineo, but conceives a violent passion for Lelia, mistaking her for a man. In the third act Fabritio arrives at Modena, when mistakes arise owing to the close resemblance there is between Fabritio and his sister in her male attire. Ultimately recognitions take place; the affections of Isabella are easily transferred from Lelia to Fabritio, and Flamineo takes to his bosom the affectionate and faithful Lelia. * * * We have in the Italian play, a subordinate character named Pasquella, to whom Maria corresponds; and in the subordinate incidents we find Fabritio mistaken in the street for Lelia by the servant of Isabella, who takes him to her mistress's house, exactly as Sebastian is taken for Viola, and led to the house of Olivia. . . . . The name of *Fabian* given by Shakespeare to one of his characters was probably suggested to him by the name of *Fabia*, which Lelia in the Italian play assumed in her disguise. *Malvolio* is a happy adaptation from *Malevolti*, a character in the *Il Sacrificio*. A phrase occurring in a long prologue or preface prefixed to this play in the Italian [*la Notte di Beffana*] appears to me to have suggested the title 'Twelfth-Night.'"

Persons Represented.

ORSINO, *Duke of* Illyria.
SEBASTIAN, *a Young Gentleman, brother to* Viola.
ANTONIO, *a Sea Captain, friend to* Sebastian.
A Sea Captain, friend to Viola.
CURIO, VALENTINE, } *Lords attending on the* Duke.
Sir TOBY BELCH, *Uncle to the Lady* Olivia.
Sir ANDREW AGUECHEEK.
MALVOLIO, *Steward to* Olivia.

FABIAN, CLOWN, } *Servants to* Olivia.

OLIVIA, *a rich Countess.*
VIOLA, *in love with the* Duke.
MARIA, Olivia's *woman.*

Lords, Priests, Sailors, Officers, Musicians, and other Attendants.

SCENE,—*A City in* Illyria, *and the Sea-coast near it.*

ACT I.

SCENE I.—*An Apartment in the Duke's Palace.*

Enter DUKE, CURIO, *and other* Lords; Musicians *attending.*

DUKE. If music be the food of love, play on;
Give me excess of it; that surfeiting,
The appetite may sicken, and so die.——
That strain again; it had a dying fall:
O, it came o'er my ear, like the sweet sound [a]
That breathes upon a bank of violets,

[a] *O, it came o'er my ear, like the sweet* sound—] So the early text, but Pope changed *sound* to *south*, and the alteration has been approved, perhaps too readily, by nearly every editor and critic since his time; at all events, if *south* were the poet's word, he must have employed it, not in the sense Pope intended of *south-wind*, but as *south*, *sowth*, or *sough* is used in the North, to signify the soft whisper of the breeze:—

"The soft *south* of the swyre, and sound of the stremes,
The sweit savour of the swairde, and singing of fewlis,
Might comfort any creature of the kyn of Adam."
Dunbar, MAITLAND'S POEMS, p. 64.

Stealing, and giving odour!—Enough; no more:
'T is not so sweet now, as it was before.
O spirit of love, how quick and fresh art thou!
That, notwithstanding thy capacity
Receiveth as the sea, nought enters there,
Of what validity and pitch soe'er,
But falls into abatement and low price,
Even in a minute! so full of shapes is fancy,
That it alone is high-fantastical.

CUR. Will you go hunt, my lord?

DUKE. What? Curio.

CUR. The hart.

DUKE. Why, so I do, the noblest that I have:
O, when mine eyes did see Olivia first,
Methought, she purg'd the air of pestilence!
That instant was I turn'd into a hart;
And my desires, like fell and cruel hounds,
E'er since pursue me.—

Enter VALENTINE.

How now! what news from her?

VAL. So please my lord, I might not be admitted,
But from her handmaid do return this answer:
The element itself, till seven years' heat,
Shall not behold her face at ample view;
But, like a cloistress, she will veiled walk,
And water once a day her chamber round
With eye-offending brine: all this to season
A brother's dead love, which she would keep fresh
And lasting in her sad remembrance.

DUKE. O, she that hath a heart of that fine frame
To pay this debt of love but to a brother,
How will she love, when the rich golden shaft
Hath kill'd the flock of all affections else
That live in her!—when liver, brain, and heart,
These sovereign thrones, are all supplied and fill'd—
Her sweet perfection,[a]—with one self king!—
Away before me to sweet beds of flowers;
Love-thoughts lie rich, when canopied with bowers.
[*Exeunt.*

SCENE II.—*The Sea-coast.*

Enter VIOLA, Captain, *and* Sailors.

VIO. What country, friends, is this?

CAP. This is Illyria, lady.

VIO. And what should I do in Illyria?
My brother he is in Elysium.
Perchance, he is not drown'd:—what think you, [sailors?

CAP. It is perchance, that you yourself were sav'd.

VIO. O my poor brother! and so perchance may he be. [chance,

CAP. True, madam: and, to comfort you with
Assure yourself, after our ship did split,
When you, and those poor number sav'd with you,
Hung on our driving boat, I saw your brother,
Most provident in peril, bind himself
(Courage and hope both teaching him the practice)
To a strong mast, that liv'd upon the sea;
Where, like Arion* on the dolphin's back,
I saw him hold acquaintance with the waves,
So long as I could see.

VIO. For saying so, there's gold:
Mine own escape unfoldeth to my hope,—
Whereto thy speech serves for authority,—
The like of him. Know'st thou this country?

CAP. Ay, madam, well; for I was bred and born
Not three hours' travel from this very place.

VIO. Who governs here?

CAP. A noble duke, in nature as in name.

VIO. What is his name?

CAP. Orsino.

VIO. Orsino! I have heard my father name him:
He was a bachelor then.

CAP. And so is now, or was so very late;
For but a month ago I went from hence,
And then 'twas fresh in murmur (as, you know,
What great ones do, the less will prattle of),
That he did seek the love of fair Olivia.

VIO. What's she?

CAP. A virtuous maid, the daughter of a count
That died some twelvemonth since; then leaving her
In the protection of his son, her brother,
Who shortly also died: for whose dear love,
They say, she hath abjur'd the company
And sight[b] of men.

VIO. O, that I served that lady,
And might not be deliver'd to the world,
Till I had made mine own occasion mellow
What my estate is!

CAP. That were hard to compass;
Because she will admit no kind of suit,
No, not the duke's.

---

[a] —— *when liver, brain, and heart,*
These sovereign thrones, are all supplied and fill'd—
Her sweet perfection,—*with one self king!*]

The old copy has, "Her sweet *perfections*," a slight but unfortunate misprint, which totally destroys the meaning of the poet. The passage should be read,—

"——When liver, brain, and heart,
These sovereign thrones, are all supplied and fill'd
With one self king,—her sweet perfection."

The "sweet perfection" not being, as Steevens conjectured, her *liver*, *brain*, and *heart*, but her husband, her "one self [or single] king." According to the doctrine of Shakespeare's time, a female was imperfect, her nature undeveloped, until by marriage she was incorporated with the other sex.

"———— and as one glorious flame,
Meeting another, grows the same:"

(*) Old text, *Orion*.

The writers of the period abound in allusions to this belief:—

"Marriage their object is; their *being* then,
And now *perfection*, they receive from men."
OVERBURY'S "*Wife*"

See also Donne's "Epithalamium made at Lincoln's Inn," in which this, the predominating idea on such occasions, is made the burden of every stanza:—

"Weep not, nor blush, here is no grief nor shame,
To-day put on *perfection*, and a woman's name."

[b] ——— *the* company
And sight *of men.*]

The old text runs:—

"———— *the sight*
And company," &c.

Hanmer made the necessary transposition.

VIO. There is a fair behaviour in thee, captain;
And though that nature with a beauteous wall
Doth oft close in pollution, yet of thee
I will believe thou hast a mind that suits
With this thy fair and outward character.
I pr'ythee, (and I'll pay thee bounteously,)
Conceal me what I am; and be my aid
For such disguise as, haply, shall become
The form of my intent. I'll serve this duke;
Thou shalt present me as an eunuch to him,
It may be worth thy pains; for I can sing,
And speak to him in many sorts of music,
That will allow me very worth his service.
What else may hap, to time I will commit;
Only shape thou thy silence to my wit.

CAP. Be you his eunuch, and your mute I'll be:
When my tongue blabs, then let mine eyes not see!

VIO. I thank thee: lead me on. [*Exeunt.*

SCENE III.—*A Room in* Olivia's *House.*

Enter Sir TOBY BELCH *and* MARIA.

SIR TO. What a plague means my niece, to take the death of her brother thus? I am sure care's an enemy to life.

MAR. By my troth, sir Toby, you must come in earlier o' nights; your cousin, my lady, takes great exceptions to your ill hours.

SIR TO. Why, let her except before excepted.

MAR. Ay, but you must confine yourself within the modest limits of order.

SIR TO. *Confine!* I'll confine myself no finer than I am: these clothes are good enough to drink in, and so be these boots too:—an they be not, let them hang themselves in their own straps.

MAR. That quaffing and drinking will undo you: I heard my lady talk of it yesterday; and of a foolish knight that you brought in one night here to be her wooer.

SIR TO. Who? Sir Andrew Aguecheek?

MAR. Ay, he.

SIR TO. He's as tall[a] a man as any's in Illyria.

MAR. What's that to the purpose?

SIR TO. Why, he has three thousand ducats a year.

MAR. Ay, but he'll have but a year in all these ducats; he's a very fool and a prodigal.

[a] *He's* as tall *a man*—] That is, as *able a* man. "*A tall man of his hands*, meant a good fighter: *a tall man of his tongue*, a licentious speaker; and *a tall man of his trencher*, a hearty feeder."—GIFFORD.

SIR To. Fie, that you'll say so! he plays o' the viol-de-gamboys,(1) and speaks three or four languages word for word without book, and hath all the good gifts of nature.

MAR. He hath, indeed,—almost natural: for, besides that he's a fool, he's a great quarreller; and, but that he hath the gift of a coward to allay the gust he hath in quarrelling, 'tis thought among the prudent, he would quickly have the gift of a grave.

SIR To. By this hand, they are scoundrels and substractors, that say so of him. Who are they?

MAR. They that add moreover, he's drunk nightly in your company.

SIR To. With drinking healths to my niece; I'll drink to her, as long as there is a passage in my throat and drink in Illyria. He's a coward, and a coystril,[a] that will not drink to my niece, till his brains turn o' the toe like a parish-top.(2) What, wench! *Castiliano vulgo;*[b] for here comes sir Andrew Agueface.

Enter Sir ANDREW AGUECHEEK.

SIR AND. Sir Toby Belch! how now, sir Toby Belch!

SIR To. Sweet sir Andrew!

SIR AND. Bless you, fair shrew.

MAR. And you too, sir.

SIR To. Accost, sir Andrew, accost.

SIR AND. What's that?

SIR To. My niece's chamber-maid.

SIR AND. Good mistress Accost, I desire better acquaintance.

MAR. My name is Mary, sir.

SIR AND. Good mistress Mary Accost,——

[a] Coystril,—] A mean groom or peasant; derived, it is thought, from the Low Latin, *Coterellus*.

[b] *Castiliano vulgo;*] Warburton proposed, "*Castiliano-volto*, put on your *Castilian*, that is, your grave looks;" but Maria appears already to have been more serious than suited Sir Toby's humour.

Sir To. You mistake, knight: *accost* is front her, board her, woo her, assail her.

Sir And. By my troth, I would not undertake her in this company. Is that the meaning of *accost?*

Mar. Fare you well, gentlemen.

Sir To. An thou let part so, sir Andrew, would thou might'st never draw sword again.

Sir And. An you part so, mistress, I would I might never draw sword again. Fair lady, do you think you have fools in hand?

Mar. Sir, I have not you by the hand.

Sir And. Marry, but you shall have, and here's my hand.

Mar. Now, sir, thought is free: I pray you, bring your hand to the buttery-bar,(3) and let it drink.

Sir And. Wherefore, sweet heart? what's your metaphor?

Mar. It's dry, sir.[a]

Sir And. Why, I think so: I am not such an ass, but I can keep my hand dry. But what's your jest?

Mar. A dry jest, sir.

Sir And. Are you full of them?

Mar. Ay, sir; I have them at my fingers' ends: marry, now I let go your hand, I am barren. [*Exit* Maria.

a *It's* dry, *sir.*] As a moist hand was commonly accounted to denote an amatory disposition, a dry one was considered symptomatic of debility.

Sir To. O knight, thou lack'st a cup of canary: when did I see thee so put down?

Sir And. Never in your life, I think, unless you see canary put me down. Methinks sometimes I have no more wit than a Christian or an ordinary man has: but I am a great eater of beef, and I believe that does harm to my wit.

Sir To. No question.

Sir And. An I thought that, I'd forswear it. I'll ride home to morrow, sir Toby.

Sir To. *Pourquoi*, my dear knight?

Sir And. What is *pourquoi?* do or not do? I would I had bestowed that time in the tongues, that I have in fencing, dancing, and bear-baiting: O, had I but followed the arts!

Sir To. Then hadst thou had an excellent head of hair.

Sir And. Why, would that have mended my hair?

Sir To. Past question; for thou seest, it will not curl by[b] nature.

Sir And. But it becomes me well enough, does 't not?

Sir To. Excellent! it hangs like flax on a distaff; and I hope to see a huswife take thee between her legs and spin it off.

Sir And. Faith, I'll home to-morrow, sir Toby: your niece will not be seen; or if she be,

b *It will not* curl by *nature.*] The old text reads, it will not *cool my* nature. Corrected by Theobald.

it's four to one she'll none of me; the count himself, here hard by, wooes her.

SIR TO. She'll none o' the count; she'll not match above her degree, neither in estate, years, nor wit; I have heard her swear't. Tut, there's life in't, man.

SIR AND. I'll stay a month longer. I am a fellow o' the strangest mind i' the world; I delight in masques and revels sometimes altogether.

SIR TO. Art thou good at these kick-shaws, knight?

SIR AND. As any man in Illyria, whatsoever he be, under the degree of my betters; and yet I will not compare with an old man.

SIR TO. What is thy excellence? in a galliard, knight?

SIR AND. Faith, I can cut a caper.

SIR TO. And I can cut the mutton to't.

SIR AND. And I think I have the back-trick, simply as strong as any man in Illyria.

SIR TO. Wherefore are these things hid? wherefore have these gifts a curtain before 'em? are they like to take dust, like mistress Mall's picture? (4) why dost thou not go to church in a galliard, and come home in a coranto? My very walk should be a jig; I would not so much as make water, but in a sink-a-pace. What dost thou mean? is it a world to hide virtues in? I did think, by the excellent constitution of thy leg, it was formed under the star of a galliard.

SIR AND. Ay, 'tis strong, and it does indifferent well in a flame-coloured* stock. Shall we set about some revels?

SIR TO. What shall we do else? were we not born under Taurus?

SIR AND. Taurus? that's† sides and heart.

SIR TO. No, sir; it is legs and thighs. Let me see thee caper: ha! higher: ha, ha!—excellent! [*Exeunt.*

SCENE IV.—*A Room in the* Duke's *Palace.*

Enter VALENTINE, *and* VIOLA *in man's attire.*

VAL. If the duke continues these favours towards you, Cesario, you are like to be much advanced; he hath known you but three days, and already you are no stranger.

VIO. You either fear his humour or my negligence, that you call in question the continuance of his love: is he inconstant, sir, in his favours?

VAL. No, believe me.

VIO. I thank you. Here comes the count.

Enter DUKE, CURIO, *and* Attendants.

DUKE. Who saw Cesario, ho?

VIO. On your attendance, my lord; here.

DUKE. Stand you awhile aloof.—Cesario,
Thou know'st no less but all; I have unclasp'd
To thee the book even of my secret soul:
Therefore, good youth, address thy gait unto her;
Be not denied access, stand at her doors,
And tell them, there thy fixed foot shall grow,
Till thou have audience.

VIO. Sure, my noble lord,
If she be so abandon'd to her sorrow
As it is spoke, she never will admit me.

DUKE. Be clamorous, and leap all civil bounds,
Rather than make unprofited return.

VIO. Say, I do speak with her, my lord, what then?

DUKE. O, then unfold the passion of my love,
Surprise her with discourse of my dear faith:
It shall become thee well to act my woes;
She will attend it better in thy youth,
Than in a nuncio* of more grave aspect.

VIO. I think not so, my lord.

DUKE. Dear lad, believe it;
For they shall yet belie thy happy years,
That say thou art a man: Diana's lip
Is not more smooth and rubious; thy small pipe
Is as the maiden's organ, shrill, and sound,
And all is semblative a woman's part.
I know thy constellation is right apt
For this affair:—some four or five attend him;
All, if you will; for I myself am best,
When least in company: prosper well in this,
And thou shalt live as freely as thy lord,
To call his fortunes thine.

VIO. I'll do my best,
To woo your lady: yet, [*Aside.*] a barful strife!
Whoe'er I woo, myself would be his wife.
[*Exeunt.*

SCENE V.—*A Room in* Olivia's *House.*

Enter MARIA *and* Clown.(5)

MAR. Nay, either tell me where thou hast been, or I will not open my lips so wide as a bristle may enter, in way of thy excuse: my lady will hang thee for thy absence.

CLO. Let her hang me: he, that is well hanged in this world, needs to fear no colours.[a]

MAR. Make that good.

CLO. He shall see none to fear.

(*) Old text, *dam'd colour'd*. (†) Old text, *That*.

(*) Old copy, *nuntio's*.

[a] *Needs* to fear no colours.] Nares conjectures that to *fear no colours* was originally a military expression for *fear no enemy*. Maria suggests the same thing, but the point of the allusion here, and in other instances of this "skipping dialogue," is lost to us.

MAR. A good lenten* answer: I can tell thee where that saying was born, of, *I fear no colours.*

CLO. Where, good mistress Mary?

MAR. In the wars; and that may you be bold to say in your foolery.

CLO. Well, God give them wisdom that have it; and those that are fools, let them use their talents.

MAR. Yet you will be hanged for being so long absent; or, to be turned away,—is not that as good as a hanging to you?

CLO. Many a good hanging prevents a bad marriage; and, for turning away, let summer bear it out.

MAR. You are resolute, then?

CLO. Not so neither, but I am resolved on two points.

MAR. That, if one break, the other will hold; or, if both break, your gaskins [a] fall.

CLO. Apt, in good faith; very apt! Well, go thy way; if sir Toby would leave drinking, thou wert as witty a piece of Eve's flesh as any in Illyria.

MAR. Peace, you rogue, no more o' that. Here comes my lady: make your excuse wisely, you were best. [*Exit.*

CLO. Wit, and 't be thy will, put me into good fooling! Those wits, that think they have thee, do very oft prove fools; and I, that am sure I lack thee, may pass for a wise man: for what says Quinapalus? Better a witty fool than a foolish wit.

Enter OLIVIA, MALVOLIO, *and* Attendants.

God bless thee, lady!

OLI. Take the fool away.

CLO. Do you not hear, fellows? take away the lady.

OLI. Go to, you're a dry fool; I'll no more of you: besides, you grow dishonest.

CLO. Two faults, madonna, that drink and good counsel will amend: for give the dry fool drink, then is the fool not dry; bid the dishonest man mend himself; if he mend, he is no longer dishonest; if he cannot, let the botcher mend him: any thing that's mended is but patched: virtue that transgresses is but patched with sin; and sin that amends is but patched with virtue. If that this simple syllogism will serve, so; if it will not, what remedy? As there is no true cuckold but calamity, so beauty's a flower.—The lady bade take away the fool; therefore, I say again, take her away.

OLI. Sir, I bade them take away you.

CLO. Misprision in the highest degree!—Lady, *Cucullus non facit monachum;* that's as much to say as,[b] I wear not motley in my brain. Good madonna, give me leave to prove you a fool.

OLI. Can you do it?

CLO. Dexterously, good madonna.

OLI. Make your proof.

CLO. I must catechize you for it, madonna; good my mouse of virtue, answer me.

OLI. Well, sir, for want of other idleness, I'll bide your proof.

CLO. Good madonna, why mournest thou?

OLI. Good fool, for my brother's death.

CLO. I think his soul is in hell, madonna.

OLI. I know his soul is in heaven, fool.

CLO. The more fool, madonna, to mourn for your brother's soul being in heaven. Take away the fool, gentlemen.

OLI. What think you of this fool, Malvolio? doth he not mend?

MAL. Yes, and shall do till the pangs of death shake him: infirmity, that decays the wise, doth ever make the better fool.

CLO. God send you, sir, a speedy infirmity, for the better increasing your folly! Sir Toby will be sworn that I am no fox; but he will not pass his word for two pence that you are no fool.

OLI. How say you to that, Malvolio?

MAL. I marvel your ladyship takes delight in such a barren rascal; I saw him put down the other day with an ordinary fool,[c] that has no more brain than a stone. Look you now, he's out of his guard already; unless you laugh and minister occasion to him, he is gagged. I protest, I take these wise men, that crow so at these set kind of fools, no better than the fools' zanies.

OLI. O, you are sick of self-love, Malvolio, and taste with a distempered appetite. To be generous, guiltless, and of free disposition, is to take those things for bird-bolts, that you deem cannon-bullets: there is no slander in an allowed fool, though he do nothing but rail; nor no railing in a known discreet man, though he do nothing but reprove.

CLO. Now Mercury endue thee with leasing,[d] for thou speakest well of fools.

(*) Old copy, *lenton.*

[a] *Or, if both* [points] break, your gaskins fall.] See note (e), p. 250, Vol. I.

[b] *That's as much to* say as,—] In modern editions this is usually printed in conformity with modern construction,—"That's as much *as to say;*" but the form in the text was not uncommon in old language:—"And yet it is said,—labour in thy vocation; which is *as much to say as,*" &c.—"Henry VI." (Part Second), Act IV. Sc. 2.

[c] *An* ordinary *fool,*—] An *ordinary* fool may mean a *common* fool; but more probably, as Shakespeare had always an eye to the manners of his own countrymen, he referred to a jester hired to make sport for the diners at a public ordinary.

[d] *Now Mercury endue thee with* leasing, for thou speakest well of fools.] The humour of this is not very conspicuous even by the light of Johnson's comment,—"May Mercury teach thee to lie, since thou liest in favour of fools!"

Re-enter MARIA.

MAR. Madam, there is at the gate a young gentleman, much desires to speak with you.

OLI. From the count Orsino, is it?

MAR. I know not, madam; 'tis a fair young man, and well attended.

OLI. Who of my people hold him in delay?

MAR. Sir Toby, madam, your kinsman.

OLI. Fetch him off, I pray you; he speaks nothing but madman: fie on him! [*Exit* MARIA.] Go you, Malvolio: if it be a suit from the count, I am sick, or not at home; what you will, to dismiss it. [*Exit* MALVOLIO.] Now you see, sir, how your fooling grows old, and people dislike it.

CLO. Thou hast spoke for us, madonna, as if thy eldest son should be a fool,—whose skull Jove cram with brains! for here he comes, one of thy kin, has a most weak *pia mater*.

Enter Sir TOBY BELCH.

OLI. By mine honour, half drunk.—What is he at the gate, cousin?

SIR TO. A gentleman.

OLI. A gentleman! what gentleman?

SIR TO. 'Tis a gentleman here—a plague o' these pickle-herring!—How now, sot!

CLO. Good sir Toby!——

OLI. Cousin, cousin, how have you come so early by this lethargy?

SIR TO. Lechery! I defy lechery. There's one at the gate.

OLI. Ay, marry; what is he?

SIR TO. Let him be the devil, an he will, I care not: give me faith, say I. Well, it's all one. [*Exit.*

OLI. What's a drunken man like, fool?

CLO. Like a drowned man, a fool, and a madman: one draught above heat makes him a fool; the second mads him; and a third drowns him.

OLI. Go thou and seek the crowner, and let him sit o' my coz; for he's in the third degree of drink,—he's drowned: go, look after him.

CLO. He is but mad yet, madonna; and the fool shall look to the madman. [*Exit* Clown.

Re-enter MALVOLIO.

MAL. Madam, yond young fellow swears he will speak with you. I told him you were sick; he takes on him to understand so much, and therefore comes to speak with you: I told him you were asleep; he seems to have a fore-knowledge of that too, and therefore comes to speak with you. What is to be said to him, lady? he's fortified against any denial.

OLI. Tell him, he shall not speak with me.

MAL. H'as been told so; and he says, he'll stand at your door like a sheriff's post,(6) and be the supporter to a bench, but he'll speak with you.

OLI. What kind o' man is he?

MAL. Why, of man kind.

OLI. What manner of man?

MAL. Of very ill manner; he'll speak with you, will you or no.

OLI. Of what personage and years is he?

MAL. Not yet old enough for a man, nor young enough for a boy; as a squash is before 'tis a peascod, or a codling when 'tis almost an apple: 'tis with him in standing water, between boy and man. He is very well-favoured, and he speaks very shrewishly; one would think his mother's milk were scarce out of him.

OLI. Let him approach; call in my gentlewoman.

MAL. Gentlewoman, my lady calls. [*Exit.*

Re-enter MARIA.

OLI. Give me my veil: come, throw it o'er my face;
We'll once more hear Orsino's embassy.

Enter VIOLA.*

VIO. The honourable lady of the house, which is she?

OLI. Speak to me, I shall answer for her: your will?

VIO. Most radiant, exquisite, and unmatchable beauty,—I pray you tell me if this be the lady of the house, for I never saw her: I would be loth to cast away my speech; for, besides that it is excellently well penned, I have taken great pains to con it. Good beauties, let me sustain no scorn; I am very comptible,[a] even to the least sinister usage.

OLI. Whence came you, sir?

VIO. I can say little more than I have studied, and that question's out of my part. Good gentle one, give me modest assurance if you be the lady of the house, that I may proceed in my speech.

OLI. Are you a comedian?

VIO. No, my profound heart: and yet, by the very fangs of malice I swear, I am not that I play. Are you the lady of the house?

OLI. If I do not usurp myself, I am.

VIO. Most certain, if you are she, you do usurp yourself; for what is yours to bestow is not yours to reserve. But this is from my commission: I will on with my speech in your praise, and then show you the heart of my message.

(*) Old copy, *Violenta.*

[a] Comptible,—] This must mean *impressible, susceptive, sensible.*

OLI. Come to what is important in't: I forgive you the praise.

VIO. Alas, I took great pains to study it, and 'tis poetical.

OLI. It is the more like to be feigned: I pray you, keep it in. I heard you were saucy at my gates, and allowed your approach rather to wonder at you than to hear you. If you be not[a] mad, be gone; if you have reason, be brief: 'tis not that time of moon with me to make one in so skipping a dialogue.

MAR. Will you hoist sail, sir? here lies your way.

VIO. No, good swabber; I am to hull here a little longer.—Some mollification for your giant, sweet lady.

OLI. Tell me your mind.

VIO. I am a messenger.[b]

OLI. Sure, you have some hideous matter to deliver, when the courtesy of it is so fearful. Speak your office.

VIO. It alone concerns your ear. I bring no overture of war, no taxation of homage; I hold the olive in my hand: my words are as full of peace as matter.

OLI. Yet you began rudely. What are you? what would you?

VIO. The rudeness that hath appeared in me nave I learned from my entertainment. What I am, and what I would, are as secret as maidenhead: to your ears, divinity; to any other's, profanation.

OLI. Give us the place alone: we will hear this divinity. [*Exit* MARIA.] Now, sir, what is your text?

VIO. Most sweet lady,——

OLI. A comfortable doctrine, and much may be said of it. Where lies your text?

VIO. In Orsino's bosom.

OLI. In his bosom! in what chapter of his bosom?

VIO. To answer by the method, in the first of his heart.

OLI. O, I have read it; it is heresy. Have you no more to say?

VIO. Good madam, let me see your face.

OLI. Have you any commission from your lord to negotiate with my face? you are now out of your text: but we will draw the curtain, and show you the picture. Look you, sir, such a one I was this present: is't not well done? [*Unveiling.*

VIO. Excellently done, if God did all.

OLI. 'Tis in grain, sir; 'twill endure wind and weather.

VIO. 'Tis beauty truly blent, whose red and white
Nature's own sweet and cunning hand laid on:
Lady, you are the cruel'st she alive,
If you will lead these graces to the grave,
And leave the world no copy.

OLI. O, sir, I will not be so hard-hearted; I will give out divers schedules of my beauty: it shall be inventoried, and every particle and utensil, labelled to my will: as, *item*, two lips indifferent red; *item*, two grey eyes, with lids to them; *item*, one neck, one chin, and so forth. Were you sent hither to *praise*[c] me?

VIO. I see you what you are,—you are too proud;
But, if you were the devil, you are fair.
My lord and master loves you: O, such love
Could be but recompens'd, though you were crown'd
The nonpareil of beauty!

OLI. How does he love me?

VIO. With adorations, with* fertile tears,
With groans that thunder love, with sighs of fire.

OLI. Your lord does know my mind, I cannot love him:
Yet I suppose him virtuous, know him noble,
Of great estate, of fresh and stainless youth;
In voices well divulg'd, free, learn'd, and valiant,
And, in dimension and the shape of nature,
A gracious person; but yet I cannot love him;
He might have took his answer long ago.

VIO. If I did love you in my master's flame,
With such a suffering, such a deadly life,
In your denial I would find no sense;
I would not understand it.

OLI. Why, what would you?

VIO. Make me a willow cabin at your gate,
And call upon my soul within the house;
Write loyal cantons of contemned love,
And sing them loud even in the dead of night;
Holla your name to the reverberate hills,
And make the babbling gossip of the air
Cry out, *Olivia!* O, you should not rest
Between the elements of air and earth,
But you should pity me.

OLI. You might do much. What is your parentage?

VIO. Above my fortunes, yet my state is well:
I am a gentleman.

OLI. Get you to your lord;
I cannot love him: let him send no more;
Unless, perchance, you come to me again,
To tell me how he takes it. Fare you well:
I thank you for your pains: spend this for me.

VIO. I am no fee'd post, lady; keep your purse;

---

a *If you be* not *mad,*—] We should perhaps read—"If you be *but* mad," &c. that is, "*If you are a mere madman, begone,*" &c. No two words are more frequently confounded in these plays than *not* and *but*.

b OLI. Tell me your mind.
VIO. I am a messenger.]

In the old copy these lines are annexed to the preceding speech, thus,—"VIO. . . Some mollification for your Giant, sweete Ladie; tell me your minde, I am a messenger."

c *To* praise *me?*] That is, to *value*, to *appraise* me.

(*) Old copy omits, *with*.

My master, not myself, lacks recompense.
Love make his heart of flint, that you shall love;
And let your fervour, like my master's, be
Plac'd in contempt! Farewell, fair cruelty. [*Exit.*

OLI. *What is your parentage?*
Above my fortunes, yet my state is well;
I am a gentleman.——I'll be sworn thou art;
Thy tongue, thy face, thy limbs, actions, and spirit,
Do give thee five-fold blazon:—not too fast:—soft! soft!
Unless the master were the man.—How now?
Even so quickly may one catch the plague?
Methinks, I feel this youth's perfections,
With an invisible and subtle stealth,
To creep in at mine eyes. Well, let it be.—
What ho, Malvolio!—

Re-enter MALVOLIO.

MAL. Here, madam, at your service.

OLI. Run after that same peevish messenger,
The county's man; he left this ring behind him
Would I or not; tell him, I'll none of it.
Desire him not to flatter with his lord,
Nor hold him up with hopes; I am not for him:
If that the youth will come this way to-morrow,
I'll give him reasons for 't. Hie thee, Malvolio.

MAL. Madam, I will. [*Exit.*

OLI. I do I know not what; and fear to find
Mine eye too great a flatterer for my mind.
Fate, show thy force: ourselves we do not owe;
What is decreed must be;—and be this so!
[*Exeunt.*

ACT II.

SCENE I.—*The Sea-coast.*

Enter ANTONIO *and* SEBASTIAN.

ANT. Will you stay no longer? nor will you not that I go with you?

SEB. By your patience, no: my stars shine darkly over me; the malignancy of my fate might perhaps distemper yours; therefore I shall crave of you your leave, that I may bear my evils alone: it were a bad recompense for your love, to lay any of them on you.

ANT. Let me yet know of you, whither you are bound.

SEB. No, sooth, sir; my determinate voyage is mere extravagancy. But I perceive in you so excellent a touch of modesty, that you will not extort from me what I am willing to keep in; therefore it charges me in manners the rather to express myself. You must know of me, then, Antonio, my name is Sebastian, which I called Roderigo; my father was that Sebastian of Messaline, whom I know you have heard of: he left behind him myself and a sister, both born in an hour: if the heavens had been pleased, would we had so ended! but you, sir, altered that; for, some hour before you took me from the breach of the sea was my sister drowned.

ANT. Alas the day!

SEB. A lady, sir, though it was said she much resembled me, was yet of many accounted beautiful: but, though I could not, with such estimable wonder, over-far believe that, yet thus far I will boldly publish her—she bore a mind that envy could not but call fair. She is drowned already, sir, with salt water, though I seem to drown her remembrance again with more.

ANT. Pardon me, sir, your bad entertainment.

SEB. O, good Antonio, forgive me your trouble!

ANT. If you will not murder me for my love, let me be your servant.

SEB. If you will not undo what you have done, that is, kill him whom you have recovered, desire it not. Fare ye well at once: my bosom is full of kindness; and I am yet so near the manners of my mother, that upon the least occasion more, mine eyes will tell tales of me. I am bound to the count Orsino's court: farewell. [*Exit.*

ANT. The gentleness of all the gods go with thee!
I have many enemies in Orsino's court,
Else would I very shortly see thee there:
But, come what may, I do adore thee so,
That danger shall seem sport, and I will go. [*Exit.*

SCENE II.—*A Street.*

Enter VIOLA; MALVOLIO *following*.

MAL. Were not you even now with the countess Olivia?

VIO. Even now, sir; on a moderate pace I have since arrived but hither.

MAL. She returns this ring to you, sir; you might have saved me my pains, to have taken it away yourself. She adds, moreover, that you should put your lord into a desperate assurance she will none of him: and one thing more, that you be never so hardy to come again in his affairs, unless it be to report your lord's taking of this. Receive it so.

VIO. She took the ring of me;—I'll none of it.

MAL. Come, sir, you peevishly threw it to her; and her will is, it should be so returned: if it be worth stooping for, there it lies in your eye; if not, be it his that finds it. [*Exit.*

VIO. I left no ring with her. What means this lady?
Fortune forbid, my outside have not charm'd her!
She made good view of me; indeed, so much,
That methought her eyes had lost her tongue,
For she did speak in starts distractedly.
She loves me, sure; the cunning of her passion
Invites me in this churlish messenger.
None of my lord's ring! why, he sent her none.
I am the man! If it be so,—as 'tis,—
Poor lady, she were better love a dream.
Disguise, I see, thou art a wickedness,
Wherein the pregnant enemy does much.
How easy is it for the proper-false
In women's waxen hearts to set their forms!
Alas, our* frailty is the cause, not we!
For, such as we are made of,† such we be.
How will this fadge? My master loves her dearly,
And I, poor monster, fond as much on him.
And she, mistaken, seems to dote on me:
What will become of this! As I am man,
My state is desperate for my master's love;
As I am woman—now alas the day!—
What thriftless sighs shall poor Olivia breathe!
O time, thou must untangle this, not I;
It is too hard a knot for me t' untie! [*Exit.*

SCENE III.—*A Room in* Olivia's *House.*

Enter Sir TOBY BELCH *and Sir* ANDREW AGUE-CHEEK.

SIR TO. Approach, sir Andrew: not to be a-bed after midnight, is to be up betimes; and *diluculo surgere*, thou knowest,——

SIR AND. Nay, by my troth, I know not: but I know, to be up late is to be up late.

SIR TO. A false conclusion; I hate it as an unfilled can. To be up after midnight, and to go to bed then, is early: so that, to go to bed after midnight, is to go to bed betimes. Does not our life[a] consist of the four elements?

SIR AND. Faith, so they say, but I think it rather consists of eating and drinking.

SIR TO. Thou'rt a scholar; let us therefore eat and drink.—Marian, I say!——a stoop of wine!

SIR AND. Here comes the fool, i' faith.

Enter Clown.

CLO. How now, my hearts! Did you never see the picture of we three? (1)

SIR TO. Welcome, ass. Now let's have a catch.

SIR AND. By my troth, the fool has an excellent breast.[b] I had rather than forty shillings I had such a leg, and so sweet a breath to sing, as the fool has. In sooth, thou wast in very gracious fooling last night, when thou spok'st of Pigrogromitus, of the Vapians passing the equinoctial of Queubus; (2) 'twas very good, i' faith. I sent thee sixpence for thy leman:[c] hadst it?

CLO. I did impeticos thy gratillity; for Malvolio's nose is no whipstock: my lady has a white hand, and the Myrmidons are no bottle-ale houses.

SIR AND. Excellent! Why, this is the best fooling, when all is done. Now, a song.

SIR TO. Come on; there is sixpence for you: let's have a song.

SIR AND. There's a testril of me too: if one knight give a——

CLO. Would you have a love-song, or a song of good life?[d]

SIR TO. A love-song, a love-song.

SIR AND. Ay, ay; I care not for good life.

SONG.

CLO. *O mistress mine, where are you roaming?*
O, stay and hear; your true-love's coming,
That can sing both high and low:
Trip no further, pretty sweeting;
Journeys end in lovers' meeting,
Every wise man's son doth know.

SIR AND. Excellent good, i' faith!

SIR TO. Good, good.

(*) Old copy, *O*. (†) Old text, *if*; corrected by Tyrwhitt.

[a] *Does not our* life *consist of the four elements?*] The old copy has *lives*, and the modern lection is, "*Do* not our *lives*," &c.; but see sir Andrew's rejoinder:—"I think, *it* rather consists," &c.

[b] *An excellent* breast.] *Breast* meant *voice*. The phrase is so common in our old writers that it would be superfluous to cite examples of its use in this sense.

[c] *Sixpence for thy* leman:] The old copy reads *lemon*. *Leman* signified *sweet-heart* or *mistress*.

[d] A song of good life?] That is, a *moral* song.

CLO. *What is love? 't is not hereafter;*
Present mirth hath present laughter;
What's to come is still unsure:
In delay there lies no plenty;
Then come kiss me, sweet-and-twenty:[a]
Youth's a stuff will not endure.

SIR AND. A mellifluous voice, as I am true knight.

SIR TO. A contagious breath.

SIR AND. Very sweet and contagious, i'faith.

SIR TO. To hear by the nose, it is dulcet in contagion. But shall we make the welkin dance indeed? Shall we rouse the night-owl in a catch that will draw three souls out of one weaver? shall we do that?

SIR AND. An you love me, let's do't: I am dog at a catch.

CLO. By'r lady, sir, and some dogs will catch well.

SIR AND. Most certain. Let our catch be, *Thou knave.*(3)

CLO. *Hold thy peace, thou knave,* knight? I shall be constrained in't to call thee *knave,* knight.

SIR AND. 'T is not the first time I have constrained one to call me knave. Begin, fool; it begins, *Hold thy peace.*

CLO. I shall never begin, if I hold my peace.

SIR AND. Good, i'faith! Come, begin.
[*They sing a catch.*

Enter MARIA.

MAR. What a caterwauling do you keep here! If my lady have not called up her steward, Malvolio, and bid him turn you out of doors, never trust me.

SIR TO. My lady's a Cataian, we are politicians; Malvolio's a Peg a-Ramsey,(4) and *Three merry men be we.*(5) Am not I consanguineous? am I not of her blood? Tilly-vally; *lady! There dwelt a man in Babylon, lady, lady!*(6)
[*Singing.*

CLO. Beshrew me, the knight's in admirable fooling.

SIR AND. Ay, he does well enough, if he be disposed, and so do I too; he does it with a better grace, but I do it more natural.

SIR TO. *O, the twelfth day of December,*—
[*Singing.*

MAR. For the love o' God, peace!

Enter MALVOLIO.

MAL. My masters, are you mad? or what are you? Have you no wit, manners, nor honesty, but to gabble like tinkers at this time of night? Do ye make an alehouse of my lady's house, that ye squeak out your coziers'[b] catches without any mitigation or remorse of voice? Is there no respect of place, persons, nor time, in you?

SIR TO. We did keep time, sir, in our catches. Sneck-up.[c]

MAL. Sir Toby, I must be round with you. My lady bade me tell you, that, though she harbours you as her kinsman, she's nothing allied to your disorders. If you can separate yourself and your misdemeanours, you are welcome to the house; if not, an it would please you to take leave of her, she is very willing to bid you farewell.

SIR TO. *Farewell, dear heart, since I must needs be gone.*[d](7) [*Singing.*

MAL. Nay, good sir Toby.

CLO. *His eyes do show his days are almost done.* [*Singing.*

MAL. Is't even so?

SIR TO. *But I will never die.* [*Singing.*

CLO. Sir Toby, there you lie.

MAL. This is much credit to you.

SIR TO. *Shall I bid him go?* [*Singing.*

CLO. *What an if you do?* [*Singing.*

SIR TO. *Shall I bid him go, and spare not?*
[*Singing.*

CLO. *O no, no, no, no, you dare not.*
[*Singing.*

SIR TO. Out o' tune, sir?[e] ye lie.—Art any more than a steward? Dost thou think, because thou art virtuous, there shall be no more cakes and ale?

CLO. Yes, by Saint Anne; and ginger shall be hot i'the mouth too.

SIR TO. Thou'rt i'the right.—Go sir, rub your chain with crumbs.[f] A stoop of wine, Maria!

---

a Sweet-and-twenty:] A proverbial endearment; thus in "The Merry Devil of Edmonton," "—— his little wanton wagtailes, his *sweet and twenties,* his pretty pinckineyd pigsnies," &c.

b Coziers' *catches*—] A *cozier* meant a botcher of clothes or shoes.

c Sneck-up.] A contemptuous exclamation, equivalent to "go hang:"—

"And now, helter-skelter, to th' rest of the house:
The most are good fellows, and love to carouse;
Who's not may go *sneck-up;* he's not worth a louse
That stops a health i' th' round."

Song by Patrick Carey, "Come, faith, since I'm parting." (See CHAPPELL'S *Popular Music of the Olden Time,* Vol. I. p. 289.)

d Farewell, dear heart, &c.] This and the subsequent lines sung by sir Toby and the Clown are modified snatches of an ancient ballad, which will be found in the Illustrative Comments on this comedy.

e *Out o' tune, sir?*] Very needlessly changed to "Out of *time!*" in most editions. Sir Toby desires an excuse for insulting the Steward, and finds it in pretending he had decried their singing.

f Rub your chain with crumbs.] The steward's badge of office formerly was a gold chain, and the usual mode of cleaning plate was by rubbing it with crumbs. See Webster's play of "The Duchess of Malfy:"—"Yea, and the chippings of the butlery fly after him, to *scouer his gold chain.*"

Mal. Mistress Mary, if you prized my lady's favour at any thing more than contempt, you would not give means for this uncivil rule; she shall know of it, by this hand. [*Exit.*

Mar. Go shake your ears.

Sir And. 'Twere as good a deed as to drink when a man's a-hungry, to challenge him the field, and then to break promise with him, and make a fool of him.

Sir To. Do't, knight; I'll write thee a challenge: or I'll deliver thy indignation to him by word of mouth.

Mar. Sweet sir Toby, be patient for to-night; since the youth of the count's was to-day with my lady, she is much out of quiet. For monsieur Malvolio, let me alone with him: if I do not gull him into a nay-word,[a] and make him a common

[a] Nay word,—] *By-word;* the old copy has, *ayword.*

recreation, do not think I have wit enough to lie straight in my bed: I know I can do it.

SIR TO. Possess us, possess us; tell us something of him.

MAR. Marry, sir, sometimes he is a kind of puritan.

SIR AND. O, if I thought that, I'd beat him like a dog!

SIR TO. What, for being a puritan? thy exquisite reason, dear knight?

SIR AND. I have no exquisite reason for't, but I have reason good enough.

MAR. The devil a puritan that he is, or any thing constantly, but a time-pleaser; an affectioned[a] ass, that cons state without book, and utters it by great swarths:[b] the best persuaded of himself, so crammed, as he thinks, with excellencies, that it is his ground of faith, that all, that look on him, love him; and on that vice in him will my revenge find notable cause to work.

SIR TO. What wilt thou do?

MAR. I will drop in his way some obscure epistles of love; wherein, by the colour of his beard, the shape of his leg, the manner of his gait, the expressure of his eye, forehead, and complexion, he shall find himself most feelingly personated: I can write very like my lady, your niece; on a forgotten matter we can hardly make distinction of our hands.

SIR TO. Excellent! I smell a device.

SIR AND. I have't in my nose too.

SIR TO. He shall think by the letters that thou wilt drop, that they come from my niece, and that she's in love with him?

MAR. My purpose is, indeed, a horse of that colour.

SIR AND. And your horse now would make him an ass.

MAR. Ass, I doubt not.

SIR AND. O, 'twill be admirable.

MAR. Sport royal, I warrant you: I know my physic will work with him. I will plant you two, and let the fool make a third, where he shall find the letter; observe his construction of it. For this night, to bed, and dream on the event. Farewell. [*Exit.*

SIR TO. Good night, Penthesilea.

SIR AND. Before me, she's a good wench.

SIR TO. She's a beagle, true-bred, and one that adores me; what o' that?

SIR AND. I was adored once too.

SIR TO. Let's to bed, knight.—Thou hadst need send for more money.

SIR AND. If I cannot recover your niece, I am a foul way out.

SIR TO. Send for money, knight; if thou hast her not i' the end, call me cut.[c]

SIR AND. If I do not, never trust me, take it how you will.

SIR TO. Come, come; I'll go burn some sack, 'tis too late to go to bed now: come, knight; come, knight. [*Exeunt.*

SCENE IV.—*A Room in the* Duke's *Palace.*

Enter DUKE, VIOLA, CURIO, *and others.*

DUKE. Give me some music.—Now, good morrow, friends:—
Now, good Cesario, but that piece of song,
That old and antique song we heard last night;
Methought it did relieve my passion much,
More than light airs, and recollected terms
Of these most brisk and giddy-paced times:—
Come, but one verse.

CUR. He is not here, so please your lordship, that should sing it.

DUKE. Who was it?

CUR. Feste, the jester, my lord; a fool that the lady Olivia's father took much delight in: he is about the house.

DUKE. Seek him out:—and play the tune the while. [*Exit* CURIO.—*Music.*
Come hither, boy; if ever thou shalt love,
In the sweet pangs of it, remember me:
For such as I am, all true lovers are,—
Unstaid and skittish in all motions else,
Save, in the constant image of the creature
That is belov'd.—How dost thou like this tune?

VIO. It gives a very echo to the seat
Where Love is thron'd.

DUKE. Thou dost speak masterly:
My life upon't, young though thou art, thine eye
Hath staid upon some favour[d] that it loves;—
Hath it not, boy?

VIO. A little, by your favour.

DUKE. What kind of woman is't?

VIO. Of your complexion.

DUKE. She is not worth thee, then. What years, i'faith?

VIO. About your years, my lord.

DUKE. Too old, by heaven: let still the woman take
An elder than herself; so wears she to him,

---

[a] Affectioned—] That is, *affected.*

[b] *Great* swarths:] A *swarth* is explained to mean as much corn or grass as a mower cuts down at one sweep of his scythe.

[c] Call me cut.] *Call me cut* is a phrase not unfrequent in our old plays; so, in the Interlude of "Nature:'—
"Yf thou se him not take his way,
Call me cut, when thou metest me another day."
It appears to be synonymous with the "call me *horse*" of Falstaff, and, Malone suggests, was probably an abbreviation of *curtal.*

[d] Favour—] *Countenance.* In her reply, Viola employs the word in a double sense.

So sways she level in her husband's heart:
For, boy, however we do praise ourselves,
Our fancies are more giddy and unfirm,
More longing, wavering, sooner lost and worn,[a]
Than women's are.

VIO. I think it well, my lord.

DUKE. Then let thy love be younger than thyself,
Or thy affection cannot hold the bent:
For women are as roses, whose fair flower,
Being once display'd, doth fall that very hour.

VIO. And so they are: alas, that they are so;—
To die, even when they to perfection grow!

Re-enter CURIO *and* Clown.

DUKE. O fellow, come, the song we had last night,—
Mark it, Cesario; it is old and plain:
The spinsters and the knitters in the sun,
And the free maids that weave their thread with bones,
Do use to chant it; it is silly sooth,
And dallies with the innocence of love,
Like the old age.

CLO. Are you ready, sir?

DUKE. Ay; pr'ythee, sing. [*Music.*

SONG.

CLO. *Come away, come away, death,*
And in sad cypress let me be laid;
Fly away, fly* breath;*
I am slain by a fair cruel maid.
My shroud of white, stuck all with yew,
O, prepare it!
My part of death, no one so true
Did share it.

Not a flower, not a flower sweet,
On my black coffin let there be strown;
Not a friend, not a friend greet
My poor corpse, where my bones shall be thrown:
A thousand thousand sighs to save,
Lay me, O, where
Sad true lover ne'er find my grave,
To weep there! (8)

DUKE. There's for thy pains.

CLO. No pains, sir; I take pleasure in singing, sir.

DUKE. I'll pay thy pleasure then.

CLO. Truly, sir, and pleasure will be paid, one time or another.

DUKE. Give me now leave to leave thee.

CLO. Now, the melancholy god protect thee; and the tailor make thy doublet of changeable taffeta, for thy mind is a very opal![b]—I would have men of such constancy put to sea, that their business might be everything, and their intent everywhere; for that's it that always makes a good voyage of nothing.—Farewell. [*Exit* Clown.

DUKE. Let all the rest give place.—
[*Exeunt* CURIO *and* Attendants.
Once more, Cesario,
Get thee to yond same sovereign cruelty:
Tell her, my love, more noble than the world,
Prizes not quantity of dirty lands;
The parts that fortune hath bestow'd upon her,
Tell her, I hold as giddily as fortune;
But 'tis that miracle and queen of gems,
That nature pranks her in, attracts my soul.

VIO. But if she cannot love you, sir?

DUKE. I* cannot be so answer'd.

VIO. Sooth, but you must.
Say that some lady, as, perhaps, there is,
Hath for your love as great a pang of heart
As you have for Olivia: you cannot love her;
You tell her so: must she not, then, be answer'd?

DUKE. There is no woman's sides,
Can bide the beating of so strong a passion
As love doth give my heart: no woman's heart
So big, to hold so much; they lack retention.
Alas, their love may be call'd appetite,—
No motion of the liver, but the palate,—
That suffer surfeit, cloyment, and revolt;
But mine is all as hungry as the sea,
And can digest as much: make no compare
Between that love a woman can bear me,
And that I owe Olivia.

VIO. Ay, but I know,—

DUKE. What dost thou know?

VIO. Too well what love women to men may owe:
In faith, they are as true of heart as we.
My father had a daughter lov'd a man,
As it might be, perhaps, were I a woman,
I should your lordship.

DUKE. And what's her history?

VIO. A blank, my lord. She never told her love,
But let concealment, like a worm i' the bud,
Feed on her damask cheek: she pin'd in thought;
And, with a green and yellow melancholy,
She sat like Patience on a monument,
Smiling at grief. Was not this love indeed?
We men may say more, swear more, but, indeed,
Our shows are more than will; for still we prove

(*) Old text, *Fye—fie.*

[a] *Sooner lost and* worn,—] Johnson proposed to read *won* for *worn*, and perhaps rightly.

(*) Old text, *It.*

[b] *For thy mind is a very* opal!] The *opal* being a stone which varies its hues according to the different lights in which it is seen.

Much in our vows, but little in our love.

DUKE. But died thy sister of her love, my boy?

VIO. I am all the daughters of my father's house,
And all the brothers too;—and yet I know not:—
Sir, shall I to this lady?

DUKE. Ay, that's the theme.
To her in haste; give her this jewel; say,
My love can give no place, bide no denay.

[*Exeunt.*

SCENE V.—Olivia's *Garden.*

Enter Sir TOBY BELCH, *Sir* ANDREW AGUE-CHEEK, *and* FABIAN.

SIR TO. Come thy ways, signior Fabian.

FAB. Nay, I'll come; if I lose a scruple of this sport, let me be boiled to death with melancholy.

SIR TO. Wouldst thou not be glad to have the niggardly rascally sheep-biter come by some notable shame?

FAB. I would exult, man: you know, he brought me out o' favour with my lady, about a bear-baiting here.

SIR TO. To anger him, we'll have the bear again; and we will fool him black and blue:—shall we not, sir Andrew?

SIR AND. An we do not, it is pity of our lives.

SIR TO. Here comes the little villain.

Enter MARIA.

How now, my nettle[a] of India?

MAR. Get ye all three into the box-tree: Malvolio's coming down this walk; he has been yonder i' the sun, practising behaviour to his own shadow this half hour: observe him, for the love of mockery; for I know this letter will make a

---

[a] *My* nettle *of India?*] So the second folio. That of 1623 has *mettle*, which in most of the modern editions is changed into *metal*, and explained to mean *gold*. By the *nettle of India*, Steevens says, is meant a zoophyte, called *Urtica Marina*, abounding in the Indian seas. "Quæ tacta totius corporis pruritum quendam excitat, unde nomen Urticæ est sortita."—FRANZII, *Hist. Animal.* 1665, p. 620. This plant is likewise mentioned in Greene's "Card of Fancie," 1608:—"The *flower of India*, pleasant to be seen, but whoso smelleth to it feeleth present smart."

contemplative idiot of him. Close, in the name of jesting! [*The men hide themselves.*] Lie thou there; [*Throws down a letter.*] for here comes the trout that must be caught with tickling.

[*Exit* MARIA.

Enter MALVOLIO.

MAL. 'Tis but fortune; all is fortune. Maria once told me she did affect me: and I have heard herself come thus near, that, should she fancy, it should be one of my complexion. Besides, she uses me with a more exalted respect than any one else that follows her. What should I think on't?

SIR TO. Here's an over-weening rogue!

FAB. O, peace! Contemplation makes a rare turkey-cock of him; how he jets under his advanced plumes!

SIR AND. 'Slight, I could so beat the rogue!

SIR TO. Peace! I say.

MAL. To be count Malvolio;—

SIR TO. Ah, rogue!

SIR AND. Pistol him, pistol him.

SIR TO. Peace, peace!

MAL. There is example for't; the lady of the Strachy [a] married the yeoman of the wardrobe.

SIR AND. Fie on him, Jezabel!

FAB. O, peace! now he's deeply in; look how imagination blows him.

MAL. Having been three months married to her, sitting in my state,—

SIR TO. O, for a stone-bow,(9) to hit him in the eye!

MAL. Calling my officers about me, in my branched velvet gown; having come from a day-bed, where I have left Olivia sleeping,—

SIR TO. Fire and brimstone!

FAB. O, peace, peace.

MAL. And then to have the humour of state: and after a demure travel of regard,—telling them, I know my place, as I would they should do theirs—to ask for my kinsman Toby;—

SIR TO. Bolts and shackles!

FAB. O, peace, peace, peace! now, now.

MAL. Seven of my people, with an obedient start, make out for him: I frown the while; and, perchance, wind up my watch, or play with some rich jewel. Toby approaches; court'sies there to me,—

SIR TO. Shall this fellow live?

FAB. Though our silence be drawn from us with cars,[b] yet peace.

MAL. I extend my hand to him thus,—quenching my familiar smile with an austere regard of control,—

SIR TO. And does not Toby take you a blow o' the lips then?

MAL. Saying, *Cousin Toby, my fortunes having cast me on your niece, give me this prerogative of speech,*—

SIR TO. What, what?

MAL. *You must amend your drunkenness.*

SIR TO. Out, scab!

FAB. Nay, patience, or we break the sinews of our plot.

MAL. *Besides, you waste the treasure of your time with a foolish knight;*—

SIR AND. That's me, I warrant you.

MAL. *One sir Andrew:*—

SIR AND. I knew, 'twas I; for many do call me fool.

MAL. What employment have we here?

[*Taking up the letter.*

FAB. Now is the woodcock near the gin.

SIR TO. O, peace! and the spirit of humours intimate reading aloud to him!

MAL. By my life, this is my lady's hand: these be her very *C*'s, her *U*'s, and her *T*'s; and thus makes she her great *P*'s. It is, in contempt of question, her hand.

SIR AND. Her *C*'s, her *U*'s, and her *T*'s: why that?

MAL. [*Reads.*] *To the unknown beloved, this, and my good wishes:* her very phrases!—By your leave, wax.—Soft!—and the impressure her Lucrece, with which she uses to seal: 'tis my lady. To whom should this be?

FAB. This wins him, liver and all.

MAL. [*Reads.*] *Jove knows, I love:*
But who?
Lips do not move:
No man must know.

No man must know.—What follows? the numbers altered!—*No man must know*:—if this should be thee, Malvolio!

SIR TO. Marry, hang thee, brock!

MAL. [*Reads.*]

I may command where I adore;
But silence, like a Lucrece' knife,
With bloodless stroke my heart doth gore;
M, O, A, I, *doth sway my life.*

FAB. A fustian riddle!

SIR TO. Excellent wench, say I.

MAL. *M, O, A, I,*(10) *doth sway my life.*—Nay, but first, let me see,—let me see,—let me see.

FAB. What dish of poison has she dressed him!

[a] *The lady of the* Strachy—] The allusion is obviously to some old story in which a lady of distinction married a person much beneath her, but who she was, and whether *Strachy* was her name, her family, or her occupation, are as much a mystery now as they were a century ago.

[b] *With* cars,—] For *cars*, an undoubted misprint, Hanmer gave "*by th' ears*;" Johnson proposed "with *carts*;" Tyrwhitt, "with *cables*;" Mr. Singer, "*tears*;" and Mr. Sidney Walker, "with *racks*;" which last we consider preferable to any suggestion yet offered.

SIR TO. And with what wing the stannyel* checks at it!

MAL. *I may command where I adore.* Why, she may command me: I serve her; she is my lady. Why, this is evident to any formal capacity; there is no obstruction in this;—and the end,—what should that alphabetical position portend? if I could make that resemble something in me,—Softly!—*M, O, A, I.*—

(*) Old text, *stallion;* corrected by Hanmer.

SIR TO. O, ay! make up that:—he is now at a cold scent.

FAB. Sowter will cry upon't, for all this, though it be as rank as a fox.

MAL. *M*,—Malvolio;—*M*,—why, that begins my name.

FAB. Did not I say, he would work it out? the cur is excellent at faults.

MAL. *M*,—but then there is no consonancy in the sequel; that suffers under probation: *A* should follow, but *O* does.

FAB. And *O* shall end, I hope.

SIR TO. Ay, or I'll cudgel him, and make him cry *O!*

MAL. And then *I* comes behind.

FAB. Ay, an you had any eye behind you, you might see more detraction at your heels than fortunes before you.

MAL. *M, O, A, I*;—This simulation is not as the former:—and yet, to crush this a little, it would bow to me, for every one of these letters are in my name. Soft! here follows prose.—[*Reads.*] *If this fall into thy hand, revolve. In my stars I am above thee; but be not afraid of greatness: some are born** *great, some achieve greatness, and some have greatness thrust upon 'em. Thy Fates open their hands; let thy blood and spirit embrace them. And, to inure thyself to what thou art like to be, cast thy humble slough and appear fresh. Be opposite with a kinsman, surly with servants: let thy tongue tang arguments of state; put thyself into the trick of singularity: she thus advises thee that sighs for thee. Remember who commended thy yellow stockings, and wished to see thee ever cross-gartered; I say, remember. Go to; thou art made, if thou desirest to be so; if not, let me see thee a steward still, the fellow of servants, and not worthy to touch Fortune's fingers. Farewell. She that would alter services with thee,*

THE FORTUNATE UNHAPPY.

Day-light and champian discovers not more: this is open. I will be proud, I will read politic authors, I will baffle sir Toby, I will wash off gross acquaintance, I will be point-de-vice, the very man. I do not now fool myself, to let imagination jade me: for every reason excites to this, that my lady loves me. She did commend my yellow stockings of late, she did praise my leg being cross-gartered; and in this she manifests herself to my love, and, with a kind of injunction, drives me to these habits of her liking. I thank my stars, I am happy. I will be strange, stout, in yellow stockings, and cross-gartered, even with the swiftness of putting on. Jove, and my stars be praised!—Here is yet a postscript. [*Reads.*] *Thou canst not choose but know who I am. If thou entertainest my love, let it appear in thy smiling; thy smiles become thee well: therefore in my presence still smile, dear my sweet, I pr'ythee.* Jove, I thank thee.—I will smile: I will do every thing that thou wilt have me. [*Exit.*

FAB. I will not give my part of this sport for a pension of thousands to be paid from the Sophy.

SIR TO. I could marry this wench for this device,—

SIR AND. So could I too.

SIR TO. And ask no other dowry with her, but such another jest.

SIR AND. Nor I neither.

FAB. Here comes my noble gull-catcher.

Re-enter MARIA.

SIR TO. Wilt thou set thy foot o' my neck?

SIR AND. Or o' mine either?

SIR TO. Shall I play my freedom at tray-trip,[a] and become thy bond-slave?

SIR AND. I'faith, or I either?

SIR TO. Why, thou hast put him in such a dream, that, when the image of it leaves him, he must run mad.

MAR. Nay, but say true; does it work upon him?

SIR TO. Like aqua-vitæ with a midwife.

MAR. If you will, then, see the fruits of the sport, mark his first approach before my lady: he will come to her in yellow stockings, and 'tis a colour she abhors, and cross-gartered, a fashion she detests; and he will smile upon her, which will now be so unsuitable to her disposition, being addicted to a melancholy as she is, that it cannot but turn him into a notable contempt: if you will see it, follow me.

SIR TO. To the gates of Tartar,[b] thou most excellent devil of wit!

SIR AND. I'll make one too. [*Exeunt.*

(*) Old text, *become*.

[a] *Tray-trip*,—] A game similar to, if not the same as, our backgammon.

[b] Tartar,—] *Tartarus*. So in "Henry V." Act II. Sc. 2:—

"He might return to vasty *Tartar* back."

ACT III.

SCENE I.—Olivia's *Garden.*

Enter VIOLA, *and* Clown *with a tabor.*(1)

VIO. 'Save thee, friend, and thy music: dost thou live by thy tabor?

CLO. No, sir, I live by the church.

VIO. Art thou a churchman?

CLO. No such matter, sir; I do live by the church, for I do live at my house, and my house doth stand by the church.

VIO. So thou may'st say, the king lies by a beggar, if a beggar dwell near him; or the church stands by thy tabor, if thy tabor stand by the church.

CLO. You have said, sir.—To see this age!—A sentence is but a cheveril glove[a] to a good wit; how quickly the wrong side may be turned outward!

VIO. Nay, that's certain; they, that dally nicely with words, may quickly make them wanton.

CLO. I would, therefore, my sister had had no name, sir.

VIO. Why, man?

CLO. Why, sir, her name's a word; and to dally with that word, might make my sister wanton: but, indeed, words are very rascals, since bonds disgraced them.

VIO. Thy reason, man?

CLO. Troth, sir, I can yield you none without words; and words are grown so false, I am loth to prove reason with them.

VIO. I warrant thou art a merry fellow, and carest for nothing.

CLO. Not so, sir, I do care for something: but in my conscience, sir, I do not care for you; if that be to care for nothing, sir, I would it would make you invisible.

VIO. Art not thou the lady Olivia's fool?

CLO. No, indeed, sir; the lady Olivia has no folly: she will keep no fool, sir, till she be married; and fools are as like husbands as pilchards are to herrings,—the husband's the bigger; I am, indeed, not her fool, but her corrupter of words.

VIO. I saw thee late at the count Orsino's.

CLO. Foolery, sir, does walk about the orb, like the sun; it shines everywhere. I would be sorry, sir, but the fool should be as oft with your master as with my mistress: I think, I saw your wisdom there.

a *Cheveril* glove—] See note (e), p. 180, Vol. I.

VIO. Nay, an thou pass upon me, I'll no more with thee. Hold, there's expenses for thee.

CLO. Now Jove, in his next commodity of hair, send thee a beard!

VIO. By my troth, I'll tell thee,—I am almost sick for one; though I would not have it grow on my chin. Is thy lady within?

CLO. Would not a pair of these have bred, sir?

VIO. Yes, being kept together, and put to use.

CLO. I would play lord Pandarus of Phrygia, sir, to bring a Cressida to this Troilus.

VIO. I understand you, sir; 't is well begged.

CLO. The matter, I hope, is not great, sir, begging but a beggar; Cressida was a beggar. My lady is within, sir. I will construe to them whence you come; who you are, and what you would, are out of my welkin,—I might say, element, but the word is over-worn. [*Exit.*

VIO. This fellow's wise enough to play the fool;
And to do that well craves a kind of wit;
He must observe their mood on whom he jests,
The quality of persons, and the time;
And, like the haggard, check at every feather
That comes before his eye. This is a practice,
As full of labour as a wise man's art:
For folly, that he wisely shows, is fit;
But wise men,* folly-fallen, quite taint their wit.

Enter Sir TOBY BELCH *and Sir* ANDREW AGUECHEEK.

SIR TO. 'Save you, gentleman.

VIO. And you, sir.

SIR AND. *Dieu vous garde, monsieur.*

VIO. *Et vous aussi; votre serviteur.*

SIR AND. I hope, sir, you are, and I am yours.

SIR TO. Will you encounter the house? my niece is desirous you should enter, if your trade be to her.

VIO. I am bound to your niece, sir: I mean, she is the list of my voyage.

SIR TO. Taste[a] your legs, sir, put them to motion.

VIO. My legs do better understand me, sir, than I understand what you mean by bidding me *taste* my legs.

SIR TO. I mean, to go, sir, to enter.

VIO. I will answer you with gait and entrance:—but we are prevented.

(*) Old text, *mens.*

[a] Taste—] *Taste* was frequently employed in the old writers as *test*, or *try*. Steevens gives an apt example from Chapman's translation of the Odyssey:—

"——— he now began
To *taste* the bow, the sharp shaft took, tugg'd hard."—*Book* 21.

But Sir Toby uses it as he does *encounter the house*, and as the Clown adopts *welkin* and *element*, to ridicule the fantastic jargon of the Euphuists.

Enter OLIVIA *and* MARIA.

Most excellent accomplished lady, the heavens rain odours on you!

SIR AND. That youth's a rare courtier! *Rain odours!* well.

VIO. My matter hath no voice, lady, but to your own most pregnant and vouchsafed ear.

SIR AND. *Odours, pregnant,* and *vouchsafed:*—I'll get 'em all three ready.*

OLI. Let the garden-door be shut, and leave me to my hearing.

[*Exeunt Sir* TOBY, *Sir* ANDREW, *and* MARIA.

Give me your hand, sir.

VIO. My duty, madam, and most humble service.

OLI. What is your name?

VIO. Cesario is your servant's name, fair princess.

OLI. My servant, sir! 'Twas never merry world,
Since lowly feigning was call'd compliment:
You're servant to the count Orsino, youth.

VIO. And he is yours, and his must needs be yours;
Your servant's servant is your servant, madam.

OLI. For him, I think not on him: for his thoughts,
Would they were blanks, rather than fill'd with me!

VIO. Madam, I come to whet your gentle thoughts
On his behalf:—

OLI. O, by your leave, I pray you,—
I bade you never speak again of him:
But, would you undertake another suit,
I had rather hear you to solicit that
Than music from the spheres.

VIO. Dear lady,——

OLI. Give me leave, beseech you: I did send,
After the last enchantment you did here,
A ring in chase of you; so did I abuse
Myself, my servant, and, I fear me, you:
Under your hard construction must I sit,
To force that on you, in a shameful cunning,
Which you knew none of yours: what might you think?
Have you not set mine honour at the stake,
And baited it with all the unmuzzled thoughts
That tyrannous heart can think? To one of your receiving
Enough is shown; a cyprus,[b] not a bosom,
Hides my heart. So, let me hear you speak.

(*) Old text, *already.*

[b] Cyprus,—] *Cyprus*, or *cipress*, was a thin, transparent stuff, similar to that now called *crape.*

VIO. I pity you.

OLI. That's a degree to love.

VIO. No, not a grise;[a] for 't is a vulgar proof,
That very oft we pity enemies.

OLI. Why, then, methinks, 't is time to smile again.
O world, how apt the poor are to be proud!
If one should be a prey, how much the better
To fall before the lion than the wolf! [*Clock strikes.*
The clock upbraids me with the waste of time.—
Be not afraid, good youth, I will not have you:
And yet, when wit and youth is come to harvest,
Your wife is like to reap a proper man:
There lies your way, due west.

VIO. Then westward-ho!—(2)
Grace and good disposition 'tend your ladyship!
You'll nothing, madam, to my lord by me?

OLI. Stay:
I pr'ythee, tell me what thou think'st of me.

VIO. That you do think you are not what you are.

OLI. If I think so, I think the same of you.

VIO. Then think you right; I am not what I am.

OLI. I would you were as I would have you be!

VIO. Would it be better, madam, than I am?
I wish it might; for now I am your fool.

OLI. [*Aside.*] O, what a deal of scorn looks beautiful
In the contempt and anger of his lip!
A murd'rous guilt shows not itself more soon
Than love that would seem hid: love's night is noon.
Cesario, by the roses of the spring,
By maidhood, honour, truth, and every thing,
I love thee so, that maugre all thy pride,
Nor wit, nor reason, can my passion hide.
Do not extort thy reasons from this clause,
For that I woo, thou therefore hast no cause:
But, rather, reason thus with reason fetter,—
Love sought is good, but given unsought, is better.

VIO. By innocence I swear, and by my youth,
I have one heart, one bosom, and one truth,—
And that no woman has; nor never none
Shall mistress be of it, save I alone.
And so adieu, good madam; never more
Will I my master's tears to you deplore.

OLI. Yet come again: for thou perhaps, may'st move
That heart, which now abhors, to like his love.
[*Exeunt.*

SCENE II.—*A Room in* Olivia's *House.*

Enter Sir TOBY BELCH, *Sir* ANDREW AGUE-CHEEK, *and* FABIAN.

SIR AND. No, faith, I'll not stay a jot longer.

SIR TO. Thy reason, dear venom, give thy reason.

FAB. You must needs yield your reason, Sir Andrew.

SIR AND. Marry, I saw your niece do more favours to the count's serving-man, than ever she bestowed upon me; I saw 't i' the orchard.

SIR TO. Did she see thee[b] the while, old boy? tell me that.

SIR AND. As plain as I see you now.

FAB. This was a great argument of love in her toward you.

SIR AND. 'Slight! will you make an ass o' me?

FAB. I will prove it legitimate, sir, upon the oaths of judgment and reason.

SIR TO. And they have been grand-jurymen, since before Noah was a sailor.

FAB. She did show favour to the youth in your sight, only to exasperate you, to awake your dormouse valour, to put fire in your heart, and brimstone in your liver. You should then have accosted her; and with some excellent jests, fire-new from the mint, you should have banged the youth into dumbness. This was looked for at your hand, and this was balked: the double gilt of this opportunity you let time wash off, and you are now sailed into the north of my lady's opinion; where you will hang like an icicle on a Dutchman's beard, unless you do redeem it by some laudable attempt, either of valour or policy.

SIR AND. And 't be any way, it must be with valour; for policy I hate: I had as lief be a Brownist(3) as a politician.

SIR TO. Why then, build me thy fortunes upon the basis of valour. Challenge me the count's youth to fight with him; hurt him in eleven places; my niece shall take note of it; and assure thyself, there is no love-broker in the world can more prevail in man's commendation with woman, than report of valour.

FAB. There is no way but this, sir Andrew.

SIR AND. Will either of you bear me a challenge to him?

SIR TO. Go, write it in a martial hand; be curst[c] and brief; it is no matter how witty, so it be eloquent and full of invention; taunt him with the licence of ink: if thou *thou'st*(4) him some thrice, it shall not be amiss; and as many lies as will lie in thy sheet of paper, although the sheet were big enough for the bed of Ware in England, set 'em down; go, about it. Let there be gall enough in thy ink, though thou write, with a goose-pen, no matter; about it.

SIR AND. Where shall I find you?

SIR TO. We'll call thee at the *cubiculo*:[d] go.
[*Exit Sir* ANDREW.

FAB. This is a dear manakin to you, sir Toby.

---

[a] *A* grise;] A *step.* Thus in "Othello," Act I. Sc. 3:—
"Which, as a *grise*, or step, may help these lovers."

[b] *Did she see* thee *the while,*—] *Thee* was added by Rowe.
[c] Curst—] *Curst* means *churlish, cross-grained.*
[d] The cubiculo:] We should surely read "*thy* cubiculo."

SIR TO. I have been dear to him, lad,—some two thousand strong, or so.

FAB. We shall have a rare letter from him: but you'll not deliver it.

SIR TO. Never trust me then; and by all means stir on the youth to an answer. I think oxen and wainropes cannot hale them together. For Andrew, if he were opened, and you find so much blood in his liver as will clog the foot of a flea, I'll eat the rest of the anatomy.

FAB. And his opposite,[a] the youth, bears in his visage no great presage of cruelty.

SIR TO. Look where the youngest wren of nine* comes.

Enter MARIA.

MAR. If you desire the spleen, and will laugh yourselves into stitches, follow me. Yond gull, Malvolio, is turned heathen, a very renegado; for there is no Christian, that means to be saved by believing rightly, can ever believe such impossible passages of grossness. He's in yellow stockings!

SIR TO. And cross gartered?

MAR. Most villainously; like a pedant that keeps a school i' the church.[b]—I have dogged him, like his murderer. He does obey every point of the letter that I dropped to betray him: he does smile his face into more lines than are in the new map, with the augmentation of the Indies: (5) you have not seen such a thing as 'tis; I can hardly forbear hurling things at him. I know my lady will strike him; if she do, he'll smile, and take't for a great favour.

SIR TO. Come, bring us, bring us where he is. [*Exeunt.*

SCENE III.—*A Street.*

Enter SEBASTIAN *and* ANTONIO.

SEB. I would not, by my will, have troubled you;
But, since you make your pleasure of your pains,
I will no further chide you.

ANT. I could not stay behind you; my desire,
More sharp than filed steel, did spur me forth;
And not all love to see you, (though so much,
As might have drawn one to a longer voyage,)
But jealousy what might befall your travel,
Being skilless in these parts; which to a stranger,
Unguided, and unfriended, often prove
Rough and unhospitable: my willing love,
The rather by these arguments of fear,
Set forth in your pursuit.

SEB. My kind Antonio,
I can no other answer make, but thanks,
And thanks, and ever thanks; and oft good turns[c]
Are shuffled off with such uncurrent pay:
But, were my worth, as is my conscience, firm,
You should find better dealing. What's to do?
Shall we go see the reliques of this town?

ANT. To-morrow, sir; best first go see your lodging.

SEB. I am not weary, and 'tis long to night:
I pray you let us satisfy our eyes
With the memorials and the things of fame,
That do renown this city.

ANT. Would you'd pardon me;
I do not without danger walk these streets:
Once, in a sea-fight, 'gainst the count his gallies,
I did some service; of such note, indeed,
That, were I ta'en here, it would scarce be answer'd.

SEB. Belike you slew great number of his people?

ANT. The offence is not of such a bloody nature;
Albeit the quality of the time and quarrel
Might well have given us bloody argument.
It might have since been answer'd in repaying
What we took from them; which, for traffic's sake,
Most of our city did: only myself stood out;
For which, if I be lapsed in this place,
I shall pay dear.

SEB. Do not, then, walk too open.

ANT. It doth not fit me. Hold, sir, here's my purse.
In the south suburbs, at the Elephant,
Is best to lodge: I will bespeak our diet,
Whiles you beguile the time and feed your know-[ledge,
With viewing of the town; there shall you have me.

SEB. Why I your purse?

ANT. Haply your eye shall light upon some toy
You have desire to purchase; and your store,
I think, is not for idle markets, sir.

SEB. I'll be your purse bearer, and leave you for an hour.

ANT. To the Elephant.—

SEB. I do remember. [*Exeunt.*

SCENE IV.—Olivia's *Garden.*

Enter OLIVIA *and* MARIA.

OLI. [*Aside.*] I have sent after him: he says he'll come;—
How shall I feast him? what bestow of[d] him?

(*) Old text, *mine.*

[a] Opposite,—] *Opponent, antagonist.*

[b] *Like a pedant that keeps a school* i' the church.] This passage may help to enlighten another in "Love's Labour's Lost," Act V. Sc. 1:—"Do you not educate youth at the *charge*-house on the top of the hill?" where *charge* is most probably a misprint for *church.*

[c] And thanks, and ever thanks; and oft good turns—] In the old copy this stands:—
"And thankes: and ever oft good turnes," &c.
The repetition was suggested by Theobald.

[d] *What bestow* of *him?*] That is, *on* him. *Of* for *on*, *to* for *with*, and the like, are archaisms repeatedly found in works of the time.

For youth is bought more oft than begg'd or borrow'd.
I speak too loud.——
Where is Malvolio?—he is sad and civil,[a]
And suits well for a servant with my fortunes:—
Where is Malvolio? [manner.

MAR. He's coming, madam; but in very strange
He is sure possessed, madam.

OLI. Why, what's the matter? does he rave?

MAR. No, madam, he does nothing but smile: your ladyship were best to have some guard about you, if he come; for, sure, the man is tainted in his wits.

OLI. Go call him hither. [*Exit* MARIA.] I'm as mad as he,
If sad and merry madness equal be.—

Re-enter MARIA, *with* MALVOLIO.

How now, Malvolio!

MAL. Sweet lady, ho, ho. [*Smiles fantastically.*

OLI. Smil'st thou?
I sent for thee upon a sad occasion.

MAL. Sad, lady? I could be sad: this does make some obstruction in the blood, this cross-gartering; but what of that? if it please the eye of one, it is with me as the very true sonnet is, *Please one, and please all.*(6)

OLI. Why, how dost thou, man? what is the matter with thee?

MAL. Not black in my mind, though yellow in my legs. It did come to his hands, and commands shall be executed. I think we do know the sweet Roman hand.

OLI. Wilt thou go to bed, Malvolio?

MAL. To bed! ay, sweet-heart; and I'll come to thee.

OLI. God comfort thee! Why dost thou smile so, and kiss thy hand so oft?

MAR. How do you, Malvolio?

MAL. At your request! Yes; nightingales answer daws.

MAR. Why appear you with this ridiculous boldness before my lady?

MAL. *Be not afraid of greatness*:—'twas well writ.

OLI. What meanest thou by that, Malvolio?

MAL. *Some are born great,*—

OLI. Ha!

MAL. *Some achieve greatness,*—

OLI. What sayest thou?

MAL. *And some have greatness thrust upon them.*

OLI. Heaven restore thee!

MAL. *Remember who commended thy yellow stockings*;—

OLI. Thy[b] yellow stockings!

MAL. *And wished to see thee cross-gartered.*

OLI. Cross-gartered!

MAL. *Go to, thou art made, if thou desirest to be so*;—

OLI. Am I made?

MAL. *If not, let me see thee a servant still.*

OLI. Why, this is very midsummer madness.

Enter Servant.

SER. Madam, the young gentleman of the count Orsino's is returned; I could hardly entreat him back: he attends your ladyship's pleasure.

OLI. I'll come to him. [*Exit* Servant.] Good Maria, let this fellow be looked to. Where's my cousin Toby? Let some of my people have a special care of him; I would not have him miscarry for the half of my dowry.

[*Exeunt* OLIVIA *and* MARIA.

MAL. Oh, ho! do you come near me now? no worse man than sir Toby to look to me? This concurs directly with the letter: she sends him on purpose, that I may appear stubborn to him; for she incites me to that in the letter. *Cast thy humble slough,* says she;—*be opposite with a kinsman, surly with servants,—let thy tongue tang** *with arguments of state,—put thyself into the trick of singularity*;—and, consequently, sets down the manner how; as, a sad face, a reverend carriage, a slow tongue, in the habit of some sir of note, and so forth. I have limed her; but it is Jove's doing, and Jove make me thankful! And, when she went away now, *Let this fellow be looked to*: *fellow!* not Malvolio, nor after my degree, but, *fellow*. Why, everything adheres together; that no dram of a scruple, no scruple of a scruple, no obstacle, no incredulous or unsafe circumstance,—What can be said? Nothing, that can be, can come between me and the full prospect of my hopes. Well, Jove, not I, is the doer of this, and he is to be thanked.

Re-enter MARIA, *with Sir* TOBY BELCH *and* FABIAN.

SIR TO. Which way is he, in the name of sanctity? If all the devils in hell be drawn in little, and Legion himself possessed him, yet I'll speak to him.

---

[a] *He is* sad *and* civil,—] Interpreted to import solemn and *grave*, which is mere tautology. *Civil* here means *tart, sour, bitter*; see note (a), p. 707, Vol. I. Thus in "The Scornful Lady" of Beaumont and Fletcher:—

> "If he be *civil*, not your powder'd sugar,
> Nor your raisins, shall persuade the captain
> To live a coxcomb with him."

(*) Old copy, *langer*.

[b] Thy *yellow stockings!*] Mr. Lettsom suggested, we should read, "*My* yellow stockings!" since Olivia has no idea that Malvolio is quoting the letter.

FAB. Here he is, here he is.—How is't with you, sir? how is't with you, man?

MAL. Go off; I discard you; let me enjoy my private; go off.

MAR. Lo, how hollow the fiend speaks within him! did not I tell you?—Sir Toby, my lady prays you to have a care of him.

MAL. Ah, ah! does she so?

SIR TO. Go to, go to; peace, peace; we must deal gently with him; let me alone. How do you, Malvolio? how is't with you? What, man! defy the devil: consider, he's an enemy to mankind.

MAL. Do you know what you say?

MAR. La you, an you speak ill of the devil, how he takes it at heart! Pray God, he be not bewitched!

FAB. Carry his water to the wise woman.

MAR. Marry, and it shall be done to-morrow morning, if I live. My lady would not lose him for more than I'll say.

MAL. How now, mistress!

MAR. O lord!

SIR TO. Pr'ythee, hold thy peace; this is not the way: do you not see, you move him? let me alone with him.

FAB. No way but gentleness: gently, gently: the fiend is rough, and will not be roughly used.

SIR TO. Why, how now, my bawcock! how dost thou, chuck?

MAL. Sir!

SIR TO. Ay, Biddy, come with me. What, man! 'tis not for gravity to play at cherry-pit with Satan: hang him, foul collier!

MAR. Get him to say his prayers; good sir Toby, get him to pray.

MAL. My prayers, minx!

MAR. No, I warrant you, he will not hear of godliness.

MAL. Go, hang yourselves all! you are idle shallow things; I am not of your element; you shall know more hereafter. [*Exit.*

SIR TO. Is't possible?

FAB. If this were played upon a stage now, I could condemn it as an improbable fiction.

SIR TO. His very genius hath taken the infection of the device, man.

MAR. Nay, pursue him now; lest the device take air, and taint.

FAB. Why, we shall make him mad indeed.

MAR. The house will be the quieter.

SIR TO. Come, we'll have him in a dark room, and bound. My niece is already in the belief that he 's mad; we may carry it thus, for our pleasure and his penance, till our very pastime, tired out of breath, prompt us to have mercy on him: at which time we will bring the device to the bar, and crown thee for a finder of madmen.—But see, but see.

FAB. More matter for a May morning.

Enter Sir ANDREW AGUECHEEK.

SIR AND. Here's the challenge, read it; I warrant there's vinegar and pepper in't.

FAB. Is't so saucy?

SIR AND. Ay, is 't, I warrant him: do but read.

SIR TO. Give me. [*Reads*] *Youth, whatsoever thou art, thou art but a scurvy fellow.*

FAB. Good, and valiant.

SIR TO. [*Reads.*] *Wonder not, nor admire not in thy mind, why I do call thee so, for I will show thee no reason for't.*

FAB. A good note: that keeps you from the blow of the law.

SIR TO. [*Reads.*] *Thou comest to the lady Olivia, and in my sight she uses thee kindly: but thou liest in thy throat;*[a] *that is not the matter I challenge thee for.*

FAB. Very brief, and to exceeding good sense—less.

SIR TO. [*Reads.*] *I will way-lay thee going home; where if it be thy chance to kill me,—*

FAB. Good.

SIR TO. [*Reads.*] *Thou killest me like a rogue and a villain.*

FAB. Still you keep o' the windy side of the law:[b] good.

SIR TO. [*Reads.*] *Fare thee well; and God have mercy upon one of our souls! He may have mercy upon mine; but my hope is better, and so look to thyself. Thy friend, as thou usest him, and thy sworn enemy,*

ANDREW AGUECHEEK.

SIR TO. If this letter move him not, his legs cannot: I'll give't him.

MAR. You may have very fit occasion for't; he is now in some commerce with my lady, and will by and by depart.

SIR TO. Go, sir Andrew; scout me for him at the corner of the orchard, like a bum-bailie: so soon as ever thou seest him, draw; and, as thou drawest, swear horrible; for it comes to pass oft, that a terrible oath, with a swaggering accent sharply twanged off, gives manhood more approbation than ever proof itself would have earned him. Away!

SIR AND. Nay, let me alone for swearing. [*Exit.*

SIR TO. Now will not I deliver his letter: for the behaviour of the young gentleman gives him out to be of good capacity and breeding; his employment between his lord and my niece confirms no less; therefore this letter, being so excellently ignorant, will breed no terror in the youth,—he will find it comes from a clodpole. But, sir, I will deliver his challenge by word of mouth; set upon Aguecheek a notable report of valour; and drive the gentleman, (as I know his youth will aptly receive it,) into a most hideous opinion of his rage, skill, fury, and impetuosity. This will so fright them both, that they will kill one another by the look, like cockatrices.

FAB. Here he comes with your niece: give them way till he take leave, and presently after him.

SIR TO. I will meditate the while upon some horrid message for a challenge.

[*Exeunt Sir* TOBY, FABIAN, *and* MARIA.

Re-enter OLIVIA, *with* VIOLA.

OLI. I have said too much unto a heart of stone,
And laid mine honour too unchary out:*
There's something in me that reproves my fault;
But such a headstrong potent fault it is,
That it but mocks reproof.

VIO. With the same 'haviour that your passion bears,
Go on my master's griefs.

OLI. Here, wear this jewel for me,—'tis my picture;
Refuse it not; it hath no tongue to vex you:
And, I beseech you, come again to-morrow.
What shall you ask of me that I'll deny,
That honour, sav'd, may upon asking give?

VIO. Nothing but this—your true love for my master.

OLI. How with mine honour may I give him that
Which I have given to you?

VIO. I will acquit you.

OLI. Well, come again to-morrow: fare thee well;
A fiend like thee might bear my soul to hell!
[*Exit.*

Re-enter Sir TOBY BELCH *and* FABIAN.

SIR TO. Gentleman, God save thee.

VIO. And you, sir.

SIR TO. That defence thou hast, betake thee to't: of what nature the wrongs are thou hast done him, I know not; but thy intercepter, full of despite, bloody as the hunter, attends thee at the orchard-end: dismount thy tuck,[c] be yare[d] in thy preparation, for thy assailant is quick, skilful, and deadly.

VIO. You mistake, sir, I am sure; no man hath any quarrel to me; my remembrance is very free and clear from any image of offence done to any man.

SIR TO. You'll find it otherwise, I assure you: therefore, if you hold your life at any price, betake you to your guard; for your opposite hath in him what youth, strength, skill, and wrath, can furnish man withal.

(*) Old text, *on't*.

[a] *Thou* liest in thy throat;] See note (2), p. 626, Vol. I.

[b] Still you keep o' the windy side of the law:] Fabian alludes to a ridiculous distinction in the Rules of the Duello, which is aptly explained in the note just mentioned, at page 626, Vol. I. where it will be remarked that to tell a man, "thou liest by the throat," or even, "thou liest by the throat, like a rogue," was an offence expiable without resort to combat; but to say, "thou liest by the throat, like a rogue, *as thou art*," was an affront to be atoned for only by blood.

[c] Dismount thy tuck,—] *Draw thy rapier.*

[d] Yare—] *Yare* means *brisk, nimble.*

VIO. I pray you, sir, what is he?

SIR TO. He is knight, dubbed with unhatched[a] rapier and on carpet consideration; (7) but he is a devil in private brawl; souls and bodies hath he divorced three; and his incensement at this moment is so implacable, that satisfaction can be none but by pangs of death and sepulchre: hob, nob,[b] is his word; give't or take't.

VIO. I will return again into the house, and desire some conduct[c] of the lady. I am no fighter. I have heard of some kind of men that put quarrels purposely on others, to taste[d] their valour: belike this is a man of that quirk.

SIR TO. Sir, no; his indignation derives itself out of a very competent injury; therefore, get you on, and give him his desire. Back you shall not to the house, unless you undertake that with me, which with as much safety you might answer him; therefore, on, or strip your sword stark naked; for meddle you must, that's certain, or forswear to wear iron about you.

VIO. This is as uncivil as strange. I beseech

[a] *Dubbed with* unhatched *rapier*—] From the context it would appear that Malone was right in thinking we ought to read *an hatch'd* rapier, that is, a rapier, the hilt of which was richly inlaid and ornamented. The ordinary lection is *unhacked* rapier.

[b] Hob, nob,—] The same as *Habbe* or *Nabbe*, have or not have, hit or miss. "The citizens in their rage * * * shot *habbe* or *nabbe* at random."—HOLINSHED.

[c] Some conduct—] Some *conductor*.

[d] *To taste their valour:*] See note (a), p. 256.

you, do me this courteous office, as to know of the knight what my offence to him is; it is something of my negligence, nothing of my purpose.

SIR TO. I will do so.—Signior Fabian, stay you by this gentleman till my return.

[*Exit Sir* TOBY.

VIO. Pray you, sir, do you know of this matter?

FAB. I know the knight is incensed against you, even to a mortal arbitrement; but nothing of the circumstance more.

VIO. I beseech you, what manner of man is he?

FAB. Nothing of that wonderful promise, to read him by his form, as you are like to find him in the proof of his valour. He is, indeed, sir, the most skilful, bloody, and fatal opposite that you could possibly have found in any part of Illyria. Will you walk towards him? I will make your peace with him, if I can.

VIO. I shall be much bound to you for't: I am one that would rather go with sir priest than sir knight: I care not who knows so much of my mettle. [*Exeunt.*

SCENE V.—*The Street adjoining* Olivia's *Garden.*

Enter Sir TOBY BELCH *and Sir* ANDREW AGUECHEEK.

SIR TO. Why, man, he's a very devil; I have not seen such a firago. I had a pass with him, rapier, scabbard, and all, and he gives me the stuck-in,[a] with such a mortal motion, that it is inevitable; and on the answer, he pays you as surely as your feet hit the ground they step on: they say, he has been fencer to the Sophy.

SIR AND. Pox on't, I'll not meddle with him.

SIR TO. Ay, but he will not now be pacified: Fabian can scarce hold him yonder.

SIR AND. Plague on't; an I thought he had been valiant and so cunning in fence, I'd have seen him damned ere I'd have challenged him. Let him let the matter slip, and I'll give him my horse, grey Capilet.

SIR TO. I'll make the motion: stand here, make a good show on't; this shall end without the perdition of souls. [*Aside.*] Marry, I'll ride your horse as well as I ride you.

Enter FABIAN *and* VIOLA.

I have his horse [*To* FAB.] to take up the quarrel;
I have persuaded him the youth's a devil.

[a] Stuck-in,—] A corruption of the Italian fencing term, *stoccata.*

FAB. He is as horribly conceited of him, and pants and looks pale, as if a bear were at his heels.

SIR TO. [*To* VIO.] There's no remedy, sir; he will fight with you for his oath sake: marry, he hath better bethought him of his quarrel, and he finds that now scarce to be worth talking of: therefore draw, for the supportance of his vow; he protests, he will not hurt you.

VIO. Pray God defend me! A little thing would make me tell them how much I lack of a man.

[*Aside.*

FAB. Give ground, if you see him furious.

SIR TO. Come, sir Andrew, there's no remedy; the gentleman will, for his honour's sake, have one bout with you: he cannot by the duello avoid it: but he has promised me, as he is a gentleman and a soldier, he will not hurt you. Come on: to't.

SIR AND. Pray God, he keep his oath!

[*Draws.*

VIO. I do assure you 'tis against my will.

[*Draws.*

Enter ANTONIO.

ANT. Put up your sword.—If this young gentleman
Have done offence, I take the fault on me;
If you offend him, I for him defy you. [*Drawing.*

SIR TO. You, sir! why what are you?

ANT. One, sir, that for his love dares yet do more
Than you have heard him brag to you he will.

SIR TO. Nay, if you be an undertaker,[b] I am for you. [*Draws.*

FAB. O good sir Toby, hold! here come the officers.

SIR TO. I'll be with you anon. [*To* ANTONIO.

VIO. Pray, sir, put your sword up, if you please.

[*To Sir* ANDREW.

SIR AND. Marry, will I, sir;—and, for that I promised you, I'll be as good as my word: he will bear you easily, and reins well.

Enter two Officers.

1 OFF. This is the man; do thy office.

2 OFF. Antonio, I arrest thee at the suit
Of count Orsino.

ANT. You do mistake me, sir.

1 OFF. No, sir, no jot; I know your favour well,
Though now you have no sea-cap on your head.—
Take him away; he knows I know him well.

ANT. I must obey.—This comes [*To* VIO.] with seeking you;—

[b] *An* undertaker,—] One who *undertakes* the quarrel of another.

But there's no remedy; I shall answer it.
What will you do, now my necessity
Makes me to ask you for my purse? It grieves [me
Much more for what I cannot do for you,
Than what befals myself. You stand amaz'd;
But be of comfort.

2 OFF. Come, sir, away.

ANT. I must entreat of you some of that money.

VIO. What money, sir?
For the fair kindness you have show'd me here,
And, part, being prompted by your present trouble,
Out of my lean and low ability
I'll lend you something: my having is not much;
I'll make division of my present with you:
Hold, there's half my coffer.

ANT. Will you deny me now?
Is't possible that my deserts to you
Can lack persuasion? Do not tempt my misery,
Lest that it make me so unsound a man
As to upbraid you with those kindnesses
That I have done for you.

VIO. I know of none;
Nor know I you by voice, or any feature:
I hate ingratitude more in a man,
Than lying, vainness, babbling, drunkenness,
Or any taint of vice, whose strong corruption
Inhabits our frail blood.

ANT. O heavens themselves!

2 OFF. Come, sir, I pray you, go.

ANT. Let me speak a little. This youth that you see here
I snatch'd one half out of the jaws of death;
Reliev'd him with such sanctity of love,—
And to his image, which methought did promise
Most venerable worth, did I devotion.

1 OFF. What's that to us? The time goes by; away!

ANT. But, O, how vile an idol proves this god!—
Thou hast, Sebastian, done good feature shame.—
In nature there's no blemish but the mind,
None can be call'd deform'd but the unkind:[a]
Virtue is beauty; but the beauteous-evil
Are empty trunks, o'erflourish'd by the devil.

1 OFF. The man grows mad; away with him!
Come, come, sir.

ANT. Lead me on.

[*Exeunt* Officers *with* ANTONIO.

VIO. Methinks his words do from such passion fly,
That he believes himself; so do not I.
Prove true, imagination, O, prove true,
That I, dear brother, be now ta'en for you.

SIR TO. Come hither, knight; come hither, Fabian; we'll whisper o'er a couple or two of most sage saws.

VIO. He nam'd Sebastian; I my brother know
Yet living in my glass; even such, and so,
In favour was my brother; and he went
Still in this fashion, colour, ornament,—
For him I imitate: O, if it prove,
Tempests are kind, and salt waves fresh in love!

[*Exit.*

SIR TO. A very dishonest paltry boy, and more a coward than a hare: his dishonesty appears in leaving his friend here in necessity, and denying him; and for his cowardship, ask Fabian.

FAB. A coward, a most devout coward, religious in it.

SIR AND. 'Slid, I'll after him again, and beat him.

SIR TO. Do; cuff him soundly, but never draw thy sword.

SIR AND. An I do not,— [*Exit.*

FAB. Come, let's see the event.

SIR TO. I dare lay any money 'twill be nothing yet. [*Exeunt.*

[a] *The* unkind:] The *unnatural.*

ACT IV.

SCENE I.—*The Street before* Olivia's *House.*

Enter SEBASTIAN *and* Clown.

CLO. Will you make me believe that I am not sent for you?

SEB. Go to, go to, thou art a foolish fellow; Let me be clear of thee.

CLO. Well held out, i'faith! No, I do not know you; nor I am not sent to you by my lady, to bid you come speak with her; nor your name is not master Cesario; nor this is not my nose neither.—Nothing that is so is so.

SEB. I pr'ythee, vent thy folly somewhere else: Thou know'st not me.

CLO. *Vent* my folly! he has heard that word of

some great man, and now applies it to a fool. *Vent* my folly! I am afraid this great lubber the world will prove a cockney.[a]—I pr'ythee now, ungird thy strangeness, and tell me what I shall *vent* to my lady; shall I *vent* to her that thou art coming?

SEB. I pr'ythee, foolish Greek, depart from me;
There's money for thee; if you tarry longer,
I shall give worse payment.

CLO. By my troth, thou hast an open hand.—These wise men, that give fools money, get themselves a good report—after fourteen years' purchase.[b]

Enter Sir ANDREW AGUECHEEK.

SIR AND. Now, sir, have I met you again? there's for you. [*Striking* SEBASTIAN.

SEB. Why, there's for thee, and there, and there.—
Are all the people mad? [*Beating Sir* ANDREW.

Enter Sir TOBY BELCH *and* FABIAN.

SIR TO. Hold, sir! or I'll throw your dagger o'er the house.

CLO. This will I tell my lady straight: I would not be in some of your coats for two-pence. [*Exit.*

SIR TO. Come on, sir; hold! [*Holding* SEBASTIAN.

SIR AND. Nay, let him alone, I'll go another way to work with him; I'll have an action of battery against him, if there be any law in Illyria: though I struck him first, yet it's no matter for that.

SEB. Let go thy hand!

SIR TO. Come, sir, I will not let you go. Come, my young soldier, put up your iron: you are well fleshed; come on.

SEB. I will be free from thee. [*Liberates himself.*] What wouldst thou now?
If thou dar'st tempt me further, draw thy sword. [*Draws.*

SIR TO. What, what? Nay, then I must have an ounce or two of this malapert blood from you. [*Draws.*

Enter OLIVIA.

OLI. Hold, Toby; on thy life, I charge thee, hold!

SIR TO. Madam—

OLI. Will it be ever thus? Ungracious wretch,
Fit for the mountains and the barbarous caves,
Where manners ne'er were preach'd! out of my sight!—
Be not offended, dear Cesario!—
Rudesby, be gone!—I pr'ythee, gentle friend,
[*Exeunt Sir* TOBY, *Sir* ANDREW, *and* FABIAN.
Let thy fair wisdom, not thy passion, sway
In this uncivil and unjust extent
Against thy peace. Go with me to my house;
And hear thou there how many fruitless pranks
This ruffian hath botch'd up, that thou thereby
May'st smile at this: thou shalt not choose but go;
Do not deny. Beshrew his soul for me,
He started one poor heart of mine in thee.[c]

SEB. What relish is in this? how runs the stream?
Or I am mad, or else this is a dream:—
Let fancy still my sense in Lethe steep;
If it be thus to dream, still let me sleep![d]

OLI. Nay, come, I pr'ythee: would thou'dst be rul'd by me.

SEB. Madam, I will.

OLI. O, say so, and so be! [*Exeunt.*

SCENE II.—*A Room in* Olivia's *House.*

Enter MARIA *and* Clown.

MAR. Nay, I pr'ythee, put on this gown and this beard; make him believe thou art sir Topas the curate; do it quickly; I'll call sir Toby the whilst. [*Exit* MARIA.

CLO. Well, I'll put it on, and I will dissemble myself in't; and I would I were the first that ever dissembled in such a gown. I am not tall[e] enough to become the function well; nor lean enough to be thought a good student; but to be said an honest man and a good housekeeper, goes as fairly as to say a careful man and a great scholar. The competitors enter.[f]

---

[a] I am afraid this great lubber the world will prove a cockney.] The point of this is not apparent. Douce conjectured we should read—"this great lubberly *word* will prove a cockney." Omitting the adjective "*great*," which may have been caught by the compositor from the line above, Douce's emendation probably gives us what the poet wrote.

[b] After fourteen years' purchase.] That is, After the *rate* of fourteen years' purchase. The current price of land in England when this play was written appears to have been twelve years' purchase; so, buying character of fools was a bad bargain.

[c] *He started one poor* heart *of mine in thee.*] Johnson was doubtful whether an ambiguity were intended between *heart* and *hart*: the hunter's technical phrase *started*, might have convinced him that the poet was playing on the word.

[d] If it be thus to dream, still let me sleep!] This speech recals that of Antipholus of Syracuse ("Comedy of Errors," Act II. Sc. 2), under similar circumstances of bewilderment:—

> "Am I in earth, in heaven, or in hell,—
> Sleeping or waking,—mad or well advis'd?
> Known unto these, and to myself disguis'd?
> I'll say as they say, and persèver so,
> And in this mist at all adventures go."

[e] *I am not* tall *enough,* &c.] For the sake of an antithesis, most modern editors read,—"I am not *fat* enough;" but "*tall*" in its ancient sense of *robust, stout, personable,* offers quite sufficient contrast to the *lean* of the next line.

[f] *The* competitors enter.] That is, the *confederates,* the *colleagues.* See note (c), p. 17, Vol. I.

Enter Sir TOBY BELCH *and* MARIA.

SIR TO. Jove bless thee, master parson.

CLO. *Bonos dies,* sir Toby; for as the old hermit of Prague, that never saw pen and ink, very wittily said to a niece of king Gorboduc, *That, that is, is:* so I, being master parson, am master parson: for what is that, but that? and is, but is?

SIR TO. To him, sir Topas.

CLO. What, ho, I say!—Peace in this prison!

SIR TO. The knave counterfeits well; a good knave.

MAL. [*In an inner chamber.*] Who calls there?

CLO. Sir Topas the curate, who comes to visit Malvolio the lunatic.

MAL. [*Within.*] Sir Topas, sir Topas, good sir Topas, go to my lady.

CLO. Out, hyperbolical fiend! how vexest thou this man! talkest thou nothing but of ladies?

SIR TO. Well said, master parson.

MAL. [*Within.*] Sir Topas, never was man thus wronged: good sir Topas, do not think I am mad; they have laid me here in hideous darkness.

CLO. Fie, thou dishonest Sathan! I call thee by the most modest terms; for I am one of those gentle ones that will use the devil himself with courtesy: sayest thou that house is dark?

MAL. [*Within.*] As hell, sir Topas.

CLO. Why, it hath bay-windows[a] transparent as barricadoes, and the clear-stories(1) towards the south-north are as lustrous as ebony; and yet complainest thou of obstruction?

MAL. [*Within.*] I am not mad, sir Topas; I say to you, this house is dark.

CLO. Madman, thou errest: I say, there is no darkness but ignorance; in which thou art more puzzled than the Egyptians in their fog.

MAL. [*Within.*] I say, this house is as dark as ignorance, though ignorance were as dark as hell; and I say, there was never man thus abused: I am no more mad than you are; make the trial of it in any constant question.

CLO. What is the opinion of Pythagoras concerning wild-fowl?

MAL. [*Within.*] That the soul of our grandam might haply inhabit a bird.

CLO. What thinkest thou of his opinion?

MAL. [*Within.*] I think nobly of the soul, and no way approve his opinion.

CLO. Fare thee well: remain thou still in darkness: thou shalt hold the opinion of Pythagoras, ere I will allow of thy wits; and fear to kill a woodcock, lest thou dispossess the soul of thy grandam. Fare thee well.

MAL. [*Within.*] Sir Topas, sir Topas,—

SIR TO. My most exquisite sir Topas!

CLO. Nay, I am for all waters.[b]

MAR. Thou might'st have done this without thy beard and gown; he sees thee not.

SIR TO. To him in thine own voice, and bring me word how thou findest him: I would we were well rid of this knavery. If he may be conveniently delivered, I would he were; for I am now so far in offence with my niece, that I cannot pursue with any safety this sport to* the upshot. Come by and by to my chamber.

[*Exeunt Sir* TOBY *and* MARIA.

CLO. [*Singing.*] *Hey Robin, jolly Robin,*(2)
Tell me how thy lady does.

MAL. [*Within.*] Fool,—

CLO. [*Singing.*] *My lady is unkind, perdy.*

MAL. Fool,—

CLO. [*Singing.*] *Alas, why is she so?*

MAL. Fool, I say;—

CLO. [*Singing.*] *She loves another.*—Who calls, ha?

MAL. [*Within.*] Good fool, as ever thou wilt deserve well at my hand, help me to a candle, and pen, ink, and paper; as I am a gentleman, I will live to be thankful to thee for't.

CLO. Master Malvolio!

MAL. [*Within.*] Ay, good fool.

CLO. Alas, sir, how fell you besides your five wits?

MAL. [*Within.*] Fool, there was never man so notoriously abused: I am as well in my wits, fool, as thou art.

CLO. But *as well?* then you are mad indeed, if you be no better in your wits than a fool.

MAL. [*Within.*] They have here propertied[c] me; keep me in darkness, send ministers to me, asses, and do all they can to face me out of my wits.

CLO. Advise you what you say; the minister is here.—[*As Sir* TOPAS.] Malvolio, Malvolio, thy wits the heavens restore! endeavour thyself to sleep, and leave thy vain bibble-babble.

MAL. [*Within.*] Sir Topas,——

CLO. Maintain no words with him, good fellow.[d]—Who, I, sir? not I, sir. God b'wi'you, good sir Topas.—Marry, amen.—I will, sir, I will.

MAL. [*Within.*] Fool, fool, fool, I say,—

CLO. Alas, sir, be patient. What say you, sir? I am shent for speaking to you.

(*) Old text omits, *to.*

[a] Bay-windows—] A bay-window was what we term a *bow-window*, and was so called, according to Minsheu, "because it is builded in manner of a Bay, or roade for ships, that is, round."

[b] I am for all waters.] I can play any character. A metaphor borrowed, perhaps, from the tavern:—"Hee is first broken to the sea in the Herring-man's Skiffe or Cockboate, where having learned *to brooke all waters,* and drinke as he can out of a tarrie canne," &c.—Nashe's "Lenten Stuffe," p. 27.

[c] Propertied—] *Propertied* bears here the same meaning,—that, apparently, of *circumscribed, restricted, appropriated,*—as in "King John," Act V. Sc. 2:—

"I am too high-born to be *propertied.*"

[d] Maintain no words with him, good fellow.] The clown is playing a double part, and feigns, by change of voice and language, a colloquy between Sir Topas and himself.

MAL. [*Within.*] Good fool, help me to some light and some paper; I tell thee, I am as well in my wits as any man in Illyria.

CLO. Well-a-day, that you were, sir!

MAL. [*Within.*] By this hand, I am. Good fool, some ink, paper, and light, and convey what I will set down to my lady; it shall advantage thee more than ever the bearing of letter did.

CLO. I will help you to't. But tell me true, are you not mad indeed? or do you but counterfeit?

MAL. [*Within.*] Believe me, I am not; I tell thee true.

CLO. Nay, I'll ne'er believe a madman till I see his brains. I will fetch you light, and paper, and ink.

MAL. [*Within.*] Fool, I'll requite it in the highest degree: I pr'ythee, be gone.

CLO. [*Singing.*] *I am gone, sir,*
And anon, sir,
I'll be with you again,
In a trice,
Like to the old vice,[a]
Your need to sustain;
Who, with dagger of lath,
In his rage and his wrath,
Cries, ah, ha! to the devil:
Like a mad lad,
Pare thy nails, dad,
*Adieu, goodman drivel.** [*Exit.*

SCENE III.—Olivia's *Garden.*

Enter SEBASTIAN.

SEB. This is the air; that is the glorious sun;
This pearl she gave me, I do feel't, and see't:
And though 'tis wonder that enwraps me thus,
Yet 'tis not madness. Where's Antonio, then?
I could not find him at the Elephant:
Yet there he was; and there I found this credit,[b]
That he did range the town to seek me out.
His counsel now might do me golden service:
For though my soul disputes well with my sense,
That this may be some error, but no madness,
Yet doth this accident and flood of fortune

[a] Like to the old vice,—] See note (3), p. 119.
[b] Credit,—] *Information.*

(*) Old text, *devil.*

So far exceed all instance, all discourse,
That I am ready to distrust mine eyes,
And wrangle with my reason, that persuades me
To any other trust, but that I am mad,—
Or else the lady's mad; yet, if 'twere so,
She could not sway her house, command her followers,
Take and give back affairs, and their despatch,
With such a smooth, discreet, and stable bearing,
As I perceive she does: there's something in't
That is deceivable. But here the lady comes.

Enter OLIVIA *and a* Priest.

OLI. Blame not this haste of mine. If you mean well,
Now go with me and with this holy man,
Into the chantry by: there, before him
And underneath that consecrated roof,
Plight me the full assurance of your faith;
That my most jealous and too doubtful soul
May live at peace: he shall conceal it,
Whiles[a] you are willing it shall come to note;
What time we will our celebration keep,
According to my birth.—What do you say?

SEB. I'll follow this good man, and go with you;
And, having sworn truth, ever will be true.

OLI. Then lead the way, good father;——and heavens so shine,
That they may fairly note this act of mine! [*Exeunt.*

[a] Whiles—] That is, *until.*

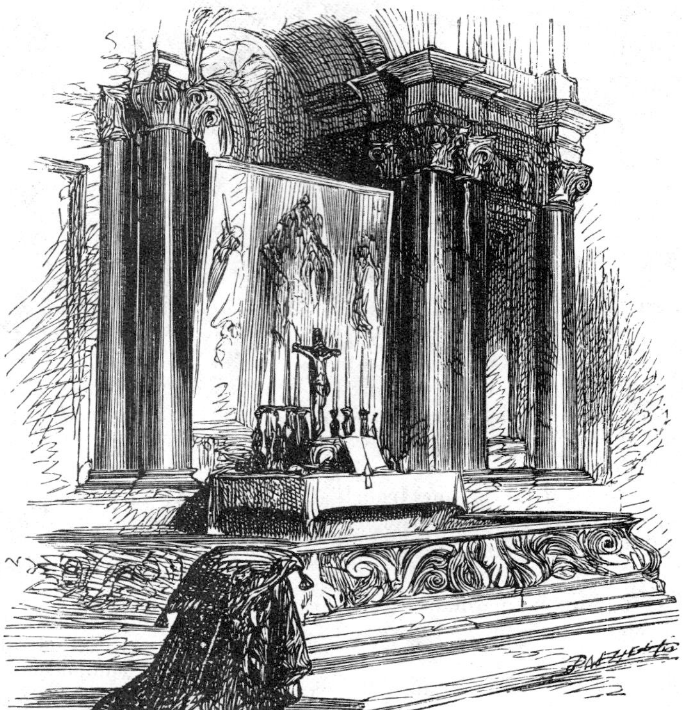

ACT V.

SCENE I.—*The Street before* Olivia's *House.*

Enter Clown *and* Fabian.

Fab. Now, as thou lovest me, let me see his letter.

Clo. Good master Fabian, grant me another request.

Fab. Any thing.

Clo. Do not desire to see this letter.

Fab. That is, to give a dog, and, in recompense, desire my dog again.

Enter Duke, Viola, Curio, *and* Attendants.

Duke. Belong you to the lady Olivia, friends?

Clo. Ay, sir; we are some of her trappings.

Duke. I know thee well; how dost thou, my good fellow?

Clo. Truly, sir, the better for my foes, and the worse for my friends.

Duke. Just the contrary; the better for thy friends.

Clo. No, sir, the worse.

Duke. How can that be?

Clo. Marry, sir, they praise me, and make an ass of me; now my foes tell me plainly I am an ass: so that by my foes, sir, I profit in the knowledge of myself; and by my friends I am abused: so that, conclusions to be as kisses,[a] if your four

[a] Conclusions to be as kisses, if your four negatives make your two affirmatives,—] A passage cited by Farmer from the tragedy of "Lust's Dominion," in some degree explains the Clown's thought:—

"*Queen.* ——— Come, let's kisse.
Moor. Away, away.
Queen. *No, no,* says *aye;* and *twice away,* sayes *stay.*"

negatives make your two affirmatives, why, then the worse for my friends, and the better for my foes.

DUKE. Why, this is excellent.

CLO. By my troth, sir, no; though it please you to be one of my friends.

DUKE. Thou shalt not be the worse for me; there's gold.

CLO. But that it would be double-dealing, sir, I would you could make it another.

DUKE. O, you give me ill counsel.

CLO. Put your grace in your pocket, sir, for this once, and let your flesh and blood obey it.

DUKE. Well, I will be so much a sinner to be a double dealer;[a] there's another.

CLO. *Primo, secundo, tertio,* is a good play; and the old saying is, the third pays for all: the *triplex,* sir, is a good tripping measure; or the bells of St. Benet, sir, may put you in mind,—one, two, three.

DUKE. You can fool no more money out of me at this throw: if you will let your lady know I am here to speak with her, and bring her along with you, it may awake my bounty further.

CLO. Marry, sir, lullaby to your bounty, till I come again. I go, sir; but I would not have you to think that my desire of having is the sin of covetousness: but, as you say, sir, let your bounty take a nap, I will awake it anon. [*Exit* Clown.

VIO. Here comes the man, sir, that did rescue me.

Enter ANTONIO *and* Officers.

DUKE. That face of his I do remember well;
Yet, when I saw it last, it was besmear'd
As black as Vulcan, in the smoke of war:
A bawbling vessel was he captain of,
For shallow draught and bulk unprizable;
With which such scatheful grapple did he make
With the most noble bottom of our fleet,
That very envy and the tongue of loss,
Cried fame and honour on him.—What's the matter?

1 OFF. Orsino, this is that Antonio
That took the Phœnix and her fraught from Candy,
And this is he that did the Tiger board,
When your young nephew Titus lost his leg:
Here in the streets, desperate of shame and state,
In private brabble did we apprehend him.

VIO. He did me kindness, sir; drew on my side;
But, in conclusion, put strange speech upon me,—
I know not what 'twas, but distraction.

DUKE. Notable pirate! thou salt-water thief!
What foolish boldness brought thee to their mercies,
Whom thou, in terms so bloody and so dear,
Hast made thine enemies?

ANT. Orsino, noble sir,
Be pleas'd that I shake off these names you give me;
Antonio never yet was thief or pirate,
Though, I confess, on base and ground enough,
Orsino's enemy. A witchcraft drew me hither:
That most ingrateful boy there by your side,
From the rude sea's enrag'd and foamy mouth
Did I redeem; a wreck past hope he was:
His life I gave him, and did thereto add
My love, without retention or restraint,
All his in dedication. For his sake,
Did I expose myself, pure for his love,
Into the danger of this adverse town;
Drew to defend him when he was beset;
Where being apprehended, his false cunning
(Not meaning to partake with me in danger)
Taught him to face me out of his acquaintance,
And grew a twenty-years-removed thing,
While one would wink; denied me mine own purse,
Which I had recommended to his use
Not half an hour before.

VIO. How can this be?

DUKE. When came he to this town?

ANT. To-day, my lord; and for three months before,
(No interim, not a minute's vacancy,)
Both day and night did we keep company.

DUKE. Here comes the countess; now heaven walks on earth.——
But for thee, fellow,—fellow, thy words are madness:
Three months this youth hath tended upon me;
But more of that anon.—Take him aside.

Enter OLIVIA *and* Attendants.

OLI. What would my lord, but that he may not have,
Wherein Olivia may seem serviceable?—
Cesario, you do not keep promise with me.

VIO. Madam!

DUKE. Gracious Olivia,——

OLI. What do you say, Cesario?——Good my lord,——

VIO. My lord would speak; my duty hushes me.

OLI. If it be aught to the old tune, my lord,
It is as fat[b] and fulsome to mine ear,
As howling after music.

DUKE. Still so cruel?

[a] A double deal r;] See note (d), p. 740, Vol. I.

[b] *It is as* fat—] *Fat*, here, means *o'ercloying, sickening.*

OLI. Still so constant, lord.
DUKE. What, to perverseness? you uncivil lady,
To whose ingrate and unauspicious altars
My soul the faithfull'st offerings hath breath'd out,
That e'er devotion tender'd! What shall I do?
OLI. Even what it please my lord, that shall become him.
DUKE. Why should I not, had I the heart to do it,
Like to th' Egyptian thief at point of death,
Kill what I love? (1) a savage jealousy
That sometime savours nobly.—But hear me this:
Since you to non-regardance cast my faith,
And that I partly know the instrument
That screws me from my true place in your favour,
Live you, the marble-breasted tyrant, still;
But this your minion, whom I know you love,
And whom, by heaven I swear, I tender dearly,
Him will I tear out of that cruel eye,
Where he sits crowned in his master's spite.—
Come, boy, with me; my thoughts are ripe in mischief:
I'll sacrifice the lamb that I do love,
To spite a raven's heart within a dove. [*Going.*
VIO. And I, most jocund, apt, and willingly,
To do you rest, a thousand deaths would die.
[*Following.*
OLI. Where goes Cesario?
VIO. After him I love
More than I love these eyes, more than my life,
More, by all mores, than e'er I shall love wife.
If I do feign, you witnesses above,
Punish my life for tainting of my love!
OLI. Ay me, detested! how am I beguil'd!
VIO. Who does beguile you? who does do you wrong?
OLI. Hast thou forgot thyself? is it so long?—
Call forth the holy father. [*Exit an* Attendant.
DUKE. Come, away! [*To* VIOLA.
OLI. Whither, my lord?—Cesario, husband, stay!
DUKE. *Husband?*
OLI. Ay, husband, can he that deny?
DUKE. Her husband, sirrah?
VIO. No, my lord, not I.
OLI. Alas, it is the baseness of thy fear
That makes thee strangle thy propriety:
Fear not, Cesario, take thy fortunes up;
Be that thou know'st thou art, and then thou art
As great as that thou fear'st.—

Re-enter Attendant, *with* Priest.

O, welcome, father!
Father, I charge thee, by thy reverence,
Here to unfold (though lately we intended
To keep in darkness, what occasion now
Reveals before 'tis ripe) what thou dost know,
Hath newly pass'd between this youth and me.
PRIEST. A contract of eternal bond of love,
Confirm'd by mutual joinder of your hands,
Attested by the holy close of lips,
Strengthen'd by interchangement of your rings: (2)
And all the ceremony of this compact
Seal'd in my function, by my testimony:
Since when, my watch hath told me, toward my grave
I have travell'd but two hours.
DUKE. O, thou dissembling cub! what wilt thou be,
When time hath sow'd a grizzle on thy case? [a]
Or will not else thy craft so quickly grow,
That thine own trip shall be thine overthrow?
Farewell, and take her; but direct thy feet
Where thou and I henceforth may never meet.
VIO. My lord, I do protest,—
OLI. O, do not swear!
Hold little faith, though thou hast too much fear.

Enter Sir ANDREW AGUECHEEK, *with his head broken.*

SIR AND. For the love of God, a surgeon! send one presently to sir Toby.
OLI. What's the matter?
SIR AND. H'as broke my head across, and has given sir Toby a bloody coxcomb too: for the love of God, your help! I had rather than forty pound I were at home.
OLI. Who has done this, sir Andrew?
SIR AND. The count's gentleman, one Cesario: we took him for a coward, but he's the very devil incardinate.
DUKE. My gentleman, Cesario?
SIR AND. 'Od's lifelings, here he is!—You broke my head for nothing; and that that I did, I was set on to do 't by sir Toby.
VIO. Why do you speak to me? I never hurt you:
You drew your sword upon me without cause;
But I bespake you fair, and hurt you not.
SIR AND. If a bloody coxcomb be a hurt, you have hurt me; I think you set nothing by a bloody coxcomb.—Here comes sir Toby, halting—you shall hear more: but if he had not been in drink, he would have tickled you othergates than he did.

Enter Sir TOBY BELCH, *drunk, led by the* Clown.

DUKE. How now, gentleman! how is't with you?
SIR TO. That's all one; h'as hurt me, and there's the end on't.—Sot, did'st see Dick surgeon, sot?

[a] Case.] An old term, not altogether disused, for *skin.*

CLO. O, he's drunk, sir Toby, an hour agone; his eyes were set at eight i' the morning.

SIR TO. Then he's a rogue, after a passy-measure's pavin;[a] I hate a drunken rogue.

OLI. Away with him! Who hath made this havoc with them?

SIR AND. I'll help you, sir Toby, because we'll be dressed together.

SIR TO. Will you help?—an ass-head and a coxcomb and a knave!—a thin-faced knave, a gull!

OLI. Get him to bed, and let his hurt be looked to.

[*Exeunt* Clown, FABIAN, *Sir* TOBY, *and Sir* ANDREW.

Enter SEBASTIAN.

SEB. I am sorry, madam, I have hurt your kinsman;
But had it been the brother of my blood,
I must have done no less with wit and safety.
You throw a strange regard upon me, and by that,
I do perceive it hath offended you;
Pardon me, sweet one, even for the vows
We made each other but so late ago.

DUKE. One face, one voice, one habit, and two persons!
A natural perspective,[b] that is and is not!

SEB. Antonio? O my dear Antonio!
How have the hours rack'd and tortur'd me,
Since I have lost thee!

ANT. Sebastian are you?

SEB. Fear'st thou that, Antonio?

ANT. How have you made division of yourself?—
An apple cleft in two is not more twin
Than these two creatures. Which is Sebastian?

OLI. Most wonderful!

SEB. Do I stand there? I never had a brother;
Nor can there be that deity in my nature,
Of here and every where. I had a sister,
Whom the blind waves and surges have devour'd:—
Of charity, what kin are you to me? [*To* VIOLA.
What countryman? what name? what parentage?

VIO. Of Messaline: Sebastian was my father;
Such a Sebastian was my brother too,
So went he suited to his watery tomb:
If spirits can assume both form and suit,
You come to fright us.

SEB. A spirit I am indeed:
But am in that dimension grossly clad,
Which from the womb I did participate.

---

[a] After *a passy-measure's pavin;*] The first folio reads, "*and* a passy measures *panyn.*" In a MS. list of old dances, Mr. Collier has found one dance called "The passinge measure Pavyon."

[b] Perspective,—] See note (4), p. 498, Vol. I.

Were you a woman, as the rest goes even,
I should my tears let fall upon your cheek,
And say—Thrice welcome, drowned Viola!
VIO. My father had a mole upon his brow,—
SEB. And so had mine.
VIO. And died that day when Viola from her birth
Had number'd thirteen years.
SEB. O, that record is lively in my soul!
He finished, indeed, his mortal act,
That day that made my sister thirteen years.
VIO. If nothing lets to make us happy both
But this my masculine usurp'd attire,
Do not embrace me, till each circumstance
Of place, time, fortune, do cohere and jump,
That I am Viola: which to confirm,
I'll bring you to a captain in this town,
Where lie my maiden weeds; by whose gentle help[a]
I was preserv'd to serve this noble count;
All the occurrence of my fortune since
Hath been between this lady and this lord.
SEB. So comes it, lady, you have been mistook: [*To* OLIVIA.
But nature to her bias drew in that.
You would have been contracted to a maid;
Nor are you therein, by my life, deceiv'd,—
You are betroth'd both to a maid and man.
DUKE. Be not amaz'd; right noble is his blood.—
If this be so, as yet the glass seems true,
I shall have share in this most happy wreck:—
Boy, thou hast said to me a thousand times, [*To* VIOLA.
Thou never shouldst love woman like to me.
VIO. And all those sayings will I over-swear;
And all those swearings keep as true in soul
As doth that orbed continent, the fire
That severs day from night.
DUKE. Give me thy hand;
And let me see thee in thy woman's weeds.
VIO. The captain that did bring me first on shore,
Hath my maid's garments: he, upon some action,
Is now in durance at Malvolio's suit,
A gentleman, and follower of my lady's.
OLI. He shall enlarge him:—fetch Malvolio hither:—
And yet, alas, now I remember me,
They say, poor gentleman, he's much distract.

Re-enter Clown, *with a letter, and* FABIAN.

A most extracting[b] frenzy of mine own
From my remembrance clearly banish'd his.—
How does he, sirrah?
CLO. Truly, madam, he holds Belzebub at the stave's end, as well as a man in his case may do: h'as here writ a letter to you, I should have given 't you to-day morning; but as a madman's epistles are no gospels, so it skills not much when they are delivered.
OLI. Open 't, and read it.
CLO. Look then to be well edified, when the fool delivers the madman: [*Reads.*] *By the Lord, madam,—*
OLI. How now! art thou mad?
CLO. No, madam, I do but read madness: an your ladyship will have it as it ought to be, you must allow *vox*.
OLI. Pr'ythee, read i' thy right wits.
CLO. So I do, madonna; but to read his right wits is to read thus: therefore perpend, my princess, and give ear.
OLI. Read it you, sirrah. [*To* FABIAN.
FAB. [*Reads.*] *By the Lord, madam, you wrong me, and the world shall know it: though you have put me into darkness, and given your drunken cousin rule over me, yet have I the benefit of my senses as well as your ladyship. I have your own letter that induced me to the semblance I put on; with the which I doubt not but to do myself much right, or you much shame. Think of me as you please. I leave my duty a little unthought of, and speak out of my injury.*
The madly-used MALVOLIO.
OLI. Did he write this?
CLO. Ay, madam.
DUKE. This savours not much of distraction.
OLI. See him deliver'd, Fabian; bring him hither. [*Exit* FABIAN.
My lord, so please you, these things further thought on,
To think me as well a sister as a wife,
One day shall crown the alliance on 't, so please you,
Here at my house, and at my proper cost.
DUKE. Madam, I am most apt to embrace your offer.—
Your master quits you; [*To* VIOLA.] and, for your service done him,—

---

[a] *Where lie my* maiden *weeds; by whose gentle help*
I was preserv'd *to serve this noble count;*]

To correct the prosody of the first line, Theobald reads, "my *maid's* weeds;" perhaps the object is attained more effectually by adding than subtracting a syllable:—

"Where lie my maiden weeds; *he* by whose gentle help," &c.

His alteration of *preferr'd* for *preserv'd* in the second line is, however, an undeniable improvement, and is almost verified by the passage in Act I. Sc. 2, where Viola tells the captain she is here speaking of,—

"I'll serve this duke:
Thou shalt *present me.*"

[b] Extracting *frenzy*—] The second folio has "*exacting*," and Mr. Collier's annotator reads "distracting;" but see the passage quoted by Malone, from "The Hystorie of Hamblet" "to try if men of great account be *extract* out of their wits;" and another, cited by Steevens, where William de Wyrcester, speaking of Henry VI. says:—"— subito cecidit in gravem infirmitatem capitis, ita quod *extractus* à mente videbatur."

So much against the mettle of your sex,
So far beneath your soft and tender breeding,
And since you call'd me master for so long,—
Here is my hand; you shall from this time be
Your master's mistress.

OLI. A sister!—you are she.

Re-enter FABIAN, *with* MALVOLIO.

DUKE. Is this the madman?

OLI. Ay, my lord, this same:—
How now, Malvolio!

MAL. Madam, you have done me wrong,
Notorious wrong.

OLI. Have I, Malvolio? no.

MAL. Lady, you have. Pray you, peruse that [letter:
You must not now deny it is your hand,—
Write from it, if you can, in hand or phrase;
Or say, 'tis not your seal, nor your invention:
You can say none of this: well, grant it then,
And tell me, in the modesty of honour,
Why you have given me such clear lights of favour;
Bade me come smiling and cross-garter'd to you;
To put on yellow stockings, and to frown
Upon sir Toby and the lighter people:
And, acting this in an obedient hope,
Why have you suffer'd me to be imprison'd,
Kept in a dark house, visited by the priest,
And made the most notorious geck and gull,
That e'er invention play'd on? tell me why.

OLI. Alas, Malvolio, this is not my writing,
Though, I confess, much like the character:
But, out of question, 'tis Maria's hand.
And now I do bethink me, it was she
First told me thou wast mad; then cam'st in [smiling,[a]
And in such forms, which here were presuppos'd
Upon thee in the letter. Pr'ythee, be content:
This practice hath most shrewdly pass'd upon thee:
But when we know the grounds and authors of it,
Thou shalt be both the plaintiff and the judge
Of thine own cause.

FAB. Good madam, hear me speak;
And let no quarrel nor no brawl to come,
Taint the condition of this present hour,
Which I have wonder'd at. In hope it shall not,
Most freely I confess, myself and Toby
Set this device against Malvolio here,
Upon some stubborn and uncourteous parts
We had conceiv'd against him: Maria writ
The letter at sir Toby's great importance;[b]
In recompense whereof he hath married her.
How with a sportful malice it was follow'd,
May rather pluck on laughter than revenge;
If that the injuries be justly weigh'd,
That have on both sides pass'd.

OLI. Alas, poor fool! how have they baffled thee!

CLO. Why, *some are born great, some achieve greatness, and some have greatness thrown*[c] *upon them.* I was one, sir, in this interlude; one sir Topas, sir; but that's all one:—*By the Lord, fool, I am not mad;*—but do you remember? *Madam, why laugh you at such a barren rascal? an you smile not, he's gagged:* and thus the whirligig of time brings in his revenges.

MAL. I'll be reveng'd on the whole pack of you! [*Exit.*

OLI. He hath been most notoriously abus'd.

DUKE. Pursue him, and entreat him to a peace:—
He hath not told us of the captain yet;
When that is known and golden time convents,
A solemn combination shall be made
Of our dear souls—Meantime, sweet sister,
We will not part from hence.—Cesario, come;
For so you shall be, while you are a man;
But when in other habits you are seen,
Orsino's mistress, and his fancy's queen.

[*Exeunt all, except the* Clown.

SONG.

CLO. *When that I was and a little tiny boy,*(3)
With hey, ho, the wind and the rain:
A foolish thing was but a toy,
For the rain it raineth every day.

But when I came to man's estate,
With hey, ho, the wind and the rain:
'Gainst knaves and thieves men shut their gate,
For the rain it raineth every day.

But when I came, alas! to wive,
With hey, ho, the wind and the rain:
By swaggering could I never thrive,
For the rain it raineth every day.

But when I came unto my beds,
With hey, ho, the wind and the rain:
With toss-pots still had drunken heads,
For the rain it raineth every day.

A great while ago the world begun,
With hey, ho, the wind and the rain:
But that's all one, our play is done,
And we'll strive to please you every day.

[*Exit.*

---

[a] Then cam'st in smiling,—] *Thou* must be understood after cam'st, "then cam'st *thou* in smiling," &c.

[b] Importance;] That is, *importunity*.

[c] *Some have greatness* thrown *upon them.*] "Query," Mr. Dyce asks, "is *thrown*, instead of 'thrust,' an oversight of the author, or an error of the scribe or printer?" We believe it to be neither one nor the other, but a purposed variation common to Shakespeare in cases of repetition, possibly from his knowing, by professional experience, the difficulty of quoting with perfect accuracy. *Thrown* occurs with precisely the same sense in Wilkins' tract of "Pericles, Prince of Tyre:"—"If the eminence of your place came unto you by descent, and the royalty of your blood, let not your life prove your birth a bastard: if it were *thrown* upon you by opinion, make good that opinion," &c.

ILLUSTRATIVE COMMENTS.

ACT I.

(1) Scene III.—*He plays o' the viol-de-gamboys.*] Mr. Gifford observes (Ben Jonson's Works, II. 125), "that a viol-de-gambo (a bass viol, as Jonson also calls it) was an indispensable piece of furniture in every fashionable house, where it hung up in the best chamber, much as the guitar does in Spain, and the violin in Italy, to be played on at will, and to fill up the void of conversation. Whoever pretended to fashion, affected an acquaintance with this instrument." The allusions to it are frequent in our old dramas: thus, in the Induction to Marston's "Malcontent," 1604:—

"Sink. Save you, coose.
Sly. O, coosin, come, you shall sit betweene my legges heare.
Sink. No, indeede, coosin, the audience then will take me for a *viol-de-gambo*, and thinke that you play upon me."

(2) Scene III.—*A parish-top.*] "A large top was formerly kept in every village, to be whipped in frosty weather, that the peasants may be kept warm by exercise, and out of mischief, while they could not work."—Steevens.

The amusement must have been very popular, being repeatedly mentioned in early books: thus, in Beaumont and Fletcher's "Thierry and Theodoret," Act II. Sc. 3:—

"——— I'll hazard
My life upon it, that a boy of twelve
Should scourge him hither like a *parish-top*,
And make him dance before you."

So also in Taylor, the Water Poet's "Jacke-a-Lent," p. 117, ed. 1630:—

"Were it not for these Netmongers, it is no flat lye to say, the Flounder might lye flat in his watry Cabin, and the Eele (whose slippery taile put mee in mind of a formall Courtiers promise) would wriggle up and downe in his muddy habitation, which would bee a great discommodity for schoole-boyes, through the want of scourges to whip Gigs and *Towne-Tops*."

(3) Scene III.—*The buttery-bar.*] This was a favourite locality in the palaces of royalty, and in the houses of the opulent. Mr. Halliwell has furnished an engraving of one still preserved at Christ Church College, Oxford; and he remarks that "this relic of ancient customs is still found in most of our ancient colleges. 'Furst every mornyng at brekefast oon chyne of beyf at our kechyn, oon chete loff and oon maunchet at our panatry barre, and a galon of ale at our *buttrye barre;* Item, at dyner, a pese of beyfe, a stroke of roste, and a reward at our said kechyn, a cast of chete bred at our panatry barre, and a galon of ale at our *buttry barre.*'—MS. dated 1522."

(4) Scene III.—*Mistress Mall's picture.*] The picture in question is supposed to be a portrait of one Mary Frith, commonly known as Mall Cut-purse, an Amazonian *bona roba,* to whom allusions innumerable are made by the dramatic and satirical writers of the period. She is said to have been born in Barbican, and to have attained to such disreputable celebrity, that about 1610 a book was published, entitled "The Madde Prancks of mery Mall of the Banckside, with her walkes in man's apparell and to what purpose, written by John Day." In the following year she was made the heroine of a comedy by Middleton and Decker, called "The Roaring Girle, or Moll Cutpurse, as it hath lately beene Acted on the Fortune-stage by the Prince his Players," on the title-page of which she is represented in her male habiliments, and smoking tobacco. About the same time she did penance at St. Paul's Cross, of which ceremony the following account is preserved in a letter from John Chamberlain to Sir Dudley Carleton, dated February 12, 1611-12:—"This last Sunday Moll Cutpurse, a notorious baggage that used to go in man's apparel, and challenged the field of diverse gallants, was brought to the same place, where she wept bitterly, and seemed very penitent; but it is since doubted she was maudlin drunk, being discovered to have tippel'd of three quarts of sack before she came to her penance." She died in 1659, and is stated to have left twenty pounds by her will for the Fleet-street conduit to run with wine when King Charles the Second returned, which happened soon after.

(5) Scene V.—*Clown.*] *Clown,* in our old plays, was the generical term for the *buffone,* or low-comedy character of the piece. Sometimes this merry-man was a mere country bumpkin, like the old shepherd's son in "The Winter's Tale;" or a shrewd rustic, like Costard in "Love's Labour's Lost;" or a witty retainer, such as Launce in "The Two Gentlemen of Verona;" and Launcelot in "The Merchant of Venice;" sometimes he was an "allowed," or hired domestic jester, like Touchstone in "As You Like it," Lavatch in "All's Well that Ends Well," and the fool in the present comedy. For a description of the sort of amusement the domestic fools were expected to afford their employers, see note (2), p. 54.

(6) Scene V.—*He says, he'll stand at your door like a sheriff's post.*] The doors of Mayors' and Sheriffs' houses were furnished with ornamented posts, on which were set up the royal and civic proclamations. It appears to have been the custom to repaint the posts whenever a new election of these officials took place: thus in "Lingua:" "Knowes he how to become a scarlet gowne? hath he a paire of *fresh posts* at his doore?" And again in "*Skialetheia, or a Shadowe of Truth,*" 1598:—

"Or like a new sherifes gate-posts, whose old faces
Are furbished over to smoothe time's disgraces."

A pair of Mayors' posts are still standing in Norwich, which, from the initials T. P. and the date 159.., are conjectured to have belonged to Thomas Pettys, who was Mayor of that city in 1592.

ACT II.

(1) SCENE III.—*Did you never see the picture of we three?*] The Clown roguishly refers to a once common sign, which represented two fools drinking, with an inscription beneath of "We *three* loggerheads be."

> "Plain home-spun stuffe shall now proceed from me,
> Much like unto the picture of *Wee Three*."
> TAYLOR'S *Farewell to the Tower-Bottles*, 1622.

There is a marginal note to this passage,—"The picture of two fooles and the third looking on, I doe fitly compare with the two black bottles and myselfe."

(2) SCENE III.—*In sooth, thou wast in very gracious fooling last night, when thou spok'st of Pigrogromitus, of the Vapians passing the equinoctial of Queubus.*] Sir Andrew's commendation calls to mind one of the most characteristic accomplishments of the wittiest domestic jesters of the sixteenth and seventeenth centuries. We say the *wittiest*, for, without distributing the Clowns of the period according to the careful classification adopted by Mr. Douce, it is evident that, in the Fool's calling, as in others, there were various degrees, and that the first-class jester of a royal or noble family ranked as much above his brother clown of the common sort, as the leading histrion of a London theatre tops the poor varlet who struts and frets his hour upon the stage at a country fair; "I marvel," says Malvolio, "that your ladyship takes delight in such a barren rascal; I saw him put down the other day with an ordinary fool, that has no more brains than a stone." All clowns were capable, more or less, of the biting sarcasms and coarse practical merriment which their vocation licensed; but few, probably, had sufficient information, not to say learning, to garnish their discourse with the mock erudition and the snatches of axiomatical philosophy exhibited by the jesters of "Twelfth Night" and "As You Like It;" and from them any reasoning admitting a sensible interpretation must not, of course, be looked for; though something may be traced in them which bears a close affinity to the fantastic extravagance and wild conceits of Rabelais. The source, however, of their sham sententiousness is of an earlier date than the romance of the great French satirist. The first known edition of that work is dated 1532; but in the library of M. de Bure were found two more ancient though undated books, entitled "*Les Chroniques de Gargantua*," which have much of this peculiar humour. The history of Gargantua, as an enormous giant, was well known too in England during the sixteenth century, though the romance relating to him contains nothing of the amusing rhodomontade indulged in by Rabelais and the humorists in question. A remote resemblance to it may be detected in some parts of the poems of Robert Longland, "The Vision and Creed of Pierce Ploughman;" and there is extant a genuine specimen of the "excellent fooling" for which the clowns of Shakespeare stand unrivalled, in the form of a mock sermon, in a manuscript of the fifteenth century, preserved in the Advocates' Library at Edinburgh, which, with other burlesques of the same date, was printed in 1841 by Mr. T. Wright, in the *Reliquiæ Antiquæ*, Vol. I. pp. 82—84. One extract from this effusion, with the orthography partly modernised, will convey no very imperfect notion of the clown's "gracious fooling" with Sir Toby and his companion knight:—"Why hopest thou not, for sooth, that there stood once a cook on St. Paul steeple top, and drew up the strapuls of his breech? How provest thou that? By all the four doctors of Wynebere hylles; that is to say, Vertas, Gadatryme, Trumpas, and Dadyl Trymsert; the which four doctors say, that there was once an old wife had a cook to her son; and he looked out of an old dove-cote, and warned and charged that no man should be so hardy neither to ride nor to go on St. Paul steeple top but if he rode on a three-footed stool, or else that he brought with him a warrant of his neck, and yet the lewd letherand lurdon went forth, and met seven acres of land betwixt Dover and Quicksand, and he brought an acre in his recke [hand-basket] from the Tower of London unto the Tower of Babilon; and, as he went by the way, he had a foul fall, and he fell down at the castle of Dover into a gruel pot, and brake both his shins. Thereof came tripping to the king of Hongre, that all people which might not lightly come to the Plain of Salisbury, but the fox and the grey convent, should pray for all the old shoe-soles that ben roasted in the king's dish on Saturday."

(3) SCENE III.—*Let our catch be, Thou knave.*] In this catch, the notes of which we append, the fun consists in the parts being so contrived that each singer in turn calls his fellow *knave*.

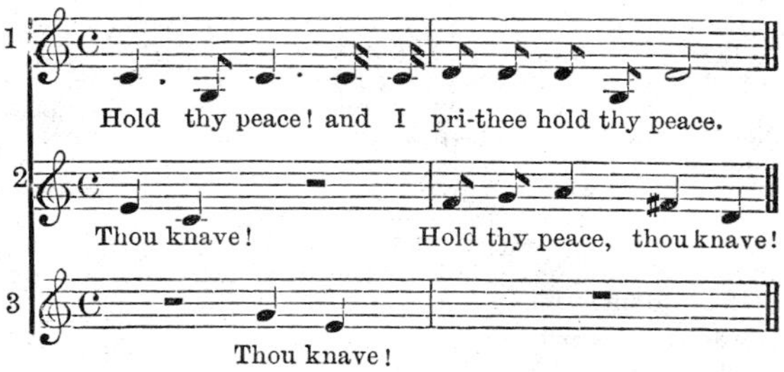

(4) SCENE III.—*Malvolio's a Peg a-Ramsey.*] The words of the old ballad of *Peg-a-Ramsey* are lost, but Mr. Chappell informs us that "there are two tunes under the name, and both as old as Shakespeare's time. The first is called *Peg-a-Ramsey* in William Ballet's Lute Book, and is given by Sir John Hawkins as the tune quoted in the text. (See the *Variorum* edition.) 'Little Pegge of Ramsie' is one of the tunes in a manuscript by Dr. Bull, which formed a part of Dr. Pepusch's, and afterwards of Dr. Kitchener's library."

(5) SCENE III.—*Three merry men be we.*] This song is mentioned in Peele's "Old Wives' Tale," 1595. Anticke, Frolicke, and Fantasticke, three adventurers, are lost in a wood in the night, and Anticke says, "Let us rehearse the old proverb:—

> "'Three merrie men, and three merrie men,
> And three merrie men be wee;
> I in the wood and thou on the ground,
> And Jacke sleeps in the tree.'"

The burden being a jovial and popular one, is continually quoted by the old play-wrights. For the tune the reader is referred to Chappell's *Popular Music of the Olden Time*, Vol. I. p. 216.

(6) SCENE III.—*There dwelt a man in Babylon, lady, lady!*] Of this long and wearisome ballad we have already given a sufficient sample (Vol. I. p. 217) in illustration of the familiar burden, "lady, lady." In a broadside preserved in the Roxburghe collection, it is headed, "An excellent Ballad, Intituled, *The constancy* of Susanna. To an excellent new tune." A "ballette of the godly constante wyse Susanna," was entered on the books of the Stationers' Company so early as 1562-3, and a play on the same subject was printed in 1578.

(7) SCENE III.—*Farewell, dear heart, since I must needs be gone.*] The ballad referred to in the note at p. 247, is printed by Percy, (Reliques, i. 205,) from an ancient miscellany, entitled "The golden Garland of princely delights."

(8) SCENE IV.—
Sad true lover ne'er find my grave,
To weep there!]

On comparing the Duke's description of that "antique song" he heard last night, with this ballad, the difference is so striking, as to beget suspicion that the latter was an interpolation and not the original song intended by the poet. It appears, indeed, to have been the privilege of the singer formerly, whenever the business of the scene required a song, to introduce one of his own choice; hence we frequently find in our old dramas, instead of the words of a ballad, merely a stage direction, "A Song," or "He sings."

(9) SCENE V.—*O, for a stone-bow, to hit him in the eye!*] "A stone-bow was a cross-bow made for propelling stones, or rather bullets, merely in contradistinction to a bow that shot arrows. 'Litle more then a yeare after I maried, I and my wife being at Skreenes with my father, (the plague being soe in London, and my building not finished,) I had exercised my-selfe with a *stone-bow* and a spar-hawke at the bush.'—*Autobiography of* SIR JOHN BRAMSTON, p. 108."—HALLIWELL.

(10) SCENE V.—*M, O, A, I, doth sway my life.*] Fustian riddles of this kind were not uncommon in Shakespeare's time, and several examples are quoted by Mr. Halliwell. Thus, in the "Squyr of Lowe Degre"—

In the myddes of your sheld ther shal be set
A ladyes head, with many a frete;
Above the head wrytten shall be
A reason for the love of me;
Both O and R shall be therein,
With A and M it shall begynne.

ACT III.

(1) SCENE I.—*Enter Clown with a tabor.*] The *tabor* was a favourite instrument with the professional fools. Most people are familiar with the print prefixed to Tarlton's Jests, 1611, in which that famous comedian is represented playing on a pipe and beating a small drum or tabor. Mr. Knight, in his "Pictorial Shakspere," has given an earlier portrait of Tarlton, (the original, apparently, of that attached to the "Jests,") which is taken from the Harleian MS. No. 3885. It is to this representation, probably, that allusion is made in "The pleasant and Stately Morall of the three Lordes and *three Ladies of London.*" By Robert Wilson, 1590. The dialogue is between Wil, Wit, Wealth (pages of the three Lords), and Simplicitie ("a poore Free man of London").

Simplicitie. "This is Tarlton's picture. Didst thou neuer know Tarlton?"
Wil. "No: what was that Tarlton? I neuer knew him."
Simplicitie. "What was he? A prentice in his youth of this honourable city, God be with him. When he was young, he was leaning to the trade that my wife vseth nowe, and I haue vsed, *vide lice shirt*, water bearing. I wis he hath tost a tankard in Cornehil er nowe: If thou knewst him not, I will not call thee ingram; but if thou knewest not him, thou knewest nobody. I warrant, her's two crackropes knew him."
Wit. "I dwelt with him."
Simplicitie. "Didst thou? now giue me thy hand: I loue thee the better."
Wit. "And I, too, sometime."
Simplicitie. "You, child! did you dwell with him sometime?"
Wit dwelt with him, indeed, as appeared by his rime, and served him well; and Wil was with him now and then. But soft: thy name is Wealth: I think in earnest he was litle acquainted with thee.
O, it was a fine fellow, as ere was borne:
There will neuer come his like while the earth can corne.
O, passing fine Tarlton! I would thou hadst liued yet."
Wealth. "He might haue some, but thou showest small wit.
There is no such finenes in the picture, that I can see."
Simplicitie. "Thou art no Cinque Port man; thou art not wit free.
The finenes was within, for without he was plaine;
But it was the merriest fellow, and had such jests in store,
That if thou hadst scene him, thou wouldst have laughed thy hart sore."

(2) SCENE I.—*Then westward-ho!*] In our poet's time the Thames formed the great highway of traffic, and "Westward, ho!" "Eastward, ho!" equivalent to the modern omnibus conductor's "West-end!" "City!" were the cries with which the watermen made its shores resound from morn till night. At that period, before the general introduction of coaches, there were not less, according to Taylor, than forty thousand of these clamorous Tritons plying their calling on the river in and near to the metropolis; and their desperate contentions to secure custom sometimes led to scenes of scandalous riot and confusion. Decker took the exclamation "Westward, ho!" for the title of a comedy, and Jonson, Chapman, and Marston adopted that of "Eastward, ho!" for one jointly written by them a few years afterwards.

(3) SCENE II.—*A Brownist.*] The *Brownists* were a sect who derived their name from Robert Browne, a gentleman of good family, and who had been educated at Cambridge. He separated from the Church, and gave great offence about 1580 by maintaining that her discipline was Popish and Antichristian, and her ministers not rightly ordained. Strype, in his life of Whitgift, relates, however, that in the year 1589 he "went off from the separation, and came into the communion of the Church."

(4) SCENE II.—*If thou* thou'st *him some thrice, it shall not be amiss.*] Theobald's conjecture that this passage was levelled at the Attorney-General Coke for his *thouing* Sir Walter Raleigh is at once put out of court since "Twelfth Night" is discovered to have been acted nearly two years before Sir Walter's trial took place. But if Theobald were ignorant of the fact, subsequent editors who have adopted his supposition ought to have known that to *thou* any body was once thought a direct mark of insult, as might be shown by a hundred examples. Mr. Singer has adduced one pertinent illustration from "The Enimie of Idlenesse," by William Fulwood, 1568: "A merchaunt having many servantes, to his chiefest may speake or wryte by this terme *you:* but to them whome he lesse esteemeth, and are more subject to correction, he may use thys terme *thou.*" The following, from the "Galateo of Maister John Della Casa, Archebishop of Beneventa," 4to. Lond. 1576, pp. 45-6, is even still more to the purpose :—

"Many times it chaunceth that men come to daggers drawing, even for this occasion alone, that one man hath not done the other, that worship and honour uppon the way, that he ought. For to saye a trueth, the power of custome is great and of much force, and would be taken for a lawe, in these cases. And that is the cause we say: *You:* to every one, that is not a man of very base calling, and in suche kinde of speach wee yealde such a one, no maner of courtesie of our owne. But if wee say: *Thou:* to suche a one, then wee disgrace him and offer him outrage and wronge: and by suche speach, seeme to make no better reconing of him, then of a knave and a clowne. * * * * So that it behoves us, hedefully to marke the doings and speache, wherewith daily practise and custome, wonteth to receave, salute, and name in our owne country, all sortes and kinds of people, and in all our familiar communication with men, let us use the same. And notwithstanding the Admerall * (as, peradventure, the maner of his time was such) in his talke with Peter the king of Aragon, did many times *Thou* him: Let us yet saye to our King, *Your* majestie: and *your* highnes: as well in speache as in writing."

---

* *Bocc. Novel. 6. Gior. 5.*

(5) SCENE II.—*The new map, with the augmentation of the Indies.*] An allusion, it is supposed, to a *multilineal* map engraved for the English translation of Linschoten's Voyages, published in 1598. Of a portion of this "new map," Mr. Knight has given a copy in his "Pictorial Shakspere," among the notes to the present play.

(6) SCENE IV.—*It is with me as the very true sonnet is,* Please one, and please all.] Of this "very true sonnet" a copy, believed to be unique, was discovered a few years ago, and is now in the possession of Mr. George Daniel. It is adorned with a rude portrait of Queen Elizabeth, with her feathered fan, starched ruff, and ample farthingale, and is said to have been the composition of her majestie's right merrie and facetious droll, Dick Tarlton. The numbers of this recovered relic are not lofty, nor the expression very felicitous; but "Please One and Please All" is worth preserving, both as an illustration of Shakespeare, and as a specimen of the quaint and simple old ballad literature of our forefathers:—

A prettie new Ballad, intytuled:
The Crowe sits upon the wall,
Please one and please all.

To the tune of, Please one and please all.

Please one and please all,
Be they great be they small,
Be they little be they lowe,
So pypeth the Crowe,
sitting upon a wall:
Please one and please all,
please one and please all.

Be they white be they black,
Have they a smock on their back,
Or a kercher on her head,
Whether they spin silke or thred,
Whatsoever they them call:
Please one and please all.

Be they sluttish be they gay,
Love they worke or love they play,
Whatsoever be theyre cheere,
Drinke they ale or drinke they beere,
Whether it be strong or small:
please one and please all.

Be they sower be they swete,
Be they shrewish be they meeke,
Weare they silke or cloth so good
Velvet bonnet or french-hood,
upon her head a cap or call:
please one and please all.

Be they halt be they lame,
Be she Lady be she dame,
If that she doo weare a pinne,
Keepe she taverne or keepe she Inne,
Either bulke bouth or stall:
please one and please all.

The goodwife I doo meane,
Be she fat or be she leane,
Whatsoever that she be,
This the Crowe tolde me,
sitting uppon a wall:
please one and please all.

If the goodwife speake aloft,
See that you then speake soft,
Whether it be good or ill,
Let her doo what she will:
and to keepe yourselfe from thrall,
please one and please all.

If the goodwife be displeased,
All the whole house is diseased,
And therefore by my will,
To please her learne the skill,
Least that she should alwaise brall:
please one and please all.

If that you bid her do ought,
If that she doo it not,
And though that you be her goodman,
You yourself must doo it then,
be it in kitchin or in hall:
please one and please all.

Let her have her owne will,
Thus the Crowe pypeth still,
Whatsoever she command,
See that you doo it out of hand,
whensoever she doth call:
please one and please all.

Be they wanton be they wilde,
Be they gentle be they milde:
Be shee white be shee browne,
Doth shee skould or doth she frowne,
Let her doo what she shall:
please one and please all.

Be she coy be she proud,
Speake she soft or speake she loud,
Be she simple be she flaunt,
Doth she trip or dooth she taunt,
the Crowe sits upon the wall:
please one and please all.

Is she huswife is she none,
Dooth she drudge dooth she grone,
Is she nimble is she quicke,
Is she short, is she thicke,
Let her be what she shall:
please one and please all.

Be she cruel be she curst,
Come she last come she first,
Be they young be they olde,
Doo they smile doo they scold,
though they doo nought at all:
please one and please all.

Though it be some Crowes guise,
Oftentimes to tell lyes,
Yet this Crowes words dooth try,
That her tale is no lye,
For thus it is and ever shall
please one and please all.

Please one and please all,
Be they great be they small,
Be they little be they lowe,
So pipeth the Crowe,
sitting upon a wall:
please one and please all,
please one and please all.

FINIS. R T

Imprinted at London for Henry Kyrkham, dwelling at the little North doore of Paules, at the syne of the blacke Boy.

(7) SCENE IV.—*On carpet consideration.*] By *carpet consideration* Shakespeare points at the *carpet knights*, or *knights of the green cloth*, as those persons were called who attained to the distinction of knighthood, not by military services, but for some real or supposed merit in their civil capacities. Of such, Francis Markham, in *The Booke of Honour*, folio 1625, p. 71, observes: "Next unto these (he had been speaking of *Dunghill*, or *Truck knights*) in degree, but not in qualitie (for these are truly for the most part vertuous and worthie), is that rank of Knights which are called *Carpet Knights*, being men who are by the prince's grace and favour made knights at home and in the time of peace, by the imposition or laying on of the king's sword, having, by some special service done to the common-wealth, or for some other particular virtues made known to the soveraigne, as also for the dignitie of their births, and in recompence of noble and famous actions done by their ancestors, deserved this great title and dignitie."

Randal Holme, in much the same terms, describes the several orders of persons eligible for the title, and speaks of it as an honourable distinction. It is plain, however, from innumerable passages in the old writers, that, to the popular idea, a *carpet knight* was synonymous then, as it is now, with an effeminate popinjay, who gained by favour what he would never have won by deeds. So, in Harrington's epigram, "Of Merit and Demerit:"—

"That captaines in those days were not regarded:
That only *Carpet-knights* were well rewarded."

Whetstone, in the story of *Rinaldo and Giletta*, in *The Rock of Regard*, 1576, says:—"Now he consults with *carpet knights* about curious masks and other delightful shewes; anon he runs unto the tailer's, to see his apparell made of the straungest and costliest fashion." And in "A Happy Husband, or Directions for a Maid to chuse her Mate, together with a Wive's Behaviour after Mariage," by Patrick Hannay, Gent. 1622, there is a full-length portrait of the character:—

"A carpet knight, who makes it his chiefe care
To trick him neatly up, and doth not spare
(Though sparing) precious time for to devoure;
Consulting with his glasse, a tedious houre

Soon flees, spent so, while each irreguler haire
His Barbor rectifies, and to seem rare,
His heat-lost lockes, to thicken closely curles,
And curiously doth set his misplac'd purles;
Powders, perfumes, and then profusely spent,
To rectifie his native, nasty sent:
This forenoones task perform'd, his way he takes,
And chamber-practis'd craving cursies makes
To each he meets; with cringes, and screw'd faces,
(Which his too partiall glasse approv'd for graces:)
Then dines, and after courts some courtly dame,
Or idle busie-bout misspending game;" &c.

ACT IV.

(1) Scene II.—*Clear-stories.*] The clear-stories are the upper story or row of windows in a church, hall, or other erection, rising clear above the adjoining parts of the building, adopted as a means of obtaining an increase of light. "Whereupon a iij thousand werkmen was werkynge iiij monethes to make it so grete in quantyte, so statly, and all with *clere-story* lyghtys, lyk a lantorne, the roffis garnyshed with sarsnettys and buddys of golde, and borderyd over all the aras over longe to dysturbe the rychnes therof."—Arnold's *Chronicle.*

(2) Scene II.—

Hey Robin, jolly Robin,
Tell me how thy lady does!]

"The original of this song is preserved in a MS. containing poems by Sir Thomas Wyatt, and is entitled 'The careful Lover complaineth, and the happy Lover counselleth:'—

A Robyn,—Jolly Robyn,
Tell me how thy leman doeth,—And thou shalt knowe of myn.
My lady is unkyinde, perde.—Alack! why is she so?
She loveth an other better than me:—And yet she will say, no.
Response. I fynde no such doubleness:—I fynde women true.
My lady loveth me dowtles,—And will change for no newe.
Le Plaintif. Thou art happy while that doeth last;—But I say, as I fynde,
That woman's love is but a blast,—And torneth with the wynde.
Response. But if thou wilt avoyde thy harme,—Lerne this lesson of me,
At others fieres thy selfe to warme,—And let them warme with the.
Le Plaintif. Suche folkes can take no harme by love,—That can abide their torn,
But I, alas, can no way prove—In love but lake and morn."—Halliwell.

ACT V.

(1) Scene I.—

Why should I not, had I the heart to do it,
Like to th' Egyptian thief at point of death,
Kill what I love?]

This relates, perhaps, as Theobald suggested, to a story found in the *Æthiopics* of Heliodorus. The *Egyptian thief* was Thyamis, a native of Memphis, and the chief of a band of robbers. Theagenes and Chariclea falling into their hands, Thyamis fell desperately in love with the lady, and would have married her. Soon after, a strong body of robbers coming down upon the band of Thyamis, he was under such apprehensions for his beloved that he had her shut up in a cave with his treasure. It was customary for those barbarians, "when they despaired of their own safety, first to make away with those whom they held dear," and desired for companions in the next life. Thyamis, therefore, benetted round with his enemies, raging with love, jealousy, and anger, betook himself to his cave; and calling aloud in the Egyptian tongue, so soon as he heard himself answered towards the mouth of the cave by a Grecian, making to the speaker by the direction of the voice, he caught her by the hair with his left hand, and (supposing her to be Chariclea) with his right hand plunged his sword into her breast.

(2) Scene I.—

A contract of eternal bond of love,
Confirm'd by mutual joinder of your hands,
Attested by the holy close of lips,
Strengthen'd by interchangement of your rings.]

The ceremony which had taken place between Olivia and Sebastian, Mr. Douce has conclusively shown, was not an actual marriage, but that which was called *espousals,* namely, a *betrothing, affiancing,* or *promise of future marriage.* "Vincent de Beauvais, a writer of the thirteenth century, in his *Speculum historiale,* lib. ix. c. 70, has defined *espousals* to be *a contract of future marriage,* made either by a simple promise, by earnest or security given, by a ring, or by an oath. During the same period, and the following centuries, we may trace several other modes of betrothing, some of which it may be worth while to describe more at large.

I. The interchangement of rings.—Thus in Chaucer's *Troilus and Creseide,* book 3:

"Soon after this they spake of sondry things
As fill to purpose of this aventure,
And playing *enterchaungeden her rings*
Of which I can not tellen no scripture."

When espousals took place at church, rings were also interchanged. According to the ritual of the Greek church, the priest first placed the rings on the fingers of the parties who afterwards exchanged them. Sometimes the man only gave a ring. * * *

II. The kiss that was mutually given. When this ceremony took place at church, the lady of course withdrew the veil which was usually worn on the occasion; when in private, the drinking of healths generally followed.

III. The joining of hands. This is often alluded to by Shakspeare himself.

IV. The testimony of witnesses. That of the priest alone was generally sufficient, though we often find many other persons attending the ceremony. The words 'there before him,' and 'he shall conceal it,' in Olivia's speech, sufficiently demonstrate that betrothing and not marriage is intended; for in the latter the presence of the priest alone would not have sufficed. In later times, espousals in the church were often prohibited in France, because instances frequently occurred where the parties, relying on the testimony of the priest, scrupled not to live together as man and wife; which gave rise to much scandal and disorder."—Douce's *Illustrations of Shakspeare,* I. 109—113.

(3) Scene I.—*When that I was and a little tiny boy.*] It is to be regretted, perhaps, that this "nonsensical ditty," as Steevens terms it, has not been long since degraded to the foot-notes. It was evidently one of those jigs, with which it was the rude custom of the Clown to gratify the groundlings upon the conclusion of a play. These absurd compositions, intended only as a vehicle for buffoonery, were usually improvisations of the singer, tagged to some popular ballad-burden—or the first lines of various songs strung together in ludicrous juxtaposition, at the end of each of which, the performer indulged in hideous grimace, and a grotesque sort of "Jump Jim Crow" dance. Of these "nonsense songs," we had formerly preserved three or four specimens, but they have unfortunately got mislaid.

CRITICAL OPINIONS

ON

TWELFTH NIGHT; OR, WHAT YOU WILL.

"*The Twelfth Night, or What you Will,* unites the entertainment of an intrigue, contrived with great ingenuity, to a rich fund of comic characters and situations, and the beauteous colours of an ethereal poetry. In most of his plays, Shakspeare treats love more as an affair of the imagination than the heart; but here he has taken particular care to remind us that, in his language, the same word, *fancy*, signified both fancy and love. The love of the music-enraptured Duke for Olivia is not merely a fancy, but an imagination; Viola appears at first to fall arbitrarily in love with the Duke, whom she serves as a page, although she afterwards touches the tenderest strings of feeling; the proud Olivia is captivated by the modest and insinuating messenger of the Duke, in whom she is far from suspecting a disguised rival, and at last, by a second deception, takes the brother for the sister. To these, which I might call ideal follies, a contrast is formed by the naked absurdities to which the entertaining tricks of the ludicrous persons of the piece give rise, under the pretext also of love: the silly and profligate knight's awkward courtship of Olivia, and her declaration of love to Viola; the imagination of the pedantic steward, Malvolio, that his mistress is secretly in love with him, which carries him so far that he is at last shut up as a lunatic, and visited by the clown in the dress of a priest. These scenes are admirably conceived, and as significant as they are laughable. If this were really, as is asserted, Shakspeare's latest work, he must have enjoyed to the last the same youthful elasticity of mind, and have carried with him to the grave the undiminished fulness of his talents."—SCHLEGEL.

"The serious and the humorous scenes are alike excellent; the former

——————' give a very echo to the seat
Where love is thron'd,'

and are tinted with those romantic hues, which impart to passion the fascinations of fancy, and which stamp the poetry of Shakespeare with a character so transcendently his own, so sweetly wild, so tenderly imaginative. Of this description are the loves of Viola and Orsino, which, though involving a few improbabilities of incident, are told in a manner so true to nature, and in a strain of such melancholy enthusiasm, as instantly put to flight all petty objections, and leave the mind wrapt in a dream of the most delicious sadness. The fourth scene of the second act more particularly breathes the blended emotions of love, of hope, and of despair, opening with a highly interesting description of the soothing effects of music in allaying the pangs of unrequited affection, and in which the attachment of Shakespeare to the simple melodies of the olden time is strongly and beautifully expressed.

"From the same source which has given birth to this delightful portion of the drama, appears to spring a large share of that rich and frolic humour which distinguishes its gayer incidents. The delusion of Malvolio, in supposing himself the object of Olivia's desires, and the ludicrous pretension of Sir Andrew Aguecheek to the same lady, fostered as they are by the comic manœuvres of the convivial Sir Toby and the keen-witted Maria, furnish, together with the professional drollery of Feste the jester, an ever-varying fund of pleasantry and mirth; scenes in which wit and raillery are finely blended with touches of original character, and strokes of poignant satire."—DRAKE.

Act II. Sc. 3.

THE FIRST PART OF

KING HENRY THE SIXTH.

THE first edition of this play known, is that of the folio 1623. It is generally supposed to be the same "*Henery the vj.*," somewhat modified and improved by Shakespeare, which is entered in Henslowe's diary as first acted on the 3rd of March, 1591–2, and to which Nash alludes in his "*Pierce Pennilesse, his Supplication to the Devil*," 1592:—"How would it have joy'd brave Talbot (the terror of the French) to thinke that after he had lyne two hundred yeare in his tombe, he should triumph againe on the stage, and have his bones new embalmed with the teares of ten thousand spectators at least, (at severall times,) who, in the tragedian that represents his person, imagine they behold him fresh bleeding." This opinion has, however, been strenuously impugned by Mr. Knight, in his able "Essay on the Three Parts of King Henry VI. and King Richard III.," wherein he attempts to show, that the present drama, as well as the two parts of the "Contention betwixt the two famous houses of Yorke and Lancaster," which Malone has been at such infinite pains to prove the works of earlier writers, are wholly the productions of Shakespeare.

The subject is of extreme difficulty, and one upon which there will always be a conflict of opinion. For our own part, we can no more agree with Mr. Knight in ascribing the piece before us solely to Shakespeare, than with Malone in the attempt to despoil him of the two parts of the "Contention." To us, in the present play, the hand of the great Master is only occasionally perceptible; while in the "Contention," it is unmistakeably visible in nearly every scene. The former was probably an early play of some inferior author, which he partly re-modelled; the latter appears to have been his first alteration of a more important production, perhaps by Marlowe, Greene, and Peele, which he subsequently re-wrote, re-christened, and divided, as it now appears, into what are called the Second and Third Parts of Henry VI.

Persons Represented.

King Henry VI.
Duke *of* Gloucester, *Uncle to the* King, *and* Protector.
Duke *of* Bedford, *Uncle to the* King, *and Regent of* France.
Thomas Beaufort, *Duke of* Exeter, *Great Uncle to the* King.
Henry Beaufort, *Great Uncle to the* King, *Bishop of* Winchester, *and afterwards* Cardinal.
John Beaufort, *Earl of* Somerset, *afterwards Duke.*
Richard Plantagenet, *Eldest Son of* Richard, *late Earl of* Cambridge ; *afterwards Duke of* York.
Earl *of* Warwick.
Earl *of* Salisbury.
Earl *of* Suffolk.
Lord Talbot, *afterwards Earl of* Shrewsbury.
Edmund Mortimer, *Earl of* March.
Sir John Fastolfe.
Sir William Lucy.
Sir William Glansdale.
Sir Thomas Gargrave.
Mayor *of* London.
Woodville, *Lieutenant of the* Tower.
Vernon, *of the* White Rose, *or* York *faction.*
Basset, *of the* Red Rose, *or* Lancaster *faction.*
A Lawyer.
Mortimer's Keepers.

Charles, *Dauphin, afterwards King of* France.
Reignier, *Duke of* Anjou, *and titular King of* Naples.
Duke *of* Burgundy.
Duke *of* Alençon.
Bastard *of* Orleans.
Governor *of* Paris.
General *of the* French Forces *in* Bourdeaux.
Master-Gunner *of* Orleans, *and his* Son.
A French Sergeant.
A Porter.
An old Shepherd, *father to* Joan la Pucelle.

Margaret, *Daughter to* Reignier ; *afterwards married to* King Henry.
Countess *of* Auvergne.
Joan la Pucelle, *commonly called* Joan of Arc.

Lords, Warders of the Tower, Heralds, Officers, Soldiers, Messengers, and various Attendants both on the English *and* French, *Fiends appearing to* La Pucelle.

SCENE,—*Partly in* England, *and partly in* France.

ACT I.

SCENE I.—Westminster Abbey.

Dead March. The corpse of King Henry *the* Fifth *discovered, lying in State; attended on by the* Dukes *of* Bedford, Gloucester, *and* Exeter; *the* Earl *of* Warwick; *the* Bishop *of* Winchester, Heralds, &c.

Bed. Hung be the heavens with black,(1) yield day to night!
Comets, importing change of times and states,
Brandish your crystal tresses in the sky,
And with them scourge the bad revolting stars,
That have consented [a] unto Henry's death!
King Henry the fifth, too famous to live long!
England ne'er lost a king of so much worth.

Glo. England ne'er had a king until his time.
Virtue he had, deserving to command:
His brandish'd sword did blind men with his beams;
His arms spread wider than a dragon's wings;
His sparkling eyes, replete with wrathful fire,
More dazzled and drove back his enemies,
Than mid-day sun, fierce bent against their faces.
What should I say? his deeds exceed all speech:
He ne'er lift up his hand but conquered.

Exe. We mourn in black, why mourn we not in blood?
Henry is dead, and never shall revive:
Upon a wooden coffin we attend;
And death's dishonourable victory
We with our stately presence glorify,
Like captives bound to a triumphant car.
What! shall we curse the planets of mishap,
That plotted thus our glory's overthrow?
Or shall we think the subtle-witted French
Conjurers and sorcerers, that, afraid of him,
By magic verses have contriv'd his end? (2)

Win. He was a king bless'd of the King of kings.
Unto the French the dreadful judgment-day
So dreadful will not be, as was his sight.
The battles of the Lord of hosts he fought:
The church's prayers made him so prosperous.

Glo. The church! where is it? Had not churchmen pray'd,
His thread of life had not so soon decay'd:

[a] Consented—] Steevens proposed to read *concented*, believing the word was not employed here in its ordinary sense, but as *concentus*.

None do you like but an effeminate prince,
Whom, like a schoolboy, you may over-awe.

WIN. Gloster, whate'er we like, thou art protector,
And lookest to command the prince and realm.
Thy wife is proud; she holdeth thee in awe,
More than God, or religious churchmen may.

GLO. Name not religion, for thou lov'st the flesh,
And ne'er throughout the year to church thou go'st,
Except it be to pray against thy foes.

BED. Cease, cease these jars, and rest your minds in peace!
Let's to the altar:—heralds, wait on us:—
Instead of gold, we'll offer up our arms,
Since arms avail not, now that Henry's dead.—
Posterity, await for wretched years,
When at their mothers' moist[a] eyes, babes shall suck;
Our isle be made a marish[b] of salt tears,
And none but women left to wail the dead.—
Henry the fifth! thy ghost I invocate;
Prosper this realm, keep it from civil broils!
Combat with adverse planets in the heavens!
A far more glorious star thy soul will make,
Than Julius Cæsar, or bright ——[c]

Enter a Messenger.

MESS. My honourable lords, health to you all!
Sad tidings bring I to you out of France,
Of loss, of slaughter, and discomfiture:
Guienne, Champaigne, Rheims, Orleans,
Paris, Guysors, Poictiers, are all quite lost.

BED. What say'st thou, man![d] before dead Henry's corse
Speak softly, or the loss of those great towns
Will make him burst his lead, and rise from death.

GLO. Is Paris lost? is Rouen yielded up?
If Henry were recall'd to life again,
These news would cause him once more yield the [ghost.

EXE. How were they lost? what treachery was us'd?

MESS. No treachery; but want of men and [money.
Among the soldiers this is muttered,—
That here you maintain several factions;
And, whilst a field should be despatch'd and fought,
You are disputing of your generals.
One would have ling'ring wars, with little cost;
Another would fly swift, but wanteth wings;
A third man* thinks, without expense at all,
By guileful fair words, peace may be obtain'd.
Awake, awake, English nobility!
Let not sloth dim your honours, new-begot:
Cropp'd are the flower-de-luces in your arms;
Of England's coat one half is cut away.

EXE. Were our tears wanting to this funeral,
These tidings would call forth her flowing tides.

BED. Me they concern; regent I am of France:—
Give me my steeled coat! I'll fight for France.—
Away with these disgraceful wailing robes!
Wounds I will lend the French, instead of eyes,
To weep their intermissive miseries.

Enter a second Messenger.

2 MESS. Lords, view these letters, full of bad mischance:
France is revolted from the English quite,
Except some petty towns of no import:
The Dauphin Charles is crowned king in Rheims;
The bastard of Orleans with him is join'd;
Reignier,† duke of Anjou, doth take his part;
The duke of Alençon flieth to his side.

EXE. The Dauphin crowned king! all fly to him!
O, whither shall we fly from this reproach?

GLO. We will not fly, but to our enemies' throats:—
Bedford, if thou be slack, I'll fight it out.

BED. Gloster, why doubt'st thou of my forwardness?
An army have I muster'd in my thoughts,
Wherewith already France is over-run.

Enter a third Messenger.

3 MESS. My gracious lords,—to add to your laments,
Wherewith you now bedew king Henry's hearse,—
I must inform you of a dismal fight,
Betwixt the stout lord Talbot and the French.

WIN. What! wherein Talbot overcame? is't so?

3 MESS. O, no; wherein Lord Talbot was o'er- [thrown:
The circumstance I'll tell you more at large.
The tenth of August last, this dreadful lord,
Retiring from the siege of Orleans,
Having full scarce six thousand in his troop,

---

[a] Moist—] The reading of the second folio: the first has *moisten'd*.

[b] Marish—] The first folio reads *Nourish*, an evident misprint, but one not lacking defenders. Our reading is Pope's, which Ritson has very well supported by a line from Kyd's "Spanish Tragedy:"

"Made mountains *marsh with spring-tides of my tears*."

(*) First folio omits, *man*. (†) Old text, *Reynold*.

[c] Or bright——] Malone conjectured that the blank arose from the transcriber's or compositor's inability to decipher the name. Johnson would fill it up with "Berenice;" while Mr. Collier's annotator reads, "Cassiopé."

[d] What say'st thou, man!] This line is invariably printed, "What say'st thou, man, before dead Henry's corse?"

By three and twenty thousand of the French
Was round encompassed and set upon:
No leisure had he to enrank his men;
He wanted pikes to set before his archers;
Instead whereof, sharp stakes, pluck'd out of hedges,
They pitched in the ground confusedly,
To keep the horsemen off from breaking in.
More than three hours the fight continued;
Where valiant Talbot, above human thought,
Enacted wonders with his sword and lance.
Hundreds he sent to hell, and none durst stand him;
Here, there, and every where, enrag'd he flew: *
The French exclaim'd, the devil was in arms;
All the whole army stood agaz'd on him:
His soldiers, spying his undaunted spirit,
A Talbot! a Talbot! cried out amain,
And rush'd into the bowels of the battle.
Here had the conquest fully been seal'd up,
If sir John Fastolfe † had not play'd the coward;
He being in the vaward,[a] (plac'd behind,
With purpose to relieve and follow them,)
Cowardly fled, not having struck one stroke.
Hence grew the general wreck and massacre;
Enclosed were they with their enemies:
A base Walloon, to win the Dauphin's grace,
Thrust Talbot with a spear into the back;
Whom all France, with their chief assembled strength,
Durst not presume to look once in the face.

BED. Is Talbot slain? then I will slay myself,
For living idly here in pomp and ease,
Whilst such a worthy leader, wanting aid,
Unto his dastard foe-men is betray'd.

3 MESS. O no, he lives; but is took prisoner,
And lord Scales with him, and lord Hungerford:
Most of the rest slaughter'd, or took, likewise.

BED. His ransom there is none but I shall pay:
I'll hale the Dauphin headlong from his throne,—
His crown shall be the ransom of my friend;
Four of their lords I'll change for one of ours,—
Farewell, my masters; to my task will I;
Bonfires in France forthwith I am to make,
To keep our great saint George's feast withal:
Ten thousand soldiers with me I will take,
Whose bloody deeds shall make all Europe quake.

3 MESS. So you had need; for Orleans is besieg'd;
The English army is grown weak and faint:
The earl of Salisbury craveth supply,
And hardly keeps his men from mutiny,
Since they, so few, watch such a multitude.

EXE. Remember, lords, your oaths to Henry sworn;
Either to quell the Dauphin utterly,
Or bring him in obedience to your yoke.

BED. I do remember it; and here take my leave,
To go about my preparation. [*Exit.*

GLO. I'll to the Tower with all the haste I can,
To view the artillery and munition;
And then I will proclaim young Henry king. [*Exit.*

EXE. To Eltham will I, where the young king is,
Being ordain'd his special governor;
And for his safety there I'll best devise. [*Exit.*

WIN. Each hath his place and function to attend:
I am left out; for me nothing remains.
But long I will not be Jack-out-of-office;
The king from Eltham I intend to steal,[b]
And sit at chiefest stern of public weal. [*Exit.*

SCENE II.—France. *Before* Orleans.

Flourish. Enter CHARLES, *with his* Forces; ALENÇON, REIGNIER, *and others.*

CHAR. Mars his true moving, even as in the heavens,
So in the earth, to this day is not known:
Late did he shine upon the English side,
Now we are victors, upon us he smiles.
What towns of any moment but we have?
At pleasure here we lie, near Orleans;
Otherwhiles, the famish'd English, like pale ghosts,
Faintly besiege us one hour in a month.

ALEN. They want their porridge, and their fat bull-beeves:
Either they must be dieted like mules,
And have their provender tied to their mouths,
Or piteous they will look, like drowned mice.

REIG. Let's raise the siege; why live we idly here?
Talbot is taken, whom we wont to fear:
Remaineth none but mad-brain'd Salisbury,
And he may well in fretting spend his gall,
Nor men, nor money, hath he to make war.

CHAR. Sound, sound alarum! we will rush on them.
Now for the honour of the forlorn French![c]—

(*) Old text, *slew*. (†) Old text, *Falstaffe*.

[a] Vaward,—] Some editors, perhaps rightly, read *rear-ward*.

[b] Steal,—] The folio has, *send*. Mason suggested, what is obvious enough, that *steal* was the poet's word; and Mr. Collier's annotator has made the same correction.

[c] *The* forlorn *French!*] The sense of *forlorn* in this place, does not appear to have been understood, and Mr. Collier's annotator proposes to read *forborne*, instead. But the old word, meaning *fore-lost*, needs no change; the Dauphin apostrophises the honour of those French who had *previously fallen*.

Him I forgive my death, that killeth me,
When he sees me go back one foot or fly.
[*Exeunt.*

Alarums; Excursions; the French *are beaten back by the* English *with great loss.*

Re-enter CHARLES, ALENÇON, REIGNIER, *and others.*

CHAR. Who ever saw the like? what men have I!—
Dogs! cowards! dastards!—I would ne'er have fled,
But that they left me 'midst my enemies.
REIG. Salisbury is a desperate homicide;
He fighteth as one weary of his life.
The other lords, like lions wanting food,
Do rush upon us as their hungry prey.
ALEN. Froissart, a countryman of ours, records,
England all Olivers and Rowlands bred,*
During the time Edward the third did reign.
More truly now may this be verified;
For none but Samsons and Goliasses,
It sendeth forth to skirmish. One to ten!
Lean raw-bon'd rascals! who would e'er suppose
They had such courage and audacity?
CHAR. Let's leave this town; for they are hair-brain'd slaves,
And hunger will enforce them to[a] be more eager:
Of old I know them; rather with their teeth
The walls they'll tear down, than forsake the siege.
REIG. I think, by some odd gimmers or device,
Their arms are set, like clocks, still to strike on;
Else ne'er could they hold out so as they do.
By my consent, we'll e'en let them alone.
ALEN. Be it so.

Enter the Bastard *of* Orleans.

BAST. Where's the prince Dauphin? I have news for him.
CHAR. Bastard of Orleans, thrice welcome to [us.
BAST. Methinks your looks are sad, your cheer appall'd;
Hath the late overthrow wrought this offence?
Be not dismay'd, for succour is at hand:
A holy maid hither with me I bring,
Which, by a vision sent to her from heaven,
Ordained is to raise this tedious siege,
And drive the English forth the bounds of France.
The spirit of deep prophecy she hath,
Exceeding the nine sibyls of old Rome;
What's past, and what's to come, she can descry.
Speak, shall I call her in? Believe my words,
For they are certain and unfallible.
CHAR. Go, call her in: [*Exit* Bastard.] but, first, to try her skill,
Reignier, stand thou as Dauphin in my place:
Question her proudly, let thy looks be stern;—
By this means shall we sound what skill she hath.
[*Retires.*

Re-enter the Bastard *of* Orleans, *with* LA PUCELLE.(3)

REIG. Fair maid, is't thou wilt do these wondrous feats?
PUC. Reignier, is't thou that thinkest to beguile [me?—
Where is the Dauphin?—Come, come from behind;
I know thee well, though never seen before.
Be not amaz'd, there's nothing hid from me:
In private will I talk with thee apart.—
Stand back, you lords, and give us leave awhile.
REIG. She takes upon her bravely at first dash.
PUC. Dauphin, I am by birth a shepherd's daughter,
My wit untrain'd in any kind of art.
Heaven and our Lady gracious hath it pleas'd
To shine on my contemptible estate:
Lo! whilst I waited on my tender lambs,
And to sun's parching heat display'd my cheeks,
God's mother deigned to appear to me;
And, in a vision full of majesty,
Will'd me to leave my base vocation,
And free my country from calamity.
Her aid she promis'd, and assur'd success:
In complete glory she reveal'd herself;
And, whereas I was black and swart before,
With those clear rays which she infus'd on me,
That beauty am I bless'd with, which you[b] see.
Ask me what question thou canst possible,
And I will answer unpremeditated:
My courage try by combat, if thou dar'st,
And thou shalt find that I exceed my sex.
Resolve[c] on this;—thou shalt be fortunate,
If thou receive me for thy warlike mate.
CHAR. Thou hast astonish'd me with thy high terms;
Only this proof I'll of thy valour make,—
In single combat thou shalt buckle with me;
And, if thou vanquishest, thy words are true;
Otherwise, I renounce all confidence.

(*) Old text, *breed.*

a To *be* more eager:] As Steevens suggested, the preposition ought to be omitted. The same redundancy is found in a subsequent line,—

"Peel'd priest, dost thou command me *to* be shut out?"

b Which you see.] Thus the second folio; the first has superfluously, "which you *may* see."

c Resolve *on this*:] Be *assured* of it.

PUC. I am prepar'd: here is my keen-edg'd sword,
Deck'd with five* flower-de-luces on each side;
The which, at Touraine, in saint Katherine's churchyard,
Out of a great deal of old iron I chose forth.

CHAR. Then come, o' God's name, I fear no woman.

PUC. And, while I live, I'll ne'er fly from a man.

[*They fight, and* LA PUCELLE *overcomes.*

CHAR. Stay, stay thy hands! thou art an amazon,
And fightest with the sword of Deborah.

PUC. Christ's mother helps me, else I were too weak.

CHAR. Whoe'er helps thee, 'tis thou that must help me:
Impatiently I burn with thy desire;
My heart and hands thou hast at once subdu'd.
Excellent Pucelle, if thy name be so,
Let me thy servant, and not sovereign, be;
'Tis the French Dauphin sueth to thee thus.

PUC. I must not yield to any rites of love,
For my profession's sacred from above:
When I have chased all thy foes from hence,
Then will I think upon a recompense.

CHAR. Mean time look gracious on thy prostrate thrall.

REIG. My lord, methinks, is very long in talk.

ALEN. Doubtless he shrives this woman to her smock,
Else ne'er could he so long protract his speech.

REIG. Shall we disturb him, since he keeps no mean?

ALEN. He may mean more than we poor men do know:
These women are shrewd tempters with their tongues.

REIG. My lord, where are you? what devise you on?
Shall we give over Orleans, or no?

PUC. Why, no, I say, distrustful recreants!
Fight till the last gasp, I will be your guard.

CHAR. What she says, I'll confirm; we'll fight it out.

PUC. Assign'd am I to be the English scourge.
This night the siege assuredly I'll raise:
Expect saint Martin's summer,[a] halcyon† days,
Since I have entered into these wars.
Glory is like a circle in the water,
Which never ceaseth to enlarge itself,
Till, by broad spreading, it disperse to nought.
With Henry's death the English circle ends;
Dispersed are the glories it included.
Now am I like that proud insulting ship,
Which Cæsar and his fortune bare at once.(4)

CHAR. Was Mahomet inspired with a dove? (5)
Thou with an eagle art inspired, then.
Helen, the mother of great Constantine,
Nor yet saint Philip's daughters, were like thee.
Bright star of Venus, fall'n down on the earth,
How may I reverently worship thee enough?

ALEN. Leave off delays, and let us raise the siege.

REIG. Woman, do what thou canst to save our honours;
Drive them from Orleans, and be immortaliz'd.

CHAR. Presently we'll try:—come, let's away about it;
No prophet will I trust, if she prove false.

[*Exeunt.*

SCENE III.—London. Tower Hill.

Enter, at the Gates, the DUKE *of* GLOUCESTER, *with his* Serving-men *in blue coats.*

GLO. I am come to survey the Tower this day;
Since Henry's death, I fear, there is conveyance.[b]—
Where be these warders, that they wait not here?
Open the gates, 'tis Gloster that calls.[c]

[Servants *knock.*

1 WARD. [*Within.*] Who's there that knocks so imperiously?

1 SERV. It is the noble duke of Gloster.

2 WARD. [*Within.*] Whoe'er he be, you may not be let in.

1 SERV. Villains, answer you so the lord protector?

1 WARD. [*Within.*] The Lord protect him! so we answer him:
We do not otherwise than we are will'd.

GLO. Who willed you? or whose will stands but mine?
There's none protector of the realm but I.—
Break up[d] the gates, I'll be your warrantize:
Shall I be flouted thus by dunghill grooms?

GLOUCESTER'S Men *rush at the* Tower *gates: and* WOODVILLE, *the* Lieutenant, *speaks within.*

WOOD. [*Within.*] What noise is this? what traitors have we here?

GLO. Lieutenant, is it you whose voice I hear?
Open the gates; here's Gloster, that would enter.

WOOD. [*Within.*] Have patience, noble duke; I may not open;
The cardinal of Winchester forbids:
From him I have express commandement,[e]
That thou, nor none of thine, shall be let in.

(*) Old copy, *fine.* (†) Old text, *halcyons.*

[a] Saint Martin's summer,—] "That is, expect *prosperity* after *misfortune*, like fair weather at Martlemas, after winter has begun."—JOHNSON.

[b] Conveyance.] *Deception, fraudulence,*—perhaps *connivance.*

[c] 'Tis Gloster that calls.] See note (b), p. 293.

[d] Break up *the gates,*—] To *break up*, meant to *break open.*

[e] Commandement,—] *Commandement*, here, as in "The Merchant of Venice," Act IV. Sc. 1—

"Be valued 'gainst your wife's commandement,"

must be pronounced as a quadrisyllable.

GLO. Faint-hearted Woodville, prizest him 'fore me?
Arrogant Winchester, that haughty prelate,
Whom Henry, our late sovereign, ne'er could brook?
Thou art no friend to God or to the king:
Open the gates, or I'll shut thee out shortly.
1 SERV. Open the gates unto the lord protector;
Or we'll burst them open, if that you come not [quickly.

Enter WINCHESTER, *with his* Serving-men *in tawny coats.*[a]

WIN. How now, ambitious Humphrey! * what means this?
GLO. Peel'd[b] priest, dost thou command me to be shut out?
WIN. I do, thou most usurping proditor,
And not protector of the king or realm.
GLO. Stand back, thou manifest conspirator;
Thou that contriv'dst to murder our dead lord;
Thou, that giv'st whores indulgences to sin:
I'll canvas[c] thee in thy broad cardinal's hat,
If thou proceed in this thy insolence.
WIN. Nay, stand thou back; I will not budge a foot;
This be Damascus,[d] be thou cursed Cain,
To slay thy brother Abel, if thou wilt.
GLO. I will not slay thee, but I'll drive thee [back:
Thy scarlet robes, as a child's bearing-cloth,
I'll use to carry thee out of this place.

(*) Old copies, *Umpheir*, and *Umpire*.

a Tawny *coats*.] A *tawny coat* was the dress worn by persons employed in the ecclesiastical courts, and by the retainers of a church dignitary. Thus, in Stow's *Chronicle*, p. 822:—"—and by the way the *bishop* of London met him, attended on by a goodly company of gentlemen in *tawny-coats*."

b Peel'd *priest*,—] In allusion to his shaven crown.

c Canvas—] That is, *toss*, as in a blanket. Thus, in "The Second Part of Henry IV." Act II. Sc. 4, when Falstaff says:—"I will toss the rogue in a blanket," Doll Tearsheet rejoins, "—if thou dost, I'll *canvas* thee between a pair of sheets."

d Damascus,—] Damascus was anciently believed to be the spot where Cain killed his brother:—"*Damascus* is as moche to saye as shedynge of blood. For there *Chaym* slowe *Abell*, and hidde hym in the sonde."—*Polychronicon*, fol. xii. quoted by Ritson.

WIN. Do what thou dar'st; I beard thee to thy face.

GLO. What! am I dar'd, and bearded to my face!—
Draw, men, for all this privileged place;
Blue-coats to tawny-coats. Priest, beware your beard;
I mean to tug it, and to cuff you soundly:
Under my feet I'll stamp thy cardinal's hat;[a]
In spite of pope or dignities of church,
Here by the cheeks I'll drag thee up and down.

WIN. Gloster, thou'lt answer this before the pope.

GLO. Winchester goose! I cry, a rope! a rope!—
Now beat them hence, why do you let them stay?—
Thee I'll chase hence, thou wolf in sheep's array.—
Out, tawny-coats!—out, scarlet hypocrite!

Here GLOUCESTER'S men *beat out the* Cardinal's men. *In the hurly-burly, enter the* Mayor *of* London *and his* Officers.

MAY. Fie, lords! that you, being supreme magistrates,
Thus contumeliously should break the peace!

GLO. Peace, mayor! thou knowest little of my wrongs:
Here's Beaufort, that regards nor God nor king,
Hath here distrain'd the Tower to his use.

WIN. Here's Gloster too,[b] a foe to citizens;
One that still motions war, and never peace,
O'ercharging your free purses with large fines;
That seeks to overthrow religion,
Because he is protector of the realm;
And would have armour here out of the Tower,
To crown himself king, and to suppress the prince.

GLO. I will not answer thee with words, but blows. [*Here they skirmish again.*

MAY. Nought rests for me, in this tumultuous strife,
But to make open proclamation:—
Come, officer; as loud as ever thou canst cry.

OFF. [*Reads.*] *All manner of men assembled here in arms this day against God's peace and the king's, we charge and command you, in his highness' name, to repair to your several dwelling-places; and not to wear, handle, or use any sword, weapon, or dagger, henceforward, upon pain of death.*

GLO. Cardinal, I'll be no breaker of the law:
But we shall meet, and break our minds at large.

WIN. Gloster, we'll meet; to thy dear[c] cost, be sure:
Thy heart-blood I will have for this day's work.

MAY. I'll call for clubs,[d] if you will not away:—
This cardinal 's more haughty than the devil.

GLO. Mayor, farewell: thou dost but what thou may'st.

WIN. Abominable Gloster! guard thy head;
For I intend to have't ere long. [*Exeunt.*

MAY. See the coast clear'd, and then we will depart.—
Good God![e] these nobles should such stomachs bear!
I myself fight not once in forty[f] year. [*Exeunt.*

SCENE IV.—France. *Before* Orleans.

Enter, on the walls, the Master-Gunner *and his* Son.

M. GUN. Sirrah, thou know'st how Orleans is besieg'd;
And how the English have the suburbs won.

SON. Father, I know; and oft have shot at them,
Howe'er, unfortunate, I miss'd my aim.

M. GUN. But now thou shalt not. Be thou rul'd by me:
Chief master-gunner am I of this town;
Something I must do to procure me grace.
The prince's espials have informed me,
How the English, in the suburbs close intrench'd,
Wont,* through a secret grate of iron bars
In yonder tower, to overpeer the city;
And thence discover how with most advantage
They may vex us with shot or with assault.
To intercept this inconvenience,
A piece of ordnance 'gainst it I have plac'd;
And fully† even these three days have I watch'd,
If I could see them. Now, boy,‡ do thou watch,
For I can stay no longer.
If thou spy'st any, run and bring me word;
And thou shalt find me at the governor's. [*Exit.*

SON. Father, I warrant you; take you no care,
I'll never trouble you, if I may spy them.

Enter, in an upper chamber of a Tower, the LORDS SALISBURY *and* TALBOT, *Sir* WILLIAM GLANSDALE, *Sir* THOMAS GARGRAVE, *and others.*

SAL. Talbot, my life, my joy, again return'd!
How wert thou handled being prisoner?

---

a *Under my feet* I'll *stamp*, &c.] So the second folio; the first reads, "*I* stamp."

b *Here's Gloster* too, *a foe to citizens;*] So the second folio; the first omits, *too*. But query, whether here, and in the line:—

"Open the gates; 'tis Gloster that calls,"

and—

"Gloster, we'll meet; to thy cost, be sure,"

we were not intended to read, *Gloucester?*

(*) Old text, *went*. (†) First folio omits, *fully*. (‡) First folio omits, *boy*.

c *To thy* dear *cost, be sure:*] The reading of the second folio; in the first, *dear* is omitted. See the preceding note.

d I'll call for clubs,—] See note (b), p. 165.

e *Good God!* these *nobles*, &c.] Here, *that* is understood,—"Good God! *that* these nobles," &c.

f Forty *year*.] That is, *many* years. See note (5), p. 150, Vol. I.

Or by what means got st thou to be releas'd?
Discourse, I pr'ythee, on this turret's top.

TAL. The duke* of Bedford had a prisoner,
Called the brave lord Ponton de Santrailles;
For him I was exchang'd and ransomed.
But with a baser man of arms by far,
Once, in contempt, they would have barter'd me:
Which I, disdaining, scorn'd: and craved death
Rather than I would be so vile†-esteem'd.
In fine, redeem'd I was as I desir'd.
But, O, the treacherous Fastolfe wounds my heart!
Whom with my bare fists I would execute,
If I now had him brought into my power.

SAL. Yet tell'st thou not how thou wert entertain'd.

TAL. With scoffs, and scorns, and contumelious taunts.
In open market-place produc'd they me,
To be a public spectacle to all;
Here, said they, is the terror of the French,
The scare-crow that affrights our children so.
Then broke I from the officers that led me;
And with my nails digg'd stones out of the ground,
To hurl at the beholders of my shame.
My grisly countenance made others fly;
None durst come near for fear of sudden death.
In iron walls they deem'd me not secure;
So great fear of my name 'mongst them was spread,
That they suppos'd I could rend bars of steel,
And spurn in pieces posts of adamant:
Wherefore a guard of chosen shot I had,
That walk'd about me every minute-while;
And if I did but stir out of my bed,
Ready they were to shoot me to the heart.

SAL. I grieve to hear what torments you endur'd;
But we will be reveng'd sufficiently.
Now, it is supper-time in Orleans:
Here, through[a] this grate, I count each one,
And view the Frenchmen how they fortify;
Let us look in, the sight will much delight thee.—
Sir Thomas Gargrave, and sir William Glansdale,
Let me have your express opinions,
Where is best place to make our battery next.

GAR. I think, at the north gate; for there stand lords.

GLAN. And I, here, at the bulwark of the bridge.

TAL. For aught I see, this city must be famish'd,
Or with light skirmishes enfeebled.[b]

[*Shot from the town.* SALISBURY *and Sir* THO. GARGRAVE *fall.*

SAL. O Lord, have mercy on us, wretched sinners!

GAR. O Lord, have mercy on me, woeful man!

TAL. What chance is this, that suddenly hath cross'd us?—
Speak, Salisbury; at least, if thou canst speak;
How far'st thou, mirror of all martial men?
One of thy eyes and thy cheek's side struck off!—
Accursed tower! accursed fatal hand,
That hath contriv'd this woeful tragedy!
In thirteen battles Salisbury o'ercame;
Henry the fifth he first train'd to the wars:
Whilst any trump did sound, or drum struck up,
His sword did ne'er leave striking in the field.—
Yet liv'st thou, Salisbury? though thy speech doth fail,
One eye thou hast, to look to heaven for grace:
The sun with one eye vieweth all the world.—
Heaven, be thou gracious to none alive,
If Salisbury wants mercy at thy hands!—
Bear hence his body; I will help to bury it.—
Sir Thomas Gargrave, hast thou any life?
Speak unto Talbot; nay, look up to him.—
Salisbury, cheer thy spirit with this comfort;
Thou shalt not die whiles——
He beckons with his hand, and smiles on me,
As who should say, *When I am dead and gone,*
Remember to avenge me on the French.—
Plantagenet, I will; and like thee, Nero,[c]
Play on the lute, beholding the towns burn:
Wretched shall France be only in my name.

[*Alarum: thunder and lightning.*

What stir is this? what tumult's in the heavens?
Whence cometh this alarum, and the noise?

Enter a Messenger.

MESS. My lord, my lord, the French have gather'd head!
The Dauphin, with one Joan la Pucelle join'd,—
A holy prophetess, new risen up,—
Is come with a great power to raise the siege.

[SALISBURY *lifts himself up and groans.*

TAL. Hear, hear, how dying Salisbury doth groan!
It irks his heart he cannot be reveng'd.—
Frenchmen, I'll be a Salisbury to you:—
Pucelle or puzzel,[d] dolphin or dogfish,
Your hearts I'll stamp out with my horse's heels,
And make a quagmire of your mingled brains.—
Convey me Salisbury into his tent,
And then we'll try what these dastard Frenchmen dare.[e] [*Exeunt, bearing out the bodies.*

(*) Old text, *Earle.* (†) Old text, *Piel'd.*

[a] *Here, through this grate, I count each one,*—] This is the reading of the first folio, although Steevens, in error, states it has *thorough;* and Mr. Knight endorses his mistake by adopting that word.

[b] Enfeebled.] Enfeebled, in this instance, must be read as a quadrisyllable.

[c] And like thee, Nero,—] The first folio omits, "*Nero;*" the second reads,—

"——and, Nero like, will," &c.

[d] Puzzel,—] *A foul drab.*

[e] And then, &c.] Steevens proposed to restore the measure of this line by omitting *and* or *these,* or by reading,—

"Then try we what these dastard Frenchmen dare."

SCENE V.—*The same.*

Before one of the Gates of Orleans.

Alarum. Skirmishings. Enter TALBOT, *pursuing the* Dauphin; *he drives him in, and exit: then enter* JOAN LA PUCELLE, *driving* Englishmen *before her, and exit after them. Then re-enter* TALBOT.

TAL. Where is my strength, my valour, and my force?
Our English troops retire, I cannot stay them;
A woman clad in armour chaseth them!
Here, here she comes:

Enter LA PUCELLE.

——I'll have a bout with thee;
Devil, or devil's dam, I'll conjure thee:
Blood will I draw on thee,[a]—thou art a witch,—
And straightway give thy soul to him thou serv'st.
PUC. Come, come, 'tis only I that must disgrace thee. [*They fight.*
TAL. Heavens, can you suffer hell so to prevail?
My breast I'll burst with straining of my courage,
And from my shoulders crack my arms asunder,
But I will chástise this high-minded strumpet.
[*They fight again.*
PUC. Talbot, farewell; thy hour is not yet come:
I must go victual Orleans forthwith.
O'ertake me, if thou canst; I scorn thy strength.
Go, go, cheer up thy hunger-starved* men;
Help Salisbury to make his testament:
This day is ours, as many more shall be.
[LA PUCELLE *enters the town, with* Soldiers.
TAL. My thoughts are whirled like a potter's wheel;
I know not where I am, nor what I do:
A witch, by fear, not force, like Hannibal,(6)
Drives back our troops, and conquers as she lists:
So bees with smoke, and doves with noisome stench,
Are from their hives and houses driven away.
They call'd us, for our fierceness, English dogs;
Now, like to whelps, we crying run away.
[*A short alarum.*
Hark, countrymen! either renew the fight,
Or tear the lions out of England's coat;
Renounce your soil, give sheep in lions' stead:
Sheep run not half so timorous[b] from the wolf,
Or horse or oxen from the leopard,
As you fly from your oft-subdued slaves.
[*Alarum. Another skirmish.*
It will not be.—Retire into your trenches:
You all consented unto Salisbury's death,
For none would strike a stroke in his revenge.—
Pucelle is enter'd into Orleans,
In spite of us, or aught that we could do.
O, would I were to die with Salisbury!
The shame hereof will make me hide my head.
[*Alarum. Retreat. Exeunt* TALBOT *and his* Forces, &c.

Flourish. Enter, on the walls, PUCELLE, CHARLES, REIGNIER, ALENÇON, *and* Soldiers.

PUC. Advance our waving colours on the walls;
Rescu'd is Orleans from the English:—[c]
Thus Joan la Pucelle hath perform'd her word.
CHAR. Divinest creature, bright Astræa's daughter,[d]
How shall I honour thee for this success?
Thy promises are like Adonis' gardens,
That one day bloom'd, and fruitful were the next.—
France, triumph in thy glorious prophetess!—
Recover'd is the town of Orleans:
More blessed hap did ne'er befall our state.
REIG. Why ring not out the bells aloud throughout the town?
Dauphin, command the citizens make bonfires,
And feast and banquet in the open streets,
To celebrate the joy that God hath given us.
ALEN. All France will be replete with mirth and joy,
When they shall hear how we have play'd the men.
CHAR. 'Tis Joan, not we, by whom the day is won;
For which I will divide my crown with her:
And all the priests and friars in my realm
Shall in procession sing her endless praise.
A statelier pyramis to her I'll rear,
Than Rhodope's of* Memphis',(7) ever was:
In memory of her, when she is dead,
Her ashes, in an urn more precious
Than the rich-jewel'd coffer of Darius,(8)
Transported shall be at high festivals
Before the kings and queens of France.
No longer on saint Denis will we cry,
But Joan la Pucelle shall be France's saint.
Come in; and let us banquet royally,
After this golden day of victory.
[*Flourish. Exeunt.*

(*) Old copy, *hungry-starved.*

(*) Old text, *or.*

[a] Blood will I draw on thee,—] It was formerly believed that drawing blood from a witch rendered her malice impotent.

[b] *So* timorous *from the wolf,*—] The old text has *trecherous*, which was corrected by Pope.

[c] From the English.—] The second folio reads,—"English *wolves;*" but, remembering what Talbot had just before said,—
"They call us, for our fierceness, English *dogs*,"
we should prefer adding *dogs*.

[d] Bright Astræa's daughter,—] So the second folio; the first omits, *bright*.

ACT II.

SCENE I.—*Before* Orleans.

Enter to the gates, a French Sergeant *and two* Sentinels.

SERG. Sirs, take your places, and be vigilant:
If any noise or soldier you perceive,
Near to the walls, by some apparent sign
Let us have knowledge at the court of guard.
1 SENT. Sergeant, you shall.—[*Exit* Sergeant.]
Thus are poor servitors
(When others sleep upon their quiet beds,)
Constrain'd to watch in darkness, rain, and cold.

Enter TALBOT, BEDFORD, BURGUNDY, *and* Forces, *with scaling ladders; their drums beating a dead march.*

TAL. Lord regent, and redoubted Burgundy,—
By whose approach the regions of Artois,
Walloon, and Picardy, are friends to us,—
This happy night the Frenchmen are secure,
Having all day carous'd and banqueted:
Embrace we, then, this opportunity;
As fitting best to quittance their deceit,
Contriv'd by art and baleful sorcery.

BED. Coward of France!—how much he wrongs his fame,—
Despairing of his own arm's fortitude,—
To join with witches and the help of hell.
BUR. Traitors have never other company.—
But what's that Pucelle, whom they term so pure?
TAL. A maid, they say.
BED. A maid! and be so martial!
BUR. Pray God, she prove not masculine ere long;
If underneath the standard of the French,
She carry armour, as she hath begun.
TAL. Well, let them practise and converse with spirits:
God is our fortress; in whose conquering name
Let us resolve to scale their flinty bulwarks.
BED. Ascend, brave Talbot; we will follow thee.
TAL. Not all together: better far, I guess,
That we do make our entrance several ways;
That, if it chance the one of us do fail,
The other yet may rise against their force.
BED. Agreed; I'll to yond corner.
BUR. And I to this.
TAL. And here will Talbot mount, or make his grave.—

Now, Salisbury! for thee, and for the right
Of English Henry, shall this night appear
How much in duty I am bound to both.

[*The* English *scale the walls, crying St. George! a Talbot! and all enter by the town.*

SENT. [*Within.*] Arm, arm! the enemy doth make assault!

The French *leap over the walls in their shirts. Enter, several ways, the* Bastard, ORLEANS, ALENÇON, REIGNIER, *half ready, and half unready.*

ALEN. How now, my lords! what, all unready[a] so?

BAST. Unready? ay, and glad we 'scap'd so well.

REIG. 'Twas time, I trow, to wake and leave our beds,
Hearing alarums at our chamber-doors.

ALEN. Of all exploits, since first I follow'd arms,
Ne'er heard I of a warlike enterprize
More venturous or desperate than this.

BAST. I think this Talbot be a fiend of hell.

REIG. If not of hell, the heavens, sure, favour him.

ALEN. Here cometh Charles; I marvel how he sped.

BAST. Tut! holy Joan was his defensive guard.

Enter CHARLES *and* LA PUCELLE.

CHAR. Is this thy cunning, thou deceitful dame?
Didst thou at first, to flatter us withal,
Make us partakers of a little gain,
That now our loss might be ten times so much?

PUC. Wherefore is Charles impatient with his friend?
At all times will you have my power alike?
Sleeping or waking, must I still prevail,
Or will you blame and lay the fault on me?—
Improvident soldiers! had your watch been good,
This sudden mischief never could have fall'n.

CHAR. Duke of Alencon, this was your default,
That, being captain of the watch to-night,
Did look no better to that weighty charge.

ALEN. Had all your quarters been as safely kept,
As that whereof I had the government,
We had not been thus shamefully surpris'd.

BAST. Mine was secure.

REIG. And so was mine, my lord.

CHAR. And, for myself, most part of all this night,
Within her quarter and mine own precinct,
I was employ'd in passing to and fro,
About relieving of the sentinels:
Then how or which way[b] should they first break in?

PUC. Question, my lords, no further of the case,
How or which way; 'tis sure they found some place
But weakly guarded, where the breach was made.
And now there rests no other shift but this,—
To gather our soldiers, scatter'd and dispers'd,
And lay new platforms[c] to endamage them.

Alarum. Enter an English Soldier *crying, a Talbot! a Talbot! They fly, leaving their clothes behind.*

SOLD. I'll be so bold to take what they have left.
The cry of Talbot serves me for a sword;
For I have loaden me with many spoils,
Using no other weapon but his name. [*Exit.*

SCENE II.—Orleans. *Within the Town.*

Enter TALBOT, BEDFORD, BURGUNDY, *a* Captain, *and others.*

BED. The day begins to break, and night is fled,
Whose pitchy mantle over-veil'd the earth.
Here sound retreat, and cease our hot pursuit.
[*Retreat sounded.*

TAL. Bring forth the body of old Salisbury,
And here advance it in the market-place,
The middle centre of this cursed town.—
Now have I paid my vow unto his soul;
For every drop of blood was drawn from him,
There hath at least five Frenchmen died to-night.
And, that hereafter ages may behold
What ruin happen'd in revenge of him,
Within their chiefest temple I'll erect
A tomb, wherein his corpse shall be interr'd:
Upon the which, that every one may read,
Shall be engrav'd the sack of Orleans,
The treacherous manner of his mournful death,
And what a terror he had been to France.
But, lords, in all our bloody massacre,
I muse we met not with the Dauphin's grace,

---

a Unready—] *Undressed.*

b *Then* how or which way—] In a note on a passage of "Richard the Second," (see p. 464, Vol. I.) where this pleonasm occurs, we expressed a suspicion that "*or which way*" was an uncancelled interlineation of the poet. We have since discovered our error. "*How or which way,*" like "Many a time and oft," was evidently an admitted phrase of old. Thus, in "All's Well that Ends Well," Act IV. Sc. 3:—"I'll take the sacrament on 't, *how and which way* you will." Again, in a curious ballad of the sixteenth century, entitled "Of Evyll Tongues," in the collection of Mr. George Daniel:—

"*Howe and which way* together they agree,
And what their talke and conference might be."

c Platforms—] *Plans, schemes.*

His new-come champion, virtuous Joan of Arc,
Nor any of his false confederates.

BED. 'Tis thought, lord Talbot, when the fight began,
Rous'd on the sudden from their drowsy beds,
They did, amongst the troops of armed men,
Leap o'er the walls for refuge in the field.

BUR. Myself (as far as I could well discern,
For smoke and dusky vapours of the night,)
Am sure I scar'd the Dauphin and his trull,
When arm in arm they both came swiftly running,
Like to a pair of loving turtle-doves,
That could not live asunder day or night.
After that things are set in order here,
We'll follow them with all the power we have.

Enter a Messenger.

MESS. All hail, my lords! Which of this princely train
Call ye the warlike Talbot, for his acts
So much applauded through the realm of France?

TAL. Here is the Talbot; who would speak with him?

MESS. The virtuous lady, countess of Auvergne,
With modesty admiring thy renown,
By me entreats, great lord, thou wouldst vouchsafe
To visit her poor castle where she lies;
That she may boast, she hath beheld the man
Whose glory fills the world with loud report.

BUR. Is it even so? Nay, then, I see, our wars
Will turn unto a peaceful comic sport,
When ladies crave to be encounter'd with.—
You may not, my lord, despise her gentle suit.

TAL. Ne'er trust me then; for when a world of men
Could not prevail with all their oratory,
Yet hath a woman's kindness over-rul'd:—
And therefore tell her I return great thanks,
And in submission will attend on her.—
Will not your honours bear me company?

BED. No, truly; it is more than manners will:
And I have heard it said, unbidden guests
Are often welcomest when they are gone.

TAL. Well then, alone, since there's no remedy,
I mean to prove this lady's courtesy.—
Come hither, captain. [*Whispers.*]—You perceive my mind.

CAPT. I do, my lord; and mean accordingly. [*Exeunt.*

SCENE III.—Auvergne. *Court of the Castle.*

Enter the COUNTESS *and her* Porter.

COUNT. Porter, remember what I give in charge;
And when you have done so, bring the keys to me.

PORT. Madam, I will. [*Exit.*

COUNT. The plot is laid: if all things fall out right,
I shall as famous be by this exploit,
As Scythian Thomyris by Cyrus' death.
Great is the rumour of this dreadful knight,
And his achievements of no less account:
Fain would mine eyes be witness with mine ears,
To give their censure of these rare reports.

Enter Messenger *and* TALBOT.

MESS. Madam, according as your ladyship desir'd,
By message crav'd, so is lord Talbot come.

COUNT. And he is welcome. What! is this the man?

MESS. Madam, it is.

COUNT. Is this the scourge of France?
Is this the Talbot, so much fear'd abroad,
That with his name the mothers still their babes?
I see report is fabulous and false:
I thought I should have seen some Hercules,
A second Hector, for his grim aspéct,
And large proportion of his strong-knit limbs.
Alas! this is a child, a silly dwarf:
It cannot be, this weak and writhled shrimp
Should strike such terror to his enemies.

TAL. Madam, I have been bold to trouble you;
But, since your ladyship is not at leisure,
I'll sort some other time to visit you. [*Going.*

COUNT. What means he now!—Go ask him whither he goes.

MESS. Stay, my lord Talbot; for my lady craves
To know the cause of your abrupt departure.

TAL. Marry, for that she's in a wrong belief,
I go to certify her, Talbot's here.

Re-enter Porter *with keys.*

COUNT. If thou be he, then art thou prisoner.

TAL. Prisoner! to whom?

COUNT. To me, blood-thirsty lord;
And for that cause I train'd thee to my house.
Long time thy shadow hath been thrall to me,
For in my gallery thy picture hangs:
But now the substance shall endure the like;
And I will chain these legs and arms of thine,
That hast by tyranny, these many years,
Wasted our country, slain our citizens,
And sent our sons and husbands captivate.

TAL. Ha, ha, ha!

COUNT. Laughest thou, wretch? thy mirth shall turn to moan.

TAL. I laugh to see your ladyship so fond,[a]

[a] Fond,—] That is, *foolish.*

To think that you have aught but Talbot's shadow
Whereon to practise your severity.

COUNT. Why, art not thou the man?

TAL. I am indeed.

COUNT. Then have I substance too.

TAL. No, no, I am but shadow of myself:
You are deceiv'd, my substance is not here;
For what you see is but the smallest part
And least proportion of humanity:
I tell you, madam, were the whole frame here,
It is of such a spacious lofty pitch,
Your roof were not sufficient to contain it.

COUNT. This is a riddling merchant for the nonce;
He will be here, and yet he is not here:
How can these contrarieties agree?

TAL. That will I show you presently.

[*He winds a horn. Drums heard; then a peal of ordnance. The gates being forced, enter* Soldiers.

How say you, madam? are you now persuaded,
That Talbot is but shadow of himself?
These are his substance, sinews, arms, and strength,
With which he yoketh your rebellious necks,
Razeth your cities, and subverts your towns,
And in a moment makes them desolate.

COUNT. Victorious Talbot! pardon my abuse:
I find, thou art no less than fame hath bruited,
And more than may be gather'd by thy shape.
Let my presumption not provoke thy wrath,
For I am sorry that with reverence
I did not entertain thee as thou art.

TAL. Be not dismay'd, fair lady; nor misconstrue
The mind of Talbot, as you did mistake
The outward composition of his body.
What you have done, hath not offended me:
No other satisfaction do I crave,
But only (with your patience) that we may
Taste of your wine, and see what cates you have;
For soldiers' stomachs always serve them well.

COUNT. With all my heart; and think me honoured
To feast so great a warrior in my house. [*Exeunt.*

SCENE IV.—London. *The* Temple Garden.

Enter the EARLS *of* SOMERSET, SUFFOLK, *and* WARWICK: RICHARD PLANTAGENET, VERNON, *and a* Lawyer.

PLAN. Great lords and gentlemen, what means this silence?
Dare no man answer in a case of truth?

SUF. Within the Temple-hall we were too loud;
The garden here is more convenient.

PLAN. Then say at once, if I maintain'd the truth,
Or else was wrangling Somerset in the error?

SUF. Faith, I have been a truant in the law,
And never yet could frame my will to it;
And, therefore, frame the law unto my will.

SOM. Judge you, my lord of Warwick, then between us.

WAR. Between two hawks, which flies the higher pitch;
Between two dogs, which hath the deeper mouth;
Between two blades, which bears the better temper;
Between two horses, which doth bear him best;
Between two girls, which hath the merriest eye;—
I have, perhaps, some shallow spirit of judgment:
But in these nice sharp quillets of the law,
Good faith, I am no wiser than a daw.

PLAN. Tut, tut, here is a mannerly forbearance:
The truth appears so naked on my side,
That any purblind eye may find it out.

SOM. And on my side it is so well apparell'd,
So clear, so shining, and so evident,
That it will glimmer through a blind man's eye.

PLAN. Since you are tongue-tied, and so loth to speak,
In dumb significants proclaim your thoughts:
Let him that is a true-born gentleman,
And stands upon the honour of his birth,
If he suppose that I have pleaded truth,
From off this briar pluck a white rose with me.

SOM. Let him that is no coward nor no flatterer,
But dare maintain the party of the truth,
Pluck a red rose from off this thorn with me.

WAR. I love no colours;[a] and, without all colour
Of base insinuating flattery,
I pluck this white rose with Plantagenet.

SUF. I pluck this red rose with young Somerset;
And say withal, I think he held the right.

VER. Stay, lords and gentlemen; and pluck no more,
Till you conclude—that he, upon whose side
The fewest roses are cropp'd from the tree,
Shall yield the other in the right opinion.

SOM. Good master Vernon, it is well objected;
If I have fewest, I subscribe in silence.

PLAN. And I.

VER. Then, for the truth and plainness of the case,
I pluck this pale and maiden blossom here,
Giving my verdict on the white rose side.

SOM. Prick not your finger as you pluck it off;
Lest, bleeding, you do paint the white rose red,
And fall on my side so, against your will.

VER. If I, my lord, for my opinion bleed,
Opinion shall be surgeon to my hurt,

[a] Colours;—] The word is employed equivocally for *artifices, specious glosses*, &c.

And keep me on the side where still I am.
SOM. Well, well, come on: who else?
LAW. Unless my study and my books be false,
The argument you held was wrong in you;
[*To* SOMERSET.
In sign whereof I pluck a white rose too.
PLAN. Now, Somerset, where is your argument?
SOM. Here, in my scabbard; meditating that,
Shall dye your white rose in a bloody red.
PLAN. Mean time, your cheeks do counterfeit our roses;
For pale they look with fear, as witnessing
The truth on our side.
SOM. No, Plantagenet,
'Tis not for fear, but anger,—that thy cheeks
Blush for pure shame to counterfeit our roses;
And yet thy tongue will not confess thy error.
PLAN. Hath not thy rose a canker, Somerset?
SOM. Hath not thy rose a thorn, Plantagenet?
PLAN. Ay, sharp and piercing, to maintain his truth;
Whiles thy consuming canker eats his falsehood.
SOM. Well, I'll find friends to wear my bleeding roses,
That shall maintain what I have said is true,
Where false Plantagenet dare not be seen.
PLAN. Now, by this maiden blossom in my hand,
I scorn thee and thy fashion,[a] peevish boy.
SUF. Turn not thy scorns this way, Plantagenet.
PLAN. Proud Poole, I will; and scorn both him and thee.
SUF. I'll turn my part thereof into thy throat.
SOM. Away, away, good William De-la-Poole!
We grace the yeoman by conversing with him.
WAR. Now, by God's will, thou wrong'st him, Somerset;
His grandfather was Lionel duke of Clarence,
Third son to the third Edward king of England:
Spring crestless yeomen from so deep a root?
PLAN. He bears him on the place's privilege,
Or durst not, for his craven heart, say thus.
SOM. By Him that made me, I'll maintain my words
On any plot of ground in Christendom:
Was not thy father, Richard earl of Cambridge,
For treason executed in our late king's days?
And, by his treason, stand'st not thou attainted,
Corrupted, and exempt from ancient gentry?

[a] *I scorn thee and thy* fashion,—] Theobald reads *faction*, we believe rightly; Plantagenet presently after says,—
"——— This pale and angry rose,——
Will I for ever, and my *faction*, wear."

His trespass yet lives guilty in thy blood;
And, till thou be restor'd, thou art a yeoman.
PLAN. My father was attached, not attainted,
Condemn'd to die for treason, but no traitor;
And that I'll prove on better men than Somerset,
Were growing time once ripen'd to my will.
For your partaker[a] Poole, and you yourself,
I'll note you in my book of memory,
To scourge you for this apprehension:[b]
Look to it well; and say you are well warn'd.
SOM. Ay, thou shalt find us ready for thee still:
And know us, by these colours, for thy foes;
For these, my friends, in spite of thee, shall wear.
PLAN. And, by my soul, this pale and angry rose,
As cognizance[c] of my blood-drinking hate,
Will I for ever, and my faction, wear,
Until it wither with me to my grave,
Or flourish to the height of my degree.
SUF. Go forward, and be chok'd with thy ambition!
And so farewell, until I meet thee next. [*Exit.*
SOM. Have with thee, Poole.—Farewell, ambitious Richard. [*Exit.*
PLAN. How I am brav'd, and must perforce endure it!
WAR. This blot, that they object against your house,
Shall be wip'd * out in the next parliament,
Call'd for the truce of Winchester and Gloster:
And if thou be not then created York,
I will not live to be accounted Warwick.
Mean time, in signal of my love to thee,
Against proud Somerset and William Poole,
Will I upon thy party wear this rose:
And here I prophecy,—this brawl to-day
Grown to this faction, in the Temple garden,
Shall send, between the red rose and the white,
A thousand souls to death and deadly night.
PLAN. Good master Vernon, I am bound to you,
That you on my behalf would pluck a flower.
VER. In your behalf still will I wear the same.
LAW. And so will I.
PLAN. Thanks, gentle sir.†
Come, let us four to dinner: I dare say,
This quarrel will drink blood another day. [*Exeunt.*

SCENE V.—*The same. A Room in the* Tower.

Enter MORTIMER,(1) *brought in a chair by* Keepers.

MOR. Kind keepers of my weak decaying age,
Let dying Mortimer here rest himself.—
Even like a man new haled from the rack,
So fare my limbs with long imprisonment:
And these grey locks, the pursuivants of death,
Nestor-like, aged in an age of care,
Argue the end of Edmund Mortimer.
These eyes,—like lamps whose wasting oil is spent,—
Wax dim, as drawing to their exigent:
Weak shoulders, overborne with burd'ning grief;
And pithless arms, like to a wither'd vine
That droops his sapless branches to the ground:—
Yet are these feet whose strengthless stay is numb,
Unable to support this lump of clay,
Swift-winged with desire to get a grave,
As witting I no other comfort have.—
But tell me, keeper, will my nephew come?
1 KEEP. Richard Plantagenet, my lord, will come:
We sent unto the Temple, to* his chamber;
And answer was return'd, that he will come.
MOR. Enough; my soul shall then be satisfied.—
Poor gentleman! his wrong doth equal mine.
Since Henry Monmouth first began to reign,
(Before whose glory I was great in arms,)
This loathsome sequestration have I had;
And even since then hath Richard been obscur'd,
Depriv'd of honour and inheritance:
But now, the arbitrator of despairs,
Just death, kind umpire of men's miseries,
With sweet enlargement doth dismiss me hence:
I would his troubles likewise were expir'd,
That so he might recover what was lost.

Enter RICHARD PLANTAGENET.

1 KEEP. My lord, your loving nephew now is come.
MOR. Richard Plantagenet, my friend, is he come?
PLAN. Ay, noble uncle, thus ignobly us'd,
Your nephew, late-despised Richard, comes.
MOR. Direct mine arms, I may embrace his neck,
And in his bosom spend my latter gasp:
O, tell me when my lips do touch his cheeks,
That I may kindly give one fainting kiss.—
And now declare, sweet stem from York's great stock,
Why didst thou say—of late thou wert despis'd?
PLAN. First, lean thine aged back against mine arm;
And, in that ease, I'll tell thee my disease.
This day, in argument upon a case,

(*) First folio, *whipt*. (†) First folio omits, *sir*.

(*) Old text, *unto*.

[a] Partaker—] *Particeps*; a *partner*, a *factionary*.
[b] Apprehension:—] *Conceit, sarcasm.* He alludes to their calling him a *yeoman*.
[c] Cognizance—] "A *badge* is called a *cognisance, à cognoscendo*, because by it such persons as do wear it upon their sleeves, their shoulders, or in their hats, are manifestly known whose servants they are. In heraldry the *cognisance* is seated upon the most prominent part of the helmet."—TOLLET.

Some words there grew 'twixt Somerset and me:
Among which terms he us'd his lavish tongue,
And did upbraid me with my father's death;
Which obloquy set bars before my tongue,
Else with the like I had requited him:
Therefore, good uncle,—for my father's sake,
In honour of a true Plantagenet,
And for alliance' sake,—declare the cause
My father, earl of Cambridge, lost his head. [me,
MOR. That cause, fair nephew, that imprison'd
And hath detain'd me all my flow'ring youth
Within a loathsome dungeon, there to pine,
Was cursed instrument of his decease. [was,
PLAN. Discover more at large what cause that
For I am ignorant, and cannot guess.
MOR. I will; if that my fading breath permit,
And death approach not ere my tale be done.
Henry the Fourth, grandfather to this king,
Depos'd his nephew [a] Richard,—Edward's son,
The first-begotten, and the lawful heir
Of Edward king, the third of that descent:
During whose reign, the Percies of the north,
Finding his usurpation most unjust,
Endeavour'd my advancement to the throne:
The reason mov'd these warlike lords to this,
Was—for that (young king* Richard thus remov'd
Leaving no heir begotten of his body,)
I was the next by birth and parentage;
For by my mother I derived am
From Lionel duke of Clarence, the† third son
To king Edward the third, whereas he,
From John of Gaunt doth bring his pedigree,
Being but fourth of that heroic line.
But mark; as, in this haughty[b] great attempt,
They laboured to plant the rightful heir,
I lost my liberty, and they their lives.
Long after this, when Henry the fifth,—
Succeeding his father Bolingbroke,—did reign,
Thy father, earl of Cambridge,—then deriv'd
From famous Edmund Langley, duke of York,—
Marrying my sister, that thy mother was,
Again, in pity of my hard distress,
Levied an army; weening to redeem
And have install'd me in the diadem:
But, as the rest, so fell that noble earl,
And was beheaded. Thus the Mortimers,
In whom the title rested, were suppress'd. [last.
PLAN. Of which, my lord, your honour is the
MOR. True; and thou seest, that I no issue have,

[a] Nephew—] Some editors read *cousin*. If *nephew* is the author's word, it must be used like the Latin *nepos*.

(*) First folio omits, *king*. (†) First folio omits, *the*.

[b] Haughty—] *High*.

And that my fainting words do warrant death;
Thou art my heir; the rest I wish thee gather:
But yet be wary in thy studious care. [me:
PLAN. Thy grave admonishments prevail with
But yet, methinks, my father's execution
Was nothing less than bloody tyranny.
MOR. With silence, nephew, be thou politic;
Strong-fixed is the house of Lancaster,
And, like a mountain, not to be remov'd.
But now thy uncle is removing hence;
As princes do their courts, when they are cloy'd
With long continuance in a settled place. [years
PLAN. O, uncle, would some part of my young
Might but redeem the passage of your age!
MOR. Thou dost, then, wrong me,—as the slaught'rer doth,
Which giveth many wounds when one will kill.
Mourn not, except thou sorrow for my good;
Only, give order for my funeral;
And so, farewell, and fair be all thy hopes!
And prosperous be thy life in peace and war!
[*Dies.*
PLAN. And peace, no war, befal thy parting soul!
In prison hast thou spent a pilgrimage,
And like a hermit overpass'd thy days.—
Well, I will lock his counsel in my breast;
And what I do imagine, let that rest.—
Keepers, convey him hence; and I myself
Will see his burial better than his life.—
[*Exeunt* Keepers, *bearing out the body of* MORTIMER.
Here dies the dusky torch of Mortimer,
Chok'd with ambition of the meaner sort:—
And, for those wrongs, those bitter injuries,
Which Somerset hath offer'd to my house,—
I doubt not, but with honour to redress;
And therefore haste I to the parliament,
Either to be restored to my blood,
Or make my ill[a] th' advantage of my good. [*Exit.*

---

a *Or make my* ill—] The old text is, "make my *will*," &c.; for the restoration of the intended antithesis, we are indebted to Theobald.

ACT III.

SCENE I.—London. *The* Parliament-House.

Flourish. Enter KING HENRY, EXETER, GLOUCESTER, WARWICK, SOMERSET, *and* SUFFOLK; *the* BISHOP *of* WINCHESTER, RICHARD PLANTAGENET, *and others.* GLOUCESTER *offers to put up a bill;* WINCHESTER *snatches it, and tears it.*

WIN. Com'st thou with deep premeditated lines,
With written pamphlets studiously devis'd?
Humphrey of Gloster, if thou canst accuse,
Or aught intend'st to lay unto my charge,
Do it without invention, suddenly;
As I with sudden and extemporal speech
Purpose to answer what thou canst object.
GLO. Presumptuous priest! this place commands my patience,
Or thou should'st find thou hast dishonour'd me.
Think not, although in writing I preferr'd
The manner of thy vile outrageous crimes,
That therefore I have forg'd, or am not able
Verbatim to rehearse the method of my pen:
No, prelate; such is thy audacious wickedness,

Thy lewd, pestiferous, and dissentious pranks,
As very infants prattle of thy pride.
Thou art a most pernicious usurer;
Froward by nature, enemy to peace;
Lascivious, wanton, more than well beseems
A man of thy profession and degree;
And for thy treachery, what's more manifest,—
In that thou laid'st a trap to take my life,
As well at London bridge, as at the Tower?
Beside, I fear me, if thy thoughts were sifted,
The king, thy sovereign, is not quite exempt
From envious malice of thy swelling heart.

WIN. Gloster, I do defy thee.—Lords, vouchsafe
To give me hearing what I shall reply.
If I were covetous, ambitious, or perverse,
As he will have me, how am I so poor?
Or how haps it, I seek not to advance
Or raise myself, but keep my wonted calling?
And for dissension, who preferreth peace
More than I do, except I be provok'd?
No, my good lords, it is not that offends;
It is not that, that hath incens'd the duke:
It is, because no one should sway but he;
No one but he should be about the king;
And that engenders thunder in his breast,
And makes him roar these accusations forth.
But he shall know I am as good—

GLO. As good!
Thou bastard of my grandfather!—

WIN. Ay, lordly sir; for what are you, I pray,
But one imperious in another's throne?

GLO. Am I not protector, saucy priest?

WIN. And am not I a prelate of the church?

GLO. Yes, as an outlaw in a castle keeps,
And useth it to patronage his theft.

WIN. Unreverent Gloster!

GLO: Thou art reverent
Touching thy spiritual function, not thy life.

WIN. Rome shall remedy this.

WAR. Roam thither then.

SOM. My lord, it were your duty to forbear.[a]

WAR. Ay, see the bishop be not overborne.

SOM. Methinks my lord should be religious,
And know the office that belongs to such.

WAR. Methinks his lordship should be humbler;
It fitteth not a prelate so to plead.

SOM. Yes, when his holy state is touch'd so near.

WAR. State holy or unhallow'd, what of that?
Is not his grace protector to the king?

PLAN. Plantagenet, I see, must hold his tongue;
Lest it be said, *Speak, sirrah, when you should;*
Must your bold verdict enter talk with lords?
Else would I have a fling at Winchester. [*Aside.*

K. HEN. Uncles of Gloster and of Winchester,
The special watchmen of our English weal;
I would prevail, if prayers might prevail,
To join your hearts in love and amity.
O, what a scandal is it to our crown,
That two such noble peers as ye should jar!
Believe me, lords, my tender years can tell,
Civil dissension is a viperous worm,
That gnaws the bowels of the commonwealth.—
[*A noise without;* "Down with the tawny coats!"
What tumult's this?

WAR. An uproar, I dare warrant,
Begun through malice of the bishop's men.
[*A noise again;* "Stones! Stones!"

Enter the Mayor *of* London, *attended.*

MAY. O, my good lords,—and virtuous Henry,—
Pity the city of London, pity us!
The bishop and the duke of Gloster's men,
Forbidden late to carry any weapon,
Have fill'd their pockets full of pebble-stones;
And banding themselves in contráry parts,
Do pelt so fast at one another's pate,
That many have their giddy brains knock'd out:
Our windows are broke down in every street,
And we, for fear, compell'd to shut our shops.

Enter, skirmishing, the Retainers *of* GLOUCESTER *and* WINCHESTER, *with bloody pates.*

K. HEN. We charge you, on allegiance to ourself,
To hold your slaught'ring hands, and keep the peace.
Pray, uncle Gloster, mitigate this strife.

1 SERV. Nay, if we be forbidden stones, we'll fall to it with our teeth.

2 SERV. Do what ye dare, we are as resolute.
[*Skirmish again.*

GLO. You of my household, leave this peevish broil,
And set this unaccustom'd fight aside.

3 SERV. My lord, we know your grace to be a man
Just and upright; and, for your royal birth,
Inferior to none but to his majesty:
And, ere that we will suffer such a prince,
So kind a father of the commonweal,
To be disgraced by an inkhorn mate,[b]
We, and our wives, and children, all will fight,
And have our bodies slaughter'd by thy foes.

---

[a] *Som.* My lord, &c.] This distribution of the speeches was made by Theobald. In the folio 1623, the dialogue runs:—
War. Roame thither then.
My Lord, it were your dutie to forbeare.
Som. I, see the Bishop be not over-borne:
Methinkes my Lord should be Religious," &c.

[b] *An* inkhorn *mate,*—] A *bookman,* a *pedant.*

1 Serv. Ay, and the very parings of our nails
Shall pitch a field[a] when we are dead.
[*Skirmish again.*
Glo. Stay, stay, I say!
An if you love me, as you say you do,
Let me persuade you to forbear a while.
K. Hen. O, how this discord doth afflict my soul!—
Can you, my lord of Winchester, behold
My sighs and tears, and will not once relent?
Who should be pitiful, if you be not?
Or who should study to prefer a peace,
If holy churchmen take delight in broils?
War. Yield, my lord protector;—yield, Winchester;—
Except you mean, with obstinate repulse,
To slay your sovereign, and destroy the realm.
You see what mischief, and what murder too,
Hath been enacted through your enmity;
Then be at peace, except ye thirst for blood.
Win. He shall submit, or I will never yield.
Glo. Compassion on the king commands me stoop,
Or, I would see his heart out, ere the priest
Should ever get that privilege of me.
War. Behold, my lord of Winchester, the duke
Hath banish'd moody discontented fury,
As by his smoothed brows it doth appear:
Why look you still so stern and tragical?
Glo. Here, Winchester, I offer thee my hand.
K. Hen. Fie, uncle Beaufort! I have heard you preach,
That malice was a great and grievous sin;
And will not you maintain the thing you teach,
But prove a chief offender in the same?

---

[a] Shall pitch a field—] To understand this allusion, it must be remembered that before beginning a battle it was customary for the archers and other foot-men to encompass themselves with sharp stakes firmly pitched in the ground, to prevent their being overpowered by the cavalry. Thus, in a previous speech, Act I. Sc. 1:—

"No leisure had he to enrank his men;
He wanted pikes to set before his archers;
Instead whereof, sharp stakes, pluck'd out of hedges,
They *pitched* in the ground confusedly,
To keep the horsemen off from breaking in."

WAR. Sweet king!—the bishop hath a kindly gird.—[a]
For shame, my lord of Winchester, relent!
What, shall a child instruct you what to do?
WIN. Well, duke of Gloster, I will yield to thee
Love for thy love; and hand for hand I give.
GLO. Ay; but, I fear me, with a hollow heart.—
See here, my friends, and loving countrymen;
This token serveth for a flag of truce,
Betwixt ourselves and all our followers:
So help me God, as I dissemble not!
WIN. [*Aside.*] So help me God, as I intend it not!
K. HEN. O loving uncle, kind duke of Gloster,
How joyful am I made by this contráct!—
Away, my masters! trouble us no more;
But join in friendship, as your lords have done.
1 SERV. Content; I'll to the surgeon's.
2 SERV. And so will I.
3 SERV. And I will see what physic the tavern affords. [*Exeunt* Mayor, Servants, *&c.*
WAR. Accept this scroll, most gracious sovereign,
Which in the right of Richard Plantagenet
We do exhibit to your majesty.
GLO. Well urg'd, my lord of Warwick;—for, sweet prince,
An if your grace mark every circumstance,
You have great reason to do Richard right:
Especially for those occasions
At Eltham-place I told your majesty.
K. HEN. And those occasions, uncle, were of force:
Therefore, my loving lords, our pleasure is,
That Richard be restored to his blood.
WAR. Let Richard be restored to his blood;
So shall his father's wrongs be recompens'd.
WIN. As will the rest, so willeth Winchester.
K. HEN. If Richard will be true, not that* alone,
But all the whole inheritance I give,
That doth belong unto the house of York,
From whence you spring by lineal descent.
PLAN. Thy humble[b] servant vows obedience,
And humble service, till the point of death.
K. HEN. Stoop then, and set your knee against my foot,
And, in reguerdon of that duty done,
I girt thee with the valiant sword of York:
Rise, Richard, like a true Plantagenet,
And rise created princely duke of York.
PLAN. And so thrive Richard, as thy foes may fall!
And as my duty springs, so perish they
That grudge one thought against your majesty!
ALL. Welcome, high prince, the mighty duke of York!

(*) First folio inserts, *all.*

[a] A kindly gird.] An *appropriate taunt; a reproach in kind.* See note (a), p. 180, Vol. I.

SOM. [*Aside.*] Perish, base prince, ignoble duke of York!
GLO. Now will it best avail your majesty,
To cross the seas, and to be crown'd in France:
The presence of a king engenders love
Amongst his subjects and his loyal friends;
As it disanimates his enemies.
K. HEN. When Gloster says the word, king Henry goes,
For friendly counsel cuts off many foes.
GLO. Your ships already are in readiness.
[*Flourish. Exeunt all except* EXETER.
EXE. Ay, we may march in England or in France,
Not seeing what is likely to ensue:
This late dissension, grown betwixt the peers,
Burns under feigned ashes of forg'd love,
And will at last break out into a flame:
As fester'd members rot but by degree,
Till bones and flesh and sinews fall away,
So will this base and envious discord breed.
And now I fear that fatal prophecy,
Which in the time of Henry, nam'd the fifth,
Was in the mouth of every sucking babe,—
That Henry, born at Monmouth, should win all,
And Henry, born at Windsor, should* lose all,
Which is so plain, that Exeter doth wish
His days may finish ere that hapless time. [*Exit.*

SCENE II.—France. *Before* Rouen.

Enter LA PUCELLE *disguised, and* Soldiers *dressed like* Countrymen, *with sacks upon their backs.*

PUC. These are the city-gates, the gates of Rouen,
Through which our policy must make a breach: (1)
Take heed, be wary how you place your words;
Talk like the vulgar sort of market-men,
That come to gather money for their corn.
If we have entrance,—as I hope we shall,—
And that we find the slothful watch but weak,
I'll by a sign give notice to our friends,
That Charles the dauphin may encounter them.
1 SOL. Our sacks shall be a mean to sack the city,
And we be lords and rulers over Rouen;
Therefore we'll knock. [*Knocks.*
GUARD. [*Within.*] *Qui est là?*
PUC. *Paysans, pauvres gens de France,*—
Poor market-folks, that come to sell their corn.

(*) First folio omits, *should.*

[b] *Thy* humble *servant*—] We incline to read, with Mr. Collier's annotator, "thy *honour'd* servant," &c.

GUARD. [*Opening the gates.*] Enter, go in; the market-bell is rung. [the ground.
PUC. Now, Rouen, I'll shake thy bulwarks to
[LA PUCELLE, *&c. enter the city.*

Enter CHARLES, *the* Bastard *of* Orleans, ALENÇON, *and* Forces.

CHAR. Saint Denis bless this happy stratagem!
And once again we'll sleep secure in Rouen.
BAST. Here enter'd Pucelle, and her practisants.
Now she is there, how will she specify
Where* is the best and safest passage in?
ALEN. By thrusting out a torch from yonder tower; [is,—
Which, once discern'd, shows that her meaning
No way to that, for weakness, which she entered.

Enter LA PUCELLE *on a battlement, holding out a burning torch.*

PUC. Behold, this is the happy wedding-torch,
That joineth Rouen unto her countrymen;
But burning-fatal to the Talbotites! [friend;
BAST. See, noble Charles, the beacon of our
The burning torch in yonder turret stands.
CHAR. Now shine it like a comet of revenge,
A prophet to the fall of all our foes! [ends;
ALEN. Defer no time, delays have dangerous
Enter, and cry—*The Dauphin!*—presently,
And then do execution on the watch. [*They enter.*

Alarums. Enter TALBOT, *and* English Soldiers *from the town.*

TAL. France, thou shalt rue this treason with thy tears,
If Talbot but survive thy treachery.—
Pucelle, that witch, that damned sorceress,
Hath wrought this hellish mischief unawares,
That hardly we escap'd the pride[a] of France.
[*Exeunt into the town.*

Alarum: excursions. Enter, from the town, BEDFORD, *brought in sick, in a chair, with* TALBOT, BURGUNDY, *and the* English Forces. *Then, enter on the walls,* LA PUCELLE, CHARLES, *the* Bastard, ALENÇON, *and others.*

PUC. Good morrow, gallants! want ye corn for bread?

(*) Old text, *Here.*

a *That hardly we escap'd the* pride *of France.*] Warburton explains *pride* to mean *haughty power.* In "Henry V." Act I. Sc. 2, we meet the same expression:—

"——could entertain
With half their forces the *full pride of France.*"

I think the duke of Burgundy will fast,
Before he'll buy again at such a rate:
'Twas full of darnel; do you like the taste?
BUR. Scoff on, vile fiend and shameless courtezan!
I trust ere long to choke thee with thine own,
And make thee curse the harvest of that corn.
CHAR. Your grace may starve, perhaps, before that time.
BED. O, let no words, but deeds, revenge this [treason!
PUC. What will you do, good grey-beard? break a lance,
And run a-tilt at death, within a chair?
TAL. Foul fiend of France, and hag of all despite,[a]
Encompass'd with thy lustful paramours!
Becomes it thee to taunt his valiant age,
And twit with cowardice a man half dead?
Damsel, I'll have a bout with you again,
Or else let Talbot perish with this shame.
PUC. Are ye so hot, sir?—yet, Pucelle, hold thy peace;
If Talbot do but thunder, rain will follow.—
[TALBOT *and the rest consult together.*
God speed the parliament! who shall be the speaker?
TAL. Dare ye come forth, and meet us in [the field?
PUC. Belike your lordship takes us then for fools,
To try if that our own be ours or no.
TAL. I speak not to that railing Hecaté,
But unto thee, Alençon, and the rest;
Will ye, like soldiers, come and fight it out?
ALEN. Signior, no.
TAL. *Signior*, hang!—base muleteers of France!
Like peasant foot-boys do they keep the walls,
And dare not take up arms like gentlemen.

[a] *Hag of* all *despite*,—] Mr. Collier's annotator substitutes, "hag of *hell's* despite;" but see "Henry VI." Pt. 3, Act II. Sc. 6:—
"That I in *all despite* might rail at him."

PUC. Away, captains! let's get us from the walls,
For Talbot means no goodness, by his looks.—
God b' wi' my lord! we came but to tell you
That we are here.
[*Exeunt* LA PUCELLE, *&c. from the walls.*

TAL. And there will we be too, ere it be long,
Or else reproach be Talbot's greatest fame!—
Vow, Burgundy, by honour of thy house,
Prick'd on by public wrongs sustain'd in France,
Either to get the town again, or die:
And I,—as sure as English Henry lives,
And as his father here was conqueror;
As sure as in this late-betrayed town
Great Cœur-de-lion's heart was buried;
So sure I swear, to get the town or die.

BUR. My vows are equal partners with thy vows.

TAL. But, ere we go, regard this dying prince,
The valiant duke of Bedford.—Come, my lord,
We will bestow you in some better place,
Fitter for sickness and for crazy age.

BED. Lord Talbot, do not so dishonour me:
Here will I sit, before the walls of Rouen,
And will be partner of your weal or woe.

BUR. Courageous Bedford, let us now persuade you.

BED. Not to be gone from hence; for once I read,
That stout Pendragon, in his litter, sick,
Came to the field, and vanquished his foes:
Methinks I should revive the soldiers' hearts,
Because I ever found them as myself.

TAL. Undaunted spirit in a dying breast!
Then be it so—heavens keep old Bedford safe!—
And now no more ado, brave Burgundy,
But gather we our forces out of hand,
And set upon our boasting enemy.
[*Exeunt into the town* BURGUNDY, TALBOT, *and* Forces, *leaving* BEDFORD *and others.*

Alarum: excursions. Enter Sir JOHN FASTOLFE, *and a* Captain.

CAP. Whither away, sir John Fastolfe, in such haste?

FAST. Whither away! to save myself by flight;
We are like to have the overthrow again.

CAP. What! will you fly, and leave lord Talbot?

FAST. Ay,
All the Talbots in the world, to save my life.
[*Exit.*

CAP. Cowardly knight! ill fortune follow thee!
[*Exit.*

Retreat: excursions. Re-enter, from the town, LA PUCELLE, ALENÇON, CHARLES, *&c., and exeunt, flying.*

BED. Now, quiet soul, depart when heaven please,
For I have seen our enemies' overthrow.
What is the trust or strength of foolish man?
They that of late were daring with their scoffs,
Are glad and fain by flight to save themselves.
[*Dies, and is carried off in his chair.*

Alarum. Re-enter TALBOT, BURGUNDY, *and others.*

TAL. Lost, and recover'd in a day again!
This is a double honour, Burgundy:
Yet heavens have glory for this victory!

BUR. Warlike and martial Talbot, Burgundy
Enshrines thee in his heart; and there erects
Thy noble deeds, as valour's monuments.

TAL. Thanks, gentle duke. But where is Pucelle now?
I think her old familiar is asleep:
Now where's the Bastard's braves, and Charles his gleeks?
What, all a-mort! Rouen hangs her head for grief,
That such a valiant company are fled.
Now will we take some order in the town,
Placing therein some expert officers;
And then depart to Paris to the king;
For there young Henry with his nobles lie.

BUR. What wills lord Talbot, pleaseth Burgundy.

TAL. But yet, before we go, let's not forget
The noble duke of Bedford, late deceas'd,
But see his exequies fulfill'd in Rouen:
A braver soldier never couched lance,
A gentler heart did never sway in court;
But kings and mightiest potentates must die,
For that's the end of human misery. [*Exeunt.*

SCENE III.—*The same. The Plains near* Rouen.

Enter CHARLES, *the* Bastard, ALENÇON, LA PUCELLE, *and* Forces.

PUC. Dismay not, princes, at this accident,
Nor grieve that Rouen is so recovered;
Care is no cure, but rather corrosive,
For things that are not to be remedied.
Let frantic Talbot triumph for a while,
And like a peacock sweep along his tail;
We'll pull his plumes, and take away his train,
If Dauphin and the rest will be but rul'd.

CHAR. We have been guided by thee hitherto,
And of thy cunning had no diffidence;
One sudden foil shall never breed distrust.

BAST. Search out thy wit for secret policies,
And we will make thee famous through the world.

ALEN. We'll set thy statue in some holy place,
And have thee reverenc'd like a blessed saint;
Employ thee then, sweet virgin, for our good.
PUC. Then thus it must be; this doth Joan devise:
By fair persuasions, mix'd with sugar'd words,
We will entice the duke of Burgundy
To leave the Talbot and to follow us.
CHAR. Ay, marry, sweeting, if we could do that,
France were no place for Henry's warriors;
Nor should that nation boast it so with us,
But be extirped from our provinces.
ALEN. For ever should they be expuls'd from France,
And not have title of an earldom here. [work,
PUC. Your honours shall perceive how I will
To bring this matter to the wished end.
[*Drum heard afar off.*
Hark! by the sound of drum you may perceive
Their powers are marching unto Paris-ward.

An English *March heard.*

There goes the Talbot, with his colours spread,
And all the troops of English after him.

A French *March. Enter the* DUKE *of* BURGUNDY *and his* Forces.

Now in the rearward comes the duke and his;
Fortune in favour makes him lag behind.
Summon a parley; we will talk with him.
[*Trumpets sound a parley.*

CHAR. A parley with the duke of Burgundy.

BUR. Who craves a parley with the Burgundy?

PUC. The princely Charles of France, thy countryman.

BUR. What say'st thou, Charles? for I am marching hence.

CHAR. Speak, Pucelle; and enchant him with thy words.

PUC. Brave Burgundy, undoubted hope of France!
Stay, let thy humble handmaid speak to thee.

BUR. Speak on; but be not over-tedious.

PUC. Look on thy country, look on fertile France,
And see the cities and the towns defac'd
By wasting ruin of the cruel foe!
As looks the mother on her lowly babe,
When death doth close his tender dying eyes,
See, see the pining malady of France;
Behold the wounds, the most unnatural wounds,
Which thou thyself hast given her woeful breast!
O, turn thy edged sword another way;
Strike those that hurt, and hurt not those that help!
One drop of blood drawn from thy country's bosom,
Should grieve thee more than streams of foreign gore;
Return thee, therefore, with a flood of tears,
And wash away thy country's stained spots!

BUR. Either she hath bewitch'd me with her words,
Or nature makes me suddenly relent.

PUC. Besides, all French and France exclaims on thee,
Doubting thy birth and lawful progeny.
Who join'st thou with, but with a lordly nation,
That will not trust thee but for profit's sake?
When Talbot hath set footing once in France,
And fashion'd thee that instrument of ill,
Who then, but English Henry, will be lord,
And thou be thrust out like a fugitive?
Call we to mind,—and mark but this for proof;—
Was not the duke of Orleans thy foe?
And was he not in England prisoner?
But, when they heard he was thine enemy,
They set him free, without his ransom paid,
In spite of Burgundy, and all his friends.
See, then, thou fight'st against thy countrymen,
And join'st with them will be thy slaughter-men.
Come, come, return; return, thou wand'ring lord;
Charles and the rest will take thee in their arms.

BUR. I am vanquished; these haughty words of hers
Have batter'd me like roaring cannon-shot,
And made me almost yield upon my knees.—
Forgive me, country, and sweet countrymen!
And, lords, accept this hearty kind embrace:
My forces and my power of men are yours;—
So, farewell, Talbot; I'll no longer trust thee.

PUC. Done like a Frenchman;—turn, and turn again!

CHAR. Welcome, brave duke! thy friendship makes us fresh.

BAST. And doth beget new courage in our breasts.

ALEN. Pucelle hath bravely play'd her part in this,
And doth deserve a coronet of gold.

CHAR. Now let us on, my lords, and join our powers,
And seek how we may prejudice the foe. [*Exeunt.*

SCENE IV.—Paris. *A Room in the Palace.*

Enter KING HENRY, GLOUCESTER, *and other* Lords, VERNON, BASSET, *&c. To them* TALBOT *and some of his* Officers.

TAL. My gracious prince,—and honourable peers,—
Hearing of your arrival in this realm,
I have a while given truce unto my wars,
To do my duty to my sovereign:
In sign whereof, this arm—that hath reclaim'd
To your obedience fifty fortresses,
Twelve cities, and seven walled towns of strength,
Beside five hundred prisoners of esteem,—
Lets fall his sword before your highness' feet;
And, with submissive loyalty of heart,
Ascribes the glory of his conquest got,
First to my God, and next unto your grace.

K. HEN. Is this the lord Talbot, uncle Gloster,
That hath so long been resident in France?

GLO. Yes, if it please your majesty, my liege.

K. HEN. Welcome, brave captain and victorious lord!
When I was young (as yet I am not old),
I do remember how my father said,
A stouter champion never handled sword.
Long since we were resolved of your truth,
Your faithful service, and your toil in war;
Yet never have you tasted our reward,
Or been reguerdon'd with so much as thanks,
Because till now we never saw your face:
Therefore, stand up; and, for these good deserts,

We here create you earl of Shrewsbury;
And in our coronation take your place.
[*Exeunt all except* VERNON *and* BASSET.
VER. Now, sir, to you, that were so hot at sea,
Disgracing of these colours that I wear
In honour of my noble lord of York,—
Dar'st thou maintain the former words thou spak'st?
BAS. Yes, sir; as well as you dare patronage
The envious barking of your saucy tongue
Against my lord, the duke of Somerset.
VER. Sirrah, thy lord I honour as he is.
BAS. Why, what is he? as good a man as York.
VER. Hark ye; not so: in witness, take ye that. [*Strikes him.*
BAS. Villain, thou know'st the law of arms is such,
That whoso draws a sword, 'tis present death;[a]
Or else this blow should broach thy dearest blood.
But I'll unto his majesty, and crave
I may have liberty to venge this wrong;
When thou shalt see I'll meet thee to thy cost.
VER. Well, miscreant, I'll be there as soon as you;
And, after, meet you sooner than you would.
[*Exeunt.*

[a] That whoso draws a sword, 'tis present death:] Meaning, possibly, that to draw a sword within the precincts of the Court was a capital offence.

ACT IV.

SCENE I.—Paris. *A Room of State in the Palace.*

Enter King Henry, Gloucester, Exeter, York, Suffolk, Somerset, Winchester, Warwick, Talbot, *the* Governor *of* Paris, *and others.*

Glo. Lord bishop, set the crown upon his head.
Win. God save king Henry, of that name the sixth!
Glo. Now, governor of Paris, take your oath,—
[Governor *kneels.*
That you elect no other king but him;
Esteem none friends but such as are his friends;
And none your foes but such as shall pretend [a]
Malicious practices against his state:
This shall ye do, so help you righteous God!
[*Exeunt* Governor *and his* Train.

Enter Sir John Fastolfe.

Fast. My gracious sovereign, as I rode from Calais,
To haste unto your coronation,
A letter was deliver'd to my hands,
Writ to your grace from the duke of Burgundy.
Tal. Shame to the duke of Burgundy and thee!
I vow'd, base knight, when I did meet thee next,
To tear the garter from thy craven's leg,
[*Plucking it off.*
(Which I have done) because unworthily
Thou wast installed in that high degree.—
Pardon me, princely Henry, and the rest:
This dastard, at the battle of Patay,*—
When but in all I was six thousand strong,
And that the French were almost ten to one,—
Before we met, or that a stroke was given,
Like to a trusty squire, did run away:
In which assault we lost twelve hundred men;
Myself, and divers gentlemen beside,
Were there surpris'd and taken prisoners.
Then judge, great lords, if I have done amiss;
Or whether that such cowards ought to wear
This ornament of knighthood, yea, or no.(1)
Glo. To say the truth, this fact was infamous,
And ill beseeming any common man,
Much more a knight, a captain, and a leader.

[a] Pretend—] *Design.*

(*) Old text, *Poictiers.*

TAL. When first this order was ordain'd, my lords,
Knights of the garter were of noble birth;
Valiant and virtuous, full of haughty courage,
Such as were grown to credit by the wars;
Not fearing death, nor shrinking for distress,
But always resolute in most [a] extremes.
He then, that is not furnish'd in this sort,
Doth but usurp the sacred name of knight,
Profaning this most honourable order;
And should (if I were worthy to be judge)
Be quite degraded, like a hedge-born swain
That doth presume to boast of gentle blood.

K. HEN. Stain to thy countrymen! thou hear'st thy doom:
Be packing therefore, thou that wast a knight;
Henceforth we banish thee, on pain of death.—
[*Exit* FASTOLFE.
And now, my* lord protector, view the letter
Sent from our uncle duke of Burgundy.

GLO. What means his grace, that he hath chang'd his style?
[*Viewing the superscription.*
No more but, plain and bluntly,—*To the king?*
Hath he forgot he is his sovereign?
Or doth this churlish superscription
Pretend [b] some alteration in good will?
What's here?—[*Reads.*] *I have, upon especial cause,*
Mov'd with compassion of my country's wreck,
Together with the pitiful complaints
Of such as your oppression feeds upon,—
Forsaken your pernicious faction,
And join'd with Charles, the rightful king of France.
O monstrous treachery! Can this be so,—
That in alliance, amity, and oaths,
There should be found such false dissembling guile?

K. HEN. What! doth my uncle Burgundy revolt?

GLO. He doth, my lord; and is become your foe.

K. HEN. Is that the worst this letter doth contain?

GLO. It is the worst, and all, my lord, he writes.

K. HEN. Why then, lord Talbot there shall talk with him,
And give him chastisement for this abuse:—
How say you, my lord? are you not content?

TAL. Content, my liege! yes; but that I am prevented,[c]
I should have begg'd I might have been employ'd.

K. HEN. Then gather strength, and march unto him straight:
Let him perceive how ill we brook his treason,
And what offence it is to flout his friends.

TAL. I go, my lord; in heart desiring still
You may behold confusion of your foes. [*Exit.*

Enter VERNON *and* BASSET.

VER. Grant me the combat, gracious sovereign!

BAS. And me, my lord, grant me the combat too!

YORK. This is my servant; hear him, noble prince!

SOM. And this is mine; sweet Henry, favour him!

K. HEN. Be patient, lords, and give them leave to speak.—
Say, gentlemen, what makes you thus exclaim?
And wherefore crave you combat? or with whom?

VER. With him, my lord; for he hath done me wrong.

BAS. And I with him; for he hath done me wrong.

K. HEN. What is that wrong whereof you both complain?
First let me know, and then I'll answer you.

BAS. Crossing the sea from England into France,
This fellow here, with envious carping tongue,
Upbraided me about the rose I wear;
Saying, the sanguine colour of the leaves
Did represent my master's blushing cheeks,
When stubbornly he did repugn the truth,
About a certain question in the law,
Argu'd betwixt the duke of York and him;
With other vile and ignominious terms:
In confutation of which rude reproach,
And in defence of my lord's worthiness,
I crave the benefit of law of arms.

VER. And that is my petition, noble lord:
For though he seem, with forged quaint conceit,
To set a gloss upon his bold intent,
Yet know, my lord, I was provok'd by him,
And he first took exceptions at this badge,
Pronouncing, that the paleness of this flower
Bewray'd[d] the faintness of my master's heart.

YORK. Will not this malice, Somerset, be left?

SOM. Your private grudge, my lord of York, will out,
Though ne'er so cunningly you smother it.

K. HEN. Good Lord! what madness rules in brain-sick men,
When, for so slight and frivolous a cause,
Such factious emulations shall arise!—
Good cousins both, of York and Somerset,
Quiet yourselves, I pray, and be at peace.

YORK. Let this dissension first be tried by fight,
And then your highness shall command a peace.

(*) First folio omits, *my*.

[a] Most *extremes.*] Mr. Collier's annotator reads "*worst* extremes."

[b] Pretend *some alteration in good will?*] *Pretend* is here equivalent to *portend*, a sense it seems sometimes to have formerly borne. Thus, in Barclay's "Ship of Fooles," fol. 129, ed. 1570, quoted by Mr. Dyce:—

"What misfortune, adversitie, or blame,
Can all the planets to man or childe *pretende*,
If God most glorious by his might us defende."

[c] Prevented,—] *Anticipated*, by the king's speech.

[d] Bewray'd—] That is, *Betrayed, betokened.*

SOM. The quarrel toucheth none but us alone;
Betwixt ourselves let us decide it, then. [merset.
YORK. There is my pledge; accept it, So-
VER. Nay, let it rest where it began at first.
BAS. Confirm it so, mine honourable lord.
GLO. Confirm it so! Confounded be your strife!
And perish ye, with your audacious prate!
Presumptuous vassals! are you not asham'd,
With this immodest clamorous outráge
To trouble and disturb the king and us?
And you, my lords,—methinks you do not well
To bear with their perverse objections;
Much less to take occasion from their mouths
To raise a mutiny betwixt yourselves:
Let me persuade you take a better course.
EXE. It grieves his highness;—good my lords, be friends. [batants.
K. HEN. Come hither, you that would be com-
Henceforth, I charge you, as you love our favour,
Quite to forget this quarrel and the cause.—
And you, my lords,—remember where we are;
In France, amongst a fickle wavering nation:
If they perceive dissension in our looks,
And that within ourselves we disagree,
How will their grudging stomachs be provok'd
To wilful disobedience, and rebel!
Beside, what infamy will there arise,
When foreign princes shall be certified,
That for a toy, a thing of no regard,
King Henry's peers and chief nobility,
Destroy'd themselves, and lost the realm of France!
O, think upon the conquest of my father;
My tender years; and let us not forego
That for a trifle that was bought with blood!
Let me be umpire in this doubtful strife.
I see no reason, if I wear this rose,
[*Putting on a red rose.*
That any one should therefore be suspicious
I more incline to Somerset than York;
Both are my kinsmen, and I love them both:
As well they may upbraid me with my crown,
Because, forsooth, the king of Scots is crown'd.
But your discretions better can persuade,
Than I am able to instruct or teach:
And therefore, as we hither came in peace,
So let us still continue peace and love.—
Cousin of York, we institute your grace
To be our regent in these parts of France:—
And, good my lord of Somerset, unite
Your troops of horsemen with his bands of foot;—
And, like true subjects, sons of your progenitors,
Go cheerfully together, and digest
Your angry choler on your enemies.
Ourself, my lord protector, and the rest,
After some respite, will return to Calais;
From thence to England; where I hope ere long
To be presented, by your victories,
With Charles, Alençon, and that traitorous rout.
[*Flourish. Exeunt* KING HENRY, GLOUCESTER, SOMERSET, WINCHESTER, SUFFOLK, *and* BASSET.
WAR. My lord of York, I promise you, the king
Prettily, methought, did play the orator.
YORK. And so he did; but yet I like it not,
In that he wears the badge of Somerset. [not;
WIN. Tush! that was but his fancy, blame him
I dare presume, sweet prince, he thought no harm.
YORK. An if I wist[a] he did!—but let it rest,
Other affairs must now be managed.
[*Exeunt* YORK, WARWICK, *and* VERNON.
EXE. Well didst thou, Richard, to suppress thy voice:
For, had the passions of thy heart burst out,
I fear we should have seen decipher'd there
More rancorous spite, more furious raging broils,
Than yet can be imagin'd or suppos'd.
But howsoe'er, no simple man that sees
This jarring discord of nobility,
This should'ring of each other in the court,
This factious bandying of their favourites,
But that[b] it doth presage some ill event.
'Tis much, when sceptres are in children's hands
But more, when envy[c] breeds unkind[d] division;
There comes the ruin, there begins confusion.
[*Exit.*

SCENE II.—France. *Before* Bourdeaux.

Enter TALBOT, *with his* Forces.

TAL. Go to the gates of Bourdeaux, trumpeter,
Summon their general unto the wall.

Trumpet sounds a parley. Enter, on the walls, the General *of the* French Forces, *and others.*

English John Talbot, captains, calls* you forth,
Servant in arms to Harry king of England;
And thus he would,—Open your city gates,
Be humble to us; call my sovereign yours,
And do him homage as obedient subjects,
And I'll withdraw me and my bloody power:
But, if you frown upon this proffer'd peace,
You tempt the fury of my three attendants,
Lean famine, quartering steel, and climbing fire;(2)*
Who, in a moment, even with the earth
Shall lay your stately and air-braving towers,
If you forsake the offer of their love.

[a] *An if I* wist *he did!*—] An if I *thought* he did, &c. The old text for *wist*, an emendation by Capell, reads *wish*.
[b] *But* that *it doth presage some ill event.*] This is very awkwardly expressed. We should perhaps read—
"But *feels* it doth presage," &c.

(*) First folio, *call*.

[c] Envy—] *Enmity*.
[d] Unkind—] *Unnatural*.

GEN. Thou ominous and fearful owl of death,
Our nation's terror, and their bloody scourge!
The period of thy tyranny approacheth.
On us thou canst not enter but by death:
For, I protest, we are well fortified,
And strong enough to issue out and fight:—
If thou retire, the Dauphin, well appointed,
Stands with the snares of war to tangle thee:
On either hand thee, there are squadrons pitch'd,
To wall thee from the liberty of flight;
And no way canst thou turn thee for redress,
But death doth front thee with apparent spoil,
And pale destruction meets thee in the face.
Ten thousand French have ta'en the sacrament,
To rive their dangerous artillery
Upon no Christian soul but English Talbot.
Lo, there thou stand'st, a breathing valiant man,
Of an invincible unconquer'd spirit!
This is the latest glory of thy praise,
That I, thy enemy, dew[a] thee withal;
For ere the glass, that now begins to run,
Finish the process of his sandy hour,
These eyes, that see thee now well coloured,
Shall see thee wither'd, bloody, pale, and dead.
[*Drum afar off.*
Hark! hark! the Dauphin's drum, a warning bell,
Sings heavy music to thy timorous soul;
And mine shall ring thy dire departure out.
[*Exeunt* General, *&c. from the walls.*

TAL. He fables not, I hear the enemy;—
Out, some light horsemen, and peruse their wings.—
O, negligent and heedless discipline!
How are we park'd and bounded in a pale,—
A little herd of England's timorous deer,
Maz'd with a yelping kennel of French curs!
If we be English deer, be, then, in blood;[b]
Not rascal-like,[c] to fall down with a pinch,
But rather moody-mad and desperate stags,
Turn on the bloody hounds with heads of steel,
And make the cowards stand aloof at bay:
Sell every man his life as dear as mine,
And they shall find dear deer of us, my friends.—
God and saint George, Talbot and England's right,
Prosper our colours in this dangerous fight!
[*Exeunt.*

SCENE III.—*Plains in* Gascony.

Enter YORK *with* Forces; *to him a* Messenger.

YORK. Are not the speedy scouts return'd again,
That dogg'd the mighty army of the Dauphin?

MESS. They are return'd, my lord; and give it out,
That he is march'd to Bourdeaux with his power,
To fight with Talbot. As he march'd along,
By your espials were discovered
Two mightier troops than that the Dauphin led;
Which join'd with him, and made their march for Bourdeaux.

YORK. A plague upon that villain Somerset,
That thus delays my promised supply
Of horsemen, that were levied for this siege!
Renowned Talbot doth expect my aid;
And I am lowted[d] by a traitor villain,
And cannot help the noble chevalier:
God comfort him in this necessity!
If he miscarry, farewell wars in France.

Enter Sir WILLIAM LUCY.

LUCY. Thou princely leader of our English strength,
Never so needful on the earth of France,
Spur to the rescue of the noble Talbot;
Who now is girdled with a waist of iron,
And hemm'd about with grim destruction.
To Bourdeaux, warlike duke! to Bourdeaux, York!
Else, farewell Talbot, France, and England's honour.

YORK. O God! that Somerset—who in proud heart
Doth stop my cornets—were in Talbot's place!
So should we save a valiant gentleman,
By forfeiting a traitor and a coward.
Mad ire and wrathful fury makes me weep,
That thus we die, while remiss traitors sleep.

LUCY. O, send some succour to the distress'd lord!

YORK. He dies, we lose; I break my warlike word:
We mourn, France smiles; we lose, they daily get;
All 'long of this vile traitor Somerset.

LUCY. Then God take mercy on brave Talbot's soul!
And on his son young John; who two hours since
I met in travel toward his warlike father!
This seven years did not Talbot see his son;
And now they meet where both their lives are done.

YORK. Alas! what joy shall noble Talbot have,
To bid his young son welcome to his grave?
Away! vexation almost stops my breath,
That sunder'd friends greet in the hour of death.—
Lucy, farewell: no more my fortune can,
But curse the cause I cannot aid the man.—
Maine, Blois, Poictiers, and Tours, are won away,
'Long all of Somerset and his delay! [*Exit.*

---

a Dew *thee withal;*] So the old text; but the modern reading *due*, in the sense of paying a deserved tribute, is, perhaps, to be preferred.

b Be, then, in blood;] See note (c), p. 71, Vol. I.

c *Not* rascal-*like,*—] *Rascal* has been before explained to be a term of the chase for a deer, lean and altogether out of condition.

d *And I am* lowted *by a traitor villain,*—] Malone interprets this:—"I am treated with contempt like a *lowt*, or low country fellow." It means, more probably, I am *left in the mire, land-lurch'd*, by a traitor, &c.

LUCY. Thus, while the vulture of sedition
Feeds in the bosom of such great commanders,
Sleeping neglection doth betray to loss
The conquest of our scarce-cold conqueror,
That ever-living man of memory,
Henry the fifth:—whiles they each other cross,
Lives, honours, lands, and all, hurry to loss. [*Exit.*

SCENE IV.—*Other Plains of* Gascony.

Enter SOMERSET, *with his* Forces; *an* Officer *of* TALBOT'S *with him.*

SOM. It is too late; I cannot send them now:
This expedition was by York and Talbot
Too rashly plotted; all our general force
Might with a sally of the very town
Be buckled with: the over-daring Talbot
Hath sullied all his gloss of former honour,
By this unheedful, desperate, wild adventure:
York set him on to fight, and die in shame,
That, Talbot dead, great York might bear the name.
OFF. Here is sir William Lucy, who with me
Set from our o'er-match'd forces forth for aid.

Enter Sir WILLIAM LUCY.

SOM. How now, sir William? whither were you sent?
LUCY. Whither, my lord? from bought and sold[a] lord Talbot;
Who, ring'd about with bold adversity,
Cries out for noble York and Somerset,
To beat assailing death from his weak legions.*
And whiles the honourable captain there
Drops bloody sweat from his war-wearied limbs,
And, in advantage lingering,[b] looks for rescue,
You, his false hopes, the trust of England's honour,
Keep off aloof with worthless emulation.
Let not your private discord keep away
The levied succours that should lend him aid,
While he, renowned noble gentleman,
Yields† up his life unto a world of odds:
Orleans the Bastard, Charles, and‡ Burgundy,
Alençon, Reignier, compass him about,
And Talbot perisheth by your default.
SOM. York set him on, York should have sent him aid.
LUCY. And York as fast upon your grace exclaims;
Swearing, that you withhold his levied horse,[c]
Collected for this expedition.
SOM. York lies; he might have sent and had the horse:
I owe him little duty, and less love,
And take foul scorn to fawn on him by sending.
LUCY. The fraud of England, not the force of France,
Hath now entrapp'd the noble-minded Talbot:
Never to England shall he bear his life;
But dies, betray'd to fortune by your strife.
SOM. Come, go; I will despatch the horsemen straight:
Within six hours they will be at his aid.
LUCY. Too late comes rescue; he is ta'en or slain:
For fly he could not, if he would have fled;
And fly would Talbot never, though he might.
SOM. If he be dead, brave Talbot, then, adieu!
LUCY. His fame lives in the world, his shame in you. [*Exeunt.*

SCENE V.—*The* English *Camp near* Bourdeaux.

Enter TALBOT *and* JOHN *his* Son.

TAL. O young John Talbot! I did send for thee
To tutor thee in stratagems of war;
That Talbot's name might be in thee reviv'd,
When sapless age and weak unable limbs,
Should bring thy father to his drooping chair.
But,—O malignant and ill-boding stars!—
Now thou art come unto a feast of death,
A terrible and unavoided[d] danger:
Therefore, dear boy, mount on my swiftest horse,
And I'll direct thee how thou shalt escape
By sudden flight: come, dally not, begone.
JOHN. Is my name Talbot? and am I your son?
And shall I fly? O, if you love my mother,
Dishonour not her honourable name,
To make a bastard and a slave of me!
The world will say—he is not Talbot's blood,
That basely fled when noble Talbot stood.
TAL. Fly to revenge my death, if I be slain.
JOHN. He that flies so will ne'er return again.
TAL. If we both stay, we both are sure to die.
JOHN. Then let me stay; and, father, do you fly:
Your loss is great, so your regard should be;
My worth unknown, no loss is known in me.

(*) Old text, *Regions.* (†) First folio, *Yield.*
(‡) First folio omits, *and.*

[a] Bought and sold—] A proverbial phrase applied to any one entrapped or made a victim of by treachery or mismanagement; it is found again in "The Comedy of Errors," Act III. Sc. 1, in "King John," Act V. Sc. 4, and in "Richard III." Act V. Sc. 3.
[b] *And, in* advantage lingering,—] Perhaps originally,—

"And, in *disadvantage ling'ring,*" &c.

[c] *His levied* horse—] In the old text, *hoast.* The correction is Hanmer's.
[d] Unavoided—] *Unavoidable,* as in "Richard III." Act IV. Sc. 1:—

"Whose *unavoided eye* is murderous."

And as in the same play, Act IV. Sc. 4:—

"All *unavoided* is the doom of destiny."

Upon my death the French can little boast;
In yours they will, in you all hopes are lost.
Flight cannot stain the honour you have won;
But mine it will, that no exploit have done:
You fled for vantage, every one will swear;
But, if I bow,[a] they'll say it was for fear.
There is no hope that ever I will stay,
If, the first hour, I shrink and run away.
Here, on my knee, I beg mortality,
Rather than life preserv'd with infamy.

TAL. Shall all thy mother's hopes lie in one tomb?

JOHN. Ay, rather than I'll shame my mother's womb.

TAL. Upon my blessing, I command thee go.

JOHN. To fight I will, but not to fly the foe.

TAL. Part of thy father may be sav'd in thee.

JOHN. No part of him but will be shame in me.

TAL. Thou never hadst renown, nor canst not lose it.

JOHN. Yes, your renowned name; shall flight abuse it?

TAL. Thy father's charge shall clear thee from that stain.

JOHN. You cannot witness for me, being slain.
If death be so apparent, then both fly.

TAL. And leave my followers here, to fight, and die?
My age was never tainted with such shame.

JOHN. And shall my youth be guilty of such blame?
No more can I be sever'd from your side,
Than can yourself yourself in twain divide:
Stay, go, do what you will, the like do I;
For live I will not, if my father die.

TAL. Then here I take my leave of thee, fair son,
Born to eclipse thy life this afternoon.
Come, side by side together live and die;
And soul with soul from France to heaven fly.
[*Exeunt.*

SCENE VI.—*A Field of Battle.*

Alarum: excursions, wherein TALBOT'S Son *is hemmed about, and* TALBOT *rescues him.*

TAL. Saint George and victory! fight, soldiers, fight!
The regent hath with Talbot broke his word,
And left us to the rage of France his sword.
Where is John Talbot?—pause, and take thy breath;
I gave thee life, and rescu'd thee from death.

JOHN. O twice my father! twice am I thy son:
The life thou gav'st me first was lost and done;
Till with thy warlike sword, despite of fate,
To my determin'd time thou gav'st new date.

TAL. When from the Dauphin's crest thy sword struck fire,
It warm'd thy father's heart with proud desire
Of bold-fac'd victory. Then leaden age,
Quicken'd with youthful spleen and warlike rage,
Beat down Alençon, Orleans, Burgundy,
And from the pride of Gallia rescu'd thee.
The ireful bastard Orleans—that drew blood
From thee, my boy, and had the maidenhood
Of thy first fight—I soon encountered;
And, interchanging blows, I quickly shed
Some of his bastard blood; and, in disgrace,
Bespoke him thus: *Contaminated, base,*
And misbegotten blood, I spill of thine,
Mean and right poor; for that pure blood of mine,
Which thou didst force from Talbot, my brave boy:—
Here purposing the Bastard to destroy,
Came in strong rescue. Speak, thy father's care,—
Art thou not weary, John? how dost thou fare?
Wilt thou yet[b] leave the battle, boy, and fly,
Now thou art seal'd the son of chivalry?
Fly to revenge my death when I am dead;
The help of one stands me in little stead.
O, too much folly is it, well I wot,
To hazard all our lives in one small boat!
If I to-day die not with Frenchmen's rage,
To-morrow I shall die with mickle age:
By me they nothing gain an if I stay,
'Tis but the short'ning of my life one day:
In thee thy mother dies, our household's name,
My death's revenge, thy youth, and England's fame:
All these, and more, we hazard by thy stay;
All these are sav'd, if thou wilt fly away.

JOHN. The sword of Orleans hath not made me smart;
These words of yours draw life-blood from my heart:
On that advantage, bought with such a shame,
(To save a paltry life, and slay bright fame,)
Before young Talbot from old Talbot fly,
The coward horse that bears me fall and die!
And like[c] me to the peasant boys of France,
To be shame's scorn, and subject of mischance!
Surely, by all the glory you have won,
An if I fly, I am not Talbot's son:
Then talk no more of flight, it is no boot;[d]
If son to Talbot die at Talbot's foot.

---

a Bow,—] Mr. Collier's annotator substitutes *fly*, and Mr. Singer, *flew*; but the *bow* of the old text, in the sense of *give way*, is no doubt the genuine word.

b Yet—] That is, *now*.

c Like *me*—] *Reduce me to the level of.*

d *It is no* boot;] *Boot* is from the Anglo-Saxon *botan, advantage, profit*, &c. *It is no boot*, means, *it is of no avail.* So, in "The Taming of the Shrew," Act V. Sc. 2:—

"Then vail your stomachs, for *it is no boot.*"

TAL. Then follow thou thy desp'rate sire of Crete,
Thou Icarus; thy life to me is sweet:
If thou wilt fight, fight by thy father's side,
And, commendable prov'd, let's die in pride.
[*Exeunt.*

SCENE VII.—*Another part of the same.*

Alarum: excursions. Enter TALBOT *wounded, supported by a* Servant.

TAL. Where is my other life?—mine own is gone;—
O, where's young Talbot? where is valiant John?—
Triumphant death, smear'd with captivity,
Young Talbot's valour makes me smile at thee!—
When he perceiv'd me shrink and on my knee,
His bloody sword he brandish'd over me,
And, like a hungry lion, did commence
Rough deeds of rage and stern impatience;
But when my angry guardant stood alone,
Tend'ring my ruin, and assail'd of none,
Dizzy-ey'd fury and great rage of heart,
Suddenly made him from my side to start
Into the clust'ring battle of the French:
And in that sea of blood my boy did drench
His overmounting spirit; and there died
My Icarus, my blossom, in his pride.
SERV. O my dear lord! lo, where your son is borne!

Enter Soldiers, *bearing the body of* JOHN TALBOT.(3)

TAL. Thou antic death, which laugh'st us here to scorn,
Anon, from thy insulting tyranny,
Coupled in bonds of perpetuity,
Two Talbots winged, through the lither [a] sky,
In thy despite, shall 'scape mortality.—

[a] *The* lither *sky,*—] This is always explained to signify the *yielding* sky; it may mean, however, the *lazy, idle* sky. *Lither* is still used in this sense in many parts of England. So in Holinshed:—"Howbeit she hath not shewed hir self so bountifull a mother in pouring forth such riches as she proveth hirself an envious stepdame, in that she instilleth in the inhabitants a drousie *lythernesse* to withdraw them from the ensearching of hir hourded and hidden jewelles."

O thou whose wounds become[a] hard-favour'd death,
Speak to thy father, ere thou yield thy breath!
Brave death by speaking, whether[b] he will or no;
Imagine him a Frenchman and thy foe.—
Poor boy! he smiles, methinks, as who should say—
Had death been French, then death had died to-day.
Come, come, and lay him in his father's arms;
My spirit can no longer bear these harms.
Soldiers, adieu! I have what I would have,
Now my old arms are young John Talbot's grave. [*Dies.*

Alarums. Exeunt Soldiers *and* Servant, *leaving the two bodies. Enter* CHARLES, ALENÇON, BURGUNDY, *the* Bastard, LA PUCELLE, *and* Forces.

CHAR. Had York and Somerset brought rescue in,
We should have found a bloody day of this.
BAST. How the young whelp of Talbot's, raging-wood,[c]
Did flesh his puny sword in Frenchmen's blood!
PUC. Once I encounter'd him, and thus I said,
Thou maiden youth, be vanquish'd by a maid:
But, with a proud majestical high scorn,
He answer'd thus; *Young Talbot was not born*
To be the pillage of a giglot[d] *wench:*
So, rushing in the bowels of the French,
He left me proudly, as unworthy fight.
BUR. Doubtless he would have made a noble knight:—
See, where he lies inhersed in the arms
Of the most bloody nurser of his harms![e]
BAST. Hew them to pieces! hack their bones asunder!
Whose life was England's glory, Gallia's wonder.
CHAR. O, no; forbear! for that which we have fled
During the life, let us not wrong it dead.

Enter Sir WILLIAM LUCY, *attended; a* French Herald *preceding.*

LUCY. Herald, conduct me to the Dauphin's tent,
To know who hath obtain'd the glory of the day.
CHAR. On what submissive message art thou sent?
LUCY. Submission, Dauphin! 'tis a mere French word;
We English warriors wot not what it means.
I come to know what prisoners thou hast ta'en,
And to survey the bodies of the dead.
CHAR. For prisoners ask'st thou? hell our prison is.
But tell me whom thou seek'st.[f]
LUCY. But where's the great Alcides of the field,
Valiant lord Talbot, earl of Shrewsbury?
Created, for his rare success in arms,
Great earl of Washford,[g] Waterford, and Valence;
Lord Talbot of Goodrig and Urchinfield,
Lord Strange of Blackmere, lord Verdun of Alton,
Lord Cromwell of Wingfield, lord Furnival of Sheffield,
The thrice victorious lord of Falconbridge,
Knight of the noble order of saint George,
Worthy saint Michael, and the golden fleece;
Great mareshal to Henry the sixth,
Of all his wars within the realm of France?
PUC. Here is a silly stately style, indeed!
The Turk, that two-and-fifty kingdoms hath,
Writes not so tedious a style as this.—
Him, that thou magnifiest with all these titles,
Stinking and fly-blown, lies here at our feet.
LUCY. Is Talbot slain,—the Frenchmen's only scourge,
Your kingdom's terror and black Nemesis?
O, were mine eyeballs into bullets turn'd,
That I, in rage, might shoot them at your faces!
O, that I could but call these dead to life!
It were enough to fright the realm of France:
Were but his picture left amongst you here,
It would amaze the proudest of you all.
Give me their bodies, that I may bear them hence,
And give them burial as beseems their worth.
PUC. I think this upstart is old Talbot's ghost,
He speaks with such a proud commanding spirit.
For God's sake, let him have 'em;* to keep them here,
They would but stink, and putrefy the air.
CHAR. Go, take their bodies hence.
LUCY. I'll bear them hence:
But from their ashes shall be rear'd[h]
A phœnix that shall make all France afeard.
CHAR. So we be rid of them, do with 'em* what thou wilt.
And now to Paris, in this conquering vein.
All will be ours, now bloody Talbot's slain. [*Exeunt.*

(*) First folio, *him.*

[a] Become *hard-favour'd death,*—] That is, *adorn, beautify,* hard-favour'd death. See note (a), p. 151.

[b] *Brave death by speaking,* whether *he will or no;*] *Whether,* in the old copies, when required to be pronounced as a monosyllable, is sometimes, but not always, contracted to *where.* In the present case it should be pronounced, if not printed, *whe'r,* or *whêr.*

[c] Raging-wood,—] That is, raging-*mad.*

[d] *A* giglot *wench*;] A *wanton* wench.

[e] *The most bloody nurser of* his *harms!*] Query "of *our* harms."

[f] But tell me whom thou seek'st.] From this imperfect line, and Lucy's abrupt inquiry, something, probably to the effect that the chief prisoners spared were present, appears to have been omitted by the transcriber or compositor.

[g] Washford,—] *Wexford* was anciently called both *Weysford* and *Washford.*

[h] But from their ashes shall be rear'd—] The deficiency in this line Pope supplied by reading,—

"But from their ashes, *Dauphin,*" &c.

Mr. Collier's annotator gives,—

"But from their *very* ashes," &c.

ACT V.

SCENE I.—London. *A Room in the Palace.*

Enter King Henry, Gloucester, *and* Exeter.

K. Hen. Have you perus'd the letters from the pope,
The emperor, and the earl of Armagnac?
Glo. I have, my lord; and their intent is this,—
They humbly sue unto your excellence,
To have a godly peace concluded of,
Between the realms of England and of France.
K. Hen. How doth your grace affect their motion?
Glo. Well, my good lord; and as the only means
To stop effusion of our Christian blood,
And stablish quietness on every side.
K. Hen. Ay, marry, uncle; for I always thought,
It was both impious and unnatural,
That such immanity[a] and bloody strife
Should reign among professors of one faith.
Glo. Beside, my lord,—the sooner to effect
And surer bind this knot of amity,—
The earl of Armagnac—near kin[b] to Charles,
A man of great authority in France,—
Proffers his only daughter to your grace
In marriage, with a large and sumptuous dowry.
K. Hen. Marriage, uncle! alas, my years are young!
And fitter is my study and my books,
Than wanton dalliance with a paramour.
Yet, call the ambassadors; and, as you please,
So let them have their answers every one:

[a] Immanity—] *Cruelty, ferocity.*
[b] *Near* kin *to Charles,*—] The old text has "near *knit* to Charles." "*Kin*" is Pope's suggestion, and it is the alteration made by Mr. Collier's annotator.

I shall be well content with any choice,
Tends to God's glory and my country's weal.

Enter a Legate *and two* Ambassadors, *with* WINCHESTER, *now* CARDINAL BEAUFORT, *in a* Cardinal's *habit.*

EXE. [*Aside.*] What! is my lord of Winchester install'd,
And call'd unto a cardinal's degree?
Then I perceive that will be verified,
Henry the fifth did sometime prophecy,—
If once he come to be a cardinal,
He'll make his cap co-equal with the crown.

K. HEN. My lords ambassadors, your several suits
Have been consider'd and debated on.
Your purpose is both good and reasonable;
And, therefore, are we certainly resolv'd
To draw conditions of a friendly peace;
Which by my lord of Winchester we mean
Shall be transported presently to France.

GLO. And for the proffer of my lord your master,—
I have inform'd his highness so at large,
As—liking of the lady's virtuous gifts,
Her beauty, and the value of her dower,—
He doth intend she shall be England's queen.

K. HEN. In argument and proof of which contráct,
Bear her this jewel, [*To the* Amb.] pledge of my affection.——
And so, my lord protector, see them guarded,
And safely brought to Dover; where, inshipp'd,
Commit them to the fortune of the sea.

[*Exeunt* KING HENRY *and* Train; GLOUCESTER, EXETER, *and* Ambassadors.

CAR. Stay, my lord legate; you shall first receive
The sum of money which I promised
Should be deliver'd to his holiness
For clothing me in these grave ornaments.

LEG. I will attend upon your lordship's leisure. [*Exit.*

CAR. Now Winchester will not submit, I trow,
Or be inferior to the proudest peer.
Humphrey of Gloster, thou shalt well perceive,
That, neither in birth, or for authority,
The bishop will be overborne by thee:
I'll either make thee stoop and bend thy knee,
Or sack this country with a mutiny. [*Exit.*

SCENE II.—France. *Plains in* Anjou.

Enter CHARLES, BURGUNDY, ALENÇON, LA PUCELLE, *and* Forces, *marching.*

CHAR. These news, my lords, may cheer our drooping spirits:
'Tis said the stout Parisians do revolt,
And turn again unto the warlike French.
ALEN. Then march to Paris, royal Charles of France,
And keep not back your powers in dalliance.
PUC. Peace be amongst them, if they turn to us.
Else, ruin combat with their palaces!

Enter a Scout.

SCOUT. Success unto our valiant general,
And happiness to his accomplices!
CHAR. What tidings send our scouts? I pr'ythee, speak.
SCOUT. The English army, that divided was
Into two parts,* is now conjoin'd in one,
And means to give you battle presently.
CHAR. Somewhat too sudden, sirs, the warning is;
But we will presently provide for them.
BUR. I trust, the ghost of Talbot is not there;
Now he is gone, my lord, you need not fear.
PUC. Of all base passions, fear is most accurs'd:—
Command the conquest, Charles, it shall be thine,
Let Henry fret, and all the world repine.
CHAR. Then on, my lords; and France be fortunate! [*Exeunt.*

SCENE III.—*The same. Before* Angiers.

Alarums: Excursions. Enter LA PUCELLE.

PUC. The regent conquers, and the Frenchmen fly.—
Now help, ye charming spells, and periapts;[a]
And ye choice spirits that admonish me,
And give me signs of future accidents— [*Thunder.*
You speedy helpers, that are substitutes
Under the lordly monarch of the north,(1)
Appear, and aid me in this enterprize!

Enter Fiends.

This speedy and quick appearance argues proof
Of your accustom'd diligence to me.
Now, ye familiar spirits, that are cull'd

(*) Old text, *parties.*

[a] *Charming spells, and* periapts;] *Periapts* or *amulets* were charms worn on the person to avert disease or danger.

Out of the powerful legions* under earth,
Help me this once, that France may get the field.
[*They walk, and speak not.*
O, hold me not with silence over-long!
Where[b] I was wont to feed you with my blood,
I'll lop a member off, and give it you,
In earnest of a further benefit;
So you do condescend to help me now.—
[*They hang their heads.*
No hope to have redress?—My body shall
Pay recompense, if you will grant my suit.
[*They shake their heads.*
Cannot my body nor blood-sacrifice,
Entreat you to your wonted furtherance?
Then take my soul,—my body, soul, and all,
Before that England give the French the foil.
[*They depart.*
See! they forsake me. Now the time is come,
That France must vail her lofty-plumed crest,
And let her head fall into England's lap.
My ancient incantations are too weak,
And hell too strong for me to buckle with:—
Now, France, thy glory droopeth to the dust.
[*Exit.*

Alarums. Enter French *and* English, *fighting.* LA PUCELLE† *and* YORK *fight hand to hand.* LA PUCELLE *is taken.*(2) *The* French *fly.*

YORK. Damsel of France, I think I have you fast:
Unchain your spirits now with spelling charms,
And try if they can gain your liberty.—
A goodly prize, fit for the devil's grace!
See, how the ugly witch doth bend her brows,
As if, with Circe, she would change my shape!
PUC. Chang'd to a worser shape thou canst not be.
YORK. O, Charles the Dauphin is a proper man;
No shape but his can please your dainty eye.
PUC. A plaguing mischief light on Charles, and thee!
And may ye both be suddenly surpriz'd
By bloody hands, in sleeping on your beds!
YORK. Fell banning hag, enchantress, hold thy tongue!
PUC. I pr'ythee, give me leave to curse a while.
YORK. Curse, miscreant, when thou comest to the stake. [*Exeunt.*

Alarums. Enter SUFFOLK, *leading in* LADY MARGARET.

SUF. Be what thou wilt, thou art my prisoner.
[*Gazes on her.*

(*) Old text, *regions.* (†) Old text, *Burgundie.*

[b] Where—] That is, *whereas.*

O fairest beauty, do not fear nor fly!
For I will touch thee but with reverent hands:
I kiss these fingers[a] for eternal peace,
And lay them gently on thy tender side.
Who art thou? say, that I may honour thee.
  MAR. Margaret my name, and daughter to a king,
The king of Naples,—whosoe'er thou art.
  SUF. An earl I am, and Suffolk am I call'd.
Be not offended, nature's miracle,
Thou art allotted to be ta'en by me:
So doth the swan her downy cygnets save,
Keeping them prisoner underneath her* wings.
Yet, if this servile usage once offend,
Go, and be free again as Suffolk's friend.
[*She turns away as going.*
O, stay!—I have no power to let her pass;
My hand would free her, but my heart says—no.

[a] I kiss these fingers—] In the modern editions, a stage direction [*Kissing her hand*] is given here, which may mislead. From the ensuing line:—

"And lay them gently *on thy tender side*,"

it would seem that Suffolk is speaking of his own hand, which he kisses in attestation of homage, and then replaces gently round the lady's waist. This view of the action is strengthened by the stage direction of the old copies:—"*Enter Suffolke with Margaret in his hand*," and by what he presently says:—

"So doth the swan her downy cygnets save,
Keeping them prisoner underneath her wings,"

and obviates the necessity of any transposition in the lines.

(*) First folio, *his*.

As plays the sun upon the glassy streams,
Twinkling another counterfeited beam,
So seems this gorgeous beauty to mine eyes.
Fain would I woo her, yet I dare not speak:
I'll call for pen and ink, and write my mind:
Fie, De la Poole! disable[a] not thyself;
Hast not a tongue? is she not here thy prisoner?[b]
Wilt thou be daunted at a woman's sight?
Ay; beauty's princely majesty is such,
Confounds the tongue, and makes the senses [rough.[c]
MAR. Say, earl of Suffolk,—if thy name be so,—
What ransom must I pay before I pass?
For I perceive I am thy prisoner.
SUF. How canst thou tell she will deny thy suit,
Before thou make a trial of her love? [*Aside.*
MAR. Why speak'st thou not? what ransom must I pay?
SUF. She's beautiful, and therefore to be woo'd:
She is a woman, therefore to be won. [*Aside.*
MAR. Wilt thou accept of ransom—yea, or no?
SUF. Fond man! remember that thou hast a wife;
Then how can Margaret be thy paramour?
[*Aside.*
MAR. I were best to leave him, for he will not hear.
SUF. There all is marr'd; there lies a cooling card. [*Aside.*
MAR. He talks at random; sure, the man is mad.
SUF. And yet a dispensation may be had.
[*Aside.*
MAR. And yet I would that you would answer me.
SUF. I'll win this lady Margaret. For whom?
Why, for my king: tush! that's a wooden[d] thing.
[*Aside.*
MAR. He talks of wood: it is some carpenter.
SUF. Yet so my fancy may be satisfied,
And peace established between these realms.
But there remains a scruple in that, too:
For though her father be the king of Naples,
Duke of Anjou and Maine, yet is he poor,
And our nobility will scorn the match. [*Aside.*
MAR. Hear ye, captain,—are you not at leisure?
SUF. It shall be so, disdain they ne'er so much:
Henry is youthful, and will quickly yield.—[*Aside.*
Madam, I have a secret to reveal.
MAR. What though I be enthrall'd, he seems a knight,
And will not any way dishonour me. [*Aside.*
SUF. Lady, vouchsafe to listen what I say.
MAR. Perhaps I shall be rescu'd by the French;
And then I need not crave his courtesy. [*Aside.*
SUF. Sweet madam, give me hearing in a cause—
MAR. Tush! women have been captivate ere now. [*Aside.*
SUF. Lady, wherefore talk you so?[e]
MAR. I cry you mercy, 'tis but *quid* for *quo*.[f]
SUF. Say, gentle princess, would you not suppose
Your bondage happy, to be made a queen?
MAR. To be a queen in bondage is more vile,
Than is a slave in base servility;
For princes should be free.
SUF. And so shall you,
If happy England's royal king be free.
MAR. Why, what concerns his freedom unto [me?
SUF. I'll undertake to make thee Henry's queen;
To put a golden sceptre in thy hand,
And set a precious crown upon thy head,
If thou wilt condescend to be my—
MAR. What?
SUF. His love.
MAR. I am unworthy to be Henry's wife.
SUF. No, gentle madam; I unworthy am
To woo so fair a dame to be his wife,
And have no portion in the choice myself.
How say you, madam; are ye so content?
MAR. An if my father please, I am content.
SUF. Then call our captains and our colours forth!—
And, madam, at your father's castle-walls
We'll crave a parley, to confer with him.
[Troops *come forward.*

A Parley sounded. Enter REIGNIER, *on the walls.*

SUF. See, Reignier, see, thy daughter prisoner!
REIG. To whom?
SUF. To me.
REIG. Suffolk, what remedy?
I am a soldier, and unapt to weep,
Or to exclaim on fortune's fickleness.
SUF. Yes, there is remedy enough, my lord:
Consent, (and, for thy honour, give consent,)
Thy daughter shall be wedded to my king;

---

[a] Disable—] That is, *disparage*. See note (e), p. 168.
[b] *Is she not here* thy prisoner?] The last two words of this line are omitted in the first folio.
[c] Ay; beauty's princely majesty is such,
Confounds the tongue, and makes the senses rough.]
This is a troublesome passage. Hanmer, for *rough*, reads *crouch*. Mr. Collier's annotator, for "makes the senses rough," proposes "*mocks the sense of touch;*" and Mr. Singer's corrector, "*wakes the sense's touch.*"
[d] Wooden—] As we now say *blockish*. So in Lily's *Galathea*, 1592:—"Would I were out of these woods, for I shall have but *wooden* luck;" and in Sidney's *Astrophel and Stella* (both quoted by Steevens):—
"Or, seeing, have so *woodden* wits as not that worth to know."
[e] Lady, wherefore talk you so?] Mr. Collier's annotator remedies the imperfection of this line by inserting "pray tell me."
[f] 'Tis but *quid* for *quo*.] Falstaff, it will be recollected, adopts the same effective course to reprove the Chief Justice for his "disease of not listening," in the "Second Part of Henry IV." Act I. Sc. 2.

Whom I with pain have woo'd and won thereto;
And this her easy-held imprisonment
Hath gain'd thy daughter princely liberty.

REIG. Speaks Suffolk as he thinks?

SUF. Fair Margaret knows,
That Suffolk doth not flatter, face, or feign.

REIG. Upon thy princely warrant, I descend,
To give thee answer of thy just demand.
[*Exit from the walls.*

SUF. And here I will expect thy coming.

Trumpets sounded. Enter REIGNIER, *below.*

REIG. Welcome, brave earl, into our territories;
Command in Anjou what your honour pleases.

SUF. Thanks, Reignier, happy for so sweet a child,
Fit to be made companion with a king:
What answer makes your grace unto my suit?

REIG. Since thou dost deign to woo her little worth,
To be the princely bride of such a lord;
Upon condition I may quietly
Enjoy mine own, the county* Maine and Anjou,
Free from oppression or the stroke of war,
My daughter shall be Henry's, if he please.

SUF. That is her ransom,—I deliver her;
And those two counties I will undertake,
Your grace shall well and quietly enjoy.

REIG. And I again,—in Henry's royal name,
As deputy unto that gracious king,—
Give thee her hand, for sign of plighted faith.

SUF. Reignier of France, I give thee kingly thanks,
Because this is in traffic of a king:—
And yet, methinks, I could be well content
To be mine own attorney in this case.— [*Aside.*
I'll over then to England with this news,
And make this marriage to be solemniz'd:
So, farewell, Reignier: set this diamond safe
In golden palaces, as it becomes.

REIG. I do embrace thee, as I would embrace
The Christian prince, king Henry, were he here.

MAR. Farewell, my lord: good wishes, praise, and prayers,
Shall Suffolk ever have of Margaret. [*Going.*

SUF. Farewell, sweet madam! But hark you, Margaret;—
No princely commendations to my king?

MAR. Such commendations as become a maid,
A virgin, and his servant, say to him.

SUF. Words sweetly plac'd and modestly† directed.
But, madam, I must trouble you again,—
No loving token to his majesty?

MAR. Yes, my good lord; a pure unspotted heart,
Never yet taint with love, I send the king.

SUF. And this withal. [*Kisses her.*

MAR. That for thyself;—I will not so presume
To send such peevish[a] tokens to a king.
[*Exeunt* REIGNIER *and* MARGARET.

SUF. O, wert thou for myself!—But, Suffolk, stay;
Thou may'st not wander in that labyrinth;
There Minotaurs and ugly treasons lurk.
Solicit Henry with her wond'rous praise:
Bethink thee on her virtues that surmount;
And [b] natural graces that extinguish art;
Repeat their semblance often on the seas,
That, when thou com'st to kneel at Henry's feet,
Thou may'st bereave him of his wits with wonder.
[*Exit.*

SCENE IV.—*Camp of the* Duke *of* York, *in* Anjou.

Enter YORK, WARWICK, *and others.*

YORK. Bring forth that sorceress, condemn'd to burn.

Enter LA PUCELLE, *guarded, and a* Shepherd.

SHEP. Ah, Joan! this kills thy father's heart outright!
Have I sought every country far and near,
And, now it is my chance to find thee out,
Must I behold thy timeless cruel death?
Ah, Joan, sweet daughter Joan, I'll die with thee!

PUC. Decrepit miser! [c] base ignoble wretch!
I am descended of a gentler blood;
Thou art no father nor no friend of mine.

SHEP. Out, out!—My lords, an please you, 'tis not so;
I did beget her, all the parish knows:
Her mother liveth yet, can testify
She was the first-fruit of my bachelorship.

WAR. Graceless! wilt thou deny thy parentage?

YORK. This argues what her kind of life hath been;—
Wicked and vile; and so her death concludes.

SHEP. Fie, Joan! that thou wilt be so obstacle![d]
God knows thou art a collop of my flesh,
And for thy sake have I shed many a tear:
Deny me not, I pr'ythee, gentle Joan.

(*) Old text, *country*. (†) First folio, *modestie*.

[a] Peevish—] *Childish, foolish.*

[b] And *natural graces*—] The first folio has "*mad* natural graces;" *and* is the emendation of Capell. Mr. Collier, on the faith of his annotator, reads "*Mid*," which he pronounces incontestable. We must take leave to differ with him, believing either *And*, or "*Her*," another substitution of the commentators, much better suited to the context.

[c] *Decrepit* miser!] *Miser* here does not imply avarice; but means a *miserable caitiff;* a sense it so commonly bore formerly that examples are needless.

[d] *So* obstacle!] An old vulgar corruption of *obstinate*.

PUC. Peasant, avaunt!—You have suborn'd this man,
Of purpose to obscure my noble birth.

SHEP. 'Tis true; I gave a noble to the priest,
The morn that I was wedded to her mother.—
Kneel down and take my blessing, good my girl.
Wilt thou not stoop? Now cursed be the time
Of thy nativity! I would the milk
Thy mother gave thee, when thou suck'dst her breast,
Had been a little ratsbane for thy sake!
Or else, when thou didst keep my lambs a-field,
I wish some ravenous wolf had eaten thee!
Dost thou deny thy father, cursed drab?
O, burn her, burn her! hanging is too good. [*Exit.*

YORK. Take her away; for she hath liv'd too long,
To fill the world with vicious qualities.

PUC. First, let me tell you whom you have condemn'd:
Not one* begotten of a shepherd swain,
But issu'd from the progeny of kings;
Virtuous, and holy; chosen from above,
By inspiration of celestial grace,
To work exceeding miracles on earth.
I never had to do with wicked spirits:
But you,—that are polluted with your lusts,
Stain'd with the guiltless blood of innocents,
Corrupt and tainted with a thousand vices,—
Because you want the grace that others have,
You judge it straight a thing impossible
To compass wonders but by help of devils.
No, misconceived![a] Joan of Arc hath been
A virgin from her tender infancy,
Chaste and immaculate in very thought;
Whose maiden blood, thus rigorously effus'd,
Will cry for vengeance at the gates of heaven.
YORK. Ay, ay;—away with her to execution!
WAR. And hark ye, sirs; because she is a maid,
Spare for no faggots, let there be enow:
Place barrels of pitch upon the fatal stake,
That so her torture may be shortened.
PUC. Will nothing turn your unrelenting hearts?—
Then, Joan, discover thine infirmity,
That warranteth by law to be thy privilege.—
I am with child, ye bloody homicides:
Murder not, then, the fruit within my womb,
Although ye hale me to a violent death.
YORK. Now heaven forefend! the holy maid with child?
WAR. The greatest miracle that e'er ye wrought!
Is all your strict preciseness come to this?
YORK. She and the Dauphin have been juggling:
I did imagine what would be her refuge.
WAR. Well, go to; we will have no bastards live;
Especially, since Charles must father it.
PUC. You are deceiv'd; my child is none of his;
It was Alençon that enjoy'd my love.
YORK. Alençon! that notorious Machiavel!
It dies, an if it had a thousand lives.
PUC. O, give me leave, I have deluded you;
'Twas neither Charles, nor yet the duke I nam'd,
But Reignier, king of Naples, that prevail'd.
WAR. A married man! that's most intolerable.
YORK. Why, here's a girl! I think, she knows not well,
There were so many, whom she may accuse.
WAR. It's sign she hath been liberal and free.
YORK. And yet, forsooth, she is a virgin pure.—
Strumpet, thy words condemn thy brat and thee:
Use no entreaty, for it is in vain.
PUC. Then lead me hence;—with whom I leave my curse;
May never glorious sun reflex his beams
Upon the country where you make abode!
But darkness and the gloomy shade of death
Environ you; till mischief and despair
Drive you to break your necks or hang yourselves.
[*Exit, guarded.*
YORK. Break thou in pieces, and consume to ashes,
Thou foul accursed minister of hell!

Enter CARDINAL BEAUFORT, *attended.*

CAR. Lord regent, I do greet your excellence
With letters of commission from the king.
For know, my lords, the states of Christendom,
Mov'd with remorse of these outrageous broils,
Have earnestly implor'd a general peace
Betwixt our nation and the aspiring French;
And here at hand the Dauphin, and his train,
Approacheth, to confer about some matter.
YORK. Is all our travail turn'd to this effect?
After the slaughter of so many peers,
So many captains, gentlemen, and soldiers,
That in this quarrel have been overthrown,
And sold their bodies for their country's benefit,
Shall we at last conclude effeminate peace?
Have we not lost most part of all the towns,
By treason, falsehood, and by treachery,
Our great progenitors had conquered?—
O, Warwick, Warwick! I foresee with grief
The utter loss of all the realm of France.
WAR. Be patient, York; if we conclude a peace,
It shall be with such strict and severe covenants,
As little shall the Frenchmen gain thereby.

Enter CHARLES, *attended;* ALENÇON, *the* BASTARD, REIGNIER, *and others.*

CHAR. Since, lords of England, it is thus agreed,
That peaceful truce shall be proclaim'd in France,
We come to be informed by yourselves
What the conditions of that league must be.
YORK. Speak, Winchester; for boiling choler chokes
The hollow passage of my prison'd[b] voice,
By sight of these our baleful enemies.
CAR. Charles, and the rest, it is enacted thus:—
That, in regard king Henry gives consent,

(*) Old text, *me*.

[a] No, misconceived! *Joan of Arc hath been*—] Steevens interprets this,—"No, ye misconceivers, ye who mistake me and my qualities." If this be the meaning, the author probably wrote:—

"*Know*, misconceived," &c.

But, perhaps, the punctuation adopted by Mr. Collier gives the true solution:—

"No; misconceived Joan of Arc hath been," &c.

[b] Prison'd *voice*.—] In the old text, "*poyson'd* voice." Theobald first substituted *prison'd*.

Of mere compassion and of lenity,
To ease your country of distressful war,
And suffer you to breathe in fruitful peace,—
You shall become true liegemen to his crown:
And, Charles, upon condition thou wilt swear
To pay him tribute, and submit thyself,
Thou shalt be plac'd as viceroy under him,
And still enjoy thy regal dignity.

ALEN. Must he be then as shadow of himself?
Adorn his temples with a coronet,
And yet, in substance and authority,
Retain but privilege of a private man?
This proffer is absurd and reasonless.

CHAR. 'Tis known already that I am possess'd
With more than half the Gallian territories,
And therein reverenc'd for their lawful king:
Shall I, for lucre of the rest unvanquish'd,
Detract so much from that prerogative,
As to be call'd but viceroy of the whole?
No, lord ambassador; I'll rather keep
That which I have, than, coveting for more,
Be cast from possibility of all.

YORK. Insulting Charles! hast thou by secret means
Us'd intercession to obtain a league,
And, now the matter grows to compromise,
Stand'st thou aloof upon comparison?
Either accept the title thou usurp'st,
Of benefit[a] proceeding from our king,
And not of any challenge of desert,
Or we will plague thee with incessant wars.

REIG. My lord, you do not well in obstinacy
To cavil in the course of this contráct:
If once it be neglected, ten to one,
We shall not find like opportunity.
[*Aside to* CHARLES.

ALEN. To say the truth, it is your policy,
To save your subjects from such massacre
And ruthless slaughters as are daily seen
By our proceeding in hostility:
And therefore take this compact of a truce,
Although you break it when your pleasure serves.
[*Aside to* CHARLES.

WAR. How say'st thou, Charles? shall our condition stand?

CHAR. It shall:
Only reserv'd, you claim no interest
In any of our towns of garrison.

YORK. Then swear allegiance to his majesty;
As thou art knight, never to disobey,
Nor be rebellious to the crown of England;
Thou, nor thy nobles, to the crown of England.—
[CHARLES *and the rest give tokens of fealty.*
So, now dismiss your army when ye please;
Hang up your ensigns, let your drums be still,
For here we entertain a solemn peace. [*Exeunt.*

[a] *Of* benefit *proceeding from our king*,—] "*Benefit* is here a term of law. Be content to live as the *beneficiary* of our king."—JOHNSON.

SCENE V.—London. *A Room in the Palace.*

Enter KING HENRY, *in conference with* SUFFOLK; GLOUCESTER *and* EXETER *following.*

K. HEN. Your wond'rous rare description, noble earl,
Of beauteous Margaret hath astonish'd me:
Her virtues, graced with external gifts,
Do breed love's settled passions in my heart:
And, like as rigour of tempestuous gusts,
Provokes the mightiest hulk against the tide;
So am I driven, by breath of her renown,
Either to suffer shipwreck, or arrive
Where I may have fruition of her love.

SUF. Tush, my good lord! this superficial tale
Is but a preface of her worthy praise:
The chief perfections of that lovely dame,
(Had I sufficient skill to utter them,)
Would make a volume of enticing lines,
Able to ravish any dull conceit.
And, which is more, she is not so divine,
So full replete with choice of all delights,
But, with as humble lowliness of mind,
She is content to be at your command;
Command, I mean, of virtuous chaste intents,
To love and honour Henry as her lord.

K. HEN. And otherwise will Henry ne'er presume.
Therefore, my lord protector, give consent,
That Margaret may be England's royal queen.

GLO. So should I give consent to flatter sin.
You know, my lord, your highness is betroth'd
Unto another lady of esteem;
How shall we, then, dispense with that contráct
And not deface your honour with reproach?

SUF. As doth a ruler with unlawful oaths;
Or one that, at a triumph having vow'd
To try his strength, forsaketh yet the lists
By reason of his adversary's odds:
A poor earl's daughter is unequal odds.
And therefore may be broke without offence.

GLO. Why, what, I pray, is Margaret more than that?
Her father is no better than an earl,
Although in glorious titles he excel.

SUF. Yes, my good* lord, her father is a king,
The king of Naples and Jerusalem;
And of such great authority in France,
As his alliance will confirm our peace,
And keep the Frenchmen in allegiance.

GLO. And so the earl of Armagnac may do,
Because he is near kinsman unto Charles.

EXE. Beside, his wealth doth warrant† liberal dower;
Where Reignier sooner will receive, than give.

(*) First folio omits, *good*. (†) First folio inserts, *a*.

SUF. A dower, my lords! disgrace not so your king,
That he should be so abject, base, and poor,
To choose for wealth, and not for perfect love.
Henry is able to enrich his queen,
And not to seek a queen to make him rich:
So worthless peasants bargain for their wives,
As market-men for oxen, sheep, or horse.
Marriage is a matter of more worth,
Than to be dealt in by attorneyship;
Not whom we will, but whom his grace affects,
Must be companion of his nuptial bed:
And therefore, lords, since he affects her most,
It[a] most of all these reasons bindeth us,
In our opinions she should be preferr'd.
For what is wedlock forced but a hell,
An age of discord and continual strife?
Whereas the contrary bringeth bliss,[b]
And is a pattern of celestial peace.
Whom should we match with Henry, being a king,
But Margaret, that is daughter to a king?
Her peerless feature, joined with her birth,
Approves her fit for none but for a king:
Her valiant courage and undaunted spirit,
(More than in women commonly is seen,)
Will answer our hope in issue of a king;
For Henry, son unto a conqueror,
Is likely to beget more conquerors,
If with a lady of so high resolve,
As is fair Margaret, he be link'd in love.
Then yield, my lords; and here conclude with me,
That Margaret shall be queen, and none but she.

K. HEN. Whether it be through force of your report,
My noble lord of Suffolk, or for that
My tender youth was never yet attaint
With any passion of inflaming love,
I cannot tell; but this I am assur'd,
I feel such sharp dissension in my breast,
Such fierce alarums both of hope and fear,
As I am sick with working of my thoughts.
Take, therefore, shipping; post, my lord, to France;
Agree to any covenants; and procure
That lady Margaret do vouchsafe to come
To cross the seas to England, and be crown'd
King Henry's faithful and anointed queen:
For your expenses and sufficient charge,
Among the people gather up a tenth.
Be gone, I say; for, till you do return,
I rest perplexed with a thousand cares.—
And you, good uncle, banish all offence:
If you do censure me by what you were,
Not what you are, I know it will excuse
This sudden execution of my will.
And so conduct me, where from company,
I may revolve and ruminate my grief. [*Exit.*

GLO. Ay, grief, I fear me, both at first and last.
[*Exeunt* GLOUCESTER *and* EXETER.

SUF. Thus Suffolk hath prevail'd: and thus he goes,
As did the youthful Paris once to Greece;
With hope to find the like event in love,
But prosper better than the Trojan did.
Margaret shall now be queen, and rule the king;
But I will rule both her, the king, and realm.
[*Exit.*

[a] It *most of all*, &c.] *It* is an addition of Rowe's; the old text exhibiting the line,

"Most of all these reasons bindeth us."

We should prefer reading, "*And* most of all," &c. conceiving Suffolk's meaning to be—since he loves her best, and we ourselves in the choice of a wife are most bound by considerations of affection, she should be preferred.

[b] *Whereas the* contrary *bringeth bliss,*—] *Contrary* must here be read as a quadrisyllable.

ILLUSTRATIVE COMMENTS.

ACT I.

(1) Scene I.—*Hung be the heavens with black.*] In our early theatres, before the introduction of movable scenery, it appears that the back and sides of the stage were usually adorned with tapestry or arras, while the internal roof, or ceiling, technically called the "Heavens," by means of blue hangings, similar perhaps to those still in use, was made to represent the actual sky. When the performance was of a tragic nature, however, the furniture of the stage partook in some degree of the sombre character of the piece, and the walls and interior covering were always hung with black. To this change in the aspect of the stage when tragedy was played, the passage in the text is one of many allusions which may be instanced from Elizabethan writers. Thus Shakespeare again, in his "Rape of Lucrece:"—

> "*Black stage* for *tragedies*, and murthers fell."

So, in the Induction to a tragedy called "A Warning for Fair Women," 1599:—

> "*Historie.* Look, Comedie. I mark'd it not till now,
> *The stage is hung with blacke*, and I perceive
> The auditors prepar'd for tragedie."

So, also, in Marston's "Insatiate Countess," Act IV.:—

> "The stage of heav'n is *hung* with solemne *black*,
> A time best fitting to act *tragedies*."

And so Sidney, in his "Arcadia," p. 125, ed. 1598:—"There arose, even with the Sunne, a vaile of darke cloudes before his face, which shortly (like inke powred into water) had *blacked over all the face of heaven;* preparing (as it were) a mournfull stage for a Tragedie to be played on." For further illustration of the practice, the reader may consult Malone's "Historical Account of the English Stage," Vol. III. p. 103 of the "Variorum" Shakespeare; and Whiter's "Specimen of a Commentary on Shakespeare," p. 156.

(2) Scene I.—
Conjurers and sorcerers, that, afraid of him,
By magic verses have contriv'd his end.]

The superstition to which Rosalind refers, "I was never so be-rhymed since Pythagoras time that I was an Irish rat," ("As You Like It," Act III. Sc. 2,) was of the same species, though of a less tragic and malignant character, as that indicated in the passage above. The rhyming rats to death was supposed to be effected partly by force of the verses employed, and partly by the solemn, ceaseless, and monotonous chant with which they were repeated. But the "magic verses" to which the death of Henry V. is here attributed were not required to be uttered in his presence: their deadly energy existing solely in the words of the imprecation and the malevolence of the reciter, which were supposed to render them effectual at any distance. Sir Philip Sidney, in his *Defence of Poesie*, says, "I will not wish you to be rimed to death as is said to be done in Ireland;" and Sir William Temple, with much probability, suggests that the practice in that country was derived from the various kinds of poetical charms employed by the Gothic races in their Runes, and the stanzas which they composed in them. The Runic letters were all believed to have different and individual powers; and some were accordingly entitled Noxious, or Bitter Runes, and to verses formed of such characters the passage in the text refers. There were, also, other Runes which would secure victory, avert misfortune, excite love, and cure disease; to which class the rat-rhymes probably belonged.

Among other reasons which might be assigned for verse being chosen as the medium for these charms, are the precise adherence to the words which was insured by the limitations of rhyme and metre; and the great assistance they afforded to the memory. The mystic language of the bards who composed these formulæ would also naturally run into rhythm and verse as being the oldest and most appropriate diction for expressing them. In the ancient epigram, called *The Poem of the Furnace,* addressed to the potters of Samos, and attributed to Homer, there is a remarkable instance of verse employed both as a blessing and a malediction; the effect of the invocation being dependent on the good or ill reward the poet met with from the workmen.

King Henry V. died at Vincennes, August 31st, 1422; but though contemporaneous historians differ as to his mortal disease, none of them attributes his death to the magical influence of conjurers and sorcerers.

(3) Scene II.—*La Pucelle.*] The Pucelle of this play is a parody on the Pucelle of history. The leading incidents in the career of this remarkable female are roughly sketched, indeed, but in the actions and speeches attributed to her we have no indication whatever of that simplicity and meekness which, in strange combination with undaunted resolution and the most reckless personal bravery, so pre-eminently distinguished the heroic Maid of Orleans. The circumstances connected with Joan's first interview with the dauphin appear to have been derived by the dramatist from Holinshed, whose narrative runs as follows:—"In time of this siege at Orleance (French stories saie) the first weeke of March 1428, unto Charles the Dolphin, at Chinon, as he was in very great care and studie how to wrestle against the English nation, by one Peter Badricourt, capteine of Vacouleur (made after marshall of France by the Dolphin's creation), was caried a young wench of an eighteene yeeres old, called Joan Are, by name of hir father (a sorie sheepheard) James of Are, and Isabell hir mother, brought up poorlie in their trade of keeping cattel, born at Domprin (therefore reported by Bale, Jone Domprin) upon Meuse in Lorraine within the diocesse of Thoule. Of favour was she counted likesome, of person stronglie made and manlie, of courage great, hardie, and stout withall, an understander of counsels though she were not at them, great semblance of chastitie both of bodie and behaviour, the name of Jesus in hir mouth about all hir businesses, humble, obedient, and fasting diverse days in the week. A person (as their bookes make hir) raised up by power divine, only for succour to the French estate, then deeplie in distresse, in whome, for planting a credit the rather, first the companie that toward the Dolphin did conduct hir, through places all dangerous, as holden by the English, where she never was afore, all the waie and by nightertale safely did she lead: then at the Dolphins sending by hir assignement, from saint Katharin's church of Fierbois in Touraine (where she never had been and knew not), in a secret place there among old iron, appointed she hir sword to be sought out and brought hir, that with five floure delices was graven on both sides, wherewith she fought and did manie slaughters by hir owne hands. In warfar rode she in armour, capapie and mustered as a man, before hir an ensigne all white, wherin was Jesus Christ painted with a floure delice in his hand.

"Unto the Dolphin into his gallerie when first she was brought, and he shadowing himselfe behind, setting other gaie lords before him to try hir cunning from all the companie, with a salutation (that indeed marred all the matter) she pickt him out alone, who thereupon had hir to the end of the gallerie, where she held him an houre in secret and private talke, that of his privie chamber was thought verie long, and therefore would have broken it off; but he made them a signe to let hir saie on."

(4) SCENE II.—

Now am I like that proud insulting ship,
Which Cæsar and his fortune bare at once.]

This may have been suggested by a passage Steevens found in Plutarch's Life of Julius Cæsar, as translated by North:—"Cæsar hearing that, straight discovered himselfe unto the maister of the pynnase, who at the first was amazed when he saw him; but Cæsar, then taking him by the hand, sayd unto him, good fellow, be of good cheere, forwardes hardily, and feare not, for *thou hast Cæsar and his fortune with thee.*"

(5) SCENE II.—*Was Mahomet inspired with a dove?*] Mahomet, it is related, had a dove, "which he used to feed with wheat out of his ear; which dove, when it was hungry, lighted on Mahomet's shoulder, and thrust its bill in to find its breakfast; Mahomet persuading the rude and simple Arabians, that it was the Holy Ghost that gave him advice."—See SIR WALTER RALEIGH'S *History of the World*, b. i. part i. ch. vi.

(6) SCENE V.—

A witch, by fear, not force, like Hannibal,
Drives back our troops, and conquers as she lists.]

Referring to Hannibal's escape by the stratagem of fixing burning twigs on the horns of oxen, as told in Livy, b. xxii. c. xvi.

(7) SCENE V.—*Than Rhodope's of Memphis.*] The old text reads:—"—— Rhodope's *or* Memphis." Capell first proposed the lection usually adopted. Of the pyramids near Memphis, Pliny records that "the fairest and most commended for workmanship was built at the cost and charges of *one Rhodope*, a verie strumpet." See also Ælian, Var. His. xiii. 33; and Strabo, xvii. p. 180.

(8) SCENE V.—*Than the rich-jewell'd coffer of Darius.*] This alludes to the costly casket which Alexander selected from the *opima spolia* of Darius at the taking of Gaza, as a befitting shrine for the Iliad of Homer. "In what price the noble poemes of *Homer* were holden with *Alexander* the great, in so much as every night they were layd under his pillow, and by day were carried in *the rich iewell cofer of Darius*, lately before vanquished by him in battaile."—PUTTENHAM'S *Arte of English Poesie*, chap. viii.

ACT II.

(1) SCENE V.—*Mortimer.*] "This Edmond Mortimer was, I believe, confounded by the author of this play, and by the old historians, with his kinsman, who was perhaps about thirty years old at his death. Edmond Mortimer was born in December, 1392, and consequently at the time of his death was thirty-two years old.

"This family had great possessions in Ireland, in consequence of the marriage of Lionel, Duke of Clarence, with the daughter of the Earl of Ulster, about 1353, and were long connected with that country. Lionel was for some time Viceroy of Ireland, and was created by his father, Edward III., Duke of *Clarence*, in consequence of possessing the honour of *Clare*, in the county of Thomond. Edmund Mortimer, Earl of March, who married Philippa, the duke's only daughter, succeeded him in the government of Ireland, and died in his office, at St. Dominick's Abbey, near Cork, in December, 1381. His son, Roger Mortimer, was twice Vicegerent of Ireland, and was slain at a place called Kenles, in Ossory, in 1398. Edmund, his son, the Mortimer of this play, was, as has been already mentioned, also Chief Governor of Ireland, in the years 1423 and 1424, and died there in 1425. His nephew and heir, Richard, Duke of York (the Plantagenet of this play), was in 1449 constituted Lord Lieutenant of Ireland, for ten years, with extraordinary powers; and his son George Duke of Clarence (who was afterwards murdered in the Tower) was born in the Castle of Dublin, in 1450. This prince filled the same office which so many of his ancestors had possessed, being constituted Chief Governor of Ireland for *life*, by his brother Edward IV. in the third year of his reign.

"Perhaps I have been mistaken in one assertion which I have made in the former part of this note; Mortimer probably did not take his title of *Clarence* from his great Irish possessions (as I have suggested), but rather from his wife's mother, Elizabeth le Clare, third daughter of Gilbert de Clare, Earl of Gloster, and sister to Gilbert de Clare, the last (of that name) Earl of Gloster, who founded Clare Hall in Cambridge.

"The error concerning Edmund Mortimer, brother-in-law to Richard, Earl of Cambridge, having been 'kept in captivity untill he died,' seems to have arisen from the legend of Richard Plantagenet, Duke of Yorke, in the 'Mirrour for Magistrates,' 1575, where the following lines are found:—

'His cursed son ensued his cruell path,
'And kept my giltlesse *cosin* strayt in *duraunce*,
'For whome my father hard entreated hath,
'But living hopelesse of his life's assuraunce,
'Hee thought it best by pollitike procuraunce
'To slay the king, and so restore his frend;
'Which brought himself to an infamous end:
'So whan King *Henry*, of that name the fifte,
'Had tane my father in his conspiracie,
'Hee, from Sir *Edmund* all the blame to shifte,
'Was fayne to say, the *French* king Charles, his alley,
'Had hyred him this trayterous act to trye;
'For which condemned shortly hee was slain,
'In helping right this was my father's gaine.'"

MALONE.

ACT III.

(1) SCENE II.—

These are the city-gates, the gates of Rouen,
Through which our policy must make a breach.]

Both Hall and Holinshed relate, in nearly the same words, a stratagem employed at the siege of Evreux in 1442, which furnished the poet with materials for this scene:—"The Frenchmen, a little before this season, had taken the town of Evreux by treason of a fisher. Sir Francis the Arragonois hearing of that chance apparelled six strong fellowes, like men of the countrie, with sacks and baskets, as cariers of corne and vittels, and sent them to the castell of Cornill, in the which diverse Englishmen were kept as prisoners, and he with an ambush of Englishmen laie in a vallie nigh to the fortresse. The six counterfet husbandmen entered the castell unsuspected, and streight came to the chamber of the capteine, and laieng hands on him, gave knowledge to them that laie in ambush to come to their aid. The which suddenlie made foorth, and entered the castell, slue and tooke all the Frenchmen, and set the Englishmen at libertie: which thing doone, they set fire in the castell, and departed to Rone with their bootie and prisoners."—HOLINSHED.

ACT IV.

(1) SCENE I.—

Or whether that such cowards ought to wear
This ornament of knighthood, yea, or no.]

The imputation of cowardice which for a short time dimmed the fame of Sir John Fastolfe, arose at the battle of Patay, where the English forces under Lord Talbot, consisting of about six thousand men, were suddenly assailed by the French, in numbers of nearly four to one. "The Englishmen had not leysure to put themselves in aray, after they had pight up their stakes before their Archers, so that there was no remedie but to fight at adventure. This battaile continued by the space of three long houres: for the Englishmen, though they were oppressed with multitude of their enimies, yet they never fled backe one foote, tyl theyr Captayne the Lord Talbot was sore wounded at the backe, and so taken. Then theyr heartes began to faint, and they fledde, in which flight were slaine above twelve hundred, and fortie taken, of whome the Lorde Talbot, the Lorde Scales, the Lord Hungerforde, and Sir Thomas Rampston, were chiefe. * * * From this battail departed, without any stroke striken, sir John Fastolfe, the same yeare for his valiantnesse elected into the order of the Garter, for which cause the Duke of Bedforde tooke from him the Image of saint George, and his Garter, though afterward, by meane of friends and apparaunt causes of good excuse, the same were to him againe delivered agaynst the mynde of the Lorde Talbot."—HOLINSHED.

(2) SCENE II.—*Lean famine, quartering steel, and climbing fire.*] So in Hall:—"The Goddesse of warre, called Bellona—hath these three *hand maides* ever of necessitie attendyng on her; *Bloud, Fire, and Famine;* whiche thre damosels be of that force and strength that every one of them alone is able and sufficient to torment and afflict a proud prince; and they all joyned together are of puissance to destroy the most populous countrey and most richest region of the world."

(3) SCENE VII.—*Enter Soldiers, bearing the body of John Talbot.*] This John Talbot was the earl's eldest son by a second wife; he was created Viscount Lisle in 1551, only two years before the engagement in which his father and he were killed. The circumstances attending the death of the "renowned Talbot" and his gallant son are graphically told by Hall:—"When the Englishmen were come to the place where the Frenchmen were encamped, in the which were iii. C peces of brasse, beside divers other small peces, and subtill Engynes to the Englishmen unknowen, and nothing suspected, they lyghted al on fote, the erle of Shrewesbury only except, which because of his age, rode on a litle hakeney, and fought fiercely with the Frenchmen, and gat thentre of their campe, and by fyne force entered into the same. This conflict continued in doubtfull judgement of victory two longe houres: duryinge which fight the lordes of Montamban and Humadayre, with a great companye of Frenchemen entered the battayle, and began a new felde, and sodaynly the gonners perceivynge the Englishmen to approche nere, discharged their ordinance, and slew iii. C persons, nere to the erle, who perceivynge the imminent ieopardy, and subtile labirynth, in the which he and hys people were enclosed and illaqueate, despisynge his owne savegarde, and desirynge the life of his entierly and welbeloved sonne the lord Lisle, willed, advertised, and counsailled hym to departe out of the felde, and to save hym selfe. But when the sonne had aunswered that it was neither honest nor natural for him, to leve his father in the extreme ieopardye of hys life, and that he would taste of that draught, which his father and parent should assay and begyn: the noble erle and comfortable caiptayn sayd to him: Oh sonne, sonne, I thy father which onely hath bene the terror and scourge of the French people so many yeres, which hath subverted so many townes, and profligate and discomfited so many of them in open battayle, and marcial conflict, neither can here dye, for the honor of my countrey, without great laude and perpetuall fame, nor flye or depart without perpetuall shame and continualle infamy. But because this is thy first iourney and enterprise, neither thy flyeng shall redounde to thy shame, nor thy death to thy glory: for as hardy a man wisely flieth, as a temerarious person folishely abidethe, therefore the fleyng of me shal be the dishonor, not only of me and my progenie, but also a discomfiture of all my company: thy departure shall save thy lyfe and make thee able another tyme, if I be slayn to revenge my death and to do honor to thy Prince and profyt to his Realme. But nature so wrought in the sonne, that neither desire of lyfe, nor thought of securitie, could withdraw or pluck him from his natural father: Who consideryng the constancy of his chyld, and the great daunger that they stode in, comforted his soldiours, cheared his capitayns, and valeantly set on his enemies, and slew of them more in number than he had in his company. But his enemies havyng a greater company of men, and more abundance of ordinaunce then before had bene sene in a battayle, fyrst shot him through the thyghe with a handgonne, and slew his horse, and cowardly killed him, lyenge on the ground, whome they never durst loke in the face, whyle he stode on his fete, and with him, there dyed manfully hys sonne the lord Lisle."

ACT V.

(1) SCENE III.—

You speedy helpers, that are substitutes
Under the lordly monarch of the north,
Appear.]

"The *monarch of the North* was Zimimar, one of the four principal devils invoked by witches. The others were, Amaimon king of the East, Gorson king of the South, and Goap king of the West. Under these devil kings were devil marquesses, dukes, prelates, knights, presidents, and earls. They are all enumerated, from Wier *De præstigiis dæmonum,* in Scot's *Discoverie of Witchcraft,* book xv. c. 2 and 3."—DOUCE.

(2) SCENE III.—*La Pucelle is taken.*] In illustration of the capture and martyrdom of this heroic female, the accompanying extracts from a brief memoir of her by Lord Mahon, (Quarterly Review, No. 138,) are well deserving perpetuation:—

"On leaving Picardy in the preceding year, Charles had confided his newly-acquired fortress of Compiègne to the charge of Guillaume de Flavy, a captain of tried bravery, but, even beyond his compeers in that age, harsh and pitiless. He was now besieged by the Duke of Burgundy, at the head of a powerful army. Joan, hearing of his danger, courageously resolved to share his fortunes, and threw herself into the place on the 24th of May, accompanied by Xaintrailles, Chabannes, Valperga, and other knights of renown. The very evening of her arrival, she headed the garrison in a sally on the side of the bridge across the Oise. She found the Burgundians scattered and unprepared; twice she drove them from their entrenchments, but, seeing their numbers increase every moment, she gave the signal to retreat, herself maintaining the post of honour, the last of the rear-guard. Never had she shown greater intrepidity; but as she approached the town-gate, she found it partly closed, so that but few could press in together; confusion spread amongst her friends, less eager to succour her than to save themselves, and she found herself surrounded by her enemies. Still she made those before her recoil, and might have effected her retreat, when an archer from Picardy, coming up from behind, seized her by her coat of crimson velvet, and drew her from her horse to the ground. She struggled to rise again, and reached the outer fosse: there, however, she was overpowered, and compelled to surrender to Lionel, a bastard of Vendone,* and a soldier in the company of John of Luxemburg. The battlements of Compiègne have long since mouldered away; choked by the fallen fragments, the fosse is once more level with the plain; even the old bridge has been replaced by another higher up the stream—yet, amidst all these manifold changes, the precise spot of the catastrophe is still pointed out by popular tradition to the passing stranger. * * * *

"The captive heroine was first conducted to the quarters of John of Luxemburg, and transferred in succession to the prisons of Beaurevoir, Arras, and Le Crotoy, at the mouth of the Somme. She made two intrepid attempts to escape. Once she had broken a passage through the wall, but was arrested on her way, and still more closely confined. Another time she threw herself headlong from the summit of her prison tower. but was taken up senseless on the ground.

* * * * * *

"The English were, however, impatient to hold the prisoner in their own hands; and, in the month of November, 1430, she was purchased from John of Luxemburg for a sum of ten thousand livres. Her cruel treatment in her new captivity is well described by M. de Barante:—'Joan was taken to Rouen, where were then the young King Henry and all the chiefs of the English. She was led into the great tower of the castle, an iron cage was made for her, and her feet were secured by a chain. The English archers who guarded her treated her with gross contumely, and more than once attempted violence towards her. Nor were they merely common soldiers who showed themselves cruel and violent towards her. The Sire de Luxembourg, whose prisoner she had been, happening to pass through Rouen, went to see her in her prison, accompanied by the Earl of Warwick and the Earl of Stafford.† "Joan," said he in jest, "I am come to put you to ransom, but you will have to promise never again to bear arms against us." "*Ah! mon Dieu,* you are laughing at me," said she, "you have neither the will nor the power to ransom me. I know well that the English will cause me to die, thinking that after my death they will win back the kingdom of France; but even were they a hundred thousand *Goddams* more than they are, they shall never have this kingdom." Incensed at these words, the Earl of Stafford drew his dagger to strike her, but was prevented by the Earl of Warwick.'

"The forebodings of the unhappy woman were but too true; her doom was indeed already sealed. * * * * On the 21st of February, 1431, Joan was brought for the first time before her judges. She underwent, nearly on successive days, fifteen examinations. The scene was the castle-chapel at Rouen; and she appeared clad, as of yore, in military attire, but loaded with chains. Undepressed either by her fallen fortunes, or by her long and cruel captivity, she displayed in her answers the same courageous spirit with which she had defended Orleans and stormed Jargeau. Nor was it courage only; her plain and clear good sense often seemed to retrieve her want of education, and to pierce through the subtle wiles and artifices elaborately prepared to ensnare her. Thus, for example, she was asked whether she knew herself to be in the grace of God? Had she answered in the affirmative, then arrogance and presumption would forthwith have been charged upon her; if in the negative, she would have been treated as guilty by her own confession. 'It is a great matter,' she said, 'to reply to such a question.' 'So great a matter,' interposed one of the assessors, touched with pity,—his name deserves to be recorded: it was Jean Fabry,—'that the prisoner is not bound in law to answer it.' 'You had better be silent,' said the Bishop of Beauvais fiercely to Fabry; and he repeated the question to Joan. 'If I am not in the grace of God,' she said, 'I pray God that it may be vouchsafed to me; if I am, I pray God that I may be preserved in it.' * * *

"The two points on which Joan's enemies and judges (the terms are here synonymous) mainly relied were—first, the 'Tree of the Fairies,' near Domremy; and secondly, the banner borne by herself in battle. Both of these it was attempted to connect with evil spirits or magical spells. As to the first, Joan replied, clearly and simply, that she had often been round the tree in procession with the other maidens of the village, but had never beheld any of her visions at that spot. With regard to the banner, she declared that she had assumed it in battle on purpose to spare the lance and the sword; that she wished not to kill any one with her own hand, and that she never had.

* * * * * *

"So plain and candid had been the general tenor of her answers, that it being referred to the assessors whether or not she should be put to the rack, in hopes of extorting further revelations, only two were found to vote in favour of this atrocious proposal. It is said that one of our countrymen present at the trial was so much struck with the evident good faith of her replies, that he could not forbear exclaiming, 'A worthy woman—if she were only English!'*

"Her judges, however, heedless of her innocence, or perhaps only the more inflamed by it, drew up twelve articles of accusation, upon the grounds of sorcery and heresy, which articles were eagerly confirmed by the University of Paris. On the 24th of May, 1431,—the very day on which Joan had been taken prisoner the year before—she was led to the churchyard before Saint Ouen, where two scaffolds had been raised; on the one stood the Cardinal of Winchester, the Bishop of Beauvais, and several prelates; the other was designed for the Maid, and for a preacher named Erard. The preacher then began his sermon, which was filled with the most vehement invectives against herself; these she bore with perfect patience; but when he came to the words: 'Your King, that heretic and that schismatic,' she could not forbear exclaiming aloud, 'Speak of me, but do not speak of the King—he is a good Christian. . . . . By my faith, sir, I can swear to you, as my life shall answer for it, that he is the noblest of all Christians, and not such as you say.' The Bishop of Beauvais, much incensed, directed the guards to stop her voice, and the preacher proceeded. At his conclusion, a formula of abjuration was presented to Joan for her signature. It was necessary, in the first place, to explain to her what was the meaning of the word abjuration; she then exclaimed that she had nothing to abjure, for that whatever she had done was at the command of God; but she was eagerly pressed with arguments and with entreaties to sign. At the same time, the prelates pointed to the public hangman, who stood close by in his car, ready to bear her away to instant death if she refused. Thus urged, Joan said at length: 'I would sign rather than burn,' and put her mark to the paper.† The object,

* Not Vendome, as most writers have supposed. The place meant is now called Wandomme, in the Département du Pas de Calais.—Quicherat, 'Procès de Jeanne d'Arc,' vol. i. p. 13.

† Not Strafford, as written by M. de Barante.

* 'C'est une bonne femme—si elle était Anglaise!' *Supplément aux Mémoires,* Collection, vol. viii. p. 294.

† Deposition, at the Trial of Revision, of Massieu, a priest and rural dean, who had stood by her side on the scaffold.—QUICHERAT, *Procès,* vol. i. p. 8.

however, was to sink her in public estimation; and with that view, by another most unworthy artifice, a much fuller and more explicit confession of her errors was afterwards made public, instead of the one which had been read to her, and which she had really signed.

"The submission of Joan having been thus extorted, the Bishop of Beauvais proceeded to pass sentence in the name of the tribunal. He announced to her, that out of 'grace and moderation' her life should be spared, but that the remainder of it must be passed in prison, 'with the bread of grief and the water of anguish for her food.'* Joan heard the sentence unmoved, saying only: 'Well, then, ye men of the church, lead me to your own prisons, and let me no longer remain in the hands of these English.' But she was taken back to the same dungeon as before.

"Nor was it designed that her life should indeed be spared. Her enemies only hoped, by a short delay and a pretended lenity, to palliate the guilt of her murder, or to heap a heavier load upon her memory. She had promised to resume a female dress; and it is related that a suit of men's apparel was placed in her cell, and her own removed during the night; so that she had no other choice next morning but to clothe herself again in the forbidden garments. Such is the common version of the story. But we greatly fear that a darker and a sadder tale remains behind. A priest, named Martin l'Advenu, who was allowed to receive her confession at this period, and to shrive her in her dying moments, was afterwards examined at the trial of revision, and declared that an English lord (*un millourt d'Angleterre*) had entered her prison and attempted violence; that, on his departure, she was found with her face disfigured and in tears; and that she had resumed men's apparel as a more effectual safeguard to her honour.†

"But whether the means employed in this infamous transaction were of fraud or of force, the object was clearly the same—to find a pretext for further rigour. For, according to the rules of the Inquisition, it was not heresy in the first instance, but only a relapse into heresy, that could be punished with death. No sooner, then, was the Bishop of Beauvais apprised of Joan's change of dress than he hastened to the prison to convict her of the fact. He asked her whether she had heard 'her Voices' again? 'I have,' answered Joan; 'St. Catherine and St. Margaret have reproved me for my weakness in signing the abjuration, and commanded me to resume the dress which I wore by the appointment of God.' This was enough; the Bishop and his compeers straightway pronounced her a heretic relapsed: no pardon could now be granted—scarce any delay allowed.

"At daybreak, on the 30th of May, her confessor, Martin l'Advenu, was directed to enter her cell and prepare her for her coming doom—to be burned alive that very day in the market-place of Rouen. At first hearing this barbarous sentence the Maid's firmness forsook her for some moments; she burst into piteous cries, and tore her hair in agony, loudly appealing to God, 'the great Judge,' against the wrongs and cruelties done her. But ere long regaining her serene demeanour, she made her last confession to the priest, and received the Holy Sacrament from his hands. At nine o'clock, having been ordered to array herself for the last time in female attire, she was placed in the hangman's car, with her confessor and some other persons, and was escorted to the place of execution by a party of English soldiers. * * * * At the market-place (it is now adorned by a statue to her memory) she found the wood ready piled, and the Bishop of Beauvais, with the Cardinal of Winchester and other prelates, awaiting their victim. First a sermon was read, and then her sentence; at this her tears flowed afresh, but she knelt down to pray with her confessor, and asked for a cross. There was none at hand, and one was sent for to a neighbouring church; meanwhile, an English soldier made another by breaking his staff asunder, and this cross she devoutly clasped to her breast. But the other soldiers were already murmuring at these long delays. 'How now, priest?' said they to l'Advenu; 'do you mean to make us dine here?' At length their fierce impatience was indulged; the ill-fated woman was bound to the stake, and upon her head was placed a mitre with the following words inscribed:—

'HERETIQUE RELAPSE, APOSTATE, IDOLATRE.'

The Bishop of Beauvais drew nigh just after the pile was kindled; 'It is you,' said she to him, 'who have brought me to this death.' To the very last, as l'Advenu states in his deposition, she continued to protest and maintain that her Voices were true and unfeigned, and that in obeying them she had obeyed the will of God. As the flames increased, she bid l'Advenu stand further from her side, but still hold the cross aloft, that her latest look on earth might fall on the Redeemer's blessed sign. And the last word which she was heard to speak ere she expired was—JESUS. Several of the prelates and assessors had already withdrawn in horror from the sight, and others were melted to tears. But the Cardinal of Winchester, still unmoved, gave orders that the ashes and bones of 'the heretic' should be collected and cast into the Seine. Such was the end of Joan of Arc—in her death the martyr, as in her life the champion, of her country."

* 'Au pain de douleurs et à l'eau d'angoisse.'—*Collection des Mémoires*, vol. viii. p. 304.

† Compare Sismondi, vol. xiii. p. 190, with the *Supplément aux Mémoires* (Collection, vol. viii. p. 304).

KING HENRY VI. PART SECOND.

Act IV. Sc. 2.

THE SECOND PART OF

KING HENRY THE SIXTH.

"THE Second Part of Henry the Sixt, with the death of the Good Duke Hvmfrey," was first printed in its complete form, in the folio of 1623. In the brief notice prefixed to the foregoing drama, we have ventured an opinion that the two plays, or one play divided into two parts, called "The First Part of the Contention," &c.* and "The True Tragedie," &c.,† afterwards published by Pavier, under the title of "The Whole Contention," &c.,‡ were not, as Malone has laboured to prove, the production of a preceding writer, but were Shakespeare's first sketches (surreptitiously and inaccurately printed) of what he subsequently re-wrote, and entitled "The Second and Third Parts of Henry VI."

In expressing this opinion, we must not be understood to go the extreme length of ascribing the whole of these two pieces to Shakespeare. Much in them unquestionably belongs to another and a very different hand; but the greater portion, especially in "The First Part of the Contention," appears to our judgment far beyond the reach of any other writer of the age. Such, too, we are pleased to find, is the view entertained by Mr. Halliwell. In his Introduction to the excellent reprint of these two dramas for the Shakespeare Society, in 1843, after a careful revision of the evidence in opposition to the claims of Shakespeare to their authorship, this judicious authority well observes:—"There are so many passages in the two plays now reprinted, that seem almost beyond the power of any of Shakespeare's predecessors or contemporaries, perhaps even not excepting Marlowe, that, as one method of explaining away the difficulties which attend a belief in Malone's theory, my conjecture that when these plays were printed in 1594 and 1595, *they included the first additions which Shakespeare made to the originals*, does not seem improbable, borne out, as it is, by an examination of the early editions. If I am so far correct, we have yet to discover the originals of the two parts of the 'Contention,' as well as that of 1 Henry VI."

* "The First part of the Contention betwixt the two famous Houses of Yorke and Lancaster, with the death of the good Duke Humphrey: And the banishment and death of the Duke of *Suffolke*, and the Tragicall end of the proud Cardinall of *Winchester*, with the notable Rebellion of *Iacke Cade: And the Duke of Yorke's first claime vnto the Crowne*. London, Printed by Thomas Creed, for Thomas Millington, and are to be sold at his shop vnder Saint Peters Church in Cornwall. 1594."

† "The True Tragedie of Richard *Duke of Yorke, and the death of* good King Henrie the Sixt, *with the whole contention betweene* the two Houses Lancaster and Yorke, as it was sundrie times acted by the Right Honourable the Earle of Pembrooke his seruants. Printed at London by P. S., for Thomas Millington, *and are to be sold at his shoppe vnder Saint Peters Church in Cornwal.* 1595."

‡ "The Whole Contention betweene the two Famous Houses, Lancaster and Yorke. With the Tragicall ends of the good Duke Humfrey, Richard Duke of Yorke, and King Henrie the sixt. Diuided into two Parts: And newly corrected and enlarged. Written by William Shakespeare, Gent. Printed at London, for T. P."

Persons Represented.

KING HENRY THE SIXTH.
HUMPHREY, *Duke of* Gloucester, *his Uncle.*
CARDINAL BEAUFORT, *Bishop of* Winchester, *Great Uncle to the* King.
RICHARD PLANTAGENET, *Duke of* York.
EDWARD *and* RICHARD, *his* Sons.
DUKE *of* SOMERSET, DUKE *of* SUFFOLK, DUKE *of* BUCKINGHAM, LORD CLIFFORD, YOUNG CLIFFORD, *his* Son, — *of the* King's *party.*
EARL *of* SALISBURY, EARL *of* WARWICK, — *of the* Yorkist *party.*
LORD SCALES, *Governor of the* Tower.
LORD SAY.
Sir HUMPHREY STAFFORD, *and his* Brother.
Sir JOHN STANLEY.
A Sea-Captain, Master, *and* Master's Mate, *and* WALTER WHITMORE.
Two Gentlemen, *Prisoners with* Suffolk.
VAUX.
HUME *and* SOUTHWELL, *two Priests.*
BOLINGBROKE, *a Conjurer.*
A Spirit *raised by him.*
THOMAS HORNER, *an Armourer.*
PETER, *his man.*
Clerk *of* Chatham.
Mayor *of* St. Alban's.
SIMPCOX, *an Impostor.*
Two Murderers.
JACK CADE, *a Rebel.*
GEORGE, JOHN, DICK, SMITH *the* Weaver, MICHAEL, *&c. his followers.*
ALEXANDER IDEN, *a* Kentish *Gentleman.*

MARGARET, *Queen to* King Henry.
ELEANOR, *Duchess of* Gloucester.
MARGERY JOURDAIN, *a Witch.*
Wife *to* Simpcox.

Lords, Ladies, and Attendants; Petitioners, Aldermen, a Herald, a Beadle, Sheriffs, and Officers; Citizens, Prentices, Falconers, Guards, Soldiers, Messengers, &c.

SCENE,—*Dispersedly in various parts of* England.

ACT I.

SCENE I.—London. *A Room of State in the Palace.*

Flourish of Trumpets: then Hautboys. Enter, on one side, KING HENRY, DUKE *of* GLOUCESTER, SALISBURY, WARWICK, *and* CARDINAL BEAUFORT; *on the other,* QUEEN MARGARET, *led in by* SUFFOLK; YORK, SOMERSET, BUCKINGHAM, *and others following.*

SUF. As by your high imperial majesty
I had in charge at my depart for France,
As procurator to your excellence,
To marry princess Margaret for your grace;
So, in the famous ancient city Tours,—
In presence of the kings of France and Sicil,
The dukes of Orleans, Calaber, Bretaigne, and Alençon,
Seven earls, twelve barons, and twenty reverend bishops,
I have perform'd my task, and was espous'd;
And humbly now upon my bended knee,

In sight of England and her lordly peers,
Deliver up my title in the queen
To your most gracious hands, that are the substance
Of that great shadow I did represent;
The happiest gift that ever marquess gave,
The fairest queen that ever king receiv'd.

K. HEN. Suffolk, arise. — Welcome, queen Margaret:
I can express no kinder sign of love,
Than this kind kiss.—O Lord, that lends me life,
Lend me a heart replete with thankfulness!
For thou hast given me, in this beauteous face,
A world of earthly blessings to my soul,
If sympathy of love unite our thoughts.

Q. MAR. Great king of England, and my gracious lord;—
The mutual conference that my mind hath had,
By day, by night; waking, and in my dreams,
In courtly company, or at my beads,—[a]
With you mine alder-liefest[b] sovereign,
Makes me the bolder to salute my king
With ruder terms, such as my wit affords
And over-joy of heart doth minister.

K. HEN. Her sight did ravish; but her grace in speech,
Her words y-clad with wisdom's majesty,
Makes me, from wondering, fall to weeping, joys;
Such is the fulness of my heart's content.—
Lords, with one cheerful voice welcome my love.

ALL. Long live queen Margaret, England's happiness!

Q. MAR. We thank you all. [*Flourish.*

SUF. My lord protector, so it please your grace,
Here are the articles of contracted peace,
Between our sovereign and the French king Charles,
For eighteen months, concluded by consent.

GLO. [*Reads.*] *Imprimis, It is agreed between the French king, Charles, and William de la Poole, marquess of Suffolk, ambassador for Henry king of England,— that the said Henry shall espouse the lady Margaret, daughter unto Reignier king of Naples, Sicilia, and Jerusalem; and crown her queen of England, ere the thirtieth of May next ensuing.—-Item,—That the duchy of Anjou and the county of Maine shall be released and delivered to the king her father*——

K. HEN. Uncle, how now!

GLO. Pardon me, gracious lord;
Some sudden qualm hath struck me at the heart,
And dimm'd mine eyes, that I can read no further.

K. HEN. Uncle of Winchester, I pray, read on.

CAR. [*Reads.*] *Item,—It is further agreed between them,— that the duchies of Anjou and Maine shall be released and delivered over to the king her father; and she sent over of the king of England's own proper cost and charges, without having any dowry.*

K. HEN. They please us well.—Lord marquess, kneel down;
We here create thee the first duke of Suffolk,
And girt thee with the sword.—Cousin of York,
We here discharge your grace from being regent
I' the parts of France, till term of eighteen months
Be full expir'd.—Thanks, uncle Winchester,
Gloster, York, Buckingham, Somerset,
Salisbury, and Warwick;
We thank you all for this great favour done,
In entertainment to my princely queen.
Come, let us in; and with all speed provide
To see her coronation be perform'd.
[*Exeunt* KING, QUEEN, *and* SUFFOLK.

GLO. Brave peers of England, pillars of the state,
To you duke Humphrey must unload his grief,—
Your grief, the common grief of all the land.
What! did my brother Henry spend his youth,
His valour, coin, and people, in the wars?
Did he so often lodge in open field,
In winter's cold and summer's parching heat,
To conquer France, his true inheritance?
And did my brother Bedford toil his wits,
To keep by policy what Henry got?
Have you yourselves, Somerset, Buckingham,
Brave York, Salisbury, and victorious Warwick,
Receiv'd deep scars in France and Normandy?
Or hath mine uncle Beaufort, and myself,
With all the learned council of the realm,
Studied so long, sat in the council-house
Early and late, debating to and fro
How France and Frenchmen might be kept in awe?
And hath his highness in his infancy
Been[c] crown'd in Paris, in despite of foes?
And shall these labours and these honours die?
Shall Henry's conquest, Bedford's vigilance,
Your deeds of war, and all our counsel die?
O, peers of England, shameful is this league!
Fatal this marriage! cancelling your fame,
Blotting your names from books of memory,
Razing the characters of your renown,
Defacing monuments of conquer'd France,
Undoing all, as all had never been!

CAR. Nephew, what means this passionate discourse,
This peroration with such circumstance?
For France, 'tis ours; and we will keep it still.

GLO. Ay, uncle, we will keep it, if we can;
But now it is impossible we should:
Suffolk, the new-made duke that rules the roast,

---

a Or at my beads,—] See note (c), p. 3, Vol. I.

b Alder-liefest—] *All-dearest; dearest of all;* a Saxon compound found in many of our early writers, from Chaucer to Shakespeare.

c Been *crown'd in Paris,*—] The old text reads "Crowned in Paris," &c. Capell added "*Been,*" as did also Mr. Collier's annotator.

Hath given the duchy of Anjou and Maine
Unto the poor king Reignier, whose large style
Agrees not with the leanness of his purse.

SAL. Now, by the death of Him that died for all,
These counties were the keys of Normandy!—
But wherefore weeps Warwick, my valiant son?

WAR. For grief that they are past recovery;
For, were there hope to conquer them again,
My sword should shed hot blood, mine eyes no tears.
Anjou and Maine! myself did win them both;
Those provinces these arms of mine did conquer:
And are the cities, that I got with wounds,
Deliver'd up again with peaceful words?
Mort Dieu!

YORK. For Suffolk's duke, may he be suffocate,
That dims the honour of this warlike isle!
France should have torn and rent my very heart,
Before I would have yielded to this league.
I never read but England's kings have had
Large sums of gold, and dowries with their wives;
And our king Henry gives away his own,
To match with her that brings no vantages.

GLO. A proper jest, and never heard before,
That Suffolk should demand a whole fifteenth
For costs and charges in transporting her!
She should have stay'd in France, and starv'd in France,
Before——

CAR. My lord of Gloster, now ye grow too hot;
It was the pleasure of my lord the king.

GLO. My lord of Winchester, I know your mind;
'Tis not my speeches that you do mislike,
But 'tis my presence that doth trouble ye.
Rancour will out: proud prelate, in thy face
I see thy fury: if I longer stay,
We shall begin our ancient bickerings.—
Lordings, farewell; and say, when I am gone,
I prophesied—France will be lost ere long. [*Exit.*

CAR. So, there goes our protector in a rage.
'Tis known to you he is mine enemy;
Nay, more, an enemy unto you all,
And no great friend, I fear me, to the king.
Consider, lords, he is the next of blood,
And heir-apparent to the English crown;
Had Henry got an empire by his marriage,
And all the wealthy kingdoms of the west,
There's reason he should he displeas'd at it.
Look to it, lords; let not his smoothing words
Bewitch your hearts; be wise and circumspect.
What though the common people favour him,
Calling him—*Humphrey, the good duke of Gloster;*
Clapping their hands, and crying with loud voice—
Jesu maintain your royal excellence!
With—*God preserve the good duke Humphrey!*
I fear me, lords, for all this flattering gloss,
He will be found a dangerous protector.

BUCK. Why should he, then, protect our sovereign,
He being of age to govern of himself?—
Cousin of Somerset, join you with me,
And all together, with the duke of Suffolk,
We'll quickly hoise duke Humphrey from his seat.

CAR. This weighty business will not brook delay;
I'll to the Duke of Suffolk presently. [*Exit.*

SOM. Cousin of Buckingham, though Humphrey's pride
And greatness of his place be grief to us,
Yet let us watch the haughty cardinal;
His insolence is more intolerable
Than all the princes in the land beside:
If Gloster be displac'd, he'll be protector.

BUCK. Or thou, or I, Somerset, will be protector,*
Despite duke Humphrey or the cardinal.
[*Exeunt* BUCKINGHAM *and* SOMERSET.

SAL. Pride went before, ambition follows him.
While these do labour for their own preferment,
Behoves it us to labour for the realm.
I never saw but Humphrey duke of Gloster
Did bear him like a noble gentleman.
Oft have I seen the haughty cardinal—
More like a soldier than a man o' the church,
As stout and proud as he were lord of all—
Swear like a ruffian, and demean himself
Unlike the ruler of a commonweal.—
Warwick, my son, the comfort of my age!
Thy deeds, thy plainness, and thy housekeeping,
Hath won the greatest favour of the commons,
Excepting none but good duke Humphrey:—
And, brother York, thy acts in Ireland,
In bringing them to civil discipline;
Thy late exploits done in the heart of France,
When thou wert regent for our sovereign;
Have made thee fear'd and honour'd of the people:—
Join we together, for the public good,
In what we can to bridle and suppress
The pride of Suffolk and the cardinal,
With Somerset's and Buckingham's ambition;
And, as we may, cherish duke Humphrey's deeds,
While they do tend the profit of the land.

WAR. So God help Warwick, as he loves the land,
And common profit of his country!

YORK. And so says York, for he hath greatest cause.

SAL. Then let's make haste away, and look unto the main.

WAR. *Unto the main!* O, father, Maine is lost,—
That Maine, which by main force Warwick did win,
And would have kept so long as breath did last!
Main chance, father, you meant; but I meant Maine,—
Which I will win from France, or else be slain.
[*Exeunt* WARWICK *and* SALISBURY.

YORK. Anjou and Maine are given to the French;
Paris is lost; the state of Normandy

(*) First folio, *protectors.*

Stands on a tickle[a] point, now they are gone :
Suffolk concluded on the articles ;
The peers agreed ; and Henry was well pleas'd
To change two dukedoms for a duke's fair daughter.
I cannot blame them all ; what is't to them ?
'T is thine they give away, and not their own.
Pirates may make cheap pennyworths of their pillage,
And purchase friends, and give to courtezans,
Still revelling, like lords, till all be gone ;
Whileas the silly owner of the goods
Weeps over them, and wrings his hapless hands,
And shakes his head, and trembling stands aloof,
While all is shar'd, and all is borne away,
Ready to starve, and dare not touch his own :
So York must sit, and fret, and bite his tongue,
While his own lands are bargain'd for and sold.
Methinks the realms of England, France, and Ire-
land,
Bear that proportion to my flesh and blood,
As did the fatal brand Althea burn'd,
Unto the prince's heart of Calydon.[b]
Anjou and Maine, both given unto the French !
Cold news for me ; for I had hope of France,
Even as I have of fertile England's soil.
A day will come when York shall claim his own ;
And therefore I will take the Nevils' parts, [phrey,
And make a show of love to proud duke Hum-
And, when I spy advantage, claim the crown,
For that's the golden mark I seek to hit :
Nor shall proud Lancaster usurp my right,
Nor hold the sceptre in his childish fist,
Nor wear the diadem upon his head,
Whose church-like humours fit* not for a crown.
Then, York, be still awhile, till time do serve :
Watch thou and wake, when others be asleep,
To pry into the secrets of the state ;
Till Henry, surfeiting in joys of love, [queen,
With his new bride and England's dear-bought
And Humphrey with the peers be fall'n at jars :
Then will I raise aloft the milk-white rose,
With whose sweet smell the air shall be perfum'd ;
And in my standard bear the arms of York,
To grapple with the house of Lancaster ; [crown,
And, force perforce, I'll make him yield the
Whose bookish rule hath pull'd fair England down.
[*Exit.*

SCENE II.—*The same. A Room in the* Duke *of* Gloucester'*s House.*

Enter GLOUCESTER *and the* DUCHESS.

DUCH. Why droops my lord, like over-ripen'd
corn,
Hanging the head at Ceres' plenteous load ?
Why doth the great duke Humphrey knit his
brows,
As frowning at the favours of the world ?
Why are thine eyes fix'd to the sullen earth,
Gazing on that which seems to dim thy sight ?
What seest thou there ? king Henry's diadem,
Enchas'd with all the honours of the world ?
If so, gaze on, and grovel on thy face,
Until thy head be circled with the same.
Put forth thy hand, reach at the glorious gold :—
What, is't too short ? I'll lengthen it with mine ;
And, having both together heav'd it up,
We'll both together lift our heads to heaven,
And never more abase our sight so low,
As to vouchsafe one glance unto the ground.

GLO. O Nell, sweet Nell, if thou dost love thy
lord,
Banish the canker of ambitious thoughts !
And may that thought, when I imagine ill
Against my king and nephew, virtuous Henry,
Be my last breathing in this mortal world !
My troublous dream* this night doth make me sad.

DUCH. What dream'd my lord ? tell me, and
I'll requite it
With sweet rehearsal of my morning's dream.

GLO. Methought this staff, mine office-badge in
court,
Was broke in twain ; by whom I have forgot,
But, as I think, it was by the cardinal ;
And on the pieces of the broken wand
Were plac'd the heads of Edmund duke of
Somerset,
And William de la Poole, first duke of Suffolk.
This was my dream ; what it doth bode, God
knows.

DUCH. Tut, this was nothing but an argument
That he that breaks a stick of Gloster's grove
Shall lose his head for his presumption.
But list to me, my Humphrey, my sweet duke :
Methought I sat in seat of majesty,
In the cathedral church of Westminster,
And in that chair where kings and queens are[c]
crown'd ;
Where[d] Henry and dame Margaret kneel'd to me,
And on my head did set the diadem.

GLO. Nay, Eleanor, then must I chide outright :
Presumptuous dame ! ill-nurtur'd Eleanor !
Art thou not second woman in the realm ;
And the protector's wife, belov'd of him ?
Hast thou not worldly pleasure at command,
Above the reach or compass of thy thought ?
And wilt thou still be hammering treachery,

(*) Old text, *fits*.

a *On a* tickle *point,*—] *Tickle* was commonly used by the old writers for *ticklish*.

b Unto the prince's heart of Calydon.] This fable is alluded to also in the "Second Part of Henry IV." Act II. Sc. 2. See note (b), p. 586, Vol. I.

(*) Old text, *dreames*.

c *Where kings and queens* are *crown'd;*] The old text has "*wer;*" an obvious misprint for *are;* witness "The Contention," which reads—

"Where Kings and Queenes *are* crownde."

d Where—] Another probable misprint for *There*.

To tumble down thy husband and thyself
From top of honour to disgrace's feet?
Away from me, and let me hear no more!

DUCH. What, what, my lord! are you so choleric
With Eleanor, for telling but her dream?
Next time I'll keep my dreams unto myself,
And not be check'd.

GLO. Nay, be not angry, I am pleas'd again.

Enter a Messenger.

MESS. My lord protector, 'tis his highness' pleasure,
You do prepare to ride unto Saint Alban's,
Whereas [a] the king and queen do mean to hawk.

GLO. I go.—Come, Nell,—thou wilt ride with us?

DUCH. Yes, my good lord, I'll follow presently.
[*Exeunt* GLOUCESTER *and* Messenger.
Follow I must; I cannot go before,
While Gloster bears this base and humble mind.
Were I a man, a duke, and next of blood,
I would remove these tedious stumbling-blocks,
And smooth my way upon their headless necks:
And, being a woman, I will not be slack
To play my part in Fortune's pageant.
Where are you there, sir John? [b] nay, fear not, man,
We are alone; here's none but thee and I.

Enter HUME.

HUME. Jesus preserve your royal majesty!

DUCH. What say'st thou? *majesty!* I am but grace.

HUME. But, by the grace of God, and Hume's advice,
Your grace's title shall be multiplied.

DUCH. What say'st thou, man? hast thou as yet conferr'd
With Margery Jourdain, the cunning witch; (1)
With Roger Bolingbroke, the conjurer?
And will they undertake to do me good?

HUME. This they have promised to show your highness,
A spirit rais'd from depth of under ground,
That shall make answer to such questions,
As by your grace shall be propounded him.

DUCH. It is enough; I'll think upon the questions:
When from Saint Alban's we do make return,
We'll see these things effected to the full.
Here, Hume, take this reward; make merry, man,
With thy confederates in this weighty cause.
[*Exit.*

HUME. Hume must make merry with the duchess' gold?
Marry, and shall. But, how now, sir John Hume!
Seal up your lips, and give no words but—mum;
The business asketh silent secrecy.
Dame Eleanor gives gold to bring the witch:
Gold cannot come amiss, were she a devil.
Yet have I gold flies from another coast;
I dare not say, from the rich cardinal,
And from the great and new-made duke of Suffolk;
Yet I do find it so: for, to be plain,
They, knowing dame Eleanor's aspiring humour,
Have hired me to undermine the duchess,
And buz these conjurations in her brain.
They say,—a crafty knave does need no broker; [c]
Yet am I Suffolk and the cardinal's broker.
Hume, if you take not heed, you shall go near
To call them both a pair of crafty knaves.
Well, so it stands; and thus I fear, at last,
Hume's knavery will be the duchess' wreck,
And her attainture will be Humphrey's fall:
Sort how it will, I shall have gold for all. [*Exit.*

SCENE III.—*The same. A Room in the Palace.*

Enter PETER, *and others, with petitions.*

1 PET. My masters, let's stand close; my lord protector will come this way by and by, and then we may deliver our supplications in the quill.[d]

2 PET. Marry, the Lord protect him, for he's a good man! Jesu bless him!

1 PET. Here a' comes, methinks, and the queen with him: I'll be the first, sure.

Enter SUFFOLK *and* QUEEN MARGARET.

2 PET. Come back, fool! this is the duke of Suffolk, and not my lord protector.

SUF. How now, fellow! wouldst any thing with me?

1 PET. I pray, my lord, pardon me! I took ye for my lord protector.

Q. MAR. [*Reading the superscription.*] *To my lord protector!* Are your supplications to his lordship? Let me see them:—what is thine?

---

[a] Whereas—] *Where* and *whereas*, like *when* and *whenas*; *while* and *whileas*, were convertible.

[b] Sir *John?*] The title *Sir*, a translation of *Dominus*, it has already been explained, was one commonly applied to certain churchmen.

[c] A crafty knave does need no broker;] This was proverbial.

[d] *In the* quill.] Mr. Dyce and Mr. Singer would read in the *coil*, or *quoil*, that is, *the stir;* while Mr. Collier's annotator substitutes "*in sequel.*" Of the two, we prefer the former, but have not sufficient confidence in either to advance it to the text.

1 Pet. Mine is, an't please your grace, against John Goodman, my lord cardinal's man, for keeping my house, and lands, and wife and all, from me.

Suf. Thy wife, too! that's some wrong, indeed.—What's yours?—What's here! [*Reads.*] *Against the duke of Suffolk, for enclosing the commons of Melford.*—How now, sir knave?

2 Pet. Alas, sir, I am but a poor petitioner of our whole township.

Peter. [*Presenting his petition.*] Against my master, Thomas Horner, for saying, that the duke of York was rightful heir to the crown.

Q. Mar. What say'st thou? did the duke of York say he was rightful heir to the crown?

Peter. That my master* was? no, forsooth: my master said, that he was; and that the king was an usurper.

Suf. Who is there? [*Enter* Servants.]—Take this fellow in, and send for his master with a pursuivant presently:—we'll hear more of your matter before the king. [*Exeunt* Servants *with* Peter.

Q. Mar. And as for you, that love to be protected
Under the wings of our protector's grace,
Begin your suits anew, and sue to him.
[*Tears the petition.*
Away, base cullions!—Suffolk, let them go.

All. Come, let's be gone. [*Exeunt* Petitioners.

(*) Old text, *Mistresse.*

Q. Mar. My lord of Suffolk, say, is this the guise,
Is this the fashion* in the court of England?
Is this the government of Britain's isle,
And this the royalty of Albion's king?
What, shall king Henry be a pupil still,
Under the surly Gloster's governance?
Am I a queen in title and in style,
And must be made a subject to a duke?
I tell thee, Poole, when in the city Tours
Thou ran'st a tilt in honour of my love,
And stol'st away the ladies' hearts of France;
I thought king Henry had resembled thee
In courage, courtship, and proportion:
But all his mind is bent to holiness,
To number *Ave-Maries* on his beads:
His champions are, the prophets and apostles;
His weapons, holy saws of sacred writ;
His study is his tilt-yard, and his loves
Are brazen images of canoniz'd saints.
I would the college of the cardinals
Would choose him pope, and carry him to Rome,
And set the triple crown upon his head;—
That were a state fit for his holiness.

Suf. Madam, be patient: as I was cause
Your highness came to England, so will I
In England work your grace's full content.

Q. Mar. Beside the haught† protector, have we Beaufort,

(*) Old text, *Fashions.* (†) First folio, *haughtie.*

The imperious churchman; Somerset, Buckingham,
And grumbling York: and not the least of these
But can do more in England than the king.

SUF. And he of these, that can do most of all,
Cannot do more in England than the Nevils:
Salisbury and Warwick are no simple peers.

Q. MAR. Not all these lords do vex me half so much
As that proud dame, the lord protector's wife.
She sweeps it through the court with troops of ladies,
More like an empress than duke Humphrey's wife.
Strangers in court do take her for the queen:
She bears a duke's revenues on her back,
And in her heart she scorns our poverty.
Shall I not live to be aveng'd on her?
Contemptuous base-born callet as she is,
She vaunted 'mongst her minions t'other day,
The very train of her worst wearing-gown
Was better worth than all my father's lands,
Till Suffolk gave two dukedoms for his daughter.

SUF. Madam, myself have lim'd a bush for her,
And plac'd a quire of such enticing birds,
That she will light to listen to the lays,
And never mount to trouble you again.
So let her rest: and, madam, list to me;
For I am bold to counsel you in this.
Although we fancy not the cardinal,
Yet must we join with him and with the lords,
Till we have brought duke Humphrey in disgrace.
As for the duke of York,—this late complaint
Will make but little for his benefit:
So, one by one, we'll weed them all at last,
And you yourself shall steer the happy helm.

Enter KING HENRY, YORK *and* SOMERSET; DUKE *and* DUCHESS *of* GLOUCESTER, CARDINAL BEAUFORT, BUCKINGHAM, SALISBURY, *and* WARWICK.

K. HEN. For my part, noble lords, I care not which;
Or Somerset or York, all's one to me.

YORK. If York have ill demean'd himself in France,
Then let him be denay'd[a] the regentship.

SOM. If Somerset be unworthy of the place,
Let York be regent; I will yield to him.

WAR. Whether your grace be worthy, yea or no,
Dispute not that York is the worthier.

CAR. Ambitious Warwick, let thy betters speak.

WAR. The cardinal's not my better in the field.

BUCK. All in this presence are thy betters, Warwick.

WAR. Warwick may live to be the best of all.

SAL. Peace, son!——and show some reason, Buckingham,
Why Somerset should be preferr'd in this.

Q. MAR. Because the king, forsooth, will have it so.

GLO. Madam, the king is old enough himself
To give his censure: these are no women's matters.

Q. MAR. If he be old enough, what needs your grace
To be protector of his excellence?

GLO. Madam, I am protector of the realm;
And, at his pleasure, will resign my place.

SUF. Resign it, then, and leave thine insolence.
Since thou wert king, (as who is king but thou?
The commonwealth hath daily run to wreck:
The Dauphin hath prevail'd beyond the seas;
And all the peers and nobles of the realm
Have been as bondmen to thy sovereignty.

CAR. The commons hast thou rack'd; the clergy's bags
Are lank and lean with thy extortions.

SOM. Thy sumptuous buildings, and thy wife's attire,
Have cost a mass of public treasury.

BUCK. Thy cruelty, in execution
Upon offenders, hath exceeded law,
And left thee to the mercy of the law.

Q. MAR. Thy sale of offices and towns in France,—
If they were known, as the suspect is great,—
Would make thee quickly hop without thy head.

[*Exit* GLOUCESTER. *The* QUEEN *drops her fan.*

Give me my fan: what, minion! can you not?

[*Gives the* DUCHESS *a box on the ear.*

I cry you mercy, madam; was it you?

DUCH. Was't I! yea, I it was, proud Frenchwoman:
Could I come near your beauty with my nails
I'd * set my ten commandments in your face.

K. HEN. Sweet aunt, be quiet; 'twas against her will.

DUCH. *Against her will!* good king, look to't in time;
She'll hamper thee, and dandle thee like a baby.
Though in this place most master wear no breeches,
She shall not strike dame Eleanor unreveng'd.

[*Exit.*

BUCK. Lord cardinal, I will follow Eleanor,
And listen after Humphrey, how he proceeds:

---

a Denay'd—] Denay was the old form of *deny*. So in "Twelfth Night," Act II, Sc. 4:—

"My love can give no place, bide no *denay*."

(*) Old text, *I could*.

She's tickled now; her fume can need* no spurs,
She'll gallop fast [a] enough to her destruction.
[*Exit.*

Re-enter GLOUCESTER.

GLO. Now, lords, my choler being over-blown,
With walking once about the quadrangle,
I come to talk of commonwealth affairs.
As for your spiteful false objections,
Prove them, and I lie open to the law:
But God in mercy so deal with my soul,
As I in duty love my king and country!
But, to the matter that we have in hand:—
I say, my sovereign, York is meetest man
To be your regent in the realm of France.
SUF. Before we make election, give me leave
To show some reason, of no little force,
That York is most unmeet of any man.
YORK. I'll tell thee, Suffolk, why I am unmeet.
First, for I cannot flatter thee in pride;
Next, if I be appointed for the place,
My lord of Somerset will keep me here,
Without discharge, money, or furniture,
Till France be won into the Dauphin's hands.
Last time, I danc'd attendance on his will
Till Paris was besieg'd, famish'd, and lost.
WAR. That I can witness; and a fouler fact
Did never traitor in the land commit.
SUF. Peace, head-strong Warwick!
WAR. Image of pride, why should I hold my peace?

Enter Servants *of* SUFFOLK, *bringing in* HORNER *and* PETER.

SUF. Because here is a man accus'd of treason;
Pray God the duke of York excuse himself!
YORK. Doth any one accuse York for a traitor?
K. HEN. What mean'st thou, Suffolk? tell me, what are these?
SUF. Please it your majesty, this is the man
That doth accuse his master of high treason:
His words were these;—that Richard, duke of York,
Was rightful heir unto the English crown;
And that your majesty was an usurper.
K. HEN. Say, man, were these thy words?
HOR. An't shall please your majesty, I never said nor thought any such matter: God is my witness, I am falsely accused by the villain.

PET. By these ten bones,[b] my lords [*holding up his hands*], he did speak them to me in the garret one night, as we were scouring my lord of York's armour.
YORK. Base dunghill villain, and mechanical,
I'll have thy head for this thy traitor's speech:—
I do beseech your royal majesty,
Let him have all the rigour of the law.
HOR. Alas, my lord, hang me if ever I spake the words. My accuser is my prentice; and when I did correct him for his fault the other day, he did vow upon his knees he would be even with me: I have good witness of this; therefore, I beseech your majesty, do not cast away an honest man for a villain's accusation.
K. HEN. Uncle, what shall we say to this in law?
GLO. This doom, my lord, if I may judge.
Let Somerset be regent o'er the French,
Because in York this breeds suspicion;
And let these have a day appointed them
For single combat in convenient place;
For he hath witness of his servant's malice:
This is the law, and this duke Humphrey's doom.
K. HEN. Then be it so.—My lord of Somerset,
We make your grace regent over the French.[c]
SOM. I humbly thank your royal majesty.
HOR. And I accept the combat willingly.
PET. Alas, my lord, I cannot fight! for God's sake, pity my case! the spite of man prevaileth against me. O Lord, have mercy upon me! I shall never be able to fight a blow: O Lord, my heart!
GLO. Sirrah, or you must fight, or else be hang'd.
K. HEN. Away with them to prison; and the day
Of combat shall be the last of the next month.—
Come, Somerset, we'll see thee sent away.
[*Exeunt.*

SCENE IV.—*The same. The* Duke *of* Gloucester's *Garden.*

Enter MARGERY JOURDAIN, HUME, SOUTHWELL, *and* BOLINGBROKE.

HUME. Come, my masters; the duchess, I tell you, expects performance of your promises.
BOLING. Master Hume, we are therefore pro-

(*) First folio, *fume needs.*

a *She'll gallop fast enough*—] In the old text, we have "*farre* enough." Corrected by Pope; and by Mr. Collier's annotator.

b By these ten bones,—] An old and a very common adjuration: thus, in the Mystery of "Candlemas-Day," 1512, quoted by Steevens:—

"But by their *bonys ten*, thei be to you untrue."

Again in Fletcher's "Monsieur Thomas," Act IV. Sc. 2:—

"By these *ten bones*, sir, if these eyes and ears
Can hear and see ——"

c Then be it so.—My lord of Somerset,
We make your grace regent over the French.]

These lines,—which are essential, since without them Somerset returns thanks for the regency before he is appointed,—were restored by Theobald from "The First Part of the Contention."

vided: will her ladyship behold and hear our exorcisms? [a]

HUME. Ay; what else? fear you not her courage.

BOLING. I have heard her reported to be a woman of an invincible spirit: but it shall be convenient, master Hume, that you be by her aloft, while we be busy below; and so, I pray you, go in God's name, and leave us. [*Exit* HUME.] Mother Jourdain, be you prostrate, and grovel on the earth:—John Southwell, read you;—and let us to our work.

Enter DUCHESS, *above.*

DUCH. Well said,[b] my masters; and welcome all. To this gear, the sooner the better.

BOLING. Patience, good lady; wizards know their times:
Deep night, dark night, the silent[c] of the night,
The time of night when Troy was set on fire;
The time when screech-owls cry, and ban-dogs howl,
And spirits walk, and ghosts break up their graves,—
That time best fits the work we have in hand.
Madam, sit you, and fear not; whom we raise,
We will make fast within a hallow'd verge.

[*Here they perform the ceremonies appertaining, and make the circle;* BOLINGBROKE *or* SOUTHWELL *reads,* Conjuro te, &c. *It thunders and lightens terribly; then the* Spirit *riseth.*

SPIR. *Adsum.*

M. JOURD. Asmath!
By the eternal God, whose name and power
Thou tremblest at, answer that I shall ask;
For, till thou speak, thou shalt not pass from hence.

SPIR. Ask what thou wilt:—that I had said and done! [d]

BOLING. *First, of the king: what shall of him become?* [*Reading out of a paper.*

SPIR. The duke yet lives that Henry shall depose;
But him outlive, and die a violent death.

[*As the* Spirit *speaks,* SOUTHWELL *writes the answer.*

BOLING. *What fates await the duke of Suffolk?*

SPIR. By water shall he die, and take his end.

---

a Exorcisms?] Mason was mistaken in asserting that Shakespeare's acceptation of *exorcise*, to raise spirits, not to lay them, was peculiar to him; it was the ordinary meaning of the word. See Minsheu, Dict. 1617. in voce "*Conjuration*," and Florio's "World of Words," 1611, under "*Esorcisma*."

b Well said,—] That is, *well done*. See note (b), p. 601, Vol. I.

c *The* silent *of the night,*—] So reads the folio 1623; but Steevens and Mason, as well as Mr. Collier's annotator, prefer the lection of the earlier version of the play,—

"—— the *silence* of the night."

d That I had said and done!] This impatience of *Asmath* is conformable to the ancient belief that spirits called to earth by spells and incantations were intolerant of question and eager to be dismissed.

BOLING. *What shall befal the duke of Somerset?*

SPIR. Let him shun castles;
Safer shall he be upon the sandy plains,
Than where castles mounted stand.—
Have done, for more I hardly can endure.

BOLING. Descend to darkness and the burning lake:
False fiend, avoid!

[*Thunder and lightning.* Spirit *descends.*

Enter YORK *and* BUCKINGHAM *hastily, with their* Guards, *and others.*

YORK. Lay hands upon these traitors and their trash.—
Beldame, I think we watch'd you at an inch.—
What, madam, are you there? The king and commonweal
Are deeply indebted for this piece of pains;

My lord protector will, I doubt it not,
See you well guerdon'd for these good deserts.

DUCH. Not half so bad as thine to England's king,
Injurious duke, that threatest where's no cause.

BUCK. True, madam, none at all: what call you this? [*Showing her the papers.*
Away with them! let them be clapp'd up close,
And kept asunder.—You, madam, shall with us:—
Stafford, take her to thee.——
We'll see your trinkets here all forthcoming;—
All, away! (2)

[*Exit* DUCHESS, *from above.* *Exeunt* Guards, *with* HUME, SOUTHWELL, BOLINGBROKE, *&c.*

YORK. Lord Buckingham, methinks, you watch'd her well:
A pretty plot, well chosen to build upon!
Now, pray, my lord, let's see the devil's writ.
What have we here? [*Reads.*
The duke yet lives that Henry shall depose;
But him outlive, and die a violent death.
Why, this is just
Aio te, Æacida, Romanos vincere posse.
Well, to the rest:
Tell me what fate awaits the duke of Suffolk?
By water shall he die, and take his end.—
What shall betide the duke of Somerset?
Let him shun castles;
Safer shall he be upon the sandy plains,
Than where castles mounted stand.
Come, come, my lords:
These oracles are hardily [a] attain'd,
And hardly understood.
The king is now in progress towards Saint Alban's,
With him the husband of this lovely lady:
Thither goes these news, as fast as horse can carry them;
A sorry breakfast for my lord protector.

BUCK. Your grace shall give me leave, my lord of York,
To be the post, in hope of his reward.

YORK. At your pleasure, my good lord.—
Who's within there, ho!

Enter a Servant.

Invite my lords of Salisbury and Warwick
To sup with me to-morrow night.—Away!
[*Exeunt.*

[a] *Are* hardily *attain'd*,—] *Hardily* is an emendation of Theobald; the old text has *hardly* both in this and the next line.

ACT II.

SCENE I.—Saint Alban's.

Enter KING HENRY, QUEEN MARGARET, GLOUCESTER, CARDINAL, *and* SUFFOLK, *with* Falconers *hollaing*.

Q. MAR. Believe me, lords, for flying at the brook,(1)
I saw not better sport these seven years' day:
Yet, by your leave, the wind was very high;
And, ten to one, old Joan had not gone out.

K. HEN. But what a point, my lord, your falcon made,
And what a pitch she flew above the rest!—
To see how God in all his creatures works!
Yea, man and birds are fain of climbing high.

SUF. No marvel, an it like your majesty,
My lord protector's hawks do tower so well;
They know their master loves to be aloft,
And bears his thoughts above his falcon's pitch.

GLO. My lord, 'tis but a base ignoble mind
That mounts no higher than a bird can soar.

CAR. I thought as much; he'd be above the clouds.

GLO. Ay, my lord cardinal,—how think you by that?
Were it not good your grace could fly to heaven?

K. HEN. The treasury of everlasting joy!

CAR. Thy heaven is on earth; thine eyes and thoughts
Beat on [a] a crown, the treasure of thy heart;
Pernicious protector, dangerous peer,
That smooth'st it so with king and commonweal!

GLO. What, cardinal, is your priesthood grown peremptory?
Tantæne animis cœlestibus iræ?
Churchmen so hot! good uncle, hide such malice;
With such holiness can you dote? [b]

SUF. No malice, sir; no more than well becomes
So good a quarrel and so bad a peer.

---

[a] Beat on *a crown*,—] Thus in "The Tempest," Act V. Sc. 1:—

"Do not infest your mind with *beating on*
The strangeness of this business."

And in "Hamlet," Act III. Sc. 1:—

"Whereon his brains still *beating*."

[b] *With such holiness can you* dote?] "Can you *do it*," is the lection of the old copies of the amended play, from which it seems impossible to extract any sense. Our reading, *dote*, is that of "The Contention," &c. 4to, 1594; and this word, in its ancient meaning *to rave, to speak madly*, is peculiarly appropriate to the context.

GLO. As who, my lord?
SUF. Why, as you, my lord;
An't like your lordly lord-protectorship.
GLO. Why, Suffolk, England knows thine insolence.
Q. MAR. And thy ambition, Gloster.
K. HEN. I pr'ythee, peace,
Good queen, and whet not on these furious peers,
For blessed are the peace-makers on earth.
CAR. Let me be blessed for the peace I make,
Against this proud protector, with my sword!
GLO. 'Faith, holy uncle, 'would 't were come to that! [*Aside to the* CARDINAL.
CAR. Marry, when thou dar'st. [*Aside to* GLO.
GLO. Make up no factious numbers for the matter;
In thine own person answer thy abuse. [*Aside to* CAR.
CAR. Ay, where thou dar'st not peep: an if thou dar'st,
This evening on the east side of the grove. [*Aside to* GLO.
K. HEN. How now, my lords!
CAR. Believe me, cousin Gloster,
Had not your man put up the fowl so suddenly,
We had had more sport.—Come with thy two-hand sword. [*Aside to* GLO.
GLO. True, uncle.
CAR. Are ye advis'd?—the east side of the grove?[a] [*Aside to* GLO.
GLO. Cardinal, I am with you. [*Aside to* CAR.
K. HEN. Why, how now, uncle Gloster!
GLO. Talking of hawking; nothing else, my lord.—
Now, by God's mother, priest, I'll shave your crown for this,
Or all my fence shall fail. [*Aside to* CAR.
CAR. *Medice teipsum;*
Protector, see to't well, protect yourself. [*Aside to* GLO.
K. HEN. The winds grow high; so do your stomachs, lords.
How irksome is this music to my heart!
When such strings jar, what hope of harmony?
I pray, my lords, let me compound this strife.

Enter an Inhabitant *of* Saint Alban's, *crying,* "A Miracle!"

GLO. What means this noise?
Fellow, what miracle dost thou proclaim?
INHAB. A miracle! a miracle!
SUF. Come to the king, and tell him what miracle.
INHAB. Forsooth, a blind man at Saint Alban's [shrine,
Within this half-hour hath receiv'd his sight;
A man that ne'er saw in his life before.
K. HEN. Now, God be prais'd! that to believing souls
Gives light in darkness, comfort in despair!

Enter the Mayor *of* St. Alban's *and his* Brethren; *and* SIMPCOX, *borne between two persons in a chair; his* Wife *and a great multitude following.*

CAR. Here come the townsmen on procession,
To present your highness with the man.
K. HEN. Great is his comfort in this earthly vale,
Although by his sight his sin be multiplied.
GLO. Stand by, my masters, bring him near the king;
His highness' pleasure is to talk with him.
K. HEN. Good fellow, tell us here the circumstance,
That we for thee may glorify the Lord.
What, hast thou been long blind, and now restor'd?
SIMP. Born blind, an't please your grace.
WIFE. Ay, indeed, was he.
SUF. What woman is this?
WIFE. His wife, an't like your worship.
GLO. Hadst thou been his mother, thou couldst have better told.
K. HEN. Where wert thou born?
SIMP. At Berwick, in the north, an't like your grace.
K. HEN. Poor soul! God's goodness hath been great to thee:
Let never day nor night unhallow'd pass,
But still remember what the Lord hath done.
Q. MAR. Tell me, good fellow, cam'st thou here by chance,
Or of devotion to this holy shrine?
SIMP. God knows, of pure devotion: being call'd
A hundred times and oft'ner, in my sleep
By good Saint Alban; who said,—*Simpcox,* come;*
Come, offer at my shrine, and I will help thee.
WIFE. Most true, forsooth; and many time and oft
Myself have heard a voice to call him so.
CAR. What, art thou lame?
SIMP. Ay, God Almighty help me!
SUF. How cam'st thou so?
SIMP. A fall off of a tree.
WIFE. A plum-tree, master.
GLO. How long hast thou been blind?
SIMP. O, born so, master.
GLO. What, and wouldst climb a tree?

[a] Are ye advis'd?—the east side of the grove?] In the old copies, this is made to form part of Gloucester's speech. Theobald properly assigned it to the Cardinal.

(*) Old text, *Symon*.

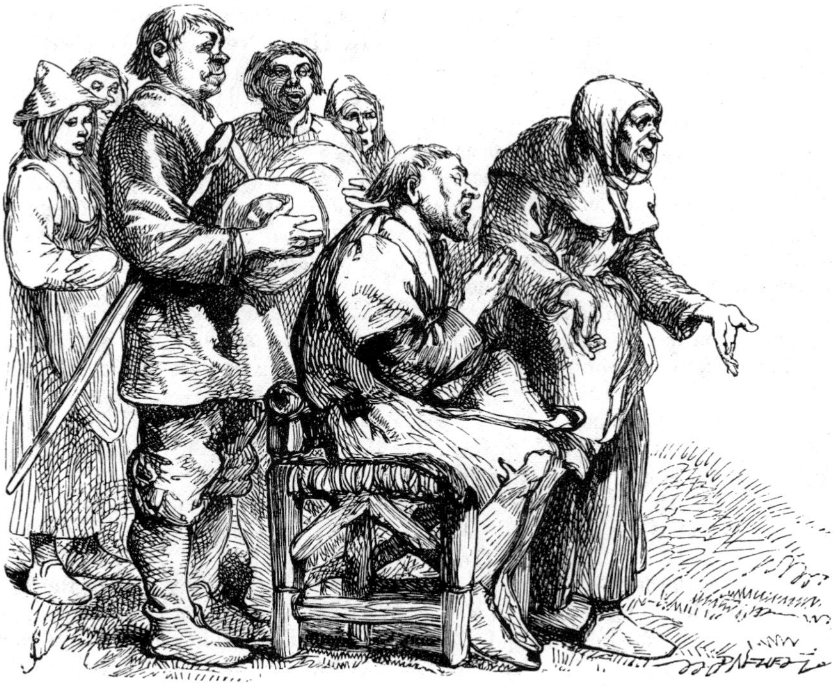

SIMP. But that in all my life, when I was a youth.

WIFE. Too true; and bought his climbing very dear.

GLO. Mass, thou lov'dst plums well, that wouldst venture so.

SIMP. Alas, good master, my wife desir'd some damsons,
And made me climb, with danger of my life.

GLO. A subtle knave! but yet it shall not serve.—
Let me see thine eyes:—wink now; now open them:—
In my opinion, yet thou seest not well.

SIMP. Yes, master, clear as day; I thank God, and Saint Alban.

GLO. Say'st thou me so? What colour is this cloak of?

SIMP. Red, master; red as blood.

GLO. Why, that's well said: what colour is my gown of?

SIMP. Black, forsooth; coal-black as jet.

K. HEN. Why, then, thou know'st what colour jet is of?

SUF. And yet, I think, jet did he never see.

GLO. But cloaks and gowns, before this day, a many.

WIFE. Never, before this day, in all his life.

GLO. Tell me, sirrah, what's my name?

SIMP. Alas, master, I know not.

GLO. What's his name?

SIMP. I know not.

GLO. Nor his?

SIMP. No, indeed, master.

GLO. What's thine own name?

SIMP. Saunder Simpcox, an if it please you, master.

GLO. Then, Saunder, sit there,[a] the lyingest knave
In Christendom. If thou hadst been born blind,
Thou mightst as well have known all our names, as thus
To name the several colours we do wear.
Sight may distinguish of colours; but suddenly
To nominate them all, it is impossible.—
My lords, Saint Alban here hath done a miracle;
And would ye not think his* cunning to be great,
That could restore this cripple to his legs again?

SIMP. O, master, that you could!

GLO. My masters of St. Alban's, have you not beadles in your town, and things called whips?

---

[a] Sit there,—] Capell reads—"sit *thou* there," and Mr. Collier's annotator restores the measure in the same way.

(*) Old text, *it*.

MAY. Yes, my lord, if it please your grace.

GLO. Then send for one presently.[a]

MAY. Sirrah, go fetch the beadle hither straight.
[*Exit an* Attendant.

GLO. Now fetch me a stool hither by and by.[b] [*A stool brought out.*] Now, sirrah, if you mean to save yourself from whipping, leap me over this stool and run away.

SIMP. Alas, master, I am not able to stand alone;
You go about to torture me in vain.

Re-enter Attendant, *with the* Beadle.

GLO. Well, sir, we must have you find your legs. Sirrah beadle, whip him till he leap over that same stool.

BEAD. I will, my lord.—Come on, sirrah: off with your doublet quickly.

SIMP. Alas, master, what shall I do? I am not able to stand.

[*After the* Beadle *hath hit him once, he leaps over the stool and runs away; and the people follow, and cry,* "A Miracle!"

K. HEN. O God, seest thou this, and bear'st so long?

Q. MAR. It made me laugh to see the villain run.

GLO. Follow the knave; and take this drab away.

WIFE. Alas, sir, we did it for pure need.

GLO. Let them be whipped through every market-town, till they come to Berwick, from whence they came.(2) [*Exeunt* Mayor, Beadle, Wife, *&c.*

CAR. Duke Humphrey has done a miracle today.

SUF. True; made the lame to leap and fly away.

GLO. But you have done more miracles than I:
You made in a day, my lord, whole towns to fly.

Enter BUCKINGHAM.

K. HEN. What tidings with our cousin Buckingham?

BUCK. Such as my heart doth tremble to unfold:
A sort[c] of naughty persons, lewdly[d] bent,—
Under the countenance and confederacy
Of lady Eleanor, the protector's wife,
The ringleader and head of all this rout,—
Have practis'd dangerously against your state,
Dealing with witches and with conjurors,
Whom we have apprehended in the fact,
Raising up wicked spirits from under ground,
Demanding of king Henry's life and death,
And other of your highness' privy council,
As more at large your grace shall understand.

CAR. And so, my lord protector, by this means
Your lady is forthcoming yet[e] at London.

---

a Presently.] *Immediately.*
b By and by.] *Directly, instantly.*

c A sort—] A *company.* d Lewdly—] *Wickedly.*
e Yet—] That is, *now.*

This news, I think, hath turn'd your weapon's edge;
'Tis like, my lord, you will not keep your hour.
[*Aside to* GLOUCESTER.

GLO. Ambitious churchman, leave to afflict my heart:
Sorrow and grief have vanquish'd all my powers:
And, vanquish'd as I am, I yield to thee,
Or to the meanest groom.

K. HEN. O God, what mischiefs work the wicked ones,
Heaping confusion on their own heads thereby!

Q. MAR. Gloster, see here the tainture of thy nest;
And look thyself be faultless, thou wert best.

GLO. Madam, for myself, to heaven I do appeal,
How I have lov'd my king and commonweal:
And, for my wife, I know not how it stands;
Sorry I am to hear what I have heard:
Noble she is; but if she have forgot
Honour and virtue, and convers'd with such
As, like to pitch, defile nobility,
I banish her my bed and company,
And give her, as a prey, to law and shame,
That hath dishonour'd Gloster's honest name.

K. HEN. Well, for this night, we will repose us here:
To-morrow toward London back again,
To look into this business thoroughly,
And call these foul offenders to their answers;
And poise the cause in justice' equal scales,
Whose beam stands sure, whose rightful cause prevails. [*Flourish. Exeunt.*

SCENE II.—London. *The* Duke *of* York's *Garden.*

Enter YORK, SALISBURY, *and* WARWICK.

YORK. Now, my good lords of Salisbury and Warwick,
Our simple supper ended, give me leave,
In this close walk, to satisfy myself,
In craving your opinion of my title,
Which is infallible, to England's crown.

SAL. My lord, I long to hear't at full.

WAR. Sweet York, begin: and if thy claim be good,
The Nevils are thy subjects to command.

YORK. Then thus—
Edward the third, my lords, had seven sons:
The first, Edward the Black Prince, prince of Wales;
The second, William of Hatfield; and the third,
Lionel, duke of Clarence; next to whom
Was John of Gaunt, the duke of Lancaster:
The fifth was Edmund Langley, duke of York;
The sixth was Thomas of Woodstock, duke of Gloster;
William of Windsor was the seventh, and last.
Edward, the Black Prince, died before his father;
And left behind him Richard, his only son,
Who, after Edward the third's death, reign'd as king;
Till Henry Bolingbroke, duke of Lancaster,
The eldest son and heir of John of Gaunt,
Crown'd by the name of Henry the fourth,
Seiz'd on the realm; depos'd the rightful king,
Sent his poor queen to France, from whence she came,
And him to Pomfret; where, as all you know,
Harmless Richard was murder'd traitorously.

WAR. Father, the duke hath told the truth;
Thus got the house of Lancaster the crown.

YORK. Which now they hold by force, and not by right;
For Richard, the first son's heir, being dead,
The issue of the next son should have reign'd.

SAL. But William of Hatfield died without an heir.

YORK. The third son, duke of Clarence (from whose line
I claim the crown), had issue—Philippe, a daughter:
Who married Edmund Mortimer, earl of March:
Edmund had issue—Roger, earl of March:
Roger had issue—Edmund, Anne, and Eleanor.

SAL. This Edmund, in the reign of Bolingbroke,
As I have read, laid claim unto the crown;
And, but for Owen Glendower, had been king,
Who kept him in captivity till he died.
But, to the rest.

YORK. His eldest sister, Anne,
My mother, being heir unto the crown,
Married Richard, earl of Cambridge; who was son
To Edmund Langley, Edward the third's fifth son.[a]
By her I claim the kingdom: she was heir
To Roger, earl of March; who was the son
Of Edmund Mortimer; who married Philippe,
Sole daughter unto Lionel, duke of Clarence:
So, if the issue of the elder son
Succeed before the younger, I am king.

WAR. What plain proceeding* is more plain than this?
Henry doth claim the crown from John of Gaunt,
The fourth son; York claims it from the third.
Till Lionel's issue fails, his should not reign:
It fails not yet, but flourishes in thee,
And in thy sons, fair slips of such a stock.—
Then, father Salisbury, kneel we together;
And, in this private plot, be we the first

(*) First folio, *proceedings.*

a Edward the third's fifth son.] In the old copies:—
"Marryed Richard, Earle of Cambridge
Who was to Edmond Langley,
Edward the thirds fift Sonnes Sonne."

That shall salute our rightful sovereign
With honour of his birthright to the crown.

BOTH. Long live our sovereign Richard, England's king!

YORK. We thank you, lords. But I am not your king
Till I be crown'd, and that my sword be stain'd
With heart-blood of the house of Lancaster;
And that's not suddenly to be perform'd,
But with advice and silent secrecy.
Do you as I do in these dangerous days,
Wink at the duke of Suffolk's insolence,
At Beaufort's pride, at Somerset's ambition,
At Buckingham, and all the crew of them,
Till they have snar'd the shepherd of the flock,
That virtuous prince, the good duke Humphrey:
'Tis that they seek; and they, in seeking that,
Shall find their deaths, if York can prophesy.

SAL. My lord, break we off; we know your mind at full.

WAR. My heart assures me that the earl of Warwick
Shall one day make the duke of York a king.

YORK. And, Nevil, this I do assure myself,—
Richard shall live to make the earl of Warwick
The greatest man in England, but the king.
[*Exeunt.*

SCENE III.—*The same. A Hall of Justice.*

Trumpets sounded. Enter KING HENRY, QUEEN MARGARET, GLOUCESTER, YORK, SUFFOLK, *and* SALISBURY; *the* DUCHESS *of* GLOUCESTER, MARGERY JOURDAIN, SOUTHWELL, HUME, *and* BOLINGBROKE, *under guard.*

K. HEN. Stand forth, dame Eleanor Cobham, Gloster's wife:
In sight of God and us, your guilt is great;
Receive the sentence of the law, for sins*
Such as by God's book are adjudg'd to death.—
You four, from hence to prison back again;
[*To* JOURDAIN, *&c.*
From thence unto the place of execution:
The witch in Smithfield shall be burn'd to ashes,
And you three shall be strangled on the gallows.—
You, madam, for you are more nobly born,
Despoiled of your honour in your life,
Shall, after three days' open penance done,
Live in your country here, in banishment,
With sir John Stanley, in the isle of Man.

DUCH. Welcome is banishment, welcome were my death.

GLO. Eleanor, the law, thou seest, hath judged thee:
I cannot justify whom the law condemns.—
[*Exeunt the* DUCHESS, *and the other prisoners, guarded.*
Mine eyes are full of tears, my heart of grief.
Ah, Humphrey, this dishonour in thine age
Will bring thy head with sorrow to the ground!—
I beseech your majesty give me leave to go;
Sorrow would solace, and mine age would ease.[a]

K. HEN. Stay, Humphrey duke of Gloster: ere thou go,
Give up thy staff; Henry will to himself
Protector be: and God shall be my hope,
My stay, my guide, and lantern to my feet;
And go in peace, Humphrey;—no less belov'd,
Than when thou wert protector to thy king.

Q. MAR. I see no reason why a king of years
Should be to be protected like a child.—
God and king Henry govern England's helm!—[b]
Give up your staff, sir, and the king his realm.

GLO. My staff!—here, noble Henry, is my staff:[c]
As willingly do I the same resign,
As ere thy father Henry made it mine;
And even as willingly at thy feet I leave it,
As others would ambitiously receive it.
Farewell, good king; when I am dead and gone,
May honourable peace attend thy throne! [*Exit.*

Q. MAR. Why, now is Henry king, and Margaret queen;
And Humphrey duke of Gloster scarce himself,
That bears so shrewd a maim; two pulls at once,—
His lady banish'd, and a limb lopp'd off;
This staff of honour raught,[d] there let it stand,
Where it best fits to be,—in Henry's hand.

SUF. Thus droops this lofty pine, and hangs his sprays;
Thus Eleanor's pride dies in her youngest[e] days.

YORK. Lords, let him go.—Please it your majesty,
This is the day appointed for the combat;
And ready are the appellant and defendant,
The armourer and his man, to enter the lists,
So please your highness to behold the fight.

Q. MAR. Ay, good my lord; for purposely therefore
Left I the court, to see this quarrel tried.

(*) Old text, *sinne.*

[a] Sorrow would solace, and mine age would ease.] That is, "Sorrow would *have* solace, and age would *have* ease."

[b] *God and king Henry govern England's* helm!] In the old text,—"England's *realme.*" The correction is Johnson's.

[c] My staff!—here, noble Henry, is my staff:] At this point Mr. Collier's annotator interpolates a line of such sheer absurdity,—

"*To think I fain would keep it makes me laugh!*"

that it is hard to believe he was not attempting a joke. This miserable puerility, we are grieved to find, Mr. Collier not only approves, but actually inserts as Shakespeare's, in his edition of the poet's works just published.

[d] Raught,—] That is, *reft, riven.*

[e] *Thus Eleanor's pride dies in her* youngest *days.*] For *youngest* Mr. Collier's annotator substitutes *proudest;* and a marginal note in Mr. Singer's copy of the second folio proposes *strongest.* The genuine word, there can be little doubt, was *haughtiest* or *proudest.*

K. HEN. O' God's name, see the lists and all things fit;
Here let them end it, and God defend the right!

YORK. I never saw a fellow worse bested,
Or more afraid to fight, than is the appellant,
The servant of this armourer, my lords.

Enter, on one side, HORNER, *and his neighbours, the former bearing his staff with a sand-bag fastened to it;*(3) *a drum before him; during the scene he drinks with so many that he becomes drunk: at the other side,* PETER *enters, with a similar staff, and a drummer before him; accompanied by* Prentices *drinking to him.*

1 NEIGH. Here, neighbour Horner, I drink to you in a cup of sack; and fear not, neighbour, you shall do well enough.

2 NEIGH. And here, neighbour, here's a cup of charneco.[a]

3 NEIGH. And here's a pot of good double-beer, neighbour: drink, and fear not your man.

HOR. Let it come, i'faith, and I'll pledge you all; and a fig for Peter!

1 PREN. Here, Peter, I drink to thee; and be not afraid.

2 PREN. Be merry, Peter, and fear not thy master: fight for credit of the prentices.

PETER. I thank you all: drink, and pray for me, I pray you; for I think I have taken my last draught in this world.—Here, Robin, an if I die, I give thee my apron; and, Will, thou shalt have my hammer:—and here, Tom, take all the money that I have.—O Lord, bless me, I pray God! for I am never able to deal with my master, he hath learnt so much fence already.

SAL. Come, leave your drinking, and fall to blows.—Sirrah, what's thy name?

PETER. Peter, forsooth.

SAL. Peter! what more?

PETER. Thump.

SAL. *Thump!* then see thou thump thy master well.

HOR. Masters, I am come hither, as it were, upon my man's instigation, to prove him a knave, and myself an honest man: and touching the duke of York, I will take my death, I never meant him any ill, nor the king, nor the queen: and therefore, Peter, have at thee with a downright blow.

YORK. Dispatch;—this knave's tongue begins [to double.
Sound, trumpets, alarum to the combatants!

[*Alarum. They fight, and* PETER *strikes down his master.*(4)

HOR. Hold, Peter, hold! I confess, I confess treason. [*Dies.*

YORK. Take away his weapon:—Fellow, thank God, and the good wine in thy master's way.

PETER. O God! have I overcome mine enemy* in this presence? O Peter, thou hast prevailed in right!

K. HEN. Go, take hence that traitor from our [sight;
For by his death we do perceive his guilt:
And God in justice hath reveal'd to us
The truth and innocence of this poor fellow,
Which he had thought to have murder'd wrongfully.—
Come, fellow, follow us for thy reward. [*Exeunt.*

SCENE IV.—*The same. A Street.*

Enter GLOUCESTER *and* Servants, *in mourning cloaks.*

GLO. Thus sometimes hath the brightest day a cloud;
And after summer evermore succeeds
Barren winter, with his wrathful nipping cold:
So cares and joys abound, as seasons fleet.—
Sirs, what's o'clock?

SERV. Ten, my lord.

GLO. Ten is the hour that was appointed me
To watch the coming of my punish'd duchess;
Uneath[b] may she endure the flinty streets,
To tread them with her tender-feeling feet.
Sweet Nell, ill can thy noble mind abrook
The abject people gazing on thy face,
With envious looks, laughing at thy shame,[c]
That erst did follow thy proud chariot-wheels,
When thou didst ride in triumph through the streets.
But, soft! I think she comes; and I'll prepare
My tear-stain'd eyes to see her miseries.

Enter the DUCHESS *of* GLOUCESTER *in a white sheet, with papers pinned upon her back, her feet bare, and a taper burning in her hand; Sir* JOHN STANLEY, *the* Sheriff, *and* Officers.

SERV. So please your grace, we'll take her from the sheriff.

GLO. No, stir not, for your lives! let her pass [by.

DUCH. Come you, my lord, to see my open shame?
Now thou dost penance too. Look, how they [gaze!
See how the giddy multitude do point,

[a] Charneco.] This is a wine often mentioned by the writers of Shakespeare's time, and so named from a village near Lisbon, where it was made.

[b] Uneath—] *Hardly, painfully, scarcely.*

[c] With envious looks, laughing at thy shame,—] So, both in the folio 1623, and in the "Contention;" but the second folio has,—"With envious looks, *still* laughing at thy shame."

(*) First folio, *Enemies.*

And nod their heads and throw their eyes on thee!
Ah, Gloster, hide thee from their hateful looks;
And, in thy closet pent up, rue my shame,
And ban thine enemies, both mine and thine.

Glo. Be patient, gentle Nell; forget this grief.

Duch. Ah, Gloster, teach me to forget myself!
For, whilst I think I am thy married wife,
And thou a prince, protector of this land,
Methinks I should not thus be led along,
Mail'd up[a] in shame, with papers on my back,
And follow'd with a rabble, that rejoice
To see my tears, and hear my deep-fet groans.
The ruthless flint doth cut my tender feet;
And when I start, the envious people laugh,
And bid me be advised how I tread.
Ah, Humphrey, can I bear this shameful yoke?
Trow'st thou that ere I'll look upon the world,
Or count them happy that enjoy the sun?
No; dark shall be my light, and night my day;
To think upon my pomp shall be my hell.
Sometime I'll say, I am duke Humphrey's wife;
And he a prince, and ruler of the land:
Yet so he rul'd, and such a prince he was,
As he stood by, whilst I, his forlorn duchess,
Was made a wonder and a pointing-stock
To every idle rascal follower.
But be thou mild, and blush not at my shame;
Nor stir at nothing, till the axe of death
Hang over thee, as, sure, it shortly will.
For Suffolk,—he that can do all in all
With her that hateth thee and hates us all,—
And York, and impious Beaufort, that false priest,
Have all lim'd bushes to betray thy wings,
And, fly thou how thou canst, they'll tangle thee:
But fear not thou, until thy foot be snar'd,
Nor never seek prevention of thy foes.

Glo. Ah, Nell, forbear! thou aimest all awry;
I must offend, before I be attainted:
And had I twenty times so many foes,
And each of them had twenty times their power,
All these could not procure me any scathe,
So long as I am loyal, true, and crimeless.

[a] Mail'd up—] *Wrapped up, inclosed.* "*Mail a hawk* is to wrap her up in a handkerchief or other cloath, that she may not be able to stir her wings or struggle."—R. Holme's *Acad. of Armory*, 1688, b. ii. p. 239, quoted by Mr. Dyce.

Wouldst have me rescue thee from this reproach?
Why, yet thy scandal were not wip'd away,
But I in danger for the breach of law.
Thy greatest help is quiet, gentle Nell:
I pray thee, sort thy heart to patience;
These few days' wonder will be quickly worn.

Enter a Herald.

HER. I summon your grace to his majesty's Parliament, holden at Bury the first of this next month.

GLO. And my consent ne'er ask'd herein before!
This is close dealing.—Well, I will be there.
[*Exit* Herald.
My Nell, I take my leave:—and, master sheriff,
Let not her penance exceed the king's commission.

SHER. An't please your grace, here my commission stays:
And sir John Stanley is appointed now
To take her with him to the isle of Man.

GLO. Must you, sir John, protect my lady here?

STAN. So am I given in charge, may't please your grace.

GLO. Entreat her not the worse, in that I pray
You use her well: the world may laugh again:[a]
And I may live to do you kindness, if
You do it her. And so, sir John, farewell.

DUCH. What! gone, my lord; and bid me not farewell!

GLO. Witness my tears, I cannot stay to speak.
[*Exeunt* GLOUCESTER *and* Servants.

DUCH. Art thou gone too? All comfort go with thee!
For none abides with me: my joy is death,—
Death, at whose name I oft have been afeard,
Because I wish'd this world's eternity.—
Stanley, I pr'ythee, go, and take me hence;
I care not whither, for I beg no favour,
Only convey me where thou art commanded.

STAN. Why, madam, that is to the isle of Man;
There to be us'd according to your state.

DUCH. That's bad enough, for I am but reproach,—
And shall I then be us'd reproachfully?

STAN. Like to a duchess, and duke Humphrey's lady,
According to that state you shall be us'd.

DUCH. Sheriff, farewell, and better than I fare,—
Although thou hast been conduct[b] of my shame!

SHER. It is my office; and, madam, pardon me.

DUCH. Ay, ay, farewell; thy office is discharg'd—
Come, Stanley, shall we go?

STAN. Madam, your penance done, throw off this sheet,
And go we to attire you for our journey.

DUCH. My shame will not be shifted with my sheet:
No, it will hang upon my richest robes,
And show itself, attire me how I can.
Go, lead the way; I long to see my prison.
[*Exeunt.*

---

a The world may laugh again:] Equivalent to, *Fortune may smile again.*
b Conduct—] *Conductor.*

ACT III.

SCENE I.—*The Abbey at* Bury St. Edmund's.

Sennet. Enter to the Parliament, King Henry, Queen Margaret, Cardinal Beaufort, Suffolk, York, Buckingham, *and others.*

K. Hen. I muse my lord of Gloster is not come;
'Tis not his wont to be the hindmost man,
Whate'er occasion keeps him from us now.

Q. Mar. Can you not see? or will ye not observe
The strangeness of his alter'd countenance?
With what a majesty he bears himself;
How insolent of late he is become,
How proud, how peremptory, and unlike himself?
We know the time since he was mild and affable;
And if we did but glance a far-off look,
Immediately he was upon his knee,
That all the court admir'd him for submission;
But meet him now, an be it in the morn,
When every one will give the time of day,
He knits his brow, and shows an angry eye,
And passeth by with stiff unbowed knee,
Disdaining duty that to us belongs.
Small curs are not regarded when they grin;
But great men tremble when the lion roars;
And Humphrey is no little man in England.
First, note, that he is near you in descent;
And should you fall, he is the next will mount.
Me seemeth then, it is no policy,—
Respecting what a rancorous mind he bears,
And his advantage following your decease,—
That he should come about your royal person,

Or be admitted to your highness' council.
By flattery hath he won the commons' hearts:
And, when he please to make commotion,
'Tis to be fear'd, they all will follow him.
Now 'tis the spring, and weeds are shallow-rooted;
Suffer them now, and they'll o'ergrow the garden,
And choke the herbs for want of husbandry.
The reverent care I bear unto my lord
Made me collect these dangers in the duke.
If it be fond, call it a woman's fear;
Which fear, if better reasons can supplant,
I will subscribe, and say I wrong'd the duke.
My lord of Suffolk,—Buckingham,—and York,—
Reprove my allegation, if you can;
Or else conclude my words effectual.

SUF. Well hath your highness seen into this duke;
And, had I first been put to speak my mind,
I think I should have told your grace's tale.
The duchess, by his subornation,
Upon my life, began her devilish practices;
Or, if he were not privy to those faults,
Yet, by reputing[a] of his high descent
As, next the king, he was successive heir,—
And such high vaunts of his nobility,—
Did instigate the bedlam brain-sick duchess
By wicked means to frame our sovereign's fall.
Smooth runs the water where the brook is deep;
And in his simple show he harbours treason:
The fox barks not when he would steal the lamb.
No, no, my sovereign; Gloster is a man
Unsounded yet, and full of deep deceit.

CAR. Did he not, contrary to form of law,
Devise strange deaths for small offences done?

YORK. And did he not, in his protectorship,
Levy great sums of money through the realm,
For soldiers' pay in France, and never sent it?
By means whereof, the towns each day revolted.

BUCK. Tut! these are petty faults to faults unknown,
Which time will bring to light in smooth duke Humphrey.

K. HEN. My lords, at once:—the care you have of us,
To mow down thorns that would annoy our foot,
Is worthy praise; but shall I speak my conscience?
Our kinsman Gloster is as innocent
From meaning treason to our royal person,
As is the sucking lamb or harmless dove:
The duke is virtuous, mild, and too well given
To dream on evil, or to work my downfall.

Q. MAR. Ah, what's more dangerous than this fond affiance!
Seems he a dove? his feathers are but borrow'd,
For he's disposed as the hateful raven.
Is he a lamb? his skin is surely lent him,
For he's inclin'd as is the ravenous wolf.*
Who cannot steal a shape that means deceit?
Take heed, my lord; the welfare of us all
Hangs on the cutting short that fraudful man.

Enter SOMERSET.

SOM. All health unto my gracious sovereign!

K. HEN. Welcome, lord Somerset. What news from France?

SOM. That all your interest in those territories
Is utterly bereft you; all is lost.

K. HEN. Cold news, lord Somerset: but God's will be done!

YORK. [*Aside.*] Cold news for me; for I had hope of France,
As firmly as I hope for fertile England.
Thus are my blossoms blasted in the bud,
And caterpillars eat my leaves away:
But I will remedy this gear ere long,
Or sell my title for a glorious grave.

Enter GLOUCESTER.

GLO. All happiness unto my lord the king!
Pardon, my liege, that I have stay'd so long.

SUF. Nay, Gloster, know, that thou art come too soon,
Unless thou wert more loyal than thou art:
I do arrest thee of high treason here.

GLO. Well, Suffolk, yet[b] thou shalt not see me blush,
Nor change my countenance for this arrest;
A heart unspotted is not easily daunted.
The purest spring is not so free from mud,
As I am clear from treason to my sovereign:
Who can accuse me? wherein am I guilty?

YORK. 'Tis thought, my lord, that you took bribes of France,
And, being protector, stay'd the soldiers' pay;
By means whereof his highness hath lost France.

GLO. Is it but thought so? What are they that think it?
I never robb'd the soldiers of their pay,
Nor ever had one penny bribe from France.
So help me God, as I have watch'd the night,—
Ay, night by night,—in studying good for England!
That doit that e'er I wrested from the king,
Or any groat I hoarded to my use,

---

[a] Reputing—] Not, as it is invariably explained, *valuing himself*, but *presuming, boasting*. See Florio's "World of Words," 1611, in voce, *Riputatione*.

[b] Yet *thou shalt not see me blush,*—] *Yet* was added in the second folio. The parallel line in the "Contention" reads,—"Why, *Suffolke's Duke*," &c.

(*) Old text, *Wolves*.

Be brought against me at my trial-day!
No; many a pound of mine own proper store,
Because I would not tax the needy commons,
Have I dispursed to the garrisons,
And never ask'd for restitution.

CAR. It serves you well, my lord, to say so much.

GLO. I say no more than truth, so help me God!

YORK. In your protectorship you did devise
Strange tortures for offenders, never heard of,
That England was defam'd by tyranny.

GLO. Why, 'tis well known, that whiles I was protector,
Pity was all the fault that was in me;
For I should melt at an offender's tears,
And lowly words were ransom for their fault.
Unless it were a bloody murderer,
Or foul felonious thief that fleec'd poor passengers,
I never gave them condign punishment:
Murder, indeed, that bloody sin, I tortur'd
Above the felon, or what trespass else.

SUF. My lord, these faults are easy, quickly answer'd:
But mightier crimes are laid unto your charge,
Whereof you cannot easily purge yourself.
I do arrest you in his highness' name;
And here commit you to my lord cardinal
To keep, until your further time of trial.

K. HEN. My Lord of Gloster, 'tis my special hope,
That you will clear yourself from all suspect;[a]
My conscience tells me you are innocent.

GLO. Ah, gracious lord, these days are dangerous!
Virtue is chok'd with foul ambition,
And charity chas'd hence by rancour's hand;
Foul subornation is predominant,
And equity exil'd your highness' land.
I know their complot is to have my life;
And, if my death might make this island happy,
And prove the period of their tyranny,
I would expend it with all willingness:
But mine is made the prologue to their play;
For thousands more, that yet suspect no peril,
Will not conclude their plotted tragedy.
Beaufort's red sparkling eyes blab his heart's malice,
And Suffolk's cloudy brow his stormy hate;
Sharp Buckingham unburdens with his tongue
The envious load that lies upon his heart;
And dogged York, that reaches at the moon,
Whose overweening arm I have pluck'd back,
By false accuse doth level at my life:—
And you, my sovereign lady, with the rest,
Causeless have laid disgraces on my head,
And with your best endeavour have stirr'd up
My liefest[b] liege to be mine enemy:—
Ay, all of you have laid your heads together
(Myself had notice of your conventicles)
And all to make away my guiltless life.
I shall not want false witness to condemn me,
Nor store of treasons to augment my guilt;
The ancient proverb will be well effected,—
A staff is quickly found to beat a dog.

CAR. My liege, his railing is intolerable:
If those that care to keep your royal person
From treason's secret knife, and traitors' rage,
Be thus upbraided, chid, and rated at,
And the offender granted scope of speech,
'Twill make them cool in zeal unto your grace.

SUF. Hath he not twit our sovereign lady here
With ignominious words, though clerkly couch'd,
As if she had suborned some to swear
False allegations to o'erthrow his state?

Q. MAR. But I can give the loser leave to chide.

GLO. Far truer spoke than meant: I lose, indeed;—
Beshrew the winners, for they play'd me false!
And well such losers may have leave to speak.

BUCK. He'll wrest the sense, and hold us here all day:—
Lord cardinal, he is your prisoner.

CAR. Sirs, take away the duke, and guard him sure.

GLO. Ah, thus king Henry throws away his crutch,
Before his legs be firm to bear his body!
Thus is the shepherd beaten from thy side,
And wolves are gnarling who shall gnaw thee first.
Ah, that my fear were false! ah, that it were!
For, good king Henry, thy decay I fear.
[*Exit guarded.*

K. HEN. My lords, what to your wisdoms seemeth best,
Do, or undo, as if ourself were here.

Q. MAR. What, will your highness leave the parliament?

K. HEN. Ay, Margaret; my heart is drown'd with grief,
Whose flood begins to flow within mine eyes;
My body round engirt with misery,—
For what's more miserable than discontent?—
Ah, uncle Humphrey! in thy face I see
The map of honour, truth, and loyalty!
And yet, good Humphrey, is the hour to come,
That e'er I prov'd thee false, or fear'd thy faith.
What lowering star now envies thy estate,
That these great lords, and Margaret our queen,
Do seek subversion of thy harmless life?
Thou never didst them wrong, nor no man wrong;
And as the butcher takes away the calf,

---

a From all suspect;] So Capell and Mr. Collier's annotator. The old copies have *suspense*.

b Liefest—] *Dearest*.

And binds the wretch, and beats it when it strays,
Bearing it to the bloody slaughter-house;
Even so, remorseless, have they borne him hence,
And as the dam runs lowing up and down,
Looking the way her harmless young one went,
And can do nought but wail her darling's loss;
Even so myself bewails good Gloster's case,
With sad unhelpful tears; and with dimm'd eyes
Look after him, and cannot do him good,—
So mighty are his vowed enemies.
His fortunes I will weep; and, 'twixt each groan,
Say—*Who's a traitor,*[a] *Gloster he is none.* [*Exit.*

Q. MAR. Free lords, cold snow melts with the sun's hot beams:
Henry my lord is cold in great affairs,
Too full of foolish pity: and Gloster's show
Beguiles him, as the mournful crocodile
With sorrow snares relenting passengers;
Or as the snake, roll'd in a flowering bank,
With shining checker'd slough, doth sting a child,
That for the beauty thinks it excellent.
Believe me, lords, were none more wise than I
(And yet herein I judge mine own wit good),
This Gloster should be quickly rid the world,
To rid us from the fear we have of him.

CAR. That he should die is worthy policy;
But yet we want a colour for his death:
'Tis meet he be condemn'd by course of law.

SUF. But, in my mind, that were no policy:
The king will labour still to save his life;
The commons haply rise to save his life;
And we have yet but trivial argument,
More than mistrust, that shows him worthy death.

YORK. So that, by this, you would not have him die.

SUF. Ah, York, no man alive so fain as I!

YORK. 'Tis York that hath more reason for his death.—
But, my lord cardinal, and you, my lord of Suffolk,—
Say as you think, and speak it from your souls,—
Wer't not all one, an empty eagle were set
To guard the chicken from a hungry kite,
As place duke Humphrey for the king's protector?

Q. MAR. So the poor chicken should be sure of death.

SUF. Madam, 'tis true: and wer't not madness then,
To make the fox surveyor of the fold?
Who being accus'd a crafty murderer,
His guilt should be but idly posted over,
Because his purpose is not executed.
No; let him die, in that he is a fox,
By nature prov'd an enemy to the flock,
Before his chaps be stain'd with crimson blood,—
As Humphrey, prov'd by reasons, to my liege.
And do not stand on quillets how to slay him:
Be it by gins, by snares, by subtlety,
Sleeping or waking, 'tis no matter how,
So he be dead; for that is good deceit
Which mates[b] him first that first intends deceit.

Q. MAR. Thrice noble Suffolk, 'tis resolutely spoke.

SUF. Not resolute, except so much were done;
For things are often spoke, and seldom meant:
But, that my heart accordeth with my tongue,—
Seeing the deed is meritorious,
And to preserve my sovereign from his foe,—
Say but the word, and I will be his priest.

CAR. But I would have him dead, my lord of Suffolk,
Ere you can take due orders for a priest.
Say, you consent, and censure well the deed,
And I'll provide his executioner,—
I tender so the safety of my liege.

SUF. Here is my hand, the deed is worthy doing.

Q. MAR. And so say I.

YORK. And I: and now we three have spoke it,
It skills[c] not greatly who impugns our doom.

Enter a Messenger.

MESS. Great lords, from Ireland am I come amain.
To signify—that rebels there are up,
And put the Englishmen unto the sword:
Send succours, lords, and stop the rage betime,
Before the wound do grow uncurable;
For, being green, there is great hope of help.

CAR. A breach, that craves a quick expedient stop!
What counsel give you in this weighty cause?

YORK. That Somerset be sent as regent thither;
'Tis meet, that lucky ruler be employ'd;
Witness the fortune he hath had in France.

SOM. If York, with all his far-fet policy,
Had been the regent there instead of me,
He never would have stay'd in France so long.

YORK. No, not to lose it all, as thou hast done:
I rather would have lost my life betimes,
Than bring a burden of dishonour home,
By staying there so long, till all were lost.
Show me one scar character'd on thy skin:
Men's flesh preserv'd so whole do seldom win.

Q. MAR. Nay, then, this spark will prove a raging fire,
If wind and fuel be brought to feed it with:—

---

[a] Who's *a traitor,*—] That is, *Whoe'er's* a traitor.

[b] Mates—] This appears to be an allusion to the check-*mate*, or stale-*mate*, in the game of chess; but it may mean merely, *confounds* or *destroys*.

[c] *It* skills *not*—] *It matters not, It is not important.* We often find to *force* bearing the same signification:—"Our enemies beare the poore people in hand that theirs is the old religion, and oures is an yesterdaies bird: but sooner or later called, *it skilleth not*, old or new, if true, *it forceth not*."—PRIME, *On Galathians*, p. 44.

No more, good York;—sweet Somerset, be still;—
Thy fortune, York, hadst thou been regent there,
Might happily have been far worse than his.

YORK. What, worse than naught? nay, then a shame take all!

SOM. And in the number, thee, that wishest shame!

CAR. My lord of York, try what your fortune is.
The uncivil kerns of Ireland are in arms,
And temper clay with blood of Englishmen:
To Ireland will you lead a band of men,
Collected choicely, from each county some,
And try your hap against the Irishmen?

YORK. I will, my lord, so please his majesty.

SUF. Why, our authority is his consent;
And what we do establish he confirms:
Then, noble York, take thou this task in hand.

YORK. I am content: provide me soldiers, lords,
Whiles I take orders for mine own affairs.

SUF. A charge, lord York, that I will see perform'd.
But now return we to the false duke Humphrey.

CAR. No more of him; for I will deal with him,
That henceforth he shall trouble us no more.
And so break off; the day is almost spent:
Lord Suffolk, you and I must talk of that event.

YORK. My lord of Suffolk, within fourteen days
At Bristol I expect my soldiers;
For there I'll ship them all for Ireland.

SUF. I'll see it truly done, my lord of York.
[*Exeunt all except* YORK.

YORK. Now, York, or never, steel thy fearful thoughts,
And change misdoubt to resolution:
Be that thou hop'st to be; or what thou art
Resign to death—it is not worth the enjoying:
Let pale-fac'd fear keep with the mean-born man,
And find no harbour in a royal heart.
Faster than spring time showers comes thought on thought,
And not a thought but thinks on dignity.
My brain, more busy than the labouring spider,
Weaves tedious snares to trap mine enemies.
Well, nobles, well, 'tis politicly done,
To send me packing with an host of men:
I fear me, you but warm the starved snake,
Who, cherish'd in your breasts, will sting your hearts.
'Twas men I lack'd, and you will give them me:
I take it kindly; yet, be well assur'd,
You put sharp weapons in a madman's hands.
Whiles I in Ireland nourish a mighty band,
I will stir up in England some black storm,
Shall blow ten thousand souls to heaven or hell:
And this fell tempest shall not cease to rage
Until the golden circuit on my head,
Like to the glorious sun's transparent beams,
Do calm the fury of this mad-bred flaw.[a]
And, for a minister of my intent,
I have seduc'd a head-strong Kentishman,
John Cade of Ashford,
To make commotion, as full well he can,
Under the title of John Mortimer.
In Ireland have I seen this stubborn Cade
Oppose himself against a troop of kerns;
And fought so long, till that his thighs with darts
Were almost like a sharp-quill'd porcupine:
And, in the end being rescu'd, I have seen him
Caper upright like a wild Mórisco,(1)
Shaking the bloody darts, as he his bells.
Full often, like a shag-hair'd crafty kern,
Hath he conversed with the enemy;
And, undiscover'd, come to me again,
And given me notice of their villanies.
This devil here shall be my substitute;
For that John Mortimer, which now is dead,
In face, in gait, in speech, he doth resemble:
By this I shall perceive the commons' mind,
How they affect the house and claim of York.
Say, he be taken, rack'd, and tortured,
I know no pain they can inflict upon him,
Will make him say I mov'd him to those arms.
Say, that he thrive (as 'tis great like he will),
Why, then from Ireland come I with my strength,
And reap the harvest which that rascal sow'd:
For, Humphrey being dead, as he shall be,
And Henry put apart, the next for me. [*Exit.*

SCENE II.—Bury. *A Room in the Palace.*

Enter certain Murderers, *hastily.*(2)

1 MUR. Run to my lord of Suffolk; let him know
We have despatch'd the duke, as he commanded.

2 MUR. O, that it were to do!—What have we done!
Didst ever hear a man so penitent?

1 MUR. Here comes my lord.

Enter SUFFOLK.

SUF. Now, sirs, have you despatch'd this thing?

1 MUR. Ay, my good lord, he's dead.

SUF. Why, that's well said. Go, get you to my house;
I will reward you for this venturous deed.
The king and all the peers are here at hand:—
Have you laid fair the bed? are all things well,
According as I gave directions?

---

[a] *Mad-bred* flaw.] *Flaw* here means a violent *gust* of wind, as in "Hamlet," Act V. Sc. 1:—

"Should patch a wall to expel the winter's *flaw!*"

1 Mur. 'Tis, my good lord.
Suf. Away! be gone. [*Exeunt* Murderers.

Trumpets sounded. Enter King Henry, Queen Margaret, Cardinal Beaufort, Somerset, Lords, *and others.*

K. Hen. Go, call our uncle to our presence straight;
Say we intend to try his grace to-day,
If he be guilty, as 'tis published.
Suf. I'll call him presently, my noble lord. [*Exit.*
K. Hen. Lords, take your places;—and, I pray you all,
Proceed no straiter 'gainst our uncle Gloster,
Than from true evidence, of good esteem,
He be approv'd in practice culpable.
Q. Mar. God forbid any malice should prevail,
That faultless may condemn a nobleman!
Pray God he may acquit him of suspicion!
K. Hen. I thank thee, Margaret;* these words content me much.—

Re-enter Suffolk.

How now! why look'st thou pale? why tremblest thou?
Where is our uncle? what's the matter, Suffolk?

(*) Old text, *Nell.*

Suf. Dead in his bed, my lord! Gloster is dead!
Q. Mar. Marry, God forefend!
Car. God's secret judgment!—I did dream to-night,
The duke was dumb, and could not speak a word. [*The* King *swoons.*
Q. Mar. How fares my lord?—Help, lords! the king is dead.
Som. Rear up his body; wring him by the nose.
Q. Mar. Run, go, help, help!—O Henry, ope thine eyes!
Suf. He doth revive again;—madam, be patient.
K. Hen. O heavenly God!
Q. Mar. How fares my gracious lord?
Suf. Comfort, my sovereign! gracious Henry, comfort!
K. Hen. What, doth my lord of Suffolk comfort me?
Came he right now to sing a raven's note,
Whose dismal tune bereft my vital powers;
And thinks he that the chirping of a wren,
By crying comfort from a hollow breast,
Can chase away the first-conceived sound?
Hide not thy poison with such sugar'd words.
Lay not thy hands on me; forbear, I say;
Their touch affrights me, as a serpent's sting.
Thou baleful messenger, out of my sight!
Upon thy eyeballs murderous tyranny
Sits in grim majesty, to fright the world.
Look not upon me, for thine eyes are wounding:—
Yet do not go away:—come, basilisk,
And kill the innocent gazer with thy sight:

For in the shade of death I shall find joy,—
In life but double death, now Gloster's dead.

Q. MAR. Why do you rate my lord of Suffolk thus?
Although the duke was enemy to him,
Yet he, most Christian-like, laments his death:
And for myself,—foe as he was to me,—
Might liquid tears, or heart-offending groans,
Or blood-consuming sighs, recall his life,
I would be blind with weeping, sick with groans,
Look pale as primrose with blood-drinking sighs,
And all to have the noble duke alive.
What know I how the world may deem of me?
For it is known we were but hollow friends;
It may be judg'd I made the duke away:
So shall my name with slander's tongue be wounded,
And princes' courts be fill'd with my reproach,
This get I by his death: ay me, unhappy!
To be a queen, and crown'd with infamy!

K. HEN. Ah, woe is me for Gloster, wretched man!

Q. MAR. Be woe for me more wretched than he is.
What, dost thou turn away, and hide thy face?
I am no loathsome leper,—look on me.
What, art thou, like the adder, waxen deaf?
Be poisonous too, and kill thy forlorn queen.
Is all thy comfort shut in Gloster's tomb?
Why, then dame Margaret* was ne'er thy joy:
Erect his statua† and worship it,
And make my image but an alehouse sign.
Was I for this nigh wreck'd upon the sea,
And twice by awkward[a] wind from England's bank
Drove back again unto my native clime?
What boded this but well-forewarning wind
Did seem to say,—Seek not a scorpion's nest,
Nor set no footing on this unkind shore!
What did I then, but curs'd the gentle[b] gusts,
And he that loos'd them from their brazen caves;
And bid them blow towards England's blessed shore,
Or turn our stern upon a dreadful rock?
Yet Æolus would not be a murderer,
But left that hateful office unto thee:
The pretty vaulting sea refus'd to drown me;
Knowing that thou wouldst have me drown'd on shore,
With tears as salt as sea, through thy unkindness:
The splitting rocks cower'd in the sinking sands,
And would not dash me with their ragged sides;
Because thy flinty heart, more hard than they,
Might in thy palace perish Margaret.*
As far as I could ken thy chalky cliffs,
When from thy shore the tempest beat us back,
I stood upon the hatches in the storm:
And when the dusky sky began to rob
My earnest-gaping sight of thy land's view,
I took a costly jewel from my neck,—
A heart it was, bound in with diamonds,—
And threw it towards thy land;—the sea receiv'd it;
And so I wish'd thy body might my heart:
And even with this I lost fair England's view,
And bid mine eyes be packing with my heart;
And call'd them blind and dusky spectacles,
For losing ken of Albion's wished coast.
How often have I tempted Suffolk's tongue
(The agent of thy foul inconstancy),
To sit and witch* me, as Ascanius did,
When he to madding Dido would unfold
His father's acts, commenc'd in burning Troy!
Am I not witch'd like her? or thou not false like him?
Ah me, I can no more! Die, Margaret!†
For Henry weeps, that thou dost live so long.

Noise without. Enter WARWICK *and* SALISBURY. *The* Commons *press to the door.*

WAR. It is reported, mighty sovereign,
That good duke Humphrey traitorously is murder'd
By Suffolk and the cardinal Beaufort's means.
The commons, like an angry hive of bees,
That want their leader, scatter up and down,
And care not who they sting in his revenge.
Myself have calm'd their spleenful mutiny,
Until they hear the order of his death.

K. HEN. That he is dead, good Warwick, 'tis too true;
But how he died, God knows, not Henry:
Enter his chamber, view his breathless corpse,
And comment then upon his sudden death.

WAR. That shall I do, my liege.—Stay, Salisbury,
With the rude multitude till I return.

[WARWICK *goes into an inner room, and* SALISBURY *retires.*

K. HEN. O thou that judgest all things, stay my thoughts!
My thoughts, that labour to persuade my soul,
Some violent hands were laid on Humphrey's life!
If my suspect be false, forgive me, God;
For judgment only doth belong to thee!
Fain would I go to chafe his paly lips
With twenty thousand kisses, and to drain[c]
Upon his face an ocean of salt tears;
To tell my love unto his dumb deaf trunk,

(*) Old text, *Elianor*. (†) Old text, *statue*.

(*) Old text, *watch*. (†) Old text, *Elinor*.

[a] Awkward *wind*—] That is, *contrary* wind. So in Marlowe's "King Edward II." Act IV. Sc. 6:—

"With *aukward* winds, and with sore tempests driven
To fall on shore."

[b] *The* gentle *gusts*,—] The gusts that kindly would have kept her from the English shore. Mr. Collier's annotator, and the old corrector of Mr. Singer's folio, however, both read *ungentle*, and they may be right.

[c] *To* drain—] Steevens and Mr. Collier's annotator substitute *rain*, which is certainly a more becoming word.

And with my fingers feel his hand unfeeling:
But all in vain are these mean obsequies;
And to survey his dead and earthy image,
What were it but to make my sorrow greater?

The folding-doors of an inner chamber are thrown open, and Gloucester *is discovered dead in his bed:* Warwick *and others standing by it.*[a]

War. Come hither, gracious sovereign, view this body.

K. Hen. That is to see how deep my grave is made;
For with his soul fled all my worldly solace,
For seeing him, I see my life in death.

War. As surely as my soul intends to live
With that dread King, that took our state upon him
To free us from his Father's wrathful curse,
I do believe that violent hands were laid
Upon the life of this thrice-famed duke!

---

[a] Warwick and others standing by it.] The whole of this direction is modern. In the old copies we find only "*Bed put forth.*"

SUF. A dreadful oath, sworn with a solemn tongue!
What instance gives lord Warwick for his vow?

WAR. See, how the blood is settled in his face!
Oft have I seen a timely-parted ghost,[a]
Of ashy semblance, meagre, pale, and bloodless,
Being all descended to the labouring heart;
Who, in the conflict that it holds with death,
Attracts the same for aidance 'gainst the enemy;
Which with the heart there cools, and ne'er returneth
To blush and beautify the cheek again.
But see, his face is black and full of blood;
His eye-balls further out than when he liv'd,
Staring full ghastly like a strangled man:
His hair uprear'd, his nostrils stretch'd with struggling;
His hands abroad display'd, as one that grasp'd
And tugg'd for life, and was by strength subdu'd.
Look on the sheets, his hair, you see, is sticking;
His well-proportion'd beard made rough and rugged,
Like to the summer's corn by tempest lodg'd.
It cannot be but he was murder'd here;
The least of all these signs were probable.(3)

SUF. Why, Warwick, who should do the duke to death?
Myself and Beaufort had him in protection;
And we, I hope, sir, are no murderers.

WAR. But both of you were vow'd duke Humphrey's foes;
And you, forsooth, had the good duke to keep:
'Tis like you would not feast him like a friend;
And 'tis well seen he found an enemy.

Q. MAR. Then you, belike, suspect these noblemen
As guilty of duke Humphrey's timeless death.

WAR. Who finds the heifer dead and bleeding fresh,
And sees fast by a butcher with an axe,
But will suspect, 't was he that made the slaughter?
Who finds the partridge in the puttock's nest,
But may imagine how the bird was dead,
Although the kite soar with unbloodied beak?
Even so suspicious is this tragedy.

Q. MAR. Are you the butcher, Suffolk? where's your knife?
Is Beaufort term'd a kite? where are his talons?

SUF. I wear no knife to slaughter sleeping men;
But here's a vengeful sword, rusted with ease,
That shall be scoured in his rancorous heart
That slanders me with murder's crimson badge:—
Say, if thou dar'st, proud lord of Warwickshire,
That I am faulty in duke Humphrey's death.

[*Exeunt* CARDINAL, SOM. *and others.*

WAR. What dares not Warwick, if false Suffolk dare him?

Q. MAR. He dares not calm his contumelious spirit,
Nor cease to be an arrogant controller,
Though Suffolk dare him twenty thousand times.

WAR. Madam, be still,—with reverence may I say;
For every word you speak in his behalf
Is slander to your royal dignity.

SUF. Blunt-witted lord, ignoble in demeanour!
If ever lady wrong'd her lord so much,
Thy mother took into her blameful bed
Some stern untutor'd churl, and noble stock
Was graft with crab-tree slip; whose fruit thou art,
And never of the Nevils' noble race.

WAR. But that the guilt of murder bucklers thee,
And I should rob the deathsman of his fee,
Quitting thee thereby of ten thousand shames;
And that my sovereign's presence makes me mild,
I would, false murderous coward, on thy knee
Make thee beg pardon for thy passed speech,
And say it was thy mother that thou meant'st,
That thou thyself wast born in bastardy:
And, after all this fearful homage done,
Give thee thy hire, and send thy soul to hell,
Pernicious blood-sucker of sleeping men!

SUF. Thou shalt be waking while I shed thy blood,
If from this presence thou dar'st go with me.

WAR. Away even now, or I will drag thee hence!
Unworthy though thou art, I'll cope with thee,
And do some service to duke Humphrey's ghost.

[*Exeunt* SUFFOLK *and* WARWICK.

K. HEN. What stronger breast-plate than a heart untainted!
Thrice is he arm'd, that hath his quarrel just;
And he but naked, though lock'd up in steel,
Whose conscience with injustice is corrupted.

[*A noise without.*

Q. MAR. What noise is this?

Re-enter SUFFOLK *and* WARWICK, *with their weapons drawn.*

K. HEN. Why, how now, lords! your wrathful weapons drawn
Here in our presence! dare you be so bold?—
Why, what tumultuous clamour have we here?

SUF. The traitorous Warwick, with the men of Bury,
Set all upon me, mighty sovereign.

[*Noise of a crowd without.*

---

[a] A timely-parted ghost,—] Though *timely* is commonly used in our ancient writers to signify *early*, it appears here to import *duly, in proper time,* as opposed to *timeless. Ghost* means *corse*, a sense in which, of old, it is found repeatedly: thus, in "The Contention:"—

"O! dismall sight, see where he breathlesse lies,
All smeard and weltred in his luke-warme blood,
Sweete father, to thy *murthred ghoast* I sweare."

Re-enter SALISBURY.

SAL. [*To those without.*] Sirs, stand apart; the king shall know your mind.—
Dread lord, the commons send you word by me,
Unless false[a] Suffolk straight be done to death,
Or banished fair England's territories,
They will by violence tear him from your palace,
And torture him with grievous ling'ring death.
They say, by him the good duke Humphrey died;
They say, in him they fear your highness' death;
And mere instinct of love and loyalty,—
Free from a stubborn opposite intent,
As being thought to contradict your liking,—
Makes them thus forward in his banishment.
They say, in care of your most royal person,
That, if your highness should intend to sleep,
And charge—that no man should disturb your rest,
In pain of your dislike, or pain of death;
Yet, notwithstanding such a strait edict,
Were there a serpent seen, with forked tongue,
That slily glided towards your majesty,
It were but necessary you were wak'd;
Lest, being suffer'd in that harmful slumber,
The mortal worm might make the sleep eternal:
And therefore do they cry, though you forbid,
That they will guard you, whêr you will or no,
From such fell serpents as false Suffolk is;
With whose envenomed and fatal sting,
Your loving uncle, twenty times his worth,
They say, is shamefully bereft of life.

COMMONS. [*Without.*] An answer from the king, my lord of Salisbury! [hinds,

SUF. 'Tis like, the commons, rude unpolish'd
Could send such message to their sovereign:
But you, my lord, were glad to be employ'd,
To show how quaint an orator you are:
But all the honour Salisbury hath won,
Is, that he was the lord ambassador,
Sent from a sort of tinkers to the king.

COMMONS. [*Without.*] An answer from the king, or we will all break in! [me,

K. HEN. Go, Salisbury, and tell them all from
I thank them for their tender loving care;
And had I not been cited so by them,
Yet did I purpose as they do entreat;
For sure, my thoughts do hourly prophesy
Mischance unto my state by Suffolk's means:
And therefore—by His majesty I swear,
Whose far unworthy deputy I am,—
He shall not breathe infection in this air,
But three days longer, on the pain of death.
[*Exit* SALISBURY.

Q. MAR. O Henry, let me plead for gentle Suffolk!

K. HEN. Ungentle queen, to call him *gentle Suffolk!*
No more, I say; if thou dost plead for him,
Thou wilt but add increase unto my wrath.
Had I but said, I would have kept my word;
But, when I swear, it is irrevocable:—
If, after three days' space, thou here be'st found
On any ground that I am ruler of,
The world shall not be ransom for thy life.—
Come, Warwick,—come, good Warwick, go with me;
I have great matters to impart to thee.
[*Exeunt* K. HENRY, WARWICK, Lords, *&c.*

Q. MAR. Mischance and sorrow go along with you!
Heart's discontent, and sour affliction,
Be playfellows to keep you company!
There's two of you; the devil make a third!
And threefold vengeance tend upon your steps!

SUF. Cease, gentle queen, these execrations,
And let thy Suffolk take his heavy leave.

Q. MAR. Fie, coward woman, and soft-hearted wretch!
Hast thou not spirit to curse thine enemies?*

SUF. A plague upon them! wherefore should I curse them?
Would curses kill, as doth the mandrake's groan,[b]
I would invent as bitter-searching terms,
As curst, as harsh, and horrible to hear,
Deliver'd strongly through my fixed teeth,
With full as many signs of deadly hate,
As lean-fac'd Envy in her loathsome cave:
My tongue should stumble in mine earnest words;
Mine eyes should sparkle like the beaten flint;
Mine hair be fix'd on end, as one distract;
Ay, every joint should seem to curse and ban:
And even now my burden'd heart would break,
Should I not curse them. Poison be their drink!
Gall, worse than gall, the daintiest that they taste!
Their sweetest shade, a grove of cypress-trees!
Their chiefest prospect, murdering basilisks!
Their softest touch, as smart as lizard's stings!
Their music, frightful as the serpent's hiss;
And boding screech-owls make the concert full!
All the foul terrors in dark-seated hell— [thyself;

Q. MAR. Enough, sweet Suffolk; thou torment'st
And these dread curses—like the sun 'gainst glass,
Or like an overcharged gun,—recoil,
And turn the force of them upon thyself. [leave?

SUF. You bade me ban, and will you bid me
Now, by the ground that I am banish'd from,
Well could I curse away a winter's night,
Though standing naked on a mountain top,
Where biting cold would never let grass grow
And think it but a minute spent in sport.

a False *Suffolk—*] So "The Contention." The folio 1623, owing, probably, to the compositor having caught the word, *Lord*, from the preceding line, has "*Lord* Suffolke," &c.

(*) Old text, *enemy*.

b The mandrake's groan,—] See note (5), p. 220, Vol. I.

Q. MAR. O, let me entreat thee, cease! Give me thy hand,
That I may dew it with my mournful tears;
Nor let the rain of heaven wet this place,
To wash away my woeful monuments.
O, could this kiss be printed in thy hand,
[*Kisses his hand.*
That thou mightst think upon these by the seal,
Through whom a thousand sighs are breath'd for thee!
So, get thee gone, that I may know my grief;
'T is but surmis'd whiles thou art standing by,
As one that surfeits, thinking on a want.
I will repeal thee, or, be well assur'd,
Adventure to be banished myself:
And banished I am, if but from thee.
Go, speak not to me:—even now be gone.—
O, go not yet!—Even thus two friends condemn'd,
Embrace, and kiss, and take ten thousand leaves,
Lother a hundred times to part than die.
Yet now farewell; and farewell life with thee!

SUF. Thus is poor Suffolk ten times banished,
Once by the king, and three times thrice by thee.
'T is not the land I care for, wert thou hence;*
A wilderness is populous enough,
So Suffolk had thy heavenly company:
For where thou art, there is the world itself,
With every several pleasure in the world;
And where thou art not, desolation.
I can no more:—live thou to joy thy life;
Myself no[a] joy in nought but that thou liv'st.

Enter VAUX.

Q. MAR. Whither goes Vaux so fast? what news, I pr'ythee?

VAUX. To signify unto his majesty,
That cardinal Beaufort is at point of death:
For suddenly a grievous sickness took him,
That makes him gasp, and stare, and catch the air,
Blaspheming God, and cursing men on earth.
Sometime he talks as if duke Humphrey's ghost
Were by his side; sometime he calls the king,
And whispers to his pillow, as to him,
The secrets of his overcharged soul:
And I am sent to tell his majesty,
That even now he cries aloud for him.

Q. MAR. Go, tell this heavy message to the king.
[*Exit* VAUX.
Ay me! what is this world! what news are these?
But wherefore grieve I at an hour's poor loss,
Omitting Suffolk's exile, my soul's treasure?
Why only, Suffolk, mourn I not for thee,
And with the southern clouds contend in tears,—
Theirs for the earth's increase, mine for my sorrows?
Now, get thee hence: the king, thou know'st, is coming;—
If thou be found by me, thou art but dead.

SUF. If I depart from thee, I cannot live:
And in thy sight to die, what were it else,
But like a pleasant slumber in thy lap?
Here could I breathe my soul into the air,
As mild and gentle as the cradle-babe,
Dying with mother's dug between its lips:
Where,[b] from thy sight, I should be raging mad,
And cry out for thee to close up mine eyes,
To have thee with thy lips to stop my mouth;
So shouldst thou either turn my flying soul,
Or I should breathe it so into thy body,
And then it liv'd in sweet Elysium.
To die by thee, were but to die in jest;
From thee to die, were torture more than death:
O, let me stay, befall what may befall!

Q. MAR. Away! Though parting be a fretful corrosive,
It is applied to a deathful wound.
To France, sweet Suffolk: let me hear from thee;
For wheresoe'er thou art in this world's globe,
I'll have an Iris that shall find thee out.

SUF. I go.

Q. MAR. And take my heart with thee.

SUF. A jewel, lock'd into the woeful'st cask
That ever did contain a thing of worth.
Even as a splitted bark, so sunder we;
This way fall I to death.

Q. MAR. This way for me.
[*Exeunt severally.*

SCENE III.—London. CARDINAL BEAUFORT'*s Bed-chamber*.

Enter KING HENRY, SALISBURY, WARWICK, *and others. The* CARDINAL *in bed;* Attendants *with him.*

K. HEN. How fares my lord? speak, Beaufort, to thy sovereign.

CAR. If thou be'st death, I'll give thee England's treasure,
Enough to purchase such another island,
So thou wilt let me live, and feel no pain.

K. HEN. Ah, what a sign it is of evil life,
Where death's approach is seen so terrible!

WAR. Beaufort, it is thy sovereign speaks to thee.

CAR. Bring me unto my trial, when you will.
Died he not in his bed? where should he die?
Can I make men live, whêr they will or no?—
O, torture me no more! I will confess.—
Alive again! then show me where he is;
I'll give a thousand pound to look upon him.—
He hath no eyes, the dust hath blinded them.—

(*) First folio, *thence*.

a *Myself* no *joy in nought*—] Mr. Collier's annotator reads,—"Myself *to* joy," &c.

b Where,—] For *whereas*.

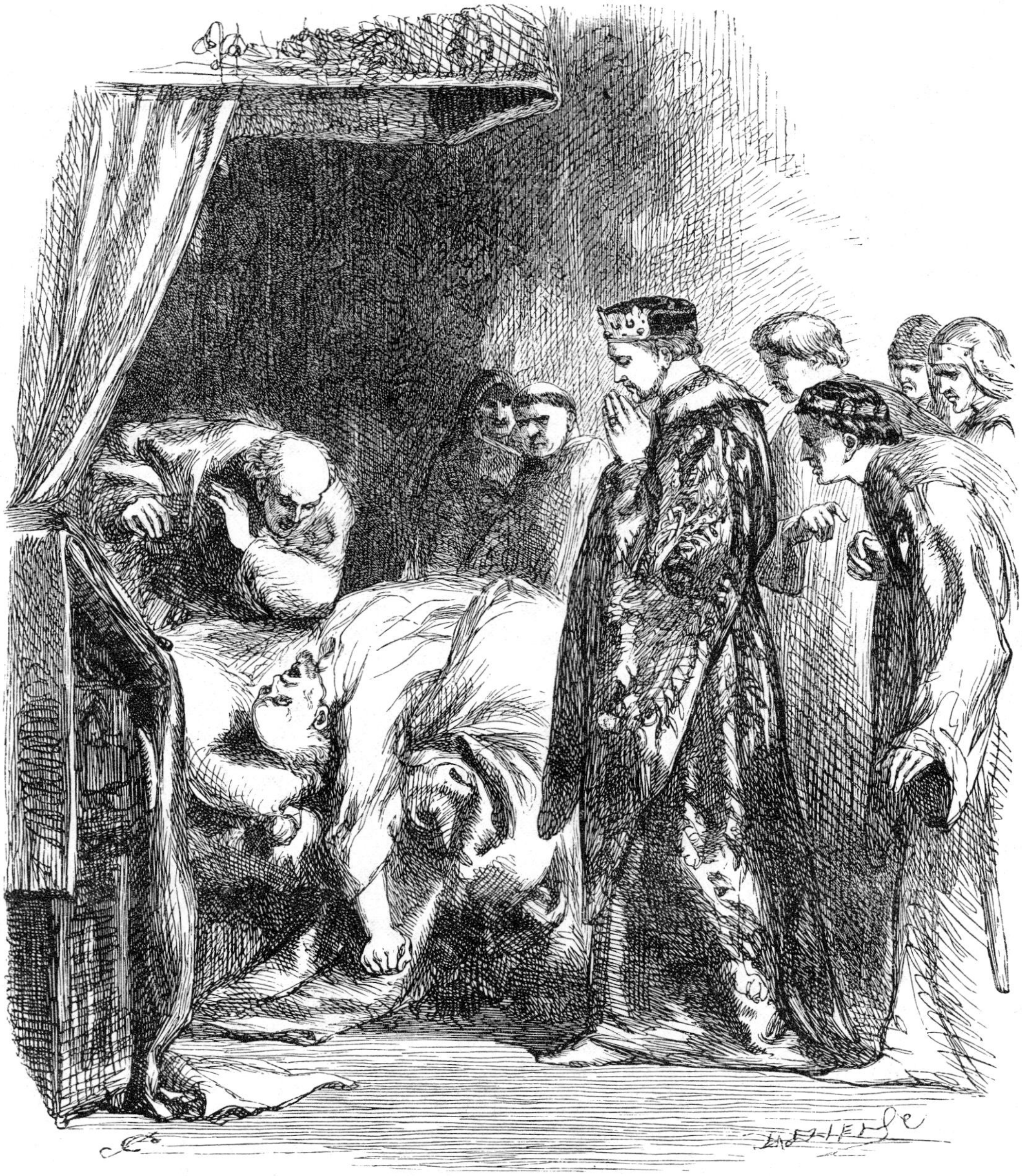

Comb down his hair; look! look! it stands upright,
Like lime-twigs set to catch my winged soul!—
Give me some drink; and bid the apothecary
Bring the strong poison that I bought of him.

K. Hen. O, thou eternal mover of the heavens,
Look with a gentle eye upon this wretch!
O, beat away the busy meddling fiend
That lays strong siege unto this wretch's soul,
And from his bosom purge this black despair!

War. See how the pangs of death do make him grin!

Sal. Disturb him not, let him pass peaceably.

K. Hen. Peace to his soul, if God's good pleasure be!
Lord cardinal, if thou think'st on heaven's bliss,
Hold up thy hand, make signal of thy hope.—
He dies, and makes no sign:—O God, forgive him!

War. So bad a death argues a monstrous life.

K. Hen. Forbear to judge, for we are sinners all.—
Close up his eyes, and draw the curtain close;
And let us all to meditation.(4) [*Exeunt.*

ACT IV.

SCENE I.—Kent. *The Sea-shore near* Dover.

Firing heard at Sea. Then enter, from a boat, a Captain,[a] *a* Master, *a* Master's Mate, WALTER WHITMORE, *and others; with them* SUFFOLK, *disguised, and other* Gentlemen, *prisoners.*

CAP. The gaudy, blabbing,[b] and remorseful[c] day
Is crept into the bosom of the sea;
And now loud-howling wolves arouse the jades
That drag the tragic melancholy night;
Who with their drowsy, slow, and flagging wings
Clip dead men's graves, and from their misty jaws
Breathe foul contagious darkness in the air.
Therefore, bring forth the soldiers of our prize;
For, whilst our pinnace anchors in the Downs,
Here shall they make their ransom on the sand,
Or with their blood stain this discolour'd shore.—
Master, this prisoner freely give I thee;—
And thou that art his mate, make boot of this;—
The other [*Pointing to* SUFFOLK.], Walter Whitmore, is thy share.

1 GENT. What is my ransom, master? let me know.

MAST. A thousand crowns, or else lay down your head.

MATE. And so much shall you give, or off goes yours.

CAP. What, think you much to pay two thousand crowns,
And bear the name and port of gentlemen?—
Cut both the villains' throats;—for die you shall;—

[a] Captain,—] So in "The Contention." The folios have *Lieutenant*, and prefix *Lieu.* to all his speeches.

[b] Blabbing,—] "The epithet *blabbing*, applied to the day by a man about to commit murder, is exquisitely beautiful. Guilt is afraid of light, considers darkness as a natural shelter, and makes night the confidante of those actions which cannot be trusted to the *tell-tale day*."—JOHNSON.

[c] Remorseful—] *Pitiful.*

The lives of those which we have lost in fight
Be counterpois'd with such a petty sum? [a]
1 GENT. I'll give it, sir; and therefore spare my life.
2 GENT. And so will I, and write home for it [straight.
WHIT. I lost mine eye in laying the prize aboard,
And therefore, to revenge it, shalt thou die;
[*To* SUF.
And so should these, if I might have my will.
CAP. Be not so rash; take ransom, let him live.
SUF. Look on my George, I am a gentleman:
Rate me at what thou wilt, thou shalt be paid.
WHIT. And so am I; my name is Walter Whitmore.
How now! why start'st thou? what, doth death [affright?
SUF. Thy name affrights me, in whose sound is death.
A cunning man did calculate my birth,
And told me—that by *water* I should die.
Yet let not this make thee be bloody-minded;
Thy name is *Gualtier*, being rightly sounded.
WHIT. *Gualtier*, or *Walter*, which it is, I care not;
Ne'er yet did base dishonour blur our name,
But with our sword we wip'd away the blot;
Therefore, when merchant-like I sell revenge,
Broke be my sword, my arms torn and defac'd,
And I proclaim'd a coward through the world!
[*Lays hold on* SUFFOLK.
SUF. Stay, Whitmore; for thy prisoner is a prince,
The duke of Suffolk, William de la Poole.
WHIT. The duke of Suffolk muffled up in rags!
SUF. Ay, but these rags are no part of the duke;
Jove sometime went disguis'd, and why not I? [b]
CAP. But Jove was never slain, as thou shalt be.
SUF. Obscure and lowly swain, king Henry's blood,[c]
The honourable blood of Lancaster,
Must not be shed by such a jaded groom.
Hast thou not kiss'd thy hand, and held my stirrup?
Bare-headed, plodded by my foot-cloth mule,
And thought thee happy when I shook my head?
How often hast thou waited at my cup,
Fed from my trencher, kneel'd down at the board,
When I have feasted with queen Margaret?
Remember it, and let it make thee crest-fall'n;
Ay, and allay this thy abortive pride:
How in our voiding-lobby hast thou stood,
And duly waited for my coming forth?
This hand of mine hath writ in thy behalf,
And therefore shall it charm thy riotous tongue.
WHIT. Speak, captain, shall I stab the forlorn swain?
CAP. First let my words stab him, as he hath me.
SUF. Base slave! thy words are blunt, and so art thou.
CAP. Convey him hence, and on our long-boat's [side
Strike off his head.
SUF. Thou dar'st not for thy own!
CAP. Yes, Poole.
SUF. Poole? [d]
CAP. Poole! Sir Poole! Lord!
Ay, kennel, puddle, sink; whose filth and dirt
Troubles the silver spring where England drinks.
Now will I dam up this thy yawning mouth,
For swallowing the treasure of the realm:
Thy lips, that kiss'd the queen, shall sweep the ground;
And thou, that smil'dst at good duke Humphrey's death,
Against the senseless winds shall grin in vain,
Who, in contempt, shall hiss at thee again:
And wedded be thou to the hags of hell,
For daring to affy a mighty lord
Unto the daughter of a worthless king,
Having neither subject, wealth, nor diadem.
By devilish policy art thou grown great,
And, like ambitious Sylla, overgorg'd
With gobbets of thy mother's bleeding* heart.
By thee, Anjou and Maine were sold to France;
The false revolting Normans, thorough thee,
Disdain to call us lord; and Picardy
Hath slain their governors, surpris'd our forts,
And sent the ragged soldiers wounded home.
The princely Warwick, and the Nevils all,—
Whose dreadful swords were never drawn in vain,—
As hating thee, are† rising up in arms:
And now the house of York—thrust from the crown,
By shameful murder of a guiltless king,
And lofty proud encroaching tyranny,—
Burns with revenging fire; whose hopeful colours
Advance our half-fac'd sun,[e] striving to shine,
Under the which is writ—*Invitis nubibus.*
The commons here in Kent are up in arms;
And, to conclude, reproach, and beggary
Is crept into the palace of our king,
And all by thee.—Away! convey him hence.

---

a The lives of those which we have lost in fight
Be counterpois'd with such a petty sum?]
Something is evidently wrong here. Rowe reads:—
"*Nor can* those lives," &c.
Capell—
"*Cannot be pois'd,*" &c.
Mr. Collier's annotator:—
"*Can* lives of those," &c.

b Jove sometime went disguis'd, and why not I?] A line found only in the earlier draft of this play—the "First Part of the Contention," but which the context renders indispensable.

(*) Old text, *Mother-bleeding.* (†) Old text, *and.*

c Obscure and lowly swain, king Henry's blood,—] In the old text this line is inadvertently given to the Captain, and *lowly* is misprinted *lowsie.*

d CAP. Yes, Poole.
SUF. Poole?]
These two speeches are only found in the "First Part of the Contention." They are obviously necessary to the dialogue.

e ——— whose hopeful colours
Advance our half-fac'd sun,—]
"Edward III. bare for his device the rays of the sun dispersing themselves out of a cloud."—CAMDEN'S *Remaines.*

SUF. O, that I were a god, to shoot forth thunder
Upon these paltry, servile, abject drudges!
Small things make base men proud: this villain here,
Being captain of a pinnace, threatens more
Than Bargulus, the strong Illyrian pirate.[a]
Drones suck not eagles' blood, but rob bee-hives.
It is impossible that I should die
By such a lowly vassal as thyself.
Thy words move rage and not remorse in me;
I go of message from the queen to France;
I charge thee, waft me safely 'cross the channel.

CAP. Walter,—

WHIT. Come, Suffolk, I must waft thee to thy [death.

SUF. *Gelidus timor occupat artus*:[b]—
It is thee I fear.

WHIT. Thou shalt have cause to fear before I leave thee.
What, are ye daunted now? now will ye stoop?

1 GENT. My gracious lord, entreat him, speak him fair.

SUF. Suffolk's imperial tongue is stern and rough,
Us'd to command, untaught to plead for favour.
Far be it we should honour such as these
With humble suit: no, rather let my head
Stoop to the block, than these knees bow to any,
Save to the God of heaven and to my king;
And sooner dance upon a bloody pole,
Than stand uncover'd to the vulgar groom.
True nobility is exempt from fear:—
More can I bear than you dare execute.

CAP. Hale him away, and let him talk no more.

SUF. Come, soldiers, show what cruelty ye can,[c]
That this my death may never be forgot!—
Great men oft die by vile Bezonians:[d]
A Roman sworder and banditto slave
Murder'd sweet Tully; Brutus' bastard hand
Stabb'd Julius Cæsar; savage islanders,
Pompey the great: and Suffolk dies by pirates.
[*Exit* SUF. *with* WHITMORE *and others.*

CAP. And as for these whose ransom we have set,
It is our pleasure one of them depart:—
Therefore come you with us, and let him go.
[*Exeunt all but the first* Gentleman.

Re-enter WHITMORE, *with* SUFFOLK'S *body.*

WHIT. There let his head and lifeless body lie,
Until the queen his mistress bury it. [*Exit.*

1 GENT. O barbarous and bloody spectacle!
His body will I bear unto the king:
If he revenge it not, yet will his friends;
So will the queen, that living held him dear.(1)
[*Exit with the body.*

SCENE II.—Blackheath.

Enter GEORGE BEVIS *and* JOHN HOLLAND.

GEO. Come, and get thee a sword, though made of a lath; they have been up these two days.

JOHN. They have the more need to sleep now, then.

GEO. I tell thee, Jack Cade the clothier means to dress the commonwealth, and turn it, and set a new nap upon it.

JOHN. So he had need, for 'tis threadbare. Well, I say it was never merry world in England since gentlemen came up.

GEO. O miserable age! Virtue is not regarded in handy-crafts-men.

JOHN. The nobility think scorn to go in leather aprons.

GEO. Nay, more, the king's council are no good workmen.

JOHN. True; and yet it is said,—*labour in thy vocation*: which is as much to say as,[e]—let the magistrates be labouring men; and therefore should we be magistrates.

GEO. Thou hast hit it: for there's no better sign of a brave mind than a hard hand.

JOHN. I see them! I see them! There's Best's son, the tanner of Wingham;—

GEO. He shall have the skins of our enemies, to make dog's leather of.

JOHN. And Dick the butcher,—

GEO. Then is sin struck down like an ox, and iniquity's throat cut like a calf.

JOHN. And Smith the weaver.

GEO. *Argo*, their thread of life is spun.

JOHN. Come, come, let's fall in with them.

Drum. Enter JACK CADE, DICK *the butcher*, SMITH *the weaver, and others in great number.*

CADE. We, John Cade, so termed of our supposed father,—

---

[a] *Than* Bargulus, *the strong Illyrian pirate.*] This noted robber, rightly *Bardyllis*, is mentioned in Cicero, *De Off. Lib. ii. cap. xi.* "*Bargulus* Illyrius latro, de quo est apud Theopompum," &c. See note on the passage in the "Variorum." The corresponding passage in "The Contention" has:—

"—— then mightie *Abradas*,
The great Masadonian pyrate."

[b] *Gelidus timor occupat artus*:—] In the first folio we have, "*Pine* gelidus," &c., which led Malone to read, "*Pene* gelidus." The editor of the second folio struck out the first word, and his example has been generally followed.

[c] Come, soldiers, &c.] A line wrongly assigned to the previous speaker in the old text.

[d] Bezonians:] See note (e), p. 621, Vol. I.

[e] *Which is* as much to say as,—] Mr. Collier adopts the modern form of the phrase, upon the authority of his annotator, "*as*," he observes, "having been misplaced in the old editions;" but, as we have before said (see note (b), p. 241), the construction found in the early copies was not unusual.

DICK. Or rather, of stealing a cade of herrings. [*Aside.*

CADE. For our enemies shall fall before us[a]—inspired with the spirit of putting down kings and princes.—Command silence.

DICK. Silence!

CADE. My father was a Mortimer,—

DICK. He was an honest man, and a good bricklayer. [*Aside.*

CADE. My mother a Plantagenet,—

DICK. I knew her well, she was a midwife. [*Aside.*

CADE. My wife descended of the Lacies,—

DICK. She was, indeed, a pedlar's daughter, and sold many laces. [*Aside.*

SMITH. But, now of late, not able to travel with her furred pack, she washes bucks here at home. [*Aside.*

CADE. Therefore am I of an honourable house.

DICK. Ay, by my faith, the field is honourable; and there was he born, under a hedge,—for his father had never a house but the cage. [*Aside.*

CADE. Valiant I am.

SMITH. 'A must needs; for beggary is valiant. [*Aside.*

CADE. I am able to endure much.

SMITH. No question of that; for I have seen him whipped three market-days together. [*Aside.*

CADE. I fear neither sword nor fire.

SMITH. He need not fear the sword, for his coat is of proof. [*Aside.*

DICK. But methinks he should stand in fear of fire, being burnt i' the hand for stealing of sheep. [*Aside.*

CADE. Be brave then; for your captain is brave, and vows reformation. There shall be in England seven half-penny loaves sold for a penny: the three-hooped pots shall have ten hoops; and I will make it felony, to drink small beer: all the realm shall be in common, and in Cheapside shall my palfrey go to grass. And when I am king,—as king I will be—

ALL. God save your majesty!

CADE. I thank you, good people—there shall be no money; all shall eat and drink on my score; and I will apparel them all in one livery, that they may agree like brothers, and worship me their lord.

DICK. The first thing we do, let's kill all the lawyers.

CADE. Nay, that I mean to do. Is not this a lamentable thing, that of the skin of an innocent lamb should be made parchment? that parchment, being scribbled o'er, should undo a man? Some say, the bee stings; but I say, 'tis the bee's wax, for I did but seal once to a thing, and I was never mine own man since. How now! who's there?

Enter some, bringing in the Clerk *of* Chatham.

SMITH. The Clerk of Chatham: he can write and read, and cast account.

CADE. O monstrous!

SMITH. We took him setting of boys' copies.

CADE. Here's a villain!

SMITH. H'as a book in his pocket with red letters in't.

CADE. Nay, then he is a conjurer.

DICK. Nay, he can make obligations, and write court-hand.

CADE. I am sorry for't: the man is a proper man, of mine honour; unless I find him guilty, he shall not die.—Come hither, sirrah, I must examine thee: what is thy name?

CLERK. Emanuel.

DICK. They use to write it on the top of letters:(2)—'twill go hard with you.

CADE. Let me alone.—Dost thou use to write thy name? or hast thou a mark to thyself, like an honest plain-dealing man?

CLERK. Sir, I thank God, I have been so well brought up that I can write my name.

ALL. He hath confessed: away with him! he's a villain and a traitor.

CADE. Away with him, I say! hang him with his pen-and-inkhorn about his neck.(3)

[*Exeunt some with the* Clerk.

Enter MICHAEL.

MICH. Where's our general?

CADE. Here I am, thou particular fellow.

MICH. Fly, fly, fly! Sir Humphrey Stafford and his brother are hard by, with the king's forces.

CADE. Stand, villain, stand, or I'll fell thee down. He shall be encountered with a man as good as himself: he is but a knight, is 'a?

MICH. No.

CADE. To equal him, I will make myself a knight presently; [*Kneels.*] rise up sir John Mortimer. [*Rises.*] Now have at him!

Enter Sir HUMPHREY STAFFORD *and* WILLIAM *his brother, with drum and* Forces.

STAF. Rebellious hinds, the filth and scum of Kent,
Mark'd for the gallows,—lay your weapons down,

---

[a] *Our enemies shall fall before us*—] Alluding, though not consistently—for the truculent rebel was no scholar—to the supposed etymology of his name, *Cade*, from *cado, to fall*. The old copies have, "*faile* before us."

Home to your cottages, forsake this groom;—
The king is merciful, if you revolt.

W. STAF. But angry, wrathful, and inclin'd to blood,
If you go forward: therefore, yield or die.

CADE. As for these silken-coated slaves, I pass not;[a]
It is to you, good people, that I speak,
O'er whom, in time to come, I hope to reign;
For I am rightful heir unto the crown.

STAF. Villain, thy father was a plasterer;
And thou thyself a shearman,—art thou not?

CADE. And Adam was a gardener.

W. STAF. And what of that?

CADE. Marry, this:—Edmund Mortimer, earl of March,
Married the duke of Clarence' daughter—did he not?

STAF. Ay, sir.

CADE. By her he had two children at one birth.

W. STAF. That's false.

CADE. Ay, there's the question; but I say, 'tis true:
The elder of them, being put to nurse,
Was by a beggar-woman stol'n away;
And, ignorant of his birth and parentage,
Became a bricklayer when he came to age:
His son am I; deny it if you can.

DICK. Nay, 'tis too true; therefore he shall be king.

SMITH. Sir, he made a chimney in my father's house, and the bricks are alive at this day to testify it; therefore deny it not.

STAF. And will you credit this base drudge's words,
That speaks he knows not what?

ALL. Ay, marry, will we; therefore get ye gone.

W. STAF. Jack Cade, the duke of York hath taught you this.

CADE. He lies, for I invented it myself. [*Aside.*—Go to, sirrah, tell the king from me, that—for his father's sake, Henry the fifth, in whose time boys went to span-counter for French crowns,—I am content he shall reign; but I'll be protector over him.

DICK. And furthermore, we'll have the lord Say's head for selling the dukedom of Maine.

CADE. And good reason, for thereby is England maimed,* and fain to go with a staff, but that my puissance holds it up. Fellow kings, I tell you that lord Say hath gelded the commonwealth, and made it an eunuch; and, more than that, he can speak French, and therefore he is a traitor.

STAF. O gross and miserable ignorance!

CADE. Nay, answer, if you can:—the Frenchmen are our enemies; go to, then, I ask but this,—can he that speaks with the tongue of an enemy be a good counsellor or no?

ALL. No, no; and therefore we'll have his head.

W. STAF. Well, seeing gentle words will not prevail,
Assail them with the army of the king.

STAF. Herald, away: and throughout every town,
Proclaim them traitors that are up with Cade;
That those, which fly before the battle ends,
May, even in their wives' and children's sight,
Be hang'd up for example at their doors:—
And you, that be the king's friends, follow me.
[*Exeunt the two* STAFFORDS, *and* Forces.

CADE. And you, that love the commons, follow me.—
Now show yourselves men; 'tis for liberty.
We will not leave one lord, one gentleman:
Spare none but such as go in clouted shoon;
For they are thrifty honest men, and such
As would (but that they dare not) take our parts.

DICK. They are all in order, and march toward us.

CADE. But then are we in order when we are most out of order. Come, march forward!
[*Exeunt.*

SCENE III.—*Another part of* Blackheath.

Alarum. The two parties enter and fight, and both the STAFFORDS *are slain.*

CADE. Where's Dick, the butcher of Ashford?

DICK. Here, sir.

CADE. They fell before thee like sheep and oxen, and thou behavedst thyself as if thou hadst been in thine own slaughter-house: therefore thus will I reward thee,—the Lent shall be as long again as it is; and thou shalt have a licence to kill for a hundred lacking one a week.[b]

DICK. I desire no more.

CADE. And, to speak truth, thou deservest no less. This monument of the victory will I bear; [*Putting on part of Sir* H. STAFFORD'S *armour.*] and the bodies shall be dragged at my horse' heels till I do come to London, where we will have the mayor's sword borne before us.

DICK. If we mean to thrive and do good, break open the gaols, and let out the prisoners.

CADE. Fear not that, I warrant thee.—Come, let's march towards London. [*Exeunt.*

(*) Old text, *main'd*.

[a] *I pass not;*] I *care* not, or, I *regard* not.

[b] *Thou shalt have a licence to kill for a hundred lacking one a week.*] The last two words are restored from "The Contention." In the reign of Elizabeth, butchers were prohibited from selling flesh-meat in Lent; "not," so the statute 5 Eliz. c. 5, expresses it, "for any superstition to be maintained in the choyce of meates," but for the double purpose of diminishing the consumption of flesh-meat (already restricted to four days in the week throughout the year), and of encouraging the fisheries, and augmenting the number of seamen. Sick and infirm people, however, unable to abstain from animal food, were dispensed by a licence from their bishop or curate, and certain butchers were specially privileged to supply a limited number each week.

SCENE IV.—London. *A Room in the Palace.*

Enter KING HENRY, *reading a supplication; the* DUKE *of* BUCKINGHAM *and* LORD SAY, *with him: at a distance* QUEEN MARGARET, *mourning over* SUFFOLK'*s head.*

Q. MAR. Oft have I heard that grief softens the mind,
And makes it fearful and degenerate;
Think therefore on revenge, and cease to weep.
But who can cease to weep, and look on this?
Here may his head lie on my throbbing breast,
But where's the body that I should embrace?

BUCK. What answer makes your grace to the rebels' supplication?

K. HEN. I'll send some holy bishop to entreat;
For God forbid, so many simple souls
Should perish by the sword! And I myself,
Rather than bloody war shall cut them short,
Will parley with Jack Cade their general.—
But stay, I'll read it over once again.

Q. MAR. Ah, barbarous villains! hath this lovely face
Rul'd, like a wandering planet, over me:
And could it not enforce them to relent,
That were unworthy to behold the same?

K. HEN. Lord Say, Jack Cade hath sworn to have thy head.

SAY. Ay, but I hope your highness shall have his.

K. HEN. How now, madam!
Still lamenting and mourning for Suffolk's death?[a]
I fear me, love, if that I had been dead,
Thou wouldest not have mourn'd so much for me.

Q. MAR. No, my love, I should not mourn, but die for thee.

Enter a Messenger.

K. HEN. How now! what news? why com'st thou in such haste?

MESS. The rebels are in Southwark: fly, my lord!
Jack Cade proclaims himself lord Mortimer,
Descended from the duke of Clarence' house;
And calls your grace usurper, openly,
And vows to crown himself in Westminster.
His army is a ragged multitude
Of hinds and peasants, rude and merciless:
Sir Humphrey Stafford and his brother's death
Hath given them heart and courage to proceed;
All scholars, lawyers, courtiers, gentlemen,
They call—false caterpillars, and intend their death.

K. HEN. O graceless men! they know not what they do.

BUCK. My gracious lord, retire to Kenilworth,
Until a power be rais'd to put them down.

Q. MAR. Ah! were the duke of Suffolk now alive,
These Kentish rebels would be soon appeas'd.

K. HEN. Lord Say, the traitor* hateth thee;
Therefore, away with us to Kenilworth.

SAY. So might your grace's person be in danger;
The sight of me is odious in their eyes;
And therefore in this city will I stay,
And live alone as secret as I may.

Enter a second Messenger.

2 MESS. Jack Cade hath gotten London-bridge;
The citizens fly and forsake their houses;
The rascal people, thirsting after prey,
Join with the traitor; and they jointly swear
To spoil the city and your royal court.

BUCK. Then linger not, my lord; away, take horse.

K. HEN. Come, Margaret; God, our hope, will succour us.

Q. MAR. My hope is gone, now Suffolk is deceas'd.

K. HEN. Farewell, my lord; [*To* LORD SAY.] trust not the Kentish rebels.

BUCK. Trust nobody, for fear you be† betray'd.

SAY. The trust I have is in mine innocence,
And therefore am I bold and resolute. [*Exeunt.*

SCENE V.—*The same. The* Tower.

Enter LORD SCALES, *and others, on the walls. Then enter certain* Citizens, *below.*

SCALES. How, now! is Jack Cade slain?

1 CIT. No, my lord, nor likely to be slain; for they have won the bridge, killing all those that withstand them. The lord mayor craves aid of your honour from the Tower, to defend the city from the rebels.

SCALES. Such aid as I can spare, you shall command;
But I am troubled here with them myself;
The rebels have assay'd to win the Tower.
But get you to Smithfield, and gather head,
And thither I will send you Matthew Gough:
Fight for your king, your country, and your lives;
And so, farewell, for I must hence again.
[*Exeunt.*

a Still lamenting and mourning for Suffolk's death?] Might we not read,
"Still mourning and lamenting Suffolk's death?"

(*) Old text, *traitors.*
(†) First folio omits, *be.*

SCENE VI.—*The same.* Cannon-street.

Enter JACK CADE, *and his* Followers. *He strikes his staff on London-stone.*

CADE. Now is Mortimer lord of this city! And here, sitting upon London-stone, I charge and command, that, of the city's cost, the pissing-conduit run nothing but claret wine this first year of our reign. And now, henceforward, it shall be treason for any that calls me other than lord Mortimer.

Enter a Soldier, *running.*

SOLD. Jack Cade! Jack Cade!

CADE. Knock him down there. [*They kill him.*

SMITH. If this fellow be wise, he'll never call you Jack Cade more; I think he hath a very fair warning.

DICK. My lord, there's an army gathered together in Smithfield.

CADE. Come then, let's go fight with them: but first, go and set London-bridge on fire; and if you can, burn down the Tower too. Come, let's away. [*Exeunt.*

SCENE VII.—*The same.* Smithfield.

Alarums. Enter, on one side, CADE *and his Company; on the other,* Citizens, *and the* KING'S Forces, *headed by* MATTHEW GOUGH. *They fight; the* Citizens *are routed, and* MATTHEW GOUGH *is slain.*

CADE. So, sirs.—Now go some and pull down the Savoy; others to the inns of court; down with them all.

DICK. I have a suit unto your lordship.

CADE. Be it a lordship, thou shalt have it for that word.

DICK. Only, that the laws of England may come out of your mouth.

JOHN. Mass, 'twill be sore law then; for he was thrust in the mouth with a spear, and 'tis not whole yet. [*Aside.*

SMITH. Nay, John, it will be stinking law; for his breath stinks with eating toasted cheese. [*Aside.*

CADE. I have thought upon it; it shall be so. Away, burn all the records of the realm: my mouth shall be the parliament of England.

JOHN. Then we are like to have biting statutes, unless his teeth be pulled out. [*Aside.*

CADE. And henceforward all things shall be in common.

Enter a Messenger.

MESS. My lord, a prize, a prize! here's the lord Say, which sold the towns in France; he that made us pay one-and-twenty fifteens,[a] and one shilling to the pound, the last subsidy.

Enter GEORGE BEVIS, *with the* LORD SAY.

CADE. Well, he shall be beheaded for it ten times.—Ah, thou say, thou serge, nay, thou buckram lord! now art thou within point-blank of our jurisdiction regal. What canst thou answer to my majesty for giving up of Normandy unto monsieur Basimecu, the dauphin of France? Be it known unto thee by these presence, even the presence of lord Mortimer, that I am the besom that must sweep the court clean of such filth as thou art. Thou hast most traitorously corrupted the youth of the realm in erecting a grammar-school; and whereas, before, our forefathers had no other books but the score and the tally, thou hast caused printing to be used; and, contrary to the king, his crown, and dignity, thou hast built a paper-mill. It will be proved to thy face that thou hast men about thee that usually talk of a noun and a verb; and such abominable words as no Christian ear can endure to hear. Thou hast appointed justices of peace, to call poor men before them about matters they were not able to answer. Moreover, thou hast put them in prison; and because they could not read, thou hast hanged them; when, indeed, only for that cause they have been most worthy to live. Thou dost ride in a foot-cloth, dost thou not?

SAY. What of that?

CADE. Marry, thou oughtest not to let thy horse wear a cloak, when honester men than thou go in their hose and doublets.

DICK. And work in their shirt too; as myself, for example, that am a butcher.

SAY. You men of Kent—

DICK. What say you of Kent?

SAY. Nothing but this: 'tis *bona terra, mala gens.*

CADE. Away with him, away with him! he speaks Latin.

SAY. Hear me but speak, and bear me where you will.
Kent, in the commentaries Cæsar writ,
Is term'd the civil'st place of all this isle:[b]
Sweet is the country, because full of riches;
The people liberal, valiant, active, wealthy;
Which makes me hope you are not void of pity.
I sold not Maine, I lost not Normandy;
Yet, to recover them, would lose my life.
Justice with favour have I always done;
Prayers and tears have mov'd me, gifts could never.
When have I aught exacted at your hands,
But[c] to maintain the king, the realm, and you?
Large gifts have I bestow'd on learned clerks,
Because my book preferr'd me to the king:
And, seeing ignorance is the curse of God,
Knowledge the wing wherewith we fly to heaven,
Unless you be possess'd with devilish spirits,
You cannot but forbear to murder me.
This tongue hath parley'd unto foreign kings
For your behoof,—

CADE. Tut! when struck'st thou one blow in the field?

SAY. Great men have reaching hands: oft have I struck
Those that I never saw, and struck them dead.

GEO. O monstrous coward! what, to come behind folks?

SAY. These cheeks are pale for watching for your good.

CADE. Give him a box o' the ear, and that will make 'em red again.

SAY. Long sitting to determine poor men's causes
Hath made me full of sickness and diseases.

CADE. Ye shall have a hempen caudle* then, and the help[d] of a hatchet.

---

a *One-and-twenty* fifteens,—] The impost called a *fifteen*, was the fifteenth part of all the personal property of each subject.

b The civil'st place of all this isle:] "*Ex his omnibus longe sunt humanissimi qui Cantium incolunt.*"—Cæsar, "De Bello Gallico," Lib. v. This passage is translated by Arthur Golding, 1565, as follows:—"Of all the inhabitantes of this isle, the *civilest* are the *Kentish folke.*"

c But *to maintain*—] In the folios,—"*Kent* to maintain," &c. The word "*But*" was substituted by Johnson.

d *The* help *of a hatchet.*] Farmer suggests that we ought to read "*pap with* a hatchet." This was a cant phrase of Shakespeare's day, and Lily has adopted it in the title of his celebrated pamphlet, "*Pap with an hatchet;* alias, a fig for my godson; or crack me this nut; or a country cuff; that is, a sound box of the ear, et cætera;" he has again introduced it, too, in his "Mother Bombie," 1594:—"They give us pap with a spoone before we can speake, and when wee speake for that we love, *pap with a hatchet.*" So also in Dent's "Plain Man's Pathway to Heaven," under "Lying:" —"their purpose was to entangle him in his words, and to entrap him, that they might catch advantage against him, and so cut his throat, and give him *pap with a hatchet.*" The *pap of a hatchet* meant, the stroke of the headsman's axe; a sa *hempen caudle*, which Cade promises with it, signified, death by the rope. The latter slang occurs, also, in the old play called, "The Downfall of Robert, Earl of Huntingdon," Act V. Sc. 1:—

"Here, Warman, put this *hempen caudle* o'er thy head.

(*) Old copies, *candle.*

DICK. Why dost thou quiver, man?

SAY. The palsy, and not fear, provokes me.

CADE. Nay, he nods at us, as who should say, I'll be even with you. I'll see if his head will stand steadier on a pole, or no. Take him away, and behead him.

SAY. Tell me wherein have I offended most?
Have I affected wealth or honour?—speak.
Are my chests fill'd up with extorted gold?
Is my apparel sumptuous to behold?
Whom have I injur'd, that ye seek my death?
These hands are free from guiltless blood-shedding,
This breast from harbouring foul deceitful thoughts.
O, let me live!

CADE. [*Aside.*] I feel remorse in myself with his words: but I'll bridle it: he shall die, an it be but for pleading so well for his life. Away with him! he has a familiar under his tongue; he speaks not o' God's name. Go, take him away, I say, and strike off his head presently; and then break into his son-in-law's house, sir James Cromer, and strike off his head, and bring them both upon two poles hither.

ALL. It shall be done.

SAY. Ah, countrymen! if when you make your prayers,
God should be so obdurate as yourselves,
How would it fare with your departed souls?
And therefore yet relent, and save my life.

CADE. Away with him! and do as I command ye. [*Exeunt some with* LORD SAY.] The proudest peer in the realm shall not wear a head on his shoulders, unless he pay me tribute; there shall not a maid be married, but she shall pay to me her maidenhead ere they have it: men shall hold of me *in capite;* and we charge and command, that their wives be as free as heart can wish, or tongue can tell.

DICK. My lord, when shall we go to Cheapside, and take up commodities upon our bills?

CADE. Marry, presently.

ALL. O brave!

Re-enter Rebels, *with the heads of* LORD SAY *and his* Son-in-law.

CADE. But is not this braver?—Let them kiss one another, for they loved well when they were

alive. Now part them again, lest they consult about the giving up of some more towns in France. Soldiers, defer the spoil of the city until night: for with these borne before us, instead of maces, will we ride through the streets; and, at every corner, have them kiss.—Away! [*Exeunt.*

SCENE VIII.—Southwark.

Alarum. Enter CADE *and all his Rabblement.*

CADE. Up Fish-street! Down Saint Magnus' corner![a] (4) Kill and knock down! Throw them into Thames!—[*A parley sounded, then a retreat.*] What noise is this I hear? Dare any be so bold to sound retreat or parley, when I command them kill?

Enter BUCKINGHAM *and old* CLIFFORD, *with* Forces.

BUCK. Ay, here they be that dare, and will disturb thee:
Know, Cade, we come ambassadors from the king
Unto the commons whom thou hast misled;
And here pronounce free pardon to them all
That will forsake thee, and go home in peace.

CLIF. What say ye, countrymen? will ye relent,
And yield to mercy, whilst 'tis offer'd you;
Or let a rebel[b] lead you to your deaths?
Who loves the king, and will embrace his pardon,
Fling up his cap, and say—*God save his majesty!*
Who hateth him, and honours not his father,
Henry the fifth, that made all France to quake,
Shake he his weapon at us, and pass by.

ALL. God save the king! God save the king!

CADE. What, Buckingham, and Clifford, are ye so brave?—And you, base peasants, do ye believe him? will you needs be hanged with your pardons about your necks? Hath my sword therefore broke through London Gates, that you should leave me at the White Hart in Southwark? I thought ye would never have given out[c] these arms, till you had recovered your ancient freedom: but you are all recreants and dastards, and delight to live in slavery to the nobility. Let them break your backs with burdens, take your houses over your heads, ravish your wives and daughters before your faces; for me,—I will make shift for one; and so—God's curse light upon you all!

---

a Up Fish-street! Down Saint Magnus' corner!] As these places are on the opposite side of the river to that on which Cade now is, we must suppose him issuing orders to different parties of his rebels as to the direction they should take.

b *Or let a* rebel *lead you to your deaths?*] So, and rightly, read Mr. Collier's and Mr. Singer's annotator. The folios have, "Or let a *rabble*," &c.

c *Have* given out, &c.] Have *given up*, have *relinquished*. To *give out*, in the sense of *resign* or *surrender*, is yet current among the vulgar.

ALL. We'll follow Cade, we'll follow Cade!
CLIF. Is Cade the son of Henry the fifth,
That thus you do exclaim you'll go with him?
Will he conduct you through the heart of France,
And make the meanest of you earls and dukes?
Alas, he hath no home, no place to fly to;
Nor knows he how to live, but by the spoil,
Unless by robbing of your friends and us.
Wer't not a shame, that whilst you live at jar,
The fearful French, whom you late vanquished,
Should make a start o'er seas, and vanquish you?
Methinks already in this civil broil,
I see them lording it in London streets,
Crying—*Viliaco!* [a] unto all they meet.
Better ten thousand base-born Cades miscarry,
Than you should stoop unto a Frenchman's mercy.
To France, to France, and get what you have lost;
Spare England, for it is your native coast:
Henry hath money, you are strong and manly;
God on our side, doubt not of victory.
ALL. A Clifford! a Clifford! we'll follow the king, and Clifford.
CADE. [*Aside.*] Was ever feather so lightly blown to and fro, as this multitude? the name of Henry the fifth hales them to an hundred mischiefs, and makes them leave me desolate. I see them lay their heads together to surprise me: my sword make way for me, for here is no staying. —In despite of the devils and hell, have through the very middest of you! and heavens and honour be witness, that no want of resolution in me, but only my followers' base and ignominious treasons, makes me betake me to my heels. [*Exit.*
BUCK. What, is he fled? Go, some, and follow him;
And he that brings his head unto the king
Shall have a thousand crowns for his reward.— [*Exeunt some of them.*
Follow me, soldiers; we'll devise a mean
To reconcile you all unto the king. [*Exeunt.*

SCENE IX.—Kenilworth Castle.

Trumpets sounded. Enter KING HENRY, QUEEN MARGARET, *and* SOMERSET, *on the terrace of the Castle.*

K. HEN. Was ever king that joy'd an earthly throne,
And could command no more content than I?
No sooner was I crept out of my cradle,
But I was made a king, at nine months old.
Was never subject long'd to be a king
As I do long and wish to be a subject.

Enter BUCKINGHAM *and* CLIFFORD.

BUCK. Health and glad tidings to your majesty!
K. HEN. Why, Buckingham, is the traitor Cade surpris'd?
Or is he but retir'd to make him strong?

Enter, below, a great number of CADE'S Followers, *with halters about their necks.*

CLIF. He's fled, my lord, and all his powers do yield;
And humbly thus, with halters on their necks,
Expect your highness' doom, of life, or death.
K. HEN. Then, heaven, set ope thy everlasting gates,
To entertain my vows of thanks and praise!—
Soldiers, this day have you redeem'd your lives,
And show'd how well you love your prince and country:
Continue still in this so good a mind,
And Henry, though he be infortunate,
Assure yourselves, will never be unkind;
And so, with thanks and pardon to you all,
I do dismiss you to your several countries.
ALL. God save the king! God save the king!

Enter a Messenger.

MESS. Please it your grace to be advertised,
The duke of York is newly come from Ireland:
And with a puissant and a mighty power,
Of gallowglasses, and stout kerns,(5)
Is marching hitherward in proud array;
And still proclaimeth, as he comes along,
His arms are only to remove from thee
The duke of Somerset, whom he terms a traitor.
K. HEN. Thus stands my state, 'twixt Cade and York, distress'd;
Like to a ship, that having 'scap'd a tempest,
Is straightway calm'd,[b] and boarded with a pirate:
But now is Cade driven back, his men dispers'd;
And now is York in arms to second him.—
I pray thee, Buckingham, go and meet him;[c]

---

[a] Viliaco!] The old copies have, *Villiago*, which Theobald transformed into *Villageois*. *Villiago*, or *Viliaco*, signifying *rascal, scoundrel*, and the like, is an epithet from the Italian, which occurs in Ben Jonson's "Every Man out of his Humour," Act V. Sc. 3, and in other of our early writers.

[b] *Is straightway* calm'd,—] This reading is derived from the fourth folio; the first has, "*calme;*" the second, "*claimd;*" the third, "*claim'd.*" Mr. Collier adopts *calm*.

[c] I pray thee, Buckingham, go and meet him;] In the Variorum this was altered to,—

" ——— go *forth* and meet him,"

and,—

" ——— go and meet *with* him."

Mr. Dyce proposes,—

" ——— go *thou* and meet him;"

and Mr. Collier's annotator,—

" ——— go *then* and meet him."

But the rhythm may be restored by the transposition of a word:—

"*Go*, I pray thee, Buckingham, and meet him."

And ask him what's the reason of these arms.
Tell him I'll send duke Edmund to the Tower;—
And, Somerset, we will commit thee thither,
Until his army be dismiss'd from him.
  Som. My lord,
I'll yield myself to prison willingly,
Or unto death, to do my country good.
  K. Hen. In any case, be not too rough in terms;
For he is fierce, and cannot brook hard language.
  Buck. I will, my lord; and doubt not so to deal,
As all things shall redound unto your good.
  K. Hen. Come, wife, let's in, and learn to govern better;
For yet may England curse my wretched reign.
[*Exeunt.*

SCENE X.—Kent. Iden's *Garden.*

Enter Cade.

Cade. Fie on ambition!* fie on myself; that have a sword, and yet am ready to famish! These five days have I hid me in these woods, and durst not peep out, for all the country is laid for me; but now am I so hungry, that if I might have a lease of my life for a thousand years, I could stay no longer. Wherefore, on a brick-wall have I climbed into this garden, to see if I can eat grass, or pick a sallet another while, which is not amiss to cool a man's stomach this hot weather. And, I think, this word sallet was born to do me good: for, many a time, but for a sallet,[a] my brain-pan had been cleft with a brown bill; and, many a time, when I have been dry, and bravely marching, it hath served me instead of a quart-pot to drink in; and now the word sallet must serve me to feed on.

Enter Iden.

Iden. Lord, who would live turmoiled in the court,
And may enjoy such quiet walks as these!
This small inheritance my father left me,
Contenteth me, and worth a monarchy.
I seek not to wax great by others' waning;*

(*) First folio, *ambitions.*

[a] Sallet,—] This feeble quibble on *sallet*, a helmet, and *salad* must have been sufficiently hackneyed. It occurs as early as 1537 in "A new Enterlude called Thersytes:"—

"Thersites. I say abyde good Mulciber, I pray ye make me a sallet.
Mulciber. Why Thersites hast thou anye wytte in thy head,
Woldest thou have a sallet nowe all the herbes are dead?
*   *   *   *   *   *
Thersites. Goddes passion, Mulciber, where is thy wit and memory?
I wolde have a sallet made of stele.
Mulciber. Whye Syr, in youre stomacke longe you shall it fele,
For stele is harde for to digest.
Thersites. Mans bones and sydes, hee is worse then a beast!
I wolde have a sallet to were on my hed."
&c. &c. &c.

(*) Old text, *warning.*

Or gather wealth, I care not with what envy;
Sufficeth that I have maintains my state,
And sends the poor well pleased from my gate.

CADE. [*Aside.*] Here's the lord of the soil come to seize me for a stray, for entering his fee-simple without leave. Ah, villain, thou wilt betray me, and get a thousand crowns of the king by carrying my head to him! but I'll make thee eat iron like an ostrich, and swallow my sword like a great pin, ere thou and I part.

IDEN. Why, rude companion, whatsoe'er thou be,
I know thee not; why, then, should I betray thee?
Is't not enough, to break into my garden,
And, like a thief, to come to rob my grounds,
Climbing my walls in spite of me the owner,
But thou wilt brave me with these saucy terms?

CADE. Brave thee! ay, by the best blood that ever was broached, and beard thee too. Look on me well: I have eat no meat these five days; yet, come thou and thy five men, and if I do not leave you all as dead as a door-nail, I pray God I may never eat grass more.

IDEN. Nay, it shall ne'er be said, while England stands,
That Alexander Iden, an esquire of Kent,
Took odds to combat a poor famish'd man.
Oppose thy steadfast-gazing eyes to mine,
See if thou canst outface me with thy looks.
Set limb to limb, and thou art far the lesser;
Thy hand is but a finger to my fist;
Thy leg a stick compared with this truncheon;
My foot shall fight with all the strength thou hast;
And if mine arm be heaved in the air,
Thy grave is digg'd already in the earth.
As for words, whose greatness answers words,
Let this my sword report what speech forbears.

CADE. By my valour, the most complete champion that ever I heard.—Steel, if thou turn the edge, or cut not out the burly-boned clown in chines of beef ere thou sleep in thy sheath, I beseech God[a] on my knees, thou mayest be turned to hobnails. [*They fight.* CADE *falls.*] O, I am slain! famine and no other hath slain me: let ten thousand devils come against me, and give me but the ten meals I have lost, and I'd defy them all. Wither, garden; and be henceforth a burying-place to all that do dwell in this house, because the unconquered soul of Cade is fled.

IDEN. Is't Cade that I have slain, that monstrous traitor?
Sword, I will hallow thee for this thy deed,
And hang thee o'er my tomb when I am dead:
Ne'er shall this blood be wiped from thy point;
But thou shalt wear it as a herald's coat,
To emblaze the honour that thy master got.

CADE. Iden, farewell; and be proud of thy victory. Tell Kent from me, she hath lost her best man, and exhort all the world to be cowards,—for I, that never feared any, am vanquished by famine, not by valour. [*Dies.*

IDEN. How much thou wrong'st me, heaven be my judge.
Die, damned wretch, the curse of her that bare thee!
And as I thrust thy body in with my sword,
So wish I, I might thrust thy soul to hell.
Hence will I drag thee headlong by the heels
Unto a dunghill, which shall be thy grave,
And there cut off thy most ungracious head;
Which I will bear in triumph to the king,
Leaving thy trunk for crows to feed upon.
[*Exit* IDEN, *dragging out the body.*

---

[a] *I beseech* God—] So "The Contention;" but in the folios, Cade is made to swear by *Jove*.

ACT V.

SCENE I.—*The same. Fields between* Dartford *and* Blackheath.

The KING'S *Camp on one side. On the other, enter* YORK *attended, with drum and colours: his* Forces *at some distance.*

YORK. From Ireland thus comes York to claim his right,
And pluck the crown from feeble Henry's head;
Ring, bells, aloud; burn, bonfires, clear and bright;
To entertain great England's lawful king!
Ah, *sancta majestas!* who would not buy thee dear?
Let them obey, that know not how to rule;
This hand was made to handle nought but gold:
I cannot give due action to my words,
Except a sword or sceptre balance it.
A sceptre shall it have,—have I a soul,—
On which I'll toss the flower-de-luce of France.

Enter BUCKINGHAM.

[*Aside.*] Whom have we here? Buckingham, to disturb me?

The king hath sent him, sure: I must dissemble.
BUCK. York, if thou meanest well, I greet thee well.
YORK. Humphrey of Buckingham, I accept thy greeting.
Art thou a messenger, or come of pleasure?
BUCK. A messenger from Henry, our dread liege,
To know the reason of these arms in peace;
Or why, thou—being a subject as I am,—
Against thy oath and true allegiance sworn,
Should raise so great a power without his leave,
Or dare to bring thy force so near the court.
YORK. Scarce can I speak, my choler is so great.
O, I could hew up rocks, and fight with flint,
I am so angry at these abject terms!
And now, like Ajax Telamonius,
On sheep or oxen could I spend my fury! *Aside.*
I am far better born than is the king;
More like a king, more kingly in my thoughts:
But I must make fair weather yet a while,
Till Henry be more weak, and I more strong.—
O* Buckingham, I pr'ythee pardon me,
That I have given no answer all this while,
My mind was troubled with deep melancholy.
The cause why I have brought this army hither,
Is to remove proud Somerset from the king,
Seditious to his grace, and to the state.
BUCK. That is too much presumption on thy part:
But if thy arms be to no other end,
The king hath yielded unto thy demand;
The duke of Somerset is in the Tower.
YORK. Upon thine honour, is he prisoner?
BUCK. Upon mine honour, he is prisoner.
YORK. Then, Buckingham, I do dismiss my powers.—
Soldiers, I thank you all; disperse yourselves:
Meet me to-morrow in Saint George's Field,
You shall have pay, and every thing you wish.
And let my sovereign, virtuous Henry,
Command my eldest son,—nay, all my sons,
As pledges of my fealty and love,
I'll send them all as willing as I live;
Lands, goods, horse, armour, any thing I have
Is his to use, so Somerset may die.
BUCK. York, I commend this kind submission:
We twain will go into his highness' tent.

Enter KING HENRY, *attended.*

K. HEN. Buckingham, doth York intend no harm to us,

(*) First folio omits, O.

That thus he marcheth with thee arm in arm?
YORK. In all submission and humility,
York doth present himself unto your highness.
K. HEN. Then what intend these forces thou dost bring?
YORK. To heave the traitor Somerset from hence;
And fight against that monstrous rebel, Cade,
Who since I heard to be discomfited.

Enter IDEN, *with* CADE'S *head.*

IDEN. If one so rude and of so mean condition,
May pass into the presence of a king,
Lo, I present your grace a traitor's head,
The head of Cade, whom I in combat slew.
K. HEN. The head of Cade!—Great God, how just art thou!
O, let me view his visage being dead,
That living wrought me such exceeding trouble.—
Tell me, my friend, art thou the man that slew him?
IDEN. I was, an't like your majesty.
K. HEN. How art thou call'd? and what is thy degree?
IDEN. Alexander Iden, that's my name;
A poor esquire of Kent, that loves his king.
BUCK. So please it you, my lord, 't were not amiss
He were created knight for his good service.
K. HEN. Iden, kneel down. [*He kneels.*] Rise up a knight.
We give thee for reward a thousand marks;
And will that thou henceforth attend on us.
IDEN. May Iden live to merit such a bounty,
And never live but true unto his liege! [*Rises.*
K. HEN. See, Buckingham! Somerset comes with the queen;
Go, bid her hide him quickly from the duke.

Enter QUEEN MARGARET *and* SOMERSET.

Q. MAR. For thousand Yorks he shall not hide his head,
But boldly stand, and front him to his face.
YORK. How now! is Somerset at liberty?
Then, York, unloose thy long-imprison'd thoughts,
And let thy tongue be equal with thy heart.
Shall I endure the sight of Somerset?—
False king! why hast thou broken faith with me,
Knowing how hardly I can brook abuse?
King did I call thee?—no, thou art not king;
Not fit to govern and rule multitudes,
Which dar'st not,—no, nor canst not rule a traitor.
That head of thine doth not become a crown;
Thy hand is made to grasp a palmer's staff,

And not to grace an awful princely sceptre.
That gold must round engirt these brows of mine;
Whose smile and frown, like to Achilles' spear,
Is able with the change to kill and cure.
Here is a hand to hold a sceptre up,
And with the same to act controlling laws.
Give place; by heaven thou shalt rule no more
O'er him whom heaven created for thy ruler.

SOM. O monstrous traitor!—I arrest thee, York,
Of capital treason 'gainst the king and crown:
Obey, audacious traitor; kneel for grace.

YORK. Wouldst have me kneel? first let me ask of these,[a]
If they can brook I bow a knee to man.—
Sirrah, call in my sons* to be my bail;
[*Exit an* Attendant.
I know, ere they will have me go to ward,
They'll pawn their swords for† my enfranchisement.

Q. MAR. Call hither Clifford; bid him come amain, [*Exit* BUCKINGHAM.[b]
To say if that the bastard boys of York
Shall be the surety for their traitor father.

YORK. O blood-bespotted Neapolitan,
Outcast of Naples, England's bloody scourge!
The sons of York, thy betters in their birth,
Shall be their father's bail; and bane to those
That for my surety will refuse the boys!
See, where they come; I'll warrant they'll make it good.

Q. MAR. And here comes Clifford, to deny their bail.

Enter EDWARD *and* RICHARD PLANTAGENET, *with* Forces, *at one side; at the other, with* Forces *also, old* CLIFFORD *and his* Son.

CLIF. Health and all happiness to my lord the king! [*Kneels.*

YORK. I thank thee, Clifford: say, what news with thee?
Nay, do not fright us with an angry look:
We are thy sovereign, Clifford,—kneel again;
For thy mistaking so, we pardon thee.

CLIF. This is my king, York,—I do not mistake;
But thou mistak'st me much to think I do:—
To Bedlam with him! is the man grown mad?

K. HEN. Ay, Clifford; a bedlam and ambitious humour
Makes him oppose himself against his king.

CLIF. He is a traitor; let him to the Tower,
And chop away that factious pate of his.

Q. MAR. He is arrested, but will not obey;
His sons, he says, shall give their words for him.

YORK. Will you not, sons?

EDW. Ay, noble father, if our words will serve.

RICH. And if words will not, then our weapons shall.

CLIF. Why, what a brood of traitors have we here!

YORK. Look in a glass, and call thy image so;
I am thy king, and thou a false-heart traitor.—
Call hither to the stake my two brave bears,
That, with the very shaking of their chains,
They may astonish these fell-lurking curs;
Bid Salisbury and Warwick come to me.

Drums. Enter WARWICK *and* SALISBURY, *with* Forces.

CLIF. Are these thy bears? we'll bait thy bears to death,
And manacle the bear-ward in their chains,
If thou dar'st bring them to the baiting-place.

RICH. Oft have I seen a hot o'erweening cur
Run back and bite, because he was withheld;
Who, being suffer'd[c] with the bear's fell paw,
Hath clapp'd his tail between his legs and cried:
And such a piece of service will you do,
If you oppose yourselves to match lord Warwick.

CLIF. Hence, heap of wrath, foul indigested lump,
As crooked in thy manners as thy shape!

YORK. Nay, we shall heat you thoroughly anon.

CLIF. Take heed, lest by your heat you burn yourselves.

K. HEN. Why, Warwick, hath thy knee forgot to bow?
Old Salisbury,—shame to thy silver hair,
Thou mad misleader of thy brain-sick son!
What, wilt thou on thy death-bed play the ruffian
And seek for sorrow with thy spectacles?—
O, where is faith! O, where is loyalty!
If it be banish'd from the frosty head,
Where shall it find a harbour in the earth?—
Wilt thou go dig a grave to find out war,
And shame thine honourable age with blood?
Why art thou old, and want'st experience?
Or wherefore dost abuse it, if thou hast it?

(*) First folio, *sonne*. (†) First folio, *of*.

a *First let me ask* of these, &c.] The old text reads, "—— of *thee*." By *these* York is supposed to mean his sons, or his forces.

b *Exit* BUCKINGHAM.] The old copies have no stage direction here; but it is evident from what the King says presently—

"*Call Buckingham*, and bid him arm himself"—

that he must have left the stage at some period of the scene. The modern editors have been equally unmindful of his *exit*.

c *Who*, being suffer'd—] That is, who being *unrestrained, unchecked*. So in Act III. Sc. 2:—

"Lest, *being suffer'd* in that harmful slumber," &c.

And in "Henry VI." Part III. Act IV. Sc. 8:—

"A little fire is quickly trodden out,
Which *being suffer'd*, rivers cannot quench."

Mr. Collier's annotator, from ignorance of the idiom, substitutes *having* for *being*; "and," Mr. C. remarks, "we may be confident, gives us the poet's language."

For shame! in duty bend thy knee to me,
That bows unto the grave with mickle age.
SAL. My lord, I have consider'd with myself
The title of this most renowned duke;
And in my conscience do repute his grace
The rightful heir to England's royal seat.
K. HEN. Hast thou not sworn allegiance unto me?
SAL. I have.
K. HEN. Canst thou dispense with heaven for such an oath?
SAL. It is great sin to swear unto a sin;
But greater sin to keep a sinful oath.
Who can be bound by any solemn vow
To do a murderous deed, to rob a man,
To force a spotless virgin's chastity,
To reave the orphan of his patrimony,
To wring the widow from her custom'd right;
And have no other reason for this wrong,
But that he was bound by a solemn oath?
Q. MAR. A subtle traitor needs no sophister.
K. HEN. Call Buckingham, and bid him arm himself.
YORK. Call Buckingham and all the friends thou hast,
I am resolv'd for death or* dignity.
CLIF. The first I warrant thee, if dreams prove true.
WAR. You were best to go to bed, and dream again,
To keep thee from the tempest of the field.
CLIF. I am resolv'd to bear a greater storm,
Than any thou canst conjure up to-day;
And that I'll write upon thy burgonet,
Might I but know thee by thy household[a] badge.
WAR. Now, by my father's badge, old Nevil's crest,
The rampant bear chain'd to the ragged staff,
This day I'll wear aloft my burgonet,
(As on a mountain-top the cedar shows
That keeps his leaves in spite of any storm,)
Even to† affright thee with the view thereof.
CLIF. And from thy burgonet I'll rend thy bear,
And tread it under foot with all contempt,
Despite the bear-ward that protects the bear.
Y. CLIF. And so to arms, victorious father,
To quell the rebels and their 'complices.
RICH. Fie! charity! for shame, speak not in spite,
For you shall sup with Jesu Christ to-night.
Y. CLIF. Foul stigmatic,[b] that's more than thou canst tell.
RICH. If not in heaven, you'll surely sup in hell. [*Exeunt severally.*

SCENE II.—Saint Alban's.

Alarums: Excursions. Enter WARWICK.

WAR. Clifford of Cumberland, 'tis Warwick calls!
And if thou dost not hide thee from the bear,
Now,—when the angry trumpet sounds alarm,
And dead men's cries do fill the empty air,—
Clifford, I say, come forth and fight with me!
Proud northern lord, Clifford of Cumberland,
Warwick is hoarse with calling thee to arms.

Enter YORK.

How now, my noble lord! what all a-foot?
YORK. The deadly-handed Clifford slew my steed,
But match to match I have encounter'd him,
And made a prey for carrion kites and crows
Even of the bonny beast he lov'd so well.

Enter CLIFFORD.

WAR. Of one or both of us the time is come.
YORK. Hold, Warwick, seek thee out some other chase,
For I myself must hunt this deer to death.
WAR. Then, nobly, York; 'tis for a crown thou fight'st.—
As I intend, Clifford, to thrive to-day,
It grieves my soul to leave thee unassail'd. [*Exit.*
CLIF. What seest thou in me, York? Why dost thou pause?
YORK. With thy brave bearing should I be in love,
But that thou art so fast mine enemy.
CLIF. Nor should thy prowess want praise and esteem,
But that 'tis shown ignobly and in treason.
YORK. So let it help me now against thy sword,
As I in justice and true right express it!
CLIF. My soul and body on the action both!—
YORK. A dreadful lay!—address thee instantly.
[*They fight, and* CLIFFORD *falls.*
CLIF. *La fin couronne les œuvres.* [*Dies.*
YORK. Thus war hath given thee peace, for thou art still.
Peace with his soul, heaven, if it be thy will! [*Exit.*

(*) Old text, *and*.

(†) Old text, *so*.

a Household *badge*.] So "The Contention." The first folio misprints *household, housed*.

b *Foul* stigmatic,—] A *stigmatic* originally signified any one marked, as a criminal punishment, with a hot iron. To appreciate the application of this term to Richard, we must call to mind the cruel belief once prevalent, that personal deformity was a brand or *stigma* set by Nature on a being, to indicate a vicious and malignant disposition.

Enter Young CLIFFORD.

Y. CLIF. Shame and confusion! all is on the rout;
Fear frames disorder, and disorder wounds
Where it should guard. O war, thou son of hell,
Whom angry heavens do make their minister,
Throw in the frozen bosoms of our part
Hot coals of vengeance!—Let no soldier fly:
He that is truly dedicate to war
Hath no self-love; nor he that loves himself,
Hath not essentially, but by circumstance,
The name of valour.—O, let the vile world end,
[*Seeing his dead father.*
And the premised flames of the last day
Knit heaven and earth together!
Now let the general trumpet blow his blast,
Particularities and petty sounds
To cease! Wast thou ordain'd, dear father,
To lose thy youth in peace, and to achieve
The silver livery of advised age;
And, in thy reverence, and thy chair-days, thus
To die in ruffian battle?—Even at this sight
My heart is turn'd to stone: and, while 'tis mine,
It shall be stony. York not our old men spares;
No more will I their babes: tears virginal
Shall be to me even as the dew to fire;
And beauty, that the tyrant oft reclaims,
Shall to my flaming wrath be oil and flax.
Henceforth I will not have to do with pity:
Meet I an infant of the house of York,
Into as many gobbets will I cut it,
As wild Medea young Absyrtus did:
In cruelty will I seek out my fame.—
Come, thou new ruin of old Clifford's house;
[*Taking up the body.*
As did Æneas old Anchises bear,
So bear I thee upon my manly shoulders;
But then Æneas bare a living load,
Nothing so heavy as these woes of mine. [*Exit.*

Enter RICHARD PLANTAGENET *and* SOMERSET, *fighting, and* SOMERSET *is killed.*

RICH. So, lie thou there;—
For underneath an alehouse' paltry sign,
The Castle in Saint Alban's, Somerset
Hath made the wizard famous in his death.—
Sword, hold thy temper: heart, be wrathful still:
Priests pray for enemies, but princes kill. [*Exit.*

Alarums: Excursions. Enter KING HENRY, QUEEN MARGARET, *and others, retreating.*

Q. MAR. Away, my lord! you are slow: for shame, away!
K. HEN. Can we outrun the heavens? Good Margaret, stay.
Q. MAR. What are you made of? you'll nor fight nor fly:
Now is it manhood, wisdom, and defence,
To give the enemy way; and to secure us
By what we can, which can no more but fly.
[*Alarum afar off.*
If you be ta'en, we then should see the bottom
Of all our fortunes: but if we haply scape
(As well we may, if not through your neglect),
We shall to London get; where you are lov'd,
And where this breach, now in our fortunes made,
May readily be stopp'd.

Re-enter Young CLIFFORD.

Y. CLIF. But that my heart's on future mischief set,
I would speak blasphemy ere bid you fly;
But fly you must; uncurable discomfit
Reigns in the hearts of all our present parts.
Away, for your relief! And we will live
To see their day, and them our fortune give:
Away, my lord, away! [*Exeunt.*

SCENE III.—*Fields near* Saint Alban's.

Alarum: Retreat. Flourish; then enter YORK, RICHARD PLANTAGENET, WARWICK, *and* Soldiers, *with drum and colours.*

YORK. Of[a] Salisbury, who can report of him,—
That winter lion, who in rage forgets
Aged contusions and all brush of time;
And, like a gallant in the brow of youth,
Repairs him with occasion? This happy day
Is not itself, nor have we won one foot,
If Salisbury be lost.
RICH. My noble father,
Three times to-day I holp him to his horse,
Three times bestrid him, thrice I led him off,
Persuaded him from any further act:
But still, where danger was, still there I met him;
And, like rich hangings in a homely house,
So was his will in his old feeble body.
But, noble as he is, look where he comes.

Enter SALISBURY.

SAL. Now, by my sword, well hast thou fought to-day;
By the mass, so did we all.—I thank you, Richard:
God knows, how long it is I have to live;
And it hath pleas'd him, that three times to-day
You have defended me from imminent death.—
Well, lords, we have not got that which we have:
'Tis not enough our foes are this time fled,
Being opposites of such repairing nature.
YORK. I know our safety is to follow them;
For, as I hear, the king is fled to London,
To call a present court of parliament.
Let us pursue him ere the writs go forth:—
What says lord Warwick? shall we after them?
WAR. After them! Nay, before them, if we can.
Now, by my hand, lords, 'twas a glorious day:
Saint Alban's battle, won by famous York,
Shall be eterniz'd in all age to come.—
Sound drum and trumpets:—and to London all:
And more such days as these to us befal! (1)
[*Exeunt.*

---

a *Of Salisbury,—*] Mr. Collier's annotator, following the earlier version of the play, which reads,—

"But did you see *old* Salisbury?"—

substitutes *old* for *of*.

ILLUSTRATIVE COMMENTS.

ACT I.

(1) Scene II.—*With Margery Jourdain, the cunning witch.*] From Ryder's *Fœdera* we find that on the ninth of May, 1432 (the 10th of Henry VI.), *Margery Jourdemayn, John Virley*, clerk, and friar *John Ashwell*, who had been confined on a charge of sorcery in the castle of Windsor, were conveyed by the Constable of the castle, Walter Hungerford, to the Council at Westminster, and were there delivered into the custody of the Lord Chancellor. The same day, upon finding securities for their good behaviour, they were discharged.

(2) Scene IV.—*All, away!*] Hall's account of the arrest and trial of the Duchess and her confederates, is as follows:—"Thys yere (1442-3), dame Elyanour Cobham, wyfe to the sayd duke, was accused of treason, for that she, by sorcery and enchauntment, entended to destroy the kyng, to thentent to advaunce and promote her husbande to the croune: upon thys she was examined in sainct Stephens chapell, before the bishop of Canterbury, and there by examinacion convict and judged to do open penaunce, in iii open places within the cytie of London, and after that adiudged to perpetuall prisone in the Isle of Man, under the kepyng of Sir Ihon Stanley, knyght. At the same season wer arrested as ayders and counsailers to the sayde duchesse, Thomas Southwel, prieste and chanon of saincte Stephens in Westmynster, Ihon Hum priest, Roger Bolyngbroke, a conyng nycromancier, and Margerie Iourdayne, surnamed the witche of Eye, to whose charge it was laied, that thei, at the request of the duchesse, had devised an image of waxe representyng the kyng, whiche by their sorcery, a litle and litle consumed, entendyng therby in conclusion to waist and destroy the kynges person, and so to bryng hym to death; for the which treison, they wer adjudged to dye, and so Margery Jordayne was brent in smithfelde, and Roger Bolyngbroke was drawen and quartered at tiborne; takyng upon his death, that there was never no suche thyng by them ymagined; Ihon Hum had his pardon, and Southwel died in the toure before execution."

ACT II.

(1) Scene I.—

——for flying at the brook,
I saw not better sport, these seven years' day.]

Thomas Nash, (not the satirical author of "Pierce Pennilesse his Supplication,") in his "Quaternio, or a Fourefold Way to a Happie Life," 1633, p. 35, affords an animated picture of the sport of hawking at water-fowl:—"And to heare an Accipitrary relate againe, how he went forth in a cleare, calme, and Sun-shine Evening, about an houre before the Sunne did usually maske himselfe, unto the River, where finding of a Mallard, he whistled off his Faulcon, and how shee flew from him as if shee would never have turned head againe, yet presently upon a shoote came in, how then by degrees, by little and little, by flying about and about, she mounted so high, until she had lessened herselfe to the view of the beholder, to the shape of a Pigeon or Partridge, and had made the height of the Moone the place of her flight, how presently upon the landing of the fowle, shee came downe like a stone and enewed it, and suddenly got up againe, and suddenly upon a second landing came downe againe, and missing of it, in the downecome recovered it, beyond expectation, to the admiration of the beholder at a long flight."

(2) Scene I.—*Let them be whipped through every market-town, till they come to Berwick, from whence they came.*] Shakespeare may have derived the incidents of the foregoing scene from a story related by Sir Thomas More as communicated to him by his father:—"I remember me that I have hard my father tell of a begger that, in Kyng Henry his daies the sixt, cam with his wife to Saint Albonis. And there was walking about the towne begging a five or six dayes before the kinges commynge thither, saienge that he was borne blinde and never sawe in hys lyfe. And was warned in hys dreame that he shoulde come out of Berwyke, where he said he had ever dwelled, to seke saynt Albon, and that he had ben at his shryne, and had not bene holpen. And therfore he woulde go seke hym at some other place, for he had hard some say sins he came, that sainct Albonys body shold be at Colon, and indede such a contencion hath ther ben. But of troth, as I am surely informed, he lieth here at Saint Albonis, saving some reliques of him, which thei there shew shrined. But to tell you forth, whan the kyng was comen, and the towne full, sodainlye thys blind man at Saint Albonis shrine had his sight agayne, and a myracle solemply rongen, and *te Deum* songen, so that nothyng was talked of in al the towne but this myracle. So happened it than that Duke Humfry of Glocester, a great wyse man and very well lerned, having great joy to se such a myracle, called the pore man unto hym. And first shewing hymselfe joyouse of Goddes glory so shewed in the gettinge of his sight, and exortinge hym to mekenes, and to none ascribing of any part the worship to himself, nor to be proued of the peoples prayse, which would call hym a good and a godly man therby. At last he loked well upon his eyen, and asked whyther he could never se nothing at al in al his life before. And whan as well his wyfe as himself affermed falsely no, than he loked advisedly upon his eien again, and said, I beleve you very wel, for me thinketh that ye cannot se well yet. Yes, sir, quoth he, I thanke God, and his holy marter, I can se nowe as well as any man. Ye can, quoth the duke; what colour is my gowne? Than anone the beggar tolde him. What coloure, quoth he, is this mans gowne? He told him also, and so forth, without any sticking, he told him the names of al the colours that coulde bee shewed him. And whan my lord saw that, he bad him walke faytoure, and made him be set openly in the stockes. For though

he could have sene soudenly by miracle, the dyfference betwene divers colours, yet coulde he not by the syght so sodenly tell the names of all these colours, but if he had knowen them before, no more than the names of al the men that he should sodenly se."

(3) SCENE III.—*Enter, on one side, Horner, &c.*] The stage direction of "The Contention" is amusing:—"*Enter at one doore the Armourer and his neighbours, drinking to him so much that he is drunken, and he enters with a drum before him, and his staffe with a sand-bag fastened to it, and at the other doore, his Man with a drum and sand-bagge, and Prentises drinking to him.*"

(4) SCENE III.—*Peter strikes down his master.*] In our illustration of the trial by battle between the Dukes of Hereford and Norfolk ("Richard the Second," Act I. Sc. 3), the combat represented in this play was especially referred to. In the former instance the duello takes place between noblemen of the first rank, in the present betwixt two persons of the lowest degree, but in both the parties are each other's equals, and in both the combat springs from an accusation of treason, which, with the appeal of murder, was always submitted to be a valid cause for permitting the Wager of Battle. The cases in question were thus far parallel, and even in the ceremonial proper to each, though widely different in the scene of action, and the habits and weapons of the combatants, there was a marked degree of similarity. The event here introduced took place early in December, 1446, and was the second appeal of treason made in that year, for which the Trial by Battle was appointed. The Prior of Kilmaine had appeached the Earl of Ormond, and "for trial thereof," says Fabian, "the place of battaill was assigned in Smithfield, and the barriers for the same there readie pight. In which meane tyme a Doctour of Divinitie, named Master Gilbert Worthington, Parsone of Saint Andrews in Holborne, and other good menne, made soche labour to the kynges counsaill, that when the daie of battaill approched, the quarell was taken into the kynges hande and there ended." The same author also records the Appeal of Treason represented in the present drama; and he, in all probability, as Mr. Douce conjectured, was Shakespeare's authority for the incident. In his Chronicle there is a blank space left for the name of the armourer, which is supplied by Holinshed. "The real names of these combatants," Mr. Douce observes, "were John Daveys and William Catour, as appears from the original precept to the sheriffs, still remaining in the Exchequer, commanding them to prepare the barriers in Smithfield for combat. The names of the sheriffs were Godfrey Boloyne and Robert Horne; and the latter, which occurs on the page of Fabian's Chronicle that records the duel, might have suggested the name of Horner to Shakespeare." The following is Fabian's narrative, by which it will be seen that the poet has historical authority for exhibiting the armourer as overcome by intoxication, though he appears to have deviated from it in making him "confess treason:"—"In this yere an armurer named . . . . was appeched of treason by a servaunte of his owne: for triall whereof a daie to them was given to fight in Smithfield. At which daie of battaill the saied armurer was overcomen and slain, and that by the misguiding of himself: for upon the morowe when he should come to the fielde, his neighbours came to him, and gave unto him so moche wine and good ale, that he was therewithe distempered, that he reeled as he went, *and so was slaine without gilt.* But that false servaunt lived not longe unpunished, for he was after hanged for felony at Tiburne." In the volume of "Illustrations of the Manners and Expences of Antient Times in England," published by Nichols, will be found the Exchequer record of the items and charges for erecting the barriers and preparing the field for this duello, amounting to £10 18*s.* 9*d.* These works occupied about a week; the barriers were brought in nine carts from Westminster, and the ground was cleared of snow, and strewed with rushes and 168 loads of sand and gravel. The account is closed with some items partly disallowed by the Barons of the Exchequer, showing that however innocent the vanquished armourer really might have been, his body was treated as that of a traitor:—"Paid to Officeres for watching of ye ded man in Smythfelde, ye same daye and ye nyghte aftyr that the bataill was doon; and for hors hyre for the Officeres at the execution doying; and for the hangmans labour,—11*s.* 6*d.* Also paid for ye cloth yat lay upon ye ded man in Smythfelde—8*d.* Also paid for 1 pole and nayllis and setting up of ye manny's hed on London bridge—8*d.*"

It is not so easy to ascertain the source whence Shakespeare derived the costume of these combatants, as it was in the case of the important personages who fought in "Richard the Second." No one of the Chronicles notices the "staff with a sand-bag fastened to it," with which Horner and Peter were to settle their differences. The weapons proper to civil persons under the rank of gentlemen, and in a case of felony, were batons of an ell in length, tipped with horn at each end, but without any iron; and square targets covered with leather. The sand-bags appear to have been attached to the batons only when the combat was assigned on a Writ of Right; which became, as Blackstone regards it, a species of cudgel-playing, the end of which was not the death of either party, but only a manifest superiority of skill. Any nice distinction as to the peculiar weapons appointed by the legal character of appeal was not to be expected in Shakespeare, especially as such disputes commonly related to questions of property, and not to criminal accusations.

ACT III.

(1) SCENE I.—*Caper upright like a wild Mórisco.*] There can be little doubt that upon the first introduction of the Moorish dance, or as it soon became corrupted *Morris* dance, the performers endeavoured, by the wildness of their gestures, by colouring their faces, and by assuming a costume which resembled that of Africa, to imitate as nearly as they could the actions and appearance of the native dancers. One peculiarity which has been already noticed (see Illustrative Comments to "All's Well that Ends Well," p. 55), and which lasted in this country as long as the Morris dance itself, was that of the dancers hanging bells about their knees, and sometimes their arms also; hence the allusion in the text to the *shaking his bells.* From some passages in our old writers, it is evident also, that in imitation of the original dancers, they were once in the habit of bearing swords, which they shook and probably clashed with vehemence, as they became excited by the motion, the noise they made, and by the plaudits of the spectators:—"There are other actions of dancing used, as of those who are represented with weapons in their hands going round in a ring capering skilfully, *shaking their weapons* after the manner of the Morris, with divers actions of meeting."—HAYDOCKE'S *Translation of Lomazzo, on Painting,* 1598.

(2) SCENE II.—*Enter certain Murderers, hastily.*] The stage direction in the folio 1623 is:—"*Enter two or three, running over the stage, from the murder of Duke* Humphrey;" but from that in the earlier version of the play, "The Contention," it is evident the murder was represented to the audience in dumb show:—"*Then the Curtaines being drawne, Duke* Humphrey *is discovered in his bed, and two men lying on his brest, and smothering him in his bed. And then enter the Duke of* Suffolke *to them.*"

(3) SCENE II.—

It cannot be but he was murder'd here;
The least of all these signs were probable.]

It is instructive and interesting also to observe the care with which this terrible picture was elaborated from what we believe to have been Shakespeare's first rough design of it in "The Contention:"—

"WAR. Oft have I seene a timely parted ghost,
Of ashie semblance, pale and bloodlesse,
But loe the blood is setled in his face,
More better coloured then when he liv'd,
His well proportioned beard made rough and sterne,
His fingers spred abroad as one that graspt for life,
Yet was by strength surprisde, the least of these are probable,
It cannot chuse but he was murthered."

An eminent medical authority makes the following observation upon the poet's description of Gloucester's death:—"My readers will smile, perhaps, to see me quoting Shakespeare among physicians and theologists; but not one of all their tribe, populous though it be, could describe so exquisitely the marks of apoplexy, conspiring with the struggles for life, and the agonies of suffocation, to deform the countenance of the dead: so curiously does our poet present to our conceptions all the signs from which it might be inferred that the good duke Humfrey had died a violent death."—BELL'S *Principles of Surgery,* 1815. ii. 557.

(4) SCENE III.—

Close up his eyes, and draw the curtain close;
And let us all to meditation.]

Every circumstance connected with a scene so universally admired as this commands attention, and no apology therefore need be offered for the introduction here of Shakespeare's original version of it as it stands in the old "Contention," or of the passage from the Chronicles on which it appears to have been based:—

"*Enter King and* Salsbury, *and then the Curtaines be drawne, and the Cardinall is discovered in his bed, raving and staring as if he were madde.*

CAR. Oh death, if thou wilt let me live but one whole yeare,
Ile give thee as much gold as will purchase such another iland.
KING. Oh see my Lord of Salsbury how he is troubled.
Lord Cardinall, remember Christ must save thy soule.
CAR. Why died he not in his bed?
What would you have me to do then?
Can I make men live whether they will or no?
Sirra, go fetch me the strong poison which the Pothicary sent me.
Oh see where Duke Humphreys ghoast doth stand,
And stares me in the face. Looke, looke, coame downe his haire,
So now hees gone againe: Oh, oh, oh.
SAL. See how the panges of death doth gripe his heart.
KING. Lord Cardinall, if thou diest assured of heavenly blisse,
Hold up thy hand and make some signe to us.
[*The Cardinall dies.*
Oh see he dies, and makes no signe at all.
Oh God forgive his soule.
SALB. So bad an ende did never none behold,
But as his death, so was his life in all.
KING. Forbeare to iudge, good Salsbury forbeare,
For God will iudge us all.
Go take him hence, and see his funerals be performde.
[*Exet omnes.*"

The account in Hall, which in all probability suggested the scene, is as follows:—"During these doynges, Henry Beaufford, byshop of Wynchester, and called the ryche Cardynall, departed out of this worlde, and was buried at Wynchester. This man was sonne to Ihon of Gaunte, duke of Lancaster, discended of an honorable lignage, but borne in Baste, more noble of bloud, then notable in learnyng, haut in stomacke, and hygh in countenaunce, ryche above measure of all men, and to fewe liberal, disdaynfull to his kynne, and dreadfull to his lovers, preferrynge money before friendshippe, many thinges begynning, and nothing perfourmyng. His covetous insaciable, and hope of long lyfe, made hym bothe to forget God, his prynce, and hym selfe, in his latter daies: for Doctor Ihon Baker, his pryvie counsailer, and hys chappellayn, wrote, that he lyeng on his death bed, said these wordes: 'Why should I dye, having so muche ryches, if the whole realme would save my lyfe, I am able either by pollicie to get it or by ryches to bye it. Fye, will not death be hyered, nor will money do nothyng? when my nephew of Bedford died, I thought myselfe halfe up the whele, but when I sawe myne other nephew of Gloucester disceased, then I thought myself able to be equale with kinges, and so thought to encrease my treasure in hoope to have worne a tryple Croune. But I se nowe the worlde faileth me, and so I am deceyved, praiyng you all to pray for me.'"

It is, perhaps, hardly necessary to add that there is no historical foundation for charging Cardinal Beaufort with complicity in the murder of Gloucester. Long before that time he had retired from public affairs, applying himself sedulously to the duties of his diocese, and distinguishing himself by many acts of munificence and charity.

ACT IV.

(1) SCENE I.—*So will the queen, that living held him dear.*] The circumstances attending the capture and murder of the Duke of Suffolk are thus briefly narrated by Hall:—"But fortune wold not that this flagitious person shoulde so escape; for when he shipped in Suffolke, entendynge to be transported into Fraunce, he was encontered with a shippe of warre appertainyng to the duke of Excester, the constable of the towre of London, called the Nicholas of the Towre. The capitayne of the same barke with small fighte entered into the duke's shyppe, and perceyving his person present, brought hym to Dover rode, and there on the one syde of a cocke bote, caused his head to be stryken of, and left his body with the heade upon the sandes of Dover, which corse was there founde by a chapelayne of his, and conveyed to Wingfelde College in Suffolke, and there buried. This ende had William de la Pole, first duke of Suffolke, as men judge by God's punyshment for above all thinges he was noted to be the very organ, engine, and diviser of the destruccion of Humfrey the good duke of Gloucester, and so the bloudde of the innocente man was with his dolorous death, recompensed and punished."

(2) SCENE II.—

Cade. *What is thy name?*
Clerk. *Emanuel.*
Dick. *They use to write it on the top of letters.*]

An exemplification of Dick's remark is found in the following letter from John Speed, the historian, to Sir Robert Cotton, written about 1609 or 1610, and published by the Camden Society in "Original Letters of Eminent Literary Men," 1843 :—

"EMANUELL.

Worshipfull Sir, my thoughts runnyng upon the well performance of this worke, and fearfull to comitt any thing disagreeing from the truth, I have sent you a coppy of some part of that which you have alredy sene, because you left in writing at the Printers that with a fast eye you had overune it, and your leasure better affording that busines in the contrey then here you had; this therefore hath caused me to send you as much as my Printer can espare, beseiching your Worshipe to read it more attentyvly, to place the Coynes, and what adicssions you will before you returne it; and I pray you to past a paper where you doe adde, and not to intirline the coppy, for somewhere we cannot read your Notes because the place geves your pene not rome to exprese your mynd. I have sent such Coynes as are cutt, and will weekly supply the same; so much therefore as you shall perfect I praye you send againe with as much speed as you can; but where you do want the Coynes, kepe that coppy still with you, untill I send them: for I shall not be sattisfied with your other directions or Mr. Coles helpe. Good Sir, afford me herein your assistance as you have begune, and remember my suit to my L. privy-seall, wherein you shall binde me in all dutifull service and affection to your Worship's command. So beseiking the Almighty to prosper our indevours I humbly take my leave, and leave your Worship to the Lordes protection. Your Worships to comand in all dutifull service, JOH. SPEED."

It is somewhat surprising that modern editors of Shakespeare, to whose research we owe so much, should have been unable to furnish a single example of the use of this prefix to letters. Warburton speaks of it as adopted only in "letters missive and such like publick acts," and Mr. Collier echoes him. This is a curious mistake. In addition to the instance cited above, we can refer to one MS. alone in the British Museum (Add. MSS. 19,400) which contains no less than fourteen private epistles headed "*Emanewell*," or "Jesus *Immanuel*." See folios 40, 47, 100, 116, 137, 142, 145, 150, 155, 163, 165, 168, 185, and 204.

(3) SCENE II. — *Hang him with his pen-and-inkhorn about his neck.*] A horn, to contain pens and ink, or a pencase and an inkhorn attached together by a cord, used formerly to be carried about by professional people, such as schoolmasters, lawyers, notaries, &c., who are always represented in ancient illuminations, pictures, and tombs, with these useful appendages hanging from their girdles. A good ideal representative of the Clerk of Chatham will be found in Waller's "Series of Monumental Brasses," from a monument, *temp.* Edward IV., in the church of St. Mary Tower, Ipswich. As more intimately connected, however, with the present drama, it is interesting to know that the identical pen-and-ink case formerly belonging to king Henry VI. still exists. It is made of leather, ornamented with the arms of England, and the rose of the House of Lancaster, surmounted by the crown. Inside are three cells, one to receive the inkstand, the other two to hold pens, &c. This curious relic is engraved in Shaw's "Dresses and Decorations of the Middle Ages."

(4) SCENE VIII.—*Up Fish-street! Down Saint Magnus' corner!*] The insurrection of Jack Cade, with all its concomitant circumstances, is told with great spirit by the old chroniclers, but at too great length to be transcribed entire: we subjoin, therefore, Holinshed's account of the fight at London-bridge :—

"The Maior and other the Magistrates of London, perceyving themselves neyther to bee sure of goodes, nor of life well warranted, determined to repulse and keepe out of their citie such a mischievous caitife and his wicked company. And to be the better able so to do, they made the lorde Scales and that renowned captaine Matthew Goughe privye both of their intent and enterprise, beseeching them of their helpe and furtherance therein. The Lord Scales promised them his aide with shooting off the artillerie in the tower, and Matthew Gough was by hym appointed to assiste the Maior and Londoners, in all that he might, and so he and other captaines, appointed for defense of the citie, tooke upon them in the night to keepe the brydge, and would not suffer the Kentishmen once to approche. The rebelles which never soundly slept for feare of soddaine chaunces, hearing that the bridge was thus kept, ran with greate haste to open that passage, where betwene both parties was a fierce and cruell fight. Matthew Gough perceiving the rebels to stand to their tackling more manfullie than he thought they would have doone, advised his companie not to advance anie further toward Southwarke, till the daie appeared, that they might see where the place of jeopardie rested, and so to provide for the same; but this little availed. For the rebels with their multitude drave backe the citizens from the stoulps at the bridgefoot to the draw bridge, and began to set fire in diverse houses. Great ruth it was to behold the miserable state, wherein some desiring to eschew the fire died upon their enimies weapon; women with children in their armes lept for feare into the river, other in a deadlie care how to save themselves, between fire, water, and sword, were in their houses choked and smothered. Yet the captains not sparing, fought on the bridge all the night valiantlie: but in conclusion the rebels gat the draw bridge, and drouned many, and slew John Sutton, alderman, and Robert Heysand, a hardie citizen, with manie other, beside Matthew Gough, a man of great wit, and much experience in feates of chivalry, the which in continual warres had spent his time in service of the king and his father.

"This sore conflict endured in doubtfull wise on the bridge, till nine of the clocke in the morning; for sometime the Londoners were beaten backe to sainte Magnus corner; and suddenelie againe, the rebels were repulsed to the stoulpes in Southwarke, so that both parts beeing faint and wearie, agreed to leave off from fighting till the next day, uppon condition that neyther Londoners should passe into Southwarke, nor Kentishmen into London. Upon this abstinence, this rakehell capteine for making him more friends, brake up the gailes of the kings Bench and Marshalsie, and so were manie mates set at libertie verie meet for his matters in hand."—HOLINSHED, *sub anno* 1450.

(5) SCENE IX.—

The duke of York is newly come from Ireland:
And with a puissant and a mighty power,
Of gallowglasses, and stout kerns,
Is marching hitherward in proud array.]

The only distinction between these formidable mercenaries, whose wild appearance and ferocious habits are specially depicted by English writers of the time of Elizabeth, was that the kerns were light, and the gallowglasses heavy, armed foot soldiers; the principal weapon of the former being a dart, which, an eye-witness of their prowess assures us, they wielded with such force as to pierce through both the chain and plate armour of their antagonists.* The gallowglass, chosen for his size and strength, was armed with a shirt of mail, a skull cap, and a gallowglass axe. Savage and merciless in warfare,

"—— the gallowglass, the kerne,
Yield or not yield, whomso they take they slay,"†

they were a terror at home in times of peace. "The kerne," says Barnaby Riche in his Description of Ireland, 1610, p. 37, "are the very drosse and scum of the countrey, a generation of villaines not worthy to live; these be they that live by robbing and spoiling the poore countreyman, that maketh him many times to buy bread to give unto them, though he want for himselfe and his poore children. These are they, that are ready to run out with everie rebell, and these are the verie hags of hell, fit for nothing but the gallows."

* French Metrical History of the Deposition of Richard II. *Archæologia*, xx. p. 33.
† Mirrour for Magistrates.

ACT V.

(1) Scene III.—

Sound drum and trumpets:—and to London all:
And more such days as these to us befal!]

The first battle of St. Alban's, fought on Thursday, 22nd May, 1455, is thus described by Holinshed. "The king enformed hereof, assembled lykewise a great host, and meaning to meet with the Duke, rather in the north parts than about London, where it was thought he had too many friends, with great speede, and small lucke, being accompanied with the Dukes of Somerset and Buckingham, the Erles of Pembroke, Stafford, Northumberland, Devonshire, Dorset, and Wiltshire, the Lords Clifford, Sudley, Berneis, Roos, and others, beeing in all above two thousande men of warre, departed from Westminster the twentith, or, as some have, the one and twentith of May, and lay the first night at Wadford. Of whose doings the duke of Yorke by espials having still advertisement, with all his power, being not past three thousande men (as some write), coasted the countrey, and came to the toune of Saint Albons, the third day next ensuing. The king there had pight his standerte in a place called Goslowe, otherwise Sandiford, in Saint Peeters streete: the Lord Clifforde kept the barriers of the toune, to stop that the Duke, being assembled in Keye field, should not enter the toune. * * * The king, when first he heard of the Dukes approche, sent to him messengers, as the Duke of Buckingham and others, to understand what he meant by his comming, thus furnished after the manner of warre. The Duke of Buckingham, doing his message as hee had in commaundement, was answered by the Duke of Yorke and his complices, that they were all of them the king's faithfull liege subjects, and intended no harme to him at all: but the cause of our comming (saie they) is not in meaning anie hurt to his person. But let that wicked and naughtie man the duke of Somerset be delivered unto us, who hath lost Normandie, and taken no regard to the preservation of Gascoigne; and furthermore hath brought the realme into this miserable estate: that where it was the floure of nations, and the princesse of provinces, now is it haled into desolation and spoile, not so dreadfull by malice of forren enimie, that indeed utterlie (as yee knowe) seeketh our ruine, as by the intollerable outrages of him that so long ago and even still appeares to have sworne the confusion of our king and realme. If it therefore please the king to deliver that bad man into our hands, we are readie without trouble or breach of peace, to returne into our countrie. But if the king be not minded so to do, because he cannot misse him; let him understand, that we will rather die in the field, than suffer such a mischeefe unredressed.

"The king, advertised of this aunswere, more wilfull than reasonable, chose rather to trie battell than deliver the duke of Somerset to his enimies. Whereof they ascertained made no longer staie, but straightway sounded the trumpet to battell, or rather as Hall hath, while King Henry sent forth his ambassadors to treate of peace at the one end of the toune, the Erle of Warwike, with his Marchmen, entred at the other end, and fiercely setting on the king's foreward, within a small tyme discomfited the same. The place where they first brake into the towne was about the middle of saint Peter's street. The fight for a time was ryghte sharp and cruell, for the Duke of Somerset, with the other lords, coming to the succours of their companions, that were put to the worse, did what they could to beate back the enimies, but the Duke of York sent ever fresh men to succour the wearie, and to supplie the places of them that were hurt, by which policie, the king's army was finally brought to confusion, and all the chiefetaines of the fielde slaine and beaten doune. For there dyed under the sign of the Castell, Edmund Duke of Somerset, who, as hath bin reported, was warned long before to avoid all castels: and beside hym laye Henry the second of that name Earle of Northumberland, Humfrey erle of Stafford, son to the Duke of Buckingham, John Lord Clifford, sir Barthram Antwisell knight, a Norman born (who forsaking his native countrie to continue in his loiall obedience to king Henrie, came over to dwell here in England when Normandie was lost), William Zouch, John Boutreux, Rafe Babthorp, with his sonne, William Corwin, William Cotton, Gilbert Faldinger, Reginald Griffon, John Dawes, Elice Wood, John Eith, Rafe Woodward, Gilbert Skarlock, and Rafe Willoughbie esquires, with many other, in all to the number of eight thousand, as Edward Hall saith in his chronicle: if there escaped not a fault in the impression, as 8000 for 800, sith hundreds in verie deed would better agree with the number of the kings whole power, which he brought with him to that battell, being not manie above two thousand, as by writers appeareth.

"Humfrey, duke of Buckingham, being wounded, and James Butler, Earle of Ormond and Wiltshire, and Thomas Thorpe lord cheefe baron of the escheker, seeing fortune thus to bee against them, left the king alone and with a number fledde away. Those that thus fled, made the best shift they could to get awaie through gardens and backesides, through shrubs, hedges, and woods, seeking places where to hide themselves, untill that dangerous tempest of the battell were overblowne. Diverse of the kings house also, that could better skill to plaie the courtiers than warriors, fled with the first; and those of the east parts of the realme were likewise noted of too much lacke of courage, for their speedie withdrawing themselves, and leaving the king in danger of his adversaries, who, perceyving hys men thus fledde from him, withdrewe into a poor mans house to save himselfe from the shot of arrowes, that flew about his eares as thicke as snowe."

Act V. Sc. 5.

THE THIRD PART OF

KING HENRY THE SIXTH.

THIS tragedy was first printed in its present form, in the folio of 1623. It is an enlarged and improved version by Shakespeare, of "The True Tragedie of Richard, Duke of Yorke," &c. before adverted to, as that, we conceive, was an alteration and improvement by him of an earlier drama, the work of one or more of his contemporaries.

From the circumstance of Robert Greene's paraphrasing a line of "The True Tragedy:"—

"O, tiger's hart, wrapt in a woman's hide;"

when reflecting on Shakespeare, in his "Groatsworth of Wit," 1592,* and of some resemblances between passages in his acknowledged dramas and passages in "The True Tragedy," it may be inferred that he had some share in the production of the piece or pieces, on which were based "The First Part of the Contention," and "The True Tragedie of Richard, Duke of Yorke." This deduction is strengthened by a passage in "Greene's Funeralls, By R. B. Gent." 4to. Lond. 1594, a small tract of twelve leaves preserved in the Bodleian Library:—

"Greene is the pleasing Obiect of an eie;
Greene pleasde the eies of all that lookt upon him.
Greene is the ground of everie Painter's die;
Greene gave the ground to all that wrote upon him.
Nay, more, the men that so Eclipst his fame,
Purloynde his Plumes, can they deny the same?"

* "Yes, trust them not: for there is an upstart crow beautified with our feathers, that with his *Tygre's heart wrapt in a player's hyde*, supposes hee is as well able to bombast out a blanke verse as the best of you; and, being an absolute Johannes Factotum, is, in his own conceyt, the onely Shake-scene in a countrey."

Persons Represented.

KING HENRY THE SIXTH.
EDWARD, *Prince of* Wales, *his* Son.
LEWIS XI., *King of* France.
DUKE *of* SOMERSET, DUKE *of* EXETER, EARL *of* OXFORD, EARL *of* NORTHUMBERLAND, EARL *of* WESTMORELAND, LORD CLIFFORD, } *On* King Henry's *side.*
RICHARD PLANTAGENET, *Duke of* York.
EDWARD, *Earl of* March, *afterwards* King Edward IV., GEORGE, *afterwards Duke of* Clarence, RICHARD, *afterwards Duke of* Gloucester, } *his* Sons.
EDMUND, *Earl of* Rutland,
DUKE *of* NORFOLK.
MARQUIS *of* MONTAGUE.
EARL *of* WARWICK.
EARL *of* PEMBROKE.
LORD HASTINGS.
LORD STAFFORD.
Sir JOHN MORTIMER, *Sir* HUGH MORTIMER, } *Uncles to the Duke of* York.
HENRY, *Earl of* Richmond, *a Youth.*
LORD RIVERS, *Brother to* Lady Grey.
Sir WILLIAM STANLEY.
Sir JOHN MONTGOMERY.
Sir JOHN SOMERVILLE.
Tutor *to* Rutland.
Mayor *of* York.
Lieutenant *of the* Tower.
A Nobleman.
Two Keepers.
A Huntsman.
A Son *that killed his* Father.
A Father *that killed his* Son.

QUEEN MARGARET.
LADY GREY, *afterwards Queen to* Edward IV.
BONA, *Sister to the* French *Queen.*

Soldiers, and other Attendants on King Henry *and* King Edward, *Messengers, Watchmen, &c.*

SCENE,—*During part of the Third Act, in* France; *during the rest of the Play, in* England.

ACT I.

SCENE I.—London. *The* Parliament-House.

Drums. Some Soldiers *of* YORK'*s party break in. Then enter the* DUKE *of* YORK, EDWARD, RICHARD, NORFOLK, MONTAGUE, WARWICK, *and others, with white roses in their hats.*

WAR. I wonder how the king escap'd our hands.
YORK. While we pursu'd the horsemen of the north,
He slily stole away, and left his men:
Whereat the great lord of Northumberland,
Whose warlike ears could never brook retreat,
Cheer'd up the drooping army; and himself,
Lord Clifford, and lord Stafford, all abreast,
Charg'd our main battle's front, and, breaking in,
Were by the swords of common soldiers slain.
EDW. Lord Stafford's father, duke of Buckingham,
Is either slain, or wounded dangerous:
I cleft his beaver with a downright blow;
That this is true, father, behold his blood.
[*Showing his bloody sword.*
MONT. And, brother, here's the earl of Wiltshire's blood, [*To* YORK, *showing his.*
Whom I encounter'd as the battles join'd.
RICH. Speak thou for me, and tell them what I did.
[*Throwing down the* DUKE *of* SOMERSET'*s head.*
YORK. Richard hath best deserv'd of all my sons.
But, is your grace dead, my lord of Somerset?
NORF. Such hope have all the line of John of Gaunt!
RICH. Thus do I hope to shake king Henry's [head.
WAR. And so do I.—Victorious prince of York,
Before I see thee seated in that throne
Which now the house of Lancaster usurps,

I vow by heaven these eyes shall never close.
This is the palace of the fearful king,
And this the regal seat: possess it, York;
For this is thine, and not king Henry's heirs'.

YORK. Assist me then, sweet Warwick, and I will;
For hither we have broken in by force.

NORF. We'll all assist you; he that flies shall die.

YORK. Thanks, gentle Norfolk:—stay by me, my lords;
And, soldiers, stay, and lodge by me this night.

WAR. And, when the king comes, offer him no violence,
Unless he seek to thrust you out perforce.
[*The* Soldiers *retire.*

YORK. The queen, this day, here holds her parliament,
But little thinks we shall be of her council:
By words or blows here let us win our right.

RICH. Arm'd as we are, let's stay within this house.

WAR. The bloody parliament shall this be call'd,
Unless Plantagenet, duke of York, be king,
And bashful Henry depos'd, whose cowardice
Hath made us bywords to our enemies.

YORK. Then leave me not, my lords; be resolute,
I mean to take possession of my right.

WAR. Neither the king, nor he that loves him best,
The proudest he that holds up Lancaster,
Dares stir a wing, if Warwick shake his bells.
I'll plant Plantagenet, root him up who dares:—
Resolve thee, Richard; claim the English crown.
[WARWICK *leads* YORK *to the throne, who seats himself.*

Flourish. Enter KING HENRY, CLIFFORD, NORTHUMBERLAND, WESTMORELAND, EXETER, *and others, with red roses in their hats.*

K. HEN. My lords, look where the sturdy rebel sits,
Even in the chair of state! belike he means
(Back'd by the power of Warwick, that false peer,)
To aspire unto the crown, and reign as king.—
Earl of Northumberland, he slew thy father;—
And thine, lord Clifford; and you both have vow'd revenge
On him, his sons, his favourites, and his friends.

NORTH. If I be not, heavens be reveng'd on me!

CLIF. The hope thereof makes Clifford mourn in steel.

WEST. What, shall we suffer this? let's pluck him down:
My heart for anger burns; I cannot brook it.

K. HEN. Be patient, gentle earl of Westmoreland.

CLIF. Patience is for poltroons,[a] such as he;
He durst not sit there, had your father liv'd.
My gracious lord, here in the parliament
Let us assail the family of York.

NORTH. Well hast thou spoken, cousin; be it so.

K. HEN. Ah, know you not the city favours them,
And they have troops of soldiers at their beck?

EXE. But when the duke is slain, they'll quickly fly.[b]

K. HEN. Far be the thought of this from Henry's heart,
To make a shambles of the parliament-house!
Cousin of Exeter, frowns, words, and threats
Shall be the war that Henry means to use.—
[*They advance to the* DUKE.
Thou factious duke of York, descend my throne,
And kneel for grace and mercy at my feet;
I am thy sovereign.

YORK. I am thine.[c]

EXE. For shame, come down: he made thee duke of York.

YORK. 'Twas my inheritance, as the earldom[d] was.

EXE. Thy father was a traitor to the crown.

WAR. Exeter, thou art a traitor to the crown,
In following this usurping Henry.

CLIF. Whom should he follow but his natural king?

WAR. True, Clifford; and[e] that's Richard, duke of York.

K. HEN. And shall I stand, and thou sit in my throne?

YORK. It must and shall be so: content thyself.

WAR. Be duke of Lancaster, let him be king.

WEST. He is both king and duke of Lancaster;
And that the lord of Westmoreland shall maintain.

WAR. And Warwick shall disprove it. You forget
That we are those which chas'd you from the field
And slew your fathers, and with colours spread,
March'd through the city to the palace-gates.

NORTH. Yes,[f] Warwick, I remember it to my grief;
And, by his soul, thou and thy house shall rue it.

WEST. Plantagenet, of thee, and these thy sons,
Thy kinsmen, and thy friends, I'll have more lives
Than drops of blood were in my father's veins.

CLIF. Urge it no more; lest that, instead of words,

---

[a] Patience is for poltroons,—] An old Italian proverb says the same:—"*Pazienza è pasto di poltroni.*"

[b] But when, &c.] In the folio 1623, this is assigned to Westmoreland: in "The True Tragedy," 1595, it has, rightly, the prefix, *Exeter.*

[c] I am thine.] "The True Tragedy" reads:—"Thou art deceiv'd: I am thine," which Malone adopts.

[d] *As the* earldom *was.*] For *earldom,* "The True Tragedy" has *kingdome.*

[e] And *that's Richard,*—] *And,* omitted in the folio, 1623, is restored from "The True Tragedy."

[f] Yes, *Warwick,*—] The earlier version reads, "*No,* Warwick," which is preferable.

I send thee, Warwick, such a messenger
As shall revenge his death before I stir.
WAR. Poor Clifford! how I scorn his worthless threats!
YORK. Will you we show our title to the crown?
If not, our swords shall plead it in the field.
K. HEN. What title hast thou, traitor, to the crown?
Thy[a] father was, as thou art, duke of York;
Thy grandfather, Roger Mortimer, earl of March:
I am the son of Henry the fifth,
Who made the dauphin and the French to stoop,
And seiz'd upon their towns and provinces.
WAR. Talk not of France, sith thou hast lost it all.
K. HEN. The lord protector lost it, and not I;
When I was crown'd, I was but nine months old.
RICH. You are old enough now, and yet, methinks you lose:—
Father, tear the crown from the usurper's head.
EDW. Sweet father, do so; set it on your head.
MONT. Good brother [*To* YORK.], as thou lov'st and honour'st arms,
Let's fight it out, and not stand cavilling thus.
RICH. Sound drums and trumpets, and the king will fly.
YORK. Sons, peace!
K. HEN. Peace thou! and give king Henry leave to speak.
WAR. Plantagenet shall speak first: hear him, lords,
And be you silent and attentive too,
For he that interrupts him shall not live.
K. HEN. Think'st thou that I will leave my kingly throne,
Wherein my grandsire and my father sat?
No: first shall war unpeople this my realm;
Ay, and their colours—often borne in France,
And now in England to our heart's great sorrow,—
Shall be my winding-sheet.—Why faint you, lords?
My title's good, and better far than his.
WAR. Prove it, Henry, and thou shalt be king.
K. HEN. Henry the fourth by conquest got the crown.
YORK. 'Twas by rebellion against his king.
K. HEN. [*Aside.*] I know not what to say; my title's weak.
Tell me, may not a king adopt an heir?
YORK. What then?
K. HEN. An if he may, then am I lawful king:
For Richard, in the view of many lords,
Resign'd the crown to Henry the fourth,
Whose heir my father was, and I am his.
YORK. He rose against him, being his sovereign,
And made him to resign his crown perforce.

[a] Thy father—] In the folio 1623, "*My* father," &c., corrected from "The True Tragedy."

WAR. Suppose, my lords, he did it unconstrain'd,
Think you 'twere prejudicial to his crown?
EXE. No; for he could not so resign his crown,
But that the next heir should succeed and reign.
K. HEN. Art thou against us, duke of Exeter?
EXE. His is the right, and therefore pardon me.
YORK. Why whisper you, my lords, and answer not?
EXE. My conscience tells me, he is lawful king.
K. HEN. [*Aside.*] All will revolt from me and turn to him.
NORTH. Plantagenet, for all the claim thou lay'st,
Think not that Henry shall be so depos'd.
WAR. Depos'd he shall be, in despite of all.
NORTH. Thou art deceiv'd: 'tis not thy southern power
Of Essex, Norfolk, Suffolk, nor of Kent,—
Which makes thee thus presumptuous and proud,—
Can set the duke up in despite of me.
CLIF. King Henry, be thy title right or wrong,
Lord Clifford vows to fight in thy defence:
May that ground gape and swallow me alive,
Where I shall kneel to him that slew my father!
K. HEN. O Clifford, how thy words revive my heart!
YORK. Henry of Lancaster, resign thy crown:—
What mutter you, or what conspire you, lords?
WAR. Do right unto this princely duke of York,
Or I will fill the house with armed men,
And o'er the chair of state, where now he sits,
Write up his title with usurping blood.
[*He stamps, and the* Soldiers *show themselves.*
K. HEN. My lord of Warwick, hear but one word;—
Let me for this my life-time reign as king.
YORK. Confirm the crown to me and to mine heirs,
And thou shalt reign in quiet while thou liv'st.
K. HEN. I am content: Richard Plantagenet,
Enjoy the kingdom after my decease.
CLIF. What wrong is this unto the prince your son!
WAR. What good is this to England and himself!
WEST. Base, fearful, and despairing Henry!
CLIF. How hast thou injur'd both thyself and us!
WEST. I cannot stay to hear these articles.
NORTH. Nor I.
CLIF. Come, cousin, let us tell the queen these news.
WEST. Farewell, faint-hearted and degenerate king,
In whose cold blood no spark of honour bides.
NORTH. Be thou a prey unto the house of York,
And die in bands, for this unmanly deed!

CLIF. In dreadful war mayst thou be overcome!
Or live in peace, abandon'd and despis'd!
[*Exeunt* NORTHUMBERLAND, CLIFFORD, *and* WESTMORELAND.

WAR. Turn this way, Henry, and regard them not.

EXE. They seek revenge, and therefore will not yield.

K. HEN. Ah, Exeter!

WAR. Why should you sigh, my lord?

K. HEN. Not for myself, lord Warwick, but my son,
Whom I unnaturally shall disinherit.
But, be it as it may:—I here entail
The crown to thee, and to thine heirs for ever; (1)
Conditionally, that here thou take an oath
To cease this civil war, and, whilst I live,
To honour me as thy king and sovereign,
And neither by treason nor hostility,
To seek to put me down, and reign thyself.

YORK. This oath I willingly take, and will perform. [*Coming from the throne.*

WAR. Long live king Henry!—Plantagenet, embrace him.

K. HEN. And long live thou, and these thy forward sons!

YORK. Now York and Lancaster are reconcil'd.

EXE. Accurs'd be he that seeks to make them foes!
[*Sennet. The* Lords *come forward.*

YORK. Farewell, my gracious lord; I'll to my castle.

WAR. And I'll keep London with my soldiers.

NORF. And I to Norfolk with my followers.

MONT. And I unto the sea, from whence I came.
[*Exeunt* YORK *and his* Sons, WARWICK, NORFOLK, MONTAGUE, Soldiers, *and* Attendants.

K. HEN. And I, with grief and sorrow, to the court.

EXE. Here comes the queen, whose looks bewray[a] her anger:
I'll steal away.

K. HEN. Exeter, so will I. [*Going.*

Enter QUEEN MARGARET, *and the* PRINCE *of* WALES.

Q. MAR. Nay, go not from me; I will follow thee.

K. HEN. Be patient, gentle queen, and I will stay.

Q. MAR. Who can be patient in such extremes?
Ah, wretched man! would I had died a maid,
And never seen thee, never borne thee son,
Seeing thou hast prov'd so unnatural a father!
Hath he deserv'd to lose his birthright thus?
Hadst thou but lov'd him half so well as I,
Or felt that pain which I did for him once,
Or nourish'd him, as I did with my blood,—
Thou wouldst have left thy dearest heart-blood there,
Rather than have made that savage duke thine heir,
And disinherited thine only son.

PRINCE. Father, you cannot disinherit me:
If you be king, why should not I succeed?

K. HEN. Pardon me, Margaret;—pardon me, sweet son;—
The earl of Warwick and the duke enforc'd me.

Q. MAR. Enforc'd thee! art thou king, and wilt be forc'd?
I shame to hear thee speak. Ah, timorous wretch!
Thou hast undone thyself, thy son, and me,
And given unto the house of York such head,
As thou shalt reign but by their sufferance.
To entail him and his heirs unto the crown,
What is it, but to make thy sepulchre,
And creep into it far before thy time?
Warwick is chancellor, and the lord of Calais;
Stern Falconbridge (2) commands the narrow seas;
The duke is made protector of the realm;
And yet shalt thou be safe? such safety finds
The trembling lamb, environed with wolves.
Had I been there, which am a silly woman,
The soldiers should have toss'd me on their pikes,
Before I would have granted to that act.
But thou preferr'st thy life before thine honour:
And, seeing thou dost, I here divorce myself,
Both from thy table, Henry, and thy bed,
Until that act of parliament be repeal'd,
Whereby my son is disinherited.
The northern lords that have forsworn thy colours
Will follow mine, if once they see them spread;
And spread they shall be, to thy foul disgrace,
And utter ruin of the house of York.
Thus do I leave thee.—Come, son, let's away;
Our army's ready; come, we'll after them.

K. HEN. Stay, gentle Margaret, and hear me speak.

Q. MAR. Thou hast spoke too much already; get thee gone.

K. HEN. Gentle son Edward, thou wilt stay with me?

Q. MAR. Ay, to be murder'd by his enemies.

PRINCE. When I return with victory from[b] the field,
I'll see your grace: till then, I'll follow her.

Q. MAR. Come, son, away! we may not linger thus.
[*Exeunt* QUEEN MARGARET *and the* PRINCE.

K. HEN. Poor queen! how love to me and to her son,
Hath made her break out into terms of rage!

---

a Bewray—] That is, *disclose, discover.*

b From *the field,*—] So the early version; the folio 1623, by mistake, prints, "*to* the field."

Reveng'd may she be on that hateful duke,
Whose haughty spirit, winged with desire,
Will cost[a] my crown, and, like an empty eagle,
Tire[b] on the flesh of me and of my son!
The loss of those three lords torments my heart:
I'll write unto them, and entreat them fair;—
Come, cousin, you shall be the messenger.
EXE. And I, I hope, shall reconcile them all.
[*Exeunt.*

SCENE II.—*A Room in* Sandal Castle, *near* Wakefield, *in* Yorkshire.

Enter EDWARD, RICHARD, *and* MONTAGUE.

RICH. Brother, though I be youngest, give me leave.
EDW. No, I can better play the orator.
MONT. But I have reasons strong and forcible.

Enter YORK.

YORK. Why, how now, sons and brother! at a strife?
What is your quarrel? how began it first?
EDW. No quarrel, but a slight contention.
YORK. About what?
RICH. About that which concerns your grace and us—
The crown of England, father, which is yours.
YORK. Mine, boy? not till king Henry be dead.
RICH. Your right depends not on his life or death.
EDW. Now you are heir, therefore enjoy it now:
By giving the house of Lancaster leave to breathe,
It will outrun you, father, in the end.
YORK. I took an oath, that he should quietly reign.
EDW. But, for a kingdom, any oath may be broken:
I'd break a thousand oaths to reign one year.
RICH. No; God forbid your grace should be forsworn.
YORK. I shall be, if I claim by open war.
RICH. I'll prove the contrary, if you'll hear me speak.
YORK. Thou canst not, son; it is impossible.
RICH. An oath is of no moment, being not took[c]
Before a true and lawful magistrate,
That hath authority over him that swears:
Henry had none, but did usurp the place;
Then, seeing 'twas he that made you to depose,
Your oath, my lord, is vain and frivolous.
Therefore, to arms! and, father, do but think,
How sweet a thing it is to wear a crown,
Within whose circuit is Elysium,
And all that poets feign of bliss and joy.
Why do we linger thus? I cannot rest,
Until the white rose that I wear, be dy'd
Even in the lukewarm blood of Henry's heart.
YORK. Richard, enough; I will be king, or die.—
Brother, thou shalt to London presently,
And whet on Warwick to this enterprise.—
Thou, Richard, shalt to the duke of Norfolk,
And tell him privily of our intent.—
You, Edward, shall unto my lord Cobham,
With whom the Kentishmen will willingly rise:
In them I trust; for they are soldiers,
Witty, courteous, liberal, full of spirit.—
While you are thus employ'd, what resteth more,
But that I seek occasion how to rise,
And yet the king not privy to my drift,
Nor any of the house of Lancaster?

Enter a Messenger.[d]

But, stay; what news? Why com'st thou in such post?
MESS. The queen with all the northern earls and lords,
Intend here to besiege you in your castle:
She is hard by with twenty thousand men;
And therefore fortify your hold, my lord.
YORK. Ay, with my sword. What! think'st thou that we fear them?—
Edward and Richard, you shall stay with me;—
My brother Montague shall post to London:
Let noble Warwick, Cobham, and the rest,
Whom we have left protectors of the king,
With powerful policy strengthen themselves,
And trust not simple Henry nor his oaths.
MONT. Brother, I go; I'll win them, fear it not:
And thus most humbly I do take my leave. [*Exit.*

Enter Sir JOHN *and Sir* HUGH MORTIMER.

YORK. Sir John, and sir Hugh Mortimer, mine uncles!
You are come to Sandal in a happy hour;
The army of the queen mean to besiege us.
SIR JOHN. She shall not need, we'll meet her in the field.
YORK. What, with five thousand men?

---

[a] *Will* cost *my crown,*—] Warburton suggested *coast* for cost. To *coast* means to *keep alongside*: but in that sense it seems as little applicable to the context as the word it would displace.

[b] Tire *on the flesh of me,* &c.] To *tire* is to *peck* as birds do; and generally implies to tear and rend the food. Steevens quotes an apt example of the word used in this sense from Decker's "Match Me in London," 1631:—

"—— the vulture *tires*
Upon the eagle's heart."

And Mr. Collier another from *Histriomastix*, 1610, Sig. F. 3:—

"O, how this vulture, vile ambition,
Tires on the heart of greatnesse, and *devours*."

[c] *Being not* took—] "The True Tragedy," with more propriety, reads:—"Being not *sworne*."

[d] Enter a Messenger.] The folio 1623 has, "*Enter Gabriel.*" *Gabriel* is supposed to have been the Christian name of the actor who performed the part.

RICH. Ay, with five hundred, father, for a need:
A woman's general; what should we fear?
[*A march afar off.*
EDW. I hear their drums; let's set our men in order;
And issue forth, and bid them battle straight.
YORK. Five men to twenty!—though the odds be great,
I doubt not, uncle, of our victory.
Many a battle have I won in France,
Whenas the enemy hath been ten to one;
Why should I not now have the like success?
[*Alarum. Exeunt.*

SCENE III.—*Plains near* Sandal Castle.

Alarum: Excursions. Enter RUTLAND *and his* Tutor.

RUT. Ah, whither shall I fly to 'scape their hands?
Ah, tutor! look where bloody Clifford comes!

Enter CLIFFORD *and* Soldiers.

CLIF. Chaplain, away! thy priesthood saves thy life.
As for the brat of this accursed duke,
Whose father slew my father,—he shall die.
TUTOR. And I, my lord, will bear him company.
CLIF. Soldiers, away with him.
TUTOR. Ah, Clifford! murder not this innocent child,
Lest thou be hated both of God and man.
[*Exit, forced off by* Soldiers.
CLIF. How now! is he dead already? or, is it fear
That makes him close his eyes?—I'll open them.
RUT. So looks the pent-up lion o'er the wretch
That trembles under his devouring paws:
And so he walks, insulting o'er his prey;
And so he comes, to rend his limbs asunder.—
Ah, gentle Clifford, kill me with thy sword,
And not with such a cruel threat'ning look!
Sweet Clifford, hear me speak before I die!—
I am too mean a subject for thy wrath;
Be thou reveng'd on men, and let me live.

CLIF. In vain thou speak'st, poor boy; my father's blood
Hath stopp'd the passage where thy words should enter.
RUT. Then let my father's blood open it again;
He is a man, and, Clifford, cope with him.
CLIF. Had I thy brethren here, their lives and thine
Were not revenge sufficient for me;
No, if I digg'd up thy forefathers' graves,
And hung their rotten coffins up in chains,
It could not slake mine ire, nor ease my heart.
The sight of any of the house of York
Is as a fury to torment my soul;
And till I root out their accursed line,
And leave not one alive, I live in hell.
Therefore—— [*Lifting his hand.*
RUT. O, let me pray before I take my death!—
To thee I pray; sweet Clifford, pity me!
CLIF. Such pity as my rapier's point affords.
RUT. I never did thee harm; why wilt thou slay me?
CLIF. Thy father hath.
RUT. But 'twas ere I was born.
Thou hast one son,—for his sake pity me,
Lest in revenge thereof,—sith God is just,—
He be as miserably slain as I.
Ah, let me live in prison all my days,
And when I give occasion of offence,
Then let me die, for now thou hast no cause.
CLIF. No cause!
Thy father slew my father; therefore, die.(3)
[*Stabs him.*
RUT. *Di faciant, laudis summa sit ista tuæ!*[a]
[*Dies.*
CLIF. Plantagenet! I come, Plantagenet!
And this thy son's blood cleaving to my blade
Shall rust upon my weapon, till thy blood,
Congeal'd with this, do make me wipe off both.
[*Exit.*

SCENE IV.—*Another part of the Plains.*

Alarum. Enter YORK.

YORK. The army of the queen hath got the field:
My uncles both are slain in rescuing me;
And all my followers to the eager foe
Turn back, and fly, like ships before the wind,
Or lambs pursu'd by hunger-starved wolves.
My sons—God knows what hath bechanced them;
But this I know,—they have demean'd themselves
Like men born to renown by life or death.
Three times did Richard make a lane to me,
And thrice cried,—*Courage, father! fight it out!*
And full as oft came Edward to my side,
With purple falchion, painted to the hilt
In blood of those that had encounter'd him:
And when the hardiest warriors did retire,
Richard cried,—*Charge! and give no foot of ground!*
And cried,—*A crown, or else a glorious tomb!*
A sceptre, or an earthly sepulchre!
With this we charg'd again: but, out alas!
We bodg'd[b] again; as I have seen a swan
With bootless labour swim against the tide,
And spend her strength with over-matching waves.
[*A short alarum.*
Ah, hark! the fatal followers do pursue,
And I am faint, and cannot fly their fury:
And were I strong, I would not shun their fury:
The sands are number'd that make up my life!
Here must I stay, and here my life must end.

Enter QUEEN MARGARET, CLIFFORD, NORTHUMBERLAND, *and* Soldiers.

Come, bloody Clifford,—rough Northumberland.—
I dare your quenchless fury to more rage;
I am your butt, and I abide your shot.
NORTH. Yield to our mercy, proud Plantagenet.
CLIF. Ay, to such mercy as his ruthless arm,
With downright payment, show'd unto my father.
Now Phaeton hath tumbled from his car,
And made an evening at the noontide prick.
YORK. My ashes, as the phœnix, may bring forth
A bird that will revenge upon you all:
And in that hope I throw mine eyes to heaven,
Scorning whate'er you can afflict me with.
Why come you not? what! multitudes, and fear?
CLIF. So cowards fight when they can fly no further;
So doves do peck the falcon's piercing talons;
So desperate thieves, all hopeless of their lives,
Breathe out invectives 'gainst the officers.
YORK. O, Clifford, but bethink thee once again,
And in thy thought o'er-run my former time;
And, if thou canst for blushing, view this face,
And bite thy tongue, that slanders him with cowardice,
Whose frown hath made thee faint and fly ere this!
CLIF. I will not bandy with thee word for word,
But buckle[c] with thee blows, twice two for one.
[*Draws.*

---

[a] *Di faciant*, &c.] This line, from Ovid's "Epist. *Phillis ad. Demophoon*," is quoted also by Nash in his "*Have With You to Saffron Walden*, or Gabriel Harvey's Hunt Is Up," &c., 1596.

[b] Bodg'd—] This is usually explained to be a misprint for *budged*, or *botched;* but *bodg'd* is the genuine word, and means *bungled*. Thus in Florio's "Worlde of Wordes," 1598, *Sbozzi* is translated "*bodges*, or bunger-like workes."

[c] Buckle—] So "The True Tragedy:" the folios have "*buckler*."

Q. MAR. Hold, valiant Clifford! for a thousand causes,
I would prolong awhile the traitor's life:—
Wrath makes him deaf:—speak thou, Northumberland.

NORTH. Hold, Clifford! do not honour him so much,
To prick thy finger, though to wound his heart:
What valour were it, when a cur doth grin,
For one to thrust his hand between his teeth,
When he might spurn him with his foot away?
It is war's prize to take all vantages;
And ten to one is no impeach of valour.

[*They lay hands on* YORK, *who struggles.*

CLIF. Ay, ay, so strives the woodcock with the gin.

NORTH. So doth the coney struggle in the net.

[YORK *is taken prisoner.*

YORK. So triumph thieves upon their conquer'd booty;
So true men yield, with robbers so o'ermatch'd.

NORTH. What would your grace have done unto him now?

Q. MAR. Brave warriors, Clifford and Northumberland,
Come, make him stand upon this molehill here,
That raught[a] at mountains with outstretched arms,
Yet parted but the shadow with his hand.—
What! was it you that would be England's king?
Was't you that revell'd in our parliament,
And made a preachment of your high descent?
Where are your mess[b] of sons to back you now,
The wanton Edward, and the lusty George?
And where's that valiant crook-back prodigy,
Dicky, your boy, that with his grumbling voice,
Was wont to cheer his dad in mutinies?
Or, with the rest, where is your darling Rutland?
Look, York; I stain'd this napkin with the blood
That valiant Clifford, with his rapier's point,
Made issue from the bosom of the boy:
And if thine eyes can water for his death,
I give thee this to dry thy cheeks withal.
Alas, poor York! but that I hate thee deadly,
I should lament thy miserable state.
I pr'ythee, grieve, to make me merry, York:
What, hath thy fiery heart so parch'd thine entrails,
That not a tear can fall for Rutland's death?
Why art thou patient, man? thou shouldst be mad,
And I, to make thee mad, do mock thee thus.
Stamp, rave, and fret, that I may sing and dance.
Thou wouldst be fee'd, I see, to make me sport:
York cannot speak, unless he wear a crown.—
A crown for York!—and, lords, bow low to him.—
Hold you his hands, whilst I do set it on.—
[*Putting a paper crown on his head.*
Ay, marry, sir, now looks he like a king!
Ay, this is he that took king Henry's chair;
And this is he was his adopted heir.—
But how is it that great Plantagenet
Is crown'd so soon, and broke his solemn oath?
As I bethink me, you should not be king
Till our king Henry had shook hands with death.
And will you pale[c] your head in Henry's glory,
And rob his temples of the diadem,
Now in his life, against your holy oath?
O, 'tis a fault too-too unpardonable!—
Off with the crown; and, with the crown, his head!
And, whilst we breathe, take time to do him dead.

CLIF. That is my office, for my father's sake.

Q. MAR. Nay, stay; let's hear the orisons he makes.

YORK. She-wolf of France, but worse than wolves of France,
Whose tongue more poisons than the adder's tooth!
How ill-beseeming is it in thy sex
To triumph, like an Amazonian trull,
Upon their woes, whom fortune captivates!
But that thy face is, vizard-like, unchanging,
Made impudent with use of evil deeds,
I would assay, proud queen, to make thee blush:
To tell thee whence thou cam'st, of whom deriv'd,
Were shame enough to shame thee, wert thou not shameless.
Thy father bears the type[d] of king of Naples,
Of both the Sicils, and Jerusalem;
Yet not so wealthy as an English yeoman.
Hath that poor monarch taught thee to insult?
It needs not, nor it boots thee not, proud queen;
Unless the adage must be verified,—
That beggars mounted run their horse to death.
'Tis beauty that doth oft make women proud;
But God he knows, thy share thereof is small:
'Tis virtue that doth make them most admir'd;
The contrary doth make thee wonder'd at:
'Tis government[e] that makes them seem divine;
The want thereof makes thee abominable:
Thou art as opposite to every good,
As the Antipodes are unto us,
Or as the south to the septentrion.[f]
O tiger's heart wrapp'd in a woman's hide!
How couldst thou drain the life-blood of the child,
To bid the father wipe his eyes withal,
And yet be seen to bear a woman's face?
Women are soft, mild, pitiful, and flexible;
Thou stern, obdurate, flinty, rough, remorseless.
Bidd'st thou me rage? why now thou hast thy wish:
Wouldst have me weep? why now thou hast thy will:
For raging wind blows up incessant showers,
And when the rage allays, the rain begins.
These tears are my sweet Rutland's obsequies,
And every drop cries vengeance for his death,—
'Gainst thee, fell Clifford,—and thee, false Frenchwoman.

---

[a] Raught—] *Reached, grasped.*

[b] *Your* mess *of sons*—] "A *mess*," Mr. Collier remarks, "is four; and at this day in the inns of Court a mess consists of four persons dining together—the origin probably being, that dinner for four was of old served in messes, or portions calculated for that number. York's 'mess of sons' consisted of Edward, George, Richard, and Edmund, Earl of Rutland."

[c] Pale—] That is, *impale*. In "The True Tragedy" the line runs:—

"And will you *impale* your head with Henrie's glorie."

[d] *The* type—] Meaning the *crown*, or distinguishing mark of royalty. The word occurs again in "Richard III." Act IV. Sc. 4:—

"The high imperial *type* of this earth's glory."

And we more than suspect that in the well-known passage in "Macbeth," Act IV. Sc. 1:—

"—— What is this,
That rises like the issue of a king;
And wears upon his baby-brow the round
And *top* of sovereignty?"

top is a mere misprint for *type*, and that the poet's lection was—

"——the round
And *type* of sovereignty?"

[e] Government—] *Moderation, self-denial, forbearance.*

[f] Septentrion.] The North. *Septentrio.*

NORTH. Beshrew me, but his passions move me so,
That hardly can I check my eyes from tears.

YORK. That face of his the hungry cannibals
Would not have touch'd, would not have stain'd with blood:
But you are more inhuman, more inexorable,—
O, ten times more,—than tigers of Hyrcania.
See, ruthless queen, a hapless father's tears:
This cloth thou dipp'dst in blood of my sweet boy,
And I with tears do wash the blood away.
Keep thou the napkin, and go boast of this:
[*He gives back the handkerchief.*
And, if thou tell'st the heavy story right,
Upon my soul, the hearers will shed tears;
Yea, even my foes will shed fast-falling tears,
And say,—*Alas, it was a piteous deed!*—
There, take the crown, and, with the crown, my curse;
[*Throwing off the paper crown.*
And, in thy need, such comfort come to thee,
As now I reap at thy too cruel hand!—
Hard-hearted Clifford, take me from the world;
My soul to heaven, my blood upon your heads!

NORTH. Had he been slaughter-man to all my kin,
I should not for my life but weep with him,
To see how inly sorrow gripes his soul.

Q. MAR. What, weeping-ripe, my lord Northumberland?
Think but upon the wrong he did us all,
And that will quickly dry thy melting tears.

CLIF. Here's for my oath, here's for my father's death. [*Stabbing him.*

Q. MAR. And here's to right our gentle-hearted king. [*Stabbing him.*

YORK. Open thy gate of mercy, gracious God!
My soul flies through these wounds to seek out thee. [*Dies.*

Q. MAR. Off with his head, and set it on York gates;
So York may overlook the town of York.
[*Flourish. Exeunt.*

ACT II.

SCENE I.—*A Plain near* Mortimer*'s* Cross, *in* Herefordshire.

Drums. Enter Edward *and* Richard, *with their* Forces *marching.*

Edw. I wonder, how our princely father 'scap'd;
Or whether he be 'scap'd away or no
From Clifford's and Northumberland's pursuit;
Had he been ta'en, we should have heard the news;
Had he been slain, we should have heard the news;
Or, had he 'scap'd, methinks we should have heard
The happy tidings of his good escape.—
How fares my brother? why is he so sad?
Rich. I cannot joy, until I be resolv'd
Where our right valiant father is become.
I saw him in the battle range about,
And watch'd him how he singled Clifford forth.
Methought he bore him in the thickest troop
As doth a lion in a herd of neat:
Or as a bear, encompass'd round with dogs,—
Who having pinch'd a few, and made them cry,
The rest stand all aloof, and bark at him.
So far'd our father with his enemies;
So fled his enemies my warlike father;
Methinks 'tis prize[a] enough to be his son.—
See how the morning opes her golden gates,
And takes her farewell of the glorious sun!
How well resembles it the prime of youth,
Trimm'd like a younker, prancing to his love!
Edw. Dazzle mine eyes, or do I see three suns?[b]
Rich. Three glorious suns, each one a perfect sun:
Not separated with the racking clouds,
But sever'd in a pale clear-shining sky.
See, see! they join, embrace, and seem to kiss,
As if they vow'd some league inviolable:
Now are they but one lamp, one light, one sun!
In this the heaven figures some event.
Edw. 'Tis wondrous strange, the like yet never heard of.
I think it cites us, brother, to the field,—
That we, the sons of brave Plantagenet,
Each one already blazing by our meeds,[c]

[a] Prize *enough*—] That is, *privilege* enough. So in Sc. 4:—
"It is war's *prize* to take all vantages."

[b] *Do I see* three suns?] So in Holinshed:—"—at which tyme the *son* (as some write) appeared to the Earle of March like *three sunnes*, and sodainely joyned altogither in one, uppon whiche sight hee tooke suche courage, that he fiercely setting on his enemyes put them to flight; and for this cause menne ymagined that he gave the sun in his full bryghtnesse for his badge or cognizance."

[c] *Our* meeds,—] Our *deserts*, our *merits*.

Should, notwithstanding, join our lights together,
And over-shine the earth, as this the world.
Whate'er it bodes, henceforward will I bear
Upon my target three fair shining suns.
RICH. Nay, bear three daughters:—by your leave I speak it,
You love the breeder better than the male.

Enter a Messenger.

But what art thou, whose heavy looks foretell
Some dreadful story hanging on thy tongue?
MESS. Ah, one that was a woeful looker on,
Whenas the noble duke of York was slain,
Your princely father and my loving lord!
EDW. O, speak no more! for I have heard too much.
RICH. Say how he died, for I will hear it all.
MESS. Environed he was with many foes;
And stood against them as the hope of Troy
Against the Greeks that would have enter'd Troy.
But Hercules himself must yield to odds;
And many strokes, though with a little axe,
Hew down and fell the hardest-timber'd oak.
By many hands your father was subdu'd;
But only slaughter'd by the ireful arm
Of unrelenting Clifford, and the queen,—
Who crown'd the gracious duke in high despite;
Laugh'd in his face; and, when with grief he wept,
The ruthless queen gave him to dry his cheeks,
A napkin steeped in the harmless blood
Of sweet young Rutland, by rough Clifford slain:
And, after many scorns, many foul taunts,
They took his head, and on the gates of York
They set the same; and there it doth remain,
The saddest spectacle that e'er I view'd. [upon,—
EDW. Sweet duke of York, our prop to lean
Now thou art gone, we have no staff, no stay!—
O Clifford, boist'rous Clifford, thou hast slain
The flower of Europe for his chivalry;
And treacherously hast thou vanquish'd him,
For, hand to hand, he would have vanquish'd thee!—
Now my soul's palace is become a prison:
Ah, would she break from hence, that this my body
Might in the ground be closed up in rest!
For never henceforth shall I joy again,
Never, O never, shall I see more joy!
RICH. I cannot weep; for all my body's moisture
Scarce serves to quench my furnace-burning heart:
Nor can my tongue unload my heart's great burden;
For self-same wind that I should speak withal,
Is kindling coals that fire all my breast, [quench.
And burn me up with flames, that tears would
To weep, is to make less the depth of grief:
Tears, then, for babes; blows and revenge for me!—
Richard, I bear thy name, I'll venge thy death,
Or die renowned by attempting it. [with thee;
EDW. His name that valiant duke hath left
His dukedom and his chair with me is left.
RICH. Nay, if thou be that princely eagle's bird,
Show thy descent by gazing 'gainst the sun: (1)
For chair and dukedom, throne and kingdom, say
Either that is thine, or else thou wert not his.

March. Enter WARWICK *and* MONTAGUE, *with* Forces.

WAR. How now, fair lords! what fare? what news abroad? [recount
RICH. Great lord of Warwick, if we should
Our baleful news, and at each word's deliverance,
Stab poniards in our flesh till all were told,
The words would add more anguish than the wounds.
O valiant lord, the duke of York is slain!
EDW. O Warwick! Warwick! that Plantagenet,
Which held thee dearly as his soul's redemption,
Is by the stern lord Clifford done to death.
WAR. Ten days ago I drown'd these news in tears;
And now, to add more measure to your woes,
I come to tell you things sith then befall'n.
After the bloody fray at Wakefield fought,
Where your brave father breath'd his latest gasp,
Tidings, as swiftly as the posts could run,
Were brought me of your loss and his depart.
I, then in London, keeper of the king,
Muster'd my soldiers, gather'd flocks of friends,
And very well appointed, as I thought,[a] [queen,
March'd toward Saint Alban's to intercept the
Bearing the king in my behalf along:
For by my scouts I was advertised,
That she was coming with a full intent
To dash our late decree in parliament,
Touching king Henry's oath, and your succession.
Short tale to make,—we at Saint Alban's met,
Our battles join'd, and both sides fiercely fought:
But whether 'twas the coldness of the king,
Who look'd full gently on his warlike queen,
That robb'd my soldiers of their heated spleen,
Or whether 'twas report of her success,
Or more than common fear of Clifford's rigour,
Who thunders to his captives—*blood and death*,
I cannot judge: but, to conclude with truth,
Their weapons like to lightning came and went;
Our soldiers'—like the night-owl's lazy flight,

[a] And very well appointed, as I thought,—] This line, which is found only in "The True Tragedy," appears to have been inadvertently omitted in the folio 1623.

Or like a lazy thresher[a] with a flail,—
Fell gently down, as if they struck their friends.
I cheer'd them up with justice of our cause,
With promise of high pay and great rewards;
But all in vain; they had no heart to fight,
And we, in them, no hope to win the day.
So that we fled: the king unto the queen;
Lord George your brother, Norfolk, and myself,
In haste, post-haste, are come to join with you;
For in the marches here, we heard you were,
Making another head to fight again. [Warwick?

EDW. Where is the duke of Norfolk, gentle
And when came George from Burgundy to England? [soldiers:

WAR. Some six miles off the duke is with the
And for your brother, he was lately sent
From your kind aunt, duchess of Burgundy,
With aid of soldiers to this needful war. [fled:

RICH. 'Twas odds, belike, when valiant Warwick
Oft have I heard his praises in pursuit,
But ne'er till now, his scandal of retire. [hear;

WAR. Nor now my *scandal*, Richard, dost thou
For thou shalt know this strong right hand of mine
Can pluck the diadem from faint Henry's head,
And wring the awful sceptre from his fist,
Were he as famous and as bold in war,
As he is fam'd for mildness, peace, and prayer.

RICH. I know it well, lord Warwick: blame me not;
'Tis love I bear thy glories makes me speak.
But, in this troublous time what's to be done?
Shall we go throw away our coats of steel,
And wrap our bodies in black mourning gowns,
Numb'ring our Ave-Maries with our beads?
Or shall we on the helmets of our foes
Tell our devotion with revengeful arms?
If for the last, say—*Ay*, and to it, lords.

WAR. Why, therefore Warwick came to seek you out;
And therefore comes my brother Montague.
Attend me, lords. The proud insulting queen,
With Clifford and the haught Northumberland,
And of their feather, many more* proud birds,
Have wrought the easy-melting king like wax.
He swore consent to your succession,
His oath enrolled in the parliament;
And now to London all the crew are gone,
To frustrate both his oath, and what beside
May make against the house of Lancaster.
Their power, I think, is thirty thousand strong:
Now, if the help of Norfolk and myself,
With all the friends that thou, brave earl of March,
Amongst the loving Welshmen canst procure,
Will but amount to five and twenty thousand,
Why, *Via!* to London will we march amain;[b]
And once again bestride our foaming steeds,
And once again cry—*Charge!* upon our foes,
But never once again turn back, and fly.

RICH. Ay, now methinks I hear great Warwick speak:
Ne'er may he live to see a sunshine day,
That cries—*Retire*, if Warwick bid him stay.

EDW. Lord Warwick, on thy shoulder will I lean;
And when thou fall'st[c] (as God forbid the hour!)
Must Edward fall, which peril heaven forefend!

WAR. No longer earl of March, but duke of York;
The next degree is England's royal throne:
For king of England shalt thou be proclaim'd
In every borough as we pass along;
And he that throws not up his cap for joy,
Shall for the fault make forfeit of his head.
King Edward,—valiant Richard,—Montague,—
Stay we no longer dreaming of renown,
But sound the trumpets, and about our task.

RICH. Then, Clifford, were thy heart as hard as steel
(As thou hast shown it flinty by thy deeds),
I come to pierce it,—or to give thee mine.

EDW. Then strike up, drums;—God and Saint George, for us!

Enter a Messenger.

WAR. How now! what news? [by me,

MESS. The duke of Norfolk sends you word
The queen is coming with a puissant host;
And craves your company for speedy counsel.

WAR. Why then it sorts: brave warriors, let's away. [*Exeunt.*

SCENE II.—*Before* York.

Enter KING HENRY, QUEEN MARGARET, *the* PRINCE *of* WALES, CLIFFORD, *and* NORTHUMBERLAND, *with* Forces.

Q. MAR. Welcome, my lord, to this brave town of York.
Yonder's the head of that arch-enemy,
That sought to be encompass'd with your crown:
Doth not the object cheer your heart, my lord?

(*) Old text, *moe.*

[a] *Or like a* lazy *thresher*—] The repetition of *lazy* was no doubt an error of the transcriber or compositor. In "The True Tragedy" we have—"Or like *an idle* thresher," &c.

[b] *Why, Via! to London will we march* amain;] The word "amain" is restored from "The True Tragedy." It probably dropped out of the folio at press.

[c] *When thou* fall'st, &c.] *Fall'st,* which seems called for by the—"Must Edward *fall*"—of the succeeding line, was an emendation by Malone; the folio 1623 reading *fail'st,* and "The True Tragedy" *faints.*

K. Hen. Ay, as the rocks cheer them that fear
their wreck ;—
To see this sight, it irks my very soul.—
Withhold revenge, dear God ! 'tis not my fault,
Not wittingly have I infring'd my vow.
Clif. My gracious liege, this too much lenity
And harmful pity must be laid aside.
To whom do lions cast their gentle looks ?
Not to the beast that would usurp their den.
Whose hand is that the forest bear doth lick ?
Not his that spoils her young before her face.
Who 'scapes the lurking serpent's mortal sting ?
Not he that sets his foot upon her back.
The smallest worm will turn being trodden on ;
And doves will peck in safeguard of their brood.
Ambitious York did level at thy crown,
Thou smiling, while he knit his angry brows :
He, but a duke, would have his son a king,
And raise his issue, like a loving sire ;
Thou, being a king, bless'd with a goodly son,

Didst yield consent to disinherit him,
Which argued thee a most unloving father.
Unreasonable creatures feed their young;
And though man's face be fearful to their eyes,
Yet, in protection of their tender ones,
Who hath not seen them (even with those wings
Which sometime they have us'd with fearful flight),
Make war with him that climb'd unto their nest,
Off'ring their own lives in their young's defence?
For shame, my liege, make them your precedent!
Were it not pity that this goodly boy
Should lose his birthright by his father's fault,
And long hereafter say unto his child,—
What my great-grandfather and grandsire got,
My careless father fondly gave away!
Ah, what a shame were this! Look on the boy;
And let his manly face, which promiseth
Successful fortune, steel thy melting heart,
To hold thine own, and leave thine own with him.

K. HEN. Full well hath Clifford play'd the orator,
Inferring arguments of mighty force.
But, Clifford, tell me, didst thou never hear
That things ill got had ever bad success?
And happy always was it for that son,
Whose father for his hoarding went to hell?(2)
I'll leave my son my virtuous deeds behind;
And would my father had left me no more!
For all the rest is held at such a rate,
As brings a thousand-fold more care to keep,
Than in possession any jot of pleasure.—
Ah, cousin York! would thy best friends did know,
How it doth grieve me that thy head is here!

Q. MAR. My lord, cheer up your spirits; our foes are nigh,
And this soft courage[a] makes your followers faint.
You promis'd knighthood to our forward son;
Unsheathe your sword, and dub him presently.—
Edward, kneel down.

K. HEN. Edward Plantagenet, arise a knight;
And learn this lesson,—draw thy sword in right.

PRINCE. My gracious father, by your kingly leave,
I'll draw it as Apparent to the crown,
And in that quarrel use it to the death.

CLIF. Why, that is spoken like a toward prince.

Enter a Messenger.

MESS. Royal commanders, be in readiness;
For, with a band of thirty thousand men,
Comes Warwick, backing of the duke of York:
And in the towns, as they do march along,
Proclaims him king, and many fly to him:
Darraign[b] your battle, for they are at hand.

CLIF. I would your highness would depart the field;
The queen hath best success when you are absent.(3)

Q. MAR. Ay, good my lord, and leave us to our fortune.

K. HEN. Why, that's my fortune too; therefore I'll stay.

NORTH. Be it with resolution, then, to fight.

PRINCE. My royal father, cheer these noble lords,
And hearten those that fight in your defence:
Unsheathe your sword, good father; cry, *Saint George!*

March. Enter EDWARD, GEORGE, RICHARD, WARWICK, NORFOLK, MONTAGUE, *and* Soldiers.

EDW. Now, perjur'd Henry! wilt thou kneel for grace,
And set thy diadem upon my head;
Or bide the mortal fortune of the field?

Q. MAR. Go, rate thy minions, proud insulting boy!
Becomes it thee to be thus bold in terms
Before thy sovereign and thy lawful king!

EDW. I am his king, and he should bow his knee;
I was adopted heir by his consent:
Since when,[c] his oath is broke; for, as I hear,
You that are king, though he do wear the crown,
Have caus'd him, by new act of parliament,
To blot out me, and put his own son in.

CLIF. And reason too;
Who should succeed the father but the son?

RICH. Are you there, butcher?—O, I cannot speak!

CLIF. Ay, crook-back; here I stand to answer thee,
Or any he the proudest of thy sort.

RICH. 'Twas you that kill'd young Rutland, was it not?

CLIF. Ay, and old York, and yet not satisfied.

RICH. For God's sake, lords, give signal to the fight.

WAR. What say'st thou, Henry: wilt thou yield the crown?

Q. MAR. Why, how now, long-tongu'd Warwick! dare you speak?
When you and I met at Saint Alban's last,
Your legs did better service than your hands.

WAR. Then 'twas my turn to fly, and now 'tis thine.

CLIF. You said so much before, and yet you fled.

---

[a] *And this soft* courage—] Mason and Mr. Collier's annotator would read *carriage* for *courage*: but *courage* here means *mettle, heart, spirit.*

[b] Darraign—] That is, *boldly prepare.*

[c] Since when, &c.] From this point the speech, both in "The True Tragedy," and in the folio, 1623, is assigned to Clarence, except that in the former the last line reads:—
"To blot *our brother out,*" &c.

WAR. 'Twas not your valour, Clifford, drove me thence.
NORTH. No, nor your manhood that durst make you stay.
RICH. Northumberland, I hold thee reverently;—
Break off the parley; for scarce I can refrain
The execution of my big-swoln heart
Upon that Clifford, that cruel child-killer.
CLIF. I slew thy father,—call'st thou him a child?
RICH. Ay, like a dastard, and a treacherous coward,
As thou didst kill our tender brother, Rutland;
But ere sunset I'll make thee curse the deed.
K. HEN. Have done with words, my lords, and hear me speak.
Q. MAR. Defy them, then, or else hold close thy lips.
K. HEN. I pr'ythee, give no limits to my tongue:
I am a king, and privileg'd to speak.
CLIF. My liege, the wound that bred this meeting here
Cannot be cur'd by words; therefore be still.
RICH. Then, executioner, unsheathe thy sword;
By Him that made us all, I am resolv'd,
That Clifford's manhood lies upon his tongue.
EDW. Say, Henry, shall I have my right or no?
A thousand men have broke their fasts to-day,
That ne'er shall dine unless thou yield the crown.
WAR. If thou deny, their blood upon thy head;
For York in justice puts his armour on.
PRINCE. If that be right which Warwick says is right,
There is no wrong, but everything is right.
RICH. Whoever got thee,[a] there thy mother stands;
For, well I wot, thou hast thy mother's tongue.
Q. MAR. But thou art neither like thy sire nor dam;

---

a Whoever got thee, &c.] This speech in the folios has the prefix *War.*, but in "The True Tragedy" it is rightly given to Richard.

But like a foul mis-shapen stigmatic,[a]
Mark'd by the destinies to be avoided,
As venom toads, or lizards' dreadful stings.
RICH. Iron of Naples hid with English gilt,
Whose father bears the title of a king
(As if a channel[b] should be call'd the sea),
Sham'st thou not, knowing whence thou art extraught,
To let thy tongue detect[c] thy base-born heart?
EDW. A wisp of straw[d] were worth a thousand crowns,
To make this shameless callet know herself.—
Helen of Greece was fairer far than thou,
Although thy husband may be Menelaus;
And ne'er was Agamemnon's brother wrong'd
By that false woman, as this king by thee.
His father revell'd in the heart of France,
And tam'd the king, and made the dauphin stoop;
And, had he match'd according to his state,
He might have kept that glory to this day;
But when he took a beggar to his bed,
And grac'd thy poor sire with his bridal-day,
Even then that sunshine brew'd a shower for him,
That wash'd his father's fortunes forth of France,
And heap'd sedition on his crown at home.
For what hath broach'd this tumult but thy pride?
Hadst thou been meek, our title still had slept,
And we, in pity of the gentle king,
Had slipp'd our claim until another age.
GEO. But when we saw our sunshine made thy spring,
And that thy summer bred us no increase,
We set the axe to thy usurping root;
And though the edge hath something hit ourselves,
Yet, know thou, since we have begun to strike,
We'll never leave till we have hewn thee down,
Or bath'd thy growing with our heated bloods.
EDW. And, in this resolution, I defy thee;
Not willing any longer conference,
Since thou deniest* the gentle king to speak.—
Sound trumpets!—Let our bloody colours wave!—
And either victory, or else a grave.
Q. MAR. Stay, Edward,—
EDW. No, wrangling woman, we'll no longer stay;
These words will cost ten thousand lives this day.
[*Exeunt.*

SCENE III.—*A Field of Battle between* Towton *and* Saxton, *in* Yorkshire.(4)

Alarums: Excursions. Enter WARWICK.

WAR. Forespent with toil, as runners with a race,
I lay me down a little while to breathe;
For strokes receiv'd, and many blows repaid,
Have robb'd my strong-knit sinews of their strength,
And, spite of spite, needs must I rest awhile.

Enter EDWARD, *running.*

EDW. Smile, gentle heaven! or strike, ungentle death!
For this world frowns, and Edward's sun is clouded.
WAR. How now, my lord! what hap? what hope of good?

Enter GEORGE.

GEO. Our hap is loss, our hope but sad despair;
Our ranks are broke, and ruin follows us:
What counsel give you? whither shall we fly?
EDW. Bootless is flight,—they follow us with wings;
And weak we are, and cannot shun pursuit.

Enter RICHARD.

RICH. Ah, Warwick, why hast thou withdrawn thyself?
Thy brother's blood the thirsty earth hath drunk,
Broach'd with the steely point of Clifford's lance;
And, in the very pangs of death, he cried,—
Like to a dismal clangor heard from far,—
Warwick, revenge! brother, revenge my death!
So underneath the belly of their steeds,
That stain'd their fetlocks in his smoking blood,
The noble gentleman gave up the ghost.
WAR. Then let the earth be drunken with our blood:
I'll kill my horse, because I will not fly.
Why stand we like soft-hearted women here,
Wailing our losses, whiles the foe doth rage;
And look upon, as if the tragedy
Were play'd in jest by counterfeiting actors?
Here on my knee I vow to God above,
I'll never pause again, never stand still,
Till either death hath clos'd these eyes of mine,
Or fortune given me measure of revenge!
EDW. O Warwick, I do bend my knee with thine;
And in this vow do chain my soul to thine!—
And, ere my knee rise from the earth's cold face,
I throw my hands, mine eyes, my heart to thee,

(*) First folio, *denied'st.*

[a] Stigmatic,—] See note (b), p. 389.
[b] Channel—] That is, *kennel.* Thus in Marlowe's "Edward II."—
"Here's *channel*-water, as our charge is given."
[c] Detect—] *Exhibit, display.*
[d] A wisp of straw—] From several passages in the old writers, it would appear that one punishment for a scold was to crown her with a *wisp of straw.* Thus in "A Dialogue between John and Jone, Striving who shall Wear the Breeches,"—Pleasures of poetry, bl. l. no date (quoted by Malone):—
"And make me promise, never more
That thou shalt mind to beat me;
For feare thou *weare the wispe*, good wife."

Thou setter-up and plucker-down of kings,—
Beseeching thee, if with thy will it stands,
That to my foes this body must be prey,—
Yet that thy brazen gates of heaven may ope,
And give sweet passage to my sinful soul!—
Now, lords. take leave until we meet again,
Where'er it be, in heaven or in earth.

RICH. Brother, give me thy hand;—and, gentle Warwick,
Let me embrace thee in my weary arms:
I, that did never weep, now melt with woe,
That winter should cut off our spring-time so.

WAR. Away, away! Once more, sweet lords, farewell.

GEO. Yet let us all together to our troops,
And give them leave to fly that will not stay;
And call them pillars that will stand to us;
And, if we thrive, promise them such rewards
As victors wear at the Olympian games:
This may plant courage in their quailing breasts;
For yet is hope of life and victory.—
Foreslow no longer, make we hence amain.
[*Exeunt.*

SCENE IV.—*Another part of the Field.*

Excursions. *Enter* RICHARD *and* CLIFFORD.

RICH. Now, Clifford, I have singled thee alone:
Suppose this arm is for the duke of York,
And this for Rutland; both bound to revenge,
Wert thou environ'd with a brazen wall.

CLIF. Now, Richard, I am with thee here alone:
This is the hand that stabb'd thy father York;
And this the hand that slew thy brother Rutland;
And here's the heart that triumphs in their death,
And cheers these hands that slew thy sire and brother,
To execute the like upon thyself;
And so, have at thee!

[*They fight.* WARWICK *enters;* CLIFFORD *flies.*

RICH. Nay, Warwick, single out some other chase;
For I myself will hunt this wolf to death. [*Exeunt.*

SCENE V.—*Another part of the Field.*

Alarum. *Enter* KING HENRY.

K. HEN. This battle fares like to the morning's war,
When dying clouds contend with growing light,
What time the shepherd, blowing of his nails,
Can neither call it perfect day nor night.
Now sways it this way, like a mighty sea
Forc'd by the tide to combat with the wind;
Now sways it that way, like the self-same sea
Forc'd to retire by fury of the wind:
Sometime the flood prevails, and then the wind;
Now, one the better, then, another best;
Both tugging to be victors, breast to breast,
Yet neither conqueror nor conquered:
So is the equal poise of this fell war.
Here on this molehill will I sit me down.
To whom God will, there be the victory!
For Margaret my queen, and Clifford too,
Have chid me from the battle; swearing both,
They prosper best of all when I am thence.
Would I were dead! if God's good will were so;
For what is in this world but grief and woe?
O God! methinks it were a happy life
To be no better than a homely swain;
To sit upon a hill, as I do now,
To carve out dials quaintly, point by point,
Thereby to see the minutes how they run,—
How many make the hour full complete;
How many hours bring about the day;
How many days will finish up the year;
How many years a mortal man may live.
When this is known, then to divide the times,—
So many hours must I tend my flock;
So many hours must I take my rest;
So many hours must I contemplate;
So many hours must I sport myself;
So many days my ewes have been with young;
So many weeks ere the poor fools will yean;
So many years[a] ere I shall shear the fleece:
So minutes, hours, days, months, and years,
Pass'd over to the end they were created,
Would bring white hairs unto a quiet grave.
Ah, what a life were this! how sweet! how lovely!
Gives not the hawthorn-bush a sweeter shade
To shepherds, looking on their silly sheep,
Than doth a rich embroider'd canopy
To kings, that fear their subjects' treachery?
O, yes, it doth; a thousand fold, it doth!
And to conclude,—the shepherd's homely curds,
His cold thin drink out of his leather bottle,
His wonted sleep under a fresh tree's shade,
All which secure and sweetly he enjoys,
Is far beyond a prince's delicates,
His viands sparkling in a golden cup,
His body couched in a curious bed,
When care, mistrust, and treason wait on him.

Alarum. *Enter a* Son *that hath killed his* Father, *bringing in the body.*

SON. Ill blows the wind that profits nobody.—
This man, whom hand to hand I slew in fight,

[a] *So many* years—] Rowe altered *years* to *months*, and Mr. Collier's annotator makes the same change. Malone explains *years* to mean—"The years which must elapse between the time of the yeaning of the ewes, and the lambs arriving to such a state as to admit of being shorn."

May be possessed with some store of crowns:
And I, that haply take them from him now,
May yet ere night yield both my life and them
To some man else, as this dead man doth me.—
Who's this?—O God! it is my father's face,
Whom in this conflict I unwares have kill'd.
O heavy times, begetting such events!
From London by the king was I press'd forth;
My father, being the earl of Warwick's man,
Came on the part of York, press'd by his master;
And I, who at his hands receiv'd my life,
Have by my hands of life bereaved him.—
Pardon me, God,—I knew not what I did!—
And pardon, father, for I knew not thee!—
My tears shall wipe away these bloody marks,
And no more words till they have flow'd their fill.

K. HEN. O piteous spectacle! O bloody times!
Whiles lions war and battle for their dens,
Poor harmless lambs abide their enmity.—
Weep, wretched man, I'll aid thee tear for tear;
And let our hearts and eyes, like civil war,
Be blind with tears, and break o'ercharg'd with grief.

Enter a Father, *that hath killed his* Son, *bringing in the body.*

FATH. Thou that so stoutly hast resisted me,
Give me thy gold, if thou hast any gold;
For I have bought it with an hundred blows.—
But let me see:—is this our foeman's face?
Ah, no, no, no, it is mine only son!
Ah, boy, if any life be left in thee,
Throw up thine eye! see, see what showers arise,
Blown with the windy tempest of my heart,
Upon thy wounds, that kill mine eye and heart!—
O, pity, God, this miserable age!—
What stratagems, how fell, how butcherly,
Erroneous, mutinous, and unnatural,
This deadly quarrel daily doth beget!—
O boy, thy father gave thee life too soon,
And hath bereft thee of thy life too late!

K. HEN. Woe above woe! grief more than common grief!
O, that my death would stay these ruthful deeds!—
O pity, pity, gentle heaven, pity!—
The red rose and the white are on his face,
The fatal colours of our striving houses:
The one his purple blood right well resembles,
The other his pale cheeks, methinks, presenteth:
Wither one rose, and let the other flourish!
If you contend, a thousand lives must wither.

SON. How will my mother for a father's death,
Take on with me, and ne'er be satisfied!

FATH. How will my wife for slaughter of my son,
Shed seas of tears, and ne'er be satisfied!

K. HEN. How will the country for these woeful chances,
Misthink the king, and not be satisfied!

SON. Was ever son so ru'd a father's death?

FATH. Was ever father so bemoan'd his son?

K. HEN. Was ever king so griev'd for subjects' woe?
Much is your sorrow; mine, ten times so much.

SON. I'll bear thee hence, where I may weep my fill. [*Exit with the body.*

FATH. These arms of mine shall be thy winding-sheet;
My heart, sweet boy, shall be thy sepulchre,—
For from my heart thine image ne'er shall go;
My sighing breast shall be thy funeral bell;
And so obsequious[a] will thy father be,
Men[b] for the loss of thee, having no more,
As Priam was for all his valiant sons.
I'll bear thee hence; and let them fight that will,
For I have murder'd where I should not kill. [*Exit with the body.*

K. HEN. Sad-hearted men, much overgone with care,
Here sits a king more woeful than you are.

Alarums: Excursions. Enter QUEEN MARGARET, *the* PRINCE *of* WALES, *and* EXETER.

PRINCE. Fly, father, fly! for all your friends are fled,
And Warwick rages like a chafed bull:
Away! for death doth hold us in pursuit.

Q. MAR. Mount you, my lord; towards Berwick post amain:
Edward and Richard, like a brace of greyhounds
Having the fearful flying hare in sight,
With fiery eyes sparkling for very wrath,
And bloody steel grasp'd in their ireful hands,
Are at our backs; and therefore hence amain.

EXE. Away! for vengeance comes along with them:
Nay, stay not to expostulate,—make speed,
Or else come after; I'll away before.

---

[a] Obsequious—] *Obsequious* here appears to signify *funereal, engrossed by death's rites.*

[b] Men *for the loss of thee,*—] The commentators, with one accord, pronounce *Men* to be a misprint: and Rowe reads:—

"*Sad* for the loss," &c.

a change generally adopted, until Mr. Dyce proposed, a few years since, to substitute,—

"*E'en* for the loss," &c.

Of the two, we prefer Mr. Dyce's emendation, but are unwilling to expel the original word, because it again occurs with equal ambiguity in "Love's Labour's Lost" (see note (b), p. 78, Vol. I.), and in Ben Jonson's "Every Man in His Humour," Act IV. Sc. 4:—"I was going along in the street, thinking nothing, when, of a sudden, a voice calls, *Mr. Knowell's man!* another cries, *Soldier!* and thus half a dozen of them, till they had call'd me within a house, where I no sooner came, but they seem'd *men,* and out flew all their rapiers at my bosom;" and it may possibly have once borne the meaning of *demented, frenzied,* and the like.

K. HEN. Nay, take me with thee, good sweet Exeter:
Not that I fear to stay, but love to go
Whither the queen intends. Forward; away!
[*Exeunt.*

SCENE VI.—*Another part of the Field.*

A loud Alarum. Enter CLIFFORD, *wounded.*

CLIF. Here burns my candle out,—ay, here it dies,
Which, whiles it lasted, gave king Henry light.
O, Lancaster, I fear thy overthrow
More than my body's parting with my soul!
My love and fear glued many friends to thee;
And, now I fall, thy tough commixtures melt,
Impairing Henry, strength'ning mis-proud York.
The common people swarm like summer flies: [a]
And whither fly the gnats but to the sun?
And who shines now but Henry's enemies?
O Phœbus, hadst thou never given consent
That Phaeton should check thy fiery steeds,
Thy burning car never had scorch'd the earth!
And Henry, hadst thou sway'd as kings should do,
Or as thy father and his father did,
Giving no ground unto the house of York,
They never then had sprung like summer flies; [b]
I, and ten thousand in this luckless realm,
Had left no mourning widows for our death,
And thou this day hadst kept thy chair in peace.
For what doth cherish weeds but gentle air?
And what makes robbers bold but too much lenity?
Bootless are plaints, and cureless are my wounds:
No way to fly, nor strength to hold out flight;
The foe is merciless, and will not pity;
For at their hands I have deserv'd no pity.
The air hath got into my deadly wounds,
And much effuse of blood doth make me faint:
Come, York, and Richard, Warwick, and the rest,
I stabb'd your fathers' bosoms,—split my breast.
[*Faints.*

Alarum and retreat. Enter EDWARD, GEORGE, RICHARD, MONTAGUE, WARWICK, *and* Soldiers.

EDW. Now breathe we, lords; good fortune bids us pause,
And smooth the frowns of war with peaceful looks.—
Some troops pursue the bloody-minded queen,
That led calm Henry, though he were a king,—
As doth a sail, fill'd with a fretting gust,
Command an argosy—to stem the waves.
But think you, lords, that Clifford fled with them?

WAR. No, 'tis impossible he should escape:
For, though before his face I speak the words,
Your brother Richard mark'd him for the grave,
And, wheresoe'er he is, he's surely dead.
[CLIFFORD *groans, and dies.*

EDW. Whose soul is that which takes her heavy leave?

RICH. A deadly groan, like life and death's departing.

EDW. See who it is: and, now the battle's ended,
If friend or foe, let him be gently us'd.[c]

RICH. Revoke that doom of mercy, for 'tis Clifford;
Who not contented that he lopp'd the branch
In hewing Rutland when his leaves put forth,
But set his murdering knife unto the root
From whence that tender spray did sweetly spring,—
I mean our princely father, duke of York.

WAR. From off the gates of York fetch down the head,
Your father's head, which Clifford placed there:
Instead whereof, let this supply the room;
Measure for measure must be answered.

EDW. Bring forth that fatal screech-owl to our house,
That nothing sung but death to us and ours:
Now death shall stop his dismal threat'ning sound,
And his ill-boding tongue no more shall speak.
[*Attendants bring the body forward.*

WAR. I think his understanding is bereft:—
Speak, Clifford, dost thou know who speaks to thee?—
Dark cloudy death o'ershades his beams of life,
And he nor sees, nor hears us what we say.

RICH. O, would he did! and so, perhaps, he doth:
'Tis but his policy to counterfeit,
Because he would avoid such bitter taunts
Which in the time of death he gave our father.

GEO. If so thou think'st, vex him with eager[d] words.

RICH. Clifford! ask mercy, and obtain no grace.

EDW. Clifford! repent in bootless penitence.

WAR. Clifford! devise excuses for thy faults.

---

a The common people swarm like summer flies:] This line, so necessary to the context, by some inadvertence was omitted in the folio. Theobald restored it from "The True Tragedy."

b They never then had sprung like summer flies;] This is not found in "The True Tragedy;" it was probably intended to be cancelled in the folio, and the line accidentally omitted above to be introduced.

c If friend or foe, let him be gently us'd.] The distribution of the three last speeches is that of "The True Tragedy;" in the folio they are apportioned thus:—

"RICH. Whose soule is that which takes hir heavy leave?
A deadly grone, like life and deaths departing.
See who it is.
ED. And now the Battailes ended,
If Friend or Foe, let him be gently used."

d Eager *words.*] *Biting, sour* words.

GEO. While we devise fell tortures for thy faults.

RICH. Thou didst love York, and I am son to York.

EDW. Thou pitied'st Rutland, I will pity thee.

GEO. Where 's captain Margaret, to fence you now?

WAR. They mock thee, Clifford! swear as thou wast wont.

RICH. What, not an oath? nay, then the world goes hard,
When Clifford cannot spare his friends an oath:—
I know by that he 's dead; and, by my soul,
If this right hand would buy two hours' life,
That I in all despite might rail at him,
This hand should chop it off; and with the issuing blood
Stifle the villain, whose unstanched thirst
York and young Rutland could not satisfy.

WAR. Ay, but he's dead: off with the traitor's head,
And rear it in the place your father's stands.—
And now to London with triumphant march,
There to be crowned England's royal king.
From whence shall Warwick cut the sea to France,
And ask the lady Bona for thy queen:
So shalt thou sinew both these lands together;
And, having France thy friend, thou shalt not dread
The scatter'd foe that hopes to rise again;
For though they cannot greatly sting to hurt,
Yet look to have them buz, to offend thine ears.
First, will I see the coronation;
And then to Brittany I'll cross the sea,
To effect this marriage, so it please my lord.

EDW. Even as thou wilt, sweet Warwick, let it be,
For in thy shoulder do I build my seat;
And never will I undertake the thing,
Wherein thy counsel and consent is wanting.—
Richard, I will create thee duke of Gloster;
And George, of Clarence;—Warwick, as ourself,
Shall do, and undo, as him pleaseth best.

RICH. Let me be duke of Clarence; George, of Gloster;
For Gloster's dukedom is too ominous.(5)

WAR. Tut, that 's a foolish observation;
Richard, be duke of Gloster. Now to London,
To see these honours in possession.

[*Exeunt.*

ACT III.

SCENE I.—*A Chace in the North of* England.

Enter two Keepers,[a] *with cross-bows in their hands.*

1 Keep. Under this thick-grown brake we'll shroud ourselves;
For through this laund[b] anon the deer will come;
And in this covert will we make our stand,
Culling the principal of all the deer.
2 Keep. I'll stay above the hill, so both may [shoot.
1 Keep. That cannot be; the noise of thy cross-bow
Will scare the herd, and so my shoot is lost.
Here stand we both, and aim we at the best:
And, for the time shall not seem tedious,
I'll tell thee what befel me on a day,
In this self-place where now we mean to stand.
2 Keep. Here comes a man; let's stay till he be pass'd.

Enter King Henry, *disguised, with a prayer-book.*

K. Hen. From Scotland am I stol'n, even of pure love,(1)
To greet mine own land with my wishful sight.
No, Harry, Harry, 't is no land of thine;
Thy place is fill'd, thy sceptre wrung from thee,

---

[a] Enter two Keepers, &c.] So "The True Tragedy:" the direction in the folio is, "*Enter Sinklo, and Humfrey,*" &c.; and these names are prefixed to the corresponding speeches throughout the scene. Sincklo and Humphrey were probably the actors who personated the two keepers. The former is mentioned again in "The Taming of the Shrew" (see note (a), p. 229, Vol. I.), and in "Henry IV." Part II. Act IV. Sc. 4.

[b] Laund—] A *lawn*, or *plain between woods.*

Thy balm wash'd off, wherewith thou wast anointed:
No bending knee will call thee Cæsar now,
No humble suitors press to speak for right,
No, not a man comes for redress of thee,
For how can I help them, and not myself?

1 KEEP. Ay, here's a deer whose skin's a keeper's fee:
This is the *quondam* king; let's seize upon him.

K. HEN. Let me embrace these sour adversities;[a]
For wise men say it is the wisest course.

2 KEEP. Why linger we? let us lay hands upon him.

1 KEEP. Forbear awhile; we'll hear a little more.

K. HEN. My queen and son are gone to France for aid;
And, as I hear, the great commanding Warwick
Is thither gone, to crave the French king's sister
To wife for Edward: if this news be true,
Poor queen and son, your labour is but lost;
For Warwick is a subtle orator,
And Lewis a prince soon won with moving words.
By this account, then, Margaret may win him,
For she's a woman to be pitied much:
Her sighs will make a battery in his breast,
Her tears will pierce into a marble heart;
The tiger will be mild, whiles she doth mourn,
And Nero will be tainted with remorse,
To hear, and see, her plaints, her brinish tears.
Ay, but she's come to beg; Warwick, to give:
She, on his left side, craving aid for Henry,
He, on his right, asking a wife for Edward.
She weeps, and says her Henry is depos'd;
He smiles, and says his Edward is install'd;
That she, poor wretch, for grief can speak no more,
Whiles Warwick tells his title, smooths the wrong,
Inferreth arguments of mighty strength;
And, in conclusion, wins the king from her,
With promise of his sister, and what else,
To strengthen and support king Edward's place.
O Margaret, thus 't will be; and thou, poor soul,
Art then forsaken, as thou went'st forlorn!

2 KEEP. Say, what art thou, that[b] talk'st of kings and queens?

K. HEN. More than I seem, and less than I was born to:
A man at least, for less I should not be;
And men may talk of kings, and why not I?

2 KEEP. Ay, but thou talk'st as if thou wert a king.

K. HEN. Why, so I am, in mind; and that's enough.

2 KEEP. But, if thou be a king, where is thy crown?

K. HEN. My crown is in my heart, not on my head;
Not deck'd with diamonds, and Indian stones,
Nor to be seen: my crown is call'd content,—
A crown it is that seldom kings enjoy.

2 KEEP. Well, if you be a king crown'd with content,
Your crown, content, and you, must be contented
To go along with us: for, as we think,
You are the king, king Edward hath depos'd;
And we his subjects, sworn in all allegiance,
Will apprehend you as his enemy.

K. HEN. But did you never swear, and break an oath?

2 KEEP. No, never such an oath; nor will not now.

K. HEN. Where did you dwell, when I was king of England?

2 KEEP. Here in this country, where we now remain.

K. HEN. I was anointed king at nine months old;
My father, and my grandfather, were kings;
And you were sworn true subjects unto me:
And, tell me then, have you not broke your oaths?

1 KEEP. No;
For we were subjects but while you were king.

K. HEN. Why, am I dead? do I not breathe a man?
Ah, simple men, you know not what you swear!
Look, as I blow this feather from my face,
And as the air blows it to me again,
Obeying with my wind when I do blow,
And yielding to another when it blows,
Commanded always by the greater gust,
Such is the lightness of you common men.
But do not break your oaths; for, of that sin
My mild entreaty shall not make you guilty.
Go where you will, the king shall be commanded;
And be you kings; command, and I'll obey.

1 KEEP. We are true subjects to the king, king Edward.

K. HEN. So would you be again to Henry,
If he were seated as king Edward is.

1 KEEP. We charge you, in God's name, and in[c] the king's,
To go with us unto the officers.

K. HEN. In God's name, lead; your king's name be obey'd;
And what God will, that let your king perform;
And what he will, I humbly yield unto. [*Exeunt.*

---

[a] These *sour* adversities;] A reading of Pope's, and Mr. Collier's annotator. In the folio 1623, we have "*the* sower *Adversaries*," &c.

[b] *Say, what art thou*, that *talk'st*—] The word *that*, omitted in the folio, is restored from the corresponding line of "The True Tragedy."

[c] *And* in *the king's*,—] The folio 1623 ads, "——and the king's." Rowe first supplied the preposition *in*.

SCENE II.—London. *A Room in the Palace.*

Enter KING EDWARD, GLOUCESTER, CLARENCE, *and* LADY GREY.

K. EDW. Brother of Gloster, at Saint Albans' field
This lady's husband, sir John* Grey, was slain,
His lands[a] then seiz'd on by the conqueror:
Her suit is now, to repossess those lands;
Which we in justice cannot well deny,
Because in quarrel of the house of York
The worthy gentleman did lose his life.(2)

GLO. Your highness shall do well, to grant her suit;
It were dishonour to deny it her.

K. EDW. It were no less; but yet I'll make a pause.

GLO. Yea! is it so? [*Aside to* CLAR.
I see, the lady hath a thing to grant,
Before the king will grant her humble suit.

CLAR. He knows the game; how true he keeps the wind! [*Aside to* GLO.

GLO. Silence! [*Aside to* CLAR.

K. EDW. Widow, we will consider of your suit;
And come some other time to know our mind.

L. GREY. Right gracious lord, I cannot brook delay:
May it please your highness to resolve me now,
And what your pleasure is, shall satisfy me.

GLO. [*Aside.*] Ay, widow? then I'll warrant you all your lands,
An if what pleases him shall pleasure you.
Fight closer, or, good faith, you'll catch a blow.

CLAR. I fear her not, unless she chance to fall. [*Aside to* GLO.

GLO. God forbid that! for he'll take vantages. [*Aside to* CLAR.

K. EDW. How many children hast thou, widow? tell me.

CLAR. I think, he means to beg a child of her. [*Aside to* GLO.

GLO. Nay, whip me then;[b] he'll rather give her two. [*Aside to* CLAR.

L. GREY. Three, my most gracious lord.

GLO. You shall have four, if you'll be rul'd by him. [*Aside.*

K. EDW. 'Twere pity they should lose their father's lands.

L. GREY. Be pitiful, dread lord, and grant it then.

K. EDW. Lords, give us leave; I'll try this widow's wit.

GLO. [*Aside.*] Ay, good leave have you; for you will have leave,
Till youth take leave and leave you to the crutch.
[GLO. *and* CLAR. *stand aloof.*

K. EDW. Now tell me, madam, do you love your children?

L. GREY. Ay, full as dearly as I love myself.

K. EDW. And would you not do much to do them good?

L. GREY. To do them good, I would sustain some harm.

K. EDW. Then get your husband's lands, to do them good.

L. GREY. Therefore I came unto your majesty.

K. EDW. I'll tell you how these lands are to be got.

L. GREY. So shall you bind me to your highness' service.

K. EDW. What service wilt thou do me, if I give them?

L. GREY. What you command, that rests in me to do.

K. EDW. But you will take exceptions to my boon.

L. GREY. No, gracious lord, except I cannot do it.

K. EDW. Ay, but thou canst do what I mean to ask.

L. GREY. Why, then I will do what your grace commands.

GLO. He plies her hard; and much rain wears the marble. [*Aside to* CLAR.

CLAR. As red as fire! nay, then her wax must melt. [*Aside to* GLO.

L. GREY. Why stops my lord? shall I not hear my task?

K. EDW. An easy task; 'tis but to love a king.

L. GREY. That's soon perform'd, because I am a subject.

K. EDW. Why then, thy husband's lands I freely give thee.

L. GREY. I take my leave with many thousand thanks.

GLO. [*Aside.*] The match is made; she seals it with a curt'sy.

K. EDW. But stay thee,—'tis the fruits of love I mean.

L. GREY. The fruits of love I mean, my loving liege.

K. EDW. Ay, but, I fear me, in another sense.
What love, think'st thou, I sue so much to get?

L. GREY. My love till death, my humble thanks, my prayers,
That love, which virtue begs, and virtue grants.

K. EDW. No, by my troth, I did not mean such love.

L. GREY. Why, then you mean not as I thought you did.

(*) Old text, *Richard*.

[a] *His* lands—] Thus "The True Tragedy." The folio 1623 has "*land*."

[b] Nay, whip me then;] So "The True Tragedy." The folio has "Nay, then whip me."

K. Edw. But now you partly may perceive my mind.

L. Grey. My mind will never grant what I perceive
Your highness aims at, if I aim aright.

K. Edw. To tell thee plain, I aim to lie with thee.

L. Grey. To tell you plain, I had rather lie in prison.

K. Edw. Why, then thou shalt not have thy husband's lands.

L. Grey. Why, then mine honesty shall be my dower;
For by that loss I will not purchase them.

K. Edw. Therein thou wrong'st thy children mightily.

L. Grey. Herein your highness wrongs both them and me.
But, mighty lord, this merry inclination
Accords not with the sadness of my suit;
Please you dismiss me, either with ay, or no.

K. Edw. *Ay*, if thou wilt say ay, to my request;
No, if thou dost say no, to my demand.

L. Grey. Then, *no*, my lord. My suit is at an end.

Glo. The widow likes him not, she knits her brows. [*Aside to* Clar.

Clar. He is the bluntest wooer in Christendom. [*Aside to* Glo.

K. Edw. [*Aside.*] Her looks do argue her replete with modesty;

Her words do show her wit incomparable;
All her perfections challenge sovereignty:
One way, or other, she is for a king;
And she shall be my love, or else my queen.—
Say that king Edward take thee for his queen?

L. GREY. 'Tis better said than done, my gracious lord:
I am a subject fit to jest withal,
But far unfit to be a sovereign.

K. EDW. Sweet widow, by my state I swear to thee,
I speak no more than what my soul intends;
And that is, to enjoy thee for my love.

L. GREY. And that is more than I will yield unto:
I know I am too mean to be your queen;
And yet too good to be your concubine.

K. EDW. You cavil, widow; I did mean, my queen.

L. GREY. 'Twill grieve your grace, my sons should call you father.

K. EDW. No more, than when my daughters call thee mother.
Thou art a widow, and thou hast some children;
And, by God's mother, I, being but a bachelor,
Have other some: why, 'tis a happy thing
To be the father unto many sons.
Answer no more, for thou shalt be my queen.

GLO. The ghostly father now hath done his shrift. [*Aside to* CLAR.

CLAR. When he was made a shriver, 'twas for shift. [*Aside to* GLO.

K. EDW. Brothers, you muse what chat we two have had.

GLO. The widow likes it not, for she looks very sad.

K. EDW. You'd think it strange if I should marry her.

CLAR. To whom, my lord?

K. EDW. Why, Clarence, to myself.

GLO. That would be ten days wonder, at the least.

CLAR. That's a day longer than a wonder lasts.

GLO. By so much is the wonder in extremes.

K. EDW. Well, jest on, brothers: I can tell you both,
Her suit is granted for her husband's lands.

Enter a Nobleman.

NOB. My gracious lord, Henry your foe is taken,
And brought your prisoner to your palace gate.

K. EDW. See that he be convey'd unto the Tower:—
And go we, brothers, to the man that took him,
To question of his apprehension.—
Widow, go you along;—lords, use her honourably.[a]

[*Exeunt* K. EDWARD, L. GREY, CLARENCE, *and* Nobleman.

GLO. Ay, Edward will use women *honourably.*
Would he were wasted, marrow, bones, and all,
That from his loins no hopeful branch may spring,
To cross me from the golden time I look for!
And yet, between my soul's desire, and me,
(The lustful Edward's title buried,)
Is Clarence, Henry, and his son young Edward,
And all the unlook'd-for issue of their bodies,
To take their rooms, ere I can place myself:
A cold premeditation for my purpose!
Why, then, I do but dream on sovereignty;
Like one that stands upon a promontory,
And spies a far-off shore where he would tread,
Wishing his foot were equal with his eye,
And chides the sea that sunders him from thence,
Saying—he'll lade it dry to have his way:
So do I wish the crown, being so far off;
And so I chide the means that keep me from it;
And so I say—I'll cut the causes off,
Flattering me with impossibilities.—
My eye's too quick, my heart o'erweens too much,
Unless my hand and strength could equal them.
Well, say there is no kingdom, then, for Richard;
What other pleasure can the world afford?
I'll make my heaven in a lady's lap,
And deck my body in gay ornaments,
And witch sweet ladies with my words and looks.
O miserable thought! and more unlikely
Than to accomplish twenty golden crowns!
Why, love forswore me in my mother's womb:
And, for I should not deal in her soft laws,
She did corrupt frail nature with some bribe
To shrink mine arm up like a wither'd shrub;
To make an envious mountain on my back,
Where sits deformity to mock my body;
To shape my legs of an unequal size;
To disproportion me in every part,
Like to a chaos, or an unlick'd bear-whelp,
That carries no impression like the dam.
And am I, then, a man to be belov'd?
O, monstrous fault, to harbour such a thought!
Then, since this earth affords no joy to me,
But to command, to check, to o'erbear such
As are of better person than myself,
I'll make my heaven—to dream upon the crown;
And, whiles I live, to account this world but hell,
Until my misshap'd trunk, that bears this head,
Be round impaled with a glorious crown.
And yet I know not how to get the crown,
For many lives stand between me and home:
And I,—like one lost in a thorny wood,
That rents the thorns, and is rent with the thorns,

[a] *Use her honourably.*] The folio 1623 reads *honourable*, in this instance probably through negligence, as "The True Tragedy" has "honourably," and Gloucester, in the next line, repeats that word.

Seeking a way, and straying from the way,
Not knowing how to find the open air,
But toiling desperately to find it out,—
Torment myself to catch the English crown:
And from that torment I will free myself,
Or hew my way out with a bloody axe.
Why, I can smile, and murder whiles I smile;
And cry content to that which grieves my heart,
And wet my cheeks with artificial tears,
And frame my face to all occasions.
I'll drown more sailors than the mermaid shall;
I'll slay more gazers than the basilisk;
I'll play the orator as well as Nestor,
Deceive more slily than Ulysses could,
And, like a Sinon, take another Troy:
I can add colours to the cameleon,
Change shapes with Proteus for advantages,
And set the murd'rous Machiavel to school.
Can I do this, and cannot get a crown?
Tut! were it farther off, I'll pluck it down.
[*Exit.*

SCENE III.—France. *A Room in the Palace.*

Flourish. Enter KING LEWIS *and* LADY BONA, *attended; the* KING *takes his state. Then enter* QUEEN MARGARET, PRINCE EDWARD *her* Son, *and the* EARL *of* OXFORD.

K. LEW. Fair queen of England, worthy Margaret, [*Rising.*
Sit down with us; it ill befits thy state
And birth, that thou should'st stand, while Lewis doth sit.

Q. MAR. No, mighty king of France; now Margaret
Must strike her sail, and learn awhile to serve
Where kings command. I was, I must confess,
Great Albion's queen in former golden days;
But now mischance hath trod my title down,
And with dishonour laid me on the ground,
Where I must take like seat unto my fortune,
And to my humble seat conform myself.

K. LEW. Why, say, fair queen, whence springs this deep despair?

Q. MAR. From such a cause as fills mine eyes with tears,
And stops my tongue, while heart is drown'd in cares.

K. LEW. Whate'er it be, be thou still like thyself,
And sit thee by our side: yield not thy neck
[*Seats her by him.*
To fortune's yoke, but let thy dauntless mind
Still ride in triumph over all mischance.
Be plain, queen Margaret, and tell thy grief;
It shall be eas'd, if France can yield relief.

Q. MAR. Those gracious words revive my drooping thoughts,
And give my tongue-tied sorrows leave to speak.
Now, therefore, be it known to noble Lewis,—
That Henry, sole possessor of my love,
Is, of a king, become a banish'd man,
And forc'd to live in Scotland a forlorn;
While proud ambitious Edward, duke of York,
Usurps the regal title, and the seat
Of England's true-anointed lawful king.
This is the cause, that I, poor Margaret,—
With this my son, prince Edward, Henry's heir,—
Am come to crave thy just and lawful aid;
And if thou fail us, all our hope is done:
Scotland hath will to help, but cannot help;
Our people and our peers are both misled,
Our treasure seiz'd, our soldiers put to flight,
And, as thou seest, ourselves in heavy plight.

K. LEW. Renowned queen, with patience calm the storm,
While we bethink a means to break it off.

Q. MAR. The more we stay, the stronger grows our foe.

K. LEW. The more I stay, the more I'll succour thee.

Q. MAR. O, but impatience waiteth on true sorrow!
And see, where comes the breeder of my sorrow.

Enter WARWICK, *attended.*

K. LEW. What's he, approacheth boldly to our presence?

Q. MAR. Our earl of Warwick, Edward's greatest friend.

K. LEW. Welcome, brave Warwick! what brings thee to France?
[*Descending from his state.* QUEEN MARGARET *rises.*

Q. MAR. Ay, now begins a second storm to rise;
For this is he that moves both wind and tide.

WAR. From worthy Edward, king of Albion,
My lord and sovereign, and thy vowed friend,
I come,—in kindness and unfeigned love,—
First, to do greetings to thy royal person,
And, then, to crave a league of amity;
And lastly, to confirm that amity
With nuptial knot, if thou vouchsafe to grant
That virtuous lady Bona, thy fair sister,
To England's king in lawful marriage.

Q. MAR. [*Aside.*] If that go forward, Henry's hope is done.

WAR. And, gracious madam, [*To* BONA.] in our king's behalf,
I am commanded, with your leave and favour,
Humbly to kiss your hand, and with my tongue
To tell the passion of my sovereign's heart;

Where fame, late entering at his heedful ears,
Hath plac'd thy beauty's image and thy virtue.
Q. Mar. King Lewis,—and lady Bona,—hear me speak,
Before you answer Warwick. His demand
Springs not from Edward's well-meant honest love,
But from deceit, bred by necessity:
For how can tyrants safely govern home,
Unless abroad they purchase great alliance?
To prove him tyrant, this reason may suffice,—
That Henry liveth still: but were he dead,
Yet here prince Edward stands, king Henry's son.
Look therefore, Lewis, that by this league and marriage
Thou draw not on thy danger and dishonour:
For though usurpers sway the rule awhile,
Yet heavens are just, and time suppresseth wrongs.
War. Injurious Margaret!
Prince. And why not queen?
War. Because thy father Henry did usurp,
And thou no more art prince than she is queen.
Oxf. Then Warwick disannuls great John of Gaunt,
Which did subdue the greatest part of Spain;
And, after John of Gaunt, Henry the fourth,
Whose wisdom was a mirror to the wisest;
And, after that wise prince, Henry the fifth,
Who by his prowess conquered all France:
From these our Henry lineally descends.
War. Oxford, how haps it, in this smooth discourse,
You told not how, Henry the sixth hath lost
All that which Henry the fifth had gotten?
Methinks these peers of France should smile at that.
But for the rest,—you tell a pedigree
Of threescore and two years; a silly time
To make prescription for a kingdom's worth.
Oxf. Why, Warwick, canst thou speak against thy liege,
Whom thou obeyed'st thirty and six years,
And not bewray thy treason with a blush?
War. Can Oxford, that did ever fence the right,
Now buckler falsehood with a pedigree?
For shame! leave Henry, and call Edward king.
Oxf. Call him my king, by whose injurious doom

My elder brother, the lord Aubrey Vere,
Was done to death? and more than so, my father,
Even in the downfall of his mellow'd years,
When nature brought him to the door of death?
No, Warwick, no; while life upholds this arm,
This arm upholds the house of Lancaster.

WAR. And I the house of York.

K. LEW. Queen Margaret, prince Edward, and Oxford,
Vouchsafe, at our request, to stand aside,
While I use further conference with Warwick.

Q. MAR. Heavens grant that Warwick's words bewitch him not!
[*Retiring with the* PRINCE *and* OXFORD.

K. LEW. Now, Warwick, tell me, even upon thy conscience,
Is Edward your true king? for I were loth
To link with him that were not lawful chosen.

WAR. Thereon I pawn my credit and mine honour.

K. LEW. But is he gracious in the people's eye?

WAR. The more, that Henry was unfortunate.

K. LEW. Then further,—all dissembling set aside,
Tell me for truth the measure of his love
Unto our sister Bona.

WAR. Such it seems,
As may beseem a monarch like himself.
Myself have often heard him say, and swear,—
That this his love was an eternal[a] plant;
Whereof the root was fix'd in virtue's ground,
The leaves and fruit maintain'd with beauty's sun;
Exempt from envy, but not from disdain,
Unless the lady Bona quit his pain.

K. LEW. Now, sister, let us hear your firm resolve.

BONA. Your grant, or your denial, shall be mine:—
Yet I confess, [*To* WAR.] that often ere this day,
When I have heard your king's desert recounted,
Mine ear hath tempted judgment to desire.

K. LEW. Then, Warwick, thus,—our sister shall be Edward's;
And now forthwith shall articles be drawn
Touching the jointure that your king must make,
Which with her dowry shall be counterpois'd:—
Draw near, queen Margaret; and be a witness,
That Bona shall be wife to the English king.

PRINCE. To Edward, but not to the English king.

Q. MAR. Deceitful Warwick! it was thy device
By this alliance to make void my suit;
Before thy coming, Lewis was Henry's friend.

K. LEW. And still is friend to him and Margaret:
But if your title to the crown be weak,—
As may appear by Edward's good success,—
Then 't is but reason that I be releas'd
From giving aid, which late I promised.
Yet shall you have all kindness at my hand,
That your estate requires, and mine can yield.

WAR. Henry now lives in Scotland, at his ease,
Where having nothing, nothing can he lose.
And as for you yourself, our *quondam* queen,—
You have a father able to maintain you;
And better 'twere you troubled him than France.

Q. MAR. Peace, impudent and shameless Warwick, peace![b]
Proud setter-up and puller-down of kings!
I will not hence, till with my talk and tears,
Both full of truth, I make king Lewis behold
Thy sly conveyance, and thy lord's false love;
For both of you are birds of self-same feather.
[*A horn sounded without.*

K. LEW. Warwick, this is some post to us, or thee.

Enter a Messenger.

MESS. My lord ambassador, these letters are for you,
Sent from your brother, marquis Montague.—
These from our king unto your majesty.—
And, madam, [*To* MARG.] these for you; from whom, I know not.
[*All read their letters.*

OXF. I like it well, that our fair queen and mistress
Smiles at her news, while Warwick frowns at his.

PRINCE. Nay, mark, how Lewis stamps as he were nettled:
I hope all's for the best.

K. LEW. Warwick, what are thy news? and yours, fair queen?

Q. MAR. Mine, such as fill my heart with unhop'd joys.

WAR. Mine, full of sorrow and heart's discontent.

K. LEW. What! has your king married the lady Grey?
And now, to soothe your forgery and his,
Sends me a paper to persuade me patience?
Is this the alliance that he seeks with France?
Dare he presume to scorn us in this manner?

Q. MAR. I told your majesty as much before:
This proveth Edward's love, and Warwick's honesty.

WAR. King Lewis, I here protest,—in sight of heaven,
And by the hope I have of heavenly bliss,—
That I am clear from this misdeed of Edward's;
No more my king! for he dishonours me,
But most himself, if he could see his shame.—
Did I forget, that by the house of York
My father came untimely to his death?
Did I let pass the abuse done to my niece?

[a] *An* eternal *plant;*] Thus "The True Tragedy;" *eternal* in the folio 1623 is misprinted "*externall.*"

[b] *Shameless Warwick,* peace!] The second *peace* is not found in the folio 1623, but was supplied by that of 1632.

Did I impale him with the regal crown?
Did I put Henry from his native right,
And am I guerdon'd at the last with shame?
Shame on himself! for my desert is honour:
And, to repair my honour lost for him,
I here renounce him, and return to Henry.—
My noble queen, let former grudges pass,
And henceforth I am thy true servitor;
I will revenge his wrong to lady Bona,
And replant Henry in his former state.

Q. MAR. Warwick, these words have turn'd my hate to love;
And I forgive and quite forget old faults,
And joy that thou becom'st king Henry's friend.

WAR. So much his friend, ay, his unfeigned friend,
That if king Lewis vouchsafe to furnish us
With some few bands of chosen soldiers,
I'll undertake to land them on our coast,
And force the tyrant from his seat by war.
'T is not his new-made bride shall succour him:
And as for Clarence,—as my letters tell me,
He's very likely now to fall from him,
For matching more for wanton lust than honour,
Or than for strength and safety of our country.

BONA. Dear brother, how shall Bona be reveng'd,
But by thy help to this distressed queen?

Q. MAR. Renowned prince, how shall poor Henry live,
Unless thou rescue him from foul despair?

BONA. My quarrel and this English queen's are one.

WAR. And mine, fair lady Bona, joins with yours.

K. LEW. And mine, with hers, and thine, and Margaret's.
Therefore, at last, I firmly am resolv'd
You shall have aid.

Q. MAR. Let me give humble thanks for all at once.

K. LEW. Then England's messenger, return in post,
And tell false Edward, thy supposed king,—
That Lewis of France is sending over masquers,
To revel it with him and his new bride:
Thou seest what's pass'd, go fear[a] thy king withal.

BONA. Tell him, in hope he'll prove a widower shortly,
I'll* wear the willow garland for his sake.

Q. MAR. Tell him, my mourning weeds are laid aside,
And I am ready to put armour on.

WAR. Tell him from me, that he hath done me wrong,
And therefore I'll uncrown him, ere't be long.
There's thy reward; be gone. [*Exit* MESS.

K. LEW. But, Warwick,
Thou and Oxford, with five thousand men,
Shall cross the seas, and bid false Edward battle:
And, as occasion serves, this noble queen
And prince shall follow with a fresh supply.
Yet, ere thou go, but answer me one doubt;—
What pledge have we of thy firm loyalty?

WAR. This shall assure my constant loyalty;—
That if our queen and this young prince agree,
I'll join mine eldest daughter, and my joy,
To him forthwith in holy wedlock bands.

Q. MAR. Yes, I agree, and thank you for your motion:—
Son Edward, she is fair and virtuous,
Therefore delay not, give thy hand to Warwick;
And, with thy hand, thy faith irrevocable,
That only Warwick's daughter shall be thine.

PRINCE. Yes, I accept her, for she well deserves it;
And here, to pledge my vow, I give my hand.
[*Gives his hand to* WARWICK.

K. LEW. Why stay we now? These soldiers shall be levied,
And thou, lord Bourbon, our high-admiral,
Shall waft them over with our royal fleet.—
I long till Edward fall by war's mischance,
For mocking marriage with a dame of France.
[*Exeunt all except* WARWICK.

WAR. I came from Edward as ambassador,(3)
But I return his sworn and mortal foe:
Matter of marriage was the charge he gave me,
But dreadful war shall answer his demand.
Had he none else to make a stale,[b] but me?
Then none but I shall turn his jest to sorrow.
I was the chief that rais'd him to the crown,
And I'll be chief to bring him down again:
Not that I pity Henry's misery,
But seek revenge on Edward's mockery. [*Exit.*

a *Go* fear—] That is, go *fright*. This active sense of *fear* was very common, and has before been noticed.

b *A* stale,—] That is, a *stalking-horse*, a *decoy*, a *pretence*. See note (5), p. 742, Vol. I.

(*) First folio, *I*.

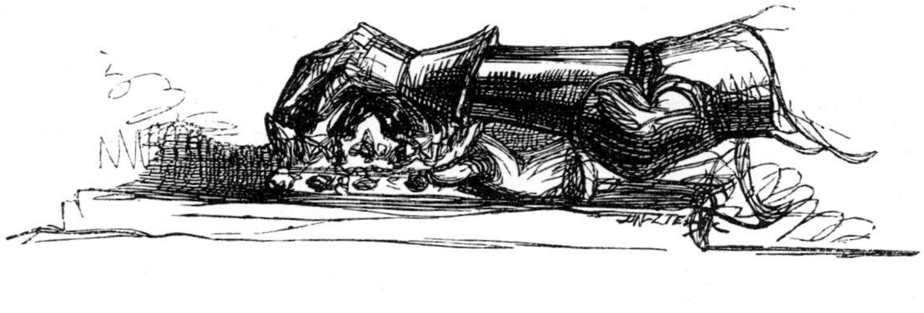

ACT IV.

SCENE I.—London. *A Room in the Palace.*

Enter Clarence, Gloucester, Somerset, Montague, *and others.*

Glo. Now tell me, brother Clarence, what think you
Of this new marriage with the lady Grey?
Hath not our brother made a worthy choice?

Clar. Alas, you know, 'tis far from hence to France;
How could he stay till Warwick made return?

Som. My lords, forbear this talk; here comes the king.

Glo. And his well-chosen bride.

Clar. I mind to tell him plainly what I think.

Flourish. Enter King Edward, *attended;* Lady Grey, *as* Queen; Pembroke, Stafford, Hastings, *and others.*[a]

K. Edw. Now, brother of Clarence, how like you our choice,
That you stand pensive, as half malcontent?

Clar. As well as Lewis of France, or the earl of Warwick;
Which are so weak of courage and in judgment,
That they'll take no offence at our abuse.

K. Edw. Suppose they take offence without a cause,
They are but Lewis and Warwick; I am Edward,
Your king and Warwick's, and must have my will.

Glo. And shall have[b] your will, because our king:
Yet hasty marriage seldom proveth well.

K. Edw. Yea, brother Richard, are you offended too?

Glo. Not I:
No; God forbid, that I should wish them sever'd
Whom God hath join'd together; ay, and 'twere pity
To sunder them that yoke so well together.

---

[a] *Enter, &c.*] The folio 1623 adds to the list of characters who enter, the direction, "*foure* stand *on one side, and foure on the other.*"

[b] And shall have, &c.] Rowe improved the measure by reading—"And *you* shall have," &c.

K. EDW. Setting your scorns and your mislike aside,
Tell me some reason why the lady Grey
Should not become my wife, and England's queen:—
And you too, Somerset and Montague,
Speak freely what you think.
CLAR. Then this is mine opinion,—that king Lewis
Becomes your enemy, for mocking him
About the marriage of the Lady Bona.
GLO. And Warwick, doing what you gave in charge,
Is now dishonoured by this new marriage.
K. EDW. What if both Lewis and Warwick be appeas'd,
By such invention as I can devise?
MONT. Yet to have join'd with France in such alliance,
Would more have strengthen'd this our commonwealth
'Gainst foreign storms, than any home-bred marriage.
HAST. Why, knows not Montague, that of itself
England is safe, if true within itself?
MONT. Yes;[a] but the safer when 'tis back'd with France.
HAST. 'Tis better using France than trusting France:
Let us be back'd with God, and with the seas
Which he hath given for fence impregnable,
And with their helps only defend ourselves;
In them and in ourselves our safety lies.
CLAR. For this one speech, lord Hastings well deserves
To have the heir of the lord Hungerford.
K. EDW. Ay, what of that? it was my will and grant;
And for this once my will shall stand for law.
GLO. And yet, methinks, your grace hath not done well,
To give the heir and daughter of lord Scales
Unto the brother of your loving bride;
She better would have fitted me, or Clarence:
But in your bride you bury brotherhood.
CLAR. Or else you would not have bestow'd the heir
Of the lord Bonville on your new wife's son,
And leave your brothers to go speed elsewhere.
K. EDW. Alas, poor Clarence! is it for a wife
That thou art malcontent? I will provide thee.
CLAR. In choosing for yourself, you show'd your judgment:
Which being shallow, you shall give me leave
To play the broker in mine own behalf;
And, to that end, I shortly mind to leave you.
K. EDW. Leave me, or tarry, Edward will be king,
And not be tied unto his brothers' will.
Q. ELIZ. My lords, before it pleas'd his majesty
To raise my state to title of a queen,
Do me but right, and you must all confess
That I was not ignoble of descent;
And meaner than myself have had like fortune.
But as this title honours me and mine,
So your dislikes, to whom I would be pleasing,
Do cloud my joys with danger and with sorrow.
K. EDW. My love, forbear to fawn upon their frowns:
What danger or what sorrow can befall thee,
So long as Edward is thy constant friend,
And their true sovereign, whom they must obey?
Nay, whom they shall obey, and love thee too,
Unless they seek for hatred at my hands;
Which if they do, yet will I keep thee safe,
And they shall feel the vengeance of my wrath.
GLO. [*Aside.*] I hear, yet say not much, but think the more.

Enter a Messenger.

K. EDW. Now, messenger, what letters, or what news,
From France?
MESS. My sovereign liege, no letters, and few words;
But such as I, without your special pardon,
Dare not relate.
K. EDW. Go to, we pardon thee: therefore, in brief,
Tell me their words as near as thou canst guess them.
What answer makes king Lewis unto our letters?
MESS. At my depart, these were his very words;
Go tell false Edward, thy[b] *supposed king,—*
That Lewis of France is sending over masquers,
To revel it with him and his new bride.
K. EDW. Is Lewis so brave? belike, he thinks me Henry.
But what said lady Bona to my marriage?
MESS. These were her words, utter'd with mild disdain;
Tell him, in hope he'll prove a widower shortly,
I'll wear the willow garland for his sake.

---

[a] Yes; &c.] So the second folio; the first omits "*Yes.*"
[b] Thy *supposed king,—*] The folio 1623 has "*the* supposed," &c.; but "*thy*" is the reading of "The True Tragedy;" and in the previous scene Lewis says, "*thy* supposed king."

K. Edw. I blame not her, she could say little less;
She had the wrong. But what said Henry's queen?
For I have heard that she was there in place.
Mess. *Tell him*, quoth she, *my mourning weeds are done,*
And I am ready to put armour on.
K. Edw. Belike, she minds to play the Amazon.
But what said Warwick to these injuries?
Mess. He, more incens'd against your majesty
Than all the rest, discharg'd me with these words;
Tell him from me, that he hath done me wrong,
And therefore I'll uncrown him, ere't be long.
K. Edw. Ha! durst the traitor breathe out so proud words?
Well, I will arm me, being thus forewarn'd:
They shall have wars, and pay for their presumption.
But say, is Warwick friends with Margaret?
Mess. Ay, gracious sovereign; they are so link'd in friendship,
That young prince Edward marries Warwick's daughter.
Clar. Belike, the elder; Clarence will have the younger.
Now, brother king, farewell, and sit you fast,
For I will hence to Warwick's other daughter;
That, though I want a kingdom, yet in marriage
I may not prove inferior to yourself.—
You, that love me and Warwick, follow me.
[*Exit* Clarence, *and* Somerset *follows.*
Glo. Not I:
My thoughts aim at a further matter;
I stay not for the love of Edward, but the crown.
[*Aside.*
K. Edw. Clarence and Somerset both gone to Warwick!
Yet am I arm'd against the worst can happen;
And haste is needful in this desperate case.—
Pembroke and Stafford, you in our behalf
Go levy men, and make prepare for war;
They are already, or quickly will be landed:
Myself in person will straight follow you.
[*Exeunt* Pembroke *and* Stafford.
But, ere I go, Hastings and Montague,
Resolve my doubt; you twain, of all the rest,
Are near to Warwick, by blood, and by alliance:
Tell me if you love Warwick more than me?
If it be so, then both depart to him;
I rather wish you foes than hollow friends;
But if you mind to hold your true obedience,
Give me assurance with some friendly vow,
That I may never have you in suspect.
Mont. So God help Montague, as he proves true!
Hast. And Hastings, as he favours Edward's cause!
K. Edw. Now, brother Richard, will you stand by us?
Glo. Ay, in despite of all that shall withstand you.
K. Edw. Why so! then am I sure of victory.
Now therefore let us hence; and lose no hour,
Till we meet Warwick with his foreign power.
[*Exeunt.*

SCENE II.—*A Plain in* Warwickshire.

Enter Warwick *and* Oxford, *with* French *and other* Forces.

War. Trust me, my lord, all hitherto goes well;
The common people by numbers swarm to us.

Enter Clarence *and* Somerset.

But see where Somerset and Clarence come!
Speak suddenly, my lords,—are we all friends?
Clar. Fear not that, my lord.
War. Then, gentle Clarence, welcome unto Warwick;—
And welcome, Somerset:—I hold it cowardice,
To rest mistrustful where a noble heart
Hath pawn'd an open hand in sign of love;
Else might I think that Clarence, Edward's brother,
Were but a feigned friend to our proceedings:
But welcome, sweet Clarence; my daughter shall be thine.
And now what rests but, in night's coverture,
Thy brother being carelessly encamp'd,
His soldiers lurking in the towns* about,
And but attended by a simple guard,
We may surprise and take him at our pleasure?
Our scouts have found the adventure very easy:
That as Ulysses, and stout Diomede,
With sleight and manhood stole to Rhesus' tents,
And brought from thence the Thracian fatal steeds;
So we, well cover'd with the night's black mantle,
At unawares may beat down Edward's guard,
And seize himself;—I say not, slaughter him,
For I intend but only to surprise[a] him.—
You that will follow me to this attempt,
Applaud the name of Henry, with your leader.
[*They all cry,* "Henry!"
Why, then, let's on our way in silent sort:
For Warwick and his friends, God and saint George!
[*Exeunt.*

[a] Surprise *him.*—] That is, *capture* him: a sense of the word *surprise*, now obsolete.

(*) Old text, *Towne.*

SCENE III.—Edward's *Camp, near* Warwick.

Enter certain Watchmen, *to guard the* KING's *tent.*

1 WATCH. Come on, my masters, each man take his stand:
The king, by this, is set him down to sleep.

2 WATCH. What, will he not to bed?

1 WATCH. Why, no; for he hath made a solemn vow
Never to lie and take his natural rest,
Till Warwick or himself be quite suppress'd.

2 WATCH. To-morrow, then, belike, shall be the day,
If Warwick be so near as men report.

3 WATCH. But say, I pray, what nobleman is that,
That with the king here resteth in his tent?
1 WATCH. 'Tis the lord Hastings, the king's chiefest friend.
3 WATCH. O, is it so? But why commands the king
That his chief followers lodge in towns about him,
While he himself keeps in the cold field?
2 WATCH. 'Tis the more honour, because more dangerous.
3 WATCH. Ay, but give me worship and quietness;
I like it better than a dangerous honour:
If Warwick knew in what estate he stands,
'Tis to be doubted, he would waken him.
1 WATCH. Unless our halberds did shut up his passage.
2 WATCH. Ay, wherefore else guard we his royal tent,
But to defend his person from night-foes?

Enter, in silence, WARWICK, CLARENCE, OXFORD, SOMERSET, *and* Forces.

WAR. This is his tent; and see, where stand his guard.
Courage, my masters! honour now, or never!
But follow me, and Edward shall be ours.
1 WATCH. Who goes there?
2 WATCH. Stay, or thou diest!

[WARWICK, *and the rest, cry all*—"Warwick! Warwick!" *and set upon the* Guard; *who fly, crying*—"Arm! Arm!" WARWICK, *and the rest, following them.*
The drum beating, and trumpet sounding, re-enter WARWICK, *and the rest, bringing the* KING *out in his gown, sitting in a chair:* GLOUCESTER *and* HASTINGS *fly.*

SOM. What are they that fly there?
WAR. Richard and Hastings: let them go; here is the duke.
K. EDW. The duke! why, Warwick, when we parted last,[a]
Thou call'dst me king!
WAR. Ay, but the case is alter'd:
When you disgrac'd me in my embassade,
Then I degraded you from being king,
And come now to create you duke of York.
Alas! how should you govern any kingdom,
That know not how to use ambassadors;
Nor how to be contented with one wife;
Nor how to use your brothers brotherly;
Nor how to study for the people's welfare;
Nor how to shroud yourself from enemies?
K. EDW. Yea, brother of Clarence, art thou here too?
Nay, then I see, that Edward needs must down.—
Yet, Warwick, in despite of all mischance,
Of thee thyself, and all thy complices,
Edward will always bear himself as king:
Though Fortune's malice overthrow my state,
My mind exceeds the compass of her wheel.
WAR. Then, for his mind, be Edward England's king: [*Takes off his crown.*
But Henry now shall wear the English crown,
And be true king indeed;—thou but the shadow.—
My lord of Somerset, at my request,
See that forthwith duke Edward be convey'd
Unto my brother, archbishop of York.
When I have fought with Pembroke and his fellows,
I'll follow you, and tell what answer
Lewis, and the lady Bona, send to him:—
Now, for a while, farewell, good duke of York.
K. EDW. What fates impose, that men must needs abide;
It boots not to resist both wind and tide.
[*Exit, led out;* SOMERSET *with him.*
OXF. What now remains, my lords, for us to do,
But march to London with our soldiers?
WAR. Ay, that's the first thing that we have to do;
To free king Henry from imprisonment,
And see him seated in the regal throne. [*Exeunt.*

SCENE IV.—London. *A Room in the Palace.*

Enter QUEEN ELIZABETH *and* RIVERS.

RIV. Madam, what makes you in this sudden change?
Q. ELIZ. Why, brother Rivers, are you yet to learn
What late misfortune is befallen king Edward?
RIV. What, loss of some pitch'd battle against Warwick?
Q. ELIZ. No, but the loss of his own royal person.
RIV. Then, is my sovereign slain?
Q. ELIZ. Ay, almost slain, for he is taken prisoner;
Either betray'd by falsehood of his guard,
Or by his foe surpris'd at unawares:
And, as I further have to understand,
Is new committed to the bishop of York,
Fell Warwick's brother, and by that our foe.
RIV. These news, I must confess, are full of grief;

a *When we parted* last,—] So reads "The True Tragedy;" in the folio 1623, *last* appears to have been accidentally omitted.

Yet, gracious madam, bear it as you may:
Warwick may lose, that now hath won the day.

Q. ELIZ. Till then, fair hope must hinder life's decay;
And I the rather wean me from despair,
For love of Edward's offspring in my womb:
This is it that makes me bridle passion,
And bear with mildness my misfortune's cross;
Ay, ay, for this I draw in many a tear,
And stop the rising of blood-sucking sighs,
Lest with my sighs or tears I blast or drown
King Edward's fruit, true heir to the English crown.

RIV. But, madam, where is Warwick then become?

Q. ELIZ. I am informed that he comes towards London,
To set the crown once more on Henry's head:
Guess thou the rest; king Edward's friends must down.
But, to prevent the tyrant's violence,
(For trust not him that hath once broken faith,)
I'll hence forthwith unto the sanctuary,
To save at least the heir of Edward's right;
There shall I rest secure from force and fraud.
Come, therefore, let us fly while we may fly;
If Warwick take us, we are sure to die. [*Exeunt.*

SCENE V.—*A Park near* Middleham Castle *in* Yorkshire.

Enter GLOUCESTER, HASTINGS, *Sir* WILLIAM STANLEY, *and others.*

GLO. Now, my lord Hastings, and sir William Stanley,
Leave off to wonder why I drew you hither,
Into this chiefest thicket of the park.
Thus stands* the case: you know our king, my brother,
Is prisoner to the bishop here, at whose hands
He hath good usage and great liberty;
And often, but attended with weak guard,
Comes† hunting this way to disport himself.
I have advertis'd him by secret means,
That if about this hour he make this way,
Under the colour of his usual game,
He shall here find his friends, with horse and men,
To set him free from his captivity.

Enter KING EDWARD *and a* Huntsman.

HUNT. This way, my lord, for this way lies the game.

K. EDW. Nay, this way, man; see, where the huntsmen stand.—
Now, brother of Gloster, lord Hastings, and the rest,
Stand you thus close, to steal the bishop's deer?

GLO. Brother, the time and case requireth haste;
Your horse stands ready at the park corner.

K. EDW. But whither shall we then?

HAST. To Lynn, my lord; and ship* from thence to Flanders.

GLO. Well guess'd, believe me; for that was my meaning.

K. EDW. Stanley, I will requite thy forwardness.

GLO. But wherefore stay we? 'tis no time to talk.

K. EDW. Huntsman, what say'st thou? wilt thou go along?

HUNT. Better do so, than tarry and be hang'd.

GLO. Come then, away! let's have no more ado.

K. EDW. Bishop, farewell: shield thee from Warwick's frown,
And pray that I may repossess the crown. [*Exeunt.*

SCENE VI.—*A Room in the* Tower.

Enter KING HENRY, CLARENCE, WARWICK, SOMERSET, *Young* RICHMOND, OXFORD, MONTAGUE, Lieutenant *of the* Tower, *and* Attendants.

K. HEN. Master lieutenant, now that God and friends
Have shaken Edward from the regal seat,
And turn'd my captive state to liberty,
My fear to hope, my sorrows unto joys,—
At our enlargement what are thy due fees?

LIEU. Subjects may challenge nothing of their sovereigns;
But if an humble prayer may prevail,
I then crave pardon of your majesty.

K. HEN. For what, lieutenant? for well using me?
Nay, be thou sure, I'll well requite thy kindness,
For that it made my imprisonment a pleasure:
Ay, such a pleasure as incaged birds
Conceive, when, after many moody thoughts,
At last, by notes of household harmony,
They quite forget their loss of liberty.—
But, Warwick, after God, thou sett'st me free,
And chiefly therefore I thank God and thee;
He was the author, thou the instrument.
Therefore, that I may conquer fortune's spite,
By living low, where fortune cannot hurt me,
And that the people of this blessed land
May not be punish'd with my thwarting stars,—
Warwick, although my head still wear the crown,
I here resign my government to thee,
For thou art fortunate in all thy deeds.

(*) First folio, *stand*. (†) First folio, *Come*.

(*) First folio, *shipt*.

WAR. Your grace hath still been fam'd for virtuous;
And now may seem as wise as virtuous,
By spying and avoiding fortune's malice,
For few men rightly temper with the stars:[a]
Yet in this one thing let me blame your grace,
For choosing me when Clarence is in place.

CLAR. No, Warwick, thou art worthy of the sway,
To whom the heavens, in thy nativity,
Adjudg'd an olive branch and laurel crown,
As likely to be blest in peace and war;
And therefore I yield thee my free consent.

WAR. And I choose Clarence only for protector.

K. HEN. Warwick and Clarence, give me both your hands;
Now join your hands and with your hands your hearts,
That no dissension hinder government:
I make you both protectors of this land,
While I myself will lead a private life,
And in devotion spend my latter days,
To sin's rebuke, and my Creator's praise.

WAR. What answers Clarence to his sovereign's will?

CLAR. That he consents, if Warwick yield consent;
For on thy fortune I repose myself.

WAR. Why then, though loth, yet must I be content:
We'll yoke together, like a double shadow
To Henry's body, and supply his place;
I mean, in bearing weight of government,
While he enjoys the honour and his ease.
And, Clarence, now then it is more than needful
Forthwith that Edward be pronounc'd a traitor,
And all his lands and goods be confiscate.[b]

CLAR. What else? and that succession be determin'd.

WAR. Ay, therein Clarence shall not want his part.

K. HEN. But, with the first of all your chief affairs,
Let me entreat, (for I command no more,)
That Margaret your queen, and my son Edward,
Be sent for, to return from France with speed:
For till I see them here, by doubtful fear
My joy of liberty is half eclips'd.

CLAR. It shall be done, my sovereign, with all speed.

K. HEN. My lord of Somerset, what youth is that,
Of whom you seem to have so tender care?

SOM. My liege, it is young Henry, earl of Richmond.(1)

K. HEN. Come hither, England's hope:—if secret powers
[*Lays his hand on his head.*
Suggest but truth to my divining thoughts,
This pretty lad will prove our country's bliss.
His looks are full of peaceful majesty;
His head by nature fram'd to wear a crown,
His hand to wield a sceptre; and himself
Likely in time to bless a regal throne.
Make much of him, my lords; for this is he,
Must help you more than you are hurt by me.

Enter a Messenger.

WAR. What news, my friend? [brother,

MESS. That Edward is escaped from your
And fled, as he hears since, to Burgundy.

WAR. Unsavoury news! but how made he escape? [Gloster,

MESS. He was convey'd by Richard duke of
And the lord Hastings, who attended him
In secret ambush on the forest side,
And from the bishop's huntsmen rescu'd him;
For hunting was his daily exercise. [charge.—

WAR. My brother was too careless of his
But let us hence, my sovereign, to provide
A salve for any sore that may betide.
[*Exeunt* KING HENRY, WAR., CLAR., Lieut. *and* Attendants.

SOM. My lord, I like not of this flight of Edward's,
For doubtless Burgundy will yield him help,
And we shall have more wars before't be long.
As Henry's late presaging prophecy
Did glad my heart with hope of this young Richmond,
So doth my heart misgive me, in these conflicts
What may befall him, to his harm and ours:
Therefore, lord Oxford, to prevent the worst,
Forthwith we'll send him hence to Brittany,
Till storms be past of civil enmity.

OXF. Ay; for, if Edward repossess the crown,
'Tis like that Richmond with the rest shall down.

SOM. It shall be so; he shall to Brittany.
Come, therefore, let's about it speedily. [*Exeunt.*

SCENE VII.—*Before* York.

Enter KING EDWARD, GLOUCESTER, HASTINGS, *and* Forces.

K. EDW. Now, brother Richard, lord Hastings, and the rest;
Yet, thus far, fortune maketh us amends,

---

[a] For few men rightly temper with the stars:] This means, apparently,—few men accept their destiny without complaint.

[b] *And all his lands and goods be confiscate.*] The first folio omits *be*, which was supplied by Malone; the second reads—
"—— and Goods *confiscated.*"

And says, that once more I shall interchange
My waned state for Henry's regal crown.
Well have we pass'd, and now repass'd the seas,
And brought desired help from Burgundy:
What then remains, we being thus arriv'd
From Ravenspurg haven before the gates of York,
But that we enter, as into our dukedom?

GLO. The gates made fast!—Brother, I like not this;
For many men that stumble at the threshold,
Are well foretold that danger lurks within.

K. EDW. Tush, man! abodements must not now affright us:
By fair or foul means we must enter in,
For hither will our friends repair to us.

HAST. My liege, I'll knock once more to summon them.

Enter, on the Walls, the Mayor *of* York, *and* Aldermen.

MAY. My lords, we were forewarned of your coming,
And shut the gates for safety of ourselves;
For now we owe allegiance unto Henry.

K. EDW. But, master mayor, if Henry be your king,
Yet Edward, at the least, is duke of York.

MAY. True, my good lord; I know you for no less.

K. EDW. Why, and I challenge nothing but my dukedom,
As being well content with that alone.

GLO. But when the fox hath once got in his nose,
He'll soon find means to make the body follow. [*Aside.*

HAST. Why, master mayor, why stand you in a doubt?
Open the gates; we are king Henry's friends.

MAY. Ay, say you so? the gates shall then be open'd. [*Exeunt from above.*

GLO. A wise stout captain, and persuaded soon![a]

HAST. The good old man would fain that all were well,
So 'twere not 'long of him: but, being enter'd,
I doubt not, I, but we shall soon persuade
Both him and all his brothers unto reason.

Enter the Mayor *and* Aldermen, *below.*

K. EDW. So, master mayor: these gates must not be shut,
But in the night, or in the time of war.
What! fear not, man, but yield me up the keys; [*Takes his keys.*
For Edward will defend the town, and thee,
And all those friends that deign to follow me.

Drum. Enter MONTGOMERY, *and* Forces, *marching.*

GLO. Brother, this is sir John Montgomery,
Our trusty friend, unless I be deceiv'd.

[a] Persuaded soon!] The old text has—"soon persuaded;" Pope made the transposition, which, as Steevens remarked, requires no apology.

K. Edw. Welcome, sir John! but why come you in arms?

Mont. To help king Edward in his time of storm, As every loyal subject ought to do.

K. Edw. Thanks, good Montgomery; but we now forget Our title to the crown, and only claim Our dukedom, till God please to send the rest.

Mont. Then fare you well, for I will hence again; I came to serve a king, and not a duke,— Drummer, strike up, and let us march away.

[*A march begun.*

K. Edw. Nay, stay, sir John, awhile; and we'll debate, By what safe means the crown may be recovered.

Mont. What talk you of debating? in few words, If you'll not here proclaim yourself our king, I'll leave you to your fortune, and be gone To keep them back that come to succour you: Why shall we fight,[a] if you pretend no title?

Glo. Why, brother, wherefore stand you on nice points?

K. Edw. When we grow stronger, then we'll make our claim: Till then, 'tis wisdom to conceal our meaning.

Hast. Away with scrupulous wit! now arms must rule.

Glo. And fearless minds climb soonest unto crowns. Brother, we will proclaim you out of hand; The bruit thereof will bring you many friends.

K. Edw. Then be it as you will; for 'tis my right, And Henry but usurps the diadem.

---

a *Why shall we fight,*—] Malone prints this, "Why *should* we fight," &c., whereupon Mr. Collier very properly asks, "Why vary at all from the text?" a question, which, in all courtesy, we might take the liberty of retorting upon Mr. Collier himself, since, in addition to the manifold variations he has thought proper to introduce into this play on the authority of his annotator, he has several times departed from the old text without a syllable of explanation; for instance, in Act I. Sc. 1, the folio 1623 reads:—

"Unless he seek to thrust you out *perforce*."

Mr. Collier has—

"—— to thrust you out *by force*."

In Act II. Sc. 1, in the folio 1623 we have—

"Amongst the loving Welshmen *canst* procure."

In Mr. Collier's edition, "— *can* procure."

In Act II. Sc. 5, in the folio 1623 it is—

"Was ever father so bemoaned *his* son?"

In Mr. Collier, "— *a* son?"

In Act II. Sc. 6, the folio 1623 has—

"Which, *whiles* it lasted," &c.

Mr. Collier reads, "— *while* it lasted."

In Act IV. Sc. 8, the folio 1623 has—

"*Shalt* stir up," "*shalt* find," and "*shalt* muster."

While Mr. Collier reads,—

"*Shall* stir up," "*shall* find," and "*shall* muster."

These deviations are not, certainly, of great importance, though of quite as much as Malone's change of *shall* to *should*.

MONT. Ay, now my sovereign speaketh like himself;
And now will I be Edward's champion.
HAST. Sound, trumpet; Edward shall be here proclaim'd:—
Come, fellow-soldier, make thou proclamation.
[*Gives him a paper. Flourish.*
SOLD. [Reads.] *Edward the fourth, by the grace of God, king of England and France, and lord of Ireland, &c.*
MONT. And whosoe'er gainsays king Edward's right,
By this I challenge him to single fight.
[*Throws down his gauntlet.*
ALL. Long live Edward the fourth!
K. EDW. Thanks, brave Montgomery;—and thanks unto you all:
If fortune serve me, I'll requite this kindness.
Now, for this night, let's harbour here in York,
And when the morning sun shall raise his car
Above the border of this horizon,
We'll forward towards Warwick and his mates;
For well I wot that Henry is no soldier.—
Ah, froward Clarence!—how evil it beseems thee,
To flatter Henry, and forsake thy brother!
Yet, as we may, we'll meet both thee and Warwick.—
Come on, brave soldiers; doubt not of the day,
And, that once gotten, doubt not of large pay.
[*Exeunt.*

SCENE VIII.—London. *A Room in the Palace.*

Enter KING HENRY, WARWICK, CLARENCE, MONTAGUE, EXETER, *and* OXFORD.[a]

WAR. What counsel, lords? Edward from Belgia,
With hasty Germans and blunt Hollanders,
Hath pass'd in safety through the narrow seas,
And with his troops doth march amain to London;
And many giddy people flock to him.
OXF. Let's levy men, and beat him back again.[b]
CLAR. A little fire is quickly trodden out,
Which being suffer'd, rivers cannot quench.
WAR. In Warwickshire I have true-hearted friends,
Not mutinous in peace, yet bold in war;
Those will I muster up:—and thou, son Clarence,
Shalt stir up in Suffolk, Norfolk, and in Kent,
The knights and gentlemen to come with thee:—
Thou, brother Montague, in Buckingham,
Northampton, and in Leicestershire, shalt find
Men well inclin'd to hear what thou command'st:—
And thou, brave Oxford, wondrous well belov'd,
In Oxfordshire shalt muster up thy friends.—
My sovereign, with the loving citizens,—
Like to his island, girt in with the ocean,
Or modest Dian, circled with her nymphs,—
Shall rest in London, till we come to him.—
Fair lords, take leave, and stand not to reply.—
Farewell, my sovereign.
K. HEN. Farewell, my Hector, and my Troy's true hope.
CLAR. In sign of truth, I kiss your highness' hand.
K. HEN. Well-minded Clarence, be thou fortunate!
MONT. Comfort, my lord;—and so I take my leave.
OXF. And thus [*Kissing* HENRY'*s hand.*] I seal my truth, and bid adieu.
K. HEN. Sweet Oxford, and my loving Montague,
And all at once,[c] once more a happy farewell.
WAR. Farewell, sweet lords: let's meet at Coventry.
[*Exeunt* WAR., CLAR., OXF., *and* MONT.
K. HEN. Here at the palace will I rest a while.
Cousin of Exeter, what thinks your lordship?
Methinks the power that Edward hath in field,
Should not be able to encounter mine.
EXE. The doubt is, that he will seduce the rest.
K. HEN. That's not my fear; my meed[d] hath got me fame:
I have not stopp'd mine ears to their demands,
Nor posted off their suits with slow delays;
My pity hath been balm to heal their wounds,
My mildness hath allay'd their swelling griefs,
My mercy dried their water-flowing tears;
I have not been desirous of their wealth,
Nor much oppress'd them with great subsidies,(2)
Nor forward of revenge, though they much err'd:
Then why should they love Edward more than me?
No, Exeter, these graces challenge grace;
And, when the lion fawns upon the lamb,
The lamb will never cease to follow him.
[*Shout without,* "A Lancaster! A Lancaster!"
EXE. Hark, hark, my lord! what shouts are these?

---

[a] Exeter, *and Oxford.*] The folio 1623, for *Exeter*, has mistakenly *Somerset.*

[b] Let's levy men, and beat him back again.] In the folio 1623, this line is given to the King; but the modern editors, who assigned it to a more warlike character, were probably right. It is not consonant with Henry's pacific nature, nor indeed becoming to one who has just before abdicated his sovereignty in everything but the name, that he might—

"—— lead a private life,
And in devotion spend [his] latter days."

[c] And all at once,—] See note ([a]), p. 65.

[d] *My* meed—] My *merit*, as in a former passage, Act II. Sc. 1:

"Each one already blazing by our *meeds.*"

Enter KING EDWARD, GLOUCESTER, *and* Soldiers.

K. EDW. Seize on the shame-fac'd Henry, bear him hence,
And once again proclaim us king of England!—
You are the fount, that makes small brooks to flow;
Now stops thy spring; my sea shall suck them dry,
And swell so much the higher by their ebb.—
Hence with him to the Tower; let him not speak.
[*Exeunt some with* KING HENRY.
And, lords, towards Coventry bend we our course,
Where peremptory Warwick now remains:
The sun shines hot, and, if we use delay,
Cold biting winter mars our hop'd-for hay.

GLO. Away betimes, before his forces join,
And take the great-grown traitor unawares:
Brave warriors, march amain towards Coventry.
[*Exeunt.*

ACT V.

SCENE I.—Coventry.

Enter, upon the Walls, WARWICK, *the* Mayor *of* Coventry, *two* Messengers, *and others.*

WAR. Where is the post, that came from valiant Oxford?
How far hence is thy lord, mine honest fellow?

1 MESS. By this at Dunsmore, marching hitherward.

WAR. How far off is our brother Montague?—
Where is the post that came from Montague?

2 MESS. By this at Daintry, with a puissant troop.

Enter Sir JOHN SOMERVILLE.

WAR. Say, Somerville, what says my loving son?
And, by thy guess, how nigh is Clarence now?

SOM. At Southam I did leave him with his forces,
And do expect him here some two hours hence.
[*Drum heard.*

WAR. Then Clarence is at hand, I hear his drum.

SOM. It is not his, my lord; here Southam lies:
The drum your honour hears, marcheth from Warwick.

WAR. Who should that be? belike, unlook'd-for friends.

SOM. They are at hand, and you shall quickly know.

March. Enter KING EDWARD, GLOUCESTER, *and* Forces.

K. EDW. Go, trumpet, to the walls, and sound a parle. [*Flourish.*

GLO. See how the surly Warwick mans the wall.

WAR. O, unbid spite! is sportful Edward come?
Where slept our scouts, or how are they seduc'd,
That we could hear no news of his repair?

K. EDW. Now, Warwick, wilt thou ope the city gates,
Speak gentle words, and humbly bend thy knee,

Call Edward king, and at his hands beg mercy?
And he shall pardon thee these outrages.
WAR. Nay, rather, wilt thou draw thy forces hence,
Confess who set thee up and pluck'd thee down,
Call Warwick patron, and be penitent?
And thou shalt still remain the duke of York.
GLO. I thought, at least, he would have said—the king;
Or did he make the jest against his will?
WAR. Is not a dukedom, sir, a goodly gift?
GLO. Ay, by my faith, for a poor earl to give:
I'll do thee service for so good a gift.
WAR. 'Twas I, that gave the kingdom to thy brother.
K. EDW. Why, then 'tis mine, if but by Warwick's gift.
WAR. Thou art no Atlas for so great a weight:
And, weakling, Warwick takes his gift again;
And Henry is my king, Warwick his subject.
K. EDW. But Warwick's king is Edward's prisoner:
And gallant Warwick, do but answer this,—
What is the body when the head is off?
GLO. Alas, that Warwick had no more forecast,
But, whiles he thought to steal the single ten,
The king was slily finger'd from the deck![a]
You left poor Henry at the bishop's palace,
And, ten to one, you'll meet him in the Tower.
K. EDW. 'Tis even so; yet you are Warwick still.
GLO. Come, Warwick, take the time; kneel down, kneel down:
Nay, when?[b] strike now, or else the iron cools.
WAR. I had rather chop this hand off at a blow,
And with the other fling it at thy face,
Than bear so low a sail, to strike to thee.
K. EDW. Sail how thou canst, have wind and tide thy friend;
This hand, fast wound about thy coal-black hair,
Shall, whiles thy head is warm, and new cut off,
Write in the dust this sentence with thy blood,—
Wind-changing Warwick now can change no more.

Enter OXFORD, *with* Forces, *drum, and colours.*

WAR. O cheerful colours! see, where Oxford comes!
OXF. Oxford, Oxford, for Lancaster!
[*He and his* Forces *enter the city.*
GLO. The gates are open, let us enter too.
K. EDW. So other foes may set upon our backs.
Stand we in good array; for they, no doubt,
Will issue out again and bid us battle:
If not, the city being but of small defence,
We'll quickly rouse the traitors in the same.
WAR. O, welcome, Oxford! for we want thy help.

Enter MONTAGUE, *with* Forces, *drum, and colours.*

MONT. Montague, Montague, for Lancaster!
[*He and his* Forces *enter the city.*
GLO. Thou and thy brother both shall buy this treason
Even with the dearest blood your bodies bear.
K. EDW. The harder match'd, the greater victory:
My mind presageth happy gain and conquest.

Enter SOMERSET, *with* Forces, *drum, and colours.*

SOM. Somerset, Somerset, for Lancaster!
[*He and his* Forces *enter the city.*
GLO. Two of thy name, both dukes of Somerset,
Have sold their lives unto the house of York;
And thou shalt be the third, if this sword hold.

Enter CLARENCE, *with* Forces, *drum, and colours.*

WAR. And lo, where George of Clarence sweeps along,
Of force enough to bid his brother battle;
With whom an* upright zeal to right prevails,
More than the nature of a brother's love:—
Come, Clarence, come; thou wilt, if Warwick call.
CLAR. Father of Warwick, know you what this means?
[*Taking the red rose out of his hat.*[c]
Look, here I throw my infamy at thee!
I will not ruinate my father's house,
Who gave his blood to lime the stones together,
And set up Lancaster. Why trow'st thou, Warwick,
That Clarence is so harsh, so blunt,[d] unnatural,
To bend the fatal instruments of war

(*) First folio, *in*.

[a] *The king was slily finger'd from the* deck!] A pack of cards was formerly termed a *deck of cards*; thus, in "Selimus, Emperor of the Turks," 1594, quoted by Steevens:—

"Well, if I chance but once to get the *deck*
To deal about and shuffle as I would."

[b] *Nay,* when?] This expression of impatience occurs again in "Richard the Second," and in "The Taming of the Shrew." See note (f), p. 449, Vol. I.

[c] *Taking the red rose out of his hat.*] The folio has no stage direction here, and but for "The True Tragedy," which reads, "*Sound a Parlie, and* Richard *and* Clarence *whispers togither, and then* Clarence *takes his red Rose out of his hat and throwes it at* Warwicke," it would have been difficult to guess what Clarence did on saying,—

"Look, here I throw my infamy at thee!"

[d] Blunt,—] That is, *dull, insensible.*

Against his brother and his lawful king?
Perhaps, thou wilt object my holy oath:
To keep that oath, were more impiety
Than Jephtha's,* when he sacrific'd his daughter.
I am so sorry for my trespass made,
That, to deserve well at my brother's hands,
I here proclaim myself thy mortal foe;
With resolution, wheresoe'er I meet thee,
(As I will meet thee, if thou stir abroad,)
To plague thee for thy foul misleading me.
And so proud-hearted Warwick, I defy thee,
And to my brother turn my blushing cheeks.—
Pardon me, Edward, I will make amends;—
And, Richard, do not frown upon my faults,
For I will henceforth be no more unconstant.

K. EDW. Now welcome more, and ten times more belov'd,
Than if thou never hadst deserv'd our hate.

GLO. Welcome, good Clarence; this is brother-like.

WAR. O passing[a] traitor, perjur'd, and unjust!

K. EDW. What, Warwick, wilt thou leave the town, and fight?
Or shall we beat the stones about thine ears?

WAR. Alas, I am not coop'd here for defence!
I will away towards Barnet presently,
And bid thee battle, Edward, if thou dar'st.

K. EDW. Yes, Warwick, Edward dares, and leads the way:—
Lords, to the field! saint George, and victory!
[*March. Exeunt.*

SCENE II.—*A Field of Battle near* Barnet.

Alarums and Excursions. Enter KING EDWARD, *bringing in* WARWICK *wounded.*

K. EDW. So, lie thou there: die thou, and die our fear;
For Warwick was a bug, that fear'd us all.[b]—
Now, Montague, sit fast; I seek for thee,
That Warwick's bones may keep thine company.
[*Exit.*

WAR. Ah, who is nigh? come to me, friend or foe,
And tell me who is victor, York, or Warwick?
Why ask I that? my mangled body shows,
My blood, my want of strength, my sick heart shows,
That I must yield my body to the earth,
And, by my fall, the conquest to my foe.
Thus yields the cedar to the axe's edge,
Whose arms gave shelter to the princely eagle,
Under whose shade the ramping lion slept,
Whose top-branch overpeer'd Jove's spreading tree,
And kept low shrubs from winter's powerful wind.
These eyes, that now are dimm'd with death's black veil,
Have been as piercing as the mid-day sun,
To search the secret treasons of the world:
The wrinkles in my brows, now fill'd with blood,
Were liken'd oft to kingly sepulchres;
For who liv'd king, but I could dig his grave?
And who durst smile when Warwick bent his brow?
Lo, now my glory smear'd in dust and blood!
My parks, my walks, my manors that I had,
Even now forsake me; and of all my lands,
Is nothing left me, but my body's length!
Why, what is pomp, rule, reign, but earth and dust?
And, live we how we can, yet die we must.

Enter OXFORD *and* SOMERSET.

SOM. Ah, Warwick, Warwick! wert thou as we are,
We might recover all our loss again!
The queen from France hath brought a puissant power;
Even now we heard the news: ah, couldst thou fly!

WAR. Why, then I would not fly.—Ah, Montague,
If thou be there, sweet brother, take my hand,
And with thy lips keep in my soul awhile!
Thou lov'st me not; for, brother, if thou didst,
Thy tears would wash this cold congealed blood,
That glues my lips, and will not let me speak.
Come quickly, Montague, or I am dead.

SOM. Ah, Warwick! Montague hath breath'd his last;
And to the latest gasp, cried out for Warwick,
And said—*Commend me to my valiant brother.*
And more he would have said; and more he spoke,
Which sounded like a cannon in a vault,
That mought[c] not be distinguish'd; but, at last,
I well might hear, deliver'd with a groan,—
O, farewell, Warwick!

WAR. Sweet rest his soul!—Fly, lords, and save yourselves;

(*) Old text, *Iephah.*

[a] Passing—] *Surpassing, exceeding, egregious, wondrous.* See note (c), p. 644, Vol. I.

[b] *Warwick was a* bug, *that* fear'd *us all.*—] Meaning, Warwick was a *bugbear*, a *goblin*, a *bogie* that *appalled* us all. So in "The Taming of the Shrew," Act I. Sc. 2,—"Tush! tush! *fear* boys with *bugs.*"

[c] *That* mought *not be distinguish'd;*] This ancient use of the preterite tense of *might*, has been overlooked by all the editors.

For Warwick bids you all farewell, to meet in heaven. [*Dies.*

OXF. Away, away, to meet the queen's great power!

[*Exeunt, bearing off* WARWICK'S *body.*

SCENE III.—*Another part of the Field.*

Flourish. Enter KING EDWARD *in triumph; with* CLARENCE, GLOUCESTER, *and the rest.*

K. EDW. Thus far our fortune keeps an upward course,
And we are grac'd with wreaths of victory.
But in the midst of this bright-shining day,
I spy a black, suspicious, threat'ning cloud,
That will encounter with our glorious sun,
Ere he attain his easeful western bed:
I mean, my lords,—those powers, that the queen
Hath rais'd in Gallia, have arriv'd our coast,
And, as we hear, march on to fight with us.

CLAR. A little gale will soon disperse that cloud,
And blow it to the source from whence it came:
Thy very beams will dry those vapours up,
For every cloud engenders not a storm.

GLO. The queen is valu'd thirty thousand strong,
And Somerset, with Oxford, fled to her:
If she have time to breathe, be well assur'd,
Her faction will be full as strong as ours.

K. EDW. We are advértis'd by our loving friends,
That they do hold their course toward Tewksbury:
We, having now the best at Barnet field,
Will thither straight, for willingness rids way;
And, as we march, our strength will be augmented
In every county as we go along.—
Strike up the drum! cry—Courage! and away.

[*Exeunt.*

SCENE IV.—*Plains near* Tewksbury.

March. Enter QUEEN MARGARET, PRINCE EDWARD, SOMERSET, OXFORD, *and* Soldiers.

Q. MAR. Great lords, wise men ne'er sit and wail their loss,
But cheerly seek how to redress their harms.
What though the mast be now blown over-board,
The cable broke, the holding anchor lost,
And half our sailors swallow'd in the flood?
Yet lives our pilot still: is't meet that he
Should leave the helm, and, like a fearful lad,
With tearful eyes add water to the sea,
And give more strength to that which hath too much;
Whiles, in his moan, the ship splits on the rock,
Which industry and courage might have sav'd?
Ah, what a shame! ah, what a fault were this!
Say, Warwick was our anchor; what of that?
And Montague our top-mast; what of him?
Our slaughter'd friends the tackles; what of these?
Why, is not Oxford here another anchor?
And Somerset another goodly mast?
The friends of France our shrouds and tacklings?
And, though unskilful, why not Ned and I
For once allow'd the skilful pilot's charge?
We will not from the helm to sit and weep;
But keep our course, though the rough wind say no,
From shelves and rocks that threaten us with wreck.
As good to chide the waves, as speak them fair.
And what is Edward but a ruthless sea?
What Clarence but a quicksand of deceit?
And Richard but a ragged fatal rock?
All these the enemies to our poor bark.
Say, you can swim; alas, 'tis but awhile:
Tread on the sand; why, there you quickly sink:
Bestride the rock; the tide will wash you off,
Or else you famish,—that's a threefold death.
This speak I, lords, to let you understand,
If case some one of you would fly from us,
That there's no hop'd-for mercy with the brothers,
More than with ruthless waves, with sands, and rocks.
Why, courage, then! what cannot be avoided,
'T were childish weakness to lament, or fear.

PRINCE. Methinks, a woman of this valiant spirit
Should, if a coward heard her speak these words,
Infuse his breast with magnanimity,
And make him, naked, foil a man at arms.
I speak not this, as doubting any here,
For did I but suspect a fearful man,
He should have leave to go away betimes,
Lest, in our need, he might infect another,
And make him of like spirit to himself.
If any such be here,—as God forbid!—
Let him depart before we need his help.

OXF. Women and children of so high a courage,
And warriors faint! why, 'twere perpetual shame.—
O, brave young prince! thy famous grandfather
Doth live again in thee: long may'st thou live,
To bear his image, and renew his glories!

SOM. And he that will not fight for such a hope,
Go home to bed, and, like the owl by day,
If he arise, be mock'd and wonder'd at.

Q. MAR. Thanks, gentle Somerset;—sweet Oxford, thanks.

PRINCE. And take his thanks, that yet hath nothing else.

Enter a Messenger.

MESS. Prepare you, lords, for Edward is at hand,
Ready to fight; therefore be resolute.
OXF. I thought no less: it is his policy,
To haste thus fast, to find us unprovided.
SOM. But he's deceiv'd; we are in readiness.
Q. MAR. This cheers my heart, to see your forwardness.
OXF. Here pitch our battle, hence we will not [budge.

Flourish and march. Enter, at a distance, KING EDWARD, CLARENCE, GLOUCESTER, *and* Forces.

K. EDW. Brave followers, yonder stands the thorny wood,
Which, by the heavens' assistance, and your strength,
Must by the roots be hewn up yet ere night.
I need not add more fuel to your fire,
For, well I wot, ye blaze to burn them out:
Give signal to the fight, and to it, lords!
Q. MAR. Lords, knights, and gentlemen, what I should say,
My tears gainsay; for every word I speak,
Ye see, I drink the water of mine eyes.[a]
Therefore, no more but this:—Henry, your sovereign,
Is prisoner to the foe; his state usurp'd,
His realm a slaughter-house, his subjects slain,
His statutes cancell'd, and his treasure spent;
And yonder is the wolf, that makes this spoil.
You fight in justice: then, in God's name, lords,
Be valiant, and give signal to the fight.
[*Exeunt both Armies.*

SCENE V.—*Another part of the same.*

Alarums; Excursions; and afterwards a retreat. Then enter KING EDWARD, CLARENCE, GLOUCESTER, *and* Forces; *with* QUEEN MARGARET, OXFORD, *and* SOMERSET, *Prisoners.*

K. EDW. Now, here a period of tumultuous broils.
Away with Oxford to Hammes' castle straight:
For Somerset, off with his guilty head.
Go, bear them hence; I will not hear them speak.
OXF. For my part, I'll not trouble thee with words.

[a] Mine eyes.] So "The True Tragedy;" the folio 1623 reads, "my eye."

SOM. Nor I, but stoop with patience to my fortune.
[*Exeunt* OXFORD *and* SOMERSET, *guarded.*
Q. MAR. So part we sadly in this troublous world,
To meet with joy in sweet Jerusalem.
K. EDW. Is proclamation made, that who finds Edward,
Shall have a high reward, and he his life?
GLO. It is; and, lo, where youthful Edward comes!

Enter Soldiers, *with* PRINCE EDWARD.

K. EDW. Bring forth the gallant, let us hear him speak.
What! can so young a thorn begin to prick?—
Edward, what satisfaction canst thou make,
For bearing arms, for stirring up my subjects,
And all the trouble thou hast turn'd me to?
PRINCE. Speak like a subject, proud ambitious York!
Suppose that I am now my father's mouth;
Resign thy chair, and where I stand kneel thou,
Whilst I propose the self-same words to thee,
Which, traitor, thou wouldst have me answer to.
Q. MAR. Ah, that thy father had been so resolv'd!
GLO. That you might still have worn the petticoat,
And ne'er have stol'n the breech from Lancaster.
PRINCE. Let Æsop fable in a winter's night;
His currish riddles sort not with this place.
GLO. By heaven, brat, I'll plague ye for that word.
Q. MAR. Ay, thou wast born to be a plague to men.
GLO. For God's sake, take away this captive scold.
PRINCE. Nay, take away this scolding crookback rather.
K. EDW. Peace, wilful boy, or I will charm your tongue.
CLAR. Untutor'd lad, thou art too malapert.
PRINCE. I know my duty; you are all undutiful:
Lascivious Edward,—and thou perjur'd George,—
And thou misshapen Dick,—I tell ye all,
I am your better, traitors as ye are;—
And thou usurp'st my father's right and mine.
K. EDW. Take that, the likeness of this railer here. [*Stabs him.*
GLO. Sprawl'st thou? take that, to end thy agony. [*Stabs him.*
CLAR. And there's for twitting me with perjury.
[*Stabs him.*
Q. MAR. O, kill me too!
GLO. Marry, and shall. [*Offers to kill her.*

K. EDW. Hold, Richard, hold! for we have done too much.

GLO. Why should she live, to fill the world with [words?

K. EDW. What! doth she swoon? use means for her recovery.

GLO. Clarence, excuse me to the king my brother;
I'll hence to London on a serious matter:
Ere ye come there, be sure to hear some news.

CLAR. What? what?

GLO. The* Tower, the Tower! [*Exit.*

Q. MAR. O, Ned, sweet Ned! speak to thy mother, boy!
Canst thou not speak?—O traitors! murderers!—
They that stabb'd Cæsar shed no blood at all,
Did not offend, nor were not worthy blame,
If this foul deed were by to equal it.
He was a man; this, in respect, a child;
And men ne'er spend their fury on a child.
What's worse than murderer, that I may name it?
No, no; my heart will burst, an if I speak:—
And I will speak, that so my heart may burst.—
Butchers and villains! bloody cannibals!
How sweet a plant have you untimely cropp'd!
You have no children, butchers! if you had,
The thought of them would have stirr'd up remorse:
But if you ever chance to have a child,
Look in his youth to have him so cut off,
As, deathsmen, you have rid[a] this sweet young prince!

K. EDW. Away with her! go, bear her hence perforce.

Q. MAR. Nay, never bear me hence, despatch me here;
Here sheathe thy sword, I'll pardon thee my death:
What! wilt thou not?—then, Clarence, do it thou.

CLAR. By heaven, I will not do thee so much ease.

Q. MAR. Good Clarence, do; sweet Clarence, do thou do it.

CLAR. Didst thou not hear me swear I would not do it?

Q. MAR. Ay, but thou usest to forswear thyself:
'Twas sin before, but now 'tis charity.
What! wilt thou not? where is that devil's butcher,[b]
Hard-favour'd Richard? Richard, where art thou?
Thou art not here: Murder is thy alms-deed;
Petitioners for blood thou ne'er putt'st back.

K. EDW. Away, I say! I charge ye, bear her hence.

Q. MAR. So come to you, and yours, as to this prince! [*Exit, led out.*

K. EDW. Where's Richard gone?

CLAR. To London, all in post; and, as I guess,
To make a bloody supper in the Tower.

K. EDW. He's sudden, if a thing comes in his head.
Now march we hence: discharge the common sort
With pay and thanks, and let's away to London,
And see our gentle queen how well she fares;
By this, I hope, she hath a son for me. [*Exeunt.*

SCENE VI.—London. *A Room in the* Tower.

KING HENRY *is discovered sitting with a book in his hand, the* Lieutenant *attending. Enter* GLOUCESTER.

GLO. Good day, my lord. What, at your book so hard?

K. HEN. Ay, my good lord: my lord, I should say rather;
'Tis sin to flatter, *good* was little better:
Good Gloster, and good devil, were alike,
And both preposterous; therefore, not good lord.

GLO. Sirrah, leave us to ourselves: we must confer. [*Exit* Lieutenant.

K. HEN. So flies the reckless shepherd from the wolf:
So first the harmless sheep doth yield his fleece,
And next his throat unto the butcher's knife.—
What scene of death hath Roscius now to act?

GLO. Suspicion always haunts the guilty mind;
The thief doth fear each bush an officer.

K. HEN. The bird, that hath been limed in a bush,
With trembling wings misdoubteth every bush:
And I, the hapless male to one sweet bird,
Have now the fatal object in my eye,
Where my poor young was lim'd, was caught, and kill'd.

GLO. Why, what a peevish fool was that of Crete,
That taught his son the office of a fowl!
And yet, for all his wings, the fool was drown'd.

K. HEN. I, Dædalus; my poor boy, Icarus;
Thy father, Minos, that denied our course;
The sun, that sear'd the wings of my sweet boy,
Thy brother Edward; and thyself, the sea,
Whose envious gulf did swallow up his life.

(*) First folio omits, *The.*

[a] Rid *this sweet young prince!*] One sense of *rid* was to *destroy;* so in Scene 3 of the present Act,

"—for willingness *rids* way."

And in "The Tempest," Act I. Sc. 2:—

"—The red plague *rid* you."

[b] That devil's butcher,—] In the folio 1623, the line is encumbered by the addition of "Richard;" but as it is not found in the corresponding line of the earlier version, it was probably only an inadvertent repetition.

Ah, kill me with thy weapon, not with words!
My breast can better brook thy dagger's point,
Than can my ears that tragic history.—
But wherefore dost thou come? is't for my life?
GLO. Think'st thou I am an executioner?
K. HEN. A persecutor, I am sure, thou art;
If murdering innocents be executing,
Why, then thou art an executioner.
GLO. Thy son I kill'd for his presumption.
K. HEN. Hadst thou been kill'd when first thou didst presume,
Thou hadst not liv'd to kill a son of mine.
And thus I prophesy,—that many a thousand,
Which now mistrust no parcel of my fear,
And many an old man's sigh, and many a widow's,
And many an orphan's water-standing eye,—
Men for their sons', wives for their husbands',
And[a] orphans for their parents' timeless death,—

[a] And *orphans*, &c.] *And* is found only in the second folio, which amends the preceding line also, by reading, "—for their husbands' *fate*."

Shall rue the hour that ever thou wast born.
The owl shriek'd at thy birth, an evil sign;
The night-crow cried, aboding[a] luckless time;
Dogs howl'd, and hideous tempest shook down trees;
The raven rook'd[b] her on the chimney's top,
And chattering pies in dismal discords sung.
Thy mother felt more than a mother's pain,
And yet brought forth less than a mother's hope;
To wit, an indigest deformed lump,[c]
Not like the fruit of such a goodly tree.
Teeth hadst thou in thy head when thou wast born,
To signify, thou cam'st to bite the world:
And, if the rest be true which I have heard,
Thou cam'st—

GLO. I'll hear no more;—die, prophet, in thy speech! [*Stabs him.*
For this, amongst the rest, was I ordain'd.

K. HEN. Ay, and for much more slaughter after this.
O, God forgive my sins, and pardon thee! (1) [*Dies.*

GLO. What, will the aspiring blood of Lancaster
Sink in the ground? I thought it would have mounted.
See how my sword weeps for the poor king's death!
O, may such purple tears be alway shed
From those that wish the downfall of our house!—
If any spark of life be yet remaining,
Down, down to hell; and say I sent thee thither,
[*Stabs him again.*
I, that have neither pity, love, nor fear.—
Indeed, 'tis true that Henry told me of;
For I have often heard my mother say
I came into the world with my legs forward:
Had I not reason, think ye, to make haste,
And seek their ruin that usurp'd our right?
The midwife wonder'd and the women cried,
O, Jesus bless us, he is born with teeth!
And so I was; which plainly signified
That I should snarl, and bite, and play the dog.
Then, since the heavens have shap'd my body so,
Let hell make crook'd my mind to answer it.
I have no brother, I am like no brother:
And this word *love*, which greybeards call divine,
Be resident in men like one another,
And not in me; I am myself alone.—
Clarence, beware; thou keep'st me from the light;
But I will sort a pitchy day for thee:
For I will buz abroad such prophecies,
That Edward shall be fearful of his life;
And then, to purge his fear, I'll be thy death.
King Henry, and the prince his son, are gone:
Clarence, thy turn is next; and then the rest;
Counting myself but bad, till I be best.—
I'll throw thy body in another room,
And triumph, Henry, in thy day of doom.
[*Exit, bearing the body.*

SCENE VII.—*The same. A Room in the Palace. Flourish.* KING EDWARD *discovered sitting on his throne;* QUEEN ELIZABETH *with the infant* PRINCE *carried by a* Nurse, CLARENCE, GLOUCESTER, HASTINGS, *and others, near him.*

K. EDW. Once more we sit in England's royal throne,
Re-purchas'd with the blood of enemies.
What valiant foemen, like to autumn's corn,
Have we mow'd down in tops of all their pride!
Three dukes of Somerset, threefold renown'd *
For hardy and undoubted champions:
Two Cliffords, as the father and the son,
And two Northumberlands; two braver men
Ne'er spurr'd their coursers at the trumpet's sound:
With them, the two brave bears, Warwick and Montague,
That in their chains fetter'd the kingly lion,
And made the forest tremble when they roar'd.
Thus have we swept suspicion from our seat,
And made our footstool of security.—
Come hither, Bess, and let me kiss my boy:—
Young Ned, for thee, thine uncles and myself
Have in our armours watch'd the winter's night;
Went all afoot in summer's scalding heat,
That thou mightst repossess the crown in peace;
And of our labours thou shalt reap the gain.

GLO. I'll blast his harvest, if your head were laid;
For yet I am not look'd on in the world.
This shoulder was ordain'd so thick, to heave;
And heave it shall some weight, or break my back:—
Work thou the way,—and that shalt execute.[d]
[*Aside.*

K. EDW. Clarence and Gloster, love my lovely queen;
And kiss † your princely nephew, brothers both.

CLAR. The duty, that I owe unto your majesty,
I seal upon the lips of this sweet babe.

K. EDW. Thanks, noble Clarence; worthy brother, thanks.[e]

---

[a] Aboding—] *Foreboding, portending.*
[b] *The raven* rook'd her—] To *ruck*, or to *rook*, means to *squat down*, or *lodge*, or *roost*.
[c] *To wit, an* indigest *deformed lump,*—] The folio 1623 reads, "—an *indigested and* deformed lumpe." "The True Tragedy," "—an *undigest created* lumpe." We adopt the slight change made by Malone, a change made also by Mr. Collier's annotator.
[d] Work thou the way,—and that shalt execute.] *Thou* refers to the speaker's *head; that*, to his arm or shoulder. Some copies of the folio 1623 read, "*add* that shalt," &c.
[e] In the folio 1623 this line, which there begins,—"*Thanke* Noble Clarence," &c., has the prefix *Cla.* In "The True Tragedy" it is given to the Queen.

(*) Old text, *Renowne.* (†) First folio, *'tis.*

GLO. And, that I love the tree from whence thou sprang'st,
Witness the loving kiss I give the fruit:—
To say the truth, so Judas kiss'd his master;
And cried—*all hail!* whenas he meant—all harm. [*Aside.*

K. EDW. Now am I seated as my soul delights,
Having my country's peace and brothers' loves.

CLAR. What will your grace have done with Margaret?
Reignier, her father, to the king of France
Hath pawn'd the Sicils and Jerusalem,
And hither have they sent it for her ransom.

K. EDW. Away with her, and waft her hence to France.—
And now what rests, but that we spend the time
With stately triumphs, mirthful comic shows,
Such as befit the pleasure of the court?—
Sound drums and trumpets!—farewell sour annoy!
For here, I hope, begins our lasting joy. [*Exeunt.*

ILLUSTRATIVE COMMENTS.

ACT I.

(1) Scene I.—

—— I here entail
The crown to thee, and to thine heirs for ever.]

This compromise is an historical fact; and, from the following account, extracted from a MS. in the British Museum (Harl. C. 7), appears to have been the result of long and frequent debates in parliament. "On halmesse evyn, abowt thre after noyne, comyn into the Comowne Howus, the Lordys spiritual and temporal, excepte the Kyng, the Duk of York, and hys sonys; And the Chawnceler reherset the debate had bytwyn owre soveren Lord the Kyng and the Duk of York upon the tytelys of Inglond, Fraunce, and the Lordschep of Erlond, wyche mater was debat, arguet, and disputet by the seyd lordes spiritual and temporal byfore owre soveren Lord and the Duk of York longe and diverse tymys. And at the last, by gret avyce and deliberacion, and by the assent of owre soveryn Lord and the Duk of York, and alle the lordes spiritual and temporal ther assemelyd by vertu of thys present parlement, assentyt, agreyt, and acordyt, that owre sovereyne Lord the Kyng schal pessabylly and quyetly rejoys and possesse the crowne of Inglond and of Fraunce, and the Lordchip of Irlond, with al hys preemynences, prerogatyves, and liberteys during hys lyf. And that after hys desese, the coroun, etc., schal remayne to Rychard Duk of York, as rythe inheryt to hym and to hys issue, prayng and desyring ther the comownes of Inglond, be vertu of thys present parlement assemylet, to comyne the seyd mater, and to gyff therto her assent. The whyche comyns, after the mater debatet, comynt, grawntyt, and assentyt to the forseyd premisses. And ferthermore was granted and assentyt, that the seyd Duk of York, the Erl of March, and of Rutlond, schul be sworne that they schuld not compas ne conspyrene the kynges deth ne hys hurt duryng hys lyf. Ferthermore the forseyd Duk schulde be had, take and reportyt as eyr apparent prince and ryth inheryter to the crowne aboveseyd. Ferthermore for to be had and take tresoun to ymagine or compas the deth or the hurt of the seyd Duk, wythe othyr prerogatyves as long to the prince and eyr parawnt. And ferthermore the seyd Duk and hys sonys schul have of the Kyng yerly ten thousand marces, that is to sey, to hemself five thousand, to the Erl of Marche three thousand, the Erl of Rutlond two thousand marces. And alle these mateyrs agreyd, assentyt, and inactyt by the auctoritie of thys present parlement. And ferthermore, the statutes mad in the tyme of Kyng Herry the fowrth, wherby the croune was curtaylet to hys issu male, utterly anullyd and evertyth, wyth alle other statutes and grantys mad by the seyd Kynges days, Kyng Herry the V. and King Herry the vj^te^, in the infforsyng of the tytel of Kyng Herry the fourth in general."

(2) Scene I.—*Stern Falconbridge.*] "The person here meant was Thomas Nevil, bastard son to the lord Fauconbridge. 'A man (says Hall) of no lesse corage then audacitie, who for his evel condicions was such an apte person, that a more meter could not be chosen to set all the worlde in a broyle, and to put the estate of the realme on an yl hazard.' He had been appointed by Warwick vice-admiral of the sea, and had in charge so to keep the passage between Dover and Calais, that none which either favoured King Henry or his friends should escape untaken or undrowned: such at least were his instructions, with respect to the friends and favourers of King Edward, after the rupture between him and Warwick. On Warwick's death, he fell into poverty, and robbed, both by sea and land, as well friends as enemies. He once brought his ships up the Thames, and with a considerable body of the men of Kent and Essex, made a spirited assault on the City, with a view to plunder and pillage, which was not repelled but after a sharp conflict, and the loss of many lives; and, had it happened at a more critical period, might have been attended with fatal consequences to Edward. After roving on the sea some little time longer, he ventured to land at Southampton, where he was taken and beheaded."—Ritson.

(3) Scene III.—*Thy father slew my father; therefore, die.*] "While this battaill was in fightyng, a prieste called sir Robert Aspall, chappelain and schole master to the yong erle of Rutland ii. sonne to the above named duke of Yorke, scarce of the age of .xii. yeres, a faire gentleman, and a maydenlike person, perceivyng that flight was more savegard, then tariyng, bothe for him and his master, secretly conveyed therle out of the felde, by the lord Cliffordes bande, toward the towne, but or he coulde enter into a house, he was by the sayd lord Clifford espied, folowed, and taken, and by reson of his apparell, demaunded what he was. The yong gentelman dismaied, had not a word to speake, but kneled on his knees imploryng mercy, and desiryng grace, both with holding up his handes and making dolorous countinance, for his speache was gone for feare. Save him sayde his Chappelein, for he is a princes sonne, and peradventure may do you good hereafter. With that word, the lord Clifford marked him and sayde: by Gods blode, thy father slew myne, and so wil I do the and all thy kyn, and with that woord, stacke the erle to the hart with his dagger, and bad his Chappeleyn bere the erles mother and brother worde what he had done, and sayde. In this acte the lord Clyfford was accompted a tyraunt, and no gentelman, for the propertie of the Lyon, which is a furious and an unreasonable beaste, is to be cruell to them that withstande hym, and gentle to such as prostrate or humiliate them selfes before him."—Hall.

ACT II.

(1) SCENE I.—

Nay, if thou be that princely eagle's bird,
Show thy descent by gazing 'gainst the sun.]

The opinion that the eagle, of all birds, possessed the faculty of gazing undazzled at the blazing sun, is of very high antiquity. Pliny relates that it exposes its brood to this test as soon as hatched, to prove if they be genuine or not. Chaucer refers to the belief in the "Assemblie of Foules:"—

"There mighten men the royal egal find,
That with his sharp look persith the sonne."

As does Spenser, in the "Hymn of Heavenly Beauty:"—

"Mount up aloft, through heavenly contemplation,
From this dark world, whose damps the soul do blind.
And like the native brood of eagles kind,
On that bright sun of glory fix thyne eyes,
Clear'd from gross mists of frail infirmitys."

(2) SCENE II.—

And happy always was it for that son,
Whose father for his hoarding went to hell?]

An allusion to a trite proverb: "Happy is the child whose father went to the devil." "It hath beene an olde proverbe, that happy is that sonne whose father goes to the devill: meaning by thys allegoricall kind of speech, that such fathers as seeke to inrich theyr sonnes by covetousnes, by briberie, purloyning, or by any other sinister meanes, suffer not onely affliction of mind, as greeved with insatietie of getting, but wyth danger of soule, as a just reward for such wretchednesse."—GREENE'S *Royal Exchange,* 4to. Lond. 1590.

(3) SCENE II.—

I would your highness would depart the field;
The queen hath best success when you are absent.]

"Happy was the Quene in her two battayls, but unfortunate was the King in al his enterprises, for wher his person was presente, ther victory fled ever from him to the other parte, and he commonly was subdued and vanqueshed."—HALL.

Drayton, in "The Miseries of Queen Margaret," calls attention to this general belief in the luckless fortunes of the King:—

"Some think that Warwick had not lost the day,
But that the King into the field he brought;
For with the worse that side went still away
Which had King Henry with them when they fought.
Upon his birth so sad a curse there lay,
As that he never prospered in aught.
The queen won two, among the loss of many,
Her husband absent; present, never any."

(4) SCENE III.—*A Field of Battle* between Towton and Saxton, in Yorkshire.] The following is Hall's narrative of the memorable battle of Towton; "a battle," Carte observes, which "decided the fate of the house of Lancaster, overturning in one day an usurpation strengthened by near sixty-two years' continuance, and established Edward on the throne of England." "The same day, about .ix. of the clocke, whiche was the .xxix. day of Marche, beyng Palmsundaye, bothe the hostes approched in a playn felde, between Towton and Saxton. When eche parte perceyved other, thei made a great shoute, and at the same instante time, their fell a small snyt or snow, which by violence of the wynd was driven into the faces of them, which were of kyng Henries parte, so that their sight was somewhat blemeshed and minished. The lord Fawnconbridge, which led the forward of kyng Edwardes battail (as before is rehersed) being a man of great polecie, and of much experience in marciall feates, caused every archer under his standard, to shot one flyght (which before he caused them to provide) and then made them to stand still. The Northrenmen, feling the shoot, but by reason of the snow, not wel vewyng the distaunce betwene them and their enemies, like hardy men shot their schiefe arrowes as fast as thei might, but al their shot was lost, and their labor vayn for they came not nere the Southermen by .xl. taylors yerdes. When their shot was almost spent, the lord Fawconbridge marched forwarde with his archers, which not onely shot their awne whole sheves, but also gathered the arrowes of their enemies, and let a great parte of them flye agaynst their awne masters, and another part thei let stand on the ground, which sore noyed the legges of the owners, when the battayle joyned. The erle of Northumberland, and Andrew Trolope, which were chefetayns of Kyng Henries vangard, seynge their shot not to prevayle, hasted forward to joine with their enemies you may besure the other part nothing retarded, but valeauntly foughte with their enemies. This battayl was sore foughten, for hope of life was set on side on every parte and takynge of prisoners was proclaymed as a great offence, by reason wherof every man determined, either to conquere or to dye in the felde. This deadly battayle and bloudy conflicte, continued .x. houres in doubtfull victorie. The one parte some time flowyng, and some time ebbyng, but in conclusion, kyng Edward so coragiously comforted his men, refreshyng the wery, and helping the wounded, that the other part was discomfited and overcome, and lyke men amased, fledde toward Tadcaster bridge to save them selfes: but in the meane way there is a litle broke called Cocke not very broade, but of a great deapnes, in the whiche, what for hast of escapyng, and what for feare of folowers, a great number were drent and drowned, in so much that the common people there affirme, that men alyve passed the ryver upon dead carcasis, and that the great ryver of Wharfe, which is the great sewer of that broke, and of all the water comyng from Towton, was colored with bloude."

(5) SCENE VI.—*For Gloster's dukedom is too ominous.*] So Hall:—"It seemeth to many men that the name and title of Gloucester hath bene unfortunate and unluckie to diverse, whiche for their honor have bene erected by creation of princes to that stile and dignitie; as Hugh Spencer, Thomas of Woodstocke, son to Kynge Edward the thirde, and this duke Humphrey; whiche three persons by miserable death finished their daies; and after them King Richard the iii. also duke of Gloucester, in civil warre was slaine and confounded; so that this name of Gloucester is taken for an unhappie and unfortunate stile, as the proverbe speaketh of Sejanes horse, whose ryder was ever unhorsed, and whose possessor was ever brought to miserie."

ACT III.

(1) SCENE I.—*From Scotland am I stol'n, even of pure love, &c.*] "And on that parte that marched upon Scotlande, he laied watches and espialles, that no persone should go out of the realme to kyng Henry and his company, which then laye soiornyng in Scotlande; but whatsoever ieoperdy or peryll might bee construed or demed to have insued by the meanes of kyng Henry, all suche doubtes were now shortly resolved and determined, and all feare of his doynges were clerely put under and extinct; for he hymselfe, whether he were past all feare, or was not well stablished in his perfite mynde, or could not long kepe hymselfe secrete, in a disguysed apparell boldely entered into Englande. He was no soner entered, but he was knowen and taken of one Cantlowe, and brought towarde the kyng, whom the erle of Warwicke met on the waie, by the kynges commaundement, and brought hym through London to the towre, and there he was laied in sure holde."—HALL.

(2) SCENE II.—

Because in quarrel of the house of York
The worthy gentleman did lose his life.]

This is an error. Sir John Grey fell at the second battle of St. Alban's, while fighting, not on the side of York, but Lancaster; a fact of which Shakespeare was subsequently aware, since, in "Richard III." Act I. Sc. 3, Richard, addressing Queen Elizabeth, remarks,—

"In all which time, you, and your husband Grey,
Were factious *for the house of Lancaster*;—
And, Rivers, so were you:—was not your husband
In *Margaret's battle* at Saint Alban's slain?"

It may not be out of place to introduce here a portion of Hall's description of King Edward's first interview with the lady Grey, upon which the present scene was founded:—

"The king being on huntyng in the forest of Wychwod besyde Stonnystratforde, came for his recreacion to the mannor of Grafton, where the duches of Bedford sojorned, then wyfe to sir Richard Wodvile, lord Ryvers, on whom then was attendyng a doughter of hers, called dame Elizabeth Greye, wydow of sir Ihon Grey knight, slayn at the last battell of saincte Albons, by the power of kyng Edward. This wydow havyng a suyt to the king, either to be restored by hym to some thyng taken from her, or requyring hym of pitie, to have some augmentacion to her livyng, founde such grace in the kynges eyes, that he not onely favored her suyte, but much more phantasied her person, for she was a woman more of formal countenaunce, then of excellent beautie, but yet of such beautie and favor, that with her sober demeanure, lovely lokyng, and femynyne smylyng, (neither to wanton nor to humble) besyde her toungue so eloquent, and her wit so pregnant, she was able to ravishe the mynde of a meane person, when she allured, and made subject to her, the hart of so great a king. After that kyng Edward had well considered all the linyamentes of her body, and the wise and womanly demeanure that he saw in her, he determined first to attempt, if he might provoke her to be his sovereigne lady, promisyng her many giftes and fayre rewardes, affirmynge farther, that if she woulde therunto condiscend, she myght so fortune of his peramour and concubyne, to be chaunged to his wyfe and lawfull bedfelow: whiche demaunde she so wisely and with so covert speache aunswered and repugned, affirmynge that as she was for his honor farre unable to be hys spouse and bedfelow: So for her awne poore honestie, she was to good to be either hys concubyne, or sovereigne lady: that where he was a littell before heated with the dart of Cupid, he was nowe set all on a hote burnyng fyre, what for the confidence that he had in her perfyte constancy, and the trust that he had in her constant chastitie, and without any farther deliberacion, he determined with him selfe clerely to marye with her, after that askyng counsaill of them, whiche he knewe neither woulde nor once durst impugne his concluded purpose. But the duches of Yorke hys mother letted it as much as in her lay alledgyng a precontract made by hym with the lady Lucye, and divers other lettes: al which doubtes were resolved, and all thinges made clere and all cavillacions avoyded. And so, privilie in a mornyng he maried her at Grafton, where he first phantasied her visage."

(3) SCENE III.—

I came from Edward as ambassador,
But I return his sworn and mortal foe.]

Shakespeare s relation of Warwick's embassy and commission, and the rupture between king Edward and him in consequence of the former's marriage with lady Grey, are strictly accordant with the statements of Hall and Holinshed; but, as Ritson observes, "later as well as earlyer writers, of better authority, incline us to discredit the whole; and to refer the rupture between the king and his political creator to causes which have not reached posterity, or to that jealousy and ingratitude so natural, perhaps, to those who are under great obligations, too great to be discharged. '*Beneficia* (says Tacitus) *eò usque læta sunt, dum videntur exsolvi posse: ubi multum antevenere, pro gratiâ odium redditur.*'"

Hall's narration of the circumstances, which appears to have been that adopted by the poet, is as follows:—

"The same yere he [Warwick] cam to kyng Lewes the .xi. then beyng Frenche kyng, liying at Tours, and with greate honor was there received, and honorably interteined: of whom, for kyng Edward his master, he demaunded to have in mariage the lady Bona, doughter to Lewes duke of Savoy, and suster to the lady Carlot, then French Quene, beyng then in the Frenche court. This mariage semeth pollitiquely devised, and of an high imaginacion to be invented, if you will well consider, the state and condicion of king Edwardes affaires, which at this time, had kyng Henry the vi. in safe custody, in the strong toure of London, and the moste parte of his adherentes, he had as he thought, either profligated or extinct, Quene Margaret onely except, and Prince Edward her sonne, which wer then sojornyng at Angiers, with old Duke Reiner of Anjow her father, writyng hymself kyng of Naples, Scicile, and Jerusalem, having as much profites of the letters of his glorious stile, as rentes and revenues out of the said large and riche realmes and dominions, (because the kyng of Arragon toke the profites of the same, and would make no accompt therof to duke Reiner). Kyng Edward therfore thought it necessary, to have affinitie in Fraunce, and especially by the Quenes suster: which Quene although she ruled not the kyng her husband, (as many women do) yet he of a certain especiall humilitie, was more content to have her favor and folowe her desire, (for wedded men oftentymes doubt stormes) rather then to have a lowryng countenaunce, and a ringing peale, when he should go to his rest and quietnes: trusting that by this mariage, quene Margarete (whom the same Quene Carlot litle or nothyng regarded, although her father was called a kyng and she a quene, and none of both having subjectes, profites, nor dominions) should have no aide, succor, nor any comfort of the French king, nor of none of his frendes nor alies, wherfore quene Carlot much desirous to advance her blod and progenie, and especially to so great a prince as kyng Edward was, obteyned both the good will of the kyng her husband, and also of her syster, so that the matrimony on that syde was clerely assented to. * * * * * * * * * * *

But when the erle of Warwycke had perfit knowledge by the letters of his trusty frendes, that kyng Edward had gotten him a new wyfe, and that all that he had done with kyng Lewes in his ambassade for the conjoynyng of this new affinitie, was both frustrate and vayn, he was earnestly moved and sore chafed with the chaunce, and thought it necessarye that king Edward should be deposed from his croune and royal dignitie, as an inconstant prince, not worthy of such a kyngly office. All men for the most parte agre, that this mariage was the only cause, why the erle of Warwycke bare grudge, and made warre on kynge Edwarde. Other affirme that ther wer other causes, which added to this, made the fyre to flame, which before was but a litell smoke."

ACT IV.

(1) Scene VI.—*My liege, it is young Henry, earl of Richmond.*] "Henry, Earl of Richmond, was the son of Edmond and Margaret, daughter to John the first 'Duke of Somerset.' Edmond, Earl of Richmond, was half-brother to King Henry the Sixth, being the son of that king's mother, Queen Catharine, by her second husband, Owen Teuther, or Tudor, who was taken prisoner at the battle of Mortimer's Cross, and soon afterwards beheaded at Hereford.

"Henry the Seventh, to show his gratitude to Henry the Sixth for this early presage in his favour, solicited Pope Julius to canonize him as a saint; but, either Henry would not pay the money demanded, or, as Bacon supposes, the Pope refused, lest, 'as Henry was reputed in the world abroad but for a simple man, the estimation of that kind of honour might be diminished, if there were not a distance kept between *innocents* and saints.'"—Malone.

(2) Scene VIII.—

I have not been desirous of their wealth,
Nor much oppress'd them with great subsidies.]

In speaking of the impost called a *fifteen*, or *fifteenth* (see note (a), p. 380), we described it as a tax of the fifteenth part of all the personal property of each subject; but we should have added that, subsequently to the 8th of Edward III., when a taxation was made upon all the cities, towns, boroughs, &c., by compositions, the fifteenth became a sum certain, namely, the fifteenth part of their then existing value. The distinction between the taxes called fifteenths and tenths (*quindismes* and *dismes*), and the subsidy, in later times, Camden expresses thus:—"A fifteen and a tenth (that I may note it for forrainers' sakes) is a certain taxation upon every city, borough, and town; not every particular man, but in general in respect of the fifteenth part of the wealth of the place. A *subsidy* we call that which is imposed upon every man, being cessed by the powle, man by man, according to the valuation of their goods and lands."

ACT V.

(1) Scene VI.—*O, God forgive my sins, and pardon thee!*] The circumstances attending the death of Henry VI. are involved in deep obscurity. The balance of testimony supports the popular tradition that he was murdered on the night of Edward's entry into London, 21st May, 1471:—"And the same nyghte that Kynge Edwarde came to Londone, Kynge Herry, beynge inwarde in presone in the Toure of Londone, was putt to dethe, the xxj. day of Maij, on a tywesday nyght, betwyx xj. and xij. of the cloke, beynge thenne at the Toure the Duke of Gloucetre, brothere to Kynge Edwarde, and many other; and one the morwe he was chestyde and brought to Paulys, and his face was opyne that every manne myghte see hyme; and in hys lyinge he bledde one the pament ther; and afterward at the Blake Fryres was broughte, and ther he blede new and fresche; and from thens he was caryed to Chyrchsey abbey in a bote, and buryed there in oure Lady chapelle."

Dr. Warkworth, whose chronicle furnishes the above extract, was a contemporary writer, Master of St. Peter's College, Cambridge, from 1473 to 1498, and a man of learning and ability. Fabyan, a citizen of London in the time of Henry the Seventh, is more explicit:—"Of the death of this Prynce dyverse tales were tolde: but the most common fame wente, that he was stykked with a dagger by the handes of the Duke of Gloucester."

On the other hand, the Yorkist party contended that the deposed monarch died of grief and melancholy:—"In every party of England, where any commotion was begonne for Kynge Henry's party, anone they were rebuked, so that it appered to every mann at eye the sayde partie was extincte and repressed for evar, without any mannar hope of agayne quikkening: utterly despaired of any maner of hoope or releve. The certaintie of all whiche came to the knowledge of the sayd Henry, late called Kyng, being in the Tower of London; not havynge, afore that, knowledge of the saide matars, he toke it to so great dispite, ire, and indingnation, that, of pure displeasure, and melencoly, he dyed the xxiij day of the monithe of May. Whom the kynge dyd to be browght to the friers prechars at London, and there, his funerall service donne, to be caried, by watar, to an Abbey upon Thamys syd, xvj myles from London, called Chartsey, and there honorably enteryd."—*Arrivall of Edward IV.*

CRITICAL OPINIONS

ON THE

THREE PARTS OF KING HENRY VI.

"SHAKSPEARE'S choice fell first on this period of English history, so full of misery and horrors of every kind, because the pathetic is naturally more suitable than the characteristic to a young poet's mind. We do not yet find here the whole maturity of his genius, yet certainly its whole strength. Careless as to the apparent unconnectedness of contemporary events, he bestows little attention on preparation and development: all the figures follow in rapid succession, and announce themselves emphatically for what we ought to take them; from scenes where the effect is sufficiently agitating to form the catastrophe of a less extensive plan, the poet perpetually hurries us on to catastrophes still more dreadful.

"The *First Part* contains only the first forming of the parties of the White and Red Rose, under which blooming ensigns such bloody deeds were afterwards perpetrated; the varying results of the war in France principally fill the stage. The wonderful saviour of her country, Joan of Arc, is pourtrayed by Shakspeare with an Englishman's prejudices: yet he at first leaves it doubtful whether she has not in reality a heavenly mission; she appears in the pure glory of virgin heroism; by her supernatural eloquence (and this circumstance is of the poet's invention) she wins over the Duke of Burgundy to the French cause; afterwards, corrupted by vanity and luxury, she has recourse to hellish fiends, and comes to a miserable end. To her is opposed Talbot, a rough iron warrior, who moves us the more powerfully, as, in the moment when he is threatened with inevitable death, all his care is tenderly directed to save his son, who performs his first deeds of arms under his eye. After Talbot has in vain sacrificed himself, and the Maid of Orleans has fallen into the hands of the English, the French provinces are completely lost by an impolitic marriage; and with this the piece ends. The conversation between the aged Mortimer in prison, and Richard Plantagenet, afterwards Duke of York, contains an exposition of the claims of the latter to the throne: considered by itself, it is a beautiful tragic elegy.

"In the *Second Part*, the events more particularly prominent are the murder of the honest Protector, Gloucester, and its consequences; the death of Cardinal Beaufort; the parting of the Queen from her favourite Suffolk, and his death by the hands of savage pirates; then the insurrection of Jack Cade under an assumed name, and at the instigation of the Duke of York. The short scene where Cardinal Beaufort, who is tormented by his conscience on account of the murder of Gloucester, is visited on his death-bed by Henry VI., is sublime beyond all praise. Can any other poet be named who has drawn aside the curtain of eternity at the close of this life with such overpowering and awful effect? And yet it is not mere horror with which the mind is filled, but solemn emotion; a blessing and a curse stand side by side; the pious King is an image of the heavenly mercy which, even in the sinner's last moments, labours to enter into his soul. The adulterous passion of Queen Margaret and Suffolk is invested with tragical dignity, and all low and ignoble ideas carefully kept out of sight. Without attempting to gloss over the crime of which both are guilty, without seeking to remove our disapprobation of this criminal love, he still, by the magic force of expression, contrives to excite in us a sympathy with their sorrow. In the insurrection of Cade he has delineated the conduct of a popular demagogue, the fearful ludicrousness of the anarchical tumult of the people, with such convincing truth, that one would believe he was an eye-witness of many of the events of our age, which, from ignorance of history, have been considered as without example.

"The civil war only begins in the Second Part; in the *Third* it is unfolded in its full destructive fury. The picture becomes gloomier and gloomier; and seems at last to be painted rather with blood than with colours. With horror we behold fury giving birth to fury, vengeance to vengeance, and see that when all the bonds of human society are violently torn asunder, even noble matrons became hardened to cruelty. The most bitter contempt is the portion of the unfortunate; no one affords to his enemy that pity which he will himself shortly stand in need of. With all, party is family, country, and religion, the only spring of action. As York, whose ambition is coupled with noble qualities, prematurely perishes, the object of the whole contest is now either to support an imbecile king, or to place on the throne a luxurious monarch, who shortens the dear-bought possession by the gratification of an insatiable voluptuousness. For this the celebrated and magnanimous Warwick spends his chivalrous life; Clifford revenges the death of his father with blood-thirsty filial love; and Richard, for the elevation of his brother, practises those dark deeds by which he is soon after to pave the way to his own greatness. In the midst of the general misery, of which he has been the innocent cause, King Henry appears like the powerless image of a saint, in whose wonder-working influence no man any longer believes: he can but sigh and weep over the enormities which he witnesses. In his simplicity, however, the gift of prophecy is lent to this pious king: in the moment of his death, at the close of this great tragedy, he prophesies a still more dreadful tragedy with which futurity is pregnant, as much distinguished for the poisonous wiles of cold-blooded wickedness as the former for deeds of savage fury."—SCHLEGEL.

Act IV. Sc. 3

TIMON OF ATHENS.

"The Life of Tymon of Athens" appeared first in the folio of 1623. At what period it was written we have no evidence, though Malone assigns it to the year 1610. The story, originally derived from Lucian, was a popular one in Shakespeare's time, and must have been known to him from its forming the subject of a novel in Paynter's "Palace of Pleasure," and from the account of Timon given in North's translation of Plutarch. The immediate archetype of the play, however, was probably some old and now lost drama, remodelled and partially re-written by our author, but of which he permitted much of the rude material to remain, with scarcely any alteration.

It is upon this theory alone we find it possible to reconcile the discordance between the defective plan, and the faultless execution of particular parts,—between the poverty and negligence observable in some scenes, and the grandeur and consummate finish displayed in others. The basis of Shakespeare's "Timon" was long supposed to be an anonymous piece, the manuscript of which was in the possession of Mr. Strutt, and is now the property of Mr. Dyce. But this manuscript was printed, in 1842, for the Shakespeare Society; and although it is found to have one character, Laches, who is a coarse counterpart to the faithful steward, Flavius, and two or three incidents, particularly that of the mock banquet, where the misanthrope regales his parasites with stones, painted to look like artichokes, which correspond in some measure with transactions in the piece before us, there is not the slightest reason for believing Shakespeare ever saw it. These resemblances are no doubt merely owing to both plays being founded on a common origin; for the subject was evidently familiar to the stage long before we can suppose Shakespeare to have produced his version. In Guilpin's Collection of Epigrams and Satires, called "Skialetheia," 1598, we have in Epigram 52:—

"Like hate-man Timon in his cell he sits,"

which, as Mr. Collier says, apparently points to some scene wherein Timon had been represented; and he is again mentioned, in a way to show that his peculiarities were well understood, in the play of "Jack Drum's Entertainment," printed in 1601:—"*But if all the brewers' jades in the town can drag me from the love of myself, they shall do more than e'er the seven wise men of Greece could. Come, come; now I'll be as sociable as Timon of Athens.*"

Persons Represented.

TIMON, *a noble* Athenian.

LUCIUS, LUCULLUS, SEMPRONIUS,	*Lords, and flatterers of* Timon.

VENTIDIUS, *one of* Timon's *false Friends.*
ALCIBIADES, *an* Athenian *General.*
APEMANTUS, *a churlish Philosopher.*
FLAVIUS, *Steward to* Timon.
Poet, Painter, Jeweller, *and* Merchant.
An old Athenian.

FLAMINIUS, LUCILIUS, SERVILIUS,	*Servants to* Timon.
CAPHIS, PHILOTUS, TITUS, LUCIUS, HORTENSIUS, *And others,*	*Servants to* Timon's *Creditors.*

A Page, *a* Fool, *Three* Strangers.

PHRYNIA, TIMANDRA,	*Mistresses to* ALCIBIADES.

CUPID, *and* Amazons *in the Masque.*

Other Lords, Senators, Officers, Soldiers, Banditti, and Attendants.

SCENE,—ATHENS, *and the Woods adjoining.*

ACT I.

SCENE I.—Athens. *A Hall in* Timon's *House.*

Enter Poet *and* Painter.

POET. Good day, sir.
PAIN. I am glad you're well.
POET. I have not seen you long; how goes the world?
PAIN. It wears, sir, as it grows.
POET. Ay, that's well known:
But what particular rarity? what strange,
Which manifold record not matches?—See,

Enter Jeweller, Merchant, *and others, at several doors.*

Magic of bounty! all these spirits thy power
Hath conjur'd to attend. I know the merchant.
PAIN. I know them both; the other's a jeweller.
MER. O, 'tis a worthy lord!
JEW. Nay, that's most fix'd.
MER. A most incomparable man; breath'd, as it were,
To an untirable and continuate goodness,
He passes.[a]

---

a —— breath'd, as it were,
To an untirable and continuate goodness,
He passes.]

In the accepted reading of this passage, a colon is placed after "goodness," and the phrase "He passes," interpreted to mean, he *surpasses* or *exceeds*, is made a separate member of the sentence. From the expressions "breath'd" and "untirable," it may well be questioned, however, whether "He passes" should not be immediately connected with what goes before, and be understood in the same sense, of *runs*, which it bears in "Henry V." Act II. Sc. 1:—"*He passes* some humours and careers."

JEW. I have a jewel here—
MER. O, pray, let's see't: for the lord Timon, sir?
JEW. If he will touch the estimate: but, for that—
POET. [*Reciting aside.*] *When we for recompense have prais'd the vile,*
It stains the glory in that happy verse
Which aptly sings the good.
MER. 'Tis a good form.
[*Looking at the jewel.*
JEW. And rich: here is a water, look ye.
PAIN. You are rapt, sir, in some work, some dedication
To the great lord.
POET. A thing slipp'd idly from me.
Our poesy is as a gum, which oozes [a]
From whence 'tis nourished. The fire i' the flint
Shows not, till it be struck; our gentle flame
Provokes itself, and, like the current, flies
Each bound it chafes.* What have you there?
PAIN. A picture, sir.—When comes your book forth?
POET. Upon the heels of my presentment, sir.
Let's see your piece.
PAIN. 'Tis a good piece.
POET. So 'tis: this comes off well and excellent.
PAIN. Indifferent.
POET. Admirable! how this grace
Speaks his own standing! what a mental power
This eye shoots forth! how big imagination
Moves in this lip! to the dumbness of the gesture
One might interpret.
PAIN. It is a pretty mocking of the life.
Here is a touch; is't good?
POET. I'll say of it,
It tutors nature: artificial strife
Lives in these touches, livelier than life.

Enter certain Senators, *and pass over.*

PAIN. How this lord is follow'd!
POET. The senators of Athens:—happy men! [b]
PAIN. Look, more!†
POET. You see this confluence, this great flood of visitors.
I have, in this rough work, shap'd out a man,
Whom this beneath world doth embrace and hug
With amplest entertainment: my free drift
Halts not particularly, but moves itself
In a wide sea of wax: [c] no levelled malice
Infects one comma in the course I hold;
But flies an eagle flight, bold, and forth on,
Leaving no track behind.
PAIN. How shall I understand you?
POET. I'll unbolt to you.
You see how all conditions, how all minds,
(As well of glib and slippery creatures, as
Of grave and austere quality) tender down
Their services to lord Timon: his large fortune,
Upon his good and gracious nature hanging,
Subdues and properties [d] to his love and tendance
All sorts of hearts; yea, from the glass-fac'd flatterer
To Apemantus, that few things loves better
Than to abhor himself; even he drops down
The knee before him, and returns in peace,
Most rich in Timon's nod.
PAIN. I saw them speak together.
POET. Sir, I have upon a high and pleasant hill,
Feign'd Fortune to be thron'd: the base o' the mount
Is rank'd with all deserts, all kind of natures,
That labour on the bosom of this sphere
To propagate their states: amongst them all,
Whose eyes are on this sovereign lady fix'd,
One do I personate of lord Timon's frame,
Whom Fortune with her ivory hand wafts to her;
Whose present grace to present slaves and servants
Translates his rivals.
PAIN. 'Tis conceiv'd to scope.
This throne, this Fortune, and this hill, methinks,
With one man beckon'd from the rest below,
Bowing his head against the steepy mount
To climb his happiness, would be well express'd
In our condition. [e]
POET. Nay, sir, but hear me on:
All those which were his fellows but of late,
(Some better than his value,) on the moment
Follow his strides, his lobbies fill with tendance,
Rain sacrificial whisperings in his ear,
Make sacred even his stirrup, and through him
Drink the free air,—
PAIN. Ay, marry, what of these?
POET.—When Fortune, in her shift and change of mood,
Spurns down her late beloved, all his dependants,
Which labour'd after him to the mountain's top,
Even on their knees and hands,* let him slip [f] down,
Not one accompanying his declining foot.
PAIN. 'Tis common:
A thousand moral paintings I can show,
That shall demonstrate these quick blows of fortune's
More pregnantly than words. Yet you do well,

(*) Old text, *chases*. (†) Old text, *moe*.

(*) First folio, *hand*.

[a] *Our poesy is as a* gum, *which* oozes—] In the old text the latter portion of this line is ludicrously misprinted, "—as a *Gowne*, which *uses*," &c. Pope corrected *gowne* to "gum," and Johnson very happily changed *uses* to "oozes."

[b] *Happy* men!] Theobald reads "happy *man*," perhaps rightly.

[c] *In a wide sea of* wax:] The allusion is presumed to point to the Roman practice of writing on waxen tablets: a practice prevalent in England until about the end of the fourteenth century; but the word *wax* is more probably a misprint, though not certainly, for *verse*, which Mr. Collier's annotator substitutes for it.

[d] Properties—] *Appropriates*. See note (c), p. 268.

[e] *In our* condition.] *Condition* here means, *profession* or *art*.

[f] *Let him* slip *down*,—] The old text has, "let him *sit* downe;" the necessary alteration was made by Rowe.

To show lord Timon that mean eyes have seen
The foot above the head.

Trumpets sound. Enter TIMON,(1) *attended; the* Servant *of* VENTIDIUS *talking with him.*[a]

TIM. Imprison'd is he, say you?
VEN. SERV. Ay, my good lord: five talents is his debt;
His means most short, his creditors most strait:
Your honourable letter he desires
To those have shut him up; which failing,
Periods his comfort.
TIM. Noble Ventidius! Well,
I am not of that feather to shake off
My friend when he most needs me.[b] I do know him
A gentleman that well deserves a help,
Which he shall have: I'll pay the debt, and free [him.

[a] Talking with him.] The old stage direction is, "*Trumpets sound. Enter Lord Timon, addressing himselfe curteously to every Sutor.*"

[b] *When he* most needs *me.*] So the folio 1664; that of 1623 reads:—
"——when he *must neede* me."

VEN. SERV. Your lordship ever binds him.
TIM. Commend me to him: I will send his ransom;
And, being enfranchis'd, bid him come to me:—
'T is not enough to help the feeble up,
But to support him after.—Fare you well.
VEN. SERV. All happiness to your honour! [*Exit.*

Enter an old Athenian.

OLD ATH. Lord Timon, hear me speak.
TIM. Freely, good father.
OLD ATH. Thou hast a servant nam'd Lucilius.
TIM. I have so: what of him?
OLD ATH. Most noble Timon, call the man before thee.
TIM. Attends he here, or no?—Lucilius!

Enter LUCILIUS.

LUC. Here, at your lordship's service.
OLD. ATH. This fellow here, lord Timon, this thy creature,
By night frequents my house. I am a man
That from my first have been inclin'd to thrift;
And my estate deserves an heir more rais'd,
Than one which holds a trencher.
TIM. Well; what further?
OLD ATH. One only daughter have I, no kin else,
On whom I may confer what I have got:
The maid is fair, o' the youngest for a bride,
And I have bred her at my dearest cost,
In qualities of the best. This man of thine
Attempts her love: I pr'ythee, noble lord,
Join with me to forbid him her resort;
Myself have spoke in vain.
TIM. The man is honest.
OLD ATH. Therefore he will be, Timon: [a]
His honesty rewards him in itself,
It must not bear my daughter.
TIM. Does she love him?
OLD ATH. She is young and apt:
Our own precedent passions do instruct us
What levity's in youth.
TIM. [*To* LUCILIUS.] Love you the maid?
LUC. Ay, my good lord, and she accepts of it.
OLD ATH. If in her marriage my consent be missing,
I call the gods to witness, I will choose
Mine heir from forth the beggars of the world,
And dispossess her all.
TIM. How shall she be endow'd,
If she be mated with an equal husband?
OLD ATH. Three talents on the present; in future, all.
TIM. This gentleman of mine hath serv'd me long;
To build his fortune I will strain a little,
For 'tis a bond in men. Give him thy daughter:
What you bestow, in him I'll counterpoise,
And make him weigh with her.
OLD ATH. Most noble lord,
Pawn me to this your honour, she is his.
TIM. My hand to thee; mine honour on my promise.
LUC. Humbly I thank your lordship: never may
That state or fortune fall into my keeping,
Which is not ow'd to you!
[*Exeunt* LUCILIUS *and old* Athenian.
POET. Vouchsafe my labour, and long live your lordship!
TIM. I thank you; you shall hear from me anon:
Go not away.—What have you there, my friend?
PAIN. A piece of painting, which I do beseech
Your lordship to accept.
TIM. Painting is welcome.
The painting is almost the natural man;
For since dishonour traffics with man's nature,
He is but outside: these pencill'd figures are
Even such as they give out. I like your work;
And you shall find I like it: wait attendance
Till you hear further from me.
PAIN. The gods preserve ye!
TIM. Well fare you, gentleman: give me your hand;
We must needs dine together.—Sir, your jewel
Hath suffered under praise.
JEW. What, my lord! dispraise?
TIM. A mere satiety of commendations.
If I should pay you for't as 'tis extoll'd,
It would unclew me quite.
JEW. My lord, 'tis rated
As those which sell would give: but you well know,
Things of like value, differing in the owners,
Are prized by their masters: [b] believe't, dear lord,
You mend the jewel by the wearing it.
TIM. Well mock'd.
MER. No, my good lord; he speaks the common tongue,
Which all men speak with him.
TIM. Look, who comes here: will you be chid?

---

[a] Therefore he will be, Timon:] The meaning is not apparent. Malone construes it,—"Therefore he will continue to be so, and is sure of being sufficiently rewarded by the consciousness of virtue." But this, too, is inexplicit. We should perhaps read,—"Therefore he will be Timon's," &c., that is, he will continue to be in the service of so noble a master, and thus, his virtue will reward itself: or it is possible the words, "Therefore he will be," may originally have formed part of Timon's speech, and the dialogue have run thus:—

TIMON. The man is honest,
Therefore he will be——
OLD ATH. Timon,
His honesty rewards him in itself,
It must not bear my daughter.

In a text so lamentably imperfect as that of the present play, a more than ordinary licence of conjecture is permissible.

[b] Are prized by their masters:] "Are rated according to the esteem in which their possessor is held."—JOHNSON.

Enter APEMANTUS.(2)

JEW. We 'll bear, with your lordship.
MER. He'll spare none.
TIM. Good morrow to thee, gentle Apemantus!
APEM. Till I be gentle, stay thou for thy good morrow;
When thou art Timon's dog, and these knaves honest.
TIM. Why dost thou call them knaves? thou know'st them not.
APEM. Are they not Athenians?
TIM. Yes.
APEM. Then I repent not.
JEW. You know me, Apemantus?
APEM. Thou know'st I do; I call'd thee by thy name.
TIM. Thou art proud, Apemantus.
APEM. Of nothing so much, as that I am not like Timon.
TIM. Whither art going?
APEM. To knock out an honest Athenian's brains.
TIM. That's a deed thou'lt die for.
APEM. Right, if doing nothing be death by the law.
TIM. How likest thou this picture, Apemantus?
APEM. The best, for the innocence.
TIM. Wrought he not well, that painted it?
APEM. He wrought better that made the painter; and yet he's but a filthy piece of work.
PAIN. You are a dog.
APEM. Thy mother's of my generation; what's she, if I be a dog?
TIM. Wilt dine with me, Apemantus?
APEM. No; I eat not lords.
TIM. An thou shouldst, thou'dst anger ladies.
APEM. O, they eat lords; so they come by great bellies.
TIM. That's a lascivious apprehension.
APEM. So thou apprehend'st it, take it for thy labour.[a]

[a] So thou apprehend'st it, take it, &c] That is, In whatever sense thou apprehend'st it, take it, &c.

TIM. How dost thou like this jewel, Apemantus?

APEM. Not so well as plain-dealing, which will not cost * a man a doit.

TIM. What dost thou think 'tis worth?

APEM. Not worth my thinking.—How now, poet!

POET. How now, philosopher!

APEM. Thou liest.

POET. Art not one?

APEM. Yes.

POET. Then I lie not.

APEM. Art not a poet?

POET. Yes.

APEM. Then thou liest: look in thy last work, where thou hast feigned him a worthy fellow.

POET. That's not feigned; he is so.

APEM. Yes, he is worthy of thee, and to pay thee for thy labour: he that loves to be flattered is worthy o' the flatterer. Heavens, that I were a lord!

TIM. What wouldst do then, Apemantus?

APEM. Even as Apemantus does now,—hate a lord with my heart.

TIM. What, thyself?

APEM. Ay.

TIM. Wherefore?

APEM. That I had no angry wit to be a lord.—[a] Art not thou a merchant?

MER. Ay, Apemantus.

APEM. Traffic confound thee, if the gods will not!

MER. If traffic do it, the gods do it.

APEM. Traffic's thy god, and thy god confound thee!

Trumpet sounds. Enter a Servant.

TIM. What trumpet's that?

SERV. 'T is Alcibiades, and some twenty horse,
All of companionship.

TIM. Pray, entertain them; give them guide to us.— [*Exeunt some* Attendants.
You must needs dine with me.—Go not you hence,
Till I have thank'd you; and † when dinner's done,
Show me this piece.—I am joyful of your sights.—

Enter ALCIBIADES, *with his* Company.

Most welcome, sir! [*They salute.*

APEM. So, so; there!—[b]
Aches contract and starve your supple joints!—
That there should be small love 'mongst these sweet knaves,
And all this court'sy! The strain of man's bred out
Into baboon and monkey.

ALCIB. Sir, you have sav'd my longing, and I feed
Most hungerly on your sight.

TIM. Right welcome, sir!
Ere we depart,[c] we'll share a bounteous time
In different pleasures. Pray you, let us in.
[*Exeunt all except* APEMANTUS.

Enter Two Lords.

1 LORD. What time o' day is't, Apemantus?

APEM. Time to be honest.

1 LORD. That time serves still.

APEM. The most accursed thou, that still omitt'st it.

2 LORD. Thou art going to lord Timon's feast?

APEM. Ay; to see meat fill knaves, and wine heat fools.

2 LORD. Fare thee well, fare thee well.

APEM. Thou art a fool to bid me farewell twice.

2 LORD. Why, Apemantus?

APEM. Shouldst have kept one to thyself, for I mean to give thee none.

1 LORD. Hang thyself!

APEM. No, I will do nothing at thy bidding; make thy requests to thy friend.

2 LORD. Away, unpeaceable dog, or I'll spurn thee hence!

APEM. I will fly, like a dog, the heels o' the ass. [*Exit.*

1 LORD. He's opposite to humanity. Come,* shall we in,
And taste lord Timon's bounty? he outgoes
The very heart of kindness.

2 LORD. He pours it out; Plutus, the god of gold,
Is but his steward: no meed,[d] but he repays

(*) Old text, *cast*. (†) First folio omits, *and*.

(*) First folio, *Comes*.

[a] That I had no angry wit to be a lord.—] This appears to be an incorrigible corruption. Warburton proposed, "That I had *so hungry* a wit to be a lord." Mason—"That I had *an* angry *wish* to be a lord." And Mr. Collier's annotator reads, "That I had *so hungry* a *wish* to be a lord." No one of these, or of many other emendations which have been proposed, is sufficiently plausible to deserve a place in the text. We leave the passage, therefore, as it stands in the old copy, merely suggesting that *be* may have been misprinted for *bay*; "That I had no angry wit to *bay* a lord." The meaning being, he should hate himself, because, by his elevation, he had lost the privilege of reviling rank. In a subsequent scene, he says,—"No, I'll nothing: for, if I should be bribed too, there would be none left to rail upon thee;" &c.

[b] So, so; there! &c.] This speech is printed as prose in the old text, and begins, "So, so; *their* Aches contract," &c. The present arrangement was made by Capell.

[c] Depart,—] *Separate, part.*

[d] Meed—] Here, as in other places, Shakespeare uses *meed* in the sense of *merit*, or *desert*. See "Henry VI. Part III." Act II. Sc. 1:—

"Each one already blazing by our *meeds*."

And a passage in Act IV. Sc. 8, of the same play,—

"That's not my fear; my *meed* hath got me fame."

So also in "Hamlet," Act V. Sc. 2:—

"——but in the imputation laid on him by them, in his *meed* he's unfellowed."

Sevenfold above itself; no gift to him,
But breeds the giver a return, exceeding
All use of quittance.[a]

1 LORD. The noblest mind he carries,
That ever govern'd man.

2 LORD. Long may he live in fortunes! Shall we in?

1 LORD. I'll keep you company. [*Exeunt.*

SCENE II.—*The same. A Room of State in* Timon's *House.*

Hautboys playing loud music. A great banquet served in; FLAVIUS *and others attending; then enter* TIMON, ALCIBIADES, Lords, Senators, *and* VENTIDIUS. *Then comes, dropping after all,* APEMANTUS, *discontentedly, like himself.*

VEN. Most honour'd Timon,
It hath pleas'd the gods to remember my father's age,
And call him to long peace.
He is gone happy, and has left me rich:
Then, as in grateful virtue I am bound
To your free heart, I do return those talents,
Doubled with thanks and service, from whose help
I deriv'd liberty.

TIM. O, by no means;
Honest Ventidius, you mistake my love;
I gave it freely ever, and there's none
Can truly say he gives, if he receives:
If our betters play at that game, we must not dare
To imitate them; faults that are rich are fair.

VEN. A noble spirit.

[*They all stand ceremoniously looking on* TIMON.

TIM. Nay, my lords, ceremony was but devis'd at first,
To set a gloss on faint deeds, hollow welcomes,
Recanting goodness, sorry ere 'tis shown;
But where there is true friendship, there needs none.
Pray, sit; more welcome are ye to my fortunes,
Than my fortunes to me. [*They sit.*

1 LORD. My lord, we always have confess'd it.

APEM. Ho, ho, *confess'd it!* hang'd it, have you not?[b]

TIM. O, Apemantus!—you are welcome.

APEM. No, you shall not make me welcome:
I come to have thee thrust me out of doors.

TIM. Fie, thou 'rt a churl; you 've got a humour there
Does not become a man, 't is much to blame:—
They say, my lords, *ira furor brevis est,*
But yond' man is ever[c] angry.
Go, let him have a table by himself;
For he does neither affect company,
Nor is he fit for it, indeed.

APEM. Let me stay at thine apperil, Timon;
I come to observe; I give thee warning on't.

TIM. I take no heed of thee; thou art an Athenian, therefore welcome: I myself would have no power: pr'ythee, let my meat make thee silent.

APEM. I scorn thy meat; 't would choke me, for I should ne'er flatter thee. O you gods! what a number of men eat Timon, and he sees 'em not! It grieves me to see so many dip their meat in one man's blood; and all the madness is, he cheers them up too.
I wonder men dare trust themselves with men:
Methinks they should invite them without knives;
Good for their meat, and safer for their lives.
There's much example for't; the fellow that sits next him, now parts bread with him, pledges the breath of him in a divided draught, is the readiest man to kill him: it has been proved. If I were a huge man, I should fear to drink at meals;
Lest they should spy my windpipe's dangerous notes:
Great men should drink with harness on their throats.

TIM. My lord, in heart; and let the health go round.

2 LORD. Let it flow this way, my good lord.

APEM. *Flow this way!*
A brave fellow!—he keeps his tides well. Timon,[d]
Those healths will make thee and thy state look ill.
Here's that, which is too weak to be a sinner,[e]
Honest water, which ne'er left man i' the mire:
This and my food are equals; there's no odds.
Feasts are too proud to give thanks to the gods.

APEMANTUS' GRACE.

Immortal gods, I crave no pelf;
I pray for no man but myself:
Grant I may never prove so fond,
To trust man on his oath or bond;
Or a harlot, for her weeping;
Or a dog, that seems a-sleeping;
Or a keeper with my freedom;
Or my friends, if I should need 'em.
Amen. So fall to 't:
Rich men sin, and I eat root.
[*Eats and drinks.*

Much good dich thy good heart, Apemantus!

---

a All use of quittance.] All customary requital.

b Confess'd it! hang'd it, *have you not?*] An allusion, not unfrequent with the writers of the Elizabethan era, to a familiar proverbial saying, "Confess and be hang'd." Shakespeare again refers to it in "Othello," Act IV. Sc. 1:—

"——to *confess, and be hang'd* for his labour."

c *But yond' man is* ever *angry.*] The original reads, *verie* angry; corrected by Rowe.

d Timon,—] In the old text, *Timon* is printed at the end of the following line. Capell made the transposition.

e *Here's that, which is too weak to be a* sinner,—] For *sinner*, Mr. Collier's annotator reads *fire*.

TIM. Captain Alcibiades, your heart's in the field now.

ALCIB. My heart is ever at your service, my lord.

TIM. You had rather be at a breakfast of enemies, than a dinner of friends.

ALCIB. So they were bleeding-new, my lord, there's no meat like 'em; I could wish my best friend at such a feast.

APEM. Would all those flatterers were thine enemies then, that then thou mightst kill 'em, and bid me to 'em!

1 LORD. Might we but have that happiness, my lord, that you would once use our hearts, whereby we might express some part of our zeals, we should think ourselves for ever perfect.

TIM. O, no doubt, my good friends, but the gods themselves have provided that I shall have much help from you: how had you been my friends else? why have you that charitable title from thousands, did not you chiefly belong to my heart? I have told more of you to myself, than you can with modesty speak in your own behalf; and thus far I confirm you. O, you gods, think I, what need we have any friends, if we should ne'er have need of 'em? they were the most needless creatures living, should we ne'er have use for 'em;[a] and would most resemble sweet instruments hung up in cases, that keep their sounds to themselves. Why, I have often wished myself poorer, that I might come nearer to you. We are born to do benefits; and what better or properer can we call our own, than the riches of our friends? O, what a precious comfort 'tis, to have so many, like brothers, commanding one another's fortunes! O joy,* e'en made away ere't can be born! Mine eyes cannot hold out water, methinks; to forget their faults, I drink to you.

APEM. Thou weepest to make them drink, Timon.

2 LORD. Joy had the like conception in our eyes,
And, at that instant, like a babe, sprung up.

APEM. Ho, ho! I laugh to think that babe a bastard.

3 LORD. I promise you, my lord, you mov'd me much.

APEM. *Much!*[b] [*Tucket sounded.*

TIM. What means that trump?—

Enter a Servant.

How now?

SERV. Please you, my lord, there are certain ladies most desirous of admittance.

TIM. Ladies! what are their wills?

SERV. There comes with them a forerunner, my lord, which bears that office, to signify their pleasures.

TIM. I pray, let them be admitted.

Enter CUPID.

CUP. Hail to thee, worthy Timon;—and to all
That of his bounties taste!—The five best senses
Acknowledge thee their patron; and come freely
To gratulate thy plenteous bosom: the ear,
Taste, touch, smell, pleas'd from thy table rise;[c]
They only now come but to feast thine eyes.

TIM. They are welcome all; let 'em have kind admittance:
Music, make their welcome. [*Exit* CUPID.

1 LORD. You see, my lord, how ample you're belov'd.

Music. Re-enter CUPID, *with a masque of* Ladies *as* Amazons, *with lutes in their hands, dancing and playing.*

APEM. Hoy day, what a sweep of vanity comes this way!
They dance! they are mad women.
Like madness is the glory of this life,
As this pomp shows to a little oil and root.[d]
We make ourselves fools, to disport ourselves;
And spend our flatteries, to drink those men,
Upon whose age we void it up again,
With poisonous spite and envy.
Who lives, that's not depraved or depraves?
Who dies, that bears not one spurn to their graves
Of their friends' gift?
I should fear those that dance before me now,
Would one day stamp upon me: 't has been done;
Men shut their doors against a setting sun.

The Lords *rise from table, with much adoring of* TIMON; *and to show their loves, each singles out an* Amazon, *and all dance, men with women, a lofty strain or two to the hautboys, and cease.*

TIM. You have done our pleasures much grace, fair ladies,

(*) Old text, *ioyes.*

[a] Should we ne'er have use for 'em.] Either this or the previous clause,—"if we should ne'er have need of 'em," was probably intended to be cancelled.

[b] Much!] This contemptuous expression, or epithet, occurs again in the "Second Part of Henry IV." Act II. Sc. 4.

[c] —— The ear,
Taste, touch, smell, pleas'd from thy table rise;]
Corruptly given in the old text:—
"There tast, touch all, pleas'd from thy Table rise:"
Warburton made the happy emendation now universally accepted.

[d] As this pomp shows to a little oil and root.] A line so inexplicable and obtrusive as part of the speech, that we could almost believe it to have been originally a stage direction:—

"They dance! they are mad women:
Like madness is the glory of this life!
[*As this pomp shows, take a little oil and root.*
We make ourselves fools," &c.

Set a fair fashion on our entertainment,
Which was not half so beautiful and kind;
You have added worth unto 't, and lustre,
And entertain'd me with mine own device;
I am to thank you for it.

1 LADY.* My lord, you take us even at the best.

APEM. Faith, for the worst is filthy; and would not hold taking, I doubt me.

TIM. Ladies, there is an idle banquet attends you:
Please you to dispose yourselves.

ALL LAD. Most thankfully, my lord.
[*Exeunt* CUPID *and* Ladies.

TIM. Flavius,——

FLAV. My lord.

TIM. The little casket bring me hither.

FLAV. Yes, my lord.—More jewels yet!
There is no crossing him in 's humour; [*Aside.*
Else I should tell him well, i'faith, I should:[a]
When all's spent, he'd be cross'd then, an he could.
'Tis pity bounty had not eyes behind,
That man might ne'er be wretched for his mind.
[*Fetches the casket.*

1 LORD. Where be our men?

SERV. Here, my lord, in readiness.

2 LORD. Our horses!

TIM. O my friends,
I have one word to say to you.—Look you, my good lord,
I must entreat you honour me so much
As to advance this jewel; accept it and wear it,
Kind my lord.

1 LORD. I am so far already in your gifts,—

ALL. So are we all.

Enter a Servant.

SERV. My lord, there are certain nobles of the senate newly alighted, and come to visit you.

TIM. They are fairly welcome.

FLAV. I beseech your honour,
Vouchsafe me a word; it does concern you near.

TIM. Near! why then another time I'll hear thee:
I pr'ythee, let's be provided to show them entertainment.

FLAV. [*Aside.*] I scarce know how.

(*) Old text, 1 *Lord*.

[a] There is no crossing him in 's humour;
Else I should tell him well, i'faith, I should:
When all's spent, he'd be cross'd then, an he could.]

In the second line we adopt the punctuation of the old copy, which, from not perceiving the sense of *tell*, that is, *rate*, or *call to account*, modern editors have oddly altered to,—

"Else I should tell him,—well,—i' faith, I should."

The word *crossing* induced the irresistible paragram on *tell*, and a still further quibble on *cross'd*, which is to be understood, both in the sense of *thwarted* and have *crosses*, or money. For examples cf. a similar equivoque, see note (c), p. 56, Vol. I., and note (a), p. 141 of the present Volume.

Enter another Servant.

2 SERV. May it please your honour, lord Lucius,
Out of his free love, hath presented to you
Four milk-white horses, trapp'd in silver.

TIM. I shall accept them fairly: let the presents
Be worthily entertain'd.—

Enter a third Servant.

How now! what news?

3 SERV. Please you, my lord, that honourable gentleman, lord Lucullus, entreats your company to-morrow to hunt with him; and has sent your honour two brace of greyhounds.

TIM. I'll hunt with him; and let them be receiv'd,
Not without fair reward.

FLAV. [*Aside.*] What will this come to?
He commands us to provide, and give great gifts,
And all out of an empty coffer.—
Nor will he know his purse; or yield me this,
To show him what a beggar his heart is,
Being of no power to make his wishes good;
His promises fly so beyond his state,
That what he speaks is all in debt, he owes for every word;
He is so kind, that he now pays interest for't;
His land's put to their books. Well, would I were
Gently put out of office, before I were forc'd out!
Happier is he that has no friend to feed,
Than such that do e'en enemies exceed.
I bleed inwardly for my lord. [*Exit.*

TIM. You do yourselves much wrong, you bate too much of your own merits.—Here, my lord, a trifle of our love.

2 LORD. With more than common thanks I will receive it.

3 LORD. O, he's the very soul of bounty!

TIM. And now I remember, my lord, you gave good words the other day of a bay courser I rode on: 'tis yours, because you liked it.

2 LORD. O, I beseech you, pardon me, my lord, in that.

TIM. You may take my word, my lord; I know, no man can justly praise, but what he does affect: I weigh my friend's affection with mine own; I'll tell you true. I'll call to you.

ALL LORDS. O, none so welcome.

TIM. I take all and your several visitations
So kind to heart, 'tis not enough to give;
Methinks, I could deal kingdoms to my friends,
And ne'er be weary.—Alcibiades,
Thou art a soldier, therefore seldom rich,
It comes in charity to thee; for all thy living
Is 'mongst the dead; and all the lands thou hast
Lie in a pitch'd field.

ALCIB. Ay, defiled land, my lord.

1 LORD. We are so virtuously bound,—

TIM. And so
Am I to you.

2 LORD. So infinitely endear'd,—

TIM. All to you.—Lights, more lights!

1 LORD. The best of happiness, honour, and fortunes,
Keep with you, lord Timon!

TIM. Ready for his friends.

[*Exeunt* ALCIBIADES, Lords, *&c.*

APEM. What a coil's here.
Serving of becks,[a] and jutting out of bums!
I doubt whether their legs[b] be worth the sums
That are given for 'em. Friendship's full of dregs:
Methinks, false hearts should never have sound legs.
Thus honest fools lay out their wealth on court'sies.

TIM. Now, Apemantus, if thou wert not sullen,
I would be good to thee.

APEM. No, I'll nothing: for, if I should be bribed too, there would be none left to rail upon thee; and then thou wouldst sin the faster. Thou givest so long, Timon, I fear me thou wilt give away thyself in paper[c] shortly: what need these feasts, pomps, and vain glories?

TIM. Nay, an you begin to rail on society once, I am sworn not to give regard to you. Farewell; and come with better music. [*Exit.*

APEM. So thou wilt not hear me now,[d] thou shalt not then; I'll lock thy heaven from thee.
O, that men's ears should be
To counsel deaf, but not to flattery! [*Exit.*

---

a Becks,—] *Becks* here mean *bows.*

b *I doubt whether their* legs, &c.] To make *a leg,* meant formerly to make an *obeisance.* Apemantus, perhaps, intends a play upon the word.

c In paper—] In *paper* is supposed to mean in *securities.*

d So thou wilt not—] That is, *As* thou wilt not, &c.

ACT II.

SCENE I.—Athens. *A Room in a* Senator*'s House.*

Enter a Senator *with papers in his hand.*

SEN. And late, five thousand;—to Varro and to Isidore
He owes nine thousand;—besides my former sum,
Which makes it five and twenty.—Still in motion
Of raging waste! It cannot hold; it will not.
If I want gold, steal but a beggar's dog,
And give it Timon, why, the dog coins gold:
If I would sell my horse, and buy ten[a] more*
Better than he, why, give my horse to Timon,
Ask nothing, give it him, it foals me straight,
Ten[b] able horses: no porter[c] at his gate;
But rather one that smiles, and still invites
All that pass by. It cannot hold; no reason
Can found† his state in safety. Caphis, ho!
Caphis, I say!

Enter CAPHIS.

CAPH. Here, sir; what is your pleasure?

SEN. Get on your cloak, and haste you to lord Timon;
Impórtune him for my monies; be not ceas'd
With slight denial; nor then silenc'd, when—
Commend me to your master—and the cap
Plays in the right hand, thus:—but tell him, sirrah,*
My uses cry to me, I must serve my turn
Out of mine own; his days and times are past,
And my reliances on his fracted dates
Have smit my credit: I love and honour him;
But must not break my back to heal his finger:
Immediate are my needs; and my relief
Must not be toss'd and turn'd to me in words,

(*) Old text, *moe*. (†) Old text, *sound*.

(*) First folio omits, *sirrah*.

[a] Ten—] This is Pope's emendation, the old text having "twenty."

[b] Ten—] So Theobald. The old text reads—"*And* able horses."

[c] No porter—] From what follows we may suspect the original had "no *grim* porter."

But find supply immediate. Get you gone:
Put on a most importunate aspéct,
A visage of demand; for, I do fear,
When every feather sticks in his own wing,
Lord Timon will be left a naked gull,
Which flashes now a phœnix. Get you gone.

CAPH. I go, sir.

SEN. Take the bonds along with you,[a]
And have the dates in compt.[b]

CAPH. I will, sir.

SEN. Go.

[*Exeunt.*

SCENE II.—*The same. A Hall in* Timon's *House.*

Enter FLAVIUS, *with many bills in his hand.*

FLAV. No care, no stop! so senseless of expense
That he will neither know how to maintain it,
Nor cease his flow of riot: takes no account
How things go from him; nor resumes[c] no care
Of what is to continue; never mind
Was to be so unwise, to be so kind.
What shall be done? he will not hear, till feel:
I must be round with him, now he comes from hunting.
Fie, fie, fie, fie!

Enter CAPHIS, *and the* Servants *of* ISIDORE *and* VARRO.

CAPH. Good even, Varro:[d] what,
You come for money?

VAR. SERV. Is't not your business too?

CAPH. It is;—and yours too, Isidore?

ISID. SERV. It is so.

CAPH. Would we were all discharg'd!

VAR. SERV. I fear it.

CAPH. Here comes the lord.

Enter TIMON, ALCIBIADES, Lords, &c.

TIM. So soon as dinner's done, we'll forth again,
My Alcibiades.—With me? what is your will?

CAPH. My lord, here is a note of certain dues.

TIM. Dues! whence are you?

CAPH. Of Athens here, my lord.

TIM. Go to my steward.

CAPH. Please it your lordship, he hath put me off,
To the succession of new days, this month:
My master is awak'd by great occasion,
To call upon his own; and humbly prays you,
That with your other noble parts you'll suit,
In giving him his right.

TIM. Mine honest friend,
I pr'ythee, but repair to me next morning.

CAPH. Nay, good my lord,—

TIM. Contain thyself, good friend.

VAR. SERV. One Varro's servant, my good lord,—

ISID SERV. From Isidore;
He humbly prays your speedy payment,—

CAPH. If you did know, my lord, my master's wants,—

VAR. SERV. 'Twas due on forfeiture, my lord, six weeks and past.

ISID. SERV. Your steward puts me off, my lord, and I
Am sent expressly to your lordship.—

TIM. Give me breath:—
I do beseech you, good my lords, keep on;
I'll wait upon you instantly.

[*Exeunt* ALCIBIADES *and* Lords.

Come hither: pray you, [*To* FLAVIUS.
How goes the world, that I am thus encounter'd
With clamorous demands of date-broke* bonds,
And the detention of long-since-due debts,
Against my honour?

FLAV. Please you, gentlemen,
The time is unagreeable to this business:
Your importunacy cease till after dinner;
That I may make his lordship understand
Wherefore you are not paid.

TIM. Do so, my friends:—
See them well entertained. [*Exit* TIMON.

FLAV. Pray, draw near.

[*Exit* FLAVIUS.

Enter APEMANTUS *and* Fool.

CAPH. Stay, stay, here comes the fool with Apemantus; let's have some sport with 'em.

VAR. SERV. Hang him, he'll abuse us.

ISID. SERV. A plague upon him, dog!

VAR. SERV. How dost, fool?

APEM. Dost dialogue with thy shadow?

---

[a] CAPH. I go, sir.
SEN. Take the bonds, &c.]

The old copies read,—

CAPH. I go sir.
SEN. *I go sir?*
Take the bonds, &c.

The repetition of "I go, sir," was, in all probability, an error of the copyist or compositor.

[b] *And have the dates in* compt.] Theobald's amendment of the old text, which reads—

"And have the dates in. *Come.*"

(*) Old text, *debt, broken*.

[c] *Nor* resumes no care, &c.] The old text reads—"nor *resume* no care," &c., for which Mr. Collier's annotator, with much plausibility, substitutes,—"no *reserves*, no care," &c., according to Mr. Collier's last edition of Shakespeare; or, "no *reserve;* no care," &c., if we are to believe his monovolume edition, and the supplemental volume of "Notes and Emendations," &c.

[d] *Good even*, Varro:] The old stage direction is, "*Enter Caphis, Isidore, and Varro;*" the two latter, though addressed by their masters' names, it is clear, from what follows, are only servants.

VAR. SERV. I speak not to thee.

APEM. No; 'tis to thyself.—Come away. [*To the* Fool.

ISID. SERV. [*To* VAR. SERV.] There's the fool hangs on your back already.

APEM. No, thou stand'st single, thou art not on him yet.

CAPH. Where's the fool now?

APEM. He last asked the question.—Poor rogues, and usurers' men! bawds between gold and want!

ALL SERV. What are we, Apemantus?

APEM. Asses.

ALL SERV. Why?

APEM. That you ask me what you are, and do not know yourselves.—Speak to 'em, fool.

FOOL. How do you, gentlemen?

ALL SERV. Gramercies, good fool: how does your mistress?

FOOL. She's e'en setting on water to scald such chickens as you are. Would we could see you at Corinth!

APEM. Good! gramercy.

FOOL. Look you, here comes my mistress'* page.

Enter Page.

PAGE. [*To the* Fool.] Why, how now, captain! what do you in this wise company? How dost thou, Apemantus?

APEM. Would I had a rod in my mouth, that I might answer thee profitably.

PAGE. Pr'ythee, Apemantus, read me the superscription of these letters; I know not which is which.

APEM. Canst not read?

PAGE. No.

APEM. There will little learning die, then, that day thou art hanged. This is to lord Timon; this to Alcibiades. Go; thou wast born a bastard, and thou'lt die a bawd.

PAGE. Thou wast whelped a dog, and thou shalt famish a dog's death. Answer not, I am gone. [*Exit* Page.

APEM. E'en so thou out-runn'st grace. Fool, I will go with you to lord Timon's.

FOOL. Will you leave me there?

APEM. If Timon stay at home.—You three serve three usurers?

ALL SERV. Ay; would they served us!

APEM. So would I,—as good a trick as ever hangman served thief.

FOOL. Are you three usurers' men?

ALL SERV. Ay, fool.

FOOL. I think no usurer but has a fool to his servant: my mistress is one, and I am her fool. When men come to borrow of your masters, they approach sadly, and go away merry; but they enter my mistress'* house merrily, and go away sadly: The reason of this?

VAR. SERV. I could render one.

APEM. Do it then, that we may account thee a whoremaster and a knave; which, notwithstanding, thou shalt be no less esteemed.

VAR. SERV. What is a whoremaster, fool?

FOOL. A fool in good clothes, and something like thee. 'T is a spirit: sometime, it appears like a lord; sometime, like a lawyer; sometime, like a philosopher, with two stones more† than his artificial one: he is very often like a knight; and, generally, in all shapes that man goes up and down in from fourscore to thirteen, this spirit walks in.

VAR. SERV. Thou art not altogether a fool.

FOOL. Nor thou altogether a wise man: as much foolery as I have, so much wit thou lackest.

APEM. That answer might have become Apemantus.

ALL SERV. Aside, aside; here comes lord Timon.

APEM. Come with me, fool, come.

FOOL. I do not always follow lover, elder brother, and woman; sometime, the philosopher. [*Exeunt* APEMANTUS *and* Fool.

Re-enter TIMON *and* FLAVIUS.

FLAV. Pray you, walk near; I'll speak with you anon. [*Exeunt* Servants.

TIM. You make me marvel: wherefore, ere this time,
Had you not fully laid my state before me,
That I might so have rated my expense,
As I had leave of means.

FLAV. You would not hear me;
At many leisures I propos'd.‡

TIM. Go to:
Perchance some single vantages you took,
When my indisposition put you back;
And that unaptness made your minister,[a]
Thus to excuse yourself.

FLAV. O my good lord!
At many times I brought in my accounts,[b]
Laid them before you, you would throw them off,
And say, you found § them in mine honesty.
When, for some trifling present, you have bid me
Return so much,[c] I have shook my head and wept;
Yea, 'gainst the authority of manners, pray'd you

(*) Old text, *Masters*.

[a] *And that unaptness made your minister,*—] That unaptness *became*, or *was* made, &c.

[b] At many times I brought in my accounts,—] The import is, "At many times *when* I brought in my accounts," &c.

(*) Old text, *Masters*. (†) First folio, *moe*. (‡) First folio, *propose*. (§) First folio, *sound*.

[c] *Return* so much—] As Malone observes, he does not mean so *great* a sum, but a certain sum, as it might happen to be.

To hold your hand more close: I did endure
Not seldom, nor no slight checks, when I have
Prompted you, in the ebb of your estate,
And your great flow of debts. My dear-lov'd* lord,
Though you hear now, too late! yet now's a time,
The greatest of your having lacks a half
To pay your present debts.
TIM. Let all my land be sold.
FLAV. 'Tis all engag'd, some forfeited and gone;
And what remains will hardly stop the mouth
Of present dues: the future comes apace:
What shall defend the interim? and at length
How goes our reckoning!
TIM. To Lacedæmon did my land extend.
FLAV. O my good lord, the world is but a word:
Were it all yours to give it in a breath,
How quickly were it gone!
TIM. You tell me true.[a]
FLAV. If you suspect my husbandry or falsehood,
Call me before the exactest auditors,
And set me on the proof. So the gods bless me,
When all our offices have been oppress'd
With riotous feeders; when our vaults have wept
With drunken spilth of wine; when every room
Hath blaz'd with lights, and bray'd with minstrelsy;
I have retir'd me to a wasteful cock,
And set mine eyes at flow.[b]
TIM. Pr'ythee, no more.

(*) First folio omits, *dear*.

a *You* tell *me true.*] That is, you *estimate* or *rate* me truly. So in a previous scene, Act I. Sc. 2:—

"I'll *tell* you true. I'll call to you."

b *I have retir'd me to a* wasteful cock,
And set mine eyes at flow.]

This is one of those humiliating passages occasionally found in the first folio, the meaning of which, from no involution or abstruseness of language in the poet, but through some trivial error on the part of copyist or compositor, has foiled the penetration of every commentator. Pope boldly cut the knot by reading "lonely room" for "wasteful cock," but this daring substitution never got beyond his own edition. Hanmer explained the doubtful words to signfy "a cock-loft or garret, lying in waste;" (!) and Mr. Collier's annotator changes "wasteful cock" to "wasteful *nook;*" an alteration not likely to fare better than Pope's, since everybody who reads the context feels, we apprehend, instinctively, that "a wasteful cock," *i.e.* the tap of a wine butt turned on to waste, is an image so peculiarly suitable in the steward's picture of profligate dissipation, that it must be right. In default of any satisfactory explication, we hazard a suggestion that the passage might originally have been printed thus,—

"———So the gods bless me,
When all our offices have been oppress'd
With riotous feeders; when our vaults have wept
With drunken spilth of wine; when every room
Hath blaz'd with lights, and bray'd with minstrelsy,
I have retir'd (me too a wasteful cock,)
And set mine eyes at flow."

FLAV. Heavens, have I said, the bounty of this lord!
How many prodigal bits have slaves and peasants,
This night englutted! Who is not Timon's?
What heart, head, sword, force, means, but is lord Timon's?
Great Timon! noble, worthy, royal Timon!
Ah! when the means are gone, that buy this praise,
The breath is gone whereof this praise is made:
Feast-won, fast-lost; one cloud of winter showers,
These flies are couch'd.

TIM. Come, sermon me no further:
No villainous bounty yet hath pass'd my heart;
Unwisely, not ignobly, have I given.
Why dost thou weep? Canst thou the conscience lack,
To think I shall lack friends? Secure[a] thy heart;
If I would broach the vessels of my love,
And try the argument of hearts by borrowing,
Men and men's fortunes could I frankly use,
As I can bid thee speak.

FLAV. Assurance bless your thoughts!

TIM. And, in some sort, these wants of mine are crown'd,
That I account them blessings; for by these
Shall I try friends: you shall perceive, how you
Mistake my fortunes; I am wealthy in my friends.—
Within there,—Flaminius!* Servilius!

Enter FLAMINIUS, SERVILIUS, *and other* Servants.

SERV. My lord? my lord?—

TIM. I will despatch you severally.—You, to lord Lucius,—to lord Lucullus you; I hunted with his honour to-day;—you, to Sempronius; commend me to their loves; and, I am proud, say, that my occasions have found time to use 'em toward a supply of money: let the request be fifty talents.

FLAM. As you have said, my lord.

FLAV. Lord Lucius and Lucullus? hum! [*Aside.*

TIM. Go you, sir, [*To another* Serv.] to the senators,
Of whom, even to the state's best health, I have
Deserv'd this hearing, bid 'em send o' the instant
A thousand talents to me.

FLAV. I have been bold
(For that I knew it the most general way)
To them to use your signet and your name;
But they do shake their heads, and I am here
No richer in return.

TIM. Is't true? can't be?

FLAV. They answer, in a joint and corporate voice,
That now they are at fall—want treasure—cannot
Do what they would—are sorry—you are honourable,—
But yet they could have wish'd—they know not—
Something hath been amiss—a noble nature
May catch a wrench—would all were well—'tis pity;—
And so, intending[b] other serious matters,
After distasteful looks, and these hard fractions,
With certain half-caps, and cold-moving nods,
They froze me into silence.

TIM. You gods, reward them!—
Pr'ythee, man, look cheerly. These old fellows
Have their ingratitude in them hereditary:
Their blood is cak'd, 'tis cold, it seldom flows;
'Tis lack of kindly warmth they are not kind;
And nature, as it grows again toward earth,
Is fashion'd for the journey, dull, and heavy.—
Go to Ventidius:—[*To a* Serv.] Pr'ythee, [*To* FLAVIUS.] be not sad,
Thou art true and honest: ingeniously[c] I speak,
No blame belongs to thee:—[*To* Serv.] Ventidius lately
Buried his father, by whose death he's stepp'd
Into a great estate: when he was poor,
Imprison'd, and in scarcity of friends,
I clear'd him with five talents: greet him from me;
Bid him suppose some good necessity
Touches his friend, which craves to be remember'd
With those five talents:—that had,—[*To* FLAV.] give it these fellows
To whom 'tis instant due. Ne'er speak, or think,
That Timon's fortunes 'mong his friends can sink.

FLAV. I would I could not think it; that thought is bounty's foe;
Being free itself, it thinks all others so. [*Exeunt.*

(*) Old text, *Flavius.*

[a] Secure *thy heart;*] *Assure, make confident,* thy heart.

[b] Intending—] That is, *pretending.* So in "Richard III." Act III. Sc. 5,—

"Tremble and start at wagging of a straw,
Intending deep suspicion."

[c] Ingeniously—] The use of *ingenious* where we now employ *ingenuous* was not uncommon formerly. Thus in "The Taming of the Shrew," Act I. Sc. 1,—

"Here let us breathe and haply institute
A course of learning, and *ingenious* studies."

ACT III.

SCENE I.—Athens. *A Room in* Lucullus' *House.*

Flaminius *waiting.* *Enter a* Servant *to him.*

Serv. I have told my lord of you; he is coming down to you.

Flam. I thank you, sir.

Enter Lucullus.

Serv. Here's my lord.

Lucul. [*Aside.*] One of lord Timon's men! a gift, I warrant. Why, this hits right; I dreamt of a silver basin and ewer to-night. Flaminius, honest Flaminius; you are very respectively welcome, sir.—Fill me some wine.—[*Exit* Servant.] And how does that honourable, complete, free-hearted gentleman of Athens, thy very bountiful good lord and master?

Flam. His health is well, sir.

Lucul. I am right glad that his health is well, sir: and what hast thou there under thy cloak, pretty Flaminius?

Flam. 'Faith, nothing but an empty box, sir; which, in my lord's behalf, I come to entreat your honour to supply; who, having great and instant occasion to use fifty talents, hath sent to your lordship to furnish him; nothing doubting your present assistance therein.

Lucul. La, la, la, la,—*nothing doubting*, says he? Alas, good lord! a noble gentleman 'tis, if he would not keep so good a house. Many a time and often I have dined with him, and told him on't; and come again to supper to him, of purpose to have him spend less, and yet he would embrace no counsel, take no warning by my coming. Every man has his fault, and honesty[a] is his; I have told him on't, but I could never get him from it.

Re-enter Servant, *with wine.*

SERV. Please your lordship, here is the wine.

LUCUL. Flaminius, I have noted thee always wise. Here's to thee.

FLAM. Your lordship speaks your pleasure.

LUCUL. I have observed thee always for a towardly prompt spirit,—give thee thy due,—and one that knows what belongs to reason; and canst use the time well, if the time use thee well: good parts in thee.—Get you gone, sirrah.—[*To the* Servant, *who goes out.*]—Draw nearer, honest Flaminius. Thy lord's a bountiful gentleman; but thou art wise, and thou knowest well enough, although thou comest to me, that this is no time to lend money; especially upon bare friendship, without security. Here's three solidares for thee; good boy, wink at me, and say, thou sawest me not. Fare thee well.

FLAM. Is't possible the world should so much differ;
And we alive that liv'd? Fly, damned baseness,
To him that worships thee.
[*Throwing back the money.*

LUCUL. Ha! now I see thou art a fool, and fit for thy master. [*Exit* LUCULLUS.

FLAM. May these add to the number that may scald thee!
Let molten coin be thy damnation,
Thou disease of a friend, and not himself!
Has friendship such a faint and milky heart,
It turns in less than two nights? O you gods,
I feel my master's passion! This slave
Unto his honour, has my lord's meat in him:[b]
Why should it thrive, and turn to nutriment,
When he is turn'd to poison?
O, may diseases only work upon't! [nature
And, when he's sick to death, let not that part of
Which my lord paid for, be of any power
To expel sickness, but prolong his hour! [*Exit.*

SCENE II.—*The same. A Public Place.*

Enter LUCIUS, *with Three* Strangers.

LUC. Who? the lord Timon? he is my very good friend, and an honourable gentleman.

1 STRAN. We know him for no less, though we are but strangers to him: but I can tell you one thing, my lord, and which I hear from common rumours;—now lord Timon's happy hours are done and past, and his estate shrinks from him.

LUC. Fie no, do not believe it; he cannot want for money.

2 STRAN. But believe you this, my lord, that, not long ago, one of his men was with the lord Lucullus, to borrow so many talents;[c] nay, urged extremely for't, and showed what necessity belonged to't, and yet was denied.

LUC. How!

2 STRAN. I tell you, denied, my lord.

LUC. What a strange case was that! now, before the gods, I am ashamed on't. Denied that honourable man! there was very little honour showed in't. For my own part, I must needs confess, I have received some small kindnesses from him, as money, plate, jewels, and such-like trifles, nothing comparing to his; yet, had he mistook him, and sent to me, I should ne'er have denied his occasion so many talents.

Enter SERVILIUS.

SER. See, by good hap, yonder's my lord; I have sweat to see his honour.—My honoured lord,— [*To* LUCIUS.

LUC. Servilius! you are kindly met, sir. Fare thee well:—commend me to thy honourable, virtuous lord, my very exquisite friend.

SER. May it please your honour, my lord hath sent—

LUC. Ha! what has he sent? I am so much endeared to that lord; he's ever sending: how shall I thank him, think'st thou? and what has he sent now?

SER. H'as only sent his present occasion now, my lord; requesting your lordship to supply his instant use with so many talents.

LUC. I know his lordship is but merry with me;
He cannot want fifty-five hundred talents.

SER. But in the mean time he wants less, my lord.
If his occasion were not virtuous,
I should not urge it half so faithfully.

LUC. Dost thou speak seriously, Servilius?

SER. Upon my soul, 'tis true, sir.

LUC. What a wicked beast was I to disfurnish

---

a Honesty—] *Honesty* here signifies, *liberality.*

b *This* slave
Unto his honour, *has my lord's meat in him:*]
Pope, who has been followed in some later editions, printed,—
"———This slave
Unto *this hour* has," &c.
Mr. Collier's annotator substitutes,—
"———This slave
Unto his *humour* has," &c.
And Mr. Dyce thinks there is "a high probability that the true reading is,"—
"This *slander*
Unto his honour has," &c.
If any change be really needed, we would read,—
"This slave
Unto dishonour has," &c.

c So many *talents;*] That is, *certain* talents. The expression occurs twice again in the present scene. See also note (c), p. 473.

myself against such a good time, when I might have shown myself honourable! how unluckily it happened, that I should purchase the day before for a little part,[a] and undo a great deal of honour.—Servilius, now before the gods, I am not able to do; the more beast, I say:—I was sending to use lord Timon myself, these gentlemen can witness; but I would not, for the wealth of Athens, I had done it now. Commend me bountifully to his good lordship; and I hope, his honour will conceive the fairest of me, because I have no power to be kind:—and tell him this from me, I count it one of my greatest afflictions, say, that I cannot pleasure such an honourable gentleman. Good Servilius, will you befriend me so far, as to use mine own words to him?

SER. Yes, sir, I shall.

LUC. I'll look you out a good turn, Servilius.— [*Exit* SERVILIUS.

True, as you said, Timon is shrunk indeed;
And he that's once denied will hardly speed.
[*Exit* LUCIUS.

1 STRAN. Do you observe this, Hostilius?

2 STRAN. Ay, too well.

1 STRAN. Why this is the world's soul; and just of the same piece
Is every flatterer's spirit.[b] Who can call him his friend,
That dips in the same dish? for, in my knowing,
Timon has been this lord's father,
And kept his credit with his purse;
Supported his estate; nay, Timon's money
Has paid his men their wages. He ne'er drinks,
But Timon's silver treads upon his lip;
And yet, (O, see the monstrousness of man
When he looks out in an ungrateful shape!)
He does deny him, in respect of his,
What charitable men afford to beggars.

3 STRAN. Religion groans at it.

---

[a] *A little* part,—] *Part* seems a palpable misprint. We should, perhaps, as Mason suggested, read, "a little *port*," that is, *ostentation, show*, and the like. Theobald proposed, "a little *dirt*." Johnson, "a little *park*."

[b] Spirit.] An emendation by Theobald; the old text has, *sport*.

1 STRAN. For mine own part,
I never tasted Timon in my life,
Nor came any of his bounties over me,
To mark me for his friend; yet, I protest,
For his right noble mind, illustrious virtue,
And honourable carriage,
Had his necessity made use of me,
I would have put my wealth into donation,
And the best half should have return'd to him,
So much I love his heart: but, I perceive,
Men must learn now with pity to dispense,
For policy sits above conscience. [*Exeunt.*

SCENE III.—*The same. A Room in* Sempronius' *House.*

Enter SEMPRONIUS, *and a* Servant *of* TIMON'*s.*

SEM. Must he needs trouble me in't?—hum!—'bove all others?
He might have tried lord Lucius or Lucullus;
And now Ventidius is wealthy too,
Whom he redeem'd from prison: all these
Owe their estates unto him.

SERV. My lord,
They have all been touch'd, and found base metal;
For they have all denied him!

SEM. How! have they denied him?
Has Ventidius and Lucullus denied him?
And does he send to me? Three? hum!—
It shows but little love or judgment in him.
Must I be his last refuge? His friends, like physicians,
Thrice[a] give him over; must I take the cure upon me?
H'as much disgrac'd me in't; I'm angry at him,
That might have known my place: I see no sense for't,
But his occasions might have woo'd me first;
For, in my conscience, I was the first man
That e'er received gift from him:
And does he think so backwardly of me now,
That I'll requite it last? No: so it may prove
An argument of laughter to the rest,
And amongst lords I[b] be thought a fool.
I had rather than the worth of thrice the sum,
H'ad sent to me first, but for my mind's sake;
I'd such a courage to do him good. But now return,
And with their faint reply this answer join;
Who bates mine honour, shall not know my coin. [*Exit.*

SERV. Excellent! Your lordship's a goodly villain. The devil knew not what he did when he made man politic,—he crossed himself by't: and I cannot think, but, in the end, the villainies of man will set him clear. How fairly this lord strives to appear foul! takes virtuous copies to be wicked; like those that, under hot ardent zeal, would set whole realms on fire. Of such a nature is his politic love.
This was my lord's best hope; now all are fled,
Save the gods only:* now his friends are dead,
Doors, that were ne'er acquainted with their wards
Many a bounteous year, must be employ'd
Now to guard sure their master.
And this is all a liberal course allows;
Who cannot keep his wealth must keep his house. [*Exit.*

SCENE IV.—*The same. A Hall in* Timon'*s House.*

Enter Two Servants *of* VARRO, *and the* Servant *of* LUCIUS, *meeting* TITUS, HORTENSIUS, *and other* Servants *of* TIMON'*s* Creditors, *waiting his coming out.*

1 VAR. SERV. Well met; good-morrow, Titus and Hortensius.

TIT. The like to you, kind Varro.

HOR. Lucius?
What, do we meet together?

LUC. SERV. Ay, and, I think,
One business does command us all; for mine
Is money.

TIT. So is theirs and ours.

Enter PHILOTUS.

LUC. SERV. And sir Philotus too!

PHI. Good day at once.

LUC. SERV. Welcome, good brother.
What do you think the hour?

PHI. Labouring for nine.

LUC. SERV. So much?

PHI. Is not my lord seen yet?

LUC. SERV. Not yet.

PHI. I wonder on't; he was wont to shine at seven.

---

a ——— *His friends, like physicians,*
Thrice *give him over;*]

Thrice is an emendation of Johnson's; the old text having *Thrive.*

b ——— *So* it *may prove*
An argument of laughter to the rest,
And amongst lords I *be thought a fool;*]

I was introduced by the second folio. We believe, however, the original error arose from the trifling misprint of *it* for *I*, and that the passage once stood,—

" ——— So *I* may prove
An argument of laughter to the rest,
And amongst lords be thought a fool."

Compare: "Well, if ever thou dost fall from this faith, *thou wilt prove a notable argument.*"—*Much Ado about Nothing,* Act I. Sc. 1. The same misprint occurs in "King John," Act I. Sc. 1:—

"*It* would not be sir Nob in any case;"

which, in the second folio, is corrected to,—

"*I* would not be," &c.

(*) Old text, *onely the Gods.*

LUC. SERV. Ay, but the days are wax'd shorter with him:
You must consider that a prodigal course
Is like the sun's, but not like his recoverable.
I fear, 'tis deepest winter in lord Timon's purse;
That is, one may reach deep enough, and yet
Find little.

PHI. I am of your fear for that.

TIT. I'll show you how to observe a strange event.
Your lord sends now for money.

HOR. Most true, he does.

TIT. And he wears jewels now of Timon's gift,
For which I wait for money.

HOR. It is against my heart.

LUC. SERV. Mark, how strange it shows,
Timon in this should pay more than he owes:
And e'en as if your lord should wear rich jewels,
And send for money for 'em.

HOR. I am weary of this charge, the gods can witness:
I know my lord hath spent of Timon's wealth,
And now ingratitude makes it worse than stealth.

1 VAR. SERV. Yes, mine's three thousand crowns: what's yours?

LUC. SERV. Five thousand mine.

1 VAR. SERV. 'Tis much deep: and it should seem by the sum,
Your master's confidence was above mine;
Else, surely, his had equall'd.

Enter FLAMINIUS.

TIT. One of lord Timon's men.

LUC. SERV. Flaminius! sir, a word: pray, is my lord ready to come forth?

FLAM. No, indeed, he is not.

TIT. We attend his lordship; pray, signify so much.

FLAM. I need not tell him that; he knows you are too diligent. [*Exit* FLAMINIUS.

Enter FLAVIUS, *in a cloak, muffled.*

LUC. SERV. Ha! is not that his steward muffled so?
He goes away in a cloud: call him, call him.

TIT. Do you hear, sir?

1 VAR. SERV. By your leave, sir,—

FLAV. What do ye ask of me, my friend?

TIT. We wait for certain money here, sir.

FLAV. Ay, if money were as certain as your waiting,
'T were sure enough.
Why then preferr'd you not your sums and bills,
When your false masters ate of my lord's meat?
Then they could smile, and fawn upon his debts,
And take down the interest into their gluttonous maws.
You do yourselves but wrong to stir me up;
Let me pass quietly:
Believe't, my lord and I have made an end;
I have no more to reckon, he to spend.

LUC. SERV. Ay, but this answer will not serve.

FLAV. If 'twill not serve, 'tis not so base as you;
For you serve knaves. [*Exit.*

1 VAR. SERV. How! what does his cashier'd worship mutter?

2 VAR. SERV. No matter what; he's poor, and that's revenge enough. Who can speak broader than he that has no house to put his head in? such may rail against great buildings.

Enter SERVILIUS.

TIT. O, here's Servilius; now we shall know some answer.

SER. If I might beseech you, gentlemen, to repair some other hour, I should derive much from it: for, take it of my soul, my lord leans wondrously to discontent. His comfortable temper has forsook him; he's much out of health, and keeps his chamber.

LUC. SERV. Many do keep their chambers are not sick:
And, if it be so far beyond his health,
Methinks he should the sooner pay his debts,
And make a clear way to the gods.

SER. Good gods!

TIT. We cannot take this for answer, sir.

FLAM. [*Without.*] Servilius, help!—my lord! my lord!

Enter TIMON, *in a rage;* FLAMINIUS *following.*

TIM. What, are my doors oppos'd against my passage?
Have I been ever free, and must my house
Be my retentive enemy, my gaol?
The place which I have feasted, does it now,
Like all mankind, show me an iron heart?

LUC. SERV. Put in now, Titus.

TIT. My lord, here is my bill.

LUC. SERV. Here's mine.

HOR. SERV. And mine, my lord.[a]

BOTH VAR. SERV. And ours, my lord.

PHI. All our bills.

TIM. Knock me down with 'em:[b] cleave me to [the girdle.

LUC. SERV. Alas! my lord,—

TIM. Cut my heart in sums.

TIT. Mine, fifty talents.

TIM. Tell out my blood.

LUC. SERV. Five thousand crowns, my lord.

TIM. Five thousand drops pays that.—
What yours?—and yours?

1 VAR. SERV. My lord,—

2 VAR. SERV. My lord,—

TIM. Tear me, take me, and the gods fall upon you! [*Exit.*

HOR. 'Faith, I perceive our masters may throw their caps at their money; these debts may well be called desperate ones, for a madman owes 'em. [*Exeunt.*

Re-enter TIMON *and* FLAVIUS.

TIM. They have e'en put my breath from me, the slaves.
Creditors!—devils.

FLAV. My dear lord,—

TIM. What if it should be so?

FLAV. My lord,—

TIM. I'll have it so. My steward!

FLAV. Here, my lord.

TIM. So fitly? Go, bid all my friends again,
Lucius, Lucullus, and Sempronius;[c] all:
I'll once more feast the rascals.

FLAV. O my lord,
You only speak from your distracted soul;
There is not so much left, to furnish out
A moderate table.

TIM. Be't not in thy care;
Go, I charge thee; invite them all: let in the tide
Of knaves once more; my cook and I'll provide. [*Exeunt.*

SCENE V.—*The same. The* Senate-House.

The Senate *sitting.*

1 SEN. My lord, you have my voice to it; the fault's bloody; 'tis necessary he should die: nothing emboldens sin so much as mercy.

2 SEN. Most true; the law shall bruise him.*

Enter ALCIBIADES, *attended.*

ALCIB. Honour, health, and compassion to the senate!

1 SEN. Now, captain?

ALCIB. I am an humble suitor to your virtues;
For pity is the virtue of the law,
And none but tyrants use it cruelly.
It pleases time and fortune to lie heavy
Upon a friend of mine, who, in hot blood,
Hath stepp'd into the law, which is past depth
To those that, without heed, do plunge into 't.
He is a man, setting his fate aside,
Of comely virtues:
Nor did he soil the fact with cowardice,
(An † honour in him which buys out his fault,)
But with a noble fury and fair spirit,

---

[a] And mine, my lord.] The old copies assign this speech to 1 Varro. Capell correctly gave it to the servant of Hortensius, because Varro's two servants proffer their bills immediately afterwards.

[b] PHI. All our bills.
TIM. Knock me down with 'em:]
Again the inveterate conceit on *bill* a weapon, and *bill* a paper!

(*) Old text, *'em.* (†) Old text, *And.*

[c] Lucius, Lucullus, and Sempronius; all:] The folio 1623 has,
"——— and Sempronius *Vllorxa:* All,"
but, as *Ullorxa* is utterly unintelligible, and overloads the line, we adopt the example set by the editor of the second folio, and expunge it from the text.

Seeing his reputation touch'd to death,
He did oppose his foe:
And with such sober and unnoted passion
He did behave[a] his anger ere 'twas spent,
As if he had but prov'd an argument.
1 SEN. You undergo too strict a paradox,[b]
Striving to make an ugly deed look fair:
Your words have took such pains, as if they
labour'd [relling
To bring manslaughter into form, and set quar-
Upon the head of valour; which, indeed,
Is valour misbegot, and came into the world
When sects and factions were newly born:
He's truly valiant, that can wisely suffer
The worst that man can breathe;
And make his wrongs his outsides,
To wear them like his raiment, carelessly;
And ne'er prefer his injuries to his heart,
To bring it into danger.
If wrongs be evils, and enforce us kill,
What folly 'tis to hazard life for ill?
ALCIB. My lord,— [clear:
1 SEN. You cannot make gross sins look
To revenge is no valour, but to bear. [me,
ALCIB. My lords, then, under favour, pardon
If I speak like a captain.—
Why do fond men expose themselves to battle,

[a] *He did* behave *his anger*—] *Behave*, in its ancient sense of *control*, was substituted by Rowe, in place of *behoove*, which is the word in the old copies; but, with Malone, we doubt the text is not yet right.

And not endure all threats? sleep upon it,
And let the foes quietly cut their throats,
Without repugnancy? If there be
Such valour in the bearing, what make we
Abroad? why then, women are more valiant
That stay at home, if bearing carry it;
And the ass more captain than the lion;
The felon* loaden with irons wiser than the judge,
If wisdom be in suffering. O my lords,
As you are great, be pitifully good:
Who cannot condemn rashness in cold blood?
To kill, I grant, is sin's extremest gust;
But, in defence, by mercy, 'tis most just.
To be in anger is impiety;
But who is man that is not angry?
Weigh but the crime with this.
2 SEN. You breathe in vain.
ALCIB. In vain! his service done
At Lacedæmon, and Byzantium,
Were a sufficient briber for his life.
1 SEN. What's that?
ALCIB. Why, I † say, my lords, h'as done fair
service,
And slain in fight many of your enemies:
How full of valour did he bear himself
In the last conflict, and made plenteous wounds!
2 SEN. He has made too much plenty with 'em,‡

(*) Old text, *fellow*. (†) First folio omits, *I*. (‡) First folio, *him*.

[b] *You* undergo *too* strict *a paradox*,—] You *undertake* too *harsh* a paradox.

He's a sworn rioter: he has a sin that often
Drowns him, and takes his valour prisoner:
If there were no foes, that were enough
To overcome him: in that beastly fury
He has been known to commit outrages,
And cherish factions: 't is inferr'd to us,
His days are foul, and his drink dangerous.

1 SEN. He dies.

ALCIB. Hard fate! he might have died in war.
My lords, if not for any parts in him,
(Though his right arm might purchase his own time,
And be in debt to none,) yet, more to move you,
Take my deserts to his, and join 'em both:
And for I know your reverend ages love security,
I'll pawn my victories, all my honour to you,
Upon his good returns.
If by this crime he owes the law his life,
Why, let the war receive't in valiant gore;
For law is strict, and war is nothing more.

1 SEN. We are for law,—he dies; urge it no more,
On height of our displeasure: friend or brother,
He forfeits his own blood that spills another.

ALCIB. Must it be so? it must not be. My lords,
I do beseech you, know me.

2 SEN. How!

ALCIB. Call me to your remembrances.

3 SEN. What!

ALCIB. I cannot think but your age has forgot me;
It could not else be I should prove so base,
To sue, and be denied such common grace:
My wounds ache at you.

1 SEN. Do you dare our anger?
'T is in few words, but spacious in effect;
We banish thee for ever.

ALCIB. Banish me!
Banish your dotage; banish usury,
That makes the senate ugly.

1 SEN. If, after two days' shine, Athens contain thee,
Attend our weightier judgment. And, not to swell our spirit,
He shall be executed presently. [*Exeunt* Senators.

ALCIB. Now the gods keep you old enough; that you may live
Only in bone,[a] that none may look on you!
I'm worse than mad: I have kept back their foes,
While they have told their money, and let out
Their coin upon large interest; I myself,
Rich only in large hurts;—all those, for this?
Is this the balsam that the usuring senate
Pours into captains' wounds? Banishment!
It comes not ill; I hate not to be banish'd;
It is a cause worthy my spleen and fury,
That I may strike at Athens. I'll cheer up
My discontented troops, and lay for hearts.
'T is honour with most lands to be at odds;
Soldiers should brook as little wrongs as gods.
[*Exit.*

SCENE VI.—*The same. A magnificent Room in* Timon's *House.*

Music. Tables set out: Servants *attending. Enter divers* Lords, *at several doors.*

1 LORD. The good time of day to you, sir.

2 LORD. I also wish it to you. I think this honourable lord did but try us this other day.

1 LORD. Upon that were my thoughts tiring,[b] when we encountered: I hope, it is not so low with him, as he made it seem in the trial of his several friends.

2 LORD. It should not be, by the persuasion of his new feasting.

1 LORD. I should think so. He hath sent me an earnest inviting, which many my near occasions did urge me to put off; but he hath conjured me beyond them, and I must needs appear.

2 LORD. In like manner was I in debt to my importunate business, but he would not hear my excuse. I am sorry, when he sent to borrow of me, that my provision was out.

1 LORD. I am sick of that grief too, as I understand how all things go.

2 LORD. Every man here's so. What would he have borrowed of you?

1 LORD. A thousand pieces.

2 LORD. A thousand pieces!

1 LORD. What of you?

3 LORD. He sent to me, sir,—Here he comes.

Enter TIMON *and* Attendants.

TIM. With all my heart, gentlemen both:—and how fare you?

1 LORD. Ever at the best, hearing well of your lordship.

2 LORD. The swallow follows not summer more willing than we your lordship.

a *That you may live*
Only in bone, that none may look on you!]
What living *in bone* may mean, and why when ossified these aged senators should become invisible, are beyond our comprehension; though we make the avowal with diffidence, because previous editors print the passage without any misgiving apparently as to its integrity. Hamlet, speaking to Ophelia of her father, says,—"Let the doors be shut upon him, that he play the fool nowhere *but in's own house*," and it may be questionable whether "*only in bone*" is not a typographical error for *only at home*, or *only in doors*.

b Tiring,—] That is, *pecking*, as a bird at its prey.

Tim. [*Aside.*] Nor more willingly leaves winter; such summer-birds are men.—Gentlemen, our dinner will not recompense this long stay: feast your ears with the music awhile, if they will fare so harshly o' the trumpet's sound: we shall to 't presently.

1 Lord. I hope it remains not unkindly with your lordship, that I returned you an empty messenger.

Tim. O, sir, let it not trouble you.

2 Lord. My noble lord,—

Tim. Ah, my good friend! what cheer?

2 Lord. My most honourable lord, I am e'en sick of shame, that, when your lordship this other day sent to me, I was so unfortunate a beggar.

Tim. Think not on't, sir.

2 Lord. If you had sent but two hours before,—

Tim. Let it not cumber your better remembrance.—Come, bring in all together.

[*The Banquet brought in.*

2 Lord. All covered dishes!

1 Lord. Royal cheer, I warrant you.

3 Lord. Doubt not that, if money and the season can yield it.

1 Lord. How do you? what's the news?

3 Lord. Alcibiades is banished; hear you of it?

1 & 2 Lord. Alcibiades banished!

3 Lord. 'Tis so, be sure of it.

1 Lord. How! how!

2 Lord. I pray you, upon what?

Tim. My worthy friends, will you draw near?

3 Lord. I'll tell you more anon. Here's a noble feast toward.

2 Lord. This is the old man still.

3 Lord. Will't hold? will't hold?

2 Lord. It does: but time will—and so—

3 Lord. I do conceive.

Tim. Each man to his stool, with that spur as he would to the lip of his mistress: your diet shall be in all places alike. Make not a city feast of it, to let the meat cool ere we can agree upon the first place: sit, sit. The gods require our thanks.—

You great benefactors, sprinkle our society with thankfulness. For your own gifts, make yourselves praised; but reserve still to give, lest your deities be despised. Lend to each man enough, that one need not lend to another; for, were your godheads to borrow of men, men would forsake the gods. Make the meat be beloved, more than the man that gives it. Let no assembly of twenty be without a score of villains: if there sit twelve women at the table, let a dozen of them be—as they are.—The rest of your fees,[a] *O gods,—the senators of Athens, together with the common lag*[b] *of people,—what is amiss in them, you gods make*

[a] *The rest of your* fees,—] Warburton proposed *foes;* but Capell explained "The rest of your *fees*" to mean, "forfeits due to your vengeance."

[b] Lag—] So Rowe. The old text has "*legge,*" for which Mr. Collier's annotator substitutes "*tag.*"

suitable for destruction. For these my present friends,—as they are to me nothing, so in nothing bless them, and to nothing are they welcome.

Uncover, dogs, and lap.
[*The dishes, uncovered, are full of warm water.*
SOME SPEAK. What does his lordship mean?
SOME OTHER. I know not.
TIM. May you a better feast never behold,
You knot of mouth-friends! smoke and luke-warm water
Is your perfection. This is Timon's last;
Who, stuck and spangled with your* flatteries,
Washes it off, and sprinkles in your faces
[*Throwing water in their faces.*
Your reeking villainy. Live loath'd, and long,
Most smiling, smooth, detested parasites,
Courteous destroyers, affable wolves, meek bears;
You fools of fortune, trencher-friends, time's flies,
Cap-and-knee slaves, vapours, and minute-jacks!
Of man and beast the infinite malady
Crust you quite o'er!—What, dost thou go?
Soft, take thy physic first—thou too,—and thou;—
[*Throws the dishes at them, and drives them out.*
Stay, I will lend thee money, borrow none.—
What, all in motion? Henceforth be no feast,
Whereat a villain's not a welcome guest.
Burn, house! sink, Athens! henceforth hated be
Of Timon, man and all humanity! (1) [*Exit.*

Re-enter the Lords, *with other* Lords *and* Senators.

1 LORD. How now, my lords!
2 LORD. Know you the quality of lord Timon's fury?
3 LORD. Push! did you see my cap?
4 LORD. I have lost my gown.
3 LORD. He's but a mad lord, and nought but humour sways him. He gave me a jewel the other day, and now he has beat it out of my hat:—did you see my jewel?
4 LORD. Did you see my cap?
2 LORD. Here 'tis.
4 LORD. Here lies my gown.
1 LORD. Let's make no stay.
2 LORD. Lord Timon's mad.
3 LORD. I feel't upon my bones.
4 LORD. One day he gives us diamonds, next day stones.[a] (2) [*Exeunt.*

(*) Old text, *you with.*

[a] *One day he gives us diamonds, next day* stones.] It has been inferred from the mention of *stones* in this line that Shakespeare was not unacquainted with the old Academic drama noticed in the Introduction, where "painted stones" form part of the banquet; but the traces of a feebler hand than his are so evident and so frequent in the present play, that we think, with Mr. Knight, the dialogue which concludes this act was probably a portion of the old piece, which, recast and improved by Shakespeare, forms the tragedy before us. When, in remodelling the stage business, he caused the feast to consist of warm water in lieu of stones, he perhaps neglected to cancel the line above.

ACT IV.

SCENE I.—*Without the Walls of* Athens.

Enter TIMON.

TIM. Let me look back upon thee. O thou wall,
That girdlest(*) in those wolves, dive in the earth,
And fence not Athens! Matrons, turn incontinent!
Obedience fail in children! slaves and fools,
Pluck the grave wrinkled senate from the bench,
And minister in their steads! to general filths
Convert[a] o'the instant, green virginity!
Do't in your parents' eyes! bankrupts, hold fast;
Rather than render back, out with your knives,
And cut your trusters' throats! bound servants, steal!
Large-handed robbers your grave masters are,
And pill by law! maid, to thy master's bed;—
Thy mistress is o' the brothel! son(*) of sixteen,
Pluck the lin'd crutch from thy old limping sire,
With it beat out his brains! piety, and fear,
Religion to the gods, peace, justice, truth,
Domestic awe, night-rest, and neighbourhood,
Instruction, manners, mysteries, and trades,
Degrees, observances, customs, and laws,
Decline to your confounding contraries,
And yet[b] confusion live!—Plagues, incident to men,
Your potent and infectious fevers heap
On Athens, ripe for stroke! thou cold sciatica,

(*) Old text, *girdles*.

(*) First folio, *Some*.

[a] Convert *o' the instant, green virginity!*] That is, *turn* yourself, green virginity, into, &c.

[b] *And* yet *confusion live!*] So the old text. The usual modern reading is,—"And *let* confusion live!" but *yet* has here the sense we have shown it to bear in many other passages, of *now*, and any change detracts from the emphasis and grandeur of the climax.

Cripple our senators, that their limbs may halt
As lamely as their manners! lust and liberty
Creep in the minds and marrows of our youth,
That 'gainst the stream of virtue they may strive,
And drown themselves in riot! itches, blains,
Sow all the Athenian bosoms, and their crop
Be general leprosy! breath infect breath;
That their society, as their friendship, may
Be merely poison! Nothing I'll bear from thee,
But nakedness, thou détestable town!
Take thou that too, with multiplying bans!
Timon will to the woods; where he shall find
The unkindest beast more kinder than mankind.
The gods confound (hear me, you good gods all,)
The Athenians both within and out that wall!
And grant, as Timon grows, his hate may grow
To the whole race of mankind, high and low!
Amen. [*Exit.*

SCENE II.—Athens. *A Room in* Timon's *House.*

Enter FLAVIUS, *with two or three* Servants.

1 SERV. Hear you, master steward, where's our master?
Are we undone? cast off? nothing remaining?
FLAV. Alack, my fellows, what should I say to you?
Let me be recorded by the righteous gods,
I am as poor as you.
1 SERV. Such a house broke!
So noble a master fall'n! All gone! and not
One friend to take his fortune by the arm,
And go along with him!
2 SERV. As we do turn our backs
From[a] our companion thrown into his grave,
So his familiars to his buried fortunes

---

[a] *As we do turn our backs*
From *our companion thrown into his grave,*
So his familiars to *his buried fortunes*
Slink all away;]

Mason proposed, with reason, that *from* and *to* in this passage should change places.

Slink all away; leave their false vows with him,
Like empty purses pick'd: and his poor self,
A dedicated beggar to the air,
With his disease of all-shunn'd poverty,
Walks, like contempt, alone.—More of our fellows.

Enter other Servants.

FLAV. All broken implements of a ruin'd house.
3 SERV. Yet do our hearts wear Timon's livery,
That see I by our faces; we are fellows still,
Serving alike in sorrow: leak'd is our bark;
And we, poor mates, stand on the dying deck,
Hearing the surges threat: we must all part
Into this sea of air.
FLAV. Good fellows all,
The latest of my wealth I'll share amongst you.
Wherever we shall meet, for Timon's sake,
Let's yet be fellows; let's shake our heads, and say,
As 'twere a knell unto our master's fortunes,
We have seen better days. Let each take some;
[*Giving them money.*
Nay, put out all your hands. Not one word more:
Thus part we rich in sorrow, parting poor.
[*Servants embrace, and part several ways.*
O, the fierce wretchedness that glory brings us!
Who would not wish to be from wealth exempt,
Since riches point to misery and contempt?
Who'd be so mock'd with glory? or so[a] live
But in a dream of friendship?
To have his pomp, and all what state compounds,[b]
But only painted, like his varnish'd friends?
Poor honest lord, brought low by his own heart;
Undone by goodness! Strange, unusual blood,[c]
When man's worst sin is, he does too much good!
Who, then, dares to be half so kind again?
For bounty, that makes gods, does still mar men.
My dearest lord,—bless'd, to be most accurs'd,
Rich, only to be wretched;—thy great fortunes
Are made thy chief afflictions. Alas, kind lord!
He's flung in rage from this ingrateful seat
Of monstrous friends:
Nor has he with him to supply his life,
Or that which can command it.
I'll follow, and inquire him out:
I'll ever serve his mind with my best will;
Whilst I have gold, I'll be his steward still. [*Exit.*

SCENE III.—*The Woods.*

Enter TIMON, *with a spade.*

TIM. O blessed breeding sun, draw from the earth
Rotten humidity; below thy sister's orb
Infect the air! Twinn'd brothers of one womb,—
Whose procreation, residence, and birth,
Scarce is dividant,—touch them with several fortunes;
The greater scorns the lesser: not nature,
To whom all sores lay siege, can bear great fortune,
But by contempt of nature.
Raise me this beggar, and demit[d] that lord;
The senator* shall bear contempt hereditary,
The beggar native honour.
It is the pasture lards the rother's[e] sides,
The want that makes him lean.† Who dares, who dares,
In purity of manhood stand upright,
And say, *This man's a flatterer?* if one be,
So are they all; for every grise of fortune
Is smooth'd[f] by that below: the learned pate
Ducks to the golden fool: all is oblique;‡
There's nothing level in our cursed natures,
But direct villainy. Therefore, be abhorr'd
All feasts, societies, and throngs of men!
His semblable, yea, himself, Timon disdains:
Destruction fang mankind!—Earth, yield me roots!
[*Digging.*
Who seeks for better of thee, sauce his palate
With thy most operant poison!—What is here?
Gold? yellow, glittering, precious gold? No, gods,
I am no idle[g] votarist. Roots, you clear heavens!
Thus much of this will make black, white; foul, fair;
Wrong, right; base, noble; old, young; coward, valiant.
Ha, you gods! why this? what this, you gods? why this
Will lug your priests and servants from your sides;
Pluck stout[h] men's pillows from below their heads:
This yellow slave
Will knit and break religions; bless the accurs'd;
Make the hoar leprosy ador'd; place thieves,
And give them title, knee, and approbation,

[a] *Or* so *live*—] The old text has,—"or *to* live," which is unintelligible. The slight change of *so* for *to* occurred to us many years ago, and we are glad to find it recently proposed by Mr. Grant White, in his entertaining and suggestive book, called "Shakespeare's Scholar," &c., p. 393.

[b] *And all what state* compounds,—] Mr. Collier's annotator reads,—"All state *comprehends.*"

[c] *Strange, unusual* blood,—] *Blood* is here supposed to signify *propensity* or *disposition;* but we suspect it to be one of several misprints by which this speech is depraved.

[d] *Raise me this beggar, and* demit *that lord;*] The old text has—"deny't that, lord," which, notwithstanding Mr. Dyce pronounces it "unquestionably right," we believe to be certainly wrong, and a mere misprint for *demit*, of old spelt *demyt*, from the Latin *demitto*, to depress or cast down.

[e] *It is the pasture lards the* rother's *sides,*—] *Rother* is an emendation by Mr. Singer; the first folio reading,—

"It is the Pastour Lards, the *Brothers* sides."

[f] *Is* smooth'd *by that below:*] After all that has been written upon this passage, the sense of *smooth'd* here remains to be explained. It means, *fawned on, beslavered,* &c.

[g] *I am no* idle *votarist.*] Mr. Collier's annotator reads, "*idol* votarist;" but *idle* here, as in "Hamlet," Act III. Sc. 3, and in other places, means *mad-brained, demented.*

[h] *Pluck* stout *men's pillows from below their heads:*] Hanmer was surely right in substituting *sick* for stout: the allusion is to an atrocious practice attributed to nurses of sometimes accelerating the dissolution of their patients by drawing away the pillows from beneath their heads.

(*) Old text, *Senators.* (†) First folio, *leave.* (‡) First folio, *All's obliquie.*

With senators on the bench: this is it,
That makes the wappen'd widow wed again;
She, whom the spital-house, and ulcerous sores
Would cast the gorge at, this embalms and spices
To the April day again. Come, damned earth,
Thou common whore of mankind, that putt'st odds
Among the rout of nations, I will make thee
Do thy right nature.—[*March afar off.*]—Ha! a drum!—Thou'rt quick,
But yet I'll bury thee: thou'lt go, strong thief,
When gouty keepers of thee cannot stand:—
Nay, stay thou out for earnest.
[*Laying aside some gold.*

Enter ALCIBIADES, *with drum and fife, in warlike manner;* PHRYNIA *and* TIMANDRA.

ALCIB. What art thou there? speak.
TIM. A beast, as thou art. The canker gnaw thy heart,
For showing me again the eyes of man!
ALCIB. What is thy name? Is man so hateful to thee,
That art thyself a man?
TIM. I am *misanthropos*, and hate mankind.(1)
For thy part, I do wish thou wert a dog,
That I might love thee something.
ALCIB. I know thee well;
But in thy fortunes am unlearn'd and strange.
TIM. I know thee too; and more than that I know thee,
I not desire to know. Follow thy drum;
With man's blood paint the ground, gules, gules:
Religious canons, civil laws are cruel;
Then what should war be? This fell whore of thine
Hath in her more destruction than thy sword,
For all her cherubin look.
PHRY. Thy lips rot off!
TIM. I will not[a] kiss thee; then the rot returns
To thine own lips again.
ALCIB. How came the noble Timon to this change?
TIM. As the moon does, by wanting light to give:
But then renew I could not, like the moon;
There were no suns to borrow of.
ALCIB. Noble Timon, what friendship may I do thee?
TIM. None, but to maintain my opinion.
ALCIB. What is it, Timon?
TIM. Promise me friendship, but perform none: if thou wilt not[b] promise, the gods plague thee, for thou art a man! if thou dost perform, confound thee, for thou art a man!

ALCIB. I have heard in some sort of thy miseries.
TIM. Thou saw'st them, when I had prosperity.
ALCIB. I see them now; then was a blessed time.
TIM. As thine is now, held with a brace of harlots.
TIMAN. Is this the Athenian minion, whom the world
Voic'd so regardfully?
TIM. Art thou Timandra?
TIMAN. Yes.
TIM. Be a whore still: they love thee not that use thee;
Give them diseases, leaving with thee their lust.
Make use of thy salt hours: season the slaves
For tubs and baths; bring down rose-cheeked youth
To the tub-fast, and the diet.
TIMAN. Hang thee, monster!
ALCIB. Pardon him, sweet Timandra; for his wits
Are drown'd and lost in his calamities.—
I have but little gold of late, brave Timon,
The want whereof doth daily make revolt
In my penurious band: I have heard, and griev'd,
How cursed Athens, mindless of thy worth,
Forgetting thy great deeds, when neighbour states,
But for thy sword and fortune, trod upon them,—
TIM. I pr'ythee beat thy drum, and get thee gone.
ALCIB. I am thy friend, and pity thee, dear Timon.
TIM. How dost thou pity him whom thou dost trouble?
I had rather be alone.
ALCIB. Why, fare thee well:
Here's some gold for thee.
TIM. Keep it, I cannot eat it.
ALCIB. When I have laid proud Athens on a heap,—
TIM. Warr'st thou 'gainst Athens?
ALCIB. Ay, Timon, and have cause.
TIM. The gods confound them all in thy conquest;
And thee after, when thou hast conquered!
ALCIB. Why me, Timon?
TIM. That, by killing of villains,
Thou wast born to conquer my country.
Put up thy gold; go on,—here's gold,—go on;
Be as a planetary plague, when Jove
Will o'er some high-vic'd city hang his poison
In the sick air: let not thy sword skip one:
Pity not honour'd age for his white beard,—
He is an usurer: strike me the counterfeit matron:—
It is her habit only that is honest,
Herself's a bawd: let not the virgin's cheek

[a] *I will* not *kiss thee;*] We should perhaps read, "I will *but* kiss thee."

[b] *If thou wilt* not *promise,*—] Here again *not* appears to be a misprint for *but*.

Make soft thy trenchant sword; for those milk paps,
That through the window-bars* bore at men's eyes,[a]
Are not within the leaf of pity writ,
But set them down horrible traitors: spare not the babe,
Whose dimpled smiles from fools exhaust their mercy;
Think it a bastard, whom the oracle
Hath doubtfully pronounc'd thy† throat shall cut,
And mince it sans remorse: swear against objects;
Put armour on thine ears and on thine eyes,
Whose proof, nor yells of mothers, maids, nor babes,
Nor sight of priests in holy vestments bleeding,
Shall pierce a jot. There's gold to pay thy soldiers:
Make large confusion; and, thy fury spent,
Confounded be thyself! Speak not, be gone.

ALCIB. Hast thou gold yet? I'll take the gold thou giv'st me,
Not all thy counsel.

TIM. Dost thou, or dost thou not, heaven's curse upon thee!

PHRY. & TIMAN. Give us some gold, good Timon: hast thou more?

TIM. Enough to make a whore forswear her trade,
And to make whores, a bawd. Hold up, you sluts,
Your aprons mountant: you are not oathable,—
Although I know you'll swear, terribly swear,
Into strong shudders and to heavenly agues,
The immortal gods that hear you,—spare your oaths,
I'll trust to your conditions: be whores still;
And he whose pious breath seeks to convert you,
Be strong in whore, allure him, burn him up;
Let your close[b] fire predominate his smoke
And be no turncoats: yet may your pains, six months,
Be quite contrary: and thatch your poor thin roofs
With burdens of the dead;—some that were hang'd,
No matter:—wear them, betray with them: whore still;
Paint till a horse may mire upon your face:
A pox of wrinkles!

PHRY. & TIMAN. Well, more gold;—what then?
Believe't, that we'll do anything for gold.

TIM. Consumptions sow
In hollow bones of man; strike their sharp shins,
And mar men's spurring. Crack the lawyer's voice,
That he may never more false title plead,
Nor sound his quillets shrilly: hoar the flamen,[c]
That scolds* against the quality of flesh,
And not believes himself: down with the nose,
Down with it flat; take the bridge quite away
Of him that, his particular to foresee,
Smells from the general weal: make curl'd-pate ruffians bald;
And let the unscarr'd braggarts of the war
Derive some pain from you: plague all;
That your activity may defeat and quell
The source of all erection.—There's more gold:—
Do you damn others, and let this damn you,
And ditches grave you all!

PHRY. & TIMAN. More counsel with more money, bounteous Timon.

TIM. More whore, more mischief first; I have given you earnest.

ALCIB. Strike up the drum, towards Athens! Farewell, Timon;
If I thrive well, I'll visit thee again.

TIM. If I hope well, I'll never see thee more.

ALCIB. I never did thee harm.

TIM. Yes, thou spok'st well of me.

ALCIB. Call'st thou that harm?

TIM. Men daily find it. Get thee away,
And take thy beagles with thee.

ALCIB. We but offend him.—
Strike!

[*Drum beats. Exeunt* ALCIBIADES, PHRYNIA, *and* TIMANDRA.

TIM. That nature, being sick of man's unkindness,
Should yet be hungry!—Common mother, thou,—(2) [*Digging.*
Whose womb unmeasurable, and infinite breast,
Teems, and feeds all; whose self-same mettle,
Whereof thy proud child, arrogant man, is puff'd,
Engenders the black toad and adder blue,
The gilded newt and eyeless venom'd worm,
With all the abhorred births below crisp heaven
Whereon Hyperion's quick'ning fire doth shine,—
Yield him, who all thy† human sons doth‡ hate,
From forth thy plenteous bosom, one poor root!
Ensear thy fertile and conceptious womb,

(*) Old text, *Barne.* (†) Old text, *the.*

(*) Old text, *scold'st.* (†) Old text, *the.* (‡) Old text, *do.*

[a] ——For those milk-paps,
That through the window-bars bore at men's eyes,—]

Johnson interprets this, "The virgin that shows her bosom through the lattice of her chamber!" and although we have two pages of commentary on the subject in the "Variorum," no writer there has exposed the absurdity of this explanation. The "window-bars" in question meant the cross-bars or lattice-work worn, as we see it in the Swiss women's dress, across the breasts. In modern times, these bars have always a bodice of satin, muslin, or other material beneath them; at one period they crossed the nude bosom.

[b] *Let your* close *fire*—] *Close*, of old, among other significations, meant *wanton*, *lascivious*, &c., of which none of the commentators seem to have been aware, and of which even Gifford was ignorant; vide Vol. II. p. 300, of Ben Jonson's Works on the passage:—"I am to say to you these ladies are not of that *close* and open behaviour as haply you may suspend."

[c] Hoar the flamen,—] Infect with the *hoar*, or white, *leprosy*, the priest, &c.

Let it no more bring out ingrateful man!
Go great with tigers, dragons, wolves, and bears;
Teem with new monsters, whom thy upward face
Hath to the marbled mansion all above
Never presented!—O, a root,—dear thanks!
Dry up thy marrows, vines, and plough-torn leas;
Whereof ingrateful man, with liquorish draughts,
And morsels unctuous, greases his pure mind,
That from it all consideration slips!—
More man? Plague! plague!

Enter APEMANTUS.

APEM. I was directed hither: men report,
Thou dost affect my manners, and dost use them.

TIM. 'T is then, because thou dost not keep a dog
Whom I would imitate: consumption catch thee!

APEM. This is in thee a nature but infected;
A poor unmanly melancholy, sprung
From change of fortune.* Why this spade? this place?
This slave-like habit? and these looks of care?
Thy flatterers yet wear silk, drink wine, lie soft;
Hug their diseas'd perfumes, and have forgot
That ever Timon was. Shame not these woods,
By putting on the cunning of a carper.
Be thou a flatterer now, and seek to thrive
By that which has undone thee: hinge thy knee,
And let his very breath, whom thou 'lt observe,
Blow off thy cap: praise his most vicious strain,
And call it excellent: thou wast told thus;
Thou gav'st thine ears, (like tapsters that bad[a] welcome,)
To knaves and all approachers: 'tis most just
That thou turn rascal; hadst thou wealth again,
Rascals should have't. Do not assume my likeness.

TIM. Were I like thee, I'd throw away myself.

APEM. Thou hast cast away thyself, being like thyself
A madman so long, now a fool: what, think'st
That the bleak air, thy boisterous chamberlain,
Will put thy shirt on warm? Will these moss'd[b] trees,
That have outliv'd the eagle, page thy heels,
And skip when thou point'st out? Will the cold brook,
Candied with ice, caudle thy morning taste,
To cure thy o'er-night's surfeit? call the creatures,
Whose naked natures live in all the spite
Of wreakful heaven; whose bare unhoused trunks,
To the conflicting elements expos'd,
Answer mere nature, bid them flatter thee;
O! thou shalt find—

TIM. A fool of thee: depart.

APEM. I love thee better now than e'er I did.

TIM. I hate thee worse.

APEM. Why?

TIM. Thou flatterest misery.

APEM. I flatter not, but say thou art a caitiff.

TIM. Why dost thou seek me out?

APEM. To vex thee.

TIM. Always a villain's office, or a fool's.
Dost please thyself in't?

APEM. Ay.

TIM. What! a knave too?

APEM. If thou didst put this sour-cold habit on
To castigate thy pride, 't were well: but thou
Dost it enforcedly; thou 'dst courtier be again,
Wert thou not beggar. Willing misery
Outlives incertain pomp, is crown'd before:
The one is filling still, never complete;
The other, at high wish: best state, contentless,
Hath a distracted and most wretched being,
Worse than the worst, content.
Thou shouldst desire to die, being miserable.

TIM. Not by his breath that is more miserable.
Thou art a slave, whom Fortune's tender arm
With favour never clasp'd, but bred a dog.
Hadst thou, like us from our first swath, proceeded
The sweet degrees that this brief world affords,
To such as may the passive drugs[c] of it
Freely command, thou wouldst have plung'd thyself
In general riot; melted down thy youth
In different beds of lust; and never learn'd
The icy precepts of respect, but follow'd
The sugar'd game before thee. But myself,
Who had the world as my confectionary;
The mouths, the tongues, the eyes, and hearts of men
At duty, more than I could frame employment;
That numberless upon me stuck, as leaves
Do on the oak, have with one winter's brush
Fell from their boughs, and left me open, bare
For every storm that blows;—I, to bear this,
That never knew but better, is some burden:
Thy nature did commence in sufferance, time
Hath made thee hard in't. Why shouldst thou hate men?
They never flatter'd thee: what hast thou given?

(*) Old text, *future*.

a *Like tapsters that* bad *welcome*,—] Thus the first folio, which, from not perceiving that *bad* meant the *bad* of society, *bad people*, later editors have changed to,—"like tapsters that *bid* welcome," &c.

b *Will these* moss'd *trees*,—] The old text has, *moyst* trees. The emendation, which was made by Hanmer, is strengthened by the line in, "As you Like It," Act IV. Sc. 3:—

"Under an oak, whose boughs were *moss'd* with age."

c *Passive* drugs—] That is, *drudges*. Mr. Collier's annotator gives, "passive *dugs*."

If thou wilt curse,—thy father, that poor rag,[a]
Must be thy subject; who, in spite, put stuff
To some she-beggar, and compounded thee
Poor rogue hereditary. Hence! be gone!—
If thou hadst not been born the worst of men,
Thou hadst been a knave and flatterer.

APEM. Art thou proud yet?

TIM. Ay, that I am not thee.

APEM. I, that I was no prodigal.

TIM. I, that I am one now;
Were all the wealth I have shut up in thee,
I'd give thee leave to hang it. Get thee gone.—
That the whole life of Athens were in this!
Thus would I eat it. [*Eating a root.*

APEM. Here; I will mend thy feast.
[*Offering him something.*

TIM. First mend my * company, take away thyself.

APEM. So I shall mend mine own, by the lack of thine.

TIM. 'T is not well mended so, it is but botch'd;
If not, I would it were.

APEM. What wouldst thou have to Athens?

TIM. Thee thither in a whirlwind. If thou wilt,
Tell them there I have gold; look, so I have.

APEM. Here is no use for gold.

TIM. The best, and truest:
For here it sleeps, and does no hired harm.

APEM. Where liest o' nights, Timon?

TIM. Under that's above me.
Where feed'st thou o' days, Apemantus?

APEM. Where my stomach finds meat; or, rather, where I eat it.

TIM. Would poison were obedient, and knew my mind!

APEM. Where wouldst thou send it?

TIM. To sauce thy dishes.

APEM. The middle of humanity thou never knewest, but the extremity of both ends. When thou wast in thy gilt and thy perfume, they mocked thee for too much curiosity;[b] in thy rags thou knowest none, but art despised for the contrary. There's a medlar for thee, eat it.

TIM. On what I hate I feed not.

APEM. Dost hate a medlar?

TIM. Ay, though[c] it look like thee.

APEM. An thou hadst hated meddlers sooner, thou shouldst have loved thyself better now. What man didst thou ever know unthrift, that was beloved after his means?

TIM. Who, without those means thou talkest of, didst thou ever know beloved?

APEM. Myself.

TIM. I understand thee; thou hadst some means to keep a dog.

APEM. What things in the world canst thou nearest compare to thy flatterers?

TIM. Women nearest; but men, men are the things themselves. What wouldst thou do with the world, Apemantus, if it lay in thy power?

APEM. Give it the beasts, to be rid of the men.

TIM. Wouldst thou have thyself fall in the confusion of men, and remain a beast with the beasts?

APEM. Ay, Timon.

TIM. A beastly ambition, which the gods grant thee to attain to! If thou wert the lion, the fox would beguile thee: if thou wert the lamb, the fox would eat thee: if thou wert the fox, the lion would suspect thee, when, peradventure, thou wert accused by the ass: if thou wert the ass, thy dulness would torment thee; and still thou livedst but as a breakfast to the wolf: if thou wert the wolf, thy greediness would afflict thee, and oft thou shouldst hazard thy life for thy dinner: wert thou the unicorn, pride and wrath would confound thee,(3) and make thine own self the conquest of thy fury: wert thou a bear, thou wouldst be killed by the horse; wert thou a horse, thou wouldst be seized by the leopard; wert thou a leopard, thou wert german to the lion, and the spots of thy kindred were jurors on thy life: all thy safety were remotion, and thy defence, absence. What beast couldst thou be, that were not subject to a beast? and what a beast art thou already, that seest not thy loss in transformation?

APEM. If thou couldst please me with speaking to me, thou mightst have hit upon it here: the commonwealth of Athens is become a forest of beasts.

TIM. How has the ass broke the wall, that thou art out of the city?

APEM. Yonder comes a poet and a painter: the plague of company light upon thee! I will fear to catch it, and give way: when I know not what else to do, I'll see thee again.

(*) Old copies, *thy*.

[a] *That poor* rag.—] Mr. Singer's corrected second folio reads, "poor *rogue*," a substitution also proposed by Johnson; but, as Mr. Dyce remarks, "*rag* occurs elsewhere in our author as a term of contempt; and it was formerly a very common one."

[b] Curiosity;] *Finical refinement.*

[c] *Ay,* though *it look like thee.*] Johnson observes on this speech,—"Timon here supposes that an objection against hatred, which through the whole tenor of the conversation appears an argument for it. One would have expected him to have answered:—

'*Yes*, for it looks like thee.'"

The remark is just, if we accept the word *though* in its ordinary sense; but in this place and elsewhere it appears to import, *if* or *since*. Compare,—

"My lips are no common, *though* several they be."
Love's Labour's Lost, Act II. Sc. 1.

And,—

"No marvel, *though* you bite so sharp at reasons,
You are so empty of them."
Troilus and Cressida, Act II. Sc. 1.

TIM. When there is nothing living but thee, thou shalt be welcome. I had rather be a beggar's dog, than Apemantus.

APEM. Thou art the cap of all the fools alive.

TIM. Would thou wert clean enough to spit upon!

APEM. A plague on thee, thou art too bad to curse!

TIM. All villains that do stand by thee are pure.

APEM. There is no leprosy but what thou speak'st.

TIM. If I name thee.—
I'll beat thee, but I should infect my hands.

APEM. I would my tongue could rot them off!

TIM. Away, thou issue of a mangy dog!

Choler does kill me that thou art alive;
I swoon to see thee.
APEM. Would thou wouldst burst!
TIM. Away,
Thou tedious rogue! I am sorry I shall lose
A stone by thee. [*Throws a stone at him.*
APEM. Beast!
TIM. Slave!
APEM. Toad!
TIM. Rogue, rogue, rogue!
[APEMANTUS *retreats backward, as going.*
I am sick of this false world; and will love nought
But even the mere necessities upon it.
Then, Timon, presently prepare thy grave;
Lie where the light foam of the sea may beat
Thy grave-stone daily: make thine epitaph,
That death in me at others' lives may laugh.
O thou sweet king-killer, and dear divorce
[*Looking on the gold.*
'Twixt natural son and sire!* thou bright defiler
Of Hymen's purest bed! thou valiant Mars!
Thou ever young, fresh, lov'd, and delicate wooer,
Whose blush doth thaw the consecrated snow
That lies on Dian's lap! thou visible god,
That solder'st close impossibilities,
And mak'st them kiss! that speak'st with every tongue,
To every purpose! O thou touch of hearts!
Think, thy slave man rebels; and by thy virtue
Set them into confounding odds, that beasts
May have the world in empire!
APEM. Would 'twere so!—
But not till I am dead.—I'll say thou'st gold:
Thou wilt be throng'd to shortly.
TIM. Throng'd to!
APEM. Ay.
TIM. Thy back, I pr'ythee.
APEM. Live, and love thy misery!
TIM. Long live so, and so die!—I am quit.—
[*Exit* APEMANTUS.
More things like men?—Eat, Timon, and abhor them.[a]

Enter Banditti.

1 BAN. Where should he have this gold? It is some poor fragment, some slender ort of his remainder: the mere want of gold, and the falling-from of his friends, drove him into this melancholy.

2 BAN. It is noised he hath a mass of treasure.

3 BAN. Let us make the assay upon him; if he care not for't, he will supply us easily; if he covetously reserve it, how shall's get it?

2 BAN. True; for he bears it not about him, 'tis hid.

1 BAN. Is not this he?
BANDITTI. Where?
2 BAN. 'T is his description.
3 BAN. He; I know him.
BANDITTI. Save thee, Timon.
TIM. Now, thieves!
BANDITTI. Soldiers, not thieves.
TIM. Both too; and women's sons.
BANDITTI. We are not thieves, but men that much do want.
TIM. Your greatest want is, you want much of meat. [roots;
Why should you want? Behold, the earth hath
Within this mile break forth a hundred springs;
The oaks bear mast, the briars scarlet hips;
The bounteous housewife, Nature, on each bush
Lays her full mess before you. Want! why want?
1 BAN. We cannot live on grass, on berries, water,
As beasts, and birds, and fishes.
TIM. Nor on the beasts themselves, the birds, and fishes;
You must eat men. Yet thanks I must you con,
That you are thieves profess'd; that you work not
In holier shapes: for there is boundless theft
In limited professions. Rascal thieves,
Here's gold: go, suck the subtle blood o' the grape,
Till the high fever seethe your blood to froth,
And so 'scape hanging: trust not the physician;
His antidotes are poison, and he slays
More* than you rob: take wealth and lives together;
Do villainy,† do, since you protest to do't,
Like workmen. I'll example you with thievery:
The sun's a thief, and with his great attraction
Robs the vast sea: the moon's an arrant thief,
And her pale fire she snatches from the sun:
The sea's a thief, whose liquid surge resolves
The moon into salt tears: the earth's a thief,
That feeds and breeds by a composture stol'n
From general excrement: each thing's a thief;(4)
The laws, your curb and whip, in their rough power
Have uncheck'd theft. Love not yourselves; away;
Rob one another;—there's more gold:—cut throats;
All that you meet are thieves: to Athens go,
Break open shops; nothing can you steal,
But thieves do lose it: steal not[b] less, for this
I give you; and gold confound you howsoe'er!
Amen. [TIMON *retires to his cave.*

(*) Old text, *Sunne and fire.*

(*) Old text, *Moe.* (†) Old text, *Villaine.*

[a] More things like men, &c.] In the old copies, this line, which runs,—
"*Mo* things like men,
Eate Timon, and abhorre *then*,"
is assigned to Apemantus.

[b] *Steal* not *less*,—] *Not*, which is omitted in the old copies, was first supplied by Rowe.

3 Ban. H'as almost charmed me from my profession, by persuading me to it.

1 Ban. 'Tis in the malice of mankind that he thus advises us; not to have us thrive in our mystery.

2 Ban. I'll believe him as an enemy, and give over my trade.

1 Ban. Let us first see peace in Athens: there is no time so miserable but a man may be true.[a]

[*Exeunt* Banditti.

Enter Flavius.

Flav. O you gods!
Is yond despis'd and ruinous man my lord?
Full of decay and failing? O monument
And wonder of good deeds evilly bestow'd!
What an alteration of honour
Has desperate want made!
What viler thing upon the earth, than friends
Who can bring noblest minds to basest ends!
How rarely does it meet with this time's guise,
When man was wish'd to love his enemies:
Grant I may ever love, and rather woo
Those that would mischief me, than those that do!
H'as caught me in his eye: I will present
My honest grief unto him; and, as my lord,
Still serve him with my life.—My dearest master!

[a] True.] That is, *honest.*

Timon *comes forward from his cave.*

Tim. Away! what art thou?
Flav. Have you forgot me, sir?
Tim. Why dost ask that? I have forgot all men;
Then, if thou grant'st* thou'rt a man, I have forgot thee.
Flav. An honest poor servant of yours.
Tim. Then I know thee not:
I ne'er had honest man about me, I;
All I kept were knaves, to serve in meat to villains.
Flav. The gods are witness,
Ne'er did poor steward wear a truer grief
For his undone lord, than mine eyes for you.
Tim. What, dost thou weep?—Come nearer then;—I love thee,
Because thou art a woman, and disclaim'st
Flinty mankind; whose eyes do never give,
But thorough lust and laughter. Pity's sleeping:
Strange times, that weep with laughing, not with weeping!
Flav. I beg of you to know me, good my lord,
To accept my grief, and, whilst this poor wealth lasts,
To entertain me as your steward still.
Tim. Had I a steward
So true, so just, and now so comfortable?

(*) Old text, *grunt'st.*

It almost turns my dangerous nature wild.[a]
Let me behold thy face.—Surely, this man
Was born of woman.—
Forgive my general and exceptless rashness,
You perpetual-sober gods! I do proclaim
One honest man,—mistake me not,—but one;
No more, I pray,—and he's a steward.—
How fain would I have hated all mankind,
And thou redeem'st thyself: but all, save thee,
I fell with curses.
Methinks thou art more honest now than wise;
For, by oppressing and betraying me,
Thou mightst have sooner got another service:
For many so arrive at second masters,
Upon their first lord's neck. But tell me true,
(For I must ever doubt, though ne'er so sure,)
Is not thy kindness subtle, covetous,
If not a usuring kindness, and, as rich men deal gifts,
Expecting in return twenty for one?

FLAV. No, my most worthy master; in whose breast
Doubt and suspect, alas, are plac'd too late:
You should have fear'd false times, when you did feast:
Suspect still comes where an estate is least.
That which I show, heaven knows, is merely love,
Duty and zeal to your unmatched mind,
Care of your food and living: and, believe it,
My most honour'd lord,
For any benefit that points to me,
Either in hope or present, I'd exchange
For this one wish,—that you had power and wealth
To requite me, by making rich yourself.

TIM. Look thee, 'tis so!—Thou singly honest man,
Here, take:—the gods out of my misery
Have sent thee treasure. Go, live rich and happy;
But thus condition'd; thou shalt build from men;
Hate all, curse all: show charity to none;
But let the famish'd flesh slide from the bone,
Ere thou relieve the beggar: give to dogs
What thou deniest to men; let prisons swallow 'em,
Debts wither 'em to nothing: be men like blasted woods,
And may diseases lick up their false bloods!
And so, farewell, and thrive.

FLAV. O, let me stay,
And comfort you, my master.

TIM. If thou hat'st curses,
Stay not; fly, whilst thou'rt bless'd and free:
Ne'er see thou man, and let me ne'er see thee.

[*Exit* FLAVIUS. TIMON *retires into his cave.*

[a] Wild.] Hanmer and Warburton read *mild*, and the same word is suggested by Mr. Collier's annotator.

ACT V.

SCENE I.—*Before* Timon's *Cave.*

Enter Poet *and* Painter; Timon *behind, unseen by them.*

Pain. As I took note of the place, it cannot be far where he abides.

Poet. What's to be thought of him? Does the rumour hold for true, that he's so full of gold?

Pain. Certain: Alcibiades reports it; Phrynia and Timandra had gold of him: he likewise enriched poor straggling soldiers with great quantity: 'tis said he gave unto his steward a mighty sum.

Poet. Then this breaking of his has been but a try for his friends.

Pain. Nothing else; you shall see him a palm in Athens again, and flourish with the highest. Therefore 'tis not amiss we tender our loves to him, in this supposed distress of his: it will show honestly in us; and is very likely to load our purposes with what they travail for, if it be a just and true report that goes of his having.

Poet. What have you now to present unto him?

Pain. Nothing at this time but my visitation: only I will promise him an excellent piece.

Poet. I must serve him so too,—tell him of an intent that's coming toward him.

Pain. Good as the best. Promising is the very air o' the time; it opens the eyes of expectation: performance is ever the duller for his act; and, but in the plainer and simpler kind of people, the deed of saying[a] is quite out of use. To promise, is most courtly and fashionable: performance is a kind of will or testament, which argues a great sickness in his judgment that makes it.

TIM. Excellent workman! thou canst not paint a man so bad as is thyself.

POET. I am thinking what I shall say I have provided for him: it must be a personating of himself: a satire against the softness of prosperity, with a discovery of the infinite flatteries that follow youth and opulency.

TIM. Must thou needs stand for a villain in thine own work? wilt thou whip thine own faults in other men? Do so, I have gold for thee.

POET. Nay, let's seek him:
Then do we sin against our own estate,
When we may profit meet, and come too late.

PAIN. True;—
When the day serves, before black-corner'd[b] night,
Find what thou want'st by free and offer'd light.[c]
Come.

TIM. I'll meet you at the turn.—What a god's gold,
That he is worshipp'd in a baser temple
Than where swine feed!
'Tis thou that rigg'st the bark, and plough'st the foam;
Settlest admired reverence in a slave:
To thee be worship!* and thy saints for aye
Be crown'd with plagues, that thee alone obey!—
Fit I meet them. [*Advancing.*

POET. Hail, worthy Timon!

PAIN. Our late noble master!

TIM. Have I once liv'd to see two honest men?

POET. Sir,
Having often of your open bounty tasted,
Hearing you were retir'd, your friends fall'n off,
Whose thankless natures—O abhorred spirits!—
Not all the whips of heaven are large enough—
What! to you,
Whose star-like nobleness gave life and influence
To their whole being! I am rapt, and cannot cover
The monstrous bulk of this ingratitude
With any size of words.

TIM. Let it go naked, men may see't the better:
You that are honest, by being what you are,
Make them best seen and known.

PAIN. He and myself
Have travail'd in the great shower of your gifts,
And sweetly felt it.

TIM. Ay, you are honest men.†

PAIN. We are hither come to offer you our service.

TIM. Most honest men! Why, how shall I requite you?
Can you eat roots, and drink cold water? no.

BOTH. What we can do, we'll do, to do you service.

TIM. You're honest men: you've heard that I have gold;
I am sure, you have: speak truth: you're honest men.

PAIN. So it is said, my noble lord: but therefore
Came not my friend nor I.

TIM. Good honest men!—Thou draw'st a counterfeit
Best in all Athens: thou'rt, indeed, the best;
Thou counterfeit'st most lively.

PAIN. So, so, my lord.

TIM. Even so, sir, as I say.—And, for thy fiction, [*To the* Poet.
Why, thy verse swells with stuff so fine and smooth,
That thou art even natural in thine art.—
But, for all this, my honest-natur'd friends,
I must needs say you have a little fault:
Marry, 'tis not monstrous in you; neither wish I
You take much pains to mend.

BOTH. Beseech your honour,
To make it known to us.

TIM. You'll take it ill.

BOTH. Most thankfully, my lord.

TIM. Will you, indeed?

BOTH. Doubt it not, worthy lord.

TIM. There's ne'er a one of you but trusts a knave,
That mightily deceives you.

BOTH. Do we, my lord?

TIM. Ay, and you hear him cog, see him dissemble,
Know his gross patchery, love him, feed him,
Keep in your bosom: yet remain assur'd,
That he's a made-up villain.[d]

PAIN. I know none such, my lord.

POET. Nor I.

TIM. Look you, I love you well; I'll give you gold,
Rid me these villains from your companies:
Hang them or stab them, drown them in a draught,
Confound them by some course, and come to me,
I'll give you gold enough.

BOTH. Name them, my lord, let's know them.

TIM. You that way, and you this,—but two in company:—
Each man apart, all single and alone,

(*) Old text, *worshipt*. (†) First folio, *man*.

a The deed of saying—] In other words, the *performance of promise*.

b *Black*-corner'd night,—] For this strange expression, a correspondent of Steevens' proposed to read, "black-*cover'd* night." Mr. Dyce suggests "black-*curtain'd* night."

c When the day serves, &c.] This couplet should be assigned to the Poet, to whom it undoubtedly belongs.

d *A* made-up *villain.*] A *finished*, or *accomplished* villain.

Yet an arch-villain keeps him company.
If, where thou art, two villains shall not be,
[*To the* Painter.
Come not near him.—If thou wouldst not reside
[*To the* Poet.
But where one villain is, then him abandon.—
Hence! pack! there's gold, you came for gold, ye slaves:
You have done[a] work for me, there's payment: hence!
You are an alchemist, make gold of that:—
Out, rascal dogs!
[*Beats them out, and then retires into his cave.*

Enter FLAVIUS, *and Two* Senators.

FLAV. It is vain that you would speak with Timon;
For he is set so only to himself,
That nothing but himself, which looks like man,
Is friendly with him.
1 SEN. Bring us to his cave:
It is our part, and promise to the Athenians,
To speak with Timon.
2 SEN. At all times alike
Men are not still the same: 'twas time and griefs
That fram'd him thus: time, with his fairer hand,
Offering the fortunes of his former days,
The former man may make him. Bring us to him,
And chance* it as it may.
FLAV. Here is his cave.—
Peace and content be here![b] Lord Timon! Timon!
Look out, and speak to friends: the Athenians,
By two of their most reverend senate, greet thee:
Speak to them, noble Timon.

TIMON *comes from the cave.*

TIM. Thou sun, that comfort'st, burn!—Speak, and be hang'd:
For each true word, a blister! and each false
Be as a cauterizing† to the root o'the tongue,
Consuming it with speaking!
1 SEN. Worthy Timon,—
TIM. Of none but such as you, and you of Timon.
2 SEN. The senators of Athens greet thee, Timon.
TIM. I thank them; and would send them back the plague,
Could I but catch it for them.

---

[a] *You have* done *work for me,*—] So Malone: the folios read,—

"You have worke for me," &c.

(*) First folio, *chanc'd.* (†) First folio, *cantherizing.*

[b] Peace and content be here!] This speech would be more appropriate to one of the Senators.

1 SEN. O, forget
What we are sorry for ourselves in thee.
The senators, with one consent of love,
Entreat thee back to Athens; who have thought
On special dignities, which vacant lie
For thy best use and wearing.

2 SEN. They confess,
Toward thee, forgetfulness too general, gross:
Which now the public body,—which doth seldom
Play the recanter,—feeling in itself
A lack of Timon's aid, hath sense* withal
Of it own fall,[a] restraining aid to Timon;

[a] *Of* it *own* fall,—] We should perhaps read,—"Of it own *fault.*" Every editor for *it*, here and in other instances, silently substitutes *its*; but see note (3), p. 330, Vol. I.

(*) Old text, *since*.

And send forth us, to make their sorrow'd render,
Together with a recompense more fruitful
Than their offence can weigh down by the dram;
Ay, even such heaps and sums of love and wealth,
As shall to thee blot out what wrongs were theirs,
And write in thee the figures of their love,
Ever to read them thine.

TIM. You witch me in it;
Surprise me to the very brink of tears:
Lend me a fool's heart and a woman's eyes,
And I'll beweep these comforts, worthy senators.

1 SEN. Therefore, so please thee to return with us,
And of our Athens (thine and ours) to take
The captainship, thou shalt be met with thanks,
Allow'd with absolute power, and thy good name
Live with authority:—so soon we shall drive back
Of Alcibiades the approaches wild;
Who, like a boar too savage, doth root up
His country's peace.

2 SEN. And shakes his threat'ning sword
Against the walls of Athens.

1 SEN. Therefore, Timon,—

TIM. Well, sir, I will,—therefore, I will, sir,—thus,—
If Alcibiades kill my countrymen,
Let Alcibiades know this of Timon,
That Timon—cares not. But if he sack fair Athens,
And take our goodly aged men by the beards,
Giving our holy virgins to the stain
Of contumelious, beastly, mad-brain'd war;
Then, let him know,—and tell him Timon speaks it,
In pity of our aged and our youth,
I cannot choose but tell him, that—I care not,
And let him take't at worst; for their knives care not,
While you have throats to answer: for myself,
There's not a whittle in the unruly camp,
But I do prize it at my love, before

The reverend'st throat in Athens. So I leave you
To the protection of the prosperous gods,
As thieves to keepers.
FLAV. Stay not, all's in vain.
TIM. Why, I was writing of my epitaph;
It will be seen to-morrow; my long sickness
Of health and living, now begins to mend,
And nothing brings me all things. Go, live still;
Be Alcibiades your plague, you his,—
And last so long enough!
1 SEN. We speak in vain.
TIM. But yet I love my country, and am not
One that rejoices in the common wreck,
As common bruit doth put it.
1 SEN. That's well spoke.
TIM. Commend me to my loving countrymen,—
1 SEN. These words become your lips as they pass through them.
2 SEN. And enter in our ears like great triúmphers
In their applauding gates.
TIM. Commend me to them;
And tell them that, to ease them of their griefs,
Their fears of hostile strokes, their aches, losses,
Their pangs of love, with other incident throes
That nature's fragile vessel doth sustain
In life's uncertain voyage, I will some kindness do them,—
I'll teach them to prevent wild Alcibiades' wrath.
2 SEN. I like this well; he will return again.
TIM. I have a tree, which grows here in my close,
That mine own use invites me to cut down,
And shortly must I fell it; tell my friends,
Tell Athens, in the sequence of degree,
From high to low throughout, that whoso please
To stop affliction, let him take his haste,[a]
Come hither, ere my tree hath felt the axe,
And hang himself.—I pray you, do my greeting.
FLAV. Trouble him no further, thus you still shall find him.
TIM. Come not to me again: but say to Athens,
Timon hath made his everlasting mansion
Upon the beached verge of the salt flood;
Who once a day with his embossed froth
The turbulent surge shall cover; thither come,
And let my grave-stone be your oracle.—
Lips, let sour * words go by, and language end:
What is amiss, plague and infection mend!
Graves only be men's works, and death their gain!
Sun, hide thy beams! Timon hath done his reign.
[*Exit* TIMON.
1 SEN. His discontents are unremovably
Coupled to nature.
2 SEN. Our hope in him is dead: let us return,
And strain what other means is left unto us
In our dear peril.
2 SEN. It requires swift foot. [*Exeunt.*

SCENE II.—*The Walls of* Athens.

Enter Two Senators, *and a* Messenger.

1 SEN. Thou hast painfully discover'd; are his files
As full as thy report?
MESS. I have spoke the least:
Besides, his expedition promises
Present approach.
2 SEN. We stand much hazard, if they bring not Timon.
MESS. I met a courier, one mine ancient friend;
Whom, though in general part we were oppos'd,
Yet our old love made a particular force,[b]
And made us speak like friends:—this man was riding
From Alcibiades to Timon's cave,
With letters of entreaty, which imported
His fellowship i' the cause against your city,
In part for his sake mov'd.
1 SEN. Here come our brothers.

Enter Senators *from* TIMON.

3 SEN. No talk of Timon, nothing of him expect.—
The enemy's drum is heard, and fearful scouring
Doth choke the air with dust. In, and prepare;
Ours is the fall, I fear, our foes the snare.
[*Exeunt.*

(*) Old copy, *foure.*

a Take his haste,—] To *take time*, is to go leisurely about a business; to *take haste* is to perform it expeditiously. Mr. Collier's annotator suggests,—"take his *halter.*"

b *Whom, though in general part we were oppos'd,*
Yet our old love made *a particular* force,
And made us speak like friends:—]

The second line is unquestionably corrupt; Hanmer endeavoured to restore the sense by printing,—

"*And*, though in general part we were oppos'd,
Yet our old love *had* a particular force," &c.

And Mr. Singer by reading,—

"*When*, though *on several* part we were oppos'd,
Yet our old love *had* a particular force."

We conceive the errors to lurk in the words *made* and *force*, the former having been caught by the compositor from the following line, and would read,—

"Whom, though in general part we were oppos'd,
Yet our old love *took* a particular *truce*,
And made us speak like friends."

To *take a truce* was an every-day expression in our author's time, and has been adopted by him more than once; thus, in "King John," Act III. Sc. 1:—

"With my vex'd spirits I cannot *take a truce.*"

And in "Troilus and Cressida," Act II. Sc. 3:—

"——*Took a truce*, and did him service."

SCENE III.—*The Woods.* Timon's *Cave, and a rough Tomb near it.*

Enter a Soldier, *seeking* TIMON.

SOLD. By all description this should be the place.
Who's here? speak, ho!—No answer? What is this?
[*Reads.*] TIMON IS DEAD!—*who*[a] *hath outstretch'd his span,—*
Some beast—read this; there does not live a man.[b]
Dead, sure, and this his grave: what's on this tomb
I cannot read; the character I'll take with wax;
Our captain hath in every figure skill;[c]
An ag'd interpreter, though young in days:
Before proud Athens he's set down by this,
Whose fall the mark of his ambition is. [*Exit.*

SCENE IV.—*Before the Walls of* Athens.

Trumpets sound. Enter ALCIBIADES *and* Forces.

ALCIB. Sound to this coward and lascivious town
Our terrible approach. [*A parley sounded.*

Enter Senators *on the Walls.*

Till now you have gone on, and fill'd the time
With all licentious measure, making your wills
The scope of justice; till now, myself, and such
As slept within the shadow of your power,
Have wander'd with our travers'd arms, and breath'd
Our sufferance vainly: now the time is flush,
When crouching marrow, in the bearer strong,
Cries, of itself, *No more!* now breathless wrong
Shall sit and pant in your great chairs of ease;
And pursy insolence shall break his wind
With fear and horrid flight.
1 SEN. Noble and young,
When thy first griefs were but a mere conceit,
Ere thou hadst power, or we had cause of fear,
We sent to thee; to give thy rages balm,
To wipe out our ingratitude with loves
Above their quantity.
2 SEN. So did we woo
Transformed Timon to our city's love,
By humble message and by promis'd means;
We were not all unkind, nor all deserve
The common stroke of war.
1 SEN. These walls of ours
Were not erected by their hands from whom
You have receiv'd your grief: nor are they such,
That these great towers, trophies, and schools should fall
For private faults in them.
2 SEN. Nor are they living
Who were the motives that you first went out;
Shame, that they wanted cunning,[d] in excess
Hath broke their hearts. March, noble lord,
Into our city with thy banners spread:
By decimation, and a tithed death,
(If thy revenges hunger for that food,
Which nature loathes,) take thou the destin'd tenth;
And by the hazard of the spotted die,
Let die the spotted.
1 SEN. All have not offended;
For those that were, it is not square,[e] to take,
On those that are, revenge: crimes, like lands,
Are not inherited. Then, dear countryman,
Bring in thy ranks, but leave without thy rage:
Spare thy Athenian cradle, and those kin
Which, in the bluster of thy wrath, must fall,
With those that have offended: like a shepherd,
Approach the fold, and cull the infected forth,
But kill not all together.
2 SEN. What thou wilt,
Thou rather shalt enforce it with thy smile,
Than hew to't with thy sword.
1 SEN. Set but thy foot
Against our rampir'd gates, and they shall ope;
So thou wilt send thy gentle heart before,
To say, thou'lt enter friendly.
2 SEN. Throw thy glove,
Or any token of thine honour else,
That thou wilt use the wars as thy redress,
And not as our confusion, all thy powers
Shall make their harbour in our town, till we
Have seal'd thy full desire.
ALCIB. Then there's my glove;

---

a Who *hath,* &c.] That is, *whoever* hath, &c.

b TIMON IS DEAD!—*who hath outstretch'd his span,—*
Some beast—read this; there does not live a man.]

Of the many erroneous interpretations of Shakespeare's text for which his commentators are responsible, none, perhaps, is so remarkable, and, at the same time, so supremely ridiculous, as that into which they have lapsed with regard to the above passage. Not perceiving—what it seems scarcely possible from the lines themselves and their context to miss—that this couplet is an inscription by Timon to indicate his death, and point to the epitaph on his tomb, they have invariably printed it as a portion of the soldier's speech, and thus represented him as misanthropical as the hero of the piece! Nor was this absurdity sufficient: as, says Warburton, "The soldier had yet only seen the rude pile of earth heaped up for Timon's grave, and not the *inscription* upon it," we should read:

"Some beast *rear'd* this;"—

and he prints it accordingly. And because "our poet certainly would not make the soldier call on a beast to read the inscription *before* he had informed the audience that he could not read it himself; which he does *afterwards,*" Malone adopts Warburton's reading, and every editor since follows his judicious example! What is still more amusing, too, Mr. Collier, who has claimed for his mysterious annotator three-fourths of the most acute of modern emendations, assigns this precious "restoration" to him also! We are curious to know whether he derived it from some manuscript copy of the play, or merely from the traditions of the stage.

c Our captain hath in every figure skill;] We are obviously to understand that the insculpture on the tomb, unlike the inscription which he has just read, is in a language the soldier was unacquainted with.

d *Cunning,*—] That is, wisdom, foresight.

e Square,—] *Equitable.*

Descend,* and open your uncharged ports:
Those enemies of Timon's, and mine own,
Whom you yourselves shall set out for reproof,
Fall, and no more: and,—to atone your fears
With my more noble meaning,—not a man
Shall pass his quarter, or offend the stream
Of regular justice in your city's bounds,
But shall be render'd,[a] to your public laws
At heaviest answer.

BOTH. 'T is most nobly spoken.

ALCIB. Descend, and keep your words.

[*The* Senators *descend, and open the Gates.*

Enter a Soldier.

SOLD. My noble general, Timon is dead;
Entomb'd upon the very hem o' the sea:
And on his grave-stone this insculpture; which
With wax I brought away, whose soft impression
Interprets for my poor ignorance.

ALCIB. [Reads.] *Here lies a wretched corse, of wretched soul bereft.*
Seek not my name: a plague consume you wicked caitiffs left!
Here lie I Timon; who, alive, all living men did hate:
Pass by, and curse thy fill; but pass, and stay not here thy gait.
These well express in thee thy latter spirits:
Though thou abhorr'dst in us our human griefs,
Scorn'dst our brain's flow, and those our droplets which
From niggard nature fall, yet rich conceit
Taught thee to make vast Neptune weep for aye
On thy low grave, on faults forgiven. Dead
Is noble Timon; of whose memory
Hereafter more.—Bring me into your city,
And I will use the olive with my sword:
Make war breed peace; make peace stint war; make each
Prescribe to other, as each other's leech.—
Let our drums strike. [*Exeunt.*

(*) First folio, *Defend*.

[a] Render'd,—] A correction by Mason, the first folio reading,—
"But shall be *remedied to*," &c.
And the second,—
"But shall be *remedied by*," &c.

ILLUSTRATIVE COMMENTS.

ACT I.

(1) SCENE I.—*Enter* TIMON.] It is so interesting to contrast Shakespeare's exalted conception of Timon's character with the popular idea of the misanthrope in his time, that we need ask no indulgence for reprinting the once familiar story on which, it is believed, the present play was based.

THE TWENTY-EIGHTH NOUELL.

Of the straunge and beastlie nature of Timon of Athens, enemie to mankinde, with his death, buriall, and Epitaphe.

Al the beastes of the worlde do apply theimselues to other beastes of theyr kind, Timon of Athens onely excepted: of whose straunge nature Plutarche is astonied, in the life of Marcus Antonius. Plato and Aristophanes do report his marveylous nature, because he was a man but by shape onely, in qualities hee was the capitall enemie of mankinde, which he confessed franckely vtterly to abhorre and hate. He dwelt alone in a litle cabane in the fieldes not farre from Athenes, separated from all neighbours and company; he neuer wente to the citie, or to any other habitable place, except he were constrayned: he could not abide any mans company and conuersation: he was neuer seen to goe to any mannes house, ne yet would suffer them to come to him. At the same time there was in Athenes another of like qualitie, called Apemantus, of the very same nature, differente from the naturall kinde of man, and lodged likewise in the middes of the fields. On a day they two being alone together at dinner, Apemantus said vnto him: "O Timon, what a pleasant feast is this, and what a merie companie are wee, being no more but thou and I." "Naie (quoth Timon) it would be a merie banquet in deede, if there were none here but my selfe."

Wherein he shewed how like a beast (in deede) he was: for he could not abide any other man, being not able to suffer the company of him, which was of like nature. And if by chaunce hee happened to goe to Athenes, it was onelye to speake with Alcibiades, who then was an excellente captaine there, whereat many did marueile: and therefore Apemantus demaunded of him, why he spake to no man, but to Alcibiades. "I speake to him sometimes," said Timon, "because I know that by his occasion, the Atheniens shall receiue great hurt and trouble." Which wordes many times he told to Alcibiades himselfe. He had a garden adioyning to his house in the fields, wherin was a figge tree, wheruppon many desperate men ordinarily did hange themselues: in place whereof, he purposed to set vp a house, and therefore was forced to cutte it donne, for which cause hee went to Athenes, and in the markette place, hee called the people about him, saying that hee had newes to tell them: when the people vnderstoode that he was about to make a discourse vnto them, which was wont to speake to no man, they marueiled, and the citizens on every part of the citie, ranne to heare him: to whom he saide, that he purposed to cutte doune his figge tree, to builde a house vpon the place where it stoode. "Wherefore (quoth he) if there be any man amonges you all in this company, that is disposed to hange himselfe, let him come betimes, before it be cutte doune." Hauing thus bestowed his charitie amonges the people, hee returned to his lodging, wher he liued a certaine time after, without alteration of nature; and because that nature chaunged not in his life time, he would not suffer that death should alter, or varie the same: for like as he liued a beastly and churlish life, euen so he required to haue his funerall done after that maner. By his last will he ordeined himselfe to be interred vpon the sea shore, that the waues and surges might beate and vexe his dead carcas. Yea, and that if it were possible, his desire was to be buried in the depth of the sea: causing an epitaphe to be made, wherin was described the qualities of his brutishe life. Plutarche also reporteth an other to be made by Calimachus, much like to that which Timon made himselfe, whose owne soundeth to this effect in Englishe verse.

My wretched catife dayes,
Expired now and past:
My carren corps intered here,
Is fast in grounde:
In waltring waues of swel-
ling sea by surges cast,
My name if thou desire,
The gods thee doe confounde.

PAYNTER'S *Palace of Pleasure*, Tom. I.

(2) SCENE I.—*Enter* APEMANTUS.] The name and disposition of this cynic were probably borrowed by the original author of the play from Paynter's novel, though he appears to have caught some hints for the delineation from the following lively scene in Lucian's Dialogues:—

Mercury. You Fellow, with the Scrip over your shoulder, stand forth, and walke round the Assembly. O yes, I sell a stout, ver tuous, well-bred, free mortall. Who buyes him?

Merchant. Do you sell a Free-man, Cryer?

Mercury. Yes. * * *

Merchant. To what imployment may a man put such a slovenly ill-lookt fellow, unlesse he should make him a Delver, or Water-bearer?

Mercury. That's not all, set him to keep your house, you will need no Dogs. His name is Dogge.

Merchant. What s his Countrey or Profession?

Mercury. You were best to ask him.

Merchant. I fear his crabbed, grimme looks, least he should bark, if I should draw neer, and bite me. Do you not see how he lifts his Staffe, and bends his Brows, and how threatningly, and Cholerick he looks?

Mercury. Fear him not, he is very tame.

Merchant. Of what Countrey are you, my Friend

Diogenes. Of all Countreys.

* * * * * * * * * *

Merchant. Well, sir, if I should buy you, what will you teach me?

* * * * * * * * * *

Diogenes. The things which you are chiefly to learn, are to be impudent, bold, to barke without distinction at all, both Kinges, and private men. A way to make them regard and admire you, for a valiant man. Let your speech be Barbarous, and your Elocution rude, and Artlesse, like a dogge. Let your look be forced and your Gate be agreeable to your look. In a word, let your whole behaviour be beastly and savage. Be Modesty, Gentlenesse, and moderation far from you, and all blushing quite blotted out of your face. You are to frequent, also, populous places, and there to walk alone, and unaccompanied, and neither to salute acquaintance or stranger, for that were to destroy your Empire. * * * Hereby you will neither need Education or Studies, or such like trifles, but will arrive at glory a more compendious way. Though you be an Idiot, or Tanner, or Salter, or Mason, or Banker, yet these are no hindrances, why you should not be admired, if you have impudence, and boldnesse, and can artificially rayle.—*From the "Sale of Philosophers," in Lucian's Dialogues, translated by Jasper Mayne*, 1638, *published* 1664, *pp.* 383-4.

ACT III.

(1) Scene VI.—

Burn, house! sink, Athens! henceforth hated be
Of Timon, man and all humanity!]

The circumstances which led to Timon's self-expulsion, and many of the incidents in his subsequent career, are touched on, though slightly, in the following passage from Plutarch's Life of Antony:—"Antonius, he forsooke the citie and companie of his frendes, and built him a house in the sea, by the Ile of Pharos, upon certaine forced mountes which he caused to be cast into the sea, and dwelt there, as a man that banished him selfe from all mens companie: saying that he would lead Timons life, bicause he had the like wrong offered him, that was affore offered unto Timon: and that for the unthankefulnes of those he had done good unto, and whom he tooke to be his frendes, he was angry with all men, and would trust no man. This Timon was a citizen of Athens, that lived about the warre of Peloponnesus, as appeareth by Plato, and Aristophanes commedies: in the which they mocked him, calling him a vyper, and malicious man unto mankind, to shunne all other mens companies, but the companie of young Alcibiades, a bolde and insolent youth, whom he woulde greatly feast, and make much of, and kissed him very gladly. Apemantus wondering at it, asked him the cause what he ment to make so muche of that young man alone, and to hate all others: Timon aunswered him, I do it, sayd he, bicause I know that one day he shall do great mischiefe unto the Athenians. This Timon sometimes would have Apemantus in his companie, bicause he was much like to his nature and condicions, and also followed him in maner of life. On a time when they solemnly celebrated the feasts called Choæ at Athens (to wit, the feasts of the dead, where they make sprincklings and sacrifices for the dead), and that they two then feasted together by them selves, Apemantus said unto the other: O, here is a trimme banket Timon. Timon aunswered againe, yea said he, so thou wert not here. It is reported of him also, that this Timon on a time (the people being assembled in the market place about dispatch of some affaires) got up into the pulpit for Orations, where the Orators commonly use to speake unto the people: and silence being made, everie man listning to heare what he would say, bicause it was a wonder to see him in that place: at length he began to speake in this maner. My Lordes of Athens, I have a litle yard in my house where there groweth a figge tree, on the which many citizens have hanged them selves: and bicause I meane to make some building upon the place, I thought good to let you all understand it, that before the figge tree be cut downe, if any of you be desperate, you may there in time goe hang your selves. He dyed in the citie of Hales, and was buried upon the sea side. Nowe it chaunced so, that the sea getting in, it compassed his tombe rounde about, that no man coulde come to it: and upon the same was wrytten this epitaphe.

Heere lyes a wretched corse, of wretched soule bereft,
Seeke not my name: a plague consume you wicked wretches left.

It is reported, that Timon him selfe when he lived made this epitaphe: for that which is commonly rehearsed was not this, but made by the poet Callimachus.

Heere lye I Timon who alive all living men did hate,
Passe by, and curse thy fill: but passe, and stay not heere thy gate.

North's *Plutarch:* ed. 1579, p. 1003.

(2) Scene VI.—*One day he gives us diamonds, next day stones.*] Subjoined is the scene from the old manuscript play, before mentioned, to which Shakespeare or his predecessor is supposed to have been indebted for the idea of the mock banquet in Act III.:—

Tim. Why doe yee not fall to? I am at home:
Ile standing suppe, or walking, if I please.—
Laches, bring here the artichokes with speede.—
Eutrapelus, Demeas, Hermogenes,
I'le drinke this cuppe, a healthe to all your healths!
Lach. Converte it into poison, O yee gods!
Let it bee ratsbane to them! [*Aside.*
Gelas. What, wilt thou have the legge or els the winge?
Eutr. Carve yee that capon.
Dem. I will cutte him up,
And make a beaste of him.
Phil. Timon, this healthe to thee.
Tim. Ile pledge you, sir.
These artichokes doe noe mans pallat please.
Dem. I love them well, by Jove.
Tim. Here, take them, then.
[*Stones painted like to them; and throwes them at them.*
Nay, thou shalt have them, thou and all of yee!
Yee wicked, base, perfidious rascalls,
Think yee my hate's soe soone extinguished?
[Timon *beates* Herm. *above all the reste.*
Dem. O my heade!
Herm. O my cheekes!
Phil. Is this a feaste?
Gelas. Truly, a stony one.
Stilpo. Stones sublunary have the same matter with the heavenly.
Tim. If I Joves horridde thunderbolte did holde
Within my hande, thus, thus would I darte it! [*Hee hitts* Herm.
Herm. Woe and alas, my braines are dashed out!
Gelas. Alas, alas, twill never bee my happe
To travaile now to the Antipodes!
Ah, that I had my Pegasus but here!
I'de fly away, by Jove. [*Exeunt all except* Tim. *and* Lach.
Tim. Yee are a stony generation,
Or harder, if ought harder may bee founde;
Monsters of Scythia inhospitall,
Nay, very divells, hatefull to the gods.
Lach. Master, they are gone.

Act IV. Sc. 5.

ACT IV.

(1) Scene III.—*I am* misanthropos, *and hate mankind.*] The epithet, *misanthropos*, was perhaps taken, as Malone conjectured, from a marginal note in North's translation of Plutarch's Life of Antony: "Antonius followeth the life and example of Timon *Misanthropus*, the Athenian;" or it might have been derived by the original author of this drama, from the subjoined soliloquy in "Lucian:"—

"I will purchase the whole confines of this countrey, and build a towre over my treasure big enough for myself alone to live in, and which I purpose shall be my sepulchre at my death; and for the remainder of my ensuing life, I will resolve upon these rules, to accompany no man, to take notice of no man, and to live in contempt of all men: the title of friend, or guest, or companion, or the altar of mercy, are but meer toyes, not worth a straw to be talkt of: to be sorry for him that weeps, or help him that wants, shall be a transgression and breach of our laws: I will eat alone as wolves do, and have but one friend in the world to bear me company, and that shall be Timon; all others shall be enemies and traitors, and to have speech with any of them, an absolute piacle [enormity]: If I do but see a man, that day shall be dismal and accursed: I will make no difference between them and statues of stone and brass: I will admit no messenger from them, nor contract any truce with them, but solitariness shall be the main limit betwixt me and them; to be of the same tribe, the same fraternity, the same people, or the same countrey, shall be but poor and unprofitable terms, to be respected by none but fools; let Timon alone be rich, and live in despight of all other; let him revel alone by himself, far from flattery and odious commendations; let him sacrifice to the gods, and make good chear alone, as a neighbour conjoyned only to himself, discarding all other; and let it be further enacted, that it shall be lawful for him only to shake himself by the hand, that is, either when he is about to die, or to set a crown upon his head; and the welcomest name to him in the world is to be called *Man-hater.*"—HICKES' *Lucian*, fol. 1663, p. 174.

(3) SCENE III.—

——— *Common mother, thou,—*
Whose womb unmeasurable, and infinite breast.]

Warburton conjectured this image was borrowed from the ancient statues of Diana Ephesia Multimammia, called παναίολος φύσις πάντων Μήτηρ; see Montfauçon, "l'Antiquité Expliquée," lib. iii. ch. xv.

(4) SCENE III.—*Wert thou the unicorn, pride and wrath would confound thee, and make thine own self the conquest of thy fury.*] An allusion to the notion once current, that this fabulous animal, in the impetuosity of its attack, would sometimes strike its horn into the root of a tree so deeply, as to become transfixed:—"He is an enemy to the lions, wherefore as soon as ever a lion seeth a unicorn, he runneth to a tree for succour, that so when the unicorn maketh force at him, he may not only avoid his horn, but also destroy him; for the unicorn in the swiftness of his course runneth against the tree, wherein his sharp horn sticketh fast, then when the lion seeth the unicorn fastened by the horn, without all danger he falleth upon him and killeth him. These things are reported by the King of Œthiopia, in an Hebrew epistle unto the Bishop of Rome."—TOPSEL'S *History of Four-footed Beasts,* ed. 1658, p. 557.

So too Spenser:—

"Like as a lion whose imperial power
A proud rebellious Vnicorn defies,
To avoid the rash assault and wrathful stour
Of his fierce foe, him to a tree applies;
And when him running in full course he spies,
He slips aside; the whiles the furious beast
His precious horn, sought of his enemies,
Strikes in the stock, ne thence can be releast,
But to the mighty Victor yields a bounteous feast."
Faëry Queen, b. ii. Canto V. st. 5.

(4) SCENE III.—*Each thing's a thief.*] Timon's magnificent exemplifications of thievery, like others of a less elevated and universal kind, which are to be found in writers of his period, had their origin probably in Anacreon's graceful ode, beginning—Η γη μελαινα πινει.

Thus in the old play of Albumazar, quoted by Steevens:—

"The world 's a theatre of theft: great rivers
Rob smaller brooks, and them the ocean.
And in this world of ours, this microcosm,
Guts from the stomach steal; and what they spare
The Meseraicks filch, and lay 't i' the liver;
Where (lest it should be found) turn'd to red nectar,
'T is by a thousand thievish veins convey'd,
And hid in flesh, nerves, bones, muscles and sinews,
In tendons, skin, and hair; so that the property
Thus altered, the theft can never be discover'd.
Now all these pilfries, couch'd, and compos'd in order,
Frame thee and me; Man 's a quick mass of thievery."

In farther illustration of the same idea, an antiquarian correspondent supplies the following lines, which, however, though bearing the early date of 1590, are, it is plain, but of comparatively modern composition:—

"*Certaine fine Thoughtes gathered oute of the Greeke and Romane Authours, and done into English.* 1590.

AN EPIGRAM ON THEEUES.

(1.)

Eache Thing that liues of somewhat else
Becomes the Foode or Prey:
So if it were that *Nature* tells
To take whene're we may.
For worldlie superfluitie
Here is a sure reliefe;
When euerie Thing is made to be
A Giver, or a Theefe.

(2.)

A glorious Robber is the *Sunne,*
For with his vaste attracte
Hee robbes the boundlesse sea: the *Moone*
From him steales Lighte to acte
O're the broade *Earthe,* and *Ocean* too:
Whilst the rapacious *Maine*
Absorbs the Vapoures, Mists, and Dewe
To yielde the *Cloudes* their Raine.

(3.)

The brutish *Earthe* can little give
From her composture rude:
Though some there be ordaind to live
Upon *Earthes* foulest foode.
Is all *Creation* then but fedde
By Spoile, his Life to gaine?
Nay,—all Things liuing be but made
Eache other to maintaine."

CRITICAL OPINIONS ON TIMON OF ATHENS.

"Timon of Athens, of all the works of Shakspeare, possesses most the character of satire:—a laughing satire in the picture of the parasites and flatterers, and Juvenalian in the bitterness of Timon's imprecations on the ingratitude of a false world. The story is very simply treated, and is definitely divided into large masses:—in the first act, the joyous life of Timon, his noble and hospitable extravagance, and around him the throng of suitors of every description; in the second and third acts, his embarrassment, and the trial which he is thereby reduced to make of his supposed friends, who all desert him in the hour of need;—in the fourth and fifth acts, Timon's flight to the woods, his misanthropical melancholy, and his death. The only thing which may be called an episode is the banishment of Alcibiades, and his return by force of arms. However, they are both examples of ingratitude,—the one of a state towards its defender, and the other of private friends to their benefactor. As the merits of the General towards his fellow-citizens suppose more strength of character than those of the generous prodigal, their respective behaviours are not less different: Timon frets himself to death, Alcibiades regains his lost dignity by force. If the poet very properly sides with Timon against the common practice of the world, he is, on the other hand, by no means disposed to spare Timon. Timon was a fool in his generosity; in his discontent he is a madman; he is everywhere wanting in the wisdom which enables a man in all things to observe the due measure. Although the truth of his extravagant feelings is proved by his death, and though when he digs up a treasure he spurns the wealth which seems to tempt him, we yet see distinctly enough that the vanity of wishing to be singular, in both the parts that he plays, had some share in his liberal self-forgetfulness, as well as in his anchoritical seclusion. This is particularly evident in the incomparable scene where the cynic Apemantus visits Timon in the wilderness. They have a sort of competition with each other in their trade of misanthropy: the Cynic reproaches the impoverished Timon with having been merely driven by necessity to take to the way of living which he himself had long been following of his free choice, and Timon cannot bear the thought of being merely an imitator of the Cynic. In such a subject as this, the due effect could only be produced by an accumulation of similar features; still, in the variety of the shades, an amazing degree of understanding has been displayed by Shakspeare. What a powerfully diversified concert of flatteries and of empty testimonies of devotedness! It is highly amusing to see the suitors, when the ruined circumstances of their patron had dispersed, immediately flock to him again when they learn that he has been revisited by fortune. On the other hand, in the speeches of Timon, after he is undeceived, all hostile figures of speech are exhausted,—it is a dictionary of eloquent imprecations."
—Schlegel.

Act IV. Sc. 2.

KING RICHARD THE THIRD.

THE earliest known copy of this popular tragedy is a quarto published in 1597, entitled,—"The Tragedy of King Richard the Third. Containing, His treacherous Plots against his brother Clarence: the pittiefull murther of his innocent nephewes: His tyrannicall vsurpation: with the whole course of his detested life, and most deserued death. As it hath beene lately acted by the Right honourable the Lord Chamberlaine, his seruants. At London, Printed by Valentine Sims, for Andrew Wise, dwelling in Paules Church-yard, at the signe of the Angell, 1597." In 1598, another edition appeared bearing the same title, and in addition the author's name, "William Shake-speare." The next impression, brought out in 1602, professes to be "Newly augmented;" this was followed by a fourth in 1605, and a fifth in 1613, which was the last quarto copy prior to the publication of the folio in 1623. Subsequently, three other quarto editions, dated respectively 1624, 1629, and 1634, were published, not one of which however, it is noticeable, contains the passages first found in the folio. Although an historical piece on the same subject,—"*The True Tragedie of Richard the Third: wherein is showne the death of Edward the fourth, with the smothering of the two young Princes in the Tower: with a lamentable ende of Shores wife, an example for all wicked women. And lastly, the conjunction and ioyning of the two noble houses, Lancaster and Yorke. As it was playd by the Queenes Maiesties Players,*"—was issued in 1594, there are no proofs that Shakespeare has any obligations to it: his only authorities appear to have been the old chroniclers.

Malone has remarked that the textual variations between the quarto version of this play and the folio are more numerous than in any other of our author's works. This is true, and the diversity has proved, and will continue to prove, a source of incalculable trouble and perpetual dispute to his editors, since, although it is admitted by every one properly qualified to judge, that a reasonably perfect text can only be formed from the two versions, there will always be a conflict of opinions regarding some of the readings. Upon the whole, we prefer the quarto text, though execrably deformed by printing-office blunders, and can by no means acquiesce in the decision that those passages found only in the folio are "additions" made by the poet, subsequent to the publication of the early quartos. On the contrary, we believe those very passages to have been structural portions of the piece, and the real additions to be the terse and vigorous bits of dialogue peculiar to the quartos. Is it credible that so accomplished a master of stage-craft as Shakespeare, after witnessing the representation of Richard the Third, would have added above eighty lines to the longest scene in this or perhaps any other play? Is it not far more probable that these lines in Act IV., those touching the young prince's train in Act II., the nine in Gloucester's mock reply to the Mayor and Buckingham, and some others, formed originally part of the text and were omitted to accelerate the action, and afford space for the more lively and dramatic substitutions which are met with in the quartos alone? But although in these and a few other instances the folio copy appears to have been an earlier one than that used by the printers of the quartos, it must be admitted that there are numerous places in which the text of the former has undergone minute and careful correction, and where, both in rhythm and in language, it is superior to the previous editions.

Malone conjectured that Shakespeare wrote "Richard the Third" in 1593; the received impression at the present day is, that he produced it very shortly before its first publication in 1597.

Persons Represented.

King Edward the Fourth.
Edward, *Prince of* Wales, *afterwards* King Edward V. } *Sons to the* King.
Richard, *Duke of* York, } *Sons to the* King.
George, *Duke of* Clarence, } *Brothers to the* King.
Richard, *Duke of* Gloucester, *afterwards* King Richard III. } *Brothers to the* King.
A Young Son *of* Clarence.
Henry, *Earl of* Richmond, *afterwards* King Henry VII.
Cardinal Bourchier, *Archbishop of* Canterbury.
Thomas Rotherham, *Archbishop of* York.
John Morton, *Bishop of* Ely.
Duke *of* Buckingham.
Duke *of* Norfolk.
Earl *of* Surrey, *his Son.*
Earl Rivers, *Brother to* King Edward's *Queen.*
Marquis *of* Dorset, *and* Lord Grey, *her Sons.*
Earl *of* Oxford.
Lord Hastings.
Lord Stanley.
Lord Lovel.
Sir Thomas Vaughan.
Sir Richard Ratcliff.
Sir William Catesby.
Sir James Tyrrel.
Sir James Blount.
Sir Walter Herbert.
Sir Robert Brakenbury, *Lieutenant of the* Tower.
Christopher Urswick, *a Priest.*
Another Priest.
Lord Mayor *of* London.
Sheriff *of* Wiltshire.

Elizabeth, *Queen of* King Edward IV.
Margaret, *Widow of* King Henry VI.
Duchess *of* York, *Mother to* King Edward IV., Clarence, *and* Gloucester.
Lady Anne, *Widow of* Edward *Prince of* Wales, *Son to* King Henry VI.; *afterwards married to the Duke of* Gloucester.
A Young Daughter *of* Clarence.

Lords, and other Attendants; two Gentlemen, a Pursuivant, Scrivener, Citizens, Murderers, Messengers, Ghosts, Soldiers, &c.

SCENE,—England.

ACT I.

SCENE I.—London. *A Street.*

Enter GLOUCESTER.(1)

GLO. Now is the winter of our discontent
Made glorious summer by this sun of York;
And all the clouds, that lour'd upon our house,
In the deep bosom of the ocean buried.
Now are our brows bound with victorious wreaths;
Our bruised arms hung up for monuments;
Our stern alarums chang'd to merry meetings,
Our dreadful marches to delightful measures.
Grim-visag'd war hath smooth'd his wrinkled front;

And now,—instead of mounting barbed steeds,
To fright the souls of fearful adversaries,—
He capers nimbly in a lady's chamber,
To the lascivious pleasing of a lute.[a]
But I,—that am not shap'd for sportive tricks,
Nor made to court an amorous looking-glass;
I, that am rudely stamp'd, and want love's majesty,
To strut before a wanton ambling nymph;
I, that am curtail'd of this fair proportion,
Cheated of feature by dissembling nature,
Deform'd, unfinish'd, sent before my time
Into this breathing world, scarce half made up,
And that so lamely and unfashionable,
That dogs bark at me, as I halt by them;—
Why I, in this weak piping time of peace,
Have no delight to pass away the time;
Unless to spy* my shadow in the sun,
And descant on mine own deformity:
And therefore,—since I cannot prove a lover,
To entertain these fair well-spoken days,—
I am determined to prove a villain,
And hate the idle pleasures of these days.
Plots have I laid, inductions dangerous,
By drunken prophecies, libels, and dreams,
To set my brother Clarence and the king,
In deadly hate the one against the other:
And, if king Edward be as true and just,
As I am subtle, false, and treacherous,
This day should Clarence closely be mew'd up,
About a prophecy, which says that G
Of Edward's heirs the murderer shall be.
Dive, thoughts, down to my soul! here Clarence comes.

Enter CLARENCE, *guarded, and* BRAKENBURY.

Brother, good day: what means this armed guard,
That waits upon your grace?
CLAR. His majesty,
Tendering my person's safety, hath appointed
This conduct to convey me to the Tower.
GLO. Upon what cause?
CLAR. Because my name is George.
GLO. Alack, my lord, that fault is none of yours;
He should for that commit your godfathers:—
O, belike his majesty hath some intent,
That you shall† be new-christen'd in the Tower.
But what's the matter, Clarence? may I know?
CLAR. Yea, Richard, when I know; for,‡ I protest,
As yet I do not: but, as I can learn,
He hearkens after prophecies and dreams;
And from the cross-row plucks the letter G,

(*) First folio, *see*. (†) First folio, *should*. (‡) First folio, *but*.

a *Of* a lute.] In the quartos, *lute* is misprinted *love*.
b *That* tempers *him to this extremity*.] So the first quarto, 1597. The folio 1623 reads:—
"That *tempts* him to this *harsh* extremity."

And says a wizard told him that by G
His issue disinherited should be;
And for my name of George begins with G,
It follows in his thought that I am he:
These, as I learn, and such like toys as these,
Have* mov'd his highness to commit me now.
GLO. Why this it is, when men are rul'd by women:—
'Tis not the king that sends you to the Tower;
My lady Grey his wife, Clarence, 'tis she,
That tempers him to this extremity.[b]
Was it not she, and that good man of worship,
Antony Woodville, her brother there,
That made him send lord Hastings to the Tower,
From whence this present day he is delivered?
We are not safe, Clarence; we are not safe.
CLAR. By heaven, I think there is no man secure,
But the queen's kindred, and night-walking heralds
That trudge betwixt the king and mistress Shore.
Heard you not, what an humble suppliant
Lord Hastings was to her for his delivery?[c]
GLO. Humbly complaining to her deity
Got my lord chamberlain his liberty.
I'll tell you what,—I think it is our way,
If we will keep in favour with the king,
To be her men, and wear her livery:
The jealous o'er-worn widow and herself,
Since that our brother dubb'd them gentlewomen,
Are mighty gossips in this† monarchy.
BRAK. I beseech your graces both to pardon me;
His majesty hath straitly given in charge,
That no man shall have private conference
(Of what degree soever) with his‡ brother.
GLO. Even so, an please your worship; Brakenbury,
You may partake of anything we say:
We speak no treason, man;—we say, the king
Is wise and virtuous; and his noble queen
Well struck in years, fair, and not jealous:—
We say that Shore's wife hath a pretty foot,
A cherry lip, a bonny eye, a passing pleasing tongue;
And that the queen's kindred are made gentlefolks:
How say you, sir? can you deny all this?
BRAK. With this, my lord, myself have nought to do.
GLO. Naught to do with mistress Shore? I tell thee, fellow,
He that doth naught with her, excepting one,
Were best to do it secretly, alone.

(*) First folio, *Hath*. (†) First folio, *our*. (‡) First folio, *your*.

c Lord Hastings was to her for his delivery?] The folio reads,—
"Lord Hastings was, for her delivery."

BRAK. What one, my lord?
GLO. Her husband, knave:—wouldst thou betray me?
BRAK. I* beseech your grace to pardon me; and, withal,
Forbear your conference with the noble duke.
CLAR. We know thy charge, Brakenbury, and will obey.
GLO. We are the queen's abjects, and must obey.
Brother, farewell; I will unto the king;
And whatsoe'er you will employ me in,—
Were it to call king Edward's widow, sister—
I will perform it to enfranchise you.
Meantime, this deep disgrace in brotherhood,
Touches me deeper than you can imagine.
CLAR. I know it pleaseth neither of us well.
GLO. Well, your imprisonment shall not be long;
I will deliver you, or† lie for you:[a]
Meantime, have patience.
CLAR. I must perforce:[b] farewell.
[*Exeunt* CLARENCE, BRAKENBURY, *and* Guard.
GLO. Go, tread the path that thou shalt ne'er return!
Simple, plain Clarence, I do love thee so,
That I will shortly send thy soul to heaven,
If heaven will take the present at our hands.—
But who comes here? the new-deliver'd Hastings!

Enter HASTINGS.

HAST. Good time of day unto my gracious lord!
GLO. As much unto my good lord chamberlain!
Well are you welcome to this open air.
How hath your lordship brook'd imprisonment?
HAST. With patience, noble lord, as prisoners must:
But I shall live, my lord, to give them thanks,
That were the cause of my imprisonment.
GLO. No doubt, no doubt; and so shall Clarence too;
For they that were your enemies are his,
And have prevail'd as much on him as you.
HAST. More pity that the eagle‡ should be mew'd,
While§ kites and buzzards prey§ at liberty.
GLO. What news abroad?
HAST. No news so bad abroad as this at home;—
The king is sickly, weak, and melancholy,
And his physicians fear him mightily.

GLO. Now, by Saint Paul, this[c] news is bad indeed.
O, he hath kept an evil diet long,
And over-much consum'd his royal person;
'Tis very grievous to be thought upon.
What,* is he in his bed?
HAST. He is.
GLO. Go you before, and I will follow you.
[*Exit* HASTINGS.
He cannot live, I hope; and must not die
Till George be pack'd with post-horse up to heaven.
I'll in, to urge his hatred more to Clarence,
With lies well steel'd with weighty arguments;
And if I fail not in my deep intent,
Clarence hath not another day to live:
Which done, God take king Edward to his mercy,
And leave the world for me to bustle in!
For then I'll marry Warwick's youngest daughter:
What though I kill'd her husband and her father;
The readiest way to make the wench amends,
Is to become her husband and her father:
The which will I; not all so much for love
As for another secret close intent,
By marrying her, which I must reach unto.
But yet I run before my horse to market:
Clarence still breathes, Edward still lives and reigns;
When they are gone, then must I count my gains.
[*Exit.*

SCENE II.—*The same. Another Street.*

Enter the corpse of KING HENRY *the* SIXTH, *borne upon a hearse,* Gentlemen *bearing halberds, to guard it; and* LADY ANNE *as mourner.*

ANNE. Set down, set down your honourable load,—
If honour may be shrouded in a hearse,—
Whilst I awhile obsequiously[d] lament
The untimely fall of virtuous Lancaster.—
Poor key-cold figure of a holy king!
Pale ashes of the house of Lancaster!
Thou bloodless remnant of that royal blood!
Be it lawful that I invocate thy ghost,
To hear the lamentations of poor Anne,
Wife to thy Edward, to thy slaughter'd son,
Stabb'd by the self-same hand that made these wounds!†
Lo, in those windows, that let forth thy life,
I pour the helpless balm of my poor eyes:—

(*) First folio inserts, *do.* (†) First folio inserts, *else.*
(‡) First folio, *eagles.* (§) First folio, *Whiles—play.*

[a] *Or* lie *for you*:] Or lie imprisoned in your stead.
[b] *Must* perforce:] In allusion to the popular saying,—"*Patience upon force* is a medicine for a mad dog."

(*) First folio, *Where.* (†) Quartos, *holes.*

[c] *Now, by Saint* Paul, this *news*, &c.] So the quartos. The folio 1623 has,—"Now by *S Iohn, that* Newes," &c.
[d] Obsequiously *lament*—] That is, *funereally* lament.

Curs'd be the hand, that made these fatal holes!
Curs'd be the heart, that had the heart to do it![a]
[Cursed the blood, that let this blood from hence![b]]
More direful hap betide that hated wretch,
That makes us wretched by the death of thee,
Than I can wish to adders, spiders, toads,[c]
Or any creeping venom'd thing that lives!
If ever he have child, abortive be it,
Prodigious, and untimely brought to light,
Whose ugly and unnatural aspéct
May fright the hopeful mother at the view;
[And that be heir to his unhappiness![d]]
If ever he have wife, let her be made
As* miserable by the death of him,
As† I am made by my young lord and thee!—
Come, now towards Chertsey with your holy load,
Taken from Paul's to be interred there;
And still, as you are weary of the‡ weight,
Rest you, whiles I lament king Henry's corse.
[*Bearers take up the corpse, and move forward.*

Enter GLOUCESTER.

GLO. Stay, you that bear the corse, and set it down.
ANNE. What black magician conjures up this fiend,
To stop devoted charitable deeds?
GLO. Villains, set down the corse; or, by Saint Paul,
I'll make a corse of him that disobeys!
1 GENT. My lord, stand back, and let the coffin pass.
GLO. Unmanner'd dog! stand§ thou when I command:
Advance thy halberd higher than my breast,
Or by Saint Paul, I'll strike thee to my foot,
And spurn upon thee, beggar, for thy boldness.
[*Bearers set down the hearse.*
ANNE. What, do you tremble? are you all afraid?
Alas, I blame you not, for you are mortal,
And mortal eyes cannot endure the devil.—
Avaunt, thou dreadful minister of hell!
Thou hadst but power over his mortal body,
His soul thou canst not have; therefore, be gone.
GLO. Sweet saint, for charity, be not so curst.
ANNE. Foul devil, for God's sake, hence, and trouble us not;
For thou hast made the happy earth thy hell,
Fill'd it with cursing cries and deep exclaims.
If thou delight to view thy heinous deeds,
Behold this pattern of thy butcheries:—
O, gentlemen, see, see! dead Henry's wounds
Open their congeal'd mouths and bleed afresh.(2)—
Blush, blush, thou lump of foul deformity;
For 'tis thy presence that exhales this blood
From cold and empty veins, where no blood dwells;
Thy deed,* inhuman and unnatural,
Provokes this deluge most unnatural.—
O God, which this blood mad'st, revenge his death!
O earth, which this blood drink'st, revenge his death!
Either, heaven, with lightning strike the murderer dead,
Or, earth, gape open wide, and eat him quick,[e]
As thou didst swallow up this good king's blood,
Which his hell-govern'd arm hath butchered!
GLO. Lady, you know no rules of charity,
Which renders good for bad, blessings for curses.
ANNE. Villain, thou know'st no† law of God nor man;
No beast so fierce, but knows some touch of pity.
GLO. But I know none, and therefore am no beast.
ANNE. O wonderful, when devils tell the truth!
GLO. More wonderful, when angels are so angry.—
Vouchsafe, divine perfection of a woman,
Of these supposed evils,‡ to give me leave,
By circumstance, but to acquit myself.
ANNE. Vouchsafe, diffus'd infection of a man,
For§ these known evils, but to give me leave,
By circumstance, to curse thy cursed self.
GLO. Fairer than tongue can name thee, let me have
Some patient leisure to excuse myself.
ANNE. Fouler than heart can think thee, thou canst make
No excuse current, but to hang thyself.
GLO. By such despair, I should accuse myself.
ANNE. And, by despairing, shouldst|| thou stand excus'd
For doing worthy vengeance on thyself,
Which¶ didst unworthy slaughter upon others.
GLO. Say, that I slew them not?
ANNE. Why, then, they are not dead:[f]
But dead they are, and, devilish slave, by thee.
GLO. I did not kill your husband.

(*) First folio, *More*. (†) First folio, *Than*.
(‡) First folio, *this*. (§) First folio, *Stand'st*.

a Curs'd be the hand, that made these fatal holes!
Curs'd be the heart, that had the heart to do it!]
The folio gives these lines as follows:—

"O cursed be the hand that made these holes:
Cursed the Heart, that had the heart to do it."

b Cursed the blood, &c.] A line not in the quartos.

(*) First folio, *Deeds*. (†) First folio, *nor*.
(‡) First folio, *crimes*. (§) First folio, *Of*.
(||) First folio, *shalt*. (¶) First folio, *That*.

c *Than I can wish to* adders, spiders, toads,—] Thus the quartos; the folio reads,—"to *Wolves, to* Spiders," &c.
d And that be, &c.] A line omitted in the quartos.
e *And eat him* quick,—] That is, swallow him *alive*.
f Why, then, they are not dead: &c.] The folio has,—

"Then say they were not slaine."

ANNE. Why, then he is alive.
GLO. Nay, he is dead; and slain by Edward's hand.*
ANNE. In thy foul throat thou liest; queen Margaret saw
Thy murderous falchion smoking in his blood;
The which thou once did bend against her breast,
But that thy brothers beat aside the point.
GLO. I was provoked by her slanderous tongue,
Which† laid their guilt upon my guiltless shoulders.
ANNE. Thou wast provoked by thy bloody mind,
Which† never dreamt[a] on aught but butcheries:
Didst thou not kill this king?
GLO. I grant ye.
ANNE. Dost *grant* me, hedge-hog? then, God grant me too,
Thou mayst be damned for that wicked deed!
O, he was gentle, mild, and virtuous!
GLO. The fitter‡ for the King of heaven that hath him.
ANNE. He is in heaven, where thou shalt never come.
GLO. Let him thank me, that holp to send him thither;
For he was fitter for that place than earth.
ANNE. And thou unfit for any place but hell.
GLO. Yes, one place else, if you will hear me name it.
ANNE. Some dungeon.
GLO. Your bed-chamber.
ANNE. Ill rest betide the chamber where thou liest!
GLO. So will it, madam, till I lie with you.
ANNE. I hope so.
GLO. I know so.—But, gentle lady Anne,—
To leave this keen encounter of our wits,
And fall somewhat§ into a slower method;—
Is not the causer of the timeless deaths
Of these Plantagenets, Henry, and Edward,
As blameful as the executioner?
ANNE. Thou wast the cause, and most accurs'd [effect.
GLO. Your beauty was the cause of that effect;
Your beauty, which† did haunt me in my sleep,
To undertake the death of all the world,
So I might live|| one hour in your sweet bosom.
ANNE. If I thought that, I tell thee, homicide,
These nails should rend¶ that beauty from my cheeks.
GLO. These eyes could not endure that beauty's wreck.[b]
You should not blemish it, if I stood by:
As all the world is cheered by the sun,
So I by that; it is my day, my life.
ANNE. Black night o'ershade thy day, and death thy life!
GLO. Curse not thyself, fair creature; thou art both.
ANNE. I would I were, to be reveng'd on thee.
GLO. It is a quarrel most unnatural,
To be reveng'd on him that loveth thee.
ANNE. It is a quarrel just and reasonable,
To be reveng'd on him that slew* my husband.
GLO. He that bereft thee, lady, of thy husband,
Did it to help thee to a better husband.
ANNE. His better doth not breathe upon the earth.
GLO. He lives that loves you† better than he could.
ANNE. Name him.
GLO. Plantagenet.
ANNE. Why, that was he.
GLO. The self-same name, but one of better nature.
ANNE. Where is he?
GLO. Here! [*She spits at him.*] Why dost thou spit at me?
ANNE. Would it were mortal poison, for thy sake!
GLO. Never came poison from so sweet a place.
ANNE. Never hung poison on a fouler toad.
Out of my sight! thou dost infect mine eyes.
GLO. Thine eyes, sweet lady, have infected mine.
ANNE. Would they were basilisks, to strike thee dead!
GLO. I would they were, that I might die at once;
For now they kill me with a living death.
Those eyes of thine from mine have drawn salt tears,
Sham'd their aspéct‡ with store of childish drops:
[These eyes, which never shed remorseful tear,—[c]
No, when my father York and Edward wept,
To hear the piteous moan that Rutland made,
When black-fac'd Clifford shook his sword at him:
Nor when thy warlike father, like a child,
Told the sad story of my father's death,
And twenty times made pause, to sob, and weep,
That all the standers-by had wet their cheeks,
Like trees bedash'd with rain: in that sad time,
My manly eyes did scorn an humble tear;
And what these sorrows could not thence exhale,
Thy beauty hath, and made them blind with weeping.]
I never sued to friend nor enemy;

(*) First folio, *hands*. (†) First folio, *That*. (‡) First folio, *better*. (§) First folio, *something*. (||) Quartos, *rest*. (¶) First folio, *rent*.

a Which *never* dreamt—] In the folio,—"*That* never *dream'st*."

b These eyes, &c.] This passage is misprinted in the quartos,—
"These eies could *never* endure *sweet* beauties wrack,
You should not blemish *them* if I stood by."

(*) First folio, *kill'd*. (†) First folio, *thee*. (‡) First folio, *aspects*.

c These eyes, which never shed remorseful tear,—] This and the eleven following lines are omitted in the quarto copies.

My tongue could never learn sweet soothing[a] words;
But now thy beauty is propos'd my fee,
My proud heart sues, and prompts my tongue to speak.
[*She looks scornfully at him.*

Teach not thy lip[b] such scorn; for it was made
For kissing, lady, not for such contempt.
If thy revengeful heart cannot forgive,
Lo here I lend thee this sharp-pointed sword;
Which if thou please to hide in this true breast,*
And let the soul forth that adoreth thee,

[a] *Sweet* soothing words;] The folio reads,—
"—— sweet *smoothing word.*"
[b] Teach not thy lip, &c.] The quartos less elegantly read,—
"Teach not thy *lips* such scorne, for *they* were made—"

(*) Quartos, *bosome.*

I lay it naked to thy deadly stroke,
And humbly beg the death upon my knee.
[*Lays his breast open.*
Nay, do not pause; 't was I that kill'd your husband;—
[*She offers at it with his sword.*
But 'twas thy beauty that provoked me.
Nay, now despatch; 'twas I that kill'd king Henry;—[a]
[*She again offers at his breast.*
But 't was thy heavenly face that set me on.
[*She lets fall the sword.*
Take up the sword again, or take up me.

ANNE. Arise, dissembler; though I wish thy death,
I will not be thy executioner.

GLO. Then bid me kill myself, and I will do it.

ANNE. I have already.

GLO. Tush,* that was in thy rage:
Speak it again, and, even with the word,
This hand, which for thy love did kill thy love,
Shall for thy love kill a far truer love;
To both their deaths shalt thou be accessory.

ANNE. I would I knew thy heart.

GLO. 'T is figur'd in my tongue.

ANNE. I fear me both are false.

GLO. Then never man was true.

ANNE. Well, well, put up your sword.

GLO. Say then, my peace is made.

ANNE. That shall you† know hereafter.

GLO. But shall I live in hope?

ANNE. All men, I hope, live so.

GLO. Vouchsafe to wear this ring.

ANNE. To take, is not to give.[b]
[*Puts on the ring.*

GLO. Look, how this‡ ring encompasseth thy finger,
Even so thy breast encloseth my poor heart;
Wear both of them, for both of them are thine.
And if thy poor devoted suppliant § may
But beg one favour at thy gracious hand,
Thou dost confirm his happiness for ever.

ANNE. What is it?

GLO. That it may please you leave these sad designs
To him that hath more || cause to be a mourner,
And presently repair to Crosby-place: ¶ (3)
Where—after I have solemnly interr'd,
At Chertsey monast'ry, this noble king,
And wet his grave with my repentant tears,—
I will with all expedient[c] duty see you:
For divers unknown reasons, I beseech you,
Grant me this boon.

ANNE. With all my heart; and much it joys me too,
To see you are become so penitent.—
Tressel and Berkley, go along with me.

GLO. Bid me farewell.

ANNE. 'T is more than you deserve:
But since you teach me how to flatter you,
Imagine I have said farewell already.
[*Exeunt* LADY ANNE, TRESSEL, *and* BERKLEY.

GLO. Sirs, take up the corse.[d]

GEN. Towards Chertsey, noble lord?

GLO. No, to White-friars; there attend my coming.
[*Exeunt the rest with the corpse.*
Was ever woman in this humour woo'd?
Was ever woman in this humour won?
I'll have her,—but I will not keep her long.
What! I, that kill'd her husband and his father,
To take her in her heart's extremest hate,
With curses in her mouth, tears in her eyes,
The bleeding witness of her * hatred by;
Having God, her conscience, and these bars against me,
And I no thing[e] to back my suit withal,
But the plain devil and dissembling looks,
And yet to win her,—all the world to nothing! Ha!
Hath she forgot already that brave prince,
Edward, her lord, whom I, some three months since,
Stabb'd in my angry mood at Tewksbury?
A sweeter and a lovelier gentleman,—
Fram'd in the prodigality of nature,
Young, valiant, wise, and, no doubt, right royal,—
The spacious world cannot again afford:
And will she yet debase† her eyes on me,
That cropp'd the golden prime of this sweet prince,
And made her widow to a woeful bed?
On me, whose all not equals Edward's moiety?
On me, that halt,‡ and am unshapen § thus?
My dukedom to a beggarly denier,[f]
I do mistake my person all this while:
Upon my life, she finds, although I cannot,
Myself to be a marvellous proper man.
I'll be at charges for a looking glass;
And entertain some score or two of tailors,
To study fashions to adorn my body:
Since I am crept in favour with myself,
I will maintain it with a|| little cost.

(*) First folio omits, *Tush.* (†) First folio, *shalt thou.*
(‡) First folio, *my.* (§) First folio, *Servant.*
(||) First folio, *most.* (¶) First folio, *Crosbie House.*

a 'T was I that killed king Henry,—] In the folio, this and the two preceding lines run thus,—

"Nay do not pause: For I did kill King Henrie,
But 't was thy Beautie that provoked me.
Nay now dispatch: 'T was I that stabb'd young Edward," &c.

(*) First folio, *my.* (†) First folio, *abase.*
(‡) First folio, *halts.* (§) First folio, *mishapen.*
(||) First folio, *some.*

b To take, is not to give.—] This line is not in the folio, which also errs in attributing to Anne the preceding line.
c Expedient—] For *expeditious.*
d Sirs, take up the corse.—] This line is omitted in the folio.
e *And I* no thing—] In the folio, "And I, *no Friends*—"
f *A beggarly* denier,—] A *denier* is the twelfth part of a French *sous.*

But, first, I'll turn yon fellow in his grave;
And then return lamenting to my love.—
Shine out, fair sun, till I have bought a glass,
That I may see my shadow as I pass. [*Exit.*

SCENE III.—*The same. A Room in the Palace.*

Enter QUEEN ELIZABETH, LORD RIVERS, *and* LORD GREY.

RIV. Have patience, madam; there's no doubt, his majesty
Will soon recover his accustom'd health.
GREY. In that you brook it ill, it makes him worse:
Therefore, for God's sake, entertain good comfort,
And cheer his grace with quick and merry words.*
Q. ELIZ. If he were dead, what would betide of† me?
GREY. No other harm but loss of such a lord.
Q. ELIZ. The loss of such a lord includes all harm.‡
GREY. The heavens have bless'd you with a goodly son,
To be your comforter when he is gone.
Q. ELIZ. Ah, he is young; and his minority
Is put unto the trust of Richard Gloster,
A man that loves not me, nor none of you.
RIV. Is it concluded he shall be protector?
Q. ELIZ. It is determin'd, not concluded yet:
But so it must be, if the king miscarry.
GREY. Here come the lords§ of Buckingham and Stanley.[a]

Enter BUCKINGHAM *and* STANLEY.[a]

BUCK. Good time of day unto your royal grace!
STAN. God make your majesty joyful as you have been!
Q. ELIZ. The countess Richmond, good my lord of Stanley,
To your good prayer will scarcely say amen.
Yet, Stanley, notwithstanding she's your wife,
And loves not me, be you, good lord, assur'd,
I hate not you for her proud arrogance.
STAN. I do beseech you, either not believe
The envious slanders of her false accusers;
Or, if she be accus'd on true report,
Bear with her weakness, which, I think, proceeds
From wayward sickness, and no grounded malice.
Q. ELIZ. Saw you the king to-day, my lord of Stanley?
STAN. But now, the duke of Buckingham and I
Are come from visiting his majesty.
Q. ELIZ. What likelihood of his amendment, lords?
BUCK. Madam, good hope; his grace speaks cheerfully.
Q. ELIZ. God grant him health! did you confer with him?
BUCK. Madam, we did:* he desires to make atonement
Betwixt† the duke of Gloster and your brothers,
And betwixt† them and my lord chamberlain;
And sent to warn them to his royal presence.
Q. ELIZ. Would all were well!—but that will never be;—
I fear our happiness is at the height.

Enter GLOUCESTER, HASTINGS, *and* DORSET.

GLO. They do me wrong, and I will not endure it:—
Who are they that complain ‡ unto the king,
That I, forsooth, am stern, and love them not?
By holy Paul, they love his grace but lightly,
That fill his ears with such dissentious rumours.
Because I cannot flatter, and speak § fair,
Smile in men's faces, smooth, deceive, and cog,
Duck with French nods and apish courtesy,[b]
I must be held a rancorous enemy.
Cannot a plain man live, and think no harm,
But thus his simple truth must be abus'd
By || silken, sly, insinuating Jacks?
GREY. To whom¶ in all this presence speaks your grace?
GLO. To thee, that hast nor honesty nor grace.
When have I injur'd thee? when done thee wrong?—
Or thee?—or thee?—or any of your faction?
A plague upon you all! His royal grace,—
Whom God preserve better than you would wish!—
Cannot be quiet scarce a breathing-while,
But you must trouble him with lewd complaints.

(*) First folio, *eyes*. (†) First folio, *on*.
(‡) First folio, *harmes*. (§) First folio, *the lord*.

[a] Stanley.] He is styled *Derby* in the old copies; but he was not created Earl of Derby until after Henry VII. came to the throne.

[b] Duck with French nods and apish courtesy,—] "An importation of artificial manners seems to have afforded our ancient poets a never failing topick of invective. So, in A Tragical Discourse of the Haplesse Man's Life, by Churchyard, 1593:—

'We make a legge, and kisse the hand withall,
(A *French* device, nay sure a Spanish tricke)
And speake in print, and say loe at your call
I will remaine your owne both dead and quicke.
A courtier so can give a lobbe a licke,
And dress a dolt in motley for a while,
And so in sleeve at silly woodcocke smile.'"
STEEVENS.

(*) First folio, *I madam*. (†) First folio, *Betweene*.
(‡) First folio, *Who is it that complains*.
(§) First folio, *look*. (||) First folio, *with*.
(¶) First folio, *who*.

Q. ELIZ. Brother of Gloster, you mistake the matter:
The king, of* his own royal disposition,
And not provok'd by any suitor else;
Aiming, belike, at your interior hatred,
Which† in your outward action shows itself,
Against my children, brothers, and myself,
Makes him to send, that thereby he may gather
The ground of your ill-will, and so remove it.[a]

GLO. I cannot tell;[b]—the world is grown so bad,
That wrens make prey where eagles dare not perch:
Since every Jack became a gentleman,
There's many a gentle person made a Jack.

Q. ELIZ. Come, come, we know your meaning, brother Gloster;
You envy my advancement, and my friends';
God grant we never may have need of you!

GLO. Meantime, God grants that we‡ have need of you:
Our brother is imprison'd by your means,
Myself disgrac'd, and the nobility
Held in contempt; whilst many fair§ promotions
Are daily given to ennoble those
That scarce, some two days since, were worth a noble.

Q. ELIZ. By Him that rais'd me to this careful height
From that contented hap which I enjoy'd,
I never did incense his majesty
Against the duke of Clarence, but have been
An earnest advocate to plead for him.
My lord, you do me shameful injury,
Falsely to draw me in these vile suspects.

GLO. You may deny that you were not the cause ||
Of my lord Hastings' late imprisonment.

RIV. She may, my lord; for—

GLO. *She may*, lord Rivers!—why, who knows not so?
She may do more, sir, than denying that:
She may help you to many fair preferments;
And then deny her aiding hand therein,
And lay those honours on your high deserts.¶
What may she not? *She may*,—ay, marry, may she,—

RIV. What, *marry, may she?*

GLO. *What, marry, may she?* marry with a king,
A bachelor,** a handsome stripling too:
I wis your grandam had a worser match.

Q. ELIZ. My lord of Gloster, I have too long borne
Your blunt upbraidings and your bitter scoffs;
By heaven, I will acquaint his majesty,
With those gross taunts I often* have endur'd.
I had rather be a country servant-maid,
Than a great queen, with this condition—
To be thus taunted, scorn'd, and baited at:—[c]
Small joy have I in being England's queen.

Enter QUEEN MARGARET, *behind.*

Q. MAR. [*Aside.*] And lessen'd be that small, God, I beseech thee!†
Thy honour, state, and seat, is due to me.

GLO. What! threat you me with telling of the king?
Tell him and spare not; look, what have I said[d]
I will avouch‡ in presence of the king:
[I dare adventure to be sent to the Tower.][e]
'T is time to speak,—my pains are quite forgot.

Q. MAR. [*Aside.*] Out, devil! I§ remember them too well:
Thou slew'st || my husband Henry in the Tower,
And Edward, my poor son, at Tewksbury.

GLO. Ere you were queen, ay, or your husband king,
I was a pack-horse in his great affairs;
A weeder-out of his proud adversaries,
A liberal rewarder of his friends;
To royalize his blood, I spilt¶ mine own.

Q. MAR. [*Aside.*] Yea, and much better blood than his or thine.

GLO. In all which time, you and your husband Grey
Were factious for the house of Lancaster;—
And, Rivers, so were you.—Was not your husband
In Margaret's battle at Saint Albans slain?
Let me put in your minds, if you forget,
What you have been ere this, and what you are;
Withal, what I have been, and what I am.

Q. MAR. [*Aside.*] A murd'rous villain, and so still thou art.

GLO. Poor Clarence did forsake his father Warwick,
Ay, and forswore himself,—which Jesu pardon!—

Q. MAR. [*Aside.*] Which God revenge!

GLO. To fight on Edward's party for the crown;
And, for his meed, poor lord, he is mew'd up:
I would to God my heart were flint, like Edward's,
Or Edward's soft and pitiful, like mine;
I am too childish-foolish for this world.

Q. MAR. [*Aside.*] Hie thee to hell for shame, and leave the world,
Thou cacodæmon! there thy kingdom is.

(*) First folio, *on.* (†) First folio, *That.*
(‡) First folio, *I.* (§) First folio, *while great.*
(||) First folio, *meane.* (¶) First folio, *desert.*
(**) First folio inserts, *and.*

(*) First folio, *that oft I.* (†) First folio, *him.*
(‡) First folio, *avouch't.* (§) First folio inserts, *do.*
(||) First folio, *kill'dst.* (¶) First folio, *spent.*

[a] *Makes him to send, that* thereby he may gather
The ground of your ill-will, and so remove it.]

In the folio, this is reduced to a single line,—

"Makes him to send, that *he may learne the ground.*"

[b] I cannot tell;—] I cannot account for it, I cannot make it out. See note (d), p. 577, Vol. I.

[c] To be thus taunted, scorn'd, and baited at:—] The folio has,—"To be *so* baited, scorn'd, and *stormed* at."

[d] Tell him, and spare not; &c.] This line is omitted in the folio.

[e] I dare adventure to be sent to the Tower.] A line which is only in the folio.

RIV. My lord of Gloster, in those busy days,
Which here you urge to prove us enemies,
We follow'd then our lord, our lawful* king;
So should we you, if you should be our king.
GLO. If I should be?—I had rather be a pedlar:
Far be it from my heart, the thought of it!†
Q. ELIZ. As little joy, my lord, as you suppose
You should enjoy, were you this country's king,—
As little joy may you suppose in me,
That I enjoy, being the queen thereof.
Q. MAR. [*Aside.*] As‡ little joy enjoys the queen thereof;
For I am she, and altogether joyless.
I can no longer hold me patient.— [*Advancing.*
Hear me, you wrangling pirates, that fall out
In sharing that which you have pill'd[a] from me!
Which of you trembles not that looks on me?
If not, that I being§ queen, you bow like subjects;
Yet that, by you depos'd, you quake like rebels?—
O,‖ gentle villain, do not turn away!
GLO. Foul wrinkled witch, what mak'st thou in my sight?
Q. MAR. But repetition of what thou hast [marr'd;
That will I make, before I let thee go.
[GLO. Wert thou not banished,[b] on pain of death?
Q. MAR. I was; but I do find more pain in banishment,
Than death can yield me here by my abode.]
A husband and a son thou ow'st to me,—
And thou, a kingdom;—all of you, allegiance:
This sorrow that I have, by right is yours;
And all the pleasures you usurp are mine.
GLO. The curse my noble father laid on thee,—
When thou didst crown his warlike brows with paper,
And with thy scorn drew'st rivers from his eyes;
And then, to dry them, gav'st the duke a clout
Steep'd in the faultless blood of pretty Rutland;—
His curses, then from bitterness of soul
Denounc'd against thee, are all fallen upon thee;
And God, not we, hath plagu'd[c] thy bloody deed.
Q. ELIZ. So just is God to right the innocent.
HAST. O, 'twas the foulest deed to slay that babe,
And the most merciless that e'er was heard of!
RIV. Tyrants themselves wept when it was reported.
DORS. No man but prophesied revenge for it.
BUCK. Northumberland, then present, wept to see it.
Q. MAR. What! were you snarling all before [I came,
Ready to catch each other by the throat,
And turn you all your hatred now on me?
Did York's dread curse prevail so much with heaven,
That Henry's death, my lovely Edward's death,
Their kingdom's loss, my woeful banishment,
Could* all but answer for that peevish brat?
Can curses pierce the clouds and enter heaven?—
Why, then give way, dull clouds, to my quick curses!—[d]
If† not by war, by surfeit die your king,
As ours by murder, to make him a king!
Edward thy son, which‡ now is prince of Wales,
For Edward my§ son, which‡ was prince of Wales,
Die in his youth by like untimely violence!
Thyself a queen, for me that was a queen,
Outlive thy glory, like my wretched self!
Long mayst thou live to wail thy children's loss;‖
And see another, as I see thee now,
Deck'd in thy glory,¶ as thou'rt stall'd in mine!
Long die thy happy days before thy death;
And, after many lengthen'd hours of grief,
Die neither mother, wife, nor England's queen!—
Rivers and Dorset, you were standers by,—
And so wast thou, lord Hastings,—when my son
Was stabb'd with bloody daggers; God, I pray him,
That none of you may live his natural age,
But by some unlook'd accident cut off!
GLO. Have done thy charm, thou hateful wither'd hag!
Q. MAR. And leave out thee? stay, dog, for thou shalt hear me.
If heaven have any grievous plague in store,
Exceeding those that I can wish upon thee,
O, let them keep it till thy sins be ripe,
And then hurl down their indignation
On thee, the troubler of the poor world's peace!
The worm of conscience still be-gnaw thy soul!
Thy friends suspect for traitors while thou liv'st,
And take deep traitors for thy dearest friends!
No sleep close up that deadly eye of thine,
Unless it be while some tormenting dream
Affrights thee with a hell of ugly devils!
Thou elvish-mark'd, abortive, rooting hog!
Thou that wast seal'd in thy nativity
The slave of nature and the son of hell!

(*) First folio, *soveraigne*. (†) First folio, *thereof*. (‡) Old text, *A*. (§) First folio, *am*. (‖) First folio, *Ah*.

(*) First folio, *Should*. (†) First folio, *Though*. (‡) First folio, *that*. (§) First folio, *our*. (‖) First folio, *death*. (¶) First folio, *rights*.

a *That which you have* pill'd *from me!*] *Pilled* is the same as pillaged. To *pill*, means literally to *peel*, or *strip* off the rind or skin.

b Wert thou not banished, &c.] This, and the two lines following, are not in the quartos.

c Plagu'd—] In our early language to *plague* meant to *punish*. Thus, in "King John," Act II. Sc. 1:—

"That he's not only *plagued* for her sin,
But God hath made her sin and her the *plague*
On this removed issue."

d Why, then give way, dull clouds, to my quick curses!—] This line serves to show that the accepted explanation of "lither sky" in the "First Part of Henry VI." is erroneous. Instead of *yielding* sky, it certainly meant *heavy, lazy* sky. See note (a), p. 320.

Thou slander of thy mother's heavy* womb!
Thou loathed issue of thy father's loins!
Thou rag of honour! thou detested—

GLO. Margaret.

Q. MAR. Richard!

GLO. Ha?

Q. MAR. I call thee not.

GLO. I cry thee mercy then; for I did think,
That thou hadst[a] call'd me all these bitter names.

Q. MAR. Why so I did; but look'd for no reply.
O, let me make the period to my curse!

GLO. 'Tis done by me, and ends in—Margaret.

Q. ELIZ. Thus have you breath'd your curse against yourself.

Q. MAR. Poor painted queen, vain flourish of my fortune!
Why strew'st thou sugar on that bottled[b] spider,
Whose deadly web ensnareth thee about?
Fool, fool! thou whett'st a knife to kill thyself.
The time will come when thou shalt wish for me
To help thee curse that pois'nous† bunch-back'd toad.[c]

HAST. False-boding woman, end thy frantic curse,
Lest to thy harm thou move our patience.

Q. MAR. Foul shame upon you! you have all mov'd mine.

RIV. Were you well serv'd, you would be taught your duty.

Q. MAR. To serve me well, you all should do me duty,
Teach me to be your queen, and you my subjects:
O, serve me well, and teach yourselves that duty!

DORS. Dispute not with her, she is lunatic.

Q. MAR. Peace, master marquis, you are malapert:
Your fire-new stamp of honour is scarce current:
O, that your young nobility could judge,
What 'twere to lose it, and be miserable!
They that stand high have mighty‡ blasts to shake them;
And if they fall, they dash themselves to pieces.

GLO. Good counsel, marry;—learn it, learn it, marquis.

DORS. It touches you, my lord, as much as me.

GLO. Yea,§ and much more: but I was born so high,
Our aiery buildeth in the cedar's top,
And dallies with the wind, and scorns the sun.

Q. MAR. And turns the sun to shade;—alas! alas!—
Witness my sun, now in the shade of death,
Whose bright out-shining beams thy cloudy wrath
Hath in eternal darkness folded up.
Your aiery buildeth in our aiery's nest:—
O God, that seest it, do not suffer it;
As it was* won with blood, lost be it so!

BUCK. Peace, peace, for shame, if not for charity.

Q. MAR. Urge neither charity nor shame to me;
Uncharitably with me have you dealt,
And shamefully by you my hopes† are butcher'd.
My charity is outrage, life my shame,—
And in that shame still live my sorrow's rage!

BUCK. Have done, have done.

Q. MAR. O princely Buckingham, I‡ kiss thy hand,
In sign of league and amity with thee:
Now fair befall thee, and thy princely§ house!
Thy garments are not spotted with our blood,
Nor thou within the compass of my curse.

BUCK. Nor no one here; for curses never pass
The lips of those that breathe them in the air.

Q. MAR. I'll not believe‖ but they ascend the sky,
And there awake God's gentle-sleeping peace.
O Buckingham, take heed of yonder dog;
Look, when he fawns, he bites; and when he bites,
His venom tooth will rankle to the death:
Have not to do with him, beware of him;
Sin, death, and hell, have set their marks on him,
And all their ministers attend on him.

GLO. What doth she say, my lord of Buckingham?

BUCK. Nothing that I respect, my gracious lord.

Q. MAR. What, dost thou scorn me for my gentle counsel?
And soothe the devil that I warn thee from?
O, but remember this another day,
When he shall split thy very heart with sorrow,
And say, poor Margaret was a prophetess!—
Live each of you the subjects to his hate,
And he to yours, and all of you to God's! [*Exit.*

HAST. My hair doth stand on end to hear her curses.

RIV. And so doth mine; I wonder¶ she's at liberty.

GLO. I cannot blame her: by God's holy mother,
She hath had too much wrong, and I repent
My part thereof that I have done to her.

(*) First folio, *heavie Mothers*. (†) Quartos, *poisoned*.
(‡) First folio, *many*. (§) First folio, *I*.

(*) First folio, *is*. (†) First folio, *my hopes by you*.
(‡) First folio, *Ile*. (§) First folio, *noble*.
(‖) First folio, *I will not thinke*. (¶) First folio, *I muse why*.

a ——— for I did think,
That thou hadst—]
The reading of the folio: the quartos have,—
"———for I had thought
Thou hadst," &c.

b Bottled *spider*,—] That is, *swollen, bloated*, spider.

c *The time will come when thou shalt wish for me
To help thee curse* that, &c.]
So the quartos The folio reads,—
"The *day* will come *that* thou shalt wish for me
To help thee curse *this*," &c.

Q. ELIZ. I never did her any, to my knowledge.
GLO. Yet you have all the vantage of her wrong.
I was too hot to do somebody good,
That is too cold in thinking of it now.
Marry, as for Clarence, he is well repaid;
He is frank'd up to fatting[a] for his pains;—
God pardon them that are the cause of it!*
RIV. A virtuous and a christian-like conclusion,
To pray for them that have done scath to us.
GLO. [*Aside.*[b]] So do I ever, being well advis'd;—
For had I curs'd now, I had curs'd myself.

Enter CATESBY.

CATES. Madam, his majesty doth call for you,—
And for your grace,—and you, my noble lords.[c]
Q. ELIZ. Catesby, we† come:—lords, will you go with us?†
RIV. Madam, we will attend[d] your grace.
[*Exeunt all except* GLOUCESTER.
GLO. I do the wrong, and first begin to brawl.
The secret mischiefs that I set abroach,
I lay unto the grievous charge of others.
Clarence,—whom I, indeed, have laid‡ in darkness,—
I do beweep to many simple gulls;
Namely, to Hastings, Stanley, Buckingham;
And say—it is§ the queen and her allies
That stir the king against the duke my brother.
Now they believe it; and withal whet me
To be reveng'd on Rivers, Vaughan,|| Grey:
But then I sigh, and, with a piece of scripture,
Tell them that God bids us do good for evil:
And thus I clothe my naked villainy
With old odd¶ ends, stol'n out** of holy writ;
And seem a saint, when most I play the devil.—
But soft! here come my executioners.—

Enter two Murderers.

How now, my hardy, stout, resolved mates!
Are ye now going to despatch this deed?††

1 MURD. We are, my lord; and come to have the warrant,
That we may be admitted where he is.
GLO. Well thought upon; I have it here about me: [*Gives the warrant.*
When you have done, repair to Crosby-place.
But, sirs, be sudden in the execution,
Withal obdurate; do not hear him plead,
For Clarence is well spoken, and perhaps,
May move your hearts to pity, if you mark him.
1 MURD. Tut, tut, my lord, we will not stand to prate,
Talkers are no good doers; be assur'd,
We go to use our hands, and not our tongues.
GLO. Your eyes drop* millstones, when fools' eyes drop tears:[e]
I like you, lads;—about your business [straight;
Go, go, dispatch.
1 MURD. We will, my noble lord.[f]] [*Exeunt.*

SCENE IV.—*The same. A Room in the* Tower.

Enter CLARENCE *and* BRAKENBURY.

BRAK. Why looks your grace so heavily to-day?
CLAR. O, I have pass'd a miserable night,
So full of ugly sights, of ghastly dreams,[g]
That, as I am a christian-faithful man,
I would not spend another such a night,
Though 'twere to buy a world of happy days;—
So full of dismal terror was the time!
BRAK. What was your dream? I long to hear you tell it.[h]
CLAR. Methought, I was embark'd for Burgundy;[i]
And in my company my brother Gloster;
Who from my cabin tempted me to walk
Upon the hatches; thence† we look'd toward England,
And cited up a thousand fearful‡ times,

(*) First folio, *thereof.* (†) First folio, *I—mee.*
(‡) First folio, *cast.* (§) First folio, *And tell them 't is.*
(||) First folio, *Dorset.* (¶) First folio, *odde old.*
(**) First folio, *forth.* (††) First folio, *thing.*

(*) First folio, *fall.* (†) First folio, *there.*
(‡) First folio, *heavy.*

a *He is* frank'd up to fatting—] He is *styed* up. Speaking of hogs, in his Description of Britaine, Holinshed says, "The husbandmen and farmers never *fraunke* them above three or four months, in which time he is dyeted with otes and peason, and lodged on the bare planches of an uneasie coate."—Book III. p. 1096.

b *Aside*] The old copies rarely direct a speech to be spoken aside: appended to this passage, the folio has, "*Speakes to himselfe.*"

c *And* you, *my* noble lords.] So the first quarto 1597: the folio reads, "and *yours* my *gracious Lord.*"

d Madam we will attend your grace.] The folio has, "We wait upon your Grace."

e Your eyes drop millstones, when fools' eyes drop tears:] A proverbial expression, which occurs in the tragedy of "Cæsar and Pompey," 1607:—

"Men's eyes must *mill-stones* drop, when fools shed tears."

f We will, my noble lord.] In the quartos the scene ends with Gloucester saying:—

"——about *your business.*"

A more becoming termination than for an inferior actor to have the last word.

g Of ugly sights, of ghastly dreams,—] The folio gives, "*of fearefull Dreames, of ugly sights.*"

h *What was your dream?* I long to hear you tell it.] In the folio the line stands,—

"What was your dream, *my lord, I pray you tel me.*"

i Methought, I was embark'd for Burgundy;] The folio reads,—

"*Me thoughts that I had broken from the Tower,*
And was embark'd to crosse to Burgundy."

During the wars of York and Lancaster
That had befall'n us. As we pac'd along
Upon the giddy footing of the hatches,
Methought that Gloster stumbled; and, in stumbling,*
Struck me, that thought to stay him, overboard,
Into the tumbling billows of the main.
Lord! Lord! † methought, what pain it was to drown!
What dreadful noise of waters in mine ears!
What ugly sights ‡ of death within mine eyes!
Methought,§ I saw a thousand fearful wrecks;
Ten thousand men that fishes gnaw'd upon;
Wedges of gold, great anchors, heaps of pearl,
Inestimable stones, unvalued[a] jewels,
All scatter'd in the bottom of the sea.
Some lay in dead men's skulls; and, in those ‖ holes
Where eyes did once inhabit, there were crept
(As 't were in scorn of eyes) reflecting gems,
Which ¶ woo'd the slimy bottom of the deep,
And mock'd the dead bones that lay scatter'd by.

BRAK. Had you such leisure in the time of death,
To gaze upon these secrets of the deep?

CLAR. Methought I had; for still the envious flood
Kept in my soul,[b] and would not let it forth
To seek ** the empty, vast, and wand'ring air;
But smother'd it within my panting bulk,
Which ¶ almost burst to belch it in the sea.

BRAK. Awak'd you not in this sore agony?

CLAR. O, no, my dream was lengthen'd after life;
O, then began the tempest of my soul!
I pass'd, methought, the melancholy flood,
With that grim †† ferryman which poets write of,
Unto the kingdom of perpetual night.
The first that there did greet my stranger soul,
Was my great father-in-law, renowned Warwick;
Who cried ‡‡ aloud,—*What scourge for perjury*
Can this dark monarchy afford false Clarence?
And so he vanish'd: then came wand'ring by
A shadow like an angel, with bright hair
Dabbled in blood; and he shriek'd out aloud,—
Clarence is come,—false, fleeting, perjur'd Clarence,
That stabb'd me in the field by Tewksbury;—
*Seize on him, furies, take him to your torments!**—
With that, methought, a legion of foul fiends
Environ'd me, and howled in mine ears
Such hideous cries, that, with the very noise,
I trembling wak'd, and, for a season after,
Could not believe but that I was in hell;—
Such terrible impression made the † dream.

BRAK. No marvel, lord, though[c] it affrighted you;
I promise you, I am afraid to hear you tell it.[d]

CLAR. O Brakenbury, ‡ I have done these things,—
Which now bear[e] evidence against my soul,—
For Edward's sake; and see how he requites me!—
[O God! if my deep prayers cannot appease thee,
But thou wilt be aveng'd on my misdeeds,
Yet execute thy wrath in me alone:
O, spare my guiltless wife, and my poor children!—][f]
I pray thee, gentle keeper, stay by me,[g]
My soul is heavy, and I fain would sleep.

BRAK. I will, my lord; God give your grace good rest!— [CLARENCE *sleeps.*
Sorrow breaks seasons and reposing hours,
Makes the night morning, and the noon-tide night.
Princes have but their titles for their glories,
An outward honour for an inward toil;
And, for unfelt imagination,§
They often feel a world of restless cares:
So that, between their titles and low name,
There's nothing differs but the outward fame.

Enter the two Murderers.

In God's name what are you, and how came you hither?

1 MURD. I would speak with Clarence, and I came hither on my legs.

BRAK. Yea, are ye so brief?

2 MURD. O, sir, 't is better to be brief than tedious:—

(*) First folio, *falling*. (†) First folio, *O Lord*.
(‡) First folio, *sights of ugly*. (§) First folio, *methoughts*.
(‖) First folio, *the*. (¶) First folio, *who*.
(**) First folio, *find*. (††) First folio, *sowre*.
(‡‡) First folio, *spake*.

a Unvalued—] That is, *invaluable*.

b ——for still the envious flood
Kept *in my soul*,—]

The folio reads,—

"——and often did I strive
To *yeeld the Ghost; but* still the envious Flood
Stop't in my soule," &c.

(*) First folio, *unto Torment*. (†) First folio, *my*.
(‡) First folio, *Ah, Keeper, Keeper*. (§) First folio, *imaginations*.

c *No marvel, lord*, though *it affrighted you;*] See note (d), p. 492.

d I promise you, *I am afraid*, &c.] In the folio, "I am affraid (*me thinkes*) to hear," &c.

e Which *now* bear *evidence*—] The folio has, "*That* now *give* evidence," &c.

f O God! if my deep prayers, &c.] The four lines composing this prayer are not found in the quartos.

g I pray thee, gentle keeper, stay by me.] In the folio,—

"Keeper, I prythee sit by me a-while."

Show him our commission; talk no more.[a]

[*A paper is delivered to* BRAKENBURY, *who reads it.*

BRAK. I am, in this, commanded to deliver
The noble duke of Clarence to your hands:—
I will not reason what is meant hereby,
Because I will be guiltless of * the meaning.
Here are the keys,—there sits the duke asleep:
I'll to his majesty and certify his grace
That thus I have resign'd my place to you.[b]

1 MURD. Do so;† it is a point of wisdom:

[*Exit* BRAKENBURY.

2 MURD. What, shall we stab him as he sleeps?

1 MURD. No; then he'll say, 't was done cowardly, when he wakes.

2 MURD. *When he wakes!* why, fool,‡ he shall never wake till the great judgment day.

1 MURD. Why, then he'll say, we stabbed him sleeping.

2 MURD. The urging of that word, *judgment*, hath bred a kind of remorse in me.

1 MURD. What! art thou afraid?

2 MURD. Not to kill him, having a warrant for it; § but to be damned for killing him, from || which no warrant can defend us.

[1 MURD. I thought thou hadst been resolute.

2 MURD. So I am, to let him live.][c]

1 MURD. I'll back to the duke of Gloucester, and tell him so.

2 MURD. Nay, I pr'ythee, stay a little: I hope my holy ¶ humour will change; it was wont to hold me but while one could tell twenty.

1 MURD. How dost thou feel thyself now?

2 MURD. Faith,** some certain dregs of conscience are yet within me.

1 MURD. Remember our reward, when the deed's done.

2 MURD. Zounds,†† he dies; I had forgot the reward.

1 MURD. Where is thy conscience now?

2 MURD. In the duke of Gloucester's purse.

1 MURD. So,‡‡ when he opens his purse to give us our reward, thy conscience flies out.

2 MURD. Let it go;[d] there's few or none will entertain it.

1 MURD. How if it come to thee again?

2 MURD. I'll not meddle with it, it is a dangerous thing,* it makes a man a coward; a man cannot steal, but it accuseth him; he † cannot swear, but it checks him; he † cannot lie with his neighbour's wife, but it detects him: 't is a blushing shame-faced spirit, that mutinies in a man's bosom; it fills one † full of obstacles: it made me once restore a purse of gold, that I found; it beggars any man that keeps it: it is turned out of all ‡ towns and cities for a dangerous thing; and every man that means to live well, endeavours to trust to himself, and live without it.

1 MURD. Zounds,§ it is even now at my elbow, persuading me not to kill the duke.

2 MURD. Take the devil in thy mind, and believe him not; he would insinuate with thee but to make thee sigh.

1 MURD. I am strong-framed, he cannot prevail with me.[e]

2 MURD. Spoke like a tall fellow, || that respects his ¶ reputation. Come, shall we fall to work?

1 MURD. Take him over** the costard with the hilts of thy sword, and then throw him into the malmsey-butt in the next room.

2 MURD. O excellent device! and make a sop of him.[f]

1 MURD. Hark! he stirs. Shall I strike?

1 MURD. No, first let's reason with him.

CLAR. [*Awaking.*] Where art thou, keeper? give me a cup of wine.

1 MURD. You shall have wine enough, my lord, anon.

CLAR. In God's name, what art thou?

1 MURD. A man, as you are.

CLAR. But not, as I am, royal.

1 MURD. Nor you, as we are, loyal.

CLAR. Thy voice is thunder, but thy looks are humble.

(*) First folio, *from*. (†) First folio, *You may sir.*
(‡) First folio omits, *when he wakes*, and *fool*.
(§) First folio omits, *for it*. (||) First folio inserts, *the*.
(¶) First folio, *this passionate humor of mine*.
(**) First folio omits, *Faith*. (††) First folio, *Come*.
(‡‡) First folio omits, *So*.

[a] Talk no more.] In the folio, the dialogue begins thus,—

"1 MUR. Ho, who's heere?
BRA. What would'st thou Fellow? And how camm'st thou hither.
2 MUR. I would speak with Clarence, and I came hither on my Legges.
BRA. What so breefe?
1 'T is better (Sir) then to be tedious:
Let him see our Commission, and talke no more."

[b] Here are the keys,—there sits the duke asleep:
I'll to his majesty and certify his grace
That thus I have resign'd my place to you.]

(*) First folio omits, *it is a dangerous thing*.
(†) First folio, *a man*. (‡) First folio omits, *all*.
(§) First folio omits, *Zounds*. (||) First folio, *man*.
(¶) First folio, *thy*. (**) First folio, *on*.

So the quartos: the folio gives,—

"There lies the Duke asleepe, and there the Keyes.
Ile to the King and signifie to him
That thus I have resign'd to you my charge."

[c] To let him live.] The lines in brackets are omitted in the quartos.

[d] Let it go;] The folio has, "*T is no matter;* let it goe."

[e] *I am strong*-framed, &c.] So the folio text; the quartos read, "*Tut*, I am strong *in fraud;* he cannot prevail with me, *I warrant thee.*"

[f] And make a sop of him.] The folio continues the dialogue thus:—

"1. Soft, he wakes.
2. Strike.
1. No, wee'l reason with him."

MURD. My voice is now the king's, my looks mine own.

CLAR. How darkly and how deadly dost thou speak!
[Your eyes do menace me: why look you pale?][a]
Tell me who are you? wherefore come you hither?

BOTH MURD. To, to, to,—

CLAR. To murder me?

BOTH MURD. Ay, ay.

CLAR. You scarcely have the hearts to tell me so,
And therefore cannot have the hearts to do it.
Wherein, my friends, have I offended you?

1 MURD. Offended us you have not, but the king.

CLAR. I shall be reconcil'd to him again.

2 MURD. Never, my lord; therefore prepare to die.

CLAR. Are you call'd forth from out a world of men,[b]
To slay the innocent? What is my offence?
Where is the evidence that doth accuse me?
What lawful quest have given their verdict up
Unto the frowning judge? or who pronounc'd
The bitter sentence of poor Clarence' death?
Before I be convict by course of law,
To threaten me with death is most unlawful.
I charge you, as you hope to have redemption
By Christ's dear blood shed for our grievous sins,[c]
That you depart, and lay no hands on me;
The deed you undertake is damnable.

1 MURD. What we will do, we do upon command.

2 MURD. And he that hath commanded is the* king.

CLAR. Erroneous vassal!† the great King of kings
Hath in the table of his law commanded,
That thou shalt do no murder; wilt thou‡ then
Spurn at his edict, and fulfil a man's?
Take heed; for he holds vengeance in his hand,
To hurl upon their heads that break his law.

2 MURD. And that same vengeance doth he hurl§ on thee,
For false forswearing, and for murder too:
Thou didst receive the holy || sacrament,
To fight in quarrel of the house of Lancaster.

1 MURD. And, like a traitor to the name of God,
Didst break that vow; and with thy treacherous blade
Unripp'dst the bowels of thy sovereign's son.

---

[a] Your eyes do menace me: why look you pale?] This line is omitted in the quartos, possibly because Clarence had just before said,—"thy looks are humble," and the next in the folio reads,—

"Who sent you hither? Wherefore do you come?"

[b] *Are you* call'd *forth* from out *a world of men*,—] The folio has,—

"Are you *drawne* forth *among* a world of men."

[c] *I charge you, as you hope* to have redemption
By Christ's dear blood shed for our grievous sins,—] So the quartos: the folio poorly reads,—

"I charge you, as you hope *for any goodnesse*,"

and omits the emphatic line which follows.

(*) First folio, *our*. (†) First folio, *Vassals*. (‡) First folio, *will you*. (§) Quartos, *throw*. (||) First folio omits, *holy*.

2 MURD. Whom thou wert* sworn to cherish and defend. [law to us,
1 MURD. How canst thou urge God's dreadful
When thou hast broke it in such dear degree?
CLAR. Alas! for whose sake did I that ill deed?
For Edward, for my brother, for his sake:
Why, sirs,† he sends you not to murder me for this;
For in this‡ sin he is as deep as I.
If God will be avenged for the deed,
[O, know you yet, he doth it publicly;][a]
Take not the quarrel from his powerful arm;
He needs no indirect nor§ lawless course,
To cut off those that have offended him.
1 MURD. Who made thee then a bloody minister,
When gallant-springing, brave Plantagenet,
That princely novice, was struck dead by thee?
CLAR. My brother's love, the devil, and my rage. [faults,
1 MURD. Thy brother's love, our duty, and thy
Provoke us hither now to slaughter thee.
CLAR. If you do love my brother, hate not me;
I am his brother, and I love him well.
If you are hir'd for meed, go back again,
And I will send you to my brother Gloster;
Who shall reward you better for my life,
Than Edward will for tidings of my death.
2 MURD. You are deceiv'd, your brother Gloster hates you. [dear:
CLAR. O, no, he loves me, and he holds me
Go you to him from me.
BOTH MURD. Ay, so we will. [York
CLAR. Tell him, when that our princely father
Bless'd his three sons with his victorious arm,
And charg'd us from his soul to love each other,[b]
He little thought of this divided friendship:
Bid Gloster think of this, and he will weep.
1 MURD. Ay, mill-stones; as he lesson'd us to weep.
CLAR. O, do not slander him, for he is kind.
1 MURD. Right; as snow in harvest.—Come, you deceive yourself;
'Tis he that sends us to destroy you here.[c]

(*) First folio, *wast*. (†) First folio omits, *Why, sirs*.
(‡) First folio, *that*. (§) First folio, *or*.

a O, know you yet, he doth it publicly;] A line omitted in the quartos.
b And charg'd us, &c.] This line is not in the folio.
c 'Tis he that sends us to destroy you here.] In the quartos,—
"'Tis he hath sent us hither now to slaughter thee."
d Ay, thus, and thus! [*Stabs him.*] if this will not serve,—] The confusion observable in the latter portion of this scene as it is presented in the folio, is confirmatory, perhaps, of our theory that the text of "Richard III." in that edition is made up in parts from an earlier manuscript than that from which the quartos were printed. In the passages under consideration, the player-editors have retained five lines, beginning,—"Which of you, if you were a prince's son," that were apparently the poet's first sketch of a speech for Clarence, and which he no doubt intended to be superseded by his after-thought, and this retention has reduced the trialogue to chaos. Let any one compare the following transcript of the speeches, as they stand in the folio, with the concise and lucid colloquy of the quartos, and he will not find it difficult to determine which text bears the latest marks of the

CLAR. It cannot be; for he bewept my fortune,
And hugg'd me in his arms, and swore, with sobs,
That he would labour my delivery.
1 MURD. Why, so he doth, when he delivers you
From this earth's thraldom to the joys of heaven.
2 MURD. Make peace with God, for you must die, my lord.
CLAR. Hast thou that holy feeling in thy soul,
To counsel me to make my peace with God,
And art thou yet to your own soul so blind,
That thou wilt war with God by murdering me?—
Ah, sirs, consider, they that set you on
To do this deed, will hate you for this deed.
2 MURD. What shall we do?
CLAR. Relent, and save your souls.
1 MURD. Relent! 'tis cowardly, and womanish.
CLAR. Not to relent, is beastly, savage, devilish.—
My friend, I spy some pity in thy looks;
O, if thine eye be not a flatterer,
Come thou on my side, and entreat for me,
A begging prince what beggar pities not?
1 MURD. Ay, thus, and thus! [*Stabs him.*] if this will not serve,[d]
I'll chop thee in the malmsey-butt in the next room.(4)
2 MURD. A bloody deed, and desperately perform'd!
How fain, like Pilate, would I wash my hands
Of this most grievous guilty murder done![e] (5)
1 MURD. Why dost not thou help me?
By heavens, the duke shall know how slack thou art.*
2 MURD. I would he knew that I had sav'd his brother!
Take thou the fee, and tell him what I say;
For I repent me that the duke is slain. [*Exit.*
1 MURD. So do not I; go, coward as thou art.—
Now, must I† hide his body in some hole,
Until the duke take order for his burial:
And when I have my meed, I must away;
For this will out, and here I must not stay.
[*Exit with the body.*

(*) First folio, *you have beene*. (†) First folio, *Well Ile go*.

author's hand:—
"2 MUR. What shall we do?
CLA. Relent, and save your soules;
Which of you, if you were a Princes Sonne,
Being pent from Liberty, as I am now,
If two such murtherers as your selves came to you,
Would not intreat for life, as you would begge
Were you in my distresse.
1 MUR. Relent? no: 'T is cowardly and womanish.
CLA. Not to relent, is beastly, savage, divellish:
My Friend, I spy some pitty in thy lookes:
O, if thine eye be not a Flatterer,
Come thou on my side, and intreate for mee,
A begging Prince, what begger pitties not.
2 MURD. Looke behinde you, my Lord.
1 MURD. Take that, and that, if all this will not do, [*Stabs him.*
Ile drowne you in the Malmesey-But within."
e *Of this most grievous* guilty *murder* done!] The folio reads,—
"Of this most greevous murther."

ACT II.

SCENE I.—*The same. A Room in the Palace.*

Enter KING EDWARD (*led in sick*), QUEEN ELIZABETH, DORSET, RIVERS, HASTINGS, BUCKINGHAM, GREY, *and others.*

K. EDW. Why, so :—now have I done a good day's work ;—
You peers, continue this united league:
I every day expect an embassage
From my Redeemer to redeem me hence ;
And now in * peace my soul shall part to heaven,
Since I have set † my friends at peace on earth.
Rivers, and Hastings, ‡ take each other's hand ;
Dissemble not your hatred, swear your love.

RIV. By heaven, my soul § is purg'd from grudging hate,
And with my hand I seal my true heart's love.

HAST. So thrive I, as I truly swear the like !

K. EDW. Take heed you dally not before your king,
Lest he, that is the supreme King of kings,
Confound your hidden falsehood, and award
Either of you to be the other's end.

HAST. So prosper I, as I swear perfect love !

RIV. And I, as I love Hastings with my heart !

K. EDW. Madam, yourself are * not exempt in † this,—
Nor you, son Dorset,—Buckingham, nor you ;—
You have been factious one against the other.
Wife, love lord Hastings, let him kiss your hand ;
And what you do, do it unfeignedly.

(*) First folio, *more to.* (†) First folio, *made.*
(‡) First folio, *Dorset and Rivers.* (§) Quartos, *heart.*

(*) First folio, *is.*
(†) First folio, *from.*

Q. ELIZ. There, Hastings;—I will never more remember
Our former hatred, so thrive I, and mine!
[K. EDW. Dorset, embrace him,—Hastings, love lord marquis.][a]
DORS. This interchange of love, I here protest,
Upon my part shall be inviolable.
HAST. And so swear I. [*They embrace.*
K. EDW. Now, princely Buckingham, seal thou this league
With thy embracements to my wife's allies,
And make me happy in your unity.
BUCK. Whenever Buckingham doth turn his hate
On you or yours,* [*To the* QUEEN.] but with all duteous love
Doth cherish you and yours, God punish me
With hate in those where I expect most love!
When I have most need to employ a friend,
And most assured that he is a friend,
Deep, hollow, treacherous, and full of guile,
Be he unto me! this do I beg of heaven,
When I am cold in zeal,† to you or yours!
[*Embracing* RIVERS, *&c.*
K. EDW. A pleasing cordial, princely Buckingham,
Is this thy vow unto my sickly heart.
There wanteth now our brother Gloster here,
To make the perfect‡ period of this peace.
BUCK. And, in good time, here comes the noble duke.[b]

Enter GLOUCESTER.

GLO. Good morrow to my sovereign king, and queen;
And, princely peers, a happy time of day!
K. EDW. Happy, indeed, as we have spent the day:—
Brother,§ we have done deeds of charity;
Made peace of enmity, fair love of hate,
Between these swelling wrong-incensed peers.
GLO. A blessed labour, my most sovereign liege.||
Among this princely heap, if any here,
By false intelligence, or wrong surmise,
Hold me a foe; if I unwittingly,¶ or in my rage,
Have aught committed that is hardly borne
By** any in this presence, I desire
To reconcile me to his friendly peace:
'Tis death to me to be at enmity;
I hate it, and desire all good men's love.—
First, madam, I entreat true peace of you,
Which I will purchase with my duteous service;—
Of you, my noble cousin Buckingham,
If ever any grudge were lodg'd between us;—
Of you, lord Rivers,—and lord Grey of you,[c]
That all without desert have frown'd on me;—
Dukes, earls, lords, gentlemen; indeed, of all.
I do not know that Englishman alive,
With whom my soul is any jot at odds,
More than the infant that is born to-night;
I thank my God for my humility.(1)
Q. ELIZ. A holy day shall this be kept hereafter:—
I would to God, all strifes were well compounded.—
My sovereign liege,* I do beseech your majesty†
To take our brother Clarence to your grace.
GLO. Why, madam, have I offer'd love for this,
To be so flouted in this royal presence?
Who knows not that the gentle duke is dead?
[*They all start.*
You do him injury to scorn his corse.
K. EDW. Who knows not he is dead! who knows he is?
Q. ELIZ. All-seeing heaven, what a world is this!
BUCK. Look I so pale, lord Dorset, as the rest?
DORS. Ay, my good lord; and no one‡ in this presence,
But his red colour hath forsook his cheeks.
K. EDW. Is Clarence dead? the order was revers'd.
GLO. But he, poor soul,‡ by your first order died,
And that a winged Mercury did bear;
Some tardy cripple bore§ the countermand,
That came too lag to see him buried.—
God grant that some, less noble and less loyal,
Nearer in bloody thoughts, but || not in blood,
Deserve not worse than wretched Clarence did,
And yet go current from suspicion!

Enter STANLEY.

STAN. A boon, my sovereign, for my service done!
K. EDW. I pr'ythee peace; my soul is full of [sorrow.
STAN. I will not rise, unless your highness grant.¶

(*) First folio, *Upon your grace.* (†) First folio, *love.* (‡) First folio, *blessed.* (§) First folio, *Gloster.* (||) First folio, *Lord.* (¶) First folio, *unwillingly.* (**) First folio, *To.*

a —Hastings, love lord marquis.] A line omitted in the quartos.
b *Here comes* the noble duke.] So the quartos. The folio reads,—
"Here comes *Sir Richard Ratcliffe, and the Duke.*"
c Of you, lord Rivers,—and lord Grey of you,—] The folio reads,—
"Of you and you, Lord Rivers and of Dorset,"
and adds, after the next line,—
"Of you, Lord Woodvill, and Lord Scales of you."

(*) First folio, *Lord.* (†) First folio, *Highnesse.* (‡) First folio, *man.* (§) First folio, *bare.* (||) First folio, *and.* (¶) First folio, *heare me.*

K. EDW. Then say at once, what is it thou demand'st.*
STAN. The forfeit, sovereign, of my servant's life;
Who slew to-day a riotous gentleman,
Lately attendant on the duke of Norfolk.
K. EDW. Have I a tongue to doom my brother's death,
And shall that tongue give pardon to a slave?
My brother slew† no man, his fault was thought,
And yet his punishment was cruel‡ death.
Who sued to me for him? who, in my rage,§
Kneel'd at my feet, and bade me be advis'd?
Who spoke of brotherhood? who spoke of love?
Who told me how the poor soul did forsake
The mighty Warwick, and did fight for me?
Who told me, in the field by‖ Tewksbury,
When Oxford had me down, he rescu'd me,
And said, *Dear brother, live, and be a king*?
Who told me, when we both lay in the field
Frozen almost to death, how he did lap me
Even in his garments, and did give himself,
All thin and naked, to the numb-cold night?
All this from my remembrance brutish wrath
Sinfully pluck'd, and not a man of you
Had so much grace to put it in my mind.
But when your carters or your waiting-vassals
Have done a drunken slaughter, and defac'd
The precious image of our dear Redeemer,
You straight are on your knees for pardon, pardon!
And I, unjustly too, must grant it you:—
But for my brother not a man would speak,—
Nor I (ungracious) speak unto myself
For him, poor soul.—The proudest of you all
Have been beholden to him in his life;
Yet none of you would once plead¶ for his life,—
O God! I fear, thy justice will take hold
On me and you, and mine and yours for this!—
Come, Hastings, help me to my closet. Ah, poor Clarence!
[*Exeunt* KING, QUEEN, HASTINGS, RIVERS, DORSET, *and* GREY.
GLO. This is the fruit** of rashness!—Mark'd you not,
How that the guilty kindred of the queen
Look'd pale when they did hear of Clarence' death?
O, they did urge it still unto the king!
God will revenge it. But come, let's in*
To comfort Edward with our company?[a]
[*Exeunt.*

SCENE II.—*The same.*

Enter the DUCHESS *of* YORK, *with a* SON *and* DAUGHTER *of* CLARENCE.

SON. Tell me, good grandam,† is our father dead?
DUCH. No, boy.
DAUGH. Why do you wring your hands,[b] and beat your breast?
And cry—*O Clarence, my unhappy son!*
SON. Why do you look on us, and shake your head,
And call us—*wretches, orphans, castaways*,
If that our noble father be‡ alive?
DUCH. My pretty cousins, you mistake me much;§
I do lament the sickness of the king,
As loth to lose him, not your father's death;
It were lost sorrow, to wail one that's lost.
SON. Then, grandam, you conclude that he is dead.[c]
The king mine uncle is to blame for this:‖
God will revenge it; whom I will importune
With daily¶ prayers all to that effect.
[DAUGH. And so will I.][d]
DUCH. Peace, children, peace! the king doth love you well:
Incapable and shallow innocents,
You cannot guess who caus'd your father's death.
SON. Grandam, we can: for my good uncle Gloster
Told me, the king, provoked** by the queen,
Devis'd impeachments to imprison him:
And when my uncle told me so, he wept,
And pitied me, and kindly kiss'd my cheek;[e]
Bade me rely on him as on my father,
And he would love me dearly as his†† child.
DUCH. Ah, that deceit should steal such gentle shape,
And with a virtuous vizor hide foul guile!‡‡
He is my son, ay, and therein my shame,
Yet from my dugs he drew not this deceit.

(*) First folio, *requests*. (†) First folio, *kill'd*.
(‡) First folio, *bitter*. (§) First folio, *wrath*.
(‖) First folio, *at*. (¶) First folio, *beg*.
(**) First folio, *fruits*.

[a] To comfort Edward with our company?] The folio adds,—
"BUC. We wait upon your grace;"
which may have been omitted, like the Murderers' "We will, my noble lord," Act I. Sc. 3, to give what is technically called the "exit" to the chief performer.

[b] Why do you wring your hands, and beat your breast?] In the folio,—
"Why do weepe so oft?" &c.

[c] Then, grandam, you conclude that he is dead.] The folio reads,—"Then you conclude, (*my* grandam) he is dead."

(*) First folio, *Come, lords, will you go*.
(†) *Good grandam tell us*. (‡) First folio, *were*.
(§) First folio, *both*. (‖) First folio, *it*.
(¶) First folio, *earnest*. (**) First folio, *provok'd to it*.
(††) First folio, *a*. (‡‡) First folio, *deepe vice*.

[d] And so will I.] Omitted in the quartos.

[e] And when my uncle told me so, he wept,
And pitied me, and kindly kiss'd my cheek;]
The quartos tamely read,—
"And when *he* told me so he wept,
And *hugd me in his arms* and kindly kist my *cheeke*."

SON. Think you, my uncle did dissemble, grandam?
DUCH. Ay, boy.
SON. I cannot think it. Hark! what noise is this?

Enter QUEEN ELIZABETH, *distractedly, with her hair dishevelled;* RIVERS *and* DORSET *following her.*

Q. ELIZ. Who,* who shall hinder me to wail and weep,
To chide my fortune, and torment myself?
I'll join with black despair against my soul,
And to myself become an enemy.
DUCH. What means this scene of rude impatience?
Q. ELIZ. To make an act of tragic violence:—
Edward, my lord, your* son, our king, is dead.—
Why grow the branches when the root is gone?
Why wither not the leaves that want their sap?—[a]
If you will live, lament; if die, be brief,
That our swift-winged souls may catch the king's;
Or, like obedient subjects, follow him
To his new kingdom of perpetual rest.[b]
DUCH. Ah, so much interest have I† in thy sorrow,
As I had title in thy noble husband!
I have bewept a worthy husband's death,
And liv'd with looking on his images:
But now two mirrors of his princely semblance
Are crack'd in pieces by malignant death;
And I for comfort have but one false glass,
Which‡ grieves me when I see my shame in him.
Thou art a widow; yet thou art a mother,
And hast the comfort of thy children left:

(*) First folio, *Ah!*

a Why grow the branches when the root is gone?
Why wither not the leaves that want their sap?—]
The quartos, less musically, read,—
"Why grow the branches, now the roote is withred?
Why wither not the leaves, the sap being gone?"

(*) First folio, *thy.* (†) First folio omits, *I.* (‡) First folio, *That.*

b *To his new kingdom of* perpetual rest.] So the quarto. The folio has,—
"To his new kingdom of *nere-changing night.*"

But death hath snatch'd my husband[a] from mine arms,
And pluck'd two crutches from my feeble hands,
Clarence, and Edward. O, what cause have I,
(Thine being but a moiety of my moan,)
To over-go thy plaints,* and drown thy cries?

SON. Ah, aunt! you wept not for our father's death!
How can we aid you with our kindred tears?

DAUGH. Our fatherless distress was left unmoan'd;
Your widow-dolour likewise be unwept!

Q. ELIZ. Give me no help in lamentation,
I am not barren to bring forth complaints:†
All springs reduce their currents to mine eyes,
That I, being govern'd by the wat'ry moon,
May send forth plenteous tears to drown the world!
Ah, for my husband, for my dear lord Edward!

CHIL. Ah, for our father, for our dear lord Clarence!

DUCH. Alas, for both, both mine, Edward and Clarence!

Q. ELIZ. What stay had I but Edward? and he's gone.

CHIL. What stay had we but Clarence? and he's gone.

DUCH. What stays had I but they? and they are gone.

Q. ELIZ. Was never widow, had so dear a loss!

CHIL. Were never orphans, had so dear a loss!

DUCH. Was never mother, had so dear a loss!
Alas! I am the mother of these moans!‡
Their woes are parcell'd, mine are§ general.
She for an Edward weeps, and so do I;
I for a Clarence weep,|| so doth not she:
These babes for Clarence weep, and so do I:
I for an Edward weep, so do not they:—[b]
Alas! you three, on me threefold distress'd,
Pour all your tears, I am your sorrow's nurse,
And I will pamper it with lamentation.

[DORS. Comfort, dear mother; God is much displeas'd,
That you take with unthankfulness his doing:
In common worldly things, 'tis call'd ungrateful,
With dull unwillingness to repay a debt,
Which with a bounteous hand was kindly lent;
Much more, to be thus opposite with heaven,
For it requires the royal debt it lent you.

RIV. Madam, bethink you, like a careful mother,
Of the young prince your son: send straight for him,
Let him be crown'd; in him your comfort lives:
Drown desperate sorrow in dead Edward's grave,
And plant your joys in living Edward's throne.[c]]

Enter GLOUCESTER, BUCKINGHAM, STANLEY, HASTINGS, RATCLIFF, *and others*.

GLO. Sister, have comfort: all of us have cause
To wail the dimming of our shining star;
But none can cure their* harms by wailing them.—
Madam, my mother, I do cry you mercy,
I did not see your grace:—humbly on my knee
I crave your blessing.

DUCH. God bless thee, and put meekness in thy breast,
Love, charity, obedience, and true duty!

GLO. Amen; [*Aside.*] and make me die a good old man!—
That is the butt-end of a mother's blessing.
I marvel why† her grace did leave it out.

BUCK. You cloudy princes and heart-sorrowing peers,
That bear this mutual heavy load of moan,
Now cheer each other in each other's love:
Though we have spent our harvest of this king,
We are to reap the harvest of his son.
The broken rancour of your high swoln hearts,‡
But lately splinted,§ knit, and join'd together,
Must gently be preserv'd, cherish'd, and kept:
Me seemeth good, that, with some little train,
Forthwith from Ludlow the young prince be fetch'd||
Hither to London, to be crown'd our king.

[RIV. Why with some little train, my lord of Buckingham?[d]

BUCK. Marry, my lord, lest, by a multitude,
The new-heal'd wound of malice should break out,
Which would be so much the more dangerous,
By how much the estate is green, and yet ungovern'd:
Where every horse bears his commanding rein,
And may direct his course as please himself,
As well the fear of harm, as harm apparent,
In my opinion, ought to be prevented.

(*) First folio, *woes*. (†) Quartos, *laments*. (‡) First folio, *Greefes*. (§) First folio, *is*. (||) First folio, *weepes*.

(*) First folio, *helpe our*. (†) First folio, *that*. (‡) First folio, *hates*. (§) First folio, *splinter'd*. (||) First folio, *fet*.

a My husband—] The quartos erroneously read, "My children."

b These babes for Clarence weep, and so do I:
I for an Edward weep, so do not they:—]

The folio text, through an oversight of the compositor, occasioned by the recurrence of the same word in both lines, reads,—

"These Babes for Clarence weepe, so do not they."

c In living Edward's throne.] This, and the preceding speech, are omitted in the quartos.

d Why with some little train, &c.] These speeches, down to where Hastings replies, "And so say I," are omitted in the quartos.

GLO. I hope the king made peace with all of us,
And the compact is firm, and true, in me.

RIV. And so in me, and so, I think, in all:
Yet, since it is but green, it should be put
To no apparent likelihood of breach,
Which, haply, by much company might be urg'd:
Therefore I say with noble Buckingham,
That it is meet so few should fetch the prince.

HAST. And so say I.][a]

GLO. Then be it so; and go we to determine
Who they shall be that straight shall post to Ludlow.*
Madam,—and you my mother,†—will you go
To give your censures in this weighty‡ business?

BOTH. With all our hearts.[b]

[*Exeunt all except* BUCKINGHAM *and* GLOUCESTER.

BUCK. My lord, whoever journeys to the prince,
For God's sake, let not us two be behind: §
For, by the way, I'll sort occasion,
As index to the story we late talk'd of,
To part the queen's proud kindred from the prince.

GLO. My other self, my counsel's consistory,
My oracle, my prophet!—My dear cousin,
I, as a child, will go by thy direction.
Toward Ludlow* then, for we'll not stay behind.
[*Exeunt.*

SCENE III.—*The same. A Street.*

Enter two Citizens, *meeting.*

1 CIT. Neighbour, well met: † whither away so fast?

2 CIT. I promise you, I scarcely know myself.

1 CIT. Hear you the news abroad?

2 CIT. Ay,‡ that the king is dead.

1 CIT. Bad § news, by'r lady; seldom comes the better:[c]
I fear, I fear, 'twill prove a giddy world.

(*) First folio, *London.* (†) First folio, *sister.*
(‡) First folio omits, *weighty.* (§) First folio, *stay at home.*

(*) First folio, *London.*
(†) First folio, *Good morrow, Neighbour.*
(‡) First folio, *Yes.* (§) First folio, *Ill.*

a And so say I.] The foregoing, and some other passages omitted in the quartos, are invariably assumed to be additions made to the play subsequent to the publication of the early quartos. We have already—in the Introductory Notice—expressed our dissent to this postulate; and we have only to add that, in the present instance, as in another—Act IV. Sc. 4, where, in one speech, there are no less than fifty-five lines not found in the quartos—not only is there no indication whatever of interpolation, but the lines supposed to be added appear, to us at least, absolutely essential to the integrity of the dialogue.

b With all our hearts.] This line is not in the folio.

c Seldom comes the better:] A proverbial saying, of which examples are abundant in our early writers.

Enter another Citizen.

3 CIT. Good morrow, neighbours.
Doth this news hold[a] of good king Edward's death?
1 CIT. Ay, sir, it is too true; God help the while!
3 CIT. Then, masters, look to see a troublous world.
1 CIT. No, no; by God's good grace his son shall reign.
3 CIT. Woe to that land that's govern'd by a child.
2 CIT. In him there is a hope of government,
Which, in his nonage, council under him,
And, in his full and ripen'd years, himself,
No doubt, shall then, and till then, govern well.
1 CIT. So stood the state, when Henry the sixth
Was crown'd in Paris but at nine months old.
3 CIT. Stood the state so? no, no, good friends, God wot;
For then this land was famously enrich'd
With politic grave counsel; then the king
Had virtuous uncles to protect his grace.
1 CIT. Why, so hath this, both by his father and mother.
3 CIT. Better it were they all came by his father;
Or by his father there were none at all:
For emulation, now who shall be nearest,
Will touch us all too near, if God prevent not.
O, full of danger is the duke of Gloster;
And the queen's sons and brothers haught and proud:[b]
And were they to be rul'd, and not to rule,
This sickly land might solace as before.
1 CIT. Come, come, we fear the worst; all will be well.
3 CIT. When clouds appear,* wise men put on their cloaks;
When great leaves fall, then winter is at hand;
When the sun sets, who doth not look for night?
Untimely storms make men expect a dearth:
All may be well; but, if God sort it so,
'Tis more than we deserve, or I expect.
2 CIT. Truly, the souls † of men are full of dread: ‡
You cannot reason almost with a man
That looks not heavily, and full of fear.§

(*) First folio, *are seen*. (†) First folio, *hearts*.
(‡) First folio, *feare*. (§) First folio, *dread*.

a Doth this news hold—] In the folio the colloquy on the entrance of the third citizen runs:—
"3. Neighbours, God speed.
1. Give you good morrow, Sir.
3. Doth *the* newes hold," &c.

b And the queen's sons and brothers haught and proud:] So the folio. The quartos, unmetrically,—
"And the queenes kindred hautie and proude."

c Last night, I heard, they lay at Northampton,
At Stony-Stratford will they be to-night:] In the folio the places are reversed; a clear though minute indication that the quarto text was in parts a corrected one. See Malone's note in the Variorum edition, xix. pp. 88—9.

3 CIT. Before the times* of change, still is it so:
By a divine instinct men's minds mistrust
Ensuing† danger; as, by proof, we see
The waters swell before a boist'rous storm.
But leave it all to God. Whither away?
2 CIT. Marry, we were sent for to the justices.
3 CIT. And so was I; I'll bear you company.
[*Exeunt.*

SCENE IV.—*The same. A Room in the Palace.*

Enter the ARCHBISHOP *of* YORK, *the young* DUKE *of* YORK, QUEEN ELIZABETH, *and the* DUCHESS *of* YORK.

ARCH. Last night, I heard, they lay at Northampton,
At Stony-Stratford will they be‡ to-night:[c]
To-morrow, or next day, they will be here.
DUCH. I long with all my heart to see the prince;
I hope he is much grown since last I saw him.
Q. ELIZ. But I hear, no; they say, my son of York
Hath almost overta'en him in his growth.
YORK. Ay, mother, but I would not have it so.
DUCH. Why, my young§ cousin, it is good to grow.
YORK. Grandam, one night as we did sit at supper,
My uncle Rivers talk'd how I did grow
More than my brother: *Ay*, quoth my uncle Gloster,
Small herbs have grace, great weeds do grow apace:
And since, methinks, I would not grow so fast,
Because sweet flowers are slow, and weeds make haste.
DUCH. Good faith, good faith, the saying did not hold
In him that did object the same to thee:
He was the wretched'st thing when he was young,
So long a growing and so leisurely,
That, if this were a rule, he should be gracious.[d]
ARCH. And so, no doubt, he is, my gracious madam.[e]
DUCH. I hope, he is; but yet let mothers doubt.
YORK. Now, by my troth, if I had been remember'd,
I could have given my uncle's grace a flout,

(*) First folio, *dayes*. (†) First folio, *Pursuing*.
(‡) First folio, *they do rest* (§) First folio, *good*.

d That, if this were a rule, &c.] The folio reads,—
"That if his rule were true."

e The quartos have,—
"Why madame, so no doubt he is."

That should have nearer touch'd his growth than he did mine.[a]

Duch. How, my pretty* York? I pr'ythee let me hear it.

York. Marry, they say my uncle grew so fast
That he could gnaw a crust at two hours old;
'T was full two years ere I could get a tooth.
Grandam, this would have been a biting[b] jest.

Duch. I pr'ythee, pretty York, who told thee this?

York. Grandam, his nurse.

Duch. His nurse! why she was dead ere thou wast born.

York. If 't were not she, I cannot tell who told me.

Q. Eliz. A parlous boy:—go to, you are too shrewd.

Arch. Good madam, be not angry with the child.

Q. Eliz. Pitchers have ears.

Arch. Here comes your son,[c] lord marquis Dorset.

Enter Dorset.

What news, lord marquis?

Dors. Such news, my lord, as grieves me to unfold.

Q. Eliz. How fares the prince?

Dors. Well, madam, and in health.

Duch. What is the news then?

Dors. Lord Rivers, and lord Grey,[d] are sent to Pomfret,
With* them sir Thomas Vaughan, prisoners.

Duch. Who hath committed them?

Dors. The mighty dukes,
Gloster and Buckingham.

Arch. For what offence?

Dors. The sum of all I can, I have disclos'd:
Why or for what, these† nobles were committed,
Is all unknown to me, my gracious lord.

Q. Eliz. Ay me, I see the downfall of our‡ house!
The tiger now hath seiz'd the gentle hind;
Insulting tyranny begins to jet§

(*) First folio, *yong*.

(*) First folio, *And with*. (†) First folio, *the*.
(‡) First folio, *ruine of my*. (§) First folio, *Iutt*.

a That should, &c.] The folio reading is,—
"To touch his growth, neerer then he toucht mine."

b *A* biting *jest*.] The quartos spoil the jest by reading, *prettie*.

c Here comes your son, &c.] In the folio we read as follows:—
"*Enter a Messenger*.
Arch. Here comes a Messenger. What Newes?
Mes. Such newes my Lord, as greeves me to report.
Qu. How doth the Prince?
Mes. Well Madam, and in health.
Dut. What is thy Newes?"

d Lord Rivers, and Lord Grey, &c.] Perhaps Capell's rhythmical arrangement of these lines might be adopted with advantage.
"Lord Rivers, and lord Grey,
Are sent to Pomfret, prisoners; and with them,
Sir Thomas Vaughan."

Upon the innocent and awless throne :—
Welcome destruction, blood, and massacre !
I see, as in a map, the end of all.
DUCH. Accursed and unquiet wrangling days,
How many of you have mine eyes beheld !
My husband lost his life to get the crown ;
And often up and down my sons were toss'd,
For me to joy, and weep, their gain and loss :
And being seated, and domestic broils
Clean over-blown, themselves, the conquerors,
Make war upon themselves ; brother to brother,
Blood to blood, self against self :—O, preposterous
And frantic outrage, end thy damned spleen ;
Or let me die, to look on death* no more !

Q. ELIZ. Come, come, my boy, we will to sanctuary.—
Madam, farewell.
DUCH. Stay, I will go with you.
Q. ELIZ. You have no cause.[a]
ARCH. My gracious lady, go,
[*To the* QUEEN.
And thither bear your treasure and your goods.
For my part, I'll resign unto your grace
The seal I keep ; and so betide to me,
As well I tender you and all of yours !
Come,* I'll conduct you to the sanctuary.(2)
[*Exeunt.*

(*) First folio, *earth.*

a Madam, farewell.
DUCH. Stay, I will go with you.
Q. ELIZ. You have no cause.]

(*) First folio, *Go.*

In the quartos the dialogue run thus :—
"QU. Come, come, my boy, we will to sanctuarie.
DUT. Ile go along with you."

ACT III.

SCENE I.—London. *A Street.*

Trumpets sound. Enter the PRINCE *of* WALES, GLOUCESTER, BUCKINGHAM, CARDINAL BOURCHIER, *and others.*

BUCK. Welcome, sweet prince, to London, to your chamber.(1)

GLO. Welcome, dear cousin, my thought's sovereign:
The weary way hath made you melancholy.

PRINCE. No, uncle; but our crosses on the way
Have made it tedious, wearisome, and heavy:
I want more uncles here to welcome me.

GLO. Sweet prince, the untainted virtue of your years
Hath not yet div'd into the world's deceit;
Nor* more can you distinguish of a man,
Than of his outward show; which, God he knows,
Seldom or never jumpeth with the heart.
Those uncles which you want were dangerous;
Your grace attended to their sugar'd words,
But look'd not on the poison of their hearts:
God keep you from them, and from such false friends!

PRINCE. God keep me from false friends! but they were none.

GLO. My lord, the mayor of London comes to greet you.

Enter the Lord Mayor, *and his* Train.

MAY. God bless your grace with health and happy days!

PRINCE. I thank you, good my lord;—and thank you all.—[a]
I thought my mother, and my brother York,
Would long ere this have met us on the way:—
Fie, what a slug is Hastings, that he comes not
To tell us whether they will come or no!

BUCK. And, in good time, here comes the sweating lord.

Enter HASTINGS.

PRINCE. Welcome, my lord: what, will our mother come?

HAST. On what occasion, God he knows, not I,
The queen your mother, and your brother York,
Have taken sanctuary: the tender prince
Would fain have come with me to meet your grace,
But by his mother was perforce withheld.

BUCK. Fie, what an indirect and peevish course
Is this of hers!—Lord cardinal, will your grace
Persuade the queen to send the duke of York
Unto his princely brother presently?
If she deny,—lord Hastings, go with him,
And from her jealous arms pluck him perforce.

CAR. My lord of Buckingham, if my weak oratory
Can from his mother win the duke of York,
Anon expect him here: but if she be obdurate
To mild entreaties, God in heaven* forbid
We should infringe the holy privilege
Of blessed sanctuary! not for all this land
Would I be guilty of so deep† a sin.

BUCK. You are too senseless-obstinate,[b] my lord,
Too ceremonious, and traditional,
Weigh it but with the grossness[c] of this age: (2)
You break not sanctuary in seizing him;
The benefit thereof is always granted
To those whose dealings have deserv'd the place,
And those who have the wit to claim the place:
This prince hath neither claim'd it, nor deserv'd it;
And therefore, in mine opinion, cannot have it:
Then, taking him from thence that is not there,
You break no privilege nor charter there.
Oft have I heard of sanctuary-men;
But sanctuary-children, ne'er till now.

CAR. My lord, you shall o'errule my mind for once.—
Come on, lord Hastings, will you go with me?

HAST. I go, my lord.

PRINCE. Good lords, make all the speedy haste you may.
[*Exeunt* CARDINAL *and* HASTINGS.
Say, uncle Gloster, if our brother come,
Where shall we sojourn till our coronation?

GLO. Where it seems‡ best unto your royal self.
If I may counsel you, some day or two,
Your highness shall repose you at the Tower:
Then where you please, and shall be thought most fit
For your best health and recreation.

PRINCE. I do not like the Tower, of any place:—
Did Julius Cæsar build that place, my lord?

GLO. He did, my gracious lord, begin that place;
Which since succeeding ages have re-edified.

PRINCE. Is it upon record, or else reported
Successively from age to age, he built it?

BUCK. Upon record, my gracious lord.

PRINCE. But say, my lord, it were not register'd;
Methinks the truth should live from age to age,
As 't were retail'd to all posterity,
Even to the general all-ending§ day.

GLO. [*Aside.*] So wise, so young, they say, do ne'er live long.

PRINCE. What say you, uncle?

GLO. I say, without characters, fame lives long.—

(*) First folio, *No.*

[a] And thank you all.] Here, in all modern editions, we find a stage direction, "*Exeunt* Mayor, &c.;" but query, upon what authority, and with what necessity, is this important official so abruptly dismissed?

[b] *Too* senseless-*obstinate,*—] A misprint probably for *needless*-obstinate.

(*) First folio omits, *in heaven.* (†) First folio, *great.*
(‡) First folio, *think'st.*
(§) First folio, *generall ending day.*

c Grossness of this age:] The quarto, 1622, reads, "*greatness* of *his* age;" Warburton, "*the greenness* of *his* age;" and Mr. Collier's annotator, "the *goodness* of *his* age." See note on the passage in the Illustrative Comments to Act III.

Thus, like the formal Vice, Iniquity,
I moralize two meanings in one word.[a] [*Aside.*
PRINCE. That Julius Cæsar was a famous man;
With what his valour did enrich his wit,
His wit set down to make his valour live:
Death makes no conquest of this* conqueror;
For now he lives in fame, though not in life.—
I'll tell you what, my cousin Buckingham—
BUCK. What, my gracious lord?
PRINCE. An if I live until I be a man,
I'll win our ancient right in France again,
Or die a soldier, as I liv'd a king.
GLO. [*Aside.*] Short summers lightly[b] have a forward spring.
BUCK. Now, in good time, here comes the duke of York.

Enter YORK, HASTINGS, *and the* CARDINAL.

PRINCE. Richard of York! how fares our loving† brother?
YORK. Well, my dread ‡ lord; so must I call you now.
PRINCE. Ay, brother,—to our grief, as it is yours:
Too late[c] he died, that might have kept that title,
Which by his death hath lost much majesty.
GLO. How fares our cousin, noble lord of York?
YORK. I thank you, gentle uncle. O, my lord,
You said that idle weeds are fast in growth:
The prince my brother hath outgrown me far.
GLO. He hath, my lord.
YORK. And therefore is he idle?
GLO. O, my fair cousin, I must not say so.
YORK. Then he is more beholden to you than I?
GLO. He may command me as my sovereign;
But you have power in me as in a kinsman.
YORK. I pray you, uncle, give me this dagger.
GLO. My dagger, little cousin? with all my heart.
PRINCE. A beggar, brother?
YORK. Of my kind uncle, that I know will give;
And being but a toy, which is no grief to give.
GLO. A greater gift than that I'll give my cousin.
YORK. A greater gift! O, that's the sword to it?
GLO. Ay, gentle cousin, were it light enough.
YORK. O then, I see, you'll part but with light gifts;
In weightier things you'll say a beggar nay.
GLO. It is too weighty for your grace to wear.
YORK. I weigh it lightly, were it heavier.
GLO. What, would you have my weapon, little lord?
YORK. I would, that I might thank you as * you call me.
GLO. How?
YORK. *Little.*
PRINCE. My lord of York will still be cross in talk;—
Uncle, your grace knows how to bear with him.
YORK. You mean, to bear me, not to bear with me:—
Uncle, my brother mocks both you and me;
Because that I am little, like an ape,
He thinks that you should bear me on your shoulders.
BUCK. With what a sharp provided[d] wit he reasons!
To mitigate the scorn he gives his uncle,
He prettily and aptly taunts himself:
So cunning and so young is wonderful.
GLO. My lord, will't please you pass along?
Myself, and my good cousin Buckingham,
Will to your mother, to entreat of her,
To meet you at the Tower, and welcome you.
YORK. What, will you go unto the Tower, my lord?
PRINCE. My lord protector needs † will have it so.
YORK. I shall not sleep in quiet at the Tower.
GLO. Why, what should you fear?
YORK. Marry, my uncle Clarence' angry ghost;
My grandam told me he was murder'd there.
PRINCE. I fear no uncles dead.
GLO. Nor none that live, I hope.
PRINCE. An if they live, I hope I need not fear.
But come, my lord, and with a heavy heart,
Thinking on them, go I unto the Tower.
[*Sennet. Exeunt* PRINCE, YORK, HASTINGS, CARDINAL, *and* Attendants.

(*) First folio, *his.* (†) First folio, *Noble.* (‡) First folio, *deare.*

(*) First folio repeats, *as.* (†) First folio omits, *needs.*

a Thus, like the formal Vice, Iniquity,
I moralize two meanings in one word.]

On what expression does the equivocation of Gloucester depend? Johnson thinks he alludes to the line,—

"So wise, so young, they say, do ne'er live long."

In which he conceals under a proverb, his design of hastening the Prince's death. Mason conceives the ambiguity to lie in the words "live long," and Warburton adopts the extraordinary change of,—

" —— *formal-wise Antiquity*"!

May he not refer to the double sense of the word *characters*, which signifies both the signs by which we communicate ideas, and the good or evil qualities which distinguish us? For an account of the *Vice*, see note (5), p. 658, Vol. I.

b Lightly—] *Commonly, usually.*

c Too late—] That is, too *recently*, too *lately*.

d Provided *wit*—] A wit furnished him beforehand. Buckingham suspects the young prince had been instigated by the Queen to mock his uncle Gloucester,—

"Think you, my lord, this little prating York
Was not incensed by his subtle mother,
To taunt and scorn you thus opprobriously

BUCK. Think you, my lord, this little prating York
Was not incensed by his subtle mother,
To taunt and scorn you thus opprobriously?

GLO. No doubt, no doubt: O, 't is a parlous boy;
Bold, quick, ingenious, forward, capable;
He 's all the mother's, from the top to toe.

BUCK. Well, let them rest.—Come hither, Catesby,
Thou 'rt sworn as deeply to effect what we intend,
As closely to conceal what we impart:
Thou know'st our reasons urg'd upon the way;—
What think'st thou? is it not an easy matter
To make William lord Hastings of our mind,
For the instalment of this noble duke
In the seat royal of this famous isle?

CATE. He for his father's sake so loves the prince,
That he will not be won to aught against him.

BUCK. What think'st thou then of Stanley? will not he?*

CATE. He will do all in all as Hastings doth.

BUCK. Well then, no more but this: go, gentle Catesby,
And, as it were far off, sound thou lord Hastings,
How he doth stand affected to our purpose;
[And summon him to-morrow to the Tower,
To sit about the coronation.][a]
If thou dost find him tractable to us,
Encourage him, and show† him all our reasons:
If he be leaden, icy, cold, unwilling,
Be thou so too, and so break off your‡ talk,
And give us notice of his inclination:
For we to-morrow hold divided councils,(3)
Wherein thyself shalt highly be employ'd.

GLO. Commend me to lord William; tell him, Catesby,
His ancient knot of dangerous adversaries
To-morrow are let blood at Pomfret-castle;
And bid my friend,§ for joy of this good news,
Give mistress Shore one gentle kiss the more.

BUCK. Good Catesby, go, effect this business soundly.

CATE. My good lords both, with all the heed I may.||

GLO. Shall we hear from you, Catesby, ere we sleep?

CATE. You shall, my lord.

GLO. At Crosby-place,* there shall you find us both. [*Exit* CATESBY.

BUCK. Now, my lord, what shall we do, if we perceive
William† lord Hastings will not yield to our complots?

GLO. Chop off his head, man;—somewhat we will do:—[b]
And, look, when I am king, claim thou of me
The earldom of Hereford, and‡ the moveables
Whereof the king my brother stood§ possess'd.

BUCK. I 'll claim that promise at your grace's hand.

GLO. And look to have it yielded with all willingness.||
Come, let us sup betimes, that afterwards
We may digest our complots in some form.
[*Exeunt.*

SCENE II.—*Before* Lord Hastings' *House.*

Enter a Messenger.

MESS. What ho! My lord!— [*Knocking.*

HAST. [*Within.*] Who knocks at the door?

MESS. A messenger from the lord Stanley.[c]

HAST. [*Within.*] What is 't o'clock?

MESS. Upon the stroke of four.

Enter HASTINGS.

HAST. Cannot thy master¶ sleep these tedious nights?

MESS. So it should seem** by that I have to say.
First, he commends him to your noble self.††

HAST. And‡‡ then?

MESS. Then certifies your lordship, that this night
He dreamt the boar had rased off his helm:
Besides, he says, there are two councils held; §§
And that may be determin'd at the one,
Which may make you and him to rue at the other.
Therefore he sends to know your lordship's pleasure,—
If you will presently take horse with him,

(*) Quartos, *what will he.* (†) First folio, *tell.* (‡) First folio, *the.* (§) First folio, *Lord.* (||) First folio, *can.*

a About the coronation.] These two lines are only found in the folio. In the quartos, the speech is in other respects slightly varied,—

"Well, then no more but this:
Go, gentle Catesby, and as it were afarre off,
Sound thou lord Hastings how he stands affected
Unto our purpose, if he be willing,
Encourage him," &c.

b Chop off his head, man;—somewhat *we will* do:—] This is the spirited version of the quarto text: the folio sadly mars Gloucester's energy by reading,—

"*Chop off his head; Something* wee will *determine.*"

(*) First folio, *Crosby-House.* (†) First folio omits, *William.* (‡) First folio inserts, *all.* (§) First folio, *was.* (||) First folio, *kindness.* (¶) First folio, *my lord Stanley* (**) First folio, *appeares.* (††) Quartos, *lordship.* (‡‡) First folio, *What.* (§§) First folio, *kept.*

c A messenger from the lord Stanley.] In the folio, the scene begins,—

"MESS. My Lord, my Lord.
HAST. Who knockes?
MESS. One from the Lord Stanley."

And with all speed post with him toward the north,
To shun the danger that his soul divines.
HAST. Go, fellow, go, return unto thy lord;
Bid him not fear the separated councils: *
His honour and myself are at the one;
And at the other is my good friend Catesby;
Where nothing can proceed, that toucheth us,
Whereof I shall not have intelligence.
Tell him his fears are shallow, wanting† instance:
And for his dreams, I wonder he's so fond‡
To trust the mockery of unquiet slumbers:
To fly the boar, before the boar pursues,
Were to incense the boar to follow us,
And make pursuit where he did mean no chase.
Go, bid thy master rise and come to me;
And we will both together to the Tower,
Where, he shall see, the boar will use us kindly.
MESS. My gracious lord, I'll § tell him what you say. [*Exit.*

Enter CATESBY.

CATE. Many good morrows to my noble lord!
HAST. Good morrow, Catesby; you are early stirring:
What news, what news, in this our tottering state?
CATE. It is a reeling world, indeed, my lord;
And, I believe, will never stand upright,
Till Richard wear the garland of the realm.
HAST. How! *wear the garland!* dost thou mean the crown?
CATE. Ay, my good lord.
HAST. I'll have this crown of mine cut from my shoulders,
Ere I will || see the crown so foul misplac'd.
But canst thou guess that he doth aim at it?
CATE. Ay, on my life; and hopes to find you forward
Upon his party, for the gain thereof:
And thereupon he sends you this good news,—
That this same very day your enemies,
The kindred of the queen, must die at Pomfret.
HAST. Indeed, I am no mourner for that news,
Because they have been still my enemies:¶
But that I'll give my voice on Richard's side,
To bar my master's heirs in true descent,
God knows I will not do it to the death.

(*) First folio, *Councell.* (†) First folio, *without.*
(‡) First folio, *simple.* (§) First folio, *Ile goe, my Lord, and.*
(||) First folio, *Before Ile.* (¶) First folio, *adversaries.*

[a] I tell thee, Catesby,—] In the folio there is no break in Hastings' speech, which stands,—

" *Well*, Catesby, ere a fort-night make me older,
Ile send," &c.

[b] *As dear* as you do *yours;*] The quartos' reading, which certainly expresses the speaker's meaning more lucidly than the curt lection of the folio,—

" My Lord, I hold my Life as deare as yours."

CATE. God keep your lordship in that gracious mind!
HAST. But I shall laugh at this à twelve-month hence,—
That they, who* brought me in my master's hate,
I live to look upon their tragedy.
I tell thee, Catesby,[a]—
CATE. What, my lord.
HAST. Ere a fortnight make me older,
I'll send some packing that yet think not on 't.
CATE. 'Tis a vile thing to die, my gracious lord,
When men are unprepar'd, and look not for it.
HAST. O monstrous, monstrous! and so falls it out
With Rivers, Vaughan, Grey: and so 'twill do
With some men else, that think themselves as safe
As thou and I, who, as thou know'st, are dear
To princely Richard and to Buckingham.
CATE. The princes both make high account of you,—
[*Aside.*] For they account his head upon the bridge.
HAST. I know they do; and I have well deserv'd it.

Enter STANLEY.

Come on, come on,† where is your boar-spear, man?
Fear you the boar, and go so unprovided?
STAN. My lord, good morrow;—good morrow, Catesby;—
You may jest on, but by the holy rood,
I do not like these several councils, I.
HAST. My lord, I hold my life as dear as you do yours;[b]
And never, in my life I do protest,
Was it more precious to me than[c] 'tis now:
Think you, but that I know our state secure,
I would be so triumphant as I am?
STAN. The lords at Pomfret, when they rode from London,
Were jocund, and suppos'd their states were sure,
And they, indeed, had no cause to mistrust;
But yet, you see, how soon the day o'ercast;
This sudden stab of rancour I misdoubt;
Pray God, I say, I prove a needless coward!
But come, my lord, shall we to the Tower?
HAST. I go; but stay, hear you not the news?[d]
This day those men you talk of are beheaded.

(*) First folio, *which.* (†) Quartos, *What my L.*

[c] *And never, in my* life *I do protest,*
Was it more precious to me than *'t is now:*]

The folio has,—

" And never in my *dayes*, I doe protest,
Was it *so* precious to me, *as* 't is now."

[d] Hear you not the news?] The folio reads,—

" What, shall we toward the Tower? the day is spent.
HAST. Come, come, have with you:
Wot you what, my Lord,
To-day the Lords you talke of, are beheaded."

STAN. They, for their truth, might better wear their heads,
Than some that have accus'd them wear their hats.—
But come, my lord, let's away.

Enter a Pursuivant.

HAST. Go you before, I'll follow presently.
[*Exeunt* STANLEY *and* CATESBY.
Well met![a] how goes the world with thee?
PURS. The better that your lordship please to ask.
HAST. I tell thee, man, 'tis better with me now,
Than when I met thee* last where now we meet:
Then was I going prisoner to the Tower,
By the suggestion of the queen's allies;
But now, I tell thee, (keep it to thyself,)
This day those enemies are put to death,
And I in better state than ere I was.
PURS. God hold it to your honour's good content!
HAST. Gramercy, fellow: there, drink that for me. [*Throwing him his purse.*
PURS. I thank your honour. [*Exit.*

Enter a Priest.

PR. Well met, my lord; I am glad to see your honour.
HAST. I thank thee, good sir John, with all my heart.
I am beholden to you for your last exercise;[b]
Come the next sabbath, and I will content you.[c]

Enter BUCKINGHAM.

BUCK. How now, lord chamberlain, what, talking with a priest?[d]
Your friends at Pomfret, they do need the priest;
Your honour hath no shriving work in hand.
HAST. Good faith, and when I met this holy man,
Those† men you talk of came into my mind.—
What, go you to the Tower, my lord?
BUCK. I do, but long, my lord, I shall not stay:[e]
I shall return before your lordship thence.

(*) First folio, *thou met'st me.* (†) First folio, *The.*

[a] Well met!] The folio has,—
"Goe on before, Ile talke with this good fellow."

[b] For your last exercise;] This is given somewhat differently in the folio,—
"PRIEST. Well met, my Lord, I am glad to see your Honor.
HAST. I thank thee, good Sir John, with all my heart.
I am in your debt, for your last Exercise," &c.

[c] I will content you.] In the folio, we have,—
"PRIEST. Ile wait upon your Lordship;"
but as the words are immediately after given to Hastings, Theobald, Malone, and others conceive, what is highly probable, they were inserted twice by mistake.

[d] How now, lord chamberlain, what, talking with a priest?] The folio has,—
"What, talking with a Priest, Lord Chamberlaine?"

[e] What, go you to the Tower, my lord?

HAST. Nay, like enough, for I stay dinner there.
BUCK. [*Aside.*] And supper too, although thou know'st it not.
Come, shall we go along?*
[HAST. I'll wait upon your lordship.][f]
[*Exeunt.*

SCENE III.—Pomfret. *Before the Castle.*

Enter RATCLIFF, *with a guard, conducting* RIVERS, GREY, *and* VAUGHAN *to execution.*

RAT. Come, bring forth the prisoners.[g]
RIV. Sir Richard Ratcliff, let me tell thee this,—
To-day shalt thou behold a subject die,
For truth, for duty, and for loyalty.
GREY. God keep† the prince from all the pack of you!
A knot you are of damned blood-suckers.[h]
RIV. O Pomfret, Pomfret! O thou bloody prison,
Fatal and ominous to noble peers!
Within the guilty closure of thy walls,
Richard the second here was hack'd to death:
And, for more slander to thy dismal seat,
We give thee up‡ our guiltless blood to drink.
GREY. Now Margaret's curse is fallen upon our heads,
[When she exclaim'd on Hastings, you, and I,][i]
For standing by when Richard stabb'd her son.
RIV. Then curs'd she Richard, then curs'd she Buckingham,
Then curs'd she Hastings:—O, remember, God,
To hear her prayer for them, as now for us!
And for my sister and her princely sons,
Be satisfied, dear God, with our true blood,
Which, as thou know'st, unjustly must be spilt!
RAT. Come, come, dispatch, the limit of your lives is out.[k]
RIV. Come, Grey,—come, Vaughan,—let us all§ embrace:
And take our leave until we meet in heaven.[l]
[*Exeunt.*

(*) First folio, *will you goe?* (†) First folio, *blesse.*
(‡) First folio, *to thee.* (§) First folio, *here.*

BUCK. I do, but long, my lord, I shall not stay:] In the folio we read,—
"What, goe you toward the Tower?
BUC. I doe, my Lord, but long I cannot stay there."

[f] I'll wait upon your lordship.] A line omitted in the quartos.

[g] Come, bring forth the prisoners.] This line is not in the folio.

[h] Blood-suckers.] After this, in the folio, are the following lines:—
"VAUGH. You live, that shall cry woe for this heereafter.
RAT. Dispatch, the limit of your Lives is out."

[i] When she exclaim'd on Hastings, you, and I,—] A line not found in the quartos.

[k] Come, come, dispatch, &c.] The folio has,—
"Make haste, the houre of death is expiate."

[l] And take our leave *until we meet in heaven.*] The folio reads,—"Farewell, until we meet *againe* in Heaven."

SCENE IV.—London. *A Room in the* Tower.

BUCKINGHAM, STANLEY, HASTINGS, *the* BISHOP *of* ELY, CATESBY, LOVEL, *and others, sitting at a table:* Officers *of the council attending.*

HAST. My lords, at once,* the cause why we are met
Is, to determine of the coronation:
In God's name, say,† when is this‡ royal day?

BUCK. Are§ all things fitting‖ for that‡ royal time?

STAN. They are;¶ and wants but nomination.

ELY. To-morrow then I guess a happy time.**

BUCK. Who knows the lord protector's mind herein?
Who is most inward with the noble duke?

ELY. Your grace, we think, should soonest know his mind.[a]

BUCK. Who? I, my lord? we know each other's faces;
But for our hearts, he knows no more of mine,
Than I of yours; nor I no more of his, than you of mine: [b]—
Lord Hastings, you and he are near in love.

HAST. I thank his grace, I know he loves me well;
But, for his purpose in the coronation,
I have not sounded him, nor he delivered

(*) First folio, *Now Noble Peeres.* (†) First folio, *speake.* (‡) First folio, *the.* (§) First folio, *Is.* (‖) First folio, *ready.* (¶) Old text, *It is.* (**) First folio, *I judge a happie day.*

a Your grace, we think, should soonest know his mind.] This line is thus lamely printed in the quartos:—

"Why you my Lo: me thinks you should soonest know his mind."

b — than you of mine:—] In the folio, the foregoing stands as follows:—

"We know each others Faces: for our Hearts,
He knowes no more of mine, then I of yours,
Or I of his, my Lord, then you of mine."

His gracious pleasure any way therein:
But you, my noble* lords, may name the time,
And in the duke's behalf I'll give my voice,
Which, I presume, he'll take in gentle part.

ELY. Now in good† time, here comes the duke himself.

Enter GLOUCESTER.

GLO. My noble lords and cousins all, good morrow:
I have been long a sleeper; but, I trust,
My absence doth neglect no great design
Which by my presence might have been concluded.

BUCK. Had you not come upon your cue, my lord,
William lord Hastings had pronounc'd your part,—
I mean your voice,—for crowning of the king.

GLO. Than my lord Hastings no man might be bolder;
His lordship knows me well, and loves me well.—
My lord of Ely, when I was last in Holborn,
I saw good strawberries in your garden there;
I do beseech you send for some of them.

ELY. Marry and will, my lord, with all my heart. [*Exit* ELY.

GLO. Cousin of Buckingham, a word with you. [*Takes him aside.*
Catesby hath sounded Hastings in our business,
And finds the testy gentleman so hot,
That he will lose his head ere give consent,
His master's son, as worshipfully he terms it,
Shall lose the royalty of England's throne.

BUCK. Withdraw yourself awhile, I'll go with you.
[*Exeunt* GLOUCESTER *and* BUCKINGHAM.

STAN. We have not yet set down this day of triumph.
To-morrow, in my judgment, is too sudden;
For I myself am not so well provided,
As else I would be, were the day prolong'd.

Re-enter BISHOP *of* ELY.

ELY. Where is my lord protector?‡
I have sent for these strawberries.

HAST. His grace looks cheerfully and smooth this morning;
There's some conceit or other likes him well,
When he doth bid* good morrow with such spirit.
I think there's ne'er a man in Christendom,
That can less hide[a] his love or hate than he;
For by his face straight shall you know his heart.

STAN. What of his heart perceive you in his face,
By any likelihood† he show'd to-day?

HAST. Marry, that with no man here he is offended;
For, if he were, he would have shown it in his looks.

STAN. Ay, pray God he be not, I say.[b]

Re-enter GLOUCESTER *and* BUCKINGHAM.

GLO. I pray you all, tell me what they deserve,[c]
That do conspire my death with devilish plots
Of damned witchcraft; and that have prevail'd
Upon my body with their hellish charms?

HAST. The tender love I bear your grace, my lord,
Makes me most forward in this noble‡ presence
To doom the offenders: whosoe'er they be,
I say, my lord, they have deserved death.

GLO. Then be your eyes the witness of this ill,§
See|| how I am bewitch'd; behold mine arm
Is, like a blasted sapling, wither'd up:
This is that¶ Edward's wife, that monstrous witch,
Consorted with that harlot, strumpet Shore,
That by their witchcraft thus have marked me.

HAST. If they have done this deed, my noble lord,—

GLO. *If!* thou protector of this damned strumpet,
Talk'st thou to me of *ifs!*—Thou art a traitor!—
Off with his head!—now, by Saint Paul I swear,
I will not dine until I see the same!—
Some see it done;—[d]
The rest, that love me, rise and follow me.
[*Exeunt all, except* HASTINGS, CATESBY, *and* LOVEL.

HAST. Woe, woe, for England! not a whit for me;
For I, too fond, might have prevented this.
Stanley did dream the boar did rase his helm;[e]
But I disdain'd it and did scorn to fly.

(*) First folio, *Honorable*. (†) First folio, *In happie*. (‡) First folio, *the Duke of Gloster*.

(*) First folio, *that he bids*. (†) First folio, *livelyhood*. (‡) First folio, *princely*. (§) First folio, *their evil*. (||) First folio, *Looke*. (¶) First folio, *And this is*.

a That can less hide—] In the folio,—

"Can lesser hide," &c.

b Ay, pray God he be not, I say.] A line not found in the folio.

c —what they deserve,—] This is lamely printed in the quartos,—

"I pray you all, what do they deserve," &c.

d Some see it done;—] The folio has,—

"Lovel and Ratcliffe, looke that it be done;"

but, as Ratcliff was engaged at the time in attending the execution of Rivers, Grey, and Vaughan, he could not be present in the Tower. The inconsistency is avoided in the quartos; and probably arose in the folio from the actor who personated Ratcliff being cast to "double" with that character the part of an attendant on the duke of Gloucester.

e Stanley did dream, &c.] The folio reads,—

"Stanley did dreame, the Bore did *rowse our Helmes*,
And I did scorne it, and disdaine to flye."

Three times to-day my foot-cloth horse did stumble,
And started when he look'd upon the Tower,
As loth to bear me to the slaughter-house.
O, now I need the priest that spake to me:
I now repent I told the pursuivant,
As 't were* triumphing at† mine enemies,
How they‡ at Pomfret bloodily were butcher'd,
And I myself secure in grace and favour.
O, Margaret, Margaret, now thy heavy curse
Is lighted on poor Hastings' wretched head.

CATE. Dispatch, my lord; § the duke would be at dinner:
Make a short shrift, he longs to see your head.

HAST. O momentary grace of mortal men,
Which we more hunt for than the grace of God!
Who builds his hope in air of your fair || looks,
Lives like a drunken sailor on a mast,
Ready with every nod to tumble down
Into the fatal bowels of the deep.

[LOV. Come, come, dispatch; 'tis bootless to exclaim.

HAST. O, bloody Richard!—miserable England!
I prophesy the fearfull'st time to thee,
That ever wretched age hath look'd upon.—][a]
Come, lead me to the block; bear him my head:
They smile at me who shortly shall be dead.(4)

[*Exeunt.*

SCENE V.—*The same. The* Tower *Walls.*

Enter GLOUCESTER *and* BUCKINGHAM, *in rusty armour,*(5) *marvellous ill-favoured.*

GLO. Come, cousin, canst thou quake, and change thy colour,
Murder thy breath in middle of a word,—
And then again begin, and stop again,
As if thou wert¶ distraught and mad with terror?

BUCK. Tut, I can counterfeit the deep tragedian;
Speak and look back, and pry on every side;
[Tremble and start at wagging of a straw,][b]
Intending deep suspicion: ghastly looks
Are at my service, like enforced smiles;
And both are ready in their offices,
To grace my stratagems,—[c]

GLO. Here comes the mayor!

Enter the Lord Mayor *and* CATESBY.

BUCK. Let me alone to entertain him. Lord mayor!—

GLO. Look to the drawbridge there!

BUCK. The reason we have sent for you—

GLO. Catesby, overlook the walls.

BUCK. Hark! I hear a drum.

GLO. Look back! defend thee,—here are enemies!

BUCK. God and our innocency defend us!

GLO. Be patient; they are friends: Ratcliff and Lovel.[d]

Enter LOVEL *and* RATCLIFF, *with* HASTINGS' *head.*

LOV. Here is the head of that ignoble traitor,
The dangerous and unsuspected Hastings.

GLO. So dear I lov'd the man, that I must weep.
I took him for the plainest harmless man,
That breath'd upon this* earth a christian;
Made him my book, wherein my soul recorded
The history of all her secret thoughts:
So smooth he daub'd his vice with show of virtue,
That, his apparent open guilt omitted,—
I mean his conversation with Shore's wife,—
He liv'd from all attainder of suspect.†

BUCK. Well, well, he was the covert'st shelter'd traitor
That ever liv'd.—
Would you imagine, or almost believe,
Wer't not, that by great preservation
We live to tell it, that the subtle traitor
This day had plotted, in the council-house,
To murder me and my good lord of Gloster?

MAY. Had he done so?

GLO. What! think ye we are Turks, or infidels?
Or that we should, against the form of law,
Proceed thus rashly in the villain's death,
But that the extreme peril of the case,
The peace of England and our persons' safety,
Enforc'd us to this execution?

MAY. Now, fair befall you! he deserv'd his death;
And you, my good lords,‡ both, have well proceeded,
To warn false traitors from the like attempts.

(*) First folio, *too.* (†) First folio, *how.* (‡) First folio, *To-day.* (§) First folio, *Come, come, dispatch.* (||) First folio, *good.* (¶) First folio, *were.*

a That ever wretched age hath look'd upon.—] This and the three lines preceding it are found only in the folio.

b Tremble and start at wagging of a straw,—] A line not given in the quartos.

c To grace my stratagems,—] The folio reads, "*At any time* to grace," &c.; and adds, "But what, is Catesby gone?" to which Gloucester replies, "He is, and see he brings the Maior along."

(*) First folio, *the.* (†) First folio, *suspects.* (‡) First folio, *your good Graces.*

d Be patient; they are friends: Ratcliff and Lovel.] This short episode with the Lord Mayor is thus varied in the folio:—

"BUCK. Lord Maior.
RICH. Looke to the Draw-Bridge there.
BUCK. Hearke, a Drumme.
RICH. Catesby, o're-looke the Walls.
BUCK. Lord Maior, the reason we have sent.
RICH. Looke back, defend thee, here are Enemies.
BUCK. God and our Innocencie defend, and guard us."

I never look'd for better at his hands,
After he once fell in with mistress Shore.
GLO. Yet had not we determin'd he should die,
Until your lordship came to see his end;
Which now the loving haste of these our friends,
Somewhat* against our meaning,* hath† prevented:
Because, my lord, we would have had you heard
The traitor speak, and timorously confess
The manner and the purpose of his treasons;
That you might well have signified the same
Unto the citizens, who haply may
Misconstrue us in him, and wail his death.
MAY. But, my good lord, your grace's word‡ shall serve,
As well as I had seen, and heard him speak:
And do not doubt, right noble princes both,
But I'll acquaint our duteous citizens
With all your just proceedings in this case.
GLO. And to that end we wish'd your lordship here,
To avoid the censures of the carping world.
BUCK. But§ since you come too late of our intent,
Yet witness what you hear we did intend:
And so, my good lord mayor, we bid farewell.
[*Exit* Lord Mayor.
GLO. Go after, after, cousin Buckingham.
The mayor towards Guildhall hies him in all post:—
There, at your meet'st advantage|| of the time,
Infer the bastardy of Edward's children:
Tell them, how Edward put to death a citizen,
Only for saying he would make his son
Heir to the crown; meaning, indeed, his house,
Which, by the sign thereof, was termed so.
Moreover, urge his hateful luxury,
And bestial appetite in change of lust;
Which stretch'd unto their servants, daughters, wives,
Even where his lustful¶ eye, or savage heart,
Without control, listed** to make a prey.
Nay, for a need, thus far come near my person:—
Tell them, when that my mother went with child
Of that unsatiate Edward, noble York
My princely father then had wars in France;
And, by true computation of the time,
Found that the issue was not his begot;
Which well appeared in his lineaments,
Being nothing like the noble duke my father:
But†† touch this sparingly, as 'twere far off;
Because you know, my lord. my mother lives.

BUCK. Fear* not, my lord, I'll play the orator,
As if the golden fee for which I plead,
Were for myself.[a]
GLO. If you thrive well, bring them to Baynard's castle,
Where you shall find me well accompanied,
With reverend fathers and well-learned bishops.
BUCK. I go; and, towards three or four o'clock,
Look for the news that the Guildhall affords.
[*Exit.*
[GLO. Go, Lovel, with all speed to doctor Shaw,—
Go thou [*To* CATESBY.] to friar Penker;†—bid them both
Meet me within this hour at Baynard's castle.][b]
[*Exeunt* LOVEL, RATCLIFF, *and* CATESBY.
Now will I in,‡ to take some privy order
To draw the brats of Clarence out of sight;
And to give notice,§ that no manner of person[c]
Have any time recourse unto the princes.
[*Exit.*

SCENE VI.—*The same. A Street.*

Enter a Scrivener.

SCRIV. This|| is the indictment of the good lord Hastings,
Which in a set hand fairly is engross'd,
That it may be this day¶ read o'er in Paul's.
And mark how well the sequel hangs together:—
Eleven hours I** spent to write it o'er,
For yesternight by Catesby was it brought†† me;
The precedent was full as long a doing,
And yet within these five hours Hastings liv'd,(6)
Untainted, unexamin'd, free, at liberty.
Here's a good world the while!—Why‡‡ who's so gross,
That cannot see this palpable device?
Yet who so blind,§§ but says he sees it not?
Bad is the world; and all will come to nought,
When such ill dealing must be seen in thought.
[*Exit.*

SCENE VII.—*The same. Court of* Baynard's Castle.

Enter GLOUCESTER *and* BUCKINGHAM, *meeting.*

GLO. How now, how now! what say the citizens?

(*) First folio, *Something—meanings.*
(†) Old text, *have.*
(‡) First folio, *words.*
(§) First folio, *Which.*
(||) First folio, *meetest vantage.*
(¶) First folio, *raging.*
(**) First folio, *lusted.*
(††) First folio, *Yet.*

a Were for myself.] The folio adds,—
"And so, my Lord adue."

b At Baynard's castle.] This and the two foregoing lines are not in the quartos.

(*) First folio, *Doubt.*
(†) First folio, *Peuker.*
(‡) First folio, *goe.*
(§) First folio, *order.*
(||) First folio, *Here.*
(¶) First folio, *to day.*
(**) First folio inserts, *have.*
(††) First folio, *sent.*
(‡‡) First folio omits, *Why.*
(§§) First folio, *bold.*

c That no manner of person—] In the folio,—"No manner person."

BUCK. Now by the holy mother of our Lord,
The citizens are mum, say not a word.
GLO. Touch'd you the bastardy of Edward's children?
BUCK. I did; with [his contract with lady Lucy,
And his contract by deputy in France:][a]
The unsatiate greediness of his desire,
And his enforcement of the city wives;
His tyranny for trifles; his own bastardy,—
As being got, your father then in France;
[And his resemblance, being not like the duke.][b]
Withal, I did infer your lineaments,—
Being the right idea of your father,
Both in your form and nobleness of mind:
Laid open all your victories in Scotland,
Your discipline in war, wisdom in peace,
Your bounty, virtue, fair humility;
Indeed, left nothing fitting for your purpose,
Untouch'd, or slightly handled, in discourse.
And, when my oratory drew toward end,
I bade* them, that did love their country's good,
Cry—*God save Richard, England's royal king!*
GLO. And did they so?
BUCK. No, so God help me, they spake not a word;[c]
But, like dumb statuas, or breathing stones,
Gaz'd† on each other, and look'd deadly pale.
Which when I saw, I reprehended them;
And ask'd the mayor what meant this wilful silence:
His answer was,—the people were not wont‡
To be spoke to but by the recorder.
Then he was urg'd to tell my tale again;—
Thus saith the duke, thus hath the duke inferr'd;
But nothing spoke in warrant from himself.
When he had done, some followers of mine own,
At lower end of the hall, hurl'd up their caps,
And some ten voices cried, *God save king Richard!*
[And thus I took the vantage of those few,—][d]
Thanks, gentle citizens and friends, quoth I;
This general applause and cheerful shout,
Argues your wisdom and your love to Richard:
And even here brake off, and came away.
GLO. What tongueless blocks were they! would they not speak?
BUCK. No, by my troth, my lord.[e]
GLO. Will not the mayor then, and his brethren, come?
BUCK. The mayor is here at hand; intend[f] some fear;
Be not you spoke with but by mighty suit:
And look you get a prayer-book in your hand,
And stand between two churchmen, good my lord;
For on that ground I'll build* a holy descant:
And be not easily won to our requests;
Play the maid's part, still answer nay, and take it.
GLO. I go; and if you plead as well for them,
As I can say nay to thee for myself,
No doubt we bring it to a happy issue.
BUCK. Go, go, up to the leads; the lord mayor knocks. [*Exit* GLOUCESTER.

Enter the Lord Mayor, Aldermen, *and* Citizens.

Welcome, my lord: I dance attendance here;
I think the duke will not be spoke withal.—

Enter CATESBY.

Now, Catesby,—what says your lord to my request?[g]
CATE. He doth entreat your grace, my noble lord,
To visit him to-morrow, or next day:
He is within, with two right reverend fathers,
Divinely bent to meditation;
And in no worldly suit† would he be mov'd,
To draw him from his holy exercise.
BUCK. Return, good Catesby, to thy lord again;‡
Tell him, myself, the mayor and citizens,§
In deep designs, in matter of great moment,
No less importing than our general good,
Are come to have some conference with his grace.
CATE. I'll signify so much unto him straight. [*Exit.*
BUCK. Ah, ha, my lord, this prince is not an Edward!
He is not lolling‖ on a lewd day-bed,¶
But on his knees at meditation;
Not dallying with a brace of courtezans,
But meditating with two deep divines;
Not sleeping to engross his idle body,
But praying to enrich his watchful soul:
Happy were England, would this virtuous prince
Take on his grace the sovereignty thereof;
But, sure,[h] I fear, we shall not win him to it.

(*) First folio, *bid*. (†) First folio, *Star'd*. (‡) First folio, *used*.

[a] His contract with lady Lucy,
And his contract by deputy in France:]
Omitted in the quartos.
[b] And his resemblance, being not like the duke.] This line also is found only in the folio.
[c] —they spake not a word;] Omitted in the quartos.
[d] And thus I took the vantage of those few,—] A line omitted in the quartos.
[e] No, by my troth, my lord.] Only in the quartos.

(*) First folio, *make*. (†) First folio, *suites*. (‡) First folio, *the gracious Duke*. (§) First folio, *Aldermen*. (‖) Old text, *lulling*. (¶) First folio, *Love-Bed*.

[f] Intend—] That is, *pretend*.
[g] Now, Catesby,—what says your lord to my request?] So the folio. In the quartos, Buckingham is made to say,—
"Here comes his servant: how now Catesby, what sayes he?"
[h] *But*, sure, *I fear*,—] Mr. Collier's annotator reads very plausibly,—
"But *sore* I fear."

MAY. Marry, God forbid* his grace should say us nay!
BUCK. I fear, he will: here Catesby comes again;—

Re-enter CATESBY.

Now, Catesby, what says his grace?
CATE. He wonders to what end you have assembled
Such troops of citizens to come to him,
His grace not being warn'd thereof before:
He fears, my lord, you mean no good to him.
BUCK. Sorry I am my noble cousin should
Suspect me, that I mean no good to him:
By heaven, we come to him in perfect love;
And so once more return and tell his grace.
[*Exit* CATESBY.
When holy and devout religious men
Are at their beads, 'tis much to draw them thence;
So sweet is zealous contemplation.

Enter GLOUCESTER *in a gallery above, between two* Bishops. CATESBY *returns.*

MAY. See, where he stands between two clergymen![a]
BUCK. Two props of virtue for a christian prince,
To stay him from the fall of vanity:
[And, see, a book of prayer in his hand,
True ornaments to know a holy man.—][b]
Famous Plantagenet, most gracious prince,
Lend favourable ear to our requests;
And pardon us the interruption
Of thy devotion and right christian zeal.
GLO. My lord, there needs no such apology;
I rather do beseech you pardon me,[c]
Who, earnest in the service of my God,
Neglect† the visitation of my friends.
But, leaving this, what is your grace's pleasure?
BUCK. Even that, I hope, which pleaseth God above,
And all good men of this ungovern'd isle.
GLO. I do suspect I have done some offence,
That seems disgracious in the city's eye;
And that you come to reprehend my ignorance.
BUCK. You have, my lord: would it might please your grace,
On our entreaties, to amend your fault!
GLO. Else wherefore breathe I in a christian land?
BUCK. Know then, it is your fault that you [resign
The supreme seat, the throne majestical,
The scepter'd office of your ancestors,
[Your state of fortune and your due of birth,][d]
The lineal glory of your royal house,
To the corruption of a blemish'd stock:
Whiles, in the mildness of your sleepy thoughts,
Which here we waken to our country's good,
The noble isle doth want her* proper limbs;
Her* face defac'd with scars of infamy,
Her* royal stock graft with ignoble plants,
And almost shoulder'd in the swallowing gulf
Of dark forgetfulness and deep oblivion.
Which to recure, we heartily solicit
Your gracious self to take on you the charge
And kingly government of this your land;—
Not as protector, steward, substitute,
Or lowly factor for another's gain;
But as successively, from blood to blood,
Your right of birth, your empery, your own.
For this, consorted with the citizens,
Your very worshipful and loving friends,
And by their vehement instigation,
In this just suit† come I to move your grace.
GLO. I cannot tell, if to depart in silence,
Or bitterly to speak in your reproof,
Best fitteth my degree or your condition:
[If, not to answer,—you might haply think,
Tongue-tied ambition, not replying, yielded
To bear the golden yoke of sovereignty,
Which fondly you would here impose on me;
If to reprove you for this suit of yours,
So season'd with your faithful love to me,
Then, on the other side, I check'd my friends.
Therefore,—to speak, and to avoid the first;
And then, in speaking, not to incur the last,—
Definitively thus I answer you.][e]
Your love deserves my thanks; but my desert
Unmeritable, shuns your high request.
First, if all obstacles were cut away,
And that my path were even to the crown,
As the ripe revenue and due of birth;
Yet so much is my poverty of spirit,
So mighty and so many my defects,
That I would rather hide me from my greatness,—
Being a bark to brook no mighty sea,—
Than in my greatness covet to be hid,
And in the vapour of my glory smother'd.
But, God be thank'd, there is no need of me;
(And much I need to help you, were there need.)
The royal tree hath left us royal fruit,
Which, mellow'd by the stealing hours of time,
Will well become the seat of majesty,

(*) First folio, *defend.* (†) First folio, *Deferr'd.*

a See, where he stands between two clergymen!] The folio slightly varies this to,—

"See where his Grace stands, tweene two Clergiemen!"

b And, see, &c.] The lines in brackets are found only in the folio.

(*) First folio, *His.* (†) First folio, *Cause.*

c *I rather do beseech you pardon me,*—] So the quartos: the folio reads, I *doe* beseech *your Grace to* pardon me.
d Your state of fortune and your due of birth,—] A line omitted in the quartos.
e Definitively thus I answer you.] This and the preceding nine lines are not in the quartos.

And make, no doubt, us happy by his reign.
On him I lay that you would lay on me,
The right and fortune of his happy stars;
Which God defend that I should wring from him!
  BUCK. My lord, this argues conscience in your grace;
But the respects thereof are nice and trivial,
All circumstances well considered.
You say that Edward is your brother's son;
So say we too, but not by Edward's wife:
For first was he contráct to lady Lucy,—
Your mother lives a witness to his vow,—
And afterward by substitute betroth'd
To Bona, sister to the king of France.
These both put off, a poor petitioner,
A care-craz'd mother to a many sons,
A beauty-waning and distressed widow,
Even in the afternoon of her best days,
Made prize and purchase of his wanton eye,
Seduc'd the pitch and height of his degree
To base declension and loath'd bigamy:[a]
By her, in his unlawful bed, he got
This Edward, whom our manners call—the prince.
More bitterly could I expostulate,
Save that, for reverence to some alive,
I give a sparing limit to my tongue.

a Loath'd bigamy:] *Bigamy*, Blackstone remarks, which differed from *polygamy*, or having two wives at once, consisted in either marrying two virgins successively, or once marrying a widow, and was made unlawful and infamous by a canon of the Council of Lyons, A.D. 1274.

Then, good my lord, take to your royal self
This proffer'd benefit of dignity:
If not to bless us and the land withal,
Yet to draw forth your noble ancestry
From the corruption of abusing times,
Unto a lineal true-derived course. [you.

MAY. Do, good my lord; your citizens entreat

BUCK. Refuse not, mighty lord, this proffer'd love.

CATE. O, make them joyful, grant their lawful suit!

GLO. Alas, why would you heap those cares* on me?
I am unfit for state and majesty:
I do beseech you, take it not amiss,
I cannot nor I will not yield to you.

BUCK. If you refuse it,—as in love and zeal,
Loth to depose the child, your brother's son;
As well we know your tenderness of heart,
And gentle, kind, effeminate remorse,
Which we have noted in you to your kindred,
And equally, indeed, to all estates,—
Yet know, whê'r you accept our suit or no,
Your brother's son shall never reign our king;
But we will plant some other in the throne,
To the disgrace and downfall of your house.
And, in this resolution, here we leave you;—
Come, citizens, we will entreat no more.[a]

[*Exeunt* BUCK. *and* Cit.

CATE. Call them† again, sweet prince, accept their suit;
If you deny them, all the land will rue it.

GLO. Will you enforce me to a world of cares?
Call them again; I am not made of stone,‡

(*) First folio, *this Care*. (†) First folio, *him*. (‡) First folio, *Stones*.

[a] Come, citizens, we will entreat no more.] The quartos give this line with an oath:—

"Come citizens, zounds Ile intreat no more."

But penetrable to your kind entreaties,

[*Exit* CATESBY.

Albeit against my conscience and my soul.—

Re-enter BUCKINGHAM, *and the rest.*

Cousin of Buckingham,—and sage, grave men,—
Since you will buckle fortune on my back,
To bear her burden, whê'r I will or no,
I must have patience to endure the load:
But if black scandal or foul-fac'd reproach,
Attend the sequel of your imposition,
Your mere enforcement shall acquittance me
From all the impure blots and stains thereof;
For God he knows,* and you may partly see,
How far I am from the desire of this.

MAY. God bless your grace! we see it, and will say it.

GLO. In saying so, you shall but say the truth.

BUCK. Then I salute you with this royal title,—
Long live king Richard, England's worthy king!

ALL. Amen.

BUCK. To-morrow may it please you to be crown'd?

GLO. Even when you please, since† you will have it so.

BUCK. To-morrow then we will attend your grace;
And so, most joyfully, we take our leave.

GLO. Come, let us to our holy work again:—

[*To the* Bishops.

Farewell, my cousin;‡—farewell, gentle friends.

[*Exeunt.*

(*) First folio, *doth know*. (†) First folio, *for*. (‡) First folio, *Cousins*.

To which Richard answers,

"O do not sweare, my lord of Buckingham."

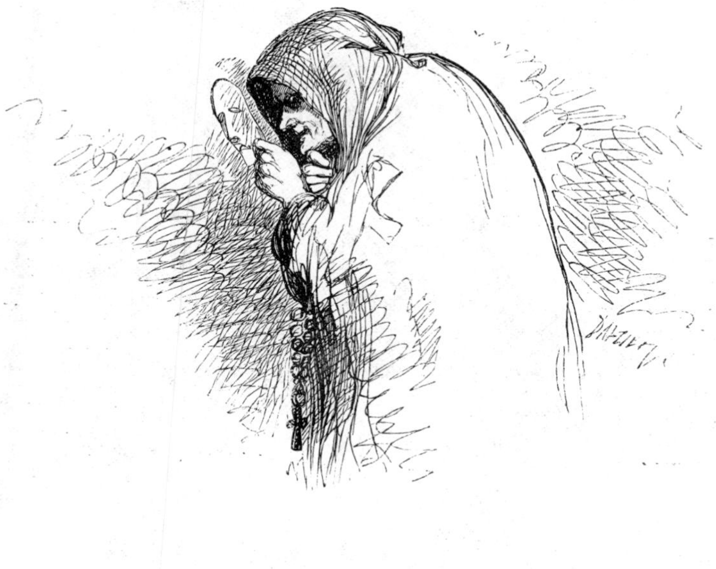

ACT IV.

SCENE I.—London. *Before the* Tower.

Enter, on one side, QUEEN ELIZABETH, *the* DUCHESS *of* YORK, *and* MARQUIS *of* DORSET; *on the other,* ANNE DUCHESS *of* GLOUCESTER, *leading* LADY MARGARET PLANTAGENET, CLARENCE'S *young daughter.*

DUCH. Who meets us here? my niece Plantagenet?[a]

Q. ELIZ. Sister, well met! whither away so fast?

ANNE. No farther than the Tower; and, as I guess,

[a] Who meets us here? my niece Plantagenet?] The opening of this scene is thus exhibited in the folio text:—

"DUCH. YORKE. Who meets us heere?
My Neece *Plantagenet*,
Led in the hand of her kind Aunt of Gloster?
Now, for my Life, shee's wandring to the Tower,
On pure hearts love, to greet the tender Prince.
Daughter, well met.
ANNE. God give your Graces both, a happie
And a ioyfull time of day.
QU. As much to you, good Sister: whither away?
ANNE. No farther then the Tower," &c.

Upon the like devotion as yourselves,
To gratulate the tender * princes there.
  Q. ELIZ. Kind sister, thanks; we'll enter all together:
And, in good time, here the lieutenant comes.—

Enter BRAKENBURY.

Master lieutenant, pray you, by your leave,
How fares the prince ? [a]
  BRAK. Well, madam, and in health; but by your leave,
I may not suffer you to visit him;
The king hath straightly charg'd the contrary.
  Q. ELIZ. *The king!* who's that?
  BRAK. I cry you mercy,† I mean the lord protector.
  Q. ELIZ. The lord protect him from that kingly title!
Hath he set bounds betwixt ‡ their love and me?
I am their mother; who should keep§ me from them?
  DUCH. I am their father's mother, and || will see them.
  ANNE. Their aunt I am in law, in love their mother;
Then fear not thou; I'll bear thy blame,[b]
And take thy office from thee, on my peril.
  BRAK. No, madam, no, I may not leave it so;
I am bound by oath, and therefore pardon me.
[*Exit* BRAK.

Enter STANLEY.

  STAN. Let me but meet you, ladies, one hour hence,
And I'll salute your grace of York as mother,
And reverend looker-on of two fair queens.—
Come, madam, you must straight to Westminster,
[*To the* DUCHESS *of* GLOUCESTER.
There to be crowned Richard's royal queen.
  Q. ELIZ. O,¶ cut my lace asunder!
That my pent heart may have some scope to beat,
Or else I swoon with this dead-killing news.[c]
  DORS. Madam, have comfort: how fares your grace?
  Q. ELIZ. O Dorset, speak not to me, get thee hence,*
Death and destruction dog thee at the† heels;
Thy mother's name is ominous to children:
If thou wilt outstrip death, go cross the seas,
And live with Richmond, from the reach of hell.
Go, hie thee, hie thee from this slaughter-house,
Lest thou increase the number of the dead;
And make me die the thrall of Margaret's curse,—
Nor mother, wife, nor England's counted queen.
  STAN. Full of wise care is this your counsel, madam:—
Take all the swift advantage of the time; ‡
You shall have letters from me to my son
To meet you on the way and welcome you: [d]
Be not ta'en tardy by unwise delay.
  DUCH. O ill-dispersing wind of misery!—
O my accursed womb, the bed of death;
A cockatrice hast thou hatch'd to the world,
Whose unavoided eye is murderous!
  STAN. Come, madam, come; I in all haste was sent.
  ANNE. And I in § all unwillingness will go.—
O, would to God that the inclusive verge
Of golden metal that must round my brow,
Were red-hot steel, to sear me to the brain! || (1)
Anointed let me be with deadly poison,¶
And die, ere men can say—God save the queen
  Q. ELIZ. Alas!** poor soul, I envy not thy glory;
To feed my humour, wish thyself no harm.
  ANNE. No! why?—When he that is my husband now,
Came to me, as I follow'd Henry's corse;
When scarce the blood was well wash'd from his hands,
Which issu'd from my other angel husband,
And that dead†† saint which then I weeping follow'd;
O, when, I say, I look'd on Richard's face,
This was my wish,—*Be thou*, quoth I, *accurs'd,*
For making me, so young, so old a widow!
And, when thou wedd'st, let sorrow haunt thy bed;
And be thy wife (if any be so mad)
As‡‡ miserable by the life§§ of thee,
As|| || thou hast made me by my dear lord's death!
Lo, ere I can repeat this curse again,

(*) First folio, *gentle*. (†) First folio omits, *I cry you mercy*. (‡) First folio, *betweene*. (§) First folio, *shall barre*. (||) First folio, *I*. (¶) First folio, *Ah*.

(*) First folio, *gone*. (†) First folio, *thy*. (‡) First folio, *howres*. (§) First folio, *with*. (||) First folio, *Braines*. (¶) First folio, *Venome*. (**) First folio, *Goe, goe*. (††) First folio, *deare*. (‡‡) First folio, *More*. (§§) Quartos, *death*. (|| ||) First folio, *Then*.

[a] How fares the prince? &c.] So the quartos; the corresponding passage in the folio reads:—

"How doth the Prince, and my young sonne of Yorke?
  LIEU. Right well, deare Madame: by your patience,
I may not suffer you to visit them,
The King hath strictly charg'd the contrary."

[b] *Then* fear not thou;] The folio reads, Then *bring me to their sights*.

[c] Or else I swoon with this dead-killing news.] In the folio, Anne here exclaims,—

"Despightfull tidings, O unpleasing newes."

And Dorset resumes,—

"Be of good cheare: Mother, how fares your Grace

[d] *To meet you on the way*, and welcome you:] So the quartos: in the folio,—

"*In your behalfe*, to meet you on the way."

E'en in so short a space,* my woman's heart
Grossly grew captive to his honey words,
And prov'd the subject of mine own soul's curse:
Which ever since hath kept† mine eyes from rest;
For never yet one hour in his bed
Have I enjoy'd‡ the golden dew of sleep,
But have been waked by his timorous dreams.[a]
Besides, he hates me for my father Warwick;
And will, no doubt,§ shortly be rid of me.

Q. ELIZ. Alas, poor soul! I pity thy complaints.[b]

ANNE. No more than from || my soul I mourn for yours.

Q. ELIZ. Farewell, thou woeful welcomer of glory!

ANNE. Adieu, poor soul, that tak'st thy leave of it!

DUCH. Go thou to Richmond, and good fortune guide thee!— [*To* DORSET.
Go thou to Richard, and good angels tend thee!— [*To* ANNE.
Go thou to sanctuary, and good thoughts possess thee! [*To* Q. ELIZABETH.
I to my grave, where peace and rest lie with me!
Eighty odd years of sorrow have I seen,
And each hour's joy wreck'd with a week of teen.

[Q. ELIZ. Stay yet;[c] look back with me unto the Tower.—
Pity, you ancient stones, those tender babes,
Whom envy hath immur'd within your walls!
Rough cradle for such little pretty ones!
Rude ragged nurse, old sullen play-fellow
For tender princes, use my babies well!
So foolish sorrow bids your stones farewell.]
[*Exeunt.*

SCENE II.—*The same. A Room of State in the Palace.*

Flourish of trumpets. RICHARD, *crowned;*[d] BUCKINGHAM, CATESBY, *a* Page, *and others.*

K. RICH. Stand all apart.—Cousin of Buckingham,[e]
Give me thy hand. [RICH. *ascends the throne.*
Thus high, by thy advice
And thy assistance, is king Richard seated:—
But shall we wear these honours* for a day,
Or shall they last, and we rejoice in them?

BUCK. Still live they, and for ever may they† last!

K. RICH. O,‡ Buckingham, now do I play the touch,
To try if thou be current gold indeed:—
Young Edward lives;—think now what I would say.§

BUCK. Say on, my gracious sovereign.[f]

K. RICH. Why, Buckingham, I say I would be king.

BUCK. Why so you are, my thrice-renowned liege. ||

K. RICH. Ha! am I king? 'T is so:—but Edward lives.

BUCK. True, noble prince.

K. RICH. O bitter consequence,
That Edward still should live,—*true, noble prince!*—
Cousin, thou wert¶ not wont to be so dull:—
Shall I be plain? I wish the bastards dead;
And I would have it suddenly perform'd.
What say'st thou now? speak suddenly, be brief.

BUCK. Your grace may do your pleasure.

K. RICH. Tut, tut, thou art all ice, thy kindness freezeth:
Say, have I thy consent that they shall die?

BUCK. Give me some breath, some little pause, my lord,[g]
Before I positively speak herein:**
I will resolve your grace immediately.[h]
[*Exit* BUCK.

CATE. The king is angry; see, he bites†† his lip. [*Aside.*

K. RICH. I will converse with iron-witted fools, [*Descends from his throne.*
And unrespective boys; none are for me,
That look into me with considerate eyes:—
High-reaching Buckingham grows circumspect.—
Boy,—

PAGE. My lord?

K. RICH. Know'st thou not any whom corrupting gold
Would‡‡ tempt unto a close exploit of death?

PAGE. I know a discontented gentleman,

(*) First folio, *Within so small a time.*
(†) First folio, *hitherto hath held.* (‡) First folio, *Did I enioy.*
(§) Quartos omit, *no doubt.* (||) First folio, *with.*

a But have been waked by his timorous dreams.] In the folio,—
"But with his timorous Dreames was still awak'd."

b Alas, *poor* soul! *I pity thy* complaints.] So the quarto: the folio version reads,—
"Poore *heart adieu,* I pittie thy *complaining.*"

c Stay yet; &c.] This speech is omitted in the quartos.

d RICHARD, *crowned;*] "Enter Richard in pompe" is the stage direction of the folio.

e Cousin of Buckingham,—] The folio adds,—
"BUCK. My gracious Soveraigne."

(*) First folio, *Glories.* (†) First folio, *let them.*
(‡) First folio, *Ah.* (§) First folio, *speake.*
(||) First folio, *Lord.* (¶) First folio, *wast.*
(**) First folio, *in this.* (††) First folio, *gnawes.*
(‡‡) First folio, *Will.*

f *Say on, my* gracious sovereign.] The folio reads,—
"Say on my *loving Lord.*"

g *Give me some breath, some* little *pause,* my *lord,*—] So the quarto: the folio has,—
"Give me some *litle* breath, some pawse, *deare* Lord."

h *I will resolve* your grace immediately.] In the folio,—
"I will resolve *you herein presently.*"

Whose humble means match not his haughty mind:*
Gold were as good as twenty orators,
And will, no doubt, tempt him to any thing.
K. RICH. What is his name?
PAGE. His name, my lord, is Tyrrel.
K. RICH. Go, call him hither presently.[a]—
[*Exit* Page.
The deep-revolving witty Buckingham
No more shall be the neighbour to my counsel:†
Hath he so long held out with me untir'd,
And stops he now for breath?*

Enter STANLEY.

How now, what news with you?[b]
STAN. Know, my loving lord,
The marquis Dorset, as I hear, is fled
To Richmond, in the parts where he abides.
K. RICH. Catesby?

(*) First folio, *spirit*. (†) First folio, *counsailes*.

(*) First folio adds, *Well, be it so.*

[a] *Go, call him hither presently.*] That is, *immediately*. The folio has, "I partly know the man: goe call him hither, Boy."

[b] How now, what news with you?] The abrupt exclamation of the quarto: the folio reads, *How now, Lord Stanley, what's the news?* But Stanley's answer in the latter edition seems preferable to the quarto, which has,—

"My lord, I hear the marquesse Dorset
Is fled to Richmond, in those parts beyond the seas where he abides."

CATE. My lord?
K. RICH. Rumour it abroad,[a]
That Anne, my wife, is sick, and like to die;
I will take order for her keeping close.
Inquire me out some mean born* gentleman,
Whom I will marry straight to Clarence' daughter:—
The boy is foolish, and I fear not him.—(2)
Look, how thou dream'st!—I say again, give out,
That Anne my wife† is sick, and like to die:
About it; for it stands me much upon,
To stop all hopes whose growth may damage me.— [*Exit* CATESBY.
I must be married to my brother's daughter,
Or else my kingdom stands on brittle glass:—
Murder her brothers, and then marry her!
Uncertain way of gain! But I am in
So far in blood, that sin will pluck on sin.
Tear-falling pity dwells not in this eye.—

Re-enter Page, *with* TYRREL.

Is thy name Tyrrel?
TYR. James Tyrrel, and your most obedient subject.
K. RICH. Art thou, indeed?
TYR. Prove me, my gracious sovereign.‡
K. RICH. Dar'st thou resolve to kill a friend of mine?
TYR. Please you; but I had rather kill two enemies.
K. RICH. Why, then thou hast it; two deep enemies,
Foes to my rest, and my sweet sleep's disturbers
Are they that I would have thee deal upon:—
Tyrrel, I mean those bastards in the Tower.
TYR. Let me have open means to come to them,
And soon I'll rid you from the fear of them.
K. RICH. Thou sing'st sweet music. Come§ hither, Tyrrel;
Go, by this token:—rise, and lend thine ear: [*Whispers.*
There is no more but so:—say, it is done,
And I will love thee, and prefer thee too.[b]
TYR. 'Tis done, my gracious lord.
K. RICH. Shall we hear from thee, Tyrrel, ere we sleep?
TYR. You shall, my lord. [*Exit.*

Re-enter BUCKINGHAM.

BUCK. My lord, I have consider'd in my mind
The late request that you did sound me in.
K. RICH. Well, let that pass.* Dorset is fled to Richmond.
BUCK. I hear that† news, my lord.
K. RICH. Stanley, he is your wife's son:—well, look to‡ it.
BUCK. My lord, I claim the gift, my due by promise,
For which your honour and your faith is pawn'd;
The earldom of Hereford, and the moveables,
The which you promised I should possess.[c] (3)
K. RICH. Stanley, look to your wife; if she convey
Letters to Richmond, you shall answer it.
BUCK. What says your highness to my just demand?§
K. RICH. As I remember||—Henry the sixth
Did prophesy, that Richmond should be king,
When Richmond was a little peevish boy.
A king!—perhaps—perhaps—¶
BUCK. My lord,—[d]
K. RICH. How chance the prophet could not at that time
Have told me, I being by, that I should kill him?
BUCK. My lord, your promise for the earldom,—
K. RICH. Richmond!—When last I was at Exeter,
The mayor in courtesy showed me the castle,
And call'd it—Rouge-mont; at which name, I started,
Because a bard of Ireland told me once,
I should not live long after I saw Richmond.
BUCK. My lord,—
K. RICH. Ay, what's o'clock?
BUCK. I am thus bold to put your grace in mind
Of what you promis'd me.
K. RICH. Well, but what's o'clock?

(*) First folio, *poore.* (†) First folio, *Queene.*
(‡) First folio, *Lord.* (§) First folio, *Hearke, come.*

a K. RICH. *Catesby?*
CATE. My lord?
K. RICH. *Rumour it abroad,*
That Anne, my wife, is sick, and like to die;]
So the quarto: the folio reads,—
"RICH. *Come hither* Catesby, rumor it abroad,
That Anne my Wife is *very grievous* sicke."

b *And I will love thee, and prefer thee* too.] The folio reads, "preferre thee *for it;*" and in place of the three lines that follow makes Tyrrel answer only,—
"I will dispatch it straight."

(*) First folio, *rest.* (†) First folio, *the.*
(‡) First folio, *unto.* (§) First folio, *request.*
(||) First folio, *I doe remember me.*
(¶) First folio, *perhaps,* once only.

c The *which you promised I* should *possess.*] In the folio,—
"Which you *have* promised I *shall* possesse."

d BUCK. My lord,—] The characteristic and dramatic portion of the scene that follows is entirely omitted in the folio, where Buckingham is made to say,—
"May it please you to resolve me in my suit?"—
and the King immediately answers,—
"Thou troublest me," &c.

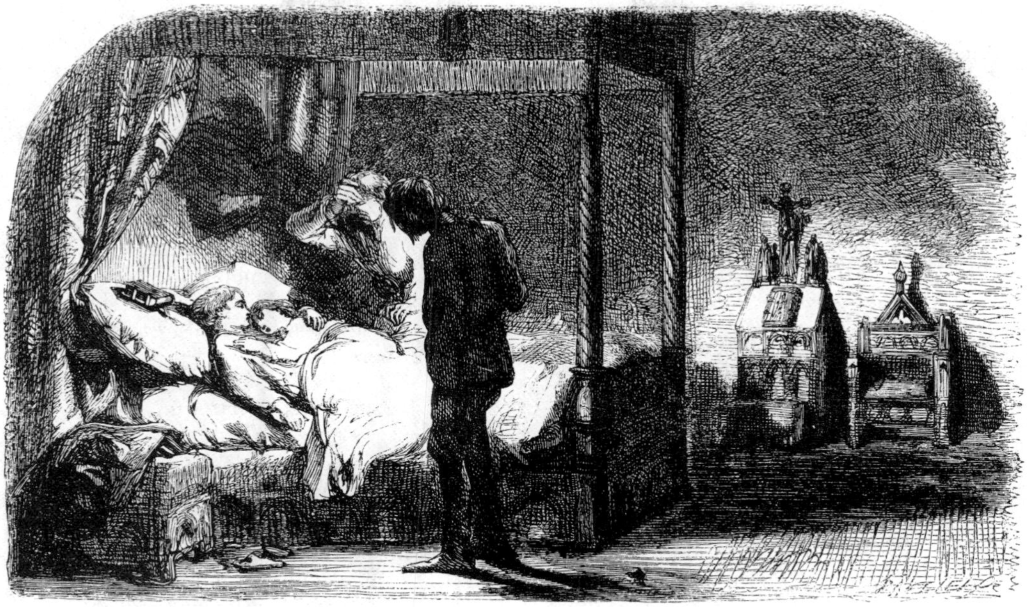

BUCK. Upon the stroke of ten.
K. RICH. Well, let it strike.
BUCK. Why let it strike?
K. RICH. Because that, like a jack, thou keep'st the stroke
Betwixt thy begging and my meditation.
I am not in the giving vein to-day.
BUCK. Why, then resolve me whe'r you will, or no.
K. RICH. Tut, tut,* thou troublest me; I am not in the vein.
[*Exeunt* K. RICHARD *and* Train.
BUCK. Is it even so?[a] repays he my true† service
With such‡ contempt? made I him king for this?
O, let me think on Hastings; and be gone
To Brecknock, while my fearful head is on!
[*Exit.*

SCENE III.—*The same.*

Enter TYRREL.

TYR. The tyrannous and bloody deed§ is done,—
The most arch-act ‖ of piteous massacre,
That ever yet this land was guilty of.
Dighton, and Forrest, whom I did suborn
To do this ruthless* piece of butchery,
Albeit they were flesh'd villains, bloody dogs,
Melting † with tenderness and mild compassion,
Wept like two children in their death's sad story.
Lo, thus, quoth Dighton, *lay those tender* ‡ *babes,*—
Thus, thus, quoth Forrest, *girdling one another*
Within their innocent alabaster§ *arms:*
Their lips like four red roses on a stalk,
Which, in their summer beauty, kiss'd each other.(4) [b]
A book of prayers on their pillow lay;
Which once, ‖ quoth Forrest, *almost chang'd my mind;*
But, O, the devil—there the villain stopp'd;
When Dighton thus told on,—*we smothered*
The most replenished sweet work of nature,
That from the prime creation e'er she fram'd.—
Hence both are gone with conscience and remorse
They could not speak; and so I left them both,
To bear this tidings to the bloody king.
And here he comes:—

(*) First folio omits, *Tut, tut.* (†) First folio, *deepe.*
(‡) Quartos insert, *deepe.* (§) First folio, *Act.*
(‖) First folio, *deed.*

a Is it even so?] The folio reads, "*And is it thus?*"

b *Their lips* like *four red roses on a stalk,*
Which, *in their summer beauty, kiss'd each other.*]

(*) First folio, *peece of ruthfull.* (†) First folio, *Melted.*
(‡) First folio, *the gentle.*
(§) First folio, *Alablaster innocent.* (‖) First folio, *one.*

The folio lection is,—

"Their lips *were* foure red Roses on a stalke,
And in their Summer Beauty kist each other."

Enter KING RICHARD.

All hail,* my sovereign liege!†
K. RICH. Kind Tyrrel, am I happy in thy news?
TYR. If to have done the thing you gave in [charge
Beget your happiness, be happy then,
For it is done, my lord.‡
K. RICH. But didst thou see them dead?
TYR. I did, my lord.
K. RICH. And buried, gentle Tyrrel?
TYR. The chaplain of the Tower hath buried them;
But how, or in what place,[a] I do not know.
K. RICH. Come to me, Tyrrel, soon at§ after-supper,
And || thou shalt tell the process of their death.
Mean time but think how I may do thee good,
And be inheritor of thy desire.
Farewell, till then.
[TYR. I humbly take my leave.][b]
[*Exit* TYRREL.
K. RICH. The son of Clarence have I pent up close;
His daughter meanly have I match'd in marriage;
The sons of Edward sleep in Abraham's bosom,
And Anne my wife hath bid the¶ world good night.
Now, for I know the Bretagne Richmond aims
At young Elizabeth, my brother's daughter,
And, by that knot, looks proudly on the crown,
To her go I, a jolly thriving wooer.

Enter CATESBY.

CATE. My lord,—
K. RICH. Good news or bad,** that thou com'st in so bluntly?
CATE. Bad news, my lord: Ely †† is fled to [Richmond;
And Buckingham, back'd with the hardy Welshmen,
Is in the field, and still his power increaseth.
K. RICH. Ely with Richmond troubles me more near,
Than Buckingham and his rash-levied strength.‡‡
Come,—I have heard§§ that fearful commenting
Is leaden servitor to dull delay;
Delay leads |||| impotent and snail-pac'd beggary:
Then fiery expedition be my wing,
Jove's Mercury and herald for a king!
Go muster men: my counsel is my shield;
We must be brief, when traitors brave the field.
[*Exeunt.*

(*) First folio, *health*.
(†) First folio, *Lord*.
(‡) First folio omits, *my lord*.
(§) First folio, *and*.
(||) First folio, *When*.
(¶) First folio, *this*.
(**) First folio, *Good or bad news*.
(††) First folio, *Mourton*.
(‡‡) Quarto, *army*.
(§§) First folio, *learn'd*.
(||||) First folio, *leds*.

[a] *But* how, or in what place,—] In the folio, But *where* (*to say the truth*.)

SCENE IV.—*The same. Before the Palace.*

Enter QUEEN MARGARET.

Q. MAR. So; now prosperity begins to mellow,
And drop into the rotten mouth of death.
Here in these confines slily have I lurk'd,
To watch the waning of mine enemies.
A dire induction am I witness to,
And will to France; hoping the consequence
Will prove as bitter, black, and tragical.—
Withdraw thee, wretched Margaret; who comes here? [*Retires.*

Enter QUEEN ELIZABETH *and the* DUCHESS *of* YORK.

Q. ELIZ. Ah, my poor princes! ah, my tender babes!
My unblown* flowers, new-appearing sweets!
If yet your gentle souls fly in the air,
And be not fix'd in doom perpetual,
Hover about me with your airy wings,
And hear your mother's lamentation!
Q. MAR. [*Aside.*] Hover about her! say, that right for right
Hath dimm'd your infant morn to aged night.
DUCH. So many miseries have craz'd my voice,
That my woe-wearied tongue is still and mute,—
Edward Plantagenet, why art thou dead?
Q. MAR. [*Aside.*] Plantagenet doth quit Plantagenet.
Edward, for Edward, pays a dying debt.
Q. ELIZ. Wilt thou, O God, fly from such gentle lambs,
And throw them in the entrails of the wolf?
When didst thou sleep, when such a deed was done?
Q. MAR. [*Aside.*] When holy Harry died, and my sweet son.
DUCH. Blind sight, dead life,† poor mortal-living ghost,
Woe's scene, world's shame, grave's due by life usurp'd,
[Brief abstract and record of tedious days,][c]
Rest thy unrest on England's lawful earth,
[*Sitting down.*
Unlawfully made drunk with innocent blood!
Q. ELIZ. O,‡ that thou wouldst as soon afford a grave,
As thou canst yield a melancholy seat!

(*) First folio, *unblowed*.
(†) First folio, *Dead life, blind sight*.
(‡) First folio, *Ah*.

[b] I humbly take my leave.] Omitted in the quartos.
[c] Brief abstract and record of tedious days,—] This line is omitted in the quartos.

Then would I hide my bones, not rest them here!
O,* who hath any cause to mourn but I? †
[*Sitting down by her.*

Q. MAR. [*Coming forward.*] If ancient sorrow be most reverent,
Give mine the benefit of seniory, ‡
And let my griefs frown on the upper hand.
If sorrow can admit society,
[*Sitting down with them.*
Tell o'er your woes again by viewing mine:—[a]
I had an Edward, till a Richard kill'd him;
I had a Henry, § till a Richard kill'd him:
Thou hadst an Edward, till a Richard kill'd him;
Thou hadst a Richard, till a Richard kill'd him.

DUCH. I had a Richard too, and thou didst kill him;
I had a Rutland too, thou holp'st || to kill him.

Q. MAR. Thou hadst a Clarence too, till ¶ Richard kill'd him.
From forth the kennel of thy womb hath crept
A hell-hound that doth hunt us all to death:
That dog, that had his teeth before his eyes,
To worry lambs, and lap their gentle blood;
That foul defacer of God's handy-work;[b]
Thy womb let loose, to chase us to our graves.—
O upright, just, and true-disposing God,
How do I thank thee, that this carnal cur
Preys on the issue of his mother's body,
And makes her pew-fellow with others' moan!

DUCH. O, Harry's wife, triumph not in my woes!
God witness with me, I have wept for thine.

Q. MAR. Bear with me; I am hungry for revenge,
And now I cloy me with beholding it.
Thy Edward he is dead, that stabb'd** my Edward;
Thy other Edward dead, to quit my Edward;
Young York he is but boot, because both they
Match †† not the high perfection of my loss.
Thy Clarence he is dead that kill'd ‡‡ my Edward;
And the beholders of this tragic §§ play,
The adulterate Hastings, Rivers, Vaughan, Grey,
Untimely smother'd in their dusky graves.
Richard yet lives, hell's black intelligencer;
Only reserv'd their factor, to buy souls,
And send them thither: but at hand, at hand,
Ensues his piteous and unpitied end:
Earth gapes, hell burns, fiends roar, saints pray,
To have him suddenly convey'd from hence:—
Cancel his bond of life, dear God, I pray,
That I may live to* say, The dog is dead!

Q. ELIZ. O, thou didst prophesy the time would come,
That I should wish for thee to help me curse
That bottled spider, that foul bunch-back'd toad.

Q. MAR. I call'd thee then, vain flourish of my fortune;
I call'd thee then, poor shadow, painted queen;
The presentation of but what I was,
The flattering index of a direful pageant,
One heav'd a-high, to be hurl'd down below:
A mother only mock'd with two sweet † babes;
A dream of what thou wast; a breath, a bubble;[c]
A sign of dignity, a garish flag,
To be the aim of every dangerous shot;
A queen in jest, only to fill the scene.
Where is thy husband now? where be thy brothers?
Where be thy children? ‡ wherein dost thou joy?
Who sues to thee and cries[d]—*God save the queen?*
Where be the bending peers that flatter'd thee?
Where be the thronging troops that follow'd thee?
Decline all this, and see what now thou art.
For happy wife, a most distressed widow;
For joyful mother, one that wails the name;
For queen, a very caitiff crown'd with care:[e]
For one being sued to, one that humbly sues;
For one commanding all, obey'd of none.
For one that scorn'd at me, now scorn'd of me;
Thus hath the course of justice wheel'd § about,
And left thee but a very prey to time;
Having no more but thought of what thou wert, ||
To torture thee the more, being what thou art.
Thou didst usurp my place, and dost thou not
Usurp the just proportion of my sorrow?
Now thy proud neck bears half my burden'd yoke;
From which even here I slip my weary neck, ¶
And leave the burden of it all on thee.
Farewell, York's wife, and queen of sad mischance;
These English woes shall make me smile in France.

(*) First folio, *Ah.* (†) First folio, *wee.* (‡) First folio, *signeurie.* (§) First folio, *Husband.* (||) First folio, *hop'st.* (¶) First folio, *And.* (**) First folio, *kill'd.* (††) First folio, *Matcht.* (‡‡) First folio, *stab'd.* (§§) First folio, *franticke.*

a Tell o'er your woes again by viewing mine:] This line is omitted in the folio.

b That foul defacer of God's handy-work;] Here, in the folio, follow these two lines—

"That reignes in gauled eyes of weeping soules:
That excellent grand Tyrant of the earth."

c ——— a breath, a bubble;
A sign of dignity, a garish flag,
To be the aim of every dangerous shot;]

The folio text arranges these lines thus:—

" ——— a garish Flagge
To be the ayme of every dangerous Shot;
A signe of Dignity, a Breath, a Bubble."

d *Who sues* to thee *and* cries—] In the folio,
"Who sues, *and kneeles* and *sayes*."

e For queen, a very caitiff crown'd with care: &c.] The folio reads:—

"For one being sued too, one that humbly sues:
For Queene, a very Caytiffe, crown'd with care:
For she that scorn'd at me, now scorn'd of me:
For she being feared of all, now fearing one:
For she commanding all, obey'd of none."

(*) First folio, *and.* (†) First folio, *faire.* (‡) First folio, *two Sonnes.* (§) First folio, *whirl'd.* (||) Old text, *art,—wast.* (¶) First folio, *wearied head.*

Q. ELIZ. O thou well skill'd in curses, stay awhile,
And teach me how to curse mine enemies.
Q. MAR. Forbear to sleep the night, and fast the day;
Compare dead happiness with living woe;
Think that thy babes were fairer* than they were,
And he, that slew them, fouler than he is:
Bettering thy loss makes the bad-causer worse;
Revolving this will teach thee how to curse.
Q. ELIZ. My words are dull, O, quicken them with thine!
Q. MAR. Thy woes will make them sharp, and pierce like mine. [*Exit* Q. MARGARET.
DUCH. Why should calamity be full of words?
Q. ELIZ. Windy attorneys to their client† woes,
Airy succeeders of intestate‡ joys,
Poor breathing orators of miseries!
Let them have scope; though what they do§ impart
Help not at all,|| yet do they ease the heart.
DUCH. If so, then be not tongue-tied: go with me,
And in the breath of bitter words let's smother
My damned son, that thy two sweet sons smother'd.
I hear his drum,¶—be copious in exclaims.

Drums and Trumpets. Enter KING RICHARD *and his* Train, *marching.*

K. RICH. Who intercepts me in my expedition?
DUCH. O, she that might have intercepted thee,—
By strangling thee in her accursed womb,—
From all the slaughters, wretch, that thou hast done.
Q. ELIZ. Hid'st thou that forehead with a golden crown, [right,
Where** should be graven,†† if that right were
The slaughter of the prince that ow'd that crown,
And the dire death of my poor‡‡ sons and brothers?
Tell me, thou villain-slave, where are my children?
DUCH. Thou toad! thou toad! where is thy brother Clarence?
And little Ned Plantagenet, his son?

(*) First folio, *sweeter*. (†) First folio, *Clients*.
(‡) First folio, *intestine*. (§) First folio, *will*.
(||) First folio, *nothing els*.
(¶) First folio, *The Trumpet sounds*.
(**) First folio, *Where't*. (††) First folio, *branded*.
(‡‡) Quartos, *two*.

a Where is kind Hastings, Rivers, Vaughan, Grey?] This inquiry is distributed in the folio between the two ladies:—

"QU. Where is *the gentle* Rivers, Vaughan, Gray?
DUT. Where is kinde Hastings?"

b Which cannot brook the accent of reproof.] The following unimportant lines here occur in the folio:—

"DUT. O let me speake.
RICH. Do then, but Ile not heare."

c *In* anguish, pain, *and agony*.] In the folio, "in *torment* and *in* agony."

Q. ELIZ. Where is kind Hastings, Rivers, Vaughan, Grey?[a]
K. RICH. A flourish, trumpets!—strike alarum, drums!
Let not the heavens hear these tell-tale women
Rail on the Lord's anointed: strike, I say!— [*Flourish. Alarums.*
Either be patient, and entreat me fair,
Or with the clamorous report of war
Thus will I drown your exclamations.
DUCH. Art thou my son?
K. RICH. Ay, I thank God, my father, and yourself.
DUCH. Then patiently hear my impatience.
K. RICH. Madam, I have a touch of your condition,
Which* cannot brook the accent of reproof.[b]
DUCH. I will be mild and gentle in my speech.†
K. RICH. And brief, good mother, for I am in haste.
DUCH. Art thou so hasty? I have stay'd for thee,
God knows, in anguish, pain, and agony.[c]
K. RICH. And came I not at last to comfort you?
DUCH. No, by the holy rood! thou know'st it well,
Thou cam'st on earth to make the earth my hell.
A grievous burden was thy birth to me;
Tetchy and wayward was thy infancy;
Thy school-days frightful, desperate, wild, and furious;
Thy prime of manhood, daring, bold, and venturous;
Thy age confirm'd, proud, subtle, bloody, treacherous,[d]
What comfortable hour canst thou name,
That ever grac'd me in‡ thy company?
K. RICH. 'Faith, none, but Humphrey Hour,(5) that call'd your grace
To break fast once, forth of my company.
If I§ be so disgracious in your sight,||
Let me march on, and not offend you, madam.—
Strike up the drum.
DUCH. O, hear me speak; for I shall never see thee more.[e]

(*) First folio, *That*. (†) First folio, *words*.
(‡) First folio, *with*. (§) Quartos, *it*.
(||) First folio, *eye*.

d *Thy age confirm'd, proud, subtle, bloody, treacherous,*—] The folio reads, "subtle, *slye, and* bloody," and adds a line,—

"*More milde, but yet more harmfull; Kinde in hatred.*"

e DUCH. O, hear me speak; for I shall never see thee more.
K. RICH. Come, come, you are too bitter.]

In the folio:—

"DUT. I prythee heare me speake.
RICH. You speake too bitterly.
DUT. Heare me a word:
For I shall never speake to thee againe."

K. Rich. Come, come, you are too bitter.

Duch. Either thou wilt die, by God's just ordinance,
Ere from this war thou turn a conqueror;
Or I with grief and éxtreme age shall perish,
And never look upon* thy face again.
Therefore, take with thee my most heavy† curse;
Which, in the day of battle, tire thee more,
Than all the cómplete armour that thou wear'st!
My prayers on the adverse party fight;
And there the little souls of Edward's children
Whisper the spirits of thine enemies,
And promise them success and victory.
Bloody thou art, bloody will be thy end;
Shame serves thy life, and doth thy death attend.
[*Exit.*

(*) First folio, *never more behold.* (†) First folio, *greevous.*

Q. ELIZ. Though far more cause, yet much less spirit to curse
Abides in me; I say *Amen* to all.* [*Going.*
K. RICH. Stay, madam, I must speak † a word with you.
Q. ELIZ. I have no more sons of the royal blood,
For thee to murder: ‡ for my daughters, Richard,—
They shall be praying nuns, not weeping queens;
And therefore level not to hit their lives.
K. RICH. You have a daughter call'd Elizabeth,
Virtuous and fair, royal and gracious.
Q. ELIZ. And must she die for this? O, let her live,
And I'll corrupt her manners, stain her beauty;
Slander myself as false to Edward's bed;
Throw over her the veil of infamy:
So she may live unscarr'd from § bleeding slaughter,
I will confess she was not Edward's daughter!
K. RICH. Wrong not her birth, she is of royal blood.[a]
Q. ELIZ. To save her life, I'll say she is not so.
K. RICH. Her life is only || safest in her birth.
Q. ELIZ. And only in that safety died her brothers.
K. RICH. Lo, at their birth good stars were opposite.
Q. ELIZ. No, to their lives bad ¶ friends were contrary.
K. RICH. All unavoided[b] is the doom of destiny.
Q. ELIZ. True, when avoided grace makes destiny:
My babes were destin'd to a fairer death,
If grace had bless'd thee with a fairer life.
[K. RICH. You speak as if that I had slain my cousins.
Q. ELIZ. *Cousins*, indeed; and by their uncle cozen'd
Of comfort, kingdom, kindred, freedom, life.
Whose hands soever lanc'd** their tender hearts,
Thy head, all indirectly, gave direction:
No doubt the murderous knife was dull and blunt,
Till it was whetted on thy stone-hard heart,
To revel in the entrails of my lambs.
But that still use of grief makes wild grief tame,
My tongue should to thy ears not name my boys,
Till that my nails were anchor'd in thine eyes;
And I, in such a desperate bay of death,
Like a poor bark, of sails and tackling reft,
Rush all to pieces on thy rocky bosom.][c]
K. RICH. Madam, so thrive I in my enterprize,
And dangerous success of bloody wars,
As I intend more good to you and yours,
Than ever you or yours were by me wrong'd!*
Q. ELIZ. What good is cover'd with the face of heaven,
To be discover'd, that can do me good?
K. RICH. The advancement of your children, gentle † lady.
Q. ELIZ. Up to some scaffold, there to lose their heads?
K. RICH. No, to the‡ dignity and height of honour,§
The high imperial type of this earth's glory.
Q. ELIZ. Flatter my sorrows || with report of it;
Tell me, what state, what dignity, what honour,
Canst thou demise to any child of mine?
K. RICH. Even all I have; ay, and myself and all,
Will I withal endow a child of thine;
So in the Lethe of thy angry soul
Thou drown the sad remembrance of those wrongs,
Which thou supposest I have done to thee.
Q. ELIZ. Be brief, lest that the process of thy kindness
Last longer telling than thy kindness' date.
K. RICH. Then know, that from my soul I love thy daughter.
Q. ELIZ. My daughter's mother thinks it with her soul.
K. RICH. What do you think?
Q. ELIZ. That thou dost love my daughter, from thy soul:
So, from thy soul's love, didst thou love her brothers;
And, from my heart's love, I do thank thee for it.
K. RICH. Be not so hasty to confound my meaning:
I mean, that with my soul I love thy daughter,
And do intend to make her queen of England.
Q. ELIZ. Say ¶ then, who dost thou mean shall be her king?
K. RICH. Even he that makes her queen; who else should be?
Q. ELIZ. What, thou?
K. RICH. Even so: how think you of it?
Q. ELIZ. How canst thou woo her?
K. RICH. That would I** learn of you,
As one being best acquainted with her humour.
Q. ELIZ. And wilt thou learn of me?
K. RICH. Madam, with all my heart.
Q. ELIZ. Send to her, by the man that slew her brothers,
A pair of bleeding hearts; thereon engrave,

(*) First folio, *her*. (†) First folio, *talke*. (‡) First folio, *slaughter*. (§) First folio, *of*. (||) First folio, *safest onely*. (¶) First folio, *ill*. (**) Old text, *lanch'd*.

a *She is* of royal blood.] So the quarto; the folio has, "She is *a Royall Princesse*."

b *All* unavoided *is the doom,* &c.] That is, All *unavoidable*.

(*) First folio, *and yours by me were harm'd*. (†) Quartos, *mightie*. (‡) First folio, *Unto the*. (§) First folio, *Fortune*. (||) First folio, *sorrow*. (¶) First folio, *Well*. (**) First folio, *I would*.

c Rush all to pieces on thy rocky bosom.] The lines within brackets are not in the quartos.

Edward and York; then, haply, will she weep:
Therefore present to her,—as sometime Margaret
Did to thy father, steep'd in Rutland's blood,—
A handkerchief; [which, say to her, did drain
The purple sap from her sweet brother's body,] [a]
And bid her dry* her weeping eyes therewith.†
If this inducement force‡ her not to love,
Send her a story of thy noble acts; [b]
Tell her, thou mad'st away her uncle Clarence,
Her uncle Rivers; yea,§ and, for her sake,
Mad'st quick conveyance with her good aunt Anne.

K. RICH. You mock me, madam; this is not the way
To win your daughter.

Q. ELIZ. There is no other way;
Unless thou couldst put on some other shape,
And not be Richard that hath done all this.

[K. RICH. Say, that I did all this for love of her?

Q. ELIZ. Nay, then indeed, she cannot choose but hate [c] thee,
Having bought love with such a bloody spoil.

K. RICH. Look, what is done cannot be now amended:
Men shall deal unadvisedly sometimes,
Which after-hours gives leisure to repent.
If I did take the kingdom from your sons,
To make amends, I'll give it to your daughter.
If I have kill'd the issue of your womb,
To quicken your increase, I will beget
Mine issue of your blood upon your daughter.
A grandam's name is little less in love,
Than is the doting title of a mother;
They are as children but one step below,
Even of your mettle, of your very blood;
Of all one pain, save for a night of groans
Endur'd of her, for whom you bid like sorrow.
Your children were vexation to your youth,
But mine shall be a comfort to your age.
The loss you have is but a son being king,
And by that loss your daughter is made queen.
I cannot make you what amends I would,
Therefore accept such kindness as I can.
Dorset your son, that, with a fearful soul,
Leads discontented steps in foreign soil,
This fair alliance quickly shall call home
To high promotions and great dignity:
The king, that calls your beauteous daughter, wife,
Familiarly shall call thy Dorset, brother;
Again shall you be mother to a king,
And all the ruins of distressful times
Repair'd with double riches of content.
What! we have many goodly days to see:
The liquid drops of tears that you have shed,
Shall come again, transform'd to orient pearl;
Advantaging their loan,* with interest
Of ten-times-double gain of happiness.
Go then, my mother, to thy daughter go;
Make bold her bashful years with your experience;
Prepare her ears to hear a wooer's tale;
Put in her tender heart the aspiring flame
Of golden sovereignty; acquaint the princess
With the sweet silent hours of marriage joys:
And when this arm of mine hath chástised
The petty rebel, dull-brain'd Buckingham,
Bound with triumphant garlands will I come,
And lead thy daughter to a conqueror's bed;
To whom I will retail my conquest won,
And she shall be sole victress, Cæsar's Cæsar.

Q. ELIZ. What were I best to say? her father's brother
Would be her lord? or shall I say, her uncle?
Or, he that slew her brothers and her uncles?
Under what title shall I woo for thee,
That God, the law, my honour, and her love,
Can make seem pleasing to her tender years?] [d]

K. RICH. Infer fair England's peace by this alliance.

Q. ELIZ. Which she shall purchase with still-lasting war.

K. RICH. Say that the king, which may command,[e] entreats.

Q. ELIZ. That at her hands, which the king's King forbids.

K. RICH. Say she shall be a high and mighty queen.

Q. ELIZ. To wail† the title, as her mother doth.

K. RICH. Say I will love her everlastingly.

Q. ELIZ. But how long shall that title, *ever*, last?

K. RICH. Sweetly in force unto her fair life's end.

Q. ELIZ. But how long fairly shall her sweet life last?

K. RICH. So‡ long as heaven and nature lengthens it.

Q. ELIZ. As long as hell and Richard likes of it.

K. RICH. Say, I, her sovereign, am her subject love.§

Q. ELIZ. But she, your subject, loaths such sovereignty.

K. RICH. Be eloquent in my behalf to her.

Q. ELIZ. An honest tale speeds best, being plainly told.

(*) First folio, *wipe*. (†) First folio, *withall*.
(‡) First folio, *move*. (§) First folio, *I*.

a ——— which, say to her, did drain
The purple sap from her sweet brother's body,—]
These words are omitted in the quartos.

b *A* story *of thy noble* acts;] So the quartos: the folio has, "a *Letter* of thy Noble *deeds*."

c *She cannot choose but* hate *thee*,—] A misprint probably, as Mason and Steevens surmised, for "*—have* thee," or, as Tyrwhitt conjectured, for "*—love* thee."

(*) Old text, *Loue*. (†) First folio, *vaile*.
(‡) First folio, *As*. (§) First folio, *low*.

d Can make seem pleasing to her tender years?] The fifty-five lines inclosed in brackets are found only in the folio. See note (a), p. 534, and the Introductory Notice.

e Say that *the king*, which *may command*,—] In the folio,—"*Tell her*, the King *that* may command,—" &c.

K. RICH. Then, in plain terms, tell her* my loving tale.
Q. ELIZ. Plain and not honest is too harsh a style.
K. RICH. Madam,† your reasons are too shallow and too quick.
Q. ELIZ. O, no, my reasons are too deep and dead;—
Too deep and dead, poor infants, in their graves.
K. RICH. Harp not on that string, madam; that is past.
Q. ELIZ. Harp on it still shall I, till heart-strings break.[a]
K. RICH. Now, by my George, my garter, and my crown,—
Q. ELIZ. Profan'd, dishonour'd, and the third usurp'd.
K. RICH. I swear—
Q. ELIZ. By nothing; for this is no oath.
Thy George, profan'd, hath lost his holy‡ honour;
Thy garter, blemish'd, pawn'd his knightly virtue;
Thy crown, usurp'd, disgrac'd his kingly glory:§
If something thou wilt || swear to be believ'd,
Swear then by something that thou hast not wrong'd.
K. RICH. Now by the world,—
Q. ELIZ. 'Tis full of thy foul wrongs.
K. RICH. My father's death,—
Q. ELIZ. Thy life hath that¶ dishonour'd.
K. RICH. Then, by myself,—
Q. ELIZ. Thyself thyself mis-usest.[b]
K. RICH. Why then, by God,**—
Q. ELIZ. God's** wrong is most of all.
If thou hadst fear'd†† to break an oath by‡‡ Him,
The unity the king thy brother[c] made,
Had not been broken, nor my brother slain.
If thou hadst fear'd to break an oath by Him,
The imperial metal, circling now thy brow, §§
Had grac'd the tender temples of my child;
And both the princes had been breathing here,
Which now, two[d] tender play-fellows |||| for dust,
Thy broken faith hath made a¶¶ prey for worms.
What canst thou swear by now?[e]
K. RICH. The time to come.

(*) First folio, *plainly to her, tell.*
(†) First folio omits, *Madam.*
(‡) First folio, *Lordly.*
(§) Quarto, *dignitie.*
(||) First folio, *would'st.*
(¶) First folio, *it.*
(**) First folio, *Heaven—Heavens.*
(††) First folio, *didd'st feare.*
(‡‡) First folio, *with.*
(§§) First folio, *head.*
(||||) First folio, *Bed-fellowes.*
(¶¶) First folio, *the.*

[a] Harp on it still shall I, till heart-strings break.] In the folio, the Queen's answer precedes Richard's speech, which is accidentally omitted in the quartos.

[b] K. RICH. Then, by myself,—
Q. ELIZ. Thyself thyself mis-usest.]
In the folio, which reads, "Thy Selfe, *is selfe misus'd,*" this oath and the Queen's *repartee* immediately follow the line,—
"Swear then by something that thou hast not wrong'd."

[c] *The unity the king* thy brother *made,*
Had not been *broken, nor my* brother slain.]
In the quartos, *thy*, in the first line, is misprinted *my*: the folio reads,—

Q. ELIZ. That thou hast wronged in the time o'er-past;
For I myself have many tears to wash
Hereafter time, for time past wrong'd by thee.
The children live, whose parents* thou hast slaughter'd,
Ungovern'd youth, to wail it in† their age:
The parents live, whose children thou hast butcher'd,
Old wither'd‡ plants, to wail it with their age.
Swear not by time to come; for that thou hast
Misus'd ere us'd, by times mis-us'd o'er-past.§
K. RICH. As I intend to prosper, and repent!
So thrive I in my dangerous attempt ||
Of hostile arms! myself myself confound!
[Heaven and fortune bar me happy hours![f]]
Day, yield me not thy light; nor, night, thy rest!
Be opposite all planets of good luck
To my proceeding! if, with pure¶ heart's love,
Immaculate devotion, holy thoughts,
I tender not thy beauteous princely daughter!
In her consists my happiness and thine;
Without her, follows to this land and me,
To thee, herself, and many a christian soul,[g]
Death,** desolation, ruin, and decay:
It cannot be avoided but by this;
It will not be avoided but by this.
Therefore, dear†† mother, (I must call you so,)
Be the attorney of my love to her.
Plead what I will be, not what I have been;
Not my deserts, but what I will deserve:
Urge the necessity and state of times,
And be not peevish-fond‡‡ in great designs.
Q. ELIZ. Shall I be tempted of the devil thus?
K. RICH. Ay, if the devil tempt you to do good.
Q. ELIZ. Shall I forget myself to be myself?
K. RICH. Ay, if your self's remembrance wrong yourself.
Q. ELIZ. But§§ thou didst kill my children.
K. RICH. But in your daughter's womb I'll |||| bury them:
Where, in that nest of spicery, they shall¶¶ breed
Selves of themselves, to your recomforture.
Q. ELIZ. Shall I go win my daughter to thy will?

(*) First folio, *Fathers.*
(†) First folio, *with.*
(‡) First folio, *barren.*
(§) First folio, *ill-us'd repast.*
(||) First folio, *Affayres.*
(¶) First folio, *deere.*
(**) Quarto, *Sad.*
(††) Quarto, *good.*
(‡‡) First folio, *peevish found.*
(§§) First folio, *Yet.*
(||||) First folio, *I bury.*
(¶¶) First folio, *will.*

"The unity the King *my husband* made
Thou had'st not broken, nor my *Brothers died.*"

[d] Two *tender play-fellows*—] *Two* in this passage is unquestionably an error for *too.*

[e] What canst thou swear by now?] Omitted in the quartos.

[f] Heaven and fortune bar me happy hours!] This line is not in the quarto.

[g] *Without her, follows to* this land and me,
To thee, herself, *and many a christian soul,*—]
In the folio, the arrangement is slightly altered.—
"Without her, followes to *my selfe, and thee;*
Her selfe, the Land," &c.

K. RICH. And be a happy mother by the deed.
Q. ELIZ. I go.—Write to me very shortly,
[And you shall understand from me her mind.][a]
K. RICH. Bear her my true love's kiss, and so farewell.
[*Kissing her. Exit* Q. ELIZABETH.
Relenting fool, and shallow, changing woman!

Enter RATCLIFF; CATESBY *following*.

[How now! what news?][b]
RAT. My gracious* sovereign, on the western coast
Rideth a puissant navy; to the shore†
Throng many doubtful hollow-hearted friends,
Unarm'd, and unresolv'd to beat them back:
'Tis thought that Richmond is their admiral;
And there they hull, expecting but the aid
Of Buckingham to welcome them ashore.
K. RICH. Some light-foot friend post to the duke of Norfolk:—
Ratcliff, thyself,—or Catesby; where is he?
CATE. Here, my good lord.
K. RICH. Catesby, fly to the duke.
[CATE. I will, my lord, with all convenient haste.
K. RICH. Ratcliff,‡ come hither:][c] post to Salisbury;
When thou com'st thither—Dull unmindful villain, [*To* CATESBY.
Why stay'st thou here, and go'st not to the duke?
CATE. First, mighty liege, tell me your highness' pleasure,
What from your grace I shall deliver § him.
K. RICH. O, true, good Catesby;—bid him levy straight
The greatest strength and power ‖ he can make,
And meet me suddenly at Salisbury.
CATE. I go. [*Exit.*
RAT. What, may it please you, shall I do at Salisbury?
K. RICH. Why, what wouldst thou do there, before I go?
RAT. Your highness told me, I should post before.
K. RICH. My mind is chang'd.—

Enter STANLEY.

Stanley, what news with you?
STAN. None good, my liege, to please you with the hearing;
Nor none so bad, but well may be reported.
K. RICH. Hoyday, a riddle! neither good nor bad!
What need'st thou run so many miles about,
When thou mayst tell thy tale the nearest way?
Once more, what news?
STAN. Richmond is on the seas.
K. RICH. There let him sink, and be the seas on him!
White-liver'd runagate! what doth he there?
STAN. I know not, mighty sovereign, but by guess.
K. RICH. Well, as you guess?
STAN. Stirr'd up by Dorset, Buckingham, and Morton,
He makes for England, here to claim the crown.
K. RICH. Is the chair empty? is the sword unsway'd?
Is the king dead? the empire unpossess'd?
What heir of York is there alive but we?
And who is England's king but great York's heir?
Then, tell me, what makes he upon the seas?
STAN. Unless for that, my liege, I cannot guess.
K. RICH. Unless for that he comes to be your liege,
You cannot guess wherefore the Welshman comes?
Thou wilt revolt, and fly to him, I fear.
STAN. No, mighty liege;* therefore mistrust me not.
K. RICH. Where is thy power then, to beat him back?
Where be thy tenants and thy followers?
Are they not now upon the western shore,
Safe-cónducting the rebels from their ships?
STAN. No, my good lord, my friends are in the north.
K. RICH. Cold friends to me: what do they in the north,
When they should serve their sovereign in the west?
STAN. They have not been commanded, mighty king:
Pleaseth your majesty to give me leave,
I'll muster up my friends, and meet your grace,
Where, and what time, your majesty shall please.
K. RICH. Ay, thou wouldst be gone to join with Richmond:
But I'll not trust thee.
STAN. Most mighty sovereign,
You have no cause to hold my friendship doubtful;
I never was, nor never will be false.
K. RICH. Go then, and muster men: but leave behind
Your son, George Stanley: look your heart be firm,
Or else his head's assurance is but frail.
STAN. So deal with him as I prove true to you.
[*Exit* STANLEY.

(*) First folio, *Most mightie*. (†) First folio, *our shores*.
(‡) Old text, *Catesby*. (§) First folio inserts, *to*.
(‖) First folio inserts, *that*.

[a] And you shall understand from me her mind.] The quartos omit this line.

(*) First folio, *my good Lord*.

[b] How now! what news?] Omitted in the quarto.
[c] I will, my lord, with all convenient haste.
K. RICH. Ratcliff, come hither:] Not in the quartos

Enter a Messenger.

MESS. My gracious sovereign, now in Devonshire,
As I by friends am well advértisèd,
Sir Edward Courtney, and the haughty prelate,
Bishop of Exeter, his elder brother,
With many more* confederates, are in arms.

Enter a second Messenger.

2 MESS. In Kent, my liege, the Guildfords are in arms;
And every hour more competitors
Flock to the rebels, and their power grows strong.

Enter a third Messenger.

3 MESS. My lord, the army of great Buckingham—
K. RICH. Out on ye, owls! nothing but songs of death? [*Striking him.*
There, take thou that, till thou bring better news.
3 MESS. The news I have to tell your majesty,
Is, that by sudden floods and fall of waters,
Buckingham's army is dispers'd and scatter'd;
And he himself wander'd away alone,
No man knows whither.
K. RICH. I cry thee mercy:
There is my purse, to cure that blow of thine.
Hath any well-advised friend proclaim'd
Reward to him that brings the traitor in?
3 MESS. Such proclamation hath been made, my liege.†

Enter a fourth Messenger.

4 MESS. Sir Thomas Lovel and lord marquis Dorset,
'T is said, my liege, in Yorkshire are in arms.
But this good comfort bring I to your highness,—
The Bretagne navy is dispers'd by tempest:
Richmond, in Dorsetshire, sent out a boat
Unto the shore, to ask those on the banks,
If they were his assistants, yea, or no;
Who answer'd him, they came from Buckingham
Upon his party: he, mistrusting them,
Hois'd sail, and made his course again for Bretagne.

(*) First folio, *moe*. (†) First folio, *Lord*.

[a] Sir Christopher Urswick.] Chaplain to Margaret, countess of Richmond, and afterwards grand almoner to Henry the Seventh, by whom he was held in great esteem. He died in 1521, at Hackney, of which place he was rector, where a monument still remains to his memory.

K. RICH. March on, march on, since we are up in arms;
If not to fight with foreign enemies,
Yet to beat down these rebels here at home.

Re-enter CATESBY.

CATE. My liege, the duke of Buckingham is taken,
That is the best news; that the earl of Richmond
Is with a mighty power landed at Milford,
Is colder news, but yet they must be told.
K. RICH. Away towards Salisbury! while we reason here,
A royal battle might be won and lost:—
Some one take order Buckingham be brought
To Salisbury;—the rest march on with me.
[*Flourish. Exeunt.*

SCENE V.—*A Room in* Lord Stanley's *House.*

Enter STANLEY *and Sir* CHRISTOPHER URSWICK.[a]

STAN. Sir Christopher, tell Richmond this from me:—
That, in the sty of this most bloody* boar,
My son George Stanley is frank'd up in hold;
If I revolt, off goes young George's head;
The fear of that withholds† my present aid.
So get thee gone; commend me to thy lord:
Tell him‡ the queen hath heartily consented
He should espouse Elizabeth her daughter.
But, tell me, where is princely Richmond now?
CHRIS. At Pembroke, or at Ha'rford-west, in Wales.
STAN. What men of name resort to him?
CHRIS. Sir Walter Herbert, a renowned soldier;
Sir Gilbert Talbot, sir William Stanley;
Oxford, redoubted Pembroke, sir James Blunt,
And Rice ap Thomas, with a valiant crew;
And many more of noble fame§ and worth:
And towards London do they bend their power,
If by the way they be not fought withal.
STAN. Well, hie thee to thy lord; I kiss his hand:
These letters‖ will resolve him of my mind.
Farewell. [*Exeunt.*

(*) First folio, *the most deadly*. (†) First folio, *holds off*.
(‡) First folio, *Withall say, that*.
(§) First folio, *other of great name*. (‖) First folio, *My Letter*.

ACT V.

SCENE I.—Salisbury. *An open Place.*

Enter the Sheriff, *and the* Guard, *with* BUCKINGHAM, *led to execution.*

BUCK. Will not king Richard let me speak with him?
SHER. No, my good lord; therefore be patient.
BUCK. Hastings, and Edward's children, Rivers, Grey,*
Holy king Henry, and thy fair son Edward,
Vaughan, and all that have miscarried
By underhand corrupted foul injustice,
If that your moody discontented souls
Do through the clouds behold this present hour,
Even for revenge mock my destruction!—
This is All-souls' day, fellows,† is it not?
SHER. It is, my lord.‡
BUCK. Why, then All-souls' day is my body's doomsday.
This is the day which, in king Edward's time,
I wish'd might fall on me, when I was found
False to his children or* his wife's allies:
This is the day wherein I wish'd to fall
By the false faith of him I trusted most;†
This, this All-souls' day to my fearful soul,
Is the determin'd respite of my wrongs.
That high All-seer which I dallied with,
Hath turn'd my feigned prayer on my head,
And given in earnest what I begg'd in jest.
Thus doth he force the swords of wicked men
To turn their own points on‡ their masters' bosom:§
Now‖ Margaret's curse falls heavy on my neck,—
When he, quoth she, *shall split thy heart with sorrow,*
Remember Margaret was a prophetess.—
Come, sirs, convey me to the block of shame,[a]
Wrong hath but wrong, and blame the due of blame. [*Exeunt.*

(*) First folio, *Gray and Rivers*. (†) First folio, *Fellow*. (‡) First folio omits, *my lord*.

[a] *Come, sirs, convey me to the block of shame,*—] The folio reading is,—
"Come *leade* me *Officers*," &c.

(*) First folio, *and*. (†) First folio, *whom most I trusted*. (‡) First folio, *in*. (§) First folio, *bosomes*. (‖) First folio, *Thus*.

SCENE II.—*A Plain near* Tamworth.

Enter, with drum and colours, RICHMOND, OXFORD, *Sir* JAMES BLUNT, *Sir* WALTER HERBERT, *and others, with* Forces, *marching.*

RICHM. Fellows in arms, and my most loving friends,
Bruis'd underneath the yoke of tyranny,
Thus far into the bowels of the land
Have we march'd on without impediment;
And here receive we from our father Stanley
Lines of fair comfort and encouragement.
The wretched, bloody, and usurping boar,
That spoil'd your summer fields and fruitful vines,
Swills your warm blood like wash, and makes his trough
In your embowell'd bosoms,—this foul swine
Lies* now even in the centre of this isle,
Near to the town of Leicester, as we learn:
From Tamworth thither is but one day's march.
In God's name, cheerly on, courageous friends,
To reap the harvest of perpetual peace
By this one bloody trial of sharp war!

OXF. Every man's conscience is a thousand swords,†
To fight against that bloody‡ homicide.

HERB. I doubt not but his friends will turn to us.

BLUNT. He hath no friends but what are friends for fear;
Which in his dearest need will fly from him.

RICHM. All for our vantage. Then, in God's name, march:
True hope is swift, and flies with swallow's wings,
Kings it makes gods, and meaner creatures kings.
[*Exeunt.*

SCENE III.—Bosworth Field.

Enter KING RICHARD, *and* Forces; *the* DUKE *of* NORFOLK, EARL *of* SURREY, *and others.*

K. RICH. Here pitch our tents,§ even here in Bosworth field.—
My lord of Surrey, why look you so sad?

SUR. My heart is ten times lighter than my looks.

K. RICH. My lord of Norfolk,—

(*) First folio, *Is.* (†) First folio, *men.*
(‡) First folio, *this guilty.* (§) First folio, *Tent.*

a *Up with* my *tent* there!—Valiant *gentlemen,*—] The corresponding line in the folio is:—

"Up with *the* Tent: *Come Noble* Gentlemen."

b And you, Sir Walter Herbert, &c.] This and the preceding line are found only in the folio.

NOR. Here, most gracious liege.

K. RICH. Norfolk, we must have knocks, ha! must we not?

NOR. We must both give and take, my loving lord.

K. RICH. Up with my tent! here will I lie to-night;
[Soldiers *begin to set up the* KING'S *tent.*
But where to-morrow?—Well, all 's one for that.—
Who hath descried the number of our foe?*

NOR. Six or seven thousand is their utmost power.

K. RICH. Why, our battalia trebles that account:
Besides, the king's name is a tower of strength,
Which they upon the adverse faction want.—
Up with my tent there!—Valiant gentlemen,[a]
Let us survey the vantage of the field;†—
Call for some men of sound direction:—
Let's want‡ no discipline, make no delay;
For, lords, to-morrow is a busy day. [*Exeunt.*

Enter, on the other side of the field, RICHMOND, *Sir* WILLIAM BRANDON, OXFORD, *Sir* JAMES BLUNT, *and other* Officers. *Some of the* Soldiers *pitch* RICHMOND'S *tent.*

RICHM. The weary sun hath made a golden set,
And, by the bright track§ of his fiery car,
Gives token of a goodly day to-morrow.—
Sir William Brandon, you shall bear my standard.—
[My lord of Oxford,—you, sir William Brandon,—
And you, sir Walter Herbert, stay with me:][b]
The earl of Pembroke keep ‖ his regiment;
Good captain Blunt, bear my good night to him,
And by the second hour in the morning
Desire the earl to see me in my tent:
Yet one thing more, good Blunt, before thou goest;[c]—
Where is lord Stanley quarter'd, do you know?

BLUNT. Unless I have mista'en his colours much,
(Which well I am assur'd I have not done,)
His regiment lies half a mile at least
South from the mighty power of the king.

RICHM. If without peril it be possible,
Sweet Blunt, make some good means to speak with him,
And give him from me this most needful scroll.¶

BLUNT. Upon my life, my lord, I'll undertake it;

(*) First folio, *the Traitors.* (†) First folio, *ground.*
(‡) First folio, *lacke.* (§) First folio, *Tract.*
(‖) First folio, *keepes.* (¶) First folio, *Note.*

c *Good* Blunt, before thou goest;—] The folio reads,—"Good *Captaine do for me.*"

[And so, God give you quiet rest to-night!][a]
RICHM. Good night, good captain Blunt.
Give me some ink and paper in my tent;[b]
I'll draw the form and model of our battle,
Limit each leader to his several charge,
And part in just proportion our small power.
Come, gentlemen,
Let us consult upon to-morrow's business;
In to my tent, the air* is raw and cold.
[*They withdraw into the tent.*

Enter, to his tent, KING RICHARD, NORFOLK, RATCLIFF, *and* CATESBY.

RICH. What is 't o'clock?
CATE. It's supper time, my lord;
It's six† o'clock.
K. RICH. I will not sup to-night.—
Give me some ink and paper.—
What, is my beaver easier than it was?
And all my armour laid into my tent?
CATE. It is, my liege; and all things are in readiness.
K. RICH. Good Norfolk, hie thee to thy charge;
Use careful watch, choose trusty sentinels.
NOR. I go, my lord.
K. RICH. Stir with the lark to-morrow, gentle Norfolk.
NOR. I warrant you, my lord. [*Exit.*
K. RICH. Ratcliff,—
RAT. My lord?
K. RICH. Send out a pursuivant-at-arms
To Stanley's regiment; bid him bring his power
Before sun-rising, lest his son George fall
Into the blind cave of eternal night.—
Fill me a bowl of wine.—Give me a watch:—[c]
[*To* CATESBY.
Saddle white Surrey for the field to-morrow.—
Look that my staves be sound, and not too heavy.
Ratcliff,—
RAT. My lord?
K. RICH. Saw'st thou‡ the melancholy lord Northumberland?
RAT. Thomas the earl of Surrey, and himself,
Much about cock-shut time, from troop to troop,
Went through the army, cheering up the soldiers.
K. RICH. So; I am satisfied. Give me a bowl of wine:
I have not that alacrity of spirit,
Nor cheer of mind, that I was wont to have.—
Set it down.—Is ink and paper ready?
RAT. It is, my lord.

K. RICH. Bid my guard watch; leave me.
Ratcliff, about the mid of night, come to my tent
And help to arm me.—Leave me, I say.
[KING RICHARD *retires into his tent.*
Exeunt RATCLIFF *and* CATESBY.

RICHMOND'*s tent opens, and discovers him, and his* Officers, *&c.*

Enter STANLEY.

STAN. Fortune and victory sit on thy helm!
RICHM. All comfort that the dark night can afford,
Be to thy person, noble father-in-law!
Tell me, how fares our loving* mother?
STAN. I, by attorney, bless thee from thy mother,
Who prays continually for Richmond's good:
So much for that.—The silent hours steal on,
And flaky darkness breaks within the east.
In brief, for so the season bids us be,
Prepare thy battle early in the morning;
And put thy fortune to the arbitrement
Of bloody strokes and mortal-staring war,[d]
I, as I may, (that which I would, I cannot,)
With best advantage will deceive the time,
And aid thee in this doubtful shock of arms:
But on thy side I may not be too forward,
Lest, being seen, thy brother, tender George,
Be executed in his father's sight.(1)
Farewell: the leisure and the fearful time
Cuts off the ceremonious vows of love,
And ample interchange of sweet discourse,
Which so long sunder'd friends should dwell upon;
God give us leisure for these rites of love!
Once more, adieu:—be valiant, and speed well!
RICHM. Good lords, conduct him to his regiment:
I'll strive, with troubled thoughts,† to take a nap;
Lest leaden slumber peise me down to-morrow,
When I should mount with wings of victory:
Once more, good night, kind lords and gentlemen.—
[*Exeunt* Officers, *&c. with* STANLEY.
O Thou, whose captain I account myself,
Look on my forces with a gracious eye!
Put in their hands thy bruising irons of wrath,
That they may crush down with a heavy fall
The usurping helmets of our adversaries!
Make us thy ministers of chastisement,
That we may praise thee in thy victory!
To thee I do commend my watchful soul,

(*) First folio, *Dew*. (†) First folio, *nine*. (‡) First folio omits, *thou*.

(*) First folio, *Noble*. (†) First folio, *noise*.

a And so, God give you quiet rest to-night!] Omitted in the quartos.
b Give me some ink and paper in my tent;] In the folio, this and the three following lines are introduced into Richmond's previous speech after the words,—"Sir William Brandon, you shall bear my standard."
c A watch:—] Probably, a *watch-light*, or candle marked in sections to denote the lapse of time.
d *And* mortal-staring *war*,—] Query, *mortal-stabbing*?

Ere I let fall the windows of mine eyes;
Sleeping, and waking, O, defend me still!
[*Sleeps.*

The Ghost *of* Prince Edward, *son to* Henry *the* Sixth, *rises between the two tents.*

Ghost. [*To* K. Rich.] Let me sit heavy on thy soul to-morrow!
Think, how thou stabb'dst me in my prime of youth
At Tewksbury; despair, therefore, and die!—
[*To* Richmond.] Be cheerful, Richmond, for the wronged souls
Of butcher'd princes fight in thy behalf:
King Henry's issue, Richmond, comforts thee.

The Ghost *of* King Henry *the* Sixth *rises.*

Ghost. [*To* K. Rich.] When I was mortal, my anointed body
By thee was punched full of deadly* holes:

(*) First folio omits, *deadly*.

Think on the Tower and me; despair, and die!
Harry the sixth bids thee despair and die!—
[*To* RICHMOND.] Virtuous and holy, be thou conqueror!
Harry, that prophesied thou shouldst be king,
Doth comfort thee in thy* sleep; live, and flourish!

The Ghost *of* CLARENCE *rises.*

GHOST. [*To* K. RICH.] Let me sit heavy on† thy soul to-morrow!
I, that was wash'd to death with fulsome wine;
Poor Clarence, by thy guile betray'd to death!
To-morrow in the battle think on me,
And fall thy edgeless sword; despair, and die!—
[*To* RICHMOND.] Thou offspring of the house of Lancaster,
The wronged heirs of York do pray for thee;
Good angels guard thy battle! live and flourish!

The Ghosts *of* RIVERS, GREY, *and* VAUGHAN *rise.*

RIV. [*To* K. RICH.] Let me sit heavy on† thy soul to-morrow,
Rivers, that died at Pomfret! despair, and die!
GREY. [*To* K. RICH.] Think upon Grey, and let thy soul despair!
VAUGH. [*To* K. RICH.] Think upon Vaughan, and, with guilty fear,
Let fall thy lance![a] despair, and die!—
ALL. [*To* RICHMOND.] Awake! and think our wrongs in Richard's bosom
Will conquer him!—awake, and win the day!

The Ghost *of* HASTINGS *rises.*

GHOST. [*To* K. RICH.] Bloody and guilty, guiltily awake;
And in a bloody battle end thy days!
Think on lord Hastings; despair, and die!—
[*To* RICHMOND.] Quiet untroubled soul, awake, awake!
Arm, fight, and conquer, for fair England's sake!

The Ghosts *of the two young* Princes *rise.*

GHOSTS. [*To* K. RICH.] Dream on thy cousins smother'd in the Tower;
Let us be lead‡ within thy bosom, Richard,
And weigh thee down to ruin, shame, and death!
Thy nephews' souls bid§ thee despair and die!—
[*To* RICHMOND.] Sleep, Richmond, sleep in peace, and wake in joy;
Good angels guard thee from the boar's annoy!
Live, and beget a happy race of kings!
Edward's unhappy sons do bid thee flourish!

The Ghost *of* QUEEN ANNE *rises.*

GHOST. [*To* K. RICH.] Richard, thy wife, that wretched Anne thy wife,
That never slept a quiet hour with thee,(2)
Now fills thy sleep with perturbations:
To-morrow in the battle think on me,
And fall thy edgeless sword; despair, and die!—
[*To* RICHMOND.] Thou, quiet soul, sleep thou a quiet sleep;
Dream of success and happy victory;
Thy adversary's wife doth pray for thee!

The Ghost *of* BUCKINGHAM *rises.*

GHOST. [*To* K. RICH.] The first was I that help'd thee to the crown;
The last was I that felt thy tyranny:
O, in the battle think on Buckingham,
And die in terror of thy guiltiness!
Dream on, dream on, of bloody deeds and death;
Fainting, despair; despairing, yield thy breath!—
[*To* RICHMOND.] I died for hope ere I could lend thee aid:
But cheer thy heart, and be thou not dismay'd:
God and good angels fight on Richmond's side;
And Richard fall in height of all his pride!

[*The* Ghosts *vanish.* KING RICHARD *starts out of his dream.*

K. RICH. Give me another horse!—bind up my wounds!—
Have mercy, Jesu!—Soft! I did but dream.—
O coward conscience, how dost thou afflict me!—
The lights burn blue.—It is now* dead midnight.
Cold fearful drops stand on my trembling flesh.
What, do I fear myself? there's none else by:
Richard loves Richard; that is, I am I.
Is there a murderer here? No;—yes; I am:
Then fly. What, from myself? great reason: why?
Lest I revenge. What, myself, upon myself?
Alack, I love myself. Wherefore? for any good
That I myself have done unto myself?
O, no! alas, I rather hate myself,
For hateful deeds committed by myself!
I am a villain: yet I lie, I am not.
Fool, of thyself speak well:—fool, do not flatter.
My conscience hath a thousand several tongues,
And every tongue brings in a several tale,

(*) First folio omits, *thy*. (†) First folio, *in*.
(‡) First folio, *laid*. (§) First folio, *soule bids*.

(*) First folio, *not*.

a Let fall thy lance!] Mr. Collier's annotator reads, we believe rightly,—
"Let fall thy *pointless* lance!" &c.

And every tale condemns me for a villain.
Perjury, perjury,* in the high'st degree,
Murder, stern murder, in the dir'st degree;
All several sins, all us'd in each degree,
Throng† to the bar, crying all,—Guilty! guilty!
I shall despair:—there is no creature loves me;
And if I die, no soul shall pity me:—
Nay, wherefore should they? since that I myself
Find in myself no pity to myself.
Methought the souls of all that I had murdered
Came to my tent; and every one did threat
To-morrow's vengeance on the head of Richard.

Enter RATCLIFF.

RAT. My lord,—
K. RICH. Who's there?
RAT. My lord; 'tis I.[a] The early village cock
Hath twice done salutation to the morn;
Your friends are up, and buckle on their armour.
K. RICH. O, Ratcliff, I have dream'd a fearful dream!—
What thinkest thou? will our friends prove all true?
RAT. No doubt, my lord.[b]

(*) First folio, *perjury*, once only.
(†) First folio inserts, *all*.

a My lord; 'tis I.] The old texts read,—"*Ratcliffe*, my Lord, 'tis I." Capell expelled the redundant word; but it has been reinserted by subsequent editors.

b No doubt, my lord.] Richard's speech, and Ratcliff's answer, are omitted in the folio.

K. RICH. O Ratcliff, I fear, I fear,—
RAT. Nay, good my lord, be not afraid of shadows.
K. RICH. By the apostle Paul, shadows to-night
Have struck more terror to the soul of Richard,
Than can the substance of ten thousand soldiers,
Armed in proof, and led by shallow Richmond!
It is not yet near day. Come, go with me;
Under our tents I'll play the eaves-dropper,*
To hear if any mean to shrink from me.
[*Exeunt* KING RICHARD *and* RATCLIFF.

Enter OXFORD *and others.*

LORDS. Good morrow, Richmond!
RICHM. Cry mercy, lords, and watchful gentlemen,
That you have ta'en a tardy sluggard here.
LORDS. How have you slept, my lord?
RICHM. The sweetest sleep, and fairest-boding dreams,
That ever enter'd in a drowsy head,
Have I since your departure, had, my lords.
Methought, their souls, whose bodies Richard murder'd,
Came to my tent, and cried on victory.[a]
I promise you, my heart is very jocund
In the remembrance of so fair a dream.
How far into the morning is it, lords?
LORDS. Upon the stroke of four.
RICHM. Why, then 'tis time to arm, and give direction.— [*Advances to the* Troops.
More than I have said, loving countrymen,
The leisure and enforcement of the time
Forbids to dwell upon: yet remember this,—
God and our good cause fight upon our side;
The prayers of holy saints and wronged souls,
Like high-rear'd bulwarks, stand before our faces;
Richard except, those whom we fight against,
Had rather have us win than him they follow.
For what is he they follow? truly, gentlemen,
A bloody tyrant and a homicide;
One rais'd in blood, and one in blood establish'd;
One that made means to come by what he hath,
And slaughter'd those that were the means to help him;
A base foul stone, made precious by the foil†
Of England's chair, where he is falsely set;
One that hath ever been God's enemy:
Then, if you fight against God's enemy,
God will, in justice, ward you as his soldiers;
If you do sweat‡ to put a tyrant down,
You sleep in peace, the tyrant being slain;
If you do fight against your country's foes,
Your country's fat shall pay your pains the hire;
If you do fight in safeguard of your wives,
Your wives shall welcome home the conquerors;
If you do free your children from the sword,
Your children's children quit it in your age.
Then, in the name of God, and all these rights,
Advance your standards, draw your willing swords:
For me, the ransom of my bold attempt
Shall be this cold corpse on the earth's cold face;
But if I thrive, the gain of my attempt
The least of you shall share his part thereof.
Sound, drums and trumpets, bold* and cheerfully;
God, and Saint George! (3) Richmond, and victory!
[*Exeunt.*

Re-enter KING RICHARD, RATCLIFF, Attendants, *and* Forces.

K. RICH. What said Northumberland as touching Richmond?
RAT. That he was never trained up in arms.
K. RICH. He said the truth; and what said Surrey then?
RAT. He smil'd and said, *The better for our purpose.*
K. RICH. He was i' the right; and so, indeed, it is. [*Clock strikes.*
Tell the clock there.—Give me a calendar.—
Who saw the sun to-day?
RAT. Not I, my lord.
K. RICH. Then he disdains to shine; for, by the book,
He should have brav'd the east an hour ago:
A black day will it be to somebody.—
Ratcliff,—
RAT. My lord?
K. RICH. The sun will not be seen to-day;
The sky doth frown and lour upon our army.
I would these dewy tears were from the ground.
Not shine to-day! Why, what is that to me,
More than to Richmond? for the self-same heaven
That frowns on me, looks sadly upon him.

Enter NORFOLK.

NOR. Arm, arm, my lord! the foe vaunts in the field.
K. RICH. Come, bustle, bustle;—caparison my horse;—
Call up lord Stanley, bid him bring his power:—
I will lead forth my soldiers to the plain,
And thus my battle shall be ordered.—
My forward shall be drawn out all† in length,
Consisting equally of horse and foot;

(*) First folio, *Ease-dropper.* (†) First folio, *soyle.* (‡) First folio, *sweare.*

(*) Old text, *boldly.* (†) First folio omits, *out all.*

[a] *And* cried on victory.] This has been needlessly changed to "cried *out* victory," or printed, "—cried—On! victory!" To *cry on* anything was a familiar expression formerly; thus, in "Hamlet," Act V. Sc. 2, "This quarry *cries on* havoc;" and in "Othello," Act V. Sc. 1, "—whose noise is this that *cries on* murder?"

Our archers shall be placed in the midst:
John duke of Norfolk, Thomas earl of Surrey,
Shall have the leading of the foot and horse.
They thus directed, we will follow
In the main battle; whose puissance on either side
Shall be well winged with our chiefest horse.
This, and Saint George to boot!—What think'st thou, Norfolk?

NOR. A good direction, warlike sovereign.—
This found I on my tent this morning.
[*Giving a scroll.*

K. RICH. [Reads.]
Jockey of Norfolk, be not too bold,*
For Dickon thy master is bought and sold.
A thing devised by the enemy.—
Go, gentlemen, every man unto† his charge:
Let not our babbling dreams affright our souls;
Conscience is but a word that cowards use,[a]
Devis'd at first to keep the strong in awe;
Our strong arms be our conscience, swords our law.
March on, join bravely, let us to't pell-mell;
If not to heaven, then hand in hand to hell.—
What shall I say more than I have inferr'd?
Remember whom you are to cope withal;—
A sort of vagabonds, rascals, and run-aways,
A scum of Bretagnes, and base lackey peasants,
Whom their o'er-cloyed country vomits forth
To desperate ventures‡ and assur'd destruction.
You sleeping safe, they bring to you§ unrest;
You having lands, and bless'd with beauteous wives,
They would restrain the one, distain the other.
And who doth lead them but a paltry fellow,
Long kept in Bretagne at our mother's cost?[b]
A milk-sop, one that never in his life
Felt so much cold as over shoes in snow?
Let's whip these stragglers o'er the seas again;
Lash hence these over-weening rags of France,
These famish'd beggars, weary of their lives;
Who, but for dreaming on this fond exploit,
For want of means, poor rats, had hang'd themselves:
If we be conquer'd, let men conquer us,
And not these bastard Bretagnes, whom our fathers
Have in their own land beaten, bobb'd, and thump'd,
And, on record, left them the heirs of shame.
Shall these enjoy our lands? lie with our wives?
Ravish our daughters?—Hark! I hear their drum.
[*Drum afar off.*
Fight, ‖ gentlemen of England!—fight, bold ¶ yeomen! (4)
Draw, archers, draw your arrows to the head!—
Spur your proud horses hard, and ride in blood;—
Amaze the welkin with your broken staves!—

(*) First folio, *so.* (†) First folio, *to.* (‡) Old text, *Adventures.* (§) First folio, *you to.* (‖) First folio, *Right.* (¶) Old text, *boldly.*

a Conscience is but a word that cowards use,—] The folio reads, "*For* conscience is a word," &c.

Enter a Messenger.

What says lord Stanley? will he bring his power?

MESS. My lord, he doth deny to come.

K. RICH. Off with his son George's head!

NOR. My lord, the enemy is pass'd the marsh;
After the battle let George Stanley die.

K. RICH. A thousand hearts are great within my bosom:
Advance our standards! set upon our foes!
Our ancient word of courage, fair Saint George,
Inspire us with the spleen of fiery dragons!
Upon them! Victory sits on our helms.* [*Exeunt.*

SCENE IV.—*Another part of the Field.*

Alarum. Excursions. Enter NORFOLK, *and* Forces; *to him* CATESBY.

CATE. Rescue! my lord of Norfolk, rescue! rescue!
The king enacts more wonders than a man,
Daring an opposite to every danger;
His horse is slain, and all on foot he fights,
Seeking for Richmond in the throat of death:
Rescue, fair lord, or else the day is lost!

Alarum. Enter KING RICHARD.

K. RICH. A horse! a horse! my kingdom for a horse!

CATE. Withdraw, my lord, I'll help you to a horse.

K. RICH. Slave, I have set my life upon a cast,
And I will stand the hazard of the die!
I think there be six Richmonds in the field;
Five have I slain to-day instead of him:—
A horse! a horse! my kingdom for a horse!
[*Exeunt.*

SCENE V.—*Another part of the Field.*

Alarums. Enter, from opposite sides, KING RICHARD *and* RICHMOND; *they fight, and exeunt fighting. Retreat and flourish. Then re-enter* RICHMOND, *with* STANLEY *bearing the crown, and divers other* Lords, *and* Forces.

RICHM. God and your arms be prais'd, victorious friends;
The day is ours, the bloody dog is dead! (4)

STAN. Courageous Richmond, well hast thou acquit thee!
Lo here this† long-usurped royalty,‡

(*) First folio, *helpes.* (†) First folio, *these.* (‡) Old text, *Royalties.*

b *At our* mother's *cost?*] It should be, "our *brother's* cost." Shakespeare fell into the error by following a particular edition of Holinshed, wherein *brother* is misprinted *moother.*

From the dead temples of this bloody wretch
Have I pluck'd off, to grace thy brows withal;
Wear it, enjoy it,* and make much of it.

RICHM. Great God of heaven, say *Amen* to all!—
But, tell me is young George Stanley living?

STAN. He is, my lord, and safe in Leicester town,
Whither, if it please you, we may now withdraw us.[a]

RICHM. What men of name are slain on either side?

STAN. John duke of Norfolk, Walter lord Ferrers,
Sir Robert Brakenbury, and sir William Brandon.

RICHM. Inter their bodies as becomes† their births.
Proclaim a pardon to the soldiers fled,
That in submission will return to us;
And then, as we have ta'en the sacrament,
We will unite the white rose and the red:—
Smile heaven upon this fair conjunction,
That long hath‡ frown'd upon their enmity!—
What traitor hears me, and says not,—*Amen?*
England hath long been mad, and scarr'd herself;
The brother blindly shed the brother's blood,
The father rashly slaughter'd his own son,
The son, compell'd, been butcher to the sire;
All this divided York and Lancaster,
Divided, in their dire division.—
O, now, let Richmond and Elizabeth,
The true succeeders of each royal house,
By God's fair ordinance conjoin together!
And let their* heirs (God, if thy will be so,)
Enrich the time to come with smooth-fac'd peace,
With smiling plenty, and fair prosperous days!
Abate the edge of traitors, gracious Lord,
That would reduce these bloody days again,
And make poor England weep in streams of blood!
Let them not live to taste this land's increase,
That would with treason wound this fair land's peace!
Now civil wounds are stopp'd, peace lives agen;
That she may long live here, God say *Amen!*

[*Exeunt.*

(*) First folio omits, *enjoy it.* (†) Old text, *become.* (‡) First folio, *have.*

(*) First folio, *thy.*

[a] *Whither, if it please you, we may now withdraw us.*] The folio reads,—
"Whither (if *you please*) we may withdraw us."

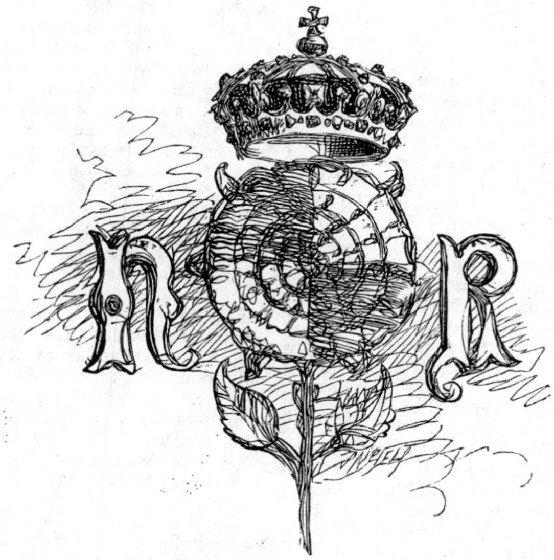

ILLUSTRATIVE COMMENTS.

ACT I.

(1) SCENE I.—*Enter* GLOUCESTER.] In the broad outlines of Richard's person and character, Shakespeare has closely adhered to the description of the usurper, by Sir Thomas More, as he found it in the Chronicles of Hall and Holinshed.

"Richarde the third sonne [of Richard Plantagenet duke of York], of whom we now entreate, was in witte and courage egall with either of them, in bodye and prowesse farre under them both [his brothers Edward and Clarence], litle of stature, ill fetured of limmes, croke backed, his left shoulder much higher then his right, hard favoured of visage, and such as is in states called warlye, in other menne otherwise;* he was malicious, wrathfull, envious, and from afore his birth ever frowarde. It is for trouth reported, that the Duches his mother had so muche a doe in her travaile, that she coulde not bee delivered of hym uncutte, and that hee came into the worlde with the feete forwarde, as menne bee borne outwarde, and (as the fame runneth) also not untothed: whether menne of hatred reporte above the trouthe, or elles that nature chaunged her course in hys beginnynge, whiche in the course of his lyfe many thynges unnaturallye committed. None evill captaine was hee in the warre, as to whiche, his disposicion was more metely then for peace. Sundrye victories hadde he, and sometime overthrowes, but never in defaulte as for his owne persone, either of hardinesse or polytike order. Free was he called of dispence, and sommewhat above his power liberall, with large giftes he get hym unstedfaste frendeshippe, for whiche hee was faine to pil and spoyle in other places, and get hym stedfast hatred. He was close and secrete, a deepe dissimuler, lowlye of counteynaunce, arrogant of heart, outwardely coumpinable where he inwardely hated, not letting to kisse whom he thoughte to kyll, dispitious and cruell, not for evill will alway, but ofter for ambicion and either for the suretie or encrease of his estate. Frende and fooe was muche what indifferent, where his advauntage grewe, he spared no mannes deathe whose life withstode his purpose. He slewe with his owne handes king Henry the sixt, being prisoner in the Tower as men constantly saye, and that without commaundemente or knowledge of the kyng, which woulde undoubtedly yf he had entended that thing, have appointed that bocherly office to some other, then his owne borne brother. Some wise menne also wene, that his drifte covertly convayde lacked not in helpyng furth his brother of Clarence to his death, whiche he resisted openly, howbeit somewhat (as menne demed) more faintly then he that wer hartely minded to his welth. And they that thus deme, think that he long time in king Edwardes life, fore-thought to be kyng in case that the king his brother (whose life he looked that evil dyete shoulde shorten) shoulde happen to decease (as in dede he did) while his chyldren were yonge. And thei deme that for thys intente he was gladde of his brothers death the Duke of Clarence, whose life must nedes have hindered him so entendynge, whither the same Duke of Clarence hadde kepte him true to his Nephew the yonge king or enterprised to be kyng himselfe. But of al this pointe is there no certaintie and whoso divineth uppon coniectures, may as wel shote to farre as to short."—SIR T. MORE, *Life of kyng Rycharde the thirde.* Lond. fo. 1557, fo. 37.

* "Such as in estates is called a warlyke visage, and emonge common persones a crabbed face."—HALL.

(2) SCENE II.—

Dead Henry's wounds
Open their congeal'd mouths and bleed afresh.]

An allusion to the once prevalent superstition that the body of a murdered person always bled at the touch or on the approach of the murderer:—"For as in a secret murther, if the deade carcase be at any time thereafter handled by the murtherer, it will gush out of bloud, as if the blud wer crying to the heaven for revenge of the murtherer."—K. JAMES, *Demonologie,* 4to. 1597, p. 80.

At Hertford assizes, 4 Car. I. the following was taken by Sir John Maynard, serjeant-at-law, from the deposition of the minister of the parish where a murder was committed:—"That the body being taken out of the grave thirty days after the party's death, and lying on the grass, and the four defendants (suspected of murdering her) being required, each of them touched the dead body, whereupon the brow of the dead, which before was of a livid and carrion colour, began to have a dew or gentle sweat arise on it, which increased by degrees, till the sweat ran down in drops on the face, the brow turned to a lively and fresh colour, and the deceased opened one of her eyes and shut it again three several times; she likewise thrust out the ring or marriage finger three times and pulled it in again, and the finger dropt blood on the grass."—*See the Gentleman's Magazine, Sept.* 1731.

(3) SCENE II.—*Crosby-place.*] So called because built by Sir John Crosby, grocer and woolman, upon ground leased to him in 1466, for ninety-nine years by Alice Ashfield, prioress of St. Helen's. In the year 1470, being then an alderman, he was elected sheriff, and in that character went out to meet Edward IV. on that monarch's coming to London, 21st May, 1471. On this occasion he received the honour of knighthood. His effigy in the neighbouring church of St. Helen bears the Yorkish collar of roses and suns; and his attachment to that house explains why Gloucester held his "divided councils" in Crosby-place. "For by little and little," says Holinshed, "all folke with drewe from the Tower, and drew unto Crosbies in Bishopsgate Street, where the Protector kept his household."

The mansion was spacious and very beautiful. Its noble hall, still existing, is fifty feet long, twenty-seven broad, and forty feet high, and its roof is considered to be one of the finest specimens of timber-work known. Among the distinguished possessors of Crosby-place, was Sir Thomas More, who here wrote his "Life of King Richard the Third."

(4) SCENE IV.—*I'll chop thee in the malmsey-butt in the next room.*] Though the ancient chroniclers concur in

alleging Clarence to have been drowned in a butt of malmsey wine, the story is now believed to be apocryphal. In the "Mirror for Magistrates," he is made to relate his murder thus:—

"And, covertly, within the tower they calde
A guest to geve such verdite as they should:
Who, what with feare and what with favour thralde,
Durst not pronounce but as my brethren would:
And though my false accusers never could
Prove ought they sayd, I guiltlesse was condemned:
Such verdites passe where iustice is contemned.

This feat atchived, yet could they not for shame
Cause mee bee kild by any common way,
But like a wolfe the tyrant Richard came,
(My brother nay my butcher I may say)
Unto the tower when all men were away,
Save such as were provided for the feate:
Who in this wise did strangely mee entreate.

His purpose was with a prepared string
To strangle mee: but I bestird mee so,
That by no force they could mee therto bring,
Which caused him that purpose to forgo:
Howbeit they bound mee, whether I would or no,
And in a but of malmsey standing by,
Newe christned mee, because I should not cry."

(5) SCENE IV.—

How fain, like Pilate, would I wash my hands
Of this most grievous guilty murder done!]

The authority upon which Shakespeare imputed to Richard the murder of his brother Clarence, was not merely the popular tradition of his own day, but the statements of the old chroniclers upon whom he relied for historic information. Walpole conjectured, from a passage in the "Chronicle of England," that the real cause of Gloucester's animosity to Clarence was the latter's unwillingness to share with him that moiety of the estate of the great Earl of Warwick, to which Gloucester became entitled on his marriage with the younger sister of the Duchess of Clarence. Mr. Sharon Turner, however, observes that there is a Patent Roll which records "great grievances" at this time existing between Clarence and the Queen's brother, Lord Rivers. The Act of his Attainder charges him with purposing treason against the Queen and her son and great part of the nobles of the land; and his confiscated estates were chiefly given to Lord Rivers, and the stewardship and marriage of his heir to the Queen's son, the Marquis of Dorset. The parties, therefore, who most profited by Clarence's death, were really the friends of the Queen and the political opponents of the Duke of Gloucester.

"In the .xvii. yere of kyng Edward, there fel a sparcle of privy malice, betwene the kyng and his brother, the duke of Clarence. Whether it rose of old grudges before tyme passed, or were it newly kyndled and set a fyre by the Quene or her bloud, which were ever mistrustyng and prively barkynge at the kynges lignage, or were he desirous to reigne after hys brother: to men that have thereof made large inquisicion, of suche as were of no small authoritie in those dayes, the certayntie therof was hyd, and coulde not truely be disclosed, but by coniectures, which as often deceyve the imaginacions of fantastical folke, as declare treuth to them in their conclusion. The fame was that the kyng or the Quene, or bothe, sore troubled with a folish Prophesye, and by reason therof, began to stomacke and grevously to grudge agaynst the duke. The effect of which was, after king Edward should reigne, one whose first letter of hys name shoulde be a G., and because the devel is wont with such wytchcraftes to wrappe and illaqueat the myndes of men, which delyte in such develyshe fantasyes, they sayd afterward that that Prophesie lost not hys effect, when after kyng Edward, Glocester usurped hys kyngdome.

Other allege this to be the cause of his death: That of late, the old rancor betwene them beyng newly revived (The which betwene no creatures can be more vehement then betwene bretherne, especially when it is fermely radicate), the duke beyng destitute of a wyfe, by the meanes of lady Margaret duches of Burgoyn, hys syster, procured to have the lady Marye, daughter and heyre to duke Charles her husbande, to bee geven to hym in matrimony: which mariage kynge Edward (envyenge the felicitie of hys brother) bothe agaynesayed and disturbed. Thys privy displeasure was openly appeased, but not inwardly forgotten, nor outwardly forgeven, for that, not withstandyng a servaunt of the Dukes was sodainly accused (I can not say of treuth, or untruely suspected by the Dukes enemyes) of poysonyng, sorcery, or inchauntment, and thereof condempned, and put to taste the paynes of death. The duke, whiche myght not suffer the wrongfull condemnacion of hys man (as he in his conscience adiudged) nor yet forbere, nor paciently suffer the unjust handelyng of hys trusty servaunt, dayly dyd oppugne, and wyth yll woordes murmur at the doyng thereof. The king much greved and troubled with hys brothers dayly querimonye, and continuall exclamacion, caused hym to be apprehended, and cast into the Towre, where he beynge taken, adjudged for a Traytor, was prively drouned in a But of Malvesey.

But sure it is, that although kyng Edward were consentyng to his death and destruccion, yet he muche did bothe lamente hys infortunate chaunce, and repent hys sodayne execucion. In asmuche, that when any person sued to hym for Pardon or remission, of any malefactor condempned to the punyshment of death, he woulde accustomably saye, and openly speke, O infortunate brother for whose lyfe not one creatoure woulde make intercession, openly spekyng, and apparantly meanynge, that by the meanes of some of the nobilitie, he was circumvented, and brought to his confusion."—HALL.

ACT II.

(1) SCENE I.—*I thank my God for my humility.*] Milton, in his "Iconoclastes," has this observation:—

"The deepest policy of a Tyrant hath bin ever to counterfet Religious. And *Aristotle* in his Politics, hath mentiond that special craft among twelve other tyrannical *Sophisms*. Neither want wee examples. * * * From Stories of this nature both Ancient and Modern which abound, the Poets also, and som English, have bin in this point so mindfull of *Decorum*, as to put never more pious words in the mouth of any person, then of a Tyrant. I shall not instance an abstruse Author, wherein the King might be less conversant, but one whom wee well know was the Closet Companion of these his solitudes, *William Shakespeare*; who introduces the Person of Richard the third speaking in as high a strain of pietie and mortification, as is utterd in any passage of this Book; and sometimes to the same sense and purpose with some words in this place, *I intended*, saith he, *not onely to oblige my Freinds, but mine Enemies.* The like saith *Richard*, *Act.* 2. *Scen.* 1.

I doe not know that Englishman alive,
With whom my soule is any jott at odds,
More then the Infant that is borne to-night;
I thank my God for my humilitie.

Other stuff of this sort may be read throughout the whole Tragedie, wherein the Poet us'd not much licence in departing from the truth of History, which delivers him a deep dissembler, not of his affections only, but of Religion. ΕΙΚΟΝΟΚΛΑΣΤΗΣ. *The Author I. M.*, Lond. 4to. 1649, p. 11.

(2) SCENE IV.—*Come, I'll conduct you to the sanctuary.*] "These tidynges came hastely to the quene before mydnighte, by a very sore reporte that the kynge her sonne was taken and that her brother and her other sonne and other her frendes were arested and sent, no man wyste whether. With this heavy tidynges the quene bewayled her chyldes ruyne, her frendes mischaunce, and her owne infortune, curssyng the tyme that ever she was persuaded to leave the gatherynge of people to brynge up the kynge with a great powre, but that was passed, and therfore now she toke her younger sonne the duke of Yorke and her doughters, and went out of the palays of Westminster into the sanctuary, and there lodged in the abbotes place, and she and all her chyldren and compaignie were regestred for sanctuarye-persons. The same night there came to doctor Rotheram Archebyshop of Yorke and lorde Chauncelour, a messenger from the lorde Chambrelayne to Yorke place besyde Westminster: the messenger was broughte to the bisshoppes bedsyde and declared to him that the dukes were gone backe with the young kyng to Northampton, and declared further, that the lorde Hastynges his maister sent hym worde that he shoulde feare nothyng, for all should be well. (Wel quod the Archebishop) be it as wel as it wyl, it wyll never be so wel as we have sene it, and then the messenger departed. Wherupon the bishop called up all his servauntes and toke with hym the great seale and came before day to the quene, about whom he found much hevynesse, rumble, haste, busynesse, conveighaunce, and cariage of her stuffe into sanctuarye, every man was busy to carye, beare and conveigh stuffe, chestes and fardelles, no man was unoccupied, and some caried more then they were commaunded to another place.

The quene sat alone belowe on the rushes all desolate and dismayde, whom the Archebishoppe comforted in the best maner that he coulde, shewyng her that the matter was nothyng so sore as she tooke it for, and that he was putte in good hope and out of feare by the message sent to hym from the lord Hastynges. 'A wo worth hym' quod the quene, 'for it is he that goeth about to destroy me and my blodde.' 'Madame,' quod he, 'be of good comforte and I assure you, yf they croune any other kynge then your sonne whom they now have, we shal on the morow croune his brother whom you have here with you. And here is the greate seale, which in likewyse as your noble husband delivered it to me, so I deliver it to you to the use of your sonne,' and therwith delivered her the greate seale and departed home in the dawning of the day. And when he opened his wyndowes and loked on the Temys, he might see the river full of boates, of the duke of Gloucester his servauntes watchyng, that no person should go to sanctuary, nor none should passe unserched." —HALL.

ACT III.

(1) SCENE I.—*Welcome, sweet prince, to London, to your chamber.*] London was anciently called *Camera Regis;*—a name of which Buckingham took advantage in his speech to the citizens upon the death of Hastings:—"The prince by this noble citye as his *special chamber*, and the well renowned citye of this realme, much honorable fame receiveth among all other nacions."* The best explanation of the term is given in Ben Jonson's "Part of King James's Entertainment in passing to his coronation, through the City of London, on Thursday the 15th of March 1603:—

At Fen-Church.

The scene presented it self in a square and flat upright, like to the side of a city: the top thereof, above the vent and crest, adorned with houses, towers and steeples, set off in prospective. Upon the battlements in a great capital letter was inscribed,

LONDINIUM:

According to Tacitus, *Annal.* lib. 14. * * * Beneath that in a less and different character, was written

CAMERA REGIA,

which title immediately after the Norman conquest it began to have; and by the indulgence of successive princes, hath been hitherto continued. In the frieze over the gate it seemeth to speak this verse:

PAR DOMUS HÆC CŒLO,
SED MINOR EST DOMINO.

Taken out of Martial (lib. 8. epig. 36) and implying that though this city (for the state and magnificence) might by hyperbole be said to touch the stars, and reach up to heaven, yet was it far inferior to the master thereof, who was his Majesty; and in that respect unworthy to receive him. The highest person advanced therein, was

MONARCHIA BRITANNICA;

and fitly; applying to the abovementioned title of the city, THE KING'S CHAMBER, and therefore here placed as in the proper seat of the empire."

(2) SCENE I.—

You are too senseless-obstinate, my lord,
Too ceremonious, and traditional,
Weigh it but with the grossness of this age.]

Buckingham's reasons against the young duke of York's right to enjoy the privilege of sanctuary, were first set forth by Sir Thomas More, and were copied by Hall and Holinshed, from one or other of whom the poet took them:—

"'Womanish feare, naie womanish frowardnes' (quod the duke of Buckingham) * * * 'I ensure you faithfully for my mynde, I will rather (maugre her stomacke) fetche hym away then leave him there till her frowardnesse or fond feare conveie him awaye. And yet will I break no sanctuary, for verely sithe the privilege of that place and other of that sorte have so long continued, I would not goe about to breake it, but if they were now to begynne I would not be he that should make them. Yet wyll not I say nay but it is a deede of pitie that such men as the chaunce of the sea or their evill debters have brought into povertie, should have some place of refuge to kepe in their bodies out of the daunger of their cruell creditours. And if it fortune the croune to come in question, as it hath done before this tyme, while eche parte taketh other for traytours, I thinke it necessarye to have a place of refuge for bothe: But as for theves and murtherers whereof these places be full, and whiche never falle from their crafte after they once falle therunto, it is pytee that ever Sanctuary

* Sir Thomas Moré's Life of King Richard III. fo. 63.

should serve them, and in especiall wylful murtherers whom God commaundeth to be taken from the aulter and to be put to death. * * * Nowe loke how fewe sanctuary menne there be whome necessitie or misfortune compelled to go thether. And then see on the other syde what a sort there be commonly therein of suche whome wylful unthriftynes hath brought to naught? What a rable of theves, murtherers, and malicious heinous traitours be, and that in twoo places specially; the one at the elbow of the cytee and the other in the very bowels. I dare well a vowe it, if you waye the good that they do, with the hurt that commeth of them, ye shall finde it muche better to lose bothe then to have bothe. And this I saye, although they were not abused (as they now be and so long have bene) that I feare me ever they will be, while men be afeard to set to their hands to the amendmente, as though God and saincte Peter were the patrons of ungracious livynge. Nowe unthriftes riot and ronne in debte upon boldnes of these places; yea, and riche men ronne thyther with poore mens goodes: there they buylde, there they spend and bid their creditours goo whystle. Mens wyves ronne thither with their husbandes plate and saye they dare not abyde with their husbandes for betynge; theves brynge thither stollen goodes and lyve thereon. There devise they new robberies nightely, and steale out and rob, reave and kylle menne, and come againe into those places as though those places gave them not onely a savegard for the harme that they have dooen but a licence also to do more mischief. * * * Where a manne is by lawfull meanes in peril there nedeth he the tuition of some speciall privilege which is the onely grounde of all sanctuaries; from which necessitee this noble prince is farre, whose love to his kynge, nature and kinred proveth: whose innocencie to all the worlde, his tender youth affirmeth, and so sanctuarye, as for hym is not necessary, ner none he can have. Men come not to sanctuary as they come to baptisme, to require it by his godfathers; he must aske it himselfe that must have it; and reason, sithe no maune hath cause to have it but whose conscience of his owne faute maketh him have nede to require it. What will then hath yonder babe, which yf he had discretion to require it, if nede were, I dare say would be now right angry with them that kepe him there. * * * And if nobody may be taken out of sanctuary because he saieth he will abide there, then yf a child will take sanctuary because he feareth to go to schoole, his master must lette him alone. And as simple as that example is, yet is there lesse reason in our case then in it, for there, though it be a childish feare, yet is there at the least some feare, and herein is no feare at all. *And verily I have hearde of sanctuary menne, but I never hearde before of sanctuary children:* and therefore as for the conclusion of my minde, whosoever may deserve to have nede of it, if thei thynke it for their suretee, let them kepe it. * * * And he that taketh one out of sanctuarye to doe him goode, I saie plainly, he breaketh no sanctuary.' "—HALL.

(3) SCENE I.—*For we to-morrow hold divided councils.*] This is correspondent with historical fact:—

"And when they were thus at a point betweene themselves [Richard and Buckingham] they went about to prepare for the coronation of the young king, as they would have it seeme. And that they might turne both the eies and minds of men from perceiving of their drifts otherwhere, the lords being sent for from all parts of the realme, came thicke to that solemnitie. But the protector and the duke, after that they had sent the lord cardinall, the archbishope of Yorke then lord chancellor, the bishop of Elie, the lord Stanleie, and the lord Hastings then lord chamberlaine, with manie other noble men to common and devise about the coronation in one place, as fast were they in an other place, contriving the contrarie, and to make the protector king.

To which councell albeit there were adhibited verie few, and they were secret: yet began there here and there abouts, some maner of muttering among the people, as though all should not long be well, though they neither wist what they feared, nor wherefore; were it, that before such great things, mens hearts of a secret instinct of nature misgive them; as the sea without winde swelleth of himselfe sometime before a tempest; or were it that some one man, happilie somewhat perceiving, filled manie men with suspicion, though he shewed few men what he knew. Howbeit somewhat the dealing it selfe made men to muse on the matter, though the councell were close. For by little and little all folke withdrew from the Tower, and drew unto Crosbies in Bishops gates street, where the protector kept his houshold. The protector had the resort, the king in maner desolate.

While some for their businesse made sute to them that had the dooing, some were by their freends secretlie warned, that it might happilie turne them to no good to be too much attendant about the king without the protectors appointment, which remooved also diverse of the princes old servants from him, and set new about him. Thus manie things comming togither, partlie by chance, partlie of purpose, caused at length not common people onelie, that woond with the wind, but wise men also, and some lords eke to marke the matter and muse thereon; so farre foorth that the lord Stanleie that was after earle of Derbie, wiselie mistrusted it, and said unto the lord Hastings, that he much misliked these two severall councels. 'For while we' (quoth he) 'talke of one matter in the tone place, little wot we wherof they talke in the tother place.' "—HOLINSHED.

(4) SCENE IV.—

Come, lead me to the block; bear him my head:
They smile at me who shortly shall be dead.]

The leading incidents connected with the sudden impeachment and execution of Hastings, are borrowed, probably through Holinshed, from the following relation of them by Sir Thomas More:—

Many Lordes assembled in the tower, and there sat in counsaile, devising the honourable solempnite of the kinges coronacion, of which the time appointed then so nere approched; that the pageauntes and suttelties were in making day and night at Westminster, and much vitaile killed therfore, that afterward was cast away. These lordes so sytting togyther comoning of thys matter, the protectour came in among them, fyrst aboute ix. of the clock, saluting them curtesly, and excusing hymself that he had bene so long, saieng merely that he had bene a slepe that day. And after a little talking with them, he sayd unto the Bishop of Elye: my lord you have very good strawberies at your gardayne in Holberne, I require you let us have a messe of them. Gladly my lord, quod he, woulde God I had some better thing as redy to your pleasure as that. And therewith in al the hast he sent hys servant for a messe of strauberies. The protectour sette the lordes fast in comoning, and thereupon prayeng them to spare hym for a little while, departed thence. And sone after one hower betwene x. and xi. he returned into the chamber among them, al changed with a wonderful soure angrye countenaunce, knitting the browes, frowning and froting and knawing on hys lippes, and so sat hym downe in hys place: al the lords much dismaied and sore merveiling of this manner of sodaine chaunge, and what thing should him aile. Then when he had sitten still a while, thus he began: what were they worthy to have, that compasse and ymagine the distruccion of me, being so nere of blood unto the kyng and protectour of his riall persone and his realme. At this question, al the lordes sat sore astonied, musyng much by whome thys question should be ment, of which every man wyst himselfe clere. Then the lord chamberlen, as he for the love betwene them thoughte he might be boldest with him, aunswered and sayd, that thei wer worthye to bee punished as heighnous traitors whatsoever they were. And al the other affirmed the same. That is (quod he) yonder sorceres my brothers wife and other with her, meaning the quene. At these wordes many of the other Lordes were gretly abashed that favoured her. But the lord Hastings was in his minde better content, that it was moved by her, then by any other whom he loved better. Albeit hys harte somewhat grudged, that he was not afore, made of counsell in this mater as he was of the takyng of her kynred, and of their putting to death, which were by his assent before, devised to bee byhedded at Pountfreit this selfe same day, in which he was not ware that it was by other devised, that himself should the same day be behedded at London. Then said the protectour: ye shal al se in what wyse that sorceres and that other witch of her counsel, Shoris wife wyth their affynite, have by their sorcery and witchcraft wasted my body. And therwyth he plucked up hys doublet sleve to his elbow upon his left arme, where he shewed a werish withered arme and small, as it was never other. And therupon every mannes mind sore misgave them, well perceiving that this mater was but a quarel. For wel thei wist, that the quene was to wise to go about any such folye. And also if she woold, yet wolde she of all folke leste make Shoris wyfe of counsaile, whom of al women she most hated, as that concubine whom the king her husband had most loved. And also no man was ther present but wel knew that his arme was ever such since his birth. Natheles the lorde Chamberlen (which from the death of king Edward kept Shoris wife, on whom he somewhat doted in the kinges life, saving as it is said he that while forbare her of reverence towarde hys king, or els of a certaine kinde of fidelite to hys frend) aunswered and sayd: certainly my lorde if they have so heinously done, thei be worthy heinouse punishmente. What, quod the protectour, thou servest me I wene with *iffes* and with *andes*, I tel the thei have so done, and that I will make good on thy body, traitour. And therwith as in a great anger, he clapped his fiste upon the borde a great rappe. At which token given, one cried treason without the chambre. Therwith a dore clapped, and in come ther rushing men in harneys as many as the chambre might hold. And anon the protectour sayd to the lorde Hastinges: I arest the, traitour. What me, my Lorde, quod he. Yea the, traitour, quod the protectour. And a nother let flee at the Lorde Standley which shronke at the stroke and fel under the table, or els his hed had bene clefte to the tethe; for as shortely as he shranke, yet ranne the blood about hys eares. Then were they al quickly bestowed in diverse chambres, except the lorde Chamberlen, whom the protectour bade spede and shryve hym a pace, for by saynt Poule (quod he) I wil not to dinner til I se thy hed of. It boted him not to aske why, but hevely he toke a priest at adventure, and made a short shrift, for a longer would not be suffered, the protectour made so much hast to dyner: which he might not go to til this wer done for saving of his othe. So was he brought forthe into the grene beside the chappel within the tower, and his head laid down upon a long log of tymbre, and there striken of, and afterward his body with the hed entred at Windsore beside the body of kinge Edward, whose both soules our lord pardon."—MORE.

(5) SCENE V.—*Enter* GLOUCESTER *and* BUCKINGHAM, *in rusty armour, marvellous ill-favoured.*] An historical fact. "Nowe flewe the fame of thys lordes death through the cytie and farther about, lyke a wynde in every mans eare, but the Protectour immediately after dyner (entendyng to set some colour upon the matter) sent in all the haste for many substancial men out of the cytie into the Towre, and at their comming him selfe with the Duke of Buckyngham stode, harnessed in olde evill favoured briganders, such as no man would wene that they would have vouchesafed to have put on their backes, excepte some sodeyne necessitie had constraigned them. Then the lord protector shewed them, that the lord Hastynges and other of his conspiracy had contrived to have sodeynly destroyed hym and the Duke of Buckyngham there the same daie in counsail, and what they entended farther, was yet not well knowen, of whiche their treason he had never knowlege before .x. of the clocke the same forenone, which sodeyn feare drave them to put on suche harnesse as came next to their handes for their defence, and so God holpe them, that the mischiefe turned upon them that woulde have done it, and thus he required them to report. Every man answered fayre, as though no man mistrusted the matter, which of trueth no man beleved."—HALL.

(6) SCENE VI.—*And yet within these five hours Hastings liv'd.*] So Hall, who follows Sir Thomas More:—"Nowe was thys proclamacion made within twoo houres after he was beheaded, and it was so curiously endyted and so fayre writen in Parchment in a fayre sette hande, and therewith of it selfe so long a processe, that every chyld might perceyve that it was prepared and studyed before (and as some men thought, by Catesby) for all the tyme betwene hys death and the proclamacion proclaimyng, coulde skant have suffyced unto the bare wrytyng alone, albeit that it had bene on paper and scribeled furthe in haste at adventure. So that upon the proclaimyng thereof, one that was scolemayster at Paules standyng by and comparyng the shortenesse of the tyme with the length of the matter sayed to theim that stoode aboute hym, here is a gaye goodly cast, foule cast awaye for hast. And a marchaunte that stoode by hym sayed that it was wrytten by inspiracyon and prophesye."—HALL.

ACT IV.

(1) SCENE I.—*Were red-hot steel, to sear me to the brain!*] The ancient mode of punishing a regicide, or one who attempted to deprive a lawful monarch of his realm, was to crown him with a coronet of iron made red-hot. In Goulart's "Admirable and Memorable Histories," 1607, it is related that John, the son of Vaivode Stephen, after defeating the army of Hungarian peasants, called Croisadoes, in 1514, caused their general to be stript naked, and the executioner to set a crown of "hot burning iron" upon his head. Other instances of this horrible torture, which was, probably, first derived from the Northern nations, are referred to in the notes to the Variorum Shakespeare, Edit. 1821, p. 153, Vol. XIX.

(2) SCENE II.—*The boy is foolish, and I fear not him.*] Edward, Earl of Warwick, the unhappy son of Clarence, was imprisoned by Gloucester at Sherif-hutton Castle; whence, the day after the battle of Bosworth, he was removed, by the order of Richmond, to the Tower. There he remained in captivity until the year 1499, when he was barbarously executed on Tower Hill. Owing to his long confinement, and the consequent neglect of his education, he is said by the historians to have become idiotic at the time of his death:—"Edouardus Varvici comes in carcere ab incunabulis extra hominum ferarumque conspectum nutritus, qui gallinam ab ansere non facile internoscerit, cum nullo suo delicto supplicium quærere posset, alieno ad id tractus est."—POLYDORE VIRGIL.

(3) SCENE II.—
The earldom of Hereford, and the moveables,
The which you promised I should possess.]

"At Northhampton the duke met with the protector himselfe with three hundred horses, and from thence still continued with him partner of all his devises, till that after his coronation, they departed (as it seemed) verie great freends at Glocester. From whense as soone as the duke came home, he so lightlie turned from him, and so highlie conspired against him, that a man would marvell whereof the change grew. And surelie the occasion of their variance is of diverse men diverselie reported.

Some have I heard say, that the duke a little before his coronation, among other things, required of the protector the duke of Hereford's lands, to the whiche he pretended himselfe just inheritor. And forsomuch as the title which he claimed by inheritance, was somewhat interlaced with the title to the crowne by the line of King Henrie before deprived, the protector conceived such indignation, that he rejected the dukes request with many spitefull and minatorie words. Which so wounded his heart with hatred and mistrust, that he never after coulde endure to looke aright on king Richard, but ever feared his owne life."—HOLINSHED.

(4) SCENE III.—

Their lips like four red roses on a stalk,
Which, in their summer beauty, kiss'd each other.]

It is thought that Shakespeare had here in his mind an old ballad of "The most cruel Murther of Edward V." &c. which is printed in "The Golden Garland of Princely Delight:"—

"When these sweet children thus were lain in bed,
And to the Lord their hearty prayers had said,
Sweet slumbring sleep then closing up their eyes,
Each folded in the other's arms then lies."

(5) SCENE IV.—*Humphrey Hour.*] This expression has been controverted; Steevens conjectured the poet designed to mark the hour at which the good Duchess was as hungry as the followers of Duke Humphrey, and he quotes a passage from Decker's pamphlet, "The Guls Hornbooke," 1609, in explanation of the phrase, "dining with Duke Humphrey," the meaning of which is now familiar to everybody. Malone supposes *Humphrey Hour* "is merely used in ludicrous language for *hour*, like *Tom Troth*, for *truth*, and twenty more such terms." We apprehend Steevens's surmise is nearer the true solution, and that *Humphrey hour* was nothing more than a cant phrase for *eating hour*.

ACT V.

(1) SCENE III.—

Lest, being seen, thy brother, tender George,
Be executed in his father's sight.]

"The lorde Stanleie was afraid, least if he should seeme openlie to be a fautor, or aider to the earle his sonne in law, before the day of the battell, that king Richard, which yet utterly did not put him in diffidence and mistrust, would put to some cruell death his sonne and heir apparant, George lord Strange, whome king Richard (as you have heard before) kept with him as a pledge or hostage, to the intent that the lord Stanleie his father should attempt nothing prejudiciall to him."—HOLINSHED.

(2) SCENE III.—

Richard, thy wife, that wretched Anne thy wife,
That never slept a quiet hour with thee.]

Malone observes that Shakespeare was probably thinking of Sir Thomas More's animated description of Richard:—

"I have heard by credible report of such as were secrete with his chamberers, that after this abhominable deede done, he never hadde quiet in his minde, hee never thought himself sure. Where he went abrode, his eyen whirled about, his body privily fenced, his hand ever on his dager, his countenance and maner like one alway ready to strike againe, he tooke ill rest a nightes, lay long wakyng and musing, sore weried with care and watch, rather slumbred then slept, troubled wyth fearful dreames, sodainly sommetyme sterte up, leape out of his bed and runne about the chamber, so was his restles herte continually tossed and tumbled with the tedious impression and stormy remembrance of his abhominable dede."—MORE.

(3) SCENE III.—*God, and Saint George!*] "*Saint George* was the common cry of the English soldiers when they charged the enemy. The author of the old Arte of Warre, printed in the latter end of Queen Elizabeth's reign, formally enjoins the use of this cry among his military laws, p. 84:—

'*Item*, that all souldiers entring into battaile, assault, skirmish, or other faction of armes, shall have for their common cry and word, *Saint George, forward, or upon them, Saint George*, whereby the souldiour is much comforted, and the enemy dismaied by calling to minde the ancient valour of England, which with that name has so often been victorious; and therefore he, who upon any *sinister zeale*, shall *maliciously* omit so fortunate a name, shall be *severely punished* for his obstinate *erroneous* heart, and perverse mind.'"

(4) SCENE V.—*The day is ours, the bloody dog is dead!*] The old chroniclers furnish a very long but spirited account of the decisive battle which terminated Richard's career. We append some extracts:—

"In the meane ceason kyng Richard (whiche was appoynted nowe to finyshe his last laboure by the very devine justice and providence of God, whiche called hym to condigne punyshement for his scelerate merites and myscheveous desertes) marched to a place mete for twoo battayles to encountre by a village called Bosworth, not farre from Leycester, and there he pitched his felde, refreshed his souldioures and toke his rest. The fame went that he had the same night a dreadfull and a terrible dreame, for yt semed to hym beynge a slepe, that he sawe diverse ymages like terrible develles whiche pulled and haled hym, not sufferynge hym to take any quyet or rest. The whiche straunge vision not so sodenily strake his heart with a sodeyn feare, but it stuffed his hed, and troubled his mynde with many dreadfull and busy Imaginacions. For incontynent after, his heart beynge almost damped, he pronosticated before the doubtfull chaunce of the battaile to come, not usynge the alacrite and myrth of mynde and of countenaunce as he was accustomed to do before he came toward the battaile. And leaste that it might be suspected that he was abasshed for feare of his enemyes, and for that cause looked so piteously, he recyted and declared to his famylyer frendes in the morenynge hys wonderfull visyon and terrible dreame. But I thynke this was no dreame, but a punction and pricke of his synfull conscyence."

After detailing the speeches first of king Richard, and then of Richmond, Hall proceeds:—

"He had scantly finyshed his saienge, but the one armye espyed the other, lord how hastely the souldioures buckled their healmes, how quikly the archers bent ther bowes and frushed their feathers, how redely the byllmen shoke their bylles and proved their staves, redy to approche and joyne when the terrible trompet should sound the bluddy blast to victorie or deathe. Betwene both armies ther was a great marrysse which therle of Richemond left on his right hand, for this entent that it should be on that syde a defence for his parte, and in so doyng he had the sonne at his backe and in the faces of his enemies. When kynge Richard saw the earles compaignie was passed the marresse, he commaunded with al hast to sett upon them, then the trompettes blew and the souldiours showted, and the kyngs archers couragiously let fly there arrowes ; the erles bowmen stode not still but paied them home againe. The terrible shot ons passed, the armies joyned, and came to hand strokes, where nother swerde nor byll was spared, at whiche encounter the lord Stanley joyned with therle. The earl of Oxforde in the meane season feryng lest while his compaignie was fightyng, thei should be compassed and circumvented with the multitude of his enemies, gave commaundement in every ranke that no man should be so hardy as go above .x. fote from the standard, whiche commaundement ons knowen thei knyte themselves together, and ceased a littel from fightyng. * * * While the two forwardes thus mortallye fought, eche entendyng to vanquishe and convince the other, kyng Richard was admonished by his explorators and espialles, that therle of Richmond accompaignied with a small nomber of men of armes was not farre of, and as he approched and marched toward him, he perfitely knew his personage by certaine demonstracions and tokens whiche he had learned and knowen of other. And being inflamed with ire and vexed with outrageous malice, he put his spurres to his horse, and rode out of the syde of the range of his battaile, levyng the avant gardes fightyng, and lyke a hungery lion ran with spere in rest toward hym. Therle of Richmonde perceyved wel the king furiusly commyng towarde hym, and by cause the whole hope of his welth and purpose was to be determined by battaill, he gladlye proferred to encountre with him body to body and man to man. Kyng Richard sett on so sharpely at the first brount that he overthrew therles standarde, and slew Sir William Brandon his standarde bearer (whiche was father to Sir Charles Brandon by kynge Hery the .VIII. created duke of Suffolke) and matched hand to hand with Sir Jhon Cheinye, a man of great force and strength which would have resisted hym, and the saied Jhon was by hym manfully overthrowen, and so he makyng open passage by dent of swerde as he went forwarde, therle of Richmond withstode his violence and kept hym at the swerdes poincte without avantage longer than his compaignions other thought or judged, which beyng almost in dispaire of victorie, were sodainly recomforted by Sir William Stanley, whiche came to succours with .iii. thousande tall men, at whiche very instant kynge Richardes men were dryven backe and fledde, and he him selfe manfully fyghtynge in the mydell of his enemies was slaine and brought to his death as he worthely had deserved."—HALL.

CRITICAL OPINIONS

ON

KING RICHARD THE THIRD.

"THE part of 'Richard III.' has become highly celebrated in England from its having been filled by excellent performers, and this has naturally had an influence on the admiration of the piece itself, for many readers of Shakspeare stand in want of good interpreters of the poet to understand him properly. This admiration is certainly in every respect well founded, though I cannot help thinking there is an injustice in considering the three parts of 'Henry the Sixth' as of little value compared with 'Richard the Third.' These four plays were undoubtedly composed in succession, as is proved by the style and the spirit in the handling of the subject: the last is definitely announced in the one which precedes it, and is also full of references to it: the same views run through the series; in a word, the whole make together only one single work. Even the deep characterization of Richard is by no means the exclusive property of the piece which bears his name: his character is very distinctly drawn in the two last parts of 'Henry the Sixth;' nay, even his first speeches lead us already to form the most unfavourable anticipations of his future conduct. He lowers obliquely like a dark thunder-cloud on the horizon, which gradually approaches nearer and nearer, and first pours out the devastating elements with which it is charged when it hangs over the heads of mortals. Two of Richard's most significant soliloquies which enable us to draw the most important conclusions with regard to his mental temperament, are to be found in 'The Last Part of Henry the Sixth.' As to the value and the justice of the actions to which passion impels us, we may be blind, but wickedness cannot mistake its own nature; Richard, as well as Iago, is a villain with full consciousness. That they should say this in so many words, is not perhaps in human nature: but the poet has the right in soliloquies to lend a voice to the most hidden thoughts, otherwise the form of the monologue would, generally speaking, be censurable.* Richard's deformity is the expression of his internal malice, and perhaps in part the effect of it: for where is the ugliness that would not be softened by benevolence and openness? He, however, considers it as an iniquitous neglect of nature, which justifies him in taking his revenge on that human society from which it is the means of excluding him. Hence these sublime lines:

> And this word love, which greybeards call divine,
> Be resident in men like one another,
> And not in me. I am myself alone.

Wickedness is nothing but selfishness designedly unconscientious; however it can never do altogether without the form at least of morality, as this is the law of all thinking beings,—it must seek to found

---

* What, however, happens in so many tragedies, where a person is made to avow himself a villain to his confidants, is most decidedly unnatural. He will, indeed, announce his way of thinking, not, however, under damning names, but as something that is understood of itself, and is equally approved of by others.

its depraved way of acting on something like principles. Although Richard is thoroughly acquainted with the blackness of his mind and his hellish mission, he yet endeavours to justify this to himself by a sophism: the happiness of being beloved is denied to him; what then remains to him but the happiness of ruling? All that stands in the way of this must be removed. This envy of the enjoyment of love is so much the more natural in Richard, as his brother Edward, who besides preceded him in the possession of the crown, was distinguished by the nobleness and beauty of his figure, and was an almost irresistible conqueror of female hearts. Notwithstanding his pretended renunciation, Richard places his chief vanity in being able to please and win over the women, if not by his figure at least by his insinuating discourse. Shakspeare here shows us, with his accustomed acuteness of observation, that human nature, even when it is altogether decided in goodness or wickedness, is still subject to petty infirmities. Richard's favourite amusement is to ridicule others, and he possesses an eminent satirical wit. He entertains at bottom a contempt for all mankind: for he is confident of his ability to deceive them, whether as his instruments or his adversaries. In hypocrisy he is particularly fond of using religious forms, as if actuated by a desire of profaning in the service of hell the religion whose blessings he had inwardly abjured.

"So much for the main features of Richard's character. The play named after him embraces also the latter part of the reign of Edward IV., in the whole a period of eight years. It exhibits all the machinations by which Richard obtained the throne, and the deeds which he perpetrated to secure himself in its possession, which lasted, however, but two years. Shakspeare intended that terror rather than compassion should prevail throughout this tragedy: he has rather avoided than sought the pathetic scenes which he had at command. Of all the sacrifices to Richard's lust of power, Clarence alone is put to death on the stage: his dream excites a deep horror, and proves the omnipotence of the poet's fancy: his conversation with the murderers is powerfully agitating; but the earlier crimes of Clarence merited death, although not from his brother's hand. The most innocent and unspotted sacrifices are the two princes: we see but little of them, and their murder is merely related. Anne disappears without our learning any thing farther respecting her: in marrying the murderer of her husband, she had shown a weakness almost incredible. The parts of Lord Rivers, and other friends of the queen, are of too secondary a nature to excite a powerful sympathy; Hastings, from his triumph at the fall of his friend, forfeits all title to compassion; Buckingham is the satellite of the tyrant, who is afterwards consigned by him to the axe of the executioner. In the background the widowed Queen Margaret appears as the fury of the past, who invokes a curse on the future: every calamity which her enemies draw down on each other, is a cordial to her revengeful heart. Other female voices join, from time to time, in the lamentations and imprecations. But Richard is the soul, or rather the dæmon, of the whole tragedy. He fulfils the promise which he formerly made of leading the murderous Machiavel to school. Notwithstanding the uniform aversion with which he inspires us, he still engages us in the greatest variety of ways by his profound skill in dissimulation, his wit, his prudence, his presence of mind, his quick activity, and his valour. He fights at last against Richmond like a desperado, and dies the honourable death of a hero on the field of battle. Shakspeare could not change this historical issue, and yet it is by no means satisfactory to our moral feelings, as Lessing, when speaking of a German play on the same subject, has very judiciously remarked. How has Shakspeare solved this difficulty? By a wonderful invention he opens a prospect into the other world, and shows us Richard in his last moments already branded with the stamp of reprobation. We see Richard and Richmond in the night before the battle sleeping in their tents; the spirits of the murdered victims of the tyrant ascend in succession, and pour out their curses against him, and their blessings on his adversary. These apparitions are properly but the dreams of the two generals represented visibly. It is no doubt contrary to probability that their tents should only be separated by so small a space; but Shakspeare could reckon on poetical spectators who were ready to take the breadth of the stage for the distance between two hostile camps, if for such indulgence they were to be recompensed by beauties of so sublime a nature as this series of spectres and Richard's awakening soliloquy. The catastrophe of 'Richard the Third' is, in respect of the external events, very like that of 'Macbeth:' we have only to compare the thorough difference of handling them to be convinced that Shakspeare has most accurately observed poetical justice in the genuine sense of the word, that is, as signifying the revelation of an invisible blessing or curse which hangs over human sentiments and actions."—SCHLEGEL.

"The character of Richard the Third, which had been opened in so masterly a manner in the 'Concluding Part of Henry the Sixth,' is, in this play, developed in all its horrible grandeur. It is, in fact, the picture of a demoniacal incarnation, moulding the passions and foibles of mankind, with superhuman precision, to its own iniquitous purposes. Of this isolated and peculiar state of being Richard himself seems sensible, when he declares—

I have no brother, I am like no brother:
And this word love, which greybeards call divine,
Be resident in men like one another,
And not in me; I am myself alone.

"From a delineation like this, Milton must have caught many of the most striking features of his Satanic portrait. The same union of unmitigated depravity and consummate intellectual energy characterises both, and renders what would otherwise be loathsome and disgusting, an object of sublimity and shuddering admiration.

"Richard, stript as he is of all the softer feelings, and all the common charities of humanity, possessed of

neither pity, love, nor fear,

and loaded with every dangerous and dreadful vice, would, were it not for his unconquerable powers of mind, be insufferably revolting. But, though insatiate in his ambition, envious and hypocritical in his disposition, cruel, bloody, and remorseless in all his deeds, he displays such an extraordinary share of cool and determined courage, such alacrity and buoyancy of spirit, such constant self-possession, such an intuitive intimacy with the workings of the human heart, and such matchless skill in rendering them subservient to his views, as so far to subdue our detestation and abhorrence of his villany, that we at length contemplate this fiend in human shape with a mingled sensation of intense curiosity and grateful terror.

"The task, however, which Shakspeare undertook was, in one instance, more arduous than that which Milton subsequently attempted; for, in addition to the hateful constitution of Richard's moral character, he had to contend also against the prejudices arising from personal deformity, from a figure

———curtail'd of it's fair proportion,
Cheated of feature by dissembling nature,
Deform'd, unfinish'd, sent before it's time
Into this breathing world, scarce half made up.

and yet, in spite of these striking personal defects, which were considered, also, as indicatory of the depravity and wickedness of his nature, the poet has contrived, through the medium of the high mental endowments just enumerated, not only to obviate disgust, but to excite extraordinary admiration.

"One of the most prominent and detestable vices, indeed, in Richard's character, his hypocrisy, connected, as it always is, in his person, with the most profound skill and dissimulation, has, owing to the various parts which it induces him to assume, most materially contributed to the popularity of this play, both on the stage and in the closet. He is one who can

———frame his face to all occasions,

and accordingly appears, during the course of his career, under the contrasted forms of a subject and a monarch, a politician and a wit, a soldier and a suitor, a sinner and a saint; and in all with such apparent ease and fidelity to nature, that while to the explorer of the human mind he affords, by his penetration and address, a subject of peculiar interest and delight, he offers to the practised performer a study well calculated to call forth his fullest and finest exertions. He, therefore, whose histrionic powers are adequate to the just exhibition of this character, may be said to have attained the highest honours of his profession; and, consequently, the popularity of 'Richard the Third,' notwithstanding the moral enormity of its hero, may be readily accounted for, when we recollect that, the versatile and consummate hypocrisy of the tyrant has been embodied by the talents of such masterly performers as Garrick, Kemble, Cooke, and Kean.

"So overwhelming and exclusive is the character of Richard, that the comparative insignificancy of all the other persons of the drama may be necessarily inferred; they are reflected to us, as it were, from his mirror, and become more or less important, and more or less developed, as he finds it necessary to act upon them; so that our estimate of their character is entirely founded on his relative conduct, through which we may very correctly appreciate their strength or weakness.

"The only exception to this remark is in the person of Queen Margaret, who, apart from the agency of Richard, and dimly seen in the darkest recesses of the picture, pours forth, in union with the deep tone of this tragedy, the most dreadful curses and imprecations; with such a wild and prophetic fury, indeed, as to involve the whole scene in tenfold gloom and horror.

"We have to add that the moral of this play is great and impressive. Richard, having excited a general sense of indignation, and a general desire of revenge, and, unaware of his danger from having lost, through familiarity with guilt, all idea of moral obligation, becomes at length the victim of his own enormous crimes; he falls not unvisited by the terrors of conscience, for, on the eve of danger and of death, the retribution of another world is placed before him; the spirits of those whom he had murdered reveal the awful sentence of his fate, and his bosom heaves with the infliction of eternal torture."—DRAKE.

Act V. Sc. 1.

MEASURE FOR MEASURE.

THIS play was first printed in the folio of 1623, and is supposed, upon the slight foundation of two or three doubtful allusions to contemporary events, to have been written in 1603. The fact of its having been played before the Court on St. Stephen's night, December 26, 1604, which is gathered from Tylney's account of the expenses of The Revels from the end of October, 1604, to the end of the same month, 1605:—

"By his Ma[tes.] plaiers. On St. Stivens Night in the Hall, A Play called Mesur for Mesur"—

proves it to have been written before that date, and this really is all that is known with certainty respecting the period of its production. The plot appears to have been taken from Whetstone's drama, in two parts, called "The right excellent and famous Historye of Promos and Cassandra," &c. 1578, of which the "Argument" is as follows:—

"In the cyttie of Julio (sometimes vnder the dominion of Coruinus Kinge of Hungarie and Boemia) there was a law, that what man so euer committed adultery should lose his head, and the woman offender should weare some disguised apparel during her life, to make her infamouslye noted. This seuere lawe, by the fauour of some mercifull magistrate, became little regarded vntill the time of Lord Promos auctority; who conuicting a yong gentleman named Andrugio of incontinency, condemned both him and his minion to the execution of this statute. Andrugio had a very vertuous and beawtiful gentlewoman to his sister, named Cassandra: Cassandra to enlarge her brothers life, submitted an humble petition to the Lord Promos: Promos regarding her good behauiours, and fantasying her great beawtie, was much delighted with the sweete order of her talke; and, doying good that euill might come thereof, for a time he repryu'd her brother; but, wicked man, tourning his liking vnto vnlawfull lust, he set downe the spoile of her honour raunsome for her brothers life. Chaste Cassandra, abhorring both him and his sute, by no perswasion would yeald to this raunsome: but in fine, wonne with the importunitye of hir brother (pleading for life) vpon these conditions she agreede to Promos; first that he should pardon her brother, and after marry her. Promos, as feareles in promisse as carelesse in performance, with sollemne vowe sygned her conditions: but worse then any infydel, his will satisfyed, he performed neither the one nor the other; for, to keepe his aucthoritye vnspotted with fauour, and to preuent Cassandraes clamors, he commaunded the gayler secretly to present Cassandra with her brothers head. The gayler, with the outcryes of Andrugio [*sic*], abhorryng Promos lewdenes, by the prouidence of God prouided thus for his safety. He presented Cassandra with a felon's head newlie executed, who (being mangled, knew it not from her brothers, by the gayler who was set at libertie) was so agreeued at this trecherye, that, at the pointe to kyl her selfe, she spared that stroke to be auenged of Promos: and deuisyng a way, she concluded to make her fortunes knowne vnto the kinge. She (executinge this resolution) was so highly fauoured of the king, that forthwith he hasted to do justice on Promos: whose judgement was, to marrye Cassandra to repaire her crased honour; which donne, for his hainous offence he should lose his head. This maryage solempnised, Cassandra, tyed in the greatest bondes of affection to her husband, became an earnest suter for his life: the kinge (tendringe the generall benefit of the common weale before her special ease, although he fauoured her much,) would not graunt her sute. Andrugio (disguised amonge the company) sorrowing the griefe of his sister, bewrayde his safetye, and craued pardon. The kinge, to renowne the vertues of Cassandra, pardoned both him and Promos. The circumstances of this rare historye in action lyuelye foloweth."

Whetstone was indebted for the story, of which he afterwards introduced a prose narrative in his "Heptameron of Civil Discourses," 1582, to Giraldi Cinthio's *Hecatommithi,*—Parte Seconda, Deca. viii. Novella 5 :—

"Juriste è mandato da Massamiano Imperadore in Ispruchi, ove fà prendere un giovane violatore di una vergine, e condannalo a morte: la sorella cerca di liberarlo: Juriste da speranza alla donna di pigliarla per moglie, e di darle libero il fratello: ella con lui si giace, e la notte istessa Juriste fà tagliar al giovane la testa, e la manda alla sorella. Ella ne fà querela all' Imperadore, il quale fà sposare ad Juriste la donna; poscia lo fà dare ad essere ucciso: la donna lo libera, e con lui si vive amorevolissimamente."

Persons Represented.

VINCENTIO, *the Duke.*
ANGELO, *the Deputy.*
ESCALUS, *an Ancient Lord.*
CLAUDIO, *a Young Gentleman.*
LUCIO, *a Fantastic.*
Two other like Gentlemen.
Provost.
THOMAS, } *Two Friars.*
PETER, }
A Justice.
ELBOW, *a simple Constable.*

FROTH, *a foolish Gentleman.*
POMPEY, *Servant to* Mistress Overdone.
ABHORSON, *an Executioner.*
BARNARDINE, *a dissolute Prisoner.*

ISABELLA, *Sister to* Claudio.
MARIANA, *betrothed to* Angelo.
JULIET, *beloved of* Claudio.
FRANCISCA, *a Nun.*
Mistress OVERDONE, *a Bawd.*

Lords, Gentlemen, Guards, Officers, and other Attendants.

SCENE—VIENNA

ACT I.

SCENE I.—*An Apartment in the* Duke's *Palace.*

Enter Duke, Escalus, Lords, *and* Attendants.

Duke. Escalus!
Escal. My lord.
Duke. Of government the properties to unfold,
Would seem in me to affect speech and discourse;
Since I am put to know, that your own science
Exceeds, in that, the lists of all advice
My strength can give you: then no more remains,
But that, to your sufficiency, as your worth is able,
And let them work.[a] The nature of our people,
Our city's institutions, and the terms
For common justice, you're as pregnant in
As art and practice hath enriched any
That we remember. There is our commission,
[*Giving it.*
From which we would not have you warp.—Call hither,
I say, bid come before us Angelo.—
[*Exit an* Attendant.
What figure of us think you he will bear?
For you must know, we have with special soul
Elected him our absence to supply,
Lent him our terror, drest him with our love,

a ——Then no more remains,
But that, to your sufficiency, as your worth is able,
And let them work.]

Malone was perhaps right in suspecting some omission here; though the transposition of a single word will restore the passage to sense: we might read

——"Then no more remains,
But that, [*Tendering his Commission.*] to your sufficiency;
And, as your worth is able, let them work."

And given his deputation all the organs
Of our own power: what think you of it?
ESCAL. If any in Vienna be of worth
To undergo such ample grace and honour,
It is lord Angelo.
DUKE. Look where he comes.

Enter ANGELO.

ANG. Always obedient to your grace's will,
I come to know your pleasure.
DUKE. Angelo,
There is a kind of character in thy life,
That to the observer doth thy history
Fully unfold. Thyself and thy belongings
Are not thine own so proper, as to waste
Thyself upon thy virtues, them* on thee.
Heaven doth with us as we with torches do,
Not light them for themselves; for if our virtues
Did not go forth of us, 'twere all alike
As if we had them not. Spirits are not finely touch'd,
But to fine issues; nor nature never lends
The smallest scruple of her excellence,
But, like a thrifty goddess, she determines
Herself the glory of a creditor,
Both thanks and use.[a] But I do bend my speech
To one that can my part in him advértise:
Hold, therefore.—Angelo,
In our remove be thou at full ourself;
Mortality and mercy in Vienna
Live in thy tongue and heart: old Escalus,
Though first in question, is thy secondary:
Take thy commission. [*Giving it.*
ANG. Now, good my lord,
Let there be some more test made of my metal,
Before so noble and so great a figure
Be stamp'd upon it.
DUKE. No more evasion:
We have with a leaven'd and prepared choice
Proceeded to you; therefore take your honours.
Our haste from hence is of so quick condition,
That it prefers itself, and leaves unquestion'd
Matters of needful value. We shall write to you,
As time and our concernings shall importune,
How it goes with us; and do look to know
What doth befall you here. So, fare you well:
To the hopeful execution do I leave you
Of your commissions.
ANG. Yet, give leave, my lord,
That we may bring you something on the way.
DUKE. My haste may not admit it;
Nor need you, on mine honour, have to do
With any scruple: your scope is as mine own,
So to enforce or qualify the laws
As to your soul seems good. Give me your hand.
I'll privily away: I love the people,
But do not like to stage me to their eyes:
Though it do well, I do not relish well
Their loud applause, and *aves* vehement,
Nor do I think the man of safe discretion,
That does affect it. Once more, fare you well.
ANG. The heavens give safety to your purposes!
ESCAL. Lead forth, and bring you back in happiness!
DUKE. I thank you. Fare you well. [*Exit.*
ESCAL. I shall desire you, sir, to give me leave
To have free speech with you; and it concerns me
To look into the bottom of my place:
A power I have, but of what strength and nature
I am not yet instructed.
ANG. 'Tis so with me. Let us withdraw together,
And we may soon our satisfaction have
Touching that point.
ESCAL. I'll wait upon your honour.
[*Exeunt.*

SCENE II.—*A Street.*

Enter LUCIO *and two* Gentlemen.

LUCIO. If the duke, with the other dukes, come not to composition with the king of Hungary, why then, all the dukes fall upon the king.

1 GENT. Heaven grant us its peace, but not the king of Hungary's!

2 GENT. Amen.

LUCIO. Thou concludest like the sanctimonious pirate, that went to sea with the Ten Commandments, but scraped one out of the table.

2 GENT. *Thou shalt not steal?*

LUCIO. Ay, that he razed.

1 GENT. Why, 'twas a commandment to command the captain and all the rest from their functions: they put forth to steal. There 's not a soldier of us all, that, in the thanksgiving before meat, doth relish the petition well that prays for peace.

2 GENT. I never heard any soldier dislike it.

LUCIO. I believe thee; for I think thou never wast where grace was said.

2 GENT. No? a dozen times at least.

1 GENT. What, in metre?

LUCIO. In any proportion or in any language.

1 GENT. I think, or in any religion.

LUCIO. Ay, why not? Grace is grace, despite of all controversy: as for example,—thou thyself art a wicked villain, despite of all grace.

(*) Old text, *they*.

[a] Use.] *Use* formerly signified *interest of money.*

1 GENT. Well, there went but a pair of shears between us.[a]

LUCIO. I grant; as there may between the lists and the velvet: thou art the list.

1 GENT. And thou the velvet: thou art good velvet; thou'rt a three-piled piece, I warrant thee. I had as lief be a list of an English kersey, as be piled, as thou art piled, for a French velvet. Do I speak feelingly now?

LUCIO. I think thou dost; and, indeed, with most painful feeling of thy speech: I will out of thine own confession, learn to begin thy health; but, whilst I live, forget to drink after thee.

1 GENT. I think I have done myself wrong, have I not?

2 GENT. Yes, that thou hast, whether thou art tainted or free.

LUCIO. Behold, behold, where madam Mitigation comes!

1 GENT. I have purchased as many diseases under her roof, as come to—[b]

2 GENT. To what, I pray?

---

[a] There went but a pair of shears between us.] An early proverbial saying to the effect, that there was little difference between them; they were both of a piece. "The thanksgiving" to which the same speaker refers just before as distasteful to every soldier, because it prays for peace, appears to have been overlooked by all the commentators. It is found in ancient rituals in the very words of the text, "Heaven grant us its peace." And in a collection of devotions, entitled *Preces Privatæ*, published and established by the authority of Queen Elizabeth in 1564, the title directs that "the Acts of Thanksgiving in Eating shall always be concluded by these short prayers."—"Deus servet Ecclesiam—Regem vel Reginam custodiat—Consiliarios ejus regat—Populum universum tueatur—*et Pacem nobis donet perpetuam*. Amen."

[b] I have purchased, &c.] This, in the old copies, forms part of Lucio's speech, though it obviously belongs to the first Gentleman

LUCIO. Judge.

2 GENT. To three thousand dollars[a] a year.

1 GENT. Ay, and more.

LUCIO. A French crown more.

2 GENT. Thou art always figuring diseases in me; but thou art full of error,—I am sound.

LUCIO. Nay, not as one would say, healthy; but so sound as things that are hollow: thy bones are hollow; impiety has made a feast of thee.

Enter MISTRESS OVERDONE.

1 GENT. How now! which of your hips has the most profound sciatica?

MRS. OV. Well, well; there's one yonder arrested and carried to prison, was worth five thousand of you all.

2 GENT. Who's that, I pray thee?

MRS. OV. Marry, sir, that's Claudio; signior Claudio.

1 GENT. Claudio to prison! 't is not so.

MRS. OV. Nay, but I know, 'tis so: I saw him arrested; saw him carried away; and, which is more, within these three days his head to be chopped off.

LUCIO. But, after all this fooling, I would not have it so. Art thou sure of this?

MRS. OV. I am too sure of it; and it is for getting madam Julietta with child.

LUCIO. Believe me, this may be: he promised to meet me two hours since, and he was ever precise in promise-keeping.

2 GENT. Besides, you know, it draws something near to the speech we had to such a purpose.

1 GENT. But, most of all, agreeing with the proclamation.

LUCIO. Away! let's go learn the truth of it.

[*Exeunt* LUCIO *and* Gentlemen.

MRS. OV. Thus, what with the war, what with the sweat, what with the gallows, and what with poverty, I am custom-shrunk.

Enter POMPEY.(1)

How now! what's the news with you?

POM. Yonder man is carried to prison.

MRS. OV. Well; what has he done?

POM. A woman.

MRS. OV. But what's his offence?

POM. Groping for trouts in a peculiar river.

MRS. OV. What, is there a maid with child by him?

POM. No; but there's a woman with maid by him: you have not heard of the proclamation, have you?

MRS. OV. What proclamation, man?

POM. All houses in the suburbs[b] of Vienna must be plucked down.

MRS. OV. And what shall become of those in the city?

POM. They shall stand for seed: they had gone down too, but that a wise burgher put in for them.

MRS. OV. But shall all our houses of resort in the suburbs be pulled down?

POM. To the ground, mistress.

MRS. OV. Why, here's a change indeed in the commonwealth! What shall become of me?

POM. Come; fear not you: good counsellors lack no clients: though you change your place, you need not change your trade; I'll be your tapster still. Courage! there will be pity taken on you: you that have worn your eyes almost out in the service, you will be considered.

MRS. OV. What's to do here, Thomas Tapster? let's withdraw.

POM. Here comes signior Claudio, led by the provost to prison; and there's madam Juliet.

[*Exeunt.*

Enter Provost, CLAUDIO, JULIET, *and* Officers.[c]

CLAUD. Fellow, why dost thou show me thus
to the world?
Bear me to prison, where I am committed.

PROV. I do it not in evil disposition,
But from lord Angelo by special charge.

CLAUD. Thus can the demi-god Authority
Make us pay down for our offence by weight.—
The sword of heaven;[d] on whom it will, it will;
On whom it will not, so; yet still 'tis just.

Re-enter LUCIO *and* Gentlemen.

LUCIO. Why, how now, Claudio! whence comes this restraint?

CLAUD. From too much liberty, my Lucio,
liberty:

---

a *To three thousand dollars a year.*] The same sorry play on "dollar" and *dolour* occurs in "The Tempest," Act II. Sc. 1, and in "King Lear," Act II. Sc. 4.

b All houses in the suburbs, &c.] Some critics would read, "All *bawdy*-houses," &c., needlessly; for "*suburb* houses," like "*suburb* wenches," were all "in an ill name."

c Enter Provost, &c.] This is marked in the folio as a new scene, but wrongly, as there is no change of locality. In the same text, too, Lucio and the two Gentlemen are set down as if entering with the Provost, &c.; but this was only in accordance with the old stage practice of indicating at the beginning of a scene all the characters required to take part in it.

d The sword of heaven;] The old text reads,—"The *words* of heaven;" but Claudio is apparently contrasting the capriciousness of earthly punishments with the ever just award of Heaven. This ingenious and easy alteration was suggested by Dr. Roberts, of Eton.

As surfeit is the father of much fast,
So every scope by the immoderate use
Turns to restraint. Our natures do pursue,
Like rats that ravin down their proper bane,
A thirsty evil, and when we drink, we die.

LUCIO. If I could speak so wisely under an arrest, I would send for certain of my creditors: and yet, to say the truth, I had as lief have the foppery of freedom, as the morality* of imprisonment.—What's thy offence, Claudio?

CLAUD. What but to speak of would offend again.

LUCIO. What, is't murder?

CLAUD. No.

LUCIO. Lechery?

CLAUD. Call it so.

PROV. Away, sir! you must go.

CLAUD. One word, good friend.—Lucio, a word with you. [*Takes him aside.*

LUCIO. A hundred, if they'll do you any good.—Is lechery so looked after?

CLAUD. Thus stands it with me:—upon a true contráct,
I got possession of Julietta's bed:
You know the lady; she is fast my wife,
Save that we do the denunciation[a] lack
Of outward order: this we came not to,
Only for propagation of a dower
Remaining in the coffer of her friends,
From whom we thought it meet to hide our love
Till time had made them for us.(2) But it chances,
The stealth of our most mutual entertainment
With character too gross is writ on Juliet.

LUCIO. With child, perhaps?

CLAUD. Unhappily, even so.
And the new deputy now for the duke,—
Whether it be the fault and glimpse of newness,
Or whether that the body public be
A horse whereon the governor doth ride,
Who, newly in the seat, that it may know
He can command, lets it straight feel the spur;
Whether the tyranny be in his place,
Or in his eminence that fills it up,
I stagger in;—but this new governor
Awakes me all the enrolled penalties,
Which have, like unscour'd armour, hung by the wall
So long, that nineteen zodiacs have gone round,
And none of them been worn; and, for a name,
Now puts the drowsy and neglected act
Freshly on me:—'tis surely for a name.

LUCIO. I warrant it is; and thy head stands so tickle on thy shoulders, that a milk-maid, if she be in love, may sigh it off. Send after the duke, and appeal to him.

CLAUD. I have done so, but he's not to be found.
I pr'ythee, Lucio, do me this kind service:—
This day my sister should the cloister enter,
And there receive her approbation:
Acquaint her with the danger of my state;
Implore her, in my voice, that she make friends
To the strict deputy; bid herself assay him:
I have great hope in that; for in her youth
There is a prone[b] and speechless dialect,
Such as moves men; beside, she hath prosperous art
When she will play with reason and discourse,
And well she can persuade.

LUCIO. I pray she may: as well for the encouragement of the like, which else would stand under grievous imposition, as for the enjoying of thy life, who I would be sorry should be thus foolishly lost at a game of tick-tack. I'll to her.

CLAUD. I thank you, good friend Lucio.

LUCIO. Within two hours.

CLAUD. Come, officer; away!
[*Exeunt.*

SCENE III.—*A Monastery.*

Enter DUKE *and* FRIAR THOMAS.

DUKE. No, holy father; throw away that thought;
Believe not that the dribbling dart of Love
Can pierce a cómplete bosom. Why I desire thee
To give me secret harbour, hath a purpose
More grave and wrinkled than the aims and ends
Of burning youth.

FRI. T. May your grace speak of it?

DUKE. My holy sir, none better knows than you
How I have ever lov'd the life remov'd;
And held in idle price to haunt assemblies,

(*) Old text, *mortality*.

[a] *Save that we do the* denunciation *lack*, &c.] *Denunciation* here means neither more nor less than *annunciation* or *pronunciation*. In Todd's edition of Johnson's Dictionary, under *Denunciation*, an example is quoted from Hall's *Cases of Conscience*, which places this beyond question;—"This publick and reiterated *denunciation* of banns before matrimony," &c.

[b] —— *for in her youth*
There is a prone *and speechless dialect*, &c.]

The word *prone*, in the sixteenth century, bore more than one meaning, which it has now lost. In its primitive sense it signifies bending forward, and metaphorically—to be much inclined to certain actions or passions; but in the "Lucrece," as Malone observes, Shakespeare uses it as equivalent to ardent, headstrong, &c.:—

"O that *prone* lust should stain so pure a bed!"

and again in "Cymbeline,"—"I never saw any one so *prone*," &c. In the lines we are now considering, however, the poet has obviously intended it to imply a power of bending or inclining another by the exertion of a strong yet silent personal influence.

Where youth, and cost, and witless bravery keeps.[a]
I have deliver'd to lord Angelo—
A man of stricture and firm abstinence—
My absolute power and place here in Vienna,
And he supposes me travell'd to Poland;
For so I have strew'd it in the common ear,
And so it is receiv'd. Now, pious sir,
You will demand of me why I do this?

Fri. T. Gladly, my lord.

Duke. We have strict statutes and most biting laws,—
The needful bits and curbs to headstrong steeds,—*
Which for these fourteen years we have let sleep;†
Even like an o'ergrown lion in a cave,
That goes not out to prey. Now, as fond fathers,
Having bound up the threat'ning twigs of birch,
Only to stick it in their children's sight
For terror, not to use, in time the rod
Becomes[b] more mock'd, than fear'd; so our decrees,
Dead to infliction, to themselves are dead,
And liberty plucks justice by the nose;
The baby beats the nurse, and quite athwart
Goes all decorum.

Fri. T. It rested in your grace
To unloose this tied-up justice when you pleas'd;
And it in you more dreadful would have seem'd,
Than in lord Angelo.

Duke. I do fear, too dreadful:
Sith 't was my fault to give the people scope,
'T would be my tyranny to strike and gall them
For what I bid them do: for we bid this be done,
When evil deeds have their permissive pass,
And not the punishment. Therefore, indeed, my father,
I have on Angelo impos'd the office;
Who may, in the ambush of my name, strike home,
And yet my nature never in the fight,
To do in slander.[c] And to behold his sway,
I will, as 't were a brother of your order,
Visit both prince and people: therefore, I pr'ythee,
Supply me with the habit, and instruct me
How I may formally in person bear

(*) Old text, *weedes*. (†) Old text, *slip*.

a Where . . . *and* witless bravery keeps.] That is, *where senseless ostentation dwells*. *And* is added from the second folio.

b Becomes—] The old text reads,—

"—— in time the rod
More mock'd, than fear'd."

For *becomes* we are indebted to Pope, who probably derived it from the corresponding passage in Davenant's "Law against Lovers," a piece made up from "Measure for Measure" and "Much Ado about Nothing,"—

"Till it in time *become* more," &c.

c Who may, in the ambush of my name, strike home,
And yet my nature never in the fight,
To do in slander.]

So the old text, corruptly without doubt. Hanmer attempted to obtain sense by reading,—

"Never in the *sight*,
To do *it* slander."

We should prefer,—

"And yet my nature never *win* the fight
To *die* in slander."

Like a true friar. More* reasons for this action,
At our more leisure shall I render you;
Only, this one:—lord Angelo is precise;
Stands at a guard with envy; scarce confesses
That his blood flows, or that his appetite
Is more to bread than stone: hence shall we see,
If power change purpose, what our seemers be.
[*Exeunt.*

SCENE IV.—*A Nunnery.*

Enter ISABELLA *and* FRANCISCA.

ISAB. And have you nuns no farther privileges?
FRAN. Are not these large enough?
ISAB. Yes, truly; I speak not as desiring more,
But rather wishing a more strict restraint
Upon the sisterhood, the votarists of Saint Clare.
LUCIO. [*Without.*] Ho! peace be in this place!
ISAB. Who's that which calls?
FRAN. It is a man's voice. Gentle Isabella,
Turn you the key, and know his business of him;
You may, I may not; you are yet unsworn.
When you have vow'd, you must not speak with men,
But in the presence of the prioress:
Then, if you speak, you must not show your face;
Or, if you show your face, you must not speak.
He calls again; I pray you, answer him. [*Exit.*
ISAB. Peace and prosperity! Who is't that calls?

Enter LUCIO.

LUCIO. Hail, virgin, if you be,—as those cheek-roses
Proclaim you are no less! Can you so stead me,
As bring me to the sight of Isabella,
A novice of this place, and the fair sister
To her unhappy brother Claudio?
ISAB. Why her *unhappy* brother? let me ask;
The rather, for I now must make you know
I am that Isabella and his sister.
LUCIO. Gentle and fair, your brother kindly greets you.
Not to be weary with you, he's in prison.
ISAB. Woe me! for what?
LUCIO. For that which, if myself might be his judge,
He should receive his punishment in thanks:
He hath got his friend with child.
ISAB. Sir, make me not your story.[a]
LUCIO. 'Tis true. I would not—though 'tis my familiar sin

(*) Old text, *Moe.*

[a] *Sir, make me not your story.*] Davenant in his play, "A Law against Lovers," reads here *scorne* for *story*, and Mr. Collier's annotator adopts the same alteration. We retain the old lection, not for the reason assigned by Steevens, that *make me*, according to a common mode of phraseology in the poet's day, might mean, "*invent not* your story," but because *story* may without much licence be used to signify *jest* or *laughing-stock*.

With maids to seem the lapwing, and to jest,
Tongue far from heart—play with all virgins so:
I hold you as a thing enskied and sainted;
By your renouncement, an immortal spirit;
And to be talk'd with in sincerity,
As with a saint.

ISAB. You do blaspheme the good in mocking me.

LUCIO. Do not believe it. Fewness and truth,[a] 'tis thus:—
Your brother and his lover have embrac'd:
As those that feed grow full; as blossoming time,
That from the seedness the bare fallow brings
To teeming foison,[b] even so her plenteous womb
Expresseth his full tilth and husbandry.

ISAB. Some one with child by him!—My cousin Juliet?

LUCIO. Is she your cousin?

ISAB. Adoptedly; as school-maids change their names
By vain, though apt, affection.

LUCIO. She it is.

ISAB. O, let him marry her!

LUCIO. This is the point.
The duke is very strangely gone from hence,
Bore many gentlemen, myself being one,
In hand, and hope of action; but we do learn,
By those that know the very nerves of state,
His givings-out* were of an infinite distance
From his true-meant design. Upon his place,
And with full line of his authority,
Governs lord Angelo; a man whose blood
Is very snow-broth; one who never feels
The wanton stings and motions of the sense,
But doth rebate and blunt his natural edge
With profits of the mind, study and fast.
He—to give fear to use and liberty,
Which have for long run by the hideous law,
As mice by lions—hath pick'd out an act,
Under whose heavy sense your brother's life
Falls into forfeit: he arrests him on it,
And follows close the rigour of the statute,
To make him an example. All hope is gone,
Unless you have the grace by your fair prayer
To soften Angelo; and that's my pith of business
'Twixt you and your poor brother.

ISAB. Doth he so seek his life?

LUCIO. Has censur'd him[c] already:
And, as I hear, the provost hath a warrant
For his execution.

ISAB. Alas! what poor ability 's in me
To do him good?

LUCIO. Assay the power you have.

ISAB. My power! Alas, I doubt,—

LUCIO. Our doubts are traitors,
And make us lose the good we oft might win,
By fearing to attempt. Go to lord Angelo,
And let him learn to know, when maidens sue,
Men give like gods; but when they weep and kneel,
All their petitions are as freely theirs
As they themselves would owe[d] them.

ISAB. I'll see what I can do.

LUCIO. But speedily.

ISAB. I will about it straight;
No longer staying but to give the mother
Notice of my affair. I humbly thank you:
Commend me to my brother; soon at night
I'll send him certain word of my success.

LUCIO. I take my leave of you.

ISAB. Good sir, adieu.
[*Exeunt severally.*

(*) Old text, *giving out.*

a Fewness and truth,—] That is, in few words and true.

b Foison,—] *Foison,* as signifying *plenty, abundance,* was used metaphorically for *Autumn.*

c Censur'd him—] Pronounced judgment on him. Judged him.

d *Would* owe *them.*] That is, would *have* or *possess* them.

ACT II.

SCENE I.—*A Hall in* Angelo's *House.*

Enter ANGELO, ESCALUS, *a* Justice, Provost, Officers, *and other* Attendants.

ANG. We must not make a scare-crow of the law,
Setting it up to fear the birds of prey,
And let it keep one shape, till custom make it
Their perch, and not their terror.

ESCAL. Ay, but yet
Let us be keen, and rather cut a little, [man,
Than fall, and bruise to death. Alas, this gentle-
Whom I would save, had a most noble father!

Let but your honour know,—
Whom I believe to be most straight in virtue,—
That, in the working of your own affections,
Had time coher'd with place or place with wishing,
Or that the resolute acting of your* blood
Could have attain'd the effect of your own purpose,
Whether you had not some time in your life,
Err'd in this point which now you censure him,[a]
And pull'd the law upon you.

ANG. 'T is one thing to be tempted, Escalus,
Another thing to fall. I not deny,
The jury, passing on the prisoner's life,
May in the sworn twelve have a thief or two
Guiltier than him they try. What 's open made to justice,
That justice seizes: what know the laws,
That thieves do pass on[b] thieves? 'T is very pregnant,
The jewel that we find, we stoop and take 't,
Because we see it; but what we do not see
We tread upon, and never think of it.
You may not so extenuate his offence
For[c] I have had such faults; but rather tell me
When I, that censure him, do so offend,
Let mine own judgment pattern out my death,
And nothing come in partial. Sir, he must die.

ESCAL. Be it as your wisdom will.

ANG. Where is the provost?

PROV. Here, if it like your honour.

ANG. See that Claudio
Be executed by nine to-morrow morning:
Bring him his confessor, let him be prepar'd,
For that's the utmost of his pilgrimage.
[*Exit* Provost.

ESCAL. Well, heaven forgive him! and forgive us all!
Some rise by sin, and some by virtue fall:
Some run from brakes of vice,[d] and answer none;
And some condemned for a fault alone.

Enter ELBOW *and* Officers, *with* FROTH *and* POMPEY.

ELB. Come, bring them away: if these be good people in a common-weal that do nothing but use their abuses in common houses, I know no law: bring them away.

ANG. How now, sir! What's your name? and what's the matter?

ELB. If it please your honour, I am the poor duke's constable, and my name is Elbow; I do lean upon justice, sir, and do bring in here before your good honour two notorious benefactors.

ANG. Benefactors! Well; what benefactors are they? are they not malefactors?

ELB. If it please your honour, I know not well what they are; but precise villains they are, that I am sure of, and void of all profanation in the world that good Christians ought to have.

ESCAL. This comes off well: here's a wise officer.

ANG. Go to:—what quality are they of? Elbow is your name? why dost thou not speak, Elbow?

POM. He cannot, sir: he's out at elbow.

ANG. What are you, sir?

ELB. He, sir! a tapster, sir; parcel-bawd; one that serves a bad woman, whose house, sir, was, as they say, plucked down in the suburbs; and now she professes a hot-house, which, I think, is a very ill house too.

ESCAL. How know you that?

ELB. My wife, sir, whom I detest before heaven and your honour,—

ESCAL. How! thy wife?

ELB. Ay, sir;—whom, I thank heaven, is an honest woman,—

ESCAL. Dost thou detest her therefore?

ELB. I say, sir, I will detest myself also, as well as she, that this house, if it be not a bawd's house, it is pity of her life, for it is a naughty house.

ESCAL. How dost thou know that, constable?

ELB. Marry, sir, by my wife; who, if she had been a woman cardinally given, might have been accused in fornication, adultery, and all uncleanliness there.

ESCAL. By the woman's means?

ELB. Ay, sir, by mistress Overdone's means; but as she spit in his face, so she defied him.

POM. Sir, if it please your honour, this is not so.

ELB. Prove it before these varlets here, thou honourable man; prove it.

ESCAL. [*To* ANGELO.] Do you hear how he misplaces?

POM. Sir, she came in great with child, and longing—saving your honour's reverence—for stewed prunes:—sir, we had but two in the house, which at that very distant time stood, as it were,

(*) Old text, *our*.

a Which now you censure him,—] Here *for* must be understood:—"*for* which now you censure him."

b Pass on—] As Malone observes, *To pass on* is a forensic term; it occurs again in "King Lear," Act II. Sc. 7:—

"Though well we may not *pass upon* his life
Without the form of justice."

c For—] That is, *Because*.

d *Some run from brakes of* vice,—] The old text has, "brakes of *Ice*:" *vice* is an emendation of Rowe. If this be the true word, the allusion may be either to the instrument of torture termed a "brake;" or by "*brakes* of vice" may be meant, as Steevens conjectured, a number, a *thicket* of vices. It is by no means certain, however, that we have yet got either the poet's expression or meaning in this difficult passage.

in a fruit-dish, a dish of some three-pence,—your honours have seen such dishes; they are not China dishes, but very good dishes,—

ESCAL. Go to, go to: no matter for the dish, sir.

POM. No, indeed, sir, not of a pin; you are therein in the right;—but to the point. As I say, this mistress Elbow, being, as I say, with child, and being great bellied, and longing, as I said, for prunes, and having but two in the dish, as I said, master Froth here, this very man, having eaten the rest, as I said, and, as I say, paying for them very honestly;—for, as you know, master Froth, I could not give you three-pence again,—

FROTH. No, indeed.

POM. Very well;—you being then, if you be remembered, cracking the stones of the foresaid prunes,—

FROTH. Ay, so I did indeed.

POM. Why very well;—I telling you then, if you be remembered, that such a one and such a one, were past cure of the thing you wot of, unless they kept very good diet, as I told you,—

FROTH. All this is true.

POM. Why, very well then,—

ESCAL. Come, you are a tedious fool: to the purpose.—What was done to Elbow's wife, that he hath cause to complain of? Come me to what was done to her.

POM. Sir, your honour cannot come to that yet.

ESCAL. No, sir, nor I mean it not.

POM. Sir, but you shall come to it, by your honour's leave. And, I beseech you, look into master Froth here, sir; a man of fourscore pound a year, whose father died at Hallowmas:—was't not at Hallowmas, master Froth?

FROTH. All-hallownd eve.

POM. Why, very well; I hope here be truths. He, sir, sitting, as I say, in a lower chair, sir;—'twas in the Bunch of Grapes, where, indeed, you have a delight to sit, have you not?—

FROTH. I have so: because it is an open room, and good for winter.[a]

POM. Why, very well, then: I hope here be truths.

ANG. This will last out a night in Russia,
When nights are longest there: I'll take my leave,
And leave you to the hearing of the cause;
Hoping you'll find good cause to whip them all.

ESCAL. I think no less; good morrow to your lordship. [*Exit* ANGELO.
Now, sir, come on: what was done to Elbow's wife, once more?

POM. *Once*, sir! there was nothing done to her once.

ELB. I beseech you, sir, ask him what this man did to my wife.

POM. I beseech your honour, ask me.

ESCAL. Well, sir, what did this gentleman to her?

POM. I beseech you, sir, look in this gentleman's face.—Good master Froth, look upon his honour; 'tis for a good purpose.—Doth your honour mark his face?

ESCAL. Ay, sir, very well.

POM. Nay, I beseech you, mark it well.

ESCAL. Well, I do so.

POM. Doth your honour see any harm in his face?

ESCAL. Why, no.

POM. I'll be supposed upon a book, his face is the worst thing about him. Good, then; if his face be the worst thing about him, how could master Froth do the constable's wife any harm? I would know that of your honour.

ESCAL. He's in the right.—Constable, what say you to it?

ELB. First, an it like you, the house is a respected house; next, this is a respected fellow; and his mistress is a respected woman.

POM. By this hand, sir, his wife is a more respected person than any of us all.

ELB. Varlet, thou liest! thou liest, wicked varlet! the time is yet to come that she was ever respected with man, woman, or child.

POM. Sir, she was respected with him before he married with her.

ESCAL. Which is the wiser here? Justice, or Iniquity?[b]—Is this true?

ELB. O thou caitiff! O thou varlet! O thou wicked Hannibal! I respected with her before I was married to her!—If ever I was respected with her, or she with me, let not your worship think me the poor duke's officer.—Prove this, thou wicked Hannibal, or I'll have mine action of battery on thee.

ESCAL. If he took you a box o' the ear, you might have your action of slander too.

ELB. Marry, I thank your good worship for it. What is't your worship's pleasure I shall do with this wicked caitiff?

ESCAL. Truly, officer, because he hath some offences in him that thou wouldst discover if thou couldst, let him continue in his courses till thou knowest what they are.

ELB. Marry, I thank your worship for it.—Thou seest, thou wicked varlet, now, what's come upon thee: thou art to *continue* now, thou varlet; thou art to *continue*.

ESCAL. [*To* FROTH.] Where were you born, friend?

---

a An open room, and good for winter.] Master Froth may have been intended to blunder, otherwise we should have suspected *for* was a misprint.

b Justice, or Iniquity?] *Justice* and *Iniquity* were characters in the old Moralities.

FROTH. Here in Vienna, sir.

ESCAL. Are you of fourscore pounds a year?

FROTH. Yes, an't please you, sir.

ESCAL. So.—[*To* POMPEY.] What trade are you of, sir?

POM. A tapster; a poor widow's tapster.

ESCAL. Your mistress' name?

POM. Mistress Overdone.

ESCAL. Hath she had any more than one husband?

POM. Nine, sir; Overdone by the last.

ESCAL. Nine!—Come hither to me, master Froth. Master Froth, I would not have you acquainted with tapsters: they will draw you, master Froth, and you will hang them: get you gone, and let me hear no more of you.

FROTH. I thank your worship. For mine own part, I never come into any room in a taphouse, but I am drawn in.

ESCAL. Well, no more of it, master Froth: farewell. [*Exit* FROTH.]—Come you hither to me, master tapster. What's your name, master tapster?

POM. Pompey.

ESCAL. What else?

POM. Bum, sir.

ESCAL. Troth, and your bum is the greatest thing about you; so that, in the beastliest sense, you are Pompey the Great. Pompey, you are partly a bawd, Pompey, howsoever you colour it in being a tapster: are you not? come, tell me true: it shall be the better for you.

POM. Truly, sir, I am a poor fellow that would live.

ESCAL. How would you live, Pompey? by being a bawd? What do you think of the trade, Pompey? is it a lawful trade?

POM. If the law would allow it, sir.

ESCAL. But the law will not allow it, Pompey; nor it shall not be allowed in Vienna.

POM. Does your worship mean to geld and splay all the youth of the city?

ESCAL. No, Pompey.

POM. Truly, sir, in my poor opinion, they will to't then. If your worship will take order for the drabs and the knaves, you need not to fear the bawds.

ESCAL. There are pretty orders beginning, I can tell you: it is but heading and hanging.

POM. If you head and hang all that offend that way but for ten year together, you'll be glad to give out a commission for more heads: if this law hold in Vienna ten year, I'll rent the fairest house in it after threepence a bay:[a] if you live to see this come to pass, say Pompey told you so.

ESCAL. Thank you, good Pompey; and, in requital of your prophecy, hark you:—I advise you, let me not find you before me again upon any complaint whatsoever; no, not for dwelling where you do: if I do, Pompey, I shall beat you to your tent, and prove a shrewd Cæsar to you; in plain dealing, Pompey, I shall have you whipped: so, for this time, Pompey, fare you well.

POM. I thank your worship for your good counsel; [*Aside.*] but I shall follow it, as the flesh and fortune shall better determine.
Whip me! No, no; let carman whip his jade;
The valiant heart's not whipt out of his trade. [*Exit.*

ESCAL. Come hither to me, master Elbow; come hither, master constable. How long have you been in this place of constable?

ELB. Seven year and a half, sir.

ESCAL. I thought, by your* readiness in the office, you had continued in it some time; you say, seven years together?

ELB. And a half, sir.

ESCAL. Alas, it hath been great pains to you! They do you wrong to put you so oft upon't: are there not men in your ward sufficient to serve it?

ELB. Faith, sir, few of any wit in such matters: as they are chosen, they are glad to choose me for them: I do it for some piece of money, and go through with all.

ESCAL. Look you bring me in the names of some six or seven, the most sufficient of your parish.

ELB. To your worship's house, sir?

ESCAL. To my house; fare you well. [*Exit* ELBOW.
What's o'clock, think you?

JUST. Eleven, sir.

ESCAL. I pray you home to dinner with me.

JUST. I humbly thank you.

ESCAL. It grieves me for the death of Claudio;
But there's no remedy.

JUST. Lord Angelo is severe.

ESCAL. It is but needful:
Mercy is not itself, that oft looks so;
Pardon is still the nurse of second woe:
But yet,—poor Claudio!—There is no remedy.—
Come, sir. [*Exeunt.*

SCENE II.—*Another Room in the same.*

Enter Provost *and a* Servant.

SERV. He's hearing of a cause; he will come straight:
I'll tell him of you.

---

[a] *Threepence* a bay:] Pope and Mr. Collier's annotator read,—"threepence *a day;*" but "a bay of building," which Coles in his Dictionary explains—*mensura viginti quatuor pedum*—was a common expression in reference to the measurement of a building's frontage. Pompey means he would rent the best house in the city after the rate of threepence for every twenty-four feet of frontage.

(*) Old text, *the.*

PROV. Pray you, do. [*Exit* Servant.] I'll know
His pleasure; may be he will relent. Alas,
He hath but as offended in a dream!
All sects, all ages smack of this vice; and he
To die for it!—

Enter ANGELO.

ANG. Now, what's the matter, provost?
PROV. Is it your will Claudio shall die to-morrow?
ANG. Did not I tell thee yea? hadst thou not order?
Why dost thou ask again?
PROV. Lest I might be too rash:
Under your good correction, I have seen,
When, after execution, judgment hath
Repented o'er his doom.
ANG. Go to; let that be mine:
Do you your office, or give up your place,
And you shall well be spar'd.
PROV. I crave your honour's pardon.—
What shall be done, sir, with the groaning Juliet?
She's very near her hour.
ANG. Dispose of her
To some more fitter place, and that with speed.

Re-enter Servant.

SERV. Here is the sister of the man condemn'd
Desires access to you.
ANG. Hath he a sister?
PROV. Ay, my good lord; a very virtuous maid,
And to be shortly of a sisterhood,
If not already.
ANG. Well, let her be admitted. [*Exit* Servant.
See you the fornicatress be remov'd:
Let her have needful, but not lavish, means;
There shall be order for it.

Enter ISABELLA *and* LUCIO.

PROV. Save your honour! [*Offering to retire.*
ANG. Stay a little while.—[*To* ISAB.] You're welcome: what's your will?
ISAB. I am a woeful suitor to your honour,
Please but your honour hear me.
ANG. Well; what's your suit?
ISAB. There is a vice that most I do abhor,
And most desire should meet the blow of justice;
For which I would not plead, but that I must;
For which I must not plead, but that I am
At war 'twixt will and will not.
ANG. Well; the matter?
ISAB. I have a brother is condemn'd to die:
I do beseech you, let it be his fault,
And not my brother.
PROV. [*Aside.*] Heaven give thee moving graces!
ANG. Condemn the fault, and not the actor of it?
Why, every fault's condemn'd ere it be done:
Mine were the very cipher of a function,
To fine the fault,* whose fine stands in record,
And let go by the actor.
ISAB. O just but severe law!
I had a brother, then.—Heaven keep your honour! [*Retiring.*
LUCIO. [*Aside to* ISAB.] Give't not o'er so: to him again, entreat him;
Kneel down before him, hang upon his gown:
You are too cold; if you should need a pin,
You could not with more tame a tongue desire it:
To him, I say.
ISAB. Must he needs die?
ANG. Maiden, no remedy.
ISAB. Yes; I do think that you might pardon him,
And neither heaven nor man grieve at the mercy.
ANG. I will not do't.
ISAB. But can you, if you would?
ANG. Look, what I will not, that I cannot do.
ISAB. But might you do't, and do the world no wrong,
If so your heart were touch'd with that remorse
As mine is to him?
ANG. He's sentenc'd: 'tis too late.
LUCIO. [*Aside to* ISAB.] You are too cold.
ISAB. Too late! why, no; I, that do speak a word,
May call it back[a] again. Well believe this,
No ceremony that to great ones 'longs,
Not the king's crown nor the deputed sword,
The marshal's truncheon nor the judge's robe,
Become them with one half so good a grace
As mercy does. If he had been as you, and you as he,
You would have slipp'd like him; but he, like you
Would not have been so stern.
ANG. Pray you, begone.
ISAB. I would to heaven I had your potency,
And you were Isabel! should it then be thus?
No; I would tell what 'twere to be a judge,
And what a prisoner.
LUCIO. [*Aside to* ISAB.] Ay, touch him; there's the vein.
ANG. Your brother is a forfeit of the law,
And you but waste your words.
ISAB. Alas! alas!
Why, all the souls that were were forfeit once;
And He that might the vantage best have took,
Found out the remedy. How would you be,

---

[a] *May call it back again.*] The word *back*, perhaps accidentally omitted in the folio 1623, was inserted by the editor of the second folio.

(*) Old text, *faults*.

If He, which is the top of judgment,[a] should
But judge you as you are? O, think on that,
And mercy then will breathe within your lips,
Like man new made!

ANG. Be you content, fair maid,
It is the law, not I, condemns* your brother:
Were he my kinsman, brother, or my son,
It should be thus with him:—he must die to-morrow.

ISAB. To-morrow! O, that's sudden! Spare him, spare him!—
He's not prepar'd for death. Even for our kitchens
We kill the fowl of season: shall we serve heaven
With less respect than we do minister
To our gross selves? Good, good my lord, bethink [you:
Who is it that hath died for this offence?
There's many have committed it.

LUCIO. [*Aside.*] Ay, well said.

ANG. The law hath not been dead, though it hath slept:
Those many had not dar'd to do that evil,
If the first that did the edict infringe,
Had answer'd for his deed: now 'tis awake;
Takes note of what is done, and, like a prophet,
Looks in a glass, that shows what future evils
(Either new,* or by remissness new-conceiv'd,
And so in progress to be hatch'd and born,)
Are now to have no súccessive degrees,
But ere† they live to end.

ISAB. Yet show some pity.

ANG. I show it most of all when I show justice;
For then I pity those I do not know,
Which a dismiss'd offence would after gall;
And do him right that, answering one foul wrong,
Lives not to act another. Be satisfied;
Your brother die to-morrow: be content;

(*) First folio, *condemne*.

(*) Old text, *now*. (†) Old text, *here*.

a *The* top of judgment,—] Mr. Dyce, in illustration of this expression, aptly quotes the following line from Dante's *Purgatorio*, c. VI. 28:—
"Chè *cima di giudicio* non s'avvalla," &c.

ISAB. So you must be the first that gives this sentence,
And he that suffers. O, it is excellent
To have a giant's strength; but it is tyrannous
To use it like a giant!

LUCIO. [*Aside to* ISAB.] That's well said.

ISAB. Could great men thunder
As Jove himself does, Jove would ne'er be quiet,
For every pelting, petty officer
Would use his heaven for thunder;
Nothing but thunder.—Merciful heaven!
Thou rather with thy sharp and sulphurous bolt
Splitt'st the unwedgeable and gnarled oak,
Than the soft myrtle; but man, proud man!
Dress'd in a little brief authority,—
Most ignorant of what he's most assur'd,
His glassy essence,—like an angry ape,
Plays such fantastic tricks before high heaven,
As make the angels weep; who, with our spleens,
Would all themselves laugh mortal.

LUCIO. [*Aside to* ISAB.] O, to him, to him, wench! he will relent:
He's coming; I perceive't.

PROV. [*Aside.*] Pray heaven she win him!

ISAB. We cannot weigh our brother with ourself:[a]
Great men may jest with saints; 'tis wit in them,
But in the less foul profanation.

LUCIO. [*Aside to* ISAB.] Thou'rt i' the right, girl; more o' that.

ISAB. That in the captain's but a choleric word,
Which in the soldier is flat blasphemy.

LUCIO. [*Aside to* ISAB.] Art avis'd o' that? more on't.

ANG. Why do you put these sayings upon me?

ISAB. Because authority, though it err like others,
Hath yet a kind of med'cine in itself,
That skins the vice o' the top. Go to your bosom;
Knock there, and ask your heart what it doth know
That's like my brother's fault: if it confess
A natural guiltiness such as is his,
Let it not sound a thought upon your tongue
Against my brother's life.

ANG. [*Aside.*] She speaks, and 'tis such sense,
That my sense breeds with it. [*To* ISAB.] Fare you well.

ISAB. Gentle my lord, turn back.

ANG. I will bethink me:—come again to-morrow. [turn back.

ISAB. Hark, how I'll bribe you: good my lord,

ANG. How! bribe me!

ISAB. Ay, with such gifts, that heaven shall share with you.

LUCIO. [*Aside.*] You had marr'd all else.

ISAB. Not with fond shekels* of the tested gold,
Or stones, whose rates are either rich or poor
As fancy values them; but with true prayers,
That shall be up at heaven, and enter there
Ere sunrise,—prayers from preserved souls,
From fasting maids, whose minds are dedicate
To nothing temporal.

ANG. Well; come to me to-morrow.

LUCIO. [*Aside to* ISAB.] Go to; 'tis well: away!

ISAB. Heaven keep your honour safe!

ANG. [*Aside.*] Amen:
For I am that way going to temptation,
Where prayers cross.[b]

ISAB. At what hour to-morrow
Shall I attend your lordship?

ANG. At any time 'fore noon.

ISAB. Save your honour!

[*Exeunt* ISABELLA, LUCIO, *and* Provost.

ANG. From thee,—even from thy virtue!—
What's this? what's this? Is this her fault or mine?
The tempter or the tempted, who sins most, ha?
Not she; nor doth she tempt; but it is I
That, lying by the violet in the sun,
Do, as the carrion does, not as the flower,
Corrupt with virtuous season. Can it be
That modesty may more betray our sense
Than woman's lightness? Having waste ground enough,
Shall we desire to raze the sanctuary,
And pitch our evils there?[c] O, fie, fie, fie!
What dost thou, or what art thou, Angelo?
Dost thou desire her foully for those things
That make her good? O, let her brother live!
Thieves for their robbery have authority,
When judges steal themselves. What, do I love her,
That I desire to hear her speak again,
And feast upon her eyes? What is't I dream on?
O cunning enemy, that, to catch a saint,
With saints dost bait thy hook! Most dangerous
Is that temptation that doth goad us on
To sin in loving virtue; never could the strumpet,
With all her double vigour, art and nature,
Once stir my temper; but this virtuous maid
Subdues me quite: ever, till now,
When men were fond, I smil'd, and wonder'd how.

[*Exit.*

---

[a] *We cannot weigh our brother with* ourself:] Warburton, perhaps rightly, reads *yourself*.

[b] For I am that way going to temptation,
Where prayers cross.]
The following is Henley's interpretation of this somewhat obscure passage:—"The petition of the Lord's Prayer—'lead us not into temptation'—is here considered as crossing or intercepting the onward way in which Angelo was going; this appointment of his for the morrow's meeting being a premeditated exposure of himself to temptation, which it was the general object of prayer to thwart."

(*) Old text, *sickles*.

[c] Shall we desire to raze the sanctuary,
And pitch our evils there?]
"The desecration of edifices devoted to religion, by converting them to the most abject purposes of nature, was an Eastern method of expressing contempt."—HENLEY. So in 2 Kings, ch. x. v. 27:—"And they brake down the image of Baal, and brake down the house of Baal, and made it a draught house unto this day;" or, as the Douay version of 1609 reads,—"and made a jakes in its place unto this day."

SCENE III.—*A Room in a Prison.*

Enter, severally, DUKE, *disguised as a Friar, and* PROVOST.

DUKE. Hail to you, provost! so I think you are.
PROV. I am the provost. What's your will, good friar?
DUKE. Bound by my charity, and my blessed order,
I come to visit the afflicted spirits
Here in the prison: do me the common right
To let me see them, and to make me know
The nature of their crimes, that I may minister
To them accordingly.
PROV. I would do more than that, if more were needful.
Look; here comes one,—a gentlewoman of mine,
Who, falling in the flames[a] of her own youth,
Hath blister'd her report; she is with child,
And he that got it, sentenc'd—a young man
More fit to do another such offence,
Than die for this.

Enter JULIET.

DUKE. When must he die?
PROV. As I do think, to-morrow.—
[*To* JULIET.] I have provided for you: stay a while,
And you shall be conducted.
DUKE. Repent you, fair one, of the sin you carry?
JULIET. I do, and bear the shame most patiently.
DUKE. I'll teach you how you shall arraign your conscience,
And try your penitence, if it be sound,
Or hollowly put on.
JULIET. I'll gladly learn.
DUKE. Love you the man that wrong'd you?
JULIET. Yes, as I love the woman that wrong'd him.
DUKE. So, then, it seems, your most offenceful act
Was mutually committed?
JULIET. Mutually.
DUKE. Then was your sin of heavier kind than his.
JULIET. I do confess it, and repent it, father.
DUKE. 'Tis meet so, daughter: but lest you do repent,
As that the sin hath brought you to this shame,—
Which sorrow is always toward ourselves, not heaven,
Showing we would not spare heaven,[b] as we love it,
But as we stand in fear,—
JULIET. I do repent me, as it is an evil,
And take the shame with joy.
DUKE. There rest.

[a] *Who, falling in the* flames *of her own youth,*
Hath blister'd her report.]
The old text, which reads *flawes*, was first corrected by Davenant, in his "Law against Lovers."

[b] *Showing we would not* spare *heaven,*—] This suspicious expression Capell interprets.—"spare to *offend* heaven." Mr. Collier's annotator, with more plausibility, changes it to "*serve* heaven," &c.

Your partner, as I hear, must die to-morrow,
And I am going with instruction to him.
Grace go with you![a] *Benedicite!* [*Exit.*

JULIET. *Must die to-morrow!* O, injurious love,[b]
That respites me a life, whose very comfort
Is still a dying horror!

PROV. 'T is pity of him. [*Exeunt.*

SCENE IV.—*A Room in* Angelo's *House.*

Enter ANGELO.

ANG. When I would pray and think, I think and pray
To several subjects: heaven hath my empty words,
Whilst my invention,[c] hearing not my tongue,
Anchors on Isabel. Heaven in my mouth,
As if I did but only chew his name,
And in my heart the strong and swelling evil
Of my conception. The state, whereon I studied,
Is like a good thing, being often read,
Grown sear'd* and tedious; yea, my gravity,
Wherein—let no man hear me—I take pride,
Could I, with boot, change for an idle plume,
Which the air beats for vain. O place! O form!
How often dost thou with thy case, thy habit,
Wrench awe from fools, and tie the wiser souls
To thy false seeming! Blood, thou art blood:
Let's write good angel on the devil's horn,
'T is not the devil's crest.

Enter Servant.

How now! who's there?

SERV. One Isabel, a sister,
Desires access to you.

ANG. Teach her the way. [*Exit* SERV.] O heavens!
Why does my blood thus muster to my heart,
Making both it unable for itself,
And dispossessing all my other parts
Of necessary fitness?
So play the foolish throngs with one that swoons;
Come all to help him, and so stop the air
By which he should revive: and even so
The general,[d] subject to a well-wish'd king,
Quit their own part, and in obsequious fondness
Crowd to his presence, where their untaught love
Must needs appear offence.

Enter ISABELLA.

How now, fair maid?

ISAB. I am come to know your pleasure.

ANG. That you might know it, would much better please me,
Than to demand what 't is. Your brother cannot live.

ISAB. Even so.—Heaven keep your honour! [*Retiring.*

ANG. Yet may he live a while; and, it may be,
As long as you or I: yet he must die.

ISAB. Under your sentence?

ANG. Yea.

ISAB. When, I beseech you? that in his reprieve,
Longer or shorter, he may be so fitted,
That his soul sicken not.

ANG. Ha! fie, these filthy vices! It were as good
To pardon him that hath from nature stol'n
A man already made, as to remit
Their saucy sweetness, that do coin heaven's image
In stamps that are forbid: 't is all as easy
Falsely to take away a life true made,
As to put metal in restrained means,
To make a false one.

ISAB. 'T is set down so in heaven, but not in earth.

ANG. Say you so? then I shall pose you quickly.
Which had you rather,—that the most just law
Now took your brother's life, or,* to redeem him,
Give up your body to such sweet uncleanness
As she that he hath stain'd?

ISAB. Sir, believe this,
I had rather give my body than my soul.

ANG. I talk not of your soul: our compell'd sins
Stand more for number than for accompt.

ISAB. How say you?

ANG. Nay, I'll not warrant that; for I can speak
Against the thing I say. Answer to this:—
I, now the voice of the recorded law,
Pronounce a sentence on your brother's life:
Might there not be a charity in sin,
To save this brother's life?

ISAB. Please you to do't,
I'll take it as a peril to my soul,
It is no sin at all, but charity.

ANG. Pleas'd you to do't, at peril of your soul,
Were equal poise of sin and charity.

ISAB. That I do beg his life, if it be sin,

(*) Old text, *eard.*

(*) Old text, *and.*

[a] Grace go with you!] A benediction Ritson proposed to give to Juliet; regulating the dialogue thus,—

"JUL. Grace go with you!
DUKE. *Benedicite!*"

[b] *O, injurious love,*—] Hanmer reads.—"injurious *law.*" but *love* in this place appears to mean, *kindness*, or *mercy*, and need not be changed.

[c] Invention,—] That is, *imagination.*

[d] *The* general,—] The *multitude*, or *people.*

Heaven, let me bear it! you granting of my suit,
If that be sin, I'll make it my morn-prayer
To have it added to the faults of mine,
And nothing of your answer.

ANG. Nay, but hear me.
Your sense pursues not mine: either you are ignorant,
Or seem so, crafty;[a] and that is not good.

ISAB. Let me* be ignorant and in nothing good,
But graciously to know I am no better.

ANG. Thus wisdom wishes to appear most bright,
When it doth tax itself; as these black masks
Proclaim an enshield beauty ten times louder
Than beauty could, displayed.—But mark me:
To be received plain, I'll speak more gross:
Your brother is to die.

ISAB. So.

ANG. And his offence is so, as it appears,
Accountant to the law upon that pain.

ISAB. True.

ANG. Admit no other way to save his life,—
As I subscribe not that, nor any other,
But in the loss[b] of question—that you, his sister,
Finding yourself desir'd of such a person,
Whose credit with the judge, or own great place,
Could fetch your brother from the manacles
Of the all-binding† law; and that there were
No earthly mean to save him, but that either
You must lay down the treasures of your body
To this supposed, or else to let him suffer;
What would you do?

ISAB. As much for my poor brother as myself:
That is, were I under the terms of death,
The impression of keen whips I'd wear as rubies,
And strip myself to death, as to a bed
That longing have[c] been sick for ere I'd yield
My body up to shame.

ANG. Then must your brother die.

ISAB. And 'twere the cheaper way:
Better it were a brother died at once,
Than that a sister, by redeeming him,
Should die for ever.

ANG. Were not you, then, as cruel, as the sentence
That you have slander'd so?

ISAB. Ignomy in ransom, and free pardon,
Are of two houses: lawful mercy is
Nothing akin‡ to foul redemption.

ANG. You seem'd of late to make the law a tyrant;
And rather prov'd the sliding of your brother
A merriment than a vice.

ISAB. O, pardon me, my lord; it oft falls out,
To have what we would have, we speak not what we mean:
I something do excuse the thing I hate,
For his advantage that I dearly love.

ANG. We are all frail.

ISAB. Else let my brother die,
If not a feodary, but only he,
Owe, and succeed thy weakness.[d]

ANG. Nay, women are frail too.

ISAB. Ay, as the glasses where they view themselves;
Which are as easy broke as they make forms.
Women!—Help heaven! men their creation mar
In profiting by them. Nay, call us ten times frail,
For we are soft as our complexions are,
And credulous to false prints.

ANG. I think it well;
And from this testimony of your own sex,—
Since, I suppose, we are made to be no stronger
Than faults may shake our frames,—let me be bold;—
I do arrest your words. Be that you are,
That is, a woman; if you be more, you're none;
If you be one,—as you are well express'd
By all external warrants,—show it now,
By putting on the destin'd livery.

ISAB. I have no tongue but one: gentle my lord,
Let me intreat you speak the former language.

ANG. Plainly conceive, I love you.

ISAB. My brother did love Juliet;
And you tell me that he shall die for it.

ANG. He shall not, Isabel, if you give me love.

ISAB. I know your virtue hath a licence in 't,
Which seems a little fouler than it is,
To pluck on others.

ANG. Believe me, on mine honour,
My words express my purpose.

ISAB. Ha! little honour to be much believ'd,
And most pernicious purpose!—Seeming, seeming!—

(*) First folio omits, *me*. (†) Old text, *all-building*. (‡) Old text, *kin*.

a *Or seem so*, crafty;] Meaning, "or seem so, *being* crafty." Davenant reads *craftily*, an emendation generally, and perhaps rightly, adopted by modern editors.

b *But in the* loss *of question*—] This may mean, *in the absence of topics for conversation*; but with Johnson we apprehend *loss* to be a misprint for *toss*. To *toss* an argument, or to *toss* logic is a phrase not yet quite obsolete.

c *That longing* have *been sick for*—] *Have*, in this passage, by a not unfrequent ellipsis, is used for *I have*.]

d If not a feodary, but only he,
Owe, and succeed thy weakness.]

The meaning is plain, though the language is perplexed:—If frailty is not man's common portion, if my brother, instead of being a mere *feodary* or *vassal*, like other men, possess it solely as his heritage, then let him die. *Feodary*, however, is explained by the commentators to mean an associate or companion, and the sense is said to be,—"If my brother alone offend, if he have no *feodary* (companion or associate), let him die." The words, "*Owe*, and *succeed*," which imply possession and inheritance, somewhat militate against this interpretation of the passage.

I will proclaim thee, Angelo; look for 't:
Sign me a present pardon for my brother,
Or with an outstretch'd throat I 'll tell the world aloud
What man thou art.

ANG. Who will believe thee, Isabel?
My unsoil'd name, the austereness of my life,
My vouch against you, and my place i' the state,
Will so your accusation overweigh,
That you shall stifle in your own report,
And smell of calumny. I have begun,
And now I give my sensual race the rein:
Fit thy consent to my sharp appetite;
Lay by all nicety and prolixious blushes,
That banish what they sue for; redeem thy brother
By yielding up thy body to my will,
Or else he must not only die the death,
But thy unkindness shall his death draw out
To ling'ring sufferance. Answer me to-morrow,
Or, by the affection that now guides me most,
I'll prove a tyrant to him. As for you,
Say what you can, my false o'erweighs your true. [*Exit.*

ISAB. To whom should I complain? did I tell this,
Who would believe me? O perilous mouths,
That bear in them one and the self-same tongue,
Either of condemnation or approof;
Bidding the law make court'sy to their will;
Hooking both right and wrong to the appetite,
To follow as it draws! I'll to my brother:
Though he hath fall'n by prompture of the blood,
Yet hath he in him such a mind of honour,
That had he twenty heads to tender down
On twenty bloody blocks, he'd yield them up,
Before his sister should her body stoop
To such abhorr'd pollution.
Then, Isabel, live chaste, and, brother, die:
More than our brother is our chastity.
I'll tell him yet of Angelo's request,
And fit his mind to death, for his soul's rest. [*Exit.*

ACT III.

SCENE I.—*A Room in the Prison.*

Enter, to CLAUDIO, *the* DUKE, *disguised as before, and* Provost.

DUKE. So, then, you hope of pardon from lord Angelo?

CLAUD. The miserable have no other medicine,
But only hope:
I have hope to live, and am prepar'd to die.

DUKE. Be absolute for death; either death or life
Shall thereby be the sweeter. Reason thus with life:—
If I do lose thee, I do lose a thing
That none but fools would keep: a breath thou art,
Servile to all the skyey influences
That do* this habitation, where thou keep'st,
Hourly afflict: merely, thou art death's fool;(1)
For him thou labour'st by thy flight to shun,
And yet runn'st toward him still. Thou art not noble;
For all the accommodations that thou bear'st
Are nurs'd by baseness. Thou art by no means valiant,
For thou dost fear the soft and tender fork
Of a poor worm. Thy best of rest is sleep,
And that thou oft provok'st; yet grossly fear'st
Thy death, which is no more. Thou'rt not thyself;
For thou exist'st on many a thousand grains
That issue out of dust. Happy thou art not;

(*) Old text, *dost*.

For what thou hast not, still thou striv'st to get,
And what thou hast, forgett'st. Thou art not certain;
For thy complexion shifts to strange effects,[a]
After the moon. If thou art rich, thou'rt poor;
For, like an ass whose back with ingots bows,
Thou bear'st thy heavy riches but a journey,
And death unloads thee. Friend hast thou none;
For thine own bowels, which do call thee sire,*
The mere effusion of thy proper loins,
Do curse the gout, serpigo,[b] and the rheum,
For ending thee no sooner. Thou hast nor youth nor age,
But, as it were, an after-dinner's sleep,
Dreaming on both; for all thy blessed youth
Becomes as aged,[c] and doth beg the alms
Of palsied eld; and when thou art old and rich,
Thou hast neither heat, affection, limb, nor beauty,
To make thy riches pleasant. What 's yet in this
That bears the name of life? Yet in this life
Lie hid more thousand deaths: yet death we fear,
That makes these odds all even.

CLAUD. I humbly thank you.
To sue to live, I find I seek to die;
And, seeking death, find life: let it come on.

ISAB. [*Without.*] What, ho! Peace here; grace and good company!

PROV. Who's there? come in: the wish deserves a welcome.

DUKE. Dear sir, ere long I'll visit you again.

CLAUD. Most holy sir, I thank you.

Enter ISABELLA.

ISAB. My business is a word or two with Claudio.

PROV. And very welcome.—Look, signior, here's your sister.

DUKE. Provost, a word with you.

PROV. As many as you please.

DUKE. Bring me to hear them speak, where I may be conceal'd.[d]

[*Exeunt* DUKE *and* PROVOST.

CLAUD. Now, sister, what 's the comfort?

ISAB. Why, as all comforts are; most good, most good indeed.
Lord Angelo, having affairs to heaven,
Intends you for his swift ambassador,
Where you shall be an everlasting lieger:[e]
Therefore your best appointment make with speed;
To-morrow you set on.

CLAUD. Is there no remedy?

ISAB. None:—but such remedy as, to save a head,
To cleave a heart in twain.

CLAUD. But is there any?

ISAB. Yes, brother, you may live:
There is a devilish mercy in the judge,
If you'll implore it, that will free your life,
But fetter you till death.

CLAUD. Perpetual durance?

ISAB. Ay, just; perpetual durance,—a restraint,
Though* all the world's vastidity you had,
To a determin'd scope.

CLAUD. But in what nature?

ISAB. In such a one as, you consenting to't,
Would bark your honour from that trunk you bear,
And leave you naked.

CLAUD. Let me know the point.

ISAB. O, I do fear thee, Claudio; and I quake,
Lest thou a feverous life shouldst entertain,
And six or seven winters more respect
Than a perpetual honour. Dar'st thou die?
The sense of death is most in apprehension;
And the poor beetle that we tread upon,
In corporal sufferance finds a pang as great
As when a giant dies.

CLAUD. Why give you me this shame?
Think you I can a resolution fetch
From flowery tenderness? If I must die,
I will encounter darkness as a bride,
And hug it in mine arms.

ISAB. There spake my brother! there my father's grave
Did utter forth a voice! Yes, thou must die:

(*) Old text, *fire*.

[a] *Strange* effects,—] Johnson proposed to read, *affects*, that is, *affections*, *passions* of mind, perhaps rightly; but *effects*, in the sense of *results*, *consequences*, *conclusions*, affords a reasonable meaning.

[b] Serpigo,—] *Leprosy*. The folios read, *Sapego* and *Sarpego*.

[c] "—— for all thy blessed youth
Becomes as aged, and doth beg the alms
Of palsied eld;]

With all respect for Johnson's defence of the old text, we must confess there appears much force in Warburton's objection to the logic of this passage; but his remedy, which is to read,—

"—— for *pall'd*, thy *blazed* youth
Becomes *assuaged*, and *both* beg," &c.

is not admissible. With much less violence to the original, and with advantage, perhaps, to the reasoning, we might read,—

(*) Old text, *through*.

"—— for all thy blessed youth
Becomes *engaged*, and doth beg the alms
Of palsied eld;"

taking *engaged* in the sense of enthralled by debt and lack of means; a sense it bears in the following passage,—

"I have *engag'd* myself to a dear friend,
Engag'd my friend to his mere enemy,
To feed my means."
Merchant of Venice, Act III. Sc. 2.

[d] Bring me to hear them speak, where I may be conceal'd.] The first folio reads,—"Bring *them* to heare *me* speak, where I may be conceald;" and the second,—"Bring *them* to speake, where I may be conceal'd, *yet heare them*."

[e] *An everlasting* lieger:] A *lieger* meant an ambassador permanently resident at a foreign court.

Thou art too noble to conserve a life
In base appliances. This outward-sainted deputy—
Whose settled visage and deliberate word
Nips youth i'the head, and follies doth emmew [a]
As falcon doth the fowl—is yet a devil;
His filth within being cast, he would appear
A pond as deep as hell.

CLAUD. The rev'rend [b] Angelo?

ISAB. O, 'tis the cunning livery of hell,
The damned'st body to invest and cover
In rev'rend [b] guards! Dost thou think, Claudio,—
If I would yield him my virginity,
Thou might'st be freed!

CLAUD. O, heavens! it cannot be.

ISAB. Yes, he would give't thee, from this rank offence,
So to offend him still. This night 's the time
That I should do what I abhor to name,
Or else thou diest to-morrow.

CLAUD. Thou shalt not do't.

ISAB. O, were it but my life,
I'd throw it down for your deliverance
As frankly as a pin!

CLAUD. Thanks, dear Isabel.

ISAB. Be ready, Claudio, for your death to-morrow.

CLAUD. Yes.—Has he affections in him,
That thus can make him bite the law by the nose,
When he would force it? Sure, it is no sin;
Or of the deadly seven it is the least.

ISAB. Which is the least?

CLAUD. If it were damnable, he being so wise,
Why would he for the momentary trick
Be perdurably fin'd?—O Isabel!

ISAB. What says my brother?

CLAUD. Death is a fearful thing.

ISAB. And shamed life a hateful.

CLAUD. Ay, but to die, and go we know not where;
To lie in cold obstruction and to rot;
This sensible warm motion to become
A kneaded clod; and the delighted spirit
To bathe in fiery floods, or to reside
In thrilling region of thick-ribbed ice;
To be imprison'd in the viewless winds,
And blown with restless violence round about
The pendent world; or to be worse than worst
Of those that lawless and incertain thoughts *
Imagine howling!—'tis too horrible!
The weariest and most loathed worldly life,
That age, ache, penury,† and imprisonment

---

a *And follies doth* emmew
As falcon doth the fowl—]
To *emmew* or *enmew* is a hawking technical, and as here used signifies, we believe, to paralyse and disable, as the falcon does the frightened bird over and around which it wheels preparatory to making the deadly swoop by which the prey is transfixed.

b *The* rev'rend *Angelo?* . . . rev'rend *guards!*] Of this passage Johnson remarks,—"The first folio has, in both places, *prenzie*, from which the other folios made *princely*, and every editor may make what he can." The word we adopt, though bearing upon the face of it little resemblance to *prenzie*, will be found upon transposing the letters to be not very dissimilar; while as regards the requirements of the sense, it seems preferable to *princely*, or *priestly*, or *precise*, each of which has found advocates, and a place in one or other of the modern editions.

(*) Old text, *thought*. (†) First folio, *periury*.

Can lay on nature, is a paradise
To what we fear of death.

ISAB. Alas! alas!

CLAUD. Sweet sister, let me live:
What sin you do to save a brother's life,
Nature dispenses with the deed so far
That it becomes a virtue.

ISAB. O, you beast!
O, faithless coward! O, dishonest wretch!
Wilt thou be made a man out of my vice?
Is't not a kind of incest, to take life
From thine own sister's shame? What should I think?
Heaven shield, my mother play'd my father fair!
For such a warped slip of wilderness[a]
Ne'er issu'd from his blood. Take my defiance;
Die! perish! might but my bending down
Reprieve thee from thy fate, it should proceed:
I'll pray a thousand prayers for thy death,—
No word to save thee.

CLAUD. Nay, hear me, Isabel.

ISAB. O, fie, fie, fie!
Thy sin's not accidental, but a trade.
Mercy to thee would prove itself a bawd:
'Tis best that thou diest quickly. [*Going.*

CLAUD. O, hear me, Isabella!

Re-enter DUKE, *the* Provost *following.*

DUKE. Vouchsafe a word, young sister; but one word.

ISAB. What is your will?

DUKE. Might you dispense with your leisure, I would by and by have some speech with you: the satisfaction I would require is likewise your own benefit.

ISAB. I have no superfluous leisure; my stay must be stolen out of other affairs; but I will attend you a while.

DUKE. [*Aside to* CLAUDIO.] Son, I have overheard what hath passed between you and your sister. Angelo had never the purpose to corrupt her; only he hath made an assay of her virtue, to practise his judgment with the disposition of natures: she, having the truth of honour in her, hath made him that gracious denial which he is most glad to receive. I am confessor to Angelo, and I know this to be true; therefore prepare yourself to death. Do not satisfy your resolution with hopes that are fallible: to-morrow you must die; go to your knees, and make ready.

CLAUD. Let me ask my sister pardon. I am so out of love with life, that I will sue to be rid of it.

DUKE. Hold you there: farewell. [*Exit* CLAUDIO.] Provost, a word with you.

PROV. What's your will, father?

DUKE. That now you are come, you will be gone. Leave me a while with the maid: my mind promises with my habit no loss shall touch her by my company.

PROV. In good time. [*Exit* Provost.

DUKE. The hand that hath made you fair hath made you good: the goodness that is cheap in beauty makes beauty brief in goodness; but grace, being the soul of your complexion, shall keep the body of it ever fair. The assault that Angelo hath made to you, fortune hath conveyed to my understanding; and, but that frailty hath examples for his falling, I should wonder at Angelo. How will you do to content this substitute, and to save your brother?

ISAB. I am now going to resolve him: I had rather my brother die by the law, than my son should be unlawfully born. But O, how much is the good duke deceived in Angelo! If ever he return, and I can speak to him, I will open my lips in vain, or discover his government.

DUKE. That shall not be much amiss; yet, as the matter now stands, he will avoid your accusation,—he made trial of you only.—Therefore fasten your ear on my advisings: to the love I have in doing good a remedy presents itself. I do make myself believe, that you may most uprighteously do a poor wronged lady a merited benefit; redeem your brother from the angry law; do no stain to your own gracious person; and much please the absent duke, if peradventure he shall ever return to have hearing of this business.

ISAB. Let me hear you speak further. I have spirit to do any thing that appears not foul in the truth of my spirit.

DUKE. Virtue is bold, and goodness never fearful. Have you not heard speak of Mariana, the sister of Frederick the great soldier who miscarried at sea?

ISAB. I have heard of the lady, and good words went with her name.

DUKE. She should this Angelo have married; was affianced to her by* oath, and the nuptial appointed: between which time of the contract and limit of the solemnity, her brother Frederick was wrecked at sea, having in that perished vessel the dowry of his sister. But mark how heavily this befel to the poor gentlewoman: there she lost a noble and renowned brother, in his love toward her ever most kind and natural; with him the portion and sinew of her fortune, her marriage-

[a] Wilderness—] *Wildness. Wilderness* in this sense is met with in many of the old poets.

(*) First folio omits, *by*.

dowry; with both, her combinate[a] husband, this well-seeming Angelo.

ISAB. Can this be so? did Angelo so leave her?

DUKE. Left her in her tears, and dried not one of them with his comfort; swallowed his vows whole, pretending in her discoveries of dishonour: in few, bestowed her on her own lamentation, which she yet wears for his sake, and he, a marble to her tears, is washed with them, but relents not.

ISAB. What a merit were it in death to take this poor maid from the world! What corruption in this life, that it will let this man live!—But how out of this can she avail?

DUKE. It is a rupture that you may easily heal; and the cure of it not only saves your brother, but keeps you from dishonour in doing it.

ISAB. Show me how, good father.

DUKE. This fore-named maid hath yet in her the continuance of her first affection: his unjust unkindness, that in all reason should have quenched her love, hath, like an impediment in the current, made it more violent and unruly. Go you to Angelo; answer his requiring with a plausible obedience: agree with his demands to the point; only refer yourself to this advantage,—first, that your stay with him may not be long; that the time may have all shadow and silence in it; and the place answer to convenience. This being granted, in course and now follows all:—we shall advise this wronged maid to stead up your appointment, go in your place; if the encounter acknowledge itself hereafter, it may compel him to her recompense; and here, by this, is your brother saved, your honour untainted, the poor Mariana advantaged, and the corrupt deputy scaled.[b] The maid will I frame and make fit for his attempt. If you think well to carry this, as you may, the doubleness of the benefit defends the deceit from reproof. What think you of it?

ISAB. The image of it gives me content already; and I trust it will grow to a most prosperous perfection.

DUKE. It lies much in your holding up. Haste you speedily to Angelo: if for this night he entreat you to his bed, give him promise of satisfaction. I will presently to Saint Luke's; there, at the moated grange, resides this dejected Mariana: at that place call upon me, and dispatch with Angelo, that it may be quickly.

ISAB. I thank you for this comfort. Fare you well, good father. [*Exeunt severally.*

[a] Combinate *husband,*—] *Elected* or *contracted* husband.

[b] *And the corrupt deputy* scaled.] It is doubtful whether *scaled* in this place signifies *stripped* and *exposed,* or *reached,* or *brought to justice* by being metaphorically *weighed.* It may be indeed only a misprint for *sealed,* in the sense of *stamped,* as in "Richard III." Act I. Sc. 3:—

"Thou that wast *seal'd* in thy nativity
The slave of nature," &c.

SCENE II.[c]—*The Street before the Prison.*

Enter on one side, DUKE, *disguised as before; on the other,* ELBOW, *and* Officers *with* POMPEY.

ELB. Nay, if there be no remedy for it, but that you will needs buy and sell men and women like beasts, we shall have all the world drink brown and white bastard.

DUKE. O, heavens! what stuff is here?

POM. 'Twas never merry world since, of two usuries, the merriest was put down, and the worser allowed by order of law a furred gown to keep him warm; and furred with fox and lamb-skins too, to signify that craft, being richer than innocency, stands for the facing.

ELB. Come your way, sir.—Bless you, good father friar!

DUKE. And you, good brother father. What offence hath this man made you, sir?

ELB. Marry, sir, he hath offended the law: and, sir, we take him to be a thief too, sir; for we have found upon him, sir, a strange pick-lock, which we have sent to the deputy.

DUKE. Fie, sirrah! a bawd, a wicked bawd!
The evil that thou causest to be done,
That is thy means to live. Do thou but think
What 'tis to cram a maw or clothe a back
From such a filthy vice: say to thyself,—
From their abominable and beastly touches
I drink, I eat, array* myself, and live.
Canst thou believe thy living is a life,
So stinkingly depending? Go mend, go mend.

POM. Indeed, it does stink in some sort, sir; but yet, sir, I would prove—

DUKE. Nay, if the devil have given thee proofs for sin,
Thou wilt prove his.—Take him to prison, officer:
Correction and instruction must both work,
Ere this rude beast will profit.

ELB. He must before the deputy, sir; he has given him warning: the deputy cannot abide a whoremaster: if he be a whoremonger, and comes before him, he were as good go a mile on his errand.

DUKE. That we were all, as some would seem to be,

(*) Old text, *away.*

[c] Scene II.] In the old copies no change of scene is indicated, they merely give "*Exit*" [Isabella]; and when she has left the stage, the audience, as Mr. Dyce observes, were to suppose that the scene changed from the interior to the outside of the prison.

Free* from our faults, as[a] faults from seeming, free!

Elb. His neck will come to your waist,—a cord, sir.[b]

Pom. I spy comfort: I cry, bail! Here's a gentleman, and a friend of mine.

Enter Lucio.

Lucio. How now, noble Pompey! What, at the wheels of Cæsar! Art thou led in triumph? What, is there none of Pygmalion's images, newly made woman, to be had now, for putting the hand in the pocket and extracting it† clutched? What reply, ha? What say'st thou to this tune, matter, and method? Is't not drowned i' the last rain, ha? What say'st thou, trot? Is the world as it was, man? Which is the way? Is it sad, and few words? or how? The trick of it?

Duke. Still thus, and thus; still worse!

Lucio. How doth my dear morsel, thy mistress? Procures she still, ha!

Pom. Troth, sir, she hath eaten up all her beef, and she is herself in the tub.

Lucio. Why, 'tis good; it is the right of it; it must be so: ever your fresh whore and your powdered bawd: an unshunned consequence; it must be so. Art going to prison, Pompey?

Pom. Yes, faith, sir.

Lucio. Why, 'tis not amiss, Pompey. Farewell: go, say, I sent thee thither. For debt, Pompey? or how?

Elb. For being a bawd, for being a bawd.

Lucio. Well, then, imprison him: if imprisonment be the due of a bawd, why, 'tis his right: bawd is he doubtless, and of antiquity too; bawd-born.—Farewell, good Pompey. Commend me to the prison, Pompey: you will turn good husband now, Pompey; you will keep the house.

Pom. I hope, sir, your good worship will be my bail.

Lucio. No, indeed, will I not, Pompey; it is not the wear.[c] I will pray, Pompey, to increase your bondage: if you take it not patiently, why, your mettle is the more. Adieu, trusty Pompey. —Bless you, friar.

Duke. And you.

Lucio. Does Bridget paint still, Pompey, ha?

Elb. Come your ways, sir; come.

(*) First folio omits, *Free*. (†) Old copies omit, *it*.

[a] *Free from our faults*, as *faults from seeming*, free!] As this stands, the meaning is not very apparent. We might read,—

"Free from our faults, *or* faults from seeming, free!"

Would we were either exempt from faults altogether, as some pretend to be, or that they were not hidden by a semblance of virtue.

[b] His neck will come to your waist,—a cord,—] This desperate witticism depends on the hempen girdle which the duke, as a friar, wore.

[c] *Not the* wear.] Not the *fashion*.

POM. You will not bail me then, sir?

LUCIO. *Then*, Pompey? nor now.—What news abroad, friar? what news?

ELB. Come your ways, sir; come.

LUCIO. Go,—to kennel, Pompey, go.

[*Exeunt* ELBOW, *and* Officers, *with* POMPEY.

What news, friar, of the duke?

DUKE. I know none; can you tell me of any?

LUCIO. Some say he is with the emperor of Russia; other some, he is in Rome: but where is he, think you?

DUKE. I know not where; but wheresoever, I wish him well.

LUCIO. It was a mad fantastical trick of him to steal from the state, and usurp the beggary he was never born to. Lord Angelo dukes it well in his absence; he puts transgression to't.

DUKE. He does well in't.

LUCIO. A little more lenity to lechery would do no harm in him: something too crabbed that way, friar.

DUKE. It is too general a vice, and severity must cure it.

LUCIO. Yes, in good sooth, the vice is of a great kindred; it is well allied: but it is impossible to extirp it quite, friar, till eating and drinking be put down. They say, this Angelo was not made by man and woman, after this downright way of creation: is it true, think you?

DUKE. How should he be made, then?

LUCIO. Some report, a sea-maid spawned him: some, that he was begot between two stock-fishes. But it is certain, that when he makes water, his urine is congealed ice: that I know to be true; and he is a motion ungenerative,[a] that's infallible.

DUKE. You are pleasant, sir, and speak apace.

LUCIO. Why, what a ruthless thing is this in him, for the rebellion of a cod-piece to take away the life of a man! Would the duke that is absent have done this? Ere he would have hanged a man for the getting a hundred bastards, he would have paid for the nursing a thousand: he had some feeling of the sport; he knew the service, and that instructed him to mercy.

DUKE. I never heard the absent duke much detected[b] for women: he was not inclined that way.

LUCIO. O, sir! you are deceived.

DUKE. 'Tis not possible.

LUCIO. Who? not the duke? yes, your beggar of fifty; and his use was to put a ducat in her clack-dish: the duke had crotchets in him. He would be drunk too; that let me inform you.

DUKE. You do him wrong, surely.

LUCIO. Sir, I was an inward[c] of his. A shy fellow was the duke; and I believe I know the cause of his withdrawing.

DUKE. What, I pr'ythee, might be the cause?

LUCIO. No,—pardon:—'tis a secret must be locked within the teeth and the lips; but this I can let you understand,—the greater file of the subject held the duke to be wise.

DUKE. Wise! why, no question but he was.

LUCIO. A very superficial, ignorant, unweighing fellow.

DUKE. Either this is envy in you, folly, or mistaking: the very stream of his life, and the business he hath helmed, must, upon a warranted need, give him a better proclamation. Let him be but testimonied in his own bringings-forth, and he shall appear to the envious a scholar, a statesman, and a soldier. Therefore, you speak unskilfully; or, if your knowledge be more, it is much darkened in your malice.

LUCIO. Sir, I know him, and I love him.

DUKE. Love talks with better knowledge, and knowledge with dearer* love.

LUCIO. Come, sir, I know what I know.

DUKE. I can hardly believe that, since you know not what you speak. But, if ever the duke return (as our prayers are he may), let me desire you to make your answer before him. If it be honest you have spoke, you have courage to maintain it: I am bound to call upon you; and, I pray you, your name?

LUCIO. Sir, my name is Lucio; well known to the duke.

DUKE. He shall know you better, sir, if I may live to report you.

LUCIO. I fear you not.

DUKE. O, you hope the duke will return no more, or you imagine me too unhurtful an opposite. But, indeed, I can do you little harm; you'll forswear this again.

LUCIO. I'll be hanged first: thou art deceived in me, friar. But no more of this. Canst thou tell if Claudio die to-morrow or no?

DUKE. Why should he die, sir?

LUCIO. Why? for filling a bottle with a tun-dish.[d] I would the duke we talk of, were returned again: this ungenitured agent will unpeople the province with continency; sparrows must not build in his house-eaves, because they are lecherous. The duke yet would have dark deeds darkly answered; he would never bring them to light: would he were returned! Marry, this Claudio is condemned for untrussing. Farewell, good friar; I pr'ythee, pray for me. The duke, I say to thee again,

---

[a] *A motion* ungenerative,—] The old text has,—"a motion *generative*," corrected by Theobald.

[b] Detected *for women*:] That is, *accused* on account of women.

[c] *An* inward—] A *familiar*, an *intimate*.

(*) Old text, *deare*.

[d] A tun-dish.] An old Warwickshire name for a funnel.

would eat mutton on Fridays. He's now past it; yet[a] and I say to thee, he would mouth with a beggar, though she smelt brown bread and garlic: say, that I said so. Farewell. [*Exit.*

DUKE. No might nor greatness in mortality
Can censure 'scape: back-wounding calumny
The whitest virtue strikes. What king so strong,
Can tie the gall up in the slanderous tongue?—
But who comes here?

Enter ESCALUS, Provost, *and* Officers, *with* MISTRESS OVERDONE.

ESCAL. Go: away with her to prison!

MRS. OV. Good my lord, be good to me! your honour is accounted a merciful man: good my lord!

ESCAL. Double and treble admonition, and still forfeit in the same kind? This would make mercy swear and play the tyrant.

PROV. A bawd of eleven years' continuance, may it please your honour.

MRS. OV. My lord, this is one Lucio's information against me. Mistress Kate Keepdown was with child by him in the duke's time; he promised her marriage: his child is a year and a quarter old, come Philip and Jacob. I have kept it myself; and see how he goes about to abuse me!

ESCAL. That fellow is a fellow of much licence:—let him be called before us.—Away with her to prison! Go to: no more words. [*Exeunt* Officers, *with* MISTRESS OVERDONE.
Provost, my brother Angelo will not be altered; Claudio must die to-morrow: let him be furnished with divines, and have all charitable preparation. If my brother wrought by my pity, it should not be so with him.

PROV. So please you, this friar hath been with him, and advised him for the entertainment of death.

ESCAL. Good even, good father.

DUKE. Bliss and goodness on you!

ESCAL. Of whence are you?

DUKE. Not of this country, though my chance is now
To use it for my time: I am a brother
Of gracious order, late come from the See,
In special business from his holiness.

ESCAL. What news abroad i' the world?

DUKE. None, but that there is so great a fever on goodness, that the dissolution of it must cure it: novelty is only in request; and* it is as dangerous to be aged in any kind of course, as it is virtuous to be constant[b] in any undertaking: there is scarce truth enough alive to make societies secure, but security enough to make fellowships accursed.[c] Much upon this riddle runs the wisdom of the world. This news is old enough, yet it is every day's news. I pray you, sir, of what disposition was the duke?

ESCAL. One that, above all other strifes, contended especially to know himself.

DUKE. What pleasure was he given to?

ESCAL. Rather rejoicing to see another merry, than merry at any thing which professed to make him rejoice: a gentleman of all temperance. But leave we him to his events, with a prayer they may prove prosperous; and let me desire to know how you find Claudio prepared. I am made to understand that you have lent him visitation.

DUKE. He professes to have received no sinister measure from his judge, but most willingly humbles himself to the determination of justice; yet had he framed to himself, by the instruction of his frailty, many deceiving promises of life, which I, by my good leisure, have discredited to him, and now is he resolved to die.

ESCAL. You have paid the heavens your function, and the prisoner the very debt of your calling. I have laboured for the poor gentleman to the extremest shore of my modesty; but my brother justice have I found so severe, that he hath forced me to tell him he is indeed—justice.

DUKE. If his own life answer the straitness of his proceeding, it shall become him well; wherein if he chance to fail, he hath sentenced himself.

ESCAL. I am going to visit the prisoner. Fare you well.

DUKE. Peace be with you!
[*Exeunt* ESCALUS *and* Provost.
He, who the sword of heaven will bear,
Should be as holy as severe;
Pattern in himself to know,
Grace to stand, and virtue go;
More nor less to others paying,
Than by self offences weighing.
Shame to him whose cruel striking
Kills for faults of his own liking!
Twice treble shame on Angelo,
To weed my vice and let his grow!
O, what may man within him hide,
Though angel on the outward side!
How may likeness, made in crimes,
Making practice on the times,
To draw with idle spiders' strings

(*) Old text inserts, *as.*

[a] He's now past it: yet and I say to thee, &c.] Hanmer altered this to—

"He's *not* past it yet; and, I say to thee," &c.

[b] *As it is virtuous to be* constant in any undertaking:] Is it not plain the poet wrote, *inconstant?* What possible sense can be extracted from the passage as it stands?

[c] But security enough to make fellowships accursed.] The allusion, Malone says, is "to those legal securities into which *fellowship* leads men to enter for each other."

Most pond'rous and substantial things ! [a]
Craft against vice I must apply :
With Angelo to-night shall lie
His old betrothed but despis'd ;
So disguise shall, by the disguis'd,
Pay with falsehood false exacting,
And perform an old contracting.

[*Exit.*

[a] Most pond'rous and substantial things !] This speech is disfigured by a cluster of errors: in the third line, for "know," which is an evident misprint, we propose to substitute *show;* in the thirteenth, "made," we think with Malone, is a typographical slip for *wade;* as "Making," in the next line, appears to be for *Masking*. Adopting these slight changes, and reading, "*So* draw," instead of "*To* draw," in the fifteenth line, the sense becomes perfectly intelligible :—

"He who the sword of heaven will bear,
Should be as holy as severe ;
Pattern in himself to show
Grace to stand, and virtue go ;

(That is, to show grace how to stand and virtue how to go.)

More nor less to others paying,
Than by self offences weighing.
Shame to him whose cruel striking
Kills for faults of his own liking !
Twice treble shame on Angelo,
To weed my vice and let his grow !
O, what may man within him hide
Though angel on the outward side !
How may likeness wade in crimes !

(*Likeness* means *false seeming.*)

Masking, practice on the times !

(That is, *How may masking practice,* &c.)

So draw with idle spider's strings
Most pond'rous and substantial things !"

ACT IV.

SCENE I.—*A Room in* Mariana's *House.*

MARIANA *discovered sitting: a* BOY *singing.*

SONG.

Take, O, take those lips away,
That so sweetly were forsworn;
And those eyes, the break of day,
Lights that do mislead the morn:
But my kisses bring again,
bring again,
Seals of love, but seal'd in vain,
seal'd in vain.(1)

MARI. Break off thy song, and haste thee quick away:
Here comes a man of comfort, whose advice
Hath often still'd my brawling discontent.— [*Exit* BOY.

Enter DUKE, *disguised as before.*

I cry you mercy, sir; and well could wish
You had not found me here so musical:
Let me excuse me, and believe me so,—
My mirth it much displeas'd, but pleas'd my woe.

DUKE. 'Tis good; though music oft hath such a charm,
To make bad good, and good provoke to harm.—
I pray you, tell me, hath any body inquired for me here to-day? much upon this time have I promised here to meet.

MARI. You have not been inquired after: I have sat here all day.

DUKE. I do constantly believe you.—The time is come even now. I shall crave your forbearance a little: may be I will call upon you anon, for some advantage to yourself.

MARI. I am always bound to you. [*Exit.*

Enter ISABELLA.

DUKE. Very well met, and welcome.
What is the news from this good deputy?

ISAB. He hath a garden circummur'd with brick,
Whose western side is with a vineyard back'd;
And to that vineyard is a planched gate,
That makes his opening with this bigger key:
This other doth command a little door,
Which from the vineyard to the garden leads;
There have I made my promise upon the heavy middle of the night to call upon him.[a]

DUKE. But shall you on your knowledge find this way?

ISAB. I have ta'en a due and wary note upon't:
With whispering and most guilty diligence,
In action all of precept, he did show me
The way twice o'er.

DUKE. Are there no other tokens
Between you 'greed, concerning her observance?

ISAB. No, none, but only a repair i' the dark;
And that I have possess'd him my most stay
Can be but brief; for I have made him know
I have a servant comes with me along,
That stays upon me; whose persuasion is,
I come about my brother.

DUKE. 'Tis well borne up.
I have not yet made known to Mariana
A word of this.—What, ho! within! come forth.

Re-enter MARIANA.

I pray you, be acquainted with this maid;
She comes to do you good.

ISAB. I do desire the like.

DUKE. Do you persuade yourself that I respect you?

MARI. Good friar, I know you do, and have[b] found it.

DUKE. Take, then, this your companion by the hand,
Who hath a story ready for your ear.
I shall attend your leisure: but make haste;
The vaporous night approaches.

MARI. Will't please you walk aside?
[*Exeunt* MARIANA *and* ISABELLA.

DUKE. O place and greatness! millions of false eyes
Are stuck upon thee! Volumes of report
Run with these false and most contrarious quests*
Upon thy doings! thousand escapes of wit
Make thee the father of their idle dream,
And rack thee in their fancies!

Re-enter MARIANA *and* ISABELLA.

Welcome! How agreed?

ISAB. She'll take the enterprise upon her, father,
If you advise it.

DUKE. It is not my consent,
But my entreaty too.

ISAB. Little have you to say,
When you depart from him, but, soft and low,
Remember now my brother.

MARI. Fear me not.

DUKE. Nor, gentle daughter, fear you not at all.
He is your husband on a pre-contràct:
To bring you thus together, 'tis no sin,
Sith that the justice of your title to him
Doth flourish the deceit. Come, let us go:
Our corn's to reap, for yet our tilth's† to sow.
[*Exeunt.*

SCENE II.—*A Room in the Prison.*

Enter Provost *and* POMPEY.

PROV. Come hither, sirrah. Can you cut off a man's head?

POM. If the man be a bachelor, sir, I can; but if he be a married man, he is his wife's head, and I can never cut off a woman's head.

PROV. Come, sir, leave me your snatches, and yield me a direct answer. To-morrow morning are to die Claudio and Barnardine: here is in our prison a common executioner, who in his office lacks a helper: if you will take it on you to assist him, it shall redeem you from your gyves; if not, you shall have your full time of imprisonment, and your deliverance with an unpitied whipping, for you have been a notorious bawd.

POM. Sir, I have been an unlawful bawd, time out of mind; but yet I will be content to be a lawful hangman. I would be glad to receive some instruction from my fellow partner.

PROV. What ho, Abhorson! where's Abhorson, there?

---

[a] There have I made my promise upon the heavy middle of the night to call upon him.] This is printed thus, as verse, in the old copies,—
"There have I made my promise upon the
Heavy middle of the night to call upon him."

(*) First folio, *Quest*. (†) Old text, *Tithes*.

[b] And have found it.] We should perhaps read,—"and have *oft* found it," &c.

Enter Abhorson.

Abhor. Do you call, sir?

Prov. Sirrah, here's a fellow will help you to-morrow in your execution. If you think it meet, compound with him by the year, and let him abide here with you; if not, use him for the present, and dismiss him. He cannot plead his estimation with you; he hath been a bawd.

Abhor. A bawd, sir, fie upon him! he will discredit our mystery.

Prov. Go to, sir; you weigh equally: a feather will turn the scale. [*Exit.*

Pom. Pray, sir, by your good favour,—for, surely, sir, a good favour[a] you have, but that you have a hanging look,—do you call, sir, your occupation a *mystery?*

Abhor. Ay, sir; a mystery.

Pom. Painting, sir, I have heard say, is a mystery; and your whores, sir, being members of my occupation, using painting, do prove my occupation a mystery; but what mystery there should be in hanging, if I should be hanged, I cannot imagine.

Abhor. Sir, it is a mystery.

Pom. Proof?

Abhor. Every true man's apparel fits your thief.

a Favour—] That is, *countenance, aspect.*

POM. If it be too little for your thief, your true man thinks it big enough; if it be too big for your thief, your thief thinks it little enough: so, every true man's apparel fits your thief.[a]

Re-enter Provost.

PROV. Are you agreed?

POM. Sir, I will serve him; for I do find, your hangman is a more penitent trade than your bawd; he doth oftener ask forgiveness.

PROV. You, sirrah, provide your block and your axe to-morrow four o'clock.

ABHOR. Come on, bawd; I will instruct thee in my trade: follow.

POM. I do desire to learn, sir; and I hope, if you have occasion to use me for your own turn, you shall find me yare;[b] for, truly, sir, for your kindness I owe you a good turn.

PROV. Call hither Barnardine and Claudio:
[*Exeunt* POMPEY *and* ABHORSON.
The one has my pity; not a jot the other,
Being a murderer, though he were my brother.

Enter CLAUDIO.

Look, here's the warrant, Claudio, for thy death:
'T is now dead midnight, and by eight to-morrow
Thou must be made immortal. Where's Barnardine?

CLAUD. As fast lock'd up in sleep, as guiltless [labour,
When it lies starkly in the traveller's bones:
He will not wake.

PROV. Who can do good on him?
Well, go; prepare yourself. [*Knocking without.*]
But hark, what noise?
Heaven give your spirits comfort!—[*Exit* CLAUDIO.]
By and by!—
I hope it is some pardon or reprieve
For the most gentle Claudio.—

Enter DUKE, *disguised as before.*

Welcome, father.

DUKE. The best and wholesom'st spirits of the night
Envelop you, good provost! Who call'd here of [late?

PROV. None, since the curfew rung.

DUKE. Not Isabel?

PROV. No.

DUKE. They will, then, ere't be long.

PROV. What comfort is for Claudio?

DUKE. There's some in hope.

PROV. It is a bitter deputy.

DUKE. Not so, not so: his life is parallel'd
Even with the stroke[c] and line of his great justice.
He doth with holy abstinence subdue
That in himself which he spurs on his power
To qualify in others: were he meal'd[d] with that
Which he corrects, then were he tyrannous;
But this being so, he's just.—[*Knocking without.*]
Now are they come.— [*Exit* Provost.
This is a gentle provost: seldom when
The steeled gaoler is the friend of men.
[*Knocking.*
How now! what noise? That spirit's possessed with haste,
That wounds the unsisting[e] postern with these strokes.

PROV. [*Without. Speaking to one at the door.*]
There he must stay until the officer
Arise to let him in: he is call'd up.

Re-enter Provost.

DUKE. Have you no countermand for Claudio yet,
But he must die to-morrow?

PROV. None, sir, none.

DUKE. As near the dawning, provost, as it is,
You shall hear more ere morning.

PROV. Happily,
You something know; yet I believe there comes
No countermand: no such example have we:
Besides, upon the very siege[f] of justice,
Lord Angelo hath to the public ear
Profess'd the contrary.—

Enter a Messenger.

This is his lordship's* man.

DUKE. And here comes Claudio's pardon.[g]

MESS. My lord hath sent you this note; and by me this further charge,—that you swerve not from the smallest article of it, neither in time, matter, or other circumstance. Good morrow; for, as I take it, it is almost day.

PROV. I shall obey him. [*Exit* Messenger.

DUKE. [*Aside.*] This is his pardon; purchas'd by such sin,
For which the pardoner himself is in.
Hence hath offence his quick celerity,

---

a —every true man's apparel fits your thief.] This is the division of the dialogue in the old copies. In modern editions, this speech of Pompey's forms part of Abhorson's, perhaps rightly.

b Yare;] *Ready, nimble.*

c Stroke—] Stroke means *rule*, and not, as it has always been understood, "a stroke of a pen."!

d Meal'd—] *Mingled, compounded.*

e Unsisting—] So the old text. Blackstone suggested it came from *sisto*, to stand still, and signified, "never at rest." It is more probably a misprint.

f Siege—] *Seat.*

g And here comes Claudio's pardon.] In the old copies this line is given to the Provost and the preceding one to the Duke; a manifest mistake.

(*) Old text, *Lords man.*

When it is borne in high authority:
When vice makes mercy, mercy's so extended,
That for the fault's love is the offender friended.—
Now, sir, what news?

PROV. I told you: lord Angelo, belike thinking me remiss in mine office, awakens me with this unwonted putting on; methinks strangely, for he hath not used it before.

DUKE. Pray you, let's hear.

PROV. [Reads.] *Whatsoever you may hear to the contrary, let Claudio be executed by four of the clock; and in the afternoon Barnardine. For my better satisfaction, let me have Claudio's head sent me by five. Let this be duly performed; with a thought that more depends on it than we must yet deliver. Thus fail not to do your office, as you will answer it at your peril.*
What say you to this, sir?

DUKE. What is that Barnardine, who is to be executed in the afternoon?

PROV. A Bohemian born, but here nursed up and bred: one that is a prisoner nine years old.[a]

DUKE. How came it that the absent duke had not either delivered him to his liberty or executed him? I have heard it was ever his manner to do so.

PROV. His friends still wrought reprieves for him: and, indeed, his fact, till now in the government of lord Angelo, came not to an undoubtful proof.

DUKE. It is now apparent?

PROV. Most manifest, and not denied by himself.

DUKE. Hath he borne himself penitently in prison? How seems he to be touched?

PROV. A man that apprehends death no more dreadfully but as a drunken sleep; careless, reckless, and fearless of what's past, present, or to come; insensible of mortality, and desperately mortal.

DUKE. He wants advice.

PROV. He will hear none. He hath evermore had the liberty of the prison; give him leave to escape hence, he would not: drunk many times a day, if not many days entirely drunk. We have very oft awaked him, as if to carry him to execution, and showed him a seeming warrant for it; it hath not moved him at all.

DUKE. More of him anon. There is written in your brow, provost, honesty and constancy: if I read it not truly, my ancient skill beguiles me; but, in the boldness of my cunning,[b] I will lay myself in hazard. Claudio, whom here you have warrant to execute is no greater forfeit to the law than Angelo who hath sentenced him. To make you understand this in a manifested effect, I crave but four days' respite, for the which you are to do me both a present and a dangerous courtesy.

PROV. Pray, sir, in what?

DUKE. In the delaying death.

PROV. Alack! how may I do it,—having the hour limited, and an express command, under penalty, to deliver his head in the view of Angelo? I may make my case as Claudio's, to cross this in the smallest.

DUKE. By the vow of mine order I warrant you: if my instructions may be your guide, let this Barnardine be this morning executed, and his head borne to Angelo.

PROV. Angelo hath seen them both, and will discover the favour.

DUKE. O death's a great disguiser; and you may add to it. Shave the head, and tie the beard; and say it was the desire of the penitent to be so bared before his death: you know the course is common. If anything fall to you upon this, more than thanks and good fortune, by the Saint whom I profess, I will plead against it with my life.

PROV. Pardon me, good father; it is against my oath.

DUKE. Were you sworn to the duke, or to the deputy?

PROV. To him, and to his substitutes.

DUKE. You will think you have made no offence, if the duke avouch the justice of your dealing.

PROV. But what likelihood is in that?

DUKE. Not a resemblance, but a certainty. Yet since I see you fearful, that neither my coat, integrity, nor persuasion, can with ease attempt you, I will go further than I meant, to pluck all fears out of you. Look you, sir, here is the hand and seal of the duke: you know the character, I doubt not; and the signet is not strange to you.

PROV. I know them both.

DUKE. The contents of this is the return of the duke: you shall anon over-read it at your pleasure, where you shall find, within these two days he will be here. This is a thing that Angelo knows not, for he this very day receives letters of strange tenour; perchance, of the duke's death; perchance, entering into some monastery; but, by chance, nothing of what is writ.[c] Look, the unfolding star calls up the shepherd. Put not yourself into amazement how these things should be: all difficulties are but easy when they are known. Call your executioner, and off with Barnardine's head: I will give him a present shrift, and advise him for a better place. Yet you are amazed; but this shall absolutely resolve you. Come away; it is almost clear dawn. [*Exeunt.*

---

[a] A prisoner nine years old.] That is, has been imprisoned for nine years.

[b] The boldness of my cunning—] In the *assurance* of my *sagacity*.

[c] By *chance, nothing of what is* writ.] That is, nothing of what is *truth*, or *gospel:* so in "Pericles," Act II. (Gower)—

"Thinks all is *writ* he spoken can."

From not understanding this sense of the word, some modern editors propose to read, with Warburton,—"nothing of what is *here* writ," and to make the Duke point to the letter in his hand. Mr. Collier indeed suggests the possibility that "writ" ought to be *right!*

SCENE III.—*Another Room in the same.*

Enter POMPEY.

POM. I am as well acquainted[a] here, as I was in our house of profession: one would think it were mistress Overdone's own house, for here be many of her old customers. First, here's young master Rash; he's in for a commodity of brown paper and old ginger,(2) nine-score and seventeen pounds; of which he made five marks, ready money: marry, then ginger was not much in request, for the old women were all dead. Then is there here one master Caper, at the suit of master Threepile the mercer, for some four suits of peach-coloured satin, which now peaches him a beggar. Then have we here young Dizzy, and young master Deepvow, and master Copperspur, and master Starvelackey, the rapier and dagger-man, and young Dropheir that killed lusty Pudding, and master Forthright the tilter, and brave master Shoetie the great traveller, and wild Halfcan that stabbed Pots, and, I think, forty more; all great doers in our trade, and are now *for the Lord's sake*.(3)

Enter ABHORSON.

ABHOR. Sirrah, bring Barnardine hither.

POM. Master Barnardine! you must rise and be hanged, master Barnardine.

ABHOR. What, ho, Barnardine!

BARNAR. [*Within.*] A pox o' your throats! Who makes that noise there? what are you?

POM. Your friend,* sir; the hangman. You must be so good, sir, to rise and be put to death.

BARNAR. [*Within.*] Away, you rogue, away! I am sleepy.

ABHOR. Tell him, he must awake, and that quickly too.

POM. Pray, master Barnardine, awake till you are executed, and sleep afterwards.

ABHOR. Go in to him, and fetch him out.

POM. He is coming, sir, he is coming; I hear his straw rustle.

ABHOR. Is the axe upon the block, sirrah?

POM. Very ready, sir.

Enter BARNARDINE.

BARNAR. How now, Abhorson! what's the news with you?

ABHOR. Truly, sir, I would desire you to clap into your prayers; for, look you, the warrant's come.

BARNAR. You rogue, I have been drinking all night; I am not fitted for't.

POM. O, the better, sir; for he that drinks all night, and is hanged betimes in the morning, may sleep the sounder all the next day.

ABHOR. Look you, sir; here comes your ghostly father: do we jest now, think you?

Enter DUKE, *disguised as before.*

DUKE. Sir, induced by my charity, and hearing how hastily you are to depart, I am come to advise you, comfort you, and pray with you.

BARNAR. Friar, not I: I have been drinking hard all night, and I will have more time to prepare me, or they shall beat out my brains with billets. I will not consent to die this day, that's certain.

DUKE. O, sir, you must; and therefore, I beseech you
Look forward on the journey you shall go.

BARNAR. I swear, I will not die to-day for any man's persuasion.

DUKE. But hear you,—

BARNAR. Not a word: if you have any thing to say to me, come to my ward; for thence will not I to-day. [*Exit.*

DUKE. Unfit to live, or die: O, gravel heart!—
After him, fellows: bring him to the block.
[*Exeunt* ABHORSON *and* POMPEY.

Enter Provost.

PROV. Now, sir; how do you find the prisoner?

DUKE. A creature unprepar'd, unmeet for death;
And to transport him in the mind he is,
Were damnable.

PROV. Here in the prison, father,
There died this morning of a cruel fever
One Ragozine, a most notorious pirate,
A man of Claudio's years; his beard and head,
Just of his colour. What if we do omit
This reprobate till he were well inclin'd,
And satisfy the deputy with the visage
Of Ragozine, more like to Claudio?

DUKE. O, 'tis an accident that heaven provides!
Dispatch it presently; the hour draws on
Prefix'd by Angelo: see this be done,
And sent according to command, whiles I
Persuade this rude wretch willingly to die.

PROV. This shall be done, good father, presently.
But Barnardine must die this afternoon;
And how shall we continue Claudio,

(*) Old text, *friends*.

[a] I am as well acquainted—] That is, as well furnished with acquaintance.

To save me from the danger that might come,
If he were known alive?
DUKE. Let this be done. [Claudio:
Put them in secret holds, both Barnardine and
Ere twice the sun hath made his journal greeting,
To yonder generation you shall find
Your safety manifested.[a]
PROV. I am your free dependant.
DUKE. Quick, despatch, and send the head to
Angelo. [*Exit* Provost.
Now will I write letters to Angelo,—
The provost, he shall bear them,—whose contents
Shall witness to him I am near at home,
And that, by great injunctions, I am bound
To enter publicly: him I'll desire
To meet me at the consecrated fount,
A league below the city; and from thence,
By cold gradation and well-balanc'd* form,
We shall proceed with Angelo.

Re-enter Provost *with* Ragozine's *head.*

PROV. Here is the head; I'll carry it myself.
DUKE. Convenient is it. Make a swift return,
For I would commune with you of such things
That want no ear but yours.
PROV. I'll make all speed.
[*Exit.*
ISAB. [*Without.*] Peace, ho, be here! [know,
DUKE. The tongue of Isabel.—She's come to
If yet her brother's pardon be come hither;
But I will keep her ignorant of her good,
To make her heavenly comforts of despair,
When it is least expected.

---

a Ere twice the sun hath made his journal greeting,
To yonder generation you shall find
Your safety manifested.]

The usual reading is that introduced by Hanmer,—

"Ere twice the sun hath made his journal greeting
To th' *under* generation, you shall find," &c.

(*) Old text, *weale-ballanc'd.*

Messrs. Knight, Collier, and Singer, however, have—

"Ere twice the sun hath made his journal greeting
To yonder generation, you shall find," &c.

The meaning we take to be simply, *ere two days, you shall find your safety manifested to the outer world.*

Enter ISABELLA.

ISAB. Ho! by your leave.

DUKE. Good morning to you, fair and gracious daughter.

ISAB. The better, given me by so holy a man.
Hath yet the deputy sent my brother's pardon?

DUKE. He hath releas'd him, Isabel, from the world:
His head is off, and sent to Angelo.

ISAB. Nay, but it is not so.

DUKE. It is no other.
Show your wisdom, daughter, in your close patience.

ISAB. O, I will to him, and pluck out his eyes!

DUKE. You shall not be admitted to his sight.

ISAB. Unhappy Claudio! Wretched Isabel!
Injurious world! Most damned Angelo!

DUKE. This nor hurts him, nor profits you a jot:
Forbear it therefore; give your cause to heaven.
Mark what I say, which you shall find
By every syllable a faithful verity.
The duke comes home to-morrow;—nay, dry [your eyes:
One of our covent,[a] and his confessor,
Gives me this instance: already he hath carried
Notice to Escalus and Angelo;
Who do prepare to meet him at the gates,
There to give up their power. If you can, pace your wisdom
In that good path that I would wish it go;
And you shall have your bosom on this wretch,
Grace of the duke, revenges to your heart,
And general honour.

ISAB. I am directed by you.

DUKE. This letter, then, to friar Peter give;
'Tis that he sent me of the duke's return:
Say, by this token, I desire his company
At Mariana's house to-night. Her cause and yours
I'll perfect him withal; and he shall bring you
Before the duke; and to the head of Angelo
Accuse him home and home. For my poor self,
I am combined by a sacred vow,
And shall be absent. Wend you with this letter:

[a] Covent,—] The older form of the word *convent*.

Command these fretting waters from your eyes
With a light heart; trust not my holy order,
If I pervert your course.—Who's here?

Enter LUCIO.

LUCIO. Good even.—
Friar, where's the provost?

DUKE. Not within, sir.

LUCIO. O, pretty Isabella, I am pale at mine heart to see thine eyes so red: thou must be patient. I am fain to dine and sup with water and bran; I dare not for my head fill my belly; one fruitful meal would set me to't. But they say the duke will be here to-morrow. By my troth, Isabel, I loved thy brother: if the old fantastical duke of dark corners had been at home, he had lived. [*Exit* ISABELLA.

DUKE. Sir, the duke is marvellous little beholden to your reports; but the best is, he lives not in them.

LUCIO. Friar, thou knowest not the duke so well as I do: he's a better woodman[a] than thou takest him for.

DUKE. Well, you'll answer this one day. Fare ye well.

LUCIO. Nay, tarry; I'll go along with thee: I can tell thee pretty tales of the duke.

DUKE. You have told me too many of him already, sir, if they be true; if not true, none were enough.

LUCIO. I was once before him for getting a wench with child.

DUKE. Did you such a thing?

LUCIO. Yes, marry, did I; but I was fain to forswear it; they would else have married me to the rotten medlar.

DUKE. Sir, your company is fairer than honest. Rest you well.

LUCIO. By my troth, I'll go with thee to the lane's end: if bawdy talk offend you, we'll have very little of it. Nay, friar, I am a kind of burr; I shall stick. [*Exeunt.*

SCENE IV.—*A Room in* Angelo's *House.*

Enter ANGELO *and* ESCALUS.

ESCAL. Every letter he hath writ hath disvouched other.

ANG. In most uneven and distracted manner. His actions show much like to madness: pray heaven his wisdom be not tainted! And why meet him at the gates, and re-deliver[b] our authorities there?

ESCAL. I guess not.

ANG. And why should we proclaim it in an hour before his entering, that if any crave redress of injustice, they should exhibit their petitions in the street?

ESCAL. He shows his reason for that;—to have a dispatch of complaints, and to deliver us from devices hereafter, which shall then have no power to stand against us.

ANG. Well, I beseech you, let it be proclaim'd.
Betimes i' the morn, I'll call you at your house.
Give notice to such men of sort and suit
As are to meet him.

ESCAL. I shall, sir: fare you well.

ANG. Good night.— [*Exit* ESCALUS.
This deed unshapes me quite, makes me unpregnant,[c]
And dull to all proceedings. A deflower'd maid!
And by an eminent body that enforc'd
The law against it!—But that her tender shame
Will not proclaim against her maiden loss,
How might she tongue me! Yet reason dares her no;[d]
For my authority rears[e] of a credent bulk
That no particular scandal once can touch,
But it confounds the breather. He should have liv'd,
Save that his riotous youth, with dangerous sense,
Might in the times to come have ta'en revenge,
By so receiving a dishonour'd life
With ransom of such shame. Would yet he had liv'd!
Alack, when once our grace we have forgot,
Nothing goes right! we would, and we would not.
[*Exit.*

SCENE V.—*An open Place without the City.*

Enter DUKE, *in his own habit, and* FRIAR PETER.

DUKE. These letters at fit time deliver me:
[*Giving letters.*
The provost knows our purpose and our plot.
The matter being afoot, keep your instruction,
And hold you ever to our special drift,

---

a Woodman—] A cant term for a wencher.

b Re-deliver—] The first folio has *reliver;* the second, *deliver.*

c Unpregnant,—] *Inapt, unable.*

d Yet reason dares her no;] The meaning seems to be, reason overawes, or frights her *not* to impeach me.

e *For my authority* rears of *a credent bulk*—] The old copies have,—

"For my authority *beares* of a credent bulke," &c.

which is plainly wrong. In modern editions the reading is,—

"For my authority bears *off* a credent bulk," &c.

or

"—————— bears so credent bulk," &c.

and Mr. Collier's annotator suggests,

"—————— bears *such* a credent bulk."

For the substitution of *rears* for *bears* we are responsible.

Though sometimes you do blench from this to that,
As cause doth minister. Go, call at Flavius'* house,
And tell him where I stay: give the like notice
To Valentinus,† Rowland, and to Crassus,
And bid them bring the trumpets to the gate;
But send me Flavius first.

F. PETER. It shall be speeded well.
[*Exit* F. PETER.

Enter VARRIUS.

DUKE. I thank thee, Varrius; thou hast made good haste:
Come, we will walk. There's other of our friends
Will greet us here anon, my gentle Varrius.
[*Exeunt.*

SCENE VI.—*Street near the City Gate.*

Enter ISABELLA *and* MARIANA.

ISAB. To speak so indirectly I am loth:
I would say the truth; but to accuse him so,
That is your part; yet I am advis'd to do it;
He says, to veil full[a] purpose.

MARI. Be rul'd by him.

ISAB. Besides, he tells me that, if peradventure
He speak against me on the adverse side,
I should not think it strange; for 'tis a physic,
That's bitter to sweet end.

MARI. I would friar Peter—

ISAB. O, peace! the friar is come.

Enter FRIAR PETER.

F. PETER. Come, I have found you out a stand most fit,
Where you may have such vantage on the duke,
He shall not pass you. Twice have the trumpets sounded:
The generous[b] and gravest citizens
Have hent[c] the gates, and very near upon
The duke is ent'ring: therefore, hence, away!
[*Exeunt.*

(*) Old text, *Flavia's*. (†) Old text, *Valencius*.

a To veil full purpose.] Theobald, whose lection has been generally adopted, reads,—"to 'vailful purpose."

b Generous—] In the Latin sense, as in "Othello," Act III. Sc. 3,—
"——the *generous* islanders," &c.

c Hent—] From the Saxon *hentan*, to *take, catch*, or *lay hold of*.

ACT V.

SCENE I.—*A public Place near the City Gate.*

MARIANA (*veiled*), ISABELLA, *and* FRIAR PETER, *at a distance. Enter from one side,* DUKE, VARRIUS, Lords; *from the other,* ANGELO, ESCALUS, LUCIO, Provost, Officers, *and* Citizens.

DUKE. My very worthy cousin, fairly met:—
Our old and faithful friend, we are glad to see you.

ANG. and ESCAL. Happy return be to your royal grace!

DUKE. Many and hearty thankings to you both.
We have made inquiry of you; and we hear
Such goodness of your justice, that our soul
Cannot but yield you forth to public thanks,
Forerunning more requital.

ANG. You make my bonds still greater.
DUKE. O, your desert speaks loud; and I should wrong it,
To lock it in the wards of covert bosom,
When it deserves, with characters of brass,
A forted residence 'gainst the tooth of time,
And razure of oblivion. Give me your hand,
And let the subject see, to make them know
That outward courtesies would fain proclaim
Favours that keep within.—Come, Escalus;
You must walk by us on our other hand:—
And good supporters are you.

FRIAR PETER *and* ISABELLA *come forward.*

F. PETER. Now is your time: speak loud, and kneel before him.
ISAB. Justice, O royal duke! Vail your regard
Upon a wronged, I would fain have said, a maid!
O worthy prince, dishonour not your eye
By throwing it on any other object,
Till you have heard me in my true complaint,
And given me justice, justice, justice, justice!
DUKE. Relate your wrongs: in what? by whom? be brief.
Here is lord Angelo shall give you justice:
Reveal yourself to him.
ISAB. O, worthy duke!
You bid me seek redemption of the devil:
Hear me yourself; for that which I must speak
Must either punish me, not being believ'd,
Or wring redress from you: hear me, O, hear me, here!
ANG. My lord, her wits, I fear me, are not firm:
She hath been a suitor to me for her brother,
Cut off by course of justice,—
ISAB. *By course of justice!*
ANG. And she will speak most bitterly and strange.
ISAB. Most strange, but yet most truly, will I speak:
That Angelo's forsworn, is it not strange?
That Angelo's a murderer, is't not strange?
That Angelo is an adulterous thief,
An hypocrite, a virgin-violator,
Is it not strange and strange?
DUKE. Nay, it is ten times strange.
ISAB. It is not truer he is Angelo,
Than this is all as true as it is strange:
Nay, it is ten times true; for truth is truth
To the end of reckoning.
DUKE. Away with her!—Poor soul,
She speaks this in the infirmity of sense.
ISAB. O prince, I cōnjure thee, as thou believ'st
There is another comfort than this world,
That thou neglect me not, with that opinion
That I am touch'd with madness! Make not impossible
That which but seems unlike: 'tis not impossible,
But one, the wicked'st caitiff on the ground,
May seem as shy, as grave, as just, as absolute,
As Angelo; even so may Angelo,
In all his dressings, characts, titles, forms,
Be an arch-villain: believe it, royal prince:
If he be less, he's nothing; but he's more,
Had I more name for badness.
DUKE. By mine honesty,
If she be mad,—as I believe no other,—
Her madness hath the oddest frame of sense,
Such a dependency of thing on thing,
As e'er[a] I heard in madness.
ISAB. O, gracious duke,
Harp not on that; nor do not banish reason
For inequality; but let your reason serve
To make the truth appear where it seems hid,
And hide the false seems true.
DUKE. Many that are not mad,
Have, sure, more lack of reason.—What would you say?
ISAB. I am the sister of one Claudio,
Condemn'd upon the act of fornication
To lose his head; condemn'd by Angelo:
I, in probation of a sisterhood,
Was sent to by my brother; one Lucio,
As then the messenger—
LUCIO. That's I, an't like your grace:
I came to her from Claudio, and desir'd her
To try her gracious fortune with lord Angelo,
For her poor brother's pardon.
ISAB. That's he, indeed.
DUKE. You were not bid to speak.
LUCIO. No, my good lord;
Nor wish'd to hold my peace.
DUKE. I wish you now, then;
Pray you, take note of it; and when you have
A business for yourself, pray heaven you then
Be perfect.
LUCIO. I warrant your honour.
DUKE. The warrant's for yourself: take heed to it.
ISAB. This gentleman told somewhat of my tale,—
LUCIO. Right.
DUKE. It may be right; but you are i' the wrong
To speak before your time.—Proceed.
ISAB. I went
To this pernicious caitiff deputy,—
DUKE. That's somewhat madly spoken.
ISAB. Pardon it:
The phrase is to the matter.
DUKE. Mended again: the matter;—proceed.
ISAB. In brief,—to set the needless process by,

a As e'er—] We agree in thinking with Malone that Shakespeare wrote:—
"As *ne'er* I heard in madness."

How I persuaded, how I pray'd, and kneel'd,
How he refell'd[a] me, and how I replied,—
For this was of much length,—the vile conclusion
I now begin with grief and shame to utter:
He would not, but by gift of my chaste body
To his concupiscible intemperate lust,
Release my brother; and, after much debatement,
My sisterly remorse[b] confutes mine honour,
And I did yield to him: but the next morn betimes,
His purpose surfeiting, he sends a warrant
For my poor brother's head.

DUKE. This is most likely!

ISAB. O, that it were as like as it is true![c]

DUKE. By heaven, fond wretch! thou know'st not what thou speak'st,
Or else thou art suborn'd against his honour
In hateful practice.[d] First, his integrity
Stands without blemish: next, it imports no reason,
That with such vehemency he should pursue
Faults proper to himself; if he had so offended,
He would have weigh'd thy brother by himself,
And not have cut him off. Some one hath set you on:
Confess the truth, and say by whose advice
Thou cam'st here to complain.

ISAB. And is this all?
Then, O, you blessed ministers above,
Keep me in patience, and, with ripen'd time,
Unfold the evil which is here wrapt up
In countenance!—Heaven shield your grace from woe,
As I, thus wrong'd, hence unbelieved go!

DUKE. I know you'd fain be gone.—An officer!
To prison with her!—Shall we thus permit
A blasting and a scandalous breath to fall
On him so near us? This needs must be a practice.—
Who knew of your intent and coming hither?

ISAB. One that I would were here, friar Lodowick.

DUKE. A ghostly father, belike.—Who knows that Lodowick?

LUCIO. My lord, I know him; 'tis a meddling friar;
I do not like the man: had he been lay, my lord,
For certain words he spake against your grace
In your retirement, I had swinged him soundly.

DUKE. Words against me! this a good friar,[e] belike!
And to set on this wretched woman here
Against our substitute!—Let this friar be found.

LUCIO. But yesternight, my lord, she and that friar,
I saw them at the prison: a saucy friar,
A very scurvy fellow.

F. PETER. Bless'd be your royal grace!
I have stood by, my lord, and I have heard
Your royal ear abus'd. First, hath this woman
Most wrongfully accus'd your substitute,
Who is as free from touch or soil with her,
As she from one ungot.

DUKE. We did believe no less.
Know you that friar Lodowick that she speaks of?

F. PETER. I know him for a man divine and holy;
Not scurvy, nor a temporary meddler,
As he's reported by this gentleman;
And, on my trust, a man that never yet
Did, as he vouches, misreport your grace.

LUCIO. My lord, most villainously; believe it.

F. PETER. Well, he in time may come to clear himself;
But at this instant he is sick, my lord,
Of a strange fever. Upon his mere request,—
Being come to knowledge that there was complaint
Intended 'gainst lord Angelo,—came I hither,
To speak, as from his mouth, what he doth know
Is true and false; and what he with his oath,
And all probation, will make up full clear,
Whensoever he's convented.[f] First, for this woman,—
To justify this worthy nobleman,
So vulgarly and personally accus'd,
Her shall you hear disproved to her eyes,
Till she herself confess it.

DUKE. Good friar, let's hear it.

[ISABELLA *is carried off guarded; and* MARIANA *comes forward.*

Do you not smile at this, lord Angelo?—
O heaven, the vanity of wretched fools!—
Give us some seats.—Come, cousin Angelo;
In this I'll be impartial;[g] be you judge
Of your own cause.—Is this the witness, friar?
First, let her show her face, and after speak.

MARI. Pardon, my lord, I will not show my face,
Until my husband bid me.

DUKE. What, are you married?

MARI. No, my lord.

DUKE. Are you a maid?

MARI. No, my lord.

DUKE. A widow then?

MARI. Neither, my lord.

DUKE. Why, you are nothing then:—neither maid, widow, nor wife?

LUCIO. My lord, she may be a punk; for many of them are neither maid, widow, nor wife.

---

a Refell'd *me*,—] *Refuted* me.
b Remorse—] *Pity*.
c O, that it were as like as it is true!] Malone's explanation of this appears the right one;—"O, that it had as much of the *likeness*, or *appearance*, as it has of the *reality* of truth!"
d Practice.] *Conspiracy, collusion.*

e This a good friar,—] Meaning, "This *is* a good friar;" an habitual turn of expression in old language.
f Convented.] That is, *summoned, cited*.
g I'll be impartial;] Although *impartial* is sometimes used by our old writers for *most partial*, it means in this place no more than *neutral*.

DUKE. Silence that fellow: I would, he had some cause
To prattle for himself.
LUCIO. Well, my lord.
MARI. My lord, I do confess I ne'er was married;
And, I confess, besides, I am no maid: [not
I have known my husband, yet my husband knows
That ever he knew me.
LUCIO. He was drunk then, my lord: it can be no better.
DUKE. For the benefit of silence, would thou wert so too!
LUCIO. Well, my lord.
DUKE. This is no witness for lord Angelo.
MARI. Now I come to't, my lord:
She that accuses him of fornication,
In self-same manner doth accuse my husband;
And charges him, my lord, with such a time
When I'll depose I had him in mine arms
With all the effect of love.
ANG. Charges she more than me?
MARI. Not that I know.
DUKE. No? you say your husband.
MARI. Why, just, my lord, and that is Angelo,
Who thinks he knows that he ne'er knew my body,
But knows he thinks that he knows Isabel's.
ANG. This is a strange abuse.[a]—Let's see thy face.
MARI. My husband bids me; now I will unmask. [*Unveiling.*
This is that face, thou cruel Angelo,
Which once thou swor'st was worth the looking on:
This is the hand, which, with a vow'd contráct,
Was fast belock'd in thine: this is the body
That took away the match from Isabel,
And did supply thee at thy garden-house
In her imagin'd person.
DUKE. Know you this woman?
LUCIO. Carnally, she says.
DUKE. Sirrah, no more!
LUCIO. Enough, my lord. [woman;
ANG. My lord, I must confess I know this
And five years since there was some speech of marriage
Betwixt myself and her; which was broke off,
Partly for that her promised proportions
Came short of composition; but, in chief,
For that her reputation was disvalued
In levity: since which time of five years [her,
I never spake with her, saw her, nor heard from
Upon my faith and honour.
MARI. Noble prince,
As there comes light from heaven, and words from breath,
As there is sense in truth, and truth in virtue,
I am affianc'd this man's wife as strongly
As words could make up vows: and, my good lord,
But Tuesday night last gone, in's garden-house,
He knew me as a wife. As this is true,
Let me in safety raise me from my knees,
Or else for ever be confixed here,
A marble monument!
ANG. I did but smile till now:
Now, good my lord, give me the scope of justice;
My patience here is touch'd. I do perceive,
These poor informal[b] women are no more
But instruments of some more mightier member,
That sets them on: let me have way, my lord,
To find this practice out.
DUKE. Ay, with my heart;
And punish them to your height of pleasure.—
Thou foolish friar; and thou pernicious woman,
Compáct with her that's gone, think'st thou thy oaths, [saint,
Though they would swear down each particular
Were testimonies against his worth and credit,
That's seal'd in approbation?—You, lord Escalus,
Sit with my cousin: lend him your kind pains
To find out this abuse, whence 'tis deriv'd.—
There is another friar that set them on;
Let him be sent for.
F. PETER. Would he were here, my lord! for he, indeed,
Hath set the women on to this complaint:
Your provost knows the place where he abides,
And he may fetch him.
DUKE. Go, do it instantly.—
[*Exit* Provost.
And you, my noble and well-warranted cousin,
Whom it concerns to hear this matter forth,[c]
Do with your injuries as seems you best,
In any chastisement: I for a while
Will leave you; but stir not you, till you have well
Determined upon these slanderers.
ESCAL. My lord, we'll do it throughly.—[*Exit* DUKE.] Signior Lucio, did not you say you knew that friar Lodowick to be a dishonest person?
LUCIO. *Cucullus non facit monachum:* honest in nothing but in his clothes; and one that hath spoke most villainous speeches of the duke.
ESCAL. We shall entreat you to abide here till he come, and enforce them against him: we shall find this friar a notable fellow.
LUCIO. As any in Vienna, on my word.
ESCAL. Call that same Isabel here once again: I would speak with her. [*Exit an* Attendant.] Pray you, my lord, give me leave to question; you shall see how I'll handle her.

[a] A *strange* abuse.] Abuse here seems to imply *delusion*, or *deception;* as in "Macbeth," Act III. Sc. 4:—
"——— my strange and *self-abuse.*"

[b] Informal—] *Deranged, infatuated.*
[c] *To hear this matter* forth,—] That is, to hear it *out.*

LUCIO. Not better than he, by her own report.

ESCAL. Say you?

LUCIO. Marry, sir, I think, if you handled her privately, she would sooner confess: perchance, publicly, she'll be ashamed.

ESCAL. I will go darkly to work with her.

LUCIO. That's the way; for women are light at midnight.

Re-enter Officers *with* ISABELLA.

ESCAL. [*To* ISABELLA.] Come on, mistress: here's a gentlewoman denies all that you have said.

LUCIO. My lord, here comes the rascal I spoke of; here, with the provost.

ESCAL. In very good time:—speak not you to him till we call upon you.

LUCIO. Mum.

Re-enter DUKE, *disguised as a Friar, and* Provost.

ESCAL. Come, sir: did you set these women on to slander lord Angelo? they have confessed you did.

DUKE. 'Tis false.

ESCAL. How! know you where you are?

DUKE. Respect to your great place! and let the devil
Be sometime honour'd for his burning throne!—
Where is the duke? 'tis he should hear me speak.

ESCAL. The duke's in us, and we will hear you speak:
Look you speak justly.

DUKE. Boldly, at least.—But, O, poor souls,
Come you to seek the lamb here of the fox?
Good night to your redress! Is the duke gone?
Then is your cause gone too. The duke's unjust,
Thus to retort your manifest appeal,
And put your trial in the villain's mouth,
Which here you come to accuse.

LUCIO. This is the rascal; this is he I spoke of.

ESCAL. Why, thou unreverend and unhallow'd friar,
Is't not enough thou hast suborn'd these women
To accuse this worthy man, but, in foul mouth,
And in the witness of his proper ear,
To call him villain? and then to glance from him
To the duke himself, to tax him with injustice?—
Take him hence; to the rack with him!—We'll touse you
Joint by joint, but we will know his[a] purpose.—
What? unjust!

DUKE. Be not so hot; the duke dare
No more stretch this finger of mine, than he
Dare rack his own: his subject am I not,
Nor here provincial.[b] My business in this state
Made me a looker-on here in Vienna,
Where I have seen corruption boil and bubble,
Till it o'er-run the stew: laws for all faults,
But faults so countenanc'd, that the strong statutes
Stand like the forfeits in a barber's shop,
As much in mock as mark.(1)

ESCAL. Slander to the state! Away with him to prison!

ANG. What can you vouch against him, signior Lucio?
Is this the man that you did tell us of?

LUCIO. 'Tis he, my lord.—Come hither, goodman bald-pate: do you know me?

DUKE. I remember you, sir, by the sound of your voice: I met you at the prison, in the absence of the duke.

LUCIO. O, did you so? and do you remember what you said of the duke?

DUKE. Most notedly, sir.

LUCIO. Do you so, sir? and was the duke a fleshmonger, a fool, and a coward, as you then reported him to be?

DUKE. You must, sir, change persons with me, ere you make that my report: you, indeed, spoke so of him; and much more, much worse.

LUCIO. O, thou damnable fellow! did not I pluck thee by the nose, for thy speeches?

DUKE. I protest, I love the duke as I love myself.

ANG. Hark how the villain would close[c] now, after his treasonable abuses!

ESCAL. Such a fellow is not to be talked withal—away with him to prison!—where is the provost?—away with him to prison! lay bolts enough upon him: let him speak no more.—Away with those giglots too, and with the other confederate companion!

[*The* Provost *lays hand on the* DUKE.

DUKE. Stay, sir; stay a while.

ANG. What! resists he?—Help him, Lucio.

LUCIO. Come, sir; come, sir; come, sir; foh, sir! Why, you bald-pated, lying rascal! you must be hooded, must you? Show your knave's visage, with a pox to you! show your sheep-biting face, and be hanged an hour! Will't not off?

[*Pulls off the Friar's hood, and discovers the* DUKE.

---

[a] —his purpose.] Capell reads, "—*this* purpose," and Mr. Collier's annotator, "—*your* purpose," but Boswell suggested that, after threatening the supposed Friar, Escalus addresses the close of the sentence to the bystanders.

[b] *Nor here* provincial.] Nor within the ecclesiastical jurisdiction of the *province*.

[c] Close—] So the old copies. In Mr. Collier's annotated folio, the word is changed to *gloze*.

DUKE. Thou art the first knave, that e'er made* a duke.—
First, provost, let me bail these gentle three.—
Sneak not away, sir; [*To* LUCIO.] for the friar and you
Must have a word anon.—Lay hold on him.
LUCIO. This may prove worse than hanging.
DUKE. [*To* ESCALUS.] What you have spoke, I pardon; sit you down:—
We'll borrow place of him:— [*To* ANGELO.] sir, by your leave.
Hast thou or word, or wit, or impudence,
That yet can do thee office? If thou hast,
Rely upon it till my tale be heard,
And hold no longer out.
ANG. O, my dread lord,
I should be guiltier than my guiltiness,
To think I can be undiscernible,
When I perceive your grace, like power divine,
Hath look'd upon my passes![a] Then, good prince,
No longer session hold upon my shame,
But let my trial be mine own confession:
Immediate sentence then, and sequent death,
Is all the grace I beg.
DUKE. Come hither, Mariana.—
Say, wast thou e'er contracted to this woman?
ANG. I was, my lord.
DUKE. Go take her hence, and marry her instantly.—
Do you the office, friar; which consummate,
Return him here again.—Go with him, provost.
[*Exeunt* ANGELO, MARIANA, FRIAR PETER, *and* Provost.
ESCAL. My lord, I am more amaz'd at his dishonour,
Than at the strangeness of it.
DUKE. Come hither, Isabel.
Your friar is now your prince: as I was then
Advértising and holy to your business,
Not changing heart with habit, I am still
Attorney'd at your service.
ISAB. O, give me pardon,
That I, your vassal, have employ'd and pain'd
Your unknown sovereignty!
DUKE. You are pardon'd, Isabel:
And now, dear maid, be you as free to us.
Your brother's death, I know, sits at your heart;
And you may marvel why I obscur'd myself,
Labouring to save his life, and would not rather
Make rash demonstrance[b] of my hidden power,
Than let him so be lost. O, most kind maid!
It was the swift celerity of his death,
Which I did think with slower foot came on,
That brain'd my purpose: but, peace be with him!
That life is better life, past fearing death,
Than that which lives to fear: make it your comfort,
So happy is your brother.
ISAB. I do, my lord.

Re-enter ANGELO, MARIANA, FRIAR PETER, *and* Provost.

DUKE. For this new-married man, approaching here,
Whose salt imagination yet hath wrong'd
Your well-defended honour, you must pardon
For Mariana's sake: but as he adjudg'd your brother,—
Being criminal, in double violation
Of sacred chastity, and of promise-breach
Thereon dependent,—for your brother's life,
The very mercy of the law cries out
Most audible, even from his proper tongue,
An Angelo for Claudio, death for death!
Haste still pays haste, and leisure answers leisure;
Like doth quit like, and Measure still for Measure.
Then, Angelo, thy fault[c] thus manifested,—
Which, though thou wouldst deny, denies thee vantage,—
We do condemn thee to the very block
Where Claudio stoop'd to death, and with like haste.—
Away with him!
MARI. O, my most gracious lord,
I hope you will not mock me with a husband!
DUKE. It is your husband mock'd you with a husband:
Consenting to the safeguard of your honour,
I thought your marriage fit; else imputation,
For that he knew you, might reproach your life,
And choke your good to come. For his possessions,
Although by confiscation* they are ours,
We do instate and widow you withal,
To buy you a better husband.
MARI. O, my dear lord,
I crave no other, nor no better man.
DUKE. Never crave him; we are definitive.
MARI. Gentle my liege,— [*Kneeling.*
DUKE. You do but lose your labour.
Away with him to death!—[*To* LUCIO.] Now, sir, to you.
MARI. O, my good lord!—Sweet Isabel, take my part;
Lend me your knees, and all my life to come
I'll lend you all my life to do you service.

(*) Old text, *ere mad'st*.

(*) First folio, *confutation*.

a *Hath looked upon my* passes!] *Passes*, if not a typographical mistake, as we have sometimes suspected it to be, for *lapses*, may mean *courses*, from the French *passées*.

b Demonstrance—] In the old text, *remonstrance;* the correction was made by Malone.

c —*thy* fault thus *manifested*,—] *Fault* is an emendation of Mr. Dyce. The old copies have *fault's*.

DUKE. Against all sense you do impórtune her:
Should she kneel down in mercy of this fact,
Her brother's ghost his paved bed would break,
And take her hence in horror.

MARI. Isabel,
Sweet Isabel, do yet but kneel by me:
Hold up your hands, say nothing,—I'll speak all.
They say, best men are moulded out of faults,
And, for the most, become much more the better
For being a little bad: so may my husband.
O, Isabel! will you not lend a knee?

DUKE. He dies for Claudio's death.

ISAB. Most bounteous sir, [*Kneeling.*
Look, if it please you, on this man condemn'd,
As if my brother liv'd: I partly think,
A due sincerity govern'd his deeds,
Till he did look on me: since it is so,
Let him not die. My brother had but justice,
In that he did the thing for which he died:
For Angelo,
His act did not o'ertake his bad intent;
And must be buried but as an intent
That perish'd by the way: thoughts are no subjects;
Intents but merely thoughts.

MARI. Merely, my lord.

DUKE. Your suit's unprofitable: stand up, I say.—
I have bethought me of another fault.—
Provost, how came it Claudio was beheaded
At an unusual hour?

PROV. It was commanded so.

DUKE. Had you a special warrant for the deed?

PROV. No, my good lord; it was by private message.

DUKE. For which I do discharge you of your office:
Give up your keys.

PROV. Pardon me, noble lord:
I thought it was a fault, but knew it not;
Yet did repent me, after more advice:
For testimony whereof, one in the prison,
That should by private order else have died,
I have reserv'd alive.

DUKE. What's he?

PROV. His name is Barnardine.

DUKE. I would thou hadst done so by Claudio.—
Go, fetch him hither; let me look upon him.
[*Exit* Provost.

ESCAL. I am sorry, one so learned and so wise
As you, lord Angelo, have still appear'd,
Should slip so grossly, both in the heat of blood,
And lack of temper'd judgment afterward.

ANG. I am sorry that such sorrow I procure;
And so deep sticks it in my penitent heart,
That I crave death more willingly than mercy;
'T is my deserving, and I do entreat it.

Re-enter Provost, *with* BARNARDINE, CLAUDIO, *muffled, and* JULIET.

DUKE. Which is that Barnardine?

PROV. This, my lord.

DUKE. There was a friar told me of this man.—
Sirrah, thou art said to have a stubborn soul,
That apprehends no further than this world,
And squar'st thy life according. Thou'rt condemn'd;
But, for those earthly faults, I quit them all,
And pray thee, take this mercy to provide
For better times to come.—Friar, advise him;
I leave him to your hand.—What muffled fellow's that?

PROV. This is another prisoner that I sav'd,
Who should have died when Claudio lost his head;
As like almost to Claudio as himself.
[*Unmuffles* CLAUDIO.

DUKE. [*To* ISABELLA.] If he be like your brother, for his sake
Is he pardon'd; and, for your lovely sake,
Give me your hand, and say you will be mine,
He is my brother too: but fitter time for that.—
By this lord Angelo perceives he's safe:
Methinks I see a quick'ning in his eye.—
Well, Angelo, your evil quits[a] you well:
Look that you love your wife; her worth, worth yours.—
I find an apt remission in myself;
And yet here's one in place I cannot pardon.—
[*To* LUCIO.] You, sirrah, that knew me for a fool, a coward,
One all of luxury,[b] an ass, a madman:
Wherein have I deserved* so of you,
That you extol me thus?

LUCIO. Faith, my lord, I spoke it but according to the trick. If you will hang me for it, you may; but I had rather it would please you I might be whipped.

DUKE. Whipp'd first, sir, and hang'd after.—
Proclaim it, provost, round about the city,
If any woman's† wrong'd by this lewd fellow,
—As I have heard him swear himself there's one
Whom he begot with child,—let her appear,
And he shall marry her: the nuptial finish'd,
Let him be whipp'd and hang'd.

LUCIO. I beseech your highness, do not marry me to a whore! Your highness said even now, I

---

[a] *Your evil* quits *you well*:] That is, *requites* you well: you receive good for evil.

[b] Luxury,—] *Concupiscence.*

(*) Old text, *so deserv'd.*

(†) Old text, *woman.*

made you a duke: good my lord, do not recompense me in making me a cuckold.

DUKE. Upon mine honour, thou shalt marry her.
Thy slanders I forgive; and therewithal
Remit thy other forfeits.—Take him to prison;
And see our pleasure herein executed.

LUCIO. Marrying a punk, my lord, is pressing to death, whipping, and hanging.

DUKE. Slandering a prince deserves it.—

[*Exeunt* Officers *with* LUCIO.

She, Claudio, that you wrong'd, look you restore.—
Joy to you, Mariana!—Love her, Angelo:
I have confess'd her, and I know her virtue.—
Thanks, good friend Escalus, for thy much goodness:
There's more behind that is more gratulate.—
Thanks, provost, for thy care and secrecy;
We shall employ thee in a worthier place.—
Forgive him, Angelo, that brought you home
The head of Ragozine for Claudio's:
The offence pardons itself.—Dear Isabel,
I have a motion much imports your good;
Whereto if you'll a willing ear incline,
What's mine is yours, and what is yours is mine.—
So, bring us to our palace; where we'll show
What's yet behind, that's* meet you all should know. [*Exeunt.*

(*) First folio, *that*.

ILLUSTRATIVE COMMENTS.

ACT I.

(1) Scene II.—*Enter* Pompey.] The original stage direction is "Enter Clown." Of this character Mr. Douce remarks,—"The clown in this play officiates as the tapster of a brothel; whence it has been concluded that he is not a domestic fool, nor ought to appear in the dress of that character. A little consideration will serve to shew that the opinion is erroneous, that *this* clown is *altogether* a domestic fool, and that he should be habited accordingly. In Act II. Sc. 1, Escalus calls him a *tedious fool,* and *Iniquity,* a name for one of the old stage buffoons. He tells him that he will have him *whipt,* a punishment that was very often inflicted on fools. In *Timon of Athens,* we have a *strumpet's fool,* and a similar character is mentioned in the first speech in *Antony and Cleopatra.* But if any one should still entertain a doubt on the subject, he may receive the most complete satisfaction by an attentive examination of ancient prints, many of which will furnish instances of the common use of the domestic fool in brothels."—*Illustrations of Shakespeare,* I. 151.

(2) Scene II.—

> —— *this we came not to,*
> *Only for* propagation of a dower
> *Remaining in the coffer of her friends,*
> *From whom we thought it meet to hide our love*
> *Till time had made them for us.*]

If *propagation* be the poet's word, its most literal meaning, that is, to increase or multiply, seems to furnish the real and natural sense of this much-disputed passage. The dowry of Julietta was "at use" in the coffer of her friends until her authorised marriage should require it to be paid. The *principal,* therefore, was a fixed sum, but the "propagation" of the "dower" expressed the increase of it as added to that principal by the extension of the time in which it lay at interest in the hands of the lady's friends. It is very probable that, in the sixteenth and seventeenth centuries, this was not an uncommon contrivance for improving the portions of unmarried women; and, wherever it could be safely and legally adopted, it was a great protection to their property against the feudal claims of wardship. With respect to the sense of the word *propagation,* as implying the increase of money by interest, there is a pertinent illustration in "Twelfth Night," Act III. Sc. 1, where the Clown says to Viola,—

> "Would not a pair of these have bred, sir?"

and she replies,—

> "Yes, being kept together, and put to use."

Sometimes, however, the improvement of the dowry was not assured by the accumulation of periodical interest; but was left altogether dependent on the good will of a relation. There is an instance of this power being given, in the will of Humphrey de Bohun, Earl of Hereford and Essex, 1361; one of the bequests of which is to "Thomasine Belle, xl marks, [6*l.* 13*s.* 4*d.*] for her marriage, *or more, if she be well married.*" But, in the testament of Henry, the last Lord Grey of Codnor, dated Sept. 10th, 1492, there occurs an instance, perhaps still more to the purpose. The testator is directing the payment of several bequests to his illegitimate children, and he orders that his cousin, Sir Thomas Barrow, should pay 100*l.* to two of them, named Richard Grey, and "the Greater Harry;" or else, *that the land of his part stand still in feoffees'* hands, "till Two Hundred Marks [33*l.* 6*s.* 8*d.*] be raised and paid to the marriage of the said two children."

Still, after all the endeavours to impart a meaning to the word "propagation" in this passage, the expression is so peculiar that it will be suspected. Malone proposed to read, "for *prorogation;*" and Mr. Collier's annotator, "for *procuration.*" Query, is the disputed word a misprint for *propugnation?*—

> "Only for *propugnation* [that is, *defence,* or *preservation*] of a dower,"—

Shakespeare uses the word in this sense elsewhere:—

> "What *propugnation* is in one man's valour."
> *Troilus and Cressida,* Act II. Sc. 2.

ACT III.

(1) Scene I.—

> —— *merely, thou art death's fool.*]

Here, as in a passage of "Pericles," Act III. Sc. 2,—

> "A more content in course of true delight
> Than to be thirsty after tottering honour,
> Or tie my treasure up in silken bags
> To please the *fool and death,*"—

Steevens and Douce conceive the general idea was suggested by the ancient dance of Machabre, or, as it is commonly called, Dance of Death; "that curious pageant of mortality which, during the middle ages, was so great a favourite as to be perpetually exhibited to the people either in the sculpture and painting of ecclesiastical buildings, or in the books adapted to the service of the church." * But, notwithstanding such eminent authority, it may well be questioned whether Shakespeare's allusion is not rather to some old stage representation, familiar to his auditory, where the Devil and the Fool; Death and the Fool; and Time and the Fool,—

> "—— and Life, *Time's fool*"—*First Part of Henry IV.* Act V. Sc. 4.

were in turn brought into ludicrous collision for the entertainment of the spectators.

* Douce's Illustrations of Shakespeare, I. 130.

ACT IV.

(1) SCENE I.—

Take, O, take those lips away,
That so sweetly were forsworn;
And those eyes, the break of day,
Lights that do mislead the morn:
But my kisses bring again, bring again,
Seals of love, but seal'd in vain, seal'd in vain.]

In the edition of our poet's poems, printed in 1640, this beautiful song, with a second stanza,—

"Hide, oh, hide those hills of snow,
Which thy frozen bosom bears,
On whose tops the pinks that grow
Are of those that April wears;
But first set my poor heart free,
Bound in those icy chains by thee"—

is assigned to Shakespeare. Both stanzas, however, are given in Fletcher's play of "The Bloody Brother;" and as the first is evidently intended to be sung by a female, and the second as plainly designed for a man, it has been conjectured that the one was written by Shakespeare for the present scene, and the other added in "The Bloody Brother," by Fletcher. "The first," Mr. R. G. White remarks, "is animated purely by sentiment; the second, delicately beautiful as it is, is the expression of a man carried captive solely through his sense of beauty. The first breathes woman's wasted love; the second, man's disappointed passion. The first could not have been written by Fletcher; the second would not have been written by Shakespeare, as a companion to the first." *

(2) SCENE III.—*First, here's young master Rash; he's in for a commodity of brown paper and old ginger.*] It was the custom of money-lenders in Shakespeare's time, as now, in making advances to improvident young men, to compel them to take a part of the loan in goods, frequently of the most worthless kind. The practice, no doubt, originated in a desire to evade the penalties for usury, and must have reached an alarming height, as the old writers make it a perpetual mark for satire. In Lodge's and Greene's "Looking Glasse for London and Englande," 1598, an unhappy victim who is urged by the usurer for repayment of his debt remonstrates thus, "I pray you sir consider that my losse was great by the commoditie I tooke up; you know sir I borrowed of you forty pounds, whereof I had ten pounds in money, and thirtie pounds in *Lute strings*, which when I came to sell againe, I could get but five pounds for them, so had I sir, but fifteene pounds for my fortie: In consideration of this ill bargaine, I pray you sir give me a month longer." That the commodity sometimes consisted partly or entirely of *brown paper*, is established by a profusion of passages from writers of the period; thus, in Greene's "Quip for an Upstart Courtier," 1592:—"For the Marchant delivered the Yron, Tin, Lead, hops, Sugars, Spices, Oiles, *browne paper*, or whatsoever else, from sixe moneths to sixe moneths: whiche when the poore Gentleman came to sell againe, hee coulde not make threescore and ten in the hundred beside the usury."

Again, in his "Defence of Coney-catching," 1592:—"If he borrow a hundred pound, he shall have forty in silver, and three score in wares; as lute strings, hobby horses, or *brown paper*."

So, also, in Davenport's comedy, "A New Tricke to cheat the Divell," 1639:—

"—— Th' have bin so bit already
With taking up *Commodities of browne paper*,
Buttons past fashion, silkes, and Sattins,
Babies, and Childrens Fiddles, with like trash
Tooke up at a deare rate, and sold for trifles."

(3) SCENE III.—*And are now for the Lord's sake.*] "Charity for the Lord's sake" was the form of supplication used by imprisoned debtors to the passers-by:—

"Good gentle writers, *for the Lord's sake, for the Lord's sake,*
Like Ludgate prisoner, lo, I begging, make
My mone." DAVIES'S *Epigrams*, 1611.

In illustration of the custom and the language used, Mr. Singer adduces a curious passage from Baret's "Alvearie," 1573, under the word "*Interest*, or the borrowing of usurie money wherewith to pay my debt:"—"And therefore methinke it is prettily sayd in Grammar that *Interest* will be joyned with *Mea, Tua, Sua, Nostra, Vestra*, and *Cuia*, only in the ablative case, because they are pronouns possessives. For how great soever his possessions, goodes, or lands be that haunteth the company of this impersonall, if now perchance he be able to kepe three persons, at length he shall not be able to kepe one: yea he himselfe shall shortly become such an impersonall, that he shall be counted as nobody, without any countenance, credit, person, or estimation among men. And when he hath thus filched, and fleeced his *possessive* so long till he hath made him as rich as a new shorn sheepe, then will he turn him to commons *into Ludgate:* where for his ablative case he shall have a dative cage, *craving and crying at the grate, your worships' charitie* FOR THE LORDS SAKE."

* Shakespeare's Scholar, p. 165-6.

ACT V.

(1) SCENE I.—

Stand like the forfeits in a barber's shop,
As much in mock as mark.]

In his review of Dr. Johnson's edition of Shakespeare, Kenrick introduced a metrical list of these forfeits, which he professed to quote from recollection of a table he had seen hung up in a barber's shop either at Malton, or Thirsk, in Yorkshire. Steevens boldly pronounced the version to be a forgery; but, although Dr. Kenrick's memory probably betrayed him in two or three particulars, there are some grounds for believing his list to be in the main a veritable relic of old times. It runs thus:—

RULES FOR SEEMLY BEHAVIOUR.

First come, first serve.—Then come not late;
And, when arrived, keep your state;
For he, who from these rules shall swerve,
Must pay the forfeits.—So, observe.

I.

Who enters here with boots and spurs,
Must keep his nook; for, if he stirs,
And gives, with armed heel, a kick,
A pint he pays for every prick.

II.

Who rudely takes another's turn,
A forfeit mug may manners learn.

III.

Who reverentless shall swear or curse,
Must lug seven farthings from his purse.

IV.

Who checks the barber in his tale
Must pay for each a pot of ale.

V.

Who will, or can, not miss his hat
While trimming, pays a pint for that.

VI.

And he who can, or will, not pay,
Shall hence be sent half trimm'd away;
For, will-he, nill-he, if in fault,
He forfeit must, in meal or malt.
But mark,—who is already in drink,
The cannikin must never clink.

CRITICAL OPINIONS

ON

MEASURE FOR MEASURE.

"In 'Measure for Measure' Shakspeare was compelled, by the nature of the subject, to make his poetry more familiar with criminal justice than is usual with him. All kinds of proceedings connected with the subject, all sorts of active or passive persons, pass in review before us: the hypocritical Lord Deputy, the compassionate Provost, and the hard-hearted Hangman; a young man of quality who is to suffer for the seduction of his mistress before marriage, loose wretches brought in by the police, nay, even a hardened criminal, whom even the preparations for his execution cannot awaken out of his callousness. But yet, notwithstanding this agitating truthfulness, how tender and mild is the pervading tone of the picture! The piece takes improperly its name from punishment; the true significance of the whole is the triumph of mercy over strict justice; no man being himself so free from errors as to be entitled to deal it out to his equals. The most beautiful embellishment of the composition is the character of Isabella, who, on the point of taking the veil, is yet prevailed upon by sisterly affection to tread again the perplexing ways of the world, while, amid the general corruption, the heavenly purity of her mind is not even stained with one unholy thought: in the humble robes of the novice she is a very angel of light. When the cold and stern Angelo, heretofore of unblemished reputation, whom the Duke has commissioned, during his pretended absence, to restrain, by a rigid administration of the laws, the excesses of dissolute immorality, is even himself tempted by the virgin charms of Isabella, supplicating for the pardon of her brother Claudio, condemned to death for a youthful indiscretion; when at first, in timid and obscure language, he insinuates, but at last impudently avouches his readiness to grant Claudio's life to the sacrifice of her honour; when Isabella repulses his offer with a noble scorn; in her account of the interview to her brother, when the latter at first applauds her conduct, but at length, overcome by the fear of death, strives to persuade her to consent to dishonour;—in these masterly scenes, Shakspeare has sounded the depths of the human heart. The interest here reposes altogether on the represented action; curiosity contributes nothing to our delight, for the Duke, in the disguise of a Monk, is always present to watch over his dangerous representative, and to avert every evil which could possibly be apprehended; we look to him with confidence for a happy result. The Duke acts the part of the Monk naturally, even to deception; he unites in his person the wisdom of the priest and the prince. Only in his wisdom he is too fond of round-about ways; his vanity is flattered with acting invisibly like an earthly providence; he takes more pleasure in overhearing his subjects than governing them in the customary way of princes. As he ultimately extends a free pardon to all the guilty, we do not see how his original purpose, in committing the execution of the laws to other hands, of restoring their strictness, has in any wise been accomplished. The poet might have had this irony in view, that of the numberless slanders of the Duke, told him by the petulant Lucio, in ignorance of the person whom he is addressing, that at least which regarded his singularities and whims was not wholly without foundation. It is deserving of remark, that Shakspeare, amidst the rancour of religious parties, takes a delight in painting the condition of a monk, and always represents his influence as beneficial. We find in him none of the black and knavish monks, which an enthusiasm for Protestantism, rather than poetical inspiration, has suggested to some of our modern poets. Shakspeare merely gives his monks an inclination to busy themselves in the affairs of others, after renouncing the world for themselves; with respect, however, to pious frauds, he does not represent them as very conscientious. Such are the parts acted by the monk in 'Romeo and Juliet,' and another in 'Much Ado about Nothing,' and even by the Duke, whom, contrary to the well-known proverb, the cowl seems really to make a monk."—SCHLEGEL.

"Of 'Measure for Measure,' independent of the comic characters, which afford a rich fund of entertainment, the great charm springs from the lovely example of female excellence in the person of Isabella. Piety, spotless purity, tenderness combined with firmness, and an eloquence the most persuasive, unite to render her singularly interesting and attractive. To save the life of her brother, she hastens to quit the peaceful seclusion of her convent, and moves amid the votaries of corruption and hypocrisy, amid the sensual, the vulgar, and the profligate, as a being of a higher order, as a ministering spirit from the throne of grace. Her first interview with Angelo, and the immediately subsequent one with Claudio, exhibit, along with the most engaging feminine diffidence and modesty, an extraordinary display of intellectual energy, of dexterous argument, and of indignant contempt. Her pleadings before the lord deputy are directed with a strong appeal both to his understanding and his heart, while her sagacity and address in the communication of the result of her appointment with him to her brother, of whose weakness and irresolution she is justly apprehensive, are, if possible, still more skilfully marked, and add another to the multitude of instances which have established for Shakspeare an unrivalled intimacy with the finest feelings of our nature.

"The page of poetry, indeed, has not two nobler passages to produce, than those which paint the suspicions of Isabella, as to the fortitude of her brother, her encouragement of his nascent resolution, and the fears which he subsequently entertains of the consequences of dissolution.

"On learning the terms which would effect his liberation, his astonishment and indignation are extreme, and he exclaims with vehemence to his sister,—

Thou shalt not do't;

but no sooner does this burst of moral anger subside, than the natural love of existence returns, and he endeavours to impress Isabella, under the wish of exciting her to the sacrifice demanded for his preservation, with the horrible possibilities which may follow the extinction of this state of being, an enumeration which makes the blood run chill."—DRAKE.

Act III. Sc. 2.

KING HENRY THE EIGHTH.

"The Famous History of The Life of King Henry the Eight" was first printed, it is believed, in the folio of 1623. The date of its production is uncertain. Some editors, including Theobald and Malone, contend that it was written before the death of Elizabeth, and that the complimentary address to her successor—

> "Nor shall this peace sleep with her; but as when
> The bird of wonder dies, the maiden phœnix,
> Her ashes new create another heir,
> As great in admiration as herself;
> So shall she leave her blessedness to one
> (When heaven shall call her from this cloud of darkness)
> Who from the sacred ashes of her honour
> Shall star-like rise, as great in fame as she was,
> And so stand fix'd"—

was interpolated on the play being revived for presentation before King James. Messrs. Dyce, Collier, and others, on the contrary, conjecture it was produced after the accession of James, and in confirmation of this opinion adduce the following Memorandum from the Registers of the Stationers' Company:—

"12 Feb 1604 [1605].

"Nath. Butter] Yf he get good allowance for the Enterlude of K. Henry 8th before he begyn to print it, and then procure the wardens hands to yt for the entrance of yt, he is to have the same for his copy."

This insertion, supposed by many to refer to Rowley's piece, "When you see me you know me," which was published in the same year, and is founded on events and characters in the reign of Henry the Eighth, they think pertains to the present play. Although both parties maintain their theory with confidence, the evidence, external or intrinsic, in favour of either appears too slight and speculative to warrant a decision. One fact seems established, namely, that there was a play upon the same subject at least as early as Shakespeare's "Henry the Eighth," presumably before; for in Henslowe's Diary, pp. 189, 198, 221, &c., are notices regarding two pieces, consisting of a first and second part, written in 1601, the one entitled "The Rising of Cardinal Wolsey," and the other, "Cardinal Wolsey," on which an exceptional amount of money was expended for costume and decoration. There is a probability, too, that at one period "Henry the Eighth" bore a double title, and was known as "Henry the Eighth, or All is True." The grounds for supposing so are these. On the 29th of June, 1613, the Globe theatre on Bankside was totally destroyed, owing to the thatch of the roof being fired by the wadding of some "chambers," or small cannon, discharged during a performance. According to Howes, the continuator of Stow's Chronicle, this catastrophe occurred at the representation of "Henry the Eighth." The same fact is recorded in a MS. letter from Thomas Lorkin to Sir Thomas Puckering, dated the very day after the fire:— * * * * "No longer since than yesterday, while Bourbege his companie were acting at y^e^ Globe the play of Hen = 8. and there shooting of certayne chambers in way of triumph, the fire catch'd, and fastened upon the thatch of the house and there burned so furiously, as it consumed the whole house and all in lesse then two houres;" &c.—MSS. Harl. 7002. But Sir Henry Wotton, writing on the 2d of July in the same year, and describing this calamity, says it took place during the acting of "a *new play*, called, *All is true*, representing some principal pieces of the Reign of Henry the 8th."—*Reliquiæ* (edit. 1672, p. 425). There appears to be no doubt that the play in question, which Sir Henry terms *new*, probably because it was revived with *new* dresses, *new* prologue, epilogue, &c. &c., was our author's "Henry the Eighth," and the discrepancy as to the title might have arisen from the circumstance, just hinted at, of its having originally borne a double one.

Persons Represented.

King Henry the Eighth.
Cardinal Wolsey.
Cardinal Campeius.
Capucius, *Ambassador from the* Emperor Charles V.
Cranmer, *Archbishop of* Canterbury.
Duke *of* Norfolk.
Duke *of* Buckingham.
Duke *of* Suffolk.
Earl *of* Surrey.
Lord Chamberlain.
Lord Chancellor.
Gardiner, King's Secretary, *afterwards* Bishop *of* Winchester.
Bishop *of* Lincoln.
Lord Abergavenny.
Lord Sands.
Sir Henry Guilford.
Sir Thomas Lovell.
Sir Anthony Denny.
Sir Nicholas Vaux.
Secretaries *to* Wolsey.
Cromwell, *Servant to* Wolsey, *afterwards* King's Secretary.
Griffith, *Gentleman-Usher to* Queen Katharine.
Gentleman *of the* King's.
Gentleman *of the* Queen's.
Three Gentlemen.
Doctor Butts, *Physician to the* King.
Garter King-at-Arms.
Surveyor *to the* Duke *of* Buckingham.
Brandon, *and a* Sergeant-at-Arms.
Door-keeper *of the Council Chamber.*
Porter, *and his* Man.
Page *to* Gardiner.
A Crier.

Queen Katharine, *Wife to* King Henry; *afterwards divorced.*
Anne Bullen, *her Maid of Honour; afterwards* Queen.
An Old Lady, *Friend to* Anne Bullen.
Patience, *Woman to* Queen Katharine.

Several Lords and Ladies in the dumb shows; Women attending upon the Queen; Spirits, which appear to her; Scribes, Officers, Guards, and other Attendants.

SCENE,—*Chiefly in* London *and* Westminster; *once at* Kimbolton.

PROLOGUE.

I come no more to make you laugh; things now,
That bear a weighty and a serious brow,
Sad, and high-working,[a] full of state and woe,
Such noble scenes as draw the eye to flow,
We now present. Those that can pity, here
May, if they think it well, let fall a tear;
The subject will deserve it. Such as give
Their money out of hope they may believe,
May here find truth too. Those that come to see
Only a show or two, and so agree
The play may pass, if they be still and willing,
I'll undertake may see away their shilling
Richly in two short hours. Only they,
That come to hear a merry bawdy play,
A noise of targets, or to see a fellow
In a long motley coat, guarded with yellow,
Will be deceiv'd: for, gentle hearers, know,
To rank our chosen truth with such a show
As fool and fight is, beside forfeiting
Our own brains, and the opinion that we bring,
(To make that only true we now intend,)
Will leave us never an understanding friend.
Therefore, for goodness' sake, and as you are known
The first and happiest hearers of the town,
Be sad, as we would make ye: think ye see
The very persons of our noble story,
As they were living; think you see them great,
And follow'd with the general throng and sweat
Of thousand friends; then, in a moment, see
How soon this mightiness meets misery!
And, if you can be merry then, I'll say
A man may weep upon his wedding-day.[b]

---

[a] *Sad*, and high-working,—] The old, and every modern copy, read—

"Sad, high, and working;"

but see,—

"Then let not this Divinitie in earth
(Deare Prince) be sleighted, as she were the birth
Of idle Fancie; *since she workes so hie.*"
Epistle Dedicatorie to Chapman's "Iliads of Homer."

[b] Upon his wedding-day.] The conjecture of Johnson and Farmer, that Ben Jonson furnished the prologue and epilogue to this play, is strongly borne out, not only by their general style and structure, but by particular expressions in them also. As Johnson observes, there is in Shakespeare's dramas so much of "fool and fight," that it is not probable he would animadvert so severely on the introduction of such characters and incidents.

ACT I.

SCENE I.—London. *An Ante-chamber in the Palace.*

Enter, on one side, the DUKE *of* NORFOLK; *on the other, the* DUKE *of* BUCKINGHAM, *and the* LORD ABERGAVENNY.

BUCK. Good morrow, and well met. How have ye done,
Since last we saw in France?
NORF. I thank your grace,
Healthful; and ever since a fresh admirer
Of what I saw there.
BUCK. An untimely ague
Stay'd me a prisoner in my chamber, when

Those suns of glory, those two lights of men,
Met in the vale of Andren.[a]

NORF. 'Twixt Guynes and Arde:
I was then present, saw them salute on horseback;
Beheld them, when they 'lighted, how they clung
In their embracement, as they grew together;
Which had they, what four thron'd ones could have weigh'd
Such a compounded one?

BUCK. All the whole time
I was my chamber's prisoner.

NORF. Then you lost
The view of earthly glory: men might say,
Till this time pomp was single, but now married
To one above itself. Each following day
Became the next day's master, till the last
Made former wonders its: to-day, the French,
All clinquant, all in gold, like heathen gods,
Shone down the English; and, to-morrow, they
Made Britain, India: every man that stood,
Show'd like a mine. Their dwarfish pages were
As cherubins, all gilt: the madams too,
Not us'd to toil, did almost sweat to bear
The pride upon them, that their very labour
Was to them as a painting: now this masque
Was cried incomparable; and the ensuing night
Made it a fool and beggar. The two kings,
Equal in lustre, were now best, now worst,
As presence did present them; him in eye,
Still him in praise: and, being present both,
'Twas said, they saw but one; and no discerner
Durst wag his tongue in censure.[b] When these suns
(For so they phrase 'em) by their heralds challeng'd
The noble spirits to arms, they did perform
Beyond thought's compass; that former fabulous story,
Being now seen possible enough, got credit,
That Bevis was believ'd.(1)

BUCK. O, you go far.

NORF. As I belong to worship, and affect
In honour honesty, the tract of every thing
Would by a good discourser lose some life,
Which action's self was tongue to. All was royal;[c]
To the disposing of it nought rebell'd,
Order gave each thing view; the office did
Distinctly his full function.

BUCK. Who did guide?
I mean, who set the body and the limbs
Of this great sport together, as you guess?

NORF. One, certes, that promises no element[d]
In such a business.

BUCK. I pray you, who, my lord?

NORF. All this was order'd by the good discretion
Of the right-reverend cardinal of York.

BUCK. The devil speed him! no man's pie is [freed
From his ambitious finger. What had he
To do in these fierce vanities? I wonder
That such a keech[e] can with his very bulk
Take up the rays o' the beneficial sun,
And keep it from the earth.

NORF. Surely, sir,
There 's in him stuff that puts him to these ends:
For,—being not propp'd by ancestry, whose grace
Chalks successors their way; nor call'd upon
For high feats done to the crown; neither allied
To eminent assistants; but, spider-like,
Out of his self drawing web,—he gives us note,—[f]
The force of his own merit makes his way;
A gift that heaven gives for him,[g] which buys
A place next to the king.

ABER. I cannot tell
What heaven hath given him,—let some graver eye
Pierce into that;—but I can see his pride
Peep through each part of him: whence has he that?
If not from hell, the devil is a niggard;
Or has given all before, and he begins
A new hell in himself.

BUCK. Why the devil,
Upon this French going-out, took he upon him,
Without the privity o' the king, to appoint
Who should attend on him? He makes up the file
Of all the gentry; for the most part such
To whom as great a charge as little honour
He meant to lay upon: and his own letter,
The honourable board of council out,
Must fetch him in, he papers.[h]

---

[a] Andren.] So in the original, and so also in Holinshed, whom Shakespeare followed. The valley of *Ardren* lies between Guynes and Ardres; and, at the period alluded to, the former belonged to the English, and the latter to the French.

[b] *Durst wag his tongue* in censure.] That is, in *judging* either superior to the other.

[c] All was royal;] These words and the remainder of the speech are in the old copies given to Buckingham.

[d] No element—] No *rudimentary* knowledge even.

[e] Keech—] See note (e), p. 530, Vol. I.

[f] Out of his self drawing web,—he gives us note,—] The old text reads:—

"Out of his Selfe-drawing Web. O gives us note," &c.

Steevens surmised that the manuscript had, "*'A* gives us note," which the compositor mistook for "*O* gives us note." This is not improbable; but the expression, "*self-drawing* web," which every editor adopts without comment, appears to us an error likewise. The sense is better and more clearly expressed by omitting the hyphen.

[g] A gift that heaven gives for him, &c.] This is a very doubtful line. Mr. Collier's annotator changes it to—

"A gift that heaven *gives him, and* which buys;"

but if such licentious alterations were permissible, it would be easy to improve on this emendation.

[h] "—— *and his own letter,*
The honourable board of council out,
Must fetch him in, he papers.]

By "The honourable board of council out," is meant, without concurrence of the council; but what are we to understand by the expression in the last line,—"*he papers?*" In sheer despair, Pope threw out a suggestion that *papers* was here a verb.—"whom he *papers down*," and succeeding editors have been content with the explication; yet what thinking reader can ever believe this is what Shakespeare intended? From the context, see especially the two next speeches, it would seem that the sense requires a synonyme for the verb *beggars*,—"whom he *beggars*," or impoverishes; it is then possible that the meaningless *papers* is a misprint, and that we should read:—

"——— And his own letter,
Must fetch him in, he *paupers*."

ABER. I do know
Kinsmen of mine, three at the least, that have
By this so sicken'd their estates, that never
They shall abound as formerly.
BUCK. O, many
Have broke their backs with laying manors on 'em
For this great journey. What did this vanity
But minister communication of
A most poor issue? [a]
NORF. Grievingly I think,
The peace between the French and us not values
The cost that did conclude it.
BUCK. Every man,
After the hideous storm that follow'd, was
A thing inspir'd; and, not consulting, broke
Into a general prophecy,—That this tempest,
Dashing the garment of this peace, aboded
The sudden breach on't.
NORF. Which is budded out;
For France hath flaw'd the league, and hath attach'd
Our merchants' goods at Bourdeaux.
ABER. Is it therefore
The ambassador is silenc'd?
NORF. Marry, is't.
ABER. A proper title of a peace; and purchas'd
At a superfluous rate!
BUCK. Why, all this business
Our reverend cardinal carried.
NORF. Like it your grace,[b]
The state takes notice of the private difference
Betwixt you and the cardinal. I advise you,
(And take it from a heart that wishes towards you
Honour and plenteous safety,) that you read
The cardinal's malice and his potency
Together: to consider further, that
What his high hatred would effect, wants not
A minister in his power. You know his nature,
That he's revengeful; and I know his sword
Hath a sharp edge: it's long, and 't may be said,
It reaches far; and where 'twill not extend,
Thither he darts it. Bosom up my counsel,
You'll find it wholesome. Lo, where comes that rock
That I advise your shunning.

Enter CARDINAL WOLSEY (*the purse borne before him*), *certain of the* Guard, *and two* Secretaries *with papers. The* CARDINAL *in his passage fixeth his eye on* BUCKINGHAM, *and* BUCKINGHAM *on him, both full of disdain.*

WOL. The duke of Buckingham's surveyor, ha?
Where's his examination?
1 SECR. Here, so please you.
WOL. Is he in person ready?
1 SECR. Ay, please your grace.
WOL. Well, we shall then know more; and Buckingham
Shall lessen this big look.
[*Exeunt* CARDINAL *and Train.*
BUCK. This butcher's cur is venom-mouth'd,* and I
Have not the power to muzzle him; therefore best
Not wake him in his slumber. A beggar's book [c]
Out-worths a noble's blood.
NORF. What, are you chaf'd?
Ask God for temperance; that's the appliance only,
Which your disease requires.
BUCK. I read in's looks
Matter against me; and his eye revil'd
Me, as his abject object: at this instant
He bores [d] me with some trick: he's gone to the king;
I'll follow, and out-stare him.
NORF. Stay, my lord,
And let your reason with your choler question
What 'tis you go about: to climb steep hills,
Requires slow pace at first: anger is like
A full-hot horse, who being allow'd his way,
Self-mettle tires him. Not a man in England
Can advise me like you: be to yourself
As you would to your friend.
BUCK. I'll to the king;
And from a mouth of honour quite cry down
This Ipswich fellow's insolence; or proclaim
There's difference in no persons.
NORF. Be advis'd;
Heat not a furnace for your foe so hot
That it do singe yourself: we may outrun,
By violent swiftness, that which we run at,
And lose by over-running. Know you not,

---

a But minister communication of
A most poor issue?]

That is, But furnish *discourse* on the poverty of its result. *Communication* in the sense of *talk*, or *discourse*, is found so repeatedly in writers of Shakespeare's time, that the passage would hardly have required explanation, if the commentators had not overlooked this meaning of the word, and Mr. Collier, in adopting "consummation,"—a reading of his annotator,—had not pronounced the old text "little better than nonsense."

b Like it your grace,—] Equivalent to "An it like your grace."

(*) Old text, *venom'd-mouth'd*.

c A beggar's book
Out-worths a noble's blood.]

It may be we should read, "a beggar's look;" it was the *look* which Wolsey threw on Buckingham, that chafed his "blood:"—

"——— his eye revil'd
Me, as his abject object."

d *He* bores *me with some trick:*] According to Johnson, He *stabs* or *wounds* me with some artifice or fiction. Rather, He *undermines* me with some device.

The fire that mounts the liquor till't run o'er,
In seeming to augment it wastes it? Be advis'd:
I say again, there is no English soul
More stronger to direct you than yourself,
If with the sap of reason you would quench,
Or but allay, the fire of passion.

BUCK. Sir, I am thankful to you; and I'll go along
By your prescription:—but this top-proud fellow,
(Whom from the flow of gall I name not, but
From sincere motions,) by intelligence,
And proofs as clear as founts in Júly, when
We see each grain of gravel, I do know
To be corrupt and treasonous.

NORF. Say not, *treasonous*.

BUCK. To the king I'll say't; and make my vouch as strong
As shore of rock. Attend. This holy fox,
Or wolf, or both,—for he is equal ravenous
As he is subtle, and as prone to mischief
As able to perform 't; his mind and place
Infecting one another, yea, reciprocally,—
Only to show his pomp as well in France
As here at home, suggests the king our master
To this last costly treaty, the interview,
That swallow'd so much treasure, and like a glass
Did break i' the rinsing:—*

NORF. Faith, and so it did.

BUCK. Pray, give me favour, sir—this cunning cardinal
The articles o' the combination drew
As himself pleas'd; and they were ratified,
As he cried, *Thus let be*, to as much end
As give a crutch to the dead: but our count-cardinal
Has done this, and 'tis well; for worthy Wolsey,
Who cannot err, he did it. Now this follows,
(Which, as I take it, is a kind of puppy
To the old dam, treason,)—Charles the emperor,
Under pretence to see the queen his aunt,
(For 'twas indeed his colour; but he came
To whisper Wolsey,) here makes visitation:
His fears were, that the interview betwixt
England and France might, through their amity,
Breed him some prejudice; for from this league
Peep'd harms that menac'd him: he† privily
Deals with our cardinal; and, as I trow,—
Which I do well, for, I am sure,—the emperor
Paid ere he promis'd; whereby his suit was granted
Ere it was ask'd; but when the way was made,
And pav'd with gold, the emperor thus desir'd;—
That he would please to alter the king's course,

(*) Old text, *wrenching*. (†) First folio omits, *he*.

[a] Mistaken—] Misapprehended.

[b] The business present:] That is, I am sorry, since it is to see you deprived of liberty, that I am a witness of this business.

And break the foresaid peace. Let the king know
(As soon he shall by me) that thus the cardinal
Does buy and sell his honour as he pleases,
And for his own advantage.

NORF. I am sorry
To hear this of him; and could wish he were
Something mistaken[a] in't.

BUCK. No, not a syllable;
I do pronounce him in that very shape
He shall appear in proof.

Enter BRANDON; *a* Sergeant-at-arms *before him, and two or three of the* Guard.

BRAN. Your office, sergeant; execute it.

SERG. Sir,
My lord the duke of Buckingham, and earl
Of Hereford, Stafford, and Northampton, I
Arrest thee of high treason, in the name
Of our most sovereign king.

BUCK. Lo, you, my lord,
The net has fall'n upon me! I shall perish
Under device and practice.

BRAN. I am sorry,
To see you ta'en from liberty, to look on
The business present:[b] 'tis his highness' pleasure,
You shall to the Tower.

BUCK. It will help me nothing
To plead mine innocence; for that dye is on me
Which makes my whit'st part black. The will of heaven
Be done in this and all things!—I obey.—
O my lord Aberga'ny, fare you well!

BRAN. Nay, he must bear you company.—The king [*To* ABERGAVENNY.
Is pleas'd you shall to the Tower, till you know
How he determines further.

ABER. As the duke said,
The will of heaven be done, and the king's pleasure
By me obey'd!

BRAN. Here is a warrant from
The king, to attach lord Montacute; and the bodies
Of the duke's cónfessor, John de la Car,
One Gilbert Peck, his chancellor,*—

BUCK. So, so;
These are the limbs o' the plot:—no more, I hope?

BRAN. A monk o' the Chartreux.

BUCK. O, Nicholas† Hopkins?

BRAN. He.

(*) Old text, *Councellour*. (†) Old text, *Michaell*.

BUCK. My surveyor is false; the o'er-great cardinal
Hath show'd him gold: my life is spann'd already:
I am the shadow of poor Buckingham,
Whose figure even this instant cloud puts on,
By dark'ning my clear sun.[a]—My lord,* farewell.
[*Exeunt.*

SCENE II.—*The same. The Council Chamber.*

Cornets. Enter KING HENRY, CARDINAL WOLSEY, *the* Lords *of the* Council, *Sir* THOMAS LOVELL, Officers, *and* Attendants. *The* KING *enters leaning on the* CARDINAL'*s shoulder.*

K. HEN. My life itself, and the best heart of it,
Thanks you for this great care: I stood i' the level
Of a full-charg'd confederacy, and give thanks
To you that chok'd it.—Let be call'd before us
That gentleman of Buckingham's: in person
I'll hear him his confessions justify;
And point by point the treasons of his master
He shall again relate.

The KING *takes his state. The* Lords *of the* Council *take their several places. The* CARDINAL *places himself under the* KING'*s feet, on his right side.*

A noise without, crying, "Room for the Queen." *Enter the* QUEEN, *ushered by the* DUKES *of* NORFOLK *and* SUFFOLK: *she kneels. The* KING *riseth from his state, takes her up, kisses, and placeth her by him.*

Q. KATH. Nay, we must longer kneel; I am a suitor.
K. HEN. Arise, and take place by us:—half your suit
Never name to us; you have half our power:
The other moiety, ere you ask, is given;
Repeat your will, and take it.
Q. KATH. Thank your majesty.
That you would love yourself, and in that love
Not unconsider'd leave your honour, nor
The dignity of your office, is the point
Of my petition.
K. HEN. Lady mine, proceed.
Q. KATH. I am solicited, not by a few,
And those of true condition, that your subjects
Are in great grievance: there have been commissions
Sent down among 'em, which hath flaw'd the heart
Of all their loyalties:—wherein, although,
My good lord cardinal, they vent reproaches
Most bitterly on you, as putter-on[b]
Of these exactions, yet the king our master,
(Whose honour heaven shield from soil!) even he escapes not
Language unmannerly, yea, such which breaks
The sides of loyalty, and almost appears
In loud rebellion.
NORF. Not *almost* appears,—
It doth appear; for, upon these taxations,
The clothiers all, not able to maintain
The many to them 'longing, have put off
The spinsters, carders, fullers, weavers, who,
Unfit for other life, compell'd by hunger
And lack of other means, in desperate manner
Daring the event to the teeth, are all in uproar,
And danger serves among them.
K. HEN. *Taxation!*
Wherein? and what taxation?—My lord cardinal,
You that are blam'd for it alike with us,
Know you of this taxation?
WOL. Please you, sir,
I know but of a single part, in aught
Pertains to the state; and front but in that file
Where others tell steps with me.
Q. KATH. No, my lord,
You know no more than others: but you frame
Things, that are known alike, which are not wholesome
To those which would not know them, and yet must
Perforce be their acquaintance. These exactions,
Whereof my sovereign would have note, they are
Most pestilent to the hearing; and, to bear 'em,
The back is sacrifice to the load. They say
They are devis'd by you; or else you suffer
Too hard an exclamation.
K. HEN. Still *exaction!*
The nature of it? In what kind, let's know,
Is this exaction?
Q. KATH. I am much too venturous
In tempting of your patience; but am bolden'd
Under your promis'd pardon. The subjects' grief
Comes through commissions, which compel from each
The sixth part of his substance, to be levied
Without delay; and the pretence for this
Is nam'd, your wars in France: this makes bold mouths:
Tongues spit their duties out, and cold hearts freeze

(*) Old text, *Lords.*

a I am the shadow of poor Buckingham,
Whose figure even this instant cloud puts on,
By dark'ning my clear sun.]

A very difficult passage, of which, no explanation yet attempted affords an intelligible meaning. Our idea of it is, that by *figure* is meant his own form, and that the expression "cloud puts on," signifies *assumes obscurity*; or possibly, *is eclipsed by cloud.*

b Putter-on—] *Contriver, deviser.* So in "The Winter's Tale," Act II. Sc. 1:—

"You are abus'd, and by some *putter-on.*"

Allegiance in them; their curses now,
Live where their prayers did; and it's come to pass,
This[a] tractable obedience is a slave
To each incensed will. I would your highness
Would give it quick consideration, for
There is no primer business.[b]
K. HEN. By my life,
This is against our pleasure.
WOL. And for me,
I have no further gone in this, than by
A single voice; and that not pass'd me but
By learned approbation of the judges. If I am
Traduc'd by ignorant tongues, which neither know
My faculties nor person, yet will be
The chronicles of my doing,—let me say,
'Tis but the fate of place, and the rough brake
That virtue must go through. We must not stint
Our necessary actions, in the fear
To cope malicious censurers; which ever,
As ravenous fishes, do a vessel follow
That is new trimm'd, but benefit no further
Than vainly longing. What we oft do best,
By sick interpreters, once weak ones, is
Not ours, or not allow'd; what worst, as oft,

a This *tractable obedience* is a slave—] So the old text. Rowe reads,—

"*That* tractable obedience," &c.

And Mr. Collier's annotator,—

"*Their* tractable obedience," &c.

b No primer business.] The old copies have "basenesse," which was corrected in Southern's copy of the fourth folio.

Hitting a grosser quality, is cried up
For our best act. If we shall stand still,
In fear our motion will be mock'd or carp'd at,
We should take root here where we sit, or sit
State-statues only.

K. HEN. Things done well,
And with a care, exempt themselves from fear;
Things done without example, in their issue
Are to be fear'd. Have you a precedent
Of this commission? I believe, not any.
We must not rend our subjects from our laws,
And stick them in our will. Sixth part of each?
A trembling[a] contribution! Why, we take
From every tree, lop,[b] bark, and part o' the timber;
And, though we leave it with a root, thus hack'd,
The air will drink the sap. To every county
Where this is question'd send our letters, with
Free pardon to each man that has denied
The force of this commission: pray, look to't;
I put it to your care.

WOL. A word with you. [*To the* Secretary.
Let there be letters writ to every shire,
Of the king's grace and pardon. The griev'd commons
Hardly conceive of me; let it be nois'd,
That through our intercession this revokement
And pardon comes: I shall anon advise you
Further in the proceeding. [*Exit* Secretary.

Enter Surveyor.

Q. KATH. I am sorry that the duke of Buckingham
Is run in your displeasure.

K. HEN. It grieves many:
The gentleman is learn'd, and a most rare speaker;
To nature none more bound; his training such,
That he may furnish and instruct great teachers,
And never seek for aid out of himself. Yet see,
When these so noble benefits shall prove
Not well dispos'd, the mind growing once corrupt,
They turn to vicious forms, ten times more ugly
Than ever they were fair. This man so complete,—
Who was enroll'd 'mongst wonders, and when we,
Almost with ravish'd list'ning, could not find
His hour of speech a minute—he, my lady,
Hath into monstrous habits put the graces
That once were his, and is become as black
As if besmear'd in hell. Sit by us; you shall hear
(This was his gentleman in trust) of him
Things to strike honour sad.—Bid him recount
The fore-recited practices; whereof
We cannot feel too little, hear too much.

WOL. Stand forth, and with bold spirit relate what you,
Most like a careful subject, have collected
Out of the duke of Buckingham.

K. HEN. Speak freely.

SURV. First,—it was usual with him, every day
It would infect his speech,—that if the king
Should without issue die, he'd* carry it so
To make the sceptre his: these very words
I have heard him utter to his son-in law,
Lord Aberga'ny; to whom by oath he menac'd
Revenge upon the cardinal.

WOL. Please your highness, note
This dangerous conception in this point:
Not friended by his wish to your high person,
His will is most malignant; and it stretches
Beyond you, to your friends.

Q. KATH. My learn'd lord cardinal,
Deliver all with charity.

K. HEN. Speak on:
How grounded he his title to the crown,
Upon our fail? to this point hast thou heard him
At any time speak aught?

SURV. He was brought to this
By a vain prophecy of Nicholas Hopkins.[c]

K. HEN. What was that Hopkins?

SURV. Sir, a Chartreux friar,
His cónfessor; who fed him every minute
With words of sovereignty.

K. HEN. How know'st thou this?

SURV. Not long before your highness sped to France,
The duke being at the Rose,[d] within the parish
Saint Lawrence Poultney, did of me demand
What was the speech amongst the Londoners
Concerning the French journey: I replied,
Men fear'd † the French would prove perfidious,
To the king's danger. Presently the duke
Said, 'twas the fear, indeed; and that he doubted
'Twould prove the verity of certain words
Spoke by a holy monk; *that oft*, says he,
Hath sent to me, wishing me to permit
John de la Car, my chaplain, a choice hour
To hear from him a matter of some moment:
Whom after under the confession's ‡ *seal*
He solemnly had sworn, that what he spoke
My chaplain to no creature living, but
To me, should utter, with demure confidence
This pausingly ensued,—Neither the king nor's heirs,

(*) Old text, *hee'l.* (†) Old text, *feare.* (‡) Old text, *Commissions.*

a *A trembling contribution!*] Mr. Collier's annotator would change this to,—
"*A trebling contribution.*"

b Lop,—] *Lop* is the technical term for the *branches*, or faggot wood, of a tree, distinct from the trunk or timber.

c Nicholas Hopkins.] The old text has Nicholas *Henton;* and Hopkins was sometimes so named from the convent of Henton, near Bristol.

d The Rose,—] A house belonging to the Duke of Buckingham, part of which is now the Merchant Taylors' School, in Suffolk-lane, Thames-street.

(Tell you the duke) shall prosper: bid him strive
To gain[a] *the love of the commonalty; the duke*
Shall govern England.

Q. KATH. If I know you well,
You were the duke's surveyor, and lost your office
On the complaint o' the tenants: take good heed
You charge not in your spleen a noble person,
And spoil your nobler soul! I say, take heed;
Yes, heartily beseech you.

K. HEN. Let him on.—
Go forward.

SURV. On my soul, I'll speak but truth.
I told my lord the duke, by the devil's illusions
The monk might be deceiv'd; and that 'twas dangerous
For him* to ruminate on this so far, until
It forg'd him some design, which, being believ'd,
It was much like to do: he answer'd, *Tush!*
It can do me no damage: adding further,
That, had the king in his last sickness fail'd,
The cardinal's and sir Thomas Lovell's heads
Should have gone off.

K. HEN. Ha! what, so rank? Ah-ha!
There's mischief in this man:—canst thou say further?

SURV. I can, my liege.

K. HEN. Proceed.

SURV. Being at Greenwich,
After your highness had reprov'd the duke
About sir William Blomer,—

K. HEN. I remember
Of such a time:—being my sworn servant,
The duke retain'd him his.—But on; what hence?

SURV. *If, quoth he, I for this had been committed,*
As, to the Tower, I thought,[b]*—I would have play'd*
The part my father meant to act upon
The usurper Richard; who, being at Salisbury,
Made suit to come in's presence; which if granted,
As he made semblance of his duty, would
Have put his knife into him.

K. HEN. A giant traitor!

WOL. Now, madam, may his highness live in freedom,
And this man out of prison?

Q. KATH. God mend all!

K. HEN. There's something more would out of thee; what say'st?

SURV. After—*the duke his father,*—with the *knife,*—
He stretch'd him, and, with one hand on his dagger,
Another spread on's breast, mounting his eyes,
He did discharge a horrible oath; whose tenour
Was,—were he evil us'd, he would outgo
His father by as much as a performance
Does an irresolute purpose.

K. HEN. There's his period,
To sheath his knife in us. He is attach'd;
Call him to present trial: if he may
Find mercy in the law, 'tis his; if none,
Let him not seek't of us: by day and night,
He's traitor to the height![c] [*Exeunt.*

SCENE III.—*The same. A Room in the Palace.*

Enter the Lord Chamberlain *and* LORD SANDS.

CHAM. Is't possible, the spells of France should juggle
Men into such strange mysteries?

SANDS. New customs,
Though they be never so ridiculous,
Nay, let'em be unmanly, yet are follow'd.

CHAM. As far as I see, all the good our English
Have got by the late voyage, is but merely
A fit or two o'the face;[d] but they are shrewd ones;
For when they hold 'em, you would swear directly,
Their very noses had been counsellors
To Pepin or Clotharius, they keep state so.

SANDS. They have all new legs, and lame ones; one would take it,
That never saw 'em pace before, the spavin,
Or* springhalt, reign'd among 'em.

CHAM. Death! my lord,
Their clothes are after such a pagan cut too,†
That, sure, they've worn out christendom.

Enter Sir THOMAS LOVELL.

How now!
What news, sir Thomas Lovell?

LOV. Faith, my lord,
I hear of none, but the new proclamation
That's clapp'd upon the court-gate.

CHAM. What is't for?

LOV. The reformation of our travell'd gallants,
That fill the court with quarrels, talk, and tailors.

CHAM. I'm glad 't is there: now I would pray our monsieurs
To think an English courtier may be wise,
And never see the Louvre.

LOV. They must either

(*) Old text, *this*.

[a] *To gain—*] The word *gain* was first supplied by the folio of 1685.

[b] As, to the Tower, I thought,—] That is, "To the Tower, as I thought." Similar inversions continually occur in old authors.

(*) Old text, *A*. (†) Old text, *too't*.

[c] He's traitor to the height!] Mr. Collier's annotator proposes to read,—
"He *is a daring* traitor to the height."

[d] A fit or two o' the face;] A *grimace* or two.

(For so run the conditions) leave those remnants
Of fool and feather, that they got in France,
With all their honourable points of ignorance
Pertaining thereunto, as fights and fireworks;
Abusing better men than they can be,
Out of a foreign wisdom; renouncing clean
The faith they have in tennis, and tall stockings,
Short blister'd breeches, and those types of travel,
And understand again like honest men;
Or pack to their old playfellows: there, I take it,
They may, *cum privilegio*, wear* away
The lag end of their lewdness, and be laugh'd at.

SANDS. 'T is time to give 'em physic, their diseases
Are grown so catching.

CHAM. What a loss our ladies
Will have of these trim vanities!

LOV. Ay, marry,
There will be woe indeed, lords: the sly whoresons
Have got a speeding trick to lay down ladies;
A French song and a fiddle has no fellow.

SANDS. The devil fiddle 'em! I am glad they are going,
(For, sure, there's no converting of 'em;) now
An honest country lord, as I am, beaten
A long time out of play, may bring his plain-song,
And have an hour of hearing; and, by'r-lady,
Held current music too.

CHAM. Well said, lord Sands;
Your colt's tooth is not cast yet.

SANDS. No, my lord;
Nor shall not, while I have a stump.

CHAM. Sir Thomas,
Whither were you a-going?

LOV. To the cardinal's;
Your lordship is a guest too?

CHAM. O, 'tis true:
This night he makes a supper, and a great one,
To many lords and ladies; there will be
The beauty of this kingdom, I'll assure you.

LOV. That churchman bears a bounteous mind indeed,
A hand as fruitful as the land that feeds us;
His dews fall everywhere.

CHAM. No doubt he's noble;
He had a black mouth that said other of him.

SANDS. He may, my lord,—has wherewithal; in him
Sparing would show a worse sin than ill doctrine:
Men of his way should be most liberal,
They are set here for examples.

CHAM. True, they are so;
But few now give so great ones. My barge stays;
Your lordship shall along.—Come, good sir Thomas,
We shall be late else; which I would not be,
For I was spoke to, with sir Henry Guilford,
This night to be comptrollers.

SANDS. I am your lordship's.
[*Exeunt.*

SCENE IV.—*The same. The Presence Chamber in* York-Place.

Hautboys. A small table under a state for the CARDINAL, *a longer table for the guests. Enter, on one side,* ANNE BULLEN, *and divers* Lords, Ladies, *and* Gentlewomen, *as guests; on the other, enter Sir* HENRY GUILFORD.

GUIL. Ladies, a general welcome from his grace
Salutes ye all: this night he dedicates
To fair content and you: none here, he hopes,
In all this noble bevy, has brought with her
One care abroad; he would have all as merry
As, first[a] good company, good wine, good welcome,
Can make good people.—

Enter the Lord Chamberlain, LORD SANDS, *and Sir* THOMAS LOVELL.

O, my lord, you 're tardy;
The very thought of this fair company
Clapp'd wings to me.

CHAM. You are young, sir Harry Guilford.

SANDS. Sir Thomas Lovell, had the cardinal
But half my lay-thoughts in him, some of these
Should find a running banquet ere they rested,
I think, would better please 'em: by my life,
They are a sweet society of fair ones.

LOV. O, that your lordship were but now confessor
To one or two of these!

SANDS. I would I were;
They should find easy penance.

LOV. Faith, how easy?

SANDS. As easy as a down-bed would afford it.

CHAM. Sweet ladies, will it please you sit?—Sir Harry,
Place you that side; I'll take the charge of this:
His grace is ent'ring.—Nay, you must not freeze;
Two women plac'd together makes cold weather:—
My lord Sands, you are one will keep 'em waking;
Pray sit between these ladies.

SANDS. By my faith,

(*) First folio, *wee*.

a As, first good company,—] It may be doubted whether "first" is not one of the innumerable errors with which the text of this piece is disfigured; unless we are to read, "first-good," that is, *first-rate*, "company," of which compound no other example has yet been discovered.

And thank your lordship.—By your leave, sweet ladies:
[*Seats himself between* ANNE BULLEN *and another lady.*
If I chance to talk a little wild, forgive me;
I had it from my father.
ANNE. Was he mad, sir?
SANDS. O, very mad, exceeding mad, in love too:
But he would bite none; just as I do now,—
He would kiss you twenty with a breath.
[*Kisses her.*
CHAM. Well said, my lord.—
So, now you're fairly seated.—Gentlemen,
The penance lies on you, if these fair ladies
Pass away frowning.
SANDS. For my little cure,
Let me alone.

Hautboys. Enter CARDINAL WOLSEY *attended, and takes his state.*

WOL. Y'are welcome, my fair guests: that noble lady,
Or gentleman, that is not freely merry,
Is not my friend: this, to confirm my welcome,
And to you all, good health. [*Drinks.*
SANDS. Your grace is noble:
Let me have such a bowl may hold my thanks,
And save me so much talking.
WOL. My lord Sands,
I am beholden to you: cheer your neighbours.—
Ladies, you are not merry;—gentlemen,
Whose fault is this?
SANDS. The red wine first must rise
In their fair cheeks, my lord; then we shall have 'em
Talk us to silence.
ANNE. You are a merry gamester,
My lord Sands.
SANDS. Yes, if I make my play.
Here's to your ladyship; and pledge it, madam,
For 'tis to such a thing,—
ANNE. You cannot show me.
SANDS. I told your grace they would talk anon.
[*Drum and trumpets; chambers*[a] *discharged without.*
WOL. What's that?
CHAM. Look out there, some of ye.
[*Exit a* Servant.
WOL. What warlike voice,
And to what end is this?—Nay, ladies, fear not;
By all the laws of war you're privileg'd.

Re-enter Servant.

CHAM. How now! what is't?
SERV. A noble troop of strangers,—
For so they seem: they've left their barge, and landed;
And hither make, as great ambassadors
From foreign princes.
WOL. Good lord chamberlain,
Go, give 'em welcome; you can speak the French tongue;
And, pray receive 'em nobly, and conduct 'em
Into our presence, where this heaven of beauty
Shall shine at full upon them.—Some attend him.—
[*Exit* Chamberlain, *attended. All rise, and tables removed.*
You have now a broken banquet; but we'll mend it.
A good digestion to you all: and, once more,
I shower a welcome on ye;—welcome all!

Hautboys. Enter the KING *and others, as masquers, habited like shepherds; ushered by the* Lord Chamberlain. *They pass directly before the* CARDINAL, *and gracefully salute him.*

A noble company! what are their pleasures?
CHAM. Because they speak no English, thus they pray'd
To tell your grace;—That, having heard by fame
Of this so noble and so fair assembly
This night to meet here, they could do no less,
Out of the great respect they bear to beauty,
But leave their flocks; and, under your fair conduct,
Crave leave to view these ladies, and entreat
An hour of revels with 'em.
WOL. Say, lord chamberlain,
They have done my poor house grace; for which I pay 'em
A thousand thanks, and pray 'em take their pleasures.
[Ladies *chosen for the dance. The* KING *chooses* ANNE BULLEN.
K. HEN. The fairest hand I ever touch'd! O, beauty,
Till now I never knew thee! [*Music. Dance.*
WOL. My lord,—
CHAM. Your grace?
WOL. Pray, tell 'em thus much from me:
There should be one amongst 'em, by his person,
More worthy this place than myself; to whom,

---

[a] *Chambers*—] These are small pieces of ordnance, employed on occasions of rejoicing, as the sovereign's birthday, &c. Their discharges in this scene were, it is supposed, the occasion of the fire which destroyed the Globe Theatre in 1613. See the Introductory Notice.

If I but knew him, with my love and duty
I would surrender it.
CHAM. I will, my lord.
[*Whispers the* Masquers.
WOL. What say they?
CHAM. Such a one, they all confess,
There is, indeed; which they would have your grace
Find out, and he will take it.
WOL. Let me see then.—
[*Comes from his state.*
By all your good leaves, gentlemen;—here I'll make
My royal choice.
K. HEN. You have found him, cardinal:
[*Unmasking.*
You hold a fair assembly; you do well, lord:
You are a churchman, or, I'll tell you, cardinal,
I should judge now unhappily.[a]

[a] Unhappily.] *Wickedly, mischievously, equivocally.*

WOL. I am glad
Your grace is grown so pleasant.
K. HEN. My lord chamberlain,
Pr'ythee, come hither: what fair lady's that?
CHAM. An't please your grace, sir Thomas Bullen's daughter,
The viscount Rochford,—one of her highness' women.
K. HEN. By heaven, she is a dainty one.—Sweetheart,
I were unmannerly to take you out,
And not to kiss you.[a]—A health, gentlemen!
Let it go round.
WOL. Sir Thomas Lovell, is the banquet ready
I' the privy chamber?
LOV. Yes, my lord.
WOL. Your grace,
I fear, with dancing is a little heated.
K. HEN. I fear, too much.
WOL. There's fresher air, my lord,
In the next chamber.
K. HEN. Lead in your ladies, every one.—Sweet partner,
I must not yet forsake you:—let's be merry,
Good my lord cardinal; I have half a dozen healths
To drink to these fair ladies, and a measure
To lead 'em once again; and then let's dream
Who's best in favour.—Let the music knock it.(2)
[*Exeunt, with trumpets.*

[a] And not to kiss you—] A kiss, Steevens observes, was formerly the established fee of a lady's partner in the dance; which, he might have added, the lady acknowledged with a curtsey:—

"—— if he have privilege
To kiss another lady, she may say
He does salute her and return a curtsey,
To shew her breeding."
SHIRLEY'S *play of "The Ball,"* Act I Sc. 2.

ACT II.

SCENE I.—London. *A Street.*

Enter two Gentlemen, *meeting.*

1 Gent. Whither away so fast?
2 Gent. O,—God save you!
E'en to the hall, to hear what shall become
Of the great duke of Buckingham.
1 Gent. I'll save you
That labour, sir. All's now done but the ceremony
Of bringing back the prisoner.
2 Gent. Were you there?
1 Gent. Yes, indeed was I.
2 Gent. Pray speak what has happen'd?
1 Gent. You may guess quickly what.
2 Gent. Is he found guilty?
1 Gent. Yes, truly is he, and condemn'd upon't.
2 Gent. I am sorry for 't.
1 Gent. So are a number more.
2 Gent. But, pray, how pass'd it?
1 Gent. I'll tell you in a little. The great duke
Came to the bar; where, to his accusations
He pleaded still, not guilty, and alleg'd
Many sharp reasons to defeat the law.
The king's attorney, on the contrary,
Urg'd on the examinations, proofs, confessions
Of divers witnesses; which the duke desir'd
To have[a] brought, *vivâ voce*, to his face:
At which appear'd against him, his surveyor,
Sir Gilbert Peck his chancellor, and John Car,
Confessor to him; with that devil-monk,
Hopkins, that made this mischief.
2 Gent. That was he,
That fed him with his prophecies?
1 Gent. The same.
All these accus'd him strongly; which he fain
Would have flung from him, but, indeed, he could not:
And so his peers, upon this evidence,
Have found him guilty of high treason. Much
He spoke, and learnedly, for life; but all
Was either pitied in him or forgotten.
2 Gent. After all this, how did he bear himself?
1 Gent. When he was brought again to the bar,—to hear
His knell rung out, his judgment,—he was stirr'd
With such an agony, he sweat extremely,
And something spoke in choler, ill, and hasty:

[a] *To* have *brought*, &c.] The folio 1623, and the two following editions, read, "To *him* brought," &c.; an error first corrected in the folio of 1685.

But he fell to himself again, and sweetly
In all the rest show'd a most noble patience.(1)

2 Gent. I do not think he fears death.

1 Gent. Sure, he does not;
He never was so womanish; the cause
He may a little grieve at.

2 Gent. Certainly,
The cardinal is the end of this.

1 Gent. 'Tis likely,
By all conjectures: first, Kildare's attainder,
Then deputy of Ireland; who remov'd,
Earl Surrey was sent thither, and in haste too,
Lest he should help his father.

2 Gent. That trick of state
Was a deep envious one.

1 Gent. At his return,
No doubt, he will requite it. This is noted,
And generally,—whoever the king favours,
The cardinal instantly will find employment,
And far enough from court too.

2 Gent. All the commons
Hate him perniciously, and, o' my conscience,
Wish him ten fathom deep: this duke as much
They love and dote on; call him, bounteous Buckingham,
The mirror of all courtesy,—

1 Gent. Stay there, sir,
And see the noble ruin'd man you speak of.

Enter Buckingham *from his arraignment; Tipstaves before him; the axe with the edge towards him; Halberds on each side: with him, Sir* Thomas Lovell, *Sir* Nicholas Vaux, *Sir* William* Sands, *and common people.*

2 Gent. Let's stand close, and behold him.

Buck. All good people,
You that thus far have come to pity me,
Hear what I say, and then go home and lose me.
I have this day receiv'd a traitor's judgment,
And by that name must die; yet, heaven bear witness—
And if I have a conscience let it sink me,
Even as the axe falls, if I be not faithful!—
The law I bear no malice for my death;
It has done, upon the premises, but justice;
But those that sought it I could wish more christians:
Be what they will, I heartily forgive 'em:
Yet let 'em look they glory not in mischief,
Nor build their evils on the graves of great men;[a]
For then my guiltless blood must cry against 'em.
For further life in this world I ne'er hope,
Nor will I sue, although the king have mercies
More than I dare make faults. You few that lov'd me,
And dare be bold to weep for Buckingham,
His noble friends and fellows, whom to leave
Is only bitter to him, only dying,
Go with me, like good angels, to my end;
And, as the long divorce of steel falls on me,
Make of your prayers one sweet sacrifice,
And lift my soul to heaven.—Lead on, o' God's name.

Lov. I do beseech your grace, for charity,
If ever any malice in your heart
Were hid against me, now to forgive me frankly.

Buck. Sir Thomas Lovell, I as free forgive you,
As I would be forgiven: I forgive all;
There cannot be those numberless offences
'Gainst me, that I cannot take peace with: no black envy[b]
Shall mark* my grave.—Commend me to his grace;
And, if he speak of Buckingham, pray, tell him,
You met him half in heaven: my vows and prayers
Yet are the king's; and, till my soul forsake,
Shall cry for blessings on him: may he live
Longer than I have time to tell his years!
Ever belov'd and loving may his rule be!
And when old time shall lead him to his end,
Goodness and he fill up one monument!

Lov. To the water side I must conduct your grace;
Then give my charge up to sir Nicholas Vaux,
Who undertakes you to your end.

Vaux. Prepare there,
The duke is coming: see the barge be ready;
And fit it with such furniture as suits
The greatness of his person.

Buck. Nay, sir Nicholas,
Let it alone; my state now will but mock me.
When I came hither, I was lord high constable,
And duke of Buckingham; now, poor Edward Bohun:
Yet I am richer than my base accusers,
That never knew what truth meant: I now seal it;
And with that blood will make 'em one day groan for't.
My noble father, Henry of Buckingham,

(*) Old text, *Walter*.

(*) Old text, *make*.

a Nor build their evils, &c.] See note (c), p. 605.

b ——— *no black* envy
Shall mark *my grave.*—]
Envy very commonly, in our old writers, bears the sense sometimes conveyed by *invidia;* though the distinction between *envy,* in its ordinary signification, and *hatred*, was perfectly understood.—"Besides this, beasts have *hate*, but not *envy*, and that comes bicause, not having the discourse of reason, they cannot judge of the felicitie of other."—*Fearful Fancies of the Florentine Cooper*, 4to. 1599.

Who first rais'd head against usurping Richard,
Flying for succour to his servant Banister,
Being distress'd, was by that wretch betray'd,
And without trial fell; God's peace be with him!
Henry the seventh succeeding, truly pitying
My father's loss, like a most royal prince,
Restor'd me to my honours, and, out of ruins,
Made my name once more noble. Now his son,
Henry the eighth, life, honour, name, and all
That made me happy, at one stroke has taken
For ever from the world. I had my trial,
And, must needs say, a noble one; which makes me
A little happier than my wretched father:
Yet thus far we are one in fortunes,—both
Fell by our servants, by those men we lov'd most;
A most unnatural and faithless service!
Heaven has an end in all: yet, you that hear me,
This from a dying man receive as certain:—
Where you are liberal of your loves and counsels,
Be sure you be not loose; for those you make friends,
And give your hearts to, when they once perceive
The least rub in your fortunes, fall away
Like water from ye, never found again
But where they mean to sink ye. All good people,
Pray for me! I must now forsake ye; the last hour
Of my long weary life is come upon me.
Farewell: and when you would say something that is sad,
Speak how I fell.—I have done; and God forgive me! [*Exeunt* BUCKINGHAM *and Train.*

1 GENT. O, this is full of pity!—Sir, it calls,
I fear, too many curses on their heads,
That were the authors.

2 GENT. If the duke be guiltless,
'Tis full of woe: yet I can give you inkling
Of an ensuing evil, if it fall,
Greater than this.

1 GENT. Good angels keep it from us!
What may it be? you do not doubt my faith, sir?

2 GENT. This secret is so weighty, 'twill require
A strong faith to conceal it.

1 GENT. Let me have it;
I do not talk much.

2 GENT. I am confident;
You shall, sir: did you not of late days hear
A buzzing of a separation
Between the king and Katharine?

1 GENT. Yes, but it held not:
For when the king once heard it, out of anger
He sent command to the lord mayor straight
To stop the rumour, and allay those tongues
That durst disperse it.

2 GENT. But that slander, sir,
Is found a truth now: for it grows again
Fresher than e'er it was; and held for certain
The king will venture at it. Either the cardinal,
Or some about him near, have, out of malice
To the good queen, possess'd him with a scruple
That will undo her: to confirm this too,
Cardinal Campeius is arriv'd, and lately;
As all think, for this business.

1 GENT. 'Tis the cardinal;
And merely to revenge him on the emperor,
For not bestowing on him, at his asking,
The archbishopric of Toledo, this is purpos'd.

2 GENT. I think you have hit the mark: but is't not cruel,
That she should feel the smart of this? The cardinal
Will have his will, and she must fall.

1 GENT. 'Tis woeful.
We are too open here to argue this;
Let's think in private more. [*Exeunt.*

SCENE II.—*The same. An Antechamber in the Palace.*

Enter the Lord Chamberlain, *reading a letter.*

MY LORD,—*The horses your lordship sent for, with all the care I had, I saw well chosen, ridden, and furnished. They were young and handsome, and of the best breed in the north. When they were ready to set out for London, a man of my lord cardinal's, by commission and main power, took 'em from me; with this reason,—His master would be served before a subject, if not before the king; which stopped our mouths, sir.*

I fear he will, indeed: well, let him have them;
He will have all, I think.

Enter the DUKES *of* NORFOLK *and* SUFFOLK.

NORF. Well met, my lord chamberlain.

CHAM. Good day to both your graces.

SUF. How is the king employ'd?

CHAM. I left him private,
Full of sad thoughts and troubles.

NORF. What's the cause?

CHAM. It seems the marriage with his brother's wife
Has crept too near his conscience.

SUF. No, his conscience
Has crept too near another lady.

NORF. 'Tis so;
This is the cardinal's doing, the king-cardinal:
That blind priest, like the eldest son of fortune,

Turns what he list. The king will know him one day.

SUF. Pray God, he do! he'll never know himself else.

NORF. How holily he works in all his business!
And with what zeal! for, now he has crack'd the league
Between us and the emperor, the queen's great nephew,
He dives into the king's soul, and there scatters
Dangers, doubts, wringing of the conscience,
Fears, and despairs,—and all these for his marriage:
And out of all these to restore the king,
He counsels a divorce; a loss of her,
That, like a jewel, has hung twenty years
About his neck, yet never lost her lustre;
Of her that loves him with that excellence
That angels love good men with; even of her
That, when the greatest stroke of fortune falls,
Will bless the king: and is not this course pious?

CHAM. Heaven keep me from such counsel! 'T is most true,
These news are everywhere; every tongue speaks 'em,
And every true heart weeps for't: all that dare
Look into these affairs, see this main end,—
The French king's sister. Heaven will one day open
The king's eyes, that so long have slept upon
This bold bad man.

SUF. And free us from his slavery.

NORF. We had need pray,
And heartily, for our deliverance;
Or this imperious man will work us all
From princes into pages: all men's honours
Lie like one lump before him, to be fashion'd
Into what pitch he please.

SUF. For me, my lords,
I love him not, nor fear him; there's my creed:
As I am made without him, so I'll stand,
If the king please; his curses and his blessings
Touch me alike, they're breath I not believe in.
I knew him, and I know him; so I leave him
To him that made him proud, the pope.

NORF. Let's in;
And with some other business put the king
From these sad thoughts, that work too much upon him:—
My lord, you'll bear us company?

CHAM. Excuse me;
The king has sent me otherwhere: besides,
You'll find a most unfit time to disturb him:
Health to your lordships.

NORF. Thanks, my good lord chamberlain.
[*Exit* Lord Chamberlain.

NORFOLK *opens a folding-door. The* KING *is discovered sitting, and reading pensively.*

SUF. How sad he looks! sure, he is much afflicted.

K. HEN. Who's there, ha?
NORF. Pray God he be not angry.
K. HEN. Who's there, I say? How dare you thrust yourselves
Into my private meditations?
Who am I, ha?
NORF. A gracious king, that pardons all offences
Malice ne'er meant: our breach of duty this way,
Is business of estate; in which we come
To know your royal pleasure.
K. HEN. Ye are too bold;
Go to; I'll make ye know your times of business:
Is this an hour for temporal affairs, ha?—

Enter WOLSEY *and* CAMPEIUS.

Who's there? my good lord cardinal?—O my Wolsey,
The quiet of my wounded conscience,
Thou art a cure fit for a king.—You're welcome,
[*To* CAMPEIUS.
Most learned reverend sir, into our kingdom;
Use us and it.—My good lord, have great care
I be not found a talker. [*To* WOLSEY.
WOL. Sir, you cannot.
I would your grace would give us but an hour
Of private conference.
K. HEN. We are busy; go.
[*To* NORFOLK *and* SUFFOLK.
NORF. This priest has no pride in him?
SUF. Not to speak of;
I would not be so sick though for his place:
But this cannot continue.
NORF. If it do,
I'll venture one have-at-him.[a]
SUF. I another.
[*Aside to each other.*]
[*Exeunt* NORFOLK *and* SUFFOLK.
WOL. Your grace has given a precedent of wisdom
Above all princes, in committing freely
Your scruple to the voice of Christendom:
Who can be angry now? what envy reach you?
The Spaniard, tied by blood and favour to her,
Must now confess, if they have any goodness,
The trial just and noble. All the clerks,
I mean the learned ones, in christian kingdoms,
Have their free voices—Rome, the nurse of judgment,
Invited by your noble self, hath sent,
One general tongue unto us, this good man,
This just and learned priest, cardinal Campeius,—
Whom once more I present unto your highness.

[a] *I'll venture one* have-at-him] The second folio reads, "one *heave* at him."

K. HEN. And once more in mine arms I bid him welcome,
And thank the holy conclave for their loves;
They have sent me such a man I would have wish'd for.
CAM. Your grace must needs deserve all strangers' loves,
You are so noble. To your highness' hand
I tender my commission;—by whose virtue,
(The court of Rome commanding) you, my lord
Cardinal of York, are join'd with me their servant
In the unpartial judging of this business.
K. HEN. Two equal men. The queen shall be acquainted
Forthwith for what you come.—Where's Gardiner?
WOL. I know your majesty has always lov'd her
So dear in heart, not to deny her that
A woman of less place might ask by law,—
Scholars allow'd freely to argue for her.
K. HEN. Ay, and the best she shall have; and my favour
To him that does best; God forbid else. Cardinal,
Pry'thee, call Gardiner to me, my new secretary;
I find him a fit fellow. [*Exit* WOLSEY.

Re-enter WOLSEY *with* GARDINER.

WOL. [*Aside to* GARD.] Give me your hand: much joy and favour to you;
You are the king's now.
GARD. [*Aside to* WOL.] But to be commanded
For ever by your grace, whose hand has rais'd me.
K. HEN. Come hither, Gardiner.
[*They converse apart.*
CAM. My lord of York, was not one doctor Pace
In this man's place before him?
WOL. Yes, he was.
CAM. Was he not held a learned man?
WOL. Yes, surely.
CAM. Believe me, there's an ill opinion spread, then,
Even of yourself, lord cardinal.
WOL. How! of me?
CAM. They will not stick to say, you envied him;
And fearing he would rise, he was so virtuous,
Kept him a foreign man still; which so griev'd him,
That he ran mad, and died.
WOL. Heaven's peace be with him!
That's christian care enough: for living murmurers
There's places of rebuke. He was a fool;
For he would needs be virtuous: that good fellow,
If I command him, follows my appointment;
I will have none so near else. Learn this, brother,
We live not to be grip'd by meaner persons.
K. HEN. Deliver this with modesty to the queen.
[*Exit* GARDINER.

The most convenient place that I can think of,
For such receipt of learning, is Black-Friars;
There ye shall meet about this weighty business.—
My Wolsey, see it furnish'd.—O, my lord,
Would it not grieve an able man to leave
So sweet a bedfellow? But, conscience, conscience,—
O, 'tis a tender place! and I must leave her.
[*Exeunt.*

SCENE III.—*The same. An Ante-chamber in the* Queen's *Apartments.*

Enter ANNE BULLEN *and an old* Lady.

ANNE. Not for that neither;—here's the pang that pinches:—
His highness having liv'd so long with her, and she
So good a lady that no tongue could ever
Pronounce dishonour of her,—by my life,
She never knew harm-doing;—O now, after
So many courses of the sun enthron'd,
Still growing in a majesty and pomp,—the which
To leave's* a thousand-fold more bitter, than
'Tis sweet at first to acquire,—after this process,
To give her the avaunt! it is a pity
Would move a monster.

OLD L. Hearts of most hard temper
Melt and lament for her.

ANNE. O, God's will! much better
She ne'er had known pomp; though 't be temporal,
Yet, if that quarrel,[a] Fortune, do divorce

[a] *Yet, if that* quarrel, *Fortune,—*] "She calls Fortune *a quarrel* or arrow, from her striking so deep and suddenly," says Warburton. Hanmer reads, "That *quarr'ler* fortune;" an emendation on a par with Warburton's portentous gloss. Mr. Collier's annotator suggests, "that *cruel* fortune," which is as miserably prosaic and commonplace as may be. Shakespeare has elsewhere characterised her humorous ladyship as, "*strumpet* Fortune," "*harlot* Fortune," and, which is the same thing, "*giglot* Fortune;" and may here have employed a kindred epithet—*squirrel*, which, in his day, was not unfrequently applied to vicious women. Thus, in Rowland's "Looke To It: for, Ile Stab Ye," 1604:—

"Thou that within thy Table hast set down,
The names of all the *Squirrils* in the towne."

(*) Old text, *leave*.

It from the bearer, 'tis a sufferance, panging
As soul and body's severing.

OLD L. Alas, poor lady!
She's a stranger now again.

ANNE. So much the more
Must pity drop upon her. Verily,
I swear, 'tis better to be lowly born,
And range with humble livers in content,
Than to be perk'd up in a glist'ring grief,
And wear a golden sorrow.

OLD L. Our content
Is our best having.

ANNE. By my troth and maidenhead,
I would not be a queen.

OLD L. Beshrew me, I would,
And venture maidenhead for't; and so would you,
For all this spice of your hypocrisy:
You, that have so fair parts of woman on you,
Have too a woman's heart; which ever yet
Affected eminence, wealth, sovereignty;
Which, to say sooth, are blessings; and which gifts
(Saving your mincing) the capacity
Of your soft cheveril[a] conscience would receive,
If you might please to stretch it.

ANNE. Nay, good troth,—

OLD L. Yes, troth, and troth,—you would not be a queen?

ANNE. No, not for all the riches under heaven.

OLD L. 'Tis strange; a three-pence bow'd would hire me,[b]
Old as I am, to queen it: but, I pray you,
What think you of a duchess? have you limbs
To bear that load of title?

ANNE. No, in truth.

OLD L. Then you are weakly made: pluck off a little;[c]
I would not be a young count in your way,
For more than blushing comes to: if your back
Cannot vouchsafe this burden, 'tis too weak
Ever to get a boy.

ANNE. How you do talk!
I swear again, I would not be a queen
For all the world.

OLD L. In faith, for little England
You'd venture an emballing: I myself
Would for Carnarvonshire, although there 'long'd
No more to the crown but that.—Lo, who comes here?

Enter the Lord Chamberlain.

CHAM. Good morrow, ladies. What were't worth to know
The secret of your conference?

ANNE. My good lord,
Not your demand; it values not your asking:
Our mistress' sorrows we were pitying.

CHAM. It was a gentle business, and becoming
The action of good women: there is hope
All will be well.

ANNE. Now, I pray God, amen!

CHAM. You bear a gentle mind, and heavenly blessings
Follow such creatures. That you may, fair lady,
Perceive I speak sincerely, and high note's
Ta'en of your many virtues, the king's majesty
Commends his good opinion of you to you,[d] and
Does purpose honour to you no less flowing
Than marchioness of Pembroke; to which title
A thousand pound a year, annual support,
Out of his grace he adds.(2)

ANNE. I do not know,
What kind of my obedience I should tender;
More than my all is nothing: nor my prayers
Are not words duly hallow'd, nor my wishes
More worth than empty vanities; yet prayers and wishes
Are all I can return. Beseech your lordship,
Vouchsafe to speak my thanks and my obedience,
As from a blushing handmaid, to his highness;
Whose health and royalty I pray for.

CHAM. Lady,
I shall not fail to approve the fair conceit
The king hath of you.—[*Aside.*] I have perus'd her well;
Beauty and honour in her are so mingled,
That they have caught the king: and who knows yet,
But from this lady may proceed a gem
To lighten all this isle?—I'll to the king,
And say I spoke with you.

ANNE. My honour'd lord.
[*Exit* Lord Chamberlain.

OLD L. Why, this it is; see, see!
I have been begging sixteen years in court,
(Am yet a courtier beggarly,) nor could
Come pat betwixt too early and too late,
For any suit of pounds: and you, O fate!
A very fresh-fish here, (fie, fie, fie upon

---

a *Soft* cheveril *conscience*—] *Cheveril* is kid-skin leather. See note (e), p. 180, Vol. I.

b *A three-pence* bow'd *would* hire *me*,—] *Bow'd* means *bent*: it is spelt *bowed* in modern editions; but Mr. Dyce is right in saying *hire* should, in this place, be pronounced as a dissyllable.

c Pluck off a little;] Let us come down a little; if you will neither queen it nor be a duchess, perhaps you have strength enough to bear the honours of a countess. This is Steevens' explanation, and it appears to be the true one.

d Commends his good opinion of you to you,—] So the old text. The usual reading is,—

"Commends his good opinion to you."

It is highly probable that the words "to you" or "of you" were mistakenly interpolated by the compositor.

This compell'd fortune!) have your mouth fill'd up,
Before you open it.

ANNE. This is strange to me.

OLD L. How tastes it? is it bitter? forty pence, no.[a]
There was a lady once, ('t is an old story)
That would not be a queen, that would she not,
For all the mud in Egypt: have you heard it?

ANNE. Come, you are pleasant.

OLD L. With your theme, I could
O'ermount the lark. The marchioness of Pembroke!
A thousand pounds a year for pure respect!
No other obligation! By my life,
That promises more* thousands: honour's train
Is longer than his foreskirt. By this time,
I know your back will bear a duchess;—say,
Are you not stronger than you were?

ANNE. Good lady,
Make yourself mirth with your particular fancy,
And leave me out on't. Would I had no being,
If this salute[b] my blood a jot; it faints me,
To think what follows.
The queen is comfortless, and we forgetful
In our long absence: pray, do not deliver
What here you have heard to her.

OLD L. What do you think me?

[*Exeunt.*

SCENE IV.—*The same. A Hall in* Black-Friars.

Trumpets, sennet, and cornets. Enter two Vergers, *with short silver wands; next them, two* Scribes, *in the habits of doctors; after them, the* ARCHBISHOP *of* CANTERBURY *alone; after him, the* BISHOPS *of* LINCOLN, ELY, ROCHESTER, *and* SAINT ASAPH; *next them, with some small distance, follows a* Gentleman, *bearing the purse, with the great seal, and a cardinal's hat; then two* Priests, *bearing each a silver cross; then a* Gentleman-usher *bare-headed, accompanied with a* Sergeant-at-arms, *bearing a silver mace; then two* Gentlemen, *bearing two great silver pillars;*(3) *after them, side by side, the two* Cardinals, WOLSEY *and* CAMPEIUS; *two* Noblemen *with the sword and mace. Then enter the* KING *and* QUEEN, *and their Trains. The* KING *takes place*[c] *under the cloth of state; the two* Cardinals *sit under him, as judges. The* QUEEN *takes place at some distance from the* KING. *The* Bishops *place themselves on each side the court in manner of a consistory; between them, the* Scribes. *The* Lords *sit next the* Bishops. *The* Crier *and the rest of the* Attendants *stand in convenient order about the stage.*

WOL. Whilst our commission from Rome is read,
Let silence be commanded.

K. HEN. What's the need?
It hath already publicly been read,
And on all sides the authority allow'd;
You may, then, spare that time.

WOL. Be't so.—Proceed.

SCRIBE. Say, Henry king of England, come into the court.

CRIER. *Henry king of England, come into the court.*

K. HEN. Here.

SCRIBE. Say, Katharine queen of England, come into the court.

CRIER. *Katharine queen of England, come into the court!*

[*The* QUEEN *makes no answer, rises out of her chair, goes about the court, comes to the* KING, *and kneels at his feet; then speaks.*]

Q. KATH. Sir, I desire you do me right and justice;
And to bestow your pity on me; for
I am a most poor woman, and a stranger,
Born out of your dominions; having here
No judge indifferent,[d] nor no more assurance
Of equal friendship and proceeding. Alas, sir,
In what have I offended you? what cause
Hath my behaviour given to your displeasure,
That thus you should proceed to put me off,
And take your good grace from me? Heaven witness,
I have been to you a true and humble wife,
At all times to your will conformable:
Ever in fear to kindle your dislike,
Yea, subject to your countenance,—glad or sorry,
As I saw it inclin'd. When was the hour
I ever contradicted your desire,
Or made it not mine too? Or which of your friends
Have I not strove to love, although I knew
He were mine enemy? what friend of mine,
That had to him deriv'd your anger, did I

(*) Old text, *mo.*

a Forty pence, no.] That is, I'd wager forty-pence, it does not. Steevens has cited several passages to show that *forty pence,* or *three and fourpence,* was a proverbial expression for any small wager or sum.

b If *this* salute *my blood a jot;*] Some critics have made a difficulty of the word *salute* in this passage; and Mr. Collier's annotator substitutes *elate. Salute* here means *move* or *exhilarate.* So, in our author's Sonnets (cxxi.):—

"For why should others' false adulterate eyes
Give *salutation* to my sportive blood?"

c Place—] *Place* of old meant something more emphatic than mere *seat;* it implied the *appropriate seat.* We have it in "The Merchant of Venice," where the Duke bids Portia, the supposed young judge, take his "place," which is the judgment-seat, beneath the Duke's throne.

d Indifferent,—] *Impartial.*

Continue in my liking? nay, gave[a] notice
He was from thence discharg'd? Sir, call to mind
That I have been your wife, in this obedience,
Upward of twenty years, and have been blest
With many children by you: if, in the course
And process of this time, you can report,
And prove it too, against mine honour aught,
My bond to wedlock, or my love and duty,
Against your sacred person, in God's name,
Turn me away; and let the foul'st contempt
Shut door upon me, and so give me up
To the sharp'st kind of justice. Please you, sir,
The king, your father, was reputed for
A prince most prudent, of an excellent
And unmatch'd wit and judgment: Ferdinand,
My father, king of Spain, was reckon'd one

a Nay, gave notice—] It has been suggested that Shakespeare probably wrote, "nay, gave *not* notice," &c.

The wisest prince, that there had reign'd by many
A year before: it is not to be question'd
That they had gather'd a wise council to them
Of every realm, that did debate this business,
Who deem'd our marriage lawful: wherefore I humbly
Beseech you, sir, to spare me, till I may
Be by my friends in Spain advis'd; whose counsel
I will implore: if not, i' the name of God,
Your pleasure be fulfill'd!

WOL. You have here, lady,
(And of your choice) these reverend fathers; men
Of singular integrity and learning,
Yea, the elect o' the land, who are assembled
To plead your cause: it shall be therefore bootless,
That longer you desire[a] the court; as well
For your own quiet, as to rectify
What is unsettled in the king.

CAM. His grace
Hath spoken well, and justly: therefore, madam,
It's fit this royal session do proceed;
And that, without delay, their arguments
Be now produc'd, and heard.

Q. KATH. Lord cardinal,—
To you I speak.

WOL. Your pleasure, madam?

Q. KATH. Sir,
I am about to weep; but, thinking that
We are a queen, (or long have dream'd so) certain
The daughter of a king, my drops of tears
I'll turn to sparks of fire.

WOL. Be patient yet.

Q. KATH. I will, when you are humble; nay, before,
Or God will punish me. I do believe,
Induc'd by potent circumstances, that
You are mine enemy; and make my challenge,
You shall not be my judge; for it is you
Have blown this coal betwixt my lord and me,—
Which God's dew quench!—Therefore I say again,
I utterly abhor, yea, from my soul
Refuse you for my judge; whom, yet once more,
I hold my most malicious foe, and think not
At all a friend to truth.

WOL. I do profess,
You speak not like yourself; who ever yet
Have stood to charity, and display'd the effects
Of disposition gentle, and of wisdom
O'ertopping woman's power. Madam, you do me wrong:
I have no spleen against you, nor injustice
For you or any: how far I have proceeded,
Or how far further shall, is warranted
By a commission from the consistory,
Yea, the whole consistory of Rome. You charge me
That I have blown this coal: I do deny it:
The king is present: if it be known to him
That I gainsay my deed, how may he wound,
And worthily, my falsehood! yea, as much
As you have done my truth. If[b] he know
That I am free of your report, he knows,
I am not of your wrong. Therefore in him
It lies to cure me: and the cure is, to
Remove these thoughts from you: the which before
His highness shall speak in, I do beseech
You, gracious madam, to unthink your speaking,
And to say so no more.

Q. KATH. My lord, my lord,
I am a simple woman, much too weak
To oppose your cunning. You're meek and humble-mouth'd;
You sign your place and calling, in full seeming,
With meekness and humility; but your heart
Is cramm'd with arrogancy, spleen, and pride.
You have, by fortune and his highness' favours,
Gone slightly o'er low steps; and now are mounted
Where powers are your retainers; and your words,[c]
Domestics to you, serve your will, as't please
Yourself pronounce their office. I must tell you,
You tender more your person's honour, than
Your high profession spiritual: that again
I do refuse you for my judge; and here,
Before you all, appeal unto the pope,
To bring my whole cause 'fore his holiness,
And to be judg'd by him.

[*She curtsies to the* KING, *and retires.*

CAM. The queen is obstinate,
Stubborn to justice, apt to accuse it, and
Disdainful to be tried by't; 'tis not well.
She's going away.

K. HEN. Call her again.

CRIER. *Katharine queen of England, come into the court.*

GRIF. Madam, you are call'd back.

Q. KATH. What need you note it? pray you, keep your way:
When you are call'd, return.—Now the Lord help,

---

a Desire *the court;*] The fourth folio has, "*defer* the court."
b If he know, &c.] Rowe reads, "*But* if he know," &c.
c *Your* words,—] Tyrwhitt believed "words" to be a misprint for *wards;* and that the queen referred to the young men of family whom Wolsey employed in domestic services.

They vex me past my patience!—Pray you, pass on:
I will not tarry; no, nor ever more,
Upon this business, my appearance make
In any of their courts.(4)
[*Exeunt* QUEEN, GRIFFITH, *and* Attendants.

K. HEN. Go thy ways, Kate:
That man i' the world who shall report he has
A better wife, let him in nought be trusted,
For speaking false in that. Thou art, alone,
(If thy rare qualities, sweet gentleness,
Thy meekness saint-like, wife-like government,—
Obeying in commanding,—and thy parts,
Sovereign and pious else, could speak thee out)
The queen of earthly queens.—She's noble born;
And, like her true nobility, she has
Carried herself towards me.

WOL. Most gracious sir,
In humblest manner I require your highness,
That it shall please you to declare, in hearing
Of all these ears, (for where I am robb'd and bound,
There must I be unloos'd; although not there
At once and fully satisfied) whether ever I
Did broach this business to your highness, or
Laid any scruple in your way, which might
Induce you to the question on't? or ever
Have to you,—but with thanks to God for such
A royal lady,—spake one the least word, that might
Be to the prejudice of her present state,
Or touch of her good person?

K. HEN. My lord cardinal,
I do excuse you; yea, upon mine honour,
I free you from't. You are not to be taught
That you have many enemies, that know not
Why they are so, but, like to village curs,
Bark when their fellows do: by some of these
The queen is put in anger. You're excus'd:
But will you be more justified? you ever
Have wish'd the sleeping of this business; never
Desir'd it to be stirr'd; but oft have hinder'd, oft,
The passages made toward it:—on my honour,
I speak my good lord cardinal to this point,
And thus far clear him. Now, what mov'd me to't,—
I will be bold with time and your attention:—
Then mark the inducement. Thus it came;—give heed to't:—
My conscience first receiv'd a tenderness,
Scruple, and prick, on certain speeches utter'd
By the bishop of Bayonne, then French ambassador;
Who had been hither sent on the debating
A* marriage, 'twixt the duke of Orleans and
Our daughter Mary: i' the progress of this business,
Ere a determinate resolution, he
(I mean the bishop) did require a respite;
Wherein he might the king his lord advértise
Whether our daughter were legitimate,
Respecting this our marriage with the dowager,
Sometimes our brother's wife. This respite shook
The bosom of my conscience, enter'd me,
Yea, with a splitting* power, and made to tremble
The region of my breast; which forc'd such way
That many maz'd considerings did throng,
And press'd in with this caution. First, methought,
I stood not in the smile of heaven; who had
Commanded nature, that my lady's womb,
If it conceiv'd a male child by me, should
Do no more offices of life to't, than
The grave does to the dead: for her male issue
Or died where they were made, or shortly after
This world had air'd them: hence I took a thought,
This was a judgment on me; that my kingdom,—
Well worthy the best heir o' the world,—should not
Be gladded in't by me: then follows, that
I weigh'd the danger which my realms stood in
By this my issue's fail; and that gave to me
Many a groaning throe. Thus hulling[a] in
The wild sea of my conscience, I did steer
Toward this remedy, whereupon we are
Now present here together; that's to say,
I meant to rectify my conscience,—which
I then did feel full sick, and yet not well,—
By all the reverend fathers of the land
And doctors learn'd.—First I began in private
With you, my lord of Lincoln; you remember
How under my oppression I did reek,
When I first mov'd you.

LIN. Very well, my liege.

K. HEN. I have spoke long; be pleas'd yourself to say
How far you satisfied me.

LIN. So please your highness,
The question did at first so stagger me,—
Bearing a state of mighty moment in't,
And consequence of dread,—that I committed
The daring'st counsel which I had to doubt;
And did entreat your highness to this course,
Which you are running here.

K. HEN. I then mov'd you,
My lord of Canterbury; and got your leave
To make this present summons.—Unsolicited
I left no reverend person in this court;

(*) Old text, *And*.

(*) First folio, *spitting*.

[a] Hulling—] Tossing to and fro, like a ship.

But by particular consent proceeded,
Under your hands and seals: therefore, go on;
For no dislike i' the world against the person
Of the good queen, but the sharp thorny points
Of my alleged reasons, drive this forward:
Prove but our marriage lawful, by my life,
And kingly dignity, we are contented
To wear our mortal state to come, with her,
Katharine our queen, before the primest creature
That's paragon'd o' the world.

CAM. So please your highness,
The queen being absent, 'tis a needful fitness
That we adjourn this court till further day:
Meanwhile must be an earnest motion
Made to the queen, to call back her appeal
She intends unto his holiness.

[*They rise to depart.*

K. HEN. [*Aside.*] I may perceive,
These cardinals trifle with me: I abhor
This dilatory sloth, and tricks of Rome.—
My learn'd and well-beloved servant, Cranmer,
Pr'ythee return! with thy approach, I know,
My comfort comes along.—Break up the court:
I say, set on.

[*Exeunt, in manner as they entered.*

ACT III.

SCENE I.—London. *Palace at* Bridewell. *A Room in the* Queen's *Apartment.*

The QUEEN *and some of her* Women *at work.*

Q. KATH. Take thy lute, wench: my soul grows sad with troubles;
Sing, and disperse 'em, if thou canst: leave working.

SONG.

Orpheus, with his lute, made trees,
And the mountain-tops that freeze,
Bow themselves, when he did sing:
To his music, plants and flowers
Ever sprung; as sun and showers
There had made a lasting spring.
Every thing that heard him play,
Even the billows of the sea,
Hung their heads, and then lay by.
In sweet music is such art;
Killing care and grief of heart,
Fall asleep, or, hearing, die.

Enter a Gentleman.

Q. KATH. How now!
GENT. An't please your grace, the two great cardinals
Wait in the presence.
Q. KATH. Would they speak with me?
GENT. They will'd me say so, madam.
Q. KATH. Pray their graces

To come near. [*Exit* Gent.] What can be their business
With me, a poor weak woman, fall'n from favour?
I do not like their coming:—now I think on 't,
They should be good men; their affairs as righteous:
But all hoods make not monks.

Enter WOLSEY *and* CAMPEIUS.

WOL. Peace to your highness!
Q. KATH. Your graces find me here part of a housewife;
I would be all, against the worst may happen.
What are your pleasures with me, reverend lords?
WOL. May it please you, noble madam, to withdraw
Into your private chamber, we shall give you
The full cause of our coming.
Q. KATH. Speak it here;
There's nothing I have done yet, o' my conscience,
Deserves a corner: would all other women
Could speak this with as free a soul as I do!
My lords, I care not, (so much I am happy
Above a number,) if my actions
Were tried by every tongue, every eye saw 'em,
Envy and base opinion set against 'em,
I know my life so even. If your business
Seek me out, and that way I am wife in,
Out with it boldly; truth loves open dealing.
WOL. *Tanta est ergà te mentis integritas, regina serenissima,*—
Q. KATH. O, good my lord, no Latin;
I am not such a truant since my coming,
As not to know the language I have liv'd in:
A strange tongue makes my cause more strange, suspicious;
Pray, speak in English: here are some will thank you,
If you speak truth, for their poor mistress' sake;—
Believe me, she has had much wrong: lord cardinal,
The willing'st sin I ever yet committed,
May be absolv'd in English.
WOL. Noble lady,
I am sorry my integrity should breed
(And service to his majesty and you)
So deep suspicion, where all faith was meant.
We come not by the way of accusation,
To taint that honour every good tongue blesses,
Nor to betray you any way to sorrow,—
You have too much, good lady:—but to know
How you stand minded in the weighty difference
Between the king and you; and to deliver,
Like free and honest men, our just opinions,
And comforts to your* cause.

(*) First folio, *our*.

CAM. Most honour'd madam,
My lord of York,—out of his noble nature,
Zeal and obedience he still bore your grace,—
Forgetting, like a good man, your late censure
Both of his truth and him, (which was too far)—
Offers, as I do, in a sign of peace,
His service and his counsel.
Q. KATH. [*Aside.*] To betray me.—
My lords, I thank you both for your good wills,
Ye speak like honest men, (pray God, ye prove so!)
But how to make ye suddenly an answer,
In such a point of weight, so near mine honour,
(More near my life, I fear,) with my weak wit,
And to such men of gravity and learning,
In truth, I know not. I was set at work
Among my maids; full little, God knows, looking
Either for such men or such business.
For her sake that I have been, (for I feel
The last fit of my greatness,) good your graces,
Let me have time and counsel for my cause:
Alas! I am a woman, friendless, hopeless!
WOL. Madam, you wrong the king's love with these fears;
Your hopes and friends are infinite.
Q. KATH. In England,
But little for my profit: can you think, lords,
That any Englishman dare give me counsel?
Or be a known friend, 'gainst his highness' pleasure,
(Though he be grown so desperate to be honest)
And live a subject? Nay, forsooth, my friends,
They that must weigh out[a] my afflictions,
They that my trust must grow to, live not here;
They are, as all my other comforts, far hence,
In mine own country, lords.
CAM. I would your grace
Would leave your griefs, and take my counsel.
Q. KATH. How, sir?
CAM. Put your main cause into the king's protection;
He's loving, and most gracious: 'twill be much
Both for your honour better and your cause;
For if the trial of the law o'ertake ye,
You'll part away disgrac'd.
WOL. He tells you rightly.
Q. KATH. Ye tell me what ye wish for both,—my ruin:
Is this your christian counsel? out upon ye!
Heaven is above all yet; there sits a Judge,
That no king can corrupt.
CAM. Your rage mistakes us.
Q. KATH. The more shame for ye; holy men I thought ye,
Upon my soul, two reverend cardinal virtues;
But cardinal sins and hollow hearts I fear ye:
Mend 'em for shame, my lords. Is this your comfort?

a Weigh out—] Probably for *outweigh*.

The cordial that ye bring a wretched lady?
A woman lost among ye, laugh'd at, scorn'd?
I will not wish ye half my miseries,
I have more charity: but say, I warn'd ye;
Take heed, for heaven's sake take heed, lest at once
The burden of my sorrows fall upon ye.

WOL. Madam, this is a mere distraction;
You turn the good we offer into envy.

Q. KATH. Ye turn me into nothing: woe upon ye,
And all such false professors! Would you have me
(If you have any justice, any pity;
If ye be any thing but churchmen's habits)
Put my sick cause into his hands that hates me?
Alas! has banish'd me his bed already,—
His love, too long ago! I am old, my lords,
And all the fellowship I hold now with him
Is only my obedience. What can happen
To me above this wretchedness? all your studies
Make me a curse like this?

CAM. Your fears are worse.

Q. KATH. Have I liv'd thus long—(let me speak myself,
Since virtue finds no friends)—a wife, a true one?
A woman (I dare say, without vain-glory)
Never yet branded with suspicion?
Have I with all my full affections
Still met the king? lov'd him next heaven? obey'd him?
Been, out of fondness, superstitious to him?
Almost forgot my prayers to content him?
And am I thus rewarded? 't is not well, lords.
Bring me a constant woman to her husband,
One that ne'er dream'd a joy beyond his pleasure;
And to that woman, when she has done most,
Yet will I add an honour,—a great patience.

WOL. Madam, you wander from the good we aim at.

Q. KATH. My lord, I dare not make myself so guilty,
To give up willingly that noble title
Your master wed me to: nothing but death
Shall e'er divorce my dignities.

WOL. Pray, hear me.

Q. KATH. Would I had never trod this English earth,
Or felt the flatteries that grow upon it!
Ye have angels' faces,[a] but heaven knows your hearts.
What will become of me now, wretched lady!
I am the most unhappy woman living.—
Alas, poor wenches, where are now your fortunes? [*To her* Women.
Shipwreck'd upon a kingdom, where no pity,
No friends, no hope; no kindred weep for me,
Almost no grave allow'd me:—like the lily,
That once was mistress of the field and flourish'd,
I'll hang my head and perish.

WOL. If your grace
Could but be brought to know our ends are honest,
You'd feel more comfort: why should we, good lady,
Upon what cause, wrong you? alas, our places,
The way of our profession is against it;
We are to cure such sorrows, not to sow 'em.
For goodness' sake, consider what you do;
How you may hurt yourself, ay, utterly
Grow from the king's acquaintance, by this carriage.
The hearts of princes kiss obedience,
So much they love it; but to stubborn spirits
They swell, and grow as terrible as storms.
I know you have a gentle, noble temper,
A soul as even as a calm: pray, think us
Those we profess, peace-makers, friends, and servants.

CAM. Madam, you'll find it so. You wrong your virtues
With these weak women's fears: a noble spirit,
As yours was put into you, ever casts
Such doubts, as false coin, from it. The king loves you;
Beware you lose it not: for us, if you please
To trust us in your business, we are ready
To use our utmost studies in your service.

Q. KATH. Do what ye will, my lords: and, pray, forgive me,
If I have us'd myself unmannerly;
You know I am a woman, lacking wit
To make a seemly answer to such persons.
Pray, do my service to his majesty:
He has my heart yet; and shall have my prayers
While I shall have my life. Come, reverend fathers,
Bestow your counsels on me: she now begs,
That little thought, when she set footing here,
She should have bought her dignities so dear.(1) [*Exeunt.*

SCENE II.—*The same. Ante-chamber to the* King's *Apartment.*

Enter the DUKE *of* NORFOLK, *the* DUKE *of* SUFFOLK, *the* EARL *of* SURREY, *and the* Lord Chamberlain.

NORF. If you will now unite in your complaints,
And force them with a constancy, the cardinal
Cannot stand under them: if you omit
The offer of this time, I cannot promise

[a] Ye have angels' faces,—] A reference, belike, to the old quibble attributed to Augustine,—"non *Angli* sed *Angeli.*"

But that you shall sustain more new disgraces,
With these you bear already.
SUR. I am joyful
To meet the least occasion that may give me
Remembrance of my father-in-law, the duke,
To be reveng'd on him.
SUF. Which of the peers
Have uncontemn'd gone by him, or at least
Strangely neglected? when did he regard
The stamp of nobleness in any person,
Out of himself? (2)
CHAM. My lords, you speak your pleasures:
What he deserves of you and me I know;
What we can do to him, (though now the time
Gives way to us,) I much fear. If you cannot
Bar his access to the king, never attempt
Any thing on him; for he hath a witchcraft
Over the king in 's tongue.
NORF. O, fear him not;
His spell in that is out: the king hath found
Matter against him that for ever mars
The honey of his language. No, he's settled,
Not to come off, in his displeasure.
SUR. Sir,
I should be glad to hear such news as this,
Once every hour.
NORF. Believe it, this is true.
In the divorce his contrary proceedings
Are all unfolded; wherein he appears,
As I would wish mine enemy.
SUR. How came
His practices to light?
SUF. Most strangely.
SUR. O, how, how?
SUF. The cardinal's letters to the pope miscarried,
And came to the eye o' the king; wherein was read,
How that the cardinal did entreat his holiness
To stay the judgment o' the divorce; for if
It did take place, *I do*, quoth he, *perceive*
My king is tangled in affection to
A creature of the queen's, lady Anne Bullen.
SUR. Has the king this?
SUF. Believe it.
SUR. Will this work?
CHAM. The king in this perceives him, how he coasts
And hedges his own way. But in this point
All his tricks founder, and he brings his physic
After his patient's death; the king already
Hath married the fair lady.
SUR. Would he had!
SUF. May you be happy in your wish, my lord!
For, I profess, you have it.
SUR. Now, all my joy
Trace the conjunction!
SUF. My Amen to 't!
NORF. All men's!
SUF. There's order given for her coronation:
Marry, this is yet but young, and may be left
To some ears unrecounted.—But, my lords,
She is a gallant creature, and complete
In mind and feature: I persuade me, from her
Will fall some blessing to this land, which shall
In it be memoriz'd.

SUR. But, will the king
Digest this letter of the cardinal's?
The Lord forbid!
NORF. Marry, Amen!
SUF. No, no;
There be more wasps that buz about his nose,
Will make this sting the sooner. Cardinal Campeius
Is stol'n away to Rome; hath ta'en no leave;
Has left the cause o' the king unhandled; and
Is posted, as the agent of our cardinal,
To second all his plot. I do assure you
The king cried *Ha!* at this.
CHAM. Now, God incense him,
And let him cry *Ha,* louder!
NORF. But, my lord,
When returns Cranmer?
SUF. He is return'd, in his opinions; which
Have satisfied the king for his divorce,
Together with all famous colleges
Almost in Christendom: shortly, I believe,
His second marriage shall be publish'd, and
Her coronation. Katharine no more
Shall be call'd, queen, but princess dowager,
And widow to prince Arthur.
NORF. This same Cranmer's
A worthy fellow, and hath ta'en much pain
In the king's business.
SUF. He has, and we shall see him
For it, an archbishop.
NORF. So I hear.
SUF. 'T is so.—
The cardinal!

Enter WOLSEY *and* CROMWELL.

NORF. Observe, observe, he's moody.
WOL. The packet, Cromwell,
Gave't you the king?
CROM. To his own hand, in's bedchamber.
WOL. Look'd he o' the inside of the paper?
CROM. Presently
He did unseal them: and the first he view'd,
He did it with a serious mind; a heed
Was in his countenance. You he bade
Attend him here this morning.
WOL. Is he ready to come abroad?
CROM. I think by this, he is.
WOL. Leave me a while.—
[*Exit* CROMWELL.
It shall be to the duchess of Alençon,
The French king's sister: he shall marry her.—
Anne Bullen! No; I'll no Anne Bullens for him:
There's more in't than fair visage.—Bullen!
No, we'll no Bullens.—Speedily I wish
To hear from Rome.—The marchioness of Pembroke!
NORF. He's discontented.
SUF. May be, he hears the king
Does whet his anger to him.
SUR. Sharp enough,
Lord, for thy justice!
WOL. The late queen's gentlewoman; a knight's daughter,
To be her mistress' mistress! the queen's queen!—
This candle burns not clear:[a] 'tis I must snuff it;
Then, out it goes. What though I know her virtuous,
And well-deserving? yet I know her for
A spleeny Lutheran; and not wholesome to
Our cause, that she should lie i' the bosom of
Our hard-rul'd king. Again, there is sprung up
An heretic, an arch one, Cranmer; one
Hath crawl'd into the favour of the king,
And is his oracle.
NORF. He is vex'd at something.
SUR. I would, 't were something that would fret the string,
The master-cord on's heart!
SUF. The king, the king!

Enter the KING, *reading a schedule, and* LOVELL.

K. HEN. What piles of wealth hath he accumulated
To his own portion! and what expense by the hour
Seems to flow from him! How, i' the name of thrift,
Does he rake this together!—Now, my lords,—
Saw you the cardinal?
NORF. My lord, we have
Stood here observing him: some strange commotion
Is in his brain: he bites his lip, and starts;
Stops on a sudden, looks upon the ground,
Then lays his finger on his temple; straight
Springs out into fast gait; then, stops again,
Strikes his breast hard; and anon, he casts
His eye against the moon: in most strange postures
We have seen him set himself.
K. HEN. It may well be,
There is a mutiny in's mind. This morning
Papers of state he sent me to peruse,
As I requir'd; and wot you what I found
There?—on my conscience, put unwittingly;—
Forsooth, an inventory, thus importing,—
The several parcels of his plate, his treasure,
Rich stuffs, and ornaments of household; which
I find at such proud rate, that it out-speaks
Possession of a subject.

[a] This candle burns not clear:] There may be a play intended on the word *Bullen*, which is said to have been an ancient provincial name for a candle.

NORF. It's heaven's will,
Some spirit put this paper in the packet,
To bless your eye withal.
K. HEN. If we did think
His contemplation were above the earth,
And fix'd on spiritual object, he should still
Dwell in his musings; but I am afraid
His thinkings are below the moon, not worth
His serious considering.
[*He takes his seat and whispers* LOVELL, *who goes to* WOLSEY.
WOL. Heaven forgive me!—
Ever God bless your highness!
K. HEN. Good my lord,
You are full of heavenly stuff, and bear the inventory
Of your best graces in your mind; the which
You were now running o'er: you have scarce time
To steal from spiritual leisure a brief span,
To keep your earthly audit: sure in that
I deem you an ill husband, and am glad
To have you therein my companion.
WOL. Sir,
For holy offices I have a time; a time
To think upon the part of business which
I bear i' the state; and nature does require
Her times of preservation, which, perforce,
I, her frail son, amongst my brethren mortal,
Must give my tendance to.
K. HEN. You have said well.
WOL. And ever may your highness yoke together,
As I will lend you cause, my doing well
With my well saying!
K. HEN. 'T is well said again,
And 'tis a kind of good deed to say well;
And yet, words are no deeds. My father lov'd you:
He said he did; and with his deed did crown
His word upon you. Since I had my office,
I have kept you next my heart; have not alone

Employ'd you where high profits might come home,
But par'd my present havings, to bestow
My bounties upon you.

WOL. [*Aside.*] What should this mean?

SUR. [*Aside to others.*] The Lord increase this business!

K. HEN. Have I not made you
The prime man of the state? I pray you, tell me,
If what I now pronounce you have found true:
And, if you may confess it, say withal,
If you are bound to us, or no. What say you?

WOL. My sovereign, I confess, your royal graces,
Shower'd on me daily, have been more than could
My studied purposes requite; which went
Beyond all man's endeavours:—my endeavours
Have ever come too short of my desires,
Yet fil'd* with my abilities:[a] mine own ends
Have been mine so, that evermore they pointed
To the good of your most sacred person and
The profit of the state. For your great graces
Heap'd upon me, poor undeserver, I
Can nothing render but allegiant thanks,
My prayers to heaven for you; my loyalty,
Which ever has and ever shall be growing,
Till death, that winter, kill it.

K. HEN. Fairly answered;
A loyal and obedient subject is
Therein illustrated: the honour of it
Does pay the act of it; as, i'the contrary,
The foulness is the punishment. I presume,
That, as my hand has open'd bounty to you,
My heart dropp'd love, my power rain'd honour, more
On you than any; so your hand and heart,
Your brain, and every function of your power,
Should, notwithstanding that your bond of duty,
As 'twere in love's particular, be more
To me, your friend, than any.

WOL. I do profess
That for your highness' good I ever labour'd
More than mine own; that am, have, and will be,[b]
Though all the world should crack their duty to you,
And throw it from their soul; though perils did
Abound as thick as thought could make them, and
Appear in forms more horrid, yet my duty,
As doth a rock against the chiding flood,
Should the approach of this wild river break,
And stand unshaken yours.

K. HEN. 'Tis nobly spoken:—
Take notice, lords, he has a loyal breast,
For you have seen him open't.—Read o'er this;
[*Giving him papers.*
And after, this: and then to breakfast with
What appetite you have.

[*Exit, frowning upon the* CARDINAL: *the* Nobles *throng after him, smiling and whispering.*

WOL. What should this mean?
What sudden anger's this? how have I reap'd it?
He parted frowning from me, as if ruin
Leap'd from his eyes: so looks the chafed lion
Upon the daring huntsman that has gall'd him;
Then makes him nothing. I must read this paper;
I fear, the story of his anger.—'Tis so;
This paper has undone me:—'tis the account
Of all that world of wealth I have drawn together
For mine own ends; indeed, to gain the popedom,
And fee my friends in Rome. O negligence,
Fit for a fool to fall by! what cross devil
Made me put this main secret in the packet
I sent the king?—Is there no way to cure this?
No new device to beat this from his brains?
I know 'twill stir him strongly; yet I know
A way, if it take right, in spite of fortune
Will bring me off again. What's this—*To the Pope?*
The letter, as I live, with all the business
I writ to's holiness. Nay then, farewell!
I have touch'd the highest point of all my greatness;
And, from that full meridian of my glory,
I haste now to my setting; I shall fall
Like a bright exhalation in the evening,
And no man see me more.

Re-enter the DUKES *of* NORFOLK *and* SUFFOLK, *the* EARL *of* SURREY, *and the* Lord Chamberlain.

NORF. Hear the king's pleasure, cardinal, who commands you
To render up the great seal presently
Into our hands; and to confine yourself
To Asher-house, my lord of Winchester's,
Till you hear further from his highness.

WOL. Stay,—
Where's your commission, lords? words cannot carry
Authority so weighty.

(*) Old text, *fill'd.*

[a] Yet fil'd with my abilities:] Yet march'd an equal pace with my abilities.

[b] That am, have, and will be,—] A *crux* of the first magnitude. Mr. Singer proposes to make all "congruous and clear," by reading,—

"—— that *I* am *true*, and will be."

And Mr. Collier hopes to have rendered the passage intelligible by changing *am* to "aim," inserting *I* before *have*, and omitting *be*,—

"—— that *aim* I have, and will."

But neither of these alterations carries conviction; and perhaps our suggestion that the passage may have originally stood,—

"—— *to* that *I* am *slave* and will be."

or

"—— *to* that I'm *slave* and will be,"—

is not a whit more feasible.

SUF. Who dare cross 'em,
Bearing the king's will from his mouth expressly?
WOL. Till I find more than will or words to do it,
(I mean your malice) know, officious lords,
I dare and must deny it. Now I feel
Of what coarse metal ye are moulded,—envy.
How eagerly ye follow my disgraces,
As if it fed ye! and how sleek and wanton
Ye appear in every thing may bring my ruin!
Follow your envious courses, men of malice;
You have christian warrant for 'em, and, no doubt,
In time will find their fit rewards. That seal,
You ask with such a violence, the king
(Mine and your master) with his own hand gave me:
Bade me enjoy it, with the place and honours,
During my life; and, to confirm his goodness,
Tied it by letters-patents:[a]—now, who'll take it?
SUR. The king, that gave it.
WOL. It must be himself, then.
SUR. Thou art a proud traitor, priest.
WOL. Proud lord, thou liest!
Within these forty[b] hours Surrey durst better
Have burnt that tongue than said so.
SUR. Thy ambition,
Thou scarlet sin, robb'd this bewailing land
Of noble Buckingham, my father-in-law:
The heads of all thy brother cardinals
(With thee, and all thy best parts bound together)
Weigh'd not a hair of his. Plague of your policy!
You sent me deputy for Ireland;
Far from his succour, from the king, from all
That might have mercy on the fault thou gav'st him;
Whilst your great goodness, out of holy pity,
Absolv'd him with an axe.
WOL. This, and all else
This talking lord can lay upon my credit,
I answer is most false. The duke by law
Found his deserts: how innocent I was

a Tied it by letters-patents:—] This is sometimes printed, letters-*patent;* but the old text is the language of the poet's time.

b Forty hours—] Meaning, within some hours. See note (5), p. 150, Vol. I.

From any private malice in his end,
His noble jury and foul cause can witness.
If I lov'd many words, lord, I should tell you,
You have as little honesty as honour,
That, in the way of loyalty and truth
Toward the king, my ever royal master,
Dare mate a sounder man than Surrey can be,[a]
And all that love his follies.

SUR. By my soul,
Your long coat, priest, protects you; thou shouldst feel
My sword i' the life-blood of thee else.—My lords,
Can ye endure to hear this arrogance?
And from this fellow? If we live thus tamely,
To be thus jaded by a piece of scarlet,
Farewell nobility; let his grace go forward,
And dare us with his cap, like larks.[b]

WOL. All goodness
Is poison to thy stomach.

SUR. Yes, that goodness
Of gleaning all the land's wealth into one,
Into your own hands, cardinal, by extortion;
The goodness of your intercepted packets,
You writ to the pope against the king: your goodness,
Since you provoke me, shall be most notorious.—
My lord of Norfolk,—as you are truly noble,
As you respect the common good, the state
Of our despis'd nobility, our issues,
Who,* if he live, will scarce be gentlemen,—
Produce the grand sum of his sins, the articles
Collected from his life:—I'll startle you
Worse than the sacring bell, when the brown wench
Lay kissing in your arms, lord cardinal.

WOL. How much, methinks, I could despise this man,
But that I am bound in charity against it!

NORF. Those articles, my lord, are in the king's hand:
But, thus much, they are foul ones.

WOL. So much fairer
And spotless shall mine innocence arise,
When the king knows my truth.

SUR. This cannot save you:
I thank my memory, I yet remember
Some of these articles; and out they shall.
Now, if you can, blush and cry *guilty*, cardinal,
You'll show a little honesty.

WOL. Speak on, sir,
I dare your worst objections: if I blush,
It is to see a nobleman want manners.

SUR. I had rather want those than my head. Have at you!
First, that without the king's assent or knowledge,
You wrought to be a legate, by which power
You maim'd the jurisdiction of all bishops.

NORF. Then, that in all you writ to Rome, or else
To foreign princes, *Ego et Rex meus*
Was still inscrib'd; in which you brought the king
To be your servant.

SUF. Then, that without the knowledge
Either of king or council, when you went
Ambassador to the emperor, you made bold
To carry into Flanders the great seal.

SUR. *Item*, you sent a large commission
To Gregory de Cassalis,* to conclude,
Without the king's will or the state's allowance,
A league between his highness and Ferrara.

SUF. That, out of mere ambition, you have caus'd
Your holy hat to be stamp'd on the king's coin.

SUR. Then, that you have sent innumerable substance,
(By what means got, I leave to your own conscience)
To furnish Rome, and to prepare the ways
You have[c] for dignities; to the mere undoing
Of all the kingdom. Many more there are;
Which, since they are of you, and odious,
I will not taint my mouth with.

CHAM. O my lord,
Press not a falling man too far! 'tis virtue:
His faults lie open to the laws; let them,
Not you, correct him. My heart weeps to see him
So little of his great self.

SUR. I forgive him.

SUF. Lord cardinal, the king's further pleasure is,—
Because all those things you have done of late
By your power legatine† within this kingdom,
Fall into the compass of a *præmunire*,—
That therefore such a writ be sued against you,
To forfeit all your goods, lands, tenements,
Chattels,‡ and whatsoever, and to be
Out of the king's protection:—this is my charge.

NORF. And so we'll leave you to your meditations,
How to live better. For your stubborn answer

(*) First folio, *Whom*.

(*) Old text, *Cassado*. (†) Folios, *Legative, Legantine.* (‡) Old text, *Castles*.

a If I lov'd many words, lord, I should tell you,
You have as little honesty as honour,
That, in the way of loyalty and truth
Toward the king, my ever royal master,
Dare mate a sounder man than Surrey can be,
And all that love his follies.]

Theobald inserted *I* after "That," in the third line,—

"That *I* in the way," &c.

The pronoun would be more in place, perhaps, before "dare," in a subsequent line,—

"*I* dare mate a sounder man," &c.

unless, indeed, the construction has been altogether mistaken, and means, You have as little honesty and honour that dare mate (*i.e. assail, impugn, confound*) a sounder man than yourself for pursuing the course of loyalty and truth towards his king.

b And dare us with his cap, like larks.] "It is well known that the hat of a cardinal is scarlet; and that one of the methods of *daring* larks was by small mirrors fastened on scarlet cloth, which engaged the attention of these birds, while the fowler drew his net over them."—STEEVENS.

c *You* have, &c.] Query, You *pave*, &c.?

About the giving back the great seal to us,
The king shall know it, and, no doubt, shall thank you.
So, fare you well, my little good lord cardinal.
[*Exeunt all except* WOLSEY.

WOL. So, farewell to the *little good* you bear me.
Farewell! a long farewell to all my greatness!
This is the state of man; to-day he puts forth
The tender leaves of hope;* to-morrow blossoms,
And bears his blushing honours thick upon him;
The third day comes a frost, a killing frost;
And,—when he thinks, good easy man, full surely
His greatness is a-ripening,—nips his root,
And then he falls, as I do. I have ventur'd,
Like little wanton boys that swim on bladders,
This many summers in a sea of glory;
But far beyond my depth: my high-blown pride
At length broke under me; and now has left me,
Weary and old with service, to the mercy
Of a rude stream, that must for ever hide me.
Vain pomp and glory of this world, I hate ye!
I feel my heart new open'd. O, how wretched
Is that poor man that hangs on princes' favours!
There is, betwixt that smile we would aspire to,
That sweet aspéct of princes, and their ruin,
More pangs and fears than wars or women have;
And when he falls, he falls like Lucifer,
Never to hope again.—

Enter CROMWELL, *amazedly.*

Why, how now, Cromwell!

CROM. I have no power to speak, sir.

WOL. What, amaz'd
At my misfortunes? can thy spirit wonder,
A great man should decline? Nay, an you weep,
I am fall'n indeed.

CROM. How does your grace?

WOL. Why, well;
Never so truly happy, my good Cromwell.
I know myself now, and I feel within me
A peace above all earthly dignities,
A still and quiet conscience. The king has cur'd me,
I humbly thank his grace; and from these shoulders,
These ruin'd pillars, out of pity, taken
A load would sink a navy,—too much honour:
O, 'tis a burden, Cromwell, 'tis a burden,
Too heavy for a man that hopes for heaven!

CROM. I am glad your grace has made that right use of it.

WOL. I hope I have: I am able now, methinks,
(Out of a fortitude of soul I feel,)

(*) Old text, *hopes.*

To endure more miseries and greater far,
Than my weak-hearted enemies dare offer.—
What news abroad?

CROM. The heaviest and the worst
Is your displeasure with the king.

WOL. God bless him!

CROM. The next is, that sir Thomas More is chosen
Lord Chancellor in your place.

WOL. That's somewhat sudden:—
But he's a learned man. May he continue
Long in his highness' favour, and do justice
For truth's sake and his conscience; that his bones,
When he has run his course and sleeps in blessings,
May have a tomb of orphans' tears wept on 'em*!
What more?

CROM. That Cranmer is return'd with welcome,
Install'd lord archbishop of Canterbury.

WOL. That's news indeed.

CROM. Last, that the lady Anne,
Whom the king hath in secrecy long married,
This day was viewed in open as his queen,
Going to chapel; and the voice is now
Only about her coronation.

WOL. There was the weight that pull'd me down. O Cromwell,
The king has gone beyond me; all my glories
In that one woman I have lost for ever:
No sun shall ever usher forth mine honours,
Or gild again the noble troops that waited
Upon my smiles. Go, get thee from me, Cromwell;
I am a poor fall'n man, unworthy now
To be thy lord and master: seek the king;
(That sun, I pray, may never set!) I have told him
What, and how true thou art: he will advance thee;
Some little memory of me will stir him
(I know his noble nature) not to let
Thy hopeful service perish too: good Cromwell,
Neglect him not; make use[a] now, and provide
For thine own future safety.

CROM. O my lord,
Must I then leave you? must I needs forego
So good, so noble, and so true a master?
Bear witness, all that have not hearts of iron,
With what a sorrow Cromwell leaves his lord.—
The king shall have my service, but my prayers
For ever and for ever shall be yours.

WOL. Cromwell, I did not think to shed a tear
In all my miseries; but thou hast forc'd me,
Out of thy honest truth, to play the woman.
Let's dry our eyes: and thus far hear me, Cromwell;
And,—when I am forgotten, as I shall be;
And sleep in dull cold marble, where no mention
Of me more must be heard of,—say, I taught thee,
Say, Wolsey,—that once trod the ways of glory,

(*) Old text, *him.*

[a] Use—] *Interest.*

And sounded all the depths and shoals of honour,—
Found thee a way, out of his wreck, to rise in;
A sure and safe one, though thy master miss'd it.
Mark but my fall, and that that ruin'd me.
Cromwell, I charge thee, fling away ambition;
By that sin fell the angels, how can man, then,
The image of his Maker, hope to win by it?
Love thyself last: cherish those hearts that hate[a]
thee;
Corruption wins not more than honesty.
Still in thy right hand carry gentle peace,
To silence envious tongues. Be just, and fear not:
Let all the ends thou aim'st at, be thy country's,
Thy God's, and truth's; then if thou fall'st, O
Cromwell,
Thou fall'st a blessed martyr! Serve the king;
And,—pr'ythee, lead me in:
There take an inventory of all I have;
To the last penny, 'tis the king's: my robe,
And my integrity to heaven, is all
I dare now call mine own. O Cromwell, Cromwell!
Had I but serv'd my God with half the zeal
I serv'd my king, he would not in mine age
Have left me naked to mine enemies.

CROM. Good sir, have patience.

WOL. So I have. Farewell
The hopes of court! my hopes in heaven do dwell.
[*Exeunt.*

[a] *Cherish those hearts that* hate *thee;*] Warburton supposes, and very plausibly, that the poet wrote, "Cherish those hearts that *wait* thee;" that is, thy dependants.

ACT IV.

SCENE I.—*A Street in* Westminster.

Enter two Gentlemen, *meeting.*

1 Gent. You are well met once again.
2 Gent. So are you.
1 Gent. You come to take your stand here, and behold
The lady Anne pass from her coronation?
2 Gent. 'T is all my business. At our last encounter,
The duke of Buckingham came from his trial.
1 Gent. 'T is very true: but that time offer'd sorrow;
This, general joy.
2 Gent. 'T is well: the citizens,
I am sure, have shown at full their royal minds
(As, let 'em have their rights, they are ever forward)
In celebration of this day with shows,
Pageants, and sights of honour.
1 Gent. Never greater,
Nor, I'll assure you, better taken, sir.
2 Gent. May I be bold to ask what that contains,
That paper in your hand?
1 Gent. Yes; 't is the list
Of those that claim their offices this day,
By custom of the coronation.
The duke of Suffolk is the first, and claims
To be high-steward; next, the duke of Norfolk,
He to be earl marshal; you may read the rest.
2 Gent. I thank you, sir; had I not known those customs,
I should have been beholden to your paper.
But, I beseech you, what 's become of Katharine,
The princess dowager? how goes her business?

1 GENT. That I can tell you too. The archbishop
Of Canterbury, accompanied with other
Learned and reverend fathers of his order,
Held a late court at Dunstable, six miles off
From Ampthill, where the princess lay; to which
She was often cited by them, but appear'd not:
And, to be short, for not appearance and
The king's late scruple, by the main assent
Of all these learned men she was divorc'd,
And the late marriage[a] made of none effect:
Since which she was remov'd to Kimbolton,*
Where she remains now, sick.
2 GENT. Alas, good lady!— [*Trumpets.*
The trumpets sound: stand close, the queen is coming.

THE ORDER OF THE PROCESSION.

A lively flourish of trumpets; then, enter

1. *Two judges.*
2. *Lord Chancellor, with purse and mace before him.*
3. *Choristers singing.* [*Music.*
4. *Mayor of London, bearing the mace. Then Garter, in his coat of arms, and on his head a gilt copper crown.*
5. *Marquis Dorset, bearing a sceptre of gold, on his head a demi-coronal of gold. With him, the Earl of Surrey, bearing the rod of silver with the dove, crowned with an earl's coronet. Collars of SS.*
6. *Duke of Suffolk, in his robe of estate, his coronet on his head, bearing a long white wand, as high-steward. With him, the Duke of Norfolk, with the rod of marshalship, a coronet on his head. Collars of SS.*
7. *A canopy borne by four of the Cinque-ports; under it, the Queen in her robe, her hair richly adorned with pearl, crowned. On each side of her, the Bishops of London and Winchester.*
8. *The old Duchess of Norfolk, in a coronal of gold, wrought with flowers, bearing the Queen's train.*
9. *Certain Ladies or Countesses, with plain circlets of gold without flowers.*

2 GENT. A royal train, believe me.—These I know;—
Who's that, that bears the sceptre?
1 GENT. Marquis Dorset:
And that the earl of Surrey, with the rod.
2 GENT. A bold brave gentleman. That should be
The duke of Suffolk.
1 GENT. 'T is the same,—high-steward.
2 GENT. And that my lord of Norfolk?
1 GENT. Yes.
2 GENT. Heaven bless thee!
[*Looking on the* QUEEN.
Thou hast the sweetest face I ever look'd on.—
Sir, as I have a soul, she is an angel;
Our king has all the Indies in his arms,
And more and richer, when he strains that lady:
I cannot blame his conscience.
1 GENT. They that bear
The cloth of honour over her, are four barons
Of the Cinque-ports.
2 GENT. Those men are happy; and so are all are near her.—
I take it, she that carries up the train,
Is that old noble lady, duchess of Norfolk.
1 GENT. It is; and all the rest are countesses.
2 GENT. Their coronets say so. These are stars, indeed;
And sometimes falling ones.
1 GENT. No more of that.

Exit Procession, with a great flourish of trumpets.

Enter a third Gentleman.

God save you, sir! where have you been broiling?
3 GENT. Among the crowd i' the abbey; where a finger
Could not be wedg'd in more: I am stifled
With the mere rankness of their joy.
2 GENT. You saw
The ceremony?
3 GENT. That I did.
1 GENT. How was it?
3 GENT. Well worth the seeing.
2 GENT. Good sir, speak it to us.
3 GENT. As well as I am able. The rich stream
Of lords and ladies, having brought the queen
To a prepar'd place in the choir, fell off
A distance from her; while her grace sat down
To rest awhile, some half an hour or so,
In a rich chair of state, opposing freely
The beauty of her person to the people,—
Believe me, sir, she is the goodliest woman
That ever lay by man,—which when the people
Had the full view of, such a noise arose
As the shrouds make at sea in a stiff tempest,
As loud, and to as many tunes: hats, cloaks,
(Doublets, I think,) flew up; and had their faces
Been loose, this day they had been lost. Such joy

(*) Old text, *Kymmalton.*

[a] *And the late marriage,* &c.] That is, Steevens says, "the marriage lately considered a valid one." Does it not mean, rather, the second or later marriage, contradistinguished from her first union?

I never saw before. Great-bellied women,
That had not half a week to go, like rams
In the old time of war, would shake the press,
And make 'em reel before 'em. No man living
Could say, *This is my wife*, there; all were woven
So strangely in one piece.
2 GENT. But what follow'd?
3 GENT. At length her grace rose, and with modest paces
Came to the altar; where she kneel'd, and, saint-like,
Cast her fair eyes to heaven, and pray'd devoutly.
Then rose again, and bow'd her to the people:
When by the archbishop of Canterbury
She had all the royal makings of a queen;
As, holy oil, Edward Confessor's crown,
The rod, and bird of peace, and all such emblems
Laid nobly on her: which perform'd, the choir,
With all the choicest music of the kingdom,
Together sung *Te Deum*. So she parted,
And with the same full state pac'd back again
To York-place, where the feast is held.
1 GENT. Sir, you must no more call it York-place, that is past:
For, since the cardinal fell, that title 's lost;
'T is now the king's, and call'd Whitehall.
3 GENT. I know it;
But 't is so lately alter'd, that the old name
Is fresh about me.
2 GENT. What two reverend bishops
Were those that went on each side of the queen?
3 GENT. Stokesly and Gardiner; the one, of Winchester,
(Newly preferr'd from the king's secretary,)
The other, London.
2 GENT. He of Winchester
Is held no great good lover of the archbishop's,
The virtuous Cranmer.
3 GENT. All the land knows that:
However, yet there is no great breach; when it comes,
Cranmer will find a friend will not shrink from him.
2 GENT. Who may that be, I pray you?
3 GENT. Thomas Cromwell;
A man in much esteem with the king, and truly
A worthy friend.—The king
Has made him master o' the jewel-house,
And one, already, of the privy-council.
2 GENT. He will deserve more.
3 GENT. Yes, without all doubt.—
Come, gentlemen, ye shall go my way, which
Is to the court, and there ye shall be my guests;
Something I can command. As I walk thither,
I 'll tell ye more.
BOTH. You may command us, sir.
[*Exeunt.*

SCENE II.[a]—Kimbolton.

Enter KATHARINE, *Dowager, sick; led between* GRIFFITH *and* PATIENCE, *one of her women.*

GRIF. How does your grace?
KATH. O, Griffith, sick to death!
My legs, like loaden branches, bow to the earth,
Willing to leave their burden. Reach a chair;—
So,—now, methinks, I feel a little ease.
Didst thou not tell me, Griffith, as thou ledd'st* me,
That the great child of honour, cardinal Wolsey,
Was dead?
GRIF. Yes, madam; but, I think,† your grace,
Out of the pain you suffer'd, gave no ear to 't.
KATH. Pr'ythee, good Griffith, tell me how he died:
If well, he stepp'd before me, happily,
For my example.
GRIF. Well, the voice goes, madam:
For after the stout earl Northumberland
Arrested him at York, and brought him forward
(As a man sorely tainted) to his answer,
He fell sick suddenly, and grew so ill
He could not sit his mule.
KATH. Alas, poor man!
GRIF. At last, with easy roads, he came to Leicester,
Lodg'd in the abbey; where the reverend abbot,
With all his covent, honourably receiv'd him;
To whom he gave these words,—*O, father abbot,*
An old man, broken with the storms of state,
Is come to lay his weary bones among ye;
Give him a little earth for charity! (1)
So went to bed; where eagerly his sickness
Pursu'd him still; and, three nights after this,
About the hour of eight, (which he himself
Foretold should be his last) full of repentance,
Continual meditations, tears, and sorrows,
He gave his honours to the world again,
His blessed part to heaven,(2) and slept in peace.
KATH. So may he rest; his faults lie gently on him!
Yet thus far, Griffith, give me leave to speak him,
And yet with charity.—He was a man
Of an unbounded stomach,[b] ever ranking
Himself with princes; one that, by suggestion,

a Scene II.] "This scene is above any other part of Shakspeare's tragedies, and perhaps above any scene of any other poet, tender and pathetick, without gods, or furies, or poisons, or precipices, without the help of romantic circumstances, without improbable sallies of poetical lamentation, and without any throes of tumultuous misery."—JOHNSON.

(*) Old text, *lead'st*. (†) First folio, *thanke*.

b Of *an unbounded* stomach,—] Of unlimited *haughtiness* or *pride*. "This cardinal," says Holinshed, "was of a great stomach, for he computed himself equal with princes, and by craftie suggestions got into his hands innumerable treasure."

Tied[a] all the kingdom: simony was fair play;
His own opinion was his law: i' the presence
He would say untruths; and be ever double,
Both in his words and meaning: he was never,
But where he meant to ruin, pitiful:
His promises were, as he then was, mighty;
But his performance, as he is now, nothing:
Of his own body he was ill, and gave
The clergy ill example.

GRIF. Noble madam,
Men's evil manners live in brass; their virtues
We write in water. May it please your highness
To hear me speak his good now?

KATH. Yes, good Griffith;
I were malicious else.

GRIF. This cardinal,
Though from an humble stock, undoubtedly
Was fashion'd to much honour from his cradle.[b]
He was a scholar, and a ripe and good one;
Exceeding wise, fair-spoken, and persuading:
Lofty and sour to them that lov'd him not;
But to those men that sought him, sweet as summer.
And though he were unsatisfied in getting,
(Which was a sin) yet in bestowing, madam,
He was most princely: ever witness for him
Those twins of learning, that he rais'd in you,
Ipswich and Oxford! one of which fell with him,
Unwilling to outlive the good that rear'd it;[c]
The other, though unfinish'd, yet so famous,
So excellent in art, and still so rising,
That Christendom shall ever speak his virtue.
His overthrow heap'd happiness upon him;
For then, and not till then, he felt himself,
And found the blessedness of being little:
And, to add greater honours to his age
Than man could give him, he died fearing God.

KATH. After my death I wish no other herald,
No other speaker of my living actions,
To keep mine honour from corruption,
But such an honest chronicler as Griffith.
Whom I most hated living, thou hast made me,
With thy religious truth and modesty,
Now in his ashes honour: peace be with him!—
Patience, be near me still, and set me lower:
I have not long to trouble thee.—Good Griffith,
Cause the musicians play me that sad note

---

[a] Tied *all the kingdom:*] Hanmer reads, "*tyth'd* all the kingdom;" we incline to believe, rightly.

[b] Was fashion'd to much honour from his cradle.] The old text has a full point after honour, beginning a new sentence with,

"—— From his cradle
He was a scholar."

[c] *The good that* rear'd *it;*] The old copies have, "the good that *did* it;" which Pope altered to, "the good *he* did it;" and Mr. Collier's annotator to, "the good *man* did it." The slight change we have made, conceiving *did* to be a misprint for *rear'd*, may perhaps be thought to give a better sense, and to be more like the phraseology of Shakespeare. By *good*, must be understood the personification of *goodness;* the word occurs again in "Pericles," with the same meaning, Act II. (Gower)—

"The *good*, in conversation
Is still at Tharsus," &c.

I nam'd my knell, whilst I sit meditating
On that celestial harmony I go to.
[*Sad and solemn music.*

GRIF. She is asleep:—good wench, let's sit down quiet,
For fear we wake her;—softly, gentle Patience.

The vision.[a] *Enter, solemnly tripping one after another, six personages, clad in white robes, wearing on their heads garlands of bays, and golden vizards on their faces; branches of bays or palm in their hands. They first congee unto her, then dance; and, at certain changes, the first two hold a spare garland over her head; at which, the other four make reverend curtsies; then the two that held the garland deliver the same to the other next two, who observe the same order in their changes, and holding the garland over her head: which done, they deliver the same garland to the last two, who likewise observe the same order: at which, (as it were by inspiration) she makes in her sleep signs of rejoicing, and holdeth up her hands to heaven: and so in their dancing they vanish, carrying the garland with them. The music continues.*

[a] *The vision.*] The elaborate stage directions in this play exhibit no traces of Shakespeare's hand, and are foreign to his custom. They were most likely the work of some one upon whom devolved the arrangement of the pageantry. Of the present "vision," Malone remarks, "I do not believe the author wrote one word."

KATH. Spirits of peace, where are ye? are ye all gone?
And leave me here in wretchedness behind ye?
GRIF. Madam, we are here.
KATH. It is not you I call for:
Saw ye none enter since I slept?
GRIF. None, madam.
KATH. No! Saw you not, even now, a blessed troop
Invite me to a banquet; whose bright faces
Cast thousand beams upon me, like the sun?
They promis'd me eternal happiness;
And brought me garlands, Griffith, which I feel
I am not worthy yet to wear: I shall, assuredly.
GRIF. I am most joyful, madam, such good dreams
Possess your fancy.
KATH. Bid the music leave,
They are harsh and heavy to me. [*Music ceases.*
PAT. Do you note
How much her grace is alter'd on the sudden?
How long her face is drawn? how pale she looks,
And of an earthy cold![a] Mark her eyes!
GRIF. She is going, wench; pray, pray.
PAT. Heaven comfort her!

Enter a Messenger.

MESS. An't like your grace,—
KATH. You are a saucy fellow:
Deserve we no more reverence?
GRIF. You are to blame,
Knowing she will not lose her wonted greatness,
To use so rude behaviour: go to, kneel.
MESS. I humbly do entreat your highness' pardon;
My haste made me unmannerly. There is staying
A gentleman, sent from the king, to see you.
KATH. Admit him entrance, Griffith: but this fellow
Let me ne'er see again.
[*Exeunt* GRIFFITH *and* Messenger.

Re-enter GRIFFITH, *with* CAPUCIUS.

If my sight fail not,
You should be lord ambassador from the emperor,
My royal nephew, and your name Capucius.
CAP. Madam, the same,—your servant.
KATH. O, my lord,
The times and titles now are alter'd strangely
With me, since first you knew me. But, I pray you,
What is your pleasure with me?
CAP. Noble lady,
First, mine own service to your grace; the next,
The king's request that I would visit you;
Who grieves much for your weakness, and by me
Sends you his princely commendations,
And heartily entreats you take good comfort.
KATH. O, my good lord, that comfort comes too late;
'Tis like a pardon after execution:
That gentle physic, given in time, had cur'd me;
But now I am past all comforts here, but prayers.
How does his highness?
CAP. Madam, in good health.
KATH. So may he ever do! and ever flourish,
When I shall dwell with worms, and my poor name
Banish'd the kingdom!—Patience, is that letter,
I caus'd you write, yet sent away?
PAT. No, madam.
[*Giving it to* KATHARINE.
KATH. Sir, I most humbly pray you to deliver
This to my lord the king.
CAP. Most willing, madam.
KATH. In which I have commended to his goodness
The model of our chaste loves, his young daughter,—
The dews of heaven fall thick in blessings on her!—
Beseeching him to give her virtuous breeding,
(She is young, and of a noble modest nature,—
I hope she will deserve well) and a little
To love her for her mother's sake, that lov'd him,
Heaven knows how dearly. My next poor petition
Is, that his noble grace would have some pity
Upon my wretched women, that so long
Have follow'd both my fortunes faithfully:
Of which there is not one, I dare avow,
(And now I should not lie) but will deserve,
For virtue and true beauty of the soul,
For honesty and decent carriage,
A right good husband, let him be a noble;[b]
And, sure, those men are happy that shall have 'em.
The last is, for my men;—they are the poorest,
But poverty could never draw 'em from me;—
That they may have their wages duly paid 'em,
And something over to remember me by;

---

[a] And of an earthy cold!] The line is imperfect. Should we read—
"*Her hand* of an earthy cold!"?
or
"And *feels* of an earthy cold!"?
Mr. Collier's annotator would supply the deficiency by reading,—
"And of an earthy *coldness*."

[b] Let him be a noble;] That is, Even though he were a nobleman.

If heaven had pleas'd to have given me longer life
And able means, we had not parted thus.
These are the whole contents:—and, good my lord,
By that you love the dearest in this world,
As you wish christian peace to souls departed,
Stand these poor people's friend, and urge the king
To do me this last right.(3)

CAP. By heaven, I will;
Or let me lose the fashion of a man!

KATH. I thank you, honest lord. Remember me
In all humility unto his highness:
Say his long trouble now is passing
Out of this world: tell him, in death I bless'd him,
For so I will.—Mine eyes grow dim.—Farewell,
My lord.—Griffith, farewell.—Nay, Patience,
You must not leave me yet: I must to bed;
Call in more women.—When I am dead, good wench,
Let me be us'd with honour; strew me over
With maiden flowers, that all the world may know
I was a chaste wife to my grave: embalm me,
Then lay me forth: although unqueen'd, yet like
A queen, and daughter to a king, inter me.
I can no more.—

[*Exeunt*, KATHARINE *supported by* PATIENCE.

ACT V.

SCENE I.—London. *A Gallery in the Palace.*

Enter GARDINER, Bishop *of* Winchester, *a* Page *with a torch before him.*

GAR. It's one o'clock, boy, is't not?
BOY. It hath struck.
GAR. These should be hours for necessities,
Not for delights; times to repair our nature
With comforting repose, and not for us
To waste these times.

Enter Sir THOMAS LOVELL.

Good hour of night, sir Thomas.
Whither so late?
LOV. Came you from the king, my lord?
GAR. I did, sir Thomas; and left him at primero
With the duke of Suffolk.
LOV. I must to him, too,
Before he go to bed. I'll take my leave.
GAR. Not yet, sir Thomas Lovell. What's the matter?
It seems you are in haste: an if there be
No great offence belongs to't, give your friend
Some touch of your late business: affairs, that walk
(As they say spirits do) at midnight, have
In them a wilder nature, than the business
That seeks dispatch by day.
LOV. My lord, I love you;
And durst commend a secret to your ear
Much weightier than this work. The queen's in labour,
They say, in great extremity; and fear'd,
She'll with the labour end.
GAR. The fruit she goes with
I pray for heartily; that it may find
Good time, and live: but for the stock, sir Thomas,
I wish it grubb'd up now.
LOV. Methinks, I could
Cry the Amen; and yet my conscience says
She's a good creature, and, sweet lady, does
Deserve our better wishes.
GAR. But, sir, sir,—
Hear me, sir Thomas: you're a gentleman
Of mine own way; I know you wise, religious;
And, let me tell you, it will ne'er be well,—
'Twill not, sir Thomas Lovell, take't of me,—
Till Cranmer, Cromwell, her two hands, and she,
Sleep in their graves.

LOV. Now, sir, you speak of two
The most remark'd i' the kingdom. As for Cromwell,—
Beside that of the jewel-house, he's* made master
O'the rolls, and the king's secretary; further, sir,
Stands in the gap and trade of more preferments,
With which the time† will load him. The archbishop
Is the king's hand and tongue; and who dare speak
One syllable against him?

GAR. Yes, yes, sir Thomas,
There are that dare; and I myself have ventur'd
To speak my mind of him: and, indeed, this day,
(Sir, I may tell it you I think) I have
Incens'd[a] the lords o' the council, that he is
(For so I know he is, they know he is)
A most arch heretic, a pestilence
That does infect the land: with which they, mov'd,
Have broken with the king; who hath so far
Given ear to our complaint, (of his great grace
And princely care; foreseeing those fell mischiefs
Our reasons laid before him) hath commanded,
To-morrow morning to the council-board
He be convented.[b] He's a rank weed, sir Thomas,
And we must root him out. From your affairs
I hinder you too long: good night, sir Thomas.

LOV. Many good nights, my lord; I rest your servant. [*Exeunt* GARDINER *and* Page.

As LOVELL *is going out, enter the* KING *and the* DUKE *of* SUFFOLK.

K. HEN. Charles, I will play no more to-night;
My mind's not on't, you are too hard for me.

SUF. Sir, I did never win of you before.

K. HEN. But little, Charles;
Nor shall not, when my fancy's on my play.—
Now, Lovell, from the queen what is the news?

LOV. I could not personally deliver to her
What you commanded me, but by her woman
I sent your message; who return'd her thanks
In the great'st humbleness, and desir'd your highness
Most heartily to pray for her.

K. HEN. What say'st thou, ha?
To pray for her? what, is she crying out?

LOV. So said her woman; and that her sufferance made
Almost each pang a death.

K. HEN. Alas, good lady!

SUF. God safely quit her of her burden, and
With gentle travail, to the gladding of
Your highness with an heir!

K. HEN. 'Tis midnight, Charles;
Pr'ythee, to bed; and in thy prayers remember
The estate of my poor queen. Leave me alone;
For I must think of that which company
Would not be friendly to.

SUF. I wish your highness
A quiet night, and my good mistress will
Remember in my prayers.

K. HEN. Charles, good night.—
[*Exit* SUFFOLK.

Enter Sir ANTHONY DENNY.

Well, sir, what follows?

DEN. Sir, I have brought my lord the archbishop,
As you commanded me.

K. HEN. Ha! Canterbury?

DEN. Ay, my good lord.

K. HEN. 'Tis true: where is he, Denny?

DEN. He attends your highness' pleasure.

K. HEN. Bring him to us.
[*Exit* DENNY.

LOV. [*Aside.*] This is about that which the bishop spake;
I am happily come hither.

Re-enter DENNY *with* CRANMER.

K. HEN. Avoid the gallery.
[LOVELL *seems to stay.*
Ha!—I have said.—Be gone.
What!— [*Exeunt* LOVELL *and* DENNY.

CRAN. I am fearful:—wherefore frowns he thus?
'Tis his aspect of terror. All's not well.

K. HEN. How now, my lord? you do desire to know
Wherefore I sent for you.

CRAN. It is my duty,
To attend your highness' pleasure.

K. HEN. Pray you, arise,
My good and gracious lord of Canterbury.
Come, you and I must walk a turn together;
I have news to tell you: come, come, give me your hand.
Ah, my good lord, I grieve at what I speak,
And am right sorry to repeat what follows:
I have, and most unwillingly, of late

(*) Old text, *is*. (†) Old text, *Lime*.

[a] Incens'd—] That is, *prompted*.

[b] Convented.] *Summoned, convened.* So in "Coriolanus," Act II. Sc. 2:—
"—— We are *convented*
Upon a pleasing treaty."

Heard many grievous, I do say, my lord,
Grievous complaints of you; which, being consider'd,
Have mov'd us and our council, that you shall
This morning come before us; where, I know,
You cannot with such freedom purge yourself,
But that, till further trial in those charges
Which will require your answer, you must take
Your patience to you, and be well contented
To make your house our Tower: you a brother of us,
It fits we thus proceed, or else no witness
Would come against you.

CRAN. I humbly thank your highness;
And am right glad to catch this good occasion
Most throughly to be winnow'd, where my chaff
And corn shall fly asunder: for I know,
There's none stands under more calumnious tongues,
Than I myself, poor man.

K. HEN. Stand up, good Canterbury;
Thy truth and thy integrity is rooted
In us, thy friend: give me thy hand, stand up;
Pr'ythee, let's walk. Now, by my holidame,
What manner of man are you? My lord, I look'd
You would have given me your petition, that
I should have ta'en some pains to bring together
Yourself and your accusers; and to have heard you
Without indurance,[a] further.

CRAN. Most dread liege,
The good I stand on is my truth and honesty;
If they shall fail, I, with mine enemies,
Will triumph o'er my person; which I weigh not,
Being of those virtues vacant. I fear nothing
What can be said against me.

K. HEN. Know you not
How your state stands i' the world, with the whole world?
Your enemies are many, and not small; their practices
Must bear the same proportion: and not ever
The justice and the truth o' the question carries
The due o' the verdict with it: at what ease
Might corrupt minds procure knaves as corrupt
To swear against you? such things have been done.
You are potently oppos'd; and with a malice
Of as great size. Ween you of better luck,
I mean, in perjur'd witness, than your Master,
Whose minister you are, whiles here he liv'd
Upon this naughty earth? Go to, go to;
You take a precipice* for no leap of danger,
And woo† your own destruction.

CRAN. God, and your majesty,
Protect mine innocence, or I fall into
The trap is laid for me!

K. HEN. Be of good cheer;
They shall no more prevail than we give way to.
Keep comfort to you; and this morning see
You do appear before them: if they shall chance,
In charging you with matters, to commit you,
The best persuasions to the contrary
Fail not to use, and with what vehemency
The occasion shall instruct you: if entreaties
Will render you no remedy, this ring
Deliver them, and your appeal to us
There make before them.—Look, the good man weeps!
He's honest, on mine honour. God's blest mother!
I swear he is true-hearted; and a soul
None better in my kingdom.—Get you gone,
And do as I have bid you.—[*Exit* CRANMER.] He has strangled
His language in his tears.

Enter an old Lady.

GENT. [*Without.*] Come back; what mean you?

LADY. I'll not come back; the tidings that I bring
Will make my boldness, manners.—Now, good angels
Fly o'er thy royal head, and shade thy person
Under their blessed wings!

K. HEN. Now, by thy looks
I guess thy message. Is the queen deliver'd?
Say, *Ay, and of a boy.*

LADY. Ay, ay, my liege;
And of a lovely boy:—the God of heaven
Both now and ever bless her!—'tis a girl
Promises boys hereafter. Sir, your queen
Desires your visitation, and to be
Acquainted with this stranger; 'tis as like you
As cherry is to cherry.

K. HEN. Lovell,—

Re-enter LOVELL.

LOV. Sir,

K. HEN. Give her an hundred marks. I'll to the queen. [*Exit* KING.

LADY. An hundred marks! By this light, I'll ha' more.
An ordinary groom is for such payment.
I will have more, or scold it out of him.
Said I for this, the girl was like to him?
I will have more, or else unsay't; and now
While it is hot, I'll put it to the issue. [*Exeunt.*

(*) First folio, *Precipit.* (†) First folio, *woe.*

[a] Indurance,—] *Confinement, durance.*

SCENE II.—*Lobby before the Council-Chamber.*

Enter CRANMER ; Servants, Door-keeper, *&c.* *attending.*

CRAN. I hope I am not too late ; and yet the gentleman,
That was sent to me from the council, pray'd me
To make great haste.—All fast? what means this?—Ho!
Who waits there?—Sure, you know me?

D. KEEP. Yes, my lord ;
But yet I cannot help you.

CRAN. Why?

D. KEEP. Your grace must wait till you be call'd for.

Enter Doctor BUTTS.

CRAN. So.

BUTTS. [*Aside.*] This is a piece of malice. I am glad,
I came this way so happily : the king
Shall understand it presently. [*Exit* BUTTS.

CRAN. [*Aside.*] 'T is Butts,
The king's physician ; as he pass'd along,
How earnestly he cast his eyes upon me!
Pray heaven, he sound not my disgrace! For certain,
This is of purpose laid by some that hate me,
(God turn their hearts! I never sought their malice)
To quench mine honour : they would shame to make me
Wait else at door ; a fellow-counsellor,
'Mong boys, grooms, and lackeys. But their pleasures
Must be fulfill'd, and I attend with patience.

Enter, at a window above, the KING *and* BUTTS.

BUTTS. I'll show your grace the strangest sight,—

K. HEN. What's that, Butts?

BUTTS. I think your highness saw this many a day.

K. Hen. Body o' me, where is it?
Butts. There, my lord:
The high promotion of his grace of Canterbury;
Who holds his state at door, 'mongst pursuivants,
Pages, and footboys.
K. Hen. Ha! 'tis he, indeed:
Is this the honour they do one another?
'Tis well there's one above 'em yet. I had thought
They had parted so much honesty among 'em,
At least good manners, as not thus to suffer
A man of his place, and so near our favour,
To dance attendance on their lordships' pleasures,
And at the door too, like a post with packets.
By holy Mary, Butts, there's knavery:
Let 'em alone, and draw the curtain close;
We shall hear more anon.—

THE COUNCIL-CHAMBER.[a]

Enter the Lord Chancellor, *the* Duke *of* Suffolk, *the* Duke *of* Norfolk, Earl *of* Surrey, Lord Chamberlain, Gardiner, *and* Cromwell. *The* Chancellor *places himself at the upper end of the table on the left hand; a seat being left void above him, as for the* Archbishop *of* Canterbury. *The rest seat themselves in order on each side.* Cromwell *at the lower end, as secretary.*

Chan. Speak to the business, master secretary:
Why are we met in council?
Crom. Please your honours,
The chief cause concerns his grace of Canterbury.
Gar. Has he had knowledge of it?
Crom. Yes.
Nor. Who waits there?

[a] The Council-Chamber.] There is no change of scene; but the addition of some seats and a table was made to transform a portion of the stage into the Council-Chamber. The folio gives a direction, "A Councell Table brought in with Chayres and Stooles, and placed under the State. Enter Lord Chancellour," &c.

D. KEEP. Without, my noble lords?
GAR. Yes.
D. KEEP. My lord archbishop;
And has done half an hour, to know your pleasures.
CHAN. Let him come in.
D. KEEP. Your grace may enter now.
[CRANMER *approaches the Council-table.*
CHAN. My good lord archbishop, I am very sorry
To sit here at this present, and behold
That chair stand empty: but we all are men,
In our own natures frail, and capable[a]
Of our flesh; few are angels: out of which frailty,
And want of wisdom, you, that best should teach us,
Have misdemean'd yourself, and not a little:
Toward the king first, then his laws, in filling
The whole realm, by your teaching and your chaplains,
(For so we are inform'd) with new opinions,
Divers and dangerous; which are heresies,
And, not reform'd, may prove pernicious.
GAR. Which reformation must be sudden too,
My noble lords: for those that tame wild horses
Pace 'em not in their hands to make 'em gentle,
But stop their mouths with stubborn bits, and spur 'em,
Till they obey the manage. If we suffer
(Out of our easiness, and childish pity
To one man's honour) this contagious* sickness,
Farewell all physic; and what follows then?
Commotions, uproars, with a general taint
Of the whole state: as, of late days, our neighbours,
The upper Germany, can dearly witness;
Yet freshly pitied in our memories.
CRAN. My good lords, hitherto, in all the progress
Both of my life and office, I have labour'd,
And with no little study, that my teaching,
And the strong course of my authority,
Might go one way, and safely; and the end
Was ever, to do well: nor is there living
(I speak it with a single heart, my lords)
A man that more detests, more stirs against,
Both in his private conscience and his place,
Defacers of a[b] public peace, than I do.
Pray heaven, the king may never find a heart
With less allegiance in it! Men that make
Envy and crooked malice, nourishment,
Dare bite the best. I do beseech your lordships,
That, in this case of justice, my accusers,
Be what they will, may stand forth face to face,
And freely urge against me.
SUF. Nay, my lord,
That cannot be; you are a counsellor,
And, by that virtue, no man dare accuse you.
GAR. My lord, because we have business of more moment,
We will be short with you. 'Tis his highness' [pleasure,
And our consent, for better trial of you,
From hence you be committed to the Tower;
Where, being but a private man again,
You shall know many dare accuse you boldly,
More than, I fear, you are provided for.
CRAN. Ah, my good lord of Winchester, I thank you,
You are always my good friend; if your will pass,
I shall both find your lordship judge and juror,
You are so merciful: I see your end,—
'Tis my undoing: love and meekness, lord,
Become a churchman better than ambition;
Win straying souls with modesty again,
Cast none away. That I shall clear myself,
Lay all the weight ye can upon my patience,
I make as little doubt, as you do conscience
In doing daily wrongs. I could say more,
But reverence to your calling makes me modest.
GAR. My lord, my lord, you are a sectary,
That's the plain truth; your painted gloss discovers,
To men that understand you, words and weakness.
CROM. My lord of Winchester, you're a little,
By your good favour, too sharp; men so noble,
However faulty, yet should find respect
For what they have been: 'tis a cruelty,
To load a falling man.
GAR. Good master secretary,
I cry your honour mercy; you may, worst
Of all this table, say so.
CROM. Why, my lord?
GAR. Do not I know you for a favourer
Of this new sect? ye are not sound.
CROM. *Not sound!*
GAR. Not sound, I say.
CROM. Would you were half so honest!
Men's prayers then would seek you, not their fears.
GAR. I shall remember this bold language.
CROM. Do.
Remember your bold life too.
CHAN. This is too much;[c]
Forbear, for shame, my lords.
GAR. I have done.

(*) First folio, *courageous.*

a — but we all are men,
In our own natures frail, and capable
Of our flesh; few are angels:]
Capable of our flesh, if *capable* is not, as Mason surmised, a misprint for *culpable*, or, according to Malone, an error for *incapable*, may mean susceptible of fleshly temptations. Some editors point the lines thus,—
"In our own natures frail and capable:
Of our flesh, few are angels."
Turn it as we will, however, the passage affords but a doubtful sense.

b *Defacers of a public peace,*—] Rowe reads, "of *the* public peace."

c This is too much:] In the old copies, the prefix to this and the three next speeches of the Chancellor is *Cham.* Capell first assigned them correctly.

CROM. And I.
CHAN. Then thus for you, my lord,—it stands agreed,
I take it, by all voices, that forthwith
You be convey'd to the Tower a prisoner;
There to remain till the king's further pleasure
Be known unto us:—are you all agreed, lords?
ALL. We are.
CRAN. Is there no other way of mercy,
But I must needs to the Tower, my lords?
GAR. What other
Would you expect? you are strangely troublesome.
Let some o' the guard be ready there.

Enter Guard.

CRAN. For me?
Must I go like a traitor thither?
GAR. Receive him,
And see him safe i'the Tower.
CRAN. Stay, good my lords,
I have a little yet to say. Look there, my lords;
By virtue of that ring, I take my cause
Out of the gripes of cruel men, and give it
To a most noble judge, the king my master.
CHAN. This is the king's ring.
SUR. 'Tis no counterfeit.
SUF. 'Tis the right ring, by heaven! I told ye all,
When we first put this dangerous stone a rolling,
'T would fall upon ourselves.
NORF. Do you think, my lords,
The king will suffer but the little finger
Of this man to be vex'd?
CHAN. 'Tis now too certain:
How much more is his life in value with him?
Would I were fairly out on't.
CROM. My mind gave me,
In seeking tales and informations
Against this man,—whose honesty the devil
And his disciples only envy at—
Ye blew the fire that burns ye; now have at ye!

Enter the KING, *frowning on them; he takes his seat.*

GAR. Dread sovereign, how much are we bound to heaven
In daily thanks, that gave us such a prince;
Not only good and wise, but most religious:
One that, in all obedience, makes the church
The chief aim of his honour; and, to strengthen
That holy duty, out of dear respect,
His royal self in judgment comes to hear
The cause betwixt her and this great offender.
K. HEN. You were ever good at sudden commendations,
Bishop of Winchester. But know, I come not
To hear such flattery now; and in my presence,
They are too thin and bare[a] to hide offences.
To me you cannot reach, you play the spaniel,
And think with wagging of your tongue to win me;
But, whatsoe'er thou tak'st me for, I'm sure
Thou hast a cruel nature and a bloody.—
Good man, [*To* CRANMER.] sit down. Now let me see the proudest,
He that dares most, but wag his finger at thee:
By all that's holy, he had better starve,
Than but once think this[b] place becomes thee not.
SUR. May it please your grace,—
K. HEN. No, sir, it does not please me.
I had thought I had had men of some understanding
And wisdom, of my council; but I find none.
Was it discretion, lords, to let this man,
This good man, (few of you deserve that title)
This honest man, wait like a lousy footboy
At chamber door? and one as great as you are?
Why, what a shame was this? Did my commission
Bid ye so far forget yourselves? I gave ye
Power, as he was a counsellor to try him,
Not as a groom; there's some of ye, I see,
More out of malice than integrity,
Would try him to the utmost, had ye mean;
Which ye shall never have while I live.
CHAN. Thus far,
My most dread sovereign, may it like your grace
To let my tongue excuse all. What was purpos'd,
Concerning his imprisonment, was rather
(If there be faith in men) meant for his trial,
And fair purgation to the world, than malice;—
I'm sure, in me.
K. HEN. Well, well, my lords, respect him;
Take him, and use him well, he's worthy of it.
I will say thus much for him,—if a prince
May be beholden to a subject, I
Am, for his love and service, so to him.
Make me no more ado, but all embrace him;
Be friends, for shame, my lords!—My lord of Canterbury,
I have a suit which you must not deny me;
That is, a fair young maid that yet wants baptism,
You must be godfather, and answer for her.
CRAN. The greatest monarch now alive may glory
In such an honour; how may I deserve it,
That am a poor and humble subject to you?

[a] *Thin and* bare—] The old text has, "thin and *base*." Malone made the necessary emendation.
[b] This *place*—] A correction of Rowe; the old copies having, "*his* place." By "*this* place" is undoubtedly meant the vacant seat appointed for the Archbishop of Canterbury.

K. HEN. Come, come, my lord, you'd spare your spoons; you shall have two noble partners with you; the old duchess of Norfolk, and lady marquis Dorset; will these please you?—
Once more, my lord of Winchester, I charge you,
Embrace and love this man.

GAR. With a true heart,
And brother-love, I do it.

CRAN. And let heaven
Witness, how dear I hold this confirmation.

K. HEN. Good man, those joyful tears show thy true heart:*
The common voice, I see, is verified
Of thee, which says thus, *Do my lord of Canterbury*
A shrewd turn, and he's your friend for ever.—
Come, lords, we trifle time away; I long
To have this young one made a christian.
As I have made ye one, lords, one remain;
So I grow stronger, you more honour gain.
[*Exeunt.*

SCENE III.—*The Palace Yard.*

Noise and tumult without: enter Porter, *and his* Man.

PORT. You'll leave your noise anon, ye rascals: do you take the court for Parish-garden? (1) ye rude slaves, leave your gaping.[a]

[*Without.*] Good master porter, I belong to the larder.

PORT. Belong to the gallows, and be hanged, ye rogue! is this a place to roar in?—Fetch me a dozen crab-tree staves, and strong ones; these are but switches to 'em.—I'll scratch your heads: you must be seeing christenings? do you look for ale and cakes here, you rude rascals?

MAN. Pray, sir, be patient; 't is as much impossible—
Unless we sweep 'em from the door with cannons,—
To scatter 'em, as 't is to make 'em sleep
On May-day morning; which will never be:
We may as well push against Paul's, as stir 'em.

PORT. How got they in, and be hanged?

MAN. Alas, I know not; how gets the tide in?
As much as one sound cudgel of four foot
(You see the poor remainder) could distribute,
I made no spare, sir.

PORT. You did nothing, sir.

MAN. I am not Samson, nor sir Guy, nor Colbrand, to mow 'em down before me: but, if I spared any that had a head to hit, either young or old, he or she, cuckold or cuckold-maker, let me ne'er hope to see a chine again; and that I would not for a cow, God save her![b]

[*Without.*] Do you hear, master porter?

PORT. I shall be with you presently, good master puppy.—Keep the door close, sirrah.

MAN. What would you have me do?

PORT. What should you do, but knock 'em down by the dozens? Is this Moorfields to muster in? or have we some strange Indian with the great tool come to court, the women so besiege us? Bless me, what a fry of fornication is at door! On my christian conscience, this one christening will beget a thousand; here will be father, godfather, and all together.

MAN. The spoons will be the bigger, sir. There is a fellow somewhat near the door, he should be a brazier by his face, for, o' my conscience, twenty of the dog-days now reign in 's nose; all that stand about him are under the line, they need no other penance: that fire-drake did I hit three times on the head, and three times was his nose discharged against me; he stands there, like a mortar-piece, to blow us. There was a haberdasher's wife of small wit near him, that railed upon me till her pinked porringer fell off her head, for kindling such a combustion in the state. I missed the meteor once, and hit that woman, who cried out, *Clubs!* when I might see from far some forty truncheoners draw to her succour, which were the Hope of the Strand, where she was quartered. They fell on; I made good my place; at length they came to the broomstaff to me; I defied them still; when suddenly a file of boys behind 'em, loose shot, delivered such a shower of pebbles, that I was fain to draw mine honour in, and let 'em win the work: the devil was amongst 'em, I think, surely.

PORT. These are the youths that thunder at a play-house, and fight for bitten apples; that no audience, but the Tribulation of Tower-Hill, or the Limbs of Limehouse,[c] their dear brothers, are

---

(*) First folio, *hearts.*

[a] Gaping.] One sense of this word was to *yell, shout*, or *roar*.

[b] Let me ne'er hope to see a chine again; and that I would not for a cow, God save her!] Mr. Collier's annotator very speciously alters this to,—

"Let me ne'er hope to see a *queen* again;
And that I would not for a *crown*, God save her!"

but by *chine* is meant a *chine of beef*,—

"A chine of English beef, meat for a king," &c.
GREENE'S *play of "The Old Wife's Tale," Dyce's edition*, p. 224.

And perhaps the only change demanded is to read, "*my* cow," instead of "*a* cow." The expression, "my cow, God save her!" or, "my mare, God save her!" or, "my sow, God bless her!" appears to have been proverbial; thus, in Greene and Lodge's "Looking Glasse for London and Englande," 1598,—"my blind mare, God bless her!"

[c] The Tribulation of Tower-Hill, or the Limbs of Limehouse,—] "I suspect the *Tribulation*," says Johnson, "to have been a *puritanical meeting-house;*" and all the editors concur in opinion that the author here intended a fling at some puritanical sect or sects. Surely an extraordinary mistake. Can anything be more evident than that by the "Tribulation of Tower Hill," and the "Limbs of Limehouse," are meant the turbulent and mischievous 'long-shore rabble, the only congenial audience at a play-house for their "dear brothers," "the Hope of the Strand"? See Taylor's (the Water-Poet) "Jacke-a-Lent," 1630.

able to endure. I have some of 'em in *Limbo Patrum*,[a] and there they are like to dance these three days; besides the running banquet of two beadles that is to come.

Enter the Lord Chamberlain.

CHAM. Mercy o' me, what a multitude are here!
They grow still too; from all parts they are coming,
As if we kept a fair here! Where are these porters,
These lazy knaves?—Ye've made a fine hand, fellows.
There's a trim rabble let in: are all these
Your faithful friends o' the suburbs? We shall have
Great store of room, no doubt, left for the ladies,
When they pass back from the christening.
PORT. An't please your honour,
We are but men; and what so many may do,
Not being torn a-pieces, we have done:
An army cannot rule 'em.
CHAM. As I live,
If the king blame me for't, I'll lay ye all
By the heels, and suddenly; and on your heads
Clap round fines, for neglect: ye're lazy knaves;
And here ye lie baiting of bombards,[b] when
Ye should do service. Hark! the trumpets sound;
They're come already from the christening:
Go, break among the press, and find a way out
To let the troop pass fairly; or I'll find
A Marshalsea, shall hold ye play these two months.
PORT. Make way there for the princess.
MAN. You great fellow, stand close up, or I'll make your head ache.
PORT. You i' the camlet, get up o' the rail;
I'll pick[c] you o'er the pales else. [*Exeunt.*

SCENE IV.—*The Palace.*

Enter Trumpets, sounding; then two Aldermen, Lord Mayor, Garter, CRANMER, DUKE *of* NORFOLK *with his marshal's staff*, DUKE *of* SUFFOLK, *two* Noblemen *bearing great standing-bowls for the christening gifts; then four* Noblemen *bearing a canopy, under which the* DUCHESS *of* NORFOLK, *godmother, bearing the child richly habited in a mantle, &c. Train borne by a* Lady: *then follows the* MARCHIONESS *of* DORSET, *the other godmother, and* Ladies. *The troop pass once about the stage, and* Garter *speaks.*

GART. Heaven, from thy endless goodness, send prosperous life, long, and ever happy, to the high and mighty princess of England, Elizabeth!

Flourish. Enter KING, *and Train.*

CRAN. [*Kneeling.*] And to your royal grace and the good queen,
My noble partners, and myself, thus pray;—
All comfort, joy, in this most gracious lady,
Heaven ever laid up to make parents happy,
May hourly fall upon ye!
K. HEN. Thank you, good lord archbishop:
What is her name?
CRAN. Elizabeth.
K. HEN. Stand up, lord.—
[*The* KING *kisses the child.*
With this kiss take my blessing: God protect thee!
Into whose hand I give thy life.
CRAN. Amen.
K. HEN. My noble gossips, ye have been too prodigal:
I thank ye heartily; so shall this lady,
When she has so much English.
CRAN. Let me speak, sir,
For heaven now bids me; and the words I utter
Let none think flattery, for they'll find 'em truth.
This royal infant, (heaven still move about her!)
Though in her cradle, yet now promises
Upon this land a thousand thousand blessings,
Which time shall bring to ripeness: she shall be
(But few now living can behold that goodness)
A pattern to all princes living with her,
And all that shall succeed: Saba[d] was never
More covetous of wisdom and fair virtue,
Than this pure soul shall be: all princely graces,
That mould up such a mighty piece as this is,
With all the virtues that attend the good,
Shall still be doubled on her: truth shall nurse her,
Holy and heavenly thoughts still counsel her:
She shall be lov'd and fear'd: her own shall bless her;
Her foes shake like a field of beaten corn,
And hang their heads with sorrow: good grows with her:
In her days every man shall eat in safety
Under his own vine, what he plants; and sing

a *Limbo Patrum,—*] He means locked up. To be in *limbo*, is a cant phrase for being imprisoned, at the present time, and was derived probably from the *Limbus Patrum*, the place where the Patriarchs are supposed to have awaited the resurrection.

b Baiting of bombards,—] *Bombards*, or *bumbards*, were capacious vessels, sometimes made of leather, for holding drink.

c *I'll pick you o'er the pales—*] In the old copies, "Ile *pecke* you," &c. To *pick*, or *peck*, was the same formerly as to *pitch*.

d Saba—] That is, *Sheba*:—

"Were she as chaste as was Penelope,
As wise as *Saba*," &c.
MARLOWE'S *Doctor Faustus*, Act II. Sc. 1.

The merry songs of peace to all his neighbours:
God shall be truly known; and those about her
From her shall read[a] the perfect way of honour,
And by those claim their greatness, not by blood.
Nor shall this peace sleep with her: but as when[b]
The bird of wonder dies, the maiden phœnix,
Her ashes new create another heir,
As great in admiration as herself;
So shall she leave her blessedness to one,
(When heaven shall call her from this cloud of darkness)
Who from the sacred ashes of her honour

[a] *From her shall* read *the perfect way of honour,*—] *Read,* in this place. is supposed by some editors to be a misprint for *tread;* but see note (c), p. 547, Vol. I.

[b] Nor shall this peace sleep with her: but as when, &c.] This and the following seventeen lines are generally conjectured to be an interpolation, made at some revisal of the play, after the accession of King James.

Shall star-like rise, as great in fame as she was,
And so stand fix'd: peace, plenty, love, truth, terror,
That were the servants to his chosen infant,
Shall then be his, and like a vine grow to him;
Wherever the bright sun of heaven shall shine,
His honour and the greatness of his name
Shall be, and make new nations: he shall flourish,
And, like a mountain cedar, reach his branches
To all the plains about him:—our children's children
Shall see this, and bless heaven.

K. HEN. Thou speakest wonders.

CRAN. She shall be, to the happiness of England,
An aged princess; many days shall see her,
And yet no day without a deed to crown it.
Would I had known no more! but she must die,—
She must, the saints must have her,—yet a virgin;
A most unspotted lily shall she pass
To the ground, and all the world shall mourn her.

K. HEN. O lord archbishop,
Thou hast made me now a man! never, before
This happy child, did I get any thing:
This oracle of comfort has so pleas'd me,
That when I am in heaven I shall desire
To see what this child does, and praise my Maker.—
I thank ye all,—To you, my good lord mayor,
And you good brethren, I am much beholden;
I have receiv'd much honour by your presence,
And ye shall find me thankful. Lead the way, lords;—
Ye must all see the queen, and she must thank ye,
She will be sick else. This day, no man think
H 'as business at his house; for all shall stay:
This little one shall make it holiday. [*Exeunt.*

EPILOGUE.

'T is ten to one this play can never please
All that are here: some come to take their ease,
And sleep an act or two; but those, we fear,
We 've frighted with our trumpets; so, 't is clear,
They 'll say, 't is naught: others, to hear the city
Abus'd extremely, and to cry,—*that 's witty!*
Which we have not done neither: that, I fear,
All the expected good we 're like to hear
For this play at this time, is only in
The merciful construction of good women;
For such a one we show'd 'em; if they smile,
And say, 't will do, I know, within a while
All the best men are ours; for 't is ill hap,
If they hold when their ladies bid 'em clap.

ILLUSTRATIVE COMMENTS.

ACT I.

(1) SCENE I.—*That Bevis was believ'd.*] The reader unacquainted with the stupendous exploits of this hero, should consult the elegant "Specimens of Early English Metrical Romances," by George Ellis, or the romance of "Sir Bevis of Hamptoun" itself, as printed for the Maitland Club, 1838. That belief in them demanded no ordinary degree of credulity may be surmised from the following synopsis of his last great action:—"One day, whilst Sir Bevis and Josyan were taking the pleasures of the chase, they met a messenger dispatched to Saber by his good old wife, to announce that Edgar, king of England, had deprived their son Robert of all his estates, for the purpose of enriching a wicked favourite, Sir Bryant of Cornwall. Bevis, who had bestowed these estates on Saber, considered such an act as a personal insult, and determined to accompany his friend to England at the head of a formidable army. They landed in safety at Southampton, and marching rapidly towards London, encamped at Putney. Here Sir Bevis left his troops, together with Josyan, Saber, Terry, Guy, and Mile, and taking with him only twelve knights, repaired to the king, whom he found at Westminster, and, falling on his knees, humbly requested the restoration of his estates.

"Edgar, always inclined to peace, would have been glad to consent; but his steward, Sir Bryant, observed to him that Sir Bevis was a traitor, who trained up his horses in the habit of kicking out the brains of princes, and that he was still an outlaw, whose death it was the duty of all good subjects to procure by every possible device. The king, listening to this secret enemy, gave no answer, and Sir Bevis, with his attendants, took up their lodgings in the city to await his determination: but scarcely were they arrived at their inn, when they heard that a proclamation had been issued, enjoyning the citizens to shut their gates, to barricade every street, and to seize Sir Bevis alive or dead. The knight now found it necessary to provide for his defence. Having armed himself and his followers, he sallied forth in hopes of forcing his way out of the city before the measures of security should be complete; but he immediately met the steward, Sir Bryant, at the head of two hundred soldiers—

"A stroke he set upon his crown,
That to the saddle he clave him down.
So, within a little stound,
All two hundred he slew to ground.
Thorough Goose-lane Bevis went tho,*
There was him done right mickle wo!
That lane was so narrow y-wrought,
That Sir Bevis might defend him nought.
He had wunnen into his honde
Many a batayle in sundry londe;
But he was never so careful man,
For siker of sooth,† as he was than.
When Bevis saw his men were dead,
For sorrow couthe he no rede! ‡
But Morglay his sword he drew,
And many he felled, and many he slew.
Many a man he slew tho,
And out he went with mickle wo!

(*) *Then.* (†) *For certain truth.*
(‡) *Could think of no counsel.*

"The destruction of our hero appeared inevitable, after the disastrous adventure of Goose-lane, where his twelve companions were ingloriously murdered: but to Sir Bevis, when armed with Morglay and mounted on Arundel, nothing was wanting but a theatre sufficiently spacious for the display of his valour; and this he found in the Cheap, or market-place. He was beset by innumerable crowds; but Arundel, indignant at the insolence of the plebean assailants, by kicking on one side and biting on another, dispersed them in all directions to a distance of forty feet, while his master cut off the heads of all such as were driven, by the pressure of those behind, within reach of the terrible Morglay.

"In the mean time the news of the knight's distress was spread from mouth to mouth, and it was reported to Josyan that he was actually dead. After swooning with terror, she related the circumstance to her sons, and, blinded by fear, proposed an immediate retreat. But they answered that they were resolved to seek their father alive or dead, and, hastily requesting her benediction, collected four thousand knights, and departed at full speed from Putney.

"Sir Guy bestrode a Rabyte *
That was mickle, and nought light,†
That Sir Bevis in Paynim londe
Hade i-wunnen with his honde.
A sword he tooke of mickle might,
That y-cleped Aroundight,
It was Launcelot's du Lake,
Therewith he slew the fire-drake,‡
The pomel was of charbccle § stone;
(A better sword was never none,
The Romauns tellyth as I you say,
Ne none shall till Doomesday).
And Sir Myles there bestrid
A dromounday,‖ and forth he rid.
That horse was swift as any swallow,
No man might that horse begallowe.¶

"They crossed the river without opposition under cover of the night, and having set fire to Ludgate, which was closed against them, forced their way into the city, and proceeded in search of Sir Bevis. They found him untouched by any wound, but quite exhausted by the fatigue of a battle, which had now lasted during great part of the day, and the whole of the night. Arundel, too, stood motionless, bathed to his fetlocks in blood, and surrounded by dead bodies. The day had just dawned, and a burgher of some note, well armed and mounted, made a blow at Sir Bevis, under which the hero drooped to his saddle-bows; but at the same instant Sir Guy rushed forward:

"To that burgess a stroke he sent,
Through helm and hauberk down it went;
Both man and horse, in that stound,
He cleaved down to the ground!
His swordys point to the earth went,
That fire sprang out of the pavement.

(*) *An Arabian horse.* (†) *Weak.* (‡) *Fiery dragon.*
(§) *Carbuncle.* (‖) *A war horse.* (¶) *Out-gallop.*

"The fatigued and disheartened Sir Bevis immediately recovered new life at the sight of his son's valour; Arundel, too, resumed his wonted vivacity; and when Sir Mile, who rivalled his brother in gallantry, came up with the rest of the reinforcement, the discomfiture of the assailants was soon decided.

" The blood fell on that pavement
Right down to the Temple-bar it went;
As it is said in French romaunce,
Both in Yngelonde and in Fraunce,
So many men at once were never seen dead,
For the water of Thames for blood wax red;
Fro St. Mary Bowe to London Stone,
That ilke time was housing none.

"In short, sixty thousand men were slain in this battle; after which Sir Bevis and his sons returned, crowned with victory, to their camp at Putney."

(2) SCENE IV.—*Let the music knock it.*] The particulars of this masquerade were derived immediately from Cavendish's Life of Wolsey (of which, though it was not published for many years after Shakespeare's death, there were, in his time, many manuscript copies extant) or were taken at second-hand from Holinshed:—"And when it pleased the king's majesty, for his recreation, to repair to the cardinal's house, as he did divers times in the year, at which time there wanted no preparations, or goodly furniture, with viands of the finest sort that might be provided for money or friendship. Such pleasures were then devised for the king's comfort and consolation, as might be invented, or by man's wit imagined. The banquets were set forth, with masks and mummeries, in so gorgeous a sort, and costly manner, that it was a heaven to behold. There wanted no dames, or damsels, meet or apt to dance with the maskers, or to garnish the place for the time, with other goodly disports. Then was there all kind of music and harmony set forth, with excellent voices both of men and children. I have seen the king suddenly come in thither in a mask, with a dozen of other maskers, all in garments like shepherds, made of fine cloth of gold and fine crimson satin paned, and caps of the same, with visors of good proportion of visnomy; their hairs, and beards, either of fine gold wire, or else of silver, and some being of black silk; having sixteen torch-bearers, besides their drums, and other persons attending upon them, with visors, and clothed all in satin, of the same colours. And at his coming, and before he came into the hall, ye shall understand, that he came by water to the water gate, without any noise; where, against his coming, were laid charged many chambers, and at his landing, they were all shot off, which made such a rumble in the air, that it was like thunder. It made all the noblemen, ladies, and gentlewomen, to muse what it should mean coming so suddenly, they sitting quietly at a solemn banquet; under this sort: First, ye shall perceive that the tables were set in the chamber of presence, banquet-wise covered, my Lord Cardinal sitting under the cloth of estate, and there having his service all alone; and then was there set a lady and a nobleman, or a gentleman and gentlewoman, throughout all the tables in the chamber on the one side, which were made and joined as it were but one table. All which order and device was done and devised by the Lord Sands, Lord Chamberlain to the king; and also by Sir Henry Guilford, Comptroller to the king. Then immediately after this great shot of guns, the cardinal desired the Lord Chamberlain and Comptroller, to look what this sudden shot should mean, as though he knew nothing of the matter. They thereupon looking out of the windows into Thames, returned again, and showed him, that it seemed to them there should be some noblemen and strangers arrived at his bridge, as ambassadors from some foreign prince. With that, quoth the cardinal, 'I shall desire you, because ye can speak French, to take the pains to go down into the hall to encounter and to receive them, according to their estates, and to conduct them into this chamber, where they shall see us, and all these noble personages sitting merrily at our banquet, desiring them to sit down with us, and to take part of our fare and pastime.' Then [they] went incontinent down into the hall, where they received them with twenty new torches, and conveyed them up into the chamber, with such a number of drums and fifes as I have seldom seen together, at one time in any masque. At their arrival into the chamber, two and two together, they went directly before the cardinal where he sat, saluting him very reverently; to whom the Lord Chamberlain for them said: 'Sir, for as much as they be strangers, and can speak no English, they have desired me to declare unto your Grace thus; they, having understanding of this your triumphant banquet, where was assembled such a number of excellent fair dames, could do no less, under the supportation of your good grace, but to repair hither to view as well their incomparable beauty, as for to accompany them at mumchance and then after to dance with them, and so to have of them acquaintance. And, sir, they furthermore require of your Grace license to accomplish the cause of their repair.' To whom the cardinal answered, that he was very well contented they should so do. Then the maskers went first and saluted all the dames as they sat, and then returned to the most worthiest, and there opened a cup full of gold, with crowns, and other pieces of coin, to whom they set divers pieces to cast at. Thus in this manner perusing all the ladies and gentlewomen, and to some they lost, and of some they won. And thus done, they returned unto the cardinal, with great reverence, pouring down all the crowns in the cup, which was about two hundred crowns. 'At all,' quoth the cardinal, and so cast the dice, and won them all at a cast; whereat was great joy made. Then quoth the cardinal to my Lord Chamberlain, 'I pray you,' quoth he, 'show them that it seemeth me that there should be among them some noble man, whom I suppose to be much more worthy of honour to sit and occupy this room and place than I; to whom I would most gladly, if I knew him, surrender my place according to my duty.' Then spake my Lord Chamberlain unto them in French, declaring my Lord Cardinal's mind, and they rounding him again in the ear, my Lord Chamberlain said to my Lord Cardinal, 'Sir, they confess,' quoth he, 'that among them there is such a noble personage, whom, if your Grace can appoint him from the other, he is contented to disclose himself, and to accept your place most worthily.' With that the cardinal, taking a good advisement among them, at the last, quoth he, 'Me seemeth the gentleman with the black beard should be even he.' And with that he arose out of his chair, and offered the same to the gentleman in the black beard, with his cap in his hand. The person to whom he offered then his chair was Sir Edward Neville, a comely knight of a goodly personage, that much more resembled the king's person in that mask, than any other. The king, hearing and perceiving the cardinal so deceived in his estimation and choice, could not forbear laughing; but plucked down his visor, and Master Neville's also, and dashed out with such a pleasant countenance and cheer, that all noble estates there assembled, seeing the king to be there amongst them, rejoiced very much. The cardinal eftsoons desired his highness to take the place of estate, to whom the king answered, that he would go first and shift his apparel; and so departed, and went straight into my lord's bedchamber, where was a great fire made and prepared for him; and there new apparelled him with rich and princely garments. And in the time of the king's absence, the dishes of the banquet were clean taken up, and the tables spread again with new and sweet perfumed cloths; every man sitting still until the king and his maskers came in among them again, every man being newly apparelled. Then the king took his seat under the cloth of estate, commanding no man to remove, but sit still, as they did before. Then in came a new banquet before the king's majesty, and to all the rest through the tables, wherein, I suppose, were served two hundred dishes or above, of wondrous costly meats and devices, subtilly devised. Thus passed they forth the whole night with banqueting, dancing, and other triumphant devices, to the great comfort of the king, and pleasant regard of the nobility there assembled."

ACT II.

(1) Scene I.—*In all the rest show'd a most noble patience.*] Shakespeare's account of the duke's behaviour during trial corresponds pretty closely with that of the Chronicles :—"Shortlie after that the duke had beene indicted, he was arreigned in Westminster hall before the duke of Norffolke, being made by the kings letters patents high steward of England, to accomplish the high cause of appeale of the peere or peeres of the realme, and to discerne and iudge the cause of the peeres."

The witnesses having been heard, "the lords went to councell a great while, and after tooke their places. Then said the duke of Norffolke to the duke of Suffolke ; What say you of sir Edward duke of Buckingham touching the high treasons? The duke of Suffolke answered ; He is giltie : and so said the marques and all the other earls and lords. Thus was this prince duke of Buckingham found giltie of high treason, by a duke, a marques, seven earles, and twelve barons. The duke was brought to the barre sore chafing and swet marvellouslie ; and after he had made his reverence, he paused a while. The duke of Norffolke as judge said : Sir Edward, you have heard how you be indicted of high treason, you pleaded thereto not giltie, putting your selfe to the peeres of the realme, which have found you giltie. Then the duke of Norffolke wept and said : You shall be led to the kings prison, and there laid on a hardle, and so drawne to the place of execution, and there be hanged, cut downe alive, your members cut off and cast into the fire, your bowels burnt before you, your head smitten off, and your bodie quartered and divided at the kings will, and God have mercie on your soule, Amen.

"The duke of Buckingham said, My lord of Norffolke, you have said as a traitor should be said unto, but I was never anie : but my lords I nothing maligne for that you have doone to me, but the eternall God forgive you my death, and I doo : I shall never sue to the king for life, howbeit he is a gratious prince, and more grace may come from him than I desire. I desire you my lords and all my fellowes to pray for me. Then was the edge of the axe turned towards him, and he led into a barge. Sir Thomas Lovell desired him to sit on the cushins and carpet ordeined for him. He said nay ; for when I went to Westminster I was duke of Buckingham, now I am but Edward Bohune the most caitife of the world. Thus they landed at the Temple, where received him sir Nicholas Vawse and sir William Sands baronets, and led him through the citie, who desired ever the people to pray for him, of whome some wept and lamented, and said : This is the end of evill life, God forgive him, he was a proud prince, it is pitie that he behaved him so against his king and liege lord, whome God preserve. Thus about foure of the clocke he was brought as a cast man to the Tower."—Holinshed, 1521.

(2) Scene III.—

—— to which title
A thousand pound a year, annual support,
Out of his grace he adds.]

"The King gave good testymony of his love to this lady, creating her in one day Marquesse of Pembroke (that I may use the words of the patent) for the nobylity of her stocke, excellency of her virtues and conditions, and other shewes of honesty and goodnesse worthyly to be commended in her). And giving her a patent for a 1000 pounds yerely to maynteyne this honor with. She was the first woman, I read, to have honor given to her and her heyres male."—Sir Roger Twisden's *MS. Note.*

(3) Scene IV.—*Then two Gentlemen, bearing two great silver pillars.*] In describing the pageantry of the Cardinal on state occasions, Cavendish tells us :—"And as soon as he was entered into his chamber of presence, where there was attending his coming to await upon him to Westminster Hall, as well noblemen and other worthy gentlemen, of his own family ; thus passing forth with *two great* crosses of silver borne before him ; with also *two great pillars of silver*, and his pursuivant at arms with a great mace of silver gilt. Then his gentlemen ushers cried, and said, 'Oh, my lords and masters, on before ; make way for my Lord's Grace !' Thus passed he down from his chamber through the hall ; and when he came to the hall door, there was attendant for him his mule, trapped altogether in crimson velvet, and gilt stirrups. When he was mounted, with his cross bearers and *pillar bearers*, also upon great horses trapped with [fine] scarlet : Then marched he forward," &c.

His ostentatious display of these emblems of ecclesiastical authority, though they are said to be strictly appropriate to the office of *legate à latere*, seems to have excited much ridicule and resentment. Roy, in his bitter invective against Cardinal Wolsey, entitled, *Rede me, and be nott wrothe*, thus speaks of them :—

"Before him rydeth two prestes stronge :
And they beare two crosses ryght longe,
Gapynge in every mans face :
After theym folowe two laye-men secular,
And *each of theym holdynge a pillar*,
In their hondes, steade of a mace."

And so, in the same spirit, Skelton, in his *Speke, Parrot:*—

"Such pollaxis and *pyllers*, such mulys [mules] trapte with gold ;
Sens Dewcalyon's flodde in no cronycle ys told."

(4) Scene IV.—

—— no, nor ever more,
Upon this business, my appearance make
In any of their courts.]

Here also the poet was indebted immediately, or through his customary authority, Holinshed, to Cavendish.

"The court being thus furnished and ordered, the judges commanded the crier to proclaim silence ; then was the judges' commission, which they had of the pope, published and read openly before all the audience there assembled. That done, the crier called the king, by the name of 'King Henry of England, come into the court, &c.' With that the king answered and said, 'Here, my lords !' Then he called also the queen, by the name of 'Katherine, Queen of England, come into the court, &c.' who made no answer to the same, but rose up incontinent out of her chair, where as she sat, and because she could not come directly to the king for the distance which severed them, she took pain to go about unto the king, kneeling down at his feet in the sight of all the court and assembly, to whom she said in effect, in broken English, as followeth :

"'Sir,' quoth she, 'I beseech you for all the loves that hath been between us, and for the love of God, let me have justice and right, take of me some pity and compassion, for I am a poor woman and a stranger born out of your dominion, I have here no assured friend, and much less indifferent counsel ; I flee to you as to the head of justice within this realm. Alas ! Sir, wherein have I offended you, or what occasion of displeasure? Have I designed against your will and pleasure ; intending (as I perceive) to put me from you? I take God and all the world to witness, that I have been to you a true humble and obedient wife, ever conformable to your will and pleasure, that never said or did anything to the contrary thereof, being always well pleased and contented with all things wherein you had any delight or dalliance, whether it were in little or much ; I never grudged in word or countenance, or showed a visage or spark of discontentation. I loved all those whom ye loved only for your sake, whether I had cause or no ; and whether they were my friends or my enemies. This twenty years I have been your true wife or more, and by me ye have had divers children, although it hath pleased God to call them out of this world, which hath been no default in me.

"'And when ye had me at the first, I take God to be my judge, I was a true maid without touch of man; and whether it be true or no, I put it to your conscience. If there be any just cause by the law that ye can allege against me, either of dishonesty or any other impediment to banish and put me from you, I am well content to depart to my great shame and dishonour; and if there be none, then here I most lowly beseech you let me remain in my former estate, and receive justice at your hands. The king your father was in the time of his reign of such estimation thorough the world for his excellent wisdom, that he was accounted and called of all men the second Solomon; and my father Ferdinand, King of Spain, who was esteemed to be one of the wittiest princes that reigned in Spain, many years before, were both wise and excellent kings in wisdom and princely behaviour. It is not therefore to be doubted, but that they elected and gathered as wise counsellors about them as to their high discretions was thought meet. Also, as me seemeth, there was in those days as wise, as well learned men, and men of as good judgment as be at this present in both realms, who thought then the marriage between you and me good and lawful. Therefore it is a wonder to hear what new inventions are now invented against me, that never intended but honesty. And cause me to stand to the order and judgment of this new court, wherein ye may do me much wrong, if ye intend any cruelty; for ye may condemn me for lack of sufficient answer, having no indifferent counsel, but such as be assigned me, with whose wisdom and learning I am not acquainted. Ye must consider that they cannot be indifferent counsellors for my part which be your subjects, and taken out of your own council before, wherein they be made privy, and dare not, for your displeasure, disobey your will and intent, being once made privy thereto. Therefore I most humbly require you, in the way of charity, and for the love of God, who is the just Judge, to spare me the extremity of this new court, until I may be advertised what way and order my friends in Spain will advise me to take. And if ye will not extend to me so much indifferent favour, your pleasure then be fulfilled, and to God I commit my cause!'"

ACT III.

(1) SCENE I.—*She should have bought her dignities so dear.*] The foregoing scene is almost identical with the account which Cavendish has left us of the interview between Katharine and the Cardinals:—

"And then my lord rose up, and made him ready, taking his barge, and went straight to Bath Place to the other cardinal; and so went together unto Bridewell, directly to the queen's lodging: and they, being in her chamber of presence, showed to the gentleman usher that they came to speak with the queen's grace. The gentleman usher advertised the queen thereof incontinent. With that she came out of her privy chamber with a skein of white thread about her neck, into the chamber of presence, where the cardinals were giving of attendance upon her coming. At whose coming quoth she, 'Alack, my lords, I am very sorry to cause you to attend upon me; what is your pleasure with me?' 'If it please you,' quoth my Lord Cardinal, 'to go into your privy chamber, we will show you the cause of our coming.' 'My lord,' quoth she, 'if you have any thing to say, speak it openly before all these folks; for I fear nothing that ye can say or allege against me, but that I would all the world should both hear and see it; therefore I pray you speak your minds openly.' Then began my lord to speak to her in Latin. 'Nay, good my lord,' quoth she, 'speak to me in English I beseech you; although I understand Latin.' 'Forsooth then,' quoth my lord, 'Madam, if it please your grace, we come both to know your mind, how ye be disposed to do in this matter between the king and you, and also to declare secretly our opinions and our counsel unto you, which we have intended of very zeal and obedience that we bear to your grace.' 'My lords, I thank you then,' quoth she, 'of your good wills; but to make answer to your request I cannot so suddenly, for I was set among my maidens at work, thinking full little of any such matter, wherein there needeth a longer deliberation, and a better head than mine, to make answer to so noble wise men as ye be; I had need of good counsel in this case, which toucheth me so near; and for any counsel or friendship that I can find in England, [they] are nothing to my purpose or profit. Think you, I pray you, my lords, will any Englishmen counsel or be friendly unto me against the king's pleasure, they being his subjects? Nay forsooth, my lords! and for my counsel in whom I do intend to put my trust be not here; they being in Spain, in my native country. Alas, my lords! I am a poor woman lacking both wit and understanding sufficiently to answer such approved wise men as ye be both, in so weighty a matter. I pray you to extend your good and indifferent minds in your authority unto me, for I am a simple woman, destitute and barren of friendship and counsel here in a foreign region: and as for your counsel, I will not refuse, but be glad to hear.'

"And with that, she took my lord by the hand and led him into her privy chamber with the other cardinal; where they were in long communication: we, in the other chamber, might sometime hear the queen speak very loud, but what it was we could not understand. The communication ended, the cardinals departed and went directly to the king, making to him relation of their talk with the queen; and after resorted home to their houses to supper."

(2) SCENE II.—

—— when did he regard
The stamp of nobleness in any person,
Out of himself?]

Wolsey's arrogant behaviour to all with whom he came in contact, is acknowledged even by those who were best disposed towards him: "In his time of authority and glory," says Cavendish, "he was the haughtiest man in all his proceedings that then lived." It is not to be wondered at, therefore, that his enemies and satirists should make his "high-blown pride" a frequent theme for spiteful comment, nor can it be doubted that the picture Skelton has given us of the Cardinal's overweening assumption, though grossly exaggerated, was not altogether an imaginary one:—

"The Erle of Northumberlande
Dare take nothynge on hande;
Our barons be so bolde,
Into a mouse hole they wolde
Rynne away and crepe,
Lyke a mayny of shepe:
Dare nat loke out at dur
For drede of the mastyve cur,
For drede of the bochers dogge
Wold wyrry them lyke an hogge.

For and this curre do gnar,
They must stand all a far,
To holde up their hande at the bar.

For all their noble blode
He pluckes them by the hode,
And shakes them by the eare,
And brynge[s] them in suche feare;
He bayteth them lyke a bere,
Like an oxe or a bull:
Theyr wyttes, he saith, are dull;
He sayth they have no brayne
Theyr astate to mayntayne;
And maketh them to bow theyr kne
Before his majeste.
Juges of the kynges lawes,
He countys them foles and dawes;
Sergyantes of the coyfe eke,
He sayth they are to seke
In pletynge of theyr case
At the Commune Place,
Or at the Kynges Benche;
He wryngeth them such a wrenche,
That all our learned men
Dare nat set theyr penne
To plete a trew tryall
Within Westmynster hall;
In the Chauncery where he syttes,
But suche as he admyttes
None so hardy to speke:
He sayth, thou huddypeke,
Thy lernynge is to lewde,
Thy tonge is nat well thewde,
To seke before our grace;
And openly in that place
He rages and he raves,
And calls them cankerd knaves:
Thus royally he dothe deale
Under the kynges brode seale:
And in the Checker he them cheks;
In the Star Chambre he noddis and beks,
And bereth him there so stoute,
That no man dare route,
Duke, erle, baron, nor lorde,
But to his sentence must accorde:
Whether he be knyght or squyre,
All men must folow his desyre."

"*Why Come Ye Nat To Courte?*" &c. &c.

ACT IV.

(1) SCENE II.—*Give him a little earth for charity!*] So Cavendish:—

"And the next day he took his journey with Master Kingston and the guard. And as soon as they espied their old master, in such a lamentable estate, they lamented him with weeping eyes. Whom my lord took by the hands, and divers times, by the way, as he rode, he would talk with them, sometime with one, and sometime with another; at night he was lodged at a house of the Earl of Shrewsbury's, called Hardwick Hall, very evil at ease. The next day he rode to Nottingham, and there lodged that night, more sicker, and the next day we rode to Leicester Abbey; and by the way he waxed so sick that he was divers times likely to have fallen from his mule; and being night before we came to the abbey of Leicester, where at his coming in at the gates the abbot of the place with all his convent met him with the light of many torches; whom they right honourably received with great reverence. To whom my lord said, 'Father Abbot, I am come hither to leave my bones among you,' whom they brought on his mule to the stairs foot of his chamber, and there alighted, and Master Kingston then took him by the arm and led him up the stairs; who told me afterwards that he never carried so heavy a burden in all his life. And as soon as he was in his chamber, he went incontinent to his bed, very sick."

(2) SCENE II.—*His blessed part to heaven.*] By his "blessed part" is of course meant his "*spiritual* or *immortal* part:" and we apprehend that the expression "better part," in the much-controverted passage in "As You Like It," Act III. Sc. 2:—"Atalanta's *better part,*" bears a similar signification; in proof of this may be cited the trite old epitaph mentioned by Whalley:—

"Sarah's obedience, Lydia's open heart,
And Martha's care, and Mary's *better part.*"

And the following passage from Overbury's "Characters:"—"Lastly," (he is depicting *a Melancholy Man,*) "he is a man onely in shew, but comes short of *the better part,* a whole reasonable soule, which is mans chief preeminence," &c.

(3) SCENE II.—

—— *and urge the king*
To do me this last right.]

The letter referred to in this passage, which Katharine addressed to the king a short time before her death, is preserved in Polydore Virgil's History, and has been translated as follows by Lord Herbert:—

"My most dear lord, king, and husband,—

"The hour of my death now approaching, I cannot choose but, out of the love I bear you, advise you of your soul's health, which you ought to prefer before all considerations of the world or flesh whatsoever: for which yet you have cast me into many calamities, and yourself into many troubles.—But I forgive you all, and pray God to do so likewise. For the rest, I commend unto you Mary our daughter, beseeching you to be a good father to her, as I have heretofore desired. I must entreat you also to respect my maids, and give them in marriage, (which is not much, they being but three,) and to all my other servants a year's pay besides their due, lest otherwise they should be unprovided for. Lastly, I make this vow, that mine eyes desire you above all things. Farewell."

ACT V.

(1) SCENE III.—*Parish-garden.*] This is usually printed *Paris* garden, but *Parish* was possibly the vulgar pronunciation of the word. Paris Garden was a district of St. Saviour's parish, in Southwark, wherein were two famous gardens set apart for the diversion of bear-baiting. On the 25th of May, 1599, soon after her accession to the throne, Queen Elizabeth gave a splendid dinner to the French ambassadors, who were afterwards entertained with the baiting of bulls and bears, and the queen herself stood with the ambassadors looking on the pastime till six at night. The next day, the same ambassadors went by water to Paris Garden, where they saw another baiting of bulls and of bears." (*See* NICHOLS' *Progresses,* Vol. I. p. 40.)

CRITICAL OPINIONS

ON

KING HENRY THE EIGHTH.

"SHAKSPEARE was as profound a historian as a poet; when we compare his *Henry the Eighth* with the preceding pieces, we see distinctly that the English nation during the long, peaceable, and economical reign of Henry VII., whether from the exhaustion which was the fruit of the civil wars, or from more general European influences, had made a sudden transition from the powerful confusion of the middle age, to the regular tameness of modern times. *Henry the Eighth* has, therefore, somewhat of a prosaic appearance; for Shakspeare, artist-like, adapted himself always to the quality of his materials. If others of his works, both in elevation of fancy and in energy of pathos and character, tower far above this, we have here on the other hand occasion to admire his nice powers of discrimination and his perfect knowledge of courts and the world. What tact was requisite to represent before the eyes of the queen subjects of such a delicate nature, and in which she was personally so nearly concerned, without doing violence to the truth! He has unmasked the tyrannical king, and to the intelligent observer exhibited him such as he was actually: haughty and obstinate, voluptuous and unfeeling, extravagant in conferring favours, and revengeful under the pretext of justice; and yet the picture is so dexterously handled that a daughter might take it for favourable. The legitimacy of Elizabeth's birth depended on the invalidity of Henry's first marriage, and Shakspeare has placed the proceedings respecting his separation from Catharine of Arragon in a very doubtful light. We see clearly that Henry's scruples of conscience are no other than the beauty of Anne Boleyn. Catharine is, properly speaking, the heroine of the piece; she excites the warmest sympathy by her virtues, her defenceless misery, her mild but firm opposition, and her dignified resignation. After her, the fall of Cardinal Wolsey constitutes the principal part of the business. Henry's whole reign was not adapted for dramatic poetry. It would have merely been a repetition of the same scenes: the repudiation, or the execution of his wives, and the disgrace of his most estimable ministers, which was usually soon followed by death. Of all that distinguished Henry's life, Shakspeare has given us sufficient specimens. But as, properly speaking, there is no division in the history where he breaks off, we must excuse him if he gives us a flattering compliment of the great Elizabeth for a fortunate catastrophe. The piece ends with the general joy at the birth of that princess, and with prophecies of the happiness which she was afterwards to enjoy or to diffuse. It was only by such a turn that the hazardous freedom of thought in the rest of the composition could have passed with impunity: Shakspeare was not certainly himself deceived respecting this theatrical delusion. The true conclusion is the death of Catharine, which under a feeling of this kind, he has placed earlier than was conformable to history."—SCHLEGEL.

Act II. Sc. 2.

CYMBELINE.

"The Tragedie of Cymbeline" is one of the seventeen plays, the earliest known edition of which is the folio of 1623. When produced, or when first acted, we have, as usual, no means of determining; but Malone is perhaps not far wrong in supposing it was written in 1609, as about that period there is good reason for believing Shakespeare wrote "The Tempest," and "The Winter's Tale:" and the marked similarity in the versification of those plays and that of Cymbeline, indicates that the three were composed at no distant date from each other.

The main incident of the plot—the wager on the chastity of the heroine—appears to have been taken from a story in Boccaccio (Day 2, Nov. 9), of which an abstract will be found in the "Illustrative Comments." This novel was a favourite evidently, for it has been translated and paraphrased many times. One modification of it occurs in the amusing collection of stories called, "Westward for Smelts, or The Water-mans fare of mad merry Western wenches," &c., which Steevens and Malone assert was printed in 1603. If they are correct, this *réchauffé* of Boccaccio's fable may have contributed to the composition of "Cymbeline," but no edition of it earlier than 1620, and of that only one copy, is now known to exist. The events in this story are laid in England during the reigns of Henry VI. and Edward IV., and the villain of it, instead of being conveyed to the lady's chamber in a chest (as described in the Italian and French versions), hides himself beneath her bed.

The historical facts and allusions in "Cymbeline" were seemingly derived from Holinshed; but the important and delightful episode that introduces us to Belarius and the stolen princes, we may conclude was Shakespeare's own invention; unless the germ of it were found in some older play upon which the present was founded.

Persons Represented.

CYMBELINE, King *of* Britain.

GUIDERIUS, ARVIRAGUS, } *Sons to* Cymbeline, *disguised under the names of* POLYDORE *and* CADWAL, *and supposed to be Sons to* Morgan.

CLOTEN, *Son to the* Queen *by a former Husband.*

LEONATUS POSTHUMUS, *Husband to* Imogen.

BELARIUS, *a banished Lord, disguised under the name of* MORGAN.

CORNELIUS, *a Physician.*

PISANIO.

Two British Captains.

Two British Gentlemen.

A Soothsayer.

Two British Gaolers.

CAIUS LUCIUS, *General of the* Roman *Forces.*

IACHIMO, PHILARIO, } Italian *Gentlemen.*

A Roman Captain.

A French Gentleman, *Friend of* Philario.

A Spanish Gentleman, *Friend of* Philario.

A Dutch Gentleman, *Friend of* Philario.

QUEEN, *Wife to* Cymbeline.

IMOGEN, *Daughter to* Cymbeline, *by a former* Queen.

HELEN, *a Lady attending on* Imogen.

Lords, Ladies, Roman Senators, Tribunes, Officers, Soldiers, Musicians, Messengers Apparitions, and Attendants.

SCENE,—*Sometimes in* BRITAIN, *sometimes in* ITALY.

ACT I.

SCENE I.—Britain. *The Garden of* Cymbeline's *Palace.*

Enter Two Gentlemen.

1 Gent. You do not meet a man but frowns: our bloods
No more obey the heavens, than our courtiers'—
Still seemers—do the king's.[a]

2 Gent. But what's the matter?

1 Gent. His daughter, and the heir of 's kingdom, whom
He purpos'd to his wife's sole son, (a widow
That late he married,) hath referr'd herself
Unto a poor but worthy gentleman: she 's wedded;

[a]
——— *our bloods*
No more obey the heavens, than our courtiers'—
Still seemers—*do the king's.*]

The old text of "Cymbeline," in the number and inveteracy of its corruptions, is hardly surpassed by any other play in the collection. The very opening speech presents a typographical enigma which has been the subject of critical conjecture and experiment for above a century, and remains a puzzle still:—

"You do not meet a man but Frownes.
Our bloods no more obey the Heavens
Then our Courtiers;
Still seeme, as do's the Kings."

Thus stands the passage in the folio. Amid a flood of hypothetical restorations, Tyrwhitt's proposal to omit the *s* in "King's" and to point the lines as follows,—

"——*our bloods*
No more obey the heavens, than our courtiers
Still seem, as does the *king*"—

is now generally followed, though no one perhaps ever believed or believes that this was what the poet wrote. It has been accepted only because the editors had nothing better to offer. The real blot lies, we apprehend, in the words "still seem as," which were probably misheard or misread by the compositor for "still-seemers," i.e. *ever dissemblers:* and the meaning appears to be,—Everyone you meet wears a frown; our complexions do not more sympathise with the changes of the sky, than the looks of our courtiers (those *perpetual simulators*) do with the aspect of the king. The expression "seemers" occurs again in the sense here attributed to it, in "Measure for Measure," Act I. Sc. 4:—

"——hence shall we see
If power change purpose, what our *seemers* be."

Her husband banish'd; she imprison'd: all
Is outward sorrow; though, I think, the king
Be touch'd at very heart.

2 GENT. None but the king?

1 GENT. He that hath lost her, too: so is the queen,
That most desir'd the match: but not a courtier,
Although they wear their faces to the bent
Of the king's looks, hath a heart that is not
Glad at the thing they scowl at.

2 GENT. And why so?

1 GENT. He that hath miss'd the princess is a thing
Too bad for bad report; and he that hath her,
(I mean, that married her,—alack, good man!—
And therefore banish'd) is a creature such
As, to seek through the regions of the earth
For one his like, there would be something failing
In him that should compare:—I do not think
So fair an outward, and such stuff within,
Endows a man but he.

2 GENT. You speak him far.

1 GENT. I do extend him, sir, within himself;
Crush him together, rather than unfold
His measure duly.

2 GENT. What's his name, and birth?

1 GENT. I cannot delve him to the root: his father
Was call'd Sicilius, who did join his honour,
Against the Romans, with Cassibelan;
But had his titles by Tenantius, whom
He serv'd with glory and admir'd success,—
So gain'd the sur-addition, Leonatus:
And had, besides this gentleman in question,
Two other sons, who, in the wars o' the time,
Died with their swords in hand; for which their father
(Then old and fond of issue) took such sorrow
That he quit being; and his gentle lady,
Big of this gentleman, our theme, deceas'd
As he was born. The king he takes the babe
To his protection; calls him Posthumus Leonatus;[a]
Breeds him, and makes him of his bed-chamber:
Puts to him all the learnings that his time
Could make him the receiver of; which he took,
As we do air, fast as 't was minister'd,
And in 's spring became a harvest: liv'd in court
(Which rare it is to do) most prais'd, most lov'd:
A sample to the youngest; to the more mature
A glass that feated[b] them; and to the graver
A child that guided dotards: to his mistress—
For whom he now is banish'd—her own price
Proclaims how she esteem'd him and his virtue;
By her election may be truly read
What kind of man he is.

2 GENT. I honour him
Even out of your report. But, pray you, tell me,
Is she sole child to the king?

1 GENT. His only child.
He had two sons,—if this be worth your hearing,
Mark it,—the eldest of them at three years old,
I' the swathing clothes the other, from their nursery
Were stol'n; and to this hour no guess in knowledge
Which way they went.

2 GENT. How long is this ago?

1 GENT. Some twenty years.

2 GENT. That a king's children should be so convey'd![c]
So slackly guarded, and the search so slow,
That could not trace them!

1 GENT. Howsoe'er 't is strange,
Or that the negligence may well be laugh'd at,
Yet is it true, sir.

2 GENT. I do well believe you.

1 GENT. We must forbear: here comes the gentleman,
The queen, and princess. [*Exeunt.*

Enter the QUEEN, POSTHUMUS, *and* IMOGEN.[d]

QUEEN. No, be assur'd, you shall not find me, daughter,
After the slander of most step-mothers,
Evil-ey'd unto you: you're my prisoner, but
Your gaoler shall deliver you the keys
That lock up your restraint.—For you, Posthumus,
So soon as I can win the offended king,
I will be known your advocate: marry, yet,
The fire of rage is in him; and 't were good,
You lean'd unto his sentence with what patience
Your wisdom may inform you.

POST. Please your highness,
I will from hence to-day.

QUEEN. You know the peril:—
I'll fetch a turn about the garden, pitying
The pangs of barr'd affections, though the king
Hath charg'd you should not speak together.
[*Exit* QUEEN.

IMO. O dissembling courtesy! How fine this tyrant
Can tickle where she wounds!—My dearest husband,
I something fear my father's wrath; but nothing

[a] Posthumus Leonatus;] So the old copies. In many modern editions, "Leonatus" is omitted as redundant, but the old poets not unfrequently introduce proper names without regard to the measure; occasionally indeed, as if at the discretion of the player, the name was to be spoken or not.

[b] *A glass that* feated *them;*] That *fashioned*, or *moulded* them.

[c] So convey'd!] So stolen.

[d] And Imogen.] In the old and in most of the modern editions, this is marked as a new scene, but erroneously.

(Always reserv'd my holy duty) what
His rage can do on me: you must be gone;
And I shall here abide the hourly shot
Of angry eyes; not comforted to live,
But that there is this jewel in the world,
That I may see again.

POST. My queen! my mistress!
O, lady, weep no more, lest I give cause
To be suspected of more tenderness
Than doth become a man! I will remain
The loyal'st husband that did e'er plight troth:
My residence in Rome, at one Philario's; *
Who to my father was a friend, to me
Known but by letter: thither write, my queen,
And with mine eyes I'll drink the words you send,
Though ink be made of gall.

(*) Old text, *Filorio's.*

Re-enter QUEEN.

QUEEN. Be brief, I pray you:
If the king come, I shall incur I know not
How much of his displeasure.—[*Aside.*] Yet I'll move him
To walk this way. I never do him wrong,
But he does buy my injuries to be friends;
Pays dear for my offences.[a]
POST. Should we be taking leave
As long a term as yet we have to live,
The loathness to depart would grow. Adieu!
IMO. Nay, stay a little:
Were you but riding forth to air yourself,
Such parting were too petty. Look here, love;
This diamond was my mother's: take it, heart;
But keep it till you woo another wife,
When Imogen is dead.
POST. How! how! another?—
You gentle gods, give me but this I have,
And sear[b] up my embracements from a next
With bonds of death!—Remain, remain thou here, [*Putting on the ring.*
While sense can keep it on! And sweetest, fairest,
As I my poor self did exchange for you,
To your so infinite loss; so, in our trifles
I still win of you: for my sake wear this;
It is a manacle of love; I'll place it
Upon this fairest prisoner.
[*Putting a bracelet on her arm.*
IMO. O, the gods!
When shall we see again?
POST. Alack, the king!

Enter CYMBELINE (1) *and* Lords.

CYM. Thou basest thing, avoid! hence, from my sight!
If after this command thou fraught the court
With thy unworthiness, thou diest: away!
Thou 'rt poison to my blood.
POST. The gods protect you!
And bless the good remainders of the court!
I am gone. [*Exit.*
IMO. There cannot be a pinch in death
More sharp than this is.
CYM. O disloyal thing,
That shouldst repair my youth, thou heap'st
A year's age on me!
IMO. I beseech you, sir,
Harm not yourself with your vexation:
I am senseless of your wrath; a touch more rare[c]
Subdues all pangs, all fears.
CYM. Past grace? obedience?
IMO. Past hope, and in despair; that way, past grace.
CYM. That mightst have had the sole son of my queen!
IMO. O bless'd, that I might not! I chose an eagle,
And did avoid a puttock.[d]
CYM. Thou took'st a beggar; wouldst have made my throne
A seat for baseness.
IMO. No; I rather added
A lustre to it.
CYM. O thou vile one!
IMO. Sir,
It is your fault that I have lov'd Posthumus:
You bred him as my playfellow; and he is
A man worth any woman; overbuys me
Almost the sum he pays.
CYM. What! art thou mad?
IMO. Almost, sir: heaven restore me!—Would I were
A neat-herd's daughter, and my Leonatus
Our neighbour shepherd's son!

---

[a] Pays dear for my offences.] A clause intended possibly to replace or be replaced by the words "buy my injuries to be friends:" the first thought through the carelessness of the compositor being inserted as well as the reconsidered one.

[b] *And* sear *up*—] Mr. Singer reads *seal up*, which is a plausible alteration; but we believe with Steevens and Mr. Dyce that the meaning is merely *close up*, and if any change were desirable, should prefer *cere up*. The spelling of *cere* being often *sear* formerly.

[c] A touch more rare—] This has been defined a *nobler passion*, a *higher feeling;* it meant rather a *smart* or *throe more exquisite*. *A touch* in old language was often used to express a *pang*, a *wound*, or any acute pain, moral or physical, as in the passage before us; as also in the often-quoted, but perhaps not always understood sentiment from "Troilus and Cressida," Act III. Sc. 3:

"One *touch* of Nature makes the whole world kin."

and in "Macbeth," Act III. Sc. 2,—

"——Duncan is in his grave;
After life's fitful fever he sleeps well;
Treason has done his worst; nor steel, nor poison,
Malice domestic, foreign levy, nothing,
Can *touch* him further."

Sometimes it implied a *painful sense* or *sympathy*, as in "The Tempest," Act V. Sc. 1,—

"Hast thou, which art but air, *a touch*, a feeling of their afflictions?"

And occasionally *to touch* signified to *pierce* or *prick*, as in the following examples:—

"—— Spirits are not finely *touch'd*
But to fine issues."
Measure for Measure, Act I. Sc. 1.

"Ay, *touch* him, there's the vein."
Ibid. Act II. Sc. 2.

"What villain *touch'd* his body, that did stab
And not for justice."
Julius Cæsar, Act IV. Sc. 3.

"Durst thou have look'd upon him, being awake?
And hast thou kill'd him sleeping? O brave *touch!*"
A Midsummer Night's Dream, Act III. Sc. 2.

"You *touch'd* my vein at first."
As You Like It, Act II. Sc. 7.

[d] A puttock.] A buzzard, or kite: a degenerate species of hawk.

Re-enter QUEEN.

CYM. Thou foolish thing!— [*To the* QUEEN.
They were again together: you have done
Not after our command. Away with her,
And pen her up!

QUEEN. Beseech your patience.—Peace,
Dear lady daughter, peace!—Sweet sovereign,
Leave us to ourselves; and make yourself some comfort
Out of your best advice.

CYM. Nay, let her languish
A drop of blood a day; and, being aged,
Die of this folly!
[*Exeunt* CYMBELINE *and* Lords.

QUEEN. Fie!—you must give way:

Enter PISANIO.

Here is your servant.—How now, sir! What news?

PIS. My lord your son drew on my master.

QUEEN. Ha!
No harm, I trust, is done?

PIS. There might have been,
But that my master rather play'd than fought,
And had no help of anger: they were parted
By gentlemen at hand.

QUEEN. I am very glad on 't.

IMO. Your son 's my father's friend; he takes his part.—
To draw upon an exile!—O brave sir!—
I would they were in Afric both together;
Myself by with a needle, that I might prick
The goer-back.—Why came you from your master?

PIS. On his command: he would not suffer me
To bring him to the haven: left these notes
Of what commands I should be subject to,
When 't pleas'd you to employ me.

QUEEN. This hath been
Your faithful servant: I dare lay mine honour,
He will remain so.

PIS. I humbly thank your highness.

QUEEN. Pray, walk awhile.

IMO. About some half-hour hence,
I* pray you, speak with me: you shall at least
Go see my lord aboard: for this time, leave me.
[*Exeunt.*

(*) Old copies omit, *I*.

SCENE II.—*The same. A public Place.*

Enter CLOTEN *and Two* Lords.

1 LORD. Sir, I would advise you to shift a shirt; the violence of action hath made you reek as a sacrifice: where air comes out, air comes in: there 's none abroad so wholesome as that you vent.

CLO. If my shirt were bloody, then to shift it.—Have I hurt him?

2 LORD. [*Aside.*] No, faith; not so much as his patience.

1 LORD. Hurt him! his body 's a passable carcass if he be not hurt: it is a throughfare for steel, if it be not hurt.

2 LORD. [*Aside.*] His steel was in debt; it went o' the backside the town.

CLO. The villain would not stand me.

2 LORD. [*Aside.*] No; but he fled forward still, toward your face.

1 LORD. Stand you! You have land enough of your own: but he added to your having; gave you some ground.

2 LORD. [*Aside.*] As many inches as you have oceans.—Puppies!

CLO. I would they had not come between us.

2 LORD. [*Aside.*] So would I, till you had measured how long a fool you were upon the ground.

CLO. And that she should love this fellow, and refuse me!

2 LORD. [*Aside.*] If it be a sin to make a true election, she is damned.

1 LORD. Sir, as I told you always, her beauty and her brain go not together: she 's a good sign, but I have seen small reflection of her wit.

2 LORD. [*Aside.*] She shines not upon fools, lest the reflection should hurt her.

CLO. Come, I'll to my chamber. Would there had been some hurt done!

2 LORD. [*Aside.*] I wish not so; unless it had been the fall of an ass, which is no great hurt.

CLO. You 'll go with us?

1 LORD. I'll attend your lordship.

CLO. Nay, come, let 's go together.

2 LORD. Well, my lord. [*Exeunt.*

SCENE III.—*The same. A Room in* Cymbeline's *Palace.*

Enter IMOGEN *and* PISANIO.

IMO. I would thou grew'st unto the shores o' the haven,

And questioned'st every sail: if he should write,
And I not have it, 't were a paper lost,
As offer'd mercy is.[a] What was the last
That he spake to thee?
Pis. It was, *His queen, his queen!*
Imo. Then wav'd his handkerchief?
Pis. And kiss'd it, madam.
Imo. Senseless linen! happier therein than I!—
And that was all?
Pis. No, madam; for so long
As he could make me with this* eye or ear
Distinguish him from others, he did keep
The deck, with glove, or hat, or handkerchief,
Still waving, as the fits and stirs of 's mind
Could best express how slow his soul sail'd on,
How swift his ship.
Imo. Thou shouldst have made him
As little as a crow, or less, ere left
To after-eye him.
Pis. Madam, so I did.
Imo. I would have broke mine eye-strings; crack'd them, but
To look upon him; till the diminution
Of space had pointed him sharp as my needle;
Nay follow'd him, till he had melted from
The smallness of a gnat to air; and then
Have turn'd mine eye, and wept.(2)—But, good Pisanio,
When shall we hear from him?
Pis. Be assur'd, madam,
With his next vantage.
Imo. I did not take my leave of him, but had
Most pretty things to say: ere I could tell him
How I would think on him, at certain hours,
Such thoughts, and such; or I could make him swear
The shes of Italy should not betray
Mine interest and his honour; or have charg'd him,
At the sixth hour of morn, at noon, at midnight,
To encounter me with orisons, for then
I am in heaven for him; or ere I could
Give him that parting kiss which I had set
Betwixt two charming[b] words, comes in my father,
And, like the tyrannous breathing of the north,
Shakes all our buds from growing.

(*) Old text, *his*.

a —— *'twere a paper lost,*
As offer'd *mercy is.*]
The mercy meant is that which comes too tardily, a pardon after execution; as the thought is expressed in "All's Well That Ends Well," Act V. Sc. 3:—

"Like a remorseful *pardon slowly* carried."

We should, therefore, probably eject "*offer'd*" as a misprint, and read,—

"As *deferr'd* mercy is."

b *Betwixt two* charming *words,*—] *Magical* or *enchanted* words to preserve him from evil.

Enter a Lady.

LADY. The queen, madam,
Desires your highness' company.

IMO. Those things I bid you do, get them dispatch'd.—
I will attend the queen.

PIS. Madam, I shall. [*Exeunt.*

SCENE IV.—Rome. *An Apartment in* Philario's *House.*

Enter PHILARIO, IACHIMO,[a] *a* Frenchman, *a* Dutchman, *and a* Spaniard.

IACH. Believe it, sir, I have seen him in Britain: he was then of a crescent note; expected to prove so worthy as since he hath been allowed the name of: but I could then have looked on him without the help of admiration, though the catalogue of his endowments had been tabled by his side, and I to peruse him by items.

PHI. You speak of him when he was less furnished, than now he is, with that which makes him both without and within.

FRENCH. I have seen him in France: we had very many there could behold the sun with as firm eyes as he.

IACH. This matter of marrying his king's daughter,—wherein he must be weighed rather by her value than his own,—words him, I doubt not, a great deal from the matter.

FRENCH. And then his banishment—

IACH. Ay, and the approbation of those that weep this lamentable divorce, under her colours, are wonderfully to extend him; be it but to fortify her judgment, which else an easy battery might lay flat, for taking a beggar without less[b] quality. But how comes it he is to sojourn with you? How creeps acquaintance?

PHI. His father and I were soldiers together; to whom I have been often bound for no less than my life:—here comes the Briton: let him be so entertained amongst you, as suits, with gentlemen of your knowing, to a stranger of his quality.—

Enter POSTHUMUS.

I beseech you all, be better known to this gentleman, whom I commend to you as a noble friend of mine: how worthy he is I will leave to appear hereafter, rather than story him in his own hearing.

FRENCH. Sir, we have known together in Orleans.

POST. Since when I have been debtor to you for courtesies, which I will be ever to pay, and yet pay still.

FRENCH. Sir, you o'er-rate my poor kindness: I was glad I did atone[c] my countryman and you; it had been pity you should have been put together with so mortal a purpose as then each bore, upon importance of so slight and trivial a nature.

POST. By your pardon, sir; I was then a young traveller; rather shunned[d] to go even with what I heard, than in my every action to be guided by others' experiences: but, upon my mended judgment, (if I offend not* to say it is mended,) my quarrel was not altogether slight.

FRENCH. Faith, yes, to be put to the arbitrement of swords; and by such two that would, by all likelihood, have confounded one the other, or have fallen both.

IACH. Can we, with manners, ask what was the difference?

FRENCH. Safely, I think: 't was a contention in public, which may, without contradiction, suffer the report. It was much like an argument that fell out last night, where each of us fell in praise of our country mistresses: this gentleman at that time vouching (and upon warrant of bloody affirmation) his to be more fair, virtuous, wise, chaste, constant, qualified, and less attemptable, than any the rarest of our ladies in France.

IACH. That lady is not now living; or this gentleman's opinion, by this, worn out.

POST. She holds her virtue still, and I my mind.

IACH. You must not so far prefer her 'fore ours of Italy.

POST. Being so far provoked as I was in France, I would abate her nothing, though I profess myself her adorer, not her friend.[e]

IACH. As fair, and as good,—a kind of hand-in-hand comparison,—had been something too fair,

---

[a] Iachimo,—] Probably borrowed from the Italian *Giacomo.* It should be pronounced as a trisyllable, *Yachimo.*

[b] *Without* less *quality.*] This is usually printed after Rowe "*more* quality," and that apparently, though by no means certainly, was the meaning intended. As Malone remarks, however, "whenever *less* or *more* is to be joined with a verb denoting want, or a preposition of a similar import, Shakespeare never fails to be entangled in a grammatical inaccuracy."

[c] Atone—] *Reconcile;* make *at one.*

[d] *Rather* shunned to *go even with what I heard,*—] Should we not read *sinned?* The meaning being, I was then a young traveller, and wilfully preferred rather to go by what I heard than to be guided by the experience of others.

(*) Old text omits, *not.*

[e] I would abate her nothing, though I profess myself her adorer, not her friend.] The sense of this has been somewhat misunderstood, and hence the discussion the passage has provoked. Posthumus, we apprehend, does not mean,—I avow myself, not simply her admirer, but her worshipper; but stung by the scornful tone of Iachimo's remark, he answers,—Provoked as I was in France, I would abate her nothing, though the declaration of my opinion proclaimed me her idolater rather than her lover.

and too good, for any lady in Britany. If she went before others I have seen, as that diamond of yours out-lustres many I have beheld, I could but* believe she excelled many: but I have not seen the most precious diamond that is, nor you the lady.

POST. I praised her as I rated her: so do I my stone.

IACH. What do you esteem it at?

POST. More than the world enjoys.

IACH. Either your unparagoned mistress is dead, or she 's outprized by a trifle.

POST. You are mistaken: the one may be sold, or given, or[a] if there were wealth enough for the purchase,† or merit for the gift: the other is not a thing for sale, and only the gift of the gods.

IACH. Which the gods have given you?

POST. Which, by their graces, I will keep.

IACH. You may wear her in title yours; but, you know, strange fowl light upon neighbouring ponds. Your ring may be stolen too: so, your brace of unprizable estimations, the one is but frail, and the other casual; a cunning thief, or a that-way-accomplished courtier, would hazard the winning both of first and last.

POST. Your Italy contains none so accomplished a courtier to convince[b] the honour of my mistress; if, in the holding or the loss of that, you term her frail. I do nothing doubt you have store of thieves; notwithstanding, I fear not my ring.

PHI. Let us leave here, gentlemen.

POST. Sir, with all my heart. This worthy signior, I thank him, makes no stranger of me; we are familiar at first.

IACH. With five times so much conversation, I should get ground of your fair mistress; make her go back, even to the yielding, had I admittance and opportunity to friend.

POST. No, no.

IACH. I dare thereupon pawn the moiety of my estate to your ring; which, in my opinion, o'ervalues it something: but I make my wager rather against your confidence than her reputation: and, to bar your offence herein too, I durst attempt it against any lady in the world.

POST. You are a great deal abused in too bold a persuasion; and I doubt not you sustain what you're worthy of by your attempt.

IACH. What's that?

POST. A repulse: though your attempt, as you call it, deserve more,—a punishment too.

PHI. Gentlemen, enough of this: it came in too suddenly; let it die as it was born, and, I pray you, be better acquainted.

IACH. Would I had put my estate and my neighbour's on the approbation[c] of what I have spoke!

POST. What lady would you choose to assail?

IACH. Yours; whom in constancy you think stands so safe. I will lay you ten thousand ducats to your ring, that, commend me to the court where your lady is, with no more advantage than the opportunity of a second conference, and I will bring from thence that honour of hers which you imagine so reserved.

POST. I will wage against your gold, gold to it: my ring I hold dear as my finger; 't is part of it.

IACH. You are afraid,[d] and therein the wiser. If you buy ladies' flesh at a million a dram, you cannot preserve it from tainting: but, I see you have some religion in you, that you fear.

POST. This is but a custom in your tongue; you bear a graver purpose, I hope.

IACH. I am the master of my speeches; and would undergo what's spoken, I swear.

POST. Will you?—I shall but lend my diamond till your return:—let there be covenants drawn between us: my mistress exceeds in goodness the hugeness of your unworthy thinking: I dare you to this match: here's my ring.

PHI. I will have it no lay.

IACH. By the gods, it is one.—If I bring you no sufficient testimony that I have enjoyed the dearest bodily part of your mistress, my ten thousand ducats are yours; so is your diamond too: if I come off, and leave her in such honour as you have trust in, she your jewel, this your jewel, and my gold are yours;—provided I have your commendation for my more free entertainment.

POST. I embrace these conditions; let us have articles betwixt us.—Only, thus far you shall answer: if you make your voyage upon her, and give me directly to understand you have prevailed, I am no further your enemy; she is not worth our debate: if she remain unseduced,—you not making it appear otherwise,—for your ill opinion, and the assault you have made to her chastity, you shall answer me with your sword.

IACH. Your hand,—a covenant: we will have these things set down by lawful counsel, and straight away for Britain, lest the bargain should catch cold and starve.[e] I will fetch my gold, and have our two wagers recorded.

POST. Agreed.

[*Exeunt* POSTHUMUS *and* IACHIMO.

FRENCH. Will this hold, think you?

PHI. Signior Iachimo will not from it. Pray, let us follow 'em. [*Exeunt.*

(*) Old text, *not*. (†) Old text, *purchases*.

[a] Or if there were—] That is, *either* if there were.

[b] To convince—] *Convince* here, as in many other instances, signifies, *conquer* or *overcome*.

[c] The approbation—] The proof:—So in "Henry V." Act I. Sc. 2:—

"For God doth know, how many, now in health,
Shall drop their blood in *approbation*
Of what your reverence shall incite us to."

[d] You are afraid,—] In the old copies, "You are a *Friend*."—We are not altogether satisfied with the emendation, which is Warburton's, but are unable to suggest any word more likely.

[e] *And* starve.] That is, and *perish*.

SCENE V.—Britain. *A Room in* Cymbeline's *Palace.*

Enter QUEEN, Ladies, *and* CORNELIUS.

QUEEN. Whiles yet the dew 's on ground, gather those flowers;
Make haste: who has the note of them?
1 LADY. I, madam.
QUEEN. Dispatch.— [*Exeunt* Ladies.
Now, master doctor, have you brought those drugs?
COR. Pleaseth your highness, ay: here they are, madam: [*Presenting a small box.*
But I beseech your grace, without offence—
My conscience bids me ask,—wherefore you have
Commanded of me these most poisonous compounds,
Which are the movers of a languishing death;
But though slow, deadly?
QUEEN. I wonder, doctor,
Thou ask'st me such a question. Have I not been
Thy pupil long? Hast thou not learn'd me how
To make perfumes? distil? preserve? yea, so
That our great king himself doth woo me oft
For my confections? Having thus far proceeded,—
Unless thou think'st me devilish,—is't not meet
That I did amplify my judgment in
Other conclusions?[a] I will try the forces
Of these thy compounds on such creatures as
We count not worth the hanging,—but none human,—
To try the vigour of them, and apply
Allayments to their act; and by them gather
Their several virtues and effects.
COR. Your highness
Shall from this practice but make hard your heart:
Besides, the seeing these effects will be
Both noisome and infectious.
QUEEN. O, content thee.—
[*Aside.*] Here comes a flattering rascal; upon him
Will I first work: he's for his master,
And enemy to my son.—

Enter PISANIO.

How now, Pisanio!—
Doctor, your service for this time is ended;
Take your own way.
COR. [*Aside.*] I do suspect you, madam;
But you shall do no harm.
QUEEN. Hark thee, a word.—[*To* PISANIO.
COR. [*Aside.*] I do not like her. She doth think she has
Strange ling'ring poisons: I do know her spirit,
And will not trust one of her malice with
A drug of such damn'd nature. Those she has
Will stupify and dull the sense awhile;
Which first, perchance, she'll prove on cats and dogs,
Then afterward up higher; but there is

---

[a] Conclusions?] *Experiments.*

No danger in what show of death it makes,
More than the locking up the spirits a time,
To be more fresh, reviving. She is fool'd
With a most false effect; and I the truer
So to be false with her.
QUEEN. No further service, doctor,
Until I send for thee.
COR. I humbly take my leave. [*Exit.*
QUEEN. Weeps she still, say'st thou? Dost thou think in time
She will not quench, and let instructions enter
Where folly now possesses? Do thou work:
When thou shalt bring me word she loves my son,
I'll tell thee, on the instant, thou art then
As great as is thy master: greater,—for
His fortunes all lie speechless, and his name
Is at last gasp: return he cannot, nor
Continue where he is: to shift his being
Is to exchange one misery with another;
And every day that comes, comes to decay
A day's work in him. What shalt thou expect,
To be depender on a thing that leans,—
Who cannot be new built, nor has no friends,
[*The* QUEEN *drops the box:* PISANIO *takes it up.*
So much as but to prop him?—Thou tak'st up
Thou know'st not what; but take it for thy labour:
It is a thing I made, which hath the king
Five times redeem'd from death: I do not know
What is more cordial:—nay, I pr'ythee, take it;
It is an earnest of a further good
That I mean to thee. Tell thy mistress how
The case stands with her; do't as from thyself.
Think what a chance thou changest on;[a] but think
Thou hast thy mistress still,—to boot, my son,
Who shall take notice of thee: I'll move the king
To any shape of thy preferment, such
As thou 'lt desire; and then myself, I chiefly,
That set thee on to this desert, am bound
To load thy merit richly. Call my women:
Think on my words. [*Exit* PISANIO.]—A sly and constant knave;
Not to be shak'd: the agent for his master;
And the remembrancer of her, to hold
The handfast to her lord.—I have given him that,
Which, if he take, shall quite unpeople her
Of liegers for her sweet;[b] and which she after,
Except she bend her humour, shall be assur'd
To taste of too.—

Re-enter PISANIO *and* Ladies.

So, so;—well done, well done:
The violets, cowslips, and the primroses,
Bear to my closet.—Fare thee well, Pisanio;
Think on my words. [*Exeunt* QUEEN *and* Ladies.
PIS. And shall do:
But when to my good lord I prove untrue,
I'll choke myself: there's all I'll do for you.
[*Exit.*

SCENE VI.—*The same. Another Room in the Palace.*

Enter IMOGEN.

IMO. A father cruel, and a step-dame false;
A foolish suitor to a wedded lady,
That hath her husband banish'd;—O, that husband!
My supreme crown of grief! and those, repeated
Vexations of it![c] Had I been thief-stolen,
As my two brothers, happy! but most miserable
Is the desire that's glorious. Blessed be those,
How mean soe'er, that have their honest wills,
Which seasons comfort.[d]—Who may this be? Fie!

Enter PISANIO *and* IACHIMO.

PIS. Madam, a noble gentleman of Rome,
Comes from my lord with letters.
IACH. Change you, madam?
The worthy Leonatus is in safety,
And greets your highness dearly.
[*Presents a letter.*
IMO. Thanks, good sir:
You're kindly welcome.
IACH. [*Aside.*] All of her that is out of door, most rich!
If she be furnish'd with a mind so rare,
She is alone the Arabian bird; and I
Have lost the wager. Boldness be my friend!

---

a Think what a chance thou changest on; &c.] Thus the old text, which has been changed to,—

"Think what a chance thou *chancest* on;"—

And,

"Think what a *change* thou *chancest* on."

Looking at the context, we should prefer reading,—

"Think what a chance! thou changest *one;* but think
Thou hast thy mistress still,—to boot, my son."

You only change the service of your master for mine; retain your old mistress, and have my son for friend beside. *Chance*, it must be remembered, in old language meant *fortune, luck*, &c.

b Liegers for her sweet;] This apparently signifies, ambassadors to her lover.

c —— *and those*, repeated
Vexations of it!]
Something must be wrong in this place; no one with an ear for Shakespeare's rhythm can ever believe he wrote the passage as it stands.

d Which seasons comfort.—] It is probable that the obscure clause,—"but most miserable is the desire that's glorious,"— was accidentally transposed; and the true reading,

"———Had I been thief-stolen,
As my two brothers, happy! Blessed be those,
How mean soe'er, that have their honest wills,
Which seasons comfort; but most miserable
Is the desire that's glorious."

Happy are those, however lowly, who enjoy the moderate wishes that preserve comfort; but most wretched they whose inclinations are set on grandeur.

Arm me, audacity, from head to foot!
Or, like the Parthian, I shall flying fight;
Rather, directly fly.

IMO. [*Reads.*] *** *He is one of the noblest note, to whose kindnesses I am most infinitely tied. Reflect upon him accordingly, as you value your trust*—— LEONATUS.

So far I read aloud:
But even the very middle of my heart
Is warmed by the rest, and takes* it thankfully.—
You are as welcome, worthy sir, as I
Have words to bid you, and shall find it so
In all that I can do.

IACH. Thanks, fairest lady.—
What! are men mad? Hath nature given them eyes
To see this vaulted arch, and the rich crop[a]
Of sea and land, which can distinguish 'twixt
The fiery orbs above, and the twinn'd stones
Upon the number'd[b] beach? and can we not
Partition make with spectacles so precious
'Twixt fair and foul?

IMO. What makes your admiration?

IACH. It cannot be i' the eye; for apes and monkeys,
'Twixt two such shes, would chatter this way, and
Contemn with mows the other: nor i' the judgment;
For idiots, in this case of favour, would
Be wisely definite: nor i' the appetite;
Sluttery, to such neat excellence oppos'd,
Should make desire vomit emptiness,
Not so allur'd to feed.[c]

IMO. What is the matter, trow?

IACH. The cloyed will,—
That satiate yet unsatisfied desire,
That tub both fill'd and running,—ravening first the lamb,
Longs after for the garbage.

IMO. What, dear sir,
Thus raps you? Are you well?

IACH. Thanks, madam; well.—Beseech you, sir, [*To* PISANIO.
Desire my man's abode where I did leave him:
He's strange and peevish.[d]

(*) Old text, *take*.

[a] *And the rich* crop—] Warburton reads *cope*.

[b] *Upon the* number'd *beach?*] The "*number'd* beach" is a likely misprint. Theobald changed it to,—"th' *unnumber'd* beach." Might we not read,—"the *cumber'd* beach?" taking ***number'd*** in the sense either of *rough*, *strewed*, &c. or perhaps, ***troubled?***

[c] Sluttery, to such neat excellence oppos'd,
Should make desire vomit emptiness,
Not so allur'd to feed.]

Many editors read, "vomit *to* emptiness;" and certainly if "emptiness" is Shakespeare's word, "*to*" must be understood. In the last line, a very slight change would give us the sense there required; read,—

"Not so allure't [i.e. *desire*] to feed."

[d] Strange and peevish.] That is, *foreign* and *simple*.

PIS. I was going, sir,
To give him welcome. [*Exit.*
IMO. Continues well my lord his health, beseech you?[a]
IACH. Well, madam.
IMO. Is he dispos'd to mirth? I hope he is.
IACH. Exceeding pleasant; none a stranger there
So merry and so gamesome: he is call'd
The Briton reveller.
IMO. When he was here
He did incline to sadness; and ofttimes
Not knowing why.
IACH. I never saw him sad.
There is a Frenchman his companion, one
An eminent monsieur, that, it seems, much loves
A Gallian girl at home: he furnaces
The thick sighs from him; whiles the jolly Briton—
Your lord, I mean—laughs from 's free lungs, cries,—*O,*
Can my sides hold, to think that man,—who knows,
By history, report, or his own proof,
What woman is, yea, what she cannot choose
But must be,—will his free hours languish for
Assured bondage?
IMO. Will my lord say so?
IACH. Ay, madam; with his eyes in flood with laughter:
It is a recreation to be by,
And hear him mock the Frenchman. But, heavens know,
Some men are much to blame.
IMO. Not he, I hope.
IACH. Not he: but yet heaven's bounty towards him might
Be us'd more thankfully. In himself, 't is much;
In you,—which I account his,—beyond all talents.[b]
Whilst I am bound to wonder, I am bound
To pity too.
IMO. What do you pity, sir?
IACH. Two creatures heartily.
IMO. Am I one, sir?
You look on me: what wreck discern you in me
Deserves your pity?
IACH. Lamentable! What,
To hide me from the radiant sun, and solace
I' the dungeon by a snuff?
IMO. I pray you, sir,
Deliver with more openness your answers
To my demands. Why do you pity me?
IACH. That others do—
I was about to say—enjoy your——But
It is an office of the gods to venge it,
Not mine to speak on't.
IMO. You do seem to know
Something of me, or what concerns me: pray you,—
Since doubting things go ill, often hurts more
Than to be sure they do:[c] for certainties
Either are past remedies; or, timely knowing,
The remedy then born,—discover to me
What both you spur and stop.
IACH. Had I this cheek
To bathe my lips upon; this hand, whose touch,
Whose every touch, would force the feeler's soul
To the oath of loyalty; this object, which
Takes prisoner the wild motion of mine eye,
Fixing * it only here:—should I (damn'd then)
Slaver with lips as common as the stairs
That mount the Capitol: join gripes with hands
Made hard with hourly falsehood (falsehood, as
With labour); then by-peeping[d] in an eye,
Base and unlustrous[e] as the smoky light
That 's fed with stinking tallow;—it were fit
That all the plagues of hell should at one time
Encounter such revolt.
IMO. My lord, I fear,
Has forgot Britain.
IACH. And himself. Not I,
Inclin'd to this intelligence, pronounce
The beggary of his change; but 't is your graces
That, from my mutest conscience to my tongue,
Charms this report out.
IMO. Let me hear no more.
IACH. O dearest soul, your cause doth strike my heart
With pity, that doth make me sick! A lady
So fair,—and fasten'd to an empery
Would make the great'st king double,—to be partner'd
With tomboys, hir'd with that self-exhibition[f]

---

[a] Continues well my lord his health, beseech you?] This is invariably punctuated,—

"Continues well my lord? His health, beseech you?"

But does not continue here, import, *preserve*, as in "Measure for Measure," Act IV. Sc. 3?—

"And how shall we *continue* Claudio."

[b] —— In himself, 't is much;
In you,—which I account his,—beyond all talents.]

"All talents," or we mistake, means here *incalculable riches*. The bounty of heaven towards him is great in his own endowments; in its gift of you, it is beyond all estimation. By the ordinary pointing, however,—

"In you,—which I account his, beyond all talents,—
Whilst I am bound," &c.

the word *talents* is made to signify *accomplishments*, and the whole sense of the passage miserably enfeebled.

[c] Since doubting things go ill, often hurts more
Than to be sure they do:]

Massinger was mindful of this sentiment, when in "The Emperor of the East," Act V. Sc. 3, he says:—

"———— since strong doubts are
More grievous, for the most part, than to know
A certain loss—"

[d] By-peeping—] Johnson changed this to *lie peeping;* and Mr. Collier's annotator proposes *bo-peeping*.

[e] Unlustrous—] The old text has *illustrious;* corrected by Rowe.

[f] *With that* self-exhibition—] The *self-same pension*, or *allowance*.

(*) First folio, *Fiering.*

Which your own coffers yield! with diseas'd ventures,
That play with all infirmities, for gold,
Which rottenness can lend nature! such boil'd stuff
As well might poison poison! Be reveng'd;
Or she that bore you was no queen, and you
Recoil from your great stock!

IMO. *Reveng'd!*
How should I be reveng'd? If this be true,—
As I have such a heart that both mine ears
Must not in haste abuse,—if it be true,
How should I be reveng'd?

IACH. Should he make me
Live, like Diana's priest, betwixt cold sheets,
Whiles he is vaulting variable ramps,
In your despite, upon your purse? Revenge it!
I dedicate myself to your sweet pleasure;
More noble than that runagate to your bed;
And will continue fast to your affection,
Still close as sure.

IMO. What ho, Pisanio!

IACH. Let me my service tender on your lips.

IMO. Away!—I do condemn mine ears that have
So long attended thee.—If thou wert honourable,
Thou wouldst have told this tale for virtue, not
For such an end thou seek'st,—as base as strange.
Thou wrong'st a gentleman, who is as far
From thy report, as thou from honour; and
Solicit'st here a lady that disdains
Thee and the devil alike.—What ho, Pisanio!—
The king my father shall be made acquainted
Of thy assault; if he shall think it fit,
A saucy stranger, in his court, to mart
As in a Romish stew, and to expound
His beastly mind to us,—he hath a court
He little cares for, and a daughter whom*
He not respects at all.—What ho, Pisanio!

IACH. O happy Leonatus! I may say
The credit that thy lady hath of thee
Deserves thy trust, and thy most perfect goodness
Her assur'd credit!—Blessed live you long!
A lady to the worthiest sir, that ever
Country call'd his! and you his mistress, only
For the most worthiest fit! Give me your pardon;
I have spoke this, to know if your affiance
Were deeply rooted; and shall make your lord
That which he is, new o'er: and he is one
The truest manner'd; such a holy witch,
That he enchants societies into him:[a]
Half all men's† hearts are his.

IMO. You make amends.

IACH. He sits 'mongst men, like a descended* god:
He hath a kind of honour sets him off,
More than a mortal seeming. Be not angry,
Most mighty princess, that I have adventur'd
To try your taking of a false report; which hath
Honour'd with confirmation your great judgment
In the election of a sir so rare,
Which you know, cannot err: the love I bear him
Made me to fan you thus; but the gods made you,
Unlike all others, chaffless. Pray, your pardon.

IMO. All 's well, sir: take my power i' the court for yours.

IACH. My humble thanks. I had almost forgot
To entreat your grace but in a small request,
And yet of moment too, for it concerns
Your lord, myself, and other noble friends,
Are partners in the business.[b]

IMO. Pray, what is 't?

IACH. Some dozen Romans of us, and your lord,—
The best feather of our wing,—have mingled sums
To buy a present for the emperor;
Which I, the factor for the rest, have done
In France: 't is plate of rare device, and jewels
Of rich and exquisite form; their values great;
And I am something curious, being strange,
To have them in safe stowage: may it please you
To take them in protection?

IMO. Willingly;
And pawn mine honour for their safety: since
My lord hath interest in them, I will keep them
In my bedchamber.

IACH. They are in a trunk,
Attended by my men: I will make bold
To send them to you, only for this night;
I must aboard to-morrow.

IMO. O, no, no.

IACH. Yes, I beseech; or I shall short my word,
By length'ning my return. From Gallia
I cross'd the seas on purpose and on promise
To see your grace.

IMO. I thank you for your pains;
But not away to-morrow!

IACH. O, I must, madam:
Therefore, I shall beseech you, if you please
To greet your lord with writing, do 't to-night:
I have outstood my time; which is material
To the tender of our present.

IMO. I will write.
Send your trunk to me; it shall safe be kept,
And truly yielded you. You are very welcome.
[*Exeunt.*

(*) First folio, *who*. (†) First folio, *men*. (*) First folio, *defended*.

[a] That he enchants societies into him] Malone quotes the following apposite illustration from Shakespeare's "Lover's Complaint:"—

"That he did in the general bosom reign
Of young, of old; and sexes both enchanted * * *
Consents bewitch'd, ere he desire, have granted."

[b] Are partners, &c.—] *Who* is understood,—"*Who* are partners."

ACT II.

SCENE I.—Britain. *Court before* Cymbeline's *Palace.*

Enter CLOTEN *and Two* Lords.

CLO. Was there ever man had such luck! when I kissed the jack,[a] upon an up-cast to be hit away! I had a hundred pound on 't: and then a whoreson Jackanapes must take me up for swearing; as if I borrowed mine oaths of him, and might not spend them at my pleasure.

1 LORD. What got he by that? You have broke his pate with your bowl.

2 LORD. [*Aside.*] If his wit had been like him that broke it, it would have run all out.

CLO. When a gentleman is disposed to swear, it is not for any standers-by to curtail his oaths, ha?

2 LORD. No, my lord; [*Aside.*] nor crop the ears of them.

CLO. Whoreson dog!—I give* him satisfaction? Would he had been one of my rank!

2 LORD. [*Aside.*] To have smelt like a fool.

CLO. I am not vexed more at any thing in the earth,—a pox on 't! I had rather not be so noble as I am; they dare not fight with me, because of the queen my mother: every Jack-slave hath his belly-full of fighting, and I must go up and down like a cock that nobody can match.

2 LORD. [*Aside.*] You are cock and capon too; and you crow, cock, with your comb on.[b]

CLO. Sayest thou?

1 LORD. It is not fit your* lordship should undertake every companion[c] that you give offence to.

CLO. No, I know that: but it is fit I should commit offence to my inferiors.

2 LORD. Ay, it is fit for your lordship only.[d]

CLO. Why, so I say.

1 LORD. Did you hear of a stranger that's come to court to-night? †

CLO. A stranger, and I not know on 't!

(*) First folio, *gave.*

(*) Old text, *you.* (†) Old text, *to court night.*

a When I kissed the jack,—] In the game of *Bowling*, or *Bowls*, the small bowl which is aimed at, was sometimes termed the *Block*, or the *Jack*, but more often the *Mistress.*

b And you crow, cock, with your comb on.] A *cock's comb* was one of the badges of the household fool, and hence the compound became a synonyme for simpleton.

c Companion—] A contemptuous expression, equivalent to our *low fellow.*

d Ay, it is fit for your lordship only.] This conveys a sarcasm, but Cloten understands it only in its literal sense.

2 LORD. [*Aside.*] He's a strange fellow himself, and knows it not.

1 LORD. There's an Italian come; and, 't is thought, one of Leonatus' friends.

CLO. Leonatus! a banished rascal; and he's another, whatsoever he be. Who told you of this stranger?

1 LORD. One of your lordship's pages.

CLO. Is it fit I went to look upon him? Is there no derogation in 't?

1 LORD. You cannot derogate, my lord.

CLO. Not easily, I think.

2 LORD. [*Aside.*] You are a fool granted; therefore your issues, being foolish, do not derogate.

CLO. Come, I'll go see this Italian: what I have lost to-day at bowls, I'll win to-night of him. Come, go.

2 LORD. I'll attend your lordship.

[*Exeunt* CLOTEN *and first* Lord.

That such a crafty devil as is his mother
Should yield the world this ass! a woman that
Bears all down with her brain; and this her son
Cannot take two from twenty, for his heart,
And leave eighteen. Alas, poor princess,
Thou divine Imogen, what thou endur'st!
Betwixt a father by thy step-dame govern'd;
A mother hourly coining plots; a wooer,
More hateful than the foul expulsion is
Of thy dear husband, than that horrid act
Of the divorce he'd make! The heavens hold firm
The walls of thy dear honour! keep unshak'd
That temple, thy fair mind! that thou mayst stand,
To enjoy thy banish'd lord and this great land!

[*Exit.*

SCENE II.—*The same. A Bedchamber in* Cymbeline's *Palace; in one part of it a trunk.*

IMOGEN *in her bed reading; a* Lady *attending.*

IMO. Who's there? my woman Helen?

LADY. Please you, madam.

IMO. What hour is it?

LADY. Almost midnight, madam.

IMO. I have read three hours, then: mine eyes are weak:
Fold down the leaf where I have left: to bed:
Take not away the taper, leave it burning;
And if thou canst awake by four o' the clock,
I pr'ythee, call me. Sleep hath seiz'd me wholly.

[*Exit* Lady.

To your protection I commend me, gods!
From fairies, and the tempters of the night,
Guard me, beseech ye!

[*Sleeps.* IACHIMO *steals from the trunk.*

IACH. The crickets sing, and man's o'er-labour'd sense
Repairs itself by rest. Our Tarquin thus
Did softly press the rushes, ere he waken'd
The chastity he wounded.—Cytherea,
How bravely thou becom'st thy bed! fresh lily,
And whiter than the sheets! That I might touch!
But kiss! one kiss!—Rubies unparagon'd,
How dearly they do 't!—'T is her breathing that
Perfumes the chamber thus: the flame o' the taper
Bows toward her; and would under-peep her lids,
To see the enclosed lights, now canopied
Under these windows, white, and azure lac'd
With blue of heaven's own tinct.[a]—But my design,
To note the chamber: I will write all down:—
Such, and such pictures:—there the window; such
The adornment of her bed:—the arras, figures,
Why, such, and such;—and the contents o' the story,—
Ah, but some natural notes about her body,
Above ten thousand meaner moveables
Would testify, to enrich mine inventory:—
O sleep, thou ape of death, lie dull upon her,
And be her sense but as a monument,
Thus in a chapel lying!—Come off, come off;—

[*Taking off her bracelet.*

As slippery as the Gordian knot was hard!—
'T is mine; and this will witness outwardly,
As strongly as the conscience does within,
To the madding of her lord.—On her left breast
A mole cinque-spotted, like the crimson drops
I' the bottom of a cowslip:(1) here's a voucher,
Stronger than ever law could make: this secret
Will force him think I have pick'd the lock, and ta'en
The treasure of her honour. No more.—To what end?
Why should I write this down, that's riveted,
Screw'd to my memory?—She hath been reading late
The tale of Tereus; here the leaf's turn'd down
Where Philomel gave up;—I have enough:—
To the trunk again, and shut the spring of it.—

———

[a] ——— now canopied
Under these windows, white, and azure lac'd
With blue of heaven's own tinct.]

By *windows* are meant her *eyelids.* So, in "Romeo and Juliet," Act IV. Sc. 1:—

"Thy eyes' *windows* fall,
Like death, when he shuts up the day of life."

But the beauty of this image is not enhanced by the usual punctuation:—

"——— white and azure, lac'd
With blue of heaven's own tinct."

Swift, swift, you dragons of the night, that dawning
May bare* the raven's eye! I lodge in fear;
Though this a heavenly angel, hell is here.
[*Clock strikes.*
One, two, three,—Time, time!
[*Goes into the trunk. The scene closes.*

SCENE III.—*The same. An Ante-chamber adjoining* Imogen's *Apartments.*

Enter CLOTEN *and* Lords.

1 LORD. Your lordship is the most patient man in loss, the most coldest that ever turned up ace.

CLO. It would make any man cold to lose.

1 LORD. But not every man patient after the noble temper of your lordship. You are most hot and furious when you win.

CLO. Winning will put any man into courage. If I could get this foolish Imogen, I should have gold enough. It's almost morning, is't not?

1 LORD. Day, my lord.

CLO. I would this music would come: I am advised to give her music o' mornings; they say it will penetrate.—

Enter Musicians.

Come on; tune. If you can penetrate her with your fingering, so; we'll try with tongue too: if none will do, let her remain; but I'll never give o'er. First, a very excellent good-conceited thing; after, a wonderful sweet air, with admirable rich words to it,—and then—let her consider.

SONG.

Hark! hark! the lark at heaven's gate sings, (2)
And Phœbus 'gins arise,
His steeds to water at those springs
On chalic'd flowers that lies;
And winking Mary-buds begin
To ope their golden eyes;
With everything that pretty is,[a]
My lady sweet, arise:
Arise, arise.

So, get you gone. If this penetrate, I will consider your music the better: if it do not, it is a vice* in her ears, which horse-hairs and calves'-guts

(*) Old text, *beare*.

(*) Old text, *voyce*.

[a] *With everything that pretty is,*—] Hanmer changed this to,—"With *all the things* that pretty *bin*," &c.

nor the voice of unpaved eunuch to boot, can never amend. [*Exeunt* Musicians.

2 LORD. Here comes the king.

CLO. I am glad I was up so late, for that's the reason I was up so early: he cannot choose but take this service I have done fatherly.

Enter CYMBELINE *and* QUEEN.

Good morrow to your majesty, and to my gracious mother.

CYM. Attend you here the door of our stern daughter?
Will she not forth?

CLO. I have assailed her with music,* but she vouchsafes no notice.

CYM. The exile of her minion is too new;
She hath not yet forgot him: some more time
Must wear the print of his remembrance out,†
And then she's yours.

QUEEN. You are most bound to the king,
Who lets go by no vantages that may
Prefer you to his daughter. Frame yourself
To orderly solicits;‡ and, be friended
With aptness of the season; make denials
Increase your services; so seem, as if
You were inspir'd to do those duties which
You tender to her; that you in all obey her,
Save when command to your dismission tends,
And therein you are senseless.

CLO. Senseless! not so.

Enter a Messenger.

MESS. So like you, sir, ambassadors from Rome;
The one is Caius Lucius.

CYM. A worthy fellow,
Albeit he comes on angry purpose now;
But that's no fault of his: we must receive him
According to the honour of his sender;
And towards himself, his goodness forespent on us,
We must extend our notice.—Our dear son,
When you have given good morning to your mistress,
Attend the queen and us; we shall have need
To employ you towards this Roman.—Come, our queen.
[*Exeunt* CYMBELINE, QUEEN, Lords, *and* Messenger.

CLO. If she be up, I'll speak with her; if not,
Let her lie still and dream.—By your leave, ho!—
[*Knocks.*
I know her women are about her: what
If I do line one of their hands? 'T is gold
Which buys admittance; oft it doth; yea, and makes
Diana's rangers false[a] themselves, yield up
Their deer to the stand o' the stealer; and 't is gold
Which makes the true man kill'd, and saves the thief;
Nay, sometime hangs both thief and true man: what
Can it not do and undo? I will make
One of her women lawyer to me; for
I yet not understand the case myself.—
By your leave. [*Knocks.*

Enter a Lady.

LADY. Who's there that knocks?

CLO. A gentleman.

LADY. No more?

CLO. Yes, and a gentlewoman's son.

LADY. That's more
Than some, whose tailors are as dear as yours,
Can justly boast of. What's your lordship's pleasure?

CLO. Your lady's person: is she ready?

LADY. Ay,
To keep her chamber.

CLO. There's gold for you; sell me your good report.

LADY. How! my good name? or to report of you
What I shall think is good?—The princess!

Enter IMOGEN.

CLO. Good-morrow, fairest sister; your sweet hand. [*Exit* Lady.

IMO. Good-morrow, sir. You lay out too much pains
For purchasing but trouble: the thanks I give
Is telling you that I am poor of thanks,
And scarce can spare them.

CLO. Still, I swear I love you.

IMO. If you but said so, 'twere as deep with me:
If you swear still, your recompense is still
That I regard it not.

CLO. This is no answer.

IMO. But that you shall not say, I yield being silent,
I would not speak. I pray you, spare me: 'faith,
I shall unfold equal discourtesy

(*) Old text, *musickes*. (†) First folio, *on't*. (‡) First folio, *solicity*.

a False *themselves*,—] *False* is here employed as a verb. So, in Marlowe's "Tamburlaine the Great," Part I. Act II. Sc. 2:—

"And make him *false* his faith unto the king."

To your best kindness; one of your great knowing
Should learn, being taught, forbearance.
CLO. To leave you in your madness, 't were my sin:
I will not.
IMO. Fools are not mad folks.
CLO. Do you call me fool?
IMO. As I am mad, I do:
If you'll be patient, I'll no more be mad;
That cures us both. I am much sorry, sir,
You put me to forget a lady's manners,
By being so verbal: and learn now, for all,
That I, which know my heart, do here pronounce,
By the very truth of it, I care not for you;
And am so near the lack of charity,—
To accuse myself,—I hate you; which I had rather
You felt, than make't my boast.
CLO. You sin against
Obedience, which you owe your father. For
The contract you pretend with that base wretch,—
One bred of alms, and foster'd with cold dishes,
With scraps o' the court,—it is no contract, none:
And though it be allow'd in meaner parties—
Yet who than he more mean?—to knit their souls
(On whom there is no more dependency
But brats and beggary) in self-figur'd knot;
Yet you are curb'd from that enlargement by
The consequence o' the crown; and must not soil*
The precious note of it with a base slave,
A hilding for a livery, a squire's cloth,
A pantler,—not so eminent.
IMO. Profane fellow!
Wert thou the son of Jupiter, and no more
But what thou art besides, thou wert too base
To be his groom: thou wert dignified enough,
Even to the point of envy, if 't were made
Comparative for your virtues, to be styl'd
The under-hangman of his kingdom; and hated
For being preferr'd so well.
CLO. The south-fog rot him!
IMO. He never can meet more mischance than come
To be but nam'd of thee. His meanest garment,
That ever hath but clipp'd his body, is dearer
In my respect, than all the hairs above thee,
Were they all made such men.—How now, Pisanio!

Enter PISANIO.

CLO. *His garment!* † Now, the devil—
IMO. To Dorothy my woman hie thee presently:—
CLO. *His garment!*
IMO. I am sprited with a fool;
Frighted, and anger'd worse.—Go, bid my woman
Search for a jewel, that too casually
Hath left mine arm: it was thy master's; 'shrew me,
If I would lose it for a revenue
Of any king's in Europe. I do think
I saw't this morning: confident I am
Last night 'twas on mine arm; I kiss'd it:
I hope it be not gone to tell my lord
That I kiss aught but he.
PIS. 'Twill not be lost.
IMO. I hope so: go and search. [*Exit* PISANIO.
CLO. You have abus'd me:—
His meanest garment!
IMO. Ay; I said so, sir:
If you will make't an action, call witness to't.
CLO. I will inform your father.
IMO. Your mother too:
She's my good lady; and will conceive, I hope,
But the worst of me. So I leave you,* sir,
To the worst of discontent. [*Exit.*
CLO. I'll be reveng'd:
His meanest garment!—Well. [*Exit.*

SCENE IV.—Rome. *An Apartment in* Philario's *House.*

Enter POSTHUMUS *and* PHILARIO.

POST. Fear it not, sir; I would I were so sure
To win the king, as I am bold her honour
Will remain hers.
PHI. What means do you make to him?
POST. Not any; but abide the change of time;
Quake in the present winter's state, and wish
That warmer days would come: in these sear'd hopes,[a]
I barely gratify your love; they failing,
I must die much your debtor.
PHI. Your very goodness, and your company,
O'erpays all I can do. By this, your king
Hath heard of great Augustus: Caius Lucius
Will do's commission throughly: and I think
He'll grant the tribute, send the arrearages,
Or look upon our Romans, whose remembrance
Is yet fresh in their grief.
POST. I do believe,—
Statist though I am none, nor like to be,—
That this will prove a war; and you shall hear

(*) Old text, *foyle*. (†) First folio, *garments*.

(*) Old text, *your*.

[a] *In these* sear'd hopes,—] The old text has, "*fear'd hope.*" Tyrwhitt suggested, "*sear'd hopes;*" and the emendation is confirmed both by the context, and the misprint, "Growne *feard* and tedious," of the folio in "Measure for Measure," Act II. Sc. 4.

The legions,* now in Gallia, sooner landed
In our not-fearing Britain, than have tidings
Of any penny tribute paid. Our countrymen
Are men more order'd than when Julius Cæsar
Smil'd at their lack of skill, but found their courage
Worthy his frowning at: their discipline
(Now mingled† with their courage‡) will make known
To their approvers, they are people such
That mend upon the world.
PHI. See! Iachimo!

Enter IACHIMO.

POST. The swiftest harts have posted you by land;
And winds of all the corners kiss'd your sails,
To make your vessel nimble.
PHI. Welcome, sir.
POST. I hope the briefness of your answer made
The speediness of your return.
IACH. Your lady
Is one of the fairest that I have look'd upon.
POST. And therewithal the best; or let her beauty
Look through a casement to allure false hearts,
And be false with them.
IACH. Here are letters for you.
POST. Their tenour good, I trust.
IACH. 'Tis very like.
PHI. Was Caius Lucius in the Britain court,
When you were there? [a]
IACH. He was expected then,
But not approach'd.
POST. All is well yet.
Sparkles this stone as it was wont? or is it not
Too dull for your good wearing?
IACH. If I had* lost it,
I should have lost the worth of it in gold.
I'll make a journey twice as far, to enjoy
A second night of such sweet shortness, which
Was mine in Britain; for the ring is won.
POST. The stone's too hard to come by.
IACH. Not a whit,
Your lady being so easy.
POST. Make not,† sir,
Your loss your sport: I hope you know that we
Must not continue friends.
IACH. Good sir, we must,
If you keep covenant. Had I not brought
The knowledge of your mistress home, I grant
We were to question farther: but I now

(*) Old text, *Legion*. (†) Old text, *wing-led*. (‡) Old text, *courages*.

(*) Old text, *have*. (†) First folio, *note*.

[a] Was Caius Lucius, &c.] This speech in the folio is mistakenly assigned to Posthumus.

Profess myself the winner of her honour,
Together with your ring; and not the wronger
Of her or you, having proceeded but
By both your wills.
POST. If you can make't apparent
That you have tasted her in bed, my hand
And ring is yours: if not, the foul opinion
You had of her pure honour gains or loses
Your sword or mine, or masterless leaves* both
To who shall find them.
IACH. Sir, my circumstances
Being so near the truth as I will make them,
Must first induce you to believe: whose strength
I will confirm with oath; which, I doubt not,
You'll give me leave to spare, when you shall find
You need it not.
POST. Proceed.
IACH. First, her bedchamber,—
(Where, I confess, I slept not; but profess,
Had that was well worth watching,[a]) it was hang'd
With tapestry of silk and silver; the story,
Proud Cleopatra, when she met her Roman,
And Cydnus swell'd above the banks, or for
The press of boats or pride: a piece of work
So bravely done, so rich, that it did strive
In workmanship and value; which I wonder'd
Could be so rarely and exactly wrought,
Since the true life on't was—[b]
POST. This is true;
And this you might have heard of here, by me,
Or by some other.
IACH. More particulars
Must justify my knowledge.
POST. So they must,
Or do your honour injury.
IACH. The chimney
Is south the chamber; and the chimney-piece,
Chaste Dian bathing: never saw I figures
So likely to report themselves: the cutter
Was as another Nature, dumb; outwent her,
Motion and breath left out.
POST. This is a thing
Which you might from relation likewise reap,
Being, as it is, much spoke of.
IACH. The roof o' the chamber
With golden cherubins is fretted: her andirons,—
I had forgot them,—were two winking[c] Cupids
Of silver, each on one foot standing, nicely
Depending on their brands.
POST. This is her honour!—
Let it be granted you have seen all this,—and praise
Be given to your remembrance,—the description
Of what is in her chamber nothing saves
The wager you have laid.
IACH. Then, if you can,
[*Pulling out the bracelet.*
Be pale: I beg but leave to air this jewel; see!—
And now 'tis up again: it must be married
To that your diamond; I'll keep them.
POST. Jove!—
Once more let me behold it: is it that
Which I left with her?
IACH. Sir,—I thank her,—that:
She stripp'd it from her arm; I see her yet;
Her pretty action did outsell her gift,
And yet enrich'd it too: she gave it me,
And said she priz'd it once.
POST. May be she pluck'd it off
To send it me.
IACH. She writes so to you, doth she?
POST. O, no, no, no! 'tis true. Here, take this too; [*Gives the ring.*
It is a basilisk unto mine eye,
Kills me to look on't.—Let there be no honour
Where there is beauty; truth, where semblance; love,
Where there's another man: the vows of women
Of no more bondage be, to where they are made,
Than they are to their virtues; which is nothing:—
O, above measure false!
PHI. Have patience, sir,
And take your ring again; 'tis not yet won:
It may be probable she lost it; or,
Who knows if one of her women,[d] being corrupted,
Hath stol'n it from her?
POST. Very true;
And so I hope he came by't.—Back my ring;—
Render to me some corporal sign about her,
More evident than this; for this was stol'n.
IACH. By Jupiter, I had it from her arm.
POST. Hark you, he swears! *by Jupiter*, he swears.
'Tis true;—nay, keep the ring—'tis true; I am [sure
She would not lose it: her attendants are
All sworn,(3) and honourable:—they induc'd to steal it!

(*) Old text, *leave*.

[a] Watching,—] An allusion to the practice of taming hawks by depriving them of sleep. See note (d), p. 683, Vol, I.

[b] Since the true life on't was—] Capell has,—

"Since the true life *was in it*;"

Mason would read,—

"*Such* the true life on't was;"

and Mr. Collier's annotator,—

"Since the true life on't 't was."

To any of these we should prefer,—

"Since the true life on't *has*."

But what necessity is there for change? The speech was evidently intended to be interrupted by Posthumus.

[c] Winking Cupids—] *Blind* Cupids—Cupids with *closed eyes*.

[d] *Who knows if one of her women*,—] *Of* was supplied by the second folio: the first having,—

"——— one her women."

The expression is awkward without the preposition, unless we read,—

"Who knows if one, her women being corrupted," &c.

And by a stranger!—No, he hath enjoy'd her:
The cognizance of her incontinency
Is this,—she hath bought the name of whore thus dearly.—
There, take thy hire; and all the fiends of hell
Divide themselves between you!

PHI. Sir, be patient:
This is not strong enough to be believ'd
Of one persuaded well of—

POST. Never talk on't;
She hath been colted by him.

IACH. If you seek
For further satisfying,—under her breast
(Worthy the* pressing) lies a mole, right proud
Of that most delicate lodging: by my life,
I kiss'd it; and it gave me present hunger
To feed again, though full. You do remember
This stain upon her?

POST. Ay, and it doth confirm
Another stain, as big as hell can hold,
Were there no more but it.

IACH. Will you hear more?

POST. Spare your arithmetic: never count the turns;
Once, and a million!

IACH. I'll be sworn,—

POST. No swearing.
If you will swear you have not done't, you lie;
And I will kill thee, if thou dost deny
Thou'st made me cuckold.

IACH. I'll deny nothing.

POST. O, that I had her here, to tear her limb-meal!
I will go there and do't; i' the court; before
Her father:—I'll do something— [*Exit.*

PHI. Quite besides
The government of patience!—You have won:
Let's follow him, and pervert the present wrath
He hath against himself.

IACH. With all my heart.
[*Exeunt.*

(*) Old text, *her*.

SCENE V.—*The same. Another Room in the same.*

Enter POSTHUMUS.

POST. Is there no way for men to be, but women
Must be half-workers? We are all bastards;
And that most venerable man which I
Did call my father, was I know not where
When I was stamp'd; some coiner with his tools
Made me a counterfeit: yet my mother seem'd
The Dian of that time: so doth my wife
The nonpareil of this.—O, vengeance, vengeance!—
Me of my lawful pleasure she restrain'd,
And pray'd me oft forbearance; did it with
A pudency so rosy, the sweet view on't
Might well have warm'd old Saturn; that I thought her
As chaste as unsunn'd snow:—O, all the devils!—
This yellow Iachimo, in an hour,—was't not?—
Or less,—at first? perchance he spoke not, but
Like a full-acorn'd boar, a German one,
Cried, *O!* and mounted: found no opposition
But what he look'd for should oppose, and she
Should from encounter guard.—Could I find out
The woman's part in me! for there's no motion
That tends to vice in man, but I affirm
It is the woman's part: be it lying, note it
The woman's; flattering, hers; deceiving, hers;
Lust and rank thoughts, hers, hers; revenges, hers;
Ambitions, covetings, change of prides, disdain,
Nice longing, slanders, mutability,
All faults that may be nam'd,* nay, that hell knows,
Why, hers, in part or all; but rather, all: for e'en to vice
They are not constant, but are changing still
One vice, but of a minute old, for one
Not half so old as that. I'll write against them,
Detest them, curse them:—yet 't is greater skill
In a true hate, to pray they have their will:
The very devils cannot plague them better. [*Exit.*

(*) First folio, *All faults that name.*

ACT III.

SCENE I.—Britain. *A Room of State in* Cymbeline's *Palace.*

Enter, from one side, CYMBELINE, QUEEN, CLOTEN, *and* Lords; *from the other,* CAIUS LUCIUS *and* Attendants.

CYM. Now say, what would Augustus Cæsar with us?

LUC. When Julius Cæsar,—whose remembrance yet
Lives in men's eyes, and will to ears and tongues
Be theme and hearing ever,—was in this Britain,
And conquer'd it, Cassibelan, thine uncle,—
Famous in Cæsar's praises, no whit less
Than in his feats deserving it,—for him
And his succession, granted Rome a tribute,
Yearly three thousand pounds; which by thee lately
Is left untender'd.

QUEEN. And, to kill the marvel,
Shall be so ever.

CLO. There be many Cæsars,
Ere such another Julius. Britain is
A world by itself; and we will nothing pay
For wearing our own noses.

QUEEN. That opportunity,
Which then they had to take from 's, to resume
We have again.—Remember, sir, my liege,
The kings your ancestors; together with
The natural bravery of your isle, which stands
As Neptune's park, ribbed and paled in
With rocks[a] unscaleable, and roaring waters;
With sands that will not bear your enemies' boats,
But suck them up to the top-mast. A kind of conquest
Cæsar made here; but made not here his brag
Of *Came*, and *saw*, and *overcame*: with shame,—
The first that ever touch'd him—he was carried
From off our coast, twice beaten; and his shipping,—
Poor ignorant baubles!—on our terrible seas,
Like egg-shells mov'd upon their surges, crack'd
As easily 'gainst our rocks: for joy whereof,
The fam'd Cassibelan, who was once at point,—
O, giglot Fortune!—to master Cæsar's sword,
Made Lud's town with rejoicing fires bright,
And Britons strut with courage.(1)

CLO. Come, there's no more tribute to be paid: our kingdom is stronger than it was at that time; and, as I said, there is no more such Cæsars: other of them may have crooked noses; but to owe such straight arms, none.

CYM. Son, let your mother end.

CLO. We have yet many among us can gripe as hard as Cassibelan: I do not say I am one, but I have a hand.—Why tribute? why should we pay tribute? If Cæsar can hide the sun from us with a blanket, or put the moon in his pocket, we will pay him tribute for light; else, sir, no more tribute, pray you now.

CYM. You must know,
Till the injurious Romans did extort
This tribute from us, we were free: Cæsar's ambition,—
Which swell'd so much that it did almost stretch
The sides o' the world,—against all colour, here
Did put the yoke upon 's; which to shake off
Becomes a warlike people, whom we reckon
Ourselves to be. Say then, we do, to Cæsar.[b]
Our ancestor was that Mulmutius, which
Ordain'd our laws,—whose use the sword of Cæsar
Hath too much mangled; whose repair and franchise
Shall, by the power we hold, be our good deed,
Though Rome be therefore angry;—Mulmutius made our laws,[c]
Who was the first of Britain which did put
His brows within a golden crown, and call'd
Himself a king.(2)

LUC. I am sorry, Cymbeline,
That I am to pronounce Augustus Cæsar,—
Cæsar, that hath more kings his servants than
Thyself domestic officers,—thine enemy:
Receive it from me, then:—war and confusion,
In Cæsar's name pronounce I 'gainst thee: look
For fury not to be resisted.—Thus defied,
I thank thee for myself.

CYM. Thou art welcome, Caius.
Thy Cæsar knighted me; my youth I spent
Much under him; of him I gather'd honour,
Which he to seek of me again, perforce,
Behoves me keep at utterance.[d] I am perfect[e]
That the Pannonians and Dalmatians, for
Their liberties, are now in arms,—a precedent
Which not to read would show the Britons cold:
So Cæsar shall not find them.

LUC. Let proof speak.

CLO. His majesty bids you welcome. Make pastime with us a day or two, or longer: if you seek us afterwards in other terms, you shall find us in our salt-water girdle: if you beat us out of it, it is yours; if you fall in the adventure, our crows shall fare the better for you; and there's an end.

LUC. So, sir.

CYM. I know your master's pleasure, and he mine:
All the remain is, welcome.

[*Exeunt.*

---

[a] *With* rocks *unscaleable,*—] For *rocks*, an emendation of Hanmer, the old text has, *Oakes*.

[b] "——— which to shake off
Becomes a warlike people, whom we reckon
Ourselves to be. Say then, we do, to Cæsar.]

The old text tamely, and, no doubt, erroneously, has,—

"——— whom we reckon
Ourselves to be, we do. Say then to Cæsar;"—

and this is ordinarily pointed,—

"——— whom we reckon
Ourselves to be. We do say then," &c.:—

or,—

"——— *which* we reckon
Ourselves to be. Say then," &c.

Mr. Collier's annotator very ingeniously ascribes the words "we do" to Cloten; to whom, indeed, Mr. Dyce says, "they evidently belong." It is pleasant, and generally safe, to agree with Mr. Dyce; but we cannot help thinking the words in question belong to the king's speech, but were transposed through the negligence of transcriber or compositor.

[c] Mulmutius made our laws,—] This, with the next three lines, was perhaps either a portion of the old play upon which Shakespeare founded his "Cymbeline," or of his own first sketch, and were intended to be superseded by the previous clause:—

"Our ancestor was that Mulmutius," &c.

[d] *Behoves me keep at* utterance.] Requires me to guard at the extremest peril. To fight *à l'outrance* in the tourney was to combat to the death. We meet with the same expression in "Macbeth," Act III. Sc. 1:—

"Rather than so, come fate into the list,
And champion me to the *utterance*."

[e] *I am* perfect—] I am *well assured.*

SCENE II.—*The same. Another Room in the Palace.*

Enter PISANIO, *with a letter.*

PIS. How! of adultery? Wherefore write you not
What monster 's her accuser?*—Leonatus!
O, master! what a strange infection
Is fall'n into thy ear! What false Italian
(As poisonous tongu'd as handed) hath prevail'd
On thy too ready hearing?—Disloyal! No:
She 's punish'd for her truth, and undergoes,
More goddess-like than wife-like, such assaults
As would take in some virtue.—O, my master!
Thy mind to her is now as low as were
Thy fortunes.—How! that I should murder her?
Upon the love, and truth, and vows, which I
Have made to thy command?—I, her?—her blood?
If it be so to do good service, never
Let me be counted serviceable. How look I,
That I should seem to lack humanity
So much as this fact comes to?—[*Reading.*] *Do't: the letter*
That I have sent her, by her own command
Shall give thee opportunity:—O damn'd paper!
Black as the ink that 's on thee! Senseless bauble,
Art thou a feodary[a] for this act, and look'st
So virgin-like without? Lo, here she comes:—
I am ignorant in what I am commanded.

Enter IMOGEN.

IMO. How now, Pisanio?
PIS. Madam, here is a letter from my lord.
IMO. Who? thy lord? that is my lord,—Leonatus!
O, learn'd indeed were that astronomer
That knew the stars as I his characters;
He 'd lay the future open.—You good gods,
Let what is here contain'd relish of love,
Of my lord's health, of his content,—yet not,
That we two are asunder,—let that grieve him,—
(Some griefs are med'cinable; that is one of them,
For it doth physic love;)—of his content,
All but in that!—Good wax, thy leave:—bless'd be
You bees that make these locks of counsel! Lovers,
And men in dangerous bonds, pray not alike;
Though forfeiters you cast in prison, yet
You clasp young Cupid's tables.—Good news, gods! [*Reads.*

"Justice, and your father's wrath, should he take me in his dominion, could not be so cruel to me, as you, O the dearest of creatures, would even renew me with your eyes.[b] *Take notice that I am in Cambria, at Milford-Haven: what your own love will, out of this, advise you, follow. So he wishes you all happiness, that remains loyal to his vow, and your, increasing in love,*
"LEONATUS POSTHUMUS."

O, for a horse with wings!—Hear'st thou, Pisanio?
He is at Milford-Haven: read, and tell me
How far 't is thither. If one of mean affairs
May plod it in a week, why may not I
Glide thither in a day?—Then, true Pisanio,
(Who long'st, like me, to see thy lord; who long'st,—
O, let me 'bate,—but not like me:—yet long'st,—
But in a fainter kind:—O, not like me;
For mine's beyond beyond) say, and speak thick,[c]—
Love's counsellor should fill the bores of hearing,
To the smothering of the sense,—how far it is
To this same blessed Milford: and, by the way,
Tell me how Wales was made so happy as
To inherit such a haven: but, first of all,
How we may steal from hence; and for the gap
That we shall make in time, from our hence-going
And our return, to excuse:—but first, how get hence:
Why should excuse be born or e'er begot?
We 'll talk of that hereafter. Pr'ythee, speak,
How many score* of miles may we well ride
'Twixt hour and hour?
PIS. One score 'twixt sun and sun,
Madam, 's enough for you; and too much too.
IMO. Why, one that rode to 's execution, man,

(*) Old text, *accuse;* altered by Capell.

[a] Feodary—] Feodary here can hardly mean, as Hanmer surmised, a feudal vassal, *i.e.* one holding his estate by the tenure of suit and service. One signification of the word was, an officer appointed by the Court of Wards, in Henry VIII.'s reign, to be *present with*, and *assistant to* the Escheators in every county at the finding of offices, and to give in evidence for the king. He appears to have been the Escheator's *witness;* and it is not unlikely that Shakespeare, in reference to those unpopular officials, uses the word *feodary* here, and *federary* in "The Winter's Tale," Act II. Sc. 1:—

"More, she's a traitor, and Camillo is
A *federary* with her"—

in the sense of *spy* or *intelligencer*. Mason, however, contends that the meaning of the term, in both these instances, as well as in "Measure for Measure," Act. II. Sc. 4, is no other than *confederate*, or *accomplice;*—and he may be right.

(*) First folio, *store*.

[b] Could not be so cruel to me, as you, O the dearest of creatures, would even renew me with your eyes.] Not being very intelligible, this has been diversely modified by the critics; but was it not intended to be enigmatical?

[c] *Say, and speak* thick,—] See note (c), Vol. I. p. 558.

Could never go so slow: I have heard of riding-wagers,
Where horses have been nimbler than the sands
That run i' the clock's behalf:—but this is foolery:—
Go, bid my woman feign a sickness; say
She 'll home to her father: and provide me presently
A riding suit, no costlier than would fit
A franklin's housewife.

PIS. Madam, you 're best consider.

IMO. I see before me, man: nor here, nor here,
Nor what ensues, but have a fog in them
That I cannot look through. Away, I pr'ythee;
Do as I bid thee: there 's no more to say;
Accessible is none but Milford way. [*Exeunt.*

SCENE III.—Wales. *A mountainous Country.*

Enter, from a Cave, BELARIUS, GUIDERIUS, *and* ARVIRAGUS.

BEL. A goodly day not to keep house, with such
Whose roof 's as low as ours! Stoop,[a] boys: this gate
Instructs you how to adore the heavens; and bows you
To a morning's holy office: the gates of monarchs
Are arch'd so high, that giants may jet through [b]
And keep their impious turbans on, without
Good morrow to the sun.—Hail, thou fair heaven!
We house i' the rock, yet use thee not so hardly
As prouder livers do.

GUI. Hail, heaven!

ARV. Hail, heaven!

BEL. Now for our mountain sport: up to yond hill,
Your legs are young; I 'll tread these flats. Consider,
When you above perceive me like a crow,
That it is place which lessens and sets off;
And you may then revolve what tales I have told you
Of courts, of princes, of the tricks in war:
This service is not service, so being done,
But being so allow'd: to apprehend thus,
Draws us a profit from all things we see:
And often, to our comfort, shall we find
The sharded beetle in a safer hold
Than is the full-wing'd eagle. O, this life
Is nobler, than attending for a check;
Richer, than doing nothing for a bribe; [c]
Prouder, than rustling in unpaid-for silk:
Such gain the cap of him that makes 'em* fine,
Yet keeps his book uncross'd: no life to ours.

GUI. Out of your proof you speak: we, poor unfledg'd,
Have never wing'd from view o' the nest; nor know not
What air 's from home. Haply this life is best,
If quiet life be best; sweeter to you
That have a sharper known; well corresponding
With your stiff age: but unto us it is
A cell of ignorance; travelling abed;
A prison o'er† a debtor, that not dares
To stride a limit.

ARV. What should we speak of
When we are old as you? when we shall hear
The rain and wind beat dark December, how,
In this our pinching cave, shall we discourse
The freezing hours away? We have seen nothing:
We are beastly; subtle as the fox for prey;
Like warlike as the wolf for what we eat:
Our valour is to chase what flies; our cage
We make a quire, as doth the prison'd bird,
And sing our bondage freely.

BEL. How you speak!
Did you but know the city's usuries,[d]
And felt them knowingly: the art o' the court,
As hard to leave as keep; whose top to climb
Is certain falling, or so slippery that
The fear 's as bad as falling: the toil o' the war,
A pain that only seems to seek out danger
I' the name of fame and honour; which dies i' the search,
And hath as oft a slanderous epitaph
As record of fair act; nay, many times,
Doth ill deserve by doing well; what 's worse,
Must court'sy at the censure:—O, boys, this story
The world may read in me: my body 's mark'd

(*) Old text, *him*. (†) Old text, *or*.

[a] Stoop, *boys:*] This is Hanmer's self-evident correction: the old text has, *Sleepe Boyes*.

[b] ——this gate
Instructs you how to adore the heavens; and bows you
To a morning's holy office: the gates of monarchs
Are arch'd so high, that giants may jet through
And keep their impious turbans on,—]

Webster has happily expressed a similar idea:—

"Yet stay, heaven gates are not so highly arch'd
As Princes' pallaces, they that enter there
Must go upon their knees."
Duchesse of Malfy, Act IV. Sc. 2, 4to. 1623.

[c] *Richer, than doing nothing for a* bribe;] The old text reads *Babe*, for which Rowe substituted, *bauble;* Hanmer, *bribe;* Johnson, *brabe;* and Mr. Collier's annotator, *bob*. Of these emendations, the original being of course wrong, we prefer Hanmer's *bribe;* though we have very little confidence even in that.

[d] *The city's* usuries,—] *Usuries*, in this instance, would appear to mean no more than *usages, customs*, &c.; though, in "Measure for Measure," Act III. Sc. 2, where the word occurs seemingly in the same general sense—"'Twas never merry world since, of two *usuries*, the merriest was put down, and the worser allowed by order of law a furred gown to keep him warm;"—it certainly bears a particular reference to *usury:* for what says Taylor, the water-poet, in his "Waterman's suit concerning Players," 1630?—"—— and sleepe with a quieter spirit then many of our *furre gownd mony-mongers* that are accounted good common-wealths men."

With Roman swords; and my report was once
First with the best of note: Cymbeline lov'd me;
And when a soldier was the theme, my name
Was not far off: then was I as a tree
Whose boughs did bend with fruit: but in one night,
A storm or robbery, call it what you will,
Shook down my mellow hangings, nay, my leaves,
And left me bare to weather.

GUI. Uncertain favour!

BEL. My fault being nothing,—as I have told you oft,—
But that two villains, whose false oaths prevail'd
Before my perfect honour, swore to Cymbeline
I was confederate with the Romans: so,
Follow'd my banishment; and, this twenty years,
This rock and these demesnes have been my world:
Where I have liv'd at honest freedom; paid
More pious debts to heaven than in all
The fore-end of my time.—But, up to the mountains!
This is not hunters' language:—he that strikes
The venison first shall be the lord o' the feast;
To him the other two shall minister;
And we will fear no poison, which attends

In place of greater state. I'll meet you in the valleys.
[*Exeunt* GUIDERIUS *and* ARVIRAGUS.
How hard it is to hide the sparks of nature!
These boys know little they are sons to the king;
Nor Cymbeline dreams that they are alive.
They think they are mine: and, though train'd up thus meanly
I' the cave, wherein they bow,[a] their thoughts do [hit
The roofs of palaces; and nature prompts them,
In simple and low things, to prince it much
Beyond the trick of others. This Polydore,—
The heir of Cymbeline and Britain, whom
The king his father call'd Guiderius,—Jove!
When on my three-foot stool I sit, and tell
The warlike feats I have done, his spirits fly out
Into my story: say,—*Thus mine enemy fell;*
And thus I set my foot on 's neck—even then
The princely blood flows in his cheek, he sweats,
Strains his young nerves, and puts himself in posture
That acts my words. The younger brother, Cadwal,
(Once Arviragus) in as like a figure
Strikes life into my speech, and shows much more
His own conceiving. Hark! the game is rous'd!—
O Cymbeline! heaven and my conscience knows
Thou didst unjustly banish me: whereon,
At three and two years old, I stole these babes,
Thinking to bar thee of succession, as
Thou reft'st me of my lands. Euriphile,
Thou wast their nurse; they took thee for their mother,
And every day do honour to her grave:
Myself, Belarius, that am Morgan call'd,
They take for natural father.—The game is up!
[*Exit.*

SCENE IV.—*The same. Near* Milford-Haven.

Enter PISANIO *and* IMOGEN.

IMO. Thou told'st me, when we came from horse, the place
Was near at hand:—ne'er long'd my mother so
To see me first, as I have now—Pisanio, man!
Where is Posthúmus? What is in thy mind
That makes thee stare thus? Wherefore breaks that sigh
From the inward of thee? One, but painted thus,
Would be interpreted a thing perplex'd
Beyond self-explication: put thyself
Into a 'haviour of less fear, ere wildness
Vanquish my staider senses. What's the matter?
Why tender'st thou that paper to me, with
A look untender? If't be summer news,
Smile to't before; if winterly, thou need'st
But keep that count'nance still.—My husband's [hand!
That drug-damn'd Italy hath out-craftied him,
And he's at some hard point.—Speak, man; thy tongue
May take off some extremity, which to read
Would be even mortal to me.

PIS. Please you, read;
And you shall find me, wretched man, a thing
The most disdain'd of fortune.

IMO. [Reads.] *Thy mistress, Pisanio, hath played the strumpet in my bed: the testimonies whereof lie bleeding in me. I speak not out of weak surmises, but from proof as strong as my grief, and as certain as I expect my revenge. That part, thou, Pisanio, must act for me, if thy faith be not tainted with the breach of hers. Let thine own hands take away her life: I shall give thee opportunity at Milford-Haven: she hath my letter for the purpose: where, if thou fear to strike, and to make me certain it is done, thou art the pander to her dishonour, and equally to me disloyal.*

PIS. What shall I need to draw my sword? the paper
Hath cut her throat already.—No, 'tis slander,
Whose edge is sharper than the sword; whose tongue
Outvenoms all the worms of Nile; whose breath
Rides on the posting winds, and doth belie
All corners of the world; kings, queens, and states,
Maids, matrons,—nay, the secrets of the grave
This viperous slander enters.—What cheer, madam?

IMO. False to his bed! What is it to be false?
To lie in watch there, and to think on him?
To weep 'twixt clock and clock? if sleep charge nature,
To break it with a fearful dream of him,
And cry myself awake? that's false to's bed? is it?

PIS. Alas, good lady!

IMO. I false? Thy conscience witness:— [Iachimo,
Thou didst accuse him of incontinency;
Thou then look'dst like a villain; now, methinks,
Thy favour's good enough.—Some jay of Italy,
Whose mother was her painting,[b] hath betray'd him:

---

[a] Wherein they bow,—] A correction of Warburton's: the old text having, "whereon the Bowe."

[b] Whose mother was her painting,—] The meaning, if the text be right, is, her painting was her mother, *i.e.* she is made up by art. In support of this interpretation, Steevens cites a passage from an old comedy, "—a parcel of conceited feather-caps, *whose fathers were their garments*," and the following, which we find in Middleton's play of "Michaelmas Terme," Act III. Sc. 1, is equally pertinent:—"Why should not a woman confess what she is now, since the finest are but deluding shadows, begot between tire-women and tailors? *for instance behold their parents.*" Hanmer reads, "Whose *feathers* are her painting." Capell, "Whose *feather* was her painting." And Mr. Collier's annotator proposes a change which every one must admit to be singularly striking and ingenious:—

"Some jay of Italy,
Who smothers her with painting," &c.

Poor I am stale, a garment out of fashion;
And for I am richer than to hang by the walls,
I must be ripp'd:(3)—to pieces with me!—O,
Men's vows are women's traitors! All good seeming,
By thy revolt, O husband, shall be thought
Put on for villainy; not born where't grows,
But worn a bait for ladies.

PIS. Good madam, hear me.

IMO. True honest men being heard, like false Æneas,
Were, in his time, thought false: and Sinon's weeping
Did scandal many a holy tear; took pity
From most true wretchedness: so thou, Posthumus,
Wilt lay the leaven on all proper men;
Goodly and gallant, shall be false and perjur'd,
From thy great fail.—Come, fellow, be thou honest:
Do thou thy master's bidding: when thou seest him,
A little witness my obedience: look!
I draw the sword myself: take it, and hit
The innocent mansion of my love, my heart:
Fear not; 'tis empty of all things but grief:
Thy master is not there, who was, indeed,
The riches of it: do his bidding; strike.
Thou mayst be valiant in a better cause,
But now thou seem'st a coward.

PIS. Hence, vile instrument!
Thou shalt not damn my hand.

IMO. Why, I must die;
And if I do not by thy hand, thou art
No servant of thy master's: against self-slaughter
There is a prohibition so divine
That cravens my weak hand. Come, here's my heart;
Something's afore't;*—soft, soft! we'll no defence;
Obedient as the scabbard.—What is here?
The scriptures of the loyal Leonatus,
All turn'd to heresy? Away, away,
Corruptors of my faith! you shall no more
Be stomachers to my heart! Thus may poor fools
Believe false teachers. Though those that are betray'd
Do feel the treason sharply, yet the traitor
Stands in worse case of woe; and thou, Posthumus,
That didst set up my disobedience 'gainst
The king my father, and make† me put into contempt
The suits of princely fellows, shalt hereafter find
It is no act of common passage, but
A strain of rareness: and I grieve myself,
To think when thou shalt be disedg'd by her
That now thou tir'st on, how thy memory
Will then be pang'd by me.—Pr'ythee, despatch:
The lamb entreats the butcher: where's thy knife?
Thou art too slow to do thy master's bidding,
When I desire it too.

PIS. O gracious lady,
Since I receiv'd command to do this business,
I have not slept one wink.

IMO. Do't, and to bed then.

PIS. I'll wake[a] mine eye-balls first.

IMO. Wherefore, then,
Didst undertake it? Why hast thou abus'd
So many miles with a pretence? this place?
Mine action, and thine own? our horses' labour?
The time inviting thee? the perturb'd court,
For my being absent; whereunto I never
Purpose return? Why hast thou gone so far,
To be unbent when thou hast ta'en thy stand,
The elected deer before thee?

PIS. But to win time
To lose so bad employment; in the which
I have consider'd of a course. Good lady,
Hear me with patience.

IMO. Talk thy tongue weary; speak:
I have heard I am a strumpet; and mine ear,
Therein false struck, can take no greater wound,
Nor tent to bottom that: but speak.

PIS. Then, madam,
I thought you would not back again.

IMO. Most like,—
Bringing me here to kill me.

PIS. Not so, neither:
But if I were as wise as honest, then
My purpose would prove well. It cannot be
But that my master is abus'd:
Some villain, ay, and singular in his art,
Hath done you both this cursed injury.

IMO. Some Roman courtezan.

PIS. No, on my life.
I'll give but notice you are dead, and send him
Some bloody sign of it; for 'tis commanded
I should do so: you shall be miss'd at court,
And that will well confirm it.

IMO. Why, good fellow,
What shall I do the while? where bide? how live?

(*) Old text, *a-foot*. (†) Old text, *makes*.

[a] I'll wake mine eye-balls first.] This is invariably printed after Hanmer,

"I'll wake mine eye-balls *blind* first;"

except by Mr. Collier, who adopts the almost ludicrous alteration suggested by his annotator:—

"I'll *crack* mine eye-balls first."

There is not the slightest need for change of any kind. *Wake* is a synonyme for *watch;* and to *watch* is a technical term in falconry for the cruel method of taming the newly-taken hawks, by depriving them of sleep. (See note (d), p. 683, Vol. I.) "I'll *wake* mine eye-balls," then, means, "I'll prevent sleep even by the torture of my eye-balls." The very expression, indeed, though overlooked by all the editors, occurs in "Lust's Dominion," Act I. Sc. 2:—

"———I'll *still wake*
And waste these balls of sight," &c.

See also Middleton's play of "The Roaring Girl," Act IV. Sc. 2:—

"I'll ride to Oxford, and *watch* out mine eyes,
But I will hear the Brazen-head speak."

Or in my life what comfort, when I am
Dead to my husband?

PIS. If you'll back to the court,—

IMO. No court, no father; nor no more ado
With that harsh, noble, simple, nothing,—
That Cloten, whose love-suit hath been to me
As fearful as a siege.

PIS. If not at court,
Then not in Britain must you bide.

IMO. Where then?
Hath Britain all the sun that shines? Day, night,
Are they not but in Britain? I' the world's volume
Our Britain seems as of it, but not in't;
In a great pool, a swan's nest: pr'ythee, think
There's livers out of Britain.

PIS. I am most glad
You think of other place. The ambassador,
Lucius the Roman, comes to Milford-Haven
To-morrow: now, if you could wear a mind[a]
Dark as your fortune is—and but disguise
That which, to appear itself, must not yet be
But by self-danger;—you should tread a course
Pretty,[b] and full of view: yea, haply, near
The residence of Posthumus,—so nigh at least
That, though his actions were not visible, yet
Report should render him hourly to your ear,
As truly as he moves.

IMO. O, for such means!
Though peril to my modesty, not death on't,
I would adventure.

PIS. Well, then, here's the point:
You must forget to be a woman; change
Command into obedience; fear and niceness,—
The handmaids of all women, or, more truly,
Woman it pretty self,—into a waggish courage;
Ready in gibes, quick-answer'd, saucy, and
As quarrelous as the weasel; nay, you must
Forget that rarest treasure of your cheek,
Exposing it,—but, O, the harder heart!
Alack, no remedy!—to the greedy touch
Of common-kissing Titan: and forget
Your laboursome and dainty trims, wherein
You made great Juno angry.

IMO. Nay, be brief:
I see into thy end, and am almost
A man already.

PIS. First, make yourself but like one.
Fore-thinking this, I have already fit,
('Tis in my cloak-bag) doublet, hat, hose, all
That answer to them: would you, in their serving,
And with what imitation you can borrow
From youth of such a season, 'fore noble Lucius
Present yourself, desire his service, tell him
Wherein you're happy,[c]—which will make him know,[d]
If that his head have ear in music,—doubtless
With joy he will embrace you; for he's honourable,
And, doubling that, most holy. Your means abroad,[e]
You have me, rich; and I will never fail
Beginning nor supplyment.

IMO. Thou art all the comfort
The gods will diet me with. Pr'ythee, away:
There's more to be consider'd; but we'll even
All that good time will give us: this attempt
I'm soldier to, and will abide it with
A prince's courage. Away, I pr'ythee.

PIS. Well, madam, we must take a short farewell;
Lest, being miss'd, I be suspected of
Your carriage from the court. My noble mistress,
Here is a box; I had it from the queen;
What's in't is precious; if you are sick at sea,
Or stomach-qualm'd at land, a dram of this
Will drive away distemper.—To some shade,
And fit you to your manhood:—may the gods
Direct you to the best!

IMO. Amen: I thank thee.

[*Exeunt.*

SCENE V.—Britain. *A Room in* Cymbeline's *Palace.*

Enter CYMBELINE, QUEEN, CLOTEN, LUCIUS, *and* Lords.

CYM. Thus far; and so farewell.

LUC. Thanks, royal sir.
My emperor hath wrote; I must from hence;
And am right sorry that I must report ye
My master's enemy.

---

a —— *if you could wear a* mind
Dark, &c.]

"To wear a *dark mind*," Johnson remarks, "is to carry a mind impenetrable to the search of others. *Darkness*, applied to the *mind*, is *secrecy*; applied to the *fortune*, is *obscurity*." Warburton, however, suspected "mind" to be an error of the press, and would read,—

"—— if you could wear a mien
Dark," &c.

b Pretty, *and full of view*:] Mr. Collier's annotator proposes to read,—

"*Privy, yet* full of view;"

and, but that this implies the misprinting of two words together, we should unhesitatingly adopt the emendation; for "Privy" restores sense to the passage, and may easily have been mistaken for "Pretty" in old writing, where the one was spelt "Privie," and the other "Pretie."

c *Wherein you're* happy,—] i. e. *accomplished*.

d ——— which will make him know,
If that his head have ear in music,—]

This is the reading of the old text; the modern, following Hanmer, has,—

"——— which *you'll* make him know;"

or,

"——— which *you* will make him know;"

but neither is satisfactory. We might perhaps come nearer to Shakespeare by reading,—"Which will make him *bow*," i. e. *incline, yield*, &c.; a change supported by,—

"Orpheus, with his lute, made trees,
And the mountain-tops that freeze,
Bow themselves, when he did sing."
Hen. VIII. Act III. Sc. 1.

e Abroad,—] *Disbursed, expended.*

CYM. Our subjects, sir,
Will not endure his yoke; and for ourself
To show less sovereignty than they, must needs
Appear unkinglike.
LUC. So, sir; I desire of you
A conduct over-land, to Milford-Haven.—
Madam, all joy befall your grace,—and you!
CYM. My lords, you are appointed for that office,
The due of honour in no point omit.—
So, farewell, noble Lucius.
LUC. Your hand, my lord.
CLO. Receive it friendly: but from this time forth
I wear it as your enemy.
LUC. Sir, the event
Is yet to name the winner: fare you well.
CYM. Leave not the worthy Lucius, good my lords,
Till he have cross'd the Severn.—Happiness!
[*Exeunt* LUCIUS *and* Lords.
QUEEN. He goes hence frowning: but it honours us
That we have given him cause.
CLO. 'Tis all the better;
Your valiant Britons have their wishes in it.
CYM. Lucius hath wrote already to the emperor
How it goes here. It fits us therefore ripely
Our chariots and our horsemen be in readiness:
The powers that he already hath in Gallia
Will soon be drawn to head, from whence he moves
His war for Britain.
QUEEN. 'Tis not sleepy business;
But must be look'd to speedily and strongly.
CYM. Our expectation that it would be thus
Hath made us forward. But, my gentle queen,
Where is our daughter? She hath not appear'd
Before the Roman, nor to us hath tender'd
The duty of the day: she looks* us like
A thing more made of malice than of duty:
We have noted it.—Call her before us; for
We have been too slight in sufferance.
[*Exit an* Attendant.
QUEEN. Royal sir,
Since the exile of Posthumus, most retir'd
Hath her life been: the cure whereof, my lord,
'Tis time must do. Beseech your majesty,
Forbear sharp speeches to her: she's a lady
So tender of rebukes, that words are strokes,†
And strokes death to her.

Re-enter Attendant.

CYM. Where is she, sir? How
Can her contempt be answer'd?

(*) First folio, *looke*. (†) First folio, *stroke*.

[a] For—] i.e. *because*.

ATTEN. Please you, sir,
Her chambers are all lock'd, and there's no answer
That will be given to the loud'st* of noise we make.
QUEEN. My lord, when last I went to visit her,
She pray'd me to excuse her keeping close;
Whereto constrain'd by her infirmity,
She should that duty leave unpaid to you,
Which daily she was bound to proffer: this
She wish'd me to make known; but our great court
Made me to blame in memory.
CYM. Her doors lock'd?
Not seen of late? Grant, heavens, that which I fear
Prove false! [*Exit.*
QUEEN. Son, I say, follow the king.
CLO. That man of hers, Pisanio, her old servant,
I have not seen these two days.
QUEEN. Go, look after.—[*Exit* CLOTEN.
Pisanio, thou that stand'st so for Posthumus!—
He hath a drug of mine: I pray, his absence
Proceed by swallowing that; for he believes
It is a thing most precious. But for her,
Where is she gone? Haply, despair hath seiz'd her;
Or, wing'd with fervour of her love, she's flown
To her desir'd Posthumus: gone she is,
To death, or to dishonour; and my end
Can make good use of either: she being down,
I have the placing of the British crown.

Re-enter CLOTEN.

How now, my son?
CLO. 'Tis certain she is fled:
Go in and cheer the king, he rages; none
Dare come about him.
QUEEN. All the better: may
This night forestall him of the coming day! [*Exit.*
CLO. I love and hate her: for[a] she's fair and royal,
And that she hath all courtly parts more exquisite
Than lady, ladies, woman; from every one
The best she hath, and she, of all compounded,
Outsells them all,—I love her therefore; but,
Disdaining me, and throwing favours on
The low Posthumus, slanders so her judgment,
That what's else rare is chok'd; and, in that point,
I will conclude to hate her, nay, indeed,
To be reveng'd upon her. For, when fools
Shall—

Enter PISANIO.

Who is here? What! are you packing,[b] sirrah?
Come hither: ah, you precious pander! Villain,

(*) Old text, *loud*.

[b] Packing,—] *Plotting, contriving, scheming.*

Where is thy lady? In a word! or else
Thou art straightway with the fiends.

PIS. O, good my lord!

CLO. Where is thy lady? or, by Jupiter
I will not ask again! Close villain,
I'll have this secret from thy heart, or rip
Thy heart to find it. Is she with Posthumus,
From whose so many weights of baseness cannot
A dram of worth be drawn?

PIS. Alas, my lord,
How can she be with him? When was she miss'd?
He is in Rome.

CLO. Where is she, sir? Come nearer;
No farther halting: satisfy me home
What is become of her?

PIS. O, my all-worthy lord!

CLO. All-worthy villain!
Discover where thy mistress is, at once,
At the next word,—no more of *worthy lord*,—
Speak! or thy silence on the instant is
Thy condemnation and thy death.

PIS. Then, sir,
This paper is the history of my knowledge
Touching her flight. [*Presenting a letter.*

CLO. Let's see't:—I will pursue her
Even to Augustus' throne.

PIS. [*Aside.*] Or this, or perish.
She's far enough; and what he learns by this,
May prove his travel, not her danger.

CLO. Hum!

PIS. [*Aside.*] I'll write to my lord she's dead. O Imogen,
Safe mayst thou wander, safe return agen!

CLO. Sirrah, is this letter true?

PIS. Sir, as I think.

CLO. It is Posthumus' hand; I know't.—Sirrah, if thou wouldst not be a villain, but do me true service, undergo those employments wherein I should have cause to use thee, with a serious industry,—that is, what villainy soe'er I bid thee do, to perform it directly and truly,—I would think thee an honest man; thou shouldst neither want my means for thy relief nor my voice for thy preferment.

PIS. Well, my good lord.

CLO. Wilt thou serve me?—for since patiently and constantly thou hast stuck to the bare fortune of that beggar Posthumus, thou canst not, in the course of gratitude, but be a diligent follower of mine,—wilt thou serve me?

PIS. Sir, I will.

CLO. Give me thy hand; here's my purse. Hast any of thy late master's garments in thy possession?

PIS. I have, my lord, at my lodging, the same suit he wore when he took leave of my lady and mistress.

CLO. The first service thou dost me, fetch that suit hither: let it be thy first service; go.

PIS. I shall, my lord. [*Exit.*

CLO. *Meet thee at Milford-Haven*:—I forgot to ask him one thing; I'll remember't anon:—even there, thou villain Posthumus, will I kill thee.—I would these garments were come. She said upon a time,—the bitterness of it I now belch from my heart,—that she held the very garment of Posthumus in more respect than my noble and natural person, together with the adornment of my qualities. With that suit upon my back, will I ravish her: first kill him, and in her eyes; there shall she see my valour, which will then be a torment to her contempt. He on the ground, my speech of insultment ended on his dead body,—and when my lust hath dined, (which, as I say, to vex her I will execute in the clothes that she so praised) to the court I'll knock her back, foot her home again. She hath despised me rejoicingly, and I'll be merry in my revenge.

Re-enter PISANIO, *with the clothes.*

Be those the garments?

PIS. Ay, my noble lord.

CLO. How long is 't since she went to Milford-Haven?

PIS. She can scarce be there yet.

CLO. Bring this apparel to my chamber; that is the second thing that I have commanded thee; the third is, that thou wilt be a voluntary mute to my design. Be but duteous, and true preferment shall tender itself to thee.—My revenge is now at Milford: would I had wings to follow it!—Come, and be true. [*Exit.*

PIS. Thou bidd'st me to my loss: for, true to thee
Were to prove false, which I will never be,
To him that is most true.—To Milford go,
And find not her whom thou pursu'st.—Flow, flow
You heavenly blessings on her!—This fool's speed
Be cross'd with slowness; labour be his meed!
[*Exit.*

SCENE VI.—Wales. *Before the Cave of* Belarius.

Enter IMOGEN, *in boy's clothes.*

IMO. I see a man's life is a tedious one:
I have tir'd myself; and for two nights together
Have made the ground my bed. I should be sick,

But that my resolution helps me.—Milford,
When from the mountain-top Pisanio show'd thee,
Thou wast within a ken: O Jove! I think
Foundations fly the wretched; such, I mean,
Where they should be reliev'd. Two beggars told me
I could not miss my way: will poor folks lie,
That have afflictions on them, knowing 't is
A punishment or trial? Yes; no wonder,
When rich ones scarce tell true: to lapse in fulness
Is sorer than to lie for need; and falsehood
Is worse in kings than beggars.—My dear lord!
Thou art one o' the false ones: now I think on thee,
My hunger's gone; but even before, I was
At point to sink for food.—But what is this?
Here is a path to 't: 't is some savage hold:
I were best not call; I dare not call: yet famine,
Ere clean it o'erthrow nature, makes it valiant.
Plenty, and peace, breeds cowards; hardness ever
Of hardiness is mother.—Ho! who 's here?
If any thing that 's civil, speak;—if savage—
Take or lend.—Ho!—No answer? then I 'll enter.

Best draw my sword; and if mine enemy
But fear the sword like me, he 'll scarcely look on 't.
Such a foe, good heavens! [*Goes into the cave.*

Enter BELARIUS, GUIDERIUS, *and* ARVIRAGUS.

BEL. You, Polydore, have prov'd best woodman, and
Are master of the feast: Cadwal and I
Will play the cook and servant; 't is our match:
The sweat of industry would dry and die,
But for the end it works to. Come; our stomachs
Will make what 's homely, savoury: weariness
Can snore upon the flint, when resty[a] sloth
Finds the down pillow hard.—Now, peace be here,
Poor house that keep'st thyself!
GUI. I am throughly weary.
ARV. I am weak with toil, yet strong in appetite.
GUI. There is cold meat i' the cave; we 'll browse on that
Whilst what we have kill'd be cook'd.
BEL. Stay; come not in: [*Looking in.*
But that it eats our victuals, I should think
Here were a fairy.
GUI. What 's the matter, sir?
BEL. By Jupiter, an angel! or, if not,
An earthly paragon!—Behold divineness
No elder than a boy!

Re-enter IMOGEN.

IMO. Good masters, harm me not:
Before I enter'd here, I call'd; and thought
To have begg'd or bought what I have took: good troth,
I have stolen nought; nor would not, though I had found
Gold strew'd i' the floor. Here 's money for my meat:
I would have left it on the board, so soon
As I had made my meal; and parted
With prayers for the provider.
GUI. Money, youth?
ARV. All gold and silver rather turn to dirt!
As 't is no better reckon'd, but of those
Who worship dirty gods.
IMO. I see you are angry:
Know, if you kill me for my fault, I should
Have died had I not made it.
BEL. Whither bound?
IMO. To Milford-Haven.
BEL. What's your name?
IMO. Fidele, sir: I have a kinsman who
Is bound for Italy; he embark'd at Milford;
To whom being going, almost spent with hunger,
I am fall'n in this offence.
BEL. Pr'ythee, fair youth,
Think us no churls, nor measure our good minds
By this rude place we live in. Well encounter'd!
'T is almost night: you shall have better cheer
Ere you depart; and thanks to stay and eat it.—
Boys, bid him welcome.
GUI. Were you a woman, youth,
I should woo hard but be your groom:—in honesty,
I bid for you as I'd buy.[b]
ARV. I'll make 't my comfort
He is a man; I'll love him as my brother:—
And such a welcome as I'd give to him
After long absence, such is yours:—most welcome!
Be sprightly, for you fall 'mongst friends.
IMO. 'Mongst friends,
If brothers,—[*Aside.*] Would it had been so, that they
Had been my father's sons! then had my prize
Been less; and so more equal ballasting
To thee, Posthumus.
BEL. He wrings at some distress.
GUI. Would I could free 't!
ARV. Or I; whate'er it be,
What pain it cost, what danger! Gods!
BEL. Hark, boys. [*Whispering.*
IMO. Great men,
That had a court no bigger than this cave,
That did attend themselves, and had the virtue
Which their own conscience seal'd them,—laying by
That nothing-gift of differing multitudes,—[c]
Could not out-peer these twain. Pardon me, gods!
I'd change my sex to be companion with them,
Since Leonatus' false.
BEL. It shall be so.
Boys, we 'll go dress our hunt.—Fair youth, come in:
Discourse is heavy, fasting; when we have supp'd,
We 'll mannerly demand thee of thy story,
So far as thou wilt speak it.

---

[a] Resty *sloth*—] *Dull, idle*, perhaps *uneasy*, sloth.

[b] I bid for you as I'd buy.] The old text has,—"I bid for you as *I do* buy." We are not satisfied that the present emendation, which is Tyrwhitt's, gives us what the author wrote, but have none better to offer.

[c] ——— laying by
That nothing-gift of differing multitudes,—]

Theobald reads,—"*defering* multitudes," and Hanmer and Warburton follow him. But may not the error lie in "multitudes," rather than in the preceding word? "Differing *multitudes*," or "*defering* multitudes," is a very dubious expression. Imogen is struck with the generous courtesy and spirit of the young mountaineers, and she reflects that even princes or noblemen placed as they are (setting aside the worthless consideration of *different rank*) could not outshine these peasant youths. Does it not appear, then, more than probable that Shakespeare wrote,—

"——— laying by
That nothing-gift of differing *altitudes*"?

GUI. Pray, draw near.
ARV. The night to the owl, and morn to the lark, less welcome.
IMO. Thanks, sir.
ARV. I pray, draw near. [*Exeunt.*

SCENE VII.—Rome. *A public Place.*

Enter Two Senators *and* Tribunes.

1 SEN. This is the tenour of the emperor's writ,—
That since the common men are now in action
'Gainst the Pannonians and Dalmatians,
And that the legions now in Gallia are
Full weak to undertake our wars against
The fall'n-off Britons, that we do incite
The gentry to this business. He creates
Lucius pro-consul: and to you the tribunes,
For this immediate levy, he commends[a]
His absolute commission. Long live Cæsar!
TRI. Is Lucius general of the forces?
2 SEN. Ay.
TRI. Remaining now in Gallia?
1 SEN. With those legions
Which I have spoke of, whereunto your levy
Must be supplyant: the words of your commission
Will tie you to the numbers, and the time
Of their despatch.
TRI. We will discharge our duty. [*Exeunt.*

[a] Commends—] An emendation due to Warburton, the old text reading, "commands."

ACT IV.

SCENE I.—Wales. *The Forest, near the Cave of* Belarius.

Enter Cloten.

Clo. I am near to the place where they should meet, if Pisanio have mapped it truly. How fit his garments serve me! Why should his mistress, who was made by him that made the tailor, not be fit too? the rather,—saving reverence of the word,—for 't is said, a woman's fitness comes by fits. Therein I must play the workman. I dare speak it to myself,—for it is not vain-glory for a man and his glass to confer in his own chamber,—I mean, the lines of my body are as well drawn as his; no less young, more strong, not beneath him in fortunes, beyond him in the advantage of the time, above him in birth, alike conversant in general services, and more remarkable in single oppositions:[a] yet this imperseverant[b] thing loves him in my despite. What mortality is! Posthumus, thy head, which now is growing upon thy shoulders, shall within this hour be off; thy mistress enforced; thy garments cut to pieces before thy face: and all this done, spurn her home to her father, who may, haply, be a little angry for my so rough usage; but my mother, having power of his testiness, shall turn all into my commendations. My horse is tied up safe: out, sword, and to a sore purpose! Fortune, put them into my hand! This is the very description of their meeting-place, and the fellow dares not deceive me. [*Exit.*

---

a Alike conversant in general services, and more remarkable in single oppositions:] That is, equally familiar with ordinary warfare, and more distinguished for single encounters.

b Imperseverant—] *Imperceptive, undiscerning.*

SCENE II.—*The same. Before the Cave of* Belarius.

Enter, from the Cave, BELARIUS, GUIDERIUS, ARVIRAGUS, *and* IMOGEN.

BEL. [*To* IMOGEN.] You are not well: remain here in the cave;
We'll come to you after hunting.
ARV. [*To* IMOGEN.] Brother, stay here:
Are we not brothers?
IMO. So man and man should be;
But clay and clay differs in dignity,
Whose dust is both alike. I am very sick.
GUI. Go you to hunting; I'll abide with him.
IMO. So sick I am not,—yet I am not well;
But not so citizen a wanton, as
To seem to die ere sick: so please you, leave me;
Stick to your journal course; the breach of custom
Is breach of all. I am ill, but your being by me
Cannot amend me: society is no comfort
To one not sociable: I am not very sick,
Since I can reason of it. Pray you, trust me here:
I'll rob none but myself; and let me die,
Stealing so poorly.
GUI. I love thee; I have spoke it:
How much the quantity, the weight as much,
As I do love my father.
BEL. What? how? how?
ARV. If it be sin to say so, sir, I yoke me
In my good brother's fault: I know not why
I love this youth, and I have heard you say,
Love's reason's without reason; the bier at door,
And a demand who is 't shall die, I'd say,
My father, not this youth.
BEL. [*Aside.*] O noble strain!
O worthiness of nature! breed of greatness!
Cowards father cowards, and base things sire base:
Nature hath meal and bran, contempt and grace.
I'm not their father; yet who this should be
Doth miracle itself, lov'd before me.—
'T is the ninth hour o' the morn.
ARV. Brother, farewell.
IMO. I wish ye sport.
ARV. You, health.—So please you, sir.
IMO. [*Aside.*] These are kind creatures. Gods, what lies I have heard!
Our courtiers say all's savage but at court:
Experience, O, thou disprov'st report!
The imperious seas breed monsters; for the dish,
Poor tributary rivers as sweet fish.
I am sick still, heart-sick:—Pisanio,
I'll now taste of thy drug. [*Swallows some.*
GUI. I could not stir him:
He said he was gentle, but unfortunate,
Dishonestly afflicted, but yet honest.
ARV. Thus did he answer me; yet said, hereafter
I might know more.
BEL. To the field, to the field!—
We'll leave you for this time; go in and rest.
ARV. We'll not be long away.
BEL. Pray, be not sick,
For you must be our housewife.
IMO. Well or ill,
I am bound to you.
BEL. And shalt be ever.
[*Exit* IMOGEN *into the cave.*
This youth, howe'er distress'd, appears he hath had
Good ancestors.
ARV. How angel-like he sings!
GUI. But his neat cookery! he cut our roots in characters;
And sauc'd our broths, as Juno had been sick
And he her dieter.
ARV. Nobly he yokes
A smiling with a sigh,—as if the sigh
Was that it was, for not being such a smile;
The smile mocking the sigh, that it would fly
From so divine a temple, to commix
With winds that sailors rail at.
GUI. I do note
That grief and patience, rooted in him* both,
Mingle their spurs together.
ARV. Grow, patience! †
And let the stinking elder, grief, untwine
His perishing root with the increasing vine!
BEL. It is great morning. Come, away!—
Who's there?

Enter CLOTEN.

CLO. I cannot find those runagates: that villain
Hath mock'd me:—I am faint.
BEL. *Those runagates!*
Means he not us? I partly know him; 't is
Cloten, the son o' the queen. I fear some ambush.
I saw him not these many years, and yet
I know 't is he.—We are held as outlaws:—hence!
GUI. He is but one: you and my brother search
What companies are near: pray you, away;
Let me alone with him.
[*Exeunt* BELARIUS *and* ARVIRAGUS.
CLO. Soft!—What are you
That fly me thus? some villain mountaineers?
I have heard of such.—What slave art thou?
GUI. A thing
More slavish did I ne'er, than answering
A slave, without a knock.

(*) Old text, *them.* (†) Old text, *patient.*

Clo. Thou art a robber,
A law-breaker, a villain: yield thee, thief!
Gui. To who? to thee? what art thou? Have not I
An arm as big as thine? a heart as big?
Thy words, I grant, are bigger, for I wear not
My dagger in my mouth. Say what thou art,
Why I should yield to thee?
Clo. Thou villain base,
Know'st me not by my clothes?
Gui. No, nor thy tailor, rascal,
Who is thy grandfather; he made those clothes,
Which, as it seems, make thee.
Clo. Thou precious varlet,
My tailor made them not.
Gui. Hence, then, and thank

The man that gave them thee. Thou art some fool;
I am loth to beat thee.
CLO. Thou injurious thief,
Hear but my name, and tremble.
GUI. What's thy name?
CLO. Cloten, thou villain!
GUI. Cloten, thou double villain, be thy name,
I cannot tremble at it; were 't toad, or adder, spider,
'T would move me sooner.
CLO. To thy further fear,
Nay, to thy mere confusion, thou shalt know
I'm son to the queen.
GUI. I'm sorry for 't; not seeming
So worthy as thy birth.
CLO. Art not afeard?
GUI. Those that I reverence, those I fear,—the wise:
At fools I laugh, not fear them.
CLO. Die the death!
When I have slain thee with my proper hand,
I'll follow those that even now fled hence,
And on the gates of Lud's town set your heads:
Yield, rustic mountaineer! [*Exeunt, fighting.*

Re-enter BELARIUS *and* ARVIRAGUS.

BEL. No company's abroad.
ARV. None in the world: you did mistake him, sure.
BEL. I cannot tell: long is it since I saw him,
But time hath nothing blurr'd those lines of favour
Which then he wore; the snatches in his voice,
And burst of speaking, were as his: I am absolute
'T was very Cloten.
ARV. In this place we left them:
I wish my brother make good time with him,
You say he is so fell.
BEL. Being scarce made up,
I mean to man, he had not apprehension
Of roaring terrors, for defect of judgment,
Is oft the sauce[a] of fear.—But see, thy brother.

Re-enter GUIDERIUS, *with* CLOTEN'S *head.*

GUI. This Cloten was a fool, an empty purse,—
There was no money in't: not Hercules
Could have knock'd out his brains, for he had none:
Yet I not doing this, the fool had borne
My head as I do his.
BEL. What hast thou done!
GUI. I am perfect what: cut off one Cloten's head,
Son to the queen, after his own report;
Who call'd me *traitor mountaineer;* and swore,
With his own single hand he'd take us in,
Displace our heads, where (thank * the gods!) they grow,
And set them on Lud's town.
BEL. We are all undone.
GUI. Why, worthy father, what have we to lose,
But that he swore to take, our lives? The law
Protects not us: then why should we be tender
To let an arrogant piece of flesh threat us,
Play judge and executioner, all himself,
For we do fear the law? What company
Discover you abroad?
BEL. No single soul
Can we set eye on, but in all safe reason
He must have some attendants. Though his humour[b]
Was nothing but mutation,—ay, and that
From one bad thing to worse,—not frenzy, not
Absolute madness could so far have rav'd,
To bring him here alone: although, perhaps,
It may be heard at court, that such as we
Cave here, hunt here, are outlaws, and in time
May make some stronger head: the which he hearing,
(As it is like him) might break out, and swear
He'd fetch us in; yet is't not probable
To come alone, either he so undertaking,
Or they so suffering: then on good ground we fear,
If we do fear this body hath a tail
More perilous than the head.
ARV. Let ord'nance
Come as the gods foresay it: howsoe'er,
My brother hath done well.
BEL. I had no mind
To hunt this day: the boy Fidele's sickness
Did make my way long forth.
GUI. With his own sword,
Which he did wave against my throat, I have ta'en
His head from him: I'll throw't into the creek
Behind our rock, and let it to the sea,
And tell the fishes he's the queen's son, Cloten:
That's all I reck. [*Exit.*
BEL. I fear 'twill be reveng'd:

a ——— *for defect of judgment,*
Is oft the sauce *of fear.*]
The old text has, "the *cause* of fear," the direct opposite of which is meant; this Hanmer changed to, "the *cure* of fear;" while Theobald endeavoured to impart a meaning to the passage by reading,—
"——— for *th' effect* of judgment
Is oft the cause of fear."
The difficulty appears to be attributable to a very common metathesis; the letters *s* and *c* being displaced. *Sauce,* which we take to have been the poet's word, is used here in the sense of a *corrective* or *antidote*, as in "Troilus and Cressida," Act I. Sc. 2:—
"His folly *sauced* with discretion."
In the same way, Shakespeare occasionally employs the word physic:—
"The labour we delight in *physics* pain."
Macbeth, Act II. Sc. 3.

(*) Old text, *thanks.*

b *Though his* humour—] In the old text, *honour;* the correction, which indicates itself, was made by Theobald.

Would, Polydore, thou hadst not done't! though valour
Becomes thee well enough.
ARV. Would I had done't,
So the revenge alone pursu'd me!—Polydore,
I love thee brotherly; but envy much
Thou hast robb'd me of this deed: I would revenges,
That possible strength might meet, would seek us through,
And put us to our answer.
BEL. Well, 'tis done:—
We'll hunt no more to-day, nor seek for danger
Where there's no profit. I pr'ythee, to our rock;
You and Fidele play the cooks: I'll stay
Till hasty Polydore return, and bring him
To dinner presently.
ARV. Poor sick Fidele!
I'll willingly to him: to gain his colour,
I'd let a parish of such Clotens blood,
And praise myself for charity. [*Exit.*
BEL. O thou goddess,
Thou divine Nature, how * thyself thou blazon'st
In these two princely boys! They are as gentle

(*) Old text, *thou.*

As zephyrs blowing below the violet,
Not wagging his sweet head; and yet as rough,
Their royal blood enchaf'd, as the rud'st wind,
That by the top doth take the mountain pine
And make him stoop to the vale. 'T is wonder
That an invisible instinct should frame them
To royalty unlearn'd, honour untaught,
Civility not seen from other: valour,
That wildly grows in them, but yields a crop
As if it had been sow'd! Yet still it's strange
What Cloten's being here to us portends,
Or what his death will bring us.

Re-enter GUIDERIUS.

GUI. Where's my brother?
I have sent Cloten's clotpoll down the stream,
In embassy to his mother; his body's hostage
For his return. [*Solemn music.*
BEL. My ingenious * instrument!
Hark, Polydore, it sounds! But what occasion
Hath Cadwal now to give it motion? Hark!

(*) Old text, *ingenuous.*

GUI. Is he at home?
BEL. He went hence even now.
GUI. What does he mean? since death of my dear'st mother
It did not speak before. All solemn things
Should answer solemn accidents. The matter?
Triumphs for nothing, and lamenting toys,[a]
Is jollity for apes and grief for boys.
Is Cadwal mad?
BEL. Look, here he comes,
And brings the dire occasion in his arms,
Of what we blame him for!

Re-enter ARVIRAGUS, *bearing* IMOGEN, *as dead, in his arms.*

ARV. The bird is dead
That we have made so much on. I had rather
Have skipp'd from sixteen years of age to sixty;
To have turn'd my leaping time into a crutch,
Than have seen this.
GUI. O sweetest, fairest lily!
My brother wears thee not the one half so well,
As when thou grew'st thyself.
BEL. O, melancholy—
Who ever yet could sound thy bottom? find
The ooze, to show what coast thy sluggish crare[b]
Might* easiliest harbour in?—Thou blessed thing!
Jove knows what man thou mightst have made; but ah,†
Thou diedst, a most rare boy, of melancholy!—
How found you him?
ARV. Stark,[c] as you see:
Thus smiling, as some fly had tickled slumber,
Not as death's dart, being laugh'd at: his right cheek
Reposing on a cushion.
GUI. Where?
ARV. O' the floor;
His arms thus leagu'd: I thought he slept, and put
My clouted brogues from off my feet, whose rudeness
Answer'd my steps too loud.
GUI. Why, he but sleeps:
If he be gone, he'll make his grave a bed;
With female fairies will his tomb be haunted,
And worms will not come to thee.
ARV. With fairest flowers,
Whilst summer lasts, and I live here, Fidele,
I'll sweeten thy sad grave: thou shalt not lack
The flower that's like thy face, pale primrose, nor
The azur'd hare-bell, like thy veins; no, nor
The leaf of eglantine, whom not to slander,
Out-sweeten'd not thy breath: the ruddock[d] would,
With charitable bill,—O bill, sore-shaming
Those rich-left heirs that let their fathers lie
Without a monument!—bring thee all this;
Yea, and furr'd moss besides, when flowers are none,
To winter-ground[e] thy corse.
GUI. Pr'ythee, have done;
And do not play in wench-like words with that
Which is so serious. Let us bury him,
And not protract with admiration what
Is now due debt.—To the grave!
ARV. Say, where shall 's lay him?
GUI. By good Euriphile, our mother.
ARV. Be't so:
And let us, Polydore, though now our voices
Have got the mannish crack, sing him to the ground,
As once* our mother; use like note and words,
Save that *Euriphile* must be *Fidele*.
GUI. Cadwal,
I cannot sing: I'll weep, and word it with thee;
For notes of sorrow out of tune are worse
Than priests and fanes that lie.
ARV. We'll speak it then.
BEL. Great griefs, I see, medicine the less; for Cloten
Is quite forgot. He was a queen's son, boys:
And, though he came our enemy, remember
He was paid[f] for that: though mean and mighty, rotting
Together, have one dust, yet reverence
(That angel of the world) doth make distinction
Of place 'tween high and low. Our foe was princely;
And though you took his life, as being our foe,
Yet bury him as a prince.
GUI. Pray you, fetch him hither.
Thersites' body is as good as Ajax,
When neither are alive.
ARV. If you'll go fetch him,
We'll say our song the whilst.—Brother, begin.
[*Exit* BELARIUS.
GUI. Nay, Cadwal, we must lay his head to the east:
My father hath a reason for't.
ARV. 'Tis true.
GUI. Come on then, and remove him.
ARV. So.—Begin.

(*) First folio, *Might'st*. (†) Old text, *I*.

(*) Old text inserts, *to*.

a Toys,—] *Toys* are *trifles*.
b *Sluggish* crare—] The old copies have *care*, a manifest error for *crare*, a small vessel of burthen, sometimes spelt *crayer*, *cray*, and *crea*.
c Stark,—] That is, *rigid*, *stiff*.
d The ruddock—] The *red-breast*.
e To winter-ground *thy corse*.] Mr. Collier's annotator would read, "To *winter-guard*," &c., but to *winter-ground* appears to have been a technical term for protecting a plant from the frost, by laying straw or dung over it.
f Paid—] That is, *punished*.

SONG.

GUI. Fear no more the heat o' the sun,
  Nor the furious winter's rages;
Thou thy worldly task hast done,
  Home art gone, and ta'en thy wages:
Golden lads and girls all must,
As chimney-sweepers, come to dust.[a]

ARV. Fear no more the frown o' the great,
  Thou art past the tyrant's stroke;
Care no more to clothe and eat;
  To thee the reed is as the oak:
The sceptre, learning, physic, must
All follow this, and come to dust.

GUI. Fear no more the light'ning flash,
ARV. Nor the all-dreaded thunder-stone;
GUI. Fear not slander, censure rash;
ARV. Thou hast finish'd joy and moan:
BOTH. All lovers young, all lovers must
Consign to thee, and come to dust.

GUI. No exorciser harm thee!
ARV. Nor no witchcraft charm thee!
GUI. Ghost unlaid forbear thee!
ARV. Nothing ill come near thee!
BOTH. Quiet consummation have;
And renowned be thy grave!

Re-enter BELARIUS, *with the body of* CLOTEN.

GUI. We have done our obsequies: come, lay him down.
BEL. Here's a few flowers; but about midnight, more:
The herbs that have on them cold dew o' the night
Are strewings fitt'st for graves.—Upon their faces.—
You were as flowers, now wither'd: even so
These herb'lets shall, which we upon you strew.—
Come on, away: apart upon our knees.
The ground that gave them first, has them again:
Their pleasures here are past, so is * their pain.
[*Exeunt* BELARIUS, GUIDERIUS, *and* ARVIRAGUS.

(*) Old text, *are*.

[a] Golden lads and girls all must,
As chimney-sweepers, come to dust.]

There is something so strikingly inferior both in the thoughts and expression of the concluding couplet to each stanza in this song, that we may fairly set them down as additions from the same hand which furnished the contemptible *masque* or *vision* that deforms the last act.

IMO. [*Awaking.*] Yes, sir, to Milford-Haven; which is the way?
I thank you.—By yond bush?—Pray, how far thither?
'Ods pittikins!—can it be six mile yet?—
I have gone all night:—faith, I'll lie down and [sleep.
But soft! no bedfellow:—O, gods and goddesses!
[*Seeing the body.*
These flowers are like the pleasures of the world;
This bloody man, the care on't.—I hope I dream;
For so I thought I was a cave-keeper,
And cook to honest creatures: but 'tis not so;
'Twas but a bolt of nothing, shot at nothing,
Which the brain makes of fumes: our very eyes
Are sometimes like our judgments, blind. Good faith,
I tremble still with fear: but if there be
Yet left in heaven as small a drop of pity
As a wren's eye, fear'd gods, a part of it!
The dream's here still, even when I wake; it is
Without me, as within me; not imagin'd, felt!
A headless man!—the garments of Posthumus!
I know the shape of 's leg: this is his hand;
His foot Mercurial: his Martial thigh;
The brawns of Hercules: but his Jovial face—
Murder in heaven!—How?—'Tis gone.—Pisanio,
All curses madded Hecuba gave the Greeks,
And mine to boot, be darted on thee! Thou,
Conspir'd with that irregulous[a] devil, Cloten,
Hast* here cut off my lord.—To write and read
Be henceforth treacherous!—Damn'd Pisanio
Hath with his forged letters,—damn'd Pisanio—
From this most bravest vessel of the world
Struck the main-top!—O, Posthumus! alas,
Where is thy head? where's that? Ay me! where's that?
Pisanio might have kill'd thee at the heart,
And left this head on.—How should this be? Pisanio?
'Tis he and Cloten: malice and lucre in them
Have laid this woe here. O, 't is pregnant, pregnant!
The drug he gave me, which, he said, was precious
And cordial to me, have I not found it
Murderous to the senses? That confirms it home:
This is Pisanio's deed, and Cloten's:† O!—
Give colour to my pale cheek with thy blood,
That we the horrider may seem to those
Which chance to find us: O, my lord, my lord!
[*Swoons.*

Enter LUCIUS, *a* Captain, *and other* Officers, *and a* Soothsayer.

CAP. To them, the legions garrison'd in Gallia,
After your will, have cross'd the sea; attending
You here at Milford-Haven with your ships:
They are[b] in readiness.
LUC. But what from Rome?
CAP. The senate hath stirr'd up the cónfiners
And gentlemen of Italy, most willing spirits,
That promise noble service; and they come
Under the conduct of bold Iachimo,
Sienna's brother.
LUC. When expect you them?
CAP. With the next benefit o' the wind.
LUC. This forwardness
Makes our hopes fair. Command our present numbers
Be muster'd; bid the captains look to't.—Now, sir,
What have you dream'd of late of this war's purpose?
SOOTH. Last night the very gods show'd me a vision,—
I fast and pray'd for their intelligence,—thus:—
I saw Jove's bird, the Roman eagle, wing'd
From the spungy south to this part of the west,
There vanish'd in the sunbeams: which portends,—
Unless my sins abuse my divination,—
Success to the Roman host.
LUC. Dream often so,
And never false.—Soft, ho! what trunk is here
Without his top? The ruin speaks that sometime
It was a worthy building.—How! a page!—
Or dead, or sleeping on him? But dead, rather:
For nature doth abhor to make his bed
With the defunct, or sleep upon the dead.—
Let's see the boy's face.
CAP. He's alive, my lord.
LUC. He'll then instruct us of this body.—Young one,
Inform us of thy fortunes; for it seems
They crave to be demanded. Who is this
Thou mak'st thy bloody pillow? Or who was he,
That, otherwise than noble nature did,
Hath alter'd that good picture? What's thy interest
In this sad wreck? How came it? Who is it?
What art thou?
IMO. I am nothing: or if not,
Nothing to be were better. This was my master.
A very valiant Briton and a good,
That here by mountaineers lies slain;—alas!
There is no more such masters: I may wander
From east to occident, cry out for service,
Try many, all good, serve truly, never
Find such another master.
LUC. 'Lack, good youth!
Thou mov'st no less with thy complaining, than

(*) Old text, *hath*. (†) Old text, *Cloten*.

a Irregulous—] As no other example of the word has been met with, some editors conjecture it to be a misprint. It evidently means *anomalous, mongrel, monstrous.*

b They are in readiness.] The reading of the second folio; the first having,—
"They are *heere* in readinesse."

Thy master in bleeding; say his name, good friend.

IMO. Richard du Champ.—[*Aside.*] If I do lie, and do
No harm by it, though the gods hear, I hope
They 'll pardon it. Say you, sir?

LUC. Thy name?

IMO. Fidele, sir.

LUC. Thou dost approve thyself the very same:
Thy name well fits thy faith, thy faith thy name.
Wilt take thy chance with me? I will not say
Thou shalt be so well master'd; but, be sure,
No less belov'd. The Roman emperor's letters,
Sent by a consul to me, should not sooner
Than thine own worth prefer thee. Go with me.

IMO. I 'll follow, sir. But first, an 't please the gods,
I 'll hide my master from the flies, as deep
As these poor pickaxes can dig: and when
With wild wood-leaves and weeds I have strew'd his grave,
And on it said a century of prayers,
Such as I can, twice o'er, I 'll weep and sigh;
And leaving so his service follow you,
So please you entertain me.

LUC. Ay, good youth;
And rather father thee than master thee.—My friends,
The boy hath taught us manly duties: let us
Find out the prettiest daisied plot we can,
And make him with our pikes and partisans
A grave: come, arm him.—Boy, he is preferr'd
By thee to us; and he shall be interr'd
As soldiers can. Be cheerful; wipe thine eyes:
Some falls are means the happier to arise.
[*Exeunt.*

SCENE III.—Britain. *A Room in* Cymbeline's *Palace.*

Enter CYMBELINE, Lords, PISANIO, *and other* Attendants.

CYM. Again; and bring me word how 't is with her. [*Exit an* Attendant.
A fever with the absence of her son;
A madness, of which her life 's in danger:—heavens,
How deeply you at once do touch me! Imogen,
The great part of my comfort, gone; my queen
Upon a desperate bed, and in a time
When fearful wars point at me; her son gone,
So needful for this present: it strikes me, past
The hope of comfort!—But for thee, fellow,
Who needs must know of her departure, and
Dost seem so ignorant, we 'll enforce it from thee
By a sharp torture.

PIS. Sir, my life is yours,
I humbly set it at your will: but for my mistress,
I nothing know where she remains, why gone,
Nor when she purposes return. Beseech your highness,
Hold me your loyal servant.

1 LORD. Good my liege,
The day that she was missing he was here:
I dare be bound he 's true, and shall perform
All parts of his subjection loyally. For Cloten,—
There wants no diligence in seeking him,
And will, no doubt, be found.

CYM. The time is troublesome.—
We 'll slip you for a season; but our jealousy [*To* PISANIO.
Does yet depend.

1 LORD. So please your majesty,
The Roman legions, all from Gallia drawn,
Are landed on your coast; with a supply
Of Roman gentlemen, by the senate sent.

CYM. Now for the counsel of my son and queen!
I am amaz'd with matter.

1 LORD. Good my liege,
Your preparation can affront no less
Than what you hear of: come more, for more you 're ready;
The want is, but to put those powers in motion
That long to move.

CYM. I thank you: let 's withdraw;
And meet the time as it seeks us. We fear not
What can from Italy annoy us; but
We grieve at chances here.—Away!
[*Exeunt all except* PISANIO.

PIS. I heard[a] no letter from my master since
I wrote him Imogen was slain: 't is strange:
Nor hear I from my mistress, who did promise
To yield me often tidings: neither know I
What is betid to Cloten; but remain
Perplex'd in all:—the heavens still must work:
Wherein I am false, I am honest; not true, to be true.
These present wars shall find I love my country,
Even to the note o' the king, or I 'll fall in them.
All other doubts by time let them be clear'd:
Fortune brings in some boats that are not steer'd.
[*Exit.*

SCENE IV. — Wales. *Before the Cave of* Belarius.

Enter BELARIUS, GUIDERIUS, *and* ARVIRAGUS.

GUI. The noise is round about us.

BEL. Let us from it.

---

[a] I heard no letter, &c.] Mr. Collier's annotator, rightly perhaps, suggests, "I *had* no letter," &c.

ARV. What pleasure, sir, find we * in life, to lock it
From action and adventure?
GUI. Nay, what hope
Have we in hiding us? this way, the Romans
Must or for Britons slay us, or receive us
For barbarous and unnatural revolts
During their use, and slay us after.
BEL. Sons,
We'll higher to the mountains; there secure us.
To the king's party there's no going: newness
Of Cloten's death,—we being not known, not muster'd
Among the bands,—may drive us to a render
Where we have liv'd; and so extort from 's that
Which we have done, whose answer would be death
Drawn on with torture.
GUI. This is, sir, a doubt
In such a time nothing becoming you,
Nor satisfying us.
ARV. It is not likely
That when they hear the† Roman horses neigh,
Behold their quarter'd fires, have both their eyes
And ears so cloy'd importantly as now,
That they will waste their time upon our note,
To know from whence we are.
BEL. O, I am known
Of many in the army: many years,
Though Cloten then but young, you see, not wore him
From my remembrance. And, besides, the king
Hath not deserv'd my service nor your loves;
Who find in my exile the want of breeding,

(*) First folio, *we finde*. (†) Old text, *their*.

The certainty of this hard * life; aye hopeless
To have the courtesy your cradle promis'd,
But to be still hot summer's tanlings, and
The shrinking slaves of winter.
GUI. Than be so,
Better to cease to be. Pray, sir, to the army:
I and my brother are not known; yourself
So out of thought, and thereto so o'ergrown,
Cannot be question'd.
ARV. By this sun that shines,
I'll thither: what thing is it, that I never
Did see man die! scarce ever look'd on blood,
But that of coward hares, hot goats, and venison!
Never bestrid a horse, save one, that had
A rider like myself, who ne'er wore rowel
Nor iron on his heel! I am asham'd
To look upon the holy sun, to have
The benefit of his bless'd beams, remaining
So long a poor unknown.
GUI. By heavens, I'll go:
If you will bless me, sir, and give me leave,
I'll take the better care; but if you will not,
The hazard therefore due fall on me by
The hands of Romans!
ARV. So say I,—Amen.
BEL. No reason I, since of your lives you set
So slight a valuation, should reserve
My crack'd one to more care. Have with you, boys!
If in your country wars you chance to die,
That is my bed too, lads, and there I'll lie:
Lead, lead.—[*Aside.*] The time seems long: their blood thinks scorn,
Till it fly out and show them princes born.
[*Exeunt.*

(*) First folio, *heard*.

ACT V.

SCENE I.—*The* Roman *Camp.*

Enter Posthumus, *with a bloody handkerchief.*

Post. Yea, bloody cloth, I'll keep thee; for I* wish'd
Thou shouldst be colour'd thus. You married ones,
If each of you should take this course, how many
Must murder wives much better than themselves,
For wrying but a little!—O, Pisanio!
Every good servant does not all commands;
No bond but to do just ones.—Gods! if you
Should have ta'en vengeance on my faults, I never
Had liv'd to put on this: so had you sav'd
The noble Imogen to repent; and struck
Me, wretch, more worth your vengeance. But, alack,
You snatch some hence for little faults; that's love,
To have them fall no more: you some permit

(*) Old text inserts, *am.*

To second ills with ills, each elder worse,
And make them dread it, to the doer's thrift.[a]
But Imogen is your own: do your best wills,
And make me bless'd to obey!—I am brought hither
Among the Italian gentry, and to fight
Against my lady's kingdom: 't is enough
That, Britain, I have kill'd thy mistress; peace!
I'll give no wound to thee. Therefore, good heavens,
Hear patiently my purpose:—I'll disrobe me
Of these Italian weeds, and suit myself
As does a Briton peasant: so I'll fight
Against the part I come with; so I'll die
For thee, O Imogen, even for whom my life
Is, every breath, a death: and thus, unknown,
Pitied nor hated, to the face of peril
Myself I'll dedicate. Let me make men know
More valour in me, than my habits show.
Gods, put the strength o' the Leonati in me!
To shame the guise o' the world, I will begin
The fashion,—less without and more within.
[*Exit.*

SCENE II.—*A Field between the* British *and* Roman *Camps.*

Enter, on one side, LUCIUS, IACHIMO, *and the* Roman *army; the* British *army on the other.* LEONATUS POSTHUMUS *following, like a poor soldier. They march over, and go out. Then enter again in skirmish,* IACHIMO *and* POSTHUMUS: *he vanquisheth and disarmeth* IACHIMO, *and then leaves him.*

IACH. The heaviness and guilt within my bosom
Takes off my manhood: I have belied a lady,
The princess of this country; and the air on 't
Revengingly enfeebles me; or, could this carle,
A very drudge of nature's, have subdued me,
In my profession? Knighthoods and honours, borne
As I wear mine, are titles but of scorn.
If that thy gentry, Britain, go before
This lout as he exceeds our lords, the odds
Is, that we scarce are men, and you are gods.
[*Exit.*

The Battle continues; the Britons *fly;* CYMBELINE *is taken; then enter, to his rescue,* BELARIUS, GUIDERIUS, *and* ARVIRAGUS.

BEL. Stand, stand! we have the advantage of the ground;
The lane is guarded; nothing routs us but
The villainy of our fears.
GUI. ARV. Stand, stand, and fight!

Enter POSTHUMUS, *and seconds the* Britons: *they rescue* CYMBELINE, *and exeunt. Then enter* LUCIUS, IACHIMO, *and* IMOGEN.

LUC. Away, boy, from the troops, and save thyself:
For friends kill friends, and the disorder 's such
As war were hood-wink'd.
IACH. 'T is their fresh supplies.
LUC. It is a day turn'd strangely; or betimes
Let 's reinforce, or fly. [*Exeunt.*

SCENE III.—*Another Part of the Field.*

Enter POSTHUMUS *and a* British Lord.

LORD. Cam'st thou from where they made the stand?
POST. I did;
Though you, it seems, come from the fliers.
LORD. I did.
POST. No blame be to you, sir; for all was lost,
But that the heavens fought: the king himself
Of his wings destitute, the army broken,
And but the backs of Britons seen, all flying
Through a strait lane; the enemy full-hearted,
Lolling the tongue with slaught'ring, having work
More plentiful than tools to do 't, struck down
Some mortally, some slightly touch'd, some falling
Merely through fear; that the strait pass was damm'd
With dead men hurt behind, and cowards living
To die with lengthen'd shame.

---

[a] ——— you some permit
To second ills with ills, each elder worse,
And make them dread it, to the doer's thrift.]

The commentators have found a difficulty in the words "each elder worse," contending that the last deed is not the oldest; but whether rightly or wrongly, it is certain Shakespeare so considered it; thus, in "Pericles," Act I. Sc. 2:—

"And what was first but fear, what might be done,
Grows *elder* now," &c.

The real pinch in the passage is the line,—

"And make them dread it, to the doer's thrift"—

which has been tortured into,—

"And make them *dreaded* to the doer's thrift."
"And make them *deeded* to the doer's thrift."
"And make them *trade* it to the doer's thrift."
"And make them dreaded to the doer's *shrift*."
"And make *men* dread it to the doer's thrift."

And still remains as inscrutable as ever.

LORD. Where was this lane?

POST. Close by the battle, ditch'd, and wall'd with turf;
Which gave advantage to an ancient soldier,—
An honest one, I warrant; who deserv'd
So long a breeding as his white beard came to,
In doing this for 's country:—athwart the lane,
He, with two striplings, (lads more like to run
The country base, than to commit such slaughter;
With faces fit for masks, or rather fairer
Than those for preservation cas'd, or shame)
Made good the passage; cried to those that fled,
Our Britain's harts die flying, not our men:
To darkness fleet, souls that fly backwards! Stand;
Or we are Romans, and will give you that
Like beasts, which you shun beastly; and may save,
But to look back in frown: stand! stand!—These three,
Three thousand confident, in act as many,—
For three performers are the file, when all
The rest do nothing,—with this word, *stand! stand!*
Accommodated by the place, more charming[a]
With their own nobleness, (which could have turn'd
A distaff to a lance) gilded pale looks;
Part shame, part spirit renew'd, that some, turn'd coward
But by example,—O, a sin in war,
Damn'd in the first beginners!—'gan to look
The way that they did, and to grin like lions
Upon the pikes o' the hunters. Then began
A stop i' the chaser, a retire; anon,
A rout, confusion thick: forthwith, they fly
Chickens, the way which they stoop'd* eagles; slaves,
The strides they† victors made: and now our cowards
(Like fragments in hard voyages) became
The life o' the need, having found the back-door open
Of the unguarded hearts: heavens, how they wound!
Some slain before; some dying; some their friends
O'er-borne i' the former wave; ten, chas'd by one,
Are now each one the slaughter-man of twenty:
Those that would die or ere resist are grown
The mortal bugs[b] o' the field.

LORD. This was strange chance,—
A narrow lane, an old man, and two boys! (1)

---

[a] More charming—] That is, controlling others of the Britain side, as if by enchantment.

(*) Old text, *stopt*. (†) Old text, *thee*.

[b] The mortal bugs—] *The deadly terrors*, or *bugbears*.

POST. Nay, do not wonder at it:[a] you are made
Rather to wonder at the things you hear,
Than to work any. Will you rhyme upon 't,
And vent it for a mockery? Here is one:
Two boys, an old man twice a boy, a lane,
Preserv'd the Britons, was the Romans' bane.
LORD. Nay, be not angry, sir.
POST. 'Lack, to what end!
Who dares not stand his foe, I'll be his friend:
For if he'll do, as he is made to do,
I know he'll quickly fly my friendship too.
You have put me into rhyme.
LORD. Farewell; you are angry. [*Exit.*
POST. Still going?—This is a lord! O noble misery,—
To be i' the field, and ask, what news, of me!
To-day how many would have given their honours
To have sav'd their carcases? took heel to do 't,
And yet died too? I, in mine own woe charm'd,
Could not find death where I did hear him groan;
Nor feel him where he struck: being an ugly monster,
'T is strange he hides him in fresh cups, soft beds,
Sweet words: or hath more ministers than we
That draw his knives i' the war.—Well, I will find him:
For being now a favourer to the Briton,
No more a Briton,[b] I have resum'd again
The part I came in: fight I will no more,
But yield me to the veriest hind that shall
Once touch my shoulder. Great the slaughter is
Here made by the Roman: great the answer be
Britons must take; for me, my ransom's death;
On either side I come to spend my breath;
Which neither here I'll keep, nor bear agen,
But end it by some means for Imogen.

Enter two British Captains, *and* Soldiers.

1 CAP. Great Jupiter be prais'd! Lucius is taken:
'T is thought the old man and his sons were angels.
2 CAP. There was a fourth man, in a silly[c] habit,
That gave the affront with them.
1 CAP. So 't is reported:
But none of 'em can be found.—Stand! who's there?
POST. A Roman,
Who had not now been drooping here, if seconds
Had answer'd him.
2 CAP. Lay hands on him; a dog!
A leg of Rome shall not return to tell
What crows have peck'd them here: he brags his service
As if he were of note: bring him to the king.

Enter CYMBELINE, *attended by* BELARIUS, GUIDERIUS, ARVIRAGUS, PISANIO, *and* Roman Captives. *The* Captains *present* POSTHUMUS *to* CYMBELINE, *who delivers him over to a* Gaoler. *The Scene closes.*

SCENE IV.—*A Room in a Prison.*

Enter POSTHUMUS *and two* Gaolers.

1 GAOL. You shall not now be stol'n, you have locks upon you;
So, graze as you find pasture.
2 GAOL. Ay, or a stomach.
[*Exeunt* Gaolers.
POST. Most welcome, bondage! for thou art a way,
I think, to liberty: yet am I better
Than one that's sick o' the gout, since he had rather
Groan so in perpetuity, than be cur'd
By the sure physician, death, who is the key
To unbar these locks. My conscience! thou art fetter'd
More than my shanks and wrists: you good gods, give me
The penitent instrument, to pick that bolt,
Then, free for ever! Is 't enough I am sorry?
So children temporal fathers do appease;
Gods are more full of mercy. Must I repent?
I cannot do it better than in gyves,
Desir'd, more than constrain'd: to satisfy,
If of my freedom 't is the main part, take
No stricter render of me, than my all.[d]
I know you are more clement than vile men,
Who of their broken debtors take a third,
A sixth, a tenth, letting them thrive again
On their abatement: that's not my desire

---

a Nay, *do* not *wonder at it*:] From the context it might be suspected that this was a misprint for,—

"*Ay*, do *but* wonder at it:"

for Posthumus is made to bid his hearer not do the very thing he taunts him with being born to do.

b Well, I will find him:
For being now a favourer to the Briton,
No more a Briton, I have, &c.]

Since Hanmer, who made the change, the second line has been usually printed,—

"For being now a favourer to the *Roman*."

But the meaning may be this,—I will find death; and as he is now a sparer of the Briton, I will play that part no longer, but seek him as a Roman.

c *A silly habit*,—] A *simple*, or *rustic* habit.

d Must I repent?
I cannot do it better than in gyves,
Desir'd, more than constrain'd: to satisfy,
If of my freedom 't is the main part, take
No stricter render of me, than my all.]

This passage, of which Malone supposes a line to have been omitted after "satisfy," is, we fear, hopelessly incurable.

For Imogen's dear life take mine; and though
'T is not so dear, yet 't is a life; you coin'd it:
'Tween man and man, they weigh not every stamp;
Though light, take pieces for the figure's sake:
You rather, mine being yours: and so, great powers,
If you will take this audit, take this life,
And cancel these cold bonds. O Imogen!
I'll speak to thee in silence. [*Sleeps.*

Solemn music.[a] *Enter, as in an apparition,* SICILIUS LEONATUS, *father to* POSTHUMUS, *an old man, attired like a warrior; leading in his hand an ancient matron, his wife, and mother to* POSTHUMUS, *with music before them: then, after other music, follow the two young* LEONATI, *brothers to* POSTHUMUS, *with wounds, as they died in the wars. They circle* POSTHUMUS *round, as he lies sleeping.*

SICI. No more, thou thunder-master, show
Thy spite on mortal flies;
With Mars fall out, with Juno chide,
That thy adulteries
Rates and revenges.
Hath my poor boy done aught but well,
Whose face I never saw?
I died, whilst in the womb he stay'd
Attending Nature's law:
Whose father then (as men report
Thou orphans' father art)
Thou shouldst have been, and shielded him
From this earth-vexing smart.

MOTH. Lucina lent not me her aid,
But took me in my throes;
That from me was Posthumus ripp'd,
Came crying 'mongst his foes,
A thing of pity!

SICI. Great nature, like his ancestry,
Moulded the stuff so fair,
That he deserv'd the praise o' the world,
As great Sicilius' heir.

1 BRO. When once he was mature for man,
In Britain where was he
That could stand up his parallel;
Or fruitful object be
In eye of Imogen, that best
Could deem his dignity?

MOTH. With marriage wherefore was he mock'd,
To be exil'd, and thrown
From Leonati' seat, and cast
From her his dearest one,
Sweet Imogen?

SICI. Why did you suffer Iachimo,
Slight thing of Italy,
To taint his nobler heart and brain
With needless jealousy;
And to become the geck and scorn
O' the other's villainy?

---

[a] Solemn music, &c.] By whom, or under what circumstances this pitiful mummery was foisted into the play, will probably never be known. That Shakespeare had no hand in it is certain; he, as Steevens remarks, "who has conducted his fifth act with such matchless skill, could never have designed the vision to be twice described by Posthumus, had this contemptible nonsense been previously delivered on the stage."

2 BRO. For this, from stiller seats we came,
Our parents and us twain,
That, striking in our country's cause,
Fell bravely, and were slain;
Our fealty, and Tenantius' right,
With honour to maintain.

1 BRO. Like hardiment Posthumus hath
To Cymbeline perform'd:
Then Jupiter, thou king of gods,
Why hast thou thus adjourn'd
The graces for his merits due;
Being all to dolours turn'd?

SICI. Thy crystal window ope; look * out;
No longer exercise,
Upon a valiant race, thy harsh
And potent injuries.

MOTH. Since, Jupiter, our son is good,
Take off his miseries.

SICI. Peep through thy marble mansion; help!
Or we poor ghosts will cry
To the shining synod of the rest,
Against thy deity.

2 BRO. Help, Jupiter! or we appeal,
And from thy justice fly.

JUPITER *descends in thunder and lightning, sitting upon an eagle: he throws a thunderbolt. The* Ghosts *fall on their knees.*

JUP. No more, you petty spirits of region low,
Offend our hearing; hush!—How dare you ghosts
Accuse the Thunderer, whose bolt you know,
Sky-planted, batters all rebelling coasts?
Poor shadows of Elysium, hence; and rest
Upon your never-withering banks of flowers:
Be not with mortal accidents opprest;
No care of yours it is; you know 't is ours.
Whom best I love I cross; to make my gift,
The more delay'd, delighted. Be content;
Your low-laid son our godhead will uplift:
His comforts thrive, his trials well are spent.
Our Jovial star reign'd at his birth, and in
Our temple was he married.—Rise, and fade!—
He shall be lord of lady Imogen,
And happier much by his affliction made.
This tablet lay upon his breast; wherein
Our pleasure his full fortune doth confine;
And so, away: no farther with your din
Express impatience, lest you stir up mine.—
Mount, eagle, to my palace crystalline.
[*Ascends.*

SICI. He came in thunder; his celestial breath
Was sulphurous to smell: the holy eagle
Stoop'd, as to foot us: his ascension is
More sweet than our blest fields: his royal bird
Prunes the immortal wing, and cloys his beak,
As when his god is pleas'd.

ALL. Thanks, Jupiter!

SICI. The marble pavement closes, he is enter'd
His radiant roof:—away! and, to be blest,
Let us with care perform his great behest.
[*Ghosts vanish.*

POST. [*Waking.*] Sleep, thou hast been a grandsire, and begot
A father to me: and thou hast created
A mother, and two brothers; but (O scorn!)
Gone! they went hence so soon as they were born.
And so I am awake.—Poor wretches that depend
On greatness' favour, dream as I have done;
Wake, and find nothing. But, alas, I swerve:
Many dream not to find, neither deserve,
And yet are steep'd in favours; so am I,
That have this golden chance, and know not why.
What fairies haunt this ground? A book? O rare one!
Be not, as is our fangled world, a garment
Nobler than that it covers: let thy effects
So follow, to be most unlike our courtiers,
As good as promise.

[Reads.] *Whenas a lion's whelp shall, to himself unknown, without seeking find, and be embraced by a piece of tender air; and when from a stately cedar shall be lopped branches, which, being dead many years, shall after revive, be jointed to the old stock, and freshly grow; then shall Posthumus end his miseries, Britain be fortunate, and flourish in peace and plenty.*

'T is still a dream; or else such stuff as madmen
Tongue, and brain not: either both, or nothing:
Or senseless speaking, or a speaking such
As sense cannot untie. Be what it is,
The action of my life is like it, which
I 'll keep, if but for sympathy.

Re-enter First Gaoler.

GAOL. Come, sir, are you ready for death?

POST. Over-roasted rather; ready long ago.

GAOL. Hanging is the word, sir; if you be ready for that, you are well cooked.

POST. So, if I prove a good repast to the spectators, the dish pays the shot.

GAOL. A heavy reckoning for you, sir. But the comfort is, you shall be called to no more payments, fear no more tavern bills; which are[a] often the sadness of parting, as the procuring of mirth; you come in faint for want of meat, depart reeling with too much drink; sorry that you have paid too much, and sorry that you are paid[b] too much; purse and brain both empty,—the brain the heavier for being too light, the purse too light, being drawn of heaviness: O! of this contradiction you shall now be quit.—O, the charity of a penny cord! it sums up thousands in a trice: you have

(*) First folio, *looke, looke out.*

[a] Which are—] *As* is understood:—"which are *as* often," &c.

[b] *And sorry that you are* paid *too much;*] *Paid*, here, is equivalent to the slang phrase, *to settle*, now in use; as, I've *settled* him, he's *settled*, and the like. With this import, which is that of *punished*, *paid* is often met with in old authors; we find it, among other places, in "Henry the Fourth," Part I. Act II. Sc. 4:—"two, I am sure, I have *paid*;" and again in the same scene:—"seven of the eleven I *paid*."

no true debitor and creditor but it; of what's past, is, and to come, the discharge.—Your neck, sir, is pen, book, and counters; so the acquittance follows.

POST. I am merrier to die than thou art to live.

GAOL. Indeed, sir, he that sleeps feels not the tooth-ache: but a man that were to sleep your sleep, and a hangman to help him to bed, I think he would change places with his officer; for, look you, sir, you know not which way you shall go.

POST. Yes, indeed, do I, fellow.

GAOL. Your death has eyes in 's head then; I have not seen him so pictured: you must either be directed by some that take upon them to know, or* take upon yourself that which I am sure you do not know; for, jump the after-inquiry on your own peril, and how you shall speed in your journey's end, I think you 'll never return to tell one.

POST. I tell thee, fellow, there are none want eyes to direct them the way I am going, but such as wink, and will not use them.

GAOL. What an infinite mock is this, that a man should have the best use of eyes to see the way of blindness! I am sure hanging 's the way of winking.

Enter a Messenger.

MESS. Knock off his manacles; bring your prisoner to the king.

POST. Thou bring'st good news;—I am called to be made free.

GAOL. I 'll be hanged, then.

POST. Thou shalt be then freer than a gaoler; no bolts for the dead.

[*Exeunt* POSTHUMUS *and* Messenger.

GAOL. Unless a man would marry a gallows, and beget young gibbets, I never saw one so prone. Yet, on my conscience, there are verier knaves desire to live, for all he be a Roman: and there be some of them too, that die against their wills: so should I, if I were one. I would we were all of one mind, and one mind good; O, there were desolation of gaolers and gallowses! I speak against my present profit; but my wish hath a preferment in 't. [*Exit.*

SCENE V.—Cymbeline's *Tent.*

Enter CYMBELINE, BELARIUS, GUIDERIUS, ARVIRAGUS, PISANIO, Lords, Officers, *and* Attendants.

CYM. Stand by my side, you whom the gods have made
Preservers of my throne. Woe is my heart,
That the poor soldier that so richly fought,
Whose rags sham'd gilded arms, whose naked breast
Stepp'd before targes of proof, cannot be found:
He shall be happy that can find him, if
Our grace can make him so.

BEL. I never saw
Such noble fury in so poor a thing;
Such precious deeds in one that promis'd nought
But beggary and poor looks.

CYM. No tidings of him?

PIS. He hath been search'd among the dead and living,
But no trace of him.

CYM. To my grief, I am
The heir of his reward; which I will add
To you the liver, heart, and brain of Britain,
[*To* BELARIUS, GUIDERIUS, *and* ARVIRAGUS.
By whom I grant she lives. 'T is now the time
To ask of whence you are:—report it.

BEL. Sir,
In Cambria are we born, and gentlemen:
Further to boast were neither true nor modest,
Unless I add, we are honest.

CYM. Bow your knees.
Arise, my knights o' the battle; I create you
Companions to our person, and will fit you
With dignities becoming your estates.

Enter CORNELIUS *and* Ladies.

There's business in these faces.—Why so sadly
Greet you our victory? you look like Romans,
And not o' the court of Britain.

COR. Hail, great king!
To sour your happiness, I must report
The queen is dead.

CYM. Whom worse than a physician
Would this report become? But I consider,
By med'cine life may be prolong'd, yet death
Will seize the doctor too.—How ended she?

COR. With horror, madly dying, like her life,
Which, being cruel to the world, concluded
Most cruel to herself. What she confess'd
I will report, so please you: these her women
Can trip me, if I err; who with wet cheeks
Were present when she finish'd.

CYM. Pr'ythee, say.

COR. First, she confess'd she never lov'd you; only
Affected greatness got by you, not you:
Married your royalty, was wife to your place;
Abhorr'd your person.

CYM. She alone knew this:
And, but she spoke it dying, I would not
Believe her lips in opening it. Proceed.

(*) Old text inserts, *to*.

COR. Your daughter, whom she bore in hand to love
With such integrity, she did confess
Was as a scorpion to her sight; whose life,
But that her flight prevented it, she had
Ta'en off my poison.
CYM. O most delicate fiend!
Who is 't can read a woman?—Is there more?
COR. More, sir, and worse. She did confess she had
For you a mortal mineral; which, being took,
Should by the minute feed on life, and, lingering,
By inches waste you: in which time she purpos'd,
By watching, weeping, tendance, kissing, to
O'ercome you with her show: yes,* and in time
When she had fitted you with her craft, to work
Her son into the adoption of the crown:
But, failing of her end by his strange absence,
Grew shameless-desperate: open'd, in despite
Of heaven and men, her purposes; repented
The evils she hatch'd were not effected: so,
Despairing, died.
CYM. Heard you all this, her women?
LADY. We did, so please your highness.
CYM. Mine eyes
Were not in fault, for she was beautiful;
Mine ears, that heard† her flattery; nor my heart
That thought her like her seeming: it had been vicious
To have mistrusted her: yet, O my daughter!
That it was folly in me, thou mayst say,
And prove it in thy feeling. Heaven mend all!—

Enter LUCIUS, IACHIMO, *the* Soothsayer, *and other* Roman *prisoners, guarded;* POSTHUMUS *behind, and* IMOGEN.

Thou com'st not, Caius, now for tribute; that
The Britons have raz'd out, though with the loss
Of many a bold one; whose kinsmen have made suit
That their good souls may be appeas'd with slaughter
Of you their captives, which ourself have granted:
So, think of your estate.
LUC. Consider, sir, the chance of war: the day
Was yours by accident: had it gone with us,
We should not, when the blood was cool, have threaten'd
Our prisoners with the sword. But since the gods
Will have it thus, that nothing but our lives
May be call'd ransom, let it come: sufficeth
A Roman with a Roman's heart can suffer:
Augustus lives to think on 't; and so much
For my peculiar care. This one thing only
I will entreat; my boy, a Briton born,
Let him be ransom'd: never master had
A page so kind, so duteous, diligent,
So tender over his occasions, true,
So feat, so nurse-like: let his virtue join
With my request, which, I'll make bold, your highness
Cannot deny; he hath done no Briton harm,
Though he have serv'd a Roman: save him, sir,
And spare no blood beside.
CYM. I have surely seen him:
His favour is familiar to me.
Boy, thou hast look'd thyself into my grace,
And art mine own.—I know not why, nor* wherefore,
To say, live, boy: ne'er thank thy master; live:
And ask of Cymbeline what boon thou wilt,
Fitting my bounty and thy state, I'll give it;
Yea, though thou do demand a prisoner
The noblest ta'en.
IMO. I humbly thank your highness.
LUC. I do not bid thee beg my life, good lad;
And yet I know thou wilt.
IMO. No, no: alack,
There's other work in hand: I see a thing
Bitter to me as death: your life, good master,
Must shuffle for itself.
LUC. The boy disdains me,
He leaves me, scorns me: briefly die their joys,
That place them on the truth of girls and boys.—
Why stands he so perplex'd?
CYM. What wouldst thou, boy?
I love thee more and more; think more and more
What's best to ask. Know'st him thou look'st on? speak,
Wilt have him live? Is he thy kin? thy friend?
IMO. He is a Roman; no more kin to me
Than I to your highness; who, being born your vassal,
Am something nearer.
CYM. Wherefore ey'st him so?
IMO. I'll tell you, sir, in private, if you please
To give me hearing.
CYM. Ay, with all my heart,
And lend my best attention. What's thy name?
IMO. Fidele, sir.
CYM. Thou 'rt my good youth, my page;
I'll be thy master: walk with me; speak freely.
[CYMBELINE *and* IMOGEN *converse apart.*
BEL. Is not this boy reviv'd from death?
ARV. One sand another
Not more resembles that sweet rosy lad
Who died, and was Fidele:—what think you?
GUI. The same dead thing alive.
BEL. Peace, peace! see further; he eyes us not; forbear;

(*) First folio omits, *yes.* (†) Old text, *heare.*

(*) Old text omits, *nor.*

Creatures may be alike: were 't he, I am sure
He would have spoke to us.
GUI. But we saw* him dead.
BEL. Be silent; let's see further.
PIS. [*Aside.*] It is my mistress:
Since she is living, let the time run on
To good, or bad.
[CYMBELINE *and* IMOGEN *come forward.*
CYM. Come, stand thou by our side;
Make thy demand aloud.—Sir [*To* IACHIMO.], step you forth;
Givé answer to this boy, and do it freely;
Or, by our greatness, and the grace of it,
Which is our honour, bitter torture shall
Winnow the truth from falsehood.—On,† speak to him.
IMO. My boon is, that this gentleman may render
Of whom he had this ring.
POST. [*Aside.*] What's that to him?
CYM. That diamond upon your finger, say
How came it yours?
IACH. Thou'lt torture me to leave unspoken that,
Which, to be spoke, would torture thee.
CYM. How! me?
IACH. I am glad to be constrain'd to utter that
Which[a] torments me to conceal. By villainy
I got this ring; 't was Leonatus' jewel,
Whom thou didst banish; and,—which more may grieve thee
As it doth me,—a nobler sir ne'er liv'd
'Twixt sky and ground. Wilt thou hear more, my lord?
CYM. All that belongs to this.
IACH. That paragon, thy daughter,—
For whom my heart drops blood, and my false spirits
Quail to remember,—give me leave; I faint.
CYM. My daughter! what of her? Renew thy strength:
I had rather thou shouldst live while nature will,
Than die ere I hear more: strive, man, and speak.
IACH. Upon a time,—unhappy was the clock
That struck the hour!—it was in Rome,—accurs'd
The mansion where!—'t was at a feast,—O would
Our viands had been poison'd, or, at least,
Those which I heav'd to head!—the good Posthumus!—
What should I say? he was too good, to be
Where ill men were; and was the best of all
Amongst the rar'st of good ones,—sitting sadly,
Hearing us praise our loves of Italy
For beauty that made barren the swell'd boast
Of him that best could speak; for feature, laming
The shrine of Venus, or straight-pight Minerva,
Postures beyond brief nature;[b] for condition,
A shop of all the qualities that man
Loves woman for; besides, that hook of wiving,
Fairness, which strikes the eye:—
CYM. I stand on fire:
Come to the matter.
IACH. All too soon I shall,
Unless thou wouldst grieve quickly. This Posthumus—
Most like a noble lord in love, and one
That had a royal lover—took his hint;
And, not dispraising whom we prais'd,—therein
He was as calm as virtue,—he began
His mistress' picture; which by his tongue being made,
And then a mind put in't, either our brags
Were crack'd of kitchen trulls, or his description
Prov'd us unspeaking sots.
CYM. Nay, nay, to the purpose.
IACH. Your daughter's chastity—there it begins.
He spake of her, as Dian had hot dreams,
And she alone were cold: whereat, I, wretch!
Made scruple of his praise, and wager'd with him
Pieces of gold 'gainst this, which then he wore
Upon his honour'd finger, to attain
In suit the place of 's bed, and win this ring
By hers and mine adultery: he, true knight,
No lesser of her honour confident
Than I did truly find her, stakes this ring,
And would so, had it been a carbuncle
Of Phœbus' wheel; and might so safely, had it
Been all the worth of his car. Away to Britain
Post I in this design:—well may you, sir,
Remember me at court, where I was taught
Of your chaste daughter, the wide difference
'Twixt amorous and villainous. Being thus quench'd
Of hope, not longing, mine Italian brain
'Gan in your duller Britain operate
Most vilely; for my vantage, excellent;
And, to be brief, my practice so prevail'd
That I return'd with simular proof enough
To make the noble Leonatus mad,
By wounding his belief in her renown,
With tokens thus, and thus; averring notes
Of chamber-hanging, pictures, this her bracelet,—
O, cunning, how I got it!*—nay, some marks
Of secret on her person, that he could not
But think her bond of chastity quite crack'd,

(*) First folio, *see*. (†) Old text, *One*.

(*) First folio omits, *it*.

[a] Which *torments me to conceal.*] *Which* is usually an appendage of the preceding line; we adopt the arrangement of the folio, but agree with Mr. Dyce in considering the word an impertinent addition of the transcriber or printer.

[b] —— for feature, laming
The shrine of Venus, or straight-pight Minerva,
Postures beyond brief nature;]
For grace and dignity of form, surpassing those antique statues of Venus and Minerva, whose attitudes are unattainable by nature.

I having ta'en the forfeit. Whereupon,—
Methinks, I see him now,—

POST. [*Rushing forward.*] Ay, so thou dost,
Italian fiend!—Ay me, most credulous fool,
Egregious murderer, thief, any thing
That's due to all the villains past, in being,
To come!—O, give me cord, or knife, or poison,
Some upright justicer! Thou, king, send out
For torturers ingenious: it is I
That all the abhorred things o' the earth amend,
By being worse than they. I am Posthumus,
That kill'd thy daughter:—villain-like, I lie;—
That caus'd a lesser villain than myself,
A sacrilegious thief, to do't:—the temple
Of virtue was she; yea, and she herself.
Spit, and throw stones, cast mire upon me, set
The dogs o' the street to bay me: every villain
Be called Posthumus Leonatus; and
Be villainy less than 'twas!—O Imogen!
My queen, my life, my wife! O Imogen,
Imogen, Imogen!

IMO. Peace, my lord; hear, hear!

POST. Shall's have a play of this? Thou scornful page,
There lie thy part. [*Striking her: she falls.*

PIS. O, gentlemen, help
Mine and your mistress:—O, my lord Posthumus!
You ne'er kill'd Imogen till now:—help, help!—
Mine honour'd lady!

CYM. Does the world go round?

POST. How come these staggers on me?

PIS. Wake, my mistress!

CYM. If this be so, the gods do mean to strike me
To death with mortal joy.

PIS. How fares my mistress?

IMO. O, get thee from my sight;
Thou gav'st me poison: dangerous fellow, hence!
Breathe not where princes are!

CYM. The tune of Imogen!

PIS. Lady, the gods throw stones of sulphur on me, if
That box I gave you was not thought by me
A precious thing; I had it from the queen.

CYM. New matter still?

IMO. It poison'd me.

COR. O gods!—
I left out one thing which the queen confess'd,
Which must approve thee honest: *if Pisanio
Have*, said she, *given his mistress that confection
Which I gave him for cordial, she is serv'd
As I would serve a rat.*

CYM. What's this, Cornelius?

COR. The queen, sir, very oft importun'd me
To temper poisons for her; still pretending
The satisfaction of her knowledge only
In killing creatures vile, as cats and dogs
Of no esteem: I, dreading that her purpose
Was of more danger, did compound for her
A certain stuff, which, being ta'en, would cease
The present power of life; but, in short time,
All offices of nature should again
Do their due functions.—Have you ta'en of it?

IMO. Most like I did, for I was dead.

BEL. My boys,
There was our error.

GUI. This is, sure, Fidele.

IMO. Why did you throw your wedded lady from you?
Think that you are upon a rock, and now
Throw me again. [*Embracing him.*

POST. Hang there like fruit, my soul,
Till the tree die!

CYM. How now, my flesh, my child?
What, mak'st thou me a dullard in this act?[a]
Wilt thou not speak to me?

IMO. Your blessing, sir. [*Kneeling.*

BEL. Though you did love this youth, I blame ye not;
You had a motive for't.
[*To* GUIDERIUS *and* ARVIRAGUS.

CYM. My tears that fall
Prove holy water on thee! Imogen,
Thy mother's dead.

IMO. I am sorry for't, my lord.

CYM. O, she was naught; and 'long of her it was
That we meet here so strangely: but her son
Is gone, we know not how, nor where.

PIS. My lord,
Now fear is from me, I'll speak troth. Lord Cloten,
Upon my lady's missing, came to me
With his sword drawn; foam'd at the mouth, and swore
If I discover'd not which way she was gone,
It was my instant death: by accident,
I had a feigned letter of my master's
Then in my pocket, which directed him
To seek her on the mountains near to Milford;
Where, in a frenzy, in my master's garments,
Which he inforc'd from me, away he posts
With unchaste purpose, and with oath to violate
My lady's honour: what became of him,
I further know not.

GUI. Let me end the story:
I slew him there.

CYM. Marry, the gods forefend!
I would not thy good deeds should from my lips
Pluck a hard sentence: pr'ythee, valiant youth,
Deny't again.

GUI. I have spoke it, and I did it.

CYM. He was a prince.

---

[a] What, mak'st thou me a dullard in this act?] Do you give me, in this scene, the part only of a looker-on? Shakespeare was thinking of the stage.

GUI. A most incivil one: the wrongs he did me
Were nothing prince-like; for he did provoke me
With language that would make me spurn the sea,
If it could so roar to me: I cut off his head;
And am right glad he is not standing here
To tell this tale of mine.
CYM. I am sorry* for thee.
By thine own tongue thou art condemn'd, and must
Endure our law: thou'rt dead!
IMO. That headless man
I thought had been my lord.
CYM. Bind the offender,
And take him from our presence.
BEL. Stay, sir king:
This man is better than the man he slew,
As well descended as thyself; and hath
More of thee merited than a band of Clotens
Had ever scar for.—Let his arms alone; [*To the* Guard.
They were not born for bondage.
CYM. Why, old soldier,
Wilt thou undo the worth thou art unpaid for,
By tasting[a] of our wrath? How of descent
As good as we?
ARV. In that he spake too far.
CYM. And thou shalt die for't.
BEL. We will die all three;
But I will prove, that two on's are as good
As I have given out him.—My sons, I must,
For mine own part, unfold a dangerous speech,
Though, haply, well for you.
ARV. Your danger's ours.
GUI. And our good, his.
BEL. Have at it then, by leave.
Thou hadst, great king, a subject who
Was call'd Belarius.
CYM. What of him? he's
A banish'd traitor.
BEL. He it is that hath
Assum'd this age: indeed, a banish'd man;
I know not how *a traitor*.
CYM. Take him hence;
The whole world shall not save him.
BEL. Not too hot:
First pay me for the nursing of thy sons;
And let it be confiscate all, so soon
As I've receiv'd it.
CYM. Nursing of my sons!

(*) First folio, *sorrow*.

[a] *By* tasting *of our wrath?*] "The consequence," Johnson says, "is taken for the whole action; *by tasting is by forcing us to make thee taste.*" This may be the true sense of the expression; but we have always conceived *tasting*, in this place, to mean *trying, testing*, &c., as in "Twelfth Night," Act III. Sc. 1:—

"*Taste* your legs, sir."

And again in Act III. Sc. 4:—"I have heard of some kind of men that put quarrels purposely on others, to *taste* their valour.' See also note (a), p. 256.

BEL. I am too blunt and saucy: here's my knee;
Ere I arise I will prefer [a] my sons;
Then, spare not the old father. Mighty sir,
These two young gentlemen, that call me father,
And think they are my sons, are none of mine;
They are the issue of your loins, my liege,
And blood of your begetting.
CYM. How! my issue?
BEL. So sure as you your father's. I, old Morgan,
Am that Belarius whom you sometime banish'd:
Your pleasure was my mere * offence, my punishment
Itself, and all my treason; that I suffered
Was all the harm I did. These gentle princes,—
For such and so they are,—these twenty years
Have I train'd up: those arts they have, as I
Could put into them; my breeding was, sir, as
Your highness knows. Their nurse, Euriphile,
Whom for the theft I wedded, stole these children
Upon my banishment: I mov'd her to't;
Having receiv'd the punishment before,
For that which I did then: beaten for loyalty,
Excited me to treason. Their dear loss,
The more of you 't was felt, the more it shap'd
Unto my end of stealing them. But, gracious sir,
Here are your sons again; and I must lose
Two of the sweet'st companions in the world:—
The benediction of these covering heavens
Fall on their heads like dew! for they are worthy
To inlay heaven with stars.
CYM. Thou weep'st, and speak'st.—
The service that you three have done, is more
Unlike than this thou tell'st: I lost my children;
If these be they, I know not how to wish
A pair of worthier sons.
BEL. Be pleas'd awhile.—
This gentleman, whom I call Polydore,
Most worthy prince, as yours, is true Guiderius:
This gentleman, my Cadwal, Arviragus,
Your younger princely son; he, sir, was lapp'd
In a most curious mantle, wrought by the hand
Of his queen-mother, which, for more probation,
I can with ease produce.
CYM. Guiderius had
Upon his neck a mole, a sanguine star;
It was a mark of wonder.
BEL. This is he;
Who hath upon him still that natural stamp:
It was wise Nature's end in the donation,
To be his evidence now.
CYM. O, what am I
A mother to the birth of three? Ne'er mother
Rejoic'd deliverance more.—Bless'd pray you be,

(*) First folio, *neere*.

Prefer—] *Advance.*

That, after this strange starting from your orbs,
You may reign in them now!—O, Imogen,
Thou hast lost by this a kingdom.
IMO. No, my lord;
I have got two worlds by 't.—O, my gentle brothers,
Have we thus met? O, never say hereafter
But I am truest speaker: you call'd me brother,
When I was but your sister; I you, brothers,
When you * were so indeed.
CYM. Did you e'er meet?
ARV. Ay, my good lord.
GUI. And at first meeting lov'd;
Continued so, until we thought he died.
COR. By the queen's dram she swallow'd.
CYM. O rare instinct!
When shall I hear all through? This fierce abridgment
Hath to it circumstantial branches, which
Distinction should be rich in.—Where? how liv'd you?
And when came you to serve our Roman captive?
How parted with your brothers? † how first met them?
Why fled you from the court? and whither? These,
And your three motives to the battle, with
I know not how much more, should be demanded,
And all the other by-dependencies,
From chance to chance; but nor the time, nor place,
Will serve our long inter'gatories. See,
Posthumus anchors upon Imogen;
And she, like harmless lightning, throws her eye
On him, her brothers, me, her master, hitting
Each object with a joy; the counterchange
Is severally in all. Let's quit this ground,
And smoke the temple with our sacrifices.—
Thou art my brother: so we'll hold thee ever.
[*To* BELARIUS.
IMO. You are my father too; and did relieve me,
To see this gracious season.
CYM. All o'erjoy'd,
Save these in bonds; let them be joyful too,
For they shall taste our comfort.
IMO. My good master,
I will yet do you service.
LUC. Happy be you!
CYM. The forlorn soldier that so nobly fought,
He would have well becom'd this place, and grac'd
The thankings of a king.
POST. I am, sir,
The soldier that did company these three
In poor beseeming; 'twas a fitment for
The purpose I then follow'd:—that I was he,
Speak, Iachimo: I had you down, and might
Have made you finish.

(*) Old text, *we*.
(†) Old text, *brother?*

IACH. I am down again:
[*Kneeling.*
But now my heavy conscience sinks my knee,
As then your force did. Take that life, beseech you,
Which I so often owe: but your ring first;
And here the bracelet of the truest princess
That ever swore her faith.

POST. Kneel not to me;
The power that I have on you is to spare you;
The malice towards you to forgive you: live,
And deal with others better.

CYM. Nobly doom'd;
We'll learn our freeness of a son-in-law;
Pardon's the word to all.

ARV. You holp us, sir,
As you did mean indeed to be our brother;
Joy'd are we that you are.

POST. Your servant, princes.—Good my lord of Rome,
Call forth your soothsayer: as I slept, methought,
Great Jupiter, upon his eagle back'd,
Appear'd to me, with other spritely shows
Of mine own kindred: when I wak'd, I found
This label on my bosom; whose containing
Is so from sense in hardness, that I can
Make no collection of it; let him show
His skill in the construction.

LUC. Philarmonus!

SOOTH. Here, my good lord.

LUC. Read, and declare the meaning.

SOOTH. [Reads.] *Whenas a lion's whelp shall, to himself unknown, without seeking find, and be embraced by a piece of tender air; and when from a stately cedar shall be lopped branches, which, being dead many years, shall after revive, be jointed to the old stock, and freshly grow; then shall Posthumus end his miseries, Britain be fortúnate, and flourish in peace and plenty.*[a]

Thou, Leonatus, art the lion's whelp;
The fit and apt construction of thy name,
Being *Leo-natus*, doth import so much:
The piece of tender air, thy virtuous daughter,
[*To* CYMBELINE.
Which we call *mollis aer;* and *mollis aer*
We term it *mulier:* which *mulier* I divine
Is this most constant wife; who, even now,
Answering the letter of the oracle,
Unknown to you, unsought, were clipp'd about
With this most tender air.

CYM. This hath some seeming.

SOOTH. The lofty cedar, royal Cymbeline,
Personates thee: and thy lopp'd branches point
Thy two sons forth: who, by Belarius stolen,
For many years thought dead, are now reviv'd,
To the majestic cedar join'd; whose issue
Promises Britain peace and plenty.

CYM. Well,
My peace we will begin:—and, Caius Lucius,
Although the victor, we submit to Cæsar,
And to the Roman empire; promising
To pay our wonted tribute, from the which
We were dissuaded by our wicked queen:
Whom heavens, in justice, both on her and hers,
Have laid most heavy hand.

SOOTH. The fingers of the powers above do tune
The harmony of this peace. The vision
Which I made known to Lucius, ere the stroke
Of this yet* scarce-cold battle, at this instant
Is full accomplish'd: for the Roman eagle,
From south to west on wing soaring aloft,
Lessen'd herself, and in the beams o' the sun
So vanish'd: which foreshow'd our princely eagle,
The imperial Cæsar, should again unite
His favour with the radiant Cymbeline,
Which shines here in the west.

CYM. Laud we the gods;
And let our crooked smokes climb to their nostrils
From our bless'd altars! Publish we this peace
To all our subjects. Set we forward: let
A Roman and a British ensign wave
Friendly together: so through Lud's town march;
And in the temple of great Jupiter
Our peace we'll ratify; seal it with feasts.—
Set on there!—Never was a war did cease,
Ere bloody hands were wash'd, with such a peace.
[*Exeunt.*

[a] And flourish in peace and plenty.] This precious scroll, and its equally ridiculous exposition, form an appropriate sequel to the vision, and were doubtless the work of the same accomplished hand. Mr. Collier suggests, what is extremely probable, that both scroll and vision formed part of an older play; and such riddles being extremely popular on the early stage, Shakespeare may not have liked to omit them.

(*) Old text, *yet this.*

ILLUSTRATIVE COMMENTS.

ACT I.

(1) SCENE I.—*Cymbeline.*] The historical incidents in this piece Shakespeare derived from his old authority, the pages of Holinshed; and they are supposed to occur about the twenty-fourth year of Cymbeline's reign and the forty-second year of the reign of Augustus:—

"After the death of Cassibelane, Theomantius or Tenantius the yoongest sonne of Lud, was made king of Britaine in the yeere of the world 3921, after the building of Rome 706, and before the comming of Christ 45. He is named also in one of the English chronicles Tormace: in the same chronicle it is conteined, that not he, but his brother Androgeus was king, where Geffrey of Monmouth and others testifie that Androgeus abandoned the land clerelie, and continued still at Rome, because he knew the Britains hated him for treason he had committed in aiding Julius Cesar against Cassibelane. Theomantius ruled the land in good quiet, and paid the tribute to the Romans which Cassibellane had granted, and finallie departed this life after he had reigned 22 yeares, and was buried at London.

"Kymbeline or Cimbeline the sonne of Theomantius was of the Britains made king after the deceasse of his father, in the yeare of the world 3944, after the building of Rome 728, and before the birth of our Saviour 33. This man (as some write) was brought up at Rome and there made knight by Augustus Cesar, under whome he served in the warres, and was in such favour with him, that he was at libertie to pay his tribute or not. * * * Touching the continuance of the yeares of Kymbelines reigne, some writers doo varie, but the best approoved affirme, that he reigned 35 yeares and then died, and was buried at London, leaving behind him two sonnes, Guiderius and Arviragus.

"But here it is to be noted, that although our histories doo affirme, that as well this Kymbeline, as also his father Theomantius, lived in quiet with the Romans, and continuallie to them paied the tributes which the Britains had covenanted with Julius Cesar to pay, yet we find in the Romane writers, that after Julius Cesar's death, when Augustus had taken upon him the rule of the empire, the Britains refused to paie that tribute: whereat as Cornelius Tacitus reporteth, Augustus (being otherwise occupied) was contented to winke, howbeit through earnest calling upon to recover his right by such as were desirous to see the uttermost of the British kingdome; at length, to wit, in the tenth yeare after the death of Julius Cesar, which was about the thirteenth yeare of the said Theomantius, Augustus made provision to passe with an armie over into Britaine, and was come forward upon his iourney into Gallia Celtica: or as we maie saie, into these hither parts of France. * * *

"Whether this controversie which appeareth to fall forth betwixt the Britans and Augustus, was occasioned by Kymbeline, or some other prince of the Britains, I have not to avouch: for that by our writers it is reported, that Kymbeline being brought up in Rome, and knighted in the court of Augustus, ever shewed himselfe a friend to the Romans, and chieflie was loth to breake with them, because the youth of the Britaine nation should not be deprived of the benefit to be trained and brought up among the Romans, whereby they might learne both to behave themselves like civill men, and to atteine to the knowledge of feats of warre."—HOLINSHED.

(2) SCENE III.—

—— and then
Have turn'd mine eye, and wept.]

This pathetic description was perhaps suggested by a passage from Golding's translation of "Ovid's Metamorphosis:"—

"She lifting up her watry eyes behild her husband stand
Uppon the Hatches making signes by beckening with his hand:
And she made signes to him againe. And after that the land
Was farre remooved from the ship, and that the sight began
To be unable to discerne the face of any man,
As long as ere she could she lookt upon the rowing keele
And when she could no longer time for distance ken it weele,
She looked still upon the sailes that flasked with the winde
Upon the mast. And when she could the sailes no longer find,
She gate her to her emptie bed with sad and sorie hart."
GOLDING'S *Ovid*, b. xi. (1567).

ACT II.

(1) SCENE II.—

A mole cinque-spotted, like the crimson drops
I' the bottom of a cowslip.]

This particular circumstance is only found in the Italian novel, of which the following is Skottowe's abstract:—

"Several Italian merchants met accidentally in Paris at supper, and conversed freely of their absent wives. 'I know not,' one jestingly remarked, 'how my wife conducts herself in my absence, but of this I am certain, that whenever I meet with an attractive beauty, I make the best advantage I can of the opportunity. 'And so do I,' quoth another, 'for whether I believe my wife unfaithful or not, she will be so, if she pleases.' A third said the same, and all readily coincided in the licentious opinion, except Bernabo Lomellia, of Genoa, who maintained that he had a wife perfectly beautiful, in the flower of youth, and of such indisputable chastity, that he was convinced if he were absent for ten years, she would preserve her fidelity. A young merchant of Piacenza, Ambrogiulo, was extremely facetious on the subject, and concluded some libertine remarks by offering to effect the seduction of this modern Lucretia, provided opportunity were afforded him. Bernabo answered his confident boast by the proposition of a wager, which was instantly accepted.

"According to agreement, Bernabo remained at Paris, while Ambrogiulo set out for Genoa, where his inquiries soon convinced him that Ginevra, the wife of Bernabo, had not been too highly praised, and that his wager would be lost without he could effect by stratagem what he had certainly no probability of obtaining by direct solicitation. Chance threw in his way a poor woman, often employed in the house of Ginevra, whom he secured in his interest by a bribe. Pretending unavoidable absence for a few days, the woman intreated Ginevra to take charge of a large chest till she returned. The lady consented, and the chest, with Ambrogiulo secreted in it, was placed in Ginevra's bedchamber. When the lady retired to rest, the villain crept from his concealment, and by the light of a taper, took particular notice of the pictures and furniture, and the form and situation of the apartment. Advancing to the bed, he eagerly sought for some mark about the lady's person, and at last espied a mole and tuft of golden hair upon her left breast. Then taking a ring, a purse, and other trifles, he returned to his concealment, whence he was not released till the third day, when the woman returned, and had the chest conveyed home.

"Ambrogiulo hastily summoned the merchants in Paris, who were present when the wager was laid. As a proof of his success he produced the stolen trinkets; called them gifts from the lady, and described the furniture of the bed-room. Bernabo acknowledged the correctness of the account, and confessed that the purse and ring belonged to his wife; but added, that as Ambrogiulo might have obtained his account of the room, and procured the jewels also, from some of Ginevra's servants, his claim to the money was not yet established. 'The proofs I have given,' said Ambrogiulo, 'ought to suffice; but as you call on me for more, I will silence your scepticism at once;—Ginevra has a mole on her left breast.' Bernabo's countenance testified the truth of the assertion, and he shortly acknowledged it by words: he then paid the sum he had wagered, and instantly set out for Italy."

(2) SCENE III.—*Hark! hark! the lark at heaven's gate sings, &c.*] The nightingale herself has not more happily inspired our early poets than the lark. Hear, with what melody the father of them all makes the morning songster's carol welcome the glorious sun,—

"The busy larke, messager of daye
Salueth in hire song the morwe gray:
And fyry Phebus ryseth up so bright,
That al the orient laugheth of the light."
CHAUCER's *Knightes Tale.*

Hear, too, Spenser:—

"Wake now my love, awake; for it is time,
The Rosy Morne long since left Tithones bed,
All ready to her silver coche to clyme,
And Phœbus gins to shew his glorious hed.
Hark how the cheerefull birds do chaunt theyr laies
And carroll of loves praise.
The merry Larke hir mattins sings aloft,
The thrush replyes, the Mavis descant playes,
The Ouzell shrills, the Ruddock warbles soft,
So goodly all agree with sweet consent,
To this dayes merriment."—*Epithalamion*, 1595.

Nor forget Shakespeare, again, on the same theme, in his "Venus and Adonis:"—

"Lo here the gentle lark, weary of rest,
From his moist cabinet mounts up on high,
And wakes the morning, from whose silver breast
The sun ariseth in his majesty."

Nor Milton, in his "Paradise Lost," Book V.:—

"—— ye birds
That singing *up to heaven's gate* ascend."

(3) SCENE IV.—
—— her attendants are
All sworn, and honourable.]

"It was anciently the custom for the attendants on our nobility and other great personages (as it is now for the servants of the king) to take an oath of fidelity on their entrance into office. In the household book of the 5th Earl of Northumberland (compiled A.D. 1512), it is expressly ordered [p. 49] that 'what person soever he be that commyth to my Lordes service, that incontynent after he be intred in the chequyrroull [check-roll] that he be *sworn* in the countynge-hous by a gentillman-usher or yeman-usher in the presence of the hede officers; and on theire absence before the clerke of the kechynge either by such an oath as is in the Book of Othes, yff any such [oath] be, or ells by such an oth as thei shall seyme beste by their discretion.'"—PERCY.

ACT III.

(1) SCENE I.—
The fam'd Cassibelan, who was once at point,—
O, giglot Fortune!—to master Cæsar's sword,
Made Lud's town with rejoicing fires bright,
And Britons strut with courage.]

"Thus according to that which Cesar himselfe and other authentick authors have written, was Britaine made tributarie to the Romans by the conduct of the same Cesar. But our histories farre differ from this, affirming that Cesar comming the second time, was by the Britaines with valiancie and martiall prowesse beaten and repelled, as he was at the first, and speciallie by meanes that Cassibellane had pight in the Thames great piles of trees piked with yron, through which his ships being entred the river, were perished and lost. And after his comming a land, he was vanquished in battell, and constrained to flee into Gallia with those ships that remained. For ioy of this second victorie (saith Galfrid) Cassibellane made a great feast at London, and there did sacrifice to the gods."—HOLINSHED.

The same chronicler thus accounts for the name of Lud's town:—

"Lud began his reigne, in the yeere after the creation of the world 3895, after the building of the citie of Rome 679, before the comming of Christ 72, and before the Romanes entred Britaine 19 yeeres. This Lud proved a right woorthie prince, amending the lawes of the realme that were defective, abolishing evill customs and maners used among his people, and repairing old cities and tounes which were decaied: but speciallie he delited most to beautifie and inlarge with buildings the citie of Troinovant, which he compassed with a strong wall made of lime and stone, in the best maner fortified with diverse faire towers: and in the west part of the same wall he erected a strong gate, which he commanded to be called after his name, Luds gate, and so unto this daie it is called Ludgate, (S) onelie drowned in pronuntiation of the word. * * * By reason that king Lud so much esteemed that citie before all other of his realme, inlarging it so greatlie as he did, and continuallie in manner remained there, the name was changed, so that it was called Caerlud, that to saie, Luds towne: and after by corruption of speech it was named London."—*History of England,* Book III. c. 9.

(2) SCENE I.—

—— *Mulmutius made our laws,*
Who was the first of Britain which did put
His brows within a golden crown, and call'd
Himself a king.]

"Mulmucius Dunwallo, or as other saie Dunwallo Mulmucius, the sonne of Cloton, got the upper hand of the other dukes or rulers: and after his fathers deceasse began his reigne over the whole monarchie of Britaine, in the yeere of the world 3529. * * This Mulmucius Dunwallo is named in the english chronicle Donebant, and prooved a right worthie prince. He builded within the citie of London then called Troinovant, a temple, and called it the temple of peace. * * He also made manie good lawes, which were long after used, called Mulmucius lawes, turned out of the British speech into the Latine by Gildas Priscus, and long time after translated out of latine into english by Alfred king of England, and mingled in his statutes. * * After he had established his land, and set his Britains in good and convenient order, he ordeined him by the advise of his lords a crowne of golde, and caused himselfe with greate solemnitie to be crowned, according to the custom of the pagan lawes then in use: and bicause he was the first that bare a crowne heere in Britaine, after the opinion of some writers, he is named the first king of Britaine, and all the other before rehearsed are named rulers, dukes, or governors."—HOLINSHED.

(3) SCENE IV.—

—— *a garment out of fashion;*
And for I am richer than to hang by the walls,
I must be ripp'd.]

"To 'hang by the walls,'" Steevens remarks, "does not mean, to be converted into *hangings for a room,* but to be *hung up,* as useless, among the neglected contents of a *wardrobe.* So in 'Measure for Measure:'—

'That have, like unscour'd armour, *hung by the wall.*'

"When a boy, at an ancient mansion-house in Suffolk, I saw one of these repositories, which (thanks to a succession of old maids!) had been preserved with superstitious reverence for almost a century and a half.

"Clothes were not formerly, as at present, made of slight materials, were not kept in drawers, or given away as soon as lapse of time or change of fashion had impaired their value. On the contrary, they were hung up on wooden pegs in a room appropriated to the sole purpose of receiving them; and though such cast-off things as were composed of *rich* substances were occasionally *ripped* for domestic uses (viz. mantles for infants, vests for children, and counterpanes for beds), articles of inferior quality were suffered to *hang by the walls,* till age and moths had destroyed what pride would not permit to be worn by servants or poor relations."

ACT V.

(1) SCENE III.—*A narrow lane, an old man, and two boys!*] Holinshed relates the story whence this incident is taken as having happened in Scotland during the reign of king Kenneth, A.D. 976.

"The Danes, perceiving that there was no hope of life, but in victorie, rushed forth with such violence upon their adversaries, that first the right, and then after the left wing of the Scots, was constreined to retire and flee backe, the middle warde stoutly yet keeping their ground: but the same stood in such danger, being now left naked on the sides, that the victorie must needes have remained with the Danes, had not a renewer of the battell come in time, by the appointment (as is to be thought) of almightie God.

"For as it chanced, there was in the next field at the same time an husbandman, with two of his sons busie about his worke, named Haie, a man strong and stiffe in making and shape of bodie, but indued with a valiant courage. This Haie beholding the king with the most part of the nobles, fighting with great valiancie in the middle ward, now destitute of the wings, and in great danger to be oppressed with the great violence of his enimies, caught a plow-beame in his hand, and with the same exhorting his sonnes to doo the like hasted towards the battell. * * There was neere to the place of the battell a long lane fensed on the sides with ditches and walles made of turfe, through the which the Scots which fled were beaten down by the enimies in heapes.

"Here Haie with his sonnes, supposing they might best staie the fight, placed themselves overthwart the lane, beat them backe whom they met fleeing, and spared neither friend nor fo: but downe they went all such as came within their reach, wherewith diverse hardie personages cried unto their fellowes to returne back unto the battell." —*Historie of Scotland,* fo. 155.

CRITICAL OPINIONS ON CYMBELINE.

"CYMBELINE is one of Shakspeare's most wonderful compositions. He has here combined a novel of Boccacio's with traditionary tales of the ancient Britons reaching back to the times of the first Roman emperors, and he has contrived, by the most gentle transitions, to blend together into one harmonious whole the social manners of the newest times with olden heroic deeds, and even with appearances of the gods. In the character of Imogen no one feature of female excellence is omitted: her chaste tenderness, her softness, and her virgin pride, her boundless resignation, and her magnanimity towards her mistaken husband, by whom she is unjustly persecuted, her adventures in disguise, her apparent death, and her recovery, form altogether a picture equally tender and affecting. The two Princes, Guiderius and Arviragus, both educated in the wilds, form a noble contrast to Miranda and Perdita. Shakspeare is fond of showing the superiority of the natural over the artificial. Over the art which enriches nature, he somewhere says, there is a higher art created by nature herself.* As Miranda's unconscious and unstudied sweetness is more pleasing than those charms which endeavour to captivate us by the brilliant embellishments of a refined cultivation, so in these two youths, to whom the chase has given vigour and hardihood, but who are ignorant of their high destination, and have been brought up apart from human society, we are equally enchanted by a *naïve* heroism which leads them to anticipate and to dream of deeds of valour, till an occasion is offered which they are irresistibly compelled to embrace. When Imogen comes in disguise to their cave; when, with all the innocence of childhood, Guiderius and Arviragus form an impassioned friendship for the tender boy, in whom they neither suspect a female nor their own sister; when, on their return from the chase, they find her dead, then 'sing her to the ground,' and cover the grave with flowers:—these scenes might give to the most deadened imagination a new life for poetry. If a tragical event is only apparent, in such case, whether the spectators are already aware of it or ought merely to suspect it, Shakspeare always knows how to mitigate the impression without weakening it: he makes the mourning musical, that it may gain in solemnity what it loses in seriousness. With respect to the other parts, the wise and vigorous Belarius, who, after long living as a hermit, again becomes a hero, is a venerable figure; the Italian Iachimo's ready dissimulation and quick presence of mind is quite suitable to the bold treachery which he plays; Cymbeline, the father of Imogen, and even her husband Posthumus, during the first half of the piece,

---

* The passage in Shakspeare here quoted, taken with the context, will not bear the construction of the critic. The whole runs thus:—

> " Yet nature is made better by no mean,
> But nature makes that mean: so, o'er that art
> Which you say adds to nature, is an art
> That nature makes. You see, sweet maid, we marry
> A gentler scion to the wildest stock;
> And make conceive a bark of baser kind
> By bud of nobler race: this is an art
> Which does mend nature, change it rather; but
> The art itself is nature."—*Winter's Tale*, Act IV. Sc. 3.

Shakspeare does not here mean to institute a comparison between the relative excellency of that which is innate and that which we owe to instruction; but merely says, that the instruction or art is itself a part of nature. The speech is addressed by Polyxenes to Perdita, to persuade her that the changes effected in the appearance of flowers by the art of the gardener are not to be accounted unnatural; and the expression of *making conceive a bark of baser kind by bud of nobler race* (*i.e.* engrafting), would rather lead to the inference, that the mind derived its chief value from the influence of culture.—TRANS.

are somewhat sacrificed, but this could not be otherwise: the false and wicked Queen is merely an instrument of the plot; she and her stupid son Cloten (the only comic part in the piece), whose rude arrogance is portrayed with much humour, are, before the conclusion, got rid of by merited punishment. As for the heroical part of the fable,—the war between the Romans and Britons, which brings on the *dénouement*, the poet in the extent of his plan had so little room to spare, that he merely endeavours to represent it as a mute procession. But to the last scene, where all the numerous threads of the knot are untied, he has again given its full development, that he might collect together into one focus the scattered impressions of the whole. This example and many others are a sufficient refutation of Johnson's assertion, that Shakspeare usually hurries over the conclusion of his pieces. Rather does he, from a desire to satisfy the feelings, introduce a great deal which, so far as the understanding of the *dénouement* requires, might in a strict sense be justly spared: our modern spectators are much more impatient to see the curtain drop, when there is nothing more to be determined, than those of his day could have been."—SCHLEGEL.

"This play, if not, in the construction of its fable, one of the most perfect of our author's productions, is, in point of poetic beauty, of variety and truth of character, and in the display of sentiment and emotion, one of the most lovely and interesting. Nor can we avoid expressing our astonishment at the sweeping condemnation which Johnson has passed upon it; charging its fiction with folly, its conduct with absurdity, its events with impossibility; terming its faults too evident for detection and too gross for aggravation.

"Of the enormous injustice of this sentence, nearly every page of *Cymbeline* will, to a reader of any taste or discrimination, bring the most decisive evidence. That it possesses many of the too common inattentions of Shakspeare, that it exhibits a frequent violation of costume, and a singular confusion of nomenclature, cannot be denied; but these are trifles light as air when contrasted with its merits, which are of the very essence of dramatic worth, rich and full in all that breathes of vigour, animation, and intellect, in all that elevates the fancy, and improves the heart, in all that fills the eye with tears, or agitates the soul with hope and fear.

"In possession of excellences vital as these must be deemed, cold and fastidious is the criticism that, on account of irregularities in mere technical detail, would shut its eyes upon their splendour. Nor are there wanting critics of equal learning with, and superior taste to Johnson, who have considered what he has branded with the unqualified charge of 'confusion of manners,' as forming, in a certain point of view, one of the most pleasing recommendations of the piece. It may be also remarked, that, if the unities of time and place be as little observed in this play, as in many others of the same poet, unity of character and feeling, the test of genius, and without which the utmost effort of art will ever be unavailing, is uniformly and happily supported.

"Imogen, the most lovely and perfect of Shakspeare's female characters, the pattern of connubial love and chastity, by the delicacy and propriety of her sentiments, by her sensibility, tenderness, and resignation, by her patient endurance of persecution from the quarter where she had confidently looked for endearment and protection, irresistibly seizes upon our affections; and when compelled to fly from the paternal roof, from

> "A father cruel, and a step-dame false,
> A foolish suitor to a wedded lady,
> That hath her husband banished,"

she is driven to assume, under the name of Fidele, the disguise of a page, we follow her footsteps with the liveliest interest and admiration.

"The scenes which disclose the incidents of her pilgrimage; her reception at the cave of Belarius; her intercourse with her lost brothers, who are ignorant of their birth and rank, her supposed death, funeral rites and resuscitation, are wrought up with a mixture of pathos and romantic wildness peculiarly characteristic of our author's genius, and which has had but few successful imitators. Among these few, stands pre-eminent the poet Collins, who seems to have trodden this consecrated ground with a congenial mind, and who has sung the sorrows of Fidele in strains worthy of their subject, and which will continue to charm the mind and soothe the heart 'till pity's self be dead.'

"When compared with this fascinating portrait, the other personages of the drama appear but in a secondary light. Yet are they adequately brought out, and skilfully diversified; the treacherous subtlety of Iachimo, the sage experience of Belarius, the native nobleness of heart, and innate heroism of mind, which burst forth in the vigorous sketches of Guiderius and Arviragus, the temerity, credulity, and penitence of Posthumus, the uxorious weakness of Cymbeline, the hypocrisy of his Queen, and the comic arrogance of Cloten, half fool and half knave, produce a striking diversity of action and sentiment.

"Of this latter character, the constitution has been thought so extraordinary, and involving elements of a kind so incompatible, as to form an exception to the customary integrity and consistency of our author's draughts from nature. But the following passage from the pen of an elegant female writer, will prove, that this curious assemblage of frequently opposite qualities has existed, and no doubt did exist in the days of Shakspeare:—'It is curious that Shakspeare should, in so singular a character as Cloten, have given the exact prototype of a being whom I once knew. The unmeaning frown of the countenance; the shuffling gait; the burst of voice; the bustling insignificance; the fever and ague fits of valour; the froward tetchiness; the unprincipled malice; and, what is most curious, those occasional gleams of good sense, amidst the floating clouds of folly which generally darkened and confused the man's brain; and which, in the character of Cloten, we are apt to impute to a violation of unity in character; but in the sometime Captain C——n, I saw that the portrait of Cloten was not out of nature.'

"Poetical justice has been strictly observed in this drama; the vicious characters meet the punishment due to their crimes, while virtue, in all its various degrees, is proportionably rewarded. The scene of retribution, which is the closing one of the play, is a masterpiece of skill; the development of the plot, for its fulness, completeness, and ingenuity, surpassing any effort of the kind among our author's contemporaries, and atoning for any partial incongruity which the structure or conduct of the story may have previously displayed."—DRAKE.

VOLUME THREE.

Contents.

Vol. III. Act I. Sc. 2.

THE TEMPEST.

The earliest copy of "The Tempest" known is that in the folio of 1623. To the precise date of its production we have no clue, but the following memorandum from the "Accounts of the Revels at Court," is almost positive testimony that it was written before 1611:—

By the King's Players.	Hallomas nyght was presented att Whithall before ye Kinges Matie. a play called the Tempest.

And the speech of Gonzalo, Act II. Sc. 1,—

"I' the commonwealth I would by contraries," &c.—

which is obviously taken from a passage in Florio's translation of Montaigne's Essayes, first printed in 1603, is equally decisive as to its having been written after that year. The story upon which "The Tempest" is founded, was most probably derived, according to Shakespeare's usual practice, from an existing play or from some popular chronicle or romance. Collins the poet, indeed, informed T. Warton, that he had met with a novel called *Aurelio and Isabella,* printed in Italian, Spanish, French, and English in 1588, which he conceived to have formed the basis of "The Tempest." When he spoke of the circumstance, however, Collins was labouring under mental debility, and so far as the particular novel he mentioned was concerned his memory deceived him, for the fable of Aurelio and Isabella bears no resemblance to that of the play; yet it is remarkable that a friend of James Boswell declared that he had once perused an Italian novel which answered to Collins's description. In an article on the early English and German dramas published in the New Monthly Magazine for January, 1841, Mr. Thoms pointed out a dramatic piece by Jacob Ayrer, a notary of Nürnberg, contemporary with Shakespeare, entitled *Die schöne Sidea,* (The Beautiful Sidea,) which bears some resemblance to "The Tempest," and which Tieck conjectured was a translation of some old English drama from which Shakespeare borrowed his idea. How far this is probable the reader must judge from the following outline of the German play: Ludolph having been vanquished by his rival, and with his daughter Sidea driven into a forest, rebukes her for complaining of their change of fortune, and then summons his spirit Runcifal to learn from him his future destiny and prospects of revenge. Runcifal, who is, like Ariel, somewhat "moody," announces to Ludolph that the son of his enemy will shortly become his prisoner. After a comic episode, most probably introduced by the German, we see Prince Leudegast, with his son Engelbrecht and the councillors, hunting in the same forest; when Engelbrecht and his companion Famulus, having separated from the associates, are suddenly encountered by Ludolph and his daughter. On his commanding them to yield themselves prisoners, they refuse; but on attempting to draw their swords, Ludolph renders them powerless by the touch of his magical wand, and gives the prince over to Sidea to carry logs of wood for her, and to obey her commands in all respects. The resemblance between the German and English plays is continued in a later part of the former production, when Sidea, moved by pity for the labours of Engelbrecht in carrying logs, exclaims, she would "feel great joy, if he would prove faithful to me, and take me in wedlock;" an event which, in the end, is happily brought about, and leads to the reconciliation of their parents, the rival princes.

The title of "The Tempest" is supposed by some commentators to have been determined by the shipwreck of Sir George Sommers and Sir Thomas Gates on the coast of the Bermudas in 1609;

of which an account was published by Silvester Jourdan, one of the crew, in the following year:—*A Discovery of the Barmudas; otherwise called the Isle of Divels; by Sir Thomas Gates, Sir George Sommers, and Captayne Newport, with divers others*. It is highly probable, too, that Jourdan's and other accounts of the Bermudas, by some of which they are said to be enchanted and inhabited by witches and devils, suggested the expression "still-vexed Bermoothes," and induced the poet to possess his hero with necromantic influence and supernatural agency. Mr. Hunter, in his "Disquisition on the Scene, Origin, Date, &c. of Shakspeare's Tempest," has laboured with great ingenuity to prove that the actual scene of the play was Lampedusa, "an island of the Mediterranean lying not far out of a ship's course passing from Tunis to Naples," and which is uninhabited, and supposed by sailors to be enchanted. The same idea was suggested, or occurred to Douce, who thus speaks of it:—"The Island of Lampedusa is near the coast of Tunis; and from its description, in Dapper, and the real tract of the King of Naples' voyage in Shakespeare's Tempest, will turn out to be the veritable island where he was shipwrecked, and to which Prospero had been banished, whenever the Italian novel on which the play founded shall be discovered." We fervently hope not; being contented to believe it rose, like a new Atlantis, at the summons of the poet, and when his magic work on it was done:—

"From that day forth the Isle has beene
By wandering sailors never seene:
Some say 't is buried deepe
Beneath the sea, which breakes and rores
Above its savage rockie shores,
Nor ere is known to sleepe."

Persons Represented.

ALONSO, *King of* Naples.

FERDINAND, *his Son.*

SEBASTIAN, *Brother to the King.*

PROSPERO, *the rightful Duke of* Milan.

ANTONIO, *his Brother, the Usurping Duke of* Milan.

GONZALO, *an honest old Counsellor.*

ADRIAN, FRANCISCO, } *Lords.*

STEPHANO, *a drunken Butler.*

TRINCULO, *a Jester.*

Master *of a Ship,* Boatswain, *and* Mariners.

CALIBAN, *a savage and deformed Slave.*

MIRANDA, *Daughter to* Prospero.

ARIEL, *an airy Spirit.*

JUNO, CERES, IRIS, Nymphs, Reapers, } *Spirits.*

Other Spirits *attending on* Prospero.

SCENE,—*On board a* SHIP *at* SEA; *afterwards on an* ISLAND.

ACT I.

SCENE I.—*On a Ship at Sea. A tempestuous noise of thunder and lightning heard.*

Enter a Ship-master *and a* Boatswain *severally.*

MASTER. Boatswain!

BOATS. Here, master: what cheer?

MASTER. Good, speak to the mariners: fall to't yarely,[a] or we run ourselves aground: bestir, bestir. [*Exit.*

a Yarely,—] *Briskly, nimbly, actively.*

Enter Mariners.

BOATS. Heigh, my hearts! cheerly, cheerly, my hearts! yare, yare! Take in the topsail! Tend to the master's whistle! [*Exeunt* Mariners.] Blow, till thou burst thy wind, if room enough!

Enter ALONSO, FERDINAND, SEBASTIAN, ANTONIO, GONZALO, *and others*.

ALON. Good boatswain, have care. Where's the master? Play the men.

BOATS. I pray now, keep below.

ANT. Where is the master, boson?

BOATS. Do you not hear him? You mar our labour: keep your cabins: you do assist the storm.

GON. Nay, good, be patient.

BOATS. When the sea is. Hence! what care these roarers for the name of king? To cabin: silence! trouble us not.

GON. Good, yet remember whom thou hast aboard.

BOATS. None that I more love than myself. You are a counsellor;—if you can command these elements to silence, and work the peace of the present, we will not hand a rope more; use your authority: if you cannot, give thanks you have lived so long, and make yourself ready in your cabin for the mischance of the hour, if it so hap.—Cheerly, good hearts!—Out of our way, I say. [*Exit.*

GON. I have great comfort from this fellow; methinks he hath no drowning mark upon him; his complexion is perfect gallows. Stand fast, good Fate, to his hanging! make the rope of his destiny our cable, for our own doth little advantage! If he be not born to be hanged, our case is miserable. [*Exeunt.*

Re-enter Boatswain.

BOATS. Down with the topmast! yare; lower, lower! Bring her to try with main-course![a] [*A cry within.*] A plague upon this howling! they are louder than the weather or our office.—

Re-enter SEBASTIAN, ANTONIO, *and* GONZALO.

Yet again! what do you here? shall we give o'er and drown? have you a mind to sink?

SEB. A pox o' your throat, you bawling, blasphemous, incharitable dog!

BOATS. Work you, then.

ANT. Hang, cur, hang! you whoreson, insolent noise-maker, we are less afraid to be drowned than thou art.

GON. I'll warrant him for drowning; though the ship were no stronger than a nutshell, and as leaky as an unstanched wench.

BOATS. Lay her a-hold, a-hold! set her two courses! off to sea again; lay her off!

Re-enter Mariners, *wet*.

MAR. All lost! to prayers, to prayers! all lost! [*Exeunt.*

BOATS. What, must our mouths be cold?

GON. The king and prince at prayers! let 's assist them,
For our case is as theirs.

SEB. I'm out of patience.

ANT. We are merely cheated of our lives by drunkards:—
This wide-chapp'd rascal,—would thou mightst lie drowning,
The washing of ten tides!

GON. He'll be hang'd yet,
Though every drop of water swear against it,
And gape at wid'st to glut him.

[*A confused noise within.*]—*Mercy on us!—*
We split, we split!—Farewell, my wife and children!
Farewell, brother! We split, we split, we split!—(1)
[*Exit* Boatswain.

ANT. Let's all sink with the king. [*Exit.*

SEB. Let's take leave of him. [*Exit.*

GON. Now would I give a thousand furlongs of sea for an acre of barren ground,—long heath, brown furze, anything. The wills above be done! but I would fain die a dry death. [*Exit.*

SCENE II.—*The* Island: *before the Cell of* Prospero.

Enter PROSPERO *and* MIRANDA.

MIRA. If by your art, my dearest father, you have
Put the wild waters in this roar, allay them.[b]
The sky, it seems, would pour down stinking pitch,

---

[a] Bring her to try with main-course!] It has been proposed to read, "Bring her to; try with the main-course;" but see a passage from Hakluyt's Voyages, 1598, quoted by Malone:—"and when the barke had way, we cut the hawser and so gate the sea to our friend, and *tryed out* al that day with *our maine corse.*"

[b] If by your art, my dearest father, you have
Put the wild waters in this roar, allay them.]
These lines are not metrical, and sound but gratingly on the ear. It would be an improvement perhaps if we read them thus,—
"If by your art, my dearest father, you
Have put the wild waters in this roar, allay them."

But that the sea, mounting to the welkin's cheek,[a]
Dashes the fire out. O, I have suffer'd
With those that I saw suffer! a brave vessel,
Who had, no doubt, some noble creatures* in her,
Dash'd all to pieces. O, the cry did knock
Against my very heart! Poor souls, they perish'd!
Had I been any god of power, I would
Have sunk the sea within the earth, or e'er
It should the good ship so have swallow'd, and
The fraughting souls within her.

PRO. Be collected;
No more amazement: tell your piteous heart
There's no harm done.

MIRA. O, woe the day!

PRO. No harm.
I have done nothing but in care of thee,—

(*) Old text, *creature*.

[a] —— *mounting to the welkin's* cheek,—] Although we have, in "Richard II." Act III. Sc. 2,—"the cloudy *cheeks* of heaven," and elsewhere, "welkin's face," and "heaven's face," it may well be questioned whether "cheek," in this place, is not a misprint. Mr. Collier's annotator substitutes *heat*, a change characterised by Mr. Dyce as "equally tasteless and absurd." A more appropriate and expressive word, one, too, sanctioned in some measure by its occurrence in Ariel's description of the same elemental conflict, is probably, *crack*, or *cracks*,—

"—— the fire, and *cracks*
Of sulphurous roaring, the most mighty Neptune
Seem to besiege," &c.

In Miranda's picture of the tempest, the sea is seen to storm and overwhelm the tremendous artillery of heaven; in that of Ariel, the sky's ordnance, "the fire and cracks," assault the "mighty Neptune." *Crack*, in the emphatic sense it formerly bore of *crash, discharge*, or *explosion*, is very common in our old writers thus, in Marlowe's "Tamburlaine the Great," Part I. Act IV Sc. 2,—

"As when a fiery exhalation,
Wrapt in the bowels of a freezing cloud
Fighting for passage, makes the *welkin cracke*."

Again, in some verses prefixed to Coryat's "Crudities,"—

"A skewed engine mathematicall
To draw up words that make the *welkin cracke*."

And in Taylor's *Superbiæ Flagellum*, 1630,—

"Yet every Reall heav'nly *Thundercracke*,
This Caitife in such feare and terror strake," &c.

Of thee, my dear one! thee, my daughter,—who
Art ignorant of what thou art, nought knowing
Of whence I am; nor that I am more better
Than Prospero, master of a full-poor cell,
And thy no greater father.

MIRA. More to know
Did never meddle with my thoughts.

PRO. 'T is time
I should inform thee further. Lend thy hand,
And pluck my magic garment from me.—So;
[*Lays down his robe.*
Lie there, my art.—Wipe thou thine eyes; have comfort.
The direful spectacle of the wreck, which touch'd
The very virtue of compassion in thee,
I have with such provision in mine art
So safely order'd, that there is no soul—[a]
No, not so much perdition as an hair,
Betid to any creature in the vessel
Which thou heard'st cry, which thou saw'st sink. Sit down;
For thou must now know further.

MIRA. You have often[b]
Begun to tell me what I am; but stopp'd,
And left me to a bootless inquisition,
Concluding, *Stay, not yet.*—

PRO. The hour's now come;
The very minute bids thee ope thine ear;
Obey, and be attentive. Canst thou remember
A time before we came unto this cell?
I do not think thou canst, for then thou wast not
Out three years old.[c]

MIRA. Certainly, sir, I can.

PRO. By what? by any other house or person?
Of anything the image, tell me, that
Hath kept with thy remembrance.

MIRA. 'T is far off,
And rather like a dream than an assurance
That my remembrance warrants. Had I not
Four or five women once that tended me?

PRO. Thou hadst, and more, Miranda. But how is it
That this lives in thy mind? What see'st thou else
In the dark backward and abysm of time?
If thou remember'st aught ere thou cam'st here,
How thou cam'st here thou mayst.

MIRA. But that I do not.

PRO. Twelve year since, Miranda, twelve year since,
Thy father was the duke of Milan, and
A prince of power.

MIRA. Sir, are not you my father?

PRO. Thy mother was a piece of virtue, and
She said thou wast my daughter; and thy father
Was duke of Milan; and his only heir
A princess,[d] no worse issued.

MIRA. O, the heavens!
What foul play had we, that we came from thence?
Or blessed was't we did?

PRO. Both, both, my girl:
By foul play, as thou say'st, were we heav'd thence;
But blessedly holp hither.

MIRA. O, my heart bleeds
To think o' the teen[e] that I have turn'd you to,
Which is from my remembrance! Please you, further.

PRO. My brother, and thy uncle, call'd Antonio,—
I pray thee, mark me,—that a brother should
Be so perfidious!—he whom, next thyself,
Of all the world I lov'd, and to him put
The manage of my state; as, at that time,
Through all the signiories it was the first,—
And Prospero the prime duke;—being so reputed
In dignity, and for the liberal arts
Without a parallel: those being all my study,
The government I cast upon my brother,
And to my state grew stranger, being transported
And rapt in secret studies. Thy false uncle—
Dost thou attend me?

MIRA. Sir, most heedfully.

PRO. Being once perfected how to grant suits,
How to deny them, who to advance, and who
To trash[f] for over-topping,—new created
The creatures that were mine, I say, or chang'd 'em,
Or else new form'd 'em; having both the key
Of officer and office, set all hearts i' the state
To what tune pleas'd his ear; that now he was
The ivy which had hid my princely trunk,
And suck'd my verdure out on't.—Thou attend'st not.

MIRA. O good sir, I do.

PRO. I pray thee, mark me.
I thus neglecting worldly ends, all dedicated
To closeness, and the bettering of my mind
With that, which, but by being so retir'd,
O'er-priz'd all popular rate, in my false brother
Awak'd an evil nature; and my trust,

---

a —— *that there is no* soul—] Rowe prints,—
"—— that there is no soul *lost;*"
Theobald, "that there is no *foyle;*" and Johnson, "that there is no *soil.*" We believe, notwithstanding Steevens' remark that "such interruptions are not uncommon to Shakspeare," that "soul" is a typographical error, and that the author wrote, as Capell reads,—
"—— that there is no *loss,*
No, not so much perdition as an hair
Betid to any creature," &c.

b *You have* often, &c.] Query, "You have *oft,*" &c.

c Out *three years old.*] That is, *past,* or *more than,* three years old.

d A *princess,*—] In the old text, "*And* Princesse." The correction is due to Pope.

e Teen—] *Sorrow, vexation.*

f *To* trash *for over-topping,*—] To clog or impede, lest they should run too fast. The expression *to trash* is a hunting technical. In the present day sportsmen check the speed of very fleet hounds by tying a rope, called a *dog-trash,* round their necks, and letting them trail it after them: formerly they effected the object by attaching to them a weight, sometimes called in jest a *clogdogdo.*

Like a good parent, did beget of him
A falsehood, in its contrary as great
As my trust was; which had indeed no limit,
A confidence sans bound. He being thus lorded,
Not only with what my revenue yielded,
But what my power might else exact,—like one
Who having unto truth, by telling of it,
Made such a sinner of his memory,
To credit his own lie,[a]—he did believe
He was indeed the duke; out o' the substitution,
And executing the outward face of royalty,
With all prerogative:—hence his ambition growing,—
Dost thou hear?

MIRA. Your tale, sir, would cure deafness.

PRO. To have no screen between this part he play'd
And him he play'd it for, he needs will be
Absolute Milan. Me, poor man! my library
Was dukedom large enough; of temporal royalties
He thinks me now incapable; confederates
(So dry he was for sway) with the* king of Naples,
To give him annual tribute, do him homage;
Subject his coronet to his crown, and bend
The dukedom, yet unbow'd,—alas, poor Milan!—
To most ignoble stooping.

MIRA. O the heavens!

PRO. Mark his condition, and the event; then tell me,
If this might be a brother.

MIRA. I should sin
To think but nobly of my grandmother:
Good wombs have borne bad sons.

PRO. Now the condition.
This king of Naples, being an enemy
To me inveterate, hearkens my brother's suit;
Which was, that he, in lieu[b] o' the premises
Of homage, and I know not how much tribute,
Should presently extirpate me and mine
Out of the dukedom, and confer fair Milan,
With all the honours, on my brother: whereon,
A treacherous army levied, one midnight
Fated to the purpose,[c] did Antonio open
The gates of Milan; and, i' the dead of darkness,
The ministers for the purpose hurried thence
Me, and thy crying self.

MIRA. Alack, for pity!
I, not rememb'ring how I cried out then,
Will cry it o'er again: it is a hint
That wrings my eyes to't.

PRO. Hear a little further,
And then I'll bring thee to the present business
Which now's upon us; without the which, this story
Were most impertinent.

MIRA. Wherefore did they not
That hour destroy us?

PRO. Well demanded, wench:
My tale provokes that question. Dear, they durst not,—
So dear the love my people bore me,—nor set
A mark so bloody on the business; but
With colours fairer painted their foul ends.
In few,[d] they hurried us aboard a bark,
Bore us some leagues to sea; where they prepar'd
A rotten carcass of a boat,* not rigg'd,
Nor tackle, sail, nor mast; the very rats
Instinctively have quit it: there they hoist us,
To cry to the sea that roar'd to us; to sigh
To the winds, whose pity, sighing back again,
Did us but loving wrong.

MIRA. Alack, what trouble
Was I then to you?

PRO. O, a cherubin
Thou wast that did preserve me! Thou didst smile,
Infused with a fortitude from heaven,
When I have deck'd[e] the sea with drops full salt;
Under my burthen groan'd; which rais'd in me
An undergoing stomach, to bear up
Against what should ensue.

MIRA. How came we ashore?

PRO. By Providence divine.
Some food we had, and some fresh water, that
A noble Neapolitan, Gonzalo,
Out of his charity,—who being then appointed
Master of this design,—did give us; with
Rich garments, linens, stuffs, and necessaries,
Which since have steaded much; so, of his gentleness,
Knowing I lov'd my books, he furnish'd me,
From mine own library, with volumes that
I prize above my dukedom.

MIRA. Would I might
But ever see that man!

(*) Old text omits, *the*.

(*) Old text, *Butt*.

[a] —— *like one*
Who having unto *truth, by telling of it,*
Made such a sinner of his memory,
To credit his own lie,—]

The folios have, "*into* truth," which Warburton amended; but this we suspect is not the only correction needed, the passage as it stands, though intelligible, being very hazily expressed. Mr. Collier's annotator would read,—

"—— like one
Who having *to untruth*, by telling of it," &c.

and this emendation is entitled to more respect than it has received.

[b] In lieu—] *In lieu* means here, in *guerdon*, or *consideration;* not as it usually signifies, *instead*, or *in place.*

[c] *Fated to the* purpose,—] Mr. Collier's annotator reads,—"Fated to the practice;" and as "purpose" is repeated two lines below, the substitution is an improvement.

[d] In few,—] *To be brief; in a few words.*

[e] Deck'd—] *Decked*, if not a corruption for *degged*, an old provincialism, probably meant the same, that is, *sprinkled.*

Pro. [*Aside to* Ariel, *above.*] Now I arise :—[a]
Sit still, and hear the last of our sea-sorrow.
Here in this island we arriv'd ; and here
Have I, thy schoolmaster, made thee more profit
Than other princess' can, that have more time
For vainer hours, and tutors not so careful.
Mira. Heavens thank you for't ! And now, I pray you, sir,—
For still 'tis beating in my mind,—your reason
For raising this sea-storm ?
Pro. Know thus far forth.
By accident most strange, bountiful Fortune—
Now my dear lady—hath mine enemies
Brought to this shore ; and by my prescience
I find my zenith doth depend upon
A most auspicious star, whose influence
If now I court not, but omit, my fortunes
Will ever after droop.—Here cease more questions :
Thou art inclin'd to sleep ; 't is a good dulness,
And give it way ;—I know thou canst not choose.—
[Miranda *sleeps.*
Come away, servant, come ! I am ready now :
Approach, my Ariel ; come !

Enter Ariel.(2)

Ari. All hail, great master ! grave sir, hail ! I come
To answer thy best pleasure ; be't to fly,
To swim, to dive into the fire, to ride
On the curl'd clouds,—to thy strong bidding, task
Ariel, and all his quality.
Pro. Hast thou, spirit,
Perform'd to point the tempest that I bade thee ?
Ari. To every article.
I boarded the king's ship ; now on the beak,
Now in the waist, the deck, in every cabin,
I flam'd amazement : sometime I'd divide
And burn in many places ; on the topmast,
The yards, and bowsprit,* would I flame distinctly,[b]
Then meet, and join.(3) Jove's lightnings,† the precursors
O' the dreadful thunder-claps, more momentary
And sight-outrunning were not : the fire, and cracks
Of sulphurous roaring, the most mighty Neptune
Seem to besiege, and make his bold waves tremble,
Yea, his dread trident shake.

---

a Now I arise :—] The purport of these words has never been satisfactorily explained, because they have been always understood as addressed to Miranda. If we suppose them directed not to her, but aside to Ariel, who has entered, invisible except to Prospero, after having

" Perform'd to point the tempest,"

and whose arrival occasions Prospero to operate his sleepy charm upon Miranda, they are perfectly intelligible. That they were so intended becomes almost certain from Prospero's language presently, when the charm has taken effect,—

" Come away, servant, come ! I am ready *now:*
Approach, my Ariel ; come ! "

b Distinctly,—] That is, *separately.*

(*) Old text, *Bore-spritt.* (†) Old text, *Lightening.*

PRO. My brave spirit!
Who was so firm, so constant, that this coil
Would not infect his reason?
ARI. Not a soul
But felt a fever of the mad, and play'd
Some tricks of desperation. All, but mariners,
Plung'd in the foaming brine, and quit the vessel,
Then all a-fire with me: the king's son, Ferdinand,
With hair up-staring,—then like reeds, not hair,—
Was the first man that leap'd; cried, *Hell is empty,*
And all the devils are here.
PRO. Why, that's my spirit!
But was not this nigh shore?
ARI. Close by, my master.
PRO. But are they, Ariel, safe?
ARI. Not a hair perish'd;
On their sustaining garments not a blemish,
But fresher than before: and, as thou bad'st me,
In troops I have dispers'd them 'bout the isle.
The king's son have I landed by himself;
Whom I left cooling of the air with sighs,
In an odd angle of the isle, and sitting,
His arms in this sad knot.
PRO. Of the king's ship,
The mariners, say how thou hast dispos'd,
And all the rest o' the fleet.
ARI. Safely in harbour
Is the king's ship; in the deep nook, where once
Thou call'dst me up at midnight to fetch dew
From the still-vex'd Bermoothes,(4) there she's hid:
The mariners all under hatches stow'd;
Whom, with a charm join'd to their suffer'd labour,
I have left asleep: and for the rest o' the fleet,
Which I dispers'd, they all have met again,
And are upon the Mediterranean flote,[a]
Bound sadly home for Naples,
Supposing that they saw the king's ship wreck'd,
And his great person perish.
PRO. Ariel, thy charge
Exactly is perform'd; but there's more work.
What is the time o' the day?
ARI. Past the mid season.

---

a *And are upon the Mediterranean flote,*—] Mr. Collier's annotator suggests, "And *all* upon," &c.; but what is gained by the alteration we cannot discern. *Flote* is here used substantively for *flood* or *wave,* as in the following from Middleton and Rowley's play of "The Spanish Gipsie," Act I. Sc. 5,—

"—— it did not
More check my rash attempt, than draw to ebb
The *float* of those desires."

PRO. At least two glasses—the time, 'twixt six and now—
Must by us both be spent most preciously.[a]

ARI. Is there more toil? Since thou dost give me pains,
Let me remember thee what thou hast promis'd,
Which is not yet perform'd me.

PRO. How now! moody?
What is't thou canst demand?

ARI. My liberty.

PRO. Before the time be out? no more!

ARI. I pr'ythee,
Remember, I have done thee worthy service;
Told thee no lies, made thee[b] no mistakings, serv'd
Without or grudge or grumblings: thou didst promise
To bate me a full year.

PRO. Dost thou forget
From what a torment I did free thee?

ARI. No.

PRO. Thou dost; and think'st it much to tread the ooze
Of the salt deep,
To run upon the sharp wind of the north,
To do me business in the veins o' the earth
When it is bak'd with frost.

ARI. I do not, sir.

PRO. Thou liest, malignant thing! Hast thou forgot
The foul witch Sycorax, who, with age and envy,
Was grown into a hoop? hast thou forgot her?

ARI. No, sir.

PRO. Thou hast. Where was she born? speak; tell me.

ARI. Sir, in Argier.[c]

PRO. O, was she so? I must
Once in a month recount what thou hast been,
Which thou forgett'st. This damn'd witch Sycorax,
For mischiefs manifold, and sorceries terrible
To enter human hearing, from Argier,
Thou know'st, was banish'd: for one thing she did
They would not take her life. Is not this true?

ARI. Ay, sir.

PRO. This blue-ey'd hag was hither brought with child,[d]
And here was left by the sailors: Thou, my slave,
As thou report'st thyself, wast then her servant;

---

[a] At least two glasses—the time, 'twixt six and now—
Must by us both be spent most preciously.]
By the customary punctuation of this passage, Prospero is made to ask a question and answer it. The pointing we adopt obviates this inconsistency, and renders any change in the distribution of the speeches needless.

[b] *Told thee no lies, made* thee *no mistakings, serv'd*—] The second *thee*, which overloads the line, was probably repeated by the compositor through inadvertence.

[c] Argier.] The old English name for Algiers.

[d] *This* blue-ey'd *hag*—] *Blue-ey'd* has been ably defended; but it must be confessed that *blear-ey'd*, a common epithet in our old plays, seems more applicable to the "damn'd witch Sycorax." Thus in Beaumont and Fletcher's play of "The Chances," Act IV. Sc. 2, where old Antonio bids his servant—

"Get me a conjuror,
One that can raise a water devil:
* * * * * * * *
—— any *blear-ey'd people*
With red heads, and flat noses, can perform it."

And, for thou wast a spirit too delicate
To act her earthy and abhorr'd commands,
Refusing her grand hests, she did confine thee,
By help of her more potent ministers,
And in her most unmitigable rage,
Into a cloven pine; within which rift
Imprison'd, thou didst painfully remain
A dozen years; within which space she died,
And left thee there; where thou didst vent thy groans
As fast as mill-wheels strike. Then was this island—
Save for the son that she did litter here,
A freckled whelp, hag-born—not honour'd with
A human shape.

ARI. Yes, Caliban her son.

PRO. Dull thing, I say so; he, that Caliban,
Whom now I keep in service. Thou best know'st
What torment I did find thee in; thy groans
Did make wolves howl, and penetrate the breasts
Of ever-angry bears: it was a torment
To lay upon the damn'd, which Sycorax
Could not again undo: it was mine art,
When I arriv'd, and heard thee, that made gape
The pine, and let thee out.

ARI. I thank thee, master.

PRO. If thou more murmur'st, I will rend an oak,
And peg thee in his knotty entrails, till
Thou hast howl'd away twelve winters.

ARI. Pardon, master:
I will be correspondent to command,
And do my spriting gently.

PRO. Do so; and after two days
I will discharge thee.

ARI. That's my noble master!
What shall I do? say what; what shall I do?

PRO. Go make thyself like a nymph o' the sea;
Be subject to no sight but thine and mine; invisible
To every eyeball else. Go, take this shape,
And hither come in 't: go, hence with diligence!
[*Exit* ARIEL.
Awake, dear heart, awake! thou hast slept well;
Awake!

MIRA. [*Waking.*][a] The strangeness of your story put
Heaviness in me.

PRO. Shake it off. Come on;
We'll visit Caliban, my slave, who never
Yields us kind answer.

MIRA. 'Tis a villain, sir,
I do not love to look on.

PRO. But, as 'tis,
We cannot miss[b] him: he does make our fire,
Fetch in our wood, and serves in offices
That profit us. What ho! slave! Caliban!
Thou earth, thou! speak.

CAL. [*Within.*] There's wood enough within.

PRO. Come forth, I say! there's other business for thee:
Come, thou tortoise! when?[c]

Re-enter ARIEL, *like a Water-nymph.*

[*Aside to* ARIEL.] Fine apparition! My quaint Ariel,
Hark in thine ear.

ARI. My lord, it shall be done. [*Exit.*

PRO. Thou poisonous slave, got by the devil himself
Upon thy wicked dam, come forth!

Enter CALIBAN.(5)

CAL. As wicked[d] dew as e'er my mother brush'd
With raven's feather from unwholesome fen,
Drop on you both! a south-west blow on ye,
And blister you all o'er!(6)

PRO. For this, be sure, to-night thou shalt have cramps,
Side-stitches that shall pen thy breath up; urchins[e]
Shall, for that vast[f] of night that they may work,
All exercise on thee: thou shalt be pinch'd
As thick as honeycomb, each pinch more stinging
Than bees that made 'em.

CAL. I must eat my dinner.
This island's mine, by Sycorax my mother,
Which thou tak'st from me. When thou camest first,
Thou strok'dst me, and mad'st much of me; wouldst give me
Water with berries in 't; and teach me how
To name the bigger light, and how the less,
That burn by day and night: and then I lov'd thee,
And show'd thee all the qualities o' the isle,
The fresh springs, brine pits, barren place and fertile:—
Cursed be I that did so!—All the charms
Of Sycorax, toads, beetles, bats, light on you!
For I am all the subjects that you have,

---

a MIRA. (*Waking.*)] Mr. Collier claims for his annotator the merit of having first added this not very important stage direction.

b *We cannot* miss *him:*] We cannot do without him.

c When?] See note (f), p. 449, Vol. I.

d *As* wicked *dew—*] *Wicked* here implies *baneful, pernicious;* as in opposition we hear of the *virtuous* properties of "herbs, plants, stones," &c.

e Urchins—] Hedgehogs were formerly so called: it is doubtful, however, whether *urchins* in this place does not signify some fairy beings; as in "The Merry Wives of Windsor," Act IV. Sc. 4,—

"—— we'll dress
Like *urchins*, ouphes, and fairies," &c.

f Vast *of night—*] By "*vast* of night" the poet may have meant the *chasm* or *vacuity* of night, as in "Hamlet," Act I. Sc. 2,—

"In the dead *vast* and middle of the night."

But some critics have conjectured we should read,—

"—— urchins
Shall for that, *fast* of night."

Which first was mine own king: and here you sty me
In this hard rock, whiles you do keep from me
The rest o' the island.
PRO. Thou most lying slave,
Whom stripes may move, not kindness! I have us'd thee,
Filth as thou art, with human care; and lodg'd thee
In mine own cell, till thou didst seek to violate
The honour of my child.
CAL. O ho, O ho!—would it had been done!
Thou didst prevent me; I had peopled else
This isle with Calibans.
PRO.[a] Abhorred slave,
Which any print of goodness will not take,
Being capable[b] of all ill! I pitied thee,
Took pains to make thee speak, taught thee each hour
One thing or other: when thou didst not, savage,
Know thine own meaning, but wouldst gabble like
A thing most brutish, I endow'd thy purposes
With words that made them known. But thy vile race,[c]
Though thou didst learn, had that in't which good natures
Could not abide to be with; therefore wast thou
Deservedly confin'd into this rock,
Who hadst deserv'd more than a prison.
CAL. You taught me language; and my profit on't
Is, I know how to curse. The red plague rid[d] you,
For learning me your language!
PRO. Hag-seed, hence!
Fetch us in fuel; and be quick, thou 'rt best,
To answer other business. Shrugg'st thou, malice?
If thou neglect'st, or dost unwillingly
What I command, I'll rack thee with old cramps,
Fill all thy bones with aches,[e] make thee roar,
That beasts shall tremble at thy din.

---

[a] PRO.] This speech, in the folios, has the prefix "*Mira*," but it plainly belongs to Prospero, to whom Theobald assigned it, and who has retained it ever since.

[b] *Which any print of goodness will not take,*
Being capable *of all ill!*]

Here, as in many other places, *capable* signifies *impressible, susceptible*.

[c] Race,—] That is, *Nature, essence.*

[d] *The red plague* rid *you*,—] See note (a), p. 447, Vol. II.

[e] *Fill all thy bones with aches*,—] Mr. Collier remarks that "this word, of old, was used either as a monosyllable or as a dissyllable, as the case might require." This may be questioned. "*Ake*," says Baret in his "Alvearie," "is the Verbe of the substantive *Ach*, ch being turned into k." As a *substantive*, then, the word was written *aches;* and pronounced as a dissyllable: when a *verb*, it was written *akes*, and its pronunciation was monosyllabic. This distinction is invariably marked in the old text; thus, in "Romeo and Juliet," Act II. Sc. 5, where it is a verb,—

"Lord, how my head *akes*, what a head have I."

In "Coriolanus," Act III. Sc. 1,—

"—— and my soule *akes*
To know," &c.

And in "Othello," Act IV. Sc. 2,—

"That the sense *akes* at thee."

While in every instance where it occurs as a substantive, it is spelt as in the passage above, *aches*, and should be so pronounced.

CAL. No, pray thee—
[*Aside.*] I must obey: his art is of such power,
It would control my dam's god, Setebos,(7)
And make a vassal of him.

PRO. So, slave; hence! [*Exit* CAL.

Re-enter ARIEL, *invisible, playing and singing;* FERDINAND *following.*

ARIEL'*s Song.*

Come unto these yellow sands,
And then take hands:
Court'sied when you have and kiss'd,—[a]
The wild waves whist,—
Foot it featly here and there;
*And, sweet sprites, the burden bear.**
Hark, hark!

BURDEN. *Bowgh, wowgh.* [*Dispersedly.*
The watch-dogs bark:
BURDEN. *Bowgh, wowgh.* [*Dispersedly.*
ARI. *Hark, hark! I hear*
The strain of strutting chanticleer
*Cry, cock-a-doodle-doo.**

FER. Where should this music be? i' the air, or the earth?
It sounds no more:—and sure it waits upon
Some god o' the island. Sitting on a bank,
Weeping again the king my father's wreck,
This music crept by me upon the waters,
Allaying both their fury and my passion
With its sweet air: thence I have follow'd it,
Or it hath drawn me rather:—but 't is gone.
No, it begins again.

(*) Old text, *beare the burthen.*

(a) Court'sied when you have and kiss'd,—
The wild waves whist,—
Foot it featly," &c.]

It was customary in the "good old times," for the partners in some dances to curtsy and salute before beginning; and if an allusion to these ceremonies is intended, the line,—
"The wild waves whist,"—
should be read parenthetically, in the sense of, the wild waves being hushed. The original punctuation, however,—
"Court'sied when you have, and kiss'd,
The wild waves whist:"
(when you have curtsied, and kissed the waves to peace) affords an intelligible and poetic meaning.

(*) Old text, *cock-a-didle-dowe.*

ARIEL *sings.*

Full fathom five thy father lies;
Of his bones are coral made;
Those are pearls that were his eyes:
Nothing of him that doth fade,
But doth suffer a sea-change
Into something rich and strange.
Sea-nymphs hourly ring his knell:
BURDEN. *Ding-dong.*
Hark! now I hear them,—Ding-dong, bell.

FER. The ditty does remember my drown'd father:—
This is no mortal business, nor no sound
That the earth owes:—I hear it now above me.
PRO. The fringed curtains of thine eye advance,
And say what thou seest yond.
MIRA. What is 't? a spirit?
Lord, how it looks about! Believe me, sir,
It carries a brave form:—but 't is a spirit.
PRO. No, wench; it eats, and sleeps, and hath such senses
As we have, such. This gallant which thou seest
Was in the wreck; and but he's something stain'd
With grief, that's beauty's canker, thou mightst call him
A goodly person: he hath lost his fellows,
And strays about to find 'em.
MIRA. I might call him
A thing divine; for nothing natural
I ever saw so noble.
PRO. [*Aside.*] It goes on, I see,
As my soul prompts it.—Spirit, fine spirit! I'll free thee
Within two days for this.
FER. Most sure, the goddess
On whom these airs attend!—Vouchsafe my prayer
May know if you remain upon this island;
And that you will some good instruction give
How I may bear me here: my prime request,
Which I do last pronounce, is,—O you wonder!—
If you be maid or no?
MIRA. No wonder, sir;
But certainly a maid.
FER. My language! heavens!—
I am the best of them that speak this speech,
Were I but where 't is spoken.
PRO. How! the best?
What wert thou, if the king of Naples heard thee?
FER. A single thing, as I am now, that wonders
To hear thee speak of Naples. He does hear me,
And that he does I weep: myself am Naples;
Who with mine eyes, ne'er since at ebb, beheld
The king my father wreck'd.
MIRA. Alack, for mercy!
FER. Yes, faith, and all his lords; the duke of Milan
And his brave son, being twain.
PRO. [*Aside.*] The duke of Milan
And his more braver daughter, could control[a] thee,
If now 't were fit to do't.—At the first sight
They have chang'd eyes:—delicate Ariel,
I'll set thee free for this!—A word, good sir;
I fear you have done yourself some wrong: a word.
MIRA. Why speaks my father so ungently? This
Is the third man that e'er I saw; the first
That e'er I sigh'd for: pity move my father
To be inclin'd my way!
FER. O, if a virgin,
And your affection not gone forth, I'll make you
The queen of Naples.
PRO. Soft, sir! one word more.—
[*Aside.*] They are both in either's powers; but this swift business
I must uneasy make, lest too light winning
Make the prize light.—One word more; I charge thee
That thou attend me: thou dost here usurp
The name thou ow'st not; and hast put thyself
Upon this island as a spy, to win it
From me, the lord on 't.
FER. No, as I am a man.
MIRA. There's nothing ill can dwell in such a temple:
If the ill spirit have so fair a house,
Good things will strive to dwell with 't.
PRO. Follow me.—[*To* FER.
Speak not you for him; he's a traitor.—Come,
I'll manacle thy neck and feet together:
Sea-water shalt thou drink; thy food shall be
The fresh-brook muscles, wither'd roots, and husks
Wherein the acorn cradled. Follow.
FER. No,
I will resist such entertainment, till
Mine enemy has more power.
[*Draws, and is charmed from moving.*
MIRA. O dear father,
Make not too rash a trial of him, for
He's gentle, and not fearful.[b]
PRO. What! I say,
My foot my tutor!—Put thy sword up, traitor;
Who mak'st a show, but dar'st not strike, thy conscience
Is so possess'd with guilt: come from thy ward;[c]

---

a —— *could* control *thee,*—] *Control* in its ordinary acceptation, and Shakespeare uses it in no other, seems incongruous here. Is it a misprint for *console?*

b He's gentle, and not fearful.] This may mean, he's mild and not terrible: but from the context,—

"Make not too rash a trial of him," &c.—

we believe that Smollett's interpretation is the true one,—he's of a *lofty spirit* and not to be intimidated.

c —— *thy ward;*] Thy posture of defence.

For I can here disarm thee with this stick,
And make thy weapon drop.
MIRA. Beseech you, father!—
PRO. Hence; hang not on my garments.
MIRA. Sir, have pity;
I'll be his surety.
PRO. Silence! one word more
Shall make me chide thee, if not hate thee. What!
An advocate for an impostor! hush!
Thou think'st there are no more such shapes as he,
Having seen but him and Caliban: foolish wench!
To the most of men this is a Caliban,
And they to him are angels.
MIRA. My affections
Are then most humble; I have no ambition
To see a goodlier man.
PRO. Come on: obey: [*To* FER.
Thy nerves are in their infancy again,
And have no vigour in them.
FER. So they are:
My spirits, as in a dream, are all bound up.
My father's loss, the weakness which I feel,
The wreck of all my friends, nor this man's threats,
To whom I am subdued, are but light to me,
Might I but through my prison once a day
Behold this maid: all corners else o' the earth
Let liberty make use of; space enough
Have I in such a prison.
PRO. [*Aside.*] It works.—Come on.—
Thou hast done well, fine Ariel!—Follow me.—
[*To* FER.
Hark, what thou else shalt do me. [*To* ARIEL.
MIRA. Be of comfort;
My father's of a better nature, sir,
Than he appears by speech; this is unwonted,
Which now came from him.
PRO. [*To* ARIEL.] Thou shalt be as free
As mountain winds: but then exactly do
All points of my command.
ARI. To the syllable.
PRO. Come, follow. Speak not for him.
[*Exeunt.*

ACT II.

SCENE I.—*Another Part of the* Island.

Enter ALONSO, SEBASTIAN, ANTONIO, GONZALO, ADRIAN, FRANCISCO, *and others.*

GON. Beseech you, sir, be merry: you have cause—
So have we all—of joy; for our escape
Is much beyond our loss. Our hint of woe
Is common; every day, some sailor's wife,
The masters[a] of some merchant, and the merchant,
Have just our theme of woe: but for the miracle,
I mean our preservation, few in millions
Can speak like us: then wisely, good sir, weigh
Our sorrow with our comfort.
ALON. Pr'ythee, peace.

SEB. He receives comfort like cold porridge.
ANT. The visitor will not give him o'er so.
SEB. Look, he's winding up the watch of his wit; By and by it will strike.
GON. Sir,—
SEB. One:—tell.
GON. When every grief is entertain'd that's offer'd,
Comes to the entertainer—
SEB. A dollar.
GON. Dolour[b] comes to him, indeed; you have spoken truer than you purposed.
SEB. You have ta'en it wiselier than I meant you should.

---

[a] *The* masters *of some merchant,*—] Capell reads, perhaps rightly, "The *master,*" &c.; and Steevens conjectures we should print—

"The mistress of some merchant,"

Mistress being anciently spelt, *maistresse* or *maistres.*

[b] SEB. A dollar.
GON. Dolour—]
The same quibble is found in "King Lear," Act II. Sc. 4, and in "Measure for Measure," Act I. Sc. 2.

GON. Therefore, my lord,—

ANT. Fie, what a spendthrift is he of his tongue!

ALON. I pr'ythee spare.

GON. Well, I have done: but yet—

SEB. He will be talking.

ANT. Which, of he[a] or Adrian, for a good wager, first begins to crow?

SEB. The old cock.

ANT. The cockrel.

SEB. Done: the wager?

ANT. A laughter.

SEB. A match!

ADR. Though this island seem to be desert,—

SEB. Ha, ha, ha! So, you're paid.[b]

ADR. Uninhabitable, and almost inaccessible,—

SEB. Yet,—

ADR. Yet,—

ANT. He could not miss it.

ADR. It must needs be of subtle, tender, and delicate temperance.[c]

ANT. *Temperance* was a delicate wench.

SEB. Ay, and a subtle; as he most learnedly delivered.

ADR. The air breathes upon us here most sweetly.

SEB. As if it had lungs, and rotten ones.

ANT. Or as 't were perfumed by a fen.

GON. Here is everything advantageous to life.

ANT. True; save means to live.

SEB. Of that there's none, or little.

GON. How lush[d] and lusty the grass looks! how green!

ANT. The ground, indeed, is tawny.

SEB. With an eye of green in 't.

ANT. He misses not much.

SEB. No; he doth but mistake the truth totally.

GON. But the rarity of it is—which is indeed almost beyond credit—

SEB. As many vouched rarities are.

GON. That our garments, being, as they were, drenched in the sea, hold, notwithstanding, their freshness and glosses; being rather new dyed than stained with salt water.

ANT. If but one of his pockets could speak, would it not say, he lies?

SEB. Ay, or very falsely pocket up his report.

GON. Methinks our garments are now as fresh as when we put them on first in Afric, at the marriage of the king's fair daughter Claribel to the king of Tunis.

SEB. 'Twas a sweet marriage, and we prosper well in our return.

ADR. Tunis was never graced before with such a paragon to their queen.

GON. Not since widow Dido's time.

ANT. Widow? a pox o' that! How came that widow in? Widow Dido!

SEB. What if he had said, widower Æneas too? good lord, how you take it!

ADR. Widow Dido, said you? you make me study of that: she was of Carthage, not of Tunis.

GON. This Tunis, sir, was Carthage.

ADR. Carthage?

GON. I assure you, Carthage.

ANT. His word is more than the miraculous harp.[e]

SEB. He hath raised the wall, and houses too.

ANT. What impossible matter will he make easy next?

SEB. I think he will carry this island home in his pocket, and give it his son for an apple.

ANT. And, sowing the kernels of it in the sea, bring forth more islands.

ALON. Ay![f]

ANT. Why, in good time.

GON. Sir, we were talking that our garments seem now as fresh as when we were at Tunis at the marriage of your daughter, who is now queen.

ANT. And the rarest that e'er came there.

SEB. Bate, I beseech you, widow Dido.

ANT. O, widow Dido! ay, widow Dido.

GON. Is not, sir, my doublet as fresh as the first day I wore it? I mean, in a sort.

ANT. That sort was well fish'd for.

GON. When I wore it at your daughter's marriage?

ALON. You cram these words into mine ears against
The stomach of my sense. Would I had never
Married my daughter there! for, coming thence,
My son is lost; and, in my rate, she too,
Who is so far from Italy removed,
I ne'er again shall see her. O thou mine heir
Of Naples and of Milan, what strange fish
Hath made his meal on thee?

FRAN. Sir, he may live;
I saw him beat the surges under him,
And ride upon their backs; he trod the water,
Whose enmity he flung aside, and breasted
The surge most swoln that met him; his bold head
'Bove the contentious waves he kept, and oar'd
Himself with his good arms in lusty stroke

---

a *Which*, of he *or Adrian*,—] So the old text, and rightly; compare the following from "Midsummer Night's Dream," Act III. Sc. 2:—

"Now follow, if thou dar'st to try whose right,
Of thine or mine, is most in Helena."

The usual reading is that adopted by Capell, "Which of *them*, he or Adrian," &c.; but Mr. Collier's annotator reads,—

"Which, *or* he or Adrian," &c.

b Ha, ha, ha! So, you're paid.] In the old copies, "So, you're paid," is given to Antonio, wrongly.

c Temperance.] That is, *temperature*.

d Lush—] *Succulent, juicy*.

e —— the miraculous harp.] The harp of Amphion.

f Ay!] This sigh or exclamation, which the two next speeches show indisputably to have been uttered by the king, upon awaking from his trance of grief, has hitherto, in both old and modern editions, been assigned to Gonzalo.

To the shore, that o'er his wave-worn basis bow'd,
As stooping to relieve him; I not doubt
He came alive to land.

ALON. No, no, he's gone.

SEB. Sir, you may thank yourself for this great loss,
That would not bless our Europe with your daughter,
But rather lose her to an African;
Where she, at least, is banish'd from your eye,
Who hath cause to wet the grief on't.

ALON. Pr'ythee, peace.

SEB. You were kneel'd to, and importun'd otherwise,
By all of us; and the fair soul herself
Weigh'd, between lothness and obedience, at
Which end o' the beam she'd[a] bow. We have lost your son,
I fear, for ever. Milan and Naples have
More widows in them of this business' making,
Than we bring men to comfort them:
The fault's your own.

ALON. So is the dear'st o' the loss.

GON. My lord Sebastian,
The truth you speak doth lack some gentleness,
And time to speak it in; you rub the sore,
When you should bring the plaster.

SEB. Very well.

ANT. And most chirurgeonly.

GON. It is foul weather in us all, good sir,
When you are cloudy.

SEB. *Foul weather!*

ANT. Very foul.

GON. Had I plantation of this isle, my lord,—

ANT. He'd sow't with nettle-seed.

SEB. Or docks, or mallows.

GON. —And were the king on't, what would I do?

SEB. 'Scape being drunk, for want of wine.

GON. I' the commonwealth I would by contraries
Execute all things; for no kind of traffic
Would I admit; no name of magistrate;
Letters should not be known: riches, poverty,
And use of service, none: contract, succession,
Bourn, bound of land, tilth, vineyard, none;
No use of metal, corn, or wine, or oil;
No occupation; all men idle, all;
And women too,—but innocent and pure;
No sovereignty:—

SEB. Yet he would be king on't.

ANT. The latter end of his commonwealth forgets the beginning.

GON. All things in common nature should produce,
Without sweat or endeavour: treason, felony,
Sword, pike, knife, gun, or need of any engine,
Would I not have; but nature should bring forth,
Of it own kind, all foizon,[b] all abundance,
To feed my innocent people.(1)

SEB. No marrying 'mong his subjects?

ANT. None, man; all idle,—whores and knaves.

GON. I would with such perfection govern, sir,
To excel the golden age.

SEB. Save his majesty!

ANT. Long live Gonzalo!

GON. And, do you mark me, sir?—

ALON. Pr'ythee, no more: thou dost talk nothing to me.

GON. I do well believe your highness; and did it to minister occasion to these gentlemen, who are of such sensible and nimble lungs that they always use to laugh at nothing.

ANT. 'Twas you we laugh'd at.

GON. Who, in this kind of merry fooling, am nothing to you: so you may continue, and laugh at nothing still.

ANT. What a blow was there given!

SEB. An it had not fallen flat-long.

GON. You are gentlemen of brave mettle; you would lift the moon out of her sphere, if she would continue in it five weeks without changing.

Enter ARIEL, *invisible, solemn Music playing.*

SEB. We would so, and then go a bat-fowling.(2)

ANT. Nay, good my lord, be not angry.

GON. No, I warrant you; I will not adventure my discretion so weakly. Will you laugh me asleep, for I am very heavy?

ANT. Go sleep, and hear us.

[*All sleep but* ALON., SEB., *and* ANT.

ALON. What, all so soon asleep! I wish mine eyes
Would, with themselves, shut up my thoughts: I find
They are inclin'd to do so.

SEB. Please you, sir,
Do not omit the heavy offer of it:
It seldom visits sorrow; when it doth,
It is a comforter.

ANT. We two, my lord,
Will guard your person while you take your rest,
And watch your safety.

ALON. Thank you.—Wondrous heavy.

[ALON. *sleeps.* *Exit* ARIEL.

SEB. What a strange drowsiness possesses them!

---

[a] *Which end o' the beam* she'd *bow.*] So Malone. The old text has,—
"Which end o' th' beame *should* bow."
For which Capell substituted,—
"Which end the beam should bow."
And Mr. Collier's annotator changes the "at" of the previous line to *as*,—
"—— as
Which end," &c.

[b] Foizon,—] *Abundance, plenty.*

ANT. It is the quality o' the climate.
SEB. Why
Doth it not, then, our eyelids sink? I find not
Myself dispos'd to sleep.
ANT. Nor I; my spirits are nimble.
They fell together all, as by consent;
They dropp'd, as by a thunder-stroke. What might,
Worthy Sebastian—O, what might—no more:—
And yet methinks I see it in thy face,
What thou shouldst be: the occasion speaks thee; and
My strong imagination sees a crown
Dropping upon thy head.
SEB. What, art thou waking?
ANT. Do you not hear me speak?
SEB. I do; and surely
It is a sleepy language; and thou speak'st
Out of thy sleep: what is it thou didst say?
This is a strange repose, to be asleep
With eyes wide open; standing, speaking, moving,
And yet so fast asleep.
ANT. Noble Sebastian,
Thou lett'st thy fortune sleep,—die rather; wink'st
Whiles thou art waking.
SEB. Thou dost snore distinctly;
There's meaning in thy snores.
ANT. I am more serious than my custom: you
Must be so too, if heed me; which to do
Trebles thee o'er.
SEB. Well, I am standing water.
ANT. I'll teach you how to flow.
SEB. Do so: to ebb,
Hereditary sloth instructs me.
ANT. O,
If you but knew how you the purpose cherish
Whiles thus you mock it! how, in stripping it,
You more invest it! Ebbing men, indeed,
Most often do so near the bottom run,
By their own fear or sloth.
SEB. Pr'ythee, say on:
The setting of thine eye, and cheek, proclaim
A matter from thee; and a birth, indeed,
Which throes thee much to yield.
ANT. Thus, sir:
Although this lord of weak remembrance,[a] this,—
Who shall be of as little memory
When he is earth'd,—hath here almost persuaded,—
For he 's a spirit of persuasion, only
Professes to persuade,[b]—the king his son's alive,—
'T is as impossible that he 's undrown'd,
As he that sleeps here, swims.
SEB. I have no hope
That he 's undrown'd.
ANT. O, out of that *no hope*,
What great hope have you! no hope, that way, is
Another way so high a hope, that even
Ambition cannot pierce a wink beyond,
But doubts* discovery there. Will you grant with me,
That Ferdinand is drown'd?
SEB. He 's gone.
ANT. Then, tell me,
Who 's the next heir of Naples?
SEB. Claribel.
ANT. She that is queen of Tunis; she that dwells
Ten leagues beyond man's life; she that from Naples
Can have no note, unless the sun were post,—
The man i' the moon 's too slow,—till new-born chins
Be rough and razorable; she,[c] from whom
We all were sea-swallow'd, though some cast again;
And, by that destiny,[d] to perform an act,
Whereof what 's past is prologue; what to come,
In yours and my discharge.
SEB. What stuff is this?—How say you?
'T is true, my brother's daughter 's queen of Tunis;
So is she heir of Naples; 'twixt which regions
There is some space.
ANT. A space whose every cubit
Seems to cry out, *How shall that Claribel
Measure us back to Naples? Keep in Tunis,
And let Sebastian wake!*—Say, this were death
That now hath seiz'd them; why, they were no worse
Than now they are. There be that can rule Naples
As well as he that sleeps; lords that can prate
As amply and unnecessarily
As this Gonzalo; I myself could make
A chough of as deep chat. O, that you bore
The mind that I do! what a sleep were this
For your advancement! Do you understand me?
SEB. Methinks I do.
ANT. And how does your content
Tender your own good fortune?
SEB. I remember,
You did supplant your brother Prospero.
ANT. True:

---

[a] Of weak remembrance,—] Of feeble memory.

[b] Professes to persuade,—] The entanglement in this speech may have arisen from the retention of the poet's first, as well as of his reconsidered thought. By reading the passage without the words, "Professes to persuade," as Steevens justly remarks, "nothing is wanting to its sense or metre;"

"—— hath here almost persuaded,—
For he's a spirit of persuasion only,—
The king, his son's alive," &c.

(*) Old text, *doubt*.

[c] —— she, from whom—] That is, *coming* from whom. The old text has,—

"—— she *that* from whom."

Rowe made the correction.

[d] And, by that destiny,—] We should possibly read,—

"—— though some cast again,—
And *that by* destiny,—to perform," &c.

And look how well my garments sit upon me;
Much feater than before: my brother's servants
Were then my fellows; now they are my men.

SEB. But, for your conscience,—

ANT. Ay, sir; where lies that? if it were a kibe,
'T would put me to my slipper: but I feel not
This deity in my bosom; twenty consciences,
That stand 'twixt me and Milan, candied be they,
And melt, ere they molest! Here lies your brother,—
No better than the earth he lies upon,
If he were that which now he's like, that's dead,—
Whom I, with this obedient steel, three inches of it,
Can lay to bed for ever; whiles you, doing thus,
To the perpetual wink for aye might put
This ancient morsel, this sir Prudence, who
Should not upbraid our course. For all the rest,
They'll take suggestion[a] as a cat laps milk;
They'll tell the clock to any business that
We say befits the hour.

SEB. Thy case, dear friend,
Shall be my precedent; as thou gott'st Milan,
I'll come by Naples. Draw thy sword; one stroke
Shall free thee from the tribute which thou pay'st;
And I the king shall love thee.

ANT. Draw together;
And when I rear my hand, do you the like,
To fall it on Gonzalo.

SEB. O, but one word. [*They converse apart.*

Music. Re-enter ARIEL, *invisible.*

ARI. My master through his art foresees the danger
That you, his friend, are in; and sends me forth,—
For else his project dies,—to keep them[b] living.
[*Sings in* GONZALO'*s ear.*

While you here do snoring lie,
Open-eyed Conspiracy
His time doth take:
If of life you keep a care,
Shake off slumber, and beware.
Awake! awake!

ANT. Then let us both be sudden.

GON. [*Waking.*] Now, good angels, preserve the king!
Why, how now?[c] ho, awake! Why are you drawn?
Wherefore this ghastly looking?

ALON. [*Waking.*] What's the matter?

SEB. Whiles we stood here securing your repose,
Even now, we heard a hollow burst of bellowing
Like bulls, or rather lions; did it not wake you?
It struck mine ear most terribly.

ALON. I heard nothing.

ANT. O, 't was a din to fright a monster's ear;
To make an earthquake! sure, it was the roar
Of a whole herd of lions.

ALON. Heard you this, Gonzalo?

GON. Upon mine honour, sir, I heard a humming,
And that a strange one too, which did awake me:
I shak'd you, sir, and cried; as mine eyes open'd,
I saw their weapons drawn:—there was a noise,
That's verity.[d] 'T is best we stand upon our guard,
Or that we quit this place: let's draw our weapons.

ALON. Lead off this ground; and let's make further search
For my poor son.

GON. Heavens keep him from these beasts!
For he is, sure, i' the island.

ALON. Lead away. [*Exeunt.*

ARI. Prospero my lord shall know what I have done:—
So, king, go safely on to seek thy son. [*Exit.*

SCENE II.—*Another Part of the* Island.

Enter CALIBAN, *with a burden of wood. A noise of thunder heard.*

CAL. All the infections that the sun sucks up
From bogs, fens, flats, on Prosper fall, and make him
By inch-meal a disease! His spirits hear me,
And yet I needs must curse: but they'll nor pinch,
Fright me with urchin-shows, pitch me i' the mire,
Nor lead me, like a firebrand, in the dark
Out of my way, unless he bid 'em; but
For every trifle are they set upon me,
Sometime like apes, that moe and chatter at me,
And after, bite me; then like hedgehogs, which
Lie tumbling in my barefoot way, and mount

---

[a] Suggestion—] Has before been explained to mean, *temptation.*

[b] *To keep them living.*] Mr. Dyce reads, "—— to keep *thee* living," which is preferable to any alteration of the passage yet suggested; but we are not convinced that change is required.

[c] Why, how now? ho, awake! &c.] In the old copy, and in every subsequent edition, this speech is given to the king and the next to Gonzalo, but erroneously, as we think is evident from the language, the business of the scene, and from what Gonzalo presently says:—

"—— I heard a humming,
And that a strange one too, *which did awake me:*
I shak'd you, sir, and cried; as mine eyes open'd,
I saw their weapons drawn."

[d] *That's* verity.] So Pope; the old text having, "That's *verily.*"

Their pricks at my footfall; sometime am I
All wound[a] with adders, who, with cloven tongues,
Do hiss me into madness.—Lo, now! lo!
Here comes a spirit of his; and to torment me,
For bringing wood in slowly: I 'll fall flat;
Perchance, he will not mind me.

Enter TRINCULO.

TRIN. Here 's neither bush nor shrub, to bear off any weather at all, and another storm brewing; I hear it sing i' the wind: yond same black cloud, yond huge one, looks like a foul bombard that

a All wound with—] *All encircled by.*

would shed his liquor. If it should thunder as it did before, I know not where to hide my head: yond same cloud cannot choose but fall by pailfuls.—What have we here? a man or a fish? dead or alive? A fish: he smells like a fish: a very ancient and fish-like smell; a kind of, not of the newest, poor-John. A strange fish! Were I in England now (as once I was), and had but this fish painted, not a holiday fool there but would give a piece of silver: there would this monster make a man; any strange beast there makes a man: when they will not give a doit to relieve a lame beggar, they will lay out ten to see a dead Indian.(3) Legged like a man! and his fins like arms! Warm, o' my troth! I do now let loose my opinion, hold it no longer,—this is no fish, but an islander, that hath lately suffered by a thunderbolt. [*Thunder.*] Alas, the storm is come again! my best way is to creep under his gaberdine;[a] there is no other shelter hereabout: misery acquaints a man with strange bedfellows. I will here shroud till the dregs of the storm be past.

Enter STEPHANO, *singing; a bottle in his hand.*

STE. *I shall no more to sea, to sea,*
Here shall I die ashore;—

[a] Gaberdine;] A loose over-garment, worn by the lower classes. See note (6), p. 438, Vol. I.

This is a very scurvy tune to sing at a man's funeral: well, here's my comfort. [*Drinks.*

The master, the swabber, the boatswain, and I,
The gunner, and his mate,
Lov'd Mall, Meg, and Marian, and Margery,
But none of us car'd for Kate:
For she had a tongue with a tang,
Would cry to a sailor, Go hang:
She lov'd not the savour of tar nor of pitch,
Yet a tailor might scratch her where'er she did itch;
Then to sea, boys, and let her go hang!

This is a scurvy tune too: but here's my comfort. [*Drinks.*

CAL. Do not torment me:—O!

STE. What's the matter? Have we devils here? Do you put tricks upon's with salvages and men of Inde, ha? I have not 'scaped drowning, to be afeard now of your four legs; for it hath been said, As proper a man as ever went on four legs cannot make him give ground: and it shall be said so again, while Stephano breathes at nostrils.

CAL. The spirit torments me:—O!

STE. This is some monster of the isle with four legs, who hath got, as I take it, an ague. Where the devil should he learn our language? I will

give him some relief, if it be but for that. If I can recover him, and keep him tame, and get to Naples with him, he 's a present for any emperor that ever trod on neat's-leather.

CAL. Do not torment me, pr'ythee! I'll bring my wood home faster.

STE. He 's in his fit now; and does not talk after the wisest. He shall taste of my bottle: if he have never drunk wine afore, it will go near to remove his fit. If I can recover him, and keep him tame, I will not take too much for him: he shall pay for him that hath him, and that soundly.

CAL. Thou dost me yet but little hurt; thou wilt anon, I know it by thy trembling: now Prosper works upon thee.

STE. Come on your ways; open your mouth; here is that which will give language to you, cat; open your mouth; this will shake your shaking, I can tell you, and that soundly: you cannot tell who 's your friend: open your chaps again.

TRIN. I should know that voice: it should be—but he is drowned; and these are devils:—O! defend me!—

STE. Four legs and two voices; a most delicate monster! His forward voice now, is to speak well of his friend; his backward voice is to utter foul speeches and to detract. If all the wine in my bottle will recover him, I will help his ague: Come;—Amen![a] I will pour some in thy other mouth.

TRIN. Stephano,—

STE. Doth thy other mouth call me? Mercy! mercy! This is a devil, and no monster: I will leave him: I have no long spoon.[b]

TRIN. Stephano!—if thou beest Stephano, touch me, and speak to me; for I am Trinculo,—be not afeard,—thy good friend Trinculo.

STE. If thou beest Trinculo, come forth: I'll pull thee by the lesser legs: if any be Trinculo's legs, these are they.—Thou art very Trinculo, indeed: how camest thou to be the siege of this moon-calf? can he vent Trinculos?

TRIN. I took him to be killed with a thunder-stroke:—but art thou not drowned, Stephano? I hope now, thou art not drowned. Is the storm overblown? I hid me under the dead moon-calf's gaberdine for fear of the storm. And art thou living, Stephano? O Stephano, two Neapolitans 'scaped!

STE. Pr'ythee, do not turn me about; my stomach is not constant.

CAL. [*Aside.*] These be fine things, an if they be not sprites.
That 's a brave god, and bears celestial liquor:
I will kneel to him.

STE. How didst thou 'scape? How camest thou

---

[a] Amen!] Perhaps a warning to the monster to stint his draught.

[b] I have no long spoon.] An allusion which we have had before, in "The Comedy of Errors," Act IV. Sc. 3, to the ancient proverb, "He who eats with the devil hath need of a *long spoon*."

hither? swear by this bottle, how thou camest hither. I escaped upon a butt of sack, which the sailors heaved overboard, by this bottle! which I made of the bark of a tree, with mine own hands, since I was cast ashore.

Cal. [*Aside.*] I 'll swear upon that bottle, to be thy true subject; for the liquor is not earthly.

Ste. Here; swear then how thou escapedst.

Trin. Swam ashore, man, like a duck; I can swim like a duck, I'll be sworn.

Ste. Here, kiss the book. Though thou canst swim like a duck, thou art made like a goose.

Trin. O Stephano, hast any more of this?

Ste. The whole butt, man; my cellar is in a rock by the sea-side, where my wine is hid.—How now, moon-calf? how does thine ague?

Cal. Hast thou not dropped from heaven?

Ste. Out o' the moon, I do assure thee: I was the man i' the moon when time was.

Cal. I have seen thee in her, and I do adore thee;
My mistress show'd me thee, and thy dog and thy bush.

Ste. Come, swear to that; kiss the book:—I will furnish it anon with new contents:—swear.

Trin. By this good light, this is a very shallow monster:—I afeard of him!—a very weak monster:—*The man i' the moon!*—a most poor credulous monster!—Well drawn, monster, in good sooth.

Cal. I'll show thee every fertile inch o' the island;
And I will kiss thy foot: I pr'ythee, be my god.

Trin. By this light, a most perfidious and drunken monster; when 's god 's asleep he 'll rob his bottle.

Cal. I'll kiss thy foot: I'll swear myself thy subject.

Ste. Come on then; down and swear.

Trin. I shall laugh myself to death at this puppy-headed monster: a most scurvy monster! I could find in my heart to beat him.

Ste. Come, kiss.

Trin. But that the poor monster's in drink, an abominable monster!

Cal. I'll show thee the best springs; I 'll pluck thee berries;
I 'll fish for thee, and get thee wood enough.
A plague upon the tyrant that I serve!
I 'll bear him no more sticks, but follow thee,
Thou wondrous man.

Trin. A most ridiculous monster! to make a wonder of a poor drunkard!

Cal. I pr'ythee let me bring thee where crabs grow,

And I with my long nails will dig thee pig-nuts;
Show thee a jay's nest, and instruct thee how
To snare the nimble marmozet; I 'll bring thee
To clust'ring filberds, and sometimes I 'll get thee
Young scamels[a] from the rock. Wilt thou go with
me?

STE. I pr'ythee now, lead the way, without any more talking.—Trinculo, the king and all our company else being drowned, we will inherit here.—[*To* CALIBAN.] Here; bear my bottle.—Fellow Trinculo, we 'll fill him by and by again.

CAL. *Farewell, master: farewell, farewell!*
[*Sings drunkenly.*

TRIN. A howling monster; a drunken monster!

CAL. *No more dams I 'll make for fish;*
Nor fetch in firing
At requiring,
Nor scrape trencher,[b] *nor wash dish:*
'Ban, 'Ban, Ca—Caliban
Has a new master—Get a new man.

Freedom, hey-day! hey-day,[c] *Freedom!*
Freedom, hey-day, Freedom!

STE. O brave monster! lead the way.
[*Exeunt.*

[a] *Young* scamels—] So the old text, but perhaps corruptly, since the word has not been found in any other author. Theobald changed it to *shamois*, and suggested *staniels*, that is, young hawks, and *sea-malls*, or *sea-mells*.

[b] *Nor scrape* trencher,—] The old text has, "Nor scrape *trenchering*," but, as Mr. Dyce observes, "That 'trenchering' is an error of the printer (or transcriber), occasioned by the preceding words, '*firing*' and '*requiring*,' is beyond a doubt."

[c] Hey-day! hey-day!] This appears to have been a familiar burden. Thus, in Ben Jonson's "Cynthia's Revels," Act II. Sc. 1:—

"Come follow me, my wags, and say, as I say.
There's no riches but in rags, *hey day, hey-day:*
You that profess this art, come away, come away,
And help to bear a part. *Hey-day, hey-day!*"

ACT III.

SCENE I.—*Before* Prospero's *Cell.*

Enter Ferdinand, *bearing a log.*

Fer. There be some sports are painful, and their labour
Delight in them sets off: some kinds of baseness
Are nobly undergone; and most poor matters
Point to rich ends. This my mean task
Would be as heavy to me as odious; but
The mistress which I serve quickens what 's dead,
And makes my labours pleasures: O, she is
Ten times more gentle than her father's crabbed,—
And he 's compos'd of harshness! I must remove
Some thousands of these logs, and pile them up,
Upon a sore injunction. My sweet mistress
Weeps when she sees me work; and says such baseness

Had never like executor. I forget:
But these sweet thoughts do even refresh my labour;*
Most busy felt, when I do it.[a]

Enter MIRANDA, *and* PROSPERO *following*.

MIRA. Alas, now! pray you,
Work not so hard; I would the lightning had
Burnt up those logs that you are enjoin'd to pile!
Pray, set it down, and rest you: when this burns,
'T will weep for having wearied you. My father
Is hard at study; pray, now, rest yourself;
He 's safe for these three hours.

FER. O most dear mistress,
The sun will set before I shall discharge
What I must strive to do.

MIRA. If you 'll sit down
I 'll bear your logs the while: pray give me that;
I 'll carry it to the pile.

FER. No, precious creature:
I had rather crack my sinews, break my back,
Than you should such dishonour undergo,
While I sit lazy by.

MIRA. It would become me
As well as it does you; and I should do it
With much more ease; for my good will is to it,
And yours it is against.

PRO. [*Aside.*] Poor worm, thou art infected!
This visitation shows it.

MIRA. You look wearily.

FER. No, noble mistress; 't is fresh morning with me,
When you are by at night. I do beseech you,—
Chiefly that I might set it in my prayers,—
What is your name?

MIRA. Miranda:—O my father,
I have broke your 'hest to say so!

FER. Admir'd Miranda!
Indeed the top of admiration; worth
What 's dearest to the world! Full many a lady
I have ey'd with best regard; and many a time
The harmony of their tongues hath into bondage
Brought my too diligent ear: for several virtues
Have I lik'd several women; never any
With so full soul, but some defect in her
Did quarrel with the noblest grace she ow'd,
And put it to the foil: but you, O you,
So perfect and so peerless, are created
Of every creature's best!

MIRA. I do not know
One of my sex; no woman's face remember,
Save, from my glass, mine own; nor have I seen
More that I may call men, than you, good friend,
And my dear father: how features are abroad,
I am skill-less of; but, by my modesty,
—The jewel in my dower,—I would not wish
Any companion in the world but you;
Nor can imagination form a shape,
Besides yourself, to like of. But I prattle
Something too wildly, and my father's precepts
I therein do forget.

FER. I am, in my condition,
A prince, Miranda; I do think, a king,—
I would not so!—and would no more endure
This wooden slavery, than to suffer [speak:—
The flesh-fly blow my mouth.—Hear my soul
The very instant that I saw you, did
My heart fly to your service; there resides,
To make me slave to it; and for your sake
Am I this patient log-man.

MIRA. Do you love me?

FER. O heaven! O earth! bear witness to this sound,
And crown what I profess with kind event,
If I speak true! if hollowly, invert
What best is boded me, to mischief! I,
Beyond all limit of what else i' the world,
Do love, prize, honour you.

MIRA. I am a fool,
To weep at what I am glad of.

PRO. [*Aside.*] Fair encounter
Of two most rare affections! Heavens rain grace
On that which breeds between 'em!

FER. Wherefore weep you?

MIRA. At mine unworthiness, that dare not offer
What I desire to give; and much less take
What I shall die to want. But this is trifling;
And all the more it seeks to hide itself,
The bigger bulk it shows. Hence, bashful cunning!
And prompt me, plain and holy innocence!
I am your wife, if you will marry me;
If not, I 'll die your maid: to be your fellow[b]
You may deny me; but I 'll be your servant,
Whether you will or no.

FER. My mistress, dearest!
And I thus humble ever.

(*) Old text, *labours*.

a —— I forget:
But these sweet thoughts do even refresh my labour;
***Most busy* felt, *when I do it.*]**

This is the great crux of the play. No passage in Shakespeare has occasioned more speculation, and on none has speculation proved less happy. The first folio reads, "Most busie *lest*, when I doe it;" the second, "Most busie *least* when I doe it;" Pope prints, "*Least busy* when I do it;" Theobald, "Most *busyless* when I do it;" Mr. Holt White suggests, "Most *busiest* when I do it;" and Mr. Collier's annotator, "Most busy,—*blest* when I do it." Whatever may have been the word for which "lest" was misprinted, "Most busy" and that word bore reference, unquestionably, not to Ferdinand's task, but to the sweet thoughts by which it was relieved. We have substituted *felt* as a likely word to have been mis-set "lest;" but are in doubt whether *still*, in its old sense of *ever*, *always*, is not preferable,—

"Most busy still, when I do it."

b Fellow—] That is, *companion*, *pheer*.

MIRA. My husband, then?

FER. Ay, with a heart as willing
As bondage e'er of freedom: here 's my hand.

MIRA. And mine, with my heart in 't: and now, farewell,
Till half an hour hence.

FER. A thousand thousand!

[*Exeunt* FERDINAND *and* MIRANDA *severally.*

PRO. So glad of this as they I cannot be,
Who are surpris'd with all; but my rejoicing
At nothing can be more. I 'll to my book;
For yet, ere supper-time, must I perform
Much business appertaining. [*Exit.*

SCENE II.—*Another Part of the* Island.

Enter CALIBAN *with a bottle;* STEPHANO *and* TRINCULO *following.*

STE. Tell not me;—when the butt is out we will drink water; not a drop before: therefore bear up, and board 'em.—Servant-monster, drink to me.

TRIN. *Servant-monster?* the folly of this island! They say there 's but five upon this isle: we are three of them; if the other two be brained like us, the state totters.

STE. Drink, servant-monster, when I bid thee; thy eyes are almost set in thy head.

TRIN. Where should they be set else? he were a brave monster indeed, if they were set in his tail.

STE. My man-monster hath drowned his tongue in sack: for my part, the sea cannot drown me; I swam, ere I could recover the shore, five-and-thirty leagues, off and on. By this light thou shalt be my lieutenant, monster, or my standard.

TRIN. Your lieutenant, if you list; he 's no standard.

STE. We 'll not run, monsieur Monster.

TRIN. Nor go neither: but you'll lie, like dogs; and yet say nothing neither.

STE. Moon-calf, speak once in thy life, if thou beest a good moon-calf.

CAL. How does thy honour? Let me lick thy shoe.
I 'll not serve him, he is not valiant.

TRIN. Thou liest, most ignorant monster; I am in case to justle a constable. Why, thou deboshed fish, thou, was there ever a man a coward that hath drunk so much sack as I to-day? Wilt thou tell a monstrous lie, being but half a fish, and half a monster?

CAL. Lo, how he mocks me! wilt thou let him, my lord?

TRIN. *Lord*, quoth he!—that a monster should be such a natural!

CAL. Lo, lo, again! bite him to death, I pr'ythee.

STE. Trinculo, keep a good tongue in your head; if you prove a mutineer, the next tree—the poor monster 's my subject, and he shall not suffer indignity.

CAL. I thank my noble lord. Wilt thou be pleased to hearken once again to the suit I made to thee?

STE. Marry will I: kneel and repeat it; I will stand, and so shall Trinculo.

Enter ARIEL, *invisible.*

CAL. As I told thee before, I am subject to a tyrant;—a sorcerer, that by his cunning hath cheated me of the island.

ARI. Thou liest.

CAL. Thou liest, thou jesting monkey, thou;
I would my valiant master would destroy thee:
I do not lie.

STE. Trinculo, if you trouble him any more in 's tale, by this hand, I will supplant some of your teeth.

TRIN. Why, I said nothing.

STE. Mum then, and no more.—[*To* CALIBAN.] Proceed.

CAL. I say, by sorcery he got this isle;
From me he got it. If thy greatness will
Revenge it on him—for, I know, thou dar'st;
But this thing dare not,—

STE. That 's most certain.

CAL. —Thou shalt be lord of it, and I 'll serve thee.

STE. How now shall this be compassed? Canst thou bring me to the party?

CAL. Yea, yea, my lord; I 'll yield him thee asleep,
Where thou mayst knock a nail into his head.

ARI. Thou liest; thou canst not.

CAL. What a pied[a] ninny 's this!—Thou scurvy patch!—[b]
I do beseech thy greatness, give him blows,
And take his bottle from him: when that 's gone,
He shall drink nought but brine; for I 'll not show him
Where the quick freshes are.

STE. Trinculo, run into no further danger: interrupt the monster one word further, and, by this

---

a —— *a pied ninny's this!*] An allusion to the *pied*, or party coloured dress which Trinculo, as a jester, wore.

b Patch!] See notes (b), p. 127, Vol. I., and (d), p. 372, Vol. I.

hand, I'll turn my mercy out of doors, and make a stock-fish of thee.

TRIN. Why, what did I? I did nothing; I'll go further off.

STE. Didst thou not say he lied?

ARI. Thou liest.

STE. Do I so? take thou that.

[*Strikes* TRINCULO.

As you like this, give me the lie another time.

TRIN. I did not give the lie:—out o' your wits, and hearing too?—A pox o' your bottle! this can sack and drinking do.—A murrain on your monster, and the devil take your fingers!

CAL. Ha, ha, ha!

STE. Now, forward with your tale.—Pr'ythee stand further off.

CAL. Beat him enough: after a little time, I'll beat him too.

STE. Stand further.—Come, proceed. [him

CAL. Why, as I told thee, 't is a custom with

I' the afternoon to sleep: there thou mayst brain him,
Having first seiz'd his books; or with a log
Batter his skull, or paunch him with a stake,
Or cut his wezand with thy knife. Remember,
First to possess his books; for without them
He's but a sot, as I am, nor hath not
One spirit to command: they all do hate him,
As rootedly as I:—burn but his books;
He has brave utensils,—for so he calls them,—
Which, when he has a house, he'll deck withal:
And that most deeply to consider, is
The beauty of his daughter; he himself
Calls her a nonpareil: I never saw a woman,
But only Sycorax my dam and she;
But she as far surpasseth Sycorax,
As great'st does least.

STE. Is it so brave a lass?

CAL. Ay, lord; she will become thy bed, I warrant,
And bring thee forth brave brood.

STE. Monster, I will kill this man: his daughter and I will be king and queen,—save our graces!—and Trinculo and thyself shall be viceroys.—Dost thou like the plot, Trinculo?

TRIN. Excellent.

STE. Give me thy hand; I am sorry I beat thee; but, while thou livest, keep a good tongue in thy head.

CAL. Within this half-hour will he be asleep;
Wilt thou destroy him then?

STE. Ay, on mine honour.

ARI. This will I tell my master.

CAL. Thou mak'st me merry; I am full of pleasure;
Let us be jocund: will you troll the catch
You taught me but while-ere?

STE. At thy request, monster, I will do reason, any reason:—Come on, Trinculo, let us sing.
[*Sings.*

Flout 'em, and scout 'em; and scout 'em, and flout 'em;*
Thought is free.

CAL. That's not the tune.
[ARIEL *plays the tune on a tabor and pipe.*

STE. What is this same?

TRIN. This is the tune of our catch, played by the picture of Nobody.(1)

STE. If thou beest a man, show thyself in thy likeness: if thou beest a devil, take't as thou list.

TRIN. O, forgive me my sins!

STE. He that dies pays all debts: I defy thee.
—Mercy upon us!

CAL. Art thou afeard?

STE. No, monster, not I.

CAL. Be not afeard; the isle is full of noises,
Sounds, and sweet airs, that give delight, and hurt not.
Sometimes a thousand twangling instruments
Will hum about mine ears; and sometime voices,
That, if I then had wak'd after long sleep,
Will make me sleep again: and then, in dreaming,
The clouds methought would open and show riches
Ready to drop upon me; that when I wak'd
I cried to dream again.

STE. This will prove a brave kingdom to me, where I shall have my music for nothing.

CAL. When Prospero is destroyed.

STE. That shall be by and by:[a] I remember the story.

TRIN. The sound is going away: let's follow it, and after do our work.

STE. Lead, monster; we'll follow.—I would I could see this taborer! (2) he lays it on.

TRIN. Wilt come? I'll follow, Stephano.
[*Exeunt.*

SCENE III.—*Another Part of the* Island.

Enter ALONSO, SEBASTIAN, ANTONIO, GONZALO, ADRIAN, FRANCISCO, *and others.*

GON. By'r lakin,[b] I can go no further, sir:
My old bones ache;[c] here's a maze trod, indeed,
Through forth-rights[d] and meanders! by your patience,
I needs must rest me.

ALON. Old lord, I cannot blame thee,
Who am myself attach'd with weariness,
To the dulling of my spirits: sit down and rest.
Even here I will put off my hope, and keep it
No longer for my flatterer: he is drown'd
Whom thus we stray to find; and the sea mocks
Our frustrate search on land. Well, let him go.

ANT. [*Aside to* SEB.] I am right glad that he's so out of hope.
Do not, for one repulse, forego the purpose
That you resolv'd to effect.

SEB. [*Aside to* ANT.] The next advantage
Will we take throughly.

(*) Old text, *cout.*

a By and by:] *By and by*, as well as *presently*, now implies some brief delay; but in old language they usually meant *immediately*.

b *By'r* lakin,—] A contraction of *By our ladykin*, or, little lady. It occurs in "A Midsummer Night's Dream." See note (b), p. 357, Vol. I.

c Ache;] This word is now invariably spelt thus; but formerly, when used as a verb, it took the form of "*ake*," and, as a substantive, of "*ache*." See note (e), p. 14.

d Through forth-rights and meanders!] "Mazes were of two kinds, rectangular and curvilinear; Mr. Knight gives a figure of one of the former."—SINGER.

ANT. [*Aside to* SEB.] Let it be to-night;
For now they are oppress'd with travel, they
Will not, nor cannot, use such vigilance,
As when they are fresh.
SEB. [*Aside to* ANT.] I say, to-night: no more.

Solemn and strange music; and PROSPERO *above, invisible. Enter several strange* Shapes, *bringing in a banquet; they dance about it with gentle actions of salutation; and, inviting the* KING, *&c., to eat, they depart.*

ALON. What harmony is this? my good friends, hark!
GON. Marvellous sweet music!
ALON. Give us kind keepers, heavens! What were these?
SEB. A living drollery.[a] Now I will believe
That there are unicorns; that in Arabia
There is one tree, the phœnix' throne; one phœnix
At this hour reigning there.
ANT. I'll believe both;
And what does else want credit, come to me,
And I'll be sworn 'tis true: travellers ne'er did lie,
Though fools at home condemn 'em.
GON. If in Naples
I should report this now, would they believe me?
If I should say, I saw such islanders,—*
For, certes, these are people of the island,—
Who, though they are of monstrous shape, yet, note,
Their manners are more gentle-kind, than of
Our human generation you shall find
Many, nay, almost any.
PRO. [*Aside.*] Honest lord,
Thou hast said well; for some of you there present
Are worse than devils.
ALON. I cannot too much muse,
Such shapes, such gesture, and such sound, expressing,—
Although they want the use of tongue,—a kind
Of excellent dumb discourse.
PRO. [*Aside.*] Praise in departing.[b]
FRAN. They vanish'd strangely.
SEB. No matter, since
They have left their viands behind; for we have stomachs.—
Will't please you taste of what is here?
ALON. Not I.
GON. Faith, sir, you need not fear. When we were boys,
Who would believe that there were mountaineers
Dew-lapp'd like bulls, whose throats had hanging at 'em
Wallets of flesh? or that there were such men
Whose heads stood in their breasts? which now we find,
Each putter-out of five for one[c] will bring us
Good warrant of.
ALON. I will stand to, and feed,
Although my last: no matter, since I feel
The best is past.—Brother, my lord the duke,
Stand to, and do as we.

Thunder and lightning. Enter ARIEL, *like a harpy; claps his wings upon the table, and, with a quaint device, the banquet vanishes.*

ARI. You are three men of sin, whom Destiny,—
That hath to instrument this lower world
And what is in't,—the never-surfeited sea
Hath caus'd to belch up you, and on this island
Where man doth not inhabit, you 'mongst men
Being most unfit to live. I have made you mad;
And even with such-like valour, men hang and drown
Their proper selves. [ALONSO, SEBAST., *&c. draw their swords.*] You fools! I and my fellows
Are ministers of Fate: the elements,
Of whom your swords are temper'd, may as well
Wound the loud winds, or with bemock'd-at stabs
Kill the still-closing waters, as diminish
One dowle[d] that's in my plume; my fellow ministers
Are like invulnerable. If you could hurt,
Your swords are now too massy for your strengths,
And will not be uplifted. But, remember,—
For that's my business to you,—that you three
From Milan did supplant good Prospero;
Expos'd unto the sea, which hath requit it,
Him and his innocent child: for which foul deed
The powers, delaying, not forgetting, have

(*) First folio, *Islands*.

[a] A living drollery.] A puppet-show in Shakespeare's time was called a *drollery*. This, Sebastian says, is one played by living characters.

[b] Praise in departing.] A proverbial saying, equivalent to "Await the end before you commend your entertainment." So in "The Paradise of Dainty Devises," 1596,—

"A good beginning oft we see, but seldome standing at one stay,
For few do like the meane degree, then *praise at parting* some men say."

[c] Each putter-out of five for one—] It was the custom of travellers, when about to make a long voyage, to put out, or invest, a sum of money, upon a guarantee that they should receive at the rate of five for one if they returned. This species of gambling became so much in vogue at one period that adventurers were in the practice of undertaking dangerous journeys solely upon the speculation of what their *puttings-out* would yield if they got back safe. Of course when the journey ended fatally, the money they had invested went to the party who had engaged to pay the enormous interest on it. So, in Barnaby Riche's "Faults and Nothing but Faults," 1607: "Those whipsters, that, having spent the greatest part of their patrimony in prodigality, will give out the rest of their stocke *to be paid* two or *three for one* upon their return from Rome." See also Fynes Moryson's "Itinerary," Part I., p. 198, and Taylor, the water poet's pamphlet, called "The Scourge of Basenesse: or The Old Lerry, with a new Kicksey, and a new-cum *twang*, with the old Winsey." The ancient reading is usually altered in modern editions to "Each putter-out *of one for five*," or "Each putter-out *on* five for one," but no change is called for; Shakespeare and his contemporaries commonly used *of* for *on*,—

"I'd put out moneys *of* being Mayor."
"*The Ordinary*," Act I. Sc. 1.

[d] Dowle—] Feather; or particle of down.

Incens'd the seas and shores, yea, all the creatures,
Against your peace. Thee of thy son, Alonso,
They have bereft; and do pronounce, by me,
Ling'ring perdition—worse than any death
Can be at once—shall step by step attend
You and your ways; whose wraths to guard you from,—
Which here, in this most desolate isle, else falls
Upon your heads,—is nothing but heart's sorrow,
And a clear life ensuing.

He vanishes in thunder: then, to soft music, enter the Shapes *again, and dance with mocks and mows, and carry out the table.*

PRO. [*Aside.*] Bravely the figure of this harpy hast thou
Perform'd, my Ariel; a grace it had, devouring:
Of my instruction hast thou nothing 'bated,
In what thou hadst to say: so, with good life,[a]
And observation strange, my meaner ministers
Their several kinds have done. My high charms work,
And these, mine enemies, are all knit up
In their distractions: they now are in my power;

[a] *So, with* good life,—] The expression "good life" occurs with equal ambiguity in "Twelfth Night," Act II. Sc. 3, "Would you have a love-song, or a song of *good life?*"

And in these fits I leave them, while I visit
Young Ferdinand,—whom they suppose is drown'd,—
And his and mine lov'd darling. [*Exit from above.*

GON. I' the name of something holy, sir, why stand you
In this strange stare?

ALON. O, it is monstrous! monstrous!
Methought the billows spoke, and told me of it;
The winds did sing it to me; and the thunder,
That deep and dreadful organ-pipe, pronounc'd
The name of Prosper; it did bass my trespass.
Therefore my son i' the ooze is bedded; and,
I'll seek him deeper than e'er plummet sounded,
And with him there lie mudded. [*Exit.*

SEB. But one fiend at a time,
I'll fight their legions o'er!

ANT. I'll be thy second.
[*Exeunt* SEBASTIAN *and* ANTONIO.

GON. All three of them are desperate; their great guilt,
Like poison given to work a great time after,
Now 'gins to bite the spirits.—I do beseech you,
That are of suppler joints, follow them swiftly,
And hinder them from what this ecstasy
May now provoke them to.

ADR. Follow, I pray you.
[*Exeunt.*

ACT IV.

SCENE I.—*Before* Prospero's *Cell.*

Enter PROSPERO, FERDINAND, *and* MIRANDA.

PRO. If I have too austerely punish'd you,
Your compensation makes amends; for I
Have given you here a thread[a] of mine own life,
Or that for which I live; whom once again
I tender to thy hand. All thy vexations
Were but my trials of thy love, and thou
Hast strangely stood the test: here, afore Heaven,
I ratify this my rich gift. O, Ferdinand,
Do not smile at me that I boast her off,
For thou shalt find she will outstrip all praise,
And make it halt behind her!

FER. I do believe it,
Against an oracle.

PRO. Then, as my gift,* and thine own acquisition
Worthily purchas'd, take my daughter: but
If thou dost break her virgin-knot before
All sanctimonious ceremonies may
With full and holy rite be minister'd,
No sweet aspersion shall the heavens let fall
To make this contract grow; but barren hate,
Sour-ey'd disdain, and discord, shall bestrew
The union of your bed with weeds so loathly,
That you shall hate it both: therefore take heed,
As Hymen's lamps shall light you.

FER. As I hope
For quiet days, fair issue, and long life,
With such love as 't is now,—the murkiest den,
The most oppórtune place, the strong'st suggestion
Our worser Genius can, shall never melt
Mine honour into lust; to take away

(*) Old text, *guest.*

a —*a* thread *of mine own life,*—] The folios have "*third,*" a mis-spelling, perhaps, of *thred* = *thread,* which is oftentimes found in old writers.

The edge of that day's celebration,
When I shall think, or Phœbus' steeds are founder'd,
Or Night kept chain'd below.

PRO. Fairly spoke:
Sit, then, and talk with her; she is thine own.—
What, Ariel! my industrious servant, Ariel!

Enter ARIEL.

ARI. What would my potent master? here I am.

PRO. Thou and thy meaner fellows your last service
Did worthily perform; and I must use you
In such another trick. Go, bring the rabble,[a]
O'er whom I give thee power, here, to this place:
Incite them to quick motion; for I must
Bestow upon the eyes of this young couple
Some vanity of mine art; it is my promise,
And they expect it from me.

ARI. Presently?

PRO. Ay, with a twink.

ARI. Before you can say, *Come*, and *Go*,
And breathe twice, and cry, *So, so;*
Each one, tripping on his toe,
Will be here with mop and mow.
Do you love me, master? no?

PRO. Dearly, my delicate Ariel. Do not approach
Till thou dost hear me call.

ARI. Well I conceive. [*Exit.*

PRO. Look thou be true; do not give dalliance
Too much the rein: the strongest oaths are straw
To the fire i' the blood: be more abstemious,
Or else good night your vow!

FER. I warrant you, sir;
The white-cold virgin snow upon my heart
Abates the ardour of my liver.

PRO. Well.—
Now come, my Ariel! bring a corollary,[b]
Rather than want a spirit: appear, and pertly!—
No tongue; all eyes; be silent! [*Soft music.*

A Masque. Enter IRIS.

IRIS. Ceres, most bounteous lady, thy rich leas
Of wheat, rye, barley, vetches, oats, and pease;
Thy turfy mountains, where live nibbling sheep,
And flat meads thatch'd with stover, them to keep;
Thy banks with pioned and twilled brims,[c]
Which spongy April at thy hest betrims,
To make cold nymphs chaste crowns; and thy broom groves,[d]
Whose shadow the dismissed bachelor loves,
Being lass-lorn; thy pole-clipp'd vineyard;
And thy sea-marge, steril, and rocky-hard,
Where thou thyself dost air;—the queen o' the sky,
Whose watery arch and messenger am I,
Bids thee leave these; and with her sovereign grace,
Here on this grass-plot, in this very place,
To come and sport:—her peacocks fly amain;
Approach, rich Ceres, her to entertain.

Enter CERES.

CER. Hail, many-colour'd messenger, that ne'er
Dost disobey the wife of Jupiter;
Who, with thy saffron wings, upon my flowers
Diffusest honey-drops, refreshing showers;
And with each end of thy blue bow dost crown
My bosky acres and my unshrubb'd down,
Rich scarf to my proud earth;—why hath thy queen
Summon'd me hither, to this short-grass'd green?

IRIS. A contract of true love to celebrate;
And some donation freely to estate
On the bless'd lovers.

CER. Tell me, heavenly bow,
If Venus or her son, as thou dost know
Do now attend the queen? Since they did plot
The means that dusky Dis my daughter got,
Her and her blind boy's scandal'd company
I have forsworn.

IRIS. Of her society
Be not afraid; I met her deity
Cutting the clouds towards Paphos, and her son
Dove-drawn with her. Here thought they to have done
Some wanton charm upon this man and maid,
Whose vows are, that no bed-rite shall be paid
Till Hymen's torch be lighted: but in vain,
Mars's hot minion is return'd again;
Her waspish-headed son has broke his arrows,
Swears he will shoot no more, but play with sparrows,
And be a boy right out.

CER. Highest queen of state,
Great Juno comes! I know her by her gait.

---

a The rabble,—] The inferior spirits.

b A corollary,—] An overplus.

c Thy banks with pioned and twilled brims,—] According to Henley, "*pioned* and *twilled* brims meant brims *dug* and *begrimed*." Hanmer and Steevens contend that the poet had in view the margin of a stream adorned with flowers; while Mr. Collier's annotator would read, "pioned and *tilled*," that is, cultivated "brims." We much prefer the interpretation of Hanmer and Steevens to either of the others; but have not thought it desirable to alter the old text.

d —broom groves,—] Hanmer changes this to "*brown* groves," as does Mr. Collier's annotator; and a more unhappy alteration can hardly be conceived, since it at once destroys the point of the allusion: *yellow*, the colour of the broom, being supposed especially congenial to the *lass-lorn* and *dismissed* bachelor. Thus Burton, in his "Anatomy of Melancholy," Part III. Sec. 2,—"So long as we are wooers, and may kiss and coll at our pleasure, nothing is so sweet; we are in heaven, as we think: but when we are once tied, and have lost our liberty, marriage is an hell: give me my *yellow hose* again."

Enter JUNO.

JUN. How does my bounteous sister? Go with me
To bless this twain, that they may prosperous be,
And honour'd in their issue.

SONG.

JUN. *Honour, riches, marriage-blessing,*
Long continuance, and increasing,
Hourly joys be still upon you!
Juno sings her blessings on you.

CER.[a] *Earth's increase, foison plenty,*
Barns and garners never empty;
Vines, with clust'ring bunches growing;
Plants, with goodly burden bowing;
Spring[b] *come to you, at the farthest,*
In the very end of harvest!
Scarcity and want shall shun you;
Ceres' blessing so is on you.

FER. This is a most majestic vision, and
Harmonious charmingly:[c] may I be bold
To think these spirits?

PRO. Spirits, which by mine art
I have from their confines call'd to enact
My present fancies.

FER. Let me live here ever;
So rare a wonder, and a father wise,[d]
Makes this place Paradise.

[JUNO *and* CERES *whisper, and send* IRIS *on employment.*

PRO. Sweet now, silence!
Juno and Ceres whisper seriously;
There's something else to do: hush, and be mute,
Or else our spell is marred.

IRIS. You nymphs, call'd Naiads, of the wandering* brooks,
With your sedg'd crowns, and ever-harmless looks,
Leave your crisp channels, and on this green land
Answer your summons: Juno does command:
Come, temperate nymphs, and help to celebrate
A contract of true love; be not too late.

Enter certain Nymphs.

You sun-burn'd sicklemen of August, weary,
Come hither from the furrow, and be merry;
Make holiday: your rye-straw hats put on,
And these fresh nymphs encounter every one
In country footing.

Enter certain Reapers, *properly habited; they join with the* Nymphs *in a graceful dance; towards the end whereof* PROSPERO *starts suddenly, and speaks; after which, to a strange, hollow, and confused noise, they heavily vanish.*

PRO. [*Aside.*] I had forgot that foul conspiracy
Of the beast Caliban and his confederates,
Against my life; the minute of their plot
Is almost come.—[*To the* Spirits.] Well done;—avoid!—no more!

FER. This is strange: your father's in some passion
That works him strongly.

MIRA. Never till this day,
Saw I him touch'd with anger so distemper'd.

PRO. You do look, my son, in a mov'd sort,
As if you were dismay'd: be cheerful, sir.
Our revels now are ended. These our actors,
As I foretold you, were all spirits, and
Are melted into air, into thin air:
And, like the baseless fabric of this vision,
The cloud-capp'd towers, the gorgeous palaces,
The solemn temples, the great globe itself,
Yea, all which it inherit, shall dissolve,
And, like this insubstantial pageant faded,
Leave not a rack behind.(1) We are such stuff
As dreams are made on, and our little life
Is rounded with a sleep.—Sir, I am vex'd;
Bear with my weakness; my old brain is troubled:
Be not disturb'd with my infirmity:
If you be pleas'd, retire into my cell,
And there repose; a turn or two I'll walk,
To still my beating mind.

(*) Old text, *windring.*

a CER. Earth's increase, &c.] The prefix "*Cer.*" to this part of the song is omitted by mistake in the old copies, and was first inserted by Theobald.

b Spring come to you, at the farthest,
In the very end of harvest!]

Mr. Collier's annotator would alter this, strangely enough, to, "*Rain* come to you," &c. See the "Faiery Queen," B. III. C. 6, St. 42,—

"There is continuall spring, and harvest there
Continuall, both meeting at one time."

See also Amos, c. ix. v. 13:—"Behold, the days come, saith the Lord, that the plowman shall overtake the reaper, and the treader of grapes him that soweth seed."

c Harmonious charmingly:] *Charmingly* here imports *magically*, not delightfully.

d So rare a wonder, and a father wise,
Makes this place Paradise.]

In the ancient copies this reads,—

"So rare a wondred Father, and a wise
Makes this place Paradise;"

and it is usually altered to,—

"So rare a wonder'd father and a *wife*,
Make this place Paradise."

It is pretty evident that Ferdinand expresses a compliment to father and daughter; and equally so that the lines were intended to rhyme; with the very slight change we have ventured, the passage fulfils both conditions. It is noteworthy that the same rhyme occurs in the opening stanza of our author's "Passionate Pilgrim,"—

"—— what fool is not so wise,
To break an oath, to win a paradise?"

a stanza quoted in "Love's Labour's Lost," Act IV. Sc. 3.

Fer., Mira. We wish your peace. [*Exeunt.*

Pro. Come with a thought!—I thank thee.—[a]
Ariel, come!

Enter Ariel.

Ari. Thy thoughts I cleave to. What's thy pleasure?

Pro. Spirit,
We must prepare to meet with Caliban.

Ari. Ay, my commander; when I presented Ceres,
I thought to have told thee of it; but I fear'd
Lest I might anger thee.

Pro. Say again, where didst thou leave these varlets?

Ari. I told you, sir, they were red-hot with drinking;
So full of valour that they smote the air
For breathing in their faces; beat the ground
For kissing of their feet; yet always bending
Towards their project. Then I beat my tabor,
At which, like unback'd colts, they prick'd their ears,
Advanc'd their eyelids, lifted up their noses
As they smelt music; so I charm'd their ears,
That, calf-like, they my lowing follow'd through
Tooth'd briers, sharp furzes, pricking goss, and thorns,
Which enter'd their frail shins: at last I left them
I' the filthy mantled pool beyond your cell,
There dancing up to the chins, that the foul lake
O'erstunk their feet.

Pro. This was well done, my bird.
Thy shape invisible retain thou still:
The trumpery in my house, go, bring it hither,
For stale to catch these thieves.

Ari. I go, I go. [*Exit.*

Pro. A devil, a born devil, on whose nature
Nurture can never stick; on whom my pains,
Humanely taken, all, all lost, quite lost;
And as, with age, his body uglier grows,
So his mind cankers. I will plague them all,
Even to roaring.—

Re-enter Ariel, *loaden with glistering apparel, &c.*

Come, hang them on* this line.(2)

Prospero *and* Ariel *remain invisible. Enter* Caliban, Stephano, *and* Trinculo, *all wet.*

Cal. Pray you, tread softly, that the blind mole may not
Hear a foot fall: we now are near his cell.

[a] *I thank* thee.] Steevens, rightly, we believe, considered these words to be in reply to the mutual wish of Ferdinand and Miranda, but wrongly, perhaps, altered them to, "I thank *you*." *Thee*, however ungrammatical, appears to have been sometimes used in a plural sense: thus, in "Hamlet," Act II. Sc. 2; the prince, addressing the players, says,—"I am glad to see *thee* well."

(*) Old text, *on them.*

STE. Monster, your fairy, which you say is a harmless fairy, has done little better than played the Jack with us.

TRIN. Monster, I do smell all horse-piss; at which my nose is in great indignation.

STE. So is mine.—Do you hear, monster? If I should take a displeasure against you, look you,—

TRIN. Thou wert but a lost monster.

CAL. Good my lord, give me thy favour still.
Be patient, for the prize I'll bring thee to
Shall hoodwink this mischance: therefore speak softly;—
All's hush'd as midnight yet.

TRIN. Ay, but to lose our bottles in the pool,—

STE. There is not only disgrace and dishonour in that, monster, but an infinite loss.

TRIN. That's more to me than my wetting; yet this is your harmless fairy, monster.

STE. I will fetch off my bottle, though I be o'er ears for my labour.

CAL. Pr'ythee, my king, be quiet. See'st thou here,
This is the mouth o' the cell: no noise, and enter.
Do that good mischief, which may make this island
Thine own for ever, and I, thy Caliban,
For aye thy foot-licker.

STE. Give me thy hand. I do begin to have bloody thoughts.

TRIN. O, king Stephano! O, peer! O, worthy Stephano! look what a wardrobe here is for thee!

CAL. Let it alone, thou fool; it is but trash.

TRIN. O, ho, monster! we know what belongs to a frippery:[a]—O, king Stephano!

STE. Put off that gown, Trinculo: by this hand, I'll have that gown.

TRIN. Thy grace shall have it.

CAL. The dropsy drown this fool! what do you mean,
To dote thus on such luggage? Let's alone,[b]
And do the murder first: if he awake,
From toe to crown he'll fill our skins with pinches;
Make us strange stuff.

STE. Be you quiet, monster.—Mistress line, is not this my jerkin? Now is the jerkin under the line: now, jerkin, you are like to lose your hair,[c] and prove a bald jerkin.

TRIN. Do, do: we steal by line and level, an't like your grace.

STE. I thank thee for that jest: here's a garment for't: wit shall not go unrewarded while I am king of this country. *Steal by line and level* is an excellent pass of pate; there's another garment for't.

TRIN. Monster, come, put some lime upon your fingers, and away with the rest.

CAL. I will have none on't; we shall lose our time,
And all be turn'd to barnacles,(3) or to apes
With foreheads villainous low.

STE. Monster, lay-to your fingers; help to bear this away where my hogshead of wine is, or I'll turn you out of my kingdom: go to, carry this.

TRIN. And this.

STE. Ay, and this.

A noise of Hunters *heard. Enter divers* Spirits, *in shape of hounds, and hunt them about;* PROSPERO *and* ARIEL *setting them on.*

PRO. Hey, *Mountain*, hey!

ARI. *Silver!* there it goes, *Silver!*

PRO. *Fury, Fury!* there, *Tyrant*, there! hark, hark!

[CALIBAN, STEPHANO, *and* TRINCULO *are driven out.*

Go, charge my goblins that they grind their joints
With dry convulsions; shorten up their sinews
With aged cramps; and more pinch-spotted make them,
Than pard or cat o' mountain.

ARI. Hark, they roar!

PRO. Let them be hunted soundly. At this hour
Lie at my mercy all mine enemies:
Shortly shall all my labours end, and thou
Shalt have the air at freedom: for a little,
Follow, and do me service. [*Exeunt.*

a A frippery:—] A *frippery* was the name of a shop for the sale of second-hand apparel; the proprietor of which was called a *fripper*. The chief mart of the frippers, Strype tells us, was Birchin Lane and Cornhill.

b Let's alone,—] Theobald reads, "Let's *along;*" which, if *alone* was not sometimes used in the same sense, is undoubtedly the right word: but see note (b), p. 81, Vol. I.

c —now, jerkin, you are like to lose your hair,—] A quibble on the loss of hair sometimes suffered by those who visit hot climates, and the hair clothes-line on which the "glistering apparel" is suspended.

ACT V.

SCENE I.—*Before the Cell of* Prospero.

Enter Prospero *in his magic robes, and* Ariel.

Pro. Now does my project gather to a head:
My charms crack not; my spirits obey; and Time
Goes upright with his carriage. How 's the day?
Ari. On the sixth hour; at which time, my lord,
You said our work should cease.
Pro. I did say so,
When first I rais'd the tempest. Say, my spirit,
How fares the king and 's followers?
Ari. Confin'd together,
In the same fashion as you gave in charge,
Just as you left them; all prisoners, sir,
In the line-grove[a] which weather-fends your cell;
They cannot budge till your release. The king,
His brother, and yours, abide all three distracted;
And the remainder mourning over them,
Brim-full of sorrow and dismay; but chiefly
Him that you term'd, sir, *The good old lord, Gonzalo;*
His tears run down his beard, like winter's drops
From eaves of reeds: your charm so strongly works 'em,
That if you now beheld them, your affections
Would become tender.
Pro. Dost thou think so, spirit?
Ari. Mine would, sir, were I human.
Pro. And mine shall.
Hast thou, which art but air, a touch, a feeling
Of their afflictions? and shall not myself,
One of their kind, that relish all as sharply,
Passion[b] as they, be kindlier mov'd than thou art?
Though with their high wrongs I am struck to the quick,
Yet, with my nobler reason 'gainst my fury

[a] Line-grove—] Mr. Hunter, in his "Disquisition on Shakespeare's Tempest," has clearly proved that the linden, or lime, was formerly called the "*line*-tree."

[b] Passion as they,—] We should probably read, "Passion'd as they."

Do I take part. The rarer action is
In virtue than in vengeance: they being penitent,
The sole drift of my purpose doth extend
Not a frown further. Go, release them, Ariel;
My charms I'll break, their senses I'll restore,
And they shall be themselves.

ARI. I'll fetch them, sir. [*Exit.*

PRO. Ye elves of hills, brooks, standing lakes, and groves;
And ye that on the sands with printless foot
Do chase the ebbing Neptune, and do fly him
When he comes back; you demi-puppets that
By moonshine do the green-sour ringlets make,
Whereof the ewe not bites; and you, whose pastime
Is to make midnight-mushrooms, that rejoice
To hear the solemn curfew; by whose aid—
Weak masters though ye be—I have bedimm'd
The noontide sun, call'd forth the mutinous winds,
And 'twixt the green sea and the azur'd vault
Set roaring war: to the dread rattling thunder
Have I given fire, and rifted Jove's stout oak
With his own bolt: the strong-bas'd promontory
Have I made shake; and by the spurs pluck'd up
The pine and cedar: graves, at my command,
Have wak'd their sleepers; op'd, and let them forth
By my so potent art.(1) But this rough magic
I here abjure; and, when I have requir'd
Some heavenly music,—which even now I do,—
To work mine end upon their senses that
This airy charm is for, I'll break my staff,
Bury it certain fathoms in the earth,
And, deeper than did ever plummet sound,
I'll drown my book. [*Solemn music.*

Re-enter ARIEL: *after him,* ALONSO, *with a frantic gesture, attended by* GONZALO; SEBASTIAN *and* ANTONIO *in like manner, attended by* ADRIAN *and* FRANCISCO: *they all enter the circle which* PROSPERO *had made, and there stand charmed; which* PROSPERO *observing, speaks.*

A solemn air, and the best comforter
To an unsettled fancy, cure thy brains,
Now useless, boil'd* within thy skull! There stand,
For you are spell-stopp'd.—
Holy Gonzalo, honourable man,
Mine eyes, even sociable to the show[a] of thine,
Fall fellowly drops.—The charm dissolves apace;
And as the morning steals upon the night,
Melting the darkness, so their rising senses
Begin to chase the ignorant fumes that mantle
Their clearer reason.—O, good Gonzalo,
My true preserver, and a loyal sir
To him thou follow'st! I will pay thy graces
Home, both in word and deed.—Most cruelly
Didst thou, Alonso, use me and my daughter:
Thy brother was a furtherer in the act;—
Thou art pinch'd for 't now, Sebastian.—Flesh and blood,
You brother mine, that entertain ambition,
Expell'd remorse and nature; who, with Sebastian,—
Whose inward pinches therefore are most strong,—
Would here have kill'd your king; I do forgive thee,
Unnatural though thou art.—Their understanding
Begins to swell; and the approaching tide
Will shortly fill the reasonable shore,
That now lies foul and muddy. Not one of them
That yet looks on me, or would know me:—Ariel,
Fetch me the hat and rapier in my cell;— [*Exit* ARIEL.
I will discase me, and myself present,
As I was sometime Milan:—quickly, spirit;
Thou shalt ere long be free.

ARIEL *re-enters, singing, and helps to attire* PROSPERO.

ARI. *Where the bee sucks, there suck I;*
In a cowslip's bell I lie,
There I couch when owls do cry:
On the bat's back I do fly
After summer merrily:
Merrily, merrily, shall I live now,
Under the blossom that hangs on the bough.(2)

PRO. Why, that's my dainty Ariel! I shall miss thee;
But yet thou shalt have freedom: so, so, so.—
To the king's ship, invisible as thou art:
There shalt thou find the mariners asleep
Under the hatches; the master and the boatswain,

(*) Old text, *boile.*

a Holy *Gonzalo, honourable man,*
Mine eyes, even sociable to the show *of thine,*—]

On this passage Mr. Collier has the following observations in his last edition:—"'Noble' and 'flow' are from the corrected folio, 1632, and, we may be confident, are restorations of the poet's language. Why has Prospero to call Gonzalo *holy*, as the epithet stands in the folios?—he was 'noble' and 'honourable,' but in no respect *holy*; the error of *show* for 'flow' is also transparent, and must have been occasioned chiefly by the mistake of the long *s* for *f*." In his anxiety to sustain the changes proposed by his annotator, Mr. Collier appears to have forgotten two or three facts which militate very strongly against them. In the first place, the word "*holy*," in Shakespeare's time, besides its ordinary meaning of *godly, sanctified*, and the like, signified also *pure, just, righteous*, &c.: in this sense, Leontes, in "The Winter's Tale," Act V. Sc. 1, speaks of Polixenes as "holy,"—

"You have a *holy* father,
A graceful gentleman."

In the next place, the old text has "*shew*," not *show*; and, thirdly, the misprint, if there were one, could not have been occasioned chiefly by the mistake of the long *s* for *f*, seeing the *sh* of "show" in old typography formed a single character, ſh, which was far less likely to be confounded with the type which represented "fl"—fl, than the single long *s* with *f*.

Being awake, enforce them to this place;
And presently, I pr'ythee.
ARI. I drink the air before me, and return
Or e'er your pulse twice beat. [*Exit.*
GON. All torment, trouble, wonder, and amazement
Inhabits here: some heavenly power guide us
Out of this fearful country!
PRO. Behold, sir king,
The wronged duke of Milan, Prospero:
For more assurance that a living prince
Does now speak to thee, I embrace thy body;
And to thee and thy company, I bid
A hearty welcome.
ALON. Whêr thou beest he, or no,
Or some enchanted trifle[a] to abuse me,
As late I have been, I not know: thy pulse
Beats, as of flesh and blood; and, since I saw thee,
The affliction of my mind amends, with which,
I fear, a madness held me: this must crave—
An if this be at all—a most strange story.
Thy dukedom I resign; and do entreat
Thou pardon me my wrongs.—But how should Prospero
Be living, and be here?
PRO. [*To* GON.] First, noble friend,
Let me embrace thine age, whose honour cannot
Be measur'd or confin'd.
GON. Whether this be,
Or be not, I'll not swear.
PRO. You do yet taste
Some subtleties o' the isle, that will not let you
Believe things certain.—Welcome, my friends all:—
But you, my brace of lords, were I so minded,
[*Aside to* SEBASTIAN *and* ANTONIO.
I here could pluck his highness' frown upon you,
And justify you traitors; at this time
I'll tell no tales.
SEB. [*Aside.*] The devil speaks in him.
PRO. No:—
For you, most wicked sir, whom to call brother
Would even infect my mouth, I do forgive
Thy rankest fault,—all of them; and require
My dukedom of thee, which, perforce, I know
Thou must restore.
ALON. If thou beest Prospero,
Give us particulars of thy preservation;
How thou hast met us here, who three hours since
Were wreck'd upon this shore; where I have lost—
How sharp the point of this remembrance is!—
My dear son Ferdinand.
PRO. I am woe for 't, sir.
ALON. Irreparable is the loss; and Patience
Says it is past her cure.
PRO. I rather think,
You have not sought her help; of whose soft grace,
For the like loss I have her sovereign aid
And rest myself content.
ALON. You the like loss?
PRO. As great to me, as late,—and supportable
To make the dear loss, have I means much weaker
Than you may call to comfort you,—for I
Have lost my daughter.
ALON. A daughter?
O heavens! that they were living both in Naples,
The king and queen there! that they were, I wish
Myself were mudded in that oozy bed
Where my son lies. When did you lose your daughter?
PRO. In this last tempest.—I perceive these lords
At this encounter do so much admire,
That they devour their reason, and scarce think
Their eyes do offices of truth, their words
Are natural breath: but, howsoe'er you have
Been justled from your senses, know for certain
That I am Prospero, and that very duke
Which was thrust forth of Milan; who most strangely
Upon this shore, where you were wreck'd, was landed,
To be the lord on 't. No more yet of this;
For 't is a chronicle of day by day,
Not a relation for a breakfast, nor
Befitting this first meeting. Welcome, sir;
This cell 's my court: here have I few attendants,
And subjects none abroad: pray you, look in.
My dukedom since you have given me again,
I will requite you with as good a thing;
At least, bring forth a wonder to content ye,
As much as me my dukedom.

The entrance of the Cell opens, and discovers FERDINAND *and* MIRANDA *playing at chess.*

MIRA. Sweet lord, you play me false.
FER. No, my dear'st love,
I would not for the world.
MIRA. Yes, for a score of kingdoms you should wrangle,
And I would call it fair play.
ALON. If this prove
A vision of the island, one dear son
Shall I twice lose.
SEB. A most high miracle!
FER. Though the seas threaten, they are merciful:
I have curs'd them without cause.
[*Kneels to* ALONSO.
ALON. Now all the blessings

---

[a] *Or some enchanted* trifle—] Mr. Collier's annotator substitutes *devil* for "trifle;" a change as wanton as it is foolish. *Trifle* meant *phantom;* thus, in Beaumont and Fletcher's "Bonduca," Act V. Sc. 2,—

"In love too with a *trifle* to abuse me."

Of a glad father compass thee about!
Arise, and say how thou cam'st here.
MIRA. O, wonder!
How many goodly creatures are there here!
How beauteous mankind is! O brave new world,
That has such people in 't!
PRO. 'T is new to thee.
ALON. What is this maid, with whom thou wast at play?
Your eld'st acquaintance cannot be three hours:
Is she the goddess that hath sever'd us,
And brought us thus together?
FER. Sir, she is mortal;
But, by immortal Providence, she 's mine;
I chose her, when I could not ask my father
For his advice, nor thought I had one. She
Is daughter to this famous duke of Milan,
Of whom so often I have heard renown,
But never saw before; of whom I have
Receiv'd a second life; and second father
This lady makes him to me.
ALON. I am hers:
But O, how oddly will it sound that I
Must ask my child forgiveness!
PRO. There, sir, stop;
Let us not burden our remembrances with
A heaviness that 's gone.
GON. I have inly wept,
Or should have spoke ere this.—Look down, you gods,
And on this couple drop a blessed crown!
For it is you that have chalk'd forth the way
Which brought us hither.
ALON. I say, Amen, Gonzalo!
GON. Was Milan thrust from Milan, that his issue
Should become kings of Naples? O, rejoice
Beyond a common joy! and set it down
With gold on lasting pillars,—in one voyage
Did Claribel her husband find at Tunis;
And Ferdinand, her brother, found a wife
Where he himself was lost; Prospero, his dukedom,
In a poor isle; and all of us, ourselves,
When no man was his own!
ALON. [*To* FERDINAND *and* MIRANDA.] Give me your hands:
Let grief and sorrow still embrace his heart
That doth not wish you joy!
GON. Be 't so! Amen!

Re-enter ARIEL, *with the* Master *and* Boatswain *amazedly following.*

O look, sir, look, sir! here are more of us!
I prophesied if a gallows were on land,
This fellow could not drown.—Now, blasphemy,
That swear'st grace o'erboard, not an oath on shore?
Hast thou no mouth by land? What is the news?
BOATS. The best news is that we have safely found

Our king and company: the next, our ship,—
Which, but three glasses since, we gave out split,—
Is tight, and yare, and bravely rigg'd, as when
We first put out to sea.

ARI. [*Aside to* PRO.] Sir, all this service
Have I done since I went.

PRO. [*Aside to* ARIEL.] My tricksy spirit!

ALON. These are not natural events; they strengthen,
From strange to stranger.—Say, how came you [hither?

BOATS. If I did think, sir, I were well awake,
I'd strive to tell you. We were dead of sleep,
And—how, we know not—all clapp'd under hatches,
Where, but even now, with strange and several [noises
Of roaring, shrieking, howling, jingling chains,
And more diversity of sounds, all horrible,
We were awak'd; straightway, at liberty:
Where we, in all her* trim, freshly beheld
Our royal, good, and gallant ship; our master
Capering to eye her: on a trice, so please you,
Even in a dream, were we divided from them,
And were brought moping hither.

ARI. [*Aside to* PRO.] Was't well done?

PRO. [*Aside to* ARIEL.] Bravely, my diligence.
Thou shalt be free.

ALON. This is as strange a maze as e'er men [trod;
And there is in this business more than nature
Was ever conduct of: some oracle
Must rectify our knowledge.

PRO. Sir, my liege,
Do not infest your mind with beating on
The strangeness of this business; at pick'd leisure,
Which shall be shortly, single I'll resolve you—
Which to you shall seem probable—of every
These happen'd accidents: till when, be cheerful,
And think of each thing well.—[*Aside to* ARIEL.]
Come hither, spirit;
Set Caliban and his companions free:
Untie the spell. [*Exit* ARIEL.] How fares my gracious sir?
There are yet missing of your company
Some few odd lads that you remember not.

Re-enter ARIEL, *driving in* CALIBAN, STEPHANO, *and* TRINCULO, *in their stolen apparel.*

STE. Every man shift for all the rest, and let no man take care for himself; for all is but fortune!—*Coragio*, bully-monster, *Coragio!*

TRIN. If these be true spies which I wear in my head, here's a goodly sight.

CAL. O, Setebos, these be brave spirits, indeed!
How fine my master is! I am afraid
He will chastise me.

SEB. Ha, ha!
What things are these, my lord Antonio?
Will money buy them?

ANT. Very like; one of them
Is a plain fish, and, no doubt, marketable.

PRO. Mark but the badges of these men, my lords,
Then say if they be true. This mis-shapen knave,—
His mother was a witch, and one so strong
That could control the moon,[a] make flows and ebbs,
And deal in her command, without[b] her power.
These three have robb'd me; and this demi-devil—
For he's a bastard one—had plotted with them
To take my life: two of these fellows you
Must know and own; this thing of darkness I
Acknowledge mine.

CAL. I shall be pinch'd to death.

ALON. Is not this Stephano, my drunken butler?

SEB. He is drunk now: where had he wine?

ALON. And Trinculo is reeling ripe: where should they
Find this grand liquor that hath gilded 'em?—
How cam'st thou in this pickle?

TRIN. I have been in such a pickle, since I saw you last, that, I fear me, will never out of my bones: I shall not fear fly-blowing.

SEB. Why, how now, Stephano?

STE. O, touch me not; I am not Stephano, but a cramp.

PRO. You'd be king o' the isle, sirrah?

STE. I should have been a sore one, then.

ALON. This is a strange thing as e'er I look'd on. [*Pointing to* CALIBAN.

PRO. He is as disproportion'd in his manners
As in his shape.—Go, sirrah, to my cell;
Take with you your companions; as you look
To have my pardon, trim it handsomely.

CAL. Ay, that I will; and I'll be wise hereafter,
And seek for grace. What a thrice-double ass
Was I, to take this drunkard for a god,
And worship this dull fool!

PRO. Go to; away!

ALON. Hence, and bestow your luggage where you found it.

SEB. Or stole it, rather.

[*Exeunt* CALIBAN, STEPHANO, *and* TRINCULO.

(*) Old text, *our*.

[a] His mother was a witch, and one so strong
That could control the moon,—]
So in Act II. Sc. 1, Gonzalo says, "You would lift the moon out of her *sphere*, if she would continue in it five weeks without changing." Thus, too, in Beaumont and Fletcher's play of "The Prophetess," Act II. Sc. 3,—
"—— the pale moon
Pluck'd in her silver horns, trembling for fear
That my strong spells should force her from her *sphere*."
Douce quotes a marginal note in Adlington's translation of Apuleius, 1596, 4to. which says, "Witches in old time were supposed to be of such power that they could pul downe *the moone by their inchantement*." The classical reader will remember,—
"Cantus et *è curru lunam deducere* tentat;
Et faceret, si non ære repulsa sonent."
Of Tibullus; and Virgil's
"*Carmina vel cœlo possunt deducere lunam:*" &c.

[b] *And deal in her command, without her power.*] That is, *beyond* her power. See note ([b]), p. 371, Vol. I.

PRO. Sir, I invite your highness and your train
To my poor cell, where you shall take your rest
For this one night; which (part of it) I'll waste
With such discourse as, I not doubt, shall make it
Go quick away,—the story of my life,
And the particular accidents gone by,
Since I came to this isle: and in the morn
I'll bring you to your ship, and so to Naples,
Where I have hope to see the nuptial
Of these our dear-belov'd solemnizèd;
And thence retire me to my Milan, where
Every third thought shall be my grave.

ALON. I long
To hear the story of your life, which must
Take the ear strangely.

PRO. I'll deliver all;
And promise you calm seas, auspicious gales,
And sail so expeditious, that shall catch
Your royal fleet far off.—[*Aside to* ARIEL.] My Ariel,—chick,—
That is thy charge; then to the elements!
Be free, and fare thou well!—Please you, draw near. [*Exeunt.*

EPILOGUE.

Spoken by PROSPERO.

Now my charms are all o'erthrown,
And what strength I have 's mine own,—
Which is most faint: now, 't is true,
I must be here confin'd by you,
Or sent to Naples. Let me not,
Since I have my dukedom got,
And pardon'd the deceiver, dwell
In this bare island by your spell;
But release me from my bands,
With the help of your good hands.
Gentle breath of yours my sails
Must fill, or else my project fails,
Which was to please: now I want
Spirits to enforce, art to enchant;
And my ending is despair,
Unless I be reliev'd by prayer,
Which pierces so, that it assaults
Mercy itself, and frees all faults.
As you from crimes would pardon'd be,
Let your indulgence set me free. [*Exit.*

ILLUSTRATIVE COMMENTS.

ACT I.

(1) SCENE I.—*We split, we split!*] The following observations on the maritime technicalities in this scene, are extracted from an article by Lord Mulgrave, which will be found at length in Boswell's Variorum edition of Shakespeare, 1821:—

"The first scene of The Tempest is a very striking instance of the great accuracy of Shakspeare's knowledge in a professional science, the most difficult to attain without the help of experience. He must have acquired it by conversation with some of the most skilful seamen of that time. No books had then been published on the subject.

"The succession of events is strictly observed in the natural progress of the distress described; the expedients adopted are the most proper that could have been devised for a chance of safety: and it is neither to the want of skill of the seamen, or the bad qualities of the ship, but solely to the power of Prospero, that the shipwreck is to be attributed.

"The words of command are not only strictly proper, but are only such as point the object to be attained, and no superfluous ones of detail. Shakspeare's ship was too well manned to make it necessary to tell the seamen how they were to do it, as well as what they were to do.

"He has shown a knowledge of the new improvements, as well as the doubtful points of seamanship; one of the latter he has introduced, under the only circumstance in which it was indisputable.

"The events certainly follow too near one another for the strict time of representation: but perhaps, if the whole length of the play was divided by the time allowed by the critics, the portion allotted to this scene might not be too little for the whole. But he has taken care to mark intervals between the different operations by exits.

1st Position.	*1st Position.*
Fall to 't yarely, or we run ourselves aground.	Land discovered under the lee; the wind blowing too fresh to hawl upon a wind with the topsail set.—Yare is an old sea-term for briskly, in use at that time. This first command is therefore a notice to be ready to execute any orders quickly.
2d Position.	*2d Position.*
Yare, yare! Take in the topsail! Blow, till thou burst thy wind, if room enough!	The topsail is taken in.—'Blow till thou burst thy wind, if room enough.' The danger in a good sea-boat, is only from being too near the land: this is introduced here to account for the next order.
3d Position.	*3d Position.*
Down with the topmast! * Yare; lower, lower! Bring her to try with the main-course!	The gale encreasing, the topmast is struck, to take the weight from aloft, make the ship drive less to leeward, and bear the mainsail under which the ship is laid-to.
4th Position.	*4th Position.*
Lay her a-hold, a-hold! set her two courses! off to sea again; lay her off!	The ship, having driven near the shore, the mainsail is hawled up; the ship wore, and the two courses set on the other tack, to endeavour to clear the land that way.
5th Position.	*5th Position.*
We split! we split!	The ship, not able to weather a point, is driven on shore."

(2) SCENE II.—ARIEL.] According to the system of witchcraft or magic, which formed an article of popular creed in Shakespeare's day, the elementary spirits were divided into six classes by some demonologists, and into four,—those of the *Air*, of the *Water*, of the *Fire*, and of the *Earth*,—by others. In the list of characters appended to "The Tempest" in the first folio, Ariel is called "an ayrie spirit." The particular functions of this order of beings, Burton tells us, are to cause "many tempests, thunder, and lightnings, tear oaks, fire steeples, houses, strike men and beasts, make it rain stones, &c., cause whirlwinds on a sudden, and *tempestuous storms*." But at the behest of the all-powerful magician Prospero, or by his own influence and potency, the airy spirit in a twink becomes not only a spirit of fire—one of those, according to the same authority, which "commonly work by blazing stars, fire drakes, or *ignes fatui;* * * * counterfeit suns and moons, stars oftentimes, and sit upon ship-masts"—but a *naiad*, or spirit of the water also: in fact, assumes any shape, and is visible or unseen at will.

For full particulars, *de operatione Demonum*, the reader may consult, besides the ancient writers on the subject,

* The striking the top masts was a new invention in Shakspeare's time, which he here very properly introduces. Sir Henry Manwaring says, "It is not yet agreed amongst all seamen whether it is better for a ship to hull with her topmast up or down." In the Postscript to the Seaman's Dictionary, he afterwards gives his own opinion: "If you have sea-room, it is never good to strike the topmast." Shakspeare has placed his ship in the situation in which it was indisputably right to strike the topmast, when he had not sea-room.

who are legion, *Batman uppon Bartholome his booke De proprietatibus rerum,* 1582; Scot's "Discoverie of Witchcraft," &c., 1584; "The Demonologie" of James I.; "The Anatomie of Sorcerie" by Mason, 1612; and Burton's "Anatomy of Melancholy," 1617.

(3) SCENE II.—

—— on the topmast,
The yards, and bowsprit, would I flame distinctly,
Then meet, and join.]

This, as Douce remarks, is a description of the well-known meteor, called by the several names of *Saint Helen, Saint Elm, Saint Herm, Saint Clare, Saint Peter,* and *Saint Nicholas.* "Whenever it appeared as a single flame, it was supposed by the ancients to be *Helena,* the sister of Castor and Pollux; and in this state to bring ill-luck from the calamities which this lady is known to have caused in the Trojan war. When it came double, it was called Castor and Pollux, and accounted a good omen."

Hakluyt's collection of the "Voyages, Navigations, Traffiques, and Discoveries of the English Nation," furnishes an interesting account of this meteor, as seen during the "Voyage of Robert Tomson Marchant, into Nova Hispania, in the yeere 1555:"—

"I do remember that in the great and boysterous storme of this foule weather, in the night, there came upon the toppe of our maine yarde and maine maste, a certaine little light, much like unto the light of a little candle, which the Spaniards called the *Cuerpo santo,* and saide it was *S. Elmo,* whom they take to be the advocate of sailers. * * * This light continued aboord our ship about three houres, flying from maste to maste, and from top to top: and sometime it would be in two or three places at once. I informed myself of learned men afterward what that light should be, and they said, that it was but a congelation of the winde and vapours of the sea congealed with the extremitie of the weather, which, flyinge in the winde, many times doeth chance to hit on the masts and shrowds of the ships that are at sea in foule weather. And in trueth I do take it to be so: for that I have seene the like in other ships at sea, and in sundry ships at once."—HAKLUYT, III. 450, *ed.* 1600.

(4) SCENE II.—*The still-vex'd Bermoothes.*] Shakespeare's first knowledge of the storm-vex'd coast of the Bermudas, was probably acquired from Sir Walter Raleigh's "Discoverie of the Large, Rich, and Beautiful Empire of Guiana," 1596, wherein, after speaking of the Channel of Bahama, the author adds,—"The rest of the Indies for calms, and diseases, are very troublesome; and the *Bermudas* a hellish sea, for *thunder, lightning,* and *storms.*" (See Chalmers' Apology, p. 578.) Or he might have derived his information from Hakluyt's Voyages, 1600, in which there is a description of Bermuda, by Henry May, who was shipwrecked there in 1593.

(5) SCENE II.—CALIBAN.] It has been surmised that the idea of this marvellous creation was derived from the subjoined passage in Eden's "History of Travayle in the West and East Indies," 4to., London, 1577—a book from which it is exceedingly probable that Shakespeare borrowed the names of some of the principal characters of this piece, as Alonso, Ferdinand, Sebastian, Gonzalo, Antonio, &c.

"Departyng from hence, they sayled to the 49 degree and a halfe under the pole antartike; where being wyntered, they were inforced to remayne there for the space of two monethes: all which tyme they sawe no man, excepte that one day by chaunce they espyed a man of the stature of a giant, who came to the haven *daunsing and singyng,* and shortly after seemed to cast dust over his head. The captayne sent one of his men to the shore, with the shyppe boate, who made the lyke signe of peace. The which thyng the giant seeyng, was out of feare, and came with the captayne's servaunt, to his presence, into a little ilande. When he sawe the captayne with certayne of his company about hym, he was greatly amased, and made signes, *holdyng up his hande to heaven,* signifying thereby, *that our men came from thence.* This giant was so byg, that the head of one of our men of a meane stature came but to his waste. He was of good corporature, and well made in all partes of his bodie, with a large visage painted with divers colours, but, for the most parte, yelow. Uppon his cheekes were paynted two hartes, and red circles about his eyes. The heare of his head was coloured whyte, and his apparell was the skynne of a beast sowde togeather. This beast, as seemed unto us, had a large head, and great eares lyke unto a mule, with the body of a camell and tayle of a horse. The feete of the giant were foulded in the sayde skynne, after the maner of shooes. * * * The captayne caused him to eate and drynke, and gave him many thinges, and among other a great lookyng glasse, in the which, as soone as he sawe his owne lykenesse, was sodaynly afrayde, and started backe with such violence, that hee overthrewe two that stoode nearest about him. When the captayne had thus gyven him certayne haukes belles, and other great belles, with also a lookyng glasse, a combe, and a payre of beades of glasse, he sent him to lande with foure of his owne men well armed."

(6) SCENE II.—

As wicked dew as e'er my mother brush'd
With raven's feather from unwholesome fen,
Drop on you both! a south-west blow on ye,
And blister you all o'er!]

Wicked, in the sense of *baneful, hurtful,* is often met with in old medical works applied to sores and wounds. "A wykked felone," *i.e.* a bad sore, is mentioned in a tract on hawking, MS. Harl. 2340. An analogous use of the word, *fierce, savage,* is mentioned in A Glossary of Provincial Words used in Herefordshire, 1839, p. 119, as still current.—HALLIWELL.

The following passage in *Batman uppon Bartholome his booke De proprietatibus rerum,* 1582, folio, will not only throw considerable light on these lines, but furnish at the same time grounds for a conjecture that Shakespeare was indebted to it, with a slight alteration, for the name of Caliban's mother, Sycorax the witch. "The raven is called corvus of CORAX . . . . it is said that *ravens birdes* be fed with *deaw* of heaven all the time that they have no black *feathers* by benefite of age," lib. xii. c. 10. The same author will also account for the choice which is made, in the monster's speech, of the south-west wind. "This *southern wind* is hot and moyst. . . . *Southern winds* corrupt and destroy; they heat and maketh men fall into sicknesse," lib. xi. c. 3.—DOUCE.

(7) SCENE II.—*It would control my dam's god, Setebos.*] The same work, Eden's *History of Travayle,* contains a curious notice, showing that Setebos was a mythological personage in the creed of the Patagonians:—

"The captayne retayned two of these [giants] which were youngest and beste made. He tooke them by a deceite in this maner,—that givyng them knyves, sheares, looking glasses, bells, beades of crystall and suche other trifles, he so filled theyr handes, that they could holde no more; then caused two payre of shackels of iron to be put on theyr legges, makyng signes that he would also give them those chaynes, which they lyked very wel, bycause they were made of bright and shining metall. * * * When they felte the shackels faste about theyr legges, they began to doubt; but the captayne dyd put them in comfort, and bad them stand still. In fine, when they sawe how they were deceived, they roared lyke bulles, and cryed uppon theyr *great devill, Setebos,* to helpe them. * * * They say, that when any of them dye, there appeare X or XII devils, *leaping and daunsing* about the bodie of the dead, and seeme to have their bodies paynted with divers colours, and that among other there is one seene bigger then the residue, who maketh great mirth and rejoysing. This great devyll they call Setebos."—P. 434.

ACT II.

(1) SCENE I.—

— *but nature should bring forth*
Of it own kind, all foizon, all abundance,
To feed my innocent people.]

Among the most treasured rarities in the library of the British Museum, is Shakespeare's own copy of Florio's Montaigne, 1603, with his autograph, "Willm. Shakspere," on the fly-leaf. This work, intituled, "The Essayes, or Morall, Politike and Millitarie Discourses, of Lo: Michaell de Montaigne, Knight," was evidently a favourite of the poet, and furnished him with the materials for Gonzalo's Utopian commonwealth. The passage he has adopted occurs in the thirtieth chapter of the First Book, and is headed, "Of the Caniballes:"—

"Those nations seeme therefore so barbarous unto mee, because they have received very little fashion from humane wit, and are yet neere their originall naturalitie. The lawes of nature do yet commaund them, which are but little bastardized by ours. And that with such puritie, as I am sometimes grieved the knowlege of it came no sooner to light, at what time ther were men, that better than wee could have judged of it. I am sorie, Licurgus and Plato had it not: for me seemeth that what in those nations we see by experience, doth not onlie exceede all the pictures wherewith licentious Poesie hath prowdly imbellished the golden age, and al hir quaint inventions to faine a happy condition of man, but also the conception and desire of Philosophie. They could not imagine a genuitie so pure and simple, as we see it by experience; nor ever beleeve our societie might be maintained with so little arte and humane combination. *It is a nation, would I answere Plato, that hath no kinde of traffike, no knowledge of Letters, no intelligence of numbers, no name of magistrate, nor of politike superioritie; no use of service, of riches, or of poverty; no contracts, no successions, no dividences, no occupation but idle; no respect of kinred, but common, no apparell but naturall, no manuring of lands, no use of wine, corne, or mettle. The very words that import lying, falshood, treason, dissimulation, covetousnes, envie, detraction, and pardon, were never heard of amongst them.*"

(2) SCENE I.—*We would so, and then go a bat-fowling.*] The instructions for *Bat-fowling* in Markham's "Hunger's Prevention," &c. 1600, afford an accurate description of the way in which this sport was pursued in former times:—

"For the manner of *Bat-fowling* it may be vsed either with Nettes, or without Nettes: If you vse it without Nettes (which indeede is the most common of the two) you shall then proceede in this manner. First, there shall be one to cary the cresset of fire (as was showed for the *Lowbell*) then a certain number as two, three, or foure (according to the greatnesse of your company), and these shall haue poales bound with dry round wispes of hay, straw, or such like stuffe, or else bound with pieces of Linkes, or Hurdes dipt in Pitch, Rosen, Grease, or any such like matter that will blaze. Then another company shall be armed with long poales, very rough and bushy at the vpper endes, of which the Willow, Byrche, or long Hazell are best, but indeed acording as the Country will afford, so you must be content to take.

"Thus being prepared and comming into the Bushy or rough ground where the haunts of Birds are, you shall then first kindle some of your fiers as halfe, or a third part, according as your prouision is, and then with your other bushy and rough poales you shall beat the Bushes, Trees and haunts of the Birds, to enforce them to rise, which done you shall see the Birds which are raysed, to flye and play about the lights and flames of the fier, for it is their nature through their amazednesse, and affright at the strangenes of the lightt and the extreame darknesse round about it, not to depart from it, but as it were almost to scorch their wings in the same: so that those which haue the rough bushye poales may (at their pleasures) beat them down with the same, and so take thē. Thus you may spend as much of the night as is darke, for longer is not conuenient; and doubtlesse you shall finde much pastime, and take great store of birds, and in this you shall obserue all the obseruations formerly treated of in the *Lowbell;* especially, that of silence, vntill your lights be kindled, but then you may vse your pleasure, for the noyse and the light when they are heard and seene a farre of, they make the birds sit the faster and surer.

"The byrdes which are commonly taken by this labour or exercise are, for the most part, the *Rookes, Ring-doues, Blackebirdes, Throstles, Feldyfares, Linnets, Bulfinches,* and all other Byrdes whatsoeuer that pearch or sit vpon small boughes or bushes."

(3) SCENE II.—*They will lay out ten to see a dead Indian.*] Some verses written by Henry Peacham, about the year 1609, give a curious list of most of the popular exhibitions then to be seen in the metropolis, together with a few notices of some of the sights of the country:—

"Why doe the rude vulgar so hastily post in a madnesse,
To gaze at trifles and toyes not worthy the viewing?
And thinke them happy, when may be shew'd for a penny,
The Fleet-streete mandrakes, that heavenly motion of Eltham,
Westminster monuments, and Guild-hall huge Corinæus,
That horne of Windsor (of an unicorne very likely),
The cave of Merlin, the skirts of old Tom a Lincolne.
King Johns sword at Linne, with the cup the Fraternity drinke in;
The Tombe of Beauchampe, and sword of Sir Guy a Warwicke;
The great long Dutchman, and roaring Marget a Barwicke,
The *Mummied Princes,* and Cæsars wine yet i' Dover,
Saint James his Ginney Hens, the Cassawarway moreover;
The Beaver i' the Parke (strange beast as er'e any man saw)
Downe-shearing willowes with teeth as sharpe as a hand-saw.
The Lance of John a Gaunt and Brandons still i' the Tower:
The fall of Ninive, with Norwich built in an hower!
King Henries slip-shoes, the sword of valiant Edward;
The Coventry boares-shield, and fire-workes seen but to bedward.
Drakes ship at Detford, King Richards bedsted i' Leyster,
The White Hall whale-bones, the silver Bason i' Chester:
The live-caught dog-fish, the Wolfe, and Harry the Lyon,
Hunkes of the Beare-garden, to be feared, if he be nigh on."

HALLIWELL, I. 327.

ACT III.

(1) SCENE II.—*The picture of Nobody.*] "No-body" was a ludicrous figure often found on street signs, and of which a representation is prefixed to the comedy of "No-body and Some-body," 1600. The following verses form the beginning of a popular old ballad, called "The Well-spoken Nobody," the unique copy of which, in the Miller collection at Britwell-house, supplied Mr. Halliwell with a curious engraving, showing a floor all bestrewed with domestic

utensils and implements broken to pieces, and a fantastic figure in the midst bearing a scroll with the words,—

"Nobody is my name
that beyreth every bodyes blame."

"Many speke of Roben Hoode that never shott in his bowe,
So many have layed faultes to me, which I did never knowe;
But now beholde here I am,
Whom all the worlde doeth diffame
Long hath they also skorned me,
And locked my mouthe for speking free.
As many a Godly man they have so served,
Which unto them Gods truth hath shewed;
Of such they have burned and hanged some,
That unto their ydolatrye wold not come:
The ladye Truthe they have locked in cage,
Sayeng that of her Nobody had knowledge,
For as much nowe as they name Nobodye,
I think verilye they speke of me:
Wherfore to answere I nowe beginne,—
The locke of my mouthe is opened with ginne,
Wrought by no man, but by Gods grace,
Unto whom be prayse in every place."

(2) SCENE II.—*I would I could see this taborer!*] "Several of the incidents in this scene," Steevens remarks, "viz.—Ariel's mimickry of Trinculo, the tune played on the *tabor*, and Caliban's description of the twangling instruments, &c., might have been borrowed from Marco Paolo, the old Venetian voyager; who, in lib. I. ch. 44, describing the desert of Lop, in Asia, says:—'Audiuntur ibi voces dæmonum, &c. voces fingentes eorum quos comitari se putant. Audiuntur interdum in aere concentus musicorum instrumentorum.'" This work was translated into English by John Frampton in 1579, under the title of "The Most Noble and famous Travels of Marcus Paulus, one of the Nobilitie of the State of Venice," &c., and the above passage is rendered:—"You shall heare in the ayre the sound of *tabers and other instruments,* to put the travellers in feare, &c., by evill spirites that make these soundes, and also do *call diverse of the travellers by their names,*" &c.—ch. 36, p. 32.

ACT IV.

(1) SCENE I.—

*And, like this insubstantial pageant faded,
Leave not a rack behind.*]

It is impossible to doubt that Shakespeare in this sublime passage remembered the lines in Lord Sterline's "Tragedie of Darius," 1604:—

"Let greatnesse of her glascie scepters vaunt,
Not sceptors, no, but reeds, soone brus'd, soone broken;
And let this worldlie pompe our wits inchant,
All fades, and scarcelie leaves behinde a token.
Those golden pallaces, those gorgeous halles,
With fourniture superfluouslie faire:
Those statelie courts, those sky-encountring walles,
Evanish all like vapours in the aire."

With regard to the disputed word, "*rack*," which some editors, Mr. Dyce among them, conceive to be no more than an old form of *wreck*, the reader is recommended to consult Whiter's "Specimen of a Commentary on Shakspeare," &c., pp. 194-198, and Horne Tooke's Επεα Πτερυεντα, Vol. II. pp. 389-396. To what those writers have said on the subject we have only to add, that while it is evident that by *rack* was understood the drifting vapour, or *scud* as it is now termed, it would appear that Shakespeare, in the present instance, as in another, occurring in "Antony and Cleopatra," Act IV. Sc. 12,—

"That which is now a horse, even with a thought
The *rack* dislimns," &c.

—was thinking not more of the actual clouds than of those gauzy semblances which, in the pageants of his day as in the stage-spectacles of ours, were often used partly or totally to obscure the scene behind. Ben Jonson, in the descriptions of his masques, very frequently mentions this scenic contrivance. Thus in his "Entertainment at Theobalds:"—"The King and Queen, with the princes of Wales and Lorrain, and the nobility, being entered into the gallery after dinner, there was seen nothing but a traverse of white across the room; which suddenly drawn, was discovered a gloomy obscure place, *hung all with black silks,*" &c. Again, in his "Masque of Hymen:"—"At this, the whole scene being drawn again, and *all covered with clouds, as at night,* they left off their intermixed dances, and returned to their first places."

The evanishing of the actors, then, in Prospero's pageant—who

"Melted into air, into thin air,"

—was doubtless effected by the agency of filmy curtains which, being drawn one over another to resemble the flying mists, gave to the scene an appearance of gradual dissolution; when the objects were totally hidden, the drapery was withdrawn in the same manner, veil by veil, till at length even that too had disappeared and there was left, then, not even a *rack* behind.

(2) SCENE I.—*Come, hang them on this line.*] Mr. Hunter successfully exposed the error of those editors who deemed it necessary to change the old spelling of "*line*-grove," to "*lime*-grove;" see note (a), p. 41; but to our thinking he has committed a graver mistake than theirs in his ingenious endeavour to prove that the "line" in this passage meant a *line-tree*;—"When," he observes, "Prospero says to Ariel, who comes in bringing the glittering apparel, 'Come, hang them on this line,' he means on one of the line-trees near his cell, which could hardly have been if the word of the original copies, *line-grove,* had been allowed to keep its place. But the ear having long been familiar with *lime-grove,* the word suggested not the branches of a tree so-called, but a *cord-line,* and, accordingly, when the play is represented, such a line is actually drawn across the stage, and the glittering apparel is hung upon it. Anything more remote from poetry than this can scarcely be imagined."—*Disquisition on Shakespeare's Tempest.*

However unpoetic, and perhaps, as Mr. Knight has remarked, the incidents of the scene so far as the drunken butler and his companion are concerned were purposely rendered so, it is hardly possible to conceive that the coarse jesting,—"Mistress line, is not this my jerkin? Now is the jerkin *under the line:* now, jerkin, you are like *to lose your hair,* and prove a bald jerkin;" and,—

——"we steal by *line and level,*" &c.

could have been provoked by, or indeed would have been applicable to any other object than the familiar *horse-hair* line which was formerly used to hang clothes on.

(3) SCENE I.—*And all be turn'd to barnacles.*] It was anciently believed that the barnacle shell-fish, which is found on timber exposed to the action of the sea, became, when broken off, a kind of goose. Some, indeed, supposed that the barnacles actually grew on trees, and thence dropping into the sea, became geese; and an interesting cut of these birds so growing, from a MS. of the fourteenth century, is given by Mr. Halliwell, who observes that "the

barnacle mentioned by Caliban was no doubt the tree-goose; and the true absurdity of our old writers, as Douce has observed, consisted in their believing that this bird was really produced from the shell of the fish." Innumerable allusions to this vulgar error occur in our old writers, but we will adduce only the testimony of Sir John Maundeville, who declares that in his country "—weren trees that beren a fruyt, that become briddes fleeynge; and tho that fellen into the water, lyven; and thei that fallen on the erthe, dyen anon: and thei ben right gode to mannes mete."

ACT V.

(1) Scene I.—*By my so potent art.*] This speech is founded upon the invocation of Medea in Ovid's Metamorphoses, for which it is evident, from several expressions, that Shakespeare consulted Golding's translation:—

"Ye Ayres and Windes, ye *Elves of Hilles*, of *Brookes*, of Woods alone,
Of *standing Lakes*, and of the Night, approch ye everychone.
Through helpe of whom (the crooked bankes much wondring at the thing)
I have compelled streames to run cleane backward to their spring.
By charmes I make the calm seas rough, and make the rough seas playne,
And cover all the Skie with clouds, and *chase* them thence again.
By charmes I raise and lay the windes, and burst the Viper's jaw,
And from the bowels of the earth both stones and trees do draw.
Whole woods and Forests I remoove, *I make the Mountaines shake*,
And even the earth it selfe to grone and fearefully to quake.
I call up dead men from their graves, and thee, O lightsome Moone,
I darken oft, though beaten brass abate thy perill soone:
Our Sorcerie dimmes the Morning faire, and *darks the Sun at Noone*,
The flaming breath of fierie Bulles ye quenched for my sake,
And caused their unwieldy neckes the bended yoke to take.
Among the earth-bred brothers you a *mortal warre did set*,
And brought asleepe the Dragon fell, whose eyes were never shet."
Golding's *Ovid*, lib. 7, 1567.

(2) Scene I.—*Under the blossom that hangs on the bough.*] The beautiful fancy in the second line of Ariel's song,—

"*In a cowslip's bell I lie*,"

was once supposed to have been borrowed from a stanza in Drayton's delicious "Nimphidia:"—

"At midnight the appointed hour;
And for the queen a fitting *bower*,
Quoth he, is that *fair cowslip-flower*
On Hip-cut hill that bloweth."

It is now, however, generally believed that "Nimphidia," which was not printed before 1627, was written subsequently to "The Tempest;" Malone thinks in 1612.

CRITICAL OPINIONS ON THE TEMPEST.

"It is observed of 'The Tempest,' that its plan is regular. This the author of 'The Revisal' thinks, what I think too, an accidental effect of the story, not intended or regarded by our author. But whatever might be Shakespeare's intention in forming or adopting the plot, he has made it instrumental to the production of many characters, diversified with boundless invention, and preserved with profound skill in nature, extensive knowledge of opinions, and accurate observation of life. In a single drama are here exhibited princes, courtiers, and sailors, all speaking in their real characters. There is the agency of airy spirits, and of an earthly goblin; the operations of magick; the tumults of a storm, the adventures of a desart island, the native effusion of untaught affection, the punishment of guilt, and the final happiness of the pair for whom our passions and reason are equally interested."—Johnson.

"'The Tempest,' according to all appearance, was written in Shakspeare's later days: hence most critics, on the supposition that the poet must have continued to improve with increasing maturity of mind, have honoured this piece with a marked preference over the 'Midsummer Night's Dream.' I cannot, however, altogether concur with them: the internal merit of these two works are, in my opinion, pretty nearly balanced, and a predilection for the one or the other can only be governed by personal taste. In profound and original characterisation, the superiority of 'The Tempest' is obvious: as a whole we must always admire the masterly skill which he has here displayed in the economy of his means, and the dexterity with which he has disguised his preparations,—the scaffoldings for the wonderful aërial structure.

CRITICAL OPINIONS.

"'The Tempest' has little action or progressive movement; the union of Ferdinand and Miranda is settled at their first interview, and Prospero merely throws apparent obstacles in their way; the shipwrecked band go leisurely about the island; the attempts of Sebastian and Antonio on the life of the King of Naples, and the plot of Caliban and the drunken sailors against Prospero, are nothing but a feint, for we foresee that they will be completely frustrated by the magical skill of the latter; nothing remains therefore but the punishment of the guilty by dreadful sights which harrow up their consciences, and then the discovery and final reconciliation. Yet this want of movement is so admirably concealed by the most varied display of the fascinations of poetry, and the exhilaration of mirth, the details of the execution are so very attractive, that it requires no small degree of attention to perceive that the *dénouement* is, in some degree, anticipated in the exposition. The history of the loves of Ferdinand and Miranda, developed in a few short scenes, is enchantingly beautiful: an affecting union of chivalrous magnanimity on the one part, and on the other of the virgin openness of a heart which, brought up far from the world on an uninhabited island, has never learned to disguise its innocent movements. The wisdom of the princely hermit Prospero has a magical and mysterious air; the disagreeable impression left by the black falsehood of the two usurpers is softened by the honest gossiping of the old and faithful Gonzalo; Trinculo and Stephano, two good-for-nothing drunkards, find a worthy associate in Caliban; and Ariel hovers sweetly over the whole as the personified genius of the wonderful fable.

"Caliban has become a by-word as the strange creation of a poetical imagination. A mixture of gnome and savage, half demon, half brute, in his behaviour we perceive at once the traces of his native disposition, and the influence of Prospero's education. The latter could only unfold his understanding, without, in the slightest degree, taming his rooted malignity: it is as if the use of reason and human speech were communicated to an awkward ape. In inclination Caliban is malicious, cowardly, false, and base; and yet he is essentially different from the vulgar knaves of a civilized world, as portrayed occasionally by Shakspeare. He is rude, but not vulgar; he never falls into the prosaic and low familiarity of his drunken associates, for he is, in his way, a poetical being; he always speaks in verse. He has picked up everything dissonant and thorny in language to compose out of it a vocabulary of his own; and of the whole variety of nature, the hateful, repulsive, and pettily deformed, have alone been impressed on his imagination. The magical world of spirits, which the staff of Prospero has assembled on the island, casts merely a faint reflection into his mind, as a ray of light which falls into a dark cave, incapable of communicating to it either heat or illumination, serves merely to set in motion the poisonous vapours. The delineation of this monster is throughout inconceivably consistent and profound, and, notwithstanding its hatefulness, by no means hurtful to our feelings, as the honour of human nature is left untouched.

"In the zephyr-like Ariel, the image of air is not to be mistaken, his name even bears an allusion to it; as, on the other hand, Caliban signifies the heavy element of earth. Yet they are neither of them simple, allegorical personifications, but beings individually determined. In general we find in the 'Midsummer Night's Dream,' in 'The Tempest,' in the magical part of 'Macbeth,' and wherever Shakspeare avails himself of the popular belief in the invisible presence of spirits, and the possibility of coming in contact with them, a profound view of the inward life of nature and her mysterious springs, which, it is true, can never be altogether unknown to the genuine poet, as poetry is altogether incompatible with mechanical physics, but which few have possessed in an equal degree with Dante and himself."—SCHLEGEL.

Act V. Sc. 3.

KING LEAR.

The Stationers' Registers contain the following memorandum concerning this tragedy, under the date, November 26th, 1607; "Na. Butler and Jo. Busby] Entered for their copie under t' hands of Sir Geo. Bucke, Kt. and the Wardens, a booke called Mr. Willm Shakespeare his Hystorye of Kinge Lear, as yt was played before the King's Majestie at Whitehall, upon St. Stephen's night at Christmas last, by his Majesties servants playing usually at the Globe on the Bank-side." which proves that it was acted at court, on the 26th of December 1606. In 1608, no less than three editions of it in quarto were issued, all by the same stationer. One of these is intituled,—"Mr. William Shak-speare: His True Chronicle Historie of the life and death of King Lear and his three Daughters. With the vnfortunate life of Edgar, sonne and heire to the Earle of Gloster, and his sullen and assumed humorr of Tom of Bedlam. As it was played before the kings Maiestie at Whitehall upon S. Stephens night in Christmas Hollidayes. By his Maiesties seruants playing vsually at the Gloabe, on the Bancke-side.—London, Printed for Nathaniel Butter, and are to be sold at his shop in Pauls Churchyard at the signe of the Pide Bull neere St. Austins Gate. 1608.

The two other impressions are described as,—"M. William Shake-speare, His True Chronicle History of the life and death of King Lear, and his three Daughters. With the vnfortunate life of Edgar, sonne and heire to the Earle of Glocester, and his sullen and assumed humour of Tom of Bedlam. As it was plaid before the Kings Maiesty at White-hall, vppon S. Stephens night, in Christmas Hollidaies. By his Maiesties Seruants, playing vsually at the Globe, on the Banck-side.—Printed for Nathaniel Butter. 1608."

No other edition of "King Lear" has been discovered, prior to that of the folio 1623, which differs materially from the text of the quartos, chiefly in the omission of large portions of matter found in the latter, in numberless minute verbal changes, and also by the addition of about fifty lines peculiar to itself. The omissions appear to have been made for the better adapting the piece to representation, and a careful comparison of the quarto and folio texts convinces us that, unlike that of Richard III., the text of Lear in the folio is taken from a later and revised copy of the play. Whether the curtailment is the work of the author, it is impossible now to determine; it is not always judicious, and some of the substitutions are inferior to the language they displace; yet, on the other hand, the additions which we meet with in the folio bear the undoubted mark of Shakespeare's mint, and while the metrical arrangement of the speeches in that edition has been carefully regarded, the text of the quartos is printed in parts without any observance of prosodial construction. With respect to the date of its composition, Steevens remarks, that King Lear, or at least the whole of it, could not have been written till after the publication of Harsnet's *Discovery of Popish Impostures,* in 1603, because the names of the fiends mentioned by Edgar are borrowed from that work.

The story of King Lear and his daughters was so popular in Shakespeare's time, that he may have taken it from Geoffrey of Monmouth; from the legend "How Queene Cordila *in dispaire slew her selfe,* The yeare before Christ 800," in the "Mirror for Magistrates;" from Spenser's "Fairie Queene," b. ii. c. x.; or, from Holinshed. There was, indeed, an old anonymous play on the subject, an edition of which was put forth in 1605, under the title of "The True Chronicle History of King Leir, and his Three Daughters, Gonorill, Ragan, and Cordella:" mainly in consequence it would seem of the great popularity of the present drama then "running" at the Globe theatre; the publishers probably trusting to foist the elder production upon the public as Shakespeare's work; but from this piece he appears to have derived nothing, unless, perhaps, some hint for the character of Kent.

The episode of Gloucester and his two sons was probably founded on Book II. chap. x. of Sidney's *Arcadia,* "*The pitifull state and storie of the* Paphlagonian *unkinde king, and his kind sonne;*" &c. which together with the legend of "*Queene Cordila,*" from "*The Mirror for Magistrates,*" are reprinted in Mr. Collier's "*Shakespeare's Library,*" Vol. II.

Persons Represented.

LEAR, *King of* Britain.

KING *of* FRANCE.

DUKE *of* BURGUNDY.

DUKE *of* ALBANY.

DUKE *of* CORNWALL.

EARL *of* KENT.

EARL *of* GLOUCESTER.

EDGAR, *Son to* Gloucester.

EDMUND, *natural Son to* Gloucester.

CURAN, *a Courtier.*

A Herald.

An Officer, *employed by* Edmund.

A Physician.

Gentleman *attending on* Cordelia.

OSWALD, *Steward to* Goneril.

Old Man, *Tenant to* Gloucester.

A Fool.

Servants *to* Cornwall.

GONERIL, REGAN, CORDELIA, } *Daughters to* Lear.

Knights of Lear's *train, Officers, Messengers, Soldiers, and Attendants.*

SCENE,—BRITAIN.

ACT I.

SCENE I.—*A Room of State in* King Lear's *Palace.*

Enter KENT, GLOUCESTER, *and* EDMUND.

KENT. I thought the king had more affected the duke of Albany[a] than Cornwall.

GLO. It did always seem so to us: but now, in the division of the kingdom, it appears not which of the dukes he values most; for equalities* are so weighed, that curiosity in neither can make choice of either's moiety.[b]

KENT. Is not this your son, my lord?

GLO. His breeding, sir, hath been at my charge: I have so often blushed to acknowledge him, that now I am brazed to 't.

KENT. I cannot conceive you.

GLO. Sir, this young fellow's mother could: whereupon she grew round-wombed; and had, indeed, sir, a son for her cradle ere she had a husband for her bed. Do you smell a fault?

KENT. I cannot wish the fault undone, the issue of it being so proper.

GLO. But I have, sir, a son† by order of law, some year elder than this, who yet is no dearer in my account: though this knave came something saucily into* the world before he was sent for, yet was his mother fair; there was good sport at his making, and the whoreson must be acknowledged.—Do you know this noble gentleman, Edmund?

EDM. No, my lord.

GLO. My lord of Kent: remember him hereafter as my honourable friend.

EDM. My services to your lordship.

KENT. I must love you, and sue to know you better.

EDM. Sir, I shall study deserving.

GLO. He hath been out nine years, and away he shall again.—The king is coming.

[*Trumpets sound without.*

Enter LEAR, CORNWALL, ALBANY, GONERIL, REGAN, CORDELIA, *and* Attendants.

LEAR. Attend the lords of France and Burgundy, Gloster.

(*) First folio, *qualities.* (†) First folio, *a Sonne, Sir.*

a — Albany—] Scotland was anciently called Albany.

b — can make choice of either's moiety.] "The qualities and properties of the several divisions are so weighed and balanced against one another, that the exactest scrutiny could not determine in preferring one share to the other."—WARBURTON.

(*) First folio, *to.*

Glo. I shall, my liege.
[*Exeunt* Gloucester *and* Edmund.
Lear. Meantime we shall express our darker[a] purpose.—
Give me the map there.—Know that we have divided
In three our kingdom: and 'tis our fast[b] intent
To shake all cares and business from our age;
Conferring them on younger strengths, while we
Unburden'd crawl toward death.[c]—Our son of Cornwall,
And you, our no less loving son of Albany,
We have this hour a constant will to publish
Our daughters' several dowers, that future strife
May be prevented now. The princes, France and Burgundy,
Great rivals in our youngest daughter's love,
Long in our court have made their amorous sojourn,
And here are to be answer'd.—Tell me, my daughters,
(Since now we will divest us, both of rule,
Interest of territory, cares of state,[d])
Which of you shall we say doth love us most?
That we our largest bounty may extend
Where nature doth with merit challenge.—Goneril,
Our eldest-born, speak first.
Gon. Sir, I love you more than words * can wield the matter;
Dearer than eye-sight, space, and liberty;
Beyond what can be valu'd, rich or rare;
No less than life, with grace, health, beauty, honour;
As much as child e'er lov'd, or father found;
A love that makes breath poor, and speech unable;
Beyond all manner of so much I love you.
Cord. [*Aside.*] What shall Cordelia do? † Love, and be silent.
Lear. Of all these bounds, even from this line to this,
With shadowy forests and with champains rich'd,
With plenteous rivers and wide-skirted meads,[e]
We make thee lady: to thine and Albany's issue *
Be this perpetual.—What says our second daughter,
Our dearest Regan, wife to † Cornwall? speak.‡
Reg. I am made of that self metal as my sister,
And prize me at her worth. In my true heart
I find she names my very deed of love;
Only she comes too short,—that I profess
Myself an enemy to all other joys,
Which the most precious square[f] of sense possesses,§
And find I am alone felicitate
In your dear highness' love.
Cord. [*Aside.*] Then poor Cordelia!
And yet not so; since, I am sure, my love's
More richer[g] than my tongue.
Lear. To thee and thine, hereditary ever,
Remain this ample third of our fair kingdom;
No less in space, validity, and pleasure,
Than that conferr'd on Goneril.—Now, our joy,
Although our last, not least;[h] to whose young love
The vines of France and milk of Burgundy,
Strive to be interess'd; what can you say, to draw
A third more opulent than your sisters? Speak.
Cord. Nothing, my lord.
Lear. Nothing!
Cord. Nothing.[i]
Lear. Nothing will come of nothing: speak again.
Cord. Unhappy that I am, I cannot heave
My heart into my mouth: I love your majesty
According to my bond; nor more nor less.
Lear. How, how, Cordelia! mend your speech a little,
Lest it ‖ may mar your fortunes.

(*) First folio, *word*. (†) First folio, *speake*.

a Darker *purpose*.—] *Secret, hidden* purpose.

b —fast *intent*—] The quartos read, *first* intent; but "*fast* intent," signifying *fixed, settled* intent, is, like "*darker purpose*," and "*constant* will," peculiarly in Shakespeare's manner.

c —— while we
Unburden'd crawl toward death.]

The passage commencing with these words, down to "May be prevented now," does not occur in the quartos.

d (Since now we will divest us, both of rule,
Interest of territory, cares of state,)]

The quartos omit these two lines.

e *With* shadowy *forests* and with champains rich'd,
With plenteous rivers *and wide-skirted meads*,—]

So the folio: the quartos read only,—

"With *shady forrests*, and wide-skirted meads."

f Square *of sense*—] By *square* of sense, if *square* is not a corruption, may be meant the *complement* or *compass* of sense. Mr. Collier's annotator suggests, "*sphere* of sense;" but what is "*sphere* of sense?"

g *More* richer *than my tongue*.] The folio reads, "More *ponderous*," &c.

h Although our last, not least; &c.] In the quartos this passage stands,—

"Although *the* last, not least in our deere love,
What can you say to *win* a third, more opulent
Then your sisters?"

In the folio,—

"Although our last *and* least; to whose yong love,
The Vines of France, and Milke of Burgundie,
Strive to be interest. What can you say, to draw
A third, more opilent than your Sisters? speake."

That *and* in the folio is a misprint for "but," it seems scarcely possible to doubt, yet Mr. Collier and Mr. Knight read, "our last *and* least." "Though last not least," was one of the commonest forms of expression in Shakespeare's age; in addition to the overwhelming array of examples cited in the Variorum edition of 1821, Vol. II. pp. 276-279, take the following:—

"The last, not least, of these brave bretheren."
Peele's *Polyhymnia*.

"Though I speak last, my lord, I am not least."
Middleton's *Mayor of Queenborough.*, Act I. Sc. 3.

And—

"My last is, and not least."
Beaumont and Fletcher's *Monsieur Thomas*, Act III. Sc. 1.

i Lear. Nothing!
Cord. Nothing.] Omitted in the quartos.

(*) First folio, *issues*. (†) First folio, *of*.
(‡) First folio omits, *speak*. (§) First folio, *professes*.
(‖) First folio, *you*.

CORD. Good my lord,
You have begot me, bred me, lov'd me: I
Return those duties back as are right fit,
Obey you, love you, and most honour you.
Why have my sisters husbands, if they say
They love you all? Haply, when I shall wed,
That lord, whose hand must take my plight, shall carry
Half my love with him, half my care, and duty: (1)
Sure, I shall never marry like my sisters,
To love my father all.*

LEAR. But goes thy heart with this?

CORD. Ay, good my † lord.

LEAR. So young, and so untender?

CORD. So young, my lord, and true.

(*) First folio omits, *To love my father all.*
(†) First folio, *my good.*

LEAR. Let it be so,—thy truth, then, be thy dower:
For, by the sacred radiance of the sun,
The mysteries[a] of Hecate, and the night;
By all the operation of the orbs
From whom we do exist, and cease to be,
Here I disclaim all my paternal care,
Propinquity and property of blood,
And as a stranger to my heart and me
Hold thee, from this, for ever! The barbarous Scythian,
Or he that makes his generation messes
To gorge his appetite, shall to my bosom
Be as well neighbour'd, pitied, and reliev'd,
As thou my sometime daughter:—

KENT. Good my liege,—

LEAR. Peace, Kent!
Come not between the dragon and his wrath.—
I lov'd her most, and thought to set my rest
On her kind nursery.——Hence, and avoid my sight!— [*To* CORDELIA.[b]
So be my grave my peace, as here I give
Her father's heart from her!—Call France.—Who stirs?
Call Burgundy.—Cornwall and Albany,
With my two daughters' dowers digest this * third:
Let pride, which she calls plainness, marry her.
I do invest you jointly with my power,
Pre-eminence, and all the large effects
That troop with majesty. Ourself, by monthly [course,
With reservation of an hundred knights,
By you to be sustain'd, shall our abode
Make with you by due turns.† Only we still ‡ [retain
The name, and all the additions § to a king:
The sway, revènue, execution of the rest,
Beloved sons, be yours: which to confirm,
This coronet part between you.
[*Giving the crown.*

KENT. Royal Lear,
Whom I have ever honour'd as my king,
Lov'd as my father, as my master follow'd,
As my great patron thought on in my prayers,—

LEAR. The bow is bent and drawn, make from the shaft.

KENT. Let it fall rather, though the fork invade
The region of my heart: be Kent unmannerly,
When Lear is mad. What wouldst thou do, old man?
Think'st thou, that duty shall have dread to speak,
When power to flattery bows? To plainness honour's bound,
When majesty stoops * to folly. Reverse thy doom; †
And, in thy best consideration, check
This hideous rashness: answer my life my judg- [ment,
Thy youngest daughter does not love thee least;
Nor are those empty-hearted whose low sound
Reverbs ‡ no hollowness.

LEAR. Kent, on thy life no more!

KENT. My life I never held but as a § pawn
To wage against thine enemies; ne'er fear to lose it,
Thy safety being the || motive.

LEAR. Out of my sight!

KENT. See better, Lear; and let me still remain
The true blank of thine eye.

LEAR. Now, by Apollo!—

KENT. Now, by Apollo, king,
Thou swear'st thy gods in vain.

LEAR. O, vassal! miscreant!
[*Laying his hand on his sword.*

ALB. CORN. Dear sir, forbear.[c]

KENT. Kill thy physician, and the ¶ fee bestow
Upon the foul disease. Revoke thy gift;
Or, whilst I can vent clamour from my throat,
I'll tell thee thou dost evil.

LEAR. Hear me, recreant!
On thine allegiance hear me!—
Since ** thou hast sought to make us break our vow, ††
(Which we durst never yet) and, with strain'd [pride,
To come betwixt our sentence ‡‡ and our power,
(Which nor our nature nor our place can bear)
Our potency made good, take thy reward.
Five days we do allot thee, for provision
To shield thee from diseases[d] of the world;
And, on the sixth, to turn thy hated back
Upon our kingdom: if, on the tenth day following,
Thy banish'd trunk be found in our dominions,
The moment is thy death. Away! By Jupiter,
This shall not be revok'd!

KENT. Fare thee well, king: sith thus thou wilt appear,
Freedom[e] lives hence, and banishment is here.—
The gods to their dear shelter take thee, maid,
[*To* CORDELIA.

(*) First folio, *the*. (†) First folio, *turne*.
(‡) First folio, *shall*. (§) First folio, *addition*.

[a] *The* mysteries *of Hecate*,—] The quartos read *mistresse*, the first folio, *miseries*: the correction was made in the second folio.

[b] *To* CORDELIA.] This direction is modern, and some editors contend that the words,—

"——Hence, and avoid my sight!"

are addressed to Kent. Few readers, we apprehend, will agree with them.

[c] Dear sir, forbear.—] Omitted in the quartos.

[d] *To shield thee from* diseases *of the world*;] So the quartos; the folio has—"*disasters* of the world." *Diseases*, in its old and literal sense of *discomforts*, *hardships*, and the like, is, however, much the more appropriate word.

[e] Freedom *lives hence*,—] The quartos have *Friendship* for "Freedom;" and in the next line, instead of "dear shelter," they read *protection*.

(*) First folio, *falls*. (†) First folio, *reserve thy state*.
(‡) First folio, *sounds Reverbe*. (§) First folio omits, *a*.
(||) First folio omits, *the*. (¶) First folio, *thy*.
(**) First folio, *That*. (††) First folio, *vowes*.
(‡‡) First folio, *sentences*.

That justly think'st, and hast most rightly said!—
And your large speeches may your deeds approve,
[*To* REGAN *and* GONERIL.
That good effects may spring from words of love.—
Thus Kent, O princes, bids you all adieu;
He'll shape his old course in a country new.
[*Exit.*

Flourish. Re-enter GLOUCESTER; *with* FRANCE, BURGUNDY, *and* Attendants.

GLO. Here's France and Burgundy, my noble lord.
LEAR. My lord of Burgundy,
We first address toward you, who with this king
Hath rivall'd for our daughter: what, in the least,
Will you require in present dower with her,
Or cease your quest of love?
BUR. Most royal majesty,
I crave no more than hath your highness offer'd,
Nor will you tender less.
LEAR. Right noble Burgundy,
When she was dear to us, we did hold her so;
But now her price is fall'n. Sir, there she stands;
If aught within that little seeming substance,
Or all of it, with our displeasure piec'd,
And nothing more, may fitly like your grace,
She's there, and she is yours.
BUR. I know no answer.
LEAR. Will you, with those infirmities she owes,
Unfriended, new-adopted to our hate,
Dower'd with our curse, and stranger'd with our oath,
Take her, or leave her?
BUR. Pardon me, royal sir;
Election makes not up on * such conditions.
LEAR. Then leave her, sir; for, by the power that made me,
I tell you all her wealth.—For you, great king,
[*To* FRANCE.
I would not from your love make such a stray,
To match you where I hate; therefore beseech you
To avert your liking a more worthier way,
Than on a wretch whom Nature is asham'd
Almost to acknowledge hers.
FRANCE. This is most strange,
That she, who even but now was your best † object,
The argument of your praise, balm of your age,
Most best, most ‡ dearest, should in this trice of time
Commit a thing so monstrous, to dismantle
So many folds of favour! Sure, her offence
Must be of such unnatural degree,
That monsters it, or your fore-vouch'd affection
Fall into taint; which to believe of her,
Must be a faith that reason without miracle
Should never plant in me.
COR. I yet beseech your majesty,—
If for I want that glib and oily art,
To speak and purpose not; since what I well * intend,
I'll do't before I speak,—that you make known
It is no vicious blot, murder,[a] or foulness,
No unchaste action, or dishonour'd step,
That hath depriv'd me of your grace and favour;
But even for want of that for which I am richer,—
A still-soliciting eye, and such a tongue
That I am glad I have not, though not to have it
Hath lost me in your liking.
LEAR. Better thou
Hadst not been born, than not to have pleas'd me better.
FRANCE. Is it but this? a tardiness in nature,
Which often leaves the history unspoke,
That it intends to do?—My lord of Burgundy,
What say you to the lady? Love's not love,
When it is mingled with respects,[b] that stand
Aloof from the entire point. Will you have her?
She is herself a dowry.
BUR. Royal Lear,†
Give but that portion which yourself propos'd,
And here I take Cordelia by the hand,
Duchess of Burgundy.
LEAR. Nothing: I have sworn; I am firm.
BUR. I am sorry, then, you have so lost a father
That you must lose a husband.
COR. Peace be with Burgundy!
Since that respects of fortune ‡ are his love,
I shall not be his wife.
FRANCE. Fairest Cordelia, that art most rich, being poor;
Most choice, forsaken; and most lov'd, despis'd!
Thee and thy virtues here I seize upon,
Be it lawful I take up what's cast away.
Gods, gods! 'tis strange, that from their cold'st neglect
My love should kindle to inflam'd respect.—
Thy dowerless daughter, king, thrown to my chance,
Is queen of us, of ours, and our fair France:
Not all the dukes of wat'rish Burgundy
Shall buy this unpriz'd precious maid of me.—

(*) First folio, *in*. (†) First folio omits, *best*. (‡) First folio, *The best, the*.

a *It is no vicious blot*, murder, *or foulness*,—] Mr. Collier's annotator changes this to,

"—— no vicious blot, *nor other* foulness,"

which is certainly a very plausible substitution.

(*) First folio, *will*. (†) First folio, *King*. (‡) First folio, *respect and Fortunes*.

b *When it is mingled with* respects,—] The folio reads,—

"When it is mingled with *regards*," &c.

By "respects" is meant *considerations, scruples*, &c.

Bid them farewell, Cordelia, though unkind,[a]
Thou losest here, a better-where[b] to find.

LEAR. Thou hast her, France: let her be thine; for we
Have no such daughter, nor shall ever see
That face of hers again:—therefore be gone,
Without our grace, our love, our benison.—
Come, noble Burgundy.

[*Flourish. Exeunt* LEAR, BURGUNDY, CORNWALL, ALBANY, GLOUCESTER, *and* Attendants.

FRANCE. Bid farewell to your sisters.

COR. The[c] jewels of our father, with wash'd eyes
Cordelia leaves you: I know you what you are;
And, like a sister, am most loth to call
Your faults as they are nam'd. Use* well our father:
To your professed bosoms I commit him:
But yet, alas! stood I within his grace,
I would prefer him to a better place.
So farewell to you both.

GON. Prescribe not us our duties.†

REG. Let your study
Be to content your lord: who hath receiv'd you
At fortune's alms. You have obedience scanted,
And well are worth the want that you have wanted.

COR. Time shall unfold what plighted[d] cunning hides;
Who cover‡ faults, at last shame them § derides.
Well may you prosper!

FRANCE. Come, my fair Cordelia.
[*Exeunt* FRANCE *and* CORDELIA.

GON. Sister, it is not little I have to say of what most nearly appertains to us both. I think our father will hence to-night.

REG. That's most certain, and with you; next month with us.

GON. You see how full of changes his age is; the observation we have made of it hath not || been little: he always loved our sister most; and with what poor judgment he hath now cast her off appears too grossly.

REG. 'Tis the infirmity of his age: yet he hath ever but slenderly known himself.

GON. The best and soundest of his time hath been but rash; then must we look to receive from his age,* not alone the imperfections of long-engraffed condition, but, therewithal, the unruly waywardness that infirm and choleric years bring with them.

REG. Such unconstant starts are we like to have from him, as this of Kent's banishment.

GON. There is further compliment of leave-taking between France and him. Pray you, let us hit † together: if our father carry authority with such disposition as he bears, this last surrender of his will but offend us.

REG. We shall further think of it.

GON. We must do something, and i' the heat.
[*Exeunt.*

SCENE II.—*A Hall in the* Earl *of* Gloucester's *Castle.*

Enter EDMUND, *with a letter.*

EDM. Thou, Nature, art my goddess; to thy law
My services are bound. Wherefore should I
Stand in the plague[e] of custom, and permit
The curiosity of nations to deprive[f] me,
For that I am some twelve or fourteen moonshines
Lag of a brother? Why bastard? wherefore base?
When my dimensions are as well compact,
My mind as generous, and my shape as true,
As honest madam's issue? Why brand they us
With base? with baseness? bastardy? base, base?
Who, in the lusty stealth of nature, take
More composition and fierce quality,
Than doth, within a dull, stale, tired bed,
Go to the creating a whole tribe of fops,
Got 'tween asleep and wake?—Well, then,
Legitimate Edgar, I must have your land:
Our father's love is to the bastard Edmund,
As to the legitimate: fine word,—*legitimate!*
Well, my *legitimate*, if this letter speed,
And my invention thrive, Edmund the base
Shall top the *legitimate*.[g] I grow; I prosper:—
Now, gods, stand up for bastards!

(*) First folio, *Love*. (†) First folio, *dutie*.
(‡) Old text, *covers*. (§) First folio, *at last with shame*.
(||) First folio omits, *not*.

a — *though* unkind,—] *Unkind* here signifies *unnatural*, unless France is intended to mean, "though *unkinn'd*," *i.e.* though forsaken by your kindred.

b A better-where to find.] In note (a), p. 120, Vol. I. *otherwhere* is explained *other place;* but *where* in these compounds had perhaps a significance now lost. See the old ballad, "I HAVE HOUSE AND LAND IN KENT".—

"Wherefore cease off, make no delay,
And if you'll love me, love me now,
Or else ich zeek *some oderwhere*
For I cannot come every day to woo."

c The *jewels*—] Rowe and Capell read, perhaps rightly, "*Ye* jewels." Mr. Collier's annotator, too, proposes the same alteration.

(*) First folio, *from his age to receive*. (†) First folio, *sit*.

d — *what* plighted *cunning hides;*] *Plighted*, or, as the quartos give it, *pleated* cunning, means *involved, complicated* cunning.

e — plague *of custom*,—] *Plague* may here possibly signify *place*, or *boundary*, from *plaga;* but it is a very suspicious word.

f *To* deprive *me*,—] To *deprive*, in Shakespeare's day, was sometimes synonymous to *disinherit*, as Steevens has shown, and also to—*take away*, as in "Hamlet," Act I. Scene 4,—

"And there assume some other horrible form,
Which might *deprive* your sov'reignty of reason," &c.

g *Shall* top *the legitimate*.] In the old editions we find *tooth'* and *to'th'*. The present reading was first promulgated in Edwards' "Canons of Criticism," having been communicated to the author of that pungent satire by Capell. (See "Notes and various Readings to Shakespeare," by the latter, I. 146.)

Enter GLOUCESTER.

GLO. Kent banish'd thus! and France in choler parted!
And the king gone to-night! subscrib'd * his power!
Confin'd to exhibition![a] All this done
Upon the gad![b]—Edmund, how now! what news?

EDM. So please your lordship, none.
[*Putting up the letter.*

GLO. Why so earnestly seek you to put up that letter?

(*) First folio, *Prescrib'd.*

[a] Exhibition!] That is, *allowance.* The word, in this sense, is still employed in our universities.

[b] *Upon the* gad!—] Perhaps means, upon the *spur* or *point; at the instant.*

EDM. I know no news, my lord.

GLO. What paper were you reading?

EDM. Nothing, my lord.

GLO. No? What needed, then, that terrible dispatch of it into your pocket? the quality of nothing hath not such need to hide itself. Let's see: come, if it be nothing, I shall not need spectacles.

EDM. I beseech you, sir, pardon me: it is a letter from my brother, that I have not all o'er-read; and for so much as I have perused, I find it not fit for your o'er-looking.

GLO. Give me the letter, sir.

EDM. I shall offend, either to detain or give it. The contents, as in part I understand them, are to blame.

GLO. Let's see, let's see.

EDM. I hope, for my brother's justification, he wrote this but as an essay or taste[a] of my virtue.

GLO. [Reads.] *This policy and reverence of age makes the world bitter to the best of our times; keeps our fortunes from us, till our oldness cannot relish them. I begin to find an idle and fond*[b] *bondage in the oppression of aged tyranny; who sways, not as it hath power, but as it is suffered. Come to me, that of this I may speak more. If our father would sleep till I waked him, you should enjoy half his revenue for ever, and live the beloved of your brother,* EDGAR.—
Hum—Conspiracy!—*Sleep till I waked him,—you should enjoy half his revenue,*—My son Edgar! Had he a hand to write this? a heart and brain to breed it in?—When came this to you? who brought it?

EDM. It was not brought me, my lord,—there's the cunning of it; I found it thrown in at the casement of my closet.

GLO. You know the character to be your brother's?

EDM. If the matter were good, my lord, I durst swear it were his; but, in respect of that, I would fain think it were not.

GLO. It is his.

EDM. It is his hand, my lord; but, I hope, his heart is not in the contents.

GLO. Hath* he never heretofore† sounded you in this business?

EDM. Never, my lord: but I have heard him oft maintain it to be fit, that sons at perfect age, and fathers declining,‡ the father should be as ward to the son, and the son manage his revenue.

GLO. O villain, villain!—his very opinion in the letter!—Abhorred villain! Unnatural, detested, brutish villain! worse than brutish!—Go, sirrah, seek him; I'll apprehend him:—abominable villain!—Where is he?

EDM. I do not well know, my lord. If it shall please you to suspend your indignation against my brother, till you can derive from him better testimony of his intent, you shall* run a certain course; where, if you violently proceed against him, mistaking his purpose, it would make a great gap in your own honour, and shake in pieces the heart of his obedience. I dare pawn down my life for him, that he hath writ this to feel my affection to your honour, and to no other pretence of danger.

GLO. Think you so?

EDM. If your honour judge it meet, I will place you where you shall hear us confer of this, and by an auricular assurance have your satisfaction; and that without any further delay than this very evening.

GLO. He cannot be such a monster.

EDM. Nor is not, sure.

GLO. To his father, that so tenderly and entirely loves him!—Heaven and earth![c]—Edmund, seek him out; wind me into him, I pray you: frame the business after your own wisdom. I would unstate myself, to be in a due resolution.

EDM. I will seek him, sir, presently; convey the business as I shall find means, and acquaint you withal.

GLO. These late eclipses in the sun and moon portend no good to us: though the wisdom of Nature can reason it thus and thus, yet Nature finds itself scourged by the sequent effects. Love cools, friendship falls off, brothers divide: in cities, mutinies; in countries, discord; in palaces, treason; and the bond cracked 'twixt son and father. This villain of mine comes under the prediction; there's son against father: the king falls from bias of nature; there's father against child. We have seen the best of our time: machinations, hollowness, treachery, and all ruinous disorders, follow us disquietly to our graves![d]—Find out this villain, Edmund; it shall lose thee nothing; do it carefully.—And the noble and true-hearted Kent banished! his offence, honesty!—'T is strange! [*Exit.*

EDM. This is the excellent foppery of the world, that when we are sick in fortune, (often

(*) First folio, *Has.* (†) First folio, *before.* (‡) First folio, *declined.*

(*) First folio, *shold.*

[a] *An* essay *or* taste *of my virtue.*] *Essay* was commonly used in old language for *assay*, as *taste* not unfrequently was for *test*. See note (a), p. 763, Vol. II.

[b] *An* idle *and* fond *bondage*—] That is, a *vain* and *foolish* bondage.

[c] EDM. Nor is not, sure.
GLO. To his father, that so tenderly and entirely loves him! —Heaven and earth!] These lines are only found in the quarto copies.

[d] This villain of mine——disquietly to our graves.] This passage is omitted in the quartos.

the surfeit* of our own behaviour) we make guilty of our disasters the sun, the moon, and the† stars: as if we were villains by‡ necessity; fools by heavenly compulsion; knaves, thieves, and treachers, by spherical predominance; drunkards, liars, and adulterers, by an enforced obedience of planetary influence; and all that we are evil in, by a divine thrusting on. An admirable evasion of whore-master man, to lay his goatish disposition on the charge of a star! My father compounded with my mother under the dragon's tail; and my nativity was under *ursa major;* so that it follows, I am rough and lecherous.—Tut,§ I should have been that I am, had the maidenliest star in the firmament twinkled on my bastardizing. Edgar—and|| pat he comes, like the catastrophe of the old comedy: my cue is villainous melancholy, with a sigh like Tom o' Bedlam.—

Enter EDGAR.

O, these eclipses do portend these divisions! fa, sol, la, mi.

EDG. How now, brother Edmund! what serious contemplation are you in?

EDM. I am thinking, brother, of a prediction I read this other day, what should follow these eclipses.

EDG. Do you busy yourself with that?

EDM. I promise you, the effects he writes of succeed unhappily; as of unnaturalness[a] between the child and the parent; death, dearth, dissolutions of ancient amities; divisions in state, menaces and maledictions against king and nobles; needless diffidences, banishment of friends, dissipation of cohorts, nuptial breaches, and I know not what.

EDG. How long have you been a sectary astronomical?

EDM. Come, come; when saw you my father last?

EDG. The night gone by.

EDM. Spake you with him?

EDG. Ay, two hours together.

EDM. Parted you in good terms? Found you no displeasure in him, by word nor countenance?

EDG. None at all.

EDM. Bethink yourself wherein you may have offended him: and at my entreaty forbear his presence until some little time hath qualified the heat of his displeasure; which at this instant so rageth in him, that with the mischief of your person it would scarcely allay.

EDG. Some villain hath done me wrong.

EDM. That's my fear.[b] I pray you, have a continent forbearance till the speed of his rage goes slower; and, as I say, retire with me to my lodging, from whence I will fitly bring you to hear my lord speak: pray ye, go; there's my key:—if you do stir abroad, go armed.

EDG. Armed, brother?

EDM. Brother, I advise you to the best; go armed;* I am no honest man, if there be any good meaning toward you: I have told you what I have seen and heard but faintly; nothing like the image and horror of it: pray you, away.

EDG. Shall I hear from you anon?

EDM. I do serve you in this business.— [*Exit* EDGAR.

A credulous father, and a brother noble,
Whose nature is so far from doing harms,
That he suspects none; on whose foolish honesty
My practices ride easy!—I see the business.—
Let me, if not by birth, have lands by wit:
All with me's meet, that I can fashion fit. [*Exit.*

SCENE III.—*A Room in the* Duke *of* Albany's *Palace.*

Enter GONERIL, *and* OSWALD *her* Steward.

GON. Did my father strike my gentleman for chiding of his fool?

OSW. Ay, madam.

GON. By day and night he wrongs me; every hour
He flashes into one gross crime or other,
That sets us all at odds: I'll not endure it:
His knights grow riotous, and himself upbraids us
On every trifle.—When he returns from hunting,
I will not speak with him; say I am sick:—
If you come slack of former services,
You shall do well; the fault of it I'll answer.

OSW. He's coming, madam; I hear him. [*Horns without.*

GON. Put on what weary negligence you please,
You and your fellows; I'd have it come to question:
If he distaste it, let him to my sister,
Whose mind and mine, I know, in that are one,
Not to be over-rul'd.[c] Idle old man,
That still would manage those authorities,

(*) First folio, *surfets.* (†) First folio omits, *the.* (‡) First folio, *on.* (§) First folio omits, *Tut.* (||) First folio omits, *Edgar—and.*

a —as of unnaturalness—] The folio, omitting the intervening lines, reads,—

"BAST. I promise you, the effects he writes of, succeede unhappily. When saw you my Father last?"

(*) First folio omits, *go armed.*

b That's my fear.] In the quartos, the remainder of this speech, and Edgar's reply, are omitted.

c Not to be over-rul'd.] This, and the four following lines, are omitted in the folio.

That he hath given away!—Now, by my life,
Old fools are babes again, and must be us'd
With checks as flatteries,—when they are seen abus'd.
Remember what I have said.

Osw. Well, madam.

Gon. And let his knights have colder looks among you;
What grows of it, no matter; advise your fellows so:
I would breed from hence occasions, and I shall,
That I may speak:[a]—I'll write straight to my sister,
To hold my course.—Prepare for dinner.

[*Exeunt.*

SCENE IV.—*A Hall in the same.*

Enter Kent, *disguised.*

Kent. If but as well I other accents borrow,
That can my speech diffuse,[b] my good intent
May carry through itself to that full issue
For which I raz'd my likeness.—Now, banish'd Kent,
If thou canst serve where thou dost stand condemn'd,
So may it come, thy master, whom thou lov'st,
Shall find thee full of labours.

Horns without. *Enter* Lear, Knights, *and* Attendants.

Lear. Let me not stay a jot for dinner; go, get it ready. [*Exit an* Attendant.] How now! what art thou?

Kent. A man, sir.

Lear. What dost thou profess? What wouldst thou with us?

Kent. I do profess to be no less than I seem; to serve him truly that will put me in trust; to love him that is honest; to converse with him that is wise, and says little; to fear judgment; to fight when I cannot choose; and to eat no fish.(2)

Lear. What art thou?

Kent. A very honest-hearted fellow, and as poor as the king.

Lear. If thou beest as poor for a subject, as he is for a king, thou art poor enough. What wouldst thou?

Kent. Service.

Lear. Who wouldst thou serve?

Kent. You.

Lear. Dost thou know me, fellow?

Kent. No, sir; but you have that in your countenance which I would fain call master.

Lear. What's that?

Kent. Authority.

Lear. What services canst thou do?

Kent. I can keep honest counsel, ride, run, mar a curious tale in telling it, and deliver a plain message bluntly: that which ordinary men are fit for, I am qualified in; and the best of me is,—diligence.

Lear. How old art thou?

Kent. Not so young, sir, to love a woman for singing; nor so old, to dote on her for any thing: I have years on my back forty-eight.

Lear. Follow me; thou shalt serve me, if I like thee no worse after dinner. I will not part from thee yet.—Dinner, ho, dinner!—Where's my knave? my fool? Go you and call my fool hither. [*Exit an* Attendant.

Enter Oswald.

You, you, sirrah, where's my daughter?

Osw. So please you,— [*Exit.*

Lear. What says the fellow there? Call the clotpoll back.—[*Exit a* Knight.]—Where's my fool, ho?—I think the world's asleep.—

Re-enter Knight.

How now! where's that mongrel?

Knight. He says, my lord, your daughter* is not well.

Lear. Why came not the slave back to me, when I call'd him?

Knight. Sir, he answered me in the roundest manner, he would not.

Lear. *He would not!*

Knight. My lord, I know not what the matter is; but, to my judgment, your highness is not entertained with that ceremonious affection as you were wont; there's a great abatement of kindness appears as well in the general dependants as in the duke himself also, and your daughter.

Lear. Ha! sayest thou so?

Knight. I beseech you, pardon me, my lord, if I be mistaken; for my duty cannot be silent when I think your highness wronged.

Lear. Thou but rememberest me of mine own

---

[a] I would breed from hence occasions, and I shall,
That I may speak:—]
These lines are not in the folio.

(*) First folio, *Daughters.*

[b] *That can my speech* diffuse,—] *Diffuse,* here, signifies, *disguise.*

conception: I have perceived a most faint neglect ot late; which I have rather blamed as mine own jealous curiosity than as a very pretence and purpose of unkindness: I will look further into 't.—But where's my fool? I have not seen him this two days.

Knight. Since my young lady's going into France, sir, the fool hath much pined away.

Lear. No more of that; I have noted it well.

—Go you, and tell my daughter I would speak with her.—[*Exit an* Attendant.] Go you, call hither my fool.—[*Exit an* Attendant.]

Re-enter Oswald.

O, you sir, you, come you hither, sir: who am I, sir?

Osw. My lady's father.

Lear. *My lady's father!* my lord's knave: you whoreson dog! you slave! you cur!

Osw. I am none of these, my lord; I beseech your pardon.

Lear. Do you bandy looks with me, you rascal? [*Striking him.*

Osw. I'll not be struck,* my lord.

Kent. Nor tripp'd neither, you base foot-ball player. [*Tripping up his heels.*

Lear. I thank thee, fellow; thou servest me, and I'll love thee.

Kent. Come, sir, arise, away! I'll teach you differences; away, away! If you will measure your lubber's length again, tarry: but away! go to; have you wisdom? so. [*Pushes* Oswald *out.*

Lear. Now, my friendly knave, I thank thee: there's earnest of thy service.

[*Giving* Kent *money.*

Enter Fool.

Fool. Let me hire him too;—here's my coxcomb. [*Giving* Kent *his cap.*

Lear. How now, my pretty knave! how dost thou?

Fool. Sirrah, you were best take my coxcomb.

Kent. Why, fool? [a]

Fool. Why, for taking one's part that's out of favour. Nay, an thou canst not smile as the wind sits, thou'lt catch cold shortly: there, take my coxcomb. Why, this fellow has banished two on's daughters, and did the third a blessing against his will; if thou follow him, thou must needs wear my coxcomb.—How now, nuncle! Would I had two coxcombs and two daughters!

Lear. Why, my boy?

Fool. If I gave them all my living, I'd keep my coxcombs myself. There's mine; beg another of thy daughters.

Lear. Take heed, sirrah,—the whip.

Fool. Truth's a dog must to kennel; he must be whipped out, when the lady brach may stand by the fire and stink.

Lear. A pestilent gall to me!

Fool. Sirrah, I'll teach thee a speech.

Lear. Do.

Fool. Mark it, nuncle:—

Have more than thou showest,
Speak less than thou knowest,
Lend less than thou owest,
Ride more than thou goest,
Learn more than thou trowest,[b]
Set less than thou throwest;
Leave thy drink and thy whore,
And keep in-a-door,
And thou shalt have more
Than two tens to a score.

Lear. This is nothing, fool.[c]

Fool. Then 'tis like the breath of an unfee'd lawyer,—you gave me nothing for 't. Can you make no use of nothing, nuncle?

Lear. Why, no, boy; nothing can be made out of nothing.

Fool. Pr'ythee, tell him, so much the rent of his land comes to; he will not believe a fool.

[*To* Kent.

Lear. A bitter fool!

Fool. Dost thou know the difference, my boy, between a bitter fool and a sweet one?

Lear. No, lad, teach me.[d]

Fool. That lord, that counsell'd thee
To give away thy land,
Come place him here by me,—
Or* do thou for him stand;
The sweet and bitter fool
Will presently appear;
The one in motley here,
The other found out there.

Lear. Dost thou call me fool, boy?

Fool. All thy other titles thou hast given away; that thou wast born with.

Kent. This is not altogether fool, my lord.

Fool. No, 'faith, lords and great men will not let me; if I had a monopoly out,(3) they would have part on't: and ladies† too, they will not let me have all fool to myself; they'll be snatching.—Nuncle, give me an egg, and I'll give thee two crowns.

Lear. What two crowns shall they be?

Fool. Why, after I have cut the egg i' the middle, and eat up the meat, the two crowns of the egg. When thou clovest thy crown ‡ i' the middle, and gavest away both parts, thou borest thine ass on thy back o'er the dirt: thou hadst little wit in thy bald crown, when thou gavest thy golden one away. If I speak like myself in this, let him be whipped that first finds it so.

[Singing.

Fools had ne'er less grace[e] *in a year;*
For wise men are grown foppish,
And know not how their wits to wear,
Their manners are so apish.

(*) First folio, *strucken.*

a Why, fool?] This interrogatory, in the form of, "Why, my boy?" is given in the folio to Lear; but, as Mr. Dyce observes, it is plain that the Fool addresses the King for the first time, when he says, "How now, nuncle!"

b — *than thou* trowest,—] That is, than thou *believest.*

c This is nothing, fool.] In the folio, this speech is assigned to Kent.

d No, lad, teach me.] This line and the portion of the dialogue down to and including the words in the Fool's speech, "they'll be snatching," are omitted in the folio.

(*) Old copies omit, *Or.* (†) Old copies, *loades, lodes.* (‡) First folio, *Crownes.*

e *Fools had ne'er less* grace *in a year;*] The quartos have,—

"——— ne'er less *wit* in a year;"

perhaps the true reading: as in Lyly's "Mother Bombie," 1594, we find, "I think gentlemen *had never less wit in a year.*"

LEAR. When were you wont to be so full of songs, sirrah?

FOOL. I have used it, nuncle, ever since thou madest thy daughters thy mothers: for when thou gavest them the rod, and putt'st down thine own breeches,

[Singing.

Then they for sudden joy did weep,
And I for sorrow sung,[a]
That such a king should play bo-peep,
And go the fools among.*

Pr'ythee, nuncle, keep a school-master that can teach thy fool to lie; I would fain learn to lie.

LEAR. An you lie, sirrah, we'll have you whipped.

FOOL. I marvel what kin thou and thy daughters are: they'll have me whipped for speaking true, thou'lt have me whipped for lying; and sometimes I am whipped for holding my peace. I had rather be any kind o' thing than a fool; and yet I would not be thee, nuncle; thou hast pared thy wit o' both sides, and left nothing i' the middle. Here comes one o' the parings.

Enter GONERIL.

LEAR. How now, daughter! what makes that frontlet on? (4)
Methinks † you are too much of late i' the frown.

FOOL. Thou wast a pretty fellow when thou hadst no need to care for her frowning; now thou art an O without a figure. I am better than thou art now; I am a fool, thou art nothing.—Yes, forsooth [*To* GON.], I will hold my tongue, so your face bids me, though you say nothing. Mum, mum,

He that keeps nor crust nor crumb,
Weary of all, shall want some.—

That's a sheal'd peascod. [*Pointing to* LEAR.

GON. Not only, sir, this your all-licens'd fool,
But other of your insolent retinue
Do hourly carp and quarrel; breaking forth
In rank and not-to-be-endured riots. Sir,
I had thought, by making this well known unto you,
To have found a safe redress; but now grow fearful,
By what yourself too late have spoke and done,
That you protect this course, and put it on
By your allowance; which if you should, the fault
Would not 'scape censure, nor the redresses sleep,
Which, in the tender of a wholesome weal,
Might in their working do you that offence,—
Which else were shame—that then necessity
Will call discreet proceeding.

FOOL. For you trow,* nuncle,

The hedge-sparrow fed the cuckoo so long,
That it's had it head bit off by it young.[b]

So, out went the candle, and we were left darkling.[c]

LEAR. Are you our daughter?

GON. I would you would make use of that † good wisdom
Whereof I know you are fraught; and put away
These dispositions, which of late transport you
From what you rightly are.

FOOL. May not an ass know when the cart draws the horse?—*Whoop, Jug! I love thee.*

LEAR. Does any here know me?—This is not Lear:
Does Lear walk thus? speak thus? Where are his eyes?
Either his notion weakens, his discernings
Are lethargied.—Ha! Waking?—'tis not so.—
Who is it that can tell me who I am?—

FOOL. Lear's shadow?

LEAR. I would learn that, for, by the marks of sovereignty, knowledge, and reason,[d]
I should be false persuaded I had daughters.—

FOOL. Which they will make an obedient father.[e]

LEAR. Your name, fair gentlewoman?

GON. This admiration, sir, is much o' the favour
Of other your new pranks. I do beseech you
To understand my purposes aright:
As you are old and reverend, you ‡ should be wise.
Here do you keep a hundred knights and squires;
Men so disordered, so debosh'd, and bold,
That this our court, infected with their manners,
Shows like a riotous inn: epicurism and lust
Make it more like a tavern or a brothel,
Than a grac'd palace. The shame itself doth speak
For instant remedy: be, then, desir'd
By her, that else will take the thing she begs,

(*) First folio, *Foole.* (†) First folio omits, *Methinks.*

a *Then they for sudden joy did weep,*
And I for sorrow sung," &c.]
So in Heywood's "Rape of Lucrece,"—
"When Tarquin first in court began,
And was approved King,
Some men *for sudden joy gan weep,*
And I for sorrow sing."

b That it's had it head bit off by it young.] Meaning, *That it has had its head bit off,* &c.] See note (3), Vol. I. p. 330.

c — darkling.] This word, which, like the Scotch *darklins,* implied *in the dark,* occurs again in "A Midsummer Night's Dream," Act II. Sc. 3; and is found in the ancient comedy of "Roister Doister," Act III. Sc. 1,—"He will go *darklyng* to his grave."

(*) First folio, *know.* (†) First folio, *your.* (‡) First folio omits, *you.*

d — for, by the marks of sovereignty, knowledge, and reason, I should be false persuaded," &c.] This is certainly obscure. Warburton reads, "— of sovereignty *of* knowledge," &c.; but possibly the meaning may be restored by simply omitting the comma after *sovereignty,* "— by the marks of sovereignty knowledge and reason," *i.e.* of *supreme* or *sovereign* knowledge, &c.

e — an obedient father.] This and the three preceding lines are only found in the quartos.

A little to disquantity your train;
And the remainder, that shall still depend,
To be such men as may besort your age,
Which know themselves and you.

LEAR. Darkness and devils!—
Saddle my horses! call my train together!—
Degenerate bastard! I'll not trouble thee;
Yet have I left a daughter.

GON. You strike my people; and your disorder'd rabble
Make servants of their betters.

Enter ALBANY.

LEAR. Woe, that too late repents,—[*To* ALB.] O, sir, are you come? (*)
Is it your will? Speak, sir.—Prepare my horses.—
Ingratitude! thou marble-hearted fiend,
More hideous, when thou show'st thee in a child,
Than the sea-monster!

ALB. Pray, sir, be patient.

LEAR. Detested kite! thou liest: [*To* GONERIL.
My train are men of choice and rarest parts,
That all particulars of duty know,
And in the most exact regard support
The worships of their name.—O, most small fault,
How ugly didst thou in Cordelia show!
Which, like an engine,[a] wrench'd my frame of nature
From the fix'd place; drew from my heart all love,
And added to the gall. O Lear, Lear, Lear!
Beat at this gate, that let thy folly in,
[*Striking his head.*
And thy dear judgment out!—Go, go, my people.

ALB. My lord, I am guiltless, as I am ignorant
Of what hath mov'd you.

LEAR. It may be so, my lord.—
Hear, Nature, hear; dear goddess, hear!
Suspend thy purpose, if thou didst intend
To make this creature fruitful!
Into her womb convey sterility!
Dry up in her the organs of increase;
And from her derogate body never spring
A babe to honour her! If she must teem,
Create her child of spleen; that it may live,
And be a thwart disnatur'd torment to her!
Let it stamp wrinkles in her brow of youth;
With cadent tears fret channels in her cheeks;
Turn all her mother's pains and benefits
To laughter and contempt; that she may feel
How sharper than a serpent's tooth it is
To have a thankless child!—Away, away! [*Exit.*

ALB. Now, gods that we adore, whereof comes this?

GON. Never afflict yourself to know the cause; (*)
But let his disposition have that scope
That (†) dotage gives it.

Re-enter LEAR.

LEAR. What, fifty of my followers at a clap!
Within a fortnight!

ALB. What's the matter, sir?

LEAR. I'll tell thee;—Life and death! [*To* GON.] I am asham'd
That thou hast power to shake my manhood thus:
That these hot tears, which break from me perforce,
Should make thee worth them.—Blasts and fogs upon thee!
The untented woundings[b] of a father's curse
Pierce every sense about thee!—Old fond eyes,
Beweep this cause again, I'll pluck ye out,
And cast you, with the waters that you loose,[c]
To temper clay.—Ha! is it come to this?
Let it be so; yet have I left a daughter,[d]
Who, I am sure, is kind and comfortable;
When she shall hear this of thee, with her nails
She'll flay thy wolfish visage. Thou shalt find
That I'll resume the shape which thou dost think
I have cast off for ever; thou shalt, I warrant thee. (‡)
[*Exeunt* LEAR, KENT, *and* Attendants.

GON. Do you mark that, my lord? (§)

ALB. I cannot be so partial, Goneril,
To the great love I bear you,—

GON. Pray you, content.—What, Oswald, ho!—
You, sir, more knave than fool, after your master.
[*To the* Fool.

FOOL. Nuncle Lear, nuncle Lear, tarry, and (‖) take the fool with thee.

A fox, when one has caught her,
And such a daughter,
Should sure to the slaughter,
If my cap would buy a halter:
So the fool follows after. [*Exit.*

(*) First folio omits, *O sir, are you come?*

a — an engine,—] By an *engine* is meant the instrument of torture called the *rack.*

b — untented woundings—] "*Untented* wounds," Steevens says, "may possibly signify here, such as will not admit of having a tent put into them." The expression, there can be no doubt, means *unsearchable* wounds—wounds *too deep to be probed.*

c — loose,—] That is, *discharge.*

(*) First folio, *to know more of it.* (†) First folio, *As.* (‡) First folio omits, *thou shalt, I warrant thee.* (§) First folio omits, *my lord.* (‖) First folio omits, *and.*

d —— Ha! is it come to this?
Let it be so; yet have I left a daughter,—]
This passage is formed from the two old texts; the quartos read, "Yea is it come to this? yet have I left a daughter:" the folio,—
"Ha? Let it be so,
I have another daughter."

GON. This man hath had good counsel:[a]—a hundred knights!
'T is politic and safe to let him keep
At point a hundred knights: yes, that on every dream,
Each buz, each fancy, each complaint, dislike,
He may enguard his dotage with their powers,
And hold our lives in mercy.—Oswald, I say!—

ALB. Well, you may fear too far.

GON. Safer than trust too far:
Let me still take away the harms I fear,
Not fear still to be taken: I know his heart.
What he hath utter'd I have writ my sister;
If she sustain him and his hundred knights,
When I have show'd the unfitness,—

Re-enter OSWALD.

How now, Oswald?
What, have you writ that letter to my sister?

OSW. Ay, madam.

GON. Take you some company, and away to horse;
Inform her full of my particular fear;
And thereto add such reasons of your own
As may compact it more. Get you gone;
And hasten your return.—[*Exit* OSW.] No, no, my lord,
This milky gentleness and course of yours
Though I condemn not, yet, under pardon,
You are much more attask'd* for want of wisdom,
Than prais'd for harmful mildness.

ALB. How far your eyes may pierce, I cannot tell;
Striving to better, oft we mar what's well.

GON. Nay, then—

ALB. Well, well; the event. [*Exeunt.*

SCENE V.—*Court before the Same.*

Enter LEAR, KENT, *and* Fool.

LEAR. Go you before to Gloster with these letters; acquaint my daughter no further with any thing you know, than comes from her demand out of the letter. If your diligence be not speedy, I shall be there afore you.

KENT. I will not sleep, my lord, till I have delivered your letter. [*Exit.*

FOOL. If a man's brains were in 's heels, were 't not in danger of kibes?

LEAR. Ay, boy.

FOOL. Then, I pr'ythee, be merry; thy wit shall not go slip-shod.

LEAR. Ha, ha, ha!

FOOL. Shalt see thy other daughter will use thee kindly:[b] for though she's as like this as a crab's like an apple, yet I can tell what I can tell.

LEAR. What canst tell, boy?

FOOL. She will taste as like this, as a crab does to a crab. Thou canst tell why one's nose stands i' the middle on 's face?

LEAR. No.

FOOL. Why, to keep one's eyes of either side his nose; that what a man cannot smell out, he may spy into.

LEAR. I did her wrong.—

FOOL. Canst tell how an oyster makes his shell?

LEAR. No.

FOOL. Nor I neither; but I can tell why a snail has a house.

LEAR. Why?

FOOL. Why, to put his head in; not to give it away to his daughters, and leave his horns without a case.

LEAR. I will forget my nature.—So kind a father!—Be my horses ready?

FOOL. Thy asses are gone about 'em. The reason why the seven stars are no more than seven, is a pretty reason.

LEAR. Because they are not eight?

FOOL. Yes, indeed: thou wouldst make a good fool.

LEAR. To take 't again perforce!—Monster ingratitude!

FOOL. If thou wert my fool, nuncle, I'd have thee beaten for being old before thy time.

LEAR. How's that?

FOOL. Thou shouldst not have been old, before* thou hadst been wise.

LEAR. O, let me not be mad, not mad, sweet heaven!
Keep me in temper; I would not be mad!—

Enter Gentleman.

How now! Are the horses ready?

GENT. Ready, my lord.

LEAR. Come, boy.

FOOL. She that's a maid now, and laughs at my departure,
Shall not be a maid long, unless things be cut shorter. [*Exeunt.*

(*) First folio, *at task.*

a — This man hath had good counsel:—] This and what follows down to the entrance of Oswald, are not in the quartos.

(*) First folio, *till.*

b — *thy other daughter will use thee* kindly:] *Kindly* is here used, as Malone pointed out, with the double meaning of *affectionately*, and *after her nature*, or *kind*.

ACT II.

SCENE I.—*A Court within the Castle of the* Earl *of* Gloucester.

Enter Edmund *and* Curan, *meeting.*

Edm. Save thee, Curan.

Cur. And you,* sir. I have been with your father, and given him notice that the duke of Cornwall and Regan his duchess will be here with him this night.

Edm. How comes that?

Cur. Nay, I know not. You have heard of the news abroad,—I mean the whispered ones, for they are yet but ear-kissing arguments?

Edm. Not I; pray you, what are they?

Cur. Have you heard of no likely wars toward, 'twixt the dukes of Cornwall and Albany?

Edm. Not a word.

Cur. You may do, then, in time. Fare you well, sir. [*Exit.*

Edm. The duke be here to-night? The better! best!
This weaves itself perforce into my business.
My father hath set guard to take my brother;
And I have one thing, of a queasy question,
Which I must act:—briefness and fortune, work!—
Brother, a word;—descend:—brother, I say!

(*) First folio, *your*.

Enter Edgar.

My father watches:—O, sir, fly this place;
Intelligence is given where you are hid;
You have now the good advantage of the night:—
Have you not spoken 'gainst the duke of Cornwall?
He's coming hither; now, i' the night, i' the haste,
And Regan with him; have you nothing said
Upon his party 'gainst the duke of Albany?
Advise yourself.

Edg. I am sure on't, not a word.

Edm. I hear my father coming,—pardon me;
In cunning I must draw my sword upon you:—
Draw: seem to defend yourself: now quit you well.—
Yield:—come before my father.—Light, ho, here!—
Fly, brother.—Torches! torches!—So, farewell.—
[*Exit* Edgar.
Some blood drawn on me would beget opinion
[*Wounds his arm.*
Of my more fierce endeavour: I have seen drunkards
Do more than this in sport.—Father! father!
Stop, stop! No help?

Enter GLOUCESTER, *and* Servants *with torches.*

GLO. Now, Edmund, where's the villain?
EDM. Here stood he in the dark, his sharp sword out,
Mumbling of wicked charms, cónjuring the moon
To stand auspicious mistress,—
GLO. But where is he?
EDM. Look, sir, I bleed.
GLO. Where is the villain, Edmund?
EDM. Fled this way, sir. When by no means he could—
GLO. Pursue him, ho!—Go after.—[*Exeunt some* Servants.] *By no means*, what?
EDM. Persuade me to the murder of your lordship;
But that I told him, the revenging gods
'Gainst parricides did all their thunders* bend;
Spoke, with how manifold and strong a bond
The child was bound to the father;—sir, in fine,
Seeing how loathly opposite I stood
To his unnatural purpose, in fell motion
With his prepared sword, he charges home
My unprovided body, lanc'd† mine arm:
But‡ when[a] he saw my best alarum'd spirits,
Bold in the quarrel's right, rous'd to the encounter,
Or whether gasted[b] by the noise I made,
Full suddenly he fled.
GLO. Let him fly far:
Not in this land shall he remain uncaught;
And found—despatch![c]—The noble duke my master,
My worthy arch and patron, comes to-night:
By his authority I will proclaim it,
That he which finds him shall deserve our thanks,
Bringing the murderous coward to the stake;
He that conceals him, death.
EDM. When I dissuaded him from his intent,
And found him pight[d] to do it, with curst[e] speech
I threaten'd to discover him: he replied,
Thou unpossessing bastard! dost thou think,
If I would stand against thee, would the reposal
Of any trust, virtue, or worth, in thee
Make thy words faith'd? No: what I should§ [*deny*,
(*As this I would; ay,‖ though thou didst produce*
My very character[f]) *I'd turn it all*
To thy suggestion, plot, and damned practice:
And thou must make a dullard of the world,
If they not thought the profits of my death
*Were very pregnant and potential spurs**
To make thee seek it.
GLO. Strong† and fasten'd villain!
Would he deny his letter?—I never got him.—[g]
[*Trumpets without.*
Hark, the duke's trumpets! I know not why‡ he comes.—
All ports I'll bar; the villain shall not 'scape;
The duke must grant me that: besides, his picture
I will send far and near, that all the kingdom
May have due note of him; and of my land,
Loyal and natural boy, I'll work the means
To make thee capable.

Enter CORNWALL, REGAN, *and* Attendants.

CORN. How now, my noble friend! since I came hither,
(Which I can call but now) I have heard strange news.§
REG. If it be true, all vengeance comes too short,
Which can pursue the offender. How dost, my lord?
GLO. O, madam, my old heart is crack'd,—it's crack'd!
REG. What, did my father's godson seek your life?
He whom my father nam'd? your Edgar?
GLO. O, lady, lady, shame would have it hid!
REG. Was he not companion with the riotous knights
That tend‖ upon my father?
GLO. I know not, madam: 'tis too bad, too bad.—
EDM. Yes, madam, he was of that consort.
REG. No marvel then, though he were ill affected;
'Tis they have put him on the old man's death,
To have the waste and spoil[h] of his revenues.
I have this present evening from my sister
Been well inform'd of them; and with such cautions,
That if they come to sojourn at my house,
I'll not be there.
CORN. Nor I, assure thee, Regan.—
Edmund, I hear that you have shown your father
A child-like office.
EDM. 'Twas my duty, sir.
GLO. He did bewray his practice; and receiv'd
This hurt you see, striving to apprehend him.
CORN. Is he pursu'd?
GLO. Ay, my good lord.
CORN. If he be taken, he shall never more

(*) First folio, *the thunder*. (†) First folio, *latch'd*.
(‡) First folio, *And*. (§) First folio, *should I*.
(‖) First folio omits, *ay*.

[a] *But* when, &c.] "When" is very probably a misprint for *whêr*, or *whether*.
[b] — gasted—] *Gasted*, or *ghasted*, means *affrighted, dismayed*.
[c] And found—despatch!—] Warburton reads, "And found, *dispatch'd*;" as also does Mr. Collier's annotator; but the old text is right. Thus, in "Blurt, Master Constable," Act V. Sc. 1,—
"There to find Fontinelle: found, to kill him."
[d] — pight *to do it*,—] *Pight* is *fixed, settled*.

(*) First folio, *spirits*. (†) First folio, *O strange*.
(‡) First folio, *wher*. (§) First folio, *strangenesse*.
(‖) First folio, *tended*.

[e] — curst *speech*—] *Harsh, bitter* speech.
[f] — character—] That is, *hand-writing*.
[g] I never got him.—] The folio reads,—
"Would he deny his Letter, *said he?*"
[h] — the waste and spoil—] So the first quarto; the second reads, "— *these*—and waste;" all the other ancient copies, "— th' *expence and wast*."

Be fear'd of doing harm: make your own purpose,
How in my strength you please.—For you, Edmund,
Whose virtue and obedience doth this instant
So much commend itself, you shall be ours;
Natures of such deep trust we shall much need;
You we first seize on.

EDM. I shall serve you, sir, truly,
However else.

GLO. For him I thank your grace.

CORN. You know not why we came to visit you,—

REG. Thus out of season; threading dark-eyed [night.
Occasions, noble Gloster, of some poise,*
Wherein we must have use of your advice:—
Our father he hath writ, so hath our sister,
Of differences, which I best thought it fit
To answer from[a] our home; the several messengers
From hence attend despatch. Our good old friend,
Lay comforts to your bosom; and bestow
Your needful counsel to our business,†
Which craves the instant use.

GLO. I serve you, madam:
Your graces are right welcome. [*Exeunt.*

SCENE II.—*Before* Gloucester's *Castle.*

Enter KENT *and* OSWALD, *severally.*

OSW. Good dawning to thee, friend; art of this house?

KENT. Ay.

OSW. Where may we set our horses?

KENT. I'the mire.

OSW. Pr'ythee, if thou lov'st me, tell me.

KENT. I love thee not.

OSW. Why, then, I care not for thee.

KENT. If I had thee in Lipsbury pinfold, I would make thee care for me.

OSW. Why dost thou use me thus? I know thee not.

KENT. Fellow, I know thee.

OSW. What dost thou know me for?

KENT. A knave; a rascal; an eater of broken meats; a base, proud, shallow, beggarly, three-suited, hundred-pound,[b] filthy, worsted-stocking knave; a lily-livered, action-taking whoreson, glass-gazing, superserviceable, finical rogue; one trunk-inheriting slave; one that wouldst be a bawd, in way of good service, and art nothing but the composition of a knave, beggar, coward, pandar, and the son and heir of a mongrel bitch: one whom I will beat into clamourous* whining, if thou deniest the least syllable of thy addition.

OSW. Why, what a monstrous fellow art thou, thus to rail on one that is neither known of thee nor knows thee!

KENT. What a brazen-faced varlet art thou, to deny thou knowest me! Is it two days ago,† since I tripped up thy heels, and beat thee, before the king? Draw, you rogue: for, though it be night, yet[c] the moon shines, I'll make a sop o' the moonshine of you: draw,‡ you whoreson cullionly barber-monger, draw. [*Drawing his sword.*

OSW. Away! I have nothing to do with thee.

KENT. Draw, you rascal! you come with letters against the king; and take Vanity the puppet's part, against the royalty of her father: draw, you rogue, or I'll so carbonado your shanks!—draw, you rascal! come your ways.

OSW. Help, ho! murder! help!

KENT. Strike, you slave! stand, rogue, stand! you neat[d] slave, strike! [*Beating him.*

OSW. Help, ho! murder! murder!

Enter EDMUND.

EDM. How now? what's the matter? Part.

KENT. With you, goodman boy, an § you please; come, I'll flesh you; come on, young master.

Enter CORNWALL, REGAN, GLOUCESTER, *and* Servants.

GLO. Weapons! arms! what's the matter here?

CORN. Keep peace, upon your lives!
He dies, that strikes again! what is the matter?

REG. The messengers from our sister and the king!

CORN. What is your difference? speak.

OSW. I am scarce in breath, my lord.

KENT. No marvel, you have so bestirred your valour. You cowardly rascal, nature disclaims in thee; a tailor made thee.

CORN. Thou art a strange fellow: a tailor make a man?

KENT. Ay,‖ a tailor, sir: a stone-cutter, or a

(*) First folio, *prize.* (†) First folio, *businesses.*

(*) First folio, *clamours.* (†) First folio omits, *ago.* (‡) First folio omits, *draw.* (§) First folio, *if.* (‖) First folio omits, *Ay.*

a — from our home;] *Away from* home.

b — hundred-pound,—] This epithet is found in Middleton's play of "The Phœnix," Act IV. Sc. 3,—

"—— am I used like a hundred-pound gentleman."

And in Sir Walter Raleigh's speech against Foreign Retailers (Oldys's "Life of Râleigh," p. 68), he says,—"Nay at Milan, where there are three *hundred-pound* Englishmen, they cannot so much as have a barber among them."

c — yet the moon shines,—] That is, *now* the moon shines, &c.

d — *you* neat *slave*,—] The sting in this epithet, "neat," has been quite misunderstood by the commentators, who suppose it to mean simply *mere* or *finical*. For the real allusion, see a passage in the "Winter's Tale," Act I. Sc. 2,—

"—— Come, captain,
We must be *neat;* not *neat*, but cleanly, captain;
And yet the steer, the heifer, and the calf,
Are all call'd *neat.*"

See also Taylor the Water Poet's Epigram on the husband of Mrs. Parnell,—

"Neate can he talke, and feede, and neatly tread,
Neate are his feete, but most *neate is his head.*"

painter, could not have made him so ill, though they had been but two hours at the trade.*

CORN. Speak yet, how grew your quarrel?

OSW. This ancient ruffian, sir, whose life I have spar'd,
At suit of his grey beard,—

KENT. Thou whoreson zed! thou unnecessary letter!—My lord, if you will give me leave, I will tread this unbolted villain into mortar, and daub the wall of a jakes with him.—Spare my grey beard, you wagtail?[a]

CORN. Peace, sirrah!
You beastly knave, know you no reverence?

KENT. Yes, sir, but anger hath a privilege.

CORN. Why art thou angry?

KENT. That such a slave as this should wear a sword,
Who wears no honesty. Such smiling rogues as these,
Like rats, oft bite the holy cords a-twain
Which are too intrinse t'unloose: smooth every passion
That in the natures of their lords rebels;
Bring† oil to fire, snow to the colder moods;
Renege,‡ affirm, and turn their halcyon beaks
With every gale§ and vary of their masters,
Knowing nought, like dogs, but following,—
A plague upon your epileptic visage!
Smile you my speeches, as I were a fool?
Goose, if I had you upon Sarum plain,
I'd drive ye cackling home to Camelot.(1)

CORN. What, art thou mad, old fellow?

GLO. How fell you out? say that.

KENT. No contraries hold more antipathy,
Than I and such a knave.

CORN. Why dost thou call him *knave?* What's his offence? ||

KENT. His countenance likes me not.

CORN. No more, perchance, does mine, nor his, nor hers.

KENT. Sir, 'tis my occupation to be plain;
I have seen better faces in my time,
Than stands on any shoulder that I see
Before me at this instant.

CORN. This is some fellow,
Who, having been prais'd for bluntness, doth affect
A saucy roughness, and constrains the garb
Quite from his[b] nature: he cannot flatter, he—
An honest mind and plain,—he must speak truth!
An they will take it, so; if not, he's plain.
These kind of knaves I know, which in this plainness
Harbour more craft and more corrupter ends,
Than twenty silly ducking óbservants,
That stretch their duties nicely.

KENT. Sir, in good sooth,* in sincere verity,
Under the allowance of your grand† aspéct,
Whose influence, like the wreath of radiant fire
On flickering‡ Phœbus' front,—

CORN. What mean'st by this?

KENT. To go out of my dialect, which you discommend so much. I know, sir, I am no flatterer: he that beguiled you in a plain accent, was a plain knave; which, for my part, I will not be, though I should win your displeasure to entreat me to 't.

CORN. What was the offence you gave him?

OSW. I never gave him any:
It pleas'd the king his master very late,
To strike at me, upon his misconstruction;
When he, conjunct,§ and flattering his displeasure,
Tripp'd me behind; being down, insulted, rail'd,
And put upon him such a deal of man,
That worthied him, got praises of the king
For him attempting who was self-subdu'd;
And, in the fleshment of this dread || exploit,
Drew on me here again.

KENT. None of these rogues and cowards,
But Ajax is their fool.

CORN. Fetch forth the stocks, ho!
You stubborn ancient knave, you reverend braggart,
We'll teach you—

KENT. Sir, I am too old to learn:
Call not your stocks for me: I serve the king;
On whose employment I was sent to you:
You shall do small respect,¶ show too bold malice
Against the grace and person of my master,
Stocking his messenger.

CORN. Fetch forth the stocks!—
As I have life and honour, there shall he sit till noon!

REG. *Till noon!* till night, my lord; and all night too.

KENT. Why, madam, if I were your father's dog,
You should not use me so.

REG. Sir, being his knave, I will.

CORN. This is a fellow of the self-same colour
Our sister speaks of.—Come, bring away the stocks.
[*Stocks brought in.*

GLO. Let me beseech your grace not to do so:
His fault is much,[c] and the good king his master
Will check him for't: your purpos'd low correction
Is such, as basest and contemned'st** wretches,
For pilferings and most common trespasses

(*) First folio, *two yeares oth' trade.* (†) First folio, *Being.* (‡) First folio, *Revenge.* (§) First folio, *gall.* (||) First folio, *What is his fault?*

[a] Spare my grey beard, you wagtail?] An acute stroke of nature: Kent in his rage forgets it was his life, not his beard, which the fellow pretended to have spared.

[b] *Quite from his nature:*] *His* is here used for the impersonal *its.*

(*) First folio, *faith.* (†) First folio, *great.* (‡) First folio, *flicking.* (§) First folio, *compact.* (||) First folio, *dead.* (¶) First folio, *respects.* (**) Old text, *temnest,* corrected by Capell.

[c] His fault is much,—] This speech is abridged in the folio, which reads,—

"Let me beseech your Grace, not to do so,
The King *his master needs* must take it ill."

Are punish'd with : the king must take it ill,
That he's so slightly valu'd in his messenger,
Should have him thus restrain'd.

CORN. I'll answer that.

REG. My sister may receive it much more worse,
To have her gentleman abus'd, assaulted,
For following her affairs.—Put in his legs.—[a]

[KENT *is put in the stocks.*

Come, my good* lord; away.

[*Exeunt all but* GLOUCESTER *and* KENT.

GLO. I am sorry for thee, friend; 'tis the duke's pleasure,
Whose disposition, all the world well knows,
Will not be rubb'd nor stopp'd: I'll entreat for thee.

KENT. Pray do not, sir: I have watch'd and travell'd hard;
Some time I shall sleep out, the rest I'll whistle.
A good man's fortune may grow out at heels:
Give you good morrow!

GLO. [*Aside.*] The duke's to blame in this; 'twill be ill taken. [*Exit.*

KENT. Good king, that must approve the common saw,
Thou out of heaven's benediction com'st
To the warm sun![b]
Approach, thou beacon to this under globe,
That by thy comfortable beams I may
Peruse this letter!—Nothing almost sees miracles,
But misery;—I know 't is from Cordelia;
Who hath most fortunately been inform'd
Of my obscured course, and she'll find time
From this enormous state-seeking, to give
Losses their remedies.[c]—All weary and o'er-watch'd,

(*) First folio omits, *good.*

[a] For following her affairs,—Put in his legs.—] A line not found in the folio.

[b] Thou out of heaven's benediction com'st
To the warm sun!]

This "common saw" we meet with in Heywood's "Dialogues on Proverbs,"—

"In your running from him to me, *ye runne*
Out of God's blessing into the warme sunne."

It is found also in Howell's collection of English Proverbs in his Dictionary, 1660, and there explained,—"He goes out of God's blessing to the warm sun, viz. *from good to worse.*" The application, we must suppose, is to Lear's quitting one daughter only to meet more inhospitable treatment from another.

[c] I know 't is from Cordelia;
Who hath most fortunately been inform'd
Of my obscured course, and she'll find time
From this enormous state-seeking, to give
Losses their remedies.]

Some editors have gone so far as to degrade this passage altogether from the text: Steevens and others conjecture it to be made up from fragments of Cordelia's letter. We agree with Malone that it forms no part of that letter, but are opposed to his notion that "two half lines have been lost between the words *state* and *seeking.*" The slight change of "she'll" for *shall*,—the ordinary reading being, "— and *shall* find time," &c.—appears to remove much of the difficulty; that occasioned by the corrupt words, "enormous state-seeking," will some day probably find an equally facile remedy.

Take vantage, heavy eyes, not to behold
This shameful lodging.
Fortune, good night; smile once more; turn thy wheel! [*Sleeps.*

SCENE III.—*A Wood.*

Enter EDGAR.

EDG. I heard myself proclaim'd;
And, by the happy hollow of a tree,
Escap'd the hunt. No port is free; no place,
That guard, and most unusual vigilance,
Does not attend my taking. Whiles I may scape,
I will preserve myself: and am bethought
To take the basest and most poorest shape,
That ever penury, in contempt of man,
Brought near to beast: my face I'll grime with filth;
Blanket my loins; elf all my hair* in knots;[a]
And with presented nakedness out-face
The winds and persecutions of the sky.
The country gives me proof and precedent
Of Bedlam beggars,(2) who, with roaring voices,
Strike in their numb'd and mortified bare arms
Pins, wooden pricks, nails, sprigs of rosemary;
And with this horrible object, from low farms,
Poor pelting[b] villages, sheep-cotes, and mills,
Sometime with lunatic bans, sometime with prayers,
Enforce their charity.—*Poor Turlygood!*(3) *poor Tom!*[c]
That's something yet;—Edgar I nothing am. [*Exit.*

SCENE IV.—*Before* Gloucester's *Castle.* KENT *in the Stocks.*

Enter LEAR, Gentleman, *and* Fool.

LEAR. 'Tis strange that they should so depart from home,
And not send back my messenger.†
GENT. As I learn'd,
The night before there was no purpose in them
Of this remove.

KENT. [*Waking.*] Hail to thee, noble master!
LEAR. Ha! Mak'st thou this shame thy pastime?
KENT. No, my lord.
FOOL. Ha, ha! he wears cruel[d] garters! Horses are tied by the heads, dogs and bears by the neck, monkeys by the loins, and men by the legs: when a man is* over-lusty at legs, then he wears wooden nether-stocks.[e]
LEAR. What's he, that hath so much thy place mistook,
To set thee here?
KENT. It is both he and she,—
Your son and daughter.
LEAR. No!
KENT. Yes.
LEAR. No, I say!
KENT. I say, yea.
LEAR. No, no; they would not.[f]
KENT. Yes, they have.
LEAR. By Jupiter, I swear, no!
KENT. By Juno, I swear, ay.
LEAR. They durst not do't;
They could not, would not do't; 'tis worse than murder,
To do upon respect such violent outrage:
Resolve me, with all modest haste, which way
Thou mightst deserve, or they impose, this usage,
Coming from us.
KENT. My lord, when at their home
I did commend your highness' letters to them,
Ere I was risen from the place that show'd
My duty kneeling, came there a reeking post,
Stew'd in his haste, half breathless, panting† forth
From Goneril, his mistress, salutations;
Deliver'd letters, spite of intermission,
Which presently they read: on whose‡ contents,
They summon'd up their meiny,[g] straight took horse;
Commanded me to follow, and attend
The leisure of their answer; gave me cold looks:
And meeting here the other messenger,
Whose welcome I perceiv'd had poison'd mine,
(Being the very fellow which of late
Display'd so saucily against your highness)
Having more man than wit about me, drew;
He rais'd the house with loud and coward cries:

(*) First folio, *haires.* (†) First folio, *Messengers.*

a — elf all my hair in knots;] "Hair thus knotted was vulgarly supposed to be the work of *elves* and fairies in the night. So in 'Romeo and Juliet,' Act I. Sc. 4,—

'—— plats the manes of horses in the night;
And bakes the *elf-locks* in foul sluttish hairs,
Which, once untangled, much misfortune bodes.'"
—STEEVENS.

b — pelting villages,—] That is, *paltry, pedling* villages.

c *Poor Turlygood! poor Tom!*] So Dekker, in his "Bell-man of London," says of an "Abraham-man,"—"He calls himselfe by the name of poore Tom, and comming neere any body cries out, *Poore Tom is a-cold.*"

(*) First folio omits, *is.* (†) First folio, *painting.* (‡) First folio, *those.*

d — cruel *garters!*] The same quibble on *cruel* and *crewel*, *i.e. worsted* of which stockings, *garters*, &c., were made, is found in many of our old plays.

e — nether-stocks.] Stockings were formerly called *nether-stocks*, and breeches *over-stocks* or *upper-stocks*.

f No, no; they would not.] This and the next speech are not in the folio.

g *They summon'd up their* meiny,—] *Meiny* here signifies *train* or *retinue*.

Your son and daughter found this trespass worth
The shame which here it suffers.

FOOL. Winter's not gone yet,[a] if the wild geese fly that way.

Fathers that wear rags,
Do make their children blind;
But fathers that bear bags,
Shall see their children kind.
Fortune, that arrant whore,
Ne'er turns the key to the poor.—

But, for all this, thou shalt have as many dolours[b] for thy daughters, as thou canst tell in a year.

LEAR. O, how this mother swells up toward my heart!
*Hysterica** *passio*,(4)—down, thou climbing sorrow,
Thy element's below!—Where is this daughter?

KENT. With the earl, sir, here within.

LEAR. Follow me not; stay here. [*Exit.*

GENT. Made you no more offence but what you speak of?

KENT. None.
How chance the king comes with so small a train?†

FOOL. An thou hadst been set i' the stocks for that question, thou hadst well deserved it.

KENT. Why, fool?

FOOL. We'll set thee to school to an ant, to teach thee there's no labouring i' the winter. All that follow their noses are led by their eyes but blind men; and there's not a nose among twenty but can smell him that's stinking. Let go thy hold when a great wheel runs down a hill, lest it break thy neck with following it:‡ but the great one that goes up the hill,§ let him draw thee after. When a wise man gives thee better counsel, give me mine again: I would have none but knaves follow it, since a fool gives it.

That sir which serves and seeks for gain,
And follows but for form,
Will pack when it begins to rain,
And leave thee in the storm.
But I will tarry; the fool will stay,
And let the wise man fly:
The knave turns fool that runs away;
The fool no knave, perdy.[c]

KENT. Where learned you this, fool?

FOOL. Not i' the stocks, fool.

Re-enter LEAR, *with* GLOUCESTER.

LEAR. Deny to speak with me? They are sick? they are weary?
They have travell'd all the night? Mere fetches;
The images of revolt and flying off.
Fetch me a better answer.

GLO. My dear lord,
You know the fiery quality of the duke;
How unremoveable and fix'd he is
In his own course.

LEAR. Vengeance! plague! death! confusion!—
Fiery? what quality? Why, Gloster, Gloster,
I'd speak with the duke of Cornwall and his wife.

GLO. Well, my good lord, I have inform'd them so.[d]

LEAR. *Inform'd them!* Dost thou understand me, man?

GLO. Ay, my good lord.

LEAR. The king would speak with Cornwall; the dear father
Would with his daughter speak, commands her service:†
Are they inform'd of this?—My breath and blood!—
Fiery? the fiery duke?—Tell the hot duke, that—
No, but not yet:—may be, he is not well:
Infirmity doth still neglect all office,
Whereto our health is bound; we are not ourselves,
When nature, being oppress'd, commands the mind
To suffer with the body: I'll forbear;
And am fall'n out with my more headier will,
To take the indispos'd and sickly fit
For the sound man.—Death on my state! wherefore [*Looking on* KENT.
Should he sit here? This act persuades me,
That this remotion of the duke and her
Is practice[e] only. Give me my servant forth:
Go, tell the duke and 's wife I'd speak with them,
Now, presently: bid them come forth and hear me,
Or at their chamber door I'll beat the drum
Till it cry sleep to death.[f]

GLO. I would have all well betwixt you. [*Exit.*

(*) Old copies. *Historica.* (†) First folio, *number.*
(‡) First folio omits, *it.* (§) First folio, *upward.*

a Winter's not gone yet, &c.] This speech is not found in the quartos.

b — dolours—] See note (b), p. 18.

c The knave turns fool that runs away;
The fool no knave, perdy.]

Johnson thought the sense would be mended if we read,—

"The fool turns knave that runs away;
The knave no fool, perdy."

(†) First folio, *commands, tends, service.*

d Well, my good lord, &c.] This speech and Lear's rejoinder are found only in the folio.

e *Is* practice *only.*] *Practice*, it need hardly be repeated, meant *artifice, conspiracy*, &c.

f Till it cry sleep to death.] Till the clamour of the drum destroys or is the death of sleep. The line is usually given, however,

"Till it cry, *Sleep to death!*"

that is, till it cry out, *awake no more*, and this very possibly was the poet's idea.

LEAR. O me, my heart, my rising heart!—but, down!

FOOL. Cry to it, nuncle, as the cockney[a] did to the eels when she put 'em i' the paste alive; she knapp'd 'em o' the coxcombs with a stick, and cried, *Down, wantons, down:* 't was her brother, that, in pure kindness to his horse, buttered his hay.

---

[a] — *the* cockney—] "Cockney," of old, bore more than one signification; as employed by Chaucer, in "The Reve's Tale," verse 4205,—

"And when this jape is told another day,
I sal be hald a daf, a *cokenay*,"—

it plainly means an effeminate spoony. In Dekker's "Newes from Hell," &c. 1602,—"'Tis not their fault, but our mothers', our *cockering* mothers, who for their labour made us to be called *cockneys*," it has the same import. According to Percy, whose authority is the following couplet from the ancient ballad called "The Turnament of Tottenham,"—

"At that feast were they served in rich array;
Every five and five had a *cokenay*,"—

it meant a *cook* or *scullion;* and that, perhaps, is the sense of the word in the present place.

Enter CORNWALL, REGAN, GLOUCESTER, *and* Servants.

LEAR. Good morrow to you both.
CORN. Hail to your grace!
[KENT *is set at liberty.*
REG. I am glad to see your highness.
LEAR. Regan, I think you are; I know what reason
I have to think so: if thou shouldst not be glad,
I would divorce me from thy mother's* tomb,
Sepulchring an adultress.—O, are you free?
[*To* KENT.
Some other time for that.—Beloved Regan,
Thy sister's naught: O, Regan, she hath tied
Sharp-tooth'd unkindness, like a vulture, here!—
[*Points to his heart.*
I can scarce speak to thee; thou'lt not believe,
With how deprav'd a quality—O Regan!
REG. I pray you, sir, take patience: I have hope,
You less know how to value her desert,
Than she to scant her duty.
LEAR. Say, how is that?[a]
REG. I cannot think my sister in the least
Would fail her obligation: if, sir, perchance,
She have restrain'd the riots of your followers,
'Tis on such ground, and to such wholesome end,
As clears her from all blame.
LEAR. My curses on her!
REG. O, sir, you are old;
Nature in you stands on the very verge
Of her confine: you should be rul'd, and led
By some discretion that discerns your state
Better than you yourself. Therefore, I pray you,
That to our sister you do make return;
Say you have wrong'd her, sir.†
LEAR. Ask her forgiveness?
Do you but mark how this becomes the house: (5)

Dear daughter, I confess that I am old;
Age is unnecessary: on my knees I beg, [Kneeling.
That you'll vouchsafe me raiment, bed, and food.

REG. Good sir, no more; these are unsightly tricks:
Return you to my sister.
LEAR. [*Rising.*] Never, Regan!
She hath abated me of half my train;
Look'd black upon me; struck me with her tongue,
Most serpent-like, upon the very heart:—
All the stor'd vengeances of heaven fall
On her ingrateful top! Strike her young bones,
You taking[b] airs, with lameness!
CORN. Fie, sir, fie!
LEAR. You nimble lightnings, dart your blinding flames
Into her scornful eyes! Infect her beauty,
You fen-suck'd fogs, drawn by the pow'rful sun,
To fall and blast her pride![c]
REG. O, the blest gods!
So will you wish on me, when the rash mood is on.
LEAR. No, Regan, thou shalt never have my curse;
Thy tender-hefted[d] nature shall not give
Thee o'er to harshness; her eyes are fierce, but thine
Do comfort, and not burn. 'Tis not in thee
To grudge my pleasures, to cut off my train,
To bandy hasty words, to scant my sizes,[e]
And, in conclusion, to oppose the bolt
Against my coming in: thou better know'st
The offices of nature, bond of childhood,
Effects of courtesy, dues of gratitude;
Thy half o'the kingdom hast thou not forgot,
Wherein I thee endow'd.
REG. Good sir, to the purpose.
LEAR. Who put my man i'the stocks?
[*Trumpets without.*
CORN. What trumpet's that?
REG. I know't my sister's: this approves her letter,
That she would soon be here.—

Enter OSWALD.

Is your lady come?
LEAR. This is a slave, whose easy-borrow'd pride
Dwells in the fickle grace of her he follows.—
Out, varlet, from my sight!
CORN. What means your grace?
LEAR. Who stock'd my servant? Regan, I have good hope
Thou didst not know on't.—Who comes here? O heavens,

Enter GONERIL.

If you do love old men, if your sweet sway
Allow[f] obedience, if* yourselves are old,

(*) First folio, *Mother*. (†) First folio omits, *sir*.

[a] Say, how is that?] This and the next speech are not in the quartos.

[b] *You* taking *airs,*—] To *take*, in old language, signified to *blast*, or *infect* with baneful influence. So in Act III. Sc. 4,—"Bless thee from whirlwinds, star-blasting, and *taking*."

[c] *To fall and* blast her pride!] The folio tamely reads,—

"To fall and *blister*."

(*) First folio inserts, *you*.

[d] *Thy* tender-hefted *nature*—] *Tender-hefted* is a very doubtful expression; and "tender *hested*," the reading of the quartos, is not much less so: but we have not sufficient confidence in the substitution, "tender-*hearted*," which Rowe and Pope adopt, to alter the ancient text.

[e] — *to scant my* sizes,—] "Sizes" are allowances of provision.

[f] Allow *obedience*,—] That is, *approve* obedience.

Make it your cause; send down, and take my part!—
Art not asham'd to look upon this beard?— [*To* GON.
O, Regan, will you take her by the hand?
GON. Why not by the hand, sir? How have I offended?
All's not offence, that indiscretion finds
And dotage terms so.
LEAR. O, sides, you are too tough!
Will you yet hold?—How came my man i'the stocks?
CORN. I set him there, sir: but his own disorders
Deserv'd much less advancement.
LEAR. You! did you?
REG. I pray you, father, being weak, seem so.
If, till the expiration of your month,
You will return and sojourn with my sister,
Dismissing half your train, come then to me;
I am now from home, and out of that provision
Which shall be needful for your entertainment.
LEAR. Return to her, and fifty men dismiss'd!
No, rather I abjure all roofs, and choose
To wage against the enmity o'the air;
To be a comrade with the wolf and owl,—
Necessity's sharp pinch! [a]—Return with her!
Why, the hot-blooded France, that dowerless took
Our youngest born, I could as well be brought
To knee his throne, and, squire-like, pension beg
To keep base life afoot.—Return with her!
Persuade me rather to be slave and sumpter
To this detested groom. [*Pointing to* OSWALD.
GON. At your choice, sir.
LEAR. I pr'ythee, daughter, do not make me mad:
I will not trouble thee, my child; farewell:
We'll no more meet, no more see one another:—
But yet thou art my flesh, my blood, my daughter;
Or rather a disease that's in my flesh,
Which I must needs call mine: thou art a boil,
A plague-sore, an* embossed carbuncle,
In my corrupted blood. But I'll not chide thee;
Let shame come when it will, I do not call it:
I do not bid the thunder-bearer shoot,
Nor tell tales of thee to high-judging Jove:
Mend when thou canst; be better at thy leisure:
I can be patient; I can stay with Regan,
I and my hundred knights.
REG. Not altogether so:
I look'd not for you yet, nor am provided
For your fit welcome. Give ear, sir, to my sister;
For those that mingle reason with your passion,
Must be content to think you old, and so—
But she knows what she does.
LEAR. Is this well spoken?
REG. I dare avouch it, sir: what, fifty followers?
Is it not well? What should you need of more?
Yea, or so many, sith that both charge and danger
Speak 'gainst so great a number? How, in one house,
Should many people, under two commands,
Hold amity? 'Tis hard; almost impossible.
GON. Why might not you, my lord, receive attendance
From those that she calls servants, or from mine?
REG. Why not, my lord? If then they chanc'd to slack ye,
We could control them. If you will come to me,
(For now I spy a danger) I entreat you
To bring but five and twenty; to no more
Will I give place or notice.
LEAR. I gave you all—
REG. And in good time you gave it.
LEAR.—Made you my guardians, my depositaries;
But kept a reservation to be followed
With such a number. What, must I come to you
With five and twenty? Regan, said you so?
REG. And speak 't again, my lord; no more with me.
LEAR. Those wicked creatures yet do look well-favour'd,
When others are more wicked; not being the worst
Stands in some rank of praise.—I'll go with thee; [*To* GONERIL.
Thy fifty yet doth double five and twenty,
And thou art twice her love.
GON. Hear me, my lord;
What need you five and twenty, ten, or five,
To follow in a house, where twice so many
Have a command to tend you?
REG. What need one?
LEAR. O, reason not the need: our basest beggars
Are in the poorest thing superfluous:
Allow not nature more than nature needs,
Man's life is cheap as beast's: thou art a lady;
If only to go warm were gorgeous,
Why, nature needs not what thou gorgeous wear'st,
Which scarcely keeps thee warm.—But, for true need,—
You heavens, give me that patience, patience I need! [b]

(*) First folio, *or*.

a *To be a comrade with the wolf and* owl,—
Necessity's sharp pinch !]

Mr. Collier's annotator changes this to,—

"To be a comrade with the wolf, and *howl*
Necessity's sharp pinch."

And Mr. Collier terms the alteration, "A fortunate recovery of what must have been the real language of the poet"!

b You heavens, give me that patience, patience I need!]

Mr. Collier's annotator reads,—

"—— give me *but* patience," &c.

You see me here, you gods, a poor old man,
As full of grief as age; wretched in both!
If it be you that stir these daughters' hearts
Against their father, fool me not so much
To bear it tamely; touch me with noble anger,
And let not women's weapons, water-drops,
Stain my man's cheeks!—No, you unnatural hags,
I will have such revenges on you both,
That all the world shall—I will do such things—
What they are, yet I know not;—but they shall be
The terrors of the earth. You think, I'll weep;
No, I'll not weep:—
I have full cause of weeping; but this heart
Shall break into a hundred thousand flaws,
Or ere I'll weep.—O, fool, I shall go mad!

[*Exeunt* LEAR, GLOUCESTER, KENT, *and* Fool.—*Storm heard at a distance.*

CORN. Let us withdraw, 't will be a storm.

REG. This house is little; the old man and his people
Cannot be well bestow'd.

GON. 'Tis his own blame hath put himself from rest,
And must needs taste his folly.

REG. For his particular, I'll receive him gladly,
But not one follower.

GON. So am I purpos'd,—
Where is my lord of Gloster?

CORN. Follow'd the old man forth:—he is return'd.

Re-enter GLOUCESTER.

GLO. The king is in high rage.

CORN. Whither is he going?

GLO. He calls to horse;[a] but will I know not whither.

CORN. 'Tis best to give him way; he leads himself.

GON. My lord, entreat him by no means to stay.

GLO. Alack, the night comes on, and the bleak* winds
Do sorely ruffle; for many miles about
There's scarce a bush.

REG. O, sir, to wilful men,
The injuries that they themselves procure
Must be their schoolmasters. Shut up your doors:
He is attended with a desperate train;
And what they may incense him to, being apt
To have his ear abus'd, wisdom bids fear.

CORN. Shut up your doors, my lord; 't is a wild night;
My Regan counsels well: come out o' the storm.

[*Exeunt.*

[a] CORN. Whither is he going?
GLO. He calls to horse;] Omitted in the quartos.

(*) First folio, *high*.

ACT III.

SCENE I.—*A Heath.*

A storm, with thunder and lightning. *Enter* KENT *and a* Gentleman, *meeting.*

KENT. Who 's there, besides foul weather?

GENT. One minded like the weather, most unquietly.

KENT. I know you. Where's the king?

GENT. Contending with the fretful elements;
Bids the wind blow the earth into the sea,
Or swell the curled waters 'bove the main,[a]
That things might change or cease;[b] tears his white hair,
Which the impetuous blasts, with eyeless rage,
Catch in their fury, and make nothing of;
Strives in his little world of man to out-scorn
The to-and-fro-conflicting wind and rain.
This night, wherein the cub-drawn bear would couch,
The lion and the belly-pinched wolf
Keep their fur dry, unbonneted he runs,
And bids what will take all.

KENT. But who is with him?

GENT. None but the fool; who labours to out-jest
His heart-struck injuries.

KENT. Sir, I do know you,
And dare, upon the warrant of my note,
Commend a dear thing to you. There is division,—
Although as yet the face of it be* cover'd
With mutual cunning,—'twixt Albany and Cornwall;
Who have (as who have not,[c] that their great stars
Thron'd and set high?) servants, who seem no less,

---

a *Or swell the curled waters 'bove the* main,—] That is, the *main land.*

b That things might change or cease;] The remainder of this speech is omitted in the folio.

(*) First folio, *is.*

c Who have (as who have not, &c.] This and the seven following lines are omitted in the quartos, and the remainder of the speech commencing, "But, true it is," is left out of the folio.

Which are to France the spies and speculations[a]
Intelligent of our state; what hath been seen,
Either in snuffs and packings[b] of the dukes;
Or the hard rein which both of them have borne
Against the old kind king; or something deeper,
Whereof, perchance, these are but furnishings;—[c]
But, true it is, from France there comes a power
Into this scatter'd kingdom; who already,
Wise in our negligence, have secret feet
In some of our best ports, and are at point
To show their open banner.—Now to you;
If on my credit you dare build so far
To make your speed to Dover, you shall find
Some that will thank you, making just report
Of how unnatural and bemadding sorrow
The king hath cause to plain.
I am a gentleman of blood and breeding;
And, from some knowledge and assurance, offer
This office to you.

GENT. I will talk further with you.

KENT. No, do not.
For confirmation that I am much more
Than my out-wall, open this purse, and take
What it contains. If you shall see Cordelia,
(As fear not but you shall) show her this ring;
And she will tell you who your * fellow is
That yet you do not know.—Fie on this storm!
I will go seek the king.

GENT. Give me your hand: have you no more to say?

KENT. Few words, but, to effect, more than all yet,—
That, when we have found the king, (in which your pain
That way, I'll this) he that first lights on him
Holla the other. [*Exeunt severally.*

SCENE II.—*Another part of the Heath. Storm continues.*

Enter LEAR *and* FOOL.

LEAR. Blow, winds, and crack your cheeks! rage! blow!
You cataracts and hurricanoes, spout
Till you have drench'd our steeples, drown'd † the cocks!
You sulphurous and thought-executing fires,
Vaunt-couriers to * oak-cleaving thunder-bolts,
Singe my white head! And thou, all-shaking thunder,
Strike flat the thick rotundity o' the world!
Crack nature's moulds, all germens spill at once,
That make ingrateful man!

FOOL. O nuncle, court holy-water[d] in a dry house is better than this rain-water out o' door. Good nuncle, in, and † ask thy daughters' blessing; here's a night pities neither wise men nor fools.

LEAR. Rumble thy bellyfull! Spit, fire! spout, rain!
Nor rain, wind, thunder, fire, are my daughters:
I tax not you, you elements, with unkindness;
I never gave you kingdom, call'd you children,
You owe me no subscription; then let fall
Your horrible pleasure; here I stand, your slave,
A poor, infirm, weak, and despis'd old man:—
But yet I call you servile ministers,
That have with two pernicious daughters join'd[e]
Your high-engender'd battles 'gainst a head
So old and white as this. O! O! 'tis foul!

FOOL. He that has a house to put's head in, has a good head-piece.

The cod-piece that will house,
  Before the head has any,
The head and he shall louse;—
  So beggars marry many.
The man that makes his toe
  What he his heart should make,
Shall of a corn cry woe,
  And turn his sleep to wake.

—For there was never yet fair woman, but she made mouths in a glass.

LEAR. No, I will be the pattern of all patience;
I will say nothing.

Enter KENT.

KENT. Who's there?

FOOL. Marry, here's grace and a cod-piece; that's a wise man and a fool. [night,

KENT. Alas, sir, are you here? things that love
Love not such nights as these; the wrathful skies

(*) First folio, *that*. (†) First folio, *drown*.

(*) First folio, *of*. (†) First folio omits, *and*.

a *Which are to France the spies and* speculations
Intelligent of our state;]

For "speculations" we should perhaps read *speculators*, which formerly meant *watchers, overlookers, observers*, &c. Johnson proposed *speculators*, and Mr. Singer found the correction in a marginal note of his copy of the second folio.

b *Either in* snuffs and packings *of the dukes;*] "Snuffs" mean *petty dissentions, tiffs:* and "packings" signify *plots, intrigues*, &c.

c —furnishings;—] That is, according to Steevens, *samples:* but the illustration he cites from the Epistle prefixed to Greene's "Groats-worth of Witte,"—"For to lend the world a *furnish* of witte, she lays her owne to pawne,"—is not conclusive.

d —court holy-water—] Glozing speeches. Florio translates, *Dare l'allodola*, "To *cog*, to *foist*, to *flatter*, to *give one Court-hollie water*," &c.: and *Mantellizzare*, "To *court one with faire words or give court-holy-water*"

e *That* have *with two pernicious daughters* join'd—] The folio reads,—

"That *will* with two pernicious daughters *join*," &c.

Gallow[a] the very wanderers of the dark,
And make them keep their caves: since I was man,
Such sheets of fire, such bursts of horrid thunder,
Such groans of roaring wind and rain, I never
Remember to have heard: man's nature cannot
carry
The affliction nor the fear.

LEAR. Let the great gods,
That keep this dreadful pother* o'er our heads,
Find out their enemies now. Tremble, thou wretch,
That hast within thee undivulged crimes,
Unwhipp'd of justice!—Hide thee, thou bloody
hand!
Thou perjur'd,[b] and thou simular[c] of virtue

[a] Gallow—] *Affright, terrify.*—A common provincialism at this day.

[b] *Thou* perjur'd,—] Theobald and Mr. Collier's annotator read, and perhaps rightly,—

"Thou *perjure*," &c.

See note (b), p. 75, Vol. I.

[c] —simular—] That is, *simulator, counterfeit.*

(*) First folio, *pudder.*

That art incestuous!—caitiff, to pieces shake,
That under covert and convenient seeming
Hast practis'd on man's life!—Close pent-up guilts,
Rive your concealing continents, and cry
These dreadful summoners grace!—I am a man,
More sinn'd against than sinning.

KENT. Alack, bare-headed!
Gracious my lord, hard by here is a hovel;
Some friendship will it lend you 'gainst the tempest:
Repose you there, while I to this hard house,
(More harder than the stones whereof 'tis rais'd;
Which even but now, demanding after you,
Denied me to come in) return, and force
Their scanted courtesy.

LEAR. My wits begin to turn.—
Come on, my boy: how dost, my boy? art cold?
I am cold myself.—Where is this straw, my fellow?
The art of our necessities is strange,
And can make vile things precious. Come, your hovel.—
Poor fool and knave, I have one part in my heart
That's sorry yet for thee.

FOOL. [Singing.]

He that has and a little tiny wit,—
With hey, ho, the wind and the rain,—
Must make content with his fortunes fit,
Though the rain it raineth every day.

LEAR. True, boy.—Come, bring us to this hovel.[a]

[*Exeunt* LEAR *and* KENT.

FOOL. This is a brave night to cool a courtezan.—
I'll speak a prophecy ere I go:

When priests are more in word than matter;
When brewers mar their malt with water;
When nobles are their tailors' tutors;
No heretics burn'd, but wenches' suitors:
When every case in law is right;
No squire in debt, nor no poor knight;
When slanders do not live in tongues;
Nor cutpurses come not to throngs;
When usurers tell their gold i' the field;
And bawds and whores do churches build;—
Then shall the realm of Albion
Come to great confusion:
Then comes the time, who lives to see 't,
That going shall be us'd with feet.

This prophecy Merlin shall make; for I live before his time. [*Exit.*

[a] Come, bring us to this hovel.] The remainder of the scene is only found in the folio.

SCENE III.—*A Room in* Gloucester's *Castle.*

Enter GLOUCESTER *and* EDMUND.

GLO. Alack, alack, Edmund, I like not this unnatural dealing. When I desired their leave that I might pity him, they took from me the use of mine own house; charged me, on pain of their* perpetual displeasure, neither to speak of him, entreat for him, nor† any way sustain him.

EDM. Most savage and unnatural!

GLO. Go to; say you nothing. There is division between the dukes; and a worse matter than that: I have received a letter this night;—'tis dangerous to be spoken;—I have locked the letter in my closet: these injuries the king now bears will be revenged home; there is part of a power already footed: we must incline to the king. I will seek‡ him, and privily relieve him: go you, and maintain talk with the duke, that my charity be not of him perceived: if he ask for me, I am ill, and gone to bed. If I die for it, as no less is threatened me, the king my old master must be relieved. There is strange things toward, Edmund; pray you, be careful.

[*Exit.*

EDM. This courtesy, forbid thee, shall the duke
Instantly know; and of that letter too:—
This seems a fair deserving, and must draw me
That which my father loses,—no less than all:
The younger rises when the old doth fall.

[*Exit.*

SCENE IV.—*A part of the Heath, with a Hovel.*

Enter LEAR, KENT, *and* Fool.

KENT. Here is the place, my lord; good my lord, enter:
The tyranny of the open night 's too rough
For nature to endure. [*Storm continues.*

LEAR. Let me alone.

KENT. Good my lord, enter here.

LEAR. Wilt break my heart?

KENT. I had rather break mine own. Good my lord, enter.

LEAR. Thou think'st 'tis much that this contentious storm
Invades us to the skin: so 'tis to thee;
But where the greater malady is fix'd,
The lesser is scarce felt. Thou'dst shun a bear;
But if thy§ flight lay toward the roaring sea,

(*) First folio omits, *their*. (†) First folio, *or*.
(‡) First folio, *looke*. (§) First folio, *they*.

Thou'dst meet the bear i' the mouth. When the mind's free,
The body's delicate: the tempest in my mind
Doth from my senses take all feeling else,
Save what beats there.—Filial ingratitude!
Is it not as this mouth should tear this hand
For lifting food to 't?—But I will punish home:—
No, I will weep no more.—In such a night
To shut me out!—Pour on; I will endure:—
In such a night as this!—O, Regan, Goneril!
Your old kind father, whose frank heart gave all,—
O, that way madness lies; let me shun that;
No more of that.—

KENT. Good my lord, enter here.

LEAR. Pr'ythee, go in thyself; seek thine own ease:
This tempest will not give me leave to ponder
On things would hurt me more.—But I'll go in:—

In, boy; go first.—[*To the* Fool.] You houseless poverty,—
Nay, get thee in. I'll pray, and then I'll sleep.—
[Fool *goes in.*
Poor naked wretches, wheresoe'er you are,
That bide the pelting of this pitiless storm,
How shall your houseless heads and unfed sides,
Your loop'd and window'd raggedness, defend you
From seasons such as these? O, I have ta'en
Too little care of this! Take physic, pomp;
Expose thyself to feel what wretches feel,
That thou mayst shake the superflux to them,
And show the heavens more just.

EDG. [*Within.*] Fathom and half, fathom and half! poor Tom!
[*The* Fool *runs out from the hovel.*

FOOL. Come not in here, nuncle, here's a spirit.
Help me, help me!

KENT. Give me thy hand.—Who's there?

FOOL. A spirit, a spirit; he says his name's poor Tom.

KENT. What art thou that dost grumble there i' the straw? Come forth.

Enter EDGAR, *disguised as a Madman.*

EDG. Away! the foul fiend follows me!—

*Through the sharp hawthorn blows the cold wind,**—

Hum! go to thy cold bed,[a] and warm thee.

LEAR. Hast thou given all to thy two daughters?[b]
And art thou come to this?

EDG. Who gives anything to poor Tom? whom the foul fiend hath led through fire and through flame, through ford† and whirlpool, o'er bog and quagmire; that hath laid knives under his pillow,(1) and halters in his pew; set ratsbane by his porridge; made him proud of heart, to ride on a bay trotting-horse over four-inched bridges; to course his own shadow for a traitor.—Bless thy five wits! Tom's a-cold.—O, do de, do de, do de. —Bless thee from whirlwinds, star-blasting, and taking![c] Do poor Tom some charity, whom the foul fiend vexes.—There could I have him now,—and there,—and there again,—and there.
[*Storm continues.*

LEAR. What,‡ have his daughters brought him to this pass?—
Couldst thou save nothing? Didst* thou give 'em all?

FOOL. Nay, he reserved a blanket, else we had been all shamed.

LEAR. Now, all the plagues that in the pendulous air
Hang fated o'er men's faults, light on thy daughters!

KENT. He hath no daughters, sir.

LEAR. Death, traitor! nothing could have subdu'd nature
To such a lowness, but his unkind daughters.—
Is it the fashion, that discarded fathers
Should have thus little mercy on their flesh?
Judicious punishment! 'twas this flesh begot
Those pelican daughters.

EDG. Pillicock sat on Pillicock-hill;—
Halloo, halloo, loo, loo!

FOOL. This cold night will turn us all to fools and madmen.

EDG. Take heed o' the foul fiend: obey thy parents; keep thy word justly;† swear not; commit not with man's sworn spouse; set not thy sweet heart on proud array. Tom's a-cold.

LEAR. What hast thou been?

EDG. A serving-man, proud in heart and mind; that curled my hair; wore gloves in my cap,(2) served the lust of my mistress' heart, and did the act of darkness with her; swore as many oaths as I spake words, and broke them in the sweet face of heaven: one, that slept in the contriving of lust, and waked to do it. Wine loved I deeply;‡ dice dearly; and in woman, out-paramoured the Turk: false of heart, light of ear, bloody of hand; hog in sloth, fox in stealth, wolf in greediness, dog in madness, lion in prey. Let not the creaking of shoes, nor the rustling of silks, betray thy poor heart to woman: keep thy foot out of brothels, thy hand out of plackets, thy pen from lenders' books, and defy the foul fiend.—

Still through the hawthorn blows the cold wind:
Says suum, mun, ha no nonny.

Dolphin my boy, my boy, sessa; let him trot by.
[*Storm continues.*

LEAR. Why,§ thou were better in thy‖ grave, than to answer with thy uncovered body this extremity of the skies.—Is man no more than this? Consider him well. Thou owest the worm no silk,

(*) First folio, *blow the windes.* (†) First folio, *Sword.* (‡) First folio, *Ha's his Daughters.*

(*) First folio, *Wouldst.* (†) First folio, *words Justice.* (‡) First folio, *deerely.* (§) First folio omits, *Why.* (‖) First folio, *a.*

a — *go to thy* cold *bed, and warm thee.*] The commentators, with admirable unanimity, persist in declaring this line to be a ridicule on one in "The Spanish Trajedy," Act II.—

"What outcries pluck me from my naked bed!"

But to an audience of Shakespeare's age there was nothing risible in either line. The phrase *to go to a cold bed* meant only to *go cold to bed;* to *rise from a naked bed* signified to *get up naked from bed*, and to say one *lay on a sick bed* (a form of expression far from uncommon even now) implied merely that he was lying *sick a-bed*. It is to be observed that the folio, probably by accident, as it gives the line correctly in "The Taming of the Shrew," omits the word "cold."

b Hast *thou* given *all to thy* two *daughters?*] So the quarto; the folio reads, "*Did'st* thou *give* all to thy daughters?"

c — taking!] See note (b), p. 80.

the beast no hide, the sheep no wool, the cat no perfume.—Ha! here 's three on 's are sophisticated!—Thou art the thing itself: unaccommodated man is no more but such a poor, bare, forked animal as thou art.—Off, off, you lendings!—come, unbutton here.— [*Tearing off his clothes.*

FOOL. Pr'ythee, nuncle, be contented; 't is a naughty night to swim in.—Now a little fire in a wild field were like an old lecher's heart,—a small spark, all the rest on 's body cold.—Look, here comes a walking fire.

EDG. This is the foul fiend* Flibbertigibbet:[a] he begins at curfew, and walks till the† first cock; he gives the web and the pin,[b] squints the eye, and makes the hare-lip; mildews the white wheat, and hurts the poor creature of earth.

Saint Withold footed thrice the wold;[c]
He met the night-mare, and her nine-fold;
Bid her alight,
And her troth plight,
And, aroint thee, witch, aroint thee!

KENT. How fares your grace?

Enter GLOUCESTER, *with a torch.*

LEAR. What's he?

KENT. Who's there? What is't you seek?

GLO. What are you there? Your names?

EDG. Poor Tom; that eats the swimming frog, the toad, the tadpole, the wall-newt and the water; that in the fury of his heart, when the foul fiend rages, eats cow-dung for sallets; swallows the old rat, and the ditch-dog; drinks the green mantle of the standing pool; who is whipped from tything to tything, and stocked, punished, and imprisoned; who hath had‡ three suits to his back, six shirts to his body, horse to ride, and weapon to wear,—

But mice and rats, and such small deer,
Have been Tom's food for seven long year.[d]

Beware my follower.—Peace, Smulkin; peace, thou fiend!

GLO. What, hath your grace no better company?

EDG. The prince of darkness is a gentleman; Modo he 's call'd, and Mahu.(3)

GLO. Our flesh and blood, my lord, is grown so vile,
That it doth hate what gets it.

EDG. Poor Tom's a-cold.

GLO. Go in with me; my duty cannot suffer
To obey in all your daughters' hard commands:
Though their injunction be to bar my doors,
And let this tyrannous night take hold upon you,
Yet have I ventur'd to come seek you out,
And bring you where both fire and food is ready.

LEAR. First let me talk with this philosopher.—
What is the cause of thunder?

KENT. Good my lord, take his offer; go into the house.

LEAR. I'll talk a word with this same learned Theban.—
What is your study?

EDG. How to prevent the fiend, and to kill vermin.

LEAR. Let me ask you one word in private.

KENT. Impórtune him once more to go, my lord,
His wits begin to unsettle.

GLO. Canst thou blame him?
His daughters seek his death:—ah, that good Kent!—
He said it would be thus,—poor banish'd man!—
Thou say'st the king grows mad; I'll tell thee, friend,
I am almost mad myself: I had a son,
Now outlaw'd from my blood; he sought my life,
But lately, very late: I lov'd him, friend,
No father his son dearer: true to tell thee,
[*Storm continues.*
The grief hath craz'd my wits.—What a night's this!—
I do beseech your grace,—

LEAR. O, cry you mercy, sir.—
Noble philosopher, your company.

EDG. Tom's a-cold.

GLO. In, fellow, there, into the hovel: keep thee warm.

LEAR. Come, let's in all.

KENT. This way, my lord.

LEAR. With him;
I will keep still with my philosopher.

KENT. Good my lord, soothe him; let him take the fellow.

GLO. Take him you on.

KENT. Sirrah, come on; go along with us.

LEAR. Come, good Athenian.

(*) First folio omits, *fiend*. (†) First folio, *walkes at.* (‡) First folio omits, *had*.

a — Flibbertigibbet:] See quotation from Harsnet, in the Illustrative Comments to this Act.

b — the web and the pin,—] The *cataract.* One of the meanings to *Cataratta* in Florio's Dictionary is, "A dimnesse of sight occasioned by humores hardned in the eies called a Cataract or a *pin and a web.*"

c Saint Withold *footed thrice the* wold;] The old copies have *Swithold* for "Saint Withold," and *old* at the end of the line instead of "wold." Withold was the Saint popularly invoked against the nightmare.

d *But mice and rats, and such small deer,*
Have been Tom's food for seven long year.]

This distich, Percy pointed out as part of the description in the old metrical romance of "Sir Bevis of Hamptoun," of the privation endured by that doughty champion during his seven years' imprisonment,—

"Rattes and myce and such smal dere
Was his meate that seven yere."

GLO. No words, no words: hush.

EDG. *Child Rowland to the dark tower came,*
His word was still,—Fie, foh, and fum,
I smell the blood of a British man. (4)
[*Exeunt.*

SCENE V.—*A Room in* Gloucester's *Castle.*

Enter CORNWALL *and* EDMUND.

CORN. I will have my revenge, ere I depart his house.

EDM. How, my lord, I may be censured, that nature thus gives way to loyalty, something fears me to think of.

CORN. I now perceive, it was not altogether your brother's evil disposition made him seek his death; but a provoking merit, set a-work by a reproveable badness in himself.

EDM. How malicious is my fortune, that I must repent to be just! This is the letter* he spoke of, which approves him an intelligent party to the advantages of France. O heavens! that this treason were not, or not I the detector!

CORN. Go with me to the duchess.

EDM. If the matter of this paper be certain, you have mighty business in hand.

CORN. True, or false, it hath made thee earl of Gloster. Seek out where thy father is, that he may be ready for our apprehension.

EDM. [*Aside.*] If I find him comforting the king, it will stuff his suspicion more fully.—I will perséver in my course of loyalty, though the conflict be sore between that and my blood.

CORN. I will lay trust upon thee; and thou shalt find a dearer† father in my love. [*Exeunt.*

SCENE VI.—*A Chamber in a Farm-house, adjoining the Castle.*

Enter GLOUCESTER, LEAR, KENT, Fool, *and* EDGAR.

GLO. Here is better than the open air; take it thankfully. I will piece out the comfort with what addition I can: I will not be long from you.

KENT. All the power of his wits have given way to his impatience:—the gods reward your kindness! [*Exit* GLOUCESTER.

EDG. Frateretto[a] calls me; and tells me Nero is an angler in the lake of darkness. Pray, innocent,[b] and beware the foul fiend.

FOOL. Pr'ythee, nuncle, tell me whether a madman be a gentleman or a yeoman?

LEAR. A king, a king!

FOOL. No, he's a yeoman that has a gentleman to his son; for he's a mad yeoman, that sees his son a gentleman before him.[c] [spits

LEAR. To have a thousand with red burning
Come hissing in upon 'em:—

EDG. The foul fiend bites my back.[d]

FOOL. He's mad, that trusts in the tameness of a wolf, a horse's health, a boy's love, or a whore's oath.

LEAR. It shall be done; I will arraign them straight.—
Come, sit thou here, most learned justicer;*——
[*To* EDGAR.
Thou, sapient sir, sit here. [*To the* Fool.]—Now, you she-foxes!—

EDG. Look, where he stands and glares!—
Wantest[e] thou eyes at trial, madam?

Come o'er the bourn,† Bessy, to me:—

FOOL. Her boat hath a leak,
And she must not speak
Why she dares not come over to thee.

EDG. The foul fiend haunts poor Tom in the voice of a nightingale. Hopdance cries in Tom's belly for two white herring. Croak not, black angel; I have no food for thee.

KENT. How do you, sir? Stand you not so amaz'd:
Will you lie down and rest upon the cushions?

LEAR. I'll see their trial first.—Bring in the‡ evidence.—
Thou robed man of justice, take thy place;—
[*To* EDGAR.
And thou, his yoke-fellow of equity, [*To the* Fool.
Bench by his side.—You are o' the commission,
Sit you too. [*To* KENT.

EDG. Let us deal justly.

Sleepest, or wakest thou, jolly shephĕrd?
Thy sheep be in the corn;
And for one blast of thy minikin mouth,
Thy sheep shall take no harm.[f]

Pur! the cat is grey.

(*) First folio inserts, *which*. (†) First folio, *deere*.

a Frateretto *calls me;*] See the quotation from Harsnet, in the Illustrative Comments to this Act.

b Pray, innocent,—] The term "innocent," though at first given only to idiots, came in time to be applied to professed fools.

c FOOL. No; he's a yeoman, &c.] This speech is not in the quartos.

d The foul fiend bites my back.] This, with the whole of what follows, down to, and inclusive of—

"False justicer, why hast thou let her 'scape?"

is omitted in the folio.

(*) Old text, *justice;* altered by Theobald.
(†) Old text, *broome*. (‡) Old text, *their*.

e Wantest *thou eyes at trial, madam?*] Seward, plausibly enough, would read, "*Wanton'st* thou eyes," &c.

f *Thy sheep shall take no harm.*] As "the foul fiend haunts poor Tom in the voice of a nightingale," the representative of Edgar was surely intended by Shakespeare to sing these fragments of old ballads, and not tamely recite them after the manner of the modern stage.

LEAR. Arraign her first; 'tis Goneril.—I here take my oath before this honourable assembly, she kicked the poor king her father.

FOOL. Come hither, mistress. Is your name Goneril?

LEAR. She cannot deny it.

FOOL. Cry you mercy, I took you for a joint-stool.

LEAR. And here's another, whose warp'd looks [proclaim
What store her heart is made on.—Stop her there!
Arms, arms, sword, fire!—Corruption in the place!
False justicer, why hast thou let her 'scape?

EDG. Bless thy five wits!

KENT. O pity!—Sir, where is the patience now,
That you so oft have boasted to retain?

EDG. [*Aside.*] My tears begin to take his part so much,
They'll mar my counterfeiting.

LEAR. The little dogs and all,
Tray, Blanch, and Sweet-heart, see, they bark at me.

EDG. Tom will throw his head at them.—Avaunt, you curs!

Be thy mouth or black or white,
Tooth that poisons if it bite;
Mastiff, grey-hound, mongrel grim,
Hound or spaniel, brach or lym;[a]
Or bobtail tike,* or trundle tail,—
Tom will make them† weep and wail:
For, with throwing thus my head,
Dogs leap the hatch, and all are fled.

Do de, de de. Sessa![b] Come, march to wakes and fairs and market towns.—Poor Tom, thy horn is dry.

LEAR. Then let them anatomise Regan; see what breeds about her heart.—Is there any cause in nature, that makes these hard hearts?—[*To* EDGAR.] You, sir, I entertain for one of my hundred; only I do not like the fashion of your garments: you will say they are Persian; but let them be changed.

KENT. Now, good my lord, lie here and rest awhile.

LEAR. Make no noise, make no noise; draw the curtains. So, so: we'll go to supper i' the morning.

FOOL. And I'll go to bed at noon.

Re-enter GLOUCESTER.

GLO. Come hither, friend: where is the king my master?

KENT. Here, sir; but trouble him not,—his wits are gone.

GLO. Good friend, I pr'ythee take him in thy arms;

(*) First folio, *tight*. (†) First folio, *him*.

a — *brach or* lym;] A bloodhound was formerly called a *lym* or *lyme*. In some of the old copies the word is printed *him*, in others *hym*.

b Sessa!] This word, in the old text *sese*, occurs in a previous scene, and is met with also in the Induction to "The Taming of the Shrew." Johnson explains it to be "an interjection enforcing cessation of any action, like *be quiet, have done*."

I have o'er-heard a plot of death upon him:
There is a litter ready; lay him in't,
And drive toward Dover, friend, where thou shalt
meet [master:
Both welcome and protection. Take up thy
If thou shouldst dally half an hour, his life,
With thine, and all that offer to defend him,
Stand in assured loss. Take up, take up;
And follow me, that will to some provision
Give thee quick conduct.[a]

KENT. Oppressed nature sleeps:—
This rest might yet have balm'd thy broken
senses,*
Which, if convenience will not allow,
Stand in hard cure.—Come, help to bear thy
master;
Thou must not stay behind. [*To the* Fool.

GLO. Come, come, away.

[*Exeunt* KENT, GLOUCESTER, *and* Fool,
bearing off the KING.

EDG. When we our betters see bearing our woes,
We scarcely think our miseries our foes.
Who alone suffers, suffers most i'the mind;
Leaving free things, and happy shows behind:
But then the mind much sufferance doth o'erskip,
When grief hath mates, and bearing fellowship.
How light and portable my pain seems now,
When that which makes me bend, makes the
king bow;
He childed, as I father'd!—Tom, away!
Mark the high noises; and thyself bewray,
When false opinion, whose wrong thought defiles
thee,
In thy just proof, repeals and reconciles thee.
What will hap more to-night, safe 'scape the
king!—
Lurk, lurk. [*Exit.*

SCENE VII.—*A Room in* Gloucester's Castle.

Enter CORNWALL, REGAN, GONERIL, EDMUND, *and* Servants.

CORN. Post speedily to my lord your husband; show him this letter:—the army of France is landed.—Seek out the traitor Gloster.

[*Exeunt some of the* Servants.

REG. Hang him instantly.

GON. Pluck out his eyes.

CORN. Leave him to my displeasure.—Edmund, keep you our sister company; the revenges we are bound to take upon your traitorous father are not fit for your beholding. Advise the duke, where you are going, to a most festinate preparation: we are bound to the like. Our posts shall be swift and intelligent betwixt us. Farewell, dear sister:—farewell, my lord of Gloster.

Enter OSWALD.

How now! Where's the king?

OSW. My lord of Gloster hath convey'd him
hence:
Some five or six and thirty of his knights,
Hot questrists after him, met him at gate;
Who, with some other of the lords dependants,
Are gone with him toward Dover; where they boast
To have well-armed friends.

CORN. Get horses for your mistress.

[*Exit* OSWALD.

GON. Farewell, sweet lord, and sister.

CORN. Edmund, farewell.

[*Exeunt* GONERIL *and* EDMUND.

Go, seek the traitor Gloster,
Pinion him like a thief, bring him before us.

[*Exeunt other* Servants.

Though well we may not pass[b] upon his life
Without the form of justice, yet our power
Shall do a courtesy to our wrath, which men
May blame, but not control. Who's there? The
traitor?

Re-enter Servants, *with* GLOUCESTER.

REG. Ingrateful fox! 't is he.

CORN. Bind fast his corky[c] arms.

GLO. What mean your graces?—Good my
friends, consider
You are my guests: do me no foul play, friends.

CORN. Bind him, I say. [Servants *bind him.*

REG. Hard, hard:—O filthy traitor!

GLO. Unmerciful lady as you are, I am none.

CORN. To this chair bind him.—Villain, thou
shalt find— [REGAN *plucks his beard.*

GLO. By the kind gods, 'tis most ignobly done
To pluck me by the beard.

REG. So white, and such a traitor!

GLO. Naughty[d] lady,
These hairs, which thou dost ravish from my chin,
Will quicken, and accuse thee: I am your host;
With robbers' hands my hospitable favours
You should not ruffle thus. What will you do?

CORN. Come, sir, what letters had you late
from France? [truth.

REG. Be simple-answer'd, for we know the

CORN. And what confederacy have you with
the traitors
Late footed in the kingdom?

(*) Old copy, *sinewes;* corrected by Theobald.

[a] Give thee quick conduct.] In the folio, Gloucester now adds,—"Come, come, away," and the scene closes, omitting the rest of the dialogue.

[b] — pass—] See note (b), p. 600, Vol. II.

[c] — corky arms.] That is, *dry, withered* arms.

[d] Naughty *lady*,—] See note (a), p. 421, Vol. I.

REG. To whose hands have you * sent the lunatic king? Speak.

GLO. I have a letter guessingly set down,
Which came from one that's of a neutral heart,
And not from one oppos'd.

CORN. Cunning.

REG. And false.

CORN. Where hast thou sent the king?

GLO. To Dover.

REG. Wherefore to Dover? Wast thou not charg'd at peril—

CORN. Wherefore to Dover? Let him first † answer that.

GLO. I am tied to the stake, and I must stand the course.

REG. Wherefore to Dover?

GLO. Because I would not see thy cruel nails
Pluck out his poor old eyes; nor thy fierce sister
In his anointed flesh stick boarish fangs.
The sea, with such a storm as his bare head
In hell-black night endur'd, would have buoy'd up,
And quench'd the stelled fires:
Yet, poor old heart, he holp the heavens to rain.
If wolves had at thy gate howl'd that stern time,
Thou shouldst have said, *Good porter, turn the key;*
All cruels else subscrib'd: ‡—but I shall see
The winged vengeance overtake such children.

CORN. See 't shalt thou never!—Fellows, hold the chair.—
Upon these eyes of thine I'll set my foot.

GLO. He that will think to live till he be old,
Give me some help!—O cruel!—O you gods!

REG. One side will mock another; the other too.

CORN. If you see vengeance,—

1 SERV. Hold your hand, my lord!
I have serv'd you ever since I was a child;
But better service have I never done you,
Than now to bid you hold.

REG. How now, you dog!

1 SERV. If you did wear a beard upon your chin,
I'd shake it on this quarrel. What do you mean?

CORN. My villain! [*Draws.*

(*) Old text, *you have*. (†) First folio omits, *first*. (‡) Old text, *subscribe*.

1 SERV. Nay then, come on, and take the chance of anger.

[*Draws. They fight.* CORNWALL *is wounded.*

REG. Give me thy sword. A peasant stand up thus!

[*Snatches a sword, comes behind, and stabs him.*

1 SERV. O, I am slain!—My lord, you have one eye left
To see some mischief on him:—O! [*Dies.*

CORN. Lest it see more, prevent it.—Out, vile jelly!
Where is thy lustre now?

GLO. All dark and comfortless.—Where's my son Edmund?
Edmund, enkindle all the sparks of nature,
To quit this horrid act.

REG. Out, treacherous villain!
Thou call'st on him that hates thee: it was he
That made the overture of thy treasons to us;
Who is too good to pity thee.

GLO. O my follies! Then Edgar was abus'd.—
Kind gods, forgive me that, and prosper him!

REG. Go, thrust him out at gates, and let him smell
His way to Dover.—How is 't, my lord? How look you?

CORN. I have receiv'd a hurt:—follow me, lady.—
Turn out that eyeless villain;—throw this slave
Upon the dunghill.—Regan, I bleed apace:
Untimely comes this hurt: give me your arm.

[*Exit* CORNWALL, *led by* REGAN;—Servants *unbind* GLOUCESTER, *and lead him out.* [a]

2 SERV. I'll never care what wickedness I do,
If this man come to good.

3 SERV. If she live long,
And, in the end, meet the old course of death,
Women will all turn monsters.

2 SERV. Let's follow the old earl, and get the Bedlam
To lead him where he would: his roguish madness
Allows itself to any thing.

3 SERV. Go thou; I'll fetch some flax, and whites of eggs
To apply to's bleeding face. Now, heaven help him! [*Exeunt severally.*

[a] *— and lead him out.*] In the folio the scene concludes here.

ACT IV.

SCENE I.—*The* Heath.

Enter EDGAR.

EDG. Yet better thus, and known to be contemn'd,
Than still contemn'd and flatter'd. To be worst,
The lowest and most dejected thing of fortune,
Stands still in esperance, lives not in fear:
The lamentable change is from the best;
The worst returns to laughter. Welcome then,[a]
Thou unsubstantial air that I embrace!
The wretch that thou hast blown unto the worst,
Owes nothing to thy blasts.—But who comes here?

[a] Welcome then,—] These words and the three lines which follow are omitted in the quartos.

Enter GLOUCESTER, *led by an old man.*

My father, poorly led?—World, world, O world!
But that thy strange mutations make us hate thee,
Life would not yield to age.

OLD MAN. O my good lord, I have been your tenant, and your father's tenant, these fourscore years.

GLO. Away, get thee away; good friend, be gone:
Thy comforts can do me no good at all,
Thee they may hurt.

OLD MAN. You cannot see your way.

GLO. I have no way, and therefore want no eyes;
I stumbled when I saw. Full oft 'tis seen,

Our means secure us;[a] and our mere defects
Prove our commodities.—O, dear son Edgar,
The food of thy abused father's wrath!
Might I but live to see thee in my touch,
I'd say I had eyes again!

OLD MAN. How now! Who's there?

EDG. [*Aside.*] O gods! Who is't can say *I am at the worst?*
I am worse than e'er I was;—

OLD MAN. 'Tis poor mad Tom.

EDG. [*Aside.*]—And worse I may be yet: the worst is not,
So long as we can say, *This is the worst.*

OLD MAN. Fellow, where goest?

GLO. Is it a beggar-man?

OLD MAN. Madman and beggar too.

GLO. He has some reason, else he could not beg.
I' the last night's storm I such a fellow saw;
Which made me think a man a worm: my son
Came then into my mind; and yet my mind
Was then scarce friends with him: I have heard more since.
As flies to wanton boys, are we to the gods,—
They kill us for their sport.

EDG. [*Aside.*] How should this be?—
Bad is the trade that must play Fool to sorrow,
Ang'ring itself and others.—Bless thee, master!

GLO. Is that the naked fellow?

OLD MAN. Ay, my lord.

GLO. Then, pr'ythee, get thee gone:[b] if, for my sake,
Thou wilt o'ertake us hence a mile or twain,
I' the way to Dover, do it for ancient love;
And bring some covering for this naked soul,
Who* I'll entreat to lead me.

OLD MAN. Alack, sir, he is mad.

GLO. 'Tis the times' plague, when madmen lead the blind.
Do as I bid thee, or rather do thy pleasure;
Above the rest, be gone.

OLD MAN. I'll bring him the best 'parel that I have,
Come on't what will. [*Exit.*

GLO. Sirrah, naked fellow,—

EDG. Poor Tom's a-cold.—I cannot daub it further. [*Aside.*

GLO. Come hither, fellow,—

EDG. [*Aside.*] And yet I must.—Bless thy sweet eyes, they bleed.

GLO. Know'st thou the way to Dover?

EDG. Both stile and gate, horse-way and foot-path. Poor Tom hath been scared out of his good wits: bless thee, good man's son, from the foul fiend!—five fiends have been in poor Tom at once;[c] of lust, as Obidicut; Hobbididance, prince of dumbness; Mahu, of stealing; Modo, of murder; and* Flibbertigibbet, of mopping and mowing,—who since possesses chamber-maids and waiting-women. So, bless thee, master!

GLO. Here, take this purse, thou whom the heavens' plagues
Have humbled to all strokes: that I am wretched,
Makes thee the happier:—heavens, deal so still!
Let the superfluous, and lust-dieted man,
That slaves your ordinance, that will not see
Because he doth not feel, feel your power quickly;
So distribution should undo excess,
And each man have enough.—Dost thou know [Dover?

EDG. Ay, master.

GLO. There is a cliff, whose high and bending [head
Looks fearfully in the confined deep:
Bring me but to the very brim of it,
And I'll repair the misery thou dost bear,
With something rich about me: from that place
I shall no leading need.

EDG. Give me thy arm;
Poor Tom shall lead thee. [*Exeunt.*

SCENE II.—*Before the* Duke *of* Albany's *Palace.*

Enter GONERIL *and* EDMUND; OSWALD *meeting them.*

GON. Welcome, my lord; I marvel our mild husband
Not met us on the way.—Now, where's your master?

OSW. Madam, within; but never man so chang'd.
I told him of the army that was landed;
He smil'd at it: I told him, you were coming;
His answer was, *The worse*: of Gloster's treachery,
And of the loyal service of his son,

(*) First folio, *Which.*

(*) First folio omits, *and.*

a *Our means secure us; and our mere defects Prove our commodities.*—] This was an old stumbling-block to the critics Some have altered it to,—"Our *mean secures* us," &c., that is, *our middle state keeps us in safety*: others would read,—"Our *meanness* secures us:" Johnson proposed,—"Our means *seduce* us;" or "Our *maims* secure us:" and Mr. Collier's annotator reads,—"Our *wants* secure us." All this controversy arose apparently from misapprehension of the sense in which the word "secure" is to be understood. *To secure* now means only to *protect*, to *keep safely*; but in old language it very commonly signified also, to *render us careless, over-confident, unguarded*, and this appears to be its meaning here. Thus, in Sir T. More's "Life of Edward V.":—"Oh the uncertain confidence and shortsighted knowledge of man! When this lord was most afraid, he was most secure; and when he was *secure*, danger was over his head." Again, in Judges viii. 11:—"And Gideon went up by the way of them that dwelt in tents on the east of Nobah and Jogbehah, and smote the host, for the host was *secure*."

b Then, pr'ythee, get thee gone:] So the quartos the folio reads, "Get thee *away*," &c.

c — five fiends, &c.] The remainder of the speech is not given in the folio.

When I inform'd him, then he call'd me sot,
And told me I had turn'd the wrong side out:—
What most he should dislike, seems pleasant to him;
What like, offensive.

GON. [*To* EDMUND.] Then shall you go no further.
It is the cowish terror of his spirit,
That dares not undertake: he'll not feel wrongs,
Which tie him to an answer. Our wishes on the way
May prove effects. Back, Edmund, to my brother;
Hasten his musters and conduct his powers:
I must change arms* at home, and give the distaff
Into my husband's hands. This trusty servant
Shall pass between us: ere long you are like to hear,
If you dare venture in your own behalf,
A mistress's command. Wear this; spare speech;
[*Giving a favour.*
Decline your head: this kiss, if it durst speak,
Would stretch thy spirits up into the air;—
Conceive, and fare thee well.

EDM. Yours in the ranks of death.

GON. My most dear Gloster!
[*Exit* EDMUND.
O, the difference of man and man!
To thee a woman's services are due;
My fool usurps my body.[a]

OSW. Madam, here comes my lord. [*Exit.*

Enter ALBANY.

GON. I have been worth the whistle.

ALB. O, Goneril!
You are not worth the dust which the rude wind
Blows in your face! I fear your disposition:[b]
That nature, which contemns its origin,
Cannot be border'd certain in itself;
She that herself will sliver and disbranch
From her material sap, perforce must wither,
And come to deadly use.

GON. No more! the text is foolish.

ALB. Wisdom and goodness to the vile seem vile;
Filths savour but themselves. What have you done?
Tigers, not daughters! what have you perform'd?
A father, and a gracious aged man,—
Whose reverence even the head-lugg'd bear would lick,—
Most barbarous, most degenerate!—have you madded.
Could my good brother suffer you to do it?
A man, a prince, by him so benefited!
If that the heavens do not their visible spirits
Send quickly down to tame these* vile offences,
'T will come, humanity must perforce prey on 'tself,
Like monsters of the deep.

GON. Milk-liver'd man!
That bear'st a cheek for blows, a head for wrongs;
Who hast not in thy brows an eye discerning
Thine honour from thy suffering;[c] that not know'st,
Fools do those villains pity who are punish'd
Ere they have done their mischief. Where's thy drum?
France spreads his banners in our noiseless land;
With plumed helm thy state begins to threat;[d]
Whiles thou, a moral fool, sitt'st still, and criest,
Alack! why does he so?

ALB. See thyself, devil!
Proper deformity seems not in the fiend
So horrid as in woman.

GON. O vain fool![e]

ALB. Thou changed and self-cover'd thing, for shame,
Be-monster not thy feature! Were't my fitness
To let these hands obey my blood,
They are apt enough to dislocate and tear
Thy flesh and bones:—howe'er thou art a fiend,
A woman's shape doth shield thee.

GON. Marry, your manhood now!—

Enter a Messenger.

ALB. What news?

MESS. O, my good lord, the duke of Cornwall's dead,
Slain by his servant, going to put out
The other eye of Gloster.

ALB. Gloster's eyes!

MESS. A servant that he bred, thrill'd with remorse,
Oppos'd against the act, bending his sword
To his great master; who, thereat enrag'd,†
Flew on him, and amongst them fell'd him dead;
But not without that harmful stroke, which since
Hath pluck'd him after.

ALB. This shows you are above,
You justicers,‡ that these our nether crimes

(*) First folio, *names.*

a My fool usurps my body.] The reading of the folio. The first quarto has, "*A* fool usurps my *bed;*" the second, "My *foot* usurps my *head;*" while a third gives, "My *foot* usurps my *body.*"

b I fear your disposition:] This line and all that follows, down to Goneril's speech, beginning, "Milk-liver'd man!" the folio omits.

(*) Old copies, *this, the.* (†) First folio, *threat-enrag'd.* (‡) First folio, *Iustices.*

c Thine honour from thy suffering;] In the folio, Goneril's speech ends here.

d — *thy* state *begins* to threat.] The first quarto has,—"thy state begins *thereat;*" the second, "thy *slaier* begins *threats.*"

e O vain fool!] In the folio, the Messenger enters here, and begins immediately,—"O, my good lord," &c.

So speedily can venge!—But, O poor Gloster!
Lost he his other eye?
MESS. Both, both, my lord.—
This letter, madam, craves a speedy answer;
'T is from your sister.
GON. [*Aside.*] One way I like this well;
But being widow, and my Gloster with her,
May all the building in my fancy pluck
Upon my hateful life: another way,
The news is not so tart.—I'll read, and answer. [*Exit.*
ALB. Where was his son, when they did take his eyes?
MESS. Come with my lady hither.
ALB. He is not here.
MESS. No, my good lord, I met him back again.
ALB. Knows he the wickedness?
MESS. Ay, my good lord; 't was he inform'd against him;
And quit the house on purpose that their punishment
Might have the freer course.
ALB. [*Aside.*] Gloster, I live
To thank thee for the love thou show'dst the king,
And to revenge thine eyes.—Come hither, friend;
Tell me what more thou know'st. [*Exeunt.*

SCENE III.[a]—*The* French *Camp near* Dover.

Enter KENT, *and a* Gentleman.

KENT. Why the king of France is so suddenly gone back know you the reason?
GENT. Something he left imperfect in the state, which since his coming forth is thought of; which imports to the kingdom so much fear and danger, that his personal return was most required and necessary.
KENT. Who hath he left behind him general?
GENT. The mareschal of France, Monsieur le Far.
KENT. Did your letters pierce the queen to any demonstration of grief?
GENT. Ay, sir; * she took them, read them in my presence;
And now and then an ample tear trill'd down
Her delicate cheek: it seem'd, she was a queen
Over her passion; who, most rebel-like,
Sought to be king o'er her.
KENT. O, then it mov'd her.

(*) Old text, *say:* corrected by Theobald.

a SCENE III.] This scene is found only in the quartos.
b — *a better* day:] The old text has, "a better *way*," which can hardly be what Shakespeare wrote. This has been changed to "a wetter *May*," and "a better *day;*" of the two we prefer the latter.

GENT. Not to a rage: patience and sorrow strove*
Who should express her goodliest. You have seen
Sunshine and rain at once: her smiles and tears
Were like a better day:[b] those happy smilets,
That play'd on her ripe lip, seem'd not to know
What guests were in her eyes; which parted thence,
As pearls from diamonds dropp'd.—In brief,
Sorrow would be a rarity most belov'd,
If all could so become it.
KENT. Made she no verbal question?
GENT. Faith, once or twice she heav'd the name of *father*
Pantingly forth, as if it press'd her heart;
Cried, *Sisters! sisters!—Shame of ladies! sisters!*
Kent! father! sisters! What, i' the storm? i' the night?
Let pity not be believ'd!—There she shook
The holy water from her heavenly eyes,
And clamour moisten'd: then away she started
To deal with grief alone.
KENT. It is the stars,
The stars above us, govern our conditions;
Else one self mate and mate could not beget
Such different issues.—You spoke not with her since?
GENT. No.
KENT. Was this before the king return'd?
GENT. No, since.
KENT. Well, sir, the poor distressed Lear's i' the town;
Who sometime, in his better tune, remembers
What we are come about, and by no means
Will yield to see his daughter.
GENT. Why, good sir?
KENT. A sovereign shame so elbows him: his own unkindness,
That stripp'd her from his benediction, turn'd her
To foreign casualties, gave her dear rights
To his dog-hearted daughters,—these things sting
His mind so venomously, that burning shame
Detains him from Cordelia.
GENT. Alack, poor gentleman!
KENT. Of Albany's and Cornwall's powers you heard not?
GENT. 'T is so, they are a-foot. [Lear,
KENT. Well, sir, I'll bring you to our master
And leave you to attend him: some dear cause
Will in concealment wrap me up awhile;
When I am known aright, you shall not grieve
Lending me this acquaintance. I pray you, go
Along with me. [*Exeunt.*

(*) Old text, *streme:* corrected by Pope.

SCENE IV.—*The Same. A Tent.*

Enter CORDELIA, Physician, *and* Soldiers.

COR. Alack, 'tis he; why, he was met even now
As mad as the vex'd sea; singing aloud;
Crown'd with rank fumiter, and furrow weeds,
With burdocks,[a] hemlock, nettles, cuckoo-flowers,
Darnel, and all the idle weeds that grow
In our sustaining corn.—A century send forth;
Search every acre in the high-grown field,
And bring him to our eye. [*Exit an* Officer.]—
What can man's wisdom
In the restoring his bereaved sense?
He that helps him take all my outward worth.
PHY. There is means, madam:

[a] — burdocks,—] The folio has "Hardokes," the quartos "hordocks." Farmer suggested *harlocks*, citing the following lines from Drayton,—

"The honey-suckle, the *harlocke*,
The lilly, and the lady-smocke," &c.

Our foster-nurse of nature is repose,
The which he lacks; that to provoke in him,
Are many simples operative, whose power
Will close the eye of anguish.
COR. All bless'd secrets,
All you unpublish'd virtues of the earth,
Spring with my tears! be aidant and remediate
In the good man's distress! *—Seek, seek for him;
Lest his ungovern'd rage dissolve the life
That wants the means to lead it.

Enter a Messenger.

MESS. News, madam!
The British powers are marching hitherward.
COR. 'Tis known before; our preparation stands
In expectation of them.—O dear father,
It is thy business that I go about;
Therefore great France
My mourning, and important[a] tears hath pitied.
No blown ambition doth our arms incite,
But love, dear love, and our ag'd father's right:
Soon may I hear and see him! [*Exeunt.*

SCENE V.—*A Room in* Gloucester's *Castle.*

Enter REGAN *and* OSWALD.

REG. But are my brother's powers set forth?
OSW. Ay, madam.
REG. Himself in person there?
OSW. Madam, with much ado:
Your sister is the better soldier.
REG. Lord Edmund spake not with your lord at home?
OSW. No, madam.
REG. What might import my sister's letter to him?
OSW. I know not, lady.
REG. Faith, he is posted hence on serious matter.
It was great ignorance, Gloster's eyes being out,
To let him live; where he arrives he moves
All hearts against us. Edmund, I think, is gone,
In pity of his misery, to despatch
His nighted life; moreover, to descry
The strength o'the enemy.
OSW. I must needs after him, madam, with my letter.
REG. Our troops set forth to-morrow: stay with us;
The ways are dangerous.
OSW. I may not, madam;
My lady charg'd my duty in this business.
REG. Why should she write to Edmund? Might not you
Transport her purposes by word? Belike,
Something*—I know not what:—I'll love thee much,
Let me unseal the letter.
OSW. Madam, I had rather—
REG. I know your lady does not love her husband;
I'm sure of that: and at her late being here
She gave strange œiliads[b] and most speaking looks
To noble Edmund. I know you are of her bosom.—
OSW. I, madam?
REG. I speak in understanding; you are, I know't;
Therefore I do advise you, take this note:
My lord is dead; Edmund and I have talk'd;
And more convenient is he for my hand
Than for your lady's:—you may gather more.
If you do find him, pray you, give him this;
And when your mistress hears thus much from you,
I pray, desire her call her wisdom to her.
So, fare you well.
If you do chance to hear of that blind traitor,
Preferment falls on him that cuts him off.
OSW. Would I could meet him,† madam! I would ‡ show
What party I do follow.
REG. Fare thee well. [*Exeunt.*

SCENE VI.—*The Country near* Dover.

Enter GLOUCESTER, *and* EDGAR, *dressed like a Peasant.*

GLO. When shall I come to the top of that same hill?
EDG. You do climb up it now: look, how we labour.
GLO. Methinks the ground is even.
EDG. Horrible steep.
Hark, do you hear the sea?
GLO. No, truly.
EDG. Why, then, your other senses grow imperfect
By your eyes' anguish.
GLO. So may it be, indeed:
Methinks thy voice is alter'd; and thou speak'st
In better phrase and matter than thou didst.
EDG. You're much deceiv'd; in nothing am I chang'd,
But in my garments.

(*) First folio, *desires.*

a — important *tears*—] Important for *importunate;* the folio has *importun'd.*

(*) First folio, *Some things.* (†) First folio omits, *him.* (‡) First folio, *should.*

b — œiliads,—] See note (a), p. 646, Vol. I.

GLO. Methinks you're better spoken.
EDG. Come on, sir; here's the place:—stand still.—How fearful
And dizzy 'tis, to cast one's eyes so low!
The crows and choughs, that wing the midway air,
Show scarce so gross as beetles: half way down
Hangs one that gathers samphire,—dreadful trade!
Methinks he seems no bigger than his head:
The fishermen, that walk* upon the beach,
Appear like mice; and yond tall anchoring bark,
Diminish'd to her cock; her cock, a buoy
Almost too small for sight: the murmuring surge,
That on the unnumber'd idle pebbles† chafes,
Cannot be heard so high.—I'll look no more,
Lest my brain turn, and the deficient sight
Topple down headlong.
GLO. Set me where you stand.
EDG. Give me your hand:—you are now within a foot
Of the extreme verge: for all beneath the moon
Would I not leap upright.
GLO. Let go my hand.
Here, friend, 's another purse; in it a jewel
Well worth a poor man's taking: fairies and gods,
Prosper it with thee! Go thou further off;
Bid me farewell, and let me hear thee going.
EDG. Now fare you well, good sir.
[*Seems to go.*
GLO. With all my heart.
EDG. Why I do trifle thus with his despair
Is done to cure it.
GLO. O, you mighty gods!
This world I do renounce; and, in your sights,
Shake patiently my great affliction off:
If I could bear it longer, and not fall
To quarrel with your great opposeless wills,
My snuff and loathed part of nature should
Burn itself out. If Edgar live, O, bless him!—
Now, fellow, fare thee well.
EDG. Gone, sir:—farewell.—
[GLOUCESTER *leaps, and falls along.*
And yet I know not how conceit may rob
The treasury of life, when life itself
Yields to the theft: had he been where he thought,
By this, had thought been past.—Alive or dead?
Ho, you sir! friend!—Hear you, sir?—speak!—
Thus might he pass indeed:—yet he revives.—
What are you, sir?
GLO. Away, and let me die.
EDG. Hadst thou been aught but gossamer, feathers, air,
So many fathom down precipitating,
Thou'd'st shiver'd like an egg: but thou dost breathe;
Hast heavy substance; bleed'st not; speak'st; art sound!
Ten masts at each make not the altitude,
Which thou hast perpendicularly fell!
Thy life's a miracle. Speak yet again.
GLO. But have I fall'n, or no?
EDG. From the dread summit of this chalky bourn![a]
Look up a-height;—the shrill-gorg'd lark so far
Cannot be seen or heard: do but look up.
GLO. Alack, I have no eyes.—
Is wretchedness depriv'd that benefit,
To end itself by death? 'Twas yet some comfort,
When misery could beguile the tyrant's rage,
And frustrate his proud will.
EDG. Give me your arm:
Up:—so.—How is't? Feel you your legs? You stand.
GLO. Too well, too well.
EDG. This is above all strangeness.
Upon the crown o' the cliff, what thing was that
Which parted from you?
GLO. A poor unfortunate beggar.
EDG. As I stood here below, methought his eyes
Were two full moons; he had a thousand noses,
Horns whelk'd and wav'd like the enridged* sea:
It was some fiend; therefore, thou happy father,
Think that the clearest gods, who make them honours
Of men's impossibilities, have preserv'd thee.
GLO. I do remember now: henceforth I'll bear
Affliction till it do cry out itself,
Enough, enough, and die. That thing you speak of,
I took it for a man; often 'twould say,
The fiend, the fiend! he led me to that place.
EDG. Bear free and patient thoughts.—But who comes here?

Enter LEAR, *fantastically dressed with flowers.*

The safer sense will ne'er accommodate[b]
His master thus.
LEAR. No, they cannot touch me for coining;†
I am the king himself.
EDG. O thou side-piercing sight!
LEAR. Nature's above art in that respect.—

(*) First folio, *walk'd*. (†) First folio, *Pebble*.

a — *chalky* bourn.] *Bourn* here means boundary.
b The safer sense will ne'er accommodate
His master thus.]

(*) First folio, *enraged*. (†) First folio, *crying*.

The word "safer" in this passage has been suspected; but it is certainly right, and means *sounder*. The *sound* senses of a man would never permit him to go thus grotesquely garnished.

There's your press-money.[a] That fellow handles his bow like a crow-keeper: (1) draw me a clothier's yard. (2) —Look, look, a mouse! Peace, peace;—this piece of toasted cheese will do't.—There's my gauntlet; I'll prove it on a giant.—Bring up the brown bills.[b]—O, well flown, bird!—i' the clout! i' the clout![c] hewgh!—Give the word.

EDG. Sweet marjoram.

---

[a] There's your press-money.] The allusion is probably, as Douce remarks, to the money which was paid to soldiers when they were retained in the king's service.

[b] — brown bills.—] A "bill," the old weapon of the English infantry, was a sort of battle-axe with a long handle; and "brown bills" are occasionally mentioned by writers of Shakespeare's age; thus Marlowe, in King Edward II.—

"Lo, with a band of bow-men and of pikes,
Brown bills, and targiteers."

[d] — i' the clout!] The *clout* was the centre mark in the target; what we now call the *bull's-eye;* and possibly took its name from the *clout* or pin by which the target was suspended. See note (b) p. 598, vol. I.

LEAR. Pass.

GLO. I know that voice.

LEAR. Ha! Goneril!—with a white beard!—They flattered me like a dog; and told me I had * white hairs in my beard ere the black ones were there. To say *ay*, and *no*, to every thing that I said!—*Ay* and *no* too was no good divinity. When the rain came to wet me once, and the wind to make me chatter; when the thunder would not peace at my bidding, there I found 'em, there I smelt 'em out. Go to, they are not men o' their words: they told me I was every thing; 't is a lie;—I am not ague-proof.

GLO. The trick of that voice I do well remember:
Is 't not the king?

LEAR. Ay, every inch a king!
When I do stare, see how the subject quakes.
I pardon that man's life.—What was thy cause?—
Adultery?—
Thou shalt not die: die for adultery! No:
The wren goes to 't, and the small gilded fly
Does lecher in my sight.
Let copulation thrive, for Gloster's bastard son
Was kinder to his father than my daughters
Got 'tween the lawful sheets.
To 't, luxury, pell-mell! for I lack soldiers.—
Behold yond simpering dame,
Whose face between her forks presages snow;
That minces[a] virtue, and does shake the head
To hear of pleasure's name;—
The fitchew, nor the soiled horse, goes to 't
With a more riotous appetite.
Down from the waist they are Centaurs,
Though women all above:
But to the girdle do the gods inherit,
Beneath is all the fiends'; there 's hell, there 's darkness, there is the sulphurous pit, burning, scalding, stench, consumption!—fie, fie, fie! pah, pah! Give me an ounce of civet, good apothecary, to † sweeten my imagination: there's money for thee.

GLO. O, let me kiss that hand!

LEAR. Let me wipe it first; it smells of mortality.

GLO. O ruin'd piece of nature! This great world
Shall so wear out to nought.—Dost thou know me?

LEAR. I remember thine eyes well enough. Dost thou squiny at me? No, do thy worst, blind Cupid, I'll not love.—Read thou this challenge; mark but the penning of it.

GLO. Were all the* letters suns, I could not see.

EDG. I would not take this from report;—[b]
It is, and my heart breaks at it.

LEAR. Read.

GLO. What, with the case of eyes?

LEAR. O, ho! are you there with me? No eyes in your head, nor no money in your purse? Your eyes are in a heavy case, your purse in a light: yet you see how this world goes.

GLO. I see it feelingly.

LEAR. What, art mad? A man may see how this world goes with no eyes. Look with thine ears: see how yond justice rails upon yond simple thief. Hark, in thine ear: change places; and, handy-dandy, which is the justice, which is the thief?—Thou hast seen a farmer's dog bark at a beggar?

GLO. Ay, sir.

LEAR. And the creature run from the cur? There thou mightst behold the great image of authority: a dog's obeyed in office.—
Thou rascal beadle, hold thy bloody hand!
Why dost thou lash that whore? Strip thine * own back;
Thou hotly lust'st to use her in that kind
For which thou whipp'st her. The usurer hangs the cozener.
Through tatter'd clothes small † vices do appear;
Robes and furr'd gowns hide all. Plate sin[c] with gold,
And the strong lance of justice hurtless breaks:
Arm it in rags, a pigmy's straw does pierce it.
None does offend, none,—I say, none; I'll able[d] 'em:
Take that of me, my friend, who have the power
To seal the accuser's lips. Get thee glass eyes;
And, like a scurvy politician, seem
To see the things thou dost not.—Now, now, now, now:
Pull off my boots:—harder, harder;—so.

EDG. O, matter and impertinency mix'd!
Reason in madness!

LEAR. If thou wilt weep my fortunes, take my eyes.
I know thee well enough, thy name is Gloster:
Thou must be patient; we came crying hither:
Thou know'st, the first time that we smell the air,
We wawl and cry.—I will preach to thee; mark!

GLO. Alack, alack the day!

LEAR. When we are born, we cry that we are come

(*) First folio inserts, *the*. (†) First folio omits, *to*.

(*) First folio, *thy*. (†) First folio, *great*.

[a] *That* minces *virtue*,—] That affects the coy timidity of virtue.
[b] I would not take this from report, &c.] There is some obscurity here. What is it Edgar would not take from report? He must have been aware of his father's deprivation of sight; because it is mentioned in the previous scene. We are, perhaps, to suppose the poor King exhibits the proclamation for the killing of Gloucester.
[c] Plate sin *with gold*,—] A correction by Pope and Theobald; the old text having, "*Place sinnes*." This passage down to, "To seal the accuser's lips," inclusive, is only in the folio.
[d] — able *'em*] *Qualify* them.

To this great stage of fools—This a good block :—[a]
It were a delicate stratagem, to shoe
A troop of horse with felt: I'll put 't in proof;
And when I have stol'n upon these sons-in-law,*
Then, kill, kill, kill, kill, kill, kill![b]

Enter a Gentleman *with* Attendants.

GENT. O, here he is; lay hand upon him.—Sir,
Your most dear daughter—
LEAR. No rescue? What, a prisoner? I am even
The natural Fool of fortune.—Use me well;
You shall have ransom. Let me have surgeons;
I am cut to the brains.
GENT. You shall have any thing.
LEAR. No seconds? All myself?
Why, this would make a man a man of salt,
To use his eyes for garden water-pots,
Ay, and laying autumn's dust.
GENT. Good sir,—[c]
LEAR. I will die bravely, like a † bridegroom: what!
I will be jovial; come, come; I am a king,
My ‡ masters, know you that!
GENT. You are a royal one, and we obey you.
LEAR. Then there's life in 't. Nay § an you get it, you shall get it by running. Sa, sa, sa, sa!
[*Exit, running;* Attendants *follow.*
GENT. A sight most pitiful in the meanest wretch,
Past speaking of in a king!—Thou hast one|| daughter,
Who redeems nature from the general curse
Which twain have brought her to.
EDG. Hail, gentle sir.
GENT. Sir, speed you: what's your will?
EDG. Do you hear aught, sir, of a battle toward?
GENT. Most sure and vulgar, every one hears that,
Which can distinguish sound.
EDG. But, by your favour,
How near's the other army?
GENT. Near and on speedy foot; the main descry
Stands on the hourly thought.[d]
EDG. I thank you, sir: that's all.
GENT. Though that the queen on special cause is here,
Her army is mov'd on.
EDG. I thank you, sir. [*Exit* Gent.
GLO. You ever-gentle gods, take my breath from me;
Let not my worser spirit tempt me again
To die before you please!
EDG. Well pray you, father.
GLO. Now, good sir, what are you?
EDG. A most poor man, made tame to fortune's blows;
Who, by the art of known and feeling sorrows,
Am pregnant to good pity. Give me your hand,
I'll lead you to some biding.
GLO. Hearty thanks:
The bounty and the benison of heaven
To boot, and boot!

Enter OSWALD.

OSW. A proclaim'd prize! Most happy!
That eyeless head of thine was first fram'd flesh
To raise my fortunes.—Thou old unhappy traitor,
Briefly thyself remember:—the sword is out
That must destroy thee.
GLO. Now let thy friendly hand
Put strength enough to it. [EDGAR *interposes.*
OSW. Wherefore, bold peasant,
Dar'st thou support a publish'd traitor? Hence!
Lest that the infection of his fortune take
Like hold on thee. Let go his arm.
EDG. Chill not let go, zir, without vurther 'casion.
OSW. Let go, slave, or thou diest!
EDG. Good gentleman, go your gait, and let poor volk pass. An chud ha' been zwagger'd out of my life, 'twould not ha' been zo long as 'tis by a vortnight.[e]—Nay, come not near th' old man; keep out, che vor ye, or ise try whether your costard or my ballow[f] be the harder: chill be plain with you.
OSW. Out, dunghill!
EDG. Chill pick your teeth, zir: come; no matter vor your foins.[g]
[*They fight; and* EDGAR *fells him.*

(*) First folio, *Son in Lawes.* (†) First folio inserts, *smugge.* (‡) First folio omits, *My.* (§) First folio, *Come.* (||) First folio, *a.*

a This a good block :—] "Upon the king's saying, *I will preach to thee,* the poet seems to have meant him to pull off his *hat,* and keep turning it and feeling it, in the attitude of one of the preachers of those times (whom I have seen so represented in ancient prints), till the idea of *felt,* which the good *hat* or *block* was made of, raises the stratagem in his brain of shoeing a troop of horse with a substance soft as that which he held and moulded between his hands. This makes him start from his preachment."—STEEVENS.

b — kill, kill! &c.] This was the ancient cry of assault in the English army. Shakespeare introduces it again in "Coriolanus," Act V. Sc. 5; when the conspirators attack Coriolanus.

c Ay, and laying autumn's dust.
GENT. Good sir,—]
Omitted in the folio.

d — the main descry
Stands on the hourly thought.]
The meaning appears to be, the sight of the main body is expected hourly; but the expression is as harsh and disagreeable as the speaker's "Most sure and vulgar" just before.

e — 'twould not ha' been zo long as 't is by a vortnight.—] Steevens has remarked, but the reason is unexplained, that when our ancient writers have occasion to introduce a rustic, they commonly allot him this Somersetshire dialect.

f — ballow—] In some of the provincial dialects, *ballow* means a pole or staff.

g — foins.] *Thrusts.*

OSW. Slave, thou hast slain me:—villain, take my purse;
If ever thou wilt thrive, bury my body,
And give the letters which thou find'st about me,
To Edmund earl of Gloster; seek him out
Upon the British* party:—O, untimely death!†
[*Dies.*

EDG. I know thee well: a serviceable villain;
As duteous to the vices of thy mistress,
As badness would desire.

GLO. What, is he dead?

EDG. Sit you down, father; rest you.—
Let's see his ‡ pockets: these § letters, that he speaks of,
May be my friends.—He's dead; I am only sorry
He had no other death's-man.—Let us see:—
Leave, gentle wax: and, manners, blame us not:
To know our enemies' minds, we rip their hearts;
Their papers, is more lawful.

[Reads.] *Let our reciprocal vows be remembered. You have many opportunities to cut him off: if your will want not, time and place will be fruitfully offered. There is nothing done, if he return the conqueror: then am I the prisoner, and his bed my gaol; from the loathed warmth whereof deliver me, and supply the place for your labour.*

Your (wife, so I would say,)
affectionate servant,
GONERIL.

O, undistinguish'd space of woman's will!—[a]
A plot upon her virtuous husband's life; [sands,
And the exchange, my brother!—Here, in the
Thee I'll rake up, the post unsanctified
Of murderous lechers: and, in the mature time,
With this ungracious paper strike the sight
Of the death-practis'd duke: for him 'tis well,
That of thy death and business I can tell.
[*Exit, dragging out the body.*

GLO. The king is mad: how stiff is my vile sense,
That I stand up, and have ingenious feeling
Of my huge sorrows! Better I were distract:
So should my thoughts be sever'd from my griefs,
And woes, by wrong imaginations, lose
The knowledge of themselves. [*Drum afar off.*

(*) First folio, *English*. (†) Old text repeats, *death*.
(‡) First folio, *these*. (§) First folio, *the*.

a O, undistinguish'd space of *woman's* will!—] In the quartos we read, "O undistinguisht space of womans *wit*"; in the folio, "Oh *indinguish'd* space of Womans will;" and Mr. Collier's annotator suggests, "O, *unextinguish'd blaze* of woman's will!" Whatever may have been the original lection, it was plainly an exclamation against the indiscriminate caprice of woman as exhibited by Goneril in plotting against a virtuous husband's life merely to gain a villain like Edmund, and not, as Mr. Collier asserts, against the "unextinguishable appetite" of the sex: his annotator's emendation is therefore indefensible. We should, perhaps, read, "O, *undistinguishable sense* of woman's will."

Re-enter EDGAR.

EDG. Give me your hand.
Far off, methinks, I hear the beaten drum:
Come, father, I'll bestow you with a friend.
[*Exeunt.*

SCENE VII.—*A Tent in the* French *Camp.*

LEAR *on a bed asleep;* Physician, Gentleman, *and others, attending; soft music playing.*[b]

Enter CORDELIA *and* KENT.

CORD. O thou good Kent, how shall I live and work,
To match thy goodness? My life will be too short,
And every measure fail me.

KENT. To be acknowledg'd, madam, is o'erpaid.
All my reports go with the modest truth;
Nor more nor clipp'd, but so.

CORD. Be better suited:
These weeds are memories of those worser hours;
I pr'ythee, put them off.

KENT. Pardon, dear madam;
Yet to be known, shortens my made[c] intent:
My boon I make it, that you know me not,
Till time and I think meet.

CORD. Then be't so, my good lord.—How does the king? [*To the* Physician.

PHYS. Madam, sleeps still.[d]

CORD. O you kind gods,
Cure this great breach in his abused nature!
The untun'd and jarring senses, O, wind up
Of this child-changed father!

PHYS. So please your majesty
That we may wake the king? he hath slept long.

CORD. Be govern'd by your knowledge, and proceed
I' the sway of your own will. Is he array'd?

GENT. Ay, madam; in the heaviness of sleep,
We put fresh garments on him.

PHYS. Be by, good madam, when we do awake him;
I doubt not* of his temperance.

CORD. Very well.[e]

(*) First folio omits, *not*.

b — *soft music playing.*] This part of the stage direction was judiciously interpolated by Mr. Dyce.

c — made *intent:*] This may import *purposed* intent; but Mr. Collier's annotator proposes a very plausible change—"My *main* intent."

d Madam, sleeps still.] In the folio, the Physician and Gentleman form one character; the parts were combined probably, as Mr. Collier surmises, to suit the economy of performers.

e CORD. Very well.
PHYS. Please you, draw near.—Louder the music there.]
These two speeches are not in the folio.

PHYS. Please you, draw near.—Louder the music there!
CORD. O my dear father! Restoration, hang
Thy medicine on my lips; and let this kiss
Repair those violent harms that my two sisters
Have in thy reverence made!
KENT. Kind and dear princess!
CORD. Had you not been their father, these white flakes
Had challeng'd * pity of them. Was this a face
To be oppos'd against the warring † winds?
To stand against the deep dread-bolted thunder?[a]
In the most terrible and nimble stroke
Of quick, cross-lightning? to watch (poor *perdu!*)
With this thin helm? Mine enemy's dog,
Though he had bit me, should have stood that night
Against my fire; and wast thou fain, poor father,
To hovel thee with swine, and rogues forlorn,
In short and musty straw? Alack, alack!
'T is wonder that thy life and wits at once
Had not concluded all.—He wakes; speak to him.
PHYS. Madam, do you; 'tis fittest.
CORD. How does my royal lord? How fares your majesty?
LEAR. You do me wrong to take me out o' the grave:—
Thou art a soul in bliss; but I am bound
Upon a wheel of fire, that mine own tears
Do scald like molten lead.
CORD. Sir, do you know me?
LEAR. You are a spirit, I know; when * did you die?
CORD. Still, still, far wide!
PHYS. He's scarce awake; let him alone awhile.
LEAR. Where have I been? Where am I?—Fair daylight?

(*) First folio, *Did challenge*. (†) First folio, *jarring*.

a To stand against the deep dread-bolted thunder?
In the most terrible and nimble stroke
Of quick, cross-lightning? to watch (poor *perdu!*)
With this thin helm?]
These lines are omitted in the folio.

(*) First folio, *where*.

I'm mightily abus'd.—I should e'en die with pity,
To see another thus.—I know not what to say.—
I will not swear these are my hands:—let's see,
I feel this pin prick. Would I were assur'd
Of my condition!

CORD. O, look upon me, sir,
And hold your hands* in benediction o'er me:—
No, sir,† you must not kneel.

LEAR. Pray, do not mock me:
I am a very foolish fond old man,
Fourscore and upward, not an hour more nor less;
And, to deal plainly,
I fear I am not in my perfect mind.
Methinks I should know you, and know this man;
Yet I am doubtful; for I am mainly ignorant
What place this is; and all the skill I have
Remembers not these garments; nor I know not
Where I did lodge last night.—Do not laugh at me,
For, as I am a man, I think this lady
To be my child Cordelia.

CORD. And so I am, I am.

LEAR. Be your tears wet? yes, faith. I pray, weep not:
If you have poison for me, I will drink it.
I know you do not love me; for your sisters
Have, as I do remember, done me wrong:
You have some cause, they have not.

CORD. No cause, no cause.

LEAR. Am I in France?

KENT. In your own kingdom, sir.

LEAR. Do not abuse me.

PHYS. Be comforted, good madam; the great rage,
You see, is kill'd in him: and yet it is danger
To make him even o'er the time he has lost.[a]
Desire him to go in; trouble him no more,
Till further settling.

COR. Will't please your highness walk?

LEAR. You must bear with me:
Pray you now, forget and forgive: I am old, and foolish.

[*Exeunt* LEAR, CORDELIA, Physician, *and* Attendants.[b]

GENT. Holds it true, sir, that the duke of Cornwall was so slain?

KENT. Most certain, sir.

GENT. Who is conductor of his people?

KENT. As 'tis said, the bastard son of Gloster.

GENT. They say, Edgar, his banish'd son, is with the earl of Kent in Germany.

KENT. Report is changeable. 'T is time to look about; the powers of the kingdom approach apace.

GENT. The arbitrement is like to be bloody. Fare you well, sir. [*Exit.*

KENT. My point and period will be throughly wrought,
Or well or ill, as this day's battle's fought. [*Exit.*

(*) First folio, *hand*. (†) First folio omits, *No, sir*.

a "— and yet it is danger
To make him even o'er the time he has lost.]
Omitted in the folio.

b *Exeunt* LEAR, &c.] In the folio, the scene terminates here.

ACT V.

SCENE I.—*The Camp of the* British Forces, *near* Dover.

Enter, with drum and colours, EDMUND, REGAN, Officers, Soldiers, *and others.*

EDM. Know of the duke if his last purpose hold,
Or whether since he is advis'd by aught
To change the course: he's full of alteration,
And self-reproving:—bring his constant pleasure
[*To an* Officer, *who goes out*

REG. Our sister's man is certainly miscarried.

EDM. 'Tis to be doubted, madam.

REG. Now, sweet lord,
You know the goodness I intend upon you:
Tell me,—but truly,—but then speak the truth,
Do you not love my sister?
EDM. In honour'd love.
REG. But have you never found my brother's way
To the forefended place?
EDM. That thought abuses you.[a]
REG. I am doubtful that you have been conjunct
And bosom'd with her, as far as we call hers.
EDM. No, by mine honour, madam.
REG. I never shall endure her: dear my lord,
Be not familiar with her.
EDM. Fear me* not:—
She and the duke her husband!

Enter, with drum and colours, ALBANY, GONERIL, *and* Soldiers.

GON. [*Aside.*] I had rather lose the battle,[b] than that sister
Should loosen him and me.
ALB. Our very loving sister, well be-met.—
Sir, this I hear,†—The king is come to his daughter,
With others whom the rigour of our state
Forc'd to cry out. Where I could not be honest,[c]
I never yet was valiant: for this business,
It toucheth us, as France invades our land,
Not bolds the king, with others, whom I fear,
Most just and heavy causes make oppose.
EDM. Sir, you speak nobly.
REG. Why is this reason'd?
GON. Combine together 'gainst the enemy;
For these domestic and particular broils
Are not the question here.
ALB. Let us then determine
With the ancient of war on our proceedings.
EDM. I shall attend you presently at your tent.[d]
REG. Sister, you'll go with us?
GON. No.
REG. 'Tis most convenient; pray go with us.
GON. [*Aside.*] O, ho, I know the riddle.—I will go.

As they are going out, enter EDGAR *disguised.*

EDG. If e'er your grace had speech with man so poor,
Hear me one word.
ALB. I'll overtake you.—Speak.
[*Exeunt* EDM. REG. GON. Officers, Soldiers, *and* Attendants.
EDG. Before you fight the battle, ope this letter.
If you have victory, let the trumpet sound
For him that brought it: wretched though I seem,
I can produce a champion that will prove
What is avouched there. If you miscarry,
Your business of the world hath so an end,
And machination ceases. Fortune love* you!
ALB. Stay till I've read the letter.
EDG. I was forbid it.
When time shall serve, let but the herald cry,
And I'll appear again.
ALB. Why, fare thee well; I will o'erlook thy paper. [*Exit* EDGAR.

Re-enter EDMUND.

EDM. The enemy's in view, draw up your powers.
Here is the guess of their true strength and forces
By diligent discovery;—but your haste
Is now urg'd on you.
ALB. We will greet the time. [*Exit.*
EDM. To both these sisters have I sworn my love;
Each jealous of the other, as the stung
Are of the adder. Which of them shall I take?
Both? one? or neither? Neither can be enjoy'd,
If both remain alive: to take the widow,
Exasperates, makes mad her sister Goneril;
And hardly shall I carry out my side,[e]
Her husband being alive. Now then, we'll use
His countenance for the battle; which being done,
Let her who would be rid of him devise
His speedy taking off. As for the mercy
Which he intends to Lear and to Cordelia,—
The battle done, and they within our power,
Shall never see his pardon; for my state
Stands on me to defend, not to debate. [*Exit.*

(*) First folio omits, *me*. (†) First folio, *heard*.

(*) First folio, *loves*.

a That thought abuses you.] The folio omits both this and the following speech.
b I had rather lose the battle, &c.] This speech is omitted in the folio.
c Where I could not be honest, &c.] The remainder of the speech and Edmund's answer are omitted in the folio.
d I shall attend you presently at your tent.] Omitted in the folio.
e — carry out my side,—] A metaphor from the card-table, where to *carry out a side* meant to carry out the game with your partner successfully. So to *set up a side*, was to become partners in the game; to *pull* or *pluck down a side*, was to lose it. Thus in Ben Jonson's "Silent Woman," Act III. Sc. 2,—

"Mavis and she will *set up a side*."

Thus also in Massinger's "Great Duke of Florence," Act IV. Sc. 1, where Cozimo, declining to do Petronella right in a bowl of wine, says,—

"Pray you pause a little;
If I hold your cards, I shall *pull down the side:*
I am not good at the game."

SCENE II.—*A Field between the two Camps.*

Alarum without. Enter, with drum and colours, LEAR, CORDELIA, *and their* Forces; *and exeunt.*

Enter EDGAR *and* GLOUCESTER.

EDG. Here, father, take the shadow of this tree
For your good host; pray that the right may thrive:
If ever I return to you again,
I'll bring you comfort.

GLO. Grace go with you, sir!
[*Exit* EDGAR.

Alarums; afterwards a Retreat. Re-enter EDGAR.

EDG. Away, old man!—give me thy hand,—away!
King Lear hath lost, he and his daughter ta en.
Give me thy hand; come on.

GLO. No further, sir; a man may rot even here.

EDG. What, in ill thoughts again? Men must endure
Their going hence, even as their coming hither;
Ripeness is all.—come on.

GLO. And that's true too.[a]
[*Exeunt.*

SCENE III.—*The* British *Camp near* Dover.

Enter, in conquest, with drum and colours, EDMUND; LEAR *and* CORDELIA, *as prisoners;* Officers, Soldiers, *&c.*

EDM. Some officers take them away: good guard,
Until their greater pleasures first be known
That are to censure them.

a And that's true too.] These words are not in the quartos.

COR. We're not the first
Who, with best meaning, have incurr'd the worst.
For thee, oppressed king, am I* cast down;
Myself could else out-frown false fortune's frown.—
Shall we not see these daughters and these sisters?
LEAR. No, no, no, no! Come, let's away to prison:
We two alone will sing like birds i' the cage:
When thou dost ask me blessing, I'll kneel down,
And ask of thee forgiveness. So we'll live,
And pray, and sing, and tell old tales, and laugh
At gilded butterflies, and hear poor rogues
Talk of court news; and we'll talk with them too,—
Who loses, and who wins; who's in, who's out;—
And take upon 's the mystery of things,
As if we were God's spies: and we'll wear out,
In a wall'd prison, packs and sects of great ones,
That ebb and flow by the moon.
EDM. Take them away.
LEAR. Upon such sacrifices, my Cordelia,
The gods themselves throw incense. Have I caught thee?
He that parts us shall bring a brand from heaven,
And fire us hence like foxes. Wipe thine eyes;
The goujeers [a] shall devour them, flesh and fell,
Ere they shall make us weep: we'll see 'em starve† first. Come.
[*Exeunt* LEAR *and* CORDELIA, *guarded.*
EDM. Come hither, captain; hark.
Take thou this note; [*Giving a paper.*] go, follow them to prison:
One step I have advanc'd thee; if thou dost
As this instructs thee, thou dost make thy way
To noble fortunes. Know thou this,—that men
Are as the time is: to be tender-minded
Does not become a sword:—thy great employment
Will not bear question; either say thou'lt do't,
Or thrive by other means.
OFF. I'll do't, my lord.
EDM. About it; and write happy when thou hast done.
Mark,—I say, instantly; and carry it so,
As I have set it down.
OFF. I cannot draw a cart,[b] nor eat dried oats;
If it be man's work, I will do 't. [*Exit.*

Flourish. Enter ALBANY, GONERIL, REGAN, Officers, *and* Attendants.

ALB. Sir, you have shown‡ to-day your valiant strain,
And fortune led you well: you have the captives
Who were the opposites of this day's strife:
We* do require them of you, so to use them,
As we shall find their merits and our safety
May equally determine.
EDM. Sir, I thought it fit
To send the old and miserable king
To some retention and appointed guard;†
Whose age has‡ charms in it, whose title more,
To pluck the common bosom on his side,
And turn our impress'd lances in our eyes
Which do command them. With him I sent the queen;
My reason all the same; and they are ready
To-morrow, or at further space, to appear
Where you shall hold your session.[c] At this time,
We sweat, and bleed: the friend hath lost his friend;
And the best quarrels, in the heat, are curs'd
By those that feel their sharpness;—
The question of Cordelia, and her father,
Requires a fitter place.
ALB. Sir, by your patience,
I hold you but a subject of this war,
Not as a brother.
REG. That's as we list to grace him.
Methinks our pleasure might have been demanded,
Ere you had spoke so far. He led our powers;
Bore the commission of my place and person;
The which immediacy may well stand up,
And call itself your brother.
GON. Not so hot:
In his own grace he doth exalt himself,
More than in your addition.
REG. In my rights,
By me invested, he compeers the best.
GON. That were the most, if he should husband you.[d]
REG. Jesters do oft prove prophets.
GON. Holla, holla!
That eye that told you so look'd but a-squint.
REG. Lady, I am not well; else I should answer
From a full-flowing stomach.—General,
Take thou my soldiers, prisoners, patrimony;
Dispose of them, of me; the walls are thine:[e]
Witness the world, that I create thee here
My lord and master.
GON. Mean you to enjoy him?
ALB. The let-alone lies not in your good will.
EDM. Nor in thine, lord.
ALB. Half-blooded fellow, yes.

(*) First folio, *I am.* (†) First folio, *starv'd.* (‡) First folio, *shew'd.*

a *The goujeers shall devour them,*—] The "goujeers," misprinted "good yeares" in the folio, is supposed to mean the *morbus gallicus.* Tieck, however, insists that the "good yeares" of the folio is used ironically for the bad year—the year of pestilence; and like *il mal anno* of the Italians, had been long used as a curse in England.

(*) First folio, *I.* (†) First folio omits, *and appointed guard.* (‡) First folio, *had.*

b I cannot draw a cart,—] The folio omits this speech.
c Where you shall hold your session.] In the folio the speech terminates here.
d That were the most, &c.] In the folio this is assigned to Albany.
e — the walls are thine:] So the folio; the phrase, Warburton says, signifying, *to surrender at discretion.*

REG. Let the drum strike, and prove my title thine. [*To* EDMUND.

ALB. Stay yet; hear reason.—Edmund, I arrest thee
On capital treason; and, in thine attaint,*
This gilded serpent. [*Pointing to* GON.]—For your claim, fair sister,
I bar it in the interest of my wife;
'T is she is sub-contracted to this lord,
And I, her husband, contradict your bans.
If you will marry, make your love† to me,
My lady is bespoke.

GON. An interlude!

ALB. Thou art arm'd, Gloster:—let the trumpet sound:
If none appear to prove upon thy person
Thy heinous, manifest, and many treasons,
There is my pledge; [*Throwing down a glove.*] I'll make it on thy heart,
Ere I taste bread, thou art in nothing less
Than I have here proclaim'd thee!

REG. Sick, O, sick!

GON. [*Aside.*] If not, I'll ne'er trust medicine.

EDM. There's my exchange: [*Throwing down a glove.*] what in the world he is
That names me traitor, villain-like he lies!
Call by thy trumpet: he that dares approach,
On him, on you, who not? I will maintain
My truth and honour firmly.

ALB. A herald, ho!

EDM. A herald, ho, a herald![a]

ALB. Trust to thy single virtue;[b] for thy soldiers,
All levied in my name, have in my name
Took their discharge.

REG. My sickness grows upon me.

ALB. She is not well; convey her to my tent. [*Exit* REGAN, *led.*

Enter a Herald.

Come hither, herald,—let the trumpet sound,—
And read out this.

OFF. Sound, trumpet![c] [*Trumpet sounds.*

Herald *reads.*

If any man of quality or degree within the lists of the army, will maintain upon Edmund, supposed earl of Gloucester, that he is a manifold traitor, let him appear at ‡ the third sound of the trumpet. He is bold in his defence.

EDM. Sound!* [*First trumpet.*

HER. Again. [*Second trumpet.*

HER. Again. [*Third trumpet.*

[*After a pause a trumpet answers without.*

Enter EDGAR, *armed, and preceded by a Trumpet.*

ALB. Ask him his purposes, why he appears
Upon this call o' the trumpet.

HER. What are you?
Your name, your quality? and why you answer
This present summons?

EDG. Know, my name is lost;
By treason's tooth bare-gnawn and canker-bit:
Yet am I noble as the adversary
I come to cope.

ALB. Which is that adversary?

EDG. What's he that speaks for Edmund earl of Gloster?

EDM. Himself:—what say'st thou to him?

EDG. Draw thy sword,
That, if my speech offend a noble heart,
Thy arm may do thee justice: here is mine.
Behold, it is the privilege of mine honours,[d]
My oath, and my profession. I protest,—
Maugre thy strength, youth, place,† and eminence,
Despite ‡ thy victor sword and fire-new fortune,
Thy valour and thy heart,—thou art a traitor!
False to thy gods, thy brother, and thy father;
Conspirant against this high illustrious prince;
And, from the extremest upward of thy head,
To the descent and dust below thy foot,
A most toad-spotted traitor! Say thou, *No!*
This sword, this arm, and my best spirits, are bent
To prove upon thy heart, whereto I speak,
Thou liest.

EDM. In wisdom, I should ask thy name;
But, since thy outside looks so fair and warlike,
And that thy tongue some 'say[e] of breeding breathes,
What safe and nicely I might well delay
By rule of knighthood, I disdain and spurn:
Back do I toss these treasons to thy head;
With the hell-hated lie o'erwhelm thy heart;
Which, for they yet glance by, and scarcely bruise,
This sword of mine shall give them instant way,
Where they shall rest for ever.—Trumpets, speak!
[*Alarums. They fight.* EDMUND *falls.*

ALB. Save him, save him!

GON. This is practice, Gloster;[f]
By the law of arms, thou wast not bound to answer

(*) First folio, *thy arrest.* (†) First folio, *loves.* (‡) First folio, *by.*

a EDM. A herald, ho, a herald!] Omitted in the folio.
b — virtue;] That is, *valour.*
c OFF. Sound, trumpet!] Omitted in the folio.
d *Behold, it is the privilege of* mine honours,—] The quartos read,
"Behold it is the priviledge of *my tongue*
My oath and profession, &c.

(*) First folio omits, *Edm. Sound!*
(†) First folio, *place, youth.* (‡) First folio, *Despise.*

And the folio,—
"Behold, it is *my priviledge,*
The priviledge of mine Honours,
My oath, and my profession," &c.

e — *some* 'say —] *'say* means *assay,=sample,* or *taste.*
f — practice,—] *Stratagem, machination.*

An unknown opposite; thou art not vanquish'd,
But cozen'd and beguil'd.
ALB. Shut your mouth, dame,
Or with this paper shall I stop it.—Hold, sir:
Thou worse than any name, read thine own evil:—
No tearing, lady; I perceive, you know it.
[*Gives the letter to* EDMUND.
GON. Say, if I do;—the laws are mine, not thine:
Who shall arraign me for it? [*Exit.*
ALB. Most monstrous!—
Know'st * thou this paper?
EDM. Ask me not what I know.
ALB. Go after her: she's desperate; govern her.
[*To an* Officer, *who goes out.*
EDM. What you have charg'd me with, that have I done;
And more, much more, the time will bring it out:
'T is past, and so am I.—But what art thou
That hast this fortune on me? If thou'rt noble,
I do forgive thee.
EDG. Let's exchange charity.
I am no less in blood than thou art, Edmund;
If more, the more thou hast wrong'd me.
My name is Edgar, and thy father's son.
The gods are just, and of our pleasant vices
Make instruments to plague us:
The dark and vicious place where thee he got,
Cost him his eyes.
EDM. Thou hast spoken right, 'tis true;
The wheel is come full circle, I am here.
ALB. Methought thy very gait did prophesy
A royal nobleness:—I must embrace thee;
Let sorrow split my heart, if ever I
Did hate thee or thy father!
EDG. Worthy prince, I know 't.
ALB. Where have you hid yourself?
How have you known the miseries of your father?
EDG. By nursing them, my lord.—List a brief tale;—
And, when 'tis told, O, that my heart would burst!—
The bloody proclamation to escape,
That follow'd me so near, (O, our lives' sweetness!
That we the pain of death would hourly die,
Rather than die at once!) taught me to shift
Into a madman's rags; to assume a semblance
That very dogs disdain'd: and in this habit
Met I my father with his bleeding rings,
Their precious stones new lost; became his guide,
Led him, begg'd for him, sav'd him from despair;
Never (O fault!) reveal'd myself unto him,
Until some half-hour past, when I was arm'd;
Not sure, though hoping, of this good success,
I ask'd his blessing, and from first to last
Told him my * pilgrimage: but his flaw'd heart,—
Alack, too weak the conflict to support!—
'Twixt two extremes of passion, joy and grief,
Burst smilingly.
EDM. This speech of yours hath mov'd me,
And shall perchance do good: but speak you on;
You look as you had something more to say.
ALB. If there be more, more woeful, hold it in;
For I am almost ready to dissolve,
Hearing of this.[a]
EDG. This would have seem'd a period
To such as love not sorrow; but another,
To amplify too much, would make much, more,
And top extremity.
Whilst I was big in clamour, came there in a man,
Who, having seen me in my worst estate,
Shunn'd my abhorr'd society; but then, finding
Who 't was that so endur'd, with his strong arms
He fasten'd on my neck, and bellow'd out
As he'd burst heaven; threw him † on my father;
Told the most piteous tale of Lear and him,
That ever ear receiv'd: which in recounting,
His grief grew puissant, and the strings of life
Began to crack: twice then the trumpets sounded,
And there I left him tranc'd.
ALB. But who was this?
EDG. Kent, sir, the banish'd Kent; who in disguise
Follow'd his enemy king, and did him service
Improper for a slave.

Enter a Gentleman *hastily, with a bloody knife.*

GENT. Help! help! O help!
EDG. What kind of help?
ALB. Speak, man.
EDG. What means that ‡ bloody knife?
GENT. 'T is hot, it smokes;
It came even from the heart of—O, she's dead!
ALB. Who dead? speak, man!
GENT. Your lady, sir, your lady: and her sister
By her is poison'd; she hath confess'd it.§
EDM. I was contracted to them both; all three
Now marry in an instant!
EDG. Here comes Kent.
ALB. Produce their bodies, be they alive or dead;
This judgment of the heavens, that makes us tremble,
Touches us not with pity. [*Exit* Gentleman.

(*) First folio, *O, know'st.*

a Hearing of this.] The next three speeches are omitted in the folio.

(*) First folio, *our.* (†) Old text, *me.*
(‡) First folio, *this.*
(§) First folio, *she confesses it.*

Enter KENT.

O! is this he?
The time will not allow the compliment,
Which very manners urges.
KENT. I am come
To bid my king and master aye good night;
Is he not here?
ALB. Great thing of us forgot!—
Speak, Edmund, where's the king? and where's Cordelia?—
[*The bodies of* GONERIL *and* REGAN *are brought in.*
Se'st thou this object, Kent?
KENT. Alack, why thus?
EDM. Yet Edmund was belov'd:
The one the other poison'd for my sake,
And after slew herself.

ALB. Even so.—Cover their faces.

EDM. I pant for life:—some good I mean to do,
Despite of mine own nature.—Quickly send,—
Be brief in it,—to the castle; for my writ
Is on the life of Lear and on Cordelia:—
Nay, send in time.

ALB. Run, run, O, run! [send

EDG. To who, my lord?—Who has the office?
Thy token of reprieve.

EDM. Well thought on;—take my sword,
Give it the captain.

ALB. Haste thee, for thy life. [*Exit* EDGAR.

EDM. He hath commission from thy wife and me
To hang Cordelia in the prison, and
To lay the blame upon her own despair,
That she fordid herself.

ALB. The gods defend her!—Bear him hence awhile. [EDMUND *is borne off.*

Re-enter LEAR, *bearing* CORDELIA *dead in his arms;* EDGAR, Officer, *and others following.*

LEAR. Howl, howl, howl, howl!—O, you are men of stones;
Had I your tongues and eyes, I'd use them so
That heaven's vault should crack.—She's gone for ever!—
I know when one is dead, and when one lives;
She's dead as earth.—Lend me a looking-glass;
If that her breath will mist or stain the stone,
Why, then she lives.

KENT. Is this the promis'd end?

EDG. Or image of that horror?

ALB. Fall, and cease!

LEAR. This feather stirs! she lives! if it be so,
It is a chance which does redeem all sorrows
That ever I have felt.

KENT. O my good master! [*Kneeling.*

LEAR. Pr'ythee, away.

EDG. 'Tis noble Kent, your friend.

LEAR. A plague upon you, murderers, traitors all!
I might have sav'd her; now she's gone for ever!—
Cordelia, Cordelia!—stay a little. Ha!
What is't thou say'st?—Her voice was ever soft,
Gentle, and low;—an excellent thing in woman.—
I kill'd the slave that was a-hanging thee.

OFF. 'Tis true, my lords, he did.

LEAR. Did I not, fellow?
I have seen the day, with my good biting falchion
I would have made them* skip: I am old now,
And these same crosses spoil me.—Who are you?
Mine eyes are not o'the best:—I'll tell you straight.

KENT. If fortune brag of two she lov'd and hated,
One of them we behold.

LEAR. This is a dull sight; are you not Kent?

KENT. The same;
Your servant Kent.—Where is your servant Caius?

LEAR. He's a good fellow, I can tell you that;
He'll strike, and quickly too:—he's dead and rotten.

KENT. No, my good lord; I am the very man;—

LEAR. I'll see that straight.

KENT. That, from your first of difference and decay,
Have follow'd your sad steps.

LEAR. You are welcome hither.

KENT. Nor no man else;—all's cheerless, dark, and deadly.—
Your eldest daughters have fordone themselves,
And desperately are dead.

(*) First folio, *him.*

LEAR. Ay, so I think.

ALB. He knows not what he says; and vain it is*
That we present us to him.

EDG. Very bootless.

Enter an Officer.

OFF. Edmund is dead, my lord.

ALB. That's but a trifle here.—
You lords and noble friends, know our intent,
What comfort to this great decay may come,
Shall be applied: for us, we will resign,
During the life of this old majesty,
To him our absolute power:—you, to your rights;
[*To* EDGAR *and* KENT.
With boot, and such addition as your honours
Have more than merited.—All friends shall taste
The wages of their virtue, and all foes
The cup of their deservings.—O, see, see!

LEAR. And my poor fool is hang'd! No, no, no life!
Why should a dog, a horse, a rat, have life,
And thou no breath at all? Thou'lt come no more,
Never, never, never, never, never!—
Pray you, undo this button: thank you, sir.—
Do you see this? Look on her,—look,—her lips,—
Look there! look there!— [*Dies.*

EDG. He faints!—My lord! my lord!—

KENT. Break, heart, I pr'ythee, break!

EDG. Look up, my lord.

KENT. Vex not his ghost: O, let him pass! he hates him,
That would upon the rack of this tough world
Stretch him out longer.

EDG. He is gone, indeed.

KENT. The wonder is, he hath endur'd so long:
He but usurp'd his life.

ALB. Bear them from hence.—Our present business
Is general woe.—Friends of my soul, you twain
[*To* KENT *and* EDGAR.
Rule in this realm, and the gor'd state sustain.

KENT. I have a journey, sir, shortly to go;
My master calls me;—I must not say, no.

ALB. The weight of this sad time we must obey;
Speak what we feel, not what we ought to say.
The oldest hath borne most: we that are young
Shall never see so much, nor live so long.
[*Exeunt, with a dead march.*

(*) First folio, *is it.*

ILLUSTRATIVE COMMENTS.

ACT I.

(1) SCENE I.—

—— Haply, when I shall wed,
That lord, whose hand must take my plight, shall carry
Half my love with him, half my care, and duty.]

It is not improbable that Cordelia's allusion to her future husband was derived from a story similar to that of Lear, which Camden relates of Ina, King of the West Saxons:—"Ina, King of West Saxons, had three daughters, of whom upon a time he demanded whether they did love him, and so would do during their lives, above all others: the two elder sware deepely they would; the yongest, but the wisest, told her father flatly, without flattery, 'That albeit she did love, honour, and reverence him, and so would whilst shee lived, as much as nature and daughterlie dutie at the uttermost could expect, yet she did think that one day it would come to passe that she should affect another more fervently, meaning her husband, when she were married;' who being made one flesh with her, as God by commandement had told, and nature had taught her, she was to cleave fast to, forsaking father and mother, kiffe and kinne." Or he may have remembered the reply of Cordila, in the "Mirror for Magistrates," 1587:—

"But not content with this, hee asked mee likewise
If I did not him love and honour well.
No cause (quoth I) there is I should your grace despise:
For nature so doth binde and duty mee compell,
To love you, as I ought my father, well.
Yet shortely I may chaunce, if Fortune will,
To finde in heart to beare another more good will."

(2) SCENE IV.—*And to eat no fish.*] "In Queen Elizabeth's time the Papists were esteemed, and with good reason, enemies to the government. Hence the proverbial phrase of, *He's an honest man, and eats no fish;* to signify *he's a friend to the government and a Protestant.* The eating fish, on a religious account, being then esteemed such a badge of popery, that when it was enjoined for a season by act of parliament, for the encouragement of the fish towns, it was thought necessary to declare the reason; hence it was called *Cecil's fast.*"—WARBURTON.

The Act to which Warburton refers was a Statute passed in the fifth year of Elizabeth, 1562, Cap. v. "touching Politick Constitutions for the Maintenance of the Navy," Sect. xiv.—xxiii. The fifteenth section of this Act provides, that any person eating flesh on the usual fish-days, "shall forfeit Three Pound for every time he or they shall offend; or else suffer three months close imprisonment without bail or mainprise." It is probable that the greatest objection to the Act was the order in Sect. xiv.:—"That from the Feast of St. Michael the Archangel, in the Year of our Lord God 1564, *every Wednesday in every week throughout the whole year, which heretofore hath not by the laws or customs of this realm been used and observed as a Fish-day—shall be hereafter observed and kept, as the Saturdays in every week be or ought to be.*" The penal part of this statute was mitigated in 1593, the hirty-fifth of Elizabeth, cap. vii. sect. xxii., to a forfeiture of twenty shillings or one month's imprisonment In the same Act it was provided, that all the Statutes recited in it should continue in force only until the end of the Parliament next ensuing, which met October 24th, 1597, and was dissolved February 9th, in the following year, when they were presumed to have expired. So late, however, as 1655, Izaak Walton, in the second edition of his "Complete Angler," refers to "those very few that are left, that make conscience of the laws of the nation, and of keeping days of abstinence."

(3) SCENE IV.—*If I had a monopoly out, they would have part on't.*] In the sixteenth and seventeenth centuries there were three kinds of privileges issued by the king to individuals, which, from their gross abuse, were felt to be among the most intolerable of popular grievances:—*Pre-Emption* or *Purveyance, Monopolies,* and *Patents.* The first was the royal right of buying provisions and other articles for the king's household, *first,* and in preference to all other customers, and even against the will of the vendors. This was an ancient prerogative, regulated by Magna Charta, and was not finally abrogated until the restoration of Charles II. A *Monopoly* was a privilege "for the sole buying, selling, making, working, or using of any thing; by which other persons are restrained of any freedom or liberty that they had before, or hindered in their lawful trade." These Monopolies had been carried to an outrageous extent in the reigns of Henry VII., Henry VIII., and Queen Elizabeth; and the evil was not much abated at the period when this tragedy was written; nor was it effectually remedied until the passing of the statute of the twenty-first of James, 1623. Warburton supposes that the Fool's remark conveys a satire on the corruption of the courtiers of the time, who were sharers with the patentee, on the strength of having procured his grant from the sovereign; and other commentators would read, instead of "—a monopoly *out,*" "—a monopoly *on't.*" But the real meaning appears to be, that "lords and great men," "and ladies too," were all so determinately bent on playing the fool, that, although the jester might have a monopoly for folly out,—that is, in force, and extant,—yet they would insist upon participating in the exercise of his privilege.

(4) SCENE IV.—*How now, daughter! what makes that frontlet on?*] The *frontlet* was literally, as Malone explains it, a forehead-cloth, formerly worn by ladies at night to render that part of the countenance free from wrinkles. The very remarkable effect of this band, in the contraction of the brows, may be observed in some of the monumental effigies of the fourteenth century, and especially in those small figures usually called "Weepers," which are found standing in tabernacles, on the sides of the rich altar-tombs of the same period. Lear, however, may be supposed to speak metaphorically and to refer only to Goneril's cloudy looks.

ACT II.

(1) SCENE II.—*I'd drive ye cackling home to Camelot.*] So far as there can be any identification of a modern place with an ancient name in old romances, Camelot must be regarded as that mound which Selden has described in his notes on Drayton's "Polyolbion":—"By South Cadbury is that Camelot; a hill of a mile compass at the top; four trenches encircling it; and betwixt every of them an earthen wall: the contents of it within, about twenty acres; full of ruins and reliques of old buildings.—Antique report makes this one of Arthur's places of the Round Table, as the muse here sings:—

> 'Like Camelot what place was ever yet renown'd,
> Where, as at Caerlion oft, he kept the Table Round?'"

Capell has been censured for "a mistaken theory that Camelot is a name for Winchester, one of the places where Arthur held his Round Table;" and that in which the Table itself was supposed to be preserved. The History of King Arthur was, however, so long in the completion, that, while in one chapter (xxvi.) Camelot is located in the West of England (*Somersetshire*); in another (xliv.) it is stated that Sir "Balins sword was put in marble ston, standing upright, as great as a milstone; and the stone hoved alwayes above the water, and did many yeares: and so, by adventure, it swam down the stream to the citie of *Camelot; that is, in English, Winchester.*" At a still later period, when Caxton finished the printing of the "*Mort d'Arthur,*" in 1485, he says of the hero:—"He is more spoken of beyond the sea; more books be made of his noble acts than there be in England: as well in Dutch, Italian, Spanish, and Greekish, as in French. *And yet of record remain, in witness of him in Wales, in the town of Camelot, the great stones, and marvellous works of iron lying under the ground, and royal vaults, which divers now living hath seen.*" Warburton imagines that Kent intended an allusion to some proverbial saying in the romances of Arthur; but this is hardly required for the explanation of the text. In Chapter xlix. of Arthur's History, the Quest of the White Hart is undertaken by three knights, at the wedding-feast of the king with the princess Guenever, which was held at Camelot. This adventure was encountered by Sir Gawayne, Sir Tor, and King Pellinore; and, whenever they had overcome the knights whom they engaged, the vanquished combatants were always sent "unto King Arthur, and yielded them unto his grace."

(2) SCENE III.—*Bedlam beggars.*] The Bedlam beggars proper, were such lunatics as had really been confined in Bethlem Hospital, but, owing to the want of funds to support them there longer, or from their being partially restored to their senses, were dismissed into the world, with a licence to beg. The sympathy excited by these unfortunates, occasioned many sturdy vagabonds to counterfeit and exaggerate their dress and peculiarities. Of these *soi-disant* madmen, who were distinguished among the vast community of rascaldom as *Abraham-Men*, Decker gives an animated description in his "*O per se O,*" 1612, and "The Bell-man of London," 1608:—

"The Abram Cove is a lustie strong Roague, who walketh with a Slade about his Quarrons, (a sheete about his body,) Trining, (hanging) to his hammes, bandelierewise, for all the world as Cutpurses and Theeves weare their sheetes to the Gallowes, in which their Truls are to bury them: oftentimes (because hee scornes to follow any fashions of Hose) he goes without breeches, a cut Jerkin with hanging sleeves (in imitation of our Gallants) but no Sattin or Chamblet elbowes, for both his legges and armes are bare, having no Commission to cover his body, that is to say, no shirt: A face staring like a Sarasin, his hayre long and filthily knotted, for he keepes no Barber: a good Filch (or Staffe) of growne Ash, or else Hazell, in his Famble (in his Hand) and sometimes a sharpe sticke, on which hee hangeth Ruffe-pecke (Bacon). These, walking up and downe the countrey, are more terrible to women and children, then the name of Raw-head and Bloudy-bones, Robin Good-fellow or any other Hobgobling. Crackers, tyed to a Dogges tayle, make not the poore Curre runne faster, then these Abram Ninnies doe the silly Villagers of the Country, so that when they come to any doore a begging, nothing is denyed them.

"*Their Markes.*—Some of these Abrams have the letters E and R upon their armes, some have Crosses, and some other marke, all of them carrying a blew colour; some wear an iron ring, &c. which markes are printed upon their flesh, by tying their arme hard with two strings three or foure inches asunder, and then with a sharpe Awle pricking or raizing the skinne, to such a figure or print as they best fancy, they rub that place with burnt paper * * * * and Gunpowder, which being hard rubd in, and suffered to dry, stickes in the flesh a long time after: when these markes faile, they renew them at pleasure. If you examine how these letters or figures are printed upon their armes, they will tell you it is the *Marke of Bedlam,** but the truth is, they are made as I have reported.

"And to color their villanie the better, every one of these Abrams hath a severall gesture in playing his part: some make an horrid noyse, hollowly sounding: some whoope, some hollow, some shew onely a kind of wilde distracted ugly looke, uttering a simple kinde of Mawnding, with these addition of words (Well and Wisely). Some daunce, (but keepe no measure) others leape up and downe, and fetch gambals; all their actions shew them to be as drunke as Beggers: for not to belye them, what are they but drunken Beggers? All that they begge being either Loure or Bouse (money or drinke).

"*Their Mawnd or Begging.*—The first beginnes; Good Urship, Maister, or good Urships Rulers of this place, bestow your reward on a poore man that hath lyen in *Bedlam without Bishopsgate* three yeeres, four moneths and nine dayes; And bestow one piece of your small silver towards his fees, which he is indebted there, the summe of three poundes, thirteene shillings, seaven pence, halfpenny, (or to such effect) and hath not wherewith to pay the same, but by the good help of Urshipfull and well disposed people, and God to reward them for it.

"The second beginnes: Now Dame, well and wisely: what will you give *poore Tom* now? one pound of your sheepes feathers to make poore Tom a blanket: or one cutting of your Sow side, no bigger than my arme, or one piece of your Salt meate to make poore Tom a sharing home: or one crosse of your small silver towards the buying a paire of Shooes, (well and wisely:) Ah, God blesse my good Dame, (well and wisely) give poore Tom an old sheete to keepe him from the cold, or an old dublet, or Jerkin of my Maisters, God save his life.

"Then will he daunce and sing, or use some other Anticke and ridiculous gesture, shutting up his counterfeite Puppet-play with this Epilogue or Conclusion, Good Dame give poore Tom one cup of the best drinke, (well and wisely) God save the King and his Counsell, and the Governour of this place," &c.—"*O per se O,*" 1612.

In his "Bell-man of London," he says of an *Abraham-Man:* "—he sweares he hath been in Bedlam, and will

* The real TOM O' BEDLAMS, Aubrey tells us, when they were licentiated to go a begging, had on their left arm an armilla, an iron ring for the arm, about four inches long.

talk frantickely of purpose: you see *pinnes* stuck in sundry places of his naked flesh, especially of his *armes*, which paine he gladly puts himselfe to, only to make you believe he is out of his wits. He calls himselfe by the name of *poore Tom*, and comming neere any body cries out *Poore Tom is a-cold*. Of these Abraham-Men some be exceeding merry, and doe nothing but sing songs fashioned out of their own braines; * some will dance, others will doe nothing but laugh or weepe; others are dogged and so sullen both in looke and speech, that, spying but a small companie in a house, they boldly and bluntly enter," &c.

(3) SCENE III.—*Poor Turlygood!*] "Warburton would read *Turlupin*, and Hanmer *Turluru;* but there is a better reason for rejecting both these terms than for preferring either; viz. that *Turlygood* is the *corrupted* word in *our* language. The Turlupins were a fanatical sect that overran France, Italy, and Germany, in the thirteenth and fourteenth centuries. They were at first known by the name of *Beghards*, or *Beghins*, and brethren and sisters of the free spirit. Their manners and appearance exhibited the strongest indications of lunacy and distraction. The common people alone called them *Turlupins;* a name which, though it has excited much doubt and controversy, seems obviously to be connected with the *wolvish howlings*, which these people in all probability would make when influenced by their religious ravings. Their subsequent appellation of *the fraternity of poor men*, might have been the cause why the wandering rogues, called *Bedlam beggars*, and one of whom Edgar personates, assumed or obtained the title of *Turlupins* or *Turlygoods*, especially if their mode of asking alms was accompanied by the gesticulations of madmen. *Turlupino* and *Turluru* are old Italian terms for a fool or madman; and the Flemings had a proverb, *'As unfortunate as Turlupin and his children.'*"—DOUCE.

(4) SCENE IV.—*Hysterica passio.*] The disease, called the *Mother* or *Hysterica Passio*, was not thought peculiar to females only in Shakespeare's time, and Percy thinks it probable that the poet was led to make the poor king pass off the indignant swelling of his heart for this complaint, from a passage in Harsnet's "Declaration of Popish Impostures," which he might have met with when selecting other particulars to furnish his character of Tom of Bedlam. The passage referred to occurs at p. 263, in the deposition of Richard Mainy:—"The disease I spake of was a spice of the *Mother*, wherewith I had beene troubled before my going into Fraunce." In an early part of the pamphlet, p. 25, it is said,—"Ma.: Maynie had a spice of the *Hysterica passio*, as seems from his youth, hee himselfe termes it the *Moother*, and saith that hee was much troubled with it in Fraunce, and that it was one of the causes that mooved him to leave his holy order whereinto he was initiated, and to returne into England."

(5) SCENE IV.—*Do you but mark how this becomes the house.*] Warburton explains "the house" to mean the order of families and duties of relationship; other commentators regard it as signifying a household establishment; and Capell conceives the phrase to imply fathers, as emphatically "*the house*," and not the heads merely of a family, but the especial representatives. Shakespeare, however, more than once, employs the word "house" in a genealogical sense, for the paternal line, or first house, in contradistinction to the persons descended from it, and that may possibly be its import in this instance. See note (6), p. 216, Vol. I.

ACT III.

(1) SCENE IV.—*Hath laid knives under his pillow, and halters in his pew.*] In the temptations to suicide by which Edgar pretends to have been beset by the "foul fiend," Shakespeare seems to have had in view the following passage in Harsnet's "Declaration," † &c.:—

"This examinant further saith, that one Alexander an apothecarie, having brought with him from London to Denham on a time a new halter, and two blades of knives, did leave the same upon the gallerie floare in her Maisters house. The next morning he tooke occasion to goe with this examinant into the said gallerie, where she espying the said halter and blades, asked Ma: Alexander what they did there: Hee making the matter strange, aunswered, that he saw them not, though hee looked fully upon them: she her selfe pointing to them with her finger, where they lay within a yard of them, where they stoode both together. Now (quoth this examinant) doe you not see them? and so taking them up, said, looke you heere: Ah (quoth hee) now I see them indeed, but before I could not see them: And therefore saith he, I perceave that the devil hath layd them heere, to worke some mischiefe upon you, that are possessed.

"¶Hereuppon * * a great search was made in the house, to know how the said halter and knife blades came thether: but it could not in any wise be found out, as it was pretended, till Ma: Mainy in his next fit said, as it was reported, that the devil layd them in the Gallery, that some of those that were possessed, might either hang themselves with the halter, or kil themselves with the blades."—*Examination of Friswood Williams*, p. 219.

The object of the impostures which form the subject of Dr. Harsnet's exposition, Warburton describes as follows:—

"While the Spaniards were preparing their armada against England, the jesuits were here busy at work to promote it, by making converts: one method they employed was to dispossess pretended demoniacks, by which artifice they made several hundred converts among the common people. The principal scene of this farce was laid in the family of one Mr. Edmund Peckham, a Roman-catholick, where Marwood, a servant of Antony Babington's (who was afterwards executed for treason), Trayford, an attendant upon Mr. Peckham, and Sarah and Friswood Williams, and Anne Smith, *three chambermaids* in that family, came into the priests' hands for cure. But the discipline of the patients was so long and severe, and the priests so elate and careless with their success, that the plot was discovered on the confession of the parties concerned, and the contrivers of it deservedly punished."

(2) SCENE IV.—*Wore gloves in my cap.*] Steevens remarks, "It was anciently the custom to wear *gloves* in the hat on three distinct occasions, viz. as the favour of a mistress, the memorial of a friend, and as a mark to be challenged by an enemy. Prince Henry boasts that he *will pluck a glove from the commonest creature*, and fix it in

* See note (*f*), p. 90.

† As the poet was doubtless indebted to this curious work for the names of poor Tom's evil spirits, and it has now become *rarissimus*, we append the exact title of the book, from a copy in the library of the British Museum:—

"A Declaration of egregious Popish Impostures, to withdraw the harts of her Majesties Subjects from their allegeance, and from the truth of Christian Religion professed in England, under the pretence of casting out devils. Practised by Edmunds, alias Weston a Jesuit, and divers Romish priests his wicked associates. Whereunto are annexed the Copies of the Confessions, and Examinations of the parties themselves, which were pretended to be possessed, and dispossessed, taken upon oath before her Majesties Commissioners for causes Ecclesiasticall. At London Printed by James Roberts, dwelling in Barbican 1603."—4to.

his helmet; and Tucca says to Sir Quintilian, in Decker's Satiromastix: '— Thou shalt wear her *glove* in thy worshipful *hat*, like to a leather brooch:' and Pandora, in Lyly's 'Woman in the Moon,' 1597:—

'— he that first presents me with his head,
Shall wear my *glove* in favour for the deed.'

Portia, in her assumed character, asks Bassanio for his *gloves*, which she says she will *wear for his sake:* and King Henry V. gives the pretended *glove* of Alençon to Fluellen, which afterwards occasions his quarrel with the English soldier."

There is an interesting illustration of this practice of gallantry in the life of George Clifford, third Earl of Cumberland, which has been commemorated in the fine portrait of him in the Bodleian Picture Gallery. At an audience with Elizabeth on the return of the earl from one of his voyages, she dropped her glove, which he took up and presented to her on his knee. The queen then desired him to keep it for her sake; and he adorned it richly with diamonds, and wore it ever after in the front of his hat at public ceremonies.

(3) SCENE IV.—
The prince of darkness is a gentleman;
Modo he's call'd, and Mahu.]

If the subjoined extracts from Harsnet's "Declaration" do not prove indisputably that Shakespeare was indebted to that popular book for the titles of Tom o' Bedlam's infernal spirits, we may infer that these fantastic names were quite familiar to an auditory of his time.

"Now that I have acquainted you with the names of the Maister, and his twelve disciples, the names of the places wherein, and the names of the persons upon whom these wonders were shewed: it seemes not incongruent that I relate unto you the names of the devils whom in this glorious pageant they did dispossesse. * *

"First then, to marshall them in as good order, as such disorderly cattell will be brought into, you are to understand, that there were in our possessed 5 Captaines, or Commaunders above the rest: Captaine Pippin, Marwoods devil, Captaine Philpot, Trayfords devil, Captaine *Maho*, Saras devil, Captaine *Modu*, Maynies devill, and Captaine Soforce, Anne Smiths devil. These were not all of equall authoritie, and place, but some had more, some fewer under theyr commaund. * *

"The names of the punie spirits cast out of Trayford were these, Hilco, *Smolkin*, Hillio, Hiaclito, and Lustie huffe-cap: this last seemes some swaggering punie devill, dropt out of a Tinkers budget. * *

"*Modo*, Master Maynies devill, was a graund Commaunder, Muster-maister over the Captaines of the seaven deadly sinnes: Cliton, Bernon, Hilo, Motubizanto, and the rest, himselfe a Generall of a kind and curteous disposition: so saith Sara Williams, touching this devils acquaintance with Mistres Plater, and her sister Fid.

"Sara Williams had in her at a bare word, all the devils in hell. The Exorcist askes *Maho*, Saras devil, what company he had with him, and the devil makes no bones, but tels him in flat termes, *all the devils in hell.* * *

"And if I misse not my markes, this Dictator *Modu* saith, hee had beene in Sara by the space of two yeeres, then so long hell was cleere, and had not a devill to cast at a mad dogge. And sooth I cannot much blame the devils for staying so long abroade, they had taken up an Inne, much sweeter then hell: and an hostesse that wanted neither wit, nor mirth, to give them kind welcome.

"Heere, if you please, you may take a survay of the whole regiment of hell: at least the chiefe Leaders, and officers, as we finde them enrolled by theyr names. First Killico, Hob, and a third *anonymos*, are booked doune for three graund Commaunders, every one having under him 300 attendants. * *

"*Fraterretto, Fliberdigibbet, Hoberdidance*, Tocobatto were foure devils of the round, or Morrice, whom Sara in her fits, tuned together, in measure and sweet cadence. And least you should conceive, that the devils had no musicke in hell, especially that they would go a maying without their musicke, the Fidler comes in with his Taber and Pipe, and a whole Morice after him, with motly visards for theyr better grace. These foure had forty assistants under them, as themselves doe confesse. * *

"*Maho* was generall Dictator of hell; and yet for good manners sake, hee was contented of his good nature to make shew, that himselfe was under the check of *Modu*, the graund devil in Master Maynie. These were all in poore Sara at a chop, with these the poor soule travailed up and doune full two yeeres together; so as during these two yeeres, it had beene all one to say, one is gone to hell, or hee is gone to Sara Williams: for shee poore wench had all hell in her belly."—Chap. X. pp. 45—50.

(4) SCENE IV.—
Fie, foh, and fum,
I smell the blood of a British man.]

A quotation, as Mr. Jameson has shown, in his "Illustrations of Northern Antiquities," p. 397, from an old romance, familiarly known in Shakespeare's day in this country, and still partly preserved in Scotland. The words are those uttered by Rosman, king of Elfland, when *Child Rowland*, in search of his sister, "Burd Ellen," had penetrated to the tower in which she was confined by the fairy emissaries of the Elfland monarch.—

"——— *fi, fi, fo*, and *fum!*
I smell the blood of a Christian man!
Be he dead, be he living, wi' my brand
I'll dash his harns [*brains*] frae his harn-pan."

ACT IV.

(1) SCENE VI.—*That fellow handles his bow like a crow-keeper.*] The office of "crow-keeper" was to fright the crows from the corn and fruit; for this purpose a poor rustic, who, though armed with bow and arrows, was not supposed to have much skill in archery, was sometimes employed, and at others his place was supplied by a stuffed figure, resembling a man, and armed in the same way. Ascham, in his "Toxophilus," when speaking of a lubberly shooter, has a similar comparison to that in the text:—"Another coureth downe and layeth out his buttockes, as thoughe hee should shoote at crowes."

(2) SCENE VI.—*Draw me a clothier's yard.*] That is, an arrow a clothier's yard in length. The ancient "long-bow" was about six feet in length, and the shaft over three. So, in the old ballad of "Chevy-Chace:"—

"An archar off Northomberlonde
Say slean was the lord Persè,
He bar a bende-bow in his hande,
Was made off trusti tre:

An arow, that a *cloth yarde* was lang,
To th' hard stele halyde he;
A dynt, that was both sad and soar,
He sat on Sir Hewe the Mongon-byrry.

The dynt yt was both sad and soar,
That he of Mongon-byrry sete;
The swane-fethars, that his arrowe bar,
With his hart blood the wear wete."

Again, in Drayton's "Polyolbion," song xxvi.:—

"All made of Spanish yew, their bows were wondrous strong;
They not an arrow drew, but was a *cloth-yard* long."

CRITICAL OPINIONS ON KING LEAR.

"Of all Shakspeare's plays, 'Macbeth' is the most rapid, 'Hamlet' the slowest in movement. 'Lear' combines length with rapidity,—like the hurricane and the whirlpool, absorbing while it advances. It begins as a stormy day in summer, with brightness; but that brightness is lurid, and anticipates the tempest.

"It was not without forethought, nor is it without its due significance, that the division of Lear's kingdom is, in the first six lines of the play, stated as a thing already determined in all its particulars, previously to the trial of professions, as the relative rewards of which the daughters were to be made to consider their several portions. The strange, yet by no means unnatural mixture of selfishness, sensibility, and habit of feeling, derived from and fostered by the particular rank and usages of the individual;—the intense desire of being intensely beloved,—selfish, and yet characteristic of the selfishness of a loving and kindly nature alone;—the self-supportless leaning for all pleasure on another's breast;—the craving after sympathy with a prodigal disinterestedness, frustrated by its own ostentation, and the mode and nature of its claims;—the anxiety, the distrust, the jealousy, which more or less accompany all selfish affections, and are amongst the surest contradistinctions of mere fondness from true love, and which originate Lear's eager wish to enjoy his daughters' violent professions, whilst the inveterate habits of sovereignty convert the wish into claim and positive right, and an incompliance with it into crime and treason;—these facts, these passions, these moral verities, on which the whole tragedy is founded, are all prepared for, and will to the retrospect be found implied, in these first four or five lines of the play. They let us know that the trial is but a trick; and that the grossness of the old king's rage is in part the natural result of a silly trick, suddenly and most unexpectedly baffled and disappointed.

"Having thus, in the fewest words, and in a natural reply to as natural a question, which yet answers the secondary purpose of attracting our attention to the difference or diversity between the characters of Cornwall and Albany, provided the premises and *data*, as it were, for our after-insight into the mind and mood of the person whose character, passions, and sufferings are the main subject-matter of the play;—from Lear, the *persona patiens* of his drama, Shakspeare passes without delay to the second in importance, the chief agent and prime mover, and introduces Edmund to our acquaintance, preparing us with the same felicity of judgment, and in the same easy and natural way, for his character in the seemingly casual communication of its origin and occasion. From the first drawing up of the curtain Edmund has stood before us in the united strength and beauty of earliest manhood. Our eyes have been questioning him. Gifted as he is with high advantages of person, and further endowed by nature with a powerful intellect and a strong energetic will, even without any concurrence of circumstances and accident, pride will necessarily be the sin that most easily besets him. But Edmund is also the known and acknowledged son of the princely Gloster: he, therefore, has both the germ of pride, and the conditions best fitted to evolve and ripen it into a predominant feeling. Yet, hitherto, no reason appears why it should be other than the not unusual pride of person, talent, and birth,—a pride auxiliary, if not akin to many virtues, and the natural ally of honourable impulses. But, alas! in his own presence his own father takes shame to himself for the frank avowal that he is his father; he has 'blushed so often to acknowledge him, that he is now brazed to it.' Edmund hears the circumstances of his birth spoken of with a most degrading and licentious levity. * * * This, and the consciousness of its notoriety,—the gnawing conviction that every show of respect is an effort of courtesy, which recalls, while it represses, a contrary feeling;—this is the ever-trickling flow of wormwood and gall into the wounds of pride,—the corrosive *virus* which inoculates pride with a venom not its own,—with envy, hatred, and a lust for that power which, in its blaze of radiance, would hide the dark spots on his disc,—with pangs of shame personally undeserved, and therefore felt as wrongs, and with a blind ferment of vindictive working towards the occasions and causes, especially towards a brother, whose stainless birth and lawful honours were the constant remembrancers of his own debasement, and were ever in the way to prevent all chance of its being unknown, or overlooked and forgotten.

"Kent is, perhaps, the nearest to perfect goodness in all Shakspeare's characters, and yet the most individualized. There is an extraordinary charm in his bluntness, which is that only of a nobleman arising from a contempt of overstrained courtesy; and combined with easy placability where goodness of heart is apparent. His passionate affection for, and fidelity to Lear, act on our feelings in Lear's own favour: virtue itself seems to be in company with him.

"The Steward should be placed in exact antithesis to Kent, as the only character of utter irredeemable baseness in Shakspeare. Even in this the judgment and invention of the poet are very observable; for what else could the willing tool of a Goneril be? Not a vice but this of baseness was left open to him.

"The Fool is no comic buffoon to make the groundlings laugh,—no forced condescension of Shakspeare's genius to the taste of his audience. Accordingly the poet prepares for his introduction, which he never does with any of his common clowns and fools, by bringing him into living connection with the pathos of the play. He is as wonderful a creation as Caliban;—his wild babblings, and inspired idiocy, articulate and guage the horrors of the scene.

"The monster Goneril prepares what is necessary, while the character of Albany renders a still more maddening grievance possible, namely, Regan and Cornwall in perfect sympathy of monstrosity. Not a sentiment, not an image, which can give pleasure on its own account, is admitted; whenever these creatures are introduced, and they are brought forward as little as possible, pure horror reigns throughout.

"Edgar's assumed madness serves the great purpose of taking off part of the shock which would otherwise be caused by the true madness of Lear, and further displays the profound difference between the two. In every attempt at representing madness throughout the whole range of dramatic literature, with the single exception of Lear, it is mere light-headedness, as especially in Otway. In Edgar's ravings, Shakspeare all the while lets you see a fixed purpose, a practical end in view; in Lear's, there is only the brooding of the one anguish, an eddy without progression."—COLERIDGE.

Act V. Sc. 3.

CORIOLANUS.

"THE Tragedy of Coriolanus" appears to have been first printed in the folio of 1623. In the same year, November 8th, it was entered on the Registers of the Stationers' Company by Blount and Jaggard, the publishers of the folio, as one of the copies "not formerly entered to other men." Malone ascribes it to the year 1610; but with the exception of some peculiarities in the style, which would lead us to class it among the poet's latest plays, there is not a particle of evidence, internal or extrinsic, to assist in determining within several years the date of its production. That it was written subsequently to the publication of Camden's "Remains" in 1605 is probable, from the resemblance between the following version of the famous apologue of the members' rebellion against the belly, as told by that author, and the same story in the speech of Menenius, Act I. Sc. 1; for, as Malone remarks, although Shakespeare found this fable in North's Plutarch, there are some expressions, as well as the enumeration of the functions performed by the respective instruments of the body, which he seems to have taken from Camden: *—

"All the members of the body conspired against the stomach, as against the swallowing gulfe of all their labours; for whereas the eies beheld, the eares heard, the handes laboured, the feete travelled, the tongue spake, and all partes performed their functions; onely the stomache lay ydle and consumed all. Hereuppon they joyntly agreed al to forbeare their labours, and to pine away their lazie and publike enemy. One day passed over, the second followed very tedious, but the third day was so greevous to them all, that they called a common counsel. The eyes waxed dimme, the feete could not support the bodie; the armes waxed lazie, the tongue faltered, and could not lay open the matter. Therefore they all with one accord desired the *advice* of the *heart*. There *Reason* layd open before them," &c.

So, Shakespeare:—

"There was a time, when all the body's members
Rebell'd against the belly; thus accus'd it:—
That only *like a gulph* it did remain
I' the midst o' the body, idle and inactive,
Still cupboarding the viand, never bearing

* According to Douce, Camden derived what he has related of the fable from John of Salisbury, who wrote in the reign of Henry the Second, and professes to have received it from Pope Hadrian IV.

Like labour with the rest, where the other instruments
Did *see*, and *hear, devise, instruct, walk, feel,*
And, mutually participate, did minister
Unto the appetite and affection common
Of the whole body. The belly answer'd,—
'True is it, my incorporate friends,' quoth he,
'That I receive the general food at first,—
———— but, if you do remember,
I send it through the rivers of your blood,
Even to the court, *the heart, to the seat o' the brain.'*"

In the several incidents, and in some of the principal speeches of his tragedy, as may be seen from the parallel passages at the end, Shakespeare has faithfully followed "The Life of Caius Martius Coriolanus," in Sir Thomas North's translation of Plutarch; a translation which was rendered from the French of Amyot, Bishop of Auxerre, and was first published in 1579, with the title,—"The Lives of the Noble Grecians and Romanes, compared together by that grave learned Philosopher and Historiographer Plutarke of Chæronea."

Persons Represented.

CAIUS MARCIUS CORIOLANUS, *a noble* Roman.

COMINIUS, } *Generals against the* Volscians.
TITUS LARTIUS, }

SICINIUS VELUTUS, } *Tribunes of the People.*
JUNIUS BRUTUS, }

Young MARCIUS, *Son to* Coriolanus.

MENENIUS AGRIPPA, *Friend to* Coriolanus.

NICANOR.

A Roman Herald.

TULLUS AUFIDIUS, *General of the* Volscians.

Lieutenant *to* Aufidius.

ADRIAN.

Conspirators *with* Aufidius.

A Citizen *of* Antium.

Two Volscian Guards.

VOLUMNIA, *Mother to* Coriolanus.

VIRGILIA, *Wife to* Coriolanus.

VALERIA, *Friend to* Virgilia.

Gentlewoman *attending on* Virgilia.

Roman *and* Volscian *Senators, Patricians, Ædiles, Lictors, Soldiers, Citizens, Messengers, Servants to* Aufidius, *and other Attendants.*

SCENE,—*Partly in* ROME; *and partly in the territories of the* Volscians *and* Antiates.

ACT I.

SCENE I.—Rome. *A Street.*

Enter a Company of mutinous Citizens, *with staves, clubs, and other weapons.*

1 Cit. Before we proceed any further, hear me speak.

Citizens. Speak, speak!

1 Cit. You are all resolved rather to die than to famish?

Citizens. Resolved, resolved!

1 Cit. First, you know Caius Marcius is chief enemy to the people.

Citizens. We know 't, we know 't!

1 CIT. Let us kill him, and we'll have corn at our own price. Is't a verdict?

CITIZENS. No more talking on't; let it be done: away, away!

2 CIT. One word, good citizens.

1 CIT. We are accounted poor citizens; the patricians good.[a] What authority surfeits on would relieve us: if they would yield us but the superfluity, while it were wholesome, we might guess they relieved us humanely; but they think we are too dear: the leanness that afflicts us, the object of our misery, is as an inventory to particularize their abundance; our sufferance is a gain to them.—Let us revenge this with our pikes, ere we become rakes:[b] for the gods know, I speak this in hunger for bread, not in thirst for revenge.

2 CIT. Would you proceed especially against Caius Marcius?

CITIZENS. Against him first: he's a very dog to the commonalty.

2 CIT. Consider you what services he has done for his country?

1 CIT. Very well; and could be content to give him good report for't, but that he pays himself with being proud.

2 CIT. Nay, but speak not maliciously.[c]

1 CIT. I say unto you, what he hath done famously, he did it to that end: though soft-conscienced men can be content to say it was for his country, he did it to please his mother, and to be partly proud;[d] which he is, even to the altitude of his virtue.

2 CIT. What he cannot help in his nature, you account a vice in him. You must in no way say he is covetous.

1 CIT. If I must not, I need not be barren of accusations; he hath faults, with surplus, to tire in repetition. [*Shouts without.*] What shouts are these? The other side o' the city is risen: why stay we prating here? to the Capitol!

CITIZENS. Come, come!

1 CIT. Soft! who comes here?

2 CIT. Worthy Menenius Agrippa; one that hath always loved the people.

1 CIT. He's one honest enough; would, all the rest were so!

Enter MENENIUS AGRIPPA.

MEN. What work's, my countrymen, in hand?
Where go you with bats and clubs? The matter
Speak, I pray you.

1 CIT. Our business is not unknown to the senate;[e] they have had inkling, this fortnight, what we intend to do, which now we'll show 'em in deeds. They say poor suitors have strong breaths; they shall know we have strong arms too.

MEN. Why, masters, my good friends, mine honest neighbours,
Will you undo yourselves?

1 CIT. We cannot, sir, we are undone already.

MEN. I tell you, friends, most charitable care
Have the patricians of you. For your wants,
Your suffering in this dearth, you may as well
Strike at the heaven with your staves, as lift them
Against the Roman state; whose course will on
The way it takes, cracking ten thousand curbs
Of more strong link asunder than can ever
Appear in your impediment: for the dearth,
The gods, not the patricians, make it; and
Your knees to them, not arms, must help. Alack,
You are transported by calamity
Thither where more attends you; and you slander
The helms o' the state, who care for you like fathers,
When you curse them as enemies.

1 CIT. Care for us!—True, indeed, they ne'er cared for us yet. Suffer us to famish, and their store-houses crammed with grain; make edicts for usury, to support usurers;(1) repeal daily any wholesome act established against the rich; and provide more piercing statutes daily, to chain up and restrain the poor. If the wars eat us not up, they will; and there's all the love they bear us.

MEN. Either you must
Confess yourselves wondrous malicious,
Or be accus'd of folly. I shall tell you
A pretty tale; it may be, you have heard it;
But, since it serves my purpose, I will venture
To stale 't[f] a little more.

1 CIT. Well, I'll hear it, sir: yet you must not think to fob off our disgrace with a tale: but, an't please you, deliver.

---

a — *the patricians good.*] *Good* is here used in the commercial sense, of *substance;* as in "The Merchant of Venice," Act I. Sc. 3,—

"Antonio is a *good* man."

b — *ere we become* rakes:] "As lean as a rake" is a very ancient proverb; it is found in Chaucer's Cant. Tales, l. 289,—

"Al so lene was his hors as is a *rake;*"

and Spenser has it in his "Faerie Queene," B. II. c. 11,—

"His body leane and meagre as a *rake.*"

c Nay, but speak not maliciously.] In the old text this speech has the prefix "All" to it, as if spoken by a body of the citizens, but it unquestionably belongs to the second Citizen.

d — to please his mother, and to be partly proud;] This may mean, "—*partly* to please his mother, and *because he was* proud;" but we believe the genuine text would give us, "—and to be *portly* proud."

e Our business is not unknown to the senate;] This and the subsequent speeches of the civic interlocutor, are in the old copy assigned to the *second* Citizen. Capell originally gave them to the first Citizen (though Malone, *more suo*, takes credit for it), and the previous dialogue very clearly shows the necessity of the change.

f *To* stale't *a little more.*] The folio has "To *scale't,*" for which Theobald substituted *stale't*, no doubt the genuine word. See Massinger's "Unnatural Combat," Act IV. Sc. 2,—

——"I'll not *stale* the jest
By my relation,"

and Gifford's note on that passage.

MEN. There was a time, when all the body's members
Rebell'd against the belly; thus accus'd it:—
That only like a gulf it did remain
I' the midst o' the body, idle and unactive,
Still cupboarding the viand, never bearing
Like labour with the rest, where the other instruments
Did see, and hear, devise, instruct, walk, feel,
And, mutually participate, did minister
Unto the appetite and affection common
Of the whole body. The belly answer'd,—

1 CIT. Well, sir, what answer made the belly?

MEN. Sir, I shall tell you.—With a kind of smile,
Which ne'er came from the lungs, but even thus,—
For, look you, I may make the belly smile,
As well as speak,—it tauntingly * replied
To the discontented members, the mutinous parts
That envied his receipt; even so most fitly
As you malign our senators for that
They are not such as you.—

1 CIT. Your belly's answer? What!
The kingly-crowned head, the vigilant eye,
The counsellor heart, the arm our soldier,
Our steed the leg, the tongue our trumpeter,
With other muniments and petty helps
In this our fabric, if that they—

MEN. What then?—
'Fore me, this fellow speaks!—what then? what then?

1 CIT.—Should by the cormorant belly be restrain'd,
Who is the sink o' the body,—

MEN. Well, what then?

1 CIT.—The former agents, if they did complain,
What could the belly answer?

MEN. I will tell you;
If you'll bestow a small (of what you have little)
Patience, a while, you'll† hear the belly's answer.

1 CIT. You're long about it.

MEN. Note me this, good friend;
Your most grave belly was deliberate,
Not rash like his accusers, and thus answered:—
True is it, my incorporate friends, quoth he,
That I receive the general food at first,
Which you do live upon; and fit it is,
Because I am the store-house and the shop
Of the whole body: but, if you do remember,
I send it through the rivers of your blood,
Even to the court, the heart,—to the seat o' the brain;
And, through the cranks and offices of man,
The strongest nerves and small inferior veins,
From me receive that natural competency
Whereby they live: and though that all at once,
You, my good friends,—this says the belly, mark me,—

1 CIT. Ay, sir; well, well.

MEN. *Though all at once cannot*
See what I do deliver out to each,
Yet I can make my audit up, that all
From me do back receive the flour of all,
And leave me but the bran.(2)—What say you to't?

1 CIT. It was an answer: how apply you this?

MEN. The senators of Rome are this good belly,
And you the mutinous members: for, examine
Their counsels and their cares; digest things rightly,
Touching the weal o' the common; you shall find,
No public benefit which you receive,
But it proceeds or comes from them to you,
And no way from yourselves.—What do you think,—
You, the great toe of this assembly?—

1 CIT. I *the great toe!* Why the great toe?

MEN. For that, being one o' the lowest, basest, poorest,
Of this most wise rebellion, thou go'st foremost:
Thou rascal, that art worst in blood to run,[a]
Lead'st first to win some vantage.—
But make you ready your stiff bats and clubs;
Rome and her rats are at the point of battle;
The one side must have bale.—[b]

Enter CAIUS MARCIUS.

Hail, noble Marcius!

MAR. Thanks.—What's the matter, you dissentious rogues,
That, rubbing the poor itch of your opinion,
Make yourselves scabs?

1 CIT. We have ever your good word.

MAR. He that will give good words to thee will flatter
Beneath abhorring.—What would you have, you curs,
That like nor peace nor war? the one affrights you,
The other makes you proud. He that trusts to you,

(*) Old text, *taintingly*. (†) Old text, *you'st*.

a Thou rascal, that art worst in blood to run,
Lead'st first, to win some vantage.]
"Rascal" and "in blood" being ancient terms of the chase, the former applicable to a deer, lean and out of condition, the latter signifying one full of vigour and dangerous to his hunters, Menenius is supposed to mean,—"thou, meagre wretch, least in heart and resolution, art prompt enough to lead when profit points the way." Yet, if nothing better can be extracted from these words in their metaphorical sense, we would rather understand them literally, and believe "worst" to be a misprint, as it might easily be, for *last*. The passage then becomes perfectly intelligible, and in character with the speaker:—

"Thou rascal, that art *last* in blood [that is, *into bloodshed*] to run,
Lead'st first to win some vantage."

b — bale:—] That is, *hurt, injury, calamity*.

Where he should find you lions, finds you hares;
Where foxes, geese: you are no surer, no,
Than is the coal of fire upon the ice,
Or hailstone in the sun. Your virtue is,
To make him worthy whose offence subdues him,
And curse that justice did it. Who deserves greatness,
Deserves your hate; and your affections are
A sick man's appetite, who desires most that
Which would increase his evil. He that depends
Upon your favours, swims with fins of lead,
And hews down oaks with rushes. Hang ye! Trust ye!
With every minute you do change a mind;
And call him noble that was now your hate,
Him vile that was your garland. What's the matter,
That in these several places of the city
You cry against the noble senate, who,
Under the gods, keep you in awe, which else
Would feed on one another?—What's their seeking?

MEN. For corn at their own rates; whereof, they say,
The city is well stor'd.

MAR. Hang 'em! *They say!*
They'll sit by the fire, and presume to know
What's done i' the Capitol; who's like to rise,
Who thrives, and who declines; side factions, and give out
Conjectural marriages; making parties strong,
And feebling such as stand not in their liking
Below their cobbled shoes. They say there's grain enough!
Would the nobility lay aside their ruth,
And let me use my sword, I'd make a quarry [a]

[a] —— *I'd make a* quarry
With thousands of these quarter'd slaves,—]

A "quarry," in the language of the forest, meant a pile of slaughtered game.

With thousands of these quarter'd slaves, as high
As I could pick[a] my lance.

MEN. Nay, these are almost thoroughly persuaded;
For though abundantly they lack discretion,
Yet are they passing cowardly. But, I beseech you,
What says the other troop?

MAR. They are dissolv'd: hang 'em!
They said they were an-hungry; sigh'd forth proverbs,—
That hunger broke stone walls;—that dogs must eat;—
That meat was made for mouths;—that the gods sent not
Corn for the rich men only:—with these shreds
They vented their complainings; which being answer'd,
And a petition granted them, a strange one,
(To break the heart of generosity,[b]
And make bold power look pale) they threw their caps
As they would hang them on the horns o' the moon,
Shouting* their emulation.

MEN. What is granted them?

MAR. Five tribunes to defend their vulgar wisdoms,
Of their own choice: one's Junius Brutus,
Sicinius Velutus, and I know not—'sdeath!
The rabble should have first unroof'd† the city,
Ere so prevail'd with me: it will in time
Win upon power, and throw forth greater themes
For insurrection's arguing.

MEN. This is strange.

MAR. Go, get you home, you fragments!

Enter a Messenger.

MESS. Where's Caius Marcius?

MAR. Here: what's the matter?

MESS. The news is, sir, the Volsces are in arms.

MAR. I am glad on't; then we shall have means to vent
Our musty superfluity.—See, our best elders.

Enter COMINIUS, TITUS LARTIUS, *and other* Senators; JUNIUS BRUTUS *and* SICINIUS VELUTUS.

1 SEN. Marcius, 'tis true that you have lately told us;
The Volsces are in arms.

MAR. They have a leader,
Tullus Aufidius, that will put you to't.
I sin in envying his nobility;
And were I any thing but what I am,
I would wish me only he.

COM. You have fought together.

MAR. Were half to half the world by the ears, and he
Upon my party, I'd revolt, to make
Only my wars with him: he is a lion
That I am proud to hunt.

1 SEN. Then, worthy Marcius,
Attend upon Cominius to these wars.

COM. It is your former promise.

MAR. Sir, it is;
And I am constant.—Titus Lartius,* thou
Shalt see me once more strike at Tullus' face.
What, art thou stiff? stand'st out?

TIT. No, Caius Marcius;
I'll lean upon one crutch, and fight with the other,
Ere stay behind this business.

MEN. O, true bred!

1 SEN. Your company to the Capitol; where, I know,
Our greatest friends attend us.

TIT. Lead you on:
Follow, Cominius; we must follow you;
Right worthy you priority.

COM. Noble Marcius!

1 SEN. Hence! To your homes, be gone! [*To the* Citizens.

MAR. Nay, let them follow:
The Volsces have much corn; take these rats thither,
To gnaw their garners.—Worshipful mutiners,
Your valour puts well forth: pray, follow.

[*Exeunt* Senators, COM. MAR. TIT. *and* MENEN. Citizens *steal away*.

SIC. Was ever man so proud as is this Marcius?

BRU. He has no equal.

SIC. When we were chosen tribunes for the people,—

BRU. Mark'd you his lip, and eyes?

SIC. Nay, but his taunts.

BRU. Being mov'd, he will not spare to gird the gods.

SIC. Be-mock the modest moon.

BRU. The present wars devour him! he is grown
Too proud to be so valiant.[c]

SIC. Such a nature,

(*) Old text, *Shooting*. (†) Old text, *unroo'st*.

(*) Old text, *Lucius*.

a — pick *my lance*.] That is, *pitch* my lance. The word *pick* for *pitch* is in common use still in many parts of England.

b (To break the heart of generosity,—] To crush the privileges of the nobly-born. *Generosity* is used in its primary sense. So "Othello," Act III. Sc. 3:—

"—— the *generous* islanders
By you invited, do attend your presence."

c The present wars devour him! he is grown
Too proud to be so valiant.]
The beginning of this speech, which has been explained,—his pride of military prowess in these wars devours him, we prefer to read, with Warburton, as an imprecation. The latter words appear to import,—He is grown too proud of being so valiant.

Tickled with good success, disdains the shadow
Which he treads on at noon: but I do wonder,
His insolence can brook to be commanded
Under Cominius.

BRU. Fame, at the which he aims,—
In whom already he's well grac'd,—cannot
Better be held, nor more attain'd, than by
A place below the first: for what miscarries
Shall be the general's fault, though he perform
To the utmost of a man; and giddy censure
Will then cry out of Marcius, *O, if he
Had borne the business!*

SIC. Besides, if things go well,
Opinion, that so sticks on Marcius, shall
Of his demerits[a] rob Cominius.

BRU. Come;
Half all Cominius' honours are to Marcius,
Though Marcius earn'd them not; and all his faults
To Marcius shall be honours, though, indeed,
In aught he merit not.

SIC. Let's hence, and hear
How the dispatch is made; and in what fashion,
More than his singularity,[b] he goes
Upon this present action.

BRU. Let's along. [*Exeunt.*

SCENE II.—Corioli. *The Senate-House.*

Enter TULLUS AUFIDIUS, *and certain* Senators.

1 SEN. So, your opinion is, Aufidius,
That they of Rome are enter'd in our counsels,[c]
And know how we proceed.

AUF. Is it not yours?
What ever have been thought on in this state,
That could be brought to bodily act, ere Rome
Had circumvention? 'Tis not four days gone,
Since I heard thence; these are the words:—I think
I have the letter here;—yes, here it is:— [*Reads.*
*They have press'd a power, but it is not known
Whether for east or west: the dearth is great;
The people mutinous: and it is rumour'd,
Cominius, Marcius your old enemy,
(Who is of Rome worse hated than of you)
And Titus Lartius, a most valiant Roman,
These three lead on this preparation
Whither 'tis bent: most likely 'tis for you:
Consider of it.*

1 SEN. Our army's in the field:
We never yet made doubt but Rome was ready
To answer us.

AUF. Nor did you think it folly
To keep your great pretences veil'd, till when
They needs must show themselves; which in the hatching,
It seem'd, appear'd to Rome. By the discovery,
We shall be shorten'd in our aim; which was,
To take in many towns, ere, almost, Rome
Should know we were afoot.

2 SEN. Noble Aufidius,
Take your commission; hie you to your bands;
Let us alone to guard Corioli:[d]
If they set down before's, for the remove
Bring up your army; but, I think, you'll find
They've not prepar'd for us.

AUF. O, doubt not that;
I speak from certainties. Nay, more,
Some parcels of their power are forth already,
And only hitherward. I leave your honours.
If we and Caius Marcius chance to meet,
'Tis sworn between us, we shall ever strike
Till one can do no more.

ALL. The gods assist you!

AUF. And keep your honours safe!

1 SEN. Farewell.

2 SEN. Farewell.

ALL. Farewell. [*Exeunt.*

SCENE III.—Rome. *An Apartment in* Marcius' *House.*

Enter VOLUMNIA *and* VIRGILIA: *they sit down on two low stools, and sew.*

VOL. I pray you, daughter, sing; or express yourself in a more comfortable sort: if my son were my husband, I should freelier rejoice in that absence wherein he won honour, than in the embracements of his bed where he would show most love. When yet he was but tender-bodied, and the only son of my womb; when youth with comeliness plucked all gaze his way; when, for a day of kings' entreaties, a mother should not sell him an hour from her beholding; I,—considering how honour would become such a person; that it was no better than picture-like to hang by the wall, if renown made it not stir,—was pleased to let him seek danger where he was like to find fame. To a cruel war I sent him; from whence he returned, his brows bound with oak.(3) I tell thee, daughter,—I sprang not more in joy at first hearing he was

---

a *Of his* demerits *rob Cominius.*] "Demerits" and *merits* had, of old, the same meaning, that of *deserts.*

b *More than his* singularity,—] As "singularity" formerly implied *pre-eminence,* Sicinius may mean, sarcastically,—after what fashion *beside his usual assumption of superiority.*

c — are enter'd in our counsels,—] Have penetrated into our secrets, or, are informed of our purposes.

d — Corioli;] In the folio this name is spelt "Coriolus," "Corioles," or "Carioles."

a man-child, than now in first seeing he had proved himself a man.

VIR. But had he died in the business, madam,—how then ?

VOL. Then his good report should have been my son; I therein would have found issue. Hear me profess sincerely, had I a dozen sons,—each in my love alike, and none less dear than thine and my good Marcius,—I had rather had eleven die nobly for their country, than one voluptuously surfeit out of action.

Enter a Gentlewoman.

GENT. Madam, the lady Valeria is come to visit you.

VIR. Beseech you, give me leave to retire myself.

VOL. Indeed, you shall not.

Methinks I hear hither your husband's drum;
See him pluck Aufidius down by the hair;
As children from a bear, the Volsces shunning him:
Methinks I see him stamp thus, and call thus,—
Come on, you cowards! you were got in fear,
Though you were born in Rome: his bloody brow
With his mail'd hand then wiping, forth he goes,
Like to a harvest-man, that's task'd to mow
Or all, or lose his hire.

VIR. *His bloody brow!* O, Jupiter, no blood!

VOL. Away, you fool! it more becomes a man
Than gilt his trophy: the breasts of Hecuba,
When she did suckle Hector, look'd not lovelier
Than Hector's forehead when it spit forth blood
At Grecian swords' contending.[a]—Tell Valeria,
We are fit to bid her welcome. [*Exit* Gent.

VIR. Heavens bless my lord from fell Aufidius!

VOL. He'll beat Aufidius' head below his knee,
And tread upon his neck.

---

[a] *At Grecian* swords' contending.] "Contending" is the word in the second folio; the first reads,—

"At Grecian sword. Contenning, tell Valeria," &c.

Mr. Collier's annotator proposes,

"At Grecian swords *contemning*," &c.;

and Mr. W. N. Lettsom,—

"*As* Grecian swords *contemning*."

Enter VALERIA, *attended by an* Usher, *and a* Gentlewoman.

VAL. My ladies both, good day to you.
VOL. Sweet madam.
VIR. I am glad to see your ladyship.
VAL. How do you both? you are manifest house-keepers. What are you sewing here? A fine spot, in good faith.—How does your little son?
VIR. I thank your ladyship; well, good madam.
VOL. He had rather see the swords, and hear a drum, than look upon his school-master.
VAL. O' my word, the father's son: I'll swear, 'tis a very pretty boy. O' my troth, I looked upon him o' Wednesday half an hour together: h'as such a confirmed countenance. I saw him run after a gilded butterfly; and when he caught it, he let it go again; and after it again; and over and over he comes, and up again; catched it again: or[a] whether his fall enraged him, or how 'twas, he did so set his teeth, and tear it; O, I warrant, how he mammocked it.
VOL. One of his father's moods.
VAL. Indeed la, 'tis a noble child.
VIR. A crack,[b] madam.
VAL. Come, lay aside your stitchery; I must have you play the idle huswife with me this afternoon.
VIR. No, good madam; I will not out of doors.
VAL. Not out of doors!
VOL. She shall, she shall.
VIR. Indeed, no, by your patience; I'll not over the threshold till my lord return from the wars.
VAL. Fie, you confine yourself most unreasonably: come, you must go visit the good lady that lies in.
VIR. I will wish her speedy strength, and visit her with my prayers; but I cannot go thither.
VOL. Why, I pray you?
VIR. 'Tis not to save labour, nor that I want love.
VAL. You would be another Penelope: yet, they say, all the yarn she spun in Ulysses' absence, did but fill Ithaca* full of moths. Come; I would your cambric were sensible as your finger, that you might leave pricking it for pity. Come, you shall go with us.
VIR. No, good madam, pardon me; indeed, I will not forth.
VAL. In truth la, go with me; and I'll tell you excellent news of your husband.
VIR. O, good madam, there can be none yet.
VAL. Verily, I do not jest with you; there came news from him last night.
VIR. Indeed, madam?
VAL. In earnest, it's true; I heard a senator speak it. Thus it is:—The Volsces have an army forth; against whom Cominius the general is gone, with one part of our Roman power: your lord and Titus Lartius are set down before their city Corioli; they nothing doubt prevailing, and to make it brief wars. This is true, on mine honour; and so, I pray, go with us.
VIR. Give me excuse, good madam; I will obey you in every thing hereafter.
VOL. Let her alone, lady; as she is now, she will but disease our better mirth.
VAL. In troth, I think, she would.—Fare you well then.—Come, good sweet lady.—Pr'ythee, Virgilia, turn thy solemness out o' door, and go along with us.
VIR. No, at a word, madam; indeed, I must not.
I wish you much mirth.
VAL. Well then, farewell. [*Exeunt.*

SCENE IV.—*Before* Corioli.

Enter, with Drum and Colours, MARCIUS, TITUS LARTIUS, *Officers and Soldiers.*

MAR. Yonder comes news:—a wager they have met.
LART. My horse to yours, no.
MAR. 'Tis done.
LART. Agreed.

Enter a Messenger.

MAR. Say, has our general met the enemy?
MESS. They lie in view, but have not spoke as yet.
LART. So, the good horse is mine.
MAR. I'll buy him of you.
LART. No, I'll nor sell nor give him: lend you him I will,
For half a hundred years.—Summon the town.
MAR. How far off lie these armies?
MESS. Within this mile and half.
MAR. Then shall we hear their 'larum, and they ours.—
Now, Mars, I pr'ythee, make us quick in work,

(*) Old text, *Athica.*

a — or *whether his fall enraged him,*—] *Or,* here, is probably a misprint for *and.*

b *A crack, madam.*] A "crack" is a bold, sharp boy: a *manikin.* The term occurs again in the "Second Part of Henry IV." Act III. Sc. 2:—"I saw him break Skogan's head at the court-gate, when he was a *crack,* not thus high."

That we with smoking swords may march from hence,
To help our fielded friends!—Come, blow thy blast.

They sound a parley. Enter, on the walls, some Senators *and others.*

Tullus Aufidius, is he within your walls?

1 Sen. No, nor a man that fears you less than he,
That's lesser than a little. Hark! our drums [*Drums afar off.*
Are bringing forth our youth! we'll break our walls,
Rather than they shall pound us up: our gates,
Which yet seem shut, we have but pinn'd with rushes;
They'll open of themselves. Hark you, far off! [*Alarum afar off.*
There is Aufidius; list, what work he makes
Amongst your cloven army.

Mar. O, they are at it!

Lart. Their noise be our instruction.—Ladders, ho!

The Volsces *enter and pass over the Stage.*

Mar. They fear us not, but issue forth their city.
Now put your shields before your hearts, and fight
With hearts more proof than shields.—Advance, brave Titus:
They do disdain us much beyond our thoughts,
Which makes me sweat with wrath.—Come on, my fellows;
He that retires, I'll take him for a Volsce,
And he shall feel mine edge.

Alarum, and exeunt Romans *and* Volsces, *fighting. The* Romans *are beaten back to their trenches. Re-enter* Marcius.

Mar. All the contagion of the south light on you,
You shames of Rome! you herd of [a]—Boils and plagues
Plaster you o'er; that you may be abhorr'd
Further than seen, and one infect another
Against the wind a mile! You souls of geese,

a —— you herd of—Boils and plagues
Plaster you o'er;]
The old text has,—
"—— you Heard of Byles and Plagues
Plaister you o're,"
which Mr. Collier's annotator, in utter disregard of the fine rhetorical effect produced by this suppression in the speech, mercilessly alters to,—
"—— *unheard* of boils and plagues
Plaster you o'er."

That bear the shapes of men, how have you run
From slaves that apes would beat! Pluto and hell!
All hurt behind; backs red, and faces pale
With flight and agu'd fear! Mend, and charge home,
Or, by the fires of heaven, I'll leave the foe,
And make my wars on you! look to't: come on;
If you'll stand fast, we'll beat them to their wives,
As they us to our trenches followed.*

Another Alarum. The Volsces *and* Romans *re-enter, and the fight is renewed. The* Volsces *retire into* Corioli, *and* MARCIUS *follows them to the gates.*

So, now the gates are ope:—now prove good seconds:
'Tis for the followers Fortune widens them,
Not for the fliers: (4) mark me, and do the like.
[*Enters the gates.*

1 SOL. Fool-hardiness; not I.
2 SOL. Nor I.
[*The gates are closed.*
3 SOL. See, they have shut him in.
[*Alarum continues.*
ALL. To the pot,[a] I warrant him.

Enter TITUS LARTIUS.

LART. What is become of Marcius?
ALL. Slain, sir, doubtless.
1 SOL. Following the fliers at the very heels,
With them he enters: who, upon the sudden,
Clapp'd-to their gates: he is himself alone,
To answer all the city.
LART. O noble fellow!
Who, sensible, outdares his senseless sword,
And, when it bows, stands up![b] Thou art left, Marcius:
A carbuncle entire, as big as thou art,
Were not so rich a jewel. Thou wast a soldier
Even to Cato's[c] wish, not fierce and terrible
Only in strokes; but, with thy grim looks and
The thunder-like percussion of thy sounds,
Thou mad'st thine enemies shake, as if the world
Were feverous and did tremble.

Re-enter MARCIUS, *bleeding, assaulted by the enemy.*

1 SOL. Look, sir.
LART. O, 'tis Marcius!
Let's fetch him off, or make remain alike.
[*They fight, and all enter the city.*

SCENE V.—*Within* Corioli. *A Street.*

Enter certain Romans, *with spoils.*

1 ROM. This will I carry to Rome.
2 ROM. And I this.
3 ROM. A murrain on't! I took this for silver.
[*Alarum continues afar off.*

Enter MARCIUS *and* TITUS LARTIUS, *with a trumpet.*

MAR. See here these movers, that do prize their hours[d]
At a crack'd dram! Cushions, leaden spoons,
Irons of a doit, doublets that hangmen would
Bury with those that wore them, these base slaves,
Ere yet the fight be done, pack up:—down with them!—
And hark, what noise the general makes!—To him!

(*) First folio, *followes.*

a To the pot, *I warrant him.*] Mr. Collier's annotator reads,—"To the *port*, I warrant him," and Mr. Collier defends the substitution in this wise,—"In the folio, 1623, the letter *r* had dropped out in 'port,' and it was always ridiculously misprinted *pot*,—'To the *pot*, I warrant him.' To what pot? 'To go to pot,' is certainly an old vulgarism, but here it is not 'to pot,' but 'to *the* pot,' as if some particular *pot* were intended." This is strange oblivion. "To *the* pot," as Mr. Collier, better than anyone else, ought to know, was one of the most familiar expressions in our early dramatists. Take only the following examples, from plays which that gentleman must be familiar with:—
"Thou mightest sweare, if I could, I would bring them *to the pot.*"— "New Custome," Act II. Sc. 3.
"For goes this wretch, this traitor, *to the pot.*"
G. PEELE's "Edward I." DYCE's *ed.* p. 115, Vol. I.
"—— they go *to the pot* for't."
WEBSTER's "White Devil," &c. DYCE's *ed.* p. 117, Vol. I.

b *Who*, sensible, *outdares his senseless sword,*
And, when it bows, stands up!]
The old text has,—
"Who *sensibly* ——
—— *stand'st* up."

c —— *Thou wast a soldier*
Even to Cato's *wish*:]
In the old text, "Even to *Calues* wish;" the correction, Theobald's, is established by the relative passage in North's Plutarch:—"But Martius being there [before Corioli] at that time, ronning out of the campe with a fewe men with him, he slue the first enemies he met withall, and made the rest of them staye upon a sodaine, crying out to the Romaines that had turned their backes, and calling them againe to fight with a lowde voice. For he was even such another, as *Cato* would have a souldier and a captaine to be: not only terrible and fierce to laye about him, but to make the enemie afeard with the sounde of his voyce, and grimnes of his countenaunce."

d — *that do prize their* hours—] Pope changed the word "hours" to *honours*, but, as Steevens pointed out, Shakespeare followed his authority, Plutarch.—"The eittie being taken in this sorte, the most parte of the souldiers beganne incontinently to spoyle, to carie away, and to looke up the bootie they had wonne. But Martius was marvelous angry with them, and cried out on them, that it was no *time* now to looke after spoyle, and to ronne stragling here and there to enriche themselves."

There is the man of my soul's hate, Aufidius,
Piercing our Romans: then, valiant Titus, take
Convenient numbers to make good the city;
Whilst I, with those that have the spirit, will haste
To help Cominius.

LART. Worthy sir, thou bleed'st;
Thy exercise hath been too violent for
A second course of fight.

MAR. Sir, praise me not;
My work hath yet not warm'd me: fare you well:
The blood I drop is rather physical
Than dangerous to me: to Aufidius thus
I will appear, and fight.

LART. Now the fair goddess, Fortune,
Fall deep in love with thee; and her great charms
Misguide thy opposers' swords! Bold gentleman,
Prosperity be thy page!

MAR. Thy friend no less,
Than those she placeth highest! So, farewell.

LART. Thou worthiest Marcius!—
[*Exit* MARCIUS.

Go, sound thy trumpet in the market-place;
Call thither all the officers o' the town,
Where they shall know our mind: away! [*Exeunt.*

SCENE VI.—*Near the Camp of* Cominius.

Enter COMINIUS *and Forces, retreating.*

COM. Breathe you, my friends: well fought; we are come off
Like Romans, neither foolish in our stands,
Nor cowardly in retire: believe me, sirs,
We shall be charg'd again. Whiles we have struck,
By interims and conveying gusts we have heard
The charges of our friends.—Ye[a] Roman gods,
Lead their successes as we wish our own,
That both our powers, with smiling fronts encountering,
May give you thankful sacrifice!—

Enter a Messenger.

Thy news?

MESS. The citizens of Corioli have issu'd,

a ——Ye *Roman gods,*—] "The word '*you*' in the last line," Mr. Dyce remarks, "shows that '*the* Roman gods' of the old text, is wrong."

And given to Lartius and to Marcius battle:
I saw our party to their trenches driven,
And then I came away.

COM. Though thou speak'st truth,
Methinks thou speak'st not well. How long is 't since?

MESS. Above an hour, my lord.

COM. 'T is not a mile; briefly we heard their drums:
How couldst thou in a mile confound an hour,
And bring thy news so late?

MESS. Spies of the Volsces
Held me in chase, that I was forc'd to wheel
Three or four miles about; else had I, sir,
Half an hour since brought my report.

COM. Who 's yonder,
That does appear as he were flay'd? O gods!
He has the stamp of Marcius; and I have
Before-time seen him thus.

MAR. [*without.*] Come I too late?

COM. The shepherd knows not thunder from a tabor,
More than I know the sound of Marcius' tongue
From every meaner man.

Enter MARCIUS.

MAR. Come I too late?

COM. Ay, if you come not in the blood of others,
But mantled in your own.

MAR. O! let me clip ye
In arms as sound as when I woo'd; in heart
As merry as when our nuptial day was done,
And tapers burn'd to bedward!

COM. Flower of warriors,
How is 't with Titus Lartius?

MAR. As with a man busied about decrees:
Condemning some to death, and some to exile;
Ransoming him or pitying, threat'ning the other;
Holding Corioli in the name of Rome,
Even like a fawning greyhound in the leash,
To let him slip at will.

COM. Where is that slave
Which told me they had beat you to your trenches?
Where is he? Call him hither.

MAR. Let him alone;
He did inform the truth: but for our gentlemen,
The common file, (a plague!—Tribunes for them!)
The mouse ne'er shunn'd the cat, as they did budge
From rascals worse than they.

COM. But how prevail'd you?

MAR. Will the time serve to tell? I do not think.
Where is the enemy? Are you lords o' the field?
If not, why cease you till you are so?

COM. Marcius, we have at disadvantage fought,
And did retire to win our purpose.

MAR. How lies their battle? Know you on which side
They have plac'd their men of trust?

COM. As I guess, Marcius,
Their bands i' the vaward are the Antiates*
Of their best trust; o'er them Aufidius,
Their very heart of hope.

MAR. I do beseech you,
By all the battles wherein we have fought,
By the blood we have shed together, by the vows
We have made to endure friends, that you directly
Set me against Aufidius and his Antiates:
And that you not delay the present; but,
Filling the air with swords advanc'd and darts,
We prove this very hour.

COM. Though I could wish
You were conducted to a gentle bath,
And balms applied to you, yet dare I never
Deny your asking; take your choice of those
That best can aid your action.

MAR. Those are they
That most are willing.—If any such be here,
(As it were sin to doubt) that love this painting
Wherein you see me smear'd; if any fear
Lesser † his person than an ill report;
If any think brave death outweighs bad life,
And that his country's dearer than himself;
Let him alone, or so many so minded,
Wave thus, [*Waving his sword.*] to express his disposition,
And follow Marcius.

[*They all shout, and wave their swords; take him up in their arms, and cast up their caps.*

O me, alone! make you a sword of me!
If these shows be not outward, which of you
But is four Volsces? none of you but is
Able to bear against the great Aufidius
A shield as hard as his. A certain number,
Though thanks to all, must I select from all;
The rest shall bear the business in some other fight,
As cause will be obey'd. Please you to march;
And four shall quickly draw out my command,
Which men are best inclin'd.

COM. March on, my fellows
Make good this ostentation, and you shall
Divide in all with us. [*Exeunt.*

(*) Old text, *Antients.* (†) Old text, *Lessen.*

SCENE VII.—*The Gates of* Corioli.

TITUS LARTIUS, *having set a guard upon* Corioli, *going with drum and trumpet toward* COMINIUS *and* CAIUS MARCIUS, *enters with a* Lieutenant, *a party of* Soldiers, *and a* Scout.

LART. So, let the ports be guarded: keep your duties,
As I have set them down. If I do send, dispatch
Those centuries to our aid; the rest will serve
For a short holding: if we lose the field,
We cannot keep the town.

LIEU. Fear not our care, sir.

LART. Hence, and shut your gates upon us.—
Our guider, come; to the Roman camp conduct us. [*Exeunt.*

SCENE VIII.—*A Field of Battle between the* Roman *and the* Volscian *Camps.*

Alarum. Enter from opposite sides MARCIUS *and* AUFIDIUS.

MAR. I 'll fight with none but thee; for I do hate thee
Worse than a promise-breaker.

AUF. We hate alike;
Not Afric owns a serpent I abhor
More than thy fame and envy.[a] Fix thy foot.

MAR. Let the first budger die the other's slave,
And the gods doom him after!

AUF. If I fly, Marcius,
Holla me like a hare.

MAR. Within these three hours, Tullus,
Alone I fought in your Corioli walls,
And made what work I pleas'd: 't is not my blood
Wherein thou seest me mask'd; for thy revenge
Wrench up thy power to the highest.

AUF. Wert thou the Hector,
That was the whip of your bragg'd progeny,
Thou shouldst not scape me here.—

[*They fight, and certain* Volsces *come to the aid of* AUFIDIUS.

Officious, and not valiant,—you have sham'd me
In your condemned seconds.

[*Exeunt fighting, driven out by* MARCIUS.

SCENE IX.—*The* Roman *Camp.*

Alarum. A Retreat is sounded. Flourish. Enter at one side, COMINIUS *and* Romans; *at the other side,* MARCIUS, *with his arm in a scarf, and other* Romans.

COM. If I should tell thee o'er this thy day's work,
Thou 'lt not believe thy deeds: but I 'll report it,
Where senators shall mingle tears with smiles;
Where great patricians shall attend, and shrug,
I' the end, admire; where ladies shall be frighted,
And, gladly quak'd, hear more; where the dull tribunes,
That, with the fusty plébeians, hate thine honours,
Shall say, against their hearts,—*We thank the gods,*
Our Rome hath such a soldier!—
Yet cam'st thou to a morsel of this feast,
Having fully din'd before.

Enter TITUS LARTIUS, *with his power, from the pursuit.*

LART. O general,
Here is the steed, we the caparison:
Hadst thou beheld—

MAR. Pray now, no more: my mother,
Who has a charter to extol her blood,
When she does praise me, grieves me. I have done
As you have done,—that's what I can; induc'd
As you have been,—that's for my country:
He that has but effected his good will,
Hath overta'en mine act.

COM. You shall not be
The grave of your deserving; Rome must know
The value of her own: 't were a concealment
Worse than a theft, no less than a traducement,
To hide your doings; and to silence that,
Which, to the spire and top of praises vouch'd,
Would seem but modest: therefore, I beseech you,
(In sign of what you are, not to reward
What you have done,) before our army hear me.

MAR. I have some wounds upon me, and they smart
To hear themselves remember'd.

COM. Should they not,
Well might they fester 'gainst ingratitude,
And tent themselves with death. Of all the horses,
(Whereof we have ta'en good, and good store) of all
The treasure in this field achiev'd and city,
We render you the tenth; to be ta'en forth,
Before the common distribution,
At your only choice.

MAR. I thank you, general;
But cannot make my heart consent to take
A bribe to pay my sword: I do refuse it;
And stand upon my common part with those
That have beheld the doing.

---

[a] Not Afric owns a serpent I abhor
More than thy fame and envy.]
There is probably some corruption in the second line, which would better read,—"More than thy fame *I hate* and envy." So in Plutarch—"Martius knew very well that Tullus did more *malice and envy* him than he did all the Romains besides."

[*A long flourish. They all cry* "MARCIUS! MARCIUS!" *cast up their caps and lances:* COMINIUS *and* LARTIUS *stand bare*

MAR. May these same instruments, which you profane, [shall
Never sound more! when drums and trumpets
I' the field prove flatterers, let courts and cities be
Made all of false-fac'd soothing!
When steel grows soft as the parasite's silk,
Let him be made an overture for the wars![a]
No more, I say! For that I have not wash'd
My nose that bled, or foil'd some debile wretch,—
Which, without note, here 's many else have done,—
You shout * me forth in acclamations hyperbolical;
As if I lov'd my little should be dieted
In praises sauc'd with lies.

COM. Too modest are you;
More cruel to your good report, than grateful
To us that give you truly: by your patience,
If 'gainst yourself you be incens'd, we'll put you
(Like one that means his proper[b] harm) in manacles, [known,
Then reason safely with you.—Therefore, be it
As to us, to all the world, that Caius Marcius
Wears this war's garland: in token of the which,
My noble steed, known to the camp, I give him,
With all his trim belonging; and from this time,
For what he did before Corioli, call him,
With all the applause and clamour of the host,
CAIUS MARCIUS CORIOLANUS! †—Bear
The addition nobly ever!

[*Flourish. Trumpets sound, and drums.*

ALL. Caius Marcius Coriolanus! †

COR. I will go wash;
And when my face is fair, you shall perceive
Whether I blush, or no: howbeit I thank you:—
I mean to stride your steed; and at all times,
To undercrest your good addition
To the fairness of my power.

COM. So, to our tent;
Where, ere we do repose us, we will write
To Rome of our success.—You, Titus Lartius,
Must to Corioli back: send us to Rome
The best, with whom we may articulate,[c]
For their own good and ours.

LART. I shall, my lord.

COR. The gods begin to mock me. I that now
Refus'd most princely gifts, am bound to beg
Of my lord general.

COM. Take it: 'tis yours. What is't?

COR. I sometime lay here in Corioli
At a poor man's house; he us'd me kindly:
He cried to me; I saw him prisoner;
But then Aufidius was within my view,
And wrath o'erwhelm'd my pity: I request you
To give my poor host freedom.

COM. O, well begg'd!
Were he the butcher of my son, he should
Be free as is the wind.—Deliver him, Titus.

LART. Marcius, his name?

COR. By Jupiter! forgot:—
I am weary; yea, my memory is tir'd.—
Have we no wine here?

COM. Go we to our tent:
The blood upon your visage dries; 'tis time
It should be look'd to: come. [*Exeunt.*

SCENE X.—*The Camp of the* Volsces.

A flourish. Cornets. Enter TULLUS AUFIDIUS *bloody, with two or three* Soldiers.

AUF. The town is ta'en!

1 SOL. 'Twill be deliver'd back on good condition.

AUF. *Condition!*—
I would I were a Roman; for I cannot,
Being a Volsce, be that I am.—*Condition!*
What good condition can a treaty find
I' the part that is at mercy?—Five times, Marcius,
I have fought with thee; so often hast thou beat me;
And wouldst do so, I think, should we encounter
As often as we eat.—By the elements,
If e'er again I meet him beard to beard,
He's mine, or I am his! Mine emulation
Hath not that honour in't it had; for where
I thought to crush him in an equal force,
(True sword to sword) I'll potch at him some way,
Or wrath or craft may get him.

1 SOL. He's the devil.

(*) Old text, *shoot*. (†) Old text, *Marcus Caius Coriolanus*.

a
—— when drums and trumpets shall
I' the field prove flatterers, let courts and cities be
Made all of false-fac'd soothing!
When steel grows soft as the parasite's silk,
Let him *be made* an overture *for the wars!*]

In the last line of this much-controverted passage, Warburton proposed,—

"Let *hymns* be made an overture for the wars,"

Tyrwhitt would read,—

"Let *this* [that is, silk] be made a *coverture* for the wars;"

and Mr. Collier's annotator,—

"Let *it* be made *a coverture* for the wars."

If an alteration be absolutely needed, that of "a coverture" for "an overture," understanding "him" to be used for the neuter *it*, is the least objectionable; but we are strongly disposed to think that "overture," if not a misprint for *ovation*, is employed here in the same sense, and that the meaning is,—When steel grows soft as the parasite's silk, let him be made, ***i. e. let there be made for him***, a triumph, as for a successful warrior.

b —*his* proper *harm*)—] His *peculiar* or *personal* harm.

c The best, with whom we may articulate,—] The *chief* personages of Corioli, with whom we may ***enter into articles***.

AUF. Bolder, though not so subtle. My valour's poison'd,
With only suffering stain by him; for him
Shall fly out of itself. Nor sleep nor sanctuary,
Being naked, sick. Nor fane nor Capitol,
The prayers of priests nor times of sacrifice,
Embarquements[a] all of fury, shall lift up
Their rotten privilege and custom 'gainst
My hate to Marcius! Where I find him, were it
At home, upon my brother's guard,[b] even there
Against the hospitable canon, would I
Wash my fierce hand in's heart!—Go you to the city;
Learn how 'tis held; and what they are that must
Be hostages for Rome.

1 SOL. Will not you go?

AUF. I am attended at the cypress grove: I pray you,
('Tis south the city mills) bring me word thither
How the world goes, that to the pace of it
I may spur on my journey.

1 SOL. I shall, sir. [*Exeunt.*

[a] Embarquements—] That is, *embargoes*, or *impediments*.

[b] *At home*, upon my brother's guard,—] At my own house, under the protection of my brother.

ACT II.

SCENE I.—Rome. *A public Place.*

Enter Menenius, Sicinius, *and* Brutus.

Men. The augurer tells me we shall have news to-night.

Bru. Good or bad?

Men. Not according to the prayer of the people, for they love not Marcius.

Sic. Nature teaches beasts to know their friends.

Men. Pray you, who does the wolf love?

Sic. The lamb.

Men. Ay, to devour him; as the hungry plebeians would the noble Marcius.

Bru. He's a lamb indeed, that baes like a bear.

Men. He's a bear, indeed, that lives like a lamb. You two are old men: tell me one thing that I shall ask you.

Both Tri. Well, sir.

Men. In what enormity is Marcius poor in, that you two have not in abundance?

Bru. He's poor in no one fault, but stored with all.

Sic. Especially in pride.

Bru. And topping all others in boasting.

Men. This is strange now: do you two know how you are censured here in the city, I mean of us o' the right-hand file? do you?

Both. Why, how are we censured?

Men. Because you talk of pride now,—will you not be angry?

Both. Well, well, sir, well?

Men. Why, 'tis no great matter; for a very little thief of occasion will rob you of a great deal of patience: give your dispositions the reins, and be angry at your pleasures; at the least, if you take it as a pleasure to you in being so. You blame Marcius for being proud?

Bru. We do it not alone, sir.

Men. I know you can do very little alone, for your helps are many, or else your actions would grow wondrous single: your abilities are too infant-like for doing much alone. You talk of pride: O, that you could turn your eyes toward the napes of your necks, and make but an interior survey of your good selves! O, that you could!

Bru. What then, sir?

MEN. Why, then you should discover a brace of unmeriting, proud, violent, testy magistrates, (*alias* fools) as any in Rome.

SIC. Menenius, you are known well enough too.

MEN. I am known to be a humorous patrician, and one that loves a cup of hot wine with not a drop of allaying Tiber in't; said to be something imperfect in favouring the first complaint; hasty and tinder-like upon too trivial motion;[a] one that converses more with the buttock of the night than with the forehead of the morning. What I think I utter, and spend my malice in my breath. Meeting two such weal's-men as you are, (I cannot call you Lycurguses) if the drink you give me touch my palate adversely, I make a crooked face at it. I cannot* say your worships have delivered the matter well, when I find the ass in compound with the major part of your syllables: and though I must be content to bear with those that say you are reverend grave men, yet they lie deadly that tell you have good faces. If you see this in the map of my microcosm, follows it that I am *known well enough too?* What harm can your bisson † conspectuities glean out of this character, if I be *known well enough too?*

BRU. Come, sir, come, we know you well enough.

MEN. You know neither me, yourselves, nor any thing. You are ambitious for poor knaves' caps and legs: you wear out a good wholesome forenoon in hearing a cause between an orange-wife and a fosset-seller; and then rejourn the controversy of three-pence to a second day of audience. When you are hearing a matter between party and party, if you chance to be pinched with the colic, you make faces like mummers; set up the bloody flag against all patience; and, in roaring for a chamberpot, dismiss the controversy bleeding, the more entangled by your hearing: all the peace you make in their cause is, calling both the parties knaves. You are a pair of strange ones.

BRU. Come, come, you are well understood to be a perfecter giber for the table, than a necessary bencher in the Capitol.

MEN. Our very priests must become mockers, if they shall encounter such ridiculous subjects as you are. When you speak best unto the purpose, it is not worth the wagging of your beards; and your beards deserve not so honourable a grave as to stuff a botcher's cushion, or to be entombed in an ass's pack-saddle. Yet you must be saying, Marcius is proud; who, in a cheap estimation, is worth all your predecessors since Deucalion; though, peradventure, some of the best of 'em were hereditary hangmen. God-den to your worships; more of your conversation would infect my brain, being the herdsmen of the beastly plebeians; I will be bold to take my leave of you.—

[BRUTUS *and* SICINIUS *retire.*

Enter VOLUMNIA, VIRGILIA, *and* VALERIA, *attended.*

How now, my as fair as noble ladies,—and the moon, were she earthly, no nobler,—whither do you follow your eyes so fast?

VOL. Honourable Menenius, my boy Marcius approaches;—for the love of Juno, let's go.

MEN. Ha! Marcius coming home?

VOL. Ay, worthy Menenius; and with most prosperous approbation.

MEN. Take my cap, Jupiter, and I thank thee!—Hoo! Marcius coming home!

VAL. }
VIR. } Nay, 't is true.

VOL. Look, here's a letter from him: the state hath another, his wife another; and I think there's one at home for you.

MEN. I will make my very house reel to-night:—a letter for me?

VIR. Yes, certain, there's a letter for you; I saw it.

MEN. A letter for me! it gives me an estate of seven years' health; in which time I will make a lip at the physician: the most sovereign prescription in Galen is but empiricutic,[b] and, to this preservative, of no better report than a horse-drench.—Is he not wounded? he was wont to come home wounded.

VIR. O, no, no, no!

VOL. O, he is wounded,—I thank the gods for't.

MEN. So do I too, if it be not too much:—brings 'a victory in his pocket?—the wounds become him.

(*) Old text, *can*, corrected by Theobald.
(†) Old text, *beesome*, corrected by Theobald.

a *I am known to be a humorous patrician, and one that loves a cup of hot wine with not a drop of allaying Tiber in't; said to be something imperfect in favouring* the first complaint; *hasty and tinder-like upon too trivial motion;*] The pose in this passage is the expression, "the first complaint." What is "the first complaint"? At one time we conceived the sprightly, warm-hearted old senator, among his other failings, "cried out of women," and referred to what Ben Jonson as obscurely terms "the primitive work of darkness" ("The Devil is an Ass," Act II. Sc. 2); but what militates against this supposition, and the wonderfully acute emendation of Mr. Collier's annotator,—"the *thirst* complaint," also is the doubt whether "complaint" obtained the sense of *malady* or *ailment* until many years after these plays were written. If it did not bear this meaning in Shakespeare's day, the only explanation of "something imperfect, in favouring the first complaint," appears to be that he was too apt to be led away by first impressions; to act rather upon impulse than from reflection.

b —empericutic,—] In the old text, "Emperickqutique," which Pope altered to "emperic," and for which Mr. Collier's annotator substitutes, "empiric physic."

VOL. On's brows, Menenius, he comes the third time home with the oaken garland.

MEN. Has he disciplined Aufidius soundly?

VOL. Titus Lartius writes,—they fought together, but Aufidius got off.

MEN. And 'twas time for him too, I'll warrant him that: an he had stayed by him, I would not have been so 'fidiused for all the chests in Corioli, and the gold that's in them. Is the senate possessed of this?

VOL. Good ladies, let's go.—Yes, yes, yes; the senate has letters from the general, wherein he gives my son the whole name of the war: he hath in this action outdone his former deeds doubly.

VAL. In troth, there's wondrous things spoke of him.

MEN. Wondrous! ay, I warrant you, and not without his true purchasing.

VIR. The gods grant them true!

VOL. True! pow, wow.

MEN. True! I'll be sworn they are true.—Where is he wounded?—[*To the* Tribunes.] God save your good worships! Marcius is coming home: he has more cause to be proud.—Where is he wounded?

VOL. I' the shoulder and i' the left arm: there will be large cicatrices to show the people, when he shall stand for his place. He received in the repulse of Tarquin seven hurts i' the body.

MEN. One i' the neck, and two i' the thigh,—there's nine that I know.

VOL. He had, before this last expedition, twenty-five wounds upon him.

MEN. Now it's twenty-seven: every gash was an enemy's grave. [*A shout and flourish.*] Hark! the trumpets.

VOL. These are the ushers of Marcius: before him
He carries noise, and behind him he leaves tears:
Death, that dark spirit, in's nervy arm doth lie;
Which, being advanc'd, declines; and then men die.

A Sennet. Trumpets sound. Enter COMINIUS *and* TITUS LARTIUS; *between them,* CORIOLANUS, *crowned with an oaken garland; with* Captains, Soldiers, *and a* Herald.

HER. Know, Rome, that all alone Marcius did fight
Within Corioli' gates; where he hath won,
With fame, a name to Caius Marcius; * these
In honour follows, *Coriolanus*:—*
Welcome to Rome, renowned Coriolanus! [*Flourish.*

ALL. Welcome to Rome, renowned Coriolanus!

COR. No more of this, it does offend my heart;
Pray now, no more.

COM. Look, sir, your mother!

COR. O,
You have, I know, petition'd all the gods
For my prosperity! [*Kneels.*

VOL. Nay, my good soldier, up;
My gentle Marcius, worthy Caius, and
By deed-achieving honour newly nam'd,—
What is it?—*Coriolanus* must I call thee?
But O, thy wife!—

COR. My gracious silence, hail!
Wouldst thou have laugh'd had I come coffin'd home,
That weep'st to see me triumph? Ah, my dear,
Such eyes the widows in Corioli wear,
And mothers that lack sons.

MEN. Now, the gods crown thee!

COR. And live you yet?—O my sweet lady, pardon. [*To* VALERIA.

VOL. I know not where to turn:—O, welcome home;—
And welcome, general;—and ye're welcome all.

MEN. A hundred thousand welcomes:—I could weep,
And I could laugh; I am light and heavy:—welcome:
A curse begin at very root on's heart,
That is not glad to see thee!—You are three,
That Rome should dote on: yet, by the faith of men,
We have some old crab-trees here at home, that [will not
Be grafted to your relish. Yet welcome, warriors:
We call a nettle but a nettle; and
The faults of fools, but folly.

COM. Ever right.

COR. Menenius, ever, ever.

HER. Give way there, and go on!

COR. Your hand, and yours: [*To* VIRG. *and* VOLUM.
Ere in our own house I do shade my head,
The good patricians must be visited;
From whom I have receiv'd not only greetings,
But with them change[a] of honours.

VOL. I have liv'd
To see inherited my very wishes,
And the buildings of my fancy:
Only there's one thing wanting, which I doubt not,
But our Rome will cast upon thee.

(*) Old text, *Martius Caius.*

(*) Old text, *Martius Caius Coriolanus.*

a — change *of honours.*] *Change* of honours, in the sense of additional honours, may be right, though we incline to Theobald's substitution, "*charge* of honours."

COR. Know, good mother,
I had rather be their servant in my way,
Than sway with them in theirs.
COM. On, to the Capitol!
[*Flourish. Cornets. Exeunt in state, as before. The* Tribunes *remain.*

BRU. All tongues speak of him, and the bleared sights
Are spectacled to see him: your prattling nurse
Into a rapture lets her baby cry,
While she chats him:[a] the kitchen malkin[b] pins
Her richest lockram[c] 'bout her reechy neck,

a *Into a* rapture *lets her baby cry,*
While she chats *him:*]

By "rapture" is meant *fit*. So, in "The Hospital for London's Follies," 1602, as quoted by Steevens:—"Your darling will weep itself into a *rapture*, if you take not good heed." The word "chats," in the next line, is changed to "cheers" by Mr. Collier's annotator, and to "claps" by Mr. Singer: if any alteration is desirable, "*shouts*" would perhaps be more suitable than either "cheers" or "claps." Thus, in Act I. Sc. 9, Coriolanus remonstrates,—

"——— You *shout* me forth
In acclamations hyperbolical."

b — Malkin —] See note (d), p. 213, Vol. II.

c — lockram] Lockram appears to have been a sort of cheap, coarse linen.

Clambering the walls to eye him: stalls, bulks, windows,
Are smother'd up, leads fill'd, and ridges hors'd
With variable complexions; all agreeing
In earnestness to see him: seld-shown flamens[a]
Do press among the popular throngs, and puff
To win a vulgar station: our veil'd dames
Commit the war of white and damask, in
Their nicely-gawded cheeks, to the wanton spoil
Of Phœbus' burning kisses: such a pother,
As if that whatsoever god who leads him,
Were slily crept into his human powers,
And gave him graceful posture.

SIC. On the sudden,
I warrant him consul.

BRU. Then our office may,
During his power, go sleep.

SIC. He cannot temperately transport his honours
From where he should begin and end; but will
Lose those he hath won.

BRU. In that there's comfort.

SIC. Doubt not
The commoners, for whom we stand, but they,
Upon their ancient malice, will forget,
With the least cause, these his new honours;
Which that he'll give them, make I as little question
As he is proud to do't.

BRU. I heard him swear,
Were he to stand for consul, never would he
Appear i' the market-place, nor on him put
The napless* vesture of humility;
Nor, showing (as the manner is) his wounds
To the people, beg their stinking breaths.

SIC. 'T is right.

BRU. It was his word: O, he would miss it, rather
Than carry it but by the suit of the gentry to him,
And the desire of the nobles.

SIC. I wish no better,
Than have him hold that purpose, and to put it
In execution.

BRU. 'T is most like, he will.

SIC. It shall be to him, then, as our good wills,[b]
A sure destruction.

BRU. So it must fall out
To him or our authorities. For an end,
We must suggest the people in what hatred
He still hath held them; that to's power he would
Have made them mules, silenc'd their pleaders,
And dispropertied their freedoms: holding them,
In human action and capacity,
Of no more soul nor fitness for the world,
Than camels in their war; who have their provand
Only for bearing burdens, and sore blows
For sinking under them.

SIC. This, as you say, suggested
At some time when his soaring insolence
Shall reach[c] the people, (which time shall not want,
If he be put upon 't; and that's as easy,
As to set dogs on sheep) will be his fire
To kindle their dry stubble; and their blaze
Shall darken him for ever.

Enter a Messenger.

BRU. What 's the matter?

MESS. You are sent for to the Capitol.
'T is thought that Marcius shall be consul:
I have seen the dumb men throng to see him,
And the blind to hear him speak: matrons flung gloves,
Ladies and maids their scarfs and handkerchief,
Upon him as he pass'd: the nobles bended,
As to Jove's statue; and the commons made
A shower and thunder, with their caps and shouts:
I never saw the like.

BRU. Let's to the Capitol;
And carry with us ears and eyes for the time,
But hearts for the event.

SIC. Have with you. [*Exeunt.*

SCENE II.—*The same. The* Capitol.

Enter two Officers, *to lay cushions.*

1 OFF. Come, come, they are almost here. How many stand for consulships?

2 OFF. Three, they say: but 't is thought of every one, Coriolanus will carry it.

1 OFF. That 's a brave fellow; but he 's vengeance proud, and loves not the common people.

2 OFF. Faith, there have been many great men that have flattered the people, who ne'er loved them; and there be many that they have loved, they know not wherefore: so that, if they love they know not why, they hate upon no better a ground: therefore, for Coriolanus neither to care whether they love or hate him, manifests the true knowledge he has in their disposition;

(*) Old text, *Naples*.

a — seld-shown flamens—] Priests *seldom* visible.

b — as our good wills,—] That is, as our profit requires.

c *Shall* reach *the people*,—] In the old text, "*teach* the People." The correction is Theobald's. Mr. Knight suggested, "Shall *touch* the people," which is equally probable and good.

and, out of his noble carelessness, lets them plainly see 't.

1 OFF. If he did not care whether he had their love or no, he waved indifferently 'twixt doing them neither good nor harm; but he seeks their hate with greater devotion than they can render it him; and leaves nothing undone that may fully discover him their opposite. Now, to seem to affect the malice and displeasure of the people, is as bad as that which he dislikes,—to flatter them for their love.

2 OFF. He hath deserved worthily of his country; and his ascent is not by such easy degrees as those who, having been supple and courteous to the people, bonneted,[a] without any further deed to heave[b] them at all into their estimation and report: but he hath so planted his honours in their eyes, and his actions in their hearts, that for their tongues to be silent, and not confess so much, were a kind of ingrateful injury; to report otherwise, were a malice, that, giving itself the lie, would pluck reproof and rebuke from every ear that heard it.

1 OFF. No more of him; he 's a worthy man: make way, they are coming.

A Sennet. Enter, with Lictors *before them,* COMINIUS *the* Consul, MENENIUS, CORIOLANUS, *many other* Senators, SICINIUS *and* BRUTUS. *The* Senators *take their places; the* Tribunes *take theirs also by themselves.*

MEN. Having determined of the Volsces,
And to send for Titus Lartius, it remains,
As the main point of this our after-meeting,
To gratify his noble service that hath
Thus stood for his country: therefore, please you,
Most reverend and grave elders, to desire
The present consul, and last general
In our well-found successes, to report
A little of that worthy work perform'd
By Caius Marcius Coriolanus;* whom
We meet † here, both to thank, and to remember
With honours like himself.

1 SEN. Speak, good Cominius:
Leave nothing out for length, and make us think
Rather our state 's defective for requital,
Than we to stretch it out.—Masters o' the people,
We do request your kindest ears; and, after,
Your loving motion toward the common body,
To yield what passes here.

a — bonneted,—] This is accepted as meaning, took off the cap, as in "Othello," Act I. Sc. 1, we have,—"Oft *capp'd* to him;" but it may signify,—invested with the badge of consular dignity.

(*) Old text, *Martius Caius,* &c. (†) Old text, *met.*

b — *to* heave *them*—] Pope's emendation; the old text reading, "to *have* them," &c.

SIC. We are convented
Upon a pleasing treaty; and have hearts
Inclinable to honour and advance
The theme of our assembly.
BRU. Which the rather
We shall be bless'd to do, if he remember
A kinder value of the people than
He hath hereto priz'd them at.
MEN. That 's off, that 's off;[a]
I would you rather had been silent. Please you
To hear Cominius speak?
BRU. Most willingly:
But yet my caution was more pertinent,
Than the rebuke you give it.
MEN. He loves your people;
But tie him not to be their bedfellow.—
Worthy Cominius, speak.—
[CORIOLANUS *rises, and offers to go away.*
Nay, keep your place.
1 SEN. Sit, Coriolanus; never shame to hear
What you have nobly done.
COR. Your honours' pardon;
I had rather have my wounds to heal again,
Than hear say how I got them.
BRU. Sir, I hope
My words dis-bench'd you not.
COR. No, sir: yet oft,
When blows have made me stay, I fled from words.
You sooth'd not, therefore hurt not: but your [people,
I love them as they weigh.
MEN. Pray now, sit down.
COR. I had rather have one scratch my head i' the sun
When the alarum were struck, than idly sit
To hear my nothings monster'd.
[*Exit.*
MEN. Masters of the people,
Your multiplying spawn how can he flatter,
(That's thousand to one good one) when you now see,
He had rather venture all his limbs for honour
Than one on 's* ears to hear it?—Proceed, Cominius.
COM. I shall lack voice: the deeds of Corio- [lanus
Should not be utter'd feebly.—It is held,
That valour is the chiefest virtue,
And most dignifies the haver: if it be,
The man I speak of cannot in the world
Be singly counterpois'd. At sixteen years,
When Tarquin made a head for Rome, he fought
Beyond the mark of others: our then dictator,
Whom with all praise I point at, saw him fight,
When with his Amazonian chin† he drove
The bristled lips before him: he bestrid
An o'er-press'd Roman, and i' the consul's view
Slew three opposers: Tarquin's self he met,
And struck him on his knee: in that day's feats
When he might act the woman in the scene,
He prov'd best man i' the field, and for his meed
Was brow-bound with the oak. His pupil-age
Man-enter'd thus, he waxed like a sea;
And, in the brunt of seventeen battles since,
He lurch'd all swords of the garland.[b] For this last,
Before and in Corioli, let me say,
I cannot speak him home: he stopp'd the fliers;
And by his rare example made the coward
Turn terror into sport: as weeds before
A vessel under sail, so men obey'd,
And fell below his stem: his sword, Death's stamp,
Where it did mark, it took; from face to foot
He was a thing of blood, whose every motion
Was tim'd with dying cries: alone he enter'd
The mortal gate of the city, which he painted
With shunless destiny; aidless came off,
And with a sudden re-enforcement struck
Corioli like a planet: now all's his;
When by and by the din of war 'gan pierce
His ready sense; then straight his doubled spirit
Re-quicken'd what in flesh was fatigate,
And to the battle came he; where he did
Run reeking o'er the lives of men, as if
'T were a perpetual spoil: and, till we call'd
Both field and city ours, he never stood
To ease his breast with panting.
MEN. Worthy man!
1 SEN. He cannot but with measure fit the honours
Which we devise him.
COM. Our spoils he kick'd at;
And look'd upon things precious, as they were
The common muck of the world: he covets less
Than misery itself would give; rewards
His deeds with doing them; and is content
To spend the time to end it.
MEN. He's right noble:
Let him be call'd for.
1 SEN. Call Coriolanus.
OFF. He doth appear.

Re-enter CORIOLANUS.

MEN. The senate, Coriolanus, are well pleas'd
To make thee consul.

(*) Old text, *on ones.*

(†) Old text, *Shinne.*

a That's off, that's off;] That's out of the way, not called for.

b *He* lurch'd *all swords of the garland.*] A *lurch* at cards signifies an easy victory. To lurch all swords of the garland meant then, as Malone expresses it,—"to gain from all other warriors the wreath of victory, with ease, and incontestable superiority."

COR. I do owe them still
My life and services.

MEN. It then remains,
That you do speak to the people.

COR. I do beseech you,
Let me o'er-leap that custom; for I cannot
Put on the gown, stand naked, and entreat them,
For my wounds' sake, to give their sufferage:
Please you, that I may pass this doing.

SIC. Sir, the people
Must have their voices; neither will they bate
One jot of ceremony.

MEN. Put them not to't:—
Pray you, go fit you to the custom;
And take to you, as your predecessors have,
Your honour with your form.

COR. It is a part
That I shall blush in acting, and might well
Be taken from the people.

BRU. Mark you that?

COR. To brag unto them,—thus I did, and thus;—
Show them the unaching scars which I should hide,
As if I had receiv'd them for the hire
Of their breath only!—

MEN. Do not stand upon't.—
We recommend to you, tribunes of the people,
Our purpose to them;—and to our noble consul
Wish we all joy and honour.

SEN. To Coriolanus come all joy and honour!

[*Flourish. Exeunt all except* SICINIUS *and* BRUTUS.

BRU. You see how he intends to use the people.

SIC. May they perceive's intent! He will require them,
As if he did contemn what he requested
Should be in them to give.

BRU. Come, we'll inform them
Of our proceedings here: on the market-place,
I know, they do attend us. [*Exeunt.*

SCENE III.—*The Same. The* Forum.

Enter several Citizens.

1 CIT. Once,[a] if he do require our voices, we ought not to deny him.

2 CIT. We may, sir, if we will.

3 CIT. We have power in ourselves to do it, but it is a power that we have no power to do; for if he show us his wounds, and tell us his deeds, we are to put our tongues into those wounds, and speak for them; so, if he tell us his noble deeds, we must also tell him our noble acceptance of them. Ingratitude is monstrous; and for the multitude to be ingrateful, were to make a monster of the multitude; of the which we being members, should bring ourselves to be monstrous members.

1 CIT. And to make us no better thought of, a little help will serve; for once we stood up about the corn, he himself stuck not to call us—the many-headed multitude.

3 CIT. We have been called so of many; not that our heads are some brown, some black, some auburn,* some bald, but that our wits are so diversely coloured: and truly I think, if all our wits were to issue out of one skull, they would fly east, west, north, south; and their consent of one direct way should be at once to all the points o'the compass.

2 CIT. Think you so? which way do you judge my wit would fly?

3 CIT. Nay, your wit will not so soon out as another man's will,—'tis strongly wedged up in a block-head: but if it were at liberty, 'twould, sure, southward.

2 CIT. Why that way?

3 CIT. To lose itself in a fog; where being three parts melted away with rotten dews, the fourth would return for conscience sake, to help to get thee a wife.

2 CIT. You are never without your tricks:—you may, you may.[b]

3 CIT. Are you all resolved to give your voices? But that's no matter, the greater part carries it. I say, if he would incline to the people, there was never a worthier man.—Here he comes, and in the gown of humility: mark his behaviour. We are not to stay all together, but to come by him where he stands, by ones, by twos, and by threes. He's to make his requests by particulars; wherein every one of us has a single honour, in giving him our own voices with our own tongues: therefore follow me, and I'll direct you how you shall go by him.

ALL. Content, content. [*Exeunt.*

Enter CORIOLANUS *and* MENENIUS.

MEN. O, sir, you are not right: have you not known
The worthiest men have done't?

COR. What must I say?—
I pray, sir,—Plague upon't! I cannot bring
My tongue to such a pace:——*Look, sir;*——*my wounds;*—

---

a Once,—] See note (a), p. 128, Vol. I.

b You may, you may.] This colloquialism, which, like another, sometimes heard at this day, in answer to idle badinage, "Go it, go it," appears to mean,—you have full liberty to divert yourself, occurs again in "Troilus and Cressida," Act III. Sc. 2:—

"HEL. By my troth, sweet lord, thou hast a fine forehead.
PAN. Ay, *you may, you may.*"

(*) Old text, *Abram.*

I got them in my country's service, when
Some certain of your brethren roar'd, and ran
From the noise of our own drums.

MEN. O me, the gods!
You must not speak of that: you must desire them
To think upon you.

COR. Think upon me? hang 'em!
I would they would forget me, like the virtues
Which our divines lose by 'em.

MEN. You'll mar all:
I'll leave you. Pray you, speak to 'em, I pray you,
In wholesome manner.

COR. Bid them wash their faces,
And keep their teeth clean?— [*Exit* MENENIUS.

a — *two* Citizens.] The old direction says, "Enter *three* of the Citizens," but wrongly.

Enter two Citizens.[a]

So, here comes a brace.—
You know the cause, sir, of my standing here.

1 CIT. We do, sir; tell us what hath brought you to't.

COR. Mine own desert.

2 CIT. Your own desert?

COR. Ay, not* mine own desire.

1 CIT. How! not your own desire?

COR. No, sir: 'twas never my desire yet, to trouble the poor with begging.

1 CIT. You must think, if we give you anything, we hope to gain by you.

(*) Old text, *but*.

COR. Well then, I pray, your price o' the consulship?

1 CIT. The price is, to ask it kindly.

COR. Kindly! Sir, I pray, let me ha't: I have wounds to show you, which shall be yours in private.—Your good voice, sir; what say you?

2 CIT. You shall ha't, worthy sir.

COR. A match, sir? [a]—There's in all two worthy voices begged:—I have your alms; adieu.

1 CIT. But this is something odd.

2 CIT. An 'twere to give again,—but 'tis no matter. [*Exeunt the two* Citizens.

Re-enter two other Citizens.

COR. Pray you now, if it may stand with the tune of your voices that I may be consul, I have here the customary gown.

1 CIT. You have deserved nobly of your country, and you have not deserved nobly.

COR. Your enigma?

1 CIT. You have been a scourge to her enemies, you have been a rod to her friends; you have not, indeed, loved the common people.

COR. You should account me the more virtuous, that I have not been common in my love. I will, sir, flatter my sworn brother, the people, to earn a dearer estimation of them; 'tis a condition they account gentle: and since the wisdom of their choice is rather to have my hat than my heart, I will practise the insinuating nod, and be off to them most counterfeitly; that is, sir, I will counterfeit the bewitchment of some popular man, and give it bountiful to the desirers. Therefore, beseech you, I may be consul.

2 CIT. We hope to find you our friend; and therefore give you our voices heartily.

1 CIT. You have received many wounds for your country.

COR. I will not seal your knowledge with showing them. I will make much of your voices, and so trouble you no farther.

BOTH CIT. The gods give you joy, sir, heartily! [*Exeunt.*

COR. Most sweet voices!—
Better it is to die, better to starve,
Than crave the hire* which first we do deserve.
Why in this woolvish gown [b] should I stand here,
To beg of Hob and Dick, that do† appear,
Their needless vouches? Custom calls me to't:—
What custom wills, in all things should we do't,
The dust on antique time would lie unswept,
And mountainous error be too highly heap'd
For truth to over-peer.—Rather than fool it so,
Let the high office and the honour go
To one that would do thus.—I am half through;
The one part suffer'd, the other will I do.—
Here come more voices,—

Enter three other Citizens.

Your voices! for your voices I have fought;
Watch'd for your voices; for your voices bear
Of wounds two dozen odd; battles thrice six
I have seen, and heard of; for your voices have
Done many things, some less, some more:
Your voices! Indeed, I would be consul.

1 CIT. He has done nobly, and cannot go without any honest man's voice.

2 CIT. Therefore let him be consul: the gods give him joy, and make him good friend to the people!

ALL. Amen, amen.——God save thee, noble consul! [*Exeunt* Citizens.

COR. Worthy voices!

Re-enter MENENIUS, *with* BRUTUS *and* SICINIUS.

MEN. You have stood your limitation;
And the tribunes endue you with the people's voice:
Remains that, in the official marks invested,
You anon do meet the senate.

COR. Is this done?

SIC. The custom of request you have discharg'd:
The people do admit you; and are summon'd
To meet anon, upon your approbation.

COR. Where? at the senate-house?

SIC. There, Coriolanus.

COR. May I change these garments?

SIC. You may, sir.

COR. That I'll straight do; and, knowing myself again,
Repair to the senate-house.

MEN. I'll keep you company.—Will you along?

BRU. We stay here for the people.

SIC. Fare you well.

[*Exeunt* CORIOL. *and* MENEN.

He has it now; and by his looks, methinks,
'Tis warm at 's heart.

(*) Old text, *higher*. (†) Old text, *does*.

a A match, sir?] The meaning, we take to be this: Coriolanus having won the voice of one citizen, turns to the other with the inquiry, Will you match it? and then proceeds,—"There's in all *two* worthy voices begged:" &c.

b — woolvish gown—] This is the lection of the second folio; the first has, "woolvish *tongue*," which has been emendated into "woolvish *togue*;" "*foolish toge*," and "*woolless togue*;" the last a suggestion of Mr. Collier's indefatigable annotator; but the passage appears still open to controversy. Possibly, after all that has been written about it, the term "woolvish" may have been intended to apply to the mob, and not to the vestment, and the genuine reading be, "wolfish *throng*."

BRU. With a proud heart he wore his humble weeds.
Will you dismiss the people?

Re-enter Citizens.

SIC. How now, my masters? have you chose this man?
1 CIT. He has our voices, sir.
BRU. We pray the gods, he may deserve your loves.
2 CIT. Amen, sir:—to my poor unworthy notice,
He mock'd us when he begg'd our voices.
3 CIT. Certainly,
He flouted us down-right.
1 CIT. No, 'tis his kind of speech,—he did not mock us.
2 CIT. Not one amongst us, save yourself, but says
He us'd us scornfully: he should have show'd us
His marks of merit, wounds receiv'd for 's country.

SIC. Why, so he did, I am sure.
CITIZENS. No, no; no man saw 'em.
3 CIT. He said he had wounds, which he could show in private;
And with his hat, thus waving it in scorn,
I would be consul, says he: *aged custom,*
But by your voices, will not so permit me;
Your voices therefore: when we granted that,
Here was,—*I thank you for your voices,—thank you,—*
Your most sweet voices:—now you have left your voices,
I have no further with you:—was not this mockery?
SIC. Why, either were you ignorant to see't,
Or, seeing it, of such childish friendliness
To yield your voices?
BRU. Could you not have told him,
As you were lesson'd,—when he had no power,
But was a petty servant to the state,
He was your enemy; ever spake against
Your liberties, and the charters that you bear
I' the body of the weal: and now, arriving

A place of potency, and sway o' the state,
If he should still malignantly remain
Fast foe to the plebeii, your voices might
Be curses to yourselves? You should have said,
That as his worthy deeds did claim no less
Than what he stood for, so his gracious nature
Would think upon you for your voices,
And translate his malice towards you into love,
Standing your friendly lord.

SIC. Thus to have said,
As you were fore-advis'd, had touch'd his spirit
And tried his inclination; from him pluck'd
Either his gracious promise, which you might,
As cause had call'd you up, have held him to;
Or else it would have gall'd his surly nature,
Which easily endures not article
Tying him to aught; so, putting him to rage,
You should have ta'en the advantage of his choler,
And pass'd him unelected.

BRU. Did you perceive,
He did solicit you in free contempt,
When he did need your loves; and do you think
That his contempt shall not be bruising to you,
When he hath power to crush? Why, had your bodies
No heart among you? or had you tongues to cry
Against the rectorship of judgment?

SIC. Have you, ere now, denied the asker?
And now again, of him that did not ask, but mock,
Bestow your su'd-for tongues?

3 CIT. He's not confirm'd; we may deny him yet.

2 CIT. And will deny him:
I'll have five hundred voices of that sound.

1 CIT. I twice five hundred, and their friends to piece 'em.

BRU. Get you hence instantly; and tell those friends,—
They have chose a consul, that will from them take
Their liberties; make them of no more voice
Than dogs, that are as often beat for barking,
As therefore kept to do so.

SIC. Let them assemble;
And, on a safer judgment, all revoke
Your ignorant election: enforce his pride,
And his old hate unto you: besides, forget not
With what contempt he wore the humble weed;
How in his suit he scorn'd you: but your loves,
Thinking upon his services, took from you
The apprehension of his present portance,
Which most gibingly, ungravely, he did fashion
After the inveterate hate he bears you.

BRU. Lay a fault on us, your tribunes;
That we labour'd (no impediment between)
But that you must cast your election on him.

SIC. Say, you chose him more after our commandment,
Than as guided by your own true affections; and that,
Your minds, pre-occupied with what you rather must do,
Than what you should, made you against the grain
To voice him consul: lay the fault on us.

BRU. Ay, spare us not. Say we read lectures to you
How youngly he began to serve his country,
How long continued; and what stock he springs of,—
The noble house o' the Marcians; from whence came
That Ancus Marcius, Numa's daughter's son,
Who, after great Hostilius, here was king;
Of the same house Publius and Quintus were,
That our best water brought by conduits hither;
[And Censorinus, darling of the people,] (1)
And nobly nam'd so, twice being censor,
Was his great ancestor.

SIC. One thus descended,
That hath beside well in his person wrought
To be set high in place, we did commend
To your remembrances: but you have found,
Scaling his present bearing with his past,
That he's your fixed enemy, and revoke
Your sudden approbation.

BRU. Say, you ne'er had done't,
(Harp on that still) but by our putting on:[a]
And presently, when you have drawn your number,
Repair to the Capitol.

CITIZENS. We will so: almost all repent in their election. [*Exeunt Citizens.*

BRU. Let them go on;
This mutiny were better put in hazard,
Than stay, past doubt, for greater:
If, as his nature is, he fall in rage
With their refusal, both observe and answer
The vantage of his anger.

SIC. To the Capitol:
Come; we'll be there before the stream o' the people;
And this shall seem, as partly 'tis, their own,
Which we have goaded onward. [*Exeunt.*

---

[a] — our putting on:] Our *incitation*, or *provoking*.

ACT III.

SCENE I.—*The same. A Street.*

Cornets. Enter CORIOLANUS, MENENIUS, COMINIUS, TITUS LARTIUS, Senators, *and* Patricians.

COR. Tullus Aufidius, then, had made new head?

LART. He had, my lord; and that it was [which caus'd
Our swifter composition.

COR. So, then, the Volsces stand but as at first;
Ready, when time shall prompt them, to make road
Upon's again.

COM. They are worn, lord consul, so,
That we shall hardly in our ages see
Their banners wave again.

COR. Saw you Aufidius?

LART. On safe-guard he came to me; and did curse
Against the Volsces, for they had so vilely
Yielded the town: he is retir'd to Antium.

COR. Spoke he of me?

LART. He did, my lord.

COR. How? what?

LART. How often he had met you, sword to sword:
That of all things upon the earth he hated
Your person most; that he would pawn his fortunes
To hopeless restitution, so he might
Be call'd your vanquisher.

COR. At Antium lives he?

LART. At Antium.

COR. I wish I had a cause to seek him there,
To oppose his hatred fully.—Welcome home.
[*To* LARTIUS.

Enter SICINIUS, *and* BRUTUS.

Behold, these are the tribunes of the people,
The tongues o' the common mouth: I do despise them;
For they do prank them in authority,
Against all noble sufferance.
SIC. Pass no further!
COR. Ha! what is that?
BRU. It will be dangerous to go on: no further!
COR. What makes this change?
MEN. The matter?
COM. Hath he not pass'd the noble, and the common?
BRU. Cominius, no.
COR. Have I had children's voices?
1 SEN. Tribunes, give way; he shall to the market-place.
BRU. The people are incens'd against him.
SIC. Stop!
Or all will fall in broil.
COR. Are these your herd?—
Must these have voices, that can yield them now,
And straight disclaim their tongues?—What are your offices?
You being their mouths, why rule you not their teeth?
Have you not set them on?
MEN. Be calm, be calm.
COR. It is a purpos'd thing, and grows by plot,
To curb the will of the nobility:—
Suffer't, and live with such as cannot rule,
Nor ever will be rul'd.
BRU. Call't not a plot:
The people cry you mock'd them; and of late,
When corn was given them gratis, you repin'd;
Scandal'd the suppliants for the people,—call'd them
Time-pleasers, flatterers, foes to nobleness.
COR. Why, this was known before.
BRU. Not to them all.
COR. Have you inform'd them sithence?
BRU. How! I inform them!
COR.* You are like to do such business.
BRU. Not unlike,
Each way, to better yours.
COR. Why, then, should I be consul? By yond clouds,
Let me deserve so ill as you, and make me
Your fellow tribune.
SIC. You show too much of that
For which the people stir: if you will pass
To where you are bound, you must enquire your way,
Which you are out of, with a gentler spirit;
Or never be so noble as a consul,
Nor yoke with him for tribune.
MEN. Let's be calm.
COM. The people are abus'd.—Set on.—This paltering
Becomes not Rome; nor has Coriolanus
Deserv'd this so dishonour'd rub, laid falsely
I' the plain way of his merit.
COR. Tell me of corn!
This was my speech, and I will speak't again,—
MEN. Not now, not now.
1 SEN. Not in this heat, sir, now.
COR. Now, as I live, I will.—My nobler friends,
I crave their pardons:—
For the mutable, rank-scented many,
Let them regard me as I do not flatter,
And therein behold themselves: I say again,
In soothing them, we nourish 'gainst our senate
The cockle of rebellion, insolence, sedition,
Which we ourselves have plough'd for, sow'd and scatter'd,
By mingling them with us, the honour'd number;
Who lack not virtue, no, nor power, but that
Which they have given to beggars.
MEN. Well, no more.
1 SEN. No more words, we beseech you.
COR. How! no more?
As for my country I have shed my blood,
Not fearing outward force, so shall my lungs
Coin words till their decay against those meazels,
Which we disdain should tetter us, yet sought
The very way to catch them.
BRU. You speak o' the people, as if you were a god
To punish, not a man of their infirmity.
SIC. 'Twere well, we let the people know't.
MEN. What, what? his choler?
COR. Choler! Were I as patient as the midnight sleep,
By Jove, 't would be my mind!
SIC. It is a mind
That shall remain a poison where it is,
Not poison any further.
COR. *Shall* remain—
Hear you this Triton of the minnows? mark you
His absolute *shall?*
COM. 'Twas from the canon.
COR. *Shall!*
O, good,† but most unwise patricians, why!
You grave, but reckless senators, have you thus
Given Hydra here[a] to choose an officer,
That with his peremptory *shall*, being but

(*) Old text, *Com.*
(†) Old text, *O God!*

[a] *Given Hydra here*—] Mr. Collier's annotator reads,— "Given Hydra *leave*," &c.

The horn and noise o' the monster,[a] wants not spirit
To say he'll turn your current in a ditch,
And make your channel his? If he have power,
Then vail your ignorance;[b] if none, awake
Your dangerous lenity.[c] If you are learn'd,
Be not as common[d] fools; if you are not,
Let them have cushions by you. You are plebeians,
If they be senators; and they are no less,
When, both your voices blended, the great'st taste
Most palates theirs. They choose their magistrate;
And such a one as he, who puts his *shall*,
His popular *shall*, against a graver bench
Than ever frown'd in Greece! By Jove himself,
It makes the consuls base! and my soul aches
To know, when two authorities are up,
Neither supreme, how soon confusion
May enter 'twixt the gap of both, and take
The one by t'other.

COM. Well,—on to the market-place.

COR. Whoever gave that counsel, to give forth
The corn o' the storehouse gratis, as 'twas us'd
Sometime in Greece,—

MEN. Well, well, no more of that.

COR. Though there the people had more absolute power,—
I say, they nourish'd disobedience,
Fed the ruin of the state.

BRU. Why, shall the people give
One that speaks thus their voice?

COR. I'll give my reasons,
More worthier than their voices. They know the corn
Was not our recompense, resting well assur'd
They ne'er did service for't: being press'd to the war,
Even when the navel of the state was touch'd,
They would not thread the gates;—this kind of service
Did not deserve corn gratis: being i' the war
Their mutinies and revolts, wherein they show'd
Most valour, spoke not for them: the accusation
Which they have often made against the senate,
All cause unborn, could never be the motive*
Of our so frank donation; well, what then?
How shall this bisson multitude[e] digest
The senate's courtesy? Let deeds express
What's like to be their words:—*We did request it;*
We are the greater poll, and in true fear
They gave us our demands:—thus we debase
The nature of our seats, and make the rabble
Call our cares fears; which will in time break ope
The locks o' the senate, and bring in the crows
To peck the eagles.—(1)

MEN. Come, enough.

BRU. Enough, with over-measure.

COR. No, take more:
What may be sworn by, both divine and human,
Seal what I end withal!—This double worship,—
Where one part does disdain with cause, the other
Insult without all reason; where gentry, title, wisdom,
Cannot conclude but by the yea and no
Of general ignorance,—it must omit
Real necessities, and give way the while
To unstable slightness: purpose so barr'd, it follows,
Nothing is done to purpose. Therefore, beseech you,—
You that will be less fearful than discreet;
That love the fundamental part of state,
More than you doubt the change on't; that prefer
A noble life before a long, and wish
To jump[f] a body with a dangerous physic
That's sure of death without it,—at once pluck out
The multitudinous tongue; let them not lick
The sweet which is their poison: your dishonour
Mangles true judgment, and bereaves the state
Of that integrity which should become't;
Not having the power to do the good it would,
For the ill which doth control it.

---

[a] The horn and noise o' the monster,—] In the old text, "monsters." The correction was made by Capell, and also by Mr. Collier's annotator.

[b] *If he have power,*
Then vail your ignorance;]

For "*ignorance*," Mr. Collier's annotator has "*impotence*," but *to vail* means *to lower*, and Coriolanus would hardly call upon his brother patricians *to lower* their *impotence*. The genuine word was far more probably *signorie*, or *signories*, *i.e. senatorial dignity, magistracy, sway*, &c.

[c] ——— *if none*, awake
Your dangerous lenity.]

Mr. Collier's annotator would change this to,

"——— *revoke*
Your dangerous *bounty*;"

an emendation, however clever, of very questionable propriety; for "lenity" in this place does not, perhaps, mean mildness, but *lentitude, inactivity, supineness.* So, in Plutarch's life of Coriolanus;—"For he [Marcius] alledged, that the creditors losing their money they had lost, was not the worst thing; but that the *lenity* [*i.e.* the inaction of the people when summoned to resist the enemy] was favoured, was a beginning of disobedience," &c.

[d] — as common fools;] Does not the next line,—"Let *them* have cushions," &c. instruct us to read,— "*commons*' fools"?

[e] *How shall this* bisson multitude, &c.] Notwithstanding what has been said, and much more that might be said, in support of the old reading, "bosom multiplied," as meaning, *many-stomached*, we accept this emendation of Mr. Collier's annotator, as an almost certain restoration of the poet's text.

[f] To jump *a body with a dangerous physic*—] So the old text, and so Steevens and Malone, who explain "jump" as *risk* or *hazard*. Pope's emendation is "vamp," and he is followed, among others, by Mr. Dyce and Mr. Knight. Mr, Singer reads "imp." We have not presumed to change the ancient text, but have little doubt that "To *jump*" is a misprint, and the true lection,—

"To *purge* a body with a dangerous physic," &c.

Thus in "Macbeth," Act V. Sc. 2.:—

"Meet we the medicine of the sickly weal;
And with him pour we, in our country's *purge*,
Each drop of us."

Again, in the same play, Act V. Sc. 3:—

"——— my land, find her disease
And *purge* it to a sound and pristine health."

So also, in Ben Jonson's "Catiline," Act III. Sc. 1.:—
"—— who with fire must *purge* sick Rome," &c.

(*) Old text, *native*, *corrected by Mason.*

BRU. H'as said enough.
SIC. H'as spoken like a traitor, and shall answer
As traitors do.
COR. Thou wretch, despite o'erwhelm thee!—
What should the people do with these bald tribunes?
On whom depending, their obedience fails
To the greater bench: in a rebellion,
When what's not meet, but what must be, was law,
Then were they chosen; in a better hour,
Let what is meet be said it must be meet,
And throw their power i' the dust.
BRU. Manifest treason!
SIC. This a consul? no.
BRU. The ædiles, ho!—Let him be apprehended.
SIC. Go, call the people;—[*Exit* BRUTUS.] in whose name, myself
Attach thee, as a traitorous innovator,
A foe to the public weal: obey, I charge thee,
And follow to thine answer.
COR. Hence, old goat!
SEN. AND PAT. We'll surety him.
COM. Ag'd sir, hands off.
COR. Hence, rotten thing! or I shall shake thy bones
Out of thy garments.
SIC. Help, ye citizens!

Re-enter BRUTUS, *with the* Ædiles, *and a rabble of* Citizens.

MEN. On both sides more respect.
SIC. Here's he, that would take from you all your power.
BRU. Seize him, Ædiles!
CITIZENS. Down with him! down with him!
2 SEN. Weapons, weapons, weapons!
[*They all bustle about* CORIOLANUS.
Tribunes, patricians, citizens!—what ho!—
Sicinius, Brutus, Coriolanus, citizens!
CITIZENS. Peace, peace, peace! stay, hold, peace!
MEN. What is about to be?—I am out of breath;
Confusion's near;—I cannot speak.—You, tribunes
To the people,—Coriolanus, patience:—
Speak, good Sicinius.
SIC. Hear me, people;—peace!
CITIZENS. Let's hear our tribune:—peace! Speak, speak, speak!
SIC. You are at point to lose your liberties:
Marcius would have all from you; Marcius,
Whom late you have nam'd for consul.
MEN. Fie, fie, fie!
This is the way to kindle, not to quench.
1 SEN. To unbuild the city, and to lay all flat.
SIC. What is the city, but the people?
CITIZENS. True,
The people are the city.
BRU. By the consent of all, we were establish'd
The people's magistrates.
CITIZENS. You so remain.
MEN. And so are like to do.
COM. That is the way to lay the city flat;[a]
To bring the roof to the foundation,
And bury all, which yet distinctly ranges,
In heaps and piles of ruin.
SIC. This deserves death.
BRU. Or let us stand to our authority,
Or let us lose it.—We do here pronounce,
Upon the part o' the people, in whose power
We were elected theirs, Marcius is worthy
Of present death.
SIC. Therefore, lay hold of him;
Bear him to the rock Tarpeian, and from thence
Into destruction cast him!
BRU. Ædiles, seize him!
CITIZENS. Yield, Marcius, yield!
MEN. Hear me one word.
Beseech you, tribunes, hear me but a word.
ÆDI. Peace, peace!
MEN. Be that you seem, truly your country's [friend,
And temperately proceed to what you would
Thus violently redress.
BRU. Sir, those cold ways,
That seem like prudent helps, are very poisonous
Where the disease is violent.—Lay hands upon him,
And bear him to the rock!
COR. No; I'll die here.
[*Drawing his sword.*
There's some among you have beheld me fighting;
Come, try upon yourselves what you have seen me.
MEN. Down with that sword!—Tribunes, withdraw awhile.
BRU. Lay hands upon him!
MEN. Help Marcius, help,
You that be noble! help him, young and old!
CITIZENS. Down with him, down with him!
[*In this mutiny, the* Tribunes, *the* Ædiles, *and the* People, *are beat out.*
MEN. Go, get you to your house; be gone, away!—
All will be nought else.
2 SEN. Get you gone.

---

[a] That is the way to lay the city flat;] It is usual, though in opposition to the old copies, to assign this speech to Coriolanus, on account of what Sicinius says immediately after it,—
"—— This deserves death."
But the speech is not at all characteristic of Coriolanus; and the observation of the Tribune refers to what he had previously spoken,—
"Marcius would have all from you," &c.

COR.* Stand fast;
We have as many friends as enemies.
MEN. Shall it be put to that?
1 SEN. The gods forbid!
I pr'ythee, noble friend, home to thy house;
Leave us to cure this cause.
MEN. For 'tis a sore upon us,
You cannot tent yourself: begone, 'beseech you.
COM. Come, sir, along with us.[a]
COR. I would they were barbarians, (as they are,
Though in Rome litter'd) not Romans, (as they are not,
Though calv'd i' the porch o' the Capitol)—
MEN. Be gone;
Put not your worthy rage into your tongue;
One time will owe another.
COR. On fair ground, I could beat forty of them.
MEN. I could myself take up a brace o' the best of them; yea, the two tribunes.
COM. But now 'tis odds beyond arithmetic;
And manhood is call'd foolery, when it stands
Against a falling fabric.—Will you hence,
Before the tag return? whose rage doth rend
Like interrupted waters, and o'erbear
What they are us'd to bear.
MEN. Pray you, be gone:
I'll try whether my old wit be in request
With those that have but little: this must be patch'd
With cloth of any colour.
COM. Nay, come away.
[*Exeunt* CORIOLANUS, COMINIUS, *and others.*
1 PAT. This man has marr'd his fortune.
MEN. His nature is too noble for the world:
He would not flatter Neptune for his trident,
Or Jove for's power to thunder. His heart's his mouth:
What his breast forges, that his tongue must vent;
And, being angry, does forget that ever
He heard the name of death. [*A noise without.*
Here's goodly work!
2 PAT. I would they were a-bed!
MEN. I would they were in Tiber!—What, the vengeance,
Could he not speak 'em fair?

Re-enter BRUTUS *and* SICINIUS, *with the rabble.*

SIC. Where is this viper,
That would depopulate the city,
And be every man himself?
MEN. You worthy tribunes,—
SIC. He shall be thrown down the Tarpeian rock.
With rigorous hands he hath resisted law,
And therefore law shall scorn him further trial
Than the severity of the public power,
Which he so sets at nought.
1 CIT. He shall well know,
The noble tribunes are the people's mouths,
And we their hands.
CITIZENS. He shall, sure on't.
[*Several speak together.*
MEN. Sir, sir,—
SIC. Peace!
MEN. Do not cry, *Havoc*,[b] where you should but hunt
With modest warrant.
SIC. Sir, how comes't that you have holp
To make this rescue?
MEN. Hear me speak:—
As I do know the consul's worthiness,
So can I name his faults:—
SIC. *Consul!*—what consul?
MEN. The consul Coriolanus.
BRU. He consul!
CITIZENS. No, no, no, no, no!
MEN. If, by the tribunes' leave, and yours, good people,
I may be heard, I'd crave a word or two;
The which shall turn you to no further harm,
Than so much loss of time.
SIC. Speak briefly, then;
For we are peremptory to despatch
This viperous traitor: to eject him hence,
Were but one[c] danger; and to keep him here
Our certain death; therefore, it is decreed,
He dies to-night.
MEN. Now the good gods forbid
That our renowned Rome, whose gratitude
Towards her deserved children is enroll'd
In Jove's own book, like an unnatural dam
Should now eat up her own!
SIC. He's a disease that must be cut away.
MEN. O, he's a limb that has but a disease;
Mortal, to cut it off; to cure it, easy.
What has he done to Rome that's worthy death?
Killing our enemies, the blood he hath lost,
(Which, I dare vouch, is more than that he hath,
By many an ounce) he dropp'd it for his country;
And what is left, to lose it by his country,
Were to us all, that do't and suffer it,
A brand to the end o' the world.

* Old text, *Com.*

a COM. Come, sir, along with us.] In the distribution of this and the two following speeches, we follow the arrangement proposed by Tyrwhitt. The old copies present them thus,—

"CORIO. *Come, Sir, along with us.*
MENE. *I would they were Barbarians, as they are,*
Though in Rome litter'd: not Romans, as they are not,
Though calved i' th' Porch o' th' Capitoll:
Be gone, put not your worthy Rage into your Tongue,
One time will owe another."

b — cry, *Havoc*,—] To "cry, *Havoc*," appears to have been a signal for indiscriminate slaughter; the expression occurs again in "King John," Act II. Sc. 2:—

"Cry, *Havoc*, Kings!"

and in "Julius Cæsar," Act III. Sc. 1:—

"Cry, *Havoc!* and let slip the dogs of war."

c *Were but* one *danger*;] Theobald altered this to, "— but *our* danger."

SIC. This is clean kam.[a]

BRU. Merely awry: when he did love his country,
It honour'd him.

MEN. The service of the foot
Being once gangren'd, is not then respected
For what before it was?

BRU. We'll hear no more.—
Pursue him to his house, and pluck him thence,
Lest his infection, being of catching nature,
Spread further.

MEN. One word more, one word.
This tiger-footed rage, when it shall find
The harm of unscann'd swiftness, will, too late,
Tie leaden pounds to's heels. Proceed by process;
Lest parties (as he is belov'd) break out
And sack great Rome with Romans.

BRU. If it were so,—

SIC. What do ye talk?
Have we not had a taste of his obedience?
Our Ædiles smote! ourselves resisted!—come,—

MEN. Consider this;—he has been bred i'the wars
Since he could draw a sword, and is ill school'd
In boulted language; meal and bran together
He throws without distinction. Give me leave,
I'll go to him, and undertake to bring him[b]
Where he shall answer, by a lawful form,
(In peace) to his utmost peril.

1 SEN. Noble tribunes,
It is the humane way: the other course
Will prove too bloody; and the end of it
Unknown to the beginning.

SIC. Noble Menenius,
Be you, then, as the people's officer.—
Masters, lay down your weapons.

---

[a] — clean kam.] Equivalent to *rigmarole, rhodomontade*.

[b] — to bring him—] The old text adds "in peace," which Pope omitted, as injurious to the measure, and because the words are repeated two lines below.

BRU. Go not home.
SIC. Meet on the market-place.—We'll attend you there:
Where, if you bring not Marcius, we'll proceed
In our first way.
MEN. I'll bring him to you:—
Let me desire your company: [*To the* Senators.] he must come,
Or what is worst will follow.
1 SEN. Pray you, let's to him.
[*Exeunt.*

SCENE II.—*A Room in* Coriolanus's *House.*

Enter CORIOLANUS *and* Patricians.

COR. Let them pull all about mine ears; present me
Death on the wheel, or at wild horses' heels;
Or pile ten hills on the Tarpeian rock,
That the precipitation might down stretch
Below the beam of sight; yet will I still
Be thus to them.
1 PAT. You do the nobler.
COR. I muse my mother
Does not approve me further, who was wont
To call them woollen vassals, things created
To buy and sell with groats; to show bare heads
In congregations, to yawn, be still, and wonder,
When one but of my ordinance stood up
To speak of peace or war.—

Enter VOLUMNIA.

I talk of you:
Why did you wish me milder? would you have me
False to my nature? Rather say, I play
The man I am.
VOL. O, sir, sir, sir!
I would have had you put your power well on,
Before you had worn it out.
COR. Let go.
VOL. You might have been enough the man you are,
With striving less to be so: lesser had been
The thwartings[a] of your dispositions, if
You had not show'd them how ye were dispos'd
Ere they lack'd power to cross you.
COR. Let them hang!
VOL. Ay, and burn too!

Enter MENENIUS *and* Senators.

MEN. Come, come, you have been too rough, something too rough;
You must return and mend it.
1 SEN. There's no remedy;
Unless, by not so doing, our good city
Cleave in the midst, and perish.
VOL. Pray, be counsell'd:
I have a heart as little apt as yours,
But yet a brain that leads my use of anger,
To better vantage.[b]
MEN. Well said, noble woman!
Before he should thus stoop to the herd,* but that
The violent fit o'the time craves it as physic
For the whole state, I'd put mine armour on,
Which I can scarcely bear.
COR. What must I do?
MEN. Return to the tribunes.
COR. Well, what then? what then?
MEN. Repent what you have spoke.
COR. For them?—I cannot do it to the gods;
Must I, then, do't to them?
VOL. You are too absolute;
Though therein you can never be too noble,
But when extremities speak. I have heard you say,
Honour and policy, like unsever'd friends,
I'the war do grow together: grant that, and tell me,
In peace, what each of them by the other lose,
That they combine not there.
COR. Tush, tush!
MEN. A good demand.
VOL. If it be honour in your wars to seem

(*) Old text, *heart*, corrected by Theobald.

[a] *The* thwartings—] An emendation of Theobald's, the old text having,—"The *things*," &c.

[b] I have a heart as little apt as yours,
But yet a brain that leads my use of anger,
To better vantage.]

Mr. Collier's annotator here indulges in one of his most daring flights,—the intercalation of a whole line!—rendering the passage thus,—

"I have a heart as little apt as yours,
To brook reproof without the use of anger,
But yet a brain that leads my use of anger,
To better vantage."

This interpolation, (which, by the way, has been corrupted or corrected since its publication in Mr. Collier's "Notes and Emendations," and in his Mono-volume Shakespeare, where it reads,—

"To brook *control* without the use of anger,"

we hold to be quite superfluous, and, if even a *lacuna* were manifest, to be altogether inadmissible. For admitting, which we are not guilty of, the antiquity claimed by Mr. Collier for the marginal annotations of his copy of the second folio, we agree with Mr. R. G. White (Shakespeare's Scholar, p. 76), that, "the interpolation of an entire line by one man in 1662, is as little justifiable as the interpolation of an entire scene by another man in 1762 or 1853." That there is a difficulty in the construction of the speech as it stands in the ancient text, nobody can deny. But it is surely one susceptible of a solution less perilous and arbitrary than the insertion of a new line. Mr. Singer proposed to read *soft* for "apt;" an emendation which has not been favourably received. Our own impression, long before the "Perkins folio" came to light, was that the transcriber or compositor had slightly erred in the words "as little," and that the poet probably wrote,—*of mettle, i.e. of temper*, &c.—

"I have a heart *of mettle* apt as yours,"

which naturally enough led to

"But yet a brain, that leads my use of anger,
To better vantage."

The same you are not, (which, for your best ends,
You adopt your policy) how is it less or worse,
That it shall hold companionship in peace
With honour, as in war, since that to both
It stands in like request?

COR. Why force you this?

VOL. Because,
That now it lies you on to speak to the people;
Not by your own instruction, nor by the matter
Which your heart prompts you, but with such words
That are but roted in your tongue,
Though but bastards, and syllables[a]
Of no allowance [b] to your bosom's truth.
Now, this no more dishonours you at all
Than to take in a town[c] with gentle words,
Which else would put you to your fortune, and
The hazard of much blood.—
I would dissemble with my nature, where
My fortunes and my friends at stake requir'd
I should do so in honour: I am in this,
Your wife, your son, these senators, the nobles;
And you will rather show our general louts
How you can frown, than spend a fawn upon 'em,
For the inheritance of their loves, and safeguard
Of what that want might ruin.

MEN. Noble lady!—
Come, go with us; speak fair: you may salve so,
Not what is dangerous present, but the loss
Of what is past.

VOL. I pr'ythee now, my son,
Go to them, with this bonnet in thy hand;
And thus far having stretch'd it, (here be with them) [d]
Thy knee bussing the stones, (for in such business
Action is eloquence, and the eyes of the ignorant
More learned than the ears) waving thy head,
Which often,[e] thus, correcting thy stout heart,
Now humble as the ripest mulberry
That will not hold the handling: or, say to them,
Thou art their soldier, and being bred in broils,
Hast not the soft way, which, thou dost confess,
Were fit for thee to use, as they to claim,
In asking their good loves; but thou wilt frame
Thyself, forsooth, hereafter theirs, so far
As thou hast power and person.

MEN. This but done,
Even as she speaks, why, their hearts were yours:
For they have pardons, being ask'd, as free
As words to little purpose.

VOL. Pr'ythee now,
Go, and be rul'd; although I know thou hadst rather
Follow thine enemy in a fiery gulf,
Than flatter him in a bower.—Here is Cominius.

Enter COMINIUS.

COM. I have been i'the market-place; and, sir, 'tis fit
You make strong party, or defend yourself
By calmness or by absence; all's in anger.

MEN. Only fair speech.

COM. I think 'twill serve,
If he can thereto frame his spirit.

VOL. He must, and will:—
Pr'ythee now, say you will, and go about it.

COR. Must I go show them my unbarbed sconce?
Must I with my base tongue give to my noble heart
A lie, that it must bear? Well, I will do't:
Yet were there but this single plot to lose,
This mould of Marcius, they to dust should grind it,
And throw't against the wind.—To the market-place:—
You have put me now to such a part, which never
I shall discharge to the life.

COM. Come, come, we'll prompt you.

VOL. I pr'ythee now, sweet son,—as thou hast said
My praises made thee first a soldier, so,
To have my praise for this, perform a part
Thou hast not done before.

COR. Well, I must do't:
Away, my disposition, and possess me
Some harlot's spirit! my throat of war be turn'd,
Which quired with my drum, into a pipe
Small as an eunuch, or the virgin voice
That babies lulls asleep! the smiles of knaves
Tent in my cheeks; and schoolboys' tears take up
The glasses of my sight! a beggar's tongue
Make motion through my lips; and my arm'd knees,
Who bow'd but in my stirrup, bend like his
That hath receiv'd an alms!—I will not do't;
Lest I surcease to honour mine own truth,

---

a Though but bastards, and syllables, &c.] In this speech we follow the arrangement of the old copies, which though imperfect is infinitely preferable to that adopted by all the modern editions. The verse before us is evidently corrupt; "*but*" seems to have crept in from the preceding line, and some word to have been lost; we may be permitted to guess that it originally ran,—

"*Thought's* bastards, and *persuading* syllables,"

or, "*Thought's* bastards, and *glib* syllables,"

b *Of no* allowance,—] Johnson and Capell read,—"Of no *alliance.*"

c — to take in a town—] *To take in*, meant *to win*, or *subdue*.

d — (here be with them)—] That is, adopt this action. So in Brome's comedy, "A Jovial Crew, or The Merry Beggars," Act II. Sc. 1, Springlove, describing his having solicited alms as a cripple, says,—"For here I was with him." [*Halts.*

e —— waving thy head,
Which often, &c.]

We would read,—

"—— waving thy head,—
While often, thus, correcting thy stout heart,
Now humble as the ripest mulberry
That will not hold the handling,—say to them," &c.

f — unbarbed sconce?] *Unbarbed* here means, *bare, uncovered.*

And, by my body's action, teach my mind
A most inherent baseness.

VOL. At thy choice then:
To beg of thee, it is my more dishonour
Than thou of them. Come all to ruin; let
Thy mother rather feel thy pride than fear
Thy dangerous stoutness; for I mock at death
With as big heart as thou. Do as thou list.
Thy valiantness was mine, thou suck'dst it from me;
But owe thy pride thyself.

COR. Pray, be content:
Mother, I am going to the market-place;
Chide me no more. I'll mountebank their loves,
Cog their hearts from them, and come home belov'd
Of all the trades in Rome. Look, I am going:
Commend me to my wife. I'll return consul;
Or never trust to what my tongue can do
I' the way of flattery further.

VOL. Do your will. [*Exit.*

COM. Away! the tribunes do attend you: arm yourself
To answer mildly; for they are prepar'd
With accusations, as I hear, more strong
Than are upon you yet.

COR. The word is, *mildly*:—pray you, let us go:
Let them accuse me by invention, I
Will answer in mine honour.

MEN. Ay, but mildly.

COR. Well, *mildly* be it, then; *mildly*. [*Exeunt.*

SCENE III.—*The same.* *The* Forum.

Enter SICINIUS *and* BRUTUS.

BRU. In this point charge him home,—that he affects
Tyrannical power: if he evade us there,
Enforce him with his envy to the people;
And that the spoil got on the Antiates
Was ne'er distributed.—

Enter an Ædile.

What, will he come?

ÆD. He's coming.

BRU. How accompanied?

ÆD. With old Menenius, and those senators
That always favour'd him.

SIC. Have you a catalogue
Of all the voices that we have procur'd,
Set down by the poll?

ÆD. I have; 'tis ready.

SIC. Have you collected them by tribes?

ÆD. I have.

SIC. Assemble presently the people hither:
And when they hear me say, *It shall be so*
I' the right and strength o' the commons, be it either
For death, for fine, or banishment, then let them,
If I say fine, cry *Fine*;—if death, cry *Death*;
Insisting on the old prerogative
And power i' the truth o' the cause.

ÆD. I shall inform them.

BRU. And when such time they have begun to cry,
Let them not cease, but with a din confus'd
Enforce the present execution
Of what we chance to sentence.

ÆD. Very well.

SIC. Make them be strong, and ready for this hint,
When we shall hap to give't them.

BRU. Go about it.— [*Exit* Ædile.
Put him to choler straight: he hath been us'd
Ever to conquer, and to have his worth[a]
Of contradiction: being once chaf'd he cannot
Be rein'd again to temperance; then he speaks
What's in his heart; and that is there which looks
With us to break his neck.

SIC. Well, here he comes.

Enter CORIOLANUS, MENENIUS, COMINIUS, Senators, *and* Patricians.

MEN. Calmly, I do beseech you.

COR. Ay, as an ostler, that for the poorest piece
Will bear the knave by the volume.—The honour'd gods
Keep Rome in safety, and the chairs of justice
Supplied with worthy men! plant love among's!
Throng* our large temples with the shows of peace,
And not our streets with war!

1 SEN. Amen, amen!

MEN. A noble wish.

Re-enter Ædile, *with* Citizens.

SIC. Draw near, ye people.

ÆD. List to your tribunes; audience! peace, I say!

---

a —— *to have his* worth
Of contradiction:]
So the old text. Rowe prints, "his *word* of," &c.; Capell, "his '*worth* of," understanding '*worth* to be a contraction of *pennyworth*; and Mr. Collier's annotator reads, "his *mouth* of," &c. But we are by no means convinced that any change is required.

(*) Old text, *Through*, corrected by Theobald.

COR. First, hear me speak.
BOTH TRI. Well, say.—Peace, ho!
COR. Shall I be charg'd no further than this present?
Must all determine here?
SIC. I do demand,
If you submit you to the people's voices,
Allow their officers, and are content
To suffer lawful censure for such faults
As shall be prov'd upon you?
COR. I am content.
MEN. Lo, citizens, he says he is content.
The warlike service he has done, consider; think
Upon the wounds his body bears, which show
Like graves i' the holy churchyard.
COR. Scratches with briers,
Scars to move laughter only.
MEN. Consider further,
That when he speaks not like a citizen,
You find him like a soldier: do not take
His rougher accents* for malicious sounds,
But, as I say, such as become a soldier,
Rather than envy you.
COM. Well, well, no more.
COR. What is the matter,
That being pass'd for consul with full voice,
I am so dishonour'd, that the very hour
You take it off again?
SIC. Answer to us.
COR. Say, then: 'tis true, I ought so.
SIC. We charge you, that you have contriv'd to [take

(*) Old text, *actions*, corrected by Theobald.

From Rome all season'd office, and to wind
Yourself into a power tyrannical;
For which you are a traitor to the people.
COR. How! *traitor?*
MEN. Nay, temperately: your promise.
COR. The fires i' the lowest hell fold in the people!
Call me their traitor!—Thou injurious tribune!
Within thine eyes sat twenty thousand deaths,
In thy hands clutch'd as many millions, in
Thy lying tongue both numbers, I would say,
Thou liest, unto thee, with a voice as free
As I do pray the gods!
SIC. Mark you this, people?
CITIZENS. To the rock! to the rock with him!
SIC. Peace!
We need not put new matter to his charge:
What you have seen him do, and heard him speak,
Beating your officers, cursing yourselves,
Opposing laws with strokes, and here defying
Those whose great power must try him; even this,
So criminal, and in such capital kind,
Deserves the extremest death.
BRU. But since he hath serv'd well for Rome,—
COR. What do you prate of service?
BRU. I talk of that, that know it.
COR. You?
MEN. Is this the promise that you made your mother?
COM. Know, I pray you,—
COR. I'll know no further:
Let them pronounce the steep Tarpeian death,
Vagabond exile, flaying, pent to linger
But with a grain a day,—I would not buy
Their mercy at the price of one fair word;
Nor check my courage for what they can give,
To have't with saying, Good morrow.
SIC. For that he has
(As much as in him lies) from time to time
Envied[a] against the people, seeking means
To pluck away their power; has now at last
Given hostile strokes, and that not in the presence
Of dreaded justice, but on the ministers
That do distribute it; in the name o' the people,
And in the power of us the tribunes, we,
Even from this instant, banish him our city;
In peril of precipitation
From off the rock Tarpeian, never more
To enter our Rome gates. I' the people's name,
I say it shall be so.
CITIZENS. It shall be so! it shall be so! let him away!
He's banish'd, and it shall be so!
COM. Hear me, my masters, and my common friends,—
SIC. He's sentenc'd; no more hearing.
COM. Let me speak:
I have been consul, and can show for* Rome,
Her enemies' marks upon me. I do love
My country's good with a respect more tender,
More holy, and profound, than mine own life,
My dear wife's estimate, her womb's increase,
And treasure of my loins: then if I would
Speak that—
SIC. We know your drift: speak what?
BRU. There's no more to be said, but he is banish'd,
As enemy to the people and his country:
It shall be so.
CITIZENS. It shall be so! it shall be so!
COR. You common cry[b] of curs! whose breath I hate
As reek o' the rotten fens, whose loves I prize
As the dead carcasses of unburied men
That do corrupt my air,—I banish you;
And here remain with your uncertainty!
Let every feeble rumour shake your hearts!
Your enemies, with nodding of their plumes,
Fan you into despair! Have the power still
To banish your defenders; till at length
Your ignorance, (which finds not till it feels)
Making but[c] reservation of yourselves,
(Still your own foes) deliver you,
As most abated captives, to some nation
That won you without blows! Despising,
For you, the city, thus I turn my back:
There is a world elsewhere.
[*Exeunt* CORIOLANUS, COMINIUS, MENENIUS, Senators, *and* Patricians.
ÆD. The people's enemy is gone, is gone!
CITIZENS. Our enemy is banish'd! he is gone! Hoo! hoo!
[*Shouting, and throwing up their caps.*
SIC. Go, see him out at gates, and follow him,
As he hath follow'd you, with all despite;
Give him deserv'd vexation. Let a guard
Attend us through the city.
CITIZENS. Come, come, let us see him out at gates; come:—
The gods preserve our noble tribunes!—come.
[*Exeunt.*

---

a Envied *against the people,*—] That is, Steevens explains, "behaved with signs of hatred to the people," but "envied" here is perhaps only a misprint of *Inveighed;* so in North's Plutarch, (Life of Solon):—"But Solon going up into the pulpit for orations, stoutly *inveyed* against it."

b — cry *of curs!*] *Cry* here means *pack.*

c *Making* but *reservation of yourselves,*—] This, since Capell's edition, has been invariably printed, "Making *not* reservation," &c., to the complete destruction of the sense, which manifestly is,—Banish all your defenders as you do me, till, at last, your ignorance, having reserved only your impotent selves, always your own foes, deliver you the humbled captives to some nation, &c. &c.

(*) Old text, *from,* corrected by Theobald.

ACT IV.

SCENE I.—Rome. *Before a Gate of the City.*

Enter Coriolanus, Volumnia, Virgilia, Menenius, Cominius, *and several young* Patricians.

Cor. Come, leave your tears; a brief farewell:—the Beast
With many heads butts me away.—Nay, mother,
Where is your ancient courage? you were us'd
To say extremity[a] was the trier of spirits;—
That common chances common men could bear;—
That, when the sea was calm, all boats alike
Show'd mastership in floating;—Fortune's blows,
When most struck home, being gentle wounded, craves

[a] *To say* extremity *was*—] So the second folio; the first has,—"*Extreamities* was," &c.

A noble cunning; [a]—you were us'd to load me
With precepts, that would make invincible
The heart that conn'd them.
VIR. O heavens! O heavens!
COR. Nay, I pr'ythee, woman,—
VOL. Now the red pestilence strike all trades in Rome,
And occupations perish!
COR. What, what, what!
I shall be lov'd when I am lack'd. Nay, mother,
Resume that spirit, when you were wont to say,
If you had been the wife of Hercules,
Six of his labours you'd have done, and sav'd
Your husband so much sweat.—Cominius,
Droop not; adieu.—Farewell, my wife!—my mother!
I'll do well yet.—Thou old and true Menenius,
Thy tears are salter than a younger man's,
And venomous to thine eyes.—My sometime general,
I have seen thee stern, and thou hast oft beheld
Heart-hard'ning spectacles; tell these sad women,
'Tis fond[b] to wail inevitable strokes,
As 'tis to laugh at 'em.—My mother, you wot well
My hazards still have been your solace: and
Believe't not lightly, (though I go alone,
Like to a lonely dragon, that his fen
Makes fear'd and talk'd of more than seen) your son
Will or exceed the common, or be caught
With cautelous baits and practice.[c]
VOL. My first son,
Whither wilt thou go? Take good Cominius
With thee a while: determine on some course,
More than a wild exposture to each chance
That starts i' the way before thee.
COR. O, the gods!
COM. I'll follow thee a month, devise with thee
Where thou shalt rest, that thou may'st hear of us,
And we of thee: so, if the time thrust forth
A cause for thy repeal, we shall not send
O'er the vast world to seek a single man,
And lose advantage which doth ever cool
I' the absence of the needer.
COR. Fare ye well:
Thou hast years upon thee; and thou art too full
Of the wars' surfeits, to go rove with one
That's yet unbruis'd: bring me but out at gate.—
Come, my sweet wife, my dearest mother, and
My friends of noble touch; when I am forth,
Bid me farewell, and smile. I pray you, come.
While I remain above the ground, you shall
Hear from me still; and never of me aught
But what is like me formerly.
MEN. That's worthily
As any ear can hear.—Come, let's not weep—
If I could shake off but one seven years
From these old arms and legs, by the good gods,
I'd with thee every foot!
COR. Give me thy hand:—
Come. [*Exeunt.*

SCENE II.—*The same. A Street near the Gate.*

Enter SICINIUS, BRUTUS, *and an* Ædile.

SIC. Bid them all home; he's gone, and we'll no further.—
The nobility are vex'd, whom we see have sided
In his behalf.
BRU. Now we have shown our power,
Let us seem humbler after it is done,
Than when it was a-doing.
SIC. Bid them home:
Say their great enemy is gone, and they
Stand in their ancient strength.
BRU. Dismiss them home.—
[*Exit* Ædile.
Here comes his mother.
SIC. Let's not meet her.
BRU. Why?
SIC. They say she's mad.
BRU. They have ta'en note of us:
Keep on your way.

Enter VOLUMNIA, VIRGILIA, *and* MENENIUS.

VOL. O, ye're well met: the hoarded plague o' the gods
Requite your love!
MEN. Peace, peace; be not so loud.
VOL. If that I could for weeping, you should hear,—
Nay, and you shall hear some.—Will you be gone? [*To* BRUTUS.
VIR. You shall stay too: [*To* SICIN.] I would I had the power
To say so to my husband.

---

a —— Fortune's blows,
When most struck home, being gentle wounded, craves
A noble cunning;—]

Every endeavour to elicit sense from this perplexing sentence has failed: Pope's "being *gently warded*, craves," &c.; Hanmer's "being *greatly* warded, *crave*," &c.; and Mr. Collier's "being gentle-*minded*, craves," &c., are alike disputable. At one time it struck us that the right lection was possibly,—

"—— Fortune *bows*
When most struck home; being gentle, wounded, craves," &c.

But we are now persuaded the sentiment intended is akin to that of two lines by Taylor, the Water-poet,—

"For when base Peasants shrink at Fortune's blowes,
Then *magnanimity* most richly showes,"

and has been rendered unintelligible by some omission in the text.

b *'Tis* fond—] That is, 'Tis *foolish.*

c — cautelous baits and practice.] By *insidious* baits, and *treachery.*

SIC. Are you mankind?[a]
VOL. Ay, fool; is that a shame?—Note but this, fool;
Was not a man my father? Hadst thou foxship
To banish him that struck more blows for Rome
Than thou hast spoken words?
SIC. O, blessed heavens!
VOL. More noble blows than ever thou wise words;
And for Rome's good.—I'll tell thee what;—yet go:—
Nay, but thou shalt stay too:—I would my son
Were in Arabia, and thy tribe before him,
His good sword in his hand.
SIC. What then?
VIR. *What then?*
He'd make an end of thy posterity.
VOL. Bastards and all.—
Good man, the wounds that he does bear for Rome!
MEN. Come, come, peace.
SIC. I would he had continu'd to his country
As he began, and not unknit himself
The noble knot he made.
BRU. I would he had.
VOL. *I would he had!* 'Twas you incens'd the rabble;—
Cats,[b] that can judge as fitly of his worth,
As I can of those mysteries which heaven
Will not have earth to know.
BRU. Pray, let us go.
VOL. Now, pray, sir, get you gone: [this;—
You have done a brave deed. Ere you go, hear
As far as doth the Capitol exceed
The meanest house in Rome; so far, my son
(This lady's husband here, this, do you see)
Whom you have banish'd, does exceed you all.
BRU. Well, well, we'll leave you.
SIC. Why stay we to be baited
With one that wants her wits?
VOL. Take my prayers with you.—
[*Exeunt* Tribunes.
I would the gods had nothing else to do,
But to confirm my curses! Could I meet 'em
But once a day, it would unclog my heart
Of what lies heavy to't.
MEN. You have told them home;
And, by my troth, you have cause. You'll sup with me?

[a] *Are you* mankind?] Are you *termagants, viragoes?* "A *mankind* woman," Johnson says, "is a woman with the roughness of a man, and, in an aggravated sense, a woman ferocious, violent, and eager to shed blood."

[b] Cats,—] This is an odd epithet, whether intended for the Tribunes or the rabble. Mr. Collier's annotator would substitute, *Curs*, but as Volumnia is here upbraiding them for their lack of perception, we surmise the genuine word was *Bats*, for which "Cats" is an easy misprint.

VOL. Anger's my meat; I sup upon myself,
And so shall starve with feeding.—Come, let's go:
Leave this faint puling, and lament as I do,
In anger, Juno-like. Come, come, come.

MEN. Fie, fie, fie! [*Exeunt.*

SCENE III.—*A Highway between* Rome *and* Antium.

Enter NICANOR *and* ADRIAN, *meeting.*

NIC. I know you well, sir, and you know me: your name, I think, is Adrian.

ADR. It is so, sir: truly, I have forgot you.

NIC. I am a Roman; and my services are, as you are, against 'em. Know you me yet?

ADR. Nicanor? No.

NIC. The same, sir.

ADR. You had more beard when I last saw you; but your favour is well appeared[a] by your tongue. What's the news in Rome? I have a note from the Volscian state, to find you out there: you have well saved me a day's journey.

NIC. There hath been in Rome strange insurrections: the people against the senators, patricians, and nobles.

ADR. *Hath been!* is it ended then? Our state thinks not so; they are in a most warlike preparation, and hope to come upon them in the heat of their division.

NIC. The main blaze of it is past, but a small thing would make it flame again; for the nobles receive so to heart the banishment of that worthy Coriolanus, that they are in a ripe aptness to take all power from the people, and to pluck from them their tribunes for ever. This lies glowing, I can tell you, and is almost mature for the violent breaking out.

ADR. Coriolanus banished?

NIC. Banished, sir.

ADR. You will be welcome with this intelligence, Nicanor.

NIC. The day serves well for them now. I have heard it said, the fittest time to corrupt a man's wife is when she's fallen out with her husband. Your noble Tullus Aufidius will appear well in these wars, his great opposer, Coriolanus, being now in no request of his country.

ADR. He cannot choose. I am most fortunate, thus accidentally to encounter you: you have ended my business, and I will merrily accompany you home.

NIC. I shall, between this and supper, tell you most strange things from Rome, all tending to the good of their adversaries. Have you an army ready, say you?

ADR. A most royal one: the centurions, and their charges, distinctly billeted, already in the entertainment, and to be on foot at an hour's warning.

NIC. I am joyful to hear of their readiness, and am the man, I think, that shall set them in present action. So, sir, heartily well met, and most glad of your company.

ADR. You take my part from me, sir; I have the most cause to be glad of yours.

NIC. Well, let us go together. [*Exeunt.*

SCENE IV.—Antium. *Before* Aufidius' *House.*

Enter CORIOLANUS, *in mean apparel, disguised and muffled.*

COR. A goodly city is this Antium. City,
'T is I that made thy widows; many an heir
Of these fair edifices 'fore my wars
Have I heard groan and drop: then know me not,
Lest that thy wives with spits, and boys with stones,
In puny battle slay me.—

Enter a Citizen.

Save you, sir.

CIT. And you.

COR. Direct me, if it be your will,
Where great Aufidius lies: is he in Antium?

CIT. He is, and feasts the nobles of the state at his house this night.

COR. Which is his house, beseech you?

CIT. This, here before you.

COR. Thank you, sir; farewell. [*Exit* Citizen.
O, world, thy slippery turns! Friends now fast sworn,
Whose double bosoms seem to wear one heart,
Whose hours, whose bed, whose meal and exercise,
Are still together, who twin, as 't were, in love
Unseparable, shall within this hour,
On a dissention of a doit, break out
To bitterest enmity: so, fellest foes,
Whose passions and whose plots have broke their sleep
To take the one the other, by some chance,
Some trick not worth an egg, shall grow dear friends
And interjoin their issues. So with me:—
My birth-place hate[b] I, and my love's upon
This enemy town.—I'll enter: if he slay me,

---

[a] — *your favour is well* appeared *by your tongue.*] This may import your favour is well *manifested*, or *rendered apparent*; but Johnson would read,—*affeared*, and Steevens and Mr. Collier's annotator propose, "*approved* by your tongue."

[b] *My birth-place* hate *I*,—] The old text has "— *have* I." We owe the restoration to Capell.

He does fair justice; if he give me way,
I'll do his country service. [*Exit.*

SCENE V.—*The same. A Hall in* Aufidius' *House.*

Music within. Enter a Servant.

1 SERV. Wine, wine, wine! What service is here!
I think our fellows are asleep. [*Exit.*

Enter another Servant.

2 SERV. Where's Cotus? my master calls for him.—Cotus! [*Exit.*

Enter CORIOLANUS.

COR. A goodly house:
The feast smells well; but I appear not like a guest.

Re-enter the first Servant.

1 SERV. What would you have, friend? whence are you?
Here's no place for you: pray, go to the door. [*Exit.*

COR. I have deserv'd no better entertainment,
In being Coriolanus.[a]

Re-enter second Servant.

2 SERV. Whence are you, sir? Has the porter his eyes in his head, that he gives entrance to such companions? Pray, get you out.

COR. Away!

2 SERV. *Away!* Get you away.

COR. Now thou'rt troublesome.

2 SERV. Are you so brave? I'll have you talked with anon.

Enter a third Servant. *The first meets him.*

3 SERV. What fellow's this?

[a] *In being* Coriolanus.] In obtaining his surname from the sack of Corioli.

1 SERV. A strange one as ever I looked on : I cannot get him out o' the house : pr'ythee, call my master to him.

3 SERV. What have you to do here, fellow? Pray you, avoid the house.

COR. Let me but stand ; I will not hurt your [hearth.

3 SERV. What are you?

COR. A gentleman.

3 SERV. A marvellous poor one.

COR. True, so I am.

3 SERV. Pray you, poor gentleman, take up some other station : here 's no place for you ; pray you, avoid : come.

COR. Follow your function, go and batten on cold bits. [*Pushes him away.*

3 SERV. What, will you not? Pr'ythee, tell my master what a strange guest he has here.

2 SERV. And I shall. [*Exit.*

3 SERV. Where dwellest thou?

COR. Under the canopy.

3 SERV. *Under the canopy?*

COR. Ay.

3 SERV. Where 's that?

COR. I' the city of kites and crows.

3 SERV. *I' the city of kites and crows!*—What an ass it is!—then thou dwellest with daws too?

COR. No, I serve not thy master.

3 SERV. How, sir! do you meddle with my master?

COR. Ay; 't is an honester service than to meddle with thy mistress :
Thou prat'st, and prat'st; serve with thy trencher, hence! [*Beats him away.*

Enter AUFIDIUS *and the second* Servant.

AUF. Where is this fellow?

2 SERV. Here, sir ; I'd have beaten him like a dog, but for disturbing the lords within.

AUF. Whence com'st thou? what wouldst thou? Thy name?
Why speak'st not? Speak, man : what's thy name?

COR. If, Tullus, not yet thou know'st me, [*Unmuffling.*
And, seeing me, dost not think me for the man I am,
Necessity commands me name myself.

AUF. What is thy name? [Servants *retire.*

COR. A name unmusical to the Volscians' ears,
And harsh in sound to thine.

AUF. Say, what 's thy name?
Thou hast a grim appearance, and thy face
Bears a command in 't; though thy tackle 's torn,
Thou show'st a noble vessel : what 's thy name?

COR. Prepare thy brow to frown : know'st thou me yet?

AUF. I know thee not:—thy name?

COR. My name is Caius Marcius, who hath done
To thee particularly, and to all the Volsces,
Great hurt and mischief ; thereto witness may
My surname, Coriolanus : the painful service,
The extreme dangers, and the drops of blood
Shed for my thankless country, are requited
But with that surname ; a good memory,[a]
And witness of the malice and displeasure
Which thou should'st bear me : only that name remains ;
The cruelty and envy of the people,
Permitted by our dastard nobles, who
Have all forsook me, hath devour'd the rest ;
And suffer'd me by the voice of slaves to be
Whoop'd out of Rome. Now, this extremity
Hath brought me to thy hearth ; not out of hope,
Mistake me not, to save my life ; for if
I had fear'd death, of all the men i' the world
I would have 'voided thee ; but in mere spite,
To be full quit of those my banishers,
Stand I before thee here. Then if thou hast
A heart of wreak[b] in thee, that will revenge
Thine own particular wrongs, and stop those maims
Of shame seen through thy country, speed thee straight,
And make my misery serve thy turn ; so use it,
That my revengeful services may prove
As benefits to thee ; for I will fight
Against my canker'd country with the spleen
Of all the under fiends. But if so be
Thou dar'st not this, and that to prove more fortunes
Thou'rt tir'd, then, in a word, I also am
Longer to live most weary, and present
My throat to thee and to thy ancient malice ;
Which not to cut would show thee but a fool,
Since I have ever follow'd thee with hate,
Drawn tuns of blood out of thy country's breast,
And cannot live but to thy shame, unless
It be to do thee service.

AUF. O, Marcius, Marcius,
Each word thou hast spoke hath weeded from my heart
A root of ancient envy. If Jupiter
Should from yond cloud speak divine things,
And say, '*T is true;* I'd not believe them more
Than thee, all-noble Marcius.(1)—Let me twine
Mine arms about that body, where against
My grained ash an hundred times hath broke,
And scar'd the moon with splinters! Here I clip
The anvil of my sword, and do contest
As hotly and as nobly with thy love,
As ever in ambitious strength I did
Contend against thy valour. Know thou first,[c]

a — memory,—] That is, *memorial.*
b — wreak—] *Vengeance.*
c *Know thou* first,—] *First* apparently means here *noblest,* as in the opening scene of this act, where Volumnia calls Coriolanus, "my *first* son."

I lov'd the maid I married; never man
Sigh'd truer breath; but that I see thee here,
Thou noble thing! more dances my rapt heart,
Than when I first my wedded mistress saw
Bestride my threshold. Why, thou Mars! I tell thee,
We have a power on foot; and I had purpose
Once more to hew thy target from thy brawn,
Or lose mine arm for 't: thou hast beat me out
Twelve several times, and I have nightly since
Dreamt of encounters 'twixt thyself and me;
We have been down together in my sleep,
Unbuckling helms, fisting each other's throat,
And wak'd half dead with nothing. Worthy Marcius,
Had we no other quarrel else to Rome, but that
Thou art thence banish'd, we would muster all
From twelve to seventy; and, pouring war
Into the bowels of ungrateful Rome,
Like a bold flood o'er-bear. O, come, go in,
And take our friendly senators by the hands;
Who now are here, taking their leaves of me,
Who am prepar'd against your territories,
Though not for Rome itself.

COR. You bless me, gods!

AUF. Therefore, most absolute sir, if thou wilt have
The leading of thine own revenges, take
The one half of my commission, and set down,—
As best thou art experienc'd, since thou know'st
Thy country's strength and weakness,—thine own ways;
Whether to knock against the gates of Rome,
Or rudely visit them in parts remote,
To fright them, ere destroy. But come in;
Let me commend thee first to those, that shall
Say *yea* to thy desires. A thousand welcomes!
And more a friend than e'er an enemy;
Yet, Marcius, that was much. Your hand! Most welcome!

[*Exeunt* CORIOLANUS *and* AUFIDIUS.

1 SERV. [*Advancing.*] Here's a strange alteration!

2 SERV. By my hand, I had thought to have strucken him with a cudgel; and yet my mind gave me his clothes made a false report of him.

1 SERV. What an arm he has! He turned me about with his finger and his thumb, as one would set up a top.

2 SERV. Nay, I knew by his face that there was something in him: he had, sir, a kind of face, methought,—I cannot tell how to term it.

1 SERV. He had so; looking, as it were,—— Would I were hanged, but I thought there was more in him than I could think.

2 SERV. So did I, I'll be sworn: he is simply the rarest man i' the world.

1 SERV. I think he is; but a greater soldier than he, you wot one.

2 SERV. Who? my master?

1 SERV. Nay, it's no matter for that.

2 SERV. Worth six on him.

1 SERV. Nay, not so neither; but I take him to be the greater soldier.

2 SERV. Faith, look you, one cannot tell how to say that: for the defence of a town, our general is excellent.

1 SERV. Ay, and for an assault too.

Re-enter third Servant.

3 SERV. O, slaves, I can tell you news! news, you rascals!

1 *and* 2 SERV. What, what, what? let's partake.

3 SERV. I would not be a Roman, of all nations; I had as lieve be a condemned man.

1 *and* 2 SERV. Wherefore? wherefore?

3 SERV. Why, here's he that was wont to thwack our general, Caius Marcius.

1 SERV. Why do you say, *thwack our general?*

3 SERV. I do not say, thwack our general; but he was always good enough for him.

2 SERV. Come, we are fellows and friends; he was ever too hard for him; I have heard him say so himself.

1 SERV. He was too hard for him directly, to say the truth on't: before Corioli, he scotched him and notched him like a carbonado.

2 SERV. An he had been cannibally given, he might have broiled and eaten him too.

1 SERV. But more of thy news.

3 SERV. Why, he is so made on here within, as if he were son and heir to Mars; set at upper end o' the table; no question asked him by any of the senators but they stand bald before him: our general himself makes a mistress of him; sanctifies himself with 's hand, and turns up the white o' the eye to his discourse. But the bottom of the news is, our general is cut i' the middle, and but one half of what he was yesterday; for the other has half, by the entreaty and grant of the whole table. He'll go, he says, and sowle[a] the porter of Rome gates by the ears: he will mow down all before him, and leave his passage polled.[b]

2 SERV. And he's as like to do't as any man I can imagine.

3 SERV. Do't! he will do't: for, look you, sir, he has as many friends as enemies: which friends, sir, as it were, durst not, look you, sir, show them-

---

a — sowle—] The etymology of this word is uncertain, but it is still employed in many English counties for lugging and dragging. Steevens quotes a line from Heywood's comedy, called "Love's Mistress," 1636, where it occurs,—

"Venus will *sowle me by the ears* for this."

b — polled.] *Cleared.*

selves, as we term it, his friends, whilst he's in directitude.[a]

1 SERV. *Directitude!* What's that?

3 SERV. But when they shall see, sir, his crest up again, and the man in blood,[b] they will out of their burrows, like conies after rain, and revel all with him.

1 SERV. But when goes this forward?

3 SERV. To-morrow; to-day; presently: you shall have the drum struck up this afternoon: 'tis, as it were, a parcel of their feast, and to be executed ere they wipe their lips.

2 SERV. Why, then we shall have a stirring world again. This peace is nothing but to rust iron, increase tailors, and breed ballad-makers.

1 SERV. Let me have war, say I; it exceeds peace, as far as day does night; it's spritely walking,[c] audible, and full of vent.[d] Peace is a very apoplexy, lethargy; mulled, deaf, sleepy, insensible; a getter of more bastard children than wars a destroyer of men.

2 SERV. 'Tis so: and as war, in some sort, may be said to be a ravisher, so it cannot be denied but peace is a great maker of cuckolds.

1 SERV. Ay, and it makes men hate one another.

3 SERV. Reason; because they then less need one another. The wars for my money. I hope to see Romans as cheap as Volscians.—They are rising, they are rising.

ALL. In, in, in, in! [*Exeunt.*

a —directitude.] Mr. Collier's annotator would read, *dejectitude.*

b — in blood,—] See note (c), p. 71, Vol. I.

c — *it's spritely* walking,—] That is, quick *moving*, or *marching*. The modern editors all read, "—it's spritely, *waking*," &c.

d — *full of* vent.] *Vent* is *voice, utterance.*

SCENE VI.—Rome. *A Public Place.*

Enter SICINIUS *and* BRUTUS.

SIC. We hear not of him, neither need we fear him;
His remedies are tame i' the present peace[e]
And quietness o' the people, which before
Were in wild hurry. Here do we make his friends
Blush that the world goes well; who rather had,
Though they themselves did suffer by 't, behold
Dissentious numbers pestering streets, than see
Our tradesmen singing in their shops, and going
About their functions friendly.

BRU. We stood to't in good time.—Is this Menenius?

SIC. 'T is he, 'tis he: O he is grown most kind
Of late.—Hail, sir!

Enter MENENIUS.

MEN. Hail to you both!

SIC. Your Coriolanus is not much missed but with his friends: the commonwealth doth stand; and so would do, were he more angry at it.

MEN. All's well; and might have been much better, if he could have temporized.

SIC. Where is he, hear you?

MEN. Nay, I hear nothing; his mother and his wife hear nothing from him.

e *His* remedies *are tame* i' the *present peace*—] A correction by Theobald, the old copies having,—"His remedies are tame, the present peace." Omission, however, is not, perhaps, the only defect in the line; the word "remedies" is very equivocal.

Enter three or four Citizens.

CITIZENS. The gods preserve you both!
SIC. God-den, our neighbours.
BRU. God-den to you all, god-den to you all.
1 CIT. Ourselves, our wives, and children, on our knees,
Are bound to pray for you both.
SIC. Live, and thrive!
BRU. Farewell, kind neighbours: we wish'd Coriolanus
Had lov'd you as we did.
CITIZENS. Now the gods keep you!
BOTH TRI. Farewell, farewell.
[*Exeunt* Citizens.
SIC. This is a happier and more comely time
Than when these fellows ran about the streets,
Crying confusion.
BRU. Caius Marcius was
A worthy officer i' the war; but insolent,
O'ercome with pride, ambitious past all thinking,
Self-loving,—
SIC. And affecting one sole throne,
Without assistance.
MEN. I think not so.
SIC. We should by this, to all our lamentation,
If he had gone forth consul, found it so.
BRU. The gods have well prevented it, and Rome
Sits safe and still without him.

Enter an Ædile.

ÆD. Worthy tribunes,
There is a slave, whom we have put in prison,
Reports,—the Volsces with two several powers
Are enter'd in the Roman territories;
And with the deepest malice of the war
Destroy what lies before 'em.
MEN. 'T is Aufidius,
Who, hearing of our Marcius' banishment,
Thrusts forth his horns again into the world,
Which were inshell'd when Marcius stood for Rome,
And durst not once peep out.
SIC. Come, what talk you of Marcius?
BRU. Go see this rumourer whipp'd.—It cannot be
The Volsces dare break with us.
MEN. *Cannot be!*
We have record that very well it can;
And three examples of the like have been
Within my age. But reason with the fellow,
Before you punish him, where he heard this;
Lest you shall chance to whip your information,
And beat the messenger who bids beware
Of what is to be dreaded.
SIC. Tell not me:
I know this cannot be.
BRU. Not possible.

Enter a Messenger.

MESS. The nobles, in great earnestness, are going
All to the senate house: some news is come *
That turns their countenances.
SIC. 'T is this slave,—
Go whip him 'fore the people's eyes,—his raising!
Nothing but his report!
MESS. Yes, worthy sir,
The slave's report is seconded; and more,
More fearful, is deliver'd.
SIC. What more fearful?
MESS. It is spoke freely out of many mouths,
(How probable I do not know) that Marcius,
Join'd with Aufidius, leads a power 'gainst Rome;
And vows revenge as spacious as between
The young'st and oldest thing.
SIC. This is most likely!
BRU. Rais'd only that the weaker sort may wish
Good[a] Marcius home again.
SIC. The very trick on't.
MEN. This is unlikely:
He and Aufidius can no more atone
Than violent'st contrariety.

Enter another Messenger.

MESS. You are sent for to the senate:
A fearful army, led by Caius Marcius
Associated with Aufidius, rages
Upon our territories; and have already
O'er-borne their way, consum'd with fire, and took
What lay before them.

Enter COMINIUS.

COM. O, you have made good work!
MEN. What news? what news?
COM. You have holp to ravish your own daughters, and
To melt the city leads upon your pates;
To see your wives dishonour'd to your noses;—
MEN. What's the news? what's the news?
COM. Your temples burned in their cement; and
Your franchises, whereon you stood, confin'd
Into an augre's bore.
MEN. Pray now, your news?—

---

a Good *Marcius*—] Mr. Collier's annotator proposes to read,—"God Marcius," which may be right; yet in "Macbeth," Act III. Sc. 1, when Macbeth, by way of instigating the murderers to slay Banquo, expatiates on the wrongs that chief had done them, he asks, ironically,—

"—— are you so gospell'd
To pray for this *good* man?"

(*) Old text, *comming*.

You have made fair work, I fear me.—Pray, your news?
If Marcius should be join'd with Volscians,—
COM. *If!*
He is their god; he leads them like a thing
Made by some other deity than nature,
That shapes man better: and they follow him,
Against us brats, with no less confidence,
Than boys pursuing summer butterflies,
Or butchers killing flies.
MEN. You have made good work,
You and your apron-men; you that stood so much
Upon the voice of occupation,[a] and
The breath of garlic-eaters!
COM. He'll shake your Rome about your ears.
MEN. As Hercules did shake down mellow fruit.—
You have made fair work!
BRU. But is this true, sir?
COM. Ay; and you'll look pale
Before you find it other. All the regions[b]
Do smilingly revolt; and who resist
Are only mock'd for valiant ignorance,
And perish constant fools. Who is't can blame [him?
Your enemies and his find something in him.
MEN. We are all undone, unless
The noble man have mercy.
COM. Who shall ask it?
The tribunes cannot do't for shame; the people
Deserve such pity of him as the wolf
Does of the shepherds: for his best friends, if they
Should say, *Be good to Rome*, they charg'd him even
As those should do that had deserv'd his hate,
And therein show'd like enemies.
MEN. 'Tis true:
If he were putting to my house the brand
That should consume it, I have not the face
To say, *Beseech you, cease.*—You have made fair hands,
You, and your crafts! you have crafted fair!
COM. You have brought
A trembling upon Rome, such as was never
So incapable of help.
BOTH TRI. Say not, we brought it.
MEN. How! Was it we? we lov'd him; but, like beasts
And cowardly nobles, gave way unto your clusters,
Who did hoot him out o' the city.
COM. But I fear
They'll roar him in again. Tullus Aufidius,
The second name of men, obeys his points
As if he were his officer:—desperation
Is all the policy, strength, and defence,
That Rome can make against them.

Enter a troop of Citizens.

MEN. Here come the clusters.—
And is Aufidius with him?—You are they
That made the air unwholesome, when you cast
Your stinking greasy caps in hooting
At Coriolanus' exile. Now he's coming;
And not a hair upon a soldier's head,
Which will not prove a whip: as many coxcombs
As you threw caps up will he tumble down,
And pay you for your voices. 'Tis no matter;
If he could burn us all into one coal,
We have deserv'd it.
CITIZENS. Faith, we hear fearful news.
1 CIT. For mine own part,
When I said, banish him, I said, 'twas pity.
2 CIT. And so did I.
3 CIT. And so did I; and, to say the truth, so did very many of us: that we did, we did for the best; and though we willingly consented to his banishment, yet it was against our will.
COM. Ye're goodly things, you voices!
MEN. You have made good work,
You and your cry!—Shall's to the Capitol?
COM. O, ay; what else?
[*Exeunt* COM. *and* MEN.
SIC. Go, masters, get you home; be not dismay'd:
These are a side that would be glad to have
This true, which they so seem to fear. Go home,
And show no sign of fear.
1 CIT. The gods be good to us! Come, masters, let's home. I ever said we were i' the wrong, when we banished him.
2 CIT. So did we all. But, come, let's home.
[*Exeunt* Citizens.
BRU. I do not like this news.
SIC. Nor I.
BRU. Let's to the Capitol.—Would half my wealth
Would buy this for a lie!
SIC. Pray, let us go. [*Exeunt.*

SCENE VII.—*A Camp; at a small distance from* Rome.

Enter AUFIDIUS *and his* Lieutenant.

AUF. Do they still fly to the Roman?
LIEU. I do not know what witchcraft's in him, but
Your soldiers use him as the grace 'fore meat,
Their talk at table, and their thanks at end;
And you are darken'd in this action, sir,
Even by your own.

---

a — occupation.—] That is, *mechanics, craftsmen*.

b *All the* regions—] Should perhaps be, "All the *legions*," as Mr. Collier's annotator reads it.

AUF. I cannot help it now;
Unless, by using means, I lame the foot
Of our design. He bears himself more proudlier
Even to my person, than I thought he would
When first I did embrace him; yet his nature
In that's no changeling, and I must excuse
What cannot be amended.

LIEU. Yet I wish, sir,
(I mean for your particular) you had not
Join'd in commission with him; but either
Had * borne the action of yourself, or else
To him had left it solely.

AUF. I understand thee well; and be thou sure,
When he shall come to his account, he knows not
What I can urge against him. Although it seems,
And so he thinks, and is no less apparent
To the vulgar eye, that he bears all things fairly,
And shows good husbandry for the Volscian state,
Fights dragon-like, and does achieve as soon
As draw his sword; yet he hath left undone
That which shall break his neck or hazard mine,
Whene'er we come to our account.

LIEU. Sir, I beseech you, think you he'll carry Rome?

AUF. All places yield to him ere he sits down;
And the nobility of Rome are his:
The senators and patricians love him too:
The tribunes are no soldiers; and their people
Will be as rash in the repeal, as hasty
To expel him thence. I think he'll be to Rome,
As is the ospray to the fish, who takes it
By sovereignty of nature.[a] First he was
A noble servant to them; but he could not
Carry his honours even: whether 'twas pride,
Which out of daily fortune ever taints
The happy man; whether defect of judgment,
To fail in the disposing of those chances
Which he was lord of; or whether nature,
Not to be other than one thing, not moving
From the casque to the cushion, but commanding peace
Even with the same austerity and garb
As he controll'd the war; but one of these,
(As he hath spices of them all, not all,
For I dare so far free him) made him fear'd,
So hated, and so banish'd: but he has a merit,
To choke it in the utterance.[b] So our virtues *
Lie in the interpretation of the time;
And power, unto itself most commendable,
Hath not a tomb so evident as a chair
To extol what it hath done.[c]
One fire drives out one fire; one nail, one nail;
Rights by rights founder,[d] strengths by strengths do fail.
Come, let's away. When, Caius, Rome is thine,
Thou art poor'st of all; then shortly art thou mine. [*Exeunt.*

(*) Old text, *have*.

(*) Old text, *vertue*.

a By sovereignty of nature.] The image is founded on the fabulous power attributed to the ospray, of fascinating the fish on which it preys. Thus, in Peele's play, called "The Battle of Alcazar," 1594, Act II. Sc. 1,—

"I will provide thee of a princely *osprey*,
That as she flieth over fish in pools,
The fish shall turn their glistering bellies up,
And thou shalt take thy liberal choice of all."

b —— but he has a merit,
To choke it in the utterance.]

The latter portion of this speech is miserably confused. After "So hated, and so banish'd," there is obviously a chasm, which it were vain to think of filling up.

c —— So our virtues
Lie in the interpretation of the time;
And power, unto itself most commendable,
Hath not a tomb so evident as a chair
To extol what it hath done.]

The sentiment to be conveyed was no doubt identical with that expressed in Act I. Sc. 4, of "Hamlet:"—

"So, oft it chances in particular men,
That for some vicious mole of nature in them,
* * * * *
Their virtues else (be they as pure as grace,
As infinite as man may undergo,)
Shall in the general censure take corruption
From that particular fault."

And so, proceeds Aufidius, *our very virtues appear false by the misconstruction of the age, and even authority, which can exact applause, has not a more inevitable, i.e. certain, tomb for its best actions than the very chair of triumph wherein they are extolled.*

d *Rights by rights* founder,—] The old copies have "fouler," which has been changed to,—*fouled; foul are; suffer; foil'd are;* and *falter*. The emendation we adopt is by Malone.

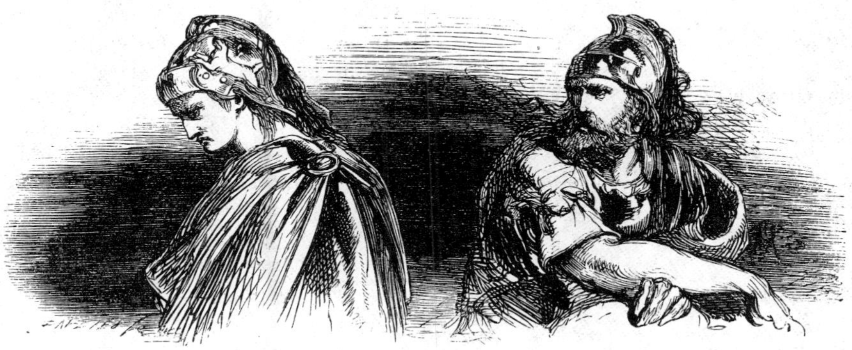

ACT V.

SCENE I.—Rome. *A Public Place.*

Enter MENENIUS, COMINIUS, SICINIUS, BRUTUS, *and Others.*

MEN. No, I'll not go: you hear what he hath said
Which was sometime his general; who lov'd him
In a most dear particular. He call'd me, father:
But what o' that? Go, you that banish'd him,
A mile before his tent fall down, and knee
The way into his mercy: nay, if he coyed
To hear Cominius speak, I'll keep at home.
COM. He would not seem to know me.
MEN. Do you hear?
COM. Yet one time he did call me by my name:
I urg'd our old acquaintance, and the drops
That we have bled together. *Coriolanus,*
He would not answer to: forbad all names;
He was a kind of nothing, titleless,
Till he had forg'd himself a name i' the fire
Of burning Rome.
MEN. Why, so! you have made good work:
A pair of tribunes that have rack'd for Rome,
To make coals cheap,—a noble memory!
COM. I minded him how royal 'twas to pardon
When it was less expected: he replied,
It was a bare[a] petition of a state
To one whom they had punish'd.

a *It was a* bare *petition of a state*
To one whom they had punish'd.]
Mason had no doubt we should read,—"It was a *base* petition;" but, even with this amendment, it is questionable if we have got what the poet wrote.

MEN. Very well:
Could he say less?
COM. I offer'd to awaken his regard
For's private friends: his answer to me was,
He could not stay to pick them in a pile
Of noisome musty chaff: he said, 'twas folly
For one poor grain or two, to leave unburnt,
And still to nose the offence.
MEN. *For one poor grain or two!*
I am one of those; his mother, wife, his child,
And this brave fellow too, we are the grains:
You are the musty chaff; and you are smelt
Above the moon. We must be burnt for you.
SIC. Nay, pray, be patient: if you refuse your aid
In this so never-heeded help, yet do not
Upbraid 's with our distress. But, sure, if you
Would be your country's pleader, your good tongue,
More than the instant army we can make,
Might stop our countryman.
MEN. No! I'll not meddle.
SIC. Pray you, go to him.
MEN. What should I do?
BRU. Only make trial what your love can do
For Rome, towards Marcius.
MEN. Well, and say that Marcius return me,
As Cominius is return'd, unheard; what then?—
But as a discontented friend, grief-shot
With his unkindness? say't be so?
SIC. Yet your good will
Must have that thanks from Rome, after the measure
As you intended well.
MEN. I'll undertake 't:
I think he'll hear me. Yet to bite his lip,
And hum at good Cominius, much unhearts me.
He was not taken well; he had not din'd:
The veins unfill'd, our blood is cold, and then
We pout upon the morning, are unapt
To give or to forgive; but when we have stuff'd
These pipes and these conveyances of our blood
With wine and feeding, we have suppler souls
Than in our priest-like fasts: therefore I'll watch him
Till he be dieted to my request,
And then I'll set upon him.
BRU. You know the very road into his kindness,
And cannot lose your way.
MEN. Good faith, I'll prove him:
Speed how it will, I shall ere long have knowledge
Of my success.[a] [*Exit.*
COM. He'll never hear him.
SIC. Not?
COM. I tell you, he does sit in gold,[b] his eye
Red as 'twould burn Rome; and his injury
The gaoler to his pity. I kneel'd before him;
'Twas very faintly he said, *Rise;* dismiss'd me
Thus, with his speechless hand: what he would do,
He sent in writing after me; what he would not,
Bound with an oath to yield to his conditions:[c]
So, that all hope is vain, unless[d] his noble mother
And his wife; who, as I hear, mean to solicit him
For mercy to his country. Therefore, let's hence,
And with our fair entreaties haste them on.
[*Exeunt.*

SCENE II.—*An advanced Post of the* Volscian *Camp before* Rome. *The* Guard *at their Stations.*

Enter to them, MENENIUS.

1 G. Stay: whence are you?
2 G. Stand, and go back.
MEN. You guard like men; 'tis well: but, by your leave,
I am an officer of state, and come
To speak with Coriolanus.
1 G. From whence?
MEN. From Rome.
1 G. You may not pass, you must return: our general
Will hear no more from thence.
2 G. You'll see your Rome embrac'd with fire, before
You'll speak with Coriolanus.
MEN. Good my friends,
If you have heard your general talk of Rome,

---

a Good faith, I'll prove him:
Speed how it will, I shall ere long have knowledge
Of my success.]

As this is invariably pointed,—

"Good faith, I'll prove him,
Speed how it will. I shall ere long," &c.

some critics have proposed to read,—

"*You* shall ere long," &c.

but the meaning of Menenius is,—I'll try him, and come what may, I shall not long be kept in suspense. "Success" has here the signification of *successo* in Italian, *i.e. event, consequence.*

b I tell you, he does sit in gold,—] The same idea, it has been noted, occurs in Homer (Iliad, viii. 442),—

"Αὐτὸς δὲ χρύσειον ἐπὶ θρόνον εὐρύοπα Ζεὺς
Ἕζετο."

which Pope renders,—

"Th' eternal Thunderer sat thron'd *in gold.*"

c —— what he would not,
Bound with an oath to yield to his conditions:]

The sense of this passage we conjecture to have been destroyed by the misprint of "his" for *no;* "his" being inadvertently caught by the transcriber from the next line. If we read,—

"—— what he would do,
He sent in writing after me; what he would not,
Bound with an oath to yield to *no* conditions,"

the meaning is clear enough,—what he would consent to, he sent in writing; what he would not, he bound himself by oath to yield on no conditions.

d — unless—] That is, *except.*

And of his friends there, it is lots to blanks,[a]
My name hath touch'd your ears; it is Menenius.

1 G. Be it so, go back; the virtue of your name
Is not here passable.

MEN. I tell thee, fellow,
Thy general is my lover: I have been
The book of his good acts, whence men have read
His fame unparallel'd, haply amplified;
For I have ever verified[b] my friends,
(Of whom he's chief) with all the size that verity
Would without lapsing suffer: nay, sometimes,
Like to a bowl upon a subtle[c] ground,
I have tumbled past the throw; and in his praise
Have almost stamp'd the leasing:[d] therefore, fellow,
I must have leave to pass.

1 G. Faith, sir, if you had told as many lies in his behalf as you have uttered words in your own, you should not pass here; no, though it were as virtuous to lie as to live chastely. Therefore, go back.

MEN. Pr'ythee, fellow, remember my name is Menenius, always factionary on the party of your general.

2 G. Howsoever you have been his liar, (as you say you have) I am one that, telling true under him, must say, you cannot pass. Therefore, go back.

MEN. Has he dined, canst thou tell? for I would not speak with him till after dinner.

1 G. You are a Roman, are you?

MEN. I am as thy general is.

1 G. Then you should hate Rome, as he does. Can you, when you have pushed out your gates the very defender of them, and, in a violent popular ignorance, given your enemy your shield, think to front his revenges with the easy[e] groans of old women, the virginal palms of your daughters, or with the palsied intercession of such a decayed dotant[f] as you seem to be? Can you think to blow out the intended fire your city is ready to flame in, with such weak breath as this? No, you are deceived; therefore, back to Rome, and prepare for your execution: you are condemned; our general has sworn you out of reprieve and pardon.

MEN. Sirrah, if thy captain knew I were here, he would use me with estimation.

---

a — lots to blanks,—] *Prizes to blanks*, everything to nothing: so in "Romeo and Juliet," Act III. Sc. 5,—

"—— and *all the world to nothing*
That he dares ne'er come back."

b *For I have ever* verified *my friends*, &c.] Hanmer gave *magnified*, and Mr. Collier's annotator has the same emendation; but perhaps the true word is *rarefied*, that is, *stretched out*. See "Love's Labour's Lost," Act IV. Sc. 2, where, for "ratified,"—"Here are only numbers *ratified*," we should also probably read *rarefied*.

c — a subtle *ground*,—] A *smooth, slippery* ground.

d — stamp'd the leasing:] "I have almost given the *lie* such a sanction as to render it current."—MALONE.

e — *the* easy *groans*—] "*Easy* groans" may mean the *slight, inconsiderable* groans; but query, *wheezy* groans?

f — a *decayed* dotant—] So the old text. Many editors, however, read *dotard*.

2 G. Come, my captain knows you not.

MEN. I mean, thy general.

1 G. My general cares not for you. Back, I say, go; lest I let forth your half pint of blood;—back,—that's the utmost of your having:—back.

MEN. Nay, but fellow, fellow,—

Enter CORIOLANUS *and* AUFIDIUS.

COR. What's the matter?

MEN. Now, you companion,[a] I'll say an errand for you; you shall know now that I am in estimation; you shall perceive that a Jack guardant cannot office me from my son Coriolanus: guess, but by* my entertainment with him, if thou standest not i'the state of hanging, or of some death more long in spectatorship, and crueller in suffering; behold now presently, and swoon for what's to come upon thee.—The glorious gods sit in hourly synod about thy particular prosperity, and love thee no worse than thy old father Menenius does! O, my son, my son! thou art preparing fire for us; look thee, here's water to quench it. I was hardly moved to come to thee; but being assured none but myself could move thee, I have been blown out of your gates with sighs; and conjure thee to pardon Rome, and thy petitionary countrymen. The good gods assuage thy wrath, and turn the dregs of it upon this varlet here;—this, who, like a block, hath denied my access to thee.

COR. Away!

MEN. How! *away?*

COR. Wife, mother, child, I know not. My affairs
Are servanted to others: though I owe
My revenge properly,[b] my remission lies
In Volscian breasts. That we have been familiar,
Ingrate forgetfulness shall poison, rather
Than pity note how much.—Therefore, be gone.
Mine ears against your suits are stronger than
Your gates against my force. Yet, for I lov'd thee,
Take this along; I writ it for thy sake,
[*Gives a letter.*
And would have sent it. Another word, Menenius,
I will not hear thee speak.—This man, Aufidius,
Was my belov'd in Rome: yet thou behold'st!—

AUF. You keep a constant temper.

[*Exeunt* CORIOLANUS *and* AUFIDIUS.

1 G. Now, sir, is your name Menenius?

2 G. 'Tis a spell, you see, of much power: you know the way home again.

1 G. Do you hear how we are shent[c] for keeping your greatness back?

2 G. What cause, do you think, I have to swoon?

MEN. I neither care for the world nor your general: for such things as you, I can scarce think there's any, ye're so slight. He that hath a will to die by himself fears it not from another: let your general do his worst. For you, be that you are, long; and your misery increase with your age! I say to you, as I was said to, Away! [*Exit.*

1 G. A noble fellow, I warrant him.

2 G. The worthy fellow is our general: he's the rock, the oak not to be wind-shaken. [*Exeunt.*

SCENE III.—*The Tent of* Coriolanus.

Enter CORIOLANUS, AUFIDIUS, *and Others.*

COR. We will before the walls of Rome to-morrow
Set down our host.—My partner in this action,
You must report to the Volscian lords, how plainly
I have borne this business.

AUF. Only their ends
You have respected; stopp'd your ears against
The general suit of Rome; never admitted
A private whisper, no, not with such friends
That thought them sure of you.

COR. This last old man,
Whom with a crack'd heart I have sent to Rome,
Lov'd me above the measure of a father;
Nay, godded me, indeed. Their latest refuge
Was to send him; for whose old love, I have
(Though I show'd sourly to him) once more offer'd
The first conditions, which they did refuse,
And cannot now accept; to grace him only
That thought he could do more, a very little
I have yielded to: fresh embassies and suits,
Nor from the state nor private friends, hereafter
Will I lend ear to.—Ha! what shout is this?
[*Shout without.*
Shall I be tempted to infringe my vow
In the same time 'tis made? I will not.—

Enter, in mourning habits, VIRGILIA, VOLUMNIA, *leading young* MARCIUS, VALERIA, *and* Attendants.

My wife comes foremost; then the honour'd mould
Wherein this trunk was fram'd, and in her hand
The grandchild to her blood. But, out, affection!
All bond and privilege of nature, break!
Let it be virtuous to be obstinate.—
What is that court'sy worth? or those doves' eyes,

(*) Old text omits, *by*.

a — companion,—] That is, as we now say, *fellow*.

b — properly,—] *Peculiarly, personally.*

c — shent—] *Disgraced.*

Which can make gods forsworn?—I melt, and am not
Of stronger earth than others.—My mother bows;
As if Olympus to a molehill should
In supplication nod; and my young boy
Hath an aspéct of intercession, which
Great nature cries, *Deny not.*—Let the Volsces
Plough Rome, and harrow Italy; I'll never
Be such a gosling to obey instinct; but stand,
As if a man were author of himself,
And knew no other kin.
VIRG. My lord and husband!
COR. These eyes are not the same I wore in Rome.
VIRG. The sorrow that delivers us thus chang'd
Makes you think so.
COR. Like a dull actor now,
I have forgot my part, and I am out,
Even to a full disgrace.—Best of my flesh,
Forgive my tyranny; but do not say,
For that, *Forgive our Romans.*—O, a kiss
Long as my exile, sweet as my revenge!
Now, by the jealous queen of heaven, that kiss
I carried from thee, dear; and my true lip
Hath virgin'd it e'er since.—You gods! I prate,*
And the most noble mother of the world
Leave unsaluted: sink, my knee, i' the earth; [*Kneels.*

(*) Old text, *pray*, corrected by Theobald.

Of thy deep duty more impression show
Than that of common sons.
VOL. O, stand up bless'd!
Whilst, with no softer cushion than the flint,
I kneel before thee; and unproperly
Show duty, as mistaken all this while
Between the child and parent. [*Kneels.*
COR. What is this?
Your knees to me? to your corrected son?
Then let the pebbles on the hungry[a] beach
Fillip the stars; then let the mutinous winds
Strike the proud cedars 'gainst the fiery sun;
Murd'ring impossibility, to make
What cannot be, slight work.
VOL. Thou art my warrior;
I holp* to frame thee.—Do you know this lady?
COR. The noble sister of Publicola,
The moon of Rome; chaste as the icicle,
That's curded by the frost from purest snow,
And hangs on Dian's temple:—dear Valeria!
VOL. This is a poor epitome of yours,
Which by the interpretation of full time
May show like all yourself.
COR. The god of soldiers,
With the consent of supreme Jove, inform
Thy thoughts with nobleness, that thou mayst prove
To shame unvulnerable, and stick i' the wars

(*) Old text, *hope*, corrected by Theobald.

a — *the* hungry *beach*—] The *sterile, unprolific* beach; or as Malone suggested, the shore *hungry* for shipwrecks. *Littus avarum.*

Like a great sea-mark, standing every flaw,
And saving those that eye thee!
VOL. Your knee, sirrah.
COR. That's my brave boy!
VOL. Even he, your wife, this lady, and myself,
Are suitors to you.
COR. I beseech you, peace:
Or, if you'd ask, remember this before,—
The things* I have forsworn to grant may never
Be held by you denials. Do not bid me
Dismiss my soldiers, or capitulate
Again with Rome's mechanics: tell me not
Wherein I seem unnatural: desire not
To allay my rages and revenges with
Your colder reasons.
VOL. O, no more, no more!
You have said you will not grant us anything;
For we have nothing else to ask, but that
Which you deny already: yet we will ask;
That, if you fail in our request,[a] the blame
May hang upon your hardness: therefore hear us.
COR. Aufidius, and you Volsces, mark; for we'll
Hear nought from Rome in private.—Your request?
VOL. Should we be silent and not speak, our raiment
And state of bodies would bewray what life
We have led since thy exile. Think with thyself,
How more unfortunate than all living women
Are we come hither: since that thy sight, which should
Make our eyes flow with joy, hearts dance with comforts,
Constrains them weep, and shake with fear and sorrow;
Making the mother, wife, and child, to see
The son, the husband, and the father, tearing
His country's bowels out. And to poor we
Thine enmity's most capital: thou barrest us
Our prayers to the gods, which is a comfort
That all but we enjoy; for how can we,
Alas! how can we for our country pray,
Whereto we are bound,—together with thy victory,
Whereto we are bound? Alack! or we must lose
The country, our dear nurse; or else thy person,
Our comfort in the country. We must find
An evident calamity,[b] though we had
Our wish, which side should win; for either thou
Must, as a foreign recreant, be led
With manacles through our streets, or else
Triumphantly tread on thy country's ruin,
And bear the palm for having bravely shed
Thy wife and children's blood. For myself, son,
I purpose not to wait on fortune till
These wars determine: if I cannot persuade thee
Rather to show a noble grace to both parts,
Than seek the end of one, thou shalt no sooner
March to assault thy country, than to tread
(Trust to't, thou shalt not) on thy mother's womb,
That brought thee to this world.
VIRG. Ay, and mine,
That brought you forth this boy, to keep your name
Living to time.
BOY. 'A shall not tread on me;
I'll run away till I am bigger, but then I'll fight.
COR. Not of a woman's tenderness to be,
Requires nor child nor woman's face to see.
I have sat too long. [*Rising.*
VOL. Nay, go not from us thus,
If it were so that our request did tend
To save the Romans, thereby to destroy
The Volsces whom you serve, you might condemn us,
As poisonous of your honour: no; our suit
Is, that you reconcile them: while the Volsces
May say, *This mercy we have show'd;* the Romans,
This we receiv'd; and each in either side
Give the *All-hail* to thee, and cry, *Be bless'd*
For making up this peace! Thou know'st, great son,
The end of war's uncertain; but this certain,
That if thou conquer Rome, the benefit
Which thou shalt thereby reap is such a name,
Whose repetition will be dogg'd with curses;
Whose chronicle thus writ,—*The man was noble,*
But with his last attempt he wip'd it out;
Destroy'd his country; and his name remains
To the ensuing age abhorr'd. Speak to me, son:
Thou hast affected the fine* strains of honour,
To imitate the graces of the gods;
To tear with thunder the wide cheeks o' the air,
And yet to charge† thy sulphur with a bolt
That should but rive an oak. Why dost not speak?
Think'st thou it honourable for a noble man
Still to remember wrongs?—Daughter, speak you;
He cares not for your weeping.—Speak thou, boy;
Perhaps thy childishness will move him more
Than can our reasons.—There's no man in the world
More bound to 's mother; yet here he lets me prate
Like one i' the stocks. Thou hast never in thy life
Show'd thy dear mother any courtesy;

(*) Old text, *thing*.

a That, if you fail in our request,—] If you fail to grant what we require. Pope and Mr. Collier's annotator read, "—if *we* fail," &c.

b *An* evident *calamity*,—] An *inevitable* calamity. So in Act IV. Sc. 7,—

"And power—
Hath not a tomb so *evident* as a chair."

(*) Old text, *five*. (†) Old text, *change*.

When she, (poor hen!) fond of no second brood,
Has cluck'd thee to the wars, and safely home,
Loaden with honour. Say my request's unjust,
And spurn me back: but, if it be not so,
Thou art not honest, and the gods will plague thee,
That thou restrain'st from me the duty, which
To a mother's part belongs.—He turns away:
Down, ladies! let us shame him with our knees.
To his surname Coriolanus 'longs more pride,
Than pity to our prayers. Down! an end:
This is the last. So, we will home to Rome,
And die among our neighbours.—Nay, behold 's;
This boy that cannot tell what he would have,
But kneels and holds up hands for fellowship,
Does reason our petition with more strength
Than thou hast to deny't.—Come, let us go:
This fellow had a Volscian to his mother;
His wife is in Corioli, and his child
Like him by chance.—Yet give us our dispatch:
I am hush'd until our city be a-fire,
And then I'll speak a little.

COR. [*After holding* VOLUMNIA *by the hand, silent.*] O mother, mother!
What have you done?—Behold! the heavens do ope,
The gods look down, and this unnatural scene
They laugh at.—O, my mother, mother! O!
You have won a happy victory to Rome;
But, for your son,—believe it, O, believe it,
Most dangerously you have with him prevail'd,
If not most mortal(1) to him! But, let it come.—
Aufidius, though I cannot make true wars,
I'll frame convenient peace. Now, good Aufidius,
Were you in my stead, would you have heard
A mother less? or granted less, Aufidius?

AUF. I was mov'd withal.

COR. I dare be sworn, you were:
And, sir, it is no little thing to make
Mine eyes to sweat compassion. But, good sir,
What peace you'll make, advise me: for my part,
I'll not to Rome, I'll back with you; and pray you,
Stand to me in this cause.—O mother! wife!

AUF. [*Aside.*] I am glad, thou hast set thy mercy and thy honour
At difference in thee: out of that I'll work
Myself a former fortune.

[*The* Ladies *make signs to* CORIOLANUS.

COR. Ay, by and by;
[*To* VOLUMNIA, VIRGILIA, *&c.*
But we will drink together; and you shall bear
A better witness back than words, which we,
On like conditions, will have counter-seal'd.
Come, enter with us. Ladies, you deserve
To have a temple built you: (2) all the swords
In Italy, and her confederate arms,
Could not have made this peace. [*Exeunt.*

SCENE IV.—Rome. *A Public Place.*

Enter MENENIUS *and* SICINIUS.

MEN. See you yond' coign o' the Capitol,—yond' corner-stone?

SIC. Why, what of that?

MEN. If it be possible for you to displace it with your little finger, there is some hope the ladies of Rome, especially his mother, may prevail with him. But I say there is no hope in 't; our throats are sentenced, and stay upon execution.

SIC. Is 't possible that so short a time can alter the condition of a man?

MEN. There is differency between a grub and a butterfly; yet your butterfly was a grub. This Marcius is grown from man to dragon: he has wings; he 's more than a creeping thing.

SIC. He loved his mother dearly.

MEN. So did he me: and he no more remembers his mother now than an eight-year-old horse. The tartness of his face sours ripe grapes: when he walks, he moves like an engine, and the ground shrinks before his treading: he is able to pierce a corslet with his eye; talks like a knell, and his hum is a battery. He sits in his state, as a thing made for Alexander. What he bids be done, is finished with his bidding. He wants nothing of a god but eternity, and a heaven to throne in.

SIC. Yes, mercy, if you report him truly.

MEN. I paint him in the character. Mark what mercy his mother shall bring from him: there is no more mercy in him than there is milk in a male tiger; that shall our poor city find: and all this is 'long of you.

SIC. The gods be good unto us!

MEN. No, in such a case the gods will not be good unto us. When we banished him, we respected not them; and, he returning to break our necks, they respect not us.

Enter a Messenger.

MESS. Sir, if you 'd save your life, fly to your house:
The plebeians have got your fellow-tribune,
And hale him up and down; all swearing, if
The Roman ladies bring not comfort home,
They 'll give him death by inches.

Enter another Messenger.

SIC. What 's the news?

MESS. Good news! good news!—the ladies have prevail'd,
The Volscians are dislodg'd, and Marcius gone!

A merrier day did never yet greet Rome,
No, not the expulsion of the Tarquins.
SIC. Friend, art thou certain this is true? is 't most certain?
SEC. MESS. As certain as I know the sun is fire:
Where have you lurk'd, that you make doubt of it?
Ne'er through an arch so hurried the blown[a] tide,
As the recomforted through the gates. Why, hark you!
[*Trumpets and hautboys sounded, and drums beaten, all together. Shouting also without.*
The trumpets, sackbuts, psalteries, and fifes,
Tabors, and cymbals, and the shouting Romans,
Make the sun dance. Hark you! [*Shouting again.*
MEN. This is good news:
I will go meet the ladies. This Volumnia
Is worth of consuls, senators, patricians,
A city full; of tribunes, such as you,
A sea and land full. You have pray'd well to-day;
This morning for ten thousand of your throats
I'd not have given a doit. Hark, how they joy!
[*Shouting and music.*
SIC. First, the gods bless you for your tidings: next,
Accept my thankfulness.
SEC. MESS. Sir, we have all
Great cause to give great thanks.
SIC. They are near the city?
SEC. MESS. Almost at point to enter.
SIC. We'll meet them, and help the joy.
[*Exeunt.*

SCENE V.—*The same. A Street near the Gate.*

Enter the Ladies, *accompanied by* Senators, Patricians, *and* People. *They pass over the stage.*

1 SEN. Behold our patroness, the life of Rome!
Call all your tribes together, praise the gods,
And make triumphant fires; strew flowers before them:
Unshout the noise that banish'd Marcius,
Repeal him with the welcome of his mother;
Cry,—*Welcome, ladies, welcome!*—
ALL. Welcome, ladies! Welcome!
[*A flourish with drums and trumpets. Exeunt.*

SCENE VI.—Corioli.[b] *A Public Place.*

Enter TULLUS AUFIDIUS, *with* Attendants.

AUF. Go tell the lords o' the city, I am here:
Deliver them this paper: having read it,
Bid them repair to the market-place; where I,
Even in theirs and in the commons' ears,
Will vouch the truth of it. Him I accuse
The city ports by this hath enter'd, and
Intends to appear before the people, hoping
To purge himself with words: dispatch.
[*Exeunt* Attendants.

Enter three or four Conspirators *of* Aufidius' *faction.*

Most welcome!
1 CON. How is it with our general?
AUF. Even so
As with a man by his own alms empoison'd,
And with his charity slain.
2 CON. Most noble sir,
If you do hold the same intent wherein
You wish'd us parties, we'll deliver you
Of your great danger.
AUF. Sir, I cannot tell;
We must proceed as we do find the people.
3 CON. The people will remain uncertain whilst
'Twixt you there's difference; but the fall of either
Makes the survivor heir of all.
AUF. I know it;
And my pretext to strike at him admits
A good construction. I rais'd him, and I pawn'd
Mine honour for his truth: who being so heighten'd,
He water'd his new plants with dews of flattery,
Seducing so my friends; and, to this end,
He bow'd his nature, never known before
But to be rough, unswayable, and free.
3 CON. Sir, his stoutness,[c]
When he did stand for consul, which he lost
By lack of stooping,—
AUF. That I would have spoke of.
Being banish'd for't, he came unto my hearth;
Presented to my knife his throat: I took him;
Made him joint-servant with me; gave him way
In all his own desires; nay, let him choose
Out of my files, his projects to accomplish,
My best and freshest men; serv'd his designments
In mine own person; holp to reap the fame
Which he did end[d] all his; and took some pride

---

a — blown *tide*,—] *Blown* tide, like "*blown* ambition," "King Lear," Act IV. Sc. 4, means "*swoll'n* tide." There is no allusion to the wind, as some commentators suppose.

b Corioli.] In all the editions, from Rowe downwards, this scene has been laid in Antium, until Mr. Singer correctly changed it to Corioli.

c Sir, his stoutness,—] A word seems to have dropped out of this line; it possibly ran originally,—"*Witness*, sir, his stoutness."

d *Which he did* end *all his;*] So the old copies. Rowe changed "end" to "make;" Mr. Collier's annotator substitutes "ear;" and Mr. Collier has a preference for *in*,—"did *in* all his;" but is not "end" an erratum for *bind?* So, in "As You Like It," Act I. Sc. 2,—

"They that reap must sheaf and *bind*."

Again, in Beaumont and Fletcher's "Bonduca," Act IV. Sc. 3,—

"—— when Rome, like reapers,
Sweat blood and spirit for a glorious harvest,
And *bound* it up, and brought it off."

And in the ancient Harvest Song,—

"Hooky, hooky, we have shorn
And *bound* what we did reap."

To do myself this wrong: till, at the last,
I seem'd his follower, not partner; and
He wag'd me with his countenance,[a] as if
I had been mercenary.
1 Con. So he did, my lord,—
The army marvell'd at it; and, in the last,
When he had carried Rome, and that we look'd
For no less spoil than glory,—
Auf. There was it,
For which my sinews shall be stretch'd upon him.
At a few drops of women's rheum, which are
As cheap as lies, he sold the blood and labour
Of our great action; therefore shall he die,
And I'll renew me in his fall. But, hark!
[*Drums and trumpets sound, with great shouts of the* People.
1 Con. Your native town you enter'd like a post,
And had no welcomes home; but he returns,
Splitting the air with noise.
2 Con. And patient fools,
Whose children he hath slain, their base throats tear
With giving him glory.
3 Con. Therefore, at your vantage,
Ere he express himself, or move the people
With what he would say, let him feel your sword,
Which we will second. When he lies along,
After your way his tale pronounc'd shall bury
His reasons with his body.[b]
Auf. Say no more;
Here come the lords.

Enter the Lords *of the city.*

Lords. You are most welcome home.
Auf. I have not deserv'd it,
But, worthy lords, have you with heed perus'd
What I have written to you?
Lords. We have.
1 Lord. And grieve to hear't.
What faults he made before the last, I think,
Might have found easy fines: but there to end,
Where he was to begin; and give away
The benefit of our levies, answering us
With our own charge; making a treaty where
There was a yielding,—this admits no excuse.
Auf. He approaches; you shall hear him.

Enter Coriolanus, *with drum and colours; a crowd of* Citizens *with him.*

Cor. Hail, lords! I am return'd your soldier;(3)
No more infected with my country's love
Than when I parted hence, but still subsisting
Under your great command. You are to know,
That prosperously I have attempted, and
With bloody passage led your wars, even to
The gates of Rome. Our spoils we have brought home
Do more than counterpoise, a full third part,
The charges of the action. We have made peace,
With no less honour to the Antiates,
Than shame to the Romans: and we here deliver,
Subscrib'd by the consuls and patricians,
Together with the seal o' the senate, what
We have compounded on.
Auf. Read it not, noble lords;
But tell the traitor, in the highest degree
He hath abus'd your powers.
Cor. *Traitor!*—How now?—
Auf. Ay, traitor, Marcius.
Cor. *Marcius!*
Auf. Ay, Marcius, Caius Marcius; dost thou think
I'll grace thee with that robbery, thy stol'n name,
Coriolanus, in Corioli?—[c]
You lords and heads o' the state, perfidiously
He has betray'd your business, and given up,
For certain drops of salt, your city Rome
(I say, your city) to his wife and mother;
Breaking his oath and resolution, like
A twist of rotten silk; never admitting
Counsel o' the war; but at his nurse's tears
He whin'd and roar'd away your victory,
That pages blush'd at him, and men of heart
Look'd wondering each at other.
Cor. Hear'st thou, Mars!
Auf. Name not the god, thou boy of tears!
Cor. Ha!
Auf. No more.
Cor. Measureless liar! thou hast made my heart
Too great for what contains it. *Boy!* O slave!—
Pardon me, lords, 'tis the first time that ever
I was forc'd to scold. Your judgments, my grave lords,
Must give this cur the lie: and his own notion
(Who wears my stripes impress'd upon him; that
Must bear my beating to his grave) shall join
To thrust the lie unto him.
1 Lord. Peace both and hear me speak.
Cor. Cut me to pieces, Volsces! men and lads,
Stain all your edges on me!—*Boy!* False hound!
If you have writ your annals true, 'tis there,
That, like an eagle in a dove-cote, I
Flutter'd* your Volscians in Corioli:
Alone I did it!—*Boy!*

---

[a] —— *and*
He wag'd *me with his* countenance,—]
This is explained,—he gave me his countenance for my wages, rewarded me with good looks. But "countenance," or we mistake, means here not looks, but *entertainment*. See note (g), p. 255, Vol. I.

[b] His reasons with his body.] In the old copies we have,—
"—— let him feele your Sword:
Which we will second, when he lies along
After your way. His Tale pronounc'd shall bury
His Reasons, with his Body."

(*) Old text, *Flatter'd*.

[c] — in Corioli?—] See note (b), in the preceding page.

AUF. Why, noble lords,
Will you be put in mind of his blind fortune,
Which was your shame, by this unholy braggart,
'Fore your own eyes and ears?

CONSPIRATORS. Let him die for't!

CITIZENS. [*Speaking promiscuously.*] Tear him to pieces!—Do it presently!—He killed my son!—my daughter!—He killed my cousin Marcus!—He killed my father!—

2 LORD. Peace, ho!—no outrage:—peace!
The man is noble, and his fame folds in
This orb o' the earth. His last offence to us
Shall have judicious hearing.—Stand, Aufidius,
And trouble not the peace.

COR. O, that I had him,
With six Aufidiuses, or more, his tribe,
To use my lawful sword!

AUF. Insolent villain!

CON. Kill, kill, kill, kill, kill him!

[AUFIDIUS *and the* Conspirators *draw, and kill* CORIOLANUS, *who falls, and* AUFIDIUS *stands on him.*

LORDS. Hold, hold, hold, hold!

AUF. My noble masters, hear me speak.

1 LORD. O Tullus!—

2 LORD. Thou hast done a deed whereat
Valour will weep.

3 LORD. Tread not upon him.—Masters all, be quiet;
Put up your swords.

AUF. My lords, when you shall know (as in this rage,
Provok'd by him, you cannot) the great danger
Which this man's life did owe you, you'll rejoice
That he is thus cut off. Please it your honours
To call me to your senate, I'll deliver
Myself your loyal servant, or endure
Your heaviest censure.

1 LORD. Bear from hence his body,
And mourn you for him: let him be regarded
As the most noble corse that ever herald
Did follow to his urn.

2 LORD. His own impatience
Takes from Aufidius a great part of blame.
Let's make the best of it.

AUF. My rage is gone,
And I am struck with sorrow.—Take him up:—
Help, three o' the chiefest soldiers; I'll be one.—
Beat thou the drum, that it speak mournfully:
Trail your steel pikes.—Though in this city he
Hath widowed and unchilded many a one,
Which to this hour bewail the injury,
Yet he shall have a noble memory.—
Assist.

[*Exeunt, bearing the body of* CORIOLANUS. *A dead march sounded.*

ILLUSTRATIVE COMMENTS.

ACT I.

(1) Scene I.—*Suffer us to famish, and their store-houses crammed with grain; make edicts for usury, to support usurers.*] The circumstances which led to the insurrection of the people in Rome at this period, and awakened their animosity in a peculiar degree against Caius Marcius, are thus related in North's translation of Plutarch, the work to which Shakespeare was indebted for all the conduct of his tragedy, and for no inconsiderable portion of its language :—

"Now he being grown to great credit and authority in Rome for his valiantnesse, it fortuned there grew sedition in the citie, bicause the Senate dyd favour the rich against the people, who did complaine of the sore oppression of userers, of whom they borrowed mony. For those that had litle, were yet spoiled of that litle they had by their creditours, for lack of ability to pay the usery : who offered their goods to be sold to them that would give most. And such as had nothing left, their bodies were layed hold on, and they were made their bondmen, notwithstanding all the wounds and cuts they shewed, which they had received in many battels, fighting for defence of their countrey and common wealth : of the which, the last warre they made was against the Sabynes, wherein they fought upon the promise the rich men had made them, that from thenceforth they would intreate them more gently, and also upon the word of *Marcus Valerius* chiefe of the Senate, who by authority of the Counsell, and in the behalfe of the rich, sayed they should performe that they had promised. But after that they had faithfully served in this last battel of al, where they overcame their enemies, seeing they were never a whit the better, nor more gently intreated, and that the Senate would give no eare to them, but made as though they had forgotten the former promise, and suffered them to be made slaves and bondmen to their creditours, and besides, to be turned out of all that ever they had : they fel then even to flat rebellion and mutinie, and to sturre up dangerous tumults within the city. The Romaines enemies hearing of this rebellion, did straight enter the teritories of Rome with a marvelous great power, spoiling and burning all as they came. Whereupon the Senate immediatly made open proclamation by sound of trumpet, that all those which were of lawfull age to cary weapon, should come and enter their names into the muster-masters book, to goe to the wars : but no man obeyed their commaundement. Wherupon their chiefe magistrates, and many of the Senate, began to be of divers opinions among themselves. For some thought it was reason, they shold somewhat yeeld to the poore peoples request, and that they should a litle qualifie the severity of the law. Other held hard against that opinion, and that was *Martius* for one. For he alledged, that the creditours losing their money they had lent, was not the worst thing that was thereby : but that the lenity that was favoured, was a beginning of disobedience, and that the proud attempt of the communalty, was to abolish law, and to bring all to confusion. Therefore he sayed, if the Senate were wise, they should betimes prevent and quench this ill favoured and worse meant beginning."

(2) Scene I.—*And leave me but the bran.*] The reader desirous of investigating the origin of the famous apologue of the belly and its members will do well to consult an article on the subject by Douce, in his "Illustrations of Shakespeare." The poet derived it apparently from Plutarch, through North's translation, and the marvellous skill with which he has varied and amplified the story will be seen from the version of it which that historian presents :—

"The Senate being afeard of their departure, dyd send unto them certaine of the pleasauntest olde men, and the most acceptable to the people among them. Of those, *Menenius Agrippa* was he, who was sent for chief man of the message from the Senate. He, after many good persuasions and gentle requests made to the people, on the behalfe of the Senate, knit up his oration in the ende, with a notable tale, in this manner. That on a time all the members of mans bodie, dyd rebell against the bellie, complaining of it, that it only remained in the middest of the bodie, without doing any thing, neither dyd beare any labour to the maintenaunce of the rest : whereas all other partes and members dyd labour paynefully, and was very carefull to satisfie the appetites and desiers of the bodie. And so the bellie, all this notwithstanding, laughed at their follie, and sayed, It is true, I first receyve all meates that norishe mans bodie : but afterwardes I send it againe to the norishment of other partes of the same. Even so (q. he) ô you, my masters, and cittizens of Rome : the reason is a like betweene the Senate and you. For matters being well digested, and their counsells throughly examined, touching the benefit of the common wealth : the Senatours are cause of the common commoditie that commeth unto every one of you."

(3) Scene III.—*His brows bound with oak.*] The oaken garland, accounted the most honourable crown among the Romans, was bestowed on him that had saved the life of a citizen :—

"But *Martius* being more inclined to the warres, then any other gentleman of his time, beganne from his childhood to give himselfe to handle weapons, and daily did exercise himselfe therein : and outward he esteemed armour to no purpose, unlesse one were naturally armed within. Moreover he did so exercise his body to hardnesse and all kinde of activitie, that he was very swift in ronning, strong in wrestling, and mightie in griping, so that no man could ever cast him. Insomuch as those that would try masteries with him for strength and nimblenesse, would say when they were overcom : that all was by reason of his naturall strength, and hardnesse of ward, that never yeelded to any paine or toyle he tooke upon him. The first time he went to the wars, being but a stripling, was when *Tarquine* surnamed the proud (that had bene king of Rome, and was driven out for his pride, after many attemps made by sundry battels to come in againe, wherein he was ever overcome) did come to Rome with all the aide of the Latines, and many other people of Italy : even as it were to set up his whole rest upon a battel by them, who with a great and mighty army had undertaken to put him into his kingdome againe, not so much to pleasure him, as to overthrow the power of the Romaines, whose greatnesse they both feared and envied. In this battell, wherein are many hote and sharpe encounters of either party, *Martius* valiantly fought in the sight of the *Dictator:* and a ROMAINE souldier being throwen to the ground even hard by him, *Martius* straight bestrid him, and slue the enemie with his owne hands that had before overthrowen the ROMAINE. Hereupon after the battell was won, the *Dictator* did not forget so noble an act, and therefore first of all he crowned *Martius* with a garland of oken boughes, For whosoever saveth the life of a ROMAINE, it is a manner among them, to honour him with such a garland."

(4) SCENE IV.—

'T is for the followers Fortune widens them,
Not for the fliers.]

So in the corresponding scene in the old translation of Plutarch :—

"Wherfore all the other VOLSCES fearing least that city should be taken by assault, they came from all parts of the countrey to save it, entending to give the ROMAINES battel before the city, and to give an onset on them in two several places. The Consul *Cominius* understanding this, devided his army also into two parts, and taking the one part with himself, he marched towards them that were drawing to the city out of the countrey: and the other part of his army he left in the campe with *Titus Lartius* (one of the valiantest men the ROMAINES had at that time) to resist those that would make any sally out of the city upon them. So the CORIOLANS making smal account of them that lay in campe before the city, made a sally out upon them, in the which at the first the CORIOLANS had the better, and drave the ROMAINES back againe into the trenches of their campe. But *Martius* being there at that time, ronning out of the campe with a few men with him, he slue the first enemies he met withall, and made the rest of them stay upon a sodain, crying out to the ROMAINES that had turned their backes, and calling them again to fight with a lowde voice. For he was even such another, as *Cato* would have a souldier and a captaine to be, not only terrible and fierce to lay about him, but to make the enemy afeard with the sound of his voice, and grimnesse of his countenaunce. Then there flocked about him immediatly, a great number of ROMAINES : whereat the enemies were so afeard, that they gave back presently.

"But *Martius* not staying so, did chase and follow them to their own gates, that fled for life. And there perceiving that the ROMAINES retired back, for the great number of darts and arrowes which flew about their eares from the wals of the city, and that there was not one man amongst them that durst venter himself to follow the flying enemies into their city, for that it was full of men of warre, very wel armed and appointed, he did incourage his fellowes with words and deeds, crying out to them, that fortune had opened the gates of the city, more for the followers then the fliers. But all this notwithstanding, few had the hearts to follow him. Howbeit *Martius* being in the throng among the enemies, thrust himself into the gates of the city, and entred the same among them that fled, without that any one of them durst at the first turne their face upon him, or offer to stay him. But he looking about him, and seeing he was entred the city with very few men to helpe him, and perceiving he was environed by his enemies that gathered round about to set upon him, did things then as it is written, wonderfull and incredible, as well for the force of his hand, as also for the agility of his body, and with a wonderfull courage and valiantnesse he made a lane through the middest of them, and overthrew also those he layed at : that some he made ronne to the furthest part of the city, and other for feare he made yeeld themselves, and to let fall their weapons before him."

(5) SCENE VI.—

As I guess, Marcius,
Their bands i' the vaward are the Antiates
Of their best trust; o'er them Aufidius,
Their very heart of hope.]

The incidents in this battle are all closely copied from Plutarch :—

"*Martius* asked him howe the order of their enemies battell was, and on which side they had placed their best fighting men. The Consul made him aunswer, that he thought the bandes which were in the voward of their battell, were those of the ANTIATES, whom they esteemed to be the warlikest men, and which for valiant courage would give no place to any of the hoast of their enemies. Then prayed *Martius*, to be set directly against them. The Consul granted him, greatly praising his courage. Then *Martius*, when both armies came almost to joyne, advanced himselfe a good space before his company, and went so fiercely to give charge on the voward that came right against him, that they could stand no longer in his hands : he made such a lane through them, and opened a passage into the battell of the enemies. But the two wings of either side turned one to the other, to compasse him in betweene them : which the Consul *Cominius* perceiving, he sent thither straight of the best souldiers he had about him. So the battell was marvelous blodie about *Martius*, and in a very short space many were slaine in the place. But in the end the ROMAINES were so strong, that they distressed the enemies, and brake their arraye : and scattering them, made them flye. Then they prayed *Martius* that he would retire to the campe, bicause they saw he was able to do no more, he was already so wearied with the great paine he had taken, and so faint with the great woundes he had upon him. But *Martius* aunswered them, that it was not for conquerours to yeeld, nor to be faint-hearted : and thereupon began afresh to chase those that fledde, untill such time as the armie of the enemies was utterly overthrowen, and numbers of them slaine and taken prisoners.

The next morning betimes, *Martius* went to the Consul, and the other ROMAINES with him. There the Consul *Cominius* going up to his chayer of state, in the presence of the whole armie, gave thanks to the gods for so great, glorious, and prosperous a victorie : then he spake to *Martius*, whose valiantnesse he commended beyond the Moone, both for that he him selfe saw him do with his eyes, as also for that *Martius* had reported unto him. So in the ende he willed *Martius*, he should choose out of all the horses they had taken of their enemies, and of all the goodes they had wonne (whereof there was great store) tenne of every sorte which he liked best, before any distribution should be made to other. Besides this great honorable offer he had made him, he gave him in testimonie that he had wonne that day the prise of prowesse above all other, a goodly horse with a capparison, and all furniture to him : which the whole army beholding, did marvellously praise and commend. But *Martius* stepping forth, told the Consul, he most thankfully accepted the gift of his horse, and was a glad man besides, that his service had deserved his general's commendation : and as for his other offer, which was rather a mercenarie reward, then an honourable recompence, he would have none of it, but was contented to have his equall part with other souldiers. Onely, this grace (sayed he) I crave and beseech you to grant me : Among the VOLSCES there is an old friend and hoast of mine, an honest wealthy man, and now a prisoner, who living before in great wealth in his owne countrie, liveth now a poore prisoner, in the hands of his enemies : and yet notwithstanding all this his misery and misfortune, it would do me great pleasure if I could save him from this one danger, to keepe him from being sold as a slave. The souldiers hearing *Martius* words, made a marvelous great shout among them, and there were more that wondred at his great contentation and abstinence, when they saw so litle covetousnesse in him, then they were that highly praised and extolled his valiantnesse. * * * * * After this shout and noise of the assembly was somewhat appeased, the Consul *Cominius* began to speake in this sort : We cannot compell *Martius* to take these gifts we offer him if he will not receive them, but we will give him such a reward for the noble service he hath done, as he cannot refuse. Therefore we do order and decree, that henceforth he be called *Coriolanus*, unlesse his valiant acts have wonne him that name before our nomination. And so ever since, he still bare the third name of *Coriolanus*.'

ACT II.

(1) SCENE III.—[*And Censorinus, darling of the people.*] This line in brackets was supplied by Pope; the original, which mentioned Censorinus, having been accidentally left out, as will at once be seen from the parallel passage in Shakespeare's authority:—"The house of the Martians at Rome was of the number of the *Patricians*, out of the which hath sprong many noble personages: whereof Ancus Martius was one, King Numaes daughters sonne, who was King of Rome after Tullus Hostilius. Of the same house were Publius, and Quintus, who brought to Rome their best water they had by conducts. *Censorinus also came of that familie*, that was so surnamed bicause the people had chosen him *Censor* twise."—NORTH'S *Plutarch*, p. 237.

ACT III.

(1) SCENE I.—

——— which will in time break ope
The locks o' the senate, and bring in the crows
To peck the eagles.]

Compare Plutarch:—"But Martius standing up on his feete, dyd somewhat sharpely take up those, who went about to gratifie the people therin: and called them people pleasers, and traitours to the nobilitie. Moreover he sayed they nourished against themselves the naughtie seede and cockle of insolencie and sedition, which had bene sowed and scattered abroade emongest the people, whom they should have cut off, if they had been wise, and have prevented their greatnes: and not (to their owne destruction) to have suffered the people to stablish a magistrate for themselves, of so great power and authority as that man had, to whom they had graunted it. Who was also to be feared, bicause he obtained what he would, and did nothing but what he listed, neither passed for any obedience to the Consuls, but lived in all liberty, acknowledging no superiour to command him, saving the only heads and authours of their faction, whom he called his magistrats. Therefore sayed he, they that gave counsell, and perswaded that the corne should be geven out to the common people *gratis*, as they used to doe in the cities of GRÆCE, where the people had more absolute power, dyd but only nourishe their disobedience, which would breake out in the ende to the utter ruine and overthrowe of the whole state. For they will not thineke it is done in recompence of their service past, sithence they know well enough they have so oft refused to goe to the warres, when they were commaunded: neither for their mutinies when they went with us, whereby they have rebelled and forsaken their countrie: neither for their accusations which their flatterers have preferred unto them, and they have received, and made good against the Senate: but they will rather judge, we give and grant them this, as abasing our selves, and standing in feare of them, and glad to flatter them every way. By this means their disobedience will still grow worse and worse: and they will never leave to practise new sedition and uprores. Therfore it were a great folly for us, me thinks to do it: yea, shall I say more? we should if we were wise, take from them the Tribuneship, which most manifestly is the embasing of the Consulship, and the cause of the division of their city. The state whereof as it standeth, is not now as it was wont to be, but becometh dismembred in two factions, which maintaines alwaies civill dissention and discord between us, and will never suffer us againe to be united into one body."

ACT IV.

(1) SCENE V.—

—— I'd not believe them more
Than thee, all-noble Marcius.]

Here, as in many other scenes in the play, the poet has followed the historian almost literally:—

"It was even twylight when he entred the cittie of ANTIUM, and many people met him in the streetes, but no man knewe him. So he went directly to *Tullus Aufidius* house, and when he came thither, he got him up straight to the chimney harthe, and sat him downe, and spake not a worde to any man, his face all muffled over. They of the house spying him, wondered what he should be, and yet they durst not byd him rise. For ill favouredly muffled and disguised as he was, yet there appeared a certaine maiestie in his countenance, and in his silence: whereupon they went to *Tullus* who was at supper, to tell him of the straunge disguising of this man. *Tullus* rose presently from the borde, and comming towards him, asked him what he was, and wherfore he came. Then *Martius* unmuffled himselfe, and after he had paused a while, making no aunswer, he sayed unto him: If thou knowest me not yet, *Tullus*, and seeing me, dost not perhappes beleeve me to be the man I am indede, I must of necessitie bewraye my selfe to be that I am. I am *Caius Martius*, who hath done to thy self particularly, and to all the VOLSCES generally, great hurte and mischief, which I cannot denie for my surname of *Coriolanus* that I beare. For I never had other benefit nor recompence, of all the true and paynefull service I have done, and the extreme daungers I have bene in, but this only surname: a good memorie and witnes of the malice and displeasure thou showldest beare me. In deede the name only remaineth with me: for the rest, the envie and crueltie of the people of ROME have taken from me, by the sufferance of the darstardly nobilitie and magistrates, who have forsaken me, and let me be banished by the people. This extremitie hath now driven me to come as a poore suter, to take thy chimney harthe, not of any hope I have to save my life thereby. For if I had feared death, I would not have come hither to have put my life in hazard: but prickt forward with spite and desire I have to be revenged of them that thus have banished me, whom now I beginne to be avenged on, putting my persone into the hands of their enemies. Wherfore, if thou hast any heart to be wrecked of the iniuries thy enemies have done thee, speed thee now, and let my misery serve thy turne, and so use it, as my service may be a benefit to the VOLSCES: promising thee, that I will fight with better good will for all you, then ever I dyd when I was against you, knowing that they fight more valiantly, who know the force of their enemy then such as have never proved it. And if it be so that thou dare not, and that thou art wearie to prove fortune any more, then am I also wearie to live any longer. And it were no wisedome in thee, to save the life of him, who hath bene heretofore thy mortall enemy, and whose service now can nothing help nor pleasure thee. *Tullus* hearing what he sayed was a marvelous glad man, and taking him by the hand, he sayed unto him: Stand up, ô *Martius*, and be of good cheare, for in profering thyselfe unto us, thou doest us great honour: and by this means thou maist hope also of greater things at all the VOLSCES hands. So he feasted him for that time, and entertained him in the honourablest manner he could, talking with him in no other matters at that present: but within few dayes after, they fell to consultation together, in what sort they should beginne their wars."

ACT V.

(1) SCENE III.—

——— *O, my mother, mother! O!*
You have won a happy victory to Rome;
But, for your son,—believe it, O, believe it,
Most dangerously you have with him prevail'd,
If not most mortal.]

This affecting interview is thus described in Plutarch:—"Nowe was *Martius* set then in his chayer of state, with all the honours of a generall, and when he had spied the women coming afarre of, he marveled what the matter ment: but afterwardes knowing his wife which came foremest, he determined at the first to persist in his obstinate and inflexible rancker. But overcomen in the ende with natural affection, and being altogether altered to see them, his harte would not serve him to tarie their comming to his chayer, but comming downe in hast, he went to meete them, and first he kissed his mother, and imbraced her a pretie while, then his wife and litle children. And nature so wrought with him, that the teares fell from his eyes, and he coulde not keepe himselfe from making much of them, but yeelded to the affection of his bloude, as if he had bene violently caried with the furie of a most swift running streame. After he had thus lovingly received them, and perceiving that his mother *Volumnia* would beginne to speak to him, he called the chiefest of the counsell of the VOLSCES to heare what she would say. Then she spake in this sort: If we held our peace (my sonne) and determined not to speake, the state of our poore bodies, and present sight of our rayment, would easely bewray to thee what life we have led at home, since thy exile and abode abroad; but thinke now with thy selfe, howe much more unfortunatly then all the women livinge, we are come hether, considering that the sight which should be most pleasaunt to all other to beholde, spitefull fortune hath made most fearefull to us: making my selfe to see my sonne, and my daughter here her husband, besieging the walls of his native countrie: so as that which is thonely comforte to all other in their adversitie and miserie, to pray unto the goddes, and to call to them for aide, is the onely thinge which plongeth us into most deepe perplexitie. For we cannot (alas) together pray, both for victorie for our countrie, and for safety of thy life also: but a worlde of grievous curses, yea more then any mortall enemie can heape uppon us, are forcibly wrapt up in our prayers. For the bitter soppe of most harde choyse is offered thy wife and children, to forgoe the one of the two: either to lose the persone of thy selfe or the nurse of their native countrie. For my selfe (my sonne) I am determined not to tarie, till fortune in my life time doe make an end of this warre. For if I cannot perswade thee, rather to doe good unto both parties, then to overthrowe and destroye the one, preferring love and nature before the malice and calamitie of warres, thou shalt see, my sonne, and trust unto it, thou shalt no sooner march forward to assault thy countrie, but thy foot shall treade upon thy mothers wombe, that brought thee first into this world. And I maye not deferre to see the day, either that my sonne be led prisoner in triumphe by his naturall countrymen, or that he himselfe do triumphe of them, and of his naturall countrie. For if it were so, that my request tended to save thy countrie, in destroying the VOLSCES, I must confesse, thou wouldest hardly and doubtfully resolve on that. For as to destroie thy natural countrie, it is altogether unmeete and unlawfull, so were it not iust, and lesse honourable, to betraye those that put their trust in thee. But my onely demaund consisteth, to make a gayle-deliverie of all evils, which delivereth equall benefite and safety, both to the one and the other, but most honourable for the VOLSCES. For it shall appeare, that having victorie in their hands, they have of speciall favour graunted us singular graces: peace, and amitie, albeit themselves have no lesse part of both, then we. Of which good, if it so come to passe, thy selfe is thonely author, and so hast thou thonely honour. But if it faile, and fall out contrarie, thy selfe alone deservedly shalt carie the shameful reproche and burden of either partie. So, though the end of warre be uncertaine, yet this notwithstanding is most certaine: that if it be thy chance to conquer, this benefite shalt thou reape of thy goodly conquest, to be chronicled the plague and destroyer of thy countrie. And if fortune also overthrowe thee, then the world will say that through desire to revenge thy private iniuries, thou hast for ever undone thy good friendes, who dyd most lovingly and curteously receive thee. *Martius* gave good eare unto his mothers wordes, without interrupting her speche at all, and after she had sayed what she would, he held his peace a prety while, and aunswered not a word. Hereupon she begane againe to speake unto him, and sayed: My sonne, why doest thou not aunswer me? doest thou thinke it good altogether to geve place unto thy choller and desire of revenge, and thinkest thou it not honestie for thee to graunt thy mother's request, in so weighty a cause? doest thou take it honorable for a noble man, to remember the wronges and iniuries done him, and doest not in like case think it an honest noble mans parte to be thankefull for the goodnes that parents doe shewe to their children, acknowledging the dutie and reverence they ought to beare unto them? No man living is more bounde to shewe himselfe thankefull in all partes and respects then thy selfe: who so unnaturally shewest all ingratitude. Moreover (my sonne) thou hast sorely taken of thy countrie, exacting grievous payments upon them, in revenge of the iniuries offered thee: besides, thou hast not hitherto shewed thy poore mother any curtesie. And therfore, it is not onely honest, but due unto me, that without compulsion I should obtaine my so iust and reasonable request of thee. But since by reason I cannot persuade thee to it, to what purpose doe I deferre my last hope? And with these wordes, herselfe, his wife, and children, fell down upon their knees before him: *Martius* seeing that, could refraine no longer, but went straight and lifte her up crying out: Oh mother, what have you done to me? And holding her hard by the right hande, oh mother, said he, you have won a happy victorie for your countrie, but mortall and unhappy for your sonne: for I see my selfe vanquished by you alone."

(2) SCENE III.—

Ladies, you deserve
To have a temple built you.]

Which, according to Plutarch, they had: dedicated to *Fortunæ muliebri*:—

"Whereupon the Senate ordeined, that the Magistrates to gratifie and honor these ladyes, should graunt them all that they would require. And they only requested that they would build a temple of *Fortune* of the women, unto the building whereof they offered them selves to defraye the whole charge of the sacrifices, and other ceremonies belonging to the service of the gods. Neverthelesse, the Senate commending their good-will and forwardnes, ordeined, that the temple and image should be made at the common charge of the cittie. Notwithstanding that, the ladyes gathered money emong them, and made with the same a second image of *Fortune*, which the ROMAINES say dyd speake as they offred her up in the temple, and dyd set her in her place."

(3) SCENE VI.—*Hail, lords! I am return'd your soldier.*] "Nowe, when *Martius* was returned againe into the citie of Antium from his voyage, *Tullus*, that hated and could no longer abide him for the fear he had of his authoritie, sought divers means to make him out of the way, thinking that if he let slippe that present time, he should never recover the like and fit occasion againe. Wherefore *Tullus*, having procured manie other of his confederacy, required *Martius* might be deposed from his estate, to render up accomptt to the VOLSCES of his charge and government. *Martius* fearing to become a private man againe under *Tullus* being Generall (whose authoritie was greater otherwise, then any other emong all the VOLSCES) answered: He was willing to geve up his charge, and would resigne it into the hands of the lordes of the VOLSCES, if they dyd al command him, as by al their commandment he received it. And moreover, that he would not refuse even at that present to geve up an accomptt unto the people, if they would tarie the hearing of it. The people hereupon called a common counsell, in which assembly there were certaine oratours appointed, that stirred up the common people against him: and when they had tolde their tales, *Martius* rose up to make them answer. Now, notwithstanding the mutinous people made a marvelous great noise, yet when they saw him, for the reverence they bare unto his valiantnesse, they quieted themselves, and gave him audience to alledge with leysure what he could for his purgation. Moreover, the honestest men of the ANTIATES, and who most rejoyced in peace, shewed by their countenaunce that they would heare him willingly, and iudge also according to their conscience. Whereupon *Tullus* fearing that if he dyd let him speake, he would prove his innocencie to the people, because emongest other things he had an eloquent tongue; besides that the first good service he had done to the people of the VOLSCES, dyd winne him more favour, then these last accusations could purchase him displeasure: and furthermore, the offence they layed to his charge, was a testimonie of the goodwill they ought him; for they would never have thought he had done them wrong for that they tooke not the cittie of ROME, if they had not bin very neare taking of it, by meanes of his approche and conduction. For these causes *Tullus* thought he might no longer delaye his presence and enterprise, neither to tarie for the mutining and rising of the common people against him: wherefore, those that were of the conspiracie, began to cry out that he was not to be heard, and that they would not suffer a traitor to usurpe tyranicall power over the tribe of the VOLSCES, who would not yeld up his state and authority. And in saying these words, they all fell upon him, and killed him in the market place, none of the people once offering to rescue him. Howbeit it is a clere case, that this murder was not generally consented unto, of the most parte of the VOLSCES: for men came out of all partes to honor his body, and dyd honourably bury him; setting up his tombe with great store of armour and spoiles, as the tombe of a worthy person and great captaine. The ROMAINES understanding of his death, shewed no other honour or malice, saving that they graunted the ladyes the request they made: that they might mourne tenne moneths for him, and that was the full time they used to weare blackes for the death of their fathers, brethren, or husbands, according to *Numa Pompilius* order, who stablished the same, as we have enlarged more amplie in the description of his life. Now *Martius* being dead, the whole state of the VOLSCES harteily wished him alive againe. For, first of all they fell out with the ÆQUES who were their friends and confederates, touching preheminence and place: and this quarrell grew on so farre betweene them, that fraies and murders fell out upon it one with another. After that the ROMAINES overcame them in battell, in which *Tullus* was slaine in the field and the flower of all their force was put to the sword: so that they were compelled to accept most shamefull conditions of peace, in yelding themselves subject unto the conquerers, and promising to be obedient at their commandement."—NORTH'S *Plutarch*.

CRITICAL OPINIONS ON CORIOLANUS.

"In the three Roman pieces, 'Coriolanus,' 'Julius Cæsar,' and 'Antony and Cleopatra,' the moderation with which Shakspeare excludes foreign appendages and arbitrary suppositions, and yet fully satisfies the wants of the stage, is particularly deserving of admiration. These plays are the very thing itself; and under the apparent artlessness of adhering closely to history as he found it, an uncommon degree of art is concealed. Of every historical transaction Shakspeare knows how to seize the true poetical point of view, and to give unity and rounding to a series of events detached from the immeasurable extent of history without in any degree changing them. The public life of ancient Rome is called up from its grave, and exhibited before our eyes with the utmost grandeur and freedom of the dramatic form, and the heroes of Plutarch are ennobled by the most eloquent poetry.

"In 'Coriolanus' we have more comic intermixtures than in the others, as the many-headed multitude plays here a considerable part; and when Shakspeare portrays the blind movements of the people in a mass, he almost always gives himself up to his merry humour. To the plebeians, whose folly is certainly sufficiently conspicuous already, the original old satirist Menenius is added by way of abundance. Droll scenes arise of a description altogether peculiar, and which are compatible only with such a political drama; for instance, when Coriolanus, to obtain the consulate, must solicit the lower order of citizens, whom he holds in contempt for their cowardice in war, but cannot so far master his haughty disposition as to assume the customary humility, and yet extorts from them their votes."—Schlegel.

* * * * "The serious and elevated persons of this drama are delineated in colours of equal, if not superior strength. The unrivalled military prowess of Coriolanus, in whose nervous arm 'Death—that dark spirit'—dwelt; the severe sublimity of his character, his stern and unbending hauteur, and his undisguised contempt of all that is vulgar, pusillanimous, and base, are brought before us with a raciness and power of impression, and, notwithstanding a very liberal use both of the sentiments and language of his Plutarch, with a freedom of outline which, even in Shakspeare, may be allowed to excite our astonishment.

"Among the female characters a very important part is necessarily attached to the person of Volumnia; the fate of Rome itself depending upon her parental influence and authority. The poet has accordingly done full justice to the great qualities which the Cheronean sage has ascribed to this energetic woman; the daring loftiness of her spirit, her bold and masculine eloquence, and, above all, her patriotic devotion, being marked by the most spirited and vigorous touches of his pencil.

"The numerous vicissitudes in the story; its rapidity of action; its contrast of character; the splendid vigour of its serious, and the satirical sharpness and relish of its more familiar scenes, together with the animation which prevails throughout all its parts, have conferred on this play, both in the closet and on the stage, a remarkable degree of attraction."—Drake.

VOL. III.

Act III Sc. 3

THE WINTER'S TALE.

THE first edition of this play known is that of the folio, 1623; and the earliest notice of its performance is an entry in the manuscript *Diary* (*Mus. Ashmol. Oxon.*) of Dr. Simon Forman, who thus describes the plot of the piece, which he witnessed at the Globe Theatre, May 15th, 1611:—

"Observe ther howe Lyontes the Kinge of Cicillia was overcom with jelosy of his wife with the Kinge of Bohemia, his frind, that came to see him, and howe he contrived his death, and wold have had his cup-berer to have poisoned, who gave the Kinge of Bohemia warning thereof and fled with him to Bohemia.

"Remember also howe he sent to the orakell of Apollo, and the aunswer of Apollo that she was giltless, and that the kinge was jelouse, &c., and howe, except the child was found againe that was loste, the kinge should die without yssue; for the child was caried into Bohemia, and there laid in a forrest, and brought up by a sheppard, and the Kinge of Bohemia, his sonn married that wentch: and howe they fled into Cicillia to Leontes, and the sheppard having showed [by] the letter of the nobleman whom Leontes sent, it was that child, and [by] the jewells found about her, she was knowen to be Leontes daughter, and was then 16. yers old.

"Remember also the rog [rogue] that cam in all tottered like roll pixci * and howe he fayned him sicke and to have him robbed of all that he had, and howe he cosoned the por man of all his money, and after cam to the shop ther [sheep sheer?] with a pedlers packe, and ther cosened them again of all their money; and how he changed apparell with the Kinge of Bomia, his sonn, and then how he turned courtier, &c. Beware of trustinge feined beggars or fawninge fellouse." †

In the same year, as we learn from a record in the Accounts of the Revels at Court, it was acted at Whitehall:—

"The kings players.	The 5th of November: A play called ye winters nightes Tayle."

[1611.]

The accounts of Lord Harrington, Treasurer of the Chamber to James I., show that it was again acted at Court, before Prince Charles, the Lady Elizabeth, and the Prince Palatine Elector, in May, 1613.

And it is further mentioned in the Office Book of Sir Henry Herbert, Master of the Revels, under the date of August the 19th, 1623:—

"For the kings players. An olde playe called Winters Tale, formerly allowed of by Sir George Bucke and likewyse by mee on Mr. Hemminges his worde that there was nothing prophane added or reformed, thogh the allowed booke was missing: and therefore I returned it without a fee, this 19th of August, 1623."

* This was no doubt some noted vagabond, whose nickname has not come down to us correctly. Mr. Collier prints it, "Coll Pipci."

† From a carefully executed copy made from the original by Mr. Halliwell.

From these facts Mr. Collier infers, and his inference is strengthened by the style of the language and the structure of the verse, that "The Winter's Tale" was a novelty at the time Forman saw it played at the Globe, and had "been composed in the autumn and winter of 1610-11, with a view to its production on the Bankside, as soon as the usual performances by the king's players commenced there."

The plot of "The Winter's Tale" is founded on a popular novel by Robert Greene, first printed in 1588, and then called "Pandosto: The Triumph of Time,"* &c., though in subsequent impressions intituled, "The History of Dorastus and Fawnia." In this tale we have the leading incidents of the play, and counterparts, though insufferably dull and coarse ones, of the principal personages. But Shakespeare has modified the crude materials of his original with such judgment, and vivified and ennobled the characters he has retained with such incomparable art, that, as usual, he may be said to have imposed rather than to have incurred an obligation by adopting them.

* "PANDOSTO THE TRIUMPH OF TIME. Wherein is Discovered by a pleasant Historie, that although by the meanes of sinister fortune, Truth may be concealed *yet by Time in spight of fortune it is most manifestly revealed. Pleasant for age to avoyde drowsie thoughts*, profitable for youth to eschue other wanton *pastimes, and bringing to both a desired content. Temporis filia veritas. By Robert Greene*, Maister of Artes in *Cambridge. Omne tulit punctum qui miscuit utile dulci.* Imprinted at London by Thomas Orwin for *Thomas Cadman*, dwelling at the Signe of the *Bible*, neere unto the North doore of Paules, 1588."

Persons Represented.

LEONTES, *King of* Sicilia.
MAMILLIUS, *Son to* Leontes.
CAMILLO, ANTIGONUS, CLEOMENES, DION, — Sicilian *Lords*.
Another Sicilian Lord.
ROGERO, *a* Sicilian *Gentleman*.
An Attendant *on the young* Prince Mamillius.
Officers *of a* Court *of* Judicature.
POLIXENES, *King of* Bohemia.
FLORIZEL, *Son to* Polixenes.
ARCHIDAMUS, *a* Bohemian *Lord*.
Paulina's Steward.
A Mariner.
Gaoler.
An old Shepherd, *reputed Father of* Perdita.
Clown, *Son to the old* Shepherd.
AUTOLYCUS, *a Rogue*.
Time, *as Chorus*.
HERMIONE, *Queen to* Leontes.
PERDITA, *Daughter to* Leontes *and* Hermione.
PAULINA, *Wife to* Antigonus.
EMILIA, Two Ladies, — *Attending on the* Queen.
MOPSA, DORCAS, — *Shepherdesses*.

Lords, Ladies, and Attendants; Satyrs for a Dance; Shepherds, Shepherdesses, Guards, &c.

SCENE,—*Sometimes in* SICILIA; *sometimes in* BOHEMIA.

ACT I.

SCENE I.—Sicilia. *An Antechamber in* Leontes' *Palace.*

Enter Camillo *and* Archidamus.

Arch. If you shall chance, Camillo, to visit Bohemia, on the like occasion whereon my services are now on foot, you shall see, as I have said, great difference betwixt our Bohemia and your Sicilia.

Cam. I think, this coming summer, the king of Sicilia means to pay Bohemia the visitation which he justly owes him.

Arch. Wherein our entertainment shall shame us, we will be justified in our loves; for, indeed,—

Cam. Beseech you,—

Arch. Verily, I speak it in the freedom of my knowledge, we cannot with such magnificence— in so rare—I know not what to say.—We will give you sleepy drinks, that your senses, unintelligent of our insufficience, may, though they cannot praise us, as little accuse us.

Cam. You pay a great deal too dear for what's given freely.

Arch. Believe me, I speak as my understanding instructs me, and as mine honesty puts it to utterance.

Cam. Sicilia cannot show himself over-kind to Bohemia. They were trained together in their childhoods; and there rooted betwixt them then such an affection which cannot choose but branch now. Since their more mature dignities and royal necessities made separation of their society, their encounters, though not personal, have been royally attorneyed, with interchange of gifts, letters, loving embassies; that they have seemed to be together, though absent; shook hands, as over a vast;[a] and embraced, as it were, from the ends of opposed winds. The heavens continue their loves!

ARCH. I think there is not in the world either malice or matter to alter it. You have an unspeakable comfort of your young prince Mamillius; it is a gentleman of the greatest promise that ever came into my note.

CAM. I very well agree with you in the hopes of him: it is a gallant child; one that, indeed, physics the subject,[b] makes old hearts fresh; they that went on crutches ere he was born, desire yet their life to see him a man.

ARCH. Would they else be content to die?

CAM. Yes; if there were no other excuse why they should desire to live.

ARCH. If the king had no son they would desire to live on crutches till he had one. [*Exeunt.*

SCENE II.—*The same. A Room of State in the Palace.*

Enter LEONTES, POLIXENES, HERMIONE, MAMILLIUS, CAMILLO, *and* Attendants.

POL. Nine changes of the wat'ry star have been
The shepherd's note, since we have left our throne
Without a burden: time as long again
Would be fill'd up, my brother, with our thanks;
And yet we should, for perpetuity,
Go hence in debt: and therefore, like a cipher,
Yet standing in rich place, I multiply,
With one we-thank-you, many thousands more
That go before it.

LEON. Stay your thanks awhile,
And pay them when you part.

POL. Sir, that's to-morrow.
I am question'd by my fears, of what may chance
Or breed upon our absence; that may blow
No sneaping winds at home, to make us say,
This is put forth too truly![c] Besides, I have stay'd
To tire your royalty.

LEON. We are tougher, brother,
Than you can put us to't.

POL. No longer stay.

LEON. One seven-night longer.

POL. Very sooth, to-morrow.

LEON. We'll part the time between's then; and in that
I'll no gainsaying.

POL. Press me not, beseech you, so;
There is no tongue that moves, none, none i' the world,
So soon as yours could win me: so it should now,
Were there necessity in your request, although
'T were needful I denied it. My affairs
Do even drag me homeward: which to hinder,
Were, in your love, a whip to me; my stay,
To you a charge and trouble: to save both,
Farewell, our brother.

LEON. Tongue-tied, our queen? speak you.

HER. I had thought, sir, to have held my peace until [sir,
You had drawn oaths from him not to stay. You,
Charge him too coldly. Tell him, you are sure
All in Bohemia's well; this satisfaction
The by-gone day proclaim'd; say this to him,
He's beat from his best ward.

LEON. Well said, Hermione.

HER. To tell he longs to see his son, were strong:
But let him say so then, and let him go;
But let him swear so, and he shall not stay,
We'll thwack him hence with distaffs.—
Yet of your royal presence [*To* POLIXENES.] I'll adventure
The borrow of a week. When at Bohemia
You take my lord, I'll give him my commission,
To let[d] him there a month, behind the gest[e]
Prefix'd for's parting: yet, good deed, Leontes,
I love thee not a jar o' the clock behind
What lady-she[f] her lord.—You'll stay?

---

[a] — *shook hands, as over a* vast;] So the first folio: that of 1632 reads,—"over a vast *sea*." The earlier lection is no doubt the true one; in "The Tempest," Act I. Sc. 2, we have, "*vast* of night;" and in "Pericles," Act III. Sc. 1,—

"The God of this great *vast*, rebuke these surges."

[b] — *one that, indeed, physics the* subject,—] "Subject," in this place, may import the people generally, as it is usually interpreted; yet from the words which immediately follow,—"makes old hearts fresh," it has perhaps a more particular meaning:—The sight and hopes of the princely boy were cordial to the afflicted, and invigorating to the old.

[c] —— *that may blow*
No sneaping winds at home, to make us say,
This is put forth too truly!]

Hanmer reads,—

"This is put forth too *early*."

And Capell,—

"This is put forth too *tardily*."

The sense appears to be,—Oh that no misfortune may occur at home to justify my apprehensions, and make me say, "I predicted too truly:" but Mr. Dyce and Mr. Collier suspect, with reason, that the passage is corrupt.

[d] *To* let—] To *stay*.

[e] — *behind* the gest—] A "*gest*" was the name of the scroll containing the route and resting-places of royalty during a "progress;" and Hermione's meaning may be,—when he visits Bohemia he shall have my licence to prolong his sojourn a month beyond the time prescribed for his departure. But *gest*, or *jest*, also signified a show or revelry, and it is not impossible that the sense intended was,—he shall have my permission to remain a month after the farewell entertainment.

[f] *What* lady-she *her lord.*—] Mr. Collier's annotator suggests, prosaically enough, "What lady *should* her lord." The difficulty in the expression arises, we apprehend, solely from the omission of the hyphen in "lady-she;" that restored, the sense is unmistakeable,—I love thee not a tick of the clock behind whatever high-born woman does her husband. So in Massinger's play of "The Bondman," Act I. Sc. 3,—

"I'll kiss him for the honour of my country,
With any she in Corinth."

POL. No, madam.
HER. Nay, but you will?
POL. I may not, verily.
HER. *Verily!*
You put me off with limber vows; but I,
Though you would seek to unsphere the stars with oaths,
Should yet say, *Sir, no going.* Verily,
You shall not go; a lady's verily's
As potent as a lord's. Will you go yet?
Force me to keep you as a prisoner,
Not like a guest; so you shall pay your fees
When you depart, and save your thanks. How say you?
My prisoner or my guest? by your dread *verily,*
One of them you shall be.
POL. Your guest then, madam:
To be your prisoner should import offending;
Which is for me less easy to commit
Than you to punish.
HER. Not your gaoler, then,
But your kind hostess. Come, I'll question you
Of my lord's tricks and yours when you were boys:
You were pretty lordings then?
POL. We were, fair queen,
Two lads that thought there was no more behind,
But such a day to-morrow as to-day,
And to be boy eternal.
HER. Was not my lord the verier wag o' the two?
POL. We were as twinn'd lambs that did frisk i' the sun,
And bleat the one at th' other: what we chang'd
Was innocence for innocence; we knew not
The doctrine of ill-doing, nor dream'd
That any did. Had we pursu'd that life,
And our weak spirits ne'er been higher rear'd
With stronger blood, we should have answer'd heaven
Boldly, *Not guilty;* the imposition clear'd,
Hereditary ours.[a]
HER. By this we gather,
You have tripp'd since.
POL. O, my most sacred lady,
Temptations have since then been born to us! for
In those unfledg'd days was my wife a girl;
Your precious self had then not cross'd the eyes
Of my young play-fellow.
HER. Grace to boot!
Of this make no conclusion, lest you say
Your queen and I are devils: yet, go on;
The offences we have made you do, we'll answer,
If you first sinn'd with us, and that with us
You did continue fault, and that you slipp'd not
With any but with us.
LEON. Is he won yet?
HER. He'll stay, my lord.
LEON. At my request he would not.
Hermione, my dear'st, thou never spok'st
To better purpose.
HER. Never?
LEON. Never, but once.
HER. What! have I twice said well? when was't before?
I pry'thee, tell me. Cram us with praise, and make us
As fat as tame things: one good deed dying tongueless,
Slaughters a thousand waiting upon that.
Our praises are our wages: you may ride us
With one soft kiss a thousand furlongs, ere
With spur we heat an acre. But to the goal;—[b]
My last good deed was to entreat his stay;
What was my first? it has an elder sister,
Or I mistake you: O, would her name were Grace!
But once before I spoke to the purpose: when?
Nay, let me have't; I long.
LEON. Why, that was when
Three crabbed months had sour'd themselves to death,
Ere I could make thee open thy white hand,
And clap thyself my love; then didst thou utter,
I am yours for ever.
HER. 'Tis Grace, indeed!—
Why, lo you now, I have spoke to the purpose twice;
The one for ever earn'd a royal husband;
The other for some while a friend.
[*Giving her hand to* POLIXENES.
LEON. [*Aside.*] Too hot, too hot!
To mingle friendship far, is mingling bloods.
I have *tremor cordis* on me,—my heart dances,—
But not for joy,—not joy.—This entertainment
May a free face put on; derive a liberty
From heartiness, from bounty, fertile bosom,[c]
And well become the agent: 't may, I grant:
But to be paddling palms and pinching fingers,
As now they are; and making practis'd smiles,
As in a looking-glass;—and then to sigh, as 't were
The mort o' the deer;[d] O, that is entertainment
My bosom likes not, nor my brows!—Mamillius,
Art thou my boy?
MAM. Ay, my good lord.

---

[a] —— the imposition clear'd,
Hereditary ours.]
That is, were the penalty remitted which we inherit from the transgression of our first parents.

[b] *With spur we* heat *an acre. But to the* goal;—] Mr. Collier's annotator substitutes,—

"With spur we *clear* an acre. But to the *good.*"

[c] — bounty, fertile bosom,—] Hanmer and Mr. Collier's annotator read,—

"— *bounty's* fertile bosom," &c.

[d] *The* mort *o' the deer;*] The mort or *mote* of the deer was a particular strain blown by the huntsmen when the deer was killed. There is perhaps, also, a latent play on the word "deer," akin to that in the ensuing speech on "neat."

LEON. I' fecks? [a]
Why, that's my bawcock. What, hast smutch'd thy nose?—
They say, it is a copy out of mine. Come, captain,
We must be neat;—not neat, but cleanly, captain:
And yet the steer, the heifer, and the calf,
Are all call'd neat.—Still virginalling
[*Observing* POLIXENES *and* HERMIONE.
Upon his palm? (1)—How now, you wanton calf?
Art thou my calf?
MAM. Yes, if you will, my lord.
LEON. Thou want'st a rough pash,[b] and the shoots that I have,
To be full like me:—yet, they say we are
Almost as like as eggs; women say so,
That will say anything: but were they false
As o'er-dyed blacks,[c] as wind, as waters;—false
As dice are to be wish'd by one that fixes
No bourn 'twixt his and mine; yet were it true
To say this boy were like me.—Come, sir page,
Look on me with your welkin eye:[d] sweet villain!
Most dear'st! my collop?—Can thy dam?—may't be
Affection thy intention stabs the centre?
Thou dost make possible things not so held?
Communicat'st with dreams?—How! can this be?—

---

[a] I' fecks?] A popular corruption of "in faith," it is supposed.

[b] — a rough pash,—] That is, a tufted *head* or *brow*.

[c] *As* o'er-dyed blacks,—] Absurdly changed by Mr. Collier's annotator to, "*our dead* blacks." "Blacks" was the common term for mourning habiliments formerly; and by "o'er-dyed blacks" were meant such garments as had become rotten and faded by frequent immersion in the dye. If any change in the text be admissible, we should read, "*oft* dyed blacks." Thus, in Webster's "Dutchess of Malfi," Act V. Sc. 2,—

"I do not think but sorrow makes her look
Like to an *oft dy'd garment*:"

[d] — welkin *eye*:] That is, sky-coloured eye.

With what's unreal thou coactive art,
And fellow'st nothing? Then 't is very credent,
Thou mayst co-join with something;[a] and thou dost,—
And that beyond commission;[b] and I find it,—
And that to the infection of my brains,
And hardening of my brows.

POL. What means Sicilia?

HER. He something seems unsettled.

POL. How, my lord!
What cheer? how is 't with you, best brother?[c]

HER. You look as if you held a brow of much distraction:
Are you mov'd, my lord? (2)

LEON. No, in good earnest.—
[*Aside.*] How sometimes nature will betray its folly,
Its tenderness, and make itself a pastime
To harder bosoms!—Looking on the lines
Of my boy's face, methought[d] I did recoil
Twenty-three years; and saw myself unbreech'd,
In my green velvet coat; my dagger muzzled,

---

a
—— Can thy dam?—may't be
Affection thy intention stabs the centre?
Thou dost make possible things not so held?
Communicat'st with dreams?—How! can this be?—
With what's unreal thou coactive art,
And fellow'st nothing? Then 't is very credent,
Thou mayst co-join with something; &c.]

"Affection" here means *imagination;* "intention" signifies *intencion* or *intensity;* and the allusion, though the commentators have all missed it, is plainly to that mysterious principle of nature by which a parent's features are transmitted to the offspring. Pursuing the train of thought induced by the acknowledged likeness between the boy and himself, Leontes asks, "Can it be possible a mother's vehement imagination should penetrate even to the womb, and there imprint upon the embryo what stamp she chooses? Such apprehensive fantasy, then," he goes on to say, "we may believe will readily co-join with something tangible, and it does," &c. &c.

b *And that beyond* commission;] "Commission" here, as in a former passage of the scene, "I'll give him my commission," means *warrant, permission, authority.*

c
POL. How, my lord!
What cheer? how is 't with you, best brother?]

"In the folio, the words 'What cheer? how is 't with you, best brother?' have the prefix 'Leo.;' Hanmer assigned them to Polixenes. Mr. Collier and Mr. Knight restore them—very injudiciously, I think—to Leontes. (I suspect that the true reading here is,—

'POL. Ho, my lord!
What cheer? how is 't with you?' &c.—

for Leontes is standing apart from Polixenes and Hermione; and 'how,' as I have already noticed, was frequently the old spelling of 'ho.'")—DYCE.

d — methought *I did recoil*—] Mr Collier, upon the strength of a MS. annotation in Lord Ellesmere's copy of the first folio, prints "*my thoughts* I did recoil;" but "methoughts" of the original was often used for "methought." So, in the folio text of "Richard III." Act I. Sc. 4,—

"*Me thoughts* that I had broken from the tower," &c.

And in the same scene,—

"*Me thoughts* I saw a thousand fearfull wrackes," &c.

Lest it should bite its master, and so prove,
As ornaments oft do, too dangerous:
How like, methought, I then was to this kernel,
This squash,[a] this gentleman:—Mine honest friend,
Will you take eggs for money?[b]

MAM. No, my lord, I'll fight.

LEON. You will? why, happy man be 's dole!—My brother,
Are you so fond of your young prince, as we
Do seem to be of ours?

POL. If at home, sir,
He's all my exercise, my mirth, my matter:
Now my sworn friend, and then mine enemy;
My parasite, mine soldier, statesman, all:
He makes a July's day short as December;
And with his varying childness cures in me
Thoughts that would thick my blood.

LEON. So stands this squire
Offic'd with me. We two will walk, my lord,
And leave you to your graver steps.—Hermione,
How thou lov'st us, show in our brother's welcome;
Let what is dear in Sicily be cheap:
Next to thyself and my young rover, he's
Apparent to my heart.[c]

HER. If you would seek us,
We are yours i' the garden: shall's attend you there?

LEON. To your own bents dispose you: you'll be found,
Be you beneath the sky.—[*Aside.*] I am angling now,
Though you perceive me not how I give line.
Go to, go to!

[*Observing* POLIXENES *and* HERMIONE.

How she holds up the neb, the bill to him!
And arms her with the boldness of a wife
To her allowing husband![d] Gone already!—

[*Exeunt* POLIXENES, HERMIONE, *and* Attendants.

Inch-thick, knee-deep, o'er head and ears a fork'd[e] one.
Go play, boy, play;—thy mother plays, and I
Play too; but so disgrac'd a part, whose issue
Will hiss me to my grave; contempt and clamour
Will be my knell.—Go play, boy, play.—There have been,
Or I am much deceiv'd, cuckolds ere now;
And many a man there is, even at this present,
(Now, while I speak this) holds his wife by th' arm,
That little thinks she has been sluic'd in's absence,
And his pond fish'd by his next neighbour, by
Sir Smile, his neighbour: nay, there's comfort in't
Whiles other men have gates, and those gates open'd,
As mine, against their will. Should all despair
That have revolted wives, the tenth of mankind
Would hang themselves. Physic for't there's none;
It is a bawdy planet, that will strike
Where 't is predominant; and 't is powerful, think it,
From east, west, north, and south: be it concluded,
No barricado for a belly; know't,
It will let in and out the enemy,
With bag and baggage: many a thousand on's
Have the disease, and feel't not.—How now, boy!

MAM. I am like you, they[f] say.

LEON. Why, that's some comfort.—
What, Camillo there?

CAM. Ay, my good lord.

LEON. Go play, Mamillius; thou'rt an honest man.— [*Exit* MAMILLIUS.
Camillo, this great sir will yet stay longer.

CAM. You had much ado to make his anchor hold:
When you cast out, it still came home.

LEON. Didst note it?

CAM. He would not stay at your petitions; made
His business more material.

LEON. Didst perceive it?—
[*Aside.*] They're here with me[g] already; whisp'ring, rounding,
Sicilia is a—so-forth: 'Tis far gone,
When I shall gust it last.—How came't, Camillo,
That he did stay?

CAM. At the good queen's entreaty.

LEON. At the queen's be't: *good* should be pertinent;
But so it is, it is not.[h] Was this taken
By any understanding pate but thine?
For thy conceit is soaking, will draw in
More than the common blocks:—not noted, is't,
But of the finer natures? by some severals

---

a *This* squash,—] A "squash" is an immature pea-pod. The word occurs again in "Twelfth Night," Act I. Sc. 5,—

"As a *squash* before it is a peascod,"

and in "A Midsummer Night's Dream," Act III. Sc. 1.

b Will you take eggs for money?] This was a proverbial phrase, implying, Will you suffer yourself to be cajoled?

c Apparent to my heart.] Nearest to my affections.

d *To her* allowing *husband!*] That is, probably, her *allowed*, her *lawful* husband.

e — *a* fork'd *one.*] A *horned* one. So, in "Othello," Act III. Sc. 3,—

"Even then this *forked* plague is fated to us
When we do quicken."

f *I am like you,* they *say.*] So the second folio; the first reads, "I am like you say."

g *They're* here with me *already;* whisp'ring, &c.] That is, say the modern editors, "Not Polixenes and Hermione, but casual observers"! or "They are aware of my condition"! Strange forgetfulness of a common form of speech. By "They're *here with me* already," the King means,—the people are already mocking me with this opprobrious gesture (the cuckold's emblem with their fingers), and whispering, &c. So in "Coriolanus," Act III. Sc. 2,—

"Go to them, with this bonnet in thy hand;
And thus far having stretch'd it, (*here be with them*).

See also note (a), p. 161 of the present Volume.

h But so it is, it is not.] But as you apply the word, it is not pertinent.

Of head-piece extraordinary? lower messes[a]
Perchance are to this business purblind? say.
CAM. *Business*, my lord? I think most understand
Bohemia stays here longer.
LEON. Ha?
CAM. Stays here longer.
LEON. Ay, but why?
CAM. To satisfy your highness, and the entreaties
Of our most gracious mistress.
LEON. *Satisfy*
The entreaties of your mistress?——*satisfy!*—
Let that suffice. I have trusted thee, Camillo,
With all the near'st things to my heart, as well
My chamber-councils, wherein, priest-like, thou
Hast cleans'd my bosom,—I from thee departed
Thy penitent reform'd: but we have been
Deceiv'd in thy integrity, deceiv'd
In that which seems so.
CAM. Be it forbid, my lord!
LEON. To bide upon't[b]—thou art not honest: or,
If thou inclin'st that way, thou art a coward,
Which hoxes[c] honesty behind, restraining
From course requir'd; or else thou must be counted
A servant grafted in my serious trust,
And therein negligent; or else a fool,
That seest a game play'd home, the rich stake [drawn,
And tak'st it all for jest.
CAM. My gracious lord,
I may be negligent, foolish, and fearful;
In every one of these no man is free,
But that his negligence, his folly, fear,
Among the infinite doings of the world,
Sometimes puts forth. In your affairs, my lord,
If ever I were wilful-negligent,
It was my folly; if industriously
I play'd the fool, it was my negligence,
Not weighing well the end; if ever fearful
To do a thing, where I the issue doubted,
Whereof the execution did cry out
Against the non-performance, 'twas a fear
Which oft infects the wisest: these, my lord,
Are such allow'd infirmities, that honesty
Is never free of. But, beseech your grace,
Be plainer with me; let me know my trespass
By its[d] own visage: if I then deny it,
'T is none of mine.
LEON. Have not you seen, Camillo,
(But that's past doubt,—you have, or your eyeglass
Is thicker than a cuckold's horn) or heard,
(For, to a vision so apparent, rumour
Cannot be mute) or thought, (for cogitation
Resides not in that man that does not think it[e])
My wife is slippery? If thou wilt confess,
(Or else be impudently negative,
To have nor eyes, nor ears, nor thought) then say
My wife's a hobbyhorse; * deserves a name
As rank as any flax-wench that puts to
Before her troth-plight: say't, and justify't.
CAM. I would not be a stander-by to hear
My sovereign mistress clouded so, without
My present vengeance taken: 'shrew my heart,
You never spoke what did become you less
Than this; which to reiterate were sin
As deep as that, though true.
LEON. Is whispering nothing?
Is leaning cheek to cheek? is meeting noses?
Kissing with inside lip? stopping the career
Of laughter with a sigh? (a note infallible
Of breaking honesty) horsing foot on foot?
Skulking in corners? wishing clocks more swift?
Hours, minutes? noon, midnight? and all eyes
Blind with the pin and web,[f] but theirs, theirs only,
That would unseen be wicked? is this nothing?
Why, then the world, and all that's in't, is nothing;
The covering sky is nothing; Bohemia nothing;
My wife is nothing; nor nothing have these nothings,
If this be nothing.
CAM. Good my lord, be cur'd
Of this diseas'd opinion, and betimes;
For 't is most dangerous.
LEON. Say it be; 'tis true.
CAM. No, no, my lord.
LEON. It is; you lie, you lie!
I say thou liest, Camillo, and I hate thee;
Pronounce thee a gross lout, a mindless slave;
Or else a hovering temporizer, that
Canst with thine eyes at once see good and evil,
Inclining to them both. Were my wife's liver
Infected as her life, she would not live
The running of one glass.
CAM. Who does infect her?
LEON. Why, he that wears her like her medal, hanging
About his neck, Bohemia: who—if I
Had servants true about me, that bare eyes
To see alike mine honour as their profits,
Their own particular thrifts, they would do that
Which should undo more doing: ay, and thou,

(*) Old text, *Holy-Horse*.

[a] — lower messes—] Meaning inferior persons; such as sat at meals below the salt.

[b] To bide upon't—] This expression appears to mean, as Mr. Dyce has shown by examples,—My abiding opinion is.

[c] — hoxes—] To *hox* or *hough* is to hamstring.

[d] — its—] The comparatively frequent use of the impersonal "its," (though, for the most part, with the apostrophe, *it's*,) in this piece, while it is found but rarely in any of the other plays; in many, not at all; may be taken as an indication that "The Winter's Tale" was one of the poet's latest productions. See note (3), p. 330, Vol. I.

[e] — that does not think it—] The lection of the second folio, at least in some copies of that edition; the first has, "—that do's not thinke," &c.

[f] — the pin and web,—] Has before been explained to mean the disorder of the sight called a cataract.

His cupbearer,—whom I from meaner form
Have bench'd, and rear'd to worship; who mayst see
Plainly, as heaven sees earth, and earth sees heaven,
How I am gallèd,—mightst bespice a cup,
To give mine enemy a lasting wink;
Which draught to me were cordial.

CAM. Sir, my lord,[a]
I could do this; and that with no rash potion,
But with a ling'ring dram, that should not work
Maliciously like poison: but I cannot
Believe this crack to be in my dread mistress,
So sovereignly being honourable.
I have lov'd thee,[b]—

LEON. Make that thy question, and go rot!
Dost think I am so muddy, so unsettled,
To appoint myself in this vexation? sully
The purity and whiteness of my sheets,—
Which to preserve is sleep; which being spotted,
Is goads, thorns, nettles, tails of wasps?
Give scandal to the blood o' the prince my son,—
Who I do think is mine, and love as mine,—
Without ripe moving to 't?—Would I do this?
Could man so blench?

CAM. I must believe you, sir;
I do; and will fetch off Bohemia for't;
Provided that, when he's remov'd, your highness
Will take again your queen as yours at first,
Even for your son's sake; and thereby for sealing
The injury of tongues, in courts and kingdoms
Known and allied to yours.

LEON. Thou dost advise me,
Even so as I mine own course have set down:
I'll give no blemish to her honour, none.

CAM. My lord,
Go then; and with a countenance as clear
As friendship wears at feasts, keep with Bohemia,
And with your queen. I am his cupbearer;
If from me he have wholesome beverage,
Account me not your servant.

LEON. This is all;—
Do't, and thou hast the one half of my heart;
Do't not, thou splitt'st thine own.

CAM. I'll do't, my lord.

LEON. I will seem friendly, as thou hast advis'd me.(3) [*Exit.*

CAM. O miserable lady!—But, for me,
What case stand I in? I must be the poisoner
Of good Polixenes; and my ground to do't
Is the obedience to a master; one,
Who, in rebellion with himself, will have
All that are his so too.—To do this deed,
Promotion follows: if I could find example
Of thousands that had struck anointed kings
And flourish'd after, I'd not do't; but since
Nor brass, nor stone, nor parchment, bears not one,
Let villainy itself forswear't. I must
Forsake the court: to do't, or no, is certain
To me a break-neck. Happy star reign now!
Here comes Bohemia.

Re-enter POLIXENES.

POL. This is strange! methinks
My favour here begins to warp. Not speak?—
Good day, Camillo.

CAM. Hail, most royal sir!

POL. What is the news i' the court?

CAM. None rare, my lord.

POL. The king hath on him such a countenance
As he had lost some province, and a region
Lov'd as he loves himself: even now I met him
With customary compliment; when he,
Wafting his eyes to the contrary, and falling
A lip of much contempt, speeds from me; and
So leaves me to consider what is breeding
That changes thus his manners.

CAM. I dare not know, my lord.

POL. How! *dare not!* do not? Do you know, and dare not
Be intelligent to me? 'Tis thereabouts;
For to yourself, what you do know, you must
And cannot say you dare not.[c] Good Camillo,
Your chang'd complexions are to me a mirror,
Which shows me mine chang'd too; for I must be
A party in this alteration, finding
Myself thus alter'd with it.

CAM. There is a sickness
Which puts some of us in distemper, but
I cannot name the disease, and it is caught
Of you that yet are well.

POL. How! caught of me?
Make me not sighted like the basilisk:
I have look'd on thousands who have sped the better
By my regard, but kill'd none so. Camillo—
As you are certainly a gentleman; thereto
Clerk-like experienc'd, which no less adorns
Our gentry than our parents' noble names,
In whose success[d] we are gentle,—I beseech you,
If you know aught which does behove my knowledge

a Sir, *my lord*,—] With his usual ignorance of Shakespearian phraseology, Mr. Collier's ever-meddling annotator, both here and in Act III. Sc. 1, where Perdita says—"Sir, my gracious lord," &c., for "Sir," reads "*Sure.*" And Mr. Collier, mindless of Paulina's "*Sir*, my liege, your eye hath too much youth," &c. in Act. V. Sc. 1, of this very play; of Prospero's,—"*Sir*, my liege, do not infest your mind," &c.; of Hamlet's,—"*Sir*, my good friend," &c., chooses to adopt the substitution, and tells us, "*Sure*" is "evidently the true text"!

b I have lov'd thee,—] These words, though forming a part of Camillo's speech in the old copies, are sometimes assigned to Leontes in modern editions.

c For to yourself, what you do know, you must
And cannot say you dare not.]

That is,—For what you know, you must not and cannot say you dare not tell yourself.

d *In whose* success *we are gentle*,—] By *succession* from whom we derive gentility.

Thereof to be inform'd, imprison't not
In ignorant concealment.

CAM. I may not answer.

POL. A sickness caught of me, and yet I well!
I must be answer'd.—Dost thou hear, Camillo?
I conjure thee, by all the parts of man
Which honour does acknowledge,—whereof the least
Is not this suit of mine,—that thou declare
What incidency thou dost guess of harm
Is creeping toward me; how far off, how near;
Which way to be prevented, if to be;
If not, how best to bear it.

CAM. Sir, I will tell you;
Since I am charg'd in honour, and by him
That I think honourable: therefore, mark my counsel,
Which must be even as swiftly follow'd as
I mean to utter it, or both yourself and me
Cry *lost*, and so good night!

POL. On, good Camillo.

CAM. I am appointed him to murder you![a]

POL. By whom, Camillo?

CAM. By the king.

POL. For what?

CAM. He thinks, nay, with all confidence, he swears,
As he had seen't, or been an instrument
To vice[b] you to't,—that you have touch'd his queen
Forbiddenly.

POL. O, then my best blood turn
To an infected jelly, and my name
Be yok'd with his that did betray the Best![c]
Turn then my freshest reputation to
A savour that may strike the dullest nostril
Where I arrive, and my approach be shunn'd,
Nay, hated too, worse than the great'st infection
That e'er was heard or read!

CAM. Swear his thought over[d]
By each particular star in heaven, and
By all their influences, you may as well
Forbid the sea for to obey the moon,
As, or by oath remove, or counsel shake
The fabric of his folly, whose foundation
Is pil'd upon his faith, and will continue
The standing of his body.

POL. How should this grow?

CAM. I know not: but I am sure 't is safer to
Avoid what's grown than question how 'tis born.
If therefore you dare trust my honesty,—
That lies enclosed in this trunk, which you
Shall bear along impawn'd,—away to-night!
Your followers I will whisper to the business;
And will, by twos and threes, at several posterns,

---

[a] I am appointed him to murder you!] I am the agent fixed upon to murder you.

[b] *To* vice *you to't*,—] To *screw* you to it. So in "Twelfth Night," Act V. Sc. 1,—

"—— I partly know the instrument
That *screws* me from my true place in your favour."

[c] Be yok'd with his that did betray the Best!] That is, with the name of Judas.

[d] Swear his thought over—] Theobald suggested,—"Swear *this though*, over," which, besides being foreign to the mode of expression in Shakespeare's time, is a change quite uncalled for; to swear over=over-swear, is merely to *out*-swear.

Clear them o' the city: for myself, I'll put
My fortunes to your service, which are here
By this discovery lost. Be not uncertain;
For, by the honour of my parents, I
Have utter'd truth; which if you seek to prove,
I dare not stand by; nor shall you be safer
Than one condemned by the king's own mouth,
Thereon his execution sworn.

POL. I do believe thee;
I saw his heart in's face. Give me thy hand;
Be pilot to me, and thy places[a] shall
Still neighbour mine. My ships are ready, and
My people did expect my hence departure
Two days ago.—This jealousy
Is for a precious creature: as she's rare,
Must it be great; and, as his person's mighty,
Must it be violent: and as he does conceive
He is dishonour'd by a man which ever
Profess'd to him, why, his revenges must
In that be made more bitter. Fear o'ershades me:
Good expedition be my friend, and comfort
The gracious queen, part of his theme, but nothing
Of his ill-ta'en suspicion![b] Come, Camillo;
I will respect thee as a father, if
Thou bear'st my life off hence: let us avoid.

CAM. It is in mine authority to command
The keys of all the posterns. Please your highness
To take the urgent hour: come, sir, away!
[*Exeunt*.(4)

a — places—] By "places" are perhaps meant *dignities*, or *honours*.

b Good expedition be my friend, and comfort
The gracious queen, part of his theme, but nothing
Of his ill-ta'en suspicion!]

Warburton gives,—

"—— and comfort
The gracious *queen's*;"

Hanmer and Mr. Collier's annotator,—

"Good expedition be my friend! Heaven comfort," &c.;

the latter substituting "dream" for "*theme*." But we are still wide—*toto cœlo, tota regione*—of the genuine text, now, it may be feared, irrecoverable.

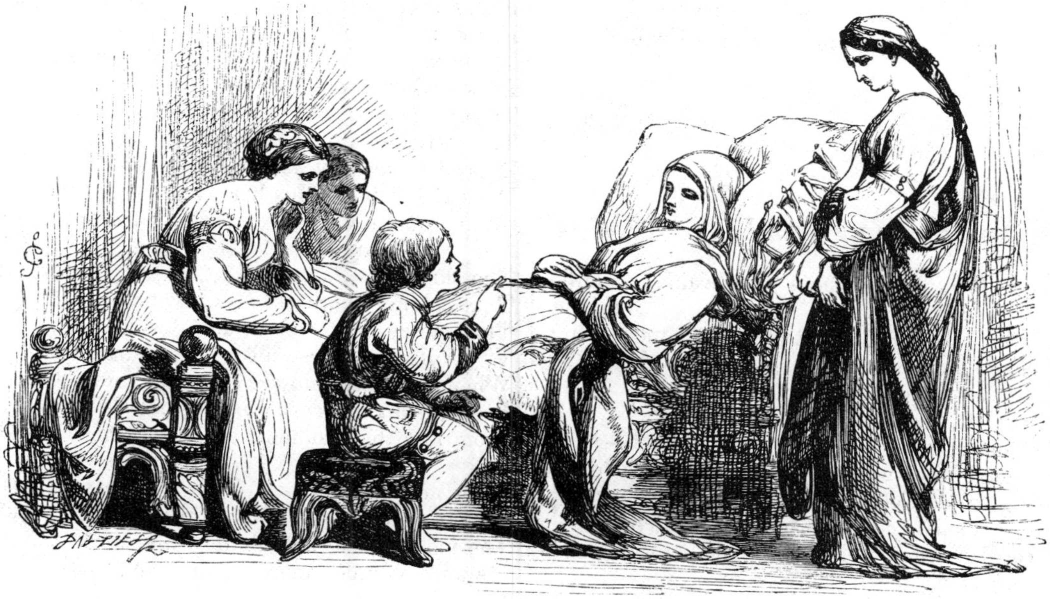

ACT II.

SCENE I.—Sicilia. *The Palace.*

Enter HERMIONE, MAMILLIUS, *and* Ladies.

HER. Take the boy to you: he so troubles me
'T is past enduring.

1 LADY. Come, my gracious lord,
Shall I be your playfellow?

MAM. No, I'll none of you.

1 LADY. Why, my sweet lord?

MAM. You'll kiss me hard, and speak to me as if
I were a baby still.—I love you better.

2 LADY. And why so, my lord?

MAM. Not for because
Your brows are blacker; yet black brows, they say,
Become some women best, so that there be not
Too much hair there, but in a semicircle,
Or a half-moon made with a pen.

2 LADY. Who taught you this? [a]

MAM. I learn'd it out of women's faces.—Pray now
What colour are your eyebrows?

1 LADY. Blue, my lord.

MAM. Nay, that's a mock: I have seen a lady's nose
That has been blue, but not her eyebrows.

2 LADY. Hark ye;
The queen your mother rounds apace: we shall
Present our services to a fine new prince
One of these days; and then you'd wanton with us,
If we would have you.

1 LADY. She is spread of late
Into a goodly bulk: good time encounter her!

HER. What wisdom stirs amongst you?—Come, sir, now
I am for you again: pray you, sit by us,
And tell's a tale.

MAM. Merry, or sad, shall't be?

HER. As merry as you will.

MAM. A sad tale's best for winter:
I have one of sprites and goblins.

HER. Let's have that, good sir.
Come on, sit down:—come on, and do your best
To fright me with your sprites; you're powerful at it.

MAM. There was a man,—

[a] Who taught you this?] It has been customary, since the time of Rowe, to read,—"Who taught *you* this?" though in the old text the pronoun is only indicated by an apostrophe.

HER. Nay, come, sit down; then on.
MAM. Dwelt by a churchyard;—I will tell it softly;
Yond crickets shall not hear it.
HER. Come on then,
And give't me in mine ear.

Enter LEONTES, ANTIGONUS, Lords, *and others.*

LEON. Was he met there? his train? Camillo with him? [never
1 LORD. Behind the tuft of pines I met them;
Saw I men scour so on their way: I ey'd them
Even to their ships.
LEON. How bless'd am I
In my just censure!—in my true opinion!—
Alack, for lesser knowledge!—how accurs'd
In being so bless'd!—There may be in the cup
A spider steep'd,[a] and one may drink, depart,[b]
And yet partake no venom; for his knowledge
Is not infected: but if one present
The abhorr'd ingredient to his eye, make known
How he hath drunk, he cracks his gorge, his sides,
With violent hefts:[c]—I have drunk, and seen the spider.
Camillo was his help in this, his pander:—
There is a plot against my life, my crown;
All's true that is mistrusted:—that false villain,
Whom I employ'd, was pre-employ'd by him:
He has discover'd my design, and I
Remain a pinch'd thing;[d] yea, a very trick
For them to play at will.—How came the posterns
So easily open?
1 LORD. By his great authority;
Which often hath no less prevail'd than so,
On your command.
LEON. I know't too well.—
Give me the boy;—I am glad you did not nurse him:
Though he does bear some signs of me, yet you
Have too much blood in him.
HER. What is this? sport?
LEON. Bear the boy hence, he shall not come about her;
Away with him!—and let her sport herself
[*Exit* MAMILLIUS, *with some of the* Attendants.
With that she's big with; for 't is Polixenes
Has made thee swell thus.
HER. But I'd say he had not,—
And I'll be sworn,—you would believe my saying,
Howe'er you lean to the nayward.
LEON. You, my lords,
Look on her, mark her well; be but about
To say, *she is a goodly lady,* and
The justice of your hearts will thereto add,
'T is pity she's not honest, honourable:
Praise her but for this her without-door form,
(Which, on my faith, deserves high speech) and straight
The shrug, the *hum,* or *ha,*—these petty brands
That calumny doth use:—O, I am out,
That mercy does; for calumny will sear
Virtue itself:—these shrugs, these hums and ha's,
When you have said *she's goodly,* come between,
Ere you can say *she's honest:* but be't known,
From him that has most cause to grieve it should be,
She's an adultress!
HER. Should a villain say so,
The most replenish'd villain in the world,
He were as much more villain: you, my lord,
Do but mistake.
LEON. You have mistook, my lady,
Polixenes for Leontes: O, thou thing,
Which I'll not call a creature of thy place,
Lest barbarism, making me the precedent,
Should a like language use to all degrees,
And mannerly distinguishment leave out
Betwixt the prince and beggar!—I have said
She's an adultress; I have said with whom:
More, she's a traitor; and Camillo is
A federary[e] with her; and one that knows
What she should shame to know herself
But with her most vile principal, that she's
A bed-swerver, even as bad as those
That vulgars give bold'st titles; ay, and privy
To this their late escape.
HER. No, by my life,
Privy to none of this! How will this grieve you
When you shall come to clearer knowledge, that
You thus have publish'd me! Gentle my lord,
You scarce can right me throughly then, to say
You did mistake.
LEON. No! if I mistake
In those foundations which I build upon,
The centre is not big enough to bear
A schoolboy's top.—Away with her to prison!
He who shall speak for her is afar off guilty
But that he speaks.

---

a A spider steep'd,—] It was a prevalent belief anciently that spiders were venomous, and that a person might be poisoned by drinking any liquid in which one was infused. From the context it would appear, however, that to render the draught fatal, the victim ought to see the spider. So, in Middleton's "No Wit, no Help like a Woman's," Act II. Sc. 1,—

"Even when my lip touch'd the contracting cup,
Even then to see the spider?"

b — *and one may drink,* depart, &c.] Mr. Collier's annotator reads,—"and one may drink *a part;*" but what Shakespeare wrote, we are persuaded, was,—

"—— and one may drink *deep o't,*
And yet partake no venom."

c — hefts:—] "Hefts" are *heavings.*

d — *a* pinch'd *thing;*] That is, a *restrained, nipped, confined* thing.

e A federary—] A supposed corruption of *feodary,* and signifying a *confederate,* or *accomplice.* See note (d), p. 608, Vol II.

HER. There's some ill planet reigns:
I must be patient till the heavens look
With an aspect more favourable.—Good my lords,
I am not prone to weeping, as our sex
Commonly are,—the want of which vain dew
Perchance shall dry your pities,—but I have
That honourable grief lodg'd here, which burns
Worse than tears drown: beseech you all, my lords,
With thoughts so qualified as your charities
Shall best instruct you, measure me;—and so
The king's will be perform'd!

LEON. Shall I be heard? [*To the* Guards.

HER. Who is't that goes with me?—Beseech your highness,
My women may be with me, for, you see,
My plight requires it.—Do not weep, good fools;
There is no cause: when you shall know your mistress
Has deserv'd prison, then abound in tears
As I come out: this action I now go on
Is for my better grace.—Adieu, my lord:
I never wish'd to see you sorry; now
I trust I shall.(1)—My women, come; you have leave.

LEON. Go, do our bidding; hence!

[*Exeunt* QUEEN *and* Ladies, *with* Guards.

1 LORD. Beseech your highness, call the queen again.

ANT. Be certain what you do, sir, lest your justice
Prove violence; in the which three great ones suffer,
Yourself, your queen, your son.

1 LORD. For her, my lord,
I dare my life lay down, and will do't, sir,
Please you to accept it, that the queen is spotless
I' the eyes of heaven and to you; I mean,
In this which you accuse her.

ANT. If it prove
She's otherwise, I'll keep my stables where
I lodge my wife; I'll go in couples with her;[a]
Than when I feel and see her, no farther trust her;
For every inch of woman in the world,
Ay, every dram of woman's flesh, is false,
If she be.

LEON. Hold your peaces.

1 LORD. Good my lord,—

ANT. It is for you we speak, not for ourselves:
You are abus'd, and by some putter-on,[b]
That will be damn'd for't; would I knew the villain,
I would land-damn[c] him. Be she honour-flaw'd,—
I have three daughters; the eldest is eleven;
The second, and the third, nine, and some five;
If this prove true, they'll pay for't: by mine honour,
I'll geld 'em all; fourteen they shall not see,
To bring false generations: they are co-heirs;
And I had rather glib myself than they
Should not produce fair issue.

LEON. Cease! no more.
You smell this business with a sense as cold
As is a dead man's nose: but I do see't and feel't,
As you feel doing thus; and see withal
The instruments that feel.[d]

ANT. If it be so,
We need no grave to bury honesty;
There's not a grain of it the face to sweeten
Of the whole dungy earth.

LEON. What! lack I credit?

1 LORD. I had rather you did lack than I, my lord,
Upon this ground; and more it would content me
To have her honour true than your suspicion,
Be blam'd for't how you might.

LEON. Why, what need we
Commune with you of this, but rather follow
Our forceful instigation? Our prerogative
Calls not your counsels; but our natural goodness
Imparts this: which, if you (or stupefied,
Or seeming so in skill[e]) cannot or will not
Relish a truth, like us, inform yourselves
We need no more of your advice: the matter,
The loss, the gain, the ordering on't, is all
Properly ours.

ANT. And I wish, my liege,
You had only in your silent judgment tried it,
Without more overture.

LEON. How could that be?
Either thou art most ignorant by age,

---

a

If it prove
She's otherwise, I'll keep my stables *where*
I lodge my wife; I'll go in couples with her;]

A prodigious amount of nonsense has been written on this unfortunate passage, but not a single editor or critic has shown the faintest perception of what it means. The accepted explanation, that by "I'll keep my stables where I lodge my wife," &c. Antigonus declares that he will have his stables in the same place with his wife; or, as some writers express it, he will "make his stable or dog-kennel of his wife's chamber"! sets gravity completely at defiance. What he means—and the excessive grossness of the idea can hardly be excused—is, unquestionably, that if Hermione be proved incontinent he should believe every woman is unchaste; his own wife as licentious as Semiramis, ("*Equum adamatum a Semiramide*," &c.—*Pliny*, l. viii. c. 42,) and where he lodged her he would "keep," that is, *guard*, or *fasten* the entry of his stables. This sense of the word "keep" is so common, even in Shakespeare, that it is amazing no one should have seen its application here. For example:—

"Dromio, *keep* the gate."—*Comedy of Errors*, Act II. Sc. 2.
"*Keep* the door close, sirrah."—*Henry VIII.* Act V. Sc. 1.
"I thank you: *keep* the door."—*Hamlet*, Act IV. Sc. 5.
"Gratiano, *keep* the house," &c.—*Othello*, Act V. Sc. 2.

b — *and by some* putter-on,—] "Putter-on" appears to have been a term of reproach, implying an *instigator*, or *plotter*. It occurs again in "Henry VIII." Act I. Sc. 2. See note (b), p. 650, Vol. II.

c — land-damn *him*.] "Land-damn" may almost with certainty be pronounced corrupt. The only tolerable attempt to extract sense from it, as it stands, is that of Rann, who conjectured that it meant "condemned to the punishment of being built up in the earth"—a torture mentioned in "Titus Andronicus," Act V. Sc. 3,—

"Set him breast-deep in earth, and famish him," &c.

d

—— and see withal
The instruments that feel.]

A stage direction of some kind is required at these words. Hanmer gives, "Laying hold of his arm;" Dr. Johnson, "Striking his brows."

e — in skill)—] That is, *cunning, design.*

Or thou wert born a fool. Camillo's flight,
Added to their familiarity,
(Which was as gross as ever touch'd conjecture,
That lack'd, sight only, nought for approbation;[a]
But only seeing, all other circumstances
Made up to the deed) doth push on this proceeding:
Yet, for a greater confirmation,
(For, in an act of this importance, 'twere
Most piteous to be wild) I have dispatch'd in post
To sacred Delphos, to Apollo's temple,
Cleomenes and Dion, whom you know
Of stuff'd sufficiency. Now, from the oracle
They will bring all; whose spiritual counsel had,
Shall stop, or spur me. Have I done well?

1 Lord. Well done, my lord.

Leon. Though I am satisfied, and need no more
Than what I know, yet shall the oracle
Give rest to the minds of others; such as he
Whose ignorant credulity will not
Come up to the truth. So have we thought it good,
From our free person she should be confin'd,
Lest that the treachery of the two fled hence
Be left her to perform. Come, follow us;
We are to speak in public; for this business
Will raise us all.

Ant. [*Aside.*] To laughter, as I take it,
If the good truth were known. [*Exeunt.*

[a] That lack'd, sight only, nought for approbation;] The meaning is,—That wanted, seeing excepted, nothing for proof.

SCENE II.—*The same. The outer Room of a Prison.*

Enter Paulina *and* Attendants.

Paul. The keeper of the prison,—call to him,
Let him have knowledge who I am.—
[*Exit an* Attendant.
Good lady!
No court in Europe is too good for thee;
What dost thou, then, in prison?

Re-enter Attendant, *with the* Gaoler.

Now, good sir,
You know me, do you not?

Gaol. For a worthy lady,
And one who much I honour.

Paul. Pray you, then,
Conduct me to the queen.

Gaol. I may not, madam: to the contrary
I have express commandment.

Paul. Here's ado,
To lock up honesty and honour from
The access of gentle visitors!—Is't lawful, pray you,
To see her women? any of them? Emilia?

Gaol. So please you, madam,
To put apart these your attendants, I
Shall bring Emilia forth.

Paul. I pray now, call her.—
Withdraw yourselves. [*Exeunt* Attendants.

GAOL. And, madam,
I must be present at your conference.

PAUL. Well, be it so, pr'ythee. [*Exit* Gaoler.
Here 's such ado to make no stain a stain,
As passes colouring.

Re-enter Gaoler, *with* EMILIA.

Dear gentlewoman,
How fares our gracious lady?

EMIL. As well as one so great and so forlorn
May hold together: on her frights and griefs,
(Which never tender lady hath borne greater)
She is, something before her time, deliver'd.

PAUL. A boy?

EMIL. A daughter; and a goodly babe,
Lusty, and like to live: the queen receives
Much comfort in 't: says, *My poor prisoner,
I am innocent as you.*

PAUL. I dare be sworn:—
These dangerous unsafe lunes[a] i' the king! beshrew them!
He must be told on 't, and he shall: the office
Becomes a woman best; I'll take 't upon me:
If I prove honey-mouth'd, let my tongue blister,
And never to my red-look'd anger be
The trumpet any more.—Pray you, Emilia,
Commend my best obedience to the queen;
If she dares trust me with her little babe,
I'll show 't the king, and undertake to be
Her advocate to the loudest. We do not know
How he may soften at the sight o' the child;
The silence often of pure innocence
Persuades, when speaking fails.

EMIL. Most worthy madam,
Your honour and your goodness is so evident,
That your free undertaking cannot miss
A thriving issue: there is no lady living
So meet for this great errand. Please your ladyship
To visit the next room, I'll presently
Acquaint the queen of your most noble offer;
Who but to-day hammer'd of this design,
But durst not tempt a minister of honour,
Lest she should be denied.

PAUL. Tell her, Emilia,
I'll use that tongue I have: if wit flow from 't,
As boldness from my bosom, let 't not be doubted
I shall do good.

EMIL. Now be you bless'd for it!
I'll to the queen: please you, come something nearer.

GAOL. Madam, if 't please the queen to send the babe,
I know not what I shall incur to pass it,
Having no warrant.

PAUL. You need not fear it, sir:
This child was prisoner to the womb, and is,
By law and process of great Nature, thence
Freed and enfranchis'd; not a party to
The anger of the king, nor guilty of,
If any be, the trespass of the queen.

GAOL. I do believe it.

PAUL. Do not you fear; upon mine honour, I
Will stand betwixt you and danger. [*Exeunt.*

SCENE III.—*The same. A Room in the Palace.*

ANTIGONUS, Lords, *and other* Attendants, *in waiting behind.*

Enter LEONTES.

LEON. Nor night nor day no rest. It is but weakness
To bear the matter thus;—mere weakness. If
The cause were not in being,—part o' the cause,
She the adultress; for the harlot king
Is quite beyond mine arm, out of the blank
And level[b] of my brain, plot-proof; but she
I can hook to me:—say that she were gone,
Given to the fire, a moiety of my rest
Might come to me again.—Who 's there?

1 ATTEND. [*Advancing.*] My lord!

LEON. How does the boy?

1 ATTEND. He took good rest to-night;
'T is hop'd his sickness is discharg'd.

LEON. To see his nobleness!
Conceiving the dishonour of his mother,
He straight declin'd, droop'd, took it deeply;
Fasten'd and fix'd the shame on 't in himself;
Threw off his spirit, his appetite, his sleep,
And downright languish'd.—Leave me solely:—go,
See how he fares. [*Exit* Attend.]—Fie, fie! no thought of him;—
The very thought of my revenges that way
Recoil upon me: in himself too mighty,
And in his parties, his alliance,—let him be,
Until a time may serve: for present vengeance,
Take it on her. Camillo and Polixenes
Laugh at me; make their pastime at my sorrow:
They should not laugh, if I could reach them; nor
Shall she, within my power.

Enter PAULINA, *with a* Child.

1 LORD. You must not enter.

PAUL. Nay, rather, good my lords, be second to me:

---

[a] These dangerous unsafe lunes—] To remedy the apparent tautology in this line, Mr. Collier's annotator would have us read, —still more tautologically,—

"These dangerous *unsane* lunes," &c.

But the old text needs no alteration; "dangerous," like its synonym "perilous," was sometimes used for *biting, caustic, mischievous;* and in some such sense may very well stand here.

[b] —— *out of the* blank
And level *of my brain,*—]

"Blank" and "level" are terms in gunnery; the former means *mark;* the latter *range.*

Fear you his tyrannous passion more, alas,
Than the queen's life? a gracious innocent soul,
More free than he is jealous.
ANT. That 's enough.
2 ATTEND. Madam, he hath not slept to-night; commanded
None should come at him.
PAUL. Not so hot, good sir;
I come to bring him sleep. 'T is such as you,—
That creep like shadows by him, and do sigh
At each his needless heavings,—such as you
Nourish the cause of his awaking: I
Do come with words as med'cinal as true,
Honest as either, to purge him of that humour
That presses him from sleep.
LEON. What* noise there ho?

(*) First folio, *who*.

PAUL. No noise, my lord; but needful conference
About some gossips for your highness.

LEON. How!—
Away with that audacious lady!—Antigonus,
I charg'd thee that she should not come about me:
I knew she would.

ANT. I told her so, my lord,
On your displeasure's peril and on mine,
She should not visit you.

LEON. What, canst not rule her?

PAUL. From all dishonesty he can: in this,
(Unless he take the course that you have done,
Commit me, for committing honour) trust it,
He shall not rule me.

ANT. La you now! you hear:
When she will take the rein, I let her run;
But she'll not stumble.

PAUL. Good my liege, I come,—
And, I beseech you, hear me, who professes
Myself your loyal servant, your physician,
Your most obedient counsellor; yet that dares
Less appear so, in comforting[a] your evils,
Than such as most seem yours:—I say, I come
From your good queen.

LEON. *Good queen!*

PAUL. Good queen, my lord, good queen: I say, good queen;
And would by combat make her good, so were I
A man, the worst about you.

LEON. Force her hence.

PAUL. Let him that makes but trifles of his eyes
First hand me: on mine own accord I'll off;
But first I'll do my errand.—The good queen,
For she is good, hath brought you forth a daughter;
Here 't is; commends it to your blessing.
[*Laying down the* Child.

LEON. Out!
A mankind[b] witch! Hence with her, out o' door:
A most intelligencing bawd!

PAUL. Not so:
I am as ignorant in that as you
In so entitling me: and no less honest[c]
Than you are mad; which is enough, I'll warrant,
As this world goes, to pass for honest.

LEON. Traitors!
Will you not push her out? Give her the bastard.—
Thou dotard [*To* ANTIGONUS.], thou art woman-tir'd,[d] unroosted
By thy dame Partlet here:—take up the bastard;
Take 't up, I say; give 't to thy crone.

PAUL. For ever
Unvenerable be thy hands, if thou
Tak'st up the princess by that forced baseness[e]
Which he has put upon 't!

LEON. He dreads his wife!

PAUL. So I would you did; then 't were past all doubt
You'd call your children yours.

LEON. A nest of traitors!

ANT. I am none, by this good light.

PAUL. Nor I; nor any,
But one, that 's here, and that 's himself; for he
The sacred honour of himself, his queen's,
His hopeful son's, his babe's, betrays to slander,
Whose sting is sharper than the sword's; and will not
(For, as the case now stands, it is a curse
He cannot be compell'd to 't) once remove
The root of his opinion, which is rotten,
As ever oak, or stone, was sound.

LEON. A callat,
Of boundless tongue, who late hath beat her husband,
And now baits me!—This brat is none of mine;
It is the issue of Polixenes:
Hence with it; and, together with the dam,
Commit them to the fire!

PAUL. It is yours;
And, might we lay the old proverb to your charge,
So like you, 't is the worse.[f]—Behold, my lords,
Although the print be little, the whole matter
And copy of the father,—eye, nose, lip;
The trick of 's frown; his forehead; nay, the valley,
The pretty dimples of his chin and cheek; his smiles;
The very mould and frame of hand, nail, finger:—
And thou, good goddess Nature, which hast made it
So like to him that got it, if thou hast
The ordering of the mind too, 'mongst all colours
No yellow in 't, lest she suspect, as he does,
Her children not her husband's!

LEON. A gross hag!—
And, losel,[g] thou art worthy to be hang'd,
That wilt not stay her tongue.

ANT. Hang all the husbands
That cannot do that feat, you'll leave yourself
Hardly one subject.

LEON. Once more, take her hence!

PAUL. A most unworthy and unnatural lord
Can do no more.

LEON. I'll have thee burn'd.

PAUL. I care not:
It is an heretic that makes the fire,
Not she which burns in 't. I'll not call you tyrant;

a — *in* comforting *your evils*,—] "Comforting" is here employed in the old and forensic sense of *encouraging, abetting*, &c.

b *A* mankind *witch!*] See note (a), p. 167.

c — honest—] That is, *chaste*.

d — woman-tir'd,—] As we say, *hen-pecked*.

e — by that forced baseness—] By that *false* appellation, *bastard*.

f And, might we lay the old proverb to your charge,
So like you, 't is the worse.—]
Overbury quotes this "old proverb" in his character of "A Sargeant":—"The devill cals him his white sonne; *he is so like him, that he is the worse for it*, and hee lokes after his father."—OVERBURY'S *Works, Ed.* 1616.

g — losel,—] Said to be derived from the Saxon *Losian*, to lose, and to mean an abandoned, worthless fellow.

But this most cruel usage of your queen
(Not able to produce more accusation
Than your own weak-hing'd fancy) something [savours
Of tyranny, and will ignoble make you,
Yea, scandalous to the world.

LEON. On your allegiance,
Out of the chamber with her! Were I a tyrant,
Where were her life? she durst not call me so,
If she did know me one. Away with her!

PAUL. I pray you, do not push me; I'll be gone.
Look to your babe, my lord; 't is yours: Jove send her
A better guiding spirit!—What needs these [hands?—
You, that are thus so tender o'er his follies,
Will never do him good, not one of you.
So, so:—farewell; we are gone. [*Exit.*

LEON. Thou, traitor, hast set on thy wife to this.—
My child? away with 't!—even thou, that hast
A heart so tender o'er it, take it hence,
And see it instantly consum'd with fire;
Even thou, and none but thou. Take it up straight:
Within this hour bring me word 't is done,
(And by good testimony) or I'll seize thy life,
With what thou else call'st thine. If thou refuse,
And wilt encounter with my wrath, say so;
The bastard brains with these my proper hands
Shall I dash out. Go, take it to the fire;
For thou sett'st on thy wife.

ANT. I did not, sir:
These lords, my noble fellows, if they please,
Can clear me in 't.

1 LORD. We can:—my royal liege,
He is not guilty of her coming hither.

LEON. You 're liars all.

1 LORD. Beseech your highness, give us better [credit:
We have always truly serv'd you; and beseech[a]
So to esteem of us: and on our knees we beg,
(As recompense of our dear services
Past and to come) that you do change this purpose,
Which being so horrible, so bloody, must
Lead on to some foul issue: we all kneel.

LEON. I am a feather for each wind that blows:—
Shall I live on, to see this bastard kneel
And call me father? Better burn it now,
Than curse it then. But be it; let it live:—
It shall not neither. You, sir, come you hither;
[*To* ANTIGONUS.
You that have been so tenderly officious
With lady Margery, your midwife, there,
To save this bastard's life,—for 't is a bastard,
So sure as this beard 's grey,[b]—what will you adventure
To save this brat's life?

ANT. Anything, my lord,
That my ability may undergo,
And nobleness impose:—at least, thus much,
I'll pawn the little blood which I have left
To save the innocent:—anything possible.

LEON. It shall be possible. Swear by this sword,
Thou wilt perform my bidding.

ANT. I will, my lord.

LEON. Mark, and perform it, seest thou; for the fail
Of any point in 't shall not only be
Death to thyself, but to thy lewd-tongu'd wife,
Whom for this time we pardon. We enjoin thee,
As thou art liegeman to us, that thou carry
This female bastard hence; and that thou bear it
To some remote and desert place, quite out
Of our dominions; and that there thou leave it,
Without more mercy, to it[c] own protection
And favour of the climate. As by strange fortune
It came to us, I do in justice charge thee,
On thy soul's peril, and thy body's torture,
That thou commend[d] it strangely to some place,
Where chance may nurse or end it. Take it up.

ANT. I swear to do this, though a present death
Had been more merciful.—Come on, poor babe:
Some powerful spirit instruct the kites and ravens
To be thy nurses! Wolves and bears, they say,
Casting their savageness aside, have done
Like offices of pity.—Sir, be prosperous
In more than this deed does require!—and blessing,
Against this cruelty, fight on thy side,
Poor thing, condemn'd to loss! (2)
[*Exit, with the* Child.

LEON. No, I'll not rear
Another's issue.

2 ATTEND. Please your highness, posts,
From those you sent to the oracle, are come
An hour since: Cleomenes and Dion,
Being well arriv'd from Delphos, are both landed,
Hasting to the court.

1 LORD. So please you, sir, their speed
Hath been beyond account.

LEON. Twenty-three days
They have been absent: 't is good speed; foretells
The great Apollo suddenly will have
The truth of this appear. Prepare you, lords;
Summon a session, that we may arraign
Our most disloyal lady; for, as she hath
Been publicly accus'd, so shall she have
A just and open trial. While she lives,
My heart will be a burden to me. Leave me;
And think upon my bidding. [*Exeunt.*

---

a — and beseech —] Here again in the old text the elision of *you* is marked by an apostrophe; thus, beseech '.

b So sure as this beard 's grey,—] Unless we read according to a marginal annotation in Lord Ellesmere's copy of the first folio, —"*thy* beard," we must suppose the king to point to, or touch the beard of Antigonus; he himself, who twenty-three years before the play began was unbreeched, could hardly have a grey beard.

c — *to it own protection*—] Although the pronoun "its" occurs more frequently in this piece than in any other of Shakespeare's plays, showing it to have been one of his last works, that now indispensable vocable was still only in its infancy; for in this drama we have "it" in the instance above, and again in Act III. Sc. 2,—
"The innocent milke in *it* most innocent mouth."

d — commend—] To *commend* was to *commit*.

ACT III.

SCENE I.—Sicilia. *A Street in some Town.*

Enter CLEOMENES *and* DION.

CLEO. The climate 's delicate; the air most sweet;
Fertile the isle; the temple much surpassing
The common praise it bears.
DION. I shall report,
For most it caught me, the celestial habits,
(Methinks I so should term them) and the reverence
Of the grave wearers. O, the sacrifice!
How ceremonious, solemn, and unearthly
It was i' the offering!
CLEO. But, of all, the burst
And the ear-deafening voice o' the oracle,
Kin to Jove's thunder, so surpris'd my sense,
That I was nothing.
DION. If the event o' the journey
Prove as successful to the queen,—O, be it so!—
As it hath been to us rare, pleasant, speedy,
The time is worth the use on 't.
CLEO. Great Apollo,
Turn all to the best! These proclamations,
So forcing faults upon Hermione,
I little like.
DION. The violent carriage of it
Will clear or end the business: when the oracle
(Thus by Apollo's great divine seal'd up)
Shall the contents discover, something rare
Even then will rush to knowledge.—Go,—fresh horses;—
And gracious be the issue! [*Exeunt.*

SCENE II.—*The same. A Court of Justice.*

LEONTES, Lords, *and* Officers *discovered, properly seated.*

LEON. This sessions (to our great grief we pronounce)
Even pushes 'gainst our heart; the party tried,
The daughter of a king, our wife, and one
Of us too much belov'd.—Let us be clear'd
Of being tyrannous, since we so openly
Proceed in justice; which shall have due course,
Even to the guilt or the purgation.——
Produce the prisoner.
OFFI. It is his highness' pleasure that the queen
Appear in person here in court.—Silence![a]

---

[a] Silence!] In the old copies this word stands as a stage direction; but that it was intended for a command, to be spoken by the officer, or by the ordinary crier, is evident. Compare the opening of the scene of Queen Katharine's trial in "Henry VIII."

Enter HERMIONE, *guarded;* PAULINA *and* Ladies, *attending.*

LEON. Read the indictment.

OFFI. [Reads.] *Hermione, queen to the worthy Leontes, king of Sicilia, thou art here accused and arraigned of high treason, in committing adultery with Polixenes, king of Bohemia; and conspiring with Camillo to take away the life of our sovereign lord the king, thy royal husband: the pretence*[a] *whereof being by circumstances partly laid open, thou, Hermione, contrary to the faith and allegiance of a true subject, didst counsel and aid them, for their better safety, to fly away by night.*

[a] — pretence—] That is, *plot, design,* &c. So, in "Macbeth," Act II. Sc. 1,—

"—— and thence
Against the undivulg'd *pretence* I fight
Of treasonous malice."

HER. Since what I am to say must be but that
Which contradicts my accusation, and
The testimony on my part no other
But what comes from myself, it shall scarce boot
me
To say, *Not guilty;* mine integrity,
Being counted falsehood, shall, as I express it,
Be so receiv'd. But thus,—If powers divine
Behold our human actions (as they do),
I doubt not, then, but innocence shall make
False accusation blush, and tyranny
Tremble at patience.—You, my lord, best know
(Who least will seem to do so) my past life
Hath been as continent, as chaste, as true,
As I am now unhappy; which is more
Than history can pattern, though devis'd
And play'd to take spectators; for behold me,—
A fellow of the royal bed, which owe

A moiety of the throne, a great king's daughter,
The mother to a hopeful prince,—here standing,
To prate and talk for life and honour 'fore
Who please to come and hear. For life, I prize it
As I weigh grief,[a] which I would spare: for honour,
'T is a derivative from me to mine,
And only that I stand for. I appeal
To your own conscience, sir, before Polixenes
Came to your court, how I was in your grace,
How merited to be so; since he came,
With what encounter so uncurrent I
Have strain'd, to appear thus:[b] if one jot beyond
The bound of honour, or in act or will
That way inclining, harden'd be the hearts
Of all that hear me, and my near'st of kin
Cry *Fie!* upon my grave!

LEON. I ne'er heard yet
That any of these bolder vices wanted
Less impudence to gainsay what they did,
Than to perform it first.

HER. That's true enough;
Though 't is a saying, sir, not due to me.

LEON. You will not own it.

HER. More than mistress of
Which comes to me in name of fault, I must not
At all acknowledge. For Polixenes,
(With whom I am accus'd) I do confess
I lov'd him,—as in honour he requir'd,—
With such a kind of love as might become
A lady like me; with a love, even such,
So and no other, as yourself commanded:
Which not to have done, I think had been in me
Both disobedience and ingratitude
To you and toward your friend; whose love had spoke,
Even since it could speak, from an infant, freely,
That it was yours. Now, for conspiracy,
I know not how it tastes; though it be dish'd
For me to try how: all I know of it,
Is that Camillo was an honest man;
And why he left your court, the gods themselves,
Wotting no more than I, are ignorant.

LEON. You knew of his departure, as you know
What you have underta'en to do in 's absence.

HER. Sir,
You speak a language that I understand not:
My life stands in the level of your dreams,[c]
Which I 'll lay down.

LEON. Your actions are my dreams;
You had a bastard by Polixenes,
And I but dream'd it:—as you were past all shame,
(Those of your fact[d] are so,) so past all truth;
Which to deny, concerns more than avails; for as
Thy brat hath been cast out, like to itself,
No father owning it, (which is, indeed,
More criminal in thee than it) so thou
Shalt feel our justice; in whose easiest passage,
Look for no less than death.(1)

HER. Sir, spare your threats;
The bug which you would fright me with, I seek.
To me can life be no commodity:
The crown and comfort of my life, your favour,
I do give lost; for I do feel it gone,
But know not how it went: my second joy,
And first-fruits of my body, from his presence
I am barr'd, like one infectious: my third comfort,
Starr'd most unluckily, is from my breast,
The innocent milk in it[e] most innocent mouth,
Hal'd out to murder: myself on every post
Proclaim'd a strumpet; with immodest hatred,
The child-bed privilege denied, which 'longs
To women of all fashion;—lastly, hurried
Here to this place, i' the open air, before
I have got strength of limit. Now, my liege,
Tell me what blessings I have here alive,
That I should fear to die? Therefore, proceed.
But yet hear this; mistake me not;—no life,—
I prize it not a straw:—but for mine honour,
(Which I would free) if I shall be condemn'd
Upon surmises,—all proofs sleeping else,
But what your jealousies awake,—I tell you
'T is rigour, and not law.—Your honours all,
I do refer me to the oracle:
Apollo be my judge! (2)

1 LORD. This your request
Is altogether just:—therefore, bring forth,
And in Apollo's name, his oracle.

[*Exeunt certain* Officers.

HER. The emperor of Russia was my father:
O, that he were alive, and here beholding
His daughter's trial! that he did but see
The flatness of my misery,—yet with eyes
Of pity, not revenge!

---

a —— *For life, I prize it*
As I weigh grief, *which I would spare:*]

It is surprising this passage should have passed without question, for "grief" must surely be an error. Hermione means that life to her is of as little estimation as the most trivial thing which she would part with; and she expresses the same sentiment shortly after, in similar terms,—

"—— no life,—
I prize it *not a straw.*"

Could she speak of "grief" as a trifle, of no moment or importance?

b With what encounter so uncurrent I
Have strain'd, to appear thus:]

This is not remarkably perspicuous; the sense appears to be,—By what unwarrantable familiarity have I lapsed, that I should be made to stand as a public criminal thus?

c — in the level—] To be *in the level* is to be within the range or compass;—"and therefore when under his covert or pertision he is gotten within his *levell* and hath the Winde fit and certaine, then hee shall make choice of his marke," &c.—MARKHAM'S *Hunger's Prevention*, 1621, p. 45.

d (*Those of your* fact—] Those of your *crime*. Thus, in "Pericles," Act IV. Sc. 3,—

"Becoming well thy *fact.*"

e — *in* it *most innocent mouth,*—] See note (b), p. 214.

Re-enter Officers, *with* CLEOMENES *and* DION.

OFFI. You here shall swear upon this sword of justice,
That you, Cleomenes and Dion, have
Been both at Delphos; and from thence have brought
This seal'd-up oracle, by the hand deliver'd
Of great Apollo's priest; and that, since then,
You have not dar'd to break the holy seal,
Nor read the secrets in 't.

CLEO. *and* DION. All this we swear.

LEON. Break up the seals, and read.

OFFI. [Reads.] *Hermione is chaste; Polixenes blameless; Camillo a true subject; Leontes a jealous tyrant; his innocent babe truly begotten; and the king shall live without an heir, if that which is lost be not found.* (3)

LORDS. Now blessed be the great Apollo!

HER. Praised!

LEON. Hast thou read truth?

OFFI. Ay, my lord; even so
As it is here set down.

LEON. There is no truth at all i' the oracle:
The sessions shall proceed: this is mere falsehood.

Enter an Attendant, *hastily.*

ATTEN. My lord the king, the king!

LEON. What is the business?

ATTEN. O sir, I shall be hated to report it!
The prince your son, with mere conceit and fear
Of the queen's speed,[a] is gone.

LEON. How! gone?

ATTEN. Is dead.

LEON. Apollo 's angry; and the heavens themselves
Do strike at my injustice. [HERMIONE *faints.*]
How now there!

PAUL. This news is mortal to the queen.—
Look down,
And see what death is doing.

LEON. Take her hence:
Her heart is but o'ercharg'd; she will recover:—
I have too much believ'd mine own suspicion:—
Beseech you tenderly apply to her
Some remedies for life.—

[*Exeunt* PAULINA *and* Ladies, *with* HERMIONE.

Apollo, pardon
My great profaneness 'gainst thine oracle!—
I 'll reconcile me to Polixenes;
New woo my queen; recall the good Camillo,
Whom I proclaim a man of truth, of mercy;
For, being transported by my jealousies
To bloody thoughts and to revenge, I chose
Camillo for the minister, to poison
My friend Polixenes: which had been done,
But that the good mind of Camillo tardied
My swift command, though I with death, and with
Reward, did threaten and encourage him,
Not doing it, and being done: he, most humane,
And fill'd with honour, to my kingly guest
Unclasp'd my practice; quit his fortunes here,
Which you knew great; and to the hazard
Of all incertainties himself commended.
No richer than his honour, how he glisters
Thorough my rust! and how his piety
Does my deeds make the blacker![b]

Re-enter PAULINA.

PAUL. Woe the while!
O, cut my lace; lest my heart, cracking it,
Break too!

1 LORD. What fit is this, good lady?

PAUL. What studied torments, tyrant, hast for me?
What wheels? racks? fires? what flaying? boiling
In leads or oils? what old or newer torture
Must I receive, whose every word deserves
To taste of thy most worst? Thy tyranny
Together working with thy jealousies,—
Fancies too weak for boys, too green and idle
For girls of nine!—O, think what they have done,
And then run mad indeed,—stark mad! for all
Thy by-gone fooleries were but spices of it.
That thou betray'dst Polixenes, 't was nothing,—
That did but show thee of a fool,[c] inconstant
And damnable[d] ingrateful; nor was 't much,
Thou wouldst have poison'd good Camillo's honour,
To have him kill a king;—poor trespasses,
More monstrous standing by: whereof I reckon
The casting forth to crows thy baby daughter,
To be or none, or little,—though a devil
Would have shed water out of fire, ere done 't;
Nor is 't directly laid to thee, the death
Of the young prince, whose honourable thoughts
(Thoughts high for one so tender) cleft the heart
That could conceive a gross and foolish sire
Blemish'd his gracious dam: this is not, no,
Laid to thy answer: but the last,—O, lords,

---

a *Of the queen's* speed,—] Of the queen's *fate, hap, fortune.*

b No richer than his honour, how he glisters
Thorough my rust! and how his piety
Does my deeds make the blacker!]

The force of this is miserably enfeebled by the punctuation heretofore adopted,—

"—— and to the hazard
Of all incertainties himself commended,
No richer than his honour. How he glisters," &c.

c That did but show thee of a fool,—] Theobald proposed to read,—"of a *soul;*" and Warburton,—"show thee *off*, a fool;" but any change would be to destroy a form of speech characteristic of the author's time; "*of* a fool," is the same as "*for* a fool."

d *And* damnable *ingrateful;*] That is, "*damnably* ingrateful."

When I have said, cry, *Woe!* [a]—the queen, the queen,
The sweet'st, dear'st creature 's dead; and vengeance for 't
Not dropp'd down yet!

1 LORD. The higher powers forbid!

PAUL. I say, she 's dead; I 'll swear 't. If word nor oath
Prevail not, go and see: if you can bring
Tincture or lustre in her lip, her eye,
Heat outwardly or breath within, I 'll serve you
As I would do the gods.—But, O, thou tyrant!
Do not repent these things; for they are heavier
Than all thy woes can stir: therefore betake thee
To nothing but despair. A thousand knees,
Ten thousand years together, naked, fasting,
Upon a barren mountain, and still winter,
In storm perpetual, could not move the gods
To look that way thou wert.

LEON. Go on, go on:
Thou canst not speak too much; I have deserv'd
All tongues to talk their bitterest.

1 LORD. Say no more;
Howe'er the business goes, you have made fault
I' the boldness of your speech.

PAUL. I am sorry for 't;
All faults I make, when I shall come to know them,
I do repent. Alas, I have show'd too much
The rashness of a woman! he is touch'd
To the noble heart.—What 's gone, and what 's past help,
Should be past grief; do not receive affliction
At my petition; [b] I beseech you, rather
Let me be punish'd, that have minded you
Of what you should forget. Now, good my liege,—
Sir, royal sir,—forgive a foolish woman:
The love I bore your queen,—lo, fool again!—
I 'll speak of her no more, nor of your children;
I 'll not remember you of my own lord,
Who is lost too: take your patience to you,
And I 'll say nothing.

LEON. Thou didst speak but well,
When most the truth; which I receive much better
Than to be pitied of thee. Pr'ythee, bring me
To the dead bodies of my queen and son:
One grave shall be for both; upon them shall
The causes of their death appear, unto
Our shame perpetual. Once a day I 'll visit
The chapel where they lie; and tears shed there
Shall be my recreation: so long as nature
Will bear up with this exercise, so long
I daily vow to use it. Come, and lead me
To these sorrows. [*Exeunt.*

SCENE III.—Bohemia. *A desert Country near the Sea.*

Enter ANTIGONUS *with the* Babe; *and a* Mariner.

ANT. Thou art perfect [c] then, our ship hath touch'd upon
The deserts of Bohemia?

MAR. Ay, my lord; and fear
We have landed in ill time: the skies look grimly,
And threaten present blusters; in my conscience,
The heavens with that we have in hand are angry,
And frown upon us.

ANT. Their sacred wills be done!—Go, get aboard;
Look to thy bark; I 'll not be long before
I call upon thee.

MAR. Make your best haste; and go not
Too far i' the land: 't is like to be loud weather;
Besides, this place is famous for the creatures
Of prey that keep upon 't.

ANT. Go thou away:
I 'll follow instantly.

MAR. I am glad at heart
To be so rid o' the business. [*Exit.*

ANT. Come, poor babe:—
I have heard (but not believ'd) the spirits o' the dead
May walk again: if such thing be, thy mother
Appear'd to me last night; for ne'er was dream
So like a waking. To me comes a creature,
Sometimes her head on one side, some, another;
I never saw a vessel of like sorrow,
So fill'd, and so becoming: [d] in pure white robes,
Like very sanctity, she did approach
My cabin where I lay; thrice bow'd before me;
And, gasping to begin some speech, her eyes
Became two spouts: the fury spent, anon
Did this break from her: *Good Antigonus,*
Since fate, against thy better disposition,

---

a When I have said, cry, *Woe!*] When I have done, do you cry, *Woe!*

b —— *do not* receive *affliction*
At my petition;]

We should perhaps read,—"do not *revive* affliction," &c., but certainly not,—

"—— do not receive affliction
At *repetition;*"

as suggested by Mr. Collier's annotator.

c *Thou art* perfect, *then*,—] "Perfect" is commonly used by our old writers for *confident, well assured;* thus in "Cymbeline," Act III. Sc. 1,—"I am *perfect* that the Pannonians and Dalmatians are—" &c.

d So fill'd, and so becoming:] Mr. Collier's annotator suggests, and Mr. Collier adopts, an alteration which at once destroys the meaning of the poet, and converts a beauteous image into one pre-eminently ludicrous:—

"So fill'd, and so o'er-running"!

"So *becoming*" here means, so *self-restrained:* not as it is usually explained, so *decent*, or so *dignified*. Compare the following in "Romeo and Juliet," Act IV. Sc. 2,—

"I met the youthful lord at Laurence' cell;
And gave him what *becomed* love I might,
Not stepping o'er the bounds of modesty."

Hath made thy person for the thrower-out
Of my poor babe, according to thine oath,
Places remote enough are in Bohemia,
There weep, and leave it, crying; and, for the babe
Is counted lost for ever, Perdita,
I pr'ythee, call't. For this ungentle business,
Put on thee by my lord, thou ne'er shalt see
Thy wife Paulina more:—and so, with shrieks,
She melted into air. Affrighted much,
I did in time collect myself; and thought
This was so, and no slumber. Dreams are toys;
Yet, for this once, yea, superstitiously,
I will be squar'd by this. I do believe
Hermione hath suffer'd death; and that
Apollo would, this being indeed the issue
Of king Polixenes, it should here be laid,
Either for life or death, upon the earth
Of its right father. Blossom, speed thee well!—
[*Laying down the* Child.
There lie; and there thy character:[a] there these;—
[*Laying down a bundle.*
Which may, if Fortune please both breed thee, (pretty!)
And still rest thine.[b]—The storm begins:—poor wretch,
That, for thy mother's fault, art thus expos'd
To loss and what may follow!—Weep I cannot,
But my heart bleeds: and most accurs'd am I
To be by oath enjoin'd to this.—Farewell!
The day frowns more and more:—thou 'rt like to have
A lullaby too rough:—I never saw
The heavens so dim by day.—
[*Noise without of* Hunters *and Dogs.*
A savage clamour!—
Well may I get aboard!—[*Sees a Bear.*] This is the chase!
I am gone for ever! [*Exit, pursued by the Bear.*

Enter an old Shepherd.

SHEP. I would there were no age between ten and three-and-twenty, or that youth would sleep out the rest; for there is nothing in the between but getting wenches with child, wronging the ancientry, stealing, fighting—Hark you now!—Would any but these boiled brains of nineteen and two-and-twenty hunt this weather? They have scared away two of my best sheep, which I fear the wolf will sooner find than the master; if any-where I have them, 't is by the sea-side, browzing of ivy.(4) Good luck, an 't be thy will!—What have we here? [*Taking up the* Babe.] Mercy on 's, a barne; a very pretty barne! A boy or a child,[c] I wonder? A pretty one; a very pretty one: sure, some scape: though I am not bookish, yet I can read waiting-gentlewoman in the scape. This has been some stair-work, some trunk-work, some behind-door-work: they were warmer that got this than the poor thing is here. I 'll take it up for pity: yet I 'll tarry till my son come; he hol-laed but even now.—Whoa, ho hoa!

CLO. [*Without.*] Hilloa, loa!

SHEP. What, art so near? If thou 'lt see a thing to talk on when thou art dead and rotten, come hither.

Enter Clown.

What ailest thou, man?

CLO. I have seen two such sights, by sea and by land!—but I am not to say it is a sea, for it is now the sky; betwixt the firmament and it you cannot thrust a bodkin's point.

SHEP. Why, boy, how is it?

CLO. I would you did but see how it chafes, how it rages, how it takes up the shore!—but that 's not to the point. O, the most piteous cry of the poor souls! sometimes to see 'em, and not to see 'em; now the ship boring the moon with her mainmast, and anon swallowed with yest and froth, as you 'd thrust a cork into a hogshead. And then for the land-service,—to see how the bear tore out his shoulder-bone; how he cried to me for help, and said his name was Antigonus, a nobleman:—but to make an end of the ship,—to see how the sea flap-dragoned it[d]:—but, first, how the poor souls roared, and the sea mocked them;—and how the poor gentleman roared, and the bear mocked him, both roaring louder than the sea or weather.

SHEP. Name of mercy! when was this, boy?

CLO. Now, now; I have not winked since I saw these sights: the men are not yet cold under

---

[a] — *thy* character:] Some ciphers and the name, "Perdita," by which the child hereafter might be recognised.

[b] Blossom, speed thee well!—
There lie; and there thy character: there these;—
Which may, if Fortune please both breed thee, (pretty!)
And still rest thine.]

The meaning is manifestly,—"Poor Blossom, good speed to thee! which may happen, despite thy present desolate condition, if Fortune please to adopt thee, (thou pretty one!) and remain thy constant friend;" the intermediate line,—"There lie," &c. being, of course, parenthetical. From the punctuation hitherto adopted,—

"Blossom, speed thee well!
There lie; and there thy character; there these;
Which may, if Fortune please, both breed thee pretty,
And still rest thine,"

the editors, one and all, must have supposed Antigonus to antici-pate that the rich clothes, &c. which he leaves with the child, might breed it beautiful and prove of permanent utility to it in its after course of life.

[c] A boy or a child, I wonder?] "I am told, that in some of our inland counties, a *female infant*, in contradistinction to a *male one*, is still termed, among the peasantry,—*a child*."—STEEVENS.

In support of this, Mr. Halliwell quotes the following from Hole's MS. Glossary of Devonshire Words, collected about 1780, "A child, a female infant."

[d] — *the sea* flap-dragoned *it*:—] This may mean,—swallowed it as our old revellers did a flap-dragon.

water, nor the bear half dined on the gentleman,—he 's at it now.

SHEP. Would I had been by, to have helped the old man!

CLO. I would you had been by the ship side, to have helped her; there your charity would have lacked footing.

SHEP. Heavy matters! heavy matters! but look thee here, boy. Now bless thyself; thou mett'st with things dying, I with things new born. Here 's a sight for thee; look thee, a bearing cloth[a] for a squire's child! look thee here! take up, take up, boy; open 't. So, let 's see:—it was told me I should be rich by the fairies; this is some changeling:—open 't. What 's within, boy?

CLO. You 're a made* old man; if the sins of

a — a bearing cloth—] The mantle in which an infant was wrapped when carried to the font to be baptized.

(*) Old text, *mad*.

your youth are forgiven you, you 're well to live. Gold! all gold!

SHEP. This is fairy gold, boy, and 't will prove so: up with it, keep it close;[a] home, home, the next[b] way. We are lucky, boy, and to be so still, requires nothing but secrecy.—Let my sheep go:—come, good boy, the next way home.

CLO. Go you the next way with your findings. I 'll go see if the bear be gone from the gentleman, and how much he hath eaten: they are never curst[c] but when they are hungry: if there be any of him left, I 'll bury it.

SHEP. That 's a good deed. If thou mayest discern by that which is left of him, what he is, fetch me to the sight of him.

CLO. Marry, will I; and you shall help to put him i' the ground.

SHEP. 'T is a lucky day, boy, and we'll do good deeds on 't. [*Exeunt.*

a This is fairy gold,——keep it close;] To divulge the possession of fairies' gifts was supposed to entail misfortune. Thus, Ben Jonson,—

"A prince's secrets are like fairy favours,
Wholesome if kept; but poison if discover'd."

b — *the* next *way*.] "The next way" meant the *nearest* way.

c — curst—] That is, *malicious, dangerous*.

ACT IV.

Enter Time, *as Chorus.*

Time. I,—that please some, try all; both joy and terror
Of good and bad;—that make and unfold error;—
Now take upon me, in the name of Time,
To use my wings. Impute it not a crime
To me or my swift passage, that I slide
O'er sixteen years, and leave the growth untried
Of that wide gap; since it is in my power
To o'erthrow law, and in one self-born hour
To plant and o'erwhelm custom. Let me pass
The same I am, ere ancient'st order was,
Or what is now receiv'd: I witness to
The times that brought them in; so shall I do
To the freshest things now reigning, and make stale
The glistering of this present, as my tale
Now seems to it. Your patience this allowing,
I turn my glass, and give my scene such growing
As you had slept between. Leontes leaving,—
The effects of his fond jealousies so grieving,
That he shuts up himself;—imagine me,
Gentle spectators, that I now may be
In fair Bohemia;[a] and remember well,
I mentioned a son o' the king's, which Florizel
I now name to you; and with speed so pace
To speak of Perdita, now grown in grace
Equal with wondering: what of her ensues
I list not prophesy; but let Time's news
Be known when 't is brought forth:—a shepherd's daughter,
And what to her adheres, which follows after,
Is the argument of Time. Of this allow,
If ever you have spent time worse ere now;
If never, yet that Time himself doth say,
He wishes earnestly you never may. [*Exit.*

a Leontes leaving,—
The effects of his fond jealousies so grieving,
That he shuts up himself;—imagine me,
Gentle spectators, that I now may be
In fair Bohemia;]

It is hardly credible that, in every edition, not excepting even that of Mr. Dyce, which is immeasurably superior to most others in the article of punctuation, these lines should stand thus,—

"— Leontes leaving
The effects of his fond jealousies; so grieving
That he shuts up himself; imagine me," &c.!

If the absurdity of representing Leontes as "leaving" the consequences of his foolish jealousies, and at the same time as so "grieving" over them that he shuts himself up, were not enough to indicate the poet's meaning, how could any editor possibly miss it who had bestowed a moment's reflection on the parallel passage in the original story?—"This epitaph being ingraven, Pandosto would once a day repaire to the tombe, and there with watry plaintes bewaile his misfortune, coveting no other companion but sorrowe, nor no other harmonie but repentance. *But leaving him to his dolorous passions, at last let us come to shewe the tragicall discourse of the young infant.*" Compare, too, the corresponding lines in Sabie's "Fisherman's Tale," 1595,—

"He having thus her funerals dispatcht,
Liv'd in vast dolour, and perpetuall griefe,
Sighing, and crying out against the Fates;
Amid these woes, whome now I meane to leave,
And make recourse unto this little babe," &c.

SCENE I.—Bohemia. *A Room in the Palace of* Polixenes.

Enter POLIXENES *and* CAMILLO.

POL. I pray thee, good Camillo, be no more importunate: 't is a sickness denying thee anything; a death to grant this.

CAM. It is fifteen years since I saw my country: though I have, for the most part, been aired abroad, I desire to lay my bones there. Besides, the penitent king, my master, hath sent for me; to whose feeling sorrows I might be some allay, or I o'erween to think so,—which is another spur to my departure.

POL. As thou lovest me, Camillo, wipe not out the rest of thy services by leaving me now: the need I have of thee, thine own goodness hath made; better not to have had thee, than thus to want thee: thou, having made me businesses which none without thee can sufficiently manage, must either stay to execute them thyself, or take away with thee the very services thou hast done; which if I have not enough considered, (as too much I cannot) to be more thankful to thee shall be my study; and my profit therein, the heaping friendships. Of that fatal country Sicilia, pr'ythee speak no more; whose very naming punishes me with the remembrance of that penitent, as thou callest him, and reconciled king, my brother; whose loss of his most precious queen and children are even now to be afresh lamented. Say to me, when sawest thou the prince Florizel, my son? Kings are no less unhappy, their issue not being gracious, than they are in losing them when they have approved their virtues.

CAM. Sir, it is three days since I saw the prince. What his happier affairs may be, are to me unknown; but I have missingly[a] noted, he is of late much retired from court, and is less frequent to his princely exercises than formerly he hath appeared.

POL. I have considered so much, Camillo, and with some care; so far, that I have eyes under my service which look upon his removedness, from whom I have this intelligence;—that he is seldom from the house of a most homely shepherd; a man, they say, that from very nothing, and beyond the imagination of his neighbours, is grown into an unspeakable estate.

CAM. I have heard, sir, of such a man, who hath a daughter of most rare note: the report of her is extended more than can be thought to begin from such a cottage.

POL. That 's likewise part of my intelligence; but[b] I fear the angle that plucks our son thither.

[a] — *but I have* missingly *noted*,—] Hanmer, with some plausibility, reads,—"*musingly* noted," and Mr. Collier's annotator proposes the same substitution.

[b] — but *I fear the angle that plucks our son thither.*] "But," in this place, is the Saxon *Botan=to boot*, and the King's meaning,—The attractions of that girl form part of my intelligence, and they are, I apprehend, the angle which draws the prince there.

Thou shalt accompany us to the place; where we will, not appearing what we are, have some question with the shepherd; from whose simplicity I think it not uneasy to get the cause of my son's resort thither. Pr'ythee, be my present partner in this business, and lay aside the thoughts of Sicilia.

CAM. I willingly obey your command.

POL. My best Camillo!—We must disguise ourselves. [*Exeunt.*

SCENE II.—*The same. A Road near the* Shepherd's *Cottage.*

Enter AUTOLYCUS, *singing.*

When daffodils begin to peer,—
With hey! the doxy over the dale,—
Why then comes in the sweet o' the year;
For the red blood reigns in the winter's pale.

The white sheet bleaching on the hedge,
With hey! the sweet birds, O, how they sing!
Doth set my pugging[a] *tooth on edge;*
For a quart of ale is a dish for a king.

The lark that tirra-lirra chants,—
With hey! with hey![b] *the thrush and the jay,—*
Are summer songs for me and my aunts,
While we lie tumbling in the hay.

I have served prince Florizel, and, in my time, wore three-pile;[c] but now I am out of service:

But shall I go mourn for that, my dear? [Singing.
The pale moon shines by night;
And when I wander here and there,
I then do most go right.

If tinkers may have leave to live,
And bear the sow-skin budget;
Then my account I well may give,
And in the stocks avouch it.

My traffic is sheets; when the kite builds, look to lesser linen. My father named me Autolycus; who, being as I am, littered under Mercury, was likewise a snapper-up of unconsidered trifles. With die and drab I purchased this caparison; and my revenue is the silly cheat:[d] gallows and knock are too powerful on the highway; beating and hanging are terrors to me; for the life to come, I sleep out the thought of it.—A prize! a prize!

Enter Clown.

CLO. Let me see:—every 'leven wether tods;[e] every tod yields—pound and odd shilling: fifteen hundred shorn, what comes the wool to?

AUT. If the springe hold, the cock's mine. [*Aside.*

CLO. I cannot do't without counters.—Let me see; what am I to buy for our sheep-shearing feast? [Reads.] *Three pound of sugar; five pound of currants; rice*——What will this sister of mine do with rice? But my father hath made her mistress of the feast, and she lays it on. She hath made me four-and-twenty nosegays for the shearers,—three-man song-men[f] all, and very good ones; but they are most of them means and bases; but one Puritan amongst them, and he sings psalms to hornpipes. I must have saffron, to colour the warden[g] pies; mace,—dates,—none, that's out of my note; [Reads.] *nutmegs, seven; a race or two of ginger;* but that I may beg;—*four pound of prunes, and as many of raisins o' the sun.*

AUT. O, that ever I was born! [*Grovelling on the ground.*

CLO. I' the name of me——

AUT. O, help me, help me! pluck but off these rags; and then, death, death!

CLO. Alack, poor soul! thou hast need of more rags to lay on thee, rather than have these off.

AUT. O, sir, the loathsomeness of them offend me more than the stripes I have received; which are mighty ones and millions.

CLO. Alas, poor man! a million of beating may come to a great matter.

AUT. I am robbed, sir, and beaten; my money and apparel ta'en from me, and these detestable things put upon me.

CLO. What by, a horse-man or a foot-man?

AUT. A foot-man, sweet sir, a foot-man.

CLO. Indeed, he should be a foot-man by the garments he has left with thee; if this be a horse-man's coat, it hath seen very hot service. Lend me thy hand, I'll help thee: come, lend me thy hand. [*Helping him up.*

AUT. O, good sir! tenderly, O!

CLO. Alas, poor soul!

AUT. O, good sir! softly, good sir! I fear, sir, my shoulder-blade is out.

CLO. How now! canst stand?

AUT. Softly, dear sir; [*Picks his pocket.*] good sir, softly. You ha' done me a charitable office.

CLO. Dost lack any money? I have a little money for thee.

AUT. No, good sweet sir; no, I beseech you, sir: I have a kinsman not past three-quarters of a mile hence, unto whom I was going; I shall there have money, or anything I want. Offer me no money, I pray you,—that kills my heart.

CLO. What manner of fellow was he that robbed you?

AUT. A fellow, sir, that I have known to go about with trol-my-dames:(1) I knew him once a servant of the prince; I cannot tell, good sir, for which of his virtues it was, but he was certainly whipped out of the court.

CLO. His vices, you would say; there's no virtue whipped out of the court: they cherish it, to make it stay there; and yet it will no more but abide.[h]

AUT. Vices, I would say, sir. I know this man well: he hath been since an ape-bearer;(2) then a process-server, a bailiff; then he compassed a motion of the Prodigal Son,(3) and married

a — pugging *tooth*—] Pugging was a cant term equivalent to *prigging*.

b *With hey!* with hey!] The second "with hey!" was added in the folio of 1632.

c — three-pile;] That is, *three-piled velvet*.

d — the silly cheat:] A technical phrase in rogues' parlance, meaning *petty theft*.

e — every 'leven wether tods;] He means, every eleven wethers *yields a tod, i. e.* twenty-eight pounds of wool.

f — three-man song-men—] Singers of songs in three parts.

g — warden *pies*;] Wardens was the old name for a species of pears.

h — and yet it will no more but abide.] Equivalent to,—And yet it will barely, or with difficulty, remain.

a tinker's wife within a mile where my land and living lies; and, having flown over many knavish professions, he settled only in rogue: some call him Autolycus.

Clo. Out upon him! prig, for my life, prig: he haunts wakes, fairs, and bear-baitings.

Aut. Very true, sir; he, sir, he; that's the rogue that put me into this apparel.

Clo. Not a more cowardly rogue in all Bohemia; if you had but looked big and spit at him, he'd have run.

Aut. I must confess to you, sir, I am no fighter; I am false of heart that way; and that he knew, I warrant him.

Clo. How do you now?

Aut. Sweet sir, much better than I was; I can stand and walk: I will even take my leave of you, and pace softly towards my kinsman's.

Clo. Shall I bring thee on the way?

Aut. No, good-faced sir; no, sweet sir.

Clo. Then fare thee well; I must go buy spices for our sheep-shearing.

Aut. Prosper you, sweet sir!—[*Exit* Clown.] —Your purse is not hot enough to purchase your spice. I'll be with you at your sheep-shearing too. If I make not this cheat bring out another, and the shearers prove sheep, let me be unrolled,[a] and my name put in the book of virtue!

[Singing.

Jog on, jog on, the foot-path way,
And merrily hent[b] *the stile-a:*
A merry heart goes all the day,
Your sad tires in a mile-a.(4) [*Exit.*

---

a — *let me be* unrolled,—] Struck off the roll of vagabonds, and entered on the book of true men.

b hent *the stile-a*:] "Hent" is from the Saxon *hentan*,—*to take*.

SCENE III.—*The same. Before a* Shepherd's *Cottage.*

Enter FLORIZEL *and* PERDITA.

FLO. These your unusual weeds to each part of you
Do give a life: no shepherdess; but Flora,
Peering in April's front. This your sheep-shearing
Is as a meeting of the petty gods,
And you the queen on't.
PER. Sir, my gracious lord,
To chide at your extremes, it not becomes me,—
O, pardon, that I name them!—your high self,
The gracious mark o' the land, you have obscur'd
With a swain's wearing; and me, poor lowly maid,
Most goddess-like prank'd up: but that our feasts
In every mess have folly, and the feeders
Digest it with a custom, I should blush
To see you so attired; swoon,[a] I think,
To show myself a glass.
FLO. I bless the time,
When my good falcon made her flight across
Thy father's ground.(5)
PER. Now Jove afford you cause!
To me, the difference forges dread; your greatness
Hath not been us'd to fear. Even now I tremble
To think your father by some accident
Should pass this way, as you did: O, the Fates!
How would he look, to see his work, so noble,
Vilely bound up? What would he say? Or how
Should I, in these my borrow'd flaunts, behold
The sternness of his presence?
FLO. Apprehend
Nothing but jollity. The gods themselves,
Humbling their deities to love, have taken
The shapes of beasts upon them: Jupiter
Became a bull, and bellow'd; the green Neptune
A ram, and bleated; and the fire-rob'd god,
Golden Apollo, a poor humble swain,
As I seem now:(6)—their transformations
Were never for a piece of beauty rarer,
Nor in a way so chaste, since my desires
Run not before mine honour, nor my lusts
Burn hotter than my faith.
PER. O, but, sir,
Your resolution cannot hold, when 't is
Oppos'd, as it must be, by the power of the king;
One of these two must be necessities,
Which then will speak,—that you must change this purpose,
Or I my life.
FLO. Thou dearest Perdita,
With these forc'd thoughts, I pr'ythee, darken not
The mirth o' the feast: or I'll be thine, my fair,
Or not my father's; for I cannot be
Mine own, nor anything to any, if
I be not thine: to this I am most constant,
Though destiny say *No.* Be merry, gentle![b]
Strangle such thoughts as these with anything
That you behold the while. Your guests are coming:
Lift up your countenance, as it were the day
Of celebration of that nuptial which
We two have sworn shall come.
PER. O, lady Fortune,
Stand you auspicious!
FLO. See, your guests approach:
Address yourself to entertain them sprightly,
And let's be red with mirth.

Enter Shepherd, *with* POLIXENES *and* CAMILLO *disguised;* Clown, MOPSA, DORCAS, *and other* Shepherds *and* Shepherdesses.

SHEP. Fie, daughter! when my old wife liv'd, upon
This day she was both pantler, butler, cook;
Both dame and servant: welcom'd all; serv'd all;
Would sing her song and dance her turn; now here,
At upper end o' the table, now, i' the middle;
On his shoulder, and his; her face o' fire
With labour, and the thing she took to quench it,
She would to each one sip. You are retir'd
As if you were a feasted one, and not
The hostess of the meeting: pray you, bid
These unknown friends to us welcome; for it is
A way to make us better friends, more known.
Come, quench your blushes, and present yourself
That which you are, mistress o' the feast: come on,
And bid us welcome to your sheep-shearing,
As your good flock shall prosper.
PER. Sir, welcome! [*To* POLIXENES.
It is my father's will I should take on me
The hostess-ship o' the day.—You're welcome, sir! [*To* CAMILLO.
Give me those flowers there, Dorcas.—Reverend sirs,

---

a —— swoon, *I think,*
To show myself a glass.]
So Hanmer; and to our mind the emendation is so convincingly true, that we are astonished it should ever have been questioned. The old copies have, "— *sworne,* I think."

b Be merry, gentle!] Mr. Collier's annotator, in his rage for reformation, changes this to, "Be merry, *girl.*" The meaning is obviously,—Be merry, gentle *one!*

For you there's rosemary and rue; these keep
Seeming and savour all the winter long:
Grace and remembrance be to you both,
And welcome to our shearing!

POL. Shepherdess,
(A fair one are you) well you fit our ages
With flowers of winter.[a]
PER. Sir, the year growing ancient,—

[a] — well *you fit our ages
With flowers of winter.*]
From the reply of Perdita, we might conjecture that Polixenes had asked reproachfully,—"*Will* you fit our ages with flowers of winter?"

Not yet on summer's death, nor on the birth
Of trembling winter,—the fairest flowers o' the season
Are our carnations, and streak'd gillyvors,[a]
Which some call nature's bastards: of that kind
Our rustic garden 's barren; and I care not
To get slips of them.

POL. Wherefore, gentle maiden,
Do you neglect them?

PER. For I have heard it said,
There is an art which, in their piedness, shares
With great creating nature.

POL. Say there be;
Yet nature is made better by no mean,
But nature makes that mean: so, o'er that art,
Which you say adds to nature, is an art
That nature makes. You see, sweet maid, we marry
A gentler scion to the wildest stock,
And make conceive a bark of baser kind
By bud of nobler race: this is an art
Which does mend nature,—change it rather; but
The art itself is nature.

PER. So it is.

POL. Then make your garden rich in gillyvors,
And do not call them bastards.

PER. I'll not put
The dibble in earth to set one slip of them;
No more than, were I painted, I would wish
This youth should say, 't were well; and only therefore
Desire to breed by me.—Here's flowers for you:
Hot lavender, mints, savory, marjoram;
The marigold,[b] that goes to bed wi' the sun,
And with him rises weeping; these are flowers
Of middle summer, and, I think, they are given
To men of middle age: ye're very welcome.

CAM. I should leave grazing, were I of your flock,
And only live by gazing.

PER. Out, alas!
You 'd be so lean, that blasts of January
Would blow you through and through.—Now, my fair'st friend,
I would I had some flowers o' the spring, that might
Become your time of day; and yours, and yours,
That wear upon your virgin branches yet
Your maidenheads growing:—O, Proserpina,(7)
For the flowers now, that, frighted, thou lett'st fall
From Dis's waggon! daffodils,
That come before the swallow dares, and take
The winds of March with beauty; violets, dim,
But sweeter than the lids of Juno's eyes,
Or Cytherea's breath; pale primroses,
That die unmarried, ere they can behold
Bright Phœbus in his strength,—a malady
Most incident to maids;—bold oxlips, and
The crown-imperial; lilies of all kinds,
The flower-de-luce being one! O, these I lack,
To make you garlands of; and, my sweet friend,
To strew him o'er and o'er!

FLO. What! like a corse?

PER. No, like a bank for love to lie and play on;
Not like a corse; or if,—not to be buried,
But quick, and in mine arms.—Come, take your flowers:
Methinks I play as I have seen them do
In Whitsun pastorals: sure, this robe of mine
Does change my disposition.

FLO. What you do
Still betters what is done. When you speak, sweet,
I 'd have you do it ever: when you sing,
I 'd have you buy and sell so; so give alms;
Pray so; and for the ordering your affairs,
To sing them too. When you do dance, I wish you
A wave o' the sea, that you might ever do
Nothing but that; move still, still so,
And own no other function: each your doing,
So singular in each particular,
Crowns what you are doing in the present deeds,
That all your acts are queens.

PER. O, Doricles!
Your praises are too large: but that your youth,
And the true blood which peeps fairly through it,[c]
Do plainly give you out an unstain'd shepherd,
With wisdom I might fear, my Doricles,
You woo'd me the false way.

FLO. I think you have
As little skill[d] to fear as I have purpose
To put you to 't.—But, come; our dance, I pray:
Your hand, my Perdita: so turtles pair,
That never mean to part.

PER. I 'll swear for 'em.

POL. This is the prettiest low-born lass that ever
Ran on the green-sward: nothing she does or seems,
But smacks of something greater than herself;
Too noble for this place.

CAM. He tells her something

a — gillyvors,—] An ancient and popular form of "gilly-flowers."

b The marigold,—] The sun-flower. "Some calle it, *Sponsus Solis*, the Spowse of the Sunne, because it sleepes and is awakened with him."—LUPTON's *Book of Notable Things*.

c And the true blood which peeps fairly through it,—] Mr. Collier's annotator, as "necessary to the measure," proposes,—"which peeps *so* fairly," &c. But the rhythm does not require the addition; we need only make a slight transposition, and read,—

"And the true blood which through it fairly peeps."

d *As little* skill—] As little *reason*, &c.

That makes her blood look out:[a] good sooth, she is
The queen of curds and cream.

CLO. Come on, strike up!

DOR. Mopsa must be your mistress: marry, garlic,
To mend her kissing with.

MOP. Now, in good time!

CLO. Not a word, a word; we stand upon our manners.—
Come, strike up! [*Music.*

Here a Dance of Shepherds *and* Shepherdesses.

POL. Pray, good shepherd, what fair swain is this
Which dances with your daughter?

SHEP. They call him Doricles; and boasts himself
To have a worthy feeding: but I have it
Upon his own report, and I believe it;
He looks like sooth. He says, he loves my daughter;
I think so too; for never gaz'd the moon
Upon the water, as he 'll stand, and read,
As 'twere, my daughter's eyes: and, to be plain,
I think there is not half a kiss to choose
Who loves another best.

POL. She dances featly.

SHEP. So she does anything; though I report it,
That should be silent: if young Doricles
Do light upon her, she shall bring him that
Which he not dreams of.

Enter a Servant.

SERV. O master, if you did but hear the pedler at the door, you would never dance again after a tabor and pipe; no, the bagpipe could not move you: he sings several tunes faster than you'll tell money: he utters them as he had eaten ballads, and all men's ears grew to his tunes.

CLO. He could never come better: he shall come in: I love a ballad but even too well, if it be doleful matter merrily set down, or a very pleasant thing indeed, and sung lamentably.

SERV. He hath songs for man or woman, of all sizes; no milliner can so fit his customers with gloves: he has the prettiest love-songs for maids; so without bawdry, which is strange; with such delicate burdens of *dildos* and *fadings: jump her and thump her;* and where some stretch-mouth'd rascal would, as it were, mean mischief, and break a foul gap[b] into the matter, he makes the maid to answer, *Whoop, do me no harm, good man;* puts him off, slights him, with *Whoop, do me no harm, good man.*

POL. This is a brave fellow.

CLO. Believe me, thou talkest of an admirable-conceited fellow. Has he any unbraided[c] wares?

SERV. He hath ribands of all the colours i' the rainbow; points,[d] more than all the lawyers in Bohemia can learnedly handle, though they come to him by the gross; inkles, caddisses,[e] cambrics, lawns; why, he sings 'em over, as they were gods or goddesses; you would think, a smock were a she-angel, he so chants to the sleeve-hand, and the work about the square[f] on 't.

CLO. Pr'ythee, bring him in; and let him approach singing.

PER. Forewarn him that he use no scurrilous words in 's tunes. [*Exit* Servant.

CLO. You have of these pedlers, that have more in them than you'd think, sister.

PER. Ay, good brother, or go about to think.

Enter AUTOLYCUS, *singing.*

Lawn as white as driven snow;
Cyprus black as e'er was crow;
Gloves as sweet as damask roses;
Masks for faces and for noses;
Bugle-bracelet, necklace-amber,
Perfume for a lady's chamber;
Golden quoifs and stomachers,
For my lads to give their dears;
Pins and poking-sticks of steel; (8)
What maids lack from head to heel:
Come, buy of me, come; come buy, come buy;
Buy, lads, or else your lasses cry: come, buy.

CLO. If I were not in love with Mopsa, thou shouldst take no money of me; but being enthralled as I am, it will also be the bondage of certain ribands and gloves.

MOP. I was promised them against the feast; but they come not too late now.

DOR. He hath promised you more than that, or there be liars.

---

a *That makes her blood look* out:] Theobald's correction; the old text having,—"look *on 't.*" The misprint was not uncommon: thus, in "Cymbeline," Act II. Sc. 3,—

"Must wear the print of his remembrance *out,*"

and in "Twelfth Night," Act III. Sc. 4,—

"And laid mine honour too unchary *out,*"

where, in both instances, the old editions have "on 't."

b — *a foul* gap—] Mr. Collier's annotator would read,—a foul *jape*, that is, a broad jest; but a "foul gap" means a gross parenthesis. See Puttenham's "Arte of Poesy," Lib. III. c. xii., under *Parenthesis*, or the Insertour.

c — unbraided *wares?*] That is, *unspoiled, unfaded*, sterling goods.

d — points,—] A quibble on "points," the laces with metal tags by which the dress was fastened up, and themes for argument.

e — inkles, caddisses,—] *Inkle* is a kind of tape; and *caddis* a narrow worsted galloon.

f — *the* square *on 't.*] The "square" appears to have signified the bosom part of the chemise, which, as we see in old pictures and engravings, was frequently ornamented with embroidery.

MOP. He hath paid you all he promised you: may be, he has paid you more;—which will shame you to give him again.

CLO. Is there no manners left among maids? will they wear their plackets where they should bear their faces? Is there not milking-time, when you are going to bed, or kiln-hole, to whistle off these secrets, but you must be tittle-tattling before all our guests? 'Tis well they are whispering. Clamour [a] your tongues, and not a word more.

[a] Clamour *your tongues,*—] Some will have this to be a corruption of *chamour* or *chaumbre*, from the French *chàmer*, to *refrain:* others suspect it to be only a misprint for *charm;* but from the following line in Taylor, the Water Poet, first cited by Mr. Hunter,—

"*Clamour* the promulgation of your tongues,"

it would seem to have been a familiar phrase.

MOP. I have done. Come, you promised me a tawdry lace [a] and a pair of sweet gloves.

CLO. Have I not told thee how I was cozened by the way, and lost all my money?

AUT. And, indeed, sir, there are cozeners abroad; therefore it behoves men to be wary.

CLO. Fear not thou, man, thou shalt lose nothing here.

AUT. I hope so, sir; for I have about me many parcels of charge.

CLO. What hast here? ballads?

MOP. Pray now, buy some: I love a ballad in print a'-life; for then we are sure they are true.

AUT. Here's one to a very doleful tune, How a usurer's wife was brought to bed of twenty money-bags at a burden; and how she longed to eat adders' heads, and toads carbonadoed.

MOP. Is it true, think you?

AUT. Very true; and but a month old.

DOR. Bless me from marrying a usurer!

AUT. Here's the midwife's name to't, one mistress Taleporter; and five or six honest wives' that were present. Why should I carry lies abroad?

MOP. Pray you now, buy it.

CLO. Come on, lay it by: and let's first see more ballads; we'll buy the other things anon.

AUT. Here's another ballad, Of a fish, that appeared upon the coast on Wednesday the fourscore of April, forty thousand fathom above water, and sung this ballad against the hard hearts of maids: (9) it was thought she was a woman, and was turned into a cold fish for she would not exchange flesh with one that loved her: the ballad is very pitiful, and as true.

DOR. Is it true too, think you?

AUT. Five justices' hands at it, and witnesses more than my pack will hold.

CLO. Lay it by too: another.

AUT. This is a merry ballad, but a very pretty one.

MOP. Let's have some merry ones.

AUT. Why, this is a passing [b] merry one, and goes to the tune of '*Two maids wooing a man:*' there's scarce a maid westward but she sings it; 't is in request, I can tell you.

MOP. We can both sing it; if thou'lt bear a part, thou shalt hear; 't is in three parts.

DOR. We had the tune on't a month ago.

AUT. I can bear my part; you must know, 't is my occupation: have at it with you.

SONG.

A. *Get you hence, for I must go;*
Where it fits not you to know.
D. *Whither?*
M. *O, whither?*
D. *Whither?*
M. *It becomes thy oath full well,*
Thou to me thy secrets tell:
D. *Me too, let me go thither.*
M. *Or thou go'st to the grange, or mill:*
D. *If to either, thou dost ill.*
A. *Neither.*
D. *What, neither?*
A. *Neither.*
D. *Thou hast sworn my love to be;*
M. *Thou hast sworn it more to me:*
Then whither go'st? say, whither?

CLO. We'll have this song out anon by ourselves: my father and the gentlemen are in sad [c] talk, and we'll not trouble them.—Come, bring away thy pack after me.—Wenches, I'll buy for you both.—Pedler, let's have the first choice.—Follow me, girls.

[*Exit with* MOPSA *and* DORCAS.

AUT. And you shall pay well for 'em.

[Singing.

Will you buy any tape,
Or lace for your cape,
My dainty duck, my dear-a?
Any silk, any thread,
Any toys for your head,
Of the new'st and fin'st, fin'st wear-a?
Come to the pedler;
Money's a meddler,
That doth utter all men's ware-a. [*Exit.*

Re-enter Servant.

SERV. Master, there is three carters, three shepherds, three neatherds, three swineherds, that have made themselves all men of hair; (10) they call themselves Saltiers: [d] and they have a dance which the wenches say is a gallimaufry of gambols, because they are not in't; but they themselves are o' the mind, (if it be not too rough for some that know little but bowling) it will please plentifully.

SHEP. Away! we'll none on't; here has been too much homely foolery already.—I know, sir, we weary you.

POL. You weary those that refresh us: pray, let's see these four threes of herdsmen.

SERV. One three of them, by their own report, sir, hath danced before the king; and not the worst of the three but jumps twelve foot and a half by the squire. [e]

SHEP. Leave your prating: since these good

[a] — a tawdry lace—] A sort of ornament worn by women round the neck or waist, and so called, it is said, after St. Audrey (Etheldreda).

[b] — *a* passing *merry one,*—] As we should now call it, a *surpassingly* merry one, an *exceeding* merry one

[c] — sad—] For *grave, serious.*

[d] — Saltiers:] The rustic's blunder for *Satyrs.*

[e] — *the* squire.] The foot-*rule:* French, *esquierre.* See note (b), p. 92, Vol. I.

men are pleased, let them come in; but quickly now.

SERV. Why, they stay at door, sir. [*Exit.*

Re-enter Servant, *with twelve* Rustics, *habited like Satyrs. They dance, and then exeunt.*

POL. O, father, you'll know more of that hereafter.—[a]
Is it not too far gone?—'T is time to part them.
[*Aside.*] He 's simple and tells much.—How now, fair shepherd?
Your heart is full of something that does take
Your mind from feasting. Sooth, when I was young,
And handed love as you do, I was wont
To load my she with knacks: I would have ransack'd
The pedler's silken treasury, and have pour'd it
To her acceptance; you have let him go,
And nothing marted with him. If your lass
Interpretation should abuse, and call this
Your lack of love or bounty, you were straited
For a reply, at least, if you make a care
Of happy holding her.

FLO. Old sir, I know
She prizes not such trifles as these are:
The gifts she looks from me are pack'd and lock'd
Up in my heart; which I have given already,
But not deliver'd.—O, hear me breathe my life
Before this ancient sir, who, it should seem,
Hath sometime lov'd! I take thy hand,—this hand,
As soft as dove's down, and as white as it,
Or Ethiopian's tooth, or the fann'd snow,
That 's bolted[b] by the northern blasts twice o'er.

POL. What follows this?—
How prettily the young swain seems to wash
The hand was fair before!—I have put you out:—
But to your protestation; let me hear
What you profess.

FLO. Do, and be witness to 't.

POL. And this my neighbour too?

FLO. And he, and more
Than he, and men,—the earth, the heavens, and all:—
That, were I crown'd the most imperial monarch,
Thereof most worthy; were I the fairest youth
That ever made eye swerve; had force and knowledge
More than was ever man's,—I would not prize them,
Without her love; for her, employ them all;
Commend them, and condemn them, to her service,
Or to their own perdition!

POL. Fairly offer'd.

CAM. This shows a sound affection.

SHEP. But, my daughter,
Say you the like to him?

PER. I cannot speak
So well, nothing so well; no, nor mean better:
By the pattern of mine own thoughts I cut out
The purity of his.

SHEP. Take hands, a bargain!—
And, friends unknown, you shall bear witness to 't:
I give my daughter to him, and will make
Her portion equal his.

FLO. O, that must be
I' the virtue of your daughter: one being dead,
I shall have more than you can dream of yet;[c]
Enough then for your wonder. But, come on,
Contract us 'fore these witnesses.

SHEP. Come, your hand;—
And, daughter, yours.

POL. Soft, swain, awhile, beseech you;
Have you a father?

FLO. I have: but what of him?

POL. Knows he of this?

FLO. He neither does nor shall.

POL. Methinks a father
Is, at the nuptial of his son, a guest
That best becomes the table. Pray you, once more;
Is not your father grown incapable
Of reasonable affairs? is he not stupid
With age and altering rheums? can he speak? hear?
Know man from man? dispute his own estate?[d]
Lies he not bed-rid? and again does nothing
But what he did, being childish?

FLO. No, good sir;
He has his health, and ampler strength indeed
Than most have of his age.

POL. By my white beard,
You offer him, if this be so, a wrong
Something unfilial: reason, my son
Should choose himself a wife; but as good reason,
The father (all whose joy is nothing else
But fair posterity) should hold some counsel
In such a business.

FLO. I yield all this;
But, for some other reasons, my grave sir,
Which 't is not fit you know, I not acquaint
My father of this business.

---

a O, father, you 'll know more of that hereafter.—] This we must suppose to be a continuation of some discourse begun between Polixenes and the old Shepherd while the dance proceeded.

b — bolted—] *Sifted.*

c —— *more than you can dream of* yet;
Enough then for your wonder.]
We have shown before, in several instances, that "yet" was frequently used in the sense of *now*. In the present passage that meaning is indispensable to the antithesis.

d — dispute his own estate?] That is, reason upon his affairs or condition. The phrase is found again in "Romeo and Juliet," Act III. Sc. 3,—

"Let me *dispute* with thee of thy *estate*."

POL. Let him know 't.
FLO. He shall not.
POL. Pr'ythee, let him.
FLO. No, he must not.
SHEP. Let him, my son; he shall not need to grieve
At knowing of thy choice.
FLO. Come, come, he must not:—
Mark our contrăct.
POL. Mark your divorce, young sir,
[*Discovering himself.*
Whom son I dare not call; thou art too base
To be acknowledg'd: thou a sceptre's heir,
That thus affect'st a sheep-hook!—Thou old traitor,
I am sorry, that, by hanging thee, I can
But shorten thy life one week.—And thou, fresh piece
Of excellent witchcraft, who, of force, must know
The royal fool thou cop'st with;—
SHEP. O, my heart!
POL. I 'll have thy beauty scratch'd with briers, and made
More homely than thy state.—For thee, fond boy,
If I may ever know thou dost but sigh
That thou no more shalt never see this knack, (as never[a]
I mean thou shalt) we 'll bar thee from succession;
Not hold thee of our blood, no, not our kin,
Far than Deucalion off;—mark thou my words;—
Follow us to the court.—Thou churl, for this time,
Though full of our displeasure, yet we free thee
From the dead blow of it.—And you, enchantment,
Worthy enough a herdsman; yea, him too,
That makes himself, but for our honour therein,
Unworthy thee,—if ever henceforth thou
These rural latches to his entrance open,
Or hoop* his body more with thy embraces,
I will devise a death as cruel for thee
As thou art tender to 't. [*Exit.*
PER. Even here undone![b]
I was not much afeard: for once or twice
I was about to speak, and tell him plainly,
The self-same sun that shines upon his court
Hides not his visage from our cottage, but
Looks on alike.—Will 't please you, sir, be gone?
[*To* FLORIZEL.
I told you what would come of this: beseech you,
Of your own state take care: this dream of mine,
Being now awake, I 'll queen it no inch farther,
But milk my ewes, and weep.

CAM. Why, how now, father!
Speak, ere thou diest.
SHEP. I cannot speak, nor think,
Nor dare to know that which I know.—O, sir,
[*To* FLORIZEL.
You have undone a man of fourscore three,
That thought to fill his grave in quiet,—yea,
To die upon the bed my father died,
To lie close by his honest bones! but now
Some hangman must put on my shroud, and lay me
Where no priest shovels in dust.—O cursed wretch!
[*To* PERDITA.
That knew'st this was the prince, and wouldst adventure
To mingle faith with him!—Undone! undone!
If I might die within this hour, I have liv'd
To die when I desire. [*Exit.*
FLO. Why look you so upon me?
I am but sorry, not afeard; delay'd,
But nothing alter'd: what I was, I am;
More straining on for plucking back; not following
My leash unwillingly.
CAM. Gracious my lord,
You know your* father's temper: at this time
He will allow no speech,—which I do guess
You do not purpose to him;—and as hardly
Will he endure your sight as yet, I fear:
Then, till the fury of his highness settle,
Come not before him.
FLO. I not purpose it.
I think, Camillo?
CAM. Even he, my lord.
PER. How often have I told you 't would be thus!
How often said, my dignity would last
But till 't were known!
FLO. It cannot fail, but by
The violation of my faith; and then
Let nature crush the sides o' the earth together,
And mar the seeds within! Lift up thy looks:—
From my succession wipe me, father! I
Am heir to my affection.
CAM. Be advis'd.
FLO. I am,—and by my fancy:[c] if my reason
Will thereto be obedient, I have reason;
If not, my senses, better pleas'd with madness,
Do bid it welcome.
CAM. This is desperate, sir.
FLO. So call it: but it does fulfil my vow,[d]
I needs must think it honesty. Camillo,
Not for Bohemia, nor the pomp that may

(*) Old text, *hope.*

a That thou no more shalt never see this knack, (as never I mean thou shalt)—]

The first "never" appears to have crept in by the inadvertence of the compositor, whose eye caught it from the end of the line.

b Even here undone!] This is the accepted punctuation, and it ought not to be lightly tampered with; yet some readers may possibly think with us that the passage would be more in harmony with the high-born spirit by which Perdita is unconsciously sustained in this terrible moment, if it were read,—

"Even here undone,
I was not much afeard; for once or twice," &c.

(*) First folio, *my.*

c — *by my* fancy:] That is, by my *love.*

d — but it does fulfil my vow,—] *As*, is understood, —"but *as* it does fulfil my vow, I needs must think it honesty."

Be thereat glean'd; for all the sun sees, or
The close earth wombs, or the profound seas hide
In unknown fathoms, will I break my oath
To this my fair belov'd: therefore, I pray you,
As you have ever been my father's honour'd friend,
When he shall miss me, (as, in faith, I mean not
To see him any more) cast your good counsels
Upon his passion. Let myself and fortune
Tug for the time to come. This you may know,
And so deliver,—I am put to sea
With her, whom here I cannot hold on shore;
And, most oppórtune to our[a] need, I have
A vessel rides fast by, but not prepar'd
For this design. What course I mean to hold
Shall nothing benefit your knowledge, nor
Concern me the reporting.

CAM. O, my lord,
I would your spirit were easier for advice,
Or stronger for your need!

FLO. Hark, Perdita.—
[*Takes her aside.*
I'll hear you by and by. [*To* CAMILLO.

CAM. He's irremoveable[b]
Resolv'd for flight. Now were I happy, if
His going I could frame to serve my turn;
Save him from danger, do him love and honour;
Purchase the sight again of dear Sicilia,
And that unhappy king, my master, whom
I so much thirst to see.

FLO. Now, good Camillo,
I am so fraught with curious business, that
I leave out ceremony. [*Going.*

CAM. Sir, I think,
You have heard of my poor services, i' the love
That I have borne your father?

FLO. Very nobly
Have you deserv'd: it is my father's music,
To speak your deeds; not little of his care
To have them recompens'd as thought on.

CAM. Well, my lord,
If you may please to think I love the king,
And, through him, what's nearest to him, which is
Your gracious self, embrace but my direction,
(If your more ponderous and settled project
May suffer alteration) on mine honour
I'll point you where you shall have such receiving
As shall become your highness; where you may
Enjoy your mistress; (from the whom, I see,
There's no disjunction to be made, but by,
As heavens forfend! your ruin) marry her;
And (with my best endeavours in your absence)
Your discontenting father strive to qualify,
And bring him up to liking.

FLO. How, Camillo,
May this, almost a miracle, be done?
That I may call thee something more than man,
And, after that, trust to thee.

CAM. Have you thought on
A place, whereto you'll go?

FLO. Not any yet:
But as the unthought-on accident is guilty
To what we wildly do, so we profess
Ourselves to be the slaves of chance, and flies
Of every wind that blows.

CAM. Then list to me:
This follows,—if you will not change your purpose,
But undergo this flight,—make for Sicilia;
And there present yourself and your fair princess,
(For so I see she must be) 'fore Leontes;
She shall be habited as it becomes
The partner of your bed. Methinks, I see
Leontes opening his free arms, and weeping
His welcomes forth; asks thee, the* son, forgiveness,
As 't were i' the father's person; kisses the hands
Of your fresh princess; o'er and o'er divides him
'Twixt his unkindness and his kindness,—the one
He chides to hell, and bids the other grow
Faster than thought or time.

FLO. Worthy Camillo,
What colour for my visitation shall I
Hold up before him?

CAM. Sent by the king your father
To greet him and to give him comforts. Sir,
The manner of your bearing towards him, with
What you, as from your father, shall deliver,
Things known betwixt us three, I'll write you down:
The which shall point you forth at every sitting
What you must say; that he shall not perceive,
But that you have your father's bosom there,
And speak his very heart.

FLO. I am bound to you:
There is some sap in this.

CAM. A course more promising
Than a wild dedication of yourselves
To unpath'd waters, undream'd shores; most certain,
To miseries enough: no hope to help you;
But, as you shake off one, to take another:
Nothing so certain as your anchors; who
Do their best office, if they can but stay you
Where you'll be loth to be: besides, you know,
Prosperity's the very bond of love,
Whose fresh complexion and whose heart together
Affliction alters.

PER. One of these is true:

---

[a] — *to our need,*—] Theobald's correction, the old copies reading, "*her* need."

[b] *He's* irremoveable
Resolv'd for flight.] "Irremoveable" is here employed adverbially; "He's *irremoveably* resolved," &c. So in Act III. Sc. 2,—"And *damnable* ungrateful."

(*) Old text, *there*.

I think affliction may subdue the cheek,
But not take in the mind.

CAM. Yea, say you so?
There shall not, at your father's house, these seven years,
Be born another such.

FLO. My good Camillo,
She is as forward of her breeding as
She is i' the rear of our birth.[a]

CAM. I cannot say, 'tis pity
She lacks instructions, for she seems a mistress
To most that teach.

PER. Your pardon, sir; for this
I'll blush you thanks.

FLO. My prettiest Perdita!—
But, O, the thorns we stand upon!—Camillo,—
Preserver of my father, now of me,
The medicine of our house!—how shall we do?
We are not furnish'd like Bohemia's son;
Nor shall appear in Sicilia.[b]

CAM. My lord,
Fear none of this: I think you know my fortunes
Do all lie there: it shall be so my care
To have you royally appointed, as if
The scene you play were mine. For instance, sir,
That you may know you shall not want,—one word. [*They talk aside.*

Enter AUTOLYCUS.

AUT. Ha, ha! what a fool Honesty is! and Trust, his sworn brother, a very simple gentleman! I have sold all my trumpery; not a counterfeit stone, not a riband, glass, pomander,[c] brooch, table-book, ballad, knife, tape, glove, shoe-tie, bracelet, horn-ring, to keep my pack from fasting; they throng who should buy first, as if my trinkets had been hallowed, and brought a benediction to the buyer: by which means I saw whose purse was best in picture; and what I saw, to my good use I remembered. My clown (who wants but something to be a reasonable man) grew so in love with the wenches' song, that he would not stir his pettitoes till he had both tune and words; which so drew the rest of the herd to me, that all their other senses stuck in ears: you might have pinched a placket, it was senseless; 't was nothing to geld a cod-piece of a purse; I would have filed keys off that hung in chains: no hearing, no feeling, but my sir's song, and admiring the nothing[d] of it. So that, in this time of lethargy, I picked and cut most of their festival purses; and had not the old man come in with a whoobub against his daughter and the king's son, and scared my choughs from the chaff, I had not left a purse alive in the whole army.

[CAM. FLO. *and* PER. *come forward.*

CAM. Nay, but my letters, by this means being there
So soon as you arrive, shall clear that doubt.

FLO. And those that you'll procure from king Leontes—

CAM. Shall satisfy your father.

PER. Happy be you!
All that you speak shows fair.

CAM. Who have we here?— [*Seeing* AUTOLYCUS.
We'll make an instrument of this; omit
Nothing may give us aid.

AUT. [*Aside.*] If they have overheard me now,——why, hanging.

CAM. How now, good fellow! why shakest thou so? Fear not, man; here's no harm intended to thee.

AUT. I am a poor fellow, sir.

CAM. Why, be so still; here's nobody will steal that from thee: yet, for the outside of thy poverty, we must make an exchange; therefore, discase thee instantly, (thou must think there's a necessity in't) and change garments with this gentleman: though the pennyworth on his side be the worst, yet hold thee, there's some boot. [*Giving money.*

AUT. I am a poor fellow, sir.—[*Aside.*] I know ye well enough.

CAM. Nay, pr'ythee, dispatch: the gentleman is half flayed already.

AUT. Are you in earnest, sir?—[*Aside.*] I smell the trick on't.

FLO. Dispatch, I pr'ythee.

AUT. Indeed, I have had earnest; but I cannot with conscience take it.

CAM. Unbuckle, unbuckle.—

[FLO. *and* AUTOL. *exchange garments.*
Fortunate mistress,—let my prophecy
Come home to ye!—you must retire yourself
Into some covert: take your sweetheart's hat
And pluck it o'er your brows; muffle your face;
Dismantle you; and, as you can, disliken
The truth of your own seeming; that you may
(For I do fear eyes over[e]) to shipboard
Get undescried.

PER. I see the play so lies
That I must bear a part.

a — i' the rear of our birth.] The original has,—"i' th' reare' our Birth."

b Nor shall appear in Sicilia.] It is usual to print this with a break after "Sicilia;" the proper remedy, we believe, is to insert "so," which appears to have dropped out at press,—"Nor shall appear *so* in Sicilia."

c — pomander,—] A *pomander* was a ball of perfumes, "*Pomme d'ambre*," carried in the pocket, worn round the neck, or suspended from the wrist.

d — *the* nothing *of it.*] It has been suggested that "nothing" in this place is a misprint for *noting*; but like *moth* for *mote*, it is only the old mode of spelling that word.

e (*For I do fear* eyes over)] Rowe reads,—"eyes over *you*;" a MS. note in Lord Ellesmere's copy of the first folio has, "eyes *ever*;" and Mr. Collier's annotator proposes the same alteration.

CAM. No remedy.—
Have you done there?
FLO. Should I now meet my father,
He would not call me son.
CAM. Nay, you shall have no hat.—
Come, lady, come.—Farewell, my friend.
AUT. Adieu, sir.
FLO. O, Perdita, what have we twain forgot!
Pray you, a word. [*They converse apart.*
CAM. [*Aside.*] What I do next, shall be to tell the king
Of this escape, and whither they are bound;
Wherein, my hope is, I shall so prevail
To force him after; in whose company
I shall re-view Sicilia, for whose sight
I have a woman's longing.
FLO. Fortune speed us!—
Thus we set on, Camillo, to the sea-side.
CAM. The swifter speed the better.
[*Exeunt* FLO. PER. *and* CAM.

AUT. I understand the business, I hear it: to have an open ear, a quick eye, and a nimble hand, is necessary for a cutpurse; a good nose is requisite also, to smell out work for the other senses. I see this is the time that the unjust man doth thrive. What an exchange had this been without boot! what a boot is here with this exchange! Sure, the gods do this year connive at us, and we may do anything *extempore*. The prince himself is about a piece of iniquity; stealing away from his father with his clog at his heels: if I thought it were a piece of honesty to acquaint the king withal, I would not do 't: I hold it the more knavery to conceal it; and therein am I constant to my profession.—Aside, aside!—here is more matter for a hot brain: every lane's end, every shop, church, session, hanging, yields a careful man work.

Enter Clown *and* Shepherd.

CLO. See, see; what a man you are now! There is no other way but to tell the king she 's a changeling, and none of your flesh and blood.

SHEP. Nay, but hear me.

CLO. Nay, but hear me.

SHEP. Go to, then.

CLO. She being none of your flesh and blood, your flesh and blood has not offended the king; and so your flesh and blood is not to be punished by him. Show those things you found about her; those secret things, all but what she has with her: this being done, let the law go whistle; I warrant you.

SHEP. I will tell the king all, every word; yea, and his son's pranks too,—who, I may say, is no honest man neither to his father nor to me, to go about to make me the king's brother-in-law.

CLO. Indeed, brother-in-law was the farthest off you could have been to him; and then your blood had been the dearer by I know how much an ounce.

AUT. [*Aside.*] Very wisely, puppies!

SHEP. Well, let us to the king; there is that in this fardel [a] will make him scratch his beard.

AUT. I know not what impediment this complaint may be to the flight of my master.

CLO. Pray heartily he be at palace.

AUT. Though I am not naturally honest, I am so sometimes by chance:—let me pocket up my pedler's excrement.[b]—[*Aside. Taking off his false beard.*] How now, rustics! whither are you bound?

SHEP. To the palace, an it like your worship.

AUT. Your affairs there? what? with whom? the condition of that fardel, the place of your dwelling, your names, your ages, of what having, breeding, and anything that is fitting to be known, discover.

CLO. We are but plain fellows, sir.

AUT. A lie; you are rough and hairy. Let me have no lying; it becomes none but tradesmen, and they often give us soldiers the lie: but we pay them for it with stamped coin, not stabbing steel; therefore they do not give us the lie.

CLO. Your worship had like to have given us one, if you had not taken yourself with the manner.

SHEP. Are you a courtier, an 't like you, sir?

AUT. Whether it like me or no, I am a courtier. See'st thou not the air of the court in these enfoldings? hath not my gait in it the measure of the court? receives not thy nose court-odour from me? reflect I not on thy baseness court-contempt? Thinkest thou, for that I insinuate, or* toze from thee thy business, I am therefore no courtier? I am courtier cap-a-pè; and one that will either push on or pluck back thy business there: whereupon I command thee to open thy affair.

SHEP. My business, sir, is to the king.

AUT. What advocate hast thou to him?

SHEP. I know not, an 't like you.

CLO. [*Aside to the* Shepherd.] Advocate 's the court-word for a pheasant; say, you have none.

SHEP. None, sir; I have no pheasant, cock nor hen.

AUT. How bless'd are we that are not simple men!

---

a — fardel—] A *bundle, pack,* or *burden.*
b — excrement.] He means *beard.* We have a similar application of the word in "Love's Labour's Lost," Act V. Sc. 1,—"and with his royal finger, thus, dally with my *excrement,* with my mustachio."

(*) Old text, *at.*

Yet nature might have made me as these are,
Therefore I'll not disdain.

CLO. This cannot be but a great courtier.

SHEP. His garments are rich, but he wears them not handsomely.

CLO. He seems to be the more noble in being fantastical: a great man, I'll warrant; I know by the picking on's teeth.

AUT. The fardel there? what's i' the fardel? Wherefore that box?

SHEP. Sir, there lies such secrets in this fardel and box, which none must know but the king; and which he shall know within this hour, if I may come to the speech of him.

AUT. Age, thou hast lost thy labour.

SHEP. Why, sir?

AUT. The king is not at the palace: he is gone aboard a new ship to purge melancholy and air himself: for if thou be'st capable of things serious, thou must know the king is full of grief.

SHEP. So 't is said, sir,—about his son, that should have married a shepherd's daughter.

AUT. If that shepherd be not in hand-fast,[a] let him fly; the curses he shall have, the tortures he shall feel, will break the back of man, the heart of monster.

CLO. Think you so, sir?

AUT. Not he alone shall suffer what wit can make heavy, and vengeance bitter; but those that are germane to him, though removed fifty times, shall all come under the hangman: which though it be great pity, yet it is necessary. An old sheep-whistling rogue, a ram-tender, to offer to have his daughter come into grace! Some say, he shall be stoned; but that death is too soft for him, say I: draw our throne into a sheep-cote! all deaths are too few, the sharpest too easy.

CLO. Has the old man e'er a son, sir, do you hear, an 't like you, sir?

AUT. He has a son,—who shall be flayed alive; then, 'nointed over with honey, set on the head of a wasp's nest; then stand till he be three quarters and a dram dead; then recovered again with aqua-vitæ, or some other hot infusion; then, raw as he is, and in the hottest day prognostication[b] proclaims, shall be set against a brick wall, the sun looking with a southward eye upon him,—where he is to behold him with flies blown to death. But what talk we of these traitorly rascals, whose miseries are to be smiled at, their offences being so capital? Tell me (for you seem to be honest plain men) what you have to the king: being something gently considered, I'll bring you where he is aboard, tender your persons to his presence, whisper him in your behalfs; and, if it be in man, besides the king, to effect your suits, here is man shall do it.

CLO. He seems to be of great authority: close with him, give him gold; and though authority be a stubborn bear, yet he is oft led by the nose with gold: show the inside of your purse to the outside of his hand, and no more ado. Remember,—stoned, and flayed alive!

SHEP. An 't please you, sir, to undertake the business for us, here is that gold I have: I'll make it as much more, and leave this young man in pawn till I bring it you.

AUT. After I have done what I promised?

SHEP. Ay, sir.

AUT. Well, give me the moiety.—Are you a party in this business?

CLO. In some sort, sir: but though my case be a pitiful one, I hope I shall not be flayed out of it.

AUT. O, that's the case of the shepherd's son;—hang him, he'll be made an example.

CLO. Comfort, good comfort! We must to the king, and show our strange sights: he must know 't is none of your daughter nor my sister; we are gone else.—Sir, I will give you as much as this old man does, when the business is performed; and remain, as he says, your pawn till it be brought you.

AUT. I will trust you. Walk before toward the sea-side; go on the right hand; I will but look upon the hedge, and follow you.

CLO. We are blessed in this man, as I may say, even blessed.

SHEP. Let's before, as he bids us: he was provided to do us good. [*Exeunt* Shepherd *and* Clown.

AUT. If I had a mind to be honest, I see Fortune would not suffer me; she drops booties in my mouth. I am courted now with a double occasion,—gold, and a means to do the prince my master good; which who knows how that may turn back to my advancement? I will bring these two moles, these blind ones, aboard him: if he think it fit to shore them again, and that the complaint they have to the king concerns him nothing, let him call me rogue for being so far officious; for I am proof against that title, and what shame else belongs to 't. To him will I present them; there may be matter in it. [*Exit.*

[a] *If that shepherd be not in* hand-fast, *let him fly;*] The only critic who has noticed the term "hand-fast" is Mr. R. G. White; and he quite mistakes its meaning. To be in "hand-fast"=*main-prize,* is to be at large only on security given.

[b] — prognostication *proclaims,*—] The hottest day predicted by the almanac. "Almanacks were in Shakespeare's time published under this title, 'An Almanack and *Prognostication* made for the year of our Lord God 1595.'"—MALONE.

ACT V.

SCENE I.—Sicilia. *A Room in the Palace of* Leontes.

Enter LEONTES, CLEOMENES, DION, PAULINA, *and others.*

CLEO. Sir, you have done enough, and have perform'd
A saint-like sorrow: no fault could you make,
Which you have not redeem'd; indeed, paid down
More penitence than done trespass: at the last,
Do as the heavens have done, forget your evil;
With them, forgive yourself.
LEON. Whilst I remember
Her and her virtues, I cannot forget
My blemishes in them; and so still think of
The wrong I did myself: which was so much,
That heirless it hath made my kingdom; and
Destroy'd the sweet'st companion that e'er man
Bred his hopes out of.
PAUL. True, too true, my lord:[a]
If, one by one, you wedded all the world,
Or from the all that are took something good,
To make a perfect woman, she, you kill'd,
Would be unparallel'd.
LEON. I think so. *Kill'd!*
She I *kill'd!* I did so: but thou strik'st me
Sorely, to say I did; it is as bitter
Upon thy tongue as in my thought. Now, good now,
Say so but seldom.
CLEO. Not at all, good lady;
You might have spoken a thousand things that would
Have done the time more benefit, and grac'd
Your kindness better.
PAUL. You are one of those
Would have him wed again.
DION. If you would not so,
You pity not the state, nor the remembrance
Of his most sovereign name; consider little
What dangers, by his highness' fail of issue,
May drop upon his kingdom, and devour
Incertain lookers-on. What were more holy

[a] True, too true, my lord:] A correction of Theobald; the old editions having,—

"Destroy'd the sweet'st Companion, that ere man
Bred his hopes out of, true.
Paul. Too true (my Lord;)"

Than to rejoice the former queen is well?[a]
What holier than,—for royalty's repair,
For present comfort and for future good,—
To bless the bed of majesty again
With a sweet fellow to 't?
PAUL. There is none worthy,
Respecting her that 's gone. Besides, the gods
Will have fulfill'd their secret purposes;
For has not the divine Apollo said,
Is 't not the tenor of his oracle,
That king Leontes shall not have an heir
Till his lost child be found? which that it shall,
Is all as monstrous to our human reason,
As my Antigonus to break his grave,
And come again to me; who, on my life,
Did perish with the infant. 'T is your counsel
My lord should to the heavens be contrary,
Oppose against their wills.—Care not for issue;
[*To* LEONTES.
The crown will find an heir. Great Alexander
Left his to the worthiest; so his successor
Was like to be the best.
LEON. Good Paulina,—
Who hast the memory of Hermione,
I know, in honour,—O, that ever I
Had squar'd me to thy counsel!—then, even now,
I might have look'd upon my queen's full eyes;
Have taken treasure from her lips,—
PAUL. And left them
More rich for what they yielded.
LEON. Thou speak'st truth.
No more such wives; therefore, no wife: one worse,
And better us'd, would make her sainted spirit
Again possess her corpse; and on this stage
(Where we offenders now) appear,[b] soul-vex'd,
And begin, *Why to me?*
PAUL. Had she such power,
She had just cause.[c]
LEON. She had; and would incense me
To murder her I married.
PAUL. I should so:
Were I the ghost that walk'd, I 'd bid you mark
Her eye; and tell me for what dull part in 't
You chose her; then I 'd shriek, that even your ears
Should rift to hear me; and the words that follow'd
Should be, *Remember mine!*
LEON. Stars, stars,
And all eyes else dead coals!—fear thou no wife;
I 'll have no wife, Paulina.
PAUL. Will you swear
Never to marry but by my free leave?
LEON. Never, Paulina; so be bless'd my spirit!
PAUL. Then, good my lords, bear witness to his oath.
CLEO. You tempt him over-much.
PAUL. Unless another,
As like Hermione as is her picture,
Affront his eye.
CLEO. Good madam,—
PAUL. I have done.[d]
Yet, if my lord will marry,—if you will, sir,
No remedy but you will,—give me the office
To choose you a queen: she shall not be so young
As was your former; but she shall be such
As, walk'd your first queen's ghost, it should take joy
To see her in your arms.
LEON. My true Paulina,
We shall not marry till thou bidd'st us.
PAUL. That
Shall be when your first queen 's again in breath;
Never till then.

Enter a Gentleman.

GENT. One that gives out himself prince Florizel,
Son of Polixenes, with his princess, (she
The fairest I have yet beheld) desires access
To your high presence.
LEON. What with him? he comes not
Like to his father's greatness: his approach,
So out of circumstance and sudden, tells us
'T is not a visitation fram'd, but forc'd
By need and accident. What train?
GENT. But few,
And those but mean.
LEON. His princess, say you, with him?
GENT. Ay, the most peerless piece of earth, I think,
That e'er the sun shone bright on.
PAUL. O, Hermione,
As every present time doth boast itself
Above a better gone, so must thy grave[e]
Give way to what 's seen now. Sir, you yourself

---

[a] — *the former queen* is well?] An expression applied to the dead: thus in "Antony and Cleopatra," Act II. Sc. 5,—

> "*Mess.* First, madam, he is *well.*
> *Cleop.* Why there's more gold.
> But, sirrah, mark, we use
> To say *the dead are well,*" &c.

See also Malone's note in the Variorum edition, Vol. XIV. p. 400.

[b]
> —— and on this stage
> (Where we offenders now) appear, &c.]

Theobald reads,—

> "—— and on this stage
> (Where we *offend her* now) appear," &c.

[c] She had just cause.] The first and second folios have,—"She had just *such* cause."

[d] PAUL. I have done.] In the old editions, the words, "I have done," form part of the preceding speech; they were properly assigned by Capell.

[e]
> —— *so must thy* grave
> *Give way to what's seen now.*]

"Grave" has been changed by some editors to *grace*, by others to *graces;* to the destruction of a very fine idea.

Have said, and writ so, (but your writing now
Is colder than that theme,) *She had not been,*
Nor was not to be equall'd;—thus your verse
Flow'd with her beauty once; 't is shrewdly ebb'd,
To say you have seen a better.

GENT. Pardon, madam;
The one I have almost forgot; (your pardon)
The other, when she has obtain'd your eye,
Will have your tongue too. This is a creature,
Would she begin a sect, might quench the zeal
Of all professors else; make proselytes
Of who she but bid follow.

PAUL. How! not women?

GENT. Women will love her, that she is a woman
More worth than any man; men, that she is
The rarest of all women.

LEON. Go, Cleomenes;
Yourself, assisted with your honour'd friends,
Bring them to our embracement.—Still 't is strange,

[*Exeunt* CLEOMENES, Lords, *and* Gentleman.

He thus should steal upon us.

PAUL. Had our prince
(Jewel of children) seen this hour, he had pair'd
Well with this lord; there was not full a month
Between their births.

LEON. Pr'ythee, no more; cease; thou know'st,
He dies to me again when talk'd of: sure,
When I shall see this gentleman, thy speeches
Will bring me to consider that which may
Unfurnish me of reason.—They are come.—

Re-enter CLEOMENES, *with* FLORIZEL *and* PERDITA.

Your mother was most true to wedlock, prince;
For she did print your royal father off,
Conceiving you: were I but twenty-one,
Your father's image is so hit in you,
His very air, that I should call you brother,
As I did him; and speak of something, wildly
By us perform'd before. Most dearly welcome!
And your fair princess,—goddess!—O, alas!
I lost a couple, that 'twixt heaven and earth
Might thus have stood, begetting wonder, as
You, gracious couple, do! and then I lost
(All mine own folly) the society,
Amity too, of your brave father, whom,
Though bearing misery, I desire my life
Once more to look on him.

FLO. By his command
Have I here touch'd Sicilia; and from him
Give you all greetings, that a king, at friend,[a]
Can send his brother: and, but infirmity
(Which waits upon worn times) hath something seiz'd
His wish'd ability, he had himself
The lands and waters 'twixt your throne and his
Measur'd to look upon you; whom he loves
(He bade me say so) more than all the sceptres,
And those that bear them, living.

LEON. O, my brother,
(Good gentleman!) the wrongs I have done thee stir
Afresh within me; and these thy offices,
So rarely kind, are as interpreters
Of my behind-hand slackness!—Welcome hither,
As is the spring to the earth. And hath he too
Expos'd this paragon to the fearful usage,
At least ungentle, of the dreadful Neptune,
To greet a man not worth her pains, much less
The adventure of her person?

FLO. Good my lord,
She came from Libya.

LEON. Where the warlike Smalus,
That noble honour'd lord, is fear'd and lov'd?

FLO. Most royal sir, from thence; from him, whose daughter
His tears proclaim'd his, parting with her: thence
(A prosperous south-wind friendly) we have cross'd,
To execute the charge my father gave me,
For visiting your highness. My best train
I have from your Sicilian shores dismiss'd;
Who for Bohemia bend, to signify
Not only my success in Libya, sir,
But my arrival, and my wife's, in safety
Here where we are.

LEON. The blessed gods
Purge all infection from our air, whilst you
Do climate here! You have a holy father,
A graceful gentleman; against whose person,
So sacred as it is, I have done sin,
For which the heavens, taking angry note,
Have left me issueless; and your father's bless'd
(As he from heaven merits it) with you,
Worthy his goodness. What might I have been,
Might I a son and daughter now have look'd on,
Such goodly things as you!

Enter a Lord.

LORD. Most noble sir,
That which I shall report will bear no credit,
Were not the proof so nigh. Please you, great sir,

---

a — *that a king, at friend,*—] This has been variously and needlessly altered; the most recent change is,—"a king *as* friend;" but "a king at friend" means a king on terms of friendship, and is as much the phraseology of Shakespeare's age as "*to* friend,"—"I know that we shall have him well to friend,"—*Julius Cæsar*, Act III. Sc. 1; "Had I admittance and opportunity to friend,"—*Cymbeline*, Act I. Sc. 4.

Bohemia greets you from himself by me;
Desires you to attach his son, who has
(His dignity and duty both cast off)
Fled from his father, from his hopes, and with
A shepherd's daughter.

LEON. Where 's Bohemia? speak!

LORD. Here in your city; I now came from him:
I speak amazedly; and it becomes
My marvel and my message. To your court
Whiles he was hast'ning, (in the chase, it seems,
Of this fair couple) meets he on the way
The father of this seeming lady, and
Her brother, having both their country quitted
With this young prince.

FLO. Camillo has betray'd me;
Whose honour and whose honesty, till now,
Endur'd all weathers.

LORD. Lay 't so to his charge;
He 's with the king your father.

LEON. Who? Camillo?

LORD. Camillo, sir; I spake with him; who now
Has these poor men in question. Never saw I
Wretches so quake: they kneel, they kiss the earth;
Forswear themselves as often as they speak:
Bohemia stops his ears, and threatens them
With divers deaths in death.

PER. O, my poor father!—
The heavens set spies upon us, will not have
Our contract celebrated.

LEON. You are married?

FLO. We are not, sir, nor are we like to be;
The stars, I see, will kiss the valleys first:—
The odds for high and low 's alike.

LEON. My lord,
Is this the daughter of a king?

FLO. She is,
When once she is my wife.

LEON. That once, I see, by your good father's speed,
Will come on very slowly. I am sorry,
Most sorry, you have broken from his liking,
Where you were tied in duty; and as sorry
Your choice is not so rich in worth as beauty,
That you might well enjoy her.

FLO. Dear, look up:
Though Fortune, visible an enemy,
Should chase us with my father, power no jot
Hath she to change our loves.—Beseech you, sir,
Remember since you ow'd no more to time
Than I do now: with thought of such affections,
Step forth mine advocate; at your request
My father will grant precious things as trifles.

LEON. Would he do so, I 'd beg your precious mistress,
Which he counts but a trifle.

PAUL. Sir, my liege,[a]
Your eye hath too much youth in 't: not a month
'Fore your queen died, she was more worth such gazes
Than what you look on now.

LEON. I thought of her,
Even in these looks I made.—But your petition [*To* FLORIZEL.
Is yet unanswer'd. I will to your father;
Your honour not o'erthrown by your desires,
I am friend to them and you: upon which errand
I now go toward him; therefore, follow me,
And mark what way I make: come, good my lord. [*Exeunt.*

SCENE II.—*The same. Before the Palace of* Leontes.

Enter AUTOLYCUS *and a* Gentleman.

AUT. Beseech you, sir, were you present at this relation?

GENT. I was by at the opening of the fardel; heard the old shepherd deliver the manner how he found it: whereupon, after a little amazedness, we were all commanded out of the chamber; only this, methought I heard the shepherd say he found the child.

AUT. I would most gladly know the issue of it.

GENT. I make a broken delivery of the business;—but the changes I perceived in the king and Camillo were very notes of admiration: they seemed almost, with staring on one another, to tear the cases of their eyes; there was speech in their dumbness, language in their very gesture; they looked as they had heard of a world ransomed, or one destroyed: a notable passion of wonder appeared in them; but the wisest beholder, that knew no more but seeing, could not say if the importance[b] were joy or sorrow,—but in the extremity of the one it must needs be.—Here comes a gentleman that happily knows more:

Enter ROGERO.

The news, Rogero?

ROG. Nothing but bonfires: the oracle is fulfilled; the king's daughter is found: such a

a Sir, my liege,—] See note (a), p. 204.

b —*if the* importance *were joy or sorrow,*—] The meaning seems to be,—A mere spectator could never have said whether their emotion were of joyful or sorrowing significance.

deal of wonder is broken out within this hour, that ballad-makers cannot be able to express it.—Here comes the lady Paulina's steward; he can deliver you more.—

Enter Paulina's Steward.

How goes it now, sir? this news, which is called true, is so like an old tale, that the verity of it is in strong suspicion: has the king found his heir?

STEW. Most true, if ever truth were pregnant by circumstance: that which you hear you'll swear you see, there is such unity in the proofs. The mantle of queen Hermione's;—her jewel about the neck of it;—the letters of Antigonus, found with it, which they know to be his character;—the majesty of the creature, in resemblance of the mother;—the affection of nobleness, which nature shows above her breeding;—and many other evidences, proclaim her with all certainty to be the king's daughter. Did you see the meeting of the two kings?

ROG. No.

STEW. Then have you lost a sight, which was to be seen, cannot be spoken of. There might you have beheld one joy crown another, so and in such manner, that it seemed sorrow wept to take leave of them,—for their joy waded in tears. There was casting up of eyes, holding up of hands, with countenance of such distraction, that they were to be known by garment, not by favour. Our king, being ready to leap out of himself for joy of his found daughter, as if that joy were now become a loss, cries, *O, thy mother, thy mother!* then asks Bohemia forgiveness; then embraces his son-in-law; then again worries he his daughter with clipping[a] her; now he thanks the old shepherd, which stands by like a weather-bitten conduit of many kings' reigns. I never heard of such another encounter, which lames report to follow it, and undoes description to do it.

ROG. What, pray you, became of Antigonus, that carried hence the child?

STEW. Like an old tale still, which will have matter to rehearse, though credit be asleep, and not an ear open. He was torn to pieces with a bear: this avouches the shepherd's son; who has not only his innocence (which seems much) to justify him, but a handkerchief and rings of his, that Paulina knows.

GENT. What became of his bark and his followers?

STEW. Wrecked the same instant of their

a — *with* clipping *her;*] That is, embracing her. So in "Coriolanus," Act I. Sc. 6,—

"O! let me *clip* ye
In arms as sound as when I woo'd."

master's death, and in the view of the shepherd: so that all the instruments which aided to expose the child, were even then lost when it was found. But, O, the noble combat that, 'twixt joy and sorrow, was fought in Paulina! She had one eye declined for the loss of her husband, another elevated that the oracle was fulfilled: she lifted the princess from the earth; and so locks her in embracing, as if she would pin her to her heart, that she might no more be in danger of losing.

GENT. The dignity of this act was worth the audience of kings and princes; for by such was it acted.

STEW. One of the prettiest touches of all, and that which angled for mine eyes, (caught the water, though not the fish) was, when at the relation of the queen's death, with the manner how she came to 't, (bravely confessed and lamented by the king) how attentiveness wounded his daughter; till, from one sign of dolour to another, she did, with an *Alas!* I would fain say, bleed tears,—for I am sure my heart wept blood. Who was most marble there changed colour; some swooned, all sorrowed: if all the world could have seen 't, the woe had been universal.

GENT. Are they returned to the court?

STEW. No: the princess hearing of her mother's statue, which is in the keeping of Paulina,—a piece many years in doing, and now newly performed by that rare Italian master, Julio Romano, who, had he himself eternity, and could put breath into his work, would beguile Nature of her custom, so perfectly he is her ape: he so near to Hermione hath done Hermione, that they say one would speak to her, and stand in hope of answer:—thither, with all greediness of affection, are they gone; and there they intend to sup.

ROG. I thought she had some great matter there in hand; for she hath privately twice or thrice a day, ever since the death of Hermione, visited that removed house. Shall we thither, and with our company piece the rejoicing?

GENT. Who would be thence that has the benefit of access? every wink of an eye, some new grace will be born: our absence makes us unthrifty to our knowledge. Let's along.

[*Exeunt.*

AUT. Now, had I not the dash of my former life in me, would preferment drop on my head. I brought the old man and his son aboard the prince; told him I heard them talk of a fardel, and I know not what; but he at that time, over-fond of the shepherd's daughter, (so he then took her to be) who began to be much sea-sick, and himself little better, extremity of weather continuing, this mystery remained undiscovered. But 't is all one to me; for had I been the finder-out of this secret, it would not have relished among my other discredits. Here come those I have done good to against my will, and already appearing in the blossoms of their fortune.

Enter Shepherd *and* Clown.

SHEP. Come, boy; I am past more children, but thy sons and daughters will be all gentlemen born.

CLO. You are well met, sir. You denied to fight with me this other day, because I was no gentleman born. See you these clothes? say, you see them not, and think me still no gentleman born: you were best say these robes are not gentlemen born. Give me the lie, do; and try whether I am not now a gentleman born.

AUT. I know you are now, sir, a gentleman born.

CLO. Ay, and have been so any time these four hours.

SHEP. And so have I, boy.

CLO. So you have:—but I was a gentleman born before my father; for the king's son took me by the hand, and called me brother; and then the two kings called my father brother; and then the prince my brother, and the princess my sister, called my father father; and so we wept,—and there was the first gentleman-like tears that ever we shed.

SHEP. We may live, son, to shed many more.

CLO. Ay; or else 't were hard luck, being in so preposterous estate as we are.

AUT. I humbly beseech you, sir, to pardon me all the faults I have committed to your worship, and to give me your good report to the prince my master.

SHEP. Pr'ythee, son, do; for we must be gentle, now we are gentlemen.

CLO. Thou wilt amend thy life?

AUT. Ay, an it like your good worship.

CLO. Give me thy hand: I will swear to the prince thou art as honest a true fellow as any is in Bohemia.

SHEP. You may say it, but not swear it.

CLO. Not swear it, now I am a gentleman? Let boors and franklins say it, I'll swear it.

SHEP. How if it be false, son?

CLO. If it be ne'er so false, a true gentleman may swear it in the behalf of his friend:—and I'll swear to the prince, thou art a tall fellow of thy hands,[a] and that thou wilt not be drunk; but I know thou art no tall fellow of thy hands, and that thou wilt be drunk; but I'll swear it; and I would thou wouldst be a tall fellow of thy hands.

a — a tall fellow of thy hands,—] See note (a), p. 237, Vol. II.

AUT. I will prove so, sir, to my power.

CLO. Ay, by any means prove a tall fellow: if I do not wonder how thou dar'st venture to be drunk, not being a tall fellow, trust me not.—Hark! the kings and the princes, our kindred, are going to see the queen's picture. Come, follow us: we'll be thy good masters. [*Exeunt.*

SCENE III.—*The same. A Chapel in* Paulina's *House.*

Enter LEONTES, POLIXENES, FLORIZEL, PERDITA, CAMILLO, PAULINA, Lords, *and* Attendants.

LEON. O, grave and good Paulina, the great comfort
That I have had of thee!

PAUL. What, sovereign sir,
I did not well, I meant well. All my services
You have paid home: but that you have vouchsaf'd,
With your crown'd brother, and these your[a] contracted
Heirs of your kingdoms, my poor house to visit,
It is a surplus of your grace, which never
My life may last to answer.

LEON. O, Paulina,
We honour you with trouble:—but we came
To see the statue of our queen: your gallery
Have we pass'd through, not without much content
In many singularities; but we saw not
That which my daughter came to look upon,
The statue of her mother.

PAUL. As she liv'd peerless,
So her dead likeness, I do well believe,
Excels whatever yet you look'd upon,
Or hand of man hath done; therefore I keep it
Lonely,* apart. But here it is—prepare

[a] *With your crown'd brother, and these* your *contracted*—] This verse reads so uncouthly that we suspect the second "your" to be an interpolation of the compositor.

(*) Old text, *Louely.*

To see the life as lively mock'd as ever
Still sleep mock'd death: behold! and say 'tis well.

[PAULINA *undraws a curtain, and discovers* HERMIONE *as a statue.*

I like your silence,—it the more shows off
Your wonder: but yet speak;—first, you, my liege.
Comes it not something near?

LEON. Her natural posture!—
Chide me, dear stone, that I may say indeed
Thou art Hermione, or rather, thou art she,
In thy not chiding,—for she was as tender
As infancy and grace.—But yet, Paulina,
Hermione was not so much wrinkled; nothing
So aged as this seems.

POL. O, not by much.

PAUL. So much the more our carver's excellence;

Which lets go by some sixteen years, and makes her
As she liv'd now.

LEON. As now she might have done,
So much to my good comfort, as it is
Now piercing to my soul. O, thus she stood,
Even with such life of majesty (warm life,
As now it coldly stands) when first I woo'd her!
I am asham'd,—does not the stone rebuke me,—
For being more stone than it?—O, royal piece,
There's magic in thy majesty; which has
My evils conjur'd to remembrance; and
From thy admiring daughter took the spirits,
Standing like stone with thee!

PER. And give me leave;
And do not say 't is superstition that
I kneel, and then implore her blessing.—Lady,
Dear queen, that ended when I but began,
Give me that hand of yours to kiss.

PAUL. O, patience!
The statue is but newly fix'd, the colour 's
Not dry.

CAM. My lord, your sorrow was too sore laid on,
Which sixteen winters cannot blow away,
So many summers dry: scarce any joy
Did ever so long live; no sorrow,
But kill'd itself much sooner.

POL. Dear my brother,
Let him that was the cause of this have power
To take off so much grief from you as he
Will piece up in himself.

PAUL. Indeed, my lord,
If I had thought the sight of my poor image
Would thus have wrought you (for the stone is mine)
I'd not have show'd it.

LEON. Do not draw the curtain!

PAUL. No longer shall you gaze on't, lest your fancy
May think anon it moves.

LEON. Let be! let be!
Would I were dead, but that, methinks, already—[a]
What was he that did make it?—See, my lord!
Would you not deem it breath'd? and that those veins
Did verily bear blood?

POL. Masterly done!
The very life seems warm upon her lip.

LEON. The fixure of her eye has motion in't,
As we are mock'd with art!

PAUL. I'll draw the curtain;
My lord's almost so far transported that
He'll think anon it lives.

LEON. O, sweet Paulina,
Make me to think so twenty years together!
No settled senses of the world can match
The pleasure of that madness. Let't alone!

PAUL. I am sorry, sir, I have thus far stirr'd you: but
I could afflict you further.

LEON. Do, Paulina!
For this affliction has a taste as sweet
As any cordial comfort.—Still, methinks,
There is an air comes from her! What fine chisel
Could ever yet cut breath? Let no man mock me,
For I will kiss her.

PAUL. Good my lord, forbear!
The ruddiness upon her lip is wet;(1)
You'll mar it, if you kiss it; stain your own
With oily painting. Shall I draw the curtain?

---

a
Let be! let be!
Would I were dead, but that, methinks, already—
What was he that did make it?—]

To a reader of taste and sensibility, the art by which the emotions of Leontes are developed in this situation, from the moment when with an apparent feeling of disappointment he first beholds the "so much wrinkled" statue, and gradually becomes impressed, amazed, enthralled, till at length, borne along by a wild, tumultuous throng of indefinable sensations, he reaches that grand climax where, in delirious rapture, he clasps the figure to his bosom and faintly murmurs,—

"O, she's warm!"

must appear consummate. Mr. Collier and his annotator, however, are not satisfied. To them the eloquent abruption,—

"— but that, methinks, already—
What was he that did make it?"

is but a blot, and so, to add "to the force and clearness of the speech of Leontes," they stem the torrent of his passion in mid-stream and make him drivel out,—

"Would I were dead, but that, methinks, already
I am but dead, stone looking upon stone."!

Can anything be viler? Conceive Leontes whimpering of himself as "dead," just when the thick pulsation of his heart could have been heard! and speaking of the statue as a "stone" at the very moment when, to his imagination, it was flesh and blood! Was it thus Shakespeare wrought? The insertion of such a line in such a place is absolutely monstrous, and implies, both in the forger and the utterer, an entire incompetence to appreciate the finer touches of his genius. But it does more, for it betrays the most discreditable ignorance of the current phraseology of the poet's time. When Leontes says,—

"Would I were dead, but that, methinks, already—"

Mr. Collier's annotator, and Mr. Collier, and all the advocates of the intercalated line, assume him to mean,—"I should desire to die, only that I am already dead or holding converse with the dead;" whereas, in fact, the expression, "*Would I were dead,*" &c. is neither more nor less than an imprecation, equivalent to—"*Would I may die,*" &c.; and the king's real meaning, in reference to Paulina's remark, that he will think *anon* it moves, is, "May I die, if I do not think it moves *already*." In proof of this, take the following examples, which might easily be multiplied a hundred-fold, of similar forms of speech:—

"—— and, *would I might be dead,*
If I in thought—" &c.
The Two Gentlemen of Verona, Act IV. Sc. 4.

"*Would I had no being,*
If this salute my blood a jot."
Henry VIII. Act II. Sc. 3.

"*The gods rebuke me, but* it is tidings
To wash the eyes of kings."
Antony and Cleopatra, Act V. Sc. 1.

"*Would I with thunder presently might die*
So I might speak."
Summer's Last Will and Testament.

"—— *Let me suffer death*
If in my apprehension—" &c.
BEAUMONT *and* FLETCHER'*s Play of The* "*Night-Walker,*" Act III. Sc. 6.

"*Would I were dead,*" &c.
"If I do know," &c.
BEN JONSON'*s Tale of a Tub*, Act II. Sc. 1.

LEON. No, not these twenty years!
PER. So long could I
Stand by, a looker-on.
PAUL. Either forbear,
Quit presently the chapel, or resolve you
For more amazement. If you can behold it,
I'll make the statue move; indeed, descend
And take you by the hand: but then you'll think
(Which I protest against) I am assisted
By wicked powers.
LEON. What you can make her do,
I am content to look on: what to speak,
I am content to hear; for 't is as easy
To make her speak as move.
PAUL. It is requir'd
You do awake your faith. Then all stand still;
Or * those that think it is unlawful business
I am about, let them depart.
LEON. Proceed!
No foot shall stir.
PAUL. Music, awake her, strike!— [*Music.*
'T is time; descend; be stone no more; approach;
Strike all that look upon with marvel! Come;
I'll fill your grave up: stir; nay, come away;
Bequeath to Death your numbness, for from him
Dear Life redeems you.—You perceive she stirs;
[HERMIONE *slowly descends from the pedestal.*
Start not; her actions shall be holy as
You hear my spell is lawful: do not shun her,
Until you see her die again; for then
You kill her double. Nay, present your hand:
When she was young you woo'd her; now in age
Is she become the suitor!
LEON. O, she 's warm! [*Embracing her.*
If this be magic, let it be an art
Lawful as eating.
POL. She embraces him!
CAM. She hangs about his neck!
If she pertain to life, let her speak too.
POL. Ay, and make 't manifest where she has liv'd,
Or how stol'n from the dead!
PAUL. That she is living,
Were it but told you, should be hooted at
Like an old tale; but it appears she lives,
Though yet she speak not. Mark a little while.—
Please you to interpose, fair madam; kneel,
And pray your mother's blessing.—Turn, good lady;
Our Perdita is found.
[*Presenting* PERDITA, *who kneels to* HERMIONE.
HER. You gods, look down,
And from your sacred vials pour your graces
Upon my daughter's head!—Tell me, mine own,
Where hast thou been preserv'd? where liv'd? how found
Thy father's court? for thou shalt hear that I,—
Knowing by Paulina that the oracle
Gave hope thou wast in being,—have preserv'd
Myself, to see the issue.
PAUL. There 's time enough for that;
Lest they desire, upon this push, to trouble
Your joys with like relation.—Go together,
You precious winners all; your exultation
Partake[a] to every one. I, an old turtle,
Will wing me to some wither'd bough, and there
My mate, that 's never to be found again,
Lament till I am lost.
LEON. O, peace, Paulina!
Thou shouldst a husband take by my consent,
As I by thine a wife: this is a match,
And made between 's by vows. Thou hast found mine;
But how, is to be question'd,—for I saw her,
As I thought, dead; and have, in vain, said many
A prayer upon her grave. I'll not seek far
(For him, I partly know his mind) to find thee
An honourable husband.—Come, Camillo,
And take her by the hand:—whose[b] worth and honesty
Is richly noted; and here justified
By us, a pair of kings.—Let 's from this place.—
What!—look upon my brother:[c]—both your pardons,
That e'er I put between your holy looks
My ill suspicion.—This your son-in-law,
And son unto the king, whom heavens directing,
Is troth-plight to your daughter.—Good Paulina,
Lead us from hence, where we may leisurely
Each one demand, and answer to his part
Perform'd in this wide gap of time, since first
We were dissever'd: hastily lead away. [*Exeunt.*

(*) Old text, *On*.

[a] Partake—] That is, *participate*.
[b] — whose *worth and honesty*, &c.] "Whose" refers to Camillo, not to Paulina.
[c] What!—look upon my brother:—] This unfolds a charming and delicate trait of action in Hermione; remembering how sixteen sad years agone her innocent freedoms with Polixenes had been misconstrued, and keenly sensible, even amidst the joy of her present restoration to child and husband, of the bitter penalty they had involved, she now turns from him, when they meet, with feelings of mingled modesty and apprehension.

ILLUSTRATIVE COMMENTS.

ACT I.

(1) SCENE II.—

—— Still virginalling
Upon his palm?]

By "virginalling," Leontes meant that Hermione was tapping or fingering on the hand of Polixenes, in the manner of a person playing on the "Virginals." This instrument, which, with the spinet and harpsichord, Mr. Chappell tells us was the precursor of the modern pianoforte, was stringed, and played on with keys, formerly called *jacks*:—

> "Where be these rascals that skip up and down,
> Faster than *virginal jacks?*"
> *Ram Alley, or Merry Tricks*, Act IV. Sc. I.

It was of an oblong shape, somewhat resembling a small square pianoforte, and, from the repeated mention of it in books of Shakespeare's age, as well as long afterwards, must have been in general vogue among the opulent. The name, as Nares supposed, was most probably derived from its being chiefly used by young girls.

(2) SCENE II.—*Are you mov'd, my lord?*] In Greene's novel, the theme of which, it will be seen from our extracts, Shakespeare pretty closely followed, except in the repulsive catastrophe, the scene of action is reversed; Pandosto [Leontes] being King of Bohemia, and Egistus [Polixenes] King of Sicilia. After describing the visit paid by the latter to Pandosto, and the "honest familiarity" which sprang up between him and Bellaria [Hermione], the novelist proceeds to expatiate on the effects of this familiarity upon the mind of Pandosto:—

"He then began to measure all their actions, and to misconstrue of their too private familiaritie, judging that it was not for honest affection, but for disordinate fancy, so that hee began to watch them more narrowly to see if he coulde gette any true and certaine proofe to confirme his doubtfull suspition. While thus he noted their lookes and gestures and suspected their thoughtes and meaninges, they two seely soules, who doubted nothing of this his treacherous intent, frequented daily eache others companie, which drave him into such a franticke passion, that he beganne to beare a secret hate to Egistus and a lowring countenance to Bellaria; who marveiling at such unaccustomed frowns, began to cast beeyond the moone, and to enter into a thousand sundrie thoughtes, which way she should offend her husband: but finding in her selfe a cleare conscience ceassed to muse, until such time as she might find fit opportunitie to demaund the cause of his dumps. In the meane time Pandostoes minde was so farre charged with jealousy, that he did no longer doubt, but was assured, (as he thought) that his friend Egistus had entered a wrong pointe in his tables, and so had played him false play."

(3) SCENE II.—

—— I'll do't, my lord.
LEON. *I will seem friendly, as thou hast advis'd me.*]

Compare the corresponding circumstances as related in the novel:—"Devising with himself a long time how he might best put away Egistus without suspition of treacherous murder, hee concluded at last to poyson him; which opinion pleasing his humour, he became resolute in his determination, and the better to bring the matter to passe he called unto him his cupbearer, with whom in secret he brake the matter, promising to him for the performance thereof to geve him a thousande crownes of yearely revenues.

"His cupbearer, eyther being of a good conscience or willing for fashion sake to deny such a bloudy request, began with great reasons to perswade Pandosto from his determinate mischief, showing him what an offence murther was to the Gods; how such unnaturall actions did more displease the heavens than men, and that causelesse cruelty did sildome or never escape without revenge: he layd before his face that Egistus was his friend, a king, and one that was come into his kingdome to confirme a league of perpetuall amitie betwixt them; that he had and did shew him a most friendly countenance; how Egistus was not onely honoured of his owne people by obedience, but also loved of the Bohemians for his curtesie, and that if he now should without any just or manifest cause poyson him, it would not onely be a great dishonour to his majestie, and a meanes to sow perpetuall enmity between the Sycilians and the Bohemians, but also his owne subjects would repine at such treacherous cruelty. These and such like perswasions of Franion (for so was his cupbearer called) could no whit prevaile to diswade him from his devellish enterprize, but remaining resolute in his determination (his fury so fired with rage as it could not be appeased with reason), he began with bitter taunts to take up his man, and to lay before him two baites, preferment and death; saying that if he would poyson Egistus he would advance him to high dignities; if he refused to doe it of an obstinate minde, no torture should be too great to requite his disobedience. Franion, seeing that to perswade Pandosto any more was but to strive against the streame, consented as soone as an opportunity would give him leave to dispatch Egistus: wherewith Pandosto remained somewhat satisfied, hoping now he should be fully revenged of such mistrusted injuries, intending also as soon as Egistus was dead to give his wife a sop of the same sawse, and so be rid of those which were the cause of his restles sorrow."

(4) SCENE II. — *Come, sir, away!* [*Exeunt.*] The betrayal of the king's jealous design is thus related in the story:—"Lingring thus in doubtfull feare, in an evening he went to Egistus lodging, and desirous to breake with him of certaine affaires that touched the king, after all were commanded out of the chamber, Franion made manifest the whole conspiracie which Pandosto had devised against him, desiring Egistus not to account him a traytor for bewraying his maisters counsaile, but to thinke that he did it for conscience: hoping that although his maister, inflamed with rage or incensed by some sinister reportes or slanderous speeches, had imagined such causelesse mischiefe, yet when time should pacifie his anger, and try those talebearers but flattering parasites, then he would count him as a faithfull servant that with such care had kept his maisters credite. Egistus had not fully heard Franion tell forth his tale, but a quaking feare possessed all his limnes, thinking that there was some treason wrought, and that Franion did but shaddow his craft with these false colours: wherefore he began to waxe in choller,

and saide that he doubted not Pandosto, sith he was his friend, and there had never as yet beene any breach of amity. He had not sought to invade his lands, to conspire with his enemies, to disswade his subjects from their allegiance; but in word and thought he rested his at all times: he knew not therefore any cause that should moove Pandosto to seeke his death, but suspected it to be a compacted knavery of the Bohemians to bring the king and him to oddes.

"Franion staying him in the middst of his talke, told him that to dally with princes was with the swannes to sing against their death, and that if the Bohemians had intended any such mischiefe, it might have beene better brought to passe then by revealing the conspiracie; therefore his Majestie did ill to misconstrue of his good meaneng, sith his intent was to hinder treason, not to become a traytor; and to confirme his promises, if it pleased his Majestie to fly into Sicilia for the safegarde of his life, hee would goe with him, and if then he found not such a practice to be pretended, let his imagined treacherie be repayed with most monstrous torments. Egistus hearing the solemne protestations of Franion, begann to consider that in love and kingdomes neither faith nor lawe is to bee respected, doubting that Pandosto thought by his death to destroy his men, and with speedy warre to invade Sicilia. These and such doubtes throughly weyghed he gave great thankes to Franion, promising if hee might with life returne to Syracusa, that he would create him a duke in Sycilia, craving his counsell how hee might escape out of the countrie."

ACT II.

(1) Scene I.—

—— Adieu, my lord:
I never wish'd to see you sorry; now
I trust I shall.]

"Whereupon he began to imagine that Franion and his wife Bellaria had conspired with Egistus, and that the fervent affection shee bare him was the onely meanes of his secret departure; in so much that incensed with rage he commaundes that his wife should be carried straight to prison untill they heard further of his pleasure. The guarde, unwilling to lay their hands one such a vertuous princesse and yet fearing the kings fury, went very sorrowfull to fulfill their charge. Comming to the queenes lodging they found her playing with her yong sonne Garinter, unto whom with teares doing the message, Bellaria, astonished at such a hard censure and finding her cleere consceence a sure advocate to pleade in her cause, went to the prison most willingly, where with sighes and teares shee past away the time till she might come to her triall.

"But Pandosto, whose reason was suppressed with rage and whose unbridled follie was incensed with fury, seeing Franion had bewrayed his secrets, and that Egistus might well be rayled on, but not revenged, determined to wreake all his wrath on poore Bellaria. He therefore caused a generall proclamation to be made through all his realme that the queene and Egistus had, by the help of Franion, not only committed most incestuous adultery, but also had conspired the kings death: whereupon the traitor Franion was fled away with Egistus, and Bellaria was most justly imprisoned. This proclamation being once blazed through the country, although the vertuous disposition of the queene did halfe discredit the contents, yet the suddaine and speedy passage of Egistus, and the secret departure of Franion, induced them (the circumstances throughly considered) to thinke that both the proclamation was true, and the king greatly injured: yet they pittyed her case, as sorrowful that so good a ladye should be crossed with such adverse fortune. But the king, whose restlesse rage would remit no pitty, thought that although he might sufficiently requite his wives falshood with the bitter plague of pinching penury, yet his minde should never be glutted with revenge till he might have fit time and opportunity to repay the treachery of Egistus with a totall injury. But a curst cow hath oftentimes short hornes, and a willing minde but a weake arme; for Pandosto, although he felt that revenge was a spurre to warre, and that envy alwaies proffereth steele, yet he saw that Egistus was not onely of great puissance and prowesse to withstand him, but had also many kings of his alliance to ayde him if neede should serve, for he married the Emperours daughter of Russia."
—*Pandosto. The Triumph of Time*, 1588.

(2) Scene III.—*Poor thing, condemn'd to loss!*] In the novel, as in the play, the unhappy queen, while in prison, gives birth to a daughter, which the king at first determines shall be burnt, but being diverted from this bloody purpose by the remonstrance of his nobles, he resolves to set the hapless infant adrift upon the sea:—"The guard left her in this perplexitie, and carried the child to the king, who quite devoide of pity commanded that without delay it should bee put in the boat, having neither saile nor other [*rudder?*] to guid it and so to be carried into the midst of the sea, and there left to the wind and wave as the destinies please to appoint. The very ship-men, seeing the sweete countenance of the yong babe, began to accuse the king of rigor, and to pity the childs hard fortune; but feare constrayned them to that which their nature did abhorre, so that they placed it in one of the ends of the boat, and with a few greene bows made a homely cabben to shrowd it as they could from wind and weather. Having thus trimmed the boat they tied it to a ship and so haled it into the mayne sea, and then cut in sunder the coarde; which they had no sooner done, but there arose a mighty tempest, which tossed the little boate so vehemently in the waves that the ship men thought it could not continue long without sincking; yea, the storm grew so great, that with much labour and perill they got to the shoare."

ACT III.

(1) Scene II.—*Look for no less than death.*] "But leaving the childe to her fortunes, againe to Pandosto, who not yet glutted with sufficient revenge desired which way he should best increase his wives calamitie. But first assembling his nobles and counsellors, hee called her for the more reproch into open court, where it was objected against her that she had committed adulterie with Egistus, and conspired with Franion to poyson Pandosto her husband, but their pretence being partely spyed, she counselled them to flie away by night for their better safety. Bellaria, who standing like a prisoner at the barre, feeling in herselfe a cleare conscience to withstand her false accusers, seeing that no lesse than death could pacifie her husbands wrath, waxed bolde and desired that

she might have lawe and justice, for mercy shee neyther craved nor hoped for; and that those perjured wretches which had falsely accused her to the king might be brought before her face to give in evidence. But Pandosto, whose rage and jealousie was such as no reason nor equitie could appease, tolde her, that for her accusers they were of such credite as their wordes were sufficient witnesse, and that the sodaine and secret flight of Egistus and Franion confirmed that which they had confessed; and as for her, it was her parte to deny such a monstrous crime, and to be impudent in forswearing the fact, since shee had past all shame in committing the fault: but her state countenaunce should stand for no coyne, for as the bastard which she bare was served, so she should with some cruell death be requited."—*Pandosto. The Triumph of Time*, 1588.

(2) Scene II.—

—— Your honours all,
I do refer me to the oracle:
Apollo be my judge!]

The extracts here given will show that in most of the incidents connected with the arraignment of the queen, the great dramatist varies but little from the story. He has made one important change, however, without which we should have lost the finest scene in the play; for in the novel the unfortunate lady, overcome with grief for the death of her eldest child, expires in the public court shortly after the response of the oracle is declared.

"The noble men which sate in judgement said that Bellaria spake reason, and intreated the king that the accusers might be openly examined and sworne, and if then the evidence were such as the jury might finde her guilty, (for seeing she was a prince she ought to be tryed by her peeres) then let her have such punishment as the extremitie of the law will assigne to such malefactors. The king presently made answere that in this case he might and would dispence with the law, and that the jury being once panneld they should take his word for sufficient evidence, otherwise he would make the proudest of them repent it. The noble men seeing the king in choler were all whist; but Bellaria, whose life then hung in the ballaunce, fearing more perpetual infamie than momentarie death, told the king if his furie might stand for a law that it were vaine to have the jury yeeld their verdict; and therefore she fell downe upon her knees, and desired the king that for the love he bare to his young sonne Garinter, whome she brought into the world, that hee would graunt her a request; which was this, that it would please his majestie to send sixe of his noble men whom he best trusted to the Isle of Delphos, there to enquire of the oracle of Apollo whether she had committed adultery with Egistus or conspired to poyson him with Franion? and if the god Apollo, who by his divine essence knew al secrets, gave answere that she was guiltie, she were content to suffer any torment were it never so terrible. The request was so reasonable that Pandosto could not for shame deny it, unlesse he would bee counted of all his subjects more wilfull than wise: he therefore agreed that with as much speede as might be there should be certaine Embassadores dispatched to the Ile of Delphos, and in the meane season he commanded that his wife should be kept in close prison."

(3) Scene II.—*And the king shall live without an heir, if that which is lost be not found.*] The answer of the oracle in the play is almost literally the same as that in the tale:—

"THE ORACLE.

"Suspition is no proofe: Jealousie is an unequal judge: Bellaria is chast: Egistus blameless: Franion a true subject: Pandosto treacherous: His babe innocent, and the king shall live long without an heire, if that which is lost be not founde."

(4) Scene III.—*They have scared away two of my best sheep,—— if anywhere I have them, 'tis by the sea-side, browzing of ivy.*] This is one of the instances, proving that Shakespeare had the novel before him while composing his drama, in which the identical expression of the original is transferred to the copy. After recounting how the babe, which had been left to the mercies of the "gastfull seas," "floated two whole daies without succour, readie at every puffe to bee drowned in the sea, till at last the tempest ceased and the little boate was driven with the tyde into the coaste of Sycilia, where sticking uppon the sandes it rested," the novelist proceeds to tell that, "It fortuned a poore mercenary sheepheard that dwelled in Sycilia, who got his living by other mens flockes, missed one of his sheepe, and thinking it had strayed into the covert that was hard by, sought very diligently to find that which he could not see, fearing either that the wolves or eagles had undone him (for he was so poore as a sheepe was halfe his substance), wandered downe toward the sea cliffes to see if perchaunce the sheepe was *browsing on the sea ivy*, whereon they greatly doe feede; but not finding her there, as he was ready to returne to his flocke hee heard a child crie, but knowing there was no house nere, he thought he had mistaken the sound and that it was the bleatyng of his sheepe. Wherefore looking more narrowely, as he cast his eye to the sea, he spyed a little boate, from whence, as he attentively listened, he might heare the cry to come. Standing a good while in a maze, at last he went to the shoare, and wading to the boate, as he looked in he saw the little babe lying al alone ready to die for hunger and colde, wrapped in a mantle of scarlet richely imbrodered with golde, and having a chayne about the necke."

ACT IV.

(1) Scene II.—*Trol-my-dames.*] A game more anciently known as "Pigeon-holes," because the balls were driven through arches on the board resembling the apertures in a dove-cote. It is mentioned in a treatise, quoted by Farmer, on "*Buckstone Bathes;*"—"The ladyes, gentle woomen, wyves, maydes, if the weather be not agreeable, may have in the ende of a benche eleven holes made, intoo the which to troule pummits, either wyolent or softe, after their own discretion: the pastyme *troule in madame* is termed;" and an illustration, showing the board and mode of play, will be found prefixed to Emblem No. II. in Quarles' "Emblems," 1635, which begins:—

"Prepost'rous fool, thou *troul'st* amiss;
Thou err'st; that's not the way, 'tis this."

(2) Scene II.—*An ape-bearer.*] In explanation of a passage in Massinger's play of "The Bondman," Act III. Sc. 3, Gifford has an amusing note on the excellence displayed by our ancestors in the education of animals:—"Banks's horse far surpassed all that have been brought up in the academy of Mr. Astley; and the apes of these days are mere clowns to their progenitors. The apes of Massinger's time were gifted with a pretty smattering of politics and philosophy. The widow Wild had one of them: 'He would *come over* for all my friends, but was the dog-

ged'st thing to my enemies; he would sit upon his tale before them, and frown like John-a-napes when the pope is named.' "—*The Parson's Wedding.*

Another may be found in *Ram Alley*:—

> "Men say you've tricks; remember, noble captain,
> You skip when I shall shake my whip. Now, sir,
> What can you do for the great Turk?
> What can you do for the Pope of Rome?
> Lo!
> He stirreth not, he moveth not, he waggeth not.
> What can you do for the town of Geneva, sirrah?
> [*Captain holds up his hand,*" &c.

The occupation of the ape-bearer, then, was to instruct apes in their tumbling, and to exhibit the learned animals for a consideration to the public. The course of tuition must have required no little patience on the part of the teacher, and great docility in the pupil; for it usually ended in giving to the ape-bearer an absolute control over the creature, which, by means of some secret correspondence between them, could be made to express either anger or good-humour at the keeper's will. This perfect mastery gave occasion for a saying attributed to James I.—"If I have Jack-a-napes, I can make him bite you; if you have Jack-a-napes, you can make him bite me." In the Induction to Ben Jonson's "Bartholomew Fair," the stage-keeper speaks of "a juggler with a well-educated ape, to come over the chain for a King of England, and back again for the prince; and sit still for the Pope and the King of Spain." This evolution of *coming over,* &c. was performed by the animal's placing his forepaws on the ground, and turning over the chain on his head, and going back again in the same fashion, as the feat is represented in an illuminated manuscript of the fourteenth century.

(3) SCENE II.—*Then he compassed a motion of the Prodigal Son.*] A "Motion," though sometimes used to denote a *puppet,* more frequently signified a *puppet-show.* In these exhibitions, the successors of the ancient Mysteries, scriptural subjects appear to have been the most attractive. In Ben Jonson's "Bartholomew Fair," Act V. Sc. I., the master of a puppet-show ejaculates,—"O, the motions that I Lanthorn Leatherhead have given light to in my time since my master, Pod, died! Jerusalem was a stately thing, and so was Nineveh and the City of Norwich, and Sodom and Gomorrah," &c. Mr. Halliwell has given an engraving representing the performance of a *Motion* of the Prodigal Son, copied from an English woodcut of the seventeenth century; and Strutt, in his "Sports and Pastimes," reprints a Bartholomew Fair showman's bill, which affords a lively picture of what a *Motion* was in later times:—"At Crawley's Booth, over against the Crown Tavern in Smithfield, during the time of Bartholomew Fair, will be presented a little opera called the Old Creation of the World, yet newly revived; with the addition of Noah's Flood; also several fountains playing water during the time of the play.—The last scene does present Noah and his family coming out of the Ark with all the beasts two and two, and all the fowls of the air seen in a prospect sitting upon trees; likewise over the Ark is seen the Sun rising in a most glorious manner: moreover, a multitude of Angels will be seen in a double rank, which presents a double prospect, one for the sun, the other for a palace, where will be seen six Angels ringing of bells.—Likewise Machines descend from above, double and treble, with Dives rising out of Hell, and Lazarus seen in Abraham's bosom," &c.

(4) SCENE II.—

> *Jog on, jog on, the foot-path way,*
> *And merrily hent the stile-a:*
> *A merry heart goes all the day,*
> *Your sad tires in a mile-a.*]

These lines are part of a song found in a collection of "Witty Ballads, Jovial Songs, and Merry Catches," called "An Antidote against Melancholy;" 1661. It is said to have been set as a round for three voices by John Hilton; and the melody, a base and accompaniment being added, is given as follows from "The Dancing Master," 1650, by Mr. Knight in his "Pictorial Shakespeare:"—

Jog on, jog on the foot - path way, And
mer - ri - ly hent the stile, O; A mer-ry heart goes
all the day, Your sad tires in a mile, O.

(5) SCENE III.—

> *I bless the time,*
> *When my good falcon made her flight across*
> *Thy father's ground.*]

So in the tale:—"It happened not long after this that there was a meeting of all the farmers daughters in Sycilia, whither Fawnia was also bidden as the mistres of the feast, who having attired her selfe in her best garments, went among the rest of her companions to the merry meeting, there spending the day in such homely pastimes as shepheards use. As the evening grew on, and their sportes ceased, ech taking their leave at other, Fawnia, desiring one of her companions to beare her companie, went home by the flocke to see if they were well folded, and as they returned it fortuned that Dorastus (who all that day had been hawking, and kilde store of game) incountred by the way these two mayds, and casting his eye sodenly on Fawnia he was halfe afraid fearing that with Acteon he had seene Diana; for he thought such exquisite perfection could not be founde in any mortall creature."

(6) SCENE III.—

> —— *The gods themselves,*
> *Humbling their deities to love, have taken*
> *The shapes of beasts upon them: Jupiter*
> *Became a bull, and bellow'd; the green Neptune*
> *A ram, and bleated; and the fire-rob'd god,*
> *Golden Apollo, a poor humble swain,*
> *As I seem now.*]

Literally, this is from the novel; but mark the change effected by the few but admirably chosen epithets:—"And yet, Dorastus, shame not at thy shepheards weede; the heavenly godes have sometime earthly thoughtes. Neptune became a ram, Jupiter a bul, Apollo a shepheard: they gods, and yet in love; and thou a man appointed to love."

(7) SCENE III.—

—— O, Proserpina,
For the flowers now, that, frighted, thou lett'st fall
From Dis's waggon !]

See the passage in Ovid's Metamorphoses, lib. v.

"—— ut summa vestem laxavit ab ora
Collecti flores tunicis cecidere remissis,—"

and the following translation by Shakespeare's contemporary, Golding:—

"Neare Enna walles there stands a lake Pergusa is the name,
Cayster heareth not more songs of swannes than doth the same.
A wood environs every side the water round about,
And with his leaves as with a veile doth keepe the sun heat out.
The boughes doo yeeld a coole fresh aire: the moistnesse of the ground
Yeelds sundrie flowers: continuall spring is all the yeare there found.
While in this garden Proserpine was taking her pastime,
In gathering either violets blew, or lillies white as lime,
And while of maidenlie desire she fild her maund and lap
Endevouring to out-gather her companions there. By hap
Dis spide her, lov'd her, caught her up, and all at once well neere:
So hastie, hot, and swift a thing is love, as may appeere.
The ladie with a wailing voice afright did often call
Her mother and her waiting maids, but mother most of all.
And as she from the upper part her garment would have rent
By chance she let her lap slip downe, and out the flowers went."

(8) SCENE III.—*Poking-sticks of steel.*] "These *poking-sticks* were heated in the fire, and made use of to adjust the plaits of ruffs. In Marston's 'Malcontent' [Act V. Sc. 3] 1604, is the following instance: 'There is such a deale a pinning these ruffes, when the fine clean fall is worth all; and again, if you should chance to take a nap in an afternoon, your falling band requires no *poking-stick* to recover his form,' &c. Again, in Middleton's comedy of 'Blurt, Master Constable' [Act III. Sc. 3], 1602: 'Your ruff must stand in print; and for that purpose, get *poking-sticks* with fair long handles, lest they scorch your [lily sweating] hands.' Again, in the Second Part of Stubbes's Anatomie of Abuses, 8vo. no date: 'They (*poking-sticks*) be made of yron and steele, and some of brasse, kept as bright as silver, yea some of silver itselfe, and it is well if in processe of time they grow not to be gold. The fashion whereafter they be made, I cannot resemble to any thing so well as to a squirt or a little squibbe which little children used to squirt out water withal; and when they come to starching and setting of their ruffes, then must this instrument be heated in the fire, the better to stiffen the ruffe,' &c."—STEEVENS.

(9) SCENE III.—*Of a fish, that appeared upon the coast on Wednesday the fourscore of April, &c.*] "The Shakesperian era was the age of ballads, broadsides, and fugitive pieces on all kinds of wonders, which were either gross exaggerations of facts or mere inventions. The present dialogue seems to be a general, not a particular, satire; but it may be curiously illustrated by an early ballad of a fish, copied from the unique exemplar preserved in the Miller collection, entitled,—'The discription of a rare or rather most monstrous fishe, taken on the east cost of Holland the xvij. of November, anno 1566.' In 1569 was published a prose broadside, containing,—'A true description of this marveilous straunge Fishe, which was taken on Thursday was sennight, the 16. day of June, this present month, in the yeare of our Lord God, 1569.—Finis, Qd. C. R.—Imprinted at London, in Fleetstreete, beneath the conduit, at the signe of Saint John Evangelist, by Thomas Colwell.' In 1604 was entered on the books of the Stationers' Company: 'A strange reporte of a monstrous *fish* that appeared in the form of a *woman*, from her waist upward, seene in the sea;' and in May of the same year, 'a ballad called a ballad of a strange and monstruous fishe seene in the sea on Friday the 17 of Febr. 1603.' In Sir Henry Herbert's office-book, which contains a register of all the shows of London from 1623 to 1642, is 'a licence to Francis Sherret to shew a *strange fish* for a yeare, from the 10th of Marche, 1635.'"—HALLIWELL.

(10) SCENE III.—*Men of hair.*] A dance in which the performers were disguised as satyrs, not unusually formed a feature of the entertainment on festival occasions in olden time, and this species of masquerade is connected with a very tragic incident, graphically told by Froissart, which occurred at the French court in 1392:—

"It fortuned that, soon after the retaining of the foresaid knight, a marriage was made in the king's house between a young knight of Vermandois and one of the queen's gentlewomen; and because they were both of the king's house, the king's uncles, and other lords, ladies, and damoiselles, made great triumph: there was the Dukes of Orléans, Berry, and Bourgoyne, and their wives, dancing and making great joy. The king made a great supper to the lords and ladies, and the queen kept her estate, desiring every man to be merry: and there was a squire of Normandy, called Hogreymen Gensay, he advised to make some pastime. The day of the marriage, which was on a Tuesday before Candlemas, he provided for a mummery against night: he devised six coats made of linen cloth, covered with pitch, and thereon flax-like hair, and had them ready in a chamber. The king put on one of them, and the Earl of Jouy, a young lusty knight, another, and Sir Charles of Poitiers the third, who was son to the earl of Valentenois, and Sir Juan of Foix another, and the son of the Lord Nanthorillet had on the fifth, and the squire himself had on the sixth; and when they were thus arrayed in these sad coats, and sewed fast in them, they seemed like wild woodhouses,* full of hair from the top of the head to the sole of the foot. This device pleased well the French king, and was well content with the squire for it. They were apparelled in these coats secretly in a chamber that no man knew thereof but such as helped them. When Sir Juan of Foix had well devised these coats, he said to the king,—'Sir, command straightly that no man approach near us with any torch or fire, for if the fire fasten in any of these coats, we shall all be burnt without remedy.' The king answered and said,—'Juan, ye speak well and wisely; it shall be done as ye have devised;' and incontinent sent for an usher of his chamber, commanding him to go into the chamber where the ladies danced, and to command all the varlets holding torches to stand up by the walls, and none of them to approach near to the woodhouses that should come thither to dance. The usher did the king's commandment, which was fulfilled. Soon after the Duke of Orléans entered into the hall, accompanied with four knights and six torches, and knew nothing of the king's commandment for the torches, nor of the mummery that was coming thither, but thought to behold the dancing, and began himself to dance. Therewith the king with the five other came in; they were so disguised in flax that no man knew them: five of them were fastened one to another; the king was loose, and went before and led the device.

"When they entered into the hall every man took so great heed to them that they forgot the torches: the king departed from his company and went to the ladies to sport with them, as youth required, and so passed by the queen and came to the Duchess of Berry, who took and held him by the arm, to know what he was, but the king would not show his name. Then the duchess said, Ye shall not escape me till I know your name. In this mean season great mischief fell on the other, and by reason of the Duke of Orléans; howbeit, it was by ignorance, and against his will, for if he had considered before the mischief that fell, he would not have done as he did for all the good in the world: but he was so desirous to know what personages the five were that danced, he put one of the torches that his servant held so near, that the heat of the fire entered into the flax (wherein if fire take there is no remedy), and suddenly was on a bright flame, and so each of them set fire on other; the pitch was so fastened to the linen cloth, and their shirts so dry and fine, and so joining to their flesh, that they began to burn and to cry for help: none durst come near them; they that did burnt their hands by reason of the heat of the pitch: one of them called

* Savages.

Nanthorillet advised him how the botry was thereby; he fled thither, and cast himself into a vessel full of water, wherein they rinsed pots, which saved him, or else he had been dead as the other were; yet he was sore hurt with the fire. When the queen heard the cry that they made, she doubted her of the king, for she knew well that he should be one of the six; therewith she fell into a swoon, and knights and ladies came and comforted her. A piteous noise there was in the hall. The Duchess of Berry delivered the king from that peril, for she did cast over him the train of her gown, and covered him from the fire. The king would have gone from her. Whither will ye go? quoth she; ye see well how your company burns. What are ye? I am the king, quoth he. Haste ye, quoth she, and get you into other apparel, and come to the queen. And the Duchess of Berry had somewhat comforted her, and had showed her how she should see the king shortly. Therewith the king came to the queen, and as soon as she saw him, for joy she embraced him and fell in a swoon; then she was borne to her chamber, and the king went with her. And the bastard of Foix, who was all on a fire, cried ever with a loud voice, Save the king, save the king! Thus was the king saved. It was happy for him that he went from his company, for else he had been dead without remedy. This great mischief fell thus about midnight in the hall of Saint Powle in Paris, where there was two burnt to death in the place, and other two, the bastard of Foix and the Earl of Jouy, borne to their lodgings, and died within two days after in great misery and pain."

ACT V.

(1) SCENE III.—*The ruddiness upon her lip is wet.*] However general the distaste for colouring sculpture in the present day, there can be no denying that the practice is of very high antiquity; since the painted low reliefs found in such profusion in the Egyptian tombs are usually assigned to the period B.C. 2400. In those remains there appears to have been the same intention as that shown in the coloured Monumental Effigies of the later middle-ages and the sixteenth century; namely, the production of a perfect and substantial image of the person represented, painted with his natural complexion and apparelled "in his habit as he lived." In this view of the custom it may be divested of much of its bad taste; especially if we suppose that really eminent artists were frequently employed as well on the painting of the figure as on the modelling and carving it. The later commentators only have taken this the true view of the statue of Hermione; though they have all pointed out the poet's error in representing Giulio Romano as a sculptor. We are inclined to doubt, however, whether Shakespeare committed any mistake upon the subject: when he calls the statue "A piece many years in doing, and now newly performed," he may have remembered that Vasari, Romano's contemporary, has recorded that "over his paintings he sometimes consumed months and even years, until they became wearisome to him." And when he represents this artist as colouring sculpture, he may have recollected the same authority states, that Giulio Romano built a house for himself in Mantua, opposite to the church of St. Barnaba. "The front of this he *adorned with a fantastic decoration of coloured stuccoes; causing it at the same time to be painted and adorned with stucco-work within.*" It will be readily admitted that when the practice of making painted effigy portraits and busts was established, the greatest talent as well as the most inferior might be employed on the colouring; and Vasari adds further, that Giulio Romano would not refuse to set his hand to the most trifling matter, when the object was to do a service to his lord or to give pleasure to his friends.

CRITICAL OPINIONS ON THE WINTER'S TALE.

"'The Winter's Tale' is as appropriately named as 'The Midsummer Night's Dream.' It is one of those tales which are peculiarly calculated to beguile the dreary leisure of a long winter evening, and are even attractive and intelligible to childhood, while, animated by fervent truth in the delineation of character and passion, and invested with the embellishments of poetry, lowering itself, as it were, to the simplicity of the subject, they transport even manhood back to the golden age of imagination. The calculation of probabilities has nothing to do with such wonderful and fleeting adventures, when all end at last in universal joy: and, accordingly, Shakspeare has here taken the greatest licence of anachronisms and geographical errors; not to mention other incongruities, he opens a free navigation between Sicily and Bohemia, makes Giulio Romano the contemporary of the Delphic oracle. The piece divides itself in some degree into two plays. Leontes becomes suddenly jealous of his royal bosom-friend Polyxenes, who is on a visit to his court; makes an attempt on his life, from which Polyxenes only saves himself by a clandestine flight;—Hermione, suspected of infidelity, is thrown into prison, and the daughter which she there brings into the world is exposed on a remote coast;—the accused queen, declared innocent by the oracle, on learning that her infant son has pined to death on her account, falls down in a swoon, and is mourned as dead by her husband, who becomes sensible, when too late, of his error: all this makes up the first three acts. The last two are separated from these by a chasm of sixteen years; but the foregoing tragical catastrophe was only apparent, and this serves to connect the two parts. The princess, who has been exposed on the coast of Polyxenes' kingdom, grows up among low shepherds; but her tender beauty, her noble manners, and elevation of sentiment, bespeak her descent; the Crown Prince Florizel, in the course of his hawking, falls in with her, becomes enamoured, and courts her in the disguise of a shepherd; at a rural entertainment Polyxenes discovers their attachment, and breaks out into a violent rage; the two lovers seek refuge from his persecutions at the court of Leontes in Sicily, where the discovery and general reconciliation take place. Lastly, when Leontes beholds, as he imagines, the statue of his lost wife, it descends from the niche: it is she herself, the still living Hermione, who has kept herself so long concealed; and the piece ends with universal rejoicing. The jealousy of Leontes is not, like that of Othello, developed through all its causes, symptoms, and variations; it is brought forward at once full grown and mature, and is portrayed as a distempered frenzy. It is a passion whose effects the spectator is more concerned with than its origin, and which does not produce the catastrophe, but merely ties the knot of the piece. In fact, the poet might perhaps have wished slightly to indicate that Hermione, though virtuous, was too warm in her efforts to please Polyxenes; and it appears as if this germ of inclination first attained its proper maturity in their children. Nothing can be more fresh and youthful, nothing at once so ideally pastoral and princely, as the love of Florizel and Perdita; of the prince, whom love converts into a voluntary shepherd; and the princess, who betrays her exalted origin without knowing it, and in whose hands nosegays become crowns. Shakspeare has never hesitated to place ideal poetry side by side of the most vulgar prose: and in the world of reality also this is generally the case. Perdita's foster-father and his son are both made simple boors, that we may the more distinctly see how all that ennobles her belongs only to herself. Autolycus, the merry pedlar and pickpocket, so inimitably portrayed, is necessary to complete the rustic feast, which Perdita on her part seems to render meet for an assemblage of gods in disguise."—SCHLEGEL.

Act IV. Sc. 4.

TROILUS AND CRESSIDA.

Fourteen years before the appearance of the folio of 1623, a quarto edition of this play was published under the title of "The Famous Historie of Troylus and Cresseid. Excellently expressing the beginning of their loves, with the conceited wooing of Pandarus Prince of Licia. Written by William Shakespeare. London Imprinted by G. Eld for R. Bonian and H. Walley, and are to be sold at the spred Eagle in Paules Church-yeard, over against the great North doore. 1609." In the same year, another edition, or rather a second issue of the above, was printed with a different title-page,—"The Historie of Troylus and Cresseida. As it was acted by the Kings Maiesties servants at the Globe. Written by William Shakespeare. London," &c. Nor is this the only diversity between the two issues, for the first contains the following curious prefatory address, which was omitted in all the subsequent copies,—

"*A never Writer to an ever Reader.* Newes.

"Eternall reader, you have heere a new play, never stal'd with the Stage, never clapper-clawd with the palmes of the vulger, and yet passing full of the palme comicall; for it is a birth of your braine, that never undertooke any thing commicall vainely: and were but the vaine names of Commedies changde for the titles of commodities, or of Playes for Pleas, you should see all those grand censors, that now stile them such vanities, flock to them for the maine grace of their gravities; especially this author's Commedies, that are so fram'd to the life, that they serve for the most common Commentaries of all the actions of our lives, shewing such a dexteritie and power of witte, that the most displeased with Playes are pleasd with his Commedies. And all such dull and heavy-witted worldlings, as were never capable of the witte of a Commedie, comming by report of them to his representations, have found that witte there that they never found in themselves, and have parted better-wittied then they came; feeling an edge of witte set upon them, more then ever they dreamd they had brain to grinde it on. So much and such savoured salt of witte is in his Commedies, that they seeme (for their height of pleasure) to be borne in that sea that brought forth Venus. Amongst all there is none more witty then this: And had I time I would comment upon it, though I know it needs not, (for so much as will make you thinke your testerne well bestowd) but for so much worth, as even poore I know to be stuft in it. It deserves such a labour, as well as the best Commedie in Terence or Plautus. And beleeve this, that when hee is gone, and his Commedies out of sale, you will scramble for them, and set up a new English Inquisition. Take this for a warning, and at the perrill of your pleasures losse, and Judgements, refuse not, nor like this the lesse for not being sullied with the smoaky breath of the multitude: but thanke fortune for the scape it hath made amongst you. Since by the grand possessors wills, I beleeve, you should have prayd for them rather then been prayd. And so I leave all such to bee prayd for (for the states of their wits healths) that will not praise it.—Vale."

From this address we may conclude that, when first published, the piece had not been acted, or only acted at court, and that, being shortly after represented on the stage, it was thought necessary to withdraw the preface, and substitute another title-page.

In Henslowe's Diary is an entry, showing that in April, 1599, Decker and Chettle were occupied in writing a play, called "Troilus and Cressida," and this may have been the "booke" recorded on the Stationers' Registers, February 7th, 1602-3,—

"Mr. Roberts] The booke of Troilus and Cressida, as yt is acted by my Lo. Chamberlens men."

Farther, as the company to which Shakespeare belonged was entitled the "Lord Chamberlain's Servants" until the year 1603, and as some parts of his "Troilus and Cressida" are evidently the production of an inferior writer, it is not at all improbable that the earlier piece formed the basis of the later one.

In the preface to his alteration of the present play, Dryden remarks that, "The original story was written by one Lollius, a Lombard, in Latin verse, and translated by Chaucer into English." "'Twere to consider too curiously," perhaps, to enter here upon the question whether "Myn auctor Lollius" were a tangible personage, or the mere creation of the old bard's fancy; we may be satisfied the plot of the drama is immediately founded upon the poem of "Troylus and Cryseyde." Upon this point there can be no reasonable doubt; and Mr. Godwin, in his "Life of Chaucer," complains, with reason, that the commentators have dealt ungenerously towards the elder poet in not acknowledging the honour conferred upon him by the immortal dramatist,—

"It would be extremely unjust to quit the consideration of Chaucer's poem of 'Troilus and Cresseide,' without noticing the high honour it has received in having been made the foundation of one of the plays of Shakespear. There seems to have been in this respect a sort of conspiracy in the commentators upon Shakespear against the glory of our old English bard. In what they have written concerning this play, they make a very slight mention of Chaucer; they have not consulted his poem for the purpose of illustrating this admirable drama; and they have agreed, as far as possible, to transfer to another author the honour of having supplied materials to the tragic artist. Dr. Johnson says, 'Shakespeare has in his story followed, for the greater part, the old book of Caxton, which was then very popular; but the character of Thersites, of which it makes no mention, is a proof that this play was written after Chapman had published his version of Homer.' Mr. Steevens asserts that 'Shakspeare received the greatest part of his materials for the structure of this play from the Troye Boke of Lydgate.' And Mr. Malone repeatedly treats the 'History of the Destruction of Troy, translated by Caxton,' as 'Shakspeare's authority' in the composition of this drama. * * * * * The fact is, that the play of Shakespear we are here considering has for its main foundation the poem of Chaucer, and is indebted for many accessory helps to the books mentioned by the commentators. * * * * *

"We are not, however, left to probability and conjecture as to the use made by Shakespear of the poem of Chaucer. His other sources were Chapman's translation of Homer, the 'Troy Book' of Lydgate, and Caxton's 'History of the Destruction of Troy.' It is well known that there is no trace of the particular story of 'Troilus and Cresseide' among the ancients. It occurs, indeed, in Lydgate and Caxton; but the name and actions of Pandarus, a very essential personage in the tale as related by Shakespear and Chaucer, are entirely wanting, except a single mention of him by Lydgate, and that with an express reference to Chaucer as his authority. Shakespear has taken the story of Chaucer with all its imperfections and defects, and has copied the series of its incidents with his customary fidelity;—an exactness seldom to be found in any other dramatic writer."

Persons Represented.

PRIAM, *King of* Troy.

HECTOR, TROILUS, PARIS, DEIPHOBUS, HELENUS, } *His Sons.*

MARGARELON, *a natural Son of* Priam.

ÆNEAS, ANTENOR, } Trojan *Commanders.*

CALCHAS, *a* Trojan *Priest, taking part with the Greeks.*

PANDARUS, *Uncle to* Cressida.

AGAMEMNON, *the* Grecian *General.*

MENELAUS, *his Brother.*

ACHILLES, ULYSSES, NESTOR, AJAX, DIOMEDES, PATROCLUS, } Grecian *Commanders.*

THERSITES, *a deformed and scurrilous* Grecian.

ALEXANDER, *Servant to* Cressida.

Servant *to* Troilus.

Servant *to* Paris.

Servant *to* Diomedes.

HELEN, *Wife to* Menelaus.

ANDROMACHE, *Wife to* Hector.

CASSANDRA, *Daughter to* Priam; *a Prophetess.*

CRESSIDA, *Daughter to* Calchas.

Trojan *and* Grecian *Soldiers, and Attendants.*

SCENE,—TROY *and the* Grecian *Camp before it.*

PROLOGUE.

In Troy, there lies the scene. From isles of Greece
The princes orgulous,[a] their high blood chaf'd,
Have to the port of Athens sent their ships,
Fraught with the ministers and instruments
Of cruel war: sixty and nine, that wore
Their crownets regal, from the Athenian bay
Put forth toward Phrygia; and their vow is made
To ransack Troy; within whose strong immures
The ravish'd Helen, Menelaus' queen,
With wanton Paris sleeps; and that's the quarrel.
To Tenedos they come;
And the deep-drawing barks* do there disgorge
Their warlike fraughtage. Now on Dardan plains
The fresh and yet unbruised Greeks do pitch
Their brave pavilions: Priam's six-gated city,
Dardan, and Tymbria, Helias, Chetas, Troien,
And Antenorides,[b] with massy staples,
And corresponsive and fulfilling bolts,
Sperr[c] up the sons of Troy.
Now expectation, tickling skittish spirits,
On one and other side, Trojan and Greek,
Sets all on hazard.—And hither am I come
A prologue arm'd,[d]—but not in confidence
Of author's pen or actor's voice; but suited
In like conditions as our argument,—
To tell you, fair beholders, that our play
Leaps o'er the vaunt[e] and firstlings of those broils,
Beginning in the middle; starting thence away
To what may be digested in a play.
Like, or find fault; do as your pleasures are;
Now good, or bad, 'tis but the chance of war.

(*) First folio, *Barke*.

a *The princes* orgulous,—] "Orgulous," from the French *Orgueilleux*, means *proud, haughty*.

b Dardan, and Tymbria, Helias, Chetas, Troien,
And Antenorides,—]

So these names are exhibited in the folio 1623, (with the exception of the last, which is there "*Antenonidus*,") a circumstance that leads us to conjecture Shakespeare had consulted Lydgate's poem called, "The hystorye, Sege and dystruccyon of Troye,"—

"The firste of all and strengest eke withall
* * * * * *
Was by the Kynge called *Dardanydes*;
And in storye lyke as it is founde,
Tymbria was named the seconde;
And the thirde called *Helyas*;
The fourthe gate highte also *Cetheas*;
The fyfte *Troiana*, the syxth *Anthonydes*," &c.—

as well as Caxton's "Recuyell of the historyes of Troye," &c., where, in the chapter headed, "How the Kynge Priam reediffied the cyte of troye," it is said, "In this Cyte were sixe pryncipall gates. of whome that one was named *dardane*. the seconde *tymbria*. the third *helyas*. the fourthe *chetas*. the fifthe *troyenne*. and the sixthe *antenorides*."

c Sperr *up the sons of Troy*.] The folio, where alone of the old editions this Prologue is given, reads, "*Stirre* up." Theobald first proposed "Sperr," an old word signifying *to shut up*, which is occasionally used by Chaucer, Spenser, and other of our early writers.

d — arm'd,—] From this it appears that the speaker of the Prologue, instead of wearing the customary black cloak, was dressed in armour,—"In like conditions as our argument."

e — *the* vaunt—] That is, the *van*, the *fore-going*, the *beginning*.

ACT I.

SCENE I.—Troy. *Before* Priam's *Palace.*

Enter TROILUS *armed, and* PANDARUS.

TRO. Call here my varlet;[a] I'll unarm again:
Why should I war without the walls of Troy,
That find such cruel battle here within?
Each Trojan that is master of his heart,
Let him to field; Troilus, alas! hath none.

PAN. Will this gear ne'er be mended?

TRO. The Greeks are strong, and skilful to their strength,
Fierce to their skill, and to their fierceness valiant;
But I am weaker than a woman's tear,
Tamer than sleep, fonder than ignorance;
Less valiant than the virgin in the night,
And skill-less as unpractis'd infancy.

PAN. Well, I have told you enough of this: for my part, I'll not meddle nor make no further. He that will have a cake out of the wheat must needs tarry the grinding.

[a] — varlet;] A "varlet" anciently signified a *footman* or *servant*.

TRO. Have I not tarried?

PAN. Ay, the grinding; but you must tarry the bolting.

TRO. Have I not tarried?

PAN. Ay, the bolting; but you must tarry the leavening.

TRO. Still have I tarried.

PAN. Ay, to the leavening; but here's yet in the word *hereafter*, the kneading, the making of the cake, the heating of the oven, and the baking; nay, you must stay the cooling too, or you may chance to burn your lips.

TRO. Patience herself, what goddess e'er she be,
Doth lesser blench [a] at sufferance than I do.
At Priam's royal table do I sit;
And when fair Cressid comes into my thoughts,—
So, traitor!—when she comes!—when is she thence? [b]

PAN. Well, she looked yesternight fairer than ever I saw her look, or any woman else.

TRO. I was about to tell thee,—when my heart,
As wedged with a sigh, would rive in twain;
Lest Hector or my father should perceive me,
I have (as when the sun doth light a storm*)
Buried this sigh in wrinkle of a smile:
But sorrow, that is couch'd in seeming gladness,
Is like that mirth fate turns to sudden sadness.

PAN. An her hair were not somewhat darker than Helen's,—well, go to,—there were no more comparison between the women,—but, for my part, she is my kinswoman; I would not, as they term it, praise her,†—but I would somebody had heard her talk yesterday, as I did. I will not dispraise your sister Cassandra's wit; but—

TRO. O Pandarus! I tell thee, Pandarus,—
When I do tell thee, there my hopes lie drown'd,
Reply not in how many fathoms deep
They lie indrench'd. I tell thee, I am mad
In Cressid's love: thou answer'st, *she is fair;*
Pour'st in the open ulcer of my heart
Her eyes, her hair, her cheek, her gait, her voice:
Handlest in thy discourse,—*O, that her hand,*[c]
In whose comparison all whites are ink,
Writing their own reproach; to whose soft seizure
The cygnet's down is harsh, and spirit of sense
Hard as the palm of ploughman!—this thou tell'st me,
As true thou tell'st me, when I say I love her;
But, saying thus, instead of oil and balm,
Thou lay'st in every gash that love hath given me
The knife that made it.

PAN. I speak no more than truth.

TRO. Thou dost not speak so much.

PAN. Faith, I'll not meddle in 't. Let her be as she is: if she be fair, 'tis the better for her; an she be not, she has the mends in her own hands.[d]

TRO. Good Pandarus,—how now, Pandarus?

PAN. I have had my labour for my travail; ill-thought on of her, and ill-thought on of you: gone between and between, but small thanks for my labour.

TRO. What, art thou angry, Pandarus? what, with me?

PAN. Because she's kin to me, therefore she's not so fair as Helen: an she were not kin to me, she would be as fair on Friday as Helen is on Sunday.[e] But what care I? I care not an she were a blackamoor; 't is all one to me.

TRO. Say I she is not fair?

PAN. I do not care whether you do or no. She's a fool to stay behind her father; let her to the Greeks; and so I'll tell her the next time I see her: for my part, I'll meddle nor make no more in the matter.

TRO. Pandarus,—

PAN. Not I.

TRO. Sweet Pandarus,—

PAN. Pray you, speak no more to me; I will leave all as I found it, and there an end.
[*Exit. An alarum.*

TRO. Peace, you ungracious clamours! peace, rude sounds!
Fools on both sides! Helen must needs be fair,
When with your blood you daily paint her thus.
I cannot fight upon this argument;
It is too starv'd a subject for my sword.
But Pandarus,—O gods, how do you plague me!
I cannot come to Cressid but by Pandar;
And he's as tetchy to be woo'd to woo,
As she is stubborn-chaste against all suit.

(*) Old text, *a-scorne*, corrected by Rowe. (†) First folio, *it*.

a — blench—] To *blench* meant to *flinch*, or *start off*. The word is found again in "The Winter's Tale," Act II. Sc. 2; in "Hamlet," Act II. Sc. 2; and in "Measure for Measure," Act IV. Sc. 5.

b — when she comes!—when is she thence?] So Rowe; the old editions having,—

"—— *then* she comes when *she is* thence."

c Handlest in thy discourse,—*O, that her hand*, &c.] This line, we surmise, has suffered from a compositor's transposition: the genuine reading, apparently, being,—

"Handlest in thy discourse her hand,—*O, that,*
In whose comparison," &c.

Unless, indeed, the words, "her hand," were intended to be repeated,—

"Handlest in thy discourse her hand—*O, that her hand*," &c.

In any case, it is evident from what follows,—"this thou tell'st me," &c.—that Troilus is repeating, or pretending to repeat, what Pandarus had said in praise of Cressida's hand; and the lines should be marked as a quotation.

d — she has the mends in her own hands.] This was a proverbial expression; the meaning,—She must make the best of it. So Burton, in his "Anatomy of Melancholy,"—"— and if men will be jealous in such cases, *the mends is in their own hands*—they must thank themselves."

e — she would be as fair on Friday as Helen is on Sunday.] We are not sure we understand this; it perhaps means,—She would be considered as fair in ordinary apparel as Helen in holiday finery.

Tell me, Apollo, for thy Daphne's love,
What Cressid is, what Pandar, and what we?
Her bed is India; there she lies, a pearl:
Between our Ilium and where she resides,
Let it be call'd the wild and wandering flood;
Ourself, the merchant; and this sailing Pandar,
Our doubtful hope, our convoy, and our bark.

Alarum. Enter ÆNEAS.

ÆNE. How now, prince Troilus! wherefore not afield?
TRO. Because not there: this woman's answer sorts,[a]
For womanish it is to be from thence.
What news, Æneas, from the field to-day?
ÆNE. That Paris is returned home, and hurt.
TRO. By whom, Æneas?
ÆNE. Troilus, by Menelaus.
TRO. Let Paris bleed: 'tis but a scar to scorn;
Paris is gor'd with Menelaus' horn. [*Alarum.*
ÆNE. Hark, what good sport is out of town to-day!
TRO. Better at home, if *would I might*, were *may.*—
But to the sport abroad;—are you bound thither?
ÆNE. In all swift haste.
TRO. Come, go we, then, together. [*Exeunt.*

SCENE II.—*The same. A Street.*

Enter CRESSIDA *and* ALEXANDER.

CRES. Who were those went by?
ALEX. Queen Hecuba and Helen.
CRES. And whither go they?
ALEX. Up to the eastern tower,
Whose height commands as subject all the vale,
To see the battle. Hector, whose patience
Is, as a virtue, fix'd, to-day was mov'd:
He chid* Andromache, and struck his armourer;
And, like as there were husbandry in war,
Before the sun rose, he was harness'd light,[b]
And to the field goes he; where every flower
Did, as a prophet, weep what it foresaw
In Hector's wrath.
CRES. What was his cause of anger?
ALEX. The noise goes, this: there is among the Greeks
A lord of Trojan blood, nephew to Hector;
They call him, Ajax.
CRES. Good; and what of him?
ALEX. They say he is a very man *per se*,
And stands alone.

CRES. So do all men,—unless they are drunk, sick, or have no legs.

ALEX. This man, lady, hath robbed many beasts of their particular additions;[c] he is as valiant as the lion, churlish as the bear, slow as the elephant: a man into whom nature hath so crowded humours, that his valour is crushed into folly, his folly sauced with discretion: there is no man hath a virtue, that he hath not a glimpse of; nor any man an attaint, but he carries some stain of it: he is melancholy without cause, and merry against the hair:[d] he hath the joints of every thing; but every thing so out of joint, that he is a gouty Briareus, many hands and no use; or purblind* Argus, all eyes and no sight.

CRES. But how should this man, that makes me smile, make Hector angry?

ALEX. They say, he yesterday coped Hector in the battle, and struck him down; the disdain† and shame whereof hath ever since kept Hector fasting and waking.

CRES. Who comes here?
ALEX. Madam, your uncle Pandarus.

Enter PANDARUS.

CRES. Hector's a gallant man.
ALEX. As may be in the world, lady.
PAN. What's that? what's that?
CRES. Good morrow, uncle Pandarus.

PAN. Good morrow, cousin Cressid: what do you talk of?—Good morrow, Alexander.—How do you, cousin? When were you at Ilium?

CRES. This morning, uncle.

PAN. What were you talking of, when I came? Was Hector armed and gone ere ye came to Ilium? Helen was not up, was she?

CRES. Hector was gone, but Helen was not up.
PAN. E'en so; Hector was stirring early.
CRES. That were we talking of, and of his anger.
PAN. Was he angry?
CRES. So he says here.

(*) First folio, *chides*.

(*) First folio, *purblinded*. (†) First folio, *disdaind*.

a — sorts,—] That is, *suits, fits, is appropriate.* As in "Henry V." Act IV. Sc. 1,—

"It *sorts* well with thy fierceness."

b *Before the sun rose*, he was harness'd light,—] Some corruption has been suspected here: and it is noticeable, that both in the quartos and folio the disputed word is spelt *lyte*, not *light*: yet the obvious meaning, that Hector was lightly armed, is sufficiently intelligible.

c — additions;] *Qualities*, or *characteristics*.

d — against the hair:] As we now say,—*against the grain*. The French have still the expression,—*à contrepoil*.

PAN. True, he was so; I know the cause too; he'll lay about him to-day, I can tell them that: and there's Troilus will not come far behind him; let them take heed of Troilus; I can tell them that too.

CRES. What, is he angry too?

PAN. Who, Troilus? Troilus is the better man of the two.

CRES. O, Jupiter! there's no comparison.

PAN. What, not between Troilus and Hector? Do you know a man, if you see him?

CRES. Ay, if I ever saw him before, and knew him.

PAN. Well, I say, Troilus is Troilus.

CRES. Then you say as I say; for, I am sure, he is not Hector.

PAN. No, nor* Hector is not Troilus, in some degrees.

CRES. 'Tis just to each of them; he is himself.

PAN. Himself! Alas, poor Troilus! I would, he were,—

CRES. So he is.

PAN. Condition, I had gone bare-foot to India.

CRES. He is not Hector.

PAN. Himself! no, he's not himself,—would 'a were himself! Well, the gods are above; time must friend or end. Well, Troilus, well,—I would, my heart were in her body!—No, Hector is not a better man than Troilus.

CRES. Excuse me.

(*) First folio, *not*.

PAN. He is elder.

CRES. Pardon me, pardon me.

PAN. The other 's not come to 't; you shall tell me another tale, when the other 's come to 't. Hector shall not have his wit* this year.

CRES. He shall not need it, if he have his own.

PAN. Nor his qualities,—

CRES. No matter.

PAN. Nor his beauty.

CRES. 'T would not become him,—his own 's better.

PAN. You have no judgment, niece: Helen herself swore the other day, that Troilus, for a brown favour, (for so 'tis, I must confess)—not brown neither—

CRES. No, but brown.

PAN. Faith, to say truth, brown and not brown.

CRES. To say the truth, true and not true.

PAN. She praised his complexion above Paris.

CRES. Why, Paris hath colour enough.

PAN. So he has.

CRES. Then Troilus should have too much: if she praised him above, his complexion is higher than his; he having colour enough, and the other higher, is too flaming a praise for a good complexion. I had as lief Helen's golden tongue had commended Troilus for a copper nose.

PAN. I swear to you, I think Helen loves him better than Paris.

CRES. Then she's a merry Greek,[a] indeed.

PAN. Nay, I am sure she does. She came to him the other day into the compassed window,—and you know he has not past three or four hairs on his chin.

CRES. Indeed, a tapster's arithmetic may soon bring his particulars therein to a total.

PAN. Why, he is very young: and yet will he, within three pound, lift as much as his brother Hector.

CRES. Is he so young a man, and so old a lifter?[b]

PAN. But, to prove to you that Helen loves him;—she came, and puts me her white hand to his cloven chin,—

CRES. Juno have mercy!—how came it cloven?

PAN. Why, you know, 'tis dimpled: I think his smiling becomes him better than any man in all Phrygia.

CRES. O, he smiles valiantly.

PAN. Does he not?

CRES. O yes, an 't were a cloud in autumn.

PAN. Why, go to then:—but to prove to you that Helen loves Troilus,—

CRES. Troilus will stand to the proof, if you'll prove it so.

PAN. Troilus! why, he esteems her no more than I esteem an addle egg.

CRES. If you love an addle egg as well as you love an idle head, you would eat chickens i' the shell.

PAN. I cannot choose but laugh, to think how she tickled his chin;—indeed, she has a marvellous white hand, I must needs confess.

CRES. Without the rack.

PAN. And she takes upon her to spy a white hair on his chain.

CRES. Alas, poor chin! many a wart is richer.

PAN. But there was such laughing! Queen Hecuba laughed, that her eyes ran o'er,—

CRES. With mill-stones.

PAN. And Cassandra laughed,—

CRES. But there was more temperate fire under the pot of her eyes;—did her eyes run o'er too?

PAN. And Hector laughed.

CRES. At what was all this laughing?

PAN. Marry, at the white hair that Helen spied on Troilus' chin.

CRES. An't had been a green hair, I should have laughed too.

PAN. They laughed not so much at the hair as at his pretty answer.

CRES. What was his answer?

PAN. Quoth she, *Here's but one and fifty hairs*[c] *on your chin, and one of them is white.*

CRES. This is her question.

PAN. That's true; make no question of that. *One and fifty hairs,* quoth he, *and one white: That white hair is my father, and all the rest are his sons. Jupiter!* quoth she, *which of these hairs is Paris, my husband? The forked one,* quoth he; *pluck 't out, and give it him.* But there was such laughing! and Helen so blushed, and Paris so chafed, and all the rest so laughed, that it passed.

CRES. So let it now; for it has been a great while going by.

PAN. Well, cousin, I told you a thing yesterday; think on't.

CRES. So I do.*

PAN. I'll be sworn 'tis true; he will weep you, an 'twere a man born in April.

CRES. And I'll spring up in his tears, an 'twere a nettle against May. [*A retreat sounded.*

PAN. Hark! they are coming from the field:

(*) Old text, *will.*—Rowe's correction.

a — a merry Greek,—] This expression, which seems to have meant a *wag,* or *humourist,* is frequently met with in old books. Our earliest English comedy, "Ralph Roister Doister," has a character, who is the droll of the piece, called "Mathewe Merygreeke." See, too, Act IV. Sc. 4, of the present play,—

"A woeful Cressid 'mongst the *merry Greeks.*"

(*) First folio, *does.*

b — *so old a* lifter?] A "lifter" was anciently a cant term for a thief; and we still retain it in *shop-lifter.*

c — one *and fifty hairs*—] The old text has, "— *two* and fifty hairs," &c., which Theobald changed, to make out the number of Priam and his fifty sons.

shall we stand up here, and see them as they pass toward Ilium? good niece, do; sweet niece Cressida.

CRES. At your pleasure.

PAN. Here, here, here's an excellent place; here we may see most bravely: I'll tell you them all by their names, as they pass by; but mark Troilus above the rest.

CRES. Speak not so loud.

ÆNEAS *passes over the stage.*

PAN. That's Æneas; is not that a brave man? he's one of the flowers of Troy, I can tell* you: but mark Troilus; you shall see anon.

ANTENOR *passes over.*

CRES. Who's that?

PAN. That's Antenor; he has a shrewd wit, I can tell you; and he's a man good enough: he's one o' the soundest judgments† in Troy, whosoever, and a proper man of person.—When comes Troilus?—I'll show you Troilus anon; if he see me, you shall see him nod at me.

CRES. Will he give you the nod?[a]

PAN. You shall see.

CRES. If he do, the rich[b] shall have more.

HECTOR *passes over.*

PAN. That's Hector, that, that, look you, that; there's a fellow!—Go thy way, Hector!—there's a brave man, niece!—O, brave Hector! (1)—Look how he looks! there's a countenance! is't not a brave man?

CRES. O, a‡ brave man!

PAN. Is 'a not? It does a man's heart good:—look you what hacks are on his helmet! look you yonder, do you see? look you there! there's no jesting: there's§ laying on, take't off who will,‖ as they say: there be hacks!

CRES. Be those with swords?

PAN. Swords! any thing, he cares not: an the devil come to him, it's all one: by God's lid, it does one's heart good.—Yonder comes Paris, yonder comes Paris: look ye yonder, niece; is't not a gallant man too, is't not?—

PARIS *passes over.*

Why, this is brave now.—Who said he came hurt home to-day? he's not hurt: why, this will do

(*) First folio omits, *tell.* (†) First folio, *judgement.*
(‡) First folio omits, *a.* (§) First folio omits, *there's.*
(‖) First folio, *ill.*

a *Will he give you the* nod?] To *give the nod* meant, we apprehend, like *to give the dor*—the using some gesture which turned the party against whom it was directed into ridicule.

Helen's heart good now, ha!—Would I could see Troilus now!—you shall see* Troilus anon.

HELENUS *passes over.*

CRES. Who's that?

PAN. That's Helenus:—I marvel where Troilus is:—that's Helenus;—I think he went not forth to-day:—that's Helenus.

CRES. Can Helenus fight, uncle?

PAN. Helenus! no:—yes, he'll fight indifferent well:—I marvel where Troilus is!—Hark! do you not hear the people cry, *Troilus?*—Helenus is a priest.

CRES. What sneaking fellow comes yonder?

TROILUS *passes over.*

PAN. Where? yonder? that's Deiphobus.—'Tis Troilus! there's a man, niece!—Hem!—Brave Troilus! the prince of chivalry!

CRES. Peace, for shame, peace!

PAN. Mark him; note† him;—O brave Troilus!—look well upon him, niece; look you how his sword is bloodied, and his helm more hacked than Hector's; and how he looks, and how he goes!—O, admirable youth! he ne'er saw three-and-twenty.—Go thy way, Troilus, go thy way!—Had I a sister were a grace, or a daughter a goddess, he should take his choice. O, admirable man! Paris?—Paris is dirt to him; and, I warrant, Helen, to change, would give an eye‡ to boot.

CRES. Here come more.

Forces *pass over the stage.*

PAN. Asses, fools, dolts! chaff and bran, chaff and bran! porridge after meat!—I could live and die i' the eyes of Troilus.—Ne'er look, ne'er look; the eagles are gone; crows and daws, crows and daws! I had rather be such a man as Troilus, than Agamemnon and all Greece.

CRES. There is among the Greeks, Achilles,—a better man than Troilus.

PAN. Achilles! a drayman, a porter, a very camel.

CRES. Well, well.

PAN. *Well, well?*—Why, have you any discretion? have you any eyes? do you know what a man is? Is not birth, beauty, good shape, dis-

(*) First folio omits, *see.* (†) First folio, *not.*
(‡) First folio, *give money.*

b *If he do, the* rich *shall have more.*] If "rich" is the genuine word, it must have conveyed some allusion now lost to us; possibly, however, it may be only a misprint for *wretch.*

course, manhood, learning, gentleness, virtue, youth, liberality, and such like,* the spice and salt that seasons a man?

CRES. Ay, a minced man: and then to be baked with no date in the pie,—for then the man's date is out.

PAN. You are such a† woman! a man knows not at what ward you lie.

CRES. Upon my back, to defend my belly; upon my wit, to defend my wiles; upon my secrecy, to defend mine honesty; my mask, to defend my beauty; and you, to defend all these: and at all these wards I lie,‡ at a thousand watches.

PAN. Say one of your watches.

CRES. Nay, I'll watch you for that; and that's one of the chiefest of them too: if I cannot ward what I would not have hit, I can watch you for telling how I took the blow; unless it swell past hiding, and then it's past watching.

PAN. You are such another!

Enter Troilus' Boy.

BOY. Sir, my lord would instantly speak with you.

PAN. Where?

BOY. At your own house; there he unarms him.[a]

PAN. Good boy, tell him I come. [*Exit* Boy.
I doubt he be hurt.—Fare ye well, good niece.

CRES. Adieu, uncle.

PAN. I'll be with you, niece, by and by.

CRES. To bring,[b] uncle.

PAN. Ay, a token from Troilus. [*Exit.*

CRES. By the same token—you are a bawd.—
Words, vows, gifts, tears, and love's full sacrifice,
He offers in another's enterprise:
But more in Troilus thousand fold I see
Than in the glass of Pandar's praise may be;
Yet hold I off. Women are angels, wooing:
Things won are done, joy's soul lies in the doing:
That she belov'd knows nought, that knows not this,—
Men prize the thing ungain'd more than it is:
That she was never yet, that ever knew
Love got so sweet, as when desire did sue:
Therefore this maxim out of love I teach,—
Achievement is command; ungain'd, beseech:[c]
Then* though my heart's content† firm love doth bear,
Nothing of that shall from mine eyes appear.
[*Exeunt.*

SCENE III.—*The* Grecian *Camp. Before* Agamemnon's *Tent.*

Trumpets. Enter AGAMEMNON, NESTOR, ULYSSES, MENELAUS, *and others.*

AGAM. Princes,
What grief hath set the jaundice on your cheeks?
The ample proposition that hope makes
In all designs begun on earth below,
Fails in the promis'd largeness: checks and disasters
Grow in the veins of actions highest rear'd;
As knots, by the conflúx of meeting sap,
Infect the sound pine, and divert his grain
Tortive and errant from his course of growth.
Nor, princes, is it matter new to us,
That we come short of our suppose so far,
That, after seven years' siege, yet Troy walls stand,
Sith every action that hath gone before,
Whereof we have record, trial did draw
Bias and thwart, not answering the aim,
And that unbodied figure of the thought
That gave't surmised shape. Why then, you princes,
Do you with cheeks abash'd behold our works;[d]
And call them shames,‡ which are, indeed, nought else
But the protractive trials of great Jove,
To find persistive constancy in men?
The fineness of which metal is not found
In Fortune's love; for then the bold and coward,
The wise and fool, the artist and unread,
The hard and soft, seem all affin'd and kin:
But, in the wind and tempest of her frown,
Distinction, with a broad§ and powerful fan,
Puffing at all, winnows the light away;
And what hath mass or matter, by itself
Lies rich in virtue and unmingled.

(*) First folio, *so forth.* (†) First folio, *such another woman.* (‡) First folio, *I lye at, at, &c.*

[a] — there he unarms him.] These words are only in the quartos.

[b] PAN. I'll be with you, niece, &c.
CRES. To bring, *uncle.*]

Mr. Dyce has supplied some examples of the peculiar expression, *to be with a person to bring,*—

"And I'll close with Bryan till I have gotten the thing
That he hath promis'd me, and then *I'll be with him to bring.*"
PEELE'S *Sir Clyomon and Sir Clamydes.*

"And here I'll have a fling at him, that's flat;
And, Balthazar, *I'll be with thee to bring.*"
KYD'S *Spanish Tragedy,* Act IV.

But the particular meaning it conveyed has yet to be disclosed.

[c] Achievement is *command; ungain'd,* beseech:] There is so much obscurity in the construction of this "maxim," that, although to us, in its terse irregularity, it appears conformable to Shakespeare's style, we are not surprised that Mr. Harness's neat substitution,—

"*Achiev'd men us* command," &c.

should be generally preferred.

[d] — *behold our* works;] Mr. Collier's annotator would read,— "— behold our *wrecks,*"—perhaps rightly.

(*) First folio, *That.* (†) First folio, *Contents.* (‡) First folio, *thinke them shame.* (§) First folio, *lowd.*

NEST. With due observance of thy godlike*
seat,
Great Agamemnon, Nestor shall apply
Thy latest words. In the reproof of chance
Lies the true proof of men: the sea being smooth,
How many shallow bauble boats dare sail
Upon her patient† breast, making their way
With those of nobler bulk!
But let the ruffian Boreas once enrage
The gentle Thetis, and, anon, behold
The strong-ribb'd bark through liquid mountains
cut,
Bounding between the two moist elements,
Like Perseus' horse: where's then the saucy boat,
Whose weak untimber'd sides but even now
Co-rivall'd greatness? either to harbour fled,

(*) First folio, *godly*. (†) Quartos, *ancient*.

Or made a toast for Neptune. Even so
Doth valour's show and valour's worth divide
In storms of Fortune: for in her ray and brightness,
The herd hath more annoyance by the brize,[a]
Than by the tiger; but when the splitting wind
Makes flexible the knees of knotted oaks,
And flies fled under shade, why, then the thing of courage,
As rous'd with rage, with rage doth sympathize,
And with an accent tun'd in self-same key,
Re-chides[b] to chiding Fortune.

ULYSS. Agamemnon,—
Thou great commander, nerve and bone of Greece,
Heart of our numbers, soul and only spirit,
In whom the tempers and the minds of all
Should be shut up,—hear what Ulysses speaks.
Besides the applause and approbation
The which,—most mighty, for thy place and sway,— [*To* AGAMEMNON.
And thou, most reverend, for thy stretch'd-out life,— [*To* NESTOR.
I give to both your speeches,—which were such,
As Agamemnon and the hand of Greece
Should hold up high in brass; and such again,
As venerable Nestor, hatch'd in silver,
Should with a bond of air (strong as the axletree
On which heaven rides) knit all the Greekish ears[c]
To his experienc'd tongue,—yet let it please both,—
Thou great, and wise,—to hear Ulysses speak.

AGAM. Speak, prince of Ithaca;[d] and be't of less expect
That matter needless, of importless burden,
Divide thy lips, than we are confident,
When rank Thersites opes his mastiff * jaws,
We shall hear music, wit, and oracle.

ULYSS. Troy, yet upon his basis, had been down,
And the great Hector's sword had lack'd a master,
But for these instances.
The specialty of rule hath been neglected:
And look how many Grecian tents do stand
Hollow upon this plain, so many hollow factions.
When that the general is not like the hive,
To whom the foragers shall all repair,
What honey is expected? Degree being vizarded,
The unworthiest shows as fairly in the mask.
The heavens themselves, the planets, and this centre,
Observe degree, priority, and place,
Insisture, course, proportion, season, form,
Office, and custom, in all line of order;
And therefore is the glorious planet, Sol,
In noble eminence enthron'd and spher'd
Amidst the other;[e] whose med'cinable eye
Corrects the ill aspécts of planets evil,
And posts, like the commandment of a king,
Sans check, to good and bad: but, when the planets,
In evil mixture, to disorder wander,(2)
What plagues and what portents! what mutiny!
What raging of the sea! shaking of earth!
Commotion in the winds! frights, changes, horrors,
Divert and crack, rend and deracinate
The unity and married calm of states
Quite from their fixure! O, when degree is shak'd,
Which is the ladder to all high designs,
The[f] enterprise is sick! How could communities,
Degrees in schools, and brotherhoods in cities,
Peaceful commérce from dividable shores,
The primogenitive[g] and due of birth,
Prerogative of age, crowns, sceptres, laurels,
But by degree, stand in authentic place?
Take but degree away, untune that string,
And, hark, what discord follows! each thing meets
In mere oppugnancy: the bounded waters
Should lift their bosoms higher than the shores,
And make a sop of all this solid globe:
Strength should be lord of imbecility,
And the rude son should strike his father dead:
Force should be right; or, rather, right and wrong
(Between whose endless jar justice resides)
Should lose their* names, and so should justice too.
Then every thing includes itself in power,
Power into will, will into appetite;
And appetite, an universal wolf,
So doubly seconded with will and power,
Must make perforce an universal prey,
And, last, eat up himself. Great Agamemnon,
This chaos, when degree is suffocate,
Follows the choking.
And this neglection of degree it is,
That by a pace goes backward, with† a purpose
It hath to climb. The general's disdain'd
By him one step below; he, by the next;
That next, by him beneath: so every step,
Exampled by the first pace that is sick

(*) Old text, *masticke*.

(*) First folio, *her*. (†) First folio, *in*.

[a] — *the* brize,—] The *horse-fly*, or *gad*.

[b] Re-chides *to chiding Fortune*.] The old text has *Retires:* for which Pope substituted *Returns*; Hanmer, *Replies*; and Mr. Dyce, *Retorts*: the two former are not sufficiently expressive, but the last will perhaps be more readily accepted than the word we have ventured to adopt.

[c] On *which* heaven rides) *knit all* the Greekish *ears*—] So the quartos: the folio reads,—

"*In* which *the Heavens ride*, knit all *Greekes* eares."

[d] Speak, prince of Ithaca; &c.] This speech is omitted in the quarto.

[e] *Amidst the* other;] Mr. Singer reads speciously, but certainly in error,—

"Amidst the *ether*."

[f] The *enterprise is sick!*] Hanmer has,—

"*Then* enterprise," &c.

[g] The primogenitive—] Mr. Collier asks, "Might we not read, *primogeniture?*"—forgetful that Rowe, Pope, Theobald, Warburton, Hanmer, and Capell all read, *primogeniture*.

Of his superior, grows to an envious fever
Of pale and bloodless emulation:
And 'tis this fever that keeps Troy on foot,
Not her own sinews. To end a tale of length,
Troy in our weakness stands,* not in her strength.

NEST. Most wisely hath Ulysses here discover'd
The fever whereof all our power is sick.

AGAM. The nature of the sickness found, Ulysses,
What is the remedy?

ULYSS. The great Achilles,—whom opinion crowns
The sinew and the forehand of our host,—
Having his ear full of his airy fame,
Grows dainty of his worth, and in his tent
Lies mocking our designs: with him, Patroclus,
Upon a lazy bed, the livelong day
Breaks scurril jests;
And with ridiculous and awkward action
(Which, slanderer, he *imitation* calls,)
He pageants us. Sometime, great Agamemnon,
Thy topless deputation he puts on;
And, like a strutting player,—whose conceit
Lies in his hamstring, and doth think it rich
To hear the wooden dialogue and sound
'Twixt his stretch'd footing and the scaffoldage,—
Such to-be-pitied and o'er-wrested[a] seeming
He acts thy greatness in: and when he speaks,
'Tis like a chime a-mending; with terms unsquar'd,
Which, from the tongue of roaring Typhon dropp'd,
Would seem† hyperboles. At this fusty stuff,
The large Achilles, on his press'd bed lolling,
From his deep chest laughs out a loud applause;
Cries—*Excellent!—'tis Agamemnon just!—*
Now play me Nestor;—hem, and stroke thy beard,
As he, being 'dress'd[b] *to some oration.*
That's done;—as near as the extremest ends
Of parallels; as like as Vulcan and his wife:
Yet god Achilles still cries, *Excellent!*
'Tis Nestor right! Now play him me, Patroclus,
Arming to answer in a night alarm.
And then, forsooth, the faint defects of age
Must be the scene of mirth; to cough and spit,
And with a palsy-fumbling on his gorget,
Shake in and out the rivet:—and at this sport
Sir Valour dies; cries, *O! enough, Patroclus;*
Or give me ribs of steel! I shall split all
In pleasure of my spleen. And in this fashion,
All our abilities, gifts, natures, shapes,
Severals and generals of grace exact,[c]
Achievements, plots, orders, preventions,
Excitements to the field, or speech for truce,
Success or loss, what is or is not, serves
As stuff for these two to make paradoxes.

NEST. And in the imitation of these twain
(Who, as Ulysses says, opinion crowns
With an imperial voice) many are infect.
Ajax is grown self-will'd; and bears his head
In such a rein, in full as proud a place
As broad Achilles:* keeps his tent like him;
Makes factious feasts; rails on our state of war,
Bold as an oracle; and sets Thersites—
A slave whose gall coins slanders like a mint—
To match us in comparisons with dirt;
To weaken and discredit our exposure,
How rank soever rounded-in with danger.

ULYSS. They tax our policy, and call it cowardice;
Count wisdom as no member of the war;
Forestall prescience, and esteem no act
But that of hand: the still and mental parts,—
That do contrive how many hands shall strike,
When fitness calls† them on; and know, by measure
Of their observant toil, the enemies' weight,—
Why, this hath not a finger's dignity:
They call this—bed-work, mappery, closet-war;
So that the ram, that batters down the wall,
For the great swing and rudeness of his poise,
They place before his hand that made the engine,
Or those that with the fineness of their souls
By reason guide his execution.

NEST. Let this be granted, and Achilles' horse
Makes many Thetis' sons. [*Trumpet sounds.*

AGAM. What trumpet? look, Menelaus.

MEN. From Troy.

Enter ÆNEAS.

AGAM. What would you 'fore our tent?

ÆNE. Is this great Agamemnon's tent, I pray you?

AGAM. Even this.

(*) First folio, *lives.* (†) First folio, *seemes.*

(*) First folio inserts, *and.* (†) First folio, *call.*

[a] — o'er-wrested *seeming*—] "O'er-wrested" means *over-wound;* the image being taken from the instrument called a *wrest,* which was used for tuning the harp. In the old copies we have, "o'er rested," and the same mistake occurs in a subsequent passage, Act III. Sc. 3, where Calchas says,—

"—— But this Antenor,
I know is such a *wrest* in their affairs," &c.—

the old text reading,—

"—— a *rest* in their affairs," &c.

[b] — *being* 'dress'd—] That is, *addrest, prepared.*

[c] Severals and generals of grace exact,—] Mr. Collier's annotator reads,—

"Severals and generals *all* grace *extract,*" &c.;—

and Mr. Singer,—

"—— *are* of grace extract."

We should prefer,—

"Severals and generals of grace *and act,*" &c.—

but are not quite convinced that any change is needed.

ÆNE. May one, that is a herald and a prince,
Do a fair message to his kingly ears?
AGAM. With surety stronger than Achilles' arm,
'Fore all the Greekish heads, which with one voice
Call Agamemnon head and general.
ÆNE. Fair leave and large security.—How may
A stranger to those most imperial looks
Know them from eyes of other mortals?
AGAM. How?
ÆNE. Ay; I ask, that I might waken reverence,
And bid the cheek be ready with a blush
Modest as morning when she coldly eyes
The youthful Phœbus:
Which is that god in office, guiding men?
Which is the high and mighty Agamemnon?
AGAM. This Trojan scorns us; or the men of Troy
Are ceremonious courtiers.
ÆNE. Courtiers as free, as debonair; unarm'd,
As bending angels; that's their fame in peace:
But when they would seem soldiers, they have galls,
Good arms, strong joints, true swords; and Jove's accord,[a]
Nothing so full of heart. But peace, Æneas,
Peace, Trojan; lay thy finger on thy lips!
The worthiness of praise distains his worth,
If that the* prais'd himself bring the praise forth:
But what the repining enemy commends,
That breath fame blows; that praise, sole pure, transcends.[b]
AGAM. Sir, you of Troy, call you yourself Æneas?
ÆNE. Ay, Greek, that is my name.
AGAM. What's your affair, I pray you?
ÆNE. Sir, pardon; 'tis for Agamemnon's ears.
AGAM. He hears nought privately that comes from Troy.
ÆNE. Nor I from Troy come not to whisper him:
I bring a trumpet to awake his ear;
To set his sense on the attentive bent,
And then to speak.
AGAM. Speak frankly as the wind;
It is not Agamemnon's sleeping hour:
That thou shalt know, Trojan, he is awake,
He tells thee so himself.
ÆNE. Trumpet, blow loud;
Send thy brass voice through all these lazy tents;
And every Greek of mettle, let him know,
What Troy means fairly shall be spoke aloud;
[*Trumpet sounds.*
We have, great Agamemnon, here in Troy
A prince call'd Hector,—Priam is his father,—
Who in this dull and long-continu'd truce
Is rusty grown; he bade me take a trumpet,
And to this purpose speak.(3) Kings, princes, lords!
If there be one among the fair'st of Greece,
That holds his honour higher than his ease;
That seeks his praise more than he fears his peril;
That knows his valour, and knows not his fear;
That loves his mistress more than in confession,
(With truant vows to her own lips he loves)
And dare avow her beauty and her worth
In other arms than hers,—to him this challenge.
Hector, in view of Trojans and of Greeks,
Shall make it good, or do his best to do it,
He hath a lady, wiser, fairer, truer,
Than ever Greek did compass in his arms;
And will to-morrow with his trumpet call,
Mid-way between your tents and walls of Troy,
To rouse a Grecian that is true in love:
If any come, Hector shall honour him;
If none, he'll say in Troy when he retires,
The Grecian dames are sun-burnt, and not worth
The splinter of a lance. Even so much.
AGAM. This shall be told our lovers, lord Æneas;
If none of them have soul in such a kind,
We left them all at home: but we are soldiers;
And may that soldier a mere recreant prove,
That means not, hath not, or is not in love!
If then one is, or hath, or means to be,
That one meets Hector; if none else, I am he.*
NEST. Tell him of Nestor, one that was a man
When Hector's grandsire suck'd: he is old now;
But if there be not in our Grecian host†
One noble man that hath one spark of fire

(*) First folio, *he*.

a —— *and Jove's* accord,
Nothing so full of heart.]

Mr. Malone had not "the smallest doubt" that the poet wrote,—

"—— and Jove's *a god*
Nothing so full of heart."

We have very grave doubts whether he wrote anything of the kind; and are equally sceptical of "*Jove's accord*" being, like Horace's "*Jove probante*," an ablative absolute, as Steevens surmised. To us, "accord" appears to be a depravation of some word signifying of old a membraneous covering or receptacle for the heart; but this word we must admit our inability to supply.

(*) First folio, *I'll be he*. (†) First folio, *mould*.

b *But what the repining enemy commends,*
That breath fame blows; that praise, sole pure, *transcends.*]

With the exception of Mr. Collier's annotator, who substitutes the senseless compound *soul-pure*, for "sole pure," the scholiasts appear to be perfectly satisfied with this passage as it stands in the ancient copies, and it would seem presumptuous, therefore, to disturb the text. At the same time, we entertain a firm conviction that Shakespeare has suffered here, as in other places, by a silly transposition of his words, and that he must have written,—

"But what the repining enemy commends,
That breath fame blows; that praise *pure Sol* transcends."

To answer for his love, tell him from me,—
I'll hide my silver beard in a gold beaver,
And in my vantbrace put this wither'd brawn;
And, meeting him, will tell him that my lady
Was fairer than his grandame, and as chaste
As may be in the world: his youth in flood,
I'll prove this truth with my three drops of blood.

ÆNE. Now heavens forbid such scarcity of youth![a]

ULYSS. Amen.

AGAM. Fair lord Æneas, let me touch your hand;
To our pavilion shall I lead you, sir.*
Achilles shall have word of this intent;
So shall each lord of Greece, from tent to tent:
Yourself shall feast with us before you go,
And find the welcome of a noble foe.

[*Exeunt all except* ULYSSES *and* NESTOR.

ULYSS. Nestor,—

NEST. What says Ulysses?

ULYSS. I have a young conception in my brain,
Be you my time to bring it to some shape.

NEST. What is't?

ULYSS. This 'tis:—
Blunt wedges rive hard knots: the seeded pride
That hath to this maturity blown up
In rank Achilles must or now be cropp'd,
Or, shedding, breed a nursery of like evil,
To overbulk us all.

NEST. Well, and how?

ULYSS. This challenge that the gallant Hector sends,
However it is spread in general name,
Relates in purpose only to Achilles.

NEST. The purpose is perspicuous even as substance,
Whose grossness little characters sum up:
And, in the publication, make no strain,
But that Achilles, were his brain as barren
As banks of Lybia,—though, Apollo knows,
'Tis dry enough,—will, with great speed of judgment,
Ay, with celerity, find Hector's purpose
Pointing on him.

ULYSS. And wake him to the answer, think you?

NEST. Yes, 'tis most meet: who may you else oppose,
That can from Hector bring his honour* off,
If not Achilles? Though't be a sportful combat,
Yet in this trial much opinion dwells;
For here the Trojans taste our dear'st repute
With their fin'st palate: and trust to me, Ulysses,
Our imputation[b] shall be oddly[c] pois'd
In this wild action; for the success,
Although particular, shall give a scantling
Of good or bad unto the general;
And in such indexes, although small pricks
To their subsequent volumes, there is seen
The baby figure of the giant mass
Of things to come at large. It is suppos'd,
He that meets Hector issues from our choice;
And choice, being mutual act of all our souls,
Makes merit her election; and doth boil,
As 'twere from forth us all, a man distill'd
Out of our virtues; who miscarrying,
What heart receives from hence the conquering part,
To steel a strong opinion to themselves?
Which entertain'd, limbs are† his instruments,[d]
In no less working than are swords and bows
Directive by the limbs.

ULYSS. Give pardon to my speech;—
Therefore 'tis meet Achilles meet not Hector.
Let us, like merchants, show our foulest wares,
And think, perchance, they'll sell; if not,
The lustre of the better yet to show,
Shall show the better.[e] Do not consent
That ever Hector and Achilles meet;
For both our honour and our shame in this
Are dogg'd with two strange followers.

NEST. I see them not with my old eyes; what are they?

ULYSS. What glory our Achilles shares from Hector,
Were he not proud, we all should share with him:
But he already is too insolent;
And we were better parch in Afric sun
Than in the pride and salt scorn of his eyes,
Should he 'scape Hector fair: if he were foil'd,
Why, then we did our main opinion crush
In taint of our best man. No, make a lottery;
And, by device, let blockish Ajax (4) draw
The sort[f] to fight with Hector: among ourselves,

(*) First folio, *first*.

(*) Quarto, *those honours*. (†) Old text inserts, *in*.

a *Now heavens* forbid *such scarcity of* youth!] The quarto reads,—Now heavens *forfend* such scarcity of *men!*

b — imputation—] Mr. Collier, following his annotator, reads, "reputation," neither being aware that "imputation" was often used in that sense: see "Hamlet," Act V. Sc. 2,—"I mean, sir, for his weapon; but in the *imputation* laid on him by them, in his meed he's unfellowed."

c — oddly—] That is, *unequally*.

d Which entertain'd, limbs are his instruments,—] This and the two following lines are omitted in the quarto.

e The lustre of the better *yet to show,*
Shall show the better.]

So the folio: the quarto reads,—

The lustre of the better shall exceed,
By showing the worse first.

f The sort—] That is, the *lot*.

Give him allowance as the worthier man,[a]
For that will physic the great Myrmidon,
Who broils in loud applause, and make him fall
His crest that prouder than blue Iris bends.
If the dull, brainless Ajax come safe off,
We'll dress him up in voices: if he fail,
Yet go we under our opinion still,
That we have better men. But, hit or miss,
Our project's life this shape of sense assumes,—
Ajax employ'd plucks down Achilles' plumes.

NEST. Ulysses,
Now I begin to relish thy advice;[b]
And I will give a taste of it forthwith
To Agamemnon: go we to him straight.
Two curs shall tame each other: pride alone
Must tarre[c] the mastiffs on, as 'twere their bone.
[*Exeunt.*

a — *as the worthier man,*—] The quarto reads,—*for the better man.*

b Ulysses,
Now *I begin to relish thy advice;*]
The old text reads,—
"*Now, Ulysses,* I begin," &c.

c — tarre—] To *tarre* means to *provoke.* See note (a), p. 311, Vol. I.

ACT II.

SCENE I.—*Another part of the* Grecian *Camp.*

Enter AJAX *and* THERSITES.(1)

AJAX. Thersites,—

THER. Agamemnon—how if he had boils, full, all over, generally?—

AJAX. Thersites,—

THER. And those boils did run?—Say so,—did not the general run then?* were not that a botchy core?[a]—

AJAX. Dog,—

THER. Then would come some matter from him; I see none now.

AJAX. Thou bitch-wolf's son, canst thou not hear? Feel, then. [*Strikes him.*

THER. The plague of Greece upon thee, thou mongrel beef-witted lord!

AJAX. Speak then, thou vinewedst[b] leaven, speak: I will beat thee into handsomeness.

THER. I shall sooner rail thee into wit and holiness: but I think thy horse will sooner con an oration than thou learn a prayer without book. Thou canst strike, canst thou? a red murrain o' thy jade's tricks!

AJAX. Toadstool! learn me the proclamation.

THER. Dost thou think I have no sense, thou strikest me thus?

AJAX. The proclamation,—

THER. Thou art proclaimed a fool, I think.

(*) First folio omits, *then*.

a — *a botchy* core?—] Query, "a botchy *cur*"?

b — vinewedst *leaven*,—] *Vinewed* is mouldy or decayed. In the folio the word is misprinted *whinid'st:* the quarto reads, "unsalted."

AJAX. Do not, porcupine,[a] do not; my fingers itch.

THER. I would thou didst itch from head to foot, and I had the scratching of thee; I would make thee the loathsomest scab in Greece. When thou art forth in the incursions, thou strikest as slow as another.[b]

AJAX. I say, the proclamation,—

THER. Thou grumblest and railest every hour on Achilles; and thou art as full of envy at his greatness as Cerberus is at Proserpina's beauty, ay, that thou barkest at him.

AJAX. Mistress Thersites!

THER. Thou shouldst strike him.

AJAX. Cobloaf!

THER. He would pun thee into shivers with his fist, as a sailor breaks a biscuit.

AJAX. You whoreson cur! [*Beating him.*

THER. Do, do![c]

AJAX. Thou stool for a witch!

THER. Ay, do, do; thou sodden-witted lord! thou hast no more brain than I have in mine elbows; an assinego[d] may tutor thee. Thou scurvy-valiant ass! thou art here but to thrash Trojans; and thou art bought and sold[e] among those of any wit, like a Barbarian slave. If thou use to beat me, I will begin at thy heel, and tell what thou art by inches, thou thing of no bowels, thou!

AJAX. You dog!

THER. You scurvy lord!

AJAX. You cur! [*Beating him.*

THER. Mars his idiot! do, rudeness! do, camel! do, do!

Enter ACHILLES *and* PATROCLUS.

ACHIL. Why, how now, Ajax! wherefore do you thus?*
How now, Thersites! what's the matter, man?

THER. You see him there, do you?

ACHIL. Ay; what's the matter?

THER. Nay, look upon him.

ACHIL. So I do; what's the matter?

THER. Nay, but regard him well.

ACHIL. *Well!* why, I do so.

THER. But yet you look not well upon him; for, whosoever you take him to be, he is Ajax.

ACHIL. I know that, fool.

THER. Ay, but that fool knows not himself.

AJAX. Therefore I beat thee.

THER. Lo, lo, lo, lo, what modicums of wit he utters! his evasions have ears thus long. I have bobbed his brain more than he has beat my bones: I will buy nine sparrows for a penny, and his *pia mater* is not worth the ninth part of a sparrow. This lord, Achilles, Ajax,—who wears his wit in his belly, and his guts in his head,—I'll tell you what I say of him.

ACHIL. What?

THER. I say, this Ajax—

[AJAX *offers to beat him,* ACHILLES *interposes.*

ACHIL. Nay, good Ajax.

THER. Has not so much wit—

ACHIL. Nay, I must hold you.

THER. As will stop the eye of Helen's needle, for whom he comes to fight.

ACHIL. Peace, fool!

THER. I would have peace and quietness, but the fool will not: he there; that he; look you there.

AJAX. O, thou damned cur! I shall—

ACHIL. Will you set your wit to a fool's?

THER. No, I warrant you; for a fool's will shame it.

PATR. Good words, Thersites.

ACHIL. What's the quarrel?

AJAX. I bade the vile owl go learn me the tenour of the proclamation, and he rails upon me.

THER. I serve thee not.

AJAX. Well, go to, go to.

THER. I serve here voluntary.

ACHIL. Your last service was sufferance, 'twas not voluntary,—no man is beaten voluntary: Ajax was here the voluntary, and you as under an impress.

THER. Even so?—a great deal of your wit, too, lies in your sinews, or else there be liars. Hector shall have a great catch, if he knock out either of your brains; 'a* were as good crack a fusty nut with no kernel.

ACHIL. What, with me too, Thersites?

THER. There's Ulysses and old Nestor,—whose wit was mouldy ere your † grandsires had nails on their toes,—yoke you like draught oxen, and make you plough up the wars.‡

ACHIL. What, what?

THER. Yes, good sooth; to, Achilles! to, Ajax! to![f]

AJAX. I shall cut out your tongue.

THER. 'Tis no matter; I shall speak as much as thou, afterwards.

(*) First folio, *this*.

(*) First folio, *he*. (†) Old text, *their*. (‡) First folio, *warre*.

a — porcupine,—] Here, as in other passages where the word occurs, it is spelt "porpentine," the old form, which ought perhaps to have been retained.

b When thou art forth in the incursions, thou strikest as slow as another.] This is omitted in the folio.

c Do, do!] An expression of contempt, which was probably accompanied by some mocking gesture or grimace.

d — *an* assinego—] "Assinego" is a Portuguese word for an ass.

e — bought and sold—] That is, *out-witted, betrayed*. See note (a), p. 318, Vol. II.

f — to, Achilles! to, Ajax! to!] *To! to!* are words of encouragement which ploughmen of old employed to their draught horses and oxen.

PATR. No more words, Thersites; peace!*

THER. I will hold my peace when Achilles' brach† bids me, shall I?

ACHIL. There's for you, Patroclus.

THER. I will see you hanged, like clotpoles, ere I come any more to your tents; I will keep where there is wit stirring, and leave the faction of fools. [*Exit.*

PATR. A good riddance.

ACHIL. Marry, this, sir, is proclaim'd through all our host:—
That Hector, by the fifth hour of the sun,
Will, with a trumpet, 'twixt our tents and Troy,
To-morrow morning call some knight to arms,
That hath a stomach; and such a one, that dare
Maintain,—I know not what; 'tis trash. Farewell.

AJAX. Farewell. Who shall answer him?

ACHIL. I know not, 'tis put to lottery; otherwise
He knew his man.

AJAX. O, meaning you?—I'll go learn more of it. [*Exeunt severally.*

SCENE II.—Troy. *A Room in* Priam's *Palace.*

Enter PRIAM, HECTOR, TROILUS, PARIS, *and* HELENUS.

PRI. After so many hours, lives, speeches spent,
Thus once again says Nestor from the Greeks:—
Deliver Helen, and all damage else—
As honour, loss of time, travail, expense,
Wounds, friends, and what else dear that is consum'd
In hot digestion of this cormorant war,—
Shall be struck off:—Hector, what say you to't?

HECT. Though no man lesser fears the Greeks than I
As far as toucheth‡ my particular,
Yet, dread Priam,
There is no lady of more softer bowels,
More spongy to suck in the sense of fear,
More ready to cry out—*Who knows what follows?*
Than Hector is. The wound of peace is surety,
Surety secure;[a] but modest doubt is call'd
The beacon of the wise, the tent that searches
To the bottom of the worst. Let Helen go:
Since the first sword was drawn about this question,
Every tithe soul, 'mongst many thousand dismes,[b]
Hath been as dear as Helen,—I mean, of ours:
If we have lost so many tenths of ours,
To guard a thing not ours, nor worth to us,
Had it our name, the value of one ten,
What merit's in that reason which denies
The yielding of her up?

TROIL. Fie, fie, my brother!
Weigh you the worth and honour of a king,
So great as our dread father, in a scale
Of common ounces? will you with counters sum
The past-proportion of his infinite?
And buckle-in a waist most fathomless
With spans and inches so diminutive
As fears and reasons? fie, for godly shame!

HEL. No marvel, though you bite so sharp at reasons,[c]
You are so empty of them. Should not our father
Bear the great sway of his affairs with reasons,
Because your speech hath none that tells him so?

TROIL. You are for dreams and slumbers, brother priest;
You fur your gloves with reason. Here are your reasons:
You know an enemy intends you harm;
You know a sword employ'd is perilous,
And reason flies the object of all harm:
Who marvels, then, when Helenus beholds
A Grecian and his sword, if he do set
The very wings of reason to his heels,
And fly like chidden Mercury from Jove,[d]
Or like a star dis-orb'd?—Nay, if we talk of reason,
Let's shut our gates, and sleep: manhood and honour
Should have hare*-hearts, would they but fat their thoughts
With this cramm'd reason: reason and respect
Make livers pale, and lustihood deject.

HECT. Brother, she is not worth what she doth cost
The holding.

TROIL. What's aught, but as 'tis valued?

HECT. But value dwells not in particular will;
It holds his estimate and dignity
As well wherein 'tis precious of itself
As in the prizer: 'tis mad† idolatry,
To make the service greater than the god;
And the will dotes, that is attributive‡
To what infectiously itself affects,
Without some image of the affected merit.

TROIL. I take to-day a wife, and my election
Is led on in the conduct of my will;
My will enkindled by mine eyes and ears,
Two traded pilots 'twixt the dangerous shores

(*) First folio omits, *peace*. (†) Old text, *brooch*. (‡) First folio, *touches*.

[a] Surety secure;] In other words, over-confident assurance.

[b] — dismes,—] *Tenths*.

[c] No marvel, though you bite so sharp at reasons, &c.] Shakespeare repeats this poor quibble on *reasons* and *raisins* more than once. See note (e), p. 144, Vol. II.

[d] And fly like chidden Mercury, &c.] This and the following line are transposed in the folio.

(*) First folio, *hard*. (†) First folio, *made*. (‡) First folio, *inclineable*.

Of will and judgment: how may I avoid,
Although my will distaste what it elected,
The wife I chose? there can be no evasion
To blench from this, and to stand firm by honour:
We turn not back the silks upon the merchant,
When we have soil'd* them; nor the remainder viands
We do not throw in unrespective sieve†
Because we now are full. It was thought meet,
Paris should do some vengeance on the Greeks:
Your breath of full consent bellied his sails;
The seas and winds (old wranglers) took a truce,
And did him service: he touch'd the ports desir'd;
And, for an old aunt,[a] whom the Greeks held captive,
He brought a Grecian queen, whose youth and freshness
Wrinkles Apollo's, and makes stale[b] the morning.
Why keep we her? the Grecians keep our aunt:
Is she worth keeping? why, she is a pearl,
Whose price hath launch'd above a thousand ships,
And turn'd crown'd kings to merchants.
If you'll avouch 'twas wisdom Paris went,
(As you must needs, for you all cried—*Go, go!*)
If you'll confess he brought home noble prize,
(As you must needs, for you all clapp'd your hands,
And cried—*Inestimable!*) why do you now
The issue of your proper wisdoms rate,
And do a deed that fortune never did,—
Beggar the estimation which you priz'd
Richer than sea and land? O, theft most base,
That we have stol'n what we do fear to keep!
But, thieves, unworthy of a thing so stol'n,
That in their country did them that disgrace,
We fear to warrant in our native place!

CAS. [*Without.*] Cry, Trojans, cry!

PRI. What noise? what shriek is this?

TROIL. 'T is our mad sister, I do know her voice.

CAS. [*Without.*] Cry, Trojans!

HECT. It is Cassandra.

(*) First folio, *spoyl'd*. (†) First folio, *same*.

[a] — an old aunt,—] This was Hesione, Priam's sister.

[b] — *makes* stale *the morning.*] The quarto reads,—"makes *pale* the morning," &c.

Enter CASSANDRA, *raving*.(2)

CAS. Cry, Trojans, cry! lend me ten thousand eyes,
And I will fill them with prophetic tears.

HECT. Peace, sister, peace!

CAS. Virgins and boys, mid-age and wrinkled eld,[a]
Soft infancy, that nothing canst* but cry,
Add to my clamour! let us pay betimes
A moiety of that mass of moan to come.
Cry, Trojans, cry! practise your eyes with tears!
Troy must not be, nor goodly Ilion stand;
Our fire-brand brother,[b] Paris, burns us all.
Cry, Trojans, cry! a Helen and a woe!
Cry, cry! Troy burns, or else let Helen go.
[*Exit*.

HECT. Now, youthful Troilus, do not these high strains
Of divination in our sister work
Some touches of remorse? or is your blood
So madly hot, that no discourse of reason,
Nor fear of bad success in a bad cause,
Can qualify the same?

TROIL. Why, brother Hector,
We may not think the justness of each act
Such and no other than event doth form it;
Nor once deject the courage of our minds,
Because Cassandra's mad; her brain-sick raptures
Cannot distaste the goodness of a quarrel,
Which hath our several honours all engag'd
To make it gracious. For my private part,
I am no more touch'd than all Priam's sons:
And Jove forbid there should be done amongst us
Such things as might offend the weakest spleen
To fight for and maintain!

PAR. Else might the world convince of levity
As well my undertakings as your counsels:
But I attest the gods, your full consent
Gave wings to my propension, and cut off
All fears attending on so dire a project.
For what, alas, can these my single arms?
What propugnation is in one man's valour,
To stand the push and enmity of those
This quarrel would excite? Yet, I protest,
Were I alone to pass[c] the difficulties,
And had as ample power as I have will,
Paris should ne'er retract what he hath done,
Nor faint in the pursuit.

PRI. Paris, you speak
Like one besotted on your sweet delights:
You have the honey still, but these the gall;
So to be valiant is no praise at all.

PAR. Sir, I propose not merely to myself
The pleasures such a beauty brings with it;
But I would have the soil of her fair rape
Wip'd off, in honourable keeping her.
What treason were it to the ransack'd queen,
Disgrace to your great worths, and shame to me,
Now to deliver her possession up
On terms of base compulsion! Can it be
That so degenerate a strain as this,
Should once set footing in your generous bosoms?
There's not the meanest spirit on our party,
Without a heart to dare, or sword to draw,
When Helen is defended; nor none so noble,
Whose life were ill bestow'd, or death unfam'd,
Where Helen is the subject: then, I say,
Well may we fight for her, whom, we know well,
The world's large spaces cannot parallel.

HECT. Paris, and Troilus, you have both said well;
And on the cause and question now in hand
Have gloz'd,—but superficially; not much
Unlike young men, whom Aristotle thought
Unfit to hear moral philosophy:[d]
The reasons you allege do more conduce
To the hot passion of distemper'd blood,
Than to make up a free determination
'Twixt right and wrong; for pleasure and revenge
Have ears more deaf than adders to the voice
Of any true decision. Nature craves
All dues be render'd to their owners; now,
What nearer debt in all humanity,
Than wife is to the husband? If this law
Of nature be corrupted through affection;
And that great minds, of partial indulgence
To their benumbed wills, resist the same;
There is a law in each well-order'd nation,
To curb those raging appetites that are
Most disobedient and refractory.
If Helen, then, be wife to Sparta's king,—
As it is known she is,—these moral laws
Of nature and of nations* speak aloud
To have her back return'd: thus to persist
In doing wrong extenuates not wrong,
But makes it much more heavy. Hector's opinion
Is this, in way of truth: yet, ne'ertheless,

(*) First folio, *can*.

[a] — *wrinkled* eld,—] The quarto has *elders*; the folio, *old*.

[b] Our fire-brand brother,—] An allusion to Hecuba having dreamed, when pregnant with Paris, she should bring forth a burning torch,—

"—— *et face prægnans*
Cisseis regina Parin creat."
Æneid, X. v. 705.

[c] — pass *the difficulties*,—] A very doubtful expression. Mr. Collier's annotator reads *poise* for "pass."

(*) First folio, *Nation*.

[d] —— not much
Unlike young men, whom Aristotle thought
Unfit to hear moral philosophy:]
Did Shakespeare find this observation in the earlier play on which he based his "Troilus and Cressida," or borrow it from Bacon, or obtain it immediately from Aristotle? The inquiry is of some importance. Aristotle speaks of politics—*τῆς πολιτικῆς οὐκ ἐστὶν οἰκεῖος ἀκροατὴς ὁ νέος*—though in the passage above, as in Bacon's "Advancement of Learning," the remark is applied to morals.

My spritely brethren, I propend to you
In resolution to keep Helen still;
For 'tis a cause that hath no mean dependance
Upon our joint and several dignities.

TROIL. Why, there you touch'd the life of our design:
Were it not glory that we more affected
Than the performance of our heaving spleens,
I would not wish a drop of Trojan blood
Spent more in her defence. But, worthy Hector,
She is a theme of honour and renown;
A spur to valiant and magnanimous deeds;
Whose present courage may beat down our foes,
And fame in time to come canónize us:
For, I presume, brave Hector would not lose
So rich advantage of a promis'd glory,
As smiles upon the forehead of this action,
For the wide world's revénue.

HECT. I am yours,
You valiant offspring of great Priamus.—
I have a roisting challenge sent amongst
The dull and factious nobles of the Greeks,
Will strike amazement to their drowsy spirits:
I was advértis'd their great general slept,
Whilst emulation in the army crept;
This, I presume, will wake him. [*Exeunt.*

SCENE III.—*The* Grecian *Camp.* *Before* Achilles' *Tent.*

Enter THERSITES.

THER. How now, Thersites! what, lost in the labyrinth of thy fury? Shall the elephant Ajax carry it thus? he beats me, and I rail at him:

O, worthy satisfaction! would it were otherwise; that I could beat him, whilst he railed at me: 'sfoot, I'll learn to conjure and raise devils, but I'll see some issue of my spiteful execrations. Then there's Achilles,—a rare enginer. If Troy be not taken till these two undermine it, the walls will stand till they fall of themselves. O, thou great thunder-darter of Olympus, forget that thou art Jove, the king of gods; and, Mercury, lose all the serpentine craft of thy *caduceus;* if ye * take not that little-little less-than-little wit from them that they have! which short-armed ignorance itself knows is so abundant scarce, it will not in circumvention deliver a fly from a spider, without drawing their† massy irons and cutting the web. After this, the vengeance on the whole camp! or, rather, the bone-ache! for that, methinks, is the curse dependant on those that war for a placket. I have said my prayers; and devil envy, say Amen.—What, ho! my lord Achilles!

Enter PATROCLUS.

PATR. Who's there? Thersites! Good Thersites, come in and rail.

THER. If I could have remembered a gilt counterfeit, thou wouldst not have slipped out of my contemplation:[a] but it is no matter; thyself upon thyself! The common curse of mankind, folly and ignorance, be thine in great revenue, heaven bless thee from a tutor, and discipline come not near thee! Let thy blood be thy direction till thy death! then if she that lays thee out says thou art a fair corse, I'll be sworn and sworn upon't, she never shrouded any but lazars. Amen.—Where's Achilles?

PATR. What, art thou devout? wast thou in ‡ prayer?

THER. Ay; the heavens hear me!

Enter ACHILLES.

ACHIL. Who's there?

PATR. Thersites, my lord.

ACHIL. Where, where?—Art thou come? Why, my cheese, my digestion, why hast thou not served thyself in to my table so many meals? Come,—what's Agamemnon?

THER. Thy commander, Achilles:—then tell me, Patroclus, what's Achilles?

PATR. Thy lord, Thersites: then tell me, I pray thee, what's thyself?

THER. Thy knower, Patroclus: then tell me, Patroclus, what art thou?

PATR. Thou mayst tell that knowest.

ACHIL. O, tell, tell.

THER. I'll decline the whole question:—Agamemnon commands Achilles; Achilles is my lord; I am Patroclus' knower; and Patroclus is a fool.

PATR. You rascal!

THER. Peace, fool! I have not done.

ACHIL. He is a privileged man.—Proceed, Thersites.

THER. Agamemnon is a fool; Achilles is a fool; Thersites is a fool; and, as aforesaid, Patroclus is a fool.

ACHIL. Derive this; come.

THER. Agamemnon is a fool to offer to command Achilles; Achilles is a fool to be commanded of Agamemnon; Thersites is a fool to serve such a fool; and Patroclus is a fool positive.

PATR. Why am I a fool?

THER. Make that demand of the prover.[b]—It suffices me thou art. Look you, who comes here?

ACHIL. Patroclus, I'll speak with nobody.—Come in with me, Thersites. [*Exit.*

THER. Here is such patchery,[c] such juggling, and such knavery! all the argument is a cuckold and a whore; a good quarrel, to draw emulous * factions, and bleed to death upon. Now the dry *serpigo* on the subject! and war and lechery confound all! [*Exit.*

Enter AGAMEMNON, ULYSSES, NESTOR, DIOMEDES, *and* AJAX.

AGAM. Where is Achilles?

PATR. Within his tent; but ill-dispos'd, my lord.

AGAM. Let it be known to him that we are here.
He shent[d] our messengers; and we lay by
Our appertainments, visiting of him:
Let him be told so; lest[e] perchance he think
We dare not move the question of our place,
Or know not what we are.

PATR. I shall so say to him. [*Exit.*

(*) First folio, *thou*. (†) First folio, *the*. (‡) First folio inserts, *a*.

a *If I could have remembered a gilt* counterfeit, *thou wouldst not have* slipped *out of my contemplation*:] A similar play on *slip* and *counterfeit*, the cant names for false pieces of money, occurs in "Romeo and Juliet:" see note (b), p. 179, Vol. I. By "contemplation," he refers to his previous devout imprecations.

b — of the prover.—] The folio reads, *to the creator*.

c — patchery,—] "Patchery" meant *roguery, villany;* not *folly*, as Mr. Collier persists in explaining it.

(*) First folio, *emulations*.

d *He* shent *our messengers;*] An emendation of Theobald; the quarto reading,—

"He *sate* our messengers," &c.;—

the folio,—

"He *sent* our messengers," &c.

e *Let him be told* so; lest *perchance he think*, &c.] From the quarto; the folio having,—

"Let him be told *of, so* perchance," &c.

ULYSS. We saw him at the opening of his tent:
He is not sick.

AJAX. Yes, lion-sick, sick of proud heart: you may call it melancholy, if you* will favour the man; but, by my head, 'tis pride: but why, why? let him show us a† cause.—A word, my lord.
[*Takes* AGAMEMNON *aside.*

NEST. What moves Ajax thus to bay at him?

ULYSS. Achilles hath inveigled his fool from him.

NEST. Who? Thersites?

ULYSS. He.

NEST. Then will Ajax lack matter, if he have lost his argument.

ULYSS. No; you see, he is his argument that has his argument,—Achilles.

NEST. All the better; their fraction is more our wish than their faction: but it was a strong composure a fool could disunite.[a]

ULYSS. The amity that wisdom knits not, folly may easily untie.—Here comes Patroclus.

NEST. No Achilles with him.

ULYSS. The elephant hath joints, but none for courtesy: his legs are legs for necessity, not for flexure.‡

Re-enter PATROCLUS.

PATR. Achilles bids me say, he is much sorry,
If any thing more than your sport and pleasure
Did move your greatness and this noble state
To call upon him; he hopes it is no other
But, for your health and your digestion sake,
An after-dinner's breath.

AGAM. Hear you, Patroclus;—
We are too well acquainted with these answers:
But his evasion, wing'd thus swift with scorn,
Cannot outfly our apprehensions.
Much attribute he hath; and much the reason
Why we ascribe it to him: yet all his virtues,—
Not virtuously on§ his own part beheld,—
Do in our eyes begin to lose their gloss;
Yea,|| like fair fruit in an unwholesome dish,
Are like to rot untasted. Go and tell him,
We came to speak with him: and you shall not sin,
If you do say we think him over-proud
And under-honest; in self-assumption greater
Than in the note of judgment; and worthier than himself
Here tend the savage strangeness he puts on,
Disguise the holy strength of their command,
And underwrite in an observing kind
His humorous predominance; yea, watch
His pettish lunes,[b] his ebbs, his flows, as if
The passage and whole carriage of this action
Rode on his tide. Go, tell him this; and add,
That, if he overhold his price so much,
We'll none of him; but let him, like an engine
Not portable, lie under this report—
Bring action hither, this cannot go to war:
A stirring dwarf we do allowance give
Before a sleeping giant:—tell him so.

PATR. I shall; and bring his answer presently.
[*Exit.*

AGAM. In second voice we'll not be satisfied;
We come to speak with him.—Ulysses, enter you.
[*Exit* ULYSSES.

AJAX. What is he more than another?

AGAM. No more than what he thinks he is.

AJAX. Is he so much? Do you not think he thinks himself a better man than I am?

AGAM. No question.

AJAX. Will you subscribe his thought, and say he is?

AGAM. No, noble Ajax; you are as strong, as valiant, as wise, no less noble, much more gentle, and altogether more tractable.

AJAX. Why should a man be proud? How doth pride grow? I know not what pride is.*

AGAM. Your mind's the clearer, Ajax, and your virtues the fairer. He that is proud eats up himself: pride is his own glass, his own trumpet, his own chronicle; and whatever praises itself but in the deed, devours the deed in the praise.

AJAX. I do hate a proud man, as I hate the engendering of toads.

NEST. [*Aside.*] Yet he loves himself: is't not strange?

Re-enter ULYSSES.

ULYSS. Achilles will not to the field to-morrow.

AGAM. What's his excuse?

ULYSS. He doth rely on none;
But carries on the stream of his dispose,
Without observance or respect of any,
In will peculiar and in self-admission.

AGAM. Why will he not, upon our fair request,
Untent his person, and share the air with us?

ULYSS. Things small as nothing, for request's sake only,
He makes important: possess'd he is with greatness;
And speaks not to himself, but with a pride
That quarrels at self-breath: imagin'd worth†
Holds in his blood such swoln and hot discourse,

(*) First folio omits, *you*. (†) First folio, *the*.
(‡) First folio, *flight*. (§) First folio, *of*.
(||) First folio inserts, *and*.

[a] *A strong* composure *a fool could disunite.*] The folio reads,—a strong *counsell that* a Foole could disunite.

(*) First folio, *what it is*. (†) First folio, *wroth*.

[b] *His pettish* lunes,—] A correction of Hanmer; the folio reading,—
"His pettish *lines*," &c.
In the quarto, the passage runs,—
"His *course and time*, his ebbs and flows, and if," &c.

That, 'twixt his mental and his active parts,
Kingdom'd Achilles in commotion rages,
And batters 'gainst itself: what should I say?
He is so plaguy-proud, that the death-tokens(3) of it
Cry—*No recovery.*

AGAM. Let Ajax go to him.—
Dear lord, go you and greet him in his tent:
'Tis said he holds you well; and will be led,
At your request, a little from himself.

ULYSS. O, Agamemnon, let it not be so!
We'll consecrate the steps that Ajax makes
When they go from Achilles: shall the proud lord,
That bastes his arrogance with his own seam,
And never suffers matter of the world
Enter his thoughts,—save such as do revolve
And ruminate himself,—shall he be worshipp'd
Of that we hold an idol more than he?
No, this thrice-worthy and right-valiant lord
Must not so stale his palm, nobly acquir'd;
Nor, by my will, assubjugate his merit,
As amply titled as Achilles is,
By going to Achilles:
That were to enlard his fat-already pride;
And add more coals to Cancer when he burns
With entertaining great Hyperion.
This lord go to him! Jupiter forbid;
And say in thunder—*Achilles go to him!*

NEST. [*Aside.*] O, this is well; he rubs the vein of him.

DIO. [*Aside.*] And how his silence drinks up this applause!

AJAX. If I go to him, with my armed fist
I'll pash him o'er the face.

AGAM. O, no, you shall not go.

AJAX. An 'a be proud with me, I'll pheeze[a] his pride:
Let me go to him.

ULYSS. Not for the worth that hangs upon our quarrel.

AJAX. A paltry, insolent fellow,—

NEST. [*Aside.*] How he describes himself!

AJAX. Can he not be sociable?

ULYSS. [*Aside.*] The raven chides blackness.

AJAX. I'll let his humours' blood.

AGAM. [*Aside.*] He will be the physician that should be the patient.

AJAX. An all men were o' my mind,—

ULYSS. [*Aside.*] Wit would be out of fashion.

AJAX. 'A should not bear it so, 'a should eat swords first: shall pride carry it?

NEST. [*Aside.*] An 'twould, you'd carry half.

ULYSS. [*Aside.*] 'A would have ten shares.

AJAX. I will knead him, I'll make him supple.

NEST. [*Aside.*] He's not yet through warm:[b] force him with praises: pour in, pour in; his ambition is dry.

ULYSS. [*To* AGAMEMNON.] My lord, you feed too much on this dislike.

NEST. Our noble general, do not do so.

DIO. You must prepare to fight without Achilles.

ULYSS. Why, 'tis this naming of him doth him harm.
Here is a man—but 'tis before his face;—
I will be silent.

NEST. Wherefore should you so?
He is not emulous, as Achilles is.

ULYSS. Know the whole world, he is as valiant.

AJAX. A whoreson dog, that shall palter thus with us! Would he were a Trojan!

NEST. What a vice were it in Ajax now—

ULYSS. If he were proud,—

DIO. Or covetous of praise,—

ULYSS. Ay, or surly borne,—

DIO. Or strange, or self-affected!

ULYSS. Thank the heavens, lord, thou art of sweet composure;
Praise him that got thee, she that gave thee suck:
Fam'd* be thy tutor, and thy parts of nature
Thrice-fam'd, beyond† all erudition:
But he that disciplin'd thy arms to fight,
Let Mars divide eternity in twain,
And give him half: and, for thy vigour,
Bull-bearing Milo his addition yield
To sinewy Ajax. I'll not praise thy wisdom,
Which, like a bourn, a pale, a shore, confines
Thy spacious and dilated parts: here's Nestor,—
Instructed by the antiquary times,
He must, he is, he cannot but be wise;—
But pardon, father Nestor, were your days
As green as Ajax', and your brain so temper'd,
You should not have the eminence of him,
But be as Ajax.

AJAX. Shall I call you father?

NEST. Ay, my good son.[c]

DIO. Be rul'd by him, lord Ajax.

ULYSS. There is no tarrying here; the hart Achilles
Keeps thicket. Please it our great‡ general
To call together all his state of war;
Fresh kings are come to Troy: to-morrow,
We must with all our main of power stand fast:
And here's a lord,—come knights from east to west,
And cull their flower, Ajax shall cope the best.

AGAM. Go we to council. Let Achilles sleep:
Light boats§ sail swift, though greater hulks‖ draw deep. [*Exeunt.*

---

a *I'll pheeze his pride:*] I'll *tickle* his pride. See note (b), p. 227, Vol. I.

b He's not yet through warm:] In the old copies these words are inadvertently ascribed to Ajax.

(*) First folio, *Fame.* (†) First folio repeats, *beyond.*
(‡) First folio omits, *great.* (§) First folio inserts, *may.*
(‖) First folio, *bulkes.*

c Ay, my good son.] In the folio, these words are attributed to Ulysses.

ACT III.

SCENE I.—Troy. *A Room in* Priam's *Palace.*

Enter PANDARUS *and a* Servant.

PAN. Friend, you,—pray you, a word: do not you follow the young lord Paris?

SERV. Ay, sir, when he goes before me.

PAN. You depend upon him, I mean?

SERV. Sir, I do depend upon the lord.

PAN. You depend upon a noble gentleman; I must needs praise him.

SERV. The lord be praised!

PAN. You know me, do you not?

SERV. Faith, sir, superficially.

PAN. Friend, know me better; I am the lord Pandarus.

SERV. I hope I shall know your honour better.

PAN. I do desire it.

SERV. You are in the state of grace.

[*Music within.*

PAN. *Grace!* not so, friend; honour and lordship are my titles.*—What music is this?

SERV. I do but partly know, sir; it is music in parts.

PAN. Know you the musicians?

SERV. Wholly, sir.

PAN. Who play they to?

SERV. To the hearers, sir.

PAN. At whose pleasure, friend?

SERV. At mine, sir, and theirs that love music.

PAN. Command, I mean, friend.

SERV. Who shall I command, sir?

PAN. Friend, we understand not one another; I am too courtly, and thou art too cunning. At whose request do these men play?

SERV. That's to't, indeed, sir: marry, sir, at the request of Paris my lord, who's there in person; with him, the mortal Venus, the heart-blood of beauty, love's invisible soul,—

PAN. Who, my cousin Cressida?

SERV. No, sir, Helen; could you not find out that by her attributes?

PAN. It should seem, fellow, that thou hast not seen the lady Cressida. I come to speak with Paris from the prince Troilus: I will make a complimental assault upon him, for my business seeths.

SERV. Sodden business! there's a stewed phrase, indeed!

Enter PARIS *and* HELEN, *attended.*

PAN. Fair be to you, my lord, and to all this fair company! fair desires, in all fair measure, fairly guide them!—especially to you, fair queen! fair thoughts be your fair pillow!

HELEN. Dear lord, you are full of fair words.

PAN. You speak your fair pleasure, sweet queen.—Fair prince, here is good broken[a] music.

PAR. You have broke it, cousin: and, by my life, you shall make it whole again; you shall piece it out with a piece of your performance.—Nell, he is full of harmony.

PAN. Truly, lady, no.

HELEN. O, sir,—

PAN. Rude, in sooth; in good sooth, very rude.

PAR. Well said, my lord! well you say so, in fits.[b]

PAN. I have business to my lord, dear queen. —My lord, will you vouchsafe me a word?

HELEN. Nay, this shall not hedge us out: we'll hear you sing, certainly.

PAN. Well, sweet queen, you are pleasant with me.—But, marry, thus, my lord,—my dear lord, and most esteemed friend, your brother Troilus—

HELEN. My lord Pandarus; honey-sweet lord,—

PAN. Go to, sweet queen, go to:—commends himself most affectionately to you,—

HELEN. You shall not bob us out of our melody; If you do, our melancholy upon your head!

PAN. Sweet queen, sweet queen; that's a sweet queen, i' faith,—

HELEN. And to make a sweet lady sad is a sour offence.

PAN. Nay, that shall not serve your turn; that shall it not, in truth, la. Nay, I care not for such words; no, no.—And, my lord, he desires you, that if the king call for him at supper, you will make his excuse.

HELEN. My lord Pandarus,—

PAN. What says my sweet queen?—my very-very sweet queen?

PAR. What exploit's in hand? where sups he to-night?

HELEN. Nay, but my lord,—

PAN. What says my sweet queen?—My cousin will fall out with you. You must not know where he sups.[c]

PAR. I'll lay my life,* with my disposer Cressida.[d]

(*) First folio, *title.*

(*) First folio omits, *I'll lay my life.*

[a] — *good* broken *music.*] *Broken* music signified the music of stringed instruments. See note (1), p. 120, Vol. II.

[b] — well *you say so, in* fits.] Paris means you speak *in music,* alluding to the "Rude, in sooth; in good sooth, very rude." "Fits" was sometimes used to denote the divisions of a song; at others, the song itself; and, occasionally, a strain of harmony.

[c] You must not know where he sups.] Both the quarto and folio give these words to Helen; indeed, we suspect the distribution of the speeches in this scene is in several instances erroneous.

[d] — with my disposer Cressida.] No scholiast has been fortunate enough to discover why Paris terms Cressida his "disposer"; and some editors transfer the speeches in which she is so called to Helen, who, it is thought, might apply the epithet in the sense of "handmaid." It seems, however, more suitable to Paris; and possibly in Shakespeare's day may have been a colloquial term for a wild, forward damsel, since we know that "*dispos'd,*" among other meanings, bore that of—inclined to wantonness. Thus, in Peele's "Edward I."—

"*Longsh.* Say any thing but so.
Once, Nell, thou gav'st me this.
Q. Elinor. I pray, let go:
Ye are *dispos'd,* I think."

In Beaumont and Fletcher's "Custom of the Country," Act I. Sc. 1,—

"*Rut.* You love a gentlewoman, a young handsome woman;
I have lov'd a thousand, not so few.
Arn. You are *dispos'd.*"

And in the same author's "Valentinian," Act II. Sc. 4,—

"*Chi.* No;
I'll make you no such promise.
Clau. If you do, sir,
Take heed you stand to't.
Chi. Wondrous merry ladies!
Lucina. The wenches are *dispos'd.*"

Mr. Dyce, who has furnished the above and other examples of this peculiar employment of the word, is probably right in supposing the Princess, in "Love's Labour's Lost," Act II. Sc. 1, so uses it, and in that case there should be no break after "*dispos'd,*—"

"*Prin.* Come, to our pavilion; Boyet is *dispos'd.*"

PAN. No, no, no such matter; you are wide; come, your disposer is sick.

PAR. Well, I'll make excuse.

PAN. Ay, good my lord. Why should you say Cressida? no, your poor disposer's sick.

PAR. I spy.

PAN. You spy! what do you spy?—Come, give me an instrument.—Now, sweet queen.

HELEN. Why, this is kindly done.

PAN. My niece is horribly in love with a thing you have, sweet queen.

HELEN. She shall have it, my lord, if it be not my lord Paris.

PAN. He! no, she'll none of him; they two are twain.

HELEN. Falling in, after falling out, may make them three.

PAN. Come, come, I'll hear no more of this; I'll sing you a song now.

HELEN. Ay, ay, pr'ythee now. By my troth, sweet lord, thou hast a fine forehead.

PAN. Ay, you may, you may.[a]

HELEN. Let thy song be love: this love will undo us all. O, Cupid, Cupid, Cupid!

PAN. Love! ay, that it shall, i' faith.

PAR. Ay, good now, love, love, nothing but love.

PAN. In good troth, it begins so:

Love, love, nothing but love, still more!
For, O, love's bow
Shoots buck and doe:
The shaft confounds
Not that it wounds,
But tickles still the sore.

These lovers cry—O! O! they die!
Yet that which seems the wound to kill,
Doth turn O! O! to ha! ha! he!
So dying love lives still:
O! O! a while, but ha! ha! ha!
O! O! groans out for ha! ha! ha!

Heigh-ho.

HELEN. In love, i' faith, to the very tip of the nose.

PAR. He eats nothing but doves, love; and that breeds hot blood, and hot blood begets hot thoughts, and hot thoughts beget hot deeds, and hot deeds is love.

PAN. Is this the generation of love? hot blood, hot thoughts, and hot deeds?—why, they are vipers: is love a generation of vipers?—Sweet lord, who's a-field to-day?

PAR. Hector, Deiphobus, Helenus, Antenor, and all the gallantry of Troy: I would fain have armed to-day, but my Nell would not have it so. How chance my brother Troilus went not?

HELEN. He hangs the lip at something;—you know all, lord Pandarus?

PAN. Not I, honey-sweet queen.—I long to hear how they sped to-day.—You'll remember your brother's excuse?

PAR. To a hair.

PAN. Farewell, sweet queen.

HELEN. Commend me to your niece.

PAN. I will, sweet queen. [*Exit.*

[*A retreat sounded.*

PAR. They're come from field: let us to Priam's hall,
To greet the warriors. Sweet Helen, I must woo you
To help unarm our Hector: his stubborn buckles,
With these your white enchanting fingers touch'd,
Shall more obey than to the edge of steel,
Or force of Greekish sinews; you shall do more
Than all the island kings,—disarm great Hector.

HELEN. 'T will make us proud to be his servant, Paris:
Yea, what he shall receive of us in duty
Gives us more palm in beauty than we have;
Yea, overshines ourself.

PAR. Sweet, above thought I love thee![b]

[*Exeunt.*

SCENE II.—*The same.* Pandarus' *Orchard.*

Enter PANDARUS *and a* Servant, *meeting.*

PAN. How now! where's thy master? at my cousin Cressida's?

SERV. No, sir; he stays for you to conduct him thither.

PAN. O, here he comes.—

Enter TROILUS.

How now, how now?

TROIL. Sirrah, walk off. [*Exit* Servant.

PAN. Have you seen my cousin?

TROIL. No, Pandarus: I stalk about her door,
Like a strange soul upon the Stygian banks
Staying for waftage. O, be thou my Charon,
And give me swift transportance to those fields,
Where I may wallow in the lily beds
Propos'd for the deserver! O, gentle Pandarus,
From Cupid's shoulder pluck his painted wings,
And fly with me to Cressid!

---

[a] Ay, you may, you may.] See note (b), p. 149.

[b] Sweet, above thought I love thee!] In the folio mistakenly assigned to Helen.

PAN. Walk here i' the orchard, I'll bring her straight. [*Exit.*

TROIL. I am giddy; expectation whirls me round.
The imaginary relish is so sweet
That it enchants my sense; what will it be,
When that the wat'ry palate tastes* indeed
Love's thrice-repured† nectar? death, I fear me;
Swooning destruction; or some joy too fine,
Too subtle-potent, tun'd‡ too sharp in sweetness,
For the capacity of my ruder powers:
I fear it much; and I do fear besides,
That I shall lose distinction in my joys;
As doth a battle, when they charge on heaps
The enemy flying.

Re-enter PANDARUS.

PAN. She's making her ready, she'll come straight: you must be witty now. She does so blush, and fetches her wind so short, as if she were frayed with a sprite: I'll fetch her. It is the prettiest villain:—she fetches her breath so short as a new-ta'en sparrow. [*Exit.*

TROIL. Even such a passion doth embrace my bosom:
My heart beats thicker than a feverous pulse;
And all my powers do their bestowing lose,
Like vassalage at unawares encountering
The eye of majesty.

Re-enter PANDARUS *with* CRESSIDA.

PAN. Come, come, what need you blush? shame's a baby.—Here she is now: swear the oaths now to her, that you have sworn to me.—What, are you gone again? you must be watched[a] ere you be made tame, must you? Come your ways, come your ways; an you draw backward, we'll put you i' the fills.[b]—Why do you not speak

(*) Old text, *pallats taste.* (†) First folio, *thrice-reputed.* (‡) First folio, *and.*

[a] — watched—] See note (a), p. 683, Vol. II.
[b] — fills.—] "Fills," or *phills*, are the *thills*, the shafts of a cart or waggon.

to her?—Come, draw this curtain, and let's see your picture. Alas the day, how loth you are to offend day-light! an 'twere dark, you'd close sooner. So, so; rub on, and kiss the mistress.(1) How now, a kiss in fee-farm! build there, carpenter; the air is sweet. Nay, you shall fight your hearts out ere I part you. The falcon as the tercel,[a] for all the ducks i' the river: go to, go to.

TROIL. You have bereft me of all words, lady.

PAN. Words pay no debts, give her deeds: but she'll bereave you o' the deeds too, if she call your activity in question. What, billing again? Here's —*In witness whereof the parties interchangeably* —Come in, come in; I'll go get a fire. [*Exit.*

CRES. Will you walk in, my lord?

TROIL. O, Cressida, how often have I wish'd me thus?

CRES. Wished, my lord?—the gods grant!—O, my lord!

TROIL. What should they grant? what makes this pretty abruption? What too curious dreg espies my sweet lady in the fountain of our love?

CRES. More dregs than water, if my fears* have eyes.

TROIL. Fears make devils of cherubins; they never see truly.

CRES. Blind fear, that seeing reason leads, finds safer† footing than blind reason stumbling without fear: to fear the worst oft cures the worst.

TROIL. O, let my lady apprehend no fear: in all Cupid's pageant there is presented no monster.

CRES. Nor nothing monstrous neither?

TROIL. Nothing, but our undertakings; when we vow to weep seas, live in fire, eat rocks, tame tigers; thinking it harder for our mistress to devise imposition enough, than for us to undergo any difficulty imposed. This is the monstruosity in love, lady,—that the will is infinite, and the execution confined; that the desire is boundless, and the act a slave to limit.

CRES. They say all lovers swear more performance than they are able, and yet reserve an ability that they never perform; vowing more than the perfection of ten, and discharging less than the tenth part of one. They that have the voice of lions and the act of hares, are they not monsters?

TROIL. Are there such? such are not we: praise us as we are tasted, allow us as we prove; our head shall go bare till merit crown it: no perfection in reversion shall have a praise in present: we will not name desert before his birth; and, being born, his addition shall be humble. Few words to fair faith: Troilus shall be such to Cressid, as what envy can say worst, shall be a mock for his truth; and what truth can speak truest, not truer than Troilus.

CRES. Will you walk in, my lord?

Re-enter PANDARUS.

PAN. What, blushing still? have you not done talking yet?

CRES. Well, uncle, what folly I commit, I dedicate to you.

PAN. I thank you for that; if my lord get a boy of you, you'll give him me. Be true to my lord: if he flinch, chide me for it.

TROIL. You know now your hostages; your uncle's word and my firm faith.

PAN. Nay, I'll give my word for her too; our kindred, though they be long ere they are wooed, they are constant, being won: they are burs, I can tell you; they'll stick where they are thrown.

CRES. Boldness comes to me now, and brings me heart:—
Prince Troilus, I have lov'd you night and day,
For many weary months.

TROIL. Why was my Cressid, then, so hard to win?

CRES. Hard to seem won; but I was won, my lord,
With the first glance that ever—pardon me;—
If I confess much, you will play the tyrant.
I love you now; but not, till now, so much
But I might master it:—in faith, I lie;
My thoughts were like unbridled children, grown*
Too headstrong for their mother:—see, we fools!
Why have I blabb'd? who shall be true to us,
When we are so unsecret to ourselves?—
But, though I lov'd you well, I woo'd you not;
And yet, good faith, I wish'd myself a man;
Or that we women had men's privilege
Of speaking first. Sweet, bid me hold my tongue;
For, in this rapture, I shall surely speak
The thing I shall repent. See, see, your silence,
Cunning† in dumbness, from my weakness draws
My very soul of counsel:[b] stop my mouth.

TROIL. And shall, albeit sweet music issues thence.

PAN. Pretty, i' faith.

CRES. My lord, I do beseech you, pardon me;
'Twas not my purpose thus to beg a kiss:

(*) Old text, *teares*. (†) First folio, *safe*.

a The falcon as the tercel,—] The meaning of this is,—The falcon (the female hawk) I'll wager to be as good as the tercel (the male hawk); in other words, I'll back my niece to be as staunch at that game as Troilus. So, in Day's old play of "The Isle of Gulls," where the characters are playing bowls,—

"*Dut.* Come, the last marke; this cast is worth all the rest.
Viol. The leader as the follower.
Lisa. Bad's the best."

Again, in "Lingua," Act I. Sc. last,—

"*Tactus.* Next after me, *I as yourself* at any time."

(*) First folio, *grow*. (†) Old text, *Comm'ng*.

b *My* very *soul of* counsel:] The folio reads,
"My soule of counsell *from me*," &c.

I am asham'd;—O, heavens! what have I done?—
For this time will I take my leave, my lord.

TROIL. Your leave, sweet Cressid?

PAN. *Leave!* an you take leave till to-morrow morning,—

CRES. Pray you, content you.

TROIL. What offends you, lady?

CRES. Sir, mine own company.

TROIL. You cannot shun yourself.

CRES. Let me go and try:
I have a kind of self resides with you;
But an unkind self, that itself will leave,
To be another's fool. I would be gone:—
Where is my wit?[a] I know not what I speak.

TROIL. Well know they what they speak, that speak so wisely.

CRES. Perchance, my lord, I show more craft than love;
And fell so roundly to a large confession,
To angle for your thoughts: but you are wise;
Or else you love not;[b] for to be wise, and love,
Exceeds man's might; that dwells with gods above.

TROIL. O, that I thought it could be in a woman,
(As, if it can, I will presume in you,)
To feed for aye her lamp and flames of love;(2)
To keep her constancy in plight and youth,
Outliving beauty's outward, with a mind
That doth renew swifter than blood decays!
Or, that persuasion could but thus convince me,—
That my integrity and truth to you
Might be affronted with the match and weight
Of such a winnow'd purity in love;
How were I then unlifted! but, alas,
I am as true as truth's simplicity,
And simpler than the infancy of truth.

CRES. In that I'll war with you.

TROIL. O, virtuous fight,
When right with right wars who shall be most right!
True swains in love shall, in the world to come,
Approve their truths by Troilus: when their rhymes,
Full of protest, of oath, and big compare,
Want similes, truth tir'd with iteration,—
As true as steel, as plantage to the moon[c]
As sun to day, as turtle to her mate,
As iron to adamant, as earth to the centre,—
Yet, after all comparisons of truth,
As truth's authentic author to be cited,
As true as Troilus shall crown up the verse,
And sanctify the numbers.

CRES. Prophet may you be!
If I be false, or swerve a hair from truth,
When time is old and hath forgot itself,
When water-drops have worn the stones of Troy,
And blind oblivion swallow'd cities up,
And mighty states charácterless are grated
To dusty nothing; yet let memory,
From false to false, among false maids in love,
Upbraid my falsehood! when they have said—as false
As air, as water, wind, or* sandy earth,
As fox to lamb, as wolf to heifer's calf,
Pard to the hind, or step-dame to her son;
Yea, let them say, to stick the heart of falsehood,
As false as Cressid.(3)

PAN. Go to, a bargain made: seal it, seal it; I'll be the witness.—Here I hold your hand; here, my cousin's. If ever you prove false one to another, since I have taken such pains to bring you together, let all pitiful goers-between be called to the world's end after my name, call them all—Pandars; let all cónstant men be Troiluses, all false women Cressids, and all brokers-between Pandars! say, *Amen.*

TROIL. Amen.

CRES. Amen.

PAN. Amen. Whereupon I will show you a chamber and a bed,[d] which bed, because it shall not speak of your pretty encounters, press it to death: away!
And Cupid grant all tongue-tied maidens here,
Bed, chamber,† Pandar to provide this gear!

[*Exeunt.*

SCENE III.—*The* Grecian *Camp.*

Flourish. Enter AGAMEMNON, ULYSSES, DIOMEDES, NESTOR, AJAX, MENELAUS, *and* CALCHAS.

CAL. Now, princes, for the service I have done you,
The advantage of the time prompts me aloud
To call for recompense. Appear it to your mind,[e]

---

a I would be gone:—
Where is my wit?]
The folio transposes these sentences.

b *Or else you love not;*] "Or, *in other words*, you love not." Such is the simple and obvious meaning, though the commentators have all overlooked it. See the notes *ad l.* in the *Variorum* Shakespeare, and in more recent editions.

c — as plantage to the moon,—] The belief in the influence of the moon upon vegetation was universally prevalent in Shakespeare's day. Farmer has illustrated this by an apt quotation from Scot's "Discovery of Witchcraft," 1584,—"The poore husbandman perceiveth that the increase of the *moone* maketh *plants* and living creatures frutefull: so as in the *full moone* they are in best strength, decaieing in the *wane*, and in the *conjunction* doo utterlie wither and vade."

(*) First folio, *as Winde, as.* (†) First folio inserts, *and.*

d — and a bed,—] Capell added these words, which, or something equivalent, appear to have been inadvertently omitted from the original text.

e Appear it to your mind, &c.] In Chapman's translation of "The Iliads of Homer," Book I., we meet a similar form of expression,—

"——(affoord
Impression of it in thy soule)."

That, through the sight I bear in things from Jove,[a]
I have abandon'd Troy, left my possession,
Incurr'd a traitor's name; expos'd myself,
From certain and possess'd conveniences,
To doubtful fortunes; sequest'ring from me all
That time, acquaintance, custom, and condition,
Made tame and most familiar to my nature;
And here, to do you service, am become
As new into the world, strange, unacquainted:
I do beseech you, as in way of taste,
To give me now a little benefit,
Out of those many register'd in promise,
Which, you say, live to come in my behalf.(4)

AGAM. What wouldst thou of us, Trojan? make demand.

CAL. You have a Trojan prisoner, call'd Antenor,
Yesterday took; Troy holds him very dear.
Oft have you (often have you thanks therefore)
Desir'd my Cressid in right great exchange,
Whom Troy hath still denied: but this Antenor,
I know, is such a wrest[b] in their affairs,
That their negotiations all must slack,
Wanting his manage; and they will almost
Give us a prince of blood, a son of Priam,
In change of him: let him be sent, great princes,
And he shall buy my daughter; and her presence
Shall quite strike off all service I have done,
In most accepted pain.[c]

AGAM. Let Diomedes bear him,
And bring us Cressid hither; Calchas shall have
What he requests of us.—Good Diomed,
Furnish you fairly for this interchange:
Withal, bring word if Hector will to-morrow
Be answer'd in his challenge: Ajax is ready.

DIO. This shall I undertake; and 'tis a burden
Which I am proud to bear.

[*Exeunt* DIOMEDES *and* CALCHAS.

Enter ACHILLES *and* PATROCLUS, *before their Tent.*

ULYSS. Achilles stands i' the entrance of his tent:—
Please it our general to pass strangely by him,
As if he were forgot;—and, princes all,
Lay negligent and loose regard upon him:—
I will come last. 'Tis like he'll question me
Why such unplausive eyes are bent, why turn'd on him:[d]
If so, I have derision med'cinable,
To use between your strangeness and his pride,
Which his own will shall have desire to drink:
It may do good: pride hath no other glass
To show itself but pride; for supple knees
Feed arrogance, and are the proud man's fees.

AGAM. We'll execute your purpose, and put on
A form of strangeness as we pass along;—
So do each lord; and either greet him not,
Or else disdainfully, which shall shake him more
Than if not look'd on. I will lead the way.

ACHIL. What, comes the general to speak with me?
You know my mind, I'll fight no more 'gainst Troy.

AGAM. What says Achilles? would he aught with us?

NEST. Would you, my lord, aught with the general?

ACHIL. No.

NEST. Nothing, my lord.

AGAM. The better.

[*Exeunt* AGAMEMNON *and* NESTOR.

ACHIL. Good day, good day.

MEN. How do you? how do you? [*Exit.*

ACHIL. What, does the cuckold scorn me?

AJAX. How now, Patroclus?

ACHIL. Good morrow, Ajax.

AJAX. Ha?

ACHIL. Good morrow.

AJAX. Ay, and good next day too. [*Exit.*

ACHIL. What mean these fellows? know they not Achilles?

PATR. They pass by strangely: they were us'd to bend,
To send their smiles before them to Achilles;
To come as humbly as they us'd to creep
To holy altars.

ACHIL. What, am I poor of late?
'Tis certain, greatness, once fall'n out with fortune,
Must fall out with men too: what the declin'd is,
He shall as soon read in the eyes of others,
As feel in his own fall: for men, like butterflies,

---

[a] *That, through the sight I bear in things* from Jove, &c.] The old copies read, "— *to* Jove," or, "— *to* love,"—it being difficult to determine whether the latter word is intended for "Jove" or "love." Rowe printed,—

"That, through the sight I bear in things to *come*," &c.

Mr. Collier's annotator reads,—

"—— *Appeal* it to your mind,
"That through the sight I bear in things *above*," &c.

The substitution of "*from*" for "to," which we have taken the liberty to make, supposing the compositor misread "frō" as *to*, receives some support from the passage in Chapman's "Iliads of Homer," Book I., where Chalcas is sent for to discover why Apollo has struck the Greeks with the plague,—

"—— Let us aske, some Prophet, Priest, or prove
Some dreame interpreter (for dreames, are often sent from Jove)," &c.

[b] — a wrest—] See note (a), p. 273.

[c] In most accepted pain.] Hanmer and Warburton read,—

"In most accepted *pay*."

[d] Why such unplausive eyes are bent, why turn'd on him:] "If the eyes were *bent* on him, they were *turn'd* on him. This tautology, therefore, together with the redundancy of the line, plainly show that we ought to read, with Sir Thomas Hanmer,—

'Why such unplausive eyes are bent on him.'"

STEEVENS.

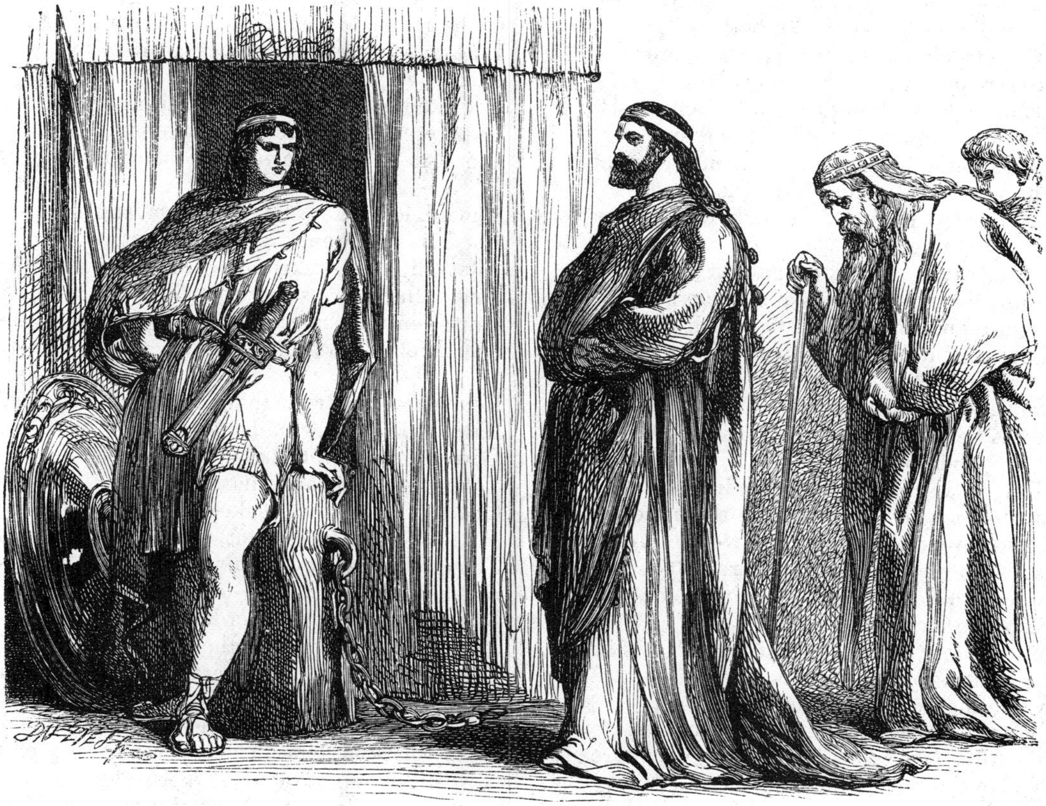

Show not their mealy wings but to the summer;
And not a man, for being simply man,
Hath any honour; but honour* for those honours
That are without him, as place, riches and favour,
Prizes of accident as oft as merit:
Which when they fall, as being slippery standers,
The love that lean'd on them as slippery too,
Do one pluck down another, and together
Die in the fall. But 'tis not so with me:
Fortune and I are friends; I do enjoy
At ample point all that I did possess,
Save these men's looks; who do, methinks, find out
Something not worth in me such rich beholding
As they have often given.—Here is Ulysses;
I'll interrupt his reading.—
How now, Ulysses!

ULYSS. Now, great Thetis' son!

ACHIL. What are you reading?

ULYSS. A strange fellow here
Writes me, That man—how dearly ever parted,[a]
How much in having, or without or in,—
Cannot make boast to have that which he hath,
Nor feels not what he owes, but by reflection;
As when his virtues shining upon others
Heat them, and they retort that heat again
To the first giver.

ACHIL. This is not strange, Ulysses.
The beauty that is borne here in the face,
The bearer knows not, but commends itself
To others' eyes:[b] nor doth the eye itself
(That most pure spirit of sense) behold itself
Not going from itself; but eye to eye oppos'd
Salutes each other with each other's form.
For speculation turns not to itself,
Till it hath travell'd, and is mirror'd there[c]
Where it may see itself: this is not strange at all.

(*) First folio, *honour'd*.

a — how dearly ever parted,—] That is, *however richly endowed*.

b To others' eyes: &c.] This and the next line are omitted in the folio.

c — and is mirror'd there—] A correction made both by Mr. Collier's and Mr. Singer's annotator; and the word "speculation" in the preceding line, which there imports *vision, espial*, and the like, renders it almost indisputably necessary. The old text reads,—

"—— and is *married* there."

ULYSS. I do not strain* at the position,—
It is familiar,—but at the author's drift:
Who, in his circumstance,[a] expressly proves—
That no man is the lord of any thing,
(Though in and of him there be† much consisting,)
Till he communicate his parts to others:
Nor doth he of himself know them for aught
Till he behold them form'd in the applause
Where they're extended; who, like an arch, reverberates
The voice again; or like a gate of steel
Fronting the sun, receives and renders back
His figure and his heat. I was much rapt in this;
And apprehended here immediately
The unknown Ajax.
Heavens, what a man is there! a very horse;
That has he knows not what. Nature, what things there are,
Most abject in regard, and dear in use!
What things again most dear in the esteem,
And poor in worth! Now shall we see to-morrow,
An act that very chance doth throw upon him,
Ajax renown'd. O, heavens, what some men do,
While some men leave to do!
How some men creep in skittish Fortune's hall,
Whiles others play the idiots in her eyes!
How one man eats into another's pride,
While pride is fasting‡ in his wantonness!
To see these Grecian lords!—why, even already
They clap the lubber Ajax on the shoulder;
As if his foot were on brave Hector's breast,
And great Troy shrieking.

ACHIL. I do believe it;
For they pass'd by me, as misers do by beggars,—
Neither gave to me good word, nor look:
What, are my deeds forgot?

ULYSS. Time hath, my lord, a wallet at his back,
Wherein he puts alms for Oblivion,
A great-siz'd monster of ingratitudes:
Those scraps are good deeds past;
Which are devour'd as fast as they are made,
Forgot as soon as done: persévérance, dear my lord,
Keeps honour bright: to have done, is to hang
Quite out of fashion, like a rusty mail
In monumental mockery. Take the instant way;
For honour travels in a strait so narrow,
Where one but goes abreast: keep, then, the path;
For emulation hath a thousand sons,
That one by one pursue: if you give way,
Or hedge aside from the direct forthright,[b]
Like to an enter'd tide, they all rush by,
And leave you hindmost;—
Or, like a gallant horse fall'n in first rank,
Lie there for pavement to the abject rear,*
O'er-run and trampled on: then what they do in present,
Though less than yours in past, must o'ertop yours:
For Time is like a fashionable host,
That slightly shakes his parting guest by the hand;
And with his arms outstretch'd, as he would fly,
Grasps-in the comer: the welcome ever smiles,
And farewell goes out sighing. O, let not virtue seek
Remuneration for the thing it was; for beauty, wit,
High birth, vigour of bone, desert in service,
Love, friendship, charity, are subjects all
To envious and calumniating time.
One touch of nature makes the whole world kin,—
That all, with one consent, praise new-born gawds,
Though they are made and moulded of things past;
And give† to dust, that is a little gilt,
More laud than gilt[c] o'erdusted.
The present eye praises the present object:
Then marvel not, thou great and cómplete man,
That all the Greeks begin to worship Ajax;
Since things in motion sooner‡ catch the eye,
Than what not stirs. The cry went once § on thee,
And still it might, and yet it may again,
If thou wouldst not entomb thyself alive,
And case thy reputation in thy tent;
Whose glorious deeds, but in these fields of late,
Made emulous missions 'mongst the gods themselves,
And drave great Mars to faction.

ACHIL. Of this my privacy
I have strong reasons.

ULYSS. But 'gainst your privacy
The reasons are more potent and heroical:
'T is known, Achilles, that you are in love
With one of Priam's daughters.

ACHIL. Ha! known?

ULYSS. Is that a wonder?
The providence that's in a watchful state,
Knows almost every grain of Plutus' ‖ gold;
Finds bottom in the uncomprehensive deeps;
Keeps place with thought, and almost, like the gods,
Does thoughts unveil in their dumb cradles.[d]

(*) First folio inserts, *it*. (†) First folio, *is*. (‡) First folio, *feasting*.

(*) Old text, *abject, neere*. (†) Old text, *goe*. (‡) First folio, *begin to*. (§) First folio, *out*. (‖) Old text, *Plutoes*.

[a] — *in his* circumstance,—] "In the detail or circumduction of his argument."—JOHNSON.

[b] — forthright,—] A *forthright* means a *strait path:* thus in the "Tempest," Act III. Sc. 3,—

" —— here's a maze trod, indeed,
Through *forthrights* and meanders!"

[c] — gilt—] Query, "— than *gold* o'erdusted"?

[d] *Does thoughts unveil in their* dumb cradles.] "Dumb cradles," the silent *incunabula* of thoughts, may be right, but the doubtful expression and the limping measure of the line instruct us to suspect some error lurks under the word "cradles," which, indeed, we once believed a misprint for *oracles*. Mr. Collier's annotator proposes to restore the sense and rhythm by reading,—

"Does thoughts unveil in their dumb *crudities*,"

and Mr. Collier actually adopts "*crudities*," and terms it a valuable emendation!

There is a mystery (with whom relation
Durst never meddle) in the soul of state;
Which hath an operation more divine,
Than breath, or pen, can give expressure to:
All the commérce that you have had with Troy,
As perfectly is ours, as yours, my lord;
And better would it fit Achilles much,
To throw down Hector, than Polyxena:
But it must grieve young Pyrrhus now at home,
When fame shall in our islands* sound her trump;
And all the Greekish girls shall tripping sing,—
Great Hector's sister did Achilles win;
But our great Ajax bravely beat down him.
Farewell, my lord: I as your lover speak;
The fool slides o'er the ice that you should break.
[*Exit.*

PATR. To this effect, Achilles, have I mov'd you:
A woman impudent and mannish grown
Is not more loath'd than an effeminate man
In time of action. I stand condemn'd for this;
They think, my little stomach to the war,
And your great love to me, restrains you thus:
Sweet, rouse yourself; and the weak wanton Cupid
Shall from your neck unloose his amorous fold,
And, like a dew-drop from the lion's mane,
Be shook to air.†

ACHIL. Shall Ajax fight with Hector?

PATR. Ay, and perhaps receive much honour by him.

ACHIL. I see my reputation is at stake;
My fame is shrewdly gor'd.

PATR. O, then beware;
Those wounds heal ill that men do give themselves:
Omission to do what is necessary
Seals a commission to a blank of danger;
And danger, like an ague, subtly taints
Even then when we sit idly in the sun.

ACHIL. Go call Thersites hither, sweet Patroclus:
I'll send the fool to Ajax, and desire him
To invite the Trojan lords after the combat,
To see us here unarm'd: I have a woman's longing,
An appetite that I am sick withal,
To see great Hector in his weeds of peace;
To talk with him, and to behold his visage,
Even to my full of view.—A labour sav'd!

Enter THERSITES.

THER. A wonder!

ACHIL. What?

(*) First folio, *her ıland.*

(†) First folio, *ayrie ayre.*

THER. Ajax goes up and down the field, asking for himself.

ACHIL. How so?

THER. He must fight singly to-morrow with Hector; and is so prophetically proud of an heroical cudgelling, that he raves in saying nothing.

ACHIL. How can that be?

THER. Why, he stalks up and down like a peacock,—a stride and a stand: ruminates, like an hostess that hath no arithmetic but her brain to set down her reckoning: bites his lip with a politic regard, as who should say—There were wit in this* head, an 'twould out; and so there is; but it lies as coldly in him as fire in a flint, which will not show without knocking. The man's undone for ever; for if Hector break not his neck i'the combat, he'll break't himself in vain-glory. He knows not me: I said, *Good morrow, Ajax;* and he replies, *Thanks, Agamemnon.* What think you of this man, that takes me for the general? He's grown a very land-fish, languageless, a monster. A plague of opinion! a man may wear it on both sides, like a leather jerkin.

ACHIL. Thou must be my ambassador to him, Thersites.

THER. Who, I? why, he'll answer nobody; he professes not answering; speaking is for beggars; he wears his tongue in's arms. I will put on his presence; let Patroclus make† demands to me, you shall see the Pageant of Ajax.

ACHIL. To him, Patroclus: tell him,—I humbly desire the valiant Ajax to invite the most valorous Hector to come unarmed to my tent; and to procure safe conduct for his person, of the magnanimous, and most illustrious, six-or-seven-times-honoured captain-general of the Grecian army, Agamemnon, &c. Do this.

PATR. Jove bless great Ajax!

THER. Hum!

PATR. I come from the worthy Achilles,—

THER. Ha!

PATR. Who most humbly desires you to invite Hector to his tent;—

THER. Hum!

PATR. And to procure safe conduct from Agamemnon.

THER. Agamemnon?

PATR. Ay, my lord.

THER. Ha!

PATR. What say you to't?

THER. God be wi' you, with all my heart.

PATR. Your answer, sir.

THER. If to-morrow be a fair day, by eleven o'clock it will go one way or other; howsoever, he shall pay for me ere he has me.

(*) First folio, *his.*

(†) First folio inserts, *his.*

PATR. Your answer, sir.

THER. Fare you well, with all my heart.

ACHIL. Why, but he is not in this tune, is he?

THER. No, but he's out o'tune thus. What music will be in him when Hector has knocked out his brains, I know not: but, I am sure, none,—unless the fiddler Apollo get his sinews to make catlings on.

ACHIL. Come, thou shalt bear a letter to him straight.

THER. Let me bear* another to his horse; for that's the more capable creature.

ACHIL. My mind is troubled, like a fountain stirr'd;
And I myself see not the bottom of it.

[*Exeunt* ACHILLES *and* PATROCLUS.

THER. Would the fountain of your mind were clear again, that I might water an ass at it! I had rather be a tick in a sheep than such a valiant ignorance. [*Exit.*

(*) First folio, *carry*.

ACT IV.

SCENE I.—Troy. *A Street.*

Enter, at one side, Æneas, *and* Servant, *with a torch; at the other,* Paris, Deiphobus, Antenor, Diomedes, *and others, with torches.*

Par. See, ho! who is that there?
Dei. 'Tis the lord Æneas.
Æne. Is the prince there in person?—
Had I so good occasion to lie long,
As you, prince Paris, nothing but heavenly business
Should rob my bed-mate of my company.
Dio. That's my mind too.—Good morrow, lord Æneas.
Par. A valiant Greek, Æneas,—take his [hand,—
Witness the process of your speech, wherein*
You told how Diomed, in a whole week by days,
Did haunt you in the field.
Æne. Health to you, valiant sir,
During all question of the gentle truce:
But when I meet you arm'd, as black defiance,
As heart can think or courage execute.
Dio. The one and other Diomed embraces.
Our bloods are now in calm; and, so long, health:
But when contention and occasion meet,
By Jove, I'll play the hunter for thy life,
With all my force,[a] pursuit, and policy.
Æne. And thou shalt hunt a lion, that will fly

---

a *With all my* force, *pursuit, and policy.*] "Force," to express physical vigour, was a word of common use in Shakespeare's day,—

"My *force* the Erymanthean bore
Should bravely overmatch."
Albions England, c. xxxvi.

but Mr. Collier's annotator, in unaccountable ignorance of its signification in this place, and in "The Winter's Tale," Act III. Sc. 3,—

"—— had *force* and knowledge
More than was ever man's;"

proposes in the above case to read,—

"With all my *fierce* pursuit," &c.

and in the other,—

"—— had *sense* and knowledge."

(*) First folio, *within*.

With his face backward.—In humane gentleness,
Welcome to Troy! now, by Anchises' life,
Welcome, indeed! By Venus' hand I swear,
No man alive can love, in such a sort,
The thing he means to kill, more excellently!

DIO. We sympathize:—Jove, let Æneas live,
If to my sword his fate be not the glory,
A thousand cómplete courses of the sun!
But, in mine emulous honour, let him die,
With every joint a wound, and that to-morrow!

ÆNE. We know each other well.

DIO. We do; and long to know each other worse.

PAR. This is the most despiteful* gentle greeting,
The noblest hateful love, that e'er I heard of.—
What business, lord, so early?

ÆNE. I was sent for to the king; but why, I know not.

PAR. His purpose meets you: 'twas to bring this Greek
To Calchas' house; and there to render him,
For the enfreed Antenor, the fair Cressid:
Let's have your company; or, if you please,
Haste there before us: I constantly do think,
(Or, rather, call my thought a certain knowledge)
My brother Troilus lodges there to-night;
Rouse him, and give him note of our approach,
With the whole quality wherefore:† I fear,
We shall be much unwelcome.

ÆNE. That I assure you;
Troilus had rather Troy were borne to Greece,
Than Cressid borne from Troy.

PAR. There is no help;
The bitter disposition of the time
Will have it so. On, lord; we'll follow you.

ÆNE. Good morrow, all. [*Exit.*

PAR. And tell me, noble Diomed—'faith, tell me true,
Even in the soul of sound good-fellowship,—
Who, in your thoughts, merits fair Helen most,
Myself or Menelaus?

DIO. Both alike:
He merits well to have her, that doth seek her
(Not making any scruple of her soilure)
With such a hell of pain and world of charge;
And you as well to keep her, that defend her
(Not palating the taste of her dishonour)
With such a costly loss of wealth and friends:
He, like a puling cuckold, would drink up
The lees and dregs of a flat tamed piece;
You, like a lecher, out of whorish loins
Are pleas'd to breed out your inheritors:
Both merits pois'd, each weighs nor less nor more;
But he as he, the‡ heavier for a whore.

(*) First folio, *despightful'st.* (†) First folio, *whereof.* (‡) First folio, *which.*

[a] *We'll* not *commend what we intend* to *sell.*] Warburton proposed,—

"—— what we intend *not* sell;"

PAR. You are too bitter to your countrywoman.

DIO. She's bitter to her country. Hear me, Paris,—
For every false drop in her bawdy veins
A Grecian's life hath sunk; for every scruple
Of her contaminated carrion weight,
A Trojan hath been slain: since she could speak,
She hath not given so many good words breath,
As for her Greeks and Trojans suffer'd death.

PAR. Fair Diomed, you do as chapmen do,
Dispraise the thing that you desire to buy:
But we in silence hold this virtue well,—
We'll not commend what we intend to sell.[a]
Here lies our way. [*Exeunt.*

SCENE II.—*The same. Court before the House of* Pandarus.

Enter TROILUS *and* CRESSIDA.

TROIL. Dear, trouble not yourself; the morn is cold.

CRES. Then, sweet my lord, I'll call mine uncle down;
He shall unbolt the gates.

TROIL. Trouble him not;
To bed, to bed: sleep kill those pretty eyes,
And give as soft attachment to thy senses,
As infants' empty of all thought!

CRES. Good morrow then.

TROIL. I pr'ythee now, to bed.

CRES. Are you a-weary of me?

TROIL. O, Cressida! but that the busy day,
Wak'd by the lark, hath rous'd the ribald crows,
And dreaming night will hide our joys* no longer,
I would not from thee.

CRES. Night hath been too brief.

TROIL. Beshrew the witch! with venomous wights she stays,
As tediously† as hell; but flies the grasps of love,
With wings more momentary-swift than thought.
You will catch cold, and curse me.

CRES. Pr'ythee, tarry;
You men will never tarry.—
O, foolish Cressid! I might have still held off,
And then you would have tarried. Hark! there's one up.

PAN. [*Within.*] What, are all the doors open here?

TROIL. It is your uncle.

CRES. A pestilence on him! now will he be mocking:
I shall have such a life,—

(*) First folio, *eyes.* (†) First folio, *hidiously.*

and Mr. Collier's annotator,—

"We'll *but* commend what we intend to sell."

The former, in all probability, is what the poet wrote.

Enter PANDARUS.

PAN. How now, how now? how go maidenheads?
—Here, you maid! where's my cousin Cressid?

CRES. Go hang yourself, you naughty mocking uncle!
You bring me to do, and then you flout me too.

PAN. To do what? to do what?—let her say what:—what have I brought you to do?

CRES. Come, come; beshrew your heart! you'll ne'er be good,
Nor suffer others.

PAN. Ha, ha! Alas, poor wretch! ah poor capocchio![a]—hast not slept to-night? would he not, a naughty man, let it sleep? a bugbear take him! (1) [*Knocking.*

[a] — ah poor capocchio!—] The old text has, "a poor chipochia." "Capocchio" is an Italian word, signifying *simpleton, innocent,* and the like.

CRES. Did not I tell you?—would he were knock'd i' the head!
Who's that at door? good uncle, go and see.—
My lord, come you again into my chamber:—
You smile, and mock me, as if I meant naughtily.

TROIL. Ha, ha!

CRES. Come, you are deceiv'd, I think of no such thing.— [*Knocking.*
How earnestly they knock!—Pray you, come in;
I would not for half Troy have you seen here.
[*Exeunt* TROILUS *and* CRESSIDA.

PAN. [*Going to the door.*] Who's there? what's the matter? will you beat down the door? How now? what's the matter?

Enter ÆNEAS.

ÆNE. Good morrow, lord, good morrow.

PAN. Who's there? my lord Æneas? By my troth, I knew you not! what news with you so early?

ÆNE. Is not prince Troilus here?

PAN. Here! what should he do here?

ÆNE. Come, he is here, my lord, do not deny him;
It doth import him much to speak with me.

PAN. Is he here, say you? 'tis more than I know, I'll be sworn:—for my own part, I came in late. What should he do here?

ÆNE. Who!—nay, then:—come, come, you'll do him wrong ere you're 'ware: you'll be so true to him, to be false to him: do not you know of him, but yet go fetch him hither; go.

As PANDARUS *is going out, re-enter* TROILUS.

TROIL. How now! what's the matter?

ÆNE. My lord, I scarce have leisure to salute you,
My matter is so rash: there is at hand
Paris your brother, and Deiphobus,
The Grecian Diomed, and our Antenor
Deliver'd to us; and for him forthwith,
Ere the first sacrifice, within this hour,
We must give up to Diomedes' hand
The lady Cressida.

TROIL. Is it concluded so?

ÆNE. By Priam, and the general state of Troy:
They are at hand, and ready to effect it.

TROIL. [*Aside.*] How my achievements mock me!—
I will go meet them: and, my lord Æneas,
We met by chance; you did not find me here.

ÆNE. Good, good, my lord; the secrets[a] of nature
Have not more gift in taciturnity.
[*Exeunt* TROILUS *and* ÆNEAS.

PAN. Is't possible? no sooner got but lost? The devil take Antenor! the young prince will go mad. A plague upon Antenor! I would, they had broke's neck!

Enter CRESSIDA.

CRES. How now? what's the matter? who was here?

PAN. Ah, ah!

CRES. Why sigh you so profoundly? where's my lord gone?
Tell me, sweet uncle, what's the matter?

PAN. Would I were as deep under the earth as I am above!

CRES. O, the gods!—what's the matter?

PAN. Pr'ythee, get thee in; would thou hadst ne'er been born! I knew thou wouldst be his death:—O, poor gentleman!—A plague upon Antenor!

CRES. Good uncle, I beseech you, on my knees
I beseech you, what's the matter?

PAN. Thou must be gone, wench, thou must be gone; thou art changed for Antenor: thou must to thy father, and be gone from Troilus; 'twill be his death; 'twill be his bane; he cannot bear it.

CRES. O, you immortal gods!—I will not go.

PAN. Thou must.

CRES. I will not, uncle: I have forgot my father;
I know no touch of consanguinity;
No kin, no love, no blood, no soul so near me
As the sweet Troilus.—O, you gods divine!
Make Cressid's name the very crown of falsehood,
If ever she leave Troilus! Time, force, and death,
Do to this body what extremes* you can;
But the strong base and building of my love
Is as the very centre of the earth,
Drawing all things to it.—I will go in and weep;—

PAN. Do, do.

CRES. Tear my bright hair, and scratch my praised cheeks;
Crack my clear voice with sobs, and break my heart
With sounding Troilus! I will not go from Troy!
[*Exeunt.*

---

a *Good, good, my lord; the* secrets *of nature*
Have not more gift in taciturnity.]

Mr. Collier's annotator, to correct the faulty measure, reads,—

"—— the secret *laws* of nature," &c.

The error, we believe, however, is in the word "secrets," which appears to have been a misprint for "*secretairs*," or *secretaries*, meaning *confidants*. Thus, in Heywood's "The Four Prentises of London," 1632,—"Prince Tancred is our royall *secretary*." Again, in Greene's "Farewell of a Friend,"—"If thy wife be wise make her thy *secretary*." Again, in Drayton's "Poly-olbion" (Notes to Song IX.),—"But in that true *secretary* of divinity and nature, Solomon," &c. So also in Ben Jonson's "Magnetic Lady," Act IV. Sc. 2,—

"If you have but a *secretary* laundress," &c.

And in the play of "The Antiquary," Act III. Sc. 1,—

"—— unless you were Time's *secretary*," &c.

(*) First folio, *extremitie*.

SCENE III.—*The same. Before* Pandarus' *House.*

Enter PARIS, TROILUS, ÆNEAS, DEIPHOBUS, ANTENOR, *and* DIOMEDES.

PAR. It is great morning; and the hour prefix'd
Of her delivery to this valiant Greek
Comes fast upon:—good my brother Troilus,
Tell you the lady what she is to do,
And haste her to the purpose.
TROIL. Walk into her house;
I'll bring her to the Grecian presently:
And to his hand when I deliver her,
Think it an altar; and thy brother Troilus
A priest, there offering to it his own* heart. [*Exit.*
PAR. I know what 'tis to love;
And would, as I shall pity, I could help!—
Please you walk in, my lords. [*Exeunt.*

SCENE IV.—*The same. A Room in* Pandarus' *House.*

Enter PANDARUS *and* CRESSIDA.

PAN. Be moderate, be moderate.
CRES. Why tell you me of moderation?
The grief is fine, full, perfect, that I taste,
And violenteth† in a sense as strong
As that which causeth it: how can I moderate it?
If I could temporize with my affection,
Or brew it to a weak and colder palate,
The like allayment could I give my grief:
My love admits no qualifying dross;‡
No more my grief, in such a precious loss.
PAN. Here, here, here he comes.—

Enter TROILUS.

Ah sweet ducks!§
CRES. O, Troilus! Troilus! [*Embracing him.*
PAN. What a pair of spectacles is here! Let me embrace too. *O, heart,*—as the goodly saying is,—

—— O, heart, O,|| heavy heart,
Why sigh'st thou without breaking?

where he answers again,

Because thou canst not ease thy smart,
By friendship nor by speaking.

There never was a truer rhyme. Let us cast away nothing, for we may live to have need of such a verse; we see it, we see it.—How now, lambs?
TROIL. Cressid, I love thee in so strain'd* a purity,
That the bless'd gods—as angry with my fancy,
More bright in zeal than the devotion which
Cold lips blow to their deities,—take thee from me.
CRES. Have the gods envy?
PAN. Ay, ay, ay, ay; 'tis too plain a case.
CRES. And is it true that I must go from Troy?
TROIL. A hateful truth.
CRES. What, and from Troilus too?
TROIL. From Troy and Troilus.
CRES. Is it possible?
TROIL. And suddenly; where injury of chance
Puts back leave-taking, justles roughly by
All time of pause, rudely beguiles our lips
Of all rejoindure, forcibly prevents
Our lock'd embrasures, strangles our dear vows
Even in the birth of our own labouring breath:
We two, that with so many thousand sighs
Did buy each other, must poorly sell ourselves
With the rude brevity and discharge of one.†
Injurious Time now, with a robber's haste,
Crams his rich thievery up, he knows not how:
As many farewells as be stars in heaven,
With distinct breath and consign'd[a] kisses to them,
He fumbles up into a loose adieu;
And scants us with a single famish'd kiss,
Distasted‡ with the salt of broken tears.
ÆNE. [*Without.*] My lord, is the lady ready?
TROIL. Hark! you are call'd: some say the Genius so
Cries, *Come!* to him that instantly must die.—
Bid them have patience; she shall come anon.
PAN. Where are my tears? rain, to lay this wind, or my heart will be blown up by the root! [*Exit.*
CRES. I must, then, to the Grecians?
TROIL. No remedy.
CRES. A woeful Cressid 'mongst the merry Greeks!
When shall we see again?[b]
TROIL. Hear me, my love: be thou but true of heart,—
CRES. I true! how now! what wicked deem is this?
TROIL. Nay, we must use expostulation kindly,
For it is parting from us:—
I speak not, *be thou true*, as fearing thee;

(*) First folio omits, *own*. (†) First folio, *And no lesse in*. (‡) First folio, *crosse*. (§) First folio, *a sweet ducke*. (||) Old text omits, *O*.

[a] — consign'd—] *Sealed*, from *consigno*.

(*) First folio, *strange*. (†) First folio, *our*. (‡) First folio, *Distasting*.

[b] When shall we see again?] In the folio, this inquiry is wrongly ascribed to Troilus.

For I will throw my glove to Death himself,
That there's no maculation in thy heart:
But, *be thou true*, say I, to fashion in
My sequent protestation; be thou true,
And I will see thee.

CRES. O, you shall be expos'd, my lord, to dangers
As infinite as imminent! but I'll be true.

TROIL. And I'll grow friend with danger. Wear this sleeve.

CRES. And you this glove. When shall I see you?

TROIL. I will corrupt the Grecian sentinels,
To give thee nightly visitation.
But yet, be true.

CRES. O, heavens!—*be true*, again?

TROIL. Hear why I speak it, love;
The Grecian youths are full of quality;
They're loving, well compos'd with gifts of nature,[a]
And flowing[b] o'er with arts and exercise;
How novelties may move, and parts with person,
Alas, a kind of godly jealousy
(Which, I beseech you, call a virtuous sin)
Makes me afeard.*

CRES. O, heavens! you love me not.

TROIL. Die I a villain then!
In this I do not call your faith in question,
So mainly as my merit: I cannot sing,
Nor heel the high lavolt, nor sweeten talk,
Nor play at subtle games; fair virtues all,
To which the Grecians are most prompt and pregnant:
But I can tell, that in each grace of these
There lurks a still and dumb-discoursive devil,
That tempts most cunningly: but be not tempted.

CRES. Do you think I will?

TROIL. No.
But something may be done that we will not:
And sometimes we are devils to ourselves,
When we will tempt the frailty of our powers,
Presuming on their changeful potency.

ÆNE. [*Without.*] Nay, good my lord,—

TROIL. Come, kiss; and let us part.

PAR. [*Without.*] Brother Troilus!

TROIL. Good brother, come you hither;
And bring Æneas and the Grecian with you.

CRES. My lord, will you be true?

TROIL. Who, I? alas, it is my vice, my fault:
Whiles others fish with craft for great opinion,
I with great truth catch mere simplicity;
Whilst some with cunning gild their copper crowns,
With truth and plainness I do wear mine bare.
Fear not my truth; the moral of my wit
Is—plain and true;—there's all the reach of it.

Enter ÆNEAS, PARIS, ANTENOR, DEIPHOBUS, *and* DIOMEDES.

Welcome, sir Diomed! here is the lady,
Which for Antenor we deliver you:
At the port, lord, I'll give her to thy hand;
And by the way possess thee what she is.
Entreat her fair; and, by my soul, fair Greek,
If e'er thou stand at mercy of my sword,
Name Cressid, and thy life shall be as safe
As Priam is in Ilion.

DIO. Fair lady Cressid,
So please you, save the thanks this prince expects:
The lustre in your eye, heaven in your cheek,
Pleads your fair usage;* and to Diomed
You shall be mistress, and command him wholly.

TROIL. Grecian, thou dost not use me courteously,
To shame the zeal† of my petition to thee,‡
In§ praising her: I tell thee, lord of Greece,
She is as far high-soaring o'er thy praises,
As thou unworthy to be call'd her servant.
I charge thee use her well, even for my charge;
For, by the dreadful Pluto, if thou dost not,
Though the great bulk Achilles be thy guard,
I'll cut thy throat!

DIO. O, be not mov'd, prince Troilus:
Let me be privileg'd by my place and message,
To be a speaker free; when I am hence,
I'll answer to my lust:[c] and know you,|| lord,
I'll nothing do on charge: to her own worth
She shall be priz'd; but that you say—Be't so,
I'll speak it in my spirit and honour,—No.

TROIL. Come, to the port.—I'll tell thee, Diomed,
This brave shall oft make thee to hide thy head.—
Lady, give me your hand; and, as we walk,
To our own selves bend we our needful talk.(2)

[*Exeunt* TROILUS, CRESSIDA, *and* DIOMEDES.
[*Trumpet heard.*

PAR. Hark! Hector's trumpet.

ÆNE. How have we spent this morning!
The prince must think me tardy and remiss,
That swore to ride before him to¶ the field.

PAR. 'Tis Troilus' fault: come, come, to field with him.

DEI. Let us make ready straight.[d]

ÆNE. Yea, with a bridegroom's fresh alacrity,
Let us address to tend on Hector's heels:
The glory of our Troy doth this day lie
On his fair worth and single chivalry. [*Exeunt.*

(*) First folio, *affraid*.

(*) First folio, *visage*. (†) Old text, *seale*. (‡) First folio, *towards*. (§) First folio, *I*. (||) First folio, *my*. (¶) First folio, *in*.

[a] *They're loving, well compos'd with gifts of nature,*—] The folio reads, *guift*; the line is omitted in the quarto.

[b] And flowing o'er, &c.] The folio reads, "*Flowing and swelling o'er*," &c.; but one or other of the words was certainly intended to be cancelled.

[c] *I'll answer to my lust*:] "Lust," in its ancient sense of *pleasure*, is intelligible; but it looks very like a misprint for *trust*.

[d] DEI. Let us make ready straight.] In the folio, where alone this line is found, the prefix is "*Dio.*"

SCENE V.—*The* Grecian *Camp.* *Lists set out.*

Enter AJAX, *armed;* AGAMEMNON, ACHILLES, PATROCLUS, MENELAUS, ULYSSES, NESTOR, *and others.*

AGAM. Here art thou in appointment fresh and fair,
Anticipating time with starting courage.[a]
Give with thy trumpet a loud note to Troy,
Thou dreadful Ajax; that the appalled air
May pierce the head of the great combatant,
And hale him hither.

AJAX. Thou, trumpet, there's my purse.
Now crack thy lungs, and split thy brazen pipe:
Blow, villain, till thy sphered bias[b] cheek
Out-swell the cholic of puff'd Aquilon:

Here art thou in appointment fresh and fair,
Anticipating time with starting courage.]
In the old copies, the passage is pointed thus absurdly,—
"Here art thou in appointment fresh and faire,
Anticipating time. With starting courage,
Give," &c.

b — *sphered* bias *cheek*—] "Swelling out," Johnson says, "like the bias of a bowl."

Come, stretch thy chest, and let thy eyes spout blood;
Thou blow'st for Hector. [*Trumpet sounds.*
ULYSS. No trumpet answers.
ACHIL. 'Tis but early days.
AGAM. Is not yond* Diomed, with Calchas' daughter?
ULYSS. 'Tis he, I ken the manner of his gait;
He rises on the toe: that spirit of his
In aspiration lifts him from the earth.

Enter DIOMEDES, *with* CRESSIDA.

AGAM. Is this the lady Cressid?
DIO. Even she.
AGAM. Most dearly welcome to the Greeks, sweet lady.
NEST. Our general doth salute you with a kiss.
ULYSS. Yet is the kindness but particular;
'Twere better, she were kiss'd in general.
NEST. And very courtly counsel: I'll begin.—
So much for Nestor.
ACHIL. I'll take that winter from your lips, fair [lady:
Achilles bids you welcome.
MEN. I had good argument for kissing once.
PATR. But that's no argument for kissing now:
For thus popp'd Paris in his hardiment;
And parted thus you and your argument.[a]
ULYSS. O, deadly gall, and theme of all our scorns!
For which we lose our heads to gild his horns.
PATR. The first was Menelaus' kiss;—this, mine:
Patroclus kisses you.
MEN. O, this is trim!
PATR. Paris and I kiss evermore for him.
MEN. I'll have my kiss, sir.—Lady, by your leave.
CRES. In kissing, do you render or receive?
PATR. Both take and give.
CRES. I'll make my match to live,
The kiss you take is better than you give;
Therefore no kiss.
MEN. I'll give you boot, I'll give you three for one.
CRES. You're an odd man; give even, or give [none.
MEN. An odd man, lady? every man is odd.
CRES. No, Paris is not; for, you know, 'tis true,
That you are odd, and he is even with you.

MEN. You fillip me o' the head.
CRES. No, I'll be sworn.
ULYSS. It were no match, your nail against his horn.—
May I, sweet lady, beg a kiss of you?
CRES. You may.
ULYSS. I do desire it.
CRES. Why, beg, then.[b]
ULYSS. Why, then, for Venus' sake, give me a kiss,
When Helen is a maid again, and his.
CRES. I am your debtor, claim it when 'tis due.
ULYSS. Never's my day, and then a kiss of you.
DIO. Lady, a word;—I'll bring you to your father. [*Exit with* CRESSIDA.
NEST. A woman of quick sense.
ULYSS. Fie, fie upon her!
There's language in her eye, her cheek, her lip,
Nay, her foot speaks; her wanton spirits look out
At every joint and motive of her body.
O, these encounterers, so glib of tongue,
That give a coasting[c] welcome ere it comes,
And wide unclasp the tables of their thoughts
To every ticklish* reader! set them down
For sluttish spoils of opportunity,
And daughters of the game. [*Trumpet without.*
ALL. The Trojans' trumpet!
AGAM. Yonder comes the troop.

Enter HECTOR, *armed;* ÆNEAS, TROILUS, *and other* Trojans, *with* Attendants.

ÆNE. Hail, all the† state of Greece! what shall be done
To him that victory commands? Or do you pur- [pose,
A victor shall be known? will you, the knights
Shall to the edge of all extremity
Pursue each other; or shall they‡ be divided
By any voice or order of the field?
Hector bade ask.
AGAM. Which way would Hector have it?
ÆNE. He cares not, he'll obey conditions.
ACHIL. 'Tis done like Hector;[d] but securely[e] done,
A little proudly, and great deal disprizing
The knight oppos'd.
ÆNE. If not Achilles, sir,
What is your name?
ACHIL. If not Achilles, nothing.

(*) First folio, *yong.*

a And parted thus you and your argument.] A line omitted in the folio.

b Why, beg, then.] Johnson proposed, for the sake of rhyme, to read,—

"Why, beg *two;*"—

and Mr. Dyce suggests,—

"Why, beg, then, *do.*"

c *That give* a coasting *welcome,* &c.] Mason conjectured we should read,—

"That give *accosting* welcome," &c.;

and Mr. Collier's annotator has,—

"That give *occasion* welcome," &c

d 'Tis done like Hector, &c.] This speech, in the old copies, is assigned to Agamemnon.

e — securely *done,*—] *Over-confidently* done.

(*) First folio, *tickling.* (†) First folio, *you.* (‡) First folio omits, *they.*

ÆNE. Therefore Achilles: but, whate'er, know this;—
In the extremity of great and little,
Valour and pride excel themselves in Hector;
The one almost as infinite as all,
The other blank as nothing. Weigh him well,
And that which looks like pride is courtesy.
This Ajax is half made of Hector's blood:
In love whereof, half Hector stays at home;
Half heart, half hand, half Hector comes to seek
This blended knight, half Trojan and half Greek.
ACHIL. A maiden battle then?—O, I perceive you.

Re-enter DIOMEDES.

AGAM. Here is sir Diomed:—go, gentle knight,
Stand by our Ajax: as you and lord Æneas
Consent upon the order of their fight,
So be it; either to the uttermost,
Or else a breath:[a] the combatants being kin,
Half stints their strife before their strokes begin.
[AJAX *and* HECTOR *enter the lists.*
ULYSS. They are oppos'd already.
AGAM. What Trojan is that same that looks so heavy?
ULYSS. The youngest son of Priam, a true knight;
Not yet mature, yet matchless; firm of word;
Speaking in deeds, and deedless in his tongue;
Not soon provok'd, nor being provok'd soon calm'd:
His heart and hand both open and both free;
For what he has he gives, what thinks, he shows;
Yet gives he not till judgment guide his bounty,
Nor dignifies an impair[b] thought with breath:
Manly as Hector, but more dangerous;
For Hector, in his blaze of wrath, subscribes
To tender objects; but he, in heat of action,
Is more vindicative than jealous love:
They call him Troilus; and on him erect
A second hope, as fairly built as Hector.
Thus says Æneas; one that knows the youth
Even to his inches, and, with private soul,
Did in great Ilion thus translate him to me.
[*Alarum.* HECTOR *and* AJAX *fight.*(3)
AGAM. They are in action.
NEST. Now, Ajax, hold thine own!
TROIL. Hector, thou sleep'st;
Awake thee!
AGAM. His blows are well dispos'd:—there, Ajax!
DIO. You must no more. [*Trumpets cease.*
ÆNE. Princes, enough, so please you.
AJAX. I am not warm yet; let us fight again.
DIO. As Hector pleases.
HECT. Why then, will I no more:—
Thou art, great lord, my father's sister's son,
A cousin-german to great Priam's seed;
The obligation of our blood forbids
A gory emulation 'twixt us twain:
Were thy commixtion Greek and Trojan so,
That thou could'st say—*This hand is Grecian all,*
And this is Trojan; the sinews of this leg
All Greek, and this all Troy; my mother's blood
Runs on the dexter cheek, and this sinister
Bounds-in my father's; by Jove multipotent,
Thou should'st not bear from me a Greekish member
Wherein my sword had not impressure made
Of our rank feud! But the just gods gainsay,
That any drop thou borrow'dst from thy mother,
My sacred aunt, should by my mortal sword
Be drained! Let me embrace thee, Ajax:
By him that thunders, thou hast lusty arms;
Hector would have them fall upon him thus:
Cousin, all honour to thee!
AJAX. I thank thee, Hector:
Thou art too gentle and too free a man:
I came to kill thee, cousin, and bear hence
A great addition earned in thy death.
HECT. Not Neoptolemus[c] so mirable
(On whose bright crest Fame with her loud'st *O-yes*
Cries, *This is he,*) could* promise to himself
A thought of added honour torn from Hector.
ÆNE. There is expectance here from both the sides,
What further you will do.
HECT. We'll answer it;
The issue is embracement:—Ajax, farewell.
AJAX. If I might in entreaties find success
(As seld I have the chance), I would desire
My famous cousin to our Grecian tents.
DIO. 'Tis Agamemnon's wish: and great Achilles
Doth long to see unarm'd the valiant Hector.
HECT. Æneas, call my brother Troilus to me:
And signify this loving interview
To the expecters of our Trojan part;
Desire them home.—Give me thy hand, my cousin:
I will go eat with thee, and see your knights.
AJAX. Great Agamemnon comes to meet us here.
HECT. The worthiest of them tell me name by name;

---

[a] *Or else a* breath:] That is, a *breathing;* a combat merely for exercise. The folio reads "breach."

[b] *Nor dignifies an* impair *thought*—] Mr. Dyce, perhaps rightly, reads,—"an *impure* thought."

[c] *Not* Neoptolemus—] By Neoptolemus was meant Achilles; the author, as Johnson conjectured, supposing, as that hero's son was Pyrrhus Neoptolemus, Neoptolemus must have been the *nomen gentilitium.*

(*) First folio, *could'st.*

But for Achilles, mine own searching eyes
Shall find him by his large and portly size.

AGAM. Worthy of arms! as welcome as to one
That would be rid of such an enemy;
But that's no welcome: understand more clear,
What's past and what's to come is strew'd with husks,
And formless ruin of oblivion;
But in this extant moment, faith and troth,
Strain'd purely from all hollow bias-drawing,
Bids thee, with most divine integrity,
From heart of very heart, great Hector, welcome!

HECT. I thank thee, most imperious Agamemnon.

AGAM. My well-fam'd lord of Troy, no less to you. [*To* TROILUS.

MEN. Let me confirm my princely brother's greeting;—
You brace of warlike brothers, welcome hither.

HECT. Whom must we answer?

ÆNE. The noble Menelaus.

HECT. O, you, my lord? by Mars his gauntlet, thanks!
Mock not, that I affect the untraded oath;
Your *quondam* wife swears still by Venus' glove:
She's well, but bade me not commend her to you.

MEN. Name her not now, sir; she's a deadly theme.

HECT. O, pardon; I offend.

NEST. I have, thou gallant Trojan, seen thee oft,
Labouring for destiny, make cruel way
Through ranks of Greekish youth: and I have seen thee,
As hot as Perseus, spur thy Phrygian steed,
Despising many forfeits and subduements,[a]
When thou hast hung thy advanced sword i' the air,
Not letting it decline on the declin'd;
That I have said to some my* standers-by,
Lo, Jupiter is yonder, dealing life!
And I have seen thee pause, and take thy breath,
When that a ring of Greeks have hemm'd thee in,
Like an Olympian wrestling: this have I seen;
But this thy countenance, still lock'd in steel,
I never saw till now. I knew thy grandsire,
And once fought with him: he was a soldier good;
But, by great Mars the captain of us all,
Never like thee! Let an old man embrace thee;
And, worthy warrior, welcome to our tents.

ÆNE. 'Tis the old Nestor.

HECT. Let me embrace thee, good old chronicle,
That hast so long walk'd hand in hand with time:—
Most reverend Nestor, I am glad to clasp thee.

NEST. I would my arms could match thee in contention,
As they contend with thee in courtesy.

HECT. I would they could.

NEST. Ha! By this white beard, I'd fight with thee to-morrow!—
Well, welcome, welcome! I have seen the time.

ULYSS. I wonder now how yonder city stands,
When we have here her base and pillar by us.

HECT. I know your favour, lord Ulysses, well.
Ah, sir, there's many a Greek and Trojan dead,
Since first I saw yourself and Diomed
In Ilion, on your Greekish embassy.

ULYSS. Sir, I foretold you then what would ensue:
My prophecy is but half his journey yet;
For yonder walls, that pertly front your town,
Yond towers, whose wanton tops do buss the clouds,
Must kiss their own feet.

HECT. I must not believe you:
There they stand yet; and modestly I think,
The fall of every Phrygian stone will cost
A drop of Grecian blood: the end crowns all;
And that old common arbitrator, Time,
Will one day end it.

ULYSS. So to him we leave it.
Most gentle and most valiant Hector, welcome:
After the general, I beseech you next
To feast with me, and see me at my tent.

ACHIL. I shall forestall thee, lord Ulysses, thou!—
Now, Hector, I have fed mine eyes on thee;
I have with exact view perus'd thee, Hector,
And quoted joint by joint.

HECT. Is this Achilles?

ACHIL. I am Achilles.

HECT. Stand fair, I pray thee: let me look on thee.

ACHIL. Behold thy fill.

HECT. Nay, I have done already.

ACHIL. Thou art too brief; I will the second time,
As I would buy thee, view thee limb by limb.

HECT. O, like a book of sport thou'lt read me o'er;
But there's more in me than thou understand'st.
Why dost thou so oppress me with thine eye?

ACHIL. Tell me you heavens, in which part of his body
Shall I destroy him? whether there, or there, or there?
That I may give the local wound a name,
And make distinct the very breach whereout
Hector's great spirit flew: answer me, heavens!

HECT. It would discredit the bless'd gods, proud man,
To answer such a question: stand again:
Think'st thou to catch my life so pleasantly,

(*) First folio, *unto my.*

a Despising many *forfeits and subduements,*—] So the quarto: the folio reads, *And seene thee scorning* forfeits, &c.

As to prenominate in nice conjecture,
Where thou wilt hit me dead?
ACHIL. I tell thee, yea.
HECT. Wert thou an* oracle to tell me so,
I'd not believe thee. Henceforth guard thee well,
For I'll not kill thee there, nor there, nor there;
But, by the forge that stithied Mars his helm,
I'll kill thee every where, yea, o'er and o'er.—
You wisest Grecians, pardon me this brag,
His insolence draws folly from my lips;
But I'll endeavour deeds to match these words,
Or may I never—
AJAX. Do not chafe thee, cousin;—
And you, Achilles, let these threats alone,
Till accident or purpose bring you to't:
You may have† every day enough of Hector,
If you have stomach; the general state, I fear,
Can scarce entreat you to be odd with him.
HECT. I pray you, let us see you in the field;
We have had pelting wars, since you refus'd
The Grecians' cause.
ACHIL. Dost thou entreat me, Hector?
To-morrow, do I meet thee, fell as death;
To-night, all friends.
HECT. Thy hand upon that match.
AGAM. First, all you peers of Greece, go to my tent;
There in the full convive we:* afterwards,
As Hector's leisure and your bounties shall
Concur together, severally entreat[a] him.—
Beat loud the tabourines, let the trumpets blow,
That this great soldier may his welcome know!
[*Exeunt all except* TROILUS *and* ULYSSES.
TROIL. My lord Ulysses, tell me, I beseech you,
In what place of the field doth Calchas keep.
ULYSS. At Menelaus' tent, most princely Troilus:
There Diomed doth feast with him to-night;
Who neither looks on heaven, nor on earth,
But gives all gaze and bent of amorous view
On the fair Cressid.
TROIL. Shall I, sweet lord, be bound to you† so much,
After we part from Agamemnon's tent,
To bring me thither?
ULYSS. You shall command me, sir.
As gentle tell me, of what honour was
This Cressida in Troy? Had she no lover there,
That wails her absence?
TROIL. O, sir, to such as boasting show their scars,
A mock is due. Will you walk on, my lord?
She was belov'd, she lov'd; she is, and doth:
But, still, sweet love is food for fortune's tooth.
[*Exeunt.*

(*) First folio, *the*. (†) First folio omits, *have*.

(*) First folio, *you*. (†) First folio, *thee*.

[a] — entreat *him*.] "Entreat" here signifies *entertain*; it is used by Achilles just above in its ordinary sense of *solicit*.

ACT V.

SCENE I.—*The* Grecian *Camp.* *Before* Achilles' *Tent.*

Enter ACHILLES *and* PATROCLUS.

ACHIL. I'll heat his blood with Greekish wine to-night,
Which with my scimitar I'll cool to-morrow.—
Patroclus, let us feast him to the height.

PATR. Here comes Thersites.

Enter THERSITES.

ACHIL. How now, thou core of envy?
Thou crusty batch of nature, what's the news?

THER. Why, thou picture of what thou seemest, and idol of idiot-worshippers, here's a letter for thee.

ACHIL. From whence, fragment?

THER. Why, thou full dish of fool, from Troy.

PATR. Who keeps the tent now?

THER. The surgeon's box, or the patient's wound.

PATR. Well said, Adversity! and what need these tricks?

THER. Pr'ythee be silent, boy; I profit not by thy talk; thou art thought to be Achilles' male varlet.[a]

PATR. *Male varlet,* you rogue! what's that?

THER. Why, his masculine whore. Now the rotten diseases of the south, the* guts-griping, ruptures, catarrhs, loads o' gravel i' the back, lethargies, cold palsies,[b] raw eyes, dirt-rotten livers, wheezing lungs, bladders full of imposthume, sciaticas, lime-kilns i' the palm, incurable bone-ache, and the rivelled fee-simple of the tetter, take and take again such preposterous discoveries!

PATR. Why thou damnable box of envy, thou, what meanest thou to curse thus?

THER. Do I curse thee?

PATR. Why, no, you ruinous butt; you whoreson indistinguishable cur, no.†

THER. No! why art thou then exasperate, thou idle immaterial skein of sleive-silk,‡ thou green

---

a — *male* varlet.] Some editors have seriously proposed to read, "male *harlot,*" not being aware that the former word often represented the latter one: thus, in Middleton's "Roaring Girl," Act I. Sc. 1,—"She's a *varlet.*" In Decker and Middleton's play called "The Honest Whore," Act I. Sc. 10, we have, indeed, the very expression of the text,—

"—— 'tis a *male varlet* sure, my lord."

b Cold palsies,—] The remainder of this unsavoury catalogue is dismissed in the folio, which reads, "cold Palsies, *and the like.*"

(*) First folio omits, *the.* (†) First folio omits, *no.* (‡) First folio, *Sleyd.*

sarcenet flap for a sore eye, thou tassel of a prodigal's purse, thou? Ah, how the poor world is pestered with such water-flies—diminutives of nature!

PATR. Out, gall!

THER. Finch egg!

ACHIL. My sweet Patroclus, I am thwarted quite
From my great purpose in to-morrow's battle.
Here is a letter from queen Hecuba;
A token from her daughter, my fair love;
Both taxing me, and gaging me to keep
An oath that I have sworn. I will not break it:
Fall Greeks; fail fame; honour or go or stay,
My major vow lies here, this I'll obey.—
Come, come, Thersites, help to trim my tent;
This night in banqueting must all be spent.—
Away, Patroclus!

[*Exeunt* ACHILLES *and* PATROCLUS.

THER. With too much blood and too little brain, these two may run mad; but if with too much brain and too little blood, they do, I'll be a curer of madmen. Here's Agamemnon,—an honest fellow enough, and one that loves quails; but he has not so much brain as ear-wax: and the goodly transformation of Jupiter there, his brother, the bull,—the primitive statue, and oblique memorial of cuckolds; a thrifty shoeing-horn in a chain, hanging at his brother's leg,—to what form but that he is, should wit larded with malice, and malice forced[a] with wit, turn him to? To an ass, were nothing; he is both ass and ox: to an ox were nothing; he is both ox and ass. To be a dog, a mule, a cat, a fitchew, a toad, a lizard, an owl, a puttock, or a herring without a roe, I would not care: but to be Menelaus,—I would conspire against destiny. Ask me not what I would be, if I were not Thersites; for I care not to be the louse of a lazar, so I were not Menelaus.—Hoy-day! spirits and fires!

Enter HECTOR, TROILUS, AJAX, AGAMEMNON, ULYSSES, NESTOR, MENELAUS, *and* DIOMEDES, *with lights.*

AGAM. We go wrong, we go wrong.

AJAX. No, yonder 'tis; there, where we see the lights.*

HECT. I trouble you.

AJAX. No, not a whit.

ULYSS. Here comes himself to guide you.

Re-enter ACHILLES.

ACHIL. Welcome, brave Hector; welcome, princes all.

(*) First folio, *light.*

a — forced—] *Stuffed.*

AGAM. So now, fair prince of Troy, I bid good night.
Ajax commands the guard to tend on you.

HECT. Thanks and good night to the Greeks' general.

MEN. Good night, my lord.

HECT. Good night, sweet Menelaus.

THER. [*Aside.*] Sweet draught:[b] *sweet*, quoth 'a! sweet sink, sweet sewer.

ACHIL. Good night, and welcome, both at once to those that go, or tarry.

AGAM. Good night.

[*Exeunt* AGAMEMNON *and* MENELAUS.

ACHIL. Old Nestor tarries; and you too, Diomed,
Keep Hector company an hour or two.

DIO. I cannot, lord; I have important business,
The tide whereof is now.—Good night, great Hector.

HECT. Give me your hand.

ULYSS. [*Aside to* TROIL.] Follow his torch, he goes
To Calchas' tent; I'll keep you company.

TROIL. Sweet sir, you honour me.

HECT. And so good night.

[*Exit* DIOMEDES; ULYSSES *and* TROILUS *following.*

ACHIL. Come, come, enter my tent.

[*Exeunt* ACHILLES, HECTOR, AJAX, *and* NESTOR.

THER. That same Diomed's a false-hearted rogue, a most unjust knave; I will no more trust him when he leers, than I will a serpent when he hisses: he will spend his mouth, and promise, like Brabbler the hound; but when he performs, astronomers foretell it;* it is prodigious, there will come some change; the sun borrows of the moon, when Diomed keeps his word. I will rather leave to see Hector, than not to dog him: they say he keeps a Trojan drab, and uses the traitor Calchas' tent: I'll after.—Nothing but lechery! all incontinent varlets! [*Exit.*

SCENE II.—*The same. Before* Calchas' *Tent.*

Enter DIOMEDES.

DIO. What, are you up here, ho? speak.

CAL. [*Within.*] Who calls?

DIO. Diomed.—Calchas, I think.—Where's your daughter?

CAL. [*Within.*] She comes to you.

(*) First folio inserts, *that.*

b *Sweet* draught:] See note (c), p. 605, Vol. II.

Enter TROILUS *and* ULYSSES, *at a distance; after them* THERSITES.

ULYSS. Stand where the torch may not discover us.

Enter CRESSIDA.

TROIL. Cressid comes forth to him!
DIO. How now, my charge?
CRES. Now, my sweet guardian!—Hark! a word with you. [*Whispers.*
TROIL. Yea, so familiar!
ULYSS. She will sing any man at first sight.
THER. [*Aside.*] And any man may sing* her, if he can take her cliff;† she's noted.
DIO. Will you remember?
CRES. Remember! yes.
DIO. Nay, but do then;
And let your mind be coupled with your words.
TROIL. What should she remember?
ULYSS. List!
CRES. Sweet honey-Greek, tempt me no more to folly.
THER. [*Aside.*] Roguery!
DIO. Nay, then,—
CRES. I'll tell you what,—
DIO. Pho, pho! come, tell a pin: you are‡ forsworn.—
CRES. In faith, I cannot: what would you have me do?
THER. [*Aside.*] A juggling trick,—to be secretly [open.
DIO. What did you swear you would bestow on me?
CRES. I pr'ythee do not hold me to mine oath;
Bid me do§ anything but that, sweet Greek.
DIO. Good night.
TROIL. Hold, patience!
ULYSS. How now, Trojan?
CRES. Diomed,—
DIO. No, no, good night: I'll be your fool no more.
TROIL. Thy better must.
CRES. Hark, one word in your ear.
TROIL. O, plague and madness!
ULYSS. You are mov'd, prince; let us depart, I pray you,
Lest your displeasure should enlarge itself
To wrathful terms: this place is dangerous;
The time right deadly; I beseech you, go.
TROIL. Behold, I pray you!
ULYSS. Now, my good lord, go off:
You flow to great distraction; come, my lord.
TROIL. I pr'ythee, stay.
ULYSS. You have not patience; come.
TROIL. I pray you, stay; by hell, and all hell's torments,*
I will not speak a word.
DIO. And so, good night.
CRES. Nay, but you part in anger.
TROIL. Doth that grieve thee?
O, wither'd truth!
ULYSS. Why, how now, lord?
TROIL. By Jove,
I will be patient.
CRES. Guardian!—why, Greek!
DIO. Pho, pho! adieu; you palter.
CRES. In faith, I do not; come hither once again.
ULYSS. You shake, my lord, at something; will you go?
You will break out.
TROIL. She strokes his cheek!
ULYSS. Come, come.
TROIL. Nay, stay; by Jove, I will not speak a word:
There is between my will and all offences
A guard of patience:—stay a little while.
THER. [*Aside.*] How the devil luxury, with his fat rump and potatoe finger, tickles these together! Fry, lechery, fry!
DIO. But will you then?
CRES. In faith, I will, la; never trust me else.
DIO. Give me some token for the surety of it.
CRES. I'll fetch you one. [*Exit.*
ULYSS. You have sworn patience.
TROIL. Fear me not, sweet lord;
I will not be myself, nor have cognition
Of what I feel; I am all patience.

Re-enter CRESSIDA.

THER. [*Aside.*] Now the pledge; now, now, now!
CRES. Here, Diomed, keep this sleeve.(1)
TROIL. O, beauty! where's thy faith?
ULYSS. My lord,—
TROIL. I will be patient; outwardly I will.
CRES. You look upon that sleeve; behold it well.—
He lov'd me—O, false wench!—Give't me again.
DIO. Whose was't?
CRES. It is no matter, now I have't again.
I will not meet with you to-morrow night:
I pr'ythee, Diomed, visit me no more.
THER. [*Aside.*] Now she sharpens;—well said, whetstone.
DIO. I shall have it.
CRES. What, this?
DIO. Ay, that.

(*) First folio, *finde*.
(†) First folio, *life*.
(‡) First folio inserts, *a*.
(§) First folio inserts, *not*.

(*) First folio, *and hell torments*.

CRES. O, all you gods!—O, pretty, pretty pledge!
Thy master now lies thinking in his bed
Of thee and me; and sighs, and takes my glove,
And gives memorial dainty kisses to it,
As I kiss thee.—Nay, do not snatch it from me;[a]
He, that takes that, doth take* my heart withal.

DIO. I had your heart before, this follows it.

TROIL. I did swear patience.

CRES. You shall not have it, Diomed; faith you shall not;
I'll give you something else.

DIO. I will have this; whose was it?

CRES. It is no matter.

DIO. Come, tell me whose it was.

CRES. 'T was one's† that lov'd me better than you will:
But, now you have it, take it.

DIO. Whose was it?

CRES. By all Diana's waiting-women yond,
And by herself, I will not tell you whose.

DIO. To-morrow will I wear it on my helm;
And grieve his spirit that dares not challenge it.

TROIL. Wert thou the devil, and wor'st it on thy horn,
It should be challeng'd!

CRES. Well, well, 't is done, 't is past;—and yet it is not;
I will not keep my word.

DIO. Why, then, farewell;
Thou never shalt mock Diomed again.

CRES. You shall not go:—one cannot speak a word,
But it straight starts you.

DIO. I do not like this fooling.

THER. [*Aside.*] Nor I, by Pluto: but that that likes not you,‡ pleases me best.

DIO. What, shall I come? the hour?

CRES. Ay, come:—O, Jove!—
Do come:—I shall be plagu'd.

DIO. Farewell till then.

CRES. Good night. I pr'ythee, come.— [*Exit* DIOMEDES.
Troilus, farewell! one eye yet looks on thee;
But with my heart the other eye doth see.—
Ah, poor our sex! this fault in us I find,
The error of our eye directs our mind:
What error leads, must err; O, then conclude,
Minds sway'd by eyes are full of turpitude. [*Exit.*

THER. [*Aside.*] A proof of strength she could not publish more,
Unless she say,—My mind is now turn'd whore.

ULYSS. All's done, my lord.

TROIL. It is.

ULYSS. Why stay we then?

TROIL. To make a recordation to my soul
Of every syllable that here was spoke.
But if I tell how these two did co-act,
Shall I not lie in publishing a truth?
Sith yet there is a credence in my heart,
An esperance so obstinately strong,
That doth invert the attest* of eyes and ears;
As if those organs had deceptious functions,
Created only to calumniate.
Was Cressid here?

ULYSS. I cannot conjure, Trojan.

TROIL. She was not, sure.

ULYSS. Most sure she was.

TROIL. Why, my negation hath no taste of madness.

ULYSS. Nor mine, my lord: Cressid was here but now.

TROIL. Let it not be believ'd for womanhood!
Think, we had mothers; do not give advantage
To stubborn critics[b]—apt, without a theme,
For depravation,—to square the general sex
By Cressid's rule: rather think this not Cressid.(2)

ULYSS. What hath she done, prince, that can soil our mothers?

TROIL. Nothing at all, unless that this were she.

THER. [*Aside.*] Will he swagger himself out on 's own eyes?

TROIL. This she? no, this is Diomed's Cressida:
If beauty have a soul, this is not she;
If souls guide vows, if vows be† sanctimony,
If sanctimony be the gods' delight,
If there be rule in unity itself,
This is not she. O, madness of discourse,
That cause sets up with and against itself! ‡
Bi-fold§ authority! where reason can revolt
Without perdition, and loss assume all reason
Without revolt; this is, and is not, Cressid!
Within my soul there doth conduce[c] a fight
Of this strange nature, that a thing inseparate
Divides more wider than the sky and earth;
And yet the spacious breadth of this division
Admits no orifice for a point, as subtle
As is Arachne's broken woof,[d] to enter.
Instance, O, instance! strong as Pluto's gates;
Cressid is mine, tied with the bonds of heaven:
Instance, O, instance! strong as heaven itself;
The bonds of heaven are slipp'd, dissolv'd, and loos'd;

(*) First folio omits, *doth*, and reads, *rakes*. (†) First folio, *one*. (‡) First folio, *me*.

(*) First folio, *that test*. (†) First folio, *are*. (‡) First folio, *thy selfe*. (§) First folio, *By foule*.

[a] Nay, do not snatch it from me;] In the old text these words are ascribed to Diomedes.

[b] — critics—] That is, *cynics*.

[c] *Within my soul there doth* conduce *a fight*—] Rowe prints *commence* for "conduce;" and certainly, the latter word, in its usual sense, is questionable.

[d] *As* is Arachne's *broken woof*, &c.] The quartos read, "*Ariachna's*" and "*Ariathna's*;" the folio, "*Ariachne's* broken woof," &c. Capell, we believe, first introduced "is," though the credit of supplying it is given to Steevens.

And with another knot, five-finger-tied,
The fractions of her faith, orts of her love,
The fragments, scraps, the bits, and greasy reliques
Of her o'er-eaten faith, are bound to Diomed.

ULYSS. May worthy Troilus be half attach'd
With that which here his passion doth express?

TROIL. Ay, Greek; and that shall be divulged well
In characters as red as Mars his heart
Inflam'd with Venus: never did young man fancy
With so eternal and so fix'd a soul.
Hark, Greek;—as much as I do Cressid love,[a]
So much by weight hate I her Diomed:
That sleeve is mine that he'll bear in his helm;
Were it a casque compos'd by Vulcan's skill,
My sword should bite it: not the dreadful spout,
Which shipmen do the hurricano call,
Constring'd in mass by the almighty sun,*
Shall dizzy with more clamour Neptune's ear
In his descent, than shall my prompted sword
Falling on Diomed.

THER. [*Aside.*] He'll tickle it for his concupy.

TROIL. O, Cressid! O, false Cressid! false, false, false!
Let all untruths stand by thy stained name,
And they'll seem glorious.

ULYSS. O, contain yourself;
Your passion draws ears hither.

Enter ÆNEAS.

ÆNE. I have been seeking you this hour, my lord:
Hector, by this, is arming him in Troy;
Ajax, your guard, stays to conduct you home.

TROIL. Have with you, prince.—My courteous lord, adieu.—
Farewell, revolted fair!—and, Diomed,
Stand fast, and wear a castle on thy head!

ULYSS. I'll bring you to the gates.

TROIL. Accept distracted thanks.

[*Exeunt* ULYSSES, TROILUS, *and* ÆNEAS.

THER. Would, I could meet that rogue Diomed! I would croak like a raven; I would bode, I would bode. Patroclus will give me any thing for the intelligence of this whore: the parrot will not do more for an almond, than he for a commodious drab. Lechery, lechery; still wars and lechery; nothing else holds fashion: a burning devil take them! [*Exit.*

(*) First folio, *Fenne.*

a — *as much* as *I do* Cressid *love,*—] The reading now usually adopted. In the quarto we have, "— as much I do Cressid love," &c., and in the folio, " — as much I doe *Cressida* love," &c.

b —— it is as lawful,
For we would give much, to use violent thefts, &c.]

The folio, in which alone this passage is found, has,—

SCENE III.—Troy. *Before* Priam's *Palace.*

Enter HECTOR *and* ANDROMACHE.

AND. When was my lord so much ungently temper'd,
To stop his ears against admonishment?
Unarm, unarm, and do not fight to-day.

HECT. You train me to offend you; get you in:*
By all† the everlasting gods, I'll go!

AND. My dreams will, sure, prove ominous to the day.

HECT. No more, I say.

Enter CASSANDRA.

CAS. Where is my brother Hector?

AND. Here, sister; arm'd, and bloody in intent:
Consort with me in loud and dear petition,
Pursue we him on knees; for I have dream'd
Of bloody turbulence, and this whole night
Hath nothing been but shapes and forms of slaughter.

CAS. O, 't is true.

HECT. Ho! bid my trumpet sound!

CAS. No notes of sally, for the heavens, sweet brother!

HECT. Begone, I say: the gods have heard me swear.

CAS. The gods are deaf to hot and peevish vows;
They are polluted offerings, more abhorr'd
Than spotted livers in the sacrifice.

AND. O, be persuaded! do not count it holy
To hurt by being just: it is as lawful,
For we would give much, to use violent thefts,[b]
And rob in the behalf of charity.

CAS. It is the purpose that makes strong the vow;
But vows to every purpose must not hold:
Unarm, sweet Hector.

HECT. Hold you still, I say
Mine honour keeps the weather of my fate:[c]
Life every man holds dear; but the dear man
Holds honour far more precious-dear than life.—

(*) First folio, *gone.* (†) First folio omits, *all.*

"—— it is as lawful,
For we would *count* give much to *as* violent thefts," &c.

We adopt the emendation proposed by Tyrwhitt; understanding "to *use* violent thefts," as, "to *practise* violent thefts."

c Mine honour keeps the weather of my fate: &c.] Equivalent to, My honour holds supremacy o'er my fate. "To keep the weather, or weather-gage," is a nautical phrase, which means, to keep to windward, and thus have the advantage.

Enter Troilus.

How now, young man! mean'st thou to fight to-day?

And. Cassandra, call my father to persuade.

[*Exit* Cassandra.

Hect. No, 'faith, young Troilus; doff thy harness, youth,
I am to-day i' the vein of chivalry:
Let grow thy sinews till their knots be strong,
And tempt not yet the brushes of the war.
Unarm thee, go; and doubt thou not, brave boy,
I'll stand to-day for thee, and me, and Troy.

Troil. Brother, you have a vice of mercy in you,
Which better fits a lion than a man.

Hect. What vice is that, good Troilus? chide me for it.

Troil. When many times the captive Grecian falls,
Even in the fan and wind of your fair sword,
You bid them rise, and live.

Hect. O, 't is fair play.

Troil. Fool's play, by heaven, Hector!

Hect. How now! how now!

Troil. For the love of all the gods,
Let's leave the hermit Pity with our mothers;
And when we have our armours buckled on,
The venom'd vengeance ride upon our swords;
Spur them to ruthful work, rein them from ruth.

Hect. Fie, savage, fie!

Troil. Hector, then 't is wars.

Hect. Troilus, I would not have you fight to-day.

Troil. Who should withhold me?
Not fate, obedience, nor the hand of Mars

Beck'ning with fiery truncheon my retire;
Not Priamus and Hecuba on knees,
Their eyes o'ergalled with recourse of tears;
Nor you, my brother, with your true sword drawn,
Oppos'd to hinder me, should stop my way,
But by my ruin.

Re-enter CASSANDRA, *with* PRIAM.

CAS. Lay hold upon him, Priam, hold him fast:
He is thy crutch; now if thou lose thy stay,
Thou on him leaning, and all Troy on thee,
Fall all together.

PRI. Come, Hector, come, go back:
Thy wife hath dream'd; thy mother hath had visions;
Cassandra doth foresee; and I myself
Am like a prophet suddenly enrapt,
To tell thee that this day is ominous:
Therefore, come back.

HECT. Æneas is a-field;
And I do stand engag'd to many Greeks,
Even in the faith of valour, to appear
This morning to them.

PRI. Ay, but thou shalt not go.

HECT. I must not break my faith.
You know me dutiful; therefore, dear sir,
Let me not shame respect; but give me leave
To take that course by your consent and voice,
Which you do here forbid me, royal Priam.

CAS. O, Priam, yield not to him!

AND. Do not, dear father.

HECT. Andromache, I am offended with you:
Upon the love you bear me, get you in.
[*Exit* ANDROMACHE.

TROIL. This foolish, dreaming, superstitious girl
Makes all these bodements.

CAS. O, farewell, dear Hector!
Look, how thou diest! look, how thy eye turns pale!
Look, how thy wounds do bleed at many vents!
Hark, how Troy roars! how Hecuba cries out!
How poor Andromache shrills her dolour forth!
Behold, distraction, frenzy, and amazement,
Like witless antics, one another meet,
And all cry—*Hector! Hector's dead!* O, Hector!

TROIL. Away! away!

CAS. Farewell.—Yet,* soft!—Hector, I take my leave:
Thou dost thyself and all our Troy deceive. [*Exit.*

HECT. You are amaz'd, my liege, at her exclaim:
Go in, and cheer the town: we'll forth, and fight;
Do deeds worth* praise, and tell you them at night.

PRI. Farewell: the gods with safety stand about thee!
[*Exeunt severally* PRIAM *and* HECTOR. *Alarums.*

TROIL. They are at it; hark! Proud Diomed, believe,
I come to lose my arm, or win my sleeve.

As TROILUS *is going out, enter, from the other side,* PANDARUS.

PAN. Do you hear, my lord? do you hear?

TROIL. What now?

PAN. Here's a letter from yond poor girl.

TROIL. Let me read.

PAN. A whoreson tisick, a whoreson rascally tisick so troubles me, and the foolish fortune of this girl; and what one thing, what another, that I shall leave you one o' these days: and I have a rheum in mine eyes too; and such an ache in my bones, that, unless a man were cursed,[a] I cannot tell what to think on't.—What says she there?

TROIL. Words, words, mere words, no matter from the heart; [*Tearing the letter.*
The effect doth operate another way.—
Go, wind, to wind, there turn and change together.—
My love with words and errors still she feeds,
But edifies another with her deeds.[b]
[*Exeunt severally.*

SCENE IV.—*Plains between* Troy *and the* Grecian *Camp.*

Alarums: Excursions. Enter THERSITES.

THER. Now they are clapper-clawing one another, I'll go look on. That dissembling abominable varlet, Diomed, has got that same scurvy doting foolish young knave's sleeve of Troy there, in his helm: I would fain see them meet; that that same young Trojan ass, that loves the whore there, might send that Greekish whoremasterly villain, with the sleeve, back to the dissembling luxurious drab, of a sleeveless errand. O' the other

(*) First folio, *yes.*

(*) First folio, *deeds of praise.*

a — cursed,—] That is, under the influence of a malediction.

b But edifies another with her deeds.] In the folio, after this couplet we have,—

"*Pand.* Why, but heare you?
Troy. Hence brother lackie; ignomie and shame
Pursue thy life, and live aye with thy name."

These lines, however, are found again towards the end of the play, and there can be no doubt were inserted here inadvertently.

side, the policy of those crafty swearing rascals,—that stale old mouse-eaten dry cheese, Nestor; and that same dog-fox, Ulysses,—is not proved worth a blackberry!—They set me up, in policy, that mongrel cur, Ajax, against that dog of as bad a kind, Achilles: and now is the cur Ajax prouder than the cur Achilles, and will not arm to-day; whereupon the Grecians begin* to proclaim barbarism, and policy grows into an ill opinion. Soft! here comes sleeve, and t'other.

Enter DIOMEDES, TROILUS *following*.

TROIL. Fly not; for shouldst thou take the river Styx,
I would swim after!
DIO. Thou dost miscall retire:
I do not fly; but advantageous care
Withdrew me from the odds of multitude:
Have at thee!

THER. [*Aside.*] Hold thy whore, Grecian!—now for thy whore, Trojan!—now the sleeve, now the sleeve!

[*Exeunt* TROILUS *and* DIOMEDES, *fighting*.

Enter HECTOR.

HECT. What art thou, Greek? art thou for Hector's match?
Art thou of blood and honour?

THER. No, no:—I am a rascal; a scurvy railing knave; a very filthy rogue.

HECT. I do believe thee;—live. [*Exit.*

THER. God-a-mercy, that thou wilt believe me; but a plague break thy neck, for frighting me! What's become of the wenching rogues? I think, they have swallowed one another: I would laugh at that miracle:—yet, in a sort, lechery eats itself. I'll seek them. [*Exit.*

SCENE V.—*Another part of the Plains.*

Enter DIOMEDES *and a* Servant.

DIO. Go, go, my servant, take thou Troilus' horse;
Present the fair steed to my lady Cressid:
Fellow, commend my service to her beauty;
Tell her I have chastis'd the amorous Trojan,
And am her knight by proof.
SERV. I go, my lord.
[*Exit.*

Enter AGAMEMNON.

AGAM. Renew, renew! The fierce Polydamus
Hath beat down Menon: bastard Margarelon
Hath Doreus prisoner;
And stands colossus-wise, waving his beam,
Upon the pashed corses of the kings
Epistrophus and Cedius: Polixenes is slain;
Amphimachus and Thoas deadly hurt;
Patroclus ta'en or slain; and Palamedes
Sore hurt and bruis'd: the dreadful Sagittary
Appals our numbers:—haste we, Diomed,
To reinforcement, or we perish all.

Enter NESTOR.

NEST. Go, bear Patroclus' body to Achilles;
And bid the snail-pac'd Ajax arm for shame.—
There is a thousand Hectors in the field:
Now here he fights on Galathe his horse,
And there lacks work; anon, he's there afoot,
And there they fly or die, like scaled[a] sculls
Before the belching whale; then is he yonder,
And there the strawy* Greeks, ripe for his edge,
Fall down before him, like the mower's swath:
Here, there, and every where, he leaves and takes;[b]
Dexterity so obeying appetite,
That what he will, he does; and does so much,
That proof is call'd impossibility.

Enter ULYSSES.

ULYSS. O, courage, courage, princes! great Achilles
Is arming, weeping, cursing, vowing vengeance:
Patroclus' wounds have rous'd his drowsy blood,
Together with his mangled Myrmidons,
That noseless, handless, hack'd and chipp'd, come to him,
Crying on Hector. Ajax hath lost a friend,
And foams at mouth, and he is arm'd, and at it,
Roaring for Troilus; who hath done to-day
Mad and fantastic execution;
Engaging and redeeming of himself,
With such a careless force and forceless care,
As if that luck, in very spite of cunning,
Bade him win all.

(*) Old text, *began*.

(*) First folio, *straying*.

a — *like* scaled sculls—] That is, like *dispersed shoals*.

b *Here, there, and every where,* he leaves and takes;] *To take* was used in the sense of to *paralyze*, to *incapacitate*: so in "Hamlet," Act I. Sc. 1,—

"—— then no planets strike,
No fairy *takes*," &c.:

so, also, in "Coriolanus," Act II. Sc. 2,—

"—— his sword, Death's stamp,
Where it did mark, it *took*;"

and we ought possibly to read,—

"Here, there, and every where, he *cleaves* and takes."

Enter AJAX.

AJAX. Troilus! thou coward Troilus! [*Exit.*
DIO. Ay, there, there.
NEST. So, so, we draw together.

Enter ACHILLES.

ACHIL. Where is this Hector?
Come, come, thou boy-queller, show thy face;
Know what it is to meet Achilles angry:—
Hector! where's Hector? I will none but Hector.
[*Exeunt.*

SCENE VI.—*Another part of the Plains.*

Enter AJAX.

AJAX. Troilus, thou coward Troilus, show thy head!

Enter DIOMEDES.

DIO. Troilus, I say! where's Troilus?
AJAX. What wouldst thou?
DIO. I would correct him.
AJAX. Were I the general, thou shouldst have my office
Ere that correction.—Troilus, I say! what, Troilus!

Enter TROILUS.

TROIL. O, traitor Diomed!—turn thy false face, thou traitor,
And pay thy life thou ow'st me for my horse!
DIO. Ha! art thou there?
AJAX. I'll fight with him alone: stand, Diomed!
DIO. He is my prize, I will not look upon.
TROIL. Come both, you cogging Greeks; have at you both! [*Exeunt, fighting.*

Enter HECTOR.

HECT. Yea, Troilus? O, well fought, my youngest brother!

Enter ACHILLES.

ACHIL. Now do I see thee, ha!—Have at thee, Hector!
HECT. Pause, if thou wilt.
ACHIL. I do disdain thy courtesy, proud Trojan.
Be happy that my arms are out of use:
My rest and negligence defends thee now,
But thou anon shalt hear of me again;
Till when, go seek thy fortune. [*Exit.*
HECT. Fare thee well:—
I would have been much more a fresher man,
Had I expected thee.—How now, my brother?

Re-enter TROILUS.

TROIL. Ajax hath ta'en Æneas; shall it be?
No, by the flame of yonder glorious heaven,
He shall not carry him; I'll be ta'en too,
Or bring him off.—Fate, hear me what I say!
I reck not though thou end my life to-day. [*Exit.*

Enter one in sumptuous armour.

HECT. Stand, stand, thou Greek; thou art a goodly mark:—
No? wilt thou not?—I like thy armour well;
I'll frush it, and unlock the rivets all,
But I'll be master of it:—wilt thou not, beast, abide?
Why then, fly on, I'll hunt thee for thy hide.
[*Exeunt.*

SCENE VII.—*Another part of the Plains.*

Enter ACHILLES, *with* Myrmidons.

ACHIL. Come here about me, you my Myrmidons;
Mark what I say.—Attend me where I wheel:
Strike not a stroke, but keep yourselves in breath;
And when I have the bloody Hector found,
Empale him with your weapons round about;
In fellest manner execute your aims.*
Follow me, sirs, and my proceedings eye:—
It is decreed—Hector the great must die.
[*Exeunt.*

SCENE VIII.—*Another part of the Plains.*

Enter MENELAUS *and* PARIS, *fighting; then* THERSITES.

THER. [*Aside.*] The cuckold and the cuckold-maker are at it. Now, bull! now, dog! 'Loo, Paris, 'loo! now my double-henned sparrow! 'loo, Paris, 'loo! The bull has the game:—ware horns, ho! [*Exeunt* PARIS *and* MENELAUS.

Enter MARGARELON.

MAR. Turn, slave, and fight.
THER. What art thou?
MAR. A bastard son of Priam's.
THER. I am a bastard too; I love bastards: I am a bastard begot, bastard instructed, bastard in mind, bastard in valour, in everything illegitimate. One bear will not bite another, and wherefore should one bastard? Take heed, the quarrel's most ominous to us: if the son of a whore fight for a whore, he tempts judgment. Farewell, bastard.
MAR. The devil take thee, coward! [*Exeunt.*

(*) First folio, *arme.*

SCENE IX.—*Another part of the Plains.*

Enter HECTOR.

HECT. Most putrified core, so fair without,
Thy goodly armour thus hath cost thy life.
Now is my day's work done; I'll take good breath:
Rest, sword; thou hast thy fill of blood and death!
[*Puts off his helmet and hangs his shield behind him.*(3)

Enter ACHILLES *and* Myrmidons.

ACHIL. Look, Hector, how the sun begins to set;
How ugly night comes breathing at his heels:
Even with the vail and darking of the sun,
To close the day up, Hector's life is done.

HECT. I am unarm'd; forego this vantage, Greek.

ACHIL. Strike, fellows, strike! this is the man I seek. [HECTOR *falls.*
So, Ilion, fall thou next!* now, Troy, sink down!
Here lies thy heart, thy sinews, and thy bone.—
On, Myrmidons; and† cry you all amain,
Achilles hath the mighty Hector slain!
[*A retreat sounded.*
Hark! a retire‡ upon our Grecian part.

(*) First folio omits, *next.* (†) First folio omits, *and.* (‡) First folio, *retreat.*

MYR. The Trojan trumpets sound the like, my lord.

ACHIL. The dragon wing of night o'erspreads the earth,
And, stickler-like,[a] the armies separates.
My half-supp'd sword, that frankly would have fed,
Pleas'd with this dainty bait,* thus goes to bed.—
[*Sheaths his sword.*
Come, tie his body to my horse's tail;
Along the field I will the Trojan trail. [*Exeunt.*

SCENE X.—*Another part of the Plains.*

Enter AGAMEMNON, AJAX, MENELAUS, NESTOR, DIOMEDES, *and others, marching. Shouts without.*

AGAM. Hark! hark! what shout is that?

NEST. Peace, drums!

[*Without.*] Achilles! Achilles! Hector's slain! Achilles!

DIO. The bruit is, Hector's slain, and by Achilles.

AJAX. If it be so, yet bragless let it be;
Great Hector was a man as good as he.

AGAM. March patiently along:—let one be sent
To pray Achilles see us at our tent.—
If in his death the gods have us befriended,
Great Troy is ours, and our sharp wars are ended.
[*Exeunt, marching.*

SCENE XI.—*Another part of the Plains.*

Enter ÆNEAS *and* Trojans.

ÆNE. Stand, ho! yet are we masters of the field:
Never go home; here starve we out the night.

Enter TROILUS.

TROIL. Hector is slain.

ALL. Hector!—The gods forbid!

TROIL. He's dead; and at the murderer's horse's tail,
In beastly sort, dragged through the shameful field.—
Frown on, you heavens, effect your rage with speed!
Sit, gods, upon your thrones, and smile at Troy!
I say, at once let your brief plagues be mercy,
And linger not our sure destructions on!

ÆNE. My lord, you do discomfort all the host.

TROIL. You understand me not that tell me so:
I do not speak of flight, of fear, of death;
But dare all imminence that gods and men
Address their dangers in. Hector is gone!
Who shall tell Priam so, or Hecuba?
Let him, that will a screech-owl aye be call'd,
Go in to Troy, and say there—*Hector's dead:*
There is a word will Priam turn to stone;
Make wells and Niobes of the maids and wives,
Cold* statues of the youth; and, in a word,
Scare Troy out of itself. But, march, away:
Hector is dead; there is no more to say.
Stay yet.—You vile abominable tents,
Thus proudly pight upon our Phrygian plains,
Let Titan rise as early as he dare,
I'll through and through you!—and thou great-siz'd coward!
No space of earth shall sunder our two hates;
I'll haunt thee like a wicked conscience still,
That mouldeth goblins swift as frenzy's thoughts.—
Strike a free march to Troy!—with comfort go:
Hope of revenge shall hide our inward woe.
[*Exeunt* ÆNEAS *and* Trojans.

As TROILUS *is going out, enter, from the other side,* PANDARUS.

PAN. But hear you, hear you!

TROIL. Hence, broker-lackey! ignomy and shame
Pursue thy life, and live aye with thy name!
[*Exit.*

PAN. A goodly med'cine for my aching bones!—O, world! world! world! thus is the poor agent despised! O, traitors and bawds, how earnestly are you set a-work, and how ill requited! Why should our endeavour be so loved,† and the performance so loathed? what verse for it? what instance for it?—Let me see:—

Full merrily the humble-bee doth sing,
Till he hath lost his honey and his sting:
And being once subdu'd in armed tail,
Sweet honey and sweet notes together fail.—

Good traders in the flesh, set this in your painted cloths.

As many as be here of Pandar's hall,
Your eyes half out weep out at Pandar's fall:
Or, if you cannot weep, yet give some groans,
Though not for me, yet for your aching bones.
Brethren and sisters of the hold-door trade,
Some two months hence my will shall here be made:
It should be now, but that my fear is this,—
Some galled goose of Winchester would hiss:
Till then I'll sweat, and seek about for eases;
And at that time bequeath you my diseases.
[*Exit.*

(*) First folio, *bed.*

(*) First folio, *Coole.* (†) First folio, *desir'd.*

[a] And, stickler-like, the armies separates.] "A *stickler* was one who stood by to part the combatants, when victory could be determined without bloodshed."—MALONE. They were so called, according to Minsheu, because they carried *sticks* or staves to interpose between the opponents.

ILLUSTRATIVE COMMENTS.

ACT I.

(1) Scene II.—*O, brave Hector!*] The hint for this scene was probably derived from the conversation in Chaucer's poem between Pandarus and Cryseide, on the qualifications of Hector and Troilus:—

" So after this, with meny wordis glade,
And frendly talis, and with mery chere,
Of this and that they pleyd, and gonnen wade
In meny an uncouthe * glad and depe matere,
As frendis done, whan they be met yfere;
Til she gan aske hym how that Hector ferd,
That was the tounys wall, and Gerkis yerd. †

" 'Ful wele I thonk it God,' quod Pandarus,
'Save in his arme he hath a lytil wound;
And eke his fressh brothir Troylus,
The wyse worthy Ector the secound,
In whom that every vertu lest abound,
In al trouthe and al gentilnes,
Wysdom, honour, fredom, and worthines.'

" 'In good faith, eme,' ‡ quod she, 'it likith me
They faryn wele, God save hem bothe two!
For truly I hold it grete deynte,
A kyngis sone in armys wele to do,
And to be of good condicions therto;
For grete power and moral vertu here
Is seldom sene yn o persone yfere.'

" 'In good faith, that is soth,' quod Pandarus;
'But, be myn heed, the kyng hath sonis twey,
That is to mene Ector and Troylus,
That certeynly, thogh that I shold dey,
They be as voyd of vices, dare I sey,
As eny man that lyvith undur the Sonne,
Her § myght is wyde know, and what they konne.

" 'Of Ector nedith no thing for to telle;
In al this world ther nys a better knyght
As he, that is of worthynes welle,
And he wel more vertu hath than myght:
This knowith meny a wyse and worthy knyght:
The same prys of Troilus I say,
God help me so, I note not such twey.'

" 'By God,' quod she, 'if Ector that is sothe,
Of Troylus the same thing trow I;
For dredles, ‖ men telle that he dothe
In armys day by day so worthily,
And berith hym here so gentilly
To every wighte, that al pris hath he
Of hem that me were levest praised be.'

" 'Ye sey right wele ywis,' ¶ quod Pandarus;
'For yesterday, who so had with hym bene,
Might have wondrid upon Troylus,
For never yet so thik a swarm of bene **
Ne flyen, as Greekis fro hym did flene;
And thurgh the feld in every wightis ere,
Ther was no cry but, "Lo Troylus is here!"

" 'Now here, now there, he huntyd hem so fast,
Ther nas but Grekys blood; and Troylus,
Now hym he hurt, and hym al doun he cast,
Ay wher he wont hit was arayed thus:
He was her dethe, and sheld of lyf for us.
That as that day ther durst none withstond,
Whil that he held his blody swerd in hond.' "

---

* Unknown. † Scourge. ‡ Uncle. § Their.
‖ Doubtless. ¶ Certainly. ** Bees.

(2) Scene III.—

—— *but, when the planets,*
In evil mixture, to disorder wander.]

In the language of astrology, by the "evil mixture" of the planets, was understood what we should now express by their *malignant conjunction.* Steevens surmised that the poet was indebted for the allusion in this passage to Spenser:—

" For who so list into the heavens looke,
And search the courses of the rowling spheares,
Shall find that from the point where they first tooke
Their setting foorth, in these few thousand yeares
They all are *wandred* much; that plaine appeares,
For that same golden fleecy ram, which bore
Phrixus and Hellé from their step-dames fears,
Hath now forgot where he was plac't of yore,
And shouldred hath the bull which faire Europa bore.

" And eke the bull hath with his bow-bent horne
So hardly butted those two twinnes of Jove,
That they have crush'd the crab, and quite him borne
Into the great Nemæan lion's grove.
So now all *range*, and do at *random rove*
Out of their proper places farre away,
And all this world with them amisse doe move,
And all his creatures from their course astray,
Till they arrive at their last ruinous decay."
Fairie Queene, Introduction to B. V. c. 1.

(3) Scene III.—

—— *he bade me take a trumpet,*
And to this purpose speak.]

Compare the challenge of Hector as given in Chapman's *Homer*:—

" Hector, with glad allowance gave, his brothers counsell eare;
And (fronting both the hoasts) advanc't, just in the midst, his speare.
The Troians instantly surceasse; the Greeks Atrides staid:
The God that bears the silver Bow, and warres triumphant Maide,
On Joves Beech, like two vultures sat, pleasd to behold both parts,
Flow in, to heare; so sternly arm'd with huge shields, helmes and darts.
And such fresh horror as you see, driven through the wrinkled waves
By rising Zephyre, under whom, the sea growes blacke, and raves:
Such did the hastie gathering troupes, of both hoasts make, to heare;
Whose tumult settl'd, twixt them both, thus spake the challenger:

'Heare Troians, and ye well arm'd Greeks, what my strong mind (diffusde
Through all my spirits) commands me speake; Saturnius hath not usde
His promist favour for our truce, but (studying both our ils)
Will never ceasse till Mars, by you, his ravenous stomacke fils,
With ruin'd Troy; or we consume, your mightie Sea borne fleet.
Amongst you all, whose breast includes, the most impulsive mind,
Let him stand forth as combattant, by all the rest designde.
Before whom thus I call high Jove, to witnesse of our strife;
If he, with home-thrust iron can reach, th' exposure of my life,
(Spoiling my armes) let him at will, convey them to his tent;
But let my body be returnd; that Troys two-sext descent
May waste it in the funerall Pile; if I can slaughter him,
(Apollo honoring me so much) Ile spoile his conquerd lim,
And beare his armes to Ilion, where in Apollos shrine
Ile hang them, as my trophies due: his body Ile resigne
To be disposed by his friends, in flamie funerals,
And honourd with erected tombe, where Hellespontus fals
Into Egæum; and doth reach, even to your navall rode;
That when our beings, in the earth, shall hide their period;
Survivers, sailing the blacke sea, may thus his name renew:
This is his monument, whose bloud, long since, illustrate Hector slew.
This shall posteritie report, and my fame never die."

(4) SCENE III.—*Blockish Ajax.*] From the subjoined description of the Ajaxes as portrayed by Lydgate, it would appear that Shakespeare, for dramatic effect, had purposely confounded Ajax Telamonius with Ajax *Oileus*:—

"Oileus Ayax was right corpulent,
To be well cladde he set al his entent
In rych aray he was ful curyous,
Although he were of body corsyous.
Of armes great with shoulders square and brode;
It was of him almost a horse lode.
High of stature, and boystous in a pres,
And of his speche rude and rechles.
Ful many worde in ydel hym asterte,
And but a coward was he of his herte.

"An other Ayax Thelamonyous
There was also dyscrete and vertuous,
Wonder fayre and semely to beholde,
Whose heyr was black and vpward ay gan folde,
In compas wise rounde as any sphere,
And of musyke was there non his pere.
Having a voyce full of melodye,
Right well entuned as by Hermonye.
And was inventife for to counterfete,
Instrumentes aswell smal as grete,
In sundry wise longyying to musyke.
And for all this yet had he good practicke
In armes eke, and was a noble knyght,
No man more orped nor hardyer for to fight.
Nor desyrous for to have vyctorye,
Devoyde of pompe, hatyng all vaynglorye,
All ydle laude spent and blowe in vayne."

"The auncient Historie and onely trewe and syncere Cronicle of the warres betwixt the Grecians and the Troyans," &c. fol. 1555. Book II. chap. 15.

ACT II.

(1) SCENE I.—THERSITES.] Hideous in person, impious and gross in speech, cowardly and vindictive by disposition, this remarkable character, by sheer intellectual vigour, seems to tower high above all the mere corporeal grace and strength by which he is surrounded; and the portrait is essentially Shakespeare's own creation, for the Thersites of Homer, on which we may suppose it founded, is nothing better than a vulgar, waspish railer, without a spark of wit or of intelligence to redeem his moral and physical obliquity:—

"—— All sate, and audience gave;
Thersites onely would speake all. A most disorderd store
Of words, he foolishly powrd out; of which his mind held more
Than it could manage; any thing, with which he could procure
Laughter, he never could containe. He should have yet been sure
To touch no kings. T' oppose their states, becomes not jesters parts.
But he, the filthiest fellow was, of all that had deserts
In Troyes brave siege: he was squint-eyd, and lame of either foote:
So crooke-backt, that he had no breast; sharp-headed, where did shoote
(Here and there sperst) thin mossie haire. He most of all envide
Ulysses and Æacides, whom still his splene would chide;
Nor could the sacred king himselfe, avoide his saucie vaine,
Against whom, since he knew the Greekes, did vehement hates sustaine
(Being angrie for Achilles wrong) he cride out; railing thus:
'Atrides! why complainst thou now? what wouldst thou more of us?
Thy tents are full of brasse, and dames; the choice of all are thine:
With whom, we must present thee first, when any townes resigne
To our invasion. Wantst thou then (besides all this) more gold
From Troyes knights, to redeeme their sonnes? whom, to be dearely sold,
I, or some other Greeke, must take? or wouldst thou yet againe,
Force from some other Lord his prise; to sooth the lusts that raigne
In thy encroching appetite? it fits no Prince to be
A Prince of ill, and governe us; or leade our progenie
By rape to ruine. O base Greekes, deserving infamie,
And ils eternall: Greekish girls, not Greekes, ye are; Come flie
Home with our ships; leave this man here, to perish with his preys,
And trie if we helpt him, or not: he wrong'd a man that weys
Farre more then he himselfe in worth: he forc't from Thetis sonne
And keepes his prise still: nor think I, that mightie man hath wonne
The stile of wrathfull worthily; he's soft, he's too remisse,
Or else Atrides, his had bene, thy last of injuries.'

Thus he the peoples Pastor chid; but straight stood up to him
Divine Ulysses; who with lookes, exceeding grave and grim,
This bitter checke gave: 'Ceasse, vaine foole, to vent thy railing vaine
On kings thus, though it serve thee well; nor think thou canst restraine,
With that thy railing facultie, their wils in least degree,
For not a worse, of all this hoast, came with our king then thee
To Troys great siege.'"—*The Iliads of Homer, &c. Done according to the Greeke, by Geo. Chapman, &c.* Book II.

(2) SCENE II.—*Enter* CASSANDRA, *raving.*] Of this circumstance, we find no hint either in Chapman's *Homer* or in Chaucer; it was probably taken, as Steevens conjectured, from a passage in Lydgate's "Auncient Historie," &c. 1555:—

"This was the noise and the pyteous crye
Of *Cassandra* that so dredefully
She gan to make aboute in every strete
Through ye towne," &c.

(3) SCENE III.—*The death-tokens of it.*] "Dr. Hodges, in his "Treatise on the Plague," says:—'Spots of a dark complexion, usually called *tokens,* and looked on as the pledges or forewarnings of *death,* are minute and distinct blasts, which have their original from within, and rise up with a little pyramidal protuberance, the pestilential poison chiefly collected at their bases, tainting the neighbouring parts, and reaching to the surface.'"—REID.

ACT III.

(1) SCENE II.—*So, so; rub on, and kiss the mistress.*] The small bowl aimed at in the game of *Bowling*, it has before been mentioned, was occasionally termed the *Mistress*. See note ([a]), p. 722, Vol. II. Perhaps the best illustration of this popular amusement and its technical phraseology, as practised in our author's day, is that given in Quarles' "Emblems" (Emb. 10, b. 1.):—

"Here's your right ground; wag gently o'er this black:
'T is a short cast; y' are quickly at the jack.
Rub, rub an inch or two; two crowns to one
On this bowl's side; blow wind, 't is fairly thrown:
The next bowl 's worse that comes; come, bowl away:
Mammon, you know the ground, untutor'd play:
Your last was gone, a yard of strength well spar'd
Had touch'd the block; your hand is still too hard.
Brave pastime, readers, to consume that day,
Which, without pastime, flies too swift away!
See how they labour; as if day and night
Were both too short to serve their loose delight:
See how their curved bodies wreath, and screw
Such antic shapes as Proteus never knew:
One raps an oath, another deals a curse;
He never better bowl'd; this never worse:
One rubs his itchless elbow, shrugs and laughs,
The other bends his beetle brows and chafes:
Sometimes they whoop, sometimes their Stygian cries
Send their black Santo's to the blushing skies:
Thus mingling humours in a mad confusion,
They make bad premises, and worse conclusion:
But where 's a palm that fortune's hand allows
To bless the victor's honourable brows?
Come, reader, come; I'll light thine eye the way
To view the prize, the while the gamesters play:
Close by the jack, behold, jill Fortune stands
To wave the game: see in her partial hands
The glorious garland's held in open show,
To cheer the lads, and crown the conqu'ror's brow.
The world 's the jack; the gamesters that contend,
Are Cupid, Mammon: that judicious fiend,
That gives the ground, is Satan: and the bowls
Are sinful thoughts; the prize, a crown for fools.
Who breathes that bowls not? What bold tongue can say
Without a blush, he has not bowl'd to-day?
It is the trade of man, and ev'ry sinner
Has play'd his rubbers: every soul's a winner.
The vulgar proverb 's crost, he hardly can
Be a good bowler and an honest man.
Good God! turn thou my Brazil* thoughts anew;
New-sole my bowls, and make their bias true.
I'll cease to game, till fairer ground be given;
Nor wish to win, until the mark be Heav'n."

(2) SCENE II.—*To feed for aye her lamp and flames of love.*] Here, as in other passages where Troilus exhibits a presentiment of his lady's inconstancy, we can trace the influence of the "Troylus and Cryseyde:"—

"But natheles, myn owene ladi bright!
Yit were it so that I wist utterly,
That I youre humble servaunt and your knyght
Were in youre herte yset so fermely,
As ye in myn, the whiche thing truly
Me lever were than this worldis tweyne,
Yit schulde I the better endure al my peyne."

And this:—

"Ye shal ek seen so many a lusti knyght,
Amonge the Grekes, ful of worthynesse;
And ech of hem, with herte, wit, and myght,
To plesen yow don alle his bisynesse,
That ye shal dullen of the rudenesse
Of us sely Troians, but if routhe
Remorde you, or vertu of your trouthe."

* The *bowls* were formerly made of what was called *Brazil* wood.

(3) SCENE II.—*As false as Cressid.*] The protestations of the fickle beauty in the old poem are not less confident; compare the following:

"To that Cryseyde answerid right anoone,
And with a sigh sche seide, 'O herte dere!
The game, ywis, so ferforthe now is gone,
That furste schal Phebus falle from his spere,
And hevene egle be as the douves fere,
And every rock out of his place sterte,
Er Troylus out of Cryseydis herte.'"

And her declaration subsequently:—

"For thylke day that I for cherisynge,
Or drede of fader, or of other wight,
Or for estat, delit, or for weddynge,
Be fals to yow, my Troylus, my knygthe,
Saturnes doughter Juno, thorugh hyre myghte,
As wood as Athamante do me dwelle
Eternaliche, in Stix, the put of Helle!

"And this, on every god celestial
I swere it yow, and ek on ech goddesse,
On every nymphe, and deyte infernal,
On satiry and fawny more and lesse,
That halve goddes ben of wildernesse;
And Attropos my thred of life to-breste,
If I be fals! Now trowe me if yow leste."

(4) SCENE III.—*Which, you say, live to come in my behalf.*] This appeal of Calchas to the Greeks recals the corresponding circumstance in Chaucer:—

"Then seyd he thus, 'Lo! lordis myn, I was
A Troyan, as it is knowe, out of drede;
And, if that yow remembre, I am Calcas,
That altherferst yaf comfort to your nede,
And tolde wele how ye sholdyn spede;
For, dredeles, thurgh you, shall, in a stound,
Ben Troy ybrent, and drewyn doun to ground.

"'And in what forme, and yn what maner wise
This toun to shent, and al your lust acheve,
Ye have, or this, wele herd me yow devise:
This knowyn ye, my lordis, as I leve;
And, for the Grekys weryn me so leve;
I come my self, in my proper persone,
To teche yow what you was best to done.

"'Havyng unto my tresour, ne my rent,
Right no regard in respect of your ese;
Thus al my good I lost, and to yow went,
Wenyng in this, my lordis, yow to plese;
But al my losse ne doth me no dissese,—
I vouchesaaf, al so wisely have I joy,
For yow to lese al that I had in Troy,—

"'Save of a doghter that I left, alas!
Slepyng at home, whan out of toun I stert.
O sterne, O cruel fadir, that I was!
How myght I in that have so hard an hert?
Alas! that I ne had her broght in her shert!
For sorow of which I wole not lyve to-morow,
But if ye, lordis, wole ruwe on my sorow.

"'For by that cause I sawe no tyme or now
Her to delivere, iche holden have my pees;
But now or nevere, if it likith you,
I may her have, for that is douteles:
O, help and grace! among all this pres,
Rewith on this old caytif in distresse,
Thurgh yow seth I am brought in wrecchidnes!

* * * * * * * * *

"Tellyng his tale alwey, this olde gray,
Humblely in his speche and loking eke,
The salte teris from his eyen tway,
Ful faste ronnen doun on either cheke;
So longe of mercy he gan hem byseke,
That, for to help hym of his sorowis sore,
They than gave hym Antenore without more."

ACT IV.

(1) SCENE II.—*A bugbear take him!*] In the banter of Pandarus here, we have arch reminiscences of his prototype in "Troylus and Cryseyde:"—

"Pandare, on morwe whiche that comen was
Unto his nece, gon hir faire to grete,
And seide, 'Al this night so reyned it, allas!
That al my drede is, that ye, nece swete,
Have litel leyser hade to slepe and mete:
Al night,' quod he, 'hath rain so do me wake,
That some of us, I trowe, her hedis ake.'

"And nigh he come and seid, 'How stant it now?
This Mey morwe, nece, how kunne ye fare?'
Cryseide answerde, 'Never the bet for yow!
Fox that ye ben, God yeve yow hertis care!
God helpe me so, yow causeth al this fare,
Trowe I,' quod sche, 'for alle youre wordis white;
O, ho so seeth you, knoweth you but alite!'"

(2) SCENE IV.—*To our own selves bend we our needful talk.*] The parting of the lovers, if not more natural, is managed with more pathos and delicacy in the elder poet:—

"Cryseyde, when she redy was to ride,
Ful sorwfully she sighte, and seyde, 'Allas!'
But forth she mot for ought that may betide,
And forth she rite ful sorwfully a pas;
There is non other remedy in this cas.
What wonder is, though that hyre soore smerte,
When she forgothe hire owne swete herte?

"This Troylus, in gise of curteysie,
With hauke on hond, and with an huge route
Of knyghtes, rood, and dide hyre compaynye,
Passynge alle the valeye fer withoute;
And ferther wold han riden, out of doute,
Ful fayne, and wo was hym to gon so soone,
But tourne he moote, and it was eke to done.

"And right with that was Antenor ycome
Oute of the Grekes oste, and every wight
Was of it glad, and seyde he was welcome;
And Troylus, al nere his herte lighte,
He peyned hym with al his fulle myght
Hym to with holde of wepynge at the leeste,
And Antenor he kyste, and made feeste.

"And therwithal he moot his leve take,
And caste his eye upon hire pitously,
And nerre he rode, his cause for to make,
To take hire by the honde al sobrely:
And, Lorde! so she gan wepen tendrely!
And he ful soft and sleighely gan hire seye,
'Now hold youre day, and do me not to deye.'

"With that his courser turned he about,
With face pale, and unto Dyomede
No worde he spak, ne non of al his route;
Of whiche the sone of Tideus tooke hede,
As he that konthe moore than the crede
In swiche a craft, and by the reyne hire hente,
And Troylus to Troye homwarde wente."

(3) SCENE V.—HECTOR *and* AJAX *fight.*] In Chapman's *Homer*, the combat is described with uncommon pomp and spirit:—

"—— This said, in bright armes shone
The good strong Ajax: who, when all his warre attire was on,
Marcht like the hugely figur'd Mars, when angry Jupiter,
With strength, on people proud of strength, sends him forth to inferre
Wreakfull contention; and comes on, with presence full of feare;
So th' Achive rampire, Telamon, did twixt the hoasts appeare:
Smil'd; yet of terrible aspect; on earth with ample pace,
He boldly stalkt, and shooke aloft his dart with deadly grace.
It did the Grecians good to see; but heartquakes shooke the joynts
Of all the Troians; Hectors selfe felt thoughts, with horrid points,
Tempt his bold bosome; but he now, must make no counterflight;
Nor (with his honour) now refuse, that had provokt the fight.
Ajax came neare; and like a towre his shield his bosome bard;
The right side brasse, and seven oxe hides within it quilted hard:
Old Tychius the best currier, that did in Hyla dwell,
Did frame it for exceeding proofe, and wrought it wondrous well.
With this stood he to Hector close, and with this Brave began:
Now Hector thou shalt clearly know, thus meeting man to man,
What other leaders arme our hoast, besides great Thetis sonne:
Who, with his hardie Lions heart, hath armies overunne.
But he lies at our crookt-sternd fleet a Rivall with our king
In height of spirit: yet to Troy, he many knights did bring,
Coequall with Eacides; all able to sustaine
All thy bold challenge can import: begin then, words are vaine.
The Helme-grac't Hector answerd him: Renowned Telamon,
Prince of the souldiers came from Greece; assay not me like one,
Yong and immartiall, with great words, as to an Amazon dame;
I have the habit of all fights; and know the bloudie frame
Of every slaughter: I well know the ready right hand charge;
I know the left, and every sway, of my securefull targe;
I triumph in the crueltie of fixed combat fight,
And manage horse to all designes; I think then with good right,
I may be confident as farre as this thy challenge goes,
Without being taxed with a vaunt, borne out with emptie showes.
But (being a souldier so renownd) I will not worke on thee,
With least advantage of that skill, I know doth strengthen me;
And so with privitie of sleight, winne that for which I strive:
But at thy best (even open strength) if my endevours thrive.
Thus sent he his long Javelin forth; it strooke his foes huge shield,
Neere to the upper skirt of brasse, which was the eighth it held.
Sixe folds th' untamed dart strooke through, and in the seventh tough hide
The point was checkt; then Ajax threw: his angry lance did glide
Quite through his bright orbicular targe, his curace, shirt of maile;
And did his manly stomachs mouth with dangerous taint assaile:
But in the bowing of himselfe, black death too short did strike.
Then both to pluck their Javelins forth, encountred Lion-like;
Whose bloudie violence is increast, by that raw food they eate:
Or Bores, whose strength, wilde nourishment, doth make so wondrous great.
Againe Priamides did wound, in midst, his shield of brasse,
Yet pierc't not through the upper plate, the head reflected was:
But Ajax (following his Lance) smote through his target quite,
And stayd bold Hector rushing in; the Lance held way outright,
And hurt his necke; out gusht the bloud; yet Hector ceast not so,
But in his strong hand tooke a Flint (as he did backwards go)
Blacke, sharpe and big, layd in the field: the sevenfold targe it smit,
Full on the bosse; and round about the brasse did ring with it.
But Ajax a farre greater stone lift up, and (wreathing round
With all his bodie layd to it) he sent it forth to wound,
And gave unmeasur'd force to it; the round stone broke within
His rundled target: his lov'd knees to languish did begin;
And he leand, stretcht out on his shield; but Phœbus raisd him streight.
Then had they layd on wounds with swords, in use of closer fight;
Unless the Heralds (messengers of Gods and godlike men)
The one of Troy, the other of Greece; had held betwixt them then
Imperiall scepters: when the one (Idæus, grave and wise)
Said to them; Now no more my sonnes: the Soveraigne of the skies
Doth love you both; both souldiers are, all witnesse with good right:
But now night lays her mace on earth; tis good t'obey the night."

ACT V.

(1) SCENE II.—*Here, Diomed, keep this sleeve.*] Steevens cites several passages from our old writers to show that it was customary for warriors to wear a lady's *sleeve* for a favour; the sleeve which Cressida bestows on Diomed, however, was that she had received from Troilus at their parting. Malone supposes it to have been such a one as was formerly used at tournaments:—"Also the deepe smocke *sleive,* which the Irish women use, they say, was old Spanish, and is used yet in Barbary; and yet that should seeme rather to be an old English fashion, for in armory the fashion of the *manche,* which is given in armes by many, being indeed nothing else but a sleive, is fashioned much like to that sleive."—SPENSER'S *View of Ireland,* p. 43, edit. 1633.

(2) SCENE II.—*Rather think this not Cressid.*] The grief of Troylus for his "light o' love" is beautifully told by the elder poet:—

"Than spak he thus:—'O, lady myn Cryseyde,
Wher is youre feith, and wher is youre beheste?
Wher is youre love, wher is youre trouth?' he seyde,
'Of Diomede have ye now al this feste!
Allas! I wold han trowed at the leste,
That, syn ye hold in trouthe to me stonde,
That ye thus holde han holden me in honde.

"'Who shal nowe trowe on any other mo?
Allas! I nevere wolde han wende, or this,
That ye, Cryseide, koude han chaunged so,
Ne but I hadde agilt, and don amys;
So cruel wende I nought youre herte, ywis,
To sle me thus! allas! youre name of trouthe
Is now fordon, and that is al my routhe.

"'Was there non other broche yow liste lete
To feffe with youre newe love,' quod he,
'But thilke broche that I, with teris wete,
You yaf, as for a remembraunce of me?
None other cause, allas! ne hadde ye,
But for despit; and ek for that ye mente
Al outrely to shewen youre entente.

"'Thorwgh which I se, that clene out of youre minde
Ye han me caste, and ne kan nor may
For al this world withinne myn herte fynde,
To unloven yow a quarter of a day;
In cursed tyme I borne was, walawey!
That yow, that dothe me al this wo endure,
Yet love I best of any creature.'"

(3) SCENE IX.—*And hangs his shield behind him.*] The circumstance of Hector being overpowered by Achilles and his followers when unarmed, the author is believed to have taken from Lydgate's poem:—

"And in this while a grekishe kinge he mette,
Were it of hap or of adventure,
The which in sothe on his cote armure
Embrouded had full many ryche stone,
That gave a lyght, when the sonne shone,
Full bryght and cleare, that joye was to sene,
For Perles white and Emerawdes grene
Full many one were therin sette.—
Of whose arraye when Hector taketh hede,
Towardes him fast gan him drawe.
And fyrst I fynde how he hath hym slawe,
And after that by force of his manheade,
He hente him up afore him on his stede,
And fast gan wyth him for to ryde
From the wardes a lytell out of syde,
At good leyser playnly, if he maye,
To spoyle him of his ryche arraye.—
On horsebacke out whan he him ladde,
Reklesly the storye maketh mynde,
He caste his shelde at his backe behynde,
To welde him selfe at more lyberte,—
So that hys brest disarmed was and bare."

CRITICAL OPINIONS ON TROILUS AND CRESSIDA

"The 'Troilus and Cressida' of Shakspeare can scarcely be classed with his dramas of Greek and Roman history; but it forms an intermediate link between the fictitious Greek and Roman histories, which we may call legendary dramas, and the proper ancient histories. There is no one of Shakspeare's plays harder to characterise. The name and the remembrances connected with it prepare us for the representation of attachment no less faithful than fervent on the side of the youth, and of sudden and shameless inconstancy on the part of the lady. And this is, indeed, as the gold thread on which the scenes are strung, though often kept out of sight and out of mind by gems of greater value than itself. But as Shakspeare calls forth nothing from the mausoleum of history, or the catacombs of tradition, without giving or eliciting some permanent and general interest, and brings forward no subject which he does not moralize or intellectualize,—so here he has drawn in Cressida the portrait of a vehement passion, that, having its true origin and proper cause in warmth of temperament, fastens on, rather than fixes to, some one object by liking and temporary preference.

'There 's language in her eye, her cheek, her lip,
Nay, her foot speaks; her wanton spirits look out
At every joint and motive of her body.'

"This Shakspeare has contrasted with the profound affection represented in Troilus, and alone worthy the name of love;—affection, passionate indeed, swoln with the confluence of youthful instincts and youthful fancy, and growing in the radiance of hope newly risen, in short enlarged by the collective sympathies of nature;—but still having a depth of calmer element in a will stronger than desire, more entire than choice, and which gives permanence to its own act by converting it into faith and duty. Hence, with excellent judgment, and with an excellence higher than mere judgment can give, at the close of the play, when Cressida has sunk into infamy below retrieval and beneath hope, the same will, which had been the substance and the basis of his love, while the restless pleasures and passionate longings, like sea-waves, had tossed but on its surface,—this same moral energy is represented as snatching him aloof from all neighbourhood with her dishonour, from all lingering fondness and languishing regrets, whilst it rushes with him into other and nobler duties, and deepens the channel which his heroic brother's death had left empty for its collected flood. Yet another secondary and subordinate purpose Shakspeare has inwoven with his delineation of these two characters,—that of opposing the inferior civilization, but purer morals, of the Trojans, to the refinements, deep policy, but duplicity and sensual corruptions, of the Greeks.

"To all this, however, so little comparative projection is given,—nay, the masterly group of Agamemnon, Nestor, and Ulysses, and, still more in advance, that of Achilles, Ajax, and Thersites, so manifestly occupy the foreground, that the subservience and vassalage of strength and animal courage to intellect and policy seems to be the lesson most often in our poet's view, and which he has taken little pains to connect with the former more interesting moral impersonated in the titular hero and heroine of the drama. But I am half inclined to believe, that Shakspeare's main object, or shall I rather say, his ruling impulse, was to translate the poetic heroes of paganism into the not less rude, but more intellectually vigorous, and more *featurely*, warriors of Christian chivalry,—and to substantiate the distinct and graceful profiles or outlines of the Homeric epic into the flesh and blood of the romantic drama,—in short, to give a grand history-piece in the robust style of Albert Durer.

"The character of Thersites, in particular, well deserves a more careful examination, as the Caliban of demagogic life;—the admirable portrait of intellectual power deserted by all grace, all moral principle, all not momentary impulse;—just wise enough to detect the weak head, and fool enough to provoke the armed fist of his betters;—one whom malcontent Achilles can inveigle from malcontent Ajax, under the one condition, that he shall be called on to do nothing but abuse and slander, and that he shall be allowed to abuse as much and as purulently as he likes, that is, as he can;—in short, a mule,—quarrelsome by the original discord of his nature,—a slave by tenure of his own baseness,—made to bray and be brayed at, to despise and be despicable."—Coleridge.

Act V. Sc. 2.

HAMLET.

On the 26th of July, 1602, a memorandum was entered on the registers of the Stationers' Company,—

> "James Roberts.] A booke, The Revenge of Hamlett prince of Denmarke, as yt was latelie acted by the Lord Chamberlayn his servantes."

This entry unquestionably refers to our author's "Hamlet," the publication of which Roberts desired to secure. As, however, an edition of the play appeared in the following year, "printed for N. L. and John Trundell," Mr. Collier conjectures that Roberts was unable to obtain such a copy of the piece as he could creditably associate his name with, but that some inferior and nameless printer, not so scrupulous, contrived to possess himself of an imperfect manuscript of it, and brought out the edition of 1603. Of this impression, one copy of which is in the library of the Duke of Devonshire, and another recently discovered has been purchased for the British Museum, the title is, "The Tragicall Historie of Hamlet Prince of Denmarke. By William Shake-speare. As it hath beene diverse times acted by his Highnesse servants in the Cittie of London: as also in the two Universities of Cambridge and Oxford, and else-where. At London printed for N. L. and John Trundell, 1603."

But, as Mr. Dyce observes, we have no proof that Roberts was not the "nameless printer" of the quarto of 1603: on the contrary, there is reason to suspect that he was, since we find that he printed the quarto of 1604 for the same Nicholas Ling who was one of the publishers of the quarto of 1603. It is of no material consequence, however, who printed that maimed and surreptitious version. What really concerns us is to know whether, making large allowance for omissions and corruptions due to the negligence of those through whose hands the manuscript passed, the edition of 1603 exhibits the play as Shakespeare first wrote it and as it was "diverse times acted." We believe it does. The internal evidence is to our judgment convincing that in this wretchedly printed copy we have the poet's first conception (written probably at an early stage of his dramatic career) of that magnificent tragedy which, remodelled and augmented, was published in 1604, under the title of, "The Tragicall Historie of Hamlet, Prince of Denmarke. By William Shakespeare. Newly imprinted and *enlarged to almost as much againe as it was*, according to the true and perfect Coppie. At London, Printed by I. R. for N. L. and are to be sold at his shoppe under Saint Dunstons Church in Fleetstreet, 1604."

Prefixed to Greene's "Menaphon. Camillas alarum to slumbering Euphues," &c. 1589, is an Epistle "To the Gentlemen Students of both Universities," by Nash, in which occurs the following passage,—"Ile turne backe to my first text, of studies of delight; and talke a little in friendship with a few of our triviall translators. It is a common practice now a daies amongst a sort of shifting companions, that runne through every arte and thrive by none, to leave the trade of *Noverint* whereto they were borne, and busie themselves with the indevours of art, that could scarcelie latinize their necke-verse if they should have neede; yet English Seneca read by candle-light yeeldes manie good sentences, as *Blould is a begger*, and so foorth: and if you intreate him faire in a frostie morning, he will affoord you whole *Hamlets*, I should say Handfulls of tragical speaches."

Here, the "shifting companions, that runne through every arte," brings so distinctly to mind the epithet, "an absolute *Johannes Fac-totum*," which Nash's sworn brother, Greene, in his

"Groats-worth of Wit," &c. 1593, applied to Shakespeare, and "the trade of *Noverint*" so well tallies with the received tradition of his having passed some time in the office of an attorney, that, *primâ facie*, the allusion to *Hamlet* would seem directly levelled at our author's tragedy. But, then, interposes a difficulty on the score of dates. Shakespeare, in 1589, was only twenty-three years of age,—too young, it may be well objected, to have earned the distinction of being satirized by Nash as having "run through every art." It is asserted, too, on good authority, that an edition of the "Menaphon." was published in 1587; and if that earlier copy contained Nash's Epistle, the probability of his referring to Shakespeare is considerably weakened. Again, in "Wits Miserie, and the Worlds Madnesse," &c. 1596, Lodge, describing a particular fiend, says, "he walks for the most part in black under colour of gravity, and looks as pale as the vizard of ye ghost which cried so miserally at ye theator like an oisterwife, *Hamlet, revenge.*"

After duly weighing the evidence on either side, we incline to agree with Mr. Dyce, that the play alluded to by Lodge and Nash was an earlier production on the same subject; though we find no cause to conclude that the first sketch of Shakespeare's "Hamlet," as published in 1603, was not the piece to which Henslowe refers in the entry connected with the performances at Newington Butts,—

"9. *of June* 1594 *at hamlet* * * * —viii. s."

The original story of "Hamlet," or "Amleth," is related by the Danish historian Saxo Grammaticus, and was adopted by Belleforest in his collection of novels, 1564. From the French of the novelist, it was rendered into English at an early date, and printed under the title of "The Hystorie of Hamblet." If there were really a tragedy of "Hamlet" anterior to the immortal drama by Shakespeare, we may reasonably assume that he derived the outline of his plot from that source. If no such play existed, he probably constructed it entirely from the rude materials furnished by "The Historie of Hamblet."

Persons Represented.

CLAUDIUS, *King of* Denmark.

HAMLET, *Son to the former, and Nephew to the present King.*

POLONIUS, *Lord Chamberlain.*

HORATIO, *Friend to* Hamlet.

LAERTES, *Son to* Polonius.

VOLTIMAND, CORNELIUS, ROSENCRANTZ, GUILDENSTERN, OSRIC, } *Courtiers.*

A Gentleman.

A Priest.

MARCELLUS, BERNARDO, FRANCISCO, } *Officers.*

REYNALDO, *Servant to* Polonius.

Players.

Two Clowns, *Grave-diggers.*

FORTINBRAS, *Prince of* Norway.

A Captain.

English Ambassadors.

GERTRUDE, *Queen of* Denmark, *and Mother to* Hamlet.

OPHELIA.

Ghost of Hamlet's *Father.*

Lords, Ladies, Officers, Soldiers, Sailors, Messengers, and other Attendants.

SCENE,—ELSINORE.

ACT I.

SCENE I.—Elsinore. *A Platform before the Castle.*

FRANCISCO *on guard.* *Enter to him* BERNARDO.

BER. Who's there?
FRAN. Nay, answer me: stand, and unfold yourself.
BER. *Long live the king!*[a]
FRAN. Bernardo?
BER. He.
FRAN. You come most carefully upon your hour.
BER. 'T is now struck twelve; get thee to bed, Francisco.
FRAN. For this relief much thanks: 'tis bitter cold,
And I am sick at heart.
BER. Have you had quiet guard?
FRAN. Not a mouse stirring.
BER. Well, good night.
If you do meet Horatio and Marcellus,
The rivals[b] of my watch, bid them make haste.
FRAN. I think I hear them.—Stand, ho!* Who's there?

Enter HORATIO *and* MARCELLUS.

HOR. Friends to this ground.
MAR. And liegemen to the Dane.
FRAN. Give you good night.
MAR. O, farewell, honest soldier:
Who hath reliev'd you?
FRAN. Bernardo has my place.
Give you good night. [*Exit.*
MAR. Holla! Bernardo!
BER. Say, what, is Horatio there?
HOR. A piece of him.
BER. Welcome, Horatio;—welcome, good Marcellus.
MAR. What, has this thing appear'd again to-night?
BER. I have seen nothing.
MAR. Horatio says, 'tis but our fantasy,
And will not let belief take hold of him,
Touching this dreaded sight, twice seen of us:

(*) The first folio omits, *ho!*

[a] *Long live the king!*] This was the watchword of the night.

[b] *The* rivals—] That is, the *associates, partners,* &c. In the quarto of 1603, the reading, indeed, is "partners."

Therefore I have entreated him along
With us to watch the minutes of this night;
That, if again this apparition come,
He may approve[a] our eyes, and speak to it.
HOR. Tush, tush! 'twill not appear.
BER. Sit down awhile;
And let us once again assail your ears,
That are so fortified against our story,
What we two nights have seen.
HOR. Well, sit we down,
And let us hear Bernardo speak of this.
BER. Last night of all,
When yond same star that's westward from the pole
Had made his course to illume that part of heaven
Where now it burns, Marcellus and myself,
The bell then beating[b] one,—
MAR. Peace! break thee off; look, where it comes again!

Enter Ghost.

BER. In the same figure, like the king that's dead.
MAR. Thou art a scholar,[c] speak to it, Horatio.
BER. Looks it not like the king? mark it, Horatio.
HOR. Most like:—it harrows me with fear and wonder.
BER. It would be spoke to.
MAR. Question it, Horatio.
HOR. What art thou, that usurp'st this time of night,
Together with that fair and warlike form
In which the majesty of buried Denmark
Did sometimes march? by heaven, I charge thee, speak!
MAR. It is offended.
BER. See! it stalks away!
HOR. Stay! speak! speak! I charge thee, speak! [*Exit* Ghost.
MAR. 'T is gone, and will not answer.
BER. How now, Horatio! you tremble, and look pale:
Is not this something more than fantasy?
What think you on 't?
HOR. Before my God, I might not this believe,
Without the sensible and true avouch
Of mine own eyes.
MAR. Is it not like the king?
HOR. As thou art to thyself:
Such was the very armour he had on,
When he* the ambitious Norway combated;
So frown'd he once, when, in an angry parle,
He smote the sledded Polacks[d] on the ice.
'T is strange.
MAR. Thus twice before, and jump[e] at this dead hour,
With martial stalk he passed through[f] our watch.
HOR. In what particular thought to work, I know not;
But in the gross and scope of mine† opinion,
This bodes some strange eruption to our state.
MAR. Good now, sit down, and tell me, he that knows,
Why this same strict and most observant watch
So nightly toils the subject of the land?
And why such daily cast of brazen cannon,
And foreign mart for implements of war;
Why such impress of shipwrights, whose sore task
Does not divide the Sunday from the week;
What might be toward that this sweaty haste
Doth make the night joint-labourer with the day:
Who is't that can inform me?
HOR. That can I;
At least, the whisper goes so. Our last king,
Whose image even but now appear'd to us,
Was, as you know, by Fortinbras of Norway,
Thereto prick'd on by a most emulate pride,
Dar'd to the combat; in which our valiant Hamlet
(For so this side of our known world esteem'd him)
Did slay this Fortinbras; who, by a seal'd compact,
Well ratified by law and heraldry,
Did forfeit, with his life, all those his lands,
Which he stood seiz'd of,‡ to the conqueror:
Against the which, a moiety competent
Was gaged by our king; which had return'd

---

a — approve—] *Corroborate, confirm, make good.*
b — beating—] The quarto, 1603, has,—

"The bell then *tolling* one,"—

which, perhaps, imparts additional solemnity to this impressive preparation for the appearance of the spectre.

c Thou art a scholar, speak to it, Horatio.] As exorcisms were usually pronounced by the clergy in Latin, the notion became current, that supernatural beings regarded only the addresses of the learned. In proof of this belief, Reed quotes the following from "The Night Walker" of Beaumont and Fletcher, Act II. Sc. 2, where Toby is scared by a supposed ghost, and exclaims,—

"Let's call the butler up, for *he speaks Latin*,
And that will daunt the devil."

— the sledded Polacks—] The *sledged Polanders;* though it may be doubtful whether the original "Pollax" was intended as the singular or plural: many editors read, "Polack."

(*) First folio omits, *he*. (†) First folio, *my*. (‡) First folio, *on*.

e — *and* jump *at this dead hour.*—] So the quartos; the folio substitutes the more modern word, *just:* but in Shakespeare's day, "jump" was the familiar term. So in Act. V. Sc. 2, of this play,—

"But since, so *jump* upon this bloody question."

So, also, in "Othello," Act II. Sc. 3,—

"—— bring him *jump* when he may Cassio find."

f *With martial stalk* he passed through *our watch.*] The reading of the earliest quarto, and presenting a finer image than that of the subsequent editions, which have,—

"—— *hath he gone by* our watch."

To the inheritance of Fortinbras,
Had he been vanquisher; as, by the same cov'nant,
And carriage of the article design'd,[a]
His fell to Hamlet. Now, sir, young Fortinbras,
Of unimproved[b] mettle hot and full,
Hath in the skirts of Norway, here and there,
Shark'd up a list of lawless* resolutes,
For food and diet, to some enterprise
That hath a stomach in't: which is no other
(As † it doth well appear unto our state,)
But to recover of us, by strong hand,
And terms compulsative, those 'foresaid lands

[a] — design'd,—] So the second folio; the previous editions having, *designe.*

[b] *Of* unimproved *mettle hot and full,*—] By *unimproved*=*unreproved,* we apprehend is meant, *insatiable, ungovernable,* as in Chapman's "Homer's Iliads," Book the Eleventh,—

" —— the King still cride, Pursue, pursue,
And all his *unreproved* hands, did blood and dust embrue."

(*) First folio, *Landlesse.* (†) First folio, *And.*

So by his father lost: and this, I take it,
Is the main motive of our preparations,
The source of this our watch, and the chief head
Of this post-haste and romage[a] in the land.
BER. I think it be no other, but e'en so:[b]
Well may it sort that this portentous figure
Comes armed through our watch; so like the king
That was and is the question of these wars.
HOR. A mote it is to trouble the mind's eye.
In the most high and palmy state of Rome,
A little ere the mightiest Julius fell,
The graves stood tenantless, and the sheeted dead
Did squeak and gibber in the Roman streets:
As stars with trains of fire and dews of blood,
Disasters in the sun; (1) and the moist star,
Upon whose influence Neptune's empire stands,
Was sick almost to dooms-day with eclipse:
And even the like precurse of fierce events,—
As harbingers preceding still the fates,
And prologue to the omen coming on,—
Have heaven and earth together demonstrated
Unto our climatures and countrymen.—
But, soft! behold! lo, where it comes again!

Re-enter Ghost.

I'll cross it, though it blast me.[c]—Stay, illusion![d]
If thou hast any sound, or use of voice,
Speak to me:
If there be any good thing to be done,
That may to thee do ease, and grace to me,
Speak to me:
If thou art privy to thy country's fate,
Which, happily, foreknowing may avoid, O, speak!
Or if thou hast uphoarded in thy life
Extorted treasure in the womb of earth,
For which, they say, you spirits oft walk in death,
[*Cock crows.*
Speak of it:—stay, and speak!—Stop it, Marcellus.

MAR. Shall I strike at it with my partisan?
HOR. Do, if it will not stand.
BER. 'Tis here!
HOR. 'Tis here!
MAR. 'Tis gone! [*Exit* Ghost.
We do it wrong, being so majestical,
To offer it the show of violence;
For it is, as the air, invulnerable,
And our vain blows malicious mockery.
BER. It was about to speak, when the cock crew.
HOR. And then it started like a guilty thing
Upon a fearful summons. I have heard,
The cock, that is the trumpet to the morn,*
Doth with his lofty and shrill-sounding throat[e]
Awake the god of day; and, at his warning,
Whether in sea or fire, in earth or air,
The extravagant and erring[f] spirit hies
To his confine: and of the truth herein,
This present object made probation.
MAR. It faded on the crowing of the cock.(2)
Some say, that ever 'gainst that season comes
Wherein our Saviour's birth is celebrated,
The bird of dawning singeth all night long:
And then, they say, no spirit dare stir † abroad;
The nights are wholesome; then no planets strike,
No fairy takes,[g] nor witch hath power to charm,
So hallow'd and so gracious is the time.
HOR. So have I heard, and do in part believe it.
But, look, the morn, in russet mantle[h] clad,
Walks o'er the dew of yon high eastern hill:[i]
Break we our watch up; and, by my advice,
Let us impart what we have seen to-night
Unto young Hamlet: for, upon my life,
This spirit, dumb to us, will speak to him:
Do you consent we shall acquaint him with it,
As needful in our loves, fitting our duty?
MAR. Let's do't, I pray: and I this morning know
Where we shall find him most conveniently.
[*Exeunt.*

---

a — romage—] *Commotion, turmoil.*

b I think it be no other, but e'en so:] This and the seventeen succeeding lines are not in the folio.

c I'll cross it, though it blast me.—] It was an ancient superstition, that any one who crossed the spot on which a spectre was seen, became subjected to its malignant influence. See Blakeway's note *ad l.* in the *Variorum* edition.

d Stay, illusion!] Attached to these words in the 1604 quarto, is a stage direction,—"*It spreads his arms.*"

e *Doth with his* lofty and shrill-sounding throat—] This is the text of the folio and all the quartos, except the first, which reads, perhaps preferably,—

"—— *early* and shrill-*crowing* throat."

f — extravagant and erring—] *Wandering* and *erratic.*

g *No fairy* takes,—] The folio inadvertently prints *talkes.* *To take* has before been explained to mean, *to paralyze, to deaden, to benumb.*

h — *in* russet mantle *clad,*—] In the recapitulation of his labours at the conclusion of the Ænead, Gawin Douglas says,—

"Quhen pale Aurora with Face lamentabill
Her *Russet Mantill* bordourit all with sabill."

i — yon high eastern hill:] The earliest quarto has,—

"—— yon hie *mountaine top;*"—

the later quartos,—

"—— yon high *eastward* hill."

We adopt the lection of the folio, as more in accordance with the poetical phraseology of the period. Thus, in Chapman's translation of the Thirteenth Book of Homer's Odyssey,—

"—— Ulysses still
An eye directed to the *eastern hill.*"

And Spenser charmingly ushers in the morn by telling us that—

"—— cheareful Chaunticlere with his note shrill
Had warned once, that Phœbus' fiery Car
In haste was climbing up the *Eastern Hill,*
Full envious that Night so long his room did fill."

(*) First folio, *day.* (†) First folio, *can walke.*

SCENE II.—*The same. A Room of State in the same.*

Enter the KING, QUEEN, HAMLET, POLONIUS, LAERTES, VOLTIMAND, CORNELIUS, Lords, *and* Attendants.

KING. Though yet of Hamlet our dear brother's death
The memory be green; and that it us befitted
To bear our hearts in grief, and our whole kingdom
To be contracted in one brow of woe;
Yet so far hath discretion fought with nature,
That we with wisest sorrow think on him,
Together with remembrance of ourselves.
Therefore our sometime sister, now our queen,
The imperial jointress of this warlike state,
Have we, as 'twere with a defeated joy,—
With one auspicious and one dropping eye,
With mirth in funeral, and with dirge in marriage,
In equal scale weighing delight and dole,—
Taken to wife: nor have we herein barr'd
Your better wisdoms, which have freely gone
With this affair along:—for all, our thanks.
Now follows, that you know, young Fortinbras,
Holding a weak supposal of our worth,
Or thinking by our late dear brother's death,
Our state to be disjoint and out of frame,
Colleagued with the dream of his advantage,—
He hath not fail'd to pester us with message,
Importing the surrender of those lands
Lost by his father, with all bonds of law,
To our most valiant brother. So much for him.—
Now for ourself, and for this time of meeting,
Thus much the business is:—we have here writ
To Norway, uncle of young Fortinbras,—
Who, impotent and bed-rid, scarcely hears

Of this his nephew's purpose,—to suppress
His further gait herein; in that the levies,
The lists, and full proportions, are all made
Out of his subject: and we here dispatch
You, good Cornelius, and you, Voltimand,
For bearers* of this greeting to old Norway;
Giving to you no further personal power
To business with the king, more than the scope
Of these dilated articles allow.
Farewell; and let your haste commend your duty.

COR., VOL. In that and all things will we show our duty.

KING. We doubt it nothing; heartily farewell.—
[*Exeunt* VOLTIMAND *and* CORNELIUS.
And now, Laertes, what's the news with you?
You told us of some suit; what is 't, Laertes?
You cannot speak of reason to the Dane,
And lose your voice: what wouldst thou beg, Laertes,
That shall not be my offer, not thy asking?
The head is not more native to the heart,
The hand more instrumental to the mouth,
Than is the throne of Denmark to thy father.
What wouldst thou have, Laertes?

LAER. Dread my lord,
Your leave and favour to return to France;
From whence though willingly I came to Denmark,
To show my duty in your coronation;
Yet now, I must confess, that duty done,
My thoughts and wishes bend again toward France,
And bow them to your gracious leave and pardon.(3)

KING. Have you your father's leave?—What says Polonius?

POL. He hath, my lord, wrung from me my slow leave
By laboursome petition; and, at last,
Upon his will I seal'd my hard consent:
I do beseech you, give him leave to go.[a]

KING. Take thy fair hour, Laertes; time be thine,
And thy best graces spend it at thy will!—
But now, my cousin Hamlet, and my son,—

HAM. [*Aside.*] A little more than kin, and less than kind.[b]

KING. How is it that the clouds still hang on you?

HAM. Not so, my lord; I am too much i' the sun.[c]

QUEEN. Good Hamlet, cast thy nighted colour [off,
And let thine eye look like a friend on Denmark.
Do not for ever with thy vailed lids
Seek for thy noble father in the dust:
Thou know'st 't is common,—all that lives must [die,
Passing through nature to eternity.

HAM. Ay, madam, it is common.

QUEEN. If it be,
Why seems it so particular with thee?

HAM. *Seems*, madam! nay, it is; I know not [seems.
'T is not alone my inky cloak, good mother,
Nor customary suits of solemn black,
Nor windy suspiration of forc'd breath,
No, nor the fruitful river in the eye,
Nor the dejected haviour of the visage,
Together with all forms, modes,* shows of grief,
That can denote me truly: these, indeed, seem,
For they are actions that a man might play:
But I have that within which passeth show;
These, but the trappings and the suits of woe.

KING. 'T is sweet and commendable in your nature, Hamlet,
To give these mourning duties to your father:
But, you must know, your father lost a father;
That father lost, lost his; and the survivor bound,
In filial obligation, for some term
To do obsequious[d] sorrow: but to perséver,
In obstinate condolement, is a course
Of impious stubbornness; 't is unmanly grief:
It shows a will most incorrect to heaven;
A heart unfortified, a mind impatient;
An understanding simple and unschool'd:
For what we know must be, and is as common
As any the most vulgar thing to sense,
Why should we, in our peevish opposition,
Take it to heart? Fie! 't is a fault to heaven,
A fault against the dead, a fault to nature,
To reason most absurd; whose common theme
Is death of fathers, and who still hath cried,
From the first corse till he that died to-day,
This must be so. We pray you, throw to earth
This unprevailing woe; and think of us
As of a father; for let the world take note,
You are the most immediate to our throne;
And with no less nobility[e] of love

(*) First folio, *bearing*.

(*) Old text, *moods*.

[a] I do beseech you, give him leave to go.] In the folio this speech is abbreviated to,—

"He hath my Lord:
I do beseech you give him leave to go."

[b] A little more than kin, and less than kind.] The meaning may perhaps be gathered from what appears to have been a proverbial saying, in Rowley's "Search for Money:"—"I would he were not so neere to us in *kindred*, then sure he would be neerer in *kindnesse*."

[c] — I am too much i'the sun.] By this, Hamlet may mean, I am too much in the way; a mote in the royal eye: but his reply is purposely enigmatical.

[d] — obsequious sorrow:] The *customary funereal* sorrow: thus, in "Titus Andronicus," Act V. Sc 3,—

"To shed *obsequious* tears upon his trunk."

[e] — with no less nobility of love—] So the Ghost,—"To me, whose *love was of that dignity*." Dr. Badham, however, proposes to read,—

"—— with *nobility no less* of love
Than that."

Than that which dearest father bears his son,
Do I impart toward you. For your intent
In going back to school in Wittenberg,
It is most retrograde to our desire:
And, we beseech you, bend you to remain
Here, in the cheer and comfort of our eye,
Our chiefest courtier, cousin, and our son.

QUEEN. Let not thy mother lose her prayers, Hamlet;
I pray thee, stay with us; go not to Wittenberg.

HAM. I shall in all my best obey you, madam.

KING. Why, 't is a loving and a fair reply:
Be as ourself in Denmark.—Madam, come;
This gentle and unforc'd accord of Hamlet
Sits smiling to my heart: in grace whereof,
No jocund health that Denmark drinks to-day,
But the great cannon to the clouds shall tell;
And the king's rouse[a] the heavens shall bruit again,
Re-speaking earthly thunder. Come away.(4)

[*Exeunt all except* HAMLET.

[a] — *the king's* rouse—] See note on the drinking terms at the end of this play.

HAM. O, that this too too[a] solid flesh would melt,
Thaw, and resolve itself into a dew!
Or that the Everlasting had not fix'd
His canon 'gainst self-slaughter! O, God! O, God!
How weary, stale, flat, and unprofitable
Seem to me all the uses of this world!
Fie on't! O, fie! 't is an unweeded garden,
That grows to seed; things rank and gross in nature
Possess it merely. That it should come to this!
But two months dead!—nay, not so much, not two;
So excellent a king; that was, to this,
Hyperion to a satyr: so loving to my mother,
That he might not beteem[b] the winds of heaven
Visit her face too roughly. Heaven and earth!
Must I remember? why, she would hang on him,
As if increase of appetite had grown
By what it fed on: and yet, within a month,—
Let me not think on't—Frailty, thy name is woman!—
A little month; or ere those shoes were old,
With which she follow'd my poor father's body,
Like Niobe, all tears;—why she, even she,—
O, God!* a beast, that wants discourse of reason,[c]
Would have mourn'd longer,—married with mine uncle,
My father's brother; but no more like my father,
Than I to Hercules: within a month:
Ere yet the salt of most unrighteous tears
Had left the flushing[d] of her galled eyes,
She married:—O, most wicked speed to post
With such dexterity to incestuous sheets,
It is not, nor it cannot come to, good;
But break, my heart,—for I must hold my tongue!

Enter HORATIO, BERNARDO, *and* MARCELLUS.

HOR. Hail to your lordship!

HAM. I am glad to see you well:
Horatio,—or I do forget myself.

HOR. The same, my lord, and your poor servant ever.

HAM. Sir, my good friend; I'll change that name with you.
And what make[e] you from Wittenberg, Horatio?—
Marcellus?

MAR. My good lord,—

HAM. I am very glad to see you.—Good even, sir,—
But what, in faith, make you from Wittenberg?

HOR. A truant disposition, good my lord.

HAM. I would not hear* your enemy say so;
Nor shall you do mine ear that violence,
To make it truster of your own report
Against yourself: I know you are no truant.
But what is your affair in Elsinore?
We'll teach you to drink deep ere you depart.[f]

HOR. My lord, I came to see your father's funeral.

HAM. I pr'ythee, do not mock me, fellow-student;
I think it was to see my mother's wedding.

HOR. Indeed, my lord, it follow'd hard upon.

HAM. Thrift, thrift, Horatio! the funeral bak'd meats (5)
Did coldly furnish forth the marriage tables.
Would I had met my dearest (6) foe in heaven
Ere ever I had † seen that day, Horatio!—
My father,—methinks, I see my father.

HOR. O, where, my lord?

HAM. In my mind's eye,[g] Horatio.

HOR. I saw him once; he was a goodly king.

HAM. He was a man, take him for all in all,
I shall not look upon his like again.

HOR. My lord, I think I saw him yesternight.

HAM. Saw who?

HOR. My lord, the king your father.

HAM. The king my father!

HOR. Season your admiration for a while
With an attentive[h] ear; till I may deliver,

(*) First folio, *heaven*.

[a] *O, that this* too too *solid flesh would melt*,—] Mr. Halliwell has proved by numberless examples, culled from our early writers, that where *too too* occurred, in the generality of cases it formed a compound word, *too-too*, and when thus connected bore the meaning of *exceeding*. The present instance, however, must be regarded as an exception to the rule. Here the repetition of *too* is not only strikingly beautiful, rhetorically, but it admirably expresses that morbid condition of the mind which makes the unhappy prince deem all the uses of the world but "weary, stale, flat, and unprofitable."

[b] — beteem—] That is, *vouchsafe*, *allow*, *suffer*, and the like.

[c] — discourse of reason,—] By "*discourse* of reason" was meant the comprehensive *range*, or *discursiveness* of reason, the retrospective and foreseeing faculties; thus in Act IV. Sc. 4, Hamlet remarks,—

"Sure he that made us with such *large discourse*,
Looking before and after, gave us not
That capability and godlike reason
To fust in us unus'd."

[d] *Had left* the *flushing*—] The quarto, 1603, reads, "— *their* flushing."

(*) First folio, *hare*. (†) First folio, *Ere I had ever*.

[e] *And what* make *you*—] We should now ask,—"What *do* you?" but the above was a household form of speech in Shakespeare's day; in the same manner, Hamlet subsequently demands of Rosencrantz and Guildenstern,—"What *make* you at Elsinore?" in "Othello," Act I. Sc. 2, Cassio inquires of Iago,—

"—— ancient, what *makes* he here?"

and in "Love's Labour's Lost," Act IV. Sc. 3, the king questions Costard,—

"—— what *makes* treason here?"

[f] We'll teach you to drink deep ere you depart.] The reading of the 1603 quarto and of the folio 1623: the other old copies have,—

"We'll teach you *for to drink* ere you depart."

[g] *In my* mind's eye, *Horatio*.] The expression was not unusual: "Ah why were the *Eyes of my Mynde* so dymned wyth the myste of fonde zeal, that I could not consyder the common Malyce of men now a dayes."—FENTON'S *Tragicall Discourses*, 4to. 1567. Again,—"Let us consider and behold with the *eyes of our soul* his long suffering will."—1 *Epistle of St. Clement*, cap. 19.

[h] — *an* attentive *ear*;] The folio and one of the quartos have,—"an *attent* ear."

Upon the witness of these gentlemen,
This marvel to you.
HAM. For God's* love, let me hear.
HOR. Two nights together had these gentlemen,
Marcellus and Bernardo, on their watch,
In the dead vast[a] and middle of the night,
Been thus encounter'd. A figure like your father,
Armed at point,[b] exactly, cap-à-pé,
Appears before them, and with solemn march
Goes slow and stately by them: thrice he walk'd
By their oppress'd and fear-surprised eyes,
Within his truncheon's length; whilst they, distill'd[c]
Almost to jelly with the act of fear,
Stand dumb, and speak not to him. This to me
In dreadful secrecy impart they did;
And I with them the third night kept the watch:
Where, as they had deliver'd, both in time,
Form of the thing, each word made true and good,
The apparition comes. I knew your father;
These hands are not more like.
HAM. But where was this?
MAR. My lord, upon the platform where we watch'd.
HAM. Did you not speak to it?
HOR. My lord, I did;
But answer made it none: yet once methought
It lifted up his[d] head, and did address
Itself to motion, like as it would speak:
But, even then, the morning cock crew loud;
And at the sound it shrunk in haste away,
And vanish'd from our sight.
HAM. 'T is very strange.
HOR. As I do live, my honour'd lord, 'tis true
And we did think it writ down in our duty
To let you know of it.
HAM. Indeed, indeed, sirs, but this troubles me.—
Hold you the watch to-night?
MAR., BER. We do, my lord.
HAM. Arm'd, say you?
MAR., BER. Arm'd, my lord.

(*) First folio, *Heavens*.

[a] *In the dead* vast, &c.] Thus the 1603 quarto; that of 1604, &c. reads,—
"In the dead *waste*," &c.;
the folio, "— dead *wast*," &c.

[b] Armed at point, *exactly, cap-à-pé*,—] So all the quartos but that of 1603; which has, "Armed *to* poynt," &c.: the folio reads, — "Arm'd at all points."

[c] —distill'd—] The reading of the quartos. The folio gives —"*bestil'd*;" and Mr. Collier's annotator substitutes *bechill'd*.

[d] *It lifted up* his *head*,—] From the quarto of 1603. The other quartos and the folio have, "— *it* head."

HAM. From top to toe?
MAR., BER. My lord, from head to foot.
HAM. Then saw you not his face?
HOR. O, yes, my lord; he wore his beaver up.
HAM. How look'd he,[a] frowningly?
HOR. A countenance more in sorrow than in anger.
HAM. Pale or red?
HOR. Nay, very pale.
HAM. And fix'd his eyes upon you?
HOR. Most constantly.
HAM. I would I had been there.
HOR. It would have much amaz'd you.
HAM. Very like, very like.—Stay'd it long?
HOR. While one with moderate haste might tell a hundred.
MAR., BER. Longer, longer.
HOR. Not when I saw it.
HAM. His beard was grizzled,*—no?
HOR. It was, as I have seen it in his life,
A sable silvered.
HAM. I'll watch to-night;
Perchance, 'twill walk† again.
HOR. I warrant you it will.
HAM. If it assume my noble father's person,
I'll speak to it, though hell itself should gape,[b]
And bid me hold my peace. I pray you all,
If you have hitherto conceal'd this sight,
Let it be tenable‡ in your silence still;
And whatsoever else shall hap to-night,
Give it an understanding, but no tongue;
I will requite your loves. So, fare ye well:
Upon the platform, 'twixt eleven and twelve,
'll visit you.
ALL. Our duty to your honour.
HAM. Your love, as mine to you:[c] farewell.
[*Exeunt* HORATIO, MARCELLUS, *and* BERNARDO.
My father's spirit in arms! all is not well;
I doubt some foul play: would the night were come!
Till then sit still, my soul: foul deeds will rise,
Though all the earth o'erwhelm them to men's eyes!

(*) First folio, *grisly*. (†) First folio, *wake*. (‡) First folio, *treble*.

[a] How look'd he,—] Thus the earliest quarto; the subsequent editions read, "*What*, look't he," &c.

[b] —— *though hell itself should* gape,
And bid me hold my peace.]

"Gape" here, perhaps, signifies *yell, howl, roar*, &c., rather than *yawn* or *open*; as in "Henry VIII." Act V. Sc. 3,—"You'll leave your noise anon, ye rascals: do you take the court for Parish-garden? Ye rude slaves, leave your *gaping*."

[c] ALL. Our duty to your honour.
HAM. Your love, as mine to you: farewell.]

In the 1603 quarto we have,—

"*All.* Our duties to your honor.
Ham. O *your loves, your loves*, as mine to you."

And the hurried repetition, "your loves, your loves," well expresses the perturbation of Hamlet at the moment, and that feverish impatience to be alone and commune with himself which he evinces whenever he is particularly moved.

SCENE III.—*A Room in* Polonius' *House.*

Enter LAERTES *and* OPHELIA.

LAER. My necessaries are embark'd; farewell:
And, sister, as the winds give benefit,
And convoy is assistant, do not sleep,
But let me hear from you.
OPH. Do you doubt that?
LAER. For Hamlet, and the trifling of his favours,
Hold it a fashion, and a toy in blood;
A violet in the youth of primy nature,
Forward,* not permanent, sweet, not lasting,
The perfume and† suppliance of a minute;
No more.
OPH. No more but so?
LAER. Think it no more:
For nature, crescent, does not grow alone
In thews and bulk; but, as this‡ temple waxes,
The inward service of the mind and soul
Grows wide withal. Perhaps he loves you now;
And now no soil nor cautel[d] doth besmirch
The virtue[e] of his will:§ but you must fear,
His greatness weigh'd, his will is not his own;
For he himself is subject to his birth:
He may not, as unvalu'd persons do,
Carve for himself; for on his choice depends
The safety and the health of the whole state;[f]
And therefore must his choice be circumscrib'd
Unto the voice and yielding of that body,
Whereof he is the head. Then if he says he loves you,
It fits your wisdom so far to believe it,
As he in his particular act and place||
May give his saying deed; which is no further
Than the main voice of Denmark goes withal.
Then weigh what loss your honour may sustain,
If with too credent ear you list his songs;
Or lose your heart; or your chaste treasure open
To his unmaster'd importunity.
Fear it, Ophelia, fear it, my dear sister;

(*) First folio, *Froward*. (†) First folio omits, *perfume and*. (‡) First folio, *his*. (§) First folio, *feare*. (||) First folio, *peculiar Sect and force*.

[d] —cautel—] *Crafty circumspection.*
[e] *The* virtue *of his will*:] *Virtue* here seems to import *essential goodness*; as we speak of the *virtues* of herbs, &c.
[f] The safety and the health of the whole state;] In the quarto of 1604, we get,—"The safety and health," &c.; "safety" being pronounced as a trisyllable. In the folio the line stands,—

"The *sanctity* and health of the *weole* State."

And keep you in* the rear of your affection,
Out of the shot and danger of desire.
The chariest maid is prodigal enough,
If she unmask her beauty to the moon:
Virtue itself scapes not calumnious strokes:
The canker galls the infants of the spring,
Too oft before their† buttons be disclos'd;
And in the morn and liquid dew of youth
Contagious blastments are most imminent.
Be wary, then; best safety lies in fear:
Youth to itself rebels, though none else near.

OPH. I shall the effect of this good lesson keep,
As watchman‡ to my heart. But, good my brother,
Do not, as some ungracious pastors do,
Show me the steep and thorny way to heaven;
Whilst, like a puff'd and reckless libertine,
Himself the primrose path of dalliance treads,
And recks not his own rede.[a]

LAER. O, fear me not.
I stay too long;—but here my father comes.—

Enter POLONIUS.

A double blessing is a double grace;
Occasion smiles upon a second leave.

POL. Yet here, Laertes! aboard, aboard, for shame!
The wind sits in the shoulder of your sail,
And you are stay'd for. There,—my blessing with you!
[*Laying his hand on* LAERTES' *head.*
And these few precepts in thy memory
See thou charácter. Give thy thoughts no tongue,
Nor any unproportion'd thought his act.
Be thou familiar, but by no means vulgar.
The friends thou hast, and their adoption tried,
Grapple them to thy soul with hoops of steel;[b]
But do not dull thy palm with entertainment
Of each new-hatch'd,§ unfledg'd comrade. Beware
Of entrance to a quarrel; but being in,
Bear't, that the opposed may beware of thee.
Give every man thine ear, but few thy voice:
Take each man's censure,[c] but reserve thy judgment.
Costly thy habit as thy purse can buy,
But not express'd in fancy; rich, not gaudy:
For the apparel oft proclaims the man;
And they in France of the best rank and station
Are of a most select and generous sheaf[d] in that.
Neither a borrower nor a lender be:
For loan oft loses both itself and friend,
And borrowing dulls the edge of husbandry.
This above all,—to thine ownself be true;
And it must follow, as the night the day,
Thou canst not then be false to any man.
Farewell; my blessing season this in thee!

LAER. Most humbly do I take my leave, my lord.

POL. The time invites you; go, your servants tend.

LAER. Farewell, Ophelia; and remember well
What I have said to you.

OPH. 'Tis in my memory lock'd,
And you yourself shall keep the key of it.

LAER. Farewell. [*Exit.*

POL. What is't, Ophelia, he hath said to you?

OPH. So please you, something touching the lord Hamlet.

POL. Marry, well bethought:
'Tis told me, he hath very oft of late
Given private time to you; and you yourself
Have of your audience been most free and bounteous:
If it be so, (as so 'tis put on me,
And that in way of caution) I must tell you,
You do not understand yourself so clearly,
As it behoves my daughter and your honour.
What is between you? give me up the truth.

OPH. He hath, my lord, of late made many tenders
Of his affection to me.

POL. *Affection!* pooh! you speak like a green girl,
Unsifted in such perilous circumstance.
Do you believe his *tenders*, as you call them?

(*) First folio, *keep within*. (†) First folio, *the*.
(‡) First folio, *watchmen*. (§) First folio, *unhatch't*.

[a] — recks not his own rede.] *Regards not his own counsel* or *advice*.

[b] — hoops of steel;] Pope substituted *hooks* for "hoops," and was followed by several of the subsequent editors.

[c] — censure,—] *Opinion, decision.*

[d] *Are of a most select and generous* sheaf *in that.*] In the quarto of 1603, this much-disputed line reads,—

"Are of a most select and generall chiefe in that:"

the after quartos,—

"Ar [and *Or*] of a most select generous cheefe in that;"

and the folio gives,—

"Are of a most select and generous cheff in that."

Rowe, the first modern editor, endeavoured to render the sense intelligible by altering the old text to,—

"Are most select and generous, chief in that;"

and his emendation has been generally adopted: Steevens proposed,—

"Select and generous, are most *choice* in that;"

while Mr. Collier's annotator has,—

"Are of a most select and generous *choice* in that."

The slight change of "sheaf" for *chiefe* or *cheff*, a change for which we alone are answerable, seems to impart a better and more poetic meaning to the passage than any variation yet suggested; and it is supported, if not established, by the following extracts from Ben Jonson,—

"Ay, and with assurance,
That it is found in noblemen and gentlemen
Of the best *sheaf*."
The Magnetic Lady, Act III. Sc. 4.

"I am so haunted at the court and at my lodging with your refined choice spirits, that it makes me clean of another garb, another *sheaf*."—*Every Man out of his Humour*, Act II. Sc. 1.

OPH. I do not know, my lord, what I should think.
POL. Marry, I'll teach you: think yourself a baby;
That you have ta'en these* tenders for true pay,
Which are not sterling. Tender yourself more dearly;
Or,—not to crack the wind of the poor phrase,
Running[a] it thus,—you 'll tender me a fool.
OPH. My lord, he hath impórtun'd me with love,
In honourable fashion.
POL. Ay, *fashion* you may call it; go to, go to.
OPH. And hath given countenance to his speech, my lord,
With almost all the holy vows of heaven.†
POL. Ay, springes to catch woodcocks. I do know,
When the blood burns, how prodigal the soul
Lends‡ the tongue vows: these blazes, daughter,
Giving more light than heat,—extinct in both,
Even in their promise, as it is a-making,—
You must not take for fire. From§ this time, daughter,
Be somewhat scanter of your maiden presence;
Set your entreatments at a higher rate,
Than a command to parley. For lord Hamlet,
Believe so much in him, that he is young;
And with a larger tether may he walk,
Than may be given you: in few, Ophelia,
Do not believe his vows; for they are brokers;
Not of that dye[b] which their investments show,
But mere implorators of unholy suits,
Breathing like sanctified and pious bonds,[c]
The better to beguile. This is for all,—
I would not, in plain terms, from this time forth,
Have you so slander[d] any moment leisure,
As to give words or talk with the lord Hamlet.
Look to 't, I charge you: come your ways.
OPH. I shall obey, my lord. [*Exeunt.*

SCENE IV.—*The Platform.*

Enter HAMLET, HORATIO, *and* MARCELLUS.

HAM. The air bites shrewdly; it is very cold.||
HOR. It is a nipping and an eager air.
HAM. What hour now?
HOR. I think it lacks of twelve.
MAR. No, it is struck.
HOR. Indeed? I heard it not: it then* draws near the season
Wherein the spirit held his wont to walk.
[*A flourish of trumpets within, and ordnance shot off.*
What does this mean, my lord?
HAM. The king doth wake to-night, and takes his rouse,
Keeps wassail,† and the swaggering up-spring reels;(7)
And, as he drains his draughts of Rhenish down,
The kettle-drum and trumpet thus bray out
The triumph of his pledge.
HOR. Is it a custom?
HAM. Ay, marry, is't:
But‡ to my mind,—though I am native here,
And to the manner born,—it is a custom
More honour'd in the breach than the observance.
This heavy-headed revel,[e] east and west
Makes us traduc'd and tax'd of other nations:
They clepe us drunkards, and with swinish phrase
Soil our addition; and, indeed, it takes
From our achievements, though perform'd at height,
The pith and marrow of our attribute.
So, oft it chances in particular men,
That for some vicious mole of nature in them,
As, in their birth, (wherein they are not guilty,
Since nature cannot choose his origin)
By the o'ergrowth of some complexion,
Oft breaking down the pales and forts of reason;
Or by some habit, that too much o'er-leavens
The form of plausive manners;—that these men,—
Carrying, I say, the stamp of one defect,
Being nature's livery, or fortune's star,—
Their§ virtues else (be they as pure as grace,
As infinite as man may undergo)
Shall in the general censure take corruption
From that particular fault:(8) the dram of eale

(*) First folio, *his*. (†) First folio, *With all the vowes of Heaven*. (‡) First folio, *Gives*. (§) First folio, *For*. (||) First folio, *is it very cold?*

[a] Running *it thus*,—] The quartos read,—"*Wrong* it thus," &c.; the folio,—"*Roaming* it thus," &c. "That 'Roaming' is a mistake for 'Running,'" Mr. Dyce remarks, "I have long been convinced; so in a line of 'King John,'—

'Say shall the current of our right *run* on?—

the folio erroneously has,—'*rome* on?' Mr. Collier also in his note on the present passage proposed '*Running;*' and I now find, from the one-volume *Shakespeare*, that his MS. corrector makes the same alteration."

[b] *Not of* that dye, &c.] Thus the quartos, 1604, &c.; but the folio has,—"Not of *the eye*," &c., which, as *eye* was occasionally employed to denote a shade of colour,—

"With an *eye* of green in 't."—*The Tempest*, Act I. Sc. 2,—

may possibly be right.

[c] — *like sanctified and pious* bonds,—] So the old editions. At one time we were strenuously in favour of Theobald's alteration, *bawds* for "bonds;" we are now persuaded the old text is right.

[d] — slander *any* moment *leisure*,]—That is, *abuse*, &c. Modern editors, with the exception of Mr. Dyce, all deviate slightly from the old text in this line by reading, "— moment's leisure."

[e] This heavy-headed revel, &c.] From these words inclusive, the remainder of the speech is omitted in the folio.

(*) First folio, *then it*. (†) First folio, *wassels*. (‡) First folio, *And*. (§) Old text, *His*, corrected by Theobald.

Doth all the noble substance of a doubt,
To his own scandal.[a]

HOR. Look, my lord, it comes!

Enter Ghost.

HAM. Angels and ministers of grace defend us!—
Be thou a spirit of health or goblin damn'd,
Bring with thee airs from heaven or blasts from hell,
Be thy intents* wicked or charitable,
Thou com'st in such a questionable shape,
That I will speak to thee: I'll call thee Hamlet,
King, father, royal Dane: O,† answer me!
Let me not burst in ignorance! but tell
Why thy canoniz'd bones, hearsèd in death,
Have burst their cerements! why the sepulchre,
Wherein we saw thee quietly in-urn'd,
Hath op'd his ponderous and marble jaws,
To cast thee up again! What may this mean,
That thou, dead corse, again in cómplete steel,
Revisit'st thus the glimpses of the moon,
Making night hideous; and we fools of nature
So horridly to shake our disposition,
With thoughts beyond the reaches of our souls?
Say, why is this? wherefore? what should we do?
[Ghost *beckons* HAMLET.

HOR. It beckons you to go away with it,
As if it some impartment did desire
To you alone.

(*) First folio, *events*. (†) First folio, *Oh, oh*.

a ——*the dram of* eale
Doth all the noble substance of a doubt,
To his own scandal.]

The meaning here is tolerably obvious; it is explained indeed by what goes before, but the diction, owing to some errors in the first and second line, has occasioned "much throwing about of brains." For "eale," two of the quartos have "ease," which probably led Theobald to print,—

"— the dram of *base*
Doth all the noble substance of *worth out*
To his own scandal."

Steevens reads,—

"— the dram of *base*
Doth all the noble substance *often dout* [i.e. *do out*]
To his own scandal."

And this is usually followed in the modern text, "ill," however, being often preferred to "base." Mason conjectured "of a doubt" was a mistake for "of't corrupt." Mr. W. N. Lettsom, too, observes, "a verb I should think must lurk under the corruption, 'a doubt,' or 'doubt,' with the signification of turn, pervert, corrupt, or the like;" and Dr. Ingleby writes, "I am convinced that 'of a doubt' is a misprint for 'derogate,' for 1st, 'of a doubt' and 'derogate' have the same number of letters; 2nd, they have the *o*, *a*, *d*, and *t* in common; and 3rd, 'derogate' is the only verb that at the same time completes the sense and preserves the metre." The suggestion of "derogate" is ingenious; but may not the construction have been this,—"The dram of base (or *ill*, or *bale*, or *lead*, or whatsoever word the compositor tortured into "eale" or "ease") doth (i.e. *doeth*, *worketh*,) all the noble substance of a pound to its own vileness"? We by no means pretend that *pound* was the actual word misrendered "doubt;" it is inserted merely because it occurs in opposition to "*dram*" in a line of Quarles' "Emblems," b. ii. E. 7,—

"Where ev'ry *dram* of gold contains a *pound* of dross,"—

and because it is extremely probable *some such* antithesis was intended here.

MAR. Look, with what courteous action
It waves* you to a more removed ground:
But do not go with it.
HOR. No, by no means.
HAM. It will not speak; then will I follow it.
HOR. Do not, my lord.
HAM. Why, what should be the fear?
I do not set my life at a pin's fee;
And for my soul, what can it do to that,
Being a thing immortal as itself?
It waves me forth again;—I'll follow it.
HOR. What if it tempt you toward the flood, my lord,
Or to the dreadful summit† of the cliff,
That beetles o'er his base into the sea,
And there assume some other horrible form,
Which might deprive your sovereignty of reason,[a]
And draw you into madness? think of it:
The very place puts toys of desperation,
Without more motive, into every brain
That looks so many fathoms to the sea,
And hears it roar beneath.[b]
HAM. It waves* me still:—
Go on; I'll follow thee.
MAR. You shall not go, my lord.
HAM. Hold off your hands!‡
HOR. Be rul'd; you shall not go.
HAM. My fate cries out,
And makes each petty artery in this body
As hardy as the Némean lion's nerve.—
[Ghost *beckons.*
Still am I call'd;—unhand me, gentlemen;—
By heaven, I'll make a ghost of him that lets[c] me!— [*Breaking from them.*
I say, away!—Go on, I'll follow thee.
[*Exeunt* Ghost *and* HAMLET.
HOR. He waxes desperate with imagination.
MAR. Let's follow; 't is not fit thus to obey him.
HOR. Have after.—To what issue will this come?
MAR. Something is rotten in the state of Denmark.
HOR. Heaven will direct it.
MAR. Nay, let's follow him.
[*Exeunt.*

(*) First folio, *wafts*. (†) Old text, *somnet*, and *Sonnet*. (‡) First folio, *hand*.

[a] *Which might* deprive your sovereignty of reason,—] Gifford was mistaken in assuming that "your sovereignty" was here merely a title of respect like "your lordship," applied to Hamlet. To *deprive your sovereignty of reason*, means to dethrone or displace your powers of reason. Warburton cites a passage from Εἰκὼν Βασιλικὴ, where the precise expression occurs: "At once to betray the *soveraignty of reason* in my own soul."

[b] And hears it roar beneath.] This and the three preceding lines are not found in the folio.

SCENE V.—*A more remote Part of the Platform.*

Enter Ghost *and* HAMLET.

HAM. Whither* wilt thou lead me? speak, I'll go no further.
GHOST. Mark me.
HAM. I will.
GHOST. My hour is almost come,
When I to sulphurous and tormenting flames
Must render up myself.
HAM. Alas, poor ghost!
GHOST. Pity me not, but lend thy serious hearing
To what I shall unfold.
HAM. Speak; I am bound to hear.
GHOST. So art thou to revenge, when thou shalt hear.
HAM. What!
GHOST. I am thy father's spirit;
Doom'd for a certain term to walk the night,
And for the day confin'd to fast in fires,[d]
Till the foul crimes done in my days of nature
Are burnt and purg'd away. But that I am forbid
To tell the secrets of my prison-house,
I could a tale unfold, whose lightest word
Would harrow up thy soul; freeze thy young blood;
Make thy two eyes, like stars, start from their spheres;
Thy knotted† and combined locks to part,
And each particular hair to stand an end,
Like quills upon the fretful porcupine;‡
But this eternal blazon must not be
To ears of flesh and blood.—List, list, O, list!—§
If thou didst ever thy dear father love,—
HAM. O, God!‖
GHOST. Revenge his foul and most unnatural murder.
HAM. *Murder!*
GHOST. Murder most foul, as in the best it is;
But this most foul, strange, and unnatural.
HAM. Haste me to know 't, that I,¶ with wings as swift
As meditation or the thoughts of love,
May sweep to my revenge.
GHOST. I find thee apt;
And duller shouldst thou be than the fat weed
That rots[e] itself in ease on Lethe wharf,

(*) First folio, *Where*. (†) First folio, *knotty*.
(‡) Old text, *Porpentine*. (§) First folio, *list Hamlet, oh list*.
(‖) First folio, *Heaven*.
(¶) First folio, *Hast, hast me to know it, That with wings*.

[c] — *that* lets *me!*—] That *hinders*, or *obstructs* me.

[d] — *confin'd to* fast in *fires*,—] The reading of all the copies, except the 1603 quarto, which has, "Confinde in flaming fire," &c. Heath proposed, "—to *lasting* fires," &c.; and the same lection is suggested by Mr. Collier's annotator.

[e] *That* rots *itself*—] The quartos all read, "*roots* itself," and it is difficult to determine which expression deserves the preference.

Wouldst thou not stir in this. Now, Hamlet, hear:
'Tis* given out that, sleeping in mine orchard,
A serpent stung me; so the whole ear of Denmark
Is by a forged process of my death
Rankly abus'd: but know, thou noble youth,
The serpent that did sting thy father's life,
Now wears his crown.

(*) First folio, *It's*.

HAM. O, my prophetic soul! mine uncle!
GHOST. Ay, that incestuous, that adulterate beast,
With witchcraft of his wit,* with traitorous gifts,
(O, wicked wit, and gifts, that have† the power
So to seduce!) won to his‡ shameful lust
The will of my most seeming-virtuous queen:
O, Hamlet, what a falling-off was there!
From me, whose love was of that dignity,

(*) Old text, *wits*. (†) First folio, *hath*. (‡) First folio, *this*.

That it went hand in hand even with the vow
I made to her in marriage; and to decline
Upon a wretch, whose natural gifts were poor
To those of mine!
But virtue, as it never will be mov'd,
Though lewdness court it in a shape of heaven;
So lust, though to a radiant angel link'd,
Will sate itself in a celestial bed,
And prey on garbage.
But, soft! methinks I scent the morning* air;
Brief let me be.—Sleeping within mine orchard,
My custom always in the afternoon,
Upon my secure[a] hour thy uncle stole,
With juice of cursed hebenon in a vial,
And in the porches of mine ears did pour
The leperous distilment; whose effect
Holds such an enmity with blood of man,
That, swift as quicksilver, it courses through
The natural gates and alleys of the body;
And, with a sudden vigour,[b] it doth posset
And curd, like eager[c] droppings into milk,
The thin and wholesome blood: so did it mine;
And a most instant tetter bark'd† about,
Most lazar-like, with vile and loathsome crust,
All my smooth body.
Thus was I, sleeping, by a brother's hand
Of life, of crown, of queen, at once despatch'd;[d]
Cut off even in the blossoms of my sin,
Unhousel'd, disappointed, unanel'd:[e]
No reckoning made, but sent to my account
With all my imperfections on my head:
O, horrible! O, horrible! most horrible![f]
If thou hast nature in thee, bear it not;
Let not the royal bed of Denmark be
A couch for luxury and damned incest.
But, howsoever thou pursu'st this act,
Taint not thy mind, nor let thy soul contrive
Against thy mother aught; leave her to heaven,
And to those thorns that in her bosom lodge,
To prick and sting her. Fare thee well at once!
The glow-worm shows the matin to be near,
And 'gins to pale his uneffectual fire: (9)
Adieu, adieu! Hamlet, remember me! [*Exit.*

HAM. O, all you host of heaven! O, earth! what else?
And shall I couple hell?—O, fie!—Hold, my heart;
And you, my sinews, grow not instant old,
But bear me stiffly up!—Remember thee!
Ay, thou poor ghost, while memory holds a seat
In this distracted globe. Remember thee!
Yea, from the table of my memory
I 'll wipe away all trivial fond records,
All saws of books, all forms, all pressures past,
That youth and observation copied there;
And thy commandment all alone shall live
Within the book and volume of my brain,
Unmix'd with baser matter: yes,* by heaven!—
O, most pernicious woman!—
O, villain, villain, smiling, damned villain!—
My tables,†—meet it is I set it down,
That one may smile, and smile, and be a villain;
At least I'm sure it may be so in Denmark; [*Writing.*
So, uncle, there you are. Now to my word;
It is, *Adieu, adieu! remember me.*
I have sworn 't.

HOR. [*Without.*] My lord, my lord,—

MAR. [*Without.*] Lord Hamlet,—

HOR. [*Without.*] Heaven secure him!

MAR. [*Without.*] So be it!

HOR. [*Without.*] Illo, ho, ho, my lord!

HAM. Hillo, ho, ho, boy! come, bird, come.[g]

Enter HORATIO *and* MARCELLUS.

MAR. How is 't, my noble lord?

HOR. What news, my lord?

HAM. O, wonderful!

HOR. Good my lord, tell it.

HAM. No; you 'll reveal it.

HOR. Not I, my lord, by heaven.

MAR. Nor I, my lord.

HAM. How say you then; would heart of man once think it?—
But you 'll be secret?—

HOR., MAR. Ay, by heaven, my lord.

HAM. There 's ne'er a villain dwelling in all Denmark—
But he 's an arrant knave.

HOR. There needs no ghost, my lord, come from the grave
To tell us this.

HAM. Why, right; you are i' the right;
And so, without more circumstance at all,
I hold it fit that we shake hands and part;
You, as your business and desire shall point you,—
For every man has business and desire,

(*) First folio, *Mornings.* (†) First folio, *bak'd.*

(*) First folio, *yes, yes.* (†) First folio repeats, *My tables.*

a — *my* secure *hour*—] My *unguarded* hour. See note (a), p. 96, of the present volume.

b — *a sudden* vigour,—] "Vigour" may be right; but *rigour* seems more suitable to the context, and more accordant with the supposed effects of narcotics formerly.

c — eager—] *Aigre, sour.*

d — despatch'd;] *Bereft.* The quarto of 1603 has "deprived;" but that hardly expresses the instantaneity of the severance so aptly as "despatch'd."

e Unhousel'd, disappointed, unanel'd:] "*Unhousel'd*" signifies without having received the eucharist; "*disappointed*" = *unappointed*, means *unprepared;* and "unanel'd" is without extreme unction.

f O, horrible! O, horrible! most horrible!] Notwithstanding the unanimity of the old copies in assigning this line to the Ghost, there can be little doubt it was intended to be spoken by Hamlet, as in acting, indeed, it usually is.

g Hillo, ho, ho, boy! come, bird, come.] These were expressions of encouragement which the falconer of old was wont to address to his hawks.

Such as it is,—and, for mine own poor part,
Look you, I 'll go pray.
HOR. These are but wild and whirling* words, my lord.
HAM. I 'm sorry they offend you, heartily;
Yes, 'faith, heartily.
HOR. There 's no offence, my lord.
HAM. Yes, by Saint Patrick, but there is, Horatio,†
And much offence too. Touching this vision here,—
It is an honest ghost, that let me tell you:
For your desire to know what is between us,
O'ermaster 't as you may. And now, good friends,
As you are friends, scholars, and soldiers,
Give me one poor request.
HOR. What is 't, my lord? we will.
HAM. Never make known what you have seen to-night.
HOR., MAR. My lord, we will not.
HAM. Nay, but swear 't.
HOR. In faith, my lord, not I!
MAR. Nor I, my lord, in faith!
HAM. Upon my sword!
MAR. We have sworn, my lord, already.
HAM. In deed, upon my sword, in deed.[a]
GHOST. [*Beneath.*] Swear!
HAM. Ah, ha, boy! say'st thou so? art thou there, true-penny?—
Come on,—you hear this fellow in the cellarage,—
Consent to swear.
HOR. Propose the oath, my lord.
HAM. Never to speak of this that you have seen,
Swear by my sword.
GHOST. [*Beneath.*] Swear!
HAM. *Hic et ubique?* then we'll shift our ground.—
Come hither, gentlemen,
And lay your hands again upon my sword:
Never to speak of this that you have heard,
Swear by my sword.

(*) First folio, *hurling*. (†) First folio, *but there is my Lord*.

[a] In deed, upon my sword, in deed.] The meaning of Hamlet unquestionably is, Not in words only, but *in act, in form;* upon the cross of my sword, pledge yourselves. The line, however, is always printed,—
"*Indeed*, upon my sword, *indeed*."

GHOST. [*Beneath.*] Swear by his sword![b]
HAM. Well said, old mole! canst work i' the earth* so fast?
A worthy pioner!—Once more remove, good friends.
HOR. O, day and night, but this is wondrous strange!
HAM. And therefore as a stranger give it welcome.
There are more things in heaven and earth, Horatio,
Than are dreamt of in your† philosophy. But come;—
Here, as before, never, so help you mercy,
How strange or odd soe'er I bear myself,—
As I, perchance, hereafter shall think meet
To put an antic disposition on,—
That you, at such times seeing me, never shall,
With arms encumber'd thus, or this‡ head-shake,
Or by pronouncing of some doubtful phrase,
As, *Well, well,*§ *we know;*—or, *We could, an if we would;*—
Or, *If we list to speak;*—or, *There be, an if they*‖ *might;*—
Or such ambiguous giving out, to note
That you know aught of me,—this not to do,
So grace and mercy at your most need help you,
Swear!
GHOST. [*Beneath.*] Swear!
HAM. Rest, rest, perturbed spirit!—So, gentlemen,
With all my love I do commend me to you:
And what so poor a man as Hamlet is
May do, to express his love and friending to you,
God willing, shall not lack. Let us go in together;
And still your fingers on your lips, I pray.
The time is out of joint:—O, cursed spite,
That ever I was born to set it right!—
Nay, come, let 's go together. [*Exeunt.*

(*) First folio, *ground*. (†) First folio, *our*.
(‡) First folio, *thus*. (§) First folio, *As well, we know*.
(‖) First folio, *there*.

[b] *Swear* by his sword!] The folio omits the words,—"by his sword."

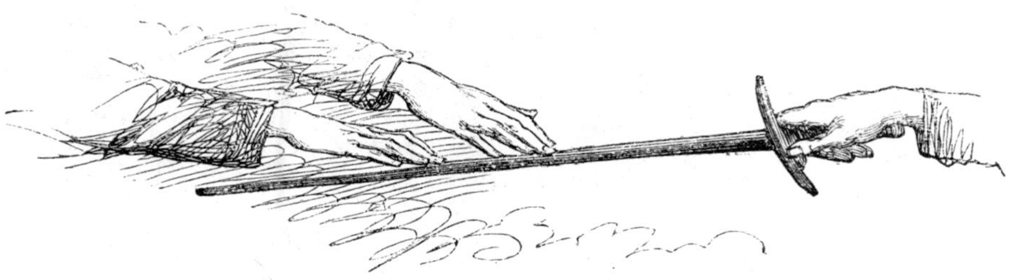

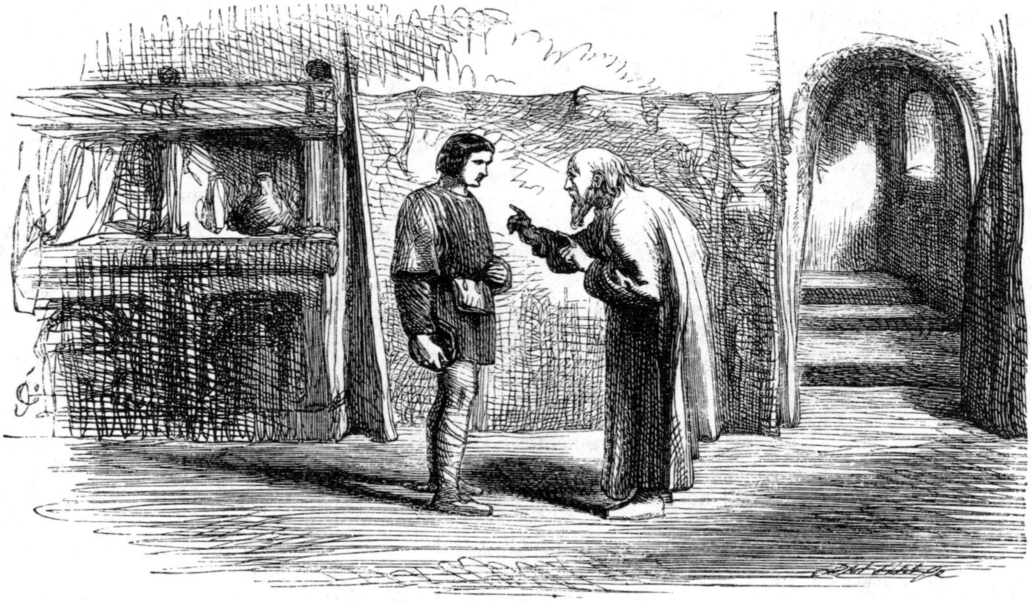

ACT II.

SCENE I.—*A Room in* Polonius' *House*.

Enter Polonius *and* Reynaldo.

Pol. Give him this* money, and these notes, Reynaldo.

Rey. I will, my lord.

Pol. You shall do marvellous wisely, good Reynaldo,
Before you visit him, to† make inquiry
Of his behaviour.

Rey. My lord, I did intend it.

Pol. Marry, well said; very well said. Look you, sir,
Inquire me first what Danskers[a] are in Paris;
And how, and who, what means, and where they keep,
What company, at what expense; and finding,
By this encompassment and drift of question,
That they do know my son, come you more nearer
Than your particular demands will touch it;
Take you, as 'twere, some distant knowledge of him;
As* thus,—*I know his father and his friends,*
And, in part, him;—do you mark this, Reynaldo?

Rey. Ay, very well, my lord.

Pol. *And, in part, him;—but,* you may say, *not well:*
But, if't be he I mean, he's very wild;
Addicted—so and so; and there put on him
What forgeries you please; marry, none so rank
As may dishonour him; take heed of that;
But, sir, such wanton, wild, and usual slips
As are companions noted and most known
To youth and liberty.

Rey. As gaming, my lord.

Pol. Ay, or drinking, fencing, swearing, quarrelling,
Drabbing:—you may go so far.

Rey. My lord, that would dishonour him.

Pol. Faith, no; as you may season it in the charge.
You must not put another scandal on him,
That he is open to incontinency;
That's not my meaning: but breathe his faults so quaintly,

(*) First folio, *his*. (†) First folio, *you*.

(*) First folio, *And*

[a] Danskers—] *Danes*

That they may seem the taints of liberty;
The flash and out-break of a fiery mind;
A savageness in unreclaimed blood,
Of general assault.

REY. But, my good lord,—

POL. Wherefore should you do this?

REY. Ay, my lord,
I would know that.

POL. Marry, sir, here's my drift;
And, I believe, it is a fetch of warrant:
You laying these slight sullies on my son,
As 'twere a thing a little soil'd i' the working,
Mark you, your party in converse, him you would sound,
Having ever seen in the prenominate crimes
The youth you breathe of guilty, be assur'd,
He closes with you in this consequence;
Good sir, or so; or *friend*, or *gentleman*,—
According to the phrase or* the addition,
Of man, and country.

REY. Very good, my lord.

POL. And then, sir, does he this,—he does—
What was I about to say? By the mass†
I was about to say something:—where did I leave?

REY. At *closes in the consequence.*
At *friend, or so, and gentleman.*

POL. At, *closes in the consequence*,—ay, marry;
He closes with you thus:—*I know the gentleman;*
I saw him yesterday, or t'other day, [*you say,*
Or then, or then; with such, or such; and, as*
There was he gaming; there o'ertook in's rouse;
There falling out at tennis; or perchance,
I saw him enter such a house of sale,—
Videlicet, a brothel,—or so forth—
See you now;
Your bait of falsehood takes this carp‡ of truth:
And thus do we of wisdom and of reach,
With windlaces, and with assays of bias,
By indirections find directions out:
So, by my former lecture and advice,
Shall you my son. You have me, have you not?

REY. My lord, I have.

POL. God be wi' you; fare you well.

REY. Good my lord!

POL. Observe his inclination in yourself.

REY. I shall, my lord.

POL. And let him ply his music.

REY. Well, my lord. [*Exit.*

POL. Farewell!—

Enter OPHELIA.

How now, Ophelia! what's the matter?

OPH. Alas, my lord, I have been so affrighted!

POL. With what, i' the name of God?*

OPH. My lord, as I was sewing in my chamber,
Lord Hamlet,—with his doublet all unbrac'd;
No hat upon his head; his stockings foul'd,
Ungarter'd, and down-gyved[a] to his ancle;
Pale as his shirt; his knees knocking each other;
And with a look so piteous in purport,
As if he had been loosed out of hell
To speak of horrors,—he comes before me.

POL. Mad for thy love!

OPH. My lord, I do not know;
But, truly, I do fear it.

POL. What said he?

OPH. He took me by the wrist, and held me hard;
Then goes he to the length of all his arm;
And, with his other hand thus o'er his brow,
He falls to such perusal of my face,
As he would draw it. Long stay'd he so;
At last,—a little shaking of mine arm,
And thrice his head thus waving up and down,—
He rais'd a sigh so piteous and profound,
That it did seem to shatter all his bulk,[b]
And end his being: that done, he lets me go:
And, with his head over his shoulder† turn'd,
He seem'd to find his way without his eyes;
For out o' doors he went without their help,
And, to the last, bended their light on me.

POL. Come,‡ go with me; I will go seek the king.
This is the very ecstasy of love;
Whose violent property fordoes itself,
And leads the will to desperate undertakings,
As oft as any passion under heaven
That does afflict our natures. I am sorry,—
What, have you given him any hard words of late?

OPH. No, my good lord; but, as you did command,
I did repel his letters, and denied
His access to me.

POL. That hath made him mad.
I am sorry that with better heed§ and judgment,
I had not quoted[c] him: I fear'd‖ he did but trifle,
And meant to wreck thee; but, beshrew my jealousy!

(*) First folio, *and.* (†) First folio omits, *By the mass.* (‡) First folio, *Cape.*

a — down-gyved to his ancle;] "*Down-gyved* means, hanging down like the loose cincture which confines the fetters round the ancles."—STEEVENS.

b — his bulk,—] Mr. Singer rightly explains "bulk" here to mean, not *all his body*, as some commentators have interpreted it, but, *his breast.* So, in Shakespeare's "Lucrece,"—

(*) First folio, *Heaven.* (†) First folio, *shoulders.* (‡) First folio omits, *Come.* (§) First folio, *speed.* (‖) First folio, *feare.*

"May feel her heart, ——
* * * * * *
Beating her *bulk*, that his hand shakes withal."

c — quoted *him:*] *To quote*, as we have seen, was not unfrequently used by Shakespeare and his contemporaries in the sense of *to look into, to scan, to mark*, &c.

It seems it is as proper to our age
To cast beyond ourselves in our opinions,
As it is common for the younger sort
To lack discretion. Come, go we to the king:
This must be known; which, being kept close, might move
More grief to hide than hate to utter love.
[*Exeunt.*

SCENE II.—*A Room in the Castle.*

Flourish. Enter KING, QUEEN, ROSENCRANTZ, GUILDENSTERN, *and* Attendants.

KING. Welcome, dear Rosencrantz and Guildenstern!
Moreover that we much did long to see you,
The need we have to use you did provoke
Our hasty sending. Something have you heard
Of Hamlet's transformation; so I call it,
Since not the exterior nor the inward man
Resembles that it was. What it should be,
More than his father's death, that thus hath put him
So much from the understanding of himself,
I cannot dream* of: I entreat you both,
That, being of so young days brought up with him,
And since so neighbour'd to his youth and humour,
That you vouchsafe your rest here in our court
Some little time: so by your companies
To draw him on to pleasures; and to gather,
So much as from occasions you may glean,
Whether aught, to us unknown, afflicts him thus,[a]
That, open'd, lies within our remedy.

QUEEN. Good gentlemen, he hath much talk'd of you;
And sure I am two men there are not living
To whom he more adheres. If it will please you
To show us so much gentry[b] and good will,
As to expend your time with us a while,
For the supply and profit of our hope,
Your visitation shall receive such thanks
As fits a king's remembrance.

ROS. Both your majesties
Might, by the sovereign power you have of us,
Put your dread pleasures more into command
Than to entreaty.

GUIL. But† we both obey;
And here give up ourselves, in the full bent,
To lay our service‡ freely at your feet,
To be commanded.

KING. Thanks, Rosencrantz and gentle Guildenstern.

QUEEN. Thanks, Guildenstern and gentle Rosencrantz:
And I beseech you instantly to visit
My too much changed son.—Go, some of you,
And bring these* gentlemen where Hamlet is.

GUIL. Heavens make our presence, and our practices,
Pleasant and helpful to him!

QUEEN. Ay,† amen!
[*Exeunt* ROSENCRANTZ, GUILDENSTERN, *and some* Attendants.

Enter POLONIUS.

POL. The ambassadors from Norway, my good lord,
Are joyfully return'd.

KING. Thou still hast been the father of good news.

POL. Have I, my lord? Assure you, my good liege,
I hold my duty, as I hold my soul,
Both to my God, and‡ to my gracious king:
And I do think (or else this brain of mine
Hunts not the trail of policy so sure
As it hath§ us'd to do) that I have found
The very cause of Hamlet's lunacy.

KING. O, speak of that; that I do long to hear.

POL. Give first admittance to the ambassadors;
My news shall be the fruit‖ to that great feast.

KING. Thyself do grace to them, and bring them in. [*Exit* POLONIUS.
He tells me, my sweet queen, that he hath found
The head and source of all your son's distemper.

QUEEN. I doubt it is no other but the main,[c]
His father's death, and our o'erhasty marriage.

KING. Well, we shall sift him.—

Re-enter POLONIUS, *with* VOLTIMAND *and* CORNELIUS.

Welcome, my¶ good friends!
Say, Voltimand, what from our brother Norway?

VOL. Most fair return of greetings and desires.
Upon our first, he sent out to suppress
His nephew's levies; which to him appear'd
To be a preparation 'gainst the Polack;

(*) First folio, *deeme.* (†) First folio omits, *But.* (‡) First folio, *Services.*

[a] Whether aught, to us unknown, afflicts him thus,—] This line, almost indispensable to the integrity of the passage, is wanting in the folio.

[b] — gentry—] *Courtesy.*

(*) First folio, *the.* (†) First folio omits, *Ay.* (‡) First folio, *one.* (§) First folio, *I have.* (‖) First folio, *Newes.* (¶) First folio omits, *my.*

[c] I doubt it is no other but the main,—] An ellipsis,—*in* being understood;—"no other but *in* the main."

But, better look'd into, he truly found
It was against your highness: whereat,—griev'd
That so his sickness, age, and impotence,
Was falsely borne in hand,—sends out arrests
On Fortinbras; which he, in brief, obeys;
Receives rebuke from Norway; and, in fine,
Makes vow before his uncle, never more
To give the assay of arms against your majesty.
Whereon old Norway, overcome with joy,
Gives him three thousand crowns in annual fee;
And his commission to employ those soldiers,
So levied as before, against the Polack:
With an entreaty, herein further shown,
[*Gives a paper.*
That it might please you to give quiet pass
Through your dominions for this* enterprise;
On such regards of safety and allowance
As therein are set down.
KING. It likes us well;
And at our more consider'd time we'll read,
Answer, and think upon this business.
Meantime we thank you for your well-took labour:

(*) First folio, *his*.

Go to your rest; at night we'll feast together:
Most welcome home!
[*Exeunt* VOLTIMAND *and* CORNELIUS.
POL. This business is* well ended.—
My liege,—and madam,—to expostulate
What majesty should be, what duty is,
Why day is day, night night, and time is time,
Were nothing but to waste night, day, and time.
Therefore, since brevity is the soul of wit,[a]
And tediousness the limbs and outward flourishes,
I will be brief: your noble son is mad:
Mad call I it; for, to define true madness,
What is't, but to be nothing else but mad?
But let that go.
QUEEN. More matter, with less art.
POL. Madam, I swear I use no art at all.
That he is mad, 't is true: 't is true 't is pity;
And pity 't is 't is true:† a foolish figure;
But farewell it, for I will use no art.
Mad let us grant him, then: and now remains,
That we find out the cause of this effect,—
Or rather say, the cause of this defect,

(*) First folio inserts, *very*. (†) First folio, *pittie it is true*.

[a] — wit,—] That is, *wisdom*.

For this effect defective comes by cause:
Thus it remains, and the remainder thus. Perpend.(1)
I have a daughter;—have, while* she is mine;[a]—
Who, in her duty and obedience, mark,
Hath given me this: now gather, and surmise.

[Reads.]—*To the celestial, and my soul's idol, the most beautified Ophelia,*—

That's an ill phrase, a vile phrase,—*beautified* is a vile phrase; but you shall hear:—Thus:†

In her excellent white bosom, these, &c.—

QUEEN. Came this from Hamlet to her?
POL. Good madam, stay awhile; I will be faithful.

[Reads.] *Doubt thou the stars are fire;*
Doubt that the sun doth move;
Doubt truth to be a liar;
But never doubt I love.

O, dear Ophelia, I am ill at these numbers; I have not art to reckon my groans: but that I love thee best, O, most best! believe it. Adieu.
Thine evermore, most dear lady, whilst this machine is to him,
HAMLET.

This, in obedience, hath my daughter show'd me:
And more above, hath his solicitings,‡
As they fell out by time, by means, and place,
All given to mine ear.
KING. But how hath she receiv'd his love?
POL. What do you think of me?
KING. As of a man faithful and honourable.
POL. I would fain prove so. But what might you think,
When I had seen this hot love on the wing,
(As I perceiv'd it, I must tell you that,
Before my daughter told me) what might you,
Or my dear majesty your queen here, think,
If I had play'd the desk or table-book;
Or given my heart a winking, mute and dumb;
Or look'd upon this love with idle sight;—
What might you think? No, I went round to work,
And my young mistress thus I did bespeak;
Lord Hamlet is a prince out of thy star;[b]
This must not be: and then I precepts gave her,
That she should lock herself from his resort,
Admit no messengers, receive no tokens.
Which done, she took the fruits of my advice;
And he, repulsed, (a short tale to make)
Fell into a sadness; then into a fast;
Thence to a watch; thence into a weakness;
Thence to a lightness; and, by this declension,
Into the madness wherein* now he raves,
And all we mourn† for.
KING. Do you think 't is this?
QUEEN. It may be very likely.
POL. Hath there been such a time, (I'd fain know that)
That I have positively said, '*T is so,*
When it prov'd otherwise?
KING. Not that I know.
POL. Take this from this, if this be otherwise:
[*Pointing to his head and shoulder.*
If circumstances lead me I will find
Where truth is hid, though it were hid indeed
Within the centre.
KING. How may we try it further?
POL. You know, sometimes he walks four[c] hours together,
Here in the lobby.
QUEEN. So he does‡ indeed.
POL. At such a time I'll loose my daughter to him:
Be you and I behind an arras; then
Mark the encounter: if he love her not,
And be not from his reason fall'n thereon,
Let me be no assistant for a state,
But§ keep a farm and carters.
KING. We will try it.
QUEEN. But look, where sadly the poor wretch comes reading.
POL. Away! I do beseech you, both away;
I'll board him presently:—O, give me leave.—
[*Exeunt* KING, QUEEN, *and* Attendants.

Enter HAMLET, *reading.*

How does my good lord Hamlet?
HAM. Well, God-'a-mercy.
POL. Do you know me, my lord?
HAM. Excellent, excellent well; you 're a fishmonger.

(*) First folio, *whil'st.* (†) First folio, *These.* (‡) First folio, *soliciting.*

(*) First folio, *whereon.* (†) First folio, *waile.* (‡) First folio, *h'as.* (§) First folio, *And.*

a — while she is mine;—] In the quarto, 1603, is added,—
"—— for that we thinke
Is surest, we often loose," &c.

b — *out of thy* star;] So all the old copies until the folio of 1632, which reads, improperly,—
"—— out of thy *sphere.*"
The meaning is, Lord Hamlet is a prince beyond the influence of the star which governs your fortunes.

c — four *hours* together,—] Hanmer and others proposed the obvious reading,—
"—— *for* hours together," &c.;—
but "four" here, as in "Coriolanus," Act I. Sc. 6,—
"And *four* shall quickly draw out my command," &c.—
and elsewhere, appears a mere colloquialism, to signify *some,* or a limited number, as "forty" is frequently used to express a great number.

POL. Not I, my lord.

HAM. Then I would you were so honest a man.

POL. Honest, my lord!

HAM. Ay, sir; to be honest, as this world goes, is to be one man picked out of ten* thousand.

POL. That 's very true, my lord.

(*) First folio, *two*.

HAM. [Reads.] *For if the sun breed maggots in a dead dog, being a god kissing carrion,*—(2) Have you a daughter?

POL. I have, my lord.

HAM. Let her not walk i' the sun: conception is a blessing; but not as your daughter may conceive:—friend, look to 't.

POL. [*Aside.*] How say you by that? Still

harping on my daughter:—yet he knew me not at first; he said I was a fishmonger: he is far gone, far gone: and truly in my youth I suffered much extremity for love; very near this. I'll speak to him again.—What do you read, my lord?

HAM. Words, words, words!

POL. What is the matter, my lord?

HAM. Between who?

POL. I mean the matter that you read,* my lord.

HAM. Slanders, sir: for the satirical rogue† says here, that old men have grey beards; that their faces are wrinkled; their eyes purging thick amber and‡ plum-tree gum; and that they have a plentiful lack of wit, together with most§ weak hams: all which, sir, though I most powerfully and potently believe, yet I hold it not honesty to have it thus set down; for you yourself, sir, should grow‖ old as I am, if, like a crab, you could go backward.

POL. [*Aside.*] Though this be madness, yet there is method in 't.—Will you walk out of the air, my lord?

HAM. Into my grave?

POL. Indeed, that is out o' the air.—[*Aside.*] How pregnant sometimes his replies are! a happiness that often madness hits on, which reason and sanity could not so prosperously be delivered of. I will leave him, and suddenly contrive the means of meeting between him and my daughter. —My honourable lord, I will most humbly take my leave of you.

HAM. You cannot, sir, take from me anything that I will more willingly part withal,—except my life, except my life, except my life.[a]

POL. Fare you well, my lord.

HAM. These tedious old fools!

Enter ROSENCRANTZ *and* GUILDENSTERN.

POL. You go to seek the¶ lord Hamlet; there he is.

ROS. [*To* POLONIUS.] God save you, sir!

[*Exit* POLONIUS.

GUIL. Mine honoured lord!—

ROS. My most dear lord!

HAM. My excellent good friends! How dost thou, Guildenstern? Ah, Rosencrantz! Good lads, how do ye both?

(*) First folio, *matter you meane.* (†) First folio, *slave.* (‡) First folio, *or.* (§) First folio omits, *most.* (‖) First folio, *be.* (¶) First folio, *my.*

[a] — except my life.] The folio reads only,—

"—— except my life, my life;"—

and Mr. Collier thinks the repetitions originated merely with the actors. To us it is evident that here, as in other places, the iteration—a well-known symptom of intellectual derangement—is purposely adopted by Hamlet to encourage the belief of his insanity. He never indulges in this cuckoo-note unless with those whom he distrusts.

ROS. As the indifferent[b] children of the earth.

GUIL. Happy, in that we are not overhappy; on Fortune's cap we are not the very button.

HAM. Nor the soles of her shoe?

ROS. Neither, my lord.

HAM. Then you live about her waist, or in the middle of her favours*?

GUIL. Faith, her privates we.

HAM. In the secret parts of Fortune? O, most true; she is a strumpet. What's the news?

ROS. None, my lord, but that the world's grown honest.

HAM. Then is dooms-day near: but your news is not true. Let me question more in particular:[c] what have you, my good friends, deserved at the hands of Fortune, that she sends you to prison hither?

GUIL. Prison, my lord?

HAM. Denmark's a prison.

ROS. Then is the world one.

HAM. A goodly one; in which there are many confines, wards, and dungeons, Denmark being one of the worst.

ROS. We think not so, my lord.

HAM. Why, then, 't is none to you; for there is nothing either good or bad, but thinking makes it so: to me it is a prison.

ROS. Why, then, your ambition makes it one; 't is too narrow for your mind.

HAM. O, God! I could be bounded in a nutshell, and count myself a king of infinite space; were it not that I have bad dreams.

GUIL. Which dreams, indeed, are ambition; for the very substance of the ambitious is merely the shadow of a dream.

HAM. A dream itself is but a shadow.

ROS. Truly, and I hold ambition of so airy and light a quality, that it is but a shadow's shadow.

HAM. Then are our beggars bodies, and our monarchs and outstretched heroes the beggars' shadows. Shall we to the court? for, by my fay, I cannot reason.

ROS., GUIL. We'll wait upon you.

HAM. No such matter: I will not sort you with the rest of my servants; for, to speak to you like an honest man, I am most dreadfully attended. But, in the beaten way of friendship, what make you at Elsinore?

ROS. To visit you, my lord: no other occasion.

HAM. Beggar that I am, I am even poor in

(*) First folio, *favour.*

[b] — indifferent—] *Moderate, medium, average,* &c.

[c] Let me question, &c.] The dialogue, from these words down to "I am most dreadfully attended," is found only in the folio.

thanks; but I thank you: and sure, dear friends, my thanks are too dear a halfpenny. Were you not sent for? Is it your own inclining? Is it a free visitation? Come, deal justly with me: come, come; nay, speak.

GUIL. What should we say, my lord?

HAM. Why anything—but[a] to the purpose. You were sent for; and there is a kind of* confession in your looks, which your modesties have not craft enough to colour: I know the good king and queen have sent for you.

ROS. To what end, my lord?

HAM. That you must teach me. But let me conjure you, by the rights of our fellowship, by the consonancy of our youth, by the obligation of our ever-preserved love, and by what more dear a better proposer could charge you withal, be even and direct with me, whether you were sent for, or no?

ROS. [*To* GUILDENSTERN.] What say you?

HAM. [*Aside.*] Nay, then, I have an eye of you.[b]—If you love me, hold not off.

GUIL. My lord, we were sent for.

HAM. I will tell you why; so shall my anticipation prevent your discovery, and your secrecy to the king and queen moult no feather.[c] I have of late, (but wherefore I know not) lost all my mirth, forgone all custom of exercises: and, indeed, it goes so heavily† with my disposition, that this goodly frame, the earth, seems to me a sterile promontory; this most excellent canopy, the air, look you,—this brave o'erhanging firmament‡—this majestical roof fretted with golden fire,—why, it appears no other thing to me than a foul and pestilent congregation of vapours. What a piece of work is a man! how noble in reason! how infinite in faculty! in form and moving how express and admirable! in action how like an angel! in apprehension how like a god! the beauty of the world! the paragon of animals! And yet, to me, what is this quintessence of dust? man delights not me; no, nor woman neither, though by your smiling you seem to say so.

ROS. My lord, there was no such stuff in my thoughts.

HAM. Why did you laugh, then,* when I said, *man delights not me?*

ROS. To think, my lord, if you delight not in man, what lenten[d] entertainment the players shall receive from you: we coted[e] them on the way; and hither are they coming, to offer you service.

HAM. He that plays the king shall be welcome,—his majesty shall have tribute of me; the adventurous knight shall use his foil and target; the lover shall not sigh gratis; the humorous[f] man shall end his part in peace; the clown shall make those laugh whose lungs are tickled o' the sere;[g] and the lady shall say her mind freely, or the blank verse shall halt for 't.—What players are they?

ROS. Even those you were wont to take such† delight in, the tragedians of the city.

HAM. How chances it they travel? their residence, both in reputation and profit, was better both ways.

ROS. I think their inhibition comes by the means of the late innovation.

HAM. Do they hold the same estimation they did when I was in the city? are they so followed?

ROS. No, indeed, they are not.

HAM. How comes it? do they grow rusty?

ROS. Nay, their endeavour keeps in the wonted pace: but there is, sir, an aiery of children, little eyases,[h] that cry out on the top of question,[i] and are most tyrannically clapped for 't: these are now the fashion; and so berattle‡ the common stages, (so they call them) that many wearing rapiers are afraid of goose-quills, and dare scarce come thither.

HAM. What, are they children? who maintains them? how are they escoted?[k] Will they pursue the quality[l] no longer than they can sing? will they not say afterwards, if they should grow themselves to common players,[m] (as it is most like,§ if their means are no better) their writers do them

(*) First folio omits, *of*. (†) First folio, *heavenly*.
(‡) First folio omits, *firmament*.

a — but *to the purpose*.] That is, *only* to the purpose.

b Nay, then, I have an eye of you.—] *I see through your purpose*, or, as the quarto of 1603 phrases it, "I see how the winde sits."

c I will tell you why; so shall my anticipation prevent your discovery, and your secrecy to the king and queen moult no feather.] The folio absurdly reads, "I will tell you why; so shall my anticipation prevent your discovery of your secricie to the King and Queen: moult no feather."

d — lenten *entertainment*—] *Meagre, stinted* entertainment, like the cheer in Lent.

e — coted *them*—] Came alongside of them.

f — *the* humorous *man*—] By the "*humorous* man" we are not to understand the funny man or jester,—he was termed "the clown,"—but the actor who personated the fantastic characters, known in Shakespeare's time as "humourists," and who, for the most part, were represented as capricious and quarrelsome.

g — tickled o' the sere;] "Tickled o' the sere,"—correctly, perhaps, "*tickle* o' the sere"—appears to signify those easily moved to the expression of mirth.

h — little eyases,—] Nestlings; unfledged hawks.

i — that cry out on the top of question,—] This is conjectured by the commentators to be an allusion to the shrill, alto voice in which the boys declaimed! The phrase, derived perhaps from the defiant crowing of a cock upon his midden, really meant, we believe, like—

"Stood challenger on mount of all the age,"

to crow over or challenge all comers to a contention. In a subsequent scene, Hamlet, speaking of the play which "pleased not the million," observes, "but it was (as I received it, and others, whose judgment in such matters *cried in the top of mine*) an excellent play," &c.; where "cried in the top" evidently means *crowed over*. Again, in Armin's "Nest of Ninnies," the author, alluding to fencers or players at single stick, talks of "making them expert *till they cry it up in the top of question*."

(*) First folio omits, *then*. (†) First folio omits, *such*.
(‡) First folio, *be-ratled*. (§) Old text, *like most*.

k — escoted?] Said to mean, *paid*; from the French *escot*, a shot or *reckoning*.

l — quality—] *Profession*, or *calling*. Here, *Histrionale studium*.

m — common players,—] As we now term them, "strolling players." "I prefix an epithite of *common*, to distinguish the base and artlesse appendants of our Citty companies, which often times start away into rusticall wanderers, and then (like Proteus) start backe again into the Citty number."—J. STEPHENS, *Essayes and Characters*, 1615, p. 301.

wrong, to make them exclaim against their own succession?

ROS. Faith, there has been much to do on both sides; and the nation holds it no sin, to tarre them to controversy; there was, for a while, no money bid for argument, unless the poet and the player went to cuffs in the question.

HAM. Is 't possible?

GUIL. O, there has been much throwing about of brains.

HAM. Do the boys carry it away?

ROS. Ay, that they do, my lord; Hercules and his load too.(3)

HAM. It is not strange; for mine uncle is king of Denmark; and those that would make mowes at him while my father lived, give twenty, forty, an hundred ducats a-piece, for his picture in little. 'S blood,* there is something in this more than natural, if philosophy could find it out.

[*Flourish of trumpets without.*

GUIL. There are the players.

HAM. Gentlemen, you are welcome to Elsinore. Your hands. Come; the appurtenance of welcome is fashion and ceremony: let me comply with you in the garb;[a] lest my extent to the players, which, I tell you, must show fairly outward, should more appear like entertainment than yours. You are welcome: but my uncle-father and aunt-mother are deceived.

GUIL. In what, my dear lord?

HAM. I am but mad north-north-west: when the wind is southerly I know a hawk from a handsaw.[b]

Enter POLONIUS.

POL. Well be with you, gentlemen!

HAM. Hark you, Guildenstern,—and you too;—at each ear a hearer; that great baby you see there is not yet out of his swathing-clouts.

ROS. Happily he 's the second time come to them; for they say an old man is twice a child.

HAM. I will prophesy he comes to tell me of the players; mark it.—You say right, sir: for o' Monday morning 't was so, indeed.

POL. My lord, I have news to tell you.

HAM. My lord, I have news to tell you. When Roscius was† an actor in Rome,—

POL. The actors are come hither, my lord.

HAM. Buz, buz![c]

POL. Upon mine honour,—

HAM. Then came* each actor on his ass,—

POL. The best actors in the world, either for tragedy, comedy, history, pastoral, pastorical-comical, historical-pastoral, tragical-historical, tragical-comical-historical-pastoral, scene-individable, or poem unlimited: Seneca cannot be too heavy, nor Plautus too light. For the law of writ and the liberty, these are the only men.

HAM. O, Jephthah, judge of Israel,—what a treasure hadst thou!

POL. What a treasure had he, my lord?

HAM. Why,

One fair daughter, and no more,
The which he loved passing well.

POL. [*Aside.*] Still on my daughter.

HAM. Am I not i' the right, old Jephthah?

POL. If you call me Jephthah, my lord, I have a daughter that I love passing well.

HAM. Nay, that follows not.

POL. What follows, then, my lord?

HAM. Why,

As by lot, God wot,

and then, you know,

It came to pass, as most like it was.(4)

The first row of the pious chanson † will show you more; for look, where my abridgment comes.[d]

Enter four or five Players.

You are welcome, masters; welcome, all:—I am glad to see thee well:—welcome, good friends.—O, my old friend! Thy face is valiant[e] since I saw thee last; comest thou to beard me in Denmark?—What! my young lady and mistress! By 'r lady, your ladyship is nearer to‡ heaven, than when I saw you last, by the altitude of a chopine.(5) Pray God, your voice, like a piece of uncurrent gold, be not cracked within the ring.(6)—Masters, you are all welcome. We 'll e'en to 't like French falconers, fly at anything we see: we 'll have a speech straight: come, give us a taste of your quality; come, a passionate speech.

(*) First folio omits, *'S blood.* (†) First folio omits, *was.*

(*) First folio, *can.* (†) First folio, *Pons Chanson.* (‡) First folio omits, *to.*

a — *let me* comply *with you in the* garb;] Let me *fraternize* or conjoin with you in the customary mode; and not, as modern editors expound it,—"Let me *compliment* with you," &c. *To comply*, literally, means *to enfold.*

b I *know a hawk from a* handsaw.] An old proverbial saying; originally,—"a hawk from a *hernshaw, i.e.* a heron; but corrupted before Shakespeare's day.

c Buz, buz!] An interjection of impatience used when any one began a story already known to the hearers.

d — for look, where my abridgment comes.] In the folio, "— My abridgements come." "Abridgment" was only another word for pastime; so, in "A Midsummer Night's Dream," Act V. Sc. 1,—

"Say, what *abridgment* have you for this evening."

e *Thy face is* valiant *since I saw thee last;*] The quartos have *valanced*. But compare the advice of Iago to Roderigo;—"Follow thou the wars; defeat thy favour with an usurped beard;" *i.e.* assume a martial aspect; and also the context in Hamlet's speech, "— comest thou to *beard* me in Denmark," where the point is lost without the fierceness implied by "valiant."

1 PLAY. What speech, my lord?

HAM. I heard thee speak me a speech once,—but it was never acted; or, if it was, not above once; for the play, I remember, pleased not the million; 't was caviare(7) to the general: but it was (as I received it, and others, whose judgment in such matters cried in the top of mine) an excellent play; well digested in the scenes; set down with as much modesty as cunning. I remember, one said there were no sallets[a] in the lines to make the matter savoury, nor no matter in the phrase that might indict the author of affectation; but called it an honest method, as wholesome as sweet, and by very much more handsome than fine.[b] One speech* in it I chiefly loved: 't was Æneas' tale to Dido; and thereabout of it especially, where he speaks of Priam's slaughter: if it live in your memory, begin at this line;—let me see, let me see;—

The rugged Pyrrhus, like the Hyrcanian beast,

—it is not so;—it begins with Pyrrhus:—

The rugged Pyrrhus,—he, whose sable arms,
Black as his purpose, did the night resemble
When he lay couched in the ominous horse,—
Hath now this dread and black complexion smear'd
With heraldry more dismal; head to foot
Now is he total gules; horridly trick'd[c]
With blood of fathers, mothers, daughters, sons,
Bak'd and impasted with the parching streets,
That lend a tyrannous and damned light
To their vile murders: roasted in wrath and fire,
And thus o'er-sized with coagulate gore,
With eyes like carbuncles, the hellish Pyrrhus
Old grandsire Priam seeks.

So proceed you.†

POL. 'Fore God, my lord, well spoken; with good accent and good discretion.

1 PLAY. Anon he finds him
Striking too short at Greeks; his antique sword,
Rebellious to his arm, lies where it falls,
Repugnant to command: unequal match'd,‡
Pyrrhus at Priam drives; in rage strikes wide;
But with the whiff and wind of his fell sword
The unnerv'd father falls. Then senseless Ilium,
Seeming to feel this § blow, with flaming top
Stoops to his base; and with a hideous crash
Takes prisoner Pyrrhus' ear: for, lo! his sword,
Which was declining on the milky head
Of reverend Priam, seem'd i' the air to stick:
So, as a painted tyrant, Pyrrhus stood;
And, like a neutral to his will and matter,
Did nothing.
But as we often see against some storm,
A silence in the heavens, the rack stand still,
The bold winds speechless, and the orb below
As hush as death, anon the dreadful thunder
Doth rend the region; so, after Pyrrhus' pause,
Aroused vengeance sets him new a-work;
And never did the Cyclops' hammers fall
On Mars his armour,* forg'd for proof eterne,
With less remorse than Pyrrhus' bleeding sword
Now falls on Priam.—
Out, out, thou strumpet, Fortune! All you gods,
In general synod, take away her power;
Break all the spokes and fellies from her wheel,
And bowl the round nave down the hill of heaven,
As low as to the fiends!

POL. This is too long.

HAM. It shall to the barber's, with your beard.—Pr'ythee, say on:—he's for a jig or a tale of bawdry, or he sleeps:—say on;—come to Hecuba.

1 PLAY. But who, O, who, had seen the mobled [d] queen—

HAM. *The mobled queen?*

POL. That's good: *mobled queen* is good.

1 PLAY. Run barefoot up and down, threat'ning the flames†
With bisson[e] rheum; a clout about that head,
Where late the diadem stood; and for a robe,
About her lank and all o'er-teemed loins
A blanket, in the alarm of fear caught up;—
Who this had seen, with tongue in venom steep'd,
'Gainst Fortune's state would treason have pronounc'd;
But if the gods themselves did see her then,
When she saw Pyrrhus make malicious sport
In mincing with his sword her husband's limbs,
The instant burst of clamour that she made,
(Unless things mortal move them not at all)
Would have made milch[f] the burning eyes of heaven,
And passion in the gods.

POL. Look, whêr he has not turned his colour, and has tears in 's eyes!—Pr'ythee,‡ no more.

HAM. 'T is well; I'll have thee speak out the rest of this§ soon.—Good my lord, will you see the players well bestowed? Do you hear? let them be well used; for they are the abstracts and brief chronicles of the time: after your death you were better have a bad epitaph than their ill report while you live.||

POL. My lord, I will use them according to their desert.

HAM. God's bodykins, man, much¶ better: use every man after his desert, and who should 'scape whipping! Use them after your own honour and dignity: the less they deserve, the more merit is in your bounty. Take them in.

POL. Come, sirs.

HAM. Follow him, friends: we'll hear a play to-morrow. [*Exit* POLONIUS *with all the* Players *except the* First.]—[*Aside to* Player.] Dost thou hear me, old friend? can you play *The Murder of Gonzago?*

1 PLAY. Ay, my lord.

(*) First folio, *One cheefe Speech.*
(†) First folio omits, *So proceed you.* (‡) First folio, *match.*
(§) First folio, *his.*

a — sallets—] So the old copies. Modern editors commonly change the word to "salt," or "salts." Mr. Singer quotes Baret: "*Sal. Salte,* a pleasante and mery word, that maketh folke to laugh, and sometimes pricketh."

b — as wholesome as sweet, and by very much more handsome than fine.] This clause is not inserted in the folio.

(*) First folio, *Armours.* (†) First folio, *flame.*
(‡) First folio, *Pray you.* (§) First folio omits, *of this*
(||) First folio, *lived.* (¶) First folio omits, *much.*

c — trick'd—] An heraldic term, meaning *blazon'd.*

d — *the* mobled *queen*—] The folio reads, *inobled.* "Mobled" appears to have been a depravation of *muffled.*

e — bisson—] *Blinding.*

f — milch—] *Moist.*

HAM. [*Aside to* Player.] We'll have 't to-morrow night. You could, for a need, study a speech of some dozen or sixteen lines, which I would set down and insert in 't, could you not?

1 PLAY. Ay, my lord.

HAM. [*Aside to* Player.] Very well.—Follow that lord; and look you mock him not. [*Exit* Player.] My good friends [*To* Ros. *and* GUIL.], I'll leave you till night: you are welcome to Elsinore.

ROS. Good my lord!

HAM. Ay, so, God be wi' you!—

[*Exeunt* ROSENCRANTZ *and* GUILDENSTERN.

Now I am alone.
O, what a rogue and peasant slave am I!
Is it not monstrous, that this player here,
But in a fiction, in a dream of passion,
Could force his soul so to his own* conceit,
That, from her working, all his visage wann'd:†
Tears in his eyes, distraction in 's aspéct,
A broken voice, and his whole function suiting
With forms to his conceit? and all for nothing!
For Hecuba!
What's Hecuba to him, or he to Hecuba,
That he should weep for her? What would he do,
Had he the motive and the cue for passion
That I have? He would drown the stage with tears,
And cleave the general ear with horrid speech;
Make mad the guilty, and appal the free,
Confound the ignorant; and amaze, indeed,
The very faculties‡ of eyes and ears. Yet I,
A dull and muddy-mettled rascal, peak,[a]
Like John-a-dreams,[b] unpregnant of my cause,
And can say nothing; no, not for a king,
Upon whose property, and most dear life,
A damn'd defeat was made. Am I a coward?
Who calls me villain? breaks my pate across?
Plucks off my beard, and blows it in my face?
Tweaks me by the nose? gives me the lie i' the throat,[c]
As deep as to the lungs? Who does me this, ha?
'Swounds,* I should take it: for it cannot be,
But I am pigeon-liver'd, and lack gall
To make oppression[d] bitter; or, ere this,
I should have fatted all the region kites
With this slave's offal:—bloody,† bawdy villain!
Remorseless, treacherous, lecherous, kindless[e] villain!
O, Vengeance!—
Why, what an ass am I! This is most brave,[f]
That I, the son of a dear father murder'd,[g]
Prompted to my revenge by heaven and hell,
Must, like a whore, unpack my heart with words,
And fall a cursing, like a very drab,
A scullion!
Fye upon 't! foh!—About, my brains!‡ I have heard
That guilty creatures, sitting at a play,
Have by the very cunning of the scene
Been struck so to the soul, that presently
They have proclaim'd their malefactions;
For murder, though it have no tongue, will speak
With most miraculous organ.(8) I'll have these players
Play something like the murder of my father,
Before mine uncle: I'll observe his looks;
I'll tent him to the quick; if he but blench,
I know my course. The spirit that I have seen
May be the devil: and the devil hath power
To assume a pleasing shape; yea, and perhaps
Out of my weakness and my melancholy,
(As he is very potent with such spirits)
Abuses me to damn me: I'll have grounds
More relative than this:—the play's the thing,
Wherein I'll catch the conscience of the king.

[*Exit.*

(*) First folio, *whole*. (†) First folio, *warm'd*. (‡) First folio, *faculty*.

a — peak,—] *Mope, pule, maunder*, and the like.

b — John-a-dreams,—] A nick-name given to any sleepy, muddle-headed, dreamy fellow.

c — the lie i' the throat,—] See note (b), p. 262, Vol. II.

d *To make* oppression *bitter;*] Mr. Collier's annotator is obtuse enough not to understand this, and actually substitutes *transgression!*

e — kindless —] *Unnatural*.

f Why what an ass am I! This is most brave,—] The folio has,—

"Who? What an Asse am I? I sure, this is most brave," &c.

The quartos, omitting "O, Vengeance!"—

"Why, what an asse am I? this is most brave," &c.

g — of a dear father murder'd, &c.] The folio misprints this,—

"That I, the Sonne of the Deere murthered;"

and the quartos 1604 and 1605 omit the word "father," much to the detriment of the passage, reading, "— of a deere murthered."

(*) First folio, *Why*. (†) First folio inserts, *a*. (‡) First folio, *braine*.

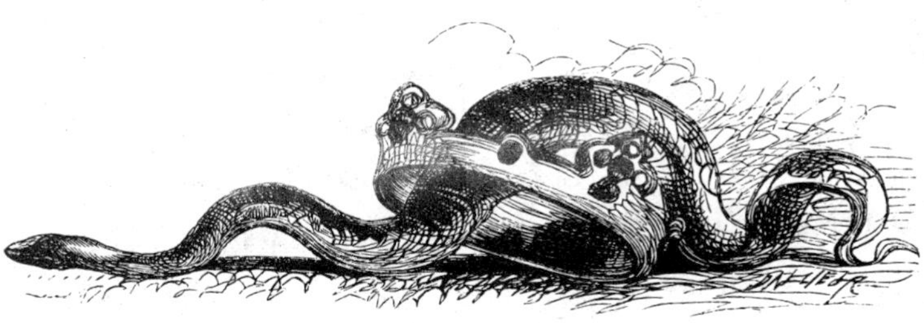

ACT III.

SCENE I.—*A Room in the Castle.*

Enter KING, QUEEN, POLONIUS, OPHELIA, ROSENCRANTZ, *and* GUILDENSTERN.

KING. And can you, by no drift of circumstance,
Get from him why he puts on this confusion;
Grating so harshly all his days of quiet
With turbulent and dangerous lunacy?
ROS. He does confess he feels himself distracted;
But from what cause he will by no means speak.
GUIL. Nor do we find him forward to be sounded;
But, with a crafty madness, keeps aloof,
When we would bring him on to some confession
Of his true state.
QUEEN. Did he receive you well?
ROS. Most like a gentleman.
GUIL. But with much forcing of his disposition.
ROS. Niggard of question; but, of our demands,
Most free in his reply.[a]
QUEEN. Did you assay him to any pastime?
ROS. Madam, it so fell out that certain players
We o'er-raught on the way: of these we told him;
And there did seem in him a kind of joy
To hear of it: they are about the court;
And, as I think, they have already order
This night to play before him.
POL. 'Tis most true:
And he beseech'd me to entreat your majesties
To hear and see the matter.
KING. With all my heart; and it doth much content me
To hear him so inclin'd.—
Good gentlemen, give him a further edge,
And drive his purpose on to these delights.
ROS. We shall, my lord.
[*Exeunt* ROSENCRANTZ *and* GUILDENSTERN.

---

[a] Niggard of question; but, of our demands,
Most free in his reply.]

Hanmer surmised we ought to read,—

"*Most free* of question; but of our demands,
Niggard in his reply."

And unless "question" is admitted to mean *argument*, his emendation yields a truer description of Hamlet's bearing towards his schoolfellows than that afforded by the old text. It should be mentioned, too, that the 1603 quarto has,—

"But still he puts us off, and by no meanes,
Would make an answere to that we exposde."

KING. Sweet Gertrude, leave us too:
For we have closely sent for Hamlet hither;
That he, as 'twere by accident, may here*
Affront[a] Ophelia.
Her father and myself,—lawful espials,—
Will so bestow ourselves, that, seeing, unseen,
We may of their encounter frankly judge;
And gather by him, as he is behav'd,
If 't be the affliction of his love or no
That thus he suffers for.

QUEEN. I shall obey you:—
And for your part, Ophelia, I do wish
That your good beauties be the happy cause
Of Hamlet's wildness; so shall I hope your virtues
Will bring him to his wonted way again,
To both your honours.

OPH. Madam, I wish it may.
[*Exit* QUEEN.

POL. Ophelia, walk you here.—Gracious, so please you,†
We will bestow ourselves.—Read on this book;
[*To* OPHELIA.
That show of such an exercise may colour
Your loneliness.—We are oft to blame in this,—
'Tis too much prov'd,—that, with devotion's visage,
And pious action, we do sugar* o'er
The devil himself.

KING. [*Aside.*] O, 'tis too† true!
How smart a lash that speech doth give my conscience!
The harlot's cheek, beautied with plast'ring art,
Is not more ugly to the thing that helps it,
Than is my deed to my most painted word:
O, heavy burden!

POL. I hear him coming; let's withdraw, my lord. [*Exeunt.*

Enter HAMLET.

HAM. To be, or not to be,—that is the question:—
Whether 'tis nobler in the mind, to suffer
The slings and arrows of outrageous fortune,
Or to take arms against a sea of troubles,[b]
And by opposing end them?—To die, to sleep,—
No more; and by a sleep to say we end
The heart-ache, and the thousand natural shocks
That flesh is heir to?—'tis a consummation

(*) First folio, *there*. (†) First folio, *ye*.

(*) First folio, *surge*. (†) First folio omits, *too*.

[a] Affront *Ophelia.*] That is, *encounter, confront, come across.*

[b] Or to take arms against a sea of troubles,—] We have been puzzled, with Dr. Johnson, to understand why commentators exhibit so much solicitude about this metaphor. As the poet has already furnished us with "a sea of joys," "a sea of glory," "a sea of conscience," "a sea of care," "a sea of wax;" and in the story on which the present piece is presumed to have been founded, we have even, "a *field* of care;" the necessity for reading, "a *siege* of troubles," with Pope; "*assail* of troubles, with Warburton; or "*assay*," with Mr. Singer, has always appeared to us very questionable. At all events, the following quotation from a work contemporary with Shakespeare, proves beyond controversy that *a sea of troubles* was a not unfamiliar figure of speech at that time:—"Cadde in *un Pelago di travagli*."—*Sansovino dell' Famiglie Illustri d'Italia*, 1609.

Devoutly to be wish'd. To die, to sleep;—
To sleep, perchance, to dream;—ay, there's the rub;
For in that sleep of death what dreams may come,
When we have shuffled off this mortal coil,
Must give us pause: there's the respect
That makes calamity of so long life;
For who would bear the whips and scorns of time,
The oppressor's wrong, the proud* man's contumely,
The pangs of dispriz'd love, the law's delay,
The insolence of office, and the spurns
That patient merit of the unworthy takes,
When he himself might his quietus make
With a bare bodkin?[a] who would fardels[b] bear,
To grunt[c] and sweat under a weary life,
But that the dread of something after death,—
The undiscover'd country, from whose bourn
No traveller returns,—puzzles the will,
And makes us rather bear those ills we have,
Than fly to others that we know not of?
Thus conscience does make cowards of us all;
And thus the native hue of resolution

(*) First folio, *poore*.

a — *a bare* bodkin?] A *bodkin* was an old term for a dagger or stiletto.

b — fardels—] *Burdens, packs.* The first folio has, "*these* fardels."

c To grunt and sweat, &c.] The expression *to grunt*, though no euphonious to modern ears, was neither disagreeable nor unusua formerly. In addition to the instances of its use before accumulated, we may add the following, perhaps the most pertinent of all, from Armin's "Nest of Ninnies:"—"How the fat fooles of this age will *gronte and sweate* under this massie burden," &c.

Is sicklied o'er with the pale cast of thought;
And enterprises of great pith[a] and moment,
With this regard, their currents turn awry,*
And lose the name of action.—Soft you now!
The fair Ophelia!—Nymph, in thy orisons
Be all my sins remember'd.

OPH. Good my lord,
How does your honour for this many a day?

HAM. I humbly thank you; well, well, well.

OPH. My lord, I have remembrances of yours,
That I have longed long to re-deliver;
I pray you, now receive them.

HAM. No, no. I never gave you aught.

OPH. My honour'd lord, you† know right well you did;
And, with them, words of so sweet breath compos'd
As made the things more rich: their perfume lost,‡
Take these again; for to the noble mind
Rich gifts wax poor when givers prove unkind.
There, my lord.

HAM. Ha, ha! are you honest?[b]

OPH. My lord?

HAM. Are you fair?

OPH. What means your lordship?

HAM. That if you be honest and fair, your honesty should admit no discourse to your beauty.

OPH. Could beauty, my lord, have better commerce than with§ honesty?

HAM. Ay, truly; for the power of beauty will sooner transform honesty from what it is to a bawd, than the force of honesty can translate beauty into his likeness: this was sometime a paradox, but now the time gives it proof. I did love you once.

OPH. Indeed, my lord, you made me believe so.

HAM. You should not have believed me: for virtue cannot so inoculate our old stock, but we shall relish of it: I lov'd you not.

OPH. I was the more deceived.

HAM. Get thee to a nunnery; why wouldst thou be a breeder of sinners? I am myself indifferent honest; but yet I could accuse me of such things, that it were better my mother had not borne me: I am very proud, revengeful, ambitious; with more offences at my beck than I have thoughts to put them in, imagination to give them shape, or time to act them in. What should such fellows as I do crawling between heaven and earth! We are arrant knaves, all; believe none of us. Go thy ways to a nunnery. Where's your father?

OPH. At home, my lord.

HAM. Let the doors be shut upon him, that he may play the fool no where* but in's own house. Farewell.

OPH. O, help him, you sweet heavens!

HAM. If thou dost marry, I'll give thee this plague for thy dowry,—be thou as chaste as ice, as pure as snow, thou shalt not escape calumny. Get thee to a nunnery, go; farewell. Or, if thou wilt needs marry, marry a fool; for wise men know well enough what monsters you make of them. To a nunnery, go; and quickly too. Farewell.

OPH. O, heavenly powers, restore him!

HAM. I have heard of your paintings too, well enough; God hath given you one face,[c] and you make yourselves another: you jig, you amble, and you lisp, and nick-name God's creatures, and make your wantonness your ignorance. Go to, I'll no more on't; it hath made me mad. I say, we will have no more marriages: those that are married already,—all but one,—shall live; the rest shall keep as they are. To a nunnery, go. [*Exit.*

OPH. O, what a noble mind is here o'erthrown!
The courtier's, scholar's, soldier's, eye, tongue, sword:[d]
The expectancy and rose of the fair state,
The glass of fashion and the mould of form,
The observ'd of all observers,—quite, quite down!
And I,† of ladies most deject and wretched,
That suck'd the honey of his music vows,
Now see that noble and most sovereign reason,
Like sweet bells jangled, out of tune and harsh;
That unmatch'd form and feature of blown youth,
Blasted with ecstasy: O, woe is me!
To have seen what I have seen, see what I see!

Re-enter KING *and* POLONIUS.

KING. Love! his affections do not that way tend;
Nor what he spake, though it lack'd form a little,

(*) First folio, *away*. (†) First folio, *I*. (‡) First folio, *then perfume left*. (§) First folio, *your*.

a — pith *and moment*,—] The quartos have, "*pitch* and moment;" which Ritson preferred, as do we, though for a different reason, he conceiving *pitch* to be an allusion "to the *pitching* or throwing the bar," we supposing it to refer to the *pitch* or summit of the falcon's flight, and "great pitch and moment" to mean great eminence and import.

b — are you honest?] That "honest" in this dialogue is equivalent to *chaste* or *virtuous*, it would be superfluous to mention but that some critics, in their strictures on the conduct of Hamlet in the present scene, appear to have forgotten it. The beginning recals to mind some passages in Shirley's play, entitled "The Royal Master," Act IV. Sc. 1,—

(*) First folio, *way*. (†) First folio, *Have I*.

"*King*. Are you honest?
Thes. Honest
King. I could have us'd the name of chaste
Or virgin; but they carry the same sense."

c *I have heard of your* paintings *too, well enough; God hath given you one* face,—] So the quartos: the folio exhibits the passage thus,—"I have heard of your *pratlings* too wel enough. God has given you one *pace*," &c.

d The courtier's, scholar's, soldier's, &c.] This is the collocation of the quarto, 1603. In the folio we have, "The courtier's, soldier's, scholar's," &c.

Was not like madness. There 's something in his soul,
O'er which his melancholy sits on brood;
And I do doubt the hatch and the disclose,
Will be some danger: which for* to prevent,
I have in quick determination
Thus set it down:—he shall with speed to England,
For the demand of our neglected tribute:
Haply, the seas, and countries different,
With variable objects, shall expel
This something-settled matter in his heart;
Whereon his brains still beating, puts him thus
From fashion of himself. What think you on't?

POL. It shall do well; but yet do I believe,
The origin and commencement of his† grief
Sprung from neglected love.—How now, Ophelia!
You need not tell us what lord Hamlet said;
We heard it all.—My lord, do as you please;
But, if you hold it fit, after the play,
Let his queen mother all alone entreat him
To show his griefs; let her be round[a] with him;
And I'll be plac'd, so please you, in the ear
Of all their conference. If she find him not,[b]
To England send him: or confine him where
Your wisdom best shall think.

KING. It shall be so:
Madness in great ones must not unwatch'd go.
[*Exeunt.*

SCENE II.—*A Hall in the same.*

Enter HAMLET, *and certain* Players.

HAM. Speak the speech, I pray you, as I pronounced it to you, trippingly on the tongue: but if you mouth it, as many of your players do, I had as lief the town-crier spoke my lines.[c] Nor do not saw the air too much with ‡ your hand, thus; but use all gently: for in the very torrent, tempest, and, as I may say, the whirlwind of your§ passion, you must acquire and beget a temperance that may give it smoothness. O, it offends me to the soul to hear‖ a robustious periwig-pated fellow tear a passion to tatters, to very rags, to split the ears of the groundlings, who, for the most part, are capable of nothing but inexplicable dumb-shows and noise: I could have such a fellow whipped for o'erdoing Termagant; it out-herods Herod:(1) pray you, avoid it.

1 PLAY. I warrant your honour.

HAM. Be not too tame neither, but let your own discretion be your tutor: suit the action to the word, the word to the action; with this special observance, that you o'erstep* not the modesty of nature; for anything so overdone is from the purpose of playing, whose end, both at the first and now, was and is, to hold, as't were, the mirror up to nature; to show virtue her own feature, scorn her own image, and the very age and body of the time his form and pressure. Now, this overdone, or come tardy off, though it make the unskilful laugh, cannot but make the judicious grieve; the censure of the which one must, in your allowance, o'erweigh a whole theatre of others. O, there be players that I have seen play,—and heard others praise, and that highly,—not to speak it profanely, that, neither having the accent of christians, nor the gait of christian, pagan, nor man,† have so strutted and bellowed, that I have thought some of Nature's journeymen had made men, and not made them well, they imitated humanity so abominably.

1 PLAY. I hope we have reformed that indifferently with us, sir.

HAM. O, reform it altogether. And let those that play your clowns speak no more than is set down for them: for there be of them, that will themselves laugh, to set on some quantity of barren spectators to laugh too; though, in the mean time, some necessary question of the play be then to be considered: that's villainous, and shows a most pitiful ambition in the fool that uses it.(2) Go, make you ready. [*Exeunt* Players.

Enter POLONIUS, ROSENCRANTZ, *and* GUILDENSTERN.

How now, my lord! will the king hear this piece of work?

POL. And the queen too, and that presently.

HAM. Bid the players make haste. [*Exit* POLONIUS.] Will you two help to hasten them?

ROS., GUIL. We will, my lord.
[*Exeunt* ROSENCRANTZ *and* GUILDENSTERN.

HAM. What, ho, Horatio!

Enter HORATIO.

HOR. Here, sweet lord, at your service.

HAM. Horatio, thou art e'en as just a man
As e'er my conversation cop'd withal.

HOR. O, my dear lord,—

HAM. Nay, do not think I flatter;
For what advancement may I hope from thee,
That no revénue hast, but thy good spirits,
To feed and clothe thee? Why should the poor be flatter'd?

(*) First folio omits, *for*. (†) First folio, *this*. (‡) First folio omits, *with*. (§) First folio omits, *your*. (‖) First folio, *see*.

[a] — *let her be* round *with him;*] Let her be *blunt, plain-spoken* with him.

[b] *If she* find *him not,*—] If she *detect* him not.

(*) First folio, *ore-stop*. (†) First folio, *or Norman*.

[c] I had as lief the town-crier spoke my lines.] So the quartos, 1604, &c. The folio reads, "I had as live the Town-Cryer *had* spoke," &c.; the quarto of 1603,—
"I'de rather heare a towne bull bellow,
Then such a fellow speake my lines," &c.

No, let the candied tongue lick* absurd pomp;
And crook the pregnant hinges of the knee,[a]
Where thrift may follow fawning.† Dost thou hear?
Since my dear soul was mistress of her‡ choice,
And could of men distinguish, her election
Hath seal'd thee for herself: for thou hast been
As one, in suffering all, that suffers nothing;
A man that fortune's buffets and rewards
Hath ta'en with equal thanks: and bless'd are those
Whose blood and judgment are so well co-mingled,
That they are not a pipe for Fortune's finger
To sound what stop she please. Give me that man
That is not passion's slave, and I will wear him
In my heart's core, ay, in my heart of heart,
As I do thee.—Something too much of this.—
There is a play to-night before the king;
One scene of it comes near the circumstance
Which I have told thee of my father's death:
I pr'ythee, when thou seest that act a-foot,
Even with the very comment of thy§ soul
Observe mine uncle: if his occulted guilt
Do not itself unkennel in one speech,
It is a damned ghost that we have seen;
And my imaginations are as foul
As Vulcan's stithy.[b] Give him heedful|| note:
For I mine eyes will rivet to his face;
And, after, we will both our judgments join
In¶ censure of his seeming.

HOR. Well, my lord:
If he steal aught the whilst this play is playing,
And scape detecting, I will pay the theft.

HAM. They are coming to the play: I must be idle:[c]
Get you a place.

Danish March. Flourish. Enter KING, QUEEN, POLONIUS, OPHELIA, ROSENCRANTZ, GUILDENSTERN, *and other* Lords *attendant, with the* Guard, *carrying torches.*

KING. How fares our cousin Hamlet?

HAM. Excellent, i' faith; of the chameleon's dish: I eat the air, promise-crammed: you cannot feed capons so.

KING. I have nothing with this answer, Hamlet; these words are not mine.

HAM. No, nor mine now.—My lord, you played once i' the university, you say? [*To* POLONIUS.

POL. That did I,* my lord; and was accounted a good actor.

HAM. And what did you enact?

POL. I did enact Julius Cæsar: I was killed i' the Capitol; Brutus killed me.

HAM. It was a brute part of him to kill so capital a calf there.—Be the players ready?

ROS. Ay, my lord; they stay upon your patience.

QUEEN. Come hither, my dear† Hamlet, sit by me.

HAM. No, good mother, here's metal more attractive.

POL. O, ho! do you mark that? [*To the* KING.

HAM. Lady, shall I lie in your lap?
[*Lying down at* OPHELIA'*s feet.*

OPH. No, my lord.

HAM. I mean, my head upon your lap?

OPH. Ay, my lord.

HAM. Do you think I meant country matters?

OPH. I think nothing, my lord.

HAM. That's a fair thought to lie between maids' legs.

OPH. What is, my lord?

HAM. Nothing.

OPH. You are merry, my lord.

HAM. Who, I?

OPH. Ay, my lord.

HAM. O, God, your only jig-maker. What should a man do but be merry? for, look you, how cheerfully my mother looks, and my father died within these‡ two hours.

OPH. Nay, 't is twice two months, my lord.

HAM. So long? Nay, then, let the devil wear black, for I'll have a suit of sables.[d] O, heavens!

(*) First folio, *like.* (†) First folio, *faining.*
(‡) First folio, *my.* (§) First folio, *my.*
(||) First folio, *needfull.* (¶) First folio, *To.*

[a] And crook the pregnant hinges of the knee,—] *Pregnant* here means *ready, supple,* &c. Quarles has the same idea,—

"My antic knees can turn upon the hinges
Of compliment, and screw a thousand cringes."
Emblems, B. IV.

b — *Vulcan's* stithy.] The *stithy* is the smith's work-place; the *stith* is his anvil.

c — *I must be* idle:] I must affect being *crazy.* We are not aware that any scholiast has pointed out the use of "idle" in the sense of *mad;* though Shakespeare so employs it several times; among others, in the quarto "Hamlet," 1603, Corambis, the Polonius of the perfect play, speaking of Hamlet's derangement, observes,—

"All this comes by love, the vemencie of love,
And when I was yong, I was very *idle,*
And suffered much *extasie* in love," &c.

Subsequently in the same edition, where the Ghost appears to Hamlet when closeted with his mother, we have the following,—

"*Queene.* But Hamlet, this is onely fantasie,
And for my love forget these *idle* fits.
Ham. Idle, no mother, my pulse doth beate like yours,
It is not *madnesse,*" &c.

(*) First folio, *I did.* (†) First folio, *good.*
(‡) First folio, *within's.*

d — for *I'll have a suit of sables.*] The favourite notion is that by "a suit of sables" is meant a dress ornamented with the costly fur called "sable." Possibly, however, the word "for" in this place, as in "Henry V." Act III. Sc. 6,—

"And, *for* achievement, offer ransom;"

and in "Antony and Cleopatra," Act IV. Sc. 9,—

"—— so bad a prayer as his was never yet *for* sleep;"

was misprinted instead of *'fore.* In the 1603 quarto of the present play, in place of "'T is not alone my *inky* cloak," &c., which is the accepted text, Hamlet is made to say, "— 't is not the *sable sute,*" &c. So also in Act IV. Sc. 7,—

"Than settled age *his sables* and his weeds."

And it is not at all improbable that in the scene before us he was intended to accompany the words, "Nay, then, let the devil wear black *'fore* I'll wear a suit of sables," with the action of flinging off his mourning cloak. Since writing the above we find that Warburton long ago suggested, "*'fore* I'll wear a suit of sables."

die two months ago, and not forgotten yet? Then there's hope a great man's memory may outlive his life half a year: but by 'r lady, he must build churches, then; or else shall he suffer not thinking on, with the hobby-horse, whose epitaph is, *For, O, for, O, the hobby-horse is forgot.*

Hautboys play. The dumb show enters.

Enter a King *and a* Queen, *very lovingly: the* Queen *embracing him, and he her.*[a] *She kneels, and makes show of protestation unto him. He takes her up, and declines his head upon her neck: lays him down upon a bank of flowers; she, seeing him asleep, leaves him. Anon comes in a fellow, takes off his crown, kisses it, pours poison in the* King's *ears, and exit. The* Queen *returns; finds the* King *dead, and makes passionate action. The Poisoner, with some two or three Mutes, comes in again, seeming to lament with her. The dead body is carried away. The Poisoner woos the* Queen *with gifts; she seems loth and unwilling awhile, but in the end accepts his love.* [*Exeunt.*

OPH. What means this, my lord?

HAM. Marry, this is miching mallecho;[b] it means mischief.

OPH. Belike, this show imports the argument of the play.

Enter Prologue.

HAM. We shall know by this fellow:* the players cannot keep counsel; they'll tell all.

OPH. Will he† tell us what this show meant?

HAM. Ay, or any show that you'll show him. Be not you ashamed to show, he'll not shame to tell you what it means.

OPH. You are naught, you are naught: I'll mark the play.

PRO. For us, and for our tragedy,
Here stooping to your clemency,
We beg your hearing patiently.

HAM. Is this a prologue, or the poesy of a ring?

OPH. 'T is brief, my lord.

HAM. As woman's love.

Enter GONZAGO *and* BAPTISTA.

GONZ. Full thirty times hath Phœbus' cart[c] gone round
Neptune's salt wash and Tellus' orbed ground;
And thirty dozen moons with borrow'd sheen,
About the world have times twelve thirties been,
Since love our hearts, and Hymen did our hands,
Unite co-mutual in most sacred bands.

BAPT. So many journeys may the sun and moon
Make us again count o'er ere love be done!
But, woe is me, you are so sick of late,
So far from cheer and from your former state,
That I distrust you. Yet, though I distrust,
Discomfort you, my lord, it nothing must:
For women's fear and love holds quantity;
In neither aught, or in extremity.
Now, what my love is, proof hath made you know;
And as my love is siz'd, my fear is so.
Where love is great,[d] the littlest doubts are fear;
Where little fears grow great, great love grows there.

GONZ. Faith, I must leave thee, love, and shortly too;
My operant powers their* functions leave to do:
And thou shalt live in this fair world behind,
Honour'd, belov'd; and haply one as kind
For husband shalt thou—

BAPT. O, confound the rest!
Such love must needs be treason in my breast:
In second husband let me be accurst!
None wed the second but who kill'd the first.

HAM. [*Aside.*] Wormwood, wormwood.

The instances that second marriage move,
Are base respects of thrift, but none of love;
A second time I kill my lord that's dead,[e]
When second husband kisses me in bed.

GONZ. I do believe you think what now you speak;
But what we do determine oft we break.
Purpose is but the slave to memory;
Of violent birth, but poor validity:
Which now, like fruit unripe, sticks on the tree;
But fall, unshaken, when they mellow be.
Most necessary 't is that we forget
To pay ourselves what to ourselves is debt:
What to ourselves in passion we propose,
The passion ending, doth the purpose lose.
The violence of either† grief or joy
Their own enactures with themselves destroy:
Where joy most revels, grief doth most lament,
Grief joys, joy grieves, on slender accident.
This world is not for aye; nor 't is not strange
That even our loves should with our fortunes change;
For 't is a question left us yet to prove,
Whether love lead fortune, or else fortune love.
The great man down, you mark his favourite flies;
The poor advanc'd makes friends of enemies.
And hitherto doth love on fortune tend:
For who not needs shall never lack a friend;
And who in want a hollow friend doth try,
Directly seasons him his enemy.
But, orderly to end where I begun,—
Our wills and fates do so contrary run,
That our devices still are overthrown;
Our thoughts are ours, their ends none of our own;
So think thou wilt no second husband wed;
But die thy thoughts when thy first lord is dead.

BAPT. Nor earth to me give‡ food, nor heaven light!
Sport and repose lock from me, day and night!
To desperation turn my trust and hope!
An anchor's[f] cheer in prison be my scope!
Each opposite, that blanks the face of joy,
Meet what I would have well, and it destroy!
Both here and hence, pursue me lasting strife,
If, once a widow, ever I be wife!

HAM. If she should break it now! [*To* OPHELIA.

(*) First folio, *these Fellowes.* (†) First folio, *they.*

[a] — *and he her.*] These words are not in the folio.

[b] — miching mallecho;] *Sneaking malefficence. To mich,* an old English verb, is *to skulk;* and *mallecho,* from the Spanish, is the same as *malefaction.*

[c] — cart—] *Car,* or *chariot.*

[d] Where love is great, &c.] This couplet is omitted in the folio.

(*) Firs folio, *my.* (†) First folio, *other.* (‡) First folio, *give me.*

[e] — *my* lord that's *dead,*—] So the quarto, 1603: the other editions have,—

"—— my *husband* dead."

[f] *An* anchor's *cheer*—] The fare of an *anchorite.* This and the preceding line are not found in the folio.

GONZ. 'Tis deeply sworn. Sweet, leave me here a while;
My spirits grow dull, and fain I would beguile
The tedious day with sleep. [*Sleeps.*
BAPT. Sleep rock thy brain,
And never come mischance between us twain! (3)
[*Exit.*

HAM. Madam, how like you this play?

QUEEN. The lady doth protest* too much, methinks.

(*) First folio, *lady protests.*

HAM. O, but she'll keep her word.

KING. Have you heard the argument? Is there no offence in 't?

HAM. No, no, they do but jest; poison in jest; no offence i' the world.

KING. What do you call the play?

HAM. The Mouse-trap. Marry, how? Tropically.[a] This play is the image of a murder done in Vienna: Gonzago is the duke's name; his wife,

[a] Tropically.] *Figuratively.*

Baptista: you shall see anon, 't is a knavish piece of work: but what of that? your majesty, and we that have free souls, it touches us not: let the galled jade wince, our withers are unwrung.

Enter LUCIANUS.

This is one Lucianus, nephew to the king.

OPH. You are as good as a chorus,* my lord.

(*) First folio, *You are a good Chorus.*

HAM. I could interpret between you and your love, if I could see the puppets dallying.

OPH. You are keen, my lord, you are keen.

HAM. It would cost you a groaning to take off my edge.

OPH. Still better, and worse.

HAM. So you must take your husbands.*—Begin, murderer;† leave thy damnable faces, and

(*) First folio, *So you mistake Husbands.* (†) First folio, *Pox, leave.*

begin.—Come;—the croaking raven doth bellow for revenge.

LUC. Thoughts black, hands apt, drugs fit, and time agreeing;
Confederate season, else no creature seeing;
Thou mixture rank, of midnight weeds collected,
With Hecate's ban thrice blasted, thrice infected,
Thy natural magic and dire property,
On wholesome life usurp immediately.
[*Pours poison in the sleeper's ears.*

HAM. He poisons him i' the garden for 's estate. His name 's Gonzago: the story is extant, and writ in choice Italian: you shall see anon how the murderer gets the love of Gonzago's wife.

OPH. The king rises!

HAM. What, frighted with false fire!

QUEEN. How fares my lord?

POL. Give o'er the play.

KING. Give me some light:—away!

ALL. Lights, lights, lights!

[*Exeunt all except* HAMLET *and* HORATIO.

HAM. *Why, let the strucken deer go weep,*
The hart ungalled play;
For some must watch, while some must sleep;
So runs the world away.—

Would not this, sir, and a forest of feathers, (if the rest of my fortunes turn Turk with me[a]) with two Provincial[b] roses on my razed[c] shoes, get me a fellowship in a cry[d] of players, sir?

HOR. Half a share.

HAM. A whole one, I.[e]

For thou dost know, O, Damon dear,
This realm dismantled was
Of Jove himself; and now reigns here
A very-very——pajock.[f]

HOR. You might have rhymed.

HAM. O, good Horatio, I 'll take the ghost's word for a thousand pound. Didst perceive?

HOR. Very well, my lord.

HAM. Upon the talk of the poisoning,—

HOR. I did very well note him.

HAM. Ah,* ha!—Come, some music! come, the recorders!—

For if the king like not the comedy,
Why then, belike,—he likes it not, perdy.—
Come, some music!

Re-enter ROSENCRANTZ *and* GUILDENSTERN.

GUIL. Good my lord, vouchsafe me a word with you.

HAM. Sir, a whole history.

GUIL. The king, sir,—

HAM. Ay, sir, what of him?

GUIL. Is, in his retirement, marvellous distempered.

HAM. With drink, sir?

GUIL. No, my lord,* with choler.

HAM. Your wisdom should show itself more richer, to signify this to his doctor; for, for me to put him to his purgation would, perhaps, plunge him into † more choler.

GUIL. Good my lord, put your discourse into some frame, and start not so wildly from my affair.

HAM. I am tame, sir:—pronounce.

GUIL. The queen, your mother, in most great affliction of spirit, hath sent me to you.

HAM. You are welcome.

GUIL. Nay, good my lord, this courtesy is not of the right breed. If it shall please you to make me a wholesome answer, I will do your mother's commandment: if not, your pardon and my return shall be the end of my business.

HAM. Sir, I cannot.

GUIL. What, my lord?

HAM. Make you a wholesome answer; my wit's diseased: but, sir, such answer ‡ as I can make you shall command; or, rather, as you say, my mother: therefore, no more, but to the matter: my mother, you say,—

ROS. Then thus she says: your behaviour hath struck her into amazement and admiration.

HAM. O, wonderful son, that can so astonish a mother!—But is there no sequel at the heels of this mother's admiration?

ROS. She desires to speak with you in her closet, ere you go to bed.

HAM. We shall obey, were she ten times our mother. Have you any further trade with us?

ROS. My lord, you once did love me.

(*) First folio, *Oh*.

(*) First folio inserts, *rather*. (†) First folio inserts, *farre*. (‡) First folio, *answers*.

a — turn Turk with me—] A popular phrase to express apostacy of any kind. Shakespeare uses it again in "Much Ado About Nothing," Act III. Sc. 4,—"Well, an you be not *turned Turk*, there's no more sailing by the star."

b Provincial *roses*—] *Provincial* roses, Mr. Douce asserts, were not so called, as Warton and others conjectured, from *Provence*, but from *Provins*, in Lower Brie, a place early celebrated for the cultivation of the flower.

c — razed *shoes*,—] The folio reads, "rac'd," and the quartos "razd;" by *razed*, if that be the true word, must be meant *slashed* or *opened* shoes. It should be noted, however, that Steevens and other critics thought that Shakespeare probably wrote *raised* shoes, *i.e.* shoes with high heels.

d — *a* cry *of players*,—] A *troop* or *company* of players.

e *A whole one*, I.] The meaning may be, "A whole one, *I say*;" but Malone's proposed emendation,—

"A whole one;—*ay*,—
For," &c.,

will strike many as the more likely reading.

f — *pajock*.] In the old copies printed *paiocke*, or *paiock*, is believed to be equivalent to *peacock*.

HAM. And do* still, by these pickers and stealers.

ROS. Good my lord, what is your cause of distemper? you do, surely,† bar the door upon‡ your own liberty, if you deny your griefs to your friend.

HAM. Sir, I lack advancement.

ROS. How can that be, when you have the voice of the king himself for your succession in Denmark?

HAM. Ay, but *While the grass grows*,—the proverb is something musty.

Re-enter Players *with* Recorders.[a]

O, the recorders: (4) let me see one.§—To withdraw with you:[b]—Why do you go about to recover the wind of me,[c] as if you would drive me into a toil?

GUIL. O, my lord, if my duty be too bold, my love is too unmannerly.

HAM. I do not well understand that. Will you play upon this pipe?

GUIL. My lord, I cannot.

HAM. I pray you.

GUIL. Believe me, I cannot.

HAM. I do beseech you.[d]

GUIL. I know no touch of it, my lord.

HAM. 'T is as easy as lying: govern these ventages with your fingers ‖ and thumb, give it breath with your mouth, and it will discourse most eloquent¶ music. Look you, these are the stops.

GUIL. But these cannot I command to any utterance of harmony; I have not the skill.

HAM. Why, look you now, how unworthy a thing you make of me! You would play upon me; you would seem to know my stops; you would pluck out the heart of my mystery; you would sound me from my lowest note to the top of my compass: and there is much music, excellent voice, in this little organ; yet cannot you make it speak.** S'blood! do you think that I am easier to be played on than a pipe? Call me what instrument you will, though you can fret[e] me, you cannot play upon me.—

Re-enter POLONIUS.

God bless you, sir!

POL. My lord, the queen would speak with you, and presently.

HAM. Do you see yonder* cloud that 's almost in shape like a camel?

POL. By the mass, and 't is† like a camel, indeed.

HAM. Methinks it is like a weasel.

POL. It is backed like a weasel.

HAM. Or like a whale.

POL. Very like a whale.

HAM. Then will I come to my mother by-and-by.—[*Aside.*] They fool me to the top of my bent.—I will come by-and-by.

POL. I will say so.

HAM. By-and-by is easily said.—[*Exit* POLONIUS.] Leave me, friends.

[*Exeunt* ROS., GUIL., HOR., *&c.*

'T is now the very witching time of night,
When churchyards yawn, and hell itself breathes out
Contagion to this world: now could I drink hot blood,
And do such bitter business[f] as the day
Would quake to look on. Soft! now to my mother.—
O, heart, lose not thy nature; let not ever
The soul of Nero enter this firm bosom:
Let me be cruel, not unnatural;
I will speak daggers to her, but use none;
My tongue and soul in this be hypocrites,—
How in my words soever she be shent,
To give them seals never, my soul, consent!

[*Exit.*

SCENE III.—*A Room in the same.*

Enter KING, ROSENCRANTZ, *and* GUILDENSTERN.

KING. I like him not; nor stands it safe with us
To let his madness range. Therefore, prepare you;
I your commission will forthwith dispatch,
And he to England shall along with you:
The terms of our estate may not endure
Hazard so dangerous as doth hourly grow
Out of his lunacies.

(*) First folio, *So I do.* (†) First folio, *freely.* (‡) First folio, *of.* (§) First folio omits, *one.* (‖) First folio, *finger.* (¶) First folio, *excellent.* (**) First folio, *make it. Why do you.*

a Re-enter, &c.] In the folio, "Enter one *with* a Recorder."

b To withdraw with you:—] Malone, to render these words intelligible, was fain to interpolate a stage direction:—[*Taking Guildenstern aside.*] Steevens conceived them to have been in reply to some gesture Guildenstern had used, and which Hamlet interpreted into a signal for him to attend the speaker into another room. We take them to be simply a direction addressed to the players who bring in the recorders, and their true reading,—"So,—[*taking a recorder*] withdraw with you." What subsequently transpires between Hamlet and his schoolfellows could hardly have taken place in presence of the players, and the disputed words may have been intended to mark the departure of the latter.

c — to recover the wind of me,—] An expression borrowed from hunting, as Mr. Singer explains, and meaning, "to get the animal pursued to run with the wind, that it may not scent the toil or its pursuers."

(*) First folio, *that.* (†) First folio, *By th' Misse, and it's.*

d I do beseech you.] Should not this be addressed, and the reply which follows be assigned, to Rosencrantz? In the quarto, 1603, the dialogue runs,—

"*Ham.* I pray will you play upon this pipe?
Ross. Alas, my lord, I cannot.
Ham. Pray will you.
Gil. I have no skill, my lord."

e — *though you can* fret *me*,—] An obvious quibble on *fret*, the stop or key of a musical instrument, and the same word in its ordinary sense of *vex, irritate*, &c.

f And do such bitter business as the day—] In the quartos,—"— such business as the *bitter day*," &c.

GUIL. We will ourselves provide:
Most holy and religious fear it is
To keep those many-many[a] bodies safe,
That live and feed upon your majesty.
ROS. The single and peculiar life is bound,
With all the strength and armour of the mind,
To keep itself from 'noyance; but much more
That spirit upon whose weal* depend and rest
The lives of many. The cease of majesty
Dies not alone; but, like a gulf, doth draw
What's near it with it: it is a massy wheel,
Fix'd on the summit of the highest mount,
To whose huge spokes ten thousand lesser things
Are mortis'd and adjoin'd; which, when it falls,
Each small annexment, petty consequence,
Attends the boist'rous ruin. Never alone
Did the king sigh, but with a general groan.
KING. Arm you, I pray you, to this speedy voyage;
For we will fetters put upon this fear,
Which now goes too free-footed.
ROS., GUIL. We will haste us.
[*Exeunt* ROSENCRANTZ *and* GUILDENSTERN.

Enter POLONIUS.

POL. My lord, he's going to his mother's closet:
Behind the arras I'll convey myself,
To hear the process; I'll warrant she'll tax him home.
And, as you said, and wisely was it said,
'T is meet that some more audience than a mother,
Since nature makes them partial, should o'erhear
The speech of vantage. Fare you well, my liege:
I'll call upon you ere you go to bed,
And tell you what I know.
KING. Thanks, dear my lord.
[*Exit* POLONIUS.
O, my offence is rank, it smells to heaven;
It hath the primal eldest curse upon 't,—
A brother's murder!—Pray can I not;
Though inclination be as sharp as will,
My stronger guilt defeats my strong intent;
And, like a man to double business bound,
I stand in pause where I shall first begin,
And both neglect. What if this cursed hand
Were thicker than itself with brother's blood,—
Is there not rain enough in the sweet heavens,
To wash it white as snow? Whereto serves mercy,
But to confront the visage of offence?
And what's in prayer but this two-fold force,—
To be forestalled ere we come to fall,
Or pardon'd being down? Then I'll look up;
My fault is past. But, O, what form of prayer
Can serve my turn? Forgive me my foul murder!—
That cannot be; since I am still possess'd
Of those effects for which I did the murder,—
My crown, mine own ambition, and my queen.
May one be pardon'd, and retain the offence?
In the corrupted currents of this world,
Offence's gilded hand may shove by justice;
And oft 't is seen the wicked prize[b] itself
Buys out the law: but 't is not so above;
There is no shuffling,—there the action lies
In his true nature; and we ourselves compell'd,
Even to the teeth and forehead of our faults,
To give in evidence. What then? what rests?
Try what repentance can: what can it not?
Yet what can it, when one can not repent?
O, wretched state! O, bosom, black as death!
O, limed soul, that struggling to be free,
Art more engag'd! Help, angels! make assay!
Bow, stubborn knees; and, heart with strings of steel,
Be soft as sinews of the new-born babe!
All may be well! [*Retires and kneels.*

Enter HAMLET.

HAM. Now might I do it pat, now he is praying;
And now I'll do 't;—and so he goes to heaven:
And so am I reveng'd:—that would be scann'd:
A villain kills my father; and, for that,
I, his sole* son, do this same villain send to heav'n.
O, this is hire and salary, not revenge.
He took my father grossly, full of bread;
With all his crimes broad blown, as flush† as May;
And how his audit stands who knows save heaven?
But, in our circumstance and course of thought,
'T is heavy with him: and am I, then, reveng'd,
To take him in the purging of his soul,
When he is fit and season'd for his passage? No!
Up, sword; and know thou a more horrid hent:[c]
When he is drunk, asleep, or in his rage;
Or in the incestuous pleasure of his bed;
At gaming, swearing; or about some act
That has no relish of salvation in 't;—

(*) First folio, *spirit*.

(*) First folio, *foule*. (†) First folio, *fresh*.

a — many-many—] This expression, signifying numberless, has hitherto been always printed "many many:" it should certainly be hyphened like *too-too, few-few, most-most*, and the like.

b — *the wicked* prize *itself*—] Mr. Collier's annotator, with abominable taste, suggests *purse* for "prize," and Mr. Collier says, "there cannot be a doubt on the propriety of the emendation"!

c — know *thou a more horrid* hent:] That is, and feel or be conscious of a more terrible *purpose*.

Then trip him, that his heels may kick at heaven;
And that his soul may be as damn'd and black,
As hell, whereto it goes. My mother stays:—
This physic but prolongs thy sickly days. [*Exit.*

The KING *rises and advances.*

KING. My words fly up, my thoughts remain below:
Words without thoughts never to heaven go. [*Exit.*

SCENE IV.—*Another Room in the same.*

Enter QUEEN *and* POLONIUS.

POL. He will come straight. Look you lay home to him;
Tell him his pranks have been too broad to bear with,
And that your grace hath screen'd and stood between
Much heat and him. I'll silence[a] me e'en here.
Pray you, be round with him.

HAM. [*Without.*] Mother, mother, mother!

QUEEN. I'll warrant you;
Fear me not:—withdraw, I hear him coming.
[POLONIUS *hides behind the arras.*(5)

Enter HAMLET.

HAM. Now, mother; what 's the matter?

QUEEN. Hamlet, thou hast thy father much offended.

HAM. Mother, you have my father much offended.

QUEEN. Come, come, you answer with an idle tongue.

---

[a] *I'll* silence *me e'en here.*] Hanmer reads, "I'll *sconce* me even here;" and perhaps rightly. Compare the corresponding passage in the quarto, 1603, "I'le *shrowde myself* behinde the Arras;" and, "Merry Wives of Windsor," Act III. Sc. 3,—"I'll *ensconce* me behind the arras."

HAM. Go, go, you question with a wicked* tongue.
QUEEN. Why, how now, Hamlet!
HAM. What 's the matter now?
QUEEN. Have you forgot me?
HAM. No, by the rood, not so:
You are the queen, your husband's brother's wife;
And,—would it† were not so!—you are my mother.
QUEEN. Nay, then, I 'll set those to you that can speak.
HAM. Come, come, and sit you down; you shall not budge;
You go not till I set you up a glass
Where you may see the inmost part of you.
QUEEN. What wilt thou do? thou wilt not murder me?—
Help, help, ho!
POL. [*Behind.*] What, ho! help, help, help!
HAM. How now! a rat? [*Draws.*] Dead! for a ducat, dead!
[*Makes a pass through the arras.*
POL. [*Behind.*] O, I am slain.
[*Falls and dies.*
QUEEN. O, me, what hast thou done?
HAM. Nay, I know not: is it the king?
QUEEN. O, what a rash and bloody deed is this!
HAM. A bloody deed!—almost as bad, good mother,
As kill a king, and marry with his brother.
QUEEN. *As kill a king!*
HAM. Ay, lady, 't was my word.—
[*Lifts up the arras and sees* POLONIUS.
Thou wretched, rash, intruding fool, farewell!
I took thee for thy better:‡ take thy fortune:
Thou find'st to be too busy is some danger.—
Leave wringing of your hands: peace! sit you down,
And let me wring your heart: for so I shall,
If it be made of penetrable stuff;
If damned custom have not braz'd it so,
That it is proof and bulwark against sense.
QUEEN. What have I done, that thou dar'st wag thy tongue
In noise so rude against me?
HAM. Such an act
That blurs the grace and blush of modesty;
Calls virtue hypocrite; takes off the rose
From the fair forehead of an innocent love,
And sets* a blister there; makes marriage vows
As false as dicers' oaths: O, such a deed
As from the body of contraction plucks
The very soul; and sweet religion makes
A rhapsody of words! heaven's face doth glow;
Yea, this solidity and compound mass,
With tristful visage, as against the doom,
Is thought-sick at the act.
QUEEN. Ay me, what act,
That roars so loud, and thunders in the index?
HAM. Look here, upon this picture, and on this,—
The counterfeit presentment of two brothers.
See, what a grace was seated on this† brow:
Hyperion's curls; the front of Jove himself;
An eye like Mars, to threaten and‡ command;
A station like the herald Mercury
New-lighted on a heaven-kissing hill;
A combination and a form, indeed,
Where every god did seem to set his seal,
To give the world assurance of a man:
This was your husband.—Look you now, what follows:
Here is your husband; like a mildew'd ear,
Blasting his wholesome brother.§—Have you eyes?
Could you on this fair mountain leave to feed,
And batten on this moor? Ha! have you eyes?
You cannot call it love; for at your age
The hey-day in the blood is tame, it 's humble,
And waits upon the judgment: and what judgment
Would step from this to this? Sense,[a] sure, you have,
Else could you not have motion: but sure, that sense
Is apoplex'd: for madness would not err;
Nor sense to ecstasy was ne'er so thrall'd
But it reserv'd some quantity of choice,
To serve in such a difference.[b] What devil was 't,
That thus hath cozen'd you at hoodman-blind?
Eyes without feeling, feeling without sight,
Ears without hands or eyes, smelling sans all,
Or but a sickly part of one true sense

(*) First folio, *an idle*. (†) First folio, *But would you*. (‡) First folio, *Betters*.

(*) First folio, *makes*. (†) First folio, *his*. (‡) First folio, *or*. (§) First folio, *breath*.

a —— Sense, *sure, you have,*
Else could you not have motion:]

The meaning we apprehend to be,—"Sense (*i.e.* the sensibility to appreciate the distinction between external objects) you must have, or you would no longer feel the *impulse of desire*. This signification of "motion" might be illustrated by numerous examples from our early writers, but the accompanying out of Shakespeare will suffice:—

" — one who never feels
The wanton stings and *motions* of the sense."
Measure for Measure, Act I. Sc. 5.

"—— A maiden never bold;
Of spirit so still and quiet, that her *motion*
Blush'd at herself."
Othello, Act I. Sc. 3.

"But we have reason to cool our raging
Motions, our carnal stings," &c.
Ibid. Act I. Sc. 3.

b To serve in such a difference.] The passage commencing "Sense, sure, you have," to these words inclusive, is not printed in the folio.

Could not so mope.[a]
O, shame! where is thy blush? Rebellious hell,
If thou canst mutine in a matron's bones,
To flaming youth let virtue be as wax,
And melt in her own fire: proclaim no shame
When the compulsive ardour gives the charge;
Since frost itself as actively doth burn,
And* reason panders will.

(*) First folio, *As*.

QUEEN. O, Hamlet, speak no more:
Thou turn'st mine eyes into my very soul;
And there I see such black and grained spots,
As will not leave their tinct.
HAM. Nay, but to live
In the rank sweat of an enseamed bed;
Stew'd in corruption; honeying and making love
Over the nasty stye,—

[a] Could not so mope.] This and the three foregoing lines are wanting in the folio.

QUEEN. O, speak to me no more!
These words, like daggers, enter in mine ears;
No more, sweet Hamlet!
HAM. A murderer and a villain!
A slave that is not twentieth part the tithe
Of your precedent lord;—a vice[a] of kings!
A cutpurse of the empire and the rule,
That from a shelf the precious diadem stole,
And put it in his pocket!
QUEEN. No more!
HAM. A king of shreds and patches!—

Enter Ghost.

Save me, and hover o'er me with your wings,
You heavenly guards!—What would your* gracious figure?
QUEEN. Alas, he 's mad!
HAM. Do you not come your tardy son to chide,
That, laps'd in time and passion, lets go by
The important acting of your dread command?
O, say!
GHOST. Do not forget: this visitation
Is but to whet thy almost blunted purpose.
But, look! amazement on thy mother sits:
O, step between her and her fighting soul,—
Conceit in weakest bodies strongest works,—
Speak to her, Hamlet.
HAM. How is it with you, lady?
QUEEN. Alas, how is 't with you,
That you do† bend your eye on vacancy,
And with the incorporal‡ air do hold discourse?
Forth at your eyes your spirits wildly peep;
And, as the sleeping soldiers in the alarm,
Your bedded hair, like life in excrements,
Starts up, and stands on end. O, gentle son,
Upon the heat and flame of thy distemper
Sprinkle cool patience. Whereon do you look?
HAM. On him! on him!—Look you, how pale he glares!
His form and cause conjoin'd, preaching to stones,
Would make them capable.[b]—Do not look upon me;
Lest with this piteous action you convert
My stern effects:[c] then what I have to do
Will want true colour; tears perchance for blood.
QUEEN. To whom do you speak this?
HAM. Do you see nothing there?
QUEEN. Nothing at all; yet all that is I see.
HAM. Nor did you nothing hear?
QUEEN. No, nothing but ourselves.
HAM. Why, look you there! look, how it steals away!
My father, in his habit as he liv'd!
Look, where he goes, even now, out at the portal!
[*Exit* Ghost.
QUEEN. This is the very coinage of your brain:
This bodiless creation ecstasy[d]
Is very cunning in.
HAM. *Ecstasy!*
My pulse as yours doth temperately keep time,
And makes as healthful music: it is not madness
That I have utter'd: bring me to the test,
And I the matter will re-word, which madness
Would gambol from. Mother, for love of grace,
Lay not that* flattering unction to your soul,
That not your trespass, but my madness speaks:
It will but skin and film the ulcerous place,
Whiles† rank corruption, mining all within,
Infects unseen. Confess yourself to heaven;
Repent what 's past; avoid what is to come;
And do not spread the compost on[e] the weeds,
To make them ranker.‡—[*Aside.*] Forgive me this, my virtue;[f]
For in the fatness of these§ pursy times,
Virtue itself of vice must pardon beg;
Yea, curb[g] and woo for leave to do him good.
QUEEN. O, Hamlet! thou hast cleft my heart in twain.
HAM. O, throw away the worser part of it,
And live the purer with the other half.
Good night: but go not to mine uncle's bed;
Assume a virtue, if you have it not.
That monster, Custom, who all sense doth eat,
Oft habits' devil, is angel yet in this,—[h]

(*) First folio, *you*. (†) First folio omits, *do*. (‡) First folio, *their corporall*.

(*) First folio, *a*. (†) First folio, *Whil'st*. (‡) First folio, *ranke*. (§) First folio, *this*.

a — *a* vice *of kings!*] A "vice" was the buffoon or clown of the older drama.

b — capable.] *Susceptible.*

c — effects:] For "effects," Mr. Singer reads, *affects*, quoting in support of his emendation,—

"—— the young *affects*
In me defunct—" &c.

d — ecstasy—] *Madness.* The quarto, 1603, exhibits this speech of the Queen very differently to the after copies; and the peculiarity is interesting in connexion with the question of her participation in the murder of her first husband:—

"Alas, it is the weaknesse of thy braine,
Which makes thy tongue to blazon thy hearts griefe:
But as I have a soule, I sweare by heaven,
I never knew of this most horride murder:
But Hamlet, this is onely fantasie,
And for my love forget these idle fits."

e — *do not spread the compost* on *the weeds,*—] The folio has,—"— *or* the weeds;" the poet's manuscript probably read, "*o'er* the weeds," &c.

f — Forgive me this, my virtue; &c.] Although the modern editors uniformly print this as if Hamlet addressed it to the Queen, nothing can be more evident than that it is an imploration to his own virtue.

g — curb—] *Bow*, or *truckle;* from the French courber.

h *That monster, Custom, who all sense doth eat,*
Oft *habits' devil*, &c.]

The reading of the old text is,—

"That monster custome, who all sense doth eate
Of habits devill," &c.;

Which has been variously modified to,—

"— who all sense doth eat
Of habits *evil*," &c.
"— who all sense doth eat,
If habit's devil," &c.;

and

"— who all sense doth eat,
Or habit's devil," &c.

The trifling change we have taken the liberty to make, while doing little violence to the original, may be thought, it is hoped, to give at least as good a meaning as any other which has been proposed.

That to the use of actions fair and good
He likewise gives a frock or livery,
That aptly is put on.[a] Refrain to-night:
And that shall lend a kind of easiness
To the next abstinence: the next more easy;
For use almost can change the stamp of nature,
And master[b] the devil, or throw him out
With wondrous potency.[c] Once more, good night:
And when you are desirous to be bless'd,
I 'll blessing beg of you.—For this same lord,
[*Pointing to* POLONIUS.
I do repent: but heaven hath pleas'd it so,
To punish me with this, and this with me,
That I must be their scourge and minister.
I will bestow him, and will answer well
The death I gave him. So, again, good night.—
I must be cruel, only to be kind:
Thus bad begins, and worse remains behind.—
One word more, good lady.[d]

QUEEN. What shall I do?

HAM. Not this, by no means, that I bid you do:
Let the bloat* king tempt you again to bed;
Pinch wanton on your cheek; call you his mouse;
And let him, for a pair of reechy kisses,
Or paddling in your neck with his damn'd fingers,
Make you to ravel all this matter out,
That I essentially am not in madness,
But mad in craft. 'T were good you let him know;
For who, that 's but a queen, fair, sober, wise,
Would from a paddock, from a bat, a gib,[e]
Such dear concernings hide? who would do so?
No, in despite of sense and secrecy,
Unpeg the basket on the house's top,
Let the birds fly, and, like the famous ape,
To try conclusions,[f] in the basket creep,
And break your own neck down.

QUEEN. Be thou assur'd, if words be made of breath,
And breath of life, I have no life to breathe
What thou hast said to me.

HAM. I must to England; you know that?

QUEEN. Alack.
I had forgot 't is so concluded on.

HAM. There 's letters seal'd: and my two schoolfellows,—
Whom I will trust as I will adders fang'd,—
They bear the mandate; they must sweep my way,
And marshal me to knavery. Let it work!
For 't is the sport to have the enginer
Hoist with his own petar: and 't shall go hard,
But I will delve one yard below their mines,
And blow them at the moon. O, 't is most sweet,
When in one line two crafts directly meet.—[g]
This man shall set me packing:
I 'll lug the guts into the neighbour room:—
Mother, good night.—Indeed, this counsellor
Is now most still, most secret, and most grave,
Who was in life a foolish prating knave.
Come, sir, to draw toward an end with you.—
Good night, mother.

[*Exeunt severally;* HAMLET *dragging out*[h] *the body of* POLONIUS.(6)

(*) First folio, *blunt*.

[a] That aptly is put on.] The passage from "That monster" to "put on" inclusive, is not in the folio.

[b] And master the devil, or throw him out—] The quartos, 1604 and 1605, present this line, "And *either* the devill," &c.; the after ones read as above, which, as it affords sense, though destructive to the metre, we retain, not, however, without acknowledging a preference for Malone's conjecture, "And either *curb* the devil," &c.

[c] With wondrous potency.] This and what precedes, from "the next more easy" inclusive, is only in the quarto copies.

[d] One word more, good lady.] Not in the folio.

[e] — a paddock—a gib,—] A "paddock" is a *toad;* for "gib," "*a cat*," see note (b), p. 512, Vol. I.

[f] — conclusions,—] *Experiments.*

[g] — directly meet.—] This, as well as the eight preceding lines, are only in the quartos.

[h] — *dragging out*—] The folio direction reads, "*tugging in*."

ACT IV.

SCENE I.—*The same.*

Enter KING, QUEEN, ROSENCRANTZ, *and* GUILDENSTERN.

KING. There's matter* in these sighs, these profound heaves,
You must translate; 't is fit we understand them.
Where is your son?

QUEEN. Bestow this place on us a little while.[a]
[*To* ROSENCRANTZ *and* GUILDENSTERN, *who exeunt.*
Ah, my good lord, what have I seen to-night!

KING. What, Gertrude? How does Hamlet?

QUEEN. Mad as the sea* and wind, when both contend
Which is the mightier: in his lawless fit,
Behind the arras hearing something stir,
He whips his rapier out, and cries, *A rat! a rat!*
And in this† brainish apprehension, kills
The unseen good old man.

KING. O, heavy deed!
It had been so with us, had we been there:
His liberty is full of threats to all;

(*) First folio, *matters.*

a Bestow this place, &c.] A line not in the folio.

(*) First folio, *seas.*

(†) First folio, *his.*

To you yourself, to us, to every one.
Alas! how shall this bloody deed be answered?
It will be laid to us, whose providence
Should have kept short, restrain'd, and out of haunt,[a]
This mad young man: but so much was our love,
We would not understand what was most fit;
But, like the owner of a foul disease,
To keep it from divulging, let* it feed
Even on the pith of life. Where is he gone?

QUEEN. To draw apart the body he hath kill'd,
O'er whom his very madness, like some ore[b]
Among a mineral[c] of metals base,
Shows itself pure; he weeps for what is done.

KING. O, Gertrude, come away!
The sun no sooner shall the mountains touch,
But we will ship him hence: and this vile deed
We must, with all our majesty and skill,
Both countenance and excuse.—Ho! Guildenstern!

Re-enter ROSENCRANTZ *and* GUILDENSTERN.

Friends both, go join you with some further aid:
Hamlet in madness hath Polonius slain,
And from his mother's closet* hath he dragg'd him:
Go, seek him out; speak fair, and bring the body
Into the chapel. I pray you, haste in this.—
[*Exeunt* ROS. *and* GUIL.
Come, Gertrude, we'll call up our wisest friends;
To let them know, both what we mean to do,
And what's untimely done: so, haply slander,—[d]
Whose whisper o'er the world's diameter,
As level as the cannon to his blank,
Transports his poison'd shot,—may miss our name,
And hit the woundless air.[e]—O, come away!
My soul is full of discord and dismay. [*Exeunt.*

SCENE II.—*Another Room in the same.*

Enter HAMLET.

HAM. Safely stowed.

ROS., GUIL. [*Without.*] Hamlet! lord Hamlet!

HAM. But soft![f] what noise? who calls on Hamlet? O, here they come.

(*) First folio, *lets*.

a — out of haunt,—] Out of *company*.

b — ore—] "Ore" is here used for *gold*, the most precious of ores.

c — mineral—] A *mine*, or rather a *metallic vein* in a mine; we should now say a *lode*.

d — so, haply slander,—] In the old copies the passage reads,—

"And let them know both what we meane to do
And whats untimely done," &c.;

the latter portion of the line having been accidentally omitted. Theobald supplied the *hiatus* by inserting "*for* haply, slander;" Malone by reading, "so *viperous* slander," &c.; we should prefer to either,—

"— *thus calumny*,—
Whose whisper," &c.

e And hit the woundless air.] These words and the three previous lines are not given in the folio.

f But soft!] Only in the quartos.

(*) First folio, *Clossets*.

Enter ROSENCRANTZ *and* GUILDENSTERN.

ROS. What have you done, my lord, with the dead body?

HAM. Compounded it with dust, whereto 'tis kin.

ROS. Tell us where 't is; that we may take it thence,
And bear it to the chapel.

HAM. Do not believe it.

ROS. Believe what?

HAM. That I can keep your counsel, and not mine own. Besides, to be demanded of a sponge!—what replication should be made by the son of a king?

ROS. Take you me for a sponge, my lord?

HAM. Ay, sir; that soaks up the king's countenance, his rewards, his authorities. But such officers do the king best service in the end: he keeps them, like an ape doth nuts,[a] in the corner of his jaw; first mouthed, to be last swallowed: when he needs what you have gleaned, it is but squeezing you, and, sponge, you shall be dry again.

ROS. I understand you not, my lord.

HAM. I am glad of it: a knavish speech sleeps in a foolish ear.

ROS. My lord, you must tell us where the body is, and go with us to the king.

HAM. The body is with the king, but the king is not with the body. The king is a thing—

GUIL. *A thing*, my lord?

HAM. Of nothing: bring me to him. Hide fox, and all after.[b] [*Exeunt.*

SCENE III.—*Another Room in the same.*

Enter KING, *attended.*

KING. I have sent to seek him, and to find the body.
How dangerous is it that this man goes loose!
Yet must not we put the strong law on him:
He 's lov'd of the distracted multitude,
Who like not in their judgment, but their eyes;
And where 't is so, the offender's scourge is weigh'd,
But never* the offence. To bear all smooth and even,
This sudden sending him away must seem
Deliberate pause: diseases desperate grown,
By desperate appliance are reliev'd,
Or not at all.

Enter ROSENCRANTZ.

How now! what hath befall'n?

ROS. Where the dead body is bestow'd, my lord,
We cannot get from him.

KING. But where is he?

ROS. Without, my lord, guarded, to know your pleasure.

KING. Bring him before us.

ROS. Ho, Guildenstern! bring in my lord.

Enter HAMLET *and* GUILDENSTERN.

KING. Now, Hamlet, where 's Polonius?

HAM. At supper.

KING. *At supper!* Where?

HAM. Not where he eats, but where he is eaten: a certain convocation of politic* worms are e'en at him. Your worm is your only emperor for diet: we fat all creatures else to fat us; and we fat ourselves† for maggots: your fat king and your lean beggar, is but variable service,—two dishes, but to one table; that 's the end.

KING. Alas, alas![c]

HAM. A man may fish with the worm that hath eat of a king; and eat of the fish that hath fed of that worm.[d]

KING. What dost thou mean by this?

HAM. Nothing but to show you how a king may go a progress through the guts of a beggar.

KING. Where is Polonius?

HAM. In heaven; send thither to see: if your messenger find him not there, seek him i' the other place yourself. But, indeed, if you find him not within‡ this month, you shall nose him as you go up the stairs into the lobby.

KING. Go seek him there. [*To some* Attendants.

HAM. He will stay till ye come. [*Exeunt* Attendants.

KING. Hamlet, this deed§ for thine especial safety,—
Which we do tender, as we dearly grieve
For that which thou hast done,—must send thee hence
With fiery quickness: therefore, prepare thyself;
The bark is ready, and the wind at help,
The associates tend, and everything is || bent
For England.

HAM. For England!

KING. Ay, Hamlet.

(*) First folio, *neerer.*

[a] — doth nuts,—] These words are restored from the 1603 quarto.

[b] Hide fox, and all after.] The early name for the boys' game, now known as *hoop*, or *hide and seek.*

[c] Alas, alas!] These exclamations, with the next speech, are only in the quartos.

(*) First folio omits, *politic.* (†) First folio, *ourselfe.* (‡) First folio omits, *within.* (§) First folio adds, *of thine.* (||) First folio, *at.*

[d] — and eat of the fish, &c.] In the quarto, 1603, this stands,—"A man may fish with the worme that hath eaten of a king, *and a beggar eate that fish which that worme hath caught.*"

HAM. Good.

KING. So is it, if thou knew'st our purposes.

HAM. I see a cherub, that sees them.*—But, come; for England!—Farewell, dear mother.

KING. Thy loving father, Hamlet!

HAM. My mother: father and mother is man and wife; man and wife is one flesh; and so, my mother.—Come, for England! [*Exit.*

KING. Follow him at foot; tempt him with speed aboard;
Delay it not; I'll have him hence to-night:
Away! for everything is seal'd and done
That else leans on the affair: pray you, make haste. [*Exeunt* Ros. *and* Guil.
And, England, if my love thou hold'st at aught,—
As my great power thereof may give thee sense,
Since yet thy cicatrice looks raw and red
After the Danish sword, and thy free awe
Pays homage to us,—thou mayst not coldly set
Our sovereign process; which imports at full,
By letters conjuring to that effect,
The present death of Hamlet. Do it, England;
For like the hectic in my blood he rages,
And thou must cure me: till I know 't is done,
Howe'er my haps, my joys were ne'er begun.
[*Exit.*

(*) First folio, *him.*

SCENE IV.—*A Plain in* Denmark.

Enter FORTINBRAS, *and* Forces, *marching.*

FOR. [*To an* Officer.] Go, captain, from me greet the Danish king;
Tell him, that, by his licence, Fortinbras
Claims the conveyance of a promis'd march
Over his kingdom. You know the rendezvous.
If that his majesty would aught with us,
We shall express our duty in his eye;
And let him know so.

CAP. I will do 't, my lord.

FOR. Go softly[a] on.
[*Exeunt* FORTINBRAS *and* Forces.

[a] *Go* softly *on.*] The folio has "safely;" but "softly," as in the quartos, meaning *slowly*, was doubtless the author's word.

Enter HAMLET, ROSENCRANTZ, GUILDENSTERN, *&c.*[a]

HAM. Good sir, whose powers are these?
CAP. They are of Norway, sir.
HAM. How purposed, sir, I pray you?
CAP. Against some part of Poland.
HAM. Who commands them, sir?
CAP. The nephew to old Norway, Fortinbras.
HAM. Goes it against the main of Poland, sir,
Or for some frontier?
CAP. Truly to speak, and with no addition,
We go to gain a little patch of ground,
That hath in it no profit but the name.
To pay five ducats, five, I would not farm it;
Nor will it yield to Norway or the Pole
A ranker rate, should it be sold in fee.
HAM. Why, then the Polack never will defend it.
CAP. Yes, 't is already garrison'd.
HAM. Two thousand souls, and twenty thousand ducats,
Will not debate the question of this straw:
This is the imposthume of much wealth and peace,
That inward breaks, and shows no cause without
Why the man dies.—I humbly thank you, sir.
CAP. God be wi' you, sir. [*Exit.*
ROS. Will 't please you go, my lord?
HAM. I will be with you straight. Go a little before.
[*Exeunt* ROSENCRANTZ *and* GUILDENSTERN.
How all occasions do inform against me,
And spur my dull revenge! What is a man,
If his chief good and market of his time,
Be but to sleep and feed? a beast, no more.
Sure, he that made us with such large discourse,
Looking before and after, gave us not
That capability and god-like reason
To fust in us unus'd. Now, whether it be
Bestial oblivion, or some craven scruple
Of thinking too precisely on the event,—
A thought which, quarter'd, hath but one part wisdom,
And ever three parts coward,—I do not know
Why yet I live to say, *This thing 's to do;*
Sith I have cause, and will, and strength, and means,
To do 't. Examples, gross as earth, exhort me:
Witness this army of such mass and charge,
Led by a delicate and tender prince;
Whose spirit, with divine ambition puff'd,
Makes mouths at the invisible event;
Exposing what is mortal and unsure
To all that fortune, death, and danger dare,
Even for an egg-shell. Rightly to be great,
Is not to stir without great argument,
But greatly to find quarrel in a straw,
When honour's at the stake. How stand I, then,
That have a father kill'd, a mother stain'd,
Excitements of my reason and my blood,
And let all sleep? while, to my shame, I see
The imminent death of twenty thousand men,
That, for a fantasy and trick of fame,
Go to their graves like beds; fight for a plot
Whereon the numbers cannot try the cause,
Which is not tomb enough and continent,
To hide the slain?—O, from this time forth,
My thoughts be bloody, or be nothing worth!
[*Exit.*

SCENE V.—Elsinore. *A Room in the Castle.*

Enter QUEEN, HORATIO, *and a* Gentleman.[b]

QUEEN. I will not speak with her.
GENT. She is importunate; indeed, distract;
Her mood will needs be pitied.
QUEEN. What would she have?
GENT. She speaks much of her father; says she hears,
There 's tricks i' the world; and hems, and beats her heart;
Spurns enviously at straws; speaks things in doubt,
That carry but half sense: her speech is nothing,
Yet the unshaped use of it doth move
The hearers to collection; they aim at it,
And botch the words up fit to their own thoughts;
Which, as her winks, and nods, and gestures yield them,
Indeed would make one think there might* be thought,[c]
Though nothing sure, yet much unhappily.
HOR. 'T were good she were spoken with; for she may strew
Dangerous conjectures in ill-breeding minds.
QUEEN. Let her come in.[d] [*Exit* HORATIO.
To my sick soul, as sin's true nature is,
Each toy seems prologue to some great amiss:
So full of artless jealousy is guilt,
It spills itself in fearing to be spilt.

(*) First folio, *would.*

[a] *Enter* HAMLET, &c.] The remainder of this scene is entirely wanting in the folio.
[b] — *and a* Gentleman.] So the quartos: the folio omits this character, and Horatio is made to speak what the former copies assign to him. We adopt the older distribution of the dialogue as the better one.
[c] — *there might be* thought,—] "Thought" is possibly a misprint, caught from the line above, for *meant*, or *seen*, or a word of like import.
[d] Let her come in.] In the quartos, these words are mistakenly attached to Horatio's speech; and in the folio, the two previous lines are assigned to the Queen.

Re-enter HORATIO *with* OPHELIA.[a]

OPH. Where is the beauteous majesty of Denmark?

QUEEN. How now, Ophelia?

OPH. [Sings.]

How should I your true love know
From another one?
By his cockle hat and staff,
And his sandal shoon.

QUEEN. Alas, sweet lady! what imports this song?

OPH. Say you? nay, pray you, mark!

[Sings.] *He is dead and gone, lady,*
He is dead and gone;
At his head a grass-green turf,
At his heels a stone.

QUEEN. Nay, but Ophelia,—

OPH. Pray you, mark!

[Sings.] *White his shroud as the mountain snow,*

Enter KING.

QUEEN. Alas, look here, my lord.

OPH. [Sings.]

Larded all with sweet flowers;*
Which bewept to the grave did† go,
With true-love showers.

KING. How do you, pretty lady?

OPH. Well, God 'ield you! They say, the owl was a baker's daughter.(1) Lord, we know what we are, but know not what we may be. God be at your table!

KING. Conceit upon her father.

OPH. Pray you, let 's have no words of this; but when they ask you what it means, say you this:

[Sings.] *To-morrow is Saint Valentine's day,*
All in the morning betime,
And I a maid at your window,
To be your Valentine.

Then up he rose, and donn'd[b] *his clothes,*
And dupp'd[c] *the chamber door;*
Let in the maid, that out a maid
Never departed more.

KING. Pretty Ophelia!

OPH. Indeed, la, without an oath, I'll make an end on't:

[Sings.] *By Gis, and by Saint Charity,*
Alack, and fie for shame!
Young men will do't, if they come to't;
By cock they are to blame.

Quoth she, before you tumbled me,
You promis'd me to wed.
So would I ha' done, by yonder sun,
An thou hadst not come to my bed.

KING. How long hath she been thus?*

OPH. I hope, all will be well. We must be patient; but I cannot choose but weep, to think they should lay him i' the cold ground.—My brother shall know of it; and so I thank you for your good counsel.—Come, my coach!—Good night, ladies; good night, sweet ladies; good night, good night. [*Exit.*

KING. Follow her close; give her good watch,
I pray you. [*Exit* HORATIO.
O, this is the poison of deep grief; it springs
All from her father's death. O, Gertrude, Gertrude,
When sorrows come, they come not single spies,
But in battalias! First, her father slain;
Next, your son gone; and he most violent author
Of his own just remove; the people muddied,
Thick and unwholesome in their thoughts and whispers,
For good Polonius' death; and we have done but greenly,[d]
In hugger-mugger[e] to inter him; poor Ophelia,
Divided from herself and her fair judgment,
Without the which we are pictures, or mere beasts:
Last, and as much containing as all these,
Her brother is in secret come from France;
Feeds† on his wonder, keeps himself in clouds,
And wants not buzzers to infect his ear
With pestilent speeches of his father's death;
Wherein necessity, of matter beggar'd,
Will nothing stick our person‡ to arraign

(*) First folio omits, *all*. (†) Old copies, *did not go*.

a — *with* OPHELIA.] The quaint direction of the quarto, 1603, is entitled to consideration from future representatives of this lovely creation, since in all probability it indicates the manner in which the author himself designed she should appear in this her greatest scene,—"*Enter Ofelia playing on a Lute, and her haire downe singing.*"

b — *donn'd*—] *To don* = to *do on*, or *put on*.

(*) First folio, *this*. (†) First folio, *Keepes*. (‡) First folio, *persons*.

c — *dupp'd*—] A contraction of *do up*; to *lift the latch*. Johnson suggested, "And *op'd*;" but compare, "What devell! iche weene the porters are drunke, wil they not *dup* the gate to-day?" —*Damon and Pythias*, 1582.

d — greenly,—] *Immaturely, unwisely*.

e — hugger-mugger—] An old word signifying *secretly, by stealth*.

In ear and ear. O, my dear Gertrude, this,
Like to a murdering-piece,[a] in many places
Gives me superfluous death. [*A noise without.*
QUEEN. Alack! what noise is this?
KING. Where are my Switzers? Let them guard the door:

Enter another Gentleman.

What is the matter?
GENT. Save yourself, my lord!
The ocean, overpeering of his list,
Eats not the flats with more impetuous* haste,
Than young Laertes, in a riotous head,
O'erbears your officers. The rabble call him lord;
And, as the world were now but to begin,
Antiquity forgot, custom not known,
The ratifiers and props of every word,
They cry, *Choose we! Laertes shall be king!*
Caps, hands, and tongues, applaud it to the clouds,
Laertes shall be king, Laertes king!
QUEEN. How cheerfully on the false trail they cry!
O, this is counter,[b] you false Danish dogs.
[*Noise without.*
KING. The doors are broke!

Enter LAERTES, *armed;* Danes *following.*

LAER. Where is this† king?—Sirs, stand you all without.
DANES. No, let's come in.
LAER. I pray you, give me leave.
DANES. We will, we will.
[*They retire without the door.*
LAER. I thank you:—keep the door.—O, thou vile king,
Give me my father!
QUEEN. Calmly, good Laertes.
LAER. That drop of blood that's calm‡ proclaims me bastard;
Cries cuckold to my father; brands the harlot
Even here, between the chaste unsmirched brow
Of my true mother!
KING. What is the cause, Laertes,
That thy rebellion looks so giant-like?—
Let him go, Gertrude; do not fear our person;
There's such divinity doth hedge a king,
That treason can but peep to what it would,
Acts little of his will.[c]—Tell me, Laertes,
Why thou art thus incensed:—let him go, Gertrude;—
Speak, man.
LAER. Where is my father?
KING. Dead.
QUEEN. But not by him.[d]
KING. Let him demand his fill.
LAER. How came he dead? I'll not be juggled with;
To hell, allegiance! vows, to the blackest devil!
Conscience and grace, to the profoundest pit!
I dare damnation: to this point I stand,
That both the worlds I give to negligence,
Let come what comes; only I'll be reveng'd
Most throughly for my father.
KING. Who shall stay you?
LAER. My will, not all the world:
And for my means, I'll husband them so well,
They shall go far with little.
KING. Good Laertes,
If you desire to know the certainty
Of your dear father's death, is't* writ in your revenge,
That, swoopstake, you will draw both friend and foe,
Winner and loser?
LAER. None but his enemies.
KING. Will you know them, then?
LAER. To his good friends thus wide I'll ope my arms;
And, like the kind life-rend'ring pelican,†
Repast them with my blood.
KING. Why, now you speak
Like a good child and a true gentleman.
That I am guiltless of your father's death,
And am most sensible in grief for it,
It shall as level to your judgment pierce,
As day does to your eye.
DANES. [*Without.*] Let her come in.
LAER. How now! what noise is that?—

Re-enter OPHELIA.

O, heat, dry up my brains! tears seven-times salt,
Burn out the sense and virtue of mine eye!—

(*) First folio, *impittious.* (†) First folio, *the.* (‡) First folio, *that calmes.*

a — a murdering-piece,—] A piece of artillery with several barrels, which discharged a hail of missiles composed of bullets, nails, old iron, and the like.

b — this is counter,—] To hunt *counter* is explained at p. 150, Vol. I. "to follow on a false scent;" it should have been added, "or to *retrace* the scent." A hound which, instead of going forward, turns and pursues the backward trail, was in the old language of the chase said to *hunt counter*.

c That treason can but peep to what it would,
Acts little of his will.]

(*) First folio, *if.* (†) First folio, *Politician.*

This is passed by the critics without comment; but we shrewdly suspect it has undergone some depravation at the hands of transcribers or compositors.

d But not by him.] In the 1603 quarto the dialogue proceeds,—

"*Laer.* Speake, say, where's my father?
King. Dead.
Laer. Who hath murdred him? speake, ile not
Be juggled with, for he is murdred.
Queene. True, but not by him."

By heaven, thy madness shall be paid by weight,
Till our scale turn the beam! O, rose of May!
Dear maid, kind sister, sweet Ophelia!—
O, heavens! is't possible, a young maid's wits
Should be as mortal as an old man's life?
Nature is fine in love: and, where 'tis fine,
It sends some precious instance of itself
After the thing it loves.

OPH. [Sings.]

They bore him barefac'd on the bier;
Hey non nonny, nonny, hey nonny;
And on his grave rains many a tear;—

Fare you well, my dove!

LAER. Hadst thou thy wits, and didst persuade revenge,
It could not move thus.

OPH. [Sings.]

You must sing, a-down a-down,
An you call him a-down-a.

O, how the wheel[a] becomes it! It is the false steward, that stole his master's daughter.

LAER. This nothing 's more than matter.

OPH. There's rosemary, that's for remembrance;

[Sings.] *Pray, love, remember:*

and there is pansies,* that's for thoughts.

LAER. A document in madness! thoughts and remembrance fitted.

OPH. There's fennel for you, and columbines:—there's rue for you; and here's some for me:—we may call it herb-grace o' Sundays:—O, you must wear your rue with a difference.—There's a daisy:(2)—I would give you some violets, but they withered all when my father died:—they say he made a good end,—

[Sings.] *For bonny sweet Robin is all my joy,*—

LAER. Thought and affliction, passion, hell itself,
She turns to favour and to prettiness.

OPH. [Sings.] *And will he not come again?*
And will he not come again?
No, no, he is dead,
Go to thy death-bed,
He never will come again.

His beard as white as snow,
All flaxen was his poll:
He is gone, he is gone,
And we cast away moan:
Gramercy on his soul!

And of all christian souls, I pray God.—God be wi' you. [*Exit.*

LAER. Do you see this, O God?†

KING. Laertes, I must commune[b] with your grief,
Or you deny me right. Go but apart,
Make choice of whom your wisest friends you will,
And they shall hear and judge 'twixt you and me:
If by direct or by collateral hand
They find us touch'd, we will our kingdom give,
Our crown, our life, and all that we call ours,
To you in satisfaction; but if not,
Be you content to lend your patience to us,
And we shall jointly labour with your soul
To give it due content.

LAER. Let this be so;
His means of death, his obscure burial—
No trophy, sword, nor hatchment, o'er his bones,
No noble rite nor formal ostentation,—
Cry to be heard, as 'twere from heaven to earth,
That I must call't* in question.

KING. So you shall;
And where the offence is let the great axe fall.
I pray you, go with me. [*Exeunt.*

SCENE VI.—*Another Room in the same.*

Enter HORATIO *and a* Servant.(3)

HOR. What are they that would speak with me?

SERV. Sailors, sir; they say, they have letters for you.

HOR. Let them come in.— [*Exit* Servant.
I do not know from what part of the world
I should be greeted, if not from lord Hamlet.

Enter Sailors.†

1 SAIL. God bless you, sir.

HOR. Let him bless thee too.

1 SAIL. He shall, sir, an't please him. There's a letter for you, sir,—it comes from the ambassador that was bound for England,—if your name be Horatio, as I am let to know it is.

HOR. [Reads.] *HORATIO, when thou shalt have overlooked this, give these fellows some means to the king; they have letters for him. Ere we were two days old at sea, a pirate of very warlike appointment gave us chace. Finding ourselves too slow of sail, we put on a compelled valour; in the grapple I boarded them; on the instant they got clear of our ship; so I alone became their prisoner. They have dealt with me like thieves of mercy; but they knew what they did; I am to do a good turn for them. Let the king have the letters I have sent; and repair thou to me with as much haste as thou wouldst fly death. I have words to speak in thine‡ ear, will make thee dumb: yet are they much too light for the bore of the matter. These good fellows will bring thee*

(*) First folio, *Paconcies*. (†) First folio, *you Gods*.

(*) First folio, *call*. (†) First folio, *Saylor*. (‡) First folio, *your*.

a — the wheel—] The "wheel" = *rota*, is another name for the *burden* or *refrain* of a ballad: it was perhaps the practice on the old stage for Ophelia to play the "wheel" upon her lute before these words.

b — *I must* commune *with your grief*,—] The folio alone reads "common," which is only the more ancient orthography of the same word.

where I am. ROSENCRANTZ *and* GUILDENSTERN *hold their course for England; of them I have much to tell thee. Farewell.*

He that thou knowest thine, HAMLET.

Come, I will give you way for these your letters;
And do't the speedier, that you may direct me
To him from whom you brought them. [*Exeunt.*

SCENE VII.—*Another Room in the same.*

Enter KING *and* LAERTES.

KING. Now must your conscience my acquittance seal,
And you must put me in your heart for friend;
Sith you have heard, and with a knowing ear,
That he which hath your noble father slain,
Pursu'd my life.
LAER. It well appears:—but tell me
Why you proceeded not against these feats,
So crimeful and so capital in nature,
As by your safety, wisdom, all things else,
You mainly were stirr'd up.
KING. O, for two special reasons;
Which may to you, perhaps, seem much unsinew'd,
But* yet to me they are strong. The queen, his mother,
Lives almost by his looks; and for myself,

(*) First folio, *and.*

(My virtue or my plague, be it either which,)
She's so conjunctive to my life and soul,
That, as the star moves not but in his sphere,
I could not but by her. The other motive,
Why to a public count I might not go,
Is the great love the general gender bear him;
Who, dipping all his faults in their affection,
Would, like the spring that turneth wood to stone,
Convert his gyves to graces; so that my arrows,
Too slightly timber'd for so loud a wind,
Would have reverted to my bow again,
And not where I had aim'd* them.
LAER. And so have I a noble father lost;
A sister driven into desperate terms,—
Whose worth,† if praises may go back again,
Stood challenger on mount of all the age
For her perfections:—but my revenge will come.
KING. Break not your sleeps for that: you must not think
That we are made of stuff so flat and dull,
That we can let our beard be shook with danger,
And think it pastime. You shortly shall hear more:
I lov'd your father, and we love ourself;
And that, I hope, will teach you to imagine,—

Enter a Messenger.

How now! what news?
MESS. Letters, my lord, from Hamlet:
This to your majesty; this to the queen.

(*) First folio, *arm'd.* (†) First folio, *Who was.*

KING. From Hamlet! who brought them?
MESS. Sailors, my lord, they say: I saw them not.
They were given to me by Claudio, he received them
Of him that brought them.*
KING. Laertes, you shall hear them:—
Leave us. [*Exit* Messenger.

[Reads.] *High and mighty,—You shall know I am set naked on your kingdom. To-morrow shall I beg leave to see your kingly eyes: when I shall, first asking your pardon thereunto, recount the occasions of my sudden and more strange return.*
HAMLET.

What should this mean? Are all the rest come back?
Or is it some abuse, and† no such thing?
LAER. Know you the hand?
KING. 'Tis Hamlet's character.—*Naked,*—
And in a postscript here, he says, *alone!*
Can you advise me?
LAER. I'm lost in it, my lord. But let him come!
It warms the very sickness in my heart,
That I shall live and tell him to his teeth,
Thus diddest thou![a]
KING. If it be so, Laertes,—
As how should it be so? how otherwise?—
Will you be rul'd by me?
LAER. Ay, my lord,‡
So§ you will not o'er-rule me to a peace.
KING. To thine own peace. If he be now return'd,—
As checking[b] at his voyage, and that he means
No more to undertake it,—I will work him
To an exploit, now ripe in my device,
Under the which he shall not choose but fall;
And for his death no wind of blame shall breathe;
But even his mother shall uncharge the practice,
And call it accident.
LAER. My lord, I will be rul'd;
The rather, if you could devise it so,
That I might be the organ.
KING. It falls right.
You have been talk'd of since your travel much,
And that in Hamlet's hearing, for a quality
Wherein, they say, you shine: your sum of parts
Did not together pluck such envy from him,
As did that one; and that, in my regard,
Of the unworthiest siege.[c]
LAER. What part is that, my lord?
KING. A very riband in the cap of youth,
Yet needful too; for youth no less becomes
The light and careless livery that it wears,
Than settled age his sables and his weeds,
Importing health and graveness.[d]—Two months since,*
Here was a gentleman of Normandy,—
I've seen myself, and served against, the French,
And they can[e] well on horseback: but this gallant
Had witchcraft in't; he grew into his seat;
And to such wondrous doing brought his horse,
As he had been incorps'd and demi-natur'd
With the brave beast: so far he topp'd† my thought,
That I, in forgery of shapes and tricks,
Come short of what he did.
LAER. A Norman was't?
KING. A Norman.
LAER. Upon my life, Lamond.
KING. The very same.
LAER. I know him well: he is the brooch, indeed,
And gem of all the‡ nation.
KING. He made confession of you;
And gave you such a masterly report,
For art and exercise in your defence,[f]
And for your rapier most especially,
That he cried out, 'twould be a sight indeed,
If one could match you: the scrimers[g] of their nation,
He swore, had neither motion, guard, nor eye,
If you oppos'd them.[h] Sir, this report of his
Did Hamlet so envenom with his envy,
That he could nothing do, but wish and beg
Your sudden coming o'er, to play with him.
Now, out of this,—
LAER. What§ out of this, my lord?
KING. Laertes, was your father dear to you?
Or are you like the painting of a sorrow,
A face without a heart?
LAER. Why ask you this?

(*) This hemistich is omitted in the first folio.
(†) First folio, *Or.* (‡) First folio omits, *Ay, my lord.*
(§) First folio, *If so you'l.*

a *Thus diddest thou!*] The reading of the 1603 quarto is,—
"That I shall live to tell him, *thus he dies,*"
which by some may be thought superior.

b *As* checking *at his voyage,*—] *To check,* a technical phrase from falconry, means to *fly from* or *shy at.* "— For who knows not, quoth she, that this hawk which comes now so fair to the first, may to-morrow *check* at the lure."—HINDE'S *Eliosto Libidinoso,* 1606, quoted by Steevens. Again, in Massinger's play of "The Unnatural Combat," Act V. Sc. 2,—
"—— and there's something here that tells me
I stand accomptable for greater sins
I never *check'd* at."

(*) First folio, *Some two Monthes hence.* (†) First folio, *past.*
(‡) First folio, *our.* (§) First folio, *Why.*

c *Of the* unworthiest siege.] *Siege* is *seat, place, state;* and the meaning therefore is, Of the most *ignoble rank.*

d Importing health and graveness.] These words, and the preceding lines to "And call it accident," inclusive, are not in the folio.

e *And they* can *well on horseback:*] The folio misprints this, "*ran* well."

f — defence,—] That is, *Science of Defence,* as the knowledge of sword-play was formerly called. See note 6, p. 216, Vol. I.

g — scrimers—] *Fencers,* from the French, *Escrimeur.*

h If you oppos'd them.] The passage beginning, "the scrimers," &c., is not in the folio.

KING. Not that I think you did not love your father;
But that I know love is begun by time;
And that I see, in passages of proof,
Time qualifies the spark and fire of it.
There lives within the very flame of love
A kind of wick or snuff that will abate it;
And nothing is at a like goodness still;
For goodness, growing to a plurisy,[a]
Dies in his own too-much: that we would do,
We should do when we would; for this *would* changes,
And hath abatements and delays as many
As there are tongues, are hands, are accidents;
And then this *should* is like a spendthrift* sigh,
That hurts by easing. But, to the quick o' the ulcer:—[b]
Hamlet comes back: what would you undertake,
To show yourself your father's son in deed
More than in words?

LAER. To cut his throat i' the church.

KING. No place, indeed, should murder sanctuarize;
Revenge should have no bounds. But, good Laertes,
Will you do this,[c] keep close within your chamber.
Hamlet return'd shall know you are come home:
We'll put on those shall praise your excellence,
And set a double varnish on the fame
The Frenchman gave you; bring you, in fine, together,
And wager on your heads: he, being remiss,
Most generous, and free from all contriving,
Will not peruse the foils; so that, with ease,
Or with a little shuffling, you may choose
A sword unbated,[d] and, in a pass of practice,
Requite him for your father.

LAER. I will do't:
And, for that purpose, I'll anoint my sword.
I bought an unction of a mountebank,
So mortal, that but dip† a knife in it,
Where it draws blood no cataplasm so rare,
Collected from all simples that have virtue
Under the moon, can save the thing from death
That is but scratch'd withal: I'll touch my point
With this contagion, that, if I gall him slightly,
It may be death.

KING. Let's further think of this;
Weigh what convenience both of time and means
May fit us to our shape: if this should fail,
And that our drift look through our bad performance,
'T were better not assay'd; therefore this project
Should have a back or second, that might hold,
If this should blast in proof. Soft!—let me see:—
We'll make a solemn wager on your cunnings,*—
I ha't! when in your motion you are hot and dry,
(As make your bouts more violent to that† end)
And that he calls for drink, I'll have prepar'd him
A chalice for the nonce, whereon but sipping,
If he by chance escape your venom'd stuck,[e]
Our purpose may hold there.

Enter QUEEN.

How now,[f] sweet queen?

QUEEN. One woe doth tread upon another's heel,
So fast they follow:—your sister's drown'd, Laertes.

LAER. *Drown'd!*—O, where?

QUEEN. There is a willow grows ascaunt‡ a brook,
That shows his hoar leaves in the glassy stream;
There with fantastic garlands did she come
Of crow-flowers, nettles, daisies, and long purples
That liberal shepherds give a grosser name,
But our cold maids do dead men's fingers call them:
There, on the pendent boughs her coronet weeds
Clambering to hang, an envious sliver broke;
When down the weedy trophies and herself
Fell in the weeping brook. Her clothes spread wide;
And, mermaid-like, a while they bore her up:
Which time she chanted snatches of old tunes,
As one incapable[g] of her own distress,
Or like a creature native and indu'd
Unto that element: but long it could not be,
Till that her garments, heavy with their§ drink,
Pull'd the poor wretch from her melodious lay‖
To muddy death.

LAER. Alas, then, is she drown'd?

QUEEN. Drown'd, drown'd.

LAER. Too much of water hast thou, poor Ophelia,
And therefore I forbid my tears: but yet
It is our trick; Nature her custom holds,
Let shame say what it will: when these are gone,
The woman will be out.—Adieu, my lord:—
I have a speech of fire that fain would blaze,
But that this folly drowns¶ it. [*Exit.*

KING. Let's follow, Gertrude.
How much I had to do to calm his rage!
Now fear I this will give it start again;
Therefore let's follow. [*Exeunt.*

(*) Old text, *spend-thrift's sigh*. (†) First folio, *I but dipt*.

[a] — plurisy,—] *Repletion, superfluance.* Not from πλευρῖτις, but from *plus, pluris*.

[b] But, to the quick o' the ulcer:—] This and the nine foregoing lines are not in the folio.

[c] Will you do this, &c.] That is, "If you will do this, then keep close," &c.

[d] — unbated,—] *Unblunted, without a button on the point*, as fencing foils have.

(*) First folio, *commings*. (†) First folio, *the*.
(‡) First folio, *aslant*. (§) First folio, *her*.
(‖) First folio, *buy*. (¶) First folio, *doubts*.

[e] — *venom'd* stuck,—] "Stuck." = *tuck*, is perhaps used for a sword; or it may mean a *thrust, stoccata*.

[f] *How* now, *sweet queen?*] The parallel passage in the 1603 quarto is, "*How now* Gertred, why looke you heavily?" but all subsequent editions, until the folio of 1632, omit "*now*."

[g] — incapable—] *Unsusceptible, unintelligent.*

ACT V.

SCENE I.—*A Church-Yard.*

Enter Two Clowns, *with spades, &c.*

1 Clo. Is she to be buried in christian burial that wilfully seeks her own salvation?

2 Clo. I tell thee she is; and therefore make her grave straight: the crowner hath sat on her, and finds it christian burial.

1 Clo. How can that be, unless she drowned herself in her own defence?

2 Clo. Why, 'tis found so.

1 Clo. It must be *se offendendo;* it cannot be else: for here lies the point: if I drown myself wittingly, it argues an act: and an act hath three branches; it is, to* act, to do, and to perform: argal, she drowned herself wittingly.

2 Clo. Nay, but hear you, goodman delver,—

1 Clo. Give me leave. Here lies the water; good: here stands the man; good: if the man go to this water, and drown himself, it is, will he nill he, he goes,—mark you that; but if the water come to him and drown him, he drowns not himself: argal, he that is not guilty of his own death shortens not his own life.(1)

2 Clo. But is this law?

1 Clo. Ay, marry, is't; crowner's quest-law.

2 Clo. Will you ha' the truth on't? If this had not been a gentlewoman, she should have been buried out of christian burial.

1 Clo. Why, there thou sayst: and the more pity that great folk should have countenance in this world to drown or hang themselves, more than their even[a] christian.—Come, my spade. There is no ancient gentlemen but gardeners, ditchers, and grave-makers; they hold up Adam's profession.

2 Clo. Was he a gentleman?

1 Clo. He was the first that ever bore arms.

2 Clo. Why, he had none.

1 Clo. What, art a heathen? How dost thou understand the scripture? The scripture says, Adam digged; could he dig without arms? I'll put another question to thee: if thou answerest me not to the purpose, confess thyself—

(*) First folio, *an.*

a — even *christian.*—] This old expression for *fellow* christian is frequently met with in the early English writers. See the *Variorum*, 1821, Vol. VIII. *ad l.* where several examples are cited by Steevens and Malone.

2 CLO. Go to.

1 CLO. What is he that builds stronger than either the mason, the shipwright, or the carpenter?[a]

2 CLO. The gallows-maker; for that frame outlives a thousand tenants.

1 CLO. I like thy wit well, in good faith; the gallows does well; but how does it well? it does well to those that do ill: now, thou dost ill to say the gallows is built stronger than the church; argal, the gallows may do well to thee. To 't again, come.

2 CLO. Who builds stronger than a mason, a shipwright, or a carpenter?

1 CLO. Ay, tell me that, and unyoke.[b]

2 CLO. Marry, now I can tell.

1 CLO. To 't.

2 CLO. Mass, I cannot tell.

Enter HAMLET *and* HORATIO *at a distance.*

1 CLO. Cudgel thy brains no more about it, for your dull ass will not mend his pace with beating; and when you are asked this question next, say, *a gravemaker*,—the houses that he makes last till doomsday. Go, get thee to Yaughan;[c] fetch me a stoup of liquor. [*Exit* 2 Clown.

1 Clown *digs and sings.*

In youth, when I did love, did love,(2)
Methought it was very sweet,
To contract, O, *the time, for,* ah, *my behove*
O, *methought there was nothing meet.*

HAM. Has this fellow no feeling of his business, that he sings at grave-making?

HOR. Custom hath made it in him a property of easiness.

HAM. 'T is e'en so: the hand of little employment hath the daintier sense.

1 Clown *sings.*

But age, with his stealing steps,
Hath caught me in his clutch,
And hath shipped me intil the land,
As if I had never been such.
[*Throws up a skull.*

HAM. That skull had a tongue in it, and could sing once: how the knave jowls it to the ground, as if it were Cain's jaw-bone, that did the first murder! This* might be the pate of a politician,[d] which this ass o'er-reaches;† one that could circumvent God, might it not?

HOR. It might, my lord.

HAM. Or of a courtier; which could say, *Good-morrow, sweet lord! How dost thou, good lord?* This might be my lord Such-a-one, that praised my lord Such-a-one's horse, when he meant to beg it,—might it not?

HOR. Ay, my lord.

HAM. Why, e'en so: and now my lady Worm's; chapless, and knocked about the mazzard with a sexton's spade: here's fine revolution, if we had the trick to see 't. Did these bones cost no more the breeding, but to play at loggats with 'em? mine ache to think on 't.

1 Clown *sings.*

A pick-axe, and a spade, a spade,
For and[e] *a shrouding sheet:*
O, a pit of clay for to be made
For such a guest is meet.
[*Throws up another skull.*

HAM. There's another: why might not that be the skull of a lawyer? Where be his quiddits now, his quillets, his cases, his tenures, and his tricks? why does he suffer this rude knave now to knock him about the sconce with a dirty shovel, and will not tell him of his action of battery? Hum! This fellow might be in 's time a great buyer of land, with his statutes, his recognizances, his fines, his double vouchers, his recoveries: is this the fine of his fines, and the recovery of his recoveries, to have his fine pate full of fine dirt? will his vouchers vouch him no more of his purchases, and double ones too, than the length and breadth of a pair of indentures? The very conveyances of his lands will hardly lie in this box; and must the inheritor himself have no more, ha?(3)

HOR. Not a jot more, my lord.

HAM. Is not parchment made of sheep-skins?

HOR. Ay, my lord, and of calf-skins too.

(*) First folio, *It.* (†) First folio, *o're offices.*

a What is he that builds, &c.] Queries of this description formed a favourite item in the homely festivities of our forefathers. One of the earliest collections of them known, is a little book called "Demaundes Joyous," printed in 1511, by Wynkyn de Worde, of the questions in which Steevens remarks, "The innocence may deserve a praise, which is not always due to their delicacy."

b — and unyoke.] A rustic phrase for giving over work, of which the meaning here may be, as Caldecott explains it,—"Unravel this, and your day's work is done, your team you may then unharness."

c *Go, get thee to* Yaughan;] Whether by "Yaughan" a man or place is meant, or whether the word is a corruption, we are not qualified to determine. Mr. Collier once conjectured that it "might be a misunderstood stage-direction for the 1 Clown to *yawn;*"! he now accepts the emendation of his annotator, who reads "to *yon*."

d — a politician,—] A *plotter*, a *schemer* for his own advantage; so Hotspur calls Henry the Fourth,—"this vile *politician;*" and Sir Andrew Ague-cheek, who had scant brains for circumvention, declares he "had as lief be a Brownist as a *politician*."

e For and—] "For and," as Mr. Dyce has shown, answers here to "And eke," as the line reads in a version of this song published in Percy's Relics of Ancient English Poetry,—

"*And eke* a shrowding shete."

HAM. They are sheep, and calves that seek out assurance in that. I will speak to this fellow:—Whose grave 's this, sir?

1 CLO. Mine, sir.—

Sings.] *O, a pit of clay for to be made*
For such a guest is meet.

HAM. I think it be thine, indeed; for thou liest in 't.

1 CLO. You lie out on 't, sir, and therefore it is not yours: for my part, I do not lie in 't, and yet it is mine.

HAM. Thou dost lie in 't, to be in 't, and say 't is thine: 't is for the dead, not for the quick; therefore thou liest.

1 CLO. 'T is a quick lie, sir; 't will away again, from me to you.

HAM. What man dost thou dig it for?

1 CLO. For no man, sir.

HAM. What woman, then?

1 CLO. For none, neither.

HAM. Who is to be buried in 't?

1 CLO. One that was a woman, sir; but, rest her soul, she 's dead.

HAM. How absolute the knave is! we must speak by the card,[a] or equivocation will undo us. By the lord, Horatio, these three years I have taken note of it: the age is grown so picked,[b] that the toe of the peasant comes so near the heel of the* courtier, he galls his kibe.—How long hast thou been a grave-maker?

1 CLO. Of all the days i' the year, I came to 't that day that our last king Hamlet o'ercame Fortinbras.

HAM. How long is that since?

1 CLO. Cannot you tell that? every fool can tell that: it was the very day that young Hamlet was born,—he that was mad, and sent into England.

HAM. Ay, marry, why was he sent into England?

1 CLO. Why, because he was mad: he shall recover his wits there; or if he do not, it 's no great matter there.

HAM. Why?

1 CLO. 'T will not be seen in him; there the men are as mad as he.

HAM. How came he mad?

1 CLO. Very strangely, they say.

HAM. How strangely?

1 CLO. 'Faith, e'en with losing his wits.

HAM. Upon what ground?

1 CLO. Why, here in Denmark: I have been sexton* here, man and boy, thirty years.

HAM. How long will a man lie i' the earth ere he rot?

1 CLO. I' faith, if he be not rotten before he die (as we have many pocky corses now-a-days, that will scarce hold the laying in) he will last you some eight year or nine year: a tanner will last you nine year.

HAM. Why he more than another?

1 CLO. Why, sir, his hide is so tanned with his trade, that he will keep out water a great while; and your water is a sore decayer of your whoreson dead body. Here's a skull now; this skull has lain in the earth three-and-twenty years.[c]

HAM. Whose was it?

1 CLO. A whoreson mad fellow's it was: whose do you think it was?

HAM. Nay, I know not.

1 CLO. A pestilence on him for a mad rogue! 'a poured a flagon of Rhenish on my head once. This same skull, sir, this same skull, sir, was Yorick's skull, the king's jester.

HAM. This?

1 CLO. E'en that.

HAM. Let me see. [*Takes the skull.*]—Alas, poor Yorick!—I knew him, Horatio; a fellow of infinite jest, of most excellent fancy: he hath borne me on his back a thousand times; and now, how abhorred in my imagination it is![d] my gorge rises at it. Here hung those lips that I have kissed I know not how oft.—Where be your gibes now? your gambols? your songs? your flashes of merriment, that were wont to set the table on a roar? Not† one now, to mock your own grinning?‡ quite chap-fallen? Now get you to my lady's chamber, and tell her, let her paint an inch thick, to this favour she must come; make her laugh at that.—Prythee, Horatio, tell me one thing.

HOR. What 's that, my lord?

HAM. Dost thou think Alexander looked o' this fashion i' the earth?

HOR. E'en so.

HAM. And smelt so?—pah!

[*Puts down the skull.*

HOR. E'en so, my lord.

HAM. To what base uses we may return, Horatio! Why may not imagination trace the noble dust of Alexander, till he find it stopping a bung-hole?

(*) First folio, *heeles of our*.

[a] We must speak by the card.] *To speak by the card* is explained to be a metaphor from the seaman's card or chart; it is rather an allusion to the *card* and *calendar* of etiquette, or *book of manners*, of which more than one were published during Shakespeare's age.

[b] —*so* picked,—] That is, so *refined*, so *fastidious*, so *precise*.

[c] —three-and-twenty years.] The quarto 1603 reads,—

"Here's a scull hath bin here this *dozen yeare*,
Let me see, I ever since our last king *Hamlet*
Slew *Fortenbrasse* in combat."

(*) First folio, *sixteene*. (†) First folio, *No*. (‡) First folio, *Ieering*.

[d] —and now how abhorred in my imagination it is!] The folio has,—"And how abhorred my Imagination is," &c.

HOR. 'T were to consider too curiously, to consider so.

HAM. No, faith, not a jot; but to follow him thither with modesty enough, and likelihood to lead it: as thus;—Alexander died, Alexander was buried, Alexander returneth into dust; the dust is earth; of earth we make loam; and why of that loam, whereto he was converted, might they not stop a beer-barrel?

Imperious[a] Cæsar, dead and turn'd to clay,
Might stop a hole to keep the wind away:
O, that that earth, which kept the world in awe,
Should patch a wall to expel the winter's flaw!—
But soft! but soft! aside:—here comes the king,

[a] Imperious *Cæsar*,—] So the quartos; the folio substituted *Imperiall*, "not knowing," perhaps, as Malone observes, "that *imperious* was used in the same sense."

Enter Priests, &c., *in procession; the corpse of* OPHELIA, LAERTES *and* Mourners *following;* KING, QUEEN, *their* Trains, *&c.*

The queen, the courtiers! Who is that they follow?
And with such maimed rites! This doth betoken,
The corse they follow did with desperate hand
Fordo its[a] own life: 't was of some estate:
Couch we awhile, and mark.
[*Retiring with* HORATIO.

LAER. What ceremony else?

HAM. That is Laertes,
A very noble youth: mark.

LAER. What ceremony else?

1 PRIEST. Her obsequies have been as far enlarg'd
As we have warrantise: her death was doubtful;
And, but that great command o'ersways the order,
She should in ground unsanctified have lodg'd
Till the last trumpet; for charitable prayer,
Shards, flints, and pebbles, should be thrown on her:
Yet here she is allow'd her virgin crants,[b]
Her maiden strewments, and the bringing home
Of bell and burial.

LAER. Must there no more be done?

1 PRIEST. *No more be done!*
We should profane the service of the dead,
To sing* a requiem, and such rest to her,
As to peace-parted souls.

LAER. Lay her i' the earth;—
And from her fair and unpolluted flesh
May violets spring!—I tell thee, churlish priest,
A minist'ring angel shall my sister be,
When thou liest howling.

HAM. What, the fair Ophelia!

QUEEN. Sweets to the sweet: farewell!
[*Scattering flowers.*
I hop'd thou shouldst have been my Hamlet's wife;
I thought thy bride-bed to have deck'd, sweet maid,
And not t' have strew'd thy grave.

LAER. O, treble woe†
Fall ten times treble on that cursed head,
Whose wicked deed thy most ingenious sense
Depriv'd thee of!—Hold off the earth a while,
Till I have caught her once more in mine arms:
[*Leaps into the grave.*

---

a — its *own life*:] So the undated quarto; the other early editions have, "*it* own life."

b — crants,—] "Crants" are crowns = *coronæ*, or garlands. The folio reads, "*Rites.*"

(*) First folio, *sage.* (†) First folio, *Oh terrible woer.*

Now pile your dust upon the quick and dead,
Till of this flat a mountain you have made,
To o'er-top old Pelion, or the skyish head
Of blue Olympus.

HAM. [*Advancing.*] What is he whose grief*
Bears such an emphasis? whose phrase of sorrow
Cónjures the wand'ring stars, and makes them stand
Like wonder-wounded hearers? This is I,
Hamlet the Dane! [*Leaps into the grave.*

LAER. The devil take thy soul! [*Grappling with him.*

HAM. Thou pray'st not well.
I pr'ythee, take thy fingers from my throat;
For † though I am not splenitive and rash,
Yet have I something in me dangerous,
Which let thy wiseness fear: away thy hand!

KING. Pluck them asunder!

QUEEN. Hamlet, Hamlet!

HOR.‡ Good my lord, be quiet.
[*The* Attendants *part them, and they come out of the grave.*

HAM. Why, I will fight with him upon this theme,
Until my eyelids will no longer wag.

QUEEN. O, my son! what theme?

HAM. I lov'd Ophelia; forty thousand brothers
Could not, with all their quantity of love,
Make up my sum.—What wilt thou do for her?

KING. O, he is mad, Laertes.

QUEEN. For love of God, forbear him.

HAM. Come, show me what thou 'lt do:
Woo't weep? woo't fight? woo't fast?§ woo't tear thyself?
Woo't drink up eisel?[a] eat a crocodile?
I 'll do 't.—Dost thou come here to whine?
To outface me with leaping in her grave?
Be buried quick with her, and so will I;
And, if thou prate of mountains, let them throw
Millions of acres on us, till our ground,
Singeing his pate against the burning zone,
Make Ossa like a wart! Nay, an thou 'lt mouth,
I 'll rant as well as thou.

QUEEN. This is mere madness,
And thus a while the fit will work on him;
Anon, as patient as the female dove,
When that her golden couplets are disclos'd,
His silence will sit drooping.[b]

HAM. Hear you, sir;
What is the reason that you use me thus?
I lov'd you ever: but it is no matter;
Let Hercules himself do what he may,
The cat will mew, and dog will have his day. [*Exit.*

KING. I pray you, good Horatio, wait upon him.— [*Exit* HORATIO.
Strengthen your patience in our last night's speech; [*To* LAERTES.
We 'll put the matter to the present push.—
Good Gertrude, set some watch over your son.— [*Exit* QUEEN.
This grave shall have a living monument:
An hour of quiet shortly shall we see;
Till then, in patience our proceeding be. [*Exeunt.*

SCENE II.—*A Hall in the Castle.*

Enter HAMLET *and* HORATIO.

HAM. So much for this, sir: now let me see the other;—
You do remember all the circumstance?

HOR. Remember it, my lord?

HAM. Sir, in my heart there was a kind of fighting,
That would not let me sleep: methought I lay
Worse than the mutines in the bilboes.[c] Rashly,
And prais'd* be rashness for it,[d]—let us know,
Our indiscretion sometimes serves us well,
When our dear plots do pall; and that should teach us,

(*) First folio, *griefes*.
(†) First folio, *Sir*.
(‡) First folio, *Gen*.
(§) First folio omits, *woo't fast?*

(*) First folio, *praise*.

a — *drink up* eisel?] The question whether Hamlet speaks here of a river (the Yssell, Issell, or Isel, has been suggested), or proposes the more practical exploit of drinking some nauseous potion, *eisel* of old being used for *wormwood* and for *vinegar*, has been fiercely disputed. Those who believe that *eisel* means a river, lay much stress on the addition, *up;* but Gifford, in a note on the phrase, "Kills them all *up*," ("Every Man in his Humour," Act IV. Sc. 5,) has satisfactorily disposed of this plea:—"— *off, out*, and *up*, are continually used by the purest and most excellent of our old writers after verbs of destroying, consuming, eating, drinking, &c.: to us, who are less conversant with the power of language, they appear, indeed, somewhat like expletives; but they undoubtedly contributed something to the force, and something to the roundness of the sentence. There is much wretched criticism on a similar expression in Shakespeare, 'Woo't *drink up* eisel?' Theobald gives the sense of the passage in a clumsy note; Hanmer, who had more taste than judgment, and more judgment than knowledge, corrupts the language as usual [he reads, '*Wilt* drink up *Nile?*']; Steevens gaily perverts the sense; and Malone, with great effort, brings the reader back to the meaning which poor Theobald had long before excogitated."

b His silence will sit drooping.] In the folio this speech is assigned to the King!

c — bilboes.] An instrument of torture, consisting of a bar of iron with fetters attached, used formerly for the punishment of sailors, and supposed to have been named from *Bilboa*, in Spain.

d And prais'd be rashness for it,—] We think, with Tyrwhitt, that *Rashly* should be joined in construction with—*in the dark grop'd I to find out them*, and the passage therefore distributed and read as follows:—

"—— Rashly
(And prais'd be rashness, for it lets us know,
Our indiscretion sometimes serves us well,
When our dear plots do pall; and that should teach us,
There's a divinity that shapes our ends,
Rough-hew them how we will;—
HOR. That is most certain—)
HAM. Up from my cabin," &c.

There's a divinity that shapes our ends,
Rough-hew[a] them how we will,—
HOR. That is most certain.
HAM. Up from my cabin,
My sea-gown scarf'd about me, in the dark
Grop'd I to find out them: had my desire;
Finger'd their packet; and, in fine, withdrew
To mine own room again: making so bold,
My fears forgetting manners, to unseal
Their grand commission; where I found, Horatio,—
O, royal knavery!—an exact command,
Larded with many several sorts of reason,
Importing Denmark's health, and England's too,
With, ho! such bugs and goblins in my life,—[b]
That, on the supervise, no leisure bated,
No, not to stay the grinding of the axe,
My head should be struck off.
HOR. Is 't possible?
HAM. Here 's the commission; read it at more leisure.
But wilt thou hear me how I did proceed?
HOR. Ay, beseech you.
HAM. Being thus be-netted round with villainies,—*
Ere I could make a prologue to my brains,
They had begun the play,—I sat me down;
Devis'd a new commission; wrote it fair:—
I once did hold it, as our statists do,
A baseness to write fair, and labour'd much
How to forget that learning; but, sir, now
It did me yeoman's service—wilt thou know
The effects of what I wrote?
HOR. Ay, good my lord.
HAM. An earnest conjuration from the king,—
As England was his faithful tributary;
As love between them as the palm should flourish;
As peace should still her wheaten garland wear,
And stand a comma[c] 'tween their amities;
And many such like *as's* of great charge,—
That on the view and know of these contents,
Without debatement further, more or less,
He should the bearers put to sudden death,
Not shriving-time allow'd.
HOR. How was this seal'd?
HAM. Why, even in that was heaven ordinant;†
I had my father's signet in my purse,
Which was the model of that Danish seal:
Folded the writ up in form of the other;
Subscrib'd it; gave 't the impression; plac'd it safely,
The changeling never known. Now, the next day
Was our sea-fight; and what to this was sequent*
Thou know'st already.
HOR. So Guildenstern and Rosencrantz go to 't.
HAM. Why, man, they did make love to this employment:
They are not near my conscience; their defeat†
Does by their own insinuation grow:
'Tis dangerous when the baser nature comes
Between the pass and fell-incensed points
Of mighty opposites.
HOR. Why, what a king is this!
HAM. Does it not, think'st thee, stand me now upon—[d]
He that hath kill'd my king, and whor'd my mother;
Popp'd in between the election and my hopes;
Thrown out his angle for my proper life,
And with such cozenage—is 't not perfect conscience,
To quit him with this arm? and is 't not to be damn'd,
To let this canker of our nature come
In further evil?
HOR. It must be shortly known to him from England,
What is the issue of the business there.
HAM. It will be short: the interim is mine;
And a man's life 's no more than to say, *One*.
But I am very sorry, good Horatio,
That to Laertes I forgot myself;
For by the image of my cause I see
The portraiture of his: I'll court[e] his favours:
But, sure, the bravery of his grief did put me
Into a towering passion.
HOR. Peace! who comes here?

Enter OSRIC.

OSR. Your lordship is right welcome back to Denmark.
HAM. I humbly thank you, sir.—Dost know this water-fly?
HOR. No, my good lord.

(*) Old text, *villaines*. (†) First folio, *ordinate*.

(*) First folio, *sement*. (†) First folio, *debate*.

[a] Rough-hew—] Farmer's assertion that these words were merely technical, and referred to the making *skewers*, has never, we believe, been contradicted; a striking proof, if so, how much the commentators on Shakespeare have yet to learn from our early literature. To *rough-hew* meant to plan or scheme, or do anything in the rough. Thus Florio interprets "Abbozzare," *to rough-hew* or *cast any first draught, to bungle up ill-favouredly:* and Baret, in his *Alvearie*, says, "To cut out grossely: to *hew rough*." "It is *rough hewed*, or squared out, or it is begun."

[b] — such bugs and goblins in my life,—] "With *such causes of error*, rising from my character and designs."—JOHNSON.

[c] *And stand a* comma *'tween their amities;*] Johnson thinks this not incapable of explanation,—"The *comma* is the note of *connection* and continuity of sentences; the *period* is the note of abruption and disjunction." To us it is much easier to believe that "comma" is a typographical slip than that Shakespeare should have chosen that point as a mark of *connection;* at the same time, having no faith in the substitution, *cement*, by Hanmer, or *commere*, by Warburton, or *co-mere* (a *boundary-stone*), by Singer, we leave the text as it stands in the old copies, simply suggesting the possibility of "comma" being a misprint for *co-mate*.

[d] Does it not, think'st thee, stand me now upon—] Equipollent to, Is it not, think you, incumbent on me?

[e] *I'll* court *his favours:*] A correction due to Rowe; the folio, in which alone the speech is found, reading, "Ile *count* his favours," &c.

HAM. Thy state is the more gracious; for 't is a vice to know him. He hath much land, and fertile; let a beast be lord of beasts, and his crib shall stand at the king's mess. 'T is a chough; but, as I say,* spacious in the possession of dirt.

OSR. Sweet lord, if your lordship† were at leisure, I should impart a thing to you from his majesty.

HAM. I will receive it with all diligence of spirit. Put your bonnet to his right use; 't is for the head.

OSR. I thank your lordship, 't is very hot.

HAM. No, believe me, 't is very cold; the wind is northerly.

OSR. It is indifferent cold, my lord, indeed.

HAM. Methinks it is very sultry and hot for my complexion.

OSR. Exceedingly, my lord; it is very sultry,—as 't were,—I cannot tell how.—But, my lord, his majesty bade me signify to you, that he has laid a great wager on your head: sir, this is the matter.

HAM. I beseech you, remember—

[HAMLET *moves him to put on his hat.*

OSR. Nay, in good faith; for mine ease, in good faith. Sir, here is newly come to court, Laertes: believe me, an absolute gentleman, full of most excellent differences, of very soft society and great showing: indeed, to speak feelingly of him, he is the card or calendar of gentry, for you shall find in him the continent of what part a gentleman would see.

HAM. Sir, his definement suffers no perdition in you;—though, I know, to divide him inventorially would dizzy the arithmetic of memory; and yet but yaw[a] neither, in respect of his quick sail. But, in the verity of extolment, I take him to be a soul of great article; and his infusion of such dearth and rareness, as, to make true diction of him, his semblable is his mirror; and who else would trace him, his umbrage, nothing more.

OSR. Your lordship speaks most infallibly of him.

HAM. The concernancy, sir?—why do we wrap the gentleman in our more rawer breath?

OSR. Sir?

HOR. Is 't not possible to understand in another[b] tongue? You will do 't, sir, really.

HAM. What imports the nomination of this gentleman?

OSR. Of Laertes?

HOR. His purse is empty already; all's golden words are spent.

HAM. Of him, sir.

OSR. I know you are not ignorant—

HAM. I would you did, sir; yet, in faith, if you did, it would not much approve me.—Well, sir.[c]

OSR. You are not ignorant of what excellence Laertes is—

HAM. I dare not confess that, lest I should compare with him in excellence; but to know a man well were to know himself.

OSR. I mean, sir, for his weapon; but in the imputation laid on him by them, in his meed[d] he 's unfellowed.[e]

HAM. What 's his weapon?

OSR. Rapier and dagger.

HAM. That 's two of his weapons: but, well.

OSR. The king, sir, hath waged with him six Barbary horses: against the which he has* imponed, as I take it, six French rapiers and poniards, with their assigns, as girdle, hangers, and† so: three of the carriages, in faith, are very dear to fancy, very responsive to the hilts, most delicate carriages, and of very liberal conceit.

HAM. What call you the carriages?

HOR. I knew you must be edified by the margent ere you had done.[f]

OSR. The carriages, sir, are the hangers.

HAM. The phrase would be more german[g] to the matter, if we could carry cannon by our sides: I would it might be hangers till then. But, on: six Barbary horses against six French swords, their assigns, and three liberal-conceited carriages: that 's the French bet against the Danish. Why is this *imponed*, as you call it?

OSR. The king, sir, hath laid, that in a dozen passes between you and him, he shall not exceed you three hits; he hath laid on‡ twelve for nine; and it§ would come to immediate trial, if your lordship would vouchsafe the answer.

HAM. How if I answer No?

OSR. I mean, my lord, the opposition of your person in trial.

HAM. Sir, I will walk here in the hall; if it please his majesty,—'t is the breathing time of day with me,—let the foils be brought; the gentleman willing, and the king hold his purpose, I will win

(*) First folio, *saw*. (†) First folio, *friendship*.

(*) First folio omits, *has*. (†) First folio, *or*.
(‡) First folio, *He hath one*. (§) First folio, *that*.

[a] — and yet but yaw neither, in respect of his quick sail.] This is not in the folio nor in the quarto of 1603. In the other quartos, except that of 1604, we have "*raw*" for "yaw," though the latter is shown by the context to be unquestionably the poet's word. To *yaw* is to stagger and vacillate, as a ship sometimes does, instead of going due on. Mr. Dyce, of course, adopts "yaw," but conceiving "yet," often written "yt," to be a misprint for *it*, he reads "— and *it*, but yaw neither," &c. which we must admit our inability to understand. "*Yet*" certainly is suspicious, but the word displaced we have always thought was *wit*, not *it*, and the drift of Hamlet's jargon to be this:—his qualifications are so numerous, and so far surpass all ordinary reckoning, that memory would grow giddy in cataloguing, and *wit* be distanced in attempting to keep pace with them.

[b] — *in* another *tongue?*] Should we not read with Johnson, "in a *mother* tongue?" or, "*in's mother* tongue?"

[c] Well, sir.] The whole of the dialogue beginning, "—Sir, here is newly come to court," &c. down to the above words, inclusive, is omitted in the folio.

[d] — meed—] *Merit, excellence.*

[e] — he's unfellowed.] This and the preceding speech are not in the folio.

[f] I knew you must be edified, &c.] Omitted in the folio.

[g] — more german—] More akin.

for him if I can; if not, I'll gain nothing but my shame and the odd hits.

OSR. Shall I re-deliver you e'en so?

HAM. To this effect, sir; after what flourish your nature will.

OSR. I commend my duty to your lordship.

HAM. Yours, yours. [*Exit* OSRIC.] He does well to commend it himself; there are no tongues else for 's turn.*

HOR. This lapwing runs away with the shell on his head.

HAM. He did comply[a] with his dug, before he sucked it. Thus has† he (and many‡ more of the same bevy, that, I know, the drossy age dotes on) only got the tune of the time, and outward habit of encounter; a kind of yesty collection, which carries them through and through the most fanned and winnowed opinions;[b] and do but blow them to their trials, the bubbles are out.

Enter a Lord.

LORD. My lord, his majesty commended him to you by young Osric, who brings back to him, that you attend him in the hall: he sends to know if your pleasure hold to play with Laertes, or that you will take longer time.

HAM. I am constant to my purposes; they follow the king's pleasure: if his fitness speaks, mine is ready, now or whensoever, provided I be so able as now.

LORD. The king, and queen, and all, are coming down.

HAM. In happy time.

LORD. The queen desires you to use some gentle entertainment to Laertes before you fall to play.

HAM. She well instructs me. [*Exit* Lord.[c]

HOR. You will lose this wager, my lord.

HAM. I do not think so; since he went into France, I have been in continual practice; I shall win at the odds. But thou wouldst not think how ill all 's§ here about my heart: but it is no matter.

HOR. Nay, good my lord,—

HAM. It is but foolery; but it is such a kind of gain-giving, as would perhaps trouble a woman.

HOR. If your mind dislike anything, obey it:|| I will forestal their repair hither, and say you are not fit.

HAM. Not a whit, we defy augury; there 's a special providence in the fall of a sparrow. If it be now, 'tis not to come: if it be not to come, it will be now; if it be not now, yet it will come: the readiness is all: since no man has aught of what he leaves, what is't to leave betimes?

Enter KING, QUEEN, LAERTES, Lords, OSRIC, *and* Attendants, *with foils, &c.*

KING. [*Taking* LAERTES *by the hand.*] Come, Hamlet, come, and take this hand from me.

HAM. [*To* LAERTES.] Give me your pardon, sir: I 've done you wrong;
But pardon 't, as you are a gentleman.
This presence knows, and you must needs have heard,
How I am punish'd with a* sore distraction.
What I have done,
That might your nature, honour, and exception,
Roughly awake, I here proclaim was madness.
Was't Hamlet wrong'd Laertes? Never, Hamlet:
If Hamlet from himself be ta'en away,
And when he 's not himself does wrong Laertes,
Then Hamlet does it not, Hamlet denies it.
Who does it then? His madness; if 't be so,
Hamlet is of the faction that is wrong'd;
His madness is poor Hamlet's enemy.
Sir, in this audience,
Let my disclaiming from a purpos'd evil
Free me so far in your most generous thoughts,
That I have shot mine arrow o'er the house,
And hurt my brother.†

LAER. I am satisfied in nature,
Whose motive, in this case, should stir me most
To my revenge: but in my terms of honour
I stand aloof; and will no reconcilement,
Till by some elder masters, of known honour,
I have a voice and precedent of peace,
To keep my name ungor'd.‡ But till that time,
I do receive your offer'd love like love,
And will not wrong it.

HAM. I do embrace it freely;
And will this brother's wager frankly play.—
Give us the foils.—Come on.

LAER. Come, one for me.

HAM. I'll be your foil, Laertes; in mine ignorance
Your skill shall, like a star i' the darkest night,
Stick fiery off indeed.

(*) First folio, *tongue*. (†) First folio, *had*.
(‡) First folio, *mine*. (§) First folio, *how all heere*.
(||) First folio omits, *it*.

[a] *He did comply with his dug,*—] Was ceremonious, or played the courtier with his dug.

[b] — *the most* fanned *and winnowed opinions;*] A lection proposed by Warburton; the quartos having—"Most *prophane* and *trennowed* [and *trennowned*] opinions;" and the folio, "most *fond* and winnowed opinions," &c.

[c] *Exit* Lord.] From the entrance of this character to his exit, the text is not found in the folio.

(*) First folio omits, *a*. (†) First folio, *Mother*.
(‡) First folio, *ungorg'd*.

LAER. You mock me, sir.

HAM. No, by this hand.

KING. Give them the foils, young Osric.—Cousin Hamlet,
You know the wager?

HAM. Very well, my lord;
Your grace hath laid the odds o' the weaker side.

KING. I do not fear it: I have seen you both:
But since he 's better'd, we have therefore odds.

LAER. This is too heavy, let me see another.

HAM. This likes me well. These foils have all a length?

OSR. Ay, my good lord.
[*They prepare to play.*

KING. Set me the stoups of wine upon that table.—
If Hamlet give the first or second hit,
Or quit in answer of the third exchange,
Let all the battlements their ordnance fire;
The king shall drink to Hamlet's better breath;
And in the cup an union[a] shall he throw,
Richer than that which four successive kings
In Denmark's crown have worn. Give me the cups;
And let the kettle to the trumpet speak,
The trumpet to the cannoneer without,
The cannons to the heavens, the heavens to earth,
Now the king drinks to Hamlet.—Come, begin;—
And you, the judges, bear a wary eye.

HAM. Come on, sir.

LAER. Come on, sir. [*They play.*

HAM. One.

LAER. No.

HAM. Judgment.

OSR. A hit, a very palpable hit.

LAER. Well;—again.

KING. Stay, give me drink.—Hamlet, this pearl is thine;
Here's to thy health.
[*Trumpets sound; and cannon shot off without.*
Give him the cup.

HAM. I'll play this bout first; set it* by awhile.—
Come.—Another hit; what say you? [*They play.*

LAER. A touch, a touch, I do confess.

KING. Our son shall win.

QUEEN. He's fat, and scant of breath.[b]—
Here, Hamlet, take my napkin, rub thy brows:[c]
The queen carouses to thy fortune, Hamlet.

HAM. Good, madam.

KING. Gertrude, do not drink.

QUEEN. I will, my lord; I pray you, pardon me.

KING. [*Aside.*] It is the poison'd cup! it is too late!

HAM. I dare not drink yet, madam; by and by.

QUEEN. Come, let me wipe thy face.

LAER. My lord, I'll hit him now.

KING. I do not think 't.

LAER. [*Aside.*] And yet 't is almost 'gainst my conscience.

HAM. Come, for the third; Laertes, you but dally;
I pray you, pass with your best violence;
I am afeard you make a wanton of me.

LAER. Say you so? come on. [*They play.*

OSR. Nothing, neither way.

LAER. Have at you now!

[LAERTES *wounds* HAMLET; *then, in scuffling, they change rapiers, and* HAMLET *wounds* LAERTES.

KING. Part them! they are incens'd.

HAM. Nay, come again. [*The* QUEEN *falls.*

OSR. Look to the queen there.—Ho![d]

HOR. They bleed on both sides!—How is it, my lord?

OSR. How is 't, Laertes?

LAER. Why, as a woodcock to mine own* springe, Osric;
I am justly kill'd with mine own treachery.

HAM. How does the queen?

KING. She swoons to see them bleed.

QUEEN. No, no, the drink, the drink!—O, my dear Hamlet!—
The drink, the drink!—I am poison'd! [*Dies.*

HAM. O, villainy!—Ho! let the door be lock'd:
Treachery! seek it out. [LAERTES *falls.*

LAER. It is here, Hamlet: Hamlet, thou art slain;
No medicine in the world can do thee good,
In thee there is not half an hour of life;
The treacherous instrument is in thy hand,
Unbated[e] and envenom'd: the foul practice
Hath turn'd itself on me; lo, here I lie,
Never to rise again! thy mother 's poison'd;—
I can no more:—the king, the king's to blame.

HAM. The point—envenom'd too!—[f]
Then, venom, to thy work. [*Stabs the* KING.

(*) First folio omits, *it*.

(*) First folio omits, *own*.

a — *an* union—] By an *union* was meant a pearl of faultless beauty; an "*orient* pearl;" ("Antony and Cleopatra," Act I. Sc. 5;) *i.e.* a pearl clear, white, and spotless.

b — He's fat, and scant of breath.—] Does the Queen refer to Hamlet or Laertes?

c Here, Hamlet, &c.] In the folio, "Heere's a Napkin, rub thy browes."

d Look to the queen there.—Ho!] The exclamation "Ho!" meaning *stop!* should perhaps be addressed to the combatants, and not, as it is always printed, to those who are to raise the Queen.

e Unbated—] See note (d), p. 385.

f The point—envenom'd too!] Why should this line invariably be printed—

"The point envenom'd too!"

as if Hamlet supposed the hilt was poison'd? Recurring to what Laertes had just said, "Unbated and envenom'd," he examines the foil, and finding the button gone, exclaims, "The point—," and then, without finishing the sentence,—"unblunted"—hurries on to—"envenom'd too!" &c. This is so obviously the sense, that one marvels it should ever have been mistaken.

OSR. *and* LORDS. Treason! treason!
KING. O, yet defend me, friends; I am but hurt.
HAM. Here, thou incestuous, murderous, damned Dane,
Drink off this potion:—is thy union here?
Follow my mother. [KING *dies.*
LAER. He is justly serv'd;
It is a poison temper'd by himself.—
Exchange forgiveness with me, noble Hamlet:
Mine and my father's death come not upon thee,
Nor thine on me! [*Dies.*
HAM. Heaven make thee free of it! I follow thee.—
I am dead, Horatio.—Wretched queen, adieu!—
You that look pale and tremble at this chance,
That are but mutes or audience to this act,
Had I but time, (as this fell sergeant, death,
Is strict in his arrest) O, I could tell you,—
But let it be.—Horatio, I am dead;
Thou liv'st; report me and my cause* aright
To the unsatisfied.
HOR. Never believe it.
I am more an antique Roman than a Dane,
Here's yet some liquor left.
HAM. As thou'rt a man,
Give me the cup; let go; by heaven I'll have 't!—
O, good Horatio, what a wounded name,
Things standing thus unknown, shall live behind me![a]
If thou didst ever hold me in thy heart,
Absent thee from felicity awhile,
And in this harsh world draw thy breath in pain,
To tell my story.
[*March afar off, and shot*† *without.*
What warlike noise is this?
OSR. Young Fortinbras, with conquest come from Poland,
To the ambassadors of England gives
This warlike volley.
HAM. O, I die, Horatio;
The potent poison quite o'er-crows my spirit;
I cannot live to hear the news from England;
But I do prophesy the election lights
On Fortinbras; he has my dying voice;
So tell him, with the occurrents, more and less,
Which have solicited.—The rest is silence.[b] [*Dies.*
HOR. Now cracks‡ a noble heart. Good night, sweet prince;
And flights of angels sing thee to thy rest!—
Why does the drum come hither? [*March without.*

(*) First folio, *causes*. (†) First folio, *shout*. (‡) First folio, *cracke*.

a — shall live behind me!] Compare ("Much Ado About Nothing," Act III. Sc. 1), "No lory *lives behind* the back of such."

Enter FORTINBRAS, *the* English Ambassadors, *and others.*

FORT. Where is this sight?
HOR. What is it ye would see?
If aught of woe or wonder, cease your search.
FORT. This* quarry cries on havoc.—O, proud death,
What feast is toward in thine eternal cell,
That thou so many princes at a shot,†
So bloodily hast struck?
1 AMB. The sight is dismal;
And our affairs from England come too late:
The ears are senseless that should give us hearing:
To tell him his commandment is fulfill'd,
That Rosencrantz and Guildenstern are dead,
Where should we have our thanks?
HOR. Not from his mouth,
Had it the ability of life to thank you:
He never gave commandment for their death.
But since, so jump upon this bloody question,
You from the Polack wars, and you from England,
Are here arriv'd, give order that these bodies
High on a stage be placed to the view;
And let me speak, to the yet unknowing world,
How these things came about: so shall you hear
Of carnal, bloody, and unnatural acts;
Of accidental judgments, casual slaughters;
Of deaths put on by cunning and forc'd cause;
And, in this upshot, purposes mistook
Fall'n on the inventors' heads: all this can I
Truly deliver.
FORT. Let us haste to hear it,
And call the noblest to the audience.
For me, with sorrow I embrace my fortune;
I have some rights of memory in this kingdom,
Which now‡ to claim my vantage doth invite me.
HOR. Of that I shall have also§ cause to speak,
And from his mouth whose voice will draw on more;
But let this same be presently perform'd,
E'en while men's minds are wild; lest more mischance,
On plots and errors, happen.
FORT. Let four captains
Bear Hamlet, like a soldier, to the stage;
For he was likely, had he been put on,
To have prov'd most royally: and, for his passage,
The soldier's music, and the rites of war,
Speak loudly for him.—
Take up the bodies:||—such a sight as this
Becomes the field, but here shows much amiss.—
Go, bid the soldiers shoot. [*A dead March.*
[*Exeunt bearing off the bodies; after which a peal of ordnance is shot off.*

(*) First folio, *His*. (†) First folio, *shoote*. (‡) First folio, *are*. (§) First folio, *alwayes*. (||) First folio, *body*.

b The rest is silence.] The folio adds, "O, o, o, o."

ILLUSTRATIVE COMMENTS.

ACT I.

(1) Scene I.—

As stars with trains of fire and dews of blood,
Disasters in the sun; and the moist star,
Upon whose influence Neptune's empire stands,
Was sick almost to dooms-day with eclipse:]

Some depravation is manifest in the first two lines, and Rowe, to connect them with what precedes, printed,—

" Stars *shone* with trains of fire, dews of blood *fall*,
Disasters *veil'd* the sun—"

Malone, with more plausibility and less violence, proposed to change "As stars" to *Astres*, observing, "The disagreeable recurrence of the word *stars* in the second line induces me to believe that *As stars*, in that which precedes, is a corruption. Perhaps Shakespeare wrote:—

" *Astres* with trains of fire,—
—— and dews of blood
Disasterous dimm'd the sun."

Following up this hint, an ingenious correspondent (A.E.B.) of *Notes and Queries*, Vol. V. No. 117, would read,—

" *Asters* with trains of fire and dews of blood,
Disasters in the sun;"—

by *disasters* understanding *spots* or *blotches*. *Astres* or *asters* is an acceptable conjecture, but we conceive the cardinal error lies in "Disasters," which conceals some verb importing the obscuration of the sun; for example,—

" Asters with trains of fire and dews of blood
Distempered the sun;"

or,—

" *Discoloured* the sun."

(2) Scene I.—

The cock, that is the trumpet to the morn,
Doth with his lofty and shrill-sounding throat
Awake the god of day; and, at his warning,
Whether in sea or fire, in earth or air,
The extravagant and erring spirit hies
To his confine: * * * *
* * * * * * *
* * *It faded on the crowing of the cock.*]

Farmer pointed attention to a hymn, *ad Gallicinium*, in Prudentius, which appositely illustrates these beautiful lines:—

" Ferunt, vagantes Dæmonas,
Lætos tenebris Noctium,
Gallo canente exterritos
Sparsim timere, et cedere.—
Hoc esse signum præscii
Norunt repromissæ Spei,
Qua nos soporis liberi
Speramus adventum Dei."

And Douce refers to another hymn formerly used in the Salisbury service, which is still more relevant:—

" Preco diei jam sonat,
Noctis profundæ pervigil;
Nocturna lux viantibus,
A nocte noctem segregans.
Hoc excitatus Lucifer,
Solvit polum caligine;
Hoc omnis errorum chorus
Viam nocendi deserit.
Gallo canente spes redit," &c.

The superstition of a phantom disappearing on the crowing of a cock, Steevens has shown to be very ancient by a passage (Vit. Apol. iv. 16) where "Philostratus giving an account of the apparition of Achilles' shade to Apollonius Tyaneus, says that it vanished with a glimmer as soon as the cock crowed."

(3) Scene II.—*And bow them to your gracious leave and pardon.*] As an instance of the minute attention with which the finished play was elaborated from the early sketch, it may be noteworthy, that in the quarto of 1603, the motive of Laertes' visit to the court is said to be desire to attend the late king's funeral,—

" *King.* And now *Laertes* what's the newes with you?
You said you had a sute what is't *Laertes?*
Lea. My gratious Lord, your favorable licence,
Now that the funerall rites are all performed,
I may have leave to go againe to *France*,
For though the favour of your grace might stay mee,
Yet something is there whispers in my hart,
Which makes my minde and spirits bend all for France."

But it evidently occurred to Shakespeare that the acknowledgment of such an object was as little consistent with the character of Laertes as it would be palatable to the living monarch, and, accordingly, in the augmented piece the reason given by Laertes for his coming is more courtier-like,—

" To show my duty in your coronation."

(4) Scene II.—*Come away.*] The dialogue between the King, the Queen, and Hamlet, in this scene was much expanded and improved after the first draft: in the new-found quarto it runs thus meagrely,—

" *King.* And now princely Sonne *Hamlet*,
What meanes these sad and melancholy moodes?
For your intent going to *Wittenberg*,
Wee hold it most unmeet and unconvenient,
Being the Joy and halfe heart of your Mother.
Therefore let mee intreat you stay in Court,
All Denmarkes hope our coosin and dearest Sonne.

Ham. My lord, ti's not the sable sute I weare:
No nor the teares that still stand in my eyes,
Nor the distracted haviour in the visage,
Nor all together mixt with outward semblance,
Is equall to the sorrow of my heart,
Him have I lost I must of force forgoe,
These but the ornaments and sutes of woe.

King. This shewes a loving care in you, Sonne *Hamlet*,
But you must thinke your father lost a father,
That father dead, lost his, and so shall be until the
Generall ending. Therefore cease laments,
It is a fault gainst heaven, fault gainst the dead,
A fault gainst nature, and in reasons
Common course most certaine,
None lives on earth, but hee is borne to die.

Que. Let not thy Mother loose her praiers *Hamlet*,
Stay here with us, go not to *Wittenberg*.

Ham. I shall in all my best obey you Madam.

King. Spoke like a kinde and a most loving Sonne,
And there's no health the King shall drinke to day,
But the great Canon to the clowdes shall tell
The rowse the King shall drinke unto Prince *Hamlet*."

(5) Scene II.—

—— the funeral bak'd meats
Did coldly furnish forth the marriage tables.]

"The practice of making entertainments at funerals which prevailed in this and other countries, and which is not even at present quite disused in some of the northern counties of England, was certainly borrowed from the *cœna feralis* of the Romans, alluded to in Juvenal's fifth satire, and in the laws of the twelve tables. It consisted of an offering of a small plate of milk, honey, wine, flowers, &c. to the ghost of the deceased. In the instances of heroes and other great characters, the same custom appears to have prevailed among the Greeks. With us the appetites of the living are consulted on this occasion. In the north this feast is called an *arval* or arvil-supper; and the loaves that are sometimes distributed among the poor, *arval-bread*."—Douce.

(6) Scene II.—

Would I had met my dearest foe in heaven
Ere ever I had seen that day.]

On this use of *dear*, some examples of which will be found at p. 449, Vol. I., Caldecott has a good note:—

"Throughout Shakespeare and all the poets of his and a much later day, we find this epithet applied to that person or thing, which, for or against us, excites the liveliest and strongest interest. It is used variously, indefinitely and metaphorically to express the warmest feelings of the soul; its nearest, most intimate, home and heartfelt emotions: and here no doubt, though, as everywhere else, more directly interpreted signifying 'veriest, extremest,' must by consequence and figuratively import 'bitterest, deadliest, most mortal.' As extremes are said in a certain sense to approximate, and are in many respects alike or the same, so this word is made in a certain sense to carry with it an union of the fiercest opposites: it is made to signify the extremes of love and hatred.

"But to suppose, with Mr. Tooke (Divers. of Purl. II. 409), that in all cases it must at that time have meant 'injurious,' as being derived from the Saxon verb *dere*, to hurt, is perfectly absurd. Dr. Johnson's derivation of the word, as used in this place, from the Latin *dirus*, is doubtless ridiculous enough: but Mr. Tooke has not produced a single instance of the use of it, *i. e.* of the adjective, in the sense upon which he insists; except, as he pretends, from our author. In the instance cited in this place by Mr. Steevens, in support of the extraordinary interpretation ('most consequential, important,') he has here and elsewhere put upon the word, 'A ring, that I must use in *deere* employment' (Rom. & Jul. sc. last), although the word is spelt after the fashion of the Saxon verb, it is impossible to interpret it 'injurious;' its meaning being most clearly, 'anxious, deeply interesting.' '*Deere* to me as are the ruddy drops that visit my sad heart.' Jul. Cæs. II. 2, Bru. cannot admit of interpretation in any other sense than that in which Gray's Bard understood it,

'*Dear* as the ruddy drops, that warm my heart.'

"In Tr. & Cr. V. 3, Andromache says,

'Consort with me in loud and *deere* petition.'

And in Hector's answer the word occurs thrice so spelt:

'Life every man holds *deere;* but the *deere* man
Holds honour far more precious, *deere*, than life.'

And it is no less than impossible, in either of these instances, to put the sense of 'injurious' upon this word. With his mind possessed by the Saxon verb, *to hurt*, Mr. Tooke seems altogether to have forgotten the existence of the epithet, which answers to the Latin word *charus*. In the same sense it is used by Puttenham: 'The lacke of life is the *dearest* detriment of any other.' Arte of Engl. Poesie, 4to. 1589, p. 182. See '*dearly*,' IV. 3, King; As you, &c. I. 3, Celia; and L. L. L. II. 1, Boyet; and '*dear* guiltiness,' Ib. V. 2, Princess. We will add from Drayton's Moses his birth, 4to. 1630, B. I. that Sarah, about to expose her child, says, she has

'—— her minde of misery compacted,
That must consent unto so *deere* a murther.'

i. e. distressing or heart-rending."

(7) Scene IV.—

The king doth wake to-night, and takes his rouse,
Keeps wassail, and the swaggering up-spring reels.]

"Wake" here means a *wake-feast* or *watch-festival*, originally a nocturnal entertainment held to celebrate the dedication of a church (*vigilia*); but it subsequently came to be used for any *night revel*. "Rouse," in reality the Danish *Ruus*, a deep draught, act of intoxication, or surfeit in drinking, was employed by our old writers with great laxity; sometimes it is used indifferently with *carouse*, to signify a bumper,—

"*Cas.* 'Fore heaven, they have given me a *rouse* already.
Mon. Good faith, a little one; not past a pint, as I am a soldier." *Othello*, Act II. Sc. 3.

Again,—

"*Nor.* I have took since supper,
A *rouse* or two too much, and, by the gods,
It warms my blood."
The Knight of Malta, Act III. Sc. 4.

While in a previous passage of the present play,—

"And the king's *rouse* the heaven shall *bruit* again,
Re-speaking earthly thunder,"—

it plainly imports not simply a deep draught, but the accompaniment of some outcry, similar, perhaps, to our "hip, hip, hurrah!"

Of "Wassail," from the Saxon *wæs hael*, abundant illustration will be found in the *Variorum* Shakespeare, and in Douce; but the expression, "swaggering up-spring reels," still admits of farther explanation. At one time it was generally believed to be a derogatory epithet applied by Hamlet to the *upstart* king, until Steevens proved by a quotation from Chapman's "Alphonsus, Emperor of Germany,"—

"We Germans have no changes in our dances;
An *almain* and an *up-spring*, that is all,"—

that a particular kind of dance was meant. *Up-spring*, indeed, is from the Anglo-Saxon, and also the Danish *Opspringer*, and the Low-Dutch *Op-springen*, to leap up; and the "upspring reels" we conceive to have been some boisterous dance in which the performers joined hands in a ring and then indulged in violent leaps and shoutings, somewhat in the manner of our leaping dances or *Hoppings* at a country wake.

(8) Scene IV.—

Shall in the general censure take corruption
From that particular fault.]

In "The Plain Man's Pathway to Heaven," of Arthur Dent, 1590, we have a dilatation of the same idea:—

"*Phil.* I do verily thus think, that as sin generally doth stain every man's good name, which all are chary and tender of; so especially it doth blot those which are in high places, and of special note for learning, wisdom, and godliness.

Theol. You have spoken most truly, and agreable to the Scriptures. For the Scriptures saith, 'As a dead fly causeth the apothecary's ointment to stink, so doth a little folly him that is in reputation for wisdom and honour:' where Solomon sheweth, That if a fly get into the apothecary's box of ointment, and die, and putrefy in it, she marreth it, though it be never so pretious: even so, if a little sin get into the heart, and break out in the forehead of a man of great fame for some singular gift, it will blear him, though he be never so excellent."

And Nash, in his "Pierce Penniless's Supplication to the Devil," 1592, complaining of drunkenness, observes:—"A mightie deformer of men's manners and features is this unnecessary vice of all others. Let him bee indued with never so manie vertues, and have as much goodly proportion and favour, as Nature can bestow upon a man, yet if hee be thirstie after his owne destruction, and hath no ioy nor comfort, but when he is drowning his soule in a gallon pot, that one beastly imperfection wil utterly obscure all that is commendable in him, and all his goode qualities sinke like lead downe to the bottome of his carrowsing cups, where they will lye, like lees and dregges, dead and unregarded of any man."

(9) SCENE V.—
The glow-worm shows the matin to be near,
And 'gins to pale his uneffectual fire.]

"It was the popular belief that ghosts could not endure the light, and consequently disappeared at the dawn of day. This superstition is derived from our northern ancestors, who held that the sun and everything containing *light or fire* had the property of expelling demons and spirits of all kinds. With them it seems to have originated in the stories that are related in the Edda concerning the battles of Thor against the giants and evil demons, wherein he made use of his dreadful mallet of iron, which he hurled against them as Jupiter did his thunderbolts against the Titans. Many of the *transparent* precious stones were supposed to have the power of expelling evil spirits; and the flint and other stones found in the tombs of the northern nations, and from which fire might be extracted, were imagined, in like manner, to be efficacious in confining the manes of the dead to their proper habitations. They were called Thor's hammers."—DOUCE.

ACT II.

(1) SCENE I.— *Perpend.*] Dr. Johnson's analysis of Polonius has been justly commended for its perspicacity and discrimination. It is certainly an admirable interpretation, and leaves us at a loss to understand how a writer who exhibits such judgment and astuteness in the delineation of this particular character should have failed so signally in his appreciation of nearly every other one of Shakespeare's, which he has attempted to unfold.

"Polonius is a man bred in courts, exercised in business, stored with observation, confident in his knowledge, proud of his eloquence, and declining into dotage. His mode of oratory is truly represented as designed to ridicule the practice of those times, of prefaces that made no introduction, and of method that embarrassed rather than explained. This part of his character is accidental, the rest is natural. Such a man is positive and confident, because he knows that his mind was once strong, and knows not that it is become weak. Such a man excels in general principles, but fails in the particular application. He is knowing in retrospect, and ignorant in foresight. While he depends upon his memory, and can draw from his repositories of knowledge, he utters weighty sentences, and gives useful counsel; but as the mind in its enfeebled state cannot be kept long busy and intent, the old man is subject to sudden dereliction of his faculties, he loses the order of his ideas, and entangles himself in his own thoughts, till he recovers the leading principle, and falls again into his former train. This idea of dotage encroaching upon wisdom, will solve all the phænomena of the character of Polonius."

(2) SCENE II.—[Reads.] *For if the sun breed maggots in a dead dog, being a god kissing carrion.*] In this passage, famous rather from the discussion it has occasioned than for any sublimity of reflection or beauty of language, we adopt the now almost universally accepted correction of Warburton—"a god" for "a good" of the old editions. At the same time we dissent *toto cœlo* from the reasoning by which he and other commentators have sought to connect "For if the sun breed maggots in a dead dog, being a god kissing carrion," with what Hamlet had previously said. The circumstance of the prince coming in reading, that he evinces the utmost intolerance of the old courtier's interruptions, and rejoices in his departure, serve, in our opinion, to show that Shakespeare intended the actor should manifest his wish to be alone, after the words, "Ay, sir; to be honest, as this world goes, is to be one man picked out of ten thousand," in the most unmistakeable manner, by walking away and appearing to resume his study:—that then, finding Polonius still watching him, he should turn sharply round with the abrupt question, "Have you a daughter?" It is this view of the stage business which prompted us to print the passage above, as something read, or affected to be read, by Hamlet,—an innovation—if it be one, (for we are ignorant whether it has been suggested previously)—that will the more readily be pardoned, since the passage as usually exhibited has hitherto defied solution.

(3) SCENE II.—*Ay, that they do, my lord; Hercules and his load too.*] The allusion is doubtless, as Steevens surmised, to the Globe Theatre on the Bankside, the sign of which was, *Hercules carrying the Globe;* and the "aiery of children," against whom this satire was levelled, were, as he observes, "the young singing men of the Chapel Royal or St. Paul's; of the former of whom, perhaps, the earliest mention occurs in an anonymous puritanical pamphlet, 1569, entitled, 'The Children of the Chapel stript and whipt:'—' Plaies will never be supprest, while her maiesties unfledged minions flaunt it in silkes and sattens; They had as well be at their popish service in the devil's garments,' &c. Again, *ibid.:* 'Even in her maiesties chapel do these pretty upstart youthes profane the Lordes day by the lascivious writhing of their tender limbes, and gorgeous decking of their apparell, in feigning bawdie fables gathered from the idolatrous heathen poets,' &c.

Concerning the performances and success of the latter in attracting the best company, I also find the following passage in 'Jack Drum's Entertainment, or Pasquil and Katherine,' 1601:—

'I sawe the *Children of Powles* last night,
And troth they pleasde me prettie, prettie well,
The Apes in time will do it hansomely.
' —— I like the audience that frequenteth there
With *much applause:* a man shall not be choakte
With the stench of garlicke, nor be pasted
To the barmy jacket of a beer-brewer.
' —— 'Tis a good gentle audience.' "

(4) SCENE II.—*It came to pass, as most like it was.*] Hamlet quotes from the opening stanza of an ancient ballad,

still preserved, and which will be found in Evans's Collection, 1810:—

> "I have read that many years agoe,
> When Jepha, judge of Israel,
> Had *one fair daughter and no more,*
> Whom *he loved passing well.*
> *As by lot, God wot,*
> *It came to passe, most like it was,*
> Great warrs there should be,
> And who should be the chiefe; but he, but he."

The subject appears to have been popular. In the Stationers' Registers, 1567-8, a ballad entitled "The song of Jefphas dowghter at his [her?] death," is licensed to Alexander Lacy; in 1624, another called "Jeffa, Judge of Israel," was entered on the same records; and from Henslowe's Diary, we learn that in May, 1602, Decker and Chettle were engaged in writing a tragedy based on the story of Jephthah.

(5) SCENE II.—*A chopine.*] *Chopines* or *chapines* were clogs with enormously thick soles, which the ladies of Spain and Italy wore on their shoes when going abroad. Coryat's account of those he saw in Venice is this: "There is one thing used of the Venetian women, and some others dwelling in the cities and townes subject to the signory of Venice, that is not to be observed (I thinke) amongst any other women in Christendome: which is so common in Venice, that no woman whatsoever goeth without it, either in her house or abroad; a thing made of wood and covered with leather of sundry colors, some with white, some redde, some yellow. It is called a Chapiney, which they weare under their shoes. Many of them are curiously painted; some also of them I have seen fairely gilt: so uncomely a thing (in my opinion) that it is pitty this foolish custom is not cleane banished and exterminated out of the citie. There are many of these Chapineys of a great heigth, even halfe a yard high, which maketh many of their women that are very short seeme much taller then the tallest women we have in England. Also I have heard that this is observed amongst them, that by how much the nobler a woman is, by so much the higher are her Chapineys. All their gentlewomen, and most of their wives and widowes that are of any wealth, are assisted and supported eyther by men or women, when they walke abroad, to the end they may not fall. They are borne up most commonly by the left arme, otherwise they might quickly take a fall."—*Crudities*, p. 262.

(6) SCENE II.—*Pray God, your voice, like a piece of uncurrent gold, be not cracked within the ring.*] Hamlet, it must be remembered, is addressing the youth who personated the female characters, and simply expresses a hope that his voice has not grown too manly to pass current for a woman's; there is not the slightest ground for suspecting any covert allusion. "It is to be observed," says Douce, "that there was a ring or circle on the coin, within which the sovereign's head was placed; if the crack extended from the edge beyond this ring, the coin was rendered unfit for currency. Such pieces were hoarded by the usurers of the time, and lent out as lawful money. Of this we are informed by Roger Fenton in his 'Treatise of Usury,' 1611, 4to. p. 23. 'A poore man desireth a goldsmith to lend him such a summe, but he is not able to pay him interest. If such as I can spare (saith the goldsmith) will pleasure you, you shall have it for three or four moneths. Now, hee hath a number of light, clipt *crackt* peeces (for such he useth to take in change with consideration for their defects:) this summe of money is repaid by the poore man at the time appointed in good lawful money. This is usurie.' And, again: 'It is a common custom of his [the usurer's] to buy up *crackt angels* at nine shillings the peece. Now, sir, if a gentleman (on good assurance) request him of mony, good sir (saith hee, with a counterfait sigh) I would be glad to please your worship, but my *good* mony is abroad, and that I have, I dare not put in your hands. The gentleman thinking this conscience, where it is subtilty, and being beside that in some necessity, ventures on the *crackt angels*, some of which cannot flie, for soldering, and paies double interest to the miser under the cloake of honesty.'"—LODGE'S *Wit's Miserie*, 1596, 4to. p. 28.

(7) SCENE II.—*'T was caviare to the general.*] The play was of too peculiar a relish, like caviare, for the palate of the multitude. *Caviare* is a preparation of sturgeon's roe; and the taste for it was considered a mark of refinement in Shakespeare's day: thus Mercury, in "Cynthia's Revels," Act II. Sc. 1, describing a coxcomb, says: "He doth learn to make strange sauces, to eat anchovies, maccaroni, bovoli, fagioli, and *caviare*," &c.

(8) SCENE II.—

> *For murder, though it have no tongue, will speak*
> *With most miraculous organ.*]

There is a curious illustration of this passage in T. Heywood's "Apology for Actors," 1612, and the same story is related in an old tragedy, called "A Warning for Fair Women," 1599:—

"At Lin, in Norfolke, the then Earl of Sussex players acting the old History of Feyer Francis, and presenting a woman who, insatiately doting on a yong gentleman (the more securely to enjoy his affection), mischievously and secretly murdered her husband, whose ghost haunted her; and, at divers times, in her most solitary and private contemplations, in most horrid and feareful shapes, appeared and stood before her. As this was acted, a toune's woman (till then of good estimation and report), finding her conscience (at this presentment) extremely troubled, suddenly skritched and cryd out, Oh! my husband, my husband! I see the ghost of my husband fiercely threatning and menacing me! At which shrill and unexpected outcry, the people about her, moov'd to a strange amazement, inquired the reason of her clamour, when presently, un-urged, she told them that seven yeares ago she, to be possest of such a gentleman (meaning him), had poysoned her husband, whose fearefull image personated it selfe in the shape of that ghost. Whereupon the murdresse was apprehended, before the justices further examined, and by her voluntary confession after condemned. That this is true, as well by the report of the actors as the records of the towne, there are many eyewitnesses of this accident yet living vocally to confirme it."

ACT III.

(1) SCENE II.—*I could have such a fellow whipped for o'erdoing Termagant; it out-herods Herod.*] In many of the early miracle plays, one of the most prominent characters was a roaring, hectoring tyrant, who made "all split," and was alike the terror and the admiration of the multitude; in some cases, this truculent monster represented *Termagant*, a supposed god of the Saracens; but more frequently he was *Herod* of Jewry. An extract from the ancient Pageant, performed at Coventry by the Shearmen and Taylors, in 1534, but the composition of which is of much earlier date, well exemplifies the saying, when any one rants and tears a passion to tatters, that he *out-herods* Herod. The entrance of Herod is announced in unintelligible *French;* after which the monarch proceeds in this wise :—

"Qui statis in Jude et Rex iseraell
And the myghttyst conquerowre that eyer walkid on grownd
For I am evyn he thatt made bothe hevin & hell
And of my mighté powar holdith vp the world rownd
Magog and madroke bothe thes did I confownde
And wt this bryght bronde there bonis I brak on sund'r
Thatt all the wyde worlde on those rappis did wond'r
I am the cawse of this grett lyght and thund'r
Ytt ys throgh my furé that they soche noyse dothe make
My feyrefull contenance the clowdis so doth incumbur
That oftymes for drede thereof the verre yerth doth quake
Loke when I wt malés* this bryght bronde doth schake
All the whole world from the north to the sowthe
I ma them dystroie wt won worde of my mowthe
To reycownt vnto you myn innewmerabull substance
Thatt were to moche for any tong to tell
For all the whole orent ys vnd'r myn obbeydeance
And prynce am I of purgatorre & cheff capten of hell
And those tyraneos trayturs be force ma I compell
Myne eñmyis to vanquese & evyn to dust them dryve
And wt a twynke of myn iee not won to be lafte alyve
Behold my contenance and my colur
Bryghtur then the sun in the meddis of the dey
Where can you haue a more grettur succur
Then to behold my person that ys soo gaye
My fawcun and my fassion with my gorgis araye
He thatt had the grace all wey thereon to thynke
Lyve then myght all wey withowt othur meyte or drynke
And thys my tryomfande fame most hylist dothe a bownde
Throgh owt this world in all reygeons abrod
Reysemelyng the favour of thatt most myght Mahownd
From Jubytor be desent† and cosyn to the grett god
And namyd the most reydowndid king eyrodde
Wyche thatt all pryncis hath vnder subjeccion
And all there whole powar under my proteccion
And therefore my hareode‡ here callid calcas
Warne thou eyery porte that noo schyppis a ryve
Nor also aleond§ stranger throg my realme pas
But théy for thére truage do pay markis fyve
Now spede thé forth hastelé
For théy thatt wyll the contraré
Apon a galowse hangid schalbe
And be Mahownde of me thé gett noo grace."

The above is copied *verbatim* from the Pageant, as it is given in Sharp's "Dissertation on the Pageants, &c. anciently performed at Coventry," with the exception of some contractions which render the original obscure.

(2) SCENE II.—*And let those that play your clowns speak no more than is set down for them:——a most pitiful ambition in the fool that uses it.*] In the 1603 quarto there follows here a passage supposed to have been levelled at the famous clown, William Kemp :—

"And then you have some agen, that keepes one sute
Of jeasts, as a man is knowne by one sute of
Apparell, and Gentlemen quotes his jeasts downe
In their tables, before they come to the play, as thus:
Cannot you stay till I eate my porrige? and, you owe me
A quarters wages: and my coate wants a cullison:
And, youre beere is sowre: and, blabbering with his lips,
And thus keeping in his cinkapase of jeasts,
When, God knows, the warme Clowne cannot make a jest,
Unless by chance, as the blinde man catcheth a hare."

(3) SCENE II.—*And never come mischance between us twain!*] In the quarto of 1603, the preceding dialogue between Gonzago and Baptista is a mere bald sketch of the subsequent version :—

"*Duke.* Full fortie yeares are past, their date is gone,
Since happy time joyn'd both our hearts as one:
And now the blood that fill'd my youthful veines,
Runnes weakely in their pipes, and all the straines,
Of musicke, which whilome pleasde mine eare,
Is now a burthen that age cannot beare:
And therefore sweete Nature must pay his due,
To heaven must I, and leave the earth with you.
Dutchesse. O say not so, lest that you kill my heart,
When death takes you, let life from me depart.
Duke. Content thy selfe, when ended is my date,
Thou maist (perchance) have a more noble mate,
More wise, more youthfull, and one.—
Dutchesse. O speake no more, for then I am accurst,
None weds the second, but she kils the first:
A second time I kill my Lord that's dead,
When second husband kisses me in bed.
Ham. O wormewood, wormewood!
Duke. I doe beleeve you sweete, what now you speake,
But what we doe determine oft we breake,
For our demises stil are overthrowne,
Our thoughts are ours, their end's none of our owne:
So thinke you will no second husband wed,
But die thy thoughts, when thy first Lord is dead.
Dutchesse. Both here and there pursue me lasting strife,
If once a widdow, ever I be wife," &c.

(4) SCENE II.—*O, the recorders.*] The best, indeed the only reliable description of these instruments, is that furnished by Mr. W. Chappell in his delightful work, called "Popular Music of the Olden Time:"—

"Old English musical instruments were commonly made of three or four different sizes, so that a player might take any of the four parts that were required to fill up the harmony. So Violins, Lutes, Recorders, Flutes, Shawms, &c. have been described by some writers in a manner which (to those unacquainted with this peculiarity) has appeared irreconcileable with other accounts. Shakespeare (in *Hamlet*) speaks of the Recorder as a little pipe, and says, in *A Midsummer Night's Dream*, 'he hath played on his prologue like a *child* on a recorder;' but in an engraving of the instrument,* it reaches from the lip to the knee of the performer; and among those left by Henry VIII. were Recorders of box, oak, and ivory, great and small, two base recorders of walnut, and one *great* base recorder. Recorders and (English) Flutes are to outward appearance the same, although Lord Bacon, in his *Natural History*, cent. iii. sec. 221, says the Recorder hath a less bore, and a greater above and below. The number of holes for the fingers is the same, and the scale, the compass, and the manner of playing, the same. Salter describes the *recorder*, from which the instrument derives its name, as situate in the upper part of it, *i.e.* between the hole below the mouth and the highest hole for the finger. He says, 'Of the kinds of music, vocal has always had the preference in esteem, and in consequence, the Recorder, as *approaching nearest to the sweet delightfulness of the voice*, ought to have first place in opinion, as we see by the universal use of it confirmed.'"

* *Malice.* † *I am descended.* ‡ *Herald.* § *Allow.*

* See "The Genteel Companion for the Recorder," by Humphrey Salter, 1683.

(5) SCENE IV.—POLONIUS *hides behind the arras.*] The incident of Polonius concealing himself to overhear the conversation between Hamlet and the Queen, was suggested by the "Hystorie of Hamblet."—"Meane time the counsell or entred secretly into the queenes chamber, and there hid himselfe behind the arras, not long before the queene and Hamblet came thither, who being craftie and pollitique, as soone as hee was within the chamber, doubting some treason, and fearing if he should speake severely and wisely to his mother touching his secret practices he should be understood, and by that means intercepted, used his ordinary manner of dissimulation, and began to come like a cocke beating with his armes (in such manner as cockes use to strike with their wings) upon the hangings of the chamber; whereby, feeling something stirring under them, he cried, A rat, a rat! and presently drawing his sworde, thrust it into the hangings; which done, pulled the counsellor (halfe dead) out by the heeles, made an end of killing him," &c.

(6) SCENE IV.—HAMLET *dragging out the body of* POLONIUS.] The earliest quarto has, "*Exit Hamlet with the dead body;*" the folio, "*Exit Hamlet tugging in Polonius.*" It is remarkable that, while nearly every department of our early literature has been ransacked to supply illustrations of Shakespeare's language and ideas, so little has been done towards their elucidation from the history of his own stage. When Hamlet, at the termination of the present scene, says, "I'll lug the guts into the neighbour room," the commentators very properly reply to the objections of those who, unacquainted with old language, complain of the grossness of expression, that the word *guts* was not by any means so offensive to delicacy formerly as it is considered now. It was commonly used, in fact, where we should employ *entrails*, and in this place really signifies no more than *lack-brain* or *shallow-pate*. But a little consideration of the exigences of the theatre in Shakespeare's time, which not only obliged an actor to play two or more parts in the same drama, but to perform such servile offices as are now done by attendants of the stage, would have enabled them to show that the line in question is a mere interpolation to afford the player an excuse for removing the body. We append a few examples where the same expedient is adopted for the same purpose. Among them the notable instance of Sir John Falstaff carrying off the body of Harry Percy on his back, an exploit as clumsy and unseemly as Hamlet's "tugging" out Polonius, and, like that, perpetuated on the modern stage only from sheer ignorance of the circumstances which originated such a practice:—

"Romeo and Juliet," Act III. Sc. 1. Death of Tybalt, Vol. I. p. 188:—

"*Prince.* Let Romeo hence in haste,
Else when he's found, that hour is his last.—
Bear hence this body, and attend our will:
Mercy but murders, pardoning those that kill."

"Richard II." Act V. Sc. 5. Death of Richard, and Exton's men. Vol. I. p. 492:—

"*Exton. This dead king to the living king I'll bear;—*
Take hence the rest and give them burial here."

"Henry IV." Act V. Sc. 4. Death of Hotspur. Vol. I. p. 560:—

"*P. Hen.* [*To* FALSTAFF.] *Come, bring your luggage nobly on your back.* * * * * * * [*Exit* FALSTAFF *bearing the body.*"

"Henry VI." Part I. Act I. Sc. 4. Death of Salisbury. Vol. II. p. 294:—

"*Talbot.* Your hearts I'll stamp out with my horse's heels,
And make a quagmire of your mingled brains.—
Convey me Salisbury into his tent,
And then we'll try what these dastard Frenchmen dare."

"Henry VI." Part I. Act II. Sc. 5. Death of Mortimer. Vol. II. p. 303:—

"*Plan.* Well, I will lock his counsel in my breast;
And what I do imagine, let that rest.—
Keepers, convey him hence; and I myself
Will see his burial better than his life.—
Here lies the dusky torch of Mortimer,
Chok'd with ambition of the meaner sort:" &c.

"Henry VI." Part I. Act IV. Sc. 7. Death of Talbot and his son. Vol. II. p. 321:—

"*Pucelle.* For God's sake, let him have 'em; to keep them here,
They would but stink and putrefy the air.
Char. Go, take their bodies hence.
Lucy. I'll bear them hence," &c.

"Henry VI." Part II. Act IV. Sc. 1. Death of Suffolk. Vol. II. p. 375:—

"*Gent.* O barbarous and bloody spectacle!
His body will I bear unto the king:
If he revenge it not, yet will his friends;
So will the queen that living held him dear. [*Exit.*"

"Henry VI." Part II. Act IV. Sc. 10. Death of Jack Cade. Vol. II. p. 385:—

"*Iden.* Die, damned wretch, the curse of her that bare thee!
And as I thrust thy body in with my sword,
So wish I, I might thrust thy soul to hell.—
Hence will I drag thee headlong by the heels
Unto a dunghill, which shall be thy grave,
And there cut off thy most ungracious head,
Which I will bear in triumph to the king,
Leaving thy trunk for crows to feed upon. [*Exit.*"

"Henry VI." Part II. Act V. Sc. 2. Old Clifford's body. Vol. II. p. 390:—

"*Young Cliff. Come thou new ruin of old Clifford's house;*
As did Æneas old Anchises bear,
So bear I thee upon my manly shoulders;
But then Æneas bare a living load,
Nothing so heavy as these woes of mine. [*Exit.*"

"Henry VI." Part III. Act II. Sc. 5. The dead father. Vol. II. p. 419:—

"*Son. I'll bear thee hence, where I may weep my fill.*"

"Henry VI." Part III. Act II. Sc. 5. The dead son. Vol. II. p. 419:—

"*Father. I'll bear thee hence; and let them fight that will,*
For I have murder'd where I should not kill."

"Henry VI." Part III. Act V. Sc. 6. Death of Henry. Vol. II. p. 449:—

"*Glo.* Clarence, thy turn is next; and then the rest;
Counting myself but bad, till I be best.—
I'll throw thy body in another room,
And triumph, Henry, in thy day of doom."

"Richard III." Act III. Sc. 4. Death of Clarence. Vol. II. p. 528:—

"*1 Murd. Now must I hide his body in some hole*
Until the duke take order for his burial."

"King Lear," Act IV. Sc. 6. Death of Oswald. Vol. III. p. 105:—

"*Edg. Here in the sands,*
Thee I'll rake up, the post unsanctified
Of murderous lechers."

"Troilus and Cressida," Act V. Sc. 9. Death of Hector. Vol. III. p. 318:—

"*Achil. Come, tie his body to my horse's tail;*
Along the field I will the Trojan trail."

"Julius Cæsar," Act III. Sc. 2. Cæsar's body exhibited in the Forum:—

"*1 Cit.* Away, away!
We'll burn his body in the holy place,
And with the brands fire the traitors' houses.
Take up the body."

"Julius Cæsar," Act V. Sc. 5. Brutus' body. (End of play):—

> "*Oct. Within my tent his bones to-night shall lie,*
> *Most like a soldier, order'd honourably.*"

"Antony and Cleopatra," Act IV. Sc. 9. Death of Enobarbus:—

> "1 *Sold.* The hand of death hath raught him. Hark, the drums
> Demurely wake the sleepers. *Let us bear him*
> *To the court of guard;* he is of note: our hour
> Is fully out.
> 3 *Sold.* Come on then,
> He may recover yet. [*Exeunt with body.*"

"Antony and Cleopatra," Act IV. Sc. 12. The dying Antony:—

> "Take me up,
> I have led you oft; carry me now, good friends,
> And have my thanks for all. [*Exeunt with* ANTONY."

These instances from Shakespeare alone, and they could easily be multiplied, will suffice to bring into view one of the inconveniences to which the elder dramatists were subject through the paucity of actors; and, at the same time, by exhibiting the mode in which they endeavoured to obviate the difficulty, may afford a key to many passages and incidents that before appeared anomalous.

ACT IV.

(1) SCENE V.—*They say, the owl was a baker's daughter.*] This alludes to a tradition still current in some parts of England: "Our Saviour went into a baker's shop where they were baking, and asked for some bread to eat. The mistress of the shop immediately put a piece of dough into the oven to bake for him; but was reprimanded by her daughter, who, insisting that the piece of dough was too large, reduced it to a very small size. The dough, however, immediately afterwards began to swell, and presently became of a most enormous size. Whereupon the baker's daughter cried out, 'Heugh, heugh, heugh,' which owl-like noise probably induced our Saviour, for her wickedness, to transform her into that bird."

(2) SCENE V.—*There's rosemary, that's for remembrance; * * * and there is pansies, that's for thoughts. * * * * * There's fennel for you, and columbines:—there's rue for you;*—&c. &c.] There is method in poor Ophelia's distribution. She presents to each the herb popularly appropriate to his age or disposition. To Laertes, whom in her distraction she probably confounds with her lover, she gives "rosemary" as an emblem of his faithful remembrance:—

> "Rosemarie is for remembrance
> Betweene us daie and night,
> Wishing that I might alwaies have
> You present in my sight."
> *A Handefull of Pleasant Delites*, &c. 1584.

And "pansies," to denote love's "thoughts" or *troubles*:—

> "I pray what flowers are these?
> The *panzie* this;
> O, that's for lovers' *thoughts*."
> *All Fools*, Act II. Sc. 1.

For the King she has "fennel," signifying *flattery* and *lust;* and "columbines," which marked *ingratitude;* while for the Queen and for herself she reserves the herb of sorrow, "rue," which she reminds her Majesty may be worn by her "with a difference," *i.e.* not as an emblem of grief alone, but to indicate *contrition;*—"some of them smil'd and said, *Rue* was called *Herbe grace,* which though they scorned in their youth, they might wear in their age, and that it was never too late to say *Miserere.*"—GREENE'S *Quip for an Upstart Courtier.*

(3) SCENE VI.—*Enter* HORATIO *and a* Servant.] In the quarto, 1603, at this period of the action there is a scene between the Queen and Horatio, not a vestige of which is retained in the after copies. Like every other part of that curious edition, it is grievously deformed by misprints and mal-arrangement of the verse; but, as exhibiting the poet's earliest conception of the Queen's character, is much too precious to be lost.

> "*Enter* HORATIO *and the* QUEENE.
>
> *Hor.* Madame, your sonne is safe arriv'de in *Denmarke*,
> This letter I even now receiv'd of him,
> Whereas he writes how he escap't the danger,
> And subtle treason that the king had plotted,
> Being crossed by the contention of the windes,
> He found the Packet sent to the king of *England*,
> Wherein he saw himselfe betray'd to death,
> As at his next conversion with your grace,
> He will relate the circumstance at full.
> *Queene.* Then I perceive there's treason in his lookes
> That seem'd to sugar o're his villanie:
> But I will soothe and please him for a time,
> For murderous mindes are alwayes jealous,
> But know not you *Horatio* where he is?
> *Hor.* Yes, Madame, and he hath appoynted me
> To meete him on the east side of the Cittie
> To morrow morning.
> *Queene.* O faile not, good *Horatio*, and withall, commend me
> A mothers care to him, bid him a while
> Be wary of his presence, lest that he
> Faile in that he goes about.
> *Hor.* Madam, never make doubt of that:
> I thinke by this the news be come to court:
> He is arriv'de, observe the king, and you shall
> Quickely finde, Hamlet being here,
> Things fell not to his minde.
> *Queene.* But what became of *Gilderstone* and *Rossencraft?*
> *Hor.* He being set ashore, they went for *England*,
> And in the Packet there writ down that doome
> To be perform'd on them poynted for him:
> And by great chance he had his father's Seale,
> So all was done without discoverie.
> *Queene.* Thankes be to heaven for blessing of the prince,
> *Horatio* once againe I take my leave,
> With thousand mothers blessings to my sonne.
> *Horat.* Madam adue."

ACT V.

(1) Scene I.—*Argal, he that is not guilty of his own death shortens not his own life.*] Sir John Hawkins suggested that Shakespeare here designed a ridicule on the legal and logical subtleties enunciated in the case of Dame Hale, as reported in Plowden's Commentaries. The case was this: her husband, Sir James Hale, committed suicide by drowning himself in a river, and the point argued was whether by this act a lease which he died possessed of did not accrue to the Crown. It must be admitted that the clown's, "If I drown myself wittingly, it argues an act; and an act hath three branches;" reads amazingly like a satire on the following:—Serjeant Walsh said that —"The act consists of three parts. The first is the imagination, which is a reflection or meditation of the mind, whether or no it is convenient for him to destroy himself, and what way it can be done. The second is the resolution, which is the determination of the mind to destroy himself, and to do it in this or that particular way. The third is the perfection, which is the execution of what the mind has resolved to do. And this perfection consists of two parts, viz. the beginning and the end. The beginning is the doing of the act which causes the death, and the end is the death, which is only a sequel to the act." &c. &c.

Nor would it be easy to find a better parallel for,—"Here lies the water; good: here stands the man; good: if the man go to this water, and drown himself, it is, will he nill he, he goes,—mark you that; but if the water come to him and drown him, he drowns not himself:" &c.—than what follows, in the argument of the judges, viz. Weston, Anthony Brown, and Lord Dyer, "Sir James Hale was dead, and how came he to his death? It may be answered By drowning. And who drowned him? Sir James Hale. And when did he drown him? In his lifetime. So that Sir James Hale being alive, caused Sir James Hale to die; and the act of the living man was the death of the dead man. And then for this offence it is reasonable to punish the living man who committed the offence, and not the dead man." &c.

(2) Scene I.—*In youth, when I did love, did love, &c.*] The three stanzas sung by the grave-digger are a barbarous version of a sonnet said to have been written by Lord Vaux, one copy of which, with music, has been discovered by Dr. Rimbault, in MS. Sloane, No. 4900: another, unaccompanied by music, is in the Harleian MSS. No. 1703. The whole poem, too, may be seen in Tottel's Miscellany, 1557, and has been reprinted in Percy's Reliques, Vol. I. p. 190, Edition 1812, and in Bell's Edition, 1854, where the words are thus given:—

"The Aged Lover Renounceth Love.

"I loathe that I did love,
  In youth that I thought sweet,
As time requires for my behove,
  Methinks they are not meet.

"My lusts they do me leave,
  My fancies all are fled,
And track of time begins to weave
  Grey hairs upon my head.

"For Age with stealing steps
  Hath clawed me with his crutch,
And lusty Life away she leaps
  As there had been none such.

"My Muse doth not delight
  Me as she did before;
My hand and pen are not in plight,
  As they have been of yore.

"For Reason me denies
  This youthly idle rhyme;
And day by day to me she cries,
  'Leave off these toys in time.'

"The wrinkles in my brow,
  The furrows in my face
Say, limping Age will lodge him now
  Where Youth must give him place.

"The harbinger of Death
  To me I see him ride,
The cough, the cold, the gasping breath
  Doth bid me to provide

"A pickaxe and a spade,
  And eke a shrouding sheet,
A house of clay for to be made
  For such a guest most meet.

"Methinks I hear the clerk,
  That knolls the careful knell,
And bids me leave my woeful work,
  Ere Nature me compel.

"My keepers knit the knot
  That Youth did laugh to scorn,
Of me that clean shall be forgot,
  As I had not been born.

"Thus must I Youth give up,
  Whose badge I long did wear;
To them I yield the wanton cup,
  That better may it bear.

"Lo, here the bared skull,
  By whose bald sign I know,
That stooping Age away shall pull
  Which youthful years did sow.

"For Beauty with her band
  These crooked cares hath wrought,
And shipped me into the land
  From whence I first was brought.

"And ye that bide behind,
  Have ye none other trust,
As ye of clay were cast by kind,
  So shall ye waste to dust."

(3) Scene I.—*And must the inheritor himself have no more, ha?*] We have something very like these reflections in Thomas Randolph's comedy of "The Jealous Lovers," played before Charles the Second at Cambridge, and published at Oxford, 1668:—

"*Sexton.* [*Shewing a skull.*] This was a poetical noddle. O the sweet lines, choice language, eloquent figures, besides the jests, half jests, quarter jests, and quibbles that have come out of these chaps that yawn so! He has not so much as a new-coined complement to procure him a supper. The best friend he has may walk by him now, and yet have ne'er a jeer put upon him. His mistris had a little dog, deceased the other day, and all the wit in his noddle could not pump out an elegie to bewail it. He has been my tenant this seven years, and in all that while I never heard him rail against the times, or complain of the neglect of learning. Melpomene and the rest of the Muses have a good turn on't that he's dead; for while he lived, he ne'er left calling upon 'em. He was buried (as most of the tribe) at the charge of the parish: and is happier dead than alive; for he has now as much money as the best in the company,—and yet has left off the poetical way of begging, called borrowing."—Act IV. Sc. 3.

Again, in the next scene:—

"*Sexton.* Look here; this is a lawyer's skull. There was a tongue in 't once, a damnable eloquent tongue, that would almost have perswaded any man to the gallows. This was a turbulent busie fellow, till Death gave him his *Quietus est;* and yet I ventured to rob him of his gown, and the rest of his habiliments, to the very buckram bag, not leaving him so much as a poor halfpeny to pay for his waftage, and yet the good man nere repin'd at it.—Now a man may clap you o'th' coxcomb with his spade, and never stand in fear of an action of battery."

CRITICAL OPINIONS ON HAMLET.

"THE seeming inconsistencies in the conduct and character of Hamlet have long exercised the conjectural ingenuity of critics; and, as we are always loth to suppose that the cause of defective apprehension is in ourselves, the mystery has been too commonly explained by the very easy process of setting it down as in fact inexplicable, and by resolving the phenomenon into a misgrowth, or *lusus*, of the capricious and irregular genius of Shakspeare. The shallow and stupid arrogance of these vulgar and indolent decisions, I would fain do my best to expose. I believe the character of Hamlet may be traced to Shakspeare's deep and accurate science in mental philosophy. Indeed, that this character must have some connexion with the common fundamental laws of our nature, may be assumed from the fact, that Hamlet has been the darling of every country in which the literature of England has been fostered. In order to understand him, it is essential that we should reflect on the constitution of our own minds. Man is distinguished from the brute animals in proportion as thought prevails over sense; but in the healthy processes of the mind, a balance is constantly maintained between the impressions from outward objects and the inward operations of the intellect;—for if there be an overbalance in the contemplative faculty, man thereby becomes the creature of mere meditation, and loses his natural power of action. Now, one of Shakspeare's modes of creating characters is, to conceive any one intellectual or moral faculty in morbid excess, and then to place himself, Shakspeare, thus mutilated or diseased, under given circumstances. In Hamlet, he seems to have wished to exemplify the moral necessity of a due balance between our attention to the objects of our senses, and our meditation on the workings of our minds,—an *equilibrium* between the real and the imaginary worlds. In Hamlet, this balance is disturbed; his thoughts and the images of his fancy are far more vivid than his actual perceptions; and his very perceptions, instantly passing through the medium of his contemplations, acquire, as they pass, a form and a colour not naturally their own. Hence we see a great, an almost enormous, intellectual activity, and a proportionate aversion to real action consequent upon it, with all its symptoms and accompanying qualities. This character Shakspeare places in circumstances under which it is obliged to act on the spur of the moment. Hamlet is brave and careless of death; but he vacillates from sensibility, and procrastinates from thought, and loses the power of action in the energy of resolve. Thus it is that this tragedy presents a direct contrast to that of 'Macbeth;' the one proceeds with the utmost slowness, the other with a crowded and breathless rapidity.

"The effect of this overbalance of the imaginative power is beautifully illustrated in the everlasting broodings and superfluous activities of Hamlet's mind, which, unseated from its healthy relation, is constantly occupied with the world within, and abstracted from the world without,—giving substance to shadows, and throwing a mist over all common-place actualities. It is the nature of thought to be indefinite;—definiteness belongs to external imagery alone. Hence it is that the sense of sublimity arises, not from the sight of an outward object, but from the beholder's reflection upon it;—not from the sensuous impression, but from the imaginative reflex. Few have seen a celebrated waterfall without feeling something akin to disappointment; it is only subsequently that the image comes back full into the mind, and brings with it a train of grand or beautiful associations. Hamlet feels this; his senses are in a state of trance, and he looks upon external things as hieroglyphics. His soliloquy,—

'O! that this too too solid flesh would melt,' &c.—

springs from that craving after the indefinite—for that which is not—which most easily besets men of genius; and the self-delusion common to this temper of mind is finely exemplified in the character which Hamlet gives of himself,—

> '—— It cannot be
> But I am pigeon-livered, and lack gall
> To make oppression bitter.'

He mistakes the seeing his chains for the breaking them; delays action till action is of no use; and dies the victim of mere circumstance and accident."—COLERIDGE.

"'Hamlet' is singular in its kind; a tragedy of thought, inspired by continual and never-satisfied meditation on human destiny and the dark perplexity of the events of this world, and calculated to call forth the very same meditation in the minds of the spectators. This enigmatical work resembles those irrational equations in which a fraction of unknown magnitude always remains, that will in no way admit of solution. Much has been said, much written, on this piece, and yet no thinking head, who anew expresses himself on it, will (in his view of the connexion and the signification of all the parts) entirely coincide with his predecessors. What naturally most astonishes us is, the fact that with such hidden purposes—with a foundation laid in such unfathomable depth, the whole should, at a first view, exhibit an extremely popular appearance. The dread appearance of the Ghost takes possession of the mind and the imagination almost at the very commencement; then the play within the play, in which, as in a glass, we see reflected the crime, whose fruitlessly attempted punishment constitutes the subject-matter of the piece; the alarm with which it fills the King; Hamlet's pretended, and Ophelia's real madness; her death and burial; the meeting of Hamlet and Laertes at her grave; their combat, and the grand determination; lastly, the appearance of the young hero Fortinbras, who, with warlike pomp, pays the last honours to an extinct family of kings; the interspersion of comic characteristic scenes with Polonius, the courtiers, and the gravediggers, which have all of them their signification,—all this fills the stage with an animated and varied movement. The only circumstance from which this piece might be judged to be less theatrical than other tragedies of Shakspeare is, that in the last scenes the main action either stands still or appears to retrograde. This, however, was inevitable, and lay in the nature of the subject. The whole is intended to show that a calculating consideration, which exhausts all the relations and possible consequences of a deed, must cripple the power of acting; as Hamlet himself expresses it,—

> 'And thus the native hue of resolution
> Is sicklied o'er with the pale cast of thought;
> And enterprises of great pith and moment,
> With this regard, their currents turn awry,
> And lose the name of action.'

With respect to Hamlet's character: I cannot, as I understand the poet's views, pronounce altogether so favourable a sentence upon it as Goethe does. He is, it is true, of a highly cultivated mind, a prince of royal manners, endowed with the finest sense of propriety, susceptible of noble ambition, and open in the highest degree to an enthusiastic admiration of that excellence in others of which he himself is deficient. He acts the part of madness with unrivalled power, convincing the persons who are sent to examine into his supposed loss of reason, merely by telling them unwelcome truths, and rallying them with the most caustic wit. But in the resolutions which he so often embraces and always leaves unexecuted, his weakness is too apparent: he does himself only justice when he implies that there is no greater dissimilarity than between himself and Hercules. He is not solely impelled by necessity to artifice and dissimulation, he has a natural inclination for crooked ways; he is a hypocrite towards himself; his far-fetched scruples are often mere pretexts to cover his want of determination: thoughts, as he says on a different occasion, which have

> '—— but one part wisdom
> And ever three parts coward.'

He has been chiefly condemned both for his harshness in repulsing the love of Ophelia, which he himself had cherished, and for his insensibility at her death. But he is too much overwhelmed with his own sorrow to have any compassion to spare for others; besides, his outward indifference gives us by no means the measure of his internal perturbation. On the other hand, we evidently perceive in him a malicious joy, when he has succeeded in getting rid of his enemies, more through necessity and accident, which alone are able to impel him to quick and decisive measures, than by the merit of his own courage, as he himself confesses after the murder of Polonius, and with respect to Rosencrantz and Guildenstern. Hamlet has no firm belief either in himself or in anything else: from expressions of religious confidence he passes over to sceptical doubts; he believes in the Ghost of his father as long as he sees it, but as soon as it has disappeared, it appears to him almost in the light of a deception.* He has even gone so far as to say, 'there is nothing either good or bad, but thinking makes it so;' with him the poet loses himself here in labyrinths of thought, in which neither end nor beginning is discoverable. The stars themselves, from the course of events, afford no answer to the question so urgently proposed to them. A voice from another world, commissioned, it would appear, by heaven, demands vengeance for a monstrous enormity, and the demand remains without effect; the criminals are at last punished, but, as it were, by an accidental blow, and not in the solemn way requisite to convey to the world a warning example of justice; irresolute foresight, cunning treachery, and impetuous rage, hurry on to a common destruction; the less guilty and the innocent are equally involved in the general ruin. The destiny of humanity is there exhibited as a gigantic Sphinx, which threatens to precipitate into the abyss of scepticism all who are unable to solve her dreadful enigmas.

"As one example of the many niceties of Shakspeare which have never been understood, I may allude to the style in which the player's speech about Hecuba is conceived. It has been the subject of much controversy among the commentators, whether this was borrowed by Shakspeare from himself or from another, and whether, in the praise of the piece of which it is supposed to be a part, he was speaking seriously, or merely meant to ridicule the tragical bombast of his contemporaries. It seems never to have occurred to them that this speech must not be judged of by itself, but in connexion with the place where it is introduced. To distinguish it in the play itself as dramatic poetry, it was necessary that it should rise above the dignified poetry of the former in the same proportion that generally theatrical elevation soars above simple nature. Hence Shakspeare has composed the play in 'Hamlet' altogether in sententious rhymes full of antitheses. But this solemn and measured tone did not suit a speech in which violent emotion ought to prevail, and the poet had no other expedient than the one of which he made choice—overcharging the pathos. The language of the speech in question is certainly falsely emphatical; but yet this fault is so mixed up with true grandeur, that a player practised in artificially calling forth in himself the emotion he is imitating, may certainly be carried away by it. Besides, it will hardly be believed that Shakspeare knew so little of his art, as not to be aware that a tragedy in which Æneas had to make a lengthy epic relation of a transaction that happened so long before as the destruction of Troy, could neither be dramatical nor theatrical."—SCHLEGEL.

"Conceive a prince, such as is here painted, and that his father suddenly dies. Ambition and the love of rule are not the passions that inspire him. As a king's son he would have been contented; but now he is first constrained to consider the difference which separates a sovereign from a subject. The crown was not hereditary; yet a longer possession of it by his father would have strengthened the pretensions of an only son, and secured his hopes of the succession. In place of this, he now beholds himself excluded by his uncle, in spite of specious promises, most probably for ever. He is now poor in goods and favour, and a stranger in the scene which from youth he had looked upon as his inheritance. His temper here assumes its first mournful tinge. He feels that now he is not more—that he is less—than a private nobleman; he offers himself as the servant of every one; he is not courteous and condescending, he is needy and degraded.

"His past condition he remembers as a vanished dream. It is in vain that his uncle strives to cheer him,—to present his situation in another point of view. The feeling of his nothingness will not leave him.

"The second stroke that came upon him wounded deeper, bowed still more. It was the marriage of his mother. The faithful tender son had yet a mother, when his father passed away. He hoped, in the company of his surviving noble-minded parent, to reverence the heroic form of the departed; but his mother too he loses, and it is something worse than death that robs him of her. The trustful image, which a good child loves to form of its parents, is gone. With the dead there is no help; on the living no hold. She also is a woman, and her name is Frailty, like that of all her sex.

"Now first does he feel himself completely bent and orphaned; and no happiness of life can repay what he has lost. Not reflective or sorrowful by nature, reflection and sorrow have become for him a

* "It has been censured as a contradiction, that Hamlet in the soliloquy on self-murder should say,—

'The undiscover'd country, from whose bourn
No traveller returns—'

for was not the Ghost a returned traveller? Shakspeare, however, purposely wished to show, that Hamlet could not fix himself in any conviction of any kind whatever."

heavy obligation. It is thus that we see him first enter on the scene. Figure to yourselves this youth, this son of princes; conceive him vividly, bring his state before your eyes, and then observe him when he learns that his father's spirit walks; stand by him in the terrors of the night, when the venerable ghost itself appears before him. A horrid shudder passes over him; he speaks to the mysterious form; he sees it beckon him; he follows it and hears. The fearful accusation of his uncle rings in his ears; the summons to revenge, and the piercing, oft-repeated prayer, 'Remember me!'

"And when the ghost has vanished, who is it that stands before us? A young hero panting for vengeance? A prince by birth, rejoicing to be called to punish the usurper of his crown? No! trouble and astonishment take hold of the solitary young man: he grows bitter against smiling villains, swears that he will not forget the spirit, and concludes with the significant ejaculation,—

'The time is out of joint: O cursed spite,
That ever I was born to set it right!'

In these words, I imagine, will be found the key to Hamlet's whole procedure. To me it is clear that Shakspeare meant, in the present case, to represent the effects of a great action laid upon a soul unfit for the performance of it. In this view the whole piece seems to me to be composed. There is an oak-tree planted in a costly jar, which should have borne only pleasant flowers in its bosom;—the roots expand, the jar is shivered.

"A lovely, pure, noble, and most moral nature, without the strength of nerve which forms a hero, sinks beneath a burden which it cannot bear, and must not cast away. All duties are holy for him; the present is too hard. Impossibilities have been required of him;—not in themselves impossibilities, but such for him. He winds, and turns, and torments himself; he advances and recoils; is ever put in mind, ever puts himself in mind; at last does all but lose his purpose from his thoughts; yet still without recovering his peace of mind."—Goethe.

"This is that Hamlet the Dane whom we read of in our youth, and whom we seem almost to remember in our after years;—he who made that famous soliloquy on life, who gave the advice to the players, who thought 'this goodly frame, the earth, a sterile promontory, and this brave o'erhanging firmament, the air—this majestical roof fretted with golden fire, a foul and pestilent congregation of vapours;' whom 'man delighted not, nor woman neither;' he who talked with the gravediggers, and moralised on Yorick's skull; the schoolfellow of Rosencrantz and Guildenstern at Wittenberg; the friend of Horatio; the lover of Ophelia; he that was mad and sent to England; the slow avenger of his father's death; who lived at the court of Horwendillus five hundred years before we were born, but all whose thoughts we seem to know as well as we do our own, because we have read them in Shakespeare.

"Hamlet is a name; his speeches and sayings but the idle coinage of the poet's brain. What, then, are they not real? They are as real as our own thoughts; their reality is in the reader's mind. It is *we* who are Hamlet. This play has a prophetic truth, which is above that of history. Whoever has become thoughtful and melancholy through his own mishaps or those of others; whoever has borne about with him the clouded brow of reflection, and thought himself 'too much i' the sun;' whoever has seen the golden lamp of day dimmed by envious mists rising in his own breast, and could find in the world before him only a dull blank with nothing left remarkable in it; whoever has known 'the pangs of despised love, the insolence of office, or the spurns which patient merit of the unworthy takes;' he who has felt his mind sink within him, and sadness cling to his heart like a malady, who has had his hopes blighted and his youth staggered by the apparitions of strange things; who cannot be well at ease while he sees evil hovering near him like a spectre; whose powers of action have been eaten up by thought,—he to whom the universe seems infinite, and himself nothing; whose bitterness of soul makes him careless of consequences, and who goes to a play as his best resource to shove off, to a second remove, the evils of life, by a mock-representation of them—this is the true Hamlet."—Hazlitt.

Act III. Sc. 1.

JULIUS CÆSAR.

THIS tragedy, there can be no reasonable doubt, was first published in the folio collection of 1623, where it is printed with, for that volume, a remarkable exemption from typographical inaccuracies. The date of its production is less certain. Malone, in his "Attempt to ascertain the order in which the Plays of Shakespeare were written," concludes that it could not have been composed before 1607; but, as his argument mainly rests upon the fact that a tragedy with the same title by William Alexander, afterwards Earl of Sterline, was printed in London that year,* from which he conjectured Shakespeare had derived one or two ideas, it cannot be regarded as satisfactory. Upon safer grounds, we think, Mr. Collier believes that Shakespeare's "Julius Cæsar" was written and acted before 1603. In Act V. Sc. 5, it will be remembered, Antony pays a beautiful tribute to the character of Brutus,—

> "His life was gentle; and *the elements*
> *So mix'd in him,* that Nature might stand up
> And say to all the world, *This was a man!*"

Referring to this passage, Mr. Collier observes, "In Drayton's 'Barons' Wars,' Book III. edit. 8vo. 1603, p. 61, we meet with the subsequent stanza. The author is speaking of Mortimer:—

> "'Such one he was, of him we boldly say,
> In whose rich soul all sovereign powers did suit,
> In whom in peace *th' elements all lay*
> *So mix'd,* as none could sovereignty impute;
> As all did govern, yet all did obey:
> His lively temper was so absolute,
> That't seem'd, when heaven his model first began,
> In him it show'd *perfection of a man.*'

Italic type is hardly necessary to establish that one poet must have availed himself, not only of the thought, but of the very words of the other. The question is, was Shakespeare indebted to Drayton, or Drayton to Shakespeare? We shall not enter into general probabilities, founded upon the original and exhaustless stores of the mind of our great dramatist, but advert to a few dates, which, we think, warrant the conclusion that Drayton, having heard 'Julius Cæsar' at a theatre, or seen it in manuscript, before 1603, applied to his own purpose, perhaps unconsciously, what, in fact, belonged to another poet.

"Drayton's 'Barons' Wars' first appeared in 1596, 4to., under the title of 'Mortimeriados.' Malone had a copy without date, and he and Steevens erroneously imagined that the poem had been originally printed in 1598. In the 4to. of 1596, and in the undated edition, it is not divided into books, and is in seven-line stanzas; and what is there said of Mortimer bears no likeness whatever to Shakespeare's expressions in 'Julius Cæsar.' Drayton afterwards changed the title from 'Mortimeriados' to 'The Barons' Wars,' and remodelled the whole historical poem, altering the stanza from the English ballad form to the Italian *ottava rima.* This course he took before 1603, when it came out in octavo, with the stanza first quoted, which contains so marked a similarity to the lines from 'Julius Cæsar.' We apprehend that he did so, because he had heard or seen Shakespeare's tragedy before 1603; and we think that strong presumptive

* It was published in Scotland, of which Malone was not aware, three years before.

proof that he was the borrower and not Shakespeare, is derived from the fact, that in the subsequent impressions of the 'Barons' Wars,' in 1605, 1607, 1608, 1610, and 1613, the stanza remained precisely as in the edition of 1603: but in 1619, after Shakespeare's death and before 'Julius Cæsar' was printed, Drayton made even a nearer approach to the words of his original, thus:—

"'He was a man, then boldly dare to say,
In whose rich soul the virtues well did suit;
In whom *so mix'd the elements did lay,*
That none to one could sovereignty impute;
As all did govern, so did all obey:
He of a temper was so absolute,
As that it seem'd, when *Nature* him began,
She meant to show *all that might be in man.*'"

We think it will be admitted that Mr. Collier has made out a very strong case,—all but proved, indeed, that in this instance Drayton was the borrower, and, as a consequence, that Shakespeare's tragedy is of an earlier date by some years than Malone and others had supposed.

The material incidents of this tragedy appear to have been derived from North's translation of Plutarch; but as there was a Latin play upon the subject of Cæsar—"Epilogus Cæsaris Interfecti," &c.—written by Dr. Richard Eedes, which was played at Christ's Church Coll., Oxford, in 1582, and an old anonymous play in English, of the same age, it is possible that Shakespeare may have incurred some obligations to one or both of these.

Persons Represented.

JULIUS CÆSAR.

OCTAVIUS CÆSAR, MARCUS ANTONIUS, M. ÆMIL. LEPIDUS, } *Triumvirs, after the death of* Julius Cæsar.

CICERO, PUBLIUS, POPILIUS LENA; *Senators.*

MARCUS BRUTUS, CASSIUS, CASCA, CINNA, TREBONIUS, LIGARIUS, DECIUS BRUTUS, METELLUS CIMBER, } *Conspirators against* Julius Cæsar.

FLAVIUS *and* MARULLUS, *Tribunes.*

ARTEMIDORUS, *a Sophist of* Cnidos.

CINNA, *a Poet. Another* Poet.

A Soothsayer.

LUCILIUS, TITINIUS, MESSALA, YOUNG CATO, *and* VOLUMNIUS; *Friends to* Brutus *and* Cassius.

VARRO, CLITUS, CLAUDIUS, STRATO, LUCIUS, DARDANIUS; *Servants to* Brutus.

PINDARUS, *Servant to* Cassius.

CALPHURNIA, *Wife to* Julius Cæsar.

PORTIA, *Wife to* Brutus.

Senators, Citizens, Guards, Attendants, &c.

SCENE,—*During a great part of the Play at* ROME; *afterwards at* SARDIS; *and near* PHILIPPI.

ACT I.

SCENE I.—Rome. *A Street.*

Enter FLAVIUS, MARULLUS,[a] *and a rabble of* Citizens.

FLAV. Hence! home, you idle creatures, get you home;
Is this a holiday? What! know you not,
Being mechanical, you ought not walk
Upon a labouring day, without the sign
Of your profession?—Speak, what trade art thou?

1 CIT. Why, sir, a carpenter.

MAR. Where is thy leather apron and thy rule?
What dost thou with thy best apparel on?—
You, sir, what trade are you?

2 CIT. Truly, sir, in respect of a fine workman, I am but, as you would say, a cobbler.

MAR. But what trade art thou? Answer me directly.[b]

2 CIT. A trade, sir, that I hope I may use with a safe conscience; which is, indeed, sir, a mender of bad soles.

MAR. What trade, thou knave? thou naughty knave, what trade?[c]

2 CIT. Nay, I beseech you, sir, be not out with me: yet if you be out, sir, I can mend you.

MAR. What meanest thou by that? *Mend* me, thou saucy fellow?

2 CIT. Why, sir, cobble you.

---

[a] MARULLUS,—] A correction first made by Theobald, the old text having throughout, *Murellus*.

[b] — directly.] *Explicitly, without ambiguity.*

[c] What trade, thou knave? &c.] In the old copies this speech is erroneously assigned to Flavius.

FLAV. Thou art a cobbler, art thou?

2 CIT. Truly, sir, all that I live by is with the awl: I meddle with no tradesman's matters, nor women's matters, but with awl.[a] I am, indeed, sir, a surgeon to old shoes; when they are in great danger, I re-cover them. As proper men as ever trod upon neat's-leather have gone upon my handiwork.

FLAV. But wherefore art not in thy shop to-day?
Why dost thou lead these men about the streets?

2 CIT. Truly, sir, to wear out their shoes, to get myself into more work. But, indeed, sir, we make holiday, to see Cæsar, and to rejoice in his triumph.

MAR. Wherefore rejoice? What conquest brings he home?[b]
What tributaries follow him to Rome,
To grace in captive bonds his chariot-wheels?
You blocks, you stones, you worse than senseless things!
O, you hard hearts, you cruel men of Rome,
Knew you not Pompey? Many a time and oft
Have you climb'd up to walls and battlements,
To towers and windows, yea, to chimney-tops,
Your infants in your arms, and there have sat
The live-long day, with patient expectation,
To see great Pompey pass the streets of Rome:
And when you saw his chariot but appear,
Have you not made an universal shout
That Tiber trembled underneath her banks,
To hear the replication of your sounds,
Made in her concave shores?
And do you now put on your best attire?
And do you now cull out a holiday?
And do you now strew flowers in his way,
That comes in triumph over Pompey's blood?
Be gone!
Run to your houses, fall upon your knees,
Pray to the gods to intermit the plague
That needs must light on this ingratitude.

FLAV. Go, go, good countrymen, and, for this fault,
Assemble all the poor men of your sort;
Draw them to Tiber banks, and weep your tears
Into the channel, till the lowest stream
Do kiss the most exalted shores of all.—
[*Exeunt* Citizens.
See, whêr their basest metal be not mov'd;
They vanish tongue-tied in their guiltiness.
Go you down that way towards the Capitol;
This way will I: disrobe the images,
If you do find them deck'd with ceremonies.[c]

MAR. May we do so?
You know it is the feast of Lupercal.

FLAV. It is no matter; let no images
Be hung with Cæsar's trophies. I 'll about,
And drive away the vulgar from the streets:
So do you too, where you perceive them thick.
These growing feathers pluck'd from Cæsar's wing
Will make him fly an ordinary pitch;
Who else would soar above the view of men,
And keep us all in servile fearfulness. [*Exeunt.*

SCENE II.—*The same. A public Place.*

Enter, in procession, with music, CÆSAR; ANTONY, *for the course;* CALPHURNIA, PORTIA, DECIUS, CICERO, BRUTUS, CASSIUS, *and* CASCA, *a great crowd following; among them a* Soothsayer.

CÆS. Calphurnia,—

CASCA. Peace, ho! Cæsar speaks.
[*Music ceases.*

CÆS. Calphurnia,—

CAL. Here, my lord.

CÆS. Stand you directly in Antonius' way,
When he doth run his course.(1)—Antonius,—

ANT. Cæsar, my lord.

CÆS. Forget not, in your speed, Antonius,
To touch Calphurnia; for our elders say,
The barren, touched in this holy chase,
Shake off their sterile curse.

ANT. I shall remember:
When Cæsar says, *Do this*, it is perform'd.

CÆS. Set on; and leave no ceremony out.
[*Music.*

SOOTH. Cæsar!

CÆS. Ha! Who calls?

CASCA. Bid every noise be still:—peace yet again![d] [*Music ceases.*

CÆS. Who is it in the press that calls on me?
I hear a tongue, shriller than all the music,
Cry, *Cæsar*. Speak; Cæsar is turn'd to hear.

SOOTH. Beware the ides of March.

CÆS. What man is that?

---

[a] I meddle with no tradesman's matters, &c.] Farmer conjectured that the true reading is, "I meddle with no trade, man's matters," &c.; and, substituting *trades* for trade, we incline to his opinion.

[b] Wherefore rejoice? &c.] "This was in the beginning of B. C. 44 (A. U. C. 709), when Cæsar, having returned from Spain in the preceding October, after defeating the sons of Pompey at the Battle of Munda (fought 17 March, B. C. 45), had been appointed Consul for the next ten years, and Dictator for life. The festival of the Lupercalia, at which he was offered and declined the crown, was celebrated 13th February, B. C. 44, and he was assassinated 15th March following, being then in his fifty-sixth year."—CRAIK'S *English of Shakespeare*, p. 71.

[c] — *with* ceremonies.] See note (c), p. 23, Vol. II.

[d] Bid every noise be still:—peace yet again!] If this did not originally form a continuation of Cæsar's previous speech, the regulation we presume to have been:—

"CASCA. Bid every noise be still:—peace yet!
CÆS. Again!
Who is it," &c.

BRU. A soothsayer, bids you beware the ides of March.
CÆS. Set him before me; let me see his face.
CAS. Fellow, come from the throng: look upon Cæsar.
CÆS. What say'st thou to me now? speak once again.
SOOTH. Beware the Ides[a] of March.
CÆS. He is a dreamer; let us leave him;—pass.
[*Sennet. Exeunt all but* BRUTUS *and* CASSIUS.
CAS. Will you go see the order of the course?
BRU. Not I.
CAS. I pray you, do.
BRU. I am not gamesome: I do lack some part
Of that quick spirit that is in Antony.
Let me not hinder, Cassius, your desires;
I 'll leave you.
CAS. Brutus, I do observe you now of late:
I have not from your eyes that gentleness
And show of love as I was wont to have:
You bear too stubborn and too strange a hand
Over your friend that loves you.
BRU. Cassius,
Be not deceiv'd: if I have veil'd my look,
I turn the trouble of my countenance
Merely[b] upon myself. Vexed I am,
Of late, with passions of some difference,
Conceptions only proper to myself,
Which give some soil, perhaps, to my behaviours;
But let not therefore my good friends be griev'd,
(Among which number, Cassius, be you one)
Nor construe any further my neglect,
Than that poor Brutus, with himself at war,
Forgets the shows of love to other men.
CAS. Then, Brutus, I have much mistook your passion;
By means whereof this breast of mine hath buried
Thoughts of great value, worthy cogitations.
Tell me, good Brutus, can you see your face?
BRU. No, Cassius: for the eye sees not itself,
But by reflection by[c] some other things.
CAS. 'T is just:
And it is very much lamented, Brutus,
That you have no such mirrors as will turn
Your hidden worthiness into your eye,
That you might see your shadow. I have heard,
Where many of the best respect in Rome,
(Except immortal Cæsar) speaking of Brutus,
And groaning underneath this age's yoke,
Have wish'd that noble Brutus had his eyes.
BRU. Into what dangers would you lead me, Cassius,
That you would have me seek into myself
For that which is not in me?
CAS. Therefore, good Brutus, be prepar'd to hear:
And, since you know you cannot see yourself
So well as by reflection, I, your glass,
Will modestly discover to yourself
That of yourself which you yet know not of.
And be not jealous on me, gentle Brutus:
Were I a common laugher,[d] or did use
To stale with ordinary oaths my love
To every new protester; if you know
That I do fawn on men, and hug them hard,
And after scandal them; or if you know
That I profess myself in banqueting
To all the rout, then hold me dangerous.
[*Flourish and shout.*
BRU. What means this shouting? I do fear the people
Choose Cæsar for their king.
CAS. Ay, do you fear it?
Then must I think you would not have it so.
BRU. I would not, Cassius; yet I love him well.—
But wherefore do you hold me here so long?
What is it that you would impart to me?
If it be aught toward the general good,
Set honour in one eye, and death i' the other,
And I will look on both indifferently:
For, let the gods so speed me as I love
The name of honour more than I fear death.
CAS. I know that virtue to be in you, Brutus,
As well as I do know your outward favour.
Well, honour is the subject of my story.—
I cannot tell what you and other men
Think of this life; but, for my single self,
I had as lief not be as live to be
In awe of such a thing as I myself.
I was born free as Cæsar; so were you:
We both have fed as well; and we can both
Endure the winter's cold as well as he;
For once, upon a raw and gusty day,
The troubled Tiber chafing with her shores,
Cæsar said to me, *Dar'st thou, Cassius, now,*
Leap in with me into this angry flood,
And swim to yonder point?—Upon the word,
Accoutred as I was, I plunged in,
And bade him follow: so, indeed, he did.
The torrent roar'd; and we did buffet it
With lusty sinews; throwing it aside
And stemming it with hearts of controversy:
But ere we could arrive the point propos'd,

---

a *The* Ides *of March.*] The Ides (*Idus*) fell on the 15th of March, May, July, and October, and on the 13th of the remaining months.

b Merely—] *Purely, solely, entirely.*

c *But by reflection* by *some other things.*] Here, not improbably, the poet wrote,—

"— *of* some other things,"

or,—

"—*from* some other things,"

the second "by" in the old text being an accidental repetition of the compositor.

d *Were I a common* laugher,—] Rowe's correction; the old copy having, "Laughter." As Mr. Craik remarks, neither word seems to be quite satisfactory.

Cæsar cried, *Help me, Cassius, or I sink.*
I, as Æneas, our great ancestor,
Did from the flames of Troy upon his shoulder
The old Anchises bear, so from the waves of Tiber
Did I the tired Cæsar: and this man
Is now become a god; and Cassius is
A wretched creature, and must bend his body
If Cæsar carelessly but nod on him.
He had a fever when he was in Spain,
And, when the fit was on him, I did mark
How he did shake: 't is true, this god did shake:
His coward lips did from their colour fly;
And that same eye whose bend doth awe the world
Did lose his lustre: I did hear him groan:
Ay, and that tongue of his, that bade the Romans
Mark him, and write his speeches in their books,
Alas! it cried, *Give me some drink, Titinius,*
As a sick girl. Ye gods, it doth amaze me,
A man of such a feeble temper should
So get the start of the majestic world,
And bear the palm alone. [*Flourish, and shout.*

BRU. Another general shout!
I do believe that these applauses are
For some new honours that are heap'd on Cæsar.

CAS. Why, man, he doth bestride the narrow world
Like a Colossus; and we petty men
Walk under his huge legs, and peep about
To find ourselves dishonourable graves.
Men at some time are masters of their fates:
The fault, dear Brutus, is not in our stars,
But in ourselves, that we are underlings.
Brutus, and *Cæsar*: what should be in that *Cæsar?*
Why should that name be sounded more than yours?
Write them together, yours is as fair a name;
Sound them, it doth become the mouth as well;
Weigh them, it is as heavy; conjure with 'em,
Brutus will start a spirit as soon as *Cæsar*.
Now, in the names of all the gods at once,
Upon what meat does this our Cæsar feed,
That he is grown so great? Age, thou art sham'd!
Rome, thou hast lost the breed of noble bloods!
When went there by an age, since the great flood,
But it was fam'd with more than with one man?
When could they say, till now, that talk'd of Rome,
That her wide walks[a] encompass'd but one man?
Now is it Rome indeed, and room enough
When there is in it but one only man.
O, you and I have heard our fathers say,
There was a Brutus once that would have brook'd
The eternal devil to keep his state in Rome,
As easily as a king!

BRU. That you do love me, I am nothing jealous;
What you would work me to, I have some aim;
How I have thought of this, and of these times,
I shall recount hereafter; for this present,
I would not, so with love I might entreat you,
Be any further mov'd. What you have said,
I will consider; what you have to say,
I will with patience hear; and find a time
Both meet to hear and answer such high things.
Till then, my noble friend, chew upon this;
Brutus had rather be a villager,
Than to repute himself a son of Rome
Under these hard conditions as this time
Is like to lay upon us.

CAS. I am glad that my weak words
Have struck but thus much show of fire from Brutus.

BRU. The games are done, and Cæsar is returning.

CAS. As they pass by, pluck Casca by the sleeve;
And he will, after his sour fashion, tell you
What has proceeded worthy note to-day.

Re-enter CÆSAR *and his* Train.

BRU. I will do so:—but, look you, Cassius,
The angry spot doth glow on Cæsar's brow,
And all the rest look like a chidden train:
Calphurnia's cheek is pale; and Cicero
Looks with such ferret and such fiery eyes,
As we have seen him in the Capitol,
Being cross'd in conference by some senators.

CAS. Casca will tell us what the matter is.

CÆS. Antonius,—

ANT. Cæsar.

CÆS. Let me have men about me that are fat;
Sleek-headed men, and such as sleep o' nights:
Yond Cassius has a lean and hungry look;
He thinks too much: such men are dangerous.[b]

ANT. Fear him not, Cæsar, he's not dangerous;
He is a noble Roman, and well given.

---

[a] — *wide* walks—] Modern editors nearly all adopt the emendation, wide *walls*, proposed by Rowe, but the original, "wide *walks*," *i.e.* "spacious bounds," ought not to be displaced.

"In the time of civill warres the souldiers of the Castell and chanons of Old Sarum fell at ods, insomuch that after other bralles they fell at last to sad blowes. It happened therefore in a rogation weeke that the clergie going in solemne procession a controversie fell betweene them about certeine *walkes and limits* which the one side claimed and the other denied. Such also was the hot entertainment on ech part, that at the last the Castellanes espieng their time, gate betweene the cleargie and the towne, and so cotled them as they returned homeward, that they feared anie more to gang about their *bounds* for a yeare.—HOLINSHED'S *Description of Britaine*, p. 57.

[b] Let me have men about me that are fat;" &c.] So in North's translation of Plutarch's Life of Julius Cæsar:—"Cæsar also had Cassius in great jealousie, and suspected him much: whereupon he said on a time to his friends, what wil Cassius do, thinke ye? I like not his pale lookes. Another time when Cæsars friends complained unto him of Antonius and Dolabella, that they pretended some mischiefe towards him, he answered them again, As for those fat men and smooth combed heads, quoth he, I never reckon of them; but these pale visaged and carion leane people, I feare them most, meaning Brutus and Cassius."

CÆS. Would he were fatter!—but I fear him not:
Yet if my name were liable to fear,
I do not know the man I should avoid
So soon as that spare Cassius. He reads much;
He is a great observer, and he looks
Quite through the deeds of men: he loves no plays,
As thou dost, Antony; he hears no music:
Seldom he smiles; and smiles in such a sort
As if he mock'd himself, and scorn'd his spirit
That could be mov'd to smile at any-thing.
Such men as he be never at heart's ease
Whiles they behold a greater than themselves;
And therefore are they very dangerous.
I rather tell thee what is to be fear'd
Than what I fear,—for always I am Cæsar.
Come on my right hand, for this ear is deaf,
And tell me truly what thou think'st of him.
[*Exeunt* CÆSAR *and his* Train. CASCA *stays behind*.

CASCA. You pull'd me by the cloak; would you speak with me?

BRU. Ay, Casca; tell us what hath chanc'd to-day,
That Cæsar looks so sad?

CASCA. Why, you were with him, were you not?

BRU. I should not, then, ask Casca what had chanc'd.

CASCA. Why, there was a crown offered him: and being offered him, he put it by with the back of his hand, thus; and then the people fell a shouting.

BRU. What was the second noise for?

CASCA. Why, for that too.

CAS. They shouted thrice: what was the last cry for?

CASCA. Why, for that too.

BRU. Was the crown offered him thrice?

CASCA. Ay, marry, was't, and he put it by thrice, every time gentler than other; and at every putting-by, mine honest neighbours shouted.

CAS. Who offered him the crown?

CASCA. Why, Antony.

BRU. Tell us the manner of it, gentle Casca.

CASCA. I can as well be hanged as tell the manner of it: it was mere foolery; I did not mark it. I saw Mark Antony offer him a crown;—yet 'twas not a crown neither, 'twas one of these coronets;—and, as I told you, he put it by once; but for all that, to my thinking, he would fain have had it. Then he offered it to him again; then he put it by again: but, to my thinking, he was very loth to lay his fingers off it. And then he offered it the third time; he put it the third time by: and still as he refused it, the rabblement shouted,[a] and clapped their chapped hands, and threw up their

[a] — *the rabblement* shouted,—] This emendation is due to Hanmer, the first three folios having *howted*, and the fourth *houted*.

sweaty nightcaps, and uttered such a deal of stinking breath because Cæsar refused the crown, that it had almost choked Cæsar;(2) for he swooned, and fell down at it: and for mine own part, I durst not laugh, for fear of opening my lips, and receiving the bad air.

CAS. But, soft, I pray you: what, did Cæsar swoon?

CASCA. He fell down in the market-place, and foamed at mouth, and was speechless.

BRU. 'Tis very like,—he hath the falling sickness.

CAS. No, Cæsar hath it not; but you, and I,
And honest Casca, we have the falling sickness.

CASCA. I know not what you mean by that; but, I am sure, Cæsar fell down. If the tag-rag people did not clap him and hiss him, according as he pleased and displeased them, as they use to do the players in the theatre, I am no true man.

BRU. What said he when he came unto himself?

CASCA. Marry, before he fell down, when he perceived the common herd was glad he refused the crown, he plucked me ope his doublet, and offered them his throat to cut!—An I had been a man of any occupation,[a] if I would not have taken him at a word, I would I might go to hell among the rogues:—and so he fell. When he came to himself again, he said, If he had done or said any-thing amiss, he desired their worships to think it was his infirmity. Three or four wenches, where I stood, cried *Alas, good soul!*—and forgave him with all their hearts: but there's no heed to be taken of them; if Cæsar had stabbed their mothers they would have done no less.

BRU. And after that, he came, thus sad, away?

CASCA. Ay.

CAS. Did Cicero say anything?

CASCA. Ay, he spoke Greek.

CAS. To what effect?

CASCA. Nay, an I tell you that I'll ne'er look you i' the face again: but those that understood him smiled at one another, and shook their heads; but, for mine own part, it was Greek to me. I could tell you more news too: Marullus and Flavius, for pulling scarfs off Cæsar's images, are put to silence. Fare you well. There was more foolery yet, if I could remember it.

CAS. Will you sup with me to-night, Casca?

CASCA. No, I am promised forth.

CAS. Will you dine with me to-morrow?

CASCA. Ay, if I be alive, and your mind hold, and your dinner worth the eating.

CAS. Good; I will expect you.

CASCA. Do so: farewell both. [*Exit.*

BRU. What a blunt fellow is this grown to be!
He was quick mettle when he went to school.

CAS. So is he now, in execution
Of any bold or noble enterprise,
However he puts on this tardy form.
This rudeness is a sauce to his good wit,
Which gives men stomach to digest his words
With better appetite.

BRU. And so it is. For this time I will leave you:
To-morrow, if you please to speak with me,
I will come home to you; or, if you will,
Come home to me, and I will wait for you.

CAS. I will do so:—till then, think of the world.
[*Exit* BRUTUS.
Well, Brutus, thou art noble; yet, I see
Thy honourable metal may be wrought
From that it is dispos'd: therefore it is meet
That noble minds keep ever with their likes;
For who so firm that cannot be seduc'd?
Cæsar doth bear me hard;[b] but he loves Brutus:
If I were Brutus now, and he were Cassius,
He should not humour me. I will this night,
In several hands, in at his windows throw,
As if they came from several citizens,
Writings, all tending to the great opinion
That Rome holds of his name; wherein obscurely
Cæsar's ambition shall be glanced at:
And, after this, let Cæsar seat him sure;
For we will shake him, or worse days endure.
[*Exit.*

SCENE III.—*The same. A Street.*

Thunder and lightning. Enter, from opposite sides, CASCA, *with his sword drawn, and* CICERO.

CIC. Good even, Casca: brought you Cæsar home?
Why are you breathless? and why stare you so?

CASCA. Are not you mov'd, when all the sway of earth
Shakes like a thing unfirm? O, Cicero,
I have seen tempests, when the scolding winds
Have riv'd the knotty oaks; and I have seen
The ambitious ocean swell, and rage, and foam,
To be exalted with the threat'ning clouds:

---

[a] An I had been a man of any occupation,—] If I had been one of the mechanics.

[b] *Cæsar* doth bear me hard:] The commentators appear to have overlooked the exact force of this. It is an expression borrowed, we believe, from horsemanship, equivalent, literally, to, *keeps a tight rein upon me*, and, metaphorically, to, *does not trust me*, or *fears*, or *doubts me:* so Antony, in Act III. Sc. 1, says,—

"—— if you bear me hard,"
(*i.e.* if you fear to trust me)
"Now, whilst your purpled hands do reek and smoke,
Fulfil your pleasure."

Compare also, Act I. Sc. 2,—

"*You bear too stubborn and too strange a hand*
Over your friend that loves you."

But never till to-night, never till now,
Did I go through a tempest dropping fire.
Either there is a civil strife in heaven;
Or else the world, too saucy with the gods,
Incenses them to send destruction.

CIC. Why, saw you anything more wonderful?

CASCA. A common slave (you know him well by sight)
Held up his left hand, which did flame and burn
Like twenty torches join'd; and yet his hand,
Not sensible of fire, remain'd unscorch'd.[a]
Besides, (I have not since put up my sword)
Against the Capitol I met a lion,
Who glar'd* upon me, and went surly by
Without annoying me: and there were drawn
Upon a heap a hundred ghastly women,
Transformed with their fear; who swore they saw
Men, all in fire, walk up and down the streets.
And yesterday the bird of night did sit,
Even at noon-day, upon the market-place,
Hooting and shrieking. When these prodigies
Do so conjointly meet, let not men say
These are their reasons,—they are natural;
For, I believe, they are portentous things
Unto the climate that they point upon.

CIC. Indeed, it is a strange disposed time:
But men may construe things after their fashion,
Clean from the purpose of the things themselves.
Comes Cæsar to the Capitol to-morrow?

CASCA. He doth; for he did bid Antonius
Send word to you he would be there to-morrow.

CIC. Good night, then, Casca: this disturbed sky
Is not to walk in.

CASCA. Farewell, Cicero. [*Exit* CICERO.

Enter CASSIUS.

CAS. Who's there?

CASCA. A Roman.

CAS. Casca, by your voice.

CASCA. Your ear is good. Cassius, what night is this![b]

CAS. A very pleasing night to honest men.

CASCA. Who ever knew the heavens menace so?

(*) Old text, *glaz'd*.

a A common slave (you know him well by sight)
Held up his left hand, &c.]
"A slave of the souldiers that did cast a marvellous burning flame out of his hands, insomuch as they that saw it thought he had been burnt; but when the fire was out, it was found that he had no hurt."—*Life of Julius Cæsar in North's Plutarch.*

b — what night is this!] Simply, "what *a* night is this!" the omission of the article being not at all uncommon in such exclamations. In proof of this Mr. Dyce quotes,—

"*What fool* is she, that knows I am a maid,
And would not force the letter to my view!"
Two Gentlemen of Verona, Act I. Sc. 2

And,—

"*Fab. What dish* of poison has she dressed him!
Sir To. And with *what wing* the stannyel checks at it!"
Twelfth Night, Act II. Sc. 5.

CAS. Those that have known the earth so full of faults.
For my part, I have walk'd about the streets,
Submitting me unto the perilous night;
And, thus unbraced, Casca, as you see,
Have bar'd my bosom to the thunder-stone:[a]
And when the cross blue lightning seem'd to open
The breast of heaven, I did present myself
Even in the aim and very flash of it.

CASCA. But wherefore did you so much tempt the heavens?
It is the part of men to fear and tremble,
When the most mighty gods, by tokens, send
Such dreadful heralds to astonish us.

CAS. You are dull, Casca; and those sparks of life
That should be in a Roman you do want,
Or else you use not. You look pale, and gaze,
And put on fear, and cast yourself in wonder,
To see the strange impatience of the heavens:
But if you would consider the true cause
Why all these fires, why all these gliding ghosts,
Why birds and beasts, from quality and kind;[b]
Why old men fools,[c] and children calculate;
Why all these things change from their ordinance,
Their natures, and pre-formed faculties,
To monstrous[d] quality;—why, you shall find,
That heaven hath infus'd them with these spirits,
To make them instruments of fear and warning
Unto some monstrous state.
Now could I, Casca, name to thee a man
Most like this dreadful night,
That thunders, lightens, opens graves, and roars
As doth the lion in the Capitol,—
A man no mightier than thyself or me,
In personal action; yet prodigious[e] grown,
And fearful, as these strange eruptions are.

CASCA. 'Tis Cæsar that you mean; is it not, Cassius?

CAS. Let it be who it is: for Romans now
Have thews and limbs like to their ancestors,
But, woe the while! our fathers' minds are dead,
And we are govern'd with our mothers' spirits;
Our yoke and sufferance show us womanish.

CASCA. Indeed, they say the senators to-morrow
Mean to establish Cæsar as a king;
And he shall wear his crown by sea and land,
In every place, save here in Italy.

CAS. I know where I will wear this dagger then;
Cassius from bondage will deliver Cassius:
Therein, ye gods, you make the weak most strong;
Therein, ye gods, you tyrants do defeat:
Nor stony tower, nor walls of beaten brass,
Nor airless dungeon, nor strong links of iron,
Can be retentive to the strength of spirit;
But life, being weary of these worldly bars,
Never lacks power to dismiss itself.
If I know this, know all the world besides,
That part of tyranny that I do bear
I can shake off at pleasure. [*Thunder still.*

CASCA. So can I:
So every bondman in his own hand bears
The power to cancel his captivity.

CAS. And why should Cæsar be a tyrant, then?
Poor man! I know he would not be a wolf,
But that he sees the Romans are but sheep:
He were no lion, were not Romans hinds.
Those that with haste will make a mighty fire
Begin it with weak straws: what trash is Rome,
What rubbish, and what offal, when it serves
For the base matter to illuminate
So vile a thing as Cæsar!—but, O, grief!
Where hast thou led me? I, perhaps, speak this
Before a willing bondman; then I know
My answer must be made: but I am arm'd,
And dangers are to me indifferent.

CASCA. You speak to Casca; and to such a man
That is no fleering tell-tale. Hold my hand:
Be factious for redress of all these griefs;
And I will set this foot of mine as far
As who goes farthest.

CAS. There's a bargain made.
Now know you, Casca, I have mov'd already
Some certain of the noblest-minded Romans,
To undergo with me an enterprise
Of honourable-dangerous consequence;
And I do know, by this, they stay for me
In Pompey's porch: for now, this fearful night,
There is no stir or walking in the streets;
And the complexion of the element
In favour's like[f] the work we have in hand,
Most bloody, fiery, and most terrible.

CASCA. Stand close awhile, for here comes one in haste.

CAS. 'Tis Cinna,—I do know him by his gait;
He is a friend.

Enter CINNA.

Cinna, where haste you so?

CIN. To find out you. Who's that? Metellus Cimber?

---

a — the thunder-stone:] "The thunder-stone is the imaginary produce of the thunder, which the ancients called *Brontia*, mentioned by Pliny (N. H. xxxvii. 10) as a species of gem, and as that which, falling with the lightning, does the mischief."—CRAIK.

b Why birds and beasts, from quality and kind;] That is, why they reverse their habits and nature.

c Why old men fools, and children calculate;] The old copy points thus,—

"Why old men, fools, and children calculate;"

but the punctuation we adopt, which was long ago suggested by Blackstone, clearly gives the sense and antithesis intended, *i.e.* why we have all these fires, &c. why old men, in spite of their experience, have turned fools, and children prophesy.

d — monstrous—] *unnatural, ominously prophetic.*

e — prodigious—] *Portentous, ominous.*

f In favour's *like*—] This is Johnson's reading. The folio has, "Is Favors, like," &c. Capell proposed, "Is *favoured* like;" Rowe, "*Is feverous* like," &c.; and Mr. Hunter would substitute "*It favours* like," &c.

CAS. No, it is Casca; one incorporate
To our attempts. Am I not stay'd for, Cinna?
CIN. I am glad on't. What a fearful night is this!
There's two or three of us have seen strange sights.
CAS. Am I not stay'd for? tell me.
CIN. Yes, you are.
O, Cassius, if you could
But win the noble Brutus to our party—[a]
CAS. Be you content, good Cinna; take this paper,
And look you lay it in the prætor's chair,
Where Brutus may but find it;[b] and throw this
In at his window; set this up with wax
Upon old Brutus' statue: all this done,
Repair to Pompey's porch, where you shall find us.
Is Decius Brutus and Trebonius there?
CIN. All but Metellus Cimber; and he's gone
To seek you at your house. Well, I will hie,
And so bestow these papers as you bade me.
CAS. That done, repair to Pompey's theatre.
[*Exit* CINNA.
Come, Casca, you and I will yet, ere day,
See Brutus at his house: three parts of him
Is ours already; and the man entire,
Upon the next encounter, yields him ours.
CASCA. O, he sits high in all the people's hearts:
And that which would appear offence in us,
His countenance, like richest alchemy,
Will change to virtue and to worthiness.(3)
CAS. Him, and his worth, and our great need of him,
You have right well conceited. Let us go,
For it is after midnight; and, ere day,
We will awake him, and be sure of him. [*Exeunt.*

[a] O, Cassius, if you could
But win the noble Brutus to our party—]
In the folio this speech runs, or rather hobbles, thus,—
"Yes, you are. O Cassius,
If you could but winne the noble Brutus
To our party—"
And in modern editions the arrangement is,—
"Yes
You are. O Cassius, if you could but win
The noble Brutus to our party."
which is intolerable; or, as given by Mr. Knight,—
"Yes, you are.
O, Cassius, if you could but win the noble Brutus
To our party;"
which is not much better. We adopt the distribution of the lines proposed by Mr. Craik, though even this will hardly satisfy the requirements of an ear accustomed to Shakespearian rhythm.

[b] Where Brutus may but find it;] We should now say, "Where *only* Brutus may find it."

ACT II.

SCENE I.—*The same.* Brutus's *Orchard.*

Enter Brutus.

Bru. What, Lucius! ho!—
I cannot, by the progress of the stars,
Give guess how near to day.—Lucius, I say!—
I would it were my fault to sleep so soundly.—
When, Lucius, when?[a] awake, I say! what, Lucius!

[a] When, Lucius, when?] See note (f), p. 449, Vol. I.

Enter LUCIUS.

LUC. Call'd you, my lord?
BRU. Get me a taper in my study, Lucius:
When it is lighted, come and call me here.
LUC. I will, my lord. [*Exit.*
BRU. It must be by his death: and, for my part,
I know no personal cause to spurn at him,
But for the general,—he would be crown'd:[a]
How that might change his nature, there 's the question.
It is the bright day that brings forth the adder;
And that craves wary walking. Crown him?—that;—
And then, I grant, we put a sting in him,
That at his will he may do danger[b] with.
The abuse of greatness is, when it disjoins
Remorse from power: and, to speak truth of Cæsar,
I have not known when his affections sway'd
More than his reason. But 't is a common proof,
That lowliness is young ambition's ladder,
Whereto the climber-upward turns his face;
But when he once attains the upmost round,
He then unto the ladder turns his back,
Looks in the clouds, scorning the base degrees
By which he did ascend: so Cæsar may;
Then, lest he may, prevent.[c] And, since the quarrel
Will bear no colour for the thing he is,
Fashion it thus;—that what he is, augmented,
Would run to these and these extremities:
And therefore think him as a serpent's egg,
Which, hatch'd, would, as his kind,[d] grow mischievous;
And kill him in the shell.

Re-enter LUCIUS.

LUC. The taper burneth in your closet, sir.
Searching the window for a flint, I found
[*Giving a letter.*
This paper, thus seal'd up; and, I am sure,
It did not lie there when I went to bed.

BRU. Get you to bed again, it is not day.
Is not to-morrow, boy, the ides[e] of March?
LUC. I know not, sir.
BRU. Look in the calendar, and bring me word.
LUC. I will, sir. [*Exit.*
BRU. The exhalations, whizzing in the air,
Give so much light, that I may read by them.
[*Opens the letter and reads.*
"Brutus, thou sleep'st; awake! and see thyself.
Shall Rome, &c. Speak, strike, redress!"—
Brutus, thou sleep'st; awake!—
Such instigations have been often dropp'd
Where I have took them up.
Shall Rome, &c. Thus must I piece it out;
Shall Rome stand under one man's awe? What Rome?
My ancestors did from the streets of Rome
The Tarquin drive, when he was call'd a king.
Speak, strike, redress!—Am I entreated
To speak, and strike? O, Rome! I make thee promise,
If the redress will follow, thou receivest
Thy full petition at the hand of Brutus! (1)

Re-enter LUCIUS.

LUC. Sir, March is wasted fourteen[f] days.
[*Knocking without.*
BRU. 'T is good. Go to the gate; somebody knocks.— [*Exit* LUCIUS.
Since Cassius first did whet me against Cæsar
I have not slept.
Between the acting of a dreadful thing
And the first motion, all the interim is
Like a phantasma, or a hideous dream:
The Genius and the mortal instruments
Are then in council; and the state of man,[g]
Like to a little kingdom, suffers then
The nature of an insurrection.

Re-enter LUCIUS.

LUC. Sir, 'tis your brother[h] Cassius at the door,
Who doth desire to see you.
BRU. Is he alone?
LUC. No, sir, there are more[i] with him.

---

a
I know no personal cause to spurn at him,
But for the general,—he would be crown'd:]

This may either mean,—I know no personal cause of enmity against him; only the general, *i.e.* the public good; or,—I know no personal cause, &c. only the general one, that he would be crowned.

b — *he may do* danger *with.*] He may do *damage*, or *mischief* with.

c — prevent.] We have before explained that *to prevent* (*prævenire*) in Shakespeare's day was always employed in the sense of *to come before*, or *anticipate*; whether the purpose of *prevention* were to hinder or to aid.

d — as his kind,—] *According to his nature*; or, *like his species.*

e — *the* ides *of March?*] In the folio, "the *first* of March:" corrected by Theobald.

f — fourteen days.] So Theobald. In the folio, "*fifteene* dayes."

g — and the state of man,—] The original has,—"of *a* man;" Mr. Craik advocates the retention of the article; Mr. Dyce omits it, as having "evidently crept in by the mistake of the transcriber or compositor."

h — *your* brother *Cassius*—] Cassius married Junia, the sister of Brutus.

i — *there are* more *with him.*] Mr. Craik, here and in other passages where it occurs, retains the old form, *mo*; at one time we were inclined to do so likewise, but, upon consideration, thought it better to abide by this orthography only when it was demanded by the verse.

BRU. Do you know them?

LUC. No, sir; their hats are pluck'd about their ears,
And half their faces buried in their cloaks,
That by no means I may discover them
By any mark of favour.

BRU. Let 'em enter.— [*Exit* LUCIUS.
They are the faction. O, Conspiracy!
Sham'st thou to show thy dangerous brow by night,
When evils are most free? O, then, by day
Where wilt thou find a cavern dark enough
To mask thy monstrous visage? Seek none, Conspiracy;
Hide it in smiles and affability:
For if thou path,[a] thy native semblance on,
Not Erebus itself were dim enough
To hide thee from prevention.

Enter CASSIUS, CASCA, DECIUS, CINNA, METELLUS CIMBER, *and* TREBONIUS.

CAS. I think we are too bold upon your rest:
Good-morrow, Brutus; do we trouble you?

BRU. I have been up this hour; awake all night.
Know I these men that come along with you?

CAS. Yes, every man of them; and no man here
But honours you; and every one doth wish
You had but that opinion of yourself
Which every noble Roman bears of you.
This is Trebonius.

BRU. He is welcome hither.

CAS. This, Decius Brutus.

BRU. He is welcome too.

CAS. This, Casca; this, Cinna; and this, Metellus Cimber.

---

a — *if thou* path,—] "Path" is perhaps obscure, and the examples of its employment as a verb, which Steevens adduced, are hardly to the point; but who for a moment could admit the possibility that *put*, as Coleridge suggested, was the genuine word?

BRU. They are all welcome.—
What watchful cares do interpose themselves
Betwixt your eyes and night?
CAS. Shall I entreat a word?
[BRUTUS *and* CASSIUS *retire.*
DEC. Here lies the east: doth not the day break here?
CASCA. No.
CIN. O, pardon, sir, it doth; and yon grey lines,
That fret the clouds, are messengers of day.
CASCA. You shall confess that you are both deceiv'd.
Here, as I point my sword, the sun arises;
Which is a great way growing on the south,
Weighing the youthful season of the year.
Some two months hence, up higher toward the north
He first presents his fire; and the high east
Stands, as the Capitol, directly here.
BRU. [*Advancing.*] Give me your hands all over, one by one.
CAS. [*Advancing.*] And let us swear our resolution.
BRU. No, not an oath: if not the face[a] of men,
The sufferance of our souls, the time's abuse,—
If these be motives weak, break off betimes,
And every man hence to his idle bed;[b]
So let high-sighted tyranny range on,
Till each man drop by lottery. But if these,
As I am sure they do, bear fire enough
To kindle cowards, and to steel with valour
The melting spirits of women; then, countrymen,
What need we any spur, but our own cause,
To prick us to redress? what other bond
Than secret[c] Romans, that have spoke the word,
And will not palter? and what other oath,
Than honesty to honesty engag'd,
That this shall be, or we will fall for it?
Swear priests, and cowards, and men cautelous,
Old feeble carrions, and such suffering souls
That welcome wrongs; unto bad causes swear
Such creatures as men doubt: but do not stain
The even[d] virtue of our enterprise,
Nor the insuppressive mettle of our spirits,
To think that or our cause or our performance
Did need an oath; when every drop of blood
That every Roman bears, and nobly bears,
Is guilty of a several bastardy,
If he do break the smallest particle
Of any promise that hath pass'd from him.
CAS. But what of Cicero? shall we sound him?
I think he will stand very strong with us.
CASCA. Let us not leave him out.
CIN. No, by no means.
MET. O, let us have him; for his silver hairs
Will purchase us a good opinion,
And buy men's voices to commend our deeds:
It shall be said, his judgment rul'd our hands;
Our youths, and wildness, shall no whit appear,
But all be buried in his gravity.
BRU. O, name him not; let us not break with him;[e]
For he will never follow anything
That other men begin.
CAS. Then leave him out.
CASCA. Indeed he is not fit.
DEC. Shall no man else be touch'd but only Cæsar?
CAS. Decius, well urg'd:—I think it is not meet,
Mark Antony, so well belov'd of Cæsar,
Should outlive Cæsar: we shall find of him
A shrewd contriver; and, you know, his means,
If he improve them, may well stretch so far
As to annoy us all: which to prevent,
Let Antony and Cæsar fall together.
BRU. Our course will seem too bloody, Caius Cassius,
To cut the head off, and then hack the limbs,—
Like wrath in death, and envy[f] afterwards;
For Antony is but a limb of Cæsar.
Let 's be sacrificers, but not butchers, Caius.
We all stand up against the spirit of Cæsar;
And in the spirit of men there is no blood:
O, that we, then, could come by Cæsar's spirit,
And not dismember Cæsar! But, alas,
Cæsar must bleed for it! And, gentle friends,
Let 's kill him boldly, but not wrathfully;
Let 's carve him as a dish fit for the gods,
Not hew him as a carcase fit for hounds:
And let our hearts, as subtle masters do,
Stir up their servants to an act of rage,
And after seem to chide 'em. This shall make
Our purpose necessary, and not envious:
Which so appearing to the common eyes,
We shall be call'd purgers, not murderers.[g]
And for Mark Antony, think not of him;
For he can do no more than Cæsar's arm,
When Cæsar's head is off.
CAS. Yet I fear him:
For in the ingrafted love he bears to Cæsar,—

---

a — *the* face *of men,*—] If "face" be right, though it reads dubiously, we are perhaps to understand the general gloom observable on men's countenances: Warburton proposed *fate*, Mason *faith*, and Malone *faiths*.

b — *his* idle *bed;*] His bed of indolence; see note (a), p. 88 of present volume.

c — secret *Romans,*—] "Secret" is here employed with strict classical accuracy for *separated, set apart;* and hence, *dedicated*, or *devoted* to a particular purpose. So Milton, "Paradise Lost," B. I. l. 6,—

"—— On the *secret* top
Of Oreb or of Sinai."

d *The* even *virtue*—] The *just*, or *equitable, quality.*

e — let us not break with him;] Let us not open the matter to him.

f — envy—] *Envy* in this place, as usual, means *hatred* or *malice.*

g *We shall be* call'd purgers, *not murderers.*] Query?—"We shall be *purgers call'd,*" &c.

BRU. Alas, good Cassius, do not think of him:
If he love Cæsar, all that he can do
Is to himself,—take thought,[a] and die for Cæsar:
And that were much he should; for he is given
To sports, to wildness, and much company.
TREB. There is no fear in him;[b] let him not die;
For he will live, and laugh at this hereafter.
[*Clock strikes.*
BRU. Peace! count the clock.
CAS. The clock hath stricken three.
TREB. 'T is time to part.
CAS. But it is doubtful yet,
Whether Cæsar will come forth to-day, or no;
For he is superstitious grown of late;
Quite from the main opinion he held once
Of fantasy, of dreams, and ceremonies;[c]
It may be, these apparent[d] prodigies,
The unaccustom'd terror of this night,
And the persuasion of his augurers,
May hold him from the Capitol to-day.
DEC. Never fear that: if he be so resolv'd
I can o'ersway him: for he loves to hear
That unicorns may be betray'd with trees,
And bears with glasses, elephants with holes,[e]
Lions with toils, and men with flatterers:
But when I tell him he hates flatterers,
He says he does,—being then most flattered.
Let me work;
For I can give his humour the true bent,
And I will bring him to the Capitol.
CAS. Nay, we will all of us be there to fetch him.
BRU. By the eighth hour: is that the uttermost?
CIN. Be that the uttermost, and fail not then.
MET. Caius Ligarius doth bear Cæsar hard,[f]
Who rated him for speaking well of Pompey;
I wonder none of you have thought of him.
BRU. Now, good Metellus, go along by[g] him:
He loves me well, and I have given him reasons;
Send him but hither, and I'll fashion him.
CAS. The morning comes upon 's: we'll leave you, Brutus:—
And, friends, disperse yourselves: but all remember
What you have said, and show yourselves true Romans.
BRU. Good gentlemen, look fresh and merrily;
Let not our looks put on our purposes;
But bear it as our Roman actors do,
With untir'd spirits and formal constancy:
And so, good-morrow to you every one.
[*Exeunt all except* BRUTUS.
Boy! Lucius!—Fast asleep? It is no matter;
Enjoy the honey-heavy dew of slumber:
Thou hast no figures nor no fantasies,
Which busy care draws in the brains of men;
Therefore thou sleep'st so sound.

Enter PORTIA.

POR. Brutus, my lord!
BRU. Portia, what mean you? wherefore rise you now?
It is not for your health thus to commit
Your weak condition to the raw cold morning.
POR. Nor for yours neither. You've ungently, Brutus,
Stole from my bed: and yesternight, at supper,
You suddenly arose, and walk'd about,
Musing and sighing, with your arms across:
And when I ask'd you what the matter was,
You star'd upon me with ungentle looks:
I urg'd you further; then you scratch'd your head,
And too impatiently stamp'd with your foot:
Yet I insisted, yet you answer'd not;
But, with an angry wafture of your hand,
Gave sign for me to leave you: so I did;
Fearing to strengthen that impatience
Which seem'd too much enkindled; and withal
Hoping it was but an effect of humour,
Which sometime hath his hour with every man.
It will not let you eat, nor talk, nor sleep;
And, could it work so much upon your shape,
As it hath much prevail'd on your condition,[h]
I should not know you, Brutus. Dear my lord,
Make me acquainted with your cause of grief.
BRU. I am not well in health, and that is all.
POR. Brutus is wise, and were he not in health,
He would embrace the means to come by it.
BRU. Why, so I do:—good Portia, go to bed.
POR. Is Brutus sick,—and is it physical[i]
To walk unbraced, and suck up the humours
Of the dank morning? What, is Brutus sick,—
And will he steal out of his wholesome bed,
To dare the vile contagion of the night,
And tempt the rheumy and unpurged air
To add unto his sickness? No, my Brutus;

---

a — take thought,—] Abandon himself to grief.
b — no fear in him;] That is, no cause of fear in him.
c — ceremonies;] See note (c), p. 23, Vol. II.
d — apparent—] *Manifest, evident.*
e That unicorns may be betray'd with trees,
And bears with glasses, elephants with holes,—]
For an account of the manner in which unicorns are related to have been captured, see note (4), p. 507, Vol. II. Bears, Steevens says, were surprised by means of a mirror, which they would gaze on, affording their pursuers an opportunity of taking the surer aim; and elephants were seduced into pitfalls, lightly covered with hurdles and turf. See Pliny's *Natural History*, Book VIII.
f — doth bear Cæsar hard,—] See note (b), p. 418.
g — *go along* by *him;*] *By his house*, Malone says.
h — condition,—] *Temper, disposition.*
i — *is it* physical—] Is it *medicinal.*

You have some sick offence within your mind,
Which, by the right and virtue of my place,
I ought to know of: and, upon my knees,
I charm[a] you, by my once-commended beauty,
By all your vows of love, and that great vow
Which did incorporate and make us one,
That you unfold to me, yourself, your half,
Why you are heavy; and what men to-night
Have had resort to you,—for here have been
Some six or seven, who did hide their faces
Even from darkness.

BRU. Kneel not, gentle Portia.

POR. I should not need, if you were gentle, Brutus.
Within the bond of marriage, tell me, Brutus,
Is it excepted I should know no secrets
That appertain to you? Am I yourself
But, as it were, in sort or limitation,—

[a] I charm you,—] I *conjure* you.

To keep[a] with you at meals, comfort your bed,
And talk to you sometimes? Dwell I but in the suburbs
Of your good pleasure? If it be no more,
Portia is Brutus' harlot, not his wife.

BRU. You are my true and honourable wife:
As dear to me as are the ruddy drops
That visit my sad heart.

POR. If this were true, then should I know this secret.
I grant I am a woman; but withal,
A woman that lord Brutus took to wife:
I grant I am a woman; but withal,
A woman, well-reputed Cato's daughter.[b]
Think you I am no stronger than my sex,
Being so father'd and so husbanded?
Tell me your counsels, I will not disclose 'em:
I have made strong proof of my constancy,
Giving myself a voluntary wound
Here, in the thigh: can I bear that with patience,
And not my husband's secrets?(2)

BRU. O, ye gods,
Render me worthy of this noble wife!—
[*Knocking without.*
Hark, hark! one knocks: Portia, go in a while;
And by and by thy bosom shall partake
The secrets of my heart:
All my engagements I will construe to thee,
All the charactery[c] of my sad brows:—
Leave me with haste.—Lucius, who 's that knocks?
[*Exit* PORTIA.

Enter LUCIUS, *followed by* LIGARIUS.

LUC. Here is a sick man that would speak with you.

BRU. Caius Ligarius, that Metellus spake of.—
Boy, stand aside.—Caius Ligarius! how?

LIG. Vouchsafe good morrow from a feeble tongue.

BRU. O, what a time have you chose out, brave Caius,
To wear a kerchief! (3) Would you were not sick!

LIG. I am not sick, if Brutus have in hand
Any exploit worthy the name of honour.

BRU. Such an exploit have I in hand, Ligarius,
Had you a healthful ear to hear of it.

LIG. By all the gods that Romans bow before,
I here discard my sickness! Soul of Rome!
Brave son, deriv'd from honourable loins!
Thou, like an exorcist, hast conjur'd up
My mortified spirit. Now bid me run,
And I will strive with things impossible;
Yea, get the better of them. What 's to do?

BRU. A piece of work that will make sick men whole.

LIG. But are not some whole that we must make sick?

BRU. That must we also. What it is, my Caius,
I shall unfold to thee, as we are going
To whom it must be done.

LIG. Set on your foot;
And, with a heart new-fir'd, I follow you,
To do I know not what: but it sufficeth
That Brutus leads me on.

BRU. Follow me then.
[*Exeunt.*

SCENE II.—*The same. A Hall in* Cæsar's *Palace.*

Thunder and lightning. Enter CÆSAR.

CÆS. Nor heaven nor earth have been at peace to-night:
Thrice hath Calphurnia in her sleep cried out,
Help, ho! they murder Cæsar!—Who 's within?

Enter a Servant.

SERV. My lord?

CÆS. Go bid the priests do present sacrifice,
And bring me their opinions of success.

SERV. I will, my lord. [*Exit.*

Enter CALPHURNIA.

CAL. What mean you, Cæsar? think you to walk forth?
You shall not stir out of your house to-day.

CÆS. Cæsar shall forth: the things that threaten'd me
Ne'er look'd but on my back; when they shall see
The face of Cæsar, they are vanished.

CAL. Cæsar, I never stood on ceremonies,
Yet now they fright me. There is one within,
Besides the things that we have heard and seen,

---

[a] *To keep with you*, &c.] To live with, to keep company with.

[b] —— but withal,
A woman, well-reputed Cato's daughter.]
The customary pointing of this latter line is not satisfactory; it is usually printed,—
"A woman well-reputed; Cato's daughter."
But regarding what immediately precedes and follows, does she not mean,—
"A woman, well-reputed Cato's daughter,"?
that is, A woman, daughter of the much-esteemed Cato? There is a marked propriety, then, in her asking,—
"Think you I am no stronger than my sex,
Being so father'd and so husbanded?"

[c] *All the* charactery *of my sad brows*:—] All that is written in my melancholy aspect.

Recounts most horrid sights seen by the watch.
A lioness hath whelped in the streets;
And graves have yawn'd, and yielded up their dead;
Fierce fiery warriors fight [a] upon the clouds,
In ranks and squadrons and right form of war,
Which drizzled blood upon the Capitol;
The noise of battle hurtled in the air,
Horses did* neigh, and dying men did groan;
And ghosts did shriek and squeal about the streets.
O, Cæsar, these things are beyond all use,
And I do fear them! (4)

CÆS. What can be avoided
Whose end is purpos'd by the mighty gods?
Yet Cæsar shall go forth; for these predictions
Are to the world in general as to Cæsar.

CAL. When beggars die, there are no comets seen;
The heavens themselves blaze forth the death of princes.

CÆS. Cowards die many times before their deaths;
The valiant never taste of death but once.
Of all the wonders that I yet have heard,
It seems to me most strange that men should fear;
Seeing that death, a necessary end,
Will come when it will come.—

Re-enter Servant.

What say the augurers?

SERV. They would not have you to stir forth to-day.
Plucking the entrails of an offering forth,
They could not find a heart within the beast.

CÆS. The gods do this in shame of cowardice:
Cæsar should be a beast without a heart,
If he should stay at home to-day for fear.

(*) First folio, *do*.

[a] *Fierce fiery warriors* fight *upon the clouds,*—] Mr. Dyce conceives the word "fight" to be an error for "fought;" "since we cannot suppose that here the poet used 'fight' as a past tense."

No, Cæsar shall not: Danger knows full well
That Cæsar is more dangerous than he:
We are[a] two lions litter'd in one day,
And I the elder and more terrible;—
And Cæsar shall go forth.
CAL. Alas, my lord,
Your wisdom is consum'd in confidence.
Do not go forth to-day: call it my fear
That keeps you in the house, and not your own.
We 'll send Mark Antony to the senate-house;
And he shall say you are not well to-day:
Let me, upon my knee, prevail in this.
CÆS. Mark Antony shall say I am not well;
And, for thy humour, I will stay at home.

Enter DECIUS.

Here 's Decius Brutus, he shall tell them so.
DEC. Cæsar, all hail! good morrow, worthy Cæsar:
I come to fetch you to the senate-house.
CÆS. And you are come in very happy time,
To bear my greeting to the senators,
And tell them that I will not come to-day:
Cannot, is false; and that I dare not, falser:
I will not come to-day,—tell them so, Decius.
CAL. Say he is sick.
CÆS. Shall Cæsar send a lie?
Have I in conquest stretch'd mine arm so far,
To be afeard to tell grey-beards the truth?
Decius, go tell them Cæsar will not come.
DEC. Most mighty Cæsar, let me know some cause,
Lest I be laugh'd at when I tell them so.
CÆS. The cause is in my will,—I will not come;
That is enough to satisfy the senate.
But, for your private satisfaction,
Because I love you, I will let you know,—
Calphurnia here, my wife, stays me at home:
She dreamt, to-night she saw my statua,
Which, like a fountain with an hundred spouts,
Did run pure blood; and many lusty Romans
Came smiling, and did bathe their hands in it:
And these does she apply for warnings, and portents,
And evils imminent; and on her knee
Hath begg'd that I will stay at home to-day.
DEC. This dream is all amiss interpreted;
It was a vision fair and fortunate:
Your statue spouting blood in many pipes,
In which so many smiling Romans bath'd,
Signifies that from you great Rome shall suck
Reviving blood; and that great men shall press
For tinctures, stains, relics, and cognizance.
This by Calphurnia's dream is signified.
CÆS. And this way have you well expounded it.
DEC. I have, when you have heard what I can say:
And know it now,—the senate have concluded
To give, this day, a crown to mighty Cæsar.
If you shall send them word you will not come,
Their minds may change. Besides, it were a mock
Apt to be render'd, for some one to say,
Break up the senate till another time,
When Cæsar's wife shall meet with better dreams.
If Cæsar hide himself, shall they not whisper,
Lo, Cæsar is afraid?
Pardon me, Cæsar; for my dear-dear love
To your proceeding[b] bids me tell you this;
And reason to my love is liable.[c]
CÆS. How foolish do your fears seem now, Calphurnia!
I am ashamed I did yield to them.—
Give me my robe, for I will go:—

Enter PUBLIUS, BRUTUS, LIGARIUS, METELLUS, CASCA, TREBONIUS, *and* CINNA.

And look where Publius is come to fetch me.
PUB. Good morrow, Cæsar.
CÆS. Welcome, Publius.—
What, Brutus, are you stirr'd so early too?—
Good morrow, Casca.—Caius Ligarius,
Cæsar was ne'er so much your enemy
As that same ague which hath made you lean.—
What is 't o'clock?
BRU. Cæsar, 't is strucken eight.
CÆS. I thank you for your pains and courtesy.

Enter ANTONY.

See! Antony, that revels long o' nights,
Is notwithstanding up.—Good morrow, Antony.
ANT. So to most noble Cæsar.
CÆS. Bid them prepare within:—
I am to blame to be thus waited for.—
Now, Cinna:—now, Metellus:—what, Trebonius!
I have an hour's talk in store for you;
Remember that you call on me to-day:
Be near me, that I may remember you.
TREB. Cæsar, I will:—[*Aside.*] and so near will I be,

---

[a] *We are two lions,* &c.] The old reading is, "We *heare*," &c., for which Theobald printed "We *were*," &c., and this until recently has been the ordinary text; at the present time, however, Upton's emendation, "We *are*," &c., is very justly preferred.

[b] *To your* proceeding—] To your *advancement.*

[c] And reason to my love is liable.] Mr. Craik explains this:—"My reason where you are concerned is subject to, and is overborne by, my affection."

That your best friends shall wish I had been further.

CÆS. Good friends, go in, and taste some wine with me;
And we, like friends, will straightway go together.

BRU. [*Aside.*] That every like is not the same, O, Cæsar,
The heart of Brutus yearns to think upon!
[*Exeunt.*

SCENE III.—*The same. A street near the* Capitol.

Enter ARTEMIDORUS, *reading a paper.*

ART. *Cæsar, beware of Brutus; take heed of Cassius; come not near Casca; have an eye to Cinna; trust not Trebonius; mark well Metellus Cimber; Decius Brutus loves thee not; thou hast wronged Caius Ligarius. There is but one mind in all these men, and it is bent against Cæsar. If thou beest not immortal, look about you: security gives way to conspiracy.*[a] *The mighty gods defend thee! Thy lover,*[b]

ARTEMIDORUS.

Here will I stand till Cæsar pass along,
And as a suitor will I give him this.
My heart laments that virtue cannot live
Out of the teeth of emulation.
If thou read this, O, Cæsar, thou mayst live;
If not, the Fates with traitors do contrive.[c] [*Exit.*

SCENE IV.—*The same. Another part of the same Street, before the House of* Brutus.

Enter PORTIA *and* LUCIUS.

POR. I pr'ythee, boy, run to the senate-house;
Stay not to answer me, but get thee gone:
Why dost thou stay?

[a] Security gives way to, &c.] The meaning is, over-confidence affords a passage, &c.

[b] Thy lover,—] It need hardly be repeated that "lover" was formerly equivalent to friend.

[c] — contrive.] See note (a), p. 429, Vol. II.

LUC. To know my errand, madam.
POR. I would have had thee there, and here again,
Ere I can tell thee what thou shouldst do there.—
O, constancy, be strong upon my side!
Set a huge mountain 'tween my heart and tongue!
I have a man's mind, but a woman's might.
How hard it is for women to keep counsel!—
Art thou here yet?
LUC. Madam, what should I do?
Run to the Capitol, and nothing else?
And so return to you, and nothing else?
POR. Yes, bring me word, boy, if thy lord look well,
For he went sickly forth: and take good note
What Cæsar doth, what suitors press to him.
Hark, boy! what noise is that?
LUC. I hear none, madam.
POR. Pr'ythee, listen well.
I heard a bustling rumour, like a fray,
And the wind brings it from the Capitol.
LUC. 'Sooth, madam, I hear nothing.

Enter Soothsayer.

POR. Come hither, fellow: which way hast thou been?
SOOTH. At mine own house, good lady.
POR. What is't o'clock?
SOOTH. About the ninth hour, lady.
POR. Is Cæsar yet gone to the Capitol?
SOOTH. Madam, not yet: I go to take my stand,
To see him pass on to the Capitol.
POR. Thou hast some suit to Cæsar, hast thou not?
SOOTH. That I have, lady: if it will please Cæsar
To be so good to Cæsar as to hear me,
I shall beseech him to befriend himself.
POR. Why, know'st thou any harm 's intended towards him?
SOOTH. None that I know will be, much that I fear may chance.
Good morrow to you. Here the street is narrow:
The throng that follows Cæsar at the heels,
Of senators, of prætors, common suitors,
Will crowd a feeble man almost to death:
I'll get me to a place more void, and there
Speak to great Cæsar as he comes along. [*Exit.*
POR. I must go in.—Ay me! how weak a thing
The heart of woman is! O Brutus!
The heavens speed thee in thine enterprise!
Sure, the boy heard me:—Brutus hath a suit
That Cæsar will not grant.—O, I grow faint.—
Run, Lucius, and commend me to my lord;
Say I am merry: come to me again,
And bring me word what he doth say to thee.
[*Exeunt severally.*

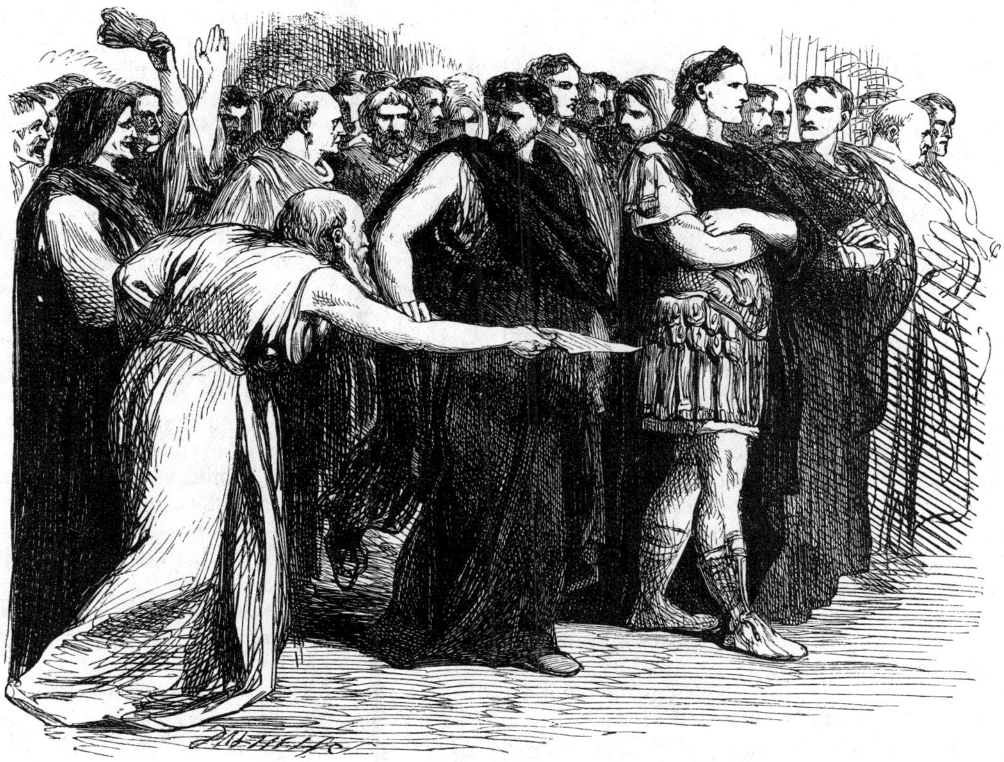

ACT III.

SCENE I.—*The same. The* Capitol; *the* Senate *sitting.*

A crowd of people in the Street leading to the Capitol; *among them* ARTEMIDORUS *and the* Soothsayer. *Flourish. Enter* CÆSAR, BRUTUS, CASSIUS, CASCA, DECIUS, METELLUS, TREBONIUS, CINNA, ANTONY, LEPIDUS, POPILIUS, PUBLIUS, *and others.*

CÆS. The ides of March are come.
SOOTH. Ay, Cæsar; but not gone.
ART. Hail, Cæsar! read this schedule.
DEC. Trebonius doth desire you to o'er-read,
At your best leisure, this his humble suit.
ART. O, Cæsar, read mine first; for mine's a suit
That touches Cæsar nearer: read it, great Cæsar.
CÆS. What touches us ourself shall be last serv'd.[a]
ART. Delay not, Cæsar; read it instantly.
CÆS. What, is the fellow mad?
PUB. Sirrah, give place.
CAS. What, urge you your petitions in the street?
Come to the Capitol.

CÆSAR *enters the* Capitol, *the rest following. All the* Senators *rise.*

POP. I wish your enterprise to-day may thrive.
CAS. What enterprise, Popilius?

---

a What touches us ourself shall be last serv'd.] Here Mr. Craik, to our surprise, adopts the specious sophistication of Mr. Collier's annotator,—

"*That* touches us? Ourself shall be last served,"—

with the remark,—"To *serve*, or attend to, a *person* is a familiar form of expression; to speak of a *thing* as *served*, in the sense of attended to, would, it is apprehended, be unexampled." But there is nothing uncommon or improper in speaking of a dinner or of a dish as *served*, and it is in this sense, we believe, the verb is used in the present case.

POP. Fare you well.
[*Advances to* CÆSAR.

BRU. What said Popilius Lena?

CAS. He wish'd, to-day our enterprise might thrive.
I fear our purpose is discovered.

BRU. Look, how he makes to Cæsar: mark him.

CAS. Casca, be sudden, for we fear prevention.—
Brutus, what shall be done? If this be known,
Cassius or Cæsar never shall turn back,
For I will slay myself.

BRU. Cassius, be constant.[a]
Popilius Lena speaks not of our purposes;
For, look, he smiles, and Cæsar doth not change.

CAS. Trebonius knows his time; for, look you, Brutus,
He draws Mark Antony out of the way.
[*Exeunt* ANTONY *and* TREBONIUS. CÆSAR *and the* Senators *take their seats.*

DEC. Where is Metellus Cimber? Let him go,
And presently prefer his suit to Cæsar.

BRU. He is address'd:[b] press near and second him.

CIN. Casca, you are the first that rears your hand.

CASCA. Are we all ready?[c]

CÆS. What is now amiss
That Cæsar and his senate must redress?

MET. Most high, most mighty, and most puissant Cæsar,
Metellus Cimber throws before thy seat
An humble heart,— [*Kneeling.*

CÆS. I must prevent thee, Cimber.
These couchings[d] and these lowly courtesies
Might fire the blood of ordinary men,
And turn pre-ordinance and first decree
Into the law* of children. Be not fond,
To think that Cæsar bears such rebel blood
That will be thaw'd from the true quality
With that which melteth fools; I mean, sweet words,
Low-crooked[e] court'sies, and base spaniel-fawning.
Thy brother by decree is banished;
If thou dost bend, and pray, and fawn for him,
I spurn thee like a cur out of my way.
Know, Cæsar doth not wrong; nor without cause
Will he be satisfied.(1)

MET. Is there no voice more worthy than my own,
To sound more sweetly in great Cæsar's ear,
For the repealing of my banish'd brother?

BRU. I kiss thy hand, but not in flattery, Cæsar;
Desiring thee that Publius Cimber may
Have an immediate freedom of repeal.

CÆS. What, Brutus!

CAS. Pardon, Cæsar: Cæsar, pardon:
As low as to thy foot doth Cassius fall,
To beg enfranchisement for Publius Cimber.

CÆS. I could be well mov'd, if I were as you;
If I could pray to move, prayers would move me:
But I am constant as the northern star,
Of whose true-fix'd and resting quality
There is no fellow in the firmament.
The skies are painted with unnumber'd sparks,
They are all fire, and every one doth shine;
But there's but one in all doth hold his place:
So, in the world,—'tis furnish'd well with men,
And men are flesh and blood, and apprehensive;
Yet, in the number, I do know but one
That unassailable holds on his rank,
Unshak'd of motion: and that I am he
Let me a little show it, even in this,—
That I was constant Cimber should be banish'd,
And constant do remain to keep him so.

CIN. O, Cæsar—

CÆS. Hence! wilt thou lift up Olympus?

DEC. Great Cæsar,—

CÆS. Doth not Brutus bootless kneel?

CASCA. Speak, hands, for me!

[CASCA *stabs* CÆSAR *in the neck.* CÆSAR *catches hold of his arm; and is then stabbed by several other* Conspirators, *and at last by* MARCUS BRUTUS.

CÆS. *Et tu, Brute?*(2)—Then fall, Cæsar!
[*Dies. The* Senators *and people retire in confusion.*

CIN. Liberty! Freedom! Tyranny is dead!—
Run hence, proclaim, cry it about the streets.

CAS. Some to the common pulpits, and cry out,
Liberty, freedom, and enfranchisement!

BRU. People, and senators, be not affrighted;
Fly not; stand still:—ambition's debt is paid.

CASCA. Go to the pulpit, Brutus.

DEC. And Cassius too.

BRU. Where's Publius?

CIN. Here, quite confounded with this mutiny.

MET. Stand fast together, lest some friend of Cæsar's
Should chance—

BRU. Talk not of standing.—Publius, good cheer;
There is no harm intended to your person,
Nor to no Roman else: so tell them, Publius.

CAS. And leave us, Publius; lest that the people,
Rushing on us, should do your age some mischief.

(*) Old text, *lane*.

a — *be* constant.] Be *firm, steady, self-possessed.*

b — address'd:] *Prepared, ready.*

c CASCA. Are we all ready?] In the old copy these words begin Cæsar's speech; there can be little doubt that Mr. Collier's annotator was right in assigning them to Casca.

d — couchings—] Hanmer changed this to *crouchings;* but *couching* had of old the same meaning as *crouching.*

e Low-crooked *court'sies,*—] That is, *low-crouched,* or *low-bowed* court'sies.

BRU. Do so;—and let no man abide[a] this deed,
But we the doers.

Re-enter TREBONIUS.

CAS. Where is Antony?
TRE. Fled to his house amaz'd:
Men, wives, and children stare, cry out, and run
As it were doomsday.
BRU. Fates! we will[b] know your pleasures:—
That we shall die, we know; 'tis but the time,
And drawing days out, that men stand upon.
CAS.[c] Why, he that cuts off twenty years of life
Cuts off so many years of fearing death.
BRU. Grant that, and then is death a benefit:
So are we Cæsar's friends, that have abridg'd
His time of fearing death.—Stoop, Romans, stoop,
And let us bathe our hands in Cæsar's blood
Up to the elbows, and besmear our swords:
Then walk we forth, even to the market-place,
And, waving our red weapons o'er our heads,
Let's all cry, *Peace, Freedom, and Liberty!*
CAS. Stoop, then, and wash.—How many ages hence
Shall this our lofty scene be acted over
In states * unborn and accents yet unknown!
BRU. How many times shall Cæsar bleed in sport,
That now on Pompey's basis lies † along,
No worthier than the dust!
CAS. So oft as that shall be,
So often shall the knot of us be call'd
The men that gave their country liberty.
DEC. What, shall we forth?
CAS. Ay, every man away:
Brutus shall lead; and we will grace his heels
With the most boldest and best hearts of Rome.
BRU. Soft! who comes here?

Enter a Servant.

A friend of Antony's.
SERV. Thus, Brutus, did my master bid me kneel;
Thus did Mark Antony bid me fall down;
And, being prostrate, thus he bade me say:—
Brutus is noble, wise, valiant, and honest;
Cæsar was mighty, bold, royal, and loving:
Say I love Brutus, and I honour him;
Say I fear'd Cæsar, honour'd him, and lov'd him.
If Brutus will vouchsafe that Antony
May safely come to him, and be resolv'd
How Cæsar hath deserv'd to lie in death,
Mark Antony shall not love Cæsar dead
So well as Brutus living; but will follow
The fortunes and affairs of noble Brutus,
Thorough the hazards of this untrod state,
With all true faith. So says my master Antony.
BRU. Thy master is a wise and valiant Roman;
I never thought him worse.
Tell him, so please him come unto this place,
He shall be satisfied; and, by my honour,
Depart untouch'd.
SERV. I'll fetch him presently. [*Exit.*
BRU. I know that we shall have him well to friend.[d]
CAS. I wish we may: but yet have I a mind
That fears him much; and my misgiving still[e]
Falls shrewdly to the purpose.
BRU. But here comes Antony.—

Re-enter ANTONY.

Welcome, Mark Antony.
ANT. O, mighty Cæsar! dost thou lie so low?
Are all thy conquests, glories, triumphs, spoils,
Shrunk to this little measure?—Fare thee well.—
I know not, gentlemen, what you intend,
Who else must be let blood, who else is rank:[f]
If I myself, there is no hour so fit
As Cæsar's death's hour; nor no instrument
Of half that worth as those your swords, made rich
With the most noble blood of all this world.
I do beseech ye, if you bear me hard,[g]
Now, whilst your purpled hands do reek and smoke,
Fulfil your pleasure. Live a thousand years,
I shall not find myself so apt to die;
No place will please me so, no mean of death,
As here by Cæsar, and by you cut off,
The choice and master spirits of this age.
BRU. O, Antony! beg not your death of us.
Though now we must appear bloody and cruel,
As, by our hands and this our present act,
You see we do; yet see you but our hands,
And this the bleeding business they have done:
Our hearts you see not,—they are pitiful;
And pity to the general wrong of Rome
(As fire drives out fire, so pity, pity)
Hath done this deed on Cæsar. For your part,
To you our swords have leaden points, Mark Antony:

(*) First folio, *State*. (†) First folio, *lye*.

a — *let no man* abide *this deed,*—] Let no man pay the penalty for, or stand the consequences of this deed.

b *Fates! we* will *know your pleasures:*—] We should perhaps read, "We *well* know," &c. Compare, "King Lear," Act III. Sc. 1,—

"—— then let fall
Your horrible *pleasure*."

c CAS.] The folio has the prefix *Cask*.

d — to *friend*.] Equivalent to, *for* friend.

e —— *and my misgiving* still
Falls shrewdly to the purpose.]

My misgiving *always*, or *ever*, falls, &c.

f — *who else* is rank:] Who else is *too high-topped*; of *too luxuriant growth*.

g — if you bear me hard,—] *Vide* note (b), p. 418.

Our arms, in strength of malice,[a] and our hearts
Of brothers' temper, do receive you in
With all kind love, good thoughts, and reverence.
CAS. Your voice shall be as strong as any man's
In the disposing of new dignities.
BRU. Only be patient till we have appeas'd
The multitude, beside themselves with fear,
And then we will deliver you the cause,
Why I, that did love Cæsar when I struck him,
Have thus proceeded.
ANT. I doubt not of your wisdom.
Let each man render me his bloody hand:
First, Marcus Brutus, will I shake with you;—
Next, Caius Cassius, do I take your hand;—
Now, Decius Brutus, yours;—now yours, Metellus;—
Yours, Cinna;—and, my valiant Casca, yours;—
Though last, not least in love, yours, good Trebonius.
Gentlemen all,—alas! what shall I say?
My credit now stands on such slippery ground,
That one of two bad ways you must conceit me,
Either a coward or a flatterer.—
That I did love thee, Cæsar, O, 'tis true:
If, then, thy spirit look upon us now,
Shall it not grieve thee dearer than thy death,
To see thy Antony making his peace,
Shaking the bloody fingers of thy foes,
Most noble! in the presence of thy corse?
Had I as many eyes as thou hast wounds,
Weeping as fast as they stream forth thy blood,
It would become me better than to close
In terms of friendship with thine enemies.
Pardon me, Julius!—Here wast thou bay'd, brave hart;
Here didst thou fall; and here thy hunters stand,
Sign'd in thy spoil, and crimson'd in thy lethe.[b]—
O world! thou wast the forest to this hart;
And this, indeed, O, world! the heart of thee.—
How like a deer, strucken by many princes,
Dost thou here lie!
CAS. Mark Antony,—
ANT. Pardon me, Caius Cassius:
The enemies of Cæsar shall say this;
Then, in a friend, it is cold modesty.
CAS. I blame you not for praising Cæsar so;
But what compáct mean you to have with us?
Will you be prick'd in number of our friends;
Or shall we on, and not depend on you?
ANT. Therefore I took your hands; but was, indeed,
Sway'd from the point, by looking down on Cæsar.
Friends[c] am I with you all, and love you all;
Upon this hope, that you shall give me reasons
Why and wherein Cæsar was dangerous.
BRU. Or else were this a savage spectacle:
Our reasons are so full of good regard,
That were you, Antony, the son of Cæsar,
You should be satisfied.
ANT. That's all I seek:
And am moreover suitor that I may
Produce his body to the market-place;
And in the pulpit, as becomes a friend,
Speak in the order of his funeral.[d]
BRU. You shall, Mark Antony.
CAS. Brutus, a word with you.—
[*Aside to* BRUTUS.] You know not what you do: do not consent
That Antony speak in his funeral:
Know you how much the people may be mov'd
By that which he will utter?
BRU. By your pardon;—
I will myself into the pulpit first,
And show the reason of our Cæsar's death:
What Antony shall speak, I will protest
He speaks by leave and by permission;
And that we are contented Cæsar shall
Have all true rites and lawful ceremonies.
It shall advantage more than do us wrong.
CAS. I know not what may fall; I like it not.
BRU. Mark Antony, here, take you Cæsar's body.
You shall not in your funeral speech blame us,
But speak all good you can devise of Cæsar;
And say you do't by our permission;
Else shall you not have any hand at all
About his funeral: and you shall speak
In the same pulpit whereto I am going,
After my speech is ended.
ANT. Be it so;
I do desire no more.
BRU. Prepare the body, then, and follow us.
[*Exeunt all except* ANTONY.
ANT. O, pardon me, thou bleeding piece of earth,

---

[a] — in strength of malice,—] For "malice," an unquestionable corruption, Mr. Collier's annotator proposes, *welcome*, a word, as Mr. Dyce remarks, which no way resembles it in the *ductus literarum*. Mr. Singer, with far more likelihood, suggests, *amity*.

[b] *Sign'd in thy spoil, and crimson'd in thy lethe.*—] The allusion is to the huntsmen's custom of tricking themselves out with the hide and antlers of the slaughtered deer and bathing their hands in its blood. Some difficulty, however, arises from the word "lethe," which, notwithstanding the assertion of Steevens that it was employed of old for *death*, has by many been pronounced a misprint. Theobald first proposed to read,—

" —— crimson'd in thy *death*."—

and this not improbably was what the poet wrote. *Blood*, it is well known, often signified *death* and *life*; we still hear, "I'll have his *blood*," for I'll take his life, or be the death of him; and in Beaumont and Fletcher's "Custom of the Country," Act V. Sc. 5, there is a passage, strikingly illustrative of the one under consideration, where "life" is used as a synonym for blood:—

"When thine own bloody sword cried out against thee,
Hatch'd in the *life* of him."

[c] Friends *am I with you all*,—] The inaccurate pluralism here, as Henley observes, "is still so prevalent, as that the omission of the anomalous *s* would give some uncouthness to the sound of an otherwise familiar expression."

[d] — *in the* order *of his funeral.*] That is, in the course of the ceremonial.

That I am meek and gentle with these butchers!
Thou art the ruins of the noblest man
That ever lived in the tide of times.
Woe to the hand that shed this costly blood!
Over thy wounds now do I prophesy,—
Which, like dumb mouths, do ope their ruby lips,
To beg the voice and utterance of my tongue,—
A curse shall light upon the limbs[a] of men;
Domestic fury and fierce civil strife
Shall cumber all the parts of Italy;
Blood and destruction shall be so in use,
And dreadful objects so familiar,
That mothers shall but smile when they behold
Their infants quarter'd with the hands of war;
All pity chok'd with custom of fell deeds:
And Cæsar's spirit, ranging for revenge,
With Até by his side come hot from hell,
Shall in these confines, with a monarch's voice,
Cry *Havoc*,[b] and let slip the dogs of war;
That this foul deed shall smell above the earth
With carrion men, groaning for burial!

Enter a Servant.

You serve Octavius Cæsar, do you not?

SERV. I do, Mark Antony.

ANT. Cæsar did write for him to come to Rome.

SERV. He did receive his letters, and is coming;
And bid me say to you by word of mouth,—
O, Cæsar!— [*Seeing the body.*

ANT. Thy heart is big; get thee apart and weep.
Passion, I see, is catching; for[c] mine eyes,
Seeing those beads of sorrow stand in thine,
Began to water. Is thy master coming?

---

a *A curse shall light upon the* limbs of *men*;] The expression "*limbs* of men," has been much disputed. Hanmer substituted "the *kind* of men;" Warburton, "the *line* of men;" Johnson proposed, "the *lives* of men;" and Mr. Collier's annotator, "the *loins* of men." The last has been pronounced by Mr. Craik to be "one of the most satisfactory and valuable emendations ever made," yet to us it appears far more probable that Shakespeare wrote,—

"A curse shall light upon the *tombs* of men;"

"Cursed be thy grave," is a common Oriental form of malediction, and in "The Merchant of Venice," Act II. Sc. 7, the old copies exhibit a misprint, "Gilded *timber*," for "Gilded *tombs*," which closely resembles that we presume to have occurred in the present instance.

b Cry *Havoc*, &c.] See note (b), p. 158.

c — for *mine eyes*,—] So the second folio; the first has,—

"—— *from* mine eyes."

SERV. He lies to-night within seven leagues of Rome.

ANT. Post back with speed, and tell him what hath chanc'd:
Here is a mourning Rome, a dangerous Rome,
No Rome of safety[a] for Octavius yet;
Hie hence, and tell him so. Yet, stay awhile;
Thou shalt not back till I have borne this corse*
Into the market-place: there shall I try,
In my oration, how the people take
The cruel issue of these bloody men;
According to the which, thou shalt discourse
To young Octavius of the state of things.
Lend me your hand.

[*Exeunt with* CÆSAR's *body*.

SCENE II.—*The same. The* Forum.

Enter BRUTUS *and* CASSIUS, *and a throng of* Citizens.

CITIZENS. We will be satisfied! let us be satisfied!

BRU. Then follow me, and give me audience, friends.—
Cassius, go you into the other street,
And part the numbers.—
Those that will hear me speak, let 'em stay here;
Those that will follow Cassius, go with him;
And public reasons shall be rendered
Of Cæsar's death.

1 CIT. I will hear Brutus speak.

2 CIT. I will hear Cassius; and compare their reasons,
When severally we hear them rendered.

[*Exit* CASSIUS, *with some of the* Citizens. BRUTUS *goes into the Rostrum*.

3 CIT. The noble Brutus is ascended: silence!

BRU. Be patient till the last.
Romans, countrymen, and lovers! hear me for my cause; and be silent, that you may hear: believe me for mine honour; and have respect to mine honour, that you may believe: censure me in your wisdom; and awake your senses, that you may the better judge. If there be any in this assembly, any dear friend of Cæsar's, to him I say, that Brutus' love to Cæsar was no less than his. If, then, that friend demand why Brutus rose against Cæsar, this is my answer,—Not that I loved Cæsar less, but that I loved Rome more. Had you rather Cæsar were living, and die all slaves; than that Cæsar were dead, to live all freemen? As Cæsar loved me, I weep for him; as he was fortunate, I rejoice at it; as he was valiant, I honour him: but, as he was ambitious, I slew him. There is tears for his love; joy for his fortune; honour for his valour; and death for his ambition. Who is here so base that would be a bondman? If any, speak; for him have I offended. Who is here so rude that would not be a Roman? If any, speak; for him have I offended. Who is here so vile that will not love his country? If any, speak; for him have I offended. I pause for a reply.(3)

CITIZENS. None, Brutus, none.

BRU. Then none have I offended. I have done no more to Cæsar than you shall do to Brutus. The question[b] of his death is enrolled in the Capitol; his glory not extenuated, wherein he was worthy; nor his offences enforced, for which he suffered death. Here comes his body, mourned by Mark Antony: who, though he had no hand in his death, shall receive the benefit of his dying, a place in the commonwealth; as which of you shall not? With this I depart,—that, as I slew my best lover[c] for the good of Rome, I have the same dagger for myself, when it shall please my country to need my death.

Enter ANTONY *and others with* CÆSAR's *body*.

CITIZENS. Live, Brutus! live, live!

1 CIT. Bring him with triumph home unto his house!

2 CIT. Give him a statue with his ancestors!

3 CIT. Let him be Cæsar!

4 CIT. Cæsar's better parts
Shall now[d] be crown'd in Brutus.

1 CIT. We'll bring him to his house with shouts and clamours.

BRU. My countrymen,—

2 CIT. Peace! silence! Brutus speaks.

1 CIT. Peace, ho!

BRU. Good countrymen, let me depart alone,
And, for my sake, stay here with Antony:
Do grace to Cæsar's corpse, and grace his speech
Tending to Cæsar's glories; which Mark Antony,
By our permission, is allow'd to make.
I do intreat you, not a man depart,
Save I alone, till Antony have spoke. [*Exit*.

(*) Old text, *course*.

a *No* Rome *of safety*—] We have the same quibble on *Rome*, the city, and *room*, an old word for *place*, in Act I. Sc. 2, and it appears to have been a familiar one of the time. Prime, in his Commentary on the Galatians, p. 122, 1587, has the expression, "Rome is too narrow a *Room* for the church of God."

b *The* question *of his death*—] *Question* here means, the motives or reasons which led to his death.

c — *my best* lover—] As we now say,—My best *friend*; so in "Coriolanus," Act V. Sc. 2,—

"—— I tell thee, fellow,
Thy general is my *lover*:"

and in a hundred other places in these or in contemporary books.

d *Shall* now *be crown'd in Brutus*.] The old text reads,—"Shall be crowned in Brutus;" but some word, as *now*, which Pope supplied, or *all*, or *well*, must have been omitted evidently.

1 Cit. Stay, ho! and let us hear Mark Antony.
3 Cit. Let him go up into the public chair;
We'll hear him.—Noble Antony, go up.
Ant. For Brutus' sake, I am beholden to you.
[*Ascends.*
4 Cit. What does he say of Brutus?
3 Cit. He says, for Brutus' sake,
He finds himself beholden to us all.
4 Cit. 'T were best he speak no harm of Brutus here.
1 Cit. This Cæsar was a tyrant.
3 Cit. Nay, that's certain:
We are bless'd that Rome is rid of him.
2 Cit. Peace! let us hear what Antony can say.
Ant. You gentle Romans,—
Citizens. Peace, ho! let us hear him.
Ant. Friends, Romans, countrymen, lend me your ears;
I come to bury Cæsar, not to praise him.

The evil that men do lives after them;
The good is oft interred with their bones;
So let it be with Cæsar. The noble Brutus
Hath told you Cæsar was ambitious:
If it were so, it was a grievous fault;
And grievously hath Cæsar answer'd it.
Here, under leave of Brutus and the rest,
(For Brutus is an honourable man;
So are they all, all honourable men)
Come I to speak in Cæsar's funeral.
He was my friend, faithful and just to me:
But Brutus says he was ambitious;
And Brutus is an honourable man.
He hath brought many captives home to Rome,
Whose ransoms did the general coffers fill:
Did this in Cæsar seem ambitious?
When that the poor have cried, Cæsar hath wept:
Ambition should be made of sterner stuff:
Yet Brutus says he was ambitious;
And Brutus is an honourable man.
You all did see that on the Lupercal
I thrice presented him a kingly crown,
Which he did thrice refuse: was this ambition?
Yet Brutus says he was ambitious;
And, sure, he is an honourable man.
I speak not to disprove what Brutus spoke,
But here I am to speak what I do know.
You all did love him once,—not without cause;
What cause withholds you, then, to mourn for him?—
O, judgment, thou art fled to brutish beasts,
And men have lost their reason!—Bear with me;
My heart is in the coffin there with Cæsar,
And I must pause till it come back to me.

1 CIT. Methinks there is much reason in his sayings.

2 CIT. If thou consider rightly of the matter,
Cæsar has had great wrong.

3 CIT. Has he, masters?
I fear there will a worse come in his place.

4 CIT. Mark'd ye his words? He would not take the crown;
Therefore 't is certain he was not ambitious.

1 CIT. If it be found so, some will dear abide it.

2 CIT. Poor soul! his eyes are red as fire with weeping.

3 CIT. There's not a nobler man in Rome than Antony.

4 CIT. Now mark him, he begins again to speak.

ANT. But yesterday the word of Cæsar might
Have stood against the world: now lies he there,
And none so poor to do him reverence.
O, masters! if I were dispos'd to stir
Your hearts and minds to mutiny and rage,
I should do Brutus wrong, and Cassius wrong,
Who, you all know, are honourable men.
I will not do them wrong; I rather choose
To wrong the dead, to wrong myself, and you,
Than I will wrong such honourable men.
But here 's a parchment with the seal of Cæsar,—
I found it in his closet,—'t is his will:
Let but the commons hear this testament,
(Which, pardon me, I do not mean to read)
And they would go and kiss dead Cæsar's wounds,
And dip their napkins[a] in his sacred blood;
Yea, beg a hair of him for memory,
And, dying, mention it within their wills,
Bequeathing it, as a rich legacy,
Unto their issue.

4 CIT. We'll hear the will! read it, Mark Antony.

CITIZENS. The will, the will! we will hear Cæsar's will!

ANT. Have patience, gentle friends; I must not read it:
It is not meet you know how Cæsar lov'd you.
You are not wood, you are not stones, but men;
And, being men, hearing the will of Cæsar,
It will inflame you, it will make you mad:
'T is good you know not that you are his heirs;
For if you should, O, what would come of it!

4 CIT. Read the will; we'll hear it, Antony;
You shall read us the will;—Cæsar's will!

ANT. Will you be patient? Will you stay a while?
I have o'ershot myself to tell you of it:
I fear I wrong the honourable men
Whose daggers have stabb'd Cæsar; I do fear it.

4 CIT. They were traitors! *honourable men!*

CITIZENS. The will! the testament!

2 CIT. They were villains, murderers! the will! read the will!

ANT. You will compel me then, to read the will?
Then make a ring about the corpse of Cæsar,
And let me show you him that made the will.
Shall I descend? and will you give me leave?

CITIZENS. Come down.

2 CIT. Descend. [ANTONY *descends.*

3 CIT. You shall have leave.

4 CIT. A ring; stand round.

1 CIT. Stand from the hearse! stand from the body!

2 CIT. Room for Antony, most noble Antony.

ANT. Nay, press not so upon me; stand far off.

CITIZENS. Stand back! room! bear back!

ANT. If you have tears, prepare to shed them now.
You all do know this mantle: I remember
The first time ever Cæsar put it on;
'T was on a summer's evening, in his tent,
That day he overcame the Nervii:—
Look! in this place ran Cassius' dagger through:
See what a rent the envious Casca made:

[a] — napkins—] Handkerchiefs. They are still so named in Scotland.

Through this the well-beloved Brutus stabb'd;
And, as he pluck'd his cursed steel away,
Mark how the blood of Cæsar follow'd it,
As rushing out of doors, to be resolv'd
If Brutus so unkindly knock'd, or no;
For Brutus, as you know, was Cæsar's angel:
Judge, O you gods, how dearly Cæsar lov'd him!
This was the most unkindest cut of all;
For when the noble Cæsar saw him stab,
Ingratitude, more strong than traitors' arms,
Quite vanquish'd him: then burst his mighty heart;
And, in his mantle muffling up his face,
Even at the base of Pompey's statua,*
Which all the while ran blood, great Cæsar fell.
O, what a fall was there, my countrymen!
Then I, and you, and all of us fell down,
Whilst bloody treason flourish'd over us.
O, now you weep; and, I perceive, you feel
The dint of pity: these are gracious drops.
Kind souls, what, weep you when you but behold

(*) Old text, *statue*.

Our Cæsar's vesture wounded? Look you here!
Here is himself, marr'd, as you see, with traitors.

1 Cit. O, piteous spectacle!

2 Cit. O, noble Cæsar!

3 Cit. O, woful day!

4 Cit. O, traitors, villains!

1 Cit. O, most bloody sight!

2 Cit. We will be revenged: revenge! about!—seek,—burn,—fire,—kill,—slay!—let not a traitor live!

Ant. Stay, countrymen.

1 Cit. Peace, there!—hear the noble Antony.

2 Cit. We'll hear him, we'll follow him, we'll die with him!

Ant. Good friends, sweet friends, let me not stir you up
To such a sudden flood of mutiny.
They that have done this deed are honourable;—
What private griefs they have, alas! I know not
That made them do it;—they are wise and honourable,
And will, no doubt, with reasons answer you.
I come not, friends, to steal away your hearts:

I am no orator, as Brutus is;
But, as you know me all, a plain blunt man,
That love my friend; and that they know full well
That gave me public leave to speak of him.
For I have neither wit,[a] nor words, nor worth,
Action, nor utterance, nor the power of speech,
To stir men's blood: I only speak right on;
I tell you that which you yourselves do know;
Show you sweet Cæsar's wounds, poor-poor dumb mouths,
And bid them speak for me: but were I Brutus,
And Brutus Antony, there were an Antony
Would ruffle up your spirits, and put a tongue
In every wound of Cæsar, that should move
The stones of Rome to rise and mutiny.

CITIZENS. We'll mutiny!

1 CIT. We'll burn the house of Brutus!

3 CIT. Away, then! come, seek the conspirators!

ANT. Yet hear me, countrymen; yet hear me speak.

CITIZENS. Peace, ho! hear Antony, most noble Antony.

ANT. Why, friends, you go to do you know not what:
Wherein hath Cæsar thus deserv'd your loves?
Alas, you know not,—I must tell you then:—
You have forgot the will I told you of.

CITIZENS. Most true;—the will!—let's stay and hear the will!

ANT. Here is the will; and, under Cæsar's seal,
To every Roman citizen he gives,—
To every several man,—seventy-five drachmas.

2 CIT. Most noble Cæsar!—we'll revenge his death.

3 CIT. O, royal Cæsar!

ANT. Hear me with patience.

CITIZENS. Peace, ho!

ANT. Moreover, he hath left you all his walks,
His private arbours, and new-planted orchards,
On this side Tiber; he hath left them you,
And to your heirs for ever,—common pleasures,
To walk abroad, and recreate yourselves.
Here was a Cæsar! when comes such another?

1 CIT. Never, never!—Come, away, away!
We'll burn his body in the holy place,
And with the brands fire the traitors' houses.
Take up the body.

2 CIT. Go fetch fire.

3 CIT. Pluck down benches.

4 CIT. Pluck down forms, windows, anything!(4)
[*Exeunt* Citizens *with the body*.

ANT. Now let it work!—Mischief, thou art afoot,
Take thou what course thou wilt!—

Enter a Servant.

How now, fellow?

SERV. Sir, Octavius is already come to Rome.

ANT. Where is he?

SERV. He and Lepidus are at Cæsar's house.

ANT. And thither will I straight to visit him:
He comes upon a wish. Fortune is merry,
And in this mood will give us anything.

SERV. I heard him say, Brutus and Cassius
Are rid like madmen through the gates of Rome.

ANT. Belike they had some notice of the people,
How I had mov'd them. Bring me to Octavius.
[*Exeunt*.

SCENE III.—*The same. A Street.*

Enter CINNA *the Poet*.

CIN. I dreamt to-night that I did feast with Cæsar,
And things unlucky[b] charge my fantasy:
I have no will to wander forth[c] of doors,
Yet something leads me forth.

Enter Citizens.

1 CIT. What is your name?

2 CIT. Whither are you going?

3 CIT. Where do you dwell?

4 CIT. Are you a married man or a bachelor?

2 CIT. Answer every man directly.

1 CIT. Ay, and briefly.

4 CIT. Ay, and wisely.

3 CIT. Ay, and truly, you were best.

CIN. What is my name? Whither am I

---

a *For I have neither* wit,—] The folio 1623 has,—"neyther *writ*," &c.; an obvious error, which the second folio set right. See "Measure for Measure," Act V. Sc. 1,—

"Hast thou or word, or wit, or impudence,
That yet can do thee office?"

b *And things* unlucky—] The old text has, "unluckily;" which Warburton corrected to *unlucky*, the reading generally adopted. Mr. Collier's annotator, however, suggests *unlikely*, a change Mr. Craik approves, but which we believe to be certainly wrong. To dream of feasting, as Steevens showed, was inauspicious; and in North's Plutarch (Life of Brutus) we have the restored word "unlucky" used precisely as here:—"The first and chiefest, was Cæsars long tarying, who came very late to the Senate: for, because the signes of the sacrifices appeared *unluckie*, his wife Calphurnia kept him at home," &c.

c *I have no* will *to wander* forth, &c.] I have no inclination to wander out, &c.: so Shylock, in "The Merchant of Venice," Act II. Sc. 5,—

"I have no mind of feasting forth to-night:
But I will go."

going? Where do I dwell? Am I a married man or a bachelor? Then, to answer every man directly and briefly, wisely and truly;—*wisely*, I say, I am a bachelor.

2 CIT. That 's as much as to say, they are fools that marry:—you 'll bear me a bang for that, I fear. Proceed;—directly.

CIN. *Directly*, I am going to Cæsar's funeral.

1 CIT. As a friend or an enemy?

CIN. As a friend.

2 CIT. That matter is answered directly.

4 CIT. For your dwelling,—briefly.

CIN. *Briefly*, I dwell by the Capitol.

3 CIT. Your name, sir,—truly.

CIN. *Truly*, my name is Cinna.

1 CIT. Tear him to pieces! he 's a conspirator.

CIN. I am Cinna the poet, I am Cinna the poet.

4 CIT. Tear him for his bad verses, tear him for his bad verses!

CIN. I am not Cinna the conspirator.

2 CIT. It is no matter, his name 's Cinna; pluck but his name out of his heart, and turn him going.[a]

3 CIT. Tear him, tear him! Come, brands, ho! firebrands! To Brutus', to Cassius'; burn all! Some to Decius' house, and some to Casca's; some to Ligarius'! away! go! [*Exeunt.*

[a] — and turn him going.] So in "As You Like It," Act III. Sc. 1,—

"Do this expediently, *and turn him going*."

ACT IV.

SCENE I.—Rome. *A Room in* Antony's *House.*

ANTONY, OCTAVIUS, *and* LEPIDUS, *seated at a table.*

ANT. These many, then, shall die; their names are prick'd.
OCT. Your brother too must die; consent you, Lepidus?
LEP. I do consent,—
OCT. Prick him down, Antony.
LEP. Upon condition Publius shall not live,
Who is your sister's son,[a] Mark Antony.
ANT. He shall not live: look, with a spot I damn[b] him.
But, Lepidus, go you to Cæsar's house;
Fetch the will hither, and we shall determine
How to cut off some charge in legacies.
LEP. What, shall I find you here?
OCT. Or here, or at the Capitol.
[*Exit* LEPIDUS.
ANT. This is a slight unmeritable man,
Meet to be sent on errands: is it fit,
The three-fold world divided, he should stand
One of the three to share it?
OCT. So you thought him;
And took his voice who should be prick'd to die,
In our black sentence and proscription.
ANT. Octavius, I have seen more days than you:
And though we lay these honours on this man,
To ease ourselves of divers slanderous loads,
He shall but bear them as the ass bears gold,
To groan and sweat under the business,
Either led or driven, as we point the way;
And having brought our treasure where we will,
Then take we down his load, and turn him off,
Like to the empty ass, to shake his ears,
And graze in commons.
OCT. You may do your will;
But he's a tried and valiant soldier.
ANT. So is my horse, Octavius; and for that
I do appoint him store of provender:
It is a creature that I teach to fight,
To wind, to stop, to run directly on,—

---

a Who is your sister's son, Mark Antony.] This is, historically, an error. The individual meant, Lucius Cæsar, was the brother of Mark Antony's mother. Upton, therefore, concludes that Shakespeare wrote,—

" *You are his sister's son,*" &c.

b — *I* damn *him.*] I *condemn* him. So, quoted by Steevens, in "Promos and Cassandra," Part II.,—

" Vouchsafe to give my *dampned* husband lyfe."

His corporal motion govern'd by my spirit.
And, in some taste, is Lepidus but so;
He must be taught, and train'd, and bid go forth;—
A barren-spirited fellow; one that feeds
On abjects, orts,[a] and imitations,
Which, out of use and stal'd by other men,
Begin his fashion: do not talk of him,
But as a property. And now, Octavius,
Listen great things:—Brutus and Cassius
Are levying powers: we must straight make head:
Therefore let our alliance be combin'd,
Our best friends made, and our best means stretch'd out;[b]
And let us presently go sit in council,
How covert matters may be best disclos'd,
And open perils surest answered.

OCT. Let us do so: for we are at the stake,
And bay'd about with many enemies;
And some that smile have in their hearts, I fear,
Millions of mischiefs. [*Exeunt.*

SCENE II.—*Before* Brutus' *Tent, in the Camp near* Sardis.

Drum. Enter BRUTUS, LUCILIUS, LUCIUS, *and* Soldiers: TITINIUS *and* PINDARUS *meeting them.*

BRU. Stand, ho!

LUCIL. Give the word, ho! and stand.

BRU. What now, Lucilius! is Cassius near?

LUCIL. He is at hand; and Pindarus is come
To do you salutation from his master.

BRU. He greets me well.—Your master Pindarus,
In his own change, or by ill officers,
Hath given me some worthy cause to wish
Things done, undone; but, if he be at hand,
I shall be satisfied.

PIN. I do not doubt
But that my noble master will appear,
Such as he is, full of regard and honour.

BRU. He is not doubted.—A word, Lucilius;
How he receiv'd you, let me be resolv'd.

LUCIL. With courtesy and with respect enough;
But not with such familiar instances,
Nor with such free and friendly conference,
As he hath us'd of old.

BRU. Thou hast describ'd
A hot friend cooling: ever note, Lucilius,
When love begins to sicken and decay,
It useth an enforced ceremony.
There are no tricks in plain and simple faith:
But hollow men, like horses hot at hand,
Make gallant show and promise of their mettle;
But when they should endure the bloody spur,
They fall their crests, and, like deceitful jades,
Sink in the trial. Comes his army on?

LUCIL. They mean this night in Sardis to be quarter'd,
The greater part: the horse in general,
Are come with Cassius. [*March without.*

BRU. Hark! he is arriv'd:—
March gently on to meet him.

Enter CASSIUS *and* Soldiers.

CAS. Stand, ho!

BRU. Stand, ho! Speak the word along.

[*Without.*] Stand.

[*Without.*] Stand.

[*Without.*] Stand.

CAS. Most noble brother, you have done me wrong.

BRU. Judge me, you gods! wrong I mine enemies?
And, if not so, how should I wrong a brother?

CAS. Brutus, this sober form of yours hides wrongs;
And when you do them—

BRU. Cassius, be content;[c]
Speak your griefs[d] softly,—I do know you well:—
Before the eyes of both our armies here,
Which should perceive nothing but love from us,
Let us not wrangle: bid them move away;
Then in my tent, Cassius, enlarge your griefs,
And I will give you audience.

CAS. Pindarus,
Bid our commanders lead their charges off
A little from this ground.

BRU. Lucilius, do you the like; and let no man
Come to our tent, till we have done our conference.
Let Lucius and Titinius guard our door.[e] [*Exeunt.*

---

a On abjects, orts, &c.] The old text is, "—Objects, Arts," &c., but the initials *a* and *o* appear to have been transposed by the compositor. *Abjects* are things thrown away as worthless; and *orts* are scraps. There can be no necessity, therefore, to read, with Theobald and others,—

"On *abject orts*," &c.

b *Our best friends made, and* our *best* means stretch'd *out;*] This is the lection of the second folio; the first printing, lamely enough,—

"Our best friends made, our means stretch'd;"

We might read, with possibly a nearer approach to what the poet wrote,—

"Our best friends made, our *choicest* means stretch'd *out.*"

c — be content;] Be continent; be self-restrained.

d — griefs—] Grievances. So in Act I. Sc. 3,—

"Be factious for redress of all these *griefs.*"

e Lucilius, do you the like; &c.] Mr. Craik reads, with a manifest improvement of the old text,—

"*Lucius*, do you the like; and let no man
Come to our tent, till we have done our conference.
Lucilius and Titinius, guard *the* door."

By this change, the prosody of the first line is restored, and we have no longer the anomaly of an officer of rank and a serving-boy associated together to watch the door.

SCENE III.—*Within the Tent of* Brutus.

Enter Brutus *and* Cassius.

Cas. That you have wrong'd me doth appear in this,—
You have condemn'd and noted Lucius Pella,(1)
For taking bribes here of the Sardians;
Wherein my letters, praying on his side,
Because I knew the man, were slighted off.
Bru. You wrong'd yourself to write in such a case.
Cas. In such a time as this, it is not meet
That every nice offence should bear his comment.
Bru. Let[a] me tell you, Cassius, you, yourself,
Are much condemn'd to have an itching palm
To sell and mart your offices for gold
To undeservers.
Cas. I *an itching palm!*
You know that you are Brutus that speak this,
Or, by the gods, this speech were else your last!
Bru. The name of Cassius honours this corruption,
And chastisement doth therefore hide his head.
Cas. *Chastisement!*
Bru. Remember March, the ides of March remember!
Did not great Julius bleed for justice' sake?
What villain touch'd his body, that did stab,
And not for justice? What, shall one of us,
That struck the foremost man of all this world
But for supporting robbers, shall we now
Contaminate our fingers with base bribes,
And sell the mighty space of our large honours
For so much trash as may be grasped thus?—
I had rather be a dog, and bay the moon,
Than such a Roman.
Cas. Brutus, bay* not me,—
I'll not endure it: you forget yourself,
To hedge me in; I am a soldier, I,
Older in practice, abler than yourself
To make conditions.
Bru. Go to; you are not, Cassius.
Cas. I am.
Bru. I say you are not.
Cas. Urge me no more, I shall forget myself;
Have mind upon your health, tempt me no further.
Bru. Away, slight man!
Cas. Is't possible?
Bru. Hear me, for I will speak!
Must I give way and room to your rash choler?
Shall I be frighted when a madman stares?
Cas. O, ye gods! ye gods! must I endure all this?
Bru. *All this!* ay, more: fret till your proud heart break;
Go show your slaves how choleric you are,
And make your bondmen tremble. Must I budge?
Must I observe you? must I stand and crouch
Under your testy humour? By the gods,
You shall digest the venom of your spleen,
Though it do split you! for, from this day forth,
I'll use you for my mirth, yea, for my laughter,
When you are waspish.
Cas. Is it come to this?
Bru. You say you are a better soldier:
Let it appear so; make your vaunting true,
And it shall please me well: for mine own part,
I shall be glad to learn of noble[b] men.
Cas. You wrong me; every way you wrong me, Brutus;
I said an elder soldier, not a better:
Did I say, better?
Bru. If you did, I care not.
Cas. When Cæsar liv'd he durst not thus have mov'd me.
Bru. Peace, peace! you durst not so have tempted him.
Cas. I durst not?
Bru. No.
Cas. What, durst not tempt him?
Bru. For your life you durst not.
Cas. Do not presume too much upon my love;
I may do that I shall be sorry for.
Bru. You have done that you should be sorry for.
There is no terror, Cassius, in your threats;
For I am arm'd so strong in honesty,
That they pass by me as the idle wind,
Which I respect not. I did send to you
For certain sums of gold, which you denied me;—
For I can raise no money by vile means:
By heaven, I had rather coin my heart,
And drop my blood for drachmas, than to wring
From the hard hands of peasants their vile trash
By any indirection!—I did send
To you for gold to pay my legions,
Which you denied me: was that done like Cassius?
Should I have answer'd Caius Cassius so?
When Marcus Brutus grows so covetous,
To lock such rascal counters from his friends,

(*) Old text, *baite*, corrected by Theobald.

[a] Let me tell you, Cassius, &c.] This defective line has been amended, and rightly perhaps, to,—

"*Yet* let me tell you, Cassius," &c.

[b] — *of* noble *men.*] "Of *abler* men," is the reading of Mr. Collier's annotator, and looking to what Cassius had previously said,—

"I am a soldier, I,
Older in practice, *abler* than yourself," &c.—

it is a very plausible emendation.

Be ready, gods, with all your thunderbolts,
Dash him to pieces!

CAS. I denied you not.

BRU. You did.

CAS. I did not:—he was but a fool
That brought my answer back.—Brutus hath riv'd my heart:
A friend should bear his friend's infirmities,
But Brutus makes mine greater than they are.

BRU. I do not, till you practise them on me.

CAS. You love me not.

BRU. I do not like your faults.

CAS. A friendly eye could never see such faults.

BRU. A flatterer's would not, though they do appear
As huge as high Olympus.

CAS. Come, Antony, and young Octavius, come,
Revenge yourselves alone on Cassius,
For Cassius is a-weary of the world!
Hated by one he loves; brav'd by his brother;
Check'd like a bondman; all his faults observ'd,
Set in a note-book, learn'd, and conn'd by rote,
To cast into my teeth. O, I could weep
My spirit from mine eyes!—There is my dagger,
And here my naked breast; within, a heart
Dearer than Plutus'* mine, richer than gold:
If that thou be'st a Roman, take it forth;
I, that denied thee gold, will give my heart:
Strike, as thou didst at Cæsar; for, I know,
When thou didst hate him worst, thou lov'dst him better
Than ever thou lov'dst Cassius.

BRU. Sheathe your dagger:
Be angry when you will, it shall have scope;
Do what you will, dishonour shall be humour.
O, Cassius, you are yoked with a lamb,[a]—
That carries anger as the flint bears fire;
Who, much enforced, shows a hasty spark,
And straight is cold again.

CAS. Hath Cassius liv'd
To be but mirth and laughter to his Brutus,
When grief and blood, ill-temper'd,[b] vexeth him?

---

a — *you are yoked with a* lamb,—] "Lamb" can hardly have been the poet's word, and Pope, who saw its unfitness, printed *man;* but it requires a happier conjecture than this to justify an alteration of the text.

b *When grief and blood,* ill-temper'd, &c.] By ill-tempered is meant badly qualified. "The four 'humours' in a man, according to the old physicians, were blood, choler, phlegm, and melancholy. So long as these were duly mixed, all would be well."—TRENCH.

(*) Old text, *Pluto's.*

BRU. When I spoke that, I was ill-temper'd too.

CAS. Do you confess so much? Give me your hand.

BRU. And my heart too.

CAS. O, Brutus!—

BRU. What 's the matter?

CAS. Have not you love enough to bear with me,
When that rash humour which my mother gave me
Makes me forgetful?

BRU. Yes, Cassius; and, from henceforth,
When you are over-earnest with your Brutus,
He 'll think your mother chides, and leave you so. [*Noise without.*

POET. [*Without.*] Let me go in to see the generals;
There is some grudge between 'em, 't is not meet
They be alone.

LUCIL. [*Without.*] You shall not come to them.

POET. [*Without.*] Nothing but death shall stay me.

Enter POET, *followed by* LUCILIUS *and* TITINIUS.

CAS. How now! what 's the matter?

POET. For shame, you generals! what do you mean?
Love, and be friends, as two such men should be;
For I have seen more years, I'm sure, than ye.

CAS. Ha, ha! how vilely doth this cynic rhyme!

BRU. Get you hence, sirrah; saucy fellow, hence!

CAS. Bear with him, Brutus: 't is his fashion.

BRU. I 'll know his humour, when he knows his time:
What should the wars do with these jigging fools?—
Companion, hence! (2)

CAS. Away, away, be gone! [*Exit* POET.

BRU. Lucilius and Titinius, bid the commanders
Prepare to lodge their companies to-night.

CAS. And come yourselves, and bring Messala with you,
Immediately to us. [*Exeunt* LUCILIUS *and* TITINIUS.

BRU. Lucius, a bowl of wine.

CAS. I did not think you could have been so angry.

BRU. O, Cassius, I am sick of many griefs.

CAS. Of your philosophy you make no use,
If you give place to accidental evils.

BRU. No man bears sorrow better:—Portia is dead.

CAS. Ha! Portia?

BRU. She is dead.

CAS. How 'scaped I killing when I cross'd you so?—
O, insupportable and touching loss!—
Upon what sickness?

BRU. Impatient of my absence,
And grief that young Octavius with Mark Antony
Have made themselves so strong;—for with her death
That tidings came:—with this she fell distract,
And, her attendants absent, swallow'd fire.

CAS. And died so?

BRU. Even so.

CAS. O, ye immortal gods!

Enter LUCIUS, *with wine and tapers.*

BRU. Speak no more of her.—Give me a bowl of wine.—
In this I bury all unkindness, Cassius. [*Drinks.*

CAS. My heart is thirsty for that noble pledge.—
Fill, Lucius, till the wine o'erswell the cup;
I cannot drink too much of Brutus' love. [*Drinks.*

BRU. Come in, Titinius!—

Re-enter TITINIUS *with* MESSALA.

Welcome, good Messala.—
Now sit we close about this taper here,
And call in question our necessities.

CAS. Portia, art thou gone?

BRU. No more, I pray you.—
Messala, I have here received letters,
That young Octavius and Mark Antony
Come down upon us with a mighty power,
Bending their expedition toward Philippi.

MES. Myself have letters of the self-same tenor.

BRU. With what addition?

MES. That by proscription and bills of outlawry,
Octavius, Antony, and Lepidus,
Have put to death an hundred senators.

BRU. Therein our letters do not well agree;
Mine speak of seventy senators that died
By their proscriptions, Cicero being one.

CAS. Cicero one!

MES. Cicero is dead,
And by that order of proscription.—
Had you your letters from your wife, my lord?

BRU. No, Messala.

MES. Nor nothing in your letters writ of her?
BRU. Nothing, Messala.
MES. That, methinks, is strange.
BRU. Why ask you? hear you aught of her in yours?
MES. No, my lord.
BRU. Now, as you are a Roman, tell me true.
MES. Then like a Roman bear the truth I tell:
For certain she is dead, and by strange manner.
BRU. Why, farewell, Portia.—We must die, Messala:
With meditating that she must die once,
I have the patience to endure it now.
MES. Even so great men great losses should endure.
CAS. I have as much of this in art as you,
But yet my nature could not bear it so.
BRU. Well, to our work alive. What do you think
Of marching to Philippi presently?
CAS. I do not think it good.
BRU. Your reason?
CAS. This it is:—
'T is better that the enemy seek us:
So shall he waste his means, weary his soldiers,
Doing himself offence; whilst we, lying still,
Are full of rest, defence, and nimbleness.
BRU. Good reasons must, of force, give place to better.
The people 'twixt Philippi and this ground
Do stand but in a forc'd affection;
For they have grudg'd us contribution:
The enemy, marching along by them,
By them shall make a fuller number up,
Come on refresh'd, new-added,[a] and encourag'd;
From which advantage shall we cut him off,
If at Philippi we do face him there,
These people at our back.
CAS. Hear me, good brother.
BRU. Under your pardon.—You must note beside,
That we have tried the utmost of our friends,
Our legions are brim-full, our cause is ripe:
The enemy increaseth every day;
We, at the height, are ready to decline.
There is a tide in the affairs of men,
Which, taken at the flood, leads on to fortune;
Omitted, all the voyage of their life
Is bound in shallows and in miseries.
On such a full sea are we now afloat;
And we must take the current when it serves,
Or lose our ventures.
CAS. Then, with your will, go on;
We'll along ourselves, and meet them at Philippi.
BRU. The deep of night is crept upon our talk,
And nature must obey necessity;
Which we will niggard with a little rest.
There is no more to say?
CAS. No more. Good night;
Early to-morrow will we rise, and hence.
BRU. Lucius, my gown. [*Exit* LUCIUS.] Farewell, good Messala:—
Good night, Titinius:—noble, noble Cassius,
Good night, and good repose.
CAS. O, my dear brother!
This was an ill beginning of the night:
Never come such division 'tween our souls!
Let it not, Brutus.
BRU. Every thing is well.
CAS. Good night, my lord.
BRU. Good night, good brother.
TIT., MES. Good night, lord Brutus.
BRU. Farewell, every one.
[*Exeunt* CAS., TIT., *and* MES.

Re-enter LUCIUS, *with the gown.*

Give me the gown. Where is thy instrument?
LUC. Here in the tent.
BRU. What, thou speak'st drowsily?
Poor knave, I blame thee not; thou art o'er-watch'd.[b]
Call Claudius, and some other of my men;
I'll have them sleep on cushions in my tent.
LUC. Varro and Claudius!

Enter VARRO *and* CLAUDIUS.

VAR. Calls my lord?
BRU. I pray you, sirs, lie in my tent and sleep;
It may be, I shall raise you by and by
On business to my brother Cassius.
VAR. So please you, we will stand and watch your pleasure.
BRU. I will not have it so: lie down, good sirs;
It may be I shall otherwise bethink me.—
Look, Lucius, here's the book I sought for so;
I put it in the pocket of my gown.
[VAR. *and* CLAU. *lie down.*
LUC. I was sure your lordship did not give it me.
BRU. Bear with me, good boy, I am much forgetful.
Canst thou hold up thy heavy eyes awhile,
And touch thy instrument a strain or two?
LUC. Ay, my lord, an 't please you.
BRU. It does, my boy:
I trouble thee too much, but thou art willing.
LUC. It is my duty, sir.

---

a —new-added,—] Mr. Dyce and Mr. Singer read "new-*aided*;" Mr. Collier's annotator, "new-*hearted*;" but we cannot see that change of any kind is indispensable.

b — o'er-watch'd.] Kept over-much from sleep.

Bru. I should not urge thy duty past thy might;
I know young bloods look for a time of rest.
Luc. I have slept, my lord, already.
Bru. It was well done; and thou shalt sleep again;
I will not hold thee long: if I do live,
I will be good to thee. [*Music, and a Song.*
This is a sleepy tune:—O, murderous slumber!
Lay'st thou thy leaden mace upon my boy,
That plays thee music?—Gentle knave, good night;
I will not do thee so much wrong to wake thee.
If thou dost nod, thou break'st thy instrument;
I'll take it from thee: and, good boy, good night.—
Let me see, let me see;—is not the leaf turn'd down
Where I left reading? Here it is, I think.
[*Sits down.*

Enter the Ghost *of* CÆSAR.

How ill this taper burns!—Ha! who comes here?
I think it is the weakness of mine eyes
That shapes this monstrous apparition.
It comes upon me!—Art thou anything?
Art thou some god, some angel, or some devil,
That mak'st my blood cold, and my hair to stare?
Speak to me what thou art.

GHOST. Thy evil spirit, Brutus.

BRU. Why com'st thou?

GHOST. To tell thee, thou shalt see me at Philippi.

BRU. Well: then I shall see thee again? (3)

GHOST. Ay, at Philippi.

BRU. Why, I will see thee at Philippi then.— [Ghost *vanishes.*
Now I have taken heart thou vanishest:
Ill spirit, I would hold more talk with thee.—
Boy! Lucius!—Varro! Claudius!—Sirs, awake!—
Claudius!

LUC. The strings, my lord, are false.

BRU. He thinks he still is at his instrument.—
Lucius, awake!

LUC. My lord?

BRU. Didst thou dream, Lucius, that thou so criedst out?

LUC. My lord, I do not know that I did cry.

BRU. Yes, that thou didst: didst thou see anything?

LUC. Nothing, my lord.

BRU. Sleep again, Lucius.—Sirrah, Claudius!
Fellow thou! awake!

VAR. My lord?

CLAU. My lord?

BRU. Why did you so cry out, sirs, in your sleep?

VAR., CLAU. Did we, my lord?

BRU. Ay; saw you anything?

VAR. No, my lord, I saw nothing.

CLAU. Nor I, my lord.

BRU. Go and commend me to my brother Cassius;
Bid him set on his powers betimes before,
And we will follow.

VAR., CLAU. It shall be done, my lord. [*Exeunt.*

ACT V.

SCENE I.—*The Plains of* Philippi.

Enter OCTAVIUS, ANTONY, *and their* Army.

OCT. Now, Antony, our hopes are answered:
You said the enemy would not come down,
But keep the hills and upper regions;
It proves not so: their battles are at hand;
They mean to warn[a] us at Philippi here,
Answering before we do demand of them.
ANT. Tut, I am in their bosoms, and I know
Wherefore they do it: they could be content
To visit other places; and come down
With fearful bravery,[b] thinking, by this face,[c]
To fasten in our thoughts that they have courage;
But 't is not so.

Enter a Messenger.

MESS. Prepare you, generals:
The enemy comes on in gallant show;
Their bloody sign of battle is hung out,
And something to be done immediately.

ANT. Octavius, lead your battle softly on,
Upon the left hand of the even field.
OCT. Upon the right hand I; keep thou the left.
ANT. Why do you cross me in this exigent?
OCT. I do not cross you; but I will do so.
[*March.*

Drum. *Enter* BRUTUS, CASSIUS, *and their* Army; LUCILIUS, TITINIUS, MESSALA, *and others.*

BRU. They stand, and would have parley.
CAS. Stand fast, Titinius: we must out and talk.
OCT. Mark Antony, shall we give sign of battle?
ANT. No, Cæsar, we will answer on their charge.
Make forth; the generals would have some words.
OCT. Stir not until the signal.
BRU. Words before blows:—is it so, countrymen?

---

a *They mean to* warn *us*—] That is, to *summon* us. So in "Richard III." Act I. Sc. 3,—

"And sent to *warn* them to his royal presence;"

and again in "Romeo and Juliet," Act V. Sc. 3,—

"—— is as a bell
That *warns* my old age to a sepulchre."

b *With* fearful bravery,—] With alarming ostentation. Though some critics conjecture that "fearful" is not used here in its active sense, but with the ordinary meaning, full of fear.

c — by this face,—] By this *bravado*, or *brag*.

OCT. Not that we love words better, as you do.
BRU. Good words are better than bad strokes, Octavius.
ANT. In your bad strokes, Brutus, you give good words:
Witness the hole you made in Cæsar's heart,
Crying, *Long live! hail Cæsar!*
CAS. Antony,
The posture of your blows are[a] yet unknown;
But for your words, they rob the Hybla bees,
And leave them honeyless.
ANT. Not stingless too.
BRU. O, yes, and soundless too;
For you have stol'n their buzzing, Antony,
And, very wisely, threat before you sting.
ANT. Villains, you did not so, when your vile daggers
Hack'd one another in the sides of Cæsar;
You show'd your teeth like apes, and fawn'd like hounds,
And bow'd like bondmen, kissing Cæsar's feet;
Whilst damned Casca, like a cur, behind
Struck Cæsar on the neck. O, you flatterers!
CAS. *Flatterers!*—Now Brutus, thank yourself:
This tongue had not offended so to-day,
If Cassius might have rul'd.
OCT. Come, come, the cause: if arguing make us sweat,
The proof of it will turn to redder drops.
Look,—I draw a sword against conspirators;
When think you that the sword goes up again?—
Never, till Cæsar's three-and-thirty wounds
Be well aveng'd; or till another Cæsar
Have added slaughter to the sword of traitors.
BRU. Cæsar, thou canst not die by traitors' hands,
Unless thou bring'st them with thee.
OCT. So I hope;
I was not born to die on Brutus' sword.
BRU. O, if thou wert the noblest of thy strain,
Young man, thou couldst not die more honourable.
CAS. A peevish[b] schoolboy, worthless of such honour,
Join'd with a masker and a reveller!
ANT. Old Cassius still!
OCT. Come, Antony; away!—
Defiance, traitors, hurl we in your teeth!
If you dare fight to-day, come to the field;
If not, when you have stomachs.
[*Exeunt* OCTAVIUS, ANTONY, *and their* Army.
CAS. Why now, blow, wind; swell, billow; and swim, bark!
The storm is up, and all is on the hazard.
BRU. Ho, Lucilius! hark, a word with you.
LUCIL. My lord?
[BRUTUS *and* LUCILIUS *converse apart.*
CAS. Messala,—
MES. What says my general?
CAS. Messala,
This is my birthday; as this very day
Was Cassius born. Give me thy hand, Messala:
Be thou my witness that, against my will,
As Pompey was, am I compell'd to set
Upon one battle all our liberties.
You know that I held Epicurus strong,
And his opinion: now I change my mind,
And partly credit things that do presage.
Coming from Sardis, on our former[c] ensign
Two mighty eagles fell; and there they perch'd,
Gorging and feeding from our soldiers' hands,
Who to Philippi here consorted us:
This morning are they fled away and gone; (1)
And in their steads do ravens, crows, and kites,
Fly o'er our heads, and downward look on us,
As we were sickly prey; their shadows seem
A canopy most fatal, under which
Our army lies, ready to give up the ghost.
MES. Believe not so.
CAS. I but believe it partly;
For I am fresh of spirit, and resolv'd
To meet all perils very constantly.
BRU. Even so, Lucilius. [*Advancing.*
CAS. Now, most noble Brutus,
The gods to-day stand friendly, that we may,
Lovers in peace, lead on our days to age!
But, since the affairs of men rest still incertain,
Let's reason with the worst that may befall.
If we do lose this battle, then is this
The very last time we shall speak together:
What are you, then, determined to do?
BRU. Even by the rule of that philosophy
By which I did blame Cato for the death
Which he did give himself:—I know not how,
But I do find it cowardly and vile,

---

[a] *The* posture *of your blows* are *yet unknown;*] The commentators have all something to say on the grammatical irregularity in this line, but are mute upon what is of far more importance, the exceptional use of "posture." Elsewhere Shakespeare always employs the word in its ordinary sense of *attitude, position,* &c.; but here, if not a misprint, it must be taken to mean *quality* or *composition.*

[b] *A* peevish *schoolboy,*—] Although there are one or two passages in these plays where "peevish" implies *foolish, childish,* &c., the editors are certainly not justified in attributing this signification to the word in every instance where it occurs. In nine cases out of ten, indeed, the poet uses it, as here, in the sense of *headstrong, stubborn, wilful,* the meaning which it usually carried in his time. For example,—

"A *peevish,* self-will'd harlotry it is."
Romeo and Juliet, Act IV. Sc. 2.

"And when she's froward, *peevish,* sullen, sour," &c.
Taming of the Shrew, Act V. Sc. 2.

"Being wrong'd, as we are, by this *peevish* town," &c.
King John, Act II. Sc. 2.

[c] — *on our* former *ensign*—] "Former" meant *foremost* or *fore.* In proof of this, Ritson quotes the following from Adlyngton's translation of Apuleius, 1596:—"First hee instructed me to sit at the table upon my taile, and howe I should leape and daunce, holding up my *former* feete."

For fear of what might fall, so to prevent
The time[a] of life:—arming myself with patience,
To stay the providence of some high powers,
That govern us below.

CAS. Then, if we lose this battle,
You are contented to be led in triumph
Thorough the streets of Rome?

BRU. No, Cassius, no: think not, thou noble Roman,
That ever Brutus will go bound to Rome;
He bears too great a mind. But this same day
Must end that work the ides of March begun; (2)
And whether we shall meet again I know not.
Therefore our everlasting farewell take:—
For ever, and for ever, farewell, Cassius!
If we do meet again, why, we shall smile;
If not, why, then, this parting was well made.

CAS. For ever, and for ever, farewell, Brutus!
If we do meet again, we'll smile indeed;
If not, 't is true this parting was well made.

BRU. Why then, lead on.—O, that a man might know
The end of this day's business ere it come!
But it sufficeth that the day will end,
And then the end is known.—Come, ho! away!
[*Exeunt.*

SCENE II.—*The same. The Field of Battle.*

Alarum. Enter BRUTUS *and* MESSALA.

BRU. Ride, ride, Messala, ride, and give these bills
Unto the legions on the other side! [*Loud alarum.*
Let them set on at once: for I perceive
But cold demeanour in Octavius' wing,
And sudden push gives them the overthrow.
Ride, ride, Messala! let them all come down.
[*Exeunt.*

SCENE III.—*The same. Another Part of the Field.*

Alarum. Enter CASSIUS *and* TITINIUS.

CAS. O, look, Titinius, look, the villains fly!
Myself have to mine own turn'd enemy:
This ensign here of mine was turning back;[b]
I slew the coward, and did take it from him.

TIT. O, Cassius, Brutus gave the word too early:
Who, having some advantage on Octavius,
Took it too eagerly; his soldiers fell to spoil,
Whilst we by Antony are all inclos'd.

Enter PINDARUS.

PIN. Fly further off, my lord, fly further off!
Mark Antony is in your tents, my lord!
Fly therefore, noble Cassius, fly far off!

CAS. This hill is far enough. Look, look, Titinius;
Are those my tents where I perceive the fire?

TIT. They are, my lord.

CAS. Titinius, if thou lov'st me,
Mount thou my horse, and hide thy spurs in him,
Till he have brought thee up to yonder troops,
And here again; that I may rest assur'd
Whether yond troops are friend or enemy.

TIT. I will be here again, even with a thought.
[*Exit.*

CAS. Go, Pindarus, get higher on that hill;
My sight was ever thick; regard Titinius,
And tell me what thou not'st about the field.—
[*Exit* PINDARUS.
This day I breathed first: time is come round,
And where I did begin, there shall I end;[c]
My life is run his compass.—Sirrah, what news?

PIN. [*Above.*] O my lord!

CAS. What news?

PIN. [*Above.*] Titinius is inclosed round about
With horsemen that make to him on the spur;—
Yet he spurs on.—Now they are almost on him;—
Now, Titinius!—Now some 'light:—O, he 'lights too:—
He 's ta'en;—and hark! they shout for joy.
[*Shout.*

CAS. Come down, behold no more.—
O, coward that I am, to live so long,
To see my best friend ta'en before my face!

Enter PINDARUS.

Come hither, sirrah:
In Parthia did I take thee prisoner;

---

a —— to prevent
The time *of life*:—]

That is, to anticipate the natural period of existence. The expression, *time of life*, for duration of life, occurs again in "Henry IV." Part II. Act V. Sc. 2,—

"O, gentlemen, the *time of life* is short;"

a fact Mr. Craik must have forgotten when he adopted the specious modernization, "*term* of life," from Capell.

b *This* ensign *here of mine was turning back*;] "Here the term *ensign* may almost be said to be used with the double meaning of both the standard and the standard-bearer."—CRAIK.

c This day I breathed first: time is come round,
And where I did begin, there shall I end;]

It would not be difficult to find persons even now, perhaps, who indulge the visionary notion that their life will terminate on the same day of the week or month or at the same place that it began. Shakespeare seems to have been impressed by this superstition, for he has twice or thrice adverted to it. Curiously enough, too, he might have said of his own existence, "The wheel is come full circle," for he died on the same day of the same month in which he was born, and at the same place.

And then I swore thee, saving of thy life,
That whatsoever I did bid thee do
Thou shouldst attempt it. Come now, keep thine oath!
Now be a freeman; and, with this good sword,
That ran through Cæsar's bowels, search this bosom.
Stand not to answer: here, take thou the hilts;
And, when my face is cover'd, as 't is now,
Guide thou the sword.—Cæsar, thou art reveng'd,
Even with the sword that kill'd thee.(3) [*Dies.*

PIN. So, I am free; yet would not so have been,
Durst I have done my will. O, Cassius!
Far from this country Pindarus shall run,
Where never Roman shall take note of him.
[*Exit.*

Re-enter TITINIUS, *with* MESSALA.

MES. It is but change,[a] Titinius; for Octavius
Is overthrown by noble Brutus' power,
As Cassius' legions are by Antony.
TIT. These tidings will well comfort Cassius.
MES. Where did you leave him?
TIT. All disconsolate,
With Pindarus his bondman, on this hill.
MES. Is not that he that lies upon the ground?
TIT. He lies not like the living.—O, my heart!
MES. Is not that he?
TIT. No, this was he, Messala,
But Cassius is no more.—O, setting sun!
As in thy red rays thou dost sink to night,
So in his red blood Cassius' day is set,—
The sun of Rome is set! Our day is gone;
Clouds, dews, and dangers come; our deeds are done!
Mistrust of my success[b] hath done this deed.
MES. Mistrust of good success hath done this deed.
O, hateful Error, Melancholy's child!
Why dost thou show to the apt thoughts of men
The things that are not? O, Error, soon conceiv'd,
Thou never com'st unto a happy birth,
But kill'st the mother that engender'd thee.
TIT. What, Pindarus! where art thou, Pindarus?
MES. Seek him, Titinius: whilst I go to meet
The noble Brutus, thrusting this report
Into his ears: I may say, thrusting it;
For piercing steel, and darts envenomed,
Shall be as welcome to the ears of Brutus
As tidings of this sight.
TIT. Hie you, Messala,
And I will seek for Pindarus the while.
[*Exit* MESSALA.
Why didst thou send me forth, brave Cassius?
Did I not meet thy friends? and did not they
Put on my brows this wreath of victory,
And bid me give it thee? Didst thou not hear their shouts?
Alas, thou hast misconstru'd everything!
But hold thee, take this garland on thy brow;
Thy Brutus bid me give it thee, and I
Will do his bidding.—Brutus, come apace,
And see how I regarded Caius Cassius.—
By your leave, gods:—this is a Roman's part:
Come, Cassius' sword, and find Titinius' heart.
[*Dies.*

Alarum. Re-enter MESSALA, *with* BRUTUS, YOUNG CATO, STRATO, VOLUMNIUS, *and* LUCILIUS.

BRU. Where, where, Messala, doth his body lie?
MES. Lo, yonder; and Titinius mourning it.
BRU. Titinius' face is upward.
CATO. He is slain.
BRU. O, Julius Cæsar, thou art mighty yet!
Thy spirit walks abroad, and turns our swords
In our own proper entrails. [*Low alarums.*
CATO. Brave Titinius!
Look, whêr he have not crown'd dead Cassius!
BRU. Are yet two Romans living such as these?—
The[c] last of all the Romans, fare thee well!
It is impossible that ever Rome
Should breed thy fellow.—Friends, I owe more * tears
To this dead man than you shall see me pay.—
I shall find time, Cassius, I shall find time.—
Come, therefore, and to Thassos† send his body;
His funerals shall not be in our camp,
Lest it discomfort us.—Lucilius, come;
And come, young Cato; let us to the field.—
Labeo, and Flavius, set our battles on:—
'T is three o'clock; and, Romans, yet ere night
We shall try fortune in a second fight. [*Exeunt.*

SCENE IV.—*Another Part of the Field.*

Alarum. Enter, fighting, Soldiers *of both Armies; then* BRUTUS, YOUNG CATO, LUCILIUS, *and others.*

BRU. Yet, countrymen, O, yet hold up your heads!
CATO. What bastard doth not? Who will go with me?
I will proclaim my name about the field:—
I am the son of Marcus Cato, ho!
A foe to tyrants, and my country's friend;
I am the son of Marcus Cato, ho!
[*Charges the enemy.*
BRU. And I am Brutus, Marcus Brutus, I!
Brutus, my country's friend; know me for Brutus!
[*Exit, charging the enemy.* YOUNG CATO *is overpowered, and falls.*

---

[a] It is but change,—] It is no more than an exchange or alternation of mishap.

[b] *Mistrust of my* success—] By "success," in Shakespeare's time, was commonly understood *issue, consequence, result,* &c.; it might, therefore, be good (as Messala in the next line says, "Mistrust of *good* success") or ill, according to circumstances. The meaning of Titinius is, Mistrust of my fortune, or what befell me, has done this deed.

[c] The *last of all the Romans,* &c.] Rowe, who has been followed by many editors, reads, "*Thou* last," &c.

(*) First folio, *no.* (†) Old text, *Tharsus.*

LUCIL. O, young and noble Cato, art thou down?
Why, now thou diest as bravely as Titinius;
And mayst be honour'd, being Cato's son.
1 SOLD. Yield, or thou diest!
LUCIL. Only I yield to die:
There is so much that thou wilt kill me straight; [*Offering money.*
Kill Brutus, and be honour'd in his death.
1 SOLD. We must not.—A noble prisoner!
2 SOLD. Room, ho! Tell Antony, Brutus is ta'en.
1 SOLD. I'll tell the news.—Here comes the general:—

Enter ANTONY.

Brutus is ta'en, Brutus is ta'en, my lord!
ANT. Where is he?
LUCIL. Safe, Antony; Brutus is safe enough:
I dare assure thee that no enemy
Shall ever take alive the noble Brutus:
The gods defend him from so great a shame!
When you do find him, or alive or dead,
He will be found like Brutus, like himself.
ANT. This is not Brutus, friend; but, I assure you,
A prize no less in worth: keep this man safe,
Give him all kindness: I had rather have
Such men my friends than enemies.(4) Go on,
And see whêr Brutus be alive or dead;
And bring us word unto Octavius' tent
How everything is chanc'd. [*Exeunt.*

SCENE V.—*Another Part of the Field.*

Enter BRUTUS, DARDANIUS, CLITUS, STRATO, *and* VOLUMNIUS.

BRU. Come, poor remains of friends, rest on this rock.
CLI. Statilius show'd the torchlight; but, my lord,
He came not back; he is or ta'en, or slain.
BRU. Sit thee down, Clitus: slaying is the word;
It is a deed in fashion. Hark thee, Clitus.— [*Whispering him.*
CLI. What, I, my lord? No, not for all the world.
BRU. Peace, then, no words.
CLI. I'll rather kill myself.
BRU. Hark thee, Dardanius.—[*Whispers him.*
DAR. Shall I do such a deed?
CLI. O, Dardanius!
DAR. O, Clitus!
CLI. What ill request did Brutus make to thee?
DAR. To kill him, Clitus. Look, he meditates.
CLI. Now is that noble vessel full of grief,
That it runs over even at his eyes.
BRU. Come hither, good Volumnius; list a word.
VOL. What says my lord?
BRU. Why, this, Volumnius:
The ghost of Cæsar hath appear'd to me
Two several times by night,—at Sardis once,
And, this last night, here in Philippi fields.
I know my hour is come.
VOL. Not so, my lord.
BRU. Nay, I am sure it is, Volumnius.
Thou seest the world, Volumnius, how it goes;
Our enemies have beat us to the pit: [*Loud alarums.*
It is more worthy to leap in ourselves,
Than tarry till they push us. Good Volumnius,
Thou know'st that we two went to school together;
Even for that our love of old, I pr'ythee,
Hold thou my sword-hilts, whilst I run on it.
VOL. That's not an office for a friend, my lord. [*Alarum still.*
CLI. Fly, fly, my lord! there is no tarrying here.
BRU. Farewell to you;—and you;—and you, Volumnius.—
Strato, thou hast been all this while asleep;
Farewell to thee too, Strato.—Countrymen,
My heart doth joy that yet, in all my life,
I found no man but he was true to me.
I shall have glory by this losing day,
More than Octavius and Mark Antony
By this vile conquest shall attain unto.
So, fare you well at once; for Brutus' tongue
Hath almost ended his life's history:
Night hangs upon mine eyes; my bones would rest,
That have but labour'd to attain this hour.
[*Alarum. Cry within,* Fly, fly, fly!
CLI. Fly, my lord, fly!
BRU. Hence; I will follow.
[*Exeunt* CLITUS, DARDANIUS, *and* VOLUMNIUS.
I pr'ythee, Strato, stay thou by thy lord:
Thou art a fellow of a good respect;
Thy life hath had some smatch of honour in it:
Hold then my sword, and turn away thy face,
While I do run upon it. Wilt thou, Strato?
STRA. Give me your hand first: fare you well, my lord.
BRU. Farewell, good Strato.—Cæsar, now be still:
I kill'd not thee with half so good a will.
[*Runs on his sword, and dies.*(5)

Alarum. Retreat. Enter OCTAVIUS, ANTONY, MESSALA, LUCILIUS, *and* Army.

OCT. What man is that?
MES. My master's man.—Strato, where is thy master?
STRA. Free from the bondage you are in, Messala:
The conquerors can but make a fire of him;
For Brutus only overcame himself,
And no man else hath honour by his death.
LUCIL. So Brutus should be found.—I thank thee, Brutus,
That thou hast prov'd Lucilius' saying true.
OCT. All that serv'd Brutus, I will entertain them.—
Fellow, wilt thou bestow thy time with me?
STRA. Ay, if Messala will prefer me to you.
OCT. Do so, good Messala.
MES. How died my master, Strato?
STRA. I held the sword, and he did run on it.
MES. Octavius, then take him to follow thee,
That did the latest service to my master.
ANT. This was the noblest Roman of them all: (6)
All the conspirators, save only he,
Did that they did in envy of great Cæsar;
He only, in a general honest thought,
And common good to all, made one of them.
His life was gentle; and the elements
So mix'd in him, that Nature might stand up,
And say to all the world, *This was a man!*
OCT. According to his virtue let us use him,
With all respect and rites of burial.
Within my tent his bones to-night shall lie,
Most like a soldier, order'd honourably.—
So, call the field to rest: and let's away,
To part the glories of this happy day. [*Exeunt.*

ILLUSTRATIVE COMMENTS.

ACT I.

(1) SCENE II.—

Stand you directly in Antonius' way,
When he doth run his course.]

The passages from North's "Plutarch," which we have chosen to illustrate the action of this tragedy, are extracted chiefly from the lives of Julius Cæsar and Brutus; and while attesting the almost literal fidelity with which Shakespeare, in the present case, adhered to his authority, will show the unerring skill and judgment by which he was guided in his selection of incidents for representation.

"At that time the feast Lupercalia was celebrated, the which in old time, men say was the feast of shepheards or heardmen, & is much like unto the feast of the LYCÆIANS in ARCADIA. But howsoever it is, that day there are divers noble mens sons, yong men, (and some of them Magistrates themselves that govern then) which run naked through the city, striking in sport them they meet in their way, with leather thongs, haire and all on, to make them give place. And many noble women and gentlewomen also, go of purpose to stand in their way, and do put forth their hands to be stricken, as scholers hold them out to their schoolemaster, to be stricken with the ferula: perswading themselves that being with child, they shall have good delivery; and so being barren, that it wil make them to conceive with child."

(2) SCENE II.—*The rabblement shouted, and clapped their chapped hands, and threw up their sweaty nightcaps, and uttered such a deal of stinking breath because Cæsar refused the crown, that it had almost choked Cæsar.*] "*Cæsar* sate to behold that sport upon the pulpit for Orations, in a chaire of gold, apparelled in triumphant manner. *Antonius* who was Consull at that time, was one of them that ranne this holy course. So when he came into the market place, the people made a lane for him to runne at liberty, and he came to *Cæsar*, and presented him a Diademe wreathed about with laurell, Whereupon there rose a certaine crie of reioycing, not very great, done onely by a few, appointed for the purpose. But when *Cæsar* refused the Diademe, then all the people together made an outcrie of ioy. Then *Antonius* offering it him againe, there was a second shout of ioy, but yet of a few. But when *Cæsar* refused it againe the second time, then all the whole people shouted. *Cæsar* having made this proofe, found that the people did not like of it and thereupon rose out of his chaire, and commanded the crowne to be caried unto *Iupiter* in the Capitoll. After that, there were set up images of *Cæsar* in the city, with Diademes upon their heads, like kings."

(3) SCENE III.—

His countenance, like richest alchemy,
Will change to virtue and to worthiness.]

"Now when *Cassius* felt his friends, and did stirre them up against *Cæsar:* they all agreed, and promised to take part with him, so *Brutus* were the chiefe of their conspiracie. For they told him, that so high an enterprise and attempt as that, did not so much require men of manhood and courage to draw their swords, as it stood them upon to have a man of such estimation as *Brutus*, to make every man boldly thinke, that by his onely presence the fact were holy and iust, If he tooke not this course, then that they should go to it with fainter hearts; and when they had done it, they should be more fearefull, because every man would thinke that *Brutus* would not have refused to have made one with them, if the cause had been good and honest. Therefore *Cassius* considering this matter with himselfe, did first of all speake to *Brutus*, since they grew strange together for the suite they had for the Prætorship. So when he was reconciled to him againe, and that they had embraced one another, *Cassius* asked him if he were determined to be in the Senate house the first day of the moneth of March, because he heard say that *Cæsars* friendes should move the councell that day, that *Cæsar* should be called king by the Senate. *Brutus* answered him, he wold not be there. But if we be sent for (said *Cassius*) how then? For my selfe then (said *Brutus*,) I meane not to hold my peace, but to withstand it, and rather die then lose my liberty."

ACT II.

(1) SCENE I.—

If the redress will follow, thou receivest
Thy full petition at the hand of Brutus!]

"But for *Brutus*, his friends and countrimen, both by divers procurements, and sundrie rumours of the citie, and by many bils also, did openly call and procure him to do that he did. For under the image of his ancestor *Iunius Brutus*, (that drave the kings out of ROME) they wrote: O, that it pleased the gods thou wert now alive, *Brutus!* and againe, That thou wert here among us now! His tribunall or chaire, where he gave audience during the time he was Prætor, was full of such bils: *Brutus* thou art asleepe, and art not *Brutus* indeed."

(2) SCENE I.—

—— can I bear that with patience,
And not my husband's secrets?]

"His wife *Portia* was the daughter of *Cato*, whom *Brutus* maried being his cousin, not a maiden, but a young widow after the death of her first husband *Bibulus*, by whom she had also a young sonne called *Bibulus,* who afterwards wrote a booke of the acts and gestes of *Brutus,* extant at this present day. This young ladie being excellently well seene in Philosophy, loving her husband well, and being of a noble courage, as she was also wise: because she would not aske her husband what he ayled before she had made some proofe by her selfe: she tooke a little razour, such as Barbers occupie to pare mens nailes, and causing her maydes and women to go out of her chamber gave her selfe a great gash withall in her thigh, that she was straight all of a goare bloud: and incontinently after, a vehement feaver tooke her, by reason of the paine of her wound. Then perceiving her husband was marvellously out of quiet, and that he could take no rest, even in her greatest paine of all, she spake in this sort unto him: I being, ô *Brutus,* (said she) the daughter of *Cato,* was married unto thee; not to be thy bed-fellow and companion in bedde and at boord onely, like a harlot, but to be partaker also with thee of thy good and evill fortune. Now for thy selfe, I can find no cause of fault in thee touching our match: but for my part, how may I shew my duty towards thee, and how much I would do for thy sake, if I cannot constantly beare a secret mischance or griefe with thee, which requireth secrecie and fidelitie? I confesse, that a womans wit commonly is too weake to keepe a secret safely: but yet (*Brutus*) good education, and the company of vertuous men, have some power to reforme the defect of nature. And for my selfe, I have this benefite moreover, that I am the daughter of *Cato,* and wife of *Brutus,* This notwithstanding, I did not trust to any of these things before, until that now I have found by experience, that no paine or griefe whatsoever can overcome me. With those words shee shewed him her wound on her thigh, and told him what she had done to prove her selfe. *Brutus* was amazed to heare what she sayd unto him, and lifting up his hands to heaven, he besought the goddes to give him the grace he might bring his enterprise to so good passe, that he might be found a husband, worthy of so noble a wife as *Porcia:* so he then did comfort her the best he could."

(3) SCENE I.—

O, what a time have you chose out, brave Caius,
To wear a kerchief!]

"Now amongest *Pompeys* frends there was one called *Caius Ligarius,* who had bene accused unto *Cæsar* for taking parte with *Pompey,* and *Cæsar* discharged him. But *Ligarius* thanked not *Cæsar* so muche for his discharge, as he was offended with him for that he was brought in danger by his tyrannicall power; and therefore in his heart he was always his mortal enemy, and was besides very familiar with *Brutus,* who went to see him, being sicke in his bed, and said unto him, O *Ligarius,* in what a time art thou sicke! *Ligarius,* rising up in his bed, and taking him by the right hande, said unto him, *Brutus* (said he), if thou hast any great enterprise in hande worthy of thyself, I am whole."

(4) SCENE II.—

—— these things are beyond all use,
And I do fear them!]

"Then going to bed the same night, as his manner was, and lying with his wife *Calpurnia,* all the windows and doores of his chamber flying open, the noise awoke him, and made him afraid when he saw such light; but more, when he heard his wife *Calpurnia,* being fast asleepe, weepe and sigh, and put forth many grumbling lamentable speeches, for she dreamed that *Cæsar* was slaine, and that she had him in her armes. Others also do denie that she had any such dreame, as, amongst other, *Titus Livius* writeth that it was in this sort:—The Senate having set upon the top of *Cæsars* house, for an ornament and setting forth of the same, a certaine pinnacle, *Calpurnia* dreamed that she saw it broken downe, and that she thought she lamented and wept for it; insomuch that, *Cæsar* rising in the morning, she prayed him, if it were possible, not to go out of the doores that day, but to adjorne the session of the Senate until another day; And if that he made no reckoning of her dreame, yet that he would search further of the Soothsaiers by their sacrifices to know what should happen him that day. Thereby it seemed that *Cæsar* likewise did feare or suspect somewhat, because his wife *Calpurnia* until that time was never given to any fear and superstition; and that when he saw her so troubled in mind with this dreame she had, but much more afterwards when the soothsaiers having sacrificed many beasts one after another, told him that none did like them: then he determined to send *Antonius* to adjorne the session of the Senate. But in the meane time came *Decius Brutus,* surnamed *Albinus,* in whom *Cæsar* put such confidence that in his last will and testament he had appointed him to be his next heire, and yet was of the conspiracie with *Cassius* and *Brutus:* he, fearing that, if *Cæsar* did adjorn the session that day, the conspiracie would be betrayed, laughed at the Soothsayers, and reproved *Cæsar,* saying that he gave the Senate occasion to mislike with him, and that they might think he mocked them, considering that by his commandement they were assembled, and that they were ready willingly to grant him all things, and to proclaim him king of all the provinces of the Empire of Rome out of Italy, and that he should wear his diademe in all other places, both by sea and land. And, furthermore, that if any man should tel them from him they should depart for that present time, and return again when *Calpurnia* should have better dreames, what would his enemies and illwillers say, and how could they like of his friends words? And who could persuade them otherwise, but that they would think his dominion a slavery unto them, and tyrannical in himself? And yet, if it be so, said he, that you utterly mislike of this day, it is better that you go yourself in person, and, saluting the Senate, to dismiss them til another time. Therewithal he took *Cæsar* by the hand, and brought him out of his house."

ACT III.

(1) SCENE I.—

Know, Cæsar doth not wrong; nor without cause
Will he be satisfied.]

In his "Discoveries," speaking of Shakespeare, Ben Jonson remarks, "Many times he fell into those things, could not escape laughter: as when he said in the person of Cæsar, one speaking to him, 'Cæsar, thou dost me wrong,' he replied, 'Cæsar did never wrong but with just cause.'" In *The Induction* to "The Staple of News," he has ridiculed the expression—"Cry you mercy, *you never did wrong but with just cause.*" It is uncharitable to believe with Steevens that Jonson wilfully misquoted the passage: the very fact, indeed, of his giving it in this form after its appearance in a different one in the printed copy of the poet's plays, strengthens the probability that he quotes it as in the fervour of composition it originally slipped from Shakespeare's pen, and that he was not aware of any subsequent modification of the words.

(2) SCENE I.—*Et tu, Brute?*] The original authority for this exclamation was probably Suetonius, I. 82, who says that some have written, that when Marcus Brutus ran upon Cæsar, the latter cried out Καὶ σύ, τέκνον; *And thou too, my*

son? But the particular expression of the text may have been found in the old Latin play by Dr. Eedes; or have been taken from "The True Tragedie of Richard Duke of Yorke," &c. which forms the basis of Part III. of King Henry VI.; where we have the following line:—"Et tu, Brute? Wilt thou stab Cæsar too?" It does not occur either in the description of Cæsar's death, which Plutarch gives in the life of Marcus Brutus; or in the following account, which Shakespeare seems to have more closely followed, from the life of Julius Cæsar:—

"And one *Artemidorus* also born in the Ile of GNIDOS, a doctor of Rhetorick in the Greeke tongue, who by means of his profession was very familiar with certaine of *Brutus* confederates; and therfore knew the most part of al their practises against *Cæsar*, came and brought him a litle bill written with his owne hand, of all that he meant to tel him. He marking how *Cæsar* received all the supplications that were offered him, & that he gave them straight to his men that were about him, pressed nearer to him, and said: *Cæsar*, reade this memoriall to your selfe, and that quickly, for they be matters of great weight, and touch you nearely. *Cæsar* took it of him, but could never reade it, though he many times attempted it, for the number of people that did salute him: but holding it still in his hand, keeping it to himselfe, went on withall into the Senate house. Howbeit other are of opinion, that it was some man else that gave him that memorial, & not *Artemidorus*, who did what he could all the way as he went to give it *Cæsar*, but he was alwayes repulsed by the people. For these things, they may seeme to come by chance; but the place where the murther was prepared, & where the Senate were assembled, and where also there stood up an image of *Pompey* dedicated by himselfe amongst other ornaments which he gave unto the Theater, all these were manifest proofes, that it was the ordinance of some god, that made this treason to be executed, specially in that very place. It is also reported, that *Cassius* (though otherwise he did favour the doctrine of *Epicvrus*) beholding the image of *Pompey*, before they entred into the action of their traiterous enterprise, he did softly call upon it, to aide him: but the instant danger of the present time, taking away his former reason, did sodainly put him into a furious passion, and made him like a man halfe besides himselfe. Now *Antonius* that was a faithfull friend to *Cæsar*, and a valiant man besides of his hands, him *Decius Brutus Albinus* entertained out of the Senate house, hauing begunne a long tale of set purpose. So *Cæsar* comming into the house, all the Senate stood up on their feete to do him honour. Then part of *Brutus* companie and confederates stood round about *Cæsars* chaire, and part of them also came towards him, as though they made suite with *Metellus Cimber*, to call home his brother againe from banishment: and thus prosecuting still their suite, they followed *Cæsar* till he was set in his chaire. Who denying their petitions, and being offended with them one after another, because the more they were denied, the more they pressed upon him, and were the earnester with him, *Metellus* at length, taking his gowne with both his hands, pulled it over his necke, which was the signe given the confederates to set upon him. Then *Casca* behind him, strake him in the necke with his sword; howbeit the wond was not great nor mortall, because it seemed, the feare of such a divellish attempt did amaze him, & take his strength from him, that he killed him not at the first blow. But *Cæsar* turning straight unto him, caught hold of his sword, and held it hard, & they both cried out, *Cæsar* in latin: O vile traitor *Casca*, what doest thou? And *Casca* in Greek to his brother: Brother, help me, At yᵉ beginning of this stir, they that were present, not knowing of the conspiracie, were so amazed with the horrible sight they saw, they had no power to flie, neither to help him, nor so much as once to make an outcrie. They on yᵉ other side that had conspired his death, compassed him in on every side with their swords drawn in their hands, that *Cæsar* turned him no where, but he was stricken at by some, and stil had naked swords in his face, & was hackled & mangled among them, as a wild beast taken of hunters. For it was agreed among them, that every man should give him a wound, because al their parts shold be in this murther: and then *Brutus* himself gave him one wound about his privities. Men report also, that *Cæsar* did stil defend himself against yᵉ rest, running every way with his body: but when he saw *Brutus* with his sword drawne in his hand, then he pulled his gowne over his head, and made no more resistance, & was driven either casually or purposedly, by the counsel of the conspirators, against the base, whereupon *Pompeys* image stood which ran all of a goare bloud till he was slaine. Thus it seemed that the image tooke iust revenge of *Pompeys* enemie, being throwne down on the ground at his feet, & yeelding up the ghost there, for the number of wounds he had upon him. For it is reported, that he had three & twentie wounds upon his bodie: and divers of the conspirators did hurt themselves, striking one body with so many blowes. When *Cæsar* was slaine, the Senate (though *Brutus* stood in the middest amongst them, as though he would have said something touching this fact) presently ranne out of the house, and flying, filled all the citie with marvellous feare and tumult. Insomuch as some did shut too the doores, others forsooke their shops and ware-houses, and others ranne to the place to see what the matter was: and others also that had seene it, ran home to their houses againe."

(3) SCENE II.—*I pause for a reply.*] Steevens observes that "the speech of Brutus may be regarded rather as an imitation of the false eloquence then [Shakespeare's day] in vogue, than as a specimen of a laconick brevity." Surely not. Shakespeare here adopts the very style which the historian tells us Brutus affected:—"He was properly learned in the Latin tong, and was able to make long discourse in it: beside that he could also pleade very well in Latine. But for the Greek tong, they do note in some of his Epistles, that he counterfeited that briefe compendious maner of speech of the LACEDÆMONIANS. As when the war was begun, he wrot unto the PERGAMENIANS in this sort: I understand you have given *Dolabella* money: if you have done it willingly, you confesse you have offended me; if against your wils, shew it then by giving me willingly. Another time againe unto the SAMIANS: Your councels be long, your doings be slow, consider the end. And in another Epistle he wrote unto the PATAREIANS: The XANTHIANS, despising my goodwil, have made their country a grave of despaire, and the PATAREIANS that put themselves into my protection, have lost no iot of their liberty: and therefore whilest you have liberty, either chuse the judgement of the PATAREIANS, or the fortune of the XANTHIANS. These were *Brutus* maner of letters, which were honored for their briefnesse."

(4) SCENE II.—*Pluck down forms, windows, anything!*] Then *Antonius* thinking good his testament should be read openly, and also that his bodie should be honourably buried, and not in hugger mugger, lest the people might thereby take occasion to be worse offended if they did otherwise: *Cassius* stoutly spake against it. But *Brutus* went with the motion, and agreed unto it: wherein it seemeth he committed a second fault. For the first fault he did, was when he would not consent to his fellow conspirators, that *Antonius* should be slaine: and therefore he was iustly accused, that therby he had saved and strengthened a strong and grievous enemie of their conspiracy. The second fault was, when he agreed that *Cæsars* funerals should be as *Antonius* would have them, the which indeed marred all. For first of all, when *Cæsars* testament was openly read among them, wherby it appeared that he bequeathed unto every citizen of ROME, 75 Drachmaes a man; and that he left his gardens and arbors unto the people, which he had on this side of the river Tyber, in the place where now the temple of Fortune is built: the people then loved him, and were marvellous sorie for him. Afterwards, when *Cæsars* bodie was brought into the market place, *Antonius* making his funerall oration in praise of the dead, according to the ancient custome of ROME, and perceiving that his words moved the common people to compassion, he framed his eloquence to make their hearts yearne the more; and taking *Cæsars* gowne all bloodie in his hand, he layd it open to the sight of them

all, shewing what a number of cuts and holes it had upon it. Therewithall the people fell presently into such a rage and mutinie, that there was no more order kept amongst the common people. For some of them cried out, Kill the murtherers: others plucked up formes, tables, and stalles about the market place, as they had done before at the funerals of *Clodius*, and having laid them all on a heap together, they set them on fire, and thereupon did put the bodie of *Cæsar*, and burnt it in the mids of the most holy places. And furthermore, when the fire was throughly kindled, some here, some there, tooke burning firebrands, and ranne with them to the murtherers houses that killed him, to set them on fire. Howbeit, the conspirators fore-seeing the danger before had wisely provided for them-selves, and fledde."

ACT IV.

(1) SCENE III.—*You have condemn'd and noted Lucius Pella.*] The next day after, *Brutus*, upon complaint of the SARDIANS, did condemne and note *Lucius Pella* for a defamed person, that had beene a Prætor of the ROMAINES, and whom *Brutus* had given charge unto: for that he was accused and convicted of robbery, and pilferie in his office. This iudgement much misliked *Cassius*, because he him-selfe had secretly (not many daies before) warned two of his friends, attainted and convicted of the like offences, and openly had cleared them: but yet he did not therefore leave to employ them in any manner of service as he did before. And therefore he greatly reproved *Brutus*, for that he would shew himselfe so straight and severe, in such a time as was meeter to beare a little, then to take things at the worst. *Brutus* in contrarie manner answered, that he should remember the Ides of march, at which time they slue *Iulius Cæsar*, who neither pilled nor polled the country, but onely was a favourer and suborner of all them that did rob and spoile, by his countenance and authoritie. And if there were any occasion whereby they might honestly set aside iustice and equitie, they should have had more reason to have suffered *Cæsars* friends to have robbed and done what wrong and iniurie they had would, then to beare with their owne men. For then said he, they could but have said they had been cowards, but now they may accuse us of iniustice, beside the paines we take, and the danger we put our selves into."

(2) SCENE III.—*Companion, hence!*] "Then they began to powre out their complaints one to the other, and grew hot and loud, earnestly accusing one another, and at length fell both a weeping. Their friends that were with-out the chamber, hearing them loud within, and angry betweene themselves, they were both amazed & afraid also, lest it wold grow to further matter: but yet they were commanded, that no man should come to them. Notwith-standing one *Marcus Phaonius*, that had been a friend and follower of *Cato* while he lived, and tooke upon him to counterfeit a Philosopher, not with wisedome & discretion, but with a certaine bedlem and franticke motion: he would needs come into the chamber, though the men offered to keepe him out. But it was no boote to let *Phaonius*, when a mad moode or toy tooke him in the head: for he was a hote hastie man, and sudden in all his doings, and cared for never a Senator of them all. Now, though he used this bold manner of speech after the pro-fession of the Cynicke Phylosophers (as who would say, Dogs) yet his boldnesse did no hurt many times, because they did but laugh at him to see him so mad. This *Phaonius* at that time, in despite of the doore-keepers, came into the chamber, and with a certaine scoffing and mocking gesture, which he counterfeited of purpose, he rehearsed the verses which old *Nestor* said in *Homer:*

> *My Lords, I pray you hearken both to me.*
> *For I have seene moe yeares then suchie three.*

Cassius fell a laughing at him: but *Brutus* thrust him out of the chamber, and called him dogge, and counterfeit Cynicke."

(3) SCENE III.—*Well: then I shall see thee again?*] "But as they both prepared to passe over againe out of ASIA into EUROPE, there went a rumour that there appeared a wonderfull signe unto him. *Brutus* was a carefull man, and slept very little, both for that his diet was moderate, as also because he was continually occu-pied. He never slept in the day time, and in the night no longer then the time he was driven to be alone, and when every body else tooke their rest. But now whilest he was in warre, and his head over busily occupied to thinke of his affaires, and what would happen, after he had slumbered a little after supper, he spent all the rest of the night in dispatching of his weightiest causes; and after he had taken order for them, if he had any leisure left him, he would read some booke till the third watch of the night, at what time the Captains, pettie Captaines and Colonels, did use to come to him. So, being readie to goe into EUROPE, one night very late (when all the campe tooke quiet rest) as he was in his tent with a litle light, thinking of weighty matters, he thought he heard one come in to him, and casting his eye towards the doore of his tent, that he saw a wonderfull strange and mon-strous shape of a bodie coming towards him, and said never a word. So *Brutus* boldly asked what he was, a god or a man, and what cause brought him thither. The spirit answered him, I am thy evill spirit, *Brutus;* and thou shalt see me by the citie of PHILIPPES. *Brutus* being no otherwise affraid, replyed againe unto it: well, then I shall see thee agayne. The spirit presently vanished away; and *Brutus* called his men unto him, who tolde him that they heard no noise, nor sawe any thing at all."

ACT V.

(1) Scene I.—*This morning are they fled away and gone.*] "Whey they raised their campe, there came two Eagles that flying with a marvellous force, lighted upon two of the foremost ensignes, and alwaies followed the souldiers, which gave them meate, and fed them, untill they came neare to the citie of Philippes: and there one day onely before the battell, they both flew away. * * * Notwithstanding, being busily occupied about the ceremonies of this purgation, it is reported that there chanced certaine unluckie signes unto *Cassius*. For one of his Sergeants that caried the rods before him, brought him the garland of flowers turned backward, the which he should have worne on his head in the time of sacrificing. Moreover it is reported also, that another time before, in certaine sports & triumph where they caried an image of *Cassius* victorie, of cleane gold, it fell by chance, the man stumbling that caried it. And yet further there was seene a marvellous number of fowles of prey, that feed upon dead carcasses: & Bee hives also were found where Bees were gathered together in a certain place within the trenches of the camp: the which place the Soothsayers thought good to shut out of the precinct of the campe, for to take away the superstitious feare and mistrust men would have of it. The which began somewhat to alter *Cassius* mind from *Epicurus* opinions, and had put the souldiers also in a marvellous feare. Thereupon *Cassius* was of opinion not to trie this warre at one battell, but rather to delay time, and to draw it out in length, considering that they were the stronger in money, and the weaker in men and armor. But *Brutus* in contrary maner, did alway before and at that time also, desire nothing more, then to put all to the hazard of battell, as soone as might be possible: to the end he might either quickly restore his countrey to her former liberty, or rid him forthwith of this miserable world, being still troubled in following and maintaining of such great armies together. * * * But touching *Cassius, Messala* reporteth that he supped by himselfe in his tent with a few of his friends, & that all supper time he looked very sadly, & was ful of thoughts, although it was against his nature: and that after supper he tooke him by the hand, & holding him fast (in token of kindnesse, as his maner was) told him in Greek: *Messala,* I protest unto thee, & make thee my witnesse, that I am compelled against my mind & wil (as *Pompey* the great was) to ieopard the liberty of our country to the hazard of a battel. And yet we must be lively, & of good courage, considering our good fortune, whom we should wrong too much to mistrust her, although we follow evill counsell. *Messala* writeth, that *Cassius* having spoken these last words unto him, he bad him farewel, and willed him to come to supper to him the next night following, because it was his birth day."

(2) Scene I.—

But this same day
Must end that work the ides of March begun.]

"There *Cassius* began to speake first, and said: The gods grant us O *Brutus,* that this day we may win the field, and ever after to live all the rest of our life quietly one with another. But sith the gods have so ordained it, that the greatest and chiefest things amongst men are most uncertaine, and that if the battell fall out otherwise to day then we wish or looke for, we shall hardly meet againe, what art thou then determined to doe, to flie, or die? *Brutus* answered him, being yet but a yong man, and not over greatly experienced in the world: I trust (I know not how) a certain rule of Philosophy, by the which I did greatly blame and reprove *Cato* for killing himselfe, as being no lawfull nor godly act, touching the gods: nor concerning men, valiant; not to give place and yeeld to divine providence, & not constantly and patiently to take whatsoever it pleaseth him to send us, but to draw backe and flie: but being now in the midst of the danger, I am of a contrary mind. For if it be not the will of God that this battel fall out fortunate for us, I will looke no more for hope, neither seeke to make any new supply for war againe, but will rid me of this miserable world, and content me with my fortune. For, I gave up my life for my countrey in the Ides of March, for the which I shall live in another more glorious world."

(3) Scene III.—

—— *Cæsar, thou art reveng'd,*
Even with the sword that kill'd thee.]

"First of all he was marvellous angrie to see how *Brutus* men ran to give charge upon their enemies, and taried not for the word of the battell, nor commandement to give charge: and it grieved him beside, that after he had overcome them, his men fell straight to spoile, and were not carefull to compasse in the rest of ye enemies behind: but with tarying too long also, more then through the valiantnesse or foresight of the Captaines his enemies, *Cassius* found himselfe compassed in with the right wing of his enemies armie. Wherupon his horsmen brake immediatly, and fled for life towards the sea. Furthermore perceiving his footmen to give ground, he did what he could to keepe them from flying, and tooke an ensigne from one of the ensigne-bearers that fled, and stucke it fast at his feet: although with much ado he could scant keepe his owne guard together. So *Cassius* himselfe was at length compelled to flie, with a few about him, unto a litle hill, from whence they might easily see what was done in all the plaine: howbeit *Cassius* himselfe saw nothing, for his sight was very bad, saving that he saw (and yet with much ado) how the enemies spoiled his campe before his eyes. He saw also a great troupe of horsemen, whom *Brutus* sent to aid him, and thought that they were his enemies that followed him: but yet he sent *Titinnius,* one of them that was with him, to go and know what they were. *Brutus* horsemen saw him coming a farre off, whom when they knew that he was one of *Cassius* chiefest friends, they shouted out for ioy, and they that were familiarly acquainted with him, lighted from their horses, and went and embraced him. The rest compassed him in round about on horsback, with songs of victory & great rushing of their harnesse, so that they made all the field ring againe for ioy. But this marred all. For *Cassius* thinking indeed that *Titinnius* was taken of the enemies, he then spake these words: Desiring too much to live, I have lived to see one of my best friends taken, for my sake, before my face. After that, he got into a tent where no body was, and tooke *Pindarus* with him, one of his bondmen whom he reserved ever for such a pinch, since the cursed battell of the Parthians, where *Crassus* was slaine, though he notwithstanding scaped from that overthrow: but then casting his cloake over his head, and holding out his bare neck unto *Pindarus,* he gave him his head to be stricken off. So the head was found severed from the body: but after that time *Pindarus* was never seene more. Whereupon, some tooke occasion to say that he had slaine his maister without his commandement. By & by they knew the horsmen that came towards them, and might see *Titinnius* crowned with a garland of triumph, who came before with great speed unto *Cassius.* But when he perceived by the cries & teares of his friends which tormented themselves, the misfortune that had chanced to his Captaine *Cassius,* by mistaking, he drew out his sword, cursing himself a thousand times that he had taried so long, & so slue himselfe presently in the field. *Brutus* in the meane time came forward still, and understood also that *Cassius* had bin overthrowne: but he knew nothing of his death, till he came very neare to his campe. So when he was come thither, after he had lamented the death of *Cassius*, calling him the last of all the ROMANES; being unpossible that ROME should ever breed againe so noble and valiant a man as he: he caused his body to be buried, and sent it to the citie of THASSOS, fearing lest his funerals within his campe should cause great disorder."

(4) SCENE IV.—

I had rather have
Such men my friends than enemies.]

"There was the sonne of *Marcus Cato* slaine, valiantly fighting among the lustie youth. For notwithstanding that he was very wearie and over-harried, yet would he not therefore flie, but manfully fighting and laying about him, telling aloud his name, and also his fathers name, at length he was beaten downe amongst many other dead bodies of his enemies, which he had slaine round about him. So there were slaine in the field, all the chiefest Gentlemen and Nobilitie that were in his armie, who valiantly ranne into any danger to save *Brutus* life: amongst whom there was one of *Brutus* friends called *Lucilius*, who seeing a troupe of barbarous men, making no reckoning of all men else they met in their way, but going altogether right against *Brutus*, he determined to stay them with the hazard of his life, and being left behind, told them that he was *Brutus*: and because they should beleeve him, he prayed them to bring him to *Antonius*, for he said he was afraid of *Cæsar*, and that he did trust *Antonius* better. These barbarous men being very glad of this good hap, and thinking them selves happie men, they caried him in the night, and sent some before unto *Antonius*, to tel him of their coming. He was marvellous glad of it, and went out to meete them that brought him. Others also understanding that they had brought *Brutus* prisoner, they came from all parts of the campe to see him, some pitying his hard fortune, and others saying, that it was not done like himselfe, so cowardly to be taken alive of the barbarous people, for feare of death. When they came neare together, *Antonius* staid awhile bethinking himselfe how he should use *Brutus*. In the meane time *Lucilius* was brought to him, who with a bold countenance said: *Antonius*, I dare assure thee, that no enemie hath taken or shall take *Marcus Brutus* alive: and I beseech God keepe him from that fortune: but wheresoever he be found, alive or dead, he will be found like himselfe: and touching my selfe, I am come unto thee, having deceived these men of armes making them beleeve that I was *Brutus*, and do not refuse to suffer any torment thou wilt put me to. *Lucilius* words made them all amazed that heard him. *Antonius* on the other side, looking upon all them that had brought him, said unto them: My friends, I thinke ye are sorie you have failed of your purpose, and that you think this man hath done you great wrong: but I assure you, you have taken a better bootie then that you followed. For in stead of an enemy, you have brought me a friend: and for my part, if you had brought me *Brutus* alive, truly I can not tell what I should have done to him. For I had rather have such men as this my friends then mine enemies. Then he embraced *Lucilius*, and at that time delivered him to one of his friends in custodie; and *Lucilius* ever after served him faithfully, even to his death."

(5) SCENE V.—*Runs on his sword, and dies.*] "Now the night being farre spent, *Brutus*, as he sat, bowed towards *Clitus*, one of his men, and told him somewhat in his eare: the other aunswered him not, but fell a weeping. Thereupon he proved *Dardanus*, and sayd somewhat also to him: at length he came to *Volumnius* him selfe, and, speaking to him in Greeke, prayed him, for the studies sake which brought them acquainted together, that he would helpe him to put his hande to his sword, to thrust it in him to kill him. *Volumnius* denied his request, and so did many others; and amongest the rest, one of them sayd there was no tarying for them there, but that they must needes fly. Then *Brutus*, rising upp, we must flie in deede, said he, but it must be with our handes, not with our feete. Then taking every man by the hand, he sayd these words unto them with a cheerefull countenance. It rejoiceth my hart that not one of my friends hath failed me at my neede, and I do not complaine of my fortune, but only for my countries sake: for, as for me, I think my selfe happier than they that have over come, considering that I have a perpetuall fame of our corage and manhoode, the which our enemies the conquerors shall never attaine unto by force nor money; neither can let their posteritie to say that they, being naughtie and unjust men, have slaine good men, to usurpe tyrannical power not pertaining to them. Having sayd so, he prayed everie man to shift for themselves, and then he went a little aside with two or three only, among the which *Strato* was one, with whom he came first acquainted by the study of Rethoricke. He came as neere to him as he coulde, and taking his sword by the hilts with both his hands, and falling down upon the point of it, ran himselfe through. Others say that not he but *Strato* (at his request) held the sword in his hand, and turned his head aside, and that *Brutus* fell downe upon it, and so ranne himself through and dyed presently. *Messala*, that had bene *Brutus* great frend, became afterwards *Octavius Cæsar's* frend. So, shortly after, *Cæsar* being at good leisure, he brought *Strato*, *Brutus* frende, unto him, and weeping sayd—*Cæsar*, beholde, here is he that did the last service to my *Brutus*. *Cæsar* welcomed him at that time, and afterwards he did him as faithfull service in all his affairs as any Grecian els he had about him, until the battle of Actium."

(6) SCENE V.—*This was the noblest Roman of them all.*] "But *Brutus* in contrary manner, for his vertue and valiantnesse, was well-beloved of the people and his owne, esteemed of noblemen, and hated of no man, not so much as of his enemies; because he was a marvellous lowly and gentle person, noble minded, and would never be in any rage, nor caried away with pleasure and covetousnesse, but had ever an upright mind with him, and would never yeeld to any wrong or iniustice; the which was the chiefest cause of his fame, of his rising, & of the goodwill that every man bare him: for they were all persuaded that his intent was good. For they did not certainly beleeve, that if *Pompey* himself had overcome *Cæsar*, he would have resigned his authority to the law, but rather they were of opinion, that he would stil keepe the soveraigntie and absolute government in his hands, taking onely, to please the people, the title of Consul, or Dictator, or of some other more civill office. And as for *Cassius*, a hote, cholericke, and cruell man, that would oftentimes be caried away from iustice for gaine, it was certainly thought that he made warre, and put himselfe into sundrie dangers, more to have absolute power and authoritie, then to defend the liberty of his countrey. For, they that will also consider others, that were elder men then they, as *Cinna*, *Marinus*, & *Carbo*, it is out of doubt that the end & hope of their victorie, was to be the Lords of their countrey, and in manner they did all confesse, that they fought for the tyranny, and to be Lords of the Empire of ROME. And in contrary maner, his enemies themselves did never reprove *Brutus* for any such change or desire. For, it was said that *Antonius* spake it openly diverse times, that he thought, that of all them that had slaine *Cæsar*, there was none but *Brutus* onely that was moved to do it, as thinking the act commendable of it selfe: but that all the other conspiratours did conspire his death for some private malice or envie, that they otherwise did beare unto him."

CRITICAL OPINIONS ON JULIUS CÆSAR.

"The piece of 'Julius Cæsar,' to complete the action, requires to be continued to the fall of Brutus and Cassius. Cæsar is not the hero of the piece, but Brutus. The amiable beauty of his character, his feeling and patriotic heroism, are portrayed with peculiar care. Yet the poet has pointed out with great nicety the superiority of Cassius over Brutus in independent volition and discernment in judging of human affairs; that the latter, from the purity of his mind, and his conscientious love of justice, is unfit to be the head of a party in a state entirely corrupted; and that these very faults give an unfortunate turn to the cause of the conspirators. In the part of Cæsar, several ostentatious speeches have been censured as unsuitable. But as he never appears in action, we have no other measure of his greatness than the impression which he makes upon the rest of the characters, and his peculiar confidence in himself. In this, Cæsar was by no means deficient, as we learn from history and his own writings; but he displayed it more in the easy ridicule of his enemies than in pompous discourses. The theatrical effect of this play is injured by a partial falling off of the last two acts, compared with the preceding, in external splendour and rapidity. The first appearance of Cæsar in festal robes, when the music stops, and all are silent whenever he opens his mouth, and when the few words which he utters are received as oracles, is truly magnificent; the conspiracy is a true conspiracy, which, in stolen interviews and in the dead of night, prepares the blow which is to be struck in open day, and which is to change the constitution of the world;—the confused thronging before the murder of Cæsar, the general agitation even of the perpetrators after the deed, are all portrayed with most masterly skill; with the funeral procession and the speech of Antony, the effect reaches its utmost height. Cæsar's shade is more powerful to avenge his fall than he himself was to guard against it. After the overthrow of the external splendour and greatness of the conqueror and ruler of the world, the intrinsic grandeur of character of Brutus and Cassius is all that remains to fill the stage and occupy the minds of the spectators: suitably to their name, as the last of the Romans, they stand there, in some degree alone; and the forming a great and hazardous determination is more powerfully calculated to excite our expectation, than the supporting the consequences of the deed with heroic firmness."—SCHLEGEL.

Act IV. Sc. 1.

MACBETH.

"The Tragedie of Macbeth" appears to have been first printed in the folio of 1623. The date of its composition is not determinable. Malone, from internal probabilities, satisfied himself that it must have been written not later than 1606: his chief grounds for this conviction being two passages in the Porter's soliloquy, Act II. Sc. 3:—"Here's a farmer that hanged himself on the expectation of plenty:" and, "Here's an equivocator, that could swear in both the scales against either scale; who committed treason enough for God's sake, yet could not equivocate to heaven." In the former passage he detects an allusion to the extreme cheapness of corn in 1606, as shown by the audit book of Eton College; the latter he maintains, with great ingenuity, to be a pointed reference to the doctrine of *equivocation* avowed by Henry Garnet, superior of the order of Jesuits, on his trial for the Gunpowder Treason, in the same year. But there is, perhaps, still stronger evidence for conjecturing this tragedy was produced very early in the reign of James I., in the apparent allusion to the union of the three kingdoms under that monarch in 1604, in the words,—

"—— Some I see
That two-fold balls and treble sceptres carry."

The reference here can hardly be gainsaid, and it is certainly one not likely to have been introduced at a period at all remote from the event which it adumbrates. Still this is only surmise. The earliest tangible information regarding the chronology of "Macbeth" is that it was acted at the Globe Theatre, on the 20th of April, 1610: a fact derived from the interesting MS. Diary of Dr. Forman (*Mus. Ashmol. Oxon.*), which contains the following minute analysis of the plot:—

"In Macbeth, at the Globe, 1610, the 20th of April, Saturday, there was to be observed, first, how Macbeth and Banquo, two noblemen of Scotland, riding through a wood, there stood before them three women, Fairies, or Nymphs, and saluted Macbeth, saying three times unto him, Hail, Macbeth, King of Codor, for thou shalt be a King, but shalt beget no Kings, &c. Then, said Banquo, What! all to Macbeth and nothing to me? Yes, said the Nymphs, Hail to thee, Banquo; thou shalt beget Kings, yet be no King. And so they departed, and came to the court of Scotland, to Duncan King of Scots, and it was in the days of Edward the Confessor. And Duncan bade them both kindly welcome, and made Macbeth forthwith Prince of Northumberland; and sent him home to his own Castle, and appointed Macbeth to provide for him, for he would sup with him the next day at night, and did so.

"And Macbeth contrived* to kill Duncan, and through the persuasion of his wife did that night murder the King in his own Castle, being his guest. And there were many prodigies seen that night and the day before. And when Macbeth had murdered the King, the blood on his hands could not be washed off by any means, nor from his wife's hands, which handled the bloody daggers in hiding them, by which means they became both much amazed and affronted.

* Plotted.

"The murder being known, Duncan's two sons fled, the one to England, [the other to] Wales, to save themselves: they, being fled, were supposed guilty of the murder of their father, which was nothing so.

"Then was Macbeth crowned King, and then he, for fear of Banquo, his old companion, that he should beget kings but be no king himself, he contrived * the death of Banquo, and caused him to be murdered on the way that he rode. The night, being at supper with his noblemen, whom he had bid to a feast (to the which also Banquo should have come), he began to speak of noble Banquo, and to wish that he were there. And as he thus did, standing up to drink a carouse to him, the ghost of Banquo came and sat down in his chair behind him. And he, turning about to sit down again, saw the ghost of Banquo, which fronted him, so that he fell in a great passion of fear and fury, uttering many words about his murder, by which, when they heard that Banquo was murdered, they suspected Macbeth.

"Then Macduff fled to England, to the King's son, and so they raised an army and came to Scotland, and at Dunston Anyse overthrew Macbeth. In the mean time, while Macduff was in England, Macbeth slew Macduff's wife and children, and after, in the battle, Macduff slew Macbeth.

"Observe, also, how Macbeth's queen did rise in the night in her sleep and walk, and talked and confessed all, and the doctor noted her words."

The historical incidents of this great tragedy are contained in the *Scotorum Historiæ* of Boethius, first printed at Paris, in 1526, and afterwards translated by Bellenden into the Scottish dialect, and published in 1541. From the latter it was copied by Holinshed, and on that Chronicler's relation of the story Shakespeare based his play. The opinion once prevalent, that some portion of the poet's preternatural machinery was borrowed from Middleton's "Witch," has no longer supporters. "The Witch" is now generally thought to have been written about 1613. (See *the Illustrative Comments at the end of the Play.*)

* Plotted.

Persons Represented.

DUNCAN, *King of* Scotland.
MALCOLM, } *Sons to* Duncan.
DONALBAIN, } *Sons to* Duncan.
MACBETH, *General of the* King's *Army, afterwards* King.
BANQUO, *General of the* King's *Army.*
FLEANCE, *Son to* Banquo.
MACDUFF, LENNOX, ROSS, MENTEITH, ANGUS, CAITHNESS, } Scottish *Noblemen.*
SIWARD, *Earl of* Northumberland, *General of the* English *Forces.*
Young SIWARD, *Son to the Earl of* Northumberland.
Son *to* Macduff.
SEYTON, *an Officer attending on the* King.
An English *Doctor.*
A Scotch *Doctor.*
A Soldier.
A Porter.
An old Man.

LADY MACBETH, *afterwards* Queen.
LADY MACDUFF.
Gentlewoman, *attending on the* Queen.
HECATE.
Three Witches.

Lords, Gentlemen, Officers, Soldiers, Murderers, Attendants, and Messengers. The Ghost of Banquo, *and other Apparitions.*

SCENE,—*In the end of Act IV. in* ENGLAND; *through the rest of the Play, in* SCOTLAND.

ACT I.

SCENE I.—*An open Place. Thunder and lightning.*

Enter three Witches.

1 Witch. When shall we three meet again
In thunder, lightning, or in rain?

2 Witch. When the hurly-burly 's[a] done,
When the battle 's lost and won.

3 Witch. That will be ere the set of sun.

1 Witch. Where the place?

[a] *When the* hurly-burly 's *done,*—] The word "hurly-burly," explained by Henry Peacham in "The Garden of Eloquence," 1577, to signify *uprore* and *tumultuous stirre*, occurs in a much earlier work, More's *Utopia*, translated by Ralphe Robinson, 1551:—"Furthermore, if I should declare unto them, that all this busy preparance to war, whereby so many nations for his sake should be brought into a troublesome *hurley-burley*, when all his coffers were emptied, his treasures wasted, and his people destroyed."

2 WITCH. Upon the heath.
3 WITCH. There to meet with Macbeth.[a]
1 WITCH. I come, Graymalkin!
ALL.[b] Paddock calls:—anon!—
Fair is foul, and foul is fair:
Hover through the fog and filthy air.
[Witches *vanish.*

SCENE II.—*A Camp near* Forres. *Alarum without.*

Enter KING DUNCAN, MALCOLM, DONALBAIN, LENNOX, *with* Attendants, *meeting a bleeding* Captain.

KING. What bloody man is that? He can report,
As seemeth by his plight, of the revolt
The newest state.
MAL. This is the sergeant,[c]
Who, like a good and hardy soldier, fought
'Gainst my captivity.—Hail, brave friend!
Say to the king the knowledge of the broil,
As thou didst leave it.
CAP. Doubtful it stood;
As two spent swimmers, that do cling together
And choke their art. The merciless Macdonald
(Worthy to be a rebel,—for, to that,
The multiplying villainies of nature
Do swarm upon him) from the western isles
Of kernes and gallowglasses is supplied;
And Fortune, on his damned quarrel [d] smiling,
Show'd like a rebel's whore: but all's too weak:
For brave Macbeth, (well he deserves that name)
Disdaining Fortune, with his brandish'd steel,
Which smok'd with bloody execution,
Like valour's minion,
Carv'd out his passage till he fac'd the slave;
Which[e] ne'er shook hands, nor bade farewell to him,
Till he unseam'd him from the nave to the chaps,
And fix'd his head upon our battlements.
KING. O, valiant cousin! worthy gentleman!
CAP. As whence the sun 'gins his reflection
Shipwrecking storms and direful thunders break;[f]
So from that spring, whence comfort seem'd to come,
Discomfort swells. Mark, king of Scotland, mark!
No sooner justice had, with valour arm'd,
Compell'd these skipping kernes to trust their heels,
But the Norweyan lord, surveying vantage,
With furbish'd arms and new supplies of men,
Began a fresh assault.
KING. Dismay'd not this
Our captains, Macbeth and Banquo?
CAP. Yes:
As sparrows eagles, or the hare the lion.
If I say sooth, I must report they were
As cannons overcharg'd with double cracks; [g]
So they doubly redoubled strokes upon the foe:
Except they meant to bathe in reeking wounds,
Or memorize another Golgotha,
I cannot tell:—
But I am faint, my gashes cry for help.
KING. So well thy words become thee as thy wounds;
They smack of honour both.—Go, get him surgeons. [*Exit* Captain, *attended.*
Who comes here?
MAL. The worthy thane of Ross.
LEN. What a haste looks through his eyes!
So should he look that seems[h] to speak things strange.

Enter ROSS.*

ROSS. God save the king!
KING. Whence cam'st thou, worthy thane?
ROSS. From Fife, great king;
Where the Norweyan banners flout the sky,
And fan our people cold.
Norway himself, with terrible numbers,[i]
Assisted by that most disloyal traitor

[a] There to meet with Macbeth.] Pope, to remedy the defective verse, reads, "There *I go* to meet Macbeth;" Capell, "There to meet with *great* Macbeth;" and Steevens,—

"3 *Witch.* There to meet with—
1 *Witch.* *Whom?*
3 *Witch.* Macbeth."

[b] ALL. Paddock calls: &c.] The folio prints these lines as if spoken in chorus by the three witches; but the distribution commonly adopted by modern editors,—

"2 *Witch.* Paddock calls:—anon.—
All. Fair is foul, and foul is fair,
Hover through the fog and filthy air,"—

is certainly preferable. The dialogue throughout, with the exception of the two lines, "I come, Graymalkin!" and "Paddock calls:—anon!—" was probably intended to be sung or chaunted.

[c] *This is the* sergeant,—] *Sergeants* were not formerly the non-commissioned officers now so called, but a guard specially appointed to attend the person of the king; and, as Minsheu says, "to arrest Traytors or great men, that doe, or are like to contemne messengers of ordinarie condition, and to attend the Lord High Steward of England, sitting in judgement upon any Traytor, and such like."

[d] *And Fortune, on his damned* quarrel *smiling,* &c.] The old text has, "— damned *Quarry,*" &c.; but the fact that *quarrel*, a most appropriate word, occurs in the corresponding passage of Holinshed, is almost certain proof that the latter term is the genuine reading:—"Out of the westerne Iles there came unto him [Makdowald] a great multitude of people, offering themselves to assist him in that rebellious *quarell.*"—*History of Scotland.*

[e] Which *ne'er shook hands,* &c.] "Which" has been altered, and perhaps rightly, to *And.*

[f] — *direful thunders* break; &c.] The word *break* is wanting in the folio 1623, and was supplied by Pope out of the subsequent folios, which read, "breaking."

[g] *As cannons overcharg'd with double* cracks; &c.] Johnson interprets this, "cannon charged with double thunders;" and observes truly that cracks was a word of such emphasis and dignity, that in this play the writer terms the general dissolution of nature the *crack of doom.*

[h] — *that* seems *to speak things strange.*] Johnson proposed, "that *teems* to speak things strange;" and Mr. Collier's annotator, with characteristic vapidity, "that *comes* to speak," &c; but compare, Scene 5,—

"Which fate and metaphysical aid doth *seem*
To have thee crown'd withal."

[i] — *with* terrible numbers,—] Pope's transposition, "numbers terrible," is, prosodically, an improvement.

(*) Old text, *Enter Rosse and Angus.*

The thane of Cawdor, began a dismal conflict;
Till that Bellona's bridegroom,[a] lapp'd in proof,[b]
Confronted him with self-comparisons,
Point, against point rebellious, arm 'gainst arm,
Curbing his lavish spirit: and, to conclude,
The victory fell on us.

KING. Great happiness!

ROSS. That now
Sweno, the Norways' king, craves composition;
Nor would we deign him burial of his men,
Till he disbursed, at Saint Colmes'-inch,[c]
Ten thousand dollars to our general use.

KING. No more that thane of Cawdor shall deceive
Our bosom interest.—Go, pronounce his present death,
And with his former title greet Macbeth.

ROSS. I'll see it done.

KING. What he hath lost, noble Macbeth hath won. [*Exeunt.*

SCENE III.—*A Heath. Thunder.*

Enter the three Witches.

1 WITCH. Where hast thou been, sister?

2 WITCH. Killing swine.

3 WITCH. Sister, where thou?

1 WITCH. A sailor's wife had chestnuts in her lap,
And mounch'd, and mounch'd, and mounch'd:—
Give me, quoth I:

[a] — Bellona's bridegroom,—] By "Bellona's bridegroom" is meant, not Mars, as Steevens too hastily concluded, but the leader of the royal host, Macbeth.

[b] — proof,—] *Armour.*

[c] *Saint* Colmes'-inch,—] *Inch* or *inse* is Erse and Irish for *island*, and *Colmes'-inch*, now *Inchcomb*, is a small island in the Frith of Edinburgh, with an abbey upon it, dedicated to St. Columb. See note by Steevens *ad l.* in the *Variorum* edition.

Aroint[a] *thee, witch!* the rump-fed ronyon cries.
Her husband's to Aleppo gone, master o' the Tiger:[b]
But in a sieve I'll thither sail,(1)
And, like a rat without a tail,
I'll do, I'll do, and I'll do.
2 WITCH. I'll give thee a wind.
1 WITCH. Thou art kind.
3 WITCH. And I another.
1 WITCH. I myself have all the other;
And the very ports they blow,
All the quarters that they know
I' the shipman's card.
I will drain him dry as hay:
Sleep shall neither night nor day
Hang upon his pent-house lid;
He shall live a man forbid:[c]
Weary sev'n-nights, nine times nine,
Shall he dwindle, peak, and pine:(2)
Though his bark cannot be lost,
Yet it shall be tempest-toss'd.—
Look what I have.
2 WITCH. Show me, show me.
1 WITCH. Here I have a pilot's thumb,
Wreck'd as homeward he did come.
[*Drum without.*
3 WITCH. A drum, a drum!
Macbeth doth come.
ALL. The weird[d] sisters, hand in hand,
Posters of the sea and land,
Thus do go about, about:
Thrice to thine, and thrice to mine,
And thrice again, to make up nine:—
Peace!—the charm's wound up.

Enter MACBETH *and* BANQUO.

MACB. So foul and fair a day I have not seen.
BAN. How far is't call'd to Forres? *—What are these,
So wither'd, and so wild in their attire;
That look not like the inhabitants o' the earth,
And yet are on't?(3)—Live you? or are you aught
That man may question? You seem to understand me,
By each at once her chappy finger laying
Upon her skinny lips.—You should be women,
And yet your beards[e] forbid me to interpret
That you are so.
MACB. Speak, if you can;—what are you?
1 WITCH. All hail, Macbeth! hail to thee, thane of Glamis!
2 WITCH. All hail, Macbeth! hail to thee, thane of Cawdor!
3 WITCH. All hail, Macbeth! that shalt be king hereafter.
BAN. Good sir, why do you start; and seem to fear
Things that do sound so fair?—I' the name of truth,
Are ye fantastical,[f] or that indeed
Which outwardly ye show? My noble partner
You greet with present grace, and great prediction
Of noble having and of royal hope,
That he seems rapt withal:—to me you speak not:
If you can look into the seeds of time,
And say which grain will grow, and which will not,
Speak, then, to me, who neither beg nor fear
Your favours nor your hate.
1 WITCH. Hail!
2 WITCH. Hail!
3 WITCH. Hail!
1 WITCH. Lesser than Macbeth, and greater.
2 WITCH. Not so happy, yet much happier.
3 WITCH. Thou shalt get kings, though thou be none:
So all hail, Macbeth and Banquo!
1 WITCH. Banquo, and Macbeth, all hail!
MACB. Stay, you imperfect speakers, tell me more:
By Sinel's death, I know I am thane of Glamis;
But how of Cawdor? the thane of Cawdor lives,
A prosperous gentleman; and to be king
Stands not within the prospect of belief,
No more than to be Cawdor. Say from whence
You owe this strange intelligence? or why
Upon this blasted heath you stop our way

(*) Old text, *Soris.*

[a] Aroint *thee, witch!*] It is strange that although the word "aroint," supposed to signify *avaunt! away! begone!* occurs again in Shakespeare, "King Lear," Act III. Sc. 4,—"Aroint thee, witch, aroint thee!" no example of its employment by any other writer has yet been discovered. From this circumstance it has been supposed by some commentators to be only a misprint for *anoint*, a term consistent enough with the vulgar belief which represents witches sailing through the air on their infernal missions by the aid of unguents. Others have ingeniously suggested that "aroint thee" may be a corruption of *a rowan-tree, i.e.* the mountain ash; a tree, time out of mind, believed to be of such sovereign efficacy against the spells of witchcraft, that any one armed with a slip of it may bid defiance to the machinations of a whole troop of evil spirits. We make no question, however, that "aroint" is the genuine word: it was not likely to be thrice misprinted. And besides, there is a North-country proverb, "*Rynt ye witch!* quoth Bessie Locket to her mother," which seems to have been formed upon the exclamation in the text.

[b] Her husband's to Aleppo gone, master o' the Tiger:] Sir W. C. Trevelyan has noted that in Hakluyt's Voyages there are several letters and journals of a voyage made to Aleppo in the ship Tiger, of London, in the year 1583.

[c] — forbid:] *Forespoken, bewitched.*

[d] *The* weird *sisters.*—] *Weird* (in the old text *weyward*) from the Saxon *wyrd=fatum*, signifies *prophetic* or *fatal*. Holinshed, whom Shakespeare follows, speaking of the witches who met Macbeth, says, "— But afterwards the common opinion was that these women were either the weird sisters, that is (as we would say) the goddesses of destinie, or else some nymphes or fairies."

[e] And yet your beards forbid me to interpret
That you are so.]

Witches, according to the popular belief, were always bearded So, in "The Honest Man's Fortune," Act II. Sc. 1,—

"— and the women that
Come to us, for disguises *must wear beards;*
And that's, they say, *a token of a witch.*"

[f] — fantastical,—] *Visionary; illusions of the fantasy.*

With such prophetic greeting? Speak, I charge you. [Witches *vanish*.

BAN. The earth hath bubbles, as the water has,
And these are of them: whither are they vanish'd?

MACB. Into the air; and what seem'd corporal, melted
As breath into the wind.—Would they had stay'd!

BAN. Were such things here as we do speak about?
Or have we eaten on the insane root,[a]
That takes the reason prisoner?

MACB. Your children shall be kings.

BAN. You shall be king.

MACB. And thane of Cawdor too,—went it not so?

[a] — *the* insane *root*,—] Shakespeare is supposed to have found the name of this root in Batman's Commentary on Bartholeme *de Propriet. Rerum*:—" Henbane . . . . . is called *Insana*, mad, for the use thereof is perillous; for if it be eate or dronke, it breedeth madnesse, or slow lykenesse of sleepe. Therefore this hearb is called commonly *Mirilidium*, for it taketh away wit and reason." —*Lib*. xvii. *ch*. 87.

BAN. To the self-same tune and words.—Who 's here?

Enter ROSS *and* ANGUS.

ROSS. The king hath happily receiv'd, Macbeth,
The news of thy success: and when he reads
Thy personal venture in the rebel's fight,
His wonders and his praises do contend,
Which should be thine or his: silenc'd with that,
In viewing o'er the rest o' the self-same day,
He finds thee in the stout Norweyan ranks,
Nothing afeard of what thyself didst make,
Strange images of death. As thick as tale[a]
Came* post with post; and every one did bear
Thy praises in his kingdom's great defence,
And pour'd them down before him.
ANG. We are sent
To give thee, from our royal master, thanks;
Only to herald thee into his sight,
Not pay thee.
ROSS. And, for an earnest of a greater honour,
He bade me, from him, call thee thane of Cawdor:
In which addition, hail, most worthy thane!
For it is thine.
BAN. [*Aside.*] What! can the devil speak true?
MACB. The thane of Cawdor lives: why do you dress me
In borrow'd robes?
ANG. Who was the thane lives yet;
But under heavy judgment bears that life
Which he deserves to lose. Whêr he was combin'd
With those of Norway, or did line the rebel
With hidden help and vantage, or that with both
He labour'd in his country's wreck, I know not;
But treasons capital, confess'd, and prov'd,
Have overthrown him.
MACB. [*Aside.*] Glamis, and thane of Cawdor!
The greatest is behind.—Thanks for your pains.—
Do you not hope your children shall be kings,
When those that gave the thane of Cawdor to me,
Promis'd no less to them?
BAN. That, trusted home,
Might yet enkindle you unto the crown,
Besides the thane of Cawdor. But 't is strange:
And oftentimes, to win us to our harm,
The instruments of darkness tell us truths;
Win us with honest trifles, to betray 's
In deepest consequence.—
Cousins, a word, I pray you.
MACB. [*Aside.*] Two truths are told,
As happy prologues to the swelling act
Of the imperial theme.—I thank you, gentlemen.—
[*Aside.*] This supernatural soliciting
Cannot be ill: cannot be good:—if ill,
Why hath it given me earnest of success,
Commencing in a truth? I am thane of Cawdor:
If good, why do I yield to that suggestion[b]
Whose horrid image doth unfix my hair,
And make my seated heart knock at my ribs,
Against the use of nature? Present fears
Are less than horrible imaginings:
My thought, whose murder yet is but fantastical,
Shakes so my single[c] state of man, that function
Is smother'd in surmise; and nothing is
But what is not.
BAN. Look, how our partner 's rapt.
MACB. [*Aside.*] If chance will have me king, why, chance may crown me,
Without my stir.
BAN. New honours come upon him,
Like our strange garments, cleave not to their mould
But with the aid of use.
MACB. [*Aside.*] Come what come may,
Time and the hour[d] runs through the roughest day.
BAN. Worthy Macbeth, we stay upon your leisure.
MACB. Give me your favour:—
My dull brain was wrought with things forgotten.
Kind gentlemen, your pains are register'd
Where every day I turn the leaf to read them.—
Let us toward the king.—
Think upon what hath chanc'd; and, at more time,
The interim having weigh'd it, let us speak
Our free hearts each to other.
BAN. Very gladly.
MACB. Till then, enough.—Come, friends.
[*Exeunt.*

(*) Old text, *Can.* Corrected by Rowe.

a — *as thick as* tale—] That is—as rapid as counting. Rowe most unwarrantably changed "*tale*" to "*hail;*" and this alteration has been adopted by many editors, for no other reason, it would appear, than that the former simile was unusual, and the latter commonplace.

b — suggestion—] *Temptation.*

c — *my* single *state of man,*—] "Single" here bears the sense of *weak; my feeble government* (or *body-politic*) of man. Shakespeare's affluence of thought and language is so unbounded that he rarely repeats himself, but there is a remarkable affinity both in idea and expression between the present passage and one in Act II. Sc. 1, of "Julius Cæsar,"—

"Between the acting of a dreadful thing
And the first motion, all the interim is
Like a phantasma, or a hideous dream:
The Genius and the mortal instruments
Are then in council; *and the state of man,*
Like to a little kingdom, suffers then
The nature of an insurrection."

d Time and the hour—] Examples of this phrase may readily be found in the early writers of England. Mr. Dyce has shown that it was familiar also to those of Italy:—

"Ferminsi in un momento *il tempo e l'ore.*"
Michelagnolo,—Son. xix.

"Aspettar vuol ch' occasion gli dia,
Come dar gli potrebbe, *il tempo e l'hora.*"
Dolce,—Prime Impresse del Conte Orlando, c. xvii. p. 145, ed. 1572.

SCENE IV.—Forres. *A Room in the Palace.*

Flourish. Enter KING DUNCAN, MALCOLM, DONALBAIN, LENNOX, *and* Attendants.

KING. Is execution done on Cawdor? Are[a] not
Those in commission yet return'd?
MAL. My liege,
They are not yet come back. But I have spoke
With one that saw him die: who did report,
That very frankly he confess'd his treasons;
Implor'd your highness' pardon; and set forth
A deep repentance: nothing in his life
Became him like the leaving it; he died
As one that had been studied in his death,
To throw away the dearest thing he ow'd,
As 't were a careless trifle.[b]
KING. There 's no art
To find the mind's construction in the face:
He was a gentleman on whom I built
An absolute trust.—

Enter MACBETH, BANQUO, ROSS, *and* ANGUS.

O, worthiest cousin!
The sin of my ingratitude even now
Was heavy on me: thou art so far before,
That swiftest wing of recompense is slow
To overtake thee. Would thou hadst less deserv'd;
That the proportion both of thanks and payment
Might have been mine![c] only I have left to say,
More is thy due than more than all can pay.
MACB. The service and the loyalty I owe,
In doing it, pays itself. Your highness' part
Is to receive our duties: and our duties
Are, to your throne and state, children and servants;
Which do but what they should, by doing every-thing
Safe toward your love and honour.
KING. Welcome hither:
I have begun to plant thee, and will labour
To make thee full of growing.—Noble Banquo,
That hast no less deserv'd, nor must be known
No less to have done so: let me infold thee,
And hold thee to my heart.
BAN. There if I grow,
The harvest is your own.
KING. My plenteous joys,
Wanton in fulness, seek to hide themselves
In drops of sorrow.—Sons, kinsmen, thanes,
And you whose places are the nearest, know,
We will establish our estate upon
Our eldest, Malcolm; whom we name hereafter
The prince of Cumberland:(4) which honour must
Not, unaccompanied, invest him only,
But signs of nobleness, like stars, shall shine
On all deservers.—From hence to Inverness,
And bind us further to you.
MACB. The rest is labour, which is not us'd for you:
I 'll be myself the harbinger, and make joyful
The hearing of my wife with your approach;
So, humbly take my leave.
KING. My worthy Cawdor!
MACB. [*Aside.*] The prince of Cumberland!—that is a step
On which I must fall down, or else o'er-leap,
For in my way it lies. Stars, hide your fires!
Let not light see my black and deep desires:
The eye wink at the hand; yet let that be,
Which the eye fears, when it is done, to see!
[*Exit.*
KING. True, worthy Banquo,—he is full so valiant;
And in his commendations I am fed,—
It is a banquet to me. Let 's after him,
Whose care is gone before to bid us welcome:
It is a peerless kinsman. [*Flourish. Exeunt.*

SCENE V.—Inverness. *A Room in* Macbeth's *Castle.*

Enter LADY MACBETH, *reading a letter.*

LADY M. *They met me in the day of success;*[d] *and I have learned by the perfectest report, they have more in them than mortal knowledge. When I burned in desire to question them further, they made themselves air, into which they vanished. Whiles I stood rapt in the wonder of it, came missives*[e] *from the king, who all-hailed me,* Thane

---

[a] — Are *not*—] So the second folio; that of 1623 has, "*Or* not," &c.

[b] As 't were a careless trifle.] "The behaviour of the *thane of Cawdor* corresponds in almost every circumstance with that of the unfortunate Earl of Essex, as related by Stowe, p. 793. His asking the Queen's forgiveness, his confession, repentance, and concern about behaving with propriety on the scaffold, are minutely described by that historian. Such an allusion could not fail of having the desired effect on an audience, many of whom were eye-witnesses to the severity of that justice which deprived the age of one of its greatest ornaments, and Southampton, Shakespeare's patron, of his dearest friend."—STEEVENS.

[c] —— *Would thou hadst less deserv'd;*
That the proportion both of thanks and payment
Might have been mine!]

For "mine," which no one can for a moment doubt to be a corruption, we would suggest that the poet wrote *mean*, i.e. *equivalent, just*, and the like; the sense then being,—That the proportion both of thanks and payment might have been *equal* to your deserts.

[d] — *in the day of* success;] In this place, as in Scene 3 of the present Act,—

"The king hath happily receiv'd, Macbeth,
The news of thy *success*;"—

Shakespeare employs *success* in the sense it bears at this day; but its ordinary signification, when unaccompanied by an adjective of quality, was, as we have before said, *event, issue*, &c.

[e] missives—] *Messengers.*

of Cawdor; *by which title, before, these weird sisters saluted me, and referred me to the coming on of time, with* Hail, king that shalt be! *This have I thought good to deliver thee, my dearest partner of greatness, that thou mightst not lose the dues of rejoicing, by being ignorant of what greatness is promised thee. Lay it to thy heart, and farewell.*

Glamis thou art, and Cawdor; and shalt be
What thou art promis'd:—yet do I fear thy nature;
It is too full o' the milk of human kindness,
To catch the nearest way. Thou wouldst be great;
Art not without ambition; but without
The illness should attend it: what thou wouldst highly,
That wouldst thou holily; wouldst not play false,
And yet wouldst wrongly win: thou 'dst have, great Glamis,
That which cries, *Thus thou must do, if thou have it;*
And that which rather thou dost fear to do,
Than wishest should be undone. Hie thee hither,
That I may pour my spirits in thine ear;
And chastise with the valour of my tongue
All that impedes thee from the golden round,
Which fate and metaphysical[a] aid doth seem
To have thee crown'd withal.—

[a] — metaphysical *aid*—] *Supernatural* aid.

Enter an Attendant.

What is your tidings?
ATTEND. The king comes here to-night.
LADY M. Thou 'rt mad to say it!—
Is not thy master with him? who, were 't so,
Would have inform'd for preparation.
ATTEND. So please you, it is true:—our thane is coming:
One of my fellows had the speed of him;
Who, almost dead for breath, had scarcely more
Than would make up his message.
LADY M. Give him tending,
He brings great news. [*Exit* Attendant.
The raven himself is hoarse
That croaks the fatal entrance of Duncan
Under my battlements.[a] Come, you spirits
That tend on mortal thoughts, unsex me here;
And fill me, from the crown to the toe, top-full
Of direst cruelty! make thick my blood,
Stop up the access and passage to remorse;
That no compunctious visitings of nature
Shake my fell purpose, nor keep peace between
The effect and it! Come to my woman's breasts,
And take my milk for gall, you murdering ministers,
Wherever in your sightless substances
You wait on nature's mischief! Come, thick night,
And pall thee in the dunnest smoke of hell,
That my keen knife see not the wound it makes;
Nor heaven peep through the blanket[b] of the dark,
To cry, *Hold, hold!*—

Enter MACBETH.

Great Glamis, worthy Cawdor!
Greater than both, by the all-hail hereafter!
Thy letters have transported me beyond
This ignorant present,[c] and I feel now
The future in the instant.
MACB. My dearest love,
Duncan comes here to-night.
LADY M. And when goes hence?
MACB. To-morrow,—as he purposes.
LADY M. O, never
Shall sun that morrow see!
Your face, my thane, is as a book where men
May read strange matters:—to beguile the time,
Look like the time; bear welcome in your eye,
Your hand, your tongue: look like the innocent flower,
But be the serpent under it. He that 's coming
Must be provided for: and you shall put
This night's great business into my dispatch;
Which shall to all our nights and days to come
Give solely sovereign sway and masterdom.
MACB. We will speak further.
LADY M. Only look up clear;
To alter favour ever is to fear:
Leave all the rest to me. [*Exeunt.*

SCENE VI.—*The same. Before the Castle.*

Hautboys. Servants *of* MACBETH *attending. Enter* KING DUNCAN, MALCOLM, DONALBAIN, BANQUO, LENNOX, MACDUFF, ROSS, ANGUS, *and* Attendants.

KING. This castle hath a pleasant seat; the air
Nimbly and sweetly recommends itself
Unto our gentle senses.
BAN. This guest of summer,
The temple-haunting martlet,* does approve,
By his lov'd mansionry,[d] that the heaven's breath
Smells wooingly here: no jutty, frieze,
Buttress, nor coign of vantage, but this bird
Hath made his pendent bed and procreant cradle:
Where they most † breed and haunt, I have observ'd,
The air is delicate.(5)
KING. See, see! our honour'd hostess!—

Enter LADY MACBETH.

The love that follows us sometime is our trouble,
Which still we thank as love. Herein I teach you,
How you shall bid God eyld us for your pains,
And thank us for your trouble.
LADY M. All our service
In every point twice done, and then done double,
Were poor and single business to contend
Against those honours deep and broad wherewith
Your majesty loads our house: for those of old,

---

a — the raven himself is hoarse, &c.] "The messenger, says the servant, had hardly breath to make up his message; to which the lady answers mentally, that he may well want breath, such a message would add hoarseness to the raven. That even the bird, whose harsh voice is accustomed to predict calamities, could not *croak the entrance of* Duncan, but in a note of unwonted harshness."—JOHNSON.

b *Nor heaven peep through the* blanket *of the dark,* &c.] Mr. Collier's annotator substitutes *blankness* for the familiar "blanket" of the text; and Mr. Collier is infatuated enough to applaud this miserable perversion of the poet's language. If "blanket" is a word too coarse for the delicacy of these commentators, what say they to the following from Act III. Sc. 1, of Middleton's "Blurt Master Constable"?—

"Blest night, wrap Cynthia in *a sable sheet.*"

c — ignorant present,—] Even this fine expression has undergone mutation; some editors actually printing,—

"ignorant present *time.*"!!

d By his lov'd mansionry,—] Looking to the context,—"his pendent bed and procreant cradle," should we not read, *love-mansionry?*

(*) Old text, *Barlet.* (†) Old text, *must.*

And the late dignities heap'd up to them,
We rest your hermits.[a]

KING. Where 's the thane of Cawdor?
We cours'd him at the heels, and had a purpose
To be his purveyor: but he rides well;
And his great love, sharp as his spur, hath holp him
To his home before us. Fair and noble hostess,
We are your guest to-night.

LADY M. Your servants ever
Have theirs, themselves, and what is theirs, in compt,[b]
To make their audit at your highness' pleasure,
Still to return your own.

KING. Give me your hand:
Conduct me to mine host: we love him highly,
And shall continue our graces towards him.
By your leave, hostess. [*Exeunt.*

SCENE VII.—*The same. A Room in the Castle.*

Hautboys and torches. Enter, and pass over the stage, a Sewer, *and divers* Servants *with dishes and service. Then enter* MACBETH.

MACB. If it were done when 't is done, then 't were well
It were done quickly: if the assassination
Could trammel up the consequence, and catch,
With his surcease, success;[c] that but this blow
Might be the be-all and the end-all here,
But here, upon this bank and shoal * of time,—
We'd jump the life to come. But in these cases,
We still have judgment here; that we but teach
Bloody instructions, which, being taught, return
To plague the inventor: this[d] even-handed justice
Commends the ingredients of our poison'd chalice
To our own lips. He 's here in double trust:
First, as I am his kinsman and his subject,
Strong both against the deed; then, as his host,
Who should against his murderer shut the door,
Not bear the knife myself. Besides, this Duncan
Hath borne his faculties so meek, hath been
So clear in his great office, that his virtues
Will plead like angels, trumpet-tongu'd, against
The deep damnation of his taking-off;
And pity, like a naked new-born babe,
Striding the blast, or heaven's cherubin, hors'd
Upon the sightless couriers of the air,
Shall blow the horrid deed in every eye,
That tears shall drown the wind.—I have no spur
To prick the sides of my Intent, but only
Vaulting Ambition, which o'erleaps itself,
And falls on the other.—[e]

Enter LADY MACBETH.

How now! what news?

LADY M. He has almost supp'd. Why have you left the chamber?

MACB. Hath he ask'd for me?

LADY M. Know you not he has?

MACB. We will proceed no further in this business:
He hath honour'd me of late; and I have bought
Golden opinions from all sorts of people,
Which would be worn now in their newest gloss,
Not cast aside so soon.

LADY M. Was the hope drunk
Wherein you dress'd yourself? hath it slept since?
And wakes it now, to look so green and pale
At what it did so freely? From this time,
Such I account thy love. Art thou afeard
To be the same in thine own act and valour,
As thou art in desire? Wouldst thou have that
Which thou esteem'st the ornament of life,
And live a coward in thine own esteem;
Letting *I dare not* wait upon *I would*,
Like the poor cat i' the adage.[f]

MACB. Pr'ythee, peace:
I dare do all that may become a man;
Who dares do* more, is none.

LADY M. What beast[g] was 't then,

(*) Old text, *Schoole*, corrected by Theobald.

(*) Old text, *no.*

a — hermits.] *Beadsmen; bound to pray for your welfare.*
b — *in* compt,—] In *trust;* to be *accounted for.*
c —— *and catch,*
With his surcease, success;]
The obscurity which critics lament in this famous passage is due to themselves. If, instead of taking "success" in its modern sense of *prosperity*, they had understood it according to its usual acceptation in Shakespeare's day, as *sequel, what follows*, &c., they must have perceived at once that to "*catch*, with his surcease, *success*," is no more than an enforcement of "trammel up the consequence." The meaning obviously being,—If the assassination were an absolutely final act, and could shut up all consecution, "— be the be-all and the end-all" even of this life only,—we would run the hazard of a future state.
d — this *even-handed justice*—] Mason suggested that we might more advantageously read,—"*Thus* even-handed justice."
e "—— I have no spur
To prick the sides of my Intent, but only
Vaulting Ambition, which o'erleaps itself,
And falls on the other.—]
Malone's exposition of this troublesome passage is as follows,—"I apprehend that there is not here one long-drawn metaphor, but two distinct ones; I have no spur to prick the sides of my intent; I have nothing to *stimulate* me to the execution of my purpose but ambition, which is apt to overreach itself; this he expresses by the second image, of a person meaning to vault into his saddle, who, by taking too great a leap, will fall on the other side." This does not assist us much; still less does the fanciful suggestion to read for "itself" *its sell, i. e.* its saddle. The only resolution of the enigma which presents itself to our mind is to suppose *Intent* and *Ambition* are represented in Macbeth's disordered imagination by two steeds, the one lacking all incentive to motion, the other so impulsive that it overreaches itself and falls on its companion.
f Like the poor cat i' the adage.] *Catus amat pisces, sed non vult tingere plantas;* or, as it is rendered in Heywood's Proverbs, 1566, —"The cat would eate fishe, and would not wet her feete."
g *What* beast *was't then,* &c.] As Mr. Collier, in deference to critical opinion, has rejected from his latest edition of the poet the preposterous substitution *boast* for "beast" in this line, we are spared the necessity of citing a host of passages collected for the purpose of substantiating the original reading.

That made you break this enterprise to me?
When you durst do it, then you were a man;
And, to be more than what you were, you would
Be so much more the man. Nor time nor place
Did then adhere, and yet you would make both:
They have made themselves, and that their fitness now
Does unmake you. I have given suck, and know
How tender 't is to love the babe that milks me;
I would, while it was smiling in my face,
Have pluck'd my nipple from his boneless gums,
And dash'd the brains out, had I so sworn
As you have done to this.

MACB. If we should fail?

LADY M. We fail!
But screw your courage to the sticking place,[a]
And we'll not fail. When Duncan is asleep,
(Whereto the rather shall his day's hard journey
Soundly invite him) his two chamberlains
Will I with wine and wassail so convince,[b]
That memory, the warder of the brain,
Shall be a fume, and the receipt[c] of reason
A limbeck only: when in swinish sleep
Their drenched natures lie as in a death,
What cannot you and I perform upon
The unguarded Duncan? what not put upon
His spongy officers, who shall bear the guilt
Of our great quell?

MACB. Bring forth men-children only!
For thy undaunted mettle should compose
Nothing but males. Will it not be receiv'd,
When we have mark'd with blood those sleepy two
Of his own chamber, and us'd their very daggers,
That they have done 't?

LADY M. Who dares receive it other,
As we shall make our griefs and clamour roar
Upon his death?

MACB. I am settled, and bend up
Each corporal agent to this terrible feat.
Away, and mock the time with fairest show:
False face must hide what the false heart doth know! [*Exeunt.*

---

a — *the* sticking place,—] The *abiding place,*—

"Which flower out of my hand shall never passe,
But in my heart shall have a *sticking place.*"
The Gorgeous Gallery of Gallant Inventions.

The metaphor may have been taken from the screwing up the chords of a musical instrument.

b — so convince,—] So *subdue* or *overpower.*

c — receipt *of reason*—] *Receptacle* of reason.

ACT II.

SCENE I.—Inverness. *Court of* Macbeth*'s Castle.*

Enter BANQUO *and* FLEANCE, *with a torch.*

BAN. How goes the night, boy?
FLE. The moon is down; I have not heard the clock.
BAN. And she goes down at twelve.
FLE. I take 't, 't is later, sir.
BAN. Hold, take my sword:—there's husbandry in heaven,
Their candles are all out.—Take thee that too.—
A heavy summons lies like lead upon me,—
And yet I would not sleep:—Merciful powers,
Restrain in me the cursed thoughts that nature
Gives way to in repose!—Give me my sword,—
Who 's there?

Enter MACBETH, *and a* Servant *with a torch.*

MACB. A friend.
BAN. What, sir, not yet at rest? The king 's a-bed:
He hath been in unusual pleasure,
And sent forth great largess to your officers: *
This diamond he greets your wife withal,
By the name of most kind hostess; and shut up
In measureless content.[a]
MACB. Being unprepar'd,
Our will became the servant to defect;
Which else should free have wrought.
BAN. All 's well.—
I dreamt last night of the three weird sisters:
To you they have show'd some truth.
MACB. I think not of them;
Yet, when we can entreat an hour to serve,
We would spend it in some words upon that business,
If you would grant the time.
BAN. At your kind'st leisure.
MACB. If you shall cleave to my consent,—when 't is,
It shall make honour for you.[b]
BAN. So I lose none,
In seeking to augment it, but still keep

a —— and shut up
In easureless content.]
Shut up, meant *finished, concluded.*

b If you shall cleave to my consent,—when 't is,
It shall make honour for you.]

(*) Old text, *offices.*

This passage, we apprehend, has suffered some mutilation or corruption since it left the poet's hands. It seems impracticable to obtain a consistent meaning from the lines as they now stand.

My bosom franchis'd, and allegiance clear,
I shall be counsell'd.
MACB. Good repose, the while!
BAN. Thanks, sir; the like to you!
[*Exeunt* BANQUO *and* FLEANCE.
MACB. Go bid thy mistress, when my drink is ready,
She strike upon the bell. Get thee to bed.—
[*Exit* Servant.
Is this a dagger which I see before me,
The handle toward my hand? Come, let me clutch thee:—
I have thee not, and yet I see thee still.
Art thou not, fatal vision, sensible
To feeling as to sight? or art thou but
A dagger of the mind, a false creation,
Proceeding from the heat-oppressed brain?
I see thee yet, in form as palpable
As this which now I draw.
Thou marshall'st me the way that I was going;
And such an instrument I was to use.—
Mine eyes are made the fools o' the other senses,
Or else worth all the rest:—I see thee still;
And on thy blade and dudgeon [a] gouts of blood,
Which was not so before.—There's no such thing;
It is the bloody business which informs
Thus to mine eyes.—Now o'er the one-half world
Nature seems dead, and wicked dreams abuse
The curtain'd sleep; [b] Witchcraft celebrates
Pale Hecate's offerings; and wither'd Murder,
Alarum'd by his sentinel, the wolf,
Whose howl's his watch, thus with his stealthy pace,
With Tarquin's ravishing strides,[c] towards his design
Moves like a ghost.—Thou sure and firm-set earth,
Hear not my steps, which way they† walk, for fear
Thy very stones prate of my where-about,
And take the present horror from the time,
Which now suits with it.—Whiles I threat, he lives:
Words to the heat of deeds too cold breath gives.
[*A bell is struck.*
I go, and it is done; the bell invites me.
Hear it not, Duncan; for it is a knell
That summons thee to heaven or to hell! [*Exit.*

Enter LADY MACBETH.

LADY M. That which hath made them drunk, hath made me bold:
What hath quench'd them, hath given me fire.—
Hark!—Peace! It was the owl that shriek'd,
The fatal bellman which gives the stern'st good-night.—
He is about it: The doors are open;
And the surfeited grooms do mock their charge with snores:
I have drugg'd their possets,
That death and nature do contend about them,
Whether they live or die.
MACB. [*Within.*] Who's there?—what, ho!
LADY M. Alack! I am afraid they have awak'd,
And 't is not done:—the attempt, and not the deed,
Confounds us.—Hark!—I laid their daggers ready;
He could not miss 'em.—Had he not resembled
My father as he slept, I had done 't—My husband!

Re-enter MACBETH.

MACB. I have done the deed.—Didst thou not hear a noise?
LADY M. I heard the owl scream and the crickets cry.
Did not you speak?
MACB. When?
LADY M. Now.
MACB. As I descended?
LADY M. Ay.
MACB. Hark!—
Who lies i' the second chamber?
LADY M. Donalbain.
MACB. This is a sorry sight.
[*Looking on his hands.*
LADY M. A foolish thought, to say *a sorry sight*.
MACB. There's one did laugh in 's sleep,
And one cried, *Murder!* that they did wake each other;
I stood and heard them: but they did say their prayers,
And address'd them again to sleep.
LADY M. There are two lodg'd together.
MACB. One cried, *God bless us!* and *Amen*, the other;
As they had seen me with these hangman's hands.
Listening their fear, I could not say, *Amen*,
When they did say, *God bless us.*
LADY M. Consider it not so deeply.
MACB. But wherefore could not I pronounce *Amen?*
I had most need of blessing, and *Amen*
Stuck in my throat.

(*) Old text, *sowre*. (†) Old text, *which they may*.

[a] — dudgeon—] The wooden *haft* or *handle* of a dagger.

[b] The curtain'd sleep; Witchcraft celebrates, &c.] To perfect the measure, D'Avenant reads, "—*now* witchcraft celebrates," &c.; but Steevens' emendation, "The curtain'd *sleeper;*" &c. is more generally adopted.

[c] With Tarquin's ravishing strides,—] It is painful to reflect, that, with the exception of "Pericles," and "All's Well that Ends Well," this sublime drama is more carelessly printed in the only old edition of it we possess, than any other in the collection; there are probably not thirty consecutive lines throughout which have come down to us as the poet wrote them. In the line above, the folio reads *sides*, and this, which was corrected by Pope, it may be suspected is not the only error. "Tarquin's ravishing strides," reads very like a transposition of "Ravishing Tarquin's strides."

LADY M. These deeds must not be thought
After these ways; so, it will make us mad.
MACB. Methought, I heard a voice cry, *Sleep no more!*
Macbeth does murder sleep!—the innocent sleep;
Sleep, that knits up the ravell'd sleave[a] of care,
The death of each day's life, sore labour's bath,
Balm of hurt minds, great nature's second course,
Chief nourisher in life's feast,—

[a] — sleave—] Unwrought silk, flos silk.

LADY M. What do you mean?
MACB. Still it cried, *Sleep no more!* to all the house:
Glamis hath murder'd sleep; and therefore Cawdor
Shall sleep no more,—Macbeth shall sleep no more!
LADY M. Who was it that thus cried? Why, worthy thane,
You do unbend your noble strength, to think
So brainsickly of things.—Go, get some water,
And wash this filthy witness from your hand.—

Why did you bring these daggers from the place?
They must lie there: go carry them; and smear
The sleepy grooms with blood.

MACB. I 'll go no more:
I am afraid to think what I have done;
Look on't again I dare not.

LADY M. Infirm of purpose!
Give me the daggers: the sleeping and the dead
Are but as pictures: 't is the eye of childhood
That fears a painted devil. If he do bleed,
I'll gild the aces of the grooms withal;
For it must seem their gailt.

[*Exit. Knocking without.*

MACB. Whence is that knocking?
How is 't with me, when every noise appals me?
What hands are here? Ha! they pluck out mine eyes!
Will all great Neptune's ocean wash this blood
Clean from my hand? No; this my hand will rather

The multitudinous seas incarnadine,
Making the green—one red.

Re-enter LADY MACBETH.

LADY M. My hands are of your colour; but I shame
To wear a heart so white. [*Knocking without.*] I hear a knocking
At the south entry:—retire we to our chamber:
A little water clears us of this deed:
How easy is it then! Your constancy
Hath left you unattended.—[*Knocking without.*] Hark! more knocking:
Get on your nightgown, lest occasion call us,
And show us to be watchers:—be not lost
So poorly in your thoughts.

MACB. To know my deed, 't were best not know myself. [*Knocking without.*
Wake Duncan with thy knocking! Ay, would thou couldst! [*Exeunt.*

SCENE II.—*The same. A Hall in the Castle.*

Enter a Porter. [*Knocking without.*

PORTER. Here's a knocking, indeed! If a man were porter of hell-gate, he should have old turning the key. [*Knocking without.*] Knock, knock, knock! Who's there, i' the name of Beelzebub?—*Here's a farmer, that hanged himself on the expectation of plenty.*—Come in, Time;[a] have napkins enow about you; here you'll sweat for 't. [*Knocking without.*] Knock, knock! Who's there, i' the other devil's name?—*Faith, here's an equivocator, that could swear in both the scales against either scale; who committed treason enough for God's sake, yet could not equivocate to heaven.*—O, come in, Equivocator. [*Knocking without.*] Knock, knock, knock! Who's there?—*Faith, here's an English tailor come hither, for stealing out of a French hose.*—Come in, Tailor; here you may roast your goose. [*Knocking without.*] Knock, knock! never at quiet! What are you?—But this place is too cold for hell. I'll devil-porter it no further: I had thought to have let in some of all professions, that go the primrose way to the everlasting bonfire. [*Knocking without.*] Anon, anon! I pray you, remember the porter. [*Opens the gate.*

Enter MACDUFF *and* LENNOX.

MACD. Was it so late, friend, ere you went to bed,
That you do lie so late?

PORT. Faith, sir, we were carousing till the second cock: and drink, sir, is a great provoker of three things.

MACD. What three things does drink especially provoke?

PORT. Marry, sir, nose-painting, sleep, and urine. Lechery, sir, it provokes, and unprovokes: it provokes the desire, but it takes away the performance: therefore, much drink may be said to be an equivocator with Lechery: it makes him, and it mars him; it sets him on, and it takes him off; it persuades him, and disheartens him; makes him stand to, and not stand to; in conclusion, equivocates him in a sleep, and, giving him the lie, leaves him.

MACD. I believe drink gave thee the lie last night.

PORT. That it did, sir, i' the very throat on me: but I requited him for his lie; and, I think, being too strong for him, though he took up my legs sometime, yet I made a shift to cast him.

MACD. Is thy master stirring?—
Our knocking has awak'd him; here he comes.

Enter MACBETH.

LEN. Good morrow, noble sir!
MACB. Good morrow, both.
MACD. Is the king stirring, worthy thane?
MACB. Not yet.
MACD. He did command me to call timely on him;
I have almost slipp'd the hour.
MACB. I'll bring you to him.
MACD. I know this is a joyful trouble to you;
But yet 't is one.
MACB. The labour we delight in physics pain.
This is the door.
MACD. I'll make so bold to call,
For 't is my limited[b] service. [*Exit.*
LEN. Goes the king hence to-day?
MACB. He does:—he did appoint so.
LEN. The night has been unruly: where we lay,
Our chimneys were blown down; and, as they say,
Lamentings heard i' the air; strange screams of death;
And prophesying, with accents terrible,

---

[a] Come in, Time;] The editors concur in printing this, "Come in time;" but what meaning they attach to it none has yet explained. As we have subsequently, "Come in, Equivocator," and "Come in, Tailor," "Time" is probably intended as a whimsical appellation for the "farmer that hanged himself."

[b] —limited—] *Appointed.*

Of dire combustion and confus'd events,
New hatch'd to the woeful time.
The obscure bird clamour'd the live-long night:
Some say, the earth was feverous and did shake.

MACB. 'Twas a rough night.

LEN. My young remembrance cannot parallel
A fellow to it.

Re-enter MACDUFF.

MACD. O, horror! horror! horror!
Tongue nor heart cannot conceive nor name thee!

MACB., LEN. What 's the matter?

MACD. Confusion now hath made his masterpiece!
Most sacrilegious murder hath broke ope
The Lord's anointed temple, and stole thence
The life o' the building!

MACB. What is 't you say? *the life?*

LEN. Mean you his majesty?

MACD. Approach the chamber, and destroy your sight
With a new Gorgon:—do not bid me speak;
See, and then speak yourselves.—

[*Exeunt* MACBETH *and* LENNOX.

Awake! awake!—
Ring the alarum-bell.—Murder and treason!—
Banquo and Donalbain! Malcolm! awake!
Shake off this downy sleep, death's counterfeit,
And look on death itself!—up, up, and see
The great doom's image!—Malcolm! Banquo!
As from your graves rise up, and walk like sprites,
To countenance this horror! Ring the bell.

[*Alarum-bell rings.*

Enter LADY MACBETH.

LADY M. What 's the business,
That such a hideous trumpet calls to parley
The sleepers of the house? speak, speak!

MACD. O, gentle lady,
'T is not for you to hear what I can speak:
The repetition, in a woman's ear,
Would murder as it fell.—

Enter BANQUO.

O, Banquo! Banquo! our royal master 's murder'd!

LADY M. Woe, alas! what, in our house?

BAN. Too cruel anywhere.
Dear Duff, I pr'ythee, contradict thyself,
And say it is not so.

Re-enter MACBETH *and* LENNOX.

MACB. Had I but died an hour before this chance,
I had liv'd a blessed time; for, from this instant,
There 's nothing serious in mortality:
All is but toys: renown and grace is dead;
The wine of life is drawn, and the mere lees
Is left this vault to brag of.

Enter MALCOLM *and* DONALBAIN.

DON. What is amiss?
MACB. You are, and do not know 't:
The spring, the head, the fountain of your blood
Is stopp'd,—the very source of it is stopp'd.
MACD. Your royal father 's murder'd.
MAL. O, by whom?
LEN. Those of his chamber, as it seem'd, had done 't:
Their hands and faces were all badg'd with blood;
So were their daggers, which, unwip'd, we found
Upon their pillows: they star'd, and were distracted;
No man's life was to be trusted with them.
MACB. O, yet, I do repent me of my fury,
That I did kill them.
MACD. Wherefore did you so?
MACB. Who can be wise, amaz'd, temperate and furious,
Loyal and neutral, in a moment? No man:
The expedition of my violent love
Outrun the pauser reason.—Here lay Duncan,
His silver skin lac'd with his golden blood;
And his gash'd stabs look'd like a breach in nature
For ruin's wasteful entrance: there, the murderers,
Steep'd in the colours of their trade, their daggers
Unmannerly breech'd with gore: who could refrain
That had a heart to love, and in that heart
Courage to make 's love known?
LADY M. Help me hence, ho!
MACD. Look to the lady.
MAL. [*Aside to* DON.] Why do we hold our tongues,
That most may claim this argument for ours?
DON. [*Aside to* MAL.] What should be spoken here,
Where our fate, hid in an auger-hole,
May rush and seize us? Let 's away;
Our tears are not yet brew'd.
MAL. [*Aside to* DON.] Nor our strong sorrow
Upon the foot of motion.
BAN. Look to the lady:—
[LADY MACBETH *is carried out.*

And when we have our naked frailties hid,
That suffer in exposure, let us meet,
And question this most bloody piece of work,
To know it further. Fears and scruples shake us:
In the great hand of God I stand; and thence
Against the undivulg'd pretence I fight
Of treasonous malice!
MACD. And so do I!
ALL. So all!
MACB. Let 's briefly put on manly readiness,
And meet i' the hall together.
ALL. Well contented.
[*Exeunt all except* MALCOLM *and* DONALBAIN.
MAL. What will you do? Let 's not consort with them:
To show an unfelt sorrow is an office
Which the false man does easy. I 'll to England.
DON. To Ireland, I; our separated fortune
Shall keep us both the safer: where we are,
There 's daggers in men's smiles: the near in blood,
The nearer bloody.
MAL. This murderous shaft that 's shot
Hath not yet lighted; and our safest way
Is to avoid the aim. Therefore, to horse;
And let us not be dainty of leave-taking,
But shift away: there 's warrant in that theft
Which steals itself, when there 's no mercy left.
[*Exeunt.*

SCENE III.—*The same. Without the Castle.*

Enter ROSS *and an* Old Man.

OLD M. Threescore and ten I can remember well:
Within the volume of which time, I have seen
Hours dreadful and things strange; but this sore night
Hath trifled former knowings.
ROSS. Ah, good father,
Thou seest the heavens, as troubled with man's act,
Threaten his bloody stage: by the clock, 't is day,
And yet dark night strangles the travelling lamp:
Is 't night's predominance, or the day's shame,
That darkness does the face of earth entomb,
When living light should kiss it?
OLD M. 'T is unnatural,
Even like the deed that 's done. On Tuesday last,
A falcon, touring in her pride of place,[a]
Was by a mousing owl hawk'd at and kill'd.

[a] *A falcon, touring in her pride of place,*—] That is, *circling at her highest point of elevation.* So in Massinger's play of "The Guardian," Act I. Sc. 2,—

"Then, for an evening flight,
A tiercel gentle, which I call, my masters,
As he were sent a messenger to the moon,
In such *a place* flies, as he seems to say,
See me or see me not!"

See also note (1), p. 333, Vol. I.

Ross. And Duncan's horses, (a thing most strange and certain)
Beauteous and swift, the minions of their race,
Turn'd wild in nature, broke their stalls, flung out,
Contending 'gainst obedience, as they would
Make war with mankind.

OLD M. 'T is said they eat each other.(1)

Ross. They did so,—to the amazement of mine eyes,
That look'd upon 't.—Here comes the good Macduff.—

Enter MACDUFF.

How goes the world, sir, now?

MACD. Why, see you not?

Ross. Is 't known who did this more than bloody deed?

MACD. Those that Macbeth hath slain.

Ross. Alas, the day!
What good could they pretend?

MACD. They were suborn'd:
Malcolm and Donalbain, the king's two sons,
Are stol'n away and fled; which puts upon them
Suspicion of the deed.

Ross. 'Gainst nature still:
Thriftless ambition, that wilt ravin up
Thine own life's means!—Then 't is most like
The sovereignty will fall upon Macbeth.[a]

MACD. He is already nam'd; and gone to Scone (2)
To be invested.

Ross. Where is Duncan's body?

MACD. Carried to Colme-kill; (3)
The sacred storehouse of his predecessors,
And guardian of their bones.

Ross. Will you to Scone?

MACD. No, cousin, I'll to Fife.

Ross. Well, I will thither.

MACD. Well, may you see things well done there,—adieu,—
Lest our old robes sit easier than our new!

Ross. Farewell, father.

OLD M. God's benison go with you, and with those
That would make good of bad, and friends of foes!

[*Exeunt.*

---

a Then 'tis most like
The sovereignty will fall upon Macbeth.]
Macbeth by his birth stood next in succession to the crown after the sons of Duncan. King Malcolm, Duncan's predecessor, had two daughters, the eldest of whom, Beatrice, was the mother of Duncan; the younger, called Doada, the mother of Macbeth.

ACT III.

SCENE I.—Forres. *A Room in the Palace.*

Enter Banquo.

Ban. Thou hast it now,—king, Cawdor, Glamis, all,
As the weird women promis'd; and, I fear,
Thou play'dst most foully for 't: yet it was said
It should not stand in thy posterity;
But that myself should be the root and father
Of many kings. If there come truth from them,
(As upon thee, Macbeth, their speeches shine)
Why, by the verities on thee made good,
May they not be my oracles as well,
And set me up in hope? But, hush; no more.

Sennet sounded. Enter Macbeth, *as King;* Lady Macbeth, *as Queen;* Lennox, Ross, Lords, Ladies, *and* Attendants.

K. Macb. Here 's our chief guest.
Queen. If he had been forgotten,
It had been as a gap in our great feast,
And all-thing [a] unbecoming.
K. Macb. To-night we hold a solemn supper, sir,
And I 'll request your presence.
Ban. Let [b] your highness
Command upon me; to the which my duties

a —all-thing—] *Every-way.*

b —— Let your highness
Command upon me;]
This has been changed to, "*Lay* your highness," &c., and "*Set* your highness," &c. D'Avenant, in his alteration of the play, reads,—

"Your Majesty layes your command on me,
To which my duty is to obey."

Are with a most indissoluble tie
For ever knit.

K. MACB. Ride you this afternoon?

BAN. Ay, my good lord.

K. MACB. We should have else desir'd your good advice
(Which still hath been both grave and prosperous)
In this day's council; but we'll take to-morrow.
Is't far you ride?

BAN. As far, my lord, as will fill up the time
'Twixt this and supper: go not my horse the better,
I must become a borrower of the night
For a dark hour or twain.

K. MACB. Fail not our feast.

BAN. My lord, I will not.

K. MACB. We hear, our bloody cousins are bestow'd
In England and in Ireland; not confessing
Their cruel parricide, filling their hearers
With strange invention,—but of that to-morrow;
When therewithal, we shall have cause of state,
Craving us jointly. Hie you to horse! adieu,
Till you return at night. Goes Fleance with you?

BAN. Ay, my good lord: our time does call upon 's.

K. MACB. I wish your horses swift and sure of foot;
And so do I commend you to their backs.
Farewell. [*Exit* BANQUO.
Let every man be master of his time
Till seven at night; to make society
The sweeter welcome, we will keep ourself
Till supper-time alone: while then, God be with you!

[*Exeunt* QUEEN, Lords, Ladies, &c.

Sirrah, a word with you: attend those men our pleasure?

ATTEND. They are, my lord, without the palace gate.

K. MACB. Bring them before us.— [*Exit* Attendant.
To be thus is nothing,
But to be safely thus.[a] Our fears in Banquo
Stick deep; and in his royalty of nature[b]
Reigns that which would be fear'd: 't is much he dares;
And, to that dauntless temper of his mind,
He hath a wisdom that doth guide his valour
To act in safety. There is none but he
Whose being I do fear: and under him
My Genius is rebuk'd; as, it is said,
Mark Antony's was by Cæsar. He chid the sisters,
When first they put the name of king upon me,
And bade them speak to him; then, prophet-like,
They hail'd him father to a line of kings:
Upon my head they plac'd a fruitless crown,
And put a barren sceptre in my gripe,
Thence to be wrench'd with an unlineal hand,
No son of mine succeeding. If 't be so,
For Banquo's issue have I fil'd my mind;
For them the gracious Duncan have I murder'd:
Put rancours in the vessel of my peace,
Only for them; and mine eternal jewel
Given to the common enemy of man,
To make them kings, the seed* of Banquo kings!
Rather than so, come, Fate, into the list,
And champion me to the utterance![c]—Who 's there?—

Re-enter Attendant, *with two* Murderers.

Now go to the door, and stay there till we call.
[*Exit* Attendant.
Was it not yesterday we spoke together?

1 MUR. It was, so please your highness.

K. MACB. Well then, now
Have you consider'd of my speeches? Know
That it was he, in the times past, which held you
So under fortune; which you thought had been
Our innocent self: this I made good to you
In our last conference, pass'd in probation with you;
How you were borne in hand,[d] how cross'd, the instruments,
Who wrought with them, and all things else that might
To half a soul and to a notion craz'd
Say, *Thus did Banquo.*

1 MUR. You made it known to us.

K. MACB. I did so: and went further, which is now
Our point of second meeting. Do you find
Your patience so predominant in your nature,
That you can let this go? Are you so gospell'd,
To pray for this good man and for his issue,
Whose heavy hand hath bow'd you to the grave,
And beggar'd yours for ever?

1 MUR. We are men, my liege.

K. MACB. Ay, in the catalogue ye go for men;
As hounds, and greyhounds, mongrels, spaniels, curs,

---

a To be thus is nothing,
But to be safely thus.]
To be a king is nothing, unless to be safely one. This is out of doubt the meaning of the poet; but the modern punctuation,—
"To be thus is nothing;
But to be safely thus:—"
renders the passage quite incomprehensible.

(*) Old text, *Seedes.*

b — royalty of nature—] A form of expression correspondent to, and confirmatory of, "sovereignty of reason," and "nobility of love."

c — *to the* utterance!] From the French; *se battre à l'outrance*, to fight to extremity, to the last gasp.

d — borne in hand,—] *Encouraged by delusive promises.*

Shoughs, water-rugs, and demi-wolves, are clep'd [a]
All by the name of dogs: the valu'd file
Distinguishes the swift, the slow, the subtle,
The housekeeper, the hunter, every one
According to the gift which bounteous nature
Hath in him clos'd; whereby he does receive
Particular addition, from the bill
That writes them all alike: and so of men.
Now, if you have a station in the file,
Not i' the worst rank of manhood, say it;
And I will put that business in your bosoms
Whose execution takes your enemy off;
Grapples you to the heart and love of us,
Who wear our health but sickly in his life,
Which in his death were perfect.

2 Mur. I am one, my liege,

a — clep'd—] *Called.*

Whom the vile blows and buffets of the world
Have so incens'd, that I am reckless what I do
To spite the world.

1 MUR. And I another,
So weary with disasters, tugg'd with fortune,
That I would set my life on any chance,
To mend it, or be rid on 't.

K. MACB. Both of you know
Banquo was your enemy.

2 MUR. True, my lord.

K. MACB. So is he mine; and in such bloody distance,
That every minute of his being thrusts
Against my near'st of life: and though I could
With bare-fac'd power sweep him from my sight,
And bid my will avouch it, yet I must not,
For certain friends that are both his and mine,
Whose loves I may not drop, but wail his fall
Who I myself struck down: and thence it is
That I to your assistance do make love;
Masking the business from the common eye
For sundry weighty reasons.

2 MUR. We shall, my lord,
Perform what you command us.

1 MUR. Though our lives—

K. MACB. Your spirits shine through you. Within this hour at most,
I will advise you where to plant yourselves;
Acquaint you with the perfect spy o' the time,
The moment on 't; for 't must be done to-night,
And something from the palace; always thought
That I require a clearness:[a] and with him,
(To leave no rubs nor botches in the work)
Fleance his son, that keeps him company,
Whose absence is no less material to me
Than is his father's, must embrace the fate
Of that dark hour. Resolve yourselves apart;
I 'll come to you anon.

BOTH MUR. We are resolv'd, my lord.

K. MACB. I'll call upon you straight; abide within. [*Exeunt* Murderers.
It is concluded:—Banquo, thy soul's flight,
If it find heaven, must find it out to-night. [*Exit.*

SCENE II.—*The same. Another Room in the Palace.*

Enter QUEEN *and a* Servant.

QUEEN. Is Banquo gone from court?

SERV. Ay, madam, but returns again to-night.

QUEEN. Say to the king, I would attend his leisure
For a few words.

SERV. Madam, I will. [*Exit.*

QUEEN. Nought 's had, all 's spent,
Where our desire is got without content:
'T is safer to be that which we destroy,
Than, by destruction, dwell in doubtful joy.

Enter KING MACBETH.

How now, my lord! why do you keep alone,
Of sorriest fancies your companions making;
Using those thoughts which should indeed have died
With them they think on? Things without all remedy,
Should be without regard: what 's done is done.

K. MACB. We have scotch'd* the snake, not kill'd it;
She 'll close, and be herself; whilst our poor malice
Remains in danger of her former tooth.
But let the frame of things disjoint, both the worlds suffer,
Ere we will eat our meal in fear, and sleep
In the affliction of these terrible dreams
That shake us nightly. Better be with the dead,
Whom we, to gain our place,[b] have sent to peace,
Than on the torture of the mind to lie
In restless ecstasy. Duncan is in his grave;
After life's fitful fever he sleeps well;
Treason has done his worst: nor steel, nor poison,
Malice domestic, foreign levy, nothing,
Can touch him further!

QUEEN. Come on;
Gentle my lord, sleek o'er your rugged looks;
Be bright and jovial among your guests to-night.

K. MACB. So shall I, love; and so, I pray, be you:
Let your remembrance apply to Banquo;
Present him eminence, both with eye and tongue:
Unsafe the while, that we[c]
Must lave our honours in these flattering streams;
And make our faces vizards to our hearts,
Disguising what they are.

QUEEN. You must leave this.

K. MACB. O, full of scorpions is my mind, dear wife!
Thou know'st that Banquo, and his Fleance, lives.

QUEEN. But in them Nature's copy 's[d] not eterne.

[a] —— always thought
That I require a clearness:]
Never forgetting that I must stand clear of all suspicion.

[b] *Whom we, to gain our* place,—] So the second folio; the first reads,—"to gayne our *peace.*"

[c] Unsafe the while, that we—] Steevens conjectured that some words, which originally rendered the sentiment less obscure, had dropped out here.

[d] — Nature's copy's not eterne.] Nature's *lease* or *copy* of their lives is only temporal.

(*) Old text, *scorch'd.*

K. Macb. There's comfort yet; they are assailable;
Then be thou jocund: ere the bat hath flown
His cloister'd flight; ere, to black Hecate's summons,
The shard-borne[a] beetle, with his drowsy hums,
Hath rung night's yawning peal, there shall be done
A deed of dreadful note.

Queen. What 's to be done?

K. Macb. Be innocent of the knowledge, dearest chuck,
Till thou applaud the deed.—Come, seeling night,
Scarf up the tender eye of pitiful day;[b]
And, with thy bloody and invisible hand,
Cancel and tear to pieces that great bond
Which keeps me pale!—Light thickens; and the crow
Makes wing to the rooky wood;
Good things of day begin to droop and drowse;
Whiles night's black agents to their preys do rouse.—
Thou marvell'st at my words: but hold thee still;
Things bad begun make strong themselves by ill:
So, pr'ythee, go with me. [*Exeunt.*

[a] *The* shard-borne *beetle,—*] The *shard-borne* beetle, as Steevens has conclusively shown, is the beetle borne along the air by its *shards* or *scaly wings*.

[b] —— *Come,* seeling *night,*
Scarf up the tender eye of pitiful day;] The expression is derived from falconry. To *seel up* the eyes of a hawk was to sew the upper and under eyelids together; an operation always performed on a newly taken bird, that it might become accustomed to the hood.

SCENE III.—*The same. A Park, with a Gate leading to the Palace.*

Enter three Murderers.

1 Mur. But who did bid thee join with us?

3 Mur. Macbeth.

2 Mur. He needs not our mistrust; since he delivers
Our offices, and what we have to do,
To the direction just.

1 Mur. Then stand with us.
The west yet glimmers with some streaks of day:
Now spurs the lated traveller apace,
To gain the timely inn; and near approaches
The subject of our watch.

3 Mur. Hark! I hear horses.

Ban. [*Without.*] Give us a light there, ho!

2 Mur. Then 't is he; the rest,
That are within the note of expectation,
Already are i' the court.

1 Mur. His horses go about.

3 Mur. Almost a mile: but he does usually,

So all men do, from hence to the palace gate
Make it their walk.
2 MUR. A light, a light!
3 MUR. 'T is he.
1 MUR. Stand to 't.

Enter BANQUO *and* FLEANCE, *the latter with a torch.*

BAN. It will be rain to-night.
1 MUR. Let it come down.
[*Assaults* BANQUO.
BAN. O, treachery!—Fly, good Fleance, fly, fly, fly!
Thou mayst revenge.—O, slave! (1)
[*Dies.* FLEANCE *escapes.*[a]
3 MUR. Who did strike out the light?
1 MUR. Was 't not the way?
3 MUR. There 's but one down; the son is fled.
2 MUR. We have lost best half of our affair.
1 MUR. Well, let 's away, and say how much is done. [*Exeunt.*

SCENE IV.—*The same. A Room of State in the Palace. A Banquet prepared.*

Enter KING MACBETH, QUEEN, ROSS, LENNOX, Lords, *and* Attendants.

K. MACB. You know your own degrees, sit down: at first
And last the hearty welcome.
LORDS. Thanks to your majesty.
K. MACB. Ourself will mingle with society,
And play the humble host.
Our hostess keeps her state;[b] but, in best time,
We will require her welcome.
QUEEN. Pronounce it for me, sir, to all our friends;
For my heart speaks they are welcome.
K. MACB. See, they encounter thee with their hearts' thanks;
Both sides are even: here I 'll sit i' the midst:

Enter First Murderer, *to the door.*

Be large in mirth; anon, we 'll drink a measure
The table round.—There 's blood upon thy face.
MUR. 'T is Banquo's then.
K. MACB. 'T is better thee without than he within.
Is he despatch'd?
MUR. My lord, his throat is cut; that I did for him.
K. MACB. Thou art the best o' the cut-throats: yet he 's good,
That did the like for Fleance: if thou didst it,
Thou art the nonpareil.
MUR. Most royal sir,
Fleance is 'scap'd.
K. MACB. Then comes my fit again: I had else been perfect;
Whole as the marble, founded as the rock;
As broad and general as the casing air:
But now, I am cabin'd, cribb'd, confin'd, bound in
To saucy doubts and fears. But Banquo 's safe?
MUR. Ay, my good lord: safe in a ditch he bides,
With twenty trenched gashes on his head;
The least a death to nature.
K. MACB. Thanks for that:
There the grown serpent lies; the worm, that 's fled,
Hath nature that in time will venom breed;
No teeth for the present.—Get thee gone; to-morrow
We 'll hear ourselves again. [*Exit* Murderer.
QUEEN. My royal lord,
You do not give the cheer; the feast is sold
That is not often vouch'd, while 't is a making,
'T is given with welcome: to feed, were best at home;
From thence the sauce to meat is ceremony,
Meeting were bare without it.
K. MACB. Sweet remembrancer!—
Now, good digestion wait on appetite,
And health on both!
LEN. May 't please your highness sit?
K. MACB. Here had we now our country's honour roof'd,
Were the grac'd person of our Banquo present;
Who may I rather challenge for unkindness
Than pity for mischance!

The Ghost *of* BANQUO *rises, and sits in* MACBETH'S *place.*

ROSS. His absence, sir,
Lays blame upon his promise. Please 't your highness
To grace us with your royal company?

---

[a] FLEANCE *escapes.*] "Fleance, after the assassination of his father, fled into Wales, where, by the daughter of the Prince of that country, he had a son named Walter, who afterwards became Lord High Steward of Scotland, and from thence assumed the name of Walter Steward. From him, in a direct line, King James I. was descended; in compliment to whom our author has chosen to describe Banquo, who was equally concerned with Macbeth in the murder of Duncan, as innocent of that crime."—MALONE.

[b] — *her* state;] A *state* was a seat of dignity; usually surmounted with a canopy.

K. MACB. The table 's full!
LEN. Here is a place reserv'd, sir.
K. MACB. Where?
LEN. Here, my good lord. What is 't that moves your highness?
K. MACB. Which of you have done this?
LORDS. What, my good lord?
K. MACB. Thou canst not say I did it: never shake
Thy gory locks at me.
ROSS. Gentlemen, rise; his highness is not well.
QUEEN. Sit, worthy friends:—my lord is often thus,
And hath been from his youth: pray you, keep seat;
The fit is momentary; upon a thought[a]
He will again be well: if much you note him,
You shall offend him, and extend his passion;
Feed, and regard him not.—Are you a man?
K. MACB. Ay, and a bold one, that dare look on that
Which might appal the devil.
QUEEN. O, proper stuff!
This is the very painting of your fear:
This is the air-drawn dagger which, you said,
Led you to Duncan. O, these flaws and starts,
(Impostors to true fear)[b] would well become
A woman's story at a winter's fire,
Authoris'd by her grandam. Shame itself!
Why do you make such faces? When all 's done,
You look but on a stool.
K. MACB. Pr'ythee, see there! behold! look! lo! how say you?—
Why, what care I? If thou canst nod, speak too.—
If charnel-houses and our graves must send
Those that we bury back, our monuments
Shall be the maws of kites. [Ghost *disappears.*
QUEEN. What! quite unmann'd in folly?
K. MACB. If I stand here, I saw him.
QUEEN. Fie, for shame!
K. MACB. Blood hath been shed ere now, i' the olden time,
Ere human statute purg'd the gentle weal;
Ay, and since too, murders have been perform'd
Too terrible for the ear: the times have been,
That when the brains were out the man would die,
And there an end; but now they rise again,
With twenty mortal murders on their crowns,
And push us from our stools: this is more strange
Than such a murder is.
QUEEN. My worthy lord,
Your noble friends do lack you.
K. MACB. I do forget:—
Do not muse at me, my most worthy friends;
I have a strange infirmity, which is nothing
To those that know me. Come, love and health to all;
Then I 'll sit down.—Give me some wine, fill full:—
I drink to the general joy of the whole table
And to our dear friend Banquo, whom we miss;
Would he were here! to all, and him, we thirst,
And all to all.
LORDS. Our duties, and the pledge.

Ghost *again rises.*

K. MACB. Avaunt! and quit my sight! Let the earth hide thee!
Thy bones are marrowless, thy blood is cold;
Thou hast no speculation in those eyes
Which thou dost glare with!
QUEEN. Think of this, good peers,
But as a thing of custom: 't is no other;
Only it spoils the pleasure of the time.
K. MACB. What man dare, I dare:
Approach thou like the rugged Russian bear,
The arm'd rhinoceros, or the Hyrcan tiger;
Take any shape but that, and my firm nerves
Shall never tremble: or be alive again,
And dare me to the desert with thy sword;
If trembling I inhabit then, protest me
The baby of a girl.[c] Hence, horrible shadow!
Unreal mockery, hence!— [Ghost *disappears.*
Why, so;—being gone,
I am a man again.—Pray you, sit still.
QUEEN. You have displac'd the mirth, broke the good meeting,
With most admir'd disorder.
K. MACB. Can such things be,
And overcome us like a summer's cloud,
Without our special wonder? You make me strange
Even to the disposition that I owe,
When now I think you can behold such sights,
And keep the natural ruby of your cheeks,
When mine are * blanch'd with fear.
ROSS. What sights, my lord?

[a] — upon a thought—] "As speedily as *thought* can be exerted," Steevens says. So, in Henry IV. Pt. I. Act II. Sc. 4, "— and, with a *thought*, seven of the eleven I paid."

[b] (Impostors to true fear)—] Mr. Singer expresses astonishment "that none of the commentators should be aware that this was a form of *elliptic* expression, commonly used even at this day in the phrase, 'this is nothing *to* them,' *i.e.* in *comparison* to them." But both Steevens and Mason have pointed out this sense of the preposition *to* in their notes on the present passage.

(*) Old text, *is*.

[c] The baby of a girl.] Steevens altered the above, which is the old text, to,—"If trembling I *inhibit thee*," but we concur with Henley in thinking that "inhabit" is here used in a neutral sense, and that the original affords a better and more forcible meaning than the alteration,—"Dare me to an encounter in the desert, and if then, trembling, I keep house, proclaim me," &c.

QUEEN. I pray you, speak not; he grows worse and worse;
Question enrages him: at once, good night:—
Stand not upon the order of your going,
But go at once.

LEN. Good night, and better health
Attend his majesty!

QUEEN. A kind good night to all!
[*Exeunt* Lords *and* Attendants.

K. MACB. It will have blood they say! blood will have blood:
Stones have been known to move, and trees to speak;
Augurs, and understood relations,[a] have

[a] *Augurs*, and *understood relations*, &c.] So, unintelligibly, reads the folio. What the poet wrote we cannot doubt was,—

"Augurs *that* understood relations," &c.

which D'Avenant turned to,—

"Augurs well read in Languages of Birds," &c.

By magot-pies, and choughs, and rooks, brought forth
The secret'st man of blood.—What is the night?

QUEEN. Almost at odds with morning, which is which.

K. MACB. How say'st thou, that Macduff denies his person,
At our great bidding?[a]

QUEEN. Did you send to him, sir?

K. MACB. I hear it by the way; but I will send:
There 's not a one of them, but in his house
I keep a servant fee'd. I will to-morrow
(And betimes I will) to the weird sisters:
More shall they speak; for now I am bent to know,
By the worst means, the worst. For mine own good,
All causes shall give way; I am in blood
Stepp'd in so far, that, should I wade no more,
Returning were as tedious as go o'er:
Strange things I have in head, that will to hand;
Which must be acted ere they may be scann'd.

QUEEN. You lack the season[b] of all natures, sleep.

K. MACB. Come, we 'll to sleep. My strange and self-abuse
Is the initiate fear, that wants hard use:—
We are yet but young in deed. [*Exeunt.*

SCENE V.—*The Heath. Thunder.*

Enter HECATE,(2) *meeting the three* WITCHES.

1 WITCH. Why, how now, Hecate? you look angerly.

HEC. Have I not reason, beldams as you are,
Saucy, and over-bold? How did you dare
To trade and traffic with Macbeth,
In riddles and affairs of death;
And I, the mistress of your charms,
The close contriver of all harms,
Was never call'd to bear my part,
Or show the glory of our art?
And, which is worse, all you have done,
Hath been but for a wayward son,
Spiteful and wrathful; who, as others do,
Loves for his own ends, not for you.
But make amends now: get you gone,
And at the pit of Acheron
Meet me i' the morning; thither he
Will come to know his destiny.
Your vessels and your spells provide,
Your charms, and everything beside.
I am for the air; this night I 'll spend
Unto a dismal and a fatal end.
Great business must be wrought ere noon:
Upon the corner of the moon
There hangs a vaporous drop profound;
I 'll catch it ere it come to ground;
And that, distill'd by magic slights,
Shall raise such artificial sprites,
As, by the strength of their illusion,
Shall draw him on to his confusion.
He shall spurn fate, scorn death, and bear
His hopes 'bove wisdom, grace, and fear:
And you all know, security
Is mortals' chiefest enemy.

SONG. [*Without.*] *Come away, come away,* &c.(3)

Hark! I am call'd; my little spirit, see,
Sits in a foggy cloud, and stays for me. [*Exit.*

1 WITCH. Come, let 's make haste; she 'll soon be back again. [*Exeunt.*

SCENE VI.—Forres. *A Room in the Palace.*

Enter LENNOX, *and another* LORD.

LEN. My former speeches have but hit your thoughts,
Which can interpret farther: only, I say,
Things have been strangely borne. The gracious Duncan
Was pitied of Macbeth,—marry, he was dead:—
And the right-valiant Banquo walk'd too late.
Whom, you may say, if 't please you, Fleance kill'd,
For Fleance fled: men must not walk too late;
Who cannot[c] want the thought, how monstrous
It was for Malcolm and for Donalbain
To kill their gracious father? damned fact!
How it did grieve Macbeth! did he not straight,
In pious rage, the two delinquents tear,
That were the slaves of drink and thralls of sleep?
Was not that nobly done? Ay, and wisely too;
For 't would have anger'd any heart alive
To hear the men deny 't. So that, I say,
He has borne all things well: and I do think,
That had he Duncan's sons under his key,
(As, an 't please heaven, he shall not) they should find
What 't were to kill a father; so should Fleance.
But, peace!—for from broad words, and 'cause he fail'd
His presence at the tyrant's feast, I hear,

---

[a] How say'st thou, &c.] This has been interpreted, "What say you to the fact that Macduff refuses to appear upon our summons?"

[b] — the season—] The *preservative.*

[c] *Who* cannot *want the thought,* &c.] The sense obviously requires us to read,—"Who *can want,*" &c. *i.e.* Who *can be without,* &c.; but, as Malone remarks, Shakespeare is sometimes incorrect in these *minutiæ.*

Macduff lives in disgrace: sir, can you tell
Where he bestows himself?
LORD. The son* of Duncan,
From whom this tyrant holds the due of birth,
Lives in the English court; and is receiv'd
Of the most pious Edward with such grace,
That the malevolence of fortune nothing
Takes from his high respect: thither Macduff
Is gone to pray the holy king, upon his aid
To wake Northumberland and warlike Siward:
That, by the help of these, (with Him above
To ratify the work) we may again
Give to our tables meat, sleep to our nights;
Free from our feasts and banquets bloody knives;
Do faithful homage, and receive free honours;—
All which we pine for now: and this report

(*) Old text, *Sonnes.*

Hath so exasperate the* king, that he
Prepares for some attempt of war.
LEN. Sent he to Macduff?
LORD. He did: and with an absolute, *Sir, not I,*
The cloudy messenger turns me his back,
And hums, as who should say, *You'll rue the time*
That clogs me with this answer.
LEN. And that well might
Advise him to a caution, to hold what distance
His wisdom can provide. Some holy angel
Fly to the court of England, and unfold
His message ere he come; that a swift blessing
May soon return to this our suffering country
Under a hand accurs'd!
LORD. I'll send my prayers with him!
[*Exeunt.*

(*) Old text, *their.*

ACT IV.

SCENE I.—*A dark Cave. In the middle, a Caldron boiling. Thunder.*

Enter the three Witches.

1 Witch. Thrice the brinded cat hath mew'd.(1)
2 Witch. Thrice and once, the hedge-pig whin'd.
3 Witch. Harpier cries:—'tis time! 'tis time!
1 Witch. Round about the caldron go;
In the poison'd entrails throw.—

Toad, that under cold stone,[a]
Days and nights has thirty-one;
Swelter'd venom sleeping got,
Boil thou first i' the charmed pot!
ALL. Double, double toil and trouble;
Fire burn, and caldron bubble.
2 WITCH. Fillet of a fenny snake,
In the caldron boil and bake;
Eye of newt, and toe of frog,
Wool of bat, and tongue of dog,
Adder's fork, and blind-worm's sting,
Lizard's leg, and owlet's wing,—
For a charm of powerful trouble,
Like a hell-broth boil and bubble.
ALL. Double, double toil and trouble;
Fire burn, and caldron bubble.
3 WITCH. Scale of dragon; tooth of wolf;
Witches' mummy; maw and gulf[b]
Of the ravin'd salt-sea shark;
Root of hemlock digg'd i' the dark;
Liver of blaspheming Jew;
Gall of goat, and slips of yew
Sliver'd in the moon's eclipse;
Nose of Turk, and Tartar's lips;
Finger of birth-strangled babe
Ditch-deliver'd by a drab,—
Make the gruel thick and slab:
Add thereto a tiger's chaudron,[c]
For the ingredients of our caldron.
ALL. Double, double toil and trouble;
Fire burn, and caldron bubble.
2 WITCH. Cool it with a baboon's blood,
Then the charm is firm and good.

Enter HECATE.[d]

HEC. O, well done! I commend your pains;
And every one shall share i' the gains.
And now about the caldron sing,
Like elves and fairies in a ring,
Enchanting all that you put in.
[*Music and Song*, "Black spirits," *&c.*(2)
[*Exit.*
2 WITCH. By the pricking of my thumbs,
Something wicked this way comes:—
Open, locks,
Whoever knocks!

Enter KING MACBETH.

K. MACB. How now, you secret, black, and midnight hags!
What is't you do?
ALL. A deed without a name.
K. MACB. I conjure you, by that which you profess,
(Howe'er you come to know it) answer me,—
Though you untie the winds, and let them fight
Against the churches; though the yesty waves
Confound and swallow navigation up;
Though bladed[e] corn be lodg'd, and trees blown [down;
Though castles topple on their warders' heads;
Though palaces and pyramids do slope
Their heads to their foundations; though the treasure
Of nature's germins* tumble all together,
Even till destruction sicken,—answer me
To what I ask you.
1 WITCH. Speak.
2 WITCH. Demand.
3 WITCH. We'll answer.
1 WITCH. Say, if thou'dst rather hear it from our mouths,
Or from our masters'?
K. MACB. Call 'em, let me see 'em.
1 WITCH. Pour in sow's blood, that hath eaten
Her nine farrow; grease, that's sweaten
From the murderer's gibbet, throw
Into the flame.
ALL. Come, high or low;
Thyself and office deftly show!

Thunder. An Apparition of an armed Head rises.[f]

K. MACB. Tell me, thou unknown power,—
1 WITCH. He knows thy thought;
Hear his speech, but say thou nought.

---

[a] Toad, that under cold stone,—] The deficiency in this line has been variously supplied. D'Avenant has,—

"*This* Toad *which* under *mossy stone*," &c.

Pope,—

"Toad, that under *the* cold stone," &c.

Steevens,—

"Toad, that under *coldest* stone," &c.

We ought probably to read, with Pope, "*the* cold stone," or "*a* cold stone."

[b] — gulf—] The *throat*, the *swallow*.

[c] — chaudron,—] *Entrails.*

[d] *Enter* HECATE.] The stage direction of the folio is, "Enter Hecat, and the other three Witches," but it is very unlikely that Shakespeare purposed any addition to the original triad. Nothing is more common in our early dramas than upon the entrance of each character on a scene, for the stage direction to recapitulate the personages already there, as if they had entered at the same time with the last comer.

(*) Old text, *Germaine*, corrected by Theobald.

[e] *Though* bladed *corn be lodg'd*, &c.] Mr. Collier's annotator proposes to read, "*bleaded* corn;" and, although the impropriety of the alteration has been clearly shown, Mr. Collier has not hesitated to substitute it for the genuine word. Had he turned to chap. iv. Book I. of "Scot's Discovery of Witchcraft,"—a work the poet was undoubtedly well read in,—he would have found, among other actions imputed to witches, "that they can transferre *corn in the blade* from one place to another." And from the article on *Husbandry* in Comenius, Janua Linguarum, 1673, he might have learned that "As soon as standing corn shoots up to *a blade*, it is in danger of scathe by a tempest."

[f] — *an armed Head*—] "The armed head represents, symbolically, Macbeth's head cut off and brought to Malcolm by Macduff. The bloody child is Macduff, untimely ripped from his mother's womb. The child with a crown on his head and a bough in his hand is the royal Malcolm, who ordered his soldiers to hew them down a bough, and bear it before them to Dunsinane."—UPTON.

APP. Macbeth! Macbeth! Macbeth! beware Macduff;
Beware the thane of Fife.—Dismiss me:—enough.[a] [*Descends.*
K. MACB. Whate'er thou art, for thy good caution, thanks;
Thou hast harp'd my fear aright:—But one word more,—
1 WITCH. He will not be commanded: here's another,
More potent than the first.

Thunder. An Apparition of a bloody Child rises.

APP. Macbeth! Macbeth! Macbeth!
K. MACB. Had I three ears, I'd hear thee.
APP. Be bloody, bold, and resolute; laugh to scorn
The power of man, for none of woman born
Shall harm Macbeth. [*Descends.*
K. MACB. Then live, Macduff: what need I fear of thee?
But yet I'll make assurance double sure,
And take a bond of fate: thou shalt not live;
That I may tell pale-hearted Fear it lies,
And sleep in spite of thunder.—What is this,

Thunder. An Apparition of a Child crowned, with a tree in his hand, rises.

That rises like the issue of a king,
And wears upon his baby brow the round
And top[b] of sovereignty?
ALL. Listen, but speak not to 't.
APP. Be lion-mettled, proud; and take no care
Who chafes, who frets, or where conspirers are:
Macbeth shall never vanquish'd be, until
Great Birnam wood to high Dunsinane[c] hill
Shall come against him. [*Descends.*
K. MACB. That will never be!
Who can impress the forest; bid the tree
Unfix his earth-bound root? Sweet bodements! good!
Rebellious head[d] rise never, till the wood
Of Birnam rise, and our high-plac'd Macbeth
Shall live the lease of nature, pay his breath
To time and mortal custom.—Yet my heart
Throbs to know one thing: tell me (if your art
Can tell so much), shall Banquo's issue ever
Reign in this kingdom?
ALL. Seek to know no more.
K. MACB. I will be satisfied: deny me this,
And an eternal curse fall on you! Let me know:—
Why sinks that caldron? and what noise is this? [*Hautboys.*
1 WITCH. Show!
2 WITCH. Show!
3 WITCH. Show!
ALL. Show his eyes, and grieve his heart;
Come like shadows, so depart!

Eight Kings appear, and pass over in order, the last with a glass in his hand; BANQUO *following.*

K. MACB. Thou art too like the spirit of Banquo; down!
Thy crown does sear mine eye-balls:—and thy hair,
Thou other gold-bound brow, is like the first:—
A third is like the former.—Filthy hags!
Why do you show me this?—A fourth?—Start, eyes!—
What! will the line stretch out to the crack of doom?—
Another yet?—A seventh?—I'll see no more!—
And yet the eighth appears, who bears a glass
Which shows me many more; and some I see
That two-fold balls and treble sceptres carry.
Horrible sight!—Now, I see, 't is true;
For the blood-bolter'd[e] Banquo smiles upon me,
And points at them for his.—What, is this so?
1 WITCH. Ay, sir, all this is so:—but why
Stands Macbeth thus amazedly?—
Come, sisters, cheer we up his sprites,[f]
And show the best of our delights:
I'll charm the air to give a sound,
While you perform your antic round;

[a] Dismiss me:—enough.] See note ([d]), p. 349, Vol. II.

[b] —— *the round*
And top *of sovereignty?*]

Query, "And *type* of sovereignty?" Thus in "Henry VI." Part I. Act I. Sc. 4,—

"Thy father bears the *type* of king of Naples;"

and in "Richard III." Act IV. Sc. 4,—

"The high imperial *type* of this earth's glory."

[c] — to high Dunsinane hill—] The accent of *Dunsinane*, in this instance, is correctly placed; but Shakespeare elsewhere pronounces the word *Dunsināne*. There is authority, however, for both quantities.

[d] *Rebellious* head—] So Theobald; the old text having, "Rebellious *dead*." Mr. Collier's annotator, following Hanmer, has "Rebellion's head," a reading Mr. Dyce declares "is evidently the right one."

[e] — blood-bolter'd—] *Blood-clotted.* The term, according to Malone, is well known in Warwickshire. "When a horse, sheep, or other animal perspires much, and any of the hair or wool, in consequence of such perspiration, or any redundant humour, becomes matted in tufts with grime and sweat, he is said to be *bolter'd;* and whenever the blood issues out and coagulates, forming the locks into hard clotted bunches, the beast is said to be *blood-bolter'd.*"

[f] — sprites,—] The customary pronunciation of *spirits* in Shakespeare's time.

That this great king may kindly say,
Our duties did his welcome pay.
[*Music. The* Witches *dance, and then vanish.*

K. Macb. Where are they? Gone?—Let this pernicious hour
Stand aye accursed in the calendar!—
Come in, without there!

Enter Lennox.

Len. What's your grace's will?
K. Macb. Saw you the weird sisters?
Len. No, my lord.
K. Macb. Came they not by you?
Len. No, indeed, my lord.
K. Macb. Infected be the air whereon they ride;
And damn'd all those that trust them!—I did hear
The galloping of horse: who was't came by?
Len. 'T is two or three, my lord, that bring you word
Macduff is fled to England.
K. Macb. *Fled to England!*
Len. Ay, my good lord.
K. Macb. Time, thou anticipat'st my dread exploits!
The flighty purpose never is o'ertook,
Unless the deed go with it: from this moment,
The very firstlings of my heart shall be
The firstlings of my hand. And even now,
To crown my thoughts with acts,—be it thought and done,—
The castle of Macduff I will surprise;
Seize upon Fife; give to the edge o' the sword
His wife, his babes, and all unfortunate souls
That trace him in his line. No boasting like a fool;
This deed I 'll do before this purpose cool:
But no more sights!—Where are these gentlemen?
Come, bring me where they are. [*Exeunt.*

SCENE II.—Fife. *A Room in* Macduff's *Castle.*

Enter Lady Macduff, *her* Son, *and* Ross.

L. Macd. What had he done, to make him fly the land?
Ross. You must have patience, madam.
L. Macd. He had none;
His flight was madness. When our actions do not,
Our fears do make us traitors.
Ross. You know not
Whether it was his wisdom or his fear.
L. Macd. *Wisdom!* to leave his wife, to leave his babes,
His mansion, and his titles, in a place
From whence himself does fly? He loves us not;
He wants the natural touch: for the poor wren,
The most diminutive of birds, will fight,
Her young ones in her nest, against the owl.
All is the fear, and nothing is the love;
As little is the wisdom, where the flight
So runs against all reason.
Ross. My dearest coz,
I pray you, school yourself: but, for your husband,
He is noble, wise, judicious, and best knows
The fits o' the season. I dare not speak much further:
But cruel are the times, when we are traitors,
And do not know ourselves; when we hold rumour
From what we fear; yet know not what we fear;[a]
But float upon a wild and violent sea,
Each way, and move.—I take my leave of you:
Shall not be long but I'll be here again:
Things at the worst will cease, or else climb upward
To what they were before.—My pretty cousin,
Blessing upon you!
L. Macd. Father'd he is, and yet he's fatherless.
Ross. I am so much a fool, should I stay longer,
It would be my disgrace, and your discomfort:
I take my leave at once. [*Exit.*
L. Macd. Sirrah, your father's dead;
And what will you do now? How will you live?
Son. As birds do, mother.
L. Macd. What, with worms and flies?
Son. With what I get, I mean; and so do they.
L. Macd. Poor bird! thou'dst never fear the net nor lime,
The pit-fall nor the gin.
Son. Why should I, mother? Poor birds they are not set for.
My father is not dead, for all your saying.
L. Macd. Yes, he is dead; how wilt thou do for a father?
Son. Nay, how will you do for a husband?
L. Macd. Why, I can buy me twenty at any market.
Son. Then you'll buy 'em to sell again.
L. Macd. Thou speak'st with all thy wit; and yet, i' faith,
With wit enough for thee.
Son. Was my father a traitor, mother?
L. Macd. Ay, that he was.

---

[a] — yet know not what we fear;] "The times are cruel when we are led by our fears to believe every rumour of danger we hear, yet are not conscious to ourselves of any crime for which we should be disturbed with those fears."—Steevens.

SON. What is a traitor?

L. MACD. Why, one that swears and lies.

SON. And be all traitors that do so?

L. MACD. Every one that does so is a traitor, and must be hanged.

SON. And must they all be hanged that swear and lie?

L. MACD. Every one.

SON. Who must hang them?

L. MACD. Why, the honest men.

SON. Then the liars and swearers are fools; for there are liars and swearers enow to beat the honest men, and hang up them.

L. MACD. Now God help thee, poor monkey! But how wilt thou do for a father?

SON. If he were dead, you'd weep for him: if you would not, it were a good sign that I should quickly have a new father.

L. MACD. Poor prattler! how thou talk'st!

Enter a Messenger.

MESS. Bless you, fair dame! I am not to you known,
Though in your state of honour I am perfect.
I doubt some danger does approach you nearly:
If you will take a homely man's advice,
Be not found here; hence, with your little ones.
To fright you thus, methinks, I am too savage;
To do worse to you were fell cruelty,
Which is too nigh your person. Heaven preserve you!
I dare abide no longer. [*Exit.*

L. MACD. Whither should I fly?
I have done no harm. But I remember now
I am in this earthly world; where to do harm
Is often laudable; to do good, sometime
Accounted dangerous folly: why then, alas!
Do I put up that womanly defence,
To say I have done no harm? What are these faces?

Enter Murderers.

MUR. Where is your husband?

L. MACD. I hope, in no place so unsanctified,
Where such as thou mayst find him.

MUR. He's a traitor.

SON. Thou liest, thou shag-hair'd[a] villain!

MUR. What, you egg! [*Stabbing him.*
Young fry of treachery!

SON. He has kill'd me, mother:
Run away, I pray you. [*Dies.*

[*Exit* LADY MACDUFF, *crying* Murder! *and pursued by the* Murderers.

[a] — shag-hair'd—] The folio has, "shagge-*ear'd*," but *ear'd* is an obvious misprint of the old word *heard*=*hair'd*.

SCENE III.—England. *Before the* King's *Palace.*

Enter MALCOLM *and* MACDUFF.

MAL. Let us seek out some desolate shade, and there
Weep our sad bosoms empty.
MACD. Let us rather
Hold fast the mortal sword; and, like good men,
Bestride our down-fall'n* birthdom. Each new morn,
New widows howl; new orphans cry; new sorrows
Strike heaven on the face, that it resounds
As if it felt with Scotland, and yell'd out
Like syllable of dolour.
MAL. What I believe, I'll wail;
What know, believe; and what I can redress,
As I shall find the time to friend,[a] I will.
What you have spoke, it may be so, perchance.
This tyrant, whose sole name blisters our tongues,
Was once thought honest: you have lov'd him well;
He hath not touch'd you yet. I am young, but something
You may deserve[b] of him through me; and wisdom[c]
To offer up a weak, poor, innocent lamb,
To appease an angry god.
MACD. I am not treacherous.
MAL. But Macbeth is.
A good and virtuous nature may recoil
In an imperial charge. But I shall crave your pardon;
That which you are my thoughts cannot transpose:
Angels are bright still, though the brightest fell:
Though all things foul would wear the brows of grace,
Yet grace must still look so.
MACD. I have lost my hopes.
MAL. Perchance even there where I did find my doubts.
Why in that rawness left you wife and child,
(Those precious motives, those strong knots of love)
Without leave-taking?—I pray you,
Let not my jealousies be your dishonours,
But mine own safeties:—you may be rightly just,
Whatever I shall think.
MACD. Bleed, bleed, poor country!
Great tyranny, lay thou thy basis sure,
For goodness dare not check thee! wear thou thy wrongs,
The title is affeer'd![d]—Fare thee well, lord:
I would not be the villain that thou think'st
For the whole space that's in the tyrant's grasp,
And the rich East to boot.
MAL. Be not offended:
I speak not as in absolute fear of you.
I think our country sinks beneath the yoke;
It weeps, it bleeds: and each new day a gash
Is added to her wounds: I think, withal,
There would be hands uplifted in my right;
And here, from gracious England, have I offer
Of goodly thousands: but, for all this,
When I shall tread upon the tyrant's head,
Or wear it on my sword, yet my poor country
Shall have more vices than it had before;
More suffer, and more sundry ways than ever,
By him that shall succeed.
MACD. What should he be?
MAL. It is myself I mean: in whom I know
All the particulars of vice so grafted,
That, when they shall be open'd, black Macbeth
Will seem as pure as snow; and the poor state
Esteem him as a lamb, being compar'd
With my confineless harms.
MACD. Not in the legions
Of horrid hell, can come a devil more damn'd
In evils to top Macbeth!
MAL. I grant him bloody,
Luxurious, avaricious, false, deceitful,
Sudden,[e] malicious, smacking of every sin
That has a name: but there's no bottom, none,
In my voluptuousness: your wives, your daughters,
Your matrons, and your maids, could not fill up
The cistern of my lust; and my desire
All continent impediments would o'erbear,
That did oppose my will. Better Macbeth,
Than such an one to reign.
MACD. Boundless intemperance

(*) Old text, *downfall.*

[a] *As I shall find the time* to friend,—] The expression "to friend," meaning *propitious, assistant, favourable,* &c. occurs again in "Cymbeline," Act I. Sc. 4,—"Had I admittance and opportunity *to friend;*" and in "Julius Cæsar," Act III. Sc. 1,—"I know that we shall have him well *to friend.*" It is not uncommon in our old poets. Thus, in Spenser, "Faerie Queen," Book I. c. 1, Stanza xxviii.:—

"So forward on his way (with God *to frend*)
He passed forth;"

and also in Massinger's play of "The Roman Actor," Act I. Sc. 1,—

"—— with this assurance,
That the state, sick in him, the gods *to friend,*
Though at the worst will now begin to mend."

[b] *You may* deserve *of him through me;*] Theobald's correction, the old text having,—

"You may discerne," &c.

[c] — and wisdom—] One more of the innumerable passages in this great play which have suffered by mutilation or corruption. We ought, perhaps, to read,—

"—— and wisdom *'t is*
To offer," &c.

or,—

"—— and wisdom *bids*
To offer," &c.

[d] *The title is* affeer'd!—] To *affeer*—a legal term—signifies to *assess* or *confirm;* and the meaning of the passage may, therefore, be, "Great tyranny, be firmly seated now, since goodness dare not curb thee! Wear openly thy ill-got acquisitions, for the title to them is approved!"

[e] Sudden,—] *Impetuous, violent.*

In nature is a tyranny; it hath been
The untimely emptying of the happy throne,
And fall of many kings. But fear not yet
To take upon you what is yours: you may
Convey[a] your pleasures in a spacious plenty,
And yet seem cold, the time you may so hoodwink.
We have willing dames enough; there cannot be
That vulture in you, to devour so many
As will to greatness dedicate themselves
Finding it so inclin'd.

MAL. With this, there grows,
In my most ill-compos'd affection, such
A stanchless avarice, that, were I king,
I should cut off the nobles for their lands;
Desire his jewels, and this other's house:
And my more-having would be as a sauce
To make me hunger more; that I should forge
Quarrels unjust against the good and loyal,
Destroying them for wealth.

MACD. This avarice
Sticks deeper; grows with more pernicious root
Than summer-seeming[b] lust; and it hath been
The sword of our slain kings: yet do not fear;
Scotland hath foisons to fill up your will,
Of your mere own. All these are portable,
With other graces weigh'd.

MAL. But I have none: the king-becoming graces,
As justice, verity, temperance, stableness,
Bounty, persévérance, mercy, lowliness,
Devotion, patience, courage, fortitude,
I have no relish of them; but abound
In the division of each several crime,
Acting it many ways. Nay, had I power, I should
Pour[c] the sweet milk of concord into hell,
Uproar the universal peace, confound
All unity on earth.

MACD. O, Scotland! Scotland!

MAL. If such a one be fit to govern, speak:
I am as I have spoken.

MACD. *Fit to govern!*
No, not to live.—O, nation miserable!
With an untitled tyrant bloody-sceptred,
When shalt thou see thy wholesome days again,
Since that the truest issue of thy throne
By his own interdiction stands accurs'd,
And does blaspheme his breed?—Thy royal father
Was a most sainted king: the queen that bore thee,—
Oft'ner upon her knees than on her feet,—
Died every day she liv'd. Fare thee well!
These evils thou repeat'st upon thyself
Have banish'd me from Scotland.—O, my breast,
Thy hope ends here!

MAL. Macduff, this noble passion,
Child of integrity, hath from my soul
Wip'd the black scruples, reconcil'd my thoughts
To thy good truth and honour. Devilish Macbeth
By many of these trains hath sought to win me
Into his power; and modest wisdom plucks me
From over-credulous haste: but God above
Deal between thee and me! for even now
I put myself to thy direction, and
Unspeak mine own detraction; here abjure
The taints and blames I laid upon myself,
For strangers to my nature. I am yet
Unknown to woman; never was forsworn;
Scarcely have coveted what was mine own;
At no time broke my faith: would not betray
The devil to his fellow; and delight
No less in truth than life: my first false speaking
Was this upon myself.—What I am truly,
Is thine, and my poor country's, to command:
Whither, indeed, before thy here-approach,
Old Siward, with ten thousand warlike men,
Already at a point, was setting forth;
Now we'll together: and the chance of goodness
Belike[d] our warranted quarrel! Why are you silent?

MACD. Such welcome and unwelcome things at once,
'Tis hard to reconcile.(3)

Enter a Doctor.

MAL. Well; more anon.—Comes the king forth, I pray you?

DOCT. Ay, sir; there are a crew of wretched souls
That stay his cure: their malady convinces[e]

---

a " —— *you may*
Convey *your pleasures in a spacious plenty,*—]

For "convey," signifying to manage any thing by stealth, an admirably appropriate word here, Mr. Collier substitutes the comparatively inexpressive one *enjoy*, and styles it an "important change"! That Mr. Collier should be unacquainted with the following quotation, where "convey" occurs in precisely the same sense as Shakespeare uses it above, is pardonable,—"But verily, verily, though the adulterer do never so closely and cunningly *convey* his sin under a canopy, yet," &c.—*The Plain Man's Pathway to Heaven*, 1599:—but how comes he to have forgotten that the word is found in the corresponding passage of "The History of Makbeth," which he himself edited? Macduff there says, in reply to Malcolm's confession of immoderate sensuality, "Make thy selfe king, and I shall *conveie* the matter so wiselie, that thou shalt be so satisfied at thy pleasure in such secret wise, that no man shall be aware thereof."

b —summer-seeming lust;] Warburton proposed to read, "summer-*teeming*;" Blackstone, "summer-*seeding*;" while Steevens conjectured that "summer-seeming" might be right, and signify lust that seems as hot as summer. As Malone has quoted from Donne's Poems "winter-seeming," we are unwilling to disturb the old text, though we have a strong persuasion that the poet wrote, "summer-*seaming* lust," *i. e.* lust *fattened* by summer heat.

c Pour *the sweet milk of concord into hell,*—] By "hell," may be meant *confusion, anarchy, disorder*, and if so, we ought possibly to read, "*Sour* the sweet milk," &c.

d —— *and the chance of goodness*
Belike *our warranted quarrel!*]

This passage has been inexplicable heretofore from "Belike" being always printed as two words, *Be like*. The meaning is,—And the fortune of goodness *approve* or *favour* our justifiable quarrel.

e — convinces —] To *convince*, as we have seen before, signified to *vanquish*, to *overcome*.

The great assay of art; but, at his touch,
Such sanctity hath heaven given his hand,
They presently amend.
Mal. I thank you, doctor. [*Exit* Doctor.
Macd. What's the disease he means?
Mal. 'T is call'd the evil;
A most miraculous work in this good king;
Which often, since my here-remain in England,
I have seen him do. How he solicits heaven,
Himself best knows: but strangely-visited people,
All swoln and ulcerous, pitiful to the eye,
The mere despair of surgery, he cures;
Hanging a golden stamp about their necks,
Put on with holy prayers: and 'tis spoken,
To the succeeding royalty he leaves
The healing benediction. With this strange virtue,
He hath a heavenly gift of prophecy;
And sundry blessings hang about his throne,
That speak him full of grace.
Macd. See, who comes here?
Mal. My countryman; but yet I know him not.

Enter Ross.

Macd. My ever-gentle cousin, welcome hither.
Mal. I know him now:—good God, betimes remove
The means[a] that makes us strangers!
Ross. Sir, Amen.
Macd. Stands Scotland where it did?
Ross. Alas, poor country,—
Almost afraid to know itself! It cannot
Be call'd our mother, but our grave: where nothing,
But who knows nothing, is once seen to smile;
Where sighs, and groans, and shrieks that rent the air,
Are made, not mark'd; where violent sorrow seems
A modern ecstasy;[b] the dead man's knell
Is there scarce ask'd for who; and good men's lives
Expire before the flowers in their caps,
Dying or ere they sicken.
Macd. O, relation
Too nice, and yet too true!
Mal. What's the newest grief?
Ross. That of an hour's age doth hiss the speaker;
Each minute teems a new one.
Macd. How does my wife?
Ross. Why, well.
Macd. And all my children?
Ross. Well too.
Macd. The tyrant has not batter'd at their peace?
Ross. No; they were well at peace when I did leave 'em.

[a] *The* means—] Used perhaps as *moans*, for *woes*, *troubles*, &c. See note (b), p. 423, Vol. I.

[b] A modern ecstasy;] An ordinary excitation.

MACD. Be not a niggard of your speech; how goes 't?

ROSS. When I came hither to transport the tidings,
Which I have heavily borne, there ran a rumour
Of many worthy fellows that were out;
Which was to my belief witness'd [a] the rather,
For that I saw the tyrant's power a-foot:
Now is the time of help; your eye in Scotland
Would create soldiers, make our women fight,
To doff their dire distresses.

MAL. Be 't their comfort
We are coming thither: gracious England hath
Lent us good Siward and ten thousand men;
An older and a better soldier none
That Christendom gives out.

ROSS. Would I could answer
This comfort with the like! But I have words
That would be howl'd out in the desert air,
Where hearing should not latch [b] them.

MACD. What concern they?
The general cause? or is it a fee-grief,
Due to some single breast?

ROSS. No mind that's honest
But in it shares some woe; though the main part
Pertains to you alone.

MACD. If it be mine,
Keep it not from me, quickly let me have it.

ROSS. Let not your ears despise my tongue for ever,
Which shall possess them with the heaviest sound
That ever yet they heard.

MACD. Hum! I guess at it.

ROSS. Your castle is surpris'd; your wife and babes
Savagely slaughter'd: to relate the manner,
Were, on the quarry of these murder'd deer,
To add the death of you.

MAL. Merciful heaven!—
What, man! ne'er pull your hat upon your brows;
Give sorrow words: the grief that does not speak
Whispers the o'erfraught heart, and bids it break.

MACD. My children too?

ROSS. Wife, children, servants, all that could be found.

MACD. And I must be from thence! My wife kill'd too?

ROSS. I have said.

MAL. Be comforted:
Let's make us med'cines of our great revenge,
To cure this deadly grief.

MACD. He has no children.—All my pretty ones?
Did you say, all?—O, hell-kite!—All?
What, all my pretty chickens and their dam
At one fell swoop?

MAL. Dispute it like a man.

MACD. I shall do so;
But I must also feel it as a man:
I cannot but remember such things were,
That were most precious to me.—Did heaven look on,
And would not take their part? Sinful Macduff,
They were all struck for thee! naught that I am,
Not for their own demerits, but for mine,
Fell slaughter on their souls. Heaven rest them now!

MAL. Be this the whetstone of your sword: let grief,
Convert to anger, blunt not the heart, enrage it.

MACD. O, I could play the woman with mine eyes,
And braggart with my tongue!—But, gentle heavens,
Cut short all intermission; front to front
Bring thou this fiend of Scotland and myself;
Within my sword's length set him; if he 'scape,
Heaven forgive him too!

MAL. This tune [c] goes manly.
Come, go we to the king; our power is ready;
Our lack is nothing but our leave: Macbeth
Is ripe for shaking, and the powers above
Put on their instruments.[d] Receive what cheer you may;
The night is long that never finds the day!

[*Exeunt.*

---

[a] — to my belief witness'd—] Evidenced to my belief.

[b] — latch—] To *latch* is a provincial word, signifying the same as to *catch*.

[c] *This* tune *goes manly.*] The old text has, "time;" but though *time* and *tune*, in their musical acceptation, were often used indifferently, few will have the hardihood to dispute the fitness of Rowe's correction here.

[d] Put on their instruments.] *Incite, stir up* their instruments against the king.

ACT V.

SCENE I.—Dunsinane. *A Room in the Castle.*

Enter a Doctor *of Physic and a waiting* Gentlewoman.

DOCT. I have two nights watched with you, but can perceive no truth in your report. When was it she last walked?

GENT. Since his majesty went into the field, I have seen her rise from her bed, throw her night-gown upon her, unlock her closet, take forth paper, fold it, write upon it, read it, afterwards seal it, and again return to bed; yet all this while in a most fast sleep.

DOCT. A great perturbation in nature,—to receive at once the benefit of sleep, and do the effects of watching!—In this slumbery agitation, besides her walking and other actual performances, what, at any time, have you heard her say?

GENT. That, sir, which I will not report after her.

DOCT. You may to me; and 't is most meet you should.

GENT. Neither to you nor any one; having no witness to confirm my speech. Lo you! here she comes.

Enter QUEEN, *with a taper.*

This is her very guise; and, upon my life, fast asleep. Observe her: stand close.

DOCT. How came she by that light?

GENT. Why, it stood by her: she has light by her continually; 't is her command.

DOCT. You see, her eyes are open.

GENT. Ay, but their sense is* shut.

DOCT. What is it she does now? Look, how she rubs her hands.

GENT. It is an accustomed action with her, to seem thus washing her hands: I have known her continue in this a quarter of an hour.

QUEEN. Yet here 's a spot.

DOCT. Hark! she speaks: I will set down what comes from her, to satisfy my remembrance the more strongly.

QUEEN. Out, damned spot! out, I say!—One, two; why, then 't is time to do 't:—Hell is murky!—Fie, my lord, fie! a soldier, and afeard? What need we fear who knows it, when none can call our power to account?—Yet who would have thought the old man to have had so much blood in him?

DOCT. Do you mark that?

QUEEN. The thane of Fife had a wife; where is she now?—What, will these hands ne'er be clean?—No more o' that, my lord, no more o' that: you mar all with this starting.

DOCT. Go to, go to; you have known what you should not.

GENT. She has spoke what she should not, I am sure of that: heaven knows what she has known.

QUEEN. Here's the smell of the blood still: all the perfumes of Arabia will not sweeten this little hand. Oh! oh! oh!

DOCT. What a sigh is there! The heart is sorely charged.

GENT. I would not have such a heart in my bosom, for the dignity of the whole body.

DOCT. Well, well, well,—

GENT. Pray God it be, sir.

DOCT. This disease is beyond my practice: yet I have known those which have walked in their sleep who have died holily in their beds.

QUEEN. Wash your hands, put on your night-gown; look not so pale:—I tell you yet again, Banquo's buried; he cannot come out on's grave.

DOCT. Even so?

QUEEN. To bed, to bed; there's knocking at the gate. Come, come, come, come, give me your hand: what's done cannot be undone. To bed, to bed, to bed. [*Exit.*

DOCT. Will she go now to bed?

GENT. Directly.

DOCT. Foul whisperings are abroad: unnatural deeds
Do breed unnatural troubles: infected minds
To their deaf pillows will discharge their secrets.
More needs she the divine than the physician:—
God, God[a] forgive us all!—Look after her;
Remove from her the means of all annoyance,
And still keep eyes upon her:—so, good night:
My mind she has mated, and amaz'd my sight:
I think, but dare not speak.

GENT. Good night, good doctor. [*Exeunt.*

SCENE II.—*The Country near* Dunsinane.

Enter, with drum and colours, MENTEITH, CAITHNESS, ANGUS, LENNOX, *and* Soldiers.

MENT. The English power is near, led on by Malcolm,
His uncle Siward, and the good Macduff:
Revenges burn in them: for their dear causes
Would, to the bleeding, and the grim alarm,
Excite the mortified[b] man.

ANG. Near Birnam wood
Shall we well meet them; that way are they coming.

CAITH. Who knows if Donalbain be with his brother?

LEN. For certain, sir, he is not: I have a file
Of all the gentry: there is Siward's son,
And many unrough youths, that even now
Protest their first of manhood.

MENT. What does the tyrant?

(*) Old text, *are*.

a God, *God forgive us all!*] A misprint, probably, for "Good God," &c.

b — *the* mortified *man.*] The *ascetic*, the *anchorite*.

CAITH. Great Dunsinane he strongly fortifies:
Some say he's mad; others, that lesser hate him,
Do call it valiant fury: but, for certain,
He cannot buckle his distemper'd cause [a]
Within the belt of rule.
ANG. Now does he feel
His secret murders sticking on his hands;
Now minutely revolts upbraid his faith-breach;
Those he commands move only in command,
Nothing in love: now does he feel his title
Hang loose about him, like a giant's robe
Upon a dwarfish thief.
MENT. Who, then, shall blame
His pester'd senses to recoil and start,
When all that is within him does condemn
Itself for being there?
CAITH. Well, march we on,
To give obedience where 't is truly ow'd:
Meet we the med'cine [b] of the sickly weal;
And with him pour we, in our country's purge,
Each drop of us.
LEN. Or so much as it needs,
To dew the sovereign flower, and drown the weeds.
Make we our march towards Birnam.
[*Exeunt, marching.*

SCENE III.—Dunsinane. *A Room in the Castle.*

Enter KING MACBETH, Doctor, *and* Attendants.

K. MACB. Bring me no more reports;—let them fly all:
Till Birnam wood remove to Dunsinane,
I cannot taint with fear. What 's the boy Malcolm?
Was he not born of woman? The spirits that know
All mortal consequences have pronounc'd me thus,—
Fear not, Macbeth; no man that 's born of woman
Shall e'er have power upon thee. Then fly, false thanes,
And mingle with the English epicures:
The mind I sway by, and the heart I bear,
Shall never sag [c] with doubt nor shake with fear.—

Enter a Servant.

The devil damn thee black, thou cream-fac'd loon!
Where gott'st thou that goose look?
SERV. There is ten thousand—
K. MACB. Geese, villain?
SERV. Soldiers, sir.
K. MACB. Go, prick thy face, and over-red thy fear,
Thou lily-liver'd boy. What soldiers, patch? [d]
Death of thy soul! those linen cheeks of thine
Are counsellors to fear. What soldiers, whey-face?
SERV. The English force, so please you.
K. MACB. Take thy face hence.—
[*Exit* Servant.
Seyton!—I am sick at heart,
When I behold—Seyton, I say!—This push
Will chair [e] me ever, or dis-seat me now.
I have liv'd long enough: my way [f] of life
Is fallen into the sear, the yellow leaf;
And that which should accompany old age,
As honour, love, obedience, troops of friends,
I must not look to have; but in their stead,
Curses not loud, but deep, mouth-honour, breath,
Which the poor heart would fain deny, and dare not.—
Seyton!—

Enter SEYTON.

SEY. What is your gracious pleasure?
K. MACB. What news more?
SEY. All is confirm'd, my lord, which was reported.
K. MACB. I'll fight, till from my bones my flesh be hack'd.—
Give me my armour.
SEY. 'T is not needed yet.
K. MACB. I'll put it on.—
Send out more horses, skirr the country round;
Hang those that talk of fear.—Give me mine armour.—
How does your patient, doctor?
DOCT. Not so sick, my lord,
As she is troubled with thick-coming fancies,
That keep her from her rest.
K. MACB. Cure her of that:

[a] *He cannot buckle his distemper'd cause—*] The late Mr. S. Walker proposed *course* for "cause," but surely change may be dispensed with here.
[b] — the med'cine—] The *physician.*
[c] — sag—] *Droop, flag.*
[d] — patch?] *Fool.* See note (d), p. 372, Vol. I.
[e] *Will* chair *me ever, or dis-seat me now.*] "Chair" is an emendation due to Dr. Percy, the old text having "cheer."
[f] — way *of life—*] The arguments for and against Johnson's proposal to read "*May* of life," extend over four pages of the *Variorum* edition. It is unnecessary now to repeat them: most readers have learnt from Capell or Gifford that "way of life," the *cursus vitæ* of the Romans, is "a simple periphrasis for *life.*" Those who are unacquainted with the latter's excellent note upon this phrase, should refer to it:—Massinger's Works, Vol. IV. p. 309, ed. 1813. See also Florio's "World of Wordes," 1611, *in voce* "Guado," which "resolute John" explains to mean, among other things, "the *way*, *course*, or *race* of *man's life.*"

Canst thou not minister to a mind diseas'd;
Pluck from the memory a rooted sorrow;
Raze out the written troubles of the brain;
And, with some sweet oblivious antidote,
Cleanse the stuff'd bosom of that perilous stuff [a]
Which weighs upon the heart?

DOCT. Therein the patient
Must minister to himself.

K. MACB. Throw physic to the dogs,—I'll none of it.—
Come, put mine armour on; give me my staff:—
Seyton, send out.—Doctor, the thanes fly from me.—
Come, sir, dispatch.—If thou couldst, doctor, cast
The water of my land, find her disease,
And purge it to a sound and pristine health,
I would applaud thee to the very echo,
That should applaud again.—Pull 't off, I say.—
What rhubarb, senna,* or what purgative drug,
Would scour these English hence?—Hear'st thou of them?

DOCT. Ay, my good lord; your royal preparation
Makes us hear something.

K. MACB. Bring it after me.—
I will not be afraid of death and bane,
Till Birnam forest come to Dunsinane.
[*Exeunt all except the* Doctor.

DOCT. Were I from Dunsinane away and clear,
Profit again should hardly draw me here. [*Exit.*

SCENE IV.—*Country near* Dunsinane: *a Wood in view.*

Enter, with drum and colours, MALCOLM, *old* SIWARD *and his* Son, MACDUFF, MENTEITH, CAITHNESS, ANGUS, LENNOX, ROSS, *and* Soldiers, *marching.*

MAL. Cousins, I hope the days are near at hand,
That chambers will be safe.

MENT. We doubt it nothing.

SIW. What wood is this before us?

MENT. The wood of Birnam.

MAL. Let every soldier hew him down a bough,
And bear't before him; thereby shall we shadow
The numbers of our host, and make discovery
Err in report of us.

SOLD. It shall be done.

SIW. We learn no other, but the confident tyrant
Keeps still in Dunsinane, and will endure
Our setting down before 't.(1)

MAL. 'T is his main hope:
For where there is advantage to be given,[b]
Both more and less have given him the revolt;
And none serve with him but constrained things,
Whose hearts are absent too.

MACD. Let our just censures
Attend the true event, and put we on
Industrious soldiership.

SIW. The time approaches,
That will with due decision make us know
What we shall say we have, and what we owe.
Thoughts speculative their unsure hopes relate;
But certain issue strokes must arbitrate:
Towards which advance the war.
[*Exeunt, marching.*

SCENE V.—Dunsinane. *Within the Castle.*

Enter, with drum and colours, KING MACBETH, SEYTON, *and* Soldiers.

K. MACB. Hang out our banners on the outward walls;
The cry is still, *They come.* Our castle's strength
Will laugh a siege to scorn: here let them lie
Till famine and the ague eat them up.
Were they not forc'd[c] with those that should be ours,
We might have met them dareful, beard to beard,
And beat them backward home.
[*A cry of women within.*
What is that noise?

SEY. It is the cry of women, my good lord.
[*Exit.*

K. MACB. I have almost forgot the taste of fears:
The time has been, my senses would have cool'd
To hear a night-shriek; and my fell of hair
Would at a dismal treatise rouse and stir
As life were in't: I have supp'd full with horrors;

(*) Old text, *Cyme.*

a *Cleanse the* stuff'd *bosom of that* perilous stuff—] To avoid the disagreeable recurrence of the word "stuff," Steevens was led to read, "*foul* bosom," and he adduced in support of his emendation the line in "As You Like It," Act II. Sc. 6,—

"Cleanse the *foul* body of the infected world."

Notwithstanding Malone's defence of the repetition, we are strongly inclined to believe with Steevens that the line originally stood as he presents it, or thus,—

"Cleanse the *clogg'd* bosom of that perilous stuff," &c.; or,—

"Cleanse the stuff'd bosom of that perilous *load,*" &c.

b *For where there is advantage to be* given,
Both more and less have given him the revolt;]

Given, in the first line, is indubitably wrong, and was probably caught up by the compositor from the line which follows. Johnson suggested, "—advantage to be *gone;*" &c. Steevens, "—advantage to be *got,*" &c.; and Mr. Singer, "—advantage to be *gain'd,*" &c.

c —forc'd—] *Strengthened.* Mr. Collier's annotator reads, *farc'd!*

Direness, familiar to my slaughterous thoughts,
Cannot once start me.

Re-enter SEYTON.

Wherefore was that cry?

SEY. The queen, my lord, is dead.

K. MACB. She should have died hereafter;
There would have been a time for such a word.—
To-morrow, and to-morrow, and to-morrow,
Creeps in this petty pace from day to day,
To the last syllable of recorded time;
And all our yesterdays have lighted fools
The way to dusty death. Out, out, brief candle!
Life's but a walking shadow; a poor player,
That struts and frets his hour upon the stage,
And then is heard no more: it is a tale
Told by an idiot, full of sound and fury,
Signifying nothing.—

Enter a Messenger.

Thou com'st to use thy tongue; thy story quickly.

MESS. Gracious my lord,
I should report that which I say I saw,
But know not how to do it.

K. MACB. Well, say, sir.

MESS. As I did stand my watch upon the hill,
I look'd toward Birnam, and anon, methought
The wood began to move.

K. MACB. Liar, and slave!

MESS. Let me endure your wrath, if 't be not so:
Within this three mile may you see it coming;
I say, a moving grove.

K. MACB. If thou speak'st false,
Upon the next tree shalt thou hang alive,
Till famine cling[a] thee: if thy speech be sooth,
I care not if thou dost for me as much.—
I pull in resolution; and begin
To doubt the equivocation of the fiend,
That lies like truth: *Fear not, till Birnam wood
Do come to Dunsinane;*—and now a wood
Comes toward Dunsinane!—Arm, arm, and out!—
If this which he avouches does appear,
There is nor flying hence nor tarrying here.
I 'gin to be a-weary of the sun,
And wish the estate o' the world were now undone.—
Ring the alarum-bell!—Blow, wind! come, wrack!
At least we'll die with harness on our back.

[*Exeunt.*

SCENE VI.—*The same. A Plain before the Castle.*

Enter, with drum and colours, MALCOLM, *old* SIWARD, MACDUFF, *&c., and their* Army *with boughs.*

MAL. Now, near enough, your leafy screens throw down,

---

[a] *Till famine* cling *thee:*] To *cling* is a north-country word, and means to *starve*, to *shrivel*, to *shrink*.

And show like those you are.—You, worthy uncle,
Shall, with my cousin, your right-noble son,
Lead our first battle: worthy Macduff and we
Shall take upon 's what else remains to do,
According to our order.

SIW. Fare you well.—
Do we but find the tyrant's power to-night,
Let us be beaten, if we cannot fight.

MACD. Make all our trumpets speak; give them all breath,
Those clamorous harbingers of blood and death.
[*Exeunt. Alarums.*

SCENE VII.—*The same. Another part of the Plain.*

Enter KING MACBETH.

K. MACB. They have tied me to a stake; I cannot fly,
But, bear-like, I must fight the course.—What 's he
That was not born of woman? Such a one
Am I to fear, or none.

Enter young SIWARD.

YO. SIW. What is thy name?

K. MACB. Thou 'lt be afraid to hear it.

YO. SIW. No; though thou call'st thyself a hotter name
Than any is in hell.

K. MACB. My name 's Macbeth.

YO. SIW. The devil himself could not pronounce a title
More hateful to mine ear.

K. MACB. No, nor more fearful.

YO. SIW. Thou liest, abhorred tyrant! with my sword
I'll prove the lie thou speak'st.
[*They fight, and young* SIWARD *is slain.*

K. MACB. Thou wast born of woman.—
But swords I smile at, weapons laugh to scorn,
Brandish'd by man that 's of a woman born.
[*Exit.*

Alarums. Enter MACDUFF.

MACD. That way the noise is.—Tyrant, show thy face!
If thou be'st slain and with no stroke of mine,
My wife and children's ghosts will haunt me still.
I cannot strike at wretched kernes whose arms
Are hir'd to bear their staves: either thou, Macbeth,
Or else my sword, with an unbatter'd edge,
I sheathe again undeeded. There thou shouldst be;
By this great clatter, one of greatest note
Seems bruited.—Let me find him, Fortune!
And more I beg not. [*Exit. Alarums.*

Enter MALCOLM *and old* SIWARD.

SIW. This way, my lord;—the castle 's gently render'd:
The tyrant's people on both sides do fight;
The noble thanes do bravely in the war;
The day almost itself professes yours,
And little is to do.

MAL. We have met with foes
That strike beside us.

SIW. Enter, sir, the castle.
[*Exeunt. Alarums.*

SCENE VIII.—*The same. Another part of the Plain.*

Enter KING MACBETH.

K. MACB. Why should I play the Roman fool, and die
On mine own sword? whiles I see lives, the gashes
Do better upon them.

Enter MACDUFF.

MACD. Turn, hell-hound, turn!

K. MACB. Of all men else I have avoided thee:
But get thee back; my soul is too much charg'd
With blood of thine already.

MACD. I have no words,—
My voice is in my sword; thou bloodier villain
Than terms can give thee out! [*They fight.*

K. MACB. Thou losest labour:
As easy mayst thou the intrenchant air
With thy keen sword impress, as make me bleed:
Let fall thy blade on vulnerable crests;
I bear a charmed life, which must not yield
To one of woman born.

MACD. Despair thy charm;
And let the angel whom thou still hast serv'd
Tell thee, Macduff was from his mother's womb
Untimely ripp'd.

K. MACB. Accursed be that tongue that tells me so,
For it hath cow'd my better part (2) of man!
And be these juggling fiends no more believ'd,
That palter with us in a double sense;
That keep the word of promise to our ear,
And break it to our hope!—I 'll not fight with thee.

MACD. Then yield thee, coward,
And live to be the show and gaze o' the time.
We 'll have thee, as our rarer monsters are,
Painted upon a pole; and underwrit,
Here may you see the tyrant.

K. MACB. I will not yield,
To kiss the ground before young Malcolm's feet,
And to be baited with the rabble's curse.
Though Birnam wood be come to Dunsinane,
And thou oppos'd, being of no woman born,
Yet I will try the last:—before my body
I throw my warlike shield: lay on, Macduff;
And damn'd be him that first cries, *Hold, enough!*
[*Exeunt, fighting.*

Retreat. Flourish. Enter, with drum and colours, MALCOLM, *old* SIWARD, ROSS, LENNOX, ANGUS, CAITHNESS, MENTEITH, *and* Soldiers.

MAL. I would the friends we miss were safe arriv'd.

SIW. Some must go off; and yet, by these I see,
So great a day as this is cheaply bought.

MAL. Macduff is missing, and your noble son.

ROSS. Your son, my lord, has paid a soldier's debt;
He only liv'd but till he was a man;
The which no sooner had his prowess confirm'd
In the unshrinking station where he fought,
But like a man he died.

SIW. Then he is dead?

ROSS. Ay, and brought off the field: your cause of sorrow
Must not be measur'd by his worth, for then
It hath no end.

SIW. Had he his hurts before?

ROSS. Ay, on the front.

SIW. Why, then, God's soldier be he!
Had I as many sons as I have hairs,
I would not wish them to a fairer death:
And so, his knell is knoll'd.

MAL. He 's worth more sorrow,
And that I 'll spend for him.

SIW. He 's worth no more:
They say he parted well, and paid his score:
And so, God be with him!—Here comes newer comfort.

Re-enter MACDUFF, *with* KING MACBETH'*s head.*(3)

MACD. Hail, king! for so thou art: behold, where stands
The usurper's cursed head: the time is free!
I see thee compass'd with thy kingdom's pearl,
That speak my salutation in their minds;

Whose voices I desire aloud with mine,—
Hail, king of Scotland!

ALL. Hail, king of Scotland! [*Flourish.*

MAL. We shall not spend a large expense of time
Before we reckon with your several loves,
And make us even with you. My thanes and kinsmen,
Henceforth be earls,—the first that ever Scotland
In such an honour nam'd. What 's more to do,
Which would be planted newly with the time,—
As calling home our exil'd friends abroad
That fled the snares of watchful tyranny;
Producing forth the cruel ministers
Of this dead butcher, and his fiend-like queen,—
Who, as 't is thought, by self and violent hands
Took off her life;—this, and what needful else
That calls upon us, by the grace of Grace,
We will perform in measure, time, and place!
So, thanks to all at once, and to each one,
Whom we invite to see us crown'd at Scone.

[*Flourish. Exeunt.*

ILLUSTRATIVE COMMENTS.

ACT I.

(1) Scene III.—*But in a sieve I'll thither sail.*] In a pamphlet entitled "Newes from Scotland, declaring the damnable life and death of Doctor Fian, a notable sorcerer," &c. 1591, which professes to expose a conspiracy of two hundred witches with Dr. Fian at their head, "to bewitch and drowne" King James in the sea, we read,—

"Item—Agnis Tompson was brought again before the kings majesty and his council, and being examined of the meetings and detestable dealings of those witches, she confessed that upon the night of All-hallawn-even last she was accompanied as well with the persons aforesaid, as also with a great many other witches, to the number of two hundred, and that they altogether went by sea, each one in a *riddle* or *sieve*, and went in the same very substantially with flaggons of wine, making merry and drinking by the way in the same riddles or sieves, to the kirk of North Berwick in Lothian, and that after they had landed they took hands on the land and danced this reel or short dance, singing all with one voice,—

> "Commer goe ye before, commer goe ye,
> Gif you will not goe before, commer let me!"

(2) Scene III.—

> *Weary sev'n-nights, nine times nine,*
> *Shall he dwindle, peak, and pine.*]

For a particular account of the manner in which this mischief was sometimes effected see note (4), p. 43, Vol. I. To what is there related, we need only add the following notable charm from "Scot's Discovery of Witchcraft:"—"*A charme teaching how to hurt whom you list with images of wax*, &c. Make an image in his name, whom you would hurt or kill, of new virgine wax; under the right arme-poke whereof place a swallow's heart, and the liver under the left; then hang about the neck thereof a new thred in a new needle pricked into the member which you would have hurt, with the rehearsall of certain words:" &c.

(3) Scene III.—

> —— *What are these,*
> *So wither'd, and so wild in their attire;*
> *That look not like the inhabitants o' the earth,*
> *And yet are on't?*]

Compare Holinshed: — "It fortuned as Makbeth and Banquho journied towards Fores, where the king then laie, they went sporting by the waie togither without other companie, save onelie themselves, passing thorough the woods and fields, when suddenlie in the middest of a laund, there met them three women in strange and wild apparell, resembling creatures of elder world, whome when they attentivelie beheld, woondering much at the sight, the first of them spake and said; 'All haile Makbeth, thane of Glammis' (for he had latelie entered into that dignitie and office by the death of his father Sinell). The second of them said; 'Haile Makbeth thane of Cawdor.' But the third said; 'All haile Makbeth that héereafter shalt be king of Scotland.'

"Then Banquho; 'What manner of women (saith he) are you, that séeme so little favourable unto me, whereas to my fellow heere, besides high offices, ye assigne also the kingdome, appointing foorth nothing for me at all?' 'Yes (saith the first of them) we promise greater benefits unto thée, than unto him, for he shall reigne in déed, but with an unluckie end: neither shall he leave anie issue behind him to succéed in his place, where contrarilie thou in déed shalt not reigne at all, but of thée those shall be borne which shall governe the Scotish kingdome by long order of continuall descent.'

"Herewith the foresaid women vanished immediatlie out of their sight. This was reputed at the first but some vaine fantasticall illusion by Makbeth and Banquho, insomuch that Banquho would call Makbeth in jest, king of Scotland; and Makbeth againe would call him in sport likewise, the father of manie kings. But afterwards the common opinion was, that these women were either the weird sisters, that is (as ye would say) the goddesses of destinie, or else some nymphs or feiries, indued with knowledge of prophesie by their necromanticall science, because everie thing came to passe as they had spoken. For shortlie after, the thane of Cawdor being condemned at Fores of treason against the king committed; his lands, livings and offices were given of the kings liberalitie to Makbeth."

(4) Scene IV.—*The prince of Cumberland.*] "But shortlie after it chanced that king Duncane, having two sonnes by his wife which was the daughter of Siward earle of Northumberland, he made the elder of them called Malcolme prince of Cumberland, as it were thereby to appoint him his sucessor in the kingdome, immediatlie after his decease. Makbeth, sore troubled herewith, for that he saw by this means his hope sore hindered (where, by the old lawes of the realme, the ordinance was, that if he that should succéed were not of able age to take the charge upon himselfe, he that was next of bloud unto him should be admitted) he began to take counsell how he might usurpe the kingdome by force, having a just quarell so to doo (as he tooke the matter) for that Duncane did what in him lay to defraud him of all maner of title and claime, which he might in time to come, pretend unto the crowne."

(5) Scene VI.—

> *Where they most breed and haunt, I have observ'd,*
> *The air is delicate.*]

Sir Joshua Reynolds was struck,—as who possessing a spark of sensibility can fail to be,—with the exceeding beauty of this brief colloquy before the castle of Macbeth, and he observes on it,—"This short dialogue between Duncan and Banquo, whilst they are approaching the gates of Macbeth's castle, has always appeared to me a striking instance of what in painting is termed *repose*. Their conversation very naturally turns upon the beauty of its situation, and the pleasantness of the air; and Banquo, observing the martlets' nests in every recess of the cornice, remarks, that where those birds most breed and haunt, the air is delicate. The subject of this quiet and easy conversation gives that repose so necessary to the mind after the tumultuous bustle of the preceding scenes, and perfectly contrasts the scene of horror that immediately succeeds. It seems as if Shakspeare asked himself, What is a prince likely to say to his attendants on such an occasion? Whereas the modern writers seem, on the contrary, to be always searching for new thoughts, such as would never occur to men in the situation which is represented. This also is frequently the practice of Homer, who, from the midst of battles and horrors, relieves and refreshes the mind of the reader by introducing some quiet rural image, a picture of domestick life."

ACT II.

(1) SCENE III.—*'Tis said they eat each other.*] Very many of the incidents connected with Duncan's death are not to be found in the narrative of that event, but are taken from the Chroniclers' account of King Duffe's murder. Among them are the prodigies mentioned in this speech:—"Monstrous sightes also that were seene without the Scottishe kingdome that yeare were these, horses in Lothian being of singuler beautie and swiftnesse, did eate their owne fleshe and would in nowise taste any other meate. In Angus there was a gentlewoman brought forth a child without eyes, nose, hande, or foote. There was a Sparhauke also strangled by an Owle. Neither was it any lesse wonder that the sunne, as before is sayd, was continually covered with cloudes, for VI. moneths space: But all men understood that the abhominable murder of king Duffe was the cause hereof."

(2) SCENE III.—

He is already nam'd; and gone to Scone
To be invested.]

"Scone is well known to have early obtained historical importance. It received, it would appear, the title of the 'Royal City of Scone,' so early as A.D. 906 or 909. The Pictish Chronicle informs us that Constantine the son of Ed, and Kellach the Bishop, together with the Scots, solemnly vowed to 'observe the laws and discipline of faith, the rights of the churches and of the Gospel, on the Hill of Credulity, near the Royal City of Scoan.' If the Stone of Destiny was transferred by Kenneth Mac Alpine from Dunstaffnage in Argyleshire to Scone in A.D. 838, we may see a reason for the title 'Royal City,' which seems to have been acquired before the meeting of the Ecclesiastical Council. One of the most memorable of the combats with the Danes was fought at Collin near Scone, in the time of Donald IV. the son of Constantine II., for the possession of this stone. This must have been previous to A.D. 904, in which year Donald fell in battle at Forteviot. It is said that a religious house was established at Scone, when the stone was transferred by Kenneth Mac Alpine. During the reign of Alexander, Scone seems to have been occasionally a royal residence, and, like St. Andrews and other places in which monasteries were established, it was a market for foreign nations. Alexander addressed a writ to the merchants of England, inviting them to trade to Scone, and promising them protection on condition of their paying a custom to the monastery. This custom was an impost on all ships trading with Scone, from which it appears to have been anciently a port.

"About a mile from the river there was at a comparatively recent period a bog called the *full sea mere*, which according to tradition has been covered by the tide, and in which when digging for a pond, stones similar to those in the bed of the Tay were found. Whatever may be the value of the commonly received fact as to the transference of the fatal stone to Scone, there can be no doubt that many of the Scottish kings were inaugurated here.

"Edward I. having penetrated to the north as far as Elgin, and having reduced Baliol to a state of the most abject submission, on his return ordered the famous stone on which the Scottish kings had been wont to be crowned, to be removed from the Abbey of Scone and conveyed to Westminster, in testimony, says Hemingford, an English contemporary chronicler, of the conquest and surrender of the kingdom. The restoration of the stone, though omitted in the treaty of Northampton (1328), was stipulated by a separate instrument. The stone, as is well known, was never restored. 'This fatal stone,' says Sir Walter Scott, 'was said to have been brought from Ireland by Fergus the son of Eric, who led the Dalriads to the shores of Argyleshire. Its virtues are preserved in the celebrated leonine verse:—

Ni fallat Fatum, Scoti, quocunque locatum
Invenient lapidem, regnare tenentur ibidem.

There were Scots who hailed the accomplishment of this prophecy at the accession of James VI. to the crown of England, and exulted that, in removing their palladium, the policy of Edward resembled that which brought the Trojan horse in triumph within their walls, and which occasioned the destruction of their royal family. The stone is still preserved, and forms the support of King Edward the Confessor's chair, which the sovereign occupies at his coronation.' In preparing this chair for the coronation of her present Majesty, some small fragments of this stone were broken off."—*New Statistical Account of Scotland*, 1845, vol. x. p. 1047.

(3) SCENE III.—

—— *Where is Duncan's body?*
MACD. *Carried to Colme-kill.*]

"To the Highlanders of the present day, Iona is known as 'Innis-nan-Druidhneach,' or *the Island of the Druids*—as 'Ii-cholum-chille,' or *the Island of Colum, of the Cell, or Cemetery*, from whence the English word Icolymkill is derived.

"In Macfarlane's MS., Advocates' library, there is a description of this island by Dean Monro, who travelled through the Western isles in 1549.

"'*Colmkill.*—Narrest this be twa myles of sea, layes the Isle the Erische call it I. colmkill, that is, Sanct Colm's Isle, ane faire mayne Isle of twa myle lange, and maire and ane myle braid, fertill and fruitfull of corn and store, and guid for fishing. Within this ile there is a monastery of Mounkes and ane uther of nuns, with a paroche kirke, and sundry other chappels dotat of auld be the kings of Scotland, and be Clandonald of the Iyles. This abbay forsaid wes the cathedrall kirk of the bischops of the Iyles sen the tyme they were expulsed out of the Iyle of Man by the Englishmen; for within the Iyle of Man was the cathedrall kirke, and living of auld. Within this ile of Colmkill, there is ane sanctuary also, or kirkaird, callit in Erische, Religoram, quhilk is a very fair kirkyaird, and weill biggit about with staine and lime. Into this sanctuary there is three tombes of staine formit like litle chappels with ane braid gray marble or quhin staine in the gavile of ilk ane of the tombes. In the staine of the tomb there is written in Latin letters *Tumulus Regum Scotiæ*, that is, the tombe or grave of the Scotts kinges. Within this tombe according to our Scotts and Erische chronickles, ther layes fortyeight crouned Scotts kinges, through the quhilk this ile has beine richlie dotat be the Scots kinges, as we have said. * * * Within this sanctuarie also lyes the maist past of the Lords of the Iles with ther lynage, two clan Lynes with ther lynage, M'Kynnon and M'Guare, with ther lineages, with sundrie uthers inhabitants of the hail iles, because this sanctuary was wont to be the sepulture of the best men of all the isles; and als of our kinge's as we have said; because it was the maist honorable and anciend place that was in Scotland in thair days as we read."—*New Statistical Account of Scotland*, 1845, vol. vii. p. 313.

ACT III.

(1) SCENE III.—

—— Fly, good Fleance, fly, fly, fly!
Thou mayst revenge.—O, slave!]

The murder of Banquo is told very briefly by Holinshed :—

"The words also of the thrée weird sisters would not out of his mind, which as they promised him the kingdome, so likewise did they promise it at the same time unto the posteritie of Banquho. He willed therefore the same Banquho with his sonne named Fleance, to come to a supper that he had prepared for them, which was in déed, as he had devised, present death at the hands of certeine murderers, whom he hired to execute that déed, appointing them to meete with the same Banquho and his sonne without the palace, as they returned to their lodgings, and there to slea them, so that he would not have his house slandered, but that in time to come he might cleare himselfe, if anie thing were laid to his charge upon anie suspicion that might arise.

"It chanced yet by the benefit of the darke night, that though the father were slaine, the sonne yet by the helpe of Almightie God reserving him to better fortune, escaped that danger: and afterwards having some inkeling (by the admonition of some friends which he had in the court) how his life was sought no lesse than his fathers, who was slaine not by chance medlie (as by the handling of the matter Makbeth would have had it to appeare) but even upon a prepensed devise: whereupon to avoid further perill he fled into Wales."

(2) SCENE V.—*Enter* HECATE.] "Shakspeare seems to have been unjustly censured for introducing Hecate among the modern witches. Scot's 'Discovery of Witchcraft,' b. iii. c. ii. and c. xvi., and b. xii. c. iii., mentions it as the common opinion of all writers, that witches were supposed to have nightly 'meetings with Herodias, and the pagan gods,' and that in the night-times they ride abroad with Diana, the goddess of the pagans,' &c. Their dame or chief leader seems always to have been an old pagan, as 'the Ladie Sibylla, Minerva, or Diana.'"—TOLLET.

(3) SCENE V.—SONG. [*Without.*] *Come away, come away, &c.*] The song actually sung here we conjecture to be that given in the corresponding scene of Middleton's "Witch," and in D'Avenant's paraphrase of "Macbeth." It was probably written by Shakespeare, and derived by Middleton and D'Avenant from stage tradition, or from some less imperfect copy of "Macbeth" than is now known.

Song in "The Witch."

"Come away, come away; } in the aire
Heccat, Heccat, come away. }
Hec. I come, I come, I come,
With all the speed I may."

"Now I goe, now I flie,
Malkin my sweete spirit and I.
Oh what a daintie pleasure tis
To ride in the aire
When the moone shines faire,
And sing and daunce, and toy and kiss:
Over woods, high rocks, and mountaines,
Over seas, our mistris fountaines,
Over steepe towres and turretts
We fly by night, 'mongst troopes of spiritts.
No ring of bells to our eares sounds,
No howles of wolves, no yelpes of hounds;
No, not the noyse of water's-breache,
Or cannon's throat, our height can reache."

"The Witch" is supposed to have been written about 1613, but it was not printed before 1778. D'Avenant's alteration of "Macbeth" was printed a century earlier. From this circumstance, as well as from the differences observable in passages common to both, it may be inferred that the latter did not copy those passages from Middleton, but that each derived them from the same original. The following is D'Avenant's version of the preceding song :—

"Come away Heccate, Heccate! Oh come away:
Hec. I come, I come, with all the speed I may."

"Now I go, and now I flye
Malking my sweet Spirit and I.
O what a dainty pleasure's this,
To sail i' th' Air
While the *Moon* shines fair;
To Sing, to Toy, to Dance and Kiss,
Over Woods, high Rocks and Mountains;
Over Hills, and misty Fountains;
Over Steeples, Towers, and Turrets:
We flye by night 'mongst troops of Spirits.
No Ring of Bells to our Ears sounds,
No howles of Wolves, nor Yelps of Hounds;
No, nor the noise of Waters breach,
Nor Cannons Throats, our Height can reach."

ACT IV.

(1) SCENE I.—*Thrice the brinded cat hath mew'd.*] "Dr. Warburton has adduced classical authority for the connexion between Hecate and this animal, with a view to trace the reason why it was the agent and favourite of modern witches. It may be added, that among the Egyptians the cat was sacred to Isis or the Moon,—their Hecate or Diana, and accordingly worshipped with great honour. Many cat-idols are still preserved in the cabinets of the curious, and the sistrum or rattle used by the priests of Isis is generally ornamented with a figure of a cat with a crescent on its head."—DOUCE.

(2) SCENE I.—*Music and Song,* "Black spirits," *&c.*] This "charm song," like the song in Act III., is found both in Middleton's "Witch" and D'Avenant's alteration of "Macbeth":—

"Black Spirits, and White,
Red Spirits and Gray;
Mingle, mingle, mingle,
You that mingle may."

(3) SCENE III.—

——*Such welcome and unwelcome things at once
'Tis hard to reconcile.*]

The foregoing dialogue very closely follows Holinshed's abridgment of the Scottish history:—

"At his comming unto Malcolme, he declared into what great miserie the estate of Scotland was brought, by the detestable cruelties exercised by the tyrant Makbeth, having committed manie horrible slaughters and murders, both as well of the nobles as commons, for the which he was hated right mortallie of all his liege people, desiring nothing more than to be delivered of that intollerable and most heavie yoke of thraldome, which they sustained at such a caitaifes hands.

"Malcolme hearing Makduffes woords, which he uttered in verie lamentable sort, for méere compassion and verie ruth that pearsed his sorrowfull hart, bewailing the miserable state of his countrie, he fetched a deepe sigh; which Makduffe perceiving, began to fall most earnestlie in hand with him, to enterprise the delivering of the Scotish people out of the hands of so cruell and bloudie a tyrant, as Makbeth by too manie plaine experiments did shew himselfe to be: which was an easie matter for him to bring to passe, considering not onelie the good title he had, but also the earnest desire of the people to have some occasion ministred, whereby they might be revenged of those notable injuries, which they dailie susteined by the outragious crueltie of Makbeths misgovernance. Though Malcolme was verie sorrowfull for the oppression of his countriemen the Scots, in maner as Makduffe had declared; yet doubting whether he were come as one that ment unfeinedlie as he spake, or else as sent from Makbeth to betraie him, he thought to have some further triall, and thereupon dissembling his mind at the first, he answered as followeth.

"'I am trulie verie sorie for the miserie chanced to my countrie of Scotland, but though I have never so great affection to relieve the same, yet by reason of certeine incurable vices, which reigne in me, I am nothing meet thereto. First, such immoderate lust and voluptuous sensualitie (the abhominable founteine of all vices) followeth me, that if I were made king of Scots, I should séeke to defloure young maids and matrones, in such wise that mine intemperancie should be more importable unto you, than the bloudie tyrannie of Makbeth now is.' Heereunto Makduffe answered: 'This suerlie is a verie evill fault, for manie noble princes and kings have lost both lives and kingdomes for the same; neverthelesse there are women enow in Scotland, and therefore follow my counsell. Make thy selfe king, and I shall conveie the matter so wiselie, that thou shalt be so satisfied at thy pleasure in such secret wise, that no man shall be aware thereof.'

"Then said Malcolme, 'I am also the most avaritious creature on the earth, so that if I were king, I should séeke so manie waies to get lands and goods, that I would slea the most part of all the nobles of Scotland by surmized accusations, to the end I might injoy their lands, goods, and possessions; and therefore to shew you what mischiefe may insue on you through mine unsatiable covetousness, I will rehearse unto you a fable. There was a fox having a sore place on hir overset with a swarme of flies, that continuallie sucked out hir bloud: and when one that came by and saw this manner, demanded whether she would have the flies driven beside her, she answered no: for if these flies that are alreadie full, and by reason thereof sucke not verie egerlie, should be chased awaie, other that are emptie and fellie an hungred should light in their places, and sucke out the residue of my bloud farre more to my greevance than these, which now being satisfied doo not much annoie me. Therefore saith Malcolme, suffer me to remaine where I am, lest if I atteine to the regiment of your realme, mine unquenchable avarice may proove such; that ye would thinke the displeasures which now grieve you, should séeme easie in respect of the unmeasurable outrage, which might insue through my coming amongst you.'

"Makduffe to this made answer, 'how it was a far woorse fault than the other: for avarice is the root of all mischiefe, and for that crime the most part of our kings have béene slaine and brought to their finall end. Yet notwithstanding follow my counsell, and take upon thée the crowne. There is gold and riches inough in Scotland to satisfie thy gréedie desire.' Then said Malcolme againe, 'I am furthermore inclined to dissimulation, telling of leasings and all other kinds of deceit, so that I naturallie rejoise in nothing so much as to betraie and deceive such as put anie trust or confidence in my woords. Then sith there is nothing that more becommeth a prince than constancie, veritie, truth, and justice, with the other laudable fellowship of those faire and noble vertues which are comprehended onelie in soothfastnesse, and that lieng utterlie overthroweth the same; you sée how unable I am to governe anie province or region: and therefore sith you have remedies to cloke and hide all the rest of my other vices, I praie you find shift to cloke this vice amongst the residue.'

"Then said Makduffe: 'This yet is the woorst of all, and there I leave thee, and therefore saie; O ye unhappie and miserable Scotishmen, which are thus scourged with so manie and sundrie calamities, ech one above other! Ye have one curssed and wicked tyrant that now reigneth over you, without anie right or title, oppressing you with his most bloudie crueltie. This other that hath the right to the crowne, is so replet with the inconstant behaviour and manifest vices of Englishmen, that he is nothing woorthie to injoy it: for by his own confession he is not onelie avaritious, and given to unsatiable lust, but so false a traitor withall, that no trust is to be had unto anie woord he speaketh. Adieu Scotland, for now I account my selfe a banished man for ever, without comfort or consolation:' and with those woords the brackish teares trickled downe his chéekes verie abundantlie.

"At the last, when he was readie to depart, Malcolme tooke him by the sléeve, and said: 'Be of good comfort Makduffe, for I have none of these vices before remembred, but have jested with thée in this manner, onelie to proove thy mind: for diverse times héeretofore hath Makbeth sought by this manner of meanes to bring me into his hands, but the more slow I have shewed my selfe to condescend to thy motion and request, the more diligence shall I use in accomplishing the same.'"

ACT V.

(1) SCENE IV.—
—— the confident tyrant
Keeps still in Dunsinane, and will endure
Our setting down before't.]

"In the meane time, Malcolme purchased such favor at king Edwards hands, that old Siward earle of Northumberland was appointed with ten thousand men to go with him into Scotland, to support him in this enterprise, for recoverie of his right. After these newes were spread abroad in Scotland, the nobles drew into two severall factions, the one taking part with Makbeth, and the other with Malcolme. Héereupon insued oftentimes sundrie bickerings, and diverse light skirmishes: for those that were of Malcolmes side, would not jeopard to joine with their enimies in a pight field, till his comming out of England to their support. But after that Makbeth perceived his enimies power to increase, by such aid as came to them foorth of England with his adversarie Malcolme, he recoiled backe into Fife, there purposing to abide in campe fortified, at the castell of Dunsinane, and to fight with his enimies, if they ment to pursue him; howbeit some of his friends advised him, that it should be best for him, either to make some agréement with Malcolme, or else to fĺée with all spéed into the Iles, and to take his treasure with him, to the end he might wage sundrie great princes of the realme to take his part, and reteine strangers, in whome he might better trust than in his owne subjects, which stale dailie from him: but he had such confidence in his prophesies, that he beléeved he should never be vanquished, till Birnam wood were brought to Dunsinane; nor yet to be slaine with anie man, that should be or was borne of anie woman."

(2) SCENE VIII.—*My better part.*] The note on that long controverted expression, "Atalanta's *better part,*" in "As You Like It," having been omitted in the proper place from lack of room, it may be well to explain here that Atalanta's *better part* was not her *modesty,* nor her *heels,* nor her *wit,* as critics have variously conjectured, but simply her *spiritual part.* The old epitaph quoted by Mr. Whalley in the *Variorum* almost proves, although he was apparently unconscious of the meaning, that *better part* signified the *immortal,* the *intelligent* part:—

"She who is dead and sleepeth in this tomb,
Had Rachel's comely face, and Leah's fruitful womb:
Sarah's obedience, Lydia's open heart,
And Martha's care, and Mary's *better part.*"

But the following lines from Overbury's poem "A Wife," places this beyond doubt:—

"Or rather let me *love,* then *be in love;*
So let me chuse, as *wife* and *friend* to find,
Let me forget her *sex* when I *approve:*
Beasts likeness lies in *shape,* but *ours* in *mind:*
Our *soules no sexes* have, their love is cleane,
No *sex,* both in the *better part* are *men.*"

The Italics, we may remark, are the author's.

(3) SCENE VIII.—*Re-enter* MACDUFF, *with* KING MACBETH'*s head.*] The catastrophe is thus told by the historian:—"Malcolme following hastilie after Makbeth, came the night before the battell unto Birnam wood; and when his armie had rested a while there to refresh them, he commanded everie man to get a bough of some trée or other of that wood in his hand, as big as he might beare, and to march foorth therewith in such wise, that on the next morrow they might come closelie and without sight in this manner within view of his enimies. On the morrow when Makbeth beheld them comming in this sort, he first marvelled what the matter ment, but in the end remembred himselfe that the prophesie which he had heard long before that time, of the comming of Birnam wood to Dunsinane castell, was likelie to be now fulfilled. Neverthelesse, he brought his men in order of battell, and exhorted them to doo valiantlie, howbeit his enimies had scarselie cast from them their boughs, when Makbeth perceiving their numbers, betooke him streict to flight, whome Makduffe pursued with great hatred, even till he came unto Lunfannaine, where Makbeth perceiving that Makduffe was hard at his backe, leapt beside his horsse, saieng; 'Thou traitor, what meaneth it that thou shouldest thus in vaine follow me that am not appointed to be slaine by anie creature that is borne of a woman, come on therefore, and receive thy reward which thou hast deserved for thy paines,' and therwithall he lifted up his swoord thinking to have slaine him.

"But Makduffe quicklie avoiding from his horsse, yer he came at him, answered (with his naked swoord in his hand) saieng: 'It is true Makbeth, and now shall thine insatiable crueltie have an end, for I am even he that thy wizzards have told thée of, who was never born of my mother, but ripped out of her wombe:' therewithall he stept unto him, and slue him in the place. Then cutting his head from his shoulders, he set it upon a pole, and brought it unto Malcolme."

CRITICAL OPINIONS ON MACBETH.

"Who could exhaust the praises of this sublime work? Since 'The Eumenides' of Æschylus, nothing so grand and terrible has ever been written. The witches are not, it is true, divine Eumenides, and are not intended to be: they are ignoble and vulgar instruments of hell. A German poet, therefore, very ill understood their meaning, when he transformed them into mongrel beings, a mixture of fates, furies, and enchantresses, and clothed them with tragic dignity. Let no man venture to lay hand on Shakspeare's works thinking to improve anything essential: he will be sure to punish himself. The bad is radically odious; and to endeavour in any manner to ennoble it, is to violate the laws of propriety. Hence, in my opinion, Dante, and even Tasso, have been much more successful in their portraiture of dæmons than Milton. Whether the age of Shakspeare still believed in ghosts and witches, is a matter of perfect indifference for the justification of the use which in 'Hamlet' and 'Macbeth' he has made of pre-existing traditions. No superstition can be widely diffused without having a foundation in human nature: on this the poet builds; he calls up from their hidden abysses that dread of the unknown, that presage of a dark side of nature, and a world of spirits, which philosophy now imagines it has altogether exploded. In this manner he is in some degree both the portrayer and the philosopher of superstition; that is, not the philosopher who denies and turns it into ridicule, but, what is still more difficult, who distinctly exhibits its origin in apparently irrational and yet natural opinions. But when he ventures to make arbitrary changes in these popular traditions, he altogether forfeits his right to them, and merely holds up his own idle fancies to our ridicule. Shakspeare's picture of the witches is truly magical: in the short scenes where they enter, he has created for them a peculiar language, which, although composed of the usual elements, still seems to be a collection of formulæ of incantation. The sound of the words, the accumulation of rhymes, and the rhythmus of the verse, form, as it were, the hollow music of a dreary witch-dance. He has been abused for using the names of disgusting objects; but he who fancies the kettle of the witches can be made effective with agreeable aromatics, is as wise as those who desire that hell should sincerely and honestly give good advice. These repulsive things, from which the imagination shrinks, are here emblems of the hostile powers which operate in nature; and the repugnance of our senses is outweighed by the mental horror. With one another the witches discourse like women of the very lowest class; for this was the class to which witches were ordinarily supposed to belong: when, however, they address Macbeth they assume a loftier tone: their predictions, which they either themselves pronounce, or allow their apparitions to deliver, have all the obscure brevity, the majestic solemnity of oracles.

"We here see that the witches are merely instruments; they are governed by an invisible spirit, or the operation of such great and dreadful events would be above their sphere. With what intent did Shakspeare assign the same place to them in his play, which they occupy in the history of Macbeth as related in the old chronicles? A monstrous crime is committed: Duncan, a venerable old man, and the best of kings, is, in defenceless sleep, under the hospitable roof, murdered by his subject, whom he has loaded with honours and rewards. Natural motives alone seem inadequate, or the perpetrator must have been portrayed as a hardened villain. Shakspeare wished to exhibit a more sublime picture: an ambitious but noble hero, yielding to a deep-laid hellish temptation; and in whom all the crimes to which, in order to secure the fruits of his first crime, he is impelled by necessity, cannot altogether eradicate the stamp of native heroism. He has, therefore, given a threefold division to the guilt of that crime. The first idea comes from that being whose whole activity is guided by a lust of wickedness. The weird sisters surprise Macbeth in the moment of intoxication of victory, when his love of glory has been gratified; they cheat his eyes by exhibiting to him as the work of fate what in reality can only be accomplished by his own deed, and gain credence for all their words by the immediate fulfilment of the first prediction. The opportunity of murdering the King immediately offers; the wife of Macbeth conjures him not to let it slip; she urges him on with a fiery eloquence, which has at command all those sophisms that serve to throw a false splendour over crime. Little more than the mere execution falls to the share of Macbeth; he is driven into it, as it were, in a tumult of fascination. Repentance immediately follows, nay, even precedes the deed, and the stings of conscience leave him rest neither night nor day. But he is now fairly entangled in the snares of hell; truly frightful is it to behold that same Macbeth, who once as a warrior could spurn at death, now that he dreads the prospect of the life to come,* clinging with growing anxiety to his earthly existence the more miserable it becomes, and pitilessly removing out of the way whatever to his dark and suspicious mind seems to threaten danger. However much we may abhor his actions, we cannot altogether refuse to compassionate the state of his mind; we lament the ruin of so many noble qualities, and even in his last defence we are compelled to admire the struggle of a brave will with a cowardly conscience. We might believe that we witness in this tragedy the overruling destiny of the ancients represented in perfect accordance with their ideas: the whole originates in a supernatural influence, to which the subsequent events seem inevitably linked. Moreover, we even find here the same ambiguous oracles which, by their literal fulfilment, deceive those who confide in them. Yet it may be easily shown that the poet has, in his work, displayed more enlightened views. He wishes to show that the conflict of good and evil in this world can only take place by the permission of Providence, which converts the curse that individual mortals draw down on their heads into a blessing to others. An accurate scale is followed in the retaliation. Lady Macbeth, who of all the human participators in the king's murder is the most guilty, is thrown by the terrors of her conscience into a state of incurable bodily and mental disease; she dies, unlamented by her husband, with all the symptoms of reprobation. Macbeth is still found worthy to die the death of a hero on the field of battle. The noble Macduff is allowed the satisfaction of saving his country by punishing with his own hand the tyrant who had murdered his wife and children. Banquo, by an early death, atones for the ambitious curiosity which prompted the wish to know his glorious descendants, as he thereby has roused Macbeth's jealousy; but he preserved his mind pure from the evil suggestions of the witches: his name is blessed in his race, destined to enjoy for a long succession of ages that royal dignity which Macbeth could only hold for his own life. In the progress of the action, this piece is altogether the reverse of 'Hamlet:' it strides forward with amazing rapidity, from the first catastrophe (for Duncan's murder may be called a catastrophe) to the last. 'Thought, and done!' is the general motto; for as Macbeth says,

'The flighty purpose never is o'ertook,
Unless the deed go with it.'

In every feature we see an energetic heroic age, in the hardy North which steels every nerve. The precise duration of the action cannot be ascertained,—years perhaps, according to the story; but we know that to the imagination the most crowded time appears always the shortest. Here we can hardly conceive how so very much could ever have been compressed into so narrow a space; not merely external events,—the very inmost recesses in the minds of the dramatic personages are laid open to us. It is as if the drags were taken from the wheels of time, and they rolled along without interruption in their descent. Nothing can equal this picture in its power to excite terror. We need only allude to the circumstances attending the murder of Duncan, the dagger that hovers before the eyes of Macbeth, the vision of Banquo at the feast, the madness of Lady Macbeth; what can possibly be said on the subject that will not rather weaken the impression they naturally leave? Such scenes stand alone, and are to be found only in this poet; otherwise the tragic muse might exchange her mask for the head of Medusa."—SCHLEGEL.

* "We'd jump the life to come."

"'Macbeth' stands in contrast throughout with 'Hamlet;' in the manner of opening more especially. In the latter, there is a gradual ascent from the simplest forms of conversation to the language of impassioned intellect,—yet the intellect still remaining the seat of passion; in the former, the invocation is at once made to the imagination and the emotions connected therewith. Hence the movement throughout is the most rapid of all Shakspeare's plays, and hence, also, with the exception of the disgusting passage of the Porter (Act II. Sc. 3), which I dare pledge myself to demonstrate to be an interpolation of the actors, there is not, to the best of my remembrance, a single pun or play on words in the whole drama. I have previously given an answer to the thousand times repeated charge against Shakspeare upon the subject of his punning; and I here merely mention the fact of the absence of any puns in 'Macbeth' as justifying a candid doubt, at least, whether even in these figures of speech and fanciful modifications of language, Shakspeare may not have followed rules and principles that merit and would stand the test of philosophic examination. And hence, also, there is an entire absence of comedy, nay, even of irony and philosophic contemplation in 'Macbeth,'—the play being wholly and purely tragic. For the same cause, there are no reasonings of equivocal morality, which would have required a more leisurely state and a consequently greater activity of mind;—no sophistry of self-delusion,—except only that previously to the dreadful act, Macbeth mistranslates the recoilings and ominous whispers of conscience into prudential and selfish reasonings, and, after the deed is done, the terrors of remorse into fear from external dangers,—like delirious men who run away from the phantoms of their own brains, or, raised by terror to rage, stab the real object that is within their reach:—whilst Lady Macbeth merely endeavours to reconcile his and her own sinkings of heart by anticipations of the worst, and an affected bravado in confronting them. In all the rest, Macbeth's language is the grave utterance of the very heart, conscience-sick, even to the last faintings of moral death. It is the same in all the other characters. The variety arises from rage, caused ever and anon by disruption of anxious thought, and the quick transition of fear into it.

"In 'Hamlet' and 'Macbeth' the scene opens with superstition; but in each it is not merely different, but opposite. In the first it is connected with the best and holiest feelings; in the second, with the shadowy, turbulent, and unsanctified cravings of the individual will. Nor is the purpose the same; in the one the object is to excite, whilst in the other it is to mark a mind already excited.

"The Weird Sisters are as true a creation of Shakspeare's as his Ariel and Caliban,—fates, furies, and materializing witches being the elements. They are wholly different from any representation of witches in the contemporary writers, and yet presented a sufficient external resemblance to the creatures of vulgar prejudice to act immediately on the audience. Their character consists in the imaginative disconnected from the good; they are the shadowy obscure and fearfully anomalous of physical nature, the lawless of human nature,—elemental avengers without sex or kin. The true reason for the first appearance of the Witches is to strike the key-note of the character of the whole drama.

"Macbeth is described by Lady Macbeth so as at the same time to reveal her own character. Could he have everything he wanted, he would rather have it innocently;—ignorant, as alas, how many of us are, that he who wishes a temporal end for itself does in truth will the means; and hence the danger of indulging fancies. Lady Macbeth, like all in Shakspeare, is a class individualized:—of high rank, left much alone, and feeding herself with day-dreams of ambition, she mistakes the courage of fantasy for the power of bearing the consequences of the realities of guilt. Hers is the mock fortitude of a mind deluded by ambition; she shames her husband with a superhuman audacity of fancy which she cannot support, but sinks in the season of remorse, and dies in suicidal agony."—COLERIDGE.

ANTONY AND CLEOPATRA.

Act V. Sc. 2.

ANTONY AND CLEOPATRA.

No edition of this tragedy, previous to that in the folio of 1623, is now known; although, from the fact of its having been entered on the Stationers' Registers by Edward Blount, one of the publishers of the folio, in May, 1608, there is a bare possibility that an earlier impression may some day come to light. It was probably written at the latter end of the year 1607, but we have no evidence to prove when it was first acted, or, indeed, that it was acted at all. There were two preceding dramas on the subject; the "Cleopatra" of Samuel Daniel, 1594; and "The Trajedie of Antonie," a translation from the French by Lady Pembroke, 1595, to neither of which, however, was Shakespeare under any obligation, his story and incidents being evidently borrowed directly from the Life of Antonius in North's *Plutarch,* which he has followed, even to the minutest circumstances, with scrupulous fidelity. The action comprehends the events of ten years; beginning with the death of Fulvia, B.C. 40, and terminating with the overthrow of the Ptolemean dynasty, B.C. 30.

Persons Represented.

M. Antony, Octavius Cæsar, M. Æmil. Lepidus, } *Triumvirs.*

Sextus Pompeius.

Domitius Enobarbus, Ventidius, Eros, Scarus, Dercetas, Demetrius, Philo, } *Friends of* Antony.

Mecænas, Agrippa, Dolabella, Proculeius, Thyreus, Gallus, } *Friends of* Cæsar.

Menas, Menecrates, Varrius, } *Friends of* Pompey.

Taurus, *Lieutenant-General to* Cæsar.

Canidius, *Lieutenant-General to* Antony.

Silius, *an Officer in* Ventidius's *Army.*

Euphronius, *an Ambassador from* Antony *to* Cæsar.

Alexas, Mardian, Seleucus, Diomedes, } *Attendants on* Cleopatra.

A Soothsayer.

A Clown.

Cleopatra, *Queen of* Egypt.

Octavia, *Sister to* Cæsar, *and Wife of* Antony.

Charmian, Iras, } *Attendants on* Cleopatra.

Officers, Soldiers, Messengers, and other Attendants.

SCENE,—*Dispersed; in several parts of the* Roman Empire.

ACT I.

SCENE I.—Alexandria. *A Room in* Cleopatra's *Palace.*

Enter DEMETRIUS *and* PHILO.

PHI. Nay, but this dotage of our general's
O'erflows the measure: those his goodly eyes,
That o'er the files and musters of the war
Have glow'd like plated Mars, now bend, now turn,
The office and devotion of their view
Upon a tawny front: his captain's heart,
Which in the scuffles of great fights hath burst

The buckles on his breast, reneges[a] all temper,
And is become the bellows and the fan
To cool a gipsy's lust. Look, where they come!
[*Flourish without.*
Take but good note, and you shall see in him
The triple pillar of the world transform'd
Into a strumpet's fool: behold and see.

Enter ANTONY *and* CLEOPATRA, *with their* Trains; Eunuchs *fanning her.*

CLEO. If it be love indeed, tell me how much.
ANT. There's beggary in the love that can be reckon'd.
CLEO. I'll set a bourn how far to be belov'd.
ANT. Then must thou needs find out new heaven, new earth.

Enter an Attendant.

ATT. News, my good lord, from Rome.
ANT. Grates me:—the sum.
CLEO. Nay, hear them, Antony:
Fulvia perchance is angry; or, who knows
If the scarce-bearded Cæsar have not sent
His powerful mandate to you, *Do this, or this;*
Take in that kingdom, and enfranchise that;
Perform't, or else we damn[b] *thee.*
ANT. How, my love!
CLEO. Perchance,—nay, and most like,—
You must not stay here longer, your dismission
Is come from Cæsar; therefore hear it, Antony.—
Where's Fulvia's process?[c] Cæsar's, I would say.—both?—
Call in the messengers.—As I am Egypt's queen,
Thou blushest, Antony; and that blood of thine
Is Cæsar's homager; else so thy cheek pays shame
When shrill-tongu'd Fulvia scolds.—The messengers!
ANT. Let Rome in Tiber melt, and the wide arch
Of the rang'd empire fall! Here is my space.
Kingdoms are clay: our dungy earth alike
Feeds beast as man: the nobleness of life
Is to do thus; when such a mutual pair,
[*Embracing.*
And such a twain can do't, in which I bind,
On pain of punishment, the world to weet,
We stand up peerless.
CLEO. Excellent falsehood!
Why did he marry Fulvia, and not love her?—
I'll seem the fool I am not;—Antony
Will be himself.
ANT. But stirr'd by Cleopatra.—
Now, for the love of Love, and her soft hours,
Let's not confound the time with conference harsh:
There's not a minute of our lives should stretch
Without some pleasure now:—what sport to-night?
CLEO. Hear the ambassadors.
ANT. Fie, wrangling queen!
Whom everything becomes,—to chide, to laugh,
To weep; whose* every passion fully strives
To make itself, in thee, fair and admir'd!
No messenger but thine; and all alone,
To-night we'll wander through the streets, and note
The qualities of people.(1) Come, my queen;
Last night you did desire it.—Speak not to us.
[*Exeunt* ANT. *and* CLEOP., *with their* Train.
DEM. Is Cæsar with Antonius priz'd so slight?
PHI. Sir, sometimes, when he is not Antony,
He comes too short of that great property
Which still should go with Antony.
DEM. I am full sorry
That he approves the common liar,[d] who
Thus speaks of him at Rome: but I will hope
Of better deeds to-morrow. Rest you happy!
[*Exeunt.*

SCENE II.—*The same. Another Room in the Palace.*

Enter CHARMIAN, IRAS, ALEXAS, *and a* Soothsayer.[e]

CHAR. Lord Alexas, sweet Alexas, most anything Alexas, almost most absolute Alexas, where's the soothsayer that you praised so to the queen? O, that I knew this husband, which, you say, must change[f] his horns with garlands!
ALEX. Soothsayer,—
SOOTH. Your will?
CHAR. Is this the man?—Is't you, sir, that know things?

(*) First folio, *who.*

a — reneges—] That is, *denies* or *renounces*. Though odd and obsolete now, it was probably the genuine word, as in "King Lear," Act II. Sc. 2, we have,—"*Renege, affirm,*" &c.
b — damn *thee.*] *Condemn* thee.
c — process?] *Citation.*
d That he approves the common liar,—] That he confirms the reports of *Rumour*.
e *Enter* CHARMIAN, IRAS, ALEXAS, *and a* Soothsayer.] The direction of the folio is, "Enter Enobarbus, Lamprius, a Soothsayer, Rannius, Lucillius, Charmian, Iras, Mardian the Eunuch, and Alexas." And Steevens thought it possible that "Lamprius, Rannius, Lucillius," &c. might have been speakers in the scene as it was originally written by the poet, who afterwards, when omitting the speeches, forgot to erase the names.
f — change *his horns with garlands!*] So the old text; to "*change* his horns," may mean to *vary* or *garnish* them. The modern reading, however, of *charge*, suggested by Southern and Warburton, is certainly very plausible.

SOOTH. In nature's infinite book of secrecy
A little I can read.

ALEX. Show him your hand.

Enter ENOBARBUS.

ENO. Bring in the banquet quickly; wine enough
Cleopatra's health to drink.

CHAR. Good sir, give me good fortune.

SOOTH. I make not, but foresee.

CHAR. Pray, then, foresee me one.

SOOTH. You shall be yet far fairer than you are.

CHAR. He means in flesh.

IRAS. No, you shall paint when you are old.

CHAR. Wrinkles forbid!

ALEX. Vex not his prescience; be attentive.

CHAR. Hush!

SOOTH. You shall be more beloving than belov'd.

CHAR. I had rather heat my liver with drinking.

ALEX. Nay, hear him.

CHAR. Good now, some excellent fortune! Let me be married to three kings in a forenoon, and widow them all: let me have a child at fifty, to whom Herod of Jewry may do homage: find me to marry me with Octavius Cæsar, and companion me with my mistress.

SOOTH. You shall outlive the lady whom you serve.

CHAR. O excellent! I love long life better than figs.[a]

SOOTH. You have seen and prov'd a fairer former fortune
Than that which is to approach.

CHAR. Then, belike my children shall have no names:[b]—pr'ythee, how many boys and wenches must I have?

SOOTH. If every of your wishes had a womb,
And fertile[c] every wish, a million.

CHAR. Out, fool! I forgive thee for a witch.

---

[a] I love long life better than figs.] This was a proverbial saying.

[b] — my children shall have no names:] That is, be illegitimate.

[c] *And* fertile *every wish*,—] A correction of Theobald or Warburton. The old copy has, "And *foretel*," &c

ALEX. You think none but your sheets are privy to your wishes.

CHAR. Nay, come, tell Iras hers.

ALEX. We 'll know all our fortunes.

ENO. Mine, and most of our fortunes, to-night, shall be—drunk to bed.

IRAS. There 's a palm presages chastity, if nothing else.

CHAR. E'en as the o'erflowing Nilus presageth famine.

IRAS. Go, you wild bedfellow, you cannot soothsay.

CHAR. Nay, if an oily palm be not a fruitful prognostication, I cannot scratch mine ear.—Pr'ythee, tell her but a worky-day fortune.

SOOTH. Your fortunes are alike.

IRAS. But how, but how? give me particulars.

SOOTH. I have said.

IRAS. Am I not an inch of fortune better than she?

CHAR. Well, if you were but an inch of fortune better than I, where would you choose it?

IRAS. Not in my husband's nose.

CHAR. Our worser thoughts heaven mend!—Alexas,—come, his fortune, his fortune![a]—O, let him marry a woman that cannot go, sweet Isis, I beseech thee! and let her die too, and give him a worse! and let worse follow worse, till the worst of all follow him laughing to his grave, fifty-fold a cuckold! Good Isis, hear me this prayer, though thou deny me a matter of more weight; good Isis, I beseech thee!

IRAS. Amen. Dear goddess, hear that prayer of the people! for, as it is a heart-breaking to see a handsome man loose-wived, so it is a deadly sorrow to behold a foul knave uncuckolded: therefore, dear Isis, keep decorum, and fortune him accordingly!

CHAR. Amen.

ALEX. Lo, now, if it lay in their hands to make me a cuckold, they would make themselves whores, but they 'd do 't!

ENO. Hush! here comes Antony.

CHAR. Not he; the queen.

Enter CLEOPATRA.

CLEO. Saw* you my lord?

ENO. No, lady.

CLEO. Was he not here?

CHAR. No, madam.

CLEO. He was dispos'd to mirth; but on the sudden
A Roman thought hath struck him.—Enobarbus,—

ENO. Madam?

CLEO. Seek him, and bring him hither.—Where's Alexas?

ALEX. Here, at your service.—My lord approaches.

CLEO. We will not look upon him: go with us.
[*Exeunt.*

Enter ANTONY, *with a* Messenger *and* Attendants.

MESS. Fulvia thy wife first came into the field.

ANT. Against my brother Lucius?

MESS. Ay:
But soon that war had end, and the time's state
Made friends of them, jointing their force 'gainst Cæsar;
Whose better issue in the war, from Italy,
Upon the first encounter, drave them.

ANT. Well, what worst?

MESS. The nature of bad news infects the teller.

ANT. When it concerns the fool, or coward.—On:—
Things that are past are done, with me.—'T is thus,
Who tells me true, though in his tale lie death,
I hear him as he flatter'd.

MESS. Labienus
(This is stiff news) hath, with his Parthian force,
Extended[b] Asia from Euphrates;
His conquering banner shook from Syria
To Lydia and to Ionia;
Whilst—

ANT. *Antony*, thou wouldst say,—

MESS. O, my lord!

ANT. Speak to me home, mince not the general tongue;
Name Cleopatra as she 's call'd in Rome;
Rail thou in Fulvia's phrase; and taunt my faults
With such full licence as both truth and malice
Have power to utter. O, then we bring forth weeds,
When our quick winds[c] lie still; and our ills told us,
Is as our earing![d] Fare thee well a while.

MESS. At your noble pleasure. [*Exit.*

ANT. From Sicyon ho,* the news! Speak there!

1 ATT. The man from Sicyon,—is there such an one?

(*) First folio, *Saue.*

(*) Old text, *how.*

[a] Alexas,—come, his fortune, his fortune!—] The compositor of the folio, mistaking "Alexas" for the prefix to the speech, has attributed what follows to him. The error was pointed out by Theobald a century ago, and has been rectified in every edition since.

[b] Extended—] *Seized.*

[c] *When our quick* winds—] Has been changed, by Warburton, to, "When our quick *minds*," &c. perhaps without necessity. "Quick *winds*" may mean, *quickening winds;* and Johnson's explanation of the passage,—"that man, not agitated by censure, like soil not ventilated by *quick winds*, produces more evil than good,"—is possibly the true one.

[d] — earing!] *Ploughing.*

2 Att. He stays upon your will.

Ant. Let him appear.—
These strong Egyptian fetters I must break,
Or lose myself in dotage.—

Enter another Messenger.

What are you?

2 Mess. Fulvia thy wife is dead.(2)

Ant. Where died she?

2 Mess. In Sicyon:
Her length of sickness, with what else more serious
Importeth thee to know, this bears.

[*Gives a letter.*

Ant. Forbear me.—

[*Exit* Messenger.

There 's a great spirit gone! Thus did I desire it:
What our contempt * doth often hurl from us,
We wish it ours again; the present pleasure,
By revolution lowering, does become
The opposite of itself: she 's good, being gone;
The hand could pluck her back that shov'd her on.
I must from this enchanting queen break off;
Ten thousand harms, more than the ills I know,
My idleness doth hatch.—How now! Enobarbus!

Re-enter Enobarbus.

Eno. What 's your pleasure, sir?

Ant. I must with haste from hence.

(*) Old text, *contempts.*

Eno. Why, then, we kill all our women. We see how mortal an unkindness is to them; if they suffer our departure, death 's the word.

Ant. I must be gone.

Eno. Under a compelling * occasion, let women die: it were pity to cast them away for nothing; though, between them and a great cause, they should be esteemed nothing. Cleopatra, catching but the least noise of this, dies instantly; I have seen her die twenty times upon far poorer moment: I do think there is mettle in death, which commits some loving act upon her, she hath such a celerity in dying.

Ant. She is cunning past man's thought.

Eno. Alack, sir, no; her passions are made of nothing but the finest part of pure love. We cannot call her winds and waters, sighs and tears; they are greater storms and tempests than almanacs can report: this cannot be cunning in her; if it be, she makes a shower of rain as well as Jove.

Ant. Would I had never seen her!

Eno. O, sir, you had then left unseen a wonderful piece of work; which not to have been blessed withal, would have discredited your travel.

Ant. Fulvia is dead.

Eno. Sir!

Ant. Fulvia is dead.

Eno. Fulvia!

Ant. Dead.

(*) Old text inserts, *an.*

ENO. Why, sir, give the gods a thankful sacrifice. When it pleaseth their deities to take the wife of a man from him, it shows to man the tailors of the earth; comforting therein, that when old robes are worn out, there are members to make new. If there were no more women but Fulvia, then had you indeed a cut, and the case to be lamented: this grief is crowned with consolation; your old smock brings forth a new petticoat:—and, indeed, the tears live in an onion that should water this sorrow.

ANT. The business she hath broached in the state
Cannot endure my absence.

ENO. And the business you have broached here cannot be without you; especially that of Cleopatra's, which wholly depends on your abode.

ANT. No more light answers. Let our officers
Have notice what we purpose. I shall break
The cause of our expedience[a] to the queen,
And get her leave* to part. For not alone
The death of Fulvia, with more urgent touches,
Do strongly speak to us; but the letters too
Of many our contriving friends in Rome
Petition us at home. Sextus Pompeius
Hath given the dare to Cæsar, and commands
The empire of the sea: our slippery people
(Whose love is never link'd to the deserver
Till his deserts are past) begin to throw
Pompey the great, and all his dignities,
Upon his son; who, high in name and power,
Higher than both in blood and life, stands up
For the main soldier: whose quality, going on,
The sides o' the world may danger. Much is breeding,
Which, like the courser's hair,[b] hath yet but life,
And not a serpent's poison. Say, our pleasure,
To such whose place is under us, requires[c]
Our quick remove from hence.

ENO. I shall do 't. [*Exeunt.*

SCENE III.—*The same. Another Room in the same.*

Enter CLEOPATRA, CHARMIAN, IRAS, *and* ALEXAS.

CLEO. Where is he?

CHAR. I did not see him since.

CLEO. [*To* ALEX.] See where he is, who's with him, what he does:—
I did not send you:—if you find him sad,
Say I am dancing; if in mirth, report
That I am sudden sick: quick, and return.
[*Exit* ALEX.

CHAR. Madam, methinks, if you did love him dearly,
You do not hold the method to enforce
The like from him.

CLEO. What should I do, I do not?

CHAR. In each thing give him way, cross him in nothing.

CLEO. Thou teachest like a fool,—the way to lose him.

CHAR. Tempt him not so too far: I wish, forbear;[d]
In time we hate that which we often fear.
But here comes Antony.

CLEO. I am sick and sullen.

Enter ANTONY.

ANT. I am sorry to give breathing to my purpose,—

CLEO. Help me away, dear Charmian, I shall fall:
It cannot be thus long, the sides of nature
Will not sustain it.

ANT. Now, my dearest queen,—

CLEO. Pray you, stand farther from me.

ANT. What 's the matter?

CLEO. I know, by that same eye, there 's some good news.
What says the married woman?—You may go:
Would she had never given you leave to come!
Let her not say 'tis I that keep you here,—
I have no power upon you; hers you are.

ANT. The gods best know,—

CLEO. O, never was there queen
So mightily betray'd! yet at the first
I saw the treasons planted.

ANT. Cleopatra,—

CLEO. Why should I think you can be mine and true,
Though you in swearing shake the throned gods,
Who have been false to Fulvia? Riotous madness,
To be entangled with those mouth-made vows,
Which break themselves in swearing!

ANT. Most sweet queen,—

CLEO. Nay, pray you, seek no colour for your going,
But bid farewell, and go: when you su'd staying,

(*) Old text, *love*. Corrected by Pope.

a — expedience—] *Expedition.*

b Which, like the courser's hair, &c.] An allusion to the vulgar superstition that a horse hair left in water or dung became a living serpent.

c To such whose place is under us, requires, &c.] The lection of the second folio. In the first, we have,—

"To such whose *places* under us *require*," &c.

d I wish, forbear;] *I commend forbearance.*

Then was the time for words: no going then;—
Eternity was in our lips and eyes,
Bliss in our brows' bent; none our parts so poor,
But was a race of heaven:[a] they are so still,
Or thou, the greatest soldier of the world,
Art turn'd the greatest liar.

ANT. How now, lady!

CLEO. I would I had thy inches; thou shouldst know
There were a heart in Egypt.

ANT. Hear me, queen:
The strong necessity of time commands
Our services a while; but my full heart
Remains in use[b] with you. Our Italy
Shines o'er with civil swords: Sextus Pompeius
Makes his approaches to the port[c] of Rome:
Equality of two domestic powers
Breeds scrupulous faction: the hated, grown to strength,
Are newly-grown to love: the condemn'd Pompey,
Rich in his father's honour, creeps apace
Into the hearts of such as have not thriv'd
Upon the present state, whose numbers threaten;
And quietness, grown sick of rest, would purge
By any desperate change. My more particular,
And that which most with you should safe my going,
Is Fulvia's death.

CLEO. Though age from folly could not give me freedom,
It does from childishness:—can Fulvia die?

ANT. She 's dead, my queen:
Look here, and, at thy sovereign leisure, read
The garboils[d] she awak'd; at the last, best,[e]
See when and where she died.

CLEO. O, most false love!
Where be the sacred vials thou shouldst fill
With sorrowful water? Now I see, I see,
In Fulvia's death how mine receiv'd shall be.

ANT. Quarrel no more, but be prepar'd to know
The purposes I bear; which are, or cease,
As you shall give the advice. By the fire
That quickens Nilus' slime, I go from hence
Thy soldier-servant; making peace or war
As thou affect'st!

CLEO. Cut my lace, Charmian, come!—
But let it be:—I am quickly ill, and well,
So Antony loves.[f]

ANT. My precious queen, forbear;
And give true evidence[g] to his love, which stands
An honourable trial.

CLEO. So Fulvia told me.
I pr'ythee, turn aside and weep for her;
Then bid adieu to me, and say the tears
Belong to Egypt. Good now, play one scene
Of excellent dissembling; and let it look
Like perfect honour.

ANT. You 'll heat my blood: no more!

CLEO. You can do better yet; but this is meetly.

ANT. Now, by my* sword,—

CLEO. And target!—Still he mends;
But this is not the best:—look, pr'ythee, Charmian,
How this Herculean Roman does become
The carriage of his chief.[h]

ANT. I'll leave you, lady.

CLEO. Courteous lord, one word.
Sir, you and I must part,—but that 's not it:
Sir, you and I have lov'd,—but there 's not it;
That you know well: something it is I would,—
O, my oblivion is a very Antony,
And I am all forgotten!

ANT. But that your royalty
Holds idleness your subject, I should take you
For idleness itself.

CLEO. 'T is sweating labour
To bear such idleness so near the heart
As Cleopatra this. But, sir, forgive me;
Since my becomings kill me, when they do not
Eye well to you: your honour calls you hence,
Therefore be deaf to my unpitied folly,
And all the gods go with you! upon your sword

(*) First folio omits, *my*.

a — a race of heaven :] The meaning is probably—*of divine mould*, or *origin*.

b — in use—] *In possession.*

c — *the* port *of Rome* :] The *gate* of Rome.

d — garboils—] *Turmoils, commotions.*

e —— at the last, best,
See, &c.]
The commentators will have the word *best* to relate to the "good end" made by Fulvia. But it is no more than an epithet of endearment which Antony applies to Cleopatra;—read at your leisure the troubles she awakened; and at the last, *my best one*, see when and where she died.

f I am quickly ill, and well,
So Antony loves.]
This has been misconceived: "*So* Antony loves" is "*As* Antony loves," and the sense therefore,—My health is as fickle as the love of Antony.

g *And give* true evidence *to his love*, &c.] Mr. Collier's annotator, in his eagerness to confound all traces of our early language, would poorly read, "true *credence*," which, like many of his suggestions, is very specious and quite wrong. The meaning of Antony is this,—"Forbear these taunts, and demonstrate to the world your confidence in my love by submitting it freely to the *trial* of absence." In adopting his mythical corrector's "excellent emendation," Mr. Collier had, of course, forgotten that the very phrase rejected may be found in another of these plays,—

"Proceed no straiter 'gainst our uncle Gloster,
Than from *true evidence*, of good esteem,
He be approv'd," &c.—*Henry VI.* Pt. II. Act III. Sc. 2.

h *How this* Herculean *Roman does become*
The carriage of his chief.]
The old and every modern edition read, "The carriage of his *chafe*." But can any one who considers the epithet "Herculean," which Cleopatra applies to Antony, and reads the following extract from Shakespeare's authority, hesitate for an instant to pronounce *chafe* a silly blunder of the transcriber or compositor for "chief," meaning Hercules, the *head* or *principal* of the house of the Antonii? "Now it had bene a speech of old time, that the family of the *Antonij* were descended from one *Anton* the son of ***Hercules***, whereof the family took the name. *This opinion did Antonius seeke to confirme in all his doings: not only resembling him in the likenesse of his body, as we have said before, but also in **the wearing** of his garments.*"—*Life of Antonius.* NORTH'S ***Plutarch.***

Sit laurel Victory! and smooth success
Be strew'd before your feet!
ANT. Let us go. Come:
Our separation so abides, and flies,
That thou, residing here, go'st yet with me,
And I, hence fleeting, here remain with thee.
Away! [*Exeunt.*

SCENE IV.—Rome. *An Apartment in* Cæsar's *House.*

Enter OCTAVIUS CÆSAR, *reading a letter,* LEPIDUS, *and* Attendants.

CÆS. You may see, Lepidus, and henceforth know,
It is not Cæsar's natural vice to hate
Our[a] great competitor: from Alexandria
This is the news:—he fishes, drinks, and wastes
The lamps of night in revel: is not more man-like
Than Cleopatra; nor the queen of Ptolemy
More womanly than he: hardly gave audience,
Or vouchsaf'd* to think he had partners. You shall find there
A man who is the abstract † of all faults
That all men follow.
LEP. I must not think there are
Evils enow to darken all his goodness:
His faults, in him, seem as the spots of heaven,
More fiery by night's blackness; hereditary,
Rather than purchas'd; what he cannot change,
Than what he chooses.
CÆS. You are too indulgent. Let us grant, 't is not amiss
To tumble on the bed of Ptolemy;
To give a kingdom for a mirth; to sit
And keep the turn of tippling with a slave;
To reel the streets at noon, and stand the buffet
With knaves that smell of sweat; say, this becomes him,—
As his composure must be rare indeed
Whom these things cannot blemish,—yet must Antony
No way excuse his soils,[b] when we do bear
So great weight in his lightness. If he fill'd
His vacancy with his voluptuousness,
Full surfeits, and the dryness of his bones,
Call on him for 't:[c] but to confound such time,
That drums him from his sport, and speaks as loud
As his own state and ours,—'t is to be chid
As we rate boys, who, being mature in knowledge,
Pawn their experience to their present pleasure,
And so rebel to judgment.
LEP. Here's more news.

Enter a Messenger.

MESS. Thy biddings have been done; and every hour,
Most noble Cæsar, shalt thou have report
How 't is abroad. Pompey is strong at sea;
And it appears he is belov'd of those
That only have fear'd Cæsar: to the ports
The discontents repair, and men's reports
Give him much wrong'd.
CÆS. I should have known no less:—
It hath been taught us from the primal state,
That he which is was wish'd until he were:
And the ebb'd man, ne'er lov'd till ne'er worth love,
Comes dear'd* by being lack'd. This common body,
Like to a vagabond flag upon the stream,
Goes to, and back, lackeying† the varying tide,
To rot itself with motion.
MESS. Cæsar, I bring thee word,
Menecrates and Menas, famous pirates,
Make the sea serve them, which they ear[d] and wound
With keels of every kind: many hot inroads
They make in Italy; the borders maritime
Lack blood to think on 't, and flush youth revolt:
No vessel can peep forth, but 't is as soon
Taken as seen; for Pompey's name strikes more
Than could his war resisted.
CÆS. Antony,
Leave thy lascivious wassails.‡ When thou once
Wast beaten from Modena, where thou slew'st
Hirtius and Pansa, consuls, at thy heel
Did famine follow; whom thou fought'st against,
Though daintily brought up, with patience more
Than savages could suffer: thou didst drink
The stale of horses, and the gilded puddle
Which beasts would cough at: thy palate then did deign
The roughest berry on the rudest hedge;
Yea, like the stag, when snow the pasture sheets,
The barks of trees thou browsed'st; on the Alps
It is reported thou didst eat strange flesh,
Which some did die to look on: (3) and all this

(*) First folio, *vouchsafe.* (†) First folio, *abstracts.*

(*) Old text, *fear'd.* Corrected by Warburton.
(†) Old text, *lacking.* Corrected by Theobald.
(‡) Old text, *Vassailes.*

[a] Our *great competitor*:] So Heath; the old text having, "*One* great competitor."

[b] — *his* soils,—] A reading suggested by Malone in lieu of "*foyles*," the very doubtful word of the old text.

[c] Call on him for 't:] *Call him to account for it.* The change, "*Fall* on him," &c. of Mr. Collier's annotator is a modern dilution.

[d] — *they* ear—] They *plough.*

(It wounds thine honour that I speak it now)
Was borne so like a soldier, that thy cheek
So much as lank'd not.

LEP. 'T is pity of him.

CÆS. Let his shames quickly
Drive him to Rome: 't is time we twain
Did show ourselves i' the field; and to that end
Assemble we* immediate council. Pompey
Thrives in our idleness.

LEP. To-morrow, Cæsar,
I shall be furnish'd to inform you rightly
Both what by sea and land I can be able,
To front this present time.

CÆS. Till which encounter,
It is my business too. Farewell.

LEP. Farewell, my lord; what you shall know meantime
Of stirs abroad, I shall beseech you, sir,
To let me be partaker.

CÆS. Doubt not, sir;
I knew it for my bond. [*Exeunt.*

SCENE V.—Alexandria. *A Room in the Palace.*

Enter CLEOPATRA, CHARMIAN, IRAS, *and* MARDIAN.

CLEO. Charmian,—

CHAR. Madam.

CLEO. Ha, ha!—Give me to drink mandragora.

CHAR. Why, madam?

CLEO. That I might sleep out this great gap of time,
My Antony is away.

CHAR. You think of him too much.

CLEO. O, 't is treason!

CHAR. Madam, I trust not so.

CLEO. Thou, eunuch Mardian!

MAR. What's your highness' pleasure?

CLEO. Not now to hear thee sing; I take no pleasure
In aught an eunuch has. 'T is well for thee,
That, being unseminar'd, thy freer thoughts
May not fly forth of Egypt. Hast thou affections?

MAR. Yes, gracious madam.

CLEO. Indeed!

MAR. Not in deed, madam; for I can do nothing
But what indeed is honest to be done:
Yet I have fierce affections, and think
What Venus did with Mars.

CLEO. O, Charmian,
Where think'st thou he is now? Stands he, or sits he?
Or does he walk? or is he on his horse?
O, happy horse, to bear the weight of Antony!
Do bravely, horse! for wott'st thou whom thou mov'st?
The demi-Atlas of this earth, the arm
And burgonet of men.—He's speaking now,
Or murmuring, *Where's my serpent of old Nile?*
For so he calls me:—now I feed myself
With most delicious poison.—Think on me,
That am with Phœbus' amorous pinches black,
And wrinkled deep in time? Broad-fronted Cæsar,
When thou wast here above the ground, I was
A morsel for a monarch: and great Pompey
Would stand, and make his eyes grow in my brow;
There would he anchor his aspéct, and die
With looking on his life.

Enter ALEXAS.

ALEX. Sovereign of Egypt, hail!

CLEO. How much unlike art thou Mark Antony!
Yet, coming from him, that great med'cine hath
With his tinct gilded thee.—
How goes it with my brave Mark Antony?

ALEX. Last thing he did, dear queen,
He kiss'd,—the last of many doubled kisses,—
This orient[a] pearl:—his speech sticks in my heart.

CLEO. Mine ear must pluck it thence.

ALEX. *Good friend,* quoth he,
*Say, the firm Roman to great Egypt sends
This treasure of an oyster; at whose foot,
To mend the petty present, I will piece
Her opulent throne with kingdoms: all the east,
Say thou, shall call her mistress.* So he nodded,
And soberly did mount an arm-gaunt[b] steed,
Who neigh'd so high, that what I would have spoke
Was beastly dumb'd by him.[c]

(*) First folio, *me.*

a — orient—] *Pellucid, lustrous.* See note (a), p. 395.

b — *an* arm-gaunt *steed,*—] The epithet "arm-gaunt" has been fruitful of controversy. Hanmer reads *arm-girt;* Mason suggests, not unhappily, *termagant;* and Mr. Boaden, *arrogant.* If the original lection be genuine, which we doubt, "gaunt" must be understood to mean *fierce, eager;* a sense it, perhaps, bears in the following passage from Ben Jonson's "Catiline," Act III. Sc. 3,—

"—— and let
His own *gaunt* eagle fly at him, and tire."

c —— that what I would have spoke
Was beastly dumb'd by him.]

The correction of "dumb'd" for *dumbe*, the reading of the folio, was made by Theobald, and is countenanced by a passage in "Pericles," Act V. Sc. 1,— (GOWER.)

"Deep clerks she *dumbs;*" &c.

CLEO. What, was he sad or merry?
ALEX. Like to the time o' the year between the extremes
Of hot and cold, he was nor sad nor merry.
CLEO. O, well-divided disposition!—Note him,
Note him, good Charmian, 'tis the man; but note him:
He was not sad,—for he would shine on those
That make their looks by his; he was not merry,—
Which seem'd to tell them his remembrance lay
In Egypt with his joy; but between both:
O, heavenly mingle!—Be'st thou sad or merry,
The violence of either thee becomes
So[a] does it no man* else.—Mett'st thou my posts?
ALEX. Ay, madam, twenty several messengers:
Why do you send so thick?

(*) Old text, *mans*.

[a] So *does it*—] That is, *As* does it.

CLEO. Who's born that day
When I forget to send to Antony,
Shall die a beggar.—Ink and paper, Charmian.—
Welcome, my good Alexas.—Did I, Charmian,
Ever love Cæsar so?
CHAR. O, that brave Cæsar!
CLEO. Be chok'd with such another emphasis!
Say, *the brave Antony!*
CHAR. The valiant Cæsar!
CLEO. By Isis, I will give thee bloody teeth,
If thou with Cæsar paragon again
My man of men!
CHAR. By your most gracious pardon,
I sing but after you.
CLEO. My salad days;
When I was green in judgment, cold in blood:
To say as I said then!—But come, away:
Get me ink and paper: he shall have every day
A several greeting, or I'll unpeople Egypt.
[*Exeunt.*

ACT II.

SCENE I.—Messina. *A Room in* Pompey's *House.*

Enter POMPEY, MENECRATES, *and* MENAS.

POM. If the great gods be just, they shall[a] assist
The deeds of justest men.
MENE. Know, worthy Pompey,
That what they do delay, they not deny.
POM. Whiles we are suitors to their throne, decays
The thing we sue for.
MENE. We, ignorant of ourselves,
Beg often our own harms, which the wise powers
Deny us for our good; so find we profit,
By losing of our prayers.
POM. I shall do well:
The people love me, and the sea is mine;
My powers are crescent,[b] and my auguring hope
Says it will come to the full. Mark Antony
In Egypt sits at dinner, and will make
No wars without doors: Cæsar gets money where
He loses hearts: Lepidus flatters both,
Of both is flatter'd; but he neither loves,
Nor either cares for him.
MEN. Cæsar and Lepidus are in the field;
A mighty strength they carry.
POM. Where have you this? 'tis false.
MEN. From Silvius, sir.
POM. He dreams; I know they are in Rome together,
Looking for Antony. But all the charms of love,
Salt Cleopatra, soften thy wan'd lip!
Let witchcraft join with beauty, lust with both!
Tie up the libertine in a field of feasts;
Keep his brain fuming; Epicurean cooks

[a] — *they* shall *assist*—] The precision now observable in the employment of *shall* and *will* among the best writers was not regarded in Shakespeare's day. He commonly follows the old custom of using the former for the latter to denote futurity, whether in the second and third persons or in the first.

[b] *My* powers are *crescent, and my auguring hope*
Says it will come to the full.]

Theobald, for the sake of concord, reads, "My *power's a* crescent," &c., a change generally, though perhaps too readily, adopted by subsequent editors.

Sharpen with cloyless sauce his appetite;
That sleep and feeding may prorogue his honour
Even till a Lethe'd dulness—[a]

Enter VARRIUS.

How now, Varrius?

VAR. This is most certain that I shall deliver:—
Mark Antony is every hour in Rome
Expected; since he went from Egypt, 'tis
A space for farther travel.

POM. I could have given less matter
A better ear.—Menas, I did not think
This amorous surfeiter would have donn'd his helm
For such a petty war: his soldiership
Is twice the other twain: but let us rear
The higher our opinion, that our stirring
Can from the lap of Egypt's widow pluck
The ne'er-lust-wearied Antony.

MEN. I cannot hope[b]
Cæsar and Antony shall well greet together:
His wife that's dead did trespasses to Cæsar;
His brother warr'd* upon him; although, I think,
Not mov'd by Antony.

POM. I know not, Menas,
How lesser enmities may give way to greater.
Were't not that we stand up against them all,
'Twere pregnant they should square[c] between themselves;
For they have entertained cause enough
To draw their swords: but how the fear of us
May cement their divisions, and bind up
The petty difference, we yet not know.
Be 't as our gods will have 't! It only stands
Our lives upon[d] to use our strongest hands.
Come, Menas. [*Exeunt.*

SCENE II.—Rome. *A Room in the House of* Lepidus.

Enter ENOBARBUS *and* LEPIDUS.

LEP. Good Enobarbus, 'tis a worthy deed,
And shall become you well, to entreat your captain
To soft and gentle speech.

ENO. I shall entreat him
To answer like himself: if Cæsar move him,
Let Antony look over Cæsar's head,
And speak as loud as Mars. By Jupiter,
Were I the wearer of Antonius' beard,
I would not shave't to-day!

LEP. 'Tis not a time
For private stomaching.

ENO. Every time
Serves for the matter that is then born in 't.

LEP. But small to greater matters must give way.

ENO. Not if the small come first.

LEP. Your speech is passion:
But, pray you, stir no embers up. Here comes
The noble Antony.

Enter ANTONY *and* VENTIDIUS.

ENO. And yonder Cæsar.

Enter CÆSAR, MECÆNAS, *and* AGRIPPA.

ANT. If we compose well here, to Parthia!
Hark, Ventidius.

CÆS. I do not know, Mecænas; ask Agrippa.

LEP. Noble friends,
That which combin'd us was most great, and let not
A leaner action rend us. What's amiss,
May it be gently heard: when we debate
Our trivial difference loud, we do commit
Murder in healing wounds: then, noble partners,—
The rather, for I earnestly beseech,—
Touch you the sourest points with sweetest terms,
Nor curstness grow to the matter.

ANT. 'Tis spoken well.
Were we before our armies, and to fight,
I should do thus.

CÆS. Welcome to Rome.

ANT. Thank you.

CÆS. Sit.

ANT. Sit, sir.

CÆS. Nay, then.

ANT. I learn, you take things ill, which are not so,
Or being, concern you not.

CÆS. I must be laugh'd at,
If, or for nothing or a little, I
Should say myself offended; and with you,
Chiefly i'the world, more laugh'd at, that I should

(*) First folio, *wan'd*.

a —— *may* prorogue *his honour*
Even till *a Lethe'd dulness*—]

Malone would have "honour" to be a misprint for *hour;* but, however unauthorised, Shakespeare certainly uses "prorogue" here, as he employs it in "Pericles," Act V. Sc. 1,—

"—— nor taken sustenance,
But to *prorogue* his grief,"—

in the sense of *deaden* or *benumb*.

b *I cannot* hope, &c.] As in our early language, *to expect* most commonly meant *to stay* or *wait*, so *to hope* on some occasions was used where we should now adopt *to expect*.

c — square—] *Quarrel.*

d ——It only stands
Our lives upon—]

Our existence solely depends, &c., or it is incumbent on us for our lives' sake, &c.

Once name you derogately, when to sound your name
It not concern'd me.
ANT. My being in Egypt, Cæsar,
What was 't to you?
CÆS. No more than my residing here at Rome
Might be to you in Egypt: yet, if you there
Did practise on[a] my state, your being in Egypt
Might be my question.
ANT. How intend you, practis'd?
CÆS. You may be pleas'd to catch at mine intent
By what did here befal me. Your wife and brother
Made wars upon me; and their contestation
Was theme for you, you were the word of war.[b]
ANT. You do mistake your business; my brother never
Did urge me in his act: I did inquire it;
And have my learning from some true reports,
That drew their swords with you. Did he not rather
Discredit my authority with yours;
And make the wars alike against my stomach,
Having alike your cause? Of this, my letters
Before did satisfy you. If you 'll patch a quarrel,
As matter whole you have not[c] to make it with,
It must not be with this.
CÆS. You praise yourself
By laying defects of judgment to me; but
You patch'd up your excuses.
ANT. Not so, not so;
I know you could not lack, I am certain on 't,
Very necessity of this thought, that I,
Your partner in the cause 'gainst which he fought,
Could not with graceful eyes attend those wars
Which fronted mine own peace. As for my wife,
I would you had her spirit in such another:
The third o' the world is yours; which with a snaffle
You may pace easy, but not such a wife.
ENO. Would we had all such wives, that the men might go to wars with the women!
ANT. So much uncurbable, her garboils, Cæsar,
Made out of her impatience,—which not wanted
Shrewdness of policy too,—I grieving grant
Did you too much disquiet: for that, you must
But say, I could not help it.
CÆS. I wrote to you
When rioting in Alexandria; you
Did pocket up my letters, and with taunts
Did gibe my missive out of audience.
ANT. Sir,
He fell upon me ere admitted; then
Three kings I had newly feasted, and did want
Of what I was i' the morning: but, next day,
I told him of myself; which was as much
As to have ask'd him pardon. Let this fellow
Be nothing of our strife; if we contend,
Out of our question wipe him.
CÆS. You have broken
The article of your oath; which you shall never
Have tongue to charge me with.
LEP. Soft, Cæsar!
ANT. No, Lepidus, let him speak;
The honour 's sacred which he talks on now,
Supposing that I lack'd it.—But, on, Cæsar;
The article of my oath,—
CÆS. To lend me arms and aid when I requir'd them;
The which you both denied.
ANT. Neglected, rather;
And then when poison'd hours had bound me up
From mine own knowledge. As nearly as I may,
I 'll play the penitent to you; but mine honesty
Shall not make poor my greatness, nor my power
Work without it. Truth is, that Fulvia,
To have me out of Egypt, made wars here;
For which myself, the ignorant motive, do
So far ask pardon as befits mine honour
To stoop in such a case.
LEP. 'T is noble spoken.
MEC. If it might please you, to enforce no further
The griefs between ye: to forget them quite
Were to remember that the present need
Speaks to atone you.
LEP. Worthily spoken, Mecænas.
ENO. Or, if you borrow one another's love for the instant, you may, when you hear no more words of Pompey, return it again: you shall have time to wrangle in when you have nothing else to do.
ANT. Thou art a soldier only; speak no more.
ENO. That truth should be silent, I had almost forgot.
ANT. You wrong this presence; therefore speak no more.

---

[a] — practise on—] *Plot* or *intrigue against*.

[b] —— and their contestation
Was theme for you, you were the word of war.]

The meaning is apparent, though the construction is obscure and perhaps corrupt. We ought possibly to read,—

"—— and their contestation
Had you for theme," &c.

[c] *As matter whole you have* not *to make it with,*—] The negative was inserted by Rowe, and is clearly indispensable; but, to satisfy the metre, Shakespeare may have adopted the old form *n'have* instead of *have not*,—

"As matter whole you *n'have* to make it with."

So likewise in "Henry the Fifth," Act V. Sc. 2, where the original has, "—for they are all girdled with maiden walls, that war hath entered," we ought probably to read, "*n'hath* entered."

ENO. Go to then; your considerate stone.[a]
CÆS. I do not much dislike the matter, but
The manner of his speech: for 't cannot be
We shall remain in friendship, our conditions [b]
So differing in their acts. Yet, if I knew
What hoop should hold us stanch, from edge to edge
O' the world I would pursue it.
AGR. Give me leave, Cæsar,—
CÆS. Speak, Agrippa.
AGR. Thou hast a sister by the mother's side,
Admir'd Octavia: great Mark Antony
Is now a widower.
CÆS. Say not so,* Agrippa;
If Cleopatra heard you, your reproof [c]
Were well deserv'd of rashness.
ANT. I am not married, Cæsar; let me hear
Agrippa further speak.
AGR. To hold you in perpetual amity,
To make you brothers, and to knit your hearts
With an unslipping knot, take Antony
Octavia to his wife; whose beauty claims
No worse a husband than the best of men;
Whose virtue and whose general graces speak
That which none else can utter. By this marriage,
All little jealousies, which now seem great,
And all great fears, which now import their dangers,
Would then be nothing: truths would be tales,[d]
Where now half tales be truths: her love to both
Would, each to other, and all loves to both,
Draw after her. Pardon what I have spoke;
For 't is a studied, not a present thought,
By duty ruminated.(1)
ANT. Will Cæsar speak?
CÆS. Not till he hears how Antony is touch'd
With what is spoke already.
ANT. What power is in Agrippa,
If I would say, *Agrippa, be it so,*
To make this good?
CÆS. The power of Cæsar,
And his power unto Octavia.
ANT. May I never
To this good purpose, that so fairly shows,
Dream of impediment!—Let me have thy hand:
Further this act of grace; and from this hour,
The heart of brothers govern in our loves,
And sway our great designs!

(*) Old text, *say*.

a —your considerate stone.] *As silent as a stone* was an expression not unusual formerly, and the words in the text may hereafter be found to be proverbial; at present they are inexplicable.

b — conditions—] *Dispositions, natures;* thus, in "Othello," Act II. Sc. 1,—"She's full of most blessed *condition*," and again, Act IV. Sc. 1,—"and then, of so gentle a *condition*."

c —— *your* reproof
Were well deserv'd of rashness.]
Warburton's emendation of the old reading,—"your *proofe*," &c.

CÆS. There is my hand.
A sister I bequeath you, whom no brother
Did ever love so dearly: let her live
To join our kingdoms and our hearts: and never
Fly off our loves again!
LEP. Happily, amen!
ANT. I did not think to draw my sword 'gainst Pompey;
For he hath laid strange courtesies and great
Of late upon me: I must thank him only,
Lest my remembrance suffer ill report;
At heel of that, defy him.
LEP. Time calls upon 's:
Of us must Pompey presently be sought,
Or else he seeks out us.
ANT. Where lies he?
CÆS. About the Mount Misenum.*
ANT. What is his strength by land?
CÆS. Great and increasing: but by sea
He is an absolute master.
ANT. So is the fame.
Would we had spoke together! Haste we for it:
Yet, ere we put ourselves in arms, despatch we
The business we have talk'd of.
CÆS. With most gladness;
And do invite you to my sister's view,
Whither straight I 'll lead you.
ANT. Let us, Lepidus,
Not lack your company.
LEP. Noble Antony,
Not sickness should detain me.
[*Flourish. Exeunt* CÆSAR, ANT., *and* LEPIDUS.
MEC. Welcome from Egypt, sir.
ENO. Half the heart of Cæsar, worthy Mecænas!—My honourable friend, Agrippa!—
AGR. Good Enobarbus!
MEC. We have cause to be glad that matters are so well digested. You stayed well by it in Egypt.
ENO. Ay, sir; we did sleep day out of countenance, and made the night light with drinking.
MEC. Eight wild boars roasted whole at a breakfast, and but twelve persons there! is this true?
ENO. This was but as a fly by an eagle: we had much more monstrous matter of feast, which worthily deserved noting.
MEC. She 's a most triumphant lady, if report be square to her.

(*) Old text, *Mount-Mesena.*

The meaning apparently is, The reproof you would receive were well deserved *for* the rashness of your speech.

d —— *truths would* be *tales,*
Where now half tales be truths:]
Theobald, to perfect the metre, inserted *but*,—
"—— would be but tales," &c.;
and Steevens, for the same purpose, proposed,—"*as* tales." Yet the remedy most accordant with the poet's manner is to read,—
"—— truths would be *half* tales,
Where now half tales be truths."

ENO. When she first met Mark Antony, she pursed up his heart, upon the river of Cydnus.

AGR. There she appeared indeed; or my reporter devised well for her.

ENO. I will tell you.
The barge she sat in, like a burnish'd throne,
Burnt on the water: the poop was beaten gold;
Purple the sails, and so perfumed that
The winds were love-sick with them; the oars were silver,
Which to the tune of flutes kept stroke, and made
The water which they beat to follow faster,
As amorous of their strokes. For her own person,
It beggar'd all description: she did lie
In her pavilion, (cloth-of-gold of tissue)[a]
O'er-picturing that Venus where we see
The fancy outwork nature: on each side her
Stood pretty dimpled boys, like smiling Cupids,
With divers-colour'd fans, whose wind did seem
To glow* the delicate cheeks which they did cool,
And what they undid, did.[b]

AGR. O, rare for Antony!

ENO. Her gentlewomen, like the Nereides,
So many mermaids, tended her i' the eyes,
And made their bends adornings:[c] at the helm
A seeming mermaid steers; the silken tackle
Swell with the touches of those flower-soft hands,
That yarely frame the office. From the barge
A strange invisible pérfume hits the sense
Of the adjacent wharfs. The city cast
Her people out upon her; and Antony,
Enthron'd 'n the market-place, did sit alone,
Whistling to the air; which, but for vacancy,
Had gone to gaze on Cleopatra too,
And made a gap in nature.(2)

AGR. Rare Egyptian!

ENO. Upon her landing, Antony sent to her,
Invited her to supper: she replied,
It should be better he became her guest;
Which she entreated: our courteous Antony,
Whom ne'er the word of *No* woman heard speak,
Being barber'd ten times o'er, goes to the feast,
And, for his ordinary, pays his heart
For what his eyes eat only.

AGR. Royal wench!
She made great Cæsar lay his sword to bed;
He plough'd her, and she cropp'd.

ENO. I saw her once
Hop forty paces through the public street;
And having lost her breath, she spoke, and panted,
That she did make defect perfection,
And, breathless, power breathe forth.

MEC. Now Antony must leave her utterly.

ENO. Never; he will not;
Age cannot wither her, nor custom stale
Her infinite variety: other women cloy
The appetites they feed; but she makes hungry
Where most she satisfies: for vilest things
Become themselves in her, that the holy priests
Bless her when she is riggish.

MEC. If beauty, wisdom, modesty, can settle
The heart of Antony, Octavia is
A blessed lottery to him.

AGR. Let us go.—
Good Enobarbus, make yourself my guest,
Whilst you abide here.

ENO. Humbly, sir, I thank you.
[*Exeunt.*

SCENE III.—*The same. A Room in* Cæsar's *House.*

Enter CÆSAR, ANTONY, OCTAVIA *between them, and* Attendants.

ANT. The world and my great office will sometimes
Divide me from your bosom.

OCTA. All which time
Before the gods my knee shall bow my prayers
To them for you.

(*) Old text, *glove.*

a —(*cloth-of-gold* of *tissue*)—] That is, cloth-of-gold *on* a ground of tissue. The expression so repeatedly occurs in early English books that we cannot imagine how any one familiar with such reading can have missed it. And yet Mr. Collier, adopting the modernization of his annotator,—"cloth of gold *and* tissue," observes with incredible simplicity that "'cloth of gold *of* tissue,' as it stands in the old copies, is nonsense; it could not be cloth of gold if it were *of* tissue."!

b *To glow the delicate cheeks which they did cool,*
And what they undid, did.]

Johnson makes exception to the last phrase, and would read,—

"And what they *did, undid;*"

we should prefer,—

"And what they *undy'd, dy'd,*"

that is, while diminishing the colour of Cleopatra's cheeks, by cooling them, they reflected a new glow from the warmth of their own tints.

c —— tended her i' the eyes,
And made their bends adornings:]

The disputation on this *crux* in the *Variorum* extends over six closely printed pages, and though amusing, is not very instructive. For "tended her i' the eyes,"—which, if it have any sense, must signify *waited upon her in her sight,*—Mason proposed "tended her i' the *guise,*" that is, the guise of mermaids, understanding "their bends *which they made adornings*" to mean the caudal appendages which common opinion has always assigned to the descendants of Nereus! This is sufficiently absurd, and has been mercilessly ridiculed by Steevens. Warburton's suggestion to read *adorings* for "adornings" is of a very different character. By adopting this likely substitution, and supposing the not improbable transposition of "eyes" and "bends," we may at least obtain a meaning:—

"—— tended her i' the *bends,*
And made their *eyes adorings.*"

It may count for something, though not much, in favour of the transposition we assume, that in "Pericles," Act II. Sc. 4, we find,—

"That all *those eyes ador'd* them."

ANT. Good night, sir.—My Octavia,
Read not my blemishes in the world's report:
I have not kept my square; but that to come
Shall all be done by the rule. Good night, dear lady.—

OCTA. Good night, sir.[a]

CÆS. Good night.

[*Exeunt* CÆSAR *and* OCTAVIA.

Enter Soothsayer.

ANT. Now, sirrah,—you do wish yourself in Egypt?

SOOTH. Would I had never come from thence, nor you thither!

ANT. If you can, your reason?

SOOTH. I see it in my motion, have it not in my tongue: but yet hie you to Egypt again.

ANT. Say to me,
Whose fortunes shall rise higher, Cæsar's or mine?

SOOTH. Cæsar's.
Therefore, O Antony, stay not by his side:
Thy demon (that thy spirit which keeps thee) is
Noble, courageous, high, unmatchable,
Where Cæsar's is not; but, near him, thy angel
Becomes a Fear,[b] as being o'erpower'd; therefore
Make space enough between you.

ANT. Speak this no more.

SOOTH. To none but thee; no more, but when to thee.
If thou dost play with him at any game,
Thou art sure to lose; and, of that natural luck,
He beats thee 'gainst the odds: thy lustre thickens
When he shines by: I say again, thy spirit
Is all afraid to govern thee near him;
But, he away,* 't is noble.

ANT. Get thee gone:
Say to Ventidius I would speak with him:—

[*Exit* Soothsayer.

He shall to Parthia.—Be it art or hap,
He hath spoken true: the very dice obey him;
And, in our sports, my better cunning faints
Under his chance: if we draw lots, he speeds;
His cocks do win the battle still of mine,
When it is all to nought; and his quails ever
Beat mine, inhoop'd, at odds.(3) I will to Egypt:
And though I make this marriage for my peace,
I' the east my pleasure lies.—

---

[a] Good night, sir.] So the second folio; in the first, these words form a portion of Antony's speech.

[b] Becomes a Fear,—] The personification of fear renders the passage more poetical; but it may be questioned, considering the old text has, "Becomes *a feare*," whether Upton's conjectural emendation, "Becomes *afeard*," is not the true reading.

(*) Old text, *alway*.

Enter VENTIDIUS.

O, come, Ventidius,
You must to Parthia: your commission 's ready;
Follow me, and receive it. [*Exeunt.*

SCENE IV.—*The same. A Street.*

Enter LEPIDUS, MECÆNAS, *and* AGRIPPA.

LEP. Trouble yourselves no further: pray you, hasten
Your generals after.
AGR. Sir, Mark Antony
Will e'en but kiss Octavia, and we 'll follow.
LEP. Till I shall see you in your soldier's dress,
Which will become you both, farewell.
MEC. We shall,
As I conceive the journey, be at Mount[a]
Before you, Lepidus.
LEP. Your way is shorter;
My purposes do draw me much about:
You 'll win two days upon me.
MEC., AGR. Sir, good success!
LEP. Farewell. [*Exeunt.*

SCENE V.—Alexandria. *A Room in the Palace.*

Enter CLEOPATRA, CHARMIAN, IRAS, *and* ALEXAS.

CLEO. Give me some music;—music, moody food
Of us that trade in love.
ATT. The music, ho!

Enter MARDIAN.

CLEO. Let it alone; let us to billiards:
Come, Charmian.
CHAR. My arm is sore; best play with Mardian.
CLEO. As well a woman with an eunuch play'd
As with a woman.—Come, you 'll play with me, sir?
MAR. As well as I can, madam.

CLEO. And when good will is show'd, though 't come too short,
The actor may plead pardon. I 'll none now:—
Give me mine angle,—we 'll to the river: there,
My music playing far off, I will betray
Tawny-finn'd* fishes; my bended hook shall pierce
Their slimy jaws; and, as I draw them up,
I 'll think them every one an Antony,
And say, *Ah, ha! you 're caught.*
CHAR. 'T was merry when
You wager'd on your angling; when your diver
Did hang a salt-fish on his hook, which he
With fervency drew up. (4)
CLEO. That time,—O, times!—
I laugh'd him out of patience; and that night
I laugh'd him into patience; and next morn,
Ere the ninth hour, I drunk him to his bed;
Then put my tires and mantles on him, whilst
I wore his sword Philippan.[b]

Enter a Messenger.

O, from Italy!
Ram[c] thou thy fruitful tidings in mine ears,
That long time have been barren.
MESS. Madam, madam,—
CLEO. Antony's dead!—If thou say so, villain,
Thou kill'st thy mistress: but, *well and free!*
If thou so yield him, there is gold, and here
My bluest veins to kiss,—a hand that kings
Have lipp'd, and trembled kissing.
MESS. First, madam, he is well.
CLEO. Why, there 's more gold. But, sirrah, mark; we use
To say the dead are well: bring it to that,
The gold I give thee will I melt and pour
Down thy ill-uttering throat.
MESS. Good madam, hear me.
CLEO. Well, go to, I will;
But there 's no goodness in thy face: if Antony
Be free and healthful—so tart a favour[d]
To trumpet such good tidings! If not well,
Thou shouldst come like a Fury crown'd with snakes,
Not like a formal[e] man.
MESS. Will 't please you hear me
CLEO. I have a mind to strike thee ere thou speak'st:
Yet, if thou say Antony lives, 'tis well;
Or friends with Cæsar, or not captive to him,

[a] — be at Mount—] Mount Misenum. The second folio reads,—"at *the* Mount."

[b] — *his sword* Philippan.] The sword so named after the great battle of Philippi.

[c] Ram *thou,* &c.] Hanmer was of opinion Shakespeare wrote,—"*Rain* thou," &c. Assuredly not; the expression in the text is quite characteristic of the speaker.

[d] Be free and healthful—so tart a favour, &c.] Some editors, after Hanmer, print,—"*why* so tart a favour," &c.

[e] — *a* formal *man.*] A *composed, sober-minded* man. Thus in "The Comedy of Errors," Act V. Sc. 1,—

"With wholesome syrups, drugs, and holy prayers,
To make of him *a formal man* again."

(*) Old text, *Tawny fine.*

I 'll set thee in a shower of gold, and hail
Rich pearls upon thee.
MESS. Madam, he 's well.
CLEO. Well said.
MESS. And friends with Cæsar.
CLEO. Thou 'rt an honest man.
MESS. Cæsar and he are greater friends than ever.
CLEO. Make thee a fortune from me.
MESS. But yet, madam,—
CLEO. I do not like *but yet*, it does allay
The good precedence; fie upon *but yet!*
But yet is as a gaoler to bring forth
Some monstrous malefactor. Pr'ythee, friend,
Pour out the pack of matter to mine ear,
The good and bad together: he 's friends with Cæsar;
In state of health thou say'st; and thou say'st free.
MESS. *Free*, madam! no, I made no such report:
He 's bound unto Octavia.
CLEO. For what good turn?
MESS. For the best turn i' the bed.
CLEO. I am pale, Charmian.

MESS. Madam, he 's married to Octavia.
CLEO. The most infectious pestilence upon thee!
[*Strikes him down.*
MESS. Good madam, patience.
CLEO. What say you?—Hence,
[*Strikes him again.*
Horrible villain! or I 'll spurn thine eyes
Like balls before me; I 'll unhair thy head;
[*She hales him up and down.*
Thou shalt be whipp'd with wire, and stew'd in brine,
Smarting in ling'ring pickle.
MESS. Gracious madam,
I that do bring the news made not the match.
CLEO. Say 't is not so, a province I will give thee,
And make thy fortunes proud: the blow thou hadst
Shall make thy peace for moving me to rage;
And I will boot thee with what gift beside
Thy modesty can beg.
MESS. He 's married, madam.
CLEO. Rogue, thou hast liv'd too long.
[*Draws a knife.*

MESS. Nay, then I 'll run.—
What mean you, madam? I have made no fault. [*Exit.*

CHAR. Good madam, keep yourself within yourself;
The man is innocent.

CLEO. Some innocents 'scape not the thunder-bolt.—
Melt Egypt into Nile! and kindly creatures
Turn all to serpents!—Call the slave again:—
Though I am mad, I will not bite him:—call!

CHAR. He is afeard to come.

CLEO. I will not hurt him:— [*Exit* CHARMIAN.
These hands do lack nobility that they strike
A meaner than myself; since I myself
Have given myself the cause.—

Re-enter CHARMIAN *and* Messenger.

Come hither, sir.
Though it be honest, it is never good
To bring bad news: give to a gracious message
An host of tongues; but let ill tidings tell
Themselves, when they be felt.

MESS. I have done my duty.

CLEO. Is he married?
I cannot hate thee worser than I do
If thou again say *Yes.*

MESS. He 's married, madam.

CLEO. The gods confound thee! dost thou hold there still?

MESS. Should I lie, madam?

CLEO. O, I would thou didst,
So half my Egypt were submerg'd, and made
A cistern for scal'd snakes! Go, get thee hence:
Hadst thou Narcissus in thy face, to me
Thou wouldst appear most ugly. He is married?

MESS. I crave your highness' pardon.

CLEO. He is married?

MESS. Take no offence that I would not offend you:
To punish me for what you make me do
Seems much unequal: he 's married to Octavia.

CLEO. O, that his fault should make a knave of thee,
That art not what thou'rt sure of![a]—Get thee hence:
The merchandise which thou hast brought from Rome
Are all too dear for me; lie they upon thy hand,
And be undone by 'em! [*Exit* Messenger.

CHAR. Good your highness, patience.

CLEO. In praising Antony, I have disprais'd Cæsar.

CHAR. Many times, madam.

CLEO. I am paid for 't now.
Lead me from hence;
I faint:—O, Iras, Charmian!—'t is no matter.—
Go to the fellow, good Alexas; bid him
Report the feature of Octavia, her years,
Her inclination; let him not leave out
The colour of her hair:—bring me word quickly.— [*Exit* ALEXAS.
Let him for ever go:—let him not—Charmian,
Though he be painted one way like a Gorgon,
The other way 's a Mars.[b]—Bid you Alexas [*To* MARDIAN.
Bring me word how tall she is.—Pity me, Charmian,
But do not speak to me.—Lead me to my chamber. [*Exeunt.*

SCENE VI.—*Near* Misenum.

Flourish. Enter POMPEY *and* MENAS *from one side, with drum and trumpet; from the other,* CÆSAR, ANTONY, LEPIDUS, ENOBARBUS, MECÆNAS, *with* Soldiers *marching.*

POM. Your hostages I have, so have you mine;
And we shall talk before we fight.

CÆS. Most meet
That first we come to words; and therefore have
Our written purposes before us sent;
Which, if thou hast consider'd, let us know
If 't will tie up thy discontented sword,
And carry back to Sicily much tall youth
That else must perish here.

POM. To you all three,
The senators alone of this great world,
Chief factors for the gods,—I do not know
Wherefore my father should revengers want,
Having a son and friends; since Julius Cæsar,
Who at Philippi the good Brutus ghosted,
There saw you labouring for him. What was 't
That mov'd pale Cassius to conspire? and what
Made the[c] all-honour'd, honest Roman, Brutus,
With the arm'd rest, courtiers of beauteous freedom,

---

a That art not what thou 'rt sure of!—] Mason's arrangement of this passage,—
"That art not!—What? thou 'rt sure *of 't?*"
is preferred by Steevens and some later editors; but the simple change proposed, though not adopted, by Malone, is more Shakespearian,—
"That art not what thou 'rt *sore* of!"

b Though he be painted one way like a Gorgon,
The other way 's a Mars.—]
An allusion to the "double" pictures in vogue formerly, of which Burton says,—"Like those double or turning pictures; stand before which you see a fair maid, on the one side an ape, on the other an owl." And Chapman, in "All Fools," Act I. Sc. 1,—
"But like a couzening picture, which *one way*
Shows like a crow, another like a swan."

c *Made* the *all-honour'd, &c.*] "The" is inserted from the second folio.

To drench the Capitol; but that they would
Have one man but a man? And that is it
Hath made me rig my navy; at whose burden
The anger'd ocean foams; with which I meant
To scourge the ingratitude that despiteful Rome
Cast on my noble father.

CÆS. Take your time.

ANT. Thou canst not fear[a] us, Pompey, with thy sails,
We'll speak with thee at sea: at land, thou know'st
How much we do o'er-count thee.

POM. At land, indeed,
Thou dost o'er-count me of my father's house;[b]
But, since the cuckoo builds not for himself,
Remain in 't as thou mayst.

LEP. Be pleas'd to tell us
(For this is from the present) how you take
The offers we have sent you.

CÆS. There 's the point.

ANT. Which do not be entreated to, but weigh
What it is worth embrac'd.

CÆS. And what may follow,
To try a larger fortune.

POM. You have made me offer
Of Sicily, Sardinia; and I must
Rid all the sea of pirates; then, to send
Measures of wheat to Rome; this 'greed upon,
To part with unhack'd edges, and bear back
Our targes undinted.

CÆS., ANT., LEP. That 's our offer.

POM. Know then,
I came before you here, a man prepar'd
To take this offer: but Mark Antony
Put me to some impatience.—Though I lose
The praise of it by telling, you must know,
When Cæsar and your brother were at blows,
Your mother came to Sicily, and did find
Her welcome friendly.

ANT. I have heard it, Pompey;
And am well studied for a liberal thanks
Which I do owe you.

POM. Let me have your hand:
I did not think, sir, to have met you here.

ANT. The beds i' the east are soft; and thanks to you,
That call'd me, timelier than my purpose, hither;
For I have gain'd by 't.

CÆS. Since I saw you last,
There is a change upon you.

POM. Well, I know not
What counts harsh Fortune casts upon my face;
But in my bosom shall she never come,
To make my heart her vassal.

LEP. Well met here.

POM. I hope so, Lepidus.—Thus we are agreed;
I crave our composition may be written,
And seal'd between us.

CÆS. That 's the next to do.

POM. We'll feast each other ere we part; and let's
Draw lots who shall begin.

ANT. That will I, Pompey.

POM. No, Antony, take the lot: but, first or last, your fine Egyptian cookery shall have the fame. I have heard that Julius Cæsar grew fat with feasting there.

ANT. You have heard much.

POM. I have fair meanings,* sir.

ANT. And fair words to them.

POM. Then so much have I heard:—
And I have heard, Apollodorus carried—

ENO. No more of that:—he did so.

POM. What, I pray you?

ENO. A certain queen to Cæsar in a mattress.

POM. I know thee now: how far'st thou, soldier?

ENO. Well;
And well am like to do; for I perceive
Four feasts are toward.

POM. Let me shake thy hand;
I never hated thee: I have seen thee fight,
When I have envied thy behaviour.

ENO. Sir,
I never lov'd you much; but I have prais'd ye,
When you have well deserv'd ten times as much
As I have said you did.

POM. Enjoy thy plainness,
It nothing ill becomes thee.—
Aboard my galley I invite you all:
Will you lead, lords?

CÆS., ANT., LEP. Show us the way, sir.

POM. Come.

[*Exeunt all except* MENAS *and* ENOBARBUS.

MEN. [*Aside.*] Thy father, Pompey, would ne'er have made this treaty.—You and I have known, sir.

ENO. At sea, I think.

MEN. We have, sir.

ENO. You have done well by water.

MEN. And you by land.

ENO. I will praise any man that will praise me; though it cannot be denied what I have done by land.

MEN. Nor what I have done by water.

ENO. Yes, something you can deny for your own safety; you have been a great thief by sea.

MEN. And you by land.

ENO. There I deny my land service. But give me your hand, Menas: if our eyes had authority, here they might take two thieves kissing.

MEN. All men's faces are true, whatsoe'er their hands are.

---

[a] *Thou canst not* fear *us*, &c.] Thou canst not *affright* us.

[b] — my father's house;] The circumstance to which this taunt refers is told in North's Plutarch:—"Afterwards, when Pompey's house was put to open sale, Antonius bought it; but when they asked him money for it, he made it very straunge, and was offended with them."

(*) Old text, *meaning*. Corrected by Heath.

ENO. But there is never a fair woman has a true face.

MEN. No slander; they steal hearts.

ENO. We came hither to fight with you.

MEN. For my part, I am sorry it is turned to a drinking. Pompey doth this day laugh away his fortune.

ENO. If he do, sure, he cannot weep 't back again.

MEN. You 've said, sir. We looked not for Mark Antony here. Pray you, is he married to Cleopatra?

ENO. Cæsar's sister is called Octavia.

MEN. True, sir; she was the wife of Caius Marcellus.

ENO. But she is now the wife of Marcus Antonius.

MEN. Pray ye, sir?

ENO. 'T is true.

MEN. Then is Cæsar and he for ever knit together.

ENO. If I were bound to divine of this unity, I would not prophesy so.

MEN. I think the policy of that purpose made more in the marriage than the love of the parties.

ENO. I think so too. But you shall find, the band that seems to tie their friendship together will be the very strangler of their amity: Octavia is of a holy, cold, and still conversation.

MEN. Who would not have his wife so?

ENO. Not he that himself is not so; which is Mark Antony. He will to his Egyptian dish again: then shall the sighs of Octavia blow the fire up in Cæsar; and, as I said before, that which is the strength of their amity shall prove the immediate author of their variance. Antony will use his affection where it is; he married but his occasion here.

MEN. And thus it may be. Come, sir, will you aboard? I have a health for you.

ENO. I shall take it, sir; we have used our throats in Egypt.

MEN. Come, let's away. [*Exeunt.*

SCENE VII.—*On board* Pompey's *Galley, lying off* Misenum.

A banquet set out, Servants *attending. Music.*

1 SERV. Here they'll be, man. Some o' their plants[a] are ill-rooted already, the least wind i' the world will blow them down.

2 SERV. Lepidus is high-coloured.

1 SERV. They have made him drink alms-drink.[b]

2 SERV. As they pinch one another by the disposition,[c] he cries out, *no more;* reconciles them to his entreaty, and himself to the drink.

1 SERV. But it raises the greater war between him and his discretion.

2 SERV. Why this it is to have a name in great men's fellowship: I had as lief have a reed that will do me no service, as a partisan[d] I could not heave.

1 SERV. To be called into a huge sphere, and not to be seen to move in't, are the holes where eyes should be, which pitifully disaster the cheeks.

Sennet. Enter CÆSAR, ANTONY, POMPEY, LEPIDUS, AGRIPPA, MECÆNAS, ENOBARBUS, MENAS, *with other* Captains.

ANT. [*To* CÆSAR.] Thus do they, sir: they take the flow o' the Nile(5)
By certain scales i' the pyramid; they know,
By the height, the lowness, or the mean, if dearth
Or foison follow. The higher Nilus swells,
The more it promises: as it ebbs, the seedsman
Upon the slime and ooze scatters his grain,
And shortly comes to harvest.

LEP. You 've strange serpents there.

ANT. Ay, Lepidus.

LEP. Your serpent of Egypt is bred now of your mud by the operation of your sun: so is your crocodile.

ANT. They are so.

POM. Sit,—and some wine! A health to Lepidus!

LEP. I am not so well as I should be, but I'll ne'er out.

ENO. [*Aside.*] Not till you have slept; I fear me you'll be in till then.

LEP. Nay, certainly, I have heard the Ptolemies' pyramises are very goodly things; without contradiction, I have heard that.

MEN. [*Aside to* POM.] Pompey, a word.

POM. [*Aside to* MEN.] Say in mine ear: what is 't?

MEN. [*Aside to* POM.] Forsake thy seat, I do beseech thee, captain,
And hear me speak a word.

POM. [*Aside to* MEN.] Forbear me till anon.—
This wine for Lepidus!

LEP. What manner o' thing is your crocodile?

ANT. It is shaped, sir, like itself; and it is as

a —plants—] An equivoque; "plants" being used here, besides its ordinary meaning, for the soles of the feet.

b —alms-drink.] According to Warburton, "That liquor of another's share which his companion drinks to ease him."

c — *by the* disposition,—] A very questionable expression. We ought perhaps to read,—"by the *disputation*," that is, *in the controversy*.

d — a partisan—] A weapon, half pike and half halberd.

broad as it hath breadth: it is just so high as it is, and moves with it own organs: it lives by that which nourisheth it; and the elements once out of it, it transmigrates.

LEP. What colour is it of?

ANT. Of it own colour too.

LEP. 'T is a strange serpent.

ANT. 'T is so. And the tears of it are wet.

CÆS. [*Aside to* ANT.] Will this description satisfy him?

ANT. [*Aside to* CÆS.] With the health that Pompey gives him, else he is a very epicure.

POM. [*Aside to* MEN.] Go hang, sir, hang! Tell me of that? away!
Do as I bid you.—Where's this cup I call'd for?

MEN. [*Aside to* POM.] If for the sake of merit thou wilt hear me,
Rise from thy stool.

POM. [*Aside to* MEN.] I think thou'rt mad. The matter? [*Rises, and walks aside.*

MEN. I have ever held my cap off to thy fortunes.

POM. Thou hast serv'd me with much faith. What's else to say?—
Be jolly, lords.

ANT. These quicksands, Lepidus,
Keep off them, for[a] you sink.

MEN. Wilt thou be lord of all the world?

POM. What say'st thou?

MEN. Wilt thou be lord of the whole world? That's twice.

POM. How should that be?

MEN. But entertain it,
And, though thou think me poor, I am the man
Will give thee all the world.

POM. Hast thou drunk well?

MEN. No, Pompey, I have kept me from the cup.
Thou art, if thou dar'st be, the earthly Jove:
Whate'er the ocean pales, or sky inclips,
Is thine, if thou wilt ha't.

POM. Show me which way.

MEN. These three world-sharers, these competitors,
Are in thy vessel: let me cut the cable;
And, when we are put off, fall to their throats;
All there[b] is thine.

POM. Ah, this thou shouldst have done,
And not have spoke on't! In me 'tis villany;
In thee 't had been good service. Thou must know,
'T is not my profit that does lead mine honour;
Mine honour, it. Repent that e'er thy tongue
Hath so betray'd thine act: being done unknown,
I should have found it afterwards well done;
But must condemn it now.(6) Desist, and drink.

MEN. [*Aside.*] For this, I'll never follow thy pall'd fortunes more.—
Who seeks, and will not take when once 't is offer'd,
Shall never find it more.

POM. This health to Lepidus!

ANT. Bear him ashore.—I'll pledge it for him, Pompey.

ENO. Here's to thee, Menas.

MEN. Enobarbus, welcome!

POM. Fill till the cup be hid.

ENO. There's a strong fellow, Menas.
[*Pointing to the* Attendant *who carries off* LEPIDUS.

MEN. Why?

ENO. 'A bears the third part of the world, man; see'st not?

MEN. The third part, then, is * drunk: would it were all,
That it might go on wheels!

ENO. Drink thou; increase the reels.

MEN. Come.

POM. This is not yet an Alexandrian feast.

ANT. It ripens towards it.—Strike[c] the vessels, ho!—
Here is to Cæsar.

CÆS. I could well forbear 't.
It's monstrous labour when I wash my brain
And it grows† fouler.

ANT. Be a child o' the time.

CÆS. Possess it, I'll make answer:[d]
But I had rather fast from all four days,
Than drink so much in one.

ENO. [*To* ANTONY.] Ha, my brave emperor!
Shall we dance now the Egyptian Bacchanals,
And celebrate our drink?

POM. Let's ha't, good soldier.

ANT. Come, let us all take hands,
Till that the conquering wine hath steep'd our sense
In soft and delicate Lethe.

ENO. All take hands.—
Make battery to our ears with the loud music:—
The while I'll place you: then the boy shall sing;
The holding every man shall bear ‡ as loud
As his strong sides can volley.
[*Music plays.* ENOBARBUS *places them hand in hand.*

(*) Old text, *then he is.* (†) First folio, *grow.*
(‡) Old text, *beat.* Corrected by Theobald.

a — for *you sink.*] Here, possibly, as in two or three other instances, "for" is a misprint of *fore*.

b *All* there *is thine.*] Southern changed this to "All *then,*" &c., and Mr. Collier's annotator availed himself of the alteration.

c Strike *the vessels,*—] To *strike* means *to tap, to broach,* or *pierce* a cask.

d Possess *it, I'll make answer:*] There is some ambiguity in the word "possess," which, if not a misprint, is employed here in a sense we are unaccustomed to; but the meaning of the passage is plain enough. In former days it was the practice, when one good fellow drank to another, for the latter to "do him right" by imbibing a quantity of wine equal to that quaffed by the health-giver. Antony proposes a health to Cæsar, but Cæsar endeavours to excuse himself, whereupon Antony urges him by saying, "Be a child o' the time," *i. e. do as others do; indulge for once.* Cæsar then consents to pledge the health, and says "*possess* it," or *propose* it,—I'll do it justice. Mr. Collier's annotator suggests that we should read, "*Profess* it," &c.

SONG.

Come, thou monarch of the vine,
Plumpy Bacchus with pink eyne! [a]
In thy vats our cares be drown'd;
With thy grapes our hairs be crown'd;

ALL. { *Cup us, till the world go round;*
Cup us, till the world go round!

CÆS. What would you more?—Pompey, good night.—Good brother,
Let me request you off: our graver business
Frowns at this levity.—Gentle lords, let's part;
You see we have burnt our cheeks: strong Enobarb
Is weaker than the wine; and mine own tongue
Splits what it speaks: the wild disguise hath almost
Antick'd us all. What needs more words? Good night.—
Good Antony, your hand.

POM. I'll try you on the shore.

ANT. And shall, sir: give's your hand.

POM. O, Antony, you have my father's house,—
But what? we are friends: Come down into the boat.

ENO. Take heed you fall not.—

[*Exeunt* POMPEY, CÆSAR, ANTONY, *and* Attendants.

Menas, I'll not on shore.

MEN.[b] No, to my cabin.—
These drums!—these trumpets, flutes! what!—
Let Neptune hear we bid a loud farewell
To these great fellows: sound and be hang'd! sound out!

[*A flourish of trumpets, with drums.*

ENO. Ho! says 'a.—There's my cap.

MEN. Ho!—noble captain, come. [*Exeunt.*

[a] *—pink eyne!*] *Small eyes.*

[b] MEN.] By the inadvertent omission of the prefix in the old copies, this speech is made to appear a part of what Enobarbus says.

ACT III.

SCENE I. *A Plain in* Syria.

Enter Ventidius *in triumph, with* Silius, *and other* Romans, Officers *and* Soldiers: *the dead body of* Pacorus *borne before him.*

Ven. Now, darting Parthia, art thou struck; and now
Pleas'd fortune does of Marcus Crassus' death
Make me revenger.—Bear the king's son's body
Before our army.—Thy Pacorus, Orodes,[a]
Pays this for Marcus Crassus.

Sil. Noble Ventidius,
Whilst yet with Parthian blood thy sword is warm,
The fugitive Parthians follow; spur through Media,
Mesopotamia, and the shelters whither
The routed fly; so thy grand captain, Antony,
Shall set thee on triumphant chariots, and
Put garlands on thy head.

Ven. O, Silius, Silius!
I have done enough: a lower place, note well,
May make too great an act; for learn this, Silius,—
Better to leave undone, than by our deed
Acquire too high a fame when him we serve 's away.
Cæsar and Antony have ever won
More in their officer than person: Sossius,
One of my place in Syria, his lieutenant,
For quick accumulation of renown,
Which he achiev'd by the minute, lost his favour.
Who does i' the wars more than his captain can,
Becomes his captain's captain; and ambition,
The soldier's virtue, rather makes choice of loss,
Than gain which darkens him.
I could do more to do Antonius good,

[a] — Thy Pacorus, Orodes,—] Pacorus was the son of Orodes, the Parthian king.

But 't would offend him; and in his offence
Should my performance perish.

SIL. Thou hast, Ventidius, that
Without the which a soldier, and his sword,
Grants[a] scarce distinction. Thou wilt write to Antony?

VEN. I 'll humbly signify what in his name,
That magical word of war, we have effected;
How, with his banners, and his well-paid ranks,
The ne'er-yet-beaten horse of Parthia
We have jaded out o' the field.

SIL. Where is he now?

VEN. He purposeth to Athens: whither with what haste
The weight we must convey with 's will permit,
We shall appear before him.—On there! pass along! [*Exeunt.*

SCENE II.—Rome. *An Ante-Chamber in* Cæsar's *House.*

Enter AGRIPPA *and* ENOBARBUS, *meeting.*

AGR. What, are the brothers parted?

ENO. They have dispatch'd with Pompey, he is gone;
The other three are sealing. Octavia weeps
To part from Rome; Cæsar is sad; and Lepidus,
Since Pompey's feast, as Menas says, is troubled
With the green sickness.

AGR. 'T is a noble Lepidus.

ENO. A very fine one: O, how he loves Cæsar!

AGR. Nay, but how dearly he adores Mark Antony!

ENO. Cæsar? Why, he 's the Jupiter of men.

AGR. What 's Antony? The god of Jupiter.

ENO. Spake you of Cæsar? Ho! the non-pareil!

AGR. O, Antony! O, thou Arabian bird!

ENO. Would you praise Cæsar, say,—*Cæsar;* —go no further.

AGR. Indeed, he plied them both with excellent praises.

ENO. But he loves Cæsar best;—yet he loves Antony:
Ho! hearts, tongues, figures,* scribes, bards, poets, cannot
Think, speak, cast, write, sing, number,—ho!—
His love to Antony. But as for Cæsar,
Kneel down, kneel down, and wonder!

AGR. Both he loves.

ENO. They are his shards,[b] and he their beetle.
So,— [*Trumpets.*
This is to horse.—Adieu, noble Agrippa.

AGR. Good fortune, worthy soldier; and farewell. [AGRIP. *and* ENOB. *retire.*

Enter CÆSAR, ANTONY, LEPIDUS, *and* OCTAVIA.

ANT. No further, sir.

CÆS. You take from me a great part of myself;
Use me well in 't.—Sister, prove such a wife
As my thoughts make thee, and as my farthest band[c]
Shall pass on thy approof.—Most noble Antony,
Let not the piece of virtue which is set
Betwixt us as the cement of our love,
To keep it builded, be the ram to batter
The fortress of it: for better might we
Have lov'd without this mean, if on both parts
This be not cherish'd.

ANT. Make me not offended
In your distrust.

CÆS. I have said.

ANT. You shall not find,
Though you be therein curious,[d] the least cause
For what you seem to fear: so, the gods keep you,
And make the hearts of Romans serve your ends!
We will here part.

CÆS. Farewell, my dearest sister, fare thee well.
The elements be kind to thee,[e] and make
Thy spirits all of comfort! fare thee well.

OCTA. My noble brother!—

ANT. The April 's in her eyes: it is love's spring,
And these the showers to bring it on.—Be cheerful.

OCTA. Sir, look well to my husband's house; and—

CÆS. What,
Octavia?

OCTA. I 'll tell you in your ear.

ANT. Her tongue will not obey her heart, nor can

(*) Old text, *figure*.

[a] Grants scarce distinction.] The meaning seems to be, as Warburton was the first to show,—Thou hast that, (*wisdom*, or *prudence*) wanting which a soldier shows himself hardly better than his senseless sword. Mr. Collier's annotator, it should be observed, would read,—

"*Gains* scarce distinction."

[b] —*his* shards,—] His *scaly wings*. So in "Macbeth," Act III. Sc. 3,—

"The *shard-borne* beetle," &c.

[c] — band.] That is, *bond*.

[d] — curious,—] *Over punctilious*, or *scrupulous*.

[e] The elements be kind, &c.] Johnson's explanation of this wish,—"May the *elements* of the body, or principles of life, maintain such proportion and harmony as may keep you cheerful,"—has been decried as too profound, and the expression said to mean no more than,—"May the elements of air and water be kind to you." In other words,—"May you have a prosperous voyage." But there is a passage, altogether forgotten by the commentators, in "Julius Cæsar," Act V. Sc. 5, which is entirely confirmatory of Dr. Johnson's interpretation,—

"His life was gentle; and *the elements*
So mix'd in him, that Nature might stand up,
And say to all the world, *This was a man!*"

Her heart inform her tongue,—the swan's down-feather,
That stands upon the swell at full of tide,[a]
And neither way inclines.
ENO. [*Aside to* AGR.] Will Cæsar weep?
AGR. [*Aside to* ENO.] He has a cloud in's face.[b]
ENO. [*Aside to* AGR.] He were the worse for that, were he a horse;
So is he, being a man.
AGR. [*Aside to* ENO.] Why, Enobarbus?
When Antony found Julius Cæsar dead,
He cried almost to roaring; and he wept,
When at Philippi he found Brutus slain.
ENO. [*Aside to* AGR.] That year, indeed, he was troubled with a rheum;
What willingly he did confound he wail'd,
Believe 't, till I wept* too.
CÆS. No, sweet Octavia,
You shall hear from me still; the time shall not
Out-go my thinking on you.
ANT. Come, sir, come;
I 'll wrestle with you in my strength of love:
Look, here I have you;—thus I let you go,
And give you to the gods.
CÆS. Adieu; be happy!
LEP. Let all the number of the stars give light
To thy fair way!
CÆS. Farewell, farewell! [*Kisses* OCTAVIA.
ANT. Farewell!
[*Trumpets sound. Exeunt.*

SCENE III.—Alexandria. *A Room in the Palace.*

Enter CLEOPATRA, CHARMIAN, IRAS, *and* ALEXAS.

CLEO. Where is the fellow?
ALEX. Half afeard to come.
CLEO. Go to, go to:—

Enter a Messenger.

Come hither, sir.
ALEX. Good majesty,
Herod of Jewry dare not look upon you,
But when you are well pleas'd.
CLEO. That Herod's head
I 'll have: but how, when Antony is gone
Through whom I might command it?—Come thou near.
MESS. Most gracious majesty,—
CLEO. Didst thou behold Octavia?
MESS. Ay, dread queen.
CLEO. Where?
MESS. Madam, in Rome;
I look'd her in the face, and saw her led
Between her brother and Mark Antony.
CLEO. Is she as tall as me?
MESS. She is not, madam.
CLEO. Didst hear her speak? Is she shrill-tongu'd or low?
MESS. Madam, I heard her speak; she is low-voic'd.
CLEO. That 's not so good:—he cannot like her long.
CHAR. *Like her?* O, Isis! 't is impossible.
CLEO. I think so, Charmian: dull of tongue, and dwarfish!—
What majesty is in her gait? Remember,
If e'er thou look'dst on majesty.
MESS. She creeps,—
Her motion and her station are as one:
She shows a body rather than a life;
A statue than a breather.
CLEO. Is this certain?
MESS. Or I have no observance.
CHAR. Three in Egypt
Cannot make better note.
CLEO. He 's very knowing;
I do perceive 't:—there 's nothing in her yet:—
The fellow has good judgment.
CHAR. Excellent.
CLEO. Guess at her years, I pr'ythee.
MESS. Madam,
She was a widow,—
CLEO. *Widow!*—Charmian, hark.
MESS. And I do think she 's thirty.
CLEO. Bear'st thou her face in mind? is 't long or round?
MESS. Round even to faultiness.
CLEO. For the most part, too, they are foolish that are so.—
Her hair, what colour?
MESS. Brown, madam: and her forehead
As low as she would wish it.[c]
CLEO. There 's gold for thee.
Thou must not take my former sharpness ill:—
I will employ thee back again; I find thee
Most fit for business: go, make thee ready;
Our letters are prepar'd. [*Exit* Messenger.
CHAR. A proper man.

(*) Old text, *weepe*, corrected by Theobald.

[a] — at full *of tide*,—] So the second folio; the first reads, less harmoniously,—

"— at *the* full of Tide."

[b] — a cloud in 's face.] This is said of a horse which has a black or dark spot on his forehead between the eyes.

[c] *As low* as she would wish it.] "The phrase is still a cant one. I once overheard a chambermaid say of her rival—'that her legs were as thick *as she could wish them*.'"—STEEVENS.

CLEO. Indeed, he is so: I repent me much
That so I harried him. Why, methinks, by him,
This creature 's no such thing.

CHAR. Nothing, madam.

CLEO. The man hath seen some majesty, and should know.

CHAR. Hath he seen majesty? Isis else defend,
And serving you so long!

CLEO. I have one thing more to ask him yet, good Charmian:
But 't is no matter; thou shalt bring him to me
Where I will write. All may be well enough.

CHAR. I warrant you, madam.

[*Exeunt.*

SCENE IV.—Athens. *A Room in* Antony'*s House.*

Enter ANTONY *and* OCTAVIA.

ANT. Nay, nay, Octavia, not only that,—
That were excusable, that and thousands more
Of semblable import,—but he hath wag'd
New wars 'gainst Pompey; made his will, and read it
To public ear:
Spoke scantly of me: when perforce he could not
But pay me terms of honour, cold and sickly

He vented them: * most narrow measure lent me:
When the best hint was given him, he not took'd,[a]
Or did it from his teeth.[b]

OCTA. O, my good lord,
Believe not all; or if you must believe,
Stomach not all. A more unhappy lady,
If this division chance, ne'er stood between,
Praying for both parts:
The good gods will mock me presently,
When I shall pray, *O, bless my lord and husband!*
Undo that prayer, by crying out as loud,
O, bless my brother! Husband win, win brother,
Prays, and destroys the prayer; no midway
'Twixt these extremes at all.

ANT. Gentle Octavia,
Let your best love draw to that point which seeks
Best to preserve it: if I lose mine honour,
I lose myself: better I were not yours,
Than yours so[c] branchless. But, as you requested,
Yourself shall go between 's: the mean time, lady,
I 'll raise the preparation of a war
Shall stain[d] your brother: make your soonest haste;
So your desires are yours.

OCTA. Thanks to my lord.
The Jove of power make me, most weak, most weak,
Your† reconciler! Wars 'twixt you twain would be
As if the world should cleave, and that slain men
Should solder up the rift.

ANT. When it appears to you where this begins,
Turn your displeasure that way; for our faults
Can never be so equal, that your love
Can equally move with them. Provide your going;
Choose your own company, and command what cost
Your heart has‡ mind to. [*Exeunt.*

SCENE V.—*The same. Another Room in the same.*

Enter ENOBARBUS *and* EROS, *meeting.*

ENO. How now, friend Eros!

EROS. There 's strange news come, sir.

ENO. What, man?

EROS. Cæsar and Lepidus have made wars upon Pompey.

ENO. This is old: what is the success?[e]

EROS. Cæsar, having made use of him in the wars 'gainst Pompey, presently denied him rivality;[f] would not let him partake in the glory of the action: and not resting here, accuses him of letters he had formerly wrote to Pompey; upon his own appeal, seizes him: so the poor third is up, till death enlarge his confine.

ENO. Then, world, thou hast a pair of chaps,[g] no more;
And throw between them all the food thou hast,
They 'll grind the one[h] the other.—Where 's Antony?

EROS. He 's walking in the garden—thus; and spurns
The rush that lies before him; cries, *Fool Lepidus!*
And threats the throat of that his officer,
That murder'd Pompey.

ENO. Our great navy 's rigg'd.

EROS. For Italy and Cæsar. More, Domitius;
My lord desires you presently: my news
I might have told hereafter.

ENO. 'T will be naught:
But let it be.—Bring me to Antony.

EROS. Come, sir. [*Exeunt.*

SCENE VI.—Rome. *A Room in* Cæsar'*s House.*

Enter CÆSAR, AGRIPPA, *and* MECÆNAS.

CÆS. Contemning Rome, he has done all this, and more;
In Alexandria—here 's the manner of 't,—
I' the market-place, on a tribunal silver'd,
Cleopatra and himself in chairs of gold
Were publicly enthron'd: at the feet, sat
Cæsarion, whom they call my father's son,
And all the unlawful issue that their lust
Since then hath made between them. Unto her
He gave the stablishment of Egypt; made her
Of lower Syria, Cyprus, Lydia,
Absolute queen.

MEC. This in the public eye?

CÆS. I' the common show-place, where they exercise.

(*) Old text, *then*. (†) First folio, *You*. (‡) First folio, *he's*.

a — *he not* took'd,—] An emendation by Thirlby; the old lection being,—"he not *look'd*."

b *Or did it* from his teeth.] To do any thing *from the teeth*, was to do it in *pretence* only, not from the heart; thus Burton,—"friendship *from teeth outward*, counterfeit." So in "Withal's Dictionary for Children," 1616, quoted by Mr Singer, "*Lingua amicus:* A friend from the teeth outward."

c Than yours so, &c.] The text of the second folio, that of 1623 has, "*Then your* so," &c.

d — stain—] Stain, if correct, must mean *eclipse* or *cast in the shade;* a sense the word is often found to bear in old literature; but *stay*, as suggested by Boswell, is more accordant with the context, and may easily have been misprinted *stain*.

e — *what is the* success?] What *follows?* what is the *upshot?*

f — rivality;] *Participation, copartnership.*

g *Then*, world, *thou* hast *a pair of chaps*,—] A restoration by Hanmer; the old text having, "Then *would* thou *hadst* a paire," &c.

h *They'll grind* the one *the other*, &c.] Capell supplied, "*the one*," which had obviously been omitted in the early copies.

His sons he there* proclaim'd the kings† of kings:
Great Media, Parthia, and Armenia,
He gave to Alexander; to Ptolemy he assign'd
Syria, Cilicia, and Phœnicia. She
In the habiliments of the goddess Isis (1)
That day appear'd; and oft before gave audience,
As 't is reported, so.

MEC. Let Rome be thus inform'd.

AGR. Who, queasy with his insolence already,
Will their good thoughts call from him.

CÆS. The people know it; and have now receiv'd
His accusations.

AGR. Who does he accuse?

CÆS. Cæsar: and that, having in Sicily
Sextus Pompeius spoil'd, we had not rated him
His part o' the isle: then does he say, he lent me
Some shipping unrestor'd: lastly, he frets,
That Lepidus of the triumvirate
Should be depos'd; and, being, that we detain
All his revenue.

AGR. Sir, this should be answer'd.

CÆS. 'T is done already, and the messenger gone.
I have told him, Lepidus was grown too cruel;
That he his high authority abus'd,
And did deserve his change; for what I have conquer'd,
I grant him part; but then, in his Armenia,
And other of his conquer'd kingdoms, I
Demand the like.

MEC. He 'll never yield to that.

CÆS. Nor must not, then, be yielded to in this.

Enter OCTAVIA, *with her* Train.

OCTA. Hail, Cæsar, and my lord! hail, most dear Cæsar!

CÆS. That ever I should call thee, cast-away!

OCTA. You have not call'd me so, nor have you cause.

CÆS. Why have you stol'n upon us thus? You come not
Like Cæsar's sister: the wife of Antony
Should have an army for an usher, and
The neighs of horse to tell of her approach,
Long ere she did appear; the trees by the way
Should have borne men; and expectation fainted,
Longing for what it had not: nay, the dust
Should have ascended to the roof of heaven,
Rais'd by your populous troops: but you are come
A market-maid to Rome; and have prevented
The ostentation of our love, which, left unshown,
Is often left unlov'd:[a] we should have met you
By sea and land; supplying every stage
With an augmented greeting.

OCTA. Good my lord,
To come thus was I not constrain'd, but did it
On my free-will. My lord, Mark Antony,
Hearing that you prepar'd for war, acquainted
My grieved ear withal; whereon, I begg'd
His pardon for return. (2)

CÆS. Which soon he granted,
Being an obstruct[b] 'tween his lust and him.

OCTA. Do not say so, my lord.

CÆS. I have eyes upon him,
And his affairs come to me on the wind.
Where is he now?

OCTA. My lord, in Athens.

CÆS. No, my most wronged sister; Cleopatra
Hath nodded him to her. He hath given his empire
Up to a whore; who now are levying
The kings o' the earth for war: he hath assembled
Bocchus, the king of Libya; Archelaus,
Of Cappadocia; Philadelphos, king
Of Paphlagonia; the Thracian king, Adallas;
King Malchus of Arabia; king of Pont;
Herod of Jewry; Mithridates, king
Of Comagene; Polemon and Amyntas,
The kings of Mede and Lycaonia,
With a more larger list of sceptres.

OCTA. Ay me, most wretched,
That have my heart parted betwixt two friends,
That do afflict each other!

CÆS. Welcome hither:
Your letters did withhold our breaking forth;
Till we perceived, both how you were wrong'd,[c]
And we in negligent danger. Cheer your heart:
Be you not troubled with the time, which drives
O'er your content these strong necessities;
But let determin'd things to destiny
Hold unbewail'd their way. Welcome to Rome!
Nothing more dear to me. You are abus'd
Beyond the mark of thought: and the high gods,
To do you justice, make* them ministers
Of us and those that love you. Best of comfort;
And ever welcome to us!

AGR. Welcome, lady!

(*) Old text, *hither*. Corrected by Capell.
(†) Old text, *King*.

(*) First folio, *makes his*. Corrected by Capell.

a —— *which, left unshown,*
Is often left unlov'd:—]
With more likelihood we should read,—
"Is often left *unpriz'd*."
Unlov'd is a very problematical expression here, and appears to have been partly formed by the compositor from the word *love* in the preceding line.

b *Being an* obstruct, &c.] The old copies read,—"an *abstract*." For the correction we are indebted to Warburton.

c *Till we perceived, both how you were* wrong'd,
And we, &c.]
Capell's emendation of the old text,—"how you were *wrong led*," &c., and the origin, manifestly, of that proposed by Mr. Collier's annotator,—"how you were *wronged*."

MEC. Welcome, dear madam!
Each heart in Rome does love and pity you:
Only the adulterous Antony, most large
In his abominations, turns you off;
And gives his potent regiment[a] to a trull,
That noises it against us.
OCTA. Is it so, sir?
CÆS. Most certain. Sister, welcome: pray you,
Be ever known to patience. My dear'st sister!
[*Exeunt.*

SCENE VII.—Antony's *Camp near the Promontory of* Actium.

Enter CLEOPATRA *and* ENOBARBUS.

CLEO. I will be even with thee, doubt it not.
ENO. But, why, why, why?
CLEO. Thou hast forspoke[b] my being in these wars;
And say'st, it is not fit.
ENO. Well, is it, is it?
CLEO. If not denounc'd against us,[c] why should not we
Be there in person?
ENO. [*Aside.*] Well, I could reply:—
If we should serve with horse and mares together,
The horse were merely lost; the mares would bear
A soldier and his horse.
CLEO. What is 't you say?
ENO. Your presence needs must puzzle Antony;
Take from his heart, take from his brain, from 's time,
What should not then be spar'd. He is already
Traduc'd for levity: and 't is said in Rome,
That Photinus an eunuch and your maids
Manage this war.
CLEO. Sink Rome! and their tongues rot,
That speak against us! A charge we bear i' the war,
And, as the president of my kingdom, will
Appear there for a man. Speak not against it;
I will not stay behind.
ENO. Nay, I have done.
Here comes the emperor.

Enter ANTONY *and* CANIDIUS.

ANT. Is it not strange, Canidius,
That from Tarentum and Brundusium,
He could so quickly cut the Ionian sea,
And take in[d] Toryne?—You have heard on't, sweet?
CLEO. Celerity is never more admir'd
Than by the negligent.
ANT. A good rebuke,
Which might have well becom'd the best of men,
To taunt at slackness.—Canidius, we
Will fight with him by sea.
CLEO. By sea! what else?
CAN. Why will my lord do so?
ANT. For that he dares us to 't.
ENO. So hath my lord dar'd him to single fight.
CAN. Ay, and to wage this battle at Pharsalia,
Where Cæsar fought with Pompey: but these offers,
Which serve not for his vantage, he shakes off;
And so should you.
ENO. Your ships are not well mann'd,—
Your mariners are muleters,* reapers, people
Ingross'd by swift impress; in Cæsar's fleet
Are those that often have 'gainst Pompey fought:
Their ships are yare,[e] yours, heavy. No disgrace
Shall fall you for refusing him at sea,
Being prepar'd for land.
ANT. By sea, by sea.
ENO. Most worthy sir, you therein throw away
The absolute soldiership you have by land;
Distract your army, which doth most consist
Of war-mark'd footmen; leave unexecuted
Your own renowned knowledge: quite forego
The way which promises assurance: and
Give up yourself merely to chance and hazard,
From firm security.
ANT. I'll fight at sea.
CLEO. I have sixty sails, Cæsar none better.
ANT. Our overplus of shipping will we burn;
And, with the rest full-mann'd, from the head of Actium
Beat the approaching Cæsar. But if we fail,
We then can do 't at land.—

Enter a Messenger.

Thy business?
MESS. The news is true, my lord; he is descried;
Cæsar has taken Toryne.
ANT. Can he be there in person? 't is impossible;

[a] — regiment—] *Directorship, rule, command.*
[b] — forspoke—] *Prejudiced, spoken against, forbidden.*
[c] If not denounc'd against us,—] This may mean, as Malone expounds it, "If there be no particular denunciation against me," &c.; but, as more emphatic, Shakespeare perhaps wrote,—

"If not, *denounc't* against us why," &c.

(*) First folio, *Militers.*
[d] — take in—] *Conquer, overcome.* The exact sense is shown in a passage from "A Winter's Tale," Act IV. Sc. 3,—

"I think affliction may *subdue* the cheek,
But not *take in* the mind."

[e] Yare,—] *Nimble, manageable.*

Strange that his power should be.—Canidius,
Our nineteen legions thou shalt hold by land,
And our twelve thousand horse.—We 'll to our ship,
Away, my Thetis!—

Enter a Soldier.

How now, worthy soldier!

SOLD. O, noble emperor, do not fight by sea;
Trust not to rotten planks: do you misdoubt
This sword and these my wounds? (3) Let the Egyptians
And the Phœnicians go a-ducking; we
Have used to conquer, standing on the earth,
And fighting foot to foot.

ANT. Well, well, away!

[*Exeunt* ANTONY, CLEOPATRA, *and* ENOBARBUS.

SOLD. By Hercules, I think I am i' the right.

CAN. Soldier, thou art: but his whole action grows
Not in the power on 't: so our leader 's led,
And we are women's men.

SOLD. You keep by land
The legions and the horse whole, do you not?

CAN.[a] Marcus Octavius, Marcus Justeius,
Publicola, and Cælius, are for sea:
But we keep whole by land. This speed of Cæsar's
Carries beyond belief.

SOLD. While he was yet in Rome,
His power went out in such distractions[b]
As beguil'd all spies.

CAN. Who 's his lieutenant, hear you?

SOLD. They say, one Taurus.

CAN. Well I know the man.

Enter a Messenger.

MESS. The emperor calls Canidius.

CAN. With news the time 's with labour, and throes forth,
Each minute, some. [*Exeunt.*

SCENE VIII.—*A Plain near* Actium.

Enter CÆSAR, TAURUS, Officers, *and others.*

CÆS. Taurus,—

TAUR. My lord.

CÆS. Strike not by land; keep whole;
Provoke not battle till we have done at sea.
Do not exceed the prescript of this scroll:
Our fortune lies upon this jump. [*Exeunt.*

SCENE IX.—*Another Part of the Plain.*

Enter ANTONY *and* ENOBARBUS.

ANT. Set we our squadrons on yond side o' the hill,
In eye of Cæsar's battle; from which place
We may the number of the ships behold,
And so proceed accordingly. [*Exeunt.*

SCENE X.—*Another Part of the Plain.*

Enter CANIDIUS, *marching with his land* Army *one way over the stage; and* TAURUS, *the* Lieutenant *of* CÆSAR, *the other way. After their going out, is heard the noise of a sea-fight.*

Alarum. Enter ENOBARBUS.

ENO. Naught, naught, all naught! I can behold no longer:
The Antoniad, the Egyptian admiral,
With all their sixty, fly, and turn the rudder:
To see 't, mine eyes are blasted.

Enter SCARUS.

SCAR. Gods and goddesses,
All the whole synod of them!

ENO. What's thy passion?

SCAR. The greater cantle[c] of the world is lost
With very ignorance; we have kiss'd away
Kingdoms and provinces.

ENO. How appears the fight?

SCAR. On our side like the token'd pestilence,[d]
Where death is sure. Yon ribaudred[e] nag of Egypt,—
Whom leprosy o'ertake!—i' the midst o' the fight,
When vantage like a pair of twins appear'd,

---

[a] CAN.] In the ancient copies this speech has the prefix *Ven.*, an abbreviation Mr. Collier suggests for *Vennard*, the actor who may have played Canidius.

[b] — distractions—] Detachments.

[c] — cantle—] A *corner*, or *coign*. French, *chanteau, quignon; Latin, quantillum.*

[d] — *the* token'd pestilence,—] See note (3), p. 320

[e] — ribaudred nag—] This has been variously and needlessly changed to *ribald hag, ribald-rid hag*, and *ribald-rid nag. Ribaudred nag*, means filthy strumpet.

Both as[a] the same, or rather ours the elder,—
The brize[b] upon her, like a cow in June,—
Hoists sails, and flies !
ENO. That I beheld:
Mine eyes did sicken at the sight, and could not
Endure a further view.
SCAR. She once being loof'd,
The noble ruin of her magic, Antony,
Claps on his sea-wing, and, like a doting mallard,
Leaving the fight in height, flies after her:
I never saw an action of such shame;
Experience, manhood, honour, ne'er before
Did violate so itself.
ENO. Alack, alack !

Enter CANIDIUS.

CAN. Our fortune on the sea is out of breath,
And sinks most lamentably. Had our general
Been what he knew himself, it had gone well:
O, he has * given example for our flight,
Most grossly, by his own !
ENO. Ay, are you thereabouts ?
Why then, good night, indeed.
CAN. Towards Peloponnesus are they fled.
SCAR. 'T is easy to 't; and there I will attend
What further comes.
CAN. To Cæsar will I render
My legions, and my horse : six kings already
Show me the way of yielding.
ENO. I'll yet follow
The wounded chance of Antony, though my reason
Sits in the wind against me. [*Exeunt.*

SCENE XI.—Alexandria. *A Room in the Palace.*

Enter ANTONY *and* Attendants.

ANT. Hark ! the land bids me tread no more upon 't,—
It is asham'd to bear me !—Friends, come hither:
I am so lated[c] in the world, that I
Have lost my way for ever :—I have a ship
Laden with gold; take that, divide it; fly,
And make your peace with Cæsar.
ALL. *Fly !* not we.
ANT. I have fled myself; and have instructed cowards
To run and show their shoulders.—Friends, be gone;
I have myself resolv'd upon a course,
Which has no need of you; be gone:
My treasure 's in the harbour, take it.—O,
I follow'd that I blush to look upon !
My very hairs do mutiny, for the white
Reprove the brown for rashness, and they them
For fear and doting.—Friends, be gone; you shall
Have letters from me to some friends, that will
Sweep your way for you. Pray you, look not sad,
Nor make replies of loathness: take the hint
Which my despair proclaims; let that * be left
Which leaves itself: to the sea-side straightway:
I will possess you of that ship and treasure.
Leave me, I pray, a little: pray you now :—
Nay, do so; for, indeed, I have lost command,
Therefore I pray you :—I'll see you by and by.
[*Sits down.*

Enter CLEOPATRA, *led by* CHARMIAN *and* IRAS, EROS *following.*

EROS. Nay, gentle madam, to him,—comfort him.
IRAS. Do, most dear queen.
CHAR. Do! why, what else ?
CLEO. Let me sit down. O, Juno !
ANT. No, no, no, no, no !
EROS. See you here, sir ?
ANT. O fie, fie, fie !
CHAR. Madam,—
IRAS. Madam; O, good empress !—
EROS. Sir, sir,—
ANT. Yes, my lord, yes :[d]—he, at Philippi, kept
His sword e'en like a dancer,[e] while I struck
The lean and wrinkled Cassius; and 't was I
That the mad Brutus ended: he alone
Dealt on lieutenantry,[f] and no practice had
In the brave squares of war: yet now—No matter.
CLEO. Ah ! stand by.
EROS. The queen, my lord, the queen !
IRAS. Go to him, madam, speak to him;
He is unqualitied with very shame.

(*) First folio, *his ha's.*

(*) First folio, *them.*

[a] *Both* as *the same,*—] This is oddly expressed. Can "as" be a transcriber's slip for *ag'd?* The context,—"or rather ours *the elder,*"—favours the supposition.

[b] *The* brize—] The *œstrum*, or gad-fly.

[c] — lated—] *Benighted, belated;* as in "Macbeth," Act III. Sc. 3,—

"Now spurs the *lated* traveller apace."

[d] Yes, my lord, yes :—] This kind of rejoinder, sometimes in play, sometimes in petulance, is not unfrequent in our old dramas. See note (c), p, 413, Vol. I.

[e] His sword e'en like a dancer,—] See note (2), p. 55, Vol. II.

[f] Dealt on lieutenantry,—] "Dealt on lieutenantry" means, probably, as Steevens conjectured, *fought by proxy:* or it may signify *traded in war's theory:*—"I met just now a usurer, that only *deals upon* ounces."—*The Witty Fair One,* Act V. Sc. 1.

CLEO. Well then,—sustain me:—O!
EROS. Most noble sir, arise; the queen approaches;
Her head 's declin'd, and death will seize her, but[a]
Your comfort makes the rescue.
ANT. I have offended reputation,—
A most unnoble swerving.
EROS. Sir, the queen.
ANT. O, whither hast thou led me, Egypt? See,
How I convey[b] my shame out of thine eyes
By looking back what I have left behind
'Stroy'd in dishonour.
CLEO. O, my lord, my lord!

[a] — but—] *Unless.*
[b] *How I* convey, &c.] How I *pass by sleight* my shame out of thy sight, in looking another way.

Forgive my fearful sails! I little thought
You would have follow'd.

ANT. Egypt, thou knew'st too well
My heart was to thy rudder tied by the strings,
And thou shouldst tow * me after: o'er my spirit
Thy † full supremacy thou knew'st, and that
Thy beck might from the bidding of the gods
Command me.

CLEO. O, my pardon!

ANT. Now I must
To the young man send humble treaties, dodge
And palter in the shifts of lowness; who
With half the bulk o' the world play'd as I pleas'd,
Making and marring fortunes. You did know
How much you were my conqueror; and that
My sword, made weak by my affection, would
Obey it on all cause.

CLEO. Pardon, pardon!

ANT. Fall not a tear, I say; one of them rates[a]
All that is won and lost. Give me a kiss;—
Even this repays me.—We sent our schoolmaster,
Is he come back?—Love, I am full of lead.—
Some wine, within there, and our viands!—Fortune knows
We scorn her most when most she offers blows.(4)
[*Exeunt.*

SCENE XII.—Cæsar's *Camp in* Egypt.

Enter CÆSAR, DOLABELLA, THYREUS,‡ *and others.*

CÆS. Let him appear that's come from Antony.—
Know you him?

DOL. Cæsar, 'tis his schoolmaster:[b]
An argument that he is pluck'd, when hither
He sends so poor a pinion of his wing,
Which had superfluous kings for messengers,
Not many moons gone by.

Enter EUPHRONIUS.§

CÆS. Approach, and speak.

EUP. Such as I am, I come from Antony:
I was of late as petty to his ends,
As is the morn-dew on the myrtle-leaf
To his grand sea.[c]

CÆS. Be 't so:—declare thine office.

EUP. Lord of his fortunes he salutes thee, and
Requires to live in Egypt: which not granted,
He lessens his requests; and to thee sues
To let him breathe between the heavens and earth,
A private man in Athens: this for him.
Next, Cleopatra does confess thy greatness;
Submits her to thy might; and of thee craves
The circle[d] of the Ptolemies for her heirs,
Now hazarded to thy grace.

CÆS. For Antony,
I have no ears to his request. The queen
Of audience nor desire shall fail, so she
From Egypt drive her all-disgraced friend,
Or take his life there; this if she perform,
She shall not sue unheard. So to them both.

EUP. Fortune pursue thee!

CÆS. Bring him through the bands.
[*Exit* EUPHRONIUS.

[*To* THYREUS.] To try thy eloquence, now 'tis time: despatch!
From Antony win Cleopatra: promise,
And in our name, what she requires; add more,
From thine invention, offers: women are not
In their best fortunes strong; but want will perjure
The ne'er-touch'd vestal. Try thy cunning, Thyreus,
Make thine own edict for thy pains, which we
Will answer as a law.

THYR. Cæsar, I go.

CÆS. Observe how Antony becomes his flaw,[e]
And what thou think'st his very action speaks
In every power that moves.

THYR. Cæsar, I shall. [*Exeunt.*

SCENE XIII.—Alexandria. *A Room in the Palace.*

Enter CLEOPATRA, ENOBARBUS, CHARMIAN, *and* IRAS.

CLEO. What shall we do, Enobarbus?

ENO. Think,[f] and die.

CLEO. Is Antony or we in fault for this?

ENO. Antony only, that would make his will
Lord of his reason. What though you fled

(*) First folio, *stowe.*
(†) Old text, *The.* Corrected by Theobald.
(‡) Old text, *Thidias,* all through.
(§) First folio, *Ambassador from Antony.*

[a] — rates—] *Counts for, is equivalent to.*
[b] — his schoolmaster:] Euphronius was the tutor of Antony's children by Cleopatra.
[c] *To* his *grand sea.*] Here, as usual, "*his*" stands for the then rare *its;* and "*its* grand sea" imports the ocean whence the dew-drop was exhaled. See Steevens' note *ad l.* in the *Variorum.*
[d] *The* circle—] The *round and top of sovereignty,* the *diadem.*
[e] *Observe how Antony* becomes his flaw,—] This is not very clear. Johnson explains it, "how Antony conforms himself to this breach of his fortune."
[f] Think, and die.] *Despair* and die. To *take thought* was formerly an expression equivalent to, *take to heart,* or *yield to sorrow.* Thus, in "Julius Cæsar," Act II. Sc. 1.—
"—— All that he can do
Is to himself,—*take thought,* and die for Cæsar."

From that great face of war, whose several ranges[a]
Frighted each other? why should he follow?
The itch of his affection should not then
Have nick'd[b] his captainship; at such a point,
When half to half the world oppos'd, he being
The mered[c] question, 't was a shame no less
Than was his loss, to course your flying flags,
And leave his navy gazing.
CLEO. Pr'ythee, peace.

Enter ANTONY *with* EUPHRONIUS.

ANT. Is that his answer?
EUP. Ay, my lord.
ANT. The queen shall, then, have courtesy, so she will yield us up.
EUP. He says so.
ANT. Let her know 't.—
To the boy Cæsar send this grizzled head,
And he will fill thy wishes to the brim
With principalities.
CLEO. That head, my lord?
ANT. To him again: tell him, he wears the rose
Of youth upon him; from which the world should note
Something particular: his coin, ships, legions,
May be a coward's; whose ministers would prevail
Under the service of a child as soon
As i' the command of Cæsar: I dare him therefore
To lay his gay comparisons apart,
And answer me declin'd, sword against sword,
Ourselves alone. I 'll write it; follow me.
[*Exeunt* ANTONY *and* EUPHRONIUS.
ENO. [*Aside.*] Yes, like enough, high-battled Cæsar will
Unstate his happiness, and be stag'd to the show,
Against a sworder! I see men's judgments are
A parcel of their fortunes; and things outward
Do draw the inward quality after them,
To suffer[d] all alike. That he should dream,
Knowing all measures, the full Cæsar will
Answer his emptiness!—Cæsar, thou hast subdu'd
His judgment too.

Enter an Attendant.

ATT. A messenger from Cæsar.
CLEO. What, no more ceremony?—See, my women!—
Against the blown rose may they stop their nose,
That kneel'd unto the buds.—Admit him, sir.
[*Exit* Attendant.
ENO. [*Aside.*] Mine honesty and I begin to square.[e]
The loyalty well held to fools does make
Our faith mere folly:—yet he that can endure
To follow with allegiance a fall'n lord,
Does conquer him that did his master conquer,
And earns a place[f] i' the story.

Enter THYREUS.

CLEO. Cæsar's will?
THYR. Hear it apart.
CLEO. None but friends; say boldly.
THYR. So, haply, are they friends to Antony.
ENO. He needs as many, sir, as Cæsar has;
Or needs not us. If Cæsar please, our master
Will leap to be his friend: for us, you know,
Whose he is we are; and that is Cæsar's.
THYR. So.—
Thus then, thou most renown'd: Cæsar entreats,
Not to consider in what case thou stand'st,
Further than he is Cæsar.*
CLEO. Go on: right royal!
THYR. He knows that you embrace not Antony
As you did love, but as you fear'd him.
CLEO. O!
THYR. The scars upon your honour, therefore, he
Does pity, as constrained blemishes,
Not as deserv'd.
CLEO. He is a god, and knows
What is most right: mine honour was not yielded,
But conquer'd merely.
ENO. [*Aside.*] To be sure of that,
I will ask Antony.—Sir, sir, thou art so leaky,
That we must leave thee to thy sinking, for[g]
Thy dearest quit thee. [*Exit* ENOBARBUS.
THYR. Shall I say to Cæsar
What you require of him? for he partly begs
To be desir'd to give. It much would please him,
That of his fortunes you should make a staff
To lean upon: but it would warm his spirits,
To hear from me you had left Antony,
And put yourself under his shroud,[h]
The universal landlord.
CLEO. What 's your name?
THYR. My name is Thyreus.
CLEO. Most kind messenger,
Say to great Cæsar this:—in disputation[i]

---

[a] *From that great face of war, whose several* ranges—] The commentators, perhaps, have a perception of what this means, since they pass it silently; to us it is inexplicable, and we cannot choose but look on "ranges" as a misprint for the *rages* of grim-visag'd war.

[b] *Have* nick'd—] Have *emasculated*.

[c] The mered *question,*—] Possibly, the *entire*, or *sole* question; but the word reads suspiciously. Johnson suggested, "The *mooted* question," and is followed by Mr. Collier's annotator.

[d] *To suffer*—] The verb is apparently used here in an active sense, meaning to *punish* or *afflict*.

[e] — to square.] *To quarrel.*

[f] — a place—] A *seat of dignity*.

(*) First folio, *Cæsars*. Corrected in the second folio.

[g] —— for
Thy dearest quit thee.]
See note ([a]), p. 550.

[h] And put yourself under his shroud,—] Capell adds, "the great;" Mr. Collier's annotator, "who is."

[i] — *in* disputation—] Theobald reads, "in *deputation;*" we are of opinion, however, that, as in Act II. Sc. 7, *disposition* was misprinted *disputation*, the reciprocal error has been perpetrated here, and that the poet wrote, "in *disposition*," that is, *in inclination, willingly*.

I kiss his conqu'ring hand: tell him, I am prompt
To lay my crown at 's feet, and there to kneel:
Tell him, from his all-obeying breath I hear
The doom of Egypt.
THYR. 'T is your noblest course.
Wisdom and fortune combating together,
If that the former dare but what it can,
No chance may shake it. Give me grace to lay
My duty on your hand.
CLEO. Your Cæsar's father, oft,
When he hath mus'd of taking kingdoms in,
Bestow'd his lips on that unworthy place,
As it rain'd kisses.

Re-enter ANTONY *and* ENOBARBUS.

ANT. Favours, by Jove that thunders!—
What art thou, fellow?
THYR. One that but performs
The bidding of the fullest man, and worthiest
To have command obey'd.
ENO. [*Aside to* THYR.] You will be whipp'd.
ANT. Approach, there!—Ah, you kite!—Now, gods and devils!
Authority melts from me: Of late, when I cried *ho!*
Like boys unto a muss,[a] kings would start forth,
And cry, *Your will?*

Enter Attendants.

Have you no ears?
I am Antony yet. Take hence this Jack, and whip him.
ENO. [*Aside.*] 'T is better playing with a lion's whelp
Than with an old one dying.
ANT. Moon and stars!—
Whip him.—Were 't twenty of the greatest tributaries
That do acknowledge Cæsar, should I find them
So saucy with the hand of she here,—what 's her name,
Since she was Cleopatra?——Whip him, fellows,
Till, like a boy, you see him cringe his face,
And whine aloud for mercy: take him hence.
THYR. Mark Antony,—
ANT. Tug him away: being whipp'd,
Bring him again:—this[*] Jack of Cæsar's shall
Bear us an errand to him.—
[*Exeunt* Attendants, *with* THYREUS.
You were half blasted ere I knew you:—ha!
Have I my pillow left unpress'd in Rome,
Forborne the getting of a lawful race,
And by a gem of women, to be abus'd
By one that looks on feeders?[b]
CLEO. Good my lord,—
ANT. You have been a boggler ever:—
But when we in our viciousness grow hard,
(O, misery on 't!) the wise gods seel[c] our eyes;
In our own filth drop our clear judgments; make us
Adore our errors; laugh at 's, while we strut
To our confusion.
CLEO. O, is 't come to this?
ANT. I found you as a morsel cold upon
Dead Cæsar's trencher: nay, you were a fragment
Of Cneius Pompey's; besides what hotter hours,
Unregister'd in vulgar fame, you have
Luxuriously pick'd out: for, I am sure,
Though[d] you can guess what temperance should be,
You know not what it is.
CLEO. Wherefore is this?
ANT. To let a fellow that will take rewards,
And say, *God quit you!* be familiar with
My playfellow, your hand; this kingly seal,
And plighter of high hearts!—O, that I were
Upon the hill of Basan, to outroar
The horned herd! for I have savage cause;
And to proclaim it civilly, were like
A halter'd neck which does the hangman thank
For being yare about him.—

Re-enter Attendants, *with* THYREUS.

Is he whipp'd?
1 ATT. Soundly, my lord.
ANT. Cried he? and begg'd he pardon?
1 ATT. He did ask favour.
ANT. If that thy father live, let him repent
Thou wast not made his daughter; and be thou sorry
To follow Cæsar in his triumph, since
Thou hast been whipp'd for following him: henceforth,
The white hand of a lady fever thee,
Shake thou to look on 't.—Get thee back to Cæsar,
Tell him thy entertainment: look, thou say
He makes me angry with him, for he seems
Proud and disdainful, harping on what I am,
Not what he knew I was: he makes me angry;
And at this time most easy 't is to do 't,
When my good stars, that were my former guides,

(*) Old text, *The*.

[a] — a muss,—] *A scramble.*

[b] — feeders?] An old nickname for servants. Thus, in Beaumont and Fletcher's play of "The Nice Valour," Act III. Sc. 1,—
"Now servants he has kept, lusty tall *feeders*."

[c] — seel our eyes;] See note (b), p. 494.

[d] Though—] "Though" carries here the sense of *if*, or *even if*.

Have empty left their orbs, and shot their fires
Into the abysm of hell. If he mislike
My speech and what is done, tell him he has
Hipparchus, my enfranched bondman, whom
He may at pleasure whip, or hang, or torture,
As he shall like, to quit me:[a] urge it thou!
Hence with thy stripes, begone! (5)
[*Exit* THYREUS.

CLEO. Have you done yet?

ANT. Alack, our terrene moon
Is now eclips'd; and it portends alone
The fall of Antony!

CLEO. I must stay his time.

ANT. To flatter Cæsar, would you mingle eyes
With one that ties his points?

CLEO. Not know me yet?

ANT. Cold-hearted toward me?

CLEO. Ah, dear, if I be so,
From my cold heart let heaven engender hail,
And poison it in the source; and the first stone
Drop in my neck: as it determines,[b] so
Dissolve my life! The next Cæsarion smite!*
Till, by degrees, the memory of my womb,
Together with my brave Egyptians all,
By the discandying[c] of this pelleted storm,
Lie graveless,—till the flies and gnats of Nile
Have buried them for prey!

ANT. I am satisfied.
Cæsar sits down in Alexandria; where
I will oppose his fate. Our force by land
Hath nobly held; our sever'd navy too
Have knit again, and fleet,[d] threat'ning most sea-like.
Where hast thou been, my heart?—Dost thou hear, lady?
If from the field I shall return once more
To kiss these lips, I will appear in blood;
I and my sword will earn our chronicle;
There's hope in't yet.

CLEO. That's my brave lord!

ANT. I will be treble-sinew'd, hearted, breath'd,
And fight maliciously: for when mine hours
Were nice and lucky, men did ransom lives
Of me for jests; but now I'll set my teeth,
And send to darkness all that stop me.—Come,
Let's have one other gaudy[e] night: call to me
All my sad captains; fill our bowls; once more
Let's mock the midnight bell.

CLEO. It is my birthday:
I had thought to have held it poor; but, since my lord
Is Antony again, I will be Cleopatra.

ANT. We will yet do well.

CLEO. Call all his noble captains to my lord.

ANT. Do so, we'll speak to them; and to-night I'll force
The wine peep through their scars.—Come on, my queen;
There's sap in't yet. The next time I do fight,
I'll make Death love me; for I will contend
Even with his pestilent scythe.
[*Exeunt all except* ENOBARBUS.

ENO. Now he'll outstare the lightning. To be furious,
Is to be frighted out of fear; and in that mood
The dove will peck the estridge; and I see still
A diminution in our captain's brain
Restores his heart: when valour preys on* reason,
It eats the sword it fights with. I will seek
Some way to leave him. [*Exit.*

(*) First folio, *Cæsarian smile.*

(*) First folio, *prayes in reason.*

a — to quit me:] To *repay*, or *requite* me, for the indignity he receives at my hands.

b — *as it* determines,—] As it *melts away*.

c — *discandying*—] *Liquefying*. The old copies read *discandering*, "from which corruption," Theobald says, "both Dr. Thirlby and I saw we must retrieve the word with which I have reformed the text."

d — *and* fleet,—] That is, *float*, the words of old being synonymous.

e — *one other* gaudy *night*:] A *festival* night; from *gaudium*. "Gaudy days" is still a collegiate term.

ACT IV.

SCENE I.—Cæsar's *Camp before* Alexandria.

Enter Cæsar, *reading a letter;* Agrippa, Mecænas, *and others.*

Cæs. He calls me boy; and chides, as he had power
To beat me out of Egypt; my messenger
He hath whipp'd with rods; dares me to personal combat:
Cæsar to Antony!—Let the old ruffian know,
I have[a] many other ways to die; mean time,
Laugh at his challenge.

Mec. Cæsar must think,
When one so great begins to rage, he 's hunted
Even to falling. Give him no breath, but now
Make boot of his distraction:—never anger
Made good guard for itself.

Cæs. Let our best heads
Know, that to-morrow the last of many battles
We mean to fight:—within our files there are
Of those that serv'd Mark Antony but late,
Enough to fetch him in. See it done:
And feast the army; we have store to do 't,
And they have earn'd the waste. Poor Antony!
[*Exeunt.*

[a] I have, &c.] Hanmer reads, "*He hath* many," &c., as Shakespeare would have done had he not mistaken the corresponding passage of his authority, North's Plutarch:—"Antonius sent againe to chalenge Cæsar to fight with him hande to hande. Cæsar aunswerd him, that he had many other ways to die than so."

SCENE II.—Alexandria. *A Room in the Palace.*

Enter ANTONY, CLEOPATRA, ENOBARBUS, CHARMIAN, IRAS, ALEXAS, *and others.*

ANT. He will not fight with me, Domitius.
ENO. No.
ANT. Why should he not?
ENO. He thinks, being twenty times of better fortune,
He is twenty men to one.
ANT. To-morrow, soldier,
By sea and land I'll fight.—Or I will live,
Or bathe my dying honour in the blood
Shall make it live again.—Woo 't thou fight well?
ENO. I'll strike, and cry, *Take all.*
ANT. Well said; come on.—
Call forth my household servants; let 's to-night
Be bounteous at our meal.—

Enter Servants.

Give me thy hand,
Thou hast been rightly honest;—so hast thou;
Thou,—and thou,—and thou:—you have serv'd me well,
And kings have been your fellows.
CLEO. [*Aside to* ENO.] What means this?
ENO. [*Aside to* CLEO.] 'T is one of those odd tricks which sorrow shoots
Out of the mind.
ANT. And thou art honest too.
I wish I could be made so many men,
And all of you clapp'd up together in
An Antony, that I might do you service,
So good as you have done.
SERVANTS. The gods forbid!
ANT. Well, my good fellows, wait on me to-night:
Scant not my cups; and make as much of me
As when mine empire was your fellow too,
And suffer'd my command.
CLEO. [*Aside to* ENO.] What does he mean?
ENO. [*Aside to* CLEO.] To make his followers weep.
ANT. Tend me to-night;
May be it is the period of your duty:
Haply you shall not see me more; or if,
A mangled shadow: perchance to-morrow
You'll serve another master. I look on you
As one that takes his leave. Mine honest friends,
I turn you not away; but, like a master
Married to your good service, stay till death:
Tend me to-night two hours, I ask no more,
And the gods yield you for 't!
ENO. What mean you, sir,
To give them this discomfort? Look, they weep;
And I, an ass, am onion-ey'd: for shame,
Transform us not to women.
ANT. Ho, ho, ho!
Now the witch take me if I meant it thus!
Grace grow where those drops fall! My hearty friends,
You take me in too dolorous a sense;
For I spake to you for your comfort,—did desire you
To burn this night with torches: know, my hearts,
I hope well of to-morrow; and will lead you
Where rather I'll expect victorious life,
Than death and honour. Let 's to supper; come,
And drown consideration. [*Exeunt.*

SCENE III.—*The same. Before the Palace.*

Enter two Soldiers, *to their guard.*

1 SOLD. Brother, good night: to-morrow is the day.
2 SOLD. It will determine one way: fare you well.
Heard you of nothing strange about the streets?
1 SOLD. Nothing. What news?
2 SOLD. Belike 't is but a rumour.
Good night to you.
1 SOLD. Well, sir, good night.

Enter two other Soldiers.

2 SOLD. Soldiers,
Have careful watch.
3 SOLD. And you. Good night, good night.
[*The first and second go to their posts.*
4 SOLD. Here we: [*Taking their posts.*] and if to-morrow
Our navy thrive, I have an absolute hope
Our landmen will stand up.
3 SOLD. 'T is a brave army,
And full of purpose.
[*Music of hautboys under the stage.*
4 SOLD. Peace! what noise?
1 SOLD. List, list!
2 SOLD. Hark!
1 SOLD. Music i' the air!
3 SOLD. Under the earth!
4 SOLD. It signs[a] well,
Does 't not?
3 SOLD. No.
1 SOLD. Peace, I say! What should this mean?
2 SOLD. 'T is the god Hercules, whom Antony lov'd,
Now leaves him.
1 SOLD. Walk; let 's see if other watchmen
Do hear what we do.
[*They advance to another post.*

[a] It signs well,—] It is a *good sign*, an *auspicious omen.*

2 Sold. How now, masters?

Soldiers. [*Speaking together.*] How now? How now? do you hear this?

1 Sold. Ay; is't not strange?

3 Sold. Do you hear, masters? do you hear?

1 Sold. Follow the noise so far as we have quarter;
Let's see how 't will give off.

Soldiers. [*Speaking together.*] Content: 'tis strange. [*Exeunt.*

SCENE IV.—*The same. A Room in the Palace.*

Enter Antony *and* Cleopatra; Charmian, Iras, *and others, attending.*

Ant. Eros! mine armour, Eros!

Cleo. Sleep a little.

Ant. No, my chuck.—Eros, come; mine armour, Eros!

Enter EROS *with armour.*

Come, good fellow, put mine* iron on:—
If Fortune be not ours to-day, it is
Because we brave her:—come.

CLEO. Nay, I'll help too.
What's this for?

ANT. Ah, let be, let be! thou art
The armourer of my heart;—false, false; this, this.

CLEO. Sooth, la, I'll help: thus it must be.[a]

ANT. Well, well:
We shall thrive now.—Seest thou, my good fellow?
Go, put on thy defences.

EROS. Briefly, sir.

CLEO. Is not this buckled well?

ANT. Rarely, rarely;
He that unbuckles this, till we do please
To doff 't for our repose, shall hear a storm.—
Thou fumblest, Eros; and my queen's a squire
More tight at this than thou: despatch.—O, love,
That thou couldst see my wars to-day, and knew'st
The royal occupation! thou shouldst see
A workman in 't.

Enter an Officer *armed.*

Good morrow to thee; welcome:
Thou look'st like him that knows a warlike charge.
To business that we love we rise betime,
And go to 't with delight.

OFF. A thousand, sir,
Early though 't be, have on their riveted trim,
And at the port expect you.

[*Shout and flourish of trumpets without.*

Enter other Officers, *and* Soldiers.

2 OFF.† The morn is fair.—Good morrow, general.

ALL. Good morrow, general.

ANT. 'T is well blown, lads:
This morning, like the spirit of a youth
That means to be of note, begins betimes.—
So, so; come, give me that: this way; well said.—
Fare thee well, dame, whate'er becomes of me:
This is a soldier's kiss: rebukeable, [*Kisses her.*
And worthy shameful check it were, to stand
On more mechanic compliment; I'll leave thee
Now, like a man of steel.—You that will fight
Follow me close; I'll bring you to 't.—Adieu.

[*Exeunt* ANTONY, EROS, Officers, *and* Soldiers.

CHAR. Please you, retire to your chamber?

CLEO. Lead me.
He goes forth gallantly. That he and Cæsar might
Determine this great war in single fight!
Then, Antony,—but now,—Well, on. [*Exeunt.*

SCENE V.—Antony's *Camp near* Alexandria.

Trumpets sound. Enter ANTONY *and* EROS; *an* Officer *meeting them.*

OFF.* The gods make this a happy day to Antony!

ANT. Would thou and those thy scars had once prevail'd
To make me fight at land!

OFF.* Hadst thou done so,
The kings that have revolted, and the soldier
That has this morning left thee, would have still
Follow'd thy heels.

ANT. Who's gone this morning?

OFF.* Who!
One ever near thee: call for Enobarbus,
He shall not hear thee; or from Cæsar's camp
Say, *I am none of thine.*

ANT. What say'st thou?

OFF. Sir,
He is with Cæsar.

EROS. Sir, his chests and treasure
He has not with him.

ANT. Is he gone?

OFF. Most certain.

ANT. Go, Eros, send his treasure after; do it;
Detain no jot, I charge thee: write to him
(I will subscribe) gentle adieus and greetings;
Say, that I wish he never find more cause
To change a master.—O, my fortunes have
Corrupted honest men!—Despatch.—Enobarbus!

[*Exeunt.*

SCENE VI.—Cæsar's *Camp before* Alexandria.

Flourish. Enter CÆSAR, *with* AGRIPPA, ENOBARBUS, *and others.*

CÆS. Go forth, Agrippa, and begin the fight:
Our will is Antony be took alive;
Make it so known.

AGR. Cæsar, I shall. [*Exit.*

(*) Old text, *thine.* Corrected by Johnson.
(†) First folio, *Alex.*

a — thus it must be.] This and the two preceding speeches stand thus in the old copies,—

"CLEO. Nay, Ile helpe too, Anthony.
What's this for? Ah let be, let be, thou art
The Armourer of my heart: False, false: This, this,
Sooth-law Ile helpe: Thus it must bee,"

and were correctly arranged by Hanmer and Malone.

(*) First folio, *Eros.*

CÆS. The time of universal peace is near:
Prove this a prosperous day, the three-nook'd world
Shall bear the olive freely.

Enter a Messenger.

MESS. Antony
Is come into the field.
CÆS. Go, charge Agrippa
Plant those that have revolted in the van,
That Antony may seem to spend his fury
Upon himself. [*Exeunt all except* ENOBARBUS.
ENO. Alexas did revolt; and went to Jewry on
Affairs of Antony; there did persuade*
Great Herod to incline himself to Cæsar,
And leave his master Antony: for this pains,
Cæsar hath hang'd him. Canidius, and the rest
That fell away, have entertainment, but
No honourable trust. I have done ill;
Of which I do accuse myself so sorely,
That I will joy no more.

Enter a Soldier *of* CÆSAR'*s*.

SOLD. Enobarbus, Antony
Hath after thee sent all thy treasure, with
His bounty overplus: the messenger
Came on my guard; and at thy tent is now
Unloading of his mules.
ENO. I give it you.
SOLD. Mock not, Enobarbus.
I tell you true: best you saf'd the bringer
Out of the host; I must attend mine office,
Or would have done 't myself. Your emperor
Continues still a Jove. [*Exit.*
ENO. I am alone the villain of the earth,
And feel I am so most. O, Antony,
Thou mine of bounty, how wouldst thou have paid
My better service, when my turpitude
Thou dost so crown with gold! This blows[a] my heart:
If swift thought break it not, a swifter mean
Shall outstrike thought: but thought[b] will do 't, I feel.
I fight against thee!—No: I will go seek
Some ditch wherein to die; the foul'st best fits
My latter part of life. [*Exit.*

SCENE VII.—*Field of Battle between the Camps.*

Alarum. Drums and trumpets. Enter AGRIPPA *and others.*

AGR. Retire! we have engag'd ourselves too far:
Cæsar himself has work, and our oppression
Exceeds what we expected. [*Exeunt.*

Alarum. Enter ANTONY, *and* SCARUS *wounded.*

SCAR. O, my brave emperor, this is fought indeed!
Had we done so at first, we had driven them home
With clouts about their heads.
ANT. Thou bleed'st apace.
SCAR. I had a wound here that was like a T,
But now 't is made an H.[c]
ANT. They do retire.
SCAR. We'll beat 'em into bench-holes: I have yet
Room for six scotches more.

Enter EROS.

EROS. They are beaten, sir; and our advantage serves
For a fair victory.
SCAR. Let us score their backs,
And snatch 'em up, as we take hares, behind;
'T is sport to maul a runner.
ANT. I will reward thee
Once for thy spritely comfort, and ten-fold
For thy good valour. Come thee on.
SCAR. I'll halt after. [*Exeunt.*

SCENE VIII.—*Under the Walls of* Alexandria.

Alarum. Enter ANTONY, *marching;* SCARUS, *and* Forces.

ANT. We have beat him to his camp:—run one before,
And let the queen know of our gests.[d]—To-morrow,
Before the sun shall see 's, we'll spill the blood
That has to-day escap'd. I thank you all;
For doughty-handed are you, and have fought
Not as you serv'd the cause, but as 't had been
Each man's like mine; you have shown all Hectors.
Enter the city, clip your wives, your friends,
Tell them your feats; whilst they with joyful tears
Wash the congealment from your wounds, and kiss
The honour'd gashes whole.—Give me thy hand;
[*To* SCARUS.

Enter CLEOPATRA, *attended.*

To this great fairy[e] I'll commend thy acts,
Make her thanks bless thee.—O, thou day o' the world,

(*) First folio, *dissuade*.

a — blows—] *Swells.*

b — thought—] "*Thought,*" as Malone remarks, "in this passage means *melancholy.*"

c — an H.] The same play (if any were intended here) on H and *ache* occurs in "Much Ado About Nothing," Act III. Sc. 4.

d — *our* gests.—] Our *exploits.* So Theobald. The old copies have, *guests.*

e — fairy—] *Enchantress.*

Chain mine arm'd neck! leap thou, attire and all,
Through proof of harness[a] to my heart, and there
Ride on the pants triúmphing!

CLEO. Lord of lords!
O, infinite virtue! com'st thou smiling from
The world's great snare uncaught?

ANT. My nightingale,
We have beat them to their beds. What, girl! though grey
Do something mingle with our younger brown, yet ha' we
A brain that nourishes our nerves, and can
Get goal for goal of youth. Behold this man;
Commend unto his lips thy favouring hand;—
Kiss it, my warrior:—he hath fought to-day,
As if a god, in hate of mankind, had
Destroy'd in such a shape.

CLEO. I'll give thee, friend,
An armour all of gold; it was a king's.(1)

ANT. He has deserv'd it, were it carbuncled
Like holy Phœbus' car.—Give me thy hand:—
Through Alexandria make a jolly march:
Bear our hack'd targets like the men that owe them.
Had our great palace the capacity
To camp this host, we all would sup together,
And drink carouses to the next day's fate,
Which promises royal peril.—Trumpeters,
With brazen din blast you the city's ear;
Make mingle with our rattling tabourines;[b]
That heaven and earth may strike their sounds together
Applauding our approach. [*Exeunt.*

SCENE IX.—Cæsar's *Camp.*

Sentinels *at their post.*

1 SOLD. If we be not reliev'd within this hour,
We must return to the court of guard: the night
Is shiny; and they say we shall embattle
By the second hour i' the morn.

2 SOLD. This last day
Was a shrewd one to 's.

---

[a] — proof of harness—] *Armour of proof.*

[b] — tabourines;] *Tabourines* was another name for drums, and occurs again in "Troilus and Cressida," Act IV. Sc. 5,—"Beat loud the *tabourines*."

Enter ENOBARBUS.

ENO. O, bear me witness, night,—
3 SOLD. What man is this?
2 SOLD. Stand close, and list him.
ENO. Be witness to me, O, thou blessed moon,
When men revolted shall upon record
Bear hateful memory, poor Enobarbus did
Before thy face repent!—
1 SOLD. *Enobarbus!*
3 SOLD. Peace!
Hark further.
ENO. O, sovereign mistress of true melancholy,
The poisonous damp of night disponge upon me,
That life, a very rebel to my will,
May hang no longer on me: throw my heart
Against the flint and hardness of my fault;
Which, being dried with grief, will break to powder,
And finish all foul thoughts. O, Antony!
Nobler than my revolt is infamous,
Forgive me in thine own particular;
But let the world rank me in register
A master-leaver and a fugitive!
O, Antony! O, Antony! [*Dies.*
2 SOLD. Let's speak to him.
1 SOLD. Let's hear him, for the things he speaks may concern Cæsar.
3 SOLD. Let's do so. But he sleeps.
1 SOLD. Swoons rather; for so bad a prayer as his was never yet for[a] sleep.
2 SOLD. Go we to him.
3 SOLD. Awake, sir, awake! speak to us.
2 SOLD. Hear you, sir?
1 SOLD. The hand of death hath raught him!
Hark! the drums [*Drums afar off.*
Demurely [b] wake the sleepers. Let us bear him
To the court of guard; he is of note: our hour
Is fully out.
3 SOLD. Come on then;
He may recover yet. [*Exeunt with the body.*

SCENE X.—*Space between the two Camps.*

Enter ANTONY *and* SCARUS, *with* Forces *marching.*

ANT. Their preparation is to-day by sea;
We please them not by land.
SCAR. For both, my lord.
ANT. I would they'd fight i' the fire or i' the air;
We'd fight there too. But this it is; our foot
Upon the hills adjoining to the city,
Shall stay with us:—order for sea is given!
They have put forth the haven:—[c]
Where their appointment we may best discover,
And look on their endeavour. [*Exeunt.*

SCENE XI.—*Another part of the same.*

Enter CÆSAR, *with his* Forces *marching.*

CÆS. But[d] being charg'd, we will be still by land,
Which, as I take 't, we shall; for his best force
Is forth to man his galleys. To the vales!
And hold our best advantage. [*Exeunt.*

SCENE XII.—*Another part of the same.*

Enter ANTONY *and* SCARUS.

ANT. Yet they are not join'd: where yond pine does stand,
I shall discover all: I'll bring thee word
Straight, how 't is like to go. [*Exit.*
SCAR. Swallows have built
In Cleopatra's sails their nests: the augurers*
Say they know not,—they cannot tell;—look grimly,
And dare not speak their knowledge. Antony
Is valiant, and dejected; and, by starts,
His fretted fortunes give him hope, and fear,
Of what he has, and has not.
[*Alarum afar off, as at a sea-fight.*

Re-enter ANTONY.

ANT. All is lost!
This foul Egyptian hath betrayed me!
My fleet hath yielded to the foe; and yonder
They cast their caps up, and carouse together
Like friends long lost!—Triple-turn'd whore! [e] 'tis thou

(*) First folio, *auguries.*

[a] — for *sleep.*] Another instance, we apprehend, where "for" is either intended to represent *fore*, or has been misprinted instead of that word. See note (f), p. 87, Vol. II.

[b] —— *the drums*
Demurely *wake the sleepers.*]
"Demurely" in this place is more than suspicious. Mr. Collier's annotator conjectures, "*Do early;*" and Mr. Dyce, "*Do merrily,*" but neither reading is very felicitous.

[c] They have put forth the haven:] We have adopted a suggestion of Mr. Knight in printing the sentence,—
"—— order for sea is given!
They have put forth the haven:"—
parenthetically, though there can be little doubt some words after "*haven*" have been accidentally omitted. Rowe supplied the presumptive deficiency by reading, "Further on;" Capell, by "Hie we on;" Malone, by "Let's seek a spot;" Tyrwhitt, by "Let us go;" and Mr. Dyce, by "Forward now." The last, slightly altered to "forward *then,*" strikes us as preferable to any of the other additions.

[d] But *being charg'd,*—] "But" seems to be used here in its exceptive sense—*unless* or *without.*

[e] Triple-turn'd—] From Julius Cæsar to Cneius Pompey, from Pompey to Antony, and, as he suspects now, from him to Octavius Cæsar.

Hast sold me to this novice; and my heart
Makes only wars on thee.—Bid them all fly!
For when I am reveng'd upon my charm,
I have done all:—bid them all fly! be gone!
[*Exit* SCARUS.
O sun, thy uprise shall I see no more!
Fortune and Antony part here; even here
Do we shake hands.—All come to this?—The hearts
That spaniel'd* me at heels, to whom I gave
Their wishes, do discandy, melt their sweets
On blossoming Cæsar; and this pine is bark'd,
That overtopp'd them all! Betray'd I am:
O, this false soul of Egypt! this grave charm,[a]—
Whose eye beck'd forth my wars, and call'd them home;
Whose bosom was my crownet, my chief end,—
Like a right gipsy, hath, at fast and loose,[b]
Beguil'd me to the very heart of loss.—
What, Eros, Eros!

Enter CLEOPATRA.

Ah, thou spell! Avaunt!
CLEO. Why is my lord enrag'd against his love?
ANT. Vanish! or I shall give thee thy deserving,
And blemish Cæsar's triumph. Let him take thee,
And hoist thee up to the shouting plébeians:
Follow his chariot, like the greatest spot
Of all thy sex: most monster-like, be shown
For poor'st diminutives, for doits;† and let
Patient Octavia plough thy visage up
With her prepared nails. [*Exit* CLEO.] 'T is well thou 'rt gone,
If it be well to live: but better 't were
Thou fell'st into my fury, for one death
Might have prevented many.—Eros, ho!—
The shirt of Nessus is upon me:—teach me,
Alcides, thou mine ancestor, thy rage:
Let me lodge Lichas on the horns o' the moon;
And with those hands, that grasp'd the heaviest club,
Subdue my worthiest self.[c] The witch shall die!
To the young Roman boy she hath sold me, and I fall
Under this plot: she dies for 't!—Eros, ho!
[*Exit.*

SCENE XIII.—Alexandria. *A Room in the Palace.*

Enter CLEOPATRA, CHARMIAN, IRAS, *and* MARDIAN.

CLEO. Help me, my women! O, he is more mad
Than Telamon for his shield; the boar of Thessaly[d]
Was never so emboss'd.[e]
CHAR. To the monument!
There lock yourself, and send him word you are dead.
The soul and body rive not more in parting,
Than greatness going off.
CLEO. To the monument!—
Mardian, go tell him I have slain myself;
Say, that the last I spoke was, *Antony*,
And word it, pr'ythee, piteously: hence, Mardian,
And bring me how he takes my death.—
To the monument! [*Exeunt.*

SCENE XIV.—*The same. Another Room.*

Enter ANTONY *and* EROS.

ANT. Eros, thou yet behold'st me?
EROS. Ay, noble lord.
ANT. Sometime we see a cloud that's dragonish; (2)
A vapour sometime like a bear or lion,
A tower'd citadel, a pendent rock,
A forked mountain, or blue promontory
With trees upon 't, that nod unto the world,
And mock our eyes with air: thou hast seen these signs?
They are black vesper's pageants.
EROS. Ay, my lord.
ANT. That which is now a horse, even with a thought
The rack dislimns, and makes it indistinct,
As water is in water.
EROS. It does, my lord.
ANT. My good knave Eros, now thy captain is
Even such a body: here I am Antony;
Yet cannot hold this visible shape, my knave.

(*) First folio, *pannelled.* Corrected by Hanmer.
(†) Old text, *dolts.* Corrected by Warburton.

a O, this false soul of Egypt! this grave charm,—] Mr. Collier's annotator would read,—

"O, this false *spell* of Egypt, this *great* charm."

Spell is very plausible; but "*great* charm" is infinitely less expressive and appropriate than "*grave* charm," *i.e. pernicious, deadly, fatal* sorceress.

b — fast and loose,—] A cheating game similar to what is now called *pricking at the belt* or *girdle.*

c *Subdue my* worthiest self.] The commentators, excepting Hanmer, have not suspected any corruption here; but would Antony, in this hour of bitter remorse, speak of his "*worthiest self*"? He might have said, "my worthless self;" yet the context, "the witch shall die," makes it more probable he is thinking of Cleopatra, and that what the author wrote was, "Subdue my *worthless elf.*" *Elf* being synonymous with witch or fairy.

d — the boar of Thessaly—] The boar killed by Meleager.

e — emboss'd.] See note (a), p. 228, Vol. I.

I made these wars for Egypt; and the queen,—
Whose heart I thought I had, for she had mine;
Which, whilst it was mine, had annex'd unto 't
A million more, now lost,—she, Eros, has
Pack'd cards with Cæsar,* and false-play'd my glory
Unto an enemy's triumph!—
Nay, weep not, gentle Eros; there is left us
Ourselves to end ourselves.—

Enter MARDIAN.

O, thy vile lady!
She has robb'd me of my sword.

MAR. No, Antony;
My mistress lov'd thee, and her fortunes mingled
With thine entirely.

ANT. Hence, saucy eunuch; peace!
She hath betray'd me, and shall die the death.

MAR. Death of one person can be paid but once,
And that she has discharg'd. What thou wouldst do
Is done unto thy hand: the last she spake
Was, *Antony! most noble Antony!*
Then in the midst a tearing groan did break
The name of Antony; it was divided
Between her heart and lips: she render'd life,
Thy name so buried in her.

ANT. Dead, then?

MAR. Dead.

ANT. Unarm, Eros; the long day's task is done,
And we must sleep!—That thou depart'st hence safe,
Does pay thy labour richly; go.—[*Exit* MARDIAN.]
Off, pluck off!—
The seven-fold shield of Ajax cannot keep
The battery from my heart. O, cleave, my sides!
Heart, once be stronger than thy continent,
Crack thy frail case!—Apace, Eros, apace!—
No more a soldier:—bruised pieces, go;
You have been nobly borne.—From me a while.— [*Exit* EROS.
I will o'ertake thee, Cleopatra, and
Weep for my pardon. So it must be, for now
All length is torture.—Since the torch is out,
Lie down, and stray no farther. Now all labour
Mars what it does; yea, very force entangles
Itself with strength: seal then, and all is done!—
Eros!—I come, my queen:—Eros!—Stay for me:
Where souls do couch on flowers, we'll hand in hand,
And with our sprightly port make the ghosts gaze:

(*) First folio, *Cæsars*.

Dido and her Æneas shall want troops,
And all the haunt be ours.—Come, Eros, Eros!

Re-enter EROS.

EROS. What would my lord?

ANT. Since Cleopatra died,
I have liv'd in such dishonour, that the gods
Detest my baseness. I, that with my sword
Quarter'd the world, and o'er green Neptune's back
With ships made cities, condemn myself to lack
The courage of a woman; less noble mind
Than she which by her death our Cæsar tells,
I am conqueror of myself. Thou art sworn, Eros,
That, when the exigent should come, (which now
Is come indeed) when I should see behind me
The inevitable prosecution of
Disgrace and horror, that, on my command,
Thou then wouldst kill me: do 't; the time is come:
Thou strik'st not me, 't is Cæsar thou defeat'st.
Put colour in thy cheek.

EROS. The gods withhold me!
Shall I do that which all the Parthian darts,
Though enemy, lost aim, and could not?

ANT. Eros,
Wouldst thou be window'd in great Rome, and see
Thy master thus with pleach'd arms, bending down
His corrigible neck, his face subdu'd
To penetrative shame, whilst the wheel'd seat
Of fortunate Cæsar, drawn before him, branded
His baseness that ensu'd?

EROS. I would not see 't.

ANT. Come then; for with a wound I must be cur'd.
Draw that thy honest sword, which thou hast worn
Most useful for thy country.

EROS. O, sir, pardon me!

ANT. When I did make thee free, swor'st thou not then
To do this when I bade thee? Do it at once;
Or thy precedent services are all
But accidents unpurpos'd. Draw, and come.

EROS. Turn from me, then, that noble countenance,
Wherein the worship of the whole world lies.

ANT. Lo thee! [*Turning from him.*

EROS. My sword is drawn.

ANT. Then let it do at once
The thing why thou hast drawn it.

EROS. My dear master,
My captain, and my emperor, let me say,
Before I strike this bloody stroke, farewell.

ANT. 'T is said, man;—and farewell.

EROS. Farewell, great chief. Shall I strike now?

ANT. Now, Eros.

EROS. Why, there then:—[*Falls on his sword.* thus I do escape the sorrow
Of Antony's death. [*Dies.*

ANT. Thrice nobler than myself!
Thou teachest me, O, valiant Eros, what
I should, and thou couldst not. My queen and [Eros
Have, by their brave instruction, got upon me
A nobleness in record: but I will be
A bridegroom in my death, and run into 't
As to a lover's bed. Come then; and, Eros,
Thy master dies thy scholar; to do thus
[*Falling on his sword.*
I learn'd of thee.—How! not dead? not dead?—
The guard—ho!—O, despatch me.

Enter DERCETAS *and* Guard.

1 GUARD. What 's the noise?

ANT. I have done my work ill, friends: O, make an end
Of what I have begun!

2 GUARD. The star is fall'n!

1 GUARD. And time is at his period.

ALL. Alas, and woe!

ANT. Let him that loves me strike me dead.

1 GUARD. Not I.

2 GUARD. Nor I.

3 GUARD. Nor any one. [*Exeunt* Guard.

DER. Thy death and fortunes bid thy followers fly.
This sword but shown to Cæsar, with this tidings,
Shall enter me with him.

Enter DIOMEDES.

DIO. Where 's Antony?

DER. There, Diomed, there.

DIO. Lives he?
Wilt thou not answer, man? [*Exit* DERCETAS.

ANT. Art thou there, Diomed? Draw thy sword, and give me
Sufficing strokes for death.

DIO. Most absolute lord,
My mistress Cleopatra sent me to thee.

ANT. When did she send thee?

DIO. Now, my lord.
ANT. Where is she?
DIO. Lock'd in her monument. She had a prophesying fear
Of what hath come to pass: for when she saw
(Which never shall be found) you did suspect
She had dispos'd[a] with Cæsar, and that your rage
Would not be purg'd, she sent you word she was dead;
But, fearing since how it might work, hath sent
Me to proclaim the truth; and I am come,
I dread, too late.
ANT. Too late, good Diomed.—Call my guard, I pr'ythee.
DIO. What, ho! the emperor's guard! The guard, what, ho!
Come, your lord calls!

Enter some of the Guard.

ANT. Bear me, good friends, where Cleopatra bides;
'T is the last service that I shall command you.
1 GUARD. Woe, woe are we, sir, you may not live to wear
All your true followers out.
ALL. Most heavy day!
ANT. Nay, good my fellows, do not please sharp fate
To grace it with your sorrows: bid that welcome
Which comes to punish us, and we punish it
Seeming to bear it lightly. Take me up:
I have led you oft; carry me now, good friends,
And have my thanks for all.
[*Exeunt, bearing* ANTONY.

SCENE XV.—*The same. A Monument.*

Enter, above, CLEOPATRA, CHARMIAN, *and* IRAS.

CLEO. O, Charmian, I will never go from hence.
CHAR. Be comforted, dear madam.
CLEO. No, I will not:
All strange and terrible events are welcome,
But comforts we despise; our size of sorrow,
Proportion'd to our cause, must be as great
As that which makes it.—

Enter, below, DIOMEDES.

How now! is he dead?
DIO. His death 's upon him, but not dead.
Look out o' the other side your monument,
His guard have brought him thither.

Enter, below, ANTONY, *borne by the* Guard.

CLEO. O, sun,
Burn the great sphere thou mov'st in!—darkling stand
The varying shore o' the world!—O, Antony!
Antony, Antony!—Help, Charmian; help, Iras, help;—
Help, friends below;—let 's draw him hither.
ANT. Peace!
Not Cæsar's valour hath o'erthrown Antony,
But Antony's hath triumph'd on itself.
CLEO. So it should be, that none but Antony
Should conquer Antony; but woe 't is so!
ANT. I am dying,—Egypt,—dying; only
I here impórtune death a while, until
Of many thousand kisses the poor last
I lay upon thy lips.—
CLEO. I dare not, dear,
(Dear my lord, pardon,) I dare not,
Lest I be taken: not the imperious show
Of the full-fortun'd Cæsar ever shall
Be brooch'd[b] with me; if knife, drugs, serpents, have
Edge, sting, or operation, I am safe:
Your wife Octavia, with her modest eyes
And still conclusion, shall acquire no honour
Demuring upon me.—But come, come, Antony,—
Help me, my women,—we must draw thee up;—
Assist, good friends.
ANT. O, quick, or I am gone!
CLEO. Here 's sport, indeed![c]—How heavy weighs my lord!
Our strength is all gone into heaviness;
That makes the weight. Had I great Juno's power,
The strong-wing'd Mercury should fetch thee up,
And set thee by Jove's side. Yet come a little,—
Wishers were ever fools,—O, come, come, come!
[*They draw* ANTONY *up.*
And welcome, welcome! die where* thou hast liv'd!
Quicken with kissing! had my lips that power,
Thus would I wear them out.
ALL. A heavy sight!
ANT. I am dying,—Egypt,—dying;—
Give me some wine, and let me speak a little.
CLEO. No, let me speak; and let me rail so high,

[a] — dispos'd *with Cæsar,*—] See note (i), p. 563.
[b] —brooch'd—] *Adorned, decorated.* So in "Titus Andronicus," Act I. Sc. 1,—
"Sufficeth not, that we are brought to Rome
To *beautify* thy triumphs—"
[c] Here 's sport, indeed!] The pathos of this exclamation, so piteous in the contrast it implies between the fallen queen's present occupation and the diversions of her happier times, is quite lost on Mr. Collier's unsusceptible commentator, who coolly reads, "Here 's *port*, indeed."!

(*) Old text, *when*.

That the false housewife, Fortune,[a] break her wheel,
Provok'd by my offence.
  ANT. One word, sweet queen:
Of Cæsar seek your honour, with your safety.—O!
  CLEO. They do not go together.
  ANT. Gentle, hear me;
None about Cæsar trust but Proculeius.
  CLEO. My resolution and my hands I'll trust;
None about Cæsar.
  ANT. The miserable change now at my end,
Lament nor sorrow at; but please your thoughts,
In feeding them with those my former fortunes
Wherein I liv'd, the greatest prince o' the world,
The noblest; and do now not basely die,
Not cowardly put off[b] my helmet to
My countryman,—a Roman by a Roman
Valiantly vanquish'd.(3) Now, my spirit is going;—
I can no more.—
  CLEO. Noblest of men, woo't die?
Hast thou no care of me? shall I abide
In this dull world, which in thy absence is
No better than a sty?—O, see, my women,
[ANTONY *dies.*
The crown o' the earth doth melt!—My lord!—
O, wither'd is the garland of the war!
The soldier's pole is fall'n: young boys and girls
Are level now with men; the odds is gone,
And there is nothing left remarkable[c]
Beneath the visiting moon. [*Faints.*
  CHAR. O, quietness, lady!
  IRAS. She is dead too, our sovereign!
  CHAR. Lady!—
  IRAS. Madam!—
  CHAR. O madam, madam, madam!—
  IRAS. Royal Egypt!
Empress!—
  CHAR. Peace, peace, Iras!
  CLEO. No more, but e'en* a woman, and commanded
By such poor passion as the maid that milks,
And does the meanest chares.—It were for me
To throw my sceptre at the injurious gods;
To tell them that this world did equal theirs,
Till they had stol'n our jewel.—All's but nought;
Patience is sottish, and impatience does
Become a dog that's mad: then is it sin
To rush into the secret house of death,
Ere death dare come to us?—How do you, women?
What, what! good cheer! Why, how now, Charmian!
My noble girls!—Ah, women, women! look,
Our lamp is spent, it's out!—Good sirs,[d] take heart:—
We'll bury him; and then, what's brave, what's noble,
Let's do it after the high Roman fashion,
And make Death proud to take us. Come, away:—
This case of that huge spirit now is cold.—
Ah, women, women!—come; we have no friend
But resolution, and the briefest end.
[*Exeunt; those above bearing off* ANTONY'*s body.*

(*) First folio, *in*, corrected by Capell.

[a] — housewife, *Fortune*,—] "Housewife" is here used in the loose sense, which it often bore, of *hussy*, or *harlot*. So in "Henry V." Act V. Sc. 1, Pistol asks,—"Doth Fortune play the *huswife* with me now?"

[b] —— and do now not basely die,
Not cowardly put off my helmet to
My countryman,—]
Thus the *textus receptus*, but perhaps we ought to read,—
"—— and do now not basely die,
Not cowardly, *but doff* my helmet to
My countryman," &c.

[c] *And there is nothing left* remarkable—] In Shakespeare's time, the word "remarkable" bore a far more impressive and appropriate meaning than with us. It then expressed not merely observable or noteworthy, but something profoundly striking and uncommon.

[d] Good sirs, *take heart:*—] Mr. Dyce has shown that this form of addressing women was not unusual; and, consequently, that the modern stage direction here, "[To the Guard below," is improper. Thus, as quoted by Mr. Dyce from Beaumont and Fletcher's play of "The Coxcomb," Act IV. Sc. 3, the mother, speaking to Viola, Nan, and Madge, says,—
"*Sirs*, to your tasks, and shew this little novice
How to bestir herself," &c.
Again, as quoted by Mr. Dyce from the same authors' "A King and No King," Act III. Sc. 1,—
"*Spa.* I do beseech you, madam, send away
Your other women, and receive from me
A few sad words, which, set against your joys,
May make 'em shine the more.
Pan. Sirs, leave me all.
[Exeunt *Wailing-women.*

ACT V.

SCENE I.—Cæsar's *Camp before* Alexandria.

Enter Cæsar, Agrippa, Dolabella, Mecænas, Gallus, Proculeius, *and others*.

Cæs. Go to him, Dolabella, bid him yield;
Being so frustrate,[a] tell him, he mocks
The pauses that he makes.
Dol. Cæsar, I shall. [*Exit.*

Enter Dercetas, *with the sword of* Antony.

Cæs. Wherefore is that? and what art thou that dar'st
Appear thus to us?
Der. I am call'd Dercetas;
Mark Antony I serv'd, who best was worthy
Best to be serv'd: whilst he stood up and spoke,
He was my master; and I wore my life
To spend upon his haters. If thou please
To take me to thee, as I was to him
I'll be to Cæsar; if thou pleasest not,
I yield thee up my life.
Cæs. What is't thou say'st?
Der. I say, O, Cæsar, Antony is dead!
Cæs. The breaking of so great a thing should make

[a] Being so frustrate, tell him, he mocks
The pauses that he makes.]
Malone reads, "—tell him, he mocks *us by*—" &c. Steevens proposed, *frustrated*, or to read,—
"—— tell him *that* he mocks —" &c.
Mr. Collier's annotator,—
"—— tell him, that he mocks us
By—"
and Mr. Sidney Walker would adhere to the old text, but, as was not unusual with the poet's contemporaries, pronounce "frustrate" trisyllabically.

A greater crack: the round world[a]
Should have shook lions into civil streets,
And citizens to their dens:—the death of Antony
Is not a single doom; in the name lay
A moiety of the world.

DER. He is dead, Cæsar,
Not by a public minister of justice,
Nor by a hired knife; but that self hand,
Which writ his honour in the acts it did,
Hath, with the courage which the heart did lend it,
Splitted the heart.—This is his sword;
I robb'd his wound of it; behold it, stain'd
With his most noble blood.

CÆS. Look you sad, friends?
The gods rebuke me, but it is tidings
To wash the eyes of kings.

AGR.* And strange it is
That nature must compel us to lament
Our most persisted deeds.

MEC. His taints and honours
Wag'd equal with him.

AGR.† A rarer spirit never
Did steer humanity: but you, gods, will give us
Some faults to make us men.—Cæsar is touch'd.

MEC. When such a spacious mirror 's set before him,
He needs must see himself.

CÆS. O, Antony!
I have follow'd thee to this;—but we do lance
Diseases in our bodies: I must perforce
Have shown to thee such a declining day,
Or look on thine; we could not stall together
In the whole world. But yet let me lament,
With tears as sovereign as the blood of hearts,
That thou, my brother, my competitor
In top of all design, my mate in empire,
Friend and companion in the front of war,
The arm of mine own body, and the heart
Where mine his thoughts did kindle,—that our stars,
Unreconciliable, should divide
Our equalness to this.—Hear me, good friends,—

Enter a Messenger.

But I will tell you at some meeter season;
The business of this man looks out of him,
We'll hear him what he says.—Whence are you?

MESS. A poor Egyptian yet.[b] The queen my mistress,
Confin'd in all she has, her monument,
Of thy intents desires instruction,
That she preparedly may frame herself
To the way she's forc'd to.

CÆS. Bid her have good heart;
She soon shall know of us, by some of ours,
How honourable and how kindly we
Determine for her: for Cæsar cannot live*
To be ungentle.

MESS. So the gods preserve thee! [*Exit.*

CÆS. Come hither, Proculeius. Go, and say,
We purpose her no shame: give her what comforts
The quality of her passion shall require,
Lest, in her greatness, by some mortal stroke
She do defeat us; for her life in Rome
Would be eternal in our triumph: go,
And with your speediest bring us what she says,
And how you find of her.

PRO. Cæsar, I shall. [*Exit.*

CÆS. Gallus, go you along. [*Exit* GALLUS.
Where's Dolabella,
To second Proculeius?

AGR., MEC. Dolabella!

CÆS. Let him alone, for I remember now
How he's employed: he shall in time be ready.
Go with me to my tent; where you shall see
How hardly I was drawn into this war;
How calm and gentle I proceeded still
In all my writings. Go with me, and see
What I can show in this. [*Exeunt.*

SCENE II.—Alexandria. *A Room in the Monument.*

Enter CLEOPATRA, CHARMIAN, *and* IRAS.

CLEO. My desolation does begin to make
A better life. 'Tis paltry to be Cæsar;
Not being Fortune, he's but Fortune's knave,
A minister of her will: and it is great
To do that thing that ends all other deeds;
Which shackles accidents, and bolts up change;
Which sleeps, and never palates more the dug,[c]
The beggar's nurse and Cæsar's.

Enter, to the gates of the Monument, PROCULEIUS, GALLUS, *and* Soldiers.

PRO. Cæsar sends greeting to the queen of Egypt;

(*) First folio, *Dol.* (†) First folio, *Dol.*

a — the round world—] Something has evidently been lost here.

b yet.] That is, *now*.

c —— *and never palates more the* dug,
The beggar's nurse and Cæsar's.]
In the old copies we have,—
"—— and never palates more the *dung*," &c.
an obvious misprint, though not wanting defenders, which was corrected by Warburton.

(*) Old text, *leave*. Corrected by Southern.

And bids thee study on what fair demands
Thou mean'st to have him grant thee.

CLEO. What's thy name?

PRO. My name is Proculeius.

CLEO. Antony
Did tell me of you, bade me trust you; but
I do not greatly care to be deceiv'd,
That have no use for trusting. If your master
Would have a queen his beggar, you must tell him
That majesty, to keep decorum, must
No less beg than a kingdom: if he please
To give me conquer'd Egypt for my son,
He gives me so much of mine own, as I
Will kneel to him with thanks.

PRO. Be of good cheer;
You're fall'n into a princely hand, fear nothing:
Make your full reference freely to my lord,
Who is so full of grace, that it flows over
On all that need. Let me report to him
Your sweet dependency, and you shall find
A conqueror that will pray in aid for kindness,
Where he for grace is kneel'd to.

CLEO. Pray you, tell him
I am his fortune's vassal, and I send him
The greatness he has got. I hourly learn
A doctrine of obedience; and would gladly
Look him i' the face.

PRO. This I'll report, dear lady.
Have comfort, for I know your plight is pitied
Of him that caus'd it.

GAL.[a] You see how easily she may be surpris'd;

[*Here* PROCULEIUS *and two of the* Guard *ascend the Monument by a ladder placed against a window, and, having descended, come behind* CLEOPATRA. *Some of the* Guard *unbar and open the gates.*

Guard her till Cæsar come.

[*To* PROCULEIUS *and the* Guard. *Exit.*

IRAS. Royal queen!

CHAR. O, Cleopatra! thou art taken, queen!—

CLEO. Quick, quick, good hands.

[*Drawing a dagger.*

PRO. Hold, worthy lady, hold!

[*Seizes and disarms her.*

Do not yourself such wrong, who are in this
Reliev'd, but not betray'd.

CLEO. What, of death too,
That rids our dogs of languish?

PRO. Cleopatra,
Do not abuse my master's bounty by
The undoing of yourself: let the world see
His nobleness well acted, which your death
Will never let come forth.

CLEO. Where art thou, Death?
Come hither, come! come, come, and take a queen
Worth many babes and beggars!

PRO. O, temperance, lady!

CLEO. Sir, I will eat no meat, I'll not drink, sir;
If idle talk will once be accessary,[b]
I'll not sleep neither: this mortal house I'll ruin,
Do Cæsar what he can. Know, sir, that I
Will not wait pinion'd at your master's court;
Nor once be chástis'd with the sober eye
Of dull Octavia. Shall they hoist me up,
And show me to the shouting varletry
Of censuring Rome? Rather a ditch in Egypt
Be gentle grave unto me! Rather on Nilus' mud
Lay me stark nak'd, and let the water-flies
Blow me into abhorring! Rather make
My country's high pyramids my gibbet,
And hang me up in chains!

PRO. You do extend
These thoughts of horror further than you shall
Find cause in Cæsar.

Enter DOLABELLA.

DOL. Proculeius,
What thou hast done thy master Cæsar knows,
And he hath sent for thee: for[c] the queen,
I'll take her to my guard.

PRO. So, Dolabella,
It shall content me best: be gentle to her.—
To Cæsar I will speak what you shall please,

[*To* CLEOPATRA.

If you'll employ me to him.

CLEO. Say, I would die.

[*Exeunt* PROCULEIUS *and* Soldiers.

DOL. Most noble empress, you have heard of me?

CLEO. I cannot tell.

DOL. Assuredly, you know me.

CLEO. No matter, sir, what I have heard or known.—
You laugh, when boys or women tell their dreams;
Is't not your trick?

DOL. I understand not, madam.

CLEO. I dreamt there was an emperor Antony;—
O, such another sleep, that I might see
But such another man!

DOL. If it might please ye,—

CLEO. His face was as the heavens; and therein stuck

---

[a] GAL.] The prefix in the first folio is "Pro.:" in the second, "Char." Malone first assigned the speech to Gallus, and added the stage direction which follows.

[b] *If idle talk will once be* accessary,—] We adopt here Hanmer's substitution "accessary" in place of *necessary*, the reading of the old copies. The sense is plainly,—"I'll neither eat nor drink, and, if idle talk will, *for the nonce*, be assistant, I'll not sleep."

[c] —for the queen,—] The second folio reads, "*as* for."

A sun and moon, which kept their course, and lighted
The little O,[a] the earth.

DOL. Most sovereign creature,—

CLEO. His legs bestrid the ocean; his rear'd arm
Crested the world; his voice was propertied
As all the tuned spheres, and that to friends;
But when he meant to quail and shake the orb,
He was as rattling thunder. For his bounty,
There was no winter in 't; an autumn* 't was,
That grew the more by reaping. His delights
Were dolphin-like; they show'd his back above
The element they liv'd in: in his livery
Walk'd crowns and crownets; realms and islands were
As plates[b] dropp'd from his pocket.

DOL. Cleopatra,—

CLEO. Think you there was, or might be, such a man
As this I dreamt of?

DOL. Gentle madam, no.

CLEO. You lie, up to the hearing of the gods!
But, if there be, or ever were, one such,
It 's past the size of dreaming: Nature wants stuff
To vie[c] strange forms with fancy; yet, to imagine
An Antony, were Nature's piece 'gainst fancy,
Condemning shadows quite.[d]

DOL. Hear me, good madam:
Your loss is as yourself, great; and you bear it
As answering to the weight: would I might never
O'ertake pursu'd success, but I do feel,
By the rebound of yours, a grief that smites†
My very heart at root.

CLEO. I thank you, sir.
Know you what Cæsar means to do with me?

DOL. I am loth to tell you what I would you knew.

CLEO. Nay, pray you, sir,—

DOL. Though he be honourable,—

CLEO. He 'll lead me, then, in triumph?

DOL. Madam, he will; I know 't.

[*Flourish without.*

Without. Make way there,—Cæsar!

Enter CÆSAR, GALLUS, PROCULEIUS, MECÆNAS, SELEUCUS, *and* Attendants.

CÆS. Which is the queen of Egypt?

DOL. It is the emperor, madam.

[CLEOPATRA *kneels.*

CÆS. Arise, you shall not kneel:—
I pray you, rise; rise, Egypt.

CLEO. Sir, the gods
Will have it thus; my master and my lord
I must obey.

CÆS. Take to you no hard thoughts:
The record of what injuries you did us,
Though written in our flesh, we shall remember
As things but done by chance.

CLEO. Sole sir o' the world,
I cannot project mine own cause so well
To make it clear; but do confess I have
Been laden with like frailties which before
Have often sham'd our sex.

CÆS. Cleopatra, know,
We will extenuate rather than enforce:
If you apply yourself to our intents,
(Which towards you are most gentle) you shall find
A benefit in this change; but if you seek
To lay on me a cruelty, by taking
Antony's course, you shall bereave yourself
Of my good purposes, and put your children
To that destruction which I 'll guard them from,
If thereon you rely. I 'll take my leave.

CLEO. And may, through all the world: 't is yours; and we,
Your scutcheons and your signs of conquest, shall
Hang in what place you please. Here, my good lord.

CÆS. You shall advise me in all for Cleopatra.

CLEO. This is the brief of money, plate, and jewels,
I am possess'd of: 't is exactly valu'd;
Not petty things admitted.—Where 's Seleucus?

SEL. Here, madam.

CLEO. This is my treasurer; let him speak, my lord,
Upon his peril, that I have reserv'd
To myself nothing. Speak the truth, Seleucus.

SEL. Madam,
I had rather seal[e] my lips, than, to my peril,
Speak that which is not.

CLEO. What have I kept back?

SEL. Enough to purchase what you have made known.

CÆS. Nay, blush not, Cleopatra; I approve
Your wisdom in the deed.

CLEO. See, Cæsar! O, behold,
How pomp is follow'd! mine will now be yours;
And should we shift estates yours would be mine.

(*) First folio, *Antony*. Corrected by Theobald.
(†) Old text, *suites*. Corrected by Capell.

[a] *The little* O,—] The little *orb*, *circlet*, or *round*.

[b] — plates—] *Silver coin.*

[c] To vie—] *To vie* was a term at cards, and meant, particularly, to increase the stakes, and, generally, to challenge any one to a *contention*, *bet*, *wager*, &c.

[d] Condemning shadows quite.] We are not sure of having mastered the sense of this, or indeed that the text exhibits precisely what Shakespeare wrote, but the meaning apparently is, "— Nature lacks material to compete with fancy in unwonted shapes, yet the conception of an Antony was a masterpiece of Nature over fancy, abasing phantoms quite."

[e] — seal *my lips*,—] The old reading is, "*seele* my lippes," but here there is no allusion to the practice of *seeling* a hawk's *eyes*, as some editors suppose; to *seal* one's lips was a familiar expression ages before Shakespeare lived.

The ingratitude of this Seleucus does
Even make me wild:—O, slave, of no more trust
Than love that 's hir'd!—What, goest thou back? thou shalt
Go back, I warrant thee; but I 'll catch thine eyes,
Though they had wings. Slave, soulless villain, dog!
O, rarely base!

CÆS. Good queen, let us entreat you.

CLEO. O, Cæsar, what a wounding shame is this,—
That thou, vouchsafing here to visit me,
Doing the honour of thy lordliness
To one so meek,—that mine own servant should
Parcel the sum of my disgraces by
Addition of his envy! Say, good Cæsar,
That I some lady trifles have reserv'd,
Immoment toys, things of such dignity
As we greet modern[a] friends withal; and say,
Some nobler token I have kept apart
For Livia and Octavia, to induce
Their mediation; must I be unfolded
With one that I have bred? The gods! It smites me
Beneath the fall I have.—Pr'ythee, go hence;
[*To* SELEUCUS.
Or I shall show the cinders of my spirits
Through the ashes of my chance:—wert thou a man,
Thou wouldst have mercy on me.

CÆS. Forbear, Seleucus.
[*Exit* SELEUCUS.

CLEO. Be it known, that we, the greatest, are misthought
For things that others do; and, when we fall,
We answer others' merits[b] in our name,
Are therefore to be pitied.

CÆS. Cleopatra,
Not what you have reserv'd, nor what acknowledg'd,
Put we i' the roll of conquest:(1) still be 't yours,
Bestow it at your pleasure; and believe
Cæsar 's no merchant, to make prize with you
Of things that merchants sold. Therefore be cheer'd;
Make not your thoughts your prisons; no, dear queen;
For we intend so to dispose you as
Yourself shall give us counsel. Feed, and sleep:
Our care and pity is so much upon you,
That we remain your friend; and so adieu.

CLEO. My master, and my lord!

CÆS. Not so. Adieu.
[*Flourish. Exeunt* CÆSAR *and his* Train.

CLEO. He words me, girls, he words me, that I should not
Be noble to myself: but hark thee, Charmian.
[*Whispers* CHARMIAN.

IRAS. Finish, good lady; the bright day is done,
And we are for the dark.

CLEO. Hie thee again:
I have spoke already, and it is provided;
Go, put it to the haste.

CHAR. Madam, I will.

Re-enter DOLABELLA.

DOL. Where is the queen?

CHAR. Behold, sir. [*Exit.*

CLEO. Dolabella!

DOL. Madam, as thereto sworn by your command,
Which my love makes religion to obey,
I tell you this: Cæsar through Syria
Intends his journey; and, within three days,
You with your children will he send before:
Make your best use of this: I have perform'd
Your pleasure, and my promise.

CLEO. Dolabella,
I shall remain your debtor.

DOL. I your servant.
Adieu, good queen; I must attend on Cæsar.

CLEO. Farewell, and thanks. [*Exit* DOL.
Now, Iras, what think'st thou?
Thou, an Egyptian puppet, shalt be shown
In Rome, as well as I: mechanic slaves
With greasy aprons, rules, and hammers, shal
Uplift us to the view; in their thick breaths,
Rank of gross diet, shall we be enclouded,
And forc'd to drink their vapour.

IRAS. The gods forbid!

CLEO. Nay, 't is most certain, Iras:—saucy lictors
Will catch at us, like strumpets; and scald rhymers
Ballad us out o' tune: the quick[c] comedians
Extemporally will stage us, and present
Our Alexandrian revels; Antony
Shall be brought drunken forth, and I shall see
Some squeaking Cleopatra boy my greatness
I' the posture of a whore.

IRAS. O, the good gods!

CLEO. Nay, that 's certain.

IRAS. I 'll never see 't; for, I am sure, my nails
Are stronger than mine eyes.

CLEO. Why, that 's the way
To fool their preparation, and to conquer
Their most absurd[d] intents.—

---

[a] — modern *friends*—] *Ordinary, common* friends.
[b] — merits—] "Merits" is here employed for *demerits* or deserts.

[c] — *the* quick *comedians*—] The *lively, quick-witted* comedians.
[d] — absurd *intents.*—] Theobald has, "— *assur'd* intents."

Re-enter CHARMIAN.

Now, Charmian !—
Show me, my women, like a queen :—go fetch
My best attires ;—I am again for Cydnus,
To meet Mark Antony :—sirrah, Iras, go.—
Now, noble Charmian, we 'll despatch indeed :
And, when thou hast done this chare, I 'll give thee leave
To play till doomsday.—Bring our crown and all. [*Exit* IRAS.
Wherefore 's this noise? [*A noise without.*

Enter one of the Guard.

GUARD. Here is a rural fellow
That will not be denied your highness' presence ;
He brings you figs.

CLEO. Let him come in. What poor an instrument[a] [*Exit* Guard.
May do a noble deed ! he brings me liberty !
My resolution 's plac'd, and I have nothing
Of woman in me : now from head to foot
I am marble-constant ; now the fleeting moon
No planet is of mine.

Re-enter Guard, *with* Clown, *bringing in a basket.*

GUARD. This is the man.

CLEO. Avoid, and leave him. [*Exit* Guard.
Hast thou the pretty worm of Nilus there,
That kills and pains not?

CLOWN. Truly I have him : but I would not be the party that should desire you to touch him, for his biting is immortal ; those that do die of it do seldom or never recover.

CLEO. Remember'st thou any that have died on 't?

CLOWN. Very many, men and women too. I heard of one of them no longer than yesterday : a very honest woman, but something given to lie ; as a woman should not do, but in the way of honesty : how she died of the biting of it, what pain she felt,—truly, she makes a very good report o' the worm ; but he that will believe all that they say, shall never be saved by half that they do : but this is most fallible, the worm 's an odd worm.

[a] What poor an instrument—] See note (b), p. 127, Vol. II.

CLEO. Get thee hence; farewell.
CLOWN. I wish you all joy of the worm.
CLEO. Farewell. [Clown *sets down the basket.*
CLOWN. You must think this, look you, that the worm will do his kind.
CLEO. Ay, ay; farewell.
CLOWN. Look you, the worm is not to be trusted but in the keeping of wise people; for, indeed, there is no goodness in the worm.
CLEO. Take thou no care; it shall be heeded.
CLOWN. Very good. Give it nothing, I pray you, for it is not worth the feeding.
CLEO. Will it eat me?
CLOWN. You must not think I am so simple, but I know the devil himself will not eat a woman: I know that a woman is a dish for the gods, if the devil dress her not. But, truly, these same whoreson devils do the gods great harm in their women; for in every ten that they make, the devils mar five.
CLEO. Well, get thee gone; farewell.
CLOWN. Yes, forsooth; I wish you joy o' the worm. [*Exit.*

Re-enter IRAS, *with a robe, crown, &c.*

CLEO. Give me my robe, put on my crown; I have
Immortal longings in me. Now no more
The juice of Egypt's grape shall moist this lip:—
Yare, yare, good Iras; quick.—Methinks I hear
Antony call; I see him rouse himself
To praise my noble act; I hear him mock
The luck of Cæsar, which the gods give men
To excuse their after wrath:—husband, I come:
Now to that name my courage prove my title!
I am fire and air; my other elements
I give to baser life.—So,—have you done?
Come then, and take the last warmth of my lips.
Farewell, kind Charmian;—Iras, long farewell.
[*Kisses them.* IRAS *falls and dies.*[a]
Have I the aspic in my lips? Dost fall?
If thou and nature can so gently part,
The stroke of death is as a lover's pinch,
Which hurts, and is desir'd. Dost thou lie still?
If thus thou vanishest, thou tell'st the world
It is not worth leave-taking.
CHAR. Dissolve, thick cloud, and rain, that I may say,
The gods themselves do weep!
CLEO. This proves me base:
If she first meet the curled Antony,
He'll make demand of her, and spend that kiss
Which is my heaven to have.—Come, thou mortal wretch,
[*To an asp, which she applies to her breast.*
With thy sharp teeth this knot intrinsicate
Of life at once untie: poor venomous fool,
Be angry, and despatch. O, couldst thou speak,
That I might hear thee call great Cæsar, *Ass Unpolicied!*
CHAR. O, eastern star!
CLEO. Peace, peace!
Dost thou not see my baby at my breast,
That sucks the nurse asleep?
CHAR. O, break! O, break!
CLEO. As sweet as balm, as soft as air, as gentle,—
O, Antony!—Nay, I will take thee too:—
[*Applying another asp to her arm.*
What should I stay— [*Dies.*
CHAR. In this vile* world?—So, fare thee well.—
Now boast thee, Death, in thy possession lies
A lass unparallel'd!—Downy windows, close;
And golden Phœbus never be beheld
Of eyes again so royal!—Your crown's awry;†
I'll mend it, and then play.

Enter the Guard, *rushing in.*

1 GUARD. Where is the queen?
CHAR. Speak softly, wake her not.
1 GUARD. Cæsar hath sent—
CHAR. Too slow a messenger.
[*Applies an asp.*
O, come apace, despatch: I partly feel thee.
1 GUARD. Approach, ho! All's not well: Cæsar's beguil'd.
2 GUARD. There's Dolabella sent from Cæsar;—call him.
1 GUARD. What work is here!—Charmian, is this well done?
CHAR. It is well done, and fitting for a princess
Descended of so many royal kings.(2)
Ah, soldier! [*Dies.*

Re-enter DOLABELLA.

DOL. How goes it here?
2 GUARD. All dead.
DOL. Cæsar, thy thoughts
Touch their effects in this: thyself art coming
To see perform'd the dreaded act which thou
So sought'st to hinder.
Without. A way there! a way for Cæsar!

---

[a] [IRAS *falls and dies.*] "Iras must be supposed to have applied an asp to her arm while her mistress was settling her dress, or I know not why she should fall so soon."—STEEVENS.

(*) Old text, *wilde*. Corrected by Capell.
(†) Old text, *away*. Corrected by Pope.

Re-enter CÆSAR *and* Attendants.

DOL. O, sir, you are too sure an augurer:
That you did fear is done.
CÆS. Bravest at the last!
She levell'd at our purposes, and, being royal,
Took her own way.—The manner of their deaths?
I do not see them bleed.
DOL. Who was last with them?
1 GUARD. A simple countryman, that brought her figs:
This was his basket.
CÆS. Poison'd then.
1 GUARD. O, Cæsar!
This Charmian liv'd but now; she stood and spake:
I found her trimming up the diadem
On her dead mistress; tremblingly she stood,
And on the sudden dropp'd.
CÆS. O, noble weakness!—
If they had swallow'd poison 't would appear
By external swelling: but she looks like sleep,
As she would catch another Antony
In her strong toil of grace.
DOL. Here, on her breast,
There is a vent of blood, and something blown:
The like is on her arm.
1 GUARD. This is an aspic's trail: and these fig-leaves
Have slime upon them, such as the aspic leaves
Upon the caves of Nile.
CÆS. Most probable
That so she died; for her physician tells me
She hath pursu'd conclusions infinite
Of easy ways to die.—Take up her bed;
And bear her women from the monument:—
She shall be buried by her Antony:
No grave upon the earth shall clip in it
A pair so famous. High events as these
Strike those that make them; and their story is
No less in pity than his glory which
Brought them to be lamented. Our army shall,
In solemn show, attend this funeral;
And then to Rome.—Come, Dolabella, see
High order in this great solemnity. [*Exeunt.*

ILLUSTRATIVE COMMENTS.

ACT I.

(1) SCENE I.—

To-night we'll wander through the streets, and note
The qualities of people.]

The extracts selected for the illustration of this tragedy are, with two exceptions, taken from the biography of Antonius in North's translation of Plutarch.

"*Plato* writeth that there are foure kinds of flatterie: but *Cleopatra* devided it into many kinds. For she (were it in sport, or in matters of earnest) still devised sundry new delights to have *Antonius* at commandement, never leaving him night nor day, nor once letting him go out of her sight. For she would play at dice with him, drinke with him, and hunt commonly with him, and also be with him when he went to any exercise or activitie of body. And sometime also, when he would go up and downe the city disguised like a slave in the night, and would peere into poore mens windowes and their shops, and scold and braule with them within the house, *Cleopatra* would be also in a chamber maides array, and amble up and downe the streets with him, so that oftentimes *Antonius* bare away both mocks and blowes. Now though most men misliked this maner, yet the ALEXANDRIANS were commonly glad of this iolitie, and liked it well, saying very gallantly and wisely: that *Antonius* shewed them a comicall face, to wit, a merie countenance: and the ROMAINES a tragicall face, to say, a grimme look."

(2) SCENE II.—*Fulvia thy wife is dead.*] "Now *Antonius* delighting in these fond and childish pastimes, very ill newes were brought him from two places. The first from ROME, that his brother *Lucius* and *Fulvia* his wife, fell out first betweene themselves, and afterwards fell to open warre with *Cæsar*, and had brought all to nought, that they were both driven to flie out of ITALY. The second newes, as bad as the first: that *Labienus* conquered all ASIA with the army of the PARTHIANS, from the river of Euphrates, and from SYRIA, unto the country of LYDIA and IONIA. Then began *Antonius* with much ado, a litle to rouze himselfe, as if he had bene wakened out of a deepe sleepe, and as a man may say, coming out of a great drunkennesse. So, first of all he bent himselfe against the PARTHIANS, and went as farre as the country of PHOENICIA: but there he received lamentable letters from his wife *Fulvia*. Wherupon he straight returned towards ITALIE, with two hundred saile: and as he went, tooke up his friends by the way that fled out of ITALIE to come to him. By them he was informed, that his wife *Fulvia* was the only cause of this war: who being of a peevish, crooked, and troblesome nature, had purposely raised this uprore in ITALIE, in hope thereby to withdraw him from *Cleopatra*. But by good fortune his wife *Fulvia* going to meet with *Antonius*, sickned by the way, and died in the city of SICYONE."

(3) SCENE IV.—

It is reported thou didst eat strange flesh,
Which some did die to look on.]

"*Antonius* flying upon this overthrow, fell into great misery al at once: but the chiefest want of al other, and that pinched him most, was famine. Howbeit he was of such a strong nature, that by patience he would overcome any adversity, and the heavier fortune lay upon him, the more constant shewed he himself. Every man that feeleth want or adversity, knoweth by vertue and discretion what he should do: but when indeed they are overlaid with extremity, and be sore oppressed, few have the hearts to follow that which they praise and commend, and much lesse to avoid that they reprove and mislike: but rather to y[e] contrary, they yeeld to their accustomed easie life, and through faint heart, and lacke of courage, do change their first mind and purpose. And therefore it was a wonderfull example to the souldiers, to see *Antonius* that was brought up in al finenesse and superfluity, so easily to drink puddle water, and to eate wild fruits and roots: and moreover it is reported, that even as they passed the Alpes, they did eate the barkes of trees, and such beasts as never man tasted of their flesh before."

ACT II.

(1) SCENE II.—

For 't is a studied, not a present thought,
By duty ruminated.]

"Thereupon every man did set forward this mariage, hoping thereby that this lady *Octavia*, having an excellent grace, wisdome and honesty, ioyned unto so rare a beauty, when she were with *Antonius* (he loving her as so worthy a Lady deserveth) she should be a good meane to keepe good love and amity betwixt her brother and him. So when *Cæsar* and he had made the match between them, they both went to ROME about this mariage, although it was against the law, that a widow should be maried within ten moneths after her husbands death. Howbeit the Senate dispensed with the law, and so the mariage proceeded accordingly."

(2) SCENE II.—

—— *to the air; which, but for vacancy,*
Had gone to gaze on Cleopatra too,
And made a gap in nature.]

"The manner how he fell in love with her was this. *Antonius* going to make war with the PARTHIANS, sent to command *Cleopatra* to appeare personally before him when he came into CILICIA, to answer unto such accusations as were laid against her, being this: that she had aided *Cassius* and *Brutus* in their war against him. The messenger sent unto *Cleopatra* to make this summons unto her, was called *Dellius;* who when he had throughly considered her beauty, the excellent grace and sweetnesse of her tong, he nothing mistrusted that *Antonius* would do any hurt to so noble a Lady, but rather assured himself, that within few daies she should be in great favour with him. Therupon he did her great honor, and perswaded her to come into CILICIA, as honourably furnished as she could possible; and bad her not to be affraid at all of *Antonius*, for he was a more courteous Lord, then any that she had ever seene. *Cleopatra* on the other side beleeving *Dellius* words, and guessing by the former accesse and credit she had with *Iulius Cæsar* and *C. Pompey* (the son of *Pompey* the Great) only for her beauty, she began to have good hope that she might more easily win *Antonius.* For *Cæsar* and *Pompey* knew her when she was but a yong thing, and knew not then what the world meant: but now she went to *Antonius* at the age when a womans beauty is at the prime, and she also of best iudgement. So she furnished her selfe with a world of gifts, store of gold & silver, and of riches and other sumptuous ornaments, as is credible enough she might bring from so great a house, and from so wealthy & riche a realme as ÆGYPT was. But yet she caried nothing with her wherin she trusted more then in her selfe, and in the charmes and inchantment of her passing beauty and grace. Therefore when she was sent unto by diverse letters, both from *Antonius* himselfe, and also from his friends, she made so light of it, and mocked *Antonius* so much, that she disdained to set forward otherwise, but to take her barge in the river of Cydnus; the poope whereof was of gold, the sailes of purple, and the oares of silver, which kept stroke in rowing after the sound of the musicke of flutes, howboyes, cithernes, vials, and such other instruments as they played upon in the barge. And now for the person of her selfe, she was layed under a pavilion of cloth of gold of tissue, apparelled and attired like the goddesse *Venus*, commonly drawne in picture: and hard by her, on either hand of her, pretie faire boyes apparelled as Painters do set foorth god *Cupid*, with little fans in their hands, with the which they fanned wind upon her. Her Ladies and Gentlewomen also, the fairest of them were apparelled like the Nimphes *Nereides* (which are the Myrmaides of the waters) & like the *Graces;* some stearing the helme, others tending the tackle and ropes of the barge, out of the which there came a wonderfull passing sweet savour of perfumes, that perfumed the wharfes side, pestered with innumerable multitudes of people. Some of them followed the barge all along the river side: others also ranne out of the city to see her coming in. So that in the end, there ranne such multitudes of people one after another to see her, that *Antonius* was left post alone in the market place, in his Imperiall seate to give audience: and there went a rumour in the peoples mouthes, that the goddesse *Venus* was come to play with the god *Bacchus* for the generall good of all ASIA. When *Cleopatra* landed, *Antonius* sent to invite her to supper to him. But she sent him worde againe, he should do better rather to come and suppe with her, *Antonius* therefore to shew himselfe courteous unto her at her arrivall, was contented to obey her, and went to supper to her: where he found such passing sumptuous fare, that no tongue can expresse it."

(3) SCENE III.—

—— and his quails ever
Beat mine, inhoop'd, at odds.]

"With *Antonius* there was a soothsayer or astronomer of EGYPT, that coulde cast a figure and judge of mens nativities, to tell them what should happen to them. He, either to please *Cleopatra*, or else for that he founde it so by his art, told *Antonius* plainly that his fortune (which of itself was excellent good and very great) was altogether bleamished and obscured by *Cæsars* fortune: and therefore he counselled him utterly to leave his company, and to get him as farre from him as he could. For thy *Demon*, said he, (that is to say, the good angell and spirit that kepeth thee) is affraied of his: and being coragious and high when he is alone, becommeth fearefull and timerous when he cometh neare unto the other. Howsoever it was, the events ensuing proved the ÆGYPTIANS words true: for it is said, that as often as they two drew cuts for pastime, who shold have any thing, or whether they plaid at dice, *Antonius* alwaye lost. Oftentimes when they were disposed to see cock-fight, or quails that were taught to fight one with another, *Cæsars* cocks or quailes did ever overcome. The which spited *Antonius* in his mind, although he made no outward shew of it: and therfore he beleeved the ÆGYPTIAN the better. In fine, he recommended the affaires of his house unto *Cæsar*, and went out of ITALY with *Octavia* his wife, whom he caried into GRECE after he had had a daughter by her."

(4) SCENE V.—

'T was merry when
You wager'd on your angling; &c.]

"But to reckon up all the foolish sports they made, revelling in this sort, it were too fond a part of me, and therefore I will onely tell you one among the rest. On a time he went to angle for fish, and when he could take none, he was as angrie as could be, because *Cleopatra* stood by. Wherefore he secretly commanded the fishermen, that when he cast in his line, they should straight dive under the water, and put a fish on his hooke which they had taken before: and so snatched up his angling rod, & brought up a fish twise or thrise. *Cleopatra* found it straight, yet she seemed not to see it, but wondered at his excellent fishing: but when she was alone by her selfe among her owne people, she told them how it was, & bad them the next morning to be on the water to see the fishing. A number of people came to the haven, and got into the fisher boates to see this fishing. *Antonius* then threw in his line, and *Cleopatra* straight commanded one of her men to dive under water before *Antonius* men, & to put some old salt-fish upon his bait, like unto those that are brought out of the country of PONT. When he had hung the fish on his hooke, *Antonius* thinking he had taken a fish indeed, snatched up his line presently. Then they all fell a laughing. *Cleopatra* laughing also, said unto him: Leave us (my Lord) ÆGYPTIANS (which dwell in the country of PHARUS and CANOBUS) your angling rod: this is not thy profession, thou must hunt after conquering of Realmes and countries."

(5) SCENE VII.—*They take the flow o' the Nile.*] It has been suggested that Shakespeare derived his information on this subject from Philemon's translation of Pliny's Natural History, 1601:—"How high it [the Nile] riseth, is knowne by markes and measures taken of certain pits. The ordinary height of it is sixteen cubites. Under that gage the waters overflow not at all. Above that stint, there are a let and hindrance by reason that the later it is ere they bee fallen and downe againe. By these the seed-time is much of it spent, for that the earth is too wet. By the other there is none at all, by reason that the ground is drie and thirstie. The provence taketh good keepe and reckoning of both, the one as well as the other. For when it is no higher then 12 cubites, it findeth extreame famine: yea, and at 13 feeleth hunger still; 14 cubites comforts their heart, 15 bids them take no care, but 16 affordeth them plentie and delicious dainties. So soone as any part of the land is freed from the water, streight waies it is sowed."

(6) SCENE VII.—

—— Repent that e'er thy tongue
Hath so betray'd thine act: &c.]

"*Sextus Pompeius* at that time kept in SICILIA, and so made many an inrode into ITALY with a great number of pinnaces and other pirates shippes, of the which were Captaines two notable pirates, *Menas* and *Menecrates*, who so scoured all the sea thereabouts, that none durst peepe out with a saile. Furthermore, *Sextus Pompeius* had dealt very friendly with *Antonius*, for he had courteously received his mother when she fled out of ITALY with *Fulvia:* and therefore they thought good to make peace with him. So they met all three together by the mount of MISENA, upon a hill that runneth farre into the sea: *Pompey* having his shippes riding hard by at anker, and *Antonius* and *Cæsar* their armies upon the shore side, directly over against him. Now, after they had agreed that *Sextus Pompeius* should have SICILE and SARDINIA, with this condition, that he should ridde the sea of all theeves and pirates, and make it safe for passengers, and withall, that he should send a certaine of wheat to ROME: one of them did feast another, and drew cuts who should begin. It was *Pompeius* chance to invite them first. Whereupon *Antonius* asked him: And where shall we suppe? There, said *Pompey;* and shewed him his Admirall gallie which had sixe bankes of oares: That (said he) is my fathers house they have left me. He spake it to taunt *Antonius*, because he had his fathers house, that was *Pompey* the Great. So he cast ankers enow into the sea, to make his gally fast, and then built a bridge of wood to convey them to his galley, from the head of mount Misena: and there he welcomed them, and made them great cheare. Now in the midst of the feast, when they fell to be mery with *Antonius* love unto *Cleopatra, Menas* the pirate came to *Pompey*, and whispering in his eare, said unto him: Shall I cut the cables of the ankers, & make thee Lord not only of SICILE & SARDINIA, but of the whole Empire of ROME besides? *Pompey* having paused a while upon it, at length answered him: Thou shouldest have done it, and never have told it me; but now we must content us with that we have: as for my selfe, I was never taught to breake my faith, nor to be counted a traitor."

ACT III.

(1) SCENE VI.—

—— *she*
In the habiliments of the goddess Isis
That day appear'd.]

"But the greatest cause of their malice unto him, was for the division of lands he made among his children in the city of ALEXANDRIA. And to confesse a troth, it was too arrogant and insolent a part, and done (as a man would say) in derision and contempt of the ROMAINES. For he assembled all the people in the shew place, where yong men do exercise themselves, and there upon a high tribunall silvered, he set two chaires of gold, the one for himself, and the other for *Cleopatra*, and lower chaires for his children, then he openly published before the assembly, that first of all he did establish *Cleopatra* Queene of ÆGYPT, of CYPRUS, of LYDIA, and of the lower SYRIA; and at that time also *Cæsarion* king of the same Realmes. This *Cæsarion* was supposed to be the son of *Iulius Cæsar*, who had left *Cleopatra* great with child. Secondly, he called the sons he had by her, the kings of kings, and gave *Alexander* for his portion, ARMENIA, MEDIA, and PARTHIA, when he had conquered the country; and unto *Ptolomy* for his portion, PHENICIA, SYRIA, and CICILIA. And therewithall he brought out *Alexander* in a long gowne after the fashion of the MEDES with a high coptanke hat on his head, narrow in the top, as the kings of the MEDES and ARMENIANS do use to weare them: & *Ptolomy* apparelled in a cloake after the MACEDONIAN maner, with slippers on his feet and a broad hat, with a royall band or diademe. Such was the apparell and old attire of the ancient kings and successors of *Alexander* the Great. So after his sons had done their humble duties, and kissed their father and mother, presently a company of ARMENIAN souldiers set there of purpose, compassed the one about, and a like company of MACEDONIANS the other. Now for *Cleopatra*, she did not onely weare at that time (but at all other times else when she came abroad) the apparell of the goddess *Isis*, and so gave audience unto all her subiects, as a new *Isis*."

(2) SCENE VI.—

—— *whereon, I begg'd*
His pardon for return.]

"There his wife *Octavia* that came out of GRECE with him, besought him to send her unto her brother, the which he did. *Octavia* at that time was great with child, and moreover had a second daughter by him, and yet she put her self in iourny, and met with her brother *Octavius Cæsar* by the way, who brought his two chiefe friends, *Mæcenas* and *Agrippa* with him. She tooke them aside, and with all the instance she could possible, intreated them they would not suffer her that was the happiest woman of the world, to become now the most wretched & unfortunatest creature of all other. For now, said she, every mans eyes do gaze on me, that am the sister of one of the Emperours, and wife of the other. And if the worst counsel take place (which the gods forbid) and that they grow to warres: for your selves, it is uncertaine to which of them two the gods have assigned the victorie or overthrow. But for me, on which side soever the victory fall, my state can be but most miserable still."

(3) SCENE VII.—

—— *do you misdoubt*
This sword and these my wounds?]

"Now as he was setting his men in order of battell, there was a Captaine, a valiant man, that had served *Antonius* in many battels and conflicts, and had all his body hacked and cut: who, as *Antonius* passed by him, cried out unto him, and said: O noble Emperour, how commeth it to passe that you trust to these vile brittle ships? What, do you mistrust these wounds of mine, and this sword? let the ÆGYPTIANS and PHOENICIANS fight by sea, and set us on the maine land, where we use to conquer, or to be slaine on our feete. *Antonius* passed by him and said never a word, but onely beckened to him with his hand and head, as though he willed him to be of good courage, although indeed he had no great courage himselfe. For when the masters of the galleys and pilots would have let their sailes alone, he made them clap them on; saying to colour y[e] matter withal, that not one of his enemies should scape."

(4) SCENE XI.—

—— *Fortune knows*
We scorn her most when most she offers blows.]

"There *Antonius* shewed plainly, that he had not onely lost the courage and heart of an Emperour, but also of a valiant man; and that he was not his owne man (proving that true which an old man spake in mirth, That the soule of a lover lived in another body, and not in his owne;) he was so caried away with the vaine love of this woman, as if he had bene glued unto her, and that she could not have removed without moving of him also. For when he saw *Cleopatraes* ship under saile, he forgot, forsook, and betrayed them that fought for him, and imbarked upon a galley with five bankes of oares, to follow her that had already begun to overthrow him, and would in the end be his utter destruction. When she knew his galley a farre off, she lift up a signe in the poope of her ship; and so *Antonius* comming to it, was pluckt up where *Cleopatra* was: howbeit he saw her not at his first comming, nor she him, but went and sate downe alone in the prow of his ship, and said never a word, clapping his head betweene both his hands. In the meane time came certaine light brigantines of *Cæsars,* that followed him hard. So *Antonius* straight turned the prow of his ship, and presently put the rest to flight, saving one *Eurycles* a LACEDÆMONIAN, that followed him neare, and pressed upon him with great courage, shaking a dart in his hand over the prow, as though he would have throwne it unto *Antonius. Antonius* seeing him, came to the fore-castell of his ship, and asked him what he was that durst follow *Antonius* so neare? I am, answered he, *Eurycles* the son of *Lachares,* who through *Cæsars* good fortune seeketh to revenge the death of my father. This *Lachares* was condemned of fellonie, and beheaded by *Antonius.* But yet *Eurycles* durst not venture upon *Antonius* ship, but set upon the other Admirall galley (for there were two:) and fell upon him with such a blow of his brazen spurre that was so heavy and bigge, that he turned her round, and tooke her, with another that was loden with very rich stuffe and cariage. After *Eurycles* had left *Antonius,* he turned againe to his place, and sate downe, speaking never a word, as he did before: and so lived three dayes alone, without speaking to any man. But when he arrived at the head of Tænarus, there *Cleopatraes* women first brought *Antonius* and *Cleopatra* to speake together, and afterwards to sup and lie together. Then began there againe a great number of merchants ships to gather about them, and some of their friends that had escaped from this overthrow, who brought newes, that his army by sea was overthrowne, but that they thought the army by land was yet whole."

(5) SCENE XIII.—*Hence with thy stripes, begone!*] "Furthermore, *Cæsar* would not grant unto *Antonius* requests: but for *Cleopatra,* he made her answer, that he would deny her nothing reasonable, so that she would either put *Antonius* to death, or drive him out of her country. Therewithal he sent *Thyreus* one of his men unto her, a very wise and discreet man: who bringing letters of credite from a young Lord unto a noble Ladie, and that besides greatly liked her beauty, might easily by his eloquence have perswaded her. He was longer in talke with her then any man else was, and the Queene her selfe also did him great honour: insomuch as he made *Antonius* iealous of him. Whereupon *Antonius* caused him to be taken and well favouredly whipped, and so sent him unto *Cæsar:* and bad him tell him, that he made him angrie with him, because he shewed himselfe proud and disdainefull towards him; and now specially, when he was easie to be angred, by reason of his present misery. To be short, if this mislike thee (said he) thou hast *Hipparchus* one of my enfranchised bondmen with thee: hang him if thou wilt, or whippe him at thy pleasure, that we may cry quittance. From henceforth *Cleopatra,* to cleare her selfe of the suspition he had of her, made more of him than ever she did. For first of all, where she did solemnize the day of her birth very meanely and sparingly, fit for her present misfortune, she now in contrary manner did keepe it with such solemnity, that she exceeded all measure of sumptuousnes and magnificence: so that the guests that were bidden to the feasts, and came poore, went away rich."

ACT IV.

(1) SCENE VIII.—

I'll give thee, friend,
An armour all of gold; it was a king's.]

"Then he came againe to the pallace, greatly boasting of this victory, and sweetly kissed *Cleopatra,* armed as he was when he came from the fight, recommending one of his men of armes unto her, that had valiantly fought in this skirmish. *Cleopatra* to reward his manlinesse, gave him an armor and head peece of cleane gold: howbeit the man at armes when he had received this rich gift, stole away by night and went to *Cæsar. Antonius* sent again to challenge *Cæsar,* to fight with him hande to hande. *Cæsar* aunswered him, That he had many other waies to dye then so. Then *Antonius* seeing there was no way more honorable for him to dye, then fighting valiantly, he determined to set up his rest, both by sea and land. So being at supper (as is reported) he commaunded his officers and household servants that waited on him at his boord, that they should fill his cuppes full, and make as muche of him as they could: for said he, you know not whether you shall do so much for me to morrow or not, or whether you shall serve another maister: and it may be you shall see me no more, but a dead bodie. This notwithstanding, perceeving that his frends and men fell a weeping to heare him say so: to salve that he had spoken, he added this more unto it that he would leade them to battell, where he thought rather safely to returne with victory, then valiantly to die with honour. Further more the selfe same night within a little of midnight, when all the city was quiet, full of feare and sorrow, thinking what would be the issue and ende of this warre, it is said, that sodainly they heard a marvellous sweete harmony of sundry sorts of instruments of musicke, with the crie of a multitude of people, as they had been dauncing, and had sung as they use in Bacchus feastes."

(2) SCENE XIV.—*Sometime we see a cloud that's dragonish.*] To the instances of a similar thought, which are given in the *Variorum,* may be added the following, from a curious black-letter volume, entitled "A most pleasant Prospect into the Garden of Naturall Contemplation, to behold the Naturall Causes of all Kind of Meteors: &c. &c. by W. Fulke, Doctor of Divinitie. 1602." "Flying Dragons, or as Englishmen call them, fire-Drakes, be caused on this maner. When a certayne quantitie of vapors are gathered together on a heap being very neere compact, and as it were hard tempered together, this lump of vapors ascending to ye region of cold, is forcibly beaten backe, which violence of moving is sufficient to kindle it (although some men wil have it to be caused between 2 cloudes, a hote and a cold) then the highest part which was climing upward, being by reason more subtil and thin, appeareth as the Dragon's neck, smoking, for y^t^ it was lately in the repulse bowed or made crooked, to represent the Dragon's belly. The last part by ye same repulse, turned upward, maketh the tayle, both appearing smaller, for y^t^ it is further off, and also for that the cold bindeth it. This Dragon being thus caused, flieth along in ye ayre, and sometime turneth to and fro, if it meet with a cold cloud to beat it back, to ye great terrour of them that behold it, of whome some call it a fire Drake: some say it is the Devill himselfe, and so make report to other. More than 47 yeeres agoe, on May day, when many young folke went abroad early in the morning, I remember, by sixe of the clocke in the forenoone, there was newes came to London, that the Devill, the same morning, was seene flying over the Temmes: afterward came word, that hee lighted at Stratford, and was there taken and set in the Stockes, and that though he would have dissembled the matter, by turning himselfe into the likenesse of a man, yet was hee knowne well yenough by his cloven feete. I knew some then living, that went to see him, and returning,

affirmed, that hee was indeede seene flying in the ayre, but was not taken prisoner. I remember also, that some wished he had bene shot at with Gunnes or shafts, as hee flew over the Temmes. Thus doe ignorant men iudge of these things that they know not. As for this Divell, I suppose it was a flying Dragon, whereof wee speake, verie fearfull to looke upon, as though hee had life, because hee moveth, whereas hee is nothing else but clowdes and smoake, so mightie is God, that hee can feare his enemies with these and such like operations, whereof some examples may bee found in holy Scripture."

(3) Scene XV.—

—— a Roman by a Roman
Valiantly vanquish'd.]

"Then she being affraid of his furie, fled into the tombe which he had caused to be made, and there she locked the doores unto her, & shut all the springs of the lockes with great bolts, and in the meane time sent unto *Antonius* to tell him, that she was dead. *Antonius* beleeving it, said unto himselfe: What doest thou looke for further, *Antonius*, sith spitefull fortune hath taken from thee the only ioy thou hadst, for whom thou yet reservedst thy life? When he had said these words, he went into a chamber & unarmed himself, & being naked, said thus: O *Cleopatra*, it grieveth me not that I have lost thy company, for I wil not be long from thee: but I am sory, that having bene so great a Captaine & Emperor, I am indeed condemned to be iudged of lesse courage and noble mind then a woman. Now he had a man of his called *Eros*, whom he loved and trusted much, and whom he had long before caused to sweare unto him, that he should kill him when he did command him: and then he willed him to keepe his promise. His man drawing his sword, lift it up as though he had ment to have stricken his master: but turning his head at one side, he thrust his sword into himselfe, and fell downe dead at his masters foote, Then said *Antonius*: O noble *Eros*, I thanke thee for this, and it is valiantly done of thee, to shew me what I should do to my selfe, which thou couldest not doe for me. Therewithall he tooke his sword, and thrust it into his belly, and so fell downe upon a little bed. The wound he had, killed him not presently, for the bloud stinted a litle when he was laide: and when he came somewhat to himselfe againe, he prayed them that were about him, to dispatch him. But they all fled out of the chamber, and left him crying out tormenting himselfe: untill at the last there came a Secretarie unto him (called *Diomedes*) who was commanded to bring him into the tomb or monument where *Cleopatra* was. When he heard that she was alive, he very earnestly prayed his men to carie his body thither, and so he was caried in his mens armes into the entry of the monument. Notwithstanding, *Cleopatra* would not open the gates, but came to the high windowes, and cast out certaine chaines and ropes, in the which *Antonius* was trussed: and *Cleopatra* her owne selfe, with two women onely, which she had suffered to come with her into these monuments, trised *Antonius* up. They that were present to behold it, said they never saw so pitifull a sight. For they plucked up poore *Antonius* all bloudie as he was, and drawing on with pangs of death: who holding up his hands to *Cleopatra*, raised up himselfe as well as he could. It was a hard thing for these women to do, to lift him up: but *Cleopatra* stooping down with her head, putting too all her strength to her uttermost power, did lift him up with much ado, and never let go her hold, with the helpe of the women beneath that bad her be of good courage, & were as sory to see her labour so, as she her selfe. So when she had gotten him in after that sort, and laid him on a bed, she rent her garments upon him, clapping her breast, and scratching her face and stomacke. Then she dried up his bloud that had bewrayed his face, & called him her Lord, her husband, & Emperor, forgetting her own misery and calamity, for the pity and compassion she took of him. *Antonius* made her ceasse her lamenting, & called for wine, either because he was a thirst, or else for that he thought thereby to hasten his death. When he had drunke, he earnestly prayed her, and perswaded her, that she would seeke to save her life, if she could possible, without reproch & dishonour: and that chiefly she should trust *Proculeius* above any man else about *Cæsar*. And as for himselfe, that she should not lament nor sorow for the miserable change of his fortune at the end of his daies: but rather that she should thinke him the more fortunate, for the former triumphes and honors he had received; considering that while he lived, he was the noblest & greatest Prince of the world; and that now, he was overcome, not cowardly, but valiantly, a Romaine by another Romaine."

ACT V.

(1) Scene II.—

Cleopatra,
Not what you have reserv'd, nor what acknowledg'd,
Put we i' the roll of conquest.]

"At length, she gave him a briefe and memoriall of all the ready mony and treasure she had. But by chance there stood one *Seleucus* by, one of her Treasurers, who to seeme, a good servant, came straight to *Cæsar* to disprove *Cleopatra*, that she had not set in all, but kept many things back of purpose. *Cleopatra* was in such a rage with him, that she flew upon him, and tooke him by the haire of the head, and boxed him well favouredly. *Cæsar* fell a laughing & parted the fray. Alas, said she, O *Cæsar*: is not this a great shame and reproch, that thou having vouchsafed to take the paines to come unto me, and done me this honor, poore wretch, & caitife creature, brought into this pitifull and miserable state: and that mine owne servants should come now to accuse me: though it may be I have reserved some iewels and trifles meet for women, but not for me (poore soule) to set out my selfe withall, but meaning to give some pretie presents and gifts unto *Octavius* and *Livia*, that they making means and intercession for me to thee, thou mightest yet extend thy favour and mercy upon me. *Cæsar* was glad to heare her say so, perswading himselfe thereby that she had yet a desire to save her life. So he made her answer, that he did not only give her that to dispose of at her pleasure, which she had kept back, but further promised to use her more honourably and bountifully, then she would thinke for: and so he took his leave of her, supposing he had deceived her, but indeed he was deceived himselfe."

(2) Scene II.—

It is well done, and fitting for a princess
Descended of so many royal kings.]

"There was a yong Gentleman *Cornelius Dolabella*, that was one of *Cæsars* very great familiars, and besides did beare no ill will unto *Cleopatra*. He sent her word secretly (as she had requested him) that *Cæsar* determined to take his iourny through Syria, & that within three daies he would send her away before with her children. When this was told *Cleopatra*, she requested *Cæsar* that it would please him to suffer her to offer the last oblations of the dead, unto the soule of *Antonius*. This being granted her, she was caried to the place where his tombe was, and there falling downe on her knees, embracing the tombe with her women, the teares running downe her cheeks, she began to speak in this sort: O my deare Lord *Antonius*, it is not long sithence I buried thee here, being a free woman: & now I offer unto thee the funerall sprinklings and oblations, being a captive and prisoner; and yet I am forbidden and kept from tearing and murthering this captive body of mine with blowes, which they carefully guard and keepe, onely to triumph of thee: looke therefore henceforth for no other honors, offerings, nor sacrifices from me: for these are the last which *Cleopatra* can give thee, sith now they carie her away. Whilest we lived together, nothing could sever our companies: but now at our death, I feare me they will make us change our countries. For as thou being a ROMAIN, hast bene buried in ÆGYPT: even so wretched creature I an ÆGYPTIAN, shall be buried in ITALY, which shall be all the good that I have received by thy country. If therefore the gods where thou art now have any power & authority, sith our gods here have forsaken us, suffer not thy true friend and lover to be caried away alive, that in me they triumph of thee: but receive me with thee, and let me be buried in one selfe tombe with thee. For though my griefes and miseries be infinit, yet none hath grieved me more, nor that I could lesse beare withall, then this small time which I have bene driven to live alone without thee. Then having ended these dolefull plaints, and crowned the tombe with garlands & sundry nosegayes, and marvellous lovingly embraced the same, she commanded they should prepare her bath; and when she had bathed and washed herselfe, she fell to her meate, and was sumptuously served. Now whilest she was at dinner, there came a countriman and brought her a basket. The souldiers that warded at the gates, asked him straight what he had in his basket. He opened his basket, and tooke out the leaves that covered the figs, and shewed them that they were figs he brought. They all of them marvelled to see so goodly figges. The countrieman laughed to heare them, and bad them take some if they would. They beleeved he told them truly, and so bad him carie them in. After *Cleopatra* had dined, she sent a certaine table written and sealed unto *Cæsar*, and commanded them all to go out of the tombes where she was, but the two women; then she shut the doores to her. *Cæsar* when he received this table, and began to reade her lamentation and petition, requesting him that he would let her be buried with *Antonius*, found straight what she meant, and thought to have gone thither himselfe: howbeit, he sent one before in all hast that might be, to see what it was. Her death was very sodaine: for those whom *Cæsar* sent unto her, ran thither in all hast possible, and found the souldiers standing at the gate, mistrusting nothing, nor understanding of her death. But when they had opened the doores, they found *Cleopatra* starke dead, laid upon a bed of gold, attired and arrayed in her royall robes, and one of her two women, which was called *Iras*, dead at her feet: and her other woman (called *Charmion*) half dead, & trembling, trimming the Diademe which *Cleopatra* wore upon her head. One of the soldiers seeing her, angrily said unto her: Is that well done *Charmion?* Very well, said she againe, and meete for a Princesse descended from the race of so many noble Kings: she said no more, but fel down dead hard by the bed."

CRITICAL OPINIONS ON ANTONY AND CLEOPATRA.

"'ANTONY AND CLEOPATRA' may, in some measure, be considered as a continuation of 'Julius Cæsar:' the two principal characters of Antony and Augustus are equally sustained in both pieces. 'Antony and Cleopatra' is a play of great extent; the progress is less simple than in 'Julius Cæsar.' The fulness and variety of political and warlike events, to which the union of the three divisions of the Roman world under one master necessarily gave rise, were perhaps too great to admit of being clearly exhibited in one dramatic picture. In this consists the great difficulty of the historical drama:—it must be a crowded extract, and a living development of history;—the difficulty, however, has generally been successfully overcome by Shakspeare. But now many things, which are transacted in the background, are here merely alluded to, in a manner which supposes an intimate acquaintance with the history; but a work of art should contain, within itself, everything necessary for its being fully understood. Many persons of historical importance are merely introduced in passing; the preparatory and concurring circumstances are not sufficiently collected into masses to avoid distracting our attention. The principal personages, however, are most emphatically distinguished by lineament and colouring, and powerfully arrest the imagination. In Antony we observe a mixture of great qualities, weaknesses, and vices; violent ambition and ebullitions of magnanimity; we see him now sinking into luxurious enjoyment, and then nobly ashamed of his own aberrations,—manning himself to resolutions not unworthy of himself, which are always shipwrecked against the seductions of an artful woman. It is Hercules in the chains of Omphale, drawn from the fabulous heroic ages into history, and invested with the Roman costume. The seductive arts of Cleopatra are in no respect veiled over; she is an ambiguous being made up of royal pride, female vanity, luxury, inconstancy, and true attachment. Although the mutual passion of herself and Antony is without moral dignity, it still excites our sympathy as an insurmountable fascination:—they seem formed for each other, and Cleopatra is as remarkable for her seductive charms, as Antony for the splendour of his deeds. As they die for each other, we forgive them for having lived for each other. The open and lavish character of Antony is admirably contrasted with the heartless littleness of Octavius, whom Shakspeare seems to have completely seen through, without allowing himself to be led astray by the fortune and the fame of Augustus."—SCHLEGEL.

"The highest praise, or rather form of praise, of this play which I can offer in my own mind, is the doubt which the perusal always occasions in me, whether the 'Antony and Cleopatra' is not, in all exhibitions of a giant power in its strength and vigour of maturity, a formidable rival of 'Macbeth,' 'Lear,' 'Hamlet,' and 'Othello.' *Feliciter audax* is the motto for its style, comparatively with that of Shakspeare's other works, even as it is the general motto of all his works compared with those of other poets. Be it remembered, too, that this happy valiancy of style is but the representative and result of all the material excellencies so expressed.

"This play should be perused in mental contrast with 'Romeo and Juliet,'—as the love of passion and appetite opposed to the love of affection and instinct. But the art displayed in the character of Cleopatra is profound; in this, especially,—that the sense of criminality in her passion is lessened by our insight into its depth and energy, at the very moment that we cannot but perceive that the passion itself springs out of the habitual craving of a licentious nature, and that it is supported and reinforced by voluntary stimulus and sought-for associations, instead of blossoming out of spontaneous emotion.

"Of all Shakspeare's historical plays, 'Antony and Cleopatra' is by far the most wonderful. There is not one in which he has followed history so minutely, and yet there are few in which he impresses the notion of angelic strength so much,—perhaps none in which he impresses it more strongly. This is greatly owing to the manner in which the fiery force is sustained throughout, and to the numerous momentary flashes of nature counteracting the historic abstraction. As a wonderful specimen of the way in which Shakspeare lives up to the very end of this play, read the last part of the concluding scene; and if you would feel the judgment as well as the genius of Shakspeare in your heart's core, compare this astonishing drama with Dryden's 'All for Love.'"—COLERIDGE.

Act III. Sc. 1.

TITUS ANDRONICUS.

THAT Shakespeare had some share in the composition of this revolting tragedy, the fact of its appearance in the list of pieces ascribed to him by Meres, and its insertion by Heminge and Condell in the folio collection of 1623, forbids us to doubt. He may, in the dawning of his dramatic career, have written a few of the speeches, and have imparted vigour and more rhythmical freedom to others; he may have been instrumental also in putting the piece upon the stage of the company to which he then belonged; but that he had any hand in the story, or in its barbarous characters and incidents, we look upon as in the highest degree improbable. Upon this point, indeed, all his editors, from Rowe to Dyce, with the exception of Capell, Collier, and Knight, appear to be of one mind.

"On what principle the editors of the first complete edition of our poet's plays admitted this [*Titus Andronicus*] into their volume cannot now be ascertained. The most probable reason that can be assigned, is, that he wrote a few lines in it, or gave some assistance to the author in revising it, or in some other way aided him in bringing it forward on the stage. The tradition mentioned by Ravenscroft in the time of King James II. warrants us in making one or other of these suppositions. 'I have been told' (says he in his preface to an alteration of this play published in 1687) 'by some anciently conversant with the stage, that it was not originally his, but brought by a private author to be acted, and he only gave some master touches to one or two of the principal parts or characters.' * * * * *

"To enter into a long disquisition to prove this piece not to have been written by Shakspeare, would be an idle waste of time. To those who are not conversant with his writings, if particular passages were examined, more words would be necessary than the subject is worth; those who are well acquainted with his works, cannot entertain a doubt on the question. I will, however, mention one mode by which it may be easily ascertained. Let the reader only peruse a few lines of *Appius and Virginia, Tancred and Gismund, The Battle of Alcazar, Jeronimo, Selimus Emperor of the Turks, The Wounds of Civil War, The Wars of Cyrus, Locrine, Arden of Feversham, King Edward I., The Spanish Tragedy, Solyman and Perseda, King Leir*, the old *King John*, or any other of the pieces that were exhibited before the time of Shakspeare, and he will at once perceive that *Titus Andronicus* was coined in the same mint."—MALONE.

Langbaine, in his *Account of English Dramatic Poets*, 1691, says this tragedy "was first printed, 4to. Lond. 1594;" and as the Stationers' Registers show an entry made by John Danter, Feb. 6th, 1593-4, of "A booke entitled a noble Roman Historye of Tytus Andronicus," he is probably correct, though the only quarto editions at present known are of 1600 and 1611. Of its origin and date of production we know but little. When registering his claim to the "Historye of Tytus Andronicus," Danter coupled with it "the ballad thereof," and this ballad, which will be found among the Comments at the end of the piece, was at one time supposed to be the basis of the drama. It is now a moot point whether the play was founded on the ballad, or the ballad on the play. The story of Titus, however, must have been popular. It is mentioned in Painter's *Palace of Pleasure;* and there is an allusion to it in the comedy called, "A Knack to know a Knave," 1594. Moreover, from a memorandum in Henslowe's Diary, which records the acting of a drama, entitled "*Titus and Ondronicus,*" Jan. 23, 1593-4, there appears to have been another play on the subject. Is it to this piece, or to the "Titus Andronicus" attributed to Shakespeare, that Ben Jonson refers in the Induction to his "Bartholomew Fair"?—"*He that will swear,* JERONIMO *or* ANDRONICUS, *are the best plays yet, shall pass unexcepted at here, as a man whose judgment shows it is constant, and hath stood still these five-and-twenty or thirty years. Though it be an ignorance, it is a virtuous and staid ignorance; and next to truth, a confirmed error does well.*"

Persons Represented.

SATURNINUS, *Son to the late* Emperor *of* Rome, *afterwards* Emperor.

BASSIANUS, *Brother to* Saturninus.

TITUS ANDRONICUS, *a noble* Roman.

MARCUS ANDRONICUS, *Brother to* Titus.

LUCIUS, QUINTUS, MARTIUS, MUTIUS, *Sons to* Titus Andronicus.

YOUNG LUCIUS, *a Boy, Son to* Lucius.

PUBLIUS, *Son to* Marcus *the Tribune.*

ÆMILIUS, *a noble* Roman.

ALARBUS, DEMETRIUS, CHIRON, *Sons to* Tamora.

AARON, *a* Moor.

A Captain.

A Tribune.

A Messenger.

A Clown.

Romans.

Goths.

TAMORA, *Queen of the* Goths.

LAVINIA, *Daughter to* Titus Andronicus.

A Nurse.

A black Child.

Kinsmen of Titus, *Senators, Tribunes, Officers, Soldiers, and Attendants.*

SCENE,—ROME, *and the Country near it.*

ACT I.

SCENE I.—Rome. *Before the* Capitol.

The Tomb of the Andronici *appearing. Enter the* Tribunes *and* Senators, *aloft; and then enter, below,* SATURNINUS *and his* Followers *from one side, and* BASSIANUS *and his* Followers *from the other, with drum and colours.*

SAT. Noble patricians, patrons of my right,
Defend the justice of my cause with arms;
And, countrymen, my loving followers,
Plead my successive title with your swords:
I am his* first-born son, that was the last

(*) First folio, *I was the.*

That wore the imperial diadem of Rome;
Then let my father's honours live in me,
Nor wrong mine age[a] with this indignity.

BASS. Romans,—friends, followers, favourers of my right,—
If ever Bassianus, Cæsar's son,
Were gracious in the eyes of royal Rome,
Keep, then, this passage to the Capitol;
And suffer not dishonour to approach
The imperial seat, to virtue consecrate,
To justice, continence,[b] and nobility:
But let desert in pure election shine;
And, Romans, fight for freedom in your choice.

Enter MARCUS ANDRONICUS, *aloft, with the crown.*

MARC. Princes,—that strive by factions and by friends
Ambitiously for rule and empery,—
Know that the people of Rome, for whom we stand
A special party, have, by common voice,
In election for the Roman empery,
Chosen Andronicus, surnamed Pius
For many good and great deserts to Rome:
A nobler man, a braver warrior,
Lives not this day within the city walls.
He by the senate is accited[c] home,
From weary wars against the barbarous Goths;
That, with his sons, a terror to our foes,
Hath yok'd a nation strong, train'd up in arms.
Ten years are spent since first he undertook
This cause of Rome, and chastisèd with arms
Our enemies' pride: five times he hath return'd
Bleeding to Rome, bearing his valiant sons
In coffins from the field;
And now at last, laden with honour's spoils,
Returns the good Andronicus to Rome,
Renowned Titus, flourishing in arms.
Let us entreat,—by honour of his name,
Whom worthily you would have now succeed,
And in the Capitol and senate's right,
Whom you pretend to honour and adore,—
That you withdraw you, and abate your strength;
Dismiss your followers, and, as suitors should,
Plead your deserts in peace and humbleness.

SAT. How fair the tribune speaks to calm my thoughts!

BASS. Marcus Andronicus, so I do affy[d]
In thy uprightness and integrity,
And so I love and honour thee and thine,
Thy noble brother Titus and his sons,
And her to whom my thoughts are humbled all,
Gracious Lavinia, Rome's rich ornament,
That I will here dismiss my loving friends;
And to my fortunes and the people's favour
Commit my cause in balance to be weigh'd.
[*Exeunt the* Followers *of* BASSIANUS.

SAT. Friends, that have been thus forward in my right,
I thank you all, and here dismiss you all;
And to the love and favour of my country
Commit myself, my person, and the cause.
[*Exeunt the* Followers *of* SATURNINUS.
Rome, be as just and gracious unto me,
As I am confident and kind to thee.—
Open the gates[e] and let me in.

BASS. Tribunes, and me, a poor competitor.
[*Flourish.* SATURNINUS *and* BASSIANUS *go up into the* Capitol.

Enter a Captain, *and others.*

CAP. Romans, make way: the good Andronicus,
Patron of virtue, Rome's best champion,
Successful in the battles that he fights,
With honour and with fortune is return'd
From where* he circumscribed with his sword,
And brought to yoke, the enemies of Rome.

[*Drums and trumpets sound, and then enter* MARTIUS *and* MUTIUS. *After them two* Men *bearing a coffin covered with black: then* LUCIUS *and* QUINTUS. *After them* TITUS ANDRONICUS; *and then* TAMORA, *the Queen of* Goths, *with* ALARBUS, DEMETRIUS, CHIRON, AARON *the* Moor, *and other* Goths, *prisoners,* Soldiers *and* People *following. The* Bearers *set down the coffin, and* TITUS *speaks.*

TIT. Hail, Rome, victorious in thy mourning weeds!
Lo, as the bark that hath discharg'd his[f] fraught,
Returns with precious lading to the bay
From whence at first she weigh'd her anchorage,
Cometh Andronicus, bound with laurel boughs,
To re-salute his country with his tears,—
Tears of true joy for his return to Rome.—

---

[a] *Nor wrong mine* age—] My claim by *seniority*.
[b] — continence,—] That is, *temperance*. So in "Macbeth," Act IV. Sc. 3,—

"—— the king-becoming graces,
As justice, verity, *temperance*," &c.

[c] — accited—] *Summoned.*
[d] — affy—] *Confide.*

(*) First folio, *whence*.

[e] Open the gates—] Capell prints—"Open the gates, tribunes," &c. Mr. Collier's annotator suggests,—"Open the *brazen* gates," &c.
[f] — his *fraught*,—] "His" is here used for the impersona pronoun, *its*.

Thou great defender of this Capitol,
Stand gracious to the rites that we intend!—
Romans, of five-and-twenty valiant sons,
Half of the number that king Priam had,
Behold the poor remains, alive and dead!
These that survive, let Rome reward with love;
These that I bring unto their latest home,
With burial amongst their ancestors:
Here Goths have given me leave to sheathe my sword.
Titus, unkind, and careless of thine own,
Why suffer'st thou thy sons, unburied yet,
To hover on the dreadful shore of Styx?
Make way to lay them by their brethren.—[a]
[*They open the tomb.*
There greet in silence, as the dead are wont,
And sleep in peace, slain in your country's wars!
O, sacred receptacle of my joys,
Sweet cell of virtue and nobility,
How many sons of mine hast thou in store,
That thou wilt never render to me more!

LUC. Give us the proudest prisoner of the Goths,
That we may hew his limbs, and, on a pile,
Ad manes fratrum, sacrifice his flesh,
Before this earthy* prison of their bones;
That so the shadows be not unappeas'd,
Nor we disturb'd with prodigies on earth.[b]

TIT. I give him you,—the noblest that survives,
The eldest son of this distressed queen.

TAM. Stay, Roman brethren!—Gracious conqueror,
Victorious Titus, rue the tears I shed,
A mother's tears in passion for her son:
And if thy sons were ever dear to thee,
O, think my sons to be as dear to me!
Sufficeth not, that we are brought to Rome
To beautify thy triumphs and return,
Captive to thee and to thy Roman yoke;
But must my sons be slaughter'd in the streets,
For valiant doings in their country's cause?
O, if to fight for king and commonweal
Were piety in thine, it is in these!
Andronicus, stain not thy tomb with blood:
Wilt thou draw near the nature of the gods?
Draw near them, then, in being merciful:
Sweet mercy is nobility's true badge.
Thrice-noble Titus, spare my first-born son.

TIT. Patient[c] yourself, madam, and pardon me.
These are their† brethren, whom you Goths beheld
Alive and dead; and for their brethren slain
Religiously they ask a sacrifice:
To this your son is mark'd; and die he must,
To appease their groaning shadows that are gone.

LUC. Away with him! and make a fire straight;
And with our swords, upon a pile of wood,
Let's hew his limbs till they be clean consum'd.
[*Exeunt* LUCIUS, QUINTUS, MARTIUS, *and* MUTIUS, *with* ALARBUS.

TAM. O cruel, irreligious piety!

CHI. Was ever Scythia half so barbarous?

DEMET. Oppose not* Scythia to ambitious Rome.
Alarbus goes to rest; and we survive
To tremble under Titus' threatening looks.
Then, madam, stand resolv'd; but hope withal,
The self-same gods, that arm'd the queen of Troy
With opportunity of sharp revenge
Upon the Thracian tyrant in his[d] tent,
May favour Tamora, the queen of Goths,
(When Goths were Goths, and Tamora was queen)
To quit the bloody wrongs upon her foes.

Re-enter LUCIUS, QUINTUS, MARTIUS, *and* MUTIUS, *with their swords bloody.*

LUC. See, lord and father, how we have perform'd
Our Roman rites: Alarbus' limbs are lopp'd,
And entrails feed the sacrificing fire,
Whose smoke, like incense, doth perfume the sky.
Remaineth nought, but to inter our brethren,
And with loud 'larums welcome them to Rome.

TIT. Let it be so; and let Andronicus
Make this his latest farewell to their souls.
[*Flourish of trumpets, and they lay the coffin*[e] *in the tomb.*
In peace and honour rest you here, my sons;
Rome's readiest champions, repose you here in rest,
Secure from worldly chances and mishaps!
Here lurks no treason, here no envy swells,
Here grow no damned grudges;[f] here are no storms,
No noise, but silence and eternal sleep:
In peace and honour rest you here, my sons!

(*) First folio, *earthly*. (†) First folio, *the*.

[a] — brethren.] To be pronounced as a trisyllable.

[b] Nor we disturb'd with prodigies on earth.] The ancients, it need hardly be observed, held belief that the spirits of the unburied dead importuned their relatives and friends to obtain funereal rites.

[c] — Patient *yourself*,—] Steevens, among other examples of this verb, cites the following from King Edward I. 1599,—
"*Patient* your highness, 'tis but mother's love."

(*) First folio, *me*.

[d] — *in* his *tent*,—] Conceiving this to be an allusion to Polymnestor's death, as related in the *Hecuba* of Euripides, Theobald reads, "in *her* tent."

[e] — *the* coffin—] So the quartos. The folio, 1623, has, "the *coffins*;" but compare the stage direction on the entrance of Titus Andronicus.

[f] — grudges;] *Murmurs of discontent.*

Enter LAVINIA.

LAV. In peace and honour live lord Titus long;
My noble lord and father, live in fame!
Lo, at this tomb my tributary tears
I render for my brethren's obsequies:
And at thy feet I kneel, with tears of joy
Shed on the earth for thy return to Rome.
O, bless me here with thy victorious hand,
Whose fortunes Rome's best citizens applaud!
TIT. Kind Rome, that hast thus lovingly reserv'd
The cordial of mine age to glad my heart!—
Lavinia, live; outlive thy father's days,
And fame's eternal date, for virtue's praise!

Enter, below, MARCUS ANDRONICUS *and* Tribunes; *re-enter* SATURNINUS *and* BASSIANUS, *attended.*

MARC. Long live lord Titus, my beloved brother,
Gracious triumpher in the eyes of Rome!

TIT. Thanks, gentle tribune, noble brother Marcus.

MARC. And welcome, nephews, from successful wars,
You that survive, and you that sleep in fame!
Fair lords, your fortunes are alike in all,
That in your country's service drew your swords;
But safer triumph is this funeral pomp,
That hath aspir'd to Solon's happiness,
And triumphs over chance in honour's bed.—[a]
Titus Andronicus, the people of Rome,
Whose friend in justice thou hast ever been,
Send thee by me, their tribune and their trust,
This palliament of white and spotless hue,
And name thee in election for the empire,
With these our late deceased emperor's sons:
Be *candidatus*, then, and put it on,
And help to set a head on headless Rome.

TIT. A better head her glorious body fits
Than his that shakes for age and feebleness.
What[b] should I don this robe and trouble you?
Be chosen with proclamations to-day,
To-morrow yield up rule, resign my life,
And set abroad[c] new business for you all?
Rome, I have been thy soldier forty years,
And led my country's strength successfully,
And buried one-and-twenty valiant sons,
Knighted in field, slain manfully in arms,
In right and service of their noble country:
Give me a staff of honour for mine age,
But not a sceptre to control the world:
Upright he held it, lords, that held it last.

MARC. Titus, thou shalt obtain and ask[d] the empery.

SAT. Proud and ambitious tribune, canst thou tell?

TIT. Patience, prince Saturninus.

SAT. Romans, do me right;—
Patricians, draw your swords, and sheathe them not
Till Saturninus be Rome's emperor.—
Andronicus, would thou wert shipp'd to hell,
Rather than rob me of the people's hearts!

LUC. Proud Saturnine, interrupter of the good
That noble-minded Titus means to thee!

TIT. Content thee, prince, I will restore to thee
The people's hearts, and wean them from themselves.

BASS. Andronicus, I do not flatter thee,
But honour thee, and will do till I die:
My faction if thou strengthen with thy friends,[e]
I will most thankful be; and thanks to men
Of noble minds is honourable meed.

TIT. People of Rome, and noble tribunes here,
I ask your voices and your suffrages:
Will you bestow them friendly on Andronicus?

TRIBUNES. To gratify the good Andronicus,
And gratulate his safe return to Rome,
The people will accept whom he admits.

TIT. Tribunes, I thank you: and this suit I make,
That you create your emperor's eldest son,
Lord Saturnine, whose virtues will, I hope,
Reflect on Rome as Titan's rays on earth,
And ripen justice in this commonweal:
Then, if you will elect by my advice,
Crown him, and say, *Long live our emperor!*

MARC. With voices and applause of every sort,
Patricians, and plebeians, we create
Lord Saturninus Rome's great emperor;
And say, *Long live our emperor, Saturnine!*
[*A long flourish.*

SAT. Titus Andronicus, for thy favours done
To us in our election this day,
I give thee thanks in part of thy deserts,
And will with deeds requite thy gentleness:
And, for an onset, Titus, to advance
Thy name and honourable family,
Lavinia will I make my empress,[f]
Rome's royal mistress, mistress of my heart,
And in the sacred Pantheon[g] her espouse:
Tell me, Andronicus, doth this motion please thee?

TIT. It doth, my worthy lord; and in this match
I hold me highly honour'd of your grace:
And here, in sight of Rome, to Saturnine,—
King and commander of our commonweal,
The wide world's emperor,—do I consecrate
My sword, my chariot, and my prisoners;
Presents well worthy Rome's imperial lord:
Receive them, then, the tribute that I owe,
Mine honour's ensigns humbled at thy * feet.

SAT. Thanks, noble Titus, father of my life!

[a] And triumphs over chance in honour's bed.—]

"—— ultima semper
Expectanda dies homini; dicique beatus
Ante obitum nemo, supremaque funera, debet."

[b] What should I don, &c.] It is customary in cases like the present to print "What" as an exclamation, "What! should I don—" &c. though it is often only equivalent to, *For What;* or to, *Why.*

[c] *And set* abroad—] The folio of 1664 has, "set *abroach,*" &c. and the substitution is adopted by Mr. Collier's annotator.

[d] — thou shalt obtain and ask—] There is here, as Steevens remarks, somewhat too much of the *hysteron proteron.* We might, without much violence, read,—

"Ask, Titus, and thou shalt obtain the empery."

(*) First folio, *my.*

[e] — thy friends,—] A correction from the folio of 1664; the prior copies having, *friend.*

[f] — empress,—] To be read as a trisyllable.

[g] — Pantheon—] From the second folio; the earlier editions printing, *Pathan.*

How proud I am of thee and of thy gifts,
Rome shall record; and when I do forget
The least of these unspeakable deserts,
Romans, forget your fealty to me.

TIT. Now, madam, are you prisoner to an emperor; [*To* TAMORA.
To him that, for your honour and your state,
Will use you nobly and your followers.

SAT. [*Aside.*] A goodly lady, trust me; of the hue
That I would choose, were I to choose anew.—
Clear up, fair queen, that cloudy countenance:
Though chance of war hath wrought this change of cheer,
Thou com'st not to be made a scorn in Rome:
Princely shall be thy usage every way.
Rest on my word, and let not discontent
Daunt all your hopes: madam, he comforts you
Can make you greater than the queen of Goths.—
Lavinia, you are not displeas'd with this?

LAV. Not I, my lord, sith true nobility
Warrants these words in princely courtesy.

SAT. Thanks, sweet Lavinia.—Romans, let us go:
Ransomless here we set our prisoners free.
Proclaim our honours, lords, with trump and drum.

[*Flourish.* SATURNINUS *courts* TAMORA *in dumb show.*

BASS. Lord Titus, by your leave, this maid is mine. [*Seizing* LAVINIA.

TIT. How, sir! are you in earnest, then, my lord?

BASS. Ay, noble Titus, and resolv'd withal
To do myself this reason and this right.

MARC. *Suum cuique* is our Roman justice:
This prince in justice seizeth but his own.

LUC. And that he will, and shall, if Lucius live.

TIT. Traitors, avaunt!—Where is the emperor's guard?—
Treason, my lord!—Lavinia is surpris'd![a]

SAT. Surpris'd! by whom?

BASS. By him that justly may
Bear his betroth'd from all the world away.

[*Exeunt* BASSIANUS *and* MARCUS, *with* LAVINIA.

MUT. Brothers, help to convey her hence away,
And with my sword I'll keep this door safe.

[*Exeunt* LUCIUS, QUINTUS, *and* MARTIUS.

TIT. Follow, my lord, and I'll soon bring her back.

MUT. My lord, you pass not here.

TIT. What, villain boy! barr'st me my way in Rome? [*Stabbing* MUTIUS.

MUT. Help, Lucius, help! [*Dies.*

Re-enter LUCIUS.

LUC. My lord, you are unjust; and, more than so,
In wrongful quarrel you have slain your son.

TIT. Nor thou, nor he, are any sons of mine;
My sons would never so dishonour me:
Traitor, restore Lavinia to the emperor.

LUC. Dead, if you will; but not to be his wife,
That is another's lawful promis'd love. [*Exit.*

SAT. No, Titus, no; the emperor needs her not,[b]
Nor her, nor thee, nor any of thy stock:
I'll trust, by leisure, him that mocks me once;
Thee never, nor thy traitorous haughty sons,
Confederates all, thus to dishonour me.
Was there none else in Rome to make a stale[c]
But Saturnine? Full well, Andronicus,
Agree these deeds with that proud brag of thine,
That said'st, I begg'd the empire at thy hands.

TIT. O, monstrous! what reproachful words are these?

SAT. But go thy ways; go, give that changing piece
To him that flourish'd for her with his sword:
A valiant son-in-law thou shalt enjoy;
One fit to bandy with thy lawless sons,
To ruffle in the commonwealth of Rome.

TIT. These words are razors to my wounded heart.

SAT. And therefore, lovely Tamora, queen of Goths,—
That, like the stately Phœbe 'mongst her nymphs,
Dost overshine the gallant'st dames of Rome,—
If thou be pleas'd with this my sudden choice,
Behold I choose thee, Tamora, for my bride,
And will create thee empress[d] of Rome.
Speak, queen of Goths, dost thou applaud my choice?
And here I swear by all the Roman gods,—
Sith priest and holy water are so near,
And tapers burn so bright, and everything
In readiness for Hymenæus stand,—
I will not re-salute the streets of Rome,
Or climb my palace, till from forth this place
I lead espous'd my bride along with me.

TAM. And here, in sight of heaven, to Rome I swear,
If Saturnine advance the queen of Goths,

---

a — surpris'd!] *Seized unawares.*

b — the emperor needs her not,—] In the old copies this line is preceded by the following stage direction:—

Enter aloft the Emperour, with Tamora, and her two sonnes, and Aaron the Moore.

c Was there none else in Rome to make a stale—] So the second folio, except that it adds "of" to the end of the line; the earlier authorities all read,—"Was none in Rome to make a stale," &c.

d — empress—] See note (f), p. 601.

She will a handmaid be to his desires,
A loving nurse, a mother to his youth.
SAT. Ascend, fair queen, Pantheon.—Lords, accompany
Your noble emperor and his lovely bride,
Sent by the heavens for prince Saturnine,
Whose wisdom hath her fortune conquered:
There shall we consummate our spousal rites.
[*Exeunt* SAT., *attended;* TAMORA, DEMETRIUS, CHIRON; AARON, *and* Goths.
TIT. I am not bid[a] to wait upon this bride:—
Titus, when wert thou wont to walk alone,
Dishonour'd thus, and challenged of wrongs?

Re-enter MARCUS, LUCIUS, QUINTUS, *and* MARTIUS.

MARC. O, Titus, see! O, see what thou hast done!
In a bad quarrel slain a virtuous son.
TIT. No, foolish tribune, no; no son of mine,—
Nor thou, nor these, confederates in the deed
That hath dishonour'd all our family;
Unworthy brother, and unworthy sons!
LUC. But let us give him burial as becomes:
Give Mutius burial with our brethren.
TIT. Traitors, away! he rests not in this tomb:—
This monument five hundred years hath stood,
Which I have sumptuously re-edified:
Here none but soldiers and Rome's servitors
Repose in fame; none basely slain in brawls:—
Bury him where you can; he comes not here.
MARC. My lord, this is impiety in you:
My nephew Mutius' deeds do plead for him,
He must be buried with his brethren.
QUINT., MART. And shall, or him we will accompany.
TIT. *And shall!* What villain was it spake that word?
QUINT. He that would vouch 't in any place but here.
TIT. What! would you bury him in my despite?
MARC. No, noble Titus; but entreat of thee
To pardon Mutius, and to bury him.
TIT. Marcus, even thou hast struck upon my crest,
And, with these boys, mine honour thou hast wounded:
My foes I do repute you every one;
So, trouble me no more, but get you gone.
MART. He is not with[b] himself; let us withdraw.
QUINT. Not I, till Mutius' bones be buried.
[MARCUS *and the* Sons *of* TITUS *kneel.*
MARC. Brother, for in that name doth nature plead,—
QUINT. Father, and in that name doth nature speak,—
TIT. Speak thou no more, if all the rest will speed.
MARC. Renowned Titus, more than half my soul,—
LUC. Dear father, soul and substance of us all,—
MARC. Suffer thy brother Marcus to inter
His noble nephew here in virtue's nest,
That died in honour and Lavinia's cause.
Thou art a Roman,—be not barbarous:
The Greeks upon advice did bury Ajax
That slew himself; and wise* Laertes' son
Did graciously plead for his funerals:[c]
Let not young Mutius, then, that was thy joy,
Be barr'd his entrance here.
TIT. Rise, Marcus, rise:—
The dismall'st day is this that e'er I saw,
To be dishonour'd by my sons in Rome!—
Well, bury him, and bury me the next.
[*They put* MUTIUS *in the tomb.*
LUC. There lie thy bones, sweet Mutius, with thy friends,
Till we with trophies do adorn thy tomb.
ALL. [*Kneeling.*] No man shed tears for noble Mutius;
He lives in fame that died in virtue's cause.
MARC. My lord,—to step out of these dreary† dumps,—
How comes it that the subtle queen of Goths
Is of a sudden thus advanc'd in Rome?
TIT. I know not, Marcus; but I know it is;
Whether by device or no, the heavens can tell:
Is she not, then, beholden to the man
That brought her for this high good turn so far?
MAR.[d] Yes, and will nobly him remunerate.

Flourish. Re-enter SATURNINUS, TAMORA, DEMETRIUS, CHIRON, *and* AARON *from one side; from the other,* BASSIANUS *and* LAVINIA, *with others.*

SAT. So, Bassianus, you have play'd your prize!
God give you joy, sir, of your gallant bride!

(*) First folio omits, *wise.* (†) First folio, *sudden.*

[a] *I am not* bid—] See note (c), p. 406, Vol. I.
[b] *He is not* with *himself;*] Equivalent to the modern phrase,—*He is beside himself.* The folio reads,—"He is not himselfe."
[c] —— and wise Laertes' son
Did graciously plead for his funerals:]
There is here an obvious reference to an incident in the *Ajax* of Sophocles; and if, as Steevens asserts, there were no translation of that piece extant in the time of Shakespeare, we may reasonably infer that "Titus Andronicus" was written by some one acquainted with the Greek tragedies in their original language.
[d] MAR.] This line is only in the folio, and there, the prefix having been omitted, it reads as a portion of the preceding speech.

BASS. And you of yours, my lord! I say no more,
Nor wish no less; and so, I take my leave.
SAT. Traitor, if Rome have law, or we have power,
Thou and thy faction shall repent this rape.
BASS. *Rape*, call you it, my lord, to seize my own,
My true-betrothed love, and now my wife?
But let the laws of Rome determine all;
Meanwhile I am possess'd of that is mine.
SAT. 'T is good, sir: you are very short with us;
But, if we live, we'll be as sharp with you.
BASS. My lord, what I have done, as best I may,
Answer I must, and shall do with my life.
Only thus much I give your grace to know,—
By all the duties that I owe to Rome,
This noble gentleman, lord Titus here,
Is in opinion and in honour wrong'd;
That, in the rescue of Lavinia,
With his own hand did slay his youngest son,
In zeal to you, and highly mov'd to wrath
To be controll'd in that he frankly gave.
Receive him, then, to favour, Saturnine,
That hath express'd himself, in all his deeds,
A father and a friend to thee and Rome.
TIT. Prince Bassianus, leave to plead my deeds:
'T is thou and those that have dishonour'd me.
Rome, and the righteous heavens, be my judge,
How I have lov'd and honour'd Saturnine!
TAM. My worthy lord, if ever Tamora
Were gracious in those princely eyes of thine,
Then hear me speak indifferently for all;
And at my suit, sweet, pardon what is past.
SAT. What, madam! be dishonour'd openly,
And basely put it up without revenge?
TAM. Not so, my lord; the gods of Rome forfend
I should be author to dishonour you!
But on mine honour dare I undertake
For good lord Titus' innocence in all;
Whose fury, not dissembled, speaks his griefs:
Then, at my suit, look graciously on him:
Lose not so noble a friend on vain suppose,
Nor with sour looks afflict his gentle heart.—
[*Aside to* SAT.] My lord, be rul'd by me, be won at last;
Dissemble all your griefs and discontents:
You are but newly planted in your throne;
Lest, then, the people, and patricians too,
Upon a just survey, take Titus' part,
And so supplant you* for ingratitude,
(Which Rome reputes to be a heinous sin,)
Yield at entreats; and then let me alone:
I'll find a day to massacre them all,
And raze their faction and their family,
The cruel father and his traitorous sons,
To whom I sued for my dear son's life;
And make them know, what 't is to let a queen
Kneel in the streets and beg for grace in vain.—
[*Aloud.*] Come, come, sweet emperor;—come, Andronicus,—
Take up this good old man, and cheer the heart
That dies in tempest of thy angry frown.
SAT. Rise, Titus, rise; my empress hath prevail'd.
TIT. I thank your majesty, and her, my lord:
These words, these looks, infuse new life in me.
TAM. Titus, I am incorporate in Rome,
A Roman now adopted happily,
And must advise the emperor for his good.
This day all quarrels die, Andronicus;—
And let it be mine honour, good my lord,
That I have reconcil'd your friends and you.—
For you, prince Bassianus, I have pass'd
My word and promise to the emperor,
That you will be more mild and tractable.—
And fear not, lords,—and you, Lavinia,—
By my advice, all humbled on your knees,
You shall ask pardon of his majesty.
LUC.* We do; and vow to heaven, and to his highness,
That what we did was mildly as we might,
Tend'ring our sister's honour and our own.
MARC. That, on mine honour, here I do protest.
SAT. Away, and talk not; trouble us no more.—
TAM. Nay, nay, sweet emperor, we must all be friends:
The tribune and his nephews kneel for grace;
I will not be denied: sweet heart, look back.
SAT. Marcus, for thy sake, and thy brother's here,
And at my lovely Tamora's entreats,
I do remit these young men's heinous faults:
Stand up.[a]—Lavinia, though you left me like a churl,
I found a friend; and, sure as death, I swore,
I would not part a bachelor from the priest.
Come, if the emperor's court can feast two brides,
You are my guest, Lavinia, and your friends.—
This day shall be a love-day, Tamora.
TIT. To-morrow, an it please your majesty,
To hunt the panther and the hart with me,
With horn and hound, we'll give your grace *bon-jour.*
SAT. Be it so, Titus, and gramercy too. [*Exeunt.*

(*) First folio, *us.*

[a] Stand up.—] Probably, as Pope surmised, a stage direction only.

(*) First folio, *Son.*

ACT II.

SCENE I.—Rome. *Before the Palace.*

Enter Aaron.

Aaron. Now climbeth Tamora Olympus' top,
Safe out of Fortune's shot; and sits aloft,
Secure of thunder's crack or lightning flash;
Advanc'd above* pale envy's threat'ning reach.
As when the golden sun salutes the morn,
And, having gilt the ocean with his beams,
Gallops the zodiac in his glistering coach,

(*) First folio, *about*.

And overlooks the highest peering hills;
So Tamora.
Upon her wit[a] doth earthly honour wait,
And virtue stoops and trembles at her frown.
Then, Aaron, arm thy heart, and fit thy thoughts,
To mount aloft with thy imperial mistress,
And mount her pitch, whom thou in triumph long
Hast prisoner held, fetter'd in amorous chains,
And faster bound to Aaron's charming[b] eyes
Than is Prometheus tied to Caucasus.
Away with slavish weeds and servile* thoughts!
I will be bright, and shine in pearl and gold,
To wait upon this new-made empress.
To wait, said I? to wanton with this queen,
This goddess, this Semiramis, this nymph,†
This siren, that will charm Rome's Saturnine,
And see his shipwreck, and his commonweal's.—
Holla! what storm is this?

Enter DEMETRIUS *and* CHIRON, *braving.*[c]

DEMET. Chiron, thy years want wit, thy wit wants edge,
And manners, to intrude where I am grac'd;
And may, for aught thou know'st, affected be.

CHI. Demetrius, thou dost over-ween in all;
And so in this, to bear me down with braves.
'T is not the difference of a year or two
Makes me less gracious, or thee more fortunate:
I am as able and as fit as thou,
To serve, and to deserve my mistress' grace;
And that my sword upon thee shall approve,
And plead my passions for Lavinia's love.

AARON. [*Aside.*] Clubs, clubs![d] these lovers will not keep the peace.

DEMET. Why, boy, although our mother, unadvis'd,
Gave you a dancing rapier by your side,
Are you so desperate grown, to threat your friends?
Go to; have your lath glu'd within your sheath,
Till you know better how to handle it.

CHI. Meanwhile, sir, with the little skill I have,
Full well shalt thou perceive how much I dare.

DEMET. Ay, boy, grow ye so brave? [*They draw.*

AARON. [*Advancing.*] Why, how now, lords!
So near the emperor's palace dare you draw,
And maintain such a quarrel openly?
Full well I wot the ground of all this grudge:
I would not for a million of gold
The cause were known to them it most concerns;
Nor would your noble mother for much more
Be so dishonour'd in the court of Rome.
For shame, put up.

DEMET. Not I, till I have sheath'd
My rapier in his bosom, and, withal,
Thrust these reproachful speeches down his throat,
That he hath breath'd in my dishonour here.

CHI. For that I am prepar'd, and full resolv'd,—
Foul-spoken coward, that thunder'st with thy tongue,
And with thy weapon nothing dar'st perform.

AARON. Away, I say!—
Now, by the gods that warlike Goths adore,
This petty* brabble will undo us all!—
Why, lords,—and think you not how dangerous
It is to jet† upon a prince's right?
What, is Lavinia, then, become so loose,
Or Bassianus so degenerate,
That for her love such quarrels may be broach'd
Without controlment, justice, or revenge?
Young lords, beware! an should the empress know
This discord's ground, the music would not please.

CHI. I care not, I, knew she and all the world:
I love Lavinia more than all the world.

DEMET. Youngling, learn thou to make some meaner choice:
Lavinia is thine elder brother's hope.

AARON. Why, are ye mad? or know ye not, in Rome,
How furious and impatient they be,
And cannot brook competitors in love?
I tell you, lords, you do but plot your deaths
By this device.

CHI. Aaron, a thousand deaths would I propose,
To achieve her whom I ‡ love.

AARON. *To achieve her!*—how?

DEMET. Why mak'st thou it so strange?
She is a woman, therefore may be woo'd;
She is a woman, therefore may be won;[e]
She is Lavinia, therefore must be lov'd.
What, man! more water glideth by the mill
Than wots the miller of;[f] and easy it is

(*) First folio, *idle.* (†) First folio, *queen.*

(*) First folio, *pretty.* (†) First folio, *set.* (‡) First folio inserts, *do.*

[a] *Upon her* wit—] For "wit," Warburton reads,—*will*, and is followed by Mr. Collier's annotator.

[b] — charming *eyes*—] He is adverting, not to the *beauty* of his eyes, but to the quality of *fascination* which the eye was once supposed to possess. See note (b), p. 714, Vol. II.

[c] — *braving.*] *Blustering, Hectoring.*

[d] Clubs, clubs!] See note (b), p. 165, Vol. II.

[e] She is a woman, therefore may be woo'd;
She is a woman; therefore may be won;]
These lines, slightly varied, occur in the First Part of "Henry VI." Act V. Sc. 3,—

"She's beautiful, and therefore to be woo'd;
She is a woman, therefore to be won;"

from which coincidence Ritson conjectured that the author of the present play was also author of the original "Henry VI."

[f] — more water glideth by the mill, &c.] A north-country proverb,—"Much water runs by the mill that the miller wots not of."

Of a cut loaf to steal a shive,[a] we know:
Though Bassianus be the emperor's brother,
Better than he have worn Vulcan's badge.

AARON. [*Aside.*] Ay, and as good as Saturninus may.

DEMET. Then why should he despair that knows to court it
With words, fair looks, and liberality?
What, hast not thou full often struck a doe,
And borne her cleanly by the keeper's nose?

AARON. Why, then, it seems, some certain snatch or so
Would serve your turns.

CHI. Ay, so the turn were serv'd.

DEMET. Aaron, thou hast hit it.

AARON. Would you had hit it[b] too!
Then should not we be tir'd with this ado.
Why, hark ye, hark ye,—and are you such fools
To square for this? would it offend you, then,
That both should speed?[c]

CHI. Faith, not me.

DEMET. Nor me, so I were one.

AARON. For shame, be friends, and join for that you jar.
'T is policy and stratagem must do
That you affect; and so must you resolve
That what you cannot as you would achieve
You must perforce accomplish as you may.
Take this of me,—Lucrece was not more chaste
Than this Lavinia, Bassianus' love.
A speedier course than * lingering languishment
Must we pursue, and I have found the path.
My lords, a solemn hunting is in hand;
There will the lovely Roman ladies troop:
The forest walks are wide and spacious;
And many unfrequented plots there are,
Fitted by kind[d] for rape and villany:
Single you thither, then, this dainty doe,
And strike her home by force, if not by words:
This way, or not at all, stand you in hope.
Come, come, our empress, with her sacred[e] wit,
To villany and vengeance consecrate,
Will we acquaint with all that we intend;
And she shall file our engines with advice,
That will not suffer you to square yourselves,
But to your wishes' height advance you both.
The emperor's court is like the house of Fame,
The palace full of tongues, of eyes, of ears:
The woods are ruthless, dreadful, deaf, and dull:
There speak, and strike, brave boys, and take your turns;
There serve your lusts, shadow'd from heaven's eye,
And revel in Lavinia's treasury.

CHI. Thy counsel, lad, smells of no cowardice.

DEMET. *Sit fas aut nefas*, till I find the stream *
To cool this heat, a charm to calm these † fits,
Per Styga, per manes vehor. [*Exeunt.*

SCENE II.—*A Forest near* Rome.

Enter TITUS ANDRONICUS, MARCUS, LUCIUS, QUINTUS *and* MARTIUS, *with* Hunters, *&c.*

TIT. The hunt is up, the morn is bright and grey,[f]
The fields are fragrant, and the woods are green:
Uncouple here, and let us make a bay,
And wake the emperor and his lovely bride,
And rouse the prince, and ring a hunter's peal,
That all the court may echo with the noise.
Sons, let it be your charge, as it is ours,
To attend the emperor's person carefully:
I have been troubled in my sleep this night,
But dawning day new comfort hath inspir'd.

Horns wind a peal; then enter SATURNINUS, TAMORA, BASSIANUS, LAVINIA, DEMETRIUS, CHIRON, *and* Attendants.

TIT. Many good morrows to your majesty;—
Madam, to you as many and as good:—
I promised your grace a hunter's peal.

SAT. And you have rung it lustily, my lords;
Somewhat too early for new-married ladies.

BASS. Lavinia, how say you?

LAV. I say no;
I have been broad ‡ awake two hours and more.

SAT. Come on, then; horse and chariots let us have,
And to our sport. Madam, now shall ye see
Our Roman hunting. [*To* TAMORA.

(*) Old text, *this*. Corrected by Rowe.

(*) First folio, *streames*. (†) First folio, *their*. (‡) First folio omits, *broad*.

a —— *and easy it is*
Of a cut loaf to steal a shive,—]
Another northern proverb,—"It is safe taking a shive [*slice*] of a cut loaf."

b *Would you had* hit it *too!*] An allusion to the ancient ballad quoted in "Love's Labour's Lost," Act IV. Sc. 1,—"Canst thou not hit it?" See note (c), p. 70, Vol. I.

c That both should speed?] These words, though indispensable to the sense, are omitted in the folio.

d — kind—] Nature.

e — sacred *wit*,—] *Accursed* wit, say the commentators: rather, perhaps, *devoted*, *dedicated* wit. See note (c), p. 425.

f — *and* grey,—] Hanmer prints, "and *gay*," &c.; and Mr. Collier's annotator, not content with borrowing this suggestion, turns the whole speech into rhyme, thus,—

"The hunt is up, the morn is bright and *gay*,
The fields are fragrant, and the woods are *wide;*
Uncouple here and let us make a bay,
And wake the emperor and his lovely bride,
And rouse the prince, and ring a hunter's *round*,
That all the court may echo with the *sound*.
Sons, let it be your charge, *and so will I*,
To attend the emperor's person carefully:
I have been troubled in my sleep this night,
But dawning day *brought* comfort *and delight*."

MARC. I have dogs, my lord,
Will rouse the proudest panther in the chase,
And climb the highest promontory top.

TIT. And I have horse will follow where the game
Makes way, and run like swallows o'er the plain.

DEMET. Chiron, we hunt not, we, with horse nor hound;
But hope to pluck a dainty doe to ground.

[*Exeunt.*

SCENE III.—*A desert part of the Forest.*

Enter AARON, *with a bag of gold.*

AARON. He that had wit would think that I had none,
To bury so much gold under a tree,
And never after to inherit it.
Let him that thinks of me so abjectly
Know that this gold must coin a stratagem,
Which, cunningly effected, will beget
A very excellent piece of villany:
And so repose, sweet gold, for their unrest,
That have their alms out of the empress' chest.

[*Hides the gold.*

Enter TAMORA.

TAM. My lovely Aaron, wherefore look'st thou sad,
When everything doth make a gleeful boast?
The birds chant melody on every bush;

The snake ies rolled[a] in the cheerful sun;
The green leaves quiver with the cooling wind,
And make a chequer'd shadow on the ground:
Under their sweet shade, Aaron, let us sit,
And, whilst the babbling echo mocks the hounds,
Replying shrilly to the well-tun'd horns,
As if a double hunt were heard at once,
Let us sit down and mark their yelping noise;
And,—after conflict such as was suppos'd
The wand'ring prince and Dido once enjoy'd,
When with a happy storm they were surpris'd,
And curtain'd with a counsel-keeping cave,—
We may, each wreathed in the other's arms,
Our pastimes done, possess a golden slumber;
While hounds and horns and sweet melodious birds
Be unto us as is a nurse's song
Of lullaby,(1) to bring her babe asleep.

AARON. Madam, though Venus govern your desires,
Saturn is dominator over mine:
What signifies my deadly-standing eye,
My silence and my cloudy melancholy,
My fleece of woolly hair, that now uncurls
Even as an adder when she doth unroll
To do some fatal execution?
No, madam, these are no venereal signs:
Vengeance is in my heart, death in my hand,
Blood and revenge are hammering in my head.
Hark, Tamora,—the empress of my soul,
Which never hopes more heaven than rests in thee,—
This is the day of doom for Bassianus;
His Philomel must lose her tongue to-day;
Thy sons make pillage of her chastity,
And wash their hands in Bassianus' blood.
Seest thou this letter? take it up, I pray thee,
And give the king this fatal-plotted scroll.—
Now question me no more,—we are espied;
Here comes a parcel of our hopeful booty,
Which dreads not yet their lives' destruction.

TAM. Ah, my sweet Moor, sweeter to me than life!

AARON. No more, great empress,—Bassianus comes:
Be cross with him; and I'll go fetch thy sons
To back thy quarrels,* whatsoe'er they be. [*Exit.*

Enter BASSIANUS *and* LAVINIA.

BASS. Whom have we here? Rome's royal empress,
Unfurnish'd of her† well-beseeming troop?
Or is it Dian, habited like her,
Who hath abandoned her holy groves,
To see the general hunting in this forest?

TAM. Saucy controller of our private steps!
Had I the power that some say Dian had,
Thy temples should be planted presently
With horns, as was Actæon's; and the hounds
Should drive[b] upon thy new-transformed limbs,
Unmannerly intruder as thou art!

LAV. Under your patience, gentle empress,
'T is thought you have a goodly gift in horning;
And to be doubted that your Moor and you
Are singled forth to try experiments:
Jove shield your husband from his hounds to-day!
'T is pity they should take him for a stag.

BASS. Believe me, queen, your swarth Cimmerian
Doth make your honour of his body's hue,
Spotted, detested, and abominable.
Why are you sequester'd from all your train,
Dismounted from your snow-white goodly steed,
And wander'd hither to an obscure plot,
Accompanied but* with a barbarous Moor,
If foul desire had not conducted you?

LAV. And, being intercepted in your sport,
Great reason that my noble lord be rated
For sauciness.—I pray you, let us hence,
And let her 'joy her raven-colour'd love;
This valley fits the purpose passing well.

BASS. The king, my brother, shall have note† of this.

LAV. Ay, for these slips have made him noted long;
Good king, to be so mightily abus'd!

TAM. Why have I[c] patience to endure all this?

Enter DEMETRIUS *and* CHIRON.

DEMET. How now, dear sovereign, and our gracious mother!
Why doth your highness look so pale and wan?

TAM. Have I not reason, think you, to look pale?
These two have 'tic'd me hither to this place:—
A barren detested vale, you see, it is;
The trees, though summer, yet forlorn and lean,
O'ercome with moss and baleful mistletoe:
Here never shines the sun; here nothing breeds,
Unless the nightly owl or fatal raven:—
And when they show'd me this abhorred pit,
They told me here, at dead time of the night,

(*) Old text, *quarrell.* (†) First folio, *our.*

[a] — rolled—] Mr. Collier's annotator reads, *coiled;* but see Aaron's following speech,—

"Even as an adder when she doth *unroll,*" &c.

[b] — drive—] Mr. Collier's annotator proposes, *dine,* &c.; but "drive," meaning to *rush pell-mell,* is more energetic and expressive.

(*) The first folio omits, *but.*
(†) Old text, *notice.* Corrected by Theobald.

[c] Why have I patience—] So the second folio; the previous editions read,—"Why *I have,*" &c.

A thousand fiends, a thousand hissing snakes,
Ten thousand swelling toads, as many urchins,[a]
Would make such fearful and confused cries,
As any mortal body, hearing it,
Should straight fall mad, or else die suddenly.
No sooner had they told this hellish tale,
But straight they told me they would bind me here
Unto the body of a dismal yew,
And leave me to this miserable death.
And then they call'd me foul adulteress,
Lascivious Goth, and all the bitterest terms
That ever ear did hear to such effect:
And had you not by wondrous fortune come,
This vengeance on me had they executed.
Revenge it, as you love your mother's life,
Or be ye not henceforth call'd my children.

DEMET. This is a witness that I am thy son.

CHI. And this for me, struck home to show my strength.

[*They stab* BASSIANUS, *who dies.*

LAV. Ay, come, Semiramis,—nay, barbarous Tamora!
For no name fits thy nature but thy own.

TAM. Give me thy poniard;—you shall know, my boys,
Your mother's hand shall right your mother's wrong.

DEMET. Stay, madam; here is more belongs to her;
First thrash the corn, then after burn the straw:
This minion stood upon[b] her chastity,
Upon her nuptial vow, her loyalty,
And, with that painted hope,[c] braves your mightiness:
And shall she carry this unto her grave?

CHI. An if she do, I would I were an eunuch.
Drag hence her husband to some secret hole,
And make his dead trunk pillow to our lust.

TAM. But when ye have the honey ye* desire,
Let not this wasp outlive, us both to sting.

CHI. I warrant you, madam, we will make that sure.—
Come, mistress, now perforce we will enjoy
That nice preserved honesty of yours.

LAV. Oh, Tamora! thou bear'st a woman's face—

TAM. I will not hear her speak; away with her!

LAV. Sweet lords, entreat her hear me but a word.

DEMET. Listen, fair madam; let it be your glory
To see her tears, but be your heart to them
As unrelenting flint to drops of rain.

LAV. When did the tiger's young ones teach the dam?
O, do not learn[d] her wrath,—she taught it thee:
The milk thou suck'dst from her did turn to marble;
Even at thy teat thou hadst thy tyranny.—
Yet every mother breeds not sons alike;
Do thou entreat her show a woman pity.

[*To* CHIRON.

CHI. What! wouldst thou have me prove myself a bastard?

LAV. 'T is true, the raven doth not hatch a lark,
Yet have I heard,—O, could I find it now!—
The lion, mov'd with pity, did endure
To have his princely paws[e] par'd all away.
Some say that ravens foster forlorn children,
The whilst their own birds famish in their nests:
O, be to me, though thy hard heart say no,
Nothing so kind, but something pitiful!

TAM. I know not what it means:—away with her!

LAV. O, let me teach thee! For my father's sake,
That gave thee life, when well he might have slain thee,
Be not obdurate, open thy deaf ears.

TAM. Had'st thou in person ne'er offended me,
Even for his sake am I pitiless.—
Remember, boys, I pour'd forth tears in vain,
To save your brother from the sacrifice;
But fierce Andronicus would not relent:
Therefore, away with her, and use her as you will;
The worse to her, the better lov'd of me.

LAV. O, Tamora, be call'd a gentle queen,
And with thine own hands kill me in this place!
For 't is not life that I have begg'd so long;
Poor I was slain when Bassianus died.

TAM. What begg'st thou then? fond woman, let me go.

LAV. 'T is present death I beg; and one thing more
That womanhood denies my tongue to tell:
O, keep me from their worse than killing lust,
And tumble me into some loathsome pit,
Where never man's eye may behold my body!
Do this, and be a charitable murderer.

TAM. So should I rob my sweet sons of their fee:
No, let them satisfy their lust on thee.

(*) Old text, *we*.

a — urchins,—] *Hedgehogs.*

b — stood upon—] *Plumed herself*, or *presumed* upon; so in Armin's *Nest of Ninnies*, 1608,—"This jest made them laugh more, and the raythe that shee *stood upon* her marriage, and disdained all the gallants there," &c.

c — painted hope,—] *Fallacious reliance*, or *trust*. But the line has suffered mutilation, and we ought possibly to read,—

"And with that painted hope *she* braves your mightiness."

d — learn—] *Learn* is here used for *teach*.

e — paws—] Mr. Collier's annotator suggests *claws*, and but that the author in this line appears to "affect the letter," we should have thought *claws* the genuine word.

DEMET. Away! for thou hast stay'd us here too long.

LAV. No grace? no womanhood? Ah, beastly creature!
The blot and enemy to our general name!
Confusion fall—

CHI. Nay, then I'll stop your mouth.—Bring thou her husband:
This is the hole where Aaron bid us hide him.

[*Exeunt* CHIRON *and* DEMETRIUS, *the former dragging off* LAVINIA, *and the latter the body of* BASSIANUS.

TAM. Farewell, my sons; see that you make her sure:—
Ne'er let my heart know merry cheer indeed,
Till all the Andronici be made away.
Now will I hence to seek my lovely Moor,
And let my spleenful sons this trull deflour. [*Exit.*

SCENE IV.—*The same.*

Enter AARON, *with* QUINTUS *and* MARTIUS.

AARON. Come on, my lords, the better foot before:
Straight will I bring you to the loathsome pit
Where I espied the panther fast asleep.

QUINT. My sight is very dull, whate'er it bodes.

MART. And mine, I promise you; were 't not for shame,
Well could I leave our sport to sleep awhile.

[*Falls into the pit.*

QUINT. What, art thou fallen?—What subtle hole is this,
Whose mouth is cover'd with rude-growing briers,
Upon whose leaves are drops of new-shed blood,

As fresh as morning's dew distill'd on flowers?
A very fatal place it seems to me,—
Speak, brother, hast thou hurt thee with the fall?

MART. O, brother, with the dismall'st object hurt,*
That ever eye with sight made heart lament!

AARON. [*Aside.*] Now will I fetch the king to find them here,
That he thereby may give† a likely guess,
How these were they that made away his brother. [*Exit.*

MART. Why dost not comfort me and help me out
From this unhallow'd and blood-stained hole?

QUINT. I am surprised with an uncouth[a] fear;
A chilling sweat o'erruns my trembling joints;
My heart suspects more than my eye can see.

MART. To prove thou hast a true-divining heart,
Aaron and thou look down into this den,
And see a fearful sight of blood and death.

QUINT. Aaron is gone, and my compassionate heart
Will not permit mine eyes once to behold
The thing whereat it trembles by surmise:
O, tell me how it is; for ne'er till now
Was I a child, to fear I know not what.

MART. Lord Bassianus lies embrued here,
All on a heap, like to a slaughter'd lamb,
In this detested, dark, blood-drinking pit.

QUINT. If it be dark, how dost thou know 't is he?

MART. Upon his bloody finger he doth wear
A precious ring, that lightens all the hole; (2)
Which, like a taper in some monument,
Doth shine upon the dead man's earthy‡ cheeks,
And shows the ragged entrails of the pit:
So pale did shine the moon on Pyramus,
When he by night lay bath'd in maiden blood.
O, brother, help me with thy fainting hand,—
If fear hath made thee faint, as me it hath,—
Out of this fell-devouring receptacle,
As hateful as Cocytus'§ misty mouth.

QUINT. Reach me thy hand, that I may help thee out;
Or, wanting strength to do thee so much good,
I may be pluck'd into the swallowing womb
Of this deep pit, poor Bassianus' grave.
I have no strength to pluck thee to the brink.

MART. Nor I no strength to climb without thy help.

QUINT. Thy hand once more; I will not loose again,
Till thou art here aloft, or I below:
Thou canst not come to me,—I come to thee. [*Falls in.*

(*) First folio omits, *hurt*. (†) First folio, *have*.
(‡) First folio, *earthly*. (§) First folio, *Ocitus*.

Enter SATURNINUS *and* AARON.

SAT. Along with me:—I'll see what hole is here,
And what he is that now is leap'd into it.—
Say, who art thou that lately didst descend
Into this gaping hollow of the earth?

MART. The unhappy son of old Andronicus;
Brought hither in a most unlucky hour,
To find thy brother Bassianus dead.

SAT. My brother dead! I know thou dost but jest:
He and his lady both are at the lodge,
Upon the north side of this pleasant chase;
'T is not an hour since I left him there.

MART. We know not where you left him all alive,
But out, alas! here have we found him dead.

Enter TAMORA, ANDRONICUS, *and* LUCIUS.

TAM. Where is my lord the king?

SAT. Here, Tamora; though griev'd with killing grief.

TAM. Where is thy brother Bassianus?

SAT. Now to the bottom dost thou search my wound;
Poor Bassianus here lies murdered.

TAM. Then all too late I bring this fatal writ, [*Giving a letter.*
The complot of this timeless tragedy;
And wonder greatly that man's face can fold
In pleasing smiles such murderous tyranny.

SAT. [Reads.]
An if we miss to meet him handsomely,—
Sweet huntsman, Bassianus 't is we mean,—
Do thou so much as dig the grave for him;
Thou know'st our meaning. Look for thy reward
Among the nettles at the elder-tree,
Which overshades the mouth of that same pit,
Where we decreed to bury Bassianus.
Do this, and purchase us thy lasting friends.

O, Tamora, was ever heard the like?
This is the pit, and this the elder-tree:
Look, sirs, if you can find the huntsman out,
That should have murder'd Bassianus here.

AARON. My gracious lord, here is the bag of gold. [*Showing it.*

SAT. [*To* TITUS.] Two of thy whelps, fell curs of bloody kind,
Have here bereft my brother of his life.—

a — uncouth—] *Unknown.*

Sirs, drag them from the pit unto the prison;
There let them bide until we have devis'd
Some never-heard-of torturing pain for them.
TAM. What, are they in this pit? O, wondrous thing!
How easily murder is discovered!
TIT. High emperor, upon my feeble knee,
I beg this boon, with tears not lightly shed,
That this fell fault of my accursed sons,—
Accursed, if the fault* be prov'd in them—
SAT. If it be prov'd! you see it is apparent.—
Who found this letter? Tamora, was it you?
TAM. Andronicus himself did take it up.
TIT. I did, my lord: yet let me be their bail;
For, by my father's reverend tomb, I vow
They shall be ready at your highness' will,
To answer their suspicion with their lives.
SAT. Thou shalt not bail them: see thou follow me.—
Some bring the murder'd body, some the murderers:
Let them not speak a word,—the guilt is plain;
For, by my soul, were there worse end than death,
That end upon them should be executed.
TAM. Andronicus, I will entreat the king:
Fear not thy sons; they shall do well enough.
TIT. Come, Lucius, come; stay not to talk with them. [*Exeunt.*

SCENE V.—*Another part of the Forest.*

Enter DEMETRIUS *and* CHIRON, *with* LAVINIA, *her hands cut off, and her tongue cut out.*

DEMET. So now go tell, an if thy tongue can speak,
Who 't was that cut thy tongue and ravish'd thee.
CHI. Write down thy mind, bewray thy meaning so,
An if thy stumps will let thee play the scribe.
DEMET. See, how with signs and tokens she can scrowl.†
CHI. Go home, call for sweet water, wash thy hands.
DEMET. She hath no tongue to call, nor hands to wash;
And so, let 's leave her to her silent walks.
CHI. An 't were my cause,[a] I should go hang myself.
DEMET. If thou hadst hands to help thee knit the cord. [*Exeunt* DEMET. *and* CHI.

(*) Old text, *faults*. (†) First folio, *scowle*.

[a] — *my* cause,—] The modern alteration is, "my *case;*" but we have some doubts as to the necessity of the change.
[b] Which that sweet tongue hath made,—] A mutilated line.

Enter MARCUS, *from hunting.*

MARC. Who is this,—my niece,—that flies away so fast?—
Cousin, a word; where is your husband?—
If I do dream, would all my wealth would wake me!
If I do wake, some planet strike me down,
That I may slumber in eternal sleep!—
Speak, gentle niece,—what stern ungentle hands
Have lopp'd and hew'd, and made thy body bare
Of her two branches,—those sweet ornaments,
Whose circling shadows kings have sought to sleep in,
And might not gain so great a happiness
As have* thy love? Why dost not speak to me?—
Alas, a crimson river of warm blood,
Like to a bubbling fountain stirr'd with wind,
Doth rise and fall between thy rosed lips,
Coming and going with thy honey breath.
But sure some Tereus hath deflouréd thee,
And, lest thou shouldst detect him,† cut thy tongue.
Ah, now thou turn'st away thy face for shame!
And, notwithstanding all this loss of blood,—
As from a conduit with three‡ issuing spouts,—
Yet do thy cheeks look red as Titan's face
Blushing to be encounter'd with a cloud.
Shall I speak for thee? shall I say, 't is so?
O, that I knew thy heart, and knew the beast,
That I might rail at him to ease my mind!
Sorrow concealed, like an oven stopp'd,
Doth burn the heart to cinders where it is.
Fair Philomela, she but lost her tongue,
And in a tedious sampler sew'd her mind:
But, lovely niece, that mean is cut from thee;
A craftier Tereus hast thou met,§
And he hath cut those pretty fingers off,
That could have better sew'd than Philomel.
O, had the monster seen those lily hands
Tremble like aspen-leaves upon a lute,
And make the silken strings delight to kiss them,
He would not, then, have touch'd them for his life!
Or, had he heard the heavenly harmony
Which that sweet tongue hath made,[b]
He would have dropp'd his knife, and fell asleep,
As Cerberus at the Thracian poet's feet.
Come, let us go, and make thy father blind;
For such a sight will blind a father's eye:
One hour's storm will drown the fragrant meads;
What will whole months of tears thy father's eyes?
Do not draw back, for we will mourn with thee:
O, could our mourning ease thy misery! [*Exeunt.*

(*) Old text, *halfe*. Corrected by Theobald.
(†) Old text, *them*. Corrected by Rowe.
(‡) Old text, *their*. Corrected by Hanmer.
(§) First folio adds, *withall*.

ACT III.

SCENE I.—Rome. *A Street.*

Enter Senators, Tribunes, *and* Officers *of* Justice, *with* MARTIUS *and* QUINTUS *bound, passing on to the place of execution;* TITUS *going before, pleading.*

TIT. Hear me, grave fathers! noble tribunes, stay!
For pity of mine age, whose youth was spent
In dangerous wars, whilst you securely slept;
For all my blood in Rome's great quarrel shed;
For all the frosty nights that I have watch'd;
And for these bitter tears, which now you see
Filling the agèd wrinkles in my cheeks;
Be pitiful to my condemned sons,
Whose souls are not corrupted, as 't is thought.
For two-and-twenty sons I never wept,
Because they died in honour's lofty bed.
For these, tribunes,[a] in the dust I write
[*Casting himself down.*
My heart's deep languor and my soul's sad tears:
Let my tears stanch the earth's dry appetite;
My sons' sweet blood will make it shame and blush.
[*Exeunt* Senators, Tribunes, *and* Prisoners.
O, earth, I will befriend thee more with rain,
That shall distil from these two ancient urns,*
Than youthful April shall with all his showers:
In summer's drought I 'll drop upon thee still;

[a] For these, tribunes,—] The metrical deficiency in this line is supplied in the second folio by a repetition of the word "these,"—

"For these, *these* tribunes," &c.

Malone thought it more likely some epithet of respect was given to the tribunes, and accordingly he printed,—

"For these, *good* tribunes," &c.

But query,—

"For these, *O*, tribunes," &c.?

(*) Old text, *ruines*. Corrected by Hanmer.

In winter, with warm tears I 'll melt the snow,
And keep eternal spring-time on thy face,
So thou refuse to drink my dear sons' blood.

Enter LUCIUS, *with his sword drawn.*

O, reverend tribunes! O, gentle, aged men!
Unbind my sons, reverse the doom of death;
And let me say, that never wept before,
My tears are now prevailing orators!

LUC. O, noble father, you lament in vain;
The tribunes hear you* not; no man is by;
And you recount your sorrows to a stone.

TIT. Ah, Lucius, for thy brothers let me plead—
Grave tribunes, once more I entreat of you!

LUC. My gracious lord, no tribune hears you speak.

TIT. Why, 'tis no matter, man; if they did hear,
They would not mark me; or, if they did mark,
They would not pity me; yet plead I must,
And bootless unto them:
Therefore I tell my sorrows to the stones,[a]
Who, though they cannot answer my distress,
Yet in some sort they 're better than the tribunes,
For that they will not intercept my tale:
When I do weep, they, humbly at my feet,
Receive my tears, and seem to weep with me;
And, were they but attired in grave weeds,
Rome could afford no tribune like to these.
A stone is as soft wax,—tribunes more hard than stones;
A stone is silent, and offendeth not;—
And tribunes with their tongues doom men to death.— [*Rises.*
But wherefore stand'st thou with thy weapon drawn?

LUC. To rescue my two brothers from their death:
For which attempt, the judges have pronounc'd
My everlasting doom of banishment.

TIT. O, happy man! they have befriended thee.
Why, foolish Lucius, dost thou not perceive
That Rome is but a wilderness of tigers?
Tigers must prey; and Rome affords no prey
But me and mine: how happy art thou, then,
From these devourers to be banished!—
But who comes with our brother Marcus here?

Enter MARCUS *and* LAVINIA.

MARC. Titus, prepare thy aged† eyes to weep;
Or, if not so, thy noble heart to break:
I bring consuming sorrow to thine age.

TIT. Will it consume me? let me see it, then.

MARC. This was thy daughter.

TIT. Why, Marcus, so she is.

LUC. Ay me! this object kills me!

TIT. Faint-hearted boy, arise and look upon her.—
Speak, Lavinia,[b] what accursed hand
Hath made thee handless in thy father's sight?
What fool hath added water to the sea?
Or brought a faggot to bright-burning Troy?
My grief was at the height before thou cam'st,
And now, like Nilus, it disdaineth bounds.—
Give me a sword, I 'll chop off my hands too;
For they have fought for Rome, and all in vain;
And they have nurs'd this woe, in feeding life;
In bootless prayer have they been held up,
And they have serv'd me to effectless use:
Now all the service I require of them
Is, that the one will help to cut the other.—
'T is well, Lavinia, that thou hast no hands;
For hands, to do Rome service, are but vain.

LUC. Speak, gentle sister, who hath martyr'd thee?

MARC. O, that delightful engine of her thoughts,
That blabb'd them with such pleasing eloquence
Is torn from forth that pretty hollow cage,
Where, like a sweet melodious bird, it sung
Sweet varied notes, enchanting every ear!

LUC. O, say thou for her, who hath done this deed?

MARC. O, thus I found her, straying in the park,
Seeking to hide herself, as doth the deer
That hath receiv'd some unrecuring wound.

TIT. It was my deer; and he that wounded her
Hath hurt me more than had he kill'd me dead:
For now I stand as one upon a rock,
Environ'd with a wilderness of sea,
Who marks the waxing tide grow wave by wave,
Expecting ever when some envious surge
Will in his brinish bowels swallow him.
This way to death my wretched sons are gone;
Here stands my other son, a banish'd man;
And here my brother, weeping at my woes:
But that which gives my soul the greatest spurn
Is dear Lavinia, dearer than my soul.—
Had I but seen thy picture in this plight
It would have madded me: what shall I do
Now I behold thy lively[c] body so?
Thou hast no hands to wipe away thy tears;
Nor tongue to tell me who hath martyr'd thee
Thy husband he is dead, and for his death

(*) First folio omits, *you.* (†) First folio, *noble.*

[a] — to the stones, &c.] The lection of the earliest quarto; the folio has,—

"Why 'tis no matter man, if they did heare
They would not marke me: oh if they did heare
They would not pitty me.
Therefore I tell my sorrowes bootles to the stones."

[b] Speak, Lavinia, &c.] The second folio reads, and perhaps correctly,—

"Speak, *my* Lavinia," &c.

[c] — lively *body*—] That is, "*living* body." So in Massinger's "Fatal Dowry," Act II. Sc. 1,—

"That his dear father might interment have,
See, the young son enter'd a *lively* grave!"

Thy brothers are condemn'd, and dead by this.—
Look, Marcus! ah, son Lucius, look on her!
When I did name her brothers, then fresh tears
Stood on her cheeks, as doth the honey-dew
Upon a gather'd lily almost withered.

MARC. Perchance, she weeps because they kill'd her husband;
Perchance, because she knows them* innocent.

TIT. If they did kill thy husband, then be joyful,
Because the law hath ta'en revenge on them.—
No, no, they would not do so foul a deed;
Witness the sorrow that their sister makes.—
Gentle Lavinia, let me kiss thy lips,
Or make some sign how I may do thee ease:
Shall thy good uncle, and thy brother Lucius,
And thou, and I, sit round about some fountain,
Looking all downwards, to behold our cheeks
How they are stain'd like[a] meadows yet not dry,
With miry slime left on them by a flood?
And in the fountain shall we gaze so long
Till the fresh taste be taken from that clearness,
And made a brine-pit with our bitter tears?
Or shall we cut away our hands, like thine?
Or shall we bite our tongues, and in dumb shows
Pass the remainder of our hateful days?
What shall we do? let us, that have our tongues,
Plot some device of further miseries
To make us wonder'd at in time to come.

LUC. Sweet father, cease your tears; for, at your grief,
See how my wretched sister sobs and weeps.

MARC. Patience, dear niece.—Good Titus, dry thine eyes.

TIT. Ah, Marcus, Marcus! brother, well I wot
Thy napkin cannot drink a tear of mine,
For thou, poor man, hast drown'd it with thine own.

LUC. Ah, my Lavinia, I will wipe thy cheeks.

TIT. Mark, Marcus, mark! I understand her signs:
Had she a tongue to speak, now would she say
That to her brother which I said to thee:
His napkin, with his[b] true tears all bewet,
Can do no service on her sorrowful cheeks.
O, what a sympathy of woe is this,—
As far from help as limbo[c] is from bliss!

Enter AARON.

AARON. Titus Andronicus, my lord the emperor
Sends thee this word,—that if thou love thy sons,
Let Marcus, Lucius, or thyself, old Titus,
Or any one of you, chop off your hand,
And send it to the king: he for the same
Will send thee hither both thy sons alive;
And that shall be the ransom for their fault.

TIT. O, gracious emperor! O, gentle Aaron!
Did ever raven sing so like a lark,
That gives sweet tidings of the sun's uprise?
With all my heart, I'll send the emperor my hand;
Good Aaron, wilt thou help to chop it off?

LUC. Stay, father! for that noble hand of thine,
That hath thrown down so many enemies,
Shall not be sent: my hand will serve the turn:
My youth can better spare my blood than you,
And therefore mine shall save my brothers' lives.

MARC. Which of your hands hath not defended Rome,
And rear'd aloft the bloody battle-axe,
Writing destruction on the enemy's castle?[d]
O, none of both but are of high desert:
My hand hath been but idle; let it serve
To ransom my two nephews from their death,
Then have I kept it to a worthy end.

AARON. Nay, come, agree whose hand shall go along,
For fear they die before their pardon come.

MARC. My hand shall go.

LUC. By heaven, it shall not go!

TIT. Sirs, strive no more; such wither'd herbs as these
Are meet for plucking up, and therefore mine.

LUC. Sweet father, if I shall be thought thy son,
Let me redeem my brothers both from death.

MARC. And for our father's sake and mother's care,
Now let me show a brother's love to thee.

TIT. Agree between you; I will spare my hand.

LUC. Then I'll go fetch an axe.

MARC. But I will use the axe.

[*Exeunt* LUCIUS *and* MARCUS.

TIT. Come hither, Aaron; I'll deceive them both:
Lend me thy hand, and I will give thee mine.

AARON. If that be call'd deceit, I will be honest,
And never, whilst I live, deceive men so:—
[*Aside.*] But I'll deceive you in another sort,
And that you'll say, ere half an hour pass.

[*He cuts off* TITUS'*s hand.*

Re-enter LUCIUS *and* MARCUS.

TIT. Now, stay your strife: what shall be, is despatch'd:
Good Aaron, give his majesty my hand:

(*) First folio, *him.*

a — like meadows—] Old copies, "in meadows," &c. Corrected by Rowe.

b — his *true tears*—] From the fourth folio; prior editions all have,—
"— *her* true tears," &c.

c — limbo—] See note (a), p. 696, Vol. II.

d — castle?] *Helmet.*

Tell him it was a hand that warded him
From thousand dangers: bid him bury it;
More hath it merited,—that let it have.
As for my sons, say I account of them
As jewels purchas'd at an easy price;
And yet dear too, because I bought mine own.
AARON. I go, Andronicus; and, for thy hand,
Look by-and-by to have thy sons with thee:—
[*Aside.*] Their heads I mean. O, how this villany
Doth fat me with the very thoughts of it!
Let fools do good, and fair men call for grace,
Aaron will have his soul black like his face. [*Exit.*
TIT. O, here I lift this one hand up to heaven,
And bow this feeble ruin to the earth:
If any power pities wretched tears,
To that I call!—What, wilt thou kneel with me?
[*To* LAVINIA.
Do, then, dear heart, for heaven shall hear our prayers,
Or with our sighs we'll breathe the welkin dim,
And stain the sun with fog, as sometime clouds,
When they do hug him in their melting bosoms.
MARC. O, brother, speak with possibilities,
And do not break into these deep extremes.
TIT. Is not my sorrow deep, having no bottom?
Then be my passions bottomless with them.
MARC. But yet let reason govern thy lament.
TIT. If there were reason for these miseries,
Then into limits could I bind my woes:
When heaven doth weep, doth not the earth o'erflow?
If the winds rage, doth not the sea wax mad,
Threat'ning the welkin with his big-swoln face?
And wilt thou have a reason for this coil?
I am the sea; hark how her sighs do blow![a]
She is the weeping welkin, I the earth:
Then must my sea be moved with her sighs;
Then must my earth with her continual tears
Become a deluge, overflow'd and drown'd:
For why[b] my bowels cannot hide her woes,

a — *hark how her sighs do* blow!] A correction in the second folio; former copies all reading, *flow*.

b For why—] *Because.*

But like a drunkard must I vomit them.
Then give me leave; for losers will have leave
To ease their stomachs with their bitter tongues.

Enter a Messenger *with two heads and a hand.*

MESS. Worthy Andronicus, ill art thou repaid
For that good hand thou sent'st the emperor.
Here are the heads of thy two noble sons,
And here's thy hand, in scorn to thee sent back;—
Thy griefs their sports, thy resolution mock'd,
That woe is me to think upon thy woes,
More than remembrance of my father's death. [*Exit.*

MARC. Now let hot Ætna cool in Sicily,
And be my heart an ever-burning hell!
These miseries are more than may be borne.
To weep with them that weep doth ease some deal;
But sorrow flouted at is double death.

LUC. Ah, that this sight should make so deep a wound,
And yet detested life not shrink thereat!
That ever death should let life bear his name,
Where life hath no more interest but to breathe! [LAVINIA *kisses* TITUS.

MARC. Alas, poor heart, that kiss is comfortless
As frozen water to a starved snake.

TIT. When will this fearful slumber have an end?

MARC. Now farewell flattery: die Andronicus;
Thou dost not slumber: see, thy two sons' heads;
Thy warlike hand; thy mangled daughter here;
Thy other banish'd son, with this dear[a] sight
Struck pale and bloodless; and thy brother, I,
Even like a stony image, cold and numb.
Ah, now no more will I control thy* griefs:
Rent off thy silver hair, thy other hand
Gnawing with thy teeth; and be this dismal sight
The closing up of our most wretched eyes:
Now is a time to storm; why art thou still?

TIT. Ha, ha, ha!

MARC. Why dost thou laugh? it fits not with this hour.

TIT. Why, I have not another tear to shed:
Besides, this sorrow is an enemy,
And would usurp upon my watery eyes,
And make them blind with tributary tears:
Then which way shall I find Revenge's cave?
For these two heads do seem to speak to me,
And threat me, I shall never come to bliss
Till all these mischiefs be return'd again
Even in their throats that have committed them.
Come, let me see what task I have to do.—
You heavy people, circle me about,
That I may turn me to each one of you,
And swear unto my soul to right your wrongs.—
The vow is made.—Come, brother, take a head,
And in this hand the other will I bear.—
Lavinia, thou shalt be employed in these things.[b]
Bear thou my hand, sweet wench, between thy teeth.—
As for thee, boy, go, get thee from my sight;
Thou art an exile, and thou must not stay:
Hie to the Goths, and raise an army there;
And, if you love me, as I think you do,
Let's kiss and part, for we have much to do.
[*Exeunt* TITUS, MARCUS, *and* LAVINIA.

LUC. Farewell, Andronicus, my noble father,—
The woefull'st man that ever liv'd in Rome:
Farewell, proud Rome; till Lucius come again,
He leaves* his pledges, dearer than his life:
Farewell, Lavinia, my noble sister;
O, would thou wert as thou tofore hast been!
But now nor Lucius nor Lavinia lives
But in oblivion and hateful griefs.
If Lucius live, he will requite your wrongs,
And make proud Saturnine and his empress
Beg at the gates, like Tarquin and his queen.
Now will I to the Goths, and raise a power,
To be reveng'd on Rome and Saturnine. [*Exit.*

SCENE II.[c]—*A Room in* TITUS'S *House. A Banquet set out.*

Enter TITUS, MARCUS, LAVINIA, *and* YOUNG LUCIUS, *a Boy.*

TIT. So, so; now sit: and look you eat no more
Than will preserve just so much strength in us
As will revenge these bitter woes of ours.
Marcus, unknit that sorrow-wreathen knot;
Thy niece and I, poor creatures, want our hands,
And cannot passionate our tenfold grief
With folded arms. This poor right hand of mine
Is left to tyrannize upon my breast;
And† when my heart, all mad with misery,
Beats in this hollow prison of my flesh,
Then thus I thump it down.—
Thou map of woe,[d] that thus dost talk in signs! [*To* LAVINIA.
When thy poor heart beats with outrageous beating,

(*) Old text, *my*. Corrected by Theobald.

a — dear *sight*—] See note (d), p. 449, Vol. I., and note (6), p. 398, of the present volume.

b Lavinia, thou shalt be employed in these things.] So the first folio, except that by inadvertence it has *And* at the beginning of the line. The quartos read,—

"*And* Lavinia thou shalt be imployd in these *armes*," &c.

(*) Old text, *loves*. Corrected by Rowe.
(†) Old text, *who*. Corrected by Rowe.

c SCENE II.—] This scene is first given in the folio of 1623.

d *Thou* map *of woe*,—] Compare, "Richard II." Act V. Sc. 1,—

"Thou *map* of honour," &c.

Thou canst not strike it thus to make it still.
Wound it with sighing, girl, kill it with groans;
Or get some little knife between thy teeth,
And just against thy heart make thou a hole;
That all the tears that thy poor eyes let fall
May run into that sink, and, soaking in,
Drown the lamenting fool in sea-salt tears.

MARC. Fie, brother, fie! teach her not thus to lay
Such violent hands upon her tender life.

TIT. How now! has sorrow made thee dote already?
Why, Marcus, no man should be mad but I.
What violent hands can she lay on her life?
Ah, wherefore dost thou urge the name of hands;—
To bid Æneas tell the tale twice o'er,
How Troy was burnt, and he made miserable?
O, handle not the theme, to talk of hands,
Lest we remember still that we have none.—
Fie, fie, how franticly I square my talk,—
As if we should forget we had no hands,
If Marcus did not name the word of hands!—
Come, let 's fall to; and, gentle girl, eat this:—
Here is no drink!—Hark, Marcus, what she says;—
I can interpret all her martyr'd signs;—
She says she drinks no other drink but tears,
Brew'd with her sorrow, mesh'd upon her cheeks:—
Speechless complainer, I will learn thy thought;
In thy dumb action will I be as perfect
As begging hermits in their holy prayers:
Thou shalt not sigh, nor hold thy stumps to heaven,
Nor wink, nor nod, nor kneel, nor make a sign,
But I, of these, will wrest an alphabet,
And, by still practice, learn to know thy meaning.

BOY. Good grandsire, leave these bitter deep laments:
Make my aunt merry with some pleasing tale.

MARC. Alas, the tender boy, in passion mov'd,
Doth weep to see his grandsire's heaviness.

TIT. Peace, tender sapling; thou art made of tears,
And tears will quickly melt thy life away.—
[MARCUS *strikes the dish with a knife.*
What dost thou strike at, Marcus, with thy[a] knife?

MARC. At that that I have kill'd, my lord,—a fly.

TIT. Out on thee, murderer! thou kill'st my heart;
Mine eyes are[b] cloy'd with view of tyranny:
A deed of death, done on the innocent,
Becomes not Titus' brother: get thee gone;
I see thou art not for my company.

MARC. Alas, my lord, I have but kill'd a fly.

TIT. *But?* how if that fly had a father and mother?
How would he hang his slender gilded wings,
And buzz lamenting doings in the air!
Poor harmless fly!
That, with his pretty buzzing melody,
Came here to make us merry! and thou hast kill'd him.

MARC. Pardon me, sir; it was a black ill-favour'd fly,
Like to the empress' Moor; therefore I kill'd him.

TIT. O, O, O!
Then pardon me for reprehending thee,
For thou hast done a charitable deed.
Give me thy knife, I will insult on him,
Flattering myself, as if it were the Moor,
Come hither purposely to poison me.—
There 's for thyself, and that 's for Tamora.—
Ah, sirrah!
Yet, I think we are not brought so low,
But that, between us, we can kill a fly,
That comes in likeness of a coal-black Moor.

MARC. Alas, poor man! grief has so wrought on him,
He takes false shadows for true substances.

TIT. Come, take away.—Lavinia, go with me:
I 'll to thy closet; and go read with thee
Sad stories, chanced in the times of old.—
Come, boy, and go with me: thy sight is young,
And thou shalt read when mine begins* to dazzle.
[*Exeunt.*

a — thy *knife?*] "Thy" is from the second folio.
b — are *cloy'd*—] So the second folio; the first omits, "

(*) First folio, *begin*.

ACT IV.

SCENE I.—Rome. *Before* Titus's *House.*

Enter Titus *and* Marcus; *then enter* Young Lucius, *running, with his books under his arm, and* Lavinia *running after him.*

Boy. Help, grandsire, help! my aunt Lavinia
Follows me everywhere, I know not why:—
Good uncle Marcus, see how swift she comes!—
Alas, sweet aunt, I know not what you mean.

Marc. Stand by me, Lucius; do not fear thy aunt.

Tit. She loves thee, boy, too well to do thee harm.

Boy. Ay, when my father was in Rome she did.

Marc. What means my niece Lavinia by these signs?

TIT. Fear her not, Lucius:—somewhat doth she mean:—
See, Lucius, see how much she makes of thee:
Somewhither would she have thee go with her.
Ay, boy, Cornelia never with more care
Read to her sons than she hath read to thee,
Sweet poetry and Tully's Orator.

MAR.[a] Canst thou not guess wherefore she plies thee thus?

BOY. My lord, I know not, I, nor can I guess,
Unless some fit or frenzy do possess her:
For I have heard my grandsire say full oft,
Extremity of griefs would make men mad;
And I have read that Hecuba of Troy
Ran mad through sorrow: that made me to fear;
Although, my lord, I know my noble aunt
Loves me as dear as e'er my mother did,
And would not, but in fury, fright my youth:
Which made me down to throw my books, and fly,—
Causeless, perhaps.—But pardon me, sweet aunt:
And, madam, if my uncle Marcus go,
I will most willingly attend your ladyship.

MARC. Lucius, I will.

[LAVINIA *turns over the books which* LUCIUS *has let fall.*

TIT. How now, Lavinia!—Marcus, what means this?
Some book there is that she desires to see.—
Which is it, girl, of these?—Open them, boy.
But thou art deeper read, and better skill'd:
Come, and take choice of all my library,
And so beguile thy sorrow, till the heavens
Reveal the damn'd contriver of this deed.—
What book?[b]
Why lifts she up her arms in sequence thus?

MARC. I think she means that there was more than one
Confederate in the fact;—ay, more there was;
Or else to heaven she heaves them for revenge.

TIT. Lucius, what book is that she tosseth so?

BOY. Grandsire, 't is Ovid's Metamorphoses;
My mother gave it me.

MARC. For love of her that 's gone,
Perhaps, she cull'd it from among the rest.

TIT. Soft! see how[c] busily she turns the leaves!
Help her: what would she find?—Lavinia, shall I read?
This is the tragic tale of Philomel,
And treats of Tereus' treason and his rape;
And rape, I fear, was root of thine annoy.

MARC. See, brother, see! note how she quotes[d] the leaves.

TIT. Lavinia, wert thou thus surpris'd, sweet girl,
Ravish'd and wrong'd, as Philomela was?
Forc'd in the ruthless, vast, and gloomy woods?—
See, see!—Ay, such a place there is where we did hunt,
(O, had we never, never hunted there!)
Pattern'd by that the poet here describes,
By nature made for murders and for rapes.

MARC. O, why should nature build so foul a den,
Unless the gods delight in tragedies?

TIT. Give signs, sweet girl,—for here are none but friends,—
What Roman lord it was durst do the deed:
Or slunk not Saturnine, as Tarquin erst,
That left the camp to sin in Lucrece' bed?

MARC. Sit down, sweet niece;—brother, sit down by me.—
Apollo, Pallas, Jove, or Mercury,
Inspire me that I may this treason find!—
My lord, look here; look here, Lavinia.
This sandy plot is plain; guide, if thou canst,
This, after me, when[e] I have writ my name,
Without the help of any hand at all.

[*He writes his name with his staff, and guides it with his feet and mouth.*

Curs'd be that heart that forc'd us to this shift!—
Write thou, good niece, and here display, at last,
What God will have discover'd for revenge.
Heaven guide thy pen to print thy sorrows plain,
That we may know the traitors and the truth!

[*She takes the staff in her mouth, and, guiding it with her stumps, writes.*

TIT. Oh, do ye read, my lord, what she hath writ?—
Stuprum—Chiron—Demetrius.

MARC. What, what!—the lustful sons of Tamora
Performers of this heinous, bloody deed?

TIT. *Magni Dominator poli,*
Tam lentus audis scelera? tam lentus vides?

MARC. Oh, calm thee, gentle lord; although I know
There is enough written upon this earth
To stir a mutiny in the mildest thoughts,
And arm the minds of infants to exclaims.
My lord, kneel down with me; Lavinia, kneel;
And kneel, sweet boy, the Roman Hector's hope;
And swear with me,—as with the woeful fere,[f]
And father of that chaste dishonour'd dame,
Lord Junius Brutus sware for Lucrece' rape,—
That we will prosecute, by good advice,
Mortal revenge upon these traitorous Goths,
And see their blood, or die with this reproach.

TIT. 'T is sure enough, an you knew how;
But if you hunt these bear-whelps, then beware;

---

[a] MAR.] In the old editions, the prefix having been omitted, this reads as a part of the foregoing speech.

[b] What book?] The words, "What book?" are not found in the quartos.

[c] *Soft! see how busily—*] So Rowe; the ancient copies reading, "Soft, so busily," &c.

[d] — quotes—] *Scans, notes, observes.*

[e] — when—] An addition in the second folio.

[f] — fere,—] "Fere," *feer*, or *phere*, is a word of frequent occurrence in our old authors, and means *companion, husband* or *wife.*

The dam will wake, an if she wind[a] you once:
She 's with the lion deeply still in league,
And lulls him whilst she playeth on her back,
And when he sleeps will she do what she list.
You are a young huntsman, Marcus; let it alone;
And, come, I will go get a leaf of brass,
And with a gad of steel will write these words,
And lay it by: the angry northern wind
Will blow these sands like Sibyls' leaves abroad,
And where 's your lesson then?—Boy, what say you?

BOY. I say, my lord, that if were a man,
Their mother's bed chamber should not be safe,
For these bad bondmen to the yoke of Rome.

MARC. Ay, that 's my boy! thy father hath full oft
For his ungrateful country done the like.

BOY. And, uncle, so will I, an if I live.

TIT. Come, go with me into mine armoury;
Lucius, I 'll fit thee; and withal, my boy
Shall carry from me to the empress' sons
Presents that I intend to send them both:
Come, come; thou 'lt do thy message, wilt thou not?

BOY. Ay, with my dagger in their bosoms, grandsire.

TIT. No, boy, not so; I 'll teach thee another course.—
Lavinia, come.—Marcus, look to my house
Lucius and I 'll go brave it at the court;
Ay, marry, will we, sir; and we 'll be waited on.
[*Exeunt* TITUS, LAVINIA, *and* BOY.

MARC. O, heavens, can you hear a good man groan,
And not relent, or not compassion him?—
Marcus, attend him in his ecstasy,
That hath more scars of sorrow in his heart,
Than foemen's marks upon his batter'd shield;
But yet so just, that he will not revenge:—
Revenge, ye* heavens, for old Andronicus! [*Exit.*

SCENE II.—*The same. A Room in the Palace.*

Enter AARON, CHIRON, *and* DEMETRIUS *from one side; from the other* YOUNG LUCIUS *and an* Attendant, *with a bundle of weapons, and verses written upon them.*

CHI. Demetrius, here 's the son of Lucius;
He hath some message to deliver us.

AARON. Ay, some mad message from his mad grandfather.

BOY. My lords, with all the humbleness I may,
I greet your honours from Andronicus;—
[*Aside.*] And pray the Roman gods confound you both!

DEMET. Gramercy, lovely Lucius: what 's the news?

BOY. [*Aside.*] That you are both decipher'd, that's the news,[b]
For villains mark'd with rape.—May it please you,
My grandsire, well advis'd, hath sent by me
The goodliest weapons of his armoury,
To gratify your honourable youth,
The hope of Rome; for so he bade me say;
And so I do, and with his gifts present
Your lordships, that,[c] whenever you have need,
You may be armed and appointed well:
And so I leave you both:—[*Aside.*] like bloody villains. [*Exeunt* Boy *and* Attendant.

DEMET. What 's here? A scroll; and written round about?—
Let 's see:—
[Reads.] *Integer vitæ scelerisque purus,*
Non eget Mauri jaculis, nec arcu.

CHI. O, 't is a verse in Horace; I know it well:
I read it in the grammar long ago.

AARON. Ay, just—a verse in Horace;—right, you have it.—
[*Aside.*] Now, what a thing it is to be an ass!
Here 's no sound jest![d] the old man hath found their guilt,
And sends them* weapons wrapp'd about with lines,
That wound, beyond their feeling, to the quick.
But were our witty empress well a-foot,
She would applaud Andronicus' conceit.
But let her rest in her unrest awhile.—
And now, young lords, was 't not a happy star
Led us to Rome, strangers, and more than so,
Captives, to be advanced to this height?
It did me good, before the palace gate,
To brave the tribune in his brother's hearing.

DEMET. But me more good, to see so great a lord
Basely insinuate and send us gifts.

AARON. Had he not reason, lord Demetrius?
Did you not use his daughter very friendly?

DEMET. I would we had a thousand Roman dames
At such a bay, by turn to serve our lust.

CHI. A charitable wish, and full of love.

(*) Old text, *the.*

[a] — *if she* wind *you once*:] *Scent* you. The ordinary printing of this,—

"The dam will wake, *and* if she wind you once,
She 's with the lion," &c.

appears to be destructive of the sense.

(*) First folio, *the.*

[b] — that's the news,—] This line and the prefix, "*Boy,*" are omitted in the folio 1623.

[c] — that,—] In the old editions "that" is accidentally omitted.

[d] Here's no sound jest!] An ironical turn of expression, common enough in old times.

AARON. Here lacks but your mother for to say Amen.

CHI. And that would she for twenty thousand more.

DEMET. Come, let us go, and pray to all the gods
For our beloved mother in her pains.

AARON. [*Aside.*] Pray to the devils; the gods have given us over. [*Trumpets sound.*

DEMET. Why do the emperor's trumpets flourish thus?

CHI. Belike, for joy the emperor hath a son.

DEMET. Soft! who comes here?

Enter a Nurse *with a blackamoor* Child *in her arms.*

NURSE. Good morrow, lords;
O, tell me, did you see Aaron the Moor?

AARON. Well, more or less,[a] or ne'er a whit at all,
Here Aaron is; and what with Aaron now?

NURSE. O, gentle Aaron, we are all undone!
Now help, or woe betide thee evermore!

AARON. Why, what a caterwauling dost thou keep!
What dost thou wrap and fumble in thine arms?

NURSE. O, that which I would hide from heaven's eye,—
Our empress' shame, and stately Rome's disgrace!—
She is deliver'd, lords,—she is deliver'd.

AARON. To whom?

NURSE. I mean, she is brought a-bed.

AARON. Well, God give her good rest! What hath he sent her?

NURSE. A devil.

AARON. Why, then she is the devil's dam; a joyful issue.

NURSE. A joyless, dismal, black, and sorrowful issue:
Here is the babe, as loathsome as a toad
Amongst the fairest breeders of our clime.
The empress sends it thee, thy stamp, thy seal,
And bids thee christen it with thy dagger's point.

AARON. Zounds,[b] ye whore! is black so base a hue?—
Sweet blowse, you are a beauteous blossom, sure.

DEMET. Villain, what hast thou done?

AARON. That which thou canst not undo.

CHI. Thou hast undone our mother.

AARON. Villain, I have done thy mother.[c]

DEMET. And therein, hellish dog, thou hast undone.
Woe to her chance, and damn'd her loathed choice!
Accurs'd the offspring of so foul a fiend!

CHI. It shall not live.

AARON. It shall not die.

NURSE. Aaron, it must; the mother wills it so.

AARON. What, must it, nurse? then let no man but I
Do execution on my flesh and blood.

DEMET. I'll broach the tadpole on my rapier's point:—
Nurse, give it me; my sword shall soon despatch it.

AARON. Sooner this sword shall plough thy bowels up.
[*Takes the* Child *from the* Nurse, *and draws his sword.*
Stay, murderous villains! will you kill your brother?
Now, by the burning tapers of the sky,
That shone so brightly when this boy was got,
He dies upon my scimitar's sharp point
That touches this my first-born son and heir!
I tell you, younglings, not Enceladus,
With all his threat'ning band of Typhon's brood,
Nor great Alcides, nor the god of war,
Shall seize this prey out of his father's hands.
What, what! ye sanguine, shallow-hearted boys!
Ye white-lim'd(*) walls! ye ale-house painted signs!
Coal-black is better than another hue,
In that it scorns to bear another hue:
For all the water in the ocean
Can never turn the swan's black legs to white,
Although she lave them hourly in the flood.
Tell the empress from me, I am of age
To keep mine own,—excuse it how she can.

DEMET. Wilt thou betray thy noble mistress thus?

AARON. My mistress is my mistress; this, my-self,—
The vigour and the picture of my youth:
This before all the world do I prefer;
This, maugre all the world, will I keep safe,
Or some of you shall smoke for it in Rome.

DEMET. By this our mother is for ever sham'd.

CHI. Rome will despise her for this foul escape.

NURSE. The emperor, in his rage, will doom her death.

CHI. I blush to think upon this ignomy.(†)

AARON. Why, there's the privilege your beauty bears:
Fie, treacherous hue, that will betray with blushing
The close enacts and counsels of the heart!
Here's a young lad fram'd of another leer:[d]
Look, how the black slave smiles upon the father,
As who should say, *Old lad, I am thine own.*
He is your brother, lords; sensibly fed
Of that self-blood that first gave life to you;
And from that womb where you imprison'd were,
He is enfranchised and come to light:

[a] Well, more or less,—] See note (a), p. 423, Vol. I.
[b] Zounds,—] The folio 1623 has, "*Out,*" &c.
[c] — thy mother.] This line is not found in the folio.

(*) Old text, white-*limb'd*.
(†) First folio, *ignominie*.

[d] — *another* leer:] Another *complexion* or *hue*.

Nay, he is your brother by the surer side,
Although my seal be stamped in his face.

NURSE. Aaron, what shall I say unto the empress?

DEMET. Advise thee, Aaron, what is to be done,
And we will all subscribe to thy advice:
Save thou the child, so we may all be safe.

AARON. Then sit we down, and let us all consult.
My son and I will have the wind of you:
Keep there; now talk at pleasure of your safety.
[*They sit.*

DEMET. How many women saw this child of his?

AARON. Why, so, brave lords! when we join in league,
I am a lamb; but if you brave the Moor,
The chafed boar, the mountain lioness,
The ocean swells not so as Aaron storms.—
But say, again, how many saw the child?

NURSE. Cornelia the midwife and myself,
And no one else but the deliver'd empress.

AARON. The empress, the midwife, and yourself:—
Two may keep counsel when the third 's away:—
Go to the empress, tell her this I said:—
[*He stabs her. She screams and dies.*
Weke, weke!—so cries a pig prepared to the spit.

DEMET. What mean'st thou, Aaron? wherefore didst thou this?

AARON. O, lord, sir, 't is a deed of policy;
Shall she live to betray this guilt of ours,—
A long-tongued babbling gossip? No, lords, no:
And now be it known to you my full intent.
Not far, one Muliteus,[a] my countryman,
His wife but yesternight was brought to bed;
His child is like to her, fair as you are:
Go pack[b] with him, and give the mother gold,
And tell them both the circumstance of all,
And how by this their child shall be advanc'd,
And be received for the emperor's heir,
And substituted in the place of mine,
To calm this tempest whirling in the court;
And let the emperor dandle him for his own.
Hark ye, lords; ye see I have given her physic,
[*Pointing to the* Nurse.
And you must needs bestow her funeral;
The fields are near, and you are gallant grooms:
This done, see that you take no longer days,
But send the midwife presently to me.
The midwife and the nurse well made away,
Then let the ladies tattle what they please.

CHI. Aaron, I see thou wilt not trust the air with secrets.

DEMET. For this care of Tamora,
Herself and hers are highly bound to thee.
[*Exeunt* DEMETRIUS *and* CHIRON, *bearing off the dead* Nurse.

AARON. Now to the Goths, as swift as swallow flies;
There to dispose this treasure in mine arms,
And secretly to greet the empress' friends.—
Come on, you thick-lipp'd slave, I'll bear you hence;
For it is you that puts us to our shifts:
I'll make you feed on berries, and on roots,
And feed[c] on curds and whey, and suck the goat,
And cabin in a cave, and bring you up
To be a warrior, and command a camp. [*Exit.*

SCENE III.—*The same. A Public Place.*

Enter TITUS, *bearing arrows with letters on them,* MARCUS, PUBLIUS, YOUNG LUCIUS, *and other* Gentlemen *with bows.*

TIT. Come, Marcus, come:—kinsmen, this is the way.—
Sir boy, now[d] let me see your archery;
Look ye draw home enough, and 't is there straight.— [Marcus,
Terras Astræa reliquit; be you remember'd,
She 's gone, she 's fled.—Sirs, take you to your tools.—
You, cousins, shall go sound the ocean,
And cast your nets. Haply, you may catch* her in the sea;
Yet there 's as little justice as at land:—
No; Publius and Sempronius, you must do 't;
'T is you must dig with mattock and with spade,
And pierce the inmost centre of the earth;
Then, when you come to Pluto's region,
I pray you, deliver him this petition;
Tell him it is for justice and for aid,
And that it comes from old Andronicus,
Shaken with sorrows in ungrateful Rome.—
Ah, Rome!—Well, well; I made thee miserable
What time I threw the people's suffrages
On him that thus doth tyrannize o'er me.—
Go, get you gone, and pray be careful all,
And leave you not a man-of-war unsearch'd;
This wicked emperor may have shipp'd her hence;
And, kinsmen, then we may go pipe for justice.

MARC. O, Publius, is not this a heavy case,
To see thy noble uncle thus distract?

---

[a] Not far, one Muliteus, &c.] Rowe reads,—"Not far one Muliteus *lives*," &c., and Mr. Steevens proposed,—"Not far one *Muley lives*," &c.; but, as Mr. Dyce remarks, "*Muliteus his* wife" may be equivalent to "Muliteus's wife."

[b] *Go* pack *with him,*—] Go *scheme, complot, conspire* with him.

(*) First folio, *find*.

[c] And feed—] Hanmer prints, "And *feast*," &c.

[d] *Sir boy,* now—] "Now," omitted in all the earlier copies, was first added in the folio of 1632.

Pub. Therefore, my lords, it highly us concerns,
By day and night to attend him carefully;
And feed his humour kindly as we may,
Till time beget some careful remedy.

Marc. Kinsmen, his sorrows are past remedy.
Join with the Goths; and with revengeful war
Take wreak on Rome for this ingratitude,
And vengeance on the traitor Saturnine.

Tit. Publius, how now! how now, my masters!
What, have you met with her?

Pub. No, my good lord; but Pluto sends you word,
If you will have Revenge from hell, you shall:
Marry, for Justice, she is so employ'd,
He thinks, with Jove in heaven, or somewhere else,
So that perforce you must needs stay a time.

Tit. He doth me wrong to feed me with delays.
I'll dive into the burning lake below,
And pull her out of Acheron by the heels.—
Marcus, we are but shrubs, no cedars we,
No big-bon'd men, fram'd of the Cyclops' size;
But metal, Marcus, steel to the very back,
Yet wrung with wrongs more than our backs can bear:
And sith there 's no justice in earth nor hell,
We will solicit heaven, and move the gods
To send down Justice for to wreak our wrongs.—
Come, to this gear.—You are a good archer, Marcus. [*He gives them the arrows.*
Ad Jovem, that's for you;—here, *ad Apollinem*:—
Ad Martem, that 's for myself;—
Here, boy, *to Pallas*;—here, *to Mercury*:—
To Saturn,* Caius, not to Saturnine;
You were as good to shoot against the wind.—
To it, boy.—Marcus, loose when I bid.—
Of my word, I have written to effect;
There 's not a god left unsolicited.

Marc. Kinsmen, shoot all your shafts into the court:
We will afflict the emperor in his pride.

Tit. Now, masters, draw. [*They shoot.*] O, well said,[a] Lucius!
Good boy, in Virgo's lap! give it Pallas.

Marc. My lord, I aim a mile beyond the moon;
Your letter is with Jupiter by this.

Tit. Ha, ha! Publius, Publius, what hast thou done?
See, see! thou hast shot off one of Taurus' horns.

a — well said,—] A common expression, as we have seen, to signify *well done*.

*) Old text, *To Saturnine, to Caius.*

MARC. This was the sport, my lord: when Publius shot,
The Bull, being gall'd, gave Aries such a knock,
That down fell both the Ram's horns in the court;
And who should find them but the empress' villain?
She laugh'd, and told the Moor he should not choose
But give them to his master for a present.

TIT. Why, there it goes: God give his* lordship joy!

Enter the Clown, *with a basket, and two pigeons in it.*

News, news from heaven! Marcus, the post is come.—
Sirrah, what tidings? have you any letters?
Shall I have justice? what says Jupiter?

CLOWN. Ho! the gibbet-maker?[a] he says that he hath taken them down again, for the man must not be hanged till the next week.

TIT. But what says Jupiter, I ask thee?

CLOWN. Alas, sir, I know not Jupiter:
I never drank with him in all my life.

TIT. Why, villain, art not thou the carrier?

CLOWN. Ay, of my pigeons, sir; nothing else.

TIT. Why, didst thou not come from heaven?

CLOWN. From heaven! alas, sir, I never came there. God forbid I should be so bold to press to heaven in my young days! Why, I am going with my pigeons to the tribunal plebs,[b] to take up a matter of brawl betwixt my uncle and one of the emperial's men.

MARC. Why, sir, that is as fit as can be to serve for your oration; and let him deliver the pigeons to the emperor from you.

TIT. Tell me, can you deliver an oration to the emperor with a grace?

CLOWN. Nay, truly, sir, I could never say grace in all my life.

TIT. Sirrah, come hither: make no more ado,
But give your pigeons to the emperor:
By me thou shalt have justice at his hands.

(*) First folio, *your*.

a —— *what says* Jupiter?
CLOWN. *Ho! the* gibbet maker?]

The humour of this, such as it is, consists in the Clown's mistaking "Jupiter," as hurriedly pronounced by Titus, for *Gibbeter*, and not, as Steevens supposed, for *Jew Peter*.

b — tribunal plebs,—] A purposed corruption, probably, as Hanmer conjectured, for *tribunis plebis*.

Hold, hold; meanwhile, here's money for thy charges.—
Give me pen and ink.—
Sirrah, can you with a grace deliver a supplication?

CLOWN. Ay, sir.

TIT. Then here is a supplication for you. And when you come to him, at the first approach you must kneel; then kiss his foot; then deliver up your pigeons; and then look for your reward. I'll be at hand, sir; see you do it bravely.

CLOWN. I warrant you, sir, let me alone.

TIT. Sirrah, hast thou a knife? Come, let me see it.—
Here, Marcus, fold it in the oration,
For thou hast made it like an humble suppliant:—
And when thou hast given it the emperor,
Knock at my door, and tell me what he says.

CLOWN. God be with you, sir; I will. [*Exit.*

TIT. Come, Marcus, let us go.—Publius, follow me. [*Exeunt.*

SCENE IV.—*Before the Palace.*

Enter SATURNINUS, TAMORA, DEMETRIUS, CHIRON, Lords, *and others;* SATURNINUS *with the arrows in his hand that* TITUS *shot.*

SAT. Why, lords, what wrongs are these! was ever seen
An emperor in Rome thus overborne,
Troubled, confronted thus; and, for the extent
Of egal justice, us'd in such contempt?
My lords, you know, as do[a] the mightful gods,
However these disturbers of our peace
Buzz in the people's ears, there nought hath pass'd,
But even with law, against the wilful sons
Of old Andronicus. And what an if
His sorrows have so overwhelm'd his wits,—
Shall we be thus afflicted in his wreaks,[b]
His fits, his frenzy, and his bitterness?
And now he writes to heaven for his redress:
See, here's, *to Jove*, and this, *to Mercury;*
This, *to Apollo;* this, *to the god of war:*—
Sweet scrolls to fly about the streets of Rome!
What's this, but libelling against the senate,
And blazoning our injustice everywhere?
A goodly humour, is it not, my lords?
As who would say, in Rome no justice were.
But if I live, his feigned ecstasies
Shall be no shelter to these outrages;
But he and his shall know that Justice lives
In Saturninus' health; whom, if she* sleep,
He'll so awake, as she in fury shall
Cut off the proud'st conspirator that lives.

TAM. My gracious lord, my lovely Saturnine,
Lord of my life, commander of my thoughts,
Calm thee, and bear the faults of Titus' age,
The effects of sorrow for his valiant sons,
Whose loss hath pierc'd him deep, and scarr'd his heart;
And rather comfort his distressed plight,
Than prosecute the meanest or the best
For these contempts.—[*Aside.*] Why thus it shall become
High-witted Tamora to gloze with all:
But, Titus, I have touch'd thee to the quick,
Thy life-blood out:[c] if Aaron now be wise,
Then is all safe, the anchor's in the port.—

Enter Clown.

How now, good fellow! wouldst thou speak with us?

CLOWN. Yes, forsooth, an your mistership be emperial.

TAM. Empress I am, but yonder sits the emperor.

CLOWN. 'T is he.—God and saint Stephen give you good den: I have brought you a letter and a couple of pigeons here.[d]

[SATURNINUS *reads the letter.*

SAT. Go, take him away, and hang him presently.

CLOWN. How much money must I have?

TAM. Come, sirrah, you must be hanged.

CLOWN. Hanged! by 'r lady then I have brought up a neck to a fair end. [*Exit, guarded.*

SAT. Despiteful and intolerable wrongs!
Shall I endure this monstrous villany?
I know from whence this same device proceeds:
May this be borne,—as if his traitorous sons,
That died by law for murder of our brother,
Have by my means been butcher'd wrongfully?—

---

a — as do—] These words are an addition by Rowe, the line in the old text reading imperfectly,—

"My lords, you know the mightful gods."

b — *his* wreaks,—] Capell, and Mr. Collier's annotator, read, *freaks.*

c —— I have touch'd thee to the quick,
Thy life-blood out:]

Touch'd means *pricked:* I have *lanced* thy life-blood out; but as she refers, it would appear, to some plot between her paramour and her, against the life of Lucius, we ought, perhaps, to point the line thus:—

"Thy life-blood out, if Aaron now be wise:"

d — and a couple of pigeons here.] Mr. Collier's annotator presents this and the poor Clown's subsequent speech in rhyme of the following cast:—

"God and Saint Stephen
Give you good even.
I have brought you a letter,
And a couple of pigeons for want of a better."

* * * * * *

"Hang'd! By 'r lady then, friend,
I have brought my neck to a fair end."

And this, which almost caps the memorable couplet, by the same authority, in "Henry VI." Part II. Act II. Sc. 3,—

"My staff! here, noble Henry, is my staff:
To think I fain would keep it, makes me laugh,"—

Mr. Collier has the barbarity to impute to Shakespeare!

(*) Old copies, *he.*

Go, drag the villain hither by the hair;
Nor age nor honour shall shape privilege:—
For this proud mock I'll be thy slaughter-man;
Sly frantic wretch, that holp'st to make me great,
In hope thyself should govern Rome and me.

Enter ÆMILIUS.

What news with thee, Æmilius?

ÆMIL. Arm, my lords,—Rome never had more cause!
The Goths have gather'd head, and with a power
Of high-resolved men, bent to the spoil,
They hither march amain, under condúct
Of Lucius, son to old Andronicus;
Who threats, in course of this revenge, to do
As much as ever Coriolanus did.

SAT. Is warlike Lucius general of the Goths?
These tidings nip me; and I hang the head
As flowers with frost, or grass beat down with storms:
Ay, now begin our sorrows to approach:
'T is he the common people love so much!
Myself hath often heard them say,[a]
(When I have walked like a private man)
That Lucius' banishment was wrongfully,
And they have wish'd that Lucius were their emperor.

TAM. Why should you fear? is not your city strong?

SAT. Ay, but the citizens favour Lucius,
And will revolt from me to succour him.

TAM. King, be thy thoughts imperious, like thy name.
Is the sun dimm'd, that gnats do fly in it?
The eagle suffers little birds to sing,
And is not careful what they mean thereby,
Knowing that with the shadow of his wing*
He can at pleasure stint their melody:
Even so mayst thou the giddy men of Rome.
Then cheer thy spirit: for know, thou emperor,
I will enchant the old Andronicus,
With words more sweet, and yet more dangerous,
Than baits to fish, or honey-stalks to sheep;
Whenas the one is wounded with the bait,
The other rotted with delicious feed.

SAT. But he will not entreat his son for us.

TAM. If Tamora entreat him, then he will;
For I can smooth, and fill his aged ear
With golden promises, that, were his heart
Almost impregnable, his old ears deaf,
Yet should both ear and heart obey my tongue.—
Go thou before; be our ambassador;[b] [*To* ÆMILIUS.
Say that the emperor requests a parley
Of warlike Lucius, and appoint the meeting,
Even at his father's house, the old Andronicus.[c]

SAT. Æmilius, do this message honourably:
And if he stand on† hostage for his safety,
Bid him demand what pledge will please him best.

ÆMIL. Your bidding shall I do effectually. [*Exit.*

TAM. Now will I to that old Andronicus,
And temper him with all the art I have,
To pluck proud Lucius from the warlike Goths.
And now, sweet emperor, be blithe again,
And bury all thy fear in my devices.

SAT. Then go successantly,[d] and plead to‡ him. [*Exeunt.*

(*) Old text, *wings*. (†) Old text, *in*. (‡) First folio, *for*.

a Myself hath often heard them say,—] A mutilated line, which Theobald rendered whole by printing,—"Myself *have* often *over*heard," &c., and Mr. Collier's annotator would perfect by reading,—"Myself hath *very* often heard," &c.

b — be our ambassador;] The quartos have,—

"Goe thou before *to* be our Embassadour," &c.

The folio reads,—

"Goe thou before *to* our Embassadour," &c.

c — the old Andronicus.] A line found only in the 4to. 1600.

d — successantly,—] Rowe prints, *successfully;* and Capell, who is followed here by Mr. Collier's annotator, *incessantly*.

ACT V.

SCENE I.—*Plains near* Rome.

Flourish. Enter Lucius, *and an Army of* Goths, *with drum and colours.*

Luc. Approved warriors, and my faithful friends,
I have received letters from great Rome,
Which signify what hate they bear their emperor,
And how desirous of our sight they are.
Therefore, great lords, be, as your titles witness,
Imperious, and impatient of your wrongs;
And wherein Rome hath done you any scath,
Let him make treble satisfaction.

1 Goth. Brave slip, sprung from the great Andronicus,
Whose name was once our terror, now our comfort;
Whose high exploits and honourable deeds,
Ingrateful Rome requites with foul contempt,
Be bold in us; we'll follow where thou lead'st,—
Like stinging bees in hottest summer's day,
Led by their master to the flower'd fields,—
And be aveng'd on cursed Tamora.

Goths.[a] And, as he saith, so say we all with him.

Luc. I humbly thank him, and I thank you all.—
But who comes here, led by a lusty Goth?

Enter a Goth, *leading* Aaron *with his* Child *in his arms.*

2 Goth. Renowned Lucius, from our troops I stray'd,
To gaze upon a ruinous monastery;
And, as I earnestly did fix mine eye
Upon the wasted building, suddenly

[a] Goths.] The prefix being omitted in the earlier copies, this line forms part of the preceding speech there.

I heard a child cry underneath a wall.
I made unto the noise; when soon I heard
The crying babe controll'd with this discourse:—
Peace, tawny slave, half me and half thy dam!
Did not thy hue bewray whose brat thou art,
Had nature lent thee but thy mother's look,
Villain, thou mightst have been an emperor:
But where the bull and cow are both milk-white,
They never do beget a coal-black calf.
Peace, villain, peace!—even thus he rates the babe,—
For I must bear thee to a trusty Goth,
Who, when he knows thou art the empress' babe,
Will hold thee dearly for thy mother's sake.
With this, my weapon drawn, I rush'd upon him,
Surpris'd him suddenly, and brought him hither,
To use as you think needful of the man.

LUC. O, worthy Goth, this is the incarnate devil
That robb'd Andronicus of his good hand;
This is the pearl[a] that pleas'd your empress' eye!
And here's the base fruit of his burning lust.—
Say, wall-eyed slave, whither wouldst thou convey
This growing image of thy fiend-like face?
Why dost not speak? what, deaf? not a word?—
A halter, soldiers! hang him on this tree,
And by his side his fruit of bastardy.

AARON. Touch not the boy,—he is of royal blood.

LUC. Too like the sire for ever being good.—
First hang the child, that he may see it sprawl,—
A sight to vex the father's soul withal.—
Get me a ladder![b]

[*A ladder brought, which* AARON *is made to ascend.*

AARON. Lucius, save the child,
And bear it from me to the empress.
If thou do this, I'll show thee wond'rous things,
That highly may advantage thee to hear:
If thou wilt not, befall what may befall,
I'll speak no more but—vengeance rot you all!

LUC. Say on; and if it please me which thou speak'st,
Thy child shall live, and I will see it nourished.

AARON. And if it please thee! why, assure thee, Lucius,
'T will vex thy soul to hear what I shall speak;
For I must talk of murders, rapes, and massacres,
Acts of black night, abominable deeds,
Complots of mischief, treason, villanies

[a] *This is the* pearl—] An allusion to the old proverb,—"A black man is a pearl in a fair woman's eye."

[b] Get me a ladder!] These words are erroneously given to Aaron in the old copies.

Ruthful to hear, yet piteously perform'd:
And this shall all be buried by my death,
Unless thou swear to me my child shall live.

LUC. Tell on thy mind; I say thy child shall live.

AARON. Swear that he shall, and then I will begin.

LUC. Who should I swear by? thou believ'st no god;
That granted, how canst thou believe an oath?

AARON. What if I do not? as, indeed, I do not:
Yet, for I know thou art religious,
And hast a thing within thee called conscience,
With twenty popish tricks and ceremonies,
Which I have seen thee careful to observe,
Therefore I urge thy oath; for that I know
An idiot holds his bauble for a god,
And keeps the oath which by that god he swears,
To that I'll urge him:—therefore thou shalt vow
By that same god, what god soe'er it be,
That thou ador'st and hast in reverence,—
To save my boy, to nourish and bring him up;
Or else I will discover nought to thee.

LUC. Even by my god I swear to thee I will.

AARON. First know thou, I begot him on the empress.

LUC. O, most insatiate, luxurious woman!

AARON. Tut, Lucius, this was but a deed of charity
To that which thou shalt hear of me anon.
'T was her two sons that murder'd Bassianus;
They cut thy sister's tongue, and ravish'd her.
And cut her hands, and trimm'd her as thou saw'st.

LUC. O, détestable villain! call'st thou that trimming?

AARON. Why, she was wash'd, and cut, and trimm'd;

And 't was trim sport for them that had the doing of it.

LUC. O, barbarous, beastly villains, like thyself!

AARON. Indeed, I was their tutor to instruct them:
That codding spirit had they from their mother,
As sure a card as ever won the set:
That bloody mind, I think, they learn'd of me,
As true a dog as ever fought at head.—
Well, let my deeds be witness of my worth.
I train'd thy brethren to that guileful hole,
Where the dead corpse of Bassianus lay:
I wrote the letter that thy father found,
And hid the gold within the letter mention'd,
Confederate with the queen and her two sons:
And what not done, that thou hast cause to rue,
Wherein I had no stroke of mischief in it?
I play'd the cheater for thy father's hand;
And, when I had it, drew myself apart,
And almost broke my heart with extreme laughter.
I pry'd me through the crevice of a wall,
When, for his hand, he had his two sons' heads;
Beheld his tears, and laugh'd so heartily,
That both mine eyes were rainy like to his:
And when I told the empress of this sport,
She swooned almost at my pleasing tale,
And for my tidings gave me twenty kisses.

1 GOTH. What, canst thou say all this, and never blush?

AARON. Ay, like a black dog, as the saying is.

LUC. Art thou not sorry for these heinous deeds?

AARON. Ay, that I had not done a thousand more.
Even now I curse the day,—and yet I think
Few come within the* compass of my curse,—
Wherein I did not some notorious ill:
As kill a man, or else devise his death;
Ravish a maid, or plot the way to do it;
Accuse some innocent, and forswear myself;
Set deadly enmity between two friends;
Make poor men's cattle break their necks; [a]
Set fire on barns and hay-stacks in the night,
And bid the owners quench them with their tears.
Oft have I digg'd up dead men from their graves,
And set them upright at their dear friends' doors,†
Even when their sorrows almost were forgot;
And on their skins, as on the bark of trees,
Have with my knife carved in Roman letters,
Let not your sorrow die, though I am dead.
Tut, I have done a thousand dreadful things
As willingly as one would kill a fly;
And nothing grieves me heartily indeed,
But that I cannot do ten thousand more.

LUC. Bring down the devil, for he must not die
So sweet a death as hanging presently.

AARON. If there be devils, would I were a devil,
To live and burn in everlasting fire,
So I might have your company in hell,
But to torment you with my bitter tongue!

LUC. Sirs, stop his mouth, and let him speak no more.

Enter a Goth.

3 GOTH. My lord, there is a messenger from Rome
Desires to be admitted to your presence.

LUC. Let him come near.

Enter ÆMILIUS.

Welcome, Æmilius: what's the news from Rome?

ÆMIL. Lord Lucius, and you princes of the Goths,
The Roman emperor greets you all by me;
And, for he understands you are in arms,
He craves a parley at your father's house,
Willing you to demand your hostages,
And they shall be immediately deliver'd.

1 GOTH. What says our general?

LUC. Æmilius, let the emperor give his pledges
Unto my father and my uncle Marcus,
And we will come.—March! away!

[*Flourish. Exeunt.*

SCENE II.—Rome. *Before* Titus's *House.*

Enter TAMORA, DEMETRIUS, *and* CHIRON, *disguised.*

TAM. Thus, in this strange and sad habiliment,
I will encounter with Andronicus,
And say I am Revenge, sent from below
To join with him and right his heinous wrongs.
Knock at his study, where, they say, he keeps,
To ruminate strange plots of dire revenge;
Tell him Revenge is come to join with him,
And work confusion on his enemies.

[*They knock. Enter* TITUS *above.*[b]

TIT. Who doth molest my contemplation?
Is it your trick to make me ope the door,
That so my sad decrees may fly away,

(*) First folio, *few*. (†) Old text, *doore*.

[a] Make poor men's cattle break their necks;] Malone proposed to supply the omission in this line by adding,—*and die:* Mr. Dyce, by reading,—"*stray and* break their necks;" and Mr. Collier's annotator by,—"*ofttimes* break their necks."

[b] *Enter* TITUS *above.*] The old copies have, "*They knocke and Titus opens his studie dore.*"

And all my study be to no effect?
You are deceiv'd; for what I mean to do
See here in bloody lines I have set down;
And what is written shall be executed.

TAM. Titus, I am come to talk with thee.[a]

TIT. No, not a word: how can I grace my talk,
Wanting a hand to give it action?
Thou hast the odds of me; therefore no more.

TAM. If thou didst know me, thou wouldst talk with me.

TIT. I am not mad; I know thee well enough:
Witness this wretched stump, witness these crimson lines;
Witness these trenches made by grief and care;
Witness the tiring day and heavy night;
Witness all sorrow, that I know thee well
For our proud empress, mighty Tamora.
Is not thy coming for my other hand?

TAM. Know, thou sad man, I am not Tamora;
She is thy enemy, and I thy friend.
I am Revenge; sent from the infernal kingdom,
To cease the gnawing vulture of thy mind,
By working wreakful vengeance on thy* foes.
Come down, and welcome me to this world's light;
Confer with me of murder and of death.
There's not a hollow cave or lurking place,
No vast obscurity or misty vale,
Where bloody Murder or detested Rape
Can couch for fear, but I will find them out;
And in their ears tell them my dreadful name,—
Revenge,—which makes the foul offenders quake.

TIT. Art thou Revenge? and art thou sent to me
To be a torment to mine enemies?

TAM. I am: therefore come down, and welcome me.

TIT. Do me some service, ere I come to thee.
Lo, by thy side where Rape and Murder stands!
Now give some surance that thou art Revenge,—
Stab them, or tear them on thy chariot-wheels;
And then I'll come and be thy waggoner,
And whirl along with thee about the globes;
Provide thee two proper palfreys,† black as jet,
To hale thy vengeful waggon swift away,
And find out murderers‡ in their guilty caves:§
And when thy car is loaden with their heads,
I will dismount, and by the waggon-wheel
Trot, like a servile footman, all day long,
Even from Hyperion's[b] rising in the east
Until his very downfall in the sea:
And day by day I'll do this heavy task,
So thou destroy Rapine and Murder there.

TAM. These are my ministers, and come with me.

TIT. Are they[c] thy ministers? what are they call'd?

TAM. Rapine and Murder; therefore called so,
'Cause they take vengeance of such kind of men.

TIT. Good lord, how like the empress' sons they are!
And you, the empress! but we worldly men
Have miserable, mad-mistaking eyes.
O, sweet Revenge, now do I come to thee;
And, if one arm's embracement will content thee,
I will embrace thee in it by and by. [*Exit above.*

TAM. This closing with him fits his lunacy:
Whate'er I forge to feed his brain-sick fits,
Do you uphold and maintain in your speeches;
For now he firmly takes me for Revenge,
And, being credulous in this mad thought,
I'll make him send for Lucius, his son;
And, whilst I at a banquet hold him sure,
I'll find some cunning practice out of hand,
To scatter and disperse the giddy Goths,
Or, at the least, make them his enemies.—
See, here he comes, and I must ply my theme.

Enter TITUS.

TIT. Long have I been forlorn, and all for thee:
Welcome, dread Fury, to my woeful house:—
Rapine and Murder, you are welcome too:—
How like the empress and her sons you are!
Well are you fitted, had you but a Moor:—
Could not all hell afford you such a devil?—
For well I wot the empress never wags
But in her company there is a Moor;
And, would you represent our queen aright,
It were convenient you had such a devil:
But welcome, as you are. What shall we do?

TAM. What wouldst thou have us do, Andronicus?

DEMET. Show me a murderer, I'll deal with him.

CHI. Show me a villain that hath done a rape,
And I am sent to be reveng'd on him.

TAM. Show me a thousand, that have done thee wrong,
And I will be revenged on them all.

TIT. Look round about the wicked streets of Rome,
And when thou find'st a man that's like thyself,
Good Murder, stab him; he's a murderer.—
Go thou with him; and when it is thy hap
To find another that is like to thee,
Good Rapine, stab him; he's a ravisher.—
Go thou with them; and in the emperor's court

(*) First folio, *my*. (†) First folio inserts, *as*.
(‡) Old text, *murder*. (§) Old text, *cares*.

a Titus, I am come to talk with thee.] Query,—"I am *here* come"?

b Hyperion's—] So the second folio; the quartos read, "*Eptons*," and the first folio has, "*Epeons*."

c *Are* they thy ministers?] A correction of the second folio; the previous copies having, "Are *them*," &c.

There is a queen attended by a Moor;
Well mayst thou know her by thy own proportion,
For up and down[a] she doth resemble thee.
I pray thee, do on them some violent death:
They have been violent to me and mine.

TAM. Well hast thou lesson'd us; this shall we do.
But would it please thee, good Andronicus,
To send for Lucius, thy thrice-valiant son,
Who leads towards Rome a band of warlike Goths,
And bid him come and banquet at thy house;
When he is here, even at thy solemn feast,
I will bring in the empress and her sons,
The emperor himself, and all thy foes,
And at thy mercy shall they stoop and kneel,
And on them shalt thou ease thy angry heart.
What says Andronicus to this device?

TIT. Marcus! my brother! 'tis sad Titus calls.

Enter MARCUS.

Go, gentle Marcus, to thy nephew Lucius,
Thou shalt inquire him out among the Goths,
Bid him repair to me, and bring with him
Some of the chiefest princes of the Goths;
Bid him encamp his soldiers where they are.
Tell him the emperor and the empress too,
Feast at my house, and he shall feast with them.
This do thou for my love; and so let him,
As he regards his aged father's life.

MARC. This will I do, and soon return again. [*Exit.*

TAM. Now will I hence about thy business,
And take my ministers along with me.

TIT. Nay, nay, let Rape and Murder stay with me,
Or else I'll call my brother back again,
And cleave to no revenge but Lucius.

TAM. [*Aside to them.*] What say you, boys? will you abide[b] with him,
Whiles I go tell my lord the emperor,
How I have govern'd our determin'd jest?
Yield to his humour, smooth and speak him fair,
And tarry with him till I turn again.

TIT. [*Aside.*] I know them all, though they suppose me mad;
And will o'erreach them in their own devices,—
A pair of cursed hell-hounds, and their dam.

DEMET. Madam, depart at pleasure; leave us here.

TAM. Farewell, Andronicus; Revenge now goes
To lay a complot to betray thy foes.

TIT. I know thou dost; and, sweet Revenge, farewell. [*Exit* TAMORA.

CHI. Tell us, old man, how shall we be employ'd?

TIT. Tut, I have work enough for you to do.—
Publius, come hither, Caius, and Valentine!

Enter PUBLIUS *and others.*

PUB. What is your will?

TIT. Know you these two?

PUB. The empress' sons,
I take them, Chiron and[c] Demetrius.

TIT. Fie, Publius, fie! thou art too much deceiv'd,—
The one is Murder, Rape is the other's name;
And therefore bind them, gentle Publius:—
Caius and Valentine, lay hands on them.—
Oft have you heard me wish for such an hour,
And now I find it; therefore bind them sure,
And stop their mouths, if they begin to cry.[d] [*Exit.*
[PUBLIUS, *&c., lay hold on* CHIRON *and* DEMETRIUS.

CHI. Villains, forbear! we are the empress' sons.

PUB. And therefore do we what we are commanded.—
Stop close their mouths; let them not speak a word.
Is he sure bound? look that you bind them fast.

Re-enter TITUS, *with* LAVINIA, *he bearing a knife and she a basin.*

TIT. Come, come, Lavinia; look, thy foes are bound.—
Sirs, stop their mouths, let them not speak to me;
But let them hear what fearful words I utter.—
O, villains, Chiron and Demetrius!
Here stands the spring whom you have stain'd with mud;
This goodly summer with your winter mix'd.
You kill'd her husband; and for that vile fault
Two of her brothers were condemn'd to death,
My hand cut off, and made a merry jest,
Both her sweet hands, her tongue; and that more dear
Than hands or tongue, her spotless chastity,
Inhuman traitors, you constrain'd and forc'd.
What would you say, if I should let you speak?
Villains, for shame you could not beg for grace.
Hark, wretches! how I mean to martyr you.

---

[a] — up and down—] That is, *thoroughly, exactly, altogether;* see note (b), p. 13, Vol. I.

[b] *What say you, boys? will you* abide *with him,*—] The early copies have, "will you *bide* with him," but the self-evident correction, "abide," though attributed by Mr. Collier to his annotator as a novelty, is found in most editions of the last century.

[c] *I take them, Chiron* and *Demetrius.*] The conjunction, omitted in the old copies, was first restored by Theobald.

[d] And stop their mouths, if they begin to cry.] A line not printed in the folio, 1623.

This one hand yet is left to cut your throats,
Whilst that Lavinia 'tween her stumps doth hold
The basin that receives your guilty blood.
You know your mother means to feast with me,
And calls herself Revenge, and thinks me mad:—
Hark, villains! I will grind your bones to dust,
And with your blood and it I'll make a paste;
And of the paste a coffin[a] I will rear,
And make two pasties of your shameful heads;
And bid that strumpet, your unhallow'd dam,
Like to the earth, swallow her own* increase.
This is the feast that I have bid her to,
And this the banquet she shall surfeit on;
For worse than Philomel you used my daughter,
And worse than Progne I will be reveng'd.
And now prepare your throats.—Lavinia, come,
[*He cuts their throats.*
Receive the blood: and when that they are dead,
Let me go grind their bones to powder small,
And with this hateful liquor temper it;
And in that paste let their vile heads be bak'd.
Come, come, be every one officious[b]
To make this banquet; which I wish may prove
More stern and bloody than the Centaur's feast.
So:—
Now bring them in, for I will play the cook,
And see them ready 'gainst their mother comes.
[*Exeunt, bearing the dead bodies.*

SCENE III.—*Gardens of* Titus's *House. A Pavilion, with tables, &c.*

Enter LUCIUS, MARCUS, *and the* Goths, *with* AARON, *prisoner.*

LUC. Uncle Marcus, since 'tis my father's mind
That I repair to Rome, I am content.
1 GOTH. And ours with thine, befall what fortune will.
LUC. Good uncle, take you in this barbarous Moor,

(*) The first folio omits, *own*.

a — a coffin—] The crust of a raised pie was of old called the *coffin*.

b — officious—] *Serviceable, obliging.*

This ravenous tiger, this accursed devil;
Let him receive no sustenance, fetter him,
Till he be brought unto the empress' face,
For testimony of her foul proceedings:
And see the ambush of our friends be strong;
I fear the emperor means no good to us.

AARON. Some devil whisper curses in mine ear,
And prompt me, that my tongue may utter forth
The venomous malice of my swelling heart!

LUC. Away, inhuman dog! unhallow'd slave!—
Sirs, help our uncle to convey him in.
[*Exeunt* Goths, *with* AARON. *Flourish without.*
The trumpets show the emperor is at hand.

Enter SATURNINUS *and* TAMORA, *with* ÆMILIUS, Tribunes, Senators, *and others.*

SAT. What, hath the firmament more suns than one?

LUC. What boots it thee to call thyself a sun?

MARC. Rome's emperor, and nephew, break the parle;
These quarrels must be quietly debated.
The feast is ready, which the careful Titus
Hath ordain'd to an honourable end,
For peace, for love, for league, and good to Rome:
Please you, therefore, draw nigh, and take your places.

SAT. Marcus, we will.
[*Hautboys sound. The company sit down at table.*

Enter TITUS, *dressed like a cook,* LAVINIA, *with a veil over her face,* YOUNG LUCIUS, *and others.* TITUS *places the dishes on the table.*

TIT. Welcome, my gracious lord; welcome, dread queen;
Welcome, ye warlike Goths; welcome, Lucius;
And welcome, all! Although the cheer be poor,
'T will fill your stomachs, please you eat of it.

SAT. Why art thou thus attir'd, Andronicus?

TIT. Because I would be sure to have all well,
To entertain your highness and your empress.

SAT. We are beholden to you, good Andronicus.

TIT. An if your highness knew my heart, you were.—
My lord the emperor, resolve me this:
Was it well done of rash Virginius
To slay his daughter with his own right hand,
Because she was enforc'd, stain'd, and deflour'd?

SAT. It was, Andronicus.

TIT. Your reason, mighty lord?

SAT. Because the girl should not survive her shame,
And by her presence still renew his sorrows.

TIT. A reason mighty, strong, and effectual;
A pattern-precedent, and lively warrant,
For me, most wretched, to perform the like:—
Die, die, Lavinia, and thy shame with thee;
[*He kills* LAVINIA.
And, with thy shame, thy father's sorrow die!

SAT. What hast thou done, unnatural and unkind?

TIT. Kill'd her, for whom my tears have made me blind.
I am as woeful as Virginius was,
And have a thousand times more cause than he
To do this outrage;—and it is now done.[a]

SAT. What, was she ravish'd? tell, who did the deed?

TIT. Will 't please you eat?—will 't please your highness feed?

TAM. Why hast thou slain thine only daughter thus?[b]

TIT. Not I; 't was Chiron and Demetrius:
They ravish'd her, and cut away her tongue;
And they, 't was they, that did her all this wrong.

SAT. Go fetch them hither to us presently.

TIT. Why, there they are, both baked in that pie,
Whereof their mother daintily hath fed,
Eating the flesh that she herself hath bred.
'T is true, 't is true, witness my knife's sharp point!
[*Kills* TAMORA.

SAT. Die, frantic wretch, for this accursed deed!
[*Kills* TITUS.

LUC. Can the son's eye behold his father bleed?
There 's meed for meed, death for a deadly deed!
[*Kills* SATURNINUS. *A great tumult. The* People *disperse in terror.* LUCIUS, MARCUS, *and their* Partisans *ascend the steps of* Titus's *House.*

MARC. You sad-fac'd men, people and sons of Rome,
By uproars sever'd, like a flight of fowl
Scatter'd by winds and high tempestuous gusts,
O, let me teach you how to knit again
This scatter'd corn into one mutual sheaf,
These broken limbs again into one body;
Lest[c] Rome herself be bane unto herself;
And she whom mighty kingdoms court'sy to,
Like a forlorn and desperate castaway,
Do shameful execution on herself.
But if my frosty signs and chaps of age,

---

[a] — and it is now done.] A line not found in the folio.

[b] — thine only daughter thus?] The reading of the 4to. 1600; later editions omitting, "*thus.*"

[c] Lest Rome, &c.] This line, beginning, "*Let* Rome," &c. in the old copies, has the prefix, "*Roman Lord,*" in the quartos, and in the folio, "*Goth.*" Steevens observes that, as the speech proceeds in a uniform tenor, the whole probably belongs to Marcus, and to him in its entirety we assign it.

Grave witnesses of true experience,
Cannot induce you to attend my words,—
Speak, Rome's dear friend, [*To* LUCIUS.] as erst our ancestor,
When with his solemn tongue he did discourse
To love-sick Dido's sad attending ear
The story of that baleful-burning night,
When subtle Greeks surpris'd king Priam's Troy,—
Tell us what Sinon hath bewitch'd our ears,
Or who hath brought the fatal engine in
That gives our Troy, our Rome, the civil wound.—
My heart is not compact of flint nor steel,
Nor can I utter all our bitter grief,
But floods of tears will drown my oratory,
And break my very utterance, even in the time
When it should move you to attend me most.
Lending your kind* commiseration,
Here is a captain, let him tell the tale,
Your hearts will throb and weep to hear him speak.

LUC. Then,† noble auditory, be it known to you,
That cursed Chiron and Demetrius
Were they that murdered our emperor's brother;
And they it was that ravished our sister:
For their fell faults our brothers were beheaded;
Our father's tears despis'd, and basely cozen'd
Of that true hand that fought Rome's quarrel out,
And sent her enemies unto the grave.
Lastly, myself, unkindly banished,
The gates shut on me, and turn'd weeping out,
To beg relief among Rome's enemies;
Who drown'd their enmity in my true tears,
And op'd their arms to embrace me as a friend:
And I am the[a] turn'd-forth, be it known to you,
That have preserv'd her welfare in my blood,
And from her bosom took the enemy's point,
Sheathing the steel in my adventurous body.
Alas, you know I am no vaunter, I!
My scars can witness, dumb although they are,
That my report is just and full of truth.
But, soft! methinks I do digress too much,
Citing my worthless praise: O, pardon me,
For, when no friends are by, men praise themselves.

MARC. Now is my turn to speak: behold this child,—

[*Pointing to the* Child *in the arms of an* Attendant.

Of this was Tamora delivered;
The issue of an irreligious Moor,
Chief architect and plotter of these woes.
The villain is alive in Titus' house,
Damn'd[b] as he is, to witness this is true.
Now judge what cause‡ had Titus to revenge
These wrongs, unspeakable, past patience,
Or more than any living man could bear.
Now you have heard the truth, what say you, Romans?
Have we done aught amiss,—show us wherein,
And, from the place where you behold us now,
The poor remainder of Andronici
Will, hand in hand, all headlong cast us down,
And on the ragged stones beat forth our brains,
And make a mutual closure of our house.
Speak, Romans, speak! and if you say we shall,
Lo, hand in hand, Lucius and I will fall!

ÆMIL. Come, come, thou reverend man of Rome,
And bring our emperor gently in thy hand,
Lucius our emperor; for well I know
The common voice do cry, *It shall be so!*

ROMANS. Lucius, all hail, Rome's royal emperor![c]

MARC. Go, go into old Titus' sorrowful house,
And hither hale that misbelieving Moor,
To be adjudg'd some direful-slaughtering death,
As punishment for his most wicked life.

[*To* Attendants, *who go into the house.*

ROMANS. Lucius, all hail, Rome's gracious governor!

LUC. Thanks, gentle Romans: may I govern so,
To heal Rome's harms, and wipe away her woe!
But, gentle people, give me aim awhile,
For nature puts me to a heavy task;
Stand all aloof;—but, uncle, draw you near,
To shed obsequious tears upon this trunk.—
O, take this warm kiss on thy pale-cold lips,

[*Kisses* TITUS.

These sorrowful drops upon thy blood-stain'd* face,
The last true duties of thy noble son!

MARC. Tear for tear, and loving kiss for kiss,
Thy brother Marcus tenders on thy lips:
O, were the sum of these that I should pay,
Countless and infinite, yet would I pay them!

LUC. Come hither, boy; come, come, and learn of us
To melt in showers. Thy grandsire lov'd thee well:
Many a time he danc'd thee on his knee,
Sung thee asleep, his loving breast thy pillow;
Many a matter hath he told to thee,
Meet and agreeing with thine infancy;
In that respect, then, like a loving child,
Shed yet some small drops from thy tender spring,
Because kind nature doth require it so:
Friends should associate friends in grief and woe:
Bid him farewell; commit him to the grave;
Do him that kindness, and take leave of him.

(*) First folio inserts, *hand*. (†) First folio, *This*. (‡) Old text, *course*.

[a] *And I am* the turn'd-forth, &c.] So the quartos; the folio has,—"And I am turned forth," &c.

[b] Damn'd *as he is*, &c.] Theobald's emendation; the old text having, "*And* as he is."

(*) Old text, *bloud-slaine*.

[c] ROMANS. Lucius, all hail, Rome's royal emperor!] This and the subsequent line,

"Lucius, all hail, Rome's gracious governor!"

are in the old copies ascribed to Marcus; but surely in error.

BOY. O, grandsire, grandsire! even with all my heart
Would I were dead, so you did live again!—
O, lord, I cannot speak to him for weeping!
My tears will choke me, if I ope my mouth.

Re-enter Attendants, *with* AARON.

1 ROMAN. You sad Andronici, have done with woes:
Give sentence on this execrable wretch,
That hath been breeder of these dire events.

LUC. Set him breast-deep in earth, and famish him;
There let him stand, and rave, and cry for food:
If any one relieves or pities him,
For the offence he dies. This is our doom.
Some stay to see him fasten'd in the earth.

AARON. O, why should wrath be mute, and fury dumb?
I am no baby, I, that with base prayers
I should repent the evils I have done:
Ten thousand worse than ever yet I did
Would I perform, if I might have my will:
If one good deed in all my life I did,
I do repent it from my very soul.

LUC. Some loving friends convey the emperor hence,
And give him burial in his father's grave.
My father and Lavinia shall forthwith
Be closed in our household's monument:
As for that heinous tiger, Tamora,
No funeral rite, nor man in mournful weeds,
No mournful [a] bell shall ring her burial;
But throw her forth to beasts and birds of prey:
Her life was beast-like, and devoid of pity,
And, being so, shall have like want of pity.
See justice done on Aaron, that damn'd Moor,
By whom our heavy haps had their beginning:
Then, afterwards, to order well the state,
That like events may ne'er it ruinate.(1) [*Exeunt.*

[a] No mournful bell—] Query, "No solemn bell," &c.?

ILLUSTRATIVE COMMENTS.

ACT II.

(1) SCENE III.—

Be unto us as is a nurse's song
Of lullaby, to bring her babe asleep.]

Douce, in his "Illustrations of Shakspeare," has an interesting note on the burden *lullaby*.

"It would be a hopeless task to trace the origin of the northern verb *to lull*, which means *to sing gently;* but it is evidently connected with the Greek λαλέω, *loquor*, or λάλλη, the sound made by the beach at sea. Thus much is certain, that the Roman nurses used the word *lalla* to quiet their children, and that they feigned a deity called *Lallus*, whom they invoked on that occasion; the lullaby or tune itself was called by the same name. As *lallare* meant to *sing lalla*, to *lull* might in like manner denote the singing of the nurse's lullaby to induce the child to sleep. Thus in an ancient carol composed in the fifteenth century, and preserved among the Sloane MSS. No. 2593:

"'che song a slepe wt her *lullynge*
here dere sone our savyoure.'

"In another old ballad, printed by Mr. Ritson in his *Ancient Songs*, p. 198, the burden is 'lully, lully, lullaby, lullyby, sweete baby,' &c.; from which it seems probable that *lullaby* is only a comparatively modern contraction of *lully baby*, the first word being the legitimate offspring of the Roman *lalla*. In another of these pieces, still more ancient, and printed in the same collection, we have 'lullay, lullow, lully, *bewy*, lulla baw baw.'

"The Welsh appear to have been famous for their lullaby songs. Jones, in his *Arte and science of preserving bodie and soule*, 1579, 4to., says:—'The best nurses, but especially the trim and skilfull Welch women, doe use to sing some preaty sonets, wherwith their copious tong is plentifully stoared of divers pretie tunes and pleasaunt ditties, that the children disquieted might be brought to reste: but translated never so well, they want their grace in Englishe, for lacke of proper words: so that I will omit them, as I wishe they would theyr lascivious *Dymes*, wanton *Lullies*, and amorous *Englins*.'

"Mr. White, in reviewing his opinion of the etymology of *good-by*, will perhaps incline to think it a contraction, when properly written *good b'ye*, of *God be with you*, and not 'may your *house* prosper!'

"To add to the stock of our old lullaby songs, two are here subjoined. The first is from a pageant of *The slaughter of the innocents*, acted at Coventry in the reign of Henry the Eighth, by the taylors and shearers of that city, and most obligingly communicated by Mr. Sharpe. The other is from the curious volume of songs mentioned before in p. 262. Both exhibit the simplicity of ancient manners:—

"'Lully, lulla, thou littell tine childe,
By by lully lullay,
Lully lullay thou littell tyne child,
By by lully lullay.

"'O sisters too, how may we do,
For to preserve this day
This pore yongling, for whom we do singe
By by lully lullay.

"'Herod the king, in his raging,
Chargid he hath this day;
His men of might, in his owne sight,
All yonge children to slay.

"'That wo is me, pore child for thee,
And ever morne and say;
For thi parting, nether say nor sing,
By by lully lullay.'

"'By by lullaby
Rockyd I my chyld
In a drē late as I lay
Me thought I hard a maydyn say
And spak thes wordys mylde,
My lytil sone with the I play
And ever she song by lullay
Thus rockyd she hyr chyld
By by lullabi,
Rockid I my child by by.
Then merveld I ryght sore of thys
A mayde to have a chyld I wys,
By by lullay.
Thus rockyd she her chyld
By by lullaby, rockyd I my chyld.'"

(2) SCENE IV.—*A precious ring, that lightens all the hole.*] The gem supposed to possess a property of emitting native light was called a *carbuncle*, and is frequently mentioned in early books; thus, in "The Gesta Romanorum," b. vi.:—"He further beheld and saw a *carbuncle* in the hall that lighted all the house." So also in Lydgate's "Description of King Priam's Palace," L. II.:—

"And for most chefe all derkeness to confound,
A *carbuncle* was set as kyng of stones all,
To recomforte and gladden all the hall.
And to enlumine in the blacke night
With the freshnes of his ruddy light."

And so Drayton, in "The Muses' Elysium:"—

"Is that admirèd mighty stone,
The *carbuncle* that's named;
Which from it such a flaming light
And radiancy ejecteth,
That in the very darkest night
The eye to it directeth."

But the best illustration of the passage we have met with occurs in a letter from Boyle, containing "Observations on a Diamond that shines in the dark:"—"Though Vortomannus was not an eye-witness of what he relates, that the King of Pegu had a true Carbuncle of that bigness and splendour, that it shined very gloriously in the dark; and though Garcias ab Horto, the Indian Vice-Roy's physician, speaks of another carbuncle only on the report of one that he discoursed with; yet as we are not sure that these men that gave themselves out to be eye-witnesses, speak true, yet they may have done so for aught we know to the contrary. . . . . . I must not omit that some virtuosi questioning me the other day at Whitehall, and meeting amongst them an ingenious Dutch gentleman whose father was long embassador for the Netherlands in England, I learned of him that he is acquainted with a person who was admiral of the Dutch in the East Indies, and who assured this gentleman Monsieur Boreel, that at his return from thence, he brought back with him into Holland a stone which though it looked but like a pale dull diamond, yet it was a real carbuncle; and did without rubbing shine so much, that when the admiral had occasion to open a chest which he kept under deck in a dark place where it was forbidden to bring candles for fear of mischances, as soon as he opened the trunk, the stone would by its native light shine so as to illustrate a great part of it."—*Boyle's Works*, Vol. II. p. 82.

ACT V.

(1) Scene III.—
Then, afterwards, to order well the state,
That like events may ne'er it ruinate.]

The following is the ballad registered by Danton when he entered the "Historye of Tytus Andronicus" on the Stationers' Rolls. It is extracted from Percy's "Reliques of Antient Poetry," Vol. I. :—

"Titus Andronicus's Complaint.

"You noble minds and famous martiall wights,
That in defence of native country fights,
Give ear to me, that ten yeers fought for Rome,
Yet reapt disgrace at my returning home.

"In Rome I lived in fame fulle threescore yeeres,
My name beloved was of all my peeres;
Full five and twenty valiant sonnes I had,
Whose forwarde vertues made their father glad.

"For when Romes foes their warlike forces bent,
Against them stille my sonnes and I were sent;
Against the Goths full ten yeeres weary warre
We spent, receiving many a bloudy scarre.

"Just two and twenty of my sonnes were slaine
Before we did returne to Rome againe:
Of five and twenty sonnes, I brought but three
Alive the stately towers of Rome to see.

"When wars were done I conquest home did bring,
And did present my prisoners to the King.
The Queene of Goths, her sons, and eke a Moore,
Which did such murders, like was nere before.

"The emperour did make this queene his wife,
Which bred in Rome debate and deadlie strife;
The Moore, with her two sonnes did growe soe proud,
That none like them in Rome might be allowd.

"The Moore soe pleased this new-made empress' eie,
That she consented to him secretlye
For to abuse her husbands marriage bed,
And soe in time a blackamore she bred.

"Then she, whose thoughts to murder were inclined,
Consented with the Moore of bloody minde
Against myself, my kin, and all my friendes,
In cruell sort to bring them to their endes.

"Soe when in age I thought to live in peace,
Both care and griefe began then to increase:
Amongst my sonnes I had one daughter bright,
Which joy'd, and pleased best my aged sight:

"My deare Lavinia was betrothed than
To Cæsars sonne, a young and noble man:
Who in a hunting by the emperours wife
And her two sonnes, bereaved was of life.

"He being slaine was cast in cruel wise
Into a darksome den from light of skies:
The cruell Moore did come that way as then
With my three sonnes, who fell into the den.

"The Moore then fetcht the emperour with speed,
For to accuse them of that murderous deed;
And when my sonnes within the den were found,
In wrongfull prison they were cast and bound.

"But nowe, behold! what wounded most my mind,
The empresses two sonnes of savage kind
My daughter ravished without remorse,
And took away her honour, quite perforce.

"When they had tasted of soe sweete a flowre,
Fearing this sweete should shortly turne to soure,
They cutt her tongue, whereby she could not tell
How that dishonoure unto her befell.

"Then both her hands they basely cutt off quite,
Whereby their wickednesse she could not write;
Nor with her needle on her sampler sowe
The bloudye workers of her direfull woe.

"My brother Marcus found her in the wood,
Staining the grassie ground with purple bloud,
That trickled from her stumpes, and bloudlesse armes;
Noe tongue at all she had to tell her harmes.

"But when I sawe her in that woefull case,
With teares of bloud I wet mine aged face;
For my Lavinia I lamented more,
Than for my two and twenty sonnes before.

"When as I sawe she could not write nor speake,
With griefe mine aged heart began to breake;
We spred an heape of sand upon the ground,
Whereby those bloudy tyrants out we found.

"For with a staffe without the help of hand
She writt these wordes upon the plat of sand:
'The lustfull sonnes of the proud emperèsse
Are doers of this hateful wickednèsse.'

"I tore the milk-white hairs from off mine head,
I curst the houre, wherein I first was bred,
I wisht this hand, that fought for countrie's fame,
In cradle rockt, had first been stroken lame.

"The Moore delighting still in villainy,
Did say, to sett my sonnes from prison free
I should unto the king my right hand give,
And then my three imprisoned sonnes should live.

"The Moore I caused to strike it off with speede,
Whereat I grieved not to see it bleed,
But for my sonnes would willingly impart,
And for their ransome send my bleeding heart.

"But as my life did linger thus in paine,
They sent to me my bootlesse hand againe,
And therewithal the heades of my three sonnes,
Which filld my dying heart with fresher moanes.

"Then past reliefe I upp and downe did goe,
And with my teares writ in the dust my woe:
I shot my arrowes towards heaven hie,
And for revenge to hell did often crie.

"The empresse then, thinking that I was mad,
Like furies she and both her sonnes were clad,
(She nam'd Revenge, and Rape and Murder they)
To undermine and heare what I would say.

"I fed their foolish veines a certaine space,
Untill my friendes did find a secret place,
Where both her sonnes unto a post were bound,
And just revenge in cruell sort was found.

"I cut their throates, my daughter held the pan
Betwixt her stumpes, wherein the bloud it ran:
And then I ground their bones to powder small,
And made a paste for pyes streight therewithall.

"Then with [illegible] fleshe I made two mighty pyes,
And at a banquet servde in stately wise:
Before the empresse set this loathsome meat;
So of her sonnes own flesh she well did eat.

"Myself bereav'd my daughter then of life,
The empresse then I slewe with bloudy knife,
And stabb'd the emperour immediatelie
And then myself: even soe did Titus die.

"Then this revenge against the Moor was found,
Alive they sett him halfe into the ground,
Whereas he stood untill such time he starv'd,
And soe God send all murderers may be served."

CRITICAL OPINIONS ON TITUS ANDRONICUS.

"All the editors and critics agree with Mr. Theobald in supposing this play spurious. I see no reason for differing from them; for the colour of the style is wholly different from that of the other plays, and there is an attempt at regular versification, and artificial closes, not always inelegant, yet seldom pleasing. The barbarity of the spectacles, and the general massacre, which are here exhibited, can scarcely be conceived tolerable to any audience; yet we are told by Jonson, that they were not only borne, but praised. That Shakespeare wrote any part, though Theobald declares it incontestable, I see no reason for believing.

"The testimony produced at the beginning of this play, by which it is ascribed to Shakespeare, is by no means equal to the argument against its authenticity, arising from the total difference of conduct, language, and sentiments, by which it stands apart from all the rest. Meres had probably no other evidence than that of a title-page, which, though in our time it be sufficient, was then of no great authority; for all the plays which were rejected by the first collectors of Shakespeare's works, and admitted in later editions, and again rejected by the critical editors, had Shakespeare's name on the title, as we must suppose, by the fraudulence of the printers, who, while there were yet no gazettes, nor advertisements, nor any means of circulating literary intelligence, could usurp at pleasure any celebrated name. Nor had Shakespeare any interest in detecting the imposture, as none of his fame or profit was produced by the press.

"The chronology of this play does not prove it not to be Shakespeare's. If it had been written twenty-five years in 1614, it might have been written when Shakespeare was twenty-five years old. When he left Warwickshire, I know not; but at the age of twenty-five it was rather too late to fly for deer-stealing.

"Ravenscroft, who in the reign of Charles II. revised this play, and restored it to the stage, tells us in his preface, from a theatrical tradition, I suppose, which in his time might be of sufficient authority, that this play was touched in different parts by Shakespeare, but written by some other poet. I do not find Shakespeare's touches very discernible."—Johnson.

"In the course of the notes on this performance, I have pointed out a passage or two which, in my opinion, sufficiently prove it to have been the work of one who was acquainted both with Greek and Roman literature. It is likewise deficient in such internal marks as distinguish the tragedies of Shakspeare from those of other writers; I mean, that it presents no struggles to introduce the vein of humour so constantly interwoven with the business of his serious dramas. It can neither boast of his striking excellencies, nor his acknowledged defects; for it offers not a single interesting situation, a natural character, or a string of quibbles from first to last. That Shakspeare should have written without commanding our attention, moving our passions, or sporting with words, appears to me as improbable, as that he should have studiously avoided dissyllable and trisyllable terminations in this play, and in no other.

"Let it likewise be remembered that this piece was not published with the name of Shakspeare till after his death. The quarto in 1611 is anonymous.

"Could the use of particular terms employed in no other of his pieces be admitted as an argument that he was not its author, more than one of these might be found; among which is *palliament* for *robe*, a Latinism which I have not met with elsewhere in any English writer, whether ancient or modern; though it must have originated from the mint of a scholar. I may add, that 'Titus Andronicus' will be found on examination to contain a greater number of classical allusions, &c. than are scattered over all the rest of the performances on which the seal of Shakspeare is indubitably fixed.—Not to write any more *about and about* this suspected *thing*, let me observe that the glitter of a few passages in it has perhaps misled the judgment of those who ought to have known, that both sentiment and description are more easily produced than the interesting fabrick of a tragedy. Without these advantages many plays have succeeded; and many have failed, in which they have been dealt about with the most lavish profusion. It does not follow, that he who can carve a frieze with minuteness, elegance, and ease, has a conception equal to the extent, propriety, and grandeur of a temple."—STEEVENS.

Act IV. Sc. 2.

OTHELLO.

In the Registers of the Stationers, under the date, October 6th, 1621, is the following memorandum:—

"Tho. Walkely] Entered for his, to wit, under the handes of Sir George Buck and of the Wardens: The Tragedie of Othello, the Moore of Venice."

This entry was made by Walkley, preparatory to the publication of his quarto edition of the play which appeared some time in the next year, and was entitled:—"The Tragœdy of Othello, The Moore of Venice. As it hath beene diverse times acted at the Globe, and at the Black-Friers, by his Maiesties Servants. Written by William Shakespeare. London, Printed by N. O. for Thomas Walkley, and are to be sold at his shop at the Eagle and Child, in Brittans Bursse, 1622." The next quarto copy appeared in 1630, seven years after the publication of the first folio: the title-page varies from that of the quarto of 1622 only in the imprint, which reads:—"by A. M. for Richard Hawkins," &c.

Upon the supposition that a passage in Act III. Sc. 4,—

"—— the hearts of old gave hands;
But our new heraldry is hands, not hearts,"—

was a satirical allusion to the creation of the new order of Baronets by James I. in 1611, Malone at first assigned the composition of "Othello" to that year; he subsequently attributed it to 1604, because, as he remarks, "we know it to have been acted in that year;" but he has given no evidence in support of his assertion. Modern research, however, has supplied this evidence. In the "Extracts from the Accounts of the Revels at Court," edited by Mr. P. Cunningham for the Shakespeare Society, there is an entry, beginning November 1st, 1604, and terminating October 31st, 1605, from which it appears that the King's Players performed the play of *The Moor of Venis* at the Banqueting-house at Whitehall on the 1st of November (*Hallamas* Day), 1604. Mr. Collier, indeed, cites an extract from "The Egerton Papers," to show that "Othello" was acted for the entertainment of Queen Elizabeth, at the residence of Lord Ellesmere (then Sir Thomas Egerton, Lord Keeper of the Great Seal), at Harefield, on the 6th of August, 1602; but the suspicion long entertained that the Shakespearian documents in that collection are modern fabrications having now deepened almost into certainty, the extract in question is of no historical value. The earliest authentic record of the performance of "Othello," then, is that in the *Accounts of the Revels*. Six years later, we know from an interesting diary first pointed out by Sir Frederic Madden (see Note (4), p. 689, Vol. I.), that the play was acted at the Globe on the 30th of April, 1610. And upon the authority of Vertue's MS. we find that it retained its popularity in 1613, early in which year it was acted at the Court.

The story upon which this tragedy is founded is a novel in Cinthio's *Hecatommithi, Parte Prima, Deca Terza, Novella* 7, bearing the following explanatory title:—" *Un capitano Moro piglia per mogliera una cittadina Venetiana: un suo alfieri l'accusa di adulterio al marito; cerca che l'alfieri uccida colui ch'egli credea l'adultero: il capitano uccide la moglie, è accusato dall' alfieri, non confessa il Moro, ma essendovi chiari inditii è bandito; e lo scelerato alfieri, credendo nuocere ad altri, procaccia a se la morte miseramente.*" There is a French translation of Cinthio's novels by Gabriel Chappuys, Paris, 1584; but no English one of a date as early as the age of Shakespeare has come down to us.

" The time of this play may be ascertained from the following circumstances. Selymus the Second formed his design against Cyprus in 1569, and took it in 1571. This was the only attempt the Turks ever made upon that island after it came into the hands of the Venetians, (which was in the year 1473,) wherefore the time must fall in with some part of that interval. We learn from the play that there was a junction of the Turkish fleet at Rhodes, in order for the invasion of Cyprus, that it first came sailing towards Cyprus, then went to Rhodes, there met another squadron, and then resumed its way to Cyprus. These are real historical facts, which happened when Mustapha Selymus's general attacked Cyprus in May, 1570, which therefore is the true period of this performance. See Knolles's *History of the Turks*, p. 838, 846, 867."—Reed.

Persons Represented.

Duke *of* Venice.

Brabantio, *a Senator.*

Other Senators.

Gratiano, *Brother to* Brabantio.

Ludovico, *Kinsman to* Brabantio.

Othello, *a noble* Moor *in the service of the* Venetian *State.*

Cassio, *his Lieutenant.*

Iago, *his Ancient.*

Roderigo, *a* Venetian *Gentleman.*

Montano, Othello's *Predecessor in the Government of* Cyprus.

Clown, *Servant to* Othello.

Desdemona, *Daughter to* Brabantio, *and Wife to* Othello.

Emilia, *Wife to* Iago.

Bianca, *Mistress to* Cassio.

Sailor, Messengers, Herald, Officers, Gentlemen, Musicians, and Attendants.

SCENE,—*The first Act in* Venice; *during the rest of the play, at a Sea-port in* Cyprus.

ACT I.

SCENE I.—Venice. *A Street.*

Enter RODERIGO *and* IAGO.

ROD. Tush!* never tell me; I take it much unkindly
That thou, Iago, who hast had my purse
As if the strings were thine, shouldst know of this,—

IAGO. 'S blood,† but you 'll not hear me;—
If ever I did dream of such a matter,
Abhor me.

ROD. Thou told'st me, thou didst hold him in thy hate.

(*) First folio omits, *Tush.* (†) First folio omits, *'S blood.*

[a] And, in conclusion,—] This hemistich is not found in the folio 1623.

IAGO. Despise me, if I do not. Three great ones of the city,
In personal suit to make me his lieutenant,
Off-capp'd* to him:—and, by the faith of man,
I know my price, I am worth no worse a place:—
But he, as loving his own pride and purposes,
Evades them with a bombast circumstance,
Horribly stuff'd with epithets of war,
And, in conclusion,[a]
Nonsuits my mediators; for, *Certes,* says he,
I have already chose my officer.
And what was he?

(*) The quartos, *Oft capt.*

Forsooth, a great arithmetician,
One Michael Cassio, a Florentine,[a]
A fellow almost damn'd in a fair wife;[b]
That never set a squadron in the field,
Nor the division of a battle[c] knows
More than a spinster; unless the bookish theoric,
Wherein the tongued[d] consuls can propose
As masterly as he: mere prattle, without practice,
Is all his soldiership. But he, sir, had the election:
And I,—of whom his eyes had seen the proof
At Rhodes, at Cyprus, and on other grounds
Christian* and heathen,—must be be-lee'd[e] and calm'd
By debitor-and-creditor:[f] this counter-caster,
He, in good time, must his lieutenant be,
And I, (God† bless the mark!) his Moorship's ancient!

ROD. By heaven, I rather would have been his hangman.

IAGO. Why, there 's no remedy; 't is the curse of service,
Preferment goes by letter and affection,
And not by old gradation, where each second
Stood heir to the first. Now, sir, be judge yourself,
Whether I in any just term am affin'd[g]
To love the Moor.

ROD. I would not follow him, then.

IAGO. O, sir, content you;
I follow him to serve my turn upon him:
We cannot all be masters, nor all masters
Cannot be truly follow'd. You shall mark
Many a duteous and knee-crooking knave,[h]
That, doting on his own obsequious[i] bondage,
Wears out his time, much like his master's ass,
For nought but provender; and, when he 's old, cashier'd:
Whip me such honest knaves. Others there are,
Who, trimm'd in forms and visages[k] of duty,
Keep yet their hearts attending on themselves;
And, throwing but shows of service on their lords,
Do well thrive by them, and, when they have lin'd their coats,
Do themselves homage: these fellows have some soul;
And such a one do I profess myself. For, sir,
It is as sure as you are Roderigo,
Were I the Moor, I would not be Iago:
In following him, I follow but myself;
Heaven is my judge, not I for love and duty,
But seeming so, for my peculiar end:
For when my outward action doth demonstrate
The native act and figure of my heart
In compliment extern, 't is not long after
But I will wear my heart upon my sleeve
For daws to peck at. I am not what I am.

ROD. What a full[l] fortune does the thicklips owe,
If he can carry 't thus!

IAGO. Call up her father,
Rouse him:—make after him, poison his delight,
Proclaim him in the streets; incense her kinsmen,
And, though he in a fertile climate dwell,
Plague him with flies: though that his joy be joy,
Yet throw such chances[m] of vexation on 't,
As it may lose some colour.

ROD. Here is her father's house; I'll call aloud.

IAGO. Do; with like timorous accent, and dire yell

(*) First folio, *Christen'd*. (†) First folio omits, *God*.

[a] — a Florentine,—] Are we quite assured Iago means by this expression merely that Cassio was a native of Florence? The system of book-keeping called *Italian Book-keeping* came, as is well known, originally from Florence; and he may not improbably use "Florentine," as he employs "*arithmetician*," "*debitor-and-creditor*," and "*counter-caster*," in a derogatory sense to denote the mercantile origin and training which he chooses to attribute to his rival.

[b] A fellow almost damn'd in a fair wife,—] This line has perplexed the commentators not a little. Tyrwhitt's conjecture that "wife" was a misprint of *life*, and that the allusion is to the judgment denounced in the Gospel against those *of whom all men speak well*, was in high favour at one time, but has long been disregarded; the impression now is that Iago refers to a report, which he subsequently speaks of, that Cassio was on the point of marrying the courtezan Bianca. To this it is objected, and the objection seems unanswerable, that there is no reason for supposing Cassio had ever seen Bianca until they met in Cyprus. We doubt, indeed, the possibility of eliciting a satisfactory meaning from the line as it stands, and, in despair of doing so, have sometimes thought the poet must have written,—

"A fellow almost damn'd in a *fair-wife*;"

That is to say, a fellow by habit of reckoning debased almost *into a market-woman*. *In* of old was commonly used for *into*; we even still employ it so, as in the expression *to fall in love*. Compare, too, "Troilus and Cressida," Act III. Sc. 3,—

"Why, he stalks up and down like a peacock,—a stride and a stand, ruminates, like an hostess that hath no arithmetic but her brain to set down her reckoning."

[c] — *of a* battle—] Of an *army*. So in "Henry V." (Chorus) Act IV.—

"*Each battle* sees the other's umber'd face:"

And in "Richard III." Act V. Sc. 3,—

"—— we will follow
In the *main battle*."

[d] — *the* tongued *consuls*—] So the folio and the quarto 1630; the quarto of 1622 has, "*toged*." The former, as Boswell observes, agrees better with the words "mere *prattle*," &c.; but "*toged*" may have sprung from the common adage, *Cedant arma togæ*, and is equally appropriate.

[e] — *must be* be-lee'd—] The quarto 1622 has, "must be *led*," &c.; this and the imperfect measure of the line in other copies might lead us to suspect the author wrote, "must be *lee'd* and calm'd," &c.

[f] — debitor-and-creditor:] The title of certain old treatises upon commercial book-keeping. So in "Cymbeline," Act V. Sc. 4,—"You have no true debitor-and-creditor but it."

[g] — *in any just term* am affin'd—] By any moral obligation am *bound*, &c.

[h] — knave,—] "*Knave*" carries no opprobrious meaning here; it is simply *servitor*.

[i] — obsequious *bondage*,—] That is, *obedient, submissive* thraldom.

[k] *Who*, trimm'd in forms and visages *of duty*,—] Who, dress'd in *shapes and masks* of duty, &c. Mr. Collier proposes to read,—

"—— in forms and *usages* of duty,"

which the expression "*trimm'd*" negatives at once.

[l] *What a* full *fortune*—] The folio has "*fall*" for "*full*," a reading Mr. Knight prefers, although in "Cymbeline," Act V. Sc. 4, we find,—

"Our pleasure his *full fortune* doth confine;"

in "Antony and Cleopatra," Act IV. Sc. 15,—"*full-fortun'd* Cæsar;" and in D'Avenant's "Law against Lovers," Act III. Sc. 1,—"She has a *full fortune*."

[m] — chances *of vexation*—] *Crosses*, or *casualties*; the quartos read, "*changes*."

As when (by night and negligence) the fire
Is spied [a] in populous cities.

ROD. What, ho! Brabantio! Signior Brabantio, ho! [thieves!

IAGO. Awake! what, ho! Brabantio! thieves!
Look to your house, your daughter, and your bags!
Thieves! thieves!

BRABANTIO *appears above, at a window.*

BRA. What is the reason of this terrible summons?
What is the matter there?

ROD. Signior, is all your family within?

IAGO. Are your doors lock'd?

BRA. Why, wherefore ask you this?

IAGO. Zounds,* sir, you're robb'd; for shame, put on your gown;
Your heart is burst, you have lost half your soul;
Even now, now, very now, an old black ram
Is tupping your white ewe. Arise, arise!
Awake the snorting citizens with the bell,
Or else the devil will make a grandsire of you:
Arise! I say.

BRA. What, have you lost your wits?

ROD. Most reverend signior, do you know my voice?

BRA. Not I; what are you?

ROD. My name is Roderigo.

BRA. The worser welcome
I have charg'd thee not to haunt about my doors:
In honest plainness thou hast heard me say
My daughter is not for thee; and now, in madness,
(Being full of supper and distempering draughts,)
Upon malicious bravery,* dost thou come
To start my quiet.

ROD. Sir, sir, sir,—

BRA. But thou must needs be sure,
My spirit† and my place have in them‡ power
To make this bitter to thee.

ROD. Patience, good sir.

(*) First folio omits, *Zounds.*

(*) First folio, *knaverie.* (†) First folio, *spirits.* (‡) First folio, *their.*

a As when (by night and negligence) the fire
Is spied, &c.]
That is, when the fire caused by night and negligence. But query as Warburton suggested, did the poet write,—"Is *spred*," &c.?

BRA. What tell'st thou me of robbing? this is Venice;
My house is not a grange.[a]

ROD. Most grave Brabantio,
In simple and pure soul I come to you.

IAGO. Zounds,* sir, you are one of those that will not serve God, if the devil bid you. Because we come to do you service, and you think we are ruffians,[b] you'll have your daughter covered with a Barbary horse; you'll have your nephews neigh to you; you'll have coursers for cousins, and gennets for germans.

BRA. What profane wretch art thou?

IAGO. I am one, sir, that comes to tell you, your daughter and the Moor are now† making the beast with two backs.

BRA. Thou art a villain.

IAGO. You are—a senator.

BRA. This thou shalt answer; I know thee, Roderigo.

ROD. Sir, I will answer any thing. But, I beseech you,
If 't be your pleasure and most wise consent
(As partly I find it is) that your fair daughter,
At this odd-even and dull watch o' the night,
Transported,[c] with no worse nor better guard
But with a knave of common hire, a gondolier,
To the gross clasps of a lascivious Moor,—
If this be known to you, and your allowance,
We then have done you bold and saucy wrongs;
But, if you know not this, my manners tell me
We have your wrong rebuke. Do not believe
That, from the sense[d] of all civility,
I thus would play and trifle with your reverence:
Your daughter,—if you have not given her leave,—
I say again, hath made a gross revolt;
Tying her duty, beauty, wit, and fortunes,
In an extravagant[e] and wheeling[f] stranger
Of here and everywhere. Straight satisfy yourself:[g]
If she be in her chamber or your house,
Let loose on me the justice of the state
For thus deluding you.

BRA. Strike on the tinder, ho!
Give me a taper!—call up all my people!—
This accident is not unlike my dream:
Belief of it oppresses me already.—
Light, I say! light! [*Exit from above.*

IAGO. Farewell; for I must leave you:
It seems not meet, nor wholesome to my place,
To be produc'd* (as, if I stay, I shall)
Against the Moor: for, I do know, the state,—
However this may gall him with some check,—
Cannot with safety cast him; for he's embark'd
With such loud reason to the Cyprus' wars,
Which even now stand in act, that, for their souls,
Another of his fathom they have none
To lead their business: in which regard,
Though I do hate him as I do hell-pains,†
Yet, for necessity of present life,
I must show out a flag and sign of love,
Which is indeed but sign. That you shall surely find him,
Lead to the Sagittary (1) the raised search;
And there will I be with him. So, farewell.
[*Exit.*

Enter, below, BRABANTIO, *and* Servants *with torches.*

BRA. It is too true an evil: gone she is!
And what's to come of my despised time
Is nought but bitterness.—Now, Roderigo,
Where didst thou see her?—O, unhappy girl!—
With the Moor, say'st thou?—Who would be a father!—
How didst thou know 't was she?—O, she deceives me
Past thought!—What said she to you?—Get more tapers;
Raise all my kindred.—Are they married, think you?

ROD. Truly, I think they are.

BRA. O, heaven!—How got she out?—O, treason of the blood!—
Fathers, from hence trust not your daughters' minds
By what you see them act.—Are there not charms
By which the property of youth and maidhood
May be abus'd? Have you not read, Roderigo,
Of some such thing?

ROD. Yes, sir, I have indeed.

BRA. Call up my brother.—O, would you had had her!—
Some one way, some another.—Do you know
Where we may apprehend her and the Moor?

(*) First folio omits, *Zounds*. (†) First folio omits, *now*.

(*) First folio, *producted*. (†) First folio, *apines*.

a —— this is Venice;
My *house is not a* grange.]

Grange, Warton remarks, is strictly and properly the farm of a monastery. But in Lincolnshire, and in other northern counties, they call every lone house, or farm which stands solitary, a *grange*. What Brabantio means, then, is,—I am in a populous city, not in a place where robbery can be easily committed.

b — ruffians,—] Here *ruffian* is employed in its secondary sense of *roisterer*, *swash-buckler*, and the like, though its primary meaning undoubtedly was, *pander;* the Latin, "leno," the Italian, "roffiano."

c Transported,—] That is, *transported herself*. Capell, however, inserts *Be* before *transported*.

d — from the sense—] *Contrary*, or *opposed to* the sense, &c.

e — extravagant—] *Vagabond*.

f — wheeling—] Mr. Collier's annotator proposes, *wheedling* we should much prefer to read,—

"—— an extravagant and *whirling* stranger
Of here and everywhere."

g Straight satisfy yourself:] This line and the sixteen preceding lines are not in the quarto 1622.

ROD. I think I can discover him, if you please
To get good guard, and go along with me.
BRA. Pray you, lead on. At every house I'll call;
I may command at most;—Get weapons, ho!
And raise some special officers of night.*—
On, good Roderigo;—I'll deserve your pains.
[*Exeunt.*

SCENE II.—*The same. Another Street.*

Enter OTHELLO, IAGO, *and* Attendants *with torches.*

IAGO. Though in the trade of war I have slain men,
Yet do I hold it very stuff o' the conscience,
To do no contriv'd murder: I lack iniquity
Sometime to do me service. Nine or ten times
I had thought to have yerk'd him here under the ribs.
OTH. 'T is better as it is.
IAGO. Nay, but he prated,
And spoke such scurvy and provoking terms
Against your honour,
That, with the little godliness I have,
I did full hard forbear him. But, I pray you, sir,
Are you fast married? Be assur'd of this,
That the magnifico is much belov'd;
And hath, in his[a] effect, a voice potential
As double as the duke's: he will divorce you;
Or put upon you what restraint and† grievance
The law (with all his might to enforce it on)
Will give him cable.
OTH. Let him do his spite:
My services, which I have done the signiory,
Shall out-tongue his complaints. 'T is yet to know,—
Which, when I know that boasting is an honour,
I shall promulgate,—I fetch my life and being
From men of royal siege; and my demerits[b]
May speak, unbonneted, to as proud a fortune
As this that I have reach'd: for know, Iago,
But that I love the gentle Desdemona,
I would not my unhoused free condition
Put into circumscription and confine,
For the sea's worth. But, look! what lights come yond?
IAGO. Those are the raised father and his friends:
You were best go in.
OTH. Not I; I must be found
My parts, my title, and my perfect soul,
Shall manifest me rightly. Is it they?
IAGO. By Janus, I think no.

Enter CASSIO, *and certain* Officers *with torches.*

OTH. The servants of the duke! and my lieutenant!—
The goodness of the night upon you, friends!
What is the news?
CAS. The duke does greet you, general;
And he requires your haste-post-haste appearance,
Even on the instant.
OTH. What is the matter, think you?
CAS. Something from Cyprus, as I may divine:
It is a business of some heat; the galleys
Have sent a dozen sequent messengers
This very night at one another's heels;
And many of the consuls, rais'd and met,
Are at the duke's already. You have been hotly call'd for;
When, being not at your lodging to be found.
The senate hath sent about three several quests
To search you out.
OTH. 'T is well I am found by you.
I will but spend a word here in the house,
And go with you. [*Exit.*
CAS. Ancient, what makes he here
IAGO. Faith, he to-night hath boarded a land-carack;[c]
If it prove lawful prize, he's made for ever.
CAS. I do not understand.
IAGO. He's married.
CAS. To who?

Re-enter OTHELLO.

IAGO. Marry, to—Come, captain, will you go?
OTH. Have with you.
CAS. Here comes another troop to seek for you.

(*) First folio, *might*. (†) First folio, *or*.

[a] — his *effect*,—] *His* is employed for the then scarce known *its* and refers to *voice*.

[b] —— and my demerits
May speak, unbonneted, to as proud a fortune
As this that I have reach'd:]

Demerit now signifies only *ill* desert; in Shakespeare's day it was used indiscriminately for good or ill deserving. In the present instance it is apparently employed in the good sense, for Othello could hardly mean that his blemishes might stand without concealment beside the dignity he had achieved. The import we take to be,—my services when revealed (*unbonneted*), may *aspire* or *lay claim* to (*may speak to*) as proud a fortune as this which I have attained. Mr. Fuseli, however, has given another explanation, founded on the fact that at Venice the *bonnet* has always been a badge of patrician honours:—I am his equal or superior in rank; and were it not so, such are my demerits, that, *unbonneted*, without the addition of patrician or senatorial dignity, they may speak to as proud a fortune, &c. But here, too, it is indispensable for the integrity of the passage that "*speak to*" be understood in the sense just mentioned of *aspire*, or *lay claim* to.

[c] — a land-carack;] A *carack* was a ship of large burden, like the Spanish galleon; but the compound in the text appears to have been a dissolute expression, the meaning of which may be gathered from the following:—

"Here to his *Land-Friggat* hee's ferried by Charon,
He bords her: a service a hot and a rare one."
Verses prefixed to *Coryat's Crudities*.

IAGO. It is Brabantio:—general, be advis'd;
He comes to bad intent.

Enter BRABANTIO, RODERIGO, *and* Officers *with torches.*

OTH. Holla! stand there!
ROD. Signior, it is the Moor.

BRA. Down with him, thief!
[*They draw on both sides.*
IAGO. You, Roderigo! come, sir, I am for you.
OTH. Keep up your bright swords, for the dew will rust them.—
Good signior, you shall more command with years
Than with your weapons.

BRA. O, thou foul thief, where hast thou stow'd my daughter?
Damn'd as thou art, thou hast enchanted her;
For I'll refer me to all things of sense,
If she in chains of magic were not bound,[a]
Whether a maid so tender, fair, and happy,
So opposite to marriage, that she shunn'd
The wealthy curled darlings[b] of our nation,
Would ever have, to incur a general mock,
Run from her guardage to the sooty bosom
Of such a thing as thou,—to fear, not to delight.
Judge me the world, if 't is not gross in sense
That thou hast practis'd on her with foul charms;
Abus'd her delicate youth with drugs or minerals
That waken[c] motion:—I'll have 't disputed on; (2)
'T is probable, and palpable to thinking.
I therefore apprehend and do attach thee[d]
For an abuser of the world, a practiser
Of arts inhibited and out of warrant.—
Lay hold upon him; if he do resist,
Subdue him at his peril.

OTH. Hold your hands!
Both you of my inclining, and the rest:
Were it my cue to fight, I should have known it
Without a prompter.—Where* will you that I go
To answer this your charge?

BRA. To prison; till fit time
Of law, and course of direct session,
Call thee to answer.

OTH. What if I† do obey?
How may the duke be therewith satisfied,
Whose messengers are here about my side,
Upon some present business of the state,
To bring me to him?

1 OFF. 'T is true, most worthy signior,
The duke's in council, and your noble self,
I am sure is sent for.

BRA. How! the duke in council
In this time of the night!—Bring him away:
Mine's not an idle cause: the duke himself,
Or any of my brothers of the state,
Cannot but feel this wrong as 't were their own;
For if such actions may have passage free,
Bond-slaves and pagans shall our statesmen be.
[*Exeunt.*

SCENE III.—*The same. A Council Chamber.*

The DUKE, *and* Senators, *sitting;* Officers *attending.*

DUKE. There is no composition in these news
That gives them credit.

1 SEN. Indeed, they are disproportioned;
My letters say a hundred and seven galleys.

DUKE. And mine, a hundred forty.

2 SEN. And mine, two hundred:
But though they jump not on a just account,—
As in these cases, where the aim[e] reports,
'T is oft with difference,—yet do they all confirm
A Turkish fleet, and bearing up to Cyprus.

DUKE. Nay, it is possible enough to judgment
I do not so secure[f] me in the error,
But the main article I do approve
In fearful sense.

SAILOR. [*Without.*] What ho! what ho! what ho!

1 OFF. A messenger from the galleys.

Enter a Sailor.

DUKE. Now, what's the business?

SAIL. The Turkish preparation makes for Rhodes;
So was I bid report here to the state,
By signior Angelo.

DUKE. How say you by this change?

1 SEN. This cannot be,
By no assay of reason; 't is a pageant,
To keep us in false gaze. When we consider
The importancy of Cyprus to the Turk;
And let ourselves again but understand,
That as it more concerns the Turk than Rhodes,
So may he with more facile question bear it,[g]
For that it stands not in such warlike brace,
But altogether lacks the abilities
That Rhodes is dress'd in;—if we make thought of this,
We must not think the Turk is so unskilful,
To leave that latest which concerns him first,

(*) First folio, *Whether*. (†) First folio omits, *I*.

[a] If she in chains of magic were not bound,—] A line not found in the quarto 1622.

[b] — curled darlings—] "*Curled*" was an epithet characteristic of gentility. Thus D'Avenant, in "The Just Italian," Act III. Sc. 1,—

"— the *curl'd* and silken Nobles of the Town."

The folio reads, "*dearlings*."

[c] *That* waken *motion*:—] So Hanmer; the original having, "That *weakens* motion," &c. The upholders of the old reading contend that Brabantio's accusation is that the Moor, by magical devices and the administering of drugs or minerals, had weakened those natural impulses of youth and maidhood in his daughter, which, uncontrolled, would have inclined to those of her own clime, complexion, and degree; but this is expressly contradicted by what he has himself just said,—

"—— a maid so tender, fair, and happy,
So opposite to marriage, that she shunn'd
The wealthy curled darlings of our nation."

We therefore readily accept the easy emendation Hanmer offers. Brabantio's grievance, it is plain, was not that Othello had, by charms and medicines, abated the motions of Desdemona's sense, but that he had aroused and stimulated them.

[d] — and do attach thee—] The passage beginning,—"Judge me the world," to the above words inclusive, is not in the quarto 1622.

[e] — *where the* aim *reports*,—] To *aim* is to *conjecture* or *surmise*.

[f] *I do not so* secure *me in the error*,—] I do not so *over-confidently* build on the discrepancy, but that, &c.

[g] So may he with more facile question bear it,—] The remainder of the speech, after this line, is found only in the folio 1623 and the quarto 1630.

Neglecting an attempt of ease and gain,
To wake and wage a danger profitless.
DUKE. Nay, in all confidence, he 's not for Rhodes.
1 OFF. Here is more news.

Enter a Messenger.

MESS. The Ottomites, reverend and gracious,
Steering with due course toward the isle of Rhodes,
Have there injointed them with an after fleet.
1 SEN. Ay, so I thought.—How many, as you guess?
MESS. Of thirty sail: and now they do re-stem
Their backward course, bearing with frank appearance
Their purposes toward Cyprus.—Signior Montano,
Your trusty and most valiant servitor,
With his free duty, recommends you thus,
And prays you to believe[a] him.

[a] — to believe him.] Capell suggested, "to *relieve* him," and Mr. Collier's annotator follows suit.

DUKE. 'T is certain, then, for Cyprus.—
Marcus Luccicos, is not he in town?
1 SEN. He 's now in Florence.
DUKE. Write from us to him, post-post-haste despatch.
1 SEN. Here comes Brabantio and the valiant Moor.

Enter BRABANTIO, OTHELLO, IAGO, RODERIGO, *and* Officers.

DUKE. Valiant Othello, we must straight employ you
Against the general enemy Ottoman.—(3)
I did not see you; welcome, gentle signior:
[*To* BRABANTIO.
We lack'd your counsel and your help to-night.
BRA. So did I yours. Good your grace, pardon me;
Neither my place, nor aught I heard of business,
Hath rais'd me from my bed; nor doth the general care
Take hold on me; for my particular grief
Is of so flood-gate and o'erbearing nature

That it engluts and swallows other sorrows,
And it is still itself.
DUKE. Why, what 's the matter?
BRA. My daughter! O, my daughter!
DUKE *and* SEN. Dead?
BRA. Ay, to me;
She is abus'd, stol'n from me, and corrupted
By spells and medicines bought of mountebanks;
For nature so preposterously to err,
Being not deficient, blind, or lame of sense,
Sans witchcraft could not.
DUKE. Whoe'er he be that, in this foul proceeding,
Hath thus beguil'd your daughter of herself,
And you of her, the bloody book of law
You shall yourself read in the bitter letter,
After your own sense; yea, though our proper son
Stood in your action.
BRA. Humbly I thank your grace.
Here is the man, this Moor; whom now, it seems,
Your special mandate, for the state-affairs,
Hath hither brought.
DUKE *and* SEN. We are very sorry for 't.
DUKE. What, in your own part, can you say to this? [*To* OTHELLO.
BRA. Nothing, but this is so.
OTH. Most potent, grave, and reverend signiors,
My very noble and approv'd good masters,—
That I have ta'en away this old man's daughter,
It is most true; true, I have married her;
The very head and front of my offending
Hath this extent, no more. Rude am I in my speech,
And little bless'd with the soft phrase of peace;
For since these arms of mine had seven years' pith,
Till now some nine moons wasted, they have us'd
Their dearest[a] action in the tented field;
And little of this great world can I speak,
More than pertains to feats of broils and battle;
And therefore little shall I grace my cause
In speaking for myself. Yet, by your gracious patience,
I will a round unvarnish'd tale deliver
Of my whole course of love; what drugs, what charms,
What conjuration, and what mighty magic,—
For such proceeding I am charg'd withal,—
I won his daughter.
BRA. A maiden never bold;
Of spirit so still and quiet, that her motion
Blush'd at herself: and she,—in spite of nature,
Of years, of country, credit, every thing,—
To fall in love with what she fear'd to look on!
It is a judgment maim'd* and most imperfect,
That will confess perfection so could err
Against all rules of nature; and must be driven
To find out practices of cunning hell,
Why this should be. I therefore vouch again,
That with some mixtures powerful o'er the blood,
Or with some dram conjur'd to this effect,
He wrought upon her.

[a] *Their dearest action*—] See note (b), p. 398.

(*) First folio, *main'd*.

DUKE. To vouch this, is no proof,
Without more wider and more overt test
Than these thin habits and poor likelihoods
Of modern seeming do prefer against him.[a]
1 SEN. But, Othello, speak:
Did you by indirect and forced courses
Subdue and poison this young maid's affections?
Or came it by request, and such fair question
As soul to soul affordeth?
OTH. I do beseech you,
Send for the lady to the Sagittary,
And let her speak of me before her father:
If you do find me foul in her report,
The trust, the office, I do hold of you,[b]
Not only take away, but let your sentence
Even fall upon my life.
DUKE. Fetch Desdemona hither.
OTH. Ancient, conduct them; you best know the place.—
[*Exeunt* IAGO *and* Attendants.
And, till she come, as truly as to heaven
I do confess the vices of my blood,
So justly to your grave ears I'll present
How I did thrive in this fair lady's love,
And she in mine.
DUKE. Say it, Othello.
OTH. Her father lov'd me; oft invited me;
Still question'd me the story of my life,
From year to year,—the battles,* sieges, fortunes,†
That I have pass'd.
I ran it through, even from my boyish days,
To the very moment that he bade me tell it:
Wherein I spake‡ of most disastrous chances;
Of moving accidents by flood and field;
Of hair-breadth scapes i' the imminent-deadly breach;
Of being taken by the insolent foe
And sold to slavery; of my redemption thence,
And portance in my travel's§ history:
Wherein of antres vast, and deserts idle,
Rough quarries, rocks and‖ hills whose heads¶ touch heaven,
It was my hint to speak,—such was the** process;—
And of the Cannibals that each other eat,
The Anthropophagi, and men whose heads
Do grow[c] beneath their shoulders.(4) This to hear[d]
Would Desdemona seriously incline:
But still the house affairs would draw her thence;††
Which ever as she could with haste despatch,
She'd come again, and with a greedy ear
Devour up my discourse:—which I observing,
Took once a pliant hour, and found good means
To draw from her a prayer of earnest heart
That I would all my pilgrimage dilate,
Whereof by parcels she had something heard,
But not intentively:* I did consent;
And often did beguile her of her tears,
When I did speak of some distressful stroke
That my youth suffer'd. My story being done,
She gave me for my pains a world of sighs:†
She swore,—in faith, 't was strange, 't was passing strange;
'T was pitiful, 't was wondrous pitiful:—
She wish'd she had not heard it;—yet she wish'd
That heaven had made her such a man;—she thank'd me;
And bade me, if I had a friend that lov'd her,
I should but teach him how to tell my story,
And that would woo her. Upon this hint I spake:—
She lov'd me for the dangers I had pass'd;
And I lov'd her that she did pity them.
This only is the witchcraft I have us'd;—
Here comes the lady, let her witness it.

Enter DESDEMONA, IAGO, *and* Attendants.

DUKE. I think this tale would win my daughter too.—
Good Brabantio,
Take up this mangled matter at the best:
Men do their broken weapons rather use
Than their bare hands.
BRA. I pray you, hear her speak;
If she confess that she was half the wooer,
Destruction on my head, if my bad blame
Light on the man!—Come hither, gentle mistress:
Do you perceive in all this noble company
Where most you owe obedience?
DES. My noble father,
I do perceive here a divided duty:
To you, I am bound for life and education;
My life and education both do learn me
How to respect you; you are the lord of duty,—
I am hitherto your daughter: but here's my husband;
And so much duty as my mother show'd
To you, preferring you before her father,
So much I challenge that I may profess
Due to the Moor, my lord.
BRA. God be with you!—I have done.—
Please it your grace, on to the state affairs;—
I had rather to adopt a child than get it.—
Come hither, Moor:

(*) First folio, *Battaile*. (†) First folio, *Fortune*.
(‡) First folio, *spoke*. (§) First folio, *Travellours*.
(‖) First folio omits, *and*. (¶) First folio, *head*.
(**) First folio, *my*. (††) First folio, *hence*.

(*) First folio, *instinctively*. (†) First folio, *kisses*.

a — do prefer against him.] In the folio, the prefix "*Duke*" having been inadvertently omitted, this speech forms part of the one preceding.

b The trust, the office, I do hold of you,—] This line is not found in the earlier quarto.

c Do grow beneath—] The folio reads, "*Grew* beneath," &c.

d This to hear—] In the folio, "*These things* to hear," &c.

I here do give thee that with all my heart,
Which, but thou hast already, with all my heart[a]
I would keep from thee.—For your sake, jewel,
I am glad at soul I have no other child;
For thy escape would teach me tyranny,
To hang clogs on them.—I have done, my lord.

DUKE. Let me speak like yourself;[b] and lay a sentence,
Which, as a grise, or step, may help these lovers
Into your favour.*
When remedies are past, the griefs are ended
By seeing the worst, which late on hopes depended.
To mourn a mischief that is past and gone
Is the next way to draw new mischief on.
What cannot be preserv'd, when Fortune takes,
Patience her injury a mockery makes.

[a] Which, but thou hast already, with all my heart—] A line wanting in the earlier quarto.

(*) First folio omits the words, *Into your favour.*

[b] Let me speak like yourself;] He perhaps means, sententiously

The robb'd that smiles, steals something from the thief;
He robs himself that spends a bootless grief.

BRA. So let the Turk of Cyprus us beguile,
We lose it not, so long as we can smile.
He bears the sentence well, that nothing bears
But the free comfort which from thence he hears;
But he bears both the sentence and the sorrow,
That, to pay grief, must of poor patience borrow.
These sentences, to sugar, or to gall,
Being strong on both sides, are equivocal:
But words are words; I never yet did hear
That the bruis'd heart was pierced through the ear.—[a]
I humbly beseech you, proceed to the affairs of state.

DUKE. The Turk with a most mighty preparation makes for Cyprus:—Othello, the fortitude of the place is best known to you; and though we have there a substitute of most allowed sufficiency, yet opinion, a* sovereign mistress of effects, throws a more safer voice on you: you must therefore be content to slubber the gloss of your new fortunes with this more stubborn and boisterous expedition.

OTH. The tyrant custom, most grave senators,
Hath made the flinty and steel couch† of war
My thrice-driven bed of down: I do agnize[b]
A natural and prompt alacrity
I find in hardness: and do undertake
These‡ present wars against the Ottomites.
Most humbly, therefore, bending to your state,
I crave fit disposition for my wife;
Due reference of place and exhibition;
With such accommodation and besort
As levels with her breeding.

DUKE. If you please,
Be 't at her father's.[c]

BRA. I 'll not have it so.

OTH. Nor I.

DES. Nor I; I would not there reside,[d]
To put my father in impatient thoughts
By being in his eye. Most gracious duke,
To my unfolding lend your prosperous ear;
And let me find a charter in your voice,
To assist my simpleness.

DUKE. What would you, Desdemona?

DES. That I did love the Moor to live with him,
My downright violence and storm* of fortunes
May trumpet to the world: my heart's subdu'd
Even to the very quality of my lord:[e]
I saw Othello's visage in his mind;
And to his honours and his valiant parts
Did I my soul and fortunes consecrate.
So that, dear lords, if I be left behind,
A moth of peace, and he go to the war,
The rites for which† I love him are bereft me,
And I a heavy interim shall support
By his dear[f] absence. Let me go with him.

OTH. Let her have your voice.[g]
Vouch with me, heaven, I therefore beg it not,
To please the palate of my appetite;
Nor to comply with heat (the young affects
In me‡ defunct) and proper satisfaction;
But to be free and bounteous to her mind:
And heaven defend your good souls, that you think
I will your serious and great business scant
For§ she is with me: no, when light-wing'd toys
Of feather'd Cupid seel with wanton dulness
My speculative and offic'd instruments,[h]
That my disports corrupt and taint my business,
Let housewives make a skillet of my helm,
And all indign and base adversities
Make head against my estimation!

DUKE. Be it as you shall privately determine,
Either for her stay or going: the affair cries haste,
And speed must answer it.

1 SEN. You must away to-night.[i]

OTH. With all my heart.

DUKE. At nine i' the morning here we 'll meet again.—
Othello, leave some officer behind,
And he shall our commission bring to you;
With‖ such things else of quality and respect
As doth import you.

OTH. So please your grace, my ancient,
A man he is of honesty and trust,

(*) First folio inserts, *more*. (†) First folio, *Coach*. (‡) Old text, *This*.

a *That the bruis'd heart was* pierced *through the ear*,—] Following Warburton, some editors read *pieced;* but Brabantio is quoting a phrase of the age. Thus Spenser:—

"Her words * * * *
Which passing through the eares would *pierce* the heart."
The Faerie Queene, B. IV. C. 8, Stanza xxvi.

So also Drayton, in the *Baron's Warrs*, Stanza xxxvi.:—

"Are not your hearts yet *pierced* through your Ears?"

b — agnize—] *Acknowledge.*

c If you please,
Be 't at her father's.]

The folio has—"Why at her Fathers?"

d Nor I; I would not there reside, &c.] In the folio,—"Nor would I there recide," &c.

e —— my heart 's subdu'd
Even to the very quality of my lord:]

"*Quality* here means *profession*. 'I am so much enamoured of Othello, that I am even willing to endure all the inconveniences incident to a *military life*, and to attend him to the wars.'"—MALONE.

(*) Quarto 1622, *scorne*. (†) First folio, *why*. (‡) Old text, *my*. (§) First folio, *When*. (‖) First folio, *And*.

f — dear *absence*.] See note (6), p. 398.

g Let her have your voice.] The folio lection; that of the quarto 1662 is,—

"Your voices lords: beseech you let her will
Have a free way."

h My speculative and offic'd instruments,—] By "speculative and offic'd instruments" he probably means, *the organs of sight and action.*

i You must away to-night.] In the quartos, "You must hence to-night," which words are given to the Duke, and the dialogue proceeds as follows,—

"*Des.* To-night my lord?
Du. This night.
Oth. With all my heart."

To his conveyance I assign my wife,
With what else needful your good grace shall think
To be sent after me.

DUKE. Let it be so.—
Good night to every one.—And, noble signior, [*To* BRABANTIO.
If virtue no delighted[a] beauty lack,
Your son-in-law is far more fair than black.

1 SEN. Adieu, brave Moor! use Desdemona well.

BRA. Look to her, Moor, if thou hast eyes to see;[b]
She has deceiv'd her father, and may thee.
[*Exeunt* DUKE, Senators, Officers, *&c.*

OTH. My life upon her faith!—Honest Iago,
My Desdemona must I leave to thee:
I pr'ythee, let thy wife attend on her;
And bring them after in the best advantage.—
Come, Desdemona, I have but an hour
Of love, of worldly matter, and direction,
To spend with thee: we must obey the time.
[*Exeunt* OTHELLO *and* DESDEMONA.

ROD. Iago,—

IAGO. What say'st thou, noble heart?

ROD. What will I do, think'st thou?

IAGO. Why, go to bed, and sleep.

ROD. I will incontinently drown myself.

IAGO. If thou dost, I shall never love thee after. Why, thou silly gentleman!

ROD. It is silliness to live when to live is torment; and then have we a prescription to die, when death is our physician.

IAGO. O, villanous! I have looked upon the world for four times seven years; and since I could distinguish betwixt a benefit and an injury, I never found man that knew how to love himself. Ere I would say, I would drown myself for the love of a Guinea-hen, I would change my humanity with a baboon.

ROD. What should I do? I confess it is my shame to be so fond; but it is not in my virtue to amend it.

IAGO. *Virtue!* a fig! 'tis in ourselves that we are thus or thus. Our bodies are our gardens; to the which our wills are gardeners: so that if we will plant nettles, or sow lettuce; set hyssop, and weed up thyme; supply it with one gender of herbs, or distract it with many; either to have it sterile with idleness, or manured with industry; why, the power and corrigible authority of this lies in our wills. If the balance* of our lives had not one scale of reason to poise another of sensuality, the blood and baseness of our natures would conduct us to most preposterous conclusions: but we have reason to cool our raging motions, our carnal stings, our unbitted lusts; whereof I take this, that you call love, to be a sect or scion.

ROD. It cannot be.

IAGO. It is merely a lust of the blood and a permission of the will. Come, be a man: drown thyself! drown cats and blind puppies. I have professed me thy friend, and I confess me knit to thy deserving with cables of perdurable toughness. I could never better stead thee than now. Put money in thy purse; follow thou the wars; defeat thy favour[c] with an usurped beard; I say, put money in thy purse. It cannot be that Desdemona should long continue her love to the Moor,[d] —put money in thy purse,—nor he his to her: it was a violent commencement, and thou shalt see an answerable sequestration;—put but money in thy purse.—These Moors are changeable in their wills;—fill thy purse with money: the food that to him now is as luscious as locusts, shall be to him shortly as bitter as coloquintida.(5) She must change for youth: when she is sated with his body, she will find the error of her choice: she must have change, she must:[e] therefore put money in thy purse.—If thou wilt needs damn thyself, do it a more delicate way than drowning. Make all the money thou canst: if sanctimony and a frail vow, betwixt an erring barbarian and a* super-subtle Venetian, be not too hard for my wits and all the tribe of hell, thou shalt enjoy her; therefore make money. A pox of drowning thyself! it is clean out of the way: seek thou rather to be hanged in compassing thy joy, than to be drowned and go without her.

ROD. Wilt thou be fast to my hopes, if I depend on the issue?

IAGO. Thou art sure of me;—go, make money:—I have told thee often, and I re-tell thee again and again, I hate the Moor: my cause is hearted, thine hath no less reason; let us be conjunctive in our revenge against him. If thou canst cuckold him, thou dost thyself a pleasure, me a sport. There are many events in the womb of time, which will be delivered. Traverse! go; provide thy money. We will have more of this to-morrow. Adieu.

ROD. Where shall we meet i' the morning?

IAGO. At my lodging.

ROD. I'll be with thee betimes.

IAGO. Go to; farewell. Do you hear, Roderigo?

(*) First folio, *braine*.

(*) First folio omits, *a*.

a — *no* delighted *beauty lack*,—] "*Delighted*" is here used for *delighting*; the passive participle for the active.

b — if thou hast eyes to see;] The 1622 quarto reads, we think preferably,—"have a quick eye to see," &c.

c — *defeat thy* favour with an usurped beard;] *Change*, or *disfigure* thy countenance by putting on a spurious beard.

d It cannot be that Desdemona should long continue her love to the Moor,—] In the folio, "It cannot be long that Desdemona should continue," &c.

e — she must have change, she must;] These words are not in the folio.

ROD. What say you?
IAGO. No more of drowning, do you hear?
ROD. I am changed: I'll go sell all my land.[a]
IAGO. Go to; farewell! put money enough in your purse. [*Exit* RODERIGO.
Thus do I ever make my fool my purse;
For I mine own gain'd knowledge should profane,
If I would time expend with such a snipe,
But for my sport and profit.—I hate the Moor;
And it is thought abroad, that 'twixt my sheets
He* has done my office: I know not if 't be true;
But I, for mere suspicion in that kind,
Will do as if for surety. He holds me well;
The better shall my purpose work on him.
Cassio's a proper man: let me see now;—
To get his place, and to plume up my will,
A* double knavery,—How, how?—Let's see:—
After some time, to abuse Othello's ear †
That he is too familiar with his wife:—
He hath a person, and a smooth dispose,
To be suspected; fram'd to make women false.
The Moor is of a free and open nature,
That thinks men honest that but seem to be so;
And will as tenderly be led by the nose
As asses are.
I have't;—it is engender'd:—hell and night
Must bring this monstrous birth to the world's light. [*Exit.*

(*) First folio, *She*.

(*) First folio, *In* (†) First folio, *ears*.

[a] I'll go sell all my land.] The folio abbreviates the foregoing dialogue thus,—

"Do you hear, Roderigo?
Rod. Ile sell all my Land. [*Exit*."

ACT II.

SCENE I.—*A Sea-port Town in Cyprus.*

Enter MONTANO *and Two* Gentlemen.

MON. What from the cape can you discern at sea?
1 GENT. Nothing at all: it is a high-wrought flood;
I cannot, 'twixt the heaven* and the main,
Descry a sail.
MON. Methinks the wind hath spoke aloud at land;
A fuller blast ne'er shook our battlements:
If it hath ruffian'd so upon the sea,
What ribs of oak, when mountains melt on them,
Can hold the mortise? What shall we hear of this?
2 GENT. A segregation of the Turkish fleet:
For do but stand upon the foaming shore,

(*) Quarto 1622, *haven.*

The chidden billow seems to pelt the clouds;
The wind-shak'd surge, with high and monstrous mane,
Seems to cast water on the burning bear,
And quench the guards of the ever-fixed pole:
I never did like molestation view
On the enchafed flood.
MON. If that the Turkish fleet
Be not enshelter'd and embay'd, they're drown'd;
It is impossible they* bear it out.

Enter a Third Gentleman.

3 GENT. News, lads! our wars are done.
The desperate tempest hath so bang'd the Turks,
That their designment halts: a noble ship of Venice

(*) First folio, *to.*

Hath seen a grievous wreck and sufferance
On most part of their fleet.

MON. How! is this true?

3 GENT. The ship is here put in;
A Veronessa, Michael Cassio,
Lieutenant to the warlike Moor Othello,
Is come on shore: the Moor himself at sea,
And is in full commission here for Cyprus.

MON. I am glad on't; 't is a worthy governor.

3 GENT. But this same Cassio,—though he speak of comfort
Touching the Turkish loss,—yet he looks sadly,
And prays the Moor be safe; for they were parted
With foul and violent tempest.

MON. Pray heavens he be;
For I have serv'd him, and the man commands
Like a full soldier. Let 's to the sea-side,—ho!
As well to see the vessel that 's come in,
As to throw out our eyes for brave Othello,
Even till we make the main and the aerial blue,
An indistinct regard.[a]

3 GENT. Come, let 's do so;
For every minute is expectancy
Of more arrivance.*

Enter CASSIO.

CAS. Thanks, you the valiant of this warlike isle,[b]
That so approve the Moor! O, let the heavens
Give him defence against the elements,
For I have lost him on a dangerous sea!

MON. Is he well shipp'd?

CAS. His bark is stoutly timber'd, and his pilot
Of very expert and approv'd allowance;
Therefore my hopes,[c] not surfeited to death,
Stand in bold cure.

[*Without.*] A sail, a sail, a sail!

Enter a Fourth Gentleman.

CAS. What noise?

4 GENT. The town is empty; on the brow o' the sea
Stand ranks of people, and they cry—*A sail!*

CAS. My hopes do shape him for the governor. [*Guns without.*

2 GENT. They do discharge their shot of courtesy:
Our friends, at least.

CAS. I pray you, sir, go forth,
And give us truth who 't is that is arriv'd.

2 GENT. I shall. [*Exit.*

MON. But, good lieutenant, is your general wiv'd?

CAS. Most fortunately: he hath achiev'd a maid
That paragons description and wild fame;
One that excels the quirks of blazoning pens,
And in the essential vesture of creation
Does tire the ingener.—[d]

Re-enter Second Gentleman.

How now? who has put in?

2 GENT. 'T is one Iago, ancient to the general.

CAS. He has had most favourable and happy speed:
Tempests themselves, high seas, and howling winds,
The gutter'd rocks, and congregated sands,—
Traitors ensteep'd to clog* the guiltless keel,—
As having sense of beauty, do omit
Their mortal natures, letting go safely by
The divine Desdemona.

MON. What is she?

CAS. She that I spake of, our great captain's captain,
Left in the conduct of the bold Iago;
Whose footing here anticipates our thoughts
A se'nnight's speed.—Great Jove, Othello guard,
And swell his sail with thine own powerful breath,
That he may bless this bay with his tall ship,
Make love's quick pants in Desdemona's arms,
Give renew'd fire to our extincted spirits,
And bring all Cyprus comfort![e]—O, behold,

Enter DESDEMONA, EMILIA, IAGO, RODERIGO, *and* Attendants.

The riches of the ship is come on shore!
Ye men of Cyprus, let her have your knees.—
Hail to thee, lady! and the grace of heaven,

(*) First folio, *Arrivancie.*

(*) First folio, *enclog.*

[a] Even till we make the main and the aerial blue,
An indistinct regard.]
Omitted in the earlier quarto.

[b] Thanks, you the valiant of this warlike isle, &c.] The first quarto has, "Thankes *to the* valiant of this *worthy* Isle," &c.; the second quarto, "Thanks to the valiant of this isle," &c.; the folio, "Thankes you, the valiant of *the* warlike Isle," &c.

[c] Therefore my hopes, not surfeited to death,—] "Hopes," here, are *expectations* or *presentiments*. See note (b), page 540.

[d] *And in the essential vesture of creation*
Does tire the ingener.—]
The quartos read, "Does *beare all excellency* [and *excellence*];" the folio has, "Do's tyre the *Inginiver*." By "ingener" is meant, perhaps, the *painter* or *artist*. Flecknoe, as Mr. Singer has remarked, in his Discourse on the English Stage, 1664, speaking of painting, mentions "the stupendous works of your great *inginiers*." Ingenier, or ingener, was, however, a term for any ingenious person; and from a passage in "Certain Edicts from a Parliament in Eutopia, written by the Lady Southwell:"—"Item, that no Lady shall court her looking-glasse, past one houre in a day, unlesse she professe to be *an Ingenir*," it might be thought in the present instance to signify what is now called a *modiste*, or deviser of new fashions in female apparel.

[e] And bring all Cyprus comfort!—] These words are omitted in the folio.

Before, behind thee, and on every hand,
Enwheel thee round!

DES. I thank you, valiant Cassio.
What tidings can you tell me* of my lord?

CAS. He is not yet arriv'd; nor know I aught
But that he's well, and will be shortly here.

DES. O, but I fear,—How lost you company?

CAS. The great contention of the† sea and skies
Parted our fellowship:—but hark! a sail!

[*Cry without*, A sail! a sail! *Then guns heard.*

2 GENT. They give their greeting to the citadel;
This likewise is a friend.

CAS. See for the news.—

[*Exit* Gentleman.

Good ancient, you are welcome;—welcome, mistress:— [*To* EMILIA.
Let it not gall your patience, good Iago,
That I extend my manners; 't is my breeding
That gives me this bold show of courtesy.

[*Kissing her.*

IAGO. Sir,‡ would she give you so much of her lips
As of her tongue she oft bestows on me,
You'd have enough.

DES. Alas, she has no speech.

IAGO. In faith, too much;
I find it still, when I have list§ to sleep:
Marry, before your ladyship, I grant,
She puts her tongue a little in her heart,
And chides with thinking.

EMIL. You have little cause to say so.

IAGO. Come on, come on; you are pictures out of doors,‖
Bells in your parlours, wild cats in your kitchens,
Saints in your injuries, devils being offended,
Players in your housewifery, and housewives in your beds.[a]

DES. O, fye upon thee, slanderer!

IAGO. Nay, it is true, or else I am a Turk,
You rise to play, and go to bed to work.

EMIL. You shall not write my praise.

IAGO. No, let me not.

DES. What wouldst thou write of me, if thou shouldst praise me?

IAGO. O, gentle lady, do not put me to 't;
For I am nothing, if not critical.[b]

DES. Come on, assay—There's one gone to the harbour?

IAGO. Ay, madam.

DES. I am not merry; but I do beguile
The thing I am, by seeming otherwise.—
Come, how wouldst thou praise me?

IAGO. I am about it; but, indeed, my invention
Comes from my pate as birdlime does from frize,—
It plucks out brains and all: but my Muse labours,
And thus she is deliver'd.
If she be fair and wise,—fairness and wit,
The one's for use, the other useth it.

DES. Well prais'd! How if she be black and witty?

IAGO. If she be black, and thereto have a wit,
She'll find a white that shall her blackness fit.[c]

DES. Worse and worse.

EMIL. How if fair and foolish?

IAGO. She never yet was foolish that was fair;
For even her folly help'd her to an heir.

DES. These are old fond paradoxes, to make fools laugh i' the alehouse. What miserable praise hast thou for her that's foul and foolish?

IAGO. There's none so foul, and foolish thereunto,
But does foul pranks which fair and wise ones do.

DES. O, heavy ignorance!—thou praisest the worst best. But what praise couldst thou bestow on a deserving woman indeed,—one that, in the authority of her merit, did justly put on the vouch of very malice itself?[d]

IAGO. She that was ever fair, and never proud;
Had tongue at will, and yet was never loud;
Never lack'd gold, and yet went never gay;
Fled from her wish, and yet said,—*Now I may;*
She that, being anger'd, her revenge being nigh,
Bade her wrong stay, and her displeasure fly;
She that in wisdom never was so frail,
To change the cod's head for the salmon's tail;[e]
She that could think, and ne'er disclose her mind;
See suitors following, and not look behind;[f]
She was a wight, if ever such wights were,—

DES. To do what?

IAGO. To suckle fools, and chronicle small beer.

DES. O, most lame and impotent conclusion!—Do not learn of him, Emilia, though he be thy husband.—How say you, Cassio? is he not a most profane and liberal[g] counsellor?[h]

(*) First folio omits, *me*. (†) First folio omits, *the*. (‡) First folio, *For*. (§) First folio, *leave*. (‖) First folio, *doore*.

a — and housewives, &c.] Puttenham, in "The Arte of English Poesie," has something resembling this; "— we limit the comely part of a woman to consist in foure points, that is to be a shrewe in the kitchen, a saint in the church, an angell at the bourd, and an ape in the bed," &c.

b — critical.] *Cynical, censorious.*

c — *her blackness* fit.] The quarto 1622 reads,—"her blackness *hit*," perhaps for the better. See note (c), p. 70, Vol. I.

d — did justly put on the vouch of very malice itself?] Did confidently *provoke* the accusation of malice itself. To "*put* on" in the sense of to *incite*, to *provoke*, occurs also in "Macbeth," Act IV. Sc. 3,—

"—— the powers above
Put on their instruments."

Shakespeare may have been thinking on a passage in Occland's *Elizabetha*, 1582:—

"Sicut ab Invidiâ laudem decusque pararet."

e To change the cod's head for the salmon's tail;] That is, says Steevens, to exchange a delicacy for coarser fare.

f See suitors following, and not look behind;] This line is wanting in the earlier quarto.

g — liberal—] *Licentious.*

h — counsellor?] Theobald prints, "— *censurer*."

CAS. He speaks home, madam; you may relish him more in the soldier than in the scholar.

IAGO. [*Aside.*] He takes her by the palm: ay, well said,—whisper: with as little a web as this will I ensnare as great a fly as Cassio. Ay, smile upon her, do; I will gyve[a] thee in thine own courtship. You say true; 't is so, indeed: if such tricks as these strip you out of your lieutenantry, it had been better you had not kissed your three fingers so oft, which now again you are most apt to play the sir[b] in. Very good! well kissed! an excellent courtesy! 't is so, indeed. Yet again your fingers to your lips? would, they were clyster-pipes for your sake!—[*Trumpet without.*] The Moor! I know his trumpet.

CAS. 'T is truly so.

DES. Let's meet him, and receive him.

CAS. Lo, where he comes!

[a] — gyve—] *Shackle, fetter.*

[b] — *the* sir—] The *courtier*, or *gallant*.

Enter OTHELLO, *and* Attendants.

OTH. O, my fair warrior! [a]
DES. My dear Othello!
OTH. It gives me wonder great as my content,
To see you here before me. O, my soul's joy!
If after every tempest come such calms,
May the winds blow till they have waken'd death!
And let the labouring bark climb hills of seas,
Olympus-high, and duck again as low
As hell 's from heaven! If it were now to die,
'T were now to be most happy; for, I fear,
My soul hath her content so absolute,
That not another comfort like to this
Succeeds in unknown fate.
DES. The heavens forbid
But that our loves and comforts should increase,
Even as our days do grow!
OTH. Amen to that, sweet powers!—
I cannot speak enough of this content;
It stops me here; it is too much of joy:
And this, and this, the greatest discords be [*Kissing her.*
That e'er our hearts shall make!
IAGO. [*Aside.*] O, you are well tun'd now!
But I 'll set[b] down the pegs that make this music,
As honest as I am.
OTH. Come, let us to the castle.—
News, friends; our wars are done, the Turks are drown'd.
How does my old acquaintance of this isle?—
Honey, you shall be well desir'd in Cyprus;
I have found great love amongst them. O, my sweet,
I prattle out of fashion, and I dote
In mine own comforts.—I pr'ythee, good Iago,
Go to the bay, and disembark my coffers:
Bring thou the master to the citadel;
He is a good one, and his worthiness
Does challenge much respect.—Come, Desdemona,
Once more well met at Cyprus.
[*Exeunt* OTH. DES. *and* Attend.

IAGO. Do thou meet me presently at the harbour. Come hither.* If thou be'st valiant,—as, they say, base men being in love have then a nobility in their natures more than is native to them,—list me. The lieutenant to-night watches on the court of guard:—first, I must tell thee this—Desdemona is directly in love with him.

ROD. With him! why, 't is not possible.

IAGO. Lay thy finger thus, and let thy soul be instructed. Mark me with what violence she first loved the Moor, but for bragging, and telling her fantastical lies: and will she love him still for prating?* let not thy discreet heart think it. Her eye must be fed; and what delight shall she have to look on the devil? When the blood is made dull with the act of sport, there should be,—again† to inflame it, and to give satiety a fresh appetite,—loveliness in favour, sympathy in years, manners, and beauties; all which the Moor is defective in: now, for want of these required conveniences, her delicate tenderness will find itself abused, begin to heave the gorge, disrelish and abhor the Moor; very nature will instruct her in it, and compel her to some second choice. Now, sir, this granted,—as it is a most pregnant and unforced position,—who stands so eminent in the degree of this fortune as Cassio does?—a knave very voluble;[c] no further conscionable than in putting on the mere form of civil and humane seeming, for the better compassing‡ of his salt and most hidden-loose affection? why, none; why, none: a slipper and subtle knave; a finder of occasions; that has an eye can stamp and counterfeit advantages, though true advantage never present itself: a devilish knave! Besides, the knave is handsome, young, and hath all those requisites in him that folly and green minds look after: a pestilent-complete knave; and the woman hath found him already.

ROD. I cannot believe that in her; she is full of most blessed condition.[d]

IAGO. *Blessed* fig's end! the wine she drinks is made of grapes: if she had been blessed, she would never have loved the Moor: blessed pudding! Didst thou not see her paddle with the palm of his hand? didst not mark that?

ROD. Yes, that I did; but that was but courtesy.

IAGO. Lechery, by this hand! an index and obscure[e] prologue to the history of lust and foul thoughts. They met so near with their lips, that their breaths embraced together. Villanous thoughts, Roderigo! When these mutualities§ so marshal the way, hard at hand comes the master and main exercise, the incorporate conclusion.

(*) First folio, *thither*.

(*) First folio, *To love him still*, &c. (†) First folio, *a game*. (‡) First folio, *compass*. (§) First folio, *mutabilities*.

[a] *O, my fair* warrior!] "This phrase was introduced by our copiers of the French Sonnetteers. Ronsard frequently calls his mistresses *guerrieres*; and Southern, his imitator, is not less prodigal of the same appellation. Thus, in his fifth Sonnet,—

'And, my *warrier*, my light shines in thy fayre eyes.'

Again in his sixth Sonnet he uses it twice,—

'I am not, my cruell *warrier*, the Thebain,' &c.

'I came not, *my warrier*, of the blood Lidain,' &c."
STEEVENS.

[b] — set *down the pegs*—] Pope causelessly changed this to "— *let* down the pegs," &c.

[c] — voluble;] Not fluent in speech, as the word now imports, but *fickle, inconstant*.

[d] — condition.] That is, *disposition, qualities of mind*.

[e] — obscure *prologue*—] Query, "*obscene* prologue—"?

Pish!—But, sir, be you ruled by me: I have brought you from Venice. Watch you to-night; for the command, I'll lay't upon you:—Cassio knows you not:—I'll not be far from you: do you find some occasion to anger Cassio, either by speaking too loud, or tainting his discipline, or from what other course[a] you please, which the time shall more favourably minister.

ROD. Well.

IAGO. Sir, he is rash, and very sudden in choler, and haply[b] may strike at you: provoke him, that he may; for even out of that will I cause these of Cyprus to mutiny; whose qualification[c] shall come into no true taste again, but by the displanting of Cassio. So shall you have a shorter journey to your desires, by the means I shall then have to prefer them; and the impediment most profitably removed, without the which there were no expectation of our prosperity.

ROD. I will do this, if I* can bring it to any opportunity.

IAGO. I warrant thee. Meet me by and by at the citadel: I must fetch his necessaries ashore. Farewell.

ROD. Adieu. [*Exit.*

IAGO. That Cassio loves her, I do well believe it;
That she loves him, 't is apt, and of great credit:
The Moor—howbeit that I endure him not,—
Is of a constant-loving, noble nature;
And I dare think he'll prove to Desdemona
A most dear husband. Now, I do love her too;
Not out of absolute lust,—though peradventure
I stand accountant for as great a sin,—
But partly led to diet my revenge,
For that I do suspect the lusty Moor
Hath leap'd into my seat: the thought whereof
Doth, like a poisonous mineral, gnaw my inwards;
And nothing can or shall content my soul,
Till I am even'd with him, wife for wife;
Or, failing so, yet that I put the Moor
At least into a jealousy so strong
That judgment cannot cure. Which thing to do,—
If this poor trash[d] of Venice, whom I trash[e]
For his quick hunting, stand the putting on,
I'll have our Michael Cassio on the hip;
Abuse him to the Moor in the rank† garb,—
For I fear Cassio with my night-cap too;—
Make the Moor thank me, love me, and reward me,
For making him egregiously an ass,
And practising upon his peace and quiet
Even to madness. 'T is here, but yet confus'd:
Knavery's plain face is never seen till us'd. [*Exit.*

(*) First folio, *if you*. (†) First folio, *right*.

a — *what other* course—] Mr. Collier credits his annotator with the alteration of "course" to *cause;* but "cause" is the reading of the 1622 quarto.

b — and haply may strike at you: &c.] The quartos read,—"— and haply *with his truncheon* may strike at you," &c.

c — whose qualification—] Whose *temperament, crasis.*

d If this poor trash of Venice,—] The 1622 quarto reads,—

"If this poore trash of Venice, whom I crush," &c.

The folio 1623 and the quarto 1630 have,—

"If this poore Trash of Venice, whome I *trace*," &c.

Warburton prints, "*brach* of Venice" for trash of Venice, an emendation to which we cannot subscribe, although persuaded that "*trash* of Venice" is a vitiation of what the poet wrote.

e — *whom* I trash—] The folio has "— *trace;*" but "*trash,*" signifying to *clog* or *impede*, is surely the genuine word. See note (f), p. 8.

SCENE II.—*A Street.*

Enter a Herald, *with a proclamation;* People *following.*

HER. It is Othello's pleasure, our noble and valiant general, that, upon certain tidings now arrived, importing the mere perdition of the Turkish fleet, every man put himself into triumph; some to dance, some to make bonfires, each man to what sport and revels his addiction* leads him; for, besides these beneficial news, it is the celebration of his nuptial:—so much was his pleasure should be proclaimed. All offices[f] are open; and there is full liberty of feasting from this present hour of five till the bell have told eleven. Heaven† bless the isle of Cyprus, and our noble general, Othello! [*Exeunt.*

SCENE III.—*A Hall in the Castle.*

Enter OTHELLO, DESDEMONA, CASSIO, *and* Attendants.

OTH. Good Michael, look you to the guard to-night:
Let's teach ourselves that honourable stop,
Not to out-sport discretion.

CAS. Iago hath direction what to do;
But, notwithstanding, with my personal eye
Will I look to't.

OTH. Iago is most honest.
Michael, good night: to-morrow with your earliest
Let me have speech with you.—Come, my dear love,—
The purchase made, the fruits are to ensue;
[*Aside to* DESDEMONA.
That profit's yet to come 'tween me and you.—
Good night. [*Exeunt* OTH. DES. *and* Attend.

(*) First folio, *addition*. (†) First folio omits, *Heaven*.

f *All* offices *are open;*] The apartments in a great establishment, where the refreshments were prepared or distributed, were anciently known as *offices:* thus, as quoted by Malone, in "Timon of Athens," Act II. Sc. 2,—

"When all our *offices* have been oppress'd
With riotous feeders."

Enter IAGO.

CAS. Welcome, Iago; we must to the watch.

IAGO. Not this hour, lieutenant; 't is not yet ten o' the clock. Our general cast[a] us thus early for the love of his Desdemona; who let us not therefore blame: he hath not yet made wanton the night with her; and she is sport for Jove.

CAS. She 's a most exquisite lady.

IAGO. And, I 'll warrant her, full of game.

CAS. Indeed, she 's a most fresh and delicate creature.

IAGO. What an eye she has! methinks it sounds a parley of* provocation.

CAS. An inviting eye; and yet methinks right modest.

IAGO. And when she speaks, is it not an alarum to love?

CAS. She is, indeed, perfection.

IAGO. Well, happiness to their sheets! Come, lieutenant, I have a stoop of wine; and here without are a brace of Cyprus gallants that would fain have a measure to the health of black Othello.

CAS. Not to-night, good Iago; I have very poor and unhappy brains for drinking: I could well wish courtesy would invent some other custom of entertainment.

IAGO. O, they are our friends; but one cup: I 'll drink for you.

CAS. I have drunk but one cup to-night, and that was craftily qualified too, and, behold, what innovation it makes here. I am unfortunate in the infirmity, and dare not task my weakness with any more.

IAGO. What, man! 't is a night of revels: the gallants desire it.

CAS. Where are they?

IAGO. Here at the door; I pray you, call them in.

CAS. I 'll do 't; but it dislikes me. [*Exit.*

IAGO. If I can fasten but one cup upon him,
With that which he hath drunk to-night already,
He 'll be as full of quarrel and offence
As my young mistress' dog. Now, my sick fool Roderigo,
Whom love has turn'd almost the wrong side out,
To Desdemona hath to-night carous'd
Potations pottle deep; and he 's to watch:
Three lads† of Cyprus,—noble-swelling spirits,
That hold their honours in a wary distance,
The very elements of this warlike isle,—
Have I to-night fluster'd with flowing cups,
And they watch too. Now, 'mongst this flock of drunkards,
Am I to put our Cassio in some action
That may offend the isle:—but here they come:
If consequence do but approve my dream,
My boat sails freely, both with wind and stream.

(*) First folio, *to*. (†) First folio, *else*.

[a] — cast *us*—] *Dismissed* us.

Re-enter CASSIO, *followed by* MONTANO, Gentlemen, *and* Servants *with wine*.

CAS. 'Fore God,* they have given me a rouse already.

MON. Good faith, a little one; not past a pint, as I am a soldier.

IAGO. Some wine, ho!

[Sings.] *And let me the canakin clink, clink;*
And let me the canakin clink:
A soldier's a man;
O, man's life's but a span;
Why, then, let a soldier drink.

Some wine, boys!

CAS. 'Fore God,* an excellent song.

IAGO. I learned it in England, where indeed they are most potent in potting: your Dane, your German, and your swag-bellied Hollander,—Drink, ho!—are nothing to your English.

CAS. Is your Englishman so expert † in his drinking?

IAGO. Why, he drinks you, with facility, your Dane dead drunk; he sweats not to overthrow your Almain; he gives your Hollander a vomit, ere the next pottle can be filled.(1)

CAS. To the health of our general!

MON. I am for it, lieutenant; and I 'll do you justice.

IAGO. O, sweet England!

King Stephen was ‡ a worthy peer,
His breeches cost him but a crown;
He held them sixpence all too dear,
With that he call'd the tailor lown.

He was a wight of high renown,
And thou art but of low degree:
'T is pride that pulls the country down,
Then § take thine ‖ auld cloak about thee.(2)

Some wine, ho!

CAS. Why this is a more exquisite song than the other.

IAGO. Will you hear 't again?

CAS. No; for I hold him to be unworthy of his place that does those things.—Well,—God 's *

(*) First folio, *heaven*. (†) First folio, *exquisite*.
(‡) First folio inserts, *and*. (§) First folio, *and*.
(‖) First folio, *thy*.

above all; and there be souls must be saved, and there be souls must not be saved.[a]

IAGO. It's true, good lieutenant.

CAS. For mine own part,—no offence to the general, nor any man of quality,—I hope to be saved.

IAGO. And so do I too, lieutenant.

CAS. Ay, but, by your leave, not before me; the lieutenant is to be saved before the ancient. Let's have no more of this; let's to our affairs. —Forgive us our sins!—Gentlemen, let's look to our business. Do not think, gentlemen, I am drunk: this is my ancient;—this is my right hand, and this is my left:—I am not drunk now; I can stand well enough, and I speak well enough.

ALL. Excellent well.

CAS. Why, very well, then: you must not think, then, that I am drunk. [*Exit.*

MON. To the platform, masters; come, let's set the watch.

IAGO. You see this fellow that is gone before;—
He is a soldier fit to stand by Cæsar
And give direction: and do but see his vice;
'T is to his virtue a just equinox,
The one as long as the other: 't is pity of him.
I fear, the trust Othello puts him in,
On some odd time of his infirmity,
Will shake this island.

MON. But is he often thus?

IAGO. 'T is evermore the* prologue to his sleep:
He'll watch the horologe a double set,[b]
If drink rock not his cradle.

MON. It were well
The general were put in mind of it,
Perhaps he sees it not; or his good nature
Prizes the virtue that appears in Cassio,
And looks not on his evils: is not this true?

Enter RODERIGO.

IAGO. [*Aside to him.*] How now, Roderigo?
I pray you, after the lieutenant; go.
[*Exit* RODERIGO.

MON. And 't is great pity that the noble Moor
Should hazard such a place as his own second
With one of an ingraft infirmity:
It were an honest action to say so
To the Moor.

IAGO. Not I, for this fair island:
I do love Cassio well, and would do much
To cure him of this evil.—But, hark! what noise?
[*Cry without,*—Help! help![c]

(*) First folio, *his.*

[a] — and there be souls must not be saved.] This clause is omitted in the 1622 quarto.

[b] He'll watch the horologe a double set,
If drink rock not his cradle.]
He'll not sleep while the hands course twice round the clock, in other words, for twenty-four hours, unless he have drink.

[c] *Cry without,*—Help! help!] This stage direction is found only in the quartos.

Re-enter CASSIO, *pursuing* RODERIGO.

CAS. You rogue! you rascal!
MON. What's the matter, lieutenant?
CAS. A knave teach me my duty!
I'll beat the knave into a twiggen bottle.
ROD. Beat me!
CAS. Dost thou prate, rogue?
[*Striking* RODERIGO.
MON. Nay, good lieutenant;
[*Staying him.*
I pray you, sir, hold your hand.
CAS. Let me go, sir,
Or I'll knock you o'er the mazzard.
MON. Come, come, you're drunk.
CAS. Drunk! [*They fight.*[a]
IAGO. Away, I say! go out, and cry—*a mutiny!*
[*Aside to* ROD. *who goes out.*
Nay, good lieutenant,—alas, gentlemen;—
Help, ho!—Lieutenant,—sir,—Montano,—sir,—*
Help, masters!—Here's a goodly watch, indeed!
[*Bell rings.*
Who's that which rings the bell?—Diablo, ho!
The town will rise: God's will,† lieutenant, hold!
You will be sham'd‡ for ever.

Re-enter OTHELLO, *and* Attendants.

OTH. What is the matter here?
MON. Zounds,§ I bleed still! I am hurt to the death.— [*He faints.*[b]
OTH. Hold, for your lives!
IAGO. Hold, ho! Lieutenant,—sir,—Montano,—gentlemen,—
Have you forgot all sense of place and duty?[c]
Hold! the general speaks to you; hold, for shame!
OTH. Why, how now, ho! from whence ariseth this?
Are we turn'd Turks, and to ourselves do that
Which heaven hath forbid the Ottomites?
For Christian shame, put by this barbarous brawl:
He that stirs next to carve for his own rage,
Holds his soul light; he dies upon his motion.—
Silence that dreadful bell! it frights the isle
From her propriety.—What is the matter, masters?—
Honest Iago, that look'st dead with grieving,
Speak, who began this? on thy love, I charge thee.

IAGO. I do not know:—friends all but now, even now,
In quarter, and in terms like bride and groom
Devesting them for bed; and then, but now
(As if some planet had unwitted men)
Swords out, and tilting one at other's breast,
In opposition bloody. I cannot speak
Any beginning to this peevish[d] odds;
And would in action glorious I had lost
Those legs that brought me to a part of it!
OTH. How comes it, Michael, you are thus forgot?
CAS. I pray you, pardon me; I cannot speak.
OTH. Worthy Montano, you were wont* be civil;
The gravity and stillness of your youth
The world hath noted, and your name is great
In mouths of wisest censure: what's the matter,
That you unlace your reputation thus,
And spend your rich opinion[e] for the name
Of a night-brawler? give me answer to 't.
MON. Worthy Othello, I am hurt to danger;
Your officer, Iago, can inform you,—
While I spare speech, which something now offends me,—
Of all that I do know: nor know I aught
By me that's said or done amiss this night;
Unless self-charity be sometimes a vice,
And to defend ourselves it be a sin
When violence assails us.
OTH. Now, by heaven,
My blood begins my safer guides to rule;
And passion, having my best judgment collied,[f]
Assays to lead the way! If I once stir,
Or do but lift this arm, the best of you
Shall sink in my rebuke. Give me to know
How this foul rout began, who set it on;
And he that is approv'd in this offence,
Though he had twinn'd with me, both at a birth,
Shall lose me.—What! in a town of war,
Yet wild, the people's hearts brimful of fear,
To manage private and domestic quarrel,
In night, and on the court and guard of safety![g]
'T is monstrous.—Iago, who began 't?
MON. If, partially affin'd,[h] or leagu'd† in office,
Thou dost deliver more or less than truth,
Thou art no soldier.
IAGO. Touch me not so near:
I had rather have this tongue cut from my mouth,
Than it should do offence to Michael Cassio;
Yet, I persuade myself, to speak the truth

(*) First folio omits, *sir*. (†) First folio, *Fie, fie*.
(‡) First folio, *asham'd*. (§) First folio omits, *Zounds*.

[a] *They fight.*] The folio omits this direction.

[b] *He faints.*] This direction is only given in the quarto of 1630. The folio instead of it adds to Montano's speech, not as a stage direction, the words, "He dies."

[c] — *all* sense of place *and duty?*] The old copies by mistake transpose the words, "sense of place," and read, "place of sense," &c.

[d] — peevish odds;] *Headstrong*, or *perverse quarrel*.

(*) First folio inserts, *to*. (†) Old copies, *league*.

[e] — spend your rich opinion—] *Squander* your valued estimation.

[f] — collied,—] To *colly* means, literally, to *blacken*, to *smut*, and figuratively, to *darken* or *obscure*. The expression in the text occurs in Ben Jonson's "Poetaster," Act IV. Sc. 3,—"Nor thou hast not *collied* thy face enough, stinkard."

[g] — on the court and guard of safety!] Such is the lection of the old copies; the usual reading, however, is that proposed by Theobald,—"the court *of* guard *and* safety."

[h] *If*, partially affin'd,—] If, being *bound by partiality*.

Shall nothing wrong him.—This it is, general:
Montano and myself being in speech,
There comes a fellow crying out for help;
And Cassio following him with determin'd sword,
To execute upon him. Sir, this gentleman
Steps in to Cassio, and entreats his pause;
Myself the crying fellow did pursue,
Lest by his clamour (as it so fell out)
The town might fall in fright: he, swift of foot,
Outran my purpose; and I return'd the rather
For that I heard the clink and fall of swords,
And Cassio high in oath; which, till to-night,
I ne'er might say before. When I came back,
(For this was brief) I found them close together,
At blow and thrust; even as again they were
When you yourself did part them.
More of this matter cannot I report:—
But men are men; the best sometimes forget:—
Though Cassio did some little wrong to him,—
As men in rage strike those that wish them best,—
Yet, surely, Cassio, I believe, receiv'd
From him that fled some strange indignity,
Which patience could not pass.

OTH. I know, Iago,
Thy honesty and love doth mince this matter,
Making it light to Cassio.—Cassio, I love thee;
But never more be officer of mine.—

Re-enter DESDEMONA *attended.*

Look, if my gentle love be not rais'd up!—
I'll make thee an example.

DES. What 's the matter?

OTH. All 's well now, sweeting;[a]
Come away to bed.—Sir, for your hurts,
Myself will be your surgeon: lead him off.
[*To* MONTANO, *who is led off.*
Iago, look with care about the town,
And silence those whom this vile brawl distracted.—
Come, Desdemona: 't is the soldiers' life
To have their balmy slumbers wak'd with strife.
[*Exeunt all except* IAGO *and* CASSIO.

IAGO. What, are you hurt, lieutenant?

CAS. Ay, past all surgery.

IAGO. Marry, heaven forbid!

CAS. Reputation, reputation, reputation! O, I have lost my reputation! I have lost the immortal part of myself, and what remains is bestial.—My reputation, Iago, my reputation!

IAGO. As I am an honest man, I* thought you had received some bodily wound; there is more sense in that than in reputation. Reputation is an idle and most false imposition; oft got without merit, and lost without deserving: you have lost no reputation at all, unless you repute yourself such a loser. What, man! there are* ways to recover the general again: you are but now cast in his mood, a punishment more in policy than in malice; even so as one would beat his offenceless dog to affright[b] an imperious lion: sue to him again, and he 's yours.

CAS. I will rather sue to be despised, than to deceive so good a commander with so slight, so drunken, and so indiscreet an officer. Drunk? and speak parrot? and squabble? swagger? swear? and discourse fustian with one's own shadow?[c]—O, thou invisible spirit of wine, if thou hast no name to be known by, let us call thee devil!

IAGO. What was he that you followed with your sword? What had he done to you?

CAS. I know not.

IAGO. Is 't possible?

CAS. I remember a mass of things, but nothing distinctly; a quarrel, but nothing wherefore.—O, God,† that men should put an enemy in their mouths to steal away their brains! that we should, with joy, pleasance, revel, and applause, transform ourselves into beasts!

IAGO. Why, but you are now well enough: how came you thus recovered?

CAS. It hath pleased the devil Drunkenness, to give place to the devil Wrath: one unperfectness shows me another, to make me frankly despise myself.

IAGO. Come, you are too severe a moraler: as the time, the place, and the condition of this country stands, I could heartily wish this had not befallen; but, since it is as it is, mend it for your own good.

CAS. I will ask him for my place again,—he shall tell me I am a drunkard! Had I as many mouths as Hydra, such an answer would stop them all. To be now a sensible man, by and by a fool, and presently a beast! O, strange!—Every inordinate cup is unblessed, and the ingredient is a devil.

IAGO. Come, come, good wine is a good familiar creature, if it be well used; exclaim no more against it. And, good lieutenant, I think you think I love you.

CAS. I have well approved it, sir.—I drunk!

IAGO. You, or any man living may be drunk at some‡ time, man. I'll tell you what you shall do.

(*) First folio inserts, *had*.

(*) First folio inserts, *more*. (†) First folio omits, *God*. (‡) First folio, *a time*.

a All's well now, sweeting;] In the folio, Desdemona's question and the response run thus:—

"*Des.* What is the matter (Deere?)
Othe. All's well Sweeting."

b — *to* affright *an imperious lion*:] Should we not read,—"to *appease* an imperious lion:"?

c Drunk? and speak parrot? and squabble? swagger? swear? and discourse fustian with one's own shadow?—] This is all wanting in the 1622 quarto.

Our general's wife is now the general;—I may say so in this respect, for that he hath devoted and given up himself to the contemplation,—mark,—and denotement* of her parts and graces:—confess yourself freely to her; importune her help to put you in your place again: she is of so free, so kind, so apt, so blessed a disposition, she holds it a vice in her goodness not to do more than she is requested. This broken joint between you and her husband entreat her to splinter, and, my fortunes against any lay worth naming, this crack of your love shall grow stronger than it was before.

CAS. You advise me well.

IAGO. I protest, in the sincerity of love and honest kindness.

CAS. I think it freely; and betimes in the morning I will beseech the virtuous Desdemona to undertake for me: I am desperate of my fortunes if they check me here.†

IAGO. You are in the right. Good night, lieutenant; I must to the watch.

CAS. Good night, honest Iago. [*Exit* CASSIO.

IAGO. And what 's he, then, that says I play the villain?
When this advice is free I give and honest,
Probal [a] to thinking, and, indeed, the course
To win the Moor again? For 't is most easy
The inclining Desdemona to subdue
In any honest suit: she 's fram'd as fruitful
As the free elements. And then for her
To win the Moor,—were 't * to renounce his baptism,
All seals and symbols of redeemed sin,—
His soul is so enfetter'd to her love,
That she may make, unmake, do what she list,
Even as her appetite shall play the god
With his weak function. How am I, then, a villain
To counsel Cassio to this parallel course,

(*) Old text, *devotement*. Corrected by Theobald.
(†) First folio omits, *here*.

(*) First folio, *were*.

[a] Probal—] This contraction of *probable* is, as far as we know, without example.

Directly to his good? Divinity of hell!
When devils will the blackest sins put on,[a]
They do suggest[b] at first with heavenly shows,
As I do now: for whiles this honest fool
Plies Desdemona to repair his fortunes,*
And she for him pleads strongly to the Moor,
I 'll pour this pestilence into his ear,—
That she repeals him for her body's lust;
And by how much she strives to do him good,
She shall undo her credit with the Moor.
So will I turn her virtue into pitch;
And out of her own goodness make the net
That shall enmesh them all.—

Enter RODERIGO.

How now, Roderigo!

ROD. I do follow here in the chase, not like a hound that hunts, but one that fills up the cry. My money is almost spent; I have been to-night exceedingly well cudgelled; and I think the issue will be—I shall have so much experience for my pains;[c] and so, with no money at all, and a little more wit, return again to Venice.

(*) First folio, *fortune*.

a — put on,—] *Instigate, provoke.*
b — suggest—] *Tempt, entice.*

IAGO. How poor are they that have not patience!
What wound did ever heal but by degrees?
Thou know'st we work by wit, and not by witchcraft;
And wit depends on dilatory time.
Does 't not go well? Cassio hath beaten thee,
And thou, by that small hurt, hast cashier'd Cassio.
Though other things grow fair against the sun,
Yet fruits that blossom first will first be ripe.
Content thyself awhile.—By the mass,* 't is morning;
Pleasure and action make the hours seem short.—
Retire thee; go where thou art billeted:
Away, I say; thou shalt know more hereafter:
Nay, get thee gone. [*Exit* ROD.] Two things are to be done,—
My wife must move for Cassio to her mistress,
I 'll set her on;
Myself the † while to draw the Moor apart,
And bring him jump when he may Cassio find
Soliciting his wife:—ay, that 's the way;
Dull not device by coldness and delay. [*Exit.*

(*) First folio, *In troth*.
(†) Old text, *awhile*. Corrected by Theobald.

c — for my pains;] The 1622 quarto adds,—"as that comes to," &c.

ACT III.

SCENE I.—*The same. Before the Castle.*

Enter Cassio, *and some* Musicians.

Cas. Masters, play here,—I will content your pains,—
Something that's brief; and bid good-morrow, general. [*Music.*

Enter Clown.

Clo. Why, masters, have your instruments been in Naples, that they speak i' the nose thus?

1 Mus. How, sir, how!

Clo. Are these, I pray you, wind-instruments?

1 Mus. Ay, marry, are they, sir.

Clo. O, thereby hangs a tail.

1 Mus. Whereby hangs a tale, sir?

Clo. Marry, sir, by many a wind-instrument that I know. But, masters, here's money for you; and the general so likes your music, that he desires you, of all loves,[a] to make no more noise with it.

1 Mus. Well, sir, we will not.

Clo. If you have any music that may not be heard, to't again: but, as they say, to hear music the general does not greatly care.

1 Mus. We have none such, sir.

---

[a] — of all loves,—] An old adjuration found in "The Merry Wives of Windsor," Act II. Sc. 2; and in "A Midsummer Night's Dream," Act II. Sc. 3; and which the folio reading, "*for love's sake,*" well explains.

CLO. Then put up your pipes in your bag, for I'll away: go; vanish into air; away!
[*Exeunt* Musicians.

CAS. Dost thou hear, my[a] honest friend?

CLO. No, I hear not your honest friend; I hear you.

CAS. Pr'ythee, keep up thy quillets. There's a poor piece of gold for thee: if the gentlewoman that attends the general's wife[b] be stirring, tell her there's one Cassio entreats her a little favour of speech: wilt thou do this?

CLO. She is stirring, sir: if she will stir hither, I shall seem to notify unto her.

CAS. Do, good my friend.[c] [*Exit* Clown.

Enter IAGO.

In happy time, Iago.

IAGO. You have not been a-bed, then?

CAS. Why, no; the day had broke
Before we parted. I have made bold, Iago,
To send in to your wife: my suit to her
Is, that she will to virtuous Desdemona
Procure me some access.

IAGO. I'll send her to you presently;
And I'll devise a mean to draw the Moor
Out of the way, that your converse and business
May be more free.

CAS. I humbly thank you for 't. [*Exit* IAGO.]
I never knew
A Florentine more kind and honest.[d]

Enter EMILIA.

EMIL. Good morrow, good lieutenant: I am sorry
For your displeasure; but all will sure be well.
The general and his wife are talking of it,
And she speaks for you stoutly: the Moor replies,
That he you hurt is of great fame in Cyprus,
And great affinity, and that in wholesome wisdom
He might not but refuse you; but he protests he loves you,
And needs no other suitor but his likings,
To take the saf'st occasion by the front[e]
To bring you in again.

CAS. Yet, I beseech you,—
If you think fit, or that it may be done,—
Give me advantage of some brief discourse
With Desdemon alone.

EMIL. Pray you, come in;
I will bestow you where you shall have time
To speak your bosom freely.

CAS. I am much bound to you.
[*Exeunt.*

SCENE II.—*A Room in the Castle.*

Enter OTHELLO, IAGO, *and* Gentlemen.

OTH. These letters give, Iago, to the pilot;
And, by him, do my duties to the senate:
That done,—I will be walking on the works,—
Repair there to me.

IAGO. Well, my good lord, I'll do 't.

OTH. This fortification, gentlemen,—shall we see 't?

GENT. We'll wait upon your lordship.
[*Exeunt.*

SCENE III.—*The Garden of the Castle.*

Enter DESDEMONA, CASSIO, *and* EMILIA.

DES. Be thou assur'd, good Cassio, I will do
All my abilities in thy behalf.

EMIL. Good madam, do; I warrant it grieves my husband,
As if the cause were his.

DES. O, that's an honest fellow.—Do not doubt, Cassio,
But I will have my lord and you again
As friendly as you were.

CAS. Bounteous madam,
Whatever shall become of Michael Cassio,
He's never any thing but your true servant.

DES. I know 't,—I thank you. You do love my lord:
You have known him long; and be you well assur'd
He shall in strangeness stand no farther off
Than in a politic distance.

CAS. Ay, but, lady,
That policy may either last so long,
Or feed upon such nice and waterish diet,
Or breed itself so out of circumstance,*

---

[a] *Dost thou hear, my honest friend?*] So the quartos; the folio reads, "Dost thou heare *me, mine* honest friend?"

[b] — that attends the general's wife, &c.] This is according to the quartos; the folio has, "that attends the *Generall*," &c.

[c] Do, good my friend.] The folio omits this hemistich.

[d] —— I never knew
A Florentine more kind and honest.]

As Iago from various passages is known to be a Venetian, and as he calls the lieutenant "A Florentine" at the opening of the play, Cassio is supposed to mean that he never experienced more kindness and honesty even in one of his own countrymen.

[e] To take the saf'st occasion by the front—] A line not found in the folio.

(*) First folio, *circumstances*.

That, I being absent, and my place supplied,
My general will forget my love and service.

DES. Do not doubt that; before Emilia here,
I give thee warrant of thy place. Assure thee,
If I do vow a friendship I'll perform it
To the last article: my lord shall never rest;
I'll watch[a] him tame, and talk him out of patience;
His bed shall seem a school, his board a shrift;
I'll intermingle every thing he does
With Cassio's suit: therefore be merry, Cassio,
For thy solicitor shall rather die
Than give thy cause away.

EMIL. Madam, here comes my lord.

CAS. Madam, I'll take my leave.

DES. Why, stay, and hear me speak.

CAS. Madam, not now; I am very ill at ease,
Unfit for mine own purposes.

DES. Well; do your discretion. [*Exit* CASSIO.

a *I'll* watch *him tame,*—] See note d, p. 683, Vol. I.

Enter OTHELLO *and* IAGO.

IAGO. Ha! I like not that.

OTH. What dost thou say?

IAGO. Nothing, my lord: or if—I know not what.

OTH. Was not that Cassio parted from my wife?

IAGO. Cassio, my lord! No, sure, I cannot think it,
That he would steal away so guilty-like,
Seeing you* coming.

OTH. I do believe 't was he.

DES. How now, my lord!
I have been talking with a suitor here,
A man that languishes in your displeasure.

OTH. Who is't you mean?

DES. Why, your lieutenant, Cassio. Good my lord,

(*) First folio,

If I have any grace or power to move you,
His present reconciliation take;
For if he be not one that truly loves you,
That errs in ignorance, and not in cunning,
I have no judgment in an honest face:
I pr'ythee call him back.

OTH. Went he hence now?

DES. Ay, sooth; so humbled,
That he hath left part of his grief with me,
To suffer with him. Good love, call him back.

OTH. Not now, sweet Desdemon; some other time.

DES. But shall 't be shortly?

OTH. The sooner, sweet, for you.

DES. Shall 't be to-night at supper?

OTH. No, not to-night.

DES. To-morrow dinner, then?

OTH. I shall not dine at home;
I meet the captains at the citadel.

DES. Why then, to-morrow night; or Tuesday morn;
On Tuesday noon, or night; on Wednesday morn;—
I pr'ythee name the time; but let it not
Exceed three days: in faith, he's penitent;
And yet his trespass, in our common reason,—
Save that, they say, the wars must make example
Out of their* best,—is not almost a fault
To incur a private check. When shall he come?
Tell me, Othello: I wonder in my soul,
What you would ask me, that I should deny,
Or stand so mammering[a] on. What! Michael Cassio,
That came a-wooing with you; and so many a time,
When I have spoke of you dispraisingly,
Hath ta'en your part; to have so much to do
To bring him in! Trust me, I could do much,—

OTH. Pr'ythee, no more: let him come when he will;
I will deny thee nothing.

DES. Why, this is not a boon;
'T is as I should entreat you wear your gloves,
Or feed on nourishing dishes, or keep you warm,
Or sue to you to do a peculiar profit
To your own person: nay, when I have a suit
Wherein I mean to touch your love indeed,
It shall be full of poize and difficulty,[b]
And fearful to be granted.

OTH. I will deny thee nothing:
Whereon, I do beseech thee, grant me this,
To leave me but a little to myself.

DES. Shall I deny you? no: farewell, my lord.

OTH. Farewell, my Desdemona: I'll come to thee straight.

DES. Emilia, come.—Be* as your fancies teach you;
Whate'er you be, I am obedient.
[*Exit, with* EMILIA.

OTH. Excellent wretch! Perdition catch my soul,
But I do love thee! and when I love thee not,
Chaos is come again.

IAGO. My noble lord,—

OTH. What dost thou say, Iago?

IAGO. Did Michael Cassio, when you† woo'd my lady,
Know of your love?

OTH. He did, from first to last: why dost thou ask?

IAGO. But for a satisfaction of my thought;
No further harm.

OTH. Why of thy thought, Iago?

IAGO. I did not think he had been acquainted with her.

OTH. O, yes; and went between us very oft.

IAGO. Indeed!

OTH. *Indeed!* ay, indeed:—discern'st thou aught in that?
Is he not honest?

IAGO. Honest, my lord!

OTH. *Honest!* ay, *honest*.

IAGO. My lord, for aught I know.

OTH. What dost thou think?

IAGO. Think, my lord?

OTH. *Think, my lord!* By heaven he echoes me,
As if there were some monster in his thought
Too hideous to be shown!—Thou dost mean something:
I heard thee say but‡ now,—thou lik'dst not that,
When Cassio left my wife: what didst not like?
And, when I told thee he was of my counsel
In§ my whole course of wooing, thou criedst, *Indeed!*
And didst contract and purse thy brow together,
As if thou then hadst shut up in thy brain
Some horrible conceit. If thou dost love me,
Show me thy thought.

IAGO. My lord, you know I love you.

OTH. I think thou dost;
And, for I know thou 'rt full of love and honesty,
And weigh'st thy words before thou giv'st them breath,

(*) Old text, *her*.

a — mammering—] To *mammer* meant to *hesitate*, to *be in doubt*. In addition to the examples of this word which the commentators have given, the following passage may be cited from Dent's "Plain Man's Path-way to Heaven,"—"They bring such simple folke as we are, into a *mammering*."

b *It shall be full of poize and difficulty,*—] The folio has,—"— and difficult weight," &c., which, as "poize" means weight, is apparently an error, arising probably from the poet's having, in the first instance, written both *poize* and *weight*, uncertain which to adopt, and afterwards forgotten to cancel the discarded word.

(*) The quartos insert, *it*. (†) First folio, *he*. (‡) First folio, *even*. (§) First folio, *Of*.

Therefore these stops of thine fright me the more:
For such things in a false-disloyal knave
Are tricks of custom ; but in a man that 's just,
They 're close dilations,[a] working from the heart
That passion cannot rule.[b]

IAGO. For Michael Cassio,
I dare be sworn I think that he is honest.

OTH. I think so too.

IAGO. Men should be what they seem;
Or those that be not, would they might seem none !

OTH. Certain, *men should be what they seem.*

IAGO. Why then, I think Cassio 's an honest man.

OTH. Nay, yet there 's more in this ;
I pr'ythee speak to me as to thy thinkings,
As thou dost ruminate ; and give thy worst of thoughts,
The worst of words.

IAGO. Good my lord, pardon me :
Though I am bound to every act of duty,
I am not bound to that all slaves are free to.*
Utter my thoughts ? Why, say, they are vile and false,—
As where 's that palace whereinto foul things
Sometimes intrude not?—who has a breast so pure,
But some uncleanly apprehensions
Keep leets and law-days, and in session sit
With meditations lawful ?[c]

OTH. Thou dost conspire against thy friend, Iago,

---

[a] — close dilations,—] The accepted reading is "*delations*," the word being taken in its Latin sense of *accusations;* but "dilations" may be a contraction of *distillations*, and the meaning of "close dilations," *secret droppings*. In the quarto, 1622, we find, "close *denotements*."

[b] —— *working from the heart*
That passion *cannot rule.*]

Unless "*passion*" is here employed in the unusual sense of *prudence, caution,* &c., we must understand Othello to mean,—working from a heart that cannot govern its emotions.

(*) First folio omits, *to.*

[c] —— who has a breast so pure,
But some uncleanly apprehensions
Keep leets and law-days, and in session sit
With meditations lawful?]

The lection of the quartos ; the folio has,—
"—— Who ha's *that* breast so pure,
Wherein uncleanly Apprehensions
Keepe Leetes, and Law-dayes, and in Sessions sit
With meditations lawfull ? "

If thou but think'st him wrong'd, and mak'st his ear
A stranger to thy thoughts.
IAGO. I do beseech you,—
Though I perchance am vicious in my guess,
(As I confess it is my nature's plague
To spy into abuses, and oft* my jealousy
Shapes faults that are not,)—that your wisdom
From one that so imperfectly conceits,
Would take no notice; nor build yourself a trouble
Out of his scattering and unsure observance:—
It were not for your quiet nor your good,
Nor for my manhood, honesty, and wisdom,
To let you know my thoughts.
OTH. What dost thou mean?
IAGO. Good name in man and woman, dear my lord,
Is the immediate jewel of their souls:
Who steals my purse steals trash; 't is something-nothing;[a]
'T was mine, 't is his, and has been slave to [thousands;
But he that filches from me my good name,
Robs me of that which not enriches him,
And makes me poor indeed.(1)
OTH. By heaven,† I'll know thy thoughts!
IAGO. You cannot, if my heart were in your hand;
Nor shall not, whilst 't is in my custody.
OTH. Ha!
IAGO. O, beware, my lord, of Jealousy;
It is the green-ey'd monster, which doth mock[b]
The meat it feeds on: that cuckold lives in bliss
Who, certain of his fate, loves not his wronger;
But, O, what damned minutes tells he o'er,
Who dotes, yet doubts; suspects, yet soundly[c] loves!
OTH. O, misery!
IAGO. Poor and content is rich, and rich enough;
But riches fineless is as poor as winter,[d]
To him that ever fears he shall be poor:—
Good heaven, the souls of all my tribe defend
From jealousy!
OTH. Why, why is this?
Think'st thou I'd make a life of jealousy;
To follow still the changes of the moon
With fresh suspicions? No: to be once in doubt,
Is once* to be resolv'd. Exchange me for a goat,
When I shall turn the business of my soul
To such exsufflicate[e] and blown† surmises,
Matching thy inference. 'T is not to make me jealous,
To say my wife is fair, feeds well, loves company,
Is free of speech, sings, plays, and dances well;‡
Where virtue is, these are more virtuous:
Nor from mine own weak merits will I draw
The smallest fear or doubt of her revolt;
For she had eyes, and chose me. No, Iago;
I'll see before I doubt; when I doubt, prove;
And, on the proof, there is no more but this,—
Away at once with love or jealousy!
IAGO. I am glad of this; for now I shall have reason
To show the love and duty that I bear you
With franker spirit: therefore, as I am bound,
Receive it from me:—I speak not yet of proof.
Look to your wife; observe her well with Cassio;
Wear your eye§ thus,—not jealous nor secure:
I would not have your free and noble nature,
Out of self-bounty, be abus'd; look to 't:
I know our country disposition well;
In Venice they do let heaven see the pranks
They dare not show their husbands; their best conscience
Is not to leav't undone, but keep't unknown.
OTH. Dost thou say so?
IAGO. She did deceive her father, marrying you;
And when she seem'd to shake and fear your looks,
She lov'd them most.
OTH. And so she did.
IAGO. Why, go to, then;
She that, so young, could give out such a seeming,
To seel her father's eyes up, close as oak,—[f]

(*) First folio, *of*. (†) First folio omits, *By heaven*.

(*) First folio omits, *once*. (†) First folio, *blowed*.
(‡) First folio omits, *well*. (§) First folio, *eyes*.

a — *'t is* something-nothing;] This is invariably printed, "something, nothing;" but "*something-nothing*" appears to have been one of those compound epithets to which our old writers were so partial, and of which the plays before us afford very many more examples than have ever been noted. The precise meaning of the phrase it is not easy to determine, the only instance of its use we have met with being the following:—"Before this newes was stale came a taile of freshe sammon to countermand it with certaine newes of a *something nothing*, and a priest that was neither dead nor alive, but suspended between both."—*A Watch Bayte to Spare Provender*, &c. &c. 4to. 1604. It appears, however, to have been nearly equivalent to the expression, *neither here nor there*.

b O, beware, my lord, of Jealousy;
It is the green-ey'd monster, which doth mock
The meat it feeds on:]

For "mock" of all the old copies, Hanmer printed *make;* and the question what is the meat that Jealousy feeds on has never yet been settled. Some affirm it to be Love; some, Desdemona; some, *pabulum zelotypiæ*. Strange that it should have occurred to no one that the meat the monster mocks (i.e. *scoffs, gibes*, or *ridicules*,) while he feeds on it, may be his credulous victim,—that thrice-wretched mortal,—

"Who dotes, yet doubts; suspects, yet soundly loves."

c — soundly *loves!*] So the folio, in support of which Mr. Dyce quotes from "Henry V." Act V. Sc. 2,—"O, fair Katherine, if you will *love me soundly* with your French heart," &c. The quartos have,—"suspects, yet *strongly* loves;" and a few modern editions read, "*fondly* loves."

d *But* riches fineless is *as poor* as winter,—] *Riches fineless*, are treasures *endless, unnumbered*. Shakespeare before in this play uses "*riches*" as a singular,—

"The *riches* of the ship *is* come on shore."

e — exsufflicate—] This word, in the old copies spelt exufflicate, Dr. Richardson considers, not improbably, "a misprint for *exsufflate*, i.e. *efflate*, or *efflated*, puffed out, and consequently, exaggerated, extravagant," &c.

f *To seel her father's eyes up, close as* oak,—] The technical term *to seel*, which has been before explained, would lead us to suspect the poet wrote,—"close as *hawk's*."

He thought 't was witchcraft:—but I am much to blame;
I humbly do beseech you of your pardon,
For too much loving you.

OTH. I am bound to thee for ever.

IAGO. I see this hath a little dash'd your spirits.

OTH. Not a jot, not a jot.

IAGO. I' faith,* I fear it has.
I hope you will consider what is spoke
Comes from my† love;—but I do see you're mov'd:—
I am to pray you not to strain my speech
To grosser issues nor to larger reach,
Than to suspicion.

OTH. I will not.

IAGO. Should you do so, my lord,
My speech should fall into such vile success
As my thoughts aim not at.[a] Cassio's my worthy friend:—
My lord, I see you're mov'd.

OTH. No, not much mov'd:—
I do not think but Desdemona's honest.

IAGO. Long live she so! and long live you to think so!

OTH. And yet, how nature erring from itself,—

IAGO. Ay, there's the point:—as,—to be bold with you,—
Not to affect many proposed matches
Of her own clime, complexion, and degree,
Whereto we see in all things nature tends;—
Foh! one may smell in such, a will most rank,
Foul disproportions, thoughts unnatural,—
But, pardon me; I do not in position
Distinctly speak of her; though I may fear
Her will, recoiling to her better judgment,
May fall to match you with her country forms,
And happily repent.

OTH. Farewell, farewell:—
If more thou dost perceive, let me know more;—
Set on thy wife to observe.—Leave me, Iago.

IAGO. My lord, I take my leave. [*Going.*

OTH. Why did I marry?—This honest creature, doubtless,
Sees and knows more, much more, than he unfolds.

IAGO. [*Returning.*] My lord, I would I might entreat your honour
To scan this thing no farther; leave it to time:
Although 't is fit that Cassio have his place,—
For, sure, he fills it up with great ability,—
Yet, if you please to hold* him off awhile,
You shall by that perceive him and his means:
Note, if your lady strain his entertainment[b]
With any strong or vehement importunity;
Much will be seen in that. In the mean time,
Let me be thought too busy in my fears,—
As worthy cause I have to fear I am,—
And hold her free, I do beseech your honour.

OTH. Fear not my government.

IAGO. I once more take my leave. [*Exit.*

OTH. This fellow 's of exceeding honesty,
And knows all qualities, with a learned spirit
Of human dealings. If I do prove her haggard,[c]
Though that her jesses[d] were my dear heart-strings,
I'd whistle her off, and let her down the wind,
To prey at fortune.[e] Haply, for I am black,
And have not those soft parts of conversation
That chamberers have; or, for I am declin'd
Into the vale of years,—yet that's not much;—
She's gone; I am abus'd; and my relief
Must be to loathe her. O, curse of marriage,
That we can call these delicate creatures ours,
And not their appetites! I had rather be a toad,
And live upon the vapour of a dungeon,
Than keep a corner in the thing I love,
For others' uses. Yet, 't is the plague of† great ones;
Prerogativ'd are they less than the base;
'T is destiny unshunnable, like death:
Even then this forked plague[f] is fated to us
When we do quicken. Desdemona comes:
If she be false, O, then heaven mocks itself!—[g]
I'll not believe 't.

Re-enter DESDEMONA, *and* EMILIA.

DES. How now, my dear Othello!
Your dinner, and the generous islanders
By you invited, do attend your presence.

(*) First folio, *Trust me.* (†) First folio, *your.*

(*) First folio omits, *hold.* (†) First folio, *to.*

[a] As my thoughts aim not at.] The reading of the quartos: the folio has,—"which my thoughts aim'd not."

[b] — his entertainment—] His *re-instatement.* "*Entertainment* was the military term for the admission of soldiers."—JOHNSON.

[c] — haggard,—] In falconry this term was often applied to a wild, unreclaimed hawk; one accustomed to seek its own prey.

[d] — jesses—] Short thongs attached to the foot of the hawk; which the falconer twisted round his hand in holding her.

[e] I'd whistle her off, and let her down the wind,
To prey at fortune.]

"The falconers always let fly the hawk against the wind; if she flies with the wind behind her, she seldom returns. If therefore a hawk was for any reason to be dismissed, she was *let down the wind,* and from that time shifted for herself and *preyed at fortune.*"—JOHNSON.

[f] — forked plague—] Malone quotes an Epigram of Sir John Harrington which very happily illustrates this expression:—

"Actæon guiltless unawares espying
Naked Diana bathing in her bowre,
Was plagu'd with *hornes;* his dogs did him devoure;
Wherefore take heed, ye that are curious, prying,
With some such *forked plague* you be not smitten,
And in your foreheads see your faults be written."

[g] —— Desdemona comes:
If she be false, O, then, heaven mocks itself!—]

So the quartos; in the folio we have,—

"—— *Looke where she* comes
If she be false, *heaven mock'd itself.*"

OTH. I am to blame.
DES. Why do you speak so faintly?[a]
Are you not well?
OTH. I have a pain upon my forehead here.
DES. Why, that 's with watching; 't will away again:
Let me but bind it hard, within this hour
It will be well.
OTH. Your napkin is too little;
[*He puts the handkerchief from him; and it drops.*
Let it alone. Come, I'll go in with you.
DES. I am very sorry that you are not well.
[*Exeunt* OTH. *and* DES.
EMIL. I am glad I have found this napkin:
This was her first remembrance[b] from the Moor:
My wayward husband hath a hundred times
Woo'd me to steal it; but she so loves the token,—
For he conjur'd her she should ever keep it,—
That she reserves it evermore about her,
To kiss and talk to. I'll have the work ta'en out,[c]
And give 't Iago; what he will do with it,
Heaven knows, not I;
I nothing, but to please his fantasy.

Re-enter IAGO.

IAGO. How now! what do you here alone?
EMIL. Do not you chide; I have a thing for you.
IAGO. A thing for me![d]—it is a common thing—
EMIL. Ha!
IAGO. To have a foolish wife.
EMIL. O, is that all? What will you give me now
For that same handkerchief?
IAGO. What handkerchief?
EMIL. *What handkerchief?*
Why, that the Moor first gave to Desdemona;
That which so often you did bid me steal.
IAGO. Hast stolen it from her?
EMIL. No, faith;* she let it drop by negligence,
And, to the advantage, I, being here, took 't up.
Look, here it is.
IAGO. A good wench; give it me.
EMIL. What will you do with 't, that you have been so earnest
To have me filch it?
IAGO. [*Snatching it.*] Why, what's that to you?
EMIL. If it be not for some purpose of import,
Giv 't me again; poor lady! she'll run mad
When she shall lack it.
IAGO. Be not acknown[e] on 't: I have use for it.
Go, leave me. [*Exit* EMILIA.
I will in Cassio's lodging lose this napkin,
And let him find it. Trifles light as air
Are to the jealous confirmations strong
As proofs of holy writ: this may do something.
The Moor already changes with my poison:—
Dangerous conceits are, in their natures, poisons,[f]
Which at the first are scarce found to distaste,
But, with a little act upon the blood,
Burn like the mines of sulphur.—I did say so:—
Look, where he comes! Not poppy, nor mandragora,(2)
Nor all the drowsy syrups of the world,
Shall ever med'cine thee to that sweet sleep
Which thou ow'dst yesterday.

Re-enter OTHELLO.

OTH. Ha! ha! false to me?
IAGO. Why, how now, general! no more of that.
OTH. Avaunt! be gone! thou hast set me on the rack:—
I swear 'tis better to be much abus'd
Than but to know 't a little.
IAGO. How now, my lord!
OTH. What sense had I of* her stol'n hours of lust?
I saw 't not, thought it not, it harm'd not me:
I slept the next night well, was free and merry;[g]
I found not Cassio's kisses on her lips:
He that is robb'd, not wanting what is stol'n,
Let him not know 't, and he's not robb'd at all.
IAGO. I am sorry to hear this.
OTH. I had been happy, if the general camp,

(*) First folio, *but*.

(*) First folio, *in*.

[a] Why do you speak so faintly?] The quarto reads,—"Why *is* your *speech so faint?*"

[b] — remembrance—] That is, *memorial* or *forget-me-not*.

[c] — *I'll have the work* ta'en out,—] *Taken out* means *copied*. Thus in the preface to Philemon Holland's translation of Pliny, 1610: "Nicophanes (a famous painter) gave his mind wholly to antique pictures, partly to exemplifie and *take out* their patterns," &c. So also in Middleton's play of "Women beware of Women," Act I. Sc. 1,—

"—— she intends
To *take out* other works in a new sampler."

[d] A thing for me!—] The folio reads,—"*You have* a thing for me?" &c.

[e] *Be not* acknown on 't:—] The quarto 1622 has,—"Be not *you known* on 't." "Acknown" is a word far from unusual with our early authors. See the notes *ad l.* in the *Variorum*, 1821.

[f] The *Moor already changes with my* poison:—
Dangerous conceits are, in their natures, poisons,—]

The repetition of *poison* here is so inelegant that we may well suspect the word in one line was caught by the compositor's eye from the other, but it is hard to say in which the corruption lies.

[g] I slept the next night well, was free and merry;] So both the quartos. The folio reads,—

"I slept the next night well, *fed well*, was free and merrie."

Pioners[a] and all, had tasted her sweet body,
So I had nothing known. O, now, for ever
Farewell the tranquil mind! farewell content!
Farewell the plumed troops, and the big wars,
That make ambition virtue! O, farewell!
Farewell the neighing steed, and the shrill trump,
The spirit-stirring drum, the ear-piercing fife,(3)
The royal banner, and all quality,
Pride, pomp, and circumstance of glorious war!
And, O, you mortal engines, whose rude throats
The immortal Jove's dread clamours counterfeit,
Farewell! Othello's occupation 's gone!

IAGO. Is 't possible?—My lord,—

OTH. Villain, be sure thou prove my love a whore,—
Be sure of it; give me the ocular proof;
[*Seizing him by the throat.*
Or, by the worth of man's[b] eternal soul,
Thou hadst been better have been born a dog
Than answer my wak'd wrath!

IAGO. Is 't come to this?

OTH. Make me to see 't; or, at the least, so prove it,
That the probation bear no hinge nor loop
To hang a doubt on, or woe upon thy life!

IAGO. My noble lord,—

OTH. If thou dost slander her, and torture me,
Never pray more; abandon all remorse;[c]
On horror's head horrors accumulate;
Do deeds to make heaven weep, all earth amaz'd;
For nothing canst thou to damnation add,
Greater than that!

IAGO. O, grace! O, heaven forgive me!
Are you a man? have you a soul or sense?—
God be wi' you; take mine office.—O, wretched fool,
That liv'st* to make thine honesty a vice!—
O, monstrous world! Take note, take note, O, world,
To be direct and honest is not safe.—
I thank you for this profit; and from hence
I 'll love no friend, sith love breeds such offence.

OTH. Nay, stay:—thou shouldst be honest.

IAGO. I should be wise; for honesty's a fool,
And loses that it works for.

OTH. By the world,
I think my wife be honest, and think she is not;
I think that thou art just, and think thou art not!
I'll have some proof: her† name, that was as fresh
As Dian's visage, is now begrim'd and black
As mine own face.—If there be cords, or knives,
Poison, or fire, or suffocating streams,
I'll not endure it.—Would I were satisfied!

IAGO. I see, sir,* you are eaten up with passion:
I do repent me that I put it to you.
You would be satisfied?

OTH. *Would!* nay, I will.

IAGO. And may: but how? how satisfied, my lord?
Would you the supervisor† grossly gape on,—
Behold her tupp'd!‡

OTH. Death and damnation! O!

IAGO. It were a tedious difficulty, I think,
To bring them to that prospect: damn them then,
If ever mortal eyes do see them bolster
More than their own? What then? how then?
What shall I say? Where 's satisfaction?
It is impossible you should see this,
Were they as prime as goats, as hot as monkeys,
As salt as wolves in pride, and fools as gross
As ignorance made drunk. But yet, I say,
If imputation and strong circumstances,—
Which lead directly to the door of truth,—
Will give you satisfaction, you may have't.

OTH. Give me a living reason she's disloyal.

IAGO. I do not like the office:
But, sith I 'm enter'd in this cause so far,—
Prick'd to't by foolish honesty and love,—
I will go on. I lay with Cassio lately;
And, being troubled with a raging tooth,
I could not sleep.
There are a kind of men so loose of soul,
That in their sleeps will mutter their affairs;
One of this kind is Cassio:
In sleep I heard him say,—*Sweet Desdemona,*
Let us be wary, let us hide our loves.
And then, sir, would he gripe and wring my hand,
Cry,—*O, sweet creature!* and§ then kiss me hard,
As if he pluck'd up kisses by the roots,
That grew upon my lips; then|| laid his leg
Over my thigh, and sigh'd, and kiss'd;¶ and then
Cried,** *Cursed fate that gave thee to the Moor!*

OTH. O, monstrous! monstrous!

IAGO. Nay, this was but his dream.

OTH. But this denoted a foregone conclusion,
'T is a shrewd doubt, though it be but a dream.

IAGO. And this may help to thicken other proofs,
That do demonstrate thinly.

OTH. I'll tear her all to pieces.

(*) First folio, *lov'st*. (†) First folio, *my*.

(*) First folio omits, *sir*. (†) First folio, *supervision*.
(‡) Old text, *top'd* and *topt*. (§) First folio omits, *and*.
(||) First folio omits, *then*. (¶) First folio, *sigh and kiss*.
(**) First folio, *Cry*.

[a] Pioners—] The "pioners" or *pioneers* were of old the degraded soldiers. So in "The Laws and Ordinances of War," 1640, quoted by Grose,—"If a trooper shall loose his horse or hackney, or a footman any part of his arms, by negligence or lewdnesse, by dice or cardes; he or they shall remain in qualitie of *pioners*, or scavengers, till they be furnished with as good as were lost, at their own charge."

[b] — *of* man's *eternal soul*,—] The folio reads, with much less force,—

"—— of *mine* eternal soul," &c.

[c] — *abandon all* remorse;] All pity, all tenderness of feeling.

IAGO. Nay, but* be wise; yet we see nothing done;
She may be honest yet. Tell me but this,—
Have you not sometimes seen a handkerchief
Spotted with strawberries in your wife's hand?

OTH. I gave her such a one; 't was my first gift.

IAGO. I know not that: but such a handkerchief
(I am sure it was your wife's) did I to-day
See Cassio wipe his beard with.

OTH. If it be that,—

IAGO. If it be that, or any that* was hers,
It speaks against her with the other proofs.

OTH. O, that the slave had forty thousand lives,—
One is too poor, too weak for my revenge!

(*) First folio, *yet*.

(*) Old text, *it*. Corrected by Malone.

Now do I see 't is true.—Look here, Iago ;
All my fond love thus do I blow to heaven :
'T is gone !—
Arise, black Vengeance, from the hollow hell ![a]
Yield up, O, Love, thy crown and hearted throne,
To tyrannous Hate ! Swell, bosom, with thy fraught,
For 't is of aspics' tongues !

IAGO. Yet be content.

OTH. O, blood, blood, blood !

IAGO. Patience, I say ; your mind perhaps* may change.

OTH. Never, Iago. Like to the Pontic sea,
Whose icy current and compulsive course
Ne'er feels† retiring ebb, but keeps due on
To the Propontic and the Hellespont ;
Even so my bloody thoughts, with violent pace,
Shall ne'er look back, ne'er ebb to humble love,
Till that a capable and wide revenge
Swallow them up.—Now, by yond marble heaven,
In the due reverence of a sacred vow [*Kneels.*
I here engage my words.

IAGO. Do not rise yet.— [*Kneels.*
Witness, you ever-burning lights above,
You elements that clip us round about,
Witness, that here Iago doth give up
The execution of his wit, hands, heart,
To wrong'd Othello's service ! Let him command,
And to obey shall be in me remorse,
What bloody business ever !

OTH. I greet thy love,
Not with vain thanks, but with acceptance bounteous,
And will upon the instant put thee to 't :
Within these three days let me hear thee say
That Cassio 's not alive.

IAGO. My friend is dead : 't is done at your request ;
But let her live.

OTH. Damn her, lewd minx ! O, damn her ! ‡
Come, go with me apart ; I will withdraw,
To furnish me with some swift means of death
For the fair devil. Now art thou my lieutenant.

IAGO. I am your own for ever. [*Exeunt.*

SCENE IV.—*The same. Before the Castle.*

Enter DESDEMONA, EMILIA, *and* Clown.

DES. Do you know, sirrah, where lieutenant Cassio lies ?

CLO. I dare not say he lies any where.

DES. Why, man ?

CLO. He is a soldier ; and for one* to say a soldier lies, is† stabbing.

DES. Go to : where lodges he ?

CLO. To tell you where he lodges, is to tell you where I lie.

DES. Can anything be made of this ?

CLO. I know not where he lodges ; and for me to devise a lodging, and say he lies here or he lies there, were to lie in mine own throat.

DES. Can you inquire him out, and be edified by report ?

CLO. I will catechize the world for him ; that is, make questions, and by them answer.

DES. Seek him, bid him come hither ; tell him I have moved my lord on his behalf, and hope all will be well.

CLO. To do this is within the compass of man's wit ; and therefore I will attempt the doing it. [*Exit.*

DES. Where should I lose that ‡ handkerchief, Emilia ?

EMIL. I know not, madam.

DES. Believe me, I had rather have lost my purse
Full of crusadoes : (4) and, but my noble Moor
Is true of mind, and made of no such baseness
As jealous creatures are, it were enough
To put him to ill thinking.

EMIL. Is he not jealous ?

DES. Who, he ? I think the sun where he was born
Drew all such humours from him.

EMIL. Look, where he comes.

DES. I will not leave him now, till Cassio
Be call'd to him.

Enter OTHELLO.

How is 't with you, my lord ?

OTH. Well, my good lady ;—[*Aside.*] O, hardness to dissemble !—
How do you, Desdemona ?

DES. Well, my good lord.

OTH. Give me your hand : this hand is moist, my lady.

DES. It yet§ has felt no age nor known no sorrow.

OTH. This argues fruitfulness and liberal heart :—
Hot, hot, and moist : this hand of yours requires
A sequester from liberty, fasting and prayer,
Much castigation, exercise devout ;

(*) First folio omits, *perhaps*. (†) First folio, *keepes*. (‡) First folio repeats, *damn her*.

(*) First folio, *me*. (†) First folio, *'tis*. (‡) First folio, *the*. (§) First folio omits, *yet*.

[a] — the hollow hell !] The quartos, which are here generally followed, have, " — thy hollow cell ! "

For here's a young and sweating devil here,
That commonly rebels. 'T is a good hand,
A frank one.

DES. You may, indeed, say so;
For 't was that hand that gave away my heart.

OTH. A liberal hand: the hearts of old gave hands;
But our new heraldry is hands, not hearts.(5)

DES. I cannot speak of this. Come now, your promise.

OTH. What promise, chuck?

DES. I have sent to bid Cassio come speak with you.

OTH. I have a salt and sorry rheum offends me;
Lend me thy handkerchief.

DES. Here, my lord.

OTH. That which I gave you.

DES. I have it not about me.

OTH. Not?

DES. No, indeed, my lord.

OTH. That is a fault.
That handkerchief
Did an Egyptian to my mother give;
She was a charmer,[a] and could almost read
The thoughts of people: she told her, while she kept it,
'T would make her amiable, and subdue my father
Entirely to her love; but if she lost it,
Or made a gift of it, my father's eye
Should hold her loathly,* and his spirits should hunt
After new fancies. She, dying, gave it me;
And bid me, when my fate would have me wive,
To give it her. I did so: and take heed on't;
Make it a darling like your precious eye;
To lose 't or give 't away were such perdition
As nothing else could match.

DES. Is 't possible?

OTH. 'T is true: there's magic in the web of it:
A sibyl, that had number'd in the world
The sun to course two hundred compasses,
In her prophetic fury sew'd the work;
The worms were hallow'd that did breed the silk;
And it was dy'd in mummy which the skilful
Conserv'd of maidens' hearts.

DES. Indeed! is 't true?

OTH. Most veritable; therefore look to 't well.

DES. Then would to God† that I had never seen 't!

OTH. Ha! wherefore?

DES. Why do you speak so startingly and rash?

OTH. Is't lost? is't gone? speak, is't out of the way?

DES. Heaven‡ bless us!

(*) First folio, *loathed*. (†) First folio, *Heaven*.
(‡) First folio omits, *Heaven*.

[a] — a charmer,—] An enchantress; one who worked by spells and charms.

OTH. Say you?

DES. It is not lost; but what an if it were?

OTH. How!

DES. I say, it is not lost.

OTH. Fetch't, let me see't.

DES. Why, so I can, sir,* but I will not now.
This is a trick to put me from my suit:
Pray you, let Cassio be receiv'd again.

OTH. Fetch me the handkerchief: my mind misgives.

DES. Come, come;
You'll never meet a more sufficient man.

OTH. The handkerchief!

DES. I pray, talk me of Cassio.

OTH. The handkerchief! [b]

DES. A man that all his time
Hath founded his good fortunes on your love,
Shar'd dangers with you,—

OTH. The handkerchief!

DES. In sooth, you are to blame.

OTH. Away!(6) [*Exit.*

EMIL. Is not this man jealous?

DES. I ne'er saw this before.
Sure, there's some wonder in this handkerchief;
I am most unhappy in the loss of it.

EMIL. 'T is not a year or two shows us a man:
They are all but stomachs, and we all but food;
They eat us hungerly, and when they are full
They belch us.—Look you,—Cassio and my husband.

Enter CASSIO *and* IAGO.

IAGO. There is no other way: 't is she must do't:
And, lo, the happiness! go and impórtune her.

DES. How now, good Cassio! what's the news with you?

CAS. Madam, my former suit: I do beseech you,
That by your virtuous means I may again
Exist, and be a member of his love
Whom I, with all the office of my heart,
Entirely honour. I would not be delay'd:
If my offence be of such mortal kind,
That nor my service past, nor present sorrows,
Nor purpos'd merit in futurity,
Can ransom me into his love again,
But to know so must be my benefit;
So shall I clothe me in a forc'd content,
And shut myself up in some other course,
To fortune's alms.

DES. Alas, thrice-gentle Cassio!
My advocation is not now in tune;

(*) First folio omits, *sir*.

[b] DES. I pray, talk me of Cassio.
OTH. The handkerchief!]
These two speeches are omitted in the folio.

My lord is not my lord; nor should I know him,
Were he in favour as in humour alter'd.
So help me every spirit sanctified,
As I have spoken for you all my best,
And stood within the blank of his displeasure
For my free speech! You must a while be patient:
What I can do I will; and more I will
Than for myself I dare: let that suffice you.

IAGO. Is my lord angry?

EMIL. He went hence but now,
And certainly in strange unquietness.

IAGO. Can he be angry? I have seen the cannon,
When it hath blown his ranks into the air,
And, like the devil, from his very arm,
Puff'd his own brother;—and can he be angry? *
Something of moment, then: I will go meet him;
There's matter in't indeed, if he be angry.

DES. I pr'ythee, do so.—[*Exit* IAGO.] Something, sure, of state,—
Either from Venice, or some unhatch'd practice
Made démonstrable here in Cyprus to him,—
Hath puddled his clear spirit; and in such cases
Men's natures wrangle with inferior things,
Though great ones are their object. 'Tis even so;
For let our finger ache, and it indues
Our other healthful members even to a sense
Of pain. Nay, we must think men are not gods,
Nor of them look for such observancy
As fits the bridal.—Beshrew me much, Emilia,
I was (unhandsome warrior as I am)
Arraigning his unkindness with my soul;
But now I find I had suborn'd the witness,
And he's indicted falsely.

EMIL. Pray heaven it be state-matters, as you think,
And no conception nor no jealous toy
Concerning you.

DES. Alas, the day, I never gave him cause!

EMIL. But jealous souls will not be answer'd so;
They are not ever jealous for the cause,
But jealous for they're jealous: it is a monster,
Begot upon itself, born on itself.

DES. Heaven keep that† monster from Othello's mind!

EMIL. Lady, amen!

DES. I will go seek him.—Cassio, walk hereabout:
If I do find him fit, I'll move your suit,
And seek to effect it to my uttermost.

CAS. I humbly thank your ladyship.
[*Exeunt* DESDEMONA *and* EMILIA.

Enter BIANCA.

BIAN. Save you, friend Cassio!

CAS. What make you from home?
How is it with you, my most fair Bianca?
I'faith,* sweet love, I was coming to your house.

BIAN. And I was going to your lodging, Cassio.
What! keep a week away? seven days and nights?
Eight score eight hours? and lovers' absent hours,
More tedious than the dial eight score times?
O, weary reckoning!

CAS. Pardon me, Bianca;
I have this while with leaden thoughts been press'd;
But I shall, in a more continuate[a] time,
Strike off this score of absence. Sweet Bianca,
[*Giving her* Desdemona's *handkerchief.*
Take me this work out.

BIAN. O, Cassio, whence came this?
This is some token from a newer friend:
To the felt absence now I feel a cause.
Is't come to this? Well, well.

CAS. Go to, woman!
Throw your vile guesses in the devil's teeth,
From whence you have them. You are jealous now
That this is from some mistress some remembrance:
No, in good troth, Bianca.

BIAN. Why, whose is it?

CAS. I know not neither: I found it in my chamber.
I like the work well: ere it be demanded,
(As like enough it will) I'd have it copied:
Take it, and do't; and leave me for this time.

BIAN. Leave you! wherefore?

CAS. I do attend here on the general;
And think it no addition, nor my wish,
To have him see me woman'd.

BIAN. Why, I pray you?

CAS. Not that I love you not.

BIAN. But that you do not love me.
I pray you, bring me on the way a little;
And say if I shall see you soon at night.

CAS. 'Tis but a little way that I can bring you,
For I attend here: but I'll see you soon.

BIAN. 'Tis very good; I must be circumstanc'd.
[*Exeunt.*

(*) First folio, *is he angry?*

(†) First folio, *the.*

(*) First folio, *Indeed.*

a —a *more* continuate *time,*—] That is, Johnson says, a time *less interrup'ed.* The quarto 1622 has,—"A more *convenient* time."

ACT IV.

SCENE I.—*The same. Before the Castle.*

Enter OTHELLO *and* IAGO.

IAGO. Will you think so?
OTH. *Think so,* Iago!
IAGO. What,
To kiss in private?

OTH. An unauthoriz'd kiss.
IAGO. Or to be naked with her friend in bed
An hour or more, not meaning any harm?
OTH. Naked in bed, Iago, and not mean harm!
It is hypocrisy against the devil:
They that mean virtuously, and yet do so,

The devil their virtue tempts, and they tempt heaven.

IAGO. If they do nothing, 'tis a venial slip:
But if I give my wife a handkerchief,—

OTH. What then?

IAGO. Why then 'tis hers, my lord; and, being hers,
She may, I think, bestow't on any man.

OTH. She is protectress of her honour too;
May she give that?

IAGO. Her honour is an essence that's not seen;
They have it very oft that have it not:
But, for the handkerchief,—

OTH. By heaven, I would most gladly have forgot it:—
Thou saidst,—O, it comes o'er my memory,
As doth the raven o'er the infectious house,
Boding to all,—he had my handkerchief.

IAGO. Ay, what of that?

OTH. That's not so good now.

IAGO. What, if I had said I had seen him do you wrong?
Or heard him say,—as knaves be such abroad,
Who having, by their own importunate suit,
Or voluntary dotage of some mistress,
Convinced, or supplied them, cannot choose
But they must blab,—

OTH. Hath he said any thing?

IAGO. He hath, my lord; but be you well assur'd,
No more than he'll unswear.

OTH. What hath he said?

IAGO. Faith,* that he did,—I know not what he did.

OTH. What? what

IAGO. Lie—

OTH. With her?

IAGO. With her;—on her;—what you will.

OTH. *Lie with her! lie on her!*—We say lie on her, when they belie her: Lie with her! that's fulsome.—Handkerchief,—confessions,—handkerchief!—To confess, and be hanged for his labour.—First, to be hanged, and then to confess.—I tremble at it. Nature would not invest herself in such shadowing passion, without some instruction. It is not words that shake me thus:—Pish!—Noses, ears, and lips:—Is't possible?—Confess!—Handkerchief!—O, devil!(1) [*Falls in a trance.*

IAGO. Work on,
My medicine, work! Thus credulous fools are caught;
And many worthy and chaste dames even thus,
All guiltless, meet reproach.—What, ho! my lord!
My lord, I say! Othello!

Enter CASSIO.

How now, Cassio!

CAS. What is the matter?

IAGO. My lord is fall'n into an epilepsy:
This is his second fit; he had one yesterday.

CAS. Rub him about the temples.

IAGO. No, forbear:[a]
The lethargy must have his quiet course;
If not, he foams at mouth, and by and by
Breaks out to savage madness. Look, he stirs:
Do you withdraw yourself a little while,
He will recover straight: when he is gone,
I would on great occasion speak with you.— [*Exit* CASSIO.
How is it, general? have you not hurt your head?

OTH. Dost thou mock me?

IAGO. I mock you! no,* by heaven:
Would you would bear your fortune like a man!

OTH. A horned man's a monster and a beast.

IAGO. There's many a beast, then, in a populous city,
And many a civil monster.

OTH. Did he confess it?

IAGO. Good sir, be a man;
Think every bearded fellow that's but yok'd
May draw with you: there's millions now alive
That nightly lie in those unproper[b] beds,
Which they dare swear peculiar; your case is better.
O, 'tis the spite of hell, the fiend's arch-mock,
To lip a wanton in a secure couch,
And to suppose her chaste! No, let me know;
And, knowing what I am, I know what she shall be.

OTH. O, thou art wise; 'tis certain.

IAGO. Stand you awhile apart;
Confine yourself but in a patient list.
Whilst you were here, o'erwhelmed with your grief,—
A passion most unsuiting† such a man,—
Cassio came hither: I shifted him away,
And laid good 'scuse upon your ecstasy;
Bade him anon return, and here speak with me;
The which he promis'd. Do but encave yourself,
And mark the fleers, the gibes, and notable scorns,
That dwell in every region of his face;
For I will make him tell the tale anew,—
Where, how, how oft, how long ago, and when
He hath, and is again to cope your wife;
I say, but mark his gesture. Marry, patience;
Or I shall say you are all-in-all in spleen,
And nothing of a man.

(*) First folio, *why*.

[a] No, forbear:] These words are not in the folio.

(*) First folio, *not*. (†) First folio, *resulting*.

[b] — unproper—] *Common*.

OTH. Dost thou hear, Iago?
I will be found most cunning in my patience;
But—dost thou hear?—most bloody.

IAGO. That's not amiss;
But yet keep time in all. Will you withdraw?
[OTHELLO *retires.*
Now will I question Cassio of Bianca,
A housewife that, by selling her desires,
Buys herself bread and clothes: it is a creature
That dotes on Cassio,—as 'tis the strumpet's plague,
To beguile many and be beguil'd by one;—
He, when he hears of her, cannot restrain
From the excess of laughter:—here he comes:—
As he shall smile, Othello shall go mad;
And his unbookish[a] jealousy must construe*
Poor Cassio's smiles, gestures, and light behaviour,
Quite in the wrong.—

Re-enter CASSIO.

How do you now,* lieutenant?

CAS. The worser, that you give me the addition
Whose want even kills me.

IAGO. Ply Desdemona well, and you are sure on't.
Now, if this suit lay in Bianca's dower,
[*Speaking lower.*
How quickly should you speed!

CAS. Alas, poor caitiff!

OTH. [*Aside.*] Look, how he laughs already!

(*) First folio, *conserve*.

[a] — unbookish *jealousy*—] *Ignorant* jealousy.

(*) First folio omits, *now*.

IAGO. I never knew woman love man so.

CAS. Alas, poor rogue! I think, i'faith,* she loves me.

OTH. [*Aside.*] Now he denies it faintly, and laughs it out.

IAGO. Do you hear, Cassio?

OTH. [*Aside.*] Now he importunes him
To tell it o'er:—go to; well said, well said.

IAGO. She gives it out, that you shall marry her:
Do you intend it?

CAS. Ha, ha, ha!

OTH. [*Aside.*] Do you triumph, Roman? do you triumph?

CAS. I marry her!†—what, a customer![a] Pr'ythee bear some charity to my wit; do not think it so unwholesome.—Ha, ha, ha!

OTH. [*Aside.*] So, so, so, so:—they laugh that win.

IAGO. Faith,‡ the cry goes that you shall§ marry her.

CAS. Pr'ythee, say true.

IAGO. I am a very villain else.

OTH. [*Aside.*] Have you scored me?[b] Well.

CAS. This is the monkey's own giving out: she is persuaded I will marry her, out of her own love and flattery, not out of my promise.

OTH. [*Aside.*] Iago beckons‖ me; now he begins the story.

CAS. She was here even now; she haunts me in every place. I was, the other day, talking on the sea-bank with certain Venetians; and thither comes the bauble, and falls me thus about my neck,—

OTH. [*Aside.*] Crying, *O, dear Cassio!* as it were: his gesture imports it.

CAS. So hangs, and lolls, and weeps upon me; so hales¶ and pulls me:—ha, ha, ha!—

OTH. [*Aside.*] Now he tells how she plucked him to my chamber. O, I see that nose of yours, but not that dog I shall throw it to.

CAS. Well, I must leave her company.

IAGO. Before me! look, where she comes.

CAS. 'Tis such another fitchew! marry, a perfumed one.

Enter BIANCA.

—What do you mean by this haunting of me?

BIAN. Let the devil and his dam haunt you! What did you mean by that same handkerchief you gave me even now? I was a fine fool to take it. I must take out the work!—A likely piece of work, that you should find it in your chamber, and know not who left it there! This is some minx's token, and I must take out the work! There,—give it your hobby-horse:[c] wheresoever you had it, I'll take out no work on't.

CAS. How now, my sweet Bianca! how now! how now!

OTH. [*Aside.*] By heaven, that should be my handkerchief!

BIAN. An* you'll come to supper to-night you may; an* you will not, come when you are next prepared for. [*Exit.*

IAGO. After her, after her.

CAS. Faith,† I must; she'll rail in the streets else.

IAGO. Will you sup there?

CAS. Faith,‡ I intend so.

IAGO. Well, I may chance to see you; for I would very fain speak with you.

CAS. Pr'ythee, come; will you?

IAGO. Go to; say no more. [*Exit* CASSIO.

OTH. [*Advancing.*] How shall I murder him, Iago?

IAGO. Did you perceive how he laughed at his vice?

OTH. O, Iago!

IAGO. And did you see the handkerchief?

OTH. Was that mine?

IAGO. Yours, by this hand: and to see how he prizes the foolish woman your wife! she gave it him, and he hath given it his whore.

OTH. I would have him nine years a-killing.—A fine woman! a fair woman! a sweet woman!

IAGO. Nay, you must forget that.

OTH. Ay, let her rot, and perish, and be damned to-night; for she shall not live: no, my heart is turned to stone; I strike it, and it hurts my hand.—O, the world hath not a sweeter creature: she might lie by an emperor's side, and command him tasks.

IAGO. Nay, that's not your way.

OTH. Hang her! I do but say what she is:—so delicate with her needle!—an admirable musician! O, she will sing the savageness out of a bear!—Of so high and plenteous wit and invention!

IAGO. She's the worse for all this.

OTH. O, a thousand-thousand times:[d]—and then, of so gentle a condition!

(*) First folio, *indeed*. (†) First folio omits, *her*.
(‡) First folio, *Why*. (§) First folio omits, *shall*.
(‖) First folio, *becomes*. (¶) First folio, *shakes*.

[a] — a customer!] This was a cant term for a loose woman. So in "All's Well That Ends Well," Act V. Sc. 3,—
"I think thee now some common *customer*."

[b] *Have you* scored *me?*] "Scored" for *branded*, unless the word is a misprint. The quartos have *stor'd;* the folio, *scoar'd*.

[c] — hobby-horse:] Another by-word for an abandoned woman.

(*) First folio, *If*. (†) First folio omits, *Faith*.
(‡) First folio, *Yes*.

In the "Winter's Tale," Act I. Sc. 2, Leontes says,—
"My wife's a *hobby-horse;*"
and in "Love's Labour's Lost," Act III. Sc. 1, Armado asks,—
"Callest thou my love *hobby-horse?*" &c.

[d] O, a thousand-thousand times:—] The folio poorly reads,—
"O, a thousand, a thousand times:" &c.

IAGO. Ay, too gentle.

OTH. Nay, that's certain:—but yet the pity of it, Iago!—O, Iago, the pity of it, Iago!

IAGO. If you are so fond over her iniquity, give her patent to offend; for, if it touch not you, it comes near nobody.

OTH. I will chop her into messes:—cuckold me!

IAGO. O, 'tis foul in her.

OTH. With mine officer!

IAGO. That's fouler.

OTH. Get me some poison, Iago; this night:—I'll not expostulate with her, lest her body and beauty unprovide my mind again:—this night, Iago.

IAGO. Do it not with poison; strangle her in her bed, even the bed she hath contaminated.

OTH. Good, good: the justice of it pleases; very good!

IAGO. And, for Cassio,—let me be his undertaker: you shall hear more by midnight.

[*A trumpet without.*

OTH. Excellent good.—What trumpet is that same?

IAGO. Something from Venice, sure. 'T is Lodovico,
Come from the duke; and, see, your wife is with him.[a]

Enter LODOVICO, DESDEMONA, *and* Attendants.

LOD. Save you, worthy general!

OTH. With all my heart, sir.

LOD. The duke and* senators of Venice greet you. [*Gives him a packet.*

OTH. I kiss the instrument of their pleasures. [*Opens the packet, and reads.*

DES. And what's the news, good cousin Lodovico?

IAGO. I am very glad to see you, signior;
Welcome to Cyprus.

LOD. I thank you. How does lieutenant Cassio?

IAGO. Lives, sir.

DES. Cousin, there's fall'n between him and my lord
An unkind breach; but you shall make all well.

OTH. Are you sure of that?

DES. My lord?

OTH. [Reads.] *This fail you not to do, as you will—*

LOD. He did not call: he's busy in the paper.
Is there division 'twixt my lord and Cassio?

DES. A most unhappy one; I would do much
To atone them, for the love I bear to Cassio.

OTH. Fire and brimstone!

DES. My lord?

OTH. Are you wise?

DES. What, is he angry?

LOD. May be the letter mov'd him;
For, as I think, they do command him home,
Deputing Cassio in his government.

DES. Trust me, I am glad on 't.

OTH. Indeed?

DES. My lord?

OTH. I am glad to see you mad.

DES. Why, sweet Othello?

OTH. Devil! [*Striking her.*

DES. I have not deserv'd this.

LOD. My lord, this would not be believ'd in Venice,
Though I should swear I saw 't: 't is very much;
Make her amends; she weeps.

OTH. O, devil, devil!
If that the earth could teem with woman's tears,
Each drop she falls would prove a crocodile.—
Out of my sight!

DES. I will not stay to offend you. [*Going.*

LOD. Truly, an* obedient lady:—
I do beseech your lordship, call her back.

OTH. Mistress!

DES. My lord?

OTH. What would you with her, sir?

LOD. Who, I, my lord?

OTH. Ay; you did wish that I would make her turn:
Sir, she can turn, and turn, and yet go on,
And turn again; and she can weep, sir,—weep!
And she's obedient, as you say,—obedient!—
Very obedient.—Proceed you in your tears.—
Concerning this, sir,—O, well-painted passion!—
I am commanded home.—Get you away;
I'll send for you anon.—Sir, I obey the mandate,
And will return to Venice.—Hence, avaunt!
[*Exit* DESDEMONA.
Cassio shall have my place. And,—sir, to-night,
I do entreat that we may sup together:
You are welcome, sir, to Cyprus.—Goats and monkeys! [*Exit.*

LOD. Is this the noble Moor whom our full senate
Call all-in-all sufficient?—Is this the nature
Whom passion could not shake? whose solid virtue

(*) First folio inserts, *the.*

a Something from Venice, sure. 'T is Lodovico,
Come from the duke; and see, your wife is with him.]
We prefer here the lection of the quartos. The folio has,—

(*) First folio omits, *an.*

"I warrant something from Venice,
'T is Lodovico this, comes from Duke.
See, your wife's with him," &c.

The shot of accident, nor dart of chance,
Could neither graze nor pierce?
IAGO. He is much chang'd.
LOD. Are his wits safe? is he not light of brain?
IAGO. He's—that he is: I may not breathe my censure.
What he might be,—if, what he might, he is not,—
I would to heaven he were!
LOD. What, strike his wife!
IAGO. Faith, that was not so well; yet would I knew
That stroke would prove the worst.
LOD. Is it his use?
Or did the letters work upon his blood,
And new-create this* fault?
IAGO. Alas, alas!
It is not honesty in me to speak
What I have seen and known. You shall observe him;
And his own courses will denote him so,
That I may save my speech: do but go after,
And mark how he continues.
LOD. I am sorry that I am deceiv'd in him.
[*Exeunt.*

(*) First folio, *his*.

SCENE II.—*A Room in the Castle.*

Enter OTHELLO *and* EMILIA.

OTH. You have seen nothing, then?
EMIL. Nor ever heard, nor ever did suspect.
OTH. Yes, you have seen Cassio and she together.
EMIL. But then I saw no harm, and then I heard
Each syllable that breath made up between them.
OTH. What, did they never whisper?
EMIL. Never, my lord.
OTH. Nor send you out o' the way?
EMIL. Never.
OTH. To fetch her fan, her gloves, her mask, nor nothing?
EMIL. Never, my lord.
OTH. That's strange.
EMIL. I durst, my lord, to wager she is honest,
Lay down my soul at stake: if you think other,
Remove your thought,—it doth abuse your bosom.
If any wretch have put this in your head,
Let heaven requite it with the serpent's curse!
For, if she be not honest, chaste, and true,
There's no man happy; the purest of their wives
Is foul as slander.

OTH. Bid her come hither:—go.— [*Exit* EMILIA.
She says enough;—yet she 's a simple bawd
That cannot say as much. This is a subtle whore,
A closet-lock-and-key of villanous secrets:
And yet she'll kneel and pray; I have seen her do 't.

Enter DESDEMONA *with* EMILIA.

DES. My lord, what is your will?
OTH. Pray you, chuck, come hither.
DES. What is your pleasure?
OTH. Let me see your eyes;
Look in my face.
DES. What horrible fancy 's this?
OTH. Some of your function, mistress; [*To* EMILIA.
Leave procreants alone, and shut the door;
Cough, or cry *hem*, if any body come:
Your mystery, your mystery;—nay, despatch! [*Exit* EMILIA.
DES. Upon my knees, what doth your speech import?
I understand a fury in your words,
But not the words.[a]
OTH. Why, what art thou?
DES. Your wife, my lord; your true and loyal wife.
OTH. Come, swear it, damn thyself;
Lest, being like one of heaven, the devils themselves
Should fear to seize thee: therefore be double-damn'd,—
Swear—thou art honest.
DES. Heaven doth truly know it.
OTH. Heaven truly knows that thou art false as hell.
DES. To whom, my lord? with whom? how am I false?
OTH. Ah, Desdemon!—away! away! away!
DES. Alas, the heavy day!—Why do you weep?
Am I the motive of these tears, my lord?
If haply you my father do suspect
An instrument of this your calling back,
Lay not your blame on me; if you have lost him,
Why,* I have lost him too.
OTH. Had it pleas'd heaven
To try me with affliction; had he† rain'd
All kinds of sores and shames on my bare head;
Steep'd me in poverty to the very lips;
Given to captivity me and my utmost hopes;
I should have found in some place of my soul
A drop of patience: but, alas, to make me
The fixed figure of the time, for Scorn
To point his slow and moving finger at!—[b]
Yet could I bear that too; well, very well:
But there, where I have garner'd up my heart,
Where either I must live, or bear no life,—
The fountain from the which my current runs,
Or else dries up; to be discarded thence!
Or keep it as a cistern for foul toads
To knot and gender in!—turn thy complexion there,
Patience, thou young and rose-lipp'd cherubin!—
Ay, there,‡ look grim as hell!
DES. I hope my noble lord esteems me honest.
OTH. O, ay; as summer flies are in the shambles,
That quicken even with blowing. O, thou weed,
Who art so lovely fair, and smell'st so sweet,
That the sense aches at thee,—would thou hadst ne'er been born!
DES. Alas, what ignorant sin have I committed?
OTH. Was this fair paper, this most goodly book,
Made to write whore upon?—*What committed!*
Committed! O, thou public commoner!
I should make very forges of my cheeks,
That would to cinders burn up modesty,
Did I but speak thy deeds.—*What committed!*
Heaven stops the nose at it, and the moon winks;
The bawdy wind, that kisses all it meets,
Is hush'd within the hollow mine of earth,
And will not hear it.—*What committed!*—
Impudent strumpet![c]
DES. By heaven, you do me wrong!
OTH. Are not you a strumpet?
DES. No, as I am a Christian!
If to preserve this vessel for my lord
From any other foul unlawful touch,
Be not to be a strumpet, I am none.

(*) First folio omits, *Why*. (†) First folio, *they*. (‡) Old text, *I heere*. Corrected by Theobald.

[a] But not the words.] The folio omits this hemistich.

[b] The fixed figure of the time, for Scorn
To point his slow and moving finger at!—]

We adopt in this much discussed passage an emendation proposed by the Rev. J. Hunter, which involves only the transposition of the particles "for" and "of," and affords an excellent sense. The text of the folio is,—

"The fixed figure *for* the time *of* scorne,
To point his slow and moving finger at."

That of the quartos,—

"A fixed figure, for the time of scorne,
To point his slow unmoving fingers at. . . oh, oh," &c.

except that the second quarto reads "*finger*" for "*fingers*." Mr. Collier's annotator, availing himself of the obvious alteration *hand* for "*time*," which Rowe first made, and the equally obvious suggestion of Mason,—*slowly moving finger at*,—presents us with the following, which Mr. Collier says "we may reasonably believe to have been what the poet wrote,"—

"A fixed figure, for the *hand* of scorn
To point his *slowly moving finger at*."

[c] Impudent strumpet!] These words are omitted in the folio.

OTH. What, not a whore?
DES. No, as I shall be sav'd!
OTH. Is't possible?
DES. O, heaven forgive us!
OTH. I cry your mercy, then;
I took you for that cunning whore of Venice,
That married with Othello.—You, mistress,
That have the office opposite to St. Peter,
And keep the gate of hell!

Re-enter EMILIA.

You! you! ay, you!
We have done our course; there's money for your pains:
I pray you, turn the key, and keep our counsel. [*Exit.*
EMIL. Alas, what does this gentleman conceive?—
How do you, madam? how do you, my good lady?
DES. Faith, half asleep.
EMIL. Good madam, what's the matter with my lord?
DES. With who?
EMIL. Why, with my lord, madam.
DES. Who is thy lord?
EMIL. He that is yours, sweet lady.
DES. I have none: do not talk to me, Emilia;
I cannot weep; nor answer have I none,
But what should go by water. Pr'ythee, to-night
Lay on my bed my wedding sheets,—remember;—
And call thy husband hither.
EMIL. Here's a change, indeed! [*Exit.*
DES. 'Tis meet I should be us'd so, very meet.
How have I been behav'd, that he might stick
The small'st opinion on my great'st abuse?*

Re-enter EMILIA, *with* IAGO.

IAGO. What is your pleasure, madam? How is't with you?
DES. I cannot tell. Those that do teach young babes,
Do it with gentle means and easy tasks:
He might have chid me so; for, in good faith,
I am a child to chiding.
IAGO. What 's the matter, lady?
EMIL. Alas, Iago, my lord hath so bewhor'd her,
Thrown such despite and heavy terms upon her,
As true hearts cannot bear.†
DES. Am I that name, Iago?
IAGO. What name, fair lady?
DES. Such as she said my lord did say I was.
EMIL. He call'd her whore: a beggar in his drink,
Could not have laid such terms upon his callat.

(*) First folio, *least misuse.*
(†) First folio, *That true heart cannot bear it.*

IAGO. Why did he so?

DES. I do not know; I am sure I am none such.

IAGO. Do not weep, do not weep:—alas the day!

EMIL. Hath she forsook so many noble matches,
Her father, and her country, and her friends,
To be called whore? would it not make one weep?

DES. It is my wretched fortune.

IAGO. Beshrew him for't!
How comes this trick upon him?

DES. Nay, heaven doth know.

EMIL. I will be hang'd, if some eternal villain,
Some busy and insinuating rogue,
Some cogging, cozening slave, to get some office,
Have not devis'd this slander; I'll be hang'd else.

IAGO. Fie, there is no such man; it is impossible.

DES. If any such there be, heaven pardon him!

EMIL. A halter pardon him! and hell gnaw his bones!
Why should he call her whore? who keeps her company?
What place? what time? what form? what likelihood?
The Moor's abus'd by some most villanous knave,
Some base notorious knave, some scurvy fellow:—
O, heaven, that such companions[a] thou'dst unfold,
And put in every honest hand a whip,
To lash the rascals naked through the world
Even from the east to the west!

IAGO. Speak within door.

EMIL. O, fie upon them! Some such squire he was [*Aside to* IAGO.
That turn'd your wit the seamy side without,
And made you to suspect me with the Moor.

IAGO. You are a fool; go to. [*Aside to* EMILIA.

DES. Alas, Iago!
What shall I do to win my lord again?
Good friend, go to him; for, by this light of heaven,
I know not how I lost him. Here I kneel:—
If e'er my will did trespass 'gainst his love,
Either in discourse of thought or actual deed;
Or that mine eyes, mine ears, or any sense,
Delighted them in* any other form;
Or that I do not yet, and ever did,
And ever will,—though he do shake me off
To beggarly divorcement,—love him dearly,
Comfort forswear me! Unkindness may do much;
And his unkindness may defeat my life,
But never taint my love. I cannot say *whore*—
It does abhor me now I speak the word;
To do the act that might the addition earn,
Not the world's mass of vanity could make me.

(*) First folio, *or*.

[a] — companions—] *Companion* was often used in Shakespeare's time as a term of contempt, in the same sense that we now employ *fellow*. So in "Henry IV." Part II. Act II. Sc. 4,—"I scorn you, scurvy *companion*;" and again in "The Merry Wives of Windsor," Act III. Sc. 1,—"This same scall, scurvy, cogging *companion*."

IAGO. I pray you, be content; 't is but his humour;
The business of the state does him offence,
And he does chide with you.[a]

DES. If 't were no other!—

IAGO. It is but so, I warrant.
[*Trumpets without.*
Hark, how these instruments summon to supper!
The messengers of Venice stay the meat.
Go in, and weep not; all things shall be well.
[*Exeunt* DESDEMONA *and* EMILIA.

Enter RODERIGO.

How now, Roderigo!

ROD. I do not find that thou deal'st justly with me.

IAGO. What in the contrary?

ROD. Every day thou daff'st me with some device, Iago; and rather, as it seems to me now, keep'st from me all conveniency, than suppliest me with the least advantage of hope. I will, indeed, no longer endure it; nor am I yet persuaded to put up in peace what already I have foolishly suffered.

IAGO. Will you hear me, Roderigo?

ROD. Faith,* I have heard too much; for† your words and performances are no kin together.

IAGO. You charge me most unjustly.

ROD. With nought but truth. I have wasted myself out of my means. The jewels you have had from me to deliver to Desdemona would half have corrupted a votarist: you have told me she hath received them, and returned me expectations and comforts of sudden respect and acquaintance; but I find none.

IAGO. Well; go to; very well.

ROD. *Very well! go to!* I cannot go to, man; nor 't is not very well: nay, I think it is scurvy; and begin to find myself fobbed‡ in it.

IAGO. Very well.

ROD. I tell you, 't is not *very well.* I will make myself known to Desdemona: if she will return me my jewels, I will give over my suit, and repent my unlawful solicitation; if not, assure yourself I will seek satisfaction of you.

IAGO. You have said now.

ROD. Ay, and said nothing but what I protest intendment of doing.

IAGO. Why, now I see there's mettle in thee; and even from this instant do build on thee a better opinion than ever before. Give me thy hand, Roderigo: thou hast taken against me a most just exception; but yet, I protest, I have dealt most directly in thy affair.

ROD. It hath not appeared.

IAGO. I grant, indeed, it hath not appeared; and your suspicion is not without wit and judgment. But, Roderigo, if thou hast that in thee indeed, which I have greater reason to believe now than ever,—I mean purpose, courage, and valour,—this night show it; if thou the next night following enjoy not Desdemona, take me from this world with treachery, and devise engines for my life.

ROD. Well, what is it? is it within reason and compass?

IAGO. Sir, there is especial commission come from Venice, to depute Cassio in Othello's place.

ROD. Is that true? why, then Othello and Desdemona return again to Venice.

IAGO. O, no; he goes into Mauritania, and takes away with him the fair Desdemona, unless his abode be lingered here by some accident; wherein none can be so determinate as the removing of Cassio.

ROD. How do you mean, removing him?

IAGO. Why, by making him uncapable of Othello's place,—knocking out his brains.

ROD. And that you would have me to do?

IAGO. Ay, if you dare do yourself a profit and a right. He sups to-night with a harlotry,[b] and thither will I go to him:—he knows not yet of his honourable fortune,—if you will watch his going thence,—which I will fashion to fall out between twelve and one,—you may take him at your pleasure: I will be near to second your attempt, and he shall fall between us. Come, stand not amazed at it, but go along with me; I will show you such a necessity in his death, that you shall think yourself bound to put it on him. It is now high supper-time, and the night grows to waste: about it.

ROD. I will hear further reason for this.

IAGO. And you shall; be satisfied. [*Exeunt.*

SCENE III.—*Another Room in the Castle.*

Enter OTHELLO, LODOVICO, DESDEMONA, EMILIA, *and* Attendants.

LOD. I do beseech you, sir, trouble yourself no further.

OTH. O, pardon me; 't will do me good to walk.

(*) First folio omits, *Faith*. (†) First folio, *and*. (‡) Old text, *fopt*.

[a] And he does chide with you.] The folio omits these words.

[b] — *a* harlotry,—] So in "Romeo and Juliet," Act IV. Sc. 2, —"A peevish self-willed *harlotry;*" and again in "Henry IV." Part I. Act III. Sc. 1, we have the same expression.

LOD. Madam, good night; I humbly thank your ladyship.
DES. Your honour is most welcome.
OTH. Will you walk, sir?—
O,—Desdemona,—
DES. My lord?
OTH. Get you to bed on the instant; I will be returned forthwith: dismiss your attendant there; look it be done.
DES. I will, my lord.
[*Exeunt* OTHELLO, LODOVICO, *and* Attendants.
EMIL. How goes it now? he looks gentler than he did.
DES. He says he will return incontinent;
And hath commanded me to go to bed,
And bade me to dismiss you.
EMIL. Dismiss me!
DES. It was his bidding; therefore, good Emilia,
Give me my nightly wearing, and adieu:
We must not now displease him.
EMIL. I would you had never seen him!
DES. So would not I; my love doth so approve him,
That even his stubbornness, his checks, his frowns,—
Pr'ythee, unpin me,—have grace and favour in them.[a]
EMIL. I have laid those sheets you bade me on the bed.
DES. All's one.—Good faith,* how foolish are our minds!—
If I do die before thee,† pr'ythee, shroud me
In one of these same sheets.
EMIL. Come, come, you talk.
DES. My mother had a maid call'd Barbara:
She was in love; and he she lov'd prov'd mad,
And did forsake her: she had a song of *Willow*,
An old thing 'twas, but it express'd her fortune,
And she died singing it: that song to-night
Will not go from my mind; I have much to do,[b]
But to go hang my head all at one side,
And sing it like poor Barbara. Pr'ythee, despatch.
EMIL. Shall I go fetch your night-gown?
DES. No, unpin me here.—
This Lodovico is a proper man.
EMIL. A very handsome man.
DES. He speaks well.
EMIL. I know a lady in Venice would have walked barefoot to Palestine for a touch of his nether lip.

DES. [Singing.] *The poor soul sat sighing‡ by a sycamore tree,*
Sing all a green willow;
Her hand on her bosom, her head on her knee,
Sing willow, willow, willow;
The fresh streams ran by her, and murmur'd her moans;
Sing willow, willow, willow;
Her salt tears fell from her, and soften'd the stones;—
Lay by these:—
Sing willow, willow, willow;
Pr'ythee, hie thee; he'll come anon:—
Sing all a green willow must be my garland.

Let nobody blame him, his scorn I approve,—

Nay, that's not next.—Hark! who is't that knocks?
EMIL. It is the wind.
DES. *I call'd my love, false love; but what said he then?*
Sing willow, willow, willow;
If I court mo women, you'll couch with mo men.—(2)

So, get thee gone; good-night. Mine eyes do itch;
Doth that bode weeping?
EMIL. 'T is neither here nor there.
DES. I have heard it said so.—O, these men, these men!—
Dost thou in conscience think,—tell me, Emilia,—
That there be women do abuse their husbands
In such gross kind?
EMIL. There be some such, no question.
DES. Wouldst thou do such a deed for all the world?
EMIL. Why, would not you?
DES. No, by this heavenly light!
EMIL. Nor I neither by this heavenly light;
I might do't as well i' the dark.
DES. Wouldst thou do such a deed for all the world?
EMIL. The world's a huge thing: 't is a great price
For a small vice.
DES. In troth, I think thou wouldst not.
EMIL. In troth, I think I should; and undo 't, when I had done. Marry, I would not do such a thing for a joint-ring, nor for measures of lawn, nor for gowns, petticoats, nor caps, nor any petty exhibition; but, for all the whole world,—why, who would not make her husband a cuckold to make him a monarch? I should venture purgatory for 't.

(*) First folio, *Father*. (†) First folio omits, *thee*. (‡) First folio, *singing*.

[a] — in them.] These words are not in the folio.

[b] I have much to do,—] These words and what follows down to "Hark! who is't that knocks?" are not in the quarto of 1622.

DES. Beshrew me, if I would do such a wrong
For the whole world.

EMIL. Why, the wrong is but a wrong i' the world; and, having the world for your labour, 't is a wrong in your own world, and you might quickly make it right.

DES. I do not think there is any such woman.

EMIL. Yes, a dozen; and as many to the vantage, as would store the world they play'd for.
But I do think it is their husbands' faults
If wives do fall: say that they slack their duties,
And pour our treasures into foreign laps;
Or else break out in peevish jealousies,
Throwing restraint upon us; or say they strike us,
Or scant our former having in despite;
Why, we have galls; and though we have some grace,
Yet have we some revenge. Let husbands know
Their wives have sense like them: they see, and smell,
And have their palates both for sweet and sour,
As husbands have. What is it that they do
When they change us for others? Is it sport?
I think it is: and doth affection breed it?
I think it doth: is 't frailty that thus errs?
It is so too:—and have not we affections,
Desires for sport, and frailty, as men have?
Then let them use us well; else let them know,
The ills we do, their ills instruct us so.

DES. Good-night, good-night: heaven me such uses[a] send,
Not to pick bad from bad, but by bad mend!

[*Exeunt.*

[a] — *heaven me such* uses *send,*—] The quarto, 1622, has "*usage*" for "*uses;*" it may be doubted whether either is the poet's word.

ACT V.

SCENE I.—*The same. A Street.*

Enter IAGO *and* RODERIGO.

IAGO. Here, stand behind this bulk;(*) straight will he come:
Wear thy good rapier bare, and put it home.
Quick, quick; fear nothing; I'll be at thy elbow:
It makes us, or it mars us; think on that,
And fix most firm thy resolution.

ROD. Be near at hand; I may miscarry in 't.

IAGO. Here, at thy hand; be bold, and take thy stand. [*Retires to a little distance.*

ROD. I have no great devotion to the deed;
And yet he hath given me satisfying reasons:—
'T is but a man gone:—forth, my sword; he dies! [*Goes to his stand.*

IAGO. I have rubb'd this young quat[a] almost to the sense,
And he grows angry. Now, whether he kill Cassio,
Or Cassio him, or each do kill the other,

(*) First folio, *Barke.*

[a] *I have rubb'd this young* quat *almost to the* sense.—] A "*quat*" means a *pimple* or *scab*; and "to the *sense*" is to the *quick*.

Every way makes my gain: live Roderigo,
He calls me to a restitution large
Of gold and jewels that I bobb'd from him,
As gifts to Desdemona;
It must not be: if Cassio do remain,
He hath a daily beauty in his life
That makes me ugly; and, besides, the Moor
May unfold me to him; there stand I in much peril:
No, he must die:—but, so, I hear* him coming.

Enter CASSIO.

ROD. I know his gait, 't is he:—Villain, thou diest!
[*Rushes from his post, and makes a pass at* CASSIO.

CAS. That thrust had been mine enemy indeed,
But that my coat is better than thou know'st:
I will make proof ot thine.
[*Draws, and wounds* RODERIGO.

ROD. O, I am slain!
[IAGO *rushes from his post, cuts* CASSIO *behind in the leg, and exit.*

CAS. I am maim'd for ever:—Help, ho! murder! murder! [*Falls.*

(*) First folio, *heard.*

[a] And your unblest fate hies.—] The reading of the folio and the quarto of 1630; in the first quarto the text is,—
"And your fate hies apace," &c.

[b] — *no* passage?] That is, no *passengers.*

Enter OTHELLO, *at a distance.*

OTH. The voice of Cassio:—Iago keeps his word.

ROD. O, villain that I am!

OTH. 'T is even so.

CAS. O, help! ho! light! a surgeon!

OTH. 'T is he;—O, brave Iago, honest and just,
That hast such noble sense of thy friend's wrong!
Thou teachest me,—Minion, your dear lies dead,
And your unblest fate hies.[a]—Strumpet, I come!
Forth* of my heart those charms, thine eyes, are blotted;
Thy bed, lust-stain'd, shall with lust's blood be spotted. [*Exit.*

Enter LODOVICO *and* GRATIANO, *at a distance.*

CAS. What, ho! no watch? no passage?[b] murder! murder!

GRA. 'T is some mischance; the voice is very direful.

CAS. O, help!

LOD. Hark!

ROD. O, wretched villain!

LOD. Two or three groan;—it is a heavy night:[c]

(*) First folio, *For.*

[c] — it is a heavy night:] A *heavy night* is a *thick cloudy* night, as Johnson observes. The folio has,—" 'T is heavy night."

These may be counterfeits; let's think't unsafe
To come in to the cry without more help.

ROD. No body come? then shall I bleed to death.

LOD. Hark!

GRA. Here's one comes in his shirt, with light and weapons.

Re-enter IAGO, *with a light.*

IAGO. Who's there? whose noise is this that cries on murder?[a]

LOD. We do not know.

IAGO. Did* not you hear a cry?

CAS. Here, here! for heaven's sake, help me!

IAGO. What's the matter?

GRA. This is Othello's ancient, as I take it.

LOD. The same, indeed; a very valiant fellow.

IAGO. What are you here that cry so grievously?

CAS. Iago? O, I am spoil'd, undone by villains!
Give me some help.

IAGO. O, me, lieutenant! what villains have done this?

CAS. I think that one of them is hereabout,
And cannot make away.

IAGO. O, treacherous villains!—
What are you there? come in, and give some help.
[*To* LODOVICO *and* GRATIANO.

ROD. O, help me there!

CAS. That's one of them.

IAGO. O, murderous slave! O, villain!
[*Stabs* RODERIGO.

ROD. O, damn'd Iago! O, inhuman dog!—

IAGO. Kill men i' the dark!—Where be these bloody thieves?—
How silent is this town!—Ho! murder! murder!—
What may you be? are you of good or evil?

LOD. As you shall prove us, praise us.

IAGO. Signior Lodovico?

LOD. He, sir.

IAGO. I cry you mercy. Here's Cassio hurt by villains.

GRA. Cassio!

IAGO. How is't, brother?

CAS. My leg is cut in two.

IAGO. Marry, heaven forbid!—
Light, gentlemen;—I'll bind it with my shirt.

Enter BIANCA.

BIAN. What is the matter, ho? who is't that cried?

IAGO. *Who is't that cried?*

BIAN. O, my dear Cassio! my sweet Cassio!
O, Cassio! Cassio! Cassio!

IAGO. O, notable strumpet!—Cassio, may you suspect
Who they should be that have thus mangled you?

CAS. No.

GRA. I am sorry to find you thus: I have been to seek you.

IAGO. Lend me a garter:—so.—O, for a chair,
To bear him easily hence!

BIAN. Alas, he faints!—O, Cassio! Cassio! Cassio!

IAGO. Gentlemen all, I do suspect this trash
To be a party in this injury.—
Patience awhile, good Cassio.—Come, come;
Lend me a light.—Know we this face or no?
Alas! my friend and my dear countryman,
Roderigo? no:—yes, sure; O, heaven!* Roderigo.

GRA. What, of Venice?

IAGO. Even he, sir: did you know him?

GRA. Know him! ay.

IAGO. Signior Gratiano? I cry your gentle pardon;
These bloody accidents must excuse my manners,
That so neglected you.

GRA. I am glad to see you.

IAGO. How do you, Cassio?—O, a chair, a chair!

GRA. Roderigo!

IAGO. He, he, 't is he:—O, that's well said;—the chair:— [*A chair brought in.*
Some good man bear him carefully from hence;
I'll fetch the general's surgeon.—For you, mistress, [*To* BIANCA.
Save you your labour.—He that lies slain here, Cassio,
Was my dear friend: what malice was between you?

CAS. None in the world; nor do I know the man.

IAGO. [*To* BIAN.] What, look you pale?—O bear him out o' the air.—
[CASSIO *and* ROD. *are borne off.*
Stay you, good gentlemen.—Look you pale, mistress?—
Do you perceive the gastness of her eye?—
Nay, if you stare, we shall hear more anon:—
Behold her well; I pray you look upon her;
Do you see, gentlemen? nay, guiltiness will speak,
Though tongues were out of use.

Enter EMILIA.

EMIL. 'Las, what's the matter? what is the matter, husband?

IAGO. Cassio hath here been set on in the dark

(*) First folio, *Do.*

a — *that* cries on *murder?*] See note (a), p. 573, Vol. II.

(*) First folio, in place of *O, heaven*, has, *Yes 'tis.*

By Roderigo, and fellows that are scap'd:
He's almost slain, and Roderigo* dead.
EMIL. Alas, good gentleman! alas, good Cassio!
IAGO. This is the fruits of whoring.—Pr'ythee, Emilia,
Go know of Cassio where he supp'd to-night:—
What, do you shake at that?
BIAN. He supp'd at my house; but I therefore shake not.
IAGO. O, did he so? I charge you, go with me.
EMIL. Fie,† fie upon thee, strumpet!
BIAN. I am no strumpet; but of life as honest
As you that thus abuse me.
EMIL. As I? foh!‡ fie upon thee!
IAGO. Kind gentlemen, let's go see poor Cassio dress'd.—
Come, mistress, you must tell's another tale.—
Emilia, run you to the citadel,
And tell my lord and lady what hath happ'd.—
Will you go on afore?—This is the night [*Aside.*
That either makes me or fordoes me quite. [*Exeunt.*

SCENE II.—*A Bedchamber in the Castle:* DESDEMONA *in bed asleep. A light burning.*

Enter OTHELLO.

OTH. It is the cause, it is the cause, my soul,[a]—
Let me not name it to you, you chaste stars!—
It is the cause.—Yet I'll not shed her blood;
Nor scar that whiter skin of hers than snow,
And smooth as monumental alabaster.
Yet she must die, else she'll betray more men.
Put out the light, and then——put out the light![b]
If I quench thee, thou flaming minister,
I can again thy former light restore,
Should I repent me:—but once put out thy light,
Thou cunning'st pattern of excelling nature,
I know not where is that Promethean heat
That can thy light relume. When I have pluck'd thy rose,
I cannot give it vital growth again,
It needs must wither:—I'll smell it§ on the tree.— [*Kissing her.*
O, balmy breath, that dost almost persuade
Justice to break her sword!—One more, one more:—
Be thus when thou art dead, and I will kill thee,
And love thee after.—One more, and that's the last:
So sweet was ne'er so fatal. I must weep,
But they are cruel tears: this sorrow's heavenly;
It strikes where it doth love.—She wakes.
DES. Who's there? Othello?
OTH. Ay, Desdemona.
DES. Will you come to bed, my lord?
OTH. Have you pray'd to-night, Desdemon?
DES. Ay, my lord.
OTH. If you bethink yourself of any crime
Unreconcil'd as yet to heaven and grace,
Solicit for it straight.
DES. Alack, my lord, what may you mean by that?
OTH. Well, do it, and be brief; I will walk by:
I would not kill thy unprepared spirit;
No,—heaven forfend!—I would not kill thy soul.
DES. Talk you of killing?
OTH. Ay, I do.
DES. Then heaven
Have mercy on me!
OTH. Amen, with all my heart!
DES. If you say so,* I hope you will not kill me.
OTH. Hum!
DES. And yet I fear you; for you are fatal then,
When your eyes roll so: why I should fear I know not,
Since guiltiness I know not; but yet I feel I fear.
OTH. Think on thy sins.
DES. They are loves I bear to you.
OTH. Ay, and for that thou diest.
DES. That death's unnatural that kills for loving.—
Alas, why gnaw you so your nether lip?
Some bloody passion shakes your very frame:
These are portents; but yet I hope, I hope,
They do not point on me.
OTH. Peace, and be still!
DES. I will so. What's the matter?
OTH. That handkerchief, which I so lov'd and gave thee,
Thou gav'st to Cassio.
DES. No, by my life and soul!
Send for the man, and ask him.
OTH. Sweet soul, take heed,
Take heed of perjury; thou art on thy death-bed.
DES. Ay, but not yet to die.
OTH. Yes,† presently;
Therefore confess thee freely of thy sin;
For to deny each article with oath

(*) First folio inserts, *quite*. (†) First folio, *Oh*.
(‡) First folio omits, *foh!* (§) First folio, *thee*.

(*) First folio omits, *so*. (†) First folio omits, *Yes*.

[a] It is the cause, it is the cause, my soul,—] "Othello, full of horror at the cruel action which he is about to perpetrate, seems at this instant to be seeking his justification, from representing to himself the cause, *i.e.* the greatness of the provocation he had received."—STEEVENS.

[b] Put out the light, and then——put out the light!] This regulation of the line, which certainly imparts to it a spirit and beauty we miss in the old punctuation, was suggested both by Upton and Warburton, and is now very generally adopted.

Cannot remove nor choke the strong conception
That I do groan withal. Thou art to die.
DES. Then Lord* have mercy on me!
OTH. I say, amen!
DES. And have you mercy too!—I never did
Offend you in my life; never lov'd Cassio
But with such general warranty of heaven
As I might love; I never gave him token.
OTH. By heaven, I saw my handkerchief in 's hand!

(*) First folio, *O Heaven*.

O, perjur'd woman! thou dost stone my heart,
And mak'st me call what I intend to do,
A murder, which I thought a sacrifice:
I saw the handkerchief.
DES. He found it, then;
I never gave it him:—send for him hither;
Let him confess a truth.
OTH. He hath confess'd.
DES. What, my lord?
OTH. That he hath—us'd thee.
DES. How? unlawfully

OTH. Ay.
DES. He will not say so.
OTH. No, his mouth is stopp'd;
Honest Iago hath ta'en order for 't.
DES. O, my fear interprets!—what, is he dead?
OTH. Had all his hairs been lives, my great revenge
Had stomach for them all.
DES. Alas, he is betray'd, and I undone!
OTH. Out, strumpet! weep'st thou for him to my face?
DES. O, banish me, my lord, but kill me not!
OTH. Down, strumpet!
DES. Kill me to-morrow; let me live to-night!
OTH. Nay, if you strive,—
DES. But half an hour!
OTH. Being done,
There is no pause.
DES. But while I say one prayer!
OTH. It is too late. [*Smothers her.*
EMIL. [*Without.*] My lord! my lord! what ho! my lord! my lord!
OTH. What noise is this?—Not dead? not yet quite dead?
I that am cruel am yet merciful;
I would not have thee linger in thy pain:—
So, so.
EMIL. [*Without.*] What ho! my lord! my lord!
OTH. Who 's there?
EMIL. [*Without.*] O, good my lord, I would speak a word with you!
OTH. Yes:—'t is Emilia;—by and by.—She 's dead.—
'T is like she comes to speak of Cassio's death;
The noise was high.—Ha! no more moving?
Still as the grave.—Shall she come in? were 't good?—
I think she stirs again:—no.—What 's best to do?
If she come in, she 'll sure speak to my wife:
My wife! my wife! what wife?—I have no wife!
O, insupportable! O, heavy hour!
Methinks it should be now a huge eclipse
Of sun and moon, and that the affrighted globe
Should* yawn at alteration.
EMIL. [*Without.*] I do beseech you that I may speak with you,
O, good my lord!
OTH. I had forgot thee:—O, come in, Emilia:—
Soft,—by and by:—let me the curtains draw.—
Where art thou? [*Unlocks the door.*

Enter EMILIA.

What 's the matter with thee now?
EMIL. O, my good lord, yonder 's foul murder done!
OTH. What, now?
EMIL. But now, my lord!
OTH. It is the very error of the moon;
She comes more nearer earth than she was wont,
And makes men mad.
EMIL. Cassio, my lord, hath kill'd a young Venetian
Call'd Roderigo.
OTH. Roderigo kill'd!
And Cassio kill'd!
EMIL. No, Cassio is not kill'd.
OTH. Not Cassio kill'd! then murder 's out of tune,
And sweet revenge grows harsh.
DES. O, falsely, falsely murder'd!
EMIL. Alas, what cry is that?
OTH. That! what?
EMIL. Out, and alas! that was my lady's voice.—
Help! help, ho! help!—O, lady, speak again!
Sweet Desdemona! O, sweet mistress, speak!
DES. A guiltless death I die.
EMIL. O, who hath done this deed?
DES. Nobody; I myself. Farewell:
Commend me to my kind lord: O, farewell! [*Dies.*
OTH. Why, how should she be murder'd?
EMIL. Alas, who knows?
OTH. You heard* her say herself, it was not I.
EMIL. She said so: I must needs report the truth.
OTH. She 's, like a liar, gone to burning hell!
'T was I that kill'd her.
EMIL. O, the more angel she,
And you the blacker devil!
OTH. She turn'd to folly,[a] and she was a whore.
EMIL. Thou dost belie her, and thou art a devil.
OTH. She was false as water.
EMIL. Thou art rash as fire, to say
That she was false; O, she was heavenly true!
OTH. Cassio did tup her; ask thy husband else.
O, I were damn'd beneath all depth in hell,
But that I did proceed upon just grounds
To this extremity! Thy husband knew it all.
EMIL. My husband!
OTH. Thy husband.
EMIL. That she was false to wedlock?
OTH. Ay, with Cassio. Nay,† had she been true,
If heaven would make me such another world
Of one entire and perfect chrysolite,
I 'd not have sold her for it.
EMIL. My husband!
OTH. Ay, 't was he that told me‡ first;

*) First folio, *Did.*

a — to folly,—] That is, to *wantonness.*

(*) First folio, *heare.* (†) First folio omits, *Nay.*
(‡) First folio inserts, *on her.*

An honest man he is, and hates the slime
That sticks on filthy deeds.

EMIL. My husband!

OTH. What needs this iterance, woman? I say thy husband.

EMIL. O, mistress, villany hath made mocks with love!—
My husband say that* she was false?

OTH. He, woman;
I say thy husband: dost understand the word?
My friend, thy husband, honest-honest Iago.

EMIL. If he say so, may his pernicious soul
Rot half a grain a day! he lies to the heart:
She was too fond of her most filthy bargain.

OTH. Ha!

EMIL. Do thy worst;
This deed of thine is no more worthy heaven,
Than thou wast worthy her.

OTH. Peace! you were best.

EMIL. Thou hast not half that power to do me harm,
As I have to be hurt. O, gull! O, dolt!
As ignorant as dirt! thou hast done a deed,—
I care not for thy sword; I'll make thee known,
Though I lost twenty lives.—Help! help! ho! help!
The Moor hath kill'd my mistress! Murder! murder!

Enter MONTANO, GRATIANO, *and* IAGO.

MON. What is the matter?—How now, general!

EMIL. O, are you come, Iago? you have done well,
That men must lay their murders on your neck.

GRA. What is the matter?

EMIL. Disprove this villain, if thou be'st a man:
He says thou toldst him that his wife was false:
I know thou didst not, thou'rt not such a villain:
Speak, for my heart is full.

IAGO. I told him what I thought; and told no more
Than what he found himself was apt and true.

EMIL. But did you ever tell him she was false?

IAGO. I did.

EMIL. You told a lie; an odious, damned lie;
Upon my soul, a lie; a wicked lie!—
She false with Cassio!—did you say with Cassio?

IAGO. With Cassio, mistress. Go to, charm your tongue.[a]

EMIL. I will not charm my tongue; I am bound to speak:
My mistress here lies murder'd in her bed,—

ALL. O, heavens forfend!

EMIL. And your reports have set the murder on.

OTH. Nay, stare not, masters; it is true, indeed.

GRA. 'T is a strange[b] truth.

MON. O, monstrous act!

EMIL. Villany, villany, villany!
I think upon't,—I think I smell't;—O, villany!—
I thought so then;[c]—I'll kill myself for grief:—
O villany, villany!

IAGO. What, are you mad? I charge you, get you home.

EMIL. Good gentlemen, let me have leave to speak:
'T is proper I obey him, but not now.—
Perchance, Iago, I will ne'er go home.

OTH. O! O! O! [*Falling on the bed.*

EMIL. Nay, lay thee down and roar;
For thou hast kill'd the sweetest innocent,
That e'er did lift up eye.

OTH. O, she was foul!— [*Rising.*
I scarce did know you, uncle. There lies your niece,
Whose breath, indeed, these hands have newly stopp'd:
I know this act shows horrible and grim.

GRA. Poor Desdemon! I am glad thy father's dead:
Thy match was mortal to him, and pure grief
Shore his old thread in twain: did he live now,
This sight would make him do a desperate turn,
Yea, curse his better angel from his side,
And fall to reprobation.[d]

OTH. 'T is pitiful; but yet Iago knows,
That she with Cassio hath the act of shame
A thousand times committed; Cassio confess'd it:
And she did gratify his amorous works
With that recognizance and pledge of love
Which I first gave her; I saw it in his hand:
It was a handkerchief, an antique token
My father gave my mother.

(*) First folio omits, *that*.

a — charm your tongue.] A familiar expression in the poet's day, meaning restrain, or put a spell upon your tongue. So in "Henry VI." Part III. Act V. Sc. 5,—"Peace, wilful boy, or I will *charm your tongue*." See also additional examples of the phrase in the *Variorum ad l.*

b — a strange *truth*.] "Strange" is one of the many words which have lost weight and emphasis since Shakespeare's time. With us, it imports no more than *unusual, not customary*, &c.; but when Desdemona spoke of the Moor's adventures as "*strange*," she meant they were *wonderful, incredible;* and it is in this deeper sense of the word that Gratiano employs it here.

c *I thought so* then;—] "That is, at the instant when she gave Desdemona's handkerchief to Iago; for even then Emilia appears to have suspected it was sought after for no honest purpose, and therefore asks her husband—

'What will you do with it?'" &c.—STEEVENS.

d *And fall to* reprobation.] So the quartos; the folio has,—"And fail to *reprobance*."

EMIL. O, God! O, heavenly God! *
IAGO. Zounds,† hold your peace!
EMIL. 'T will out, 't will out!—I hold my peace, sir? no; ‡
No, I will speak as liberal as the north! [a]
Let heaven, and men, and devils, let them all,
All, all, cry shame against me, yet I'll speak!
IAGO. Be wise, and get you home.
EMIL. I will not.
[IAGO *offers to stab* EMILIA.
GRA. Fie!
Your sword upon a woman?
EMIL. O, thou dull Moor! that handkerchief thou speak'st of
I found by fortune, and did give my husband;
For often with a solemn earnestness,—
More than, indeed, belong'd to such a trifle,—
He begg'd of me to steal 't.
IAGO. Villanous whore!
EMIL. She give it Cassio! no, alas, I found it,
And I did give't my husband.
IAGO. Filth, thou liest!
EMIL. By heaven, I do not! I do not, gentlemen!—
O, murderous coxcomb! what should such a fool
Do with so good a wife?
[IAGO *stabs* EMILIA, *and then runs out.*
OTH. Are there no stones in heaven,
But what serve for the thunder?—Precious villain!
GRA. The woman falls! sure, he hath kill'd his wife!
EMIL. Ay, ay:—O, lay me by my mistress' side!
GRA. He's gone, but his wife's kill'd.
MON. 'Tis a notorious villain. Take you this weapon,
Which I have here§ recover'd from the Moor:
Come, guard the door without; let him not pass,
But kill him rather. I'll after that same villain,
For 'tis a damned slave.
[*Exeunt* MONTANO *and* GRATIANO.
OTH. I am not valiant neither,
But every puny whipster gets my sword.—
But why should honour outlive honesty?
Let it go all.
EMIL. What did thy song bode, lady?
Hark! canst thou hear me? I will play the swan,
And die in music;—*Willow, willow, willow.*—
[Singing.
Moor, she was chaste; she lov'd thee, cruel Moor;
So come my soul to bliss, as I speak true;
So speaking as I think, I die,*—I die! [*Dies.*
OTH. I have another weapon in this chamber,
It is† a sword of Spain, the ice-brook's temper;—
O, here it is.—Uncle, I must come forth.
GRA. [*Without.*] If thou attempt it, it will cost thee dear;
Thou hast no weapon, and perforce must suffer.
OTH. Look in upon me, then, and speak with me,
Or, naked as I am, I will assault thee.

Re-enter GRATIANO.

GRA. What is the matter?
OTH. Behold! I have a weapon;
A better never did itself sustain
Upon a soldier's thigh: I have seen the day,
That, with this little arm and this good sword,
I have made my way through more impediments
Than twenty times your stop:—but, O, vain boast!
Who can control his fate? 'tis not so now.—
Be not afraid, though you do see me weapon'd;—
Here is my journey's end, here is my butt,
And very sea-mark of my utmost sail.
Do you go back dismay'd? 'tis a lost fear;
Man but a rush [b] against Othello's breast,
And he retires:—where should Othello go?—
Now, how dost thou look now? O, ill-starr'd wench!
Pale as thy smock! when we shall meet at compt,
This look of thine will hurl my soul from heaven,
And fiends will snatch at it!—Cold, cold, my girl!
Even like thy chastity.—
O, cursed, cursed slave!—Whip me, ye devils,
From the possession of this heavenly sight!
Blow me about in winds! roast me in sulphur!
Wash me in steep-down gulfs of liquid fire!—
O, Desdemon! dead, Desdemon! dead! O, O!

Enter LODOVICO, MONTANO, CASSIO *carried in a chair, and* Officers, *with* IAGO, *prisoner.*

LOD. Where is this rash and most unfortunate man?
OTH. That's he that was Othello;—here I am.
LOD. Where is that viper? bring the villain forth.
OTH. I look down towards his feet; [c]—but that's a fable.—

(*) First folio, *Oh Heaven! oh heavenly powers!*
(†) First folio, *Come.*
(‡) First folio omits, *hold my,* and *sir? no!*
(§) First folio omits, *here.*

(*) First folio, *alas.* (†) First folio, *was.*

[a] *No, I will speak as liberal as the* north;] Thus the folio; the quarto of 1622 reads,—

" I 'le *be in speaking,* liberall as the *ayre.*"

And that of 1630 has,—

" I 'le *be in speaking* liberall as the north."

[b] *Man but a* rush against Othello's breast,—] This is an allusion to the mock tournaments in which the combatants were armed with *rushes* in place of spears.

[c] — towards his feet;—] "To see if, according to the common opinion, his feet be cloven."—JOHNSON.

If that thou be'st a devil I cannot kill thee.
[Othello *wounds* Iago.

Lod. Wrench his sword from him.

Iago. I bleed, sir; but not kill'd.

Oth. I am not sorry neither; I'd have thee live;
For, in my sense, 'tis happiness to die.

Lod. O, thou Othello, that wert* once so good,
Fall'n in the practice [a] of a damned * slave,
What shall be said to thee?

Oth. Why, any thing:
An honourable murderer, if you will;
For nought did I † in hate, but all in honour.

Lod. This wretch hath part confess'd his villany:
Did you and he consent in Cassio's death?

(*) First folio, *was*.

(*) First folio, *cursed*. (†) First folio, *I did*.

[a] — *practice*—] *Machination, stratagem.*

OTH. Ay.
CAS. Dear general, I never gave you cause.
OTH. I do believe it, and I ask your pardon.
Will you, I pray, demand that demi-devil,
Why he hath thus ensnar'd my soul and body?
IAGO. Demand me nothing: what you know, you know:
From this time forth I never will speak word.
LOD. What, not to pray?
GRA. Torments will ope your lips.
OTH. Well, thou dost best.
LOD. Sir, you shall understand what hath befall'n,
Which, as I think, you know not. Here is a letter,
Found in the pocket of the slain Roderigo;
And here another: the one of them imports
The death of Cassio to be undertook
By Roderigo.
OTH. O, villain!
CAS. Most heathenish and most gross!
LOD. Now here's another discontented paper,
Found in his pocket too; and this, it seems,
Roderigo meant to have sent this damned villain;
But that, belike, Iago in the interim
Came in and satisfied him.
OTH. O, thou pernicious caitiff!—
How came you, Cassio, by that handkerchief
That was my wife's?
CAS. I found it in my chamber;
And he himself confess'd* but even now,
That there he dropp'd it for a special purpose,
Which wrought to his desire.
OTH. O, fool! fool! fool!
CAS. There is besides, in Roderigo's letter,—
How he upbraids Iago, that he made him
Brave me upon the watch; whereon it came
That I was cast: and even but now he spake,
After long seeming dead,—Iago hurt him,
Iago set him on.
LOD. You must forsake this room, and go with us;
Your power and your command is taken off,
And Cassio rules in Cyprus. For this slave,—
If there be any cunning cruelty,
That can torment him much and hold him long,
It shall be his. You shall close prisoner rest,
Till that the nature of your fault be known
To the Venetian state.—Come, bring away.
OTH. Soft you! a word or two before you go.
I have done the state some service,(1) and they know't;—
No more of that.—I pray you, in your letters,
When you shall these unlucky deeds relate,
Speak of me as I am; nothing extenuate,
Nor set down aught in malice: then must you speak
Of one, that lov'd not wisely, but too well;
Of one, not easily jealous, but, being wrought,
Perplex'd in the extreme; of one, whose hand,
Like the base Indian,(2) threw a pearl away,
Richer than all his tribe; of one, whose subdu'd eyes,
Albeit unused to the melting mood,
Drop tears as fast as the Arabian trees
Their med'cinable gum. Set you down this;
And say, besides,—that in Aleppo once,
Where a malignant and a turban'd Turk
Beat a Venetian and traduc'd the state,
I took by the throat the circumcised dog,
And smote him—thus. [*Stabs himself.*
LOD. O, bloody period!
GRA. All that is spoke is marr'd.
OTH. I kiss'd thee ere I kill'd thee;—no way but this, [*Falling upon* DESDEMONA.
Killing myself, to die upon a kiss. [*Dies.*
CAS. This did I fear, but thought he had no weapon;
For he was great of heart.
LOD. [*To* IAGO.] O, Spartan dog,
More fell than anguish, hunger, or the sea!
Look on the tragic loading of this bed;
This is thy work:—the object poisons sight;—
Let it be hid.—Gratiano, keep the house,
And seize upon the fortunes of the Moor,
For they succeed on you.—To you, lord governor,
Remains the censure of this hellish villain;
The time, the place, the torture;—O, enforce it!
Myself will straight aboard; and, to the state,
This heavy act with heavy heart relate. [*Exeunt.*

(*) First folio inserts, *it*.

ILLUSTRATIVE COMMENTS.

ACT I.

(1) SCENE I.—*Lead to the Sagittary.*] By *the Sagittary*, Mr. Knight says, was meant the "residence at the arsenal of the commanding officers of the navy and army of the republic. The figure of an archer with his drawn bow, over the gates, still indicates the place." Others, however, conceive Iago to mean only some house of resort which bore this sign.

In Lydgate's *Auncient Historie*, &c. 1555, quoted by Steevens, is found a very circumstantial description of the Sagittary:—

"And with hym Guydo sayth that he hadde
A wonder archer of syght mervalous,
Of fourme and shap in maner monstruous:
For lyke myne auctour as I reherse can,
Fro the navel upwarde he was man,
And lower downe lyke a horse yshaped:
And thilke parte that after man was maked,
Of skinne was black and rough as any bere
Covered with here fro colde him for to were,
Passyng foule and horrible of syght,
Whose eyen twain were sparkeling as bright
As is a furneis with his rede levene,
Or the lyghtnyng that falleth from ye heaven;
Dredeful of loke, and rede as fyre of chere,
And, as I reade, he was a goode archer;
And with his bowe both at even and morowe
Upon Grekes he wrought muche sorrowe,
And gasted them with many hydous loke:
So sterne he was that many of them quoke."

(2) SCENE II.—*I'll have't disputed on.*] This is an allusion to the manner in which causes were debated by the judges according to the custom of Venice formerly, and it affords one of many proofs that before writing "Othello," Shakespeare had attentively perused Lewkenor's translation of "*The Commonwealth and Government of Venice,* written by the Cardinall Gasper Contareno," &c. 1599. From this work he obtained his information concerning those "officers of night" whom Brabantio directs to be summoned; his knowledge of the *Arsenal;* as well as several particular expressions, such as Mine *eares enclined;* doe *their countrie service; experience the mistresse of all things; serve the turne;* their *countrie customs;* and others which he has modified and transplanted into the piece. The following is Contareno's account of the way criminal questions were *disputed on* before judgment could be obtained, in the ancient legal courts of Venice:—

"The Councell being assembled, the Advocator plaieth the parte of a bitter accuser, strayning the uttermost invention of his wittes against the offender, first obiecting unto him the offence, confirming the same with witnesses, and then strengthening his obiection with probabilities and likelihoodes of coniecture: having ended his speech, the advocate of the offender pleadeth in the Clyentes behalfe: After which if any of the Advocators will speake afresh, before the Iudges give sentence, he hath libertie so to do: likewise the Lawyers of the defendant have leave to aunswere and to confute, if they can, the opposed arguments. And so of eyther side the cause is debated and tossed to and fro, till eyther the offender or the Advocator whose turne it is to speake, doth declare that he hath no more to say, which done, the offender and his advocates are commanded out of the Court, and the Advocators are shutte into a roome apart with the Iudges and their Secretaries, not any one else being suffred to be there. The Advocators first doe make a motion unto the Iudges of punishing the offender, demaunding their opinions whether they thinke him worthy of punishment or no, not naming or appointing any one certayne kinde of punishment, which custome was (in a manner) observed by the Athenians: for in *Athens* the Iudges gave two sentences, in the first eyther condemning or absolving the prisoner. If in the first hee were condemned, then was the manner of his punishment determined of in the second, as out of *Platoes* Apologie of *Socrates* may plainly bee perceived, the very like order of iudgement is that in manner which we do use: first (as I say) the Advocators make a motion unto the Iudges of punishing the offender. Then the Iudges go unto their suffrages, for by suffrages among the Venetians all things are determined. Three pots are brought forth, by the one of which the offender is condemned: by the other he is absolved in maner without any correction, & by the third are known the opinion of those, which doe seeme yet to doubt whether course is to be taken: the first of condemnation is white, the second of absolution greene, the third of doubtfulnes redde. Every of the Iudges, whether the cause be *disputed of* by the forty (as usually it is) or els that the senate be consulted with (which seldome happeneth) & that only in great and waighty causes, or whether it be by the Advocators reported over to the great councell, which is most seldome, and never but in matters exceedingly enormous, to the ende to have his suffrage undiscerned, letteth fall into whether of these three pots he pleaseth a little linnen ball: which being done, the presidents of the councell doe number the balles, and if more then the half be in favour of the prisoners liberty, he is presently pronounced free, and the request of the Advocators reiected. But if more then the half of those bals, be found in the pot of condemnation, he is presently condemned: if neither of both exceede the half, but that the greater part of the Iudges put their suffrages into the pot of doubtfulnes: then his cause is deferred over til another day, & to the better discussion of the Iudges."

(3) SCENE III.—

Valiant Othello, we must straight employ you
Against the general enemy Ottoman.]

The circumstances originating the siege of Nicosia, "the chief and richest citie of all the Island," and the ultimate conquest of Cyprus by the Turks (for there was no "segregation of the Turkish fleet" as the play supposes) are thus related by Knolles in his *Historie of the Turkes*: —

"Selymus (the second) now at peace with all the world (a thing of the Turkes not much desired) began to thinke of workes of charitie: and proposing to build a magnificent temple at Hadrianople for his owne sepulture, with a monasterie, a colledge, and an almeshouse (as had his father, and other his ancestors before him at Prusa and Constantinople, led thereunto with a vaine and superstitious devotion) was troubled with nothing more, than how to endue the same with lands and revenues sufficient for the maintenance of so great a charge: For that the Mahometan kings, are by their superstition prohibited to convert any lands or possessions to such holy uses, other than such as they have with their own sword woon from the enemies of their religion, which they may (as they are persuaded) as a most acceptable sacrifice, offer to their great prophet: which devillish persuasion, serveth as a spurre to pricke forward every of those ambitious princes to adde something to their empire. This his devout purpose once knowne, wanted not the furtherance of many ripe heads, devising some one thing, some another, as they thought best fitted his humour. But amongst many things to him presented, none pleased him so well, as the plot laid for the taking of the rich island of Cyprus from the Venetians: a conquest of itselfe sufficient, both for the eternizing of his name, and performance of his owne charitable works intended; with a large overplus, for the supplying of whatsoever wanted in his fathers like devout works at Constantinople. But that which moved him most of all, was the glorie of such a conquest, which as his flaterers bare him in hand, might make him equall with any his predecessors; who in the beginning of their raign, had usually done or attempted some notable thing against the Christians. Selymus presently commanded preparation to be made both by sea and land, for the performance of his resolution. Which was not so covertly carried in the Turkes court, but that it was discovered by M. Antonius Barbaras the Venetian embassadour; and not without cause suspected by the Venetian merchants, whom the barbarous Turks began now to cut short in their trafficke, looking big upon them, as men suddenly changed, and evill entreating them with hard speeches, the undoubted signes of greater troubles to ensue. These things and such like as were then done at Constantinople, being by letters sent in post from the embassadour, made knowne at Venice, brought a generall heavinesse upon the citie: for why that understanding and provident state, warned by their former harmes, of all others most dread the Turks forces.

"In the meane time the Senatours sitting oftentimes in counsell, were divided in opinions concerning the chief matter they consulted upon: some there were, that thought it not good to wage warre against such an invincible enemy, nor to trust upon a vaine and idle hope, neither to commit all unto the hazard of such fortune as was unto them in that warre by the enemie propounded: they alleadged that it were better to depart with Cyprus, so that they might quietly enjoy the rest, rather than to enter into armes. Others were of a contrary opinion, as that the island was by force of armes to be defended: saying that nothing could be more dishonourable, than without fight to depart with so notable a part of their Seigniorie; neither anything more commendable, than to prove all things for defence of their honour: neither would the proud Turks with whom no assured league could bee made (as they said) hold themselves content with this yeelding up of the island, by intreating of them and giving them way, become more insolent: and when they had taken Cyprus from them, would also seeke after Creete and Corcyra, & so yeelding them one thing after another, spoile themselves of all together. The matter thus debated to an fro, it was in the end resolved upon, to take up armes in defence of their honour, and by plaine force to withstand the Turke.

"The greater the danger was now feared from the angrie Turke, the more carefull were the Venetians of their state. Wherefore they forthwith sent messengers with letters unto the Governours of Cyprus, charging them with all carefulness and diligence to make themsolves readie to withstand the Turke, and to raise what power they were able in the island, not omitting any thing that might concern the good of the state: and at the same time made choice of their most valiant and expert captains both by sea and land, unto whom they committed the defence of their dispersed Seigniorie, with the leading of their forces.

"Selymus thoroughly furnished with all things necessary for the invasion of Cyprus, in the beginning of Februarie sent a great power both of horse and foot into Epyrus to forage the Venetian territorie. About the middle of Aprill following he sent Piall Bassa with four score gallies, and thirtie galliots to keep the Venetians from sending aid into Cyprus. He tooke his course to Zenos, an island of the Venetians, to have taken it from them. Piall here landing his forces, sought both by faire means & foule to have persuaded the inhabitants to have yeelded up their towne; but when he could get nothing of them but foule words againe, he began by force to assault the same. Two daies the towne was valiantly both assaulted and defended, but at length the Turks perceiving how little they prevailed, and that the defendants were resolutely set downe for the defence of themselves and their countrie; shamefully gave over the assault, and abandoning the island directed their course towards Cyprus. For Mustapha, author of that expedition, had before appointed Piall Bassa at a time prefixed, *to meet him at the Rhodes, and that he that came first should tarrie for the other, that so they might together saile into Cyprus.*

"All being now in readinesse, and a most royal gallie of wonderful greatness & beautie by the appointment of Selymus prepared for the great Bassa the Generall: he together with Haly Bassa and the rest of the fleet, departed from Constantinople, the six and twentieth of May, and at the Rhodes met with Piall as he had before appointed. The whole fleet at that time consisted of *two hundred galleys*, amongst whom were diverse galliots, and small men of warre with diverse other vessels prepared for the transportation of horses: with this fleet Mustapha kept on his course for Cyprus. They of the island in the meane time carefully attending the enemies comming from their watch towers first discovered their fleet at the west end of the island not far from Paphos: from whence the Turks turning upon the right hand, and passing the promontorie Curio, now called Del Le Gate, landed diverse of their men, who burnt and spoiled certaine villages, and with such spoile and prisoners as they had taken returned againe unto the fleet: which holding on their former course came at length to a place called Salinæ (of the abundance of salt there made) where they knew was best landing: and there in an open road came to an anchor, where the Bassaes without any resistance upon a plaine shoare landed their armie."

(4) SCENE III.—

The Anthropophagi, and men whose heads
Do grow beneath their shoulders.]

In this passage the poet had probably in his mind the marvellous account which Raleigh has given in his *Discoverie of Guiana*, 1596, of the Amazons, the cannibals, and the "Nation of people, whose heads appear not above their shoulders:" or was thinking of Pliny's description of the "Anthropophagi":—

"Above those are other Scythians called Anthropophagi, where is a country named Abarimon, within a certain vale of the mountain Imans, wherein are found savage and wild men, living and conversing usually among the brute beasts, who have their feet growing backward, and turned behind the calves of their legs, howbeit they run most swiftly. The former Anthropophagi or eaters of mans flesh whom we have placed above the north pole, tenne daies journey by land above the river Borysthenes, used to drinke out of the sculs of mens heads, and to weare the scalpes, haire and all, in steed of mandellions or stomachers before their breasts. . . . Beyond the Sciopodes westward, some there be without heads standing upon their neckes who carrie eies in their shoulders."—PLINIE'S *Natural Historie.* Book vii. ch. 2.

(5) SCENE III.—*The food that to him now is as luscious as locusts, shall be to him shortly as bitter as coloquintida.*] It is a question not easily settled whether by "locusts" Shakespeare referred to the insect, which is said to be considered a great delicacy at Tonquin, or to the fruit of the locust-tree: "That viscous substance which the pod of the locust contains, is perhaps, of all others, the most *luscious.* From its likeness to honey, in consistency and flavour, the *locust* is called the *honey*-tree also."—HENLEY.

Coloquintida, says Parkinson in his *Theatre of Plants,* "runneth with his branches upon the ground as a gourd or cowcumber doth. The fruit is small and round as a ball, green at the first on the outside, and afterwards growing to be of a browne yellow, which shell is as hard as a pompion or gourde; and is usually pared away while it is greene, the substance under it being white, very light, spongie or loose, and of an extreame bitter taste, almost indurable, and provoking loathing or casting in many that taste it."—PARKINSON'S *Theatre of Plants,* Tribe II. ch. 3.

ACT II.

(1) SCENE III.—*Why, he drinks you, with facility, your Dane dead drunk; he sweats not to overthrow your Almain; he gives your Hollander a vomit, ere the next pottle can be filled.*] The Englishman's potentiality in potting, was a common topic of satire with our old writers. In Beaumont and Fletcher's play of "The Captain," Act III. Sc. 2, Lodovico asks—

"Are the Englishmen
Such stubborn drinkers?"

And Piso answers,—

"Not a leak at sea
Can suck more liquor: you shall have their children
Christen'd in mull'd sack, and, at five years old,
Able to knock a Dane down. Take an Englishman,
And cry *St. George!* and give him but a rasher,
And you shall have him upon even terms
Defy a hogshead."

Peachem in his *Complete Gentleman,* 1622, p. 193, has a section entitled "Drinking the Plague of our English Gentry," in which he remarks:—"Within these fiftie or three-score yeares it was a rare thing with us to see a drunken man, our nation carrying the name of the most sober and temperate of any other in the world. But since we had to doe in the quarrell of the Netherlands, about the time of Sir John Norris his first being there, the custom of drinking and pledging healthes was brought over into England; wherein let the Dutch be their own judges, if we equall them not; yea I think rather excell them."

To the same effect, Heywood, in the "*Philocothonista,* or the Drunkard opened, dissected, and anatomized," 4to. London, 1635, tells us that—"There is now profest an eighth liberal art of science called *Ars Bibendi, i.e.* the Art of Drinking. The students or professors thereof call a greene garland or painted hoope hang'd out a *College:* a signe where there is lodging, man's meate, and horse meate, an *Inne of Courte,* an *Hall* or an *Hostle:* where nothing is sold but ale and tobacco, a *Grammar Schoole;* a red or blew lattice (the usual designation of an ale-house) that they terme a *Free Schoole* for all comers. The bookes which they study and whose leaves they do often turne over are for the most part three of the old translation and three of the new. Those of the old translation:—1. The *tankard:* 2. the *blacke Jacke:* 3. the *quart pot rib'd,* or *thorendell.* Those of the new be these: 1. the *jugge:* 2. the *beaker:* 3. the *double or single can* or *black pot,*" &c. See also Nash's *Pierce Pennilesse* (1592), on *De Arte Bibendi;* Barnaby Rich's *Irish Hubbub,* 1618; and Harington's *Nugæ Antiquiæ,* I. p. 348.

(2) SCENE III.—
Then take thine auld cloak about thee.]

The ballad whence the stanzas sung by Iago are taken is printed as follows in Capell's *School of Shakespeare;* it will be found also in Percy's *Reliques of Ancient Poetry.*

"TAKE THY OLD CLOAK ABOUT THEE.

"This winters weather waxeth cold
And frost doth freese on everie hill,
And Boreas blowes his blasts soe bold,
That all our cattell are like to spill; *
Bell, my wife, who loves no strife,
She sayd unto me quietlie,
Rise up, and save cow Crumbockes life,
Man, put thine old cloak about thee.

HE.

"O Bell, why dost thou flyte and scorne?
Thou kenst my cloak is very thin;
It is soe bare and overworne,
A cricke he theron cannot renn:
Then Ile noe longer borrowe nor lend,
For once Ile new appareld bee,
To-morrow Ile to towne and spend,
For Ile have a new cloake about mee.

SHE.

"Cow Crumbocke is a very good cowe,
Shee has been alwayes true to the payle,
Still has helpt us to butter and cheese I trow,
And other things she will not fayle:
I wold be loth to see her pine,
Good husband, councell take of mee,
It is not for us to goe so fine,
Then take thine old cloake about thee.

HE.

"My cloake it was a very good cloake,
Itt hath been alwayes true to the weare,
But now it is not worth a groat;
I have had it four-and-forty yeare.

* *Spill.* To spoil; to come to harm.

Sometime it was of cloth in graine,
'Tis now but a sigh-clout,* as you may see,
It will neither hold out winde nor raine;
Ile have a new cloake about mee.

SHE.

"It is four and fortye yeeres agoe
Since th' one of us the other did ken;
And we have had betwixt us twoe
Of children either nine or ten:
Wee have brought them up to women and men:
In the feare of God I trow they bee;
And why wilt thou thyselfe misken?
Man, take thine old cloake about thee.

HE.

"O Bell, my wiffe, why dost thou floute?
Now is nowe, and then was then:
Seeke now all the world throughout,
Thou kenst not clowns from gentlemen.
They are cladd in blacke, greane, yellowe, or gray,
Soe far above their own degree:
Once in my life Ile do as they,
For Ile have a new cloake about mee.

SHE.

"King Stephen was a worthy peere,
His breeches cost him but a crowne;
He held them sixpence all too deere,
Therefore he calld the taylor Lowne.
He was a wight of high renowne,
And thouse but of a low degree;
Itts pride that putts the countreye downe,
Then take thine old cloake about thee.

HE.

"Bell, my wife she loves not strife,
Yet she will lead me if she can;
And oft, to live a quiet life,
I am forced to yield, though Ime good man.
Itts not for a man with a woman to threape,*
Unlesse he first give oer the plea:
Where I began wee now mun leave,
And take mine old cloake about mee."

* *Sigh-clout.* A cloth to strain milk through.

* *To threape.* To dispute.

ACT III.

(1) SCENE III.—

But he that filches from me my good name,
Robs me of that which not enriches him,
And makes me poor indeed.]

Mr. Halliwell in his *Life of Shakespeare*, p. 190, ed. 8vo., cites the subjoined lines from a MS. entitled "The Newe Metamorphosis, or a Feaste of Fancie, or Poeticall Legendes, written by J. M. Gent, 1600," as proof that "Othello" must have been produced before that year:—

"The highwayman that robs one of his purse
Is not soe bad; nay, these are ten tymes worse!
For these doe rob men of their pretious name,
And in exchange give obliquie and shame."

But the reflection is sufficiently trite, and in both instances, as in many others where it occurs, was probably founded on the following passages:—

"Is not that *Treasure* which before all other, is most regarded of honest persons, *the good Fame of Man and Woman*, lost through whoredom?"—*Homily* XI. pt. 2.

"Now here consider that St. Paul numbreth a Scolder, Brawler, or a Picker of Quarrels, among Thieves and Idolators, and many Times there cometh less Hurt of a Thiefe than of a railing tongue. For the one taketh away a *Mans good name, the other taketh but his Riches, which is of much less Value and Estimation, than is his good name.*" —*Homily* XII. pt. 1.

(2) SCENE III.—*Not poppy, nor mandragora.*] "The herb Mandragoras some writers call Circeium: two or three roots it hath of a fleshie substance running downe into the earth almost a cubit, and a fruit or apple of the bignesse of filberds or hazel-nuts, within which there be seeds like unto the pippins of peares. . . . In some countries they venture to eat the apples or fruit thereof: but those that know not how to dresse and order them aright loose the use of their tongue thereby, and prove dumbe for the time. And verily if they be so bold as to take a great quantity thereof in drink, they are sure to die for it. Yet it may be used safely ynough for to procure sleepe if there be good regard had in the dose, that it be answerable in proportion to the strength and complexion of the patient. Also it is an ordinary thing to drink it against the poyson of serpents: likewise before the cutting, cauterizing, pricking, or launcing of any member to take away the sence or feeling of such extreme cures. And sufficient it is in some bodies to cast them into a sleepe with the smell of Mandrage."—PLINIE'S *Natural Historie*, Bk. XXV. ch. 13.

(3) SCENE III.—*The spirit-stirring drum, the ear-piercing fife.*] "In mentioning the *fife* joined with the *drum*, Shakspeare, as usual, paints from the life; those instruments accompanying each other being used in his age by the English soldiery. The *fife*, however, as a martial instrument, was afterwards entirely discontinued among our troops for many years, but at length revived in the war before the last. It is commonly supposed that our soldiers borrowed it from the Highlanders in the last rebellion: but I do not know that the *fife* is peculiar to the Scotch, or even used at all by them. It was first used within the memory of man among our troops by the British guards, by order of the Duke of Cumberland, when they were encamped at Maestricht, in the year 1747, and thence soon adopted into other English regiments of infantry. They took it from the Allies with whom they served. This instrument, accompanying the drum, is of considerable antiquity in the European armies, particularly the German. In a curious picture in the Ashmolean Museum at Oxford, painted 1525, representing the siege of Pavia by the French King, where the emperor was taken prisoner, we see *fifes* and *drums*. In an old English treatise written by William Garrard before 1587, and published by one captain Hitchcock in 1591, intituled The Art of Warre, there are several wood cuts of military evolutions, in which these instruments are both introduced. In Rymer's Fœdera, in a diary of King Henry's siege of Bulloigne,

1544, mention is made of the *drommes* and *viffleurs* marching at the head of the King's army.—Tom. xv. p. 53.

"The *drum* and *fife* were also much used at ancient festivals, shows, and processions. Gerard Leigh, in his Accidence of Armorie, printed in 1576, describing a Christmas magnificently celebrated at the Inner Temple, says, 'We entered the prince his hall, where anon we heard the noyse of *drum* and *fife*.'—P. 119.

"At a stately masque on Shrove-Sunday, 1510, in which King Henry VIII. was an actor, Holinshed mentions the entry 'of a *drum* and *fife* apparelled in white damaske and grene bonnettes.'—Chron. III. 805, col. 2. There are many more instances in Holinshed and Stow's Survey of London."—WARTON.

(4) SCENE IV.—

—— I had rather have lost my purse
Full of crusadoes.]

"The cruzado was not current, as it should seem, at Venice, though it certainly was in England in the time of Shakspeare, who has here indulged his usual practice of departing from national costume. It was of gold, and weighed two penny-weights six grains, or nine shillings English."—DOUCE, *Illustrations of Shakspeare.*

(5) SCENE IV.—

—— the hearts of old gave hands;
But our new heraldry is hands, not hearts.]

The antithesis of *hearts* and *hands* appears to have been a favourite with Shakespeare and the writers of his age: so in "The Tempest" Act III. Scene I.:—

"MIR. My husband, then?
FER. Ay, with a heart as willing
As bondage e'er of freedom: here's my *hand*.
MIR. And mine, with my *heart* in't."

So also in Warner's *Albion's England*:—

"My *hand* shall never give
My *heart*, my *heart* shall give my *hand*."

And Mr. Singer has quoted a passage from the essays of Sir William Cornwallis the younger, 1601, where we have the words in similar opposition:—"We of these later times, full of a nice curiositie, mislike all the performances of our forefathers; we say they were honest plaine men, but they want the capering wits of this ripe age. They had wont to *give their hands and hearts* together, but we think it a finer grace to looke asquint, *our hand* looking one way and *our heart* another." Warburton conjectured, and Malone at one time was of the same opinion, that the expression, "our *new heraldry*" was a satirical reflection upon King James' creation of baronets. But to this it has been objected that the new order was not created until 1611, while the play was written before November 1604; and it is in the highest degree improbable that an allusion so offensive to the king was inserted afterwards.

(6) SCENE IV.—*Away!*] The incident of the handkerchief, which Shakespeare has invested with such terrible sublimity, is derived from the novel in the *Hecatommithi*, on which this play was founded:—

"I have already said that Desdemona went frequently to the ensign's house, and passed great part of the day with his wife. The villain had observed that she often brought with her a handkerchief that the Moor had given her, and which, as it was very delicately worked in the Moorish taste, was very highly valued by them both; he determined to steal it, and by its means complete her ruin. He had a little girl of three years old that was much caressed by Desdemona; and one day, when that unhappy woman was on a visit to this villain, he took up the child in his arms and presented it to Desdemona, who received it and pressed it to her bosom. In the same instant this deceiver stole from her sash the handkerchief, with such dexterity, that she did not perceive him; and went away with it in very high spirits. Desdemona went home, and, taken up with other thoughts, never recollected her handkerchief till some days after; when, not being able to find it, she began to fear that the Moor should ask her for it, as he often did. The infamous ensign, watching his opportunity, went to the lieutenant, and, to aid his wicked purpose, left the handkerchief on his bolster. The lieutenant did not find it till the next morning, when, getting up, he set his foot upon it as it had fallen to the floor. Not being able to imagine how it came there, and knowing it to be Desdemona's, he determined to carry it back to her; and, waiting till the Moor was gone out, he went to the back-door and knocked. Fortune, who seemed to have conspired along with the ensign the death of this poor woman, brought the Moor home in the same instant. Hearing some one knock, he went to the window, and, much disturbed, asked who is there? The lieutenant hearing his voice, and fearing that when he came down he should do him some mischief, ran away without answering. The Moor came down, and finding no one either at the door or in the street, returned full of suspicion to his wife, and asked if she knew who it was that had knocked. She answered with great truth that she knew not. 'But I think,' said he, 'it was the lieutenant;'—'It might be he,' said she, 'or any one else.' The Moor checked himself at the time, though he was violently enraged, and determined to take no step without first consulting the ensign. To him he immediately went, and related what had just happened, begging him to learn from the lieutenant what he could on the subject. The ensign rejoiced much in this accident, and promised to do so. He contrived to enter into discourse with him one day in a place where the Moor might see them. He talked with him on a very different subject, laughed much, and expressed by his motions and attitudes very great surprise. The Moor as soon as he saw them separate went to the ensign, and desired to know what had passed between them. The ensign, after many solicitations, at last told him that he had concealed nothing from him. He says he has enjoyed your wife every time that you have stayed long enough from home to give him an opportunity; and that in their last interview she had made him a present of that handkerchief which you gave her when you married her.* The Moor thanked him, and thought that if his wife had no longer the handkerchief in her possession it would be a proof that the ensign had told him the truth. For which reason one day after dinner, among other subjects, he asked her for this handkerchief. The poor woman, who had long apprehended this, blushed excessively at the question, and, to hide her change of colour, which the Moor had very accurately observed, ran to her wardrobe and pretended to look for it. After having searched for some time, 'I cannot conceive,' said she, 'what is become of it! have not you taken it?' 'Had I taken it,' replied he, 'I should not have asked you for it. But you may look for it another time more at your ease.' Leaving her then, he began to reflect what would be the best way of putting to death his wife and the lieutenant, and how he might avoid being prosecuted for the murder. Thinking night and day on this subject, he could not prevent Desdemona from perceiving that his behaviour was very different from what it had been formerly. She often asked him what it was that agitated him so violently. 'You, who were once the merriest man alive, are now the most melancholy.' The Moor answered and alleged a variety of reasons, but she was not satisfied with any of them; and knowing that she had done nothing to justify so much agitation, she began to fear that he grew tired of her. She once in conversation with the ensign's wife expressed herself thus: 'I know not what to say of the Moor; he used to treat me most affectionately; and I begin to fear that my example will teach young women never to marry against their parents' consent, and the Italians in particular, not

* In the tolerably correct but far from elegant translation of W. Parr, which we adopt, the words "when you married her" (*quando la sposaste*) are inadvertently omitted.

to connect themselves with men from whom they are separated by nature, climate, education, and complexion. But as I know him to be the confidential of your husband, whom he consults on all occasions, I intreat you, if you have heard anything that might explain this mystery and be of use to me, not to deny me your assistance.' These words were accompanied with a flood of tears.

"The ensign's wife, who knew all (as her husband had in vain endeavoured to prevail upon her to become an accomplice in the murder of Desdemona), but durst tell her nothing for fear of her husband, only said, 'Take care not to give the Moor any cause for suspicion, and do all in your power to convince him of your affection and fidelity.' 'Why so I do,' said she, 'but to no purpose.' The Moor, in the meantime, did all in his power to prove what he desired not to find true, and begged the ensign to make him see the handkerchief in possession of the lieutenant. Although this was a difficult undertaking, yet the villain promised to do all in his power to give him a satisfactory proof of this. The lieutenant had a woman in the house, who was a notable embroiderer in muslin, and who, struck with the beauty of Desdemona's handkerchief, determined to copy it before it should be returned to her. She set about making one like it, and while she was at work, the ensign discovered that she sat at a window where any one who passed in the street might see her. This he took care to point out to the Moor, who was then fully persuaded that his chaste and innocent wife was an adultress. He agreed with the ensign to kill both her and the lieutenant; and, consulting together about the means, the Moor entreated him to undertake the assassination of the officer, promising never to forget so great an obligation. He refused, however, to attempt what was so very difficult and dangerous, as the lieutenant was equally brave and vigilant; but with much entreaty and considerable presents, he was prevailed on to say that he would hazard the experiment. One dark night, after taking this resolution, he observed the lieutenant coming out of the house of a female libertine where he usually passed his evenings, and assaulted him sword in hand. He struck at his legs with a view of bringing him to the ground, and with the first blow cut him quite through the right thigh."

ACT IV.

(1) SCENE I.—

Is't possible!—Confess!—Handkerchief!—O, devil!— [Falls in a trance.]

"The starts and broken reflections in this speech have something very terrible, and show the mind of the speaker to be in inexpressible agonies."—WARBURTON.

"When many confused and very interesting ideas pour in upon the mind all at once, and with such rapidity that it has not time to shape or digest them, if it does not relieve itself by tears (which we know it often does, whether for joy or grief) it produces stupefaction and fainting.

"Othello, in broken sentences, and single words, all of which have a reference to the cause of his jealousy, shows, that all the proofs are present at once to his mind, which so overpowers it, that he falls into a trance, the natural consequence."—SIR JOSHUA REYNOLDS.

(2) SCENE III.—

My mother had a maid call'd Barbara:
She was in love; and he she lov'd prov'd mad,
And did forsake her: she had a song of Willow,
An old thing 'twas, but it express'd her fortune,
And she died singing it.]

The old ballad so pathetically introduced has been reprinted by Capell and Dr. Percy from a black-letter copy in the Pepys' collection at Cambridge. The original, which we append, is the lament not of a forsaken female, but of a "lass-lorn bachelor," and Shakespeare, in adapting it for a woman, has slightly altered, and added to, the words:—

"A LOVER'S COMPLAINT, BEING FORSAKEN OF HIS LOVE.

"A poore soule sat sighing under a sicamore tree;
O willow, willow, willow!
With his hand on his bosom, his head on his knee:
O willow, willow, willow!
O willow, willow, willow!
Sing, O the greene willow shall be my garland.

"He sigh'd in his singing, and after each grone,
Come willow, &c.
I am dead to all pleasure, my true love is gone;
O willow, &c.

"My love she is turned; untrue she doth prove:
O willow, &c.
She renders me nothing but hate for my love.
O willow, &c.

"O pitty me (cried he) ye lovers, each one;
O willow, &c.
Her heart 's hard as marble; she rues not my mone.
O willow, &c.

"The cold streams ran by him, his eyes wept apace;
O willow, &c.
The salt tears fell from him, which drowned his face:
O willow, &c.

"The mute birds sate by him, made tame by his mones:
O willow, &c.
The salt tears fell from him, which softned the stones.
O willow, &c.

"Let nobody blame me, her scornes I do prove;
O willow, &c.
She was born to be faire; I, to die for her love.
O willow, &c.

"O that beauty should harbour a heart that's so hard!
O willow, &c.
My true love rejecting without all regard.
O willow, &c.

"Let love no more boast him in palace or bower;
O willow, &c.
For women are trothles, and flote in an houre.
O willow, &c.

"But what helps complaining? In vaine I complaine;
O willow, &c.
I must patiently suffer her scorne and disdaine.
O willow, &c.

"Come, all you forsaken, and sit down by me,
O willow, &c.
He that 'plaines of his false love, mine's falser than she.
O willow, &c.

"The willow wreath weare I, since my love doth fleete;
O willow, willow, willow!
A Garland for lovers forsaken most meete.
O willow, willow, willow!
O willow, willow, willow!
Sing, O the greene willow shall be my gárland."

ACT V.

(1) Scene II.—*I have done the state some service.*] The policy of the Venetian commonwealth in never permitting a citizen to have command of the army, is mentioned more than once by Contareno:—

"To exclude therfore out of our estate the danger or occasion of any such ambitious enterprises, our auncesters held it a better course to defend their dominions uppon the continent with forreyn mercenarie souldiers, than with their homeborn citizens, and to assigne them their pay and stipende out of the tributes and receipts of the Province, wherin they remayned: for it is just, and reasonable, that the souldiers shoulde be maintained at the charge of those in whose defence they are employed, and into their warfare, have many of our associates been ascribed, some of which have attained to the highest degree of commandement in our army. * * * * The Cittizens therefore of Venice, for this only course are deprived of the honors belonging to warres by land, and are contented to transferre them over to straungers to which ende there was a lawe solemnely decreede, that no gentleman of Venice should have the charge and commaundement of above five and twentie souldiers," &c.

(2) Scene II.—

> —— *of one, whose hand,*
> *Like the base* Indian, *threw a pearl away,*
> *Richer than all his tribe.*]

So the quartos. In the folio we have,—

> "Of one whose hand
> (Like the base *Iudean*) threw," &c.

Upon these two readings the commentators are at issue. Theobald, Warburton, Farmer, and Malone, all advocate *Judean*, considering that the allusion is manifestly to the story of Herod and Mariamme. This view of the passage has been very ably supported too, of late, by a correspondent in Mr. G. White's *Shakespeare's Scholar*, &c. p. 443. On the other hand, the latest editors, Messrs. Dyce, Collier, and Knight, side with Boswell, who preferred *Indian*, and adduced the following quotations, from succeeding poets, in maintenance of that lection:

> "So the *unskilfull Indian* those bright gems
> Which might adde majestie to diadems
> *'Mong the waves scatters.*"
> *Habington's Castara.—To Castara weeping.*

And—

> "Behold my queen—
> Who with no more concern I'le cast away
> *Then Indians do a pearl that ne're did know*
> *Its value.*"
> *The Woman's Conquest*, by Sir Edward Howard.

We, too, follow the quartos, but must admit that a good case has been made out for the reading of the folio.

CRITICAL OPINIONS ON OTHELLO.

"THE beauties of this play impress themselves so strongly upon the attention of the reader, that they can draw no aid from critical illustration. The fiery openness of Othello, magnanimous, artless, and credulous, boundless in his confidence, ardent in his affection, inflexible in his resolution, and obdurate in his revenge; the cool malignity of Iago, silent in his resentment, subtle in his designs, and studious at once of his interest and his vengeance; the soft simplicity of Desdemona, confident of merit, and conscious of innocence, her artless perseverance in her suit, and her slowness to suspect that she can be suspected, are such proofs of Shakespeare's skill in human nature, as, I suppose, it is vain to seek in any modern writer. The gradual progress which Iago makes in the Moor's conviction, and the circumstances which he employs to inflame him, are so artfully natural, that, though it will perhaps not be said of him as he says of himself, that he is *a man not easily jealous*, yet we cannot but pity him, when at last we find him *perplexed in the extreme*.

"There is always danger, lest wickedness, conjoined with abilities, should steal upon esteem, though it misses of approbation; but the character of Iago is so conducted, that he is, from the first scene to the last, hated and despised. Even the inferior characters of this play would be very conspicuous in any other piece, not only for their justness, but their strength. Cassio is brave, benevolent, and honest, ruined only by his want of stubbornness to resist an insidious invitation. Roderigo's suspicious credulity, and impatient submission to the cheats which he sees practised upon him, and which by persuasion he suffers to be repeated, exhibit a strong picture of a weak mind betrayed by unlawful desires to a false friend; and the virtue of Æmilia is such as we often find worn loosely, but not cast off, easy to commit small crimes, but quickened and alarmed at atrocious villanies.

"The scenes from the beginning to the end are busy, varied by happy interchanges, and regularly promoting the progression of the story; and the narrative in the end, though it tells but what is known already, yet is necessary to produce the death of Othello.

"Had the scene opened in Cyprus, and the preceding incidents been occasionally related, there had been little wanting to a drama of the most exact and scrupulous regularity."—JOHNSON.

"If 'Romeo and Juliet' shines with the colours of the dawn of morning, but a dawn whose purple clouds already announce the thunder of a sultry day, 'Othello' is, on the other hand, a strongly shaded picture: we might call it a tragical Rembrandt. What a fortunate mistake that the Moor (under which name, in the original novel, a baptized Saracen of the Northern coast of Africa was unquestionably meant), has been made by Shakspeare in every respect a negro! We recognize in Othello the wild nature of that glowing zone which generates the most deadly poisons, tamed only in appearance by the desire of fame, by foreign laws of honour, and by nobler and milder manners. His jealousy is not the jealousy of the heart, which is compatible with the tenderest feeling and adoration of the beloved object; it is of that sensual kind which, in burning climes, has given birth to the disgraceful confinement of women and many other unnatural usages. A drop of this poison flows in his veins, and sets his whole blood in the wildest ferment. The Moor *seems* noble, frank, confiding, grateful for the love shown him; and he is all this, and, moreover, a hero who spurns at danger, a worthy leader of an army, a faithful servant of the State; but the mere physical force of passion puts to flight in one moment all his acquired and mere habitual virtues, and gives the upper hand to the savage over the moral man. This tyranny of the blood over the will betrays itself even in the expression of his desire of revenge upon Cassio. In his repentance, a genuine tenderness for his murdered wife, and in the presence of the damning evidence of his deed, the painful feeling of annihilated honour at last bursts forth; and in the midst of these painful emotions, he assails himself with the rage wherewith a despot punishes a runaway slave. He suffers as a double man; at once in the higher and the lower sphere into which his being was divided. While the Moor bears the nightly colour of suspicion and deceit only on his visage, Iago is black within. He haunts Othello like his evil genius, and with his light (and therefore the more dangerous) insinuations, he leaves him no rest; it is as if by means of an unfortunate affinity, founded however in nature, this influence was by necessity more powerful over him than the voice of his good angel Desdemona. A more artful villain than this Iago was never portrayed; he spreads his nets with a skill which nothing can escape. The repugnance inspired by his aims becomes tolerable from the attention of the spectators being directed to his means: these furnish endless employment to the understanding. Cool, discontented, and morose, arrogant where he dares be so, but humble and insinuating when it suits his purposes, he is a complete master in the art of dissimulation; accessible only to selfish emotions, he is thoroughly skilled in rousing the passions of others, and of availing himself of every opening which they give him: he is as excellent an observer of men as any one can be who is unacquainted with higher motives of action from his own experience; there is always some truth in his malicious observations on them. He does not merely pretend an obdurate incredulity as to the virtue of women, he actually entertains it; and this, too, falls in with his whole way of thinking, and makes him the more fit for the execution of his purpose. As in everything he sees merely the hateful side, he dissolves in the rudest manner the charm which the imagination casts over the relation between the two sexes: he does so for the purpose of revolting Othello's senses, whose heart otherwise might easily have convinced him of Desdemona's innocence. This must serve as an excuse for the numerous expressions in the speeches of Iago from which modesty shrinks. If Shakspeare had written in our days he would not perhaps have dared to hazard them; and yet this must certainly have greatly injured the truth of his picture. Desdemona is a sacrifice without blemish. She is not, it is true, a high ideal representation of sweetness and enthusiastic passion like Juliet; full of simplicity, softness, and humility, and so innocent, that she can hardly form to herself an idea of the possibility of infidelity, she seems calculated to make the most yielding and tenderest of wives. The female propensity wholly to resign itself to a foreign destiny has led her into the only fault of her life, that of marrying without her father's consent. Her choice seems wrong; and yet she has been gained over to Othello by that which induces the female to honour in man her protector and guide,—admiration of his determined heroism, and compassion for the sufferings which he had undergone. With great art it is so contrived that from the very circumstance that the possibility of a suspicion of her own purity of motive never once enters her mind, she is the less reserved in her solicitations for Cassio, and thereby does but heighten more and more the jealousy of Othello. To throw out still more clearly the angelic purity of Desdemona, Shakspeare has in Emilia associated with her a companion of doubtful virtue. From the sinful levity of this woman, it is also conceivable that she should not confess the abstraction of the handkerchief when Othello violently demands it back: this would otherwise be the circumstance in the whole piece the most difficult to justify. Cassio is portrayed exactly as he ought to be to excite suspicion without actual guilt,—amiable and nobly disposed, but easily seduced. The public events of the first two acts show us Othello in his most glorious aspect, as the support of Venice and the terror of the Turks; they serve to withdraw the story from the mere domestic circle, just as this is done in 'Romeo and Juliet' by the dissensions between the houses of Montague and Capulet. No eloquence is capable of painting the overwhelming force of the catastrophe in 'Othello,'—the pressure of feelings which measure out in a moment the abysses of eternity."—SCHLEGEL.

"Admirable is the preparation, so truly and peculiarly Shakesperian, in the introduction of Roderigo, as the dupe on whom Iago shall first exercise his art, and in doing so display his own character. Roderigo, without any fixed principle, but not without the moral notions and sympathies with honour which his rank and connexions had hung upon him, is already well fitted and predisposed for the purpose; for very want of character and strength of passion, like wind loudest in an empty house, constitute his character. The first three lines happily state the nature and foundation of the friendship between him and Iago,—the purse,—as also the contrast of Roderigo's intemperance of mind with Iago's coolness, the coolness of a preconceiving experimenter. The mere language of protestation—

'If ever I did dream of such a matter,
Abhor me,'—

which, falling in with the associative link, determines Roderigo's continuation of complaint,—

'Thou told'st me, thou didst hold him in thy hate,'—

elicits at length a true feeling of Iago's mind, the dread of contempt habitual to those who encourage in themselves, and have their keenest pleasure in, the expression of contempt for others. Observe Iago's high self-opinion, and the moral, that a wicked man will employ real feelings, as well as assume those most alien from his own, as instruments of his purposes:—

'—— and by the faith of man
I know my price, I am worth no worse a place.'

In what follows, let the reader feel how by and through the glass of two passions, disappointed vanity and envy, the very vices of which he is complaining are made to act upon him as if they were so many excellences, and the more appropriately because cunning is always admired and wished for by minds conscious of inward weakness: but they act only by half, like music on an inattentive auditor, swelling the thoughts which prevent him from listening to it.

'ROD. What a full fortune does the *thick lips* owe
If he can carry't thus!'

Roderigo turns off to Othello; and here comes one, if not the only, seeming justification of our blackamoor or negro Othello. Even if we supposed this an uninterrupted tradition of the theatre, and that Shakespear himself, from want of scenes, and the experience that nothing could be too marked for the senses of his audience, had practically sanctioned it, would this prove aught concerning his own intention as a poet for all ages? Can we imagine him so utterly ignorant as to make a barbarous negro plead royal birth—at a time too when negroes were not known except as slaves? As for Iago's language to Brabantio, it implies merely that Othello was a Moor, that is, black. Though I think the rivalry of Roderigo sufficient to account for his wilful confusion of Moor and negro, yet, even if compelled to give this up, I should think it only adapted for the acting of the day, and should complain of an enormity built on a single word, in direct contradiction to Iago's 'Barbary Horse.' Besides, if we could in good earnest believe Shakespear ignorant of the distinction, still why should we adopt one disagreeable possibility instead of a ten times greater and more pleasing probability? It is a common error to mistake the epithets applied by the *dramatis personæ* to each other as truly descriptive of what the audience ought to see or know. No doubt Desdemona saw Othello's visage in his mind; yet, as we are constituted, and most surely as an English audience was disposed in the beginning of the seventeenth century, it would be something monstrous to conceive this beautiful Venetian girl falling in love with a veritable negro. It would argue a disproportionateness, a want of balance in Desdemona, which Shakespear does not appear to have in the least contemplated.

"Iago's speech—'Virtue? a fig! 'tis in ourselves that we are thus, or thus,' &c.—comprises the passionless character of Iago. It is all will in intellect; and therefore he is here a bold partisan of the truth, but yet of a truth converted into a falsehood by the absence of all the necessary modifications caused by the frail nature of man. And then comes the last sentiment—'Our raging motions, our carnal stings, our unbitted lusts, whereof I take this, that you call—love, to be a sect or scion!' Here is the true Iagoism of alas! how many! Note Iago's pride of mastery in the repetition of 'Go, make money!' to his anticipated dupe, even stronger than his love of lucre: and when Roderigo is completely won, when the effect has been fully produced, the repetition of triumph—'Go to; farewell; put money enough in your purse!' The remainder—Iago's soliloquy—the motive-hunting of a motiveless malignity—how awful it is! Yea, whilst he is still allowed to bear the divine image, it is too fiendish for his own steady view, for the lonely gaze of a being next to devil, and not quite devil,—and yet a character which Shakespear has attempted and executed, without disgust and without scandal!

Dr. Johnson has remarked that little or nothing is wanting to render the 'Othello' a regular tragedy, but to have opened the play with the arrival of Othello in Cyprus, and to have thrown the preceding act into the form of narration. Here then is the place to determine whether such a change would or would not be an improvement: nay (to throw down the glove with a full challenge), whether the tragedy would or not by such an arrangement become more regular—that is, more consonant with the rules dictated by universal reason, or the true common-sense of mankind, in its application to the particular case. For in all acts of judgment, it can never be too often recollected, and scarcely too often repeated, that rules are means to ends, and, consequently, that the end must be determined and understood before it can be known what the rules are or ought to be. Now, from a certain species of drama, proposing to itself the accomplishment of certain ends—these partly arising from the idea of the species itself, but in part, likewise, forced upon the dramatist by accidental circumstances beyond his power to remove or control—three rules have been abstracted;—in other words, the means most conducive to the attainment of the proposed ends have been generalized, and prescribed under the names of the three unities—the unity of time, the unity of place, and the unity of action, which last would, perhaps, have been as appropriately, as well as more intelligibly, entitled the unity of interest. With this last the present question has no immediate concern: in fact, its conjunction with the former two is a mere delusion of words. It is not properly a rule, but in itself the great end, not only of the drama, but of the epic poem, the lyric ode, of all poetry, down to the candle-flame cone of an epigram, nay, of poesy in general, as the proper generic term inclusive of all the fine arts as its species. But of the unities of time and place, which alone are entitled to the name of rules, the history of their origin will be their best criterion. You might take the Greek chorus to a place, but you could not bring a place to them without as palpable an equivoque as bringing Birnam Wood to Macbeth at Dunsinane. It was the same, though in a less degree, with regard to the unity of time:—the positive fact, not for a moment removed from the senses, the presence, I mean, of the same identical chorus, was a continued measure of time; and although the imagination may supersede perception, yet it must be granted to be an imperfection, however easily tolerated, to place the two in broad contradiction to each other. In truth, it is a mere accident of terms; for the Trilogy of the Greek theatre was a drama in three acts, and notwithstanding this, what strange contrivances as to place there are in the Aristophanic Frogs. Besides, if the law of mere actual perception is once violated, as it is repeatedly even in the Greek tragedies, why is it more difficult to imagine three hours to be three years than to be a whole day and night?

"Observe in how many ways Othello is made, first our acquaintance, then our friend, then the object of our anxiety, before the duper is to be approached! And Cassio's warm-hearted, yet perfectly disengaged, praise of Desdemona 'that paragons description and wild fame,' and sympathy with the 'most fortunately' wived Othello;—and yet Cassio is an enthusiastic admirer, almost a worshipper, of Desdemona. (O, that detestable code, that excellence cannot be loved in any form that is female, but it must needs be selfish!) Observe Othello's 'honest' and Cassio's 'bold' Iago, and Cassio's full guileless-hearted wishes for the safety and love-raptures of Othello and 'the divine Desdemona.' And also note the exquisite circumstance of Cassio's kissing Iago's wife, as if it ought to be impossible that the dullest auditor should not feel Cassio's religious love of Desdemona's purity. Iago's answers are the sneers which a proud bad intellect feels towards women, and expresses to a wife. Surely it ought to be considered a very exalted compliment to women, that all the sarcasms on them in Shakespear are put in the mouths of villains.

"Finally, Othello does not kill Desdemona in jealousy, but in a conviction forced upon him by the almost superhuman art of Iago, such a conviction as any man would and must have entertained who had believed Iago's honesty as Othello did. We, the audience, know that Iago is a villain from the beginning: but in considering the essence of the Shakesperian Othello, we must perseveringly place ourselves in his situation, and under his circumstances. Then we shall immediately feel the fundamental difference between the solemn agony of the noble Moor, and the wretched fishing jealousies of Leontes, and the morbid suspiciousness of Leonatus, who is in other respects a fine character. Othello had no life but in Desdemona:—the belief that she, his angel, had fallen from the heaven of her native innocence, wrought a civil war in his heart. She is his counterpart; and like him, is almost sanctified in our eyes by her absolute unsuspiciousness, and holy entireness of love. As the curtain drops, which do we pity the most?"—COLERIDGE.

THE POEMS

OF

WILLIAM SHAKESPEARE.

VENUS AND ADONIS.

"VILIA MIRETUR VULGUS; MIHI FLAVUS APOLLO
POCULA CASTALIA PLENA MINISTRET AQUA."—*Ovid.*

TO THE

RIGHT HONOURABLE HENRY WRIOTHESLY,

EARL OF SOUTHAMPTON, AND BARON OF TICHFIELD.

RIGHT HONOURABLE,

I know not how I shall offend in dedicating my unpolished lines to your lordship, nor how the world will censure me for choosing so strong a prop to support so weak a burden: only, if your honour seem but pleased, I account myself highly praised, and vow to take advantage of all idle hours, till I have honoured you with some graver labour. But if the first heir of my invention prove deformed, I shall be sorry it had so noble a god-father, and never after ear [a] so barren a land, for fear it yield me still so bad a harvest. I leave it to your honourable survey, and your honour to your heart's content; which I wish may always answer your own wish, and the world's hopeful expectation.

Your honour's in all duty,

WILLIAM SHAKESPEARE.

---

a *—and never after* ear *so barren a land,—*] *To ear* is *to plough* or *till:* So in "All's Well That Ends Well," Act I. Sc. 3,—"He that *ears* my land, spares my team," &c. Again in "King Richard II." Act III. Sc. 2,—

"—— and let them go
To *ear* the land that hath some hope to grow."

VENUS AND ADONIS.

THIS poem, if we are to accept the expression in the introductory epistle—"the first heir of my invention"—literally, was Shakespeare's earliest composition. Some critics conceive it to have been written, indeed, before he quitted Stratford; but the question when and where it was produced has yet to be decided. It was entered on the Stationers' Registers by Richard Field, as "licensed by the Archbishop of Canterbury, and the Wardens," in 1593, and the first edition was printed in the same year.* This edition was speedily exhausted, and a second by the same printer was put forth in 1594. This again was followed by an octavo impression in 1596, and so much was the poem in demand that it had reached a fifth edition by 1602. After this date it was often reprinted, and copies of 1616, 1620, 1624, and 1627 are still extant. Its popularity, as Mr. Collier observes, is established also by the frequent mention of it in early writers.

"In the early part of Shakspeare's life, his poems seem to have gained him more reputation than his plays;—at least they are oftener mentioned or alluded to. Thus the author of an old comedy, called *The Return from Parnassus*, written about 1602, in his review of the poets of the time, says not a word of his dramatick compositions, but allots him his portion of fame solely on account of the poems that he had produced."—MALONE.

The text adopted in the present reprint of "Venus and Adonis" is that of the first quarto, 1593, collated with the best of the later editions.

EVEN as the sun with purple-colour'd face
Had ta'en his last leave of the weeping morn,
Rose-cheek'd Adonis[a] hied him to the chase;
Hunting he lov'd, but love he laugh'd to scorn:
  Sick-thoughted Venus makes amain unto him,
  And like a bold-fac'd suitor 'gins to woo him.

"Thrice fairer than myself," thus she began,
"The field's chief flower, sweet above compare,
Stain to all nymphs, more lovely than a man,
More white and red than doves or roses are;
  Nature that made thee, with herself at strife,
  Saith that the world hath ending with thy life.

"Vouchsafe, thou wonder, to alight thy steed,
And rein his proud head to the saddle-bow;
If thou wilt deign this favour, for thy meed
A thousand honey-secrets shalt thou know:

* Entitled:— "VENUS and ADONIS.
Vilia miretur vulgus: mihi flavus Apollo
Pocula Castalia plena ministret aqua.
London Imprinted by Richard Field, and are to be sold at the signe of the white Greyhound in Paules Church-yard. 1593."

a Rose-cheek'd Adonis—] Malone has noticed the same compound epithet in "Hero and Leander,"—
"The men of wealthy Sestos every year
For his sake whom their goddess held so dear,
Rose-cheek'd Adonis, kept a solemn feast," &c.

Here come and sit, where never serpent hisses,
And being set, I'll smother thee with kisses;

"And yet not cloy thy lips with loath'd satiety,
But rather famish them amid their plenty,
Making them red and pale with fresh variety,—
Ten kisses short as one, one long as twenty:
A summer's day will seem an hour but short,
Being wasted in such time-beguiling sport."

With this she seizeth on his sweating palm,
The precedent[a] of pith and livelihood,
And, trembling in her passion, calls it balm,
Earth's sovereign salve to do a goddess good:
Being so enrag'd, desire doth lend her force
Courageously to pluck him from his horse.

Over one arm the lusty courser's rein,
Under her other was the tender boy,
Who blush'd and pouted in a dull disdain,
With leaden appetite, unapt to toy;
She red and hot as coals of glowing fire,
He red for shame, but frosty in desire.

The studded bridle on a ragged bough
Nimbly she fastens; (O, how quick is love!)
The steed is stalled up, and even now
To tie the rider she begins to prove:
Backward she push'd him, as she would be thrust,
And govern'd him in strength, though not in lust.

So soon was she along, as he was down,
Each leaning on their elbows and their hips:
Now doth she stroke his cheek, now doth he frown,
And 'gins to chide, but soon she stops his lips;
And kissing, speaks, with lustful language broken,
"If thou wilt chide, thy lips shall never open."

He burns with bashful shame; she with her tears
Doth quench the maiden burning of his cheeks:
Then with her windy sighs and golden hairs,
To fan and blow them dry again she seeks:
He saith she is immodest, blames her 'miss;[b]
What follows more she murders with a kiss.

Even as an empty eagle, sharp by fast,
Tires[c] with her beak on feathers, flesh, and bone,
Shaking her wings, devouring all in haste,
Till either gorge be stuff'd, or prey be gone;
Even so she kiss'd his brow, his cheek, his chin,
And where she ends she doth anew begin.

Forc'd to content,[d] but never to obey,
Panting he lies, and breatheth in her face;
She feedeth on the steam as on a prey,
And calls it heavenly moisture, air of grace;
Wishing her cheeks were gardens full of flowers,
So they were dew'd with such-distilling showers.

Look, how a bird lies tangled in a net,
So fasten'd in her arms Adonis lies;
Pure shame and aw'd resistance made him fret,
Which bred more beauty in his angry eyes:
Rain added to a river that is rank,[e]
Perforce will force it overflow the bank.

Still she entreats, and prettily entreats,
For to a pretty ear she tunes her tale;
Still is he sullen, still he low'rs and frets,
'Twixt crimson shame and anger ashy-pale;
Being red, she loves him best; and being white,
Her best is better'd with a more delight.

Look how he can, she cannot choose but love;
And by her fair immortal hand she swears
From his soft bosom never to remove,
Till he take truce with her contending tears,
Which long have rain'd, making her cheeks all wet;
And one sweet kiss shall pay this countless debt.

Upon this promise did he raise his chin,
Like a dive-dapper peering through a wave,
Who, being look'd on, ducks as quickly in;
So offers he to give what she did crave;
But when her lips were ready for his pay,
He winks, and turns his lips another way.

Never did passenger in summer's heat
More thirst for drink than she for this good turn:
Her help she sees, but help she cannot get;
She bathes in water, yet her[f] fire must burn:
"O, pity," 'gan she cry, "flint-hearted boy!
'T is but a kiss I beg; why art thou coy?

"I have been woo'd, as I entreat thee now,
Even by the stern and direful god of war,
Whose sinewy neck in battle ne'er did bow,
Who conquers where he comes, in every jar;
Yet hath he been my captive and my slave,
And begg'd for that which thou unask'd shalt have.

"Over my altars hath he hung his lance,
His batter'd shield, his uncontrolled crest,
And for my sake hath learn'd to sport and dance,
To toy,[g] to wanton, dally, smile, and jest;
Scorning his churlish drum, and ensign red,
Making my arms his field, his tent my bed.

---

a — precedent—] *Precedent* appears to be used here in the sense of *sign*, or *indicator*.

b — *blames her* 'miss;] *Amiss* is elsewhere employed by Shakespeare as a substantive; thus in "Hamlet," Act IV. Sc. 5,—

"Each toy seems prologue to some great *amiss*."

See also Sonnet XXXV.

c Tires—] To *tire* is to *peck*, to *tear*, to *prey*.

d *Forc'd to* content,—] *To acquiescence*.

e — *a river that is* rank,—] "*Rank*" meant *brimming*, *full*, &c. Thus in "Julius Cæsar," Act III. Sc. 1,—

"Who else must be let blood, who else is *rank*;"

unless in that passage "*rank*" expresses *too luxuriant*, too *high-topped*. So, too, in Drayton's "Barons' Wars," 1603,—

"Fetching full tides, luxurious, high, and *rank*."

f — *yet* her *fire* must burn:] So read the editions, 1593, 1594, 1596; the later copies have,—"yet *in* fire must burn."

g *To* toy,—] The reading of the two earliest copies. The later ones have, "To *coy*," &c.

"Thus he that overrul'd I oversway'd,
Leading him prisoner in a red-rose chain:
Strong-temper'd steel his stronger strength obey'd,
Yet was he servile to my coy disdain.
O, be not proud, nor brag not of thy might,
For mastering her that foil'd the god of fight!

"Touch but my lips with those fair lips of thine,—
Though mine be not so fair, yet are they red,—
The kiss shall be thine own as well as mine:—
What see'st thou in the ground? hold up thy head;
Look in mine eyeballs, there thy beauty lies;
Then why not lips on lips, since eyes in eyes?

"Art thou asham'd to kiss? then wink again,
And I will wink; so shall the day seem night;
Love keeps his revels where there are but twain;
Be bold to play, our sport is not in sight:
These blue-vein'd violets whereon we lean
Never can blab, nor know not what we mean.

"The tender spring upon thy tempting lip
Shows thee unripe; yet mayst thou well be tasted:
Make use of time, let not advantage slip;
Beauty within itself should not be wasted:
Fair flowers that are not gather'd in their prime
Rot and consume themselves in little time.

"Were I hard-favour'd, foul, or wrinkled-old,
Ill-natur'd, crooked, churlish, harsh in voice,
O'er-worn, despised, rheumatic, and cold,
Thick-sighted, barren, lean, and lacking juice,
Then mightst thou pause, for then I were not for thee;
But having no defects, why dost abhor me?

"Thou canst not see one wrinkle in my brow;
Mine eyes are grey, and bright, and quick in turning;
My beauty as the spring doth yearly grow,
My flesh is soft and plump, my marrow burning;
My smooth moist hand, were it with thy hand felt,
Would in thy palm dissolve, or seem to melt.

"Bid me discourse, I will enchant thine ear,
Or, like a fairy, trip upon the green,
Or, like a nymph, with long dishevell'd hair,
Dance on the sands, and yet no footing seen:
Love is a spirit all compact[a] of fire,
Not gross to sink, but light, and will aspire.

"Witness this primrose bank whereon I lie;
These forceless flowers like sturdy trees support me;
Two strengthless doves will draw me through the sky,
From morn till night, even where I list to sport me:
Is love so light, sweet boy, and may it be
That thou shouldst think it heavy unto thee?

"Is thine own heart to thine own face affected?
Can thy right hand seize love upon thy left?
Then woo thyself, be of thyself rejected,
Steal thine own freedom, and complain on theft.
Narcissus so himself himself forsook,
And died to kiss his shadow in the brook.

"Torches are made to light, jewels to wear,
Dainties to taste, fresh beauty for the use,
Herbs for their smell, and sappy plants to bear;
Things growing to themselves are growth's abuse:
Seeds spring from seeds, and beauty breedeth beauty,
Thou wast begot,—to get it is thy duty.

"Upon the earth's increase why shouldst thou feed,
Unless the earth with thy increase be fed?
By law of nature thou art bound to breed,
That thine may live, when thou thyself art dead;
And so, in spite of death, thou dost survive,
In that thy likeness still is left alive."

By this, the love-sick queen began to sweat,
For, where they lay, the shadow had forsook them,
And Titan, 'tired in the mid-day heat,
With burning eye did hotly overlook them;
Wishing Adonis had his team to guide,
So he were like him, and by Venus' side.

And now Adonis, with a lazy sprite,
And with a heavy, dark, disliking eye,
His lowering brows o'erwhelming his fair sight,
Like misty vapours when they blot the sky,—
Souring[b] his cheeks, cries, "Fie, no more of love!
The sun doth burn my face; I must remove."

"Ah me," quoth Venus, "young, and so unkind?
What bare excuses mak'st thou to be gone!
I'll sigh celestial breath, whose gentle wind
Shall cool the heat of this descending sun:
I'll make a shadow for thee of my hairs;
If they burn too, I'll quench them with my tears.

"The sun that shines from heaven shines but warm,
And, lo, I lie between that sun and thee!
The heat I have from thence doth little harm,
Thine eye darts forth the fire that burneth me;
And were I not immortal, life were done,
Between this heavenly and earthly sun.

"Art thou obdurate, flinty, hard as steel,
Nay, more than flint, for stone at rain relenteth?
Art thou a woman's son, and canst not feel
What' t is to love? how want of love tormenteth?
O, had thy mother borne so hard a mind,
She had not brought forth thee, but died unkind![c]

"What am I, that thou shouldst contemn[d] me this?
Or what great danger dwells upon my suit?

---

[a] — compact—] *Made up, compounded.*
[b] Souring—] Misprinted *To wring*, in the quarto, 1593.
[c] — *but died* unkind!] "Unkind" in this place is explained to mean *unnatural*, a sense we have seen the word frequently bore; but may it not signify here, *without generation: without offspring?*
[d] — contemn me this?] The edition of 1627, printed at Edinburgh, reads,—"contemn me *thus*," &c.; *this* and *thus*, however as Mr. Collier remarks, seem sometimes to have been used almost indifferently.

What were thy lips the worse for one poor kiss?
Speak, fair; but speak fair words, or else be mute:
  Give me one kiss, I'll give it thee again,
  And one for interest, if thou wilt have twain.

"Fie, lifeless picture, cold and senseless stone,
Well-painted idol, image dull and dead,
Statue, contenting but the eye alone,
Thing like a man, but of no woman bred!
  Thou art no man, though of a man's complexion,
  For men will kiss even by their own direction."

This said, impatience chokes her pleading tongue,
And swelling passion doth provoke a pause;
Red cheeks and fiery eyes blaze forth her wrong,
Being judge in love, she cannot right her cause:
  And now she weeps, and now she fain would speak,
  And now her sobs do her intendments break.

Sometimes she shakes her head, and then his hand,
Now gazeth she on him, now on the ground;
Sometimes her arms infold him like a band:
She would, he will not in her arms be bound;
  And when from thence he struggles to be gone,
  She locks her lily fingers one in one.

"Fondling," she saith, "since I have hemm'd thee here,
Within the circuit of this ivory pale,
I'll be a park,[a] and thou shalt be my deer;
Feed where thou wilt, on mountain or in dale:
  Graze on my lips; and if those hills be dry,
  Stray lower, where the pleasant fountains lie.

"Within this limit is relief enough,
Sweet bottom-grass, and high-delightful plain,
Round rising hillocks, brakes obscure and rough,
To shelter thee from tempest and from rain:
  Then be my deer, since I am such a park;
  No dog shall rouse thee, though a thousand bark."

At this Adonis smiles as in disdain,
That in each cheek appears a pretty dimple:
Love made those hollows, if himself were slain,
He might be buried in a tomb so simple;
  Foreknowing well, if there he came to lie,
  Why, there Love liv'd, and there he could not die.

These lovely caves, these round enchanting pits,
Open'd their mouths to swallow Venus' liking:
Being mad before, how doth she now for wits?
Struck dead at first, what needs a second striking?
  Poor queen of love, in thine own law forlorn,
  To love a cheek that smiles at thee in scorn!

Now which way shall she turn? what shall she say?
Her words are done, her woes the more increasing;
The time is spent, her object will away,
And from her twining arms doth urge releasing:
  "Pity," she cries, "some favour—some remorse!"
  Away he springs, and hasteth to his horse.

But, lo, from forth a copse that neighbours by,
A breeding jennet, lusty, young, and proud,
Adonis' trampling courser doth espy,
And forth she rushes, snorts, and neighs aloud:
  The strong-neck'd steed, being tied unto a tree,
  Breaketh his rein, and to her straight goes he.

Imperiously he leaps, he neighs, he bounds,
And now his woven girths he breaks asunder;
The bearing earth with his hard hoof he wounds,
Whose hollow womb resounds like heaven's thunder:
  The iron bit he crushes 'tween his teeth,
  Controlling what he was controlled with.

His ears up-prick'd; his braided hanging mane
Upon his compass'd[b] crest now stand on end;[c]
His nostrils drink the air, and forth again,
As from a furnace, vapours doth he send:
  His eye, which scornfully glisters like fire,
  Shows his hot courage and his high desire.

Sometime he trots, as if he told the steps,
With gentle majesty and modest pride;
Anon he rears upright, curvets and leaps,
As who should say, Lo, thus my strength is tried,
  And this I do to captivate the eye
  Of the fair breeder that is standing by.

What recketh he his rider's angry stir,
His flattering "Holla," or his "Stand, I say"?
What cares he now for curb or pricking spur?
For rich caparisons or trapping gay?
  He sees his love, and nothing else he sees,
  Nor nothing else with his proud sight agrees.

Look, when a painter would surpass the life,
In limning out a well-proportioned steed,
His art with nature's workmanship at strife,
As if the dead the living should exceed;
  So did this horse excel a common one,[d]
  In shape, in courage, colour, pace, and bone.

Round-hoof'd, short-jointed, fetlocks shag and long,
Broad breast, full eye, small head, and nostril wide,
High crest, short ears, straight legs, and passing strong,
Thick mane, thick tail, broad buttock, tender hide:
  Look, what a horse should have he did not lack,
  Save a proud rider on so proud a back.

Sometime he scuds far off, and there he stares;
Anon he starts at stirring of a feather;
To bid the wind a base[e] he now prepares,
And whêr he run or fly they know not whether;
  For through his mane and tail the high wind sings,
  Fanning the hairs, who wave like feather'd wings.

---

a — a *park*,—] The two first copies have "— *a park*," &c.; those subsequently published, "*the* park," &c.

b — compass'd—] *Arched*.

c — stand *on end;*] "Our author uses *mane* as composed of many hairs, as plural."—MALONE.

d —— *a common* one,
.... *pace and* bone.]
One was formerly pronounced as we now sound it in *alone*, *atone*, &c.

e To bid the wind a base—] See note (7), p. 42, Vol. I.

He looks upon his love, and neighs unto her ;
She answers him, as if she knew his mind :
Being proud, as females are, to see him woo her,
She puts on outward strangeness, seems unkind ;
Spurns at his love, and scorns the heat he feels,
Beating his kind embracements with her heels.

Then, like a melancholy malcontent,
He vails [a] his tail, that, like a falling plume,
Cool shadow to his melting buttock lent :
He stamps, and bites the poor flies in his fume.
His love, perceiving how he is enrag'd,
Grew kinder, and his fury was assuag'd.

His testy master goeth about to take him ;
When, lo, the unback'd breeder, full of fear,
Jealous of catching, swiftly doth forsake him,
With her the horse, and left Adonis there :
As they were mad, unto the wood they hie them,
Out-stripping crows that strive to over-fly them.

All swoln with chafing [b] down Adonis sits,
Banning [c] his boisterous and unruly beast :
And now the happy season once more fits,
That love-sick Love by pleading may be blest ;
For lovers say, the heart hath treble wrong
When it is barr'd the aidance of the tongue.

An oven that is stopp'd, or river stay'd,
Burneth more hotly, swelleth with more rage :
So of concealed sorrow may be said ;
Free vent of words love's fire doth assuage ;
But when the heart's attorney [d] once is mute,
The client breaks, as desperate in his suit.

He sees her coming, and begins to glow,
Even as a dying coal revives with wind,
And with his bonnet hides his angry brow ;
Looks on the dull earth with disturbed mind ;
Taking no notice that she is so nigh,
For all askance he holds her in his eye.

O, what a sight it was, wistly to view
How she came stealing to the wayward boy !
To note the fighting conflict of her hue,
How white and red each other did destroy !
But now her cheek was pale, and by and by
It flash'd forth fire, as lightning from the sky.

Now was she just before him as he sat,
And like a lowly lover down she kneels ;
With one fair hand she heaveth up his hat,
Her other tender hand his fair cheek feels :
His tenderer cheek receives her soft hand's print,
As apt as new-fall'n snow takes any dint.

O, what a war of looks was there between them !
Her eyes, petitioners, to his eyes suing ;
His eyes saw her eyes as they had not seen them ;
Her eyes woo'd still, his eyes disdain'd the wooing :
And all this dumb play had his [e] acts made plain
With tears, which, chorus-like, her eyes did rain.

Full gently now she takes him by the hand,
A lily prison'd in a gaol of snow,
Or ivory in an alabaster band ;
So white a friend engirts so white a foe :
This beauteous combat, wilful and unwilling,
Show'd like two silver doves that sit a-billing.

Once more the engine of her thoughts began :
" O, fairest mover on this mortal round,
Would thou wert as I am, and I a man,
My heart all whole as thine, thy heart my wound ;
For one sweet look thy help I would assure thee,
Though nothing but my body's bane would cure thee."

"Give me my hand," saith he, "why dost thou feel it ?"
"Give me my heart," saith she, "and thou shalt have it ;
O, give it me, lest thy hard heart do steel [f] it,
And being steel'd, soft sighs can never grave it : [g]
Then love's deep groans I never shall regard,
Because Adonis' heart hath made mine hard."

"For shame," he cries, "let go, and let me go ;
My day's delight is past, my horse is gone,
And 't is your fault I am bereft him so ;
I pray you hence, and leave me here alone ;
For all my mind, my thought, my busy care,
Is how to get my palfrey from the mare."

Thus she replies : "Thy palfrey, as he should,
Welcomes the warm approach of sweet desire :
Affection is a coal that must be cool'd ;
Else, suffer'd,[h] it will set the heart on fire :
The sea hath bounds, but deep desire hath none ;
Therefore no marvel though thy horse be gone.

"How like a jade he stood, tied to the tree,
Servilely master'd with a leathern rein !
But when he saw his love, his youth's fair fee,
He held such petty bondage in disdain ;
Throwing the base thong from his bending crest,
Enfranchising his mouth, his back, his breast.

"Who sees his true-love in her naked bed,[i]
Teaching the sheets a whiter hue than white,
But, when his glutton eye so full hath fed,
His other agents aim at like delight ?
Who is so faint that dare not be so bold
To touch the fire, the weather being cold ?

"Let me excuse thy courser, gentle boy ;
And learn of him, I heartily beseech thee,
To take advantage on presented joy;
Though I were dumb, yet his proceedings teach thee :
O, learn to love ! the lesson is but plain,
And once made perfect, never lost again."

[a] He vails his tail,—] To *vail* is to *sink*, to *lower*. So in "The Merchant of Venice," Act I. Sc. I.: "*Vailing* her high-tops lower than her ribs."

[b] —*with* chafing—] The reading of all the editions before that of 1600, which substituted *chasing*.

[c] Banning—] That is, *cursing*.

[d] —attorney—] *Advocate, pleader.*

[e] — his acts—] "His" for *its*.

[f] — do steel it,—] Harden it like steel.

[g] — grave it :] "*Engrave* it, *i.e.* make an impression on it."—STEEVENS.

[h] — suffer'd,—] *Allowed, indulged, not restrained.* See note (c), p. 388, Vol. II.

[i] — naked bed,—] See note (a), p. 88, of the present volume

"I know not love," quoth he, "nor will not know it,
Unless it be a boar, and then I chase it;
'T is much to borrow, and I will not owe it;
My love to love is love but to disgrace it;
For I have heard it is a life in death,
That laughs, that weeps, and all but with a breath.

"Who wears a garment shapeless and unfinish'd?
Who plucks the bud before one leaf put forth?
If springing things be any jot diminish'd,
They wither in their prime, prove nothing worth:
The colt that's back'd and burden'd being young,
Loseth his pride, and never waxeth strong.

"You hurt my hand with wringing; let us part,
And leave this idle theme, this bootless chat:
Remove your siege from my unyielding heart;
To love's alarms it will not ope the gate:
Dismiss your vows, your feigned tears, your flattery;
For where a heart is hard, they make no battery."

"What! canst thou talk," quoth she, "hast thou a tongue?
O, would thou hadst not, or I had no hearing!
Thy mermaid's[a] voice hath done me double wrong;
I had my load before, now press'd with bearing:
Melodious discord, heavenly tune harsh-sounding,
Ear's deep-sweet music, and heart's deep-sore wounding.

"Had I no eyes but ears, my ears would love
That inward beauty and invisible;
Or were I deaf, thy outward parts would move
Each part in me that were but sensible:
Though neither eyes nor ears, to hear nor see,
Yet should I be in love by touching thee.

"Say, that the sense of feeling were bereft me,
And that I could not see, nor hear, nor touch,
And nothing but the very smell were left me,
Yet would my love to thee be still as much;
For from the still'tory of thy face excelling
Comes breath perfum'd, that breedeth love by smelling.

"But O, what banquet wert thou to the taste,
Being nurse and feeder of the other four!
Would they not wish the feast might ever last,
And bid Suspicion double-lock the door?
Lest Jealousy, that sour unwelcome guest,
Should, by his stealing in, disturb the feast."

Once more the ruby-colour'd portal open'd,
Which to his speech did honey passage yield;
Like a red morn, that ever yet betoken'd
Wreck to the seaman, tempest to the field,
Sorrow to shepherds, woe unto the birds,
Gusts and foul flaws[b] to herdmen and to herds.

This ill presage advisedly she marketh:
Even as the wind is hush'd before it raineth,
Or as the wolf doth grin before he barketh,
Or as the berry breaks before it staineth,
Or like the deadly bullet of a gun,
His meaning struck her ere his words begun.

And at his look she flatly falleth down,
For looks kill love, and love by looks reviveth:
A smile recures the wounding of a frown;
But blessed bankrupt, that by love so thriveth!
The silly boy, believing she is dead,
Claps her pale cheek, till clapping makes it red;

And all-amaz'd brake off his late intent,
For sharply did he think to reprehend her,
Which cunning love did wittily prevent:
Fair fall the wit that can so well defend her!
For on the grass she lies as she were slain,
Till his breath breatheth life in her again.

He wrings her nose, he strikes her on the cheeks,
He bends her fingers, holds her pulses hard,
He chafes her lips; a thousand ways he seeks
To mend the hurt that his unkindness marr'd:
He kisses her; and she, by her good will,
Will never rise, so he will kiss her still.

The night of sorrow now is turn'd to day:
Her two blue windows[c] faintly she up-heaveth,
Like the fair sun, when in his fresh array
He cheers the morn, and all the earth relieveth:
And as the bright sun glorifies the sky,
So is her face illumin'd with her eye;

Whose beams upon his hairless face are fix'd,
As if from thence they borrow'd all their shine.
Were never four such lamps together mix'd,
Had not his clouded with his brows' repine;[d]
But hers, which through the crystal tears gave light,
Shone like the moon in water seen by night.

"O, where am I?" quoth she, "in earth or heaven,
Or in the ocean drench'd, or in the fire?
What hour is this? or morn or weary even?
Do I delight to die, or life desire?
But now I liv'd, and life was death's annoy;
But now I died, and death was lively joy.

"O, thou didst kill me, kill me once again:
Thy eyes' shrewd tutor, that hard heart of thine,
Hath taught them scornful tricks, and such disdain,
That they have murder'd this poor heart of mine;

[a] *Thy* mermaid's *voice*—] With our early writers, *mermaid* and *siren* were synonymous.

[b] —*foul* flaws—] Violent blasts of wind.

[c] — blue windows—] By "windows" are meant eye-lids. So in "Cymbeline," Act II. Sc. 1,—

"To see the enclosed lights, now canopied
Under these *windows*, white, and *azure* lac'd
With *blue* of heaven's own tinct."

And in "Romeo and Juliet," Act IV. Sc. 1,—

—— "Thy eyes' *windows* fall,
Like death, when he shuts up the day of life."

[d] — repine;] *Repine* is here a substantive.

And these mine eyes, true leaders to their queen,
But for thy piteous lips no more had seen.

"Long may they kiss each other, for this cure!
O, never let their crimson liveries wear!
And as they last, their verdure still endure,
To drive infection[a] from the dangerous year!
That the star-gazers, having writ on death,
May say, the plague is banish'd by thy breath.

"Pure lips, sweet seals in my soft lips imprinted,
What bargains may I make, still to be sealing?
To sell myself I can be well contented,
So thou wilt buy, and pay, and use good dealing;
Which purchase if thou make, for fear of slips
Set thy seal-manual on my wax-red lips.

"A thousand kisses buys my heart from me;
And pay them at thy leisure, one by one.
What is ten hundred kisses[b] unto thee?
Are they not quickly told, and quickly gone?
Say, for non-payment that the debt should double,[c]
Is twenty hundred kisses such a trouble?"

"Fair queen," quoth he, "if any love you owe me,
Measure my strangeness with my unripe years;
Before I know myself, seek not to know me;
No fisher but the ungrown fry forbears:
The mellow plum doth fall, the green sticks fast,
Or being early pluck'd is sour to taste.

"Look, the world's comforter, with weary gait,
His day's hot task hath ended in the west:
The owl, night's herald, shrieks,—'t is very late;
The sheep are gone to fold, birds to their nest;
And coal-black clouds that shadow heaven's light
Do summon us to part, and bid good night.

"Now let me say 'Good night,' and so say you;
If you will say so, you shall have a kiss."
"Good night," quoth she; and, ere he says "Adieu,"
The honey fee of parting tender'd is:
Her arms do lend his neck a sweet embrace;
Incorporate then they seem; face grows to face;

Till, breathless, he disjoin'd, and backward drew
The heavenly moisture, that sweet coral mouth,
Whose precious taste her thirsty lips well knew,
Whereon they surfeit, yet complain on drought:
He with her plenty press'd, she faint with dearth,
(Their lips together glu'd,) fall to the earth.

Now quick Desire hath caught the yielding prey,
And glutton-like she feeds, yet never filleth;
Her lips are conquerors, his lips obey,
Paying what ransom the insulter willeth;
Whose vulture thought doth pitch the price so high,
That she will draw his lips' rich treasure dry.

And having felt the sweetness of the spoil,
With blindfold fury she begins to forage;
Her face doth reek and smoke, her blood doth boil,
And careless lust stirs up a desperate courage;
Planting oblivion, beating reason back,
Forgetting shame's pure blush and honour's wrack.

Hot, faint, and weary, with her hard embracing,
Like a wild bird being tam'd with too much handling,
Or as the fleet-foot roe that 's tir'd with chasing,
Or like the froward infant still'd with dandling,
He now obeys, and now no more resisteth,
While she takes all she can, not all she listeth.

What wax so frozen but dissolves with tempering,
And yields at last to every light impression?
Things out of hope are compass'd oft with venturing,
Chiefly in love, whose leave[d] exceeds commission:
Affection faints not like a pale-fac'd coward,
But then woos best when most his choice is froward.

When he did frown, O, had she then gave over,
Such nectar from his lips she had not suck'd.
Foul words and frowns must not repel a lover;
What though the rose have prickles, yet 't is pluck'd:
Were beauty under twenty locks kept fast,
Yet love breaks through, and picks them all at last.

For pity now she can no more detain him;
The poor fool prays her that he may depart:
She is resolv'd no longer to restrain him;
Bids him farewell, and look well to her heart,
The which, by Cupid's bow she doth protest,
He carries thence incaged in his breast.

"Sweet boy," she says, "this night I'll waste in sorrow,
For my sick heart commands mine eyes to watch.
Tell me, Love's master, shall we meet to-morrow?
Say, shall we? shall we? wilt thou make the match?"
He tells her, no; to-morrow he intends
To hunt the boar with certain of his friends.

"The boar!" quoth she; whereat a sudden pale,
Like lawn being spread upon the blushing rose,
Usurps her cheek; she trembles at his tale,
And on his neck her yoking arms she throws:
She sinketh down, still hanging by his neck,
He on her belly falls, she on her back.

---

[a] To drive infection from the dangerous year!] An allusion to the practice of strewing apartments with strong-scented herbs in the time of the plague, to prevent infection.

[b] — *ten hundred* kisses—] So the edition of 1600; the preceding copies read,—"ten hundred *touches*."

[c] Say, for non-payment that the debt should double,—] "The poet was thinking of a conditional bond's becoming forfeited for non-payment; in which case, the entire penalty (usually the double of the principal sum lent by the obligee) was formerly recoverable at law."—MALONE.

[d] — leave—] "Leave" here means *licence*.

Now is she in the very lists of love,
Her champion mounted for the hot encounter:
All is imaginary she doth prove,
He will not manage her, although he mount her;
That worse than Tantalus' is her annoy,
To clip Elysium, and to lack her joy.

Even as poor birds, deceiv'd with painted grapes,[a]
Do surfeit by the eye and pine the maw,
Even so she languisheth in her mishaps,
As those poor birds that helpless[b] berries saw.
The warm effects which she in him finds missing,
She seeks to kindle with continual kissing.

But all in vain; good queen, it will not be:
She hath assay'd as much as may be prov'd;
Her pleading hath deserv'd a greater fee;
She 's Love, she loves, and yet she is not lov'd.
"Fie, fie," he says, "you crush me; let me go;
You have no reason to withhold me so."

"Thou hadst been gone," quoth she, "sweet boy, ere this,
But that thou told'st me thou wouldst hunt the boar.
O, be advis'd! thou know'st not what it is
With javelin's point a churlish swine to gore,
Whose tushes never-sheath'd he whetteth still,
Like to a mortal[c] butcher, bent to kill.

"On his bow-back he hath a battle set
Of bristly pikes, that ever threat his foes;
His eyes like glow-worms shine when he doth fret:
His snout digs sepulchres where'er he goes;
Being mov'd, he strikes whate'er is in his way,
And whom he strikes his cruel tushes slay.

"His brawny sides, with hairy bristles arm'd,
Are better proof than thy spear's point can enter;
His short thick neck cannot be easily harm'd;
Being ireful on the lion he will venture:
The thorny brambles and embracing bushes,
As fearful of him, part; through whom he rushes.

"Alas, he nought esteems that face of thine,
To which Love's eyes pay tributary gazes;
Nor thy soft hands, sweet lips, and crystal eyne,
Whose full perfection all the world amazes;
But having thee at vantage,—wondrous dread!—
Would root these beauties as he roots the mead.

"O, let him keep his loathsome cabin still!
Beauty hath nought to do with such foul fiends:
Come not within his danger[d] by thy will;
They that thrive well take counsel of their friends.
When thou didst name the boar, not to dissemble,
I fear'd thy fortune, and my joints did tremble.

"Didst thou not mark my face? was it not white?
Saw'st thou not signs of fear lurk in mine eye?
Grew I not faint? and fell I not downright?
Within my bosom, whereon thou dost lie,
My boding heart pants, beats, and takes no rest,
But, like an earthquake, shakes thee on my breast.

"For where Love reigns, disturbing Jealousy
Doth call himself Affection's sentinel;
Gives false alarms, suggesteth mutiny,
And in a peaceful hour doth cry, 'Kill, kill;'[e]
Distempering gentle Love in his desire,
As air and water do abate the fire.

"This sour informer, this bate-breeding spy,
This canker that eats up Love's tender spring,[f]
This carry-tale, dissentious Jealousy,
That sometime true news, sometime false doth bring,
Knocks at my heart, and whispers in mine ear,
That if I love thee, I thy death should fear:

"And more than so, presenteth to mine eye
The picture of an angry-chafing boar,
Under whose sharp fangs on his back doth lie
An image like thyself, all stain'd with gore;
Whose blood upon the fresh flowers being shed
Doth make them droop with grief and hang the head.

"What should I do, seeing thee so indeed,
That tremble at the imagination?
The thought of it doth make my faint heart bleed,
And fear doth teach it divination:
I prophesy thy death, my living sorrow,
If thou encounter with the boar to-morrow.

"But if thou needs will hunt, be rul'd by me;
Uncouple at the timorous flying hare,
Or at the fox, which lives by subtlety,
Or at the roe, which no encounter dare:
Pursue these fearful creatures o'er the downs,
And on thy well-breath'd horse keep with thy hounds.

"And when thou hast on foot the purblind hare,
Mark the poor wretch, to overshoot* his troubles,
How he outruns the wind, and with what care
He cranks and crosses with a thousand doubles:
The many musits[g] through the which he goes
Are like a labyrinth to amaze his foes.

---

a — poor birds, deceiv'd with painted grapes,—] Alluding to the famous picture by Xeuxis, in which the grapes were depicted so naturally, that the birds pecked at them.

b — helpless berries—] Berries that afford no *help*. In "The Comedy of Errors," Act I. Sc. 1, we have, "Our *helpful* ship," in the sense of *the ship that came* to *succour us*.

c — mortal—] "*Mortal*" for *deadly*.

d — his danger—] His *power*.

e — doth cry, '*Kill, kill;*'] See note (b) p. 104.

f — *Love's tender* spring,—] "Spring" here, as in a previous passage,—

"The tender *spring* upon thy tempting lip," &c.

and in "Lucrece,"—

"Unruly blasts wait on the tender *spring*," &c.

means a young *shoot*, *sprig*, or *budding*.

g — musits—] A *musit*, or *muset*, is a gap in a hedge. "We term the place where she [the hare] sitteth, her form; the place through which she goes to relief, her *musit*."—"Gentleman's Academy," 1595.

(*) Old text, *overshut*.

"Sometime he runs among a flock of sheep,
To make the cunning hounds mistake their smell,
And sometime where earth-delving conies keep,[a]
To stop the loud pursuers in their yell;
  And sometime sorteth with a herd of deer:
  Danger deviseth shifts; wit waits on fear:

"For there his smell with others being mingled,
The hot scent-snuffing hounds are driven to doubt,
Ceasing their clamorous cry till they have singled
With much ado the cold fault cleanly out;
  Then do they spend their mouths: Echo replies,
  As if another chase were in the skies.

"By this, poor Wat,[b] far off upon a hill,
Stands on his hinder legs with listening ear,
To hearken if his foes pursue him still:
Anon their loud alarums he doth hear;
  And now his grief may be compared well
  To one sore sick that hears the passing-bell.

"Then shalt thou see the dew-bedabbled wretch
Turn, and return, indenting with the way;
Each envious briar his weary legs doth scratch,
Each shadow makes him stop, each murmur stay:
  For misery is trodden on by many,
  And being low never reliev'd by any.

"Lie quietly, and hear a little more;
Nay, do not struggle, for thou shalt not rise:
To make thee hate the hunting of the boar,
Unlike myself thou hear'st me moralize,
  Applying this to that, and so to so;
  For love can comment upon every woe.

"Where did I leave?"—"No matter where," quoth he;
"Leave me, and then the story aptly ends:
The night is spent."—"Why, what of that?" quoth she.
"I am," quoth he, "expected of my friends;
  And now 't is dark, and going I shall fall."
  "In night," quoth she, "desire sees best of all.

"But if thou fall, O, then imagine this,
The earth in love with thee thy footing trips,
And all is but to rob thee of a kiss.
Rich preys make true-men[c] thieves; so do thy lips
  Make modest Dian cloudy and forlorn,
  Lest she should steal a kiss, and die forsworn.

Now of this dark night I perceive the reason:
Cynthia for shame obscures her silver shine,
Till forging Nature be condemn'd of treason,
For stealing moulds from heaven that were divine,
  Wherein she fram'd thee in high heaven's despite,
  To shame the sun by day, and her by night.

"And therefore hath she brib'd the Destinies,
To cross the curious workmanship of nature,
To mingle beauty with infirmities,
And pure perfection with impure defeature;
  Making it subject to the tyranny
  Of mad mischances and much misery;

"As burning fevers, agues pale and faint,
Life-poisoning pestilence, and frenzies wood,[d]
The marrow-eating sickness, whose attaint
Disorder breeds by heating of the blood:
  Surfeits, imposthumes, grief, and damn'd despair,
  Swear Nature's death for framing thee so fair.

"And not the least of all these maladies,
But in one minute's fight brings beauty under:
Both favour, savour, hue, and qualities,
Whereat the impartial gazer late did wonder,
  Are on the sudden wasted, thaw'd, and done,[e]
  As mountain-snow melts with the mid-day sun.

"Therefore, despite of fruitless chastity,
Love-lacking vestals, and self-loving nuns,
That on the earth would breed a scarcity
And barren dearth of daughters and of sons.
  Be prodigal: the lamp that burns by night
  Dries up his oil to lend the world his light.

"What is thy body but a swallowing grave,
Seeming to bury that posterity
Which by the rights of time thou needs must have,
If thou destroy them not in dark obscurity?
  If so, the world will hold thee in disdain,
  Sith in thy pride so fair a hope is slain.

"So in thyself thyself art made away;
A mischief worse than civil home bred strife,
Or theirs whose desperate hands themselves do slay,
Or butcher-sire, that reaves his son of life.
  Foul-cankering rust the hidden treasure frets,
  But gold that 's put to use more gold begets."

"Nay, then," quoth Adon, "you will fall again
Into your idle over-handled theme;
The kiss I gave you is bestowed in vain,
And all in vain you strive against the stream;
  For by this black-fac'd night, desire's foul nurse,
  Your treatise makes me like you worse and worse.

"If love have lent you twenty thousand tongues,
And every tongue more moving than your own,
Bewitching like the wanton mermaid's songs,
Yet from mine ear the tempting tune is blown;
  For know, my heart stands armed in mine ear,
  And will not let a false sound enter there;

"Lest the deceiving harmony should run
Into the quiet closure of my breast;
And then my little heart were quite undone,
In his bedchamber to be barr'd of rest.
  No, lady, no; my heart longs not to groan,
  But soundly sleeps, while now it sleeps alone.

"What have you urg'd that I cannot reprove?
The path is smooth that leadeth on to danger;

---

[a] — keep,—] *Dwell.*
[b] —*poor* Wat,—] "Wat" is an old provincial name for the hare.
[c] — true-men—] In the language of Shakespeare's day, honest men were termed *true-men.* Thus in "Henry IV." Pt. I. Act II. Sc. 2,—
"The thieves have bound the *true-men.*"
[d] — wood,—] *Mad, crazy.*
[e] — done,—] *Destroyed.*

I hate not love, but your device in love,
That lends embracements unto every stranger.
  You do it for increase ; O, strange excuse,
  When reason is the bawd to lust's abuse!

" Call it not love, for Love to heaven is fled,
Since sweating Lust on earth usurp'd his name ;
Under whose simple semblance he hath fed
Upon fresh beauty, blotting it with blame ;
  Which the hot tyrant stains and soon bereaves,
  As caterpillars do the tender leaves.

" Love comforteth like sunshine after rain,
But Lust's effect is tempest after sun ;
Love's gentle spring doth always fresh remain,
Lust's winter comes ere summer half be done.
  Love surfeits not; Lust like a glutton dies:
  Love is all truth ; Lust full of forged lies.

" More I could tell, but more I dare not say ;
The text is old, the orator too green :
Therefore, in sadness, now I will away ;
My face is full of shame, my heart of teen ;[a]
  Mine ears that to your wanton talk attended
  Do burn themselves for having so offended."

With this, he breaketh from the sweet embrace
Of those fair arms which bound him to her breast,
And homeward through the dark laund[b] runs apace;
Leaves Love upon her back deeply distress'd.
  Look, how a bright star shooteth from the sky,
  So glides he in the night from Venus' eye ;

Which after him she darts, as one on shore
Gazing upon a late-embarked friend,
Till the wild waves will have him seen no more,
Whose ridges with the meeting clouds contend ;
  So did the merciless and pitchy night
  Fold in the object that did feed her sight.

Whereat amaz'd, as one that unaware
Hath dropp'd a precious jewel in the flood,
Or 'stonish'd as night-wanderers often are,
Their light blown out in some mistrustful wood ;
  Even so confounded in the dark she lay,
  Having lost the fair discovery of her way.

And now she beats her heart, whereat it groans,
That all the neighbour-caves, as seeming troubled,
Make verbal repetition of her moans ;
Passion on passion deeply is redoubled:
  " Ah me ! " she cries, and twenty times, " Woe, woe ! "
  And twenty echoes twenty times cry so.

She, marking them, begins a wailing note,
And sings extemp'rally a woeful ditty ;
How love makes young men thrall, and old men dote ;
How love is wise in folly, foolish-witty :
  Her heavy anthem still concludes in " Woe,"
  And still the choir of echoes answer so.

Her song was tedious, and outwore the night,
For lovers' hours are long, though seeming short:
If pleas'd themselves, others, they think, delight
In such-like circumstance, with such-like sport:
  Their copious stories, oftentimes begun,
  End without audience, and are never done.

For who hath she to spend the night withal,
But idle, sounds-resembling, parasites ;[c]
Like shrill-tongued tapsters answering every call,
Soothing the humour of fantastic wits ?
  She says, " 'T is so : " they answer all, " 'T is so ; "
  And would say after her, if she said " No."

Lo, here the gentle lark, weary of rest,
From his moist cabinet mounts up on high,
And wakes the morning, from whose silver breast
The sun ariseth in his majesty;
  Who doth the world so gloriously behold,
  That cedar-tops and hills seem burnish'd gold.

Venus salutes him with this fair Good-morrow :—
" O, thou clear god, and patron of all light,
From whom each lamp and shining star doth borrow
The beauteous influence that makes him bright,
  There lives a son, that suck'd an earthly mother,
  May lend thee light, as thou dost lend to other."

This said, she hasteth to a myrtle grove,
Musing the morning is so much o'erworn,
And yet she hears no tidings of her love :
She hearkens for his hounds and for his horn :
  Anon she hears them chant it lustily,
  And all in haste she coasteth[d] to the cry.

And as she runs, the bushes in the way
Some catch her by the neck, some kiss her face,
Some twin'd about her thigh to make her stay ;
She wildly breaketh from their strict embrace,
  Like a milch doe, whose swelling dugs do ache,
  Hasting to feed her fawn hid in some brake.

By this, she hears the hounds are at a bay ;
Whereat she starts, like one that spies an adder
Wreath'd up in fatal folds just in his way,
The fear whereof doth make him shake and shudder;
  Even so the timorous yelping of the hounds
  Appals her senses, and her spirit[e] confounds.

For now she knows it is no gentle chase,
But the blunt boar, rough bear, or lion proud,
Because the cry remaineth in one place,
Where fearfully the dogs exclaim aloud :
  Finding their enemy to be so curst,[f]
  They all strain court'sy[g] who shall cope him first.

---

[a] — teen ;] "Teen," is *grief, sorrow.*
[b] — laund—] *Laund* and *lawn* were synonymous formerly.
[c] *But idle,* sounds-resembling, *parasites ;*] This line has always hitherto been printed,—

" But idle sounds resembling parasites : "

Yet surely Shakespeare, *more suo*, wrote,—" *sounds-resembling.*"
[d] — coasteth —] *Advanceth.*

[e] — spirit—] Here, as mostly in old verse, " spirit " must be pronounced *sprite.*
[f] — curst,—] *Fierce, irascible.*
[g] They all strain court'sy—] When any one hesitated to take the post of honour in a perilous undertaking, he was sarcastically said to *strain courtesy.* Turberville applies the expression to dogs, as Shakespeare does :—" for many hounds will *strain courtesie* at this chace."

This dismal cry rings sadly in her ear,
Through which it enters to surprise her heart;
Who, overcome by doubt and bloodless fear,
With cold-pale weakness numbs each feeling part:
Like soldiers, when their captain once doth yield,
They basely fly, and dare not stay the field.

Thus stands she in a trembling ecstasy;
Till, cheering up her senses all-dismay'd,[a]
She tells them 't is a causeless fantasy,
And childish error, that they are afraid;
Bids them leave quaking, bids them fear no more:—
And with that word she spied the hunted boar;

Whose frothy mouth, bepainted all with red,
Like milk and blood being mingled both together,
A second fear through all her sinews spread,
Which madly hurries her she knows not whither:
This way she runs, and now she will no further,
But back retires to rate the boar for murther.

A thousand spleens bear her a thousand ways;
She treads the path that she untreads again;
Her more than haste is mated with delays,
Like the proceedings of a drunken brain,
Full of respects [b] yet nought at all respecting,
In hand with all things, nought at all effecting.

Here kennell'd in a brake she finds a hound,
And asks the weary caitiff for his master;
And there another licking of his wound,
'Gainst venom'd sores the only sovereign plaster;
And here she meets another sadly scowling,
To whom she speaks, and he replies with howling.

When he hath ceas'd his ill-resounding noise,
Another flap-mouth'd mourner, black and grim,
Against the welkin volleys out his voice;
Another and another answer him,
Clapping their proud tails to the ground below,
Shaking their scratch'd ears, bleeding as they go.

Look, how the world's poor people are amaz'd
At apparitions, signs, and prodigies,
Whereon with fearful eyes they long have gaz'd,
Infusing them with dreadful prophecies;
So she at these sad signs draws up her breath,
And, sighing it again, exclaims on Death:

"Hard-favour'd tyrant, ugly, meagre, lean,
Hateful divorce of love,"—thus chides she Death,—
"Grim-grinning ghost, earth's worm, what dost thou mean
To stifle beauty and to steal his breath,
Who when he liv'd, his breath and beauty set
Gloss on the rose, smell to the violet?

"If he be dead,—O, no, it cannot be,
Seeing his beauty, thou shouldst strike at it!—
O yes, it may! thou hast no eyes to see,
But hatefully at random dost thou hit:
Thy mark is feeble age; but thy false dart
Mistakes that aim, and cleaves an infant's heart.

"Hadst thou but bid beware, then he had spoke,
And hearing him, thy power had lost his power.
The Destinies will curse thee for this stroke;
They bid thee crop a weed, thou pluck'st a flower:
Love's golden arrow at him should have fled,
And not Death's ebon dart, to strike him dead.[c]

"Dost thou drink tears, that thou provok'st such weeping?
What may a heavy groan advantage thee?
Why hast thou cast into eternal sleeping
Those eyes that taught all other eyes to see?
Now Nature cares not for thy mortal vigour,
Since her best work is ruin'd with thy rigour."

Here overcome, as one full of despair,
She vail'd her eyelids, who, like sluices, stopp'd
The crystal tide that from her two cheeks fair
In the sweet channel of her bosom dropp'd;
But through the flood-gates breaks the silver rain,
And with his strong course opens them again.

O, how her eyes and tears did lend and borrow!
Her eyes seen in the tears, tears in her eye;
Both crystals, where they view'd each other's sorrow,—
Sorrow that friendly sighs sought still to dry;
But like a stormy day, now wind, now rain,
Sighs dry her cheeks, tears make them wet again.

Variable passions throng her constant woe,
As striving who should best become her grief;
All entertain'd, each passion labours so,
That every present sorrow seemeth chief,
But none is best; then join they all together,
Like many clouds consulting for foul weather.

By this, far off she hears some huntsman hollo;
A nurse's song ne'er pleas'd her babe so well:
The dire imagination she did follow
This sound of hope doth labour to expel;
For now reviving joy bids her rejoice,
And flatters her it is Adonis' voice.

Whereat her tears began to turn their tide,
Being prison'd in her eye, like pearls in glass;
Yet sometimes falls an orient drop beside,
Which her cheek melts, as scorning it should pass,
To wash the foul face of the sluttish ground,
Who is but drunken when she seemeth drown'd.

---

[a] — all-dismay'd,—] So the two earliest editions. The impression of 1596 reads, with perhaps more emphasis, "*sore* dismay'd."

[b] Full of respects—] *Minute observances, considerations.* "This is one of our author's nice observations. No one affects more wisdom than a drunken man."—MALONE.

[c] Love's golden arrow at him should have fled,
And not Death's ebon dart, &c.]

This is a supposed allusion to the ancient apologue of Love and Death exchanging their darts by mistake. Massinger, in *The Virgin-Martyr*, Act IV. Sc. 3, refers to the same fable,—

"Strange affection!
Cupid once more hath chang'd his shafts with Death,
And kills, instead of giving life."

See Gifford's note on this passage and his extract from Johannes Secundus, in Massinger's Plays.

O, hard-believing love, how strange it seems
Not to believe, and yet too credulous!
Thy weal and woe are both of them extremes;
Despair and hope make thee ridiculous:
The one doth flatter thee in thoughts unlikely,
In likely thoughts the other kills thee quickly.

Now she unweaves the web that she hath wrought;
Adonis lives, and Death is not to blame;
It was not she that call'd him all to-naught;
Now she adds honours to his hateful name;
She clepes[a] him king of graves, and grave for kings,
Imperious supreme of all mortal things.

"No, no," quoth she, "sweet Death, I did but jest;
Yet pardon me, I felt a kind of fear
Whenas I met the boar, that bloody beast,
Which knows no pity, but is still severe;
Then, gentle shadow,—truth I must confess,—
I rail'd on thee, fearing my love's decease.

"'T is not my fault: the boar provok'd my tongue;
Be wreak'd on him, invisible commander;
'T is he, foul creature, that hath done thee wrong;
I did but act, he 's author of thy slander:
Grief hath two tongues, and never woman yet,
Could rule them both, without ten women's wit."

Thus, hoping that Adonis is alive,
Her rash suspect she doth extenuate;
And that his beauty may the better thrive,
With Death she humbly doth insinuate;
Tells him of trophies, statues, tombs, and stories[b]
His victories, his triumphs, and his glories.

"O, Jove," quoth she, "how much a fool was I,
To be of such a weak and silly mind,
To wail his death who lives, and must not die
Till mutual overthrow of mortal kind!
For he being dead, with him is beauty slain,
And, beauty dead, black chaos comes again.

"Fie, fie, fond love, thou art so full of fear
As one with treasure laden, hemm'd with thieves;
Trifles, unwitnessed with eye or ear,
Thy coward heart with false bethinking grieves."
Even at this word she hears a merry horn,
Whereat she leaps that was but late forlorn.

As falcon[c] to the lure, away she flies;
The grass stoops not, she treads on it so light;
And in her haste unfortunately spies
The foul boar's conquest on her fair delight;
Which seen, her eyes, as[d] murder'd with the view,
Like stars asham'd of day, themselves withdrew;

Or, as the snail, whose tender horns being hit,
Shrinks backward in his shelly cave with pain,
And there, all smother'd up, in shade doth sit,
Long after fearing to creep forth again;
So, at his bloody view, her eyes are fled
Into the deep-dark cabins of her head;

Where they resign their office and their light
To the disposing of her troubled brain;
Who bids them still consort with ugly night,
And never wound the heart with looks again;
Who, like a king perplexed in his throne,
By their suggestion gives a deadly groan,

Whereat each tributary subject quakes;
As when the wind, imprison'd in the ground,[e]
Struggling for passage, earth's foundation shakes,
Which with cold terror doth men's minds confound,
This mutiny each part doth so surprise,
That from their dark beds once more leap her eyes;

And, being open'd, threw unwilling light
Upon the wide wound that the boar had trench'd
In his soft flank; whose wonted lily white
With purple tears, that his wound wept, was[f] drench'd:
No flower was nigh, no grass, herb, leaf, or weed,
But stole his blood, and seem'd with him to bleed.

This solemn sympathy poor Venus noteth;
Over one shoulder doth she hang her head;
Dumbly she passions,[g] franticly she doteth;
She thinks he could not die, he is not dead:
Her voice is stopp'd, her joints forget to bow;
Her eyes are mad that they have wept till now.

Upon his hurt she looks so steadfastly
That her sight dazzling makes the wound seem three;
And then she reprehends her mangling eye
That makes more gashes where no breach should be:
His face seems twain, each several limb is doubled;
For oft the eye mistakes, the brain being troubled.

---

[a] — clepes—] *Calls.* So in "Hamlet," Act I. Sc. 4,—"They *clepe* us drunkards," &c.

[b] —— and stories
His victories,—]

The employment of *story* as a verb is not unfrequent in Shakespeare: thus, in "Cymbeline," Act I. Sc. 4,—"How worthy he is I will leave to appear hereafter, rather than *story* him in his own hearing;" and in "Lucrece,"—

"He stories to her ears her husband's fame."

We suspect, too, that in "Othello," Act IV. Sc. 4, the passage usually printed,—"Have you *scored* me?" should be read,—"Have you *storied* me?" *i.e.* have you published my shame? The word in the quartos, indeed, is *stor'd*.

[c] *As* falcon *to the lure,*—] The lection of the quarto 1600; all previous editions have, "*falcons*."

[d] — as *murder'd*—] The quarto 1593 reads *are* for "as."

[e] As when the wind, imprison'd in the ground, &c.] This calls to mind the well-known passage in "Henry IV." Part I. Act III. Scene 1,—

"—— oft the teeming earth
Is with a kind of colic pinch'd and vex'd
By the imprisoning of unruly wind
Within her womb; which, for enlargement striving,
Shakes the old beldame earth, and topples down
Steeples, and moss-grown towers."

[f] — was drench'd:] All editions prior to 1600 read,—"*had* drench'd," &c.

[g] — *she* passions,—] See note ([b]), p. 35, Vol. I

"My tongue cannot express my grief for one,
And yet," quoth she, "behold two Adons dead!
My sighs are blown away, my salt tears gone,
Mine eyes are turn'd to fire, my heart to lead:
Heavy heart's lead melt at mine eyes' red fire!
So shall I die by drops of hot desire.

"Alas, poor world, what treasure hast thou lost!
What face remains alive that's worth the viewing?
Whose tongue is music now? what canst thou boast
Of things long since, or any thing ensuing?
The flowers are sweet, their colours fresh and trim;
But true-sweet beauty liv'd and died with him.

"Bonnet nor veil henceforth no creature wear!
Nor sun nor wind will ever strive to kiss you:
Having no fair [a] to lose, you need not fear;
The sun doth scorn you, and the wind doth hiss you:
But when Adonis liv'd, sun and sharp air
Lurk'd like two thieves to rob him of his fair;

"And therefore would he put his bonnet on,
Under whose brim the gaudy sun would peep;
The wind would blow it off, and, being gone,
Play with his locks; then would Adonis weep;
And straight, in pity of his tender years,
They both would strive who first should dry his tears.

"To see his face the lion walk'd along
Behind some hedge, because he would not fear [b] him;
To recreate himself, when he hath sung,
The tiger would be tame, and gently hear him;
If he had spoke, the wolf would leave his prey,
And never fright the silly lamb that day.

"When he beheld his shadow in the brook,
The fishes spread on it their golden gills;
When he was by, the birds such pleasure took,
That some would sing, some other in their bills
Would bring him mulberries and ripe-red cherries;
He fed them with his sight, they him with berries.

"But this foul, grim, and urchin-snouted [c] boar,
Whose downward eye still looketh for a grave,
Ne'er saw the beauteous livery that he wore;
Witness the entertainment that he gave:
If he did see his face, why then I know
He thought to kiss him, and hath kill'd him so.

"'T is true, 't is true; thus was Adonis slain:
He ran upon the boar with his sharp spear,
Who did not whet his teeth at him again,
But by a kiss thought to persuade him there;
And nuzzling in his flank, the loving swine
Sheath'd, unaware, the tusk in his soft groin.

"Had I been tooth'd like him, I must confess,
With kissing him I should have kill'd him first;
But he is dead, and never did he bless
My youth with his,—the more am I accurst."
With this, she falleth in the place she stood,
And stains her face with his congealed blood.

She looks upon his lips, and they are pale;
She takes him by the hand, and that is cold;
She whispers in his ears a heavy tale,
As if they heard the woeful words she told;
She lifts the coffer-lids that close his eyes,
Where, lo, two lamps, burnt out, in darkness lies!

Two glasses, where herself herself beheld
A thousand times, and now no more reflect;
Their virtue lost, wherein they late excell'd,
And every beauty robb'd of his effect:
"Wonder of time," quoth she, "this is my spite,
That, thou being dead, the day should yet be light.

"Since thou art dead, lo, here I prophesy,
Sorrow on love hereafter shall attend!
It shall be waited on with jealousy,
Find sweet beginning, but unsavoury end;
Ne'er settled equally, but high or low;
That all love's pleasure shall not match his woe.

"It shall be fickle, false, and full of fraud;
Bud and be blasted in a breathing-while;
The bottom poison, and the top o'erstraw'd [d]
With sweets that shall the truest sight beguile:
The strongest body shall it make most weak,
Strike the wise dumb, and teach the fool to speak.

"It shall be sparing, and too full of riot;
Teaching decrepit age to tread the measures, [e]
The staring ruffian shall it keep in quiet;
Pluck down the rich, enrich the poor with treasures;
It shall be raging-mad, and silly-mild,
Make the young old, the old become a child.

"It shall suspect where is no cause of fear;
It shall not fear where it should most mistrust;
It shall be merciful, and too severe,
And most deceiving when it seems most just;
Perverse it shall be where it shows most toward,
Put fear to valour, courage to the coward.

"It shall be cause of war and dire events,
And set dissention 'twixt the son and sire;
Subject and servile to all discontents,
As dry combustious matter is to fire;
Sith in his prime death doth my love destroy,
They that love best their loves shall not enjoy.

---

[a] — fair—] That is, *beauty*. See note (b), p. 121, Vol. I.

[b] — *because he would not* fear him;] Because he would not *frighten* him: so in "Henry VI." Part III. Act III. Sc. 3,—"Go *fear* thy king withal."

[c] — urchin-snouted—] An *urchin* is a hedgehog; but it also meant an elf or mischievous sprite.

[d] — o'erstraw'd—] *O'erstrewed.*

[e] — *to tread the* measures,—] By "measures," dances of any kind are here meant, and not *grave dances suitable to age*, as some commentators explain it; the power of love is to be shown by its "confounding contraries." See note (2), p. 103, Vol. I.

By this, the boy that by her side lay kill'd
Was melted like a vapour from her sight,
And in his blood, that on the ground lay spill'd,
A purple flower sprung up, chequer'd with white,
Resembling well his pale cheeks, and the blood
Which in round drops upon their whiteness stood.

She bows her head, the new-sprung flower to smell,
Comparing it to her Adonis' breath;
And says, within her bosom it shall dwell,
Since he himself is reft from her by death:
She crops the stalk, and in the breach appears
Green dropping sap, which she compares to tears.

"Poor flower," quoth she, "this was thy father's guise,—
Sweet issue of a more sweet-smelling sire,—
For every little grief to wet his eyes:
To grow unto himself was his desire,
And so 't is thine; but know, it is as good
To wither in my breast as in his blood.

"Here was thy father's bed, here in my breast;
Thou art the next of blood, and 't is thy right:
Lo, in this hollow cradle take thy rest,
My throbbing heart shall rock thee day and night!
There shall not be one minute in an hour
Wherein I will not kiss my sweet love's flower."

Thus weary of the world, away she hies,
And yokes her silver doves; by whose swift aid
Their mistress, mounted, through the empty skies
In her light chariot quickly is convey'd;
Holding their course to Paphos, where their queen
Means to immure herself and not be seen.

FINIS.

LUCRECE.

TO THE

RIGHT HONOURABLE HENRY WRIOTHESLY,

EARL OF SOUTHAMPTON, AND BARON OF TICHFIELD.

THE love I dedicate to your Lordship is without end; whereof this pamphlet, without beginning, is but a superfluous moiety.[a] The warrant I have of your honourable disposition, not the worth of my untutored lines, makes it assured of acceptance. What I have done is yours; what I have to do is yours; being part in all I have devoted yours. Were my worth greater, my duty would show greater; meantime, as it is, it is bound to your Lordship, to whom I wish long life, still lengthened with all happiness.

Your Lordship's in all duty,

WILLIAM SHAKESPEARE.

[a] — *moiety.*] "Moiety" in Shakespeare's time was commonly used to signify any *part* or *portion* of a thing.

THE ARGUMENT.

Lucius Tarquinius,—for his excessive pride surnamed Superbus,—after he had caused his own father-in-law, Servius Tullius, to be cruelly murdered, and, contrary to the Roman laws and customs, not requiring or staying for the people's suffrages, had possessed himself of the kingdom, went, accompanied with his sons and other noblemen of Rome, to besiege Ardea. During which siege the principal men of the army meeting one evening at the tent of Sextus Tarquinius, the king's son, in their discourses after supper, every one commended the virtues of his own wife; among whom, Collatinus extolled the incomparable chastity of his wife Lucretia. In that pleasant humour they all posted to Rome; and intending, by their secret and sudden arrival, to make trial of that which every one had before avouched, only Collatinus finds his wife (though it were late in the night) spinning amongst her maids: the other ladies were all found dancing and revelling, or in several disports. Whereupon the noblemen yielded Collatinus the victory, and his wife the fame. At that time Sextus Tarquinius, being inflamed with Lucrece' beauty, yet smothering his passions for the present, departed with the rest back to the camp; from whence he shortly after privily withdrew himself, and was (according to his estate) royally entertained and lodged by Lucrece at Collatium. The same night he treacherously stealeth into her chamber, violently ravished her, and early in the morning speedeth away. Lucrece, in this lamentable plight, hastily dispatcheth messengers, one to Rome for her father, another to the camp for Collatine. They came, the one accompanied with Junius Brutus, the other with Publius Valerius; and finding Lucrece attired in mourning habit, demanded the cause of her sorrow. She, first taking an oath of them for her revenge, revealed the actor, and whole manner of his dealing, and withal suddenly stabbed herself. Which done, with one consent they all vowed to root out the whole hated family of the Tarquins; and bearing the dead body to Rome, Brutus acquainted the people with the doer and manner of the vile deed, with a bitter invective against the tyranny of the king; wherewith the people were so moved, that with one consent and a general acclamation, the Tarquins were all exiled, and the state government changed from kings to consuls.

LUCRECE.

The entry of "Lucrece" on the Registers of the Stationers is as follows:—

"9 May, 1594.
"Mr. Harrison, sen.] A booke intitled the Ravyshement of Lucrece."

In the same year the first edition was issued, with the title of "Lucrece. London. Printed by Richard Field, for Iohn Harrison, and are to be sold at the signe of the white Greyhound in Paules Church-yard, 1594." 4to. It was published again for the same bookseller in 8vo. in 1598, 1600, and 1607. In 1616 another edition, purporting to be "newly revised and corrected," was put forth; but this "corrected" edition is much more inaccurate than any of its predecessors. The next copy, which professes likewise to have been "newly revised," is dated 1624; and this is accompanied by explanatory notes, which, however, are neither interesting nor instructive.

The story on which the poem is based is told by Dion. Halicarnassensis, lib. iv. c. 72; by Livy, lib. i. c. 57, 58; and by Ovid, Fast. lib. ii. But Malone conjectures, and with probability, that the poet was indebted for his model to the legend of Lucrece as it is related in Painter's *Palace of Pleasure,* 1567.

Like his "Venus and Adonis," the "Lucrece" of Shakespeare appears to have been a universal favourite: it is mentioned by Drayton in his "Matilda," 1594; and in the commendatory verses to the poem entitled "Willobie his Avisa, or the true picture of a modest Maide, and of a chast and constant wife," 1594; by Richard Barnefield, in "A Remembrance of some English Poets," at the conclusion of his "Complaints of Poetry," 1598; and by a host of contemporary writers.

[Our text in this poem is that of the quarto 1594, collated with the subsequent impressions already mentioned.]

From the besieged Ardea all in post,
Borne by the trustless wings of false desire,
Lust-breathed Tarquin leaves the Roman host,
And to Collatium bears the lightless fire
Which, in pale embers hid, lurks to aspire,
  And girdle with embracing flames the waist
  Of Collatine's fair love, Lucrece the chaste.

Haply that name of "chaste" unhapp'ly set
This bateless edge on his keen appetite;
When Collatine unwisely did not let[a]
To praise the clear unmatched red and white
Which triumph'd in that sky of his delight,
  Where mortal stars, as bright as heaven's beauties,
  With pure aspécts did him peculiar duties.

For he the night before, in Tarquin's tent,
Unlock'd the treasure of his happy state;

[a] — *did not* let—] Did not *forbear.*

What priceless wealth the heavens had him lent
In the possession of his beauteous mate;
Reckoning his fortune at such high-proud rate,
That kings might be espoused to more fame,
But king nor peer to such a peerless dame.

O, happiness enjoy'd but of a few!
And, if possess'd, as soon decay'd and done
As is the morning's silver-melting dew
Against the golden splendour of the sun!
An expir'd date, cancell'd ere well begun:[a]
Honour and beauty, in the owner's arms,
Are weakly fortress'd from a world of harms.

Beauty itself doth of itself persuade
The eyes of men without an orator;
What needeth, then, apologies be made
To set forth that which is so singular?
Or why is Collatine the publisher
Of that rich jewel he should keep unknown
From thievish ears, because it is his own?

Perchance his boast of Lucrece' sovereignty
Suggested[b] this proud issue of a king;
For by our ears our hearts oft tainted be:
Perchance that envy of so rich a thing,
Braving compare, disdainfully did sting
His high-pitch'd thoughts, that meaner men should vaunt
That golden hap which their superiors want.

But some untimely thought did instigate
His all-too-timeless speed, if none of those:
His honour, his affairs, his friends, his state,
Neglected all, with swift intent he goes
To quench the coal which in his liver glows.[c]
O rash-false heat, wrapp'd in repentant cold,
Thy hasty spring still blasts,[d] and ne'er grows old!

When at Collatium this false lord arriv'd,
Well was he welcom'd by the Roman dame,
Within whose face beauty and virtue striv'd
Which of them both should underprop her fame:
When virtue bragg'd, beauty would blush for shame;
When beauty boasted blushes, in despite
Virtue would stain that or[e] with silver white.

But beauty, in that white intituled,
From Venus' doves doth challenge that fair field:
Then virtue claims from beauty beauty's red,
Which virtue gave the golden age to gild
Their silver cheeks, and call'd it then their shield;
Teaching them thus to use it in the fight,—
When shame assail'd, the red should fence the white.

This heraldry in Lucrece' face was seen,
Argu'd by beauty's red and virtue's white:
Of either's colour was the other queen,
Proving from world's minority their right:
Yet their ambition makes them still to fight;
The sovereignty of either being so great,
That oft they interchange each other's seat.

This silent war of lilies and of roses
Which Tarquin view'd in her fair face's field,[f]
In their pure ranks his traitor eye encloses;
Where, lest between them both it should be kill'd,
The coward captive vanquished doth yield
To those two armies that would let him go,
Rather than triumph in so false a foe.

Now thinks he that her husband's shallow tongue,—
The niggard prodigal that prais'd her so,—
In that high task hath done her beauty wrong,
Which far exceeds his barren skill to show:
Therefore that praise which Collatine doth owe,
Enchanted Tarquin answers with surmise,
In silent wonder of still-gazing eyes.

This earthly saint, adored by this devil,
Little suspecteth the false worshipper;
For unstain'd thoughts do seldom dream on evil;
Birds never lim'd no secret bushes fear:[g]
So guiltless she securely gives good cheer
And reverend welcome to her princely guest,
Whose inward ill no outward harm express'd:

For that he colour'd with his high estate,
Hiding base sin in plaits of majesty;
That nothing in him seem'd inordinate,
Save sometime too much wonder of his eye,
Which, having all, all could not satisfy;
But poorly rich, so wanteth in his store,
That, cloy'd with much, he pineth still for more.

But she, that never cop'd with stranger eyes,
Could pick no meaning from their parling looks,
Nor read the subtle-shining secrecies
Writ in the glassy margents of such books:[h]
She touch'd no unknown baits, nor fear'd no hooks;

---

[a] An expir'd date, cancell'd ere well begun:] So the four earliest editions. The 1616 impression reads more smoothly,—

"A date expir'd and cancel'd ere begun."

Our author, Malone observes, seems to have remembered Daniel's *Complaint of Rosamund*, 1592:—

"Thou must not thinke thy flowre can always flourish,
And that thy *beauty* will be still admir'd,
But that those rayes which all these flames do nourish,
Cancell'd with time will have their *date expir'd*."

[b] Suggested—] *Tempted, incited.*

[c] *To quench the coal which in his* liver *glows.*] The liver was formerly supposed to be the seat of desire.

[d] Thy hasty spring still blasts,—] Thy premature *shoots* are ever *blighted.*

[e] *Virtue would stain that* or *with silver white.*] The quarto of 1594 has, "Virtue would stain that *ore* with silver white," whence Malone happily conjectured that the true word was *or*, i.e. *gold;* and the cluster of heraldic terms in the following stanza, with the opposition of the colours, gold and silver, are to us convincing proofs that "or" is a genuine restoration.

[f] This silent war of lilies and of roses
Which Tarquin view'd in her fair face's field,—]

Compare, "Coriolanus," Act II. Sc. 1,—

"—— our veil'd dames
Commit the *war of white and damask*, in
Their nicely-gawded cheeks, to the wanton spoil
Of Phœbus' burning kisses."

[g] Birds never lim'd no secret bushes fear:] So, as Steevens notes, "Henry VI." Part III. Act V. Sc. 6,—

"The bird, that hath been *limed* in a *bush*,
With trembling wing *misdoubteth* every *bush*."

[h] *Writ in the glassy* margents *of such* books:] See note (1), p. 101, Vol. I. on the lines,—

"His face's own margent did quote such amazes,
That all eyes saw his eyes enchanted with gazes."

  Nor could she moralize[a] his wanton sight
  More than his eyes were open'd to the light.

He stories to her ears her husband's fame,
Won in the fields of fruitful Italy;
And decks with praises Collatine's high name,
Made glorious by his manly chivalry
With bruised arms and wreaths of victory:
  Her joy with heav'd-up hand she doth express,
  And, wordless, so greets heaven for his success.

Far from the purpose of his coming thither,
He makes excuses for his being there.
No cloudy show of stormy blustering weather
Doth yet in his fair welkin once appear;
Till sable Night, mother of Dread and Fear,
  Upon the world dim darkness doth display,
  And in her vaulty prison stows the Day.

For then is Tarquin brought unto his bed,
Intending[b] weariness with heavy sprite;
For, after supper, long he questioned[c]
With modest Lucrece, and wore out the night:
Now leaden slumber with life's strength doth fight;
  And every one to rest themselves betake,
  Save thieves, and cares, and troubled minds, that wake.[d]

As one of which doth Tarquin lie revolving
The sundry dangers of his will's obtaining;
Yet ever to obtain his will resolving,
Though weak-built hopes persuade him to abstaining;
Despair to gain doth traffic oft for gaining;
  And when great treasure is the meed propos'd,
  Though death be adjunct, there's no death suppos'd.

Those that much covet are with gain so fond,
That what they have not,[e] that which they possess,
They scatter and unloose it from their bond,
And so, by hoping more, they have but less;
Or, gaining more, the profit of excess
  Is but to surfeit, and such griefs sustain,
  That they prove bankrupt in this poor-rich gain.

The aim of all is but to nurse the life
With honour, wealth, and ease, in waning age;
And in this aim there is such thwarting strife,
That one for all, or all for one we gage:
As life for honour in fell battles' rage,
  Honour for wealth; and oft that wealth doth cost
  The death of all, and all together lost.

So that in venturing ill[f] we leave to be
The things we are for that which we expect;
And this ambitious-foul infirmity,
In having much, torments us with defect
Of that we have: so then we do neglect
  The thing we have, and, all for want of wit,
  Make something nothing by augmenting it.

Such hazard now must doting Tarquin make,
Pawning his honour to obtain his lust;
And for himself himself he must forsake:
Then where is truth, if there be no self-trust?
When shall he think to find a stranger just,
  When he himself himself confounds, betrays
  To slanderous tongues and wretched hateful days?

Now stole upon the time the dead of night,
When heavy sleep had clos'd up mortal eyes:
No comfortable star did lend his light,
No noise but owls' and wolves' death-boding cries;[g]
Now serves the season that they may surprise
  The silly lambs: pure thoughts are dead and still,
  While lust and murder wake to stain and kill.

And now this lustful lord leap'd from his bed,
Throwing his mantle rudely o'er his arm;
Is madly toss'd between desire and dread;
Th' one sweetly flatters, th' other feareth harm;
But honest Fear, bewitch'd with lust's foul charm,
  Doth too-too oft betake him to retire,
  Beaten away by brain-sick rude Desire.

His falchion on a flint he softly smiteth,
That from the cold stone sparks of fire do fly,
Whereat a waxen torch forthwith he lighteth,
Which must be lode-star to his lustful eye;
And to the flame thus speaks advisedly,
  "As from this cold flint I enforc'd this fire,
  So Lucrece must I force to my desire."

Here pale with fear he doth premeditate
The dangers of his loathsome enterprise,
And in his inward mind he doth debate
What following sorrow may on this arise;
Then looking scornfully, he doth despise
  His naked armour of still-slaughter'd lust,
  And justly thus controls his thoughts unjust:

"Fair torch, burn out thy light, and lend it not
To darken her whose light excelleth thine!
And die, unhallow'd thoughts, before you blot
With your uncleanness that which is divine!
Offer pure incense to so pure a shrine:

---

[a] — moralize—] *Interpret.*

[b] Intending—] *Pretending:* as in "Richard III." Act III. Sc. 5,—

> "Tremble and start at wagging of a straw,
> *Intending* deep suspicion."

[c] — questioned—] *Conversed.*

[d] And every one to rest themselves betake,
Save thieves, and cares, and troubled minds that wake.]

A passage in Barnfield's *Legend of Cassandra*, 1595, very closely resembles this:—

> "Now silent night drew on, when all things sleepe,
> Save thieves and cares."

[e] That what they have not, &c.] There is some obscurity here; should we not read,—

> "*For* what they have not, that which they possess
> They scatter," &c.?

[f] *So that in venturing* ill—] That is, by a *bad venture.* Some editors, however, think we ought to read, "— venturing *all*—"

[g] No noise but owls' and wolves' death-boding cries;] This passage might have saved Mr. Collier's annotator from the ridiculous sophistication of the kindred one in "King Lear," Act II. Sc. 4,—

> "To be a comrade with the wolf and owl,
> Necessity's sharp pinch!"

Which he has tortured into,—

> "To be a comrade of the wolf, and *howl*
> Necessity's sharp pinch."

Let fair humanity abhor the deed
That spots and stains love's modest snow-white weed.[a]

"O shame to knighthood and to shining arms!
O foul dishonour to my household's grave!
O impious act, including all foul harms!
A martial man to be soft fancy's[b] slave
True valour still a true respect should have;
Then my digression is so vile, so base,
That it will live engraven in my face.

"Yea, though I die, the scandal will survive,
And be an eye-sore in my golden coat;
Some loathsome dash the herald will contrive,[c]
To cipher me how fondly I did dote;
That my posterity, sham'd with the note,
Shall curse my bones, and hold it for no sin
To wish that I their father had not bin.

"What win I, if I gain the thing I seek?
A dream, a breath, a froth of fleeting joy.
Who buys a minute's mirth to wail a week?
Or sells eternity to get a toy?
For one sweet grape who will the vine destroy?
Or what fond beggar, but to touch the crown,
Would with the sceptre straight be strucken down?

"If Collatinus dream of my intent,
Will he not wake, and in a desperate rage
Post hither, this vile purpose to prevent?
This siege that hath engirt his marriage,
This blur to youth, this sorrow to the sage,
This dying virtue, this surviving shame,
Whose crime will bear an ever-during blame?

"O, what excuse can my invention make,
When thou shalt charge me with so black a deed?
Will not my tongue be mute, my frail joints shake,
Mine eyes forego their light, my false heart bleed?
The guilt being great, the fear doth still exceed;
And extreme fear can neither fight nor fly,
But coward-like with trembling terror die.

"Had Collatinus kill'd my son or sire,
Or lain in ambush to betray my life,
Or were he not my dear friend, this desire
Might have excuse to work upon his wife,
As in revenge or quittal of such strife:
But as he is my kinsman, my dear friend,
The shame and fault finds no excuse nor end.

"Shameful it is;—ay, if the fact be known:
Hateful it is;—there is no hate in loving:
I'll beg her love;—but she is not her own:
The worst is but denial and reproving:
My will is strong, past reason's weak removing
Who fears a sentence or an old man's saw
Shall by a painted cloth be kept in awe."[d]

Thus, graceless, holds he disputation
'Tween frozen conscience and hot-burning will,
And with good thoughts makes dispensation,
Urging the worser sense for vantage still;
Which in a moment doth confound and kill
All pure effects, and doth so far proceed,
That what is vile shows like a virtuous deed.

Quoth he, "She took me kindly by the hand,
And gaz'd for tidings in my eager eyes,
Fearing some hard news from the warlike band
Where her beloved Collatinus lies.
O, how her fear did make her colour rise!
First red as roses that on lawn we lay,
Then white as lawn, the roses took away.

"And how her hand, in my hand being lock'd,
Forc'd it to tremble with her loyal fear!
Which struck her sad, and then it faster rock'd,
Until her husband's welfare she did hear;
Whereat she smiled with so sweet a cheer,[e]
That had Narcissus seen her as she stood,
Self-love had never drown'd him in the flood.

"Why hunt I, then, for colour or excuses?
All orators are dumb when beauty pleadeth;
Poor wretches have remorse in poor abuses;
Love thrives not in the heart that shadows dreadeth:
Affection is my captain, and he leadeth;
And when his gaudy banner is display'd,
The coward fights, and will not be dismay'd.

"Then, childish fear, avaunt! debating, die!
Respect and reason, wait on wrinkled age![f]
My heart shall never countermand mine eye:
Sad[g] pause and deep regard beseem the sage;
My part is youth, and beats these from the stage:
Desire my pilot is, beauty my prize;
Then who fears sinking where such treasure lies?"

As corn o'ergrown by weeds, so heedful fear
Is almost chok'd by unresisted lust.
Away he steals with open listening ear,
Full of foul hope, and full of fond mistrust;
Both which, as servitors to the unjust,
So cross him with their opposite persuasion,
That now he vows a league, and now invasion.

Within his thought her heavenly image sits,
And in the self-same seat sits Collatine:
That eye which looks on her confounds his wits;

[a] — weed.] *Robe* or *garment*.

[b] — fancy's *slave!*] *Fancy* is *love* or *affection*.

[c] Some loathsome dash the herald will contrive,—] "In the books of heraldry a particular mark of disgrace is mentioned, by which the escutcheons of those persons were anciently distinguished, who 'discourteously used a widow, maid, or wife, against her will.'"—MALONE.

[d] Shall by a painted cloth be kept in awe.] See note (1), p. 626, Vol. I.

[e] — cheer,—] *Countenance;* as in "A Midsummer Night's Dream," Act III. Sc. 1,—

"All fancy-sick she is, and pale of *cheer*," &c.

See also note c, p. 363, Vol. I.

[f] Respect and reason, *wait on wrinkled age!*] So in "Troilus and Cressida," Act II. Sc. 2,—

"—— reason and *respect*
Make livers pale, and lustihood deject."

"Respect" in both cases meaning *self-command, prudence, cautious circumspection.*

[g] Sad *pause*—] "Sad" meant *serious, grave,* as in "The Two Gentlemen of Verona," Act I. Sc. 3,—

"—— what *sad* talk was that,
Wherewith my brother held you in the cloister?"

That eye which him beholds, as more divine,
Unto a view so false will not incline ;
But with a pure appeal seeks to the heart,
Which once corrupted takes the worser part ;

And therein heartens up his servile powers,
Who, flatter'd by their leader's jocund show,
Stuff up his lust, as minutes fill up hours ;
And as their captain, so their pride doth grow,
Paying more slavish tribute than they owe.
By reprobate desire thus madly led,
The Roman lord marcheth to Lucrece' bed.

The locks between her chamber and his will,
Each one by him enforc'd, retires his ward ; [a]
But, as they open, they all rate his ill,
Which drives the creeping thief to some regard ; [b]
The threshold grates the door to have him heard ;
Night-wand'ring weasels shriek to see him there ;
They fright him, yet he still pursues his fear.

As each unwilling portal yields him way,
Through little vents and crannies of the place
The wind wars with his torch to make him stay,
And blows the smoke of it into his face,
Extinguishing his conduct [c] in this case ;
But his hot heart, which fond desire doth scorch,
Puffs forth another wind that fires the torch ;

And being lighted, by the light he spies
Lucretia's glove, wherein her needle sticks :
He takes it from the rushes where it lies,
And griping it, the neeld [d] his finger pricks :
As who should say, This glove to wanton tricks
Is not inur'd ; return again in haste ;
Thou see'st our mistress' ornaments are chaste.

But all these poor forbiddings could not stay him ;
He in the worst sense construes their denial :
The doors, the wind, the glove, that did delay him,
He takes for accidental things of trial ;
Or as those bars which stop the hourly dial,
Who with a lingering stay his course doth let, [e]
Till every minute pays the hour his debt.

" So, so," quoth he, " these lets attend the time,
Like little frosts that sometime threat the spring,
To add a more rejoicing [f] to the prime,
And give the sneaped [g] birds more cause to sing.
Pain pays the income of each precious thing ;
Huge rocks, high winds, strong pirates, shelves and sands,
The merchant fears, ere rich at home he lands."

Now is he come unto the chamber-door,
That shuts him from the heaven of his thought,
Which with a yielding latch, and with no more,
Hath barr'd him from the blessed thing he sought.
So from himself impiety hath wrought,
That for his prey to pray he doth begin,
As if the heavens should countenance his sin.

But in the midst of his unfruitful prayer,
Having solicited th' eternal power,
That his foul thoughts might compass his fair fair, [h]
And they would stand auspicious to the hour,
Even there he starts :—quoth he, " I must deflower :
The powers to whom I pray abhor this fact, [i]
How can they, then, assist me in the act ?

" Then Love and Fortune be my gods, my guide !
My will is back'd with resolution :
Thoughts are but dreams till their effects be tried ;
The blackest sin is clear'd with absolution ;
Against love's fire fear's frost hath dissolution.
The eye of heaven is out, and misty night
Covers the shame that follows sweet delight."

This said, his guilty hand pluck'd up the latch,
And with his knee the door he opens wide.
The dove sleeps fast that this night-owl will catch :
Thus treason works ere traitors be espied.
Who sees the lurking serpent steps aside ;
But she, sound sleeping, fearing no such thing,
Lies at the mercy of his mortal sting.

Into the chamber wickedly he stalks,
And gazeth on her yet-unstained bed.
The curtains being close, about he walks,
Rolling his greedy eye-balls in his head :
By their high treason is his heart misled ;
Which gives the watch-word to his hand full soon,
To draw the cloud that hides the silver moon.

Look, as the fair and fiery-pointed sun, [k]
Rushing from forth a cloud, bereaves our sight ;
Even so, the curtain drawn, his eyes begun
To wink, being blinded with a greater light :
Whether it is that she reflects so bright,
That dazzleth them, or else some shame supposed ;
But blind they are, and keep themselves enclosed.

---

[a] — retires his *ward ;*] That is, *withdraws* from *its guard*, or *post*, or *charge.*

[b] — *to some* regard ;] To some *reflection.*

[c] — *his* conduct—] "Conduct" for *conductor ;* as in "Richard II." Act IV. Sc. 1,—"I will be his *conduct ;*" and in "Romeo and Juliet," Act III. Sc. 1,—

" Away to heaven, respective lenity,
And fire-ey'd fury be my *conduct* now ! "

[d] *And griping it, the* neeld *his finger-pricks :*] So in "A Midsummer Night's Dream," Act III. Sc. 2,—

" We, Hermia, like two artificial gods,
Have with our *neelds* created both one flower."

[e] — let,—] *Hinder, stop, obstruct.*

[f] *To add a* more *rejoicing*—] "More" for *greater*, as in "King John," Act II. Sc. 1,—

" Till your strong hand shall help to give him strength,
To make a *more* requital to your love."

[g] — sneaped *birds*—] "Sneaped" means *nipped* or *checked.* So in "The Winter's Tale," Act I. Sc. 2,—

" —— that may blow
No *sneaping* winds at home," &c.

[h] — *his fair* fair,—] His fair *beauty.*

[i] — fact,—] That is, *deed*, or *crime.* So in "Measure for Measure," Act IV. Sc. 2,—" And, indeed, his *fact*, till now, in the government of lord Angelo, never came to an undoubtful proof." Again in "Titus Andronicus," Act IV. Sc. 1,—

" I think she means that there was more than one
Confederate in the *fact.*"

[k] — fiery-pointed sun,—] Steevens suggested we should read, *fire-ypointed ;* citing Milton's,—

" Under a *star-ypointing* pyramid."

O, had they in that darksome prison died!
Then had they seen the period of their ill;
Then Collatine again, by Lucrece' side,
In his clear bed might have reposed still:
But they must ope, this blessed league to kill;
  And holy-thoughted Lucrece to their sight
  Must sell her joy, her life, her world's delight.

Her lily hand her rosy cheek lies under,
Cozening the pillow of a lawful kiss;
Who, therefore angry, seems to part in sunder,
Swelling on either side to want[a] his bliss;
Between whose hills her head entombed is:
  Where, like a virtuous monument, she lies,
  To be admir'd of lewd unhallow'd eyes.

Without the bed her other fair hand was,
On the green coverlet; whose perfect white
Show'd like an April daisy on the grass,
With pearly sweat, resembling dew of night.
Her eyes, like marigolds, had sheath'd their light,
  And canopied in darkness sweetly lay,
  Till they might open to adorn the day.

Her hair, like golden threads, play'd with her breath;
O modest wantons! wanton modesty!
Showing life's triumph in the map of death,
And death's dim look in life's mortality:
Each in her sleep themselves so beautify,
  As if between them twain there were no strife,
  But that life liv'd in death, and death in life.

Her breasts, like ivory globes circled with blue,
A pair of maiden worlds unconquered,
Save of their lord no bearing yoke they knew,
And him by oath they truly honoured.
These worlds in Tarquin new ambition bred;
  Who, like a foul usurper, went about
  From this fair throne to heave the owner out.

What could he see, but mightily he noted?
What did he note, but strongly he desir'd?
What he beheld, on that he firmly doted,
And in his will his wilful eye he tir'd.
With more than admiration he admir'd
  Her azure veins, her alabaster skin,
  Her coral lips, her snow-white dimpled chin.

As the grim lion fawneth o'er his prey,
Sharp hunger by the conquest satisfied,
So o'er this sleeping soul doth Tarquin stay,
His rage of lust by gazing qualified;[b]
Slack'd, not suppress'd; for standing by her side,
  His eye, which late this mutiny restrains,
  Unto a greater uproar tempts his veins:

And they, like straggling slaves for pillage fighting,
Obdurate vassals fell exploits effecting,
In bloody death and ravishment delighting,
Nor children's tears nor mother's groans respecting,
Swell in their pride, the onset still expecting:
  Anon his beating heart, alarum striking,
  Gives the hot charge, and bids them do their liking.

His drumming heart cheers up his burning eye,
His eye commends[c] the leading to his hand;
His hand, as proud of such a dignity,
Smoking with pride, march'd on to make his stand
On her bare breast, the heart of all her land;
  Whose ranks of blue veins, as his hand did scale,
  Left their round turrets destitute and pale.

They, mustering to the quiet cabinet
Where their dear governess and lady lies,
Do tell her she is dreadfully beset,
And fright her with confusion of their cries:
She, much amaz'd, breaks ope her lock'd-up eyes,
  Who, peeping forth this tumult to behold,
  Are by his flaming torch dimm'd and controll'd.

Imagine her as one in dead of night
From forth dull sleep by dreadful fancy waking,
That thinks she hath beheld some ghastly sprite,
Whose grim aspéct sets every joint a-shaking;
What terror 'tis! but she, in worser taking,
  From sleep disturbed, heedfully doth view
  The sight which makes supposed terror true.

Wrapp'd and confounded in a thousand fears,
Like to a new-kill'd bird she trembling lies;
She dares not look; yet, winking, there appears
Quick-shifting antics, ugly in her eyes:
Such shadows are the weak brain's forgeries:
  Who, angry that the eyes fly from their lights,
  In darkness daunts them with more dreadful sights.

His hand, that yet remains upon her breast,—
Rude ram, to batter such an ivory wall!—
May feel her heart,—(poor citizen!) distress'd,
Wounding itself to death, rise up and fall,
Beating her bulk, that his hand shakes withal.
  This moves in him more rage, and lesser pity,
  To make the breach, and enter this sweet city.

First, like a trumpet, doth his tongue begin
To sound a parley to his heartless foe;
Who o'er the white sheet peers her whiter chin,
The reason of this rash alarm to know,
Which he by dumb demeanour seeks to show;
  But she with vehement prayers urgeth still
  Under what colour he commits this ill.

Thus he replies: "The colour in thy face,—
That even for anger makes the lily pale,
And the red rose blush at her own disgrace,—
Shall plead for me, and tell my loving tale:
Under that colour am I come to scale

[a] — to want—] To *miss; to be without.* See note (c), p. 351, Vol. I.

[b] — qualified;] *Mitigated, weakened;* as in "Othello," Act II. Sc. 3,—"I have drunk but one cup to-night, and that was craftily *qualified* too," &c.

[c] — commends—] *Submits, resigns.* So in "Antony and Cleopatra," Act IV. Sc. 8,—

"*Commend* unto his lips thy favouring hand;"

and in "All's Well that Ends Well," Act V. Sc. 1,—

"*Commend* the paper to his gracious hand."

Thy never-conquer'd fort; the fault is thine,
For those thine eyes betray thee unto mine.

"Thus I forestall thee, if thou mean to chide:
Thy beauty hath ensnar'd thee to this night,
Where thou with patience must my will abide;
My will that marks thee for my earth's delight,
Which I to conquer sought with all my might;
But as reproof and reason beat it dead,
By thy bright beauty was it newly bred.

"I see what crosses my attempt will bring;
I know what thorns the growing rose defends;
I think the honey guarded with a sting;[a]
All this, beforehand, counsel comprehends:
But will is deaf, and hears no heedful friends;
Only he hath an eye to gaze on beauty,
And dotes on what he looks,[b] 'gainst law or duty.

"I have debated, even in my soul,
What wrong, what shame, what sorrow I shall breed;
But nothing can Affection's course control,
Or stop the headlong fury of his speed.
I know repentant tears ensue the deed,
Reproach, disdain, and deadly enmity;
Yet strive I to embrace mine infamy."

This said, he shakes aloft his Roman blade,
Which, like a falcon tow'ring in the skies
Coucheth the fowl below with his wings' shade,[c]
Whose crooked beak threats if he mount he dies:
So under his insulting falchion lies
Harmless Lucretia, marking what he tells,
With trembling fear, as fowl hear falcon's bells.[d]

"Lucrece," quoth he, "this night I must enjoy thee:
If thou deny, then force must work my way,
For in thy bed I purpose to destroy thee;
That done, some worthless slave of thine I'll slay,
To kill thine honour with thy life's decay;
And in thy dead arms do I mean to place him,
Swearing I slew him, seeing thee embrace him.

"So thy surviving husband shall remain
The scornful mark of every open eye;
Thy kinsmen hang their heads at this disdain,
Thy issue blurr'd with nameless bastardy:
And thou, the author of their obloquy,
Shalt have thy trespass cited up in rhymes,
And sung by children in succeeding times.

"But if thou yield, I rest thy secret friend:
The fault unknown is as a thought unacted;
A little harm, done to a great good end,
For lawful policy remains enacted.
The poisonous simple sometimes is compacted
In a pure compound; being so applied,
His venom in effect is purified.

"Then, for thy husband and thy children's sake,
Tender my suit: bequeath not to their lot
The shame that from them no device can take,
The blemish that will never be forgot;
Worse than a slavish wipe,[e] or birth-hour's blot:
For marks descried in men's nativity
Are nature's faults, not their own infamy."

Here with a cockatrice' dead-killing eye[f]
He rouseth up himself, and makes a pause;
While she, the picture of pure piety,
Like a white hind under the grype's[g] sharp claws,
Pleads, in a wilderness, where are no laws,
To the rough beast that knows no gentle right,
Nor aught obeys but his foul appetite.

But[h] when a black-fac'd cloud the world doth threat,
In his dim mist the aspiring mountains hiding,
From earth's dark womb some gentle gust doth get,
Which blows these pitchy vapours from their biding,
Hindering their present fall by this dividing;
So his unhallow'd haste her words delays,
And moody Pluto winks while Orpheus plays.

Yet, foul night-waking cat, he doth but dally,
While in his hold-fast foot the weak mouse panteth;
Her sad behaviour feeds his vulture folly,[i]
A swallowing gulf that even in plenty wanteth:
His ear her prayers admits, but his heart granteth
No penetrable entrance to her plaining:
Tears harden lust, though marble wear with raining.

Her pity-pleading eyes are sadly fix'd
In the remorseless[k] wrinkles of his face;
Her modest eloquence with sighs is mix'd,
Which to her oratory adds more grace.
She puts the period often from his place,
And 'midst the sentence so her accent breaks,
That twice she doth begin ere once she speaks.

---

[a] I think *the honey guarded with a sting;*] "*I am aware* that the honey is guarded with a sting."—MALONE.

[b] And doats on what he looks,—] *On* being understood after "looks."

[c] Coucheth the fowl below with his wings' shade,—] Compare, "Measure for Measure," Act III. Sc. 1,—

"This outward-sainted deputy—
Whose settled visage and deliberate word
Nips youth i' the head, and follies doth *enmew*
As falcon does the fowl—"

and see note *ad l.*

[d] — *as fowl hear* falcon's bells.] So in "Henry VI." Part III. Act I. Sc. 1,—

"—— nor he that loves him best,
The proudest he that holds up Lancaster,
Dares stir a wing if Warwick *shake his bells.*"

[e] *Worse than a* slavish wipe,—] According to Malone, "the brand with which slaves were marked."

[f] Here with a cockatrice' dead-killing eye—] So in "Twelfth Night," Act III. Sc. 4,—"they will *kill* one another *by the look,* like *cockatrices.*" See also note (b), p. 189, Vol. I.

[g] *Like a white hind under the* grype's *sharp claws,*—] Properly, the *grype* meant the *gryphon* or *griffin;* but the name appears to have been used for *vulture.*

[h] But *when a black-fac'd cloud*—] Malone, with doubtful propriety, substituted,—"*Look,* when a black-fac'd cloud," &c.

[i] — *his vulture* folly,—] Here "*folly*" signifies *wantonness* or *depravity;* as in "Othello," Act V. Sc. 2,—

"She turn'd to *folly,* and she was a whore."

[k] — remorseless—] *Pitiless, relentless.*

She cónjures him by high almighty Jove,
By knighthood, gentry, and sweet friendship's oath,
By her untimely tears, her husband's love,
By holy human law, and common troth,
By heaven and earth, and all the power of both,
That to his borrow'd bed he make retire,
And stoop to honour, not to foul desire.

Quoth she, "Reward not hospitality
With such black payment as thou hast pretended;[a]
Mud not the fountain that gave drink to thee;
Mar not the thing that cannot be amended;
End thy ill aim before thy shoot be ended:
He is no wood-man that doth bend his bow
To strike a poor unseasonable doe.

"My husband is thy friend,—for his sake spare me;
Thyself art mighty,—for thine own sake leave me;
Myself a weakling,—do not, then, ensnare me;
Thou look'st not like deceit,—do not deceive me.
My sighs, like whirlwinds, labour hence to heave thee:
If ever man were mov'd with woman's moans,
Be moved with my tears, my sighs, my groans:

"All which together, like a troubled ocean,
Beat at thy rocky and wreck-threatening heart,
To soften it with their continual motion;
For stones dissolv'd to water do convert.
O, if no harder than a stone thou art,
Melt at my tears, and be compassionate!
Soft pity enters at an iron gate.

"In Tarquin's likeness I did entertain thee;
Hast thou put on his shape to do him shame?
To all the host of heaven I complain me,
Thou wrong'st his honour, wound'st his princely name.
Thou art not what thou seem'st; and if the same,
Thou seem'st not what thou art, a god, a king;
For kings like gods should govern everything.

"How will thy shame be seeded in thine age,
When thus thy vices bud before thy spring!
If in thy hope thou dar'st do such outrage,
What dar'st thou not when once thou art a king?
O, be remember'd, no outrageous thing
From vassal actors can be wip'd away;
Then kings' misdeeds cannot be hid in clay.

"This deed will make thee only lov'd for fear;
But happy monarchs still are fear'd for love:
With foul offenders thou perforce must bear,
When they in thee the like offences prove:
If but for fear of this, thy will remove;
For princes are the glass, the school, the book,
Where subjects' eyes do learn, do read, do look.[b]

"And wilt thou be the school where Lust shall learn?
Must he in thee read lectures of such shame?
Wilt thou be glass wherein it shall discern
Authority for sin, warrant for blame?
To privilege dishonour in thy name,
Thou back'st reproach against long-living laud,
And mak'st fair reputation but a bawd.

"Hast thou command? by him that gave it thee,
From a pure heart command thy rebel will:
Draw not thy sword to guard iniquity,
For it was lent thee all that brood to kill.
Thy princely office how canst thou fulfil,
When, pattern'd by thy fault, foul Sin may say,
He learn'd to sin, and thou didst teach the way?

"Think but how vile a spectacle it were,
To view thy present trespass in another.
Men's faults do seldom to themselves appear;
Their own transgressions partially they smother:
This guilt would seem death-worthy in thy brother.
O, how are they wrapp'd in with infamies,
That from their own misdeeds askance their eyes!

"To thee, to thee, my heav'd-up hands appeal,
Not to seducing lust, thy rash relier;
I sue for exil'd majesty's repeal;
Let him return, and flattering thoughts retire:
His true respect will prison false desire,
And wipe the dim mist from thy doting eyne,
That thou shalt see thy state, and pity mine."

"Have done," quoth he; "my uncontrolled tide
Turns not, but swells the higher by this let.
Small lights are soon blown out, huge fires abide,
And with the wind in greater fury fret:
The petty streams that pay a daily debt
To their salt sovereign, with their fresh falls' haste,
Add to his flow, but alter not his taste."

"Thou art," quoth she, "a sea, a sovereign king;
And lo, there falls into thy boundless flood
Black lust, dishonour, shame, misgoverning,
Who seek to stain the ocean of thy blood.
If all these petty ills shall change thy good,
Thy sea within a puddle's womb is hears'd,
And not the puddle in thy sea dispers'd.

"So shall these slaves be king, and thou their slave;
Thou nobly base, they basely dignified;
Thou their fair life, and they thy fouler grave;
Thou loathed in their shame, they in thy pride:
The lesser thing should not the greater hide;
The cedar stoops not to the base shrub's foot,
But low shrubs wither at the cedar's root.

"So let thy thoughts, low vassals to thy state"—
"No more," quoth he, "by heaven, I will not hear thee!
Yield to my love; if not, enforced hate,

[a] — pretended;] *Intended*, or *purposed*.
[b] For princes are the glass, &c.]
"—— *componitur orbis*
Regis ad exemplum."

Instead of love's coy touch, shall rudely tear thee;
That done, despitefully I mean to bear thee
 Unto the base bed of some rascal groom,
 To be thy partner in this shameful doom."

This said, he sets his foot upon the light,
For light and lust are deadly enemies:
Shame folded up in blind-concealing night,
When most unseen, then most doth tyrannize.
The wolf hath seiz'd his prey, the poor lamb cries;
 Till with her own white fleece her voice controll'd
 Entombs her outcry in her lips' sweet fold:

For with the nightly linen that she wears
He pens her piteous clamours in her head;
Cooling his hot face in the chastest tears
That ever modest eyes with sorrow shed.
O, that prone[a] lust should stain so pure a bed!
 The spots whereof could weeping purify,
 Her tears should drop on them perpetually.

But she hath lost a dearer thing than life,
And he hath won what he would lose again:
This forced league doth force a further strife;
This momentary joy breeds months of pain;
This hot desire converts to cold disdain:
 Pure Chastity is rifled of her store,
 And Lust, the thief, far poorer than before.

Look, as the full-fed hound or gorged hawk,
Unapt for tender smell or speedy flight,
Make slow pursuit, or altogether balk
The prey wherein by nature they delight;
So surfeit-taking Tarquin fares this night:
 His taste delicious, in digestion souring,
 Devours his will, that liv'd by foul devouring.

O, deeper sin than bottomless conceit
Can comprehend in still imagination!
Drunken Desire must vomit his receipt,
Ere he can see his own abomination.
While Lust is in his pride, no exclamation
 Can curb his heat, or rein his rash desire,
 Till, like a jade, Self-will himself doth tire.[b]

And then with lank and lean discolour'd cheek,
With heavy eye, knit brow, and strengthless pace,
Feeble Desire, all recreant, poor, and meek,
Like to a bankrupt beggar wails his case:
The flesh being proud, Desire doth fight with Grace,
 For there it revels; and when that decays,
 The guilty rebel for remission prays.

So fares it with this faultful lord of Rome,
Who this accomplishment so hotly chas'd;
For now against himself he sounds this doom,—
That through the length of time he stands disgrac'd:
Besides, his soul's fair temple is defac'd;
 To whose weak ruins muster troops of cares,
 To ask the spotted princess how she fares.

She says, her subjects with foul insurrection
Have batter'd down her consecrated wall,
And by their mortal fault brought in subjection
Her immortality, and made her thrall
To living death and pain perpetual:
 Which in her prescience she controlled still,
 But her foresight could not forestall their will.

Even in this thought through the dark night he stealeth,
A captive victor that hath lost in gain;
Bearing away the wound that nothing healeth,
The scar that will, despite of cure, remain;
Leaving his spoil perplex'd[c] in greater pain.
 She bears the load of lust he left behind,
 And he the burden of a guilty mind.

He like a thievish dog creeps sadly thence;
She like a wearied lamb lies panting there;
He scowls, and hates himself for his offence;
She, desperate, with her nails her flesh doth tear;
He faintly flies, sweating with guilty fear;
 She stays, exclaiming on the direful night;
 He runs, and chides his vanish'd, loath'd delight.

He thence departs a heavy convertite;[d]
She there remains a hopeless cast-away;
He in his speed looks for the morning light;
She prays she never may behold the day;
"For day," quoth she, "night's scapes[e] doth open lay,
 And my true eyes have never practis'd how
 To cloak offences with a cunning brow.

"They think not but that every eye can see
The same disgrace which they themselves behold;
And therefore would they still in darkness be,
To have their unseen sin remain untold;
For they their guilt with weeping will unfold,
 And grave, like water, that doth eat in steel,
 Upon my cheeks what helpless shame I feel."

Here she exclaims against repose and rest,
And bids her eyes hereafter still be blind.
She wakes her heart by beating on her breast,
And bids it leap from thence, where it may find
Some purer chest to close so pure a mind.
 Frantic with grief, thus breathes she forth her spite
 Against the unseen secrecy of night:

---

a *O, that* prone *lust should stain so pure a bed!*] See note b, p. 595, Vol. II.

b Till, like a jade, Self-will himself doth tire.] Compare, "Henry VIII." Act I. Sc. 1,—

"—— anger is like
A full-hot horse, who being allow'd his way,
Self-mettle tires him."

c — perplex'd—] This word has no longer the force it once possessed. With Shakespeare it meant *bewildered, distracted,* sometimes *frenzied:* thus in "Othello," Act V. Sc. 2,—

"—— but, being wrought,
Perplex'd in the extreme;"

and in "Cymbeline," Act III. Sc. 4,—

"—— one, but painted thus,
Would be interpreted a thing *perplex'd*
Beyond self-explication:"

d — convertite;] A "convertite" is a *penitent,* or *convert.*

e — scapes—] *Lapses, slips:* so in "The Winter's Tale," Act III. Sc. 3,—"What have we here? Mercy on 's, a barne; a very pretty barne!—sure, some *scape:* though I am not bookish, yet I can read waiting-gentlewoman in the *scape.*"

"O comfort-killing Night, image of hell!
Dim register and notary of shame!
Black stage for tragedies and murders fell![a]
Vast sin-concealing chaos! nurse of blame!
Blind muffled bawd! dark harbour for defame!
Grim cave of death! whispering conspirator
With close-tongu'd treason and the ravisher!

"O, hateful, vaporous, and foggy Night!
Since thou art guilty of my cureless crime,
Muster thy mists to meet the eastern light,
Make war against proportion'd course of time;
Or if thou wilt permit the sun to climb
His wonted height, yet ere he go to bed,
Knit poisonous clouds about his golden head.

"With rotten damps ravish the morning air;
Let their exhal'd unwholesome breaths make sick
The life of purity, the supreme fair,
Ere he arrive his weary noon-tide prick;
And let thy misty[b] vapours march so thick,
That in their smoky ranks his smother'd light
May set at noon, and make perpetual night.

"Were Tarquin Night (as he is but Night's child),
The silver-shining queen he would distain;
Her twinkling handmaids too, by him defil'd,
Through Night's black bosom should not peep again:
So should I have copartners in my pain;
And fellowship in woe doth woe assuage,[c]
As palmers' chat makes short their pilgrimage.

"Where now I have no one to blush with me,
To cross their arms, and hang their heads with mine,
To mask their brows, and hide their infamy;
But I alone alone must sit and pine,
Seasoning the earth with showers of silver brine,
Mingling my talk with tears, my grief with groans,
Poor wasting monuments of lasting moans.

"O Night, thou furnace of foul-reeking smoke,
Let not the jealous Day behold that face
Which underneath thy black all-hiding cloak
Immodestly lies martyr'd with disgrace!
Keep still possession of thy gloomy place,
That all the faults which in thy reign are made
May likewise be sepúlchred in thy shade!

"Make me not object to the tell-tale Day!
The light will show, charácter'd in my brow,
The story of sweet chastity's decay,
The impious breach of holy wedlock vow:
Yea, the illiterate, that know not how
To 'cipher what is writ in learned books,
Will quote[d] my loathsome trespass in my looks.

"The nurse, to still her child, will tell my story,
And fright her crying babe with Tarquin's name;
The orator, to deck his oratory,
Will couple my reproach to Tarquin's shame;
Feast-finding minstrels, tuning my defame,
Will tie the hearers to attend each line,
How Tarquin wronged me, I Collatine.

"Let my good name, that senseless reputation,
For Collatine's dear love be kept unspotted:
If that be made a theme for disputation,
The branches of another root are rotted,
And undeserv'd reproach to him allotted
That is as clear from this attaint of mine,
As I, ere this, was pure to Collatine.

"O unseen shame! invisible disgrace!
O unfelt sore! crest-wounding, private scar!
Reproach is stamp'd in Collatinus' face,
And Tarquin's eye may read the mot[e] afar,
How he in peace is wounded, not in war.
Alas, how many bear such shameful blows,
Which not themselves, but he that gives them knows!

"If, Collatine, thine honour lay in me,
From me by strong assault it is bereft.
My honey lost, and I, a drone-like bee,
Have no perfection of my summer left,
But robb'd and ransack'd by injurious theft:
In thy weak hive a wandering wasp hath crept,
And suck'd the honey which thy chaste bee kept.

"Yet am I guilty of thy honour's wrack,—
Yet for thy honour did I entertain him;[f]
Coming from thee, I could not put him back,
For it had been dishonour to disdain him:
Besides, of weariness he did complain him,
And talk'd of virtue;—O, unlook'd-for evil,
When virtue is profan'd in such a devil!

---

[a] Black stage for tragedies and murders fell!] See note (1), p. 332, Vol. I.

[b] — misty *vapours*—] The first quarto reads *musty;* but the subsequent copies rightly have "misty." In support of the latter Malone adduces the following passages from preceding stanzas in this poem,—

"Muster thy *mists* to meet the eastern light,"

and,—

"—— *misty* night
Covers the shame that follows such delight;"

to which Mr. Dyce has added a line still more to the purpose from "Venus and Adonis,"—

"Like *misty vapours* when they blot the sky."

[c] And fellowship in woe doth woe assuage,—] This sentiment occurs in "King Lear," Act III. Sc. 6,—

"But then the mind much sufferance doth o'erskip,
When grief hath mates, and bearing fellowship;"

and in "Romeo and Juliet," Act III. Sc. 2,—

"—— if sour woe delight in fellowship."

[d] *Will* quote—] Will *scan* or *note.* As in "Hamlet," Act II. Sc. 1,—

"I am sorry that with better heed and judgment,
I had not *quoted* him."

[e] — *the* mot—] The "mot" is the *motto,* or *word.* Thus in "Pericles," Act II. Sc. 2,—

"The *word,* Quod me alit, me *extinguit.*"

[f] *Yet am I* guilty *of thy honour's wrack,* &c.] Malone, in opposition to the old copies, reads, "Yet am I *guiltless,*" &c.; but Boswell shows very clearly that change was uncalled for: "She is reproaching herself, at first, for having received Tarquin's visit; but instantly defends herself by saying that she did it out of respect to her husband."

"Why should the worm intrude the maiden bud?
Or hateful cuckoos hatch in sparrows' nests?
Or toads infect fair founts with venom mud?
Or tyrant folly lurk in gentle breasts?
Or kings be breakers of their own behests?
  But no perfection is so absolute,
  That some impurity doth not pollute.

"The aged man that coffers-up his gold
Is plagu'd with cramps, and gouts and painful fits;
And scarce hath eyes his treasure to behold,
But like still-pining Tantalus he sits,
And useless barns the harvest of his wits;
  Having no other pleasure of his gain
  But torment that it cannot cure his pain.

"So then he hath it, when he cannot use it,
And leaves it to be master'd by his young,
Who in their pride do presently abuse it:
Their father was too weak, and they too strong,
To hold their cursed-blessed fortune long.
  The sweets we wish for turn to loathed sours,
  Even in the moment that we call them ours.

"Unruly blasts wait on the tender spring;[a]
Unwholesome weeds take root with precious flowers;
The adder hisses where the sweet birds sing;
What virtue breeds iniquity devours:
We have no good that we can say is ours,
  But ill-annexed Opportunity
  Or kills his life or else his quality.

"O Opportunity, thy guilt is great!
'T is thou that execut'st the traitor's treason;
Thou sett'st the wolf where he the lamb may get;
Whoever plots the sin, thou 'point'st the season;
'T is thou that spurn'st at right, at law, at reason;
  And in thy shady cell, where none may spy him,
  Sits Sin, to seize the souls that wander by him.

"Thou mak'st the vestal violate her oath;
Thou blow'st the fire when temperance is thaw'd;
Thou smother'st honesty, thou murder'st troth;
Thou foul abettor! thou notorious bawd!
Thou plantest scandal, and displacest laud:
  Thou ravisher, thou traitor, thou false thief,
  Thy honey turns to gall, thy joy to grief!

"Thy secret pleasure turns to open shame,
Thy private feasting to a public fast,
Thy smoothing titles to a ragged[b] name;
Thy sugar'd tongue to bitter wormwood taste:
Thy violent vanities can never last.
  How comes it, then, vile Opportunity,
  Being so bad, such numbers seek for thee?

"When wilt thou be the humble suppliant's friend,
And bring him where his suit may be obtain'd?
When wilt thou sort[c] an hour great strifes to end?
Or free that soul which wretchedness hath chain'd?
Give physic to the sick, ease to the pain'd?
  The poor, lame, blind, halt, creep, cry out for thee;
  But they ne'er meet with Opportunity.

"The patient dies while the physician sleeps;
The orphan pines while the oppressor feeds;
Justice is feasting while the widow weeps;
Advice is sporting while infection breeds;
Thou grant'st no time for charitable deeds:
  Wrath, envy, treason, rape, and murder's rages,
  Thy heinous hours wait on them as their pages.

"When Truth and Virtue have to do with thee
A thousand crosses keep them from thy aid:
They buy thy help; but Sin ne'er gives a fee,
He gratis comes; and thou art well appaid[d]
As well to hear as grant what he hath said.
  My Collatine would else have come to me
  When Tarquin did, but he was stay'd by thee.

"Guilty thou art of murder and of theft;
Guilty of perjury and subornation;
Guilty of treason, forgery, and shift;
Guilty of incest, that abomination:
An accessary by thine inclination
  To all sins past, and all that are to come,
  From the creation to the general doom.

"Mis-shapen Time, copesmate of ugly Night,
Swift-subtle post, carrier of grisly care,
Eater of youth, false slave to false delight,
Base watch of woes, sin's pack-horse, virtue's snare;
Thou nursest all, and murder'st all that are:
  O, hear me, then, injurious-shifting Time!
  Be guilty of my death, since of my crime.

"Why hath thy servant, Opportunity,
Betray'd the hours thou gav'st me to repose?
Cancell'd my fortunes, and enchained me
To endless date of never-ending woes?
Time's office is to fine[e] the hate of foes;
  To eat up errors by opinion bred,
  Not spend the dowry of a lawful bed.

"Time's glory is to calm contending kings,
To unmask falsehood, and bring truth to light,
To stamp the seal of time in aged things,
To wake the morn, and sentinel the night,
To wrong[f] the wronger till he render right,
  To ruinate proud buildings with thy hours,
  And smear with dust their glittering-golden towers;

"To fill with worm-holes stately monuments,
To feed oblivion with decay of things,
To blot old books and alter their contents,

[a] *Unruly blasts wait on the* tender spring;] See note f, p. 728.
[b] — *a* ragged *name;*] A *beggared* name.
[c] — sort *an hour*—] *Pick out*, or *choose*, or *fit* an hour: so in "Henry VI." Part I. Act II. Sc. 3,—

"I'll *sort* some other time to visit you;"

and in "Henry VI." Part III. Act V. Sc. 6,—

"—— thou keep'st me from the light;
But I will *sort* a pitchy day for thee."

[d] — appaid—] *Pleased, satisfied.*
[e] — *to* fine *the hate of foes;*] To *fine* is to *end*. So in "Much Ado about Nothing," Act I. Sc. 1,—"And the *fine* is (for the which I may go the finer), I will live and die a bachelor:" and in "All's Well that Ends Well," Act IV. Sc. 4,—

"—— the *fine's* the crown."

[f] *To* wrong *the wronger*—] Farmer proposed,—"To *wring* the wronger," &c.

To pluck the quills from ancient ravens' wings,
To dry the old oak's sap, and cherish springs,
To spoil antiquities of hammer'd steel,
And turn the giddy round of Fortune's wheel;

"To show the beldame daughters of her daughter,
To make the child a man, the man a child,
To slay the tiger that doth live by slaughter,
To tame the unicorn and lion wild,
To mock the subtle in themselves beguil'd;
To cheer the ploughman with increaseful crops,
And waste huge stones with little water-drops.

"Why work'st thou mischief in thy pilgrimage,
Unless thou couldst return to make amends?
One poor retiring [a] minute in an age
Would purchase thee a thousand-thousand friends,
Lending him wit that to bad debtors lends:
O, this dread night, wouldst thou one hour come back,
I could prevent this storm, and shun thy wrack!

"Thou ceaseless lackey to eternity,
With some mischance cross Tarquin in his flight:
Devise extremes beyond extremity,
To make him curse this cursed crimeful night:
Let ghastly shadows his lewd eyes affright;
And the dire thought of his committed evil
Shape every bush a hideous-shapeless devil.

"Disturb his hours of rest with restless trances,
Afflict him in his bed with bedrid groans;
Let there bechance him pitiful mischances,
To make him moan, but pity not his moans:
Stone him with harden'd hearts, harder than stones;
And let mild women to him lose their mildness,
Wilder to him than tigers in their wildness.

"Let him have time to tear his curled hair,[b]
Let him have time against himself to rave,
Let him have time of Time's help to despair,
Let him have time to live a loathed slave,
Let him have time a beggar's orts to crave;
And time to see one that by alms doth live
Disdain to him disdained scraps to give.

"Let him have time to see his friends his foes,
And merry fools to mock at him resort;
Let him have time to mark how slow time goes
In time of sorrow, and how swift and short
His time of folly and his time of sport;
And ever let his unrecalling crime
Have time to wail th' abusing of his time.

"O Time, thou tutor both to good and bad,
Teach me to curse him that thou taught'st this ill!
At his own shadow let the thief run mad,
Himself himself seek every hour to kill!
Such wretched hands such wretched blood should spill;

a — retiring *minute*—] *Returning* minute.
b — *his* curled hair,—] See note b, p. 653, of the present volume.
c *As* slanderous *death's-man*—] That is, as *ignominious*, or *branded* executioner.

For who so base would such an office have
As slanderous [c] death's-man to so base a slave?

"The baser is he, coming from a king,
To shame his hope with deeds degenerate:
The mightier man, the mightier is the thing
That makes him honour'd, or begets him hate;
For greatest scandal waits on greatest state.
The moon being clouded presently [d] is miss'd,
But little stars may hide them when they list.

"The crow may bathe his coal-black wings in mire,
And unperceiv'd fly with the filth away;
But if the like the snow-white swan desire,
The stain upon his silver down will stay.
Poor grooms are sightless night, kings glorious day.
Gnats are unnoted wheresoe'er they fly,
But eagles gaz'd upon with every eye.

"Out, idle words, servants to shallow fools!
Unprofitable sounds, weak arbitrators!
Busy yourselves in skill-contending schools,
Debate where leisure serves with dull debaters;
To trembling clients be you mediators:
For me, I force [e] not argument a straw,
Since that my case is past the help of law.

"In vain I rail at Opportunity,
At Time, at Tarquin, and uncheerful Night;
In vain I cavil with my infamy,
In vain I spurn at my confirm'd despite:
This helpless smoke of words doth me no right.
The remedy indeed to do me good,
Is to let forth my foul-defiled blood.

"Poor hand, why quiver'st thou at this decree?
Honour thyself to rid me of this shame;
For if I die, my honour lives in thee;
But if I live, thou liv'st in my defame:
Since thou couldst not defend thy loyal dame,
And wast afear'd to scratch her wicked foe,
Kill both thyself and her for yielding so."

This said, from her be-tumbled couch she starteth,
To find some desperate instrument of death:
But this no-slaughter-house no tool imparteth,
To make more vent for passage of her breath,
Which, thronging through her lips, so vanisheth
As smoke from Ætna, that in air consumes,
Or that which from discharged cannon fumes.

"In vain," quoth she, "I live, and seek in vain
Some happy mean to end a hapless life.
I fear'd by Tarquin's falchion to be slain,
Yet for the self-same purpose seek a knife:
But when I fear'd I was a loyal wife:
So am I now:—O no, that cannot be;
Of that true type hath Tarquin rifled me!

"O, that is gone for which I sought to live,
And therefore now I need not fear to die.
To clear this spot by death, at least I give

d — presently—] *Immediately*.
e *I force not*—] I *regard*, or *value* not: so in "Love's Labour's Lost," Act V. Sc. 2,—

"Your oath once broke, you *force* not to forswear."

A badge of fame to slander's livery ;
A dying life to living infamy :
  Poor helpless help, the treasure stol'n away,
  To burn the guiltless casket where it lay !

"Well, well, dear Collatine, thou shalt not know
The stained taste of violated troth ;
I will not wrong thy true affection so,
To flatter thee with an infringed oath ;
This bastard graff shall never come to growth :
  He shall not boast who did thy stock pollute
  That thou art doting father of his fruit.

"Nor shall he smile at thee in secret thought,
Nor laugh with his companions at thy state ;
But thou shalt know thy interest was not bought
Basely with gold, but stol'n from forth thy gate.
For me, I am the mistress of my fate,
  And with my trespass never will dispense,
  Till life to death acquit my forc'd offence.

"I will not poison thee with my attaint,
Nor fold my fault in cleanly-coin'd excuses ;
My sable ground of sin I will not paint,
To hide the truth of this false night's abuses :
My tongue shall utter all ; mine eyes like sluices,
  As from a mountain-spring that feeds a dale,
  Shall gush pure streams to purge my impure tale."

By this, lamenting Philomel had ended
The well-tun'd warble of her nightly sorrow,
And solemn night with slow-sad gait descended
To ugly hell ; when, lo, the blushing morrow
Lends light to all fair eyes that light will borrow ;
  But cloudy Lucrece shames herself to see,
  And therefore still in night would cloister'd be.

Revealing day through every cranny spies,
And seems to point her out where she sits weeping ;
To whom she sobbing speaks : "O, eye of eyes,
Why pry'st thou through my window ? leave thy peeping ;
Mock with thy tickling beams eyes that are sleeping ;
  Brand not my forehead with thy piercing light,
  For day hath nought to do what's done by night."

Thus cavils she with everything she sees :
True grief is fond and testy as a child,
Who wayward once, his mood with nought agrees.
Old woes, not infant sorrows, bear them mild ;
Continuance tames the one ; the other wild,
  Like an unpractis'd swimmer plunging still,
  With too much labour drowns for want of skill.

So she, deep-drenched in a sea of care,
Holds disputation with each thing she views,
And to herself all sorrow doth compare ;
No object but her passion's strength renews ;
And as one shifts, another straight ensues :
  Sometime her grief is dumb, and hath no words ;
  Sometime 't is mad, and too much talk affords.

The little birds that tune their morning's joy
Make her moans mad with their sweet melody :[a]
For mirth doth search the bottom of annoy ;
Sad souls are slain in merry company ;
Grief best is pleas'd with grief's society :
  True sorrow then is feelingly suffic'd
  When with like semblance it is sympathiz'd.

'T is double death to drown in ken of shore ;
He ten times pines that pines beholding food ;
To see the salve doth make the wound ache more ;
Great grief grieves most at that would do it good ;
Deep woes roll forward like a gentle flood,
  Who, being stopp'd, the bounding banks o'erflows ;
  Grief dallied with nor law nor limit knows.

"You mocking birds," quoth she, "your tunes entomb
Within your hollow-swelling feather'd breasts,
And in my hearing be you mute and dumb ![b]
My restless discord loves no stops nor rests ;[c]
A woeful hostess brooks not merry guests :
  Relish your nimble notes to pleasing ears ;
  Distress likes dumps[d] when time is kept with tears.

"Come, Philomel, that sing'st of ravishment,
Make thy sad grove in my dishevell'd hair :
As the dank earth weeps at thy languishment,
So I at each sad strain will strain a tear,
And with deep groans the diapason bear ;
  For burden-wise I'll hum on Tarquin still,
  While thou on Tereus descant'st[e] better skill.

"And whiles against a thorn thou bear'st thy part,
To keep thy sharp woes waking, wretched I,
To imitate thee well, against my heart
Will fix a sharp knife, to affright mine eye ;
Who, if it wink, shall thereon fall and die.
  These means, as frets upon an instrument,
  Shall tune our heart-strings to true languishment.

"And for, poor bird, thou sing'st not in the day,
As shaming any eye should thee behold,
Some dark-deep desert, seated from the way,

---

[a] The little birds that tune their morning's joy
Make her moans mad with their sweet melody :]

This may have been the germ of Burns' beautiful lines in *The Banks o' Doon* :—

"How can ye chant, ye little birds,
And I sae weary, fu' o' care !
Thou'lt break my heart, thou warbling bird,
That wantons thro' the flowering thorn :
Thou minds me o' departed joys,
Departed, never to return !"

[b] — *be you* mute and dumb !] To avoid this pleonasm, the octavo of 1616 has, "— be you *ever* dumb ;" but compare, "Hamlet," Act II. Sc. , —

"Or given my heart a working, *mute and dumb*."

[c] — *no* stops *nor* rests ;] "Stops" and "rests" are technical terms in music. So in "Hamlet," Act III. Sc. 2, —"Look you, these are the *stops*." And in "Romeo and Juliet," Act II. Sc. 4,—"rests me his minim *rest*."

[d] — dumps —] See note [d], p. 204, Vol. I.

[e] — descant'st —] See note [b], p. 7, Vol. I.

That knows not parching heat nor freezing cold,
We will find out; and there we will unfold
To creatures stern sad tunes, to change their kinds:
Since men prove beasts let beasts bear gentle minds."

As the poor frighted deer, that stands at gaze,
Wildly determining which way to fly,
Or one encompass'd with a winding maze,
That cannot tread the way out readily;
So with herself is she in mutiny,
To live or die which of the twain were better,
When life is sham'd, and death reproach's debtor.

"To kill myself," quoth she, "alack! what were it,
But with my body my poor soul's pollution?
They that lose half with greater patience bear it
Than they whose whole is swallowed in confusion.
That mother tries a merciless conclusion
Who, having two sweet babes, when death takes one,
Will slay the other, and be nurse to none.

"My body or my soul, which was the dearer,
When the one pure, the other made divine?
Whose love of either to myself was nearer,
When both were kept for heaven and Collatine?
Ay me! the bark peel'd from the lofty pine,
His leaves will wither, and his sap decay;
So must my soul, her bark being peel'd away.

"Her house is sack'd, her quiet interrupted,
Her mansion batter'd by the enemy;
Her sacred temple spotted, spoil'd, corrupted,
Grossly engirt with daring infamy:
Then let it not be call'd impiety,
If in this blemish'd fort I make some hole
Through which I may convey this troubled soul.

"Yet die I will not till my Collatine
Have heard the cause of my untimely death;
That he may vow, in that sad hour of mine,
Revenge on him that made me stop my breath.
My stained blood to Tarquin I'll bequeath,
Which by him tainted shall for him be spent,
And as his due, writ in my testament.

"My honour I'll bequeath unto the knife
That wounds my body so dishonoured.
'T is honour to deprive dishonour'd life;
The one will live, the other being dead:
So of shame's ashes shall my fame be bred;
For in my death I murder shameful scorn:
My shame so dead, mine honour is new-born.

"Dear lord of that dear jewel I have lost,
What legacy shall I bequeath to thee?
My resolution, love, shall be thy boast,
By whose example thou reveng'd mayst be.
How Tarquin must be us'd, read it in me:
Myself, thy friend, will kill myself, thy foe,
And, for my sake, serve thou false Tarquin so.

"This brief abridgment of my will I make:—
My soul and body to the skies and ground;
My resolution, husband, do thou take;
Mine honour be the knife's that makes my wound;
My shame be his that did my fame confound;
And all my fame that lives disbursed be
To those that live, and think no shame of me.

"Thou, Collatine, shalt oversee[a] this will;
How I was overseen that thou shalt see it!
My blood shall wash the slander of mine ill;
My life's foul deed, my life's fair end shall free it.
Faint not, faint heart, but stoutly say, 'So be it.'
Yield to my hand; my hand shall conquer thee:
Thou dead, both die, and both shall victors be."

This plot of death when sadly she had laid,
And wip'd the brinish pearl from her bright eyes,
With untun'd tongue she hoarsely call'd her maid,
Whose swift obedience to her mistress hies;
For fleet-wing'd duty with thought's feathers flies.
Poor Lucrece' cheeks unto her maid seem so
As winter meads when sun doth melt their snow.

Her mistress she doth give demure good-morrow,
With soft-slow tongue, true mark of modesty,
And sorts a sad look to her lady's sorrow,
For why her face wore sorrow's livery;
But durst not ask of her audaciously
Why her two suns were cloud-eclipsed so,
Nor why her fair cheeks over-wash'd with woe.

But as the earth doth weep, the sun being set,
Each flower moisten'd like a melting eye;
Even so the maid with swelling drops 'gan wet
Her circled eyne, enforc'd by sympathy
Of those fair suns set in her mistress' sky,
Who in a salt-wav'd ocean quench their light,
Which makes the maid weep like the dewy night.

A pretty[b] while these pretty creatures stand,
Like ivory conduits coral cisterns filling:
One justly weeps; the other takes in hand
No cause, but company, of her drops spilling:
Their gentle sex to weep are often willing;
Grieving themselves to guess at others' smarts,
And then they drown their eyes, or break their hearts.

For men have marble, women waxen, minds,
And therefore are they form'd as marble will;
The weak oppress'd, the impression of strange kinds

[a] *Thou, Collatine, shall* oversee *this will;*] "*Overseers* were frequently added in Wills from the superabundant caution of our ancestors; but our law acknowledges no such persons, nor are they (as contradistinguished from executors) invested with any legal right whatever. In some old Wills the term *overseer* is used instead of executor."—MALONE.

It is noticeable that Shakespeare in his own will appoints John Hall, his son-in-law, and Susanna his eldest daughter, executors; and Thomas Russell and Francis Collins *overseers*.

[b] *A* pretty *while*—] A *petty* or *little* while.

Is form'd in them by force, by fraud, or skill:[a]
Then call them not the authors of their ill,
No more than wax shall be accounted evil,
Wherein is stamp'd the semblance of a devil.

Their smoothness, like a goodly champaign plain,
Lays open all the little worms that creep;
In men, as in a rough-grown grove, remain
Cave-keeping evils that obscurely sleep:
Through crystal walls each little mote will peep:
Though men can cover crimes with bold stern looks,
Poor women's faces are their own faults' books.

No man inveigh against the wither'd flower,
But chide rough winter that the flower hath kill'd:
Not that devour'd, but that which doth devour,
Is worthy blame. O, let it not be hild[b]
Poor women's faults that they are so fulfill'd[c]
With men's abuses! those proud lords, to blame,
Make weak-made women tenants to their shame.

The precedent whereof in Lucrece' view,
Assail'd by night with circumstances strong
Of present death, and shame that might ensue
By that her death, to do her husband wrong:
Such danger to resistance did belong,
That dying fear through all her body spread;
And who cannot abuse a body dead?

By this, mild patience bid fair Lucrece speak
To the poor counterfeit of her complaining:
"My girl," quoth she, "on what occasion break
Those tears from thee, that down thy cheeks are raining?
If thou dost weep for grief of my sustaining,
Know, gentle wench, it small avails my mood:
If tears could help, mine own would do me good.

"But tell me, girl, when went"—and there she stay'd
Till after a deep groan—"Tarquin from hence?"
"Madam, ere I was up," replied the maid,
"The more to blame my sluggard negligence:
Yet with the fault I thus far can dispense,—
Myself was stirring ere the break of day,
And, ere I rose, was Tarquin gone away.

"But, lady, if your maid may be so bold,
She would request to know your heaviness."
"O, peace!" quoth Lucrece; "if it should be told,
The repetition cannot make it less;
For more it is than I can well express:
And that deep torture may be call'd a hell,
When more is felt than one hath power to tell.

"Go, get me hither paper, ink, and pen,—
Yet save that labour, for I have them here.
What should I say?—One of my husband's men
Bid thou be ready, by and by, to bear
A letter to my lord, my love, my dear:
Bid him with speed prepare to carry it;
The cause craves haste, and it will soon be writ."

Her maid is gone, and she prepares to write,
First hovering o'er the paper with her quill:
Conceit and grief an eager combat fight;
What wit sets down is blotted straight with will;
This is too curious-good,[d] this blunt and ill:
Much like a press of people at a door,
Throng her inventions, which shall go before.

At last she thus begins:—"Thou worthy lord
Of that unworthy wife that greeteth thee,
Health to thy person! next vouchsafe t' afford
(If ever, love, thy Lucrece thou wilt see)
Some present speed to come and visit me.
So I commend me from our house in grief:
My woes are tedious, though my words are brief."

Here folds she up the tenour of her woe,
Her certain sorrow writ uncertainly.
By this short schedule Collatine may know
Her grief, but not her grief's true quality;
She dares not thereof make discovery,
Lest he should hold it her own gross abuse,
Ere she with blood had stain'd her stain'd excuse.

Besides, the life and feeling of her passion
She hoards, to spend when he is by to hear her;
When signs and groans and tears may grace the fashion
Of her disgrace, the better so to clear her
From that suspicion which the world might bear her.
To shun this blot, she would not blot the letter
With words, till action might become them better.

To see sad sights moves more than hear them told;
For then the eye interprets to the ear
The heavy motion that it doth behold:
When every part a part of woe doth bear,
'T is but a part of sorrow that we hear:
Deep sounds[e] make lesser noise than shallow fords,
And sorrow ebbs, being blown with wind of words.

Her letter now is seal'd, and on it writ,
"At Ardea to my lord with more than haste."
The post attends, and she delivers it,

---

[a] —— the impression of strange kinds
Is form'd in them by force, by fraud, or skill: &c.]
"Kinds" here signifies *natures*. For the sentiment, compare the following passage in "Twelfth Night," Act II. Sc. 2,—
"How easy is it for the proper-false
In women's waxen hearts to set their forms!
Alas, our frailty is the cause, not we!
For, such as we are made of, such we be."

[b] — hild—] An old form of *held*, adopted for the sake of the rhyme.

[c] — fulfill'd—] *Filled to repletion.*

[d] — *too* curious-good,—] Too *fastidiously* precise.

[e] *Deep* sounds *make lesser noise than shallow fords,*—] Malone conjectured, and with much plausibility, that the poet wrote,—"Deep *floods*," &c.

Charging the sour-fac'd groom to hie as fast
As lagging fowls before the northern blast:
Speed more than speed but dull and slow she deems:
Extremity still urgeth such extremes.

The homely villain [a] court'sies to her low;
And, blushing on her, with a steadfast eye
Receives the scroll without or yea or no,
And forth with bashful innocence doth hie.
But they whose guilt within their bosoms lie
Imagine every eye beholds their blame;
For Lucrece thought he blush'd to see her shame:

When, silly groom! God wot, it was defect
Of spirit, life, and bold audacity.
Such harmless creatures have a true respect
To talk in deeds, while others saucily
Promise more speed, but do it leisurely:
Even so this pattern of the worn-out age
Pawn'd honest looks, but laid no words to gage.

His kindled duty kindled her mistrust,
That two red fires in both their faces blaz'd;
She thought he blush'd, as knowing Tarquin's lust,
And, blushing with him, wistly on him gaz'd;
Her earnest eye did make him more amaz'd:
The more she saw the blood his cheeks replenish,
The more she thought he spied in her some blemish.

But long she thinks till he return again,
And yet the duteous vassal scarce is gone.
The weary time she cannot entertain,
For now 't is stale to sigh, to weep, and groan:
So woe hath wearied woe, moan tired moan,
That she her plaints a little while doth stay,
Pausing for means to mourn some newer way.

At last she calls to mind where hangs a piece
Of skilful painting, made for Priam's Troy;
Before the which is drawn the power of Greece,
For Helen's rape the city to destroy,
Threat'ning cloud-kissing Ilion with annoy;
Which the conceited [b] painter drew so proud,
As heaven, it seem'd, to kiss the turrets bow'd.

A thousand lamentable objects there,
In scorn of nature, art gave lifeless life:
Many a dry drop seem'd a weeping tear,
Shed for the slaughter'd husband by the wife:
The red blood reek'd to show the painter's strife;
And dying eyes gleam'd forth their ashy lights,
Like dying coals burnt out in tedious nights.

There might you see the labouring pioneer
Begrim'd with sweat, and smeared all with dust;
And from the towers of Troy there would appear
The very eyes of men through loop-holes thrust,
Gazing upon the Greeks with little lust:
Such sweet observance in this work was had,
That one might see those far-off eyes look sad.

In great commanders grace and majesty
You might behold, triúmphing in their faces;
In youth, quick bearing and dexterity;
And here and there the painter interlaces
Pale cowards, marching on with trembling paces
Which heartless peasants did so well resemble,
That one would swear he saw them quake and tremble.

In Ajax and Ulysses, O, what art
Of physiognomy might one behold!
The face of either 'cipher'd either's heart;
Their face their manners most expressly told:
In Ajax' eyes blunt rage and rigour roll'd;
But the mild glance that sly Ulysses lent,
Show'd deep regard and smiling government.[c]

There pleading might you see grave Nestor stand,
As 't were encouraging the Greeks to fight;
Making such sober action with his hand
That it beguil'd attention, charm'd the sight:
In speech, it seem'd, his beard all silver white
Wagg'd up and down, and from his lips did fly
Thin winding breath, which purl'd up to the sky.

About him were a press of gaping faces,
Which seem'd to swallow up his sound advice;
All jointly listening, but with several graces,
As if some mermaid did their ears entice;
Some high, some low; the painter was so nice,
The scalps of many, almost hid behind,
To jump up higher seem'd, to mock the mind.

Here one man's hand lean'd on another's head,
His nose being shadow'd by his neighbour's ear;
Here one, being throng'd,[d] bears back, all boll'n and red;
Another, smother'd, seems to pelt and swear;
And in their rage such signs of rage they bear,
As, but for loss of Nestor's golden words,
It seem'd they would debate with angry swords.

For much imaginary work was there;
Conceit deceitful, so compact, so kind,[e]
That for Achilles' image stood his spear,
Grip'd in an armed hand; himself, behind,
Was left unseen, save to the eye of mind:
A hand, a foot, a face, a leg, a head,
Stood for the whole to be imagined.

And from the walls of strong-besieged Troy
When their brave hope, bold Hector, march'd to field,
Stood many Trojan mothers, sharing joy
To see their youthful sons bright weapons wield;
And to their hope they such odd action yield,[f]

[a] — villain—] *Slave.*
[b] — conceited—] *Apprehensive, conceptive.*
[c] — deep regard and smiling government.] Profound observation and complacent self-control.
[d] — *being* throng'd,—] Throng'd, in the same sense of *crush'd*, or *weighed down*, occurs in "Pericles," Act I. Sc. 1,—
"The blind mole casts
Copp'd hills towards heaven, to tell the earth is *throng'd*
By man's oppression."
[e] — kind.—] *Natural.*
[f] *And to their* hope *they such* odd *action* yield,—] The meaning appears to be, that to their hope (bold Hector) they exhibited such *peculiar*, or *doubtful* action, &c.

That through their light joy seemed to appear
(Like bright things stain'd) a kind of heavy fear.

And from the strand of Dardan, where they fought,
To Simois' reedy banks the red blood ran,
Whose waves to imitate the battle sought
With swelling ridges; and their ranks began
To break upon the galled shore, and than [a]
Retire again, till, meeting greater ranks,
They join, and shoot their foam at Simois' banks.

To this well-painted piece is Lucrece come,
To find a face where all distress is stell'd.[b]
Many she sees where cares have carved some,
But none where all distress and dolour dwell'd,
Till she despairing Hecuba beheld,
Staring on Priam's wounds with her old eyes,
Which bleeding under Pyrrhus' proud foot lies.

In her the painter had anatomiz'd
Time's ruin, beauty's wreck, and grim care's reign:
Her cheeks with chaps and wrinkles were disguis'd;
Of what she was no semblance did remain:
Her blue blood chang'd to black in every vein,
Wanting the spring that those shrunk pipes had fed,
Show'd life imprison'd in a body dead.

On this sad shadow Lucrece spends her eyes,
And shapes her sorrow to the beldam's woes,
Who nothing wants to answer her but cries,
And bitter words to ban her cruel foes:
The painter was no god to lend her those;
And therefore Lucrece swears he did her wrong,
To give her so much grief, and not a tongue.

"Poor instrument," quoth she, "without a sound,
I'll tune thy woes with my lamenting tongue;
And drop sweet balm in Priam's painted wound,
And rail on Pyrrhus that hath done him wrong;
And with my tears quench Troy that burns so long;
And with my knife scratch out the angry eyes
Of all the Greeks that are thine enemies.

"Show me the strumpet that began this stir,
That with my nails her beauty I may tear.
Thy heat of lust, fond Paris, did incur
This load of wrath that burning Troy doth bear:
Thy eye kindled the fire that burneth here;
And here in Troy, for trespass of thine eye,
The sire, the son, the dame, and daughter die.

"Why should the private pleasure of some one
Become the public plague of many mo?
Let sin, alone committed, light alone
Upon his head that hath transgressed so;
Let guiltless souls be freed from guilty woe:
For one's offence why should so many fall,
To plague a private sin in general?

"Lo, here weeps Hecuba, here Priam dies,
Here manly Hector faints, here Troilus swounds,
Here friend by friend in bloody channel lies,
And friend to friend gives unadvised wounds,
And one man's lust these many lives confounds:
Had doting Priam check'd his son's desire,
Troy had been bright with fame, and not with fire."

Here feelingly she weeps Troy's painted woes:
For sorrow, like a heavy-hanging bell,
Once set on ringing, with his own weight goes;
Then little strength rings out the doleful knell:
So Lucrece, set a-work, sad tales doth tell
To pencill'd pensiveness and colour'd sorrow;
She lends them words, and she their looks doth borrow.

She throws her eyes about the painting round,
And whom she finds forlorn she doth lament.
At last she sees a wretched image bound,
That piteous looks to Phrygian shepherds lent;
His face, though full of cares, yet show'd content.
Onward to Troy with the blunt swains he goes,
So mild, that Patience seem'd to scorn his woes.

In him the painter labour'd with his skill
To hide deceit, and give the harmless show
An humble gait, calm looks, eyes wailing still,
A brow unbent, that seem'd to welcome woe;
Cheeks neither red nor pale, but mingled so
That blushing red no guilty instance [c] gave,
Nor ashy pale the fear that false hearts have.

But, like a constant and confirmed devil,
He entertain'd a show so seeming just,
And therein so ensconc'd his secret evil,
That jealousy itself could not mistrust
False-creeping craft and perjury should thrust
Into so bright a day such black-fac'd storms,
Or blot with hell-born sin such saint-like forms.

The well-skill'd workman this mild image drew
For perjured Sinon, whose enchanting story
The credulous old Priam after slew;
Whose words, like wild-fire, burnt the shining glory
Of rich-built Ilion, that the skies were sorry,
And little stars shot from their fixed places,
When their glass fell wherein they view'd their faces.

This picture she advisedly perus'd,
And chid the painter for his wondrous skill,
Saying, some shape in Sinon's was abus'd;
So fair a form lodg'd not a mind so ill:
And still on him she gaz'd, and gazing still,
Such signs of truth in his plain face she spied,
That she concludes the picture was belied.

---

a — than—] This old orthography of *then*, is adopted, like that of *hild* in a former stanza, to meet the requirements of the rhyme.

b — stell'd.] *Fixed.*

c — instance—] *Indication* or *proof.*

"It cannot be," quoth she, "that so much guile"—
She would have said "can lurk in such a look;"
But Tarquin's shape came in her mind the while,
And from her tongue "can lurk" from "cannot" took:
"It cannot be," she in that sense forsook,
And turn'd it thus,—"It cannot be, I find,
But such a face should bear a wicked mind:

"For even as subtle Sinon here is painted,
So sober-sad, so weary, and so mild,
(As if with grief or travail he had fainted)
To me came Tarquin armed; so beguil'd[a]
With outward honesty, but yet defil'd
With inward vice: as Priam him did cherish,
So did I Tarquin; so my Troy did perish.

"Look, look, how listening Priam wets his eyes,
To see those borrow'd tears that Sinon sheds!
Priam, why art thou old, and yet not wise?
For every tear he falls a Trojan bleeds:
His eye drops fire, no water thence proceeds;
Those round clear pearls of his, that move thy pity,
Are balls of quenchless fire to burn thy city.

"Such devils steal effects from lightless hell;
For Sinon in his fire doth quake with cold,
And in that cold hot-burning fire doth dwell;
These contraries such unity do hold,
Only to flatter fools, and make them bold:
So Priam's trust false Sinon's tears doth flatter,
That he finds means to burn his Troy with water."

Here, all enrag'd, such passion her assails,
That patience is quite beaten from her breast.
She tears the senseless Sinon with her nails,
Comparing him to that unhappy guest
Whose deed hath made herself herself detest:
At last she smilingly with this gives o'er;
"Fool! fool!" quoth she, "his wounds will not be sore."

Thus ebbs and flows the current of her sorrow,
And time doth weary time with her complaining.
She looks for night, and then she longs for morrow,
And both she thinks too long with her remaining:
Short time seems long in sorrow's sharp sustaining:
Though woe be heavy, yet it seldom sleeps;
And they that watch see time how slow it creeps.

Which all this time hath overslipp'd her thought,
That she with painted images hath spent;
Being from the feeling of her own grief brought
By deep surmise of others' detriment;
Losing her woes in shows of discontent.
It easeth some, though none it ever cur'd,
To think their dolour others have endur'd.

But now the mindful messenger, come back,
Brings home his lord and other company;
Who finds his Lucrece clad in mourning black;
And round about her tear-distained eye
Blue circles stream'd, like rainbows in the sky:
These water-galls[b] in her dim element
Foretell new storms to those already spent.

Which when her sad-beholding husband saw,
Amazedly in her sad face he stares:
Her eyes, though sod in tears, look'd red and raw,
Her lively colour kill'd with deadly cares.
He hath no power to ask her how she fares;
But stood, like old acquaintance in a trance,
Met far from home, wondering each other's chance.

At last he takes her by the bloodless hand,
And thus begins: "What uncouth[c] ill event
Hath thee befall'n, that thou dost trembling stand?
Sweet love, what spite hath thy fair colour spent?
Why art thou thus attir'd in discontent?
Unmask, dear-dear, this moody heaviness,
And tell thy grief, that we may give redress."

Three times with sighs she gives her sorrow fire,
Ere once she can discharge one word of woe:[d]
At length address'd[e] to answer his desire,
She modestly prepares to let them know
Her honour is ta'en prisoner by the foe;
While Collatine and his consorted lords
With sad attention long to hear her words.

And now this pale swan in her watery nest
Begins the sad dirge of her certain ending:
"Few words," quoth she, "shall fit the trespass best,
Where no excuse can give the fault amending:
In me more woes than words are now depending;
And my laments would be drawn out too long,
To tell them all with one poor tired tongue.

"Then be this all the task it hath to say:—
Dear husband, in the interest of thy bed
A stranger came, and on that pillow lay
Where thou wast wont to rest thy weary head;
And what wrong else may be imagined
By foul enforcement might be done to me,
From that, alas! thy Lucrece is not free.

"For in the dreadful dead of dark midnight,
With shining falchion in my chamber came
A creeping creature, with a flaming light,
And softly cried, 'Awake, thou Roman dame,
And entertain my love; else lasting shame
On thee and thine this night I will inflict,
If thou my love's desire do contradict.

"'For some hard-favour'd groom of thine,' quoth he,
'Unless thou yoke thy liking to my will,
I'll murder straight, and then I'll slaughter thee,

[a] — so beguil'd—] *So disguised*, or *so masked;* unless Shakespeare here confounds the passive and active participle and uses "beguil'd" for *beguiling*. The old text reads,—"*to* beguild," &c.

[b] — water-galls—] *Secondary rainbows.*

[c] — uncouth—] *Unknown, strange.*

[d] Three times with sighs she gives her sorrow fire,
Ere once she can discharge one word of woe:]
The allusion here is to the manner of discharging ancient fire-arms by means of a match.

[e] — address'd—] *Prepared, ready.*

And swear I found you where you did fulfil
The loathsome act of lust, and so did kill
The lechers in their deed: this act will be
My fame, and thy perpetual infamy.'

"With this, I did begin to start and cry;
And then against my heart he set his sword,
Swearing, unless I took all patiently,
I should not live to speak another word;
So should my shame still rest upon record,
And never be forgot in mighty Rome
Th' adulterate death of Lucrece and her groom.

"Mine enemy was strong, my poor self weak,
And far the weaker with so strong a fear:
My bloody judge forbade my tongue to speak;
No rightful plea might plead for justice there:
His scarlet lust came evidence to swear
That my poor beauty had purloin'd his eyes;
And when the judge is robb'd, the prisoner dies.

"O, teach me how to make mine own excuse!
Or, at the least, this refuge let me find,—
Though my gross blood be stain'd with this abuse,
Immaculate and spotless is my mind;
That was not forc'd; that never was inclin'd
To accessory yieldings, but still pure
Doth in her poison'd closet yet endure."

Lo, here, the hopeless merchant of this loss,
With head declin'd, and voice damm'd up with woe,
With sad-set eyes, and wretched arms across,
From lips new-waxen pale begins to blow
The grief away that stops his answer so:
But, wretched as he is, he strives in vain;
What he breathes out his breath drinks up again.

As through an arch the violent-roaring tide
Outruns the eye that doth behold his haste,
Yet in the eddy boundeth in his pride
Back to the strait that forc'd him on so fast;
In rage sent out, recall'd in rage, being past:
Even so his sighs, his sorrows, make a saw,
To push grief on, and back the same grief draw.

Which speechless woe of his poor she attendeth,
And his untimely frenzy thus awaketh:
"Dear lord, thy sorrow to my sorrow lendeth
Another power; no flood by raining slaketh.
My woe too sensible thy passion maketh
More feeling-painful: let it, then, suffice
To drown one woe, one pair of weeping eyes.

"And for my sake, when I might charm thee so,
For she that was thy Lucrece,—now attend me:
Be suddenly revenged on my foe,
Thine, mine, his own: suppose thou dost defend me
From what is past; the help that thou shalt lend me
Comes all too late, yet let the traitor die;
For sparing justice feeds iniquity.

"But ere I name him, you, fair lords," quoth she,
Speaking to those that came with Collatine,
"Shall plight your honourable faiths to me,
With swift pursuit to venge this wrong of mine;
For 't is a meritorious fair design
To chase injustice with revengeful arms:
Knights, by their oaths, should right poor ladies' harms."

At this request, with noble disposition
Each present lord began to promise aid,
As bound in knighthood to her imposition,
Longing to hear the hateful foe bewray'd:
But she, that yet her sad task hath not said,
The protestation stops. "O, speak," quoth she,
"How may this forced stain be wip'd from me?

"What is the quality of mine offence?
Being constrain'd with dreadful circumstance,
May my pure mind with the foul act dispense?
My low-declined honour to advance,
May any terms acquit me from this chance?
The poison'd fountain clears itself again;
And why not I from this compelled stain?"

With this, they all at once began to say,
Her body's stain her mind untainted clears;
While with a joyless smile she turns away
The face, that map which deep impression bears
Of hard misfortune, carv'd in it with tears.
"No, no," quoth she, "no dame, hereafter living,
By my excuse shall claim excuse's giving." [a]

Here with a sigh, as if her heart would break,
She throws forth Tarquin's name: "He! he!" she says,
But more than "he!" her poor tongue could not speak;
Till after many accents and delays,
Untimely breathings, sick and short assays,
She utters this, "He, he, fair lords, 't is he,
That guides this hand to give this wound to me!"

Even here she sheathed in her harmless breast
A harmful knife, that thence her soul unsheath'd:
That blow did bail it from the deep unrest
Of that polluted prison where it breath'd:
Her contrite sighs unto the clouds bequeath'd
Her winged sprite, and through her wounds doth fly
Life's lasting date from cancell'd destiny.

Stone-still astonish'd [b] with this deadly deed,
Stood Collatine and all his lordly crew;
Till Lucrece' father, that beholds her bleed,
Himself on her self-slaughter'd body threw;
And from the purple fountain Brutus drew
The murderous knife, and, as it left the place,
Her blood, in poor revenge, held it in chase;

[a] —— "no dame, hereafter living,
By my excuse shall claim excuse's giving."]
Compare "— *nec ulla deinde impudica exemplo Lucretiæ* vivet." Liv. lib. i. c. 58.

[b] — astonish'd—] To say we are *astonished* expresses little more now than that we are *surprised*, but formerly the meaning of *astonish* was in nearer accordance with its etymology, *attonare*, *thunderstruck*. So in Pliny, N. H. Vol. I. p. 261. "The crampe-fish, torped, knoweth her own force and power; and being herself not benummed is able to *astonish* others."

And bubbling from her breast, it doth divide
In two slow rivers, that the crimson blood
Circles her body in on every side,
Who, like a late-sack'd island, vastly stood
Bare and unpeopled in this fearful flood.
Some of her blood still pure and red remain'd,
And some look'd black, and that false Tarquin stain'd.

About the mourning and congealed face
Of that black blood a watery rigol[a] goes,
Which seems to weep upon the tainted place:
And ever since, as pitying Lucrece' woes,
Corrupted blood some watery token shows;
And blood untainted still doth red abide,
Blushing at that which is so putrified.

"Daughter, dear daughter," old Lucretius cries,
"That life was mine which thou hast here depriv'd.[b]
If in the child the father's image lies,
Where shall I live now Lucrece is unliv'd?
Thou wast not to this end from me deriv'd.
If children pre-decease progenitors,
We are their offspring, and they none of ours.

"Poor broken glass, I often did behold
In thy sweet semblance my old age new born;
But now that fair-fresh mirror, dim and old,
Shows me a bare-bon'd death by time outworn:
O, from thy cheeks my image thou hast torn,
And shiver'd all the beauty of my glass,
That I no more can see what once I was!

"O time, cease thou thy course, and last no longer,
If they surcease to be that should survive!
Shall rotten death make conquest of the stronger,
And leave the faltering feeble souls alive?
The old bees die, the young possess their hive:
Then live, sweet Lucrece, live again, and see
Thy father die, and not thy father thee!"

By this, starts Collatine as from a dream,
And bids Lucretius give his sorrow place;
And then in key-cold Lucrece' bleeding stream
He falls, and bathes the pale fear in his face,
And counterfeits to die with her a space;
Till manly shame bids him possess his breath,
And live to be revenged on her death.

The deep vexation of his inward soul
Hath serv'd a dumb arrest upon his tongue;
Who, mad that sorrow should his use control,
Or keep him from heart-easing words so long,
Begins to talk; but through his lips do throng
Weak words so thick,[c] come in his poor heart's aid,
That no man could distinguish what he said.

Yet sometime, "Tarquin," was pronounced plain,
But through his teeth, as if the name he tore.
This windy tempest, till it blow up rain,
Held back his sorrow's tide, to make it more;
At last it rains, and busy winds give o'er:
Then son and father weep with equal strife
Who should weep most, for daughter or for wife.

The one doth call her his, the other his,
Yet neither may possess the claim they lay.
The father says, "She's mine." "O, mine she is!"
Replies her husband: "do not take away
My sorrow's interest; let no mourner say
He weeps for her, for she was only mine,
And only must be wail'd by Collatine."

"O," quoth Lucretius, "I did give that life
Which she too early and too late[d] hath spill'd!"
"Woe, woe," quoth Collatine, "she was my wife,
I ow'd her, and 't is mine that she hath kill'd!"
"My daughter!" and "my wife!" with clamours fill'd
The dispers'd air, who, holding Lucrece' life,
Answer'd their cries, "my daughter!" and "my wife!"

Brutus, who pluck'd the knife from Lucrece' side,
Seeing such emulation in their woe,
Began to clothe his wit in state and pride,
Burying in Lucrece' wound his folly's show.
He with the Romans was esteemed so
As silly-jeering idiots are with kings,
For sportive words and uttering foolish things.

But now he throws that shallow habit by
Wherein deep policy did him disguise;
And arm'd his long-hid wits advisedly,
To check the tears in Collatinus' eyes.
"Thou wronged lord of Rome," quoth he, "arise;
Let my unsounded self, suppos'd a fool,
Now set thy long-experienc'd wit to school.

"Why, Collatine, is woe the cure for woe?
Do wounds help[e] wounds, or grief help grievous deeds?
Is it revenge to give thyself a blow
For his foul act by whom thy fair wife bleeds?
Such childish humour from weak minds proceeds:
Thy wretched wife mistook the matter so,
To slay herself, that should have slain her foe.

"Courageous Roman, do not steep thy heart
In such relenting dew of lamentations,
But kneel with me, and help to bear thy part,
To rouse our Roman gods with invocations,
That they will suffer these abominations,

---

[a] — rigol—] See note g, p. 612, Vol. I.

[b] — depriv'd.] *Deposed;* as in "Hamlet," Act I. Sc. 4,—

"—— some other horrible form,
Which might *deprive* your sovereignty of reason," &c.

[c] — *so* thick,—] So *rapidly*. Thus in "Cymbeline," Act III. Sc. 2,—

"—— say, and speak *thick*,
Love's counsellor should fill the bores of hearing."

[d] *Which she* too early and too late hath spill'd!] By "too late" is meant *too recently*. The same conceit is found in "Henry VI." Part III. Act II. Sc. 5,—

"O boy, thy father gave thee life *too soon*,
And hath bereft thee of thy life *too late!*"

[e] *Do wounds* help *wounds, or grief* help *grievous deeds?*] The repetition is so inelegant that we cannot but believe Shakespeare wrote,—

"Do wounds *salve* wounds," &c.

or,—

"Do wounds *heal* wounds," &c.

Since Rome herself in them doth stand disgrac'd,
By our strong arms from forth her fair streets chas'd.

"Now, by the Capitol that we adore,
And by this chaste blood so unjustly stain'd,
By heaven's fair sun that breeds the fat earth's store,
By all our country rights in Rome maintain'd,
And by chaste Lucrece' soul that late complain'd
Her wrongs to us, and by this bloody knife,
We will revenge the death of this true wife!"

This said, he struck his hand upon his breast,
And kiss'd the fatal knife to end his vow;
And to his protestation urg'd the rest,
Who, wondering at him, did his words allow:[a]
Then jointly to the ground their knees they bow;
And that deep vow, which Brutus made before,
He doth again repeat, and that they swore.

When they had sworn to this advised doom,
They did conclude to bear dead Lucrece thence;
To show her bleeding body thorough Rome,
And so to publish Tarquin's foul offence:
Which being done with speedy diligence,
The Romans plausibly[b] did give consent
To Tarquin's everlasting banishment.

[a] — allow:] *Approve.*
[b] — plausibly—] Meaning perhaps, as Steevens conjectured, *with expressions of applause.* From *Plausibilis.* So in the "Argument" of the poem: "—wherewith the people were so moved, that with one consent and a general *acclamation*, the Tarquins were all exiled," &c.

FINIS.

SONNETS.

INTRODUCTION.

The earliest known edition of Shakespeare's Sonnets is the quarto published in 1609, which commonly bears the imprint, "At London. By G. Eld for T. T. and are to be solde by William Aspley. 1609;" though, in the title-pages of some copies for "William Aspley," we have, "John Wright, dwelling at Christ Church Gate. 1609." The "T. T." for whom this edition was printed is proved by an entry on the Stationers' Registers to have been Thomas Thorpe:—

"2o. May. 1609.
"Tho. Thorpe]   A booke called Shakespeare's Sonnets."

Thorpe has prefixed to his quarto a dedication silly in form and very puzzling in expression, yet of so much interest in connexion with the party to whom Shakespeare is supposed to have addressed these effusions, that we are tempted to reprint it precisely as it stands in the original:—

TO . THE . ONLIE . BEGETTER . OF .
THESE . INSVING . SONNETS .
MR. W. H. ALL . HAPPINESSE .
AND . THAT . ETERNITIE .
PROMISED .
BY .
OUR . EVER-LIVING . POET .
WISHETH .
THE . WELL-WISHING .
ADVENTVRER . IN
SETTING .
FORTH .
T. T.

This enigmatical preamble has provoked much controversy. The first inquiry has been directed to what the writer meant by "The only begetter." By some critics the phrase has been held to signify, the sole object or inspirer of the Sonnets; while others conceive that "begetter" imports no more than the *getter* or *obtainer* of them in manuscript from the hands of the poet.* The next and more important question which this dedication has raised is, who the "only begetter" typified by the contraction, "Mr. W. H." really was. Dr. Farmer supposed him to be *William Hart*, Shakespeare's nephew; but as he was not born until 1600, and Meres speaks of the Sonnets in 1598,† this supposition may be at once dismissed. Tyrwhitt conjectured from a line in the twentieth Sonnet—

"A man in hew all *Hews* in his controwling"—

* "The *begetter* is merely the person who *gets* or *procures* a thing, with the common prefix *be* added to it. So in Decker's *Satiromastic*, 'I have some cousin-germans at court shall *beget* you the reversion of the master of the king's revels.'"—Boswell.

† "As the soule of Euphorbus was thought to live in Pythagoras, so the sweete wittie soule of Ovid lives in mellifluous and honey-tongued Shakespeare: witnes his *Venus and Adonis*, his *Lucrece*, his sugred *Sonnets* among his private friends, &c."—*Palladis Tamia*, 1598.

that the unknown might be a *William Hughes.* This hypothesis is ingenious, but, unfortunate y, if admitted, it involves the perplexing task of discovering who was *William Hughes.* Chalmers has laboured hard to prove that the whole of the Sonnets were addressed to Queen Elizabeth! Drake was convinced that the initials "W. H." should be transposed, and that they represent Henry Wriothesly, Earl of Southampton. Another and more plausible theory, first broached, we believe, by Mr. Boaden,* is that "Mr. W. H." is no other than William Herbert, Earl of Pembroke, one of "the most Noble and Incomparable Paire of Brethren," to whom the first folio was inscribed. This opinion has been taken up with great fervour by Mr. Armitage Brown,† and is very ably sustained by him. But here again we are met by a troublesome objection. Thorpe's edition, as we have seen, was not published before 1609, while William Herbert succeeded to the title of Pembroke in 1601. Is it at all probable that, at a period when the distinctions of rank were punctiliously maintained, any bookseller would have presumed to address a nobleman of such eminence as "Mr. W. H."? Let the reader determine.

Attempts have been made to illustrate Shakespeare's character, as well as his life, from his Sonnets; ‡ but nothing satisfactory in either respect has been elicited. The truth we apprehend to be, that although these poems are written in the poet's own name, and are, apparently, grounded on actual incidents in his career, they are, for the most part, if not wholly, poetical fictions. We have the authority of Meres for the fact that these productions were scattered among the poet's "private friends;" and when we find some flatly contradicting others, it is reasonable to conclude that they were written on different occasions, and with no more adaptation of fact to fancy than is usually found in imaginary compositions.§

---

* "On the Sonnets of Shakespeare, identifying the Person to whom they were addressed, and elucidating several points in the Poet's History. By James Boaden." 1838.

† Shakespeare's *Autobiographical Poems*, &c. 1838.

‡ One of the most elaborate and ingenious of these is contained in the work of Mr. Armitage Brown, already mentioned.

§ Mr. Brown is of a different opinion. He conceives the Sonnets to contain "a clear allusion to events in Shakespeare's life, or rather a history of them, with his own thoughts and feelings as comments on them." He maintains, indeed, that, correctly speaking, they are not Sonnets, but Stanzas, of which 152 out of the 154 are divisible into six separate poems, according to the following arrangement:—

FIRST POEM, Stanzas 1 to 26.—*To his friend, persuading him to marry.*

SECOND POEM, Stanzas 27 to 55.—*To his friend, who had robbed the poet of his mistress, forgiving him.*

THIRD POEM, Stanzas 56 to 77.—*To his friend, complaining of his coldness, and warning him of life's decay.*

FOURTH POEM, Stanzas 78 to 101.—*To his friend, complaining that he prefers another poet's praises, and reproving him for faults that may injure his character.*

FIFTH POEM, Stanzas 102 to 126.—*To his friend, excusing himself for having been some time silent, and disclaiming the charge of inconstancy.*

SIXTH POEM, Stanzas 127 to 152.—*To his mistress, on her infidelity.*

SONNETS.

I.

FROM fairest creatures we desire increase,[a]
That thereby beauty's rose might never die,
But as the riper should by time decease,
His tender heir might bear his memory :
But thou, contracted to thine own bright eyes,
Feed'st thy light's flame with self-substantial fuel,
Making a famine where abundance lies,
Thyself thy foe, to thy sweet self too cruel.
Thou that art now the world's fresh ornament,
And only herald to the gaudy spring,
Within thine own bud buriest thy content,
And, tender churl, mak'st waste in niggarding.[b]
Pity the world, or else this glutton be,
To eat the world's due, by the grave and thee.

II.

When forty winters shall besiege thy brow,
And dig deep trenches in thy beauty's field,
Thy youth's proud livery, so gaz'd on now,
Will be a tatter'd weed, of small worth held :
Then being ask'd where all thy beauty lies,
Where all the treasure of thy lusty days,—
To say, within thine own deep-sunken eyes,
Were an all-eating shame and thriftless praise.
How much more praise deserv'd thy beauty's use,
If thou couldst answer—" This fair child of mine
Shall sum my count, and make my old excuse,—"
Proving his beauty by succession thine !
This were to be new-made when thou art old,
And see thy blood warm when thou feel'st it cold.

III.

Look in thy glass, and tell the face thou viewest,
Now is the time that face should form another ;
Whose fresh repair if now thou not renewest,
Thou dost beguile the world, unbless some mother.
For where is she so fair whose unear'd [c] womb
Disdains the tillage of thy husbandry ?
Or who is he so fond will be the tomb
Of his self-love, to stop posterity ?
Thou art thy mother's glass, and she in thee
Calls back the lovely April of her prime :
So thou through windows of thine age shalt see,
Despite of wrinkles, this thy golden time.
But if thou live, remember'd not to be,
Die single, and thine image dies with thee.

IV.

Unthrifty loveliness, why dost thou spend
Upon thyself thy beauty's legacy ?

---

[a] From fairest creatures we desire increase,—] As Boswell remarked, the first nineteen of these Sonnets are only an expansion of the stanza in "Venus and Adonis," beginning,—

" Upon the earth's increase why shouldst thou feed,
Unless the earth with thy increase be fed?
By law of nature thou art bound to breed,
That thine may live when thou thyself art dead ;"

[b] — mak'st waste in niggarding.] Compare, "Romeo and Juliet," Act I. Sc. 1,—

" *Ben.* Then she hath sworn that she will still live chaste?
Rom. She hath, and in that *sparing* makes huge waste."

[c] — unear'd—] *Unploughed.*

Nature's bequest gives nothing, but doth lend,
And, being frank, she lends to those are free.[a]
Then, beauteous niggard, why dost thou abuse
The bounteous largess given thee to give?
Profitless usurer, why dost thou use
So great a sum of sums, yet canst not live?
For having traffic with thyself alone,
Thou of thyself thy sweet self dost deceive.
Then how, when nature calls thee to be gone,
What acceptable audit canst thou leave?
  Thy unus'd beauty must be tomb'd with thee,
  Which, used, lives th' executor to be.

V.

Those hours, that with gentle work did frame
The lovely gaze where every eye doth dwell,
Will play the tyrants to the very same,
And that unfair which fairly doth excel;
For never-resting time leads summer on
To hideous winter, and confounds him there;
Sap check'd with frost, and lusty leaves quite gone,
Beauty o'ersnow'd, and bareness everywhere:
Then, were not summer's distillation left,
A liquid prisoner pent in walls of glass,
Beauty's effect with beauty were bereft,
Nor it, nor no remembrance what it was:
  But flowers distill'd, though they with winter meet,
  Leese[b] but their show; their substance still lives sweet.

VI.

Then let not winter's ragged hand deface
In thee thy summer, ere thou be distill'd:
Make sweet some phial; treasure thou some place
With beauty's treasure, ere it be self-kill'd.
That use[c] is not forbidden usury,
Which happies those that pay the willing loan;
That 's for thyself to breed another thee,
Or ten times happier, be it ten for one;
Ten times thyself were happier than thou art,
If ten of thine ten times refigur'd thee:
Then what could death do if thou shouldst depart,
Leaving thee living in posterity?
  Be not self-will'd, for thou art much too fair
  To be Death's conquest, and make worms thine heir.

VII.

Lo, in the orient when the gracious light
Lifts up his burning head, each under eye
Doth homage to his new-appearing sight,
Serving with looks his sacred majesty;
And having climb'd the steep-up heavenly hill,
Resembling strong youth in his middle age,
Yet mortal looks adore his beauty still,
Attending on his golden pilgrimage;
But when from high-most pitch, with weary car,
Like feeble age, he reeleth from the day,
The eyes, 'fore duteous, now converted are
From his low tract, and look another way:
  So thou, thyself out-going in thy noon,
  Unlook'd on diest, unless thou get a son.

[a] — to *those are* free.] To those who are likewise *liberal*.
[b] Leese—] An antique form of *lose*.
[c] — use —] *Usance, interest of money.*

VIII.

Music to hear,[d] why hear'st thou music sadly?
Sweets with sweets war not, joy delights in joy.
Why lov'st thou that which thou receiv'st not gladly,
Or else receiv'st with pleasure thine annoy?
If the true concord of well-tuned sounds,
By unions married, do offend thine ear,
They do but sweetly chide thee, who confounds
In singleness the parts that thou shouldst bear.
Mark how one string, sweet husband to another,
Strikes each in each by mutual ordering;
Resembling sire and child and happy mother,
Who, all in one, one pleasing note do sing:
  Whose speechless song, being many, seeming one,
  Sings this to thee, "thou single wilt prove none."

IX.

Is it for fear to wet a widow's eye
That thou consum'st thyself in single life?
Ah! if thou issueless shalt hap to die,
The world will wail thee, like a makeless[e] wife;
The world will be thy widow, and still weep
That thou no form of thee hast left behind,
When every private widow well may keep,
By children's eyes, her husband's shape in mind.
Look, what an unthrift in the world doth spend
Shifts but his place, for still the world enjoys it;
But beauty's waste hath in the world an end,
And kept unus'd, the user so destroys it.
  No love toward others in that bosom sits
  That on himself such murderous shame commits.

X.

For shame, deny that thou bear'st love to any,
Who for thyself art so unprovident.
Grant, if thou wilt, thou art belov'd of many,
But that thou none lov'st is most evident;
For thou art so possess'd with murderous hate,
That 'gainst thyself thou stick'st not to conspire,
Seeking that beauteous roof to ruinate,
Which to repair should be thy chief desire.
O, change thy thought, that I may change my mind!
Shall hate be fairer lodg'd than gentle love?
Be, as thy presence is, gracious and kind,
Or to thyself, at least, kind-hearted prove:
  Make thee another self, for love of me,
  That beauty still may live in thine or thee.

XI.

As fast as thou shalt wane, so fast thou growest
In one of thine, from that which thou departest;
And that fresh blood which youngly thou bestowest,
Thou mayst call thine, when thou from youth convertest.
Herein lives wisdom, beauty, and increase;
Without this, folly, age, and cold decay:
If all were minded so, the times should cease,
And threescore year would make the world away.
Let those whom Nature hath not made for store,
Harsh, featureless, and rude, barrenly perish:

[d] Music to hear, &c.] Thou to hear whom is music, why, &c.
[e] — a makeless wife;] A *mateless* wife. *Make* and *mate* were synonyms, the former being the elder form.

Look, whom she best endow'd, she gave thee more;[a]
Which bounteous gift thou shouldst in bounty cherish;
She carv'd thee for her seal, and meant thereby
Thou shouldst print more, nor let that copy die.

XII.

When I do count the clock that tells the time,
And see the brave day sunk in hideous night;
When I behold the violet past prime,
And sable curls all[b] silver'd o'er with white;
When lofty trees I see barren of leaves,
Which erst from heat did canopy the herd,
And summer's green, all girded up in sheaves,
Borne on the bier with white and bristly beard;
Then of thy beauty do I question make,
That thou among the wastes of time must go,
Since sweets and beauties do themselves forsake,
And die as fast as they see others grow;
And nothing 'gainst Time's scythe can make defence
Save breed, to brave him when he takes thee hence.

XIII.

O, that you were yourself! but, love, you are
No longer yours than you yourself here live:
Against this coming end you should prepare,
And your sweet semblance to some other give.
So should that beauty which you hold in lease
Find no determination; then you were
Yourself again, after yourself's decease,
When your sweet issue your sweet form should bear.
Who lets so fair a house fall to decay,
Which husbandry in honour might uphold
Against the stormy gusts of winter's day,
And barren rage of death's eternal cold?
O, none but unthrifts!—dear my love, you know
You had a father; let your son say so.

XIV.

Not from the stars do I my judgment pluck;
And yet methinks I have astronomy,
But not to tell of good or evil luck,
Of plagues, of dearths, or seasons' quality:
Nor can I fortune to brief minutes tell,
'Pointing to each his thunder, rain, and wind,
Or say with princes if it shall go well,
By oft predict that I in heaven find:
But from thine eyes my knowledge I derive,
And, constant stars, in them I read such art,
As truth and beauty shall together thrive.
If from thyself to store thou wouldst convert;[c]
Or else of thee this I prognosticate,—
Thy end is truth's and beauty's doom and date.

XV.

When I consider everything that grows
Holds in perfection but a little moment,
That this huge stage presenteth nought but shows
Whereon the stars in secret influence comment;
When I perceive that men as plants decrease,
Cheered and check'd even by the self-same sky;
Vaunt in their youthful sap, at height decrease,
And wear their brave state out of memory;
Then the conceit of this inconstant stay
Sets you most rich in youth before my sight,
Where wasteful Time debateth with Decay,
To change your day of youth to sullied night;
And, all in war with Time, for love of you,
As he takes from you, I engraft you new.

XVI.

But wherefore do not you a mightier way
Make war upon this bloody tyrant, Time?
And fortify yourself in your decay
With means more blessed than my barren rhyme?
Now stand you on the top of happy hours;
And many maiden gardens, yet unset,
With virtuous wish would bear your[d] living flowers,
Much liker than your painted counterfeit:
So should the lines of life[e] that life repair,
Which this, Time's pencil, or my pupil pen,
Neither in inward worth nor outward fair,[f]
Can make you live yourself in eyes of men.
To give away yourself keeps yourself still;
And you must live, drawn by your own sweet skill.

XVII.

Who will believe my verse in time to come,
If it were fill'd with your most high deserts?
Though yet, heaven knows, it is but as a tomb
Which hides your life, and shows not half your parts.
If I could write the beauty of your eyes,
And in fresh numbers number all your graces,
The age to come would say, "This poet lies,
Such heavenly touches ne'er touch'd earthly faces."
So should my papers, yellow'd with their age,
Be scorn'd, like old men of less truth than tongue;
And your true rights be term'd a poet's rage,
And stretched metre of an antique song:
But were some child of yours alive that time,
You should live twice;—in it, and in my rhyme.

XVIII.

Shall I compare thee to a summer's day?
Thou art more lovely and more temperate:
Rough winds do shake the darling buds of May,
And summer's lease hath all too short a date:
Sometime too hot the eye of heaven shines,
And often is his gold complexion dimm'd;

---

a *Look, whom she best endow'd, she gave* thee *more;*] The original has, "gave *the* more:" Malone, who restored "thee," explains the amended line as follows:—On a survey of mankind, you will find that nature, however liberal she may have been to others, has been still more bountiful to you.

b — all *silver'd o'er with white;*] The quarto of 1609 reads,—"*or* silver'd *ore* with white;" manifestly by mistake.

c If from thyself to store thou wouldst convert;] Meaning apparently,—if instead of living single thou wouldst marry, and beget lineage.

d — *would bear* your *living flowers,*—] The reading of the quarto, which Malone, conceiving "your" to be a press error, changed to—

"—— would bear *you* living flowers."

e So should the lines of life that life repair,—] An anonymous correspondent in the *Variorum* suggests that "lines of life" are perhaps living pictures, *viz.* "children."

f — fair,—] *Beauty.*

And every fair from fair sometime declines,
By chance, or nature's changing course, untrimm'd;
But thy eternal summer shall not fade,
Nor lose possession of that fair thou owest;[a]
Nor shall Death brag thou wander'st in his shade,
When in eternal lines to time thou growest:
So long as men can breathe, or eyes can see,
So long lives this, and this gives life to thee.

XIX.

Devouring Time, blunt thou the lion's paws,[b]
And make the earth devour her own sweet brood;
Pluck the keen teeth from the fierce's tiger's jaws,
And burn the long-liv'd phœnix in her blood;
Make glad and sorry seasons as thou fleets,[c]
And do whate'er thou wilt, swift-footed Time,
To the wide world and all her fading sweets;
But I forbid thee one most heinous crime:
O, carve not with thy hours my love's fair brow,
Nor draw no lines there with thine antique pen;
Him in thy course untainted do allow,
For beauty's pattern to succeeding men.
Yet, do thy worst, old Time: despite thy wrong,
My love shall in my verse ever live young.

XX.

A woman's face, with Nature's own hand painted,
Hast thou, the master-mistress of my passion;
A woman's gentle heart, but not acquainted
With shifting change, as is false women's fashion;
An eye more bright than theirs, less false in rolling,
Gilding the object whereupon it gazeth;
A man in hue, all hues in his controlling,[d]
Which steals men's eyes, and women's souls amazeth.
And for a woman wert thou first created;
Till Nature, as she wrought thee, fell a-doting,
And, by addition, me of thee defeated,
By adding one thing to my purpose nothing.
But since she prick'd thee out for women's pleasure,
Mine be thy love, and thy love's use their treasure.

XXI.

So is it not with me as with that Muse,
Stirr'd by a painted beauty to his verse;
Who heaven itself for ornament doth use,
And every fair with his fair doth rehearse;
Making a couplement of proud compare,
With sun and moon, with earth and sea's rich gems,
With April's first-born flowers, and all things rare
That heaven's air in this huge rondure[e] hems.
O, let me, true in love, but truly write,
And then believe me, my love is as fair
As any mother's child, though not so bright
As those gold candles fix'd in heaven's air:
Let them say more that like of hearsay well;
I will not praise that purpose not to sell.[f]

XXII.

My glass shall not persuade me I am old,
So long as youth and thou are of one date;
But when in thee time's furrows I behold,
Then look I death my days should expiate.[g]
For all that beauty that doth cover thee
Is but the seemly raiment of my heart,
Which in thy breast doth live, as thine in me:
How can I, then, be elder than thou art?
O, therefore, love, be of thyself so wary,
As I, not for myself, but for thee will;
Bearing thy heart, which I will keep so chary
As tender nurse her babe from faring ill.
Presume not on thy heart when mine is slain;
Thou gav'st me thine, not to give back again.

XXIII.

As an unperfect actor on the stage,
Who with his fear is put besides his part,[h]
Or some fierce thing replete with too much rage,
Whose strength's abundance weakens his own heart;
So I, for fear of trust, forget to say
The perfect ceremony[i] of love's rite,
And in mine own love's strength seem to decay,
O'ercharg'd with burden of mine own love's might.
O, let my books be, then, the eloquence
And dumb presagers of my speaking breast;
Who plead for love, and look for recompence,
More than that tongue that more hath more express'd.
O, learn to read what silent love hath writ:
To hear with eyes belongs to love's fine wit.

XXIV.

Mine eye hath play'd the painter, and hath stell'd
Thy beauty's form in table of my heart;
My body is the frame wherein 't is held,
And pérspective it is best painter's art.
For through the painter must you see his skill,
To find where your true image pictur'd lies,
Which in my bosom's shop is hanging still,
That hath his windows glazed with thine eyes.

---

a — of *that* fair *thou* owest;] Of that *beauty* thou *possessest*.

b — *blunt thou the lion's* paws,—] See "Titus Andronicus," Act II. Sc. 3,—

"The lion, mov'd with pity, did endure
To have his princely *paws* par'd all away."

c — *as thou* fleets,—] The quarto reads,—"as thou *fleet'st*."

d *A man in hue, all* hues *in his controlling*,—] In the old copy "hues" is spelt *Hews*, whence Tyrwhitt conjectured that the mysterious individual "W. H." to whom Thorpe the bookseller dedicated these Sonnets, was a *W. Hughes*, or *Hews*. See the Introduction.

e — rondure—] This word, meaning a *round* or *belt*, occurs also in "King John," Act II. Sc. 1,—

"'T is not the *roundure* of your old-fac'd walls
Can hide you from our messengers of war."

f I will not praise that purpose not to sell.] This line adds strength to Warburton's conjecture that in "Troilus and Cressida," Act IV. Sc. 1,—

"We 'll not *commend* what we intend to *sell*,"

we ought to read,—

"—— what we intend *not* sell."

g *Then look I death my days should* expiate.] That is, *terminate*. Compare, "Richard III." Act III. Sc. 3, where the folio has,—

"Make haste, the hour of death is *expiate*."

h As an unperfect actor on the stage,
Who with his fear is put besides his part,—]

So in "Coriolanus," Act V. Sc. 3,—

"Like a dull actor now,
I have forgot my part, and I am out,
Even to a full disgrace."

i *The perfect* ceremony *of love's rite*,—] This is one of the rare instances where Shakespeare employs "ceremony" as a trisyllable.

Now see what good turns eyes for eyes have done;
Mine eyes have drawn thy shape, and thine for me
Are windows to my breast, where-through the sun
Delights to peep, to gaze therein on thee;
  Yet eyes this cunning want to grace their art,
  They draw but what they see, know not the heart.

XXV.

Let those who are in favour with their stars,
Of public honour and proud titles boast,
Whilst I, whom fortune of such triumph bars,
Unlook'd for joy in that I honour most.
Great princes' favourites their fair leaves spread
But as the marigold at the sun's eye;
And in themselves their pride lies buried,
For at a frown they in their glory die.
The painful warrior famoused for fight,[a]
After a thousand victories once foil'd,
Is from the book of honour razed quite,
And all the rest forgot for which he toil'd:
  Then happy I, that love and am belov'd
  Where I may not remove nor be remov'd.

XXVI.

Lord of my love, to whom in vassalage
Thy merit hath my duty strongly knit,
To thee I send this written embassage,
To witness duty, not to show my wit:
Duty so great, which wit so poor as mine
May make seem bare, in wanting words to show it;
But that I hope some good conceit of thine
In thy soul's thought, all naked, will bestow it;
Till whatsoever star that guides by moving,
Points on me graciously with fair aspéct,
And puts apparel on my tatter'd loving,
To show me worthy of thy [b] sweet respect:
  Then may I dare to boast how I do love thee;
  Till then not show my head where thou mayst prove me.

XXVII.

Weary with toil, I haste me to my bed,
The dear repose for limbs with travel tir'd;
But then begins a journey in my head,
To work my mind, when body's work 's expir'd:
For then my thoughts (from far where I abide)
Intend a zealous pilgrimage to thee,
And keep my drooping eyelids open wide,
Looking on darkness which the blind do see:
Save that my soul's imaginary sight
Presents thy [c] shadow to my sightless view,
Which, like a jewel hung in ghastly night,[d]
Makes black night beauteous, and her old face new.
  Lo, thus, by day my limbs, by night my mind,
  For thee and for myself no quiet find.

XXVIII.

How can I, then, return in happy plight,
That am debarr'd the benefit of rest?
When day's oppression is not eas'd by night,
But day by night, and night by day, oppress'd?
And each, though enemies to either's reign,
Do in consent shake hands to torture me;
The one by toil, the other to complain
How far I toil, still farther off from thee.
I tell the day, to please him, thou art bright,
And dost him grace when clouds do blot the heaven:
So flatter I the swart-complexion'd night,
When sparkling stars twire [e] not, thou gild'st the even.
  But day doth daily draw my sorrows longer,
  And night doth nightly make grief's strength [f] seem stronger.

XXIX.

When in disgrace with fortune and men's eyes,
I all alone beweep my outcast state,
And trouble deaf heaven with my bootless cries,
And look upon myself, and curse my fate,
Wishing me like to one more rich in hope,
Featur'd like him, like him with friends possess'd,
Desiring this man's art, and that man's scope,
With what I most enjoy contented least;
Yet in these thoughts myself almost despising,
Haply I think on thee,—and then my state
(Like to the lark at break of day arising
From sullen earth) sings hymns at heaven's gate;
  For thy sweet love remember'd such wealth brings,
  That then I scorn to change my state with kings.

XXX.

When to the sessions of sweet silent thought
I summon up remembrance of things past,
I sigh the lack of many a thing I sought,
And with old woes new wail my dear time's waste:
Then can I drown an eye, unus'd to flow,
For precious friends hid in death's dateless night,
And weep afresh love's long-since-cancell'd woe,
And moan th' expense of many a vanish'd sight:
Then can I grieve at grievances foregone,
And heavily from woe to woe tell o'er
The sad account of fore-bemoaned moan,
Which I new pay as if not paid before.
  But if the while I think on thee, dear friend,
  All losses are restor'd, and sorrows end.

XXXI.

Thy bosom is endeared with all hearts,
Which I by lacking have supposed dead;

---

a — *famoused for* fight,—] The old text has, "— for *worth*," which does not rhyme with the corresponding word "quite" in the last line. Theobald substituted "fight," and he also proposed to retain *worth*, and for *quite* to read *forth*, a circumstance Mr. Collier must have forgotten when he suggested the same correction.

b — *of* thy *sweet respect:*] The quarto reads, "of *their* sweet," &c.

c *Presents* thy *shadow*—] The quarto here exhibits the same corruption noted in the preceding Sonnet, that of *their* for "thy."

d Which, like a jewel hung in ghastly night,—] Compare, "Romeo and Julist," Act I. Sc. 5,—

"—— she hangs upon the cheek of night
As a rich jewel in an Ethiop's ear."

e — twire—] *Twinkle*, or *twitter*, or *gleam fitfully*.

f — *make grief's* strength *seem stronger.*] The old copy erroneously reads,—

"— grief's *length* seem stronger."

And there reigns love, and all love's loving parts,
And all those friends which I thought buried.
How many a holy and obsequious tear
Hath dear-religious love stol'n from mine eye,
As interest of the dead, which now appear
But things remov'd, that hidden in thee [a] lie !
Thou art the grave where buried love doth live,
Hung with the trophies of my lovers gone,
Who all their parts of me to thee did give ;
That due of many now is thine alone :
Their images I lov'd I view in thee,
And thou, all they, hast all-the-all of me.

XXXII.

If thou survive my well-contented day,
When that churl Death my bones with dust shall cover,
And shalt by fortune once more re-survey
These poor rude lines of thy deceased lover,[b]
Compare them with the bettering of the time ;
And though they be outstripp'd by every pen,
Reserve [c] them for my love, not for their rhyme,
Exceeded by the height of happier men.
O, then vouchsafe me but this loving thought,—
"Had my friend's Muse grown with this growing age,
A dearer birth than this his love had brought,
To march in ranks of better equipage :
But since he died, and poets better prove,
Theirs for their style I 'll read, his for his love."

XXXIII.

Full many a glorious morning have I seen
Flatter the mountain-tops with sovereign eye,
Kissing with golden face the meadows green,
Gilding pale streams with heavenly alchemy ;
Anon permit the basest clouds to ride
With ugly rack [d] on his celestial face,
And from the forlorn world his visage hide,
Stealing unseen to west with this disgrace :
Even so my sun one early morn did shine
With all-triumphant splendour on my brow ;
But, out, alack ! he was but one hour mine,
The region cloud hath mask'd him from me now.
Yet him for this my love no whit disdaineth ;
Suns of the world may stain when heaven's sun staineth.

XXXIV.

Why didst thou promise such a beauteous day,
And make me travel forth without my cloak,
To let base clouds o'ertake me in my way,
Hiding thy bravery in their rotten smoke ?
'T is not enough that through the cloud thou break,
To dry the rain on my storm-beaten face,
For no man well of such a salve can speak,
That heals the wound, and cures not the disgrace :
Nor can thy shame give physic to my grief ;
Though thou repent, yet I have still the loss :
Th' offender's sorrow lends but weak relief
To him that bears the strong offence's cross.[e]
Ah, but those tears are pearl which thy love sheds,
And they are rich, and ransom all ill deeds.

XXXV.

No more be griev'd at that which thou hast done :
Roses have thorns, and silver fountains mud ;
Clouds and eclipses stain both moon and sun,
And loathsome canker lives in sweetest bud.
All men make faults, and even I in this,
Authórizing thy trespass with compare,
Myself corrupting, salving thy amiss,
Excusing thy sins more than thy sins are : [f]
For to thy sensual fault I bring in sense,—
Thy adverse party is thy advocate,—
And 'gainst myself a lawful plea commence :
Such civil war is in my love and hate,
That I an accessory needs must be
To that sweet thief which sourly robs from me.

XXXVI.

Let me confess that we two must be twain,
Although our undivided loves are one ;
So shall those blots that do with me remain,
Without thy help, by me be borne alone.
In our two loves there is but one respect,
Though in our lives a separable spite,
Which though it alter not love's sole effect,
Yet doth it steal sweet hours from love's delight.
I may not evermore acknowledge thee,
Lest my bewailed guilt shonld do thee shame ;
Nor thou with public kindness honour me,
Unless thou take that honour from thy name :
But do not so ; I love thee in such sort,
As, thou being mine, mine is thy good report.

XXXVII.

As a decrepit father takes delight
To see his active child do deeds of youth,
So I, made lame by fortune's dearest [g] spite,
Take all my comfort of thy worth and truth ;

---

[a] — *hidden in* thee *lie!*] Old copy, "— in *there*."

[b] — *thy deceased lover,*—] In the perusal of these Sonnets the reader should always bear in mind that friendship in Shakespeare's day was commonly spoken of as *love*. Brutus, in "Julius Cæsar," addresses the Roman people as "Romans, countrymen, and *lovers*," and speaks of Cæsar as his "best *lover*." Portia, "Merchant of Venice," conjectures that Antonio, "being the *bosom lover*" of her husband, must needs resemble him. Ben Jonson winds up a letter to Dr. Donne by telling him he is his "true *lover*;" and subscribes himself the *lover* of Camden; and Drayton, writing to Drummond of Hawthornden, informs him that Mr. Joseph Davies is *in love* with him.

[c] Reserve *them*—] "Reserve" for *preserve;* as in "Pericles," Act IV. Sc. 1,—

"— *reserve*
That excellent complexion which did steal
The eyes of young and old."

[d] *With ugly* rack—] See note (1), p. 50, of the present volume; and compare, "Henry IV." Part I. Act I. Sc. 2,—

"—— herein will I imitate the sun,
Who doth permit the base contagious clouds
To smother up his beauty from the world," &c.

[e] — *the strong offence's* cross.] The old copy, by a palpable mistake, repeats "loss" from the corresponding line above.

[f] *Excusing* thy *sins more than* thy *sins are:*] The quarto reads, "Excusing *their* sins more than *their* sins are."

[g] So I, made lame by fortune's dearest *spite,*—] *Dearest* spite is *intensest* spite. See note [b], p. 398, of this volume. From the expression in this line, "So I, made *lame*," &c., and another in the 89th Sonnet,—

"Speak of my *lameness*, an I straight will halt,"—

some critics have maintained that the poet was actually lame ; but the expression in both instances is thought with more probability by others to be merely figurative.

For whether beauty, birth, or wealth, or wit,
Or any of these all, or all, or more,
Entitled [a] in thy parts do crowned sit,
I make my love engrafted to this store:
So then I am not lame, poor, nor despis'd,
Whilst that this shadow doth such substance give,
That I in thy abundance am suffic'd,
And by a part of all thy glory live.
Look what is best, that best I wish in thee;
This wish I have; then ten times happy me!

XXXVIII.

How can my Muse want subject to invent,
While thou dost breathe, that pour'st into my verse
Thine own sweet argument, too excellent
For every vulgar paper to rehearse?
O, give thyself the thanks, if aught in me
Worthy perusal stand against thy sight;
For who 's so dumb that cannot write to thee,
When thou thyself dost give invention light?
Be thou the tenth Muse, ten times more in worth
Than those old nine which rhymers invocate;
And he that calls on thee, let him bring forth
Eternal numbers to out-live long date.
If my slight Muse do please these curious days,
The pain be mine, but thine shall be the praise.

XXXIX.

O, how thy worth with manners may I sing,
When thou art all the better part of me?
What can mine own praise to mine own self bring?
And what is 't but mine own, when I praise thee?
Even for this let us divided live,
And our dear love lose name of single one,
That by this separation I may give
That due to thee, which thou deserv'st alone.
O absence, what a torment wouldst thou prove,
Were it not thy sour leisure gave sweet leave
To entertain the time with thoughts of love,—
Which time and thoughts so sweetly doth [b] deceive,—
And that thou teachest how to make one twain,
By praising him here who doth hence remain!

XL.

Take all my loves, my love, yea, take them all;
What hast thou then more than thou hadst before?
No love, my love, that thou mayst true love call;
All mine was thine before thou hadst this more.
Then, if for my love thou my love receivest,
I cannot blame thee for my love thou usest;
But yet be blam'd, if thou thyself [c] deceivest
By wilful taste of what thyself refusest.
I do forgive thy robbery, gentle thief,
Although thou steal thee all my poverty;
And yet, love knows, it is a greater grief
To bear love's wrong, than hate's known injury.
Lascivious grace, in whom all ill well shows,
Kill me with spites; yet we must not be foes.

XLI.

Those pretty wrongs that liberty commits
When I am sometime absent from thy heart,
Thy beauty and thy years full well befits,
For still temptation follows where thou art.
Gentle thou art, and therefore to be won,
Beauteous thou art, therefore to be assail'd; [d]
And when a woman woos, what woman's son
Will sourly leave her till she [e] have prevail'd?
Ah me! but yet thou mightst my seat forbear,
And chide thy beauty and thy straying youth,
Who lead thee in their riot even there
Where thou art forc'd to break a two-fold truth,—
Hers, by thy beauty tempting her to thee,
Thine, by thy beauty being false to me.

XLII.

That thou hast her, it is not all my grief,
And yet it may be said I lov'd her dearly;
That she hath thee, is of my wailing chief,
A loss in love that touches me more nearly.
Loving offenders, thus I will excuse ye:—
Thou dost love her, because thou know'st I love her;
And for my sake even so doth she abuse me,
Suffering my friend for my sake to approve her.
If I lose thee, my loss is my love's gain,
And losing her, my friend hath found that loss;
Both find each other, and I lose both twain,
And both for my sake lay on me this cross:
But here 's the joy,—my friend and I are one;
Sweet flattery!—then she loves but me alone.

XLIII.

When most I wink, then do mine eyes best see,
For all the day they view things unrespected; [f]
But when I sleep, in dreams they look on thee,
And, darkly bright, are bright in dark directed.
Then thou, whose shadow shadows doth make bright,
How would thy shadow's form form happy show
To the clear day with thy much clearer light,
When to unseeing eyes thy shade shines so!
How would, I say, mine eyes be blessed made
By looking on thee in the living day,
When in dead night thy [g] fair imperfect shade
Through heavy sleep on sightless eyes doth stay!
All days are nights to see [h] till I see thee,
And nights, bright days when dreams do show thee me.

---

[a] Entitled—] "*Entitled* means, I think, *ennobled*. The old copy reads, "in *their* parts."—MALONE.

[b] — doth deceive,—] In the old copy, "*dost* deceive."

[c] —*if thou* thyself deceivest—] The quarto reads, "if thou *this* self deceivest," which can hardly be right.

[d] Gentle thou art, and therefore to be won,
Beauteous thou art, therefore to be assail'd;]

Compare, "Henry VI." Part I. Act V. Sc. 3,—

"She 's beautiful, and therefore to be woo d:
She is a woman, therefore to be won."

[e] —*till* she *have prevail'd?*] The old text mistakenly has, "till *he* have prevail'd?"

[f] — *things* unrespected;] Things *unregarded*.

[g] — thy *fair*—] Old text, "*their* fair."

[h] All days are nights to see, &c.] Malone thought the true reading was, "All days are nights to *me*," &c.: but hear Steevens: "As, *fair to see* (an expression which occurs in a hundred of our old ballads) signifies *fair to sight*, so,—all days *are nights to see*, means, all days *are gloomy to behold*, i.e. *look like nights*."

XLIV.

If the dull substance of my flesh were thought,
Injurious distance should not stop my way;
For then, despite of space, I would be brought
From limits far remote, where thou dost stay.
No matter then although my foot did stand
Upon the farthest earth remov'd from thee;
For nimble thought can jump both sea and land,
As soon as think the place where he would be.
But, ah! thought kills me, that I am not thought,
To leap large lengths of miles when thou art gone,
But that, so much of earth and water wrought,[a]
I must attend time's leisure with my moan;
Receiving nought by elements so slow
But heavy tears, badges of either's woe:

XLV.

The other two, slight air and purging fire,
Are both with thee, wherever I abide;
The first my thought, the other my desire,
These present-absent with swift motion slide.
For when these quicker elements are gone
In tender embassy of love to thee,
My life, being made of four, with two alone
Sinks down to death, oppress'd with melancholy;
Until life's composition be recur'd
By those swift messengers return'd from thee,
Who even but now come back again, assur'd
Of thy[b] fair health, recounting it to me:
This told, I joy; but then no longer glad,
I send them back again, and straight grow sad.

XLVI.

Mine eye and heart are at a mortal war,
How to divide the conquest of thy sight;
Mine eye my heart thy[c] picture's sight would bar,
My heart mine eye the freedom of that right.
My heart doth plead that thou in him dost lie,—
A closet never pierc'd with crystal eyes,—
But the defendant doth that plea deny,
And says in him thy fair appearance lies.
To 'cide this title is impannelled
A quest of thoughts, all tenants to the heart;
And by their verdict is determined
The clear eye's moiety and the dear heart's part:
As thus,—mine eye's due is thine outward part,
And my heart's right thine inward love of heart.

XLVII.

Betwixt mine eye and heart a league is took,
And each doth good turns now unto the other:
When that mine eye is famish'd for a look,
Or heart in love with sighs himself doth smother,
With my love's picture then my eye doth feast,
And to the painted banquet bids my heart;
Another time mine eye is my heart's guest,
And in his thoughts of love doth share a part:
So, either by thy picture or my love,
Thyself away art present still with me;
For thou not farther than my thoughts canst move,
And I am still with them, and they with thee;
Or, if they sleep, thy picture in my sight
Awakes my heart to heart's and eye's delight.

XLVIII.

How careful was I, when I took my way,
Each trifle under truest bars to thrust,
That to my use it might unused stay
From hands of falsehood, in sure wards of trust
But thou, to whom my jewels trifles are,
Most worthy comfort, now my greatest grief,
Thou, best of dearest, and mine only care,
Art left the prey of every vulgar thief.
Thee have I not lock'd up in any chest,
Save where thou art not, though I feel thou art,
Within the gentle closure of my breast,
From whence at pleasure thou mayst come and part;
And even thence thou wilt be stol'n I fear,
For truth proves thievish for a prize so dear.

XLIX.

Against that time, if ever that time come,
When I shall see thee frown on my defects,
Whenas thy love hath cast his utmost sum,
Call'd to that audit by advis'd respects;
Against that time, when thou shalt strangely pass,
And scarcely greet me with that sun, thine eye,
When love, converted from the thing it was,
Shall reasons find of settled gravity,—[d]
Against that time do I ensconce me here
Within the knowledge of mine own desert,
And this my hand against myself uprear,
To guard the lawful reasons on thy part:
To leave poor me thou hast the strength of laws,
Since why to love I can allege no cause.

L.

How heavy do I journey on the way,
When what I seek,—my weary travel's end,—
Doth teach that ease and that repose to say,
"Thus far the miles are measur'd from thy friend!"
The beast that bears me, tired with my woe,
Plods dully[e] on, to bear that weight in me,
As if by some instinct the wretch did know
His rider lov'd not speed, being made from thee:
The bloody spur cannot provoke him on
That sometimes anger thrusts into his hide,
Which heavily he answers with a groan,
More sharp to me than spurring to his side;

---

a — so much of earth and water wrought,—] That is, being composed of so much of those dull elements.

b *Of* thy *fair health*,—] The old copy reads, "*their* fair health."

c — thy *picture's sight*—] Again, the quarto misprints *their* for "thy."

d
When love, converted from the thing it was,
Shall reasons find of settled gravity,—]

Compare, "Julius Cæsar," Act IV. Sc. 2,—

"—— ever note, Lucilius,
When love begins to sicken and decay,
It useth an enforced ceremony."

e *Plods* dully *on*,—] The old copy reads, "*duly* on," a self-correcting blunder.

For that same groan doth put this in my mind,—
My grief lies onward, and my joy behind.

LI.

Thus can my love excuse the slow offence
Of my dull bearer when from thee I speed:
From where thou art why should I haste me thence?
Till I return, of posting is no need.
O, what excuse will my poor beast then find,
When swift extremity can seem but slow?
Then should I spur, though mounted on the wind,
In winged speed no motion shall I know:
Then can no horse with my desire keep pace;
Therefore desire, of perfect'st love being made,
Shall neigh,—no dull flesh,—in his fiery race;[a]
But love, for love, thus shall excuse my jade,—
Since from thee going he went wilful-slow,
Towards thee I'll run, and give him leave to go.

LII.

So am I as the rich, whose blessed key
Can bring him to his sweet up-locked treasure,
The which he will not every hour survey,
For blunting[b] the fine point of seldom pleasure.
Therefore are feasts so solemn and so rare,
Since, seldom coming, in the long year set,
Like stones of worth they thinly placed are,
Or captain jewels in the carcanet.[c]
So is the time that keeps you, as my chest,
Or as the wardrobe which the robe doth hide,
To make some special instant special-blest,
By new unfolding his imprison'd pride.
Blessed are you, whose worthiness gives scope,
Being had, to triumph, being lack'd, to hope.

LIII.

What is your substance, whereof are you made,
That millions of strange shadows on you tend?
Since every one hath, every one, one shade,
And you, but one, can every shadow lend.
Describe Adonis, and the counterfeit[d]
Is poorly imitated after you;
On Helen's cheek all art of beauty set,
And you in Grecian tires are painted new:
Speak of the spring, and foison[e] of the year;
The one doth shadow of your beauty show,
The other as your bounty doth appear;
And you in every blessed shape we know.
In all external grace you have some part,
But you like none, none you, for constant heart.

LIV.

O, how much more doth beauty beauteous seem
By that sweet ornament which truth doth give!
The rose looks fair, but fairer we it deem
For that sweet odour which doth in it live.
The canker-blooms have full as deep a dye
As the perfumed tincture of the roses,
Hang on such thorns, and play as wantonly
When summer's breath their masked buds discloses:
But, for their virtue only is their show,
They live unwoo'd, and unrespected fade;
Die to themselves. Sweet roses do not so;
Of their sweet deaths are sweetest odours made:
And so of you, beauteous and lovely youth,
When that shall fade, by[f] verse distils your truth.

LV.

Not marble, not the gilded monuments
Of princes, shall outlive this powerful rhyme;
But you shall shine more bright in these contents
Than unswept stone, besmear'd with sluttish time.
When wasteful war shall statues overturn,
And broils root out the work of masonry,
Nor Mars his sword nor war's quick fire shall burn
The living record of your memory.
'Gainst death and all-oblivious enmity
Shall you pace forth; your praise shall still find room,
Even in the eyes of all posterity
That wear this world out to the ending doom.
So, till the judgment that yourself arise,
You live in this, and dwell in lovers' eyes.

LVI.

Sweet love, renew thy force; be it not said
Thy edge should blunter be than appetite,
Which but to-day by feeding is allay'd,
To-morrow sharpen'd in his former might:
So, love, be thou: although to-day thou fill
Thy hungry eyes, even till they wink with fullness,
To-morrow see again, and do not kill
The spirit of love with a perpetual dullness.
Let this sad interim like the ocean be
Which parts the shore, where two contracted-new
Come daily to the banks, that, when they see
Return of love, more blest may be the view;
Or[g] call it winter, which, being full of care,
Makes summer's welcome thrice more wish'd, more rare.

LVII.

Being your slave, what should I do but tend
Upon the hours and times of your desire?
I have no precious time at all to spend,
Nor services to do, till you require.
Nor dare I chide the world-without-end hour,
Whilst I, my sovereign, watch the clock for you,
Nor think the bitterness of absence sour,
When you have bid your servant once adieu;
Nor dare I question with my jealous thought
Where you may be, or your affairs suppose,

a Shall neigh,—no dull flesh,—in his fiery race;] In this line the word "neigh" is, we suspect, corrupt.

b For blunting—] For *fear of* blunting, &c.

c — captain *jewels in the* carcanet.] The *superior* jewels in the *necklace*, or *collar*.

d — counterfeit—] *Picture*.

e — foison—] "Foison" is *abundance*, and *Autumn*, as the season of plenty, is named so here.

f — by *verse distils your truth*.] Malone reads, plausibly enough, "— my *verse*," &c.; but we are not quite satisfied that the change is needed.

g Or *call it winter*,—] The old copy reads, "*As* call it," &c. For the emendation we are indebted to Tyrwhitt.

But, like a sad slave, stay and think of nought
Save, where you are how happy you make those.
So true a fool is love, that in your will,
Though you do anything, he thinks no ill.

LVIII.

That god forbid that made me first your slave,
I should in thought control your times of pleasure,
Or at your hand th' account of hours to crave,
Being your vassal, bound to stay your leisure!
O, let me suffer, being at your beck,
Th' imprison'd absence of your liberty;
And patience, tame to sufferance, bide each check,
Without accusing you of injury.
Be where you list, your charter is so strong,
That you yourself may privilege your time:
Do [a] what you will, to you it doth belong
Yourself to pardon of self-doing crime.
I am to wait, though waiting so be hell;
Not blame your pleasure, be it ill or well.

LIX.

If there be nothing new, but that which is
Hath been before, how are our brains beguil'd,
Which, labouring for invention, bear amiss
The second burden of a former child!
O, that record could with a backward look,
Even of five hundred courses of the sun,
Show me your image in some antique book,
Since mind at first in character was done! [b]
That I might see what the old world could say
To this composed wonder of your frame;
Whether we are mended, or whêr better they,
Or whether revolution be the same.
O, sure I am, the wits of former days
To subjects worse have given admiring praise!

LX.

Like as the waves make towards the pebbled shore,
So do our minutes hasten to their end;
Each changing place with that which goes before,
In sequent toil all forwards do contend.
Nativity, once in the main of light,
Crawls to maturity, wherewith being crown'd,
Crooked eclipses 'gainst his glory fight,
And Time, that gave, doth now his gift confound.
Time doth transfix the flourish set on youth,
And delves the parallels in beauty's brow;
Feeds on the rarities of nature's truth,
And nothing stands but for his scythe to mow:
And yet, to times in hope my verse shall stand,
Praising thy worth, despite his cruel hand.

LXI.

Is it thy will thy image should keep open
My heavy eyelids to the weary night?
Dost thou desire my slumbers should be broken
While shadows like to thee do mock my sight?
Is it thy spirit that thou send'st from thee
So far from home into my deeds to pry,
To find out shames and idle hours in me,
The scope and tenour of thy jealousy?
O, no! thy love, though much, is not so great;
It is my love that keeps mine eye awake;
Mine own true love that doth my rest defeat,
To play the watchman ever for thy sake:
For thee watch I whilst thou dost wake elsewhere,
From me far off, with others all-too-near.

LXII.

Sin of self-love possesseth all mine eye,
And all my soul, and all my every part;
And for this sin there is no remedy,
It is so grounded inward in my heart.
Methinks no face so gracious [c] is as mine,
No shape so true, no truth of such account;
And for myself mine own worth do define,
As I all other in all worths surmount.
But when my glass shows me myself indeed,
Beated and chapp'd with tann'd antiquity,
Mine own self-love quite contrary I read;
Self so self-loving were iniquity.
'T is thee (myself) that for myself I praise,
Painting my age with beauty of thy days.

LXIII.

Against my love shall be, as I am now,
With Time's injurious hand crush'd and o'erworn;
When hours have drain'd his blood, and fill'd his brow
With lines and wrinkles; when his youthful morn
Hath travell'd on to age's steepy [d] night;
And all those beauties whereof now he's king
Are vanishing or vanish'd out of sight,
Stealing away the treasure of his spring;
For such a time do I now fortify
Against confounding age's cruel knife,
That he shall never cut from memory
My sweet love's beauty, though my lover's life:
His beauty shall in these black lines be seen,
And they shall live, and he in them, still green.

LXIV.

When I have seen by Time's fell hand defac'd
The rich-proud cost of outworn buried age;
When sometime lofty towers I see down-raz'd,
And brass eternal slave to mortal rage;
When I have seen the hungry ocean gain
Advantage on the kingdom of the shore, [e]
And the firm soil win of the wat'ry main,
Increasing store with loss, and loss with store;

---

[a] Do *what you will*,—] So Malone, and we think correctly, though Mr. Dyce reads with the old copy,—

"—— may privilege your time
To what you will;" &c.

[b] Since mind at first in character was done!] That is, we suppose,—Since thought was first expressed in writing.

[c] — gracious—] *Beautiful*. So in "King John," Act III. Sc. 4,—

"There was not such a *gracious* creature born."

[d] — steepy *night*;] Chaucer, "Canterbury Tales," has "eyen *steep*," which his editors interpret, "eyes *deep*." We believe in both cases the word is a synonym for *black* or *dark*.

[e] When I have seen the hungry ocean gain
Advantage on the kingdom of the shore, &c.]

Compare with this fine passage a parallel one in "Henry IV." Part II. Act III. Sc. 1,—

"O God! that one might read the book of fate,
And see the revolution of the times
Make mountains level, and the continent
(Weary of solid firmness) melt itself
Into the sea! and, other times, to see
The beachy girdle of the ocean
Too wide for Neptune's hips;"

When I have seen such interchange of state,
Or state itself confounded to decay;
Ruin hath taught me thus to ruminate,—
That Time will come and take my love away.
This thought is as a death, which cannot choose
But weep to have that which it fears to lose.

LXV.

Since brass, nor stone, nor earth, nor boundless sea,
But sad mortality o'er-sways their power,
How with this rage shall beauty hold a plea,
Whose action is no stronger than a flower?
O, how shall summer's honey breath hold out
Against the wreckful siege of battering days,
When rocks impregnable are not so stout,
Nor gates of steel so strong, but Time decays?
O fearful meditation! where, alack!
Shall Time's best jewel from Time's chest lie hid?
Or what strong hand can hold his swift foot back?
Or who his spoil of [a] beauty can forbid?
O, none, unless this miracle have might,
That in black ink my love may still shine bright.

LXVI.

Tir'd with all these, for restful death I cry,—
As, to behold desert a beggar born,
And needy nothing trimm'd in jollity,
And purest faith unhappily forsworn,
And gilded honour shamefully misplac'd,
And maiden virtue rudely strumpeted,
And right perfection wrongfully disgrac'd,
And strength by limping sway disabled,
And art made tongue-tied by authority,
And folly, doctor-like, controlling skill,
And simple truth miscall'd simplicity,
And captive good attending captain ill:—
Tir'd with all these, from these would I be gone,
Save that, to die, I leave my love alone.

LXVII.

Ah, wherefore with infection should he live,
And with his presence grace impiety,
That sin by him advantage should achieve,
And lace itself with his society?
Why should false painting imitate his cheek,
And steal dead seeing [b] of his living hue?
Why should poor beauty indirectly seek
Roses of shadow, since his rose is true?
Why should he live, now Nature bankrupt is,
Beggar'd of blood to blush through lively veins?
For she hath no exchequer now but his,
And, proud of many, lives upon his gains.
O, him she stores, to show what wealth she had
In days long since, before these last so bad.

LXVIII.

Thus is his cheek the map of days outworn,
When beauty liv'd and died as flowers do now,
Before these bastard signs of fair were born,
Or durst inhabit on a living brow;
Before the golden tresses of the dead,
The right of sepulchres, were shorn away,[c]
To live a second life on second head;
Ere beauty's dead fleece made another gay:
In him those holy antique hours are seen,
Without all ornament, itself, and true,
Making no summer of another's green,
Robbing no old to dress his beauty new;
And him as for a map doth Nature store,
To show false Art what beauty was of yore.

LXIX.

Those parts of thee that the world's eye doth view
Want nothing that the thought of hearts can mend;
All tongues, the voice of souls, give thee that due,[d]
Uttering bare truth, even so as foes commend.
Thine [e] outward thus with outward praise is crown'd;
But those same tongues that give thee so thine own,
In other accents do this praise confound,
By seeing farther than the eye hath shown.
They look into the beauty of thy mind,
And that, in guess, they measure by thy deeds;
Then, churls, their thoughts, although their eyes were kind,
To thy fair flower add the rank smell of weeds:
But why thy odour matcheth not thy show,
The solve [f] is this,—that thou dost common grow.

LXX.

That thou art blam'd shall not be thy defect,
For slander's mark was ever yet the fair;
The ornament of beauty is suspect,
A crow that flies in heaven's sweetest air.
So thou be good, slander doth but approve
Thy [g] worth the greater, being woo'd of time;
For canker vice the sweetest buds doth love,
And thou present'st a pure unstained prime.
Thou hast pass'd by the ambush of young days,
Either not assail'd, or victor being charg'd;
Yet this thy praise cannot be so thy praise,
To tie up envy evermore enlarg'd:
If some suspect of ill mask'd not thy show,
Then thou alone kingdoms of hearts shouldst owe.

LXXI.

No longer mourn for me when I am dead
Than you shall hear the surly sullen bell

---

a *Or who his spoil of beauty*—] The quarto has wrongly, "his spoil *or* beauty," &c.

b — *dead* seeing—] We would read with Farmer, "— dead *seeming*," &c.

c Before the golden tresses of the dead,
The right of sepulchres, were shorn away, &c.]

See note (2), p. 439, Vol. I. on the passage,—

"So are those crisped snaky golden locks,
Which make such wanton gambols with the wind
Upon supposed fairness, often known
To be the dowry of a second head,
The scull that bred them in the sepulchre."

d — *give thee that* due,—] So Tyrwhitt, the quarto reading, "— that *end*."

e Thine *outward*—] The old text has, "*Their* outward," &c.

f *The* solve *is this*,—] A conjecture of Malone. The quarto reading, "The solye," &c.

g Thy *worth*—] The old text is, "*Their* worth," &c.

Give warning to the world that I am fled
From this vile world, with vilest worms to dwell:
Nay, if you read this line, remember not
The hand that writ it; for I love you so,
That I in your sweet thoughts would be forgot,
If thinking on me then should make you woe.
Oh, if, I say, you look upon this verse
When I perhaps compounded am with clay,
Do not so much as my poor name rehearse;
But let your love even with my life decay;
  Lest the wise world should look into your moan,
  And mock you with me after I am gone.

LXXII.

O, lest the world should task you to recite
What merit liv'd in me that you should love,
After my death, dear love, forget me quite;
For you in me can nothing worthy prove
Unless you would devise some virtuous lie,
To do more for me than mine own desert,
And hang more praise upon deceased I
Than niggard truth would willingly impart:
O, lest your true love may seem false in this,
That you for love speak well of me untrue,
My name be buried where my body is,
And live no more to shame nor me nor you.
  For I am sham'd by that which I bring forth,
  And so should you, to love things nothing worth.

LXXIII.

That time of year thou mayst in me behold
When yellow leaves, or none, or few, do hang
Upon those boughs which shake against the cold,
Bare ruin'd[a] choirs, where late the sweet birds sang.
In me thou see'st the twilight of such day
As after sunset fadeth in the west;
Which by and by black night doth take away,
Death's second self, that seals up all in rest.
In me thou see'st the glowing of such fire,
That on the ashes of his youth doth lie,
As the death-bed whereon it must expire,
Consum'd with that which it was nourish'd by.
  This thou perceiv'st, which makes thy love more strong,
  To love that well which thou must leave ere long:

LXXIV.

But be contented: when that fell arrest
Without all bail shall carry me away,
My life hath in this line some interest,
Which for memorial still with thee shall stay.
When thou reviewest this, thou dost review
The very part was consecrate to thee:
The earth can have but earth, which is his due;
My spirit is thine, the better part of me:[b]
So, then, thou hast but lost the dregs of life,
The prey of worms, my body being dead;
The coward conquest of a wretch's knife,
Too base of thee to be remembered.
  The worth of that, is that which it contains,
  And that is this, and this with thee remains.

LXXV.

So are you to my thoughts as food to life,
Or as sweet-season'd showers are to the ground;
And for the peace of you I hold such strife
As 'twixt a miser and his wealth is found;
Now proud as an enjoyer, and anon
Doubting the filching age will steal his treasure;
Now counting best to be with you alone,
Then better'd that the world may see my pleasure:
Sometime all full with feasting on your sight,
And by and by clean starved for a look;
Possessing or pursuing no delight,
Save what is had or must from you be took.
  Thus do I pine and surfeit day by day,
  Or gluttoning on all, or all away.

LXXVI.

Why is my verse so barren of new pride,
So far from variation or quick change?
Why, with the time, do I not glance aside
To new-found methods and to compounds strange?
Why write I still all one, ever the same,
And keep invention in a noted weed,[c]
That every word doth almost tell[d] my name,
Showing their birth, and where they did proceed?
O, know, sweet love, I always write of you,
And you and love are still my argument;
So all my best is dressing old words new,
Spending again what is already spent:
  For as the sun is daily new and old,
  So is my love still telling what is told.

LXXVII.

Thy glass will show thee how thy beauties wear,
Thy dial how thy precious minutes waste;
The vacant leaves thy mind's imprint will bear,
And of this book this learning mayst thou taste.
The wrinkles which thy glass will truly show,
Of mouthed graves will give thee memory;
Thou by thy dial's shady stealth mayst know
Time's thievish progress to eternity.
Look, what thy memory cannot contain,
Commit to these waste blanks,[e] and thou shalt find
Those children nurs'd, deliver'd from thy brain,
To take a new acquaintance of thy mind.
  These offices, so oft as thou wilt look,
  Shall profit thee, and much enrich thy book.

LXXVIII.

So oft have I invok'd thee for my Muse,
And found such fair assistance in my verse,
As every alien pen hath got my use,
And under thee their poesy disperse.
Thine eyes, that taught the dumb on high to sing,
And heavy ignorance aloft to fly,
Have added feathers to the learned's wing,
And given grace a double majesty.

---

[a] *Bare* ruin'd *choirs,*—] So the edition of 1640; the quarto reads, "Bare *rn'wd* quiers," &c.

[b] *My spirit is thine, the* better part *of me:*] See note (2), p. 521, of the present volume.

[c] — in a noted weed,—] "That is, in a dress by which it is always *known*, as those persons are who always wear the same colours."—STEEVENS.

[d] — *almost* tell *my name,*—] The quarto has, "*fel* my name."

[e] *Commit to these waste* blanks,—] The old copy has, "— waste *blacks.*" From this line, and the expression a few lines before, "*vacant* leaves," &c. it has been conjectured that this Sonnet was inscribed in a book with blank leaves.

Yet be most proud of that which I compile,
Whose influence is thine, and born of thee:
In others' works thou dost but mend the style,
And arts with thy sweet graces graced be;
But thou art all my art, and dost advance
As high as learning my rude ignorance.

LXXIX.

Whilst I alone did call upon thy aid,
My verse alone had all thy gentle grace;
But now my gracious numbers are decay'd,
And my sick Muse doth give another place.
I grant, sweet love, thy lovely argument
Deserves the travail of a worthier pen;
Yet what of thee thy poet doth invent,
He robs thee of, and pays it thee again.
He lends thee virtue, and he stole that word
From thy behaviour; beauty doth he give,
And found it in thy cheek; he can afford
No praise to thee but what in thee doth live.
Then thank him not for that which he doth say,
Since what he owes thee thou thyself dost pay.

LXXX.

O, how I faint when I of you do write,
Knowing a better spirit doth use your name,[a]
And in the praise thereof spends all his might,
To make me tongue-tied, speaking of your fame!
But since your worth, wide as the ocean is,
The humble as the proudest sail doth bear,
My saucy bark, inferior far to his,
On your broad main doth wilfully appear.
Your shallowest help will hold me up afloat,
Whilst he upon your soundless deep doth ride;
Or, being wreck'd, I am a worthless boat,
He of tall building and of goodly pride:
Then if he thrive, and I be cast away,
The worst was this,—my love was my decay.

LXXXI.

Or I shall live your epitaph to make,
Or you survive when I in earth am rotten;
From hence your memory death cannot take,
Although in me each part will be forgotten.
Your name from hence immortal life shall have,
Though I, once gone, to all the world must die:
The earth can yield me but a common grave,
When you entombed in men's eyes shall lie.
Your monument shall be my gentle verse,
Which eyes not yet created shall o'er-read;
And tongues to be your being shall rehearse,
When all the breathers of this world are dead;
You still shall live,—such virtue hath my pen,—
Where breath most breathes,—even in the mouths of men.

LXXXII.

I grant thou wert not married to my Muse,
And therefore mayst without attaint o'erlook
The dedicated words which writers use
Of their fair subject, blessing every book.
Thou art as fair in knowledge as in hue,
Finding thy worth a limit past my praise;
And therefore art enforc'd to seek anew
Some fresher stamp of the time-bettering days.
And do so, love; yet when they have devis'd
What strained touches rhetoric can lend,
Thou truly fair wert truly sympathiz'd
In true-plain words, by thy true-telling friend;
And their gross painting might be better us'd
Where cheeks need blood,—in thee it is abus'd.

LXXXIII.

I never saw that you did painting need,
And therefore to your fair no painting set;
I found, or thought I found, you did exceed
The barren tender of a poet's debt:
And therefore have I slept in your report,
That you yourself, being extant, well might show
How far a modern [b] quill doth come too short,
Speaking of worth, what worth in you doth grow.
This silence for my sin you did impute,
Which shall be most my glory, being dumb;
For I impair not beauty, being mute,
When others would give life, and bring a tomb.
There lives more life in one of your fair eyes
Than both your poets can in praise devise.

LXXXIV.

Who is it that says most? which can say more
Than this rich praise,—that you alone are you?
In whose confine immured is the store
Which should example where your equal grew?
Lean penury within that pen doth dwell,
That to his subject lends not some small glory;
But he that writes of you, if he can tell
That you are you, so dignifies his story.
Let him but copy what in you is writ,
Not making worse what nature made so clear,
And such a counterpart shall fame his wit,
Making his style admired every where.
You to your beauteous blessings add a curse,
Being fond on praise,[c] which makes your praises worse.

LXXXV.

My tongue-tied Muse in manners holds her still,
While comments of your praise, richly compil'd,
Reserve [d] their character with golden quill,
And precious phrase by all the Muses fil'd.
I think good thoughts, whilst others write good words,
And, like unletter'd clerk, still cry "Amen"
To every hymn that able spirit affords,
In polish'd form of well-refined pen.
Hearing you prais'd, I say, "'T is so, 't is true,"
And to the most of praise add something more;
But that is in my thought, whose love to you,
Though words come hindmost, holds his rank before.
Then others for the breath of words respect,
Me for my dumb thoughts, speaking in effect.

[a] Knowing a better spirit doth use your name,—] This "better spirit" some editors have thought was Spenser; others have conjectured Daniel or Drayton was meant, but not a particle of evidence has yet been discovered to individualize the allusion.

[b] — modern—] *Trite, ordinary.* So, in "As You Like It," Act II. Sc. 7,—

"Full of wise saws and modern instances;"

That is, wise *sayings* and *common-place examples.*

[c] *Being fond* on *praise,*—] "On" here, as was common, is printed for *of.*

[d] Reserve *their character*—] "Reserve" for preserve, as in Sonnet XXXII.—

"*Reserve* them for my love, not for their rhyme.'

LXXXVI.

Was it the proud full sail[a] of his great verse,
Bound for the prize of all-too-precious you,
That did my ripe thoughts in my brain inhearse,
Making their tomb the womb wherein they grew?
Was it his spirit, by spirits taught to write
Above a mortal pitch, that struck me dead?
No, neither he, nor his compeers by night
Giving him aid, my verse astonished.[b]
He, nor that affable-familiar ghost
Which nightly gulls him with intelligence,
As victors, of my silence cannot boast;
I was not sick of any fear from thence,
But when your countenance fil'd[c] up his line,
Then lack'd I matter; that enfeebled mine.

LXXXVII.

Farewell! thou art too dear for my possessing,
And like enough thou know'st thy estimate:
The charter of thy worth gives thee releasing;
My bonds in thee are all determinate.
For how do I hold thee but by thy granting?
And for that riches where is my deserving?
The cause of this fair gift in me is wanting,
And so my patent back again is swerving.
Thyself thou gav'st, thy own worth then not knowing,
Or me to whom thou gav'st it, else mistaking;
So thy great gift, upon misprision growing,
Comes home again, on better judgment making.
Thus have I had thee, as a dream doth flatter,
In sleep a king, but waking no such matter.

LXXXVIII.

When thou shalt be dispos'd to set me light,
And place my merit in the eye of Scorn,
Upon thy side against myself I'll fight,
And prove thee virtuous, though thou art forsworn.
With mine own weakness being best acquainted,
Upon thy part I can set down a story
Of faults conceal'd, wherein I am attainted;
That thou, in losing me, shalt win much glory:
And I by this will be a gainer too;
For bending all my loving thoughts on thee,
The injuries that to myself I do,
Doing thee vantage, double-vantage me.
Such is my love, to thee I so belong,
That for thy right myself will bear all wrong.

LXXXIX.

Say that thou didst forsake me for some fault,
And I will comment upon that offence;
Speak of my lameness, and I straight will halt,[d]
Against thy reasons making no defence.
Thou canst not, love, disgrace me half so ill,
To set a form upon desired change,
As I'll myself disgrace: knowing thy will,
I will acquaintance strangle,[e] and look strange;
Be absent from thy walks; and in my tongue
Thy sweet-beloved name no more shall dwell,
Lest I, too much profane, should do it wrong,
And haply of our old acquaintance tell.
For thee, against myself I'll vow debate,
For I must ne'er love him whom thou dost hate.

XC.

Then hate me when thou wilt; if ever, now;
Now, while the world is bent my deeds to cross,
Join with the spite of fortune, make me bow,
And do not drop in for an after-loss:
Ah, do not, when my heart hath scap'd this sorrow,
Come in the rearward[f] of a conquer'd woe!
Give not a windy night a rainy morrow,
To linger out a purpos'd overthrow.
If thou wilt leave me, do not leave me last,
When other petty griefs have done their spite,
But in the onset come; so shall I taste
At first the very worst of fortune's might;
And other strains of woe, which now seem woe,
Compar'd with loss of thee will not seem so.

XCI.

Some glory in their birth, some in their skill,
Some in their wealth, some in their body's force;
Some in their garments, though new-fangled ill;
Some in their hawks and hounds, some in their horse;[g]
And every humour hath his adjunct pleasure,
Wherein it finds a joy above the rest:
But these particulars are not my measure;
All these I better in one general best.
Thy love is better than high birth to me,
Richer than wealth, prouder than garments' cost,
Of more delight than hawks or horses be;
And, having thee, of all men's pride I boast:
Wretched in this alone, that thou mayst take
All this away, and me most wretched make.

XCII.

But do thy worst to steal thyself away,
For term of life thou art assured mine;
And life no longer than thy love will stay,
For it depends upon that love of thine.
Then need I not to fear the worst of wrongs,
When in the least of them my life hath end.
I see a better state to me belongs
Than that which on thy humour doth depend:
Thou canst not vex me with inconstant mind,
Since that my life on thy revolt doth lie.
O, what a happy title do I find,
Happy to have thy love, happy to die!
But what's so blessed-fair that fears no blot?—
Thou mayst be false, and yet I know it not:

---

a — proud full sail—] See note a, p. 70, Vol. II.

b — astonished.] See note b, p. 755, of the present volume.

c — fil'd *up his line*,—] So in Jonson's commendatory verses on Shakespeare, prefixed to the first folio,—

"In his well-torned and true-*filed* lines."

d Speak of my lameness, and I straight will halt,—] See note g, p. 765, of the present volume.

e *I will acquaintance* strangle,—] I will *smother* or *stifle* familiarity. So in "Antony and Cleopatra," Act II. Sc. 6, "— you shall find, the band that seems to tie their friendship together will be the very *strangler* of their amity."

f *Come in the* rearward *of a conquer'd woe!*] *Rearward* is literally, *rearguard*. Shakespeare uses the word again in "Henry VI." Part I. Act III. Sc. 3,—

"Now in the *rearward* comes the duke and his—"

And, in "Henry IV." Part II. Act III. Sc. 2, "— he came ever in the *rearward* of the fashion," &c.

g — horse;] That is, *horses*.

XCIII.

So shall I live, supposing thou art true,
Like a deceived husband; so love's face
May still seem love to me, though alter'd-new;
Thy looks with me, thy heart in other place:
For there can live no hatred in thine eye,
Therefore in that I cannot know thy change.
In many's looks the false heart's history
Is writ, in moods and frowns and wrinkles strange;[a]
But heaven in thy creation did decree
That in thy face sweet love should ever dwell;
Whate'er thy thoughts or thy heart's workings be,
Thy looks should nothing thence but sweetness tell.
How like Eve's apple doth thy beauty grow,
If thy sweet virtue answer not thy show!

XCIV.

They that have power to hurt and will do none,
That do not do the thing they most do show,
Who, moving others, are themselves as stone,
Unmoved, cold, and to temptation slow;
They rightly do inherit heaven's graces,
And husband nature's riches from expense;
They are the lords and owners of their faces,
Others but stewards of their excellence.
The summer's flower is to the summer sweet,
Though to itself it only live and die;
But if that flower with base infection meet,
The basest weed outbraves his dignity:
For sweetest things turn sourest by their deeds;
Lilies that fester smell far worse than weeds.[b]

XCV.

How sweet and lovely dost thou make the shame
Which, like a canker in the fragrant rose,
Doth spot the beauty of thy budding name![c]
O, in what sweets dost thou thy sins enclose!
That tongue that tells the story of thy days,
Making lascivious comments on thy sport,
Cannot dispraise but in a kind of praise;
Naming thy name blesses an ill-report.
O, what a mansion have those vices got
Which for their habitation chose out thee,[d]
Where beauty's veil doth cover every blot,
And all things turn to fair, that eyes can see!
Take heed, dear heart, of this large privilege;
The hardest knife ill-us'd doth lose his edge.

XCVI.

Some say, thy fault is youth, some, wantonness;
Some say, thy grace is youth and gentle sport;
Both grace and faults are lov'd of more and less:[e]
Thou mak'st faults graces that to thee resort.
As on the finger of a throned queen
The basest jewel will be well esteem'd,
So are those errors that in thee are seen
To truths translated, and for true things deem'd.
How many lambs might the stern wolf betray,
If like a lamb he could his looks translate!
How many gazers mightst thou lead away,
If thou wouldst use the strength of all thy state!
But do not so; I love thee in such sort,
As, thou being mine, mine is thy good report.[f]

XCVII.

How like a winter hath my absence been
From thee, the pleasure of the fleeting year!
What freezings have I felt, what dark days seen!
What old December's bareness everywhere!
And yet this time remov'd[g] was summer's time;
The teeming autumn, big with rich increase,
Bearing the wanton burden of the prime,[h]
Like widow'd wombs after their lords' decease:
Yet this abundant issue seem'd to me
But hope of orphans and unfather'd fruit;
For summer and his pleasures wait on thee,
And, thou away, the very birds are mute;
Or, if they sing, 't is with so dull a cheer,
That leaves look pale, dreading the winter's near.

XCVIII.

From you have I been absent in the spring,
When proud-pied April,[i] dress'd in all his trim,
Had put a spirit of youth in everything,
That heavy Saturn laugh'd and leap'd with him.
Yet nor the lays of birds, nor the sweet smell
Of different flowers in odour and in hue,
Could make me any summer's story tell,
Or from their proud lap pluck them where they grew:
Nor did I wonder at the lily's white,
Nor praise the deep vermilion in the rose;
They were but sweet, but figures of delight,
Drawn after you,—you pattern of all those.
Yet seem'd it winter still, and, you away,
As with your shadow I with these did play:

---

a In many's looks the false heart's history
Is writ, in moods and frowns, &c.]

The "gracious Duncan" asserts the contrary,—

"There's no art
To find the mind's construction in the face."
Macbeth, Act I. Sc. 4.

b Lilies that fester smell far worse than weeds.] This line is found also in the play of "King Edward III." 1596. It was, perhaps, a proverbial saying.

c Doth spot the beauty of thy budding name!] So in "King John," Act V. Sc. 2,—

"(I must withdraw and weep
Upon the *spot* of this enforced cause.)"

d O, what a mansion have those vices got
Which for their habitation chose out thee,—]

Compare, "The Tempest," Act I. Sc. 2,—

"There's nothing ill can dwell in such a temple:
If the ill spirit have so fair a house,
Good things will strive to dwell with 't."

e — more and less:] *Great* and *small*. As in "Henry IV." Part I. Act IV. Sc. 3,—

"The *more and less* came in with cap and knee."

f But do not so; I love thee in such sort,
As, thou being mine, mine is thy good report.]

Sonnet XXXVI. concludes with the same couplet.

g — *this time* remov'd—] This time when I was *remote*, or *apart* from thee.

h *The teeming autumn, big with rich* increase,
Bearing the wanton burden of the prime,—]

"Increase" is *produce;* and the "prime" means the spring. Compare, "A Midsummer Night's Dream," Act II. Sc. 1,—

"The spring, the summer,
The *childing* autumn, angry winter, change
Their wonted liveries; and the 'mazed world,
By their *increase*, now knows not which is which."

i *When* proud-pied *April, dress'd in all his trim,*—] *Pied* means *many-coloured*. The line recalls a charming passage in "Romeo and Juliet," Act I. Sc. 2,—

"Such comfort, as do lusty young men feel,
When *well-apparell'd* April on the heel
Of limping winter treads."

XCIX.

The forward violet thus did I chide:—
Sweet thief, whence didst thou steal thy sweet that smells,
If not from my love's breath? The purple pride
Which on thy soft cheek for complexion dwells,
In my love's veins thou hast too grossly dy'd.
The lily I condemned for thy hand,[a]
And buds of marjoram had stol'n thy hair:
The roses fearfully on thorns did stand,
One[b] blushing shame, another white despair;
A third, nor red nor white, had stol'n of both,
And to his robbery had annex'd thy breath;
But, for his theft, in pride of all his growth
A vengeful canker eat him up to death.
More flowers I noted, yet I none could see,
But sweet or colour it had stol'n from thee.

C.

Where art thou, Muse, that thou forgett'st so long
To speak of that which gives thee all thy might?
Spend'st thou thy fury on some worthless song,
Darkening thy power, to lend base subjects light?
Return, forgetful Muse, and straight redeem
In gentle numbers time so idly spent;
Sing to the ear that doth thy lays esteem
And gives thy pen both skill and argument.
Rise, resty[c] Muse, my love's sweet face survey,
If Time have any wrinkle graven there;
If any, be a satire[d] to decay,
And make Time's spoils despised everywhere.
Give my love fame faster than Time wastes life;
So thou prevent'st his scythe and crooked knife.

CI.

O, truant Muse, what shall be thy amends
For thy neglect of truth in beauty dy'd?
Both truth and beauty on my love depends;
So dost thou too, and therein dignified.
Make answer, Muse: wilt thou not haply say,
"Truth needs no colour with his colour fix'd;
Beauty no pencil, beauty's truth to lay;
But best is best, if never intermix'd?"—
Because he needs no praise, wilt thou be dumb?
Excuse not silence so; for't lies in thee
To make him much outlive a gilded tomb,
And to be prais'd of ages yet to be.
Then do thy office, Muse; I teach thee how
To make him seem long hence as he shows now.

CII.

My love is strengthen'd, though more weak in seeming;
I love not less, though less the show appear;
That love is merchandiz'd whose rich esteeming
The owner's tongue doth publish everywhere.[e]
Our love was new, and then but in the spring,
When I was wont to greet it with my lays;
As Philomel in summer's front[f] doth sing,
And stops her[g] pipe in growth of riper days:
Not that the summer is less pleasant now
Than when her mournful hymns did hush the night,
But that wild music burdens every bough,
And sweets grown common lose their dear delight.[h]
Therefore, like her, I sometime hold my tongue,
Because I would not dull you with my song.

CIII.

Alack, what poverty my Muse brings forth,
That having such a scope to show her pride,
The argument, all bare, is of more worth
Than when it hath my added praise beside!
O, blame me not, if I no more can write!
Look in your glass, and there appears a face
That over-goes my blunt invention quite,
Dulling my lines, and doing me disgrace.
Were it not sinful, then, striving to mend,
To mar the subject that before was well?[i]
For to no other pass my verses tend
Than of your graces and your gifts to tell;
And more, much more, than in your verse can sit,
Your own glass shows you when you look in it.

CIV.

To me, fair friend, you never can be old,
For as you were when first your eye I ey'd,
Such seems your beauty still. Three winters' cold
Have from the forests shook three summers' pride,
Three beauteous springs to yellow autumn turn'd
In process of the seasons have I seen,
Three April perfumes in three hot Junes burn'd,
Since first I saw you fresh, which yet are green.

---

[a] *The lily I condemned* for thy hand,—] That is, for *stealing* the *whiteness* of thy hand.

[b] One *blushing shame,* &c.] The quarto reads, evidently by mistake, "*Our* blushing," &c.

[c] *Rise,* resty *Muse,*—] "Resty" here means *idle, torpid,* &c. So in "Cymbeline," Act III. Sc. 6,—

> "—— weariness
> Can snore upon the flint, when *resty* sloth
> Finds the down pillow hard."

Though some have thought that, in the latter example, "resty" signifies *uneasy, restive.*

[d] — a satire—] A *satirist.* So in Ben Jonson's Masque called "Time Vindicated," &c.—

> "*Fame.* Who's this?
> *Ears.* 'T is Chronomastix, the brave satyr.
> *Nose.* The gentleman-like satyr, cares for nobody."

[e]
> That love is merchandiz'd whose rich esteeming
> The owner's tongue doth publish everywhere.]

Compare, "Love's Labour's Lost," Act II. Sc. 1,—

> "—— my beauty, though but mean,
> Needs not the painted flourish of your praise;
> Beauty is bought by judgment of the eye,
> Not utter'd by base sale of chapmen's tongues."

[f] — *summer's* front—] Summer's *beginning.* So, in the "Winter's Tale," Act IV. Sc. 3,—

> "—— no shepherdess; but Flora
> Peering in April's *front.*"

[g] — her *pipe*—] The old copy has, "*his* pipe;" but see in the subsequent lines, "—*her* mournful hymns," and "Therefore like *her,*" &c.

[h] But that wild music burdens every bough, &c.] So, in the "Merchant of Venice," Act V. Sc. 1,—

> "The nightingale, if she should sing by day,
> When every goose is cackling, would be thought
> No better a musician than the wren."

[i]
> —— striving to mend,
> To mar the subject that before was well?]

As in "King Lear," Act I. Sc. 4,—

> "Striving to better, oft we mar what's well."

Ah, yet doth beauty, like a dial-hand,
Steal from his figure, and no pace perceiv'd![a]
So your sweet hue, which methinks still doth stand,
Hath motion, and mine eye may be deceiv'd:
For fear of which, hear this, thou age unbred,—
Ere you were born was beauty's summer dead.

CV.

Let not my love be call'd idolatry,
Nor my beloved as an idol show,
Since all alike my songs and praises be
To one, of one, still such, and ever so.
Kind is my love to-day, to-morrow kind,
Still constant in a wondrous excellence;
Therefore my verse to constancy confin'd,
One thing expressing, leaves out difference.
Fair, kind, and true, is all my argument,—
Fair, kind, and true, varying to other words;
And in this change is my invention spent,
Three themes in one, which wondrous scope affords.
Fair, kind, and true, have often liv'd alone,
Which three till now never kept seat in one.

CVI.

When in the chronicle of wasted time
I see descriptions of the fairest wights,
And beauty making beautiful old rhyme
In praise of ladies dead and lovely knights,
Then in the blazon of sweet beauty's best,
Of hand, of foot, of lip, of eye, of brow,[b]
I see their antique pen would have express'd
Even such a beauty as you master now.
So all their praises are but prophecies
Of this our time, all you prefiguring;
And, for they look'd but with divining eyes,
They had not skill[c] enough your worth to sing:
For we, which now behold these present days,
Have eyes to wonder, but lack tongues to praise.

CVII.

Not mine own fears, nor the prophetic soul
Of the wide world dreaming on things to come,
Can yet the lease of my true love control,
Suppos'd as forfeit to a confin'd doom.
The mortal moon hath her eclipse endur'd,
And the sad augurs mock their own presage;
Incertainties now crown themselves assur'd,
And peace proclaims olives of endless age.
Now with the drops of this most balmy time
My love looks fresh, and Death to me subscribes,[d]
Since, spite of him, I'll live in this poor rhyme,
While he insults o'er dull and speechless tribes:
And thou in this shalt find thy monument,
When tyrants' crests and tombs of brass are spent.

CVIII.

What's in the brain, that ink may character,
Which hath not figur'd to thee my true spirit?
What's new to speak, what new[e] to register,
That may express my love, or thy dear merit?
Nothing, sweet boy; but yet, like prayers divine,
I must each day say o'er the very same;
Counting no old thing old, thou mine, I thine,
Even as when first I hallow'd thy fair name.
So that eternal love in love's fresh case
Weighs not the dust and injury of age,
Nor gives to necessary wrinkles place,
But makes antiquity for aye his page;
Finding the first conceit of love there bred,
Where time and outward form would show it dead.

CIX.

O, never say that I was false of heart,
Though absence seem'd my flame to qualify!
As easy might I from myself depart,
As from my soul, which in thy breast doth lie:
That is my home of love: if I have rang'd,
Like him that travels, I return again;[f]
Just to the time, not with the time exchang'd,—
So that myself bring water for my stain.
Never believe, though in my nature reign'd
All frailties that besiege all kinds of blood,
That it could so preposterously be stain'd,
To leave for nothing all thy sum of good;
For nothing this wide universe I call,
Save thou, my rose; in it thou art my all.

CX.

Alas, 't is true I have gone here and there,
And made myself a motley[g] to the view,
Gor'd mine own thoughts, sold cheap what is most dear,
Made old offences of affections new.
Most true it is that I have look'd on truth
Askance and strangely; but, by all above,
These blenches gave my heart another youth,
And worse essays prov'd thee my best of love.
Now all is done, have[h] what shall have no end:
Mine appetite I never more will grind
On newer proof, to try an older friend,
A god in love, to whom I am confin'd.
Then give me welcome, next my heaven the best,
Even to thy pure and most-most loving breast.

---

a "—— like a dial-hand,
Steal from his figure, and no pace perceiv'd!]

So in Sonnet LXXVII.—

"Thou by thy dial's shady *stealth* mayst know
Time's *thievish* progress to eternity."

b Then in the blazon of sweet beauty's best,
Of hand, of foot, of lip, of eye, of brow,—]

So in "Twelfth Night," Act I. Sc. 5,—

"Thy tongue, thy face, thy limbs, actions, and spirit,
Do give thee five-fold *blazon*."

c — skill *enough*—] An emendation due to Tyrwhitt, the old copy having, "*still* enough."

d — *and Death to me* subscribes,—] That is, *succumbs*. So in Troilus and Cressida," Act IV. Sc. 5,—

"For Hector, in his blaze of wrath, *subscribes*
To tender objects."

e *What's new to speak, what* new *to register*,—] So Malone, and perhaps rightly though some editors still follow the quarto in reading, "— what *now* to register."

f That is my home of love: if I have rang'd,
Like him that travels, I return again;]

Compare, "A Midsummer Night's Dream," Act III. Sc. 2,—

"My heart to her but as guest-wise sojourn'd;
And now to Helen is it home return'd."

g *And made myself a* motley—] As a *motley* dress was the usual garb of a jester, *motley* became in time the synonym for a *fool*.

h *Now all is done*, have *what shall have no end*:] Malone, adopting a suggestion of Tyrwhitt, prints, "— *save* what shall have no end," to the manifest improvement of the sense; but as the old reading is intelligible, we are hardly warranted in making any change.

CXI.

O, for my sake do you with [a] Fortune chide,
The guilty goddess of my harmful deeds,
That did not better for my life provide,
Than public means, which public manners breeds.
Thence comes it that my name receives a brand;
And almost thence my nature is subdu'd
To what it works in, like the dyer's hand:
Pity me, then, and wish I were renew'd;
Whilst, like a willing patient, I will drink
Potions of eisel,[b] 'gainst my strong infection;
No bitterness that I will bitter think,
Nor double penance, to correct correction.
Pity me, then, dear friend, and I assure ye,
Even that your pity is enough to cure me.

CXII.

Your love and pity doth th' impression fill
Which vulgar scandal stamp'd upon my brow;
For what care I who calls me well or ill,
So you o'er-green my bad, my good allow?
You are my all-the-world, and I must strive
To know my shames and praises from your tongue;
None else to me, nor I to none alive,
That my steel'd sense' or changes right or wrong.[c]
In so profound abysm I throw all care
Of others' voices, that my adder's sense'
To critic [d] and to flatterer stopped are.
Mark how with my neglect I do dispense:—
You are so strongly in my purpose bred,
That all the world besides methinks are [e] dead.

CXIII.

Since I left you, mine eye is in my mind;
And that which governs me to go about
Doth part his function,[f] and is partly blind,
Seems seeing, but effectually is out;
For it no form delivers to the heart
Of bird, of flower, or shape, which it doth latch: [g]
Of his quick objects hath the mind no part,
Nor his own vision holds what it doth catch;
For if it see the rud'st or gentlest sight,
The most sweet favour or deformed'st creature,
The mountain or the sea, the day or night,
The crow or dove, it shapes them to your feature:
Incapable of more, replete with you,
My most true mind thus maketh mine untrue.[h]

CXIV.

Or whether doth my mind, being crown'd with you,
Drink up the monarch's plague, this flattery?
Or whether shall I say, mine eye saith true,
And that your love taught it this alchemy,
To make of monsters and things indigest
Such cherubins as your sweet self resemble,
Creating every bad a perfect best,
As fast as objects to his beams assemble?
O, 't is the first; 't is flattery in my seeing,
And my great mind most kingly drinks it up:
Mine eye well knows what with his gust is 'greeing,
And to his palate doth prepare the cup:
If it be poison'd, 't is the lesser sin
That mine eye loves it, and doth first begin.

CXV.

Those lines that I before have writ do lie;
Even those that said I could not love you dearer:
Yet then my judgment knew no reason why
My most full flame should afterwards burn clearer.
But reckoning Time, whose million'd accidents
Creep in 'twixt vows, and change decrees of kings,
Tan sacred beauty, blunt the sharp'st intents,
Divert strong minds to the course of altering things;
Alas, why, fearing of Time's tyranny,
Might I not then say, "Now I love you best,"
When I was certain o'er incertainty,
Crowning the present, doubting of the rest?
Love is a babe; then might I not say so,
To give full growth to that which still doth grow?

CXVI.

Let me not to the marriage of true minds
Admit impediments. Love is not love
Which alters when it alteration finds,[i]
Or bends with the remover to remove:
O, no! it is an ever-fixed mark,
That looks on tempests, and is never shaken; [k]
It is the star to every wandering bark,
Whose worth's unknown, although his height be taken.

---

[a] — *do you* with *Fortune chide,*—] The quarto corruptly reads, "*wish,*" for "with." To *chide with* is to *quarrel with.* So, in "Cymbeline," Act V. Sc. 4,—

"With Mars fall out, *with* Juno *chide,*" &c.

Again, in "Othello," Act IV. Sc. 3,—

"The business of the state does him offence,
And he does *chide with* you."

[b] — eisel,—] "Eisel" is vinegar, which, as Malone remarks, was esteemed very efficacious in preventing the communication of infectious distempers.

[c] None else to me, nor I to none alive,
That my steel'd sense' or changes right or wrong.]

Steevens explains this,—"You are the only person who has power to change my stubborn resolution, *either* to what is right, or to what is wrong."

[d] — critic—] *Cynic.*

[e] — *methinks* are *dead.*] In the old copy, "Methinks *y'are* dead."

[f] Doth part his function,—] Performs part of his office.

[g] — *which it doth* latch;] To *latch* is to seize, or catch. The quarto in error reads, "doth *luck.*"

[h] My most true mind thus maketh mine untrue.] "I once suspected that Shakespeare wrote,—

'My most true mind thus makes mine *eye* untrue.'

Or,—

'*Thy* most true mind thus maketh mine untrue.'

But the text is undoubtedly right. The word *untrue* is used as a substantive. "The sincerity of my affection is the cause of my untruth," *i.e.* of my not seeing objects truly, such as they appear to the rest of mankind. So in "Measure for Measure,"—

'Say what you can, my false outweighs your *true.*'"

MALONE.

[i] Love is not love
Which alters when it alteration finds,—]

Compare, "King Lear," Act I. Sc. 1,—

"*Love's not love*
When it is mingled with regards, that stand
Aloof from th' entire point."

[k] —— it is an ever-fixed mark,
That looks on tempests, and is never shaken;]

So in "Coriolanus," Act V. Sc. 3,—

"—— and stick i' the wars
Like a great *sea-mark, standing every flaw,*
And saving those that eye thee!"

Love's not Time's fool,[a] though rosy lips and cheeks
Within his bending sickle's compass come;
Love alters not with his brief hours and weeks,
But bears it out even to the edge of doom.
If this be error, and upon me prov'd,
I never writ, nor no man ever lov'd.

CXVII.

Accuse me thus:—that I have scanted all
Wherein I should your great deserts repay;
Forgot upon your dearest love to call,
Whereto all bonds do tie me day by day;
That I have frequent been with unknown minds,
And given to time your own dear-purchas'd right;
That I have hoisted sail to all the winds
Which should transport me farthest from your sight.
Book both my wilfulness and errors down,
And on just proof surmise accumulate;
Bring me within the level of your frown,[b]
But shoot not at me in your waken'd hate;
Since my appeal says I did strive to prove
The constancy and virtue of your love.

CXVIII.

Like as, to make our appetites more keen,
With eager [c] compounds we our palate urge;
As, to prevent our maladies unseen,
We sicken to shun sickness when we purge;
Even so, being full of your ne'er-cloying sweetness,
To bitter sauces did I frame my feeding;
And, sick of welfare, found a kind of meetness
To be diseas'd, ere that there was true needing.
Thus policy in love, to anticipate
The ills that were not, grew to faults assur'd,
And brought to medicine a healthful state,
Which, rank [d] of goodness, would by ill be cur'd.
But thence I learn, and find the lesson true,
Drugs poison him that so fell sick of you.

CXIX.

What potions have I drunk of Siren tears,
Distill'd from limbecs foul as hell within,
Applying fears to hopes, and hopes to fears,
Still losing when I saw myself to win!
What wretched errors hath my heart committed,
Whilst it hath thought itself so blessed never!
How have mine eyes out of their spheres been fitted,[e]
In the distraction of this madding fever!
O, benefit of ill! now I find true
That better is by evil still made better;
And ruin'd love, when it is built anew,
Grows fairer than at first, more strong, far greater.
So I return rebuk'd to my content,
And gain by ill [f] thrice more than I have spent.

CXX.

That you were once unkind befriends me now,
And for that sorrow which I then did feel
Needs must I under my transgression bow,
Unless my nerves were brass or hammer'd steel.
For if you were by my unkindness shaken,
As I by yours, you 've pass'd a hell of time;
And I, a tyrant, have no leisure taken
To weigh how once I suffer'd in your crime.
O, that our night of woe might have remember'd [g]
My deepest sense, how hard true sorrow hits,
And soon to you, as you to me then, tender'd
The humble salve which wounded bosoms fits!
But that your trespass now becomes a fee;
Mine ransoms yours, and yours must ransom me.

CXXI.

'T is better to be vile than vile-esteem'd,
When not to be receives reproach of being,
And the just pleasure lost, which is so deem'd
Not by our feeling, but by others' seeing:
For why should others' false-adulterate eyes
Give salutation to my sportive blood? [h]
Or on my frailties why are frailer spies,
Which in their wills count bad what I think good?
No.—I am that I am; and they that level
At my abuses reckon up their own:
I may be straight, though they themselves be bevel; [i]
By their rank thoughts my deeds must not be shown;
Unless this general evil they maintain,—
All men are bad, and in their badness reign.

CXXII.

Thy gift, thy tables, are within my brain
Full character'd with lasting memory,
Which shall above that idle rank remain,
Beyond all date, even to eternity:
Or, at the least, so long as brain and heart
Have faculty by nature to subsist;
Till each to raz'd oblivion yield his part
Of thee, thy record never can be miss'd.

---

a Love 's not Time's fool,—] So, in "Henry IV." Part I. Act V. Sc. 4,—

"But thought's the slave of life, and life Time's fool."

See note *ad l.* p. 559, Vol. I.

b *Bring me within the* level *of your frown,*—] The "level" meant the range; thus, in "The Winter's Tale," Act II. Sc. 3,—

"—— for the harlot king
Is quite beyond mine arm, out of the blank
And *level* of my brain."

c — eager—] "Eager," Fr. *aigre*, is *tart, sour, poignant.* So, in "Hamlet," Act I. Sc. 5,—

"—— it doth posset
And curd, like *eager* droppings into milk."

d — rank of *goodness,*—] That is, *flush* or *brimful* of goodness. So, in "Antony and Cleopatra," Act V. Sc. 2,—

"—— their thick breaths,
Rank of gross diet."

e *How have mine eyes out of their spheres been* fitted,—] "Fitted" here means *started,* as by paroxysms. Compare, "Hamlet," Act I. Sc. 5,—

"Make thy two eyes, like stars, *start from their spheres;*"

and also, "Pericles," Act II. Sc. 1,—

"If it be a day *fits* you, scratch out of the calendar," &c.

f *And gain by* ill—] Old copy, "by *ills.*"

g — remember'd—] *Reminded.* So in "Richard III." Act II. Sc. 4,—

"—— if I had been *remember'd,*" &c.

h *Give* salutation to my sportive blood?] See note b, p. 665, Vol. II.

i — bevel;] *Crooked.*

That poor retention could not so much hold,[a]
Nor need I tallies thy dear love to score;
Therefore to give them from me was I bold,
To trust those tables that receive thee more:
To keep an adjunct to remember thee,
Were to import forgetfulness in me.

CXXIII.

No, Time, thou shalt not boast that I do change!
Thy pyramids built up with newer might
To me are nothing novel, nothing strange;
They are but dressings of a former sight.
Our dates are brief, and therefore we admire
What thou dost foist upon us that is old;
And rather make them born to our desire
Than think that we before have heard them told.
Thy registers and thee I both defy,
Not wondering at the present nor the past;
For thy records and what we see do lie,
Made more or less by thy continual haste.
This I do vow, and this shall ever be,
I will be true, despite thy scythe and thee.

CXXIV.

If my dear love were but the child of state,
It might for Fortune's bastard be unfather'd,
As subject to Time's love or to Time's hate,
Weeds among weeds, or flowers with flowers gather'd.
No, it was builded far from accident;
It suffers not in smiling pomp, nor falls
Under the blow of thralled discontent,
Whereto th' inviting time our fashion calls:
It fears not policy, that heretic,
Which works on leases of short-number'd hours,
But all alone stands hugely politic,
That it nor grows with heat nor drowns with showers.
To this I witness call the fools of time,
Which die for goodness, who have liv'd for crime.

CXXV.

Were 't aught to me I bore the canopy,
With my extern the outward honouring,
Or laid great bases for eternity,
Which prove more short than waste or ruining?
Have I not seen dwellers on form and favour
Lose all, and more, by paying too much rent,
For compound sweet forgoing simple savour,
Pitiful thrivers, in their gazing spent?
No;—let me be obsequious in thy heart,
And take thou my oblation, poor but free,
Which is not mix'd with seconds, knows no art,
But mutual render, only me for thee.
Hence, thou suborn'd informer! a true soul
When most impeach'd stands least in thy control.

CXXVI.

O thou, my lovely boy,[b] who in thy power
Dost hold Time's fickle glass, his sickle-hour;
Who hast by waning grown, and therein show'st
Thy lovers withering, as thy sweet self grow'st;
If Nature, sovereign mistress over wrack,
As thou goest onwards, still will pluck thee back,
She keeps thee to this purpose, that her skill
May time disgrace, and wretched minutes kill.
Yet fear her, O thou minion of her pleasure!
She may detain, but not still keep, her treasure:
Her audit, though delay'd, answer'd must be,
And her quietus [c] is to render thee.

CXXVII.

In the old age black was not counted fair,[d]
Or if it were, it bore not beauty's name;
But now is black beauty's successive heir,
And beauty slander'd with a bastard shame:
For since each hand hath put on nature's power,
Fairing the foul with art's false-borrow'd face,
Sweet beauty hath no name, no holy bower,
But is profan'd, if not lives in disgrace.
Therefore my mistress' eyes[e] are raven black,
Her eyes so suited; and they mourners seem
At such who, not born fair, no beauty lack,
Slandering creation with a false esteem:
Yet so they mourn, becoming of their woe,
That every tongue says beauty should look so.

CXXVIII.

How oft, when thou, my music, music play'st,
Upon that blessed wood whose motion sounds
With thy sweet fingers, when thou gently sway'st
The wiry concord that mine ear confounds,
Do I envý those jacks,[f] that nimble leap
To kiss the tender inward of thy hand,
Whilst my poor lips, which should that harvest reap,
At the wood's boldness by thee blushing stand!
To be so tickled, they would change their state
And situation with those dancing chips,
O'er whom thy[g] fingers walk with gentle gait,
Making dead wood more bless'd than living lips.
Since saucy jacks so happy are in this,
Give them thy fingers, me thy lips to kiss.

---

a That poor retention could not so much hold,—] "*That poor retention* is the table-book given to him by his friend, incapable of *retaining*, or rather of *containing*, so much as the *tablet of the brain*."—MALONE.

b O thou, my lovely boy,—] "This sonnet differs from all the others in the present collection, not being written in alternate rhymes."—MALONE.

c — quietus—] *Discharge, acquittance, release.* So in Webster's "Duchess of Malfi," Act III. Sc. 2,—

"You had the trick in audit-time to be sick,
Till I had sign'd your *quietus*."

d In the old age black was not counted fair,—] This and all the remaining Sonnets are addressed to a woman.

e *Therefore my mistress'* eyes *are raven black,*
Her eyes *so suited;*] Here we suspect the repetition of "eyes" to have been a slip of the compositor, and that the poet wrote,—

"—— my mistress' *brows* are raven black," &c.

or,—

"—— my mistress' eyes are raven black,
Her *brows* so suited," &c.

Compare, "Love's Labour's Lost," Act IV. Sc. 3,—

"O, if in black my lady's *brows* be deck'd,
It mourns, that painting, and usurping hair,
Should ravish doters with a false aspect;
And therefore is she born to make black fair."

f — *those* jacks,—] The keys of a spinnet or virginal were termed "jacks."

g — thy *fingers*—] In this, as in the last line, the old copy misprints *their* for "thy."

CXXIX.

Th' expense of spirit in a waste of shame
Is lust in action; and till action, lust
Is perjur'd, murderous, bloody, full of blame.
Savage, extreme, rude, cruel, not to trust;
Enjoy'd no sooner but despised straight;
Past reason hunted; and no sooner had,
Past reason hated, as a swallow'd bait,
On purpose laid to make the taker mad:
Mad in pursuit, and in possession so;
Had, having, and in quest to have, extreme;
A bliss in proof,—and prov'd, a[a] very woe;
Before, a joy propos'd; behind, a dream.
All this the world well knows; yet none knows well
To shun the heaven that leads men to this hell.

CXXX.

My mistress' eyes are nothing like the sun;
Coral is far more red than her lips' red:
If snow be white, why then her breasts are dun;
If hairs be wires, black wires grow on her head.
I have seen roses, damask'd red and white,
But no such roses see I in her cheeks;
And in some perfumes is there more delight
Than in the breath that from my mistress reeks.
I love to hear her speak,—yet well I know
That music hath a far more pleasing sound;
I grant I never saw a goddess go,—
My mistress, when she walks, treads on the ground:
And yet, by heaven, I think my love as rare
As any she belied with false compare!

CXXXI.

Thou art as tyrannous, so as thou art,
As those whose beauties proudly make them cruel;
For well thou know'st to my dear-doting heart
Thou art the fairest and most precious jewel.
Yet, in good faith, some say that thee behold,
Thy face hath not the power to make love groan:
To say they err, I dare not be so bold,
Although I swear it to myself alone.
And, to be sure that is not false I swear,
A thousand groans, but thinking on thy face,
One on another's neck, do witness bear
Thy black is fairest in my judgment's place.
In nothing art thou black save in thy deeds,
And thence this slander, as I think, proceeds.

CXXXII.

Thine eyes I love, and they, as pitying me,
Knowing thy heart torments[b] me with disdain,
Have put on black, and loving mourners be,
Looking with pretty ruth upon my pain.
And truly not the morning sun of heaven
Better becomes the grey cheeks of the east,
Nor that full star that ushers in the even
Doth half that glory to the sober west,
As those two mourning eyes become thy face:
O, let it then as well beseem thy heart
To mourn for me, since mourning doth thee grace,
And suit thy pity like in every part.
Then will I swear beauty herself is black,
And all they foul that thy complexion lack.

CXXXIII.

Beshrew that heart that makes my heart to groan
For that deep wound it gives my friend and me!
Is 't not enough to torture me alone,
But slave to slavery my sweet'st friend must be?
Me from myself thy cruel eye hath taken,
And my next self thou harder hast engross'd:
Of him, myself, and thee, I am forsaken;
A torment thrice three-fold thus to be cross'd.
Prison my heart in thy steel bosom's ward,
But then my friend's heart let my poor heart bail;
Who e'er keeps[c] me, let my heart be his guard;
Thou canst not then use rigour in my gaol:
And yet thou wilt; for I, being pent in thee,
Perforce am thine, and all that is in me.

CXXXIV.

So, now I have confess'd that he is thine,
And I myself am mortgag'd to thy will,
Myself I'll forfeit, so that other mine
Thou wilt restore, to be my comfort still:
But thou wilt not, nor he will not be free,
For thou art covetous, and he is kind;
He learn'd but, surety-like, to write for me,
Under that bond that him as fast doth bind.
The statute[d] of thy beauty thou wilt take,
Thou usurer, that putt'st forth all to use,
And sue a friend came debtor for my sake;
So him I lose through my unkind abuse.
Him have I lost; thou hast both him and me:
He pays the whole, and yet am I not free.

CXXXV.

Whoever hath her wish, thou hast thy *Will*,[e]
And *Will* to boot, and *Will* in over-plus;
More than enough am I that vex thee still,
To thy sweet will making addition thus.
Wilt thou, whose will is large and spacious,
Not once vouchsafe to hide my will in thine?
Shall will in others seem right gracious,
And in my will no fair acceptance shine?

a *— and* prov'd, a *very woe*;] An ingenious amendment by Malone; the quarto reading,—

"—— and *proud and* very woe."

b *Thine eyes I love, and they, as pitying me,*
Knowing thy heart torments me with disdain,
Have put on black, &c.]

In the quarto we have,—"*torment* me," &c. which many modern editors have adopted, although the self-evident correction was made a century and a half ago.

c *Who e'er* keeps *me, let my heart be his guard*;] *To keep*, means *to guard, defend.*

d *The* statute *of thy beauty*—] "*Statute* has here its legal signification, that of a security or obligation for money."—MALONE.

e — thou hast thy *Will*,—] The play upon the name of "Will" in this and the two next Sonnets obviously points to the poet's own Christian name; but it perhaps indicates also the prenomen of "the only begetter of these Sonnets," "Mr. W. H."

The sea, all water, yet receives rain still,
And, in abundance, addeth to his store;
So thou, being rich in *Will*, add to thy *Will*
One will of mine, to make thy large *Will* more.
Let no unkind, no fair beseechers kill;
Think all but one, and me in that one *Will*.

CXXXVI.

If thy soul check thee that I come so near,
Swear to thy blind soul that I was thy *Will*,
And will, thy soul knows, is admitted there;
Thus far for love, my love-suit, sweet, fulfil.
Will will fulfil the treasure of thy love,
Ay, fill it full with wills, and my will one,
In things of great receipt with ease we prove
Among a number one is reckon'd none:[a]
Then in the number let me pass untold,
Though in thy stores' account I one must be;
For nothing hold me, so it please thee hold
That nothing me, a something sweet to thee:
Make but my name thy love, and love that still,
And then thou lov'st me,—for my name is *Will*.

CXXXVII.

Thou blind fool, Love, what dost thou to mine eyes,
That they behold, and see not what they see?
They know what beauty is, see where it lies,
Yet what the best is, take the worst to be.
If eyes, corrupt by over-partial looks,
Be anchor'd in the bay where all men ride,
Why of eyes' falsehood hast thou forged hooks,
Whereto the judgment of my heart is tied?
Why should my heart think that a several plot,
Which my heart knows the wide world's common place?[b]
Or mine eyes, seeing this, say this is not,
To put fair truth upon so foul a face?
In things right-true my heart and eyes have err'd,
And to this false plague are they now transferr'd.

CXXXVIII.

When my love swears that she is made of truth[c]
I do believe her, though I know she lies,
That she might think me some untutor'd youth,
Unlearned in the world's false subtleties.
Thus vainly thinking that she thinks me young,
Although she knows my days are past the best,
Simply I credit her false-speaking tongue:
On both sides thus is simple truth suppress.
But wherefore says she not she is unjust?
And wherefore say not I that I am old?
O, love's best habit is in seeming trust,
And age in love loves not to have years told:
Therefore I lie with her and she with me,
And in our faults by lies we flatter'd be.

CXXXIX.

O, call not me to justify the wrong
That thy unkindness lays upon my heart;
Wound me not with thine eye, but with thy tongue;
Use power with power, and slay me not by art.
Tell me thou lov'st elsewhere; but in my sight,
Dear heart, forbear to glance thine eye aside:
What need'st thou wound with cunning, when thy might
Is more than my o'erpress'd defence can 'bide?
Let me excuse thee: ah, my love well knows
Her pretty looks have been mine enemies!
And therefore from my face she turns my foes,
That they elsewhere might dart their injuries:
Yet do not so; but since I am near slain,
Kill me outright with looks, and rid my pain

CXL.

Be wise as thou art cruel; do not press
My tongue-tied patience with too much disdain;
Lest sorrow lend me words, and words express
The manner of my pity-wanting pain.
If I might teach thee wit, better it were,
Though not to love, yet, love, to tell me so;—
As testy sick men, when their deaths be near,
No news but health from their physicians know;—
For, if I should despair, I should grow mad,
And in my madness might speak ill of thee:
Now this ill-wresting world is grown so bad,
Mad slanderers by mad ears believed be.
That I may not be so, nor thou belied,
Bear thine eyes straight, though thy proud heart go wide.

CXLI.

In faith, I do not love thee with mine eyes,
For they in thee a thousand errors note;
But 't is my heart that loves what they despise,
Who, in despite of view, is pleas'd to dote;
Nor are mine ears with thy tongue's tune delighted;
Nor tender feeling, to base touches prone,
Nor taste, nor smell, desire to be invited
To any sensual feast with thee alone:
But my five wits[d] nor my five senses can
Dissuade one foolish heart from serving thee,
Who leaves unsway'd the likeness of a man,
Thy proud heart's slave and vassal wretch to be:
Only my plague thus far I count my gain,
That she that makes me sin awards me pain.

CXLII.

Love is my sin, and thy dear virtue hate,
Hate of my sin, grounded on sinful loving:
O, but with mine compare thou thine own state,
And thou shalt find it merits not reproving;

---

a In things of great receipt with ease we prove
Among a number one is reckon'd none:]

Compare, "Romeo and Juliet," Act I. Sc. 2,—

"Such, amongst view of many, mine, being one,
May stand in number, though in reckoning none."

b *Why should my heart think that a* several *plot,*
Which my heart knows the wide world's common *place?*]

"*Severals*, or *several lands*," Mr. Hunter tells us, "are portions of common assigned for a term to a particular proprietor, the other commoners waiving for the time their right of common over them."

c When my love swears that she is made of truth—] This Sonnet with some variations appears to have been first printed in "The Passionate Pilgrim," 1599.

d But my five wits—] The five wits were common wit, imagination, fantasy, estimation, and memory.

Or, if it do, not from those lips of thine,
That have profan'd their scarlet ornaments,[a]
And seal'd false bonds of love as oft as mine;[b]
Robb'd others' beds' revenues of their rents.
Be it lawful I love thee, as thou lov'st those
Whom thine eyes woo as mine importune thee:
Root pity in thy heart, that, when it grows,
Thy pity may deserve to pitied be.
If thou dost seek to have what thou dost hide,
By self-example mayst thou be denied!

CXLIII.

Lo, as a careful housewife runs to catch
One of her feather'd creatures broke away,
Sets down her babe, and makes all swift despatch
In púrsuit of the thing she would have stay;
Whilst her neglected child holds her in chace,
Cries to catch her whose busy care is bent
To follow that which flies before her face,
Not prizing her poor infant's discontent;
So runn'st thou after that which flies from thee,
Whilst I thy babe chase thee afar behind;
But if thou catch thy hope, turn back to me,
And play the mother's part, kiss me, be kind:
So will I pray that thou mayst have thy *Will*,
If thou turn back, and my loud crying still.

CXLIV.

Two loves I have of comfort and despair,[c]
Which like two spirits do suggest[d] me still;
The better angel is a man right fair,
The worser spirit a woman colour'd ill.
To win me soon to hell, my female evil
Tempteth my better angel from my side,[e]
And would corrupt my saint to be a devil,
Wooing his purity with her foul pride.
And whether that my angel be turn'd fiend,
Suspect I may, yet not directly tell;
But being both from me, both to each friend,
I guess one angel in another's hell:
Yet this shall I ne'er know, but live in doubt,
Till my bad angel fire my good one out.

CXLV.

Those lips that Love's own hand did make
Breath'd forth the sound that said, "I hate,"
To me that languish'd for her sake:
But when she saw my woeful state,
Straight in her heart did mercy come,
Chiding that tongue, that ever sweet
Was us'd in giving gentle doom;
And taught it thus anew to greet;
"I hate," she alter'd with an end,
That follow'd it as gentle day
Doth follow night, who, like a fiend,
From heaven to hell is flown away;
"I hate," from hate away she threw,
And sav'd my life, saying—"not you."

CXLVI.

Poor soul, the centre of my sinful earth,
Fool'd by these rebel powers that thee array,[f]
Why dost thou pine within and suffer dearth,
Painting thy outward walls so costly gay?
Why so large cost, having so short a lease,
Dost thou upon thy fading mansion spend?
Shall worms, inheritors of this excess,
Eat up thy charge? is this thy body's end?
Then, soul, live thou upon thy servant's loss,
And let that pine to aggravate thy store;
Buy terms divine in selling hours of dross;
Within be fed, without be rich no more:
So shalt thou feed on Death, that feeds on men,
And Death once dead, there's no more dying then.

CXLVII.

My love is as a fever, longing still
For that which longer nurseth the disease;
Feeding on that which doth preserve the ill,
Th' uncertain-sickly appetite to please.
My reason, the physician to my love,
Angry that his prescriptions are not kept,
Hath left me, and I, desperate now, approve
Desire is death, which physic did except.
Past cure I am, now reason is past care,
And frantic-mad with evermore unrest;
My thoughts and my discourse as madmen's are,
At random from the truth vainly express'd;
For I have sworn thee fair, and thought thee bright,
Who art as black as hell, as dark as night.

CXLVIII.

O me, what eyes hath Love put in my head,
Which have no correspondence with true sight!
Or, if they have, where is my judgment fled,
That censures[g] falsely what they see aright?
If that be fair whereon my false eyes dote,
What means the world to say it is not so?
If it be not, then love doth well denote
Love's eye is not so true as all men's: no;[h]
How can it? O, how can Love's eye be true,
That is so vex'd with watching and with tears?
No marvel, then, though I mistake my view;
The sun itself sees not, till heaven clears.
O, cunning love! with tears thou keep'st me blind,
Lest eyes well-seeing thy foul faults should find.

---

a — their scarlet ornaments,—] So in "King Edward III." 1596,—

"—— when she grew pale,
His cheeks put on *their scarlet ornaments*."

b *And* seal'd false bonds of love *as oft as mine;*] Compare, "The Merchant of Venice," Act II. Sc. 6,—

"O, ten times faster Venus' pigeons fly
To *seal love's bonds* new made, than they are wont
To keep obliged faith unforfeited!"

c Two loves I have of comfort and despair,—] This Sonnet was printed "with a difference" in "The Passionate Pilgrim," 1599.
d — suggest *me*—] *Tempt* me.
e — *from my* side,—] The quarto has, "from my *sight;*" the genuine word, however, is found in "The Passionate Pilgrim."

f Poor soul, the centre of my sinful earth,
Fool'd by these rebel powers that thee array,—]

In the old copy the transcriber or compositor has mistakenly repeated the last three words of the preceding line, and given us,—

"My *sinful earth* these rebell powres that thee array."

The emendation, "*Fool'd* by," is Malone's.
g — censures—] *Estimates, measures.*
h Love's eye is not so true as all men's: no;] We believe with Mr. W. N. Lettsom, that a quibble was intended, and that the poet wrote,—

"Love's eye [I = ay] is not so true as all men's no."

CXLIX.

Canst thou, O cruel! say I love thee not,
When I, against myself, with thee partake? [a]
Do I not think on thee, when I forgot
Am of myself, all tyrant, for thy sake?
Who hateth thee that I do call my friend?
On whom frown'st thou that I do fawn upon?
Nay if thou low'rst on me, do I not spend
Revenge upon myself with present moan?
What merit do I in myself respect,
That is so proud thy service to despise,
When all my best doth worship thy defect,
Commanded by the motion of thine eyes?
But, love, hatė on, for now I know thy mind;
Those that can see thou lov'st, and I am blind.

CL.

O, from what power hast thou this powerful might,
With insufficiency my heart to sway?
To make me give the lie to my true sight,
And swear that brightness doth not grace the day? [b]
Whence hast thou this becoming of things ill, [c]
That in the very refuse of thy deeds
There is such strength and warrantise of skill,
That, in my mind, thy worst all best exceeds?
Who taught thee how to make me love thee more,
The more I hear and see just cause of hate?
O, though I love what others do abhor,
With others thou shouldst not abhor my state:
If thy unworthiness rais'd love in me,
More worthy I to be belov'd of thee.

CLI.

Love is too young to know what conscience is;
Yet who knows not, conscience is born of love?
Then, gentle cheater, [d] urge not my amiss,
Lest guilty of my faults thy sweet self prove:
For thou betraying me, I do betray
My nobler part to my gross body's treason;
My soul doth tell my body that he may
Triumph in love; flesh stays no farther reason;
But, rising at thy name, doth point out thee
As his triumphant prize. Proud of this pride,
He is contented thy poor drudge to be,
To stand in thy affairs, fall by thy side.
No want of conscience hold it that I call
Her "love" for whose dear love I rise and fall.

CLII.

In loving thee thou know'st I am forsworn,
But thou art twice forsworn, to me love swearing;
In act thy bed-vow broke, and new faith torn,
In vowing new hate after new love bearing.
But why of two oaths' breach do I accuse thee,
When I break twenty? I am perjured most;
For all my vows are oaths but to misuse thee,
And all my honest faith in thee is lost:
For I have sworn deep oaths of thy deep kindness,
Oaths of thy love, thy truth, thy constancy;
And, to enlighten thee, gave eyes to blindness,
Or made them swear against the thing they see;
For I have sworn thee fair,—more perjur'd I, [e]
To swear, against the truth, so foul a lie!

CLIII.

Cupid laid by his brand, and fell asleep:
A maid of Dian's this advantage found,
And his love-kindling fire did quickly steep
In a cold valley-fountain of that ground;
Which borrow'd from this holy fire of Love
A dateless-lively heat, still to endure,
And grew a seething bath, which yet men prove
Against strange maladies a sovereign cure.
But at my mistress' eye Love's brand new-fir'd,
The boy for trial needs would touch my breast;
I, sick withal, the help of bath desir'd,
And thither hied, a sad distemper'd guest,
But found no cure: the bath for my help lies
Where Cupid got new fire,—my mistress' eyes. [f]

CLIV.

The little Love-god, lying once asleep,
Laid by his side his heart-inflaming brand,
Whilst many nymphs that vow'd chaste life to keep
Came tripping by; but in her maiden hand
The fairest votary took up that fire
Which many legions of true hearts had warm'd;
And so the general of hot desire
Was sleeping by a virgin hand disarm'd.
This brand she quenched in a cool well by,
Which from Love's fire took heat perpetual,
Growing a bath and healthful remedy
For men diseas'd; but I, my mistress' thrall,
Came there for cure, and this by that I prove,
Love's fire heats water, water cools not love. [g]

---

[a] — *with thee* partake?] That is, *take part.*

[b] And swear that brightness doth not grace the day?] Compare, "Romeo and Juliet," Act III. Sc. 5,—

"I'll say, yon grey is not the morning's eye."

[c] Whence hast thou this becoming of things ill,—] Whence hast thou this power of *adorning* or *setting off*, &c.

[d] *Then, gentle* cheater,—] "Cheater" here signifies *escheator*, an official who appears to have been regarded by the common people in Shakespeare's day much the same as they now look upon an informer. See note b, p. 646, Vol. I.

[e] — more perjur'd I,—] The quarto by a palpable mistake prints,—"More periurde *eye*," &c.

[f] — *my mistress'* eyes.] The old copy has,—"my mistres *eye*."

[g] — water cools not love.] On these two last Sonnets Malone observes that "They seem to have been early essays of the poet, who perhaps had not determined which he should prefer. He hardly could have intended to send them both into the world."

A LOVER'S COMPLAINT.[a]

From off a hill whose concave womb re-worded
A plaintful story from a sistering[b] vale,
My spirits to attend this double voice accorded,
And down I laid to list the sad-tun'd tale :
Ere long espied a fickle maid full pale,
Tearing of papers, breaking rings a-twain,
Storming her world[c] with sorrow's wind and rain.

Upon her head a platted hive of straw,
Which fortified her visage from the sun,
Whereon the thought might think sometime it saw
The carcass of a beauty spent and done :
Time had not scythed all that youth begun,
Nor youth all quit ; but, spite of heaven's fell rage,
Some beauty peep'd through lattice of sear'd age.

Oft did she heave her napkin[d] to her eyne,
Which on it had conceited characters,[e]
Laund'ring the silken figures in the brine
That season'd woe had pelleted in tears,
And often reading what contents it bears ;
As often shrieking undistinguish'd woe,
In clamours of all size', both high and low.

Sometimes her levell'd eyes their carriage ride,
As they did battery to the spheres intend ;
Sometime diverted their poor balls are tied
To th' orbed earth ; sometimes they do extend
Their view right on ; anon their gazes lend
To every place at once, and, nowhere fix'd,
The mind and sight distractedly commix'd.

Her hair, nor loose nor tied in formal plat,
Proclaim'd in her a careless hand of pride ;
For some, untuck'd, descended her sheav'd hat,
Hanging her pale and pined cheek beside ;
Some in her threaden fillet still did bide,
And, true to bondage, would not break from thence,
Though slackly braided in loose negligence.

A thousand favours from a maund[f] she drew
Of amber, crystal, and of beaded[g] jet,
Which one by one she in a river threw,
Upon whose weeping margent she was set ;
Like usury, applying wet to wet,
Or monarch's hands, that let not bounty fall
Where want cries some,[h] but where excess begs all.

---

[a] "This beautiful poem was first printed in 1609, with our author's name, at the end of the quarto edition of his Sonnets. I wonder that it has not attracted the attention of some English painter, the opening being uncommonly picturesque. The figures, however, of the lady and the old man should be standing, not sitting, by the river side; Shakspeare reclining on a hill."—Malone.

[b] — *a* sistering *vale*,—] A *proximate* or *contiguous* vale, we apprehend, but the word is peculiar.

[c] — world—] *Microcosm.* Compare, "King Lear," Act III. Sc. 1,—

"Strives in his *little world* of man to outscorn
The to-and-fro-conflicting wind and rain."

[d] — napkin—] *Handkerchief.*

[e] — conceited characters,—] *Fanciful figures.*

[f] — *a* maund—] A *hand-basket.*

[g] — beaded—] The quarto reads, "*bedded.*"

[h] — cries some,—] That is, as Mr. Dyce correctly explains it, *cries for some.*

Of folded schedules had she many a one,
Which she perus'd, sigh'd, tore, and gave the flood;
Crack'd many a ring of posied gold and bone,
Bidding them find their sepulchres in mud;
Found yet more letters sadly penn'd in blood,
With sleided silk feat and affectedly
Enswath'd, and seal'd to curious secrecy.[a]

These often bath'd she in her fluxive eyes,
And often kiss'd, and often gan[b] to tear;
Cried, "O false blood, thou register of lies,
What unapproved witness dost thou bear!
Ink would have seem'd more black and damned here!"
This said, in top of rage the lines she rents,
Big discontent so breaking their contents.

A reverend man that graz'd his cattle nigh,—
Sometime a blusterer, that the ruffle knew
Of court, of city, and had let go by
The swiftest hours, observed as they flew,—
Towards this afflicted fancy fastly drew;
And, privileg'd by age, desires to know
In brief the grounds and motives of her woe.

So slides he down upon his grained bat,[c]
And comely-distant sits he by her side;
When he again desires her, being sat,
Her grievance with his hearing to divide:
If that from him there may be aught applied
Which may her suffering ecstasy[d] assuage,
'T is promis'd in the charity of age.

"Father," she says, "though in me you behold
The injury of many a blasting hour,
Let it not tell your judgment I am old;
Not age, but sorrow, over me hath power:
I might as yet have been a spreading flower,
Fresh to myself, if I had self-applied
Love to myself, and to no love beside.

"But, woe is me! too early I attended
A youthful suit (it was to gain my grace)
Of[e] one by nature's outwards so commended,
That maidens' eyes stuck over all his face:
Love lack'd a dwelling, and made him her place;[f]
And when in his fair parts she did abide,
She was new lodg'd, and newly deified.

"His browny locks did hang in crooked curls;
And every light occasion of the wind
Upon his lips their silken parcels hurls.
What 's sweet to do, to do will aptly find:
Each eye that saw him did enchant the mind;
For on his visage was in little drawn,
What largeness thinks in paradise was sawn.[g]

"Small show of man was yet upon his chin;
His phœnix[h] down began but to appear,
Like unshorn velvet, on that termless skin,
Whose bare out-bragg'd the web it seem'd to wear;
Yet show'd his visage by that cost more dear;
And nice affections wavering stood in doubt
If best were as it was, or best without.

"His qualities were beauteous as his form,
For maiden-tongu'd he was, and thereof free;
Yet, if men mov'd him, was he such a storm[i]
As oft 'twixt May and April is to see,
When winds breathe sweet, unruly though they be.
His rudeness so with his authóriz'd youth
Did livery falseness in a pride of truth.

"Well could he ride, and often men would say
'That horse his mettle from his rider takes:
Proud of subjection, noble by the sway,
What rounds, what bounds, what course, what stop he makes!'
And controversy hence a question takes,
Whether the horse by him became[k] his deed,
Or he his manage by the well-doing steed.

"But quickly on this side the verdict went;
His real habitude gave life and grace
To appertainings and to ornament,
Accomplish'd in himself, not in his case:
All aids, themselves made fairer by their place,
Came[l] for additions; yet their purpos'd trim
Piec'd not his grace, but were all grac'd by him.

"So on the tip of his subduing tongue
All kind of arguments and question deep,
All replication prompt, and reason strong,
For his advantage still did wake and sleep:
To make the weeper laugh, the laugher weep,
He had the dialect and different skill,
Catching all passions in his craft of will:[m]

"That he did in the general bosom reign
Of young, of old; and sexes both enchanted

---

a *With* sleided *silk* feat and affectedly
Enswath'd, and seal'd to curious secrecy.]

"*Sleided* silk" is *untwisted* silk; what we now term *flos* silk. "Feat" means *cleverly, nicely.* "To be convinced of the propriety of this description, let the reader consult the 'Royal Letters,' &c. in the British Museum, where he will find that anciently the ends of a narrow ribbon were placed under the *seals* of letters, to connect them more closely."—STEEVENS.

b — *and often* gan *to tear;*] A conjectural reading of Malone, the old copy having,—

"—— and often *gave* to teare," &c.

c — *his* grained bat,—] His *rough staff*, or *club*.

d — ecstasy—] *Distraction.*

e Of *one*—] The quarto reads, "*O* one," &c.

f — *her* place;] Her *seat*, her *mansion.*

g — sawn.] *Sown;* or, as some explain it, *seen*. We think the former is the true meaning.

h — phœnix *down*—] Is this corrupt? Malone supposes by "phœnix" she means *matchless, rare;* but if so, the allusion is very far-fetched.

i Yet, if men mov'd him, was he such a storm, &c.] Compare, "Antony and Cleopatra," Act V. Sc. 2,—

"—— his voice was propertied
As all the tuned spheres, and that to friends;
But when he meant to quail and shake the orb,
He was as rattling thunder."

k — became—] *Adorned, graced.*

l Came *for*—] So Malone; the quarto having, "*Can* for," &c.

m Catching all passions in his craft of will:] "These lines, in which our poet has accidentally delineated his own character as a dramatist, would have been better adapted to his monumental inscription, than such as are placed on the scroll in Westminster Abbey."—STEEVENS.

To dwell with him in thoughts, or to remain
In personal duty, following where he haunted:
Consents bewitch'd, ere he desire, have granted;
And dialogu'd for him what he would say,
Ask'd their own wills, and made their wills obey.

"Many there were that did his picture get,
To serve their eyes, and in it put their mind;
Like fools that in th' imagination set
The goodly objects which abroad they find
Of lands and mansions, theirs in thought assign'd;
And labouring in more pleasures to bestow them
Than the true gouty landlord which doth owe them:

"So many have, that never touch'd his hand,
Sweetly suppos'd them mistress of his heart.
My woeful self, that did in freedom stand,
And was my own fee-simple,[a] (not in part)
What with his art in youth, and youth in art,
Threw my affections in his charmed power,
Reserv'd the stalk, and gave him all my flower.

"Yet did I not, as some my equals did,
Demand of him, nor being desir'd yielded;
Finding myself in honour so forbid,
With safest distance I mine honour shielded:
Experience for me many bulwarks builded
Of proofs new-bleeding, which remain'd the foil
Of this false jewel, and his amorous spoil.

"But, ah, who ever shunn'd by precedent
The destin'd ill she must herself assay?
Or forc'd examples, 'gainst her own content,
To put the by-pass'd perils in her way?
Counsel may stop a while what will not stay;
For when we rage, advice is often seen
By blunting us to make our wits more keen.

"Nor gives it satisfaction to our blood,
That we must curb it upon others' proof;
To be forbid the sweets that seem so good,
For fear of harms that preach in our behoof.
O appetite, from judgment stand aloof!
The one a palate hath that needs will taste,
Though Reason weep, and cry, 'It is thy last.'

"For further[b] I could say, 'This man 's untrue,'
And knew the patterns of his foul beguiling;
Heard where his plants in others' orchards grew,
Saw how deceits were gilded in his smiling;
Knew vows were ever brokers[c] to defiling;
Thought characters and words merely but art,
And bastards of his foul adulterate heart.

"And long upon these terms I held my city,
Till thus he 'gan besiege me: 'Gentle maid,
Have of my suffering youth some feeling pity,
And be not of my holy vows afraid:
That 's to you sworn, to none was ever said;
For feasts of love I have been called unto,
Till now did ne'er invite, nor never vow.

"'All my offences that abroad you see
Are errors of the blood, none of the mind;
Love made them not; with acture[d] they may be,
Where neither party is nor true nor kind:
They sought their shame that so their shame did find;
And so much less of shame in me remains,
By how much of me their reproach contains.

"'Among the many that mine eyes have seen,
Not one whose flame my heart so much as warm'd,
Or my affection put to the smallest teen,[e]
Or any of my leisures ever charm'd:
Harm have I done to them, but ne'er was harm'd;
Kept hearts in liveries, but mine own was free,
And reign'd, commanding in his monarchy.

"'Look here what tributes wounded fancies sent me,
Of paled pearls, and rubies red as blood;
Figuring that they their passions likewise lent me
Of grief and blushes, aptly understood
In bloodless white and the encrimson'd mood;
Effects of terror and dear modesty,
Encamp'd in hearts, but fighting outwardly.

"'And, lo, behold these talents[f] of their hair,
With twisted metal amorously impleach'd,
I have receiv'd from many a several fair,—
Their kind acceptance weepingly beseech'd,—
With the annexions of fair gems enrich'd,
And deep-brain'd sonnets that did amplify
Each stone's dear nature, worth, and quality.

"'The diamond,—why, 't was beautiful and hard,
Whereto his invis'd[g] properties did tend;
The deep-green emerald, in whose fresh regard
Weak sights their sickly radiance do amend;
The heaven-hu'd sapphire and the opal blend[h]
With objects manifold; each several stone,
With wit well blazon'd, smil'd or made some moan.

"'Lo, all these trophies of affections hot,
Of pensiv'd and subdu'd desires the tender,
Nature hath charg'd me that I hoard them not,
But yield them up where I myself must render,
That is, to you, my origin and ender;
For these, of force, must your oblations be,
Since I their altar, you enpatron me.

---

[a] And was my own fee-simple,—] "Had an absolute power over myself; as large as a tenant in fee has over his estate."—MALONE.

[b] *For* further *I could say,*—] We ought probably to read,—

"For, *father*, I could say," &c.

[c] — brokers—] *Pandars.* Compare, "Hamlet," Act I. Sc. 3,—

"Do not believe his *vows*, for they are *brokers*,
Not of that dye which their investments show,
But mere implorators of *unholy suits.*"

[d] — acture—] This word is suspicious. Malone conjectures it to be synonymous with *action.*

[e] — teen,—] *Trouble, suffering.*

[f] — talents of their hair,—] "Talents" appears to be used here for *riches*, as in "Cymbeline," Act I. Sc. 6,—

"—— in himself, 't is much;
In you,—which I account his,—beyond all *talents.*"

[g] — invis'd—] *Invisible.*

[h] — blend—] "*Blend*" for *blended.*

"'O, then, advance of yours that phraseless hand,
Whose white weighs down the airy scale of praise;
Take all these similes to your own command,
Hallow'd with sighs that burning lungs did raise;
What me your minister, for you obeys,
Works under you; and to your audit comes
Their distract parcels in combined sums.

"'Lo, this device was sent me from a nun,
Or[a] sister sanctified, of holiest note;
Which late her noble suit in court did shun,
Whose rarest havings made the blossoms dote;[b]
For she was sought by spirits of richest coat,[c]
But kept cold distance, and did thence remove,
To spend her living in eternal love.

"'But, O, my sweet, what labour is 't to leave
The thing we have not, mastering what not strives,—
Paling[d] the place which did no form receive,
Playing patient sports in unconstrained gyves?
She that her fame so to herself contrives,
The scars of battle 'scapeth by the flight,
And makes her absence valiant, not her might.

"'O, pardon me, in that my boast is true;
The accident which brought me to her eye,
Upon the moment did her force subdue,
And now she would the caged cloister fly:
Religious love put out Religion's eye:
Not to be tempted, would she be immur'd,[e]
And now, to tempt all, liberty procur'd.[f]

"'How mighty then you are, O, hear me tell!
The broken bosoms that to me belong
Have emptied all their fountains in my well,
And mine I pour your ocean all among:
I strong o'er them, and you o'er me being strong,
Must for your victory us all congest,
As compound love to physic your cold breast.

"'My parts had power to charm a sacred nun,[g]
Who, disciplin'd, ay, dieted[h] in grace,
Believ'd her eyes when they to assail begun,
All vows and consecrations giving place.
O, most potential love! vow, bond, nor space,
In thee hath neither sting, knot, nor confine,
For thou art all, and all things else are thine.

"'When thou impressest, what are precepts worth
Of stale example? When thou wilt inflame,
How coldly those impediments stand forth
Of wealth, of filial fear, law, kindred, fame!
Love's arms are peace,[i] 'gainst rule, 'gainst sense, 'gainst shame,
And sweetens, in the suffering pangs it bears,
The aloes of all forces, shocks, and fears.

"'Now all these hearts that do on mine depend,
Feeling it break, with bleeding groans they pine,
And supplicant their sighs to you extend,
To leave the battery that you make 'gainst mine,
Lending soft audience to my sweet design,
And credent soul to that strong-bonded oath,
That shall prefer and undertake my troth.'

"This said, his watery eyes he did dismount,
Whose sights till then were levell'd on my face;
Each cheek a river running from a fount
With brinish current downward flow'd apace:
O, how the channel to the stream gave grace!
Who glaz'd with crystal gate the glowing roses
That flame through water which their hue encloses.

"O, father, what a hell of witchcraft lies
In the small orb of one particular tear!
But with the inundation of the eyes
What rocky heart to water will not wear?
What breast so cold that is not warmed here?
O[k] cleft effect! cold modesty, hot wrath,
Both fire from hence and chill extincture hath!

"For, lo, his passion, but an art of craft,
Even there resolv'd my reason into tears;
There my white stole of chastity I daff'd,
Shook off my sober guards and civil fears;
Appear to him, as he to me appears,
All melting; though our drops this difference bore,
His poison'd me, and mine did him restore.

"In him a plenitude of subtle matter,
Applied to cautels, all strange forms receives,
Of burning blushes, or of weeping water,
Or swooning paleness; and he takes and leaves,
In either's aptness, as it best deceives,
To blush at speeches rank,[l] to weep at woes,
Or to turn white and swoon at tragic shows;

"That not a heart which in his level came
Could scape the hail of his all-hurting aim,
Showing fair nature is both kind and tame;
And, veil'd in them, did win whom he would maim:
Against the thing he sought he would exclaim;

---

a Or *sister sanctified*,—] "The poet, I suspect, wrote, '*A* sister sanctified,' &c."—MALONE. We suspect so too.

b Whose rarest havings made the blossoms dote;] "Whose accomplishments were so extraordinary that the flower of the young nobility were passionately enamoured of her."—MALONE.

c — *richest* coat,—] "Coat," for *coat* of arms.

d Paling *the place*—] This is the reading of Malone, for "*Playing* the place," &c. of the old copy. We should prefer, "*Filling* the place," &c. The word *Playing* was evidently caught by the transcriber or compositor from the following line, and in mistakes of this description the *ductus literarum* is of little moment. In support of *Filling*, compare, Sonnet CXII.:—

"Your love and pity doth th' impression *fill*
Which vulgar scandal stamp'd upon my brow;" &c.

e — immur'd,—] The quarto has, "*enur'd*."

f — procur'd.] A correction from the edition of 1640, the quarto reading, "*procure*."

g — *a sacred* nun,—] The quarto reads, "a sacred *Sunne*," &c., a manifest error, though adopted by Malone.

h Who, disciplin'd, ay, dieted in grace,—] The old copy has,—

"Who disciplin'd *I died* in grace."

i *Love's arms are* peace,—] A palpable corruption, for which Malone proposed, "Love's arms are *proof*," &c. Steevens, "Love *aims* at peace," &c.; and Mr. Dyce conjectures, "*Love* arms *our* peace," &c.

k O cleft effect!] So Malone; the quarto reading, "*Or* cleft effect," &c.; from which, unless "effect" stands for *effectually*, it is not easy to extract any sense.

l — rank,—] *Gross.*

When he most burn'd in heart-wish'd luxury,[a]
He preach'd pure maid,[b] and prais'd cold chastity.

"Thus merely with the garment of a Grace
The naked and concealed fiend he cover'd,
That th' unexperient gave the tempter place,
Which, like a cherubin, above them hover'd.
Who, young and simple, would not be so lover'd?
Ah me! I fell; and yet do question make
What I should do again for such a sake.

"O, that infected moisture of his eye,
O, that false fire which in his cheek so glow'd,
O, that forc'd thunder from his heart did fly,
O, that sad breath his spongy lungs bestow'd,
O, all that borrow'd motion, seeming ow'd,[c]
Would yet again betray the fore-betray'd,
And new pervert a reconciled maid!"

a — luxury,—] *Lasciviousness.*

b He preached pure maid,—] This construction was not uncommon. Compare, "King John," Act II. Sc. 2,—

"He speaks plain cannon-fire, and smoke, and bounce;"

and "Henry V." Act V. Sc. 2,—

"I speak to thee plain soldier," &c.

c — *that borrow'd motion, seeming* ow'd,—] *Owed* means *possessed;* that assumed desire apparently so real.

THE PASSIONATE PILGRIM.

THE ensuing collection of irrelative poems, some probably from Shakespeare's hand, but some certainly belonging to other writers, was first published by William Jaggard, in small octavo, with the title,—"The Passionate Pilgrime. By W. Shakespeare. At London. Printed for W. Iaggard, and are to be sold by W. Leake, at the Greyhound in Paules Churchyard, 1599." In 1612 another edition was printed bearing the title of, "The Passionate Pilgrime. Or Certaine Amorous Sonnets, betweene Venus and Adonis, newly corrected and augmented. By W. Shakespere. The third Edition. Where-unto is newly added two Love-Epistles, the first from Paris to Hellen, and Hellen's answere backe againe to Paris. Printed by W. Iaggard, 1612."* The "Love Epistles" which Jaggard had the audacity to particularise in his title-page, and insert in this reprint as the works of Shakespeare, were two of Ovid's Epistles, that had been translated by Thomas Heywood, and printed with his name in his "Troja Brittannica," &c. 1609. It was not likely that Heywood would patiently submit to this flagrant injustice, and accordingly at the close of a work entitled, "The Apology for Actors," &c. which was published by him in 1612, he appended the following letter to his bookseller, Nicholas Okes:—

"To my approved good friend, Mr. Nicholas Okes.

"The infinite faults escaped in my booke of *Britaines Troy*, by the negligence of the Printer, as the misquotations, mistaking of sillables, misplacing halfe lines, coining of strange and never heard of words. These being without number, when I would have taken a particular account of the *Errata*, the Printer answered me, hee would not publishe his owne disworkemanship, but rather let his owne fault lye upon the necke of the Author: and being fearfull that others of his quality, had beene of the same nature, and condition, and finding you on the contrary, so carefull and industrious, so serious and laborious, to doe the author all the rights of the presse; I could not choose but gratulate your honest endeavours with this short remembrance. Here likewise, I must necessarily insert a manifest injury done me in that worke, by taking the two Epistles of *Paris* to *Helen*, and *Helen* to *Paris*, and printing them in a lesse volume under the name of another, which may put the world in opinion I might steal them from him; and hee, to do himselfe right, hath since published them in his owne name: but as I must acknowledge my lines not worthy his patronage under whom he hath publisht them, so the Author I know much offended with *M. Jaggard* that (altogether unknowne to him)

* Although this edition purports to be the *third*, no intermediate impression between it and the first copy is now known.

presumed to make so bold with his name. These, and the like dishonesties, I know you to be cleare of; and I could wish but to bee the happy author of so worthie a worke as I could willingly commit to your care and workmanship.

"Yours ever, THOMAS HEYWOOD."

This exposure, aided probably by the indignant remonstrance of Shakespeare, compelled Jaggard to cancel the original title-page of the 1612 edition, and substitute another, which bore no author's name. Such at least is presumed to have been the case, from the fact that Malone's copy of this edition, by the "fortunate negligence" of the old binder, contains two title-pages, one with and the other without an author's name.

I.

Did not the heavenly rhetoric of thine eye,[a]
'Gainst whom the world could not hold argument,
Persuade my heart to this false perjury?
Vows for thee broke deserve not punishment.
A woman I forswore; but, I will prove,
Thou being a goddess, I forswore not thee:
My vow was earthly, thou a heavenly love;
Thy grace being gain'd cures all disgrace in me.
My vow was breath, and breath a vapour is;
Then, thou fair sun, that on this earth doth shine,
Exhale this vapour vow; in thee it is:
If broken then, it is no fault of mine.
If by me broke, what fool is not so wise
To lose an oath to win a paradise?

II.

Sweet Cytherea, sitting by a brook,
With young Adonis, lovely-fresh and green,
Did court the lad with many a lovely look,—
Such looks as none could look but beauty's queen.
She told him stories to delight his ear;[b]
She show'd him favours to allure his eye;
To win his heart, she touch'd him here and there,—
Touches so soft still conquer chastity;—
But whether unripe years did want conceit,
Or he refus'd to take her figur'd proffer,
The tender nibbler would not touch the bait,
But smile and jest at every gentle offer:
Then fell she on her back, fair queen and toward;
He rose and ran away,—ah, fool too froward!

III.

If love make me forsworn, how shall I swear to love?[c]
O, never faith could hold, if not to beauty vow'd!
Though to myself forsworn, to thee I'll constant prove;
Those thoughts to me like oaks, to thee like osiers bow'd.
Study his bias leaves, and makes his book thine eyes,
Where all those pleasures live that art can comprehend.
If knowledge be the mark, to know thee shall suffice;
Well learned is that tongue that well can thee commend;
All ignorant that soul that sees thee without wonder;
Which is to me some praise, that I thy parts admire:
Thine eye Jove's lightning seems, thy voice his dreadful thunder,
Which, not to anger bent, is music and sweet fire.
Celestial as thou art, O, do not love that wrong,
To sing the heavens' praise with such an earthly tongue!

IV.

Scarce had the sun dried up the dewy morn,
And scarce the herd gone to the hedge for shade,
When Cytherea, all in love forlorn,
A longing tarriance for Adonis made
Under an osier growing by a brook,
A brook where Adon used to cool his spleen:
Hot was the day; she hotter that did look
For his approach, that often there had been.
Anon he comes, and throws his mantle by,
And stood stark naked on the brook's green brim:
The sun look'd on the world with glorious eye,
Yet not so wistly as this queen on him:
He, spying her, bounc'd in, whereas he stood;
"O Jove," quoth she, "why was not I a flood!"

V.

Fair is my love, but not so fair as fickle;
Mild as a dove, but neither true nor trusty;
Brighter than glass, and yet, as glass is, brittle;
Softer than wax, and yet, as iron, rusty:
A lily pale, with damask dye to grace her,
None fairer, nor none falser to deface her.

Her lips to mine how often hath she join'd,
Between each kiss her oaths of true love swearing!
How many tales to please me hath she coin'd,
Dreading my love, the loss thereof still fearing!
Yet in the midst of all her pure protestings,
Her faith, her oaths, her tears, and all were jestings.

---

[a] Did not the heavenly rhetoric of thine eye,—] This Sonnet, and two others (Nos. III. and XV.), will be found, with slight variations, in "Love's Labour's Lost." In "The Passionate Pilgrim," it is preceded by two of the Sonnets already given, No. CXXXVIII., beginning,—

"When my love swears that she is made of truth," &c.

and No. CXLIV.: "Two loves I have," &c.

[b] — *to delight his* ear;] The old text has, "ears."

[c] If love make me forsworn,—] See "Love's Labour's Lost," Act IV. Sc. 2.

She burn'd with love, as straw with fire flameth,
She burn'd out love, as soon as straw out-burneth;
She fram'd the love, and yet she foil'd the framing,
She bade love last, and yet she fell a-turning.
Was this a lover, or a lecher whether?
Bad in the best, though excellent in neither.

VI.

If music and sweet poetry agree,[a]
As they must needs, the sister and the brother,
Then must the love be great 'twixt thee and me,
Because thou lov'st the one, and I the other.
Dowland to thee is dear, whose heavenly touch
Upon the lute doth ravish human sense;
Spenser to me, whose deep conceit is such,
As, passing all conceit, needs no defence.
Thou lov'st to hear the sweet melodious sound
That Phœbus' lute, the queen of music, makes;
And I in deep delight am chiefly drown'd,
Whenas himself to singing he betakes.
One god is god of both, as poets feign;
One knight loves both, and both in thee remain.

VII.

Fair was the morn, when the fair queen of love,
* * * * * * * *[b]
Paler for sorrow than her milk-white dove,
For Adon's sake, a youngster proud and wild;
Her stand she takes upon a steep-up hill:
Anon Adonis comes with horn and hounds;
She, silly queen, with more than love's good will,
Forbade the boy he should not pass those grounds;
"Once," quoth she, "did I see a fair sweet youth
Here in these brakes deep-wounded with a boar,
Deep in the thigh, a spectacle of ruth!
See in my thigh," quoth she, "here was the sore:"
She showed hers; he saw more wounds than one,
And blushing fled, and left her all alone.

VIII.

Sweet rose, fair flower, untimely pluck'd, soon faded,
Pluck'd in the bud, and faded in the spring!
Bright orient pearl, alack! too timely shaded!
Fair creature, kill'd too soon by death's sharp sting!
Like a green plum that hangs upon a tree,
And falls, through wind, before the fall should be.

I weep for thee, and yet no cause I have;
For why[c] thou left'st me nothing in thy will:
And yet thou left'st me more than I did crave;
For why I craved nothing of thee still:
O yes, dear friend, I pardon crave of thee,—
Thy discontent thou didst bequeath to me.

IX.

Venus, with young Adonis sitting by her[d]
Under a myrtle shade, began to woo him:
She told the youngling how god Mars did try her,
And as he fell to her, so fell she to him.[e]
"Even thus," quoth she, "the warlike god embrac'd me,"[f]
And then she clipp'd Adonis in her arms;
"Even thus," quoth she, "the warlike god unlac'd me,"
As if the boy should use like loving charms;
"Even thus," quoth she, "he seized on my lips,"
And with her lips on his did act the seizure;
And as she fetched breath, away he skips,
And would not take her meaning nor her pleasure.
Ah, that I had my lady at this bay,
To kiss and clip me till I run away!

X.

Crabbed age and youth
Cannot live together:
Youth is full of pleasance,
Age is full of care;
Youth like summer morn,
Age like winter weather;
Youth like summer brave,
Age like winter bare.
Youth is full of sport,
Age's breath is short;
Youth is nimble, age is lame;
Youth is hot and bold,
Age is weak and cold;
Youth is wild, and age is tame.
Age, I do abhor thee,
Youth, I do adore thee;
O, my love, my love is young!
Age, I do defy[g] thee:—
O, sweet shepherd, hie thee!
For methinks thou stay'st too long.

XI.

Beauty is but a vain and doubtful good,
A shining gloss that fadeth suddenly;
A flower that dies when first it 'gins to bud;
A brittle glass that 's broken presently:
A doubtful good, a gloss, a glass, a flower,
Lost, faded, broken, dead within an hour!

---

[a] If music and sweet poetry agree,—] This poem, according to Mr. Collier, was published in the first edition of R. Barnfield's "Encomion of Lady Pecunia," 1598, but was omitted by the author in his edition of 1605. From which circumstance, Mr. Collier infers that it was written by Shakespeare.

[b] A line has here been lost.

[c] For why—] *Because.*

[d] Venus, with young Adonis sitting by her—] This Sonnet, with some variations, occurs in a collection of Poems by B. Griffin, called *Fidessa more Chaste then Kinde*, 1596; and there the opening line is given as in our text. "The Passionate Pilgrim" reads,—

"Venus with Adonis sitting by her," &c.

[e] *And as he fell to her, so fell she to him.*] In "The Passionate Pilgrim" this line is imperfect, "so" being omitted. The word is supplied from Griffin's *Fidessa.*

[f] "Even thus," quoth she, "the warlike god embrac'd me,"—] In the latter part of this Sonnet the version in *Fidessa* differs considerably from the one before us. There, it runs as follows:—

"'Even thus,' quoth she, 'the *wanton* god embrac'd me;'
And thus she *clasp'd* Adonis in her arms:
'Even thus,' quoth she, 'the warlike god unlac'd me,'
As if the boy should use like loving charms:
But he, a wayward boy, refus'd her offer,
And ran away, the beauteous queen neglecting;
Showing both folly to abuse her proffer,
And all his sex of cowardice detecting;
Oh, that I had my *mistress* at *that* bay,
To kiss and clip me till I ran away."

[g] —defy *thee*:—] *Renounce* or *contemn* thee. So, in "Romeo and Juliet," Act V. Sc. 3,—

"I do *defy* thy conjurations," &c.

And as goods lost are seld or never found,
As faded gloss no rubbing will refresh,
As flowers dead lie wither'd on the ground,
As broken glass no cement can redress,—
So beauty blemish'd once for ever 's lost,
In spite of physic, painting, pain, and cost.

XII.

"Good night, good rest." Ah, neither be my share!
She bade good night, that kept my rest away;
And daff'd me to a cabin hang'd with care,
To descant on the doubts of my decay.
"Farewell," quoth she, "and come again to-morrow;"
Fare well I could not, for I supp'd with sorrow.

Yet at my parting sweetly did she smile,
In scorn or friendship, nill I construe whether:
'T may be, she joy'd to jest at my exile,
'T may be, again to make me wander thither:
"Wander!" a word for shadows like myself,
As take the pain, but cannot pluck the pelf.

XIII.

Lord, how mine eyes throw gazes to the east!
My heart doth charge the watch; the morning rise
Doth cite each moving sense from idle rest.
Not daring trust the office of mine eyes,
While Philomela sits and sings, I sit and mark,
And wish her lays were tuned like the lark;

For she doth welcome daylight with her ditty,
And drives away dark dismal-dreaming night:
The night so pack'd, I post unto my pretty;
Heart hath his hope, and eyes their wished sight;
Sorrow chang'd to solace, solace mix'd with sorrow;
For why she sigh'd, and bade me come to-morrow.

Were I with her, the night would post too soon;
But now are minutes added to the hours;
To spite me now, each minute seems a moon;[a]
Yet not for me, shine sun to succour flowers!
Pack night, peep day; good day, of night now borrow;
Short, night, to-night, and length thyself to-morrow.

SONNETS TO SUNDRY NOTES OF MUSIC.

XIV.

It was a lording's daughter,
The fairest one of three,[b]
That liked of her[c] master
As well as well might be,
Till looking on an Englishman,
The fair'st that eye could see,
Her fancy fell a-turning.

Long was the combat doubtful
That love with love did fight,
To leave the master loveless,
Or kill the gallant knight:
To put in practice either,
Alas, it was a spite
Unto the silly damsel!

But one must be refused;
More mickle was the pain,
That nothing could be used
To turn them both to gain,
For of the two the trusty knight
Was wounded with disdain:
Alas, she could not help it!

Thus art, with arms contending,
Was victor of the day,
Which by a gift of learning
Did bear the maid away:
Then, lullaby, the learned man
Hath got the lady gay;
For now my song is ended.

XV.

On a day (alack the day!),[d]
Love, whose month was ever May,
Spy'd a blossom passing fair,
Playing in the wanton air:
Through the velvet leaves the wind,
All unseen, 'gan passage find;
That the lover, sick to death,
Wish'd himself the heaven's breath.

a — *each minute seems* a moon;] A correction proposed by Steevens, the old copy reading, "*an hour,*" &c.

b It was a lording's daughter,
The fairest one of three,—]

"This and the five following Sonnets are said in the old copy to have been set to musick. Mr. Oldys, in one of his MSS. says they were set by John and Thomas Morley."—MALONE.

c *That liked of* her *master*—] The late Mr. S. Walker, in his valuable work, "A Critical Examination of the Text of Shakespeare," &c. which has been published while these pages were in preparation for the press, suggests that we should read, "of *a* master;" that is, a scholar by profession, a master of arts.

d On a day (alack the day!),—] This, as we have before remarked, is one of the three Sonnets found in "Love's Labour 's Lost." It was printed also, with Shakespeare's name attached, in a collection of poems entitled, "England's Helicon," 1600, where it is entitled, *The Passionate Sheepheard's Song.*

"Air," quoth he, "thy cheeks may blow;
Air, would I might triumph so!
But, alas, my hand hath sworn
Ne'er to pluck thee from thy thorn!
Vow, alack, for youth unmeet,
Youth so apt to pluck a sweet.[a]
Thou for whom Jove would swear[b]
Juno but an Ethiope were;
And deny himself for Jove,
Turning mortal for thy love."

XVI.

My flocks feed not,[c]
My ewes breed not,
My rams speed not,
  All is amiss:
Love 's denying,[d]
Faith 's defying,
Heart's renying,[e]
  Causer of this.
All my merry jigs are quite forgot,
All my lady's love is lost, God wot:
Where her faith was firmly fix'd in love,
There a nay is plac'd without remove.
One silly cross
Wrought all my loss;
  O, frowning Fortune, cursed, fickle dame!
For now I see,
Inconstancy
  More in women than in men remain.

In black mourn I,
All fears scorn I,
Love hath forlorn me,
  Living in thrall:
Heart is bleeding,
All help needing,—
O cruel speeding!—
  Fraughted with gall!
My shepherd's pipe can sound no deal,
My wether's bell rings doleful knell;
My curtail dog, that wont to have play'd,
Plays not at all, but seems afraid;
My[f] sighs so deep,
Procure to weep,
  In howling wise, to see my doleful plight.
How sighs resound
Through heartless ground,
  Like a thousand vanquish'd men in bloody fight!

Clear wells spring not,
Sweet birds sing not,
Green plants bring not
  Forth their dye:[g]
Herds stand weeping,
Flocks all sleeping,
Nymphs back peeping
  Fearfully:
All our pleasure known to us poor swains,
All our merry meetings on the plains,
All our evening sport from us is fled,
All our love is lost, for Love is dead.
Farewell, sweet lass,[h]
Thy like ne'er was
  For a sweet content, the cause of all my moan:[i]
Poor Coridon
Must live alone,
  Other help for him I see that there is none.

XVII.

Whenas thine eye hath chose the dame,
And stall'd the deer that thou shouldst strike,
Let reason rule things worthy blame,
As well as fancy partial might:[k]
  Take counsel of some wiser head,
  Neither too young, nor yet unwed.

And when thou com'st thy tale to tell,
Smooth not thy tongue with filed[l] talk,
Lest she some subtle practice smell,—
A cripple soon can find a halt;—
  But plainly say thou lov'st her well,
  And set thy person forth to sell.[m]

What though her frowning brows be bent,
Her cloudy looks will clear[n] ere night;

---

a Youth so apt to pluck a sweet.] In "Love's Labour's Lost," we have here two lines which were omitted both in the present version and in "England's Helicon:"—

"Do not call it sin in me,
That I am forsworn for thee."

b *Thou for whom Jove would* swear—] In this line, unless some epithet to "Jove" has been lost, "swear" is employed as a dissyllable.

c My flocks feed not, &c.] These verses, under the title of *The Unknown Sheepheard's Complaint*, and subscribed *Ignoto*, are printed in "England's Helicon." They are found also, with music, in Weelkes's *Madrigals*, 1599. That Shakespeare had any hand either in them or in the poor effusion beginning, "It was a lording's daughter," &c. is inconceivable.

d Love's denying,
* * * *
Heart's renying, &c.]

"*The Passionate Pilgrim* and Weelkes's book have, 'Love is dying,' and 'Heart's *denying*.' The reading of the text is found in *England's Helicon*, except that it has, 'Love *is*,' and 'Faith *is*.'"—MALONE.

e — renying,—] *Forswearing.*

f My *sighs*—] So Weelkes's *Madrigals*. The other copies read, "*With* sighes," &c.

g Green plants bring not
Forth their dye:]

Weelkes's copy has,—

"Loud bells ring not
Cheerfully."

h — *sweet* lass,—] We follow Weelkes's *Madrigals*. The other copies read, "sweet *love*," &c.

i — *the cause of all my* moan:] So Weelkes's *Madrigals*, and "England's Helicon." "The Passionate Pilgrim" has, "my *woe*," &c.

k *As well as fancy partial* might:] This is very probably corrupt, but the change proposed by Steevens, "partial *tike*," is unendurable; and we have no faith in the reading said to be derived from a MS. of this poem in the possession of Mr. Collier,—

"As well as partial fancy like," &c.

Query,—

"As well as fancy *martial* might"?

Compare, "Lucrece,"—

"A *martial* man to be soft *fancy's* slave!"

l — filed talk,—] *Polished* diction.

m *And set* thy *person forth to* sell.] A reading supplied by a manuscript copy of this poem, of the age of Shakespeare, which Malone used. "The Passionate Pilgrim" has,—

"—— *her* person forth to *sale*."

n — *will* clear—] So the MS. just referred to. "The Passionate Pilgrim" reads, "will *calm*," &c.

And then too late she will repent,
That thus dissembled her delight;
And twice desire, ere it be day,
That which with scorn she put away.

What though she strive to try her strength,
And ban and brawl, and say thee nay,
Her feeble force will yield at length,
When craft hath taught her thus to say,—
"Had women been so strong as men,
In faith you had not had it then."

And to her will frame all thy ways;
Spare not to spend,—and chiefly there
Where thy desert may merit praise,
By ringing in thy lady's ear:
The strongest castle, tower, and town,
The golden bullet beats it down.

Serve always with assured trust,
And in thy suit be humble-true;
Unless thy lady prove unjust,
Seek never thou to choose anew:
When time shall serve, be thou not slack
To proffer, though she put thee back.

The wiles and guiles that women work,
Dissembled with an outward show,
The tricks and toys that in them lurk,
The cock that treads them shall not know.
Have you not heard it said full oft,
A woman's nay doth stand for nought?

Think women love to match with men,
And not to live so like a saint:
Here is no heaven; they holy then
Begin when age does them attaint.[a]
Were kisses all the joys in bed,
One woman would another wed.

But soft! enough,—too much I fear;
For if [b] my mistress hear my song;
She will not stick to ring [c] mine ear,
To teach my tongue to be so long;
Yet will she blush, here be it said,
To hear her secrets so bewray'd.

XVIII.

Live with me, and be my love,[d]
And we will all the pleasures prove
That hills and valleys, dales and fields,
And all the craggy mountain yields.

There will we sit upon the rocks,
And see the shepherds feed their flocks,
By shallow rivers, to whose falls
Melodious birds sing madrigals.

There will I make thee a bed of roses,
With a thousand fragrant posies,
A cap of flowers, and a kirtle,
Embroider'd all with leaves of myrtle.

A belt of straw and ivy buds,
With coral clasps and amber studs;
And if these pleasures may thee move,
Then, live with me and be my love.

LOVE'S ANSWER.

If that the world and love were young,[e]
And truth in every shepherd's tongue,
These pretty pleasures might me move
To live with thee and be thy love.

XIX.

As it fell upon a day
In the merry month of May,
Sitting in a pleasant shade
Which a grove of myrtles made,
Beasts did leap, and birds did sing,
Trees did grow, and plants did spring;
Everything did banish moan,
Save the nightingale alone:
She, poor bird, as all forlorn,
Lean'd her breast up-till a thorn,
And there sung the dolefull'st ditty,
That to hear it was great pity:
"Fie, fie, fie," now would she cry,
"Tereu, tereu!" by and by;
That to hear her so complain,
Scarce I could from tears refrain;
For her griefs, so lively shown,
Made me think upon mine own.
Ah, thought I, thou mourn'st in vain!
None takes pity on thy pain:
Senseless trees they cannot hear thee;
Ruthless beasts [f] they will not cheer thee,
King Pandion he is dead;
All thy friends are lapp'd in lead;
All thy fellow-birds do sing,
Careless of thy sorrowing.
Even so, poor bird, like thee,
None alive will pity me.[g]

XX.

Whilst as fickle Fortune smil'd,
Thou and I were both beguil'd:

---

a Begin when age does them attaint.] This is the lection of the MS. followed by Malone; it is poor stuff, but it has the advantage of being intelligible, which cannot be said of the corresponding stanza in "The Passionate Pilgrim,"—

"Think women still to strive with men,
To sin and never for to saint;
There is no heaven by holy then,
When time with age shall them attaint."

b For if—] So the MS. "The Passionate Pilgrim" reads,—"*Lest that,*" &c.

c *She will not stick to* ring mine *ear,*—] The reading of the MS. used by Malone. That of "The Passionate Pilgrim" is,—

"—— to *round me on th'* ear," &c.

d Live with me, and be my love,—] This beautiful song, which is imperfectly given here, will be found complete at p. 687, Vol. I. It is generally supposed to have been written by Marlowe.

e If that the world and love were young,—] The present version of the "Answer" is also defective. Compare the copy in "England's Helicon," where it bears the signature, often adopted by Sir Walter Raleigh, of *Ignoto.* See also Percy's "Reliques," Vol. I. p. 237, edit. 1812.

f — beasts, &c.] From the abridged version of this poem in "England's Helicon." "The Passionate Pilgrim" has "*bears,*" &c.

g Even so, poor bird, like thee,
None alive will pity me.]

This couplet, which terminates the poem in "England's Helicon," is omitted in "The Passionate Pilgrim."

Every one that flatters thee
Is no friend in misery.
Words are easy, like the wind;
Faithful friends are hard to find:
Every man will be thy friend,
Whilst thou hast wherewith to spend;
But if store of crowns be scant,
No man will supply thy want.
If that one be prodigal,
Bountiful they will him call:
And with such-like flattering,
Pity but he were a king.
If he be addict to vice,
Quickly him they will entice;
If to women he be bent,
They have him at commandement;
But if fortune once do frown,
Then farewell his great renown;
They that fawn'd on him before,
Use his company no more.
He that is thy friend indeed,
He will help thee in thy need;
If thou sorrow, he will weep;
If thou wake, he cannot sleep:
Thus of every grief in heart
He with thee doth bear a part.
These are certain signs to know
Faithful friend from flattering foe.

THE PHŒNIX AND TURTLE.

(FROM THE ADDITIONAL POEMS TO CHESTER'S
Love's Martyr, or Rosalin's Complaint, 1601.)

LET the bird of loudest lay,[a]
On the sole Arabian tree,
Herald sad and trumpet be,
To whose sound chaste wings obey.

But thou shrieking harbinger,
Foul pre-currer of the fiend,
Augur of the fever's end,[b]
To this troop come thou not near!

From this session interdict
Every fowl of tyrant wing,
Save the eagle, feather'd king:
Keep the obsequy so strict.

Let the priest in surplice white,
That defunctive music can,[c]
Be the death-divining swan,
Lest the requiem lack his right.

And thou, treble-dated crow,
That thy sable gender mak'st
With the breath thou giv'st and tak'st,
'Mongst our mourners shalt thou go.

Here the anthem doth commence:—
Love and constancy is dead;
Phœnix and the turtle fled
In a mutual flame from hence.

So they lov'd, as love in twain
Had the essence but in one;
Two distincts, division none:
Number there in love was slain.

Hearts remote, yet not asunder;
Distance, and no space was seen
'Twixt the turtle and his queen:
But[d] in them it were a wonder.

So between them love did shine,
That the turtle saw his right
Flaming in the phœnix' sight;
Either was the other's mine.

Property[e] was thus appall'd,
That the self was not the same
Single nature's[f] double name
Neither two nor one was call'd.

a Let the bird of loudest lay,—] "In 1601 a book was published, entitled 'Loves Martyr, or Rosalins Complaint, Allegorically shadowing the Truth of Love, in the constant Fate of the Phœnix and Turtle. A Poem enterlaced with much Varietie and Raritie; now first translated out of the venerable Italian Torquato Cæliano by Robert Chester. With the true Legend of famous King Arthur, the last of the nine Worthies; being the first Essay of a new British Poet: collected out of diverse authentical Records.

"'To these are added some new Compositions of several modern Writers, whose names are subscribed to their several Workes; upon the first Subject, viz. the Phœnix and Turtle.'

"Among these new compositions is the following poem, subscribed with our poet's name. The second title prefixed to these verses, is yet more full. 'Hereafter follow diverse Poetical Essaies on the former Subject, viz. the Turtle and Phœnix. Done by the best and chiefest of our modern Writers, with their Names subscribed to their particular Workes. *Never before extant.*

"'And now first consecrated by them all generally to the Love and Merit of the true-noble knight, Sir John Salisburie.'

"The principal writers associated with Shakspeare in this collection are Ben Jonson, Marston, and Chapman. The above very particular account of these verses leaves us, I think, no room to doubt of the genuineness of this little poem."—MALONE.

b Augur of the fever's end,—] Compare, "A Midsummer Night's Dream," Act V. Sc. 2,—

"Now the wasted brands do glow,
Whilst the scritch-owl, scritching loud,
Puts the wretch that lies in woe,
In remembrance of a shroud."

c *That defunctive music* can,—] That funereal music *knows*.

d But *in them*—] *Except* in them.

e Property *was thus appall'd*,—] "Property" means here *propriety*. The sense of fitness was appall'd.

f Single nature's double name—] This may be right, though we have sometimes thought the genuine reading was,—

"Single natures, double name," &c.

Reason, in itself confounded,
Saw division grow together;
To themselves yet either-neither,
Simple were so well compounded;

That it cried, How true a twain
Seemeth this concordant one!
Love hath reason, reason none,
If what parts can so remain.

Whereupon it made this threne[a]
To the phœnix and the dove,
Co-supremes and stars of love,
As chorus to their tragic scene.

[a] — threne—] A funeral song.

THRENOS.

Beauty, truth, and rarity,
Grace in all simplicity,
Here enclos'd in cinders lie.

Death is now the phœnix' nest;
And the turtle's loyal breast
To eternity doth rest,

Leaving no posterity:—
'T was not their infirmity,
It was married chastity.

Truth may seem, but cannot be;
Beauty, brag, but 't is not she;
Truth and beauty buried be.

To this urn let those repair
That are either true or fair;
For these dead birds sigh a prayer.

APPENDIXES.

SOME ACCOUNT

OF

THE LIFE OF SHAKESPEARE.

For such of the information on Shakespeare's personal history as can be deemed authentic, we are chiefly indebted to modern research. No memoir of him was published in his own time, nor do the several "Commendatory" effusions of which his contemporaries and immediate successors made him the object, imply that their writers knew aught of him except as a poet. Writing nearly a century after Shakespeare's death, Rowe was only able to fill six or seven pages with personal matter; a great portion of his "Life" being devoted to criticism. He derived his memorials from the famous actor, Betterton, who was born in 1635;[1] and what he did was serviceable as a nucleus for more extended treatises; but Betterton ought to have known Shakespeare's private history better, than from Rowe's meagre and questionable narrative he appears to have done, since he was intimately associated with Sir William Davenant (born in 1605), and was apprenticed to a bookseller named Rhodes, who in his younger days was wardrobe-keeper to the theatre in Blackfriars.

From the time of Rowe to that of Malone, great part of another century, though editions of Shakespeare's works were issued by the most distinguished literary characters of the period, and much was done to increase our knowledge of the poet, very little was added to our enlightenment respecting the man. A few odd scraps and memoranda picked out of Aubrey, Oldys, Wood and others, spring up here and there among their notes and illustrations; but of a comprehensive biography we find no trace.[2] In 1790, however, Malone published a *Life of Shakespeare*, for which, although the time for collecting accounts of private occurrences in the poet's career had passed away, every available source of intelligence regarding his public course was industriously and profitably examined. Guided by this luminary, whose services, whether as biographer or commentator, have never been adequately acknowledged, other inquirers, as Messrs. Dyce, Halliwell, Collier, and Knight, have gone over the same field, each adding something to our scanty store of information on the subject. With materials derived from these authorities, the following sketch, containing an abstract of the most essential particulars really ascertained concerning his origin, family, life, property, and character, has been compiled.

---

1 "I must own a particular obligation to him [Betterton], for the most considerable part of the passages relating to this life, which I have here transmitted to the publick; his veneration for the memory of Shakspeare having engaged him to make a journey into Warwickshire on purpose to gather up what remains he could of a name for which he had so great a veneration."—Rowe's *Life of Shakspeare.*

2 "All that insatiable curiosity and unwearied diligence have hitherto detected about Shakespeare, serves rather to disappoint and perplex us, than to furnish the slightest illustration of his character. It is not the register of his baptism, or the draft of his will, or the orthography of his name that we seek. No letter of his writing, no record of his conversation, no character of him drawn with any fullness by a contemporary, has been produced."—Hallam's *Introduction to the Literature of Europe,* ii. 176. 1843.

The family of Shakespeare, Rowe says, "as appears by the register and publick writings relating to that town [Stratford-upon-Avon], were of good figure and fashion there, and are mentioned as gentlemen." This is an error. The register styles none of the family "gentleman" except the poet himself, and even he is so distinguished only after he had returned to his native place with the glory and fortune acquired by his genius and talents. Nor is it probable that his father was originally a Stratford man. Many families of the name had long been settled in different parts of Warwickshire; as at Warwick,[3] Knowle, Rowington, Wroxhall, Hampton, Lapworth, Nuneaton and Kineton. To which of these branches the dramatist belonged, was until recently an insoluble problem. It has now been pretty clearly established, by the researches of Mr. Collier and Mr. Halliwell, that his father, John Shakespeare, was a son of Richard Shakespeare, of Snitterfield, a village three or four miles from Stratford. The evidence in favour of this descent consists in the facts, that the said Richard was a tenant of Robert Arden, whose daughter John Shakespeare married, and that the poet's uncle, Henry Shakespeare, resided at Snitterfield; but this discovery, if such it may be termed, throws little light upon the family itself, and affords no assistance in our endeavours to ascertain from which particular stock the poet's branch descended. With reference to the status of the family, it appears to have been of the class of small farmers in the villages, and of respectable shopkeepers in the towns; no proof having been found, that any public honour or private fortune was ever acquired by its members.[4]

About 1551, John Shakespeare, the father of William, settled in some kind of occupation at Stratford-upon-Avon. There is clear proof that he lived in Henley Street, where the dramatist is supposed to have been born, as early as 1552.[5] In 1556, we find him in the registers of the bailiff's court described as a *glover;* at the same time he was evidently engaged in agricultural pursuits, since he is mentioned in a deed bearing that date as "John Shakespeare, of Stratford-upon-Avon, in the county of Warwick, *yeoman*." Aubrey says he was a butcher:[6] according to Rowe, he was "a considerable dealer in wool."[7] It would be a material addition to our knowledge of William Shakespeare, if the standing and means of his father could be accurately determined. We could then understand, in some degree, what is now extremely doubtful, the manner in which the dramatist was bred and educated. From the slender facts before us, we can only suppose, that John Shakespeare was the son of a respectable farmer at Snitterfield; that he came into the borough of Stratford with a moderate inheritance at his command, and then entered into business as a local merchant; dealing in wool, gloves, timber,

---

[3] From the Survey book of the Manor of Warwick, and from the Muniments at Warwick Castle, we know that a Thomas Shakespeare was possessed of lands and tenements in Warwick, in 1594.

[4] The word *Shakespeare* has been made a subject of some discussion, perhaps more than it deserves. Guided by fac-similes of original signatures, in some cases wrongly traced, certain editors have endeavoured to give the name in the poet's own fashion. The old familiar *Shakespeare* has thus become converted into *Shackspeare, Shakspeare,* and *Shakspere*. This seems a purely idle fancy. The art of spelling was in a very primitive condition at the time of Shakespeare's signing his name, and, if he had wished to attain great accuracy in his own signature, as some of his literary sponsors have done since, he would not have found it an object very easy of accomplishment. In the different records of Warwickshire, the word is spelt in innumerable ways, appearing for instance, as Shaxper, Shaxpeer, Shakspere, Schakespere, Schakespeire, Chacsper, Shakespeyre, and Shakespeere. Whatever may have been the root and original meaning of the word (a point perhaps less obvious than the multitude suppose), it has always been held to signify a race of speare shakers, or warriors. That the poet's contemporaries interpreted it in this sense, is shown in Greene having sarcastically designated Shakespeare the only "Shake-scene," and in Ben Jonson having said of him,

"Look how the father's face
Lives in his issue; even so the race
Of Shakespeare's mind and manners brightly shines
In his well-torned and true-filed lines;
In each of which he seems to *shake a lance,*
As brandish'd at the eyes of ignorance."

Using an authority as ancient as the human imagination, Verstegan, in his *Restitution of Decayed Intelligence,* explains the word in the following grave sentence:—

"Breakspear, Shakspear and the lyke have byn surnames imposed upon the first bearers of them for valour and feates of armes."

Without implicitly assenting to this doctrine, as concerns the name in question, we may fairly act upon it so far as to spell the word in accordance with its asserted root,—Shakespeare—which seems the least affected as well as most correct practice that can be followed.

[5] From a Court Roll, dated April 29th, 1552, preserved in the Record Office, by which we learn that he with others incurred a fine of xij*d.* for a *sterquinarium* before his dwelling "in Hendley Strete *contra ordinationem curiæ.*"

[6] "His [William Shakespeare's] father was a butcher."—AUBREY'S *Mss. Mus. Ashmol. Oxon.*

[7] ROWE'S *Life of Shakspeare.*

corn and perhaps cattle. In 1557, he married Mary, daughter of Robert Arden, of Wilmecote,[8] receiving with her an estate called Ashbies, estimated to have comprised about fifty-six acres of land, and the sum of £6 13*s.* 4*d.*; together with the interest in two tenements at Snitterfield. Whatever our uncertainty regarding the rank of the Shakespeares; that of the Ardens is not doubtful. They had been landed proprietors in the parish of Aston Cantlowe for more than a century before the marriage of Shakespeare's father. They were connected with John Arden, Esquire for the Body to Henry VII.[9] On the maternal side, then, the poet was unquestionably descended from a family of long standing among that class,—the yeoman-squires of England,—who, cultivating their own estates, enjoyed perhaps a larger admixture of comfort and independence than any other of the population.

At the period of his marriage, the circumstances of John Shakespeare appear to have been prosperous. On the 2d of October, 1556, a year before he wedded Mary Arden, he purchased the copyhold of a house in Green-hill Street, and of another in Henley Street: the former having a garden and croft attached to it; the latter only a garden. He became a member of the Corporation in 1557, and in the same year was chosen Ale-taster, "an officer appointed in every court-leet, and sworn to look to the assize and goodness of bread, or ale, or beer, within the precincts of that lordship." In 1558 he was appointed one of the four constables. In 1559 he was chosen one of the four affeerors, empowered to determine the fines for offences against the bye-laws of the corporation. He was elected one of the chamberlains in 1561, and in 1565 he became alderman. From Michaelmas, 1568, to the same period of 1569, he held the chief borough office of bailiff, and in 1571 he was elected chief alderman.[10] It is reasonable to suppose, that while attaining these successive municipal distinctions, his worldly condition was easy if not affluent; but subsequent to the year 1575, in which he purchased two other houses in Henley Street, his affairs appear to have declined. In 1578 he and his wife mortgaged the estate of Ashbies to Edmund Lambert;[11] and shortly after their interest in the tenements at Snitterfield was parted with. About this time, too, John Shakespeare's attendance at the corporation became irregular. On the 19th of November, 1578, when it was required that every alderman should pay fourpence a week for the relief of the poor, John Shakespeare and Robert Bratt were exempted from the tax. In March 1578-9, when an amount of money was levied on the inhabitants of Stratford for the purchase of arms, his name occurs as a defaulter. On "Jan. 19, 28 Eliz." the return to a *distringas*, was—"quod prædictus Johannes Shackspere nihil habet unde distringi potest. Ideo fiat capias versus eundem Johannem Shackspere," &c. The following month, and again in March, a *capias* was issued against him; and in the same year another person was chosen alderman in his stead, the reason assigned being, that he "dothe not come to the halles, nor hathe not done of longe tyme." Nor are these the only indications of his fallen fortune. On "Mar. 29, 29 Eliz." he produced a writ of *habeas corpus* in the Stratford Court of Record,—"Johannes Shakesper protulit breve dominæ reginæ de habeas corpus cum causa," &c.; from which it is conjectured he was then in custody for debt.

---

[8] "She was the youngest of the seven daughters of Robert Arden by his first wife, whose maiden name is not known. His second wife, Agnes Arden, was the widow of a person named Hill: her maiden name was Webbe."—DYCE.

[9] "There is no good proof that the Robert Arden, Groom of the Chamber to Henry VII., and rewarded by that sovereign, a fact which appears from the Patent Rolls of that reign, was related to the Ardens of Wilmecote; but there can be little doubt, from the identity of coat-armour, that the latter were connected with the John Arden, Esquire for the Body to Henry VII., whose will, dated in 1526, would appear to show that the King had honoured him with visits."—HALLIWELL'S *Life of Shakespeare*, p. 17, folio ed.

[10] In 1570, he occupied a small farm called Ingon, or Ington, Meadow, for which, with its appurtenances, he paid a rent of £8 yearly. The land was only fourteen acres in extent, so that a house was probably included.

[11] Joan Arden, the sister of Mary Shakespeare, was married to an Edward Lambert.

Reversing the customary order of things, John Shakespeare, in 1596, when nearly seventy years of age, and apparently in embarrassed circumstances, applied to the Herald's College for a grant of arms. His application was successful: Dethick, the Garter King of Arms, made the grant in 1597; and a second grant, authorizing the arms of Arden to be impaled on the coat, was made by Dethick and Camden in 1599. Drafts of these two grants are still preserved: that of 1597 says, "being therefore solicited, and by credible report informed that John Shakespeare of Stratford-upon-Avon in the counte of Warwick, *whose parents and late antecessors* were for their valeant and faithfull service advanced and rewarded by the most prudent prince King Henry the Seventh of famous memorie, sythence which time they have continewed at those parts in good reputacion and credit, and that the said John having maryed Mary daughter and one of the heyrs of Robert Arden of Wilmcote, in the said counte, gent. In consideration whereof and for the encouragement of his posterite, to whom theyse achevments maie desend by the auncient custom and lawes of Armes, I have therefore assigned, graunted, &c. &c." This would be a gratifying piece of the family history were it trustworthy, but unfortunately it is of very doubtful credit. Such expressions as those respecting Shakespeare's antecessors are no guarantee that the valiant services rendered to Henry the Seventh, were any beyond the most menial offices. Independently too of this drawback, we have the evidence itself on the word of a very suspicious witness. Dethick was at a subsequent period charged, among various miscellaneous offences, with having granted arms to persons whose circumstances and position did not warrant the distinction; and this grant to John Shakespeare was one of the cases cited against him. In reply to this particular portion of the charges, he and his colleague, in "The Answer of Garter and Clarencieux Kinges of Armes, to a libellous Scrawle against certain Arms supposed to be wrongfully given," say that "the persone to whom it was granted had borne magestracy, and was justice of peace at Stratford-upon-Avon; he married the daughter and heire of Arderne, and was able to maintaine that estate."

Moreover, at the bottom of the first draft, made in 1597, Dethick had attached the following memorandum:—"This John hath a patierne thereof [*i.e.* a blazon of the arms] under Clarenc Cookes hand in paper XX years past. A justice of peace, and was baylife, officer and cheffe of the town of Stratford-upon-Avon, XV or XVI years past. That he hathe landes and tenementes of good wealth and substance, £500. That he married a daughter and heyre of Arden, a Gent. of Worship." The most curious part of this note is the reference to a prior grant twenty years before, in the time of Clarence Cooke. But no confirmation of Dethick's statement on this point has ever been found, and the story is generally regarded as fabulous. The received opinion, indeed, now is, that John Shakespeare had no hand in the business, beyond lending his name; that no arms were either sought or obtained in 1576, and that they were applied for in 1596 by, or at least for, the then opulent poet, William Shakespeare.[12]

In 1597, John Shakespeare and his wife filed a bill in Chancery, to recover the estate of Ashbies, against John Lambert, son of Edmund Lambert, to whom we have seen they mortgaged the property for the sum of £40 in 1578, conditionally, that it should revert to them if they repaid the money advanced on or before Michaelmas day, 1580. The money in discharge was duly tendered, according to the declaration of the plaintiffs, but was refused unless other monies in which they were indebted to the mortgagee were also paid. In answer

[12] "In all probability John Shakespeare sought this distinction at the instance of his son William, whose profession of actor prohibited him from directly soliciting it for himself: and we certainly need not doubt that before 1599 the prosperity of the son had secured the father, during the remainder of his days, against any recurrence of those difficulties which had so long beset him."—DYCE, *Life of Shakespeare.*

to the bill, John Lambert denied that the £40 had been tendered; and maintained, that by the death of his father, he was legally entitled to the estate. This answer was followed by a replication on the part of John and Mary Shakespeare, reiterating their former declaration of the tender and refusal of the £40 within the period specified. In what way the suit terminated is not known, but it is supposed to have been settled by private arrangement.

According to Rowe, John and Mary Shakespeare had ten children, and to this circumstance he ascribes the father's incapability of giving the poet a "better education than his own employment."[13] The register of Stratford makes the number only eight. Rowe's error probably arose from the fact of there being another John Shakespeare at Stratford, who in November, 1584, married Margery Roberts, and had three children, born respectively in 1588, 1590 and 1591.[14] Adopting the baptismal register as our guide, the following are found to have been the offspring of John and Mary Shakespeare:—

1. Joan,	baptized	Sept. 15th, 1558
2. Margaret,	—	Dec. 2d, 1562.
3. William,	—	April 26th, 1564.
4. Gilbert,	—	Oct. 13th, 1566.
5. Joan,	—	April 15th, 1569.
6. Anne,	—	Sept. 28th, 1571.
7. Richard,	—	March 11, 1573-4.
8. Edmund,	—	May 3d, 1580.

Of these children, the first Joan is supposed to have lived but a few months. Margaret and Anne are known to have died young; Gilbert, the second Joan, Richard, and Edmund I shall have occasion to mention hereafter.

From the defective manner in which ancient registers were kept—an imperfection not completely remedied until the passing of the present Registration Act—we have no certain knowledge of the day when William Shakespeare was born. The record of his baptism in the register stands as follows,—"1564, April 26, Gulielmus filius Johannes [*sic*] Shakspere;" and tradition tells us he first saw the light on the 23d of the month, three days before he was baptized.[15] A house in Henley Street has always been regarded as that in which he was born, and the legend is supported by evidence of considerable weight. His father appears to have resided in Henley Street nearly if not all his Stratford life.[16] His descendants, the Harts, lived there after him.[17] It is probable that they successively occupied the same house.

Of William Shakespeare's boyhood,[18] of his pursuits up to leaving Stratford, or of the

---

[13] *Life of Shakspeare.*

[14] It has been ascertained that the second John Shakespeare was a shoemaker, and no way related to the father of the dramatist. He is always mentioned in the parish records as plain John Shakespeare, whereas the poet's father is designated Mr. John Shakespeare, a title due to his municipal standing, if not to his position in other respects. There is also evidence to prove that the shoemaker was much the younger man of the two.

[15] "The Rev. Joseph Greene, who was master of the free-school at Stratford, several years ago made some extracts from the register of that parish, which he afterwards gave to the late James West, Esq. They were imperfect, and in other respects not quite accurate. In the margin of this paper Mr. Greene has written, opposite the entry relative to our poet's baptism, '*Born on the 23d;*' but for this, as I conceive, his only authority was the inscription on Shakespeare's tomb—'Obiit ano Do. 1616, Ætates 53, die 23 Ap.' which, however, renders the date here assigned for his birth sufficiently probable."—Malone.

[16] It is proved by a deed bearing date 14 August, 1591, that John Shakespeare then lived in Henley Street. This is a deed of conveyance from George Badger to John Couch of a messuage or tenement situate in a certain street called Henley Street, "between the house of Robert Johnson on the one part *and the house* of John Shakespeare on the other."

[17] Another deed, dated 1647, mentions "all that messuage or tenement with thappurtenances scituate and beinge in Stratford upon Avon aforesaid in a certen streete there called Henley Streete commonly called or knowne by the name of the Maidenhead, and now or late in the tenure of John Rutter or his assignes; and all that other messuage or tenements scituate and beinge in Henley Streete aforesaid *now or late in the tenure of Thomas Hart, and adjoyninge unto the said messuage or tenement called the Maidenhead.*"

[18] When Shakespeare was only nine weeks' old, the plague broke out at Stratford, and raged with such malignity, that in half a year, two hundred and thirty-eight deaths were recorded in a population that did not then reach fifteen hundred. Happily, the part of the town where Shakespeare's family resided escaped the visitation of this destructive epidemic.

motive which prompted that step, nothing positive is known. The first of his immediate successors who collected any particulars of his life was the "inveterate gossip" Aubrey, who, writing about 1680, tells us that he was the son of a butcher; adding, "and I have been told heretofore by some of the neighbours that when he was a boy he exercised his fathers trade, but when he kill'd a calfe, he wold doe it in a high style, and make a speech."[19] It is well ascertained that his father was not a butcher, but it is remarkable that the very next account we meet with says the son was. On April the 10th, 1693, one Dowdall addressed to Mr. Southwell a small treatise which the latter has endorsed, "Description of severall places in Warwickshire." In this, after describing the monumental inscription over the poet's grave, in Stratford Church, the writer observes: "The clarke that shew'd me this church is above 80 years old: he says that this Shakespear was formerly in this towne bound apprentice to a butcher, but that he run from his master to London and there was received into the play house as a serviture, and by this meanes had an opportunity to be what he afterwards prov'd."

Rowe's statement, that he was for some time sent to the Free-school,[20] is probably true. There no doubt he acquired the general rudiments of education; comprising the "small Latin and less Greek," to his possession of which, in after life, Ben Jonson bears testimony.[21]

The most interesting known circumstance in connection with Shakespeare's youth, is the custom that then prevailed of encouraging theatrical representations in provincial towns. The accounts of the Stratford chamberlains contain several notices of official money having been paid for such performances; and Willis, a contemporary of Shakespeare, born in the same year, says, in his *Mount Tabor*, "When players of enterludes come to towne, they first attend the mayor, to enform him what noblemans servants they are, and so to get licence for their publique playing; and if the mayor like the actors, or would shew respect to their lord and master, he appoints them to play their first play before himself and the aldermen and common counsell of the city; and that is called the mayors play, where every one that will comes in without money, the mayor giving the players a reward as hee thinks fit, to shew respect unto them." It appears from the records which have been preserved, that this usage was of frequent observance at Stratford; and curiously enough, the first reference to it is in 1569, the year when John Shakespeare was bailiff; his son William being then five years of age, and probably a delighted spectator of the performance. The entries in the chamberlains' account that apply to the period of his residence at Stratford are as follows:—"1569. payed to the Quene's players £9. Item, for the Quenes provysyon 3*s.* 4*d.* Item, to the Erle of Worcesters pleers 1*s.*" Four years are then skipped over, when we meet with, "1573. paid Mr. Bayly for the Erle of Lecesters players 5*s.* 8*d.*" Then, after another interval of three years, "1576. Geven my Lord of Warwicke players 18*s.* Paid the Earle of Worceter players 5*s.* 8*d.*" The entries then become more frequent, companies of performers having been retained at the public expense, twice in 1577, twice in 1579, once in 1580, twice in 1581, once each in 1582 and 3, and three times in 1584. These are all the items that relate to the present inquiry; but the whole are of interest as displaying the state of a country town in Shakespeare's time, and one of later date, 1622, "payd the Kinges players for *not* playing in the hall 6*s.*" is of ominous significance, as showing into what straits the drama fell when Puritanism began to raise its shaven, dismal

---

19 Mr. Raine conjectured that Aubrey was here alluding to an old semi-dramatic entertainment called *Killing the Calf*, in which the actor, behind a door or screen, by means of ventriloquism, went through a pretended performance of slaughtering a calf.

20 The free-school of Stratford was founded by Thomas Jolyffe, in the reign of Edward IV., and subsequently chartered by Edward VI. The successive masters from 1572 to 1578, the period during which it may be presumed that Shakespeare was a scholar there, were Thomas Hunt and Thomas Jenkins.

21 Aubrey, *Mss. Mus. Ashmol. Oxon*, states, on the authority of a Mr. "Beeston," that Shakespeare "understode Latine pretty well, for he had been in his younger yeares a schoolmaster in the countrey."

countenance. We see in these numerous entries the means by which Shakespeare may have acquired his first taste for dramatic pursuits; and who shall say that it was not an acquaintance with one of these companies of players that first took him to London?

Another circumstance which may possibly have exercised an influence on his after life was Queen Elizabeth's celebrated visit to the Castle of Kenilworth. This took place in the summer of 1575, when Shakespeare was between eleven and twelve years of age. As Stratford is only thirteen miles from Kenilworth, it is by no means unlikely that the future poet was among the spectators of those "Princely pleasures." Some writers have supposed, indeed, there is a direct allusion to Leicester's entertainment in the exquisite compliment addressed to Elizabeth in *A Midsummer Night's Dream*, Act II. Sc. 1.[22]

It was an opinion of Malone, an opinion subsequently adopted by several other critics, that some years of Shakespeare's youth were passed in an attorney's office. There can be no doubt that legal expressions are more frequent, and are used with more precision in his writings than in those of any other author of the period. If these do not prove him to have had professional training, they help to show with what masterly comprehensiveness he could deal with the peculiarities of this, as of nearly every other human pursuit.[23]

Leaving such speculations, we now come to an authentic and important incident of Shakespeare's life—his marriage. Whether glover, wool-stapler, butcher, schoolmaster, or attorney's clerk, in the autumn of 1582, while under nineteen years of age, he took to wife Anne Hathaway, the daughter of a substantial yeoman of Shottery, a hamlet adjoining Stratford.[24]

Anne Hathaway, at the supposed time of the marriage, must have been nearly eight years

---

[22] "Thou remember'st
Since once I sat upon a promontory,
And heard a mermaid, on a dolphin's back,
Uttering such dulcet and harmonious breath,
That the rude sea grew civil at her song;
And certain stars shot madly from their spheres,
To hear the sea maid's music.
That very time I saw (but thou couldst not)
Flying between the cold moon and the earth,
Cupid all arm'd: a certain aim he took
At a fair vestal, throned by the west,
And loos'd his love-shaft smartly from his bow,
As it should pierce a hundred thousand hearts:
But I might see young Cupid's fiery shaft
Quench'd in the chaste beams of the watery moon,
And the imperial votaress passed on,
In maiden meditation, fancy-free."

[23] A sarcastic passage printed by Thomas Nash, in Greene's *Menaphon*, 1589, has been thought to point at Shakespeare and his early professional occupation as a lawyer's clerk. "It is a common practice now-a-dayes, amongst a sort of shifting companions, that run through every art and thrive by none, to leave the trade of *Noverint* whereto they were borne, and busie themselves with the indevours of art, that could scarcely Latinize their neck-verse, if they should have neede: yet English Seneca, read by candle-light, yields many good sentences, as *Bloud is a Beggar*, and so forth: and if you intreat him faire in a frostie morning, he will affoord you whole *Hamlets*, I should say handfuls, of tragical speeches."

[24] Neither the date of the marriage, nor the church where the ceremony was performed, has yet transpired; but the following bond was discovered a few years ago by Sir T. Phillipps, in the registry at Worcester, and leaves no doubt that the marriage was celebrated sometime after November 28th, 1582:—"Noverint universi per præsentes nos Fulconem Sandells de Stratford in comitatu Warwici, agricolam, et Johannem Rychardson ibidem agricolam, teneri et firmiter obligari Ricardo Cosin generoso, et Roberto Warmstry notario publico, in quadraginta libris bonæ et legalis monetæ Angliæ, solvend. eisdem Ricardo et Roberto, hæred. execut. vel assignat. suis, ad quam quidem solucionem bene et fideliter faciend. obligamus nos et utrumque nostrum per se pro toto et in solid. hæred. executor. et administrator. nostros firmiter per præsentes sigillis nostris sigillat. Dat. 28 die Novem. anno regni dominæ nostræ Eliz. Dei gratia Angliæ, Franc. et Hiberniæ reginæ, fidei defensor. &c. 25°."

"The condicion of this obligacion ys suche, that if herafter there shall not appere any lawfull lett or impediment, by reason of any precontract, consanguinitie, affinitie, or by any other lawfull meanes whatsoever, but that William Shagspere one thone partie, and Anne Hathwey of Stratford in the dioces of Worcester, maiden, may lawfully solennize matrimony together, and in the same afterwardes remaine and continew like man and wiffe, according unto the lawes in that behalfe provided: and moreover, if there be not at this present time any action, sute, quarrell, or demaund, moved or depending before any Judge ecclesiasticall or temporall, for and concerning any suche lawfull lett or impediment: and moreover, if the said William Shagspere do not proceed to solemnizacion of mariadg with the said Anne Hathwey without the consent of hir frindes: and also, if the said William do, upon his owne proper costes and expences, defend and save harmles the right reverend Father in God, Lord John Bushop of Worcester, and his offycers, for licensing them the said William and Anne to be maried together with once asking of the bannes of matrimony betwene them, and for all other causes which may ensue by reason or occasion therof, that then the said obligacion to be voyd and of none effect or els to stand and abide in full force and vertue."—*The marks and seals of Sandells and Richardson.*

the senior of her husband.[25] Her father, in all probability, was Richard Hathaway,[26] whose family have held property at Shottery from the middle of the sixteenth century to the present day.[27]

The first offspring of this union, Susanna, was born in May 1583.[28] The only other issue were Hamnet and Judith, twins, who were baptized Feb. 2d. 1584–5.[29]

Shortly after the birth of these children, it seems to be agreed, that Shakespeare quitted his home and family; and there is a well-known tradition, that this important step was owing to his being detected, with other young men, in stealing deer from the park of Sir Thomas Lucy, of Charlecote. For this indiscretion,[30] he is said to have been severely punished, and to have retorted with a lampoon so bitter, that Sir Thomas redoubled his persecution and compelled him to fly.[31]

What degree of authenticity the story possesses will never probably be known. Rowe derived his version of it no doubt through Betterton; but Davies makes no allusion to the source from which he drew his information, and we are left to grope our way, so far as this important incident is concerned, mainly by the light of collateral circumstances. These, it must be admitted, serve in some respects to confirm the tradition. Shakespeare certainly quitted Stratford-upon-Avon when a young man, and it could have been no ordinary impulse which drove him to leave wife, children, friends, and occupation, to take up his abode among strangers in a distant place. Then there is the pasquinade,[32] and the unmistakeable identification of Sir Thomas Lucy as Justice Shallow in the Second Part of *Henry IV.* and in the opening

---

[25] She died, according to the brass plate over her grave in Stratford church, on "the 6th day of August, 1623, *being of the age of* 67 *yeares.*"

[26] Two precepts of the Stratford Court of Record exhibit John Shakespeare as the surety of Richard Hathaway in 1566; and prove an early connexion between the two families.

[27] A house still existing in the hamlet, though now divided into three cottages, has always passed as that in which the poet's wife resided in her maiden years. Having no evidence to the contrary, we may still look upon that habitation as the scene of Shakespeare's courtship.

[28] The record of her baptism is as follows:—"1583, *May* 26. *Susanna daughter to William Shakspere.*"

[29] The record in the register runs thus:—" 1584. *Feb.* 2. *Hamnet and Judeth* sonne and daughter to *Williã Shakspere.*"

They were doubtless christened after Hamnet Sadler, and Judith his wife; the former a baker at Stratford, to whom the poet bequeathed 36*s.* and 8*d.* to purchase a ring.

[30] Deer stealing, in Shakespeare's day, was regarded only as a youthful frolic. Antony Wood (*Athen. Oxon.* i. 371), speaking of Dr. John Thornborough, who was admitted a member of Magdalen College, Oxford, 1570, at the age of eighteen, and was successively Bishop of Limerick in Ireland, and Bishop of Bristol and Worcester in England, informs us, that he and his kinsman, Robert Pinkney, "seldom studied or gave themselves to their books, but spent their time in the *fencing-schools* and dancing-schools, in *stealing deer* and *conies,* in *hunting the hare,* and *wooing girls.*"

[31] The story is first told in print by Rowe, *Life of Shakspeare*:—"He had, by a misfortune common enough to young fellows, fallen into ill company, and, amongst them, some that made a frequent practice of deer-stealing, engaged him more than once in robbing a park that belonged to Sir Thomas Lucy, of Charlecote, near Stratford. For this he was prosecuted by that gentleman, as he thought, somewhat too severely; and, in order to revenge that ill usage, he made a ballad upon him. And though this, probably the first essay of his poetry, be lost, yet it is said to have been so very bitter, that it redoubled the prosecution against him to that degree, that he was obliged to leave his business and family in Warwickshire, for some time, and shelter himself in London."

Aubrey is silent on the subject. He only says, "This William, being inclined naturally to poetry and acting, came to London I guess about eighteen." But the deer-stealing freak and its consequences are narrated more specifically than by Rowe, in an article headed *Shakespeare* among the MS. collections of the Rev. William Fulman, who died in 1688. This learned antiquary bequeathed his papers to the Rev. Richard Davies, rector of Sapperton and Archdeacon of Litchfield, upon whose death they were presented to Corpus Christi College, Oxford. To Dr. Fulman's notes under the article *Shakespeare,* Davies has added the following:—"Much given to all unluckinesse in stealing *venison and rabbits, particularly from Sr—— Lucy, who had him oft whipt and sometimes imprisoned, and at last made him fly his native country to his great advancement: but his reveng was so great, that he is his Justice Clodpate and calls him a great man, and that, in allusion to his name, bore three louses rampant for his arms.*"

[32] According to Rowe, the ballad on Sir Thomas Lucy was lost. According to Oldys, as quoted by Steevens: "There was a very aged gentleman living in the neighbourhood of Stratford (where he died fifty years since) who had not only heard from several old people in that town of Shakspere's transgression, but could remember the first stanza of that bitter ballad, which, repeating to one of his acquaintances, he preserved it in writing, and here it is, neither better nor worse, but faithfully transcribed from the copy which his relation very courteously communicated to me:—

A parliemente member, a justice of peace,
At home a poor scare-crowe, at London an asse;
If lowsie is Lucy, as some volke miscalle it,
Then Lucy is lowsie whatever befall it:
He thinks himself greate,
Yet an asse in his state
We allowe by his ears but with asses to mate,
If Lucy is lowsie, as some volke miscalle it,
Sing lowsie Lucy, whatever befall it!"

scene of *The Merry Wives of Windsor*. The genuineness of the former may be doubted; but the ridicule in the plays betokens a latent hostility to the Lucy family which is unaccountable except upon the supposition that the deer-stealing foray is founded on facts.

Whatever the motive,—fear, distress, or ambition,—Shakespeare, it is believed, left Stratford about 1586, and found employment at some theatre in London;[33] but we have no direct proof of the year when he left his home, or of that in which he took up his abode in the metropolis. According to a document introduced by Mr. Collier, as discovered in Lord Ellesmere's muniments, he was a sharer in the Blackfriars Theatre in 1589, but this memorial, like the rest of the Shakesperian papers from the same collection, has been shown to be a rank fabrication.[34] In fact, from the baptism of his twins in 1584–5, to the latter end of the year 1592, when Green alludes to him in *A Groatsworth of Wit*, &c. his history is a blank.

It does not come within the scope of this brief memoir to enter at large into the subject of the Elizabethan theatre, but a few words respecting it are indispensable. Shakespeare in all likelihood originally joined the company playing at the Blackfriars Theatre. This company afterwards (in 1594) built another theatre, called *The Globe*, on the south bank of the Thames; using the latter, which was partially open to the air, in summer; and the former, which was *a private* or enclosed house, for winter performances. The *Blackfriars* playhouse stood in an opening still called *Playhouse Yard*, between Apothecaries' Hall and Printing-house Square. Besides these two, there were several theatres in London during Shakespeare's residence there. The principal appear to have been, *The Theatre* (so denominated probably from being the first building erected specially for scenic performances) and *The Curtain*, in Shoreditch; *The Paris Garden*, *The Rose*, *The Hope*, *The Swan*, on the Bankside, Southwark; *The Fortune*, in Golden Lane, Cripplegate; *The Red Bull*, St. John Street, Smithfield; *The Whitefriars*, near to where the gas works now stand, between the Temple and Blackfriars Bridge; and a summer theatre at *Newington Butts*.[35]

---

[33] Rowe says, "He was received into the company then in being, at first in a very mean rank;" and this tallies with the statement made by Dowdall in 1693 (See p. xx.).

In a work entitled, *Lives of the Poets of Great Britain and Ireland*, 1753, there is a life of Shakespeare, in which, for the first time, we meet with the incredible tradition of his having held the horses of gentlemen who visited the play:—

"I cannot forbear relating a story which Sir William Davenant told Mr. Betterton, *who communicated it to Mr. Rowe;* Rowe told it to Mr. Pope, and Mr. Pope told it to Dr. Newton, the late editor of Milton, and from a gentleman who heard it from him, 'tis here related. Concerning Shakespear's first appearance in the playhouse. When he came to London, he was without money and friends, and being a stranger, he knew not to whom to apply, nor by what means to support himself. At that time, coaches not being in use, and as gentlemen were accustomed to ride to the playhouse, Shakespear, driven to the last necessity, went to the playhouse door, and pick'd up a little money, by taking care of the gentlemen's horses who came to the play: he became eminent even in that profession, and was taken notice of for his diligence and skill in it; he had soon more business than he himself could manage, and at last hired boys under him, who were known by the name of Shakespear's boys. Some of the players, accidentally conversing with him, found him so acute, and master of so fine a conversation, that, struck therewith, they [introduced] and recommended him to the house, in which he was first admitted in a very low station, but he did not long remain so, for he soon distinguished himself, if not as an extraordinary actor, at least as a fine writer."

[34] It is as follows:—"These are to sertifie yor right honorable Ll that he Mates poore playeres, James Burbidge, Richard Burbidge, John Laneham, Thomas Greene, Robert Wilson, John Taylor, Anth. Wadeson, Thomas Pope, George Peele, Augustine Phillippes, Nicholas Towley, William Shakespeare, William Kempe, William Johnson, Baptiste Goodale, and Robert Armyn, being all of them sharers in the blacke Fryers playehouse, have never giuen cause of displeasure, in that they haue brought into their playes maters of state and Religion, vnfitt to be handled by them or to be presented before lewde spectators; neither hath anie complainte in that kinde ever beene preferred against them or anie of them. Wherefore they truste moste humblie in yor Ll consideracōn of their former good behaiuour, beinge at all tymes readie and willing to yeelde obedience to anie comaund whatsoever your Ll in your wisedome maye thinke in such case meete, &c.

"*Novr.* 1589."

[35] *The Phœnix*, which had formerly been a *Cockpit*, in Drury Lane, was not converted into a playhouse until after Shakespeare's retirement from London.

Edmund Howes, in his Continuation of Stow's chronicle, gives a curious summary of playhouse incidents extending over the whole of Shakespeare's time. After describing the burning of the Globe in 1613, the destruction of the Fortune by a like accident four years after, the re-building of both, and the erection of "a new fair playhouse near the Whitefriars," he says, writing in 1631, "And this is the seventeenth stage, or common playhouse, which hath been new made within the space of three score years within London and the suburbs, viz. five inns, or common hostelries turned to playhouses, one cockpit, St. Paul's singing school, one in the Blackfriars, one in the Whitefriars, which was built last of all, in the year one

Before the erection of established theatres, and long afterwards, plays were also acted in the yards of certain inns, such as the *The Bell Savage*, on Ludgate Hill; *The Cross Keys*, in Gracechurch Street; and *The Bull*, in Bishopsgate Street.

With respect to the regular theatre we are not very intimately acquainted with the details of its structure, but the interior economy appears to have resembled that of the old inn yards, and it was evidently provided with different accommodation to suit different classes of visitors. There were tiers of galleries or scaffolds, and small rooms beneath, answering to the modern *boxes*. There was the *pit*, as it was called in the private theatres, or *yard*, as it was named at the public ones. In the former, spectators were provided with seats; in the latter they were obliged to stand throughout the performance.[36] The critics, wits, and gallants were allowed stools upon the stage, for which the price was sixpence or a shilling each,[37] according to the eligibility of the situation, and they were attended by pages, who supplied them with pipes and tobacco; smoking, drinking ale, playing cards, and eating nuts and apples, always forming a portion of the entertainment at our early theatres.

The stage appliances were extremely simple. At the back of the stage there was a permanent balcony, about eight feet from the platform, in which scenes supposed to take place on towers or upper chambers were represented.[38] Suspended in front of it were curtains, and these were opened or closed as the performance required.[39] The sides and back of the stage, with the exception of that part occupied by the balcony, were hung with arras tapestry, and sometimes pictures, and the internal roof with blue drapery, except on the performance of tragedy, when the sides, back, and roof of the stage were covered with black.[40] The stage was commonly strewed with rushes, though on particular occasions it was matted over.

The performance commenced at three o'clock, in the public theatres, the signal for beginning being the third *sounding* or flourish of trumpets.[41] It was customary for the actor who spoke the prologue to be dressed in a long velvet cloak. In the early part of Shakespeare's theatrical career, the want of scenery appears to have been supplied by the primitive expedient of hanging out a board, on which was written the place where the action was to be understood as taking place. Sometimes when a change of scene was requisite, the audience were left to imagine that the actors, who still remained on the stage, had removed to the spot mentioned.[42] During the performance, the clown would frequently indulge in extemporaneous buffoonery.

---

thousand six hundred and twenty nine. All the rest not named were erected only for common playhouses, besides the new-built Bear Garden, which was built as well for plays, and fencer's prizes, as bull-baiting; besides one in former time at Newington Butts. Before the space of three score years above said [*i.e.* before 1571, when Shakespeare was seven years of age] I neither knew, heard, nor read of any such theatres, set stages, or playhouses, as have been purposely built within man's memory."

36 Hence they are termed *groundlings* by Shakespeare, and *understanding* gentlemen of the *ground* by Ben Jonson.

37 According to Malone, but there is much uncertainty on the point, the prices of admission to the best *rooms*, or boxes, was, in Shakespeare's day, a shilling; that to the galleries and pit, in the chief theatres, sixpence, in the inferior ones, twopence, and sometimes only a penny.

38 "It appears," says Malone, "from the stage-directions given in *The Spanish Tragedy*, that when a play was exhibited within a play (if I may so express myself), as is the case in that piece and in *Hamlet*, the court or audience before whom the interlude was performed sat in the balcony, or upper stage already described; and a curtain or traverse being hung across the stage, *for the nonce*, the performers entered between that curtain and the general audience, and on its being drawn, began their piece, addressing themselves to the balcony, and regardless of the spectators in the theatre, to whom their backs must have been turned during the whole of the performance."—*Historical Account of the English Stage*, p. 108.

39 I am of opinion that during Shakespeare's time there were no curtains across the proscenium.

40 The covering of the internal roof, or the roof itself, was technically termed *the heavens*. See note (1), p. 332. Vol. II.

41 There was an interval of some minutes between each sounding. See the Induction to Ben Jonson's *Poetaster* and *Cynthia's Revels*.

42 "The simplicity of the old stage in this respect, may also be clearly shown by a reference to R. Greene's *Pinner of Wakefield*, printed in 1599, where Jenkin is struck by the Shoe-maker in the street. Jenkin challenges him to come to the towns-end to fight it out; and, after some farther parley, the professor of 'the gentle craft' reminds Jenkin of his challenge:—

'Come, sir, will you come to the town's-end now?
'*Jenkin*. Aye, Sir, come.'—

and in the very next line he adds,

'Now we are at the town's-end.'

History of English Dramatic Poetry, &c. iii. 68

There was always music between the acts, and sometimes singing and dancing. And at the end of the play, after a prayer for the reigning monarch, offered by the actors on their knees,[43] the clown would entertain the audience by descanting on any *theme* which the spectators might supply, or by performing what was called a *jig*, a farcical doggrel improvisation, accompanied by dancing and singing.

During the reign of Elizabeth, plays were acted every day in the week,[44] but in the time of James I., though dramatic entertainments on Sundays were allowed at court, they were prohibited in the public theatres. As there were two sorts of theatres, there were two classes of actors. There were the regular companies, acting in the name and under the auspices of the Crown or of a man of rank and influence, such as the Queen's servants (of whom Shakespeare was one),[45] the Earl of Leicester's players; those of Lord Warwick, Lord Worcester, Lord Pembroke, &c. There were also certain private adventurers who acted without official licence, and were the subjects of prohibitory enactments. The Act of the 14th of Elizabeth (1572) operated as a protective law to the authorized companies. It was entitled an act "for the punishment of vagabonds, and for the relief of the poor and impotent." One of its provisions extends the meaning of rogues and vagabonds to "all fencers, bearwards, common-players in interludes, and minstrels, not belonging to any Baron of this realm or towards any other honorable personage of greater degree; all jugglers, pedlars, tinkers, and petty chapmen, which said fencers, bearwards, common-players in interludes, minstrels, jugglers, pedlars, tinkers, and petty chapmen shall wander abroad, and not have licence of two justices of the peace at the least, whereof one to be of the quorum, where and in what shire they shall happen to wander." This act effected no material restriction on the number of actors, for, while its provisions were evaded by numerous jugglers, minstrels, and interlude players, various companies were enrolled in the service of the nobility. The growing Puritanism of the time occasioned many attempts to be made at suppressing the drama on the part of civic authorities, both in London and elsewhere,[46] but the theatre maintained its ground through the reign of Elizabeth and for many years afterwards.

---

[43] "At the end of the piece, the actors, in noblemen's houses and in taverns, where plays were frequently performed, prayed for the health and prosperity of their patrons; and in the publick theatres, for the king and queen. This prayer sometimes made part of the epilogue. Hence, probably, as Mr. Steevens has observed, the addition of *Vivant rex et regina* to the modern playbills."—MALONE.

[44] In 1580, the magistrates of the city of London obtained from the queen a prohibition against plays on the Sabbath, which seems, however, to have continued in force but a short time.

[45] "Comedians and stage-players of former time were very poor and ignorant in respect of these of this time; but being now [1583] growne very skilfull and exquisite actors for all matters, they were entertained into the service of divers great lords: out of which companies there were twelve of the best chosen, and, at the request of Sir Francis Walsingham, they were sworn the queenes servants, and were allowed wages and liveries as groomes of the chamber: and until this year 1583, the queene had no players. Among these twelve players, were two rare men, viz. Thomas Wilson, for a quicke, delicate, refined, extemporall witt, and Richard Tarleton, for a wondrous plentifull pleasant extemporall wit, he was the wonder of his tyme. He lieth buried in Shoreditch Church."—*Stow's Chronicle, sub* 1583, ed. 1615.

[46] A few years ago, Sir Frederic Madden published the following interesting illustration of the pertinacity with which the authorities of the city of London resisted the admission of stage-players within the city. It is an original letter, preserved among the Cottonian charters, from the Mayor and Alderman to the Earl of Sussex, Lord Chamberlain, dated March 2d, 1573, refusing their consent to his lordship's request in favour of a Mr. Holmes, that he should be allowed to appoint places for plays and interludes within the city; and intimating that some previous applications of the same kind had met with a similar refusal.

[Cart. Cott. xxvi. 41.]

"*To the right honorable our singular good Lord the Erle of Sussex, Lord Chamberlan of the Quenes Maties most honorable household.*

Our dutie to yor good L. humbly done, where yor L. hath made request in favor of Mr. Holmes, for our assent that he might have the apointement of places for playes and entreludes within the citie. It may please yor L. to receive undouted assurance of or redinesse to gratifie in any thing that we reasonably may, any persone whome yor L. shal favor and comend. Howbeit this case is such and so nere touching the governance of this citie in one of the greatest maters therof, namely the assemblies of multitudes of the Quenes people; and in regard to be had to sondry inconveniences wherof the peril is continually upon everie occasion to be foreseen by the rulers of this citie, that we can not with our duties, byside the president farr extending to the hart of our liberties, well assent that the sayd apointement of places be comitted to any private persone. For which and other resonable consideracons, it hath long since pleased yor good L., among the rest of her Maties most honorable counsell, to rest satisfied with our not graunting the like to such persone as by their most honorable lettres was heretofore in like case comended unto us. Byside that if it might with reasonable convenience be graunted, great offres have ben and be made for the same, to the relefe of the

The "fellowship" which Shakespeare is supposed to have joined was originally attached to the Earl of Leicester. In 1574, it was distinguished by more illustrious patronage, a writ being issued that year to the Keeper of the Great Seal,[47] commanding him to set forth letters patent addressed to all justices of the peace, licensing and authorizing James Burbadge, John Perkyn, John Lanham, William Johnson, and Robert Wylson, servants of the Earl of Leicester, "to use, exercise and occupie the art and faculty of playeing comedies, tragedies, enterludes, stage-playes, and such other like as they have alredy used and studied, as well for the recreacion of our loving subjects, as for our solace and pleasure, when we shall think good to see them as well within our Cyty of London and the liberties of the same as throughout the realm of England." This admonition was opposed by those charged with the liberties of the City of London, and in 1575 the Common Council passed what in civic language was called an "Act," in which they saddled their licence with a condition, that the players should contribute half their receipts to charitable purposes. But in the same year Burbadge and his fellow-servants of the Earl of Leicester, through the powerful influence of their patron, obtained a patent for the erection of a theatre at Blackfriars; close to the city wall, though beyond the jurisdiction of the city authorities. Shortly afterwards they took some large premises in the precinct of the dissolved Black-friars monastery, and in spite of a vigorous opposition on the part of the inhabitants in the neighbourhood, converted them into the very theatre of which it is presumed Shakespeare became a fellow, not long after his arrival in London.

Shakespeare's first connexion with the company in the Blackfriars was probably as an actor. Of his qualifications and line of performance in this art, scarcely anything is known, though, according to Aubrey, "he did act exceedingly well."[48] Rowe says, "His name is printed, as the custom was in those times, amongst those of the other players, before some old plays, but without any particular account of what sort of parts he used to play; and though I have inquired, I could never meet with any further account of him this way, than that the top of his performance was the Ghost in his own Hamlet."[49]

Downes, the writer of the *Roscius Anglicanus*, who was prompter at one of the London theatres in 1662, speaking of Sir William Davenant's theatre in Lincoln's Inn Fields, between 1662 and 1665, remarks, "The tragedy of Hamlet, *Hamlet* being performed by Mr. Betterton. Sir William having seen Mr. Taylor of the Blackfryars company act it, who being instructed by the author, Mr. Shakespear, taught Mr. Betterton in every particle of it; which, by his exact performance of it, gained him esteem and reputation superlative to all other players."

In like manner he speaks of Betterton's having been instructed by Sir William to play Henry VIII., after the fashion of "old Mr. Lowen," who had been taught by Shakespeare

---

poore in the hospitalles, which we hold us assured that yor L. will well allow that we preferre before the benefit of any private persone. And so we comitt yor L. to the tuition of Almighty God. At London, this second of March, 1573.

Yo^r^ L. humble

	John Ryvers, Mayor.	Thomas Ramsey.
Nicholas Woodrof.	Row. Haywarde, Alder.	Wyllym Bond.
John Branche.	William Allyn, Alderman.	John Olyffe.
Anthony Gamage.	Leonell Duckett, Alder.	Rychard Pype.
Wyllm Rymptone.	Jamys Hawys, Aldarman.	Wm. Box.
Wolstan Dixe.	Ambrose Nichas, Ald.	Thomas Blanke.
	Jhon Langley, Ald."	

47 "There is a material difference between the warrant under the privy seal, and the patent under the great seal, granted upon this occasion: the former gives the players a right to perform 'as well within the city of London and liberties of the same, as elsewhere; but the latter (dated three days afterwards, viz. 10 May, 1574), omits this paragraph; and we need entertain little doubt that it was excluded at the instance of the Corporation of London, always opposed to theatrical performances."—COLLIER. *Life of Shakespeare.*

48 *Mus. Ashmol. Oxon.*

49 *Life of Shakspeare.* Capell, 1779, relates that "a traditional story was current some years ago about Stratford, that a very old man of that place, of weak intellects, being asked by some of his neighbours what he remember'd about him, answer'd that he saw him once brought on the stage upon another man's back, which answer was applied by the hearers to his having performed in this scene [Sc. 7, Act II. of *As You Like It*] in the part of Adam." For a more circumstantial account of the same legend, see the Introduction to *As You Like It*, Vol. II. p. 125.

himself. On this authority, it appears that if Shakespeare, as Rowe asserts, was not a brilliant actor, he was at any rate a skilful teacher of acting. But the testimony of Chettle, who must have seen him perform, is of far more weight than the hearsay evidence of Rowe and others; and he, in the preface to his *Kind-Harts Dreame*, which we shall have to notice presently, expressly declares that he was "excellent in the quality he professed."

The earliest conjectural allusion to Shakespeare as a dramatist which has yet been discovered in print, is contained in Spenser's *Teares of the Muses*, a poem forming part of a collection published in 1591.[50] In this poem, the Muse Thalia is introduced, lamenting the decline of the drama. After reciting how "the sweete delights of learnings treasure" have disappeared from the stage; how "unseemly Sorrow," "ugly Barbarisme," and "brutish Ignorance" in the minds of men "now tyrannize," whereas "fine Counterfesaunce," "unhurtful Sport, Delight and Laughter" used to reign supreme, she says,—

"And he, the man whom Nature selfe had made
To mock herselfe, and Truth to imitate
With kindly counter under mimick shade,
Our pleasant Willy, ah! is dead of late:
With whom all joy and jolly meriment
Is also deaded, and in dolour drent.

In stead thereof, scoffing Scurrilitie,
And scornful Follie with Contempt is crept,
Rolling in rymes of shameless ribaudrie,
Without regard or due decorum kept;
Each idle wit at will presumes to make[51]
And doth the Learned's taske upon him take.

But that same gentle Spirit, from whose pen
Large streames of honnie and sweete Nectar flowe,
Scorning the boldness of such base-borne men,
Which dare their follies forth so rashlie throwe,
Doth rather choose to sit in idle cell,
Than so himselfe to mockerie to sell."

In the first edition of his *Life of Shakspeare*, Rowe tells us "Mr. Dryden was always of opinion that these verses were meant of Shakespear:" though in a subsequent impression of the memoir Rowe omitted the statement. Modern authorities are not agreed upon the point, but the prevailing opinion is that Shakespeare could not have been the writer referred to by Spenser. The reasons for this opinion are, firstly, that he had not at the time attained a rank such as would justify the encomiums; secondly, because there is no probability of his having subsided into the condition of inertness described, and thirdly, because there are grounds for supposing the verses in question were composed before he even began to write.[52]

Without entering into the last consideration, there appears to me sufficient evidence to prove that the expressions in this poem, however suitable to the character of Shakespeare, and accordant with those employed by his contemporaries when speaking of him, were intended for

---

[50] *Complaints. Containing sundrie small Poemes of the Worlds Vanitie*, &c,

[51] That is, *to compose, to invent.*

[52] Todd, in his edition of Spenser's works, conjectures from the following address, prefixed to the collection of poems in question by the publisher, that *The Teares of the Muses* was composed about 1580:—"Since my late setting foorth of the *Faerie Queene*, finding that it hath found a favourable passage amongst you; I have sithence endeavoured by all good meanes (for the better encrease and accomplishment of your delights), to get into my handes such smale poemes of the same authors, as I heard were disperst abroad in sundrie hands, and not easie to bee come by, by himselfe; *some of them having bene diverslie imbeziled and purloyned from him since his departure over Sea. Of the which* I have by good meanes gathered togeather *these fewe parcels present*, which I have caused to bee imprinted altogeather," &c.

some other *Willy*.[53] The quotation from Chettle shows, in fact, that our poet was in the full tide of activity at the time when Spenser's hero is metaphorically described as "dead of late."

Malone is of opinion that the term *Willy* had in this instance a more particular significance, and was intended to express *Lyly* the poet, and he supports this notion by adducing many examples of a similar play on names, as *Lerinda* for Ireland, *Unio* for Juno, *Caliban* for Cannibal, *Ailgna* for Anglia, &c., all derived from the literature of Spenser's age. Todd thinks, and Mr. Dyce seems to agree with him, that *Willy* means Sir Philip Sydney, "who was a writer of masks,—who is elsewhere styled by Spenser '*gentle* shepherd of *gentlest* race,' and 'the right *gentle* minde,'—and who is lamented under the name of *Willy* in *An Eclogue* in Davison's *Poetical Rhapsody*."[54]

In the following year, we have an indisputable and most important reference to Shakespeare. On the 3d of September, 1592, at a wretched lodging, in the house of a poor shoemaker, near Dowgate, and under circumstances of privation too dreadful to dwell on, expired Robert Greene, one of the most distinguished and favourite writers of his time. The last few days of this misguided and unhappy man's existence were devoted, it is said, to the production of a small pamphlet entitled *A Groatsworth of Wit bought with a Million of Repentance*, which was published not long after by Henry Chettle. In this tract, after a long and not remarkably lucid admonition to certain of his fellow dramatists,[55] we come upon the following striking passage :—"Base-minded men all three of you, if by my misery yee bee not warned ; for unto none of you (like me) sought those burs to cleave; those puppits (I meane) that speake from our mouths, those Anticks garnisht in our colours. Is it not strange that I, to whom they all have bin beholding, is it not like that you to whom they all have bin beholding, shall (were yee in that case that I am now) be both of them at once forsaken? Yes, trust them not; for there is an upstart crow beautified with our feathers, that, with his *Tygres heart wrapt in a players hyde, supposes hee is as well able to bombast out a blanke verse as the best of you ; and beeing an absolute Johannes Fac-totum, is, in his owne conceyte, the only* SHAKE-SCENE *in a countrey.* Oh, that I might intreat your rare wittes to bee imployed in more profitable courses, and let these apes imitate your past excellence, and never more acquaynte them with your admyred inventions. I knowe the best husband of you all will never proove an usurer, and the kindest of them all will never proove a kinde nurse ; yet whilst you may, seeke you better maisters; for it is pitty men of such rare wits should bee subject to the pleasures of such rude groomes."

The allusion to Shakespeare is not to be mistaken ; and the imputation is evidently, that he had remodelled pieces originally produced by Greene, Marlowe, Lodge, and Peele, and brought them upon the stage as his own composition. It seems probable, too, by the words, "his Tygres heart wrapt in a players hyde," which is a parody upon a well-known line introduced by Shakespeare into *Henry VI.*[56] from *The True Tragedie of Richard Duke of Yorke*, that Greene refers particularly to that piece and *The First Part of the Contention betwixt the two famous Houses of Yorke and Lancaster*, on which our poet based *The Second and Third Parts of King Henry the Sixth.*

Greene's address, we learn from Chettle's epistle "To the Gentlemen Readers," prefixed to his tract called *Kind-Harts Dreame*, was resented not alone by Shakespeare, at whom the attack was levelled, but by Marlowe also, whom it charged with atheism.[57] "About three moneths since,"

---

[53] *Willy* was a mere Arcadianism for any *shepherd*, i.e. *poet*.

[54] Dyce's *Life of Shakespeare*.

[55] It is addressed "To those gentlemen his quondam acquaintance, that spend their wits in making playes, R. G. wisheth a better exercise, and wisedome to prevent his extremities," and there can be little doubt was intended for Marlowe, Lodge, and Peele.

[56] *Third Part*, Act I. Sc. 4,—
"Oh, tygers hart wrapt in a woman's hide!"

[57] "Wonder not (for with thee will I first beginne), thou famous gracer of tragedians [Marlowe], that Green, who hath said with thee, like the foole in his hearte, *There is no God*, should now give glorie unto his greatnesse," &c.

are Chettle's words, "died M. Robert Greene, leaving many papers in sundry bookesellers hands; among other, his *Groatsworth of Wit*, in which a letter written to divers play-makers is offensively by one or two of them taken; and because on the dead they cannot be avenged, they wilfully forge in their conceites a living author; and after tossing it to and fro, no remedy but it must light on me. How I have, all the time of my conversing in printing, hindred the bitter inveying against schollers, it hath been very well knowne, and how in that I dealt I can sufficiently proove. With neither of them that take offence was I acquainted, *and with one of them I care not if I never be:* the other whome at that time I did not so much spare as since I wish I had, for that, as I have moderated the heate of living writers, and might have usde my owne discretion, especially in such a case, the author beeing dead, that I did not, *I am as sorry as if the originall fault had beene my fault, because myselfe have seene his demeanor no lesse civill than he exclent in the qualitie he professes; Besides, divers of worship have reported his uprightness of dealing, which argues his honesty, and his facetious grace in writting that approoves his art.* For the first, whose learning I reverence, and, at the perusing of Greenes booke, stroke out what then in conscience I thought he in some displeasure writ, or, had it beene true, yet to publish it was intollerable; him I would wish to use me no worse than I deserve. I had onely in the copy this share; it was ilwritten, as sometime Greenes hand was none of the best; licensd it must be ere it could bee printed, which could never be if it might not be read: to be briefe, I writ it over, and, as neare as I could, followed the copy, onely in that letter I put something out, but in the whole booke not a worde in; for I protest it was all Greenes, not mine nor Maister Nashes, as some unjustly have affirmed."

The "first" person to whom this apology is directed, and for whose learning Chettle expresses his reverence, though with a disparaging qualification as to his character in general, could have been none other than Marlowe. "The other" was certainly Shakespeare, and the reference is an interesting testimony to his high reputation as a dramatist and an actor, and to his urbanity and rectitude as a man.

In 1593 our author's *Venus and Adonis*, and in 1594 his *Lucrece*, appeared, each dedicated to Henry Wriothesly, Earl of Southampton. It is impossible now to determine whether the dedication of the former work first led to the friendly intercourse which appears to have subsisted so many years between Shakespeare and this generous and amiable nobleman, or whether their acquaintance began at an earlier period of the poet's career. Mr. Collier expresses an opinion, that it was shortly after the publication of the latter poem that Lord Southampton afforded that extraordinary proof of his esteem and admiration of the poet which Rowe was the first to relate: "There is one instance so singular in the magnificence of this patron of Shakespear's, that if I had not been assured that the story was handed down by Sir William Davenant, who was probably very well acquainted with his affairs, I should not have ventured to have inserted; that my Lord Southampton, at one time, gave him a thousand pounds to enable him to go through with a purchase which he heard he had a mind to." Looking at the difference in the value of money at that time and the present, we may reasonably presume that Lord Southampton's bounty on this occasion has been magnified; but the fact that Shakespeare in little more than ten years after he quitted Stratford was in circumstances to purchase New Place, one of the best houses in his native town, very strongly confirms the general truth of the anecdote.

Whatever doubt there may be as to Spenser's referring to Shakespeare, in his *Teares of the Muses*, no one will deny the extreme probability of his doing so in another poem, entitled *Colin Clout's come Home again*, written during 1594. After enumerating under fanciful titles various poets whose real names can in many instances be determined, and respecting whom the indefatigable Malone has accumulated a mass of interesting particulars, Spenser writes :—

> "And there, though last not least, is Ætion ;
> A gentler shepheard may no where be found ;
> Whose Muse, full of high thoughts' invention,
> Doth, like himselfe, heroically sound."

The applicability of the expression "heroically sound," to the name of *Shake-spear*, as well as to the subject of his Muse, he having then produced upon the stage both *Richard II.* and *Richard III.*, is not to be gainsaid.

In what year the Globe Theatre on the Bankside was completed has not been ascertained. Malone thought it was not built long before 1596. After the opening of this house, the Lord Chamberlain's servants—the company to which Shakespeare belonged,—were in the practice of performing there in the summer, and at the Blackfriars during the winter. About the period when the former was opened, the company appear to have undertaken the task of repairing and enlarging the Blackfriars. Mr. Collier was the first to call attention to three documents professing to have connexion with this circumstance in Shakespeare's life, which, if authentic, would be important, but upon which not the slightest reliance can be placed. The first of these papers, described by Mr. Collier as in the State Paper Office, and as being "a representation from certain inhabitants of the precinct in which the playhouse was situated, not only against the completion of the work of repair and enlargement, then commenced, but against all farther performances in the theatre,"[58] is not only undiscoverable, but no record of its existence can be found in the Office mentioned. The second instrument,[59] purporting to be an answer to the

---

[58] In his recent "Inquiry into the Genuineness of the Manuscript Corrections in Mr. J. Payne Collier's Annotated Shakspere, folio, 1632; and of certain Shaksperian Documents likewise published by Mr. Collier," Mr. Hamilton remarks, with reference to this paper, "I endeavoured, but unsuccessfully, to see this 'petition of the inhabitants.' In reply to an official request for the production of the document, Charles Lechmere, Esq., Assistant Keeper of State Papers, writes, 'I have referred to the Calendar of 1596, but I do not find any entry of the Petition from the inhabitants of the Blackfriars.'"

[59] Appended is a copy of this extraordinary figment, which, if only upon the credit of the place where it was deposited, has been received without hesitation by every one as a genuine document, until the recent disclosures relative to Mr. Collier's annotated folio threw suspicion upon every Shakespearian discovery of the last forty years. It was first printed by Mr. Collier, in his *History of English Dram. Poet.* (1831), where it is preceded by the following observations :—"This remarkable paper has, perhaps, never seen the light from the moment it was presented, until it was very recently discovered. It is seven years anterior to the date of any other authentic record, which contains the name of our great dramatist," and it may warrant various conjectures as to the rank he held in the company in 1596, as a poet and as a player.

"*To the right honorable the Ll of her Maties most honorable privie Counsell.*

"The humble petition of Thomas Pope Richard Burbadge John Hemings Augustine Phillips Willm Shakespeare Willm Kempe Willm Slye Nicholas Tooley and others servantes to the right honorable the L. Chamberlaine to her Matie—

"Sheweth most humbly, that yr petitioners are owners and players of the private house or theater in the precinct and libertie of the Blackfriers, wch hath beene for manie yeares used and occupied for the playing of tragedies commedies histories enterludes and playes. That the same, by reason of having beene soe long built hath falne into great decaye, and that besides the reparation thereof, it has beene found necessarie to make the same more convenient for the entertainement of auditories comming thereto That to this end yor petitioners have all and eache of them putt down somes of money according to their shares in the saide theater, and wch they have justly and honestlie gained by the exercise of their qualitie of Stage players : but that certaine persons, (some of them of honour) inhabitantes of the precinct and libertie of the Blackfriers, have, as yor petitioners are enfourmed, besought yor honorable Lps not to permitt the saide private house anie longer to remaine open, but hereafter to be shutt upp and closed to the manifest and great injurie of yor petitioners, who have no other meanes whereby to mainteine their wives and families but by the exercise of their qualitie, as they have heretofore done. Furthermore, that in the summer season yor petitioners are able to playe at their newe-built house on the Bankside callde the Globe, but that in the winter they are compelled to come to the Blackfriers, and if yor honorable Lps give consent unto that wch is prayde against yor petitioners, they will not onely while the winter endureth loose the meanes whereby they nowe support them selves and their families, but be unable to practise them selves in anie playes or enterluds when calde upon to performe for the recreation and solace of her Matie and her honorable Court as they have beene hertofore accustomed. The humble prayer of yor petitioners therefore is, that yor honble Lps will graunt permission to finishe the reparations and alterations they have begunne, and as yor petitioners have hitherto beene well ordred in their behaviour, and just in their dealinges, that yor honourable Lps will not inhibit them from acting at their above named private house, in the precinct and libertie of the Blackfriers, and yor petitioners as in dutie most bounden will ever praye for the encreasing honour and happinesse of your honorable Lps."

The attention of the Rt. Hon. the Master of the Rolls having been called to some questionable peculiarities in this petition, he directed that an official enquiry into its authenticity should be made. The gentlemen chosen for the investigation were Sir Frederic Madden, Keeper of the MSS. at the British Museum ; Sir Francis Palgrave,

former, would, if authentic, have been what Mr. Collier describes it, "a very valuable relic," inasmuch as it would have proved that Shakespeare, about the year 1596, was an "*owner*" of the Blackfriars Theatre, but on examination by several of the most skilled paleographers, it has been denounced as spurious. The third of these papers, represented to be a note from "a person of the name of Veale" to Henslowe, and found by Mr. Collier among the Alleyn collection at Dulwich, has been sought for in vain,[60] and, I fear, like nine-tenths of the so-called "New Facts" relative to the life of Shakespeare, is not entitled to the smallest credence.

Referring to some document in his possession at the time when he wrote his "Inquiry into the Authenticity of certain Papers," &c., Malone remarks, "From a paper now before me, which formerly belonged to Edward Alleyn the player, our poet appears to have lived in Southwark, near the Bear Garden, in 1596.[61] The paper in question is now perhaps irrecoverable, but its loss is not momentous. If we have no authentic trace of Shakespeare's abode during his residence in London, we have the pleasant tradition, that once a year he made his native place his home.[62] There his family continued to reside, and it is delightful to reflect that amidst all the triumphs and temptations of his career, he kept steadily in view the prospect of one day returning, honourably independent, to spend the remainder of his life with them and the humble friends of his youth. In the year we are dwelling on, that of 1596, there was a melancholy necessity for his visiting Stratford, the loss of his only son, Hamnet, who died in his twelfth year, and was buried August 11th, 1596.[63]

From his incomings as a dramatist, an actor, and perhaps a proprietor in two prosperous theatres, Shakespeare must now have been in easy circumstances. One proof of this is, that early in 1597 he bought for sixty pounds (about £300 according to the present value of money), of William Underhill, the house called New Place, in Stratford; a house originally built by Sir Hugh Clopton in the reign of Henry VII.[64] Another proof is, that in this year John Shakespeare was enabled to tender the redemption money, £40, to recover the estate of Ashbies, for which there can be little doubt he was indebted to his son. Additional evidence of his prosperity at

---

Deputy Keeper of Public Records; T. Duffus Hardy, Esq., Assistant Keeper of Public Records; Professor Brewer, Reader at the Rolls, and Mr. Hamilton. After a minute examination of the document, these gentlemen were unanimously of the opinion recorded in the following certificate:—

"We, the undersigned, at the desire of the Master of the Rolls, have carefully examined the document hereunto annexed, purporting to be a petition to the Lords of Her Majesty's Privy Council, from Thomas Pope, Richard Burbadge, John Hemings, Augustine Phillips, William Shakespeare, William Kempe, William Slye, Nicholas Tooley, and others, in answer to a petition from the Inhabitants of the Liberty of the Blackfriars; and we are of opinion that the document in question is spurious.

30th January, 1860.

FRANCIS PALGRAVE, K.H., Deputy Keeper of H.M. Public Records.

FREDERIC MADDEN, K.H., Keeper of the MSS. British Museum.

J. S. BREWER, M.A., Reader at the Rolls.

T. DUFFUS HARDY, Assistant Keeper of Records.

N. E. S. A. HAMILTON, Assistant, Department of MSS. British Museum."

60 It was first published by Mr. Collier, in his *Life of Shakespeare,* where it reads thus:—

"Mr. Hinslowe. This is to enfourme you that my Mr., the Maister of the revelles, hath rec. from the Ll. of the counsell order that the L. Chamberlen's servauntes shall not be distourbed at the Blackefryars, according with their petition in that behalfe, but leave shall be given unto theym to make good the decaye of the saide House, butt not to make the same larger then in former tyme hath bene. From thoffice of the Revelles, this 3 of maie, 1596.

Rich. Veale."

61 This paper Mr. Collier presumes to have been a small slip which he discovered in Dulwich College, containing the following memorandum:—

"Inhabitantes of Sowtherk as have complaned, this — of Jully, 1596.

Mr. Markis
Mr. Tuppin
Mr. Langorth
Wilson the pyper
Mr. Barett
Mr. Shaksper
Phellipes
Tomson
Mother Golden, the baude
Nagges
Fillpott and no more, and soe well ended."

But I have the authority of two most eminent paleographers, who have recently examined some of the manuscripts in the Alleyn collection, for saying that this fragment, so far from being the veritable document alluded to by Malone, is "an evident modern forgery."

62 "He was wont to go to his native countrey once a yeare." Aubrey's *Mss. Mus. Ashmol. Oxon.*

63 The record of the burial in the register of Stratford Church is as follows:—

"1596, *August* 11, *Hamnet filius William Shakspere.*"

64 The note of the fine levied will be found in the *Appendix.*

this period is afforded too by a letter dated January 24th, 1597–8, from Abraham Sturley, at Stratford, to, it is supposed, Richard Quiney, in the course of which the former writes:—

"It semeth bi him that our countriman, Mr. Shakspere, is willinge to disburse some monei upon some od yarde land or other att Shottri or neare about us; he thinketh it a veri fitt patterne to move him to deale in the matter of our tithes."

The year 1598, it is believed, witnessed the first acquaintance between Shakespeare and Ben Jonson, an acquaintance honourable to both, and which there can be no doubt speedily ripened into hearty friendship. According to Rowe, Shakespeare's "acquaintance with Ben Johnson began with a remarkable piece of humanity and good nature: Mr. Johnson, who was at that time altogether unknown to the world, had offer'd one of his plays to the players, in order to have it acted, and the persons into whose hands it was put, after having turn'd it carelessly and superciliously over, were just upon returning it to him with an ill-natur'd answer, that it would be of no service to their company, when Shakespear luckily cast his eye upon it, and found something so well in it as to engage him first to read it through, and afterwards to recommend Mr. Johnson and his writings to the public." We have only Rowe's authority for this anecdote, but there seems no reason for doubting that some such passage did occur.[65] There is another agreeable tradition respecting the acquaintance of these famous "Worthies" preserved by Fuller, who, speaking of Shakespeare, says, "Many were the wit-combates betwixt him and Ben Jonson, which two I behold like a Spanish great gallion and an English man-of-war;—Master Jonson (like the former) was built far higher in learning, solid but slow in his performances; Shake-speare with the English man-of-war, lesser in bulk, but lighter in sailing, could turn with all tides, tack about and take advantage of all winds, by the quickness of his wit and invention."[66]

We now come to perhaps the most remarkable literary notice of Shakespeare by a contemporary extant. In 1598, Francis Meres published a work entitled *Palladis Tamia, Wits Treasury, being the Second Part of Wits Commonwealth*, in which occurs the following passage respecting our poet and his compositions:—

"As the soule of Euphorbus was thought to live in Pythagoras, so the sweete-wittie soule of Ovid lives in mellifluous and hony-tongued Shakespeare; witnes his *Venus and Adonis*, his *Lucrece*, his sugred *Sonnets* among his private friends, &c.

"As Plautus and Seneca are accounted the best for comedy and tragedy among the Latines, so Shakespeare among the English is the most excellent in both kinds for the stage; for comedy, witnes his *Gentlemen of Verona*, his *Errors*, his *Love Labors Lost*, his *Love Labours Wonne*, his *Midsummers Night Dreame*, and his *Merchant of Venice;* for tragedy, his *Richard the 2., Richard the 3., Henry the 4., King John, Titus Andronicus*, and his *Romeo and Juliet.*

"As Epius Stolo said that the Muses would speake with Plautus tongue, if they would speak Latin, so I say that the Muses would speak with Shakespeares fine filed phrase, if they would speake English."[67]

---

[65] Gifford rejects it disdainfully, in the belief that Jonson's *Every Man in His Humour* is the piece recorded in Henslowe's Diary, *the comedie of Umers* as acted by the Lord Admiral's men in May, 1597, but Jonson distinctly states, in the edition of his works, 1616, that *Every Man in his Humour* was first acted by the Lord Chamberlain's servants in 1598. It is noticeable that in a list of the "principal comedians" subjoined to this piece, Shakespeare's name stands first; unfortunately this list does not specify the character played by each actor, but our poet is supposed to have acted Old Knowell.

[66] *Worthies*, p. 126, A a a. ed. fol. Some of these "wit-combats" have been handed down to us, but they are not of a quality to verify their alleged parentage. For example:—"Shakespeare was god-father to one of Ben Johnsons children, and after the christning, being in a deepe study, Johnson came to cheere him up, and askt him why he was so melancholy. No, faith, Ben, sayes he, not I; but I have beene considering a great while what should be the fittest gift for me to bestow upon my god-child, and I have resolv'd at last. I prythe what? says he. Ifaith, Ben, Ile e'en give him a dowzen good Lattin spoones, and thou shalt translate them." From *Merry Passages and Jeasts, Ms. Harl.* 6395.

[67] Of the poems and plays enumerated by Meres, a small portion only, it is supposed, were in print when he wrote in 1598. Those known to have been published at that date are, the *Venus and Adonis* and *Lucrece, Richard II.*, and *Richard III., Romeo and Juliet, Titus Andronicus,* and the First Part of *Henry IV.*

This extract is of striking importance in determining the chronology of Shakespeare's dramas, and it is of equal interest in a biographical sense. It shows to what a height of reputation he had risen at the early age of thirty-four, an age when many writers have hardly begun to put forth their full powers.

The next literary allusion to our author is poetic, and occurs in a collection of *Epigrams*, published by Weever in 1599:—

"*Ad Gulielmum Shakespeare.*

Honie-tongd Shakespeare, when I saw thine issue,
I sware Apollo got them, and none other;
Their rosie-tainted features clothed in tissue,
Some heaven-born goddess said to be their mother.
Rose-cheeckt Adonis with his amber tresses,
Faire fire-hot Venus charming him to love her;
Chaste Lucretia, virgine-like her dresses,
Proud lust-stung Tarquine seeking still to prove her;
Romeo, Richard, more whose names I know not;
Their sugred tongues and power-attractive beauty
Say they are saints, although that saints they shew not,
For thousand vowes to them subjective dutie.
They burn in love, thy children, Shakespeare, let them,
Go, wo thy muse; more nymphish brood beget them."

Another memorial of this period, a letter addressed by Richard Quiney[68] to the poet himself, is considered of inestimable value, as being the only one now known to exist of all the communications he must have received:—

"Loveinge Contreyman, I am bolde of yow, as of a ffrende, craveinge yowr helpe with xxxli uppon Mr. Bushells and my securytee, or Mr. Myttons with me. Mr. Rosswell is nott come to London as yeate, and I have especiall cawse. Yow shall ffrende me muche in helpeinge me out of all the debettes I owe in London, I thanck God, and muche quiete my mynde, which wolde nott be indebeted. I am nowe towardes the Cowrte, in hope of answer for the dispatche of my buysenes. Yow shall nether loose creddytt nor monney by me, the Lorde wyllinge; and nowe butt perswade yowrselfe soe, as I hope, and yow shall nott need to feare butt with all heartie thanckefullnes I wyll holde my tyme, and content yowr ffreende, and yf we bargaine farther, yow shalbe the paie-master yowrselfe. My tyme biddes me hasten to an ende, ande soe I committ thys [to] yowr care and hope of yowr helpe. I feare I shall nott be backe thys night ffrom the Cowrte. Haste. The Lorde be with yow and with us all, Amen! ffrom the Bell in Carter Lane, the 25 October, 1598.

Yowrs in all kyndenes,

Ryc. QUYNEY.

To my loveinge good ffrende and contreyman Mr. Wm. Shackespere deliver thees."

From a subsidy roll dated Oct. 1st, 1598, discovered in the Carlton Ride Record Office by the Rev. J. Hunter, Shakespeare, it appears, was then assessed at five pounds, and subjected to a rate of thirteen shillings and fourpence, in the parish of St. Helen's, Bishopsgate:

"*Affid.* William Shakespeare, v*li.*—xiij*s.* iiij*d.*"[69]

---

[68] Richard Quiney was the father of the Thomas Quiney who subsequently married Shakespeare's youngest daughter. He was at London when the above letter was written, on business connected with the Stratford corporation, that borough having solicited Lord Treasurer Burghley for exemption from the subsidies imposed by the last Parliament, on account of the distress and poverty occasioned in the town by two recent fires.

[69] The memorandum *affid.* attached to the name is supposed to signify that he had made an affidavit of non-residence, or some ground of exemption.

On the 8th of September, 1601, is recorded the burial of the poet's father.[70] He was born, according to Malone, in or before the year 1530, and had consequently outlived the allotted threescore and ten years.[71]

In May of the succeeding year, the poet increased his property by the purchase of a hundred and seven acres of arable land, for three hundred and twenty pounds;[72] in September of the same year, he purchased a house or cottage in Dead Lane, opposite New Place, and also a messuage with barns, gardens, and orchards, of Hercules Underhill, for sixty pounds.

On the 29th of March, 1602-3, died Queen Elizabeth;[73] and Chettle in his *Englandes Mourning Garment,* complains, that Shakespeare, whom she had "graced," had not bewailed her loss in elegiac strains:—

"Nor doth the silver-tonged Melicert
Drop from his honied Muse one sable teare
To mourne her death *that graced his desert,*
And to his laies opend her *royall eare.*
Shepheard, remember our Elizabeth,
And sing her Rape done by that Tarquin, Death."

King James's partiality for the drama was manifested long before he ascended the English throne. In 1589, there is said to have been an English company, called "Her Majesties Players," at the Scottish Court. Ten years later, he licensed a company of English comedians to act at Edinburgh; and on the 9th of October, 1601, we find, from the registers of the town council of Aberdeen, that the English players received thirty-two marks as a gratuity; and on the 22d of the same month, that the freedom of the city was conferred upon "Laurence Fletcher Comedian to his Majestie."

On the 17th of May, 1603, a few days only after he reached London, the following warrant[74] under the Privy Seal was issued:—

"By the King.

"Right trusty and welbeloved Counsellor, we greete you well, and will and commaund you, that under our privie seale in your custody for the time being, you cause our letters to be derected to the keeper of our greate seale of England, commaunding him under our said greate seale, he cause our letters to be made patent in forme following. James, by the grace of God, King of England, Scotland, Fraunce, and Irland, defender of the faith, &c. To all justices, maiors, sheriffs, constables, headboroughes, and other, our officers and loving subjects greeting. Know ye, that we of our speciall grace, certaine knowledge and meere motion, have licenced and authorized, and by these presentes doe licence and authorize, these our servants, Laurence Fletcher, William Shakespeare, Richard Burbage, Augustine Phillippes, John Hemmings, Henrie Condell, William Sly, Robert Armyn, Richard Cowlye, and the rest of their associats, freely

---

70 The entry in the Stratford register is as follows:—
"1601, *Septemb.* 8, *Mr. Johañes Shakspeare.*"

71 "The latest notice of John Shakespeare hitherto met with occurs in a paper in the Council Chamber at Stratford, containing notes respecting an action of trespass brought by Edward Grevil against several burgesses of Stratford, in 1601. His name is in a list that appears amongst memoranda of the defendant's case, perhaps of the witnesses intended to be called,—'Mr. Ihon Sackesper.'"—Halliwell's *Life of Shakespeare*, p. 73, fol.

72 The indenture is "Between William Combe, of Warrwicke, in the countie of Warrwick, esquier, and John Combe, of Olde Stretford, in the countie aforesaid, gentleman, on the one partie, and William Shakespere, of Stretford-uppon-Avon, in the countie aforesaide, gentleman, on thother partye," and is dated 1st of May. The dramatist being at this time absent from Stratford, the conveyance was executed by his brother Gilbert. In the fine levied on this property in 1611, "twenty acres of pasture land" are mentioned, in addition to the hundred and seven acres of arable land. *See Appendix.*

73 One of the latest visits she paid to any of her nobility, we are told, was to Sir Thomas Egerton, Lord Keeper of the Great Seal, at Harefield, at the beginning of August, 1602, and on that occasion, according to an interlined memorandum first printed by Mr. Collier from the Egerton papers, *Othello* was acted for her entertainment:
"6 August, 1602. Rewardes to the vaulters, players, and dauncers, (of this xli. to Burbidges players for Othello), lxiiij*li.* xviij*s.* x*d.*"
It is proper to state, however, that there is ground for believing this interlineation to be a modern fabrication. See the Introduction to *Othello*, p. 645, Vol. III.

74 In the Chapter House.—The patent under the Great Seal is dated May 19th.

to use and exercise the arte and faculty of playing comedies, tragedies, histories, enterludes, moralls, pastorals, stage-plaies, and such other like, as thei have already studied, or hereafter shall use or studie, as well for the recreation of our loving subjects, as for our solace and pleasure, when we shall thinke good to see them, during our pleasure; and the said comedies, trajedies, histories, enterludes, moralls, pastoralls, stage-plaies, and such like, to shew and exercise publiquely to their best commoditie, when the infection of the plague shall decrease, as well within theire now usuall howse called the Globe, within our county of Surrey, as also within anie towne halls, or mout halls, or other convenient places within the liberties and freedome of any other citie, universitie, towne, or borough whatsoever within our said realmes and dominions: willing and commaunding you, and every of you, as you tender our pleasure, not only to permit and suffer them heerin, without any your letts, hinderances, or molestations, during our said pleasure, but also to be ayding or assisting to them yf any wrong be to them offered; and to allowe them such former courtesies, as hathe bene given to men of their place and qualitie; and also what further favour you shall shew to these our servants for our sake, we shall take kindly at your hands. And these our letters shall be your sufficient warrant and discharge in this behalfe.

"Given under our signet at our mannor of Greenewiche, the seavententh day of May in the first yeere of our raigne of England, France, and Ireland, and of Scotland the six and thirtieth."

Of the precise period when Shakespeare ceased to act we know no more than of the time when he began.[75] His name last appears in a printed list of the characters attached to Jonson's "Sejanus," published in 1603, and it is thought that he relinquished a profession to which, if the lines in Sonnet CXI.[76] express his real sentiments, he was never partial, shortly after the King's Patent was issued.[77]

In 1604, we find the poet bringing an action in the Court of Record at Stratford against Phillip Rogers for the sum of £1 15*s.* 10*d.*, the consideration being for "malt" sold and

---

[75] Among the various contributions purporting to throw light on Shakespeare's career which we owe to Mr. Collier, are two that claim attention at this stage of the biography. The first is a new reading of a letter still preserved at Dulwich College, from Mrs. Alleyn to her husband the actor, then absent on a professional expedition. The letter in question is dated October 20, 1603, and towards the end, where the paper is somewhat decayed, occurs a postscript, one paragraph of which reads thus:—

"Aboute a weeke agoe there [cam]e a youthe who saide he was
Mr. Frauncis Chalo[ner]s man . . . . ld have borrow[e]d x^s to
ought have ^ things for [h]is Mr. . . . . t hym
Cominge without . . . token . . . . d
I would have . . . .
& I bene su . . . .
and inquire after the fellow and said he had lent hym a horse. I
us feare me he gulled hym, thoughe he gulled not ^. The youthe
what was a prety youthe and hansom in appayrell, we know not ^ became
of hym. Mr. Bromffeild commendes hym: hewas heare yesterdaye. Nicke
and Jeames be well, and commend them, so dothe Mr. Cooke and his [weife.
in the kyndest sorte, and so once more in the hartiest manner
farwelle."

In Mr. Collier's transcript of the letter, as published in his *Memoirs of Edward Alleyn*, 1841, and in his *Life of Shakespeare*, 1858, the above extract is exhibited as follows:—

"Aboute a weeke a goe there came a youthe who said he was
Mr. Frauncis Chaloner who would have borrowed x. li to
have bought things for * * * and said he was known
unto you, and Mr. Shakespeare of the globe, who came
* * * said he knewe hym not, only he herde of hym that he was
a roge * * * so he was glade we did not lend him
the monney * * * Richard Johnes [went] to seeke
and inquire after the fellow, and said he had lent hym a horse. I
feare me he gulled hym, thoughe he gulled not us. The youthe
was a prety youthe, and hansom in appayrell: we knowe not what became
of hym. Mr. Benfield commendes hym; he was heare yesterdaye. Nicke
and Jeames be well, and comend them: so dothe Mr. Cooke and his wiefe
in the kyndest sorte, and so once more in the hartiest manner
farwell."

By what oversight, or from what motive, certain words which by no possibility could ever have formed part of the original were interpolated, and others which are plainly visible were omitted, I will not attempt to conjecture, but as Mr. Collier has deduced from the assumed mention of *Mr. Shakespeare of the globe* that our poet was in London at the date when this letter was written, it is proper to show that the assumption is unfounded. The other document professes to be a letter, found in the Ellesmere collection, from Daniel the poet to Sir Thomas Egerton, thanking him for his advancement to the office of Master of the Queen's Revels, and which, if genuine, would be of singular interest in relation to the life of Shakespeare (*See Appendix*). But this letter, long suspected, is now proclaimed to be a forgery.

[76] "O, for my sake do you with Fortune chide,
The guilty goddess of my harmful deeds,
That did not better for my life provide
Than public means which public manners breeds.
Thence comes it that my name receives a brand;
And almost thence my nature is subdu'd
To what it works in, like the dyer's hand."

[77] To show "that he continued a member of the company until April 9, 1604," Mr. Collier prints a list of the King's players, appended to a letter from the council to the Lord Mayor of London, where the names are thus enumerated: "Burbadge, Shakespeare, Fletcher, Phillips, Condell, Heminge, Armyn, Slye, Cowley, Hostler, Day." This list, however, *though added on to a genuine document*, has lately been pronounced a modern fiction. *See Appendix.*

delivered at several times. The following year, he made the most considerable purchase he is known to have effected, in buying the tithes of Stratford, Old Stratford, Bishopton and Welcome. Not long subsequently, we are told King James wrote to the poet with his own hand "an amicable letter," [78] and, as Mr. Dyce remarks, "the tradition is, perhaps, indirectly supported by the following entries in the *Accounts of the Revels*, which prove how highly the dramas of Shakespeare were relished at the court of James :—

The Plaiers.		*The Poets which mayd the plaies.*
By the Kings Ma^{tis} plaiers.	Hallamas day being the first of Novembar, A play in the Banketinge House att Whithall called the Moor of Venis. [Nov. 1st, 1604.]	
By his Ma^{tis} plaiers.	The Sunday ffollowinge, A Play of the Merry Wives of Winsor. [Nov. 4th, 1604.]	
By his Ma^{tis} plaiers.	On St. Stivens night in the Hall a Play called Mesur for Mesur. [Dec. 26th, 1604.]	Shaxberd.
By his Ma^{tis} plaiers.	On Inosents Night The Plaie of Errors. [Dec. 28th, 1604.]	Shaxberd.
By his Ma^{tis} plaiers.	Betwin Newers day and Twelfe day a Play of Loves Labours Lost. [1605.]	
By his Ma^{tis} plaiers.	On the 7 of January was played the play of Henry the fift. [1605.]	
By his Ma^{tis} plaiers.	On Shrovsunday A play of the Marchant of Venis. [Mar. 24th, 1605.]	Shaxberd.
By his Ma^{tis} plaiers.	On Shrovtusday A Play cauled the Martchant of Venis againe commaunded by the Kings Matie. [Mar. 26, 1605.]	Shaxberd.
	[Accounts from Oct. 31st, 1611, to Nov. 1st, 1612.]	
By the Kings players.	Hallomas nyght was presented att Whithall before ye Kinges Matie a play called the Tempest. [Nov. 1st, 1611.]	
The Kings players.	The 5th of November : A play called ye winters nightes Tayle. [1611.] [79]	

[78] "That most learned prince, and great patron of learning, King James the First, was pleased with his own hand to write an amicable letter to Mr. Shakespeare; which letter, though now lost, remained long in the hands of Sir William D'Avenant, as a credible person, now living, can testify."—Advertisement to Lintot's edition of *Shakespeare's Poems*, 1710. In a manuscript note on his copy of Fuller's *Worthies*, Oldys states that Sheffield, Duke of Buckingham, told Lintot that he had seen the letter in the possession of Sir William Davenant. Farmer conjectures that the letter was in acknowledgment of the compliment conveyed in the passage of *Macbeth*, Act IV. Sc. 1, where James is indicated as carrying "two-fold balls and treble sceptres."

[79] Cunningham's *Extracts from the Accounts of the Revels at Court*, &c.

The titles of several plays of Shakespeare occur in the *Accounts* of Lord Harrington, Treasurer of the Chamber to James I. among performances given before Prince Charles, the Lady Elizabeth, and the Prince Palatine Elector, in 1613:

"Paid to John Heminges uppon the councels warr^{t}. dated at Whitehall, xx° die Maii 1613, for presentinge before the Princes Hignes, the La. Elizabeth, and the Prince Pallatyne Elector, fowerteene severall playes, viz. one playe called Filaster, one other call'd the Knotte of Fooles, one other Much Adoe abowte Nothinge, the Mayed's Tragedie, the Merye Dyvell of Edmonton, the Tempest, a Kinge and no Kinge, the Twin's Tragedie, the Winter's Tale, Sir John Falstafe [The Merry Wives of Windsor], the Moore of Venice, the Nobleman, Cæsars Tragedye, and one other called Love lyes a Bleedinge, all wch playes weare played wthin the tyme of this accompte, viz. p^{d}. the some of iiij. (xx.) xiij. *li.* vj*s.* viij*d.*"[80]

From a retrospect of the few materials available for tracing the dramatist's career from the time when he is presumed to have left Stratford, we may conjecture him to have arrived in London about the year 1586, and to have joined some theatrical company, to which he remained permanently attached as playwright and actor until 1604. How often and in what characters he performed;[81] where he lived in London; who were his personal friends; what were his habits; what intercourse he maintained with his family; and to what degree he partook of the provincial excursions of his fellows during this period, are points on which it has been shown we have scarcely any reliable information. In about the year just named, his history, I think, reverts to Stratford; where, from the records of the town, he would appear to have then finally retired, and engaged himself actively in agricultural pursuits.[82]

On June 5th, 1607, Shakespeare's eldest daughter, Susanna, was married to John Hall, a medical practitioner at Stratford. In December of the same year his brother Edmund died, and on the 31st of that month was buried at St. Saviour's, Southwark. As he is entered in the burial register as "a player," he probably belonged to the same company as the poet.

On the 21st of Feb. 1607–8, Elizabeth Hall, the only daughter of John Hall and the poet's daughter Susanna, was baptized at Stratford. A few months later, Shakespeare lost his mother.[83]

In June of 1609, the records of Stratford show him to have brought an action, and obtained a verdict, against one John Addenbroke, for a debt of £6 and costs. Addenbroke not being

---

80 Rawlinson's *Coll.* A. 239, Bodleian Lib.

81 The following verses by Davies in his *Scourge of Folly*, have been thought to afford some countenance to a shadowy tradition that Shakespeare not unfrequently played in kingly characters:—

"*To our English Terence, Mr. Will Shakespeare.*

"Some say, good Will, which I'in sport do sing,
Had'st thou not plaid some kingly parts in sport,
Thou hadst bin a companion for a king,
And beene a king among the meaner sort.

"Some others raile; but raile as they thinke fit,
Thou hast no rayling, but a raigning wit:
And honesty thou sow'st, which they do reape,
So to increase their stocke, which they do keepe."

The natural interpretation of the second line is that Shakespeare had on some occasions acted royalty in a way to provoke the displeasure of the king. Possibly he had represented James himself upon the stage, and by so doing, given offence. In a letter from John Chamberlaine to Sir R. Winwood, dated Dec. 18th, 1604, the writer states that the king's company had much annoyed the court by acting a play on the subject of the Gowry conspiracy: "The Tragedy of Gowry, with all the action and actors, hath been twice represented by the King's players, with exceeding concourse of all sorts of people. But whether the matter or manner be not well handled, or that it be thought *unfit that princes should be played on the stage in their life-time*, I hear that some great councellors are much displeased with it, and so 'tis thought shall be forbidden."—Winwood's *Memorials*, &c. 11.41.

82 The copy of a letter discovered by Mr. Collier among the Ellesmere manuscripts, which begins, "My verie honored lord. The manie good offices I have received at your Lordships hands, which ought to make me backward in asking further favors," &c. and is signed with the initials of Lord Southampton, can no longer be admitted as evidence to the contrary, since it is now declared to be a fabrication. *See Appendix*.

Another document found by Mr. Collier in the same collection, and professing to be the draft of a warrant, January 4th, 1609-10, empowering Daborne, Shakespeare, Field, and Kirkman, to train up a company of juvenile performers; and a third found by him at Dulwich College: "A brief noat taken out of the poores booke, &c., 1609," wherein Shakespeare is assessed for the relief of the poor in Southwark, at 6*d*. per week, are equally invalid as proof of the poet's continued residence in the metropolis, both being condemned as modern inventions. *See Appendix*.

83 Her burial is entered in the register as follows:— "1608, *Septemb.* 9. *Mayry Shaxpere, Wydowe.*"

forthcoming, the suit was afterwards prosecuted against Thomas Horneby, the defendant's bail; but with what result is not shown.

At the beginning of 1613, died Richard Shakespeare, the brother to the dramatist, in his fortieth year; of his history we know even less than of the other brother's, Gilbert, whom we have seen effecting a purchase for the poet, and whose signature as witness to a deed is still extant.

In the month of March, 1612–13, Shakespeare bought a house with ground attached, near to the Blackfriars Theatre, "abutting upon a streete leading downe to Pudle Wharffe on the east part, right against the Kinges Majesties Wardrobe." The indenture of conveyance dated the 10th of March, is "Betweene Henry Walker citizein and Minstrel of London, on thone partie, and William Shakespeare of Stratford upon Avon in the countie of Warwick, gentleman, William Johnson citizein and vintener of London, John Jackson and John Hemmyng of London gentlemen, on thother partie."

Local patronage of the drama we find was neither a cause nor a consequence of Shakespeare's retirement to Stratford; on the contrary, theatrical entertainments had for some years been discouraged by the municipal authorities of that borough. So early as 1602, it was ordered 'that there shall be no pleys or enterlewedes played in the chamber, the guildhalle, nor in any parte of the howsse or courte, ffrom hensforward upon payne that whosooever of the baylief, aldermen, and burgesses of this boroughe shall gyve leave or licence thereunto, shall forfeyt for everie offence xs." But this penalty does not seem to have been efficacious, for, on the 7th of February, 1612, the corporation made the following stringent order:—

"The inconvenience of plaies being verie seriouslie considered of, with the unlawfullnes, and howe contrarie the sufferance of them is againste the orders hearetofore made, and againste the examples of other well-governed citties and burrowes, the companie heare are contented and theie conclude that the penalty of xs. imposed in Mr. Bakers yeare for breakinge the order, shall from henceforth be xli. upon the breakers of that order, and this to holde untill the nexte commen councell, and from thencforth for ever, excepted, that be then finalli revokd and made voide."

One of the best known though least authentic anecdotes of Shakespeare, is that relating to his epitaph on a gentleman named Combe. This story has been variously told; Rowe's version is as follows:—"The latter part of his life was spent, as all men of good sense will wish theirs may be, in ease, retirement, and the conversation of his friends. He had the good fortune to gather an estate equal to his occasion, and, in that, to his wish; and is said to have spent some years before his death at his native Stratford. His pleasurable wit and good nature engaged him in the acquaintance, and entitled him to the friendship, of the gentlemen of the neighbourhood. Amongst them it is a story almost still remembered in that country, that he had a particular intimacy with Mr. Combe, an old gentleman noted thereabouts for his wealth and usury. It happened that in a pleasant conversation amongst their common friends, Mr. Combe told Shakespear in a laughing manner, that he fancied he intended to write his epitaph, if he happened to outlive him; and since he could not know what might be said of him when dead, he desired it might be done immediately. Upon which, Shakespear gave him these four verses:—

'Ten in the hundred lies here ingrav'd,
'Tis a hundred to ten, his soul is not sav'd!
If any man ask, Who lies in this tomb?
Oh, ho, quoth the devil, 'tis my John-a-Combe.'[84]

---

[84] These lines, variously modified, are found in miscellanies long before Shakespeare's time.

"Ten in the hundred lies under this stone,
And a hundred to ten to the divil his gone."
Addit. MS. 15,227. *p.* 18.

But the sharpness of the satire is said to have stung the man so severely, that he never forgave it."

That the tale is not altogether destitute of foundation we may believe; but Rowe's version is certainly inaccurate. So far from Shakespeare having done what Combe "never forgave," we have the conclusive evidence of Doctors' Commons that Combe testified his cordial feelings towards the poet by a legacy in his will, and that the latter reciprocated the kindness by bequeathing his sword to Thomas Combe, the nephew of John.[85] As an act of justice to the memory of John Combe, it should be mentioned that in his will he bequeathed one hundred pounds (equal to five hundred in present money) to be lent to poor tradesmen of Stratford, and in addition, as an immediate legacy, twenty pounds to the poor of that place, together with legacies of five pounds each to the poor of Warwick and of Alcester.

About this period, we find the poet engaged in the unenviable proceedings of a Chancery suit. The action grew out of the share he had purchased of the tithes payable by the land of Stratford, and some other places. The draft of a bill presented by him, Lane, and Greene, is still in existence, but nothing further is known of the litigation. The bill alleges that these three plaintiffs had a joint interest with William Combe and various other persons in the tithes, &c. the whole being held for a term of 87 years, at a reserved rent of £27 13s. 4d. a year, but that the other parties refused to pay their proportion of this annual sum, to the injury of Shakespeare and his fellow-suitors. The draft bill is of interest in one respect; it recites that Shakespeare's income from this portion of his property was "threescore pounds" (equivalent to three hundred in our time) a year.

The same year, 1613, is memorable from the destruction of the Globe Theatre, which was burnt down on the 29th of June.[86] Whether Shakespeare was a loser by the calamity is not known; but it is conjectured that when he finally retired to his native home, he parted with all his interest in theatrical property.

During the next year, Shakespeare was concerned with the corporation of Stratford in opposing a projected enclosure of some common lands. A memorandum relating to this subject, dated 5th Sept. 1614, and headed "Auncient ffreholders in the ffields of old Stratford and Welcombe," contains, among sundry entries, the following item :—"Mr. Shakspeare 4 yard land, noe common nor grownd beyond Gospell-bushe, nor grownd in Sandfield, nor none in Slow-hill-

---

"Here lyes 10 with 100, under this stone,
And 100 to one but to th' divel hees gone."
MS. Sloane, 1489, *f.* 11.

"Who is this lyes under this hearse?
Ho, ho, quoth the divel, tis my Dr. Pearce."
MS. Sloane, 14. 89, *f.* 11.

A double epitaph, said to have been his composition, is preserved in Dugdale's *Visitation of Salop*, a MS. in the Heralds' College. Describing a monument in Tong Church to the memory of Sir Thomas Stanley, Knight, Dugdale states that "these following verses were made by William Shakespeare, the late famous tragedian :

Written upon the east end of this tombe.

"Aske who lyes here, but do not weepe;
He is not dead, he doth but sleepe.
This stony register is for his bones,
His fame is more perpetuall than these stones;
And his own goodness, with himself being gone,
Shall live when earthly monument is none."

Written upon the west end thereof.

"Not monumentall stone preserves our fame,
Nor skye-aspiring piramids our name.
The memory of him for whom this stands
Shall outlive marble and defacers' hands :
When all to time's consumption shall be given,
Stanley, for whom this stands, shall stand in heaven."

[85] Another tradition, of perhaps equal veracity with that of John Combe's epitaph, was communicated to Malone by a native of Stratford, *Life of Shakespeare*, p. 500 sqq. to the effect that Shakespeare and some of his companions having accepted the challenge of a party calling themselves the Bedford topers and sippers, to a bout of ale-bibbing, whereat the Stratfordians were overcome, Shakespeare on the occasion composed these lines :

"Piping Pebworth, Dancing Marston,
Haunted Hillborough, and Hungry Grafton,
With Dadging Exhall, Papist Wixford,
Beggarly Broom, and Drunken Bidford."

[86] According to some MS. notes in a copy of Stow's *Annales* (formerly in the possession of Mr. Pickering the bookseller): "The Globe play house on the Bank side in Southwarke was burnt downe to the ground in the yeare 1612 [1613]; and newe built up againe in the year 1613 [1614], at the great charge of King James and many noble men and others." For an account of this accident, see p. 643, Vol. II.

field beyond Bishopton, nor none in the enclosures beyond Bishopton." The landowners, it appears, were desirous of effecting certain enclosures as a means of improving their property, but their scheme was opposed by the corporation, on the plea that the inhabitants of the place had recently suffered from a disastrous fire,[87] and would be still further endamaged by the consummation of this measure. A petition was consequently addressed to the Privy Council, and the effect was an order, not only prohibiting the enclosures, but requiring William Combe, who was a chief promoter of the plan, to undo certain work which, in respect of his own property, he had begun.[88] On this business, Thomas Greene, the clerk of the corporation, and a relative of Shakespeare, was sent to London, and some memoranda made by him on the occasion are still preserved. Under date of Nov. 17th, 1614, he notes, "my cosen Shakspear[89] comyng yesterdy to Town, I went to see him how he did. He told me that they assured him they ment to inclose no further than to Gospell Bush, and so upp straight (leavying out part of the Dyngles to the ffield) to the gate in Clopton hedg, and take in Salisburyes peece; and that they mean in Aprill to survey the land, and then to gyve satisfaccion, and not before; and he and Mr. Hall say they think ther will be nothyng done at all."

Shortly after the date of this memorandum, Greene returned to Stratford, leaving the poet in London. Other notes of his prove Shakespeare's uneasiness at the projected encroachments. And that he took precautions to guard himself from loss, we have remarkable evidence in certain articles of agreement between him and William Replingham, of Great Harborough, dated the 28th of October, 1614. These articles provide that the latter shall, "uppon reasonable request, satisfie, content, and make recompense unto him the said William Shackespeare or his assignes, for all such losse, detriment, and hinderance as he the said William Shackespeare, his heires and assignes, and one Thomas Greene gent. shall or maye be thought in the viewe and judgement of foure indifferent persons, to be indifferentlie elected by the said William and William and their heires, and in default of the said William Replingham, by the said William Shackespeare or his heires onely, to survey and judge the same to sustayne or incurre for or in respecte of the increasinge of the yearlie value of the tythes they the said William Shackespeare and Thomas doe joyntlie or severallie hold and enjoy in the said fieldes or anie of them, by reason of anie inclosure or decaye of tyllage there ment and intended by the said William Replingham; and that the said William Replingham and his heires shall procure such sufficient securitie unto the said William Shackespeare and his heires for the performance of theis covenauntes, as shall bee devised by learned counsell. In witnes whereof the parties abovsaid to theis presentes interchangeablie their handes and seales have put, the daye and yeare first above wrytten.

"Sealed and delivered in the presence of us, Tho. Lucas, Jo. Rogers, Anthonie Nasshe, Mich. Olney."

In the Chamberlain's Accounts for Stratford, in 1614, there is an entry:—"Item, for on quart of sack and on quart of clarrett winne, geven to a precher at the New Place, xx*d*," which is supposed to show that Shakespeare was entertaining a preacher at the time. This is not improbable, as the custom of refreshing eminent visitors with sack and claret at the general expense was not uncommon in Stratford formerly. At the same time it is quite possible that the

---

87 It appears from a brief granted for the relief of the town shortly afterwards, that this fire, "within the space of lesse than two houres consumed and burnt fifty and fowre Dwelling Howses, many of them being very faire Houses, besides Barnes, Stables, and other Howses of Office, together with great Store of Corne, Hay, Straw, Wood and Timber therein, amounting to the value of Eight Thousand Pounds and upwards; the force of which fier was so great (the Wind sitting full upon the Towne), that it dispersed into so many places thereof, whereby the whole Towne was in very great danger to have beene utterly consumed."

88 But the poet did not live to see the issue of the contest; the prohibition and order in question not being made before 1618.

89 Greene terms Shakespeare his *cousin*, i.e. *kinsman*, but their exact relationship is unknown. In the burial register of Stratford there is an entry, "1589 [90], March 6, Thomas Greene, alias Shakspere," and the town clerk is thought to have been his son.

words "New Place," may have been intended to signify, the Chapel of the Holy Cross, contiguous to the poet's dwelling. The same year saw the publication of a poem entitled *The Ghost of Richard the Third,* by C. B. in which Richard is made to utter what Mr. Dyce pronounces "perhaps the happiest encomium that Shakespeare had yet received as a dramatist" :—

> "To him that impt my fame with Clio's quill,
> Whose magicke rais'd me from Oblivion's den,
> That writ my storie on the Muses' hill,
> And with my actions dignified his pen;
> He that from Helicon sends many a rill
> Whose nectared veines are drunke by thirstie men;
> Crown'd be his stile with fame, his head with bayes,
> And none detract, but gratulate his praise."

Early in 1616, the poet's youngest daughter, Judith, was married to Thomas Quiney, vintner and wine merchant of Stratford. The ceremony took place on the 10th of February, 1615–16, the bride being then thirty-one years of age, and her husband twenty-seven.

On the 25th of the next month, Shakespeare executed his will, which had evidently been prepared two months before: the date,—"*Vicesimo quinto die Martii,*"—having originally been "*Vicesimo quinto die Januarii.*" It declares the testator to be "in perfect health and memory;" which might be true at the time when the instrument was first drawn, but his signatures on the three sheets of paper which the will occupies, are thought to indicate much physical debility. This was his last recorded act. A few weeks later, on the 23d of April, 1616, William Shakespeare died.

Of the particular malady which deprived the world of this incomparable genius, we have no authentic information. The Rev. John Ward, who was vicar of Stratford in the seventeenth century, has left behind him a Diary, now in the library of the Medical Society of London, wherein is the following passage:—"I have heard that Mr. Shakespeare was a natural wit, without any art at all; he frequented the plays all his younger time, but in his elder days lived at Stratford and supplied the stage with two plays every year, and for itt had an allowance so large, that hee spent att the rate of 1000*l.* a-year, as I have heard. *Shakespear, Drayton, and Ben Jhonson, had a merie meeting,* and itt seems drank too hard, for Shakespear died of a feavour there contracted."[90] The statement that subsequent to his retirement from London, Shakespeare supplied the stage with two plays a-year, and lived at the rate of a thousand pounds a-year, is no doubt an exaggeration; but the carousal is not at all improbable. As Mr. Dyce remarks,—"Drayton, a native of Warwickshire, and frequently in the neighbourhood of Stratford, may fairly be presumed to have partaken at times of Shakespeare's hospitality; and Jonson, who, about two years after, wandered on foot into Scotland and back again, would think little of a journey to Stratford for the sake of visiting so dear a friend.—"

It is remarkable that the poet's son-in-law, Dr. Hall, who doubtless attended him in his last illness, and who has left observations on various medical cases within his own experience,[91] should have preserved no memorandum concerning this, the most interesting case of all.

---

[90] A note at the end of the volume says, "this booke was begunne ffeb. 14. 1661, and finished April the 25th, 1663, att Mr. Brooks his house, in Stratford uppon Avon, in Warwickshire."

[91] They were written in Latin, and published with the following title in 1657: *Select Observations on English Bodies: Or, Cures both Empericall and Historicall, performed upon very eminent Persons in desperate Diseases. First written in Latine by Mr. John Hall Physician, living at Stratford upon Avon in Warwick-shire, where he was very famous, as also in the Counties adjacent, as appeares by these Observations drawn out of severall hundreds of his as choycest. Now put into English for common benefit by James Cooke Practitioner in Physick and Chirurgery.*"

On the 25th of April,[92] all of Shakespeare that could perish was buried on the north side of the chancel of Stratford Church. A flat stone covering his grave bears the following inscription :—

"Good frend for Jesus sake forbeare,
To digg the dust encloased heare :
Bleste be y^e man y_t spares thes stones
And curst be he y^t moves my bones."[93]

The monument erected to the great dramatist's memory against the north wall of the chancel, is too well known to require description. It is said to have been executed by Gerard Johnson soon after the poet's death, and is mentioned by Leonard Digges, in his verses prefixed to the folio edition of Shakespeare's plays published in 1623. The bust which forms part of the monument must therefore be regarded as the most authentic likeness of Shakespeare we possess.[94] The inscription below it is as follows :—

"Judicio Pylium, genio Socratem, arte Maronem,
Terra tegit, populus mæret [mœret,] Olympus habet."

"Stay, passenger, why goest thou by so fast ?
Read, if thou canst, whom envious Death hath plast
Within this monument, Shakspeare, with whome
Quick nature dido whose name doth deck ye tombe
Far more then cost ; sith all y^t he hath writt,
Leaves living art but page to serve his witt.
Obiit Aío Do^i 1616
Ætatis 53, die 23 Ap."

The first folio is illustrated with a portrait, engraved by Martin Droeshout, which, though inferior as a work of art, bears a general resemblance to the bust at Stratford.[95] Unless it were a copy therefrom, the similarity would indicate a certain fidelity in both. Accompanying this print are some verses by Ben Jonson, which of themselves attest in some degree the truthfulness of the portrait :—

"This figure, that thou here seest put,
It was for gentle Shakespeare cut ;
Wherein the graver had a strife
With Nature, to out-doo the life.
O, could he but have drawne his wit
As well in brasse as he hath hit
His face, the print would then surpasse
All that was ever writ in brasse ;
But since he cannot, reader, looke
Not on his picture, but his booke."

The bequests of the poet's will have been often criticized. The interlineation, by which he leaves to his wife only the "second-best bed," has occasioned especial speculation. But

92 The record in the burial-register is :—
"1616. *April* 25. *Will' Shakspere, Gent.*"

93 Dowdall affirms that this epitaph was "made by himselfe, a little before his death."

94 "The bust is as large as life, and was originally coloured in imitation of nature : the eyes were light hazel ; the hair and beard auburn ; the doublet was scarlet ; the loose gown, without sleeves, black ; the plain band round the neck, and the wrist-bands were white : the upper part of the cushion in front of the bust was green, the under half crimson : the cord running along the cushion and the tassels were gilt. These colours were renewed in 1749 ; but Malone caused the whole to be covered over with one or more coats of white paint in 1793."—DYCE.

95 For particulars respecting the other portraits of Shakespeare, the reader is referred to,—*An Inquiry into the Authenticity of various Pictures and Prints, which, from the decease of the Poet to our own times, have been offered to the Public as Portraits of Shakespeare, &c.*, by James Boaden, 1824 : and to *An Inquiry into the History, Authenticity, and Characteristics of the Shakespeare Portraits, &c.*, by Abraham Wivell, 1827.

the credit is due to Mr. Knight of having suggested that by the law of the land, Mrs. Shakespeare had certain rights in her husband's property which required no provision in his will. The same writer has pointed out that even the express mention of the second-best bed, was anything but unkindness and insult; the best bed at that period being considered amongst the chattels which went by custom to the heir in chief.

I have now approached, not without a sense of relief, the limits apportioned to a record of the few particulars in the personal history of Shakespeare which have been discovered. But, as everybody connected with so illustrious a man possesses interest, this imperfect memoir must not close without some account, however brief, of those members of his family who survived him. His widow outlived him seven years. She was buried at Stratford on the 8th of August, 1623.[96] The inscription on the brass plate over her remains is as follows:—"Heere lyeth interred the body of Anne wife of William Shakespeare, who departed this life the 6th day of Augt. 1623, being of the age of 67 yeares.

Ubera tu, mater, tu lac vitamque dedisti:
Væ mihi, pro tanto munere saxa dabo.
Quam mallem amoveat lapidem bonus angelus ore,
Exeat Christi[97] corpus imago tua.
Sed nil vota valent: venias cito, Christe, resurget,
Clausa licet tumulo, mater et astra petet."

Shakespeare's wife makes but a small figure in this memoir. From her having been older than her husband; from certain passages in his works; from the slight notice of her in his will; from none of her family being named in that instrument; and from her having apparently lived a great part of her married life in some measure separated from him; it has been inferred that the match was not felicitous. But we have no satisfactory means of forming a judgment on the subject, and in the absence of these it is not fair to conclude that there was unhappiness or estrangement between them.[98]

His eldest daughter, Susanna, who it has been mentioned was married to Dr. John Hall inherited the bulk of his property.[99] Her daughter, and only child, Elizabeth, was born 21st of

[96] The entry of her burial in the register is peculiar:—

1623.

"8 { *Mrs. Shakespeare.*
{ *Anna uxor Richardi James.*"—

The figure represents the day of the month, but what are we to understand by the bracket? Mr. Harness is of opinion that the two names represent one person; that Mrs. Shakespeare, after the death of her husband, forgot her allegiance to his memory, and became Mrs. James. "The book," he remarks, "affords no similar instance of this mode of entry. On every occasion, when two funerals have taken place on the same day, the date is either repeated, or left blank, but this bracketing the names together—supposing Mrs. Shakespeare and Mrs. James to be different people, is altogether without a parallel. What can be the meaning of this departure from the common rule, unless it was intended to show that the two names constitute one register? Again, with hardly an exception to the contrary, all the entries on the page are in Latin; and it would not only be difficult to account for the deviation into the vulgar tongue in the case of the poet's widow, but to explain why, unless the whole register referred to one individual, the officiating minister, who described one *Anna*, at full length, as '*Uxor Richardi James*,' should have been content without describing the other *Anna* at full length also, as *Vidua Gulielmi Shakspeare.*"

[97] In MS. this line no doubt originally read as it is commonly printed, "Exeat *ut* Christi," &c., —but the "*ut*" is omitted on the brass plate.

[98] A memorial of Anne Shakespeare in connexion with the friends of her youth at Shottery, is found in the will of Thomas Whittington, a man who had been her father's shepherd. Whittington, who died in 1608, made one bequest as follows:—

"Item, I geve and bequeth unt the poore of Stratfud 40*s*., that is in the hand of Anne Shaxpere, wyfe unto Mr. Wyllyam Shaxpere, and is due debt unto me, beyng paid to mine executor by the sayd Wyllyam Shaxpere or his assignes according t the true meanyng of this my will." The money in question had probably been deposited in the hands of Mrs. Shakespeare for safe custody.

[99] "New Place, the abode of the poet's later years,—which is said to have been originally built by Sir Hugh Clopton in the reign of Henry the Seventh, and which was then known by the name of *The Great House*,—came, on Shakespeare's death, to Mrs. Hall, and, on her decease, to her only child, Elizabeth Nash, afterwards Lady Barnard. In this mansion, while it belonged to Mr. and Mrs. Nash, Queen Henrietta Maria held her court for about three weeks, during the civil wars in 1643. As directed in Lady Barnard's will, New Place was sold after the death of herself and her husband. Subsequently we find it again in the possession of the Clopton family: and in 1742 Garrick, Macklin, and Delane (the actor) were entertained by Sir Hugh Clopton, in the garden of New Place, under what was called Shakespeare's mulberry-tree. The constant tradition of Stratford declared that this celebrated tree was planted by the poet's hand: probably about 1609, as during that year an immense number of young mulberry trees was imported from France, and sent into different

February, 1607–8, and appears to have been a favourite of her grandfather, as testified by his will. Dr. Hall died in 1635,[100] leaving his property between his wife and daughter. Susanna survived him fourteen years, being buried on the 16th of July, 1649. The inscription on her tombstone, which adjoins her husband's in the chancel of Stratford Church, is as follows :—

"Heere lyeth ye body of Susanna, wife of John Hall, gent ; ye daughter of William Shakespeare, gent : : shee deceased ye 11th of July, A^o^ 1649, aged 66.

Witty above her sexe, but that's not all,
Wise to salvation was good Mistris Hall :
Something of Shakespeare was in that ; but this,
Wholy of him with whome shes now in blisse.
Then, passenger, hast ne're a tear
To weepe with her that wept with all ?
That wept, yet set herselfe to chere
Them up with comforts cordiall.
Her love shall live, her mercy spread,
When thou hast ne're a teare to shed." [101]

Elizabeth, the poet's grand-daughter, was married on the 22d of April, 1626, to Thomas Nash, son of Anthony Nash, who had an estate at Welcombe. Thomas Nash was born in 1593, he was therefore fifteen years older than his wife. He died in April,[102] 1647, leaving no issue.[103] His widow married her second husband John, afterwards Sir John, Bernard, of Abington, near Northampton. He was created a knight by Charles II., on the 25th of November, 1661. He was himself a widower, having married for his first wife a daughter of Sir Clement Edmonds, of Preston, in Northamptonshire. The Bernards were a respectable county family, having held the manor and advowson of Abington for more than two hundred years. Lady Bernard died at Abington, and was buried there on the 17th of February, 1669–70,[104] and with her passed away the last of the poet's immediate descendants, as she left no issue by her marriage with Sir John Bernard.[105] By her will, preserved in the Prerogative Court of London, Lady Bernard bequeathed legacies of forty and fifty pounds each, to six members of the Hathaway family, testifying thereby, to an affectionate regard for the memory of her grandmother, Anne Shakespeare.[106] She left the inn called the Maidenhead, and the next house

---

counties of England, by order of King James, with a view to the encouragement of the silk manufacture. Sir Hugh Clopton modernized the house by internal and external alterations. His son-in-law, Henry Talbot, Esq., sold New Place to the Rev. Francis Gastrell, Vicar of Frodsham, in Cheshire. This wealthy and unamiable clergyman, conceiving a dislike to the mulberry-tree, because it subjected him to the importunities of travellers, whose veneration for Shakespeare induced them to visit it, caused it to be cut down and cleft into pieces for fire-wood, in 1756 : the greater part of it, however, was bought by a watchmaker of Stratford, who converted every fragment into small boxes, goblets, toothpick-cases, tobacco-stoppers, &c., for which he found eager purchasers. Mr. Gastrell having quarrelled with the magistrates about parochial assessments, razed the mansion to the ground in 1759, and quitted Stratford amidst the rage and execrations of the inhabitants."—DYCE.

[100] The inscription on his tombstone reads thus :—
"Heere lyeth ye body of John Hall, gent: hee marr. Susanna ye daughter and coheire of Will. Shakespeare, gent. Hee deceased Nove^r^ 25, A^o^ 1635, aged 60.

Hallius hic situs est, medica celeberrimus arte,
Expectans regni gaudia læta Dei.
Dignus erat meritis qui Nestora vinceret annis,
In terris omnes sed rapit aqua dies.
Ne tumulo quid desit, adest fidissima conjux,
Et vitæ comitem nunc quoque mortis habet."

[101] This inscription was removed to make room for another to the memory of one Richard Watts, who died in 1707 ; but it was restored a few years ago at the expense of the Rev. William Harness.

[102] He was buried with the Shakespeares in the chancel of Stratford Church :
"Heere resteth ye body of Thomas Nashe, esq. He mar. Elizabeth, the daug. and heire of John Halle, gent. He died Aprill 4. A. 1647, aged 53.

Fata manent omnes : hunc non virtute carentem,
Ut neque divitiis, abstulit atra dies ;
Abstulit, at referet lux ultima : siste, viator ;
Si peritura paras, per male parta peris."

[103] *See Appendix.*

[104] The following is the record of her burial from the Abington register :—

"Anno D^mi^. N^n^. J. C. 1669.
Madam Elizabeth Bernard wife of Sir John Bernard Knt., was buried 17th Febr. 1669."

[105] The representatives of the poet are now the Harts, descendants from his sister Joan, who was buried at Stratford, Nov. 4, 1646.

[106] *See Appendix.*

adjoining (in Henley Street, Stratford) to Thomas Hart, grandson of Shakespeare's brother-in-law, William Hart; and to her kinsman, Edward Bagley, citizen of London, she bequeathed the residue of her property. Sir John Bernard survived his wife about four years, and was buried with her at Abington.[107]

Shakespeare's second daughter, Judith, a twin with Hamnet, was married on the 10th of February, 1616, to Thomas Quiney. She died in February, 1661–2, and was buried at Stratford; the issue of this marriage consisted of three sons, Shakespeare, Richard and Thomas, born respectively in November, 1616, February, 1617–18, and August, 1619. Of these children, Shakespeare died in May, 1617, Thomas in January, 1638, and Richard in February of the same year; no one of them having attained to man's estate; and thus absolutely terminated the poet's family in the Quiney branch.

Regarding the character and disposition of Shakespeare, the testimony of his contemporaries and the traditional accounts which have reached us, concur in extolling his integrity, ingenuousness, amiability, and lively wit. Chettle, as has been shown, acknowledges "his uprightness of dealing."[108] Jonson, in a generous burst of enthusiasm, declares him to have been "indeed honest and of an open and free nature."[109] Fuller[110] has preserved for us a pleasant tradition of his social mirth. From what has been gathered of his history, and from what we know of his works, we can ourselves attest to his having been a man of rare industry, of sedulous attention to business, of unusual skill in the direction of affairs, of the right personal ambition, of admirable judgment, and to have been pre-eminently endowed with those indefinable, but well appreciated qualities, which go to make up what Englishmen understand by the term "Gentleman." His writings prove that he was exempt from the despicable weakness of sectarian animosity, since it is left for modern Papists and Protestants to dispute whether he belonged to the one denomination or the other. That he took extended views of public affairs, is manifest by the words of universal, not of temporary application, which he has put into the mouths of his kings and statesmen, and by the felicity with which he combined great freedom of expression with abstinence from giving umbrage to the ruling authorities of his time.

A good deal of argument has been expended with the view to determine the extent of his "learning." Gildon, Sewell, Upton, Whalley and others, contend that he was a man of extensive literary attainments. Dr. Farmer, on the other hand, having shown conclusively that his plays are full of historical and other errors, and that in all cases where he had the option of resorting to ancient authors in the original or to translations, he had recourse to the latter, represents him as positively illiterate, though allowing that he "remembered, perhaps, enough of his *school-boy* learning to put the *Hig, hag, hog,* into the mouth of Sir Hugh Evans; and might pick up in the writers of the time, or the course of his conversation, a familiar phrase or two of French or Italian." The truth is probably between these extremes. Ben Jonson's evidence admits him to have had some portion of Latin, if not a smattering of Greek; and although I think he

---

[107] The entry of his burial stands thus in the register book:—

"A. D. 1673.
Sr John Bernard, Knight my noble and ever honoured Patron, was buried 5th of March 1673."

[108] See page xxix.

[109] "I remember, the players have often mentioned it as an honour to Shakespeare, that in his writing (whatsoever he penned), he never blotted out a line. My answer hath been, Would he had blotted a thousand! Which they thought a malevolent speech. I had not told posterity this, but for their ignorance, who chose that circumstance to commend their friend by, wherein he most faulted; and to justify mine own candour; for I loved the man, and do honour his memory, on this side idolatry, as much as any. He was (indeed) honest, and of an open and free nature; had an excellent phantasy, brave notions, and gentle expressions; wherein he flowed with that facility, that sometimes it was necessary he should be stopped: *Sufflaminandus erat;* as Augustus said of Haterius. His wit was in his own power:' would the rule of it have been so too! Many times he fell into those things could not escape laughter: as when he said in the person of Cæsar, one speaking to him, 'Cæsar, thou dost me wrong,' he replied, 'Cæsar did never wrong but with just cause,' and such like; which were ridiculous. But he redeemed his vices with his virtues. There was ever more in him to be praised than to be pardoned."—*Discoveries,* —*Jonson's Works,* ix. 175, Gifford's ed.

[110] See page xxxii.

had little acquaintance either with French or Italian, there is nothing to show that he had not an average amount of "schooling." A man who wrote thirty-seven plays in twenty-five years, who acted in most of them, who took a prominent part in the business of an extensive theatrical enterprise, who laboured assiduously for the improvement of his private affairs, and who by these means raised himself from a lowly position to one of wealth and influence, was not likely to prosecute a laborious study of dead or foreign languages. But that Shakespeare was intimately conversant with most branches of knowledge, that he had both read diligently and pondered deeply, that he was "an exact surveyor of the inanimate world," while he was familiar with all the varied pursuits of human-kind, cannot for a moment be denied. And if the stores of "learning" were not at his command, we have the testimony of a ripe scholar that his native force enabled him to soar far above

"—— all that insolent Greece or haughty Rome
Sent forth, or since did from their ashes come."

He found, as we know, the stage scarce emerged from barbarism; and by the vigour of his own genius, unaided by the models of the ancient theatre, he "expanded the magic circle of the drama beyond the limits that belonged to it in antiquity, made it embrace more time and locality, filled it with larger business and action, with vicissitudes of gay and serious emotion, which classical taste had kept divided; with characters which developed humanity in stronger light and subtler movements, and with a language more wildly, more playfully diversified by fancy and passion, than was ever spoken on any stage."[111]

---

111 Campbell's *Specimens of the British Poets,* Vol. I. p. 48.

SHAKESPEARE'S WILL.[1]

FROM THE ORIGINAL IN THE OFFICE OF THE PREROGATIVE COURT OF CANTERBURY.

Vicesimo quinto die Martii,[2] *Anno Regni Domini nostri Jacobi nunc Regis Angliæ, &c. decimo quarto, et Scotiæ xlix*$_{o}$. *Annoque Domini* 1616.

T. W^{mj} Shackspeare

In the name of god, Amen! I William Shackspeare of Stratford upon Avon, in the countie of warr. gent, in perfect health and memorie, god be praysed! doe make and Ordayne this my last will and testament in manner and forme followeing; That ys to saye, First I Comend my Soule into the handes of god my Creator, hoping, and assuredlie beleeving, through thonelie merites of Jesus Christe my Saviour, to be made partaker of lyfe everlastinge, And my bodye to the Earth whereof yt ys made. Item, I Gyve and bequeath unto my Daughter[3] Judyth, One hundred and Fyftie poundes of lawfull English money, to be paied unto her in manner and forme followeing, That ys to saye, One hundred poundes *in discharge of her marriage porcion* within one yeare after my deceas, with consideracion after the Rate of twoe Shillinges in the pound for soe long tyme as the same shalbe unpaied unto her after my deceas, and the Fyftie poundes Residewe thereof, upon her Surrendring *of* or gyving of such sufficient Securitie as the overseers of this my Will shall like of, to Surrender or graunte All her estate and Right that shall discend or come unto her after my desceas, or *that shee* nowe hath, of in or to one Copiehold tenemente with thappurtenaunces, lyeing and being in Stratford upon Avon aforesaied, in the saied county of warr. being parcell or holden of the mannour of Rowington, unto my Daughter Susanna Hall, and her heires for ever. Item, I Gyve and bequeath unto my saied Daughter Judith One hundred and Fyftie Poundes more, if shee, or Anie issue of her bodie, be Lyvinge att thend of three yeares next ensueing the Daie of the Date of this my Will, during which tyme my executours to paie her consideracion from my deceas according to the Rate aforesaied; And if she dye within the saied tearme without issue of her bodye, then my will ys, and I Doe gyve and bequeath One Hundred Poundes thereof to my Neece Elizabeth Hall, and the Fiftie Poundes to be sett fourth by my executours during the lief of my Sister Johane Harte, and the use and proffitt thereof Cominge, shalbe payed to my saied Sister Jone, and after her deceas the said l^{li}. shall Remaine Amongst the children of my saied Sister Equallie to be Devided Amongst them; But if my saied Daughter Judith be lyving att thend of the saied three Yeares, or anie yssue of her bodye, then my will ys, and soe I Devise and bequeath the saied Hundred and Fyftie Poundes to be sett out *by my executors and overseers* for the best benefitt of her and her issue, and *the stock* not *to be* paied unto her soe long as she shalbe marryed and Covert Baron; but my will ys, that she shall have the consideracion yearelie paied unto her during her lief, and after her deceas, the saied stock and consideracion to bee paied to her children, if she have Anie, and if not, to her executours or assignes, she lyving the saied terme after my deceas: Provided that yf such husbond as she shall att thend of the saied three yeares be marryed unto, or at anie [tyme] after, doe sufficientlie Assure unto her, and thissue of her bodie landes Awnswereable to the porcion by this my will gyven unto her, and to be adjudged soe by my executours and overseers, then my will ys, that the said Cl^{li}. shalbe paied to such husbond as shall make such assurance, to his owne use. Item, I gyve and bequeath unto my saied sister Jone xx^{li}, and all my wearing Apparrell, to be paied and delivered within one yeare after my Deceas; And I doe will and devise unto her *the house* with thappurtenaunces in Stratford, wherein she dwelleth, for her natural lief, under the yearlie rent of xij^{d}.

Item, I gyve and bequeath unto her three sonnes, William Harte, [Thomas[4]] Hart, and Michaell Harte, Fyve Poundes Apeece, to be paied within one Yeare after my decease.[5] Item, I gyve and bequeath unto *the saied*

---

[1] The will is written in the clerical hand of that period, on three sheets of paper, fastened together at top. The poet's name is signed at the bottom of the first and second sheet, and his final signature, "by me William Shakspeare," is near the middle of the third sheet. Malone was of opinion that he signed the last sheet first, and that the hand grew gradually weaker in signing the second and first pages. The words printed in Italics are those which in the original are interlined.

[2] Originally written *Januarii.*

[3] Originally *sonne and* daughter.

[4] This Christian name is omitted in the original will.

[5] The following words were here at first inserted, but afterwards cancelled: "to be sett out for her within one yeare after my deceas by my executours with thadvise and direccions of my overseers, for her best profitt, until her marriage, and then the same with the increase thereof to be paied unto her."

Elizabeth Hall[6] All my plate, *except my brod silver and gilt bole,* that I now have att the Date of this my will. Item, I gyve and bequeath unto the Poore of Stratford aforesaied tenn poundes; to Mr. Thomas Combe my Sword; to Thomas Russell, Esquier, Fyve pounds; and to Frauncis Collins of the Borough of warr. in the countie of warr. gentleman, thirteene poundes Sixe shillinges and Eight pence, to be paied within one Yeare after my Deceas. Item, I gyve and bequeath to *Hamlett*[7] *Sadler* xxvi^s viij^d, to buy him A Ringe; to *William Raynoldes, gent.* xxvi^s viij^d, *to buy him A Ringe;* to my godson William Walker xx^s in gold; to Anthonye Nashe, gent. xxvi^s viij^d; and to Mr. John Nashe, xxvi^s viij^d; *and to my Fellowes, John Hemynges, Richard Burbage, and Henry Cundell,* xxvi^s viij^a *Apeece, to buy them ringes.* Item, I Gyve, will, bequeath, and devise, unto my daughter Susanna Hall, *for better enabling of her to performe this my will, and towardes the performans thereof,* All that Capital messuage or tenemente, with thappurtenances, *in Stratford aforesaid,* Called the new place, wherein I nowe Dwell, and two Messuages or tenementes, with thappurtenaunces, scituat, lyeing, and being in Henley-streete, within the borough of Stratford aforesaied; And all my barnes, stables, Orchardes, gardens, landes, tenementes, and hereditamentes whatsoever, scituat, lyeing, and being, or to be had, Receyved, perceyved, or taken, within the townes, Hamletes, Villages, Fieldes, and groundes of Stratford upon Avon, Oldstratford, Bushopton, and Welcombe, or in anie of them, in the said countie of warr. And alsoe All that messuage or tenemente, with thappurtenaunces, wherein One John Robinson dwelleth, scituat, lyeng, and being, in the blackfriers in London nere the Wardrobe; and all other my landes, tenementes, and hereditamentes whatsoever: To have and to hold All and singular the saied premisses, with their appurtenaunces, unto the saied Susanna Hall, for and during the terme of her naturall lief; and after her deceas to the first sonne of her bodie lawfullie yssueinge, and to the heires Males of the bodie of the saied first Sonne lawfully yssueinge; and for defalt of such issue, to the second Sonne of her bodie lawfullie issueinge, and to the heires males of the bodie of the said Second Sonne lawfully yssueing; and for defalt of such heires, to the third Sonne of the bodie of the saied Susanna Lawfullie yssueinge, and to the heires males of the bodie of the saied third sonne lawfullie yssueing; And for defalt of such issue, the same soe to be and Remaine to the Fourth, Fyfth, sixte, and Seaventh sonnes of her body, lawfullie issueinge one after Another, and to the heires Males of the bodies of the said Fourth, fifth, Sixte, and Seaventh sonnes lawfullie yssueing, in such manner as yt is before Lymitted to be and Remaine to the first, second, and third Sonns of her bodie, and to their heires Males; And for defalt of such issue, the saied premisses to be and Remaine to my sayed Neece Hall, and the heires Males of her bodie lawfullie yssueing; And for defalt of such issue, to my Daughter Judith and the heires Males of her bodie lawfullie issueinge, And for defalt of such issue, to the Right heires of me the saied William Shackspeare for ever. *Item, I gyve unto my wief my second best bed, with the furniture.* Item, I gyve and bequeath to my saied Daughter Judith my broad silver gilt bole. All the rest of my goodes, Chattel, Leases, plate, Jewels, and houshold stuffe whatsoever, after my Dettes and Legacies paied, and my funerall expences discharged, I gyve, devise, and bequeath to my Sonne-in-Lawe, John Hall, gent. and my Daughter Susanna his wief, whom I ordaine and make executours of this my Last will and testament. And I doe intreat and Appoint *the saied* Thomas Russell, Esquier, and Frauncis Collins, gent. to be overseers hereof, And doe Revoke All former wills, and publishe this to be my last will and testament. In Witness whereof I have hereunto put my *hand*,[8] the Daie and Yeare first above written.

Witnes to the publyshing hereof, Fra. Collyns, Julyus Shawe, John Robinson, Hamnet Sadler, Robert Whattcott.

By me William Shakspeare.

Probatum coram Magistro Willielmo Byrde, Legum Doctore Comiss. &c. xxjj.^{do} die mensis Junii, Anno Domini 1616; *juramento Johannis Hall, unius executorum &c. cui &c. de bene &c. jurat. reservat. potestate &c. Susannæ Hall, alteri executorum &c. cum venerit petitur,* (*Inv^t. ex^t.*)

---

6 This sentence was originally only *her*.
7 Instead of *Hamlett Sadler, Mr. Richard Tyler thelder,* was first written.
8 *Seale* was originally written.

APPENDIX.

Purchase of New Place. (*See page* xxxi.)

Translation of the foot of the fine levied on the occasion of Shakespeare's purchase of this house. The original is now in the Public Record Office :—

This is the Final Agreement made in the Court of our Sovereign Lady the Queen, at Westminster, in one month from the day of St. Michael in the Forty Fourth year of the reign of Elizabeth by the grace of God of England France and Ireland Queen, Defender of the Faith &c., after the Conquest : before Edmund Anderson, Thomas Walmysley, George Kingesmyll, and Peter Warburton, Justices of our Lady the Queen, and others there then present : between William Shakespeare gentleman, Complainant and Hercules Underhill gentleman deforciant ; of one messuage, two barns, two gardens, and two orchards with appurtenances in Stretford upon Avon : whereupon a plea of Covenant was summoned between them in the same Court ; that is to say, that the aforesaid Hercules hath acknowledged the aforesaid tenements with appurtenances to be the right of the same William as those which he the same William hath of the gift of the aforesaid Hercules, and those he hath remised and quit claimed from him and his heirs to the aforesaid William and his heirs for ever : And moreover the same Hercules hath granted for him and his heirs that they will warrant to the aforesaid William and his heirs the aforesaid tenements with appurtenances, against him the aforesaid Hercules and his heirs, for ever : And for this acknowledgment, remise, quitclaim, warranty, fine and Agreement the same William hath given to the aforesaid Hercules Sixty Pounds Sterling.

Warwick.

[*On the back follow the Proclamations according to the Form of the Statute.*]

Purchase of Land from William Combe and John Combe. (*See page* xxxiv.)

The following is a translation of the foot of the fine levied on this property thirteen years after its purchase. The original is preserved in the Public Record Office :—

This is the Final Agreement made in the Court of our Sovereign Lord the King at Westminster, on the morrow of the Holy Trinity in the year of the reigns of James by the grace of God of England Scotland France and Ireland King Defender of the Faith &c. of England France and Ireland the eighth, and of Scotland the Forty Third ; before Edward Coke, Thomas Walmysley, Peter Warburton, and Thomas Foster, Justices of our Lord the King and others there then present : Between William Shakespere gentleman complainant, and William Combe Esquire and John Combe gentleman deforciants, of one hundred and seven acres of land and twenty acres of pasture with appurtenances in Old Stratford and Stratford upon Avon : whereupon a plea of Covenant was summoned between them in the same Court, that is to say, that the aforesaid William Combe and John have acknowledged the aforesaid tenements with appurtenances to be the right of him the same William Shakespere as those which the same William hath of the gift of the aforesaid William Combe and John, And those they have remised and quitclaimed from them the same William Combe and John and their heirs, to the aforesaid William Shakespeare and his heirs for ever : And moreover the same William Combe hath granted for him and his heirs that they will warrant to the aforesaid William Shakespere and his heirs the aforesaid tenements with appurtenances against him the aforesaid William Combe and his heirs for ever ; And further the same John hath granted for him and his heirs that they will warrant to the aforesaid William Shakespere and his heirs the aforesaid tenements with appurtenances against the aforesaid John and his heirs for ever : And for this Acknowledgment remise quitclaim warranties fine and agreement the same William Shakespere hath given to the aforesaid William Combe and John one hundred Pounds Sterling.

WARWICK.

[*On the back follow the Proclamations according to the Form of the Statute.*]

APPENDIX.

DOCUMENTS RELATING TO SHAKESPEARE'S ESTATES, RECENTLY DISCOVERED IN THE ROLLS CHAPEL.

SHAKESPEARE by his will dated 25 March, 1616, bequeathed, as we have seen, to his daughter, Susanna Hall, [wife of John Hall] the capital messuage in Stratford-upon-Avon, called the New Place, wherein he then dwelt, and two messuages in Henley Street within the said Borough, and all his other lands and tenements in Stratford-upon-Avon, Old Stratford, Bishopton, and Welcombe in Co: Warwick ; also all that messuage wherein John Robinson dwells, in the Blackfriars, in London, near the Wardrobe ; to hold for the term of her life, and after her decease, to the heirs male of her body ; and in default of heirs male of her body, the said premises to remain to his *niece* [grand-daughter], Elizabeth Hall, and the heirs male of her body ; for default of such issue to his daughter Judith [wife of Thomas Quiney], and the heirs male of her body, and for default of such issue to his right heirs.

This lady, Elizabeth Hall, it has been shown, at eighteen years of age became the wife of Thomas Nash, and as the three sons of Judith Quiney all died without children, the last of them in January, 1639, the poet's elder daughter Susanna Hall, her daughter, Elizabeth Nash, and her husband, Thomas Nash, suffered a Fine and Recovery in the fifteenth of Charles I., A.D. 1639-40, by which all the estates in question were confirmed to Mrs. Hall, for her life, with remainder to Mr. and Mrs. Nash, and her issue ; and in default of such issue then upon Mr. Nash.

Mr. Nash died without issue 4th April, 1647 ; having by his will dated 25th August, 1642, bequeathed all the said estate to his wife Elizabeth, for her life, and the reversionary interest thereof to his cousin Edward Nash.

Mrs. Nash, advised that her husband had no right to make such a will, as the Fine and Recovery settled the estates upon her and her issue, and considering that she might marry again and have children (being then only thirty-nine years old), refused, it seems, to carry out her husband's will. Whereupon the said Edward Nash filed his Bill in Chancery against her and others, setting out the will in question, and calling upon the Court to compel Mrs. Nash to produce and execute the same, &c.

These circumstances, and the consequent fact that by another Fine and Recovery Shakespeare's estate were again limited to his descendants, were first made public by the late Mr. Wheeler, of Stratford. Neither he, however, nor Malone, who was indefatigable in his inquiries concerning the poet's grand-daughter and the ultimate disposition of the property, was fortunate enough to find the legal papers in the suit in Chancery between Mrs. Nash and Edward Nash. The instruments in question appear to have remained untouched in their origina depository, the Rolls Chapel, for above two hundred years until a few months since, when, during some alterations in the Chapel, they were brought to light, together with the original will of Thomas Nash.[1] By the liberality of Sir John Romilly, the Right Honourable the Master of the Rolls, I am enabled to print the whole of these documents, as well as some others relating to the poet's property which have never, to my knowledge, been published.

CHANCERY PROCEEDINGS.

N. N. 17. No. 65.

The several answers of Elizabeth Nash, widowe, one of the Defend^ts. to the Bill of Complaynt of Edward Nash, Complainant.

All advantage of excepcion to the incertanties and insufficiences of the said Bill of Complaynt now and at all tymes hereafter saved and reserved unto the Defend^t. for Answer sayth : That the Complainant is Cousin to the Defend^ts. late husband Thomas Nash Esquier deceased but not heir to the said Thomas Nash, For that the said Thomas Nash hath a sister liveing whoe is one of the Defend^ts. to the said Bill of Complaynt besides other kindred whoe are nearer in blood to the said Thomas Nashe deceased than the said Complainant as the Defend^t. takes it, And the Defend^t. sayth : That the said Thomas Nash in his life tyme was seized of diverse messuages, lands, Tenem^ts. and hereditam^ts. and possesssed of a personall Estate, And that hee being soe seized and possessed made his last will and Testament in writing in or about the Twentie Fifte day of August one thousand six hundred Fortie and two and thereby Devised unto this Defend^t. and the other Defend^t. his sister and the Complainant and other persons the lands and legacies in such sort and to such purpose word for word as the Complainant hath set forth in his sayd Bill of Complaynt wch. the Complainant might well doe for that the Defend^t. gave unto the said Complainant a true coppie of the sayd last will and Testament of the said Thomas Nashe and of the Codicell to the sayd will annexed which Codicell the said Thomas Nashe made or caused to bee made in his sicknes in or about the third day of Aprill Anno Domini one thousand six hundred Fortie and seaven and published the same for as

---

[1] An abstract of Nash's will, and of a nuncupative codicil thereto, was printed by Malone. See *Variorum* edition, 1821, Vol. II. p. 619.

part of his said last will and Testamt. and to bee added to the same, And that shortly after (that is to say) in or about the Fowerth day of the same moneth the said Thomas Nashe dyed haveing in or by his said last will appoynted and made this Defendt. his sole Executrix whoe proved the said will wth. the said Codicell thereunto annexed in due forme of Lawe in the Prerogative Cort of Canterbury where the said last will and Codicell are entred and remayne upon Record amongst the Records there, to wch. the Defendt. for more certantie referreth herselfe for and concerning all and everie the matters contayned in the said will and Codicell and complayned of in or by, the said Bill of Complaynt, And the Defendt. saith: That the said messuage called the New Place in Stratford with thappurtenncs and Fower yard land in the comon fields of Old Stratford and the messuage in London neer the Wardrope there supposed to bee devized to the Complainant and his heires by the said Thomas Nashe could not bee devised given or disposed of by the said Thomas Nashe, For that the said messuage Fower yard land and house in London WERE THE INHERITANCE OF WILLIAM SHAKESPEAR THE DEFENDTS. GRANDFATHER whoe was siezed thereof in Fee simple long before the Defendts. marriage wth. the said Thomas Nashe, And being soe seized by his last will and Testamt .in writing bearing date in or about the Twentie Fifte day of March in the Fowerteenth year of the raigne of our late Soveraigne Lord King James Devised the same to Susan Hall the daughter and coheir of the said William and mother to the Defendt. for and dureing her life, And after her death to this Defendt. and the heires of her body, As in and by the said will readie to bee produced to which due referrence being had may more fully appeare, And the Defendt. saith: That the said Susans the Defendts. mother to whome the said messuage, Fower yard land and the house aforesaid was devised by the saidWilliam Shakespear is yet liveing and enjoyeth the same, And that the said Susan and the Defendt. since the death of the said Thomas Nashe have acknowledged and levyed one or more Fines and suffered a Recoverie of the said messuage called the New Place and the said Fower yard land and the house in London to the use of the said Susan the Defendts. mother for her life, And after her decease to this Defendt. and her heires for ever As was lawfull for them soe to doe which are all the Conveyances and estates that the Defendt. since the death of the said Thomas Nashe hath made granted or suffered of anie the lands mencioned in the said Bill of Complaynt And the Defendt. denies that shee hath a mind to suppresse the said last will of the said Thomas Nashe, Or that the same can bee suppressed to the knowledge of the Defendt. Or that the said Thomas Nashe made noe Codicell to his said last will Or that the said Thomas Nashe dyed without makeing any alteracion of the said will set forth by the said Complainant other then is expressed in or by the said Codicell of the said Thomas Nashe, And the Defendt. denies that shee the Defendt. or any other to her knowledge give out, that the said Thomas Nashe dyed intestate and that hee made noe will, Or that hee the said Thomas revoaked the said will and made a new will to the knowledge of the Defendt. But true it is shee the Defendt. hath given forth, That the said Thomas Nashe made the said Codicell as parte of his said last will which the Defendts proved as aforesaid, And that hee the sayd Thomas Nashe had noe power to give and devise the said messuage called the Newe Place the Fower yard Land and the house in London being the Defendts. Inheritance as aforesaid. But that the Defendt. with her said mother may dispose thereof as they please And the Defendt. denies that shee doth refuse to prove the will or to assent to such Legacies as are given to the said Complainant saveing the right and Inheritance in the said messuage Fower yard land and house in London, *And saith that shee this Defendt. hath in her hands or custodie many Deeds Evidences Writings Charters Escripts and munumts. which concerne the lands and premises which the Defendt. claymeth as her Inheritance and other the lands which are the Defendts. Joynture*[1] and are devised to her by the said Thomas Nash in or by his said last will which writings concerning the Defendts. Joynture shee may keepe for her life as shee is informed But the Defendt. is readie to produce the same by coppies or otherwise to make knowne the same to the Complainant in such manner as the Honble. Cort shall appoynt, And the Defendt. denies, that shee doth supresse or conceale the said writings or hath cancelled the same, or doth refuse to set forth the same, Or that this Defendt. doth knowe that the said writings doe concerne the Complainant dureing the Defendts. life, Or that shee this Defendt. hath made or consented to the makeing any estate of the premises to any person or persons whatsoever other then as aforesaid, Without that that anie other matter or thing materiall or effectuall in the Lawe to bee Answered unto by this Defendt. and not herein and hereby well and sufficiently Answered unto confessed traversed or denyed is true All wch. matters and thingst his Defendt. is and will bee readie to aver mayntayne and prove as this Honble. Cort shall award And humbly prayeth to bee hence dismissed wth. her reasonable costs and charges &c. &c.

Predict Def Jur xvij die Aprilis
anno r. R. Carol. xxiiij to apud
Stratford sup Avon in Com Warr.
coram

Tho: Dighton
John Eston.

[1] This declaration is interesting and important as proving that some of Shakespeare's papers were in his grand-daughter's custody after the death of her first husband, and coincides with the tradition mentioned by Sir Hugh Clopton to Macklin in 1742, that she carried away with her from Stratford many of her grandfather's manuscripts.

Veneris 11° Februarij Termino Hillarij Anno dni One thousand six hundred and forty eight

Inter Edru Nash Quer

and

Eliza Nash Deftem

Forasmuch as this Court was this present day informed by Mr. Catlin being of the Plaintiff's Counsel that the Plaintiff having exhibited his Bill into this Court to be relieved touching certain lands devised to the Defendant or her life, the remainder to the Plaintiff and his heirs the Defendant by her Answer hath confessed the having of the Original Will and the Plaintiff's estate which being an estate of an inheritance and the Defendants but an estate for life and witnesses being examined in the Cause it was prayed that the Defendant might bring the said Original Will confessed in her answer into this Court, there to remain indifferently for both parties which is ordered accordingly, unless the Defendant having notice thereof shall within a week after such notice shew unto this Court good cause to the contrary.

F. BODWELL, Clerk.

B 1648 folio 343 C.

Lune 15° May Termino Pas Anno Regni Caroli Regis 24° One thousand six hundred and forty eight.

Inter Edwardu Nashe Quer.

Elizabeth Nashe executrix Thome Nash et Thoma Withers Deftes.

Upon Motion this day made unto this Court by Mr. Catlin being of the Plaintiff's Counsel It is Ordered that process of duces tecum be awarded against the Defendants to bring into this Court the will evidences and writings confessed by their answer to be in their custody or at the return thereof to shew unto this Court good cause to the contrary.

F. BODWELL, Clerk.

B 1647 folio 573 C.

Sabbi 10° Junij Term Trin A° Rs Car 24° One thousand six hundred and forty eight.

Inter Edru. Nash Quer

Eliza Nash executrix Tho: Nash and Thoma Withers Deftes

Whereas by an order of the 15th of May last process of duces tecum was awarded against the Defendants to bring into this Court the will evidences and writings confessed by their answer to be in their custody or at the return thereof to shew unto this Court good cause to the contrary, upon opening of the matter this present day unto this Court by Mr. Dighton being of the Defendants Counsel in the presence of Mr. Chute being of the Plaintiffs Counsel and upon reading of the said Order It was alleged that the Defendant Elizabeth hath an estate for life in the Lands in question and being executrix of the said Thomas Nash hath proved the will and justifies the detaining of the said evidences in her hands for the maintenance of her title but the Plaintiffs Counsel alleging that the inheritance of the lands being in the Plaintiff the said evidences do properly belong to the Plaintiff, Whereupon and upon hearing what was alleged on either side It is Ordered that the will be brought into this Court to the end the Plaintiff may examine witnesses thereupon and then to be delivered back to the Defendant and that the Defendant shall also bring the said evidencies and writings into Court upon oath the first day of the next term there to remain for the equal benefit of both parties and shall within ten days after notice deliver unto the Plaintiff a true Schedule thereof.

F. BODWELL, Clerk.

B 1647 folio 742 C.

NASH'S WILL.

By this will, dated August 25, 1642, which appears to have been kept in the Chapel of the Rolls from the period when Mrs. Nash was ordered to produce it in Court, Thomas Nash makes the following disposition of that portion of his property in which alone we are interested,—the inheritance of the poet's grand-daughter :—

"That is to saie ffirst I give dispose and bequeath unto Elizabeth my welbeloved wife and her assignes for and duringe the terme of her naturall life in lieue of her Joynture and thirdes All that messuage or Tenemente wth thappurtenances scituate lyeinge and beinge in Stratford uppon Avon in the said County of Warwicke in a streete there called or knowen by the name of the Chappell streete and nowe in the tenure use and occupacon of one Johane Norman widowe, And alsoe one meadowe wth thappurtenances lyeinge and beinge wthin the parishe of Old Stratford in the said County of Warwicke and called or knowen by the name of the Square meadowe and lyeinge nere unto the greate stone bridge of Stratford aforesaid And nowe in the tenure use & occupacon of one Willm Abbottes Inholder And alsoe one other meadowe wth thappurtenances lyeinge and beinge wthin the parishe of old Stratford aforesaid in the said County of Warwicke and Called or knowen by the name of the Washe meadowe and lyeinge nere unto the said greate stone bridge of Stratford * * * * * * Item I give dispose and bequeath unto my loveinge kindsman Edward Nash gentleman sonne and heire of my Uncle George Nashe of London gentleman and to his heires and assignes for ever after the death and deceasse of Elizabeth my said wife All that the said messuage or Tenement wth thappurtenances scituate lyeinge and being in Stratford uppon Avon aforesaid in the said County of Warwicke in the said Streete there Called the Chappell streete and nowe in the tenure use and occupacon of the said Johane Norman And alsoe the said meadowe wth the appurtenances lyeing and beinge w^th^in the parishe of old Stratford aforesaid in the said County of Warwicke Called or knowen by the name of the square meadowe and lyeinge nere unto the said greate stone bridge of Stratford aforesaid and nowe in the tenure use and occupacon of one Willm Abbottes Inholder * * * * * Item I give dispose and bequeath unto my said kindesman Edward Nash and to his heires and assignes for ever one messuage or Tenement wth the Appurtenances comonly called or knowen by the name of the Newe place scituate lyeing and being in Stratford uppon Avon Aforesiad in the said County of Warwicke in a streete there Called or knowen by the name of the Chappell streete Togeather alsoe wth all and singuler howses outhowses barnes stables orchardes gardens easementes proffittes and Comodities to the same belonginge or in anie wise appertayninge or reputed taken esteemed or enjoyed as thereunto belonging and nowe in the tenure use and occupacon of mee the said Thomas Nashe And alsoe ffoure yard land of earrable land meadowe and pasture wth Thappurtenances lyeinge and beinge in the Comon ffieldes of old Stratford in the said County of Warwicke togeather wth all easementes proffitts Comons Comodities and hereditaments to the same ffoure yard landes or anie of them belonging or in anie wise appertayninge * * * * And alsoe one other messuage or tenement wth thappurtenances scituate lyeinge & beinge in the parishe of in London and Called or knowen by the name of the wardropp and nowe in the tenure use and occupacon of one Dickes * * * And alsoe the said messuage or tenemente wth Thappurtenances scituate lyeinge and beinge in Stratford uppon Avon aforesaid in the said County of Warwicke in the said streete there Called the Henley streete and nowe in the tenure use & occupacon of the said John Horneby blacksmith And alsoe one other messuage or Tenem^t^ w^t^ Thappurtenances scituate lyeing and being in Stratford uppon Avon aforesaid in the said County of Warwicke in a certayne street there Called the Chappell streete and nowe in the tenure use and occupacon of the said Nicholas Ingram * * * * * * All the rest and other of my goodes Chattles Cattells leases Jewells plate howsehold-stuffe and Implementes of howsehold moveable and unmoveable my debtes and legacies being paid and my funerall expences being discharged I give and bequeath unto Elizabeth my wife whom I make full and whole Executrix of this my last will and Testament And I revoke and renownce all former & other Will and Wills by mee made And I appoynt and entreate my Loveinge ffrendes Edmund Rawlins gent Willm Smith and John Easton to bee the overseers of this my last Will and Testament desiringe them to see this my last Will to bee performed soe farre as in them lyeth And for their paines therein I give them and every of them fforty shillings apeece In witness to this my Will I have putt my hand & seale the day and yeare above Written.

Tho : Nashe.

Witnesses to the sealing and publishinge hereof,

John Soch.
Michaell Johnson.
Samuell Rawlins.

THE following are translations of two Recoveries hitherto unpublished, by which Mrs. Nash, after disputing the will in question, succeeded in limiting a portion of the poet's estates to his descendants. The first refers to the land purchased by him in 1602, of William and John Combe: the other to the house in Blackfriars, bought in 1612–13. It will be observed that the parties concerned with Mrs. Nash in this confirmation of the property are two of the Hathaways, or Hathways, an additional proof, to that afforded by her will, of her friendly intercourse with the members of her grandmother's family.

RECOVERY ROLL, 23. CHARLES 1. MICHAELMAS. ROLL 103 (*on the back*).

Pleas of Land Inrolled at Westminster before Peter Phesant and John Godbold Justices of the Lord the King of the Common Pleas, of Michaelmas Term in the twenty third year of the reign of Lord Charles by the grace of God of England Scotland France and Ireland, King, Defender of the Faith, &c.

Warwick Ss. William Hathway and Thomas Hathway in their proper persons demand against Richard Lane gentleman and William Smyth gentleman, three messuages, three gardens, one hundred and seven acres of land and twenty acres of pasture with appurtenances in Stratford upon Avon, Olde Stratforde, Bishopton and Welcombe as their right and inheritance And into which the same Richard and William Smyth have not entry but after the disseisin which Hugh Hunt thereof unjustly and without judgment hath made to the aforesaid William Hathway and Thomas within thirty years &c And whereupon they say that they were seised of the tenements aforesaid with appurtenances in their demesne as of fee and right in time of peace in the time of our Lord the King that now is, by taking the profits thereof to the value &c And into which &c. And thereof they bring Suit &c.

And the aforesaid Richard and William Smyth in their proper persons come and defend their right when &c. And thereupon vouch to warrant Elizabeth Nashe widow who is present here in Court in her proper person And freely warrants the tenements aforesaid with appurtenances to them &c. And hereupon the aforesaid William Hathway and Thomas demand against the same Elizabeth tenant by her own warranty the tenements aforesaid with appurtenances in form aforesaid &c. And whereupon they say that they were seised of the tenements aforesaid with appurtenances in their demesne as of fee and right in time of peace in the time of our Lord the King that now is, by taking the profits thereof to the value &c. And into which &c. And thereof they bring Suit &c.

And the aforesaid Elizabeth Tenant by her own Warranty defends her right when &c. And thereupon further voucheth to warrant Robert Lee who is also present here in Court in his proper person And freely warrants the tenements aforesaid with appurtenances to her &c. And hereupon the aforesaid William Hathway and Thomas demand against the same Robert Tenant by his own warranty the tenements aforesaid with appurtenances in form aforesaid &c. And whereupon they say that they were seised of the tenements aforesaid with appurtenances in their demesne as of fee and right in time of peace in the time of Our Lord the King that now is by taking the profits thereof, to the value &c. And into which &c. And thereof they bring Suit &c.

And the aforesaid Robert Tenant by his own warranty defends his right when, &c. And saith that the aforesaid Hugh did not disseise the aforesaid William Hathway and Thomas of the tenements aforesaid with appurtenances as the same William Hathway and Thomas by their writ and declaration aforesaid above do suppose And of this he putteth himself upon the Country &c. And the aforesaid William Hathway and Thomas thereupon crave licence to imparl And they have it &c. And afterwards the same William Hathway and Thomas come again here into Court in this same Term in their proper persons And the aforsaid Robert although solemnly called cometh not again but departed in contempt of the Court And maketh default. Therefore it is considered that the aforesaid William Hathway and Thomas recover their seisin against the aforesaid Richard and William Smyth of the tenements aforesaid with appurtenances And that the same Richard and William Smyth have of the land of the aforesaid Elizabeth to the value &c. And that the same Elizabeth further have of the land of the aforesaid Robert to the value &c. And the same Robert in Mercy, &c. And hereupon the aforesaid William Hathway and Thomas pray a writ of our Lord the King to be directed to the Sheriff of the County aforesaid to cause full seisin of the tenements aforesaid with appurtenances to be delivered to them And it is granted to them returnable here without delay &c. Afterwards that is to say on the twenty ninth day of November in this same Term come here into Court the aforesaid William Hathway and Thomas in their proper persons And the Sheriff namely Richard Lucy Esquire now returns that he by virtue of the said writ to him directed on the twenty sixth day of November last past did cause full seisin of the tenements aforesaid with appurtenances to be delivered to the aforesaid William Hathway and Thomas as by the said writ he was commanded. &c.

Recovery Roll, 23. Charles 1. Michaelmas. Roll 103 (*on the back*).

Pleas of Land Inrolled at Westminster before Peter Phesant and John Godbold Justices of the Lord the King of the Common Pleas, of Michaelmas Term in the twenty third year of the reign of Lord Charles by the grace of God of England, Scotland, France, and Ireland, King, Defender of the Faith, &c.

London Ss. William Hathway and Thomas Hathway in their proper persons demand against Richard Lane gentleman and William Smyth gentleman, one messuage with appurtenances in the parish of St Anne Blackfriers as their right and inheritance And into which the same Richard and William Smyth have not entry but after the disseisin which Hugh Hunt thereof unjustly and without judgment hath made to the aforesaid William Hathway and Thomas within thirty years &c. And whereupon they say that they were seised of the messuage aforesaid with appurtenances in their demesne as of fee and right in time of peace in the time of our Lord the King that now is by taking the profits thereof to the value &c. And into which &c. And thereof they bring suit &c.

And the aforesaid Richard and William Smyth in their proper persons come and defend their right when &c. And thereupon vouch to warrant Elizabeth Nashe widow who is present here in Court in her proper person And freely warrants the messuage aforesaid with appurtenances to them &c. And hereupon the aforesaid William Hathway and Thomas demand against the same Elizabeth tenant by her own warranty the messuage aforesaid with appurtenances in form aforesaid &c. And whereupon they say that they were seised of the messuage aforesaid with appurtenances in their demesne as of fee and right in time of peace in the time of the Lord the King that now is by taking the profits thereof to the value &c. And into which &c. And thereof they bring suit &c.

And the aforesaid Elizabeth Tenant by her own warranty defends her right when &c. And thereupon furthei voucheth to warrant Robert Lee who is also present here in Court in his proper person And freely warrants the messuage aforesaid with appurtenances to her &c. And hereupon the aforesaid William Hathway and Thomas demand against the said Robert Tenant by his own warranty the messuage aforesaid with appurtenances in form aforesaid &c. And whereupon they say that they were seised of the messuage aforesaid with appurtenances in their demesne as of fee and right in time of peace in the time of the Lord the King that now is by taking the profits thereof to the value &c. And into which &c. And thereof they bring suit &c. And the aforesaid Robert Tenant by his own warrantry defends his right when &c. And saith that the aforesaid Hugh did not disseise the aforesaid William Hathway and Thomas of the messuage aforesaid with appurtenances as the same William Hathway and Thomas by their writ and declaration aforesaid above do suppose And of this he putteth himself upon the Country &c.

And the aforesaid William Hathway and Thomas thereupon crave leave to imparl And they have it &c. And afterwards the same William Hathway and Thomas come again here into Court in this same Term in their proper persons And the aforesaid Robert although solemnly called cometh not again but departed in contempt of the Court And maketh default.

Therefore it is considered that the aforesaid William Hathway and Thomas recover their seisin against the aforesaid Richard and William Smyth of the messuage aforesaid with appurtenances And that the same Richard and William Smyth have of the land of the aforesaid Elizabeth to the value &c. And that the same Elizabeth have lastly of the land of the aforesaid Robert to the value &c. And the same Robert in mercy &c. And hereupon the aforesaid William Hathway and Thomas pray a writ of Our Lord the King to be directed to the Sheriffs of London aforesaid to cause full seisin of the messuage aforesaid with appurtenances to be delivered to them And it is granted to them returnable here without delay &c. Afterwards, that is to say, on the Twenty ninth day of November in this same Term come here into Court the aforesaid William Hathway and Thomas in their proper persons And the Sheriffs namely Samuel Averey and John Bide now return that they by virtue of the said writ to them directed on the twenty seventh day of November last past did cause full seisin of the messuage aforesaid with appurtenances to be delivered to the aforesaid William Hathway and Thomas as by the said writ they were prayed. &c.

THE SUPPOSITITIOUS SHAKESPEARE DOCUMENTS.

In addition to the MS. annotations of Mr. Collier's "Corrected folio, 1632," and those on the margins of Lord Ellesmere's folio, 1623, every one of which has been pronounced by the most competent authority to be of quite recent fabrication, the following documents, after careful inspection, have been found to present unmistakeable evidences of being counterfeit.

In Bridgewater House.

1. Memorial of the players, James Burbidge, Richard Burbidge, John Laneham, &c. &c. November, 1589 (*See note* [34], p. xxiii.) *and* Collier's *Life of Shakespeare*, p. 82.

2. List of Claims made by R. Burbidge: Laz. Fletcher: W. Shakspeare, &c. *No date*, which Mr. Collier describes as "a paper, which shows, with great exactness and particularity, the amount of interest then claimed by each sharer, those sharers being Richard Burbadge, Laurence Fletcher, William Shakespeare, John Heminge, Henry Condell, Joseph Taylor, and Lowin, with four other persons not named, each the owner of half a share."—Collier's *Life of Shakespeare*, p. 189.

"*For avoiding of the playhouse in the Blacke Friers.*

Impr	Richard Burbidge owith the Fee, and is alsoe a sharer therein. His interest he rateth at the grosse summe of 1000 li for the Fee, and for his foure Shares the summe of 933 li 6s 8d	1933 li	6s	8d
Item	Laz Fletcher owith three shares w[ch] he rateth at 700 li, that is at 7 years purchase for eche share, or 33 li 6s 8d one year with an other.	700 li		
Item	W. Shakspeare asketh for the Wardrobe and properties of the same playhouse 500 li, and for his 4 shares, the same as his fellowes Burbidge and Fletcher, viz. 933 li 6s 8d	1433 li	6s	8d
Item	Heminges and Condell eche 2 shares	933 li	6s	8d
Item	Joseph Taylor one share and an halfe	350 li		
Item	Lowing one share and an halfe	350 li		
Item	Foure more playeres with one halfe share unto eche of them	466 li	13s	4d
	Sum[a] totalis	6166 li	13s	4d

"Moreover, the hired men of the Companie demaund some recompence for their greate losse, and the Widowes and Orphanes of players, who are paide by the Sharers at diuers rates and proporcōns, soe as in the whole it will coste the Lo. Mayor and Citizens at the least 7000 li."

3. A letter from Samuel Daniel to the Rt. Hon. Sir Thomas Egerton, from which, Mr. Collier remarks, "we may perhaps conclude that Shakespeare, as well as Michael Drayton, had been candidates for the post of Master of the Queen's revels."—*(See note 75, p. xxxv.) and* COLLIER'S *Life of Shakespeare*, p. 173.

To the Right honorable Sir Thomas Egerton, Knight, Lord Keeper of the great Seale of England.

I will not indeavour, Right honorable, to thanke you in wordes for this new great and vnlookt for favor showne vnto me, whereby I am bound to you for ever, and hope one day with true harte and simple skill to prove that I am not vnmindfull.

Most earnestly doe I wishe I could praise as your Honour has knowne to deserue, for then should I, like my maister Spencer, whose memorie your Honor cherisheth, leave behinde me some worthie worke, to be treasured by posteritie; What my pore muse could performe in haste is here set downe, and though it be farre below what other poets and better pennes have written it commeth from a gratefull harte and therefore maye be accepted. I shall now be able to liue free from those cares and troubles that hetherto haue been my continuall and wearisome companions. But a little time is paste since I was called vpon to thanke yor honor for my brothers advancement and nowe I thanke you for my owne wch double kindnes will alwaies receive double gratefullnes at both our handes.

I cannot but knowe that I am lesse deseruing then some that sued by other of the nobilitie vnto her Matie for this roome, if M. Drayton my good friend had bene chosen I should not have murmured for sure I am he wold have filled it most excellentlie: but it seemeth to myne humble iudgement that one which is the authour of playes now daylie presented on the publick stages of London and the possessor of no small gaines, and moreover himself an actor in the kinges companie of Commedias, could not with reason pretend to be mr of the Queenes Maties Reuelles for as much as he wold sometimes be asked to approue and allowe of his owne writinge. Therfore he and more of like qualitie cannot iustly be disappointed because through yor Honors gracious interposition the chance was haply myne. I owe this and all else to yor Honors and if euer I haue time and abilitie to finishe anie noble vndertaking as God graunt one daye I shall, the worke will rather be yor Honors then myne. God maketh a poet but his creation would be in vaine if patrones did not make him to liue. Yor Honor hath ever showne yor selfe the friend of desert, and pitty it were if this should be the first exception to the rule. It shall not be whiles my poore witt and strength doe remaine to me, though the verses wch I nowe sende be indeed noe proofe of myne abilitie I onely intreat yor Honor to accept the same the rather as an earnest of my good will then as an example of my good deede. In all thinges I am yor Honors

Most bounden in dutie and obseruance,
S. DANYELL.

4. A letter assumed to be from Henry Lord Southampton to the Lord Chancellor Ellesmere on behalf of Shakespeare and Burbadge. No date.—*(See note 82, p. xxxvii.) and* Collier's *Life of Shakespeare*, p. 193:—

My verie honored Lo. the manie good offices I haue receiued at yor Lps handes whh ought to make me backward in asking further favours onely imbouldeneth me to require more in the same kinde. Yor Lp wilbe warned howe hereafter you graunt anie sute seeing it draweth on more and greater demaundes: this wch now presseth is to request yor Lp in all you can to be good to the poore players of the blacke Fryers who call themselues by authoritie the Servantes of his Matie and aske for the proteccōn of their most gracious maister and Soueraigne in this the tyme of there troble. They are threatened by the Lo. Maior and Aldermen of London never friendly to their calling wth the distruccōn of their meanes of liuelihood by the pulling downe of their plaiehouse wch is a priuate theatre and hath never giuen ocasion of anger by anie disorders. These bearers are two of the chiefe of the companie, one of them by name Richard Burbidge who humblie sueth for yor Lps kinde helpe for that he is a man famous as our english Roscius one who fitteth the action to the worde and the word to the action most admira[b]ly. By the exercise of his qualitie industry and good behaviour he hath become possessed of the Blacke Fryers playhouse wch hath bene imployed for playes sithence it was builded by his Father now nere 50 yeres agone. The other is a man no whitt less deseruing fauor and my especial friende till of late an actor of good account in the cumpanie, now a sharer in the same, and writer of some of our best english playes wch as your Lp. knoweth were most singulerly liked of Quene Elizabeth when the cumpanie was called vppon to performe before her Matie at Court at Christmas and Shrove tide. His most gracious Matie King James alsoe since his coming to the crowne hath extended his Royall favour to the companie in diuers waies and at sundrie tymes. This other hath to name William Shakespeare and they are both of one countie and indeede allmost of one towne, both are right famous in their qualities though it longeth not of yor Lo. grauitie and wisdome to resort vnto the places where they are wont to delight the publique eare. Their trust and sute nowe is not to bee molested in their waye of life whereby they maintaine themselves and their wives and families (being both married and of good reputacōn) as well as the widowes and orphanes of some of their dead fellows. Yo[r] Lo. most bounden at cōm.

Copia vera.

H. S.

5. Draft of warrant appointing Robert Daborne, William Shakespeare, &c. instructors of the Children of the Queen's Revels—(*See note* [82], p. xxxvii.) *and* Collier's *Life of Shakespeare*, pp. 197-8 :—

Right trustie and well beloved &c. James, &c. To all Mayors, Sheriffes, Justices of the peace, &c. Whereas the Queene our dearest wife hath for her pleasure and recreacōn appointed her servauntes Robert Daborne &c. to prouide and bring uppe a convenient nomber of children who shalbe called the children of her Ma[tes] revelles. Knowe yee that We have appointed and authorized and by these presentes doe appoint and authorize the saide Robert Daborne, Willm Shakespeare, Nathaniel Field, and Edward Kirkham from time to time to prouide and bring vpp a convenient nomber of children, and them to instruct and exercise in the qualitie of playing Tragedies Comedies &c. by the name of the children of the reuelles to the Queene, within the blacke Fryers in our Cittie of London and els where within our realme of England. Wherefore we will and commaund you and everie of you tc permitte her said servauntes to keepe a convenient nomber of children by the name of the children of the reuelles to the Queene, and them to exercise in the qualitie of playing acording to our Royall pleasure. Provided allwayes that noe playes &c. shalbe by them presented, but such playes &c. as haue receiued the aprobacōn and allowance of our Maister of the Reuelles for the tyme being. And these our lr̄es shalbe yo[r] sufficient warraunt in this behalfe. In Witnesse whereof &c. 4° die Janii, 1609.

Bl Fr and globe	Curten and fortune	All in & neere
Wh Fr and parishe garden	Hope and Swanne	London

Proude pouertie	Engl tragedie
Widdowes mite	False Friendes
Antonio kinsmen	Hate and loue
Triumph of truth	Taming of S
Touchstone	K. Edw. 2
Mirror of life	
Grissell	Stayed.

In Dulwich College.

1. Alleyn and Kempe's Wager, which Mr. Collier introduces as follows :—

"But there is another paper of a very similar kind, apparently referring to the preceding, or to some other like contest, but containing several remarkable allusions, which Malone did not notice. Perhaps it never met his eye, or perhaps he reserved it for his Life of Shakespeare, and was unwilling to forestall that production by inserting it elsewhere. It seems to be of a later date, and it mentions not only Tarlton, Knell, and Bentley, but Kempe, Phillips, and Pope, while Alleyn's rival Burbage is sneered at as 'Roscius Richard,' and Shakespeare introduced under the name of Will, by which we have Thomas Heywood's authoritie (in his 'Hierarchie of the blessed Angels,' 1635, p. 206) for saying he was known among his companions. The paper is in verse, and runs precisely as follows :

"'Swett Nedde, nowe wynne an other wager
For thine old friende and Fellow stager ;
Tarlton himself thou dost excell,
And Bentley beate, and conquer Knell,
And nowe shall Kempe orecome aswell.
The moneys downe, the place the Hope,
Phillipes shall hide his head and Pope.
Fear not, the victorie is thyne ;
Thou still as macheles Ned shall shyne.
If Roscius Richard foames and fumes,
The globe shall have but emptie roomes ;
If thou doest act ; and Willes newe playe
Shall be rehearst some other daye.
Consent, then, Nedde ; doe us this grace :
Thou cannot faile in anie case ;
For in the triall, come what maye,
All sides shall brave Ned Allin saye.'"

Memoirs of Alleyn, p. 13, ed. J. P. Collier, 1841

2. A list of players, added to a genuine memorandum ; (*See note* [77], p. xxxv.) of which addition Mr. Collier says :—

"Malone also appears to have reserved another circumstance, of very considerable importance in relation to Shakespeare, for his life of the poet. To the last-quoted document, but in a different hand and in different ink, is appended a list of the king's players. The name of Shakespeare there occurs second, and as it could not be written at the bottom of the letter of the Council to the Lord Mayor, &c. prior to the date of that letter, it proves that up to 9th April, 1604, our great dramatist continued to be numbered among the *actors* of the company.

Hitherto the last trace we have had of Shakespeare as actually on the stage, has been as one of the performers in Ben Jonson's '*Sejanus*,' which was produced in 1603. We will insert the list as it stands at the foot of the Council's letter to the Lord Mayor, &c.

" 'Ks Comp.

Burbidge	Armyn
Shakespeare	Slye
Fletcher	Cowley
Phillips	Hostler
Condle	Day.' "
Hemminges	

COLLIER'S *Memoirs of Alleyn*, p. 68.

3. A letter from John Marston to Henslow, heralded thus :—

"The following undated note from Marston to Henslowe may not be unfitly introduced here : it refers to a play by Marston on the subject of Columbus, of which we hear on no other authority. It is one of the scraps of correspondence between Henslowe and the poets in his employ, existing at Dulwich College, of the major part of which Malone has given copies, but omitting the subsequent, which is certainly one of the most interesting of the whole collection.

" 'Mr. Hensloe, at the rose on the Bankside.

" 'If you like my play of Columbus, it is verie well and you shall give me no more than twentie poundes for it, but If nott, lett mee have it by this Bearer againe, as I knowe the kinges men will freelie give mee as much for it, and the profitts of the third daye moreover.

" 'Soe I rest yours

" 'JOHN MARSTON.' "

COLLIER'S *Memoirs of Alleyn*, p. 154.

4. A slip purporting to be a list of the inhabitants of Southwark who made a complaint,—against what is not specified,—in 1596, and which Mr. Collier's *Life of Shakespeare*, p. 126, represents as "valuable only because it proves distinctly that our great dramatist was an inhabitant of Southwark very soon after the Globe was in operation." (*See note* [61], p. xxxi.)

5. "A breif noat taken out of the poores booke, contayning the names of all thenhabitants of this Liberty which are rated and assesed to a weekely paim^t towardes the relief of the poore, as it standes now encreased, this 6° day of Aprill, 1609," &c. This document is quoted by Mr. Collier in his *Memoirs of Edward Alleyn*, p. 91, and in his *Life of Shakespeare*, p. 187, to show that Shakespeare, at the date in question, was rated to the poor of the Clink in Southwark as an "inhabitant" at 6*d*. per week. Among the names on this list are Henslowe, Alleyne, Lee, Benfield, Lowins, Towne, Jubye, Hunt, Shakespeare, and Bird, all connected with the theatres of the period. (*See note* [82], p. xxxvii.)

IN THE STATE PAPER OFFICE.

1. A petition of Thomas Pope, Richard Burbadge, John Hemings, Augustine Phillips, William Shakespeare, &c. &c. For this instrument, see note [59], p. xxx.

Although the above are all of the documents brought to light by Mr. Collier which have been subjected to paleographic examination and are condemned as spurious, they form but a small part of his discoveries which stand suspected. But as the remainder will shortly undergo investigation by skilled paleographers, it is not prudent to offer an opinion on their authenticity based only upon internal evidence.

PRELIMINARY MATTER IN THE FOLIO OF 1623.[1]

THE DEDICATION.

To the Most Noble and Incomparable Paire of Brethren. William Earle of Pembroke, &c., Lord Chamberlaine to the Kings most excellent Majesty. And Philip Earle of Montgomery, &c., Gentleman of his Majesties Bed-chamber. Both Knights of the most noble Order of the Garter, and our singular good Lords.

RIGHT HONOURABLE,

WHILST we studie to be thankful in our particular, for the many favors we have received from your LL., we are falne upon the ill fortune, to mingle two the most diverse things that can bee, feare, and rashnesse; rashnesse in the enterprize, and feare of the successe. For, when we valew the places your HH. sustaine, we cannot but know their dignity greater, then to descend to the reading of these trifles: and, while we name them trifles, we have depriv'd our selves of the defence of our Dedication. But since your LL. have beene pleas'd to thinke these trifles some-thing, heeretofore; and have prosequuted both them, and their Authour living, with so much favour: we hope, that (they out-living him, and he not having the fate, common with some, to be exequutor to his owne writings) you will use the like indulgence toward them, you have done unto their parent. There is a great difference whether any Booke choose his Patrones, or finde them: This hath done both. For, so much were your LL. likings of the severall parts, when they were acted, as before they were published, the Volume ask'd to be yours. We have but collected them, and done an office to the dead, to procure his Orphanes, Guardians; without ambition either of selfe-profit, or fame: onely to keepe the memory of so worthy a Friend, & Fellow alive, as was our SHAKESPEARE, by humble offer of his playes, to your most noble patronage. Wherein, as we have justly observed, no man to come neere your LL. but with a kind of religious addresse; it hath bin the height of our care, who are the Presenters, to make the present worthy of your HH. by the perfection. But, there we must also crave our abilities to be considerd, my Lords. We cannot go beyond our owne powers. Country hands reach foorth milke, creame, fruites, or what they have: and many Nations (we have heard) that had not gummes & incense, obtained their requests with a leavened Cake. It was no fault to approch their Gods, by what meanes they could: And the most, though meanest, of things are made more precious, when they are dedicated to Temples. In that name therefore, we most humbly consecrate to your HH. these remaines of your servant Shakespeare; that what delight is in them, may be ever your LL., the reputation his, & the faults ours, if any be committed, by a payre so carefull to shew their gratitude both to the living, and the dead, as is

Your Lordshippes most bounden,

JOHN HEMINGE,
HENRY CONDELL.

---

[1] In the preliminary matter of the first and second folio, I have thought it desirable to adhere to the old, quaint spelling, and, where the sense was not obscured by it, to the ancient punctuation also.

THE ADDRESS TO THE READER.

To the great Variety of Readers.

From the most able, to him that can but spell : There you are number'd. We had rather you were weighd. Especially, when the fate of all Bookes depends upon your capacities : and not of your heads alone, but of your purses. Well ! It is now publique, & you wil stand for your priviledges wee know : to read and censure. Do so, but buy it first. That doth best commend a Booke, the Stationer saies. Then, how odde soever your braines be, or your wisedomes, make your licence the same, and spare not. Judge your sixe-pen'orth, your shillings worth, your five shillings worth at a time, or higher, so you rise to the just rates, and welcome. But, whatever you do, Buy. Censure will not drive a Trade, or make the Jacke go. And though you be a Magistrate of wit, and sit on the Stage at *Black-Friers*, or the *Cock-pit* to arraigne Playes dailie, know, these Playes have had their triall alreadie, and stood out all Appeales; and do now come forth quitted rather by a Decree of Court, then any purchas'd Letters of commendation.

It had bene a thing, we confesse, worthie to have bene wished, that the Author himselfe had liv'd to have set forth, and overseen his owne writings ; But since it hath bin ordain'd otherwise, and he by death departed from that right, we pray you do not envie his Friends, the office of their care, and paine, to have collected & publish'd them ; and so to have publish'd them, as where (before) you were abus'd with diverse stolne, and surreptitious copies, maimed, and deformed by the frauds and stealthes of injurious impostors, that expos'd them : even those, are now offer'd to your view cur'd, and perfect of their limbes ; and all the rest, absolute in their numbers, as he conceived thē. Who, as he was a happie imitator of Nature, was a most gentle expresser of it. His mind and hand went together : And what he thought, he uttered with that easinesse, that wee have scarse received from him a blot in his papers. But it is not our province, who onelie gather his works, and give them you, to praise him. It is yours that reade him. And there we hope, to your divers capacities, you will finde enough, both to draw, and hold you : for his wit can no more lie hid, then it could be lost. Reade him, therefore ; and againe, and againe : And if then you doe not like him, surely you are in some manifest danger, not to understand him. And so we leave you to other of his Friends, whom if you need, can bee your guides : if you neede them not, you can leade yourselves, and others. And such Readers we wish him.

John Heminge,
Henrie Condell.

COMMENDATORY VERSES

PREFIXED TO THE FOLIO OF 1623.

To the Reader.[a]

THIS Figure, that thou here seest put,
It was for gentle Shakespeare cut;
Wherein the Graver had a strife
With Nature, to out-doo the life:
O, could he but have drawne his wit
As well in brasse as he hath hit
His face; the print would then surpasse
All, that was ever writ in brasse,
But, since he cannot, Reader, looke
Not on his Picture, but his Booke.—B. J.

TO THE MEMORIE *of the deceased Authour Maister* W. SHAKESPEARE.

SHAKE-SPEARE, at length thy pious fellowes give
The world thy Workes: thy Workes, by which, out-live
Thy Tombe, thy name must: when that stone is rent,
And Time dissolves thy Stratford Moniment,
Here we alive shall view thee still. This booke,
When Brasse and Marble fade, shall make thee looke
Fresh to all Ages; when Posteritie
Shall loath what 's new, thinke all is prodegie
That is not Shake-speares; ev'ry Line, each Verse,
Here shall revive, redeeme thee from thy Herse.
Nor Fire, nor cankring Age, as Naso said,
Of his, thy wit-fraught Booke shall once invade.
Nor shall I e're beleeve, or thinke thee dead
(Though mist) until our bankrout Stage be sped
(Impossible) with some new strain t' out-do
Passions of Juliet, and her Romeo;
Or till I heare a Scene more nobly take,
Then when thy half-Sword parlying Romans spake,
Till these, till any of thy Volumes rest,
Shall with more fire, more feeling be exprest,
Be sure, our Shake-speare, thou canst never dye,
But crown'd with Lawrell, live eternally.
L. DIGGES.

To the Memorie of M. W. *Shake-speare.*

WEE wondred (Shake-speare) that thou went'st so soone
From the Worlds-Stage to the Graves-Tyring-roome.
Wee thought thee dead, but this thy printed worth,
Tels thy Spectators, that thou went'st but forth
To enter with applause. An Actor's Art
Can dye, and live to acte a second part.
That 's but an Exit of Mortalitie;
This, a Re-entrance to a Plaudite.—I. M.

To the memory of my beloved, the AUTHOR,
MR. WILLIAM SHAKESPEARE,
and what he hath left us.

To draw no envy (Shakespeare) on thy name,
Am I thus ample to thy Booke and Fame;
While I confesse thy writings to be such,
As neither Man nor Muse can praise too much.
'Tis true, and all men's suffrage. But these wayes
Were not the paths I meant unto thy praise;
For seeliest Ignorance on these may light,
Which, when it sounds at best, but eccho's right;
Or blind Affection, which doth ne're advance
The truth, but gropes, and urgeth all by chance;
Or crafty Malice might pretend this praise,
And thinke to ruine where it seem'd to raise.
These are, as some infamous Baud or Whore
Should praise a Matron:—what could hurt her more?
But thou art proofe against them, and, indeed,
Above th' ill fortune of them, or the need.
I, therefore, will begin. Soule of the Age!
The applause! delight! the wonder of our Stage!
My Shakespeare, rise! I will not lodge thee by[b]
Chaucer or Spenser, or bid Beaumont lye
A little further, to make thee a roome:
Thou art a Moniment, without a tombe,
And art alive still, while thy Booke doth live,
And we have wits to read, and praise to give.
That I not mixe thee so, my braine excuses,—
I meane with great, but disproportion'd Muses;
For if I thought my judgement were of yeeres,
I should commit thee surely with thy peeres,
And tell, how farre thou didst our Lily out-shine,
Or sporting Kid, or Marlowe's mighty line.
And though thou hadst small Latine, and lesse Greeke,
From thence to honour thee, I would not seeke
For names; but call forth thund'ring Æschilus,
Euripides, and Sophocles to us,

---

[a] These lines, written by Ben Jonson, refer to, and are placed opposite, the engraved portrait of Shakespeare in the first folio.

[b] Jonson here alludes to the following lines by W. Basse, which were for some time attributed to Donne, and printed among his poems:—

"Renownèd Spenser, lie a thought more nigh
To learnèd Chaucer; and, rare Beaumont, lie
A little nearer Spenser; to make room
For Shakespeare in your three-fold four-fold tomb:
To lodge all four in one bed make a shift
Until doomsday; for hardly will a fifth,
Betwixt this day and that, by fate be slain,
For whom your curtains may be drawn again.
But if precedency in death doth bar
A fourth place in your sacred sepulchre,
Under this carvèd marble of thine own,
Sleep, rare tragedian, Shakespeare, sleep alone:
Thy unmolested peace, unsharèd cave,
Possess as lord, not tenant, of thy grave;
That unto us and others it may be
Honour hereafter to be laid by thee."

Paccuvius, Accius, him of Cordova dead,
To life againe, to heare thy Buskin tread
And shake a Stage: Or, when thy Sockes were on,
Leave thee alone for the comparison
Of all that insolent Greece or haughtie Rome
Sent forth, or since did from their ashes come.
Triumph, my Britaine! thou hast one to showe,
To whom all Scenes of Europe homage owe.
He was not of an age, but for all time!
And all the Muses still were in their prime,
When, like Apollo, he came forth to warme
Our eares, or like a Mercury to charme!
Nature her-selfe was proud of his designes,
And joy'd to weare the dressing of his lines!
Which were so richly spun, and woven so fit,
As, since, she will vouchsafe no other Wit.
The merry Greeke, tart Aristophanes,
Neat Terence, witty Plautus, now not please;
But antiquated and deserted lye,
As they were not of Natures family.
Yet must I not give Nature all; thy Art,
My gentle Shakespeare, must enjoy a part:
For though the Poets matter, Nature be,
His Art doth give the fashion. And, that he,
Who casts to write a living line, must sweat
(Such as thine are) and strike the second heat
Upon the Muses anvile: turne the same,
(And himselfe with it) that he thinkes to frame;
Or, for the lawrell, he may gain a scorne,—
For a good Poet's made, as well as borne.
And such wert thou. Looke how the father's face
Lives in his issue, even so the race
Of Shakespeares minde and manners brightly shines
In his well-torned and true-filed lines:
In each of which, he seemes to shake a Lance,
As brandish't at the eyes of Ignorance.
Sweet Swan of Avon! what a sight it were
To see thee in our waters yet appeare,
And make those flights upon the bankes of Thames,
That so did take Eliza and our James!
But stay, I see thee in the Hemisphere
Advanc'd, and made a Constellation there!
Shine forth, thou Starre of Poets, and with rage
Or influence, chide or cheere the drooping Stage;
Which, since thy flight frō hence, hath mourn'd like night,
And despaires day, but for thy Volumes light.

BEN: JONSON.

Upon the Lines and Life of the Famous Scenicke Poet,
Master WILLIAM SHAKESPEARE.

THOSE hands which you so clapt, go now and wring,
You Britaines brave; for done are Shakespeare's dayes:
His dayes are done, that made the dainty Playes
Which make the Globe of heav'n and earth to ring.
Dry'de is that veine, dry'd is the Thespian Spring,
Turn'd all to teares, and Phœbus clouds his rayes:
That corps, that coffin, now besticke those bayes,
Which crown'd him Poet first, then Poets' King.
If Tragedies might any Prologue have,
All those he made, would scarce make one to this:
Where Fame, now that he gone is to the grave,
(eath's publique tyring-house) the Nuncius is.
For, though his line of life went soone about,
The life yet of his lines shall never out.

HUGH HOLLAND.

The Workes of William Shakespeare, containing all his Comedies, Histories, and Tragedies: Truely set forth, according to their first ORIGINALL.

The Names of the Principall Actors in all these Playes.

William Shakespeare.
Richard Burbadge.
John Hemmings.
Augustine Phillips.
William Kempt.
Thomas Poope.
George Bryan,
Henry Condell.
William Slye.
Richard Cowly.
John Lowine.
Samuell Crosse.
Alexander Cooke.
Samuel Gilburne.
Robert Armin.
William Ostler.
Nathan Field.
John Underwood.
Nicholas Tooley.
William Ecclestone.
Joseph Taylor.
Robert Benfield.
Robert Goughe.
Richard Robinson.
John Shancke.
John Rice.

A Catalogue of the severall Comedies, Histories, and Tragedies contained in this Volume.

COMEDIES.

The Tempest.
The Two Gentlemen of Verona.
The Merry Wives of Windsor.
Measure for Measure.
The Comedy of Errours.
Much adoo about Nothing.
Loves Labour lost.
Midsommer Nights Dreame.
The Merchant of Venice.
As You Like It.
The Taming of the Shrew.
All is Well, that Ends Well.
Twelfe-Night, or What You Will.
The Winters Tale.

HISTORIES.

The Life and Death of King John.
The Life and Death of Richard the Second.
The First Part of King Henry the Fourth.
The Second Part of K. Henry the Fourth.
The Life of King Henry the Fift.
The First Part of King Henry the Sixt.
The Second Part of King Hen. the Sixt.
The Third Part of King Henry the Sixt.
The Life and Death of Richard the Third.
The Life of King Henry the Eight.

TRAGEDIES.[a]

The Tragedy of Coriolanus.
Titus Andronicus.
Romeo and Juliet.
Timon of Athens.
The Life and Death of Julius Cæsar.
The Tragedy of Macbeth.
The Tragedy of Hamlet.
King Lear.
Othello, the Moore of Venice.
Anthony and Cleopater.
Cymbeline King of Britaine.

ADDITIONAL COMMENDATORY POEMS

PREFIXED TO THE FOLIO EDITION OF 1632.

Upon the Effigies of my worthy Friend,
the Author,
Master William Shakespeare,
and his Workes.

SPECTATOR, this Life's Shaddow is ; To see
The truer image and a livelier he,
Turne Reader. But, observe his Comicke vaine,
Laugh, and proceed next to a Tragicke straine,
Then weep, So when thou find'st two contraries,
Two different passions from thy rapt soule rise,
Say, (who alone effect such wonders could)
Rare Shake-speare to the life thou dost behold.

An Epitaph on the admirable Dramaticke Poet,
W. Shakespeare.[b]

WHAT neede my Shakespeare for his honour'd bones
The labour of an Age in piled stones,
Or that his hallow'd Reliques should be hid
Under a star-ypointing Pyramid ?
Dear Sonne of Memory, great Heire of Fame,
What needst thou such dull witness of thy Name ?
Thou in our wonder and astonishment
Hast built thyselfe a lasting Monument :
For whil'st, to th' shame of slow-endevouring Art,
Thy easie numbers flow, and that each heart[c]
Hath from the leaves of thy unvalued[d] Booke
Those Delphicke Lines with deep Impression tooke ;
Then thou, our fancy of herself bereaving,
Dost make us Marble with too much conceiving ;
And, so Sepulcher'd, in such pompe dost lie,
That Kings for such a Tombe would wish to die.

On Worthy Master Shakespeare and his Poems.

A MIND reflecting ages past, whose cleere
And equall surface can make things appeare
Distant a Thousand yeares, and represent
Them in their lively colours, just extent.
To out-run hasty Time, retrive the fates,
Rowle backe the heavens, blow ope the iron gates
Of Death and Lethe, where (confused) lye
Great heapes of ruinous mortalitie.
In that deepe duskie dungeon to discerne
A royal Ghost from Churles ; By art to learne
The Physiognomie of shades, and give
Them suddaine birth, wondring how oft they live ;
What story coldly tells, what Poets faine
At second hand, and picture without braine,
Senselesse and soullesse showes. To give a Stage
(Ample and true with life) voice, action, age,
As Plato's yeare and new Scene of the world
Them unto us, or us to them had hurld :
To raise our auncient Soveraignes from their herse,
Make Kings his subjects ; by exchanging verse
Enlive their pale trunkes, that the present age
Joyes in their joy, and trembles at their rage :
Yet so to temper passion, that our eares
Take pleasure in their paine : And eyes in teares
Both weepe and smile : fearefull at plots so sad,
Then, laughing at our feare ; abus'd, and glad
To be abus'd ; affected with that truth
Which we perceive is false ; pleas'd in that ruth
At which we start ; and by elaborate play
Tortur'd and tickled ; by a crablike way
Time past made pastime, and in ugly sort
Disgorging up his ravaine for our sport——
——While the Plebeian Impe, from lofty throne,
Creates and rules a world, and workes upon
Mankind by secret engines ; Now to move
A chilling pitty, then a rigorous love :
To strike up and stroake down, both joy and ire ;
To steere th' affections ; and by heavenly fire
Mould us anew. Stolne from ourselves———
This, and much more which cannot bee express'd
But by himselfe, his tongue, and his own brest,
Was Shakespeare's freehold ; which his cunning braine
Improv'd by favour of the nine-fold traine,
The buskind Muse, the Commicke Queene, the grand
And lowder tone of Clio ; nimble hand,
And nimbler foote of the melodious paire,
The silver-voyced Lady ; the most faire
Calliope, whose speaking silence daunts,
And she whose prayse the heavenly body chants.
These jointly woo'd him, envying one another,
(Obey'd by all as Spouse, but lov'd as brother),
And wrought a curious robe of sable grave,
Fresh greene, and pleasant yellow, red most brave,
And constant blew, rich purple, guiltlesse white,
The lowly Russet, and the Scarlet bright ;
Branch'd and embroidred like the painted Spring,
Each leafe match'd with a flower, and each string
Of golden wire, each line of silke ; there run
Italian workes whose thred the Sisters spun ;

---

[a] *Troilus and Cressida* although not found in this list, is yet inserted in the collection. From this circumstance, and because the play has only one leaf paged, the figures of which, 79 and 80, do not correspond, any more than the signatures, with the preceding and following pages, Farmer inferred that the insertion of *Troilus and Cressida* was an after-thought of Heming and Condell. Its omission from the Catalogue may be accounted for by the supposition that the folio was printed off before the player editors had purchased the right of publishing it from Bonian and Whalley, who brought out the quarto impression in 1609.

[b] These famous lines are Milton's.

[c] The folio reads *part*, an obvious misprint for "heart," the word found in the edition of Milton's Minor Poems, 1645.

[d] — unvalued—] *Inestimable.*

And there did sing, or seeme to sing, the choyce
Birdes of a forraine note and various voyce.
Here hangs a mossey rocke ; there playes a faire
But chiding fountaine, purled : Not the ayre,
Nor cloudes nor thunder, but were living drawne,
Not out of common Tiffany or Lawne,
But fine materialls, which the Muses know,
And onely know the countries where they grow.
Now, when they could no longer him enjoy,
In mortall garments pent, " death may destroy,"
They say, " his body, but his verse shall live,
And more then nature takes, our hands shall give.
In a lesse volume, but more strongly bound,
Shakespeare shall breathe and speak, with Laurell crown'd
Which never fades. Fed with Ambrosian meate
In a well-lyned vesture, rich and neate."
So with this robe they cloath him, bid him weare it,
For time shall never staine, nor envy teare it.

The friendly admirer of his Endowments,
I. M. S.[a]

[a] The author of this magnificent tribute to the genius of Shakespeare is unknown. By some writers it has been ascribed to Milton; by others to Jasper Mayne; Mr. Boaden conjectured it was from the pen of George Chapman; and the Rev. Joseph Hunter suggests the probability that the writer was *Richard James*, author of a poem called *Iter Lancastrense*, and that the initials *I. M. S.* represented *IaMeS*.

ADDENDA AND CORRIGENDA.

VOL. I.

INTRODUCTION TO "THE TWO GENTLEMEN OF VERONA."

P. 1. "*— a work very popular in Spain towards the end of the* seventeenth *century.*" Read: "sixteenth *century.*"

LOVE'S LABOUR'S LOST.

P. 52. "*Why should I joy in any abortive birth?*
At Christmas I no more desire a rose,
Than wish a snow in May's new-fangled shows:
But like of each thing that in season grows."

"Shows" here is a manifest misprint. I would read:—
"— a snow *on* May's new-fangled *wreath.*"

P. 53, note (a). Add, after "*very small game*":—But Steevens was evidently unconscious of its being a proverbial expression. It occurs in Whetstone's "Promos and Cassandra," Part I. Act III. Sc. 6:—

"A holie hood makes not a Frier devoute
He will playe at small game, or he *sitte out.*"

Ibid. note (b). "*Mr. Collier's old annotator proposes garrulity;*"—Read: Mr. Collier's annotator proposes *garrulity*, which he borrowed no doubt from Theobald, who in 1729, suggested it to Warburton. See Nichols's *Illustrations*, Vol. II. p. 317.

P. 64, note (b). Add:—Belly-doublet is in fact nonsense. The doublets were made some without stuffing—thin bellied—and some bombasted out:—"Certain I am, there never was any kind of apparel ever invented, that could more disproportion the body of man, than these doublets with *great bellies* hanging down, and stuffed," &c. &c.—STUBBES.

Ibid. note (c). Add:—Mr. Collier's annotator reads, "By my *pain* of observation," a reading first suggested by Theobald in 1729. Nichols's *Illustrations*, Vol. II. p. 320.

P. 67. "*This senior-junior* (4) *giant-dwarf.*" Dele (4).

P. 80. "*— prisons up,*"—Read: with the old editions: *poisons up*, and, in corroboration, see Act V. Sc. 2:—

"If this, or more than this, I would deny,
To *flatter up* these powers of mine with rest,
The sudden hand of death close up mine eye:"

And, stronger still, the following from King John, Act IV. Sc. 3:—

"Put but a little water in a spoon,
And it shall be, as all the ocean,
Enough to *stifle such a villain up.*"

Ibid. "*Makes heaven drowsy with the harmony.*"
A consonant idea occurs in Shirley's "Love Tricks," Act IV. Sc. 2:—

"Those eyes that grace the day, now shine on him,
He her Endymion, she his silver moon,
The tongue that's able to rock Heaven asleep,
And make the music of the spheres stand still."

P. 83, note (c). "*— and Mr. Dyce says nothing can be more evident than that Skakespeare so wrote,*" &c. Read: and Mr. Dyce says, "Nothing can be more evident than that Shakespeare wrote," &c.

P. 84, note (e). In this note, strike out the clause, "*Hence the equivoque, which was sometimes in allusion to snuff for the nose, and sometimes to the snuff of a candle.*"

P. 85. "*And shape his service wholly to my* behests;
And make him proud to make me proud that jests!"

I would now read, *hests*, with Mr. Sidney Walker, instead of *behests.*

Ibid. "*Arm'd* in arguments;—Read: "Armed *in arguments;* &c."

Ibid. note (e). It meant I now suspect, *deeply in love*, applied to a love-sick person. In this sense it occurs in the excellent old comedy of "Roister Doister," Act I. Sc. 2.

P. 91. "*Above this world: adding thereto, morever.*" Read: "moreover."

COMEDY OF ERRORS.

P. 120, note (a). See also note (b) Vol. III. p. 62.

P. 121, note (f). But to carry out this metaphor, *serious* hours, should be *several* hours. The integrity of the allusion is destroyed by *serious.* I suspect, however, the corruption lies in the word *common.*

P. 124, note (b). So also in Ben Jonson, "Sejanus," Act V. Sc. 4:—

"Cut down,
Drusus, that upright *elm;* wither'd his *vine.*"

P. 129. "*Sing, syren,*"—Read: "*Sing,* siren."

P. 136. "*With his mace.*" It ought to have been mentioned that the sergeants carried a staff or small *mace* in their hands. See "The Example," by Shirley, Act III. Sc. 1.

THE TAMING OF THE SHREW.

P. 227, note (d). Another instance may be added from Taylor, the Water Poet's, "Anagrams and Sonnets," fol. 1630:—

"He that's a mizer all the yeere beside
Will revell now, and for no cost will spare,
A poxe hang sorrow, *let the world go slide,*
Let's eate and drinke, and cast away all care."

P. 228, note (a). Add:—By "Brach Merriman,—the poor cur is emboss'd," &c. is meant, *Couple Merriman with a female hound,*—the poor cur is, &c. So in the next line, "and couple Clowder with the deep-mouth'd brach."

P. 229, note (a). "*Sinclo to this line. Sinclo,*" &c. Read: "Sinklo *to this line.* Sinklo," &c.

P. 233. *I—wis, it is not half way to her heart.*
Dele the hyphen.

P. 239. "*My mind presumes, for his own good, and yours.*" Mr. Collier's annotator, adopting a suggestion of Theobald's, (see Nichols's *Illustrations*, Vol. II. p. 334,) reads, "*— for his own good, and* ours."

P. 246. "*In cypress chests my arras, counterpoints,*" &c.—Read: "*arras* counterpoints," &c.

P. 264. "*What! up and down, carv'd like an apple tart?*" Read: "What up and down, carv'd like an apple tart!"

P. 266, note (c). I am now partly of opinion that "expect" here means, *attend, pay attention,* and that the passage should be pointed thus,—"I cannot tell. Expect! they are busied," &c. The word occurs with this sense apparently in Jonson's Masque of "Time Vindicated."

"Hark! it is Love begins to Time. Expect. [*Music*]."

P. 272, note (a). Perhaps, after all, the old text is right, but the two words have been inadvertently made into one: "therefore, sir, *as surance,*" *i.e.* as proof.

P. 273. "*We three are married, but you two are sped.*"

Of *sped*, in this place, the commentators can make no sense. It perhaps means *promised*. See "A Proper Sonet, Intituled, Maid will you Marrie," in "the Gorgeous Gallery of Gallant Inventions," part ii. p. 48 :—

"Why then you will not wed me?—
No sure, Sir, I have *sped* me."

The lover then goes on in answer to say,

"It is a woman's honestie
To keep her *promise* faithfully."

King John.

P. 293, note (a). I now think the original text is possibly correct, and that the thought running through the passage and which sufficiently explains it, is, that there is peculiar hardship in Arthur suffering, not only for the sins of the grandmother, (which might be regarded as the common lot—"the canon of the law,") but by the instrumentality of the person whose sins were thus punished; the grandmother being the agent inflicting retribution on her grandson for her own guilt.

"I have but this to say,—
That he's not only plagued for her sin,
But God hath made her sin and her the plague
On this removed issue: plagued for her
And with [or by] her plague—her sin: his injury
Her injury—the beadle to her sin.
All [is] punished in the person of this child,
And all for her; a plague upon her."

P. 302, note (a). I am not at present so satisfied of the propriety of Mr. Dyce's ingenious emendation *uptrimmed* as I was formerly. In old times it was a custom for the bride at her wedding to wear her hair unbraided, and hanging loose over her shoulders. May not Constance by "— a new *untrimmed* bride," refer to this custom? Peacham in describing the marriage of the princess Elizabeth with the Palsgrave says that "the bride came into the chapell with a coronet of pearle on her head, and *her haire dischevelled* and hanging down over her shoulders." Compare, too, "Tancred and Gismunda," Act V. Sc. 1. :—

"So let thy tresses flaring in the wind
Untrimmed hang about thy bared neck."

P. 303, note (b). "*Against the thing thou swear'st,*" query, "swearest by"?

P. 318, note (a). "Whose *confidential parley*." Rather whose *secret dispatch*. There is an instance of *private* used substantively in Ben Jonson's "Every Man in his Humour," Act IV. Sc. 5. "I will tell you, sir, by the way of *private*, and under seal."

P. 319. "*Thou'rt damn'd as black*—" It should have been remarked that Shakespeare had here probably in his mind the old religious plays of Coventry, some of which in his boyhood he might have seen, wherein the *damned souls had their faces blackened*.

In Sharp's Dissertation on these performances, the writer speaking of "White and Black Souls," observes:—"Of these characters the number was uniformly three of each, but sometimes they are denominated 'savyd' and 'dampnyd Sowles,' instead of white and black." And in the same work we meet with,

"Itm̃ payd to iij whyte sollys vs"
"Itm̃ payd to iij blake sollys vs"
"Itm̃ for makyng and mendynge of the blakke soules hose vjd"
"p'd for blakyng the sollys fassys."

Ibid. note (c). Add the following example from Florio's "Worlde of Wordes." "Ruffare, *to rifle, to skamble.*"

P. 321, note (c). Johnson is right. Florio after explaining *Foragio* to mean fodder, &c., says it had anciently the sense of *Fuora*, which is *out, abroad, forth, &c.*

A Midsummer Night's Dream.

P. 358. In some of the early copies of this edition, a part of Bottom's speech runs, "*Ladies, fair ladies, I would wish you, I would request you, I would entreat you not to fear,*" &c. Read: "Ladies, or fair ladies, I would, wish you, or I would request you, or, I would entreat you, not to fear," &c.

P. 359. For "*Exit,*" after "thou art translated:"—Read: *Exeunt Snout and Quince.*

P. 363, note (a). "*The critical remedy applied, afforded.*" Dele *applied.*

Subsequent consideration induces me to believe that the emendation of Mr. Collier's annotator, mentioned in the above note, is uncalled for.

P. 365, note (b). "*O me! what means my love?*" I should now adhere to the old text,—

"O, me! what *news* my love?"

Mr. Collier's attempt to substantiate his annotator's reading *means* by reference to a passage in Nash and Marlowe's "Dido, Queen of Carthage," where he proposes the puerile change of "*newly* clad" for "*meanly* clad," is a signal failure. The passage in the original stands thus:—

"Achates, thou shalt be so *meanly* clad,
As sea-born nymphs shall swarm about thy ships,
And wanton mermaids court thee with sweet songs."

And *meanly* is an obvious misprint for "*mienly,*" i.e. *shapely.*

P. 377. "*For, by thy gracious, golden, glittering gleams.*" For *gleams,* I would now read with the second folio, "streams."

Merchant of Venice.

P. 417, note (f). Add: which the said corrector borrowed from Theobald. (See Nichols's *Illustrations,* Vol. II. p. 308.)

P. 419, note (a). "*For intermission,*" after all may mean, *for fear of interruption.* So in "King Lear," Act II. Sc. 4:—

"*Delivered letters spite of* intermission."

P. 421. "*How true a gentleman you send relief.*" See note (d), p. 342, Vol. I.

P. 425. "*A woollen bagpipe.*"

Mr. Collier's annotator reads, "*bollen* bagpipe," and Mr. Dyce adopts the change: for "What writer," he says, "ever used such an expression as a *woollen bagpipe?* Might we not with almost equal propriety talk of a *woollen lute,* or a *woollen fiddle?*" But see Massinger's play of "The Maid of Honour," Act IV. Sc. 4:—

"Walks she on *woollen feet?*"

Richard the Second.

P. 479. "*Great Duke of Lancaster, come to thee,*" read:— "*I come to thee.*"

Henry the Fourth. Part I.

P. 508. For "*Edward Mortimer,*" Read: "Edmund *Mortimer.*"

P. 511. After, "*spent with crying—bring in,*" insert (d).

P. 525. For "*Or prisoner's ransom,*" Read: "Of, *prisoner's ransom.*"

P. 531, note (b). Add: perhaps correctly; see "A Woman is a Weathercock," Act I. Sc. 2:—

"But did that little old dried neat's tongue, that *eel-skin* get him?"

P. 534. "*The likeness of a fat old man.*" We should read as in the quarto, "*the likeness of* an old fat man."

P. 540, note (e). Add: It meant to *mix* or *mingle:* thus, in Greene's "Quip for an Upstart Courtier:"—"You *card* your beer (if you see your guests beginning to get drunk), half small half strong." Again, in Hackluyt's Voyages, Vol. II. p. 489:—"They drinke milke, or warme blood, and for the most part *card* them both together."

P. 631, note (1). For "*Asunctus,*" read "Asunetus."

MERRY WIVES OF WINDSOR.

P. 650, note (a). The emendation of "physician" for *precisian* is really Theobald's. (See Nichols's *Illustrations*, Vol. II. p. 274.)

P. 653, note (e). An antithesis was possibly intended between *firmly* and *frailty*. The meaning being,—"Who thinks himself so secure on what is a most brittle foundation."

P. 665, note (a). Add: The meaning being—I see what you would be if Fortune were as bountiful to you as Nature has been.

VOL. II.

ALL'S WELL THAT ENDS WELL.

P. 18. "*Where hope is coldest, and despair most fits.*" Mr. Collier assigns the emendation "*fits*" for *shifts* to a MS. correction in Lord Ellesmere's folio, 1623, but it is due to Theobald. (See Nichols's *Illustrations*, Vol. II. p. 343.)

P. 23, note (a). For "*Act V. Sc. 2*," read "*Act V. Sc. 5*."

P. 40, note (a). I believe now the old text is correct; *made*, in the sense of being fortunate, is a very common expression, even at this day.

KING HENRY THE FIFTH.

P. 87, note (a). "Nook-shotten isle," means, in fact, an isle *spawned* in *a corner*. *Shotten-herring* is a herring that has spawned his roe. "Here comes Romeo without his roe."—"Romeo and Juliet," Act II. Sc. 4.

Ibid. note (f). So in the "Taming of the Shrew," Act I. Sc. 1:—

"Tranio, I burn, I pine, I perish, Tranio,
If *I achieve* not this young modest girl."

Again in "The Malcontent," Act V. Sc. 4:—

"Slave take thy life:
Wert thou defenc'd, through blood and wounds
The sternest horror of a civil fight,
Would *I atchieve* thee."

P. 92. Prefix "Cho," to the first line.

P. 108. Prefix "Cho," to the first line.

PERICLES.

P. 183. "*Her face the book of praiess*," Read: "*Her face the book of* praises."

P. 187. "*His seal'd commision*," Read: "*His seal'd* commission."

P. 192. "*If it be a day fits you, scratch out of the calendar*," &c. "Fits you," possibly means *disorders you, puts you out of sorts, wrenches you*. So in "Sonnet CXIX," "How have mine eyes out of their spheres been *fitted*," i.e. been *started, wrenched*.

P. 213, note (a). So in "Measure for Measure," Act IV. Sc. 2:—"And indeed, *his fact*, till now in the government of lord Angelo, came not to an undoubtful proof."

TWELFTH NIGHT; OR, WHAT YOU WILL.

P. 233. (Introduction.) In speaking of the Manningham *Diary*, I erred in attributing to Mr. Collier any share in the discovery of this interesting MS. I have before me now unquestionable evidence that the credit of its detection, as well as of determining its authorship, is solely due to the Rev. Joseph Hunter.

P. 249. "*Ass, I doubt not.*" This feeble pun upon the words *as* and *ass*, was an old joke. It occurs in a rare tract called, "A Pil to purge Melancholy," supposed to have been printed about 1599:—

"And for bidding me, come up *asse* into a higher roome."

P. 268, note (b). The literal meaning of "*I am for all waters*," was, undoubtedly, "I am ready for any drink." The cant term for potations, in Shakespeare's time, was *waters*; and to "breathe in your *watering*," "Henry IV." Pt. I. Act II. Sc. 5, meant to take breath while drinking. See Taylor's (The Water Poet, "Drinke and welcome, or the famous history of the most part of Drinkes in use in Greate Britaine and Ireland; with an especial Declaration of the Potency, Vertue, and Operation of our English Ale: with a description of all sorts of *Waters*," &c.

HENRY THE SIXTH. PART I.

P. 288, note (c). Add: which he took from Theobald. See Nichols's *Illustrations*, Vol. II. p. 452.

P. 289, note (a). Add: which we owe, not to Mr. Collier's annotator, but to Theobald. See Nichols's *Illustrations*, Vol. II. p. 414.

P. 320, note (a). *Lither* indisputably signified *lazy, sluggish*. See North's Plutarch, (Life of Sertorius) "— he saw that Octavius was but a slow and *lither* man." See also Florio in *voce* "*Badalone*." And compare "Why then give way, *dull* clouds, to my *quick* curses." "Richard the Third," Act I. Sc. 2.

P. 325, note (a). But yet see "Richard the Third," Act I. Sc. 3:—

"O princely Buckingham, I'll kiss *thy* hand,
In sign of league and amity with thee."

HENRY THE SIXTH. PART II.

P. 362, note (a). So in "Julius Cæsar," Act I. Sc. 2:—

"Brutus had rather be a villager,
Than to *repute* himself a son of Rome
Under these hard conditions."

TIMON OF ATHENS.

P. 500, note (a). For "*own ault*," read "*own* fault."

P. 502, note (a). I now prefer, "let him *make* his haste."

P. 507, note (4). For, "*writers of his period*," Read: "*writers of* Shakespeare's *period*." And at the end of the note add:—compare, too, the Water Poet's poem, called "A Thief," fol. 1630, p. 116.

KING RICHARD THE THIRD.

P. 575. "*Abate the edge of traitors*." Mr. Collier, upon the authority of his MS. annotator, changes "Abate" to *Rebate*, and lauds the "emendation" as indisputable. This, however, is only one of innumerable instances where the "old corrector," by the needless ejection of an ancient and appropriate word, betrays the modern character of his handy-work. "Abate" here means, *to blunt, to disedge*. So Florio, in voce, "Spontare," "*to abate the edge or point of any thing or weapon, to blunt, to unpoint*." See also, "Love's Labour's Lost," Act I. Sc. 1:—

"That honour which shall *bate* his scythe's keen edge."

MEASURE FOR MEASURE.

P. 612, note (a). The following extract from Markham's "Hunger's Prevention, or the whole Arte of Fowling, &c." 1621, substantiates the explanation given in this note. "For a Fowle is so wonderfully fearefull of a man, that albeit a Hawke *were turning over her to keepe her in awe*, yet upon the least show of a man she will rise and trust to her winges and fortune."

P. 637. "*Hark how the villain would close now.*" To the note (b) on the word "close," add: but most improperly; for "close" and not *gloze*, despite of all Mr. Collier can adduce in favour of the latter, is the genuine word. In proof of this take the following unanswerable quotations:—

"It would become me better than to *close*
In terms of friendship with thine enemies."
Julius Cæsar, Act III. Sc. 1.

"This *closing* with him fits his lunacy."
Titus Andronicus, Act V. Sc. 2.

"I will *close* with this country peasant very lovingly."
WEBSTER'S *Works, Dyce's ed.* p. 281.

"Thus cunningly she *clos'd* with him, and he conceaves her thoughts."—WARNER'S *Albion's England*.

P. 637, note (2). For "£6 13*s.* 4*d.*," read "£16 13*s.* 4*d.*" and for "£33 6*s.* 8*d.*," read "£133 6*s.* 8*d.*"

King Henry the Eighth.

P. 650. "*Things, that are known alike,* &c. Mr. Collier claims for his "corrector" the merit of reading here,—"Things, that are known *belike*, &c. but the substitution was made first by Theobald. See Nichols's *Illustrations*, Vol. II. p. 459.

P. 654, note (a). "*As first good company.*" We should, I think, read: "*As* feast, *good company.*"

P. 693, note (a). The reading of *culpable*, for "capable," which Mr. Collier assigns to his annotator, was I find originally proposed by Theobald. See Nichols's *Illustrations*, Vol. II. p. 468.

Cymbeline.

P. 712. After, "*Pays dear for my offences,*" insert [*Exit.*

P. 719, note (b). For "*number'd in the sense,*" Read: "cumber'd *in the sense.*"

VOL. III.

King Lear.

P. 58, note (b). For, "*misprint for* '*but,*'" Read: "*misprint for* 'not.'"

P. 69, note (d). I now believe "*sovereignty,*" a misprint for "*sovereignly.*"

P. 90, note (e). I should prefer, "Wantonizeth *thou at trial Madam?*"

P. 114. For, "*se'st thou this object, Kent?*" Read: "see'st *thou this object, Kent?*"

Coriolanus.

P. 136, note (a). "*Take only the following examples, from plays which that gentleman must be familiar with.*" Read: "— *must be* acquainted *with.*"

P. 146. For "*scarfs and handkerchief,*" Read: "*scarfs and* handkerchiefs."

P. 156, note (b). See Shirley's "Bird in a Cage," for a similar obscure use of the word:—

"Or for some woman's *lenity* accuse
That fair creation."

P. 161. After "*my unbarbed,*" insert (*f*).

P. 169. For, "*think our fellows are asleep,*" Read: "I *think our fellows are asleep.*"

Winter's Tale.

P. 209, note (a). After "*Pliny,*" add: *Natural History.*

P. 229, note (b). So in "Antony and Cleopatra," Act IV. Sc. 15:

"— *gentle,* hear me."

P. 241, note (a). Add: Sometimes this state was called *handling:* thus in the "London Prodigal;"—"Ay, but he is now in hucster's *handling* for (*i.e.* for fear of) running away."

P. 250. In the line "*Would I were dead, but that,*" &c. Dele the first comma.

Note (a). In addition to the examples given in this note, the following from Florio's "World of Words" deserves to be quoted. "*Poss'io morire,* an oath much used, as we say, *I would I were dead, I pray God I dye, may I dye.*"

Troilus and Cressida.

P. 272. "but, when the planets
In evil mixture, to disorder wander," &c.

Was Shakespear in this place thinking of a passage in Hooker's book "Concerning Laws, &c."? "If celestial spheres should forget their wonted motions, and by irregular volubility turn themselves any way as it might happen; if the prince of the light of heaven, which now as a giant doth run his unwearied course should, as it were, through a languishing faintness begin to stand and to rest himself; if the moon should wander from her beaten way, the times and seasons of the year blend themselves by *disorders and confused mixtures,* the winds breathe out their last gasp," &c. &c.

Hamlet.

P. 335. For, "*pray thee stay with us,*" Read: "*I pray thee stay with us.*"

P. 341, note (a). Add: So in Spenser's *Faerie Queene,* b. i. c. iii. s. 30:—

"A *dram* of sweete is worth a *pound* of sowre."

P. 358, note (b). Another example of the phrase occurs in a letter from Thomas Wilkes to the Earl of Leicester, under the date 1586 (*Egerton* MS. 1694, *British Museum*):—"I am arrived here in such a time and *sea of troubles;*" and it is employed by Spenser in the *Faerie Queene,* b. vi. c. ix. s. 31:—

"With storms of fortune and tempestuous fate,
In *seas of troubles,* and of toylesome paine."

P. 396, note (a). For "*no lory:*" read "*no* glory."

Julius Cæsar.

P. 416, note (a). If the old text required further confirmation it would be supplied by the following couplet from Daniel's "Vanity of Fame:"—

"Is this the *walke* of all your wide renowne,
This little point, this scarce discerned ile?"

P. 418, note (b). Compare likewise (which put this interpretation beyond doubt) the following lines of Sir Philip Sydney, quoted by Harington in his Ariosto (Orlando Furioso):—

"Not toying kynd, nor causlesly unkynd,
Not stirring thoughts, nor yet denying right:
Not spying faults, nor in plain errors blynd,
Never *hard hand, nor ever rains to light.*"

P. 436, note (b). So also in *the Faerie Queene,* b. i. c. i., ii., s. 20.

"— the thirsty land
Dronke up his *life.*"

Macbeth.

P. 476. "*Whose horrid image doth* unfix *my hair.*"

Query, *upfix?* That temptation whose horrid image *fixes* my *unstable* hair, and shakes my *seated* heart.

P. 477. "*The swiftest wing of recompence is slow,*" &c. The substitution of *wind* for "wing" in this line, which Mr. Collier credits his "annotator" with, was first proposed by Pope.

Antony and Cleopatra.

P. 543. For, "*Enthron'd 'n the market-place:*"—Read: "*Enthron'd i' the market-place.*"

P. 547. For, "*and therefore have:*"—Read: "*and therefore have* we."

P. 580. For, "*My country's high pyramids my gibbet:*"—Read: "*My country's high* pyramides *my gibbet.*"

Titus Andronicus.

P. 609. For, "*The snake ies rolled:*"—Read: "*The snake* lies *rolled.*"

Othello.

P. 675, note (*). After "*First folio,*" insert: "*your.*"

P. 687, line 35. For, "*Oth. What? what*" Read: "*Oth. What? what?*"

GLOSSARIAL INDEX.

GLOSSARIAL INDEX.

Barnacle, *a shell-fish*, iii. 50.
Barns, *bairns*, i. 720.
Base, *a rustic game*, i. 42.
Base-court, *lower court*, i. 474.
Bases, *an embroidered mantle, hanging from the waist to the knee, worn by knights on horseback*, also *the housings of a horse*, also *the hose*, iii. 11, 193.
Basilisco, i. 329.
Basilisks, *huge pieces of ordnance*, i. 525.
Basta, *enough*, i. 235.
Bastard, *a sweet wine*, i. 529.
Bat, *staff or club*, iii. 785.
Bate, *to flap the wings like a hawk*, i. 218.
Batlet, *a bat to beat linen with*, ii. 141.
Batten, *to feed*, iii. 370.
Battle, *an army*, ii. 92, 574, iii. 648.
Bavin, *a faggot of brushwood*, i. 540.
Bawcock, *beau coq, fine fellow*, ii. 261, iii. 200.
Bay-window, *bow-window*, ii. 268.
Bead's-man, *one whose duty is to offer up prayers for another*, i. 3, ii. 342.
Bear a brain, *to remember well*, i. 166.
Bear-garden, Parish, ii. 703.
Bear hard, *to rein in from mistrust or fear*, iii. 418, 426, 435.
Bearing-cloth, *an infant's mantle in which ‹ is carried to the font*, iii. 222.
Bear in hand, *to encourage, to buoy up*, i. 258, 575, 727, iii. 491.
Beaver, *the lower part of a helmet, sometimes used for the helmet itself*, i. 548.
Beck, *a bow*, ii. 470.
Become, *to adapt, to render fit, to adorn*, i. 31, ii. 151, 321, 783, 785.
Becoming, *self-restrained*, iii. 220.
Bed-fellow, *intimate friend*, ii. 76.
Bedlam-beggars, *mad beggars*, iii. 118.
Beetles, *overhangs*, iii. 342.
Beg a fool, *to ask in wardship*, i. 104, 120.
Begetter, *one who gets or procures*, iii. 758.
Beggar and the King, a ballad, i. 101.
Beguiled, *masked, disguised*, iii. 754.
Behave, *to control*, ii. 482.
Belike, *to favour, to approve*, iii. 506.
Be-mete, *to beat with a yard measure*, i. 264.
Bemoiled, *bedraggled*, i. 255.
Be naught a while, *a mischief on you!* ii. 128.
Bench-hole, *forica*, iii. 570.
Benefit, *a beneficiary*, ii. 330.
Benumbed, *stiff, inflexible*, iii. 281.
Bergomask, *a dance*, i. 378.
Bermoothes, the Bermudas, iii. 11, 48.
Beshrew, *to curse, to imprecate sorrow or evil on a person*, i. 85, 409.
Besmirch, *to soil, to befoul*, ii. 101, iii. 338.
Bessy, o'er the bourn, iii. 90.
Best, *best one, an epithet of endearment*, iii. 535.
Bestowed, *secreted, stowed*, i. 118.
Bestraught, *distracted*, i. 230.
Beteem, *to allow, to suffer*, i. 343, iii. 336.
Better part, *the spiritual part*, iii. 521, 771.
Better penny, *a proverbial phrase*, i. 640.
Bevel, *crooked*, iii. 778.
Bevis, Sir, ii. 699.
Bewray, *to betray, to discover*, ii. 315, 404.
Bezonian, *a term of contempt*, i. 621.
Bias, *a swelling out*, iii. 303.
Bid, *to invite*, i. 406, ii. 165, 166, iii. 603.
Bid forth, *invited out*, i. 406.
Bid the base, *to challenge in the game of "base,"* i. 42, iii. 724.
Biggin, *a coif*, i. 612.
Bilberry, *the whortleberry*, i. 682.
Bilbo, i. 642, 671.
Bilboes, *instruments of torture, fetters*, iii. 391.
Bills, to set up, *to post bills, to advertise*, i. 741.
Bills, *halberds, battle-axes*, i. 720, iii. 102.
Bird-bolt, *a description of archery*, i. 741.
Bisson, *blind*, iii. 355.
Biting the thumb, *a contemptuous action*, i. 160.
Blacks, *mourning habiliments*, iii. 200.
Blank, *a mark in gunnery*, iii. 211.
Blench, *to flinch, to start off*, ii. 628, iii. 204, 265.
Blend, *blended*, iii. 786.
Bless the bridal-bed, i. 386.
Bless the mark, i. 33, 401, iii. 648.
Block, *a hat mould*, i. 696.
Blood in, *with the blood up*, i. 71.
Blood-boltered, *clotted with blood*, iii. 502.
Blow, *to swell*, iii. 570.
Blue caps, *the Scotch*, i. 533.
Blunt, *dull, insensible*, ii. 443.
Board, *to accost*, i. 705, ii. 239.
Bob, *to rap, to hit*, i. 349, ii. 143, 574.
Bobbed, *tricked*, iii. 699.
Bodged, *bungled*, ii. 407.
Bodkin, *a stiletto, a dagger*, iii. 359.
Bodykins, God's, an oath, iii. 355.
Bolds, *emboldens*, iii. 109.
Bolted, *sifted*, iii. 235.
Boltered, *clotted*, iii. 502.
Bolters, *sieves*, i. 543.
Bolting-hutch, *the bin into which meal is bolted*, i. 534.
Bombard, or bumbard, *a barrel, a capacious vessel, sometimes of leather, for holding drink*, i. 534, ii. 696.
Bombast, *a sort of wadding used to fill out dresses*, i. 97.
Bona-robas, *women of pleasure*, i. 597.
Bone-ache, the Neapolitan, iii. 283, 308.
Boot, *help, advantage*, i. 449, ii. 319.
Boots, to give, *to sell a bargain*, i. 41.
Bordered, *restrained*, iii. 97.
Borne in hand, *encouraged by delusive promises*, iii. 491.
Borrowed, *assumed*, iii. 788.
Bosky, *woody*, i. 553.
Bots, *worms in the stomach of a horse*, i. 250, 520.
Bottled, *bloated*, ii. 523.
Bottom, *to wind round, or upon*, i. 25.
Bought and sold, *entrapped, betrayed, made a victim*, ii. 318, iii. 278.
Bourn, *boundary*, iii. 101, 359.
Bow, *yoke*, ii. 155.
Bowed, *bent*, ii. 664.
Brach, *a hound bitch*, i. 228.
Braid, *false, deceitful*, ii. 39.
Braved, *bedizened, ornamented*, i. 264, ii. 144.
Bravery, *finery, ostentation*, ii. 144, 596, iii. 452.
Braving, *blustering, hectoring*, iii. 606.
Brawl, *a dance*, i. 102.
Break a day, *to make a breach of contract*, i. 438.
Break up, *to carve*, i. 69, 406.
Break with him, *to open the subject to him*, i. 8, iii. 425.
Breast, *voice*, ii. 246.
Breath, *a breathing, a combat for exercise*, iii, 305.
Breathe in watering, *to take breath while drinking*, i. 527.
Breeched, *sheathed, mired*, iii. 488.
Breed-bate, *an exciter of quarrels*, i. 647.
Brentford, Gillian of, i. 689.
Brewer's horse, i. 542.
Brew good ale, a proverb, i. 24.
Bribe-buck, i. 681.
Brize, *the gad, or horsefly*, iii. 272, 560.
Brock, *a badger*, ii. 252.
Broken music, *the music of stringed instruments*, ii. 120, 132, iii. 287.
Broker, *a pander, a procuress, a cheat*, i. 6, 298, ii. 32, iii. 786.
Brooched, *adorned, decorated*, iii. 576.
Brooded, *watchful*, i. 305.
Broom-groves, iii. 36.
Brown-bastard, *a sweet wine*, i. 529.
Brown-bill, *a battle-axe*, iii. 102.
Brownist, *a follower of Brown, a sectary*, ii. 257, 279.
Bruit, *report*, ii. 299, 439, iii. 318, 335, 514.

Clowns or Jesters, the practice of retaining, ii. 54.
Coast, *to advance*, iii. 730.
Coat, *coat of arms*, iii. 787.
Coats in heraldry, i. 384.
Cock-a-hoop, i. 170.
Cock and pye, *a popular adjuration*, i. 631.
Cockatrice, *a fabulous monster*, i. 189, ii. 262, iii. 743.
Cockle-hat, *a pilgrim's hat*, iii. 379.
Cockney, *a spooney, a cook*, iii. 79.
Cock-shut, *twilight*, ii. 569.
Coffin, *the crust of a raised pie*, i. 264, iii. 635.
Cog, *to load dice, to cheat, to defraud*, i. 89.
Cognizance, *a badge*, ii. 301.
Coil, *trouble, turmoil*, i. 7, 82, 366, iii. 359.
Colbrand the giant, i. 289.
Cold to bed, *to thy cold bed*, i. 227.
Collied, *smutted, blackened, obscured*, i. 343, iii. 669.
Collop, iii. 200.
Colme-kill, iii. 518.
Coloquintida, *a plant bearing a bitter fruit*, iii. 710.
Colours, *artifices*, ii. 299.
Colours on sculpture, iii. 257.
Colt, *to gull*, i. 523.
Combinate, *contracted*, ii. 614.
Combination, *contract*, ii. 276.
Come away, come away, a song, iii. 519.
Come off, *to pay*, i. 676.
Comforting, *encouraging, abetting*, iii. 213.
Commend, *to commit, to submit, to resign*, ii 48, iii. 214, 571.
Commission, *warrant, authority*, iii. 201.
Commit, *to fornicate*, iii. 88.
Commodity, *advantage, self-interest*, i. 298.
Common, *public*, i. 63.
Common liar, *rumour*, iii. 530.
Common players, *strolling players*, iii. 353.
Compact, *made up, compounded*, i. 129, iii. 723.
Companion, *a low fellow*, i. 138, ii. 722, iii. 179, 694.
Company, *companion*, ii. 40, 65.
Comparative, *ready in comparisons, or similes*, i. 513, 540.
Compassed, *arched*, iii. 724.
Competitor, *coadjutor, confederate, auxiliary*, i. 17, ii. 267.
Complements, *point-de-vice manners*, i. 53, 178, ii. 77.
Comply, *to fraternise, to play the courtier*, iii. 354, 394.
Compose, *accord, agree*, iii. 540.
Composure, composture, *composition*, ii. 494, iii. 284, 536.
Compt, in, *in trust, to be accounted for*, iii. 480.
Comptible, *susceptible, sensitive*, ii. 242.
Con, *to know, to allow, to award*, ii. 41, iii. 795.
Conceit, *imagination*, i. 184, 463.
Conceited, *conceptive, apprehensive*, iii. 752.
Concent, *agreement in music*, ii. 116.
Conclusions, *experiments*, ii. 717, iii. 373.
Concolinel, i. 64, 101.
Concupy, *concupiscence*, iii. 312.
Condition, *profession or art*, ii. 462.
Condition, *nature, disposition*, i. 397, ii. 41, 135, iii. 426, 542, 665.
Conduct, *a conductor, a guide*, i. 187, 210, ii. 263, 360, iii. 741.
Coney-catch, *to cheat*, i. 269.
Coney-catcher, *a sharper, a trickster*, i. 641.
Confess and be hanged, a cant phrase, iii. 687.
Conger and fennel, i. 593.
Conjurations, *entreaties*, i. 210.
Consent, *agreement, unison*, i. 617, ii. 116.
Consigned, *sealed*, iii. 301.
Consort, *fellowship, fraternity*, i. 29, 116, 186.
Consort, *a band of musicians*, i. 26.
Conspectuity, *vision, perception*, iii. 143.
Constancy, *consistency*, i, 375, iii. 434.
Contain, *to hold, to retain*, i. 435.
Contemptible, *mocking, contemptuous*, i. 712.
Content, *acquiescence*, iii. 722.
Content, *continent, self-restrained*, iii. 445.
Continence, *temperance*, iii. 598.
Continent, *capacious*, iii. 378.
Continuate, *uninterrupted*, iii. 685.
Contraction, *marriage-contract*, iii. 370.
Contrive, *to scheme, to plot*, i. 429, ii. 95, iii. 431.
Convent, *to agree, to be convenient*, ii. 276.
Convent, *to summon, to cite*, ii. 631, 689.
Convert, *to turn*, ii. 486.
Convertite, *a penitent, a convert*, iii. 745.
Convey, *to filch, to manage by stealth*, i. 482, 706, ii. 291, 710 iii. 506, 561.
Convicted, *vanquished*, i. 306.
Convince, *to conquer*, i. 96, ii. 716, iii. 481, 506.
Convive, *to feast together*, iii. 307.
Cooling-card, ii. 326.
Copatain-hat, *a high-crowned hat*, i. 269.
Cope, *to encounter*, i. 430.
Copy, *theme*, i. 142.
Coranto, *a dance*, ii. 20, 117.
Corinth, a cant name for *a bordello*, ii. 473.
Corinthian, *a wencher*, i. 527.
Cornuto, *a cuckold*, i. 671.
Corollary, *an overplus*, iii. 36.
Corporal of the field, *an aide-de-camp*, i. 67.
Costard, *the head*, i. 65.
Coted, *came alongside*, iii. 353.
Cot-quean, *a molly-coddle*, i. 202.
Cotsale, or Cotswold Hills, i. 686.
Couching, *crouching*, iii. 434.
Counsel, in counsel, *secret, in secret*, i. 17, 640, ii. 35, iii. 132.
Countenance, *to receive, to entertain*, i. 255, ii. 127, iii. 184.
Counter, to run, *to track the scent backward*, i. 150.
Counter-caster, *a disparaging term for merchant*, iii. 648.
Counterfeit, *a portrait*, i. 418, iii. 768.
Counterfeit, *a false piece of money*, iii. 283.
Counterpoints, *counterpanes*, i. 246.
Countervail, *to make equal or equivalent*, i. 183.
County, *an earl, a peer*, i. 196, 321.
Couplement, i. 93, iii. 763.
Courage, *mettle, spirit*, ii. 415.
Course, *carrière of a horse*, i. 306.
Courser's-hair, a vulgar superstition concerning, iii. 534.
Court-cupboard, *a cabinet*, i. 169.
Court holy-water, *glozing speeches*, iii. 84.
Court of wards, i. 150.
Courts, *a term in tennis*, ii. 69.
Cousin, *a kinsman*, i. 169.
Covent, *a convent*, ii. 626.
Cover, *to prepare the table*, ii. 142.
Cower, *to bend or sink*, ii. 212.
Cowl-staff, *a pole used to carry a bucket*, i. 666.
Coystril, *a mean groom, or peasant*, ii. 217, 238.
Cozenage, *sorcery, witchcraft*, i. 149.
Cozier, *a botcher of clothes or shoes*, ii. 247.
Crack, *a manikin*, iii. 134.
Cracked coin, iii. 400.
Crants, *crowns, garlands*, iii. 390.
Crare, *a small vessel of burden*, ii. 748.
Credent, *credible, plausible*, ii. 627, iii. 201.
Credit, *information*, ii. 269.
Crescive, *increasing, growing*, ii. 65.
Crewel, *worsted*, iii. 77.
Crispian, feast of, ii. 119.
Critic, *a cynic*, iii. 311, 777.
Critical, *cynical, censorious*, iii. 663.
Crooked, *bowed or crouched*, iii. 434.
Cross, *a coin stamped with a cross*, i. 56, ii. 141, 469.
Cross, *to pass across the path of a spectre*, iii. 332.
Crow-keeper, *a scarecrow, or a rustic employed to frighten crows*, iii. 120.
Crush a cup of wine, *an invitation to a carouse*, i. 164.
Cruzado, crusado, *a gold coin so called*, iii. 712.
Cry, *a pack, a troop or company*, iii. 164, 366.
Cry aim, *to encourage*, i. 39, 293, 662.
Cry Havoc ! *a signal for indiscriminate slaughter*, i. 295, iii. 158, 437.
Cry in the top of question, *to crow over or challenge*, iii. 353.
Cry on, *to announce, to assert*, ii. 272, 573, iii. 700.
Cue, *a stage term for the last words of a speech*, i. 358.
Cuisses, *armour for the thighs*, i. 548.
Cullion, *a paltry fellow*, i. 258, ii. 83.
Cunning, *knowing, skilful*, i. 233, ii. 204, 503, 623.
Curb, *to bow or truckle*, iii. 372.

Curiosity, *finical refinement*, ii. 492.
Curious, *scrupulous, over punctilious*, i. 265, iii. 553, 751.
Curious-good, *fastidiously precise*, iii. 751.
Curious-knotted, *abounding in intricate figures*, i. 55, 475.
Curled, *an epithet of gentility*, iii. 653, 748.
Cursed, *under the influence of a malediction*, iii. 314.
Curst, *cross-grained, sour, intractable, malicious*, i. 69, 365, ii. 257, iii. 73, 223, 730.
Curtail-dog, *a halting dog*, i. 652.
Curtle-ax, *a cutlass*, ii. 99, 136.
Custard, leaping into at civic feasts, ii. 56.
Customer, *a loose woman*, ii. 52, iii. 689.
Cut and long tail, *good and bad*, i. 668.
Cyprus, or Cypress, *a stuff like crape*, ii. 256.
DAFF, or doff, *to put off*, i. 174, 731.
Dagonet, Sir, in Arthur's Show, i. 628.
Damn, *to condemn*, iii. 444, 530.
Damnable, *damnably*, iii. 219.
Dancing Horse, Bankes's, i. 100.
Dancing sword, ii. 55.
Danger, *power*, i. 426, iii. 728.
Dangerous, *biting, mischievous*, i. 53, iii. 211, 423.
Dank, *wet, rotten*, i. 176, 355, 520.
Danskers, *Danes*, iii. 346.
Dare larks, to, ii. 678.
Darius's casket, ii. 333.
Darkling, *in the dark*, i. 355.
Darraign, *boldly prepared*, ii. 415.
Daubery, *juggling*, i. 675.
Day-woman, *dairy-woman*, i. 58.
Dealt on lieutenantry, *fought by proxy*, iii. 560.
Dear, *choice, rare, momentous, extreme*, i. 59, 449, ii. 135, iii. 293, 398, 618, 655, 658, 765.
Death at the ebb of tide, a popular opinion, ii. 117.
Death rock me asleep, beginning of a ballad, i. 627.
Death's fool, ii. 637.
Death's-man, *executioner*, iii. 748.
Death-tokens, *plague-spots forewarning death*, iii. 320, 559.
Debitor-and-creditor, *the title of some old treatises on book-keeping*, iii. 648.
Deceptious, *deceiving*, iii. 311.
Decked, *sprinkled*, iii. 9.
Deck of cards, *a pack of cards*, ii. 443.
Defeat, *to disfigure the countenance*, iii. 659.
Defeatures, *ill-looks, defacement*, i. 121, 145.
Defence, *knowledge of sword-play*, i. 216, iii. 384.
Defend, *to forbid*, i. 550, 704, 729, iii. 658.
Deftly, *smartly, featly*, iii. 501.
Defunctive, *mortuary*, iii. 795.
Defy, *to contemn or spurn*, iii. 791.
Defy, *to renounce*, i. 518.
Delighted, *delighting*, iii. 659.
Demerits, *good or ill deserts*, iii. 132, 651.
Demit, *to depress or cast down*, ii. 488.
Demi-wolves, *a species of dog*, iii. 492.
Denay, *to deny*, ii. 347.
Denier, *a French coin*, ii. 519.
Denunciation, *annunciation*, ii. 595.
Depart, *to part with*, i. 62, 298.
Depart, *to separate*, ii. 466.
Deprive, *to disinherit, to depose*, iii. 62, 342, 756.
Deracinate, *to root up*, ii. 112, iii. 272.
Derne, *earnest, eager*, ii. 201.
Descant, *variation in music*, i. 7, iii. 749.
Design, *to point out, to designate*, i. 450.
Desire you of, *desire of you*, i. 361, ii. 168.
Despatched, *bereft*, iii. 344.
Destractions, *detachments*, iii. 559.
Detect, *to exhibit, to display*, ii. 417.
Determine, *to end, to melt away*, i. 614, iii. 565.
Devil, roaring, ii. 119.
Devils, aerial, i. 331.
Dewberry, a sort of *blackberry*, i. 360.
Dich, *do it*, ii. 467.
Diet, to take, *to be under regimen*, i. 10.
Difference, *distinction*, i. 696.
Diffuse, *to disguise*, iii. 66.
Diffused, *wild, irregular*, i. 677.
Dilations, *delations, accusations,distillations*, iii. 677.
Dildos and fadings, *obscene burdens of old ballads*, iii. 232.
Direct, *explicitly, without ambiguity*, iii. 413.
Disability, *disparagement*, i. 15.
Disabled, *disparaged, impugned*, ii. 168, 326.
Disappointed, *unappointed*, iii. 344.
Discandying, *liquefying*, iii. 565, 573.
Disclose, *disclosure*, iii. 361.
Dishabited, *dislodged*, i. 294.
Dislike, *to express disapprobation*, ii. 168.
Dislimn, *to render indistinct, to obliterate*, iii. 573.
Dismes, *tenths*, iii. 279.
Dismount thy tuck, *draw thy rapier*, ii. 262.
Dispark, *to destroy the enclosures of a park*, i. 468.
Dispute, *to reason*, i. 191, iii. 235.
Dispute on, *to debate a cause*, iii. 708.
Disseat, *depose*, iii. 511.
Distain, *to cloud, to cast into the shade*, ii. 213.
Distempered, *disordered*, iii. 366, 649.
Distinctly, *separately*, iii. 10.
Distractions, *detachments*, iii. 559.
Distraught, *distracted*, i. 202, ii. 546.
Division, *variation in music*, i. 194.
Do, do, *an expression of contempt*, iii. 278.
Doff, *to do off, to put off*, i. 174, 731.
Dole, *distribution*, i. 574.
Do me right, *accept my challenge*, i. 733.
Do me right, *pledge me in a bumper*, i. 621.
Don, *to put on*, iii. 379.
Done, *destroyed*, iii. 729.
Double-cracks, *double-thunder-claps*, iii. 472.
Double-dealer, *one unfaithful in love or wedlock*, i. 740, ii. 272.
Double-pictures, *pictures that showed two faces by turning*, iii. 547.
Double set, *twice round*, iii. 668.
Dout, *to extinguish*, ii. 98.
Dower, *gift*, iii. 688.
Dowle, *a feather, down*, iii. 33.
Down-gyved, *hanging down loose*, iii. 347.
Dowzabel, i. 135.
Drachma, *a Greek coin*, iii. 442, 446.
Draught-house, *forica, drain, sewer, &c.*, ii. 605, iii. 809.
Draw dry foot, *to track by the scent of the foot*, i. 150.
Drawer, *a waiter*, i. 527, 587, 656.
Drawn fox, i. 544.
Dreams, John-a-, *a sleepy, muddle-headed fellow*, iii. 356
Dress, *to address, to prepare*, ii. 93, iii. 273.
Drinking habits of Englishmen, iii. 710.
Drinking in the morning fasting, i. 687.
Drive, *to rush pell-mell*, iii. 609.
Drollery, *a puppet-show*, iii. 33.
Drugs, *drudges*, ii. 491.
Drum, John, his entertainment, ii. 56.
Ducats of Venice, i. 439.
Dudgeon, *the wooden handle of a dagger*, iii. 483.
Due, *to endue*, ii. 317.
Dullard, *a dull observer*, ii. 762.
Dumbed, *silenced, rendered mute*, iii. 537.
Dumps, *heavy, mournful tunes*, i. 204, iii. 749.
Dun out of the mire, i. 215.
Duns the mouse, a proverbial saying, i. 215.
Dupp, *to lift up, to open*, iii. 379.
Durance, *a buff leather garment usually worn by sergean* i. 150.
Durance, robe of, *cant term for imprisonment*, i. 150.
Dwell, *to abide, to continue*, i. 399.
Dyeing the hair, custom of, i. 742.
EAGER, *aigre, sour*, iii. 344, 778.
Eagles' power of gazing on the sun, ii. 452.
Ear, *to plough*, i. 471, ii. 12, iii. 532, 536, 720.
Ecstasy, *aberration of mind*, i. 138, iii. 372, 785.
Eftest, *quickest, readiest*, i. 729.
Egal, *equal*, iii. 627.
Eggs for money, will you take, a proverbial phrase, iii. 202
Egyptian thief at point of death, ii. 281.
Eisel, *wormwood, vinegar*, iii. 391, 777.
Eld, *old, old age*, iii. 281.
Elements of the body, *principles of life*, iii. 553.

Force, *to strengthen*, iii. 512.
Forced, *stuffed*, iii. 309.
Fordo, *to destroy*, iii. 115, 116, 390.
Foreslow, *to delay, to loiter*, ii. 418.
Forespoke, *prejudiced, forbidden*, iii. 558.
Forfeits, *mulcts imposed by barbers*, ii. 633, 668.
Forfend, *to forbid*, ii. 329, 366, 762, iii. 701, 704.
Forgetive, *inventive*, i. 608.
Forked, *horned*, iii. 202, 679.
Forlorn, *fore-lost*, ii. 289.
Form, *the place where a hare sits*, iii. 728.
Formal, *reasonable, sober-minded*, i. 142, iii. 545.
Former, *fore, foremost*, iii. 453.
Forth, *out*, i. 395, ii. 632, iii. 442.
Forthright, *a straight path*, iii. 294.
Fortune my Foe, i. 688.
Forty, *a word expressing an indefinite number*, i. 150. ii. 293, 677.
Foul, *plain, homely*, ii. 154.
Four, *colloquialism for some*, iii. 350.
Fox, *a cant term for a sword*, ii. 101.
Frame, *order, limit*, i. 725.
Frampold, *cantankerous*, i. 656.
Frank, *a sty*, i. 586, ii. 524.
Fraughting, *constituting the fraught or freight*, iii. 7.
Frayed, *alarmed, frightened*, iii. 289.
French brawl, *a dance*, i. 102.
Fret, *a key, and also a stop-point, of a stringed musical instrument*, i. 243, iii. 367.
Friend, *a lover*, i. 704, iii. 431.
Frippery, *a shop for second-hand apparel*, iii. 40.
From the teeth, *in pretence*, iii. 556.
Front, *beginning*, iii. 775.
Frontier, *the forehead*, i. 515.
Frontlet, *a forehead cloth worn by ladies at night*, iii. 117.
Froth and lime, *a cant phrase for a tapster*, i. 644.
Frush, *to bruise, to break*, iii. 316.
Fulfilled, *filled to repletion*, iii. 751.
Fullam, *false dice*, i. 646.
Funeral entertainments, iii. 398.
Fustian riddles, ii. 279.
Gaberdine, *a large loose cloak*, i. 438, iii. 24.
Gad, *a sharp-pointed instrument*, iii. 622.
Gadshill infested by robbers, i. 562.
Gain-giving, *misgiving*, iii. 394.
Gait, *step, progress*, i. 648, iii. 36, 334.
Galliard, *a dance*, i. 104, ii. 69.
Gallias, *a huge galley*, i. 247.
Gallimanfry, *a medley*, iii. 234.
Gallow, *to affright*, iii. 85.
Gallowglasses, *Irish foot soldiers*, ii. 395, iii. 472.
Gambling in Shakespear's time, i. 100.
Gap, *a parenthesis*, iii. 232.
Gape, *to yell, to roar*, ii. 695, iii. 338.
Gaping pigs, i. 440.
Garagantua the giant, ii. 173, 278.
Garboils, *turmoils, commotions*, iii. 535.
Garden of Belmont, i. 441.
Garish, *gaudy, blazing*, i. 188, ii. 559.
Gascoigne, Chief Justice, i. 625.
Gasted, *dismayed*, iii. 73.
Gaudy, *festival*, iii. 565.
Gaunt, *fierce, eager*, iii. 537.
Geck, *a person derided*, ii. 276, 757.
General, *the generality, the multitude*, ii. 607, iii. 400, 423.
Generous, *noble, nobly born*, ii. 628, iii. 131.
Gentle, *gentle-one, an epithet of endearment*, iii. 229.
Gentry, *courtesy*, iii. 348.
German, *akin*, iii. 393.
German clocks, their introduction into England, i. 102.
Germens, *seeds*, iii. 84, 501.
Gest, *scroll containing the route of a progress*, &c. iii. 198.
Gests, *exploits*, iii. 570.
Ghostly, *spiritual*, i. 176.
Gib, *a cat, contraction of Gilbert*, i. 512, iii. 373.
Giddy, *inconstant*, i. 740.
Giglot, *a wanton*, ii. 321.
Gillian of Brentford, i. 689.
Gillivors, *gillyflowers*, iii. 231.
Gimmal-bit, *a bit in two parts*, ii. 99
Ging, *a gang*, i. 674.
Gird, *a sarcasm, a taunt*, i. 271.
Gis, by, *by Jesus*, iii. 379.
Give aim, *to direct*, i. 39.
Give out, *to surrender, to relinquish*, ii. 382.
Give the boots, *to sell a bargain*, i. 41.
Give the bucklers, *to yield oneself vanquished*, i. 744.
Give the nod, *to ridicule by gesture*, iii. 269.
Gleek, *to flout or scorn, to jest*, i. 204, 359.
Glib, *to geld*, iii. 209.
Glorious, *ambitious, ostentatious*, ii. 718.
Gloves in the cap, custom of wearing, iii. 119.
Gloze, *to wheedle*, i. 458, iii. 627.
God bless the mark, i. 401, iii. 648.
God buy you, *God be with you*, ii. 99.
God, dig you den, *God, give you good even*, i. 69, 197.
God, 'ild you, *God reward you*, ii. 168.
God save the mark, i. 516.
God warn us, ii. 159.
Gondola, description of the, i. 439.
Gongarian, i. 644.
Good cheap, *a bon marché*, i. 543.
Good even and twenty, *a popular salutation*, i. 653.
Good goose bite not, *a proverbial saying*, i. 180.
Good leave, i. 289.
Good life, ii. 246.
Good man, *a man of substance*, i. 397, iii. 128.
Good manners, book of, ii. 173.
Good wine needs no bush, ii. 174.
Gorbellied, *pot-bellied, swag-bellied*, i. 524.
Go to the world, *a matrimonial saying*, i. 707, ii. 11, 166.
Gourds, *false dice*, i. 646.
Gouts, *drops*, iii. 483.
Government, *moderation, forbearance, self-control*, ii. 409 iii. 752.
Gracious, *loving, comely, gentle*, i. 307, 417, 724, iii. 769.
Grange, *a solitary farm or lone house*, iii. 650.
Grave, *pernicious*, fatal, iii. 573.
Graves, *armour for the legs*, i. 603.
Greenly, *immaturely unwisely*, iii. 379
Green Sleeves, a tune, i. 651, 687.
Griefs, *grievances*, i. 551, iii. 445.
Grise, a step, ii. 257.
Gross, *palpable*, ii. 13.
Groundlings, iii. 361.
Growing, *accruing*, i. 133.
Grow to a point, *come to business*, i. 346.
Grudges, *murmurs of discontent*, iii. 599.
Grype, *the gryphon, or griffin, a vulture*, iii. 743.
Guard, *to ornament with a border*, i. 311, 404.
Guidon, *a standard*, ii. 99.
Gules, in heraldry, *red*, ii. 489, iii. 355.
Gulf, *the throat, the swallow*, iii. 501.
Gull, *a young unfeathered bird*, i. 554.
Gun-stones, *black roundles, stone-shot for cannon*, ii. 116.
Gust, *taste*, ii. 238, iii. 202.
Guts, *a lack-brain, a shallow pate*, iii. 402.
Gyve, *a shackle, a fetter*, iii. 664.
Hacket, Marian of Wincot, i. 229.
Haggard, *a wild unreclaimed hawk*, i. 714, iii. 679.
Halcyon, a bird, iii. 75.
Half-faces, *meagre visages*, i. 329.
Halidom, by my, *an old oath*, i. 31.
Hall, a hall! *make room*, i. 169.
Hallowmas Beggars, i. 42.
Hand, to bear in, *to encourage, to buoy up*, i. 258, 727, iii. 491.
Handfast, *mainprize, at large on security*, iii. 241.
Handsaw, *corruption of hernshaw, or heron*, iii. 354.
Hang by the walls, *to be hung up as useless*, ii. 768.
Hangings for theatres, ii. 332.
Hangings of walls in chambers of old castles, i. 495.
Hangman, *rogue, rascal, a name given to Cupid*, i. 715.
Happy, *accomplished*, ii. 737.
Happy man be his dole, *a trite phrase*, i. 234, 524, 668.
Happy the son whose father goes to the devil, **a proverb** ii. 452.

Hard, to bear, *to mistrust, to doubt, to fear*, iii. 418, 426, 435.
Harlocks, *wild mustard*, iii. 99.
Harlotry, *a term of reproach*, i. 201, 539, iii. 695.
Harlots, *base companions, villains*, i. 144.
Harmony of the soul, i. 441.
Harness, *armour*, iii. 571.
Harrow, *to subdue, to overcome*, iii. 330.
Harry, *to harass*, iii. 555.
Has the mends in his own hands, *must make the best of it*, iii. 265.
Hat at meals, wearing the, i. 439.
Haughty, *high*, ii. 302.
Haunt, *company*, iii. 375.
Have an eye of, *to see through*, iii. 353.
Having, *fortune, revenue, possession*, i. 662, iii. 787.
Havoc, cry, *a signal for indiscriminate slaughter*, i. 295, iii. 158, 437.
Hay, *a dance*, i. 84.
Hay, the, *a fencing term*, i. 217.
Hazard, *a term in tennis*, ii. 69.
Headborough, *a constable*, i. 228.
Heaven to earth, *an asseveration*, i. 557.
Heavy night, *a thick, cloudy night*, iii. 699.
Hefts, *heavings*, iii. 208.
Hell, *a vile dungeon in a prison*, i. 150.
Helpless, *giving no help*, i. 120, iii. 728.
Hem, boys, hem! the burden of an old song, i. 627.
Hence, *henceforward*, i. 623.
Henchman, *a page*, i. 351.
Henry the Fifth's early life, i. 503.
Hent, *to take*, iii. 228.
Hent, *a purpose*, iii. 368.
Herb-grace, *rue*, iii. 382.
Hercules and his load, iii. 399.
Here be with me, *mocking me with opprobrious gestures*, iii. 202.
Hereby, *as it may happen*, i. 58.
Hermits, *beadsmen*, iii. 480.
Herne's oak, i. 690.
Hero and Leander, ii. 173.
Herod, *a tyrant of the Miracle-plays*, iii. 401.
Hest, *command*, iii. 13, 29, 36.
Hey non nonny, *old ballad burden*, iii. 381.
Hey Robin, jolly Robin, a song, i. 281.
Hide fox and all after, *the game of hide and seek*, iii. 376.
High-men, *false dice*, i. 646.
Hight, *called, named*, i. 53, 55, 376, ii. 208.
High-tides, *high-days*, i. 300.
Hild, *held*, iii. 751.
Hilding, *degenerate*, i. 573.
Hillo, ho, boy! *Falconers' encouragement to hawks*, iii. 344
Hiren, i. 591.
His, *used for the impersonal its*, i. 480, ii. 10, iii. 75, 562, 598, 651, 725.
Hit it, can you, *a song or dance*, i. 70, iii. 607, 663.
Ho! *stop!* iii. 395.
Ho! ho! ho! *a fiendish or supernatural laugh*, i. 368, 384.
Hoar, *to make white with leprosy*, ii. 490.
Hobby-horse, *a pasteboard horse in May games*, i. 102.
Hobby-horse, *a by-word for an abandoned woman*, i. 65, iii. 203, 689.
Hob nob, *hit or miss*, ii. 263.
Hold or cut bow-strings, *a term in archery*, i. 382.
Holla! *a term of the manège*, ii. 151.
Holland, price of in Shakespeare's time, i. 566.
Honesty, *chastity, liberality*, ii. 32, 131, 477, iii. 213, 360.
Hood, *in falconry, to cover the hawk's eyes with a hood*, i. 218. ii. 91.
Hoodman, Hoodman blind, *Blind man's buff*, ii. 56.
Hope, *to expect*, iii. 540, 662.
Horologe, *a clock*, iii. 668.
Hot-house, *a house of ill fame*, ii. 600.
Houses in fencing, i. 216.
Houses in heraldry, i. 217.
Housewife, *a hussy or harlot*, iii. 577.
However, *anyway*, i. 4.
Hox, *to hough, to hamstring*, iii. 203.
Hugger-mugger, *secretly, by stealth*, iii. 379.
Hull, *to toss to and fro like a ship*, ii. 668.
Humorous, *perverse, capricious*, ii. 135.
Humorous-man, *the actor who personated fantastic characters*, iii. 353.
Humour of forty fancies, i. 250.
Humour of mispunctuation, i. 385.
Humphrey Hour, ii. 581.
Hundred merry Tales, i. 705, 742.
Hunt counter, *to track the scent backward*, i. 150, 576, iii. 380.
Hunt's-up, *a term employed by hunters for morning music, a song*, i. 219.
Hurly-burly, *uproar, tumult*, iii. 471.
Hurtling, *justling*, ii. 162.
Husbandry, *thrift*, iii. 482.
Hyen, *a hyæna*, ii. 160.
Hysterica passio, *the disease called the mother*, iii. 78, 119.
I, *the old form of ay*, i. 5, iii. 782.
I cannot tell, i. 577.
Iceland, or Iland dogs, ii. 117.
Ides, *the Roman name for particular days*, iii. 415.
Idle, *crazy, wild, mad-brained*, ii. 27, 36, 488, iii. 362.
Idle, *infertile*, iii. 656.
Idle bed, *bed of idleness*, iii. 425.
I' fecks, *in faith*, iii. 200.
Ignomy, *ignominy*, i. 560.
'Ild you, *yield you, reward you*, ii. 168.
Ill, *badly*, iii. 739.
Ill-erected, *erected for evil*, i. 483.
Ill-inhabited, *ill-lodged*, ii. 153.
Ill-sorted, *ill accompanied*, i. 591.
Imbared, *to lay bare*, ii. 67.
Immanity, *cruelty, ferocity*, ii. 322.
Imp, *son*, ii. 94.
Imp, *to amend a hawk's wing*, i. 462.
Impair, *unsuitable, unbecoming*, iii. 305.
Impartial, *neutral*. ii. 631.
Impeachment, *hindrance*, ii. 89.
Impleached, *interwoven, intertwined*, iii. 786.
Imperious, *imperial*, iii. 389.
Imperseverant, *imperceptive*, ii. 743.
Importance, *significance*, iii. 245.
Important, *importunate*, i. 143, 290, 704, ii. 36, 276, iii. 100.
Impose, *bidding, requirement*, i. 31.
Impossible, *incredible*, i. 705, ii. 19.
Impress, *a device, a motto*, i. 468.
In few, *in short, in brief*, i. 237, 574, iii. 9.
In blood, *with the blood up*, i. 71.
In by the week, a saying, i. 85.
In compt, *in trust*, iii. 480.
In deed, *in fact, in form*, iii. 345.
Imputation, *reputation*, iii. 275.
In print, *precisely, to the letter*, i. 12.
In youth when I did love, a ballad, iii. 404.
Inapposite similitudes, i. 563.
Incapable, *insusceptible, unintelligent*, ii. 531, iii. 385.
Incarnadine, *encrimson*, iii. 487.
Incensed, *prompted*, ii. 689.
Inch, *island*, iii. 473.
Inclip, *to embrace*, iii. 550.
Incony, *delicate, fine, pretty*, i. 67.
Increase, *produce*, iii. 774.
Indent, *contract*, i. 516.
Indian, dead, in exhibitions, iii. 49.
Indifferent, *impartial, passable, moderate*, i. 255, 466, ii. 665, iii. 352.
Indirectly, *wrongfully*, i. 291.
Induction, *beginning, entrance*, i. 536.
Indurance, *confinement*, ii. 690.
Informal, *deranged*, ii. 632.
Ingaged, *disengaged*, ii. 50.
Ingenier, or Ingener, *an ingenious person, an artist*, iii. 662.
Ingeniously, *ingenuously*, ii. 475.
Inhabitable, *not habitable*, i. 448.
Inherit, *to obtain possession, to possess*, i. 26, 448.
Inhibit, *to prohibit*, ii. 8.
Iniquity, a Morality character, ii. 601.
Inkhorn, *a bookman, a pedant*, ii. 305.
Inkle, *a kind of tape*, iii. 232.
Inland, *opposed to upland, urbanely-bred*, ii. 144, 152.

Lip, *to kiss*, iii. 687.
Lipsbury Pinfold, iii. 74.
Lists, *enclosures*, i. 495.
Lither, *lazy, idle*, ii. 320.
Little, *miniature*, ii. 149, iii. 354.
Lively, *living*, iii. 615.
Liver, the seat of love, i. 652, 726.
Livery, to sue, i. 497.
Living, *riches, possessions, resources*, i. 436.
Lob, *clown, fool*, i. 349.
Lockram, coarse linen, iii. 145.
Locks, love-locks, the fashion of wearing, i. 743.
Locusts, *insects, or the fruit of the locust tree*, iii. 710.
Lode-star, *leading or guiding star*, i. 381.
Lodge in a warren, i. 742.
Lodged, *layed*, i. 473.
Loggats, *a game like skittles*, iii. 387.
London, the King's Chamber, ii. 578.
'Long of, *because of*, i. 61, 366, ii. 317, 438, 762, iii. 182.
Loofed, *a sea-term, signifying to bring a ship nearer the wind*, iii. 560.
Loose, *to discharge*, iii. 70.
Loose bodied gown, *dress supposed to be indicative of a loose woman*, i. 264.
Lop, *faggot wood of a tree*, ii. 652.
Lordship, *dominion*, i. 342.
Love in idleness, *a flower*, i. 234.
Lover, *a friend*, iii. 431, 438, 765.
Loves, of all, *for love's sake*, i. 356, 656, iii. 673.
Low-crouched, *low-crooked*, iii. 434.
Low-men, *false dice*, i. 646.
Lower messes, *inferior persons*, iii. 203.
Lozel, a worthless fellow, iii. 213.
Luce, *a pike*, i. 639.
Lullaby, *a burden of songs and ballads*, iii. 639.
Lunes, *lunacy, mad freaks*, i. 673, iii. 211, 284.
Lupercalia, feast of, iii. 459.
Lurch, *to gain an easy victory at cards*, iii. 148.
Lush, *succulent*, iii. 19.
Lustique, *lusty*, ii. 20.
Luxury, *concupiscence*, ii. 635.
Lym, *a bloodhound*, iii. 92.
MACULATE, *stained, spotted*, i. 57.
Made up, *finished, accomplished*, ii. 498.
Magic verses to cause death, ii. 332.
Magot-pies, *magpies*, iii. 498.
Mahomet's dove, ii. 333.
Mahu, *a fiend*, iii. 89, 96, 120.
Mailed up, *wrapped up*, ii, 359.
Main, *main land*, iii. 83.
Main of light, *flood of light*, iii. 769.
Make, *a mute*, iii. 761.
Make a leg, *to make obeisance*, ii. 470, 520.
Make all split, a nautical expression, i. 346.
Make a shaft or a bolt, *here goes, hit or miss*, i. 667.
Make, Make the door, *to do, to bar the door*, i. 128, 653, ii. 128, 160, iii. 336.
Makeless, *mateless*, iii. 761.
Malkin, *a homely wench*, ii. 213, iii. 145.
Mall, Mistress, her picture, ii. 240, 277.
Mallecho, *malefaction*, iii. 363.
Malt-worms, *drunkards*, i. 521, 593.
Mammering, *hesitating*, iii. 676.
Mammet, *a puppet, a doll*, i. 198.
Mammock, *to rend, to tear*, iii. 134.
Man in the moon, legend of the, i. 386.
Manage, *to govern*, i. 286, 474.
Mandragora, *a powerful opiate*, iii. 537, 680, 711.
Mandrake, fabulously endowed with life, i. 220, ii. 370.
Mankind-woman, *a termagant, a virago*, iii. 167, 213.
Manner, *mainour, a thing stolen*, i. 54.
Manner, with the, *in the fact*, i. 54.
Manningtree ox roasted, i. 534.
Manqueller, *manslayer*, i. 582.
Many-many, *numberless*, iii. 368.
Map, *a picture*, iii. 618.
Marches, *borders, boundaries*, ii. 68, 413.
Marchpane, *a confection*, i. 169.
Margent, *margin*, i. 101.
Marian, Maid, Robin Hood's mistress, i. 544.
Marigold, *the sunflower*, iii. 231.
Masks for ladies' faces when riding, i. 44.
Masques and triumphs, i. 44.
Match, to set a, *to plan a robbery*, i. 513.
Mate, *to confound, to bewilder, to destroy*, i. 129, ii. 364.
Material, *full of matter*, ii. 154.
Maugre, *in spite of, notwithstanding*, ii. 257, iii. 112, 623.
Maund, *a basket*, iii. 784.
Meacock, *a chicken-hearted fellow*, i. 246.
Mealed, *mingled*, ii. 622.
Mean, *a term in music*, i. 7.
Measure, *a dance*, i. 103, 704, iii. 733.
Medecin, *a physician*, iii. 511.
Meeds, *deserts, merits*, ii. 411, 440, 466, iii. 393.
Mef, *to mix, to meddle*, ii. 42.
Meiny, *retinue*, iii. 77.
Melancholy of Moor-ditch, i. 562.
Memory, *memorial*, ii. 139, iii. 170.
Men of hair, *satyrs*, iii. 256.
Mends in his own hands, *must make the best of it*, iii. 265.
Mephostophilus, *a cant word for a gaunt-faced fellow*, i. 641
Mercatanté, *a merchant*, i. 260.
Mere, *quite*, ii. 32.
Mere, *sole, absolute, certain*, ii. 631, 678, iii. 666.
Mered, *entire, sole*, iii. 563.
Merely, *entirely, absolutely*, i. 712, ii. 40, 153, iii. 415.
Merit, *guerdon, reward*, i. 454.
Mermaid, *a siren*, iii. 726.
Merry-greek, *a wag or humourist*, iii. 268.
Metaphysical, *supernatural*, iii. 478.
Mete-yard, *a measuring yard*, i. 264.
Methoughts, *methought*, iii. 201.
Mewed, a term of falconry, i. 194.
Micher, *a vagabond*, i. 533.
Miching, *skulking*, iii. 363.
Milch, *moist*, iii. 355.
Mile-end, the musters at, i. 628.
Mill-sixpences, i. 642.
Mince, *to walk affectedly, to affect coyness*, i. 680, iii. 103.
Mineral, *a metallic vein in a mine*, iii. 375.
Minikin, *a darling*, iii. 90.
Minute-jack, *a little figure that struck the quarters of th clock*, ii. 485.
Mirable, *admirable*, iii. 305.
Miscreate, *spurious*, ii. 66.
Miser, *miserable caitiff*, ii. 327.
Misprised, *mistaken*, i. 363.
Misprising, *undervaluing, despising*, i. 714, ii. 29.
Misprision, *mistake, misunderstanding*, i. 363, 515, 725.
Mispunctuation, humour of, i. 385.
'Miss, *amiss*, iii. 722.
Miss, *to dispense with*, iii. 13.
Missives, *messages*, iii. 477.
Mistaken, *misapprehended*, ii. 649.
Mistful, *ready to weep*, i. 103.
Mistress, *a bowl used in bowling*, iii. 321.
Mistress Mall's picture, ii. 277.
Mobled, *muffled*, iii. 355.
Mock, *to scoff, to gibe*, iii. 678.
Model, *a mould*, i. 471.
Modern, *ordinary, common*, i. 190, 306, iii. 507, 582, 772.
Modo, *a fiend*, iii. 89, 96, 120.
Module, *model*, i. 327, ii. 41.
Moe, *to make mouths*, iii. 22.
Moiety, *a portion, also the half*, i. 537, iii. 735.
Moist star, *the moon*, iii. 332.
Mold-warp, *the mole*, i. 538.
Mome, *a blockhead, a dolt*, i. 127.
Moment, *import*, iii. 360.
Monarcho, *a crazy Italian so called*, i. 103.
Money-lenders' brown paper, ii. 638.
Monopoly privileges, iii. 117.
Monstrous, *unnatural, ominously prophetic*, iii. 420.
Montanto, *a term of fence*, i. 696.
Month's mind, i. 42.
Moon-calf, *a false conception*, iii. 25.

Moonish, *variable, inconstant*, ii. 153.
Moralize, *to interpret*, iii. 739.
More, *greater, further*, i. 309, ii. 76, iii. 741.
More and less, *great and small*, i. 575, iii. 774.
More sacks to the mill, a game, i. 77.
Morris, *Morisco dance*, ii. 55, 393.
Morris-pike, *Moorish pike*, i. 150.
Mortal, *deadly*, iii. 728.
Mort o' the deer, a strain on the horn, iii. 199.
Mortified, *ascetic*, iii. 510.
Most an end, *constantly, perpetually*, i. 33.
Mot, *motto or word*, iii. 746.
Motion, *puppet-show or puppet*, i. 11, iii. 255.
Motion, *the impulse of desire*, iii. 370.
Motley, *a fool*, iii. 376.
Mought, *might*, ii. 444.
Mouse, *a term of endearment*, i. 84, ii. 241.
Mouse-hunt, *an animal of the weasel tribe*, i. 202.
Mousing, *gorging, devouring*, i. 295.
Mowes, *mouths, ludicrous antics*, iii. 36, 354.
Much, *an expression of contempt*, i. 590, ii. 161, 468.
Muffler, *a covering to conceal a portion of the face*, i. 688.
Mule, Bajazet's, ii. 38.
Muleters, *muleteers*, iii. 558.
Mum-budget, *a pass-word*, i. 685.
Murdered persons bleeding on the approach of the murderer, ii. 576.
Murdering-piece, *a piece of artillery with several barrels*, iii. 380.
Muscadel, *a wine used in church at marriage ceremonies*, i. 276.
Musit, or Muset, *a gap in a hedge*, iii. 728.
Muss, *a scramble*, iii. 564.
Mutines, *mutineers*, i. 330.
Mutton, laced, a cant term for a courtezan, i. 41.
My cake is dough, *a proverbial saying*, i. 234, 270.
My heart is full of woe, a tune, i. 204.
NAPKINS, *handkerchiefs*, iii. 440, 784.
Naught a while, be, *a mischief on you!* ii. 128.
Naughty, *wicked, base*, i. 421, iii. 93.
Nay-word, a watch-word, i. 680, ii. 248.
Neapolitan bone-ache, iii. 283, 308.
Near, *in close confidence*, i. 705.
Near be, ne'er the near, a proverbial phrase, i. 484.
Neat slave, *a base cow-herd*, iii. 74.
Neeld, *needle*, ii. 208, iii. 741.
Neglection, *neglect*, ii. 206, 318, iii. 272.
Neif, *fist*, i. 370, 591.
Nether-stocks, *short stockings*, i. 529, iii. 77.
Next way, *the nearest way*, i. 540, ii. 12, iii. 223.
Nice, *trivial, effeminate, dainty*, i. 187, 209, 400, 574.
Nicely, *scrupulously*, ii. 209.
Nicholas' clerks, St., *cut-purses*, i. 521.
Nick, *to mark like a fool*, i. 143.
Nick, out of all, *beyond all reckoning*, i. 30.
Nicked, *emasculated*, iii. 563.
Night-rule, *a night revel*, i. 361.
Nill, *will not*, ii. 201.
Nine men's morris, *a rustic sport*, i. 383.
Nine Worthies, pageant of, i. 104.
Noble, a coin, i. 532.
Nobody, the picture of, iii. 32, 49.
Noddy, *a game at cards*, also *a noodle, a simpleton*, i. 5.
No had, an archaic expression, i. 315.
Noise, *a band of musicians*, i. 588.
Nonce, *for the occasion*, i. 514.
Nook-shotten, *spawned in a corner*, ii. 87.
No poynt, *non point*, i. 62, 89.
Nott-pated, *round-headed*, i. 528.
Novum, *a game played with dice*, i. 93.
Nurture, *breeding*, ii. 144.
Nut-hook, *a beadle or catchpoll*, i. 622, 642.
O, *orb, circlet or round*, iii. 581.
Oaken garlands, iii. 187.
Oath of fidelity by attendants of the nobility, ii. 767.
Oaths taken on the sword, i. 497, iii. 345.
Ob, *obolum, a halfpenny*, i. 535.
Oberon, of fairy legends, i. 383.
Obidicut, *a fiend*, iii. 96.
Objected, *proposed, projected*, ii. 299.
Obsequious, *funereal*, ii. 419, 515, iii. 334.
Obsequious, *obedient, submissive*, iii. 648.
Observation, *rites or observances*, i. 371.
Observed, *respectfully treated*, i. 609, 612.
Obstacle, *corruption of obstinate*, ii. 327.
Occupation, *handicraft*, iii. 418.
Oddly, *unequally*, iii. 275.
Odds, *quarrel*, iii. 669.
Od's pittikins, *God me pity*, ii. 750.
Œiliads, *ogles*, i. 646, iii. 100.
O'erparted, *not equal to a part or character*, i. 93.
O'erraught, *over-reached, over-took*, i. 118, iii. 357.
O'erstrawed, *o'erstrewed*, iii. 733.
Oes, *circular bosses of shining metal*, i. 364.
Oes, *small-pox marks*, i. 85.
Of, *for*, iii. 219, 542.
Of all loves, *for love's sake*, i. 356, 656, iii. 673.
Offices, *the apartments in great establishments where refreshments were prepared or distributed*, iii. 666.
Old, old utis, *rare, rare fun*, i. 589, 647, 736.
On, *of*, iii. 415, 772.
On, pronounced *own*, i. 10.
Once, *for the nonce, sometimes*, i. 128, 149, 668, 700, iii. 149, 580.
One good woman in ten, ii. 54.
Oneyers, *owners*, i. 521, 564.
Oosel-cock, *the blackbird*, i. 359.
Opinion, *reputation*, i. 558.
Opposite, *adversary*, i. 603, ii. 258.
Or e'er, *before, sooner than*, i. 318, ii. 732, iii. 7, 43.
Or, ore, *gold*, iii. 375, 738.
Orbs, *field fairy-rings*, i. 348.
Order, to take, *to adapt measures*, i. 238, iii. 436.
Orgulous, *proud, haught*, iii. 263.
Orient, *pellucid, lustrous*, iii. 537.
Orthography, *orthographer*, i. 709.
Orts, *scraps*, ii. 494, iii. 445.
Ospray, *a large hawk, the sea-eagle*, iii. 175.
Ostent, *appearance, parade*, i. 404.
Otherwhere, *otherplace*, i. 120, iii. 62.
Ounce, *the lynx*, i. 354.
Ouphes, *elves, goblins*, i. 677.
Out, *past*, iii. 8.
Out of all cess, *out of all measure*, i. 520.
Out of all nick, *beyond all reckoning*, i. 30.
Out of thy star, iii. 350.
Outvied, *defeated*, i. 246.
Overflown, *flooded, drowned*, i. 370.
Overlook, *to overbear, to overcome, to bewitch*, i. 325, 416, 683.
Overscutched, i. 601.
Oversee, *to execute, or superintend the execution of a will*, iii. 750.
Overwrested, *overwound*, iii. 273.
Owches, *bosses of gold set in diamonds*, i. 589.
Owe, *to own, to possess*, i. 127, 330, 355, 479, ii. 27, 598, iii. 763.
Owen Glendower, i. 565.
Owl, the, a baker's daughter, iii. 403.
PACK, *to scheme, to complot*, iii. 624.
Packed, *confederate*, i. 734.
Packing, *plotting, chicaning*, i. 270, ii. 738, iii. 84.
Paddock, *a toad*, iii. 373, 472.
Pageant of the Nine Worthies, i. 104.
Pageants and masques, i. 44, 104.
Paid, *punished*, i. 530, ii. 748.
Painted-cloth, *hangings for rooms*, i. 93, 626, ii. 151, iii. 740.
Pajock, *peacock*, iii. 366.
Palabras, *few words*, i. 721.
Pale, *to impale*, ii. 409.
Palled, *decayed, waned*, iii. 550.
Palliament, *a robe*, iii. 601.
Pansies for thoughts, iii. 403.
Pantaloon, the Italian, i. 249, 275.
Parcel, parcel-gilt, *part, parti-gilt*, i. 582, 642.
Paris Garden for bear-baiting, ii. 703.
Parish-top for the public amusement, ii. 238, 277.
Paritor, *an apparitor*, i. 67.
Parle, *speech*, i. 5, 294, ii. 85.

Parling, *speaking*, iii. 738.
Parlous, *perilous*, i. 357.
Partake, *to impart, to participate*, ii. 185, iii. 251.
Partakè, *to take the part of*, iii. 783.
Partaker, *a partner, a factionary*, ii. 301.
Parted, *endowed, imparted*, iii. 293.
Partially, *by partiality*, iii. 669.
Partisan, *a weapon, half-pike and half-halberd*, iii. 549.
Partlet, Dame, *a name for the hen*, i. 543, iii. 213.
Pash, *head or brow*, iii. 200.
Pass, *to surpass belief or expression*, i. 644, 674, ii. 444, iii. 234.
Passado, *a term in fencing*, i. 217.
Passage, *passengers*, iii. 699.
Passionate, *perturbed, agitated*, i. 298.
Passionate Shepherd, i. 687.
Passioning, *displaying emotion*, i. 35, iii. 732.
Pass not, *regard not*, ii. 377.
Pass on, pass upon, *to sentence*, ii. 600, iii. 93.
Passy-measure's pavin, *a dance*, ii. 274.
Pastry, *the room where paste was made*, i. 202.
Patch, *fool or jester*, i. 127, 372, 407, iii. 30, 511.
Patchery, *roguery, villany*, iii. 283.
Patience perforce, an adage, i. 170, ii. 615.
Patient, *to make patient*, iii. 599.
Patine, the cover of the chalice anciently used to hold particles of the host; a plate, a round, bright object, i. 433.
Pauca, pauca verba, paucus pallabris, *few words*, i. 75, 227, 641, ii. 74.
Paul's walk, i. 575.
Pavin, *a dance*, ii. 274.
Pax, *a small metal plate which was kissed at mass*, ii. 118.
Pay, *to beat, to punish*, i. 678, ii. 748, 758.
Peak, *to mope, to pule*, iii. 356.
Peat, *a pet*, i. 233.
Pedant, *a schoolmaster*, i. 248, 249, 260.
Pedascule, *a pedant*, i. 249.
Peeled, *shaven*, ii. 292.
Peevish, *childish, simple, headstrong*, ii. 327, 719, iii. 453, 669.
Peg-a-Ramsey, a tune, ii. 278.
Peise, *to weigh down*, ii. 569.
Peised, *balanced, weighted*, i. 298, 417.
Pelleted, *formed into pellets, or little balls*, iii. 565, 784.
Pelting, *paltry, despicable*, i. 351, 459, iii. 77.
Pen-and-inkhorn, carried by professional persons, ii. 395.
Penitent, *doing penance*, i. 117.
Penny, *metaphor for money, or means generally*, i. 102.
Pensioners, *a band of gentlemen in immediate attendance on the sovereign*, i. 348, 656.
Perch, *a common measure*, ii. 201.
Perdurable, *enduring*, ii. 103, iii. 659.
Perdy, *corruption of par dieu*, i. 138.
Perfect, *confident, well-assured*, iii. 220.
Periapts, *amulets*, ii. 324.
Periwigs, worn by ladies, i. 44.
Perjure, *a perjurer*, i. 75.
Perplexed, *distracted, frenzied*, ii. 735, iii. 707, 745.
Person, *old form of parson*, i. 73.
Perspectives, to be viewed obliquely, i. 498, ii. 274.
Pert, *quick, lively, subtle*, i. 380.
Peruse, *to examine*, i. 116, iii. 385.
Pervert, *to avert*, ii. 729.
Pestered, *impeded, encumbered*, i. 515, iii. 309, 511.
Pew-fellow, *companion, sharer*, ii. 559.
Pheere, *companion, husband or wife*, iii. 621.
Pheeze, *to tickle*, i. 227, iii. 285.
Philip, *a name for the sparrow*, i. 289.
Phill-horse, *the shaft-horse*, i. 402.
Phisnomy, *physiognomy*, ii. 45.
Physical, *medicinal*, iii. 426.
Pick, *to pitch*, ii. 696, iii. 131.
Picked, *scrupulously nice*, i. 82, iii. 388.
Pick-thanks, *parasites*, i. 540.
Pickt-hatch, the manor of, i. 654.
Picture of Nobody, iii. 32, 49.
Picture of we three, ii. 278.
Pied, *party-coloured*, i. 98, iii. 774.
Pied ninny, *a jester, a fool*, iii. 30.
Pight, *fixed*, iii. 73, 318.
Pigrogromitus and the Napians, ii. 278.
Pilcher, *pilch, an outer garment of leather*, i. 186.
Pilled, *robbed, pillaged*, i. 462, ii. 522.
Pin, to cleave the, *to split the wooden pin in a target*, i. 39, 71.
Pin and web, *the cataract in the eye*, iii. 89, 203.
Pinched, *restrained, nipped*, iii. 208.
Pinfold, *a pound*, i. 5, iii. 74.
Pink eyne, *small eyes*, iii. 551.
Pioners, or pioneers, *degraded soldiers*, iii. 681.
Pip, *a spot on a card*, i. 237.
Pitch, or pith, *eminence*, iii. 360.
Pitch and pay, *pay on delivery*, ii. 78.
Pittikins, 'ods, *God me pity*, ii. 750.
Place, *abiding-place*, ii. 139.
Place, *seat of authority*, i. 426, iii. 563.
Places, *dignities, honours*, iii. 206, 563.
Placket, *a petticoat*, i. 67, iii. 88, 233, 238, 283.
Plagued, *punished*, ii. 522.
Planched, *planked, made of boards*, ii. 620.
Plantage, *the moon's influence on plants*, iii. 291.
Plantain, its medicinal use, i. 65, 164.
Plants, *the soles of the feet*, iii. 549.
Plates, *silver coin*, iii. 581.
Platforms, *plans, schemes*, ii. 297.
Plausibly, *with expressions of applause*, iii. 757.
Plausive manners, *gracious, popular, winning manners*, iii. 340.
Pleached, *intertwined*, i. 701.
Please one, and please all, a ballad, ii. 280.
Plighting troth, mode of, i. 43.
Plurisy, *repletion*, iii, 385.
Point-device, *precise, with great nicety*. i. 82, ii. 153, 254.
Point of war, *a strain of military music*, i. 603.
Points, *long tagged laces to fasten dresses*, i. 250, ii. 241, iii. 232.
Poize, *weight*, iii. 676.
Poking-sticks, *irons for setting ruffs*, iii. 256.
Polacks, *Polanders*, iii. 330.
Politician, *a schemer for his own advantage*, iii. 387.
Polled, *cleared*, iii. 171.
Pomander, *a ball of perfume*, iii. 238.
Pomewater, *a kind of apple*, i. 71.
Poor John, *hake, a fish*, i. 160.
Popinjay, *a parrot, a trifling fop*, i. 515.
Porpentine, *porcupine*, i. 129, iii. 278.
Port, *a gate*, iii. 535.
Port, *show, state, appearance*, i. 235, 395.
Portable, *bearable, supportable*, iii. 93, 506.
Portage, *portholes*, ii. 82.
Portance, *carriage, mien, bearing*, iii. 656.
Possessed, *informed*, i. 398.
Posset, a, *curdled milk*, i. 690.
Posset, *to coagulate*, i. 690.
Post, the sheriff's, ii. 277.
Potch, *to push, to thrust*, iii. 140.
Potents, *potentates*, i. 295.
Poulter, *a poulterer*, i. 534.
Pouncet-box, *scent-box*, i. 515.
Powder, *to salt*, i. 560.
Poynt no, *non point*, i. 62, 89.
Practice, *conspiracy, machination, collusion*, ii. 77, 631, iii. 78, 112, 706.
Practise on, *to plot or intrigue against*, iii. 541.
'Praise, *to appraise*, ii. 243.
Prank, *to adorn, to dress ostentatiously*, ii. 250, iii. 155, 229.
Praying at the end of performances, i. 632.
Precedent, *a sign, an indicator*, iii. 722.
Precepts, *warrants*, i. 616.
Prefer, *to advance, to promote*, i. 233, ii. 764.
Pregnancy, *ready wit*, i. 577.
Pregnant, *supple, ready*, iii. 362.
Prenominate, *forenamed*, iii. 307, 347.
Preposterous, *misplaced, inversely*, i. 248, 363, 658.
Prescription, medical, ii. 54.
Presence, *presence-chamber*, i. 210.
Presently, *immediately*, ii. 355, 555, iii. 748.
Pressed, *ready, bound, urged*, i. 395.
Pretence, *design, device*, i. 21, ii. 314, iii. 216.
Pretend, *to intend*, i. 17, iii. 744.

Pretend, *to portend*, ii. 315.
Pretty, *petty, little*, iii. 750.
Prevent, to anticipate, i. 578, ii. 315, iii. 423, 454.
Pricket, *a deer so called*, i. 103.
Prick-song, *music pricked, or noted down*, i. 178.
Priest of the town, i. 687.
Prig, *a cheat, a thief*, iii. 228.
Prime, *the spring*, iii. 774.
Primero, *an old game at cards*, i. 679, ii. 688.
Prince of cats, i. 216.
Principality, *a celestial*, i. 15.
Principals, *the strongest rafters in a building*, ii. 203.
Princox, *a coxcomb*, i. 170.
Print, in, *precisely, to the letter*, i. 12.
Prison base, or prison bars, *a game*, i. 42.
Prize, *to rate*, ii. 464.
Prize, *privilege*, ii. 411.
Probal, *probable*, iii. 671.
Proceeding, *advancement*, iii. 430.
Process, *citation*, iii. 530.
Prodigious, *monstrous, portentous*, i. 300, iii. 420.
Proface, *welcome*, i. 620.
Profane use of the sacred names, act for preventing, i. 562.
Prognostication, *almanac*, iii. 241.
Project, *to shape*, iii. 581.
Projection, *forecast, preparation*, ii. 79.
Prolixious, *coy, delaying*, ii. 609.
Prompture, *suggestion*, ii. 609.
Prone, *ardent*, ii. 595, iii. 745.
Proof, *armour*, iii. 473.
Proper, *peculiar, personal*, iii. 140, 179.
Proper-false, *handsome-false*, ii. 246.
Propertied, *circumscribed, appropriated*, ii. 268, 462.
Properties, a theatrical term, i. 347, 677.
Proposing, *discoursing*, i. 713.
Prorougue, *to deaden or benumb*, iii. 540.
Provand, *provender*, iii. 146.
Provincial, *of the ecclesiastical province*, ii. 633.
Provincial, from Provins, celebrated for roses, iii. 366.
Prune, *to plume*, i. 511, ii. 758.
Pruning, *trimming up, adorning*, i. 78.
Pucelle, La, ii. 332, 334.
Pugging, *prigging*, iii. 227.
Puke-stocking, *puce-stocking*, i. 528.
Pun, *to pound*, iii. 278.
Punk, *a prostitute*, i. 656, ii. 19, 631, 636.
Punto reverso, *in fencing, a back-handed stroke*, i. 217, 650.
Purchase, *profit, advantage*, ii. 181.
Purchase, *booty, plunder*, i. 522, 615.
Push! *pish! pshaw!* i. 731, ii. 74.
Push-pin, *a game*, i. 78.
Put on, *to incite, to provoke*, iii. 508. 663, 672.
Putter on, *a contriver, an inciter*, ii. 650, iii. 153, 209, 508.
Putter out, *an adventurer of money*, iii. 33.
Puttock, *a buzzard*, ii. 713.
Puzzel, *a foul drab*, ii. 294.
Quail, *to slacken*, ii. 139.
Quaint, *dainty, clever, nimble*, i. 264.
Quaintly, *clever, adroit*, i. 12, 21.
Qualification, *temperament*, iii. 666.
Qualify, *to mitigate, to weaken*, iii. 667, 742.
Quality, *profession, calling*, i. 29, iii. 353, 658.
Quarrels, book of, ii. 173.
Quarry, *a pile of slaughtered game*, iii. 130.
Quart d'écu, or cardecue, *a coin, the fourth part of a French gold crown*, ii. 43, 49, 56.
Quat, *a pimple or scab*, iii. 698.
Queasy, *fastidious, squeamish*, i. 708.
Quell, *murder*, iii. 481.
Quern, *a hand-mill*, i. 349.
Quest, *inquisition, inquest, jury*, ii. 527, 620, 651, 767.
Question, *to converse*, iii. 739.
Question, *motives, reason*, iii. 438.
Queubus, equinoctial of, ii. 246.
Quick, *alive, quickening, quick-witted*, ii. 516, iii. 532, 582.
Quick recreation, *lively pastime*, i. 53.
Quiddit, *a subtlety*, iii. 387.
Quietus, *discharge, acquittance*, iii. 359, 779.
Quillets, *quodlibets, quibbles*, iii. 387.
Quilt, *a flock bed*, i. 550.
Quintain, *a military exercise, a pastime*, ii. 171.
Quips, *sudden, angry gibes, scoffs*, i. 29.
Quit, *to requite*, ii. 635, iii. 565.
Quittance, *requital, to make requital*, i. 574, ii. 296, 467.
Quiver, *smart, nimble*, i. 601.
Quote, *to look into, to scan*, iii. 347, 621, 746.
R, the dog's letter, i. 217.
Rabato, or rebato, *an ornament for the neck, a kind of ruff*, i. 720.
Rabbit-sucker, *a sucking rabbit*, i. 534.
Race, *nature*, iii. 14.
Rack, *to stretch, to extend*, i. 726.
Rack, *drifting vapour, or scud*, ii. 411, iii. 50, 765.
Racked, *harassed by exactions*, ii. 347.
Rag, *a term of contempt*, ii. 492.
Ragged, *rough, rugged, base*, i. 574, 618, ii. 142.
Ragged, *beggared*, iii. 747.
Rake up, *to cover up*, iii. 105.
Rampallian, *a low, creeping, mean wretch*, i. 582.
Rank, *chorus, rhyme*, ii. 149.
Rank, *brimming, full*, iii. 722, 778.
Rankness, *riotousness*, i. 325, iii. 435.
Raps, *transports*, ii. 719.
Rapture, *a fit*, iii. 145.
Rarely, *curiously*, ii. 728.
Rascal, *a lean deer*, ii. 155, 317, iii. 129.
Rates, *counts for, is equivalent to*, iii. 562.
Rather, *hasty, quick*, i. 65.
Rats rhymed to death by charms, ii. 173, 332.
Raught, *reft, reached, grasped*, ii. 357, 409.
Ravin, *to devour greedily*, ii. 595, iii. 489.
Ravined, *ravenous*, iii. 501.
Rayed, *chafed, excoriated*, i. 254.
Razed, *slashed, opened*, iii. 366.
Razes, *roots*, i. 521.
Read, *to tread*, i. 547, ii. 697.
Rearmice, *bats*, i. 354.
Rearward, *rearguard*, iii. 773.
Reason, *to discourse*, i. 411.
Reasonable swiftness, *speed of thought*, ii. 71.
Rebate, *to blunt*, i. 51, 598.
Rebato, *a kind of ruff, an ornament for the neck*, i. 720.
Rebeck, *a sort of fiddle*, i. 205.
Receipt, *receptacle*, iii. 481.
Recheat, *a note on the horn*, i. 699.
Reck, *to regard*, iii. 339.
Record, *to chant*, i. 37, ii. 208.
Recorder, *a musical instrument resembling a flute*, iii. 401.
Recover the wind of me, *a hunting expression*, iii. 367.
Recure, *to recover*, ii. 549.
Rede, *counsel, advice*, iii. 339.
Red-lattice, *the denotement of an ale-house*, i. 586, 626.
Red-lattice phrases, *ale-house phraseology*, i. 654.
Reduce, *to restore, to bring back to a former state*, ii. 575.
Reechy, *discoloured by smoke*, i. 719.
Refelled, *refuted*, ii. 631.
Regard, *reflection, observation*, iii. 741, 752.
Regiment, *directorship, rule*, iii. 558.
Reguerdon, *recompence*, ii. 307, 312.
Relume, *to relight*, iii. 701.
Remarkable, *profoundly striking*, iii. 577.
Remember thy courtesy, *discontinue ceremony*, i. 83.
Remembered, *reminded*, iii. 778.
Remembrance, *memorial*, iii. 680.
Remonstrance, *exhibition, manifestation*, ii. 634.*
Remorse, *pity, tenderness of feeling*, i. 31, 319, ii. 373, 631, iii. 681.
Remorseless, *relentless, pitiless*, iii. 743.
Remotion, *removal*, ii. 492, iii. 78.
Removed, *remote, private*, i. 293, 343, ii. 152, 595, iii. 247.
Removes, *stages, journeys*, ii. 51.
Render, *to describe, to represent*, ii. 162.
Reneges, *denies, renounces*, iii. 75, 530.

* In the text the suggestion of Malone to read demonstrance was too hastily adopted. The right word is unquestionably "remonstrance."

Repeal, *to recall from exile, to bring back*, i. 23, 464, 472, ii. 20, 371, iii. 434.
Repetition, *recrimination*, ii. 49.
Repine, *vexation, discontent*, iii. 726.
Reproof, *refutation, disproof*, i. 540.
Repugn, *to resist*, ii. 315.
Reputing, *boasting*, ii. 362.
Reserve, *preserve*, ii. 210, iii. 765, 772.
Resolve, *be assured*, ii. 290.
Respect, *self-command, prudence*, iii. 279, 740.
Respect, *regard, consideration*, i 35, 187, 288, 433, iii. 61, 731.
Rest, *a term in music*, i. 178, iii. 749.
'Rest, *arrest*, i. 136.
Resty, *immobile, dull, uneasy*, ii. 741, iii. 775.
Retire, *to withdraw*, i. 464, iii. 741.
Retiring, *returning*, iii. 748.
Retort, *to refer back*, ii. 633.
Reverb, *to reverberate*, iii. 60.
Reverso, a term in fencing, i. 659.
Reword, *to echo*, iii. 784.
Rhodope's pyramid, ii. 333.
Rialto, the, i. 437.
Ribaudred nag, *filthy strumpet*, iii. 559.
Rich coat, *a full charged escutcheon*, iii. 787.
Rich eyes, ii. 49, 159.
Rid, *to destroy*, ii. 417, iii. 14.
Riddles, fustian, ii. 279.
Rides the wild mare, *plays at see-saw*, i. 593.
Riggish, *wanton*, iii. 543.
Right, *direct, immediate*, i. 325.
Rigol, *a circle*, i. 612, iii. 756.
Rim, *a part of the intestines*, ii. 101.
Rivage, *the shore or bank*, ii. 81.
Rivality, *participation, copartnership*, iii. 556.
Rivals, *associates, partners*, iii. 329.
Rivo, a drinking exclamation, i. 529.
Road, *a roadstead, a haven*, i. 16.
Roaring Devil, ii. 119.
Robin, hey, jolly Robin, a song, i. 281.
Robin Goodfellow, i. 382.
Rolled, *coiled*, iii. 609.
Romage, *commotion, turmoil*, iii 332.
Rondure, *a round or belt*, iii. 763.
Ronyon, *a scurvy old woman, a witch*, i. 676, iii. 474.
Rood, *the cross, the image on the cross*, i. 597.
Rook, *to squat down, to roost*, ii. 449.
Ropery, rope-tricks, *ribaldry*, i. 181, 238.
Rosemary for remembrance, iii. 403.
Rother, *red cattle*, ii. 488.
Rough-hew, *to plan, or fashion in the rough*, iii. 392.
Round, *plain spoken*, i. 120, iii. 361.
Round, roundel, roundelay, *a dance*, i. 104. 354.
Rounded, *insinuated*, i. 298.
Rounding, *whispering, insinuating*, iii. 202.
Roundure, *a circle*, i. 294.
Rouse, *a carouse, a deep draught*, iii. 398.
Royal, a coin so called, i. 532.
Royal merchants, i. 440.
Roynish, *scurvy*, ii. 138.
Ruddock, *the redbreast*, ii. 748.
Rudesby, *blusterer, swaggerer*, i. 250.
Rue, *herb-grace*, iii. 382.
Ruff, *the top of the boot turned over*, ii. 29.
Ruffian, *roisterer, swash-buckler*, iii. 650.
Ruin, *rubbish*, i. 412.
Run counter, *to follow on a false scent*, i. 150.
Rushes strewed on room floors, and on the stage, i. 168, 255, 539, ii. 723.
Sables, the wearing of, iii. 362.
Sack, sherris-sack, i. 629.
Sackerson, the name of a bear, i. 644, 686.
Sack-posset, i. 690.
Sacred, *devoted, dedicated*, iii. 425, 607.
Sacring-bell, *the bell rung on the elevation of the host*, ii. 678.
Sad, *grave, serious*, i. 8, 702, 712, iii. 234, 740.
Safe, *sound*, iii. 101.
Saffron, *the colour of Judas' hair, the dissembling colour*, ii. 45.
Sag, *to droop, to flag*, iii. 511.
Sagittary, *officers' residence at the arsen of Venice*, iii. 708.
Said, *done*, i. 601, ii. 143, 349, iii. 220.
Sail, *pomp, swell*, ii. 70, iii. 773.
Saint George, an English war cry, ii. 581.
Saint Helen Meteor, iii. 48.
Saint Jaques le grand, shrine of at Compostella, ii. 56.
Saint Nicholas, patron saint of scholars and cutpurses, i. 43 521.
Sallet, *a helmet*, ii 384.
Sallets, or salte, *Atticism, piquancy*, iii. 355.
Salt, *salt-cellar*, i. 25.
Saltiers, corruption of *satyrs*, iii. 234.
Salute, *to move, to exhilarate*, ii. 665, iii. 778.
Samingo, *San Domingo, an old burden to drinking songs*, i. 621.
Sanded, *of a sandy colour*, i. 385.
Satire, *a satirist*, iii. 775.
Saucy, *prurient*, ii 44.
'Say, *assay, taste, evidence*, iii. 112.
'Sayed, *assayed*, ii. 183, iii. 112.
Scaled, *dispersed*, iii. 315.
Scamble, *to seize, to scramble, to rifle*, i. 319, ii. 64.
Scamels, or sea-mells, *sea-birds*, iii. 27.
Scapes, *lapses, slips*, iii. 221, 745.
Scarfed bark, *vessel decorated with flags*, i. 407.
Scathe, *to damage*, i. 170.
Scogan, Henry and John, i. 627.
Sconce, *a fortification*, ii. 88.
Sconce, *the head*, i. 118, 122, iii. 161, 387.
Scone stone, iii. 518.
Score, *to mark, to brand*, i. 117, iii. 689.
Scorn it with the heels, *a manner of scornful rejection* i. 401, 721.
Scotch, *to wound, to notch*, iii. 493.
Scrimers, *fencers*, iii. 384.
Scroyles, *scabby rogues*, i 296.
Scrubbed, *stunted*, i. 434.
Sculls, *shoals*, iii. 315.
'Scuse, *excuse*, i. 430, iii. 687.
Scut, *a tail*, i. 681.
Scylla and Charybdis, i. 440.
Seals on deeds, i. 485.
Sear, *to stigmatize, to close up*, ii. 712, iii. 208.
Season, *preservative*, iii. 498.
Secret, *separated, devoted*, iii. 425, 607.
Secure, *careless, to make over-confident*, i. 487, 653, 658, 662, ii. 296, iii. 96, 279, 344.
Secure, *to assure*, ii. 475.
Securely, *carelessly, over-confidently*, i. 462, iii. 304.
Security, *carelessness, over-confidence*, i. 469, iii. 431, 498.
See, to, *to the sight*, iii. 766.
Seel, in falconry, *to sew up the eyes*, iii. 494, 564.
Seen, *versed, practised, skilled*, i. 238.
Seldom comes the better, a proverbial saying, ii. 534.
Sense, to the, *to the quick*, iii. 698.
Septentrion, *the north*, ii. 409.
Sequester, *a separation*, iii. 683.
Sere, tickled o' the, *easily moved to mirth*, iii. 353.
Sergeant, *anciently one of the king's guard*, iii. 472.
Serpigo, *leprosy*, ii. 611.
Servant, *a follower, an admirer*, i. 43.
Sessa, *be quiet*, i. 227, iii. 92.
Set, a term in music, i. 7.
Set a match, *to plan a robbery*, i. 513.
Set up his rest, *to stake all*, i. 150, 203.
Setebos, a demon, iii. 48.
Seven ages of man, ii. 172.
Several, *private*, i. 63, iii. 781.
Several, *manifold*, ii. 10.
Shale, *a case, a shell*, ii. 99.
Shards, *broken fragments*, iii. 390.
Shards, *scaly wings of a beetle*, iii. 494, 553.
Shaven Hercules, the, i. 719.
Sheaf, iii. 339.
Sheen, *brightness, splendour*, i. 349, iii. 363.
Sheep, pronounced *ship*, i. 4.
Sheer, *pure, unmixed*, i. 229, 488.
Shent, *undone, ruined, reproved*, i. 648, iii. 179, 283.

Sheriffs'-posts, for proclamations, ii. 277.
Sherris, sherris-sack, i. 629.
Ship-tire, *a fanciful head-dress for ladies*, i. 664, 688.
Shive, *a slice*, iii. 607.
Shog, *to jog off*, ii. 74, 78.
Shotten, *spawned, projected*, i. 250, ii. 87.
Shoughs, *shaggy dogs*, iii. 492.
Shoulder-clapper, *a bailiff*, i. 135.
Shove-groat, *a game*, i. 626.
Shovel-boards, *broad shillings used in the game of shove-groat*, i. 642.
Shrewd, *shrewish, mischievous*, i. 84, 234, 237, 325, 349, 366, 657, 703, ii. 169, 602, iii. 571.
Shrift, *auricular confession*, i. 161, 178, 181, 182, 201, ii. 546, 623.
Shrive, *to bring to confession and absolve*, i. 125.
Shriving-time, *time of shrift or confession*, iii. 392.
Shut-up, *finished, concluded*, iii. 482.
Shylock, derivation of the name, i. 437.
Side, *long*, i. 720.
Siege, *a seat, place, state*, ii. 622, iii. 384.
Sigh-clout, *a cloth to strain milk through*, iii. 711.
Sightless, *invisible*, iii. 479, 480.
Sightless, *unsightly*, i. 300.
Sights, *apertures for seeing through in a helmet*, i. 604.
Sign, *to give an omen*, iii. 567.
Silly, *simple, rustic*, ii. 756.
Silly cheat, *petty theft*, iii. 227.
Similitudes, inapposite, i. 563.
Simular, *counterfeit, deceitful*, ii. 761, iii. 85.
Single, *simple, feeble*, i. 578. iii. 476.
Sink-a-pace, *cinque-pace, a dance*, i. 104, 704.
Sinklo, the actor, i. 229.
Sir, a title of certain churchmen, ii. 345.
Sir, applied to nobility and royalty, iii. 204, 245.
Sir Bevis of Hamptoun, ii. 699.
Sir Dagonet in Arthur's Show, i. 628.
Sir reverence, an apology for any unseemly saying, i. 130.
Sir, the, *the gallant, the courtier*, iii. 664.
Siren's song of allurement, i. 149.
Sirs, an old form of addressing women, iii. 577.
Sithence, *since*, ii. 12.
Sit out, *refuse to play*, a card-table phrase, i. 53.
Sit thee down, sorrow, i. 56.
Sizes, *allowances*, iii. 80.
Skainsmates, *reckless fellows*, i. 181.
Skill, *cunning, design, reason*, iii. 209, 231.
Skills not, *is of no importance*, ii. 364.
Skimble-skamble, *jumbled, deranged*, i. 538.
Skinker, *drawer of liquor*, i. 527.
Skirr, *to scour*, ii. 104, iii. 511.
Slander, *to abuse*, iii. 340.
Slanderous, *ignominious, branded*, iii. 748.
Slavish wipe, *the brand of slaves*, iii. 743.
Sleave, *unwrought silk*, iii. 484.
Sledded, *sledged*, iii. 330.
Sleeve, worn as a favour by tilters and warriors, iii. 323.
Sleided, *untwisted*, ii. 208, iii. 785.
Slipper, *slippery*, iii. 665.
Slips, *counterfeit pieces of money*, i. 179, iii. 283.
Sliver, *to slit or slice*, iii. 97, 385.
Slop, *loose knee-breeches*, i. 179.
Smirched, *sullied, soiled*, i. 719, 725, ii. 85, 136.
Smoke, *to discover*, ii. 34, 38.
Smoothed, *fawned on*, ii. 488.
Smug, *spruce, smart*, i. 415, 538, iii. 104.
Sneap, *a sarcasm, a set-down*, i. 583.
Sneap, *to nip or check*, iii. 198, 741.
Sneck-up, *go hang!* ii. 247.
Snipe, *a fool, a blockhead*, iii. 660.
Snuff, take it in, *to take it in dudgeon*, i. 84, 377.
Snuffs, *tiffs*, iii. 84.
So, *as*, ii. 41, 197, 465, 470, 473, iii. 535, 538.
So like you he is the worse, a proverb, iii. 213.
Softly, *slowly*, iii. 377.
Solemn, *grave, public, accustomed*, i. 251.
Solidares, *a coin*, ii. 477.
Something-nothing, *neither here nor there*, iii. 678.
Sometimes, *formerly*, i. 396, 491.
Sonnet, Sonnets or Sonneteer, i. 709.
Sonties, *corruption of sanctities*, i. 401.
Soon at, *about*, i. 116.
Sooth, *sweetness, softness, truth*, i. 473.
Sorrow, sit thee down, i. 56.
Sorry, *dismal, sorrowful*, i. 143.
Sort, *lot*, iii. 275.
Sort, *to suit, to fit*, iii. 266, 747.
Sort, *gang, crew, company*, i. 480, ii. 355.
Sort, *rank, degree, quality*, i. 696.
Sot, *a fool*, i. 125, ii. 761.
Sowle, *to lug, to drag*, iii. 171.
Speak by the card, *to speak precisely, or according to the book of manners*, iii. 388.
Speak to, *to aspire or lay claim to*, iii. 651.
Speculation, *view, espial*, iii. 293.
Speculative instruments, *organs of vision*.
Sped, *done, settled*, i. 186.
Speed, *fortune*, iii. 219.
Sperr, *to shut up*, iii. 263.
Spill, *to spoil, to come to harm*, iii. 710.
Spirits in magic or witchcraft, iii. 47.
Spleen, *flash*, i. 297, 343, 380.
Spot, *stain*, iii. 774.
Sprag, *quick, ready, sprightly*, i. 673.
Spring, *shoot, sprig*, iii. 728, 738, 747.
Sprited, *haunted*, ii. 726.
Squandered, *dispersed*, i. 398.
Square, *equitable*, ii. 503.
Square, *a quarrel, to quarrel*, i. 349, iii. 540, 563.
Square, *a stomacher*, iii. 232.
Squash, *an immature peascod*, i. 361, iii. 202.
Squire, *a rule*, i. 92, 522, iii. 234.
Staggers, *a kind of apoplexy in horses*, i. 250.
Staggers, *perplexities, incertitudes*, ii. 23, 762.
Stain, *tinct, mark, eclipse*, ii. 8, iii. 556.
Stale, *insipid, out of date*, i. 121.
Stalking-horse of fowlers, i. 742.
Stand on, stands me upon, *it is incumbent on me*, i. 178, 467, iii. 392, 540.
Stands, or Standings, in the sport of deer-shooting, i. 600.
Stannyel, *a kind of hawk*, ii. 253.
Star Chamber, court of, i. 686.
Stark, *rigid, stiff*, ii. 748.
Starve, *to perish*, ii. 716.
State, *a chair or throne*, i. 533, iii. 495.
Statuas, *statues*, ii. 548, iii. 430, 441.
Statue, *picture, image*, i. 35.
Statute, *security, or obligation*, iii. 780.
Statute-caps, *caps worn by citizens*, i. 104.
Stay, *a check or obstacle*, i. 297.
Steel, *to harden like steel*, iii. 725.
Stelled, *fixed*, iii. 753.
Stern, *rigid, unyielding*, ii. 39.
Sternage, *steerage, course*, ii. 81.
Sticking-place, *abiding place*, iii. 481.
Stickler, *an arbitrator in combats*, iii. 318.
Stigmatical, *branded with deformity*, i. 135, ii. 389, 417.
Still, *always, ever*, i. 395, 545, 698, ii. 42, 91, 98, iii. 435.
Still an end, *constantly, perpetually*, i. 33.
Still music, *soft, subdued music*, i. 370, ii. 92, 168.
Stinted, *stopped*, i. 166.
Stith, *an anvil*, iii. 362.
Stithy, *the smith's work-shop*, iii. 362.
Stoccado, or stoccata, a term of fencing, i. 186, 659.
Stomach, *haughtiness*, ii. 683.
Stone-bow, *a cross-bow for propelling stones*, ii. 279.
Stone of destiny at Scone, iii. 518.
Stood upon, *plumed or presumed upon*, iii. 610.
Stops, *a technical term in music*, iii. 362, 367, 749.
Stout, *bold, proud*, i. 314.
Stover, *fodder*, iii. 36.
Strain, *lineage*, i. 708, ii. 79.
Strain, *turn, tendency*, i. 651, 666.
Strain courtesy, to, *to avoid the post of honour in a perilous undertaking*, iii. 730.
Strange, *wonderful, incredible*, iii. 704.

Strange, *coy* i. 175.
Strange, *foreign*, ii. 719.
Strappado, *a kind of punishment*, i. 531.
Stray shaft, mode of discovering, i. 437.
Strict, *harsh*, ii. 482.
Strike, *to tap, to broach*, iii. 550.
Stroke, *rule*, ii. 622.
Strossers, *trousers*, ii. 90.
Stuck, *a sword, a thrust*, iii. 385.
Stuck-in, *corruption of stoccata*, ii. 264.
Stuff, *luggage*, i. 140.
Stuffed, *furnished, endowed*, i. 197, 696.
Subject, *people, subjects*, iii. 198.
Subscribes, *succumbs*, iii. 305, 776.
Subsidy, *an impost*, ii. 454.
Success, *consequence, succession*, ii. 15, iii. 204, 456, 480, 556.
Sudden, *violent*, ii. 145, iii. 505.
Sue livery, to, i. 498.
Suffer, *to punish, to afflict*, iii. 563.
Suffered, *unrestrained, indulged*, ii. 388, iii. 725.
Suggesting, *enticing, tempting, seducing*, i. 17, 20, 53, 449, ii. 45, iii. 22, 476, 672, 738, 782.
Suitor, pronounced *shooter*, i. 70.
Sullen, *melancholy*, i. 286.
Sumpter, *a horse that carries provisions on a journey*, iii. 81.
Supposes, *impostors*, i. 270.
Surcease, *end*, iii. 480.
Surplice, puritan objections to the, ii. 54.
Surprise, *to capture, to seize unawares*, ii. 433, iii. 602.
Swarth, *the corn cut with one stroke of a scythe*, ii. 249.
Swasher, *swaggerer*, ii. 83.
Swashing, *crushing, smashing*, i. 160.
Swear over, *to out-swear*, iii. 205.
Sweet and twenty, *a proverbial endearment*, ii. 247.
Sweet mouth, *liquorish tooth*, i. 24.
Sweltered, *weltered*, iii. 501.
Swift, *ready*, i. 714, ii. 168.
Swinge-buckler, *a bully*, i. 597.
Sword, swearing by the, i. 497, iii. 345.
Swords for dancing with, ii. 55.
Sworn brothers, *men bound to share each other's fortunes*, i. 484, ii. 73.
Sympathy, *equality*, i. 478.
TABLE, *a table-book*, i. 18.
Table, *a picture, board or canvas on which any object is painted*, i. 297, ii. 7.
Table, in palmistry, *the palm of the hand*, i. 404.
Tabor of the clown, ii. 279.
Tabourines, *drums*, iii. 307, 571.
Tag, *the rabble*, iii. 158, 418.
Tailor cries, i. 350.
Tainture, *defilement*, ii. 256.
Take, *to bewitch, to blast, to paralyse*, i. 677, iii. 80, 88, 315, 332.
Take a truce, *to make peace*, i. 300.
Take in, *to conquer, to overcome*, iii. 558.
Take it in snuff, *to take it in dudgeon*, i. 84, 377.
Take me with you, *let me understand you*, i. 197, 534.
Take out, *to copy*, iii. 680.
Take thought, *to abandon oneself to grief*, iii. 426, 562.
Take thy old cloak about thee, iii. 710.
Taking up, *dealing*, i. 575.
Tale, *telling, counting*, iii. 476.
Talent, *a talon*, i. 73.
Talents, *riches*, ii. 720.
Tall, *able, stout, robust*, i. 648, ii. 237, 267, iii. 247.
Tallow-keech, *a round lump of tallow for the chandler*, i. 530.
Tame-cheater, *a petty rogue*, i. 590.
Tame-snake, *a poltroon*, ii. 162.
Tang, *to twang*, ii. 254, iii. 24.
Tarre, *to incite*, i. 311, iii. 276.
Tartar, *Tartarus*, ii. 77, 254.
Tasked, *taxed, challenged*, i. 551, 555.
Tassel-gentle, *the male of the goshawk*, i. 216.
Taste, *to try, to test*, ii. 256, 263, 763.
Tawdry lace, *a neck ornament*, iii. 234.
Tawny-coated followers, ii. 292.
Taxation, *sarcasm, satire*, ii. 132.
Teen, *grief, sorrow*, i. 165, iii. 8, 730.
Tell, *to rate, to number, to account*, ii. 469, 474, iii. 476.
Temperance, *temperature*, iii. 19.
Tempered, *moulded, qualified*, ii. 77, iii. 447.
Ten, a card of, *a tenth card*, i. 276.
Tender, *an offer, a promise*, i. 194.
Tender hefted, iii. 80.
Tents, *hangings*, i. 246.
Tercel, *the male hawk*, iii. 290.
Termagant, *a hectoring tyrant of the Miracle plays*, iii. 401.
Testern, tester, or teston, *a coin so called, sixpence*, i. 41.
Tharborough, *a constable*, i. 54.
Theorick, *theory*, ii. 41, 65, iii. 648.
Thews, i. 600, iii. 338, 430.
Thick, *rapidly*, ii. 732, iii. 756.
Thick-skin, *thick-head*, i. 677.
Thievery, exemplifications of, ii. 507.
Thills, *the shafts of a wagon*, iii. 289.
Thou, as a mark of insult, ii. 279.
Thou knave, a catch, ii. 278.
Though, *if, even if, since*, ii. 492, 525, iii. 564.
Thought, *melancholy*, iii. 570.
Thrasonical, *bragging, boastful*, i. 82, ii. 165.
Threape, *to dispute*, iii. 711.
Three-man beetle, *an implement for driving piles*, i. 578.
Three-men song-men, *singers of songs in three parts*, iii. 227.
Three merry men be we, the burden of a song, ii. 247, 278.
Three-pile, *three-piled velvet*, iii. 227.
Thronged, *oppressed, crushed, shrunk*, ii. 184, 192, iii. 752.
Thrummed, *made of coarse woollen*, i. 674.
Thunder-stone, *the imaginary produce of thunder*, iii. 420.
Tib, *a loose wench*, ii. 217.
Tibert, prince of cats, i. 216.
Tickle, *ticklish*, ii. 344.
Tickled o' the sere, *easily moved to mirth*, iii. 353.
Tidy, *plump*, i. 592.
Tightly, *briskly, promptly*, i. 646.
Tike, *clown, clodpole*, i. 678.
Tilly-vally, *a ludicrous interjection*, i. 590, ii. 247.
Time and the hour, iii. 476.
Timely, *in proper time*, ii. 369.
Time of life, *duration of life*, iii. 454.
Time's fool, i. 559.
Timon from the Palace of Pleasure, ii. 505.
Tire, *to peck like a bird, to tear*, ii. 405, 483, iii. 722.
Titania of fairy legends, i. 383.
To, an ellipsis for *equal to*, i. 15.
To, an ellipsis for *so as to*, i. 199.
To, to, *ploughmen's words of encouragement*, iii. 278.
To friend, *for friend, propitious*, ii. 716, iii. 435, 505.
Toasts and butter, term of contempt, i. 549.
Tokened pestilence, iii. 559.
Tokens, the Lord's, *plague spots*, i. 104, iii. 559.
Toll, ii. 51.
Tom o' Bedlams, *mad beggars*, iii. 120.
Tongs and bones music, i. 385.
Too fine, *too full of finesse*, ii. 52.
Too late, *too recently*, ii. 540, iii. 756.
Took it on his death, *an oath*, i. 287.
Too-too, *excessive, excessively*, i. 16, iii. 336.
Top, the parish, ii. 238.
Topless, *supreme*, iii. 273.
Torch-bearers to maskers, i. 215.
Tottered, *tottering*, i. 472.
Touch, *a pang, a wound, sympathy*, ii. 712.
Touch, *a touchstone*, ii. 494, 554.
Touched, *pricked*, iii. 627.
Touring, *circling*, iii. 488.
Touse, *to tug, to drag*, ii. 633.
Toward, *in preparation*, iii. 330.
Towards, *approaching, near at hand*, i. 170.
Toys, *idle rumours, tricks*, i. 289.
Tranect, *a ferry*, i. 422.
Transported, *translated, transformed*, i. 372.
Trash, *to clog, to impede*, iii. 8, 666.
Tray-trip, a game so called, ii. 254.
Treachers, *traitors*, iii. 65.
Trial by battle, i. 495, iii. 393.